Library of Congress catalog card number: 89-051542
ISBN-0-910147-15-9
1990 Printing
Printed in the United States of America

With special thanks to the World of Poetry Staff:
Barbara, Lori, Sherri, Dean, Betty, Sonia, Marie, Judy, Susan, John, Raymond, Julie, Joan, Jasen, Tim, Tina, Hahn and Derrick.

Mickie P Rouse
METAMORPHOSIS
She boards the DC-10
and flies into the night
trying to make good her escape.
But I'm not ready to set her free.

Through many calendars
superimposed
I led her down paths pencil-thin—
and I'll not yet set her free.

When she stepped off
I pulled her back too easily—
(pains in her head—
pains in her gut),
I plagued her with indecision
and I would not set her free.

But now she resists,
seems to ignore me.
Her force is overcoming mine—
she even seems to be mocking me.
I might be forced to set her free.

Nell Asher
LIFE IS A GAME
Through the years
I've come to see
That life is a game
And it's what you make of it
That stakes your claim
I've traveled roads
That were hard and rough
And I've taken paths
That held good luck
I've tried it with two
And ended as one—
But your life is the game
That stakes the claim
So keep on playing
In sunshine or rain

Willa Jansen
IT STARTS WITH COLD BITING, ICY AND DARK
It starts with cold biting, icy and dark
Empty eyes, empty heart, empty hope
But soon the sun comes warm
Like brown eyes and laugh lines
It coaxes out the buds
Coddles them in soft breezes
And lightens their colors to effervescent green
Soon the bud takes a life of its own
A leaf
Tender, still limp in springtime air
Awaiting summer's full bloom
Suddenly, under the glowing sun
The leaf reaches the richness of summertime
Full, dark and green
Green with life and love
It hangs through the balmy days
Until the brilliance of autumn
Flashes gold, red and amber
A masterpiece of color and melancholy
For soon winter and its cold will come again
But this time—this time—so will the spring.

Tracy M Craig-Clark
PRISONERS OF WAR
People who were proud to fight for our country with their very own hands
Remembering the war everyday, because prisoners they are in a very strange land,

Improper treatment they may be receiving, how this is not fair and is so wrong
Searching for answers, in their mind, why all of this is still going on,

Obligated to their country, so many years ago to fight
Now, what is their country doing to get them home and make it right,

Explanations will not help to bring them home where they should be
Results is what we want and that is what they need,

So much they have lost, so much we have gained
Out of their misery and their pain,

For when you have a chance, pray for them
Wherever they may be to bring them home again,

Around the world there are many family and friends of PRISONERS OF WAR
Refusing to give up and put it all behind a closed door.

Iris L Jones
COMMUNICATE
WHAT is all the commotion?
WHAT is all the ado?
WHEN all I really wanted,
was to talk to you.

WE share each others dreams,
OUR thoughts and wild ideas
WE'VE been through so much together,
and even shared some tears.

TELL me why is it so hard,
TO communicate this way?
JUST to sit and talk to each other
each and everyday.

Ruth Graham Woodard
ETERNITY
You ask me if I'm lonely,
And I say surely nay;
I trust you only—
You're with me all the way.

You wonder why I sit and smile,
And watch the time fly by;
I'm thinking of that one last mile,
When we rise up in the sky.

And all be joined together,
And greet each and everyone;
In everlasting fair weather,
Because of Your crucified Son.

Jewell Curry
ODE TO MY GRANDSON
Perpetual motion is a typical boy.
Making a racket is his special joy.
He'll whoop and holler, and yell and fight,
From break of dawn, to dark of night.
With shirt tail flying, pants out at the knee—
Good clothes mean nothing to him, you see.
Hair plastered with sweat, his face all red;
He never stops 'til he's sent to bed.
Then the battle is on; He'll say, "Oh Gosh!"
"Why do you always make me wash?"
"I'll get all dirty tomorrow, you know—
When the light is out, it doesn't show."
"Aw Mom, do I have to use that stuff?"
"I'm sure plain water will be enough."

So he'll grumble and gripe, and splash a bit.
Then use the towel for the rest of it.
"Aw Mom, I washed, and this ain't dirt.
I fell down and my elbow's hurt."
"I hit a rock, and then I slid—
But you should see that other kid!"
"I blacked his eye; his nose it bled,
His lips—Aw shucks! I'm going to bed."

Destiny F Voyles
PUT TO SLEEP

To; Disney, whom I love very much.

Put to sleep.
It's a silent way
to die.
You don't know what's
going on. 'Cause you're
delirious inside.

On the outside you
look normal.
On the inside you're
a mess,
It's hard to tell what's
right or wrong, when
being put to death.

Anna Maria Fantasia

Anna Maria Fantasia
FANTASY

To Nana and my family, whom I will always love.

There is a place, not far away,
Where all our dreams come true.
Where magic spreads from wizards wise
Their spells their timeless brews.
The darkest forests linger here,
yet light flows wild and free.
But just one place can this exist,
Within our fantasies.
Where heroes brave the dragons fierce
To save the princess fair,
Whose heart is known for peace and love
With lovely golden hair.
Where horses with a golden horn
Glide on wings of blue,
And swans are swimming in a pond
Amid a rainbows hue.
This place of magic, mystic lands
That's only known to me,
I wake up from my golden dream,
My life, my fantasy.

Alexis Skinner
ID
You terrorize me with dreams—
Dreaming that I am human,
Not serpent

In the darkness I ponder your proposition:

Am I not a reptile?
My eyes reflect all I see;
The serpentine flows, forever molten
Inspiring the transformation
layer after layer . . .
Yet still you accuse me of humanity
Within a cringe
Behind a shudder
Another self escapes the scales

Consuelo Harrell
MY LIFE
When I was young, so very young
Life was for my taking. Goals, I
Had none, except for fun so time
I can be wasting.

When I grew up I wasn't sure
Of what I wanted to be. So I just
Sat there all alone inside my
Misery. I knew that there were
Yesterdays and so there be
Tomorrows. So I just let time
Slip away and now I feel the sorrow.

When I was old, so very old
I think of yesterdays. Now I
Sit here all alone I think that
I can cry. For I let time slip
Away I think that I may die.

Robert B Dula
NIGHT DREAMS
You had a look in your eyes
and it was easy to see,
That you wanted nothing as much
as to make love to me.
We never left the car
as we shivered in cool air.
We made love in the front seat,
because you wanted me there.
Then late on the back deck
you give all that I need,
as we are sharing our love
at an increasing speed.
The shower is streaming,
your chest flushed in red.
We're laughing and grabbing
as we dry, rolling in bed.
The past put behind us
when two lovers we play,
but it's three in the morning
and you're ten miles away.

Christine S Harper
I HEARD THE TRAIN WHISTLE
Every time I hear a train whistle blow—I miss you so.
We used to go and watch the train when you and I were younger in spite of the day of rain.

Now years have passed. I see you standing there smiling allright.
A beautiful memory that fades in the night.
When morning comes again I feel we are together.
I hear the train whistle blow. I hear you say "We will have falling weather."

Often I go and stand near the railroad track, now I know that you have come back. I see you smile.
You have gone that extra mile to return to be with me forever and ever.

Crystel Smith
GOODBYE
You left last night not to return.
I knew that was our last night together,
but I wasn't concerned.
I've held your hand and kissed your lips for the last time.
We've had so many barriers to conquer, so many mountains to climb.
Somehow we've managed to triumph through it all;
Together we made it, not once did we fall.
Now our love must withstand the

ultimate test.
The test of time is the scarriest, I do confess.
But don't worry, my love for you will never fade;
In my heart and in my mind you will always stay.
So, when I said goodbye I didn't mean it . . . you see . . .
Goodbye is never goodbye, unless you want it to be.

Shirley Ann Redd
DON'T SHAKE HANDS!

What a con game it will lay on you, pretending to be your best friend; promising to stick by your side through situations of thick and thin. It will do just that and so much more once it seduce your confidence it will surely employ self-destruction to guard your door. Knowing of all your problems and how well they cloud your mind it will introduce you to a deceitful outlet of powers that shelters a selfish kind of love. Hypnotized and living in a daze; you are now addicted and will be manipulated to your outer limits by this fatal disguise. And whenever you lay down to sleep you will pray with hope of it's defeat. Your life as you've known it will never be the same for foolishly you have welcomed a lethal destruction to find shelter in your brain . . .

Mrs Ann Duren
MY LOVE

I lie and watch this love of mine, in the morning as he sleeps. I breathe a prayer of thanks and pray his love I'll keep. He reaches for me as he's sleeping and softly whispers my name. As I snuggle in his arms I realize once more what a shame. Of years of life I've wasted before I met this man. And yet in my heart I know it was all part of a plan. They say youth is wasted on the young and this I fully believe. For in my youth I didn't give love. I only knew how to receive. But now I give so freely the love that's in my heart. And I love him so completely, I pray we never part. But if he ever needs to be free, I know I'll just let go. And pretend it doesn't matter and never let him know. The pain that will be inside me, the way it will tear me apart. Because for the very first time, I've given love from the bottom of my heart.

Rosemary George Krieger
VIOLATED

I just can't believe—what a dreadful shock!
Is my only answer a purse with a lock?
I always try to be on guard,
But my whole body was suddenly jarred.
A victim of a pick-pocket crime . . .
This happened to me a second time.
It's a feeling you need to express
To be violated brings great distress.
What warning can I give to others
What can I say?
I'm told this terrible deed occurs many times each day.
We must all report anything suspicious
This could prevent an act that is vicious.
An incident may be very brief
But it brings long-lasting grief.
It's healthy to release anxious fears
Sometimes difficult to wipe away the tears.
To survive in a New York style world
You must always be aware
A responsibility all of us must share.
Thank God to be safe and sound
No physical damage and feet on the ground.

Ann Michele Rowland
THE FINER THINGS OF LIFE

To my niece Cindy who has filled my life with such joy and happiness. With all my love, Aunt Ann.

Children, A Husband, A Wife
A Friend, A Peer
A word of cheer,
A smile, A laugh, an embrace,
A morning dewdrop upon your face.
A moment of silence sitting by a warm fire
Holding hands in the twilight
A plane soaring higher.

The Ocean's peaceful sound
The snow falling to the ground.
The leaves crackling beneath a running fawn
The hopeful promise that comes with dawn.
A Child at prayer
The words, "I Care!"
The smiling glee in your eye
Knowing the Best is yet to come
As the years roll swiftly by!

Ruth Emma Taylor
JUST US THREE

We skipped and danced—just us three—
On the blustery shore of a salty sea—
And searched for dollars—made of sand—
Delicate shells—at the water's command—
That sail ashore on the topmost crest—
And quietly come at last to rest—
On the bosom of a glistening beach—
Yet ever just beyond our eager reach—
As we skipped and danced—just us three—
Long long ago—on the shore—of a restless sea—

Kelly Fisher
PAINT

An artist sits
Only to stare
At a canvas
That is bare

Time comes
And time goes
And the picture still
No one knows

Your voice is
All you need
For people to
Take heed

A thought turned
Into a word
Anything,
That can be heard

So draw for me a picture
If you would
One that only
You could

Wilbert B Ruff
THE POET

What a wonderful thing called poetry!
The rhyme and reason inside of me,
A recording for all to see
What has been and what can be.
With pen and paper and slight of hand,
I travel to some distant land
Where flowers bloom in winters snow;
Where rain falls on parched earth below.
The joy or sadness that I see
Live on in words that come from me.
Like a master, I direct the flow
Of places, faces, feelings I know.
Though I be a stranger, I can touch you so,
For such power with the poets go.
Then I return to my humble self.
My pen and paper lie on the shelf.
But inside of me is a small glow
Of satisfaction that we poets know.

Patricia Robertson Stem
FOREVERMORE

The day is dark.
Deep shadows extend
To all the corners of the earth.
The cries of pain and anguish
  have stilled to quiet moans and
  deep sobbing.
And through it all, the murmuring of
  His children can be heard.
"He is dead!" "He is gone!"

The sombre day is encompassed
  by the black of night.
And still, the sadness can be heard
  continuing on throughout the day to
  come.
"Alas! Alas!" The cries of helpless-ness
  can still be heard throughout the
  world.

Then suddenly, a ray of light shines brightly.
Giving hope to all the earth.
Shouts of glad Hosannas echoing throughout the land.
"My Lord!" "My Lord!"
He is alive! And so are we!

FOREVERMORE!!!

Olevia Hodge
THE WORLD LOVES A LOVER

The whole world loves a lover
Or so I've heard it said
But if you marry a lover
You will surely wish him dead.

Once you are married
His love should be only for you
If he still loves everybody
His love for you can't be true.

Love has many facets
The heart holds in store
Love for mother, father and children
And many, many more.

The love of a lover
Should be only for one
If your lover wanders
It's never any fun.

Try to find a lover
Whose love is only for you
And you will have a lover
That forever will be true.

Let the world have its lover
And bask in all its glory
When he's old and ugly
It'll be a different story.

Linda Love Warner
FINDING THE INNER PEACE

Dwell each day
  upon a peaceful scene
Allow mind and body
  to rest therein
Place thoughts gently
  upon each element
Experience fully
  noting color, scent, and feel

Bless and release
  mind distractions
Know true Being
  is light
Containing an unending Peace
  always available
When inner balance allows
  expanded perception

Margaret Ann Mills
FRIENDS

There are friends of many color,
There are friends of many creed;

But the best friend anyone can have
Is a friend when you're in need.

We had that kind of friendship in the past
A friendship we knew would always last.

Then I moved away and our friendship began to fade.

But we vowed to keep in touch,
Though other friends we made.

We had some happy times,
We had some sad times too;

But I know the Lord has blessed me
Because of a friend like you.

Huntley P Christie

Huntley P Christie
GOD'S GIFTS

To my lovely wife, the source of my life: Lerhlean Mildred Christie.

God has blessed me with a brain,
A brain to me that can't be seen,
Thoughts of this brain must be clean,
I must use this brain to honour God's name.

God has given me a mind,
An intelligent mind of the superior kind,

A mind that's pure, rich and fine,
To help my neighbor, to lead the blind.

God has given me a will,
And if His will I will fulfill,
He will abide with me still,
And protect me from all ill.

God has given me a soul that's fit for the sky,
No death can destroy it even though I die,
His mansion is prepared for me on high,
I'll claim it forever in the sweet bye-and-bye.

Dawna Osborne
WIND FROM THE SEA

I awake from the magic of the night.
A sunray fills my very soul,
With a beaming crystal light.
The wind from the sea blows soft and gentle
Through delicate lace in antique curtains.
Then like seagulls in flight,
Are lifted high and dance before me.
As a cool breath touches my face,
Nostrils fill with the sweet flavor of salinity.
In the distance can be heard;
The bounding of the main,
Touching white sands of grain,
With wet lapping kisses!
Will bovinity stand still?
My senses feel so right.
Rushing to greet the day.
On endless dreams in flight.

Roberta Spencer
FORGIVENESS

Forgiveness is a word that focuses on challenge of a solid form
Can we forget a moment that has ripped our hearts and left it torn

Can we continue on in lifes spun web, the way we did before
Can we repair the damage and lock away secrets behind closed doors

Or will we turn our hearts to stone and leave forgiveness out in the cold
Or will loves warmth bring forgiveness in and
embrace it as one of lifes treasures to hold

Mary E Coffey
RECOVERING

The sun came out again today
Did you notice all the light?
And did you hear the birds wake up?
Where do they sleep at night!!!

Have you ever paused and watched a tree
As it reaches for the sky
And tried to touch that peaceful blue
So far away,—so high

The pretty flowers everywhere
Each one a different hue
The stately mountains,—picturesque
Can all bring peace to you

The sharing of a family life
Associate,—a friend
Is all a major part of us
A means unto an end

The giving of a friendly smile
An offering of a hand
To laugh,—to cry,—to let them know
You want to understand

At one time, I had all of this
And things that I could buy
I took it all without a thought
And never questioned why

Eventually, the darkness came
'Twas not the dark of night
It was the bottom,—total loss
without a hint of light

The awful fear of hopelessness
Despair,—absence of GOD
No will to live, just one desire
To lie beneath the sod

And then the help from everyone
From those who still did care
I was the one who turned my back
But they were always there

And so today, I notice much
Also appreciate
The smallest and the least of things
I've found it's not too late

You see, I have another chance
To learn, to love, To give
I lost it once and now it's back
This time, I want to live

Mary Jo Frost
THE SEA—FIRST VISIT

I feel the wind upon my face
The sand on my bare feet.
I see the gulls that fly with grace
Out where the sand and water meet.

I hear the "slap, slap" of the waves
As they beat upon the sand
And the far off haunting sounds
Of the shrimpboats far from land.

I touch the water with my toes
And love the feel of it.
I start to walk and all at once!
I find it easier to sit.

The ocean with its mighty power
Has turned me upside down.
I scream for help, "I'm so afraid!"
It must be terrible to drown.

Then I open up my eyes and find,
The water has all gone
And I'm sitting all alone
On the sandy shore.

Martha Valencia
WHY?

For Richard, because he is the best part of my life.

The word is always why?
Why, did you let it happen?
How could it ever be?
How was it that you couldn't see,
how much you meant, and mean to me.

Donna W Paskin
THE FOOL

And there he sat, pondering his fate,
Mindless of the wasteland in his brain.
While bathed in silver sun on cloudless days,
He sighed and waited for the rain.
And as the rain fell, nourishing the land,
Sweet blossoms purpled clover fields again.
So in their midst he sat, misfortune's mate,
Perplexed, still pondering his fate.

Marie Law Haire
GARE SAINT-LAZARE (19TH CENTURY PAINTING BY EDUORD MANET)

Confinement.
Walls, locked doors.
No one escapes all.

A curious child
Wanders—
Wondering, dreaming—
Perceiving freedom
Beyond immediate confinement.

Adulthood, too often,
Brings complacency.
Walls and locked doors
Are ignored.
Is there reason to do otherwise?

Outside each wall,
Is another.
Outside each locked door,
Another.

Each door requires a unique key.
The complacent ignore.
No one obtains every key.

Terry Thompson
MY HEART

All the time that I've spent with you
I really hate the thought
That you and I are through
I know sometimes it's been tough
And there have been moments
That have been rough
All though I savor the marriage for a while
I can still sit there and smile
Because even though we are apart
You'll always be right next to my heart

Helen M Buschman

Helen M Buschman
A MOTHERS SOLILOQUY

Dedicated to my daughter Diana

The wedding dress hangs in the closet
With Its hoop-skirt ruffles and lace
As I sit here tonight alone dreaming
Of the glow on my sweet daughter's face.

Memories steal in of her child-hood
Oh! the innocent laughter and din,
A grace to charm the birds from the trees
Or loving friendship win.

Now She's building her nest with Her lover
And It's feathered deep with love;
In a bower fashioned of moon beams
Suspended from stars above

Though I haven't a part in this new scheme of things,
And would like to say I don't care,
Her mirror still gapes and the room fairly sings
Of Her presence every where.

I try to dismiss the noisy silence . . .
But try as ever I might,
My traunt heart in utter defiance
Insists on these memories tonight

Cheryl L King
REMEMBERING

I dedicate to "All My Children", Larry, Jeff, Sandy, and last, but not least, Robyn, with love.

Many things were left unsaid, bedtime stories never read.
Times I simply couldn't stay, appointments took me far away.

Then there's times you'd want to talk, throw a ball, or take a walk, and I would promise, "We'll have fun, soon as I get this project done".

So now the years have slipped away, there's no more kids around to play, no stories waiting to be read, no little ones to tuck in bed.

So, what I guess I've tried to say, please, never, ever, waste a day, for children are so very dear, let's cherish them, while they are near.

Now they've gone their separate way, there's lots of time to talk or play, and what I'd give for songs unsung, and the days when all my kids were young!

Jennifer Gerow
PAST TO PRESENT

I tried to walk the other way when I saw your face . . .
For if I didn't, I would remember your sweet
And warm embrace . . .
The night you said goodbye to me,
Is the night my heart had died . . .
For that is the first and last time,
I had ever broken down and cried . . .
I love you now more than ever,
Oh, how I love you so . . .
I guess I can't bear the thought,
Of having to let you go . . .
I should try to forget the past,
And let the present in . . .
So now I just decided that it will all begin.

Margaret Kittrell
BEAUTY OF LOVE

To Karen and Ted Martinez from your (mother) and in law.

The beauty of love is a wonderful thing
A lot of joy for two people it brings
To keep this love hold on real tight
And the love you share will carry
On through life.
It will ease a lot of trouble and strife.
It's God's own words to a man and wife

Lori R Couch
MEMORIES

He was a boy. He was a friend.
Why did his life have to end?
When I was sad or really blue
He made my smile shine brightly

through.
When the day was really bad
I was happy instead of sad.
In class one day he said to me
"I'm not afraid to be set free.
So when I die no tears you'll shed
I'm not afraid of deaths eternal bed."
Then that day he passed away
Now with God he'll always stay.

Rose Strahan
IN MY HEART
The ones I knew not were all around,
Yet my own were not in town
Lord is it this what was meant all this time?
Who is my mother?
Who is my brother?
When my children are far away.
In my heart they are there to stay
Always when we are apart,
I know they are right here in my heart.

Peggy Ambrisco
FOREVER #1
Lost to the lascivious eye is forever's end
falsely courted in a youthful, senile haze.
Teased by green ripe streams of love
and entranced by ligaments
stretched to their grace.
Decaying coffins locked in keyless, dusky vaults
and green-haired soil
camouflaged from invasive tools.
Soothing strains of voice and busy, sightless eyes
tender an ignorant bliss of
always tomorrows.
Mesmerized by false security of vital, absolute worth
exaggerated by fantasia of
eternal, earth welcome.
As yet a guileless Quietus a no-show player as we
in simplistic glee prime bodies
for the quintessential game.
Autistically unaware of rules and compulsory debt payment
we intrigue stratagems with
delusional ardor.
But as the great, dead Bard nailed it upon a time
"Lord, what fools . . . "
Thinking forfeit we pace erratic guffawing strained taunts
till tunnel-visioned eyes open in periphery.
But now too late to see the merciless champion of infinity
with hollow smirk and rasping rattle
blindside us to win again.

Karen F Johnson
FREEDOM
Watching the trees sway,
as sun shines on the ground.
See the beauty of nature,
so much life is to be found.

As the day goes on,
the animals are to release
and wander about each other
searching for their peace.

The animals in the forest
were meant to be.
Let's not bother them,
they were made to be wild and
free!

Amit Bando Padhay
BEGINNINGS
Lyrics are fine
When they mean something;
My words, like the desert winds
Build no mountain, carve no gorge
Make a fuss, with crumbling sand
Die down without a trace.

Sometimes, after a dry day (or month, or year)
I want to let out
The demon wailing the passage of my time
In a lightless space, eyes closed
Treading the flow, I dare not go
Dare not reach the calm depths below.

Be my rock
Timeless in the rapids
Cool and certain.
Like nascent moss, by your side
Making inroads to your porous heart
I will sing a different song.

Maxine Neilsen

Maxine Neilsen
MOTHER
With tenderness you nursed me
Through sickness and through strife.
With gentleness of manner
You brought cheer into my life.
Though your eyes have lost their sparkle,
Though your hair is turning gray,
And your brow has tell-tale wrinkles
Caused from worry, day by day,
You are still the same sweet Mother
With the smile that I adore.
There could never be another,
If I searched forever more.

Ivan O Baker
POETASTER'S DISASTER
There once was a poetry buff,
Who wrote rather asinine stuff.
So when he went broke,
He got up and spoke,
"This is certainly life in the rough."

Richard J Treadaway
ROSE

To my wonderful mother—Huttie Mae Treadaway

As the morning breaks and the sun comes shining thru;
My heart goes out to the one with a love so true.
I long to hold and tell you how much i care;
But something inside says i should not dare.
I watch the wind blowing through your hair;
And i smell your fragrance in the air.
Then i see tears flowing from your eyes,
And you tell me to look up in the skies.
The clouds are gathering, and the north wind starts to blow,
Our hearts cry out to each other;
For we know it will soon start to snow.
The pain is almost too great to bear
But I must go on.
Tonight my rose will be dead;
And i will be alone.

Ann Swan
MY DAUGHTER, LEEANN

To my loving daughter, Leeann, the apple of my eye.

How beautiful you are
And so full of life.
A part of me,
That was finally meant to be.
Your soft golden hair,
Sways softly with the breeze;
As you romp and play,
Without a care in the world.
You bring so much joy
To those around you.
You have brought a great
Richness to my life.
Your tender words as you embrace me and say
"I love you mommie"
You're not always sweet
As little girls should be.
Sometimes you're a little devil,
And naughty as can be.
But your my Leeann
And very precious to me.

Jennie C Melmed
SUNLIT SHALLOWS

To Caryn Gibbins—Though you are far away, you will always be near me.

The sunlight sparkles
On the gold dust 'neath the sea
Iridescent fish
Flashing by in a moment
Whirling and swirling
In the aqua brilliance
In sunlit shallows

Houston H Stanley
A CHILD IS BORN

For Olivia our child and Elsie who made her possible.

Curious faces, moans and traces of her mother come to mind
My roll as dad, I've never had, has pride,
but little time

While new to us, the obvious, seems astonishing at times
A hint of one another lets us know she's yours and mine

It may be just the kid in me or the child before my eyes
For once I know without a doubt there are
no stronger ties

The joy she brings reminds us of the price
we both must pay
Eternal dedication for a child is born today

The New Jerusalem Project Group
O' JERUSALEM

This poem is dedicated to The New Group of World Servers and Workers of The New World Religion

In lifting thee up as an International Peace City within our heart and Mind
One helps humanity walk a little further upon the path of peace.
For too long religions and nations have fought over thy glory and ignored thy bounty.
No longer must one, as a soul, be condemned to wander the corridors of time bereft of earthly guidance and one's eternal home.

Thou has been a home and true inspiration more than any other.
At times humanity has trampled thy eternal truths making thee an abysmal mire of falsehoods.
Many old and new souls have learned their needed lessons and are stepping forth to redeem thy honor in exalting thee as an
International Peace City to create World Religious unity and World Peace.

No where else have individuals and the masses been lifted up to the highest heights, but by the attainment of their salvation through thee.
Not once, but three (Jewish, Moslem, Christian) times humanity has bourne witness and been moved by revelations related to thee's sacredness.

O' Jerusalem
In raising thee from a divided and strife-torn city to the status of an
International Peace City
We raise ourselves and our world from the lowest to the highest
thereby consecrating THE NEW JERUSALEM.

William Michael Mullen
HARMONIZE

Love liberates lost souls while it also affords us the opportunity to appreciate our lives to the fullest. Come hell or high water, Love will insulate or inspire you to swim. For you, love.

Thoughts
Like shattered glass
Curse the mad-man's sanity
Pain torments
This fragmented flesh,
To whom our reality,
Is but another sliver of anguish.
Bring forth the puzzle makers,
The architect,
The brainbuilder,
Who will place the shards
Back in the window frame.
The howling cannot pierce
Re-assembled clarity.

Josephine Miceli
I WENT OUTSIDE TO CHECK THE WIND

To Margaret Spurlock, my sister To Ogla Noverola, dearest friend For love and care.

I went outside to check the wind,
Wondered what the day would bring,
Looked for God near and far,
Found Him in the morning star.

Charmaine R Vogt
TO SMALL BOYS

To Charmaine, my dear daughter

Two boys, very small.
Holding their future, within their hands.

One showing promise of scholarship,
The other promise of sportsmanship.

Small hands, guide your way,
Towards God's gifts given to thee.

For everyone from beginning to end.
Have power of greatness,
Beyond
thy
thoughts.

Brian W Osborn
WHALES
Great ripples in the water,
the flash of a tale
witnessed: the diving of a whale.

I've seen such great creatures,
indeed many times,
swimming the oceans of my mind;
personality of a puppy,
perseverance of a child.

Should I swim that water
would they treat me with kind?
Approach from the front or behind?

Ripples! Waves—Great splashes I see;
Great leaps toward the heavens
loud crashes to deep,
those heroes I feel I have known in my mind—
Great whales of the north
I knew as a child.

Should you go in to swim you may feel them beneath,
their presence often but a swell.

Like friends we have known or
dreams we have lost or
the twinkling of stars in the night.

I've known many whales in my time

Lori Mansouri
TO SAY IT WITH LOVE
To say it with love, means that it comes from the heart
To say it with love, means you will never part
To say it with love, means that you care
To say it with love, means you will always be there
To say it with love, means you will give it your all
To say it with love, means no matter how small
To say it with love, means you'll say it out loud
To say it with love, means you'll say it so proud
To say it with love, means having family and friends
To say it with love, means you hope it never ends
To say it with love, means happy not sad
To say it with love, means you take the good with the bad
To say it with love, means you will always stay
To say it with love, means you will never go away
To say it with love, means not lots of money
To say it with love, means just holding your honey
To say it with love, means a special place
To say it with love, means looking in ones face
To say it with love, means to cherish the sun
To say it with love, means having lots of fun
To say it with love, means it takes more than just one

Edith F Kilday
BLUES
I love you in every way
from morning until evening
You are in my thoughts
Why am I so blue?
For you are there and I am here, all alone.
Waiting to hear you drive
in the driveway.
Come in—put your arms, around me.
Give me that embrace, and kiss.
No-more-Blues.

Yvonne Lee Fiske
HOME SWEET HOME
When something happens
When something goes wrong,
We can't be angry
We have to be strong.

When we're on this walk of life
It is all like a story,
We have our ups and downs
And still face it with glory.

When you're on the streets
Trying to make it on your own,
Picking up pennies on sidewalks
People look at you and know you're alone.

When you know you can make it
Always reaching out for something,
But you're looking in all the wrong places
And you find you're left with nothing.

After years go by,
And you see how much you've grown,
You just can't stop thinking about
What's going on at Home Sweet Home.

Rose M Pendola
SPRING
I stood there in the doorway,
It seemed just a moment, caught in time
Forever mine, forever mine.
They sky was a shattering blue,
The trees just bursting to renew,
The grass so green, the perfection of that scene,
It had to be a dream.
And yet I knew that, by God's grace
I held that perfect moment,
The wonder of which must
have shown on my face.

James Know Millen
LEGACY
I think you were a strange, sweet child who sought
With too small hands too large imaginings
To build big worlds, bright worlds.
Time passed, time brought
Lost hopes, dead years, sad goalless wanderings.
But you had courage. Even then, distraught,
You found small stones of faith, used stuccoings
Of dreams to round the wall, and out of naught
Built a new world of loved and little things.

And now I come so late, you welcome me;
Tell me we're secret safe behind your wall;
Show me your treasures; shells, a crooked tree,
"Stay with me here," you whisper, "Share it all."

How can I hide me in your child's domain?
Or say, "Come out," and chance new grief, new pain?

Rana LaVerda Cornell
THAT LOVELY PINK ROSE!
I look out my window and what do I see?
A flower is blooming
a puzzle to me.
I wonder if a miracle to be
the lovely pink rose would
keep glowing for me?
So breezy, so delicate, so lovely and kind,
A picture that would never be erased from my mind.
That lovely pink rose!

Teresa C Jillard
A CHILD IN THE MAN
Watching you sleep
I can see the child
in the man
And the man
in the child
So peaceful and handsome you are
Lying there beside me
So sweetly asleep
When I curl my body
Up next to yours
I find comfort and protection
In the arms of my love
While the child in you
Seems to find comfort
In the company of another
That once was your stuffed bear
(or your mother)
And now is me.
Good night. Sleep well,
my sweet prince.
I love you.

Jonathan D Silver
THE GAME
On a bright day without sunshine,
at the hour before time,
the ALL THAT IS spoke and
gave out a small rhyme,

I'll make of ME playmates,
We'll have us some fun,
and as of this moment
the game has begun.

You're allowed all your freedom
to BE all that you can,
across both the physical,
and spiritual band.

But the game's NEVER over
and it cannot be called,
until that sweet moment,
when we're all ONE IN ALL.

Terry L Rivera
ATTITUDES
I heard a child say thank you
While at lunch the other day.
It shouldn't have surprised me,
But it did, I'm sorry to say.

Then a friend brought daffodils
And the sun began to shine.
It made me start to wonder
If the fault might not me mine.

Like others, was I programmed
To see the bitter and the sad?
Could I no longer recognize
The joyful and the glad?

How long since I had listened
To the birdsong greet the birth
Of a fresh new day brought forward
On our struggling, faithful earth?

If I can't solve all the problems,
Perhaps I'll dent a few.
The place to start, it seems to me,
Is a change in attitude.

Earl S Teasley

Earl S Teasley
LIGHT OF A SHADOW

I would like to dedicate this poem to Kim R. Haley for her faith in me.

In a world of shadows I have found light,
Within the realm of nothing I have found something

Can it be he who seeks from the mind, and not the soul, he who will never find the light

With the rise, and fall of each setting sun
Before our eyes is the miracle of life,
A part of life taken for granted. For without the rising of the sun we would all be in the Shadows

The soul is forever, as the body is only for now. Therefore can it be that emotions of the body is only for now and that of the soul forever?

If all that is written is true then only that which we feel from the soul is forever, and everything else is an illusion of life

Lorene McBroom
LETTING GO
The Sails glide across the blue
waters suspended in space
All alone, in gentle motions I see
reflections of your face

Suddenly, the waves get restless and
rock the beautiful yacht—
The clouds form an image of
memories with lessons to be taught

I see the eagles creating a circle that
shall cast a magic spell
And there lies secrets deep within,
too mystical to tell

The seas emotions begin to quiet in a calm breeze,
A stillness takes you to a peaceful flow
Openness to guidance surrounding
we shall know the way to go

I hear music with entity voices
reaching out to take my hand
In the clouds of pureness, my soul
begins to understand

The voyage of this long journey as
we travel and reach for stars
Is beyond man's comprehension, it
already is ours

We experience emotions straight from the heart
Lack of understanding keeps the world apart

Understanding of Love is that we let it be free
Humans on this earth have not loved unconditionally

To love is to let go and let a person be, this in our hearts
We truly need to see

We seem to hold on when we need to let go—fears,
Insecurities, no faith makes it so

We need to learn to let go—

S L Barrett
MYSTERY OF THE ROPE
The wind blows
Through the caves of my heart,
The screams of sacrificed passions.
The tears start.
My eyes behold the darkness,
Like cold steel, it impales.
My mind can not recover
All memory fails.
The death of all ambition
Like snows that melt in spring,
But no new flowers linger
To soothe the final sting.
Mediocrity it settles
And steals life's living hope,
And I, in sadness ponder,
The mystery of the rope.

Catherine A Radtke
FALSE PRETENSE
Is it fair to love you as much—
yet do without
Is it fair to want you as much—
yet go without
Is it fair, I ask, for you not to know—
for me not to tell?

Must we love just as friends
at a distance . . . not too close
A touch of the hand
a smile
a hug now and then?

Do you know
Do you feel
Do you sense
I wonder, if my eyes don't give away
this false pretense.

Mary Goff
OLD TREE
Old tree I stand in awe
And look at thee,
Thou art so tall
I am so small . . .

In winter when
The cold wind blows,
Thou shields me from
The falling snow . . .

In summertime
When day is done,
Thou shields me from
The blazing sun . . .

So many things
Thou gives to me,
Thou has been blest
Old tree, old tree . . .

Le Roy Manlove
A REBIRTH
The little worm was down on luck
and tired of crawling through
the muck.
It spun itself a place to rest;
God paid a visit to its nest.

The worm awakened; wriggled out to view
a world that had taken a
different hue.
Transformed, it stretched its wings to fly,
for it had emerged a butterfly!

Maria Kuster
WHAT AMERICA MEANS TO ME
What does America mean to me?
It means the blowing and waving of the American Flag in the breeze.
And the American Eagle flying free over the plains, the mountain tops, and the flowing rivers.

It means choosing what I want to study in school.
Where I want to live and what I want to be when I grow up.

Driving through the countryside.
Seeing the crops, and the livestock.
This is the freedom when farmers exercise their right of free enterprise.

American also beautiful grass-lands, forests, parks, and lakes I'm free to visit and enjoy anytime I choose.

America means freedom—
Freedom for me to be me.

Thomas R Witman
NORTH STAR
You are my North Star
You have guided me
When I was lost
You have brightened
Up my night sky
And in the day
Your twinkle remains in my eye
You are my North Star
As I look up and gaze upon you
And wishing the time will never come
For you to leave
Your luminous sky

For then I will grieve
But I will always remember
You once shined on me
You are my North Star
And with all your glitter
You shared with me
You are the brightest star
In my galaxy
Although our distance may be afar
You'll always be, my North Star

Mary F Schawe
TO BETTS
To Betts,
A son is great to lean on
when the going gets rough.
They're strong and sure and steady
thank God they're also tough.

But daughters Betts, are something else
I've learned thru-out the years.
They help celebrate your many joys and comfort you thru tears.

You're closer to their children
because they seem to know.
How important it is to have grandparents
help their children grow.

And as daughters become mature
and mothers mellow down.
They realize that daughters are
best friends to have around.
Lots of Love
Mom

Sonoma Young Toolson

Sonoma Young Toolson
CHINESE FORGET-ME-NOTS
Lovely little blooms of blue
I wonder when I gaze at you
Where you got your pretty faces,
Your gowns of blue with bits of laces,
Your centers all of pink and rose
Each resembles a tiny nose,
But I wonder even more, I guess,
Not only about your dainty dress
Your pretty face and rare perfume,
But how through winter's ice and snow
What miracle would make you grow
In spring.

Debra A Bain-Hatcher
MY SON
There is nothing more precious than you Little one.
Your little face brightens my day.
Your little smile lights up the way.
You're a bundle of Love.
You're a bundle of Joy.
You are my little Boy.
A precious gift sent from Heaven above.
You fill our hearts with laughter and love.
You are truly a gift sent from above.
My Son you are very much Loved!!!

Tatyana Y Goldenberg
HAUNTING VENGEANCE
Alas, my victory has come and I,
I stand above the foe whom I have slain.
I wonder why it pained to watch him die?
Why hurt for someone whom I've killed in vain?

His coward pride and greedy way of life,
Had marked him dead long 'fore he hurt me so.
His twisted mind caught me within a strife,
And trapped—I had nowhere else to go.

The shot will always echo through my mind.
The smoking gun forever will I see.
Disturbed am I for peace I never find,
And wonder I—what now becomes of me.

I did what I knew I'd to do and yet,
I know that now my sun will also set.

Alyse M Herasimchuk
SUICIDE
Taking a trip along the road,
thinking of the memories all so slow.
One by one the tears await,
only to turn into hate.
Thinking if anyone cared, or
if they even knew I had been so scared.
I started to cut thinking of heaven above: Oh Lord, Oh Lord, please take me now for I wish not another chance, just take me away from this awful romance.
Drugs it was, this awful romance, which I thought it led me somewhere, but ending up nowhere.
Now in heaven where I wished so much to be, the only thing I wish now, is what I could of seen, which was my future so far ahead of me.

Betty L Smith
INTOLERANCE
When logic is applied to matters not
Of pure intelligence: No bound
Is there to horrible error, the lot
Of Hapless man caught in this evil round.
The tyranny that we ourselves do make;
When through the logical error of hate
A Common belief as the truth we take.
Real truth in its entirety will be late.
That troubling man of truth who must dissent,
While he does not accept the status quo,
The common belief he does yet prevent,
What he still professes we would not know.
This truth of ours it will remain arrears
Unless this man recants or disappears.

Marjorie R Wiley
GOOD THOUGHTS
Any day's a good day,
To sit and reminisce.
And think about the good 'ol times,
And all the things we miss.

Good memories may fade away,
If never brought to mind.
So take a moment now and then,
And let your thoughts unwind.

Recall to mind the better times,
Even if it's been awhile.
For memories are like good friends,
They always bring a smile.

Walter J Woodman
THE CITY
The city throbs with steel-brick heart,
A massive tangled network of broken tar,
A huge dark conglomerous mass,
Of flashing lights and shining windowpanes.

Its voice, its spirit, is the gleaming head-lights of passing coughing cars.
Smoke hugs its middle in soot-gripped
Tenderness and the chimneys chug and spit the
Black heavy gases of manufactured progress.

A soft white snow descends on the city.
From the purple-gray skies it rains.
A think veiled mist blankets the sordidness
Of concrete and marble in purest virginity.

Then the first faint light of morning sun,
Cuts across the opacity and the city breathes
Again and multi-colored machines
Rip through the frozen splendour turning it to mush.

And thus it is, beginning each day,
The city learns anew, a thousand different ways
To destroy itself and the animals that
Gnaw its filthy guts.

Claudette Seals

Claudette Seals
BEST FRIENDS

This poem was written for my friend Dan who came along in life, just in time and just sweet enough, to restore my faith.

Years have gone by, I have tried to forget
that I ever knew about you.
This has proven a task too large for me
the hardest thing i've ever tried to do.

I will never forget your thoughtfulness,
your gentleness, your affection . . .
You are dependable, generous, helpful, wise
A positively choice selection.

I hope you are happy as I think of you
Your ear surgery a success,
and your marriage too.

There are no regrets for having known someone like you
My life felt rich and full with you in it.
Many thoughts of you make me feel good too.

I made a terrible mess of things at the end
I only wanted to send you home to your wife again.
I know I could never be happy at her expense
The whole thing started not to make sense.

I've settled down now, cooled out, and sort of feel reborn
I am your best friend still, you were surely mine at one time

These verses are not "Barley Corn"

Peggy Skinner
UNTITLED
The night fell like a blanket upon a sleeping child.
And as lovers awaken to be enthralled into the spell of the night,
The wrath of loneliness looms near the core of my heart.
The forgotten soul of remembrance, never recalled.
The wretched anguish leaning so near, always felt.
The tears that have died and the tears that have been shed,
Are like weights forever upon me.
And this night I remember the ultimate downfall of my world.
Like the shattering of mirrors, it tumbled.
'Tis the day when I ask, "Who am I."
And hear nothing but undistinguished silence.
"Oh won't someone pick up the pieces?"
Or shall they forever lay
Sharp and taunting, and never forgotten.

A D Mack
FRIEND
A shoulder to cry on,
An ear to lend.
A smile to lighten, brighten,
and cheer the day.

A compassionate heart,
A helping hand.
Encouraging support, no matter your stand.

A generous nature,
A giving will;
Someone to stand by you, from now until.

Warm and precious,
Loving and kind;
A multitude of thoughts to mind.

There's none so fair,
So kind, so sweet;
As a friend who's there,
When you're most in need.

If I, at all else fail,
Will You, Maker of men,
Make me successful, at being a friend.

Paula M Wise
TO BE
To be is what I've always wanted;
but somehow, I end up in the middle.
To be is what I've always seen;
but never able to touch.
To be is where I've always dreamed of;
but have never been able to see.
To be is within an arms length;
but I've never been able to touch.
To be is something I've always cried for.
To be echoes within my soul.
The strangest thing is
To be haunts my very existence.
All I want is to be me.

Dorothy Pearson Chambers
A HIDDEN MESSAGE
Queen Ann's lace is now observed all
Over God's earth
It so gently waves giving thanks
For its birth
Viewed with a purple flower by the
Side of the road
It is the more majestic and graceful
In its abode
Some say these flowers are not important
Being a weed
But God placed them here with glory for
Us to heed
It tells us that everythings is meant to
Blend as one
Regardless of stature each has beauty—
A song to be sung!

Robert C Howes Sr
CHRISTMAS
Christmas comes but once a year
bringing spiritual love and lots of cheer;
a glass of eggnog with ones so dear,
the happiness of giving with families near.
Girls and boys gets lots of toys
that clatter and clank and make other noise.
There's gaiety and laughter and smiles on their faces
as we open our presents of bright frills and laces.
The food that we eat and the things that we drink
should make our hearts warmer and make our minds think,
that we should give thanks for our gifts of love
by praying and praising our Lord up above!

Jessica Bickford
THE OLD PASTURE
The old pasture where the horse used to roam.

Oh, how it's grown. The fence is falling down.

It sort of looks kind of brown.
When I walked by the horse I used to say hi.

But now it's good-bye.

I guess that's the end of that old pasture.

Mary Ruth Easley
THAT LONELY PLACE
That lonely place where only God can be;
Where human mind fades out—
nothing can he see.
Nothing real, nothing to gain;
Only a few minutes of eradicated pain.

Then back to himself—a mental hell;
Satan laughs—he had one under his spell!

But God is more powerful—He protected His own;
He gave him light to lead him home.
He gave him thoughts to never do it again,
To not let Satan tempt him again and again.

One was saved when he accepted the light.
Many yield to Satan falling to the darkness of night.
Complete darkness—no way—not even a line,
Life on earth lost, nothing can they find!

Bobby Thoburn
A THOUGHT . . .
A thought entered into my head.
The moment was shattered, now it is dead.
Where did it go to? Where did it run?
Maybe just looking for its place in the sun.
Or forever destined to flitter and roam
It frantically searched for a brain to call home.
Oh, how I wish I had written it down.
I've searched every neuron, it just can't be found.
Now only vague memories stir in my brain
and I may never know that thought again.

Beth E Ward
THE HEAT WITHIN
I can't control the heat within,
stop it from consuming me
and making my brain cease to function
when you are anywhere near.

My breath is taken away from me,
My skin is alive
my knees are weak
and the tingling starts again.

I can't talk, or hear, or move
until you break the stare
and walk away
to leave me in a daze.

J A Hollinger
SATURATION POINT
Caring and concerned about others,
Like a twin sister to the world.
How often she's said, "if you need to talk, call."
Pressures keep mounting and friends need to unload;
They know they can cry on her shoulder—
Her shoulder, like a sponge,
absorbing the tears of frustration.
Sometimes their problems become her own.
But even she reaches the limit—the saturation point.
Do they ever stop to think:
A sponge needs to wring itself dry?

Lisa M Ruggiero
THIS MEMORY WILL REMAIN
Many children suffer the hand
of a cold hearted adult.
Can a five year old understand
something so difficult?

Yes, the child understands
the sense of wrong and right,
and wrong are the demands
she complies to every night.

For daddy will always remember
where his victim sleeps at night,
without fail he will not spare her
another night of fright.

The pain goes on forever,
the crime never revealed.
Daddy was so clever
to make sure her lips were sealed.

Her entire life will hold
the secret of such pain
and always in her mind,
this memory will remain.

Patricia A Bish
REMEMBERING
Speak softly my friend as you remind me of times so long ago.

Of sunlit mornings and starlight nights and plans of where we'd go.

Speak softly my friend as you remind me of times so long ago.

Of golden grain fields and a house on a hill and a boy I used to know.

Speak softly my friend as you remind me of times so long ago.

Of a boy's farfetched dreams of a girl down the lane and hers of him also.

Speak softly my friend as you remind me of times so long ago.

Of a boy's gentle touch and loving brown eyes and the sadness when the girl had to go.

Speak softly my friend as you remind me of times so long ago.

Of a love that's lasted a lifetime though they were always apart.

Of a love that will always be there, held closely in their hearts.

Victoria Adams
THE CLOCK
The clock ticks time silently away,
you can't go home.
Some days are just days we need to be alone.
The wheel of fortune spins around
and your fortune will be told,
an endless night of loving you for
you are more precious than gold.
God put you on this earth so you
could love before
He takes you back to His heaven
above, so darling love me so I'll
know you'll stay while the clock
ticks time silently away.

Brenda Apgar
DRAGON DREAMS
Once there was a dragon
who roamed an endless sea
the sea in which he swam
was unknown to you and me.

He lived inside a child's mind
and haunted channels there
and the little child saw him
when no one else was there.

They took, together, many trips
and journeyed far and wide
inside a magic dreamland
where only they could abide.

But then there came a day
when the boy had left this place
and the dragon still roams alone
in the vast and empty space.

Dragon dreams live on
inside many minds today
still roaming evermore
though carefully tucked away

Andrea Lea Zuberka
EVEN THOUGH WE JUST MET
Even though we just met,
We know each other so well.
I'm looking for a relationship,
With you it's hard to tell.

You seem so forward,
and I seem so shy.
Please slow down,
You're scaring me, that's why.

Please don't rush me,
I want to move slow.
The love we will build,
Was meant for us to know.

I don't want you to love me,
Then let me go.
I want this to last,
And I thought you should know.

Please give it your best,
I'll give it my best too.
If all else fails,
I'll still remember you.

Kevin Stephen Ignatious Bruce

Kevin Stephen Ignatious Bruce
AIN'T NO MOUNTAIN HIGH ENOUGH

I would like to dedicate this poem to Debbie L. McNulty of West Roxbury, Mass. We met at a Catholic orphanage called Nazareth Holy Childhood School in Jamaica Plain. She blessed my life in many ways and someday I hope she'll understand.

Velvet tears and diamond eyes.
Stars twinkle in dark blue skies.
Beyond a search there's a peak.
Many people have yet to seek.
Snow top and green valley below,

Echo's sounds as sweet as mellow.
Many people have asked to come.
But the Lord said unto them, "You
have only just begun.
Air your air, wash your water and
clean your land.
Above all, make peace and love as
smooth as sand."

Helen Walpole Brewer
DEAR JANE AUSTEN
Fondly, she is called the writer's writer,
The artist who triumphs in miniature,
Her gift Character, her discernment sure;
In England her monument is brighter
In her fame being safe in the lighter
Comedic content. Her novels a lure
To young taste, their bad taste to cure.
Our Jane is a romantic, of wit higher

Than scathing, they say; but her story-line
Of Heroine—though she disdain the term—
And Hero—though interesting is he—
Gives happy delight to the reading mind:
For Sense wars with folly in goodness firm:
Her rich small world—
Universality.

Sylvia Norris
MY DAUGHTER
Little flower, bud of my own
It is sad for me to see
How quickly time has flown
Taking my rose from me.

If I have failed at any time
To show the love in my heart,
Forgive this fault of mine
For I adored you from the start.

God gave me you, little flower,
To guide the best I could.
And with the aid of his power
I try to do as I should.

If I am wrong once in awhile,
Try to understand why,
And answer me with a smile,
For the moment passes by.

Being a mother is my role,
But being perfect is not.
Understand my human soul,
Forget things best forgot.

Love is the most important of all
And this I surely have for you.
I will always answer your call
And try to see you through.

And when at last I must go
To the garden of rest.
You and I will always know,
That I loved you best.

Tommie Hayes
RAZOR BLADE
I see a silvery devil with all sides sharp.
I see black hole hearing a golden harp.
I know not what awaits the fate as such as I, because I only see what cuts me like a KNIFE.
I want to pull that silvery devil across my aching veins, but do I want to know such as that pain.

I think I do not want to know, because what would I really show.
I think I would end the hurt, pain and despair, but what I would cause could never be repaired.
Oh, I scream so loud but no one notices and no one cares, but the silvery devil and the black hole that is beginning to snare.

Michelle Holt
NOW THAT I'M GONE
You got what you wanted
For me to go away
Never to come back
For a visit or to stay.

You just had to do it
Always having the say.
You just couldn't leave me alone
You had to have your way.

Now that I'm gone
You have nothing to fear.
For I'm not close enough
So my voice you will not hear.

I wish it didn't happen
For I am all alone.
With only a few friends
But no family of my own.

Linda I Potter Scalise
I LIVE RIGHT

With love, to my wonderful Husband, and son, Tom & Keith—whom are always there when I need you!

I live right, yet it's wrong.
I sing but, there's no song.

I talk and say, not a thing.
I hear the phone, but it doesn't ring.

I walk and yet, get nowhere.
I worry, but without a care.

I see, but still it's dark.
To me a fire, is only a spark.

I listen, but I can't hear.
It seems so far, but yet it's near.

I smell, but there is no scent.
Straight I stand, but yet I'm bent.

I eat, but there is no taste.
I go slow, but yet with haste.

I think, but without a thought.
I have nothing, but yet a lot.

I touch and cannot feel.
I live my life, but not for real!

Susan Vancelette
ESTRANGEMENT

This poem is dedicated to Laura, and to supporting friends . . . who have restored my faith in life's beneficence.

The sadness of it
Lingers on and on
Through days and nights
And weeks and months
Until I face a truth
As proved by its stubborn existence.
So determined am I
To say it holds no bearing
On the two of us
That I write of "it"
Which has died between
You and me and is now

"Marriage/ 'mar-ij/
1. an expectation 2. an exaggerated myth 3. a bond that binds until asphyxiation occurs."

Steve F Terry
WHOEVER
Meat in the smoke house,
Beans on the shelf
I'm getting tired of sleeping
By myself!

Lori Lemke
THE HURT
I know you don't believe me,
But I didn't mean to hurt you.
The look in your eyes,
Made me wish I could take back those words.
It's too late now—
I've regretted hurting you so many times.
There was no reason,
I was afraid you would hurt me first.

I think about what could've been,
And it hurts me so much.
I try to tell myself,
That it's better this way,
We weren't meant for each other.
But it just doesn't help,
Because things might have worked out—
If I gave you a chance.

Beverly Chong
DREAMS
Once I sat upon a chair,
I began to be unaware;

It was though I was dazed,
Boy, was I amazed!

To be granted three wishes
by a ghost,
And then to be greeted
with a toast.

I thought it was my lucky day,
On this fourth of May;

But all things have to be earned,
For whom it concerned.

And that's how I was blessed,
When the truth was confessed.

Bessie Williams

Bessie Williams
LIFE
Life is just a promise
Life is but a dream
Life is sometimes a mystery
Not always what it seems

Life must be treasured
Live each day in stride
Thank God for your blessings
For you only have one life

When life's treasure is over
No more can be done
You have loved abundantly
Under life's setting sun

Smile because God loves you
No matter who you are
Just like his precious child
Riding on a star

Robin L Kidd
REFLECTIONS
Look unto tomorrow
As a dream to come,
And yesterday
As a memory passed.
But don't neglect
To see the light of today.
For today can make a dream come
true,
And a memory last.

C E Elliott
NICHOLAS
Nicholas,
Whenever you return to your
homeland,
A bise, a cold breeze drifts in
Making me breathless
Clouding the enchanting forests
Nestled in my mind.

Memories of your rich green country
Dapple the edge of my soul.
The natural balance of nature, fresh
air,
Edelweiss, fields, trees, streams,
mountains.
I remember a lovely tapestry.

As you leave, a cold force marches
in.
The mountain dragons, Celts, swords
and torches
Are all jumbled in my heart and
mind.
I feel as though I am ascending the
Matterhorn.
Climbing the highest mountain of all
without you
Upward.
Possibly never to see you again.
Clouds gathering
Heavy mist blots out my visibility
But not the memory of your warm
face,
Your wise thoughts.

Your face is the birthplace of my
strength.
Your presence lives in my heart.
I remember your tradition of bravery.
I must reach the peak and descend
the towering mountain.

The cold snow cannot freeze the
burning
Trust in my heart.
I will conquer this battle
We will again reunite.

We are all people, all the same.
We all love, feel joy, experience
pain.
We must tear down the barriers
And find Peace,
If this small planet is to survive.

I recall your hūmanness
Your day to day protection of me.
You are solid, spiritual
Only good comes from you.

I will descend, unscarred.
In my panic
You are the tamer of my soul.
You will capture me in the landing
place
Of my trials.

You are my haven, my hero, my
escape.
The bise will be swept away by
A warm wind.
The fohn will carry you closer to me.
You will once again cross the
shining ocean,
And return to me with a joyous
collection
Of oneness, life, celebration, unity.

No matter which country we are
from
We will be one.
Touching, joining together.
Seeing all children as brother.
One family.

Oh Nicholas, my soul is richly
carpeted
With your garden of Peace.
We must cultivate this garden
To cover all the Earth.
The World must be blanketed with
Flowers of Peace
If we are to survive.

Dream it, enjoy it, live it.
Begin with love.
Begin with us.
Begin now, for us all.

Michael Warren Stauffer
DISTORTED, DEMONIC FIGURES
Distorted, demonic figures
riding ancient, equestrian images.
Galloping across the black plains of
my soul.
Lances and shields in hand,
wearing armor long since forged by
titans.
Screaming in archaic tongues.
Prepared to do battle . . . with who

Holy, angelic beings
riding chariots of old.
Spreading light over the blackness.
Innocence of birth,
covered in milleniums of bloodshed.
Wings spread high and far apart
prepared for battle . . .

Upon my soul, the armies meet,
light and darkness interlocked.
Chaos stirring deep within.
Forever untiring the battle is fought.
Neither defeated
Neither victorious,
and I forever the victim.

Gerald A Ritter
JANN
She cares for as a guest
her unborn child within.
Once model of a kind
having the title wife.
It's now different with her.
She has the name mother,
but model just the same,
praiseworthy effort, brave.

Cecil M Davis
THE DIARY OF OUR LIFE
Life is like a diary; we write a page
each day.
And the subjects we are using are
things we do and say.
As we write, if we would only stop
and think,
The pencils we are using are filled
with indelible ink!

We should all be careful of the
things we do and say,
For we may break a tender heart or
cause some soul to stray.
When each page is finished and
neatly filed away,
We just start another page for yet
another day.

And when this diary is finished, and
the editor reads the pages one by one,
We hope when he has read them that
he will say "well done;"
For God is our Editor and He will
carefully read it o'er.
We cannot change a single thing or
add just one page more.

Let us all be prayerful,
As we write our pages one by one,
So when our Lord has read them
He will say, "well done."

Floyd Lewis Baird Jr
THE SALT SPRAY ROSE
Sandy beaches, buried toes . . .
Will you wear this
Salt spray rose?
Fresh picked; wear it
In your hair and
I'll dream of you
On our sandy beaches
Of buried toes . . .

Marie Robinett
STROKES OF BRUSH
To see a piece of canvas bare
And picture scenes all painted
there,
'Tis gift that artists understand
When they take brush and
paints in hand
And create a likeness rare.

For no other can duplicate
Or even half appreciate
The thought that went behind it all
To make the lake or waterfall,
Or mountains tall and great.

Because with ev'ry stroke of brush
A bit of magic seems to rush
From artist heart to canvas white.
A bit of dark, a bit of light,
And, presto, meadows lush!

It doesn't always take a pro'
To take up brush and try to
show
What's deep inside a person's soul
That needs expression—half or
whole.
Just let the magic flow.

Angelia C Adams

Angelia C Adams
WHY MAN AND NOT GOD

To my sons, Rashid and Rashad, to my Mother and Father, Albert and Mildred Dudly and family. To a special friend of the family Mr. & Mrs. Cuthpert & family and all of my sisters & brothers, in Christ, most of all thank God!

Man can love you,
Man can praise you,
Man can worship you,
Man can make your dreams come
true,
Man can anoint you,
Man can make you happy too.

BUT . . .
Can man save your soul?
NO!!!
Then why not GOD?
You can do all things through Christ
Who is the head of my life.

Glenn Weaver
ONE MORE CHANCE
He lies helpless in his hospital bed
Waiting for that moment to arrive
His shaky, arthritic hand reaches
over to a small table
He picks up a chewed pencil and a
wrinkled piece of paper

And begins to write with an unsteady hand
He jots down a small paragraph
Then sets it aside, dropping the pencil on the floor
Soon after, his heart grows weak
And he falls into an everlasting sleep
A nurse, on night shift, comes quickly to his room
She yells for a doctor, but it is too late
She notices the sloppy paragraph the man had written
She begins to read:
ONE MORE CHANCE IS ALL I ASK
BRING ON THE NEW, FORGET THE PAST
A CHANCE TO PLAY MY CARDS RIGHT THIS TIME
AND ALWAYS GIVE THE NEEDY THAT EXTRA DIME
OH GOD, I DON'T KNOW WHAT WENT WRONG
BUT GIVE ME A CHANCE TO SING ANOTHER SONG
A CHANCE TO CATCH THE BIG ONE THAT GOT AWAY
OH PLEASE GOD, PLEASE LET ME STAY
A tear runs slowly down her face
And she feels cold and empty in this lonely place
With a white, tear-soaked sheet she covers him
By the way, his name was Jim.

Kathy Williams
MADNESS

What is madness? Is it a state of mind? Is it a vacation from reality? Is there no return from madness, is it a journey that takes you through the past and future at the same time? Does it give you the answers to all of life's wondrous questions? Whose to say but the mad.

Are the mad and insane people the true geniuses of our time? Are they the few gifted people of this Era? Have they discovered the reasons for our existence and not been able to cope with the reality?

Or are they people who have had conversations with beings from other worlds and come back with different minds and ways of thinking so advanced that we consider them mad because we are too primitive to understand?

Whose to say but the mad!

Missy Monnier
WEDDING DAY

Two hearts joining together as one;
The love they share cannot be undone.

It is a gift from God to be together;
Today is the day their lives begin forever.

This is the beginning of something new;
When you need something borrowed and something blue.

All this started with the gift of love;
May God give them peace by the sign of the dove.

Their love will be shown in a beautiful way;
Welcome all to their wedding day.

Mima White-Harrison
STRANGE LULLABY

O give the young man a shroud, my friend,
To wear on the day he is wed.

O the moon is covered with clouds, my friend,
And the clouds hang over our heads.

O the roads are covered with mud, my friend,
And the slime in the field is our bed.

O the ground is covered with blood, my friend,
And the river is glutted and red.

O the men will never be found, my friend,
Who cried as they begged and they bled.

O the air is filled with the sound, my friend,
Of the violent screaming of lead.

O what is that song that we hear, my friend,
When all who surround us are dead?

O why is the music so near, my friend . . .
To lull us to sleep . . . the friend said.

Magdalena Obert
START ANEW

We were together, you and I,
On a cold and frigid winter night.
Your quiet words and smile so shy,
I took home in the morning light.

Like part of a dream not quite remembered,
I thought of you once in a while.
Persistent dreams while I slumbered,
Again and again I saw your smile.

Slipped past my window winter days,
I longed for the warmth I saw in you.
Gave in to my heart, I felt betrayed,
A promise broken, to start anew.

Opening my eyes to buds on trees,
I welcome in spring the love I'd lost.
With golden threads of summer weave
With you, the warmth for winters' frost.

Waitie D Gorham
MORNING TIME

Oh! the joy of morning time
While all the world is sleeping,
Except for a few like you and me,
Who like to get up in the morning, free.

But morning time is not for everyone.
You have to wake up with the birds.
You must feel the pride of the morning hour
If you must produce with divine power.

If you feel alive, alert and well
And in full harmony with the birds,
Then join in the morning tweet,
Get going, before a full retreat.

Oh! the joy of morning time
When you're full of morning zeal.
Get going while the light does shine
And you get help from the divine.

Christopher W Grahame
TELEVISION FEVER

Like soup and noodles ladled out,
"I want my VCR!" the shout.
Remote controller's what you get:
The jam jar television set.
The emcee hosts becoming ghosts
On game shows offering the most.
They offer me a brake job toast!
The gourmet chef, the G-clef,
Country songs and singalongs.
The morning, noon and nightly news,
The Sunday basketball reviews.
See wheat bread commercials too,
Video jazz and new cat foods.
Phone in, "What you eat you are."
Advertise a sexy car!
Mini-series: money talks.
Ministries and weight-loss walks.
Antique movies lame and long
Make me mutter on and on.
Our windows on the world I've feared
Are weatherized and sales-geared.

Dora Lee Hollingsworth
THIS MARIGOLD BELONGS TO ME!

That little yellow Marigold,
With beauty that cannot be told,
Growing 'neath the window in the back,
For loving care it did not lack.
I kept the weeds out,
I watered it when days were not fair.

That little yellow Marigold
Growing 'neath the window in the back
Oh! I know others have them
and with money you can buy.
But from the day I started it,
from a tiny seed;
and hope for it to grow
I did indeed!
and daily this plant I did see.
That Little Yellow Marigold
Growing 'neath the window in the back,
For it belonged to me!

Nikki Karns
MY BEST FRIEND FROM AFAR

Orion; the constellation star
My best friend from afar
The sparkle in the sky
A nice long cry
A thought out loud
A little voice within its crowd
Tells me upon an instance
My uncalculated resistance
Betelgeuse upon his shoulder's side
The Great Nebula within his stride
He's the warrior of the celestial sphere
He who looks upon us without fear
Dictator of the winter sky
His beauty will never die
My best friend from afar
Orion the dominant constellation star

Christa G Lakaschus
THE WINDS ARE BLOWING FROM THE WEST SOME MORE

The winds are blowing from the west some more,
The waves are rolling to the ocean shores.
A mist is falling like a silver veil,
The seagulls flying in the morning spray.

The first soft finger of the light of God,
Is painting the horizon in red, yellow and gold.
Waves are singing an age old song,
From sailor lost in the early morn.

A piece of driftwood from a foreign land,
Is coming to rest in the shimmering sand.
The water is moving in a never ending way,
To cover the rocks in green, blue and grey.

A shell is laying in a yellow glow,
A crab is stumbling so very slow,
To find her way home, from the sandy shores.
Dolphins are playing their never ending game,
With a splash of grey, there goes a whale.

The seals are moving in the soft lift of dawn,
They cuddle together to keep each other warm.
A ship on the mooring is blowing a horn,
That is the ocean awakening, in the early morn.

Lu Klaers

Lu Klaers
NOVEMBER WIND

Now the November cold winds are blowing in,
whipping around corners,
pushing and tugging,
whirling and twirling,
with a wonderful nimbleness that catches me up in its brisk, crisp spirit and saying lovingly, but firmly,
"Don't hide away and let your spirits darken.
energize you body, clear your mind,
open your eyes,
there are many beautiful winter days ahead.
Many creative and wonderful things to do."
I thought why not and surrendered.
A pleasant uplifting feeling slowly
moved inside of me
And the wondrous feeling made me smile again, which brought me to reflect about a painting or two I might do.
Then the November wind swept down and
kissed me on the cheek and said,
"See, creativity does come back."

Grant H Tuckett
I ASKED WHY

We weren't put here to spend forever:
We were put here to be together.
We weren't put here to waste our talents:
We were put here to learn our balance.
We weren't put here to blame each other:
We were put here to save the bother.
We weren't put here to hurt and ache:
We were put here to grow, remake.

The simple purpose of it all
Is only not to drop the ball.

Eugenie Eberle
SANDSAIL

To my first grandchild due in November 1989

The moonlight struggles through the haze
Pervading over the sky.
The wind is high and dusty with ever changing gusts
Flapping the sails, sandsails.

The race begins, the markers set.
Between two cars the sails are met.
While skimming across am empty path
Never before on the desert, cast.

The turns are caught, if luck is right
When a two wheel slant exceeds this flight.
While other boats, not catching the puff
Fall off their course, with a maddening luff.

The sport is new, the spirit high
With mounting vibes from expatriotic cries.
For, on these Arabian Sands we bring
A whole new life beyond the nomads wildest dreams

Donald E Jones II
GRAVEYARD
In the path of battle fields,
Undead spirits live to kill.
Misled dreams that were never real.
I tripped over a dead man's hand.
Echoed screams fill the air.
Blinking faces are everywhere.
Future lives go unaware.
I tripped over a dead man's hand.
The stench of rot invades my mind.
I hold myself in another bind.
A sainted cross I look to find.
I tripped over a dead man's hand.
Reality bleeds from sutured veins.
Flooding the earth in angered rains.
Removing from time negative pains.
I tripped over a dead man's hand.
A tombstone covered in drooling sweat.
An ageless wonder he has met.
Not too late to regret.
I tripped over a dead man's hand.

Eva M Roy
MY SWEETENED CHARM
After picking up the piece of candy and putting it in my mouth,
I realized what the after effects would be,
But I continued to suck on it, like it was the end of a drought.
The sweetness from it, tasted so good, as I switched it forcefully
Over my tongue, just to get the full flavor centered
From one gum to the other. The after thought
Of my mistake, came too late to be rendered
Otherwise, because, the sweets of it became caught
In my throat, from that little piece of candy,
And with an unconscious push, it slipped down my esophagus,
And was gone. The after effects, came quickly
And to the point, for the forbidden sweetness
Was already in my stomach, and sending out an alarm
To all around, to stay away from, my sweetened charm.

Jerry Givins

Jerry Givins
WHAT IS LOVE
Love is having trust, and faith,
in the one you're with.
Love is caring, sharing, it's
not a myth.
Love is being honest, and open
with each other.
Just like you would be,
with a sister or brother.
Love is taking someone by the
hand, in their time of need.
Love is not about money,
wealth, riches, or greed.
Love is about listening, when
no-one else will.
It's not about sex, or an
occasional thrill.

Love is listening to your partner,
with an open mind.
And sharing their thoughts,
some of the time.
Love is saying you're sorry,
when you know you're wrong.
Don't beat around the bush,
with a dance and a song.
Love is knowing, when your
partner needs space,—
And leaving the past, in
its rightful place.
Love will bring pain, hurt,
and strife.
But most of all love, is
doing what's right.

Dee Overpeck
THE SWEET STRINGS, A SONG
Gently he caresses the guitar's strings,
She sings with a soft, sweet sting.
He smiles as he plays in the cold light of day, without alarm.
His friendly smile is warm & full of charm.
All is shared with those who pass—
As if a dream that will surpass.
His music is free to enjoy and be heard,
Like the soft sounds of a lovebird.
The song fills the air & gently calls
Beckoning you to listen & to its spell fall.
The energy produced by the song
Seems to capture you, to resist would be wrong.
It surrounds you till you surrender to its splendor;
You become part of the music & its tune;
It causes your heart to swoon.
There's a soothing peace
And the surrounding movement of people ceases;
The Muses have touched his soul
As his spirit seems to control
Deep, deep down to his heart.
It is apparent that he possesses the true art!

Kebra L Nider
HOMELESS MAN
As I watched a young man
on the streets of D.C.
I couldn't help but think
why him, and not me?

He fed the pigeons
and called them true friends
with their pecking and cooing
their message did send.

As I drew closer
to the man on the street
I noticed his shivering
from a lack of heat.

His clothes were tattered
a sleeping bag his bed
fruit, bread and seed
his body was fed.

I gave him five dollars
and we talked awhile
he said "God Bless You"
and we exchanged a smile.

Beverly Ann Green
JAMMIE
I have a little boy who just stays dirty. No matter how you worry. You can't get him to hurry. With one sock up and one sock down, he is always jumping around.
He's cute and mean but still a dream. Someone to spank when he's got you so crazy you just want to scream.
He's little but loud. I get mad but I'm proud, a little something in dirty jeans and a lot of good things that never shows.
But I still love him goodness knows, someday he'll be grown up and gone away and I'll miss those dirty clothes, hands and little face.
So here's to all you moms and dads if you have a little boy like this, just feed and love him and tuck him in bed. Teach him his prayers. You'll never regret the time you spent to see him grown a gentle man, wonderful and warm.

Andrea Shelby
DEPRESSION
The cold wind brushes by thee
Who cries in the night
Alone thee will scream good-bye
And sadly thee will not see the light

Laughter and smiles
Thee thinks is a game
White to black—changes
The rose will never be red again

Thee believes in the dandelions
If it is the symbol of life and death
The rising sun is the sunset
When thee takes his last breath

The cold wind brushes by thee
Who smiles in the night
For thee has survived the storm
And yet thee still does not see
the light

Jan McMillan
THE GIFT OF LOVE
I cried a tear for the passing of this year,
Love for our fellow man has seemed to disappear from this vast land.

People living on the streets sleeping only God knows where,
Eating garbage and begging for money in total despair.

Murder is becoming common, as well as robbery, alcohol and drugs,
Is this really how we want to live?

What happened to humanity, brotherhood and love.

There was a time when one helped another with no questions asked,
Was only too glad to do any little task.

We have flown to the moon because of greed and power,
While here on earth someone suffers each hour.

What a sad people are we—How can we possibly expect to be free,
When we can not even live together peacefully.

It is time we start loving each other and do all that we can,
To develop the best, caring relationship for each and every man.

A hug, a kind word, a warm embrace—to put a smile on another's face.
Love is such a simple gift: so freely can we give,
And if given from the heart; surely all would have a chance to live.

Donna Bodenman
HER NAME IS ROSANNE
Her shy smile soon disarms the most critical
And puts the embarrassed at ease;
Captivating the 'soul analytical'
With her eager desire to please.

Down's Syndrome, the label life ascribed to her,
Is a person born different than some.
The compassion she exudes from inside her
Provides tenderness, equaled by none.

Loving plans vowed for her share in our lives.
An adult now, but only in years;
As a child, trusting love and blind hope thrives—
Instinctively, faith calms her fears.

When I gaze, unobserved, on her countenance,
Unspoiled or tainted by man,
There's no doubt in my mind she's shown recompense,
As an integral part of God's plan.

In repose, glows a glimpse of her inner soul,
Reflections of His gracious hand,
As she'll be, in eternity—healed and whole!
Her dear name? It's Laura Rosanne.

George Perry
LOVELY WAY ABOUT HER
Lovely way about her
as rosemallow blooms
whose scent I savour nightfall
before the harvest moon.
Genial and lightly
her grace unfurls the morn'
resplendency abounding
like summer's vestal shore.
Tuesdays find her caroling
through August-Bebel-Ring
summoning the vireos
sunning by the spring.
Nimble, sweet and sapient
th' essence of her store
Lovely way about her . . .
need I reveal more?

Marcia R Morris
AT OUR HOUSE
We have an awful lot of love
At our house
We always pray to God above
At our house
We laugh a lot and cry some too
At our house
There's always something nice to do,
When with our regular work we're through
At our house
We never speak an unkind word
At our house
We sing sweet songs and praise the Lord
At our house
We help each other with the chores
Both in the house and out of doors
At our house
We take time out to romp and play
And have some fun most every day
At our house
Now don't you wish that you lived here
At our house?

Joyce Jackson Evans
THE SEA
Only in my dreams
Will my feet touch the sand
And I walk along the waters edge
With only the surf to make a sound.

Only in my dreams
Will I see that special sunset
Listen closely and you can hear
The sound of the sun hitting the water.

Only in my dreams
And the sweet memories
Will I smell the salty air
And hear the seagulls song.

Only in my dreams
And deep in my heart
Will I look out over the bay
To see my beloved churning sea.

Christopher Dean Browne
THE ROSE
There the rose stands in solitude and grace,
with its petals outstretched
toward the sun.
The soft touch of the petals cradles the rain drops.
The gloomy clouds block the sky,
but the red ruby rose still looks
its vibrant color.
The cool and refreshing rain seems to give the rose
nourishment.
The gray clouds part and the warm beams of the sun
bring the rose from sleepy
sadness to a joyful awakening.
The song of a nightengale sweetens the warmth of the sun.
The nightingale flys by the rose,
but knows the thorns present no
danger.
The nightingale knows that the rose would never hurt him.
The rose never tires of this peaceful life,
neither does the nightingale.
The rose leads this life in peace and harmony.

Heather A Watson
TRUE TO MYSELF
I am kind, loving, learning to be true to myself.
I wonder why we are all so afraid of something we cannot name.
I hear whispers inside my mind, late at night.
I see waves that crash against white cliffs as the sun
settles below the horizon.
I want beauty everywhere around me.
I am kind, loving, learning to be true to myself.

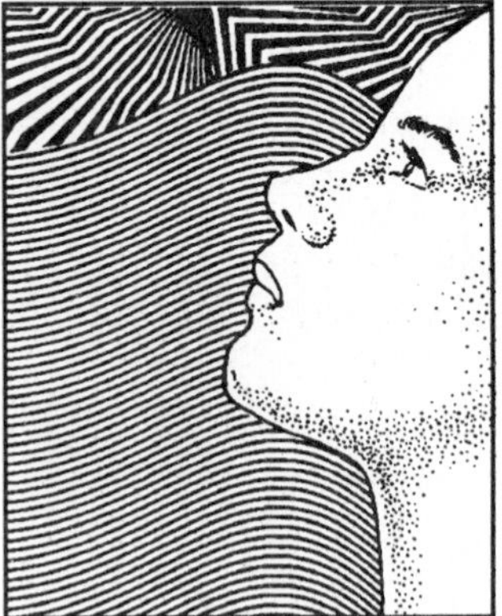

I pretend not to feel the dull, hot pain that comes of compassion.
I feel joy too strong for words, beating inside me,
like the wings of a thousand caged
doves.
I touch the music that stirs my soul, and my sorrows are
washed away by its soft caress.
I worry that I will die before I am truly alive.
I cry when one child suffers in helpless silence.
I am kind, loving, learning to be true to myself.

I understand the pain of a dream dying unspoken, locked within.
I say true love is worth any cost, and forever is not long enough
to live with love.
I dream of someone who understands the subtle and intricate melody
my heart sings.
I try to keep things in perspective at all times,
else matters become far too
confusing.
I hope to someday remove the mask I live behind and let the world know
who I truly am.
I am kind, loving, learning to be
true to myself.

Frank Roy Shapiro
REFLECTIONS OF THIS GHETTO
The Western addition of this ghetto appeared at peace in a pseudo blue light
expressing our eternal birthright, being bought at the price of our misery.

Grizzly, we now stand boldly here exposed by our addictions,
everywhere misery.
Yet special, for as we expose our essence
we are continually being reborn,
and such as an afterbirth, once essential to life,
is now waste holding on to the noise of this ghetto

reminding us continually of acrid, totalitarian concepts.
The story of the Mojave. This is loneliness.

And we slip back into the stillness of this noise
and emptiness of this anxious reclamation
almost stealing our very right to exist beyond the vibrations calming us,
though only for a time, and only if there was water in these boarded up traps.

And only if there ever was, just once, sweetness in this dry wasteland.
But on the way to sinking I wish we could dream, so many dreams.
For sometimes these dreams might become real.

Chad C Turner
SHADOWS
I see myself in shadows
On green and gold and brown.
The sky is clear,
The time is right,
And I'm the only sound.

I move ahead
With graceful speed,
Forever looking down;
For I know that soon death will come,
To whatever's on the ground.

I see a flash—
Then dive straight down;
My talons grip it tight.
Moving with the sun I head for home;
I know I'll eat tonight.

Lorinda Averill
THE ATOM BOMB
When the atom bomb hit, it shattered the earth
And then there was no hope for rebirth.
And when it hit out went a million helpless cries,
But nothing could help after mankind's lies.

How could the very men who brought the Claws of Death
knocking at our door
Be the exact same great and honest men that we
voted for?

Well, where are these fearsome leaders now?
Can't they see the destruction some how—
No dawning sun, no bright moon,
Only one big silent tomb.

Now there are no children playing
Or any hearts astraying.

Why?

Rachel Y Hellard
OUR TIME'S END
If I had a chance to see you again
Then I would never leave you my friend
I remember how you used to hate
Saying goodbye, but now it's too late
Our times will soon be coming to an end
You weren't only my love, you were my friend
You were the one who made me forget
All of those days I've come to regret
You said, "Remember love, forget about hate.
Hold me now before it's too late."
I held you then closer than before
I began to feel love like never before
I have one thing left to say to you friend
As much as I hate it, this is "our time's end".

Louise M Ballou
THE SANDS OF TIME
The sands of time
washed upon the shore.
Left a ridge
of where a wave was before.
Like a pattern of a ripple afghan
Spread before the sea.
I have returned only to find
The sand is smooth
as smooth can be.
I often wonder if I will ever see
Another afghan spread before
the sea.

Mildred E Bosnell

Mildred E Bosnell
WINTER—THRU MY WINDOW
January nine is cold and bleak,
I see no birds around;
The clouds are low and steely gray,
Deep snow is on the ground.

The trees stand black, truly forlorn,
With wildly waving limbs;
Their autumn dress that didn't last,
The memory now is dim.

I dream of spring, with its tender green,
Wish it could come today;
But I'll be content with memories lent,
And winter will melt away.

Eric S Lublin
FOREVER ENDLESS

To my parents for their love and support and to my loving girlfriend, Caterina Zuppardo I dedicate this poem of love and promise

Walking, walking down the path of life
Step by step, foot by foot walking towards an endless light
Inches to go, miles to roam to get forever home.
Searing heat blocks the way
One god knows when it will go away

Cities grow, nations aglow
Who will win the war
People never know when it's time to fold
One by one, we will go . . . over to the other side

Creatures fall, preachers call
Neither one wants to know
Young and old will never know
natures human call
Day will come, night will fall
The world wonders in a silenced dialogue

Endless night will certainly fall
When, only two men know
Only he who folds can put a hold on the final go.

Kern Conway
FIRST LOVE'S LOSS

Looking up into the sky
A star reaches out to say goodnight.
Twinkle, twinkle, it gives a smile
As if to say, just wait a while.
For underneath the dark night's sky
A broken heart begins to cry.
On that night true love was found.
Then was lost without a sound.
So naive, yet stands so tall
But not prepared to take the fall.
For giving in to love's sweet touch
She'd given all, and lost so much.
Broken hearts will always mend
But memories of him will never end.

Barbara Downs
TRY TO START THE DAY WITH A SMILE

Try to start the day with
A smile
Forgetting all the unpleasant
Things for a while
Take in each day as if it were the last
And forget all the unhappy things
That were in the past
Listen to the birds that start each
Day with a song
And no matter what else happens
Nothing can go wrong

Margie Alari Amado
FOG

To my beloved children—Margaret A. Stone, Charlene B. Davidson, Edwina L. Aylward and son Edward Guy Amado and Alari Family.

Mysterious the fog penetrating it be,
endangering ships far out at sea.
Swirling mists of fog enshrouding the
lea, instilling fear and more to be.
Sea-hardy captains dreading, the
chilling fog, gulping hot coffee to
ease their cold.
Jotting their ships progress, down in
their maritime log.
Prevailing fog of mist so thick, chills
ones body and makes one sick.
Mysterious the fog, penetrating it be,
chilling the Sea-gulls to the very
quick.
Prevailing fog so dense and cold, has
sailors wanting to stay within the
ships-hold.

Elke Zoske
LOVE AND PAIN

. . . to all women that know love and pain, and are not afraid to start all over again . . .

You and me, we fell in love, like many people do
and then the day was right and we said "I do".
There I was, inexperienced in life
and you still young and proud and so happy that I became your wife.

Why did we change through the years that past
and why did love let us down
when marriage is supposed to forever last?

Oh yes, I remember the happy moments we shared together
and sometimes we even cried when there was stormy weather.
But now we are strangers and have not much to say
yes I know it happens to so many people
but there was a time when I prayed . . .

. . . yes I prayed to be strong and understanding
but sometimes this was pending on how angry you would get,
and I cried of pain and you soon would regret.
Oh how I prayed to stand the pain
but it never seemed to cease
instead it would gain.

You never took the time to listen to me
and I felt it was a crime to be whom I supposed to be.
Perhaps I failed to be your wife, but now it's time to live my life
not only as a friend, mother, or
woman . . . but as a Human.

Warner O Schoyen
THE WITHDRAWN

Silent as shadows
They sit, huddled
Against a gray vastness.
Seeing eyes see nothing,
Hearing ears know no sound.
These are God's
Forsaken manikins
Drowned in vacuity.

Helen M Ostrom
TAX TIME

Strange how Prop Taxes can keep one awake,
Turning and flopping while the body pains,
Thinking of April when the second part's due,
One writes out the check, directly on cue.

Strange though it is, no more money is found,
To pay all the bills that grind to the ground.
One's best laid plans are never enough,
And just to survive seems to get very rough.

Income Tax seems to sorta' take second place,
And despite some reversals, some money's saved,
But when April the 10th has come and passed,
One hopes, one's roof can be saved at last!

Meanwhile, energies have been strained to the limit!
Months have passed while earning a living.
With duties pressing out the days and hours,
We greet darned taxes in time for the flowers.

Strange is that 'challenge' all the rhetoric's about!
What would one do, if not bellow and shout,
On just how unfair this world's getting to be?
But . . . look at others, one's own blessings to see.

Strange is that need for these ups and downs,
Need for Life with its feelings, its sights and sounds.

So late we get smart that at age we find youth,
And excitement of living seems to close all too soon.

Sherri Lynn Aguayo
BREEZE ON THE BAYOU

A breeze on the bayou
keeps rustling light,
The old hooty owl
he hoots to the night.

The cottonwoods whisper
a saying I love,
A whippoorwill cries
his lonely call above.

Weeping willows murmur
all ill at ease,
As the cricket's chirp echoes
through the breeze.

Silvery moonbeams
stream through the branches,
To catch a firefly
what are my chances?

I now sit down
at the still waters edge,
And listen to the music
till it's time for bed.

Katherine M Dempsey
LET'S GROW TOGETHER

I dedicate this poem to Martha Somervell. It was she that encouraged me to write my feelings on paper. I am one of her students that will never forget her.

When our love all fades away,
Only a memory will be left to stand.
I'll ponder about the day,
When your attention I'll no longer demand.

It's like the passing wind it seems,
That a bond no more remains.
The look in my eye will have no gleam,
Only tears to make a stain.

My heart will stop beating to that rhythmic tune,
Of a forever friendship that's true.
My life will proceed and I will soon,
No longer need being with you.

I want our love to stay as strong,
As the day we fell so deep.
The understanding that I long,
And your promise of love I will to keep.

So please, let's stop this useless game,
Of "hide-n-seek" with our hearts.
We are supposed to be one in the same,
Let's grow together and make a new start.

Connie J LaBenne
TO KENNETH

This poem was written for, and dedicated to, my husband, Kenneth, a Captain of the Southfield, Michigan Police Department, in celebration of our 10 year marriage.

Walks there a man in Suit of Blue,
Stalwart and fair, with heart
that is true.
Who looks at all things from both
right and left,
To pettiness and gossip, his ears
are quite deaf.
Who has such a way to tell you
you've erred,
That he leaves you with only the
thought that he cared.
Who sits not a mite in the judgement
seat,
Nor mocks he a man that still
walks the beat.
Who gives his whole being to
making things right,
And has earned deep respect
when he comes home at night.
Who knows each promotion came
straight from above,
That his knowledge and
goodness are part of God's love.
Who rarely complains at the woes of
this life,
And who could know better
than his dear loving wife.

Barbara R Williams
TRIAL SEPARATION

This man was here for thirty years
We lived, loved, hated, laughed and cried
But one was ahead, the other behind
Never beside and so something died
Can I understand it?

We are both new and old
Forging ahead and dragging our feet
Wanting to share this opening up
Sharing learning makes it complete
Can I tolerate it?

Does each new experience
Move us further apart
Or are we on parallel courses
Still guarding our heart
Can I wait?

Can we be graced by the Gods
And given another chance
To merge our new-old selves
Into a final life-long dance
Can we make it?

Janette Conger
A LETTER I WROTE

Dedicated to my husband, Ronald, whose continued belief in me, helped to give me courage.

I can't even write a letter!
Why is it so hard,
To say what I feel?
It's so easy to do,
Yet, the words are wrong.

It's almost as though,
The words are stuck inside me.
I try so cleverly,
To make them come out;
But, when I write,
It all comes out wrong.

The words are there,
On the tip of my tongue;
But, as I write,
There appears no word.

These things I've said,
Are hard to accept;
Because, once before,
I wrote a letter.

Darrel A Mason
VISIONS OF VIETNAM

Dedicated to the men and women who fought in Vietnam, and to the ones who never came home.

I see visions of the faces
of the ones,
who will never come home.

I see their eyes,
but cannot hear them speak.
Because I understand,
that they are over there
and not here.

The waves of the blue waters,
blow cold in the wind.
And the storms of our mourning,
are fresh now,
just as they were then.
Lost Saigon still weighs heavy,
on our minds.
And I still vision Kheanh.
All reminders of that troubled time.
We can't begin to imagine,
the heartaches,
or the cost.

But the good Lord knows,
as we know,

The war was not all
that we lost.

Nancy Leu Charnoski
PASTIMES

I dedicate this poem "Pastimes" to my Mom, Pauline V. Leu for all the memories. Love, Nancy

Oh, how we wish for the times that are gone
All the carefree days of the past,
When all whom we loved were with us all still
and time moved so slowly we thought it would last.
I think of the summers of the tree lined streets,
of feeding the squirrels in trees,
running at night after lightening bug flights,
and in autumn of falling red leaves.
Going to Grammas' at Christmas,
shoveling snow on the walk,
knocking down icicles hanging from eves,
knowing all of the people who lived on the block.
Memories now of long ago days,
some make us smile or cry,
Just as today in some future time,
We'll think of today
and the memories of these days gone by.

Jeri King
OUR MARRIAGE PRAYER

This poem is dedicated to my husband Randy, my most precious gift.

Thank you Lord for what you've done,
because of you we now become one.
By your love made man and wife,
with you Lord we'll share our life.
We have given our lives to you,
and each day you'll see us thru.
With you Lord at our side,
we know our love will never die.
Things now ours—not mine 'nor yours,
from you Lord all blessings pour.
Forever guide us by your love,
until we share your home above.

—amen

Randall M Walker
IF I WERE

To my mother, Thomasina, who always submits to the Lord's will and He has lifted her from her private torment.

If I were water, I would flow in the Nile
If I were brick, I'd be part of the pyramids
If I were gold, I would come from Sheba's Ophir
If I were King David, I would have married Beth-Sheba
If I were snow, I'd fall on the mountains of the moon
If I were a river they would call me the Gihon
If I were Solomon, the queen of Sheba would come see about me
If I were Jeremiah, my friend would be Ebedemelech
Even if I were with Paul in Antioch, my name is Niger
So praise ye, the Lord, praise ye the Lord!

Joanne E Vincent

Joanne E Vincent
WHAT'S IN A SMILE?

What's in a smile?
A world full of joy
That's very secure.
Also contentment
with pleasure so pure.
Happiness spreads
to others around
from simply a smile
where beauty is found.
With time there will be
far over a mile,
a more peaceful world
from merely <u>one</u> smile!

Lisa Reneé Crivello
ONE STATEMENT

Dedicated to those with whom I have spent the best years of my life with, my parents, my brother Vince, Patty, Cord, and especially you Susan. Thanks for everything all of you.

This life seems familiar
In ways, as if maybe
I have experienced it before
I would like to live it again
sometime . . .
In a different way.
Maybe it will get easier
To figure out,
I can't say for sure.
Until then I go on
Experiencing the pleasure
Of this, if ever a next one.
And so on I thought of
Things that could not yet be
Things that I have yet to see.
One statement alone,
Life as I know it,
Certainly is a story to tell.

Janice M Chang
THE MANY BLESSINGS

Every moment of my life,
I count the many blessings
you have so graciously
bestowed upon my being.
My spirits are uplifted
when I'm with you.
I feel that I can do
just about anything
life has to ask of me.
Like always,
I try to do my very best.
With your help,
it has always paid off
by giving me a sense of belonging.
I like the feeling
of being appreciated.
I will continue to help you
in any way I can
to make your life a little easier
while allowing myself to grow
intellectually and spiritually.

R Wesley Vaughan
A MIRACLE

In dedication of Debbie Michael, who showed her care.

It's a miracle to see
A rose pod from a seed
From a stony dirt heap
In the back yard.

A miracle to see
A baby blink for the first time;
And to hear him cry—
All from the love of a woman and a man.

It's a miracle,
All the wonders of God.
The stars and the sky
Blend with the colors of brush.

It's a miracle to smile,
Or have the touch of a smile tip you.
The joy it brings
Is fulfillment in itself.

A drenching drop of rain,
A bolt of lightning,
And a big gust of wind
Are all miracles of our time.

Vicky J Halliday
SPECIAL PEOPLE

To all the special people, with a special mention to Steve and Danny.

To All Those Special People, with special problems, I believe we are one. Whether it be hearing, sight, disease, mental problems, or aging, we have won.

To be ourselves without regret is a never-ending battle for us all.
Being free to accomplish for the good of just living our lives.
With the right to be ourselves, and the great fact of being alive.

To those people, who are different from us and show us we are different.
I say, what would it be like if they became like us.
Will they say they are different then, and make jokes about those special people?
The same people who make fun of special people, may find they need our help someday.

Remember the great creator created us to live in this world.
The deaf, the blind, the handicapped, people with disease, and our large population of the elderly, whose aging is their only problem,
I say, may you rise above your problems, be who you are, and that your existence in this world is more priceless than money.
There is not enough money in the world to pay for the joy each one of you Special People gives to this world.
Special people are the precious gem stones of our world, and to you all,
A Very Special Praise for standing tall and giving the greatest gift of all.
Yourself.

Beth Schepanowski
MY BEACH

Dedicated to "DAN TYE", my best friend forever. Thanks for your help, I LOVE YOU!

As I sit upon my favorite rock,
The wind sweeps through my hair.
I think about all the problems,
Life brings that I must bear.

I remember all the special nights,
That you and I had shared.
Walking along the sandy beach,
I knew you'd always be there.

As I look upon the frozen waters now,
I think back to all the fun,
We'd been through that night,
When we were together as one.

Even in winter the beach is very important to me,
Others may think it's just a rink.
But when my troubles become too much,
I need this beach and it's my place to think.

Even on the coldest wintery days,
I go to the beach among the ice and snow.
The sunsets are beautiful and maybe that's why,
My beach means more to me than you will ever know.

David J Nennich
MISSING YOU

To my first and only love . . . Though time has soiled the memories with fine dust, It shall never diminish the eternity of my feelings.

When I am emotionally adrift in the Sea of Loneliness
With its waves of depression
splashing about my sides
In some unwanted hour of darkness . . .
Or when I am as lost
As a crew-less captain sailing without his sextant,
My soul searches deep the storm's woe;
Braving the howling winds of melancholy and
Enduring the torrents of pelting emptiness and hurt
Till last it comes upon the sweet and gentle image of you
Who are life and water to my dying and thirsty spirit.
There is sweet calm as peace and tranquility precipitate
And my fractured heart is transitorily soothed
While the tears whisper their presence.
Dearest child of them all whose eyes are filled with joy

And whose love of life so wonderful
it captured the heart of this boy.
I still think of you, I can't let go,
indeed it's all too sad,
But such is life, as I'm told, and I
guess it's just too bad.
So if missing you is such a sin, then
I'm guilty as can be,
Sentenced to wanting you, for all
eternity.
And even though I have you not, I
hold oh what's so dear;
A love deep down within me, ever
existing for you.

Doris Irene Schenck
SONG OF THE WANDERING WINDS

I heard the little wandering
winds
As they sang a song today,
Sang a song of mist and rain
While the dripping cloud hung gray.

They sang a song of the great
outdoors,
Of soft wet grass and dripping
flowers,
Sang of the joy that comes
to the world
In drifting, misting showers.

The gentle winds sang as they
touched the flowers
With loving fingertip,
They sang and sighed through
rainwet trees
With flower perfumed lois.

A wet leaf dropped, and they
caught it up
And flung it across the hill.
They followed it fleet as it whirled
away,
Then all the world was still.

Carol J Kerley
THE AMERICAN SPORT

This poem is dedicated to my grandson, Andrew Keith Brown, "The American Sport"

There was a little boy named
Andrew,
from infancy to age two,
Already knew every sport on a field
or T.V.,
Such a handsome lad,
And grown up for his years,
his intelligence grew and grew,
From football, golf, basketball,
wrestling and baseball,
This child so small, knew them
all.
His enthusiasm was great, he
clapped,
he yelled, he screamed, you bet.
With a fan like Andrew he will surely
be blessed in life that maybe
An infant or a child of two will be
Watching him one day,
Repaying this Little American Sport,
Cheering him on in this same old
way.

John Lee Hunter
AMERICA'S FORGOTTEN

To my mother, Ms. Mintha Hunter, for being a strong and dedicated woman for so many years.

Who are they, they are our brothers, our sisters, our sons, our daughters, for some reason or another have gone astray, and fallen by the way side, they are America's forgotten.

As we travel to and fro, we see them in our streets, trash cans, park benches, maybe with our help, they'll rise from the pits of the slum bound streets, and face life one more time, and leave the bottom, they are truly America's forgotten.

Jo-Ann Cosentino
I REMEMBER

I dedicate this poem to my late husband, Clarence, with all my love.

I remember the day you told me
That your love for me was true.
I remember like it was yesterday
When I said I love you too.

I wish everyone could know
The kind of love we shared
A love we weren't afraid to show
With a tender touch, And loving care.

The loving moments that we knew
Brought happiness into my life
I was happiest being with you
As a friend, a lover, and wife.

Jeanne Marie Mayo
MY FRIEND SLOOPY

Dedicated to my beloved cat Sloopy

My friend Sloopy
I loved him so

Time was so short
I didn't want him to go

Winter nights I sit alone
Listening for his cry at my door
But my dear friend Sloopy . . .
Is gone forever more,

Dear friend,
Dear cat
Good-by

Joseph E Barrett
QUINTILIS

Earth's movements drive the Sun to
greater heights,
Julius, a noble Roman in his day
Who held god-hood firmly within his
sights,
Like Earth's lover would hold all life
in sway.

Though gentle lovers seek to spurn
the sun,
Brash Julius sought for new and
younger love
To join with him and Earth in the
warm fun
Shafting in fiery lances from above.

The Romans declared Julius was a
god,
So gave a month of their old year to
win
Respite when corn grows tall enough
to nod
And men dream dreams of Winter's
ice and din.

But dreams of ice and snow won't
cool the day,
The ice and snow grow liquid, flow
away.

Margaret E Smith
YOUNG FOREVER

We are the chosen.
We stand firm against the pessimism
of the world
Knowing that we can reach our
dreams,
Believing in true love,
Experiencing eternal youth.
We will never grow into the old age
of worry, of doubt, of fear.
For we are the next generation,
Our time of glory has just begun.
This time is our time—
We must experience it now while we
can,
And always believe that our hopes
for the future
Will not fade away in the sands of
Time.
We can accomplish anything—
We are the chosen.

Elinor R Adams
MY GRAMMA'S ADVICE FOR NEW BRIDES

A hungry man is an angry man.
So says the marriage book.
Keep your hubby full of all
The good things you can cook.

If he doesn't get the loving
He's looking for at home,
His eyes will start to wander,
Soon, he'll start to roam.

Be a chef in your kitchen,
A lady in your parlour.
A whore in your bedroom, and
Your troubles will get smaller.

If you follow my advice, and
To God light your candle,
There won't be anything that
You and he can't handle.

My Gramma gave me this advice
While talking late one night.
After living with my husband,
I found that she was right!

Midge Kincaid
MORNING LOVESONG

I dedicate this poem to Roger who taught me that love can be exquisite!

How sweetly doth the robin sing
As, awakening from my deep
slumber,
I first hear his melodious notes of
Spring;
But, what of my true love, I wonder.

Can he know of the poignant ache
Which my faint heart longs to quell?
Or is my love born out of an empty
faith
Languishing forlorn in a cloistered
cell.

What mattereth if the robin sings of
Undying love and eternal fidelity;
Canst lovers e'er hope to escape Fate
And overcome Love's inherent
fragility?

Yet, within my lonely room, I hear
Haunting refrains of Love's grand
fantasy;
And, suddenly, your face appears
crystal clear
Captivating my heart again with
exquisite ecstasy.

Susan Scott Abrams
SO FAR AWAY

For the one who knows me the best and is near and dear to my heart; I hope that we keep in touch.

You were mine
But that was yesterday
Now I'm alone
And you seem so far away
No recorded history
No memory
Just this empty feeling
Wrapped up inside me
Covered by a shadow
Full of doubts and fears
Erasing all of yesterday
Wiped by my tears
The hurt will pass
As yesterday fades away
And all the feelings are lost
Left in the past to decay

George T Eppley
LOVE AND TEARS

To the beautiful poetic soul of Verna Eppley

Desolation claims the right to feel
forlorn
Tears, love's cry, though reasons
favorite scorn
Profusely pouring as time commands
"Goodbye"
Hard to stop or answer the question:
Why?
Tender memories coax my
watery eyes
Confounding Puritan preference
to play wise
Siphoning off a thousand
reservoirs
Spawn a veritable river ever
more
Infinite pity for others' hapless
pathos
Calamity's legacy, lovers' tearful
loss
Hope would soothe the shocking
spicy sting
By finding a hint in the rustle of a
wing
Sublimely existing somewhere
deep in time
Beyond the reef, her Savior's
arms divine
I feed the plants for thee, dear
absentee
At least to love is prayer, though
tearful love for me

Sarah M Davis
THANK GOD FOR MY FRIEND

In memory of my son, Charles Willard Davis, who died December 29, 1987, of muscular dystrophy and pneumonia

Thank you God for sending me a
friend
Who expresses kindness and love
from deep within
A beautiful relationship we are able
to create
'Cause we have God's love which
we both appreciate

We loved each other right from the
start
And whatever we share always
comes straight from the heart
The feelings we experience all seem
so right
And I thank God for restoring my
emotional sight

Take things slow, by others I have
been told
But it's extremely difficult, since he

has such a beautiful soul
He's kind, sincere and very soft spoken
Our friendship has a bond that can never be broken

Nothing happens unless it's God's will
And no matter what happens, this way I will always feel
Having this friend makes this a better year
Filling it with love, joy and lots of good cheer

Through this friend God has removed all my sorrows
Not just for today, but for all my tomorrows
I'll keep praying right up until the end
Continuing to thank God for sending me such a friend

Hope O'Rourke

DEAR CHILD, WHY IS IT YOU HIDE?

This poem is dedicated to all Poets, for inspiration

Dear child, why is it you hide?
Bring joy forth, look inside.

It is not yours to hide away.
This gift to be given, in this way.

Let the light within you shine.
That love and joy others may find.

Maureen H Christoffelsz

HAPPY NEW YEAR '89

This year is the year there's new hope to bless
A new home, new love, new happiness
This year I know I'll get to see
My ship come in with prosperity
Each day I'll do what's best for me
And really begin to live
I'll enjoy life's trip, happy and free
And to myself I will give
Courage to cut losses, face challenges new,
This year is the year all my dreams come true
Peace, comfort and joy, and good health are mine
Here's the best to more good years
"HAPPY NEW YEAR '89"

Mary Whitenack

SELF-KNOWLEDGE

Through long love-aching,
Through despair, through dying,
Through slow heart-breaking,
Through endless bitter crying.

I went down that dark way with none beside me;
Met the end of all, naked and unarmed;
Fought, forlorn, a world of torment, anguish,
Beating out its storm upon my helpless body.

Then knew, suddenly, on a strange night
That all I had to conquer such wild terror
Stemmed from the midst of ME, a right
Inviolate, which could not yield to error.
Evil was the pain which love had brought me,
Yet Good was that which painful love had taught me.

My arms are empty, and my heart will ache
Many a long night, love, for your sake.
And know I too, softly, sadly,
I could love you rightly now and madly.
Yet, whatever, shall I cherish 'til I die
The knowing that within me, there is I.

Evan Scherman

COMMITMENT

Will you take me to be by your side?
I hope to hear you yell yes to be my bride;
You are my darling, my sweet, my pride.
Through the depths of hell which we may go through,
I will remain true, protect and love only you.
What could I do without you? I have no clue.
Through sunrise, through sunset, you and I together,
Our secrets, our thoughts will be shared now and ever.
I love only you, then, now, and no one else, NEVER.

Caryn Mendez

TIME GONE BY

I remember
Playing in the snow
Running in the yard
Sharing everything.

Why must we grow up and
Lose our innocence of childhood?

As magical as that time was,
It is gone,
And can never be returned to.

Now we are more concerned with our own lives.
Lives that have become separate,
Divided.

However old we get
Neither he nor I
Will ever forget

Because a relationship between a brother and sister
Is one of the most special things in the world.

Like playing in the snow
And running in the yard.

Naoma L Frerichs

ETERNAL FANTASY

To my son Milo J Peterson who seeks the deeper meaning of eternal knowledge.

Solitary flight in searching, cross a misty sky
Tender hurt and deepest caring, issuing the cry
Fantasy in depth and motion. Oh that man could fly!
Feathers furling, whirling, whirling o'er the mirror sea
Catching glimpse of self in motion far as eye can see
Spiraling upward, diving downward where the wave should be.

Then a rush of pearl grey feathers gliding o'er the foam
Landing silently on sea shore. Spirit coming home.
Walking awkwardly, but proudly, on the sandy loam.

Loretta Adams

THE GOLDEN TRAIL

When one day we wake to find
We've walked the golden trail
We look back to the way we were
And wish we hadn't failed

For as we live our lives each day
We really think we know
The way we live our life is right
And it's "the only way to go"

But then one day we see our life
Repeated in another
Then we know how wrong we were
As our mistakes stand out uncovered

We want to help this one like us
Whose mistakes are not all made
We want to help him change his life
Before the dues are paid

But then we realize each one of us
Must walk the golden trail
And those of us who walked before
Can't help those left to prevail

Barbara A Stripling

ANGEL TO ME

Dedicated to Charlotte Bridgewater, my angel.

An angel to me
Energy from above
Insight full of love.
Treasured thoughts we shared.
We are one in the Spirit
Chosen from above.

Our lives come together
To touch each other
In divine love.

Ansel A Walker

SHARDS OF TIME

This poem is dedicated to Nevada, a State of love, a lovely State.

As you walk the boardwalks
  of genteel Virginia City
The remnants of a once robust city
  excitement fills the need of
  many

Down the bulging formerly rich slopes
  out of sight of the curious visitor
Like little sage flats and tiny valleys
  Sprinkled with bits & pieces of
  history

Bits of "name glass and style glass"
  Lie in scintillating blankets for
  the seeker
Shards of exquisite antiques softened by
  a century's somnolent sleeper

The loving eye of a seeker seeks out
  beneath a sage root or broken
  shoe
A shard, an ethereal lady in gossamer
  clinging drapery magnificently
  hued

Precious jewel like bits enhancing Nevada
  an opalescent gem a fairy like
  shard
Sanded and formed by winds of ten decades
  resembling both an emerald and
  a ruby

The myriad of stains and peacock colors
  of glass stained by Nevada
  Minerals
The sheer excitement of the finding
  of that one so special to you

Darlene L Martin

HARMONY

To my daughter, Michelle. Whereby in her youthful innocence. Not letting me forget the meaning of life

A smooth green branch touched my face in the breeze
It was soft as it caressed my cheek
Only to bounce back as the tree regained control
And once more, the branch stood at attention
Reaching up toward the sky in praise of God
Thanking Him for the light and the warmth of life

The message of life touched upon my cheek
The harmony of all living things
Called to my attention by a single breeze
In God's splendid way of not letting us forget

Amelia E Turney (Ms Meme)

Amelia E Turney (Ms Meme)

MY BOY

To Dameon with love

He stands tall, my boy.
He looks bright.
He speaks clearly, my boy.
He's alright.

That ain't my boy
A standing on the corner.
That ain't my boy
A running in the night.

He reads them books, my boy.
He studies hard, I know.
He shows me papers, my boy.
He's smart, it shows.

Who's that screaming?
I don't know.
Who's dem policemen shooting,
Up the way?

They say it's somebody's boy.
'Tain't mine, I know, I'm sure.

Maxine Bredeman

MY COZY NOOK

I know a cozy nook
  By a babbling brook
Where all is quiet and serene;
  Where one can sit and dream

Of the things that have gone
Or those yet to come;

Thinking of far off places
And things in outer space;
Listening to the things of nature;
Rushing brook, sheep in pasture,
Hum of the busy bees
As they go from flower to
flower;

Thinking of people at a steady pace,
Nothing can quite take the place
Of my cozy nook
By the babbling brook.

Christine Cornell
MY EVERY WISH AND DREAM

To My Only Love, Bo

He's in all my dreams
I wake-up in the middle of the
night in a cold sweat
Wishing and dreaming he was
with me and near me all the
time.
I dream of what it was like when
we were together and what it
will be like when we are
together again
All of my dreams are of us
hugging, kissing and making
love
When I wake-up I sit and wish
that could happen knowing it
won't
See babe you are him and he is
you
You are my every wish and
dream
I just wanted you to know, that I
love you.

Angela Weyer
SILENT SCREAMS
Sitting in the house,
I'm all alone.
Waiting a hoping,
By the telephone.
He said he loved me
And he'd always be there,
Our love meant so much
He said he'd always care.
Silent Screams
Is all I hear.
I listen to Silent Screams
While I hold back a tear.
How could he do that?
Just turn and walk away,
He said "See ya, Baby,"
I said "That'll be the day!"
We shared our hopes
We shared our dreams,
Now I sit alone,
Listening to Silent Screams.

Charles Washington
THE GIANT BALLOON
The world is like a giant balloon,
floating in space.
Will the pace of its race, cause its
disgrace?
Or will the world float on into space,
never ending
It's race.

Tamera Rohrick
ONE NIGHT WITH YOU

To Michael—Your smile, your eyes, your touch, so true; Our love, so honest. I do love you!

One intimate journey,
Alone in the night;
The fantasy begins,
When you enter my sight.
As you stand in the shadows,
I long for your touch;
The caress of your hands,
I am craving so much.
Your touch adds a quiver,
Fingers of fire;
Exploding with passion,
And burning desire.
Your body, so sensual,
And, so full of pleasure;
The love that we make,
Is too great to measure.
With a question in mind,
As the night becomes still;
Is this just fantasy,
Or have you made it real?

S L Johnson
INSPIRATION
I was not meant
for poverty.
I am a rich woman,
trapped in the body of
a poor one.
I was meant for greatness,
I was meant to be rich.
I must fulfill my destiny,
I will be rich someday
I will show the world the life
I was meant for.
A life of worldly goods as well as
emotional fulfillment
A life of extravagant galas,
A life of beautiful clothes,
beautiful cars, beautiful people,
And most importantly, A
beautiful me.
I am full of dreams and
ambitions,
That are waiting to be
fulfilled.
I will fulfill these
dreams and ambitions.

Because I was meant
for GREATNESS.

Alice M White
THE VISIONARY
An idea grows and grows
To challenge, to nurture

A plan of action
To bring to fruition
A vision fulfilled.

Nancy Kay Baker
GOLD

TO Angel and Amy my darling daughters

As you came running up to the door,
my little girl almost four,

You held your hand out for me to
see,
In which you had a surprise for
me

A truly rare piece of beautiful gold,
As truly as beautiful as the
world is old

It was shining very, very bright,
For love had given it, its
glittering light.

But it was for my eyes and my eyes
alone,
For there in your tiny hand was
nothing more than a stone.

Rebecca Thomas
GROWING OLD
I feel myself,
growing old in my mind.
And the feeling runs deep,
down my spine.
For secretly we're all afraid,
of the day when we're old and
gray.
Our thoughts and memories,
they do fade,
And we are left with aches and pains.
While life goes by us in a daze.
We live what life is left to us.

Mary T O'Loughlin
COUNT BLESSINGS, NOT WORRIES
Life's wonders never cease.
The sky rests above us; the sun
sets and moon glows.
The beauty of a rose in full bloom
can lighten the heart's burden as
the ocean's chill can soothe the
soul.
Many are the trees so tall above
the land.
All of nature's gifts bring beauty
and contentment.
Yet man is somewhat confused
and unhappy within.
Loving yourself is the greatest
gift your heart will ever endure.
It is within this peacefulness that
every dream can come true.

Melory Gomez
GOD BLESS US ON THIS NIGHT

To Fr. Melory, OFM. For touching my life with gentle understanding, for teaching me the meaning of unselfish love, and for filling my days with happiness and a sense of belonging.

God bless us on this night, And
watch over us in our plight
for happiness, peace and love.
Let doubt not pervade our minds, In
our loneliness He is there and will
always be.
For He cares for us, as the gull
cares for the sea. And when we are
lost and are a pitiful lot, He holds us
firmly in His loving hands. And
guides us back to the road—our
Home. Where the Angels laugh, and
sing and pray.
We will find our true peace in His
Kingdom. When Life's hardships
come to us, think of the happiness
we will have then. It makes it easier
to accept the crosses He gives us to
bear. He lifts them from our
shoulders from time to time. Makes
you realize what contentment will be
When we reach our Life of
Eternity.

Lee Lashbrook
YESTERDAY

To my husband, Larry Perry

Once upon a yesterday,
I remember wagons filled with
hay—
Walking in a meadow cool with dew,
Flowers of clover casting a reddish
hue.
Drinking water from a shaded
stream,
And sitting on a bank to remember
and dream.

Dorris L Thompson
LOVING PEOPLE
Most people are wonderful.
Most people are true.
It gives us much pleasure,
When good things they do.

We love them most dearly
Because they are so nice.
They are really grand.
We admire their advice.

Love! Love! Love!
Every step of the way
Make us have pleasant thoughts
Each coming day.

J V Meade
DREAMING ABOUT WATER
A light-smear ghosting down
The channel, oily ribbons at its bows,
The huge sternwheeler
Negotiates the bend,
Wobbles darkened rowboats
Flaking paint downstream, and
refloats
Bits of beached debris. Its glow,
Like that from houses burning out,
Travels nearer on the low cloud
cover.
Carbons, heated bright, boil
Through the fretwork on its stacks,
And the paddles treadle
Sheets of brilliant nothing
Through the lucid air.

A woman's face is lit above
A table in the pilot house.
I see no other people.

The wheel goes by
Still sucking at the light.
The sounds, like hammer blows on
wood,
Come back less certainly.

R M Gordon
THE CAVE AT WAU-WAU BEACH

To Milly

Francisco, pointing 'cross the cove,
declared
"Beneath that rocky point
There is a watery cave where
mermaids sleep
And bats appoint as guards.

The water's deep and still, the
headroom low,
The inside dark and cool.
The door's a swirling pool where
fishes play.
Good swimmers here our rule."

His jeering note to me a challenge
was.
We swam across and found
The door-sized mouth waist-deep
dropped quickly off.
Inside was not a sound.

The walls were almost straight, no
handhold here,
Receding light a tease.
By jumping up my hand the ceiling
touched;
A bat that gentle breeze.

In blackness now we contact kept by
talk.
Our phosphorescent kicks
Like fireflies shone a ghostly green. I
thought,
We swim the River Styx!

Francisco up ahead called out
The right-hand wall to track.
On touching it I thought of snakes
and crabs—
So fearful, unknown, black.

The coral rocks I found like paring
knives

Cut hands and finger tips.
Francisco, waiting, spoke. "Around this turn
Just when the ceiling dips

The greenish daylight shows below your feet.
A hole leads to the sea.
The tide and mermaids here go in and out,
And so, my friends, can we!

The hole is small but big enough for one;
The passage three feet thick.
Breathe deep, dive down, swim hard and come up slow.
The walls forbid you kick.

Outside the surf is rough and hides the hole.
Keep way! To reach our cove
Swim 'round the point. There is no fear of sharks
Good luck!" And down he dove!

Francisco's disappearing legs to me
Seemed trumpeting the dare.
They gave me choice of guideless black retreat
Or forward swim with care.

A youth who fears adventure fears to live
And from the world retreats.
Although our friends turned back,
With you I go!
My wife now thrice repeats.

To me the wiggling green sunlight below
Enticed like moths the flame.
Deep breaths I took, then toward that fairy light
I dove for game or shame.

How find the hole? So deep! Beware the walls!
My muscles soon got tight
My eyes and lungs seemed crushed when like a bomb
Burst forth a world of light!

Up, up and out I swam for air and life.
How glorious the game!
I was alone at sea. The breaking waves
The rocks hid whence I came.

My lonely fear for her a moment's wait
Made long my other life.
Like Venus from the sea splashing, gasping
For air, up popped my wife!

No rest! A half-hour's swim around the point,
The jagged rocks to flee.
No flippered feet, lifesaving belt or boat.
What lucky fools were we!

Robert Perault
BLUE STREAK BUICK (A SANTA FE JOURNEY)
And as you sit across from me
Amusing yourself by yourself
I sit and watch a peaceful cemetery pass us by,
Radial thoughts gobbling up radial roads
Where whispers arise beneath the blackness
Spirits of past, princesses and warriors.
They speak to me while you guide your blue streak . . .
On and on we go—our journey of hopes
You steer the floating chariot
Amusing yourself with deserts and clouds
While all around us I see arms of vapor
And they say "join us" voices—echoes—dancing shadows
Landscapes and dreams passing us and your "Riding on a Cloud Buick"
Angel on fire in time I know you'll see, you'll hear, you'll feel
Nows tears—nows pain—nows joy—nows rainbows and waterfalls
When I am but an image, a blurred memory or a distant dream
For as you amuse yourself by yourself traveling so fast
My fantasy arms are holding you lovingly
While the "Blue Streak, Riding on a Cloud Buick"
Suspends my thoughts in time . . .

Shaun McGinley
AS THE NIGHT FALLS
As the night falls
The darkness darkens
Sounds of an echo
Shatter the consistent remarks

Regrets from the past
Result in disgust
But when one lives this way
It is clear they are just

Control now abandoned
Pandemonium begun
Blame it on the few
Run far away—just run

What causes despair
What makes one cry
Tears—they mean nothing
Only redden the eyes

Robert Perault
THE SALTON SEA-DAWN
Dawn—you danced around my waking eyes
Tempting them to capture your magnificent birth
The Horizon on fire with your new day's spirit.
Succeeding in gently touching the morning clouds
With luminescent fire red—flowing into lavender—to shades of pink—shooting across an aqua sky
Colors softening with the fading miles—
I lay in a tent in awe of your pre sunrise show
How passionate and gentle—how easily you captured my sleeping spirit from its warm dreams
Seducing my soul—my senses charged with your awesome tribute
What glorious thing has sent you here?
It's as if you travel the universe and find
Some new place to suddenly raise the curtain of day
And captivate fish—fowl—all life—and tented men.
I thank you for the journey made
For you have left behind not only an undying memory
But slipped your peace and tranquility so unassumingly and assuredly into my spirit.
Dawn—you danced around my waking eyes—
And left your magic and spirit in my soul forever
Thankyou for freely sharing with all those who were fortunate enough to see.

Eloise Skelton Forrest
THE REVOLUTION IS NOT ALWAYS FOR PUBLIC CONSUMPTION
it was so hot
my hair would have gone back,
but it was already in its natural state
a crown, woven tightly on my head.
each strand attempted to protect its underbelly
from the steamy heat and passion
we/and nature generated
that summer in chicago
when we first became lovers.

on the sands of lake michigan
protected by the darkness
of a starless illinois sky,
i learned the true association
between Black Pride
and making love.

Ernie Glavaz
LIFE
Glistening beads of softly falling rain,
shattering the nothingness of mist . . . .

Shimmering pearls of infinite beauty,
gathering the scattered reflections . . . .

Holding all that life entails
in a single,
all too brief moment . . . .

A moment of glory,
A moment of life,
A universe,
complete,
sparkling,
magnificent,

and then,

Silence . . . .

Craig Furnas
ONE DAY
I see you and the look within your eyes;
Regret and despair sadly intertwined;
Your feeble laugh—denials but a guise
To hide the change from when your sweet face shined.
Of days gone past, you think upon their bliss,
And how to live again would bring you joy.
Those days, when here, you casually dismissed;
Denying days of yore was to destroy.
We'll live again, but better than before;
Dancing, drinking, soaking up the sun.
You'll grasp the cup of life and I shall pour;
Older but wiser, fools who've finally won.
One day we'll dance upon the grave of grieving,
Elation teeming so, we'll feel we're thieving.

Brian Allen Stephens
SMILE—LIGHT

To all the good people in my life, present and past; and especially my Mom.

She's got the smile light in her eyes,
She's got the smile light in her heart;
When you meet her you will see it shine
Like I did from the very start.

Her smile light is friendly.
It's very warm and quite sincere;
It will bring you certain happiness
Whenever you see it appear.

There will be no need to worry
For she will not do you wrong;
Her love is her best asset,
Peace and harmony her song.

And she may laugh and joke a moment,
Speak of silly little things;
Before the truth sneaks in and tells you
She's an angel with no wings

That's when you'll know that she is caring
You will know that she is fair
Pretty soon you'll see her smile-light
See it shining everywhere.

Nell Donohoe
THE HELMSMAN
Steer our ship,
my helmsman,
gentle as the southern breeze,
strong as the Sequoia.

Steer us through
the shoals of life.

Save us from the storm.

Wild winds blow
that shake us.
Lightning flashes,
thunder roars beside us,
but my helmsman laughs
and steers us with a song.

Head thrown back
he laughs;
he plays the wind,
he wins the storm.

Elias Dominguez Barajas
WHEN ALL IS DONE
When all is done,
I look to the blue mountains;
knowing not what I seek.

Perhaps it is respite—
respite I desperately need.

Respite from this infectious melancholy,
which invades all I see.

Yet, they rest aloof from me.

How am I to reach them?—
perhaps only in dreams.

But when all is done
I sit and wait,
For dreams that simply—
do not come.

Litzi Hartley
THE LAST ROSE OF WINTER

For Debi Lowe . . . where are you?

I was walking outside one December morning
The chilling north wind cut me
Like a scalpel slices flesh.
Fog shrouded the winter misery.

I came across a rose—
A generous, translucent peace rose
Frozen stiff, preserved as if in glass.
Icicles hung from the fragile leaves
Each petal was glazed with frozen dew.
It had blossomed late in the summer of my youth;
It was buried by autumn leaves
The golden leaves of time
And the crimson leaves of circumstance.
The icy killer winter caught it
In its summer bloom.
I reached out carefully, as not to break a petal,
And I touched the last rose of winter.

William R Appel
THE LAST TREE

She held her ground to persevere
against the ravishing odds,
She was one of the last bulwarks
in the army of the gods.
The enemy was a multitude
trying to bear her down,
And Chaos came near her, raging—
Raging—raging—
Chaos came near her raging, and
reaching for her crown.

Sky so black with smoke, Night's
stars could not be seen;
the sun obscured.
Animals in frenzy fleeing,—
streams fought, but Chaos
undeterred
Raced on, intent upon her
surrender and destruction.
Why such anger at her, flaming?
Flaming—flaming—
The last tree was flaming; omen
of oblivion.

Dana Alex Troy Untch

Dana Alex Troy Untch
OF LOVE WE SAY

Dedicated in Living memory of Dr. William W. P. Rivers, Phd

Of love we say
'Tis no game of play
Heart to heart,
Day to day,
Love is binding in every way . . .
And what of those we call friend?
They give and take but never pretend
So few are they we can depend,
A friend is a friend is a friend . . .
Are we learning how to hate?
We block our doors and lock our gate
With family and friends we must not wait
There is no time to hesitate.
Life is short and love is great
Hold on, love long, it is our fate . . .

Karen Y Weaver
THE CORRUPTIBLE CROWN

To a life that never quite knew how to live!

Now the accolade is a faint distant echo!
The bouquets have all withered and died!
The clippings are yellow and torn with age,
And the victory went out with the tide!

Despairing—recalling the "win"—
Retelling the moment of truth—
Resurrecting and trying to beat into life
The glories of our youth!

There is no respite for the passé victor!
Gone are the host of toasts!
Lingering alone in the lengthy eve
Is the "victor" inebriated on boasts.

Great was the price—the sacrifice
To obtain the Corruptible Crown!
With one way leading back (when the top has been reached)
It's a fast one . . . . All the way DOWN!

Richard Paul
A GENTLE POOL

I am a pool,
a gentle lake
A quiet place.
Reflecting that within my realm.
I do not make,
and only see what
ever is.
I'm not a judge
of shoulds or oughts
And, if you should forget,
The ripples that are made
Belong to you.
I am a pool,
a gentle lake
I am quite simply; you.

Dr Stanley S Reyburn
ANODIC MENTALITY

Pursue life in a positive vein
Observe sunshine instead of rain
Seek out peace—instead of war
Impede spreading of a verbal
mar
Tender a helping hand to
those in need
Insist on generosity—rejecting
greed
Value friendship as the human
bond
Elevating thoughts upward like
an angel's wand

Grace D Cardinal
SOME DAY, ONE DAY

I will not see you every day
as we must be apart,
But believe me when I say
you're always in my heart.
Someday we two shall meet again
I know not how or where,
But when we do, I'll say to you
how much I really care.
Meanwhile each day and night I ask
that God will grant my prayer,
To reach the rainbow's end my dear
and find YOU waiting there!

Judy Kendrick
TWINS

To my twin brother, Jerry, with love from your bigger half.

Twins in a playpen, eight months old
The boy is watchful, the girl is bold.
Twins in a cage, crying to escape
The girl clears the top, off the back of her wombmate.
Twins in a prison, expanded a million fold
The boy is ever young, the girl has grown old.
Twins in a complex, world not their own
The boy is the master, the girl's seed yet unsown.
Twins in a puddle, of ink, guts and bone
The boy breathes freedom, the girl cries for home.
Twins in a huddle, their fears yet unknown
Whatever the outcome, they'll not be alone.

Abraham Tarsish
ANGEL'S LIGHT FALL

Dedicated to all of those who thought they may have lost their wings when in reality, they have only just learned how to fly.

Some angels may fall to the ground;
Yet, they never lose their wings.
Their radiant splendor emanates
from within
And yet, mere mortals may not see
it.
Although, some may sense the truth
Without being blinded by the light.

Rita F Harrington
THE WATCHER

To my children—Cheryl and David

I always watched for them,
Anxious if they were late.
In the winter by the window
In the summer, knowing
they would be late.
And though at times they
mocked me tenderly,
who had such foolish care,
The long way home would seem
more safe
Because I waited there,

My thoughts were all so full of
them,
I never could forget!
And so I think when I'm not
here
I'll be watching yet,
Waiting till they come to me
anxious if they're late:—
Watching from Heaven's window
Watching from Heaven's gate.

Karen Plum
TWO HORSES

Two horses black and blue. Makes me sad makes me blue. Cry all night cry all day. Makes me feel as blue as a bay. One horse was ill, one horse was still. They lay on the ground, and I felt my heart pound.

Margaret Argondizzo
CHANGES

To my Children Gina and Stacy: I hope my daily changes show the love I hold inside for you both.

My Father, you see, was a strange
kind of man.
He never, ever took me by the hand.
How I longed to hug him—
Just give him a kiss
But deep inside I knew he would just
resist.
I longed for a smile,
a kind word or a hug.
That's all I ever wanted
was just to be loved!
He is gone—not forgotten—
He is deep in my mind
Somehow I know—I've just got to
find—
That he loved me in his own way,
and try not to yearn,
For a childhood better forgotten—
finished, done
And think of my children today and
do what I wished he had done.

Anthony Steward
A LOVE DEPARTURE

This poem is dedicated in memory of Ellen Burton, Grandmother love

I just dropped a careful tear
While hugging goodbye my favorite
dear
I've just watched a fading hand
awave
While a blowing kiss it gave
In the horizon my true love slips
low
It's always so hard when it's a long
way to go
A heart it takes too much time to
heal
But it's more at ease when there's
true love to feel.

Cathy A Bryan
CAN YOU HEAR ME MOMMY?

To my precious daughters, Katrina and Natalie

My days of life are numbered now,
it's very plain to see.
I heard my Mommy talking,
and she doesn't want me.

I thought this lady loved me,
but I guess it isn't so.
How could she undertake this task
and simply let me go?

I spend my hours just wondering
what life outside might bring.
Now, all to my amazement,
life's song I will not sing.

Please, Mommy, let me live!
is all I seem to say.
But will she somehow hear my
words
before that dreadful day?

Ruth Ann Burrell Hickey
BUTTERFLY

In the butterfly I see
A fragile personality,
Flying freely through the air,
Dying soon, with none to care.
I love you gentle butterfly,
Whose colors touch both heart and
eye.

Ken Meade
AMORE WINTER

Whatever boundaries separate us
As the winter rages
Outside the icy patterns turn
Tree and tower into frozen shapes
However the inner fire of hearth

And the lovely home is compensa-
tion
You are my captive with these words
Express it clearly like tingling
chimes
O' flowered coloured lady one . . .
Who held hands in semi-darkness
Of two spirits listening to violins
Sighing out of the cool fog night
And feel the warmth of returning
dawn
When the sun blesses earth's fragile
children

Yoni Star LeGrande
WIND DANCE

To my wonderful family and friends who always told me I could do it. Love always, Yoni

---

A radiant shimmering
summer day,
on a hot, African plain.

In a thorn bush
black-faced
tiger cubs play.

Above bleached, skeleton trees
shadowed birds dance
on whisps of colored wind,

moving to the beat
of ancient music,
that blows out of forgotten hills.

Celita Cantrell Werry
THE PORTRAIT OF A HOMELY GIRL

The picture hanging on the wall
Staring down upon us all.
The sad expression in her eyes
Seems to tell us that she cries.

She watches all our fun and games
Wishing that she had a name.
The torn up dress that she wears
Shows her distress but no one cares.

Long, straight hair, never been
brushed.
Lets us know her heart is crushed.
Her heart is crushed because she's
lonely.
Tell us, God, is this girl homely?

If you don't see how this could be
true,
I'll have you know, this girl could be
you.

Gloria Johannsen
BIRTHDAYS

Teens were jeans,
Twenty . . . . . . dreams,
Thirty, a woman's best!
Oh hell, forget the rest—

Forty . . . . . . life begins,
Fifty . . . . . . who dares?
Sixty . . . . . . .who cares!
The very best age by far
Is the one right where you are!

Rosalind Gene Schmorak
MOTHER'S HANDS

Dedicated to the memory of my dear late Mother, the most charming and most spiritual person I have ever known.

We held hands
Hers were warm, gentle, loving,
They held mine tenderly
They were not old, merely frail
With light blue veins and tapering
fingers,
The moons on her nails were white
as cream
When she was young she shined
them with powder
Her delicate hands never grew
wrinkled
They caressed mine so softly
Always revealing her love,
Her sight failed
Her hearing left her
But her hands were the key
That unlocked the door to her soul.

Gretchen M Klein
ALL MY LOVE

To my John Alan, with love and respect.

All my love
is for you
All my love
can get you through
the grief you're being handed
the people who've left you stranded

All my dreams
lie with you
All my dreams
are all about you
My hopes, my fears
and any tears I shed
will be over you
I love you

J R Deardurff
EAGLE

This is dedicated to animal lovers everywhere, and to my beloved children. Val, Jamie, & April.

If I could be an Eagle
with wings that spread so proud,
I'd fly the highest hilltop
or even upon a cloud.

Like time do they fly
when they are free, to share the
wind,
And seldom do they rest
for them there is no end.

The Eagle is my idol
he's brave, bold and wise,
For he will not betray you
or tell you any lies.

When my life has ended
and darkness settles in,
I'd find another life
and be an Eagle again.

Douglas Cowan
VALENTINE'S DAY

In memory of my grandfather Albert Cohen, December 14, 1904—February 14, 1989

He lies in the hospital bed
All alone on Valentine's Day.
Always in a lot of pain, with
Nothing but death to gain.
Don't want to wait another day
Now is the last chance to say,
"I love you"
"I love you"
On this special day.
The pain is fading away,
Eyes close, breathing shallow
Heart beats shallowly
Can't open eyes or talk
Can hear everything said
Want to say more but can't
Pain and suffering a thing
of the past.
Nothing but joy to always last
At last going home free of pain.
Life's journey is now over.

S Hawkins
HELLO GEORGE

My President's Birthday is today.
I don't even know how old he is
Or would be today,
I never knew him.
And yet, his name is George.
You know him, too.
I've read about him, saw his
Reflection, his face on every
$1 bill I've held and exchanged
For food or clothes or housing.
He is my country's father,
He is my country's first.
Happy Birthday, Mr. George
Washington!
I wish I had known you,
To have shaken your hand,
To have said thanks.
Thanks for my freedom
Which I hold dear.
Thanks for my country
Which I hold dear.
Thanks Mr. President and Happy
Birthday today.

Kim Schoenberger
I'D GIVE YOU A ROSE

I'd give you a rose, if I thought
you'd take it;
I'd give you my heart, but I know
you'd break it.
I'd give you a rose, of any hue;
I'd give you the feelings, I feel for
you.
I'd give you a rose, picked from
the briar;
I'd give you my eyes, filled with
desire.
I'd give you a rose, whose petals
are soft;
I'd give you my dreams, that soar
aloft.
I'd give you a rose, with many a
thorn;
I'd give you a soul, that's been
forlorn.
I'd give you a rose, long of stem;
I'd give you the hope, to live
again.
I'd give you a rose, that's sure to
unfold;
I'd give you my mind, and its
secrets untold.
I'd give you a rose, if I thought
you'd take it;
I'd give you my heart, but I know
you'd break it.

Bernadine Larson
MY WISH

To Jack

If I could wish a wish for you
I'd wish that skies be blue
I'd wish your days be long
And full of work and joy,
I'd wish you trees of green
And flowers of every hue
A quiet brook, a shady nook
And time for many things,
I'd wish you love to last for life
Yes, longer yet than this,
A love that grows and grows each
day
And reaches perfect bliss—
All this and more I'd wish for you
If God but grant my prayer
I'd add for you a perfect faith
In Him who first loved you
A faith to see you safely through
Every stress and strife
And bring to you the perfect gift,
The gift of a perfect life.

Kathleen Carroll
TO LAURA

This poem is dedicated to the memory of my sister Laura Ann Carroll who died April 13, 1987 four days before her 25th birthday

---

You knew I always loved you
no matter how you made me feel
and now that you're gone
it doesn't seem very real.

You always told the truth
and very seldom lied,
you were the one who cheered me up
when Mom died.

And now you're with Mom
that's where God wants you, I see
You were the best sister
there ever could be.

Mercedes Tolan-Parker

Mercedes Tolan-Parker
MY BABY GIRL

To my Auntie, Sallie Bob, 87. To my baby girl, Salli-Tymna, 8 months.

My baby girl—
There's nothing like her in the whole
world!

A heavenly package that's so dear;
Bringing gentleness, warmth, and
cheer.

She's God's gift from above,
That's filled my life with so much
love.

Barbara A Newby
STAND UP AMERICA

Stand up America!
Let's get our act together.
We're foundering in a mire,
And we need a change of weather.

Let's teach our children true values.
Make them very proud to be.
A part of a great country,
For other nations to see.

There's lots of good around us,
But the bad keeps getting the fame.
Let us all pull together
And put our critics to shame.

We've gone too long as the "Great
One"
To allow a downfall now.
So let's tighten our belts, and grit our
teeth,

And make our enemies bow.

Our flag must continue to stand,
Our pioneer spirit endure.
As really true Americans,
Our intentions must be pure.

We need you America,
No matter how hard the road.
We'll come out fine, if we all try
And everyone shares the load.

No other country has it all,
As this most wondrous land.
We must fight to keep it strong,
Or freedom's our last stand.

Lena Parker
OLD AND YOUNG

To my Mom and Son. The Poem is about The Old and the Young.

When oh when did you go
walking in the rain, And squish
the mud between your toes.
A Kid again, how important to
be a Kid again.
In this world of hurry and
rush, take time out.
A clear spring brook flowing,
through a meadow of
flowers.
Little sheep grazing, on a
pasture of luscious grass.
God in all his glory
planted these things for
us to enjoy,
Why oh why is it so important for
us to succeed to buildings,
of plaster and mortar cold oh so
cold.
Good things childlike
simplicity, God's way.
Beautiful people old, walking
book of knowledge, reaching,
reaching out to young for
Love Championship.
Time out, Time out!

M W Maccree Jr
MEASURE OF LOSS
Somewhere I love
Somewhere I cry
Let the world guess at all I imply
Schizophrenia borders on genius
Yet pretend we never to change
Unconcerned for that we're unaware
"Define yourself if you dare,"
Our defenses counter,
"and condemn me not my lack of
conviction."

Building dreams
We spend the greater of our lives
Each of us in harmony
With those who share our purpose
Collectively we make up a single
entity
Ever changing to endure the ages

Mourn not our destruction
How should we cease to exist?
If all we've built is suddenly
shattered
Oh joyous time!
We begin a'new to develop our
destiny
With greater wisdom and precision
For all that was will never be lost

Doris Brown Ware
SEASONS
Big thaw, earth is in awe;
Bubbling brooks, in many nooks.
A soft breeze is blowing, life is
stirring and growing,
Spring is going,
Good-bye, goodbye!

Beautiful flowers feeding bees;
It's hot, I like the shade of the trees.
A soft breeze is blowing, school bells
will be tolling,
Summer is going,
Good-bye, good-bye!

Colored leaves, smiling from trees;
Hills high, watching the sky.
A soft breeze is blowing, it soon will
be snowing,
Autumn is going,
Good-bye, good-bye!

Moonlight bright, shining on white;
Coldest chill, from valley and hill.
A soft breeze is blowing, it's just
finished snowing.
I've waited a year,
Winter is here!

Carolyn Holleran

Carolyn Holleran
FOREVER MINE

To my Father and Mother and to all the mothers of the world

Stay close to me my little one.
To me you are so dear.
Stay close to me my little one,
Remember our hearts were near.
When you're away and others call
Remember not to fall
Just think of me and I'll be there
A million miles away. I'd care even
When you're not there
And when we met, my heart in flight
A million dreams did send.
And when we're old and stories told
Of loves both yours and mine. We'll
Sit and laugh, our hands entwined
For you're forever mine.

Toni M Price
LOVE AND WINE ARE SO MUCH ALIKE

To Don Coen and Kenny Price, (Cheers)

Love and Wine are so much alike.
It's all in the packaging, at first
the bottles are always attractive,
and the prices usually vary, but you
must shop around,
to get the best buy. For you can pay
the ultimate price,
and find that once opened, the
contents may be poisoned,
and may leave you feeling sick and
delirious.
And at this point you are blind to the
obvious.
But if you can find that certain label,
you will find
that inside, the precious nectar will
enhance every color of the rainbow.
But be careful, let it breathe, and
don't be selfish.
For this may be the last time that you
ever find such a bargain.
And if you find it, let me know
where.
I've been searching a long time for a
bottle of the good stuff.
And I would gladly pay retail.

Patricia A Williams
THE SEDUCTION
The darkness is overwhelming
Engulfing me in its entirety
Coaxing and beckoning.
Oh how I wish I was safe from it
I am not.
Now I am a part of the dark,
Part of the nothingness,
The blackness,
The evil.
It's not so bad anymore.
I have control
The blood flows at my command.
Now I am a part of the dark,
Part of the nothingness,
The blackness,
The evil.
And I am loving it.

Donald A A Leone
PROCLAMATION FOR TRUE EQUALITY
We The People, of these United
States,
friends, foes, and Loving Mates.
Are supposed to be Equal and share
the same,
Regardless, of our race, religion, or
name.

We sometimes wonder, what our
Forefathers meant.
When the Constitution was wrote,
signed, and sent.
Did they know, the fate of this Great
Nation,
To the bearers of all future
generations.

Throughout the years, as time has
passed
Many were born and then were
Classed,
From lower, to middle, to upper
we're named,
Bearing the thought we're not to be
shamed.

So life tells in many tales,
That few succeed, and many fail.
The hardships and struggles, through
the maze,
Leave many poor, hungry, and tried
with craze.

If only our leaders, could have
managed a way,
All could be treated, and helped
Equally, every day
Instead of being a poor, hungry,
homeless mass,
We would all be listed, in one Equal
Class.

Jeanne M Neville
WINTER WITHOUT SNOW

This poem is dedicated to Tom, Michael, Robbie, my loving family

As I gaze from my window
This glorious morn,

My eyes fall upon the trees
The bareness of them all.

They stare at me
As though they're waiting,

Waiting, most graciously
For the snow to fall

And blanket the ground,
Or a winter it won't be.

The days go by and still we wait
Ever so patiently,

For the beauty of winter in its
Wonderland, for everyone to see.

At last, winter has passed
A winter without snow.

Patricia Reniche
THE AMERICAN DREAM, AS THEY TOLD IT TO ME
THE AMERICAN DREAM, as they
told it to me, was a land that was
bold, energetic and free;

Where leaders were honest and
heroes were true, and never would
many be governed by few;

Where pride was a virtue, hard work
earned reward, and people gave
reverent thanks to the Lord.

I learned of this land in my classroom
at school; American savvy and God's
Golden Rule:

The perfect examples to fashion my
life—until the "real world"
introduced me to strife.

What happened to virtue and heroes
and prayer; and where's the reward
for the people who care?

Why is my country just looking
away when wrongdoers live in our
midst every day?

Where are the parents, the teachers,
the rules; what happened to family,
home and good schools?

Were parents so busy and teachers so
scared that children grew up feeling
nobody cared?

Is that why, now grown, I see only a
herd of adults whose ethical vision is
blurred?

Adam Martin
RACER
The man sits in his car.
He looks down to the end of the
hallway.
He wants to go fast.
As soon as the closet door closes,
he's going.
The door closes and he's off.
His feet spin on the carpet, and he
shoots forward.
Top speed for a quarter mile.
His chute doesn't open, he can't
stop.
Through the door, he crashes on the
bed in a ball of flame.
Laughing.

Kristian Doty
WHISPERING RAIN

To the love that left me blind

I was looking in the dictionary
And I saw the word Love
It said don't look here

Your love is gone

I remember how quickly you left
How swiftly my heart was broken
But still I hear your whisper
So softly in the falling rain
And maybe you won't be able to see
My tears that fall too

Day to day I don't go without
The pain of missing you
And why my heart won't let go
Of the love we once shared
Because it is gone

I can still hear your whisper
In the falling rain
And maybe you won't be able to see
My heart that breaks too

Tomorrow I beg the sun to shine
To warm my soul within
Because I don't want to hear your whisper
If it rains again

Nancy L Goates
LOVE ME, BE WITH ME

To Andy, thank you for being there for me all of the times I have needed you to be, you are a special person in my life.

My darling, ever so gently, cuddle me close,
speak softly into my ear;
of all that we've been through,
love me, be with me;
until heaven takes us in;
endure all we have done,
and all we have said,
in this world of sin and disgrace;
we still have each other;
together, forever.

Wanda Weiskopf
NATURAL BIRTH

Dedicated to Alder McKay

A child of nature, lulled in mother-womb
You felt the overwhelming timely urge
To leave your safe protected inner room
And face the trial that needed life's first surge
Of energy and sweet desire to thus exist
Among your kind, the evolutionary man,
Created in living mystery to perhaps enlist
Your aid in furthering the universal plan . . . .
Mother and child in league from breath to breath
Cooperating fully to bring about
The culmination of life, so cheating death
And bringing the noblest truth to all who doubt;
The necessary paths did all converge
And see your tiny infant head emerge!

Sue Theobald
CANDLE'S DANCE

To my loving husband George—For all the love, support and encouragement you give me. I love you!

A candle's flickering, ritual dance
Reflecting off the wall.
The glow upon your soft, warm skin
Wrapped in the ember's shawl.

The glistening of your silken hair
The firelight on your face.
To the song of gentle breathing
The flames keeping silent pace.

The candlesticks, now puddled wax
Their glow still in your eyes.
Blanketed within their warmth
The fire slowly dies.

Trish Fessenden
MECA—IF I COULD

This poem is dedicated to my best friend, who has cancer

If I could just tell you
What I really feel
I wouldn't write it down
But, it's no less real

If I could just show you
That I can be strong
And that, we'll get through this
No matter how long

If I could just hold you
And give you a hug
You couldn't help but feel
All of my love

If I could just wish
It would have to be
To have my friend always
Here beside me

If I could just give you
One special thing
It will be my friendship
And all the love it brings

Della Neavoll

Della Neavoll
TELL ME A STORY OLD HOUSE

This Poem is dedicated to my sisters Viva, Geneva, Arlene, and Betty who have given me years of joy.

Tell me of the family that lived on Independence St. Tell me of the people they all loved to greet.
Tell me of the Father who worked at the mill, who loved his daughters dearly and they long for him still.
Tell me of the Mother who baked bread every day, who hoed weeds in her flowerbed and taught her children how to pray.
Tell Me A Story Old House.
Where are the mud puddles that went through the road?
Running to the bus stop what memories they hold.
Where are the little girls with their laughter at play?
Have they all grown-up and moved far away?
Remember the fellows that used to call. "Hotrod," Pete, Ronnie and Paul.
Oh, those girlfriends they once knew, Emily, Kathrene, Jeanne and Sue.
TELL ME A Story Old House.
The old cellar standing out in the back, the train's whistle you could hear from the railroad track.
The father reading his bible in his old rocking chair. The little girls putting pink curlers in his graying hair.
Sunday was the Lord's Day and to worship they all went,
The little girls with their hair in curls, it was hours the mother had spent.
Tell Me A Story Old House.
The big willow tree with its branches so tall. It held many swings and was a playhouse for one and all.
Tell me of the little girl that cried so hard the night of Xmas Eve, was it because of the doll her sister brought she held upon her knee?
The rains fell through the attic and the foundation needed repair. Although the walls rang with laughter of the love that could be found there.
Tell Me A Story Old House.
What of the tear rolling down her face, as she drove back to the town to look at this place? The house was gone it was plain to see. The old house was home, our home, it was
home to me.
Tell Me A Story Old House.

CRWTH
FROM A VOID

Dedicated to Lita, Marta, Carlos

The empty page
Leers straight at me,

Commanding a verse
To titillate thee.

Cynthia Ippolito
LIFE

Life is good, Life is bad
Life is happy, Life is sad
Life is never what we want it to be, but
That's the way it has to be
We have to give, we have to take
And sometimes we make a mistake,
And when we do we have to let it be
Cause that's Life
And that's how it has to be.

Jane Sigmon
THE SELF MADE MAN

He has an air of cool, confidence and control.
Some times he seems indifferent, unyielding and cold.
Yet he can be a prankster in a childlike play.
Then he is caring and sensitive in an understanding way.

A bright and outspoken man with a "golden" tongue.
Knowing his glory and successes will be sung.
He is able to win affections and respect of most.
Everyone will praise him and he never has to boast.

He uses his humor and keen awareness to charm and seduce.
It makes everyone want to hold him and never turn him loose.
He's not afraid to be different or call attention to himself.
Using all his intellect and wit—he has no flaws left.
To manipulate people without their even knowing;
He gets just what he wants without it ever showing.
Thriving on the admiration, he enjoys it around the clock.
He's definitely a "shepherd" and not just one of the flock.

Betty Hronek
SILENT CRY

Don't look the other way,
We're crying out to you!
Don't look the other way,
There's so much you can do!

Don't overlook our bruises,
The sadness in our eyes.
The symptoms of withdrawal—
These all are silent cries.

Help us please—look and see
Reach out a helping hand.
To us, the abused children,
The neglected in this land!

We are all around you,
Tortured, sick and dying.
If you listen with your heart,
You'll hear our silent crying.

Pick up the phone or write
Someone who'll set us free
From our prison of pain and fear,
Your conscience holds the key!

Jerry W Hayes
THE MAN FROM CALVARY

They sought to punish me
but instead I was blessed,
for in my prison cell
to my saviour I confessed.

With a humbled spirit
and with swallowed pride
I asked Jesus for forgiveness
having realized why He died.

Suddenly I became aware
that my prison cell
wasn't made of concrete & steel
but of evil straight from hell.

Then Jesus came to me and said
"My friend, you are free,
for I paid for your sin
with my life at Calvary."

Tears filled my eyes
and peace filled my heart
for Jesus tore the walls of
my prison cell apart.

This you might not understand
for behind bars of steel I still lay,
because I broke the law of man
and that bill I must pay.

But my body is all
that they have locked away,
for my heart and my spirit
are free to run and to play.

Let them believe whatever
they wish about me
for what they think doesn't effect
the love of the man from Calvary.

Christina Padden
ON THEIR HEADS . . .

They said NEVER: It will never be done.
Stern, Rigid Men of black and grey flannel,
Marble faced, Ex-children of the rain
Marked this-end-up since birth,
Intangible bolts through the feet
Bore into the middle of the Earth.

But I did it, just this morning.
Defied established
Arguments and order and gravity,
I wrapped my hands about the bolts,

Pulling and twisting and wrenching,
A palpable struggle.

When the screws were loose,
The lines rent and frayed,
The glue chipped and scraped,
Ceilings razed to piles of rubble,
Something remarkable, unexplain-
able, unexpected.

These steel-jointed men
Flipped indirectly
Topsy-turvey—head-over-heels,
Circus acrobats,
Bouncing beachballs all over the
field,
Stopping only to stand
On their heads.

Ralph E Canning
THE CROSS
In the light of Jesus' victory,
Look to the cross, dear one.
He smiled that day on Calvary,
As He knew the battle was won.

Look to the cross, visualize His
smile,
See the love of glorious perfection.
His struggle with pain was mild.
With precious blood He purchased
salvation.

Victory over sin, rejoice and be glad,
Remember His promises and
continuing love.
Cherish His gift, do not be sad.
He smiles down at us from above.

He'd like the tears of those who
grieve,
To dry before the sun,
And afterglow of smiles, He'd like to
leave,
For He knew His work was done.

Bob Currie
THERE'S A BREATH ON THE WIND
there's a breath on the wind
a name.
it drifts to me in quiet times
I seek it out
when chaos rules the day
the night
the times of quiet despair
the times when I know myself
too well

there is a breath on the wind
a name
it carries no illusions
it brings not a vision
but a magic
a feather on a gentle pain
a touch
a fabric of mind once held
folded and carefully hidden
too well.

Cristiana A Roth
STRANGE DESTINATIONS
I heard the underground thoughts trip
out into your mind.
I saw the shade of your dreams
squeeze out into the time.

I felt you in a trance
As the telephone bills and tickets
Blow into distance.
I felt your grave silence
As the house mortgage and interests
Melt into disgrace.
I sensed the new, Strange
Destination
Leaving your thoughts stoned.
Then the words dragged without
inspiration,
The Day broke, the Sky burned.
I saw you passing
And I was too exhausted to breathe.
I heard you muttering
To reshape circumstances in a haze.

I can hear the rumors of the street
And there is an oddness about it.
I can feel your unmistakable scent
Brake into the unflappable
present . . .

Alyse Lynne Rubinstien
DREAM OF DREAMS
If I could dream the dream of
dreams . . .
The allusive butterfly would be mine
. . . !
Dolphins swimming in a sea of green,
I would find . . .
The unicorn would be my friend
And the humpbacks' song would
never end . . . !

If I could dream the dream of
dreams . . .
Happiness would flood the
air . . . !
All hearts would be one, would be
shared . . .
Auroras would fill the sky with light
And all of our dreams would come
true tonight . . . !

Kim Gilliland
EVENING DELIGHT
As beauty surrounds the evening sky,
With soft, pink clouds passing by,
And a cool, calm, gentle breeze
blowing,
Created by the Almighty, God all
knowing,

The world so big and strong grows
dim,
As night time slowly drifts in,
Giving an atmosphere of peace
abroad,
From the enormous pine tree, to the
moist sod,

The air grows cooler and the ground
does too,
Preparing for the early morning dew,
As the birds have stopped singing
their peaceful song,
The sound of the crickets grows very
strong,

The shining moon gives off its soft
light,
And the stars join in making it
bright,
Twinkling and sparkling as if with
joy,
Their luminous light, none can
destroy,

This atmosphere is so calm and
quiet,
Not a sign of strife or even a riot,
Every bit of creation seems, full with
grace,
And those privileged to enjoy it are
the human race.

Donna J Laughner
SERENADE IN POETRY
Softly I come to you in a poem,
I creep in with a word.
In the splendor of words unspoken,
To the timing of gifted song,
I sing into your mind,
Sounds entwined for the moment.
Then I leave you with tender
thoughts to linger,
Like the fragrances of a summer's
night.

Like a rose that has captured its
beauty,
To entice you to take leave of its
scent.
And sigh—as you behold and caress
its joy.
Like the rose, the poem has bloomed
for you.
And as you close your eyes, or turn
this page,
It will wait for another season to
enjoy.
I leave you now, may it not be
forever.
Just as the page is lost in the book,
My words are lost in your mind.
So savoring the gift to comprehend
and to hold dear,
We shall forever be, the poet and the
reader . . .
Goodbye.

Ruby W Bledsoe
THE COUNTRY STORE
Do you remember the Country Store

ah twas fifty years or more
we gathered round the old coal stove
where we went to buy apples
cinnamon and clove
Some came by buggy, others by sled
for sugar and coffee and apples so
red.
We knew everyone for miles around
no need to hurry . . . we settled
down.
We learned all the news as we
warmed our hands
how things were going in foreign
lands
We got our Mail at the Post Office
too
Paid the storekeeper when we were
through.
I miss those days at the Country
Store
and I miss those friends, who are no
more.
But we must go forward, We can't
turn back
just keep on living . . . face the fact.

We traded the Buggy, Moved to
town
Now we must hurry, scurry around.
When I remember those days gone
by
I feel sorta sad and . . . I wonder
why.

Pamela J Douglass
LIVE, LOVE, LAUGH
Live, love, laugh
Those are words of advice
Spend each moment to its fullest
You don't have to think twice

Precious are the moments
Memories will never fade
So start taking chances
Your life has not yet been made

Follow your dreams
They will lead you along the way
Listen to your heart
Let come what may

Take time out to see the ocean
Or just look at the stars
You can go as far as you want
Because life has no bars

Don't worry about your problems
They will work out in the end
Don't say "what if"
Or you will never begin

Astrida B Stahnke
WILLFULNESS
In modern poetry, he said,
avoid the oh or o.

Still . . .

I love to ornament my verse
with some spontaneous
overflow.
I like, I thought, to pin
on my vogue overcoat
an oval cameo.

Carl A Galler
AM I BLUE
Valentine; are you mine?
What do I need to do;
To get from you, the love I knew—
So briefly, and so fine?

Am I special? Am I true?
Can I and "love" endure?
Because I've known, so few who've
loved,
And I'm an open door.

Christi Henderson

Christi Henderson
KID SISTER

To my "Kid Sister", Velinda Raye H.

I have a kid sister,
Who's a big blister.
She grows on you just like a wart.
The wart grows and grows just like a
tumor.
I'd like to extract that tumor, but
Mom says, "No, she's only your kid
sister."

Louis Gates
THE AIDS RACE
Come a little closer look me in the
face
I am the AIDS virus come to kill the
human race.

You know I am out there on every
street.
I'm the AIDS virus cooking up a
treat.

I will make your friends forget you
your family turn away.
I will make you suffer every single
day.

So do not believe me and go out

tonight.
I will be there just out of sight.

You know I am here to stay.
For the cure won't be here today.

Margaret Killmer
DWARF
the dwarf dwells in the dungeon,
the dwarf dines on ducks, donuts and disgusting things;
the dwarf likes to dig and dance,
the dwarf doesn't like dogs and dinosaurs,
the dwarf killed my dog with a dagger.

Carol Abts
ONCE TOUCHED
Quietly consuming flesh and soul,
Reach boundaries of secret desire
Never felt, until overcame
Sparking a eternal fire

Demanding to be fulfilled.
Your soul can't faithfully ignore
Burning the emptiness from within
Leaving you wanting more

Although taking your breath away
You've never felt more life
For once touched by love
It may scar like a knife

Alvin Richard Doreck
SUCCESS
I can tell by your style,
that you are a successful man.
Old, but well dressed.
And with a manner grand.
But look out for me, pop.
Someday I will be at the top.
Oh, I must have had a hundred jobs.
I haven't quite got it yet.
But I've got plenty of time.
And will hit it soon, you bet.
Say, while you are doing nothing old man.
How about showing me the way, to the promised land.
What's that you say?
I passed it on the way?

Janet Austill-McCaslin
TO GRANDMA WITH LOVE
Dear Grandma I sit writing this,
wishing I was there.
So we could sit and talk awhile,
of the good times that we've shared.

We always lived so far away,
when I was growing up.
That we didn't get to talk or see,
each other near enough.

But I remember colorful balloons,
and sparkling rubber balls.
That you would bring each one of us,
when you would come to call.

Then in the mornings at your house,
up at the bar we'd sit.
Eating wheat toast and jelly,
to me was such a hit.

This poem to you I'm writing,
to show how much I care.
And especially to say thank you,
for the special times we've shared.

Clifford James McNamara
VISIONS OF DESTINY
Visions of destruction have been placed within my mind and I've seen the silver dragons soar deep within the skies.
I have seen the demons fashioned in many different ways with only one thing in common humans was their prey.
Moving as fast as lightning and making shrieking sounds as they made their lasers flash upon the ground
There were bodies of slain men laying everywhere as the smell of death and brimstone mingled through the air.
Even the whole earth trembled and woe the heavens shook, because man had forgotten the holy book, and he somehow let the devil take his very soul.
So tell me now, dear brothers, who will stroll the streets of Gold?

Kathy Miller
PARENTS
Parents are special, this is true
So here's a message from me to you.

So many nights you've stayed awake,
To cure my ills and ease my aches.
You've sacrificed for years and years,
Tended my bruises and dried my tears.

It may sometimes appear that I've forgot
How much you've done without, so I would not
I may not always say it, but, please believe
I am thankful for all that I have received.

But the thing I am most thankful for
Cannot be bought or sold in a store.
It's a debt to you I can never repay
It's The Love you give day after day.

So this is my way of making you see
I haven't forgot what you've done for me
I wrote this poem to tell you it's true
Mom and Dad I Love You

Lois C Spivey
YOUR LOVE
I am finally at peace with the world that has dealt me so much pain, but only because you came into my life and made it worth the struggle that comes with being a caring person. Your love has overwhelmed my sorrow that once ran deeper than the deepest ocean and has filled my heart with the warmth of the fire that burns within your soul.

My feelings for you are like the rays from the sun shining down upon my face, and my love for you so deep that words would merely touch the surface of excitement that comes to me when I think of you. When I touch your lips with mine, I feel the warm tears of joy welling up from my chest and flowing into my eyes, and when your hands touch me, it almost hurts, as I have longed for you.

When we finally embrace, it is as though no one else exists except you and I, with all of our love, forever.

Meg Rood
EXTERNAL BEAUTY
The sky is blue, the sun shines bright.
The birds pass by so graceful in flight.
Flowers are blooming, Children at play.
Just look and see what a wonderful day.
I sit here and watch the stream as it's flowing.
The leaves are rustling, a cool wind is blowing.
Butterflies fill the sky flying free.
I can't believe the beauty surrounding me.
A rabbit hops by and stops to pose,
in a field of green where clover grows.
The day is ending the sunsets from above.
The things that I saw filled me with love.
Nature is beautiful and should be left be!
Just like man it is meant to be free.
I think of this day and wish all people feel this way.
Nature should not be something of the past.
But if man is not wise, nature will not last.

Jan K Rainey
THE PURSUER
Like a tormented beast
Pursuing you day and night
Hounding you continually
Fright is always waiting

Hiding in the darkening shadows
Awaiting—
Awaiting the inevitable—
Its chance to consume you.

Tricia Daley
FROM BEGINNING TO END
Friends forever,
No matter what the cost
All our love,
A pure and simple honesty
A new beginning
Such sweet surroundings
All precious times together but alone
Because from beginning to end
I'll always love you

Friends can never sever
In the cold winter frost
The sign for peace is a dove
Sweet as honey that attracts a bee
Our dove flew away
You found something sweeter
But you will continually be special
Because from beginning to end
I'll always love you.

J Bradley Hoffman
ICE (THE AWAKENING OF THE SOUL)
Ice burns the briefest touch.
The finger bleeds its crimson life.
The pain consumes the mind in a golden flame, and life is banished from blackened eyes.

Hold the hair of Ice and sever the wrists upon the razor's edge.
The mind screams for its painless death;
lingers the heart for another wound.
Destroyed is the spirit, crushed within frozen walls.
The spirit strikes, biting deep the earthly throat.
The child must die for life to begin.
Enters the Ice with its burning touch.

Bring to mind the pain of Ice.
Touch the facade and know her demise.
Ice has become your essence;
tear her grip and destroy you soul.

You have become one with Ice.

Johnette English
A WINTRY WALK ON THE BEACH
I love to go walk on the beach, especially during the winter. I can dress the way I want to, and I feel the sun hitting my face keeping me warm inside.
I think about life on the beach; I look at the sea and think to myself, "Where has this water been?" Standing there, I watch and at the same time, listen to the waves come in and then turn themselves around and go back out. It makes such wonderful music.
One of the most romantic places I know of during the winter is the beach. The air is so cool and crisp. It is as if the air is talking to us, telling us just to relax and bundle up. While we are sitting down talking, the water plays its music for us.
On the beach I can see the color change. It changes from a brown sunny-crust color to a black color, almost as if death is taking it over. In other ways, it is just blossoming into one of God's most beautiful creations on this earth.

Evelyn M McNair
UNDERSTOOD
To be understood
Let life stand still

To be understood
See all life has to offer

To be understood
Enjoy all that life has bestowed you

To be understood
Understand yourself.

James T Grider
POETRY
Poetry is a good way
To tell of dreams and love,
To tell about things on this earth
And heaven up above.

Love is what makes life worthwhile,
And our dreams should be
Interwoven with our love,
As smooth as poetry.

Debra Rae Myers
NIGHT HAS FALLEN
night has fallen

music drones on and on
in the background
Lennon lives to mock me
eternally

a cold cup of bitter black coffee
imprints its image into
a letter
eternally

you staring at me staring at you
frozen on a piece of paper
by chemicals
eternally

cold fingers

throbbing chest
screaming words fill my mind
trapped by inept hands
foolish dreams in an unfit brain
senseless utterance
drivel from a babes mouth
and Eliot laughs listlessly
eternally

another night has fallen

Marsha Coller
I WISH HE HAD KISSED ME
I wish he had kissed me.
He leaned my way; I thought he
would . . .
We sat there in quiet for just a
moment
Within the cozy confines of the car.
In a brief and fleeting instant
Of exchanging our goodnights,
I paused, he waited . . .
So why did we hesitate? I really
can't say.
Why did we let that moment pass?
Was it merely shyness?
(If so, I was a fool.)
And if ever that chance comes my
way once more.
I shall not hesitate. Still,
I wish he had kissed me.

Tracy Liston

Tracy Liston
FRIENDS

To my best friends in the world, my mom and Missy Gage I appreciate you faithfulness through all the hard times thanks for putting up with me.

I don't know how we find friends.
I only know a few who are true.
Those we have are those we keep,
friends aren't won or bought, they
see a need and come to help. They
know just how you feel and they try
to understand.

They are the ones who dare to care
when the world doesn't, they share
their feelings and they open their
hearts.

They give advice but don't push,
they wait to catch you if you fail,
then they give you the inspiration to
go on.

Friends are there for you when you
want to be crazy, when you want to
cut loose;
A friend cares and shares but is also
a help to others when they are down.
I'm just glad that you're my friend.

W Notta
UNISEX
You carry your curling hair
And dashing lids in pride,
And yield your arm to me,
Which is as fresh and warm,
Only disdainfully.

The fibers of your strains,
The cells of your delicate skin
Grow and breathe like mine,
Whatever difference there,
Is not worth mentioning.

E Brian Walsh
SAND CRABS
Armed with a contented smile
and a brace of past hells survived,
He stood alone by the sea.
His torment faded
When she entered his inner space
Willingly, they lay there together
Bodies merging as one.
The gentle waves lap the shore.

Kathleen Hagen
A CHRISTIAN LIFE

Dedicated to my son John who went to be with the Lord at the age of 20 yrs. and whom I plan to see again.

This life we lead is
filled with pain;

Be it illness, injury or
loss of gain.

We work and toil each
day on this earth;

To improve our lifestyle
and add to our worth.

The thing we don't realize
until too late;

Is all our hard work
won't change our fate.

The Lord gave us the
true gift of life;

And in the end we return
out of this strife.

To the place of beginning
that's filled with pleasure and love;

And living forever with our
treasure waiting above.

Madalyn Hahn
MY DOLL OF LONG AGO
Beautiful doll of long ago
How did you age so well?
Your cheeks are as pink, and your
skin as fair
As in the days I loved you so.

You have been in a chest a long,
long time
Sleeping the years away.
Is that why you are so beautiful
now
As in the days when we loved to
play?

I believe you are even lovelier
now,
You have a very special charm.
Is it because you have lived a
long, long time
And been shielded from all
harm?

It must be because of the joy you
brought
And to the child who kept you so
well.
I would love to know your secret,
But I don't believe you are going
to tell.

Carla C DeSilva-Thurston
RUNNING SHOES
Run if you must
I must
Watch where those shoes may take
you
running for your peace of mind
running ground
What fate ran you here
and away
from where I stand
bare feet unable to catch your trail
shoes may age alone
dressed feet
you may not catch me—

Homans Donnelly
AFTER 60 YEARS A BIRTHDAY SONG
Still in the morning's mind (did we
dream the call)
"I am not in a good place these days"
"Birthdays can be an ugly job"
Grief thrown out into the night
If the answers had been better
Would I have worn this movie
actor's face
Flesh seeping through this sweet day

How much exposure can we endure?
In your town the oak murdered from
its height
A momentary pain
A piercing echo spreading desolation
We cannot hold the center

Before the dream, flickering down
the darkened garden path,
Fair haired
Where is she going, my sister?
As if we did not know, and knowing
did not know
History pacing the night
Dreaming women sitting at the
bridge table
Coming and going the Grandchild's
face
(This soft impression of loss)

Bed's a small place to die after a
lifetime of space
Lie perfectly still
That way you may not grow

John Cosgrove
FALLEN LEAVES
Once our love was tender and green
A new born leaf; quiet, serene
As the morning's golden salute
That plants in the spring its fiery
root.

Once our love's stifled cry of pain
Was silenced by a soft, spring rain.
Then the gentle wind with a sigh
Kissed our two cheeks and fanned us
dry.

One tender summer of such bliss
But alas, something went amiss.
The leaves fell from their Eden tree
Smothering the love of Eve and me.

Like an ill-fated little rhyme
Love had run the gauntlet of time.
Weary, spent, exhausted it fell
Upon the ground to wait death's
knell.

The leaves are stacked in a heap
Of memories. While two hearts weep
For one summer's lost golden rays
That faded in the autumn haze.

Clarice F Hunter
DEPRESSION
Depression is a grotesque bandit,
riding the nightmares of mistakes
long since made.
A stormy apparition, overshadowing
present hopes and dreams,
ending in grey inertia.
Clouding, delaying, obliterating
good intentions in veils of lethargy.
A cord around the neck
of mental mobility.
A despair, settling like dust
on the windowsill of the mind.
A constriction, stifling movement.
An elephant, trampling a mouse.
An acrid bile, thick and slimy,
subtly slithering like a sidewinder
into a pool of polluted water.
A twister, wriggling and writhing,
hurtling all things in its way
on a spiral of destruction.

Mrs Lorraine Reeder
ADJECTIVES
My adjectives were no longer
effective.
I set out to replace them. It was
imperative.

I found some as I approached the
bend, as I leisurely strolled down the
yellow brick road.

As I entered Fantasyland, I was
pleased to see, near at hand,
prominently established, a cluster of
trees delicately blooming with
adjectives. Within this setting which
was so tranquil, I observed that the
well-manicured lawn was—
delightful!!!

The Adjective Store held many more.
I bought a loaf of adorable and a
pound of lovable. I spread these in
layers, accent with sprigs of gracious
and luscious. Rolled up tight and tied
with an attractive bow was
magnificent and elegant. To use them
all is my intent.

I bought an ounce of atrocious for
spice.

I filled my charming little basket with
bundles of adjectives, dropped a few
on the yellow brick road on the way
back to my household.

I was ready to begin! I gently mixed
these new words and carefully folded
them all in. Then I wrapped this
poem around them.

This is not proper, but when my
poem was near completion, so that it
did not appear to be cumbersome, I
picked up a handful of happy little
commas with the tiny curly tails, and
as most of us are prone to do, without
revealing a single clue, held them up
and lightly sprinkled them over all.

Voilà a poem was born.

Margaret G Boaz
YOUNG CHILD OLDER CHILD

To: Tommy, Matt, & Nicole

From the cradle they so young
Not knowing what gift they have
brung
Little knowledge of the world
For this boy or girl
Growing up with love in home
Never knowing yet what to be
known

Then to school where learning shall
be
Seeing everything what there's to see
Drugs and sex everywhere they turn
Not knowing what they have to learn
That this is what life brings
sometimes their way.
And soon there's some who have the
price to pay.
But with hope, love, and care.
We all know there's a better world
out there.
And some will take the stand and say
We will make this a better world
someday.

John Schow
THIS MORNING
faint in fields with wind
bringing out the city to these willow
trees,
closed chambers of the heart
hushing small blood cells under
sweet reeds
in the rush of grass toward quietude,
always changing far sounds, well-
read obituaries
in the air of coming snow—a kind of
prayer
spoken from the dovecote of rural
memory.
Wishes, planets, glide past the fixed
stars
in their rising and setting. Love
moves
the Unmoved toward one face at a
clear window,
toward whatever morning strikes
with light
hours and eyelids flickering into
nothing.

Andrew F Layman
ERRATIC DESTINATION
The world, full of hope, aspiration,
and destination.
Ponder the world of life, love, and
the miserable that play.
But can one be intuitive on the
direction of travel?
For it is not he that plays this game
willingly.
One cannot assume that all the signs
of life are for the best,
or even that there is a meaning.
But in life there is one guarantee,
that is, there is another for everyone,
and that other will always be there.
If the good things are rushed,
then the bad are destined to happen.
So never rush the right,
and never foretell the wrong.
For life and love are the only things
in this world predestined.
My love for you, and your
friendship,
for these I am truly thankful.
Never forget me, for I am always
with you,
and in destiny, you with me.

Clyde R Brook
SOMEONE SPECIAL

This poem is dedicated to my best friend Michelle Hodge she gave me inspiration.

You are someone special,
No-one's special like you,
For you are very special,
For when I see you,
I can never forget you,
For I am always thinking, about you.
For you will always be,
Someone special to me.
For you came into my life,
And made my life,
More brighter each day.
You are someone special, that's
Caring, and loving, in every way.
And you are beautiful, and kind,
And sweet, and gentle.
You are a wonderful person,
To be with, and I always,
Want to be with you,
For this poem, comes
Straight from my heart.
For someone special, like you,
For you are the girl,
Of My Dreams.

Karen Walsh
BEAUTIFUL RAIN

To my darling daughter Carlie, who I hope will enjoy living even more than I.

Beautiful rain . . . you have come again . . . spreading your deep sorrow into the heart of life. And once again . . . I have the pleasure of watching your sweet tears falling from heaven and streaming down the face of the sky.
Yes, how sweet it is . . . to watch life soaking up your suffering and sharing the pain along with you. And, oh, how stirring . . . to hear you express yourself by soft and gentle weeping. Beautiful rain . . . how great a gift you have bestowed to all . . . for you have given to us sorrow . . . so we may know what it is to suffer . . . and from it . . . grow together as one.

Donna A Simmons
FUTURES SEEN

To my husband, Johnny who helped me see my future through his beautiful eyes.

Futures can't be seen when blinded
by the past,
and tomorrows are never
certain to last.

But today is what you've given me,
along with the reality—
That I again can share and feel,
all the things that are so good
and real.

When touched and kissed,
realizing that tomorrow I'll be
missed.

So just remember our thoughts are
shared,
and there's no need for you to
be so scared.

Just enjoy mile by mile.
don't forget—"Let me see your
smile".

Carl R Walkmaster
MY WIFE

Dedicated to Joann Walkmaster, my wife of 34 years

Let me ask you—what is a wife? Mine is everything to me, she is my whole life. In the beginning she was a lover and a pal, but without her my life would have been pure hell. Then came our kids and she became a wonderful mother, thru all these years there could have been no other. She was a nurse, cook, bottle washer, carpenter and maid, without her there would have been no sun—just shade. The house is empty now no more a crowd.
Our children have grown and made us so proud. The children call often with questions galore, they haven't forgot—Mom still knows more. Our time is spent together and what a time, together we stay, I knowing she is all mine. The passing years have made it clear and shown, that because of my wife the world I own. I know that I could not have made it thru life, if it had not been for that wonderful woman—my wife.

Betty Louise Domes nee Wharton Bain Jones
A LEGACY IN TIME

To my loving grand-daughter Kristin Louise Hopper (Domes)

Life is a series of endless Links.
Links of a chain, that begin at birth
And twine, connect and inter-change
From birth to death.

Ever changing experiential links
In motion, time and endless space
Formulating the human race,
Each individual so unique.

A prize to cherish, share and behold.
To look, listen and believe
In the making of an individual,
Mankind.

An honour, a privilege, available to
err,
To listen—to hear—but not to
change,
The endless race of eternity.

Humanity and in-humanity
interchange
In mankind's historic struggle.

Only the soul survives
Our eternal passing into space.
Light, buoyant, and endless infinite,
For greatness comes from the giving
heart.

Charles L Durbin
LOVE IS LIKE:
Love is like a sealed-up jug
Floating down the river—
It bobs up and down and whirls
around
But still goes on forever!

Again it's like a lovely song—
God bless the cheerful giver,
The gift is here, the giver gone
But the melody lives forever!

Again it's like a fancy coat,
Lifting spirits high!
A buffer against cold and snow
Until storms have passed you by!

The heart is an unruly member,
Having a mind of its own—
So if it belongs not to another
I'll try to make it a home!

Kimberly Daniels Alexander
DREAMSTATE
I once visited a wonderland
That had the colors
Of the rainbow,
For a riverbed.
The skies changed colors every
minute of the day,
And it seemed the stars were always
at play.
They danced around that crystal
moon; that too changed colors every
week at noon.
It was a magical, mystical land; and
I'll go back there some day—
or should I say night?
When I lay down to sleep,
When I lay down and dream.

Daniel Backus
A MAN'S NEEDS

This poem is dedicated to the love of my life, My beautiful wife, Kim.

A man needs a partner, to share in his
life, someone to stand by him, even
in hardest times,
a person who's kind, caring, and
strong,
who's willing to lend a shoulder for
him to cry upon,
someone who can calm him, when
things don't go his way,
who has a gentle smile, to get him
through the day,
a person who offers encouragement,
and a helping hand,
who looks past his faults, and sees
the heart of the man,
and finally he needs a lover, to have
and to hold,
to make him feel manly, worthy, and
bold.
All of these needs that are listed
above, are fulfilled by one woman,
the woman I love.

Ray W Lamb
THE FLOWER OF ALL SEASONS

Dedicated to Lori Jean Lamb who was taken from this world at the tender age of six.

There is a flower that always blooms
no matter what time of year.
She brings such sunshine every day
and I long to have her near.

The days are passing swiftly when
she must go her way,
To pass on this ray of sunshine to
others by the way.

Now when my journey's completed
and my earthly race is o'er,
May this sunshine that I dearly loved
shine brightly on that shore.

We have but once to live our lives
and swiftly it goes by.
So smile and love and live your all;
think not of sad good-bye.

Charles S Thompson
SUMMER FLOWERS OF LIGHT YELLOWS AND BLUES

To Becky, My Dearest Friend.

Summer flowers of light yellows and
blues.
Soft and sweet and covered with
dew.

White clouds and golden sunsets.
Cardinals and Bluebirds singing
duets.

Horses and clover on a country ride.
Puppies and rabbits with nothing to
hide.

Warm sunny days and cool summer
eves.
Watching the wind caress the trees.

Walking the banks around a pond.
Looking at turtles on a log far
beyond.

Feeding the squirrel sunflower seeds.

Wondering how simple, are their needs.

Such visions as these are nice, I confess.
But a smile and a hug from you is by far the best.

I miss you most, above all the rest.
And your happiness is my only quest.

Kathy M Croy
I WISH I WERE A LETTER

To Joan, who gave me confidence & believed in me when I didn't.

I wish I were a letter,
I could mail myself to you—
Opening up myself thru the pretty,
yet sometimes bent pages—
Where you could caress & hold me close,
as you read on & between the lines,
unable to hold back myself to you—

I wish I were a letter,
I could mail my soul to you—
Where you could read & re-read me,
to where I would always leave you with a feeling—
Sometimes joy, Sometimes sorrow,
but always, between the lines of love.

Janice Terborg
COLORLESS
The sky is blue above
The grass is green below.
For in between it's colorless
for colors do not show.

Why then do we look around us
for some color in life.
It may be lack of courage
or just this stubborn life.

To you, to me, to everyone
it's simple just to see.
Life is all in fiction
and death is all for free.

David M Macheska
TO A TELEPHONE SALESGIRL

To Liz, the telephone salesgirl of my dreams, wherever she may be.

Lovers come and go,
they always have, you know;
But lately I've been sad and feeling blue.

For I had a girl, you see
but she hung up on me
and that's the reason why I'm calling you.

You'd be under no obligation
to accept my invitation
and I hope you don't think I'm being much too bold;

but I'm reaching out, my dear,
'cause I'm all alone in here
and I know that all I need's a hand to hold.

Tod A Colby
NOVEL GIANTS
Another prod stirs the Giant awake—
Stabbing into the darkness with pen
The cyclic court is being called to order
It's time to face judgement again

Persistently connotating my name to the art
At functions I'm the lyrical bard
I live encircled by all my old works
Though they're all facing inward

Observing the merits on their tired faces
Of victories they've seen before
The battles they fight aren't in the same manner
For they just aren't winning anymore

The Giant, The General, I leave my den
Kicking up dust in my wake
Collecting the courage to face my old nemesis
And a new champion make

In another room—the quest for the weapon
Rummaging beneath piles of bills and ledger
Moving about from table to shelf
In search of the Giant's treasure

Precious pen unearthed I make the hall
Steps taken so long before
To face the ancient oaken beast
That lurks behind the Drawing Room door

Poised to strike at window side
I move to draw back the blind
Here I once scribed by morning sun
Attesting with unmolested mind

But only darkness shrouds my pallet
Turning to seek from whence shadow's cast
I behold the Behemoth National Bank
Progress erected some years past

The humbled Giant ceases the ritual
Leaving desk with curtain furled
To scrawl away in the room of reckoning
The articles now important to the world.

Lisa M Woodson
INSTINCT
Her black, shiny body
makes pantherlike movements
crawling with her belly
on the ground
she is almost unseen,
then in one swift leap
fur flies up
blood spurts
over the ground,
the rabbit is limp
Its eyes still and cold.
She drags her prey
by the neck
and lays the stiff
figure on the doorstep
meows until the offering
is noticed.
She walks triumphantly
to lay under her favorite tree
and see if the fat, red-breasted robin
will land.

Barbara Heath
MEMORIES
Lady and Fran I miss you so,
Why oh why did you have to go!

For many a year you watched over me,
You once made a prowler take to a tree.

When I came home from work at night,
You both were there, it felt so right.

I'd tell you the troubles I'd gathered that day,
You'd snuggle up close and they'd all fade away.

With you two here I was never alone,
And when I was gone you guarded our home.
We used to go for walks in the park,
If a stranger came near, you warned with a bark.

But old you got and you couldn't wait,
You had to leave for the Pearly Gate.

In Heaven I know you found your way,
Where all dogs go to romp and play.

At least I know that now you're free,
From all your pain and misery.

Oh Lady and Fran I miss you so,
No better dogs shall I ever know.

Sandra S Fisher
TO MY BATTERED DAUGHTER

To Pam

I can hear your bleeding,
I can see the pleading in your eyes,

Trying to understand,
The unthinkable.

I can feel the ache,
I can touch the hole in your heart,

You silently ask, "What did I do?,
When did it all go wrong?"

I must wait.
I must contain my terror.

Diana C VanDeusen
ICE BREAKING—1988
In the middle of the cold war
Near the center of the Arctic
Eskimos began with simple implements,
Russians finishing with a machine—
Yet, as the largest of God's kingdom
Swam out to sea
Could they fathom it was really they
Who broke the ice between two countries?

Lorraine Gautreaux

Lorraine Gautreaux
SILENT TEARS

This poem is dedicated to my sister, Connie, my inspiration.

Although you can't hear them they are there,
It's what I call a silent tear,

You can see them falling down my face,
Instead of a smile,
It's a frown in its place,

From all of the hurt through the years,
That's the cause for my silent tears,

It has been so long deep inside,
For the hurt seems never to subside,

I've tried and tried to make them disappear,
But they never go away, these silent tears,

Always living my life in sorrow,
Sometimes I dread the thought of tomorrow.

Mary F Zettler
OLD PEOPLE

My father with love

They have seen life and
Life has not always been kind
Or easy in dealing with them.

It has often pushed them
Into corners where they gather
Dust and mildew.

Like precious antiques
Their worth is seldom known
Until they, themselves, are gone.

And only then do we
Remember how very much
They were loved.

Ingrid Evyette Reeves
SLOW DOWN WORLD
Mom, Off to work,
Dad, Off to work,
Children, Off to school,
No time to care.
No time to give.
No time to talk.
No time to share.
No time to smile.
No time for me.
No time for you.
Material things, Human greed.
Material things, how much do we need?
In life the body so warm.
In death so cold.
SLOW DOWN WORLD.

Wendell R Wilson

Wendell R Wilson
WHERE WERE YOU?

This poem is dedicated to all the people of the world who have suffered social injustices.

Where were you when GOD created Man?
Were you in Russia when they invaded Afghanistan?
Where were you when JESUS was nailed to the cross?
Were you standing around?
Did your soul suffer a loss?

Where were you when they killed Martin Luther King?
Were you esthetic enough to rejoice and sing?
Where were you?
Did you fight in Vietnam?
Did you kill yellow people in the

name of Peace and UNCLE SAM?

Where were you when Nixon resigned as HEAD OF STATE?
Who is Man to attempt to escape his fate?
Where were you when Abe Lincoln died?
America, is your SOUL so black?
Have you ever cried?

Where were you when Hitler exterminated millions of Jews?
Man's inhumanity to man has not ceased.
Do you read the latest news?
Where were you when you lost your best friend?
Nothing lasts forever so prepare for THE END.

WHERE WERE YOU ???

Kathryn V Smith MA
NO TIME FOR LOVE
In the wasteland of emotions
there's no time for love
all is wasted
all is gone
emotions used and abused
battered, broken, bruised
What does this leave
but an empty shell
of what was a person
of what "I" was

Pat Sullivan
CHILD ABUSE
Oh, Daddy, please don't hurt me,
I'm just a little child,
It's only when you are drunk,
You become so wild.

I love you so very much,
And I can't understand,
You say that you love me too,
Then beat me with your hand.

When I go to bed at night,
And Mama goes to sleep,
You always come into my room,
And make promises you don't keep.

You say I must tell no one,
The things you do to me,
That it's our little secret,
And no one must hear or see.

But, Daddy, I don't understand,
If things we do are good,
Why do you say you'll beat me,
If I don't act like you say I should?

Virginia M Dwyer
REMINISCING

Love and thanks to my Mom and Dad Ginger and Ed Hornbaker.

I think of times, so far it seems,
My Mom and Dad, they made my dreams.
Her smile, that laugh, holding me tight,
Dad, never away, he kept me in sight.

Recalling the past, having memories galore,
Older now, makes me love them more.
Pictures, cards, too numerous to mention,
They always had time when I demanded attention.

May we appreciate, as I do now,
The love they gave by the sweat of their brow.
Giving of themselves so freely, so caring,
Knowing kisses and hugs, we would always be sharing.

My best friends forever, no doubt about that,
I'll love them always, wherever I'm at.
Remember now all of you, love Mom and Dad,
For if they're ever gone, you'll always be sad.

La Shawn Law
ITCHAPIE
The cowboy stands strong and tall
He's been everywhere tonight
He's got the scars to prove it all
He's always a winner in the fight

Though he may be down and weak
He stands tall and stays true
Though he's tired and wants to sleep
He fights and rides hard, and for you

He rides where the faces are so cold
He rides through town with no fears
all he wants is to go back home
He doesn't talk about what he hears

Because he's man he shows no emotion
He carries this with him where ever he goes
But he wants to share his love and devotion
But for now he will ride alone

G Roderic Durham
WHAT ARE THESE THINGS TO ME
What to me are all the things of earth?
What to me is every sight I see?
Oh, what are earthly treasures really worth
Compared to that sweet love you give to me?

What to me are all the songs they sing?
What to me are treasures bought with gold?
My heart desires, my darling, just one thing:
Your lovely form within my arms to hold.

What to me are Sun and Sky and Sea?
What to me are all the winds that blow?
Until that glad, sweet day you come to me
No rest, no peace, my heart will ever know.

Cindy Bruce
HE CARES
When we are impatient and in a hurry
It seems like God takes too long to answer.
But, if we sit back, relax and give our minds to Him,
We realize He is there.
The power of our prayers
is constantly there.
No matter what
no matter where.
Just remember,
to give to Him
And He will answer.
Sometimes it seems so slow
But, always there,
Always caring,
Always loving.
Yes, God does answer our prayers.

Wendy C Smith
MY FRIEND

To those who believed in me

Don't break her tender heart, my friend.
For it may never mend.
Don't ever tell her lies, my friend,
Once started, they'll never end.

Remember cherished moments
that she holds deep within her heart—
The simple things—a smile, a touch—
Don't tear her dreams apart.

Let her have her freedom,
A woman needs to grow,
So she can be a person
That everyone likes to know.

Don't compare her ways to someone
That you once used to know
Just love her for the woman she is
And make your new love grow.

For someday she might be gone, my friend
And you'll realize too late
That she's the one who truly loved you
With a love that wouldn't wait.

Sharlene L Miller
LOVE ME ALWAYS
Here I sit in a lonely room,
I know how it feels to be alone.
Shut up in a dark world of gloom,
I feel as tho my life is doomed.
But suddenly hope appears,
as I hear your footsteps in the hall.
My world is now bright and happy because;
I know that you will love me always.

Billy Aaron Greywolf
BIG HOUSE ON THE HILL

With love to my big sister, Ann Tipton.

Just let me slip to yesteryear, if only in my mind
To reinforce the lessons learned, from things thought left behind
I'd like to tread the barefoot path, with scent of daffodil
That led to grandpa's big white house, which stood upon the hill

Depression era then prevailed and living time was rough
Although long hours of toil stole time, for me he found enough
All childhood fears imagined real, a minor bruise or cut
I'd carry to him day or night, his door was never shut

Like on the day my robin died, I cried till my heart broke
Down through the field he watched me come, the mules stopped when he spoke
His honest-sweat soaked overalls, were cool against my cheek
His eyes grew misty like my own, when he began to speak

He told me of the master plan, that governs living things
How time on earth is meted out, to waste not what it brings
And now my years decline with time, of sixty-six and three
If I could travel back in time, I'd go to Grandpa's knee

So as you read these words I write, perceive my sorrow still
That I can't seek advice from that—big white house on the hill

Amy Lyn Pedroli
FOR MOM & DAD
When I think of my Parents
I wish they could know
How much I love them
And wish they'd never go

And yet . . . .
I know they'll always be with me
In one form or another
Through memories I have
Or feelings I've yet to discover

They're beautiful people
And I'm glad that I chose them
Because I am sure it was destined
That I love them and know them

I'm the person I am
Because of my Parents
And they'll always be in my heart
With their love and their guidance.

Alice P Ross
JUST FOR YOU
I have a red red rose,
Just for you.
Sky is blue today,
Just for you.
Sun shines every day,
Just for you.
I'll sing a pretty song,
Just for you.
I've ordered a silver moon,
Just for you.
There's a meadow of wild flowers,
Just for you .
When there's a gentle rain its,
Just for you.
A clear clean brook is,
Just for you.
This is my legacy,
Just for you.

Kenneth E Rankin
WAITING FOR THE FIRE TO GO OUT

To those not afraid to dream, especially my wife, Mae.

I'm just waiting for the fire to go out
The one that burned in my soul.
Once a bonfire, now becoming coals.
The fire's going out
And I won't relight it.

The fire's going out, my friend
And I don't care, ANYMORE.
I've been burned too many times
To stoke the embers again.

Yes, my fire's going out
I stare at it hypnotized.
Trying to find the Spark
And I shudder from its loss.

The fire's going out, my friend
That is very clear.
But I have to wonder
Is it so bad?
Now that the fire's going out.

Audnie A Sousa
THE UNIVERSE SINGS
When the night shadows start to creep—
Croaking of frogs you will hear—
Crickets and rustling of leaves—
That sound so far yet is near.—
The hoot of owls mingling with the night bird's eerie call.
And the hum of little wings that fly

'Round the waterfalls.
Listen to the sounds around you
The wild humming of the bees,
The echo of a moanful sigh
Believe what you hear and see'
When the morning shines its bright beam,
The song birds will start to sing
Ah can't you feel the rhythm
As the universe sings.
Listen to the sounds around you
The wild pounding of the breezes,
And the whispers of the trees
The murmur of running streams
And songs of larks on the wing
Ah can't you hear the rhythms
As the universe sings.
Ah can't you hear the rhythm
As the universe sings

Janet McNabb-Wiley
TENDER LOVE

Last night as you loved me,
so gentle and so new.
I never knew that love could be,
so honest and so true.

It started with a kiss of passion,
that led to so much more.
You touched me in such a fashion,
that I never had before.

The excitement was mounting,
as we continued with our play.
This love that I was counting,
was surely here to stay.

The moment was growing nearer,
as our eyes met once more.
I can say I had a little fear,
about opening my sexual door.

As ecstasy was upon me,
it sent tingles down my spine.
That this is how it could be,
A Tender Love for the first time . . .

Barbara Rae Brymer
MY SLEEP

To my Mother, Blanche Esther Johnson and to my husband, John Kenneth Brymer, Sr., For many years of encouragement and faithfulness in me.

As the trees sway to and fro
And the winds do blow
While the roosters begin to crow
  That's when I sleep.
When the baby begins to bawl
And the worms begin to crawl
And the cats begin to maul
  That's when I sleep.
Then the frogs begin to croak
And the shutters slam till broke
While the rain begins to soak
  That's when I sleep.
When my brother gets up to eat
And my folks are sound asleep
And the birds begin to peep
  That's when I sleep.
As the dog begins to bark
And the night is very dark
And the birds begin to park
  That's when I sleep.
When the stars begin to fall
And the dawn begins to call
And the fireplace burns near the hall
  That's when I sleep.
As the sun begins to shine
And the clock starts to chime
The folks begin to dine
  That's when I sleep.
As the teakettle begins to whistle
The bacon begins to sizzle
And the fog begins to drizzle
  That's when I sleep.
As the school bell begins to ding
The phone begins to ring
While my Father begins to sing
  That's when I sleep.
When noon comes around
The sun is shining on the ground
And I'm about to be crowned
  That's the end of my sleep . . .

Tracy Y Pennington
LET ME BE YOUR FRIEND.

When skies are always blue, You're always true.
When my friends seem so far away.
You're always by my side.
Whenever I'm sad, you always seem to know what to say.
When it seems that no one cares you always seem to be right there to hold my hand and say I want to be your friend trust me.
Let me walk with you through the fields. Let me love you.
Just let me be your special friend who will always love you.
No matter what.
Let me be the one to comfort you when a friend has hurt you.
Let me be the one you come to when you are lonely.
Let me be the one you tell your secrets to.
Let my shoulder be the shoulder you cry on:
Just let me be a part of you.

Deborah C Edmonds
ANOTHER PIGEON

To my children, my very special friend and my family

EARLY in the morning,
I stand on the bus stop
Watching the pigeons:
One hunts and pecks
As he thinks,
Searching for whatever
there is to eat,

Another pigeon
Flies fantail
On and off the curb,
Walking sideways-like,
A cabbage patch rhythm,
Hunting and pecking with
His beak.
He searches for whatever
There is to eat.

Early in the morning
Rain,
Glistening streets,
Light bulbs still twinkling . . .

George A Dorsey
BIRD-WATCHING

We'll need a field glass and we'll need a book—
A "field-guide," which will help identify
Some unfamiliar bird, or we can look
At diagrams, some fact to verify.
We'll need a notebook wherein we can keep
A written record of what all we see.
We may want other things, but nothing's cheap,
And some are quite expensive, you'll agree!

We might want tape recorders, microphones,
Fine cameras, blinds, and telescopes and such;
And lucky is the one who all this owns—
For field equipment we might use so much,

And more yet, but I've used so many words.
Did I forget? Oh, yes! We'll need the birds!

Barbara S Brasnick

Barbara S Brasnick
I FELL IN LOVE WITH A HANDSOME CAD

I fell in love with a handsome cad
Now I'm all alone and very sad,
As I brood about the years gone by
I greet each new day with a sigh.
Will life be good and send me a mate
What is in store for me—kind fate?
Must I remain here, night after night
Or will darkness fade and show me light.

Jan V Cloud
FROM DAD TO HIS LITTLE GIRL

To Pamela and Jeremy, Sky's brother and sister

To have a child with Down's
Is to have a kid that's proud
To show you love by the pound
Is to have SKY CLOUD around.

Bernice Stotts
THE ROSE

Our Lord has a flower garden so beautifully fair
That is tendered and kept by His infinite care.
One day He decided He'd add a rose
That's when He called her to her repose.
There in the garden He gave her a place
To stand so tall and full of grace
So there in the garden among all the others
Outstands one flower:
  The Rose, My Mother.

Robert D Barber
PROUD TO BE AMERICAN

Dedicated to my wife Jean without whom this poem would never have been printed.

Everywhere you looked, the flags were out
It made your heart pound so hard, you wanted to shout
The twenty-third Olympiad, was about to start
People came from most all the countries, just to take part

The opening ceremonies, were a beautiful sight
They lasted all day, and into the night
The pomp and pageantry, did us proud
We danced and jumped, and sang out loud

The church bells rang, and pealed in sync
It made you stop, use your head, and think
The people joined hands, as friends often do
It made you proud, you were American too

We may never hold another Olympiad here
But this one today, we'll always hold dear
For today the people came together as one
And at least for today, there was peace, and we were all one

If God is only watching us now
I know he'll be proud of us, and show us how
Love your fellow man, as a brother
Be proud and thank God, for one another

When the Olympics are done, and our friends go home
Remember them as friends, and never be alone
Be proud of your heritage, but respect others too
They may have been a friend, who has just visited you

Michael W Waddell
SUMMER SONG TO MOTHER

I'll sing my summer song
  it will make all get along

I'll make it flow, like gentle winds
  blow, as trees grow as i glow
I'll sing it nice and easy make it
  pleasing, enchanting children to
  dreaming

I'll sing my summer song
  while light sparkles across my
  eyes,
  as my shadow casts a giant upon
  the pavement that glides as i
  walk by

I'll sing my summer song
  of ice cream melting napkins
  sticking,
  lip smacking kiss's, darling
  ducks quacking,
  dog tails wagging, cats
  scrambling birds into flight,
  while waves are crashing sounds
  on sandy ground

I'll sing my summer song
  that would bend knees to the
  altar
  it would turn every bridge
  golden
  make every loving hand holding,
  molding two into one

I'll sing my summer song to
  my mother
  'cause there is no other that
  is LOVELIER!

Carol Ann Fong
WINNING

Going for the Olympic gold
whether in swimming or running
winning is the greatest thrill
that touches every man's
heart and soul

To believe in yourself
that you can
be the one
to be honor bestow
by your fellow man

To be honored
and win respect
where ever you go

Winning is the
most precious gift
that you can always cherish
and not ever forget

To break the world's record
and to win the race
that's the Olympic spirit
to be first always

Chloris B Brownell
ROSE OF SHARON
He is the Rose of Sharon,
He is the Lily white.
God gave this Child unto the world
to be a Guiding Light.

Then now again at Christmastide
we sense the Trinity.
A Bridegroom comes to claim His bride.
We know, we hear, we see!

So worship now and wonder
beside the manger stall,
that He, with birth so humble,
was sent to love us all!

Michael David Craig
GRASS

. . . for her, and the dandelion. . .

Grass
Simple pilgrims
Dressed in uniform green
Supporting the weight
Of a thousand bare feet

And you
And I
Twined about one another
Lying like snakes
In the grass.

Don G Bousquet
THE BELL
He stood on the corner ringing his bell,
A skinny little guy not dressed too well.
The uniform he wore was much too big,
had a Santa pot hooked on some kind of rig.
We were all laughing and having a time,
doing some last minute shopping,
for it was Christmas time.
He caught my eye as we rode by,
his little red nose and baggy old clothes.
Kept ringing his bell and wishing
everyone a cheery hello.
He tore me apart and made me feel small,
this skinny little guy with not much at all.
The Salvation Army was what he was in,
guess you could say he was doing his thing.
Now not a Christmas goes by that I
don't think of him, and that crazy little bell,
that goes ding a ling, ling . . . . .

Lola Mae Stevens
YEAR'S END
At times I look at the world
And am overcome with grief.
I long to hold her in my arms
To comfort, and bring relief.

The sadness and the pain she feels
Are mine to share when I see
The children of men, in the names
of strange gods, creating such misery.

She's been battered, abused and raped;
Left with raw, ugly wounds
Which she covers with time, but can't erase.
She hurts, and still she sustains,
Nourishes and gentles.

May she soon know peace.

Ken Krousey
BEE'S FISHING BAIT
Try a hula to lure the hawaiian game fish,
Throw a bone to fetch a dog fish;
Cast a rock to rile the rock bass,
Use lipstick to entice a large mouth bass.
Take a pail and scoop a snail,
A kind word will land a blue whale;
Usually catnip will bait a catfish,
An oyster will make a tasty stew dish.
Troll a karat to tempt a gold fish,
While a sunbeam can lure a sunfish;
Fling an old shoe to nail a sole,
And use a cane pole to snatch a tadpole.
Tease a rainbow trout with a fire fly,
But use an eyeglass to seize a walleye;
A hornet will paralyze a sting ray,
For dinner try a delicious crappie fillet.
Use limburger cheese to tempt a smelt, of course,
And a horse fly will annoy a lazy sea horse;
But Bee says, "A smile, a wink, and a catchy rhyme,
Will catch a sucker almost every time."

F A Thomason
THE FUNNEL
When time is laid before me, there is one thing which I see.
Possibilities
But it is too far to see and it makes me wonder where I'll be
It makes me dream of things I wish to see.
It makes me.
A pattern develops, from past actions, it forms
My future is decided from my past, you see . . .
The older I get the less unknown possibilities.
Time is a funnel which I am falling through . . . The end not yet in sight.
What I say and What I do form the section in which I have not yet fallen through.
It grows longer because of some things, and shortens when I do others
It bends and twists, bulges and shrinks, is fluid and hardened.
The beginning fades away, the future becomes a little clearer, I am a liquid with thought and sight.
Nothing stops the fall, except death.
Nothing at all.

I look outside my funnel and see those around me.
I call to some to come closer
I move away from others I see.
Then there are those who I cannot move from, those who must stay close to me.
All of the funnels are in one place
This place has no boundaries, endless space . .
Plenty of funnels though, funnels as far as I can see
And more to be.
Once in a while one passes by me,
One which I let see inside
We cross and for a second fall together as one.
We never fall too far together, the way funnels are made
it just wasn't meant to be.
Each one of us is separate, you see.
Only pieces of the funnel can break apart and join another
not the fluid which is me or she.

I believe that when it ends there is a place, a pool of these.
The fluid of which is me and the other fluids I see
Come together.
And that is where we all will be.

Floating, floating, aimlessly in a pool of funnel stuff, things which used to be.

Lauvonda M Young
REGENERATION
Give me not a winter death
of floed oaks
and denuded trees

Come for me in the spring
when scarlet tulips kindle
the emerald loam

Then with thoughts of my
imminent rebirth, I will
relinquish life.

Christy L Jones
A TENDER KISS

For Brian W. Gendron, it was destiny which united us, and The USS IOWA that took his life. This was the first poem I wrote him.

My tender, tender soft-petalled lips
Oh so yearn for a tender kiss.
But only you with gentleness,
Shall touch upon my tender lips
A soft and tender,
Tender kiss.

Sean A Miller
HEART-BROKEN
You broke my heart
One that always is true,
True to only one girl,
That one girl is you.

I love you so!
But all you can say
is the answer is no.

Through storms and hard times
my love held fast,
Now my heart is broken.
I hope it won't last!

Maybe some day I'll get over you,
On that day I'll remember
the past,
Of you and me and how love
didn't last.

Patricia Frauchiger
FREE TO LIVE
Living our lives in constant fear
That holds us hostage in its grip;
Our lives are tyrannized by fear
Of death, smothering our spirits,
Closing our minds and hearts to life.

Think of the freedom in our lives
If there were no fear deep inside,
Stifling the loving the heart strives
To give of ourselves to others,
Without fear of losing ourselves.

Life without fear of death is bold,
Unafraid to grasp each new day;
Living to depths we cannot hold
To ourselves; we must give to those
Who need, who want to know freedom.

Living without the great fear, death,
Makes us see clearly, each plateau
Of life's journey, drawing new breath
With all hope of living, being,
Free from fear of death, free to live.

Larry D Holladay

Larry D Holladay
THERE'S POWER IN A SMILE

In memory of Peggy, my first true love.

If you will smile at me,
my heart will seek to embrace
the sweet nectar of your kiss.
My arms will enfold you and the
warmth of your bosom will thrill
and excite me.

If you will smile at me,
the seed of our embrace will
blossom and produce fruit
delicate and pure. The product
of our love will grow and
enhance the purity of His gift.

If you will smile at me,
you will find me respondent to
your infinite desires and eager
to achieve the ultimate
fulfillment of your dreams.

If you will smile at me,
my life will be your life, yours
will be mine and ours will be
one. We will be as the sea is
to the shore and as the grape
is to the vine. We will drink
together and follow the sun to

enchanting places and work and
play until the day when the
physical plane of our eternal
being must fade away and
return to the soil from whence
it came.

If you will smile at me,
our love and the product of that
love will endure throughout the
trials and tribulations of
mortality and transcend into
immortality for we can be one,
If you will only smile at me!

Patricia Frauchiger

THE TWO OF US

The two of us wage war with the one
of me.
The battle tears the fabric of my life,
A futile action played with swords of
strife
That slash my body, wrench my soul
from me.
My spirit finds no place where I can
see
A path that leads me away from this
rife
Of struggles; robbing me of peace in
life.
I need to know which one of me is
free.

To find the role I need to play, to live
In harmony with a self I do not
know.
A sense of worth in what I can create
Without old strengths, without bright
mind, to give
The second me a hope, a chance to
grow,
To win the battle to forge my own
fate.

Rubye L Hundley

AUTUMN

There's a hint of frost this morn
the grass a dress of icy lace
adorn
The trees a riot of color ablaze
glows in the early autumn haze

The maples maze of orange and gold
the dogwood and sumacs red
unfold
Towering pines and firs evergreen
enhance the panoramic scene

From the Master's palette magical
colors appear
seen from distant mountains
and valleys near
Autumn is nature's canvas of lovely
scenes
picturesque portraits of an
artist's dreams

Ah Autumn! dressed in glorious
array
preens in her magnificent
display
Yes, autumn is God's universal treat
His creation perfected and
complete

Trinity Garamella

SHOULD YOU STILL LOVE HIM?

I would like to dedicate this poem to the two most important people in my life, my mother Karen Garamella and my best-friend Tina Lang.

Should you still love him when he
denies you to love another?
And then he says he's sorry,
but only wants you to love him as a
brother.
So you try to forget your love for
him.
Although it's hard to ignore how you
feel inside,
you keep trying, to save the
friendship.
Then it gets too hard to hide,
you know you'll have to get it out
somehow.
But there's only one problem, that is
what do you say when you
know he won't care?
Should you just tell him that you'll
always love him,
and that if he needs you, that you'll
always be there?
Or should you go on with a broken
heart,
pretending that it doesn't bother you,
because you knew you'd have no
chance from the very start?
I now realize that the best thing you
could do is tell him exactly
how you feel.
And then wish for at least one day,
that you'll still be around,
for your ears to hear him say,
that he loves you in return.

Ruth Poorman Eicas

SLEEPING?

To Carrie Sue—Be happy singing with the Angels.

As I lie awake in bed
Thoughts go round inside my
head,
Thoughts of paying bills and such,
What's for breakfast, what's for
lunch?

Why can't I go back to sleep?
I've said a prayer and counted
sheep,
Tossed and turned from left to right,
Will it never end, this night?

I think that I'll get out of bed
And maybe read a book
Instead of simply lying here
And wishing that the dawn was
near.

When it's time for me to rise,
To make the breakfast, exercise,
Wash the dishes, change the sheets,
That's when I am sound asleep.

Edith E Rugg

A POWERFUL FORCE

Love is as broad as the expanse of
the sky;
Sometimes clear blue, not a cloud
visible to the eye,
Sometimes a single cloud swiftly
travels by,
Sometimes clouds cover the expanse
of the sky.

Love is as deep as the ocean floor;
Sometimes in shallow places the eye
sees to the core,
Sometimes at the greatest depths, the
eye sees no more,
Sometimes the eye sees only great
billows that roar.

Love is broad and deep and always
there;
Sometimes the mind's eye sees only
the good without a care,
Sometimes the sensitive eye sees the
struggle and feels despair,
Sometimes the knowing eye clears
the air.

Love rides the winds of the blue sky;
Soars with the wind and gives a
pleasurable sigh,
Heads into the gale and rides way up
high,
Love chooses its course and ever is
nigh.

Love sails the seas of the ocean deep;
Moving quietly forward while ocean
floors sleep,
Tacking through storms its course to
keep,
Love follows the charts to be
complete.

Harry A Akers

THE GIFT OF POETRY

Many blessings are bestowed upon
me, I must confess—
Friends and Loved ones, joy and
beauty, things that I possess,
Church and home, art and music, all
Nature there to see—
Ah, but what intriguing paths I
find in Poetry!

I like to concentrate and set aside
some good time
To put an inspiration, thoughts
and words into rhyme,
Marry them to a rhythm, some
friendly pentameter,
A task not always simple for a
rank amateur.

Poetry's a special art, conferred as
God's great gift.
It turns mere thoughts to music and
gives our souls a lift.
The Poet's metaphoric phrases,
inspired and strong,
Are like color strokes on canvas,
grace notes in a song.

All the sweet and bitter yearnings of
the Human Race,
All the victories or problems
that we ever face
Will be sifted to inspire us, on into
each age
By the cosmic rhythm and music
on the Poet's page.

Harold E Williams Jr

FOR SENTIMENTAL REASONS

Verse:
For sentimental reasons
just want you to know,
that you'll be mine forever
'cause I love you so.

Darling, time and time again
I still think of you,
since you've left me here alone
feelin' very blue.

Bewitching fascination,
dream of pretty charms,
promises made together
hold you in my arms.

Chorus:
For sentimental reasons
please come back to me,
I'll build a cozy cottage
lovely sweet Marie.

For sentimental reasons
You are only mine,
some day we'll stay together
honey, all the time.

Tammi Fortino

MY DEAR FRIEND

In loving memory of Tamara Gan Raus

How I wish you were still here.
The sorrow I feel knowing I will
never see you again.
Never to see that big bright smile,
to hear the sounds of your laughter,
to feel the comfort of your voice.
I do so miss the friendship we once
shared. But having the wonderful
memories that I do is more than I
could have ever asked for.
I miss you my dear friend and I
thank you, for what a friend you
were.

Catharina Rinta

Catharina Rinta

MY TREE

I sit in your shade
when the summer is hot,
and you keep me dry in the rain,

and I watch with great sadness,
when your leaves spiral down,
and only stark branches remain.

But each beautiful Spring,
my eyes anxiously search,
for the first swelling buds overhead,

and the tender green leaves,
that will give me a sign
of new life, in a world that seemed
dead.

With a promise of summer
and all shades of green.
With a beauty so lush and so fair,

Every season a joy,
as through each passing year,
you're my strong, silent friend,
standing there.—

Maxine Parker Swanson

THE HEART YOU HOLD IN YOUR HAND

You have put the sparkle
On the dew
The sun in my sky
The moon in my night
The love in my eyes
The lilt in my voice
The spring in my step
The happiness in my heart—
You hold in your hand.

B Ewing Dreibelbis

SCORPIOPHOBIA

Sting. Un-sting.
You bring, you bring me
Fear. Runs so deep.
Staircase is steep.
Stomp you. Can't stop
Screaming. The top
Now is bottom.

I am flying.
Death-defying leap
Down staircase.
And just in case
You're not yet done
With your fun. I'm
Aimed and ready.
Holding steady.
Take your life away.

Leigh Madison
THE PAIN OF LOVE

I would like to dedicate this poem to the two most important people in my life, my mother Karen Garamella and my best-friend Tina Lang.

As I lay here I remember how it used to be,
when the one I loved was always close to me.
He was always there for me, even on the worst of days.
Then the day came for us to go our separate ways.
I wonder if he realizes the kind of love we shared together.
Our friends thought we had the type of love that lasts forever.
In my mind I know that no one could ever take his place.
The longer I am away from him the harder it gets to picture his face.
I have sat for hours by the phone hoping he would call,
then sometimes I wish I could forget about it all.
I used to think that if I got him back the pain would go away,
but now I am aware that forever it will stay.

G Jhon Kleyn
SARA
Sara rocks alone now,
Searching through the darkened window
Past the porch.

The trees in naked state
etch twisted fingers through the misty morning.

Each rhythmic swing brings winding memories of dream-clad days.
Days they would stroll, hand in hand with thoughts of endlessness.

Sara stares again, seeing ducks huddled beside the pond, without any necks.

Wrapping shawl tightly around her
She unleashes the latch; strains forward, harder still, and calls out his name.

The trees echo no reply.
Through the trees, past the pond.
Sara sees him holding out
His hands.

Herbert J Fisher
THE SNOWSHOE HARE
A ghostly shape hops o'er the snow,
Almost invisible in the cold
Moon's glow;
Its sole defence is its rapid speed
On strong legs and large feet;
Its color hides it where it is found,
By a winter white and a summer brown;
Woods are interlaced with its tracks,
In well-worn run-ways or
beaten paths;
It nibbles stems of bushes and trees,
And may gnaw bark in winter's breeze;
A cyclic mammal, the snowshoe hare,
Varies in numbers from here to there;
It provides a regular source of food
For many a predator and its brood.

Lisa Rawls
FALL LEAVES
I see the leaves
So sad and dreary
looking weary
Bitten by the wind
Coming closer to their end
They've all turned to brown
as I now look down
To see what I believe to be
A pile of dry leaves
Resting on the ground.

Ruth F Wright

Ruth F Wright
COMPANIONSHIP

To a 15 yr. girl and a 17 yr. boy, who love to farm the hills of East Tennessee, married for 55 happy years.

God united us together
In the early days of life
He wanted us to be equal yoked together
And to live our lives as man and wife.

We worked so hard from day to day
Thru all kinds of weather, side by side
The crops would fail, not much easy money.
But we looked to God, that He would provide.

God sent us out to sow the grain and seed
Among the thorns and tares
Along the way we gathered fruit
Always had plenty left over with more to spare.

When the time came for my mate to leave,
As he reached the top of the stairs,
He bowed his head, asked us all to pray.
I hope to meet him in heaven
Again up there.

Barbara Scott-Dever
BITTERSWEET LOVE

To my love, Willie Edward Dever

Oh Lord! if I could fly, I would reach above the clouds so high, away from earth's heartaches and pains, the cares of this world no longer remain.

I would go down to the depths of the sea, no more tears would there be for me, the ocean holds only peace and the calmness of the sea, if I could just be free of this bittersweet love you gave to me.

The earth is a lonely place to be, I wish there was some way I could tell you how much you mean to me, if only your heart had eyes to see, what a happy place this world would be.

No night so sweet, kind and free, are the nights you spend alone with me. In my heart there is nothing but pain, of the bittersweet love that still remains.

Jennifer Wedegis
HIS EYES
his eyes are of full moon
a deep blue shade
a twinkle
a smile

a swan on a lake over a
cool spring night
a shine
a blink

a sweet tender mood
at the break of dawn
a smooth new light
a sweet caress at
the end of night

Jerry Marie Brooks
COMFORT AND CARE

To my dear Mother and Daddy;, my sisters, Bettye, Carol and especially my brother, Robert, also my three children, Mark, Kristie and Tommy, whom I love all very much.

Where can you go when you feel so alone?
You pray to Jesus for comfort and care,
Remember His promises, what He's shown
Jesus won't let burdens be more than you can bear.

Count your blessings, instead of despair
Pray to Jesus and ask for your needs,
His will be done, accept it with care
Follow His word and to heaven it leads.

When your heart is too heavy to carry anymore
All is dark, you can't find the light,
Ask for His help, He'll be at your door
As He did promise, the dark left my sight.

I hear the birds singing, it's a new day
Happiness I feel, I wanted to share,
My faith is restored, listen to what I say
Because I prayed to Jesus for comfort and care.

Kathy Blair
MY CREED

I dedicate this poem to my Mother who sends me inspiration from her home in the clouds, and to my Father who sends me strength from his heart, on earth.

I set my feet on solid ground.
This newborn strength that
I've found
Builds the "self" I've always
dreamed
Yet couldn't touch—or so it
seemed.

I look ahead beyond the sun
To grasp my hopes—every one.
I reach and reach. I so aspire.
Never to forfeit tho' I may
tire.

The other "me" that wills to
fly
Always whispers "just one more
try."
So I trudge on in trusting
gait;
Holding on, not holding back,
And always holding straight.

Nan M McMain
FREEDOM
Who is free from care and woe?
I think the answer I must know.
Mistaken judgement by a few,
Can damage dreams of lives so new.

The young go searching for their dream.
Life, they find a bore, extreme.
Why, when a promise can't fulfill;
Their constant struggle whips their will.

Is freedom, now, an empty word?
So common, in its place is heard
A rumble against the noble deeds
Of those who died to spread its seed?

Freedom must mean something great.
For three grand men have died of late.
A President, Preacher and Bobby, too,
Were killed because they cared for you.

They knew the price one has to pay,
For freedom is not free today.
We must not lose our freedom's touch.
For those who died who have given so much.

Barrietta Killiebrew
AFRICANS TO AFRO-AMERICANS

This poem is dedicated to all people of dark color, family, friends and Vera. (Smile)

Once in our country, we ruled as prestigious kings and queens, from King Solomon to the Pharaohs of many dynasties. Where are our great royalties of riches, ideologies that weaved designed-stitches in the Hi-Tech technologies, and discovered replicas, often used today?

It was seized and utilized like our resources of gold, oil mines, precious gems, and coal. Many fortunes vanished through the embezzlement of archaeology. A study to excavate the treasures buried under sacred grounds, where our imperial ancestors' bodies lay.

A curse of greed and ignorance shattered our integrity, to sell and trade our people as slaves, to unknown foreigners, of lands far away. Is this the very reason, why apartheid has slapped our faces with disgrace and threatens our existence as a race? Who's to truly say?

Now is the time to stifle this prejudice man-made disease, which has placed peace into captivity, locked behind closed bars, and forces the hunger for war. We need ammunition to fight against the opposition. Food causes submission, and humiliation is the price we pay.

Today, it is us, who are the ones, separated by the color of our skin.

But, don't you dare grin Afro-Americans, because apartheid may have a chance to touch you again. Remember, UNITED WE STAND AND DIVIDED WE FALL. Let's pray that freedom rings to be heard and cherished by all.

Robert Paul Effler Jr
LOVE'S BEAUTY

To Wilma, My Wife and My Love

Though majesty and beauty
Oft' go hand in hand
As when a fiery sunrise
Spills gold against the land.

It cannot escape my notice
And sometimes all can see
That the smallest bit of glory
Can be deeper than the sea.

This is never more apparent
Than when your smile I see
And the universe bows its wonders
Before those you give to me.

Because there's nothing greater
Than the love I feel from you
When you hold my hand and tell me
That we are one, no longer two.

Myrtle Mae Dothager
REALITY
When I was young I had a dream
Of a country house by a tiny stream,
With flowers and trees and maybe a swing
Where all my children would play and sing.
I planned a bell hanging near the door
Whose silvery notes sounding free
Would call my little ones home to me;
And no matter where my children roam
The silver bell could bring them home.

So much for schemes of a younger time;
I've got the house, I sit in the swing
Alone with bits of a shattered dream.
Now there's no one at all in my private hell.
There's no one to call with my silver bell.

Lucia Johnson
SLOWLY

I dedicate this poem to Jason Arnold Jenkins.

my auburn beauty
for the sound of your accent
my heart gasps.
though, as a flame
your moods flutter,
I am drawn into your
trance, warm as
summer wind.
a flickering brilliance;
through sun strips
you stroll. and
beneath the spectacles
rimmed in gold,
lies a tenderness
only He can endow.

Ladisca Tegnelia
BE STILL
When you are weary,
Be still and see God.

If you are troubled,
Be still and see God.

In the winter of the spirit,
Be still and see God.

With a heavy heart, and feet of clay,
Be still and see God.

When you are discouraged,
Be still and see God.

He is alway with you, so,
Be still and know God.

Jodi LA Fountain
ALWAYS FEEL THE PAIN

To the one person who made the best summer of my life complete.

They say time heals all wounds,
but I'm not sure if it's true.
'Cause sometimes you just can't block the memories,
and there's nothing you can do.

You remember all the times you've shared,
and though you fight your tears in vain,
You can't stop the feelings creeping through,
and you'll always feel the pain.

You can't hide from it forever
when you think weak walls are strong.
Because soon the hurt will find you
and you'll realize you were wrong.

Sometimes I can't understand it
because this is the story of you and me.
What we have just isn't right,
and it can no longer be.

So I'll take each day as it may come,
and when you look back you'll find
Why, even though I still love you,
I'm leaving you behind.

Joyce L Merriweather
A PRAYER FOR JESSE AND JESLEY

For you, a father who cares. Lieutenant Jesse L. Banks, the best of Detroit's finest. "Memento 5 July 1988"

Dear God, please bless
Jesse and Jesley.
Surround them close
within your arms,
A hand from you will
prevent all harm.
For them I have much
love to share.
Given by you with
faith and care.
As children of yours please
demonstrate their way,
For without thou guidance
they tend to stray.
Thru reasons known only by you,
very special people they are to me.
Please share your love and
grant them your blessings.

Robert J Abbott
MEDITATION
The chill penetrating my jacket
Hints of transition.
The skeletal limbs reaching upward
Nearby is an outward confirmation,
That a season's end is near
And the beginning of hibernation.
From this perch—an artists view;
I have painted the scene before.
My senses are alive;
Porous to the intoxicants of nature.
So silent.
I am not moving.
It feels good to slip away
Into the surroundings.
A glance heavenward
And behold a golden halo
Spiritually placed above me.
Its perimeter: an illuminated ripple in the night,
Encircling the only light
Veiled by a wispy blanket of lace.
Does this halo of illumination
Encircle me as well?
I cannot tell.
But with every upward glance
It appears to intensify.
The rustle of a few clinging leaves
Stirs my meditation and awakens me.
Sometimes it is not a welcomed awakening.
I sense myself trembling slightly
Against a clean, stiff rush of night air.
Wait—listen:
The animals, one by one,
Wink into being.
A wise one is heard nearby;
Maybe it too senses
The cusp of seasons.
My gaze stays fixed
To this awesome ring of light
And I find myself tilting
My head in obedience to its movement.
This eye in the sky is a contradiction,
With its light pupil and dark embodiment.
But oh, what a vantage point.

Rebecca Fricker
ALL OF MY LIFE
All of my life
I've felt like a clam
With all of my feelings inside me
I was alone
But one day somebody found me
They opened me
I was special
I had a pearl

Deanne Coates
I SEE YOUR FACE BEFORE ME

To Bob: This poem is dedicated to the only man in my life

I see your face before me,
In the sunlight of the day
Your arms outstretched to hold me,
And take my cares away.
Your lips so soft and gentle,
That I no longer fear
The love I have for you my dear,
Is oh so ever near.

Manuel Almada
ONE WORD LIE EATS BABIES ALIVE
History has many pictures burned inside my brain.
Some give gentle pleasures. Some give torturing pain.
History offers an ancient scene of a soldier Hannibal
Invading ancient Rome inspired by a huge stone cannibal.

Hannibal's cannibal stone god was ancient Rome's hated Molock.
Carthage's infamous "sky scraper" with its infamous furnace of fire.
I shiver at the mental picture as Carthaginians walk
To throw living babies screaming to feed hungry Molock's fire.

Today's "civilized" history has its own baby-eating Molock.
9 black-robed "licensing" judges, highest court under the sky.
23 million mothers obeying the judges' talk . . .
23 million babies burned alive by a one-word lie.

When is a baby not a babe? We play the grisly game.
Cosmetics made of fetuses accuse no one of blame.
None hear the "fetus' silent screams" in garbage dumps decay.
Hospital furnaces burn each day fetuses and guilt away.

Above, Our Eternal Creditor eyes are growing debt.
WHO'S GOING TO PAY?

D A Bishop
SUMMER'S DAWN
When summer shadows winter's white,
When green glades dapple snows-capes blight,
When earth warmth hugs brittle ice-pond's shore;

Then life song blares its choral lore,
Then nature glows in verdant delight;

And time slides easy o'er season's relief,
And creatures hum nature's loving motif.

Lisa Barks

Lisa Barks
AN AWAKENING ROSE

In memory of my great-grandmother Cline. To my family and friends. (for you S.S. and K.W.)

The grass is not dry but covered
with dew from the youth of the morn
Sooner or later, the rose will awaken
The rose expresses much of what
we call love like no other flower tells
It has this special kind of meaning
to emotions upon its look and smell
While looking upon this beautiful

flower, it leaves all problems behind and helps you focus on the future instead of past time
Time goes by fast so hurry to see
This rose awakening to see you and me

Tonya L James
SWEET ANGEL

For Desiree, in California, who is doing much better now in 1989. Love your big sis, in Kansas, Tonya Lee.

I talked on the phone to my sister today, and as I hung up, I felt the need to pray.
Sweet little angel, trouble with her heart,
I've missed her dearly, since we've been apart.
Today is her birthday, only six years young,
I told her I loved her, though the cat had my tongue.
She had heart surgery, which should fix it all,
Soon she'll talk more, and grow real tall.
Although she still can't talk much, not much to say,
I know I'll see her again, and I long for that day.
But until then, I'll just live my life,
I think of her often, bringing me pain and strife.
My little Desiree, sweet angel is she,
My sweet little angel . . . Desiree Lee.

Mary E Siedhoff
LITTLE THINGS
An atom split, can harm a lot;
A smile can mend and heal.
A bullet can someone kill,
A hug is something we can feel.

Ricky McCormick
I NEVER KNEW
I never thought of my life of sin
Until the day I brought my Jesus in
I never felt that I was much
Until the day I felt His special touch
I never really thought of the things
He could do
Until the day when I said "Jesus, I love you"!
The Lord has done so many special things
I'm so glad for the happiness He brings
I never knew of His powers so strong
Until that day He carried me along
Through trials and troubles and heartaches too
I just look to sweet Jesus and say "I love you"!
He brings me through all terrible times
That's why I'm so proud He is mine
He died on the cross for this is true
He gave His life for me and you
I never knew He was the one
To set me free from all I've done
I praise the Lord with all my might
I praise Him always day and night!

Theodore Clay
ONCE! MIST OF TRUTH
Our knowledge.
That scholarly light at the end of the tunnel.
Gave us destiny. And, we are indebted.
And, once upon a time may prevail.
Once there was.
Does this mean a lot?
Can I have that Micro Data of spring?
Will that be an inherited legacy?

Whom shall inherit this legacy?
Tomorrow?
Oh! If, we only hadn't.
Doesn't seem to be a future.

Once! Mist of truth.
Once upon a time . . .

Pervis Ray Ford

Pervis Ray Ford
GREAT LEADERS ARE RARE

To my lovely daughter Joanese Sasha Ray Ford. Someone who I'll love always and forever. Your Father

Great leaders are rare, so I'll follow myself. Code: Chessboard Mission: Brain Drain. You'd better watch your step, you're going to fall and hurt yourself one-day. Be ready! I love you, but how can I love you, when you keep running away? Your Alibi's incomplete. I cross my heart I know why. Why do you keep running away? Ticktock, I'm looking at the clock on the wall I have no time to stall. Believe me I won't let you fall. Children of the ghetto keep your heads to the skies, and don't you cry belileve me I know why.

I watch you walk away it really doesn't have to be this way. If right or wrong you're on your own. Some good advice from Miami Vice. If you want to enjoy a quiet night tonight please stay home tonight. Cold, cold winds Evil, cold winds that blow endlessly in the night/ Real friends are like diamonds, rare! False friends are like autumn leaves, spread everywhere, never around when you need them. Never hesitate to go forward, for you will never be able to go back. Have a heart of noble courage and pursue the unknown truth. The greatest leaders of the world are the loneliest people in the world

Alice R Stoddard
AIR AILING—WATER WANTING
You, Earth People, have named me
Eagle, your national bird.
As your symbol of freedom and pride, please heed my screaming word.
The air through which I soar and on which I depend
Has now become so befouled with pollutants to offend
Intensely all living and breathing denizens of this earth;
Of clean and pure atmosphere I admit an enormous dearth.
From my tree-top aerie on this precarious perch,
I protest for myself and for my ally—the ailing birch.
In the woodlands, each tree with damaged branch, limb, twig and leaf
Silently droops and decays as the acid rain brings them to grief.
The flowers, all in bud, on the forest floor are afraid to bloom;
To do so in this contaminated air to them specifies certain doom.
On to the water supply which nurtures each fruit, nut and plant,
And in turn supports all wildlife—the contamination is blatant.
For the creatures—fish and mammal—in our river, lake and stream
The defilement has become nightmare-like—not a very pleasant dream.
As a representative of all living categories, species and sorts,
I implore you Earth People, your leaders, principals and cohorts
To act, to clean up the acid rain, to protect the ozone layer,
to end the spoilation and desecration—to hear my screaming prayer!

Jerilynn Curcio
YOUR WEDDING

To my first child, Laurie, and her new husband, Henry Turner, on their beautiful wedding, August 27, 1988.

With the passing, of each and every day,
The countdown, to your wedding, is not far away.
Problems that were, have worked their way out,
With feelings of relief, to move about,
The dresses have been ordered, and are on their way,
The D.J. chosen, with his selections to play.
The florist decided, who will make your bouquet,
And dress up the church, with a floral display.
The cake delivered, to the reception on time,
Decorated and filled, as you defined.
The limo will arrive, on your wedding day,
To usher you, and your attendants away.
The photographer started, early in the day,
To help you remember, in a special way.
Friends and relatives, come to celebrate,
The services held, for you and your mate.
You'll look so beautiful, on your wedding day,
As your dad walks you down, to give you away.
This day, you will remember, for a long time to come,
Even after, the honeymoon is done.

Amy Sinclair
SHOW ME THE WAY

For my grandmother: Someone who always believed in me; and taught me how to believe in myself.

Show me the way to trust in myself,
Lend me a helping hand.
Hold on to me forever and never let me go;
Teach me how to stand.

Through the tunnel there shines a light,
Brightly shining as the sun.
Towards it I walk, where you lead I will follow.
My life has just begun.

Many tomorrows I will face not in fear,
Living just day to day.
When my day is done, I will come home to you.
Oh Lord, please show me the way.

Tracey Wentzell
RAIN
The sweet rain falls from the sky so blue,
and brings freshness that's so pure and true.
It falls upon the big maple tree,
as I run in the rain, I feel so free.

The rain to me, is like a gentle friend,
and all my troubles, it can mend.
Together we play in the soft summer breeze,
and it falls upon me as I eat my cheese.

Without the rain, the flowers wouldn't grow,
and we would live with everlasting snow.
Without the rain, there would be no spring,
or any showers in which we sing.

The rain has a sweet, clear taste,
sometimes on the beach, we have raced.
On my face I feel the misty air,
so I know the rain will soon be here.

For now the rain has ceased to fall,
but it will be back to be welcomed by all.
And, alas, I will again run free,
with the sweet smell of freshness surrounding me.

Thora E Nelson
MY SEA
My sea is solitude—
A restless, silvered solitude.
That ebbs and flows on windrowed sands
To leave its mark on distant strands—
To meet the dunes in undulation,
All partners in pristine creation.

My sea is destiny—
Where life began to correlate
The plan of all creation.
A grain of sand, a shell, all water life.

Each working out in peace and strife
Towards that certain destiny.

My sea is peace.
Where solitude meets destiny.
Here searching souls are always blessed,
Find life and love and perfect rest.
My sea is peace, and more to me—
'Tis solitude and destiny.

Helen Strey
STAGING THE SEASONS
The MASTER of Ceremonies
reminds of RESURRECTION
so the stage hands gather to labor, with affection.
They have tirelessly worked for many a day
so enjoy each scene in this glorious array!

Winter is bowing to Spring's sunny face, waving goodbye as they embrace,
and snowflakes are melting—little buds take their place.

The cold is disappearing—the stage is re-set
as the Players don raincoats so they won't get wet!

The Spring birds are greeting their friends in the trees
while the grass below is greening and so are the leaves.

Baby bunnies bounce to the tune of the band
marching down the street—those youth look grand!

Little boys are dusting off their ball and their bat;
little girls review recipes for mud pies n' all that.

Cowboy and Indians, tree house and doll
remain on the stage through Summer and Fall.

Then—the curtain falls—and Winter blows in
as the scenes of the Seasons start over again!

The chimes from the church bell toll the true story
Thine is the Kingdom, the Power and the Glory!

Paula Leggett
SNOWFALL

I dedicate this poem to the Lord Jesus Christ, the Saviour of my life, the Author of my faith, and the Shepherd of my path. AMEN.

The snow had fallen and then the rain and sleet.
As I walked, the crisp snow crunched beneath my feet.
The sleet and rain had mixed to cover the earth with a sheet of ice.
As I gazed at the trees around me, I felt the mystery of what I saw.
Each branch and tiny twig was encased in its own diamond jacket.
The air was enchanted and I knew I was in a wonderland that only the Almighty could create.

The moon glistened high over head, giving way to ones imagination.
Picture an artist with his delicate brush, painting the tree tops with silver colors that light up the sky like bright, shiny, new coins.
Imagine, if God decided to leave His creation paralyzed to preserve it for future generations.
It would leave the world with no beautifully, colored flowers in spring and no juicy, ripen fruits for summer.
Thank God we can count on the sun coming up tomorrow to melt this dream away.

Douglas Black
THE HALLS OF THE NIGHT
On the caring daylight lies the burden of sorrow
And the ever dimming night is in all we have known.
In the midst of the dark and doom
There-in lies the dreamers tomb,
The only room he has ever known
In his life of the obscure.
As he discovers what burdens tomorrow
On his journeys through wakened fears,
He sees all threatened life
That had no love for tears,
Just because the sky never rained
Down with tears for the blood and pain,
Doesn't mean there's a life in vain,
In the halls of the night.
But life still holds on
For the truth and the courage
And for the friends we shall meet on the way,
Until then we shall live with pride
And the price to be paid inside
Is just a memory to fade within,
The halls of the night.

Carol A Lucas
DOCTOR'S CURE
Doctor Doctor can't you see
something's wrong inside of me.
My stomach felt as if it dropped;
check my pulse i think it stopped.

The doctor checked me thru and thru and said, "there's nothing wrong with you.
You must be feeling depressed and blue, so here's what i suggest you do.

Talk about what's bothering you
and the reason you're feeling blue
and once you start to talk it out
your pain will leave without a doubt."

Joyce J Miller
IF
"If" I had a son, oh I could clearly see
He would be so handsome, for he'd look a lot like me.

"If" I had a son, he'd be so perfect, bright and strong
He wouldn't have any faults and know right from wrong

"If" I had a son, I'd teach him about life and love
And that's all made possible from the man up above.

"If" I had a son, in school he would be tops in his class
For that's my son, nobody would have to ask.

"If" I had a son, understanding and discipline he would learn
And the knowledge of honor and respect he alone must earn.

He would know how to win, lose, and share
He would know that everything in life is far from fair.

He will grow up to be a doctor, lawyer or a very important man
He may even become president of this great land.

But if by chance, God's will sees that he is not perfect at birth
I would love him even more and with every inch of my soul for what it's worth

Amanda Beth Monica Chandler
LIFE IS A SAILBOAT ON THE SEA OF CURIOSITY

To Sting who is my inspiration, to my mother, father, and to my whole family and also to everyone in the world. Peace always and everywhere!

Life is a sailboat on the sea of curiosity
Tossing on the waves of a troubled mind,
Flowing with the current which must be followed,
For the future lies ahead in every changing tide

Tracy Lee Colson
MY FAITHFUL OLD FRIEND
How sorry I am to see you my faithful old friend, I know you always do what I ask . . .
For ten years behind bars helped me plan my escape and I always remain right on task . . .
What a brilliant plan I thought up with my quite clever brain, that surely would work at last . . .
To hide in a casket with a man of silent words, and who's future is now in the past . . .
You would then dig me up out of six feet of dirt, from a grave that was never meant for me . . .
But I'm running out of air because I'm still in the ground and my future is easy to see . . .
How sorry I am to see you my friend as I lie here beneath dirt and rocks . . .
How sorry I am to see you my friend, for you are the other man in this box . . .

Mildred Jarratt

Mildred Jarratt
GREAT BUT SMALL

In loving memory of my parents, John and Blanche Holloman.

Lord, when others praise me for the good deeds that I've done
I feel great.
When I feed the birds and hear their song, again,
I feel great.
When I can rest my tired feet at the end of the day . . .
I do feel great.
When I can raise my voice in a song of praise, . . . Lord, I just
Feel so great!
But, when I approach the Altar to pray . . . I feel so small,
As small as I can remember one grain of sand in this Vast Land
As small as I can remember one drop of rain in the Mighty Ocean.
When I kneel to pray, I thank You for letting me see that, I am not
So great at all.
I thank You for letting me know how small I truly am, but not so small
That, I cannot see the moon and stars, or feel the rays of the sun,
Or, to know that, You are the Greatest One, because everything I gave,
You gave it all.
Now that I know You—, Though I am small—, I DO FEEL GREAT!!!

Regina Folds
GOOD-BYE

Dedicated to: Michael Watson
Inspired By: Rick Attaway

What we had
Was special then,
But you should understand,
Now I have him.

I want to tell you
We can still be friends.
My love for him is true,
And it will never end.

So our love is dead and gone,
But we knew this would happen all along.
So don't think forever that you'll be alone.
For it to die so quick, it couldn't be that strong.

Maybe it was care, instead of love,
Because it wasn't sent from God above.
For me to have him, it had to die.
So now I bid you a final
GOOD-BYE!

Melcia L Townes
GENERATION
Enlighten, OH Generation.
Preserve your Heritage.
Complain and grumble no longer;
Proceed patiently with sincerity.
Gather thy hands together, and protect the peace and love.
Be partakers of the Bread of Life
and the joyous pleasure of the Light.

Julie Anne Cordova
TO NEED A DEEPER FEELING
Now well do you know me?
Not well I must say
Going by just what you see
Is really not okay

Don't you ever need to know
What I'm really all about?
To ask me questions in a row
And hear the answers out?

Why is it when I'm with you
You seem so far away?
You always act as though you knew
Just what I'm going to say!

A kiss and a hug are nice to get
But not when it's all day long
I like being with you yet
I feel there's something wrong

I need some more companionship,
Not just some lips to kiss
We need a closer relationship,
Not just a pretend bliss

I realize time is needed

To learn how someone thinks
To get emotions weeded
And discover all the links

I can see you've hesitated
To let me know your thoughts
So many times I've waited
And tied myself in knots

Yes we may be side by side
But mentally we're apart
No matter what is ever tried
We'll still have searching hearts

Lorena Ruth Deimer

MY ANNIVERSARY POEM

Love is a person
who loves you
Even when you are ill.

Honor, love cherish in
the marriage ceremony,
Of thirty years of a long time.

For a husband to go through illness,
and a complicated life,
Still to stick by you.

Well this marriage has lasted
Through thick and thin.

To seal with a
pretty single red
rose,
After my surgery
That's real love.

Pisa Marie Glass-Brown

Pisa Marie Glass-Brown

TEARS THAT NEVER STAIN

This empty space is such a lonely place, you know the feeling all too well

Looking for something you can't seem to find creating dreams that never sell.

You cry for love you have never known and then you cry again from pain, sometimes you cry when you have found happiness but those are tears that never stain.

We are love that keeps on growing even though we stand alone, we believe a time is coming when our love will soon be shown.

Come what may, we keep on reaching thru the tears that lead our way

When the time has come for crying think of tears that never stain.

Simon Casady

AN OCTOGENARIAN'S LAMENT

There was a time in days gone by
When I was quite a different guy.

In those old days the Christmas season
Would bring me joy beyond all reason.

I'd dream, with childish eyes aglow,
Of reindeer prancing in the snow.

I then believed in Santa Claus
Although his voice resembled pa's

But those old days have come and gone,
And though their memories linger on

And make me yearn for seasons past,
I find the pleasure does not last.

The gifts, the lights, the Christmas tree
No longer fill my heart with glee.

The thrills that once could stir my soul
No longer play that welcome role.

My appetite for myths is jaded,
And all the happy years have faded.

I think with shudders of St. Nick
And Christmas carols make me sick.

I find myself consumed with rage
At being 80 years of age!

Phyllis Newton

KISSED POPPIES

Sun paints the sky red.
At the bottom of the hills
Are fire-kissed petals.

The Spring breeze touches
Each golden gleaming blossom
Swaying gracefully.

Bees stir all around
In search of fine yellow dust
And sucks their bright eyes.

A humming bird flies
Like an arrow to the sprays
To caress the blooms.

Fog hides the red sky.
At the bottom of the hills
Are wet-kissed poppies.

Rasheeda Alia Sayles

TODAY . . .

TODAY . . .
TODAY is the future of yesterday.

CHILDREN

It's ironic that adults ask children to discipline themselves not to use drugs, yet the adults don't discipline themselves to call children "children."

THE LAND

"He that plants trees loves others besides himself."
Dismantle the guns and the tanks;
melt the metal down;
Make small hand tools and small machinery to
Farm the lands, using the water in the dams!
Use the skills done by hand, each individual taking part
In taking care of his homeland.
For "laziness travels so slowly that poverty soon overtakes him."
Learn all there is to learn, applying it to life!
It is known some "speak with a forked tongue" and will
"until the rivers run backwards."
Be not lazy; use your senses and your brain.
Reconnect with the land!

Barbara Schockaert

I BELIEVE IN ME

I dedicate this poem to my family for all their love and understanding

Let not your heart be discouraged
when all things look so dark and bleak.
Lift up your eyes and have courage
for it is just reassurance you seek.

Reassurance that you as a person
have a place in this life you can see.
But you'll know that you do when
you can say;
I truly believe in me.

When you look at the world around
you,
you may say it's so hard to endure.
But take another good look around
you
use your heart and you're bound to
see more.

You must learn to be optimistic.
Remember how to laugh and you'll
find;
that people respond well to laughter
and it does wonders for your body
and mind.

So be like the little grain of mustard
seed
and have faith in your friends and
family.
Then with the Lord's help, you'll be
reassured
and meaningfully say "I believe in
me."

Serendipity

THE JOY OF POETRY

To Joshua: in remembrance of the many, happy, bedtime hours we spent . . . rambling through the World of Poetry!

How fascinating it is to take.
A word, a dream or thought and
make
A work that pleases lover's eye
And lifts sad hearts and souls up high
On wings of words in verse and
prose . . .
That strikes the center core of
rose . . .
Or transports swiftly on fiery pen
To "The Charge of the Light
Brigade's" sad end!

The ode, the narrative, the
theme . . .
in heights and depths unplumbed
Belong to those of us who love
the songs as yet unsung . . .
Awaiting poet's pen and touch and
special gift to bring . . .
The magic Joy of Poetry that
makes our hearts to sing.

Jean Earnest

SHE CAME EVERY DAY

She came every day,
To make sure her grown up child
was safe.
Down the long leaf strewn path,
Like some midnight waif.

Always she brought something,
A shirt given her to repair,
New warm socks,
Or preserves made from pear.

She adored the small grandchild,
Whose name was the same.
Born so late in her life,
Who was not young when her child
came.

Winters rain, and sleet, and cold,
Or summers burning heat.
Spring violets picked along the way,
Or fall cookies warm and sweet.

Her steps are gone from the path
now,
Not even the prints of her shoes
remain.
Wild November rains come down,
And nothing will ever be the same.

Hazel Marie Kehrer

LOST, MY LOVE

You're gone and didn't say,
"Goodbye"
I've searched for the reason why.
Love like ours was hard to find.
We were best friends, a tie that
binds.
I miss you so with each passing day,
I'm finding it difficult to find the
way
To go on living without you.
When you were here, our love was
true.
Your life on earth, though cut short,
Was spent for me; you stole my
heart.
I wish I could have one more day
To let you know I feel this way.
You're gone and I don't know why.
For you, each day I'll try
To remember the things for which
you stood,
Holding in my heart all things that
are good.

Brenda L Frahm

LOCKED UP

The closed window, letting in
sunlight,
the walls that hold you within,
lets no freedom escape, but lingers
alone.
The cool breeze creeps through that
window,
letting you know spring is here.
The wind rustles the leaves about
as the birds pick at the ground.

The feeling of being locked up,
away from life and people,
brings forth a dream world
that you share with no one.
The wishing of being able to
touch . . .
the trees, grass and earth, to walk
the sidewalks with lovers and
friends,
brings a sadness to my heart.

To be able to sit on the ground,
next to a tree in the sunshine
with the wind softly blowing,
blowing through my hair.
To touch the fallen leaves
that lay about the cold ground . . .

Nancy E Nihart

WINDS OF FATE

To "Theo"—a friend to be remembered.

One ship drives east and another
drives west
With the selfsame winds that blow.
'Tis the set of the sails,
And not the gales,

Which tell us the way to go.
Like the winds of the sea, are the ways of fate,
As we voyage along through life,
'Tis the set of a soul
That decides its goal,
And not the calm or the strife!

Heidi Lynn Anderson
WHAT A CHILD NEEDS

To my family and friends for giving me the love I needed to grow.

Love is the sweetest gift
a man and woman share

A child is the sweetest gift
a man and woman bear

Innocence and purity are
in each boy and girl

The sweetness is so visible
within each little curl

Maturity and tenderness
are what a child learns

Along the path in life he takes
he'll learn which way to turn

Honor and respect the
child will come to grow

But love will give a child
what he needs to know.

Jonelda Bowers Sells
GENERATION GAP
Haste, my constant companion
Few my leisure moments by count;
Futile my race with Time . . .
Scarcely sipping from Life's bubbling fount.

I've never a moment to linger,
Just a blur on Life's turning page;
Hurrying, most times running
Across stepping stones of a present age.

Time and seasons are fleeting,
The journey swift as eagle's wings;
Busy years, some forgotten . . .
Lost like snow in early Spring.

But every now and then
To a country grave my footsteps go;
To kneel beside a footstone
And brush away the dust or snow.

Narrow, winding country road . . .
The golden bridge that spans the years;
A generation lately buried . . .
Demanding time for tender tears!

Laurie Ann Fleck
RELATIONSHIPS
Relationships come and go
Sometimes it's an easy flow
But other times it's hard to deal with
And may seem like a myth.
However when two people really love one another
There's no obvious cover
To hide anything
That trouble may bring
In around your years as teens
By any means
You have a lot of boy/girl friends
That you think are rated tens
But end up to be just crushes
And end up being flushes
Down the drain
Because you went by your heart not your brain
People use their hearts to pick someone
Instead of their brains to see a loser which could be done
All that I am saying is don't lay there like a mat
There are a lot of fish in the sea
Don't you see
But to find out if you really care for some body
And make sure he's no fuddy duddy
You must play the field you see
Be all you can be
Don't put on a front
Or a stunt
Let them see who you are and like what/who you are
Don't be a star
By putting on an act
Be yourself then they will let you know how they feel and react
For love isn't for sale
And once you find it, it won't let you fail
It's a true thing
And that's what a relationship brings.

Helmut Schueler

Helmut Schueler
DOGGY'S PASSPORT
World wide travel getting worse,
vacation time is running short.
Doggy need a paper sheet
signed by State Authority.

First line, first page you read,
what name is doggy's breed.
Abstract from magician text
his date of birth and sex.

They want to see in every Nation
doggy's history of vaccination.
O, is he smiling happily
second page his color photography.

Ten times biting loss of Passport
no more walking to the Airport.
When situations worsen by proofing
situation dead by shooting.

And when your doggy hits his age,
see doggy's Passport's final page.
One line for honouring your pet
write date and reason for his death.

Helen A Harris
I SANG A SONG ALL DAY TODAY
I sang a song all day today,
And when I was done, I learned to say;
How was everything for you?
And what would you have me do?
We played the game and sung our tune,
And then I waited; the answer came soon.
Give me your being, give me your soul,
None of it is yours to withhold.
My being cried, my soul then died—
A shell was left with no inside.
I sang a song all day today,
And when I was done I learned to say—

Blanche A Longres
MY DARLING DAUGHTER
Today, I watched my darling daughter
Walking up to the altar, by her father's side.
She looked beautiful . . .
In her wedding gown and lovely crown
And as she was taking her marriage vows
The memories of her childhood
Came flashing into my mind.

I remember so clearly . . .
The first time she was laid in my arms.
I wanted to see the color of her eyes
But she kept stretching and twisting her cute little mouth.

I remember too . . .
The first time I took her to school.
She kissed me goodby
And waived her hand with a big smile.
I knew then, my little girl
Would be leaving me,
To face her own world.

So today, when I saw her
Walking down from the altar
The tears I shed were tears of joy
For she looked so happy
Walking down by her husband's side.

May God's blessing
Be with them both,
For the rest of their lives.

Dolores Brand
THE FOUR SEASONS
Springtime bursts forth with beauty
Of fresh budding trees and rain,
Blue skies, the song of a robin;
New life comes to earth once again.

Then summertime brings us pleasures
Of picnics, baseball and swimming,
Mowing the yard on hot, dusty days,
Fresh fruit from the garden, canning.

In the blaze of autumn such beauty we see!
The world turns to orange, brown and gold.
And we pause to give thanks to our loving God
Who has blessed us with all we behold.

Then winter moves in with icy cold wind,
Christmas, and soft falling snow.
Earth takes its rest in a quiet peace
As we're warmed in the firelight glow.
Springtime, summertime, autumn and winter;
Each a part of God's perfect plan
To care for his earth and his people,
And bless us as only he can.

Jo B Comberiate

Jo B Comberiate
MUSIC BOX MEMORIES
I need only touch your small hand
to be in my childhood fairyland.
Beyond the rainbow over the magical seas,
starlight winks and dances to pretty melodies.
Under Heaven's dome, there I can dwell,
sharing all of God's home from a shell.

Like the sun shining through the leaves
of warmest red and gold,
Magic lanes of enchantment lead to clouds
that unfold picturesque
memories of love
And of all the hopes and dreams
that I am thinking of.

In this land of wonderment,
I can talk to God, and I'm content!
Loveliest of toys, so beautiful!
The sweetest of joys, so meaningful!
Like the bluebirds soaring in flight,
you bring back my childhood
nights with delight—

MAGIC MEMORIES! Go to sleep,
my MUSIC BOX MEMORIES!

Sister Mary Andreé OSU
DISCOVERY
Emotions turned kaleidoscope.
The world of eyes viewed yet another launch,
Frozen to its firey, fate-filled birth in progress.
Countless faces mirrored fear, anxiety and doubt.
In some, there beamed a hope, a glistening through tears,
Remembering The Challenger.

Simultaneously with countdown, rose the
Eagle, in command, majestic and serene in flight
To wing away, to cross all barriers of earth into
The great beyond.
America the beautiful stood proud.
Her spacious skies bowed low to rain down joy.
Where purple mountains glowed,
God shed His grace.

They viewed their Earth, these brave ones.
From on high they rode in paths of

glory, trekking stars.
Exhilarated with the weightless wonders, laughter, awe and peace,
Their Navigator dared to brush with golden hemlines of
The Cherubim, to join their worship of the First Great
Astronaut, circling, searching for His Astrodome.

They brought a message home with their success.
"The way is clearer, closer now, and Light in space reveals
His mystery embedded in our spirit.
It's immortality, longing for Discovery."

Ellie Koepper
MY LOVE
I give you all my love dear,
It's yours to have and hold.
The times we shared together,
Are worth much more than gold.
Whoever thought you'd be mine,
To cherish and to love,
For you were but an angel,
You came from up above.

You made me feel so happy,
And made me come alive.
Each day was filled with gladness,
The burdens I'd survive.
Along life's endless journey,
A tender interlude,
A blissful thrilling memory,
Suspends me in this mood.

Julie M Buser
MY TEDDY BEAR
He's someone that I can yell at, he doesn't get mad.
He doesn't yell back, or make me sad.
He is my teddy bear.

He keeps me company when I'm alone.
He doesn't cry or moan and groan.
He is my teddy bear.

He listens to me when I have something to say.
I get to see him everyday.
He is my teddy bear.

When I'm asleep, he's always there.
He may be old and has a tear.
He is my teddy bear.

I love him a little, I love him a lot.
He is the most precious thing I've got.
He is my teddy bear.

Janet Rae Heifner
TIDAL WAVE
The waves of the ocean are both high and low.
I guess they just don't know where to go.
So colorful blue, green, and gold,
And holds secrets left untold.
The sea is such a strange and mystic place.
For the treasure hunter would have to be brave and stare her right in the face.
The sea represents danger, death, and love.
Even though it looks so peaceful from up above.

Judith Monds
CHANCE
My life has come to an intersection, I'm confused as to which direction. All the ways look long an' never ending, of tangled problems, only pending. Shall I close my eyes an' chance blind, never looking back or behind? Unable to stand an' unable to choose. I'll flip a coin, not for heads or I'll lose. As I may not be known to everyone, or have a lot to say, but this for sure I do know, I am someone today.

H Paul Holdridge
LOVE
Love is such a wonderful thing.
Of it everyone can joyfully sing;
From the least to the smartest and greatest.
From early morning hours to the latest.

It is of inexhaustible, endless measure.
It's value is indeed a real treasure.
And though it is a gift from above,
All of us need someone, something to love.

When one is not loved, his heart longs
For someone to sing hymns and songs
About a friend or loved one so near
Who can bring his aching heart, cheer.

For all are equipped with an empty place
Until overcome by true love in a race.
And that vacancy at last is fulfilled;
The seeker is contentedly thrilled.

Melvin Manwarring
THE BIRDS
'Tis early morn—the birds
Nestled in the trees in
Our back yard begin to
Stir and fuss.

They seem to be holding a
Council and how they do
Chatter; as if to say—Does
That really matter?

Discussions over, they soon
Take wing: The ones that
Remain sometimes may sing.

Mother nature is really
Grand; but that is a part
Of God's plan.

The birds come back in early
E'en. They chatter and fuss
All over again.

The birds may chatter and fuss;
But they seem to have a plan—
Which seems lacking so much in
Modern man!

Jana K Downey
THE WIND
The wind whispered in my ear, a song,
A beautiful sound, that I so longed.
While it gently breezed past, the tops of the trees,
And playfully rustled, the new fallen leaves,
I found myself smiling, as it left me with this,
A feeling of peace, already the song, I do miss.

Rhonda Riha
A DREAM
With love to J.R., my family and friends. You've made me what I am today.

I once had a dream.
A dream of love and happiness.
In my dream, I thought the world of you.
I thought you loved me, too.
I thought, we had the same dream.
You always told me all the right things.
You convinced me you were always right.
I trusted you, because, I loved you.

Little by little, you took my heart and tore it all apart.
When there was nothing left inside of me,
you wanted more.
Now, you want me to be warm.
Now, you say you have a dream.
Now, you want me to have the same dream.
Now, my dreams are gone forever and
if I trust you,
I know, I will only have
another dream.

Diane Ratliff
CLOUDS
At 31,000 feet in the air,
I stare out the window without a care.

The fluffy white clouds spread many a mile.
I look and imagine and it makes me smile.

They could be a mattress so lumpy and soft,
For angels to fall on from aloft.

They could be a mountain all covered with snow,
When the air is cold and the North winds blow.

Or marshmallows out of a bag that was torn,
Or small, furry kittens that were just born.

They could be an ocean with whitecaps galore.
Whatever I imagine, they're something I adore.
These fluffy, white clouds as I fly above
Are something spectacular that I love.

Dean Carl Holcomb
A MEMORIAL
I dedicate this Poem to those who gave their lives for their Country.

A memorial is a tribute to a memory of long ago,
Where men lie in fields made of blood,
Giving their lives for you and for me.
For that I'm proud and free.

One day set aside in which we pay respect and give our gratitude,
I think back to a time of needless wars,
That took lives in anger, and in pride.
For that I bow my head in shame and despair.

America, home of the free and the brave,
On land in which the symbol is freedom,
I shed a tear for that young man who was of innocence, but yet had to die.
So that I may walk a free man.

William T Shrewsbury
QUESTION
As i rest
on this twig
after a long flight
through life
not knowing
what the next moment holds
among my many thoughts
happiness looms . . .
What is happiness?
i ask myself
and i answer
it is borne
out of love . . .

C Renee Layton
MOM
You are always there when I need you,
You are always there to care;
You are always there when I am hurting,
or in despair.

You try to give me your advice,
I always take it in stride;
You try to tell me its for my own good,
When I know you're really hurting inside.
You tell me things will work out for the best,
And I will forget the rest.
You tell me I'm young, I know it's true,
But when I'm older I hope I'm just like you!

There are just three little words that say
"Thanks" in so many ways;
"I LOVE YOU!" and Happy Mother's Day.

I love you,
Renee '87

Marianne Lang
stranger in town
we made our selection on the juke box
4 songs for a dollar
3 oldies for him
1 love song for me

we took our places at the bar
i looked in his eyes

he looked in a mirror

we pounded down 6 lager beers
4 for him
2 for me
and munched on pretzels
compliments of the establishment

again i tried to meet his eyes
again he looked somewhere else
at his watch
said it was getting late

time for the satin suit
and jingle bell hat
presto
a clown

he laughed
i was happy

he said we drink too much
excessively was the word

a hunk decked in guess jeans and a sassoon shirt
winked at me
across the smoke filled room
i looked somewhere else

for a third time
just trying my luck

we left
the stranger and i
and i never heard my song

Casey Parks
SUSPICIONS
Attitudes.
Open, close.
Open, close.
Breaking Points.

Say goodbye, don't you cry.
DOMINATE.
Withered, dull.
White Flag. Identity.
Sarcasm, sexual.
Shallow—lost.

Found again. Daybreak.
Questions? What?
Anger unexplained.
So sorry, no rebuttal.
No Union, clam.
Forever?

Maybe.

Past linked? Future Brides?
Brides of the past, perhaps.
Reason? Vindictive.
Obvious.

Surviving? Don't know.
Possible.

Misled? Both lanes.
Open, close.
Open, close.
No Passing. Big Fine.
Accelerate?
Yes.
Crash?
Maybe.
Burn?
Always.

Tamra Ulmer
THE FORGOTTEN STALLION
On a glorious mountain, on a glorious night
In a glorious battle, or a glorious fight.

Below the roaring thunder, below the royal sky
Stands the reddest beast there ever was, with fire in his eyes.

His world once filled with rainbows
has turned to stone and dust
And the ropes that once had tried
their luck have turned to evil rust.

The herd that he once led was strong,
but was strongly drove away.

Human drove away his herd and took all of his pride
And forgot the wild red stallion for whom no man could ride.

His color is as red as wild fire in the sky
And the wildest look upon the earth
was hid deep in his eyes.

He defeated lions and rearing
stallions and defeated mans great wealth
The only one he did not defeat was
the fire deep inside himself.

Now he rears and screams high
shrieks upon the earth below
As if he would never move through
rain, sleet, or snow.

That stallion's old and has his day,
but that fire will always burn
And those legs will always stand so strong and that land he'll always stay.
At night he'll scream his wild shrieks
to what man has taken away.

Anissa Emfinger

Anissa Emfinger
THE CREDIT CARD

A blanket of evil and darkness flows across the land. The good disappear and the wicked are left to rule the land. Some call it the Rapture, others call it the Return, but some are left unknowing and to learn too late that Christ has come back for those that would wait. For those unfortunate few that are left behind Christ gives one last chance to walk the straight and narrow line. Though it won't be easy for any child, woman or man for Satan rules this land. He'll say the easy way is to get a special kind of credit card; the kind you wear upon your hand. Though you'll find you will not want it, for the price you pay is with your soul and what you get in return is a new eternal home—one with heating, no air conditioning, oh yes, and plenty of pain; for what you've bought is an eternal damnation and burning in Hell.

For those who choose to go the straight and narrow road it won't be easy. For you see the others seem to think you're barking up the wrong tree. To them it seems that you're fighting a losing battle full of lies and at the end you lose your life for nothing. Though the battle has already been won and those who saw it are having fun in Heaven, unlike those that are down below.

Sharon A Middleton
MEMORIES OF A FAMILY REUNION
Family reunions are always fun
but remember how much more
when we were young?
The pranks we pulled, on cousins or aunts,
the laughter, the yelling, and running on the grass.

Remember the tree with the bough
shaped like a horse?
We rode the saddle, clinging to
branches as our reins.
And the cousin with braids,
that we ran away from,
straight into the electric fence?
Boy, was I stunned.

She couldn't climb trees
and didn't like haymows.
Cows scared her
but not us, we were too proud.

Now, I am older,
I sit pleasantly and chat
with aunts and uncles,
and the cousin with the braids?
Why, she's my best friend!

Valerie Finkle
AS SHE SAT IN THE DIMLY LIT ROOM
As she sat in the dimly lit room
A figure appeared out of the shadows
A tall, thin figure
His hair a light hue of brown
His eyes caught her aimlessly gazing at him
He slowly walked over
Her mind went wild with excuses
What was she to say?
What was he going to say?
Her heart was racing
Her palms were sweaty
She looked for a way out
She was trapped
Uh-Oh, he was getting closer
All of a sudden he was next to her
All she could do was smile
Here goes nothing she thought
Then it happened
He said it
The word she'd been waiting for
Hello.

Helen Price Schaefer
SUNSHINE AND SHADOW
All my songs are sad songs.
When the sun lights up the sky,
I'm much too busy living
To wonder how or why.

But when my eyes are filled with tears,
Grief opens wide the heart.
It is then the questions stir and rise
That tears the mind apart!

Margaret McNabney
THE WALNUT POT BENCH

This poem is dedicated to Stephen and Jane Layne, my Grandparents

The Walnut Pot Bench, I remember well
Could tell us many stories, could it speak
of Grandma's spotless kitchen
and the woodstove placed nearby;
The oil lamps with wicks to trim
And chimneys to be washed and shined
That bench held pots and pans
and iron skillets, black from
time and grease.

Used for making toast and hot cakes long ago;
Gingham curtains stretched before it,
Washed by Grandma many times a year
The Bench was made by Grandpa
When he built that five room house.
The two of them were married and
they moved into that home.

Children six were born there and they
lived for many years.
With the Walnut Pot Bench made by
Grandpa long years ago.

Sharon Hambrick
GONE HOME

This poem is dedicated to the memory of my son, Brad—1962-1980.

So quickly he left for Home . . .
I wasn't ready for this.
I cried:
"Lord, I'm not through with him!"
Unexpectedly my son left
in the middle of the night.
We said no good-byes.
Why did he have to leave so soon?
I need his strength;
his gentleness
and another "I love you".
God called him
and he was willing . . .
but not I.
He was only eighteen.
How I miss him!
Dear God, how I miss him!

Brandi L Erwin
ONLY BY MAGIC

For Mom—thank you for standing by me, I love you. Thanks—to all of my family.

The spring water runs down my face,
The warmth of the sun sets with grace,
The way of the lake is crystal clear,
There is no violence, there is no fear.

A light tender breeze runs through my hair,
With so much love and so much care,
All things beautiful, all things right,
And the treasures stars give at night.

This place I shall lock in my heart,
In hopes its memory shall never part,
In this land, everything's as it seems,
You reach it only by magic of your dreams.

Peter Halbrohr
YOUTH
quick batons are beating on drums
their screaming sound an explosion
in my ears
you are free master to continue
beating
to destroy all our treasures and our
peace

the intoxicating rhythm of past
desires
reappearing again breeds hope
they roll and jump and hug and fight
thousands and thousands of
youngsters are dancing

tiny atoms circulate tirelessly
tormenting everyone
our life is your life
today you are alive
tomorrow you are gone
destiny and time are our force

they do not even know
tangled in that sound
in which nerves and strings

vibrate spontaneously
that the uncertainty of existence
is just the seventh sensation
of fear and music

William Osborne
I WANT TO LOSE MYSELF

To Melody with all my heart. I love you.

I want to lose myself
Inside your eyes.
Forever and a day.
I want to sail with you
Through clear blue skies,
On rainbows we can play.

The angels will sing,
When they see,
The joy you bring,
When you're with me.

So give me your love,
To keep with mine,
And the Heavens above
For us will shine.

Viola H Woglom
A HEART THAT HAS CAUGHT IN A COBWEB

A heart that has caught in a cobweb,
That has ached with an aged oak
Creaking through a storm;
That has risen in a sparrow's song
Into melodious flight,
Will find its rest
In the dark of a light.

Enough for the eagle
The sure swift flight
Of a strong cutting wing
And an eagle sight.

But he who hears another sing
The song within his heart,
From the heart of another
Cannot rest apart.

As the curving bow in the rain
Can only find its place in the sun,
The heart can only measure its beat
In the heart of another one.

Ida-rose Machart
A FORMATION OF EAGLES

A formation of eagles
Distant thunder in the skies
Steadily moving forward
Tears pooling in his eyes

One broken soldier, caught in memory
For a moment, living through
Yesterday . . . friends lost forever
All the hell that they all knew

The thunderous roar now overhead
He could almost SEE all those he'd known
Proudly again to march among them
Past graves of wars unknown
Ten silver winged eagles
Just passing through the night
Each taking with it a memory
As each faded soon from sight

And to disappear into the shadows
On the wings on which they'd come
Rode the memories of one lone soldier
As in silence, he saluted them . . .
one by one

C D Ransom
THE WORDS

The need to write sometimes
Burns deep.
An aching so acute that it
Must be set free.
On these occasions,
The burning does burst forth
And spills the guts that
Withheld it.
Spreading itself before all,
So that mankind may see just
What it wanted to say.
Whether or not it is worth
Anything,
Makes no difference.
Just that the words are there,
That is all that matters.

Kilian Schneider
MOTHER'S LOVE

Mother's love comes down to us through the ages,
In words and songs on countless pages.
Its power and purity is hard to comprehend.
Her love and devotion is never frivolously spent.

Her life for her children she would gladly give,
So that they in happiness could live.
There is no greater love than mother's love.
Truly, it can only come from her, and God above.

God to her this maternal love has given,
To care for and protect us she seems constantly driven,
But she very seldom ever complains,
Even though we have caused her many pains.

To our mothers we can never do wrong,
This seems to be life's eternal song.
She loves us with all her heart,
From the very first day our life does start.

Dawn M Reedy
THE LOOKING GLASS

Eyes are like a looking glass.
You can see in them, but you can't interpret them.
They can tell stories, show emotions, and best of all they
can conceal the most intimate of one's self.
Only a few have the eyes of the looking glass, able to express
without a word spoken.
Eyes come in all different colors like the rainbow or better
yet ice cream flavors.
But the eyes of the person who has the looking glass never
reveals by speaking but by seeing.
The eyes are like stars which show past, present, and
deep inside the pupil lies the futures.
Some say by looking into a person's eyes who has the
looking glass aren't able to define
them in a way that only the person
with the looking glass knows.
The eyes can become shields for
protection against one or for all.
The emotions in the eyes are far more than the surface,
they lie deep inside the heart and soul
of the person.
There are only certain persons who are able to
see, feel, understand the person who
has the looking glass eyes,
but there are so few . . .

Anne Devine
THE TEENAGE YEARS

This poem is dedicated to my son William, love Mom.

Once upon a time, your parents thought of
you as their little dears,
Now, all you hear is their fears as you begin your teenage years.
When reprimanded you feel they are extremely harsh at times,
You wonder; are they the same parents who
read you nursery rhymes?
Becoming a young man or woman is a phase everyone goes through,
You may consider this a difficult time for you, all teens do.
Parents are firmer now as they adapt to the new you,
Their love and concern for you brought changes
in them too.
Some chores and small jobs you will be asked to do,
A sense of responsibility is what they're trying to instill in you.
Parenting is not an easy job, even when they are working as a team,
Your cooperation means, their hopes and your
dreams in the future will be seen.

Lorene Dunaway–O Thrower
THE VOWS THEY MADE

The wedding day of Bill and Lorene,
was March fourteen, nineteen-eighty nine . . .
She needed no whiskey. She needed no wine.
The vows they made suited her fine.

She was so happy—feeling things would turn out alright.
Neither Bill or Lorene cared to sleep much on their wedding night.

Lorene was happy to become Bill's wife, because she desired to be near
him each moment of her life.
Just being near Bill gives Lorene a thrill—
And the thrill seemed to double when she heard Bill confirming their
marriage vows with the words I will.

Orin E Needham
NEW YEAR'S RHYME

To my wife Dollie with love.

As we gaze across the valley far
And see that big bright evening star
That shines like a diamond away up high
On a blanket of velvet across the sky.

The snow on the mountain reflects the glow
Of the moon in it's heaven where we all know
The God of us all resides at home
While we across this free land roam.

We can thank the Lord for the year just past
An cheer the new that has come at last.
It's a time to count our blessings all
He bestows on us from spring till fall.

There's the rooster that crows as he greets the dawn
The flowers that bloom beside the lawn
The bird that awakes with a song in his heart
He created them all from the very start.

As the seasons change the New Year grows
Until it brings the winter snows
Then once again till the end of time
We repeat again this little rhyme.

Kathy Herreras
A MIRACLE COME TRUE

I dedicate my first published poem to my sister Laura, brother-in-law Andy and my nephew Daniel. I love you.

You are a miracle come true, a miracle that turned my whole life around.
Your precious little hands, they are so tiny and so wonderful.
You put a meaning into my life,
you're a treasure come true.
How innocent and harmful you are,
you're my whole life and I love you.
Your funny little faces, your tiny little cry, make me love you more each day.

When I hold you in my arms I cuddle you to sleep with a precious lullaby.
As you close your little eyes, and lay there asleep, you look so peaceful and carefree.
You're a miracle come true one that I will long to treasure
I'm so very proud of you. You're as beautiful as the sky and as precious as life itself.
I thank you for entering into my life and becoming my little miracle.

Irma Albury
GHETTO

To my three boys . . . Virgil, Alan and Jason Albury, with all my love, Cuca

The streets are empty and very quiet.
There are a few people hanging out.

There seems to be a certain stillness in the air.
From the far distance you hear faded

voices.
I look at the distance, kind of observing.
It seems like there isn't too much hope in the area.

The buildings are dressed to kill!
Their outfits are graffiti shaded all over them.

Their windows are like a person's eyes, except these windows are broken.

They seem so barren.

I find myself wondering of a better tomorrow,
for I know there was a better yesterday.

Grace Dombrowski Stephano

THROUGH DIFFERENT EYES

I am old you say?
I beg to differ if I may.

All you see are hairs of white,
But look at my eyes, they are so bright.

Half a century and more they've seen,
Numerous places where I've been.

All of this country and lots more
Cross land and sea and never a bore.

New York, London, Kenya too,
As far away as Timbuctoo.

Have your eyes seen all of these?
I really don't mean to tease.

But say not that I am old,
Lived many years but been so bold!

I'm ready to tackle more of life,
But let's eliminate the strife!

Some day you too shall be old
But hopefully just as bold.

Shireen Senadhira

Shireen Senadhira

FACT OF LIFE

To Neomi Abeyesundere

Mona Lisa did it
And mystified the world
Cleopatra did it
And confused all of Rome
Many women do it
And charm all around
Yet, some can do it
So it leaves you quite cold

But when it arises from the heart
Like the blooming of a rose
That's kissed by sun and dew
A glowing face and shining eyes
Sparkles so it radiates
If quick, you'll catch it too

A woman's smile
Remains unchanged
In this trouble filled world
It sustains and inspires you
Makes it all worthwhile
As when my mother smiles
It's like the sun rise on a tropic isle

Ayumi Inaba

SCARS OF CHILD ABUSE

With love to Vinh, who is always there with loving support when I need him.

There is a girl down the street,
who never plays,
never talks,
never smiles.
I only see her walking alone.
looking down.
Her big, innocent eyes
Wide with fear and—
stripped of self-esteem.
Her mouth, an old woman's mouth,
tired, grim, pinched.
Her hands,
tightly clasped fists
Her shoulders hunched
Her head bent shamefully
The drawn, pained clouds
cast across her young face
as the shadow of
Him
Looms always above.

Manulani R Daniels

T.L.C.

Dedicated to my stepmother Cynthia the one mother that was always there no matter what happened.

No
matter
how far apart
we are or how many
obstacles in between,
my T. L. C. shall go
the distance without
breaking in between.
My
tender
loving care
shall reach out
in the silence of
the night reaching
out for some one in
need.
My
heart
may not speak
in words, but my
feelings run deep.
As
they
reach out
hoping to find
some one
reaching too.

Elizabeth McManninman

PLACES AND THINGS OF THE HEART

This poem is dedicated to my husband John

A beautiful bird on the wing,
A quiet stream, a rippling spring
A walk upon a sandy shore
It lifts my heart, it makes it soar

I like to tread the busy street
And say "hello" to folk I meet
To watch a little child at play
It never fails to make my day

To travel in this lovely land
And see the sights, and understand
Each state is different, yet a part
Of this whole country, great at heart.

These are some things I like to do
Perhaps you'd like to join me too?
Even though it be down memory land
It's fun to trace your steps again.

Marlene Candler Joyner

CROSSES

To my jewels, Latryce & Yasmin Joyner

We love them
We hate them
We debase them
We elate them
We bear them
We share them
We burn them
We spurn them
We wear them
and learn them
This is a world of crosses

Elizabeth P Draper

WHY WAS YESTERDAY SO SOON A DREAM

To All Loving People Everywhere, Especially My Mother.

WHY
was
yesterday
sosoonadream
WHEN
TOMORROW
MAY
BE
what
mighthavebeen

Tamara Waltemate

Tamara Waltemate

LET'S LAST

I dedicate this poem to the precious family I made. Cynthia and Scott, Love becomes more wonderful every day!

Why is it when we are sad
we think of things past?
Be it the good or, be it the bad,
we always think of things that
we could have done, maybe said
and perhaps had.

Let's not think of that past
but, think of our future for
what it holds and it's goals
where to go and how to show,

that we cannot live in that past
but, to forever . . . LAST!

L R L Davis

FOR MEN ONLY

To my brothers Steve, Douglas, Guy, Tracy and Gary Locke

Speaking to you material men
who seek suede and leather
garments and seek other garments
for perfect pacifiers that meet
ten different desires and then
lose savor at mornings end . . .

Speaking to you 'gentle men'
as you are about town trying to
win and/or place . . . and even
trying in the midst to save face.
Assisting where you can; insisting
as you can.

Speaking to you; all of you men
to do as needed by your woman.
Please her, appease her, ease her
and at times tease her. Give her
heart's desires and love will
never lose its' fire!

Lisa Grilo

MAN OF MY DREAMS

Dedicated to Mr. Rod Stewart

How is it that we dream?
What do they all really mean?
During my sleep you enter my night,
making me feel it's gonna be alright.
Then I wake only to find,
that you were really never mine.
Though you're far away, I can almost feel you;
why, oh why, can't my dreams be true?
Every day my hope is new,
there's still a chance for me and you;
My heart knows that we'd be good,
we'd be close—I know we would.
I'm never lonely, but I just don't care,
and it's not that I want more than my share;
I just wanna love you and let you have me,
I can almost hear you say, "love me baby."
You are the man of my dreams
and I've fallen in love it seems;
So, sing to me with your eyes; let them quiet my sighs,
for I'll hold tight by all means,
to you,
the man of my dreams.

Stephen E Medlin

THE LONELY DREAMER

For Beth, you will always be in my dreams.

As I sit here all alone my mind brings back a dream. I thought i'd finally found true love but now it doesn't seem.

Once in my life I wasn't lonely, the skies were always blue. I felt that I had reached my rainbow and in it I found you.

I thought that if I told you just how I really felt. You'd come to me and love me but the cards must have misdealt.

I still dream about you and the way it might have been. I guess i'll always dream of you until the very end.

I never knew true love before until your lips met mine. I still remember how it felt and it was all too fine.

Every time I see you I can barely stand the pain. Sometimes I feel before I die I will surely go insane.

I still love you woman and not just like a friend, but for you to love me now would truly be a sin.

I'll never really understand what makes me love you so. The answer to that question, well God will only

know.
If only our paths could have crossed at a different time. I think we may have had the chance to make a perfect rhyme.
I hope your life is happy baby and I hope you dreams come true. Just think of me from time to time and remember, I Love You.

Melinda Schlehlein
THE WISE OLD TREE

To my Mother and Father, with love

As I walked through the woods,
I saw a tree.
It was no ordinary tree,
For I could see its old wise
Wrinkles in the bark.
The dry parched bark with its
Dark circles looked like eyes
That pierced deeply into mine.
I shivered.

Suddenly, a gust of wind came from
Nowhere, shaking the long old
branches.
The tree shook in the wind
And its fingers pointed—North.

The tree swayed as the zephyr
continued,
Blowing away its dry old leaves.
They crackled and crunched as they
were
Tossed about; they seemed to say . . .
"There,
There is where your destiny shall
take place."
The words faded away as the wind
grew louder and louder.
Dark clouds came overhead, telling
me a storm was brewing—
A storm, far off, in the north.

Eleanor L Smith
OUR LOVE WAS MEANT TO BE . . .

"To my boyfriend Mike," Who inspired me to write this poem with all my love.

Today our love
Is special and strong
Our love is together
Where it belongs

Our falling in love
Was meant to be
I am for you
You are for me

All I want
is to have you near
Each and every day
To love you, my dear

Never stop loving me
And wanting me near
My love for you
Will grow stronger every
year

Tami A Boss
LOST LOVE

Dedicated belatedly to my mother, Hannah, who encouraged me to express my thoughts in verse.

I have lost you
Though I have never had you
I have lost you
And all my dreams
With all my visions
Simply fade away—
For I have lost you
Though you were never mine
Alone to touch
To hold for long
On moonlit nights
When all were gone
We shared a passion—
An impossible dream—
Filled with shining stars
And the whispering wind
And the look in your eyes . . .
I will never forget—
But I have lost you
Though I have never had you.
I have lost you, my romantic friend

Debbie Schroeder
COME ON CHILD

To my mother who gave me her hand, that led me down the road of life, Thanks—Mom

Come on Child
take my hand
And we will look at life upon this
land,

We will see
through our eyes
the beauty that here lies,

We'll look at the ocean
As the waves roll in
And look at the sky, as it's always
been,

We'll roam the fields
of lovely flowers
Frolic and play for hours and hours,

We'll watch the sunrise
day after day
And the sunset in the same way,

So, come on child
And take my hand
As we have looked at life upon this
land . . .

Stephen P Redic
CAT

To Annie, my cat, for all her boundless devotion and hours of comfort.

Soft and brown bear black,
eager to be near,
I love to love you,
to scratch behind your ear.
To hear the warmth of your life,
To balance on my hands
Knowing no fear,
I love to hold you
And scratch behind an ear.
Purrs pass time,
Seasons fly,
I know, that death soon be by.
Carnivorous calm, cuddled warm,
An almost perfect career
Waiting, waiting
Waiting for me—
To scratch behind her ear.

Arthur Lazarus
CAMELOT

To JUNE. My inspiration, my love, my dear wife.

Camelot . . . a ray of sunshine in an
otherwise dark age . . .
. . . ethereal, celestial . . .
. . . instilling strong emotion in
the breast of the
romantic . . .
Camelot . . . elegant, beautiful,
resplendent, glorious,
inspiring . . .
. . . conjuring misty-eyed visions
of adventure, romance,
truth, justice, jousting
Knights upholding chivalry
and honor.
Camelot . . . has ever really lived
such a place?
. . . where Arthur ruled with the
the wisdom of a Solomon . . .
. . . whose battlements soared
majestically into the blue . . .
. . . whose colorful banners
danced in the breeze from
lofty perches, beckoning one
and all welcome.
. . . where spires and turrets,
stately tall, towered above
moated, walled city . . .
. . . whose first sight never failed
to impress and excite . . .
. . . where resided a seat of
learning, wisdom and
judiciously-applied law.
Camelot . . . if such as this did exist,
why did it not persevere?
Where did Camelot go?

Mary Esther Clauss
THE MUSIC ROLLS THROUGH MY MIND

To my dear friend who brought the music back into my life.

The music rolls through my mind,
like the hours when I am with you.
I remember you,
your warmth, your smile, your touch.
Each note rings a sense of your
presence to me.
I travel deep within each note,
like when I am lying next to you and
I travel
through each crease and fold of your
body.
The music brings you back to me
and stirs your presence ever closer.

The times apart are far and long,
but the music brings you home to
me.
To remember your touch, your sense,
your specialness,
I listen to the notes;
for each one has a part of you from
the times we were together.
The more I listen,
the more I am with you.
How special is the music.
For in the music
I find
YOU.

Paul Furman
WITH HOPE FOR TOMORROW

In memory of Scott Giantvalley

Further away than anticipated, I watched life slip toward the edge of darkness.

I could not grasp the significance of thoughts once perceived as noble truths, and yet I had been living for what seemed an eternity on borrowed lies.

I wish to purge this brain of useless drivel, give forth the waste of neuroses; they were once held as close to me as the dead layers of skin refusing to slough off.

So much with discomfort, this verse will not assuage anything in my life. Yes, a slip of attitude shows from beneath the sheath of reason; why can't I drain for good?

I will myself to meet the demands of a merciless mass; the being hasn't yet the heart or the urge.

This awful acknowledgement leaves me with the dread of being too aware . . .

Sylvia Lemmond
GOD'S PERFECTION

To My Children, George W. and Cynthia A. Schnarre

When evening comes and shadows
fall
Upon the Mountains high,
I think of all the lovely things
That rest beneath the sky.

The rose with all its color,
The leaf with it's perfection,
The rivers running never straight
Yet in the right direction,

Could you or I plan such a thing,
I doubt it very much.
You see, God's love is woven
Into everything we touch.

William Crutcher
A.R. KNEW

Dedicated to Jacques Cousteau, whose efforts to promote the protection of the global ecology have always been a quiet voice of reason in a cacophony of greed and indifference.

A season of crows twilights upon us.
Of cold, bleak fields, parched by
wind,
And the black flocks wheeling across
the winter sky.

Glossy black, nets of tangled knots
cast far into the uncertain wind.
Dark thoughts scratching at the
backs of primped skulls, lost in
desire, ignorant of need.

The dying planet orbits a sere, bitter
hydraulic star; tidal blast furnace,
frying us in our own gasses.
We knit our black inheritance, web
by web.

Down on the killed fields, the toxic
soil clutches a dead grey bush,
soaking up poisons from the root.
Riddled with webs, it claws at earth
and air—reciprocal, persistent
malice.

The watch-crow descends, eyes of
his tribe, ancestors attendant on our
battlefields.
He alights to study the dust blown
cobs where all our yesterdays, dead
dreams died.

And in the brittle branches mock full
bore limbs that once shot leaves;
now twist and rifle, clack and rot,
forkless tines in barren breeze.

Crows like wasps whose harsh cries
sting, hover and sail, true darts of
pitch,
Shadows tossed by icy gales. The
watch-crow caws, Omen's cohort
received.

Straight out of Styx to preen and
survey the fields of worms—choice
real-estate—
Left behind by darkling apes, who

put on airs and clothes and gold and fancied themselves men.

A Garden once, this field of worms—what calumnies these idiots wrought!
Who sowed their blood and then their filth, who raped their world, denied and fought.

The Dark Brotherhood knew them of old; beasts in forests running smelly wild,
Who chattered, screamed and never learned, not to shit too much on their own perch.

Lord, when cities and cruel tormented minds are run their course and fled—
Above the ignorance of man and his withered, ravaged world,

Let the empty skies disclose Your dear delightful crows.

Joanne (Hibbert) Hutson
WHEN I SLEEP

For Donald Lane Posey, you'll always be in my heart! 12-17-41 to 5-15-89 We all miss you!

At night when I sleep
My mind comes to life,
And wanders the world
With all of its strife.

I've walked through wars
With death close by,
I've stood with sickness
Its victims begging to die.

I've seen the children
With nothing to eat,
And the abuse of a child,
Death from being beat.

The political arguments
That take innocent lives,
The families of these people
Parents, children, husbands and wives.

When I wake in the morning
It's to God I pray,
That all of these things
Will someday go away!

Marlene Barry
IN SEARCH OF

For: Chad, Amber, Kristina

Does a dream without a promise, have ground to stand on its own?
Or is our strength in wishes, I've not yet been shown.
My thoughts will wander, but bear with me as I go
From the depth of my mind, to the paper and pen at flow.
I'm not trying to say any one specific thing
Just writing down my thoughts or wishes, or is it dreams?
A philosopher I'm not, but we all seem to have a need for strength
To get by without something or someone, and we go to great lengths.
Are there answers to our questions, or are we to search forever
For our dreams or wishes that we thought we'd see . . . not ever!
A dream isn't something solid to believe in
Nor is it radical, it's simply a vision.
A wish is something of the same
A desire or to long for . . . but give them no name.
The combination of all three, wish, promise or dream
Can really only become, what we make them seem.
If they are part of making us happy, and getting us through another day
Let's have the strength to combine the three and forget about . . .
"REALITY"

Barbara Garro
THE CHALLENGE OF BALANCE

To: All the dream believers
From: The dream believer behind Eclectic Envisions (The Possibilities People),

What price glory . . . to gain the world and lose life's quality!

For the gifted, who swim in a sea of uncompleted projects, who know not a separation between weekday and weekend . . .
There remains constant the challenge of balance.

Endless todays preparing for tomorrows . . .
Finding we live for a formidable future using so much of our todays in perpetual preparation that the quality of our present is strained?

For us, who dream the imponderable dreams, whose creativity flows like ocean waves ever toward shore . . .

Life in balance . . .
The greatest challenge the gifted will ever know.

Andreas Laci Gobor
WALKING OVER THE RAINBOW

This poem is dedicated to my mother Friedarike Hagen Gobot died June 17, 1988 now in Paradise

Walking over the rainbow
with tears in my eyes
because you are already gone
I try to please you all your life
I tried, I tried
but I got that feeling inside
I never did it right
Oh Mother I miss you so
since you died
I still feel your power by my side
Let's walk the rainbow together
till we find those lights
in Paradise

Evon Boykins Cortez
I'LL DO . . .

This poem is dedicated to The Boykins family, especially to my son, Christopher M. Boykins. I love all of you!!!

I'll do whatever GOD wants me to, just show me LORD what there is to do.
I'll do my best, so GOD will give me peace and rest.
I'll go where ever he sends me and help those SINNERS who plea.
Whether it's day or night . . . that's alright, because CHRIST shines within me and his light shines bright.
I'll do your will LORD, and I know I won't be bored.
If you want me to lay hands on the sick, LORD make me your pick.
If you want me to speak your word, then I'll tell those people who haven't heard.
I'll do my best, so others can also receive your peace and some rest.
If you want me to pray, LORD, I know you'll equip me the right way.
If you want me to sing, then LORD, I know this is your thing.
If you want me to shout, then I'll do it along my route.
If you want me to cry, I hope it's because of the truth and not because of a lie.
LORD, I'll do your will and pray that SATAN doesn't come to destroy, steal or kill!!!

Rock Familton

Rock Familton
A WIFE LIKE MINE

"A Wife Like Mine" is dedicated to Jinx, my reason for being, and my greatest joy in life.

If ever I were asked to name
The sweetest joy in life,
My answer would always be the same
Just being with my wife.

We all have days when all goes wrong,
When dark clouds dim the skies above
But somehow it makes a man feel strong
When he has a woman's love.

The greatest treasure isn't gold
Or glistening jewels fine
The greatest treasure isn't sold
It's given, by a wife like mine!

William Taylor
REMEMBER

This poem is dedicated to Yvonne, my loving wife.

Remember when I first met you, in a department store.
I saw you from a warehouse door.

Remember when I came up to you in the candy aisle.
On your face you had the prettiest little smile.

Remember when you made it to my trailer.
It was wonderful with me Taylor.

Remember when we got married and had our little rascals.
But still in all we still lived happy ever after—Remember.

t b thompson
HONEST JUDGEMENT

To The Unique

How do you feel when you see me?
How do you react to my name?
How do you respond to my touching?
Do you really feel happy or shame?

What is your true feelings of my being?
Do you feel safe or not?
Do you appreciate my reactions to you?
Do you really accept what you got?

Wake up and smell the coffee
Think carefully of this relation
You have to be positive in every way
To enrich our education

So, how do you feel?
Tell yourself first
Tell me second
About our turf

Sharon C Bedzyk
HOMECOMING

Dedicated to John Bedzyk, my husband, for his support and encouragement of my poetic endeavors.

We met to review our lives
our success foremost,
to praise ourselves
And propose a toast.

We saw not
but our projected egos
reflected on others
mirrored back to grow.

We came not to see
but to be seen
to applaud our
increasing self-esteem.

A mere curiosity
of others deemed,
but ourselves
crowned king or queen.

Jerry Seidenwurm
TENNIS—A GAME IN WHICH LOVE MEANS NOTHING

With loving thanks to my dear mother, who encouraged me to explore my feelings and enlightened me as to the value, and (yes) joy, of a good cry.

I want life to be a doubles match,
But my wife's decided she want to play singles.
I'd like to share the wins and losses with a partner,
But anybody on her side of the net is in the way.

Doubles enlarges the court, expands the experience
It seems to me.
But she feels she has to give up too much of herself
To work at being part of a tandem.

If I want to "play" with her,
It's got to be on the other side of the net.
And though we may try to "just volley"
We wind up being opponents.

It's not that I don't think I can cover the court.
I enjoy the challenge some of the time.

Cindy J O'Connell
YOU CAN'T STOP ME FROM LOVING YOU

This Poem Is Dedicated To Bob My One And Only, With Love Always

You should know by now
No matter what you say or do
You can't stop me from loving you

I learned from you years ago
If you love someone no one else can understand
Hold onto your dreams if you believe

I learned from the best you told me
was you
You're not going to change your
mind now
Or Are You?

If it's the only thing I keep from you,
Besides this beat up and broken heart
I guess that's what I'll hold onto

I won't let those dreams get too far
away
Who knows I may get another
chance someday
I'm holding onto my dreams and
waiting for you
Because you should know by now,
No matter what you say or do
You can't ever stop me from loving
you

Aileen Pagels
AUTUMN

To my children

The fields have turned from green to
brown,
I feel the chill of autumn's breeze.
Sweet summer you have come and
gone,
How lonely look the leafless trees.
All nature now has burrowed deep,
It seems the earth has gone to sleep.
It's now I look at crisp blue skies,
And welcome autumn with sad sighs.

Alyssa J Wilkins
DON'T EVER LOSE FAITH

This poem was written for a very special friend in her time of need. Susan, don't ever lose faith.

Don't ever lose faith, you are a
special person.
Nobody can ever take away your
dreams.
No matter all the pain you see you
must realize that there is always love
around you.
You hurt inside, but if you reach out
there will always be someone to take
your hand and accept the hurt with
you.
You feel you've lost everything, but
one day you'll wake up and see there
is so much more for you out there.
Don't ever give up on yourself.
You're worth so much more.
The pain will eventually end, you
must look at the good times and try to
focus on the love that is around you.
Don't ever feel alone, nobody is ever
alone.
Just always remember love can
conquer all and it will.
You always have friends and family,
they all love you.
You will survive and you will come
out of this as strong as you've ever
been.
Just remember one thing, fight for
yourself and never forget all the love
shared.

Mrs Susan Hansen
THE ETERNITY OF TIME

This poem is dedicated to my husband, Gary. With all my love always.

If I could dream upon a star,
I'd wish for happiness, by and far;
I'd ask for time for us to do,
Things with loved ones; if only I
knew.

Why does time go by so fast?
We'll never have each other at last.
Will time ever be ours to keep?
Or will our love always make me
weep.

If only once we could fly away,
And never once look back to stay;
I'd cherish a moment with you and
me,
And keep it forever; a memory.

Clifford Hritz
THE OTHER YEAR

To my Mother & Father—Who taught me how to forget the bad memories; and remember the good.

I remember those days clearly
as I remember my birth.
When the snow was special
not just flakes of ice.
The family pet was love.
I'll take the memories to grave
as I will take my soul.
Don't forget, or let go
the pieces of past.
Who can make you feel?
No one that way again.

Harriet Braun
EMPTY NEST

To My Children—Ross and Judi With All My Love

Rivulets drizzle—on the glass
windows where little light can pass
Looking at the colorless skies
drops form and mist my eyes,
as they trickle down my cheeks
and I wait these lonely weeks.
Straining to hear—bustle and bicker
offspring returning—sooner and
quicker.

Now bright rays hit sharply the
glass!
Bouncing through, they let sunshine
pass.
For one day—or maybe another,
Rainbowed windows for this mother.

Chris Johnson
IF I WERE A COLOR

To my mother and father Maude and Turner Maynard who taught me that love removes all barriers

If I were a Color
Which one would I be
The green of the grass
Or the blue of the sea?

If I were a Color
Selecting just one
The brown of the earth
Or the red of the sun?

If I were a Color
What if I Chose
The yellow of moonlight
Or the pink of a rose?

But God in his wisdom
Makes no such demand
We're each one a rainbow
To brighten the land

The rainbow's a promise
To state and insure
If fear is the illness
Then love is the cure.

Lessie Cantrell
MY MEDITATION

To my beloved Husband and Pastor ERNEL E. CANTRELL, And to all my Children and Grand Children.

While I was meditating this morning,
A clear picture came to me.
Of our dear loving Savior,
Hanging on a cruel tree.

Upon his head a crown of thorns,
Blood flowing down his brow.
All of us did this to him,
Still he forgives us, somehow.

I saw the holes in his hands,
And holes in his dear feet.
If you don't think that he is good,
Just taste, for he is sweet.

With a spear they pierced his side,
Then water and blood did flow.
He died upon that cruel tree,
Because he loved us so.

Thru the Holy Spirit that is so real,
As he bowed his head in shame.
He took all our sins to the Cross,
And WE are the ones to blame.

S Hoffmann
ANGRY THREADS

Mothers turn their heads.
Fathers or brothers erase, forget
The touch familial and
All too familiar.

"I didn't say 'yes', but I didn't
say 'no'.
But I wanted it over.
He stopped when Mama
Called me from her bedroom
At the other end of the
house . . ."

Critical, angry threads
Are woven into long-buried remnants
Of fear and self-neglect.
Everyone bleeds.

And everyone dreads
Their safe intimacy lost, regrets
The touch familial and
All too familiar.

Ms Micki Catoe
JUST FOR BEING YOU

I dedicate this poem to my wonderful companion and friend, Roy Huenergardt, whom truly loves and believes in me.

Like the wind that whistles.
Like the star that brightly
shines.
You my friend, I think, are
fine!

Like the flowers that bloom.
Like the colors that they
create.
To me, Friendship, is OH so
great!

Like the boat that sails.
Like the waves of the sea.
Getting to know you, is a
pleasure to me!

Like the feathers of a bird.
Like the raven and the dove.
Having true friends, fills you
with LOVE!
Like the dreams in your sleep.
Like the skies that are blue.
I want to thank-you,
JUST FOR BEING YOU!!!

Bette Stasny
METAPHORICALLY SPEAKING

With love to all the Stasny men

I'm Rip Van Winkle awake to a
world of unreal prices and
incomprehensive electronic gadgetry.
Waves of nostalgia roll me over the
sands of time.
"Why, I remember when, " is a
phrase to be stricken from your
vocabulary.
Age and wisdom are tombs of
ancient history.
Conversation is lost to that idiot
box in the corner.
Clean plates and starving
Armenians have given way to
micro waves and slamming doors.
From scratch is a lost wax
process.
The dime store is buried in the
cemetery of loose change.
TIME has been replaced by
SPEED in the dictionary of life.
I shall return to my den of
hibernation and seek simplicity in
the
dreams of yesterday.

Joseph G Kern
CAN POISON

Aluminum can
Diet Coke
Trade mark
Low Calorie Cola
Less than 1 Calorie
per serving
12 FL OZ
354 ml
CA Redemption Value
Very Low Sodium
Nutra Sweet—
Brand Sweetener
Phosphoric Acid
Citric Acid
Protein 0
Phenylketonurics:
Contains
Phenylalanine.
I ask You but one
Question—
Where is the harmful
Chemical label?
If there was one they
Would probably put it
Next to the USA Proud
Sponsor 1988 US. OLY.
Team symbol.

Keith R Yuhasz
ALZHEIMER

This poem is dedicated to every man, woman, and child that endures the wrath of disease. Not only Alzheimer's, which takes the mind, heart, and body of a person, but every disease. Soon we will overcome these obstacles.

A disease has struck
the sanctity of my soul.
Now my thoughts are amuck
and I feel ever so cold.
Who is this tear
that is shed everyday?
A world so unclear,
a life in a daze.
Is it possible to perceive
there to be a pattern
with which we are seen?

Who is this concern
standing and watching me?
I cannot fathom fear
but I can flee.
Away from all that is dear,
from all who can see.
Humanity does what can
and all a feat.
Still I wonder who I am!

Donna Marie Thorne

Donna Marie Thorne
BE POSITIVE

My beloved daughter, MARIE AVINA THORNE, who was an innocent victim of a violent crime and she is now with God. Through me she gives these words as her Victory For Humanity. She was always positive, April 19, 1967/ 4-22,89

It might be hard to be a positive person
But Christ didn't sing the blues
He is too busy bringing good news

He is a teacher in all of His ways
So we can look forward to better days

Just follow His fine example
And worship in His Tabernacle

Put His Holy Spirit in your life
And He will end your heartache and strife

Julie Estill
YOU'RE THE SEVEN WONDERS OF THE WORLD
You are the wonders of the world
You're the horizon beyond the sea
You're the oyster that holds the beautiful pearl
You're the butterfly that's just been set free.

You're the treasure down below the ocean blue
You're the stars that glitter in the night
You're the pleasant dreams that long to come true
You're the glowing moon that provides the light.

You're the shadow beneath the willow tree
You're the warmth that comes from the fire
You're the lock that has a special key
You're the happiness that everyone desires.

You're the special person that makes things so right
You're the one that holds the key to my heart
You're the one that comforts when you hold me tight
You're the one whose Love I'll always want a part.

June Wetmore
ROCK PRAIRIE LULLABY
When day fades to dusk, I'll hear again,
That beautiful, age old melody;
It's the song Nature's sung for centuries,
The lullaby of old Rock Prairie.
A whispering breeze, a babbling stream,
Twittering night birds drowsy tunes,
Low thunder's peal and falling rain
Are all part of the song that Nature croons.
A lone screech owl's mournful call
rings out like a curfew o'er the sleepy land
To tell all of Nature's little ones
Time has come to drift to slumber-land.
My cares of the day all fade away
When stars form a sparkling lace on high,
I hear our Father's benediction
In that old Rock Prairie Lullaby.

Carolyn S West
ALONE
Thru the long lonely hours of darkness,
I wander the corridors of my mind.
There stands the dark, dark doors
that I can't open for fear of what lies behind.

The bright blue globes of happiness float
Here and there, just beyond my grasp.
I feel I will drown in tears unshed there.
Then the dark whirlpool of sleep claims me.

Bridgett Hayslett
TRUE LOVE
I wish you'd whisper in my ear,
And say the words I long to hear.
Though I love you every day,
It's hard for me to say.
You want me to open up and say just how I feel,
But you have to do it, too

that's part of the deal.
I'll always want to be
your burning flame;
If it goes out I'm not to blame.
Just say it once or let me be.
I love you baby, can't you see
It's not that hard, just give it a try,
I promise I'll never ask you why.
Tell me now with all your heart,
And together we can make
A Brand new start.

Susan Sweeney
SAY YOUR PRAYERS
NOW I LAY ME DOWN TO SLEEP
Raping Babies in Their Beds
I PRAY THE LORD MY SOUL TO KEEP
Tuck Into Them Secret Dreads
IF I SHOULD DIE BEFORE I WAKE
Warping Tender Little Heads
I PRAY THE LORD MY SOUL TO TAKE

Now I Lay Me Down To Sleep
Mama knows, but all she'll say
I Pray The Lord My Soul To Keep
tell and he'll be sent away,
If I Should Die Before I Wake
please, make Daddy stop today
I Pray The Lord My Soul To Take

DADDY LAYS ME DOWN TO SLEEP
HE MAKES UP LIES THAT I MUST KEEP
I WANT TO DIE AND NEVER WAKE
I PRAY THE LORD MY SOUL TO TAKE

i pray the lord my soul to take.

Rebecca Eldridge
I LOVE YOU
I feel I'am losing you, as the days go by.
Something is Coming between us, and I don't know why.

I love you more than I could ever say, and I want you here with me, forever to stay.

But as I look into your heart, I wonder who's really there, and as I watch the way you act, I wonder if you even care.

Babe it really seems like we are falling apart,
and I don't want that to ever happen,
I truly love you deep down in my heart.

I hope and pray that things will change, and we come closer together. I love you babe and I always will forever & ever.

Felicia Whitman
TO MY LOVE MICHAEL
If roses were love,
We'd have a whole garden.
For no one loves the way we do.
Laughter and tears are our sunshine and rain;
We need both for our love to grow.

We have our good times and not-so-good times.
Just as roses have velvety petals and prickly thorns.
We are halves of the same whole;
Petals of the same rose.

I was but a tiny bud
And then, the sunshine of your love came
And my life blossomed.

We love with our whole hearts,
And that love is as sweet
As the smell of roses
On an early spring morning.

If roses were love,
I'd give you an armful every day
And pray that their perfect beauty
Would give you as much happiness
As I've found in loving you.

Debra Uhls
WORLD OF ILLUSION
Through delusions avidya we move through the world of illusion, layer our self's naked truth in fabrics of illustrious colorful lies; become less real day by day, moment by moment 'til life is deadened
And no cloth dare cover longer the death of an angry heart . . . the pain self controls' loss creates
Senseless words use seemingly envelope a false lack in communication's level
No song is sung—fresh new starts a-void-ed though costly—a lack not necessitated.
Most beautiful rose . . . careful thorn pricks blood flows wound heals and beauty's remnant intact still is the night
Like fountainhead flow to immense oceans
we course away; eternally infinite sojourn—
And thoughts too are so—
Love's definition unrevealed—
known yet unknown—
meaning confined.
So sad our limitations.

Deidre Forrester
DREAMS
You know my love for you sometimes
I wish would die
Why?
My heart has not seen so much pain
My soul has never cried so hard
I have never experienced a sense of such remorse
My love, I'd die for you
I'd cry a thousand tears
But why?
To have you hurt me again
Destroy my inner being
I guess I would
Because you're someone I can't refuse
You're someone I long to be with
But baby, I'm glad it's not my heart
that decides if I live or die
Because if it did I would die
It was a love for you and I
It was a love for all times
It was a love I guess you thought would die
So baby, I'll move on if that's what you want
I'll learn not to cry . . .
But honestly baby it's your love
I'd love to try . . .

Dr Naomi Miller Coval

Dr Naomi Miller Coval
NIGHTWIND

To my sainted mother, who taught me: love; insatiable curiosity, and charity.

The wind was a sniveling coyote last night, cracking the usual calm; or was it a learner's-cello, untuned, groaning staccato alarm? Perhaps a ship's-wail at this mirky-hour answering a fog-horn's alert; crying of petulant children who fell, attention-demanding, when hurt?
Could it be chariots, invisible, above, with screeching-brakes rounding a curve; or flocks of grey-hawks whining at field mice, capturing prey with death's verve?
It's roaring lions lazily stretching on velots, proclaiming territorial bounds; perhaps it's wild hoofbeats; red-jacketed horsemen, raced behind excited hounds?
It might be a squadron of army-jets rumbling, penciling white streaks

above clouds
However I hear its eerie lament; it's formidable, haunting, so loud!
What makes it wheeze-heavy, arouse me from sleep
with gruff voice in solo off key?
Or is it just laughter, free-wheeling thru trees, on journeys elite
and so free?
I'm awake now, it's four!
The night's rest is lost,
I'll retreat to my notebook & pen;
Let metaphors lay-bare those deceptive trombones—
sordid-concerti, again!

Estella M McGhee-Siehoff
MY LIFE

It may have been orphaned,
It may have been hated,
It may have been tormented,
It may have been impoverished,
It may have been unloved,
It may have been abused,
It may have been denied,
But it was mine, and
My life was hid in God,
For survival, and Salvation,
From sin, and redemption.

Jennifer Matney
WHO?

The tender touch of a memory
lingers and haunts my soul
I want what was had and yet to go on
I know not what I need to be whole
To question time seems inappropriate
and yet neverending in thought
what to learn is now to cope with it
and realize life is what it's not

What happened to the life I could have led
the happy side I seem to have shed
The true ones who bred me
are now dead in my life
and I know not where I was meant to be

Capable of everything yet stifled by "nothing"
Something deters from what I should be
The inherent need to define myself
questions what I'm told to be
and what is really me
The only answer that I've found to be
is that there are no real answers
and the only answers the life conceives
are what we perceive it to be

Larry Pinerski
HOOSIER SPRING

Indiana Spring is a rugged woman
With willowy, wet hair,
In mud-slinging shoes,
Too tough for scathing north winds.

She smiles dawn-dimpled
In lilac perfume,
Lies down in deep grass
Near freshwater ponds

To hear robins sing,
Watch sunnies jump
Feel shoots grow
Under corn-planting hands.

Alma 'Ray' Ferris
LOOK FOR ME THEN

When the tulip trees are blooming
and the robin sings again,
That's the time I will be coming—
Look for me then!

When the silver moon is shining
and the stars watch from above
I will hold you in my arms, dear
and tell you of my love.

How long it has been since I kissed
you and held you to my heart.
Too long it has been and I have
missed you every moment that
we've been apart.

When the lamps are lit at gloaming,
Put my supper on the stove—
Home will come this weary traveler
Back to his treasure-trove.

George A Mueller
THAT SECRET TRAVEL PROTECTION

Come, gentle spirit make my heart your home,
So my, understanding is clear.
I just should not worry what tomorrow will bring,
For, I try to fear nothing but fear.

Alone in life's darkness some footsteps make sound—
That could be just echoes of mine—
Please give me assurance, I have nothing to fear—
Or that those footsteps might be thine.

Might I feel that for sure! I'm protected?
While I drive through a red light, I'm alone.
Then, I straddle that white line in the middle,
Just trying to get safely home.

Other cars seem to be trying to scare me.
Coming close from in front and behind.
Sometimes I have trouble leaving my freeway—
Now, I just passed my own turnoff, I find.

Once more gentle leader, bring me safely home!
Where I can turn my warm blanket on.
Some mornings I wake up so early—
That the next all day I yawn and yawn.

Incidentally, I'm driving my 1912 Willies Knight. (Good car!)

Wilber Orlando Calhoun
ORIGIN, WEALTH, RESPONSIBILITY

In the beginning God
Brought forth Creation
And all that's in it.
What vast expanse of time and space,
Habitat of the human race!
In time and space, sans limiting border,
Countless worlds whirl and orbit
In meticulous order.
The atom's explosive power brings
Awareness there are NO little things.
The immutable reign of physical laws
Is enough to give the wisest pause.
Teach us Lord, to use all Thou hast wrought,
To advance Thy Kingdom, as Jesus taught;
To curb our rampant, arrogant greed;
To make wealth serve ALL human need!

Stephanie Joswick
WHAT?!

Who are you—to tell me what to do?
You can only relate,
and that is if you really try,
to what I say—in your own way.

You tell me you understand,
But by your reply, which is a demand,
you have taken my words
and forgotten my meaning.
Substituting what?
Where is my reasoning?

Please listen without the thought,
"Oh I know just how you feel,"
because then you are not listening
and what I am saying is not real.

I know when you haven't heard me speak
because questions come into your head,
and then you ask.
The answers you would already know,
if you had paid attention,
to the 'earlier show'.

Stella F Burns
I HAD A SHADOW THAT FOLLOWED ME

I had a shadow that followed me
Every where I go,
And thought of her often
More than anyone will know.
I sense her many problems
Felt them deep within,
Now I'm her shadow
Because she was my twin.

Anna Livia
SAY IT WITH LOVE

Say it with love
Again and again
Show that you care
Beyond compare.

Say it with flowers
For-get-me-nots
Show her she's needed
Never unheeded.

Say it with music
To calm her soul
Just say I love you
Enhance the glow.

Say it, just say it
Say it with love
Say it and make it
Divine as from above.

Laura G Perdue
MY HUSBAND, MY LOVE

In the spring of 1942
My love for you began
Romance blossomed, as we walked hand in hand
Down by the Old River, Dan

Every one was on the run
As World War Two, had already begun
Time was moving so fast
When we got married, I knew it would last

For a short while we were so happy and gay
Didn't know we would have to part, so soon that day
Three weeks later, you were called to serve your country
The days and nights that followed were sad and lonely

At twenty one the time seemed to drag by
All I could think of was my guy
Three years had past, A knock on my door and you were home at last
All the sadness I bore, flew away in a flash
For here was my husband I adore
America had paid a big price
The boys were home and that was nice
Laughter and joy was a delight
As our hearts went racing into the night
Everything went Zoom, Zoom, Zoom
And then came the big baby boom
The economy was first up and down
But I loved having you around
My love for you has grown
As Father Time moved on
If God calls you home first
And I am left all alone
I'll have my precious memories to live on

Madelyn LaRoche
TALENT

One has to work tenaciously
If talent is to grow.
A pulse of purpose powers one,
Makes inspiration glow.

To sing, to sculpt, to paint, to write
You must think well and choose.
Thus make each morning glad and bright
Pay gaily nature's dues.

Then in the years ahead for you
You'll know identity.
With lively senses find the clue
That solves infinity.

Stephanie D Girard
LOVE IS CONCEITED

I am the endless void that sucks power—
And I will have you.
For I have conquered countless souls before you
And when you are gone, countless more
shall follow—

I have defeated kingdoms
I have devastated empires
I have turned brother against brother, uncalculated murder . . .
I have transversed dimensions that you could never hope to comprehend.

I possess the power and wisdom of all magic and physics.
All know my name, but none know what I am—
I am more ancient than time itself.
For I am as endless as infinity
And as deep as forever . . .

Randy Wetmore
ON THE OCEAN AT SUNSET

The gentle blue waves splashed against the boat,
as the sun set, and the beautiful colors of dusk darkened.
The water became smoother,
and the sun sank deeper.
Then the stars came out one by one,
and then, it was over sunset, and all.

Betty Bragdon
I BELIEVE

Father God, I believe you are
With me in all ways.
And Father, I believe you are
The force that guides my days.
And Father, I believe that all
The things you'd have me do
Is telling me in every way
That I belong to you.
I believe that you
Have touched my life
With a loving, caring hand,
And my life is measured out by you
Like tiny grains of sand.
And Father, I believe from now
Until my life is through
That all that I accomplish
Will be sent in love from you.
'Cause Father, I believe that you
Will guide my destiny.
And my life is safe
Within your hands,
For all eternity.

Richard Houser
YOU'RE MY MOTHER NATURE

I know that you are special
I'm sure that you're the best
You're a diamond to a chunk of coal
When compared to all the rest
You're everything that's beautiful
A rose without the thorns
A lovely purple sunset
A pretty April morn
You're a tall majestic redwood
That's been there for so long
The dew on leaves in morning
The birds that sing a song
You're the snow that caps the mountains
The rivers that cross the land
The water in the oceans
The lovely desert sand
You're the meadows and the forests
And everything within
You are the drops of rain
You're a brisk refreshing wind
You're everything on God's green earth
That's beautiful kind and true
So please always remember Mom
I think the world of you

Sheila Williams Shafer
BEING BACK

"Oh, my Father up above, it's a cruel, cruel world out there. Am I to blame because my skin is dark and theirs is so fair?
A higher grade point—says they're smarter than me.
A husband or a wife—says they're more respectable than me.
A skin of white—says they're more acceptable than me.
Who are they to judge me, . . . to criticize me?
They who say you are—but, who say you can—but, who say I would—But.
Well I say to them—I am, I say to them—I can, I say to them—I Will.

I will grasp their extended, retractable hand of friendship, taking from it all that I can.

I Will turn into reality their fictitious words of encouragement and erase their knowing looks of expected failure.

I Will conquer the torment of white-controlled dreams and soothe myself with the conviction that my dreams are really self-controlled.

I Will break their invisible bonds of self-righteousness and unselfish justification for the taking of my rights to a self-fashioned life, an ounce of dignity, a sense of pride or a future made of my own accord.
I Will walk the beaten path . . . but I Will Not be beaten.
I Will play their game . . . but by my rules.
I Will reform . . . I Will Not conform.
I Will be who I Am and what I Am . . . One of God's Winners.

Claire W Coletrane
LASTING LOVE

Love waits for everyone
No matter how long it takes
So don't be impatient as you long
For a love you cannot make

Don't be afraid of a broken heart
But give it all that you've got
For love has no guarantees
As where will fall your lot

Be guided by your heart
And not by your mind
The heart searches deep within
The mind is not so kind

Don't let looks, lust, or gold
Get in the way of your hearts endeavor
For these things shall surely pass
But love can last forever

So if that special someone
Brings into your life some sorrow
Don't be fooled by circumstances
For love will last until tomorrow

Mrs Jean B Garland

Mrs Jean B Garland
CHARLESTON

If you ever visit Charleston,
You'll have memories which will last;
For the streets and architecture
Tell a history of the past.
You must ride the horse drawn coaches;
See the streets of cobblestone,
Listen as your tour guide tells you
Of the days long past and gone.
Take a walk along the coast line,
Where the ocean and two rivers meet.
See Fort Sumter in the distance,
Feel the summer breezes, sweet.
Oh 'tis such a peaceful moment,
With the sea gulls swooping down,
Water lapping at the shore line—
Of this quaint old Southern Town.
So, if you ever visit Charleston,
Relax, enjoy the sights you see.
May you feel the peace and pleasure
That my visit gave to me.

Lillian Spellman
BLESSED EASTER

Alone with God in the stillness of night
His love enfolds me—I begin to write
My thoughts are centered on coming of lent
The crucifixion of Jesus—a sad event.
The holy season of lent is upon us
Fasting—a repence—a memorial for Jesus
Good Friday—three days before Easter celebration
Our hearts filled with love and adoration.
What a vision of torture—Jesus nailed on the cross
How he must have suffered—what a loss
An execution with nails through hands and feet
A crown of thorns see him bleed.
On the third day—Jesus arose from the grave
He died for our sins—our souls to save
Forty days after Easter—Jesus ascended into Heaven
His spirit living in peace for all men.
Yes Jesus lifted me—set my conscience free
Died on the cross for you and me
This is not a myth—'tis really true
As Heavenly stars shine in skies of blue.

Pete D E Ruzzo
ONE OF THE FIVE

We care, and love,
but what does it bring?
Pain and heartbreak,
is love worth living?
When our feelings are shown,
none of them are false,
never like the others,
who lie at all costs.
When "I love you" is spoken,
we mean it so!
Why is there no return,
I want to know!
When "love" leaves
Forgotten, we fall.
and when we hit,
we don't even crawl.
To recover from Love,
takes us so long.
Why is it then,
we find love that is wrong?

I want to know!

Jan Hulbert
LIFE IS SUCH A PRECIOUS GIFT

Life is such a precious gift
It's here one day and then it's gone
What we leave is love and kindness
That's all that carries on
The gifts that we can treasure
While we're here upon this earth
Is to find someone to love and hold
To share our dreams as they unfold
The wealth that we have when we leave
Is not in dollar signs
But who will say when we are gone
What a void we've left behind

Heidi Holt DelCamp
A BIRTHDAY MESSAGE

Our lives are like the weather
Some days sunny and cheerful,
Some days rainy and gloomy,
Some days are worse than others.
Each year brings new beginnings
And new endings—
A birthday is to refresh our livelyhood
And to look forward to new days . . .
And new life!
May this Birthday
Bring to you—
A whole new light—
A whole new beginning
And a world of Happiness!
You are a unique, special person—
And a favorite of mine.
May God Bless You—
And lead you to a Bright Future!!

HAPPY BIRTHDAY!!!

Hazel C Douglas
MY VALENTINES

My Valentines throughout the years,
Have brought me joy and bitter tears.

But each one has it's own, tiny
Heart shaped home—My Heart . . .

Carmel J Kersjes
YOU ARE TO ME

You are my friend,
when others turn away.
You are my song,
when the music won't play.
You are my sunshine,
after the rain.
You are my healer,
when I feel sorrow or pain.
You are my rainbow,
when the skies are grey.
You are my clock,
keeping perfect time each day.
You are my clown,
my laughter to dry the tears.
You are my lover,
you satisfy the woman in me.
You are everything to me,
I need you till all eternity.
For a love so deeply seeded,
will forever grow.

Walden S Randall
FORTY SEVEN

Ripe,
Running a little too fat,
Middled,
Feeling the chilling edges
As the first juices cool.
The youthful threads bare from wear,
But moving nonchalantly along,
trusting.

Then,
A rip—
Torn across the grain—
Punched through roughly,
By the black branches of illness,
disfigurement,
Desertion.
The carefully assembled self
Confident cocoon pierced,
Fibers frayed, feathered,
Limply hanging.
The strings of self are broken
And the richness all runs out.

Fading patches follow the wind's fancy
Thinned fabric hugs itself
Over the holes
Sinking inward.

Until the streaks of light
On gilded waters,
The smile of a friend,
Knits the gossamers
Of ravelled edges.

Sherron A Rickman
MEMORIES

If memories were a color, I think they would definitely be blue.
Like the early morning sky, so fresh and new!!
Have you ever sat high on a cliff, just staring out to sea??

A bunch of baby tigers running after their mother,

Amazed at mother nature going to all that bother!!
You can look around for ever and ever and continuously be amazed,
The way that old girl has things arranged!!

Always stay alert and constantly be ready,
No matter how many you are fortunate enough to carry;
Memories are like the color blue;
Always and forever something very most extra special to me
and to you.

Linda J Skidmore
I THREW A TWIG IN THE RIVER ONE DAY
I threw a twig in the river one day,
and I watched as it floated
upon its way;
And I wondered what path it would take in its course
as it floated along on the
waterway's force.

Yet the twig questioned not its fate or its course
from the time that it fell from
the tree, its source,
To the time that I broke it in two with force . . .
it just went on its way, no
remorse, no remorse.

Fuel for a fire someday it will be
after washing ashore some
moonlit eve;
From earth, to fire, to air, to sea . . .
the pulsebeat of life, let it be,
let it be.

Sharon Drum
A CHRISTMAS LETTER (THE SPIRIT OF CHRISTMAS)
Dear Santa,
I'm a 30-year-old woman
That's cried many a tear,
I thought I'd take the time
To write you this year.
First of all, I'd like to thank you
For every gift you've given me.
Thank you, for the miracle (my
daughter) Candi
And my forever loving husband
Steve
Thank you for the angel my Mom
And my dearest Dad too
Mom's here loving and teaching us,
And Dad's safe there with you.
Thank you for my brothers and
sisters,
Their families, and all my
husband's family too.
I know what gift I want this
Christmas
Is to give all the thanks to you.
Let Christmas songs be heard in
all their hearts.
Like "Silent Night" and "Away In
A Manger"
'Cause my Santa isn't dressed in
red
And he's surely not a stranger.
Let the people who read this
Laugh as some may
But Santa, I know who you really
are—Jesus.
Happy Birthday
Love, Sharon Drum

Nina Groves-Walker
TWENTY-ONE LINES
Twenty one lines to journey out and back
beyond the natural borders of brain-song.
Ten drawn in the social structure
of a tribe whose narrow plane constructs
movement through a predetermined day.

Sun rays in a room of dust particles
light the automated movement of child-bearers
sucking and sweeping the earth from space.
The intelligence beamed in light and sound
configure thought beyond their knowing,

Perhaps. Perhaps,

In worship of coded experience
ten intersecting lines flash the imagery of dream's
thorough awareness of the shaman,
splitting space between Black Holes and Beatrice
gliding through the Earthly Paradise.

The rituals of a thousand visions
surround one fragile soul awaiting sacrifice
to a single laser—light of truth,
smashing the mana of particles that swarm
in the light of knowing eternity.

Caroline Shahbazian
LASTS SO LONG
A little song
During a time
Which seemed so long

Done with the pain—
The cries,
All the same

She believed in Faith
Before,
It was too late

Something within
Would not let her,
Let her give in

So, that little song
Full of Faith lasts,
Lasts so long

Eva Elizabeth Cabrera
A SONNET TO FIRST LOVE
When seeds of golden childhood have been sown,
The restless rhythm of your psyche knows,
That blushing glow of youth has boldly grown
And blossomed full, as petals of a rose:
So like a dream, that special one, so fine,
Stirs hidden depths of thoughts not felt before,
And speaks to you in music that's divine,
As bittersweet steps lead to love's fair door:
Where anguished frowns can hurt your tender heart,
Yet smiles will send you flying high and free,
And in love's nascent stage they do not part,
But thrill your life with pain and ecstasy:
And for that first and wondrous kiss, you wait
With hands entwined, half lost in love's pure state.

Robert F Moore

Robert F Moore
NATURES ANALOGY
Pure white butterfly parts its wings
To descend the mountain steep
Her wings get torn the journey slows
It takes so long to creep

The icy hands of winter
Caress the mountain top
With rosebuds frozen hard as ice
Mother earth cries out to stop

But winter is relentless
Obeying not a soul
And mother earth submits to him
With a shiver from north to south pole

Elation sends some earthquakes
To quiver down her spine
Wondering for the sake of all
Where does she draw the line

Too late she cried
The lava flowed
The season turned to spring

Paula L Anderson
A WISH
If ever there was a star
To wish upon—
To determine your fate
Before the light of dawn,
Of peace and happiness
I would surely wish of,
So that maybe everyone
Could learn to love.
I would wish that
Hearts would never be torn,
That lives would shine—
That smiles be worn.

Margaret E Krause
LOVE'S GLORY—IN ABSENTIA
This twisted life we live, we wonder, you and I
What use it is to us. To what avail we live
Each day, each week, each year to face a fruitless end.
We know the joy, the power, the glow that love can give.
But what of that? If you love me the way you say
And dream of life and love's supremest joys with me,
And want my arms to hold you, and my lips to kiss,
What joy is there for you in love that binds you endlessly
With chains that only death can part, on to a dream?
For dream it is, and ever shall be, dearest dear.
These tears you shed upon my breast, your words of grief,
Your humble, loving glance, your need to have me near;
All these I cradle in my heart, and weep with pain.
But what are tears of mine to you? You surely know
I am not yours to love, in every tear you shed
Lies the vision of my own lost love, so long ago.

Betty McNair
BOX OF DREAMS
Several locks of brown and gold,
Four baby bracelets do unfold,
A wedding ring, a picture old,
A license in a broken frame,
A dress of lace, much worn remains.

A baby shoe, a gown of blue,
A book of poetry you gave,
The locket that you had engraved,
A trinket from the home we shared,
A love note told me that you cared.

But things did change, they always do.
Now all I have is dreams of you.
So when I have no joy, it seems,
I open up my box of dreams.

Carl A Newlin
VIRGIN LOVE
Who can know the things
That move the soul to say I do
Honestly love you.

Is it like a place
That brings a smile
To a saddened face?
Or like the sound
Of a friendly voice
That's always been
A personal choice?

Can we compare it to air
That can't be seen
Oh! What does it mean?
Can love explain
Can words be found
That would trigger the same?

Or can it be
It's all in me?
It seems a shame
It's not the same
But love, can never be in vain

Johnie Ryan Evans
DEPRESSION
Crouched inside a cell of dark & cold—
An agonizing womb of fear &
pain.
Zipped up tight within myself—
I suffocate on tongue of blackest
flame.

My mind goes racing, racing on—
Oh God! Will it ever cease!
Just a little pause, God—just one minute's rest—
A small respite from this
infernal beast.

The terror, if the phone should ring—
Agonizing on each small thing
done.
Longing to walk into the world—
But having not the will—too
tired to run.

Why does someone not lend me a hand?
Does no one even know the state I'm in?
Where are all my loved ones? All my friends?
I want to live! I just cannot begin.

Teresa Chaykowsky Dedovitch
THE FARM

To my grandmothers—Stephanie and Maria, for giving me roots and for giving me a sense of my own self.

There is this place I know of,
Free of trouble, free of harm
And all who have come to know it
Know it simply as the Farm.

More than songs of birds prevail here, more than flowers bring the joy
Because a woman is just a girl here
And a man is but a boy.

It's not a farm as one knows it
It holds other graces from God above
It's not filled with crop or animals
The seeds sown here are love.

Our harvest is in our hearts as we think of days gone by
And we reap the rewards of our memories
Those that make us laugh, those that make us cry.

Ordinary it may seem
Only to the naked eye
For the souls who have walked her boundaries
Acquired an everlasting tie.

The tranquil yet chaotic place that holds some intangible charm
Is this mansion we have come to know
Simply as the Farm.

Diana Southwood
THE END
Don't try to do it all,
and carry the burden by yourself,
Because you are strong.
"Like me."
You saw where it all put me!!

Ira Curtis Fortna
WHAT MEANS THIS GLORY AROUND OUR FEET?

To my Poet—Mother, Esther Marie (Koons) Fortna, who was God's instrument to birth-rhyme in me.

"What means this Glory around our feet?"
The Shepherds say as angels they meet.
It means for them to never fear,
For news, great news, clearly they hear.
To them, to all, both far and near,
Jesus, the Savior, is born this year.

"What means this song the angles sing?"
The Shepherds say as heavens ring.
Praise to God for the new born King.
Glory and peace from heaven to earth.
Given to men because of His birth.

"What means this journey from travelers far;
Those who have followed that very bright star?"
Some men have come being dark of face,
To seek, to find, God's wonder of grace.

"What means this glory around our feet,
That on this day our Jesus we meet?"
The hustle, the rush, the deadline, the fuss,
The carols, the presents, the candle glow,
All the reflection on the pure white snow,
From Santa Claus, Hilly, to Mistletoe,
Do we really know? Do we really know?

It means that on this Holy Night,
Our blinded eyes now see the light;
Our hands once bloody never fight;
Our tongues once cursing are held tight;
Our hearts once wicked are now white.

We, who lived in darkness,
Have met the Light . . .
Even Jesus The Christ,
Sense now His heart beat
For Thy Eternity.
AMEN.

Phil Del
DEEP IN SPACE
Deep in space
there floats
the planet B2.

I heard their
race compares
to the Bronx zoo.

That's OK
with me
I'm an elephant.

Bumble bees
that pray
to the president.

14th Ave
is where
I used to dwell.

Now I live
in space
and I'm doing well.

Could you
picture me
in a snowstorm?

A dozen
harmless fleas
and some popcorn.

Eugene R Palmore
AT EASE
It happened on a clear day . . .
one where the gentle rain
came and washed away
all my fears and darkness . . .
and during a night
when the moon
rose out of the bowels of the earth
and sprayed its comforting rays
across my path,
ridding me of that anguish
which ate at me like cancer-rot.
Now I am soothed . . .
I am at peace . . .
for when the sun rose
and smiled at me,
I felt a great sense of security,
knowing that I had not died
or even cried
on that day
when I had to put my love for you . . .
in storage.

George Gordon Reader
DEATH AT WHITE LAKE
There was Death at White Lake
After Baseball and Beer
That summer night, late.

For three mothers, heartache
Accompanied the fear:
There was Death at White Lake

A boat, fools, and fate
capsized with shore near
that summer night, late.

Bottom with grapnel rake.
Feel the body tug. Here!
There was Death at White Lake.

Each man lies in state
His flesh once so dear
That summer night late.

Hail Mary! for their sake.
Hold wake at the bier.
There was Death at White Lake
That summer night, late.

Marilyn Daniels
GREAT OLD TREE

To my mother, whose love taught me to write of life and how I see it

I saw afar a great old tree, if only he could tell to me of all that climbs his limbs, of all the times they fell. If tears were shed and wars were fought, upon this land so green. I see the sky above the tree, for it seems as one to me. Against the blue so many birds I did not hear, until the tree I saw. The Mocking bird and Bob-White too, will all keep in perfect tune.

So many things I did not know, were still among us all. Magnolia trees, creeks and streams and people that always care, of each and everyone, I tell you this

I did not step back in time, although it seems to me. If we did not go so very fast, we would have seen the tree, sky and birds that sung as they flutter by. Flowers we would have stopped to smell, yes we would have known all the things that are free to be

But wait, don't give it up, look upon a childs face and touch the skin so soft. Look into the eyes of love and see if you can see

THE TREE . . .

Elizabeth Stowe
LOST AND FOUND
The Rain falls and the sun shines.
Something divine was left one lone flower, it is a gift.
Enhance the flower, bring it to life.
Finally let it go into the wilderness to be one known flower not one lone flower.

Jennie L Trimpey
THE PRICE OF LOVE
Fate brought us together and
tore us apart.
Swirling emotions flood my
mind and heart.
Miles come between us when
we need to be near.
Our love can overcome any
fear.
There are no words that
are able to explain how
I feel inside.
The only place I long to be
is standing by your side.

When I think of you I always
hear the birds sing.
I long to feel the security
which your arms bring.

JoAnn Brooks
MY PLACE
My place is here, not there.
My place is not everywhere.
My place is home
Where it's cozy and warm.

I'm there because I belong there,
And know no other place to be.
I'm there because I know my place
And it knows me.

I see a blazing fire and wind outside,
But I'm safe and warm in my place.
I see children laughing and playing
Dogs barking and leaping.
That is their place to be.

I'm looking and listening to all silent things.
I'm smiling and hoping all sorts of things.
I like my place
It's my place to be.

Donna Lee Smith
ODE TO TECHNOLOGY
How can it be advantageous
when end results are so outrageous
The risks involved we all must face
if we're to save this human race

Over there tempers flare
Every country wants their share
anxiety mounts as time stands still
who will be the first to kill

The button's pushed
it's over now
Time to take that final bow
the streets are filled with anguished cries
shrieking out their last good-byes

Lorrie Brough
A LULL IN THE BATTLE
When the silence began no one quite knew,
But the deafening stillness grew and grew.
The men stood like statues all around,
Their dead buddies about them on the ground,
Rifles held tautly, poised in mid-air,
Waiting for the enemy to come out of their lair.
Dust rose around them and remnants of fire,
Smoking wrecks of twisted steel and wire.
Hollow eyes only vacantly lit,
Weary faces lined with stubble and grit,
The scene was a scene of pain, death and horror,
Meaningful only in its meaninglessness of war.
The bombs had been dropped, the flames had been thrown,
Bayonets found their marks, each man to his own.
The last grenade had been tossed into this cave
Where the men now stood frozen.
Each had been brave.
The battle had been bloody right to the last.
No time for thinking! Each had to act fast.
Now brains began to clear the

numbness away.
But, looking around, what could a man say?
Suddenly the spell was broken by a shattering cry:
The unmistakable sound of a child . . . half sob, half sigh.
The men's muscles tightened as they looked in disbelief
At the emerging child torn by shrapnel and grief.
About ten she looked, with long black straggly hair
And large brown eyes opened wide in despair.
Only one among them knew the language she spoke,
And with a start he suddenly awoke
And rushed towards her, dropping his gun as he ran,
Putting comforting arms around her.
They moved as a man
In a body, as did he, all stunned by this grievous turn of fate.
Oh, that a child should suffer from this senseless hate!
Was this the enemy they all had fought?
Was this the enemy of whom they'd been taught?
Skin yellow, yes, but her tears were the same
As the tears they'd shed in the night without shame.
Her tears were the tears of all Mankind
For the happiness few could ever find.
She looked up at them with childish trust,
And trust them she could, as they knew she must.
War was for grown men who knew what they were doing.
They started all this mess and the bally-hooing.
How far from the parade and drill field today
With the bright uniforms and the banners so gay!
Where were the drums and horses they'd seen?
Where all the glory? . . . What did all this mean?

Mary L Sedgwick
OH NO!

SNIFFLES and SNEEZES
and early morning WHEEZES,
ACHY MUSCLES and ACHY HEAD,
all ya want to do is stay in bed,
SORE THROAT and PLUGGED EARS,
maybe it's the SUMMER COLD you feared!

Mariza Zister
I'LL SUPPORT YOU

For Brenda, who has supported my poetry with her honesty and friendship.

The sun is setting.
The gulls glide in
To argue over a hotdog left an hour before.
I wait . . . immovable,
For those who wish to pause for a time.
To gaze into the future,
Or discuss what has already passed.
The bag ladies trust me with their treasures;
Just long enough to tie a dangling shoelace.
My body is stained with tears
Someone left one day while feeling lonely.
Tom loves Cindy, carved in a heart
Remains visible on my back.
The children who played return as adults to remember.
I look old and weary.
My paint is peeling,
My legs are browned with rust.
I am just a park bench.
I can't solve your problems,
Or share in your happy times
Yet you keep coming back for support,
That only I can give you.

Leatha S Shockley

Leatha S Shockley
"I HAVE A DREAM" PROGRAM

Many years ago, Martin Luther King
Delivered a speech: "I Have a Dream!"
Little did he know that he was starting a trend
For the very rich who had money to spend.
Rich are promising poor children college free.
These children are motivated to work toward a degree.

The "I Have a Dream" program is spreading like fire.
New Yorker Eugene Lang started the blaze with his empire.
Then George Kettle, a born-again Christian, self-made man,
Promised ten per cent of his income to educate as it can.
Many—rich and not so rich—from East to West
Have promised a dream to many children with less.

Martin Luther King started the dreams;
Others are catching on—it really seems.
Now many little dreamers who are growing up
Have a chance for a future not in a rut.
Thank you God for people so giving—
Helping poor children have a chance of living.

Warren Lee Kirk
DON'T DO DRUGS

This poem is for my parents and family with all my love

There's something in our society today
And if you're smart, you will stay out if its way
It ruins lives, families, and anyone that dares to touch
And no matter how plentiful your consumption you can never get too much.
It kills the rich, poor, the famous, and the unknown
And for everyone it kills it seems two more want to get stoned
Yes drugs are something we all can live without
But if you dare try them you will find out what they're about
They'll suck you up and they'll suck you in
And before you know it it will be the END . . .

James E Epp
SOMEONE

It's strange how I feel sometimes,
I've only this meltdown for a mind,
There's something I can't seem to find.
I really need someone to hold me tight and tell me it will pass,
Into the night and love will last,
When daybreak gains the upper hand, and everything will be alright again.

For now the pain is very real,
But I've found some ways to
Reduce the panic into
A calmness I can call my own
With peace in life and joy on loan,
Until it all falls into place, and everything will be alright again.

Myldred Slesinski
SHUT-IN'S DAY

Some lonely people need loving
and once in awhile a hug.
Yes, they do live within their own four walls
and we know they are warm and snug.
These people were at one time productive
they weren't always hidden away;
But they became useless to someone,
So, we thought they should have their own day.
There are so many people shut away from the world,
And we on the outside should look in;
A visit . . . a card . . . or a letter
will put smiles on their faces again.
After years and years of working
to bring to the world their plight,
The bill finally passed in Congress—to end our tireless fight.
These shut-ins to us are precious
they are wonderful in every way.
We finally got the first Sunday in June,
as NATIONAL SHUT-IN'S DAY.
Now all will be happy to know that they
will be remembered the first Sunday in June.
After years and years of tireless work,
NATIONAL SHUT-IN'S DAY to them in a boon.

Kathleen S Hofmann
REQUIEM

You are at peace now
In your corner of the world
No cares or worries on your mind
Just fond memories left behind

Sherry Hollenbeck
TEENAGERS THOUGHTS

"What should I do?—Say yes or no?"
"If I say yes . . ?".
"If I say no . . .?".
They'll be mad if I say "yes" (Parents).
They'll be mad if I say "no" (Friends).
What should I do?
I'm confused; Sometimes happy, sometimes sad.
The good times, the bad times!
Peer pressure, Parent pressure,
Teachers arguments.
One day we're "Best Friends Forever", the next-enemies.
Goals, careers, rules, regulations.
Wars, Diseases, Bombings,
Hijackings, Famine, Inflation.
So many things to watch out for.
You can't be an individual, you must follow everyone else.
You get laughed at if you look different.
Stereotypings, Popular, Skaters,
Drugies, Bangers, nerds, Loners.
If you hang out with a certain person, you're classified as one of them.
You're a prisoner in your own mind when you're an adolescent!

Reny Lunsford
ROBIN

To my beloved 'Robin' Thank you for helping me be the person I am today.

Birds are free
Carefree and gay
Going from there to here.
Feeling the wind at the tips of your wings.
Gliding so high beyond the cloud,
Looking down upon the world,
Why so high?
Come down a bit The sun does shine.
Fly high and feel free.

I know one thing.
Be free and be happy flying so high.

I just pray that this Robin
will come flying back my way
someday.

Gail D White
THE KITE

Dedicated to my daughters, Wendy Walter and Amy Reading

That house is now all drained of kids,
Who came to watch me fly my kite.
Their dreams afloat on summer air.
To have the string I clutch so tight.

They watch it sway and climb and soar,
And ask if there is any chance
That I would let them take my place,
To make it gaily glide and dance.

I dare not look into their eyes,
I tell them, "No, this kite is mine."
And carefully watch to see it float
As I let out more length of twine.

They're too polite to say to me
What they tell one another,
"She's awfully selfish with that kite,
She's twenty-nine, and she's our Mother!"

Mrs Harley Keas
I CARE

When I awake each morning I pause to say a prayer.
A prayer to God in Heaven, to tell Him how much I care.
I care about the sunshine that brightens up my day;
The many, many blessings that God sends along my way.
I care about little children and watch them run and play.
I care about my many friends who make my life worthwhile;

The many, many precious friends
who greet me with a smile.
Have you ever stopped to think about
what real friends mean to you?
When you are discouraged, all the
things they say and do?
When they bring you a real good
cookie that they've made for you
Or when they stop and ask you if
there is anything they can do.
What is your answer?
"No, but it was sweet of you to ask
and I hope God blesses you"
When you get old and helpless as we
all will surely do,
Don't give up in despair but ask God
to help, and He will see you through.
I care about my loved ones,
friends and neighbors who enter
life's picture too;
And I know that God is there, their
strength and courage to renew.
Life's no rosey bed of roses and we
all need God to see us through.
I care because He's always there to
help each and everyone of you.
I care because too many are hungry,
homeless, lonely,
Or sad and filled with despair.
So get down on your knees, ask God
to help,
And show Him that you care.

Judia McClendon Cabets

CHRISTMAS IS A TIME OF FAITH

To Frank and all of the members of my family who are faithful in their beliefs.

Christmas is a time of faith.
Faith of the small ones
  that Santa will call,
Faith of the young ones
  the love conquers all,

Faith of the families that
  time is forever,
Faith of the elders that
  God faileth never.
Christmas is joy and
  peace and love,
Granted with grace from
  God up above.

Lisa Heinritz

DID YOU HAVE FUN LAST NIGHT?

To myself at 16 and to Jeff, living is learning

Did you have fun last night?

Were you having fun when he spilled
beer on your pants?

Was it fun when Sara called you a
pig?

Did you think she was cute when she
fell down and needed help getting
up?

Did you learn anything hearing
drunkin' stories and dirty language?

Was Lisa, the homecoming queen,
pretty when she kept belching?

What about Tom, the football star,
was he a jock when he threw up on
your car?

What about you?

Is your headache and nauseated
stomach all you have to show for the
$30 you spent?

Tell me again,

Did you have fun last night?

Christine R Dann

ONE SPECIAL NIGHT

This poem is dedicated to Michael Hartmann.

I didn't know what that night
would turn out to be
And I hope you know how much
That it meant to me

Somehow I knew
That you'd be waiting for me
And I couldn't wait
Because you're the only one I
wanted to see

Just that one look
Made me realize
That you weren't ready
To say your goodbyes

When you were holding me,
You made me feel so right
I know I will always remember
That one special night

Eloise Barclay DuBois

A SYMBOL AND A SILENT PRAYER

A wedding veil, embroidered sheets,
a baby's dress
  with hand-stitched tucks, insertion,
lace
Packed in blue tissue,
  a patch of cumulus cloud in a clear
sky,
"Fleur-de-lis"—symbol of France, a
young girl's name;
  or a blank sheet of paper awaiting
poetry—
None of these seems more pure than
a white-bearded iris
  as it blooms in May, fragile, but
Timeless as an angel's wing
  in a Giotto fresco, there in Assisi.

But so frequently, a blustering wind
or driving rain
  unexpectedly shreds the thin petals,
So when the thunderstorm subsides,
this image of God's grace
  bends forlornly in the stiff green
blades—torn, devastated,
Making no less an imprint on one's
memory
  than the face of one of El Greco's
martyred saints,
Or a white, broken cross against the
sky
  on an old adobe shrine.

So blow, wind; and come, rain; but
be more gentle.
Not until another spring will this
white iris bloom again!

Ann Rotundo

JOURNEY HOME

I'm on my long journey home.
I don't have time to stay
With you my friend
It's a long, long road I'm traveling
For I'm headed back home again
The road is long
The traveling rough
But at my journey's end
It'll be enough
To be back home
With loved ones, family and friends

And when I get home
That day will be happy, merry and
gay
We'll have a fiesta for 3 or 4 days
For I'm back home with my loved
ones to stay

So I'll be on my way
I'm headed down that road
That-a-way
I hope to see you again someday
Come see me at my journeys end
Yes, I'm on my long journey home.

Cecil A Wardell

THE CRUMBS OF LIFE

Dedicated to my only son Jimmie Lavyn Wardell, With Love And Devotion. Your Dad.

The Beautiful Cakes Have Been
Eaten,
Gone Are The Apples And Plums.
A Great CHRISTMAS Was Had,
So Don't You Feel Sad,
If You Think You Got Only The
Crumbs.

You May Think That Others
Outclass You.
Whether You Live In Mansions Or
Slums.
But When All Has Been Said, And
Others
Love Declared Dead,
CHRIST Is Still There Gathering
Crumbs.

Our Interests Have Flown To New
Regions,
New Friends And New Babies Have
Come.
But Remember HIS Love Is Not
Fleeting,
And HE Deserves More Than Our
Crumbs.

This Is The Way We Have Treated
Our SAVIOR,
Drinking And Dancing To The Blast
Of The Drums.
And As HE Asks For HIS Tithes,
With A Shrug
And A Sigh, We Throw HIM Only
Some Crumbs.

I Pray When This Life Is Over,
And My Time Of Judgement Finally
Comes.
That GOD Lets Me Take A Big Slice
Of HIS Cake,
And Don't Give Me Only Some
Crumbs.

Frank Logan

WARM

Your eyes are warm
As gentle summer rain.

Your voice a sigh
Speaks softly on,
Lifting me
  With Coaxing glee
  To looks of love.

P D Gathings Jr

OLD GRANDDAD

Old Granddad and his Kodak Disc
Is always such a pest
At every family gathering
He never seems at rest

Quietly moving among the crowd
Greeting every one there
He snaps the young and old alike
And seems to pop up everywhere
He is quite a nuisance to some
But he is always tolerated
For after all, old and senile
He should not be berated

They tell me he has quite a set
Of photos from the past
He looks at them from time to time
Re-living youth that could not last

Word comes to me he's not alone
In peeping through the pages
Of albums he has stored away
And kept throughout the ages.

Blossom Renshaw Johnson

MY RICHES

I am rich in many wonderful things,
Fiery sunsets and butterfly wings;
Rich, golden meadows and smooth
flowing streams;
High flying geese and silver
moonbeams.
Dark caverned forests and prairies so
wide;
Boundless ocean and deep, rolling
tide.
I'm wealthy in hours golden and
brown.
My future is rich and sure and sound.
I'm blessed in the warm love of
friends like you;
My storehouse holds much love for
you, too.
All my riches come from our Father
above
Granted to me by His wonderful
love.

Le

Le

WHO AM I "THE SINKING OF THE SHIP"

Who am I . . .
Dust blowing in the Wind
Felt only by the changing of the
temperature.
A constant, straight road coming
toward a bend.
No hearing of a roar, just an
occasional purr.

Who Am I . . .
Playing the fool out loud.
Shuttered away behind closed
curtains,
Buried beneath a shroud.
Leaving behind only my stains.

Telepathically viewing
Repetition of a laugh track over and
over.
The sinking of the ship.
Not a word spoken, a search for a
clover.
Dissolved! My creativity, my
originality.
  Ha!! I give no lip.

Joyce West
THE AWAKENING
I woke up this morning
Sun in my face
A feeling of warmth
Transcending through space

Spellbound, I floated
A ghost of a thing
Astounded as always
By Earth's earthly glean

Enchanted I felt
A part of this life
Abounding with pleasures
Of keenness and sight

It came to me clearly
Timeless through space
A message so urgent
No one can escape

Creation has sought
To give us new strife
For a World that cries out
For the Rebirth of Life

Glenda Diann Kerns
YOU MADE LIFE WORTH LIVING
I was so depressed and so tired of giving,
I felt that life no longer was worth living.
Then you came into my life and changed my views,
You gave me love and chased away my blues.

You woke up feelings which were asleep for years,
You filled my life with laughter and dried my tears.
You placed me on a pedestal ten feet tall,
You treated me just like a big china doll.

You sent me roses as a symbol of your love,
A love as strong as the heavens above.
You promised to live, honor, and protect me for the rest of my life,
If only I would become your loving and devoted wife.

So we strolled down that aisle, and we said, "I DO",
And now my life is filled with a love so true.
Never again will I ever be lonely,
From this day forth, "I will love you only".

Anita Gale Poole
MISSING YOU
Like an image
in two mirrors
facing each other,
you echo in my mind;
like the rippling gurgle
of water over a shoal
you flow through me,
leaving only your echo behind.

Doug Gray
IRISH BACKGROUND
I am a kid with an Irish background.
I wonder what my ancestor's house looked like,
I hear the sounds of cows mooing in an Irish field,
I see Irish kids walking down to the pond to fish.
I want to play the games Irish kids play,
I am a kid with an Irish background,
I pretend to see farmers working in their fields,
I feel like an Irish leprechaun,
I touch the tall grass in Ireland—
I cry when I hear about the hard times my ancestors had.
I am a kid with an Irish background.
I understand why they came to America—
I say that Irish have a lot of luck,
I dream of living there and walking to the marketplace—
I try to learn as much as I can about my ancestors,
I hope to someday visit Ireland,
I am a kid with an Irish background.

Rose S Vail
BLIND HANDS
The touch of a man
Blind to his own hands
Not feeling what he does

My skin grows cold
My heart-life drained
The pool of tears behind my eyes
Not seen or felt by him

Who can a man not feel his own hand?
Not know what he does?
Who robbed him of his sense of self;
slipt within his mind to rob him of his very thoughts?
His thoughts trapped within,
sigh to tell the struggle to gain freedom.

"What are you thinking?"

"I don't know."

Dawn Delynn Kinney
INSURMOUNTABLE PAIN
Stuck with this feeling of loneliness
Seems like tomorrow never comes.
This unbearable feeling of pain blinds me
and emotionally numbs.
Visions of you pour down upon me
like a shower of rain.
I am drowning myself in my feelings
coming up only for breaths of pain.
It engulfs my soul
as the sea does the sand.
To surmount this pain
Would be oh so grand.
Life is made up of circles of love
That entwine the heart and souls.
This feeling of self-indulgence
Takes me away from my dreams and goals.
The pain is psychological—
Feelings from the heart entering the mind.
If only it were scientific
Then the answers I would find.
Some day the pain will lessen,
And the sun will shine again.
Maybe I'll be able to accept you
As just a special friend.

Lori Reid
ZEBRAS
Zebras are cousins of horses you see,
They are very much different than people like me.

Tempers make them hard to train and tame,
They have many stripes that are never the same.

Found in Africa's plains, where they eat lots of grass,
Lions are their enemies, so they have to run fast.

Fifty zebras a year keep one lion well fed,
If their stripes didn't protect them, they would be dead.

In tall grasses or dry plains, zebras are hard to see,
Their stripes break up the outline of their body to a tee.
So that's what I've learned about zebras you see,
They are very much different from you and me.

Anna L Kupferschmid
A CHERISHED GIFT

Dedicated to my husband Kenny, my true love.

Love is like . . .
A rare and precious stone,
A beam of the sun,
A million dollar loan.
It gives a . . .
wonderful husband or wife,
Gleam in the eye,
Rich and glorious life.
When found it's . . .
A desired lifetime treasure,
A lifter of the spirits,
And an endless source of measure.
Love is only true!

David Bookout

David Bookout
LAUGHTER

To my children, Tevin, Tammy and Terra. A simple poem, to remind us of, the gift of laughter. Love, Dad

I'm surrounded by the laughter of children,
A day spent in the park.
In loves embrace.
My children.

How innocent their laughter is,
How few their expectations.

They view the world through special eyes.
Looking for joy, not faults.
Finding delight in each moment.
Time so happily spent.

Do you remember how it used to be?
When laughter came so easily.

Donna J Carley Tizol
ONCE IN TIME
Harmonic convergence in the Cosmos that night.
Black velvet the sky with stars shining bright.
Boundless energy in vast Heavens array.
Warm fire on Earth—Cool breeze off the Bay.
Ships glide cross the channel with colored pattern lights.
Lighthouse beacon streaks constant to aid in their plight.
Involved with my senses—feel content and secure.
To bad it wasn't made to last and endure.
Stimulating intensity—To become one with it all.
But alas, for too soon, good things did befall.

Dr Walter T St Goar
NEW MOON

To my dearest Nan—interviewer par excellence.

Your brilliant slender curvature of light
appears distinct against the autumn night
yet as we look more closely we can see
the outline of your total form-to-be;
the clear-cut silhouette which we first view
does not reliably reflect the whole of you.

New Moon, are you just telling us as best you can
how hard it is to judge our fellow man?

Melissa Anne Perdue
THE GUEST

To the Giver of all talent, I thank you.

Loneliness came to visit me
I begged her not to stay
She gazed at me and gave a laugh
But would not go away.

She tried to rule my every thought
To gain control of me
To test my strength, my will, my wit
To steal my sanity.

I set my thoughts on things gone by
And things I hoped would be
I mustered all my inner strength
To grasp reality.

Our struggle lasted days untold
And all the while she smirked
As my resolve slipped slowly by
Her evil plan had worked.

Locked in darkness, lost within
Removed from all I knew,
As for my guest, she danced away
Still others to pursue.

Gilbert S Murray
JACK FROST IS NIMBLE AND QUICK
Jack Frost, was all
the weather would call . . .
And it's a fact
he never came back
Till summer had turned to fall . . .

Jack Frost, he danced
on each tree, and its branch . . .
And it's a fact
he never came back
Till all was colored where he glanced . . .

Jack Frost, took pains

on each window and its pane . . .
And it's a fact
he never came back
Till all of them looked the
same . . .

Jack frost was host
To witches, globbins, and
ghost . . .
And its a fact
he never came back
Till Halloween nite was past . . .

Jack Frost, he rode
on a big cloud of snow
And it's a fact
he never came back
Till all was blowin far below . . .

Jack Frost, got lost
in the month of December . . .
And it's a fact
he never came back
Till late the next September . . .

Jack Frost is nimble and quick.

Tina JoAnne De Petrillo

THE UNEXPECTED

You're my inspiration Love You Always Nico, Forever Tina

You go through life
expecting wonders to mend
your broken heart
Allowing one to touch your being
and hopefully you pray it will
blossom.
Although, all that is real
is the growing strength of your
imagination.

Along life's road
appears a smile
Displaying warmth and patience
and your soul stirs with undisguised
longing
Guilt washes over your body
tormenting your thoughts
Leaving your bewildered.

Yet with the wisdom of time
the tunnel of light is found
And your heart exhales peace.

D R McCarthy

A LANDSCAPER'S LOVE

Now the tuna's under tinfoil and
one of your cats is washing herself on
my knee and
Soon the trees will be bent down by
ice storms and
The lawns are all cut and my hands
are all calloused and cut and
Scarred.
My hair's a little lighter and
My hair's a little greyer and
My hair's a little thinner.
Now the wash is mostly on the
dresser and the first
Set of Christmas lights blinks
imperfectly and soon I'll be lining up
For unemployment from the
government and
The mums are all cut down and the
mulch is all laid out and
Steaming and brown and my arms are
a little stronger and
My legs are a little stronger and my
back is a little stronger, too.
But, my appetite's larger and my sex
a little rougher and my
Skin's a little darker and my sex a
little faster and
I know you truly love me and you
suffer me silently and
Gently with quiet understanding,
But you do not suffer me
indifferently.
The ground is frozen and my motions
are frozen and
The rains are frozen and the
sunlight's frozen in my eyes.
The leaves are frozen in the mud and
my hands are frozen in my pockets,
My gloves are frozen in the truck and
the sunlight's frozen in my eyes

Mary Lou Von Meter

SUN SHINE SMILE ON ME

To All My Senior in Hamilton country With Love.

Sun shine smile on me Rainbow
makes my days
Storm cloud do not appear as long as
Sun shine smiles on me

Blue skies my whole life through.
Golden days of yesteryears. Here I
stand before you now
As long as Sunshine smile on me
Happy days I'v know a few. Sorrow
just a dade or two
Love I'v know my whole life through
And I know it because sunshine
smiles on me
Friends I have Quite a few. Family
tie old and new
And my heart does sing with joy
because sunshine smiles on me
And now I take my rest and my
Savior face I see
And he said you stand the test
And I know it because sunshine
smiles on me

William T Bruns

THE BISON

This poem is dedicated to my mother, who loved those magnificent animals of the world as she loved life itself.

They used to be great in number
As far as the eye could see,
And the sound of their thundering
hoofs
Was sweet music to the Pawnee;
The North American Bison
Is a product of our western plain,
They were vital to the Indian
Now it will never be the same;
With oversized head and very short
horns
The bison has been called a grump,
But who argues with an unfriendly
guy
Wearing a huge shaggy coat with a
hump;
The bison does have a second name
It may be important to know,
That they are also known to many
As the great American buffalo;
The bison will not rule the prairie
As they did in yesteryear,
But their struggle is well recorded
As a fighter that would not disappear.

Karyn S Brummett

ALONE

To be alone is not so bad,
Just think of all the friends you've
had,
But when it's time to die, my friend,
All by yourself, you reach the end.
Then when you're gone, and in the
ground,
The sun comes up, the earth goes
'round,
Your friends have found new friends,
you see,
But you're still there, in memory.

And only then they'll tell the tale,
Of how you fought it, tooth and nail,
You laughed and loved and lived it
all,
But by yourself you took the fall.

And when it's their turn, they will
know
It's not that bad to be alone.

Lilly L Esposito

MOUNTAIN TOP

I praise God for my gift and dedicate it all back to Him!

Mountain top—edged in lace
Formed by leafless trees, all a-row, in
place.
Sure sign of a spring profound, in
land so high—
Beauty so astounding, makes one
want to cry.

The trees thicken! A cub here—there
a fawn.
Look away to the hills, all the lace
trim is gone!
See great gifts we were given! All of
it free . . .
God keeps right on giving, 'cause He
loves you and loves me . . .

Now it's pure summer in every
direction.
The same thick trees seen in the lakes
reflection.
God's critters run hither and yon, in
one accord
They all feel so safe . . . 'cause they
belong to the Lord . . .

Judy C Osborne

MY THOUGHTS ON YOU

Your love is so warm and pure,
I hope that it will endure.
Your kiss is soft and sweet,
I tingle from my head to my feet.
Your embrace is sure and strong,
When I'm with you, nothing goes
wrong.
There's nothing more I'd rather do,
Than to be with and love you.
Although I'm your special girl,
Darling, you are my life and my
world.
Where ever I go or what ever I do,
My thought are always on you.

Sandra Knowles

REMEMBRANCE OF A STORM

Our love is like an undertow, that
pulls you out to sea
It's power can keep you or push you
back to shore
I'm afraid the strength of it is
drowning me
As I go under, I realize I want so
much more
It's like passing ships that almost
collide
That's a fear of its own kind
Especially when the ocean's so wide
Imagine the confusion it leaves in
one's mind
You search for land that may never
be there
Your mind knows the truth and still
you don't care
For what is in your heart doesn't
matter, it seems
The storm carries wild winds within
the darken sky
With a fury the rain becomes its
release
For nature has its ways, which are
ours to wonder why
Now there is stillness and everything
seems to be at peace
Where lightning has struck, a
smoldering flame shall burn
In remembrance of the storm before
For love so strong, shall always
return
But for now, I shall remain upon the
shore

Randall E Riley

DRY-ICE LADY

To the eternal Pathfinder. (Prov. 3:5-6)

Dry-ice Lady with the sad dark eyes
Would give my life to find where
your thoughts fly
Nestled deep within your tough
demeanor
Does search a soul for meadows
greener?

Would that I could be the springtime
rain
Which washes clean your auburn
pain
Or a sturdy wooden vine
Delivering you from quicksand upon
which fate would dine

But alas, foolish "Don Quixote" only
am I, errant Knight and dreamer
A tarnished but willing shield, a weak
windmill warrior
So I pray one day you will reject your
present master:
The ocean of confusion
And reclaim your rightful hopes and
dreams,
even your most precious
illusions.

Mark Meyerson

OCEAN BREEZE MEMORIES II: LAZY SUMMER

Inspired by loving parents Ann and Marty Meyerson. Dedicated to poet Mom.

The years have mellowed many
thoughts while seasons barely hear,
the rejoicing sounds embracing us all
for reasons not quite clear.
Relaxing in a quiet place,
A peaceful sort of day—
The gentle breezes soothe the soul,
Where memories drift away.
Through sparkling quencher and
splash of pool
A stretch, a yawn, —no sound,
The summer heat out lives us all
Another time around.
But when the evening sunset comes
A freshness fills the air

And tired bones from dragging days
are not so hard to bear.
Then night time sings of tired eyes
asleep by T.V. light,
As dreams replace the mellow
thoughts that wander through the
night.

Dennis L Kellogg
RIVER

To Debbie; my wife, my lover and my best friend, who above all others has put poetry into my life through her love.

The river winds
Through endless times;
Ages to eons
Bent on going
No-where,
Yet tying both ends
Of eternity.

Julie L Anderson
HIS GIFT

To my David for his belief in me.

Our Savior in a manger lay
So small and meek and mild,
While angels song in heaven above
Proclaimed the Holy Child.

A bright new star in Bethlehem
Shone o'er where Jesus lay.
A sign to all who saw it there,
A new King born today.

The light and life of all the world
In humble birth began,
But His redeeming gift of love
Fulfilled the Fathers plan.

In our hearts may we remember
That His gift is with us still,
And be a light to all the earth
As we obey His will.

Jean Michael Brownstone
ROMANTIC ENCOUNTER #2

This poem is dedicated to Stacie Leean Maxwell, George, Axl and Elton (for the name and inspiration).

Sometimes I think of how we met. It wasn't in some sleezy bar. It wasn't in some hotel room.

I thought the walks in the park were beautiful. It gave me an enlightening view. It gave me sense of direction.

I was impressed by your intellectual view of the world. Our conversations never seemed to end. Our conversations explored territories of man.

Where did we lose all of our direction and how did we wander off from one another? Will I ever see you again?

Paul Michael Papp
THE CITY

The city lain between the brown mountains and the green sea, shrouded in a gray fog of its own breath.

The city, with its arteries of concrete, and blood cells of steel and glass running throughout its vastness.

Like a colossal sleeping beast it laid, its heart beating . . . beating with the pulse of many to make the one, a sound heard by no one, but felt by all, in the city.

Always the chameleon, the city changed its color, but always remained the same.

Like great arms, the city towers of glass in a vain attempt to reach the heavens . . . blocked out the light of the eternal summer. A summer whose heat could not melt the cold blackness of the city.

For the innocent that came to the city, the city promised them the illusion of fortune, and the dream of fame, at the cost of respect and virtue.

The city gave no quarter to its lost children . . . for they did not shine with the light of self importance, but were burdened with its shadow.

The city cared little for its own past . . . to the city, its past was an unpleasant reminder of what it was once, and could never be again.

The past reflected the pride, the caring, and the warmth the city was built on.

And so one by one the palaces of dreams fell, the gardens of joy were paved over. Replaced by even more boxes of mirrored glass and steel. For the city was intoxicated by its own image.

This was the city of lost angels, of lost dreams and of lost hope . . . it was the City of L.A.

Linda M Glidden
GRACELEN

Grace & Lennita

Care you lent with loving hand
Always patience so calm and caring
The final step, a divine plan
A long journey, hope and sharing

Give the last as its best
Show all is not yet forgotten
Love in every deed and test
Life twines a road rough trodden

A peace eternal round the bend
Life's last show now is closing
Care thee who are a friend
Cry not at last the reposing

Grace thee who filled the years
and the patience shown now
unceasing
Bless those who dried my tears
and yet found the labor pleasing

Bless those who stayed it through
The times were hard and uncertain
Each day for me not you
Lifes end relief a closing curtain

JoAnn Green
WHEN I THINK OF YOU

When I think of you
I think of laughter,
sunny days,
starry nights,
fat furry puppies,
cotton candy,
long holiday weekends,
and cold beer.
I see the world
through the eyes of a child
and the work is filled
with wonder,
and joy,
and beauty.
I am the golden-haired princess
and you . . .
the knight who wears my colors
and slays dragons
in my name . . .
when I think of you.

Becki Harter
THE WRITTEN WORD

You cannot write from nothing
You must have substance
Expression of concept with emotion
Emotions with true base
You must have lived, to see, digest,
express

Writing, methods of silent expres-
sion
Escape for the taunted mind
Means for discovering of true self
Like a tool it can be useful, fulfilling

Written words
Engraved through time and perils
Used for learned instruction

When folly knocks at minds eye
One can escape into the written word
Give to it time, feeling
It takes anguish of living

Treat it as friend
Love, protect, and cherish it
And it will hold in its warmth
The labyrinths of the inquisitive mind

Karyl Irion

Karyl Irion
WHALESONG

Awesome sentience in perfect grace
Flowing blue aftertrace
Trance-like silence
In a quiet serene space.
Save the true children
Or the future misplace.

Kathy Bennett
SOUNDS OF LAUGHTER

This poem is dedicated To Keith and Melissa, With Love

I hear childrens laughter,
so far away.
The laughter I heard,
each and every day.
The laughter I hear,
is very little these days.
Since my childrens father,
came and took them away.

Nancy D Chamberlain
SOULS SACRED CONFESSION, I LOVE YOU MY FRIEND.

My senses evolve . . . like a hanging
mobile
Draw nearer my dear, and my
consciousness clears,
Love centre vibrations . . . warmly,
tenderly ascend,
Hearts common communion—I
adore you my friend.

Mountains of the spirit, rise to
beauteous summits,
The ethereal love fires, higher
sources covet
Gentle the love is, like mountain
mist covering dawn
I am swept through the heavens,
through worlds without end
While time merely stands still, I love
you my friend.

Our two forms enraptured, at times
wrapt in quiet
Minds strung out like a rosary, that
lies on soft velvet.
Our two hearts beating, to loves
mutual tune
Like churning of tides, within
bosoms of dunes.

When soul mates confide, celestrial
winds-whispering descend
Souls sacred confession . . . I need
you my friend.
Subdue me, as love fires of spirit,
rage out of control
Tenderly, with love . . . caringly
attend,
With caresses, draw nearer, love me
gently my friend.

Martine Drouin
HOLE IN MY PILLOW

To: Michael Jackson, "Le soul de ma vie" and all the children young n old . . . Luv, Martine 08-18-52

Ever wake up
N wonder,
With a mind of blurr,:
What it'd been
All about . . .
That sweet dreamin,
While eyes shut.
And body sleepin? . . .

So, discreet curiosity
Awaits, casually
As you concentrate
  But!?
To no good fate
As nothing seem to pop
No screen to be seen
No story no image
Total lack of baggage
From the night voyage
Blank page on memory stop.

What's my dream?
Where's my dream?
Where's that sheep
Which took me to sleep? . . .

Not even of the sheep,
A trace
One which took me there
An unreal place
I don't know where
On a free travel fare, I weep;
Oh no! Oh oh no!
What you notice . . .
As you straighten n sit:

What's my dream?
Where's my dream?
Where's that sheep
Which took me to sleep? . . .

No wonder!
I can't find
That picture of adventure,
No need to look again
Either
For it will be in vain,
Nothing to see!, can't be!
Oh! Oh! sorrow
Plainfully
For I miss
What I don't know!

What's my dream
Where's my dream
Where's the sheep
That took me to this sleep

  Unfair
Almost a nightmare!
My dream has evade . . .
has evade through a hole
A hole! Evade evade evade (echo)
Got a hole, a hole
In my pillow!!! . . .
As I layed peacefully
Like on a cloud,

Softly
Traveling freely
In the nite's fresh air
Imagining irreality:
The pattern of my dream
Without scheme
Was evading
disappearing
Through the hole
The hole in my pillow! . . .

What's my dream
Where's my dream
Oh sorrow
Got a hole in my pillow
Oh sorrow
Lost that dream

"Don't feel sorrow
Prepare ur tomorrow"

Ronald Lameck
ODE TO A MOONCHILD

To Diane, with bittersweet remembrance.

While walking on perception's edge in a dream,
It occurred to me;
Your love lays in twin Pandoric boxes,
Each holding the other's key.
You are the fair Artemis, scarlet queen of Gemini,
Who lives across the Milky Way—across the evening sky.
Goddess wild, of the wood, child of the moon,
A taste of your sweet absinthe has made Orion swoon.
Now past Schamballah I'll wander,
For beyond Ultima Thule,
With taurine determine to win YOU, sweet ruby-jewel.
I'll climb the snowy mountains upon the rim of space.
If King Fear should meet me there,
I'll laugh in his dead face.
A hunter on my quest I am,
The huntress I am stalking,
Do your angels whisper words to me,
Sweet words as I am walking?
"You could not seek her lest you'd found her.
She waits ahead for thee.
Heed not the doubts or disbelievers,
Ignore Persephone."
If I help you be yourself and become what you can be,
I can shatter those demon-boxes,
And free your love for me.
Then I'll string your tears among the stars
—And love you for my own.
And each day I will sing for you
The Infinity of OM.

Peggy Nevins
DEAR DAD

In memory of my beloved father William Arthur Clark 1890-1985

I'm thinking tonight of you, DEAR DAD,
Alone in your cabin home
And I know it hurt you very much
When I started out to roam.

At night when all is quiet
And stars shine bright up there;
I kneel in solemn dignity
To offer up a prayer.

I pray to GOD to keep you safe
And guide you through the years.
I pray that I might "see the light"
In answer to your prayers and tears.

Then when life's trials are over
And He sorts the good and bad;
Upon Page ONE of GOD'S tally
book
Will be your name, DEAR DAD.

Rocky Main
I SAW YOU
I saw you today
In the set wings of the hawk
In his daring but graceful dive
There was sureness of task
Then a celestial soar
I am still here—I survive

I saw you last week
In the surge of the wave
Then as you spread on the beach
Your power was there
But you—you are gone
Far from my power to reach

I see you at dawn
And late—after dusk
I see you whenever I look
This power to see
Is now part of me
Our love is all that it took.

K C Schedin
THOUGHT 1
With wisdom and unknowing acquired with age,
He gathered materials to construct his own stage.
To act out his life he would create on his own,
With the laughter and tragedy and then die alone.

The props on this stage were truly amazing,
A little of real and a lot of star gazing.
Some things that were loved, some things that were hated,
The colors of life, and some words that were stated.

The hearing of happy the deafness of sad,
The seeing of goodness the blinding of bad.
The things he kept secret the things he would tell,
A small want of heaven a small fear of hell.

An abundance of memories are left in the wings,
The laughter the friends the happy good things.
These things were not shown, which may seem uncaring,
The memories were his and were not for the sharing.

The curtain went down on this one act life play,
The same thing that happens each and every day.
To someone you know and to those that you don't,
You know that it will, and hope that it won't.

Emma S Cayo
THE CYCLE OF LIFE
His arms around
a Teddy bear,
his world of a, b, c's
wrapped-up
in a red blanket,
my son sleeps
with a future smile,
without age,
like the wind of tomorrow
between the pages
of forgotten years.
My very flesh!
An extension of what I was
and am
but will not be.
He will become himself!
An exclamation point
in times of question marks.
There . . .
Beyond the windows
of a dusty dream
and obsolete text books,
where space walks behind death
and memories are eyes
to see
through an ancient keyhole
He will, some day,
spell his generation words.
A new cycle of thought
wrapped-up
in any color blanket.
His son . . .
Himself . . .
Myself.

Grant Lessley
DESERT WINDS
Have you ever gazed at the rolling desert
And watched the whirlwind stir the restless sand?
Amazed at the silence of the eagle's flight,
Or view the beauty of the Creator's hand—
Desert winds, keep on blowing day and night,
Sometimes gentle, sometimes as high as Mars,
Too cold in winter and too harsh in summer,
Leaving your ghastly work in sandy scars.

Gone is the thunder, the rain storm is ended,
Sun comes out warm to paint the desert floor,
Birds begin to sing, fly low to the ground,
Then we feel the desert winds once more—
Desert winds, as you move the shifting sands,
On every heart you cast your magic spell,
Cactus glisten, the wild creatures listen,
What a beautiful story you can tell

Kevin D Hammon
THE NETWORK SYNAPSE
Electric dragons crackle overhead,
Changing their course for their pattern.
Searching the orders of their mission.
The complexity of conversation overwhelms.

Behind unseen cages and doors,
Where the Furies haunt the corners,
The serpents of choices and change,
Rear their distorted bodies skyward.

Each door opens a power root of others.
And others open others, and they all stand ajar.
In here, the spirits hide the flaws,
And bad memories long forgotten.

The dragons search the rooms,
For a microsegment of data.
A piece to a vast blueprint of self and time,
That's never really finished.

Like stormtroopers they hit the target
With a cool, electric precision.
The messenger turns with a prisoner
And returns to conscious Mind

And in a nanosecond you reply with your name.

Karyn S Brummett
45 MILES ALONG THE SHORE
45 miles along the shore
to see the waves
to hear the children laugh
to feel the sun
to feel how I feel with you by my side
driving me to places I love
driving me to places to love
gently, as the sun goes down
turning the sky my favorite color

I suppose you planned it this way
being such friends with the sun
as you are . . .

J R Culp
A SECOND LOOK
First time I saw you, a second look I did not take,
For I saw a friendship that we would never make,
I felt that you never could be the one for me,
You were so young, that lovers we would never be;

The more I saw you the more I wanted to know,
For now you starting looking as if in a glamor show,
The warm feeling I felt when you were near,
I loved you, but couldn't tell you because of fear;

Now there's miles between us and I want to know,
I keep asking myself, why did I have to go,
But being apart has made us closer than ever planned,
I just want to be there now to hold your hand;

For it won't be long before we're together again,
Hoping this time our relationship can truly begin,
For now I know you're the one I'm searching for,
A guy like me couldn't ask for anyone more.

Dick Robichaud
CAT'S EYES
cat's eyes
espy
do they the spirits see
floating free
mesmerized
hypnotized
as they whisper by

cat's eyes
awry
do they empathy take
ne'er to wake
with fathers
forefathers
tiptoeing by

cat's eyes
belie
do they perhaps just stare
not aware

commonplace
empty space
time passing by

cat's eyes
belie
do they perhaps just stare
not aware
commonplace
empty space
time passing by

Ted A Sloan
THE DUNCE WHO LEARNED A LESSON

This extended limerick is dedicated to Elizabeth Jayne, my 8th grade English teacher in Ashland, Ky. (1959-60) and to my nieces and nephews, Shannon, Justin, Karen, Julie, Mike and Dan Sloan.

There was a young dunce who climbed trees,
But did not employ dungarees.
He wore out the seats
Of Silky Elites,
But could not account for the breeze!

A cold he did catch and would sneeze,
But stopped to consider his knees—
To patch or to pad . . .
(God help the poor lad!)
He still did not use dungarees!

To teach him a lesson, a tree,
As big and as tall as could be,
Soon beckoned he climb
For views so sublime,
But snagged on his pants seat, you see.

He struggled and dangled all day,
With help, he escaped from the fray.
(No pun intended.)
The pants he mended,
But blue jeans he sought right away!

David W Parker

David W Parker
OKINAWA

To my family & friends that I missed while stationed in Okinawa.

Most of you don't know this place—
A place of hate, and unfriendly people.
The hardship of years past
Brings memories to the old people.

Some of you have been there—
It's in the far east,
Far away from friends and families,
Thinking of home and times you had,
Wishing your time was short
Because things are so bad.

Nothing to do, nowhere to go—
If you looked around, it really showed.
New men came day after day,
The old ones left the very same way.
And the day came when I went home,

Home to freedom of my own.

Michele Bracey
TWO APART

To my loving Quinn

Gazing on the starry night,
the moonlight beams across the sky.
I feel the warmth of your true love;
the night air coils into a sigh.

I hear the stillness in the night;
so full, yet empty, like my heart.
For now I melt with tender song,
a fear belongs while two apart.

But still your presence lingers on,
for two apart is one the same.
Yet, pain is hidden in the midst
with only true love left to blame.

Belinda Nichols-Smetana
SHOULD LOVE COME TO YOU
Should love come to you,
if only briefly . . .
like a butterfly's flight
into a darkened room . . .
and brighten your life
for only one moment . . .
and chase away sadness and gloom . . .
If you should hold love
for only one moment . . .
long enough to make you
sing one song . . .
consider yourself lucky,
regardless its ending . . .
for love chased away
darkness that long.

Herbert Potoker
THE NAMING

To our granddaughter Justine the light of our lives

In this our year of grief and strife
There came one shining light,
A little baby girl arrived
To help us make things right.

She's got a great big job to do,
She doesn't know it yet,
To fill our hearts and minds with love,
And make us all forget.

With every little smile she makes
Bad memories fade away,
She makes us think of days gone by
When hearts were young and gay.

Her eyes are bright, her face is pink,
Her little hands are strong,
She's so alert at this young age
She'll walk and talk 'ere long.

As she begins her trip through life
We'll watch with loving pride,
And should she ever need some help
We'll be there at her side.

We hope she's like her mother,
Full of wondrous dreams and hope,
And meets a guy like dear old dad,
Who'll teach her how to cope.

We've known proud moments in the past
But none are quite the same,
As when a little baby girl
Takes on her brand-new name.

So let's rejoice, as we begin
To set her on her throne,
And may this very special day
Reflect that joyous tone.

We'll beat the drums and blow the horns,
And herald our new queen,
For on this baby-naming day
She will be called "JUSTINE".

Glenda J Acker
IN THE BACK OF MY MIND
I see a place I'd like to go find
It's a beautiful place in the back of my mind.
The trees are tall and thick with leaves
There all are happy and no one grieves.

Out through the valley, homes are peaceful and quiet
You can hear laughter and joy in each at night,
And on the wide land surrounding the homes
Are beautiful crops--each having their own.

All day long birds are at play
And children there are happy and gay.
The yards of homes are filled with flowers
Where busy housewives spend stray hours.

On the hill overlooking the town
Is an old graveyard that's all run down.
The tombstones are covered with brush blown in
For up that high is a terrible wind.

Here neither man nor beast will cease to exist
For God has them all on His separate list.
One of these days I'm going to find
That beautiful place In The Back of My Mind . . .

Lillie Fialkoff Tomarin
IN MEMORIAM
Companion of my morning walks,
Missy, the cat, on your grave now stalks,
Barefooted, bathrobed, awed, not glum,
Quietly, neighborhood children come,
The curtains no longer are pushed aside,
The agile body must now reside,

The woman who hit you and sped away,
Your crumpled body must be engraved
Yet, cherished, loving and loved, forgive
From chains and restraint your youthful heart
But, well remembered, your spirit, free,
Through infinite heaven. You now may run
Your soul may cavort, jump, roll, and leap
For God has refused to put up signs,

Sleep peacefully.
Possessively.
At early hours.
Bearing flowers.
With joyous bark.
In buried dark.

First looked behind:
Upon her mind.
Her wanton deed.
By her was freed.

Unleashed, may bound
On sacred ground.
Upon a cloud,
"No dogs allowed"!

Rosie L Taylor
DON'T WORRY PRAY

This poem is in dedication to my brother, Archie Taylor

We worry about what's going to happen tomorrow
Not realizing tomorrow may never come.
We should think of the power of Jesus
Making sure what we do today is well done.

We should worry about nothing,
We should pray about everything.
When we pray we can experience the joy
Our Heavenly Father can bring.

Live one day at a time
God will take care of the next.
He has everything to give
He will give and He'll protect.

Don't worry about nothing
Worry won't help you this is true;
Instead of worrying, do some praying
Give it to God, He'll fix it for you.

Barbara Aquila Steinnagel
SHATTERED GLASS
While sitting by a window; staring through the glass . . .
Tree limbs look accusing; sunlight burning my eyes . . .
I'm caught in thoughts of my past
Wishing I had been sooner wise

In those days I was mismated
With lifeless words and selfish concern
Laughing lightly with soul-less faces
Caught in a corner in all the wrong places
Babylon clamor deafened my ear
Nothing was clear
Untouched and alone
A clingstone

Yet while believing in my own
Your truth searched the dark, deep crags and cavities
With faithful light
Your steadfastness seared the hard-baked clay
Cracking the crust of this earthen vessel
Yet leaving no scar
My heart now, soft, pliable
Willing to be shaped by Your will, Lord Jesus

Now the days of my past: just shattered glass

F Shreve
RAINBOW CITY

I dedicate this poem to my poet buddies

I'm not beggin for mercy
I'm not beggin for pity
I just want to be remembered
At rainbow city
The warmth of the heart
The warmth of the soul
I'm not lookin for favors
I'd like to write my name
On your favorite poll
Some want fortunes some gold
Some get left out in the cold
I'd like to scribble my name
On a poets honor roll
And live like a king
And swing high in the trees
Lie in bed and croon
Till there's frost on the moon
I'd like to live forever
Beneath a poets rainbow
And call it my home

Dannie Lee Carter
DAWN
Her beauty I suspect
Although, I have not seen her yet
Her voice whispers
Through the winds of my mind
And clings
Like a budding vine
Her eyes are as that of
The flaming sun
Staring deep inside
My heart is on the run
Her arms around me
Such a warm embrace
My pulse starts to race
Her charms pleasing
Her thoughts teasing
Her skin smooth
She is nobody's fool
The dusk is calm
For dawn is near
The dusk now sleeps
For dawn is here

Jennifer Chontos
THE PRECIOUS WORK OF ART
Our relationship resembled a spider's web,
An intricate mesh of woven silk.
Each fragile strand was meaningful;
Each had a part to play.
One careless move may cause collapse;
What it needed was dedication and patience.
Silken strands of thought,
Delicate threads of trust and respect
Were entwined with love and compassion.
We worked hard to make it beautiful;
Each glimmering strand was placed just so.
But it was you—it was all your fault.
You chose not to continue doing your part,
And now those loose ends dangle so far
From me to you—and heart to heart.

Larry L Wilson
GATHERING
Not unlike the air flowing through the blades of a windmill, over and over again, lifes loves flutter in turmoil.
Searching, Finding, Reaching, Catching, Releasing, after words and deeds have been thrust to the heart like the point of a foil.
Ever undecided with emotions conflicting and divided.
Crawling, walking, running and stumbling.
We make our way along the path of our lifetime.
Grasping within us tightly, the seemingly "Small to Large" remembrances the "OH" so ever shorting time, being born has provided.
As long as a word, song, place, a touch, a face, brings fondly to mind, someone.
Then we have not made our journey in mistakes, but truly in building memories, before the windmill slows, becomes still.

Frances L Porter
PSALM OF JOY
My Lord, when
I contemplate
The glory and
The wonder of
Thine awesome
Presence here
My soul sings
For my Lord, Thou art my shepherd
My salvation and my steady shield
Thou guideth me on shadowed paths
And throughout life's rocky field
Oh Lord, Thou
Art a comfort
And a hope to
Which I cling
Lord of mercy
Lord of might
Source of the
Eternal light
My happy soul
Doth sing and
Sing and sing

Blanche Eloise Higgins

Blanche Eloise Higgins
THE LOG CABIN
Many years have come and gone since,
I saw the old place today
Sagging porch, steps missing
Doors gone, broken windows
Passing years took their toll,
As Mother nature had her way
And I as a child whiled away,
Many an hour at play under the old porch in white Florida sands
So I closed my eyes
Visioned, how it used to be, with its patchie grass
This tiny portion of a life time
Amid white sands and spurs.

Corrine Ann Pavlo
RELATIONSHIP OVER

To my three joys: Susan, Michele, John "God's Gifts"

It crept gradually along the corridors of our souls
Held together by three strong bonds
Finally alone, we face each other
And we see people with no images
We see and feel it ending
we clutch at memories
Relationship over

Can it ever be what it once was
Well, what was it really
A joining of two, accepting what came along,
But, always with a yearning for something else
Relationship over

Enjoying the nurturing and loving of extensions of ourselves
But in moments alone
fighting this enjoyment, with no reason
Needing something more, but what
Relationship over

Robert Conaway
SEEDS
As you travel lifes highway,
There is one thing I know;
The harvest you reap
Is from seeds that you sow.

Just give a big smile,
And get many in return;
Give a good days work
For the money you earn.

Be honest and friendly,
Wherever you go;
And remember your harvest
Is the seeds that you sow.

Be good to your loved ones,
Let your love for them show;
Be kind to your neighbors
And your harvest will grow.

God gives us all talents,
To use wisely I know;
And remember our harvest
Is the seeds that we sow.

Donna A Lyman
YOUTH
When
you're young
you think of growing
old. You scarcely have
time to enjoy your
youth. Grow up
you're forever being
told. Your childhood
has flown by as if the years were
but pages in a book, that took only
moments to read. Now you're an
adult and a youth no more. What do
all of the years hold in store?
It's frightening, yes that is true
There's no one else
to depend on
There's only you
Is that really true?
No! I think not
for there is another
who will help
you through, open
your heart and pray
Let God be part
of your life today

Brenda Eames
UNREQUITED LOVE
I pause and watch you coming,
As you're walking through the door.
My heart speeds up its drumming,
But, as always, you just smile or nod—nothing more.

I sit and wonder how you miss
What others plainly see;
But now, I guess, it's obvious,
Romance for us was not to be.

I've lain so long awake at night,
Furtively hoping that you'd care,
And wished so hard with all my might,
With low pathetic prayer.
It hurts so much, I cannot speak,
Inside, I wince from pain.
As the tears roll slowly down my cheek
I know there's nothing I can gain.

I've realized, though, what is my fate,
And, sadly,—lesson learned,
I know no matter how long I'll wait,
My love is not returned!

Holly M Diaczuk
THE OWL
Silence so still and calm,
The darkness such a perfect black:
The owl searching for its destiny
Yet always swooping back.
It flies throughout the night
Reaching out; it survived.
With its low hollow cry
It is not alone and never deprived.
The night is its heaven of glory,
He flies like a king in the sky;
Yet some day he will not return
Or utter his lonely cry.

Chet Richards
DARWIN
Time was when Ants,
Those Miscreants,
Strode boldly 'cross the plane.

But there evolved
A beast involved
To save us from this Bane.

He cannot hide
Inflated Pride
Though justly earning Fame.

For Ants walk not
When He goes . . . ZOT.

Anteater is his Name!

Betty Ann Marron
ONE POEM ONLY
No Eliot or Allen Tate
Would ever risk poetic fate
To send in by a certain date
His thoughts, which words can celebrate

But Sandburg, Frost and all those men
Are really far beyond my Ken
I read them and my hopes just crash
But, then again, there's Ogden Nash

I'll send this in, and hope to see
A letter saying, "Golly, gee . . .
We like your work and we'll surmise
That you're about to win a prize"

What, pompous, daft and vain, you say?
Was "Wasteland" written in a day?
My stuff's more like "The Gumbie Cat"

But think what Webber did with that

This contest tempts me to create
It urges me to meditate
Upon my wish to rhyme and prate
But not for long, or I'll be late

Priscilla Davis
WHO IS SHE

To all Mothers—especially mine

As I watch from afar
this beautiful lady,
her smile is as warm
as the sun up above.

She talks to the children
who sit at her feet,
to the babe in her arms,
a sweet lullaby she sings.

Her hair is like silver
her touch like a feather,
the sun shines around her
in all kinds of weather.

The wisdom in her eyes
this love of our life,
she's a daughter, she's a mother
she's a lady, she's a wife.

Andrew H Gantt II
REDNECK FISICKS
Cose I knows
Einstein claimed kin
to Michael's son, Morley;
after all, they wuz his
relatives.

Ifn you ast me
they wuz all nuts.
God made light,
the Bible sehs so.

But wha they sehs
we makes it ourselves.
How come? Well, any
star's gleam comin or
goan, pass on by at
eggzackly the same
speed. Whuther Ise comin or
goan makes no nevamine.
As I figger it, only way
that could be wuz ifn I
was makin tha light
myself.

An everone roun here
knows I ain God for
sure.

Kathy L Fleming
DELIVERANCE

This is lovingly dedicated to those who entered my life and left magical and wondrous footprints on my soul.

I have come to regard the sea as my Friend, always constant and true. Always there when I need comforting—never turning away for the sake of "not wanting to get involved."

The sea soothes me with its calmness and serenity.
It makes me aware that the mountainous problems that I think I have are actually only fragmentations of the mind's spectrum, that can easily be dissolved, just as the wave is dissolved as it breaks against the rocks.

You are also my Friend. In essence you are the Rock of Gibraltar—steadfast. I can always be sure where I stand with you, and that is good.

Like the sea, you listen to my outcrys, and soothe me with comforting words when needed.

I have come to respect the sea—for what it is.
Likewise, I have come to respect you.
Not for what you appear to be, but what you are.

Terry Umphenour
OH GIVE THANKS
Oh, thank Thee Lord for all Thy blessings,
That help me through each day;
For my mother's love, my father's care,
And all my friends at play.

Oh, thank Thee for the clothes I wear,
So bright and new and gay;
And for my home and family,
From which I'll never stray.

Oh, thank Thee for a lovely sky,
And a deep blue sea;
For the mountains and the stars,
In a land of liberty.

Oh, thank Thee for Thy gift of faith,
Also a church in which to pray;
And for Your Holy Spirit,
That guides me on my way.

But most of all, Oh thank Thee Lord,
From my sins You've set me free;
By dying upon a lonely cross,
Your Grace You've given me.

Dennis Chatfield
I LOVE

Dedicated to the one I love, Diane.

I love the way you set my heart afire,
That proves my love is no liar.

I love your soft warm touch,
Which means I love you very much.

I love the way you laugh and smile,
Then I sit and watch you for awhile.

I love the way you run your fingers through my hair,
Then you whisper that you care.

I love the way your eyes are bright,
That makes your face shine up with light.

I love your soft and gentle voice,
Like wind through pines without a choice.

Gin Scopel
JACK'S DAD
This man I've heard of but I don't know,
he is Jack's dad and his name is Bruno.
Jack never knew his dad at all,
to take him fishing, ride a bike, or to play ball.
He never had him to sit on his lap,
to wrestle, to talk to, to ride on his back.
He missed all the good things a man tells his son,
to have courage, faith, and fights to be won.
This man gave his son such honesty,
and God did arrange it to give him to me.
Yes, Jack never knew his dad you see,
because when he died Jack was only three.

Joseph Filocomo
THE SHORES OF MAGNA GRECIA

To Jennifer

I walk along the weathered shores
Of time.
A broken column here, a pile of
Ancient stones there.
Homeric prose rides the wind
With unabashed fury.
Achilles and Hector clash
In empty caverns.
Paris' love for Helen ripples
The waves.
The receding tide reveals the
Scattered reflections of an
Amphitheater of old;
Sophocles plays to an audience
Of sea urchins and barnacles.
If you stare real hard, Ulysses
Can be seen on the hazy horizon
Sailing towards his native Ithaca.

Eleanor Horn
REFLECTIONS

To my beautiful, loving children Lillian, Donald, Gerald, Dennis

As I look out of my window
At the sky so very blue
The beauty of the flowers and trees
My thoughts have turned to you.

Do come and join me
In this world of beauteous sight—
The lovely green of rolling lawns
And bluebirds in hasty flight.

The clouds rolling lazily by,
A brilliant moon adorning the sky
Spangled with stars of lustrous light
Like diamonds encrusted in the
velvet of night.

Is it not worth a moment or two
To pause and enjoy
These wondrous gifts
So freely given to me and you.

John Tworoger

John Tworoger
GIVE SOMETHING
Give something that belongs to you,
A friendly word, a smile—
It's like a sunbeam in the blue
Out on a golden isle.

Give something to a suffering soul
That errs the same as you
And cannot find in life its goal,
Your gift will help you too.

Give something from your heart away
To save a fellow man,
A feeling of warm sympathy
Will do it now and then.

The happiness you will bestow
Today—perhaps tomorrow—
In torrents back again will flow
To help you in your sorrow.

John B Harrison
SENSELESS
I see the blue of the ocean, the blue of the sky
the blue of the bomber, consigning me to die

I hear the roar of the wind, the sharp cry of the dove
the explosion of the mortar, killing all that we love
I feel the green grass on my face, the cool breeze in my hair
the hate for my fellow man, is that really fair?

I smell the springtime coming, the smoke from the fire
the death and decay in the muck and the mire

I taste the salt of the sea, the love that I met
the tears and the blood, mixed in with my sweat

Our senses are here to enhance our true feelings
by killing the world, we can only send them reeling
It is senseless to mix beauty with suffering and pain
our lives become mangled and tears fall like rain.

Peggy Opal Snyder
THANK YOU FOR HELPING ME
What would I do without You, Lord,
To help me every day
With all the simple little tasks
That come up on my way?
You do not think I'm silly
Because I'm old and weak.
You're always there to help me,
I only have to speak.
So, thank You, Lord, for being there
To help me when I call.
Thank You for every little thing.
I love You, Lord, for all.

Bernice Houston
I FOUND THE EAGLE'S NEST

I wish to dedicate "I Found The Eagle's Nest" to the Spirit of America, as symbolized in the poem.

I went out to find the white eagle.
To sit alone in its nest;
I'd see clear skies and cooling breezes,
And peacefulness at its best.

While there I would cleanse the saddened soul,
By viewing the scenes below;
I could peek at brown bear's honey bars,
And watch sparkling streams that flow.

I ran into a most handsome lion,
Whose search was almost the same;
But his dreams were of the lion's den,
So, what is there in a name?

In his den there was such calm and fun,
Which caused my feelings to reel;
I came back home, inspired thereafter,
Found WhiteEagle on my hill.

Nancy L Rojo
WITHOUT YOU

To Jim who's made my life worthwhile

Without you
My spirit is like a tree
Dead of winter.
I need your sunshine
Of love to renew my life.

Without you
My heart is heavy
Like a weary traveler.
I need your strong embrace
To lighten the troubles I face.

Without you
My world as I see
Grows dim & cold.

I need your warmth of laughter
To undo the chill.

I need you.
For without you,
I feel I am
Nothing.

Rex E Sheffield Sr
FREEDOMS WOE

This poem is dedicated, with Love and Thanks, to my wife Gail.

Freedom is sweet and so hard earned,
Yet, more than not, haughtily spurned.
Then they take it away from you,
And you learn its precious value.

Yet, still you do not learn,
Ever more you mock and spurn!
So now the Fates have had their fill,
Can you swallow their bitter pill?

You curse the Fates, a muted mutter,
Words sane mortals dare not utter!
By the gods, you are insane!
Their awesome power you disdain!

So now, their vengeance they shall wreak,
Until you fall, so humble and meek.
Then your freedom, so grudgingly granted,
Against your right, is obscenely slanted!

Can you see, with eyes opened wide,
The troubles gathered now at your side?
Now you hang your head so low,
Ever knowing, Freedoms Woe.

June McCue
CARE
C—is for comfort
A—is for arriving to the
realization that life still holds
a future when others have
gone
R—is for romantic truth that life
can go on forever
E—is for effort to show that they
are somebody

Barbara Feene Cox
FORGET THE DAY WHEN THE SUN WAS GONE
Forget the day when the sun was gone,
Forget the cold of the lonely night long,
Forget the tears that come pouring down,
Forget the dreams as they tumble down.

Remember only the laughter and joys
Of summer picnics and children's toys,
Of life and love and toil and play,
And hope they last for many a day.

For old and cold and lonely we get,
But Dear God don't let it happen, yet.

Cheryl A Potter
EMPTY HEART
If a bird cannot fly
Or a robbin can't sing
The flowers don't bloom
A bell doesn't ring

The stars don't twinkle
The rivers don't flow
The sun doesn't shine
A moon without glow

If a road has no end
Or a hand without touch
The air has no breeze
And alot isn't much

A mouth with no smile
Dark clouds high above
To imagine these things
Is a heart without love

Shahid Maqsood
SENSITIVITY
Your preference for tender love and kisses
Over making love to me
Let's start how you feel comfortable
It's fine with me
Hopefully we shall end
How I want you to be

Roy Webster

Roy Webster
VALENTINE'S DAY

To my children and friends, "Love is what makes the world go round and will make your life worthwhile" So start sending Valentines each year

Today is the day that starts many romances,
For Valentine's cards are cupid's advances
For those who are too timid to say
"I love you"—so a card's on the way.

A card all adorned with cupids and hearts,
Is often the way a real romance starts.
A valentine card may evoke just a smile,
But to someone its message may really beguile

And change the heart of man, or a maid,
Who up to now have been somewhat afraid
To express their tender feelings in speech
But find that a valentine card is the best way to reach
The heart and the mind of the one they admire,
The one whose love they seek to acquire.
So, folks send Valentine cards every year
And you're sure to bring someone a message of cheer.

Dawn Marie Palmiero
LOVE

This poem is dedicated to the one that I love, William Demarco, for his faith inspired me.

Love is gentle, love is kind
Love is you on my mind
Loving you I'll keep you from harm.
Love is you in my arms.
Love is eternal it never
fully dies
Though it may fade from nervous alibis.
Love is good times forgetting the bad
Fighting but loving when we
make eachother mad
All these definitions may be true,
But my definition of love is
simply you.

Sylvia Johnson
SYMBOLIC

To my husband Fred and all others who seek to not judge another by what seems to be.

Said Mrs. White to Mrs. Brown
"Have a cup of tea, but don't sit down.
First come to the window and see a sad sight,
Aren't my neighbors sheets a fright?
I stand by my window and gaze everyday
And her linen is always dingy and gray!"
"Why yes" said Mrs. Brown, "they do look gray,
But there's a good reason, why they look that way
Hand me that cloth and the window spray
And now I'll whisk the dirt away!
Now look at her linen, it's so bright and clean!
And I must tell you something, as we sip our tea.
The truth of the matter: (and sometimes truth hurts)
"Mrs. White you've been gazing through your very own dirt"
Thanks for the tea, but I must get on home,
I've a lot of deep cleaning to do of my own.

Micky Woldruff
TOLL BOOTH CROSSING
Approaching the toll booth I noticed to the right, an obscure narrow unpaved road.
On the gleaming highway to the left,
I was certain to find food and rest.
Though I had lost my direction and was unsure of which way to go.
"Good Evening Sir," he said to me as I slowed my car to the gate.
"Tell me in which direction do you wish to go?"
"To the left you travel for free and go on as you please, but to
the right you must pay the toll."
That's funny I said, it doesn't seem to me that many have traveled that road.
"Most find the cost too dear, for passage to the right will cost you all that you own."
"You will relinquish to me all your worldly possessions and walk the narrow road alone."
"A mere pittance for a soul," I laughed as I handed over all that I owned.
For in choosing the narrow road, I knew with the Lord I shall never walk it alone.

Anita L Bannerman
LITTLE THINGS
A fire on a chilly night
Lightning bugs and candlelight,
New books to read, a fresh baked pie
The clear blue autumn sky.

Hearing music soft and slow
Reading poems from long ago,
Smelling balsam warm with sun
Resting after day is done.

Life's so full of lovely things
Snowy winters, golden springs,
Friends to add that special touch
How can one heart hold so much.

Susan Wilkerson
SMALL BOYS

To my small boys, Seth & Micah Wilkerson.

They churn through the door.
Like foaming ocean they arrive.
Frothing, leaving lines
upon the sand of my day.
They rumble like the ocean,
talking, sharing, cajoling.
The flotsam and jetsam of their
passing lingers on after they depart.
I laugh, and savor the memory
of the sunshine on their waves.

Wendy Marie Joice
MADNESS
"God," I said, "Answer me this:"
What is the purpose of life?
What is the purpose of death?
Why are we here on this earth?
What does this prove?
And God slowly replied:
"It proves you can live in a world of
hate—
a world filled with pain.
A world filled with lies and
sadness.
A world where no matter how
hard you try, you will never
gain.
A world where people fight each
other.
Friend against friend, brother vs.
brother.
A world of selfishness—where
everyone only cares about
themselves and no other."

"But why?" I asked, "Why are we like this?
Change us, you can do that, you
can do anything,
remember . . . God?"
God was silent. He didn't reply.
I never heard from him again.

Rod M Zinkel
THE TEAR

For Wendy Preder, My friend, For whom more than a few tears were shed.

I have come into being.

Love made me
And love will kill me.
When I began,
It was recognition of emotion,
I had barely formed.
And my existence was not known
yet.
Happiness was stored in me,

It gave me strength.
Contentment made me special,
Unlike all other.

I am filled by empathy.
Future memories nourish me.
I am part of the soul.

Now heartache manifests me
Only for a moment
Then I fall.

Harold R Snider

Harold R Snider
BIBLE TRUTHS

I heard three good sermons preached yesterday,
The best I have heard for many a day.
Now, the first one I heard was based on God's law,
Telling us how to live and correct every flaw.

The second one was entitled "God's Gift to Mankind",
The most precious gift to all God could find.
When He gave His only Son's life on Calvary
To provide us his righteousness, and from sin set us free.

The third one was on "Why We Should Tithe"
Which always helps the believer to better survive.
As we go through this life in the path we have trod,
There is no way on earth we can outgive our God.

Now these three sermons hit me pretty hard
On so many things I highly regard.
And the message I received from all three
Was just what I needed to really help me.

For I know as a Christian we sometimes grow lax,
And need to be reminded of a few facts.
So we pay more attention to what we have heard,
Especially when it comes from God's Holy Word.

Kevin Boyce
THE SEASONS

For the late Mr. & Mrs. Connel Boyce

The roses bloom in summer
The pussy willow appear in autumn
The maple leaves a' hue in the fall
The roses bloom once more in summer

Katherine Nielsen Eckhart
HE STILLED MY LONELINESS

To my dear sister, Lota May Lawrence Heigel

God seems far away up there
behind the moon, stars, the constellations
Behold—one day some time ago
—the telling not fair?
He gave me a much wanted sister
dear sweet, talented—a sensation!
We had dolls, flowers, hills, gardens,
trees, birds and love;
All the criteria children need
for learning, security and sharing our love.
Our little family was happy
through the years.
We stood by each other, no matter
excitement, surprises, joys or tears.
Now we two sisters "hold the fort"
—Montana speech—
teaching many and sharing our love
while her husband, family and I hold
her very dear.

Mina Joe A Storie
SOMETIMES WHEN I AM FEELING GOOD

This poem is dedicated to my six children, Stanley Jr., Terry, Scott, Julie, Toby and Renee

Sometimes when I am feeling good,
Enjoying life the way I should,
I think of all the living things,
And all the joys that living brings.
I think of birds and butterflies,
Of summer days, and clear blue skies.
I think of all the pretty flowers,
And wish, and wish that I had hours,
To think of all the living things,
And all the joys that living brings.

Anne Norton
PERCHERONS IN THE VILLA BORGHESE

Your corded hocks like scissors flail
dry August grass beneath your hooves.
High as my head your shoulders glow
with sweat. So lighted I can guess
the joint and how it moves,
fed by the veins that rope your flanks.
Your origin I cannot guess, nor
where you go
carrying no gear and riderless.

Are two knights somewhere being dressed
in gorget, gauntlet, cuirass, cuisse,
to sit you ponderously from a hoist,
being too heavy for the leg-up mount?
And do you see no oddity in this
parade of strollers innocent of mail,
keeping no course? Can you dismiss
so easily these sojourners who seek
no Grail?

Evelyn H Vondran
TOO SHORT A CANDLE

To my parents Aloysius and Catherine (Dietzel) Vondran who kindled the flame

It flickers and spurts;
At times it appears to engulf
A world at rest,
With an idea that has come
It takes off and burns brightly
Enthusing those it touches.
Feeding from its inner supply,
It shows the way
And promises great things.
But, alas!
Too soon the flame is gone
To another world.
One last flicker
And life has ebbed its toll.
Now only the memory lingers
Of a once bright flame,
Of a life filled with promise—
Life holds the message:

It's too short a candle!

Charles E Eagle Jr
OR IS THIS JUST A DREAM

This poem is dedicated to my Father, for being there every time I needed you. I love you!

As I lie in bed at night
And try to sleep till morning's light
I toss and turn no rest in sight
And think about my dream

A dream to last throughout my years
To see me through my doubts and fears
A goal to reach with someone dear
Or is it just a dream

A dream that only I can dream
Though others try to guide me
A dream that is my source of light
Though some they may not see

What I dream is for peace to last
That sorrow and pain will someday pass
For my children to grow as I have grown
To know the joys that I have known
Or is this just a dream

As I reflect on what I have learned
I recall how my Father had tossed and turned
So many nights he could not sleep
Could he have dreamed this dream

Lisa Deutsch
TWO DIFFERENT PEOPLE

When I look at you,
I see your blonde hair,
Your blue eyes and
Your gorgeous smile.
I envy you from afar.
I know we could never be together,
'Cause we're two different people,
That are not the same at all.
We come from two different worlds:
You have your friends
And I have mine.
Every time I see you,
It hurts because I know,
We weren't made for each other.
Somehow I know it wouldn't work out.
I wish to God things were different.
But things are as they are.
Nothing can change that.
Maybe someday,
But not now.

Sandra J Lopez
GREEN TURQUOISE SKY

To my wonderful parents, Dolores and Diego Lopez. Thank you for everything, I love you both very much. "Keep your spirits up"

Clear icy rain at my feet
Keeping the grounds so the grass will be green
Frigid morning air freezes into the flaming sun
As the splint of midnight leaves a crystal trail
The start of the day takes in nuclear fuels to wake
Dawn ridden wind sweeps away yesterday
Grey clouds gloom in faint glows
In nature's care flowers will bloom
The sun will be nailed back up again soon
White clouds will roam overhead
Painting a pleasant scene high
Turning the dreariness into wondrous
Green turquoise skies

Leslie Ann Nylen
COLDNESS CAME TO ME

To All The World With Love

In the autumn's early mourn
Trees shaken their leaves down
Howlings and whispers
Tossle the limbs
A windstorm confused
In its whirls
Tongues poison truths
And its fidelity.
A pledge of faithfulness
In the trees loyalty of standing
In observance of its duty
Leaflets in spring grow to nurture
Falls in the fall to the ground
For snow will be coming
In honorary remembrance

We shall rake the leaves
And burn them once more
For the seasons tumble galore
It shall be warm for awhile
Again in the autumn's early mourn
Coldness came to me

Hisana Afzal
THE LIGHT THAT NEVER GOES OUT

This poem shall be dedicated to Martin Gore, David Gahan, Alan Wilder, Andrew Fletcher, Morrissey, and to the memory of THE SMITHS.

Earthquake horror, thousands die
Trains collide and the dead here lie
Passenger jet bombed from sky

Alcoholic shoots his wife
Boy fourteen killed with knife
Some people have no respect for life

The malicious stare in people's eyes
Looking down on others despite their size
Racist murders, figures rise

It all seems so hopeless
It makes me want to give up
But when time has come amidst the chaos
We must remember that

There is a light that never goes out
And that is the way for the hallowed devout

In war-torn lands not far away

Annihilation is the common goal each day
As the innocent continue to pray

The hapless nations where famines blaze
Relief may come soon, prime minister says
The drought-struck land encompassed by morbid haze

The blind lead the blind in search of fame
As the story goes on, it is still the same
Hope alone won't remove their shame

It all seems so monotonous
It makes me want to give up
But when time has come amidst the confusion
We must remember that

There is a light that never goes out
And that is the thing we must never doubt

Norma C Rinie
MYSELF
Myself is there beside me now.
It was, when I could not abide
The many things inside me hides.
Myself is one so deep I keep
For those I cherish most of me.
It is the part that even they,
Of wisdom, help, assay or faith,
Can not for certain know Myself.
Myself is one of God, man, perplexity,
One of many, many in one.
Myself is often far aside
And wished it were of one quiet sound.
However Myself may go or say,
It is the best of all that may.

Margaret C Sampson
SPREAD A LITTLE SUNSHINE

To Aunt Clara Call

Spread a little sunshine
Everywhere you go.
Spread it everywhere
and God will know.

Spread it by the wayside
For a Stranger to enjoy.
Spread it in the Church yard
for every girl and boy.

Spread it on the flowers
and watch it reappear.
Spread it on your garden
and plant it every year.

For God Sent the rain
and the sunshine.
He did sow and spread.
For every little sunbeam
There's a little gold thread.

Laine Shamblin
MY ANGEL

To my loving family, and dearest friends, To L.L.: Who gave me support and love.

Cry no more Angel of life—
You walked down that path with pride.
The world you carried upon your shoulders—
Became such a heavy, heavy boulder.

The stones were thrown each one—
No direction of blame.
You pondered only in times of need—
Crying inside, tears full of greed.

You met the world the way you walked—
Tenderly you pondered silly little thoughts.
It all became just and fine, to those—
Even quietly as you strolled.

No more Angel, do you have to fear—
Those knights with their meek little spears.
No shining armour or a great white horse—
The fantasy you dreamed, you mostly lost.
The time has come to end the dreams of untruths—
So we'll cry no more my Angel, the love of my life—
Tomorrow will be yours as the universe shines so bright.

Hazel Whipple
WHEN I WAS A CHILD
When I was a child I loved the sea;
It symbolized strength untold.
The power of those surging waves
Was marvelous to behold.

When I was a child I loved the hills;
They symbolized majesty
Against an ever changing sky.
They astounded me.

I can't believe it came about these marvelous things
Without some mind to guide;
Then suddenly a spirit stirred within me
There is a God who made these things.

Rita Tritch
TIME
The clock does seem to tell us
Without a lot of trying, we simply
Have to use it wise this element
Called time.
For we cannot change it, however
Hard we try.
It's never claimed, nor thus
Regained the seconds that's
Gone by.

Fumi Migimoto
HAPPY 1989
For a year that's highly blessed
With nothing but the best
In terms of life and health
And all the worldly wealth

It's time to take some action
To make a resolution:

The Road to Success has a steep incline
Proceed with caution onward, upward
It may be rough but don't repine

Accept the challenge; don't decline
To seize any opportunity:
Take action now, to rise and shine
Time is precious; don't delay
Or sit back to fret and whine

As you reach your goal, you'll outshine
The sun atop the blessed path

SUCCESS IS ATTAINABLE . . . how divine!
in 1989

Alice Falkner

Alice Falkner
LITTLE FRIENDS
What are friends for,
Except to love, play with and adore.
I have a friend who likes to play with trains
And another who likes to walk in mud puddles after it rains.
Some friends like to play football and baseball
And others play with dolls and baby buggies, but that's not all.
They even like to climb up in tree houses real high
And some girls and boys like to fly kites 'way up in the sky.
My friends are such nice little playmates,
We get out our games, bicycles and skates.
Like I said in the beginning, what are friends for,
Except to love, play with and adore.

Traci Teague
AWAIT
As I await for the telephone to ring,
I listen to my musicbox sing;
As I watch the rains fall from the sky
Pitter patter on the wet streets,
I feel I have not talked to you in weeks;
As a tear rolls down from my eye,
the rains fall harder from the sky.

As I await for you my soul just tires,
The flames die from the fire;
The flames are burning out,
as I sit and pout;
As for I still await for the telephone to ring,
And listen to my musicbox sing.

Doris Minor
ETERNAL ROSE

To my Mother Mrs Doris Minor, the sweetest rose Jehovah God ever gave her children, Love, Sharon—Sarah—Celeste and Dick.

While walking through life's garden
I spied a rose so fair
So delicate—so lovely
Its perfume filled the air
With care I clipped this lovely flower
I'd take it home with me
I'd place it in a crystal vase
For all the world to see

Oh how I loved this lovely rose
What happiness it gave
Alas the petals withered
There was no way to save
Remembering all your fragrance
Till time took you away
Again I'll find my lovely rose
In Paradise someday.

Denise M Brady
WE BECKON FOR THE MORNING LARK
We beckon for the Morning Lark
To spread its faithful wings across the breeze
With song in heart; feather in flight
We watch this graceful bird glide gleefully through the courtyard
Soaring on a plane only our spirits can comprehend
Mortally we stand
We gaze up to catch the fragments of a dream
Drift lazily down to a world of concrete and gravity
Stare down at our lives a while longer, Morning Lark
In your freedom, stare down at our lives so we can dream
Like feathers caught in hot, summer tar
We can dream

Verna S Shellenberger
EACH DAY

Dedicated to bowling friends, Bill Dreisbach and George Boettcher

Each day when you begin;
Each thought you wish to share
Could be a peaceful thought
If God is there.

Each day when you begin;
Each deed you wish to share
Will illustrate with kindness
Your tender thought and care.

D J Bynum
REMEMBRANCE
I close my eyes and remember
One night not too long ago.
How we came and we touched
Each other's lives
And then we had to let go.
Each to our own way of living.
To obligations that each of us had.
Though now the miles may part us,
We cannot feel very sad.
The time that we had was special.
The memories are special, too.
And for all that you have given, dear friend,
I want to say "Thank you."

Stephen M Mora
MY STORY

To my children, Michelle, Lynelle, Anjanette, Stephen; my grandson Paris, and to the ladies in my life and to Elaine K., the dearest lady of them all.

I traveled many oceans, since
mountain high . . .
The Pacific, Atlantic, to China Sea,
into history in ancient seas . . .
That used to be.
Set foot in these lands of pages I
read, and remembered the
many dead of pages read.
Ruins of times before, old
customs, ancient lore still
standin,
fallen broken . . . from before.
In a country, in a country of
christian seat . . .

The hushed shuffle of their feet.
Walked the path He took . . .
weight He held upon His back,
to a hill . . . by and by!
Stood on Olive Hill to see the City
of so much pity . . . this Ancient
City.
These eyes seen beauty abound,
this heart has felt warmth
before.
This body has helped in birth of
four . . . no more!
Known a lady, two or more; loved,
I felt to be true.
These traveled eyes, traveled
heart, given a new start.
For once, I feel gentle comfort,
peace, warmth . . . . . .
Amore . . .Amore . . .Amore . . .

Charles H Johnson
ODE TO A GASTRIC TUBE

In memory of my stay in Parkview Community Hospital, Riverside, CA.—September 23 to October 10, 1985.

They put the darn thing down
through your nose,
Into your stomach, that's where it
goes!

To put it down dry makes it worse
yet.
Ask an old-timer . . . put it down
wet!

The clear plastic tube out of my
nose,
May look small to you . . . to me it's
a hose!

The stuff that comes out, easy to see,
It's all in motion, just like T.V.

Of course you can't talk, easy that is,
So please do not ask Trivia Quiz!

To swallow is bad, so you just spit,
To put up with this sure does take
grit!

And ere it comes out, you must pass
gas,
And not through your nose but out of
your ass!

There's one thing in life, you soon
get smart,
Relief is obtained when you first
fart!

Patricia Swisher
SEARCHING

To my beloved husband Bill, who encouraged and inspired me.

Up above and far away, is a place I
want to go.
I have searched my whole life thru,
looking high and looking low.
Can it be I do not see? can it be
inside of me?

My eyes just opened and now I see,
the beauty hiding inside of me.
The time has come for me to live, the
world and life has much to give.
So out I go to join life's stream and
be part of what I dream.
It's strange and new, I sometimes
fear, but the god with-in is always
near.
No time to doubt or hesitate, if I
pause now I might be late.
So watch me soar and let me fly, I
believe you must live before you
may die.

I heard the stars singing, I felt the
flowers cry.
You may know these things if you
only try.

I saw time moving forward, I
touched truth on its face.
I stepped upward and outside, into a
new place.

Erselia Montecello Barton

Erselia Montecello Barton
THE HELLION

To my husband Prof. Thomas F Barton Sr. internationally known for his many articles and books in the field of Geography, and my son dedicated to his work in human suffering is equally important to me.

How bold and cocksure I was then
In budding youth. I could not stand
Advice from father, brother or kind
friend,
Nor from a loving mother, or firm
sister's hand.
Why bother with people and such
trivial stuff
As hard-work and high-thinking-
philosophy
When money and pleasant living are
good enough?
Live while you are young, yes that is
for me!

But now, as life goes spinning by
And joints creek painfully in the
cold,
I look for love and trust in children's
eyes—
As regretfully my wasted past
unfold.
Yet—I get some pleasure in my
arthritic end
To recall the hellion I have been.

LaVone B Holt
THE FUGITIVE

We had not known how wild the
storm would be
Nor realized our timid hound would
flee
When lightning triggered a closed
door, and he
All-swift was free.

We called him, but he ran the other
way
Now wayward, knowing well that he
should stay
Yet urged by unknown demons of
the night
As he took flight.

Down roads rain-slick, through bolts
of thundering flame
His fear impelled him, drowning out
his name.
Down miles of highway, mindless,
far from home
He chose to roam.

Despairing, numb, we tried to track
his trail
Sure we had lost him, certain we
would fail;
Pursuing clues down muddy path
and lane,
We shared his pain.

We found him, finally, shadowy and
thin,
Content to follow, quieted within,
His wild adventure ended. Now I see
How much like me!

Virginia Dare Casteel
GIFT OF COLOR AND CHEER

Whoit! Cheer! Cheer! Cheer!
Wakens me in early dawn.
Purty! Sweet! Cheer! Cheer!
sing the Cardinals loud and clear
on my snowy lawn.

Against the gray sky,
amid the snow covered trees
the fiery birds fly
and their proud whistles echoe
their mates' subdued cries.

The vibrant music
and striking Winter display
is a gift of magic
brightening my drab wintry day
with color and cheer.

Gwenodine E Uber
A FRIEND

I am dedicating this poem to a dear friend, Lillian Sowl Chase, who passed away recently.

A Friend is like the sparkling dew
On the Rose at Dawn,
Refreshing where e'er you meet her
As through life you go along.

A Friend is like a precious gem
That always takes your eye,
And you thrill each time you see her
Even though you hurry by.

A Friend is part of God's Spirit
Sent down to earth from above;
Sharing each joy and sorrow,
And doing each kind deed in love.

A Friend reflects the sweetness
Of all nature in her smile.
If she's your Friend, you really know
It's Friends that make life worth-
while.

Suzanne du Vair
UNTITLED

Sink in Roses
And Heather gloom
Defunct logic
And Weather doom
Dollars don't undo
Assault from fleshly mire
You built in yourself
Archaic funeral pyre
Your fingers wrap the candle
Attempt to cradle the flame
Seeker, the Souls of others
Are more of just-the-same
Your black cloak protects
Against the winds of Bore
Your mind wracks yellowed pages
Of Infinite Wisdom yore
Yet no answer do you find
In spite of all to be
In depths you sink in Roses
While asking God to tea.

Esta Groesser Bourgoin
SKI

You start up the lift without a care,
You love the breeze blowing through
your hair.
The sun puts a glare on the snow
below,
It will be great skiing this you know.

You look down at the skiers as they
ski by,
You look back at the lodge as you
climb high.
Now you're nearing the top you're
there at last,
You ski out of your chair as it goes
past.

With poles in your hands off you go,
Gliding over the hillside covered
with snow.
You think this great as you pick up
speed,
You pass others by now you're in the
lead.

You feel light on your feet as you ski
on,
Now you're nearing the bottom,
where's the hill gone?
You feel like you're racing and you
know you've won,
You realize you've just completed
your first run.

You're waiting in line to ride up
once more,
That was a fast run that's for sure.
So the biggest run this time you want
to ski,
Because someday a champion you
want to be.

Before you know it it's time to quit,
You realize you didn't have a chance
to sit.
You look at the mountain before you
head home,
You watch it cast shadows all its
own.

It's almost as if it's begging you to
stay,
So you promise you'll be back the
very next day.
It grows dark and chilly as it closes
its door,
You whisper good good night as you
leave its floor.

Wayne S Bryant
OFF THE WALL

Popped up in my room; from a book
cover,
her nakedness was full; she said "I'm
not your lover."
Went into a church, to marry my
wonder;
disappeared again; and still it makes
me ponder.
The man is in his soul; and power
does he show;
Amazing as it seems, I had nowhere
to go.
Lying in my bed; he came into my
room,
but then the saints were there;
amazing, comfort, care.
Don't know what I did, I guess I did
it all,
Waiting for hell's fire; I saw it on the
wall.

Thou hell was long ago; a place the Evil goes;
Reality it seems, is just a dream away,
The visions were so many; they took all my love,
And then he gave me plenty, he flies like a dove.
If Jesus Christ were here, I'd kiss his feet again
But only God knows, when he'll come again

John Buld
SALOME

For Tonya

I saw Salome
dance
Under the gaze
of her loves.
And—under the guise
of dancing.
Under the gauze :
her limbs
Played everlasting
dreams.

In candelabra blaze,
in beads of
golden wax—
They pulled like the
oxen, candles.
Salome
never ended.

Joyce Keller Moore

Joyce Keller Moore
BEING STILL

This poem is dedicated to the Son of God—My Jesus—For as a child of the King of Kings and Lord of Lords, never in all my life has He not met my every need.

What shall we do when nothing seems to work for us—
One thing is for sure there is no need to get anxious, worry, or fuss.

What do we do when we find ourselves in a valley of woe
When we have little results—when we are at an all time low—

We pray and pray—and then—pray more—
But God seems far away—our knees are sore—
From kneeling day and night on our bed-side floor.

"Be Still And Know That He Is God" is really all we need to say—
And when we get still and quiet He not only will teach us to pray
But He will be in our trouble with us each and every step of the way.

His Word promises we won't have to endure more than we can stand
But with each trial and temptation we'll always feel His guiding Hand.

He also says in His Word however hurting our heartache
Never, never one of His own will He leave or forsake.

So take heart, dear one, look up—
And He will set you free.
No longer will you be overcome—
But His deliverance you'll know and see.

J Guy Kinser
LUNAR ECLIPSE
We walked on the moon today
Sassy and sure footed—
What will Celene say?
She was not there to greet us
At the temple radiant
In her silver nimbus—
Will she weep when she discovers
Foot prints in the sacred dust
Four thousand years betrayed
So true a trust?
Even yet
Will she throw her kiss to lovers
In the hope that love still covers
Pools of blood?
Does she care?
We hid in the garden tonight
Afraid and naked
To see if she was there—
And watched as red moonbeams
Breathed the air!

James E Carver
RECIFE, PERNAMBUCO
Reminiscing of breezes past, palms of hands then,
Extending of heart thoughts and life, with the music
Circulating in dances' undertoe, alone
I sift the trees, wind, waves, and people, the desire
Frothed in luxury less now a dream than burden.
Existential writers rear their ugly words, pick
Essentials apart, looming micro-scopically, bone
On blood on bygone. Tropically mesmerized, higher
Love sunburned by passion, aches pour till sullen
Intensity takes cracked promises, tries to lick
Numbness in and tan to toughness' beauty the tone.
Delicate the dedication to self, liar
Always poised to vocalize the summer that's been.

Ann M Henderson
I LONG FOR SPRING TO COME
I long for Spring to come.
The barren, winter months have possession of my soul.
I hear the frigid winds bellow in the night,
I watch as the naked trees shiver.
Spring rouses the dead! I long for Spring to come!

I long for Spring to come.
Its renaissance kindles the solemnity of winter.
I love the candor of Spring's first tulips,
their flamboyancy lifts the pallor.
Spring awakens the living! I long for Spring to come!

I long for Spring to come.
The sun thaws the icy streams, melts the ice from my soul.
I feel the cheer in Spring birds' chatter,
I gladden with every rose blossom!
Spring rouses the dead! Spring awakens the living!
I long for Spring to come!

D A Norton
YOU'LL NEVER KNOW
Overflowing with love and affection
waiting to give you my all, but
you'll never know.

During sadness and of course times of joy
I'm willing to be that shield and shoulder, but
you'll never know.

Sharing my thoughts and ideas from deep inside
dreams that we can make happen, but
you'll never know.

Cold nights and summer days
we find there's love deeper than before, but
you'll never know.

Take a chance, I promise not to fail
my words are true and my love is too, but
you'll never know.

Angela M Fasolo
JENNIFER

Dedicated to my great-niece Jennifer Anne Zurek who played Cinderella in a play when she graduated from pre-school. Her mother, Julianna made her aqua gown.

Jennifer, so sweet and precious
In her aqua flowing gown,
Is a lady who expresses
Forever a love unknown,
For she is a princess
In all the splendor of grace,
And then, what does one say
Of Jennifer, so fair of face.

Antonietta R Carroll
WHEN YOU COME NEAR ME I FEEL THE WARMTH OF YOUR SOUL

This poem is dedicated to these people that have touched my soul whether big or small: Brent, Don, JoAnne, Frank, Charlene, John D., Tom G., Jean, Jack, Deidre, Debra, Samuel, Ruby, Walter, Kathy M., Terry O., and Eugene.

When you come near me I feel the warmth of your soul,
As our bodies entangle, and our world together, begins
to unfold . . .
Our passions collide into a cosmic bond,
With such thunder and fury, we fight to hold on.
And although we are now one, we are actually two,
As we both feel the sensations of our lovemaking, reach the very core, through and through.
And even now that we have reached our highest peak,
and we can go no more,
We are still drenched in an endless intoxication of ecstasy that is so hard to endure.

Natalie Norris
LAUGHTER
Laughter's like a spring of joy
Bubbling forth in merriment—
Dancing upon the lips—
Gushing from the spirit.

Laughter's like a spring of water—
Joyous sounds like music—
Pure and beautiful as a gurgling brook
O'er the rocks—o'er the rocks of life.

Laughter's the sound of joy
That the Light of God brings forth.
Showing happiness within
That surfaces with smiles.

Comedy on the other hand
Is closer to the earthly land—
Fun and frolic bring it out
But more often like a shout.

Not the same delightful thing
That true joyousness can bring.
If all the world would laugh and sing
The gates of Heaven would open swing.

Margaret Shirley
I AM AN ISLAND
Other people have nice homes and drive waxed cars
They drive to church on Sundays
wearing
Dresses and suits, even hats and nice shoes
They wear white, and it never gets dirty . . .
They never look past thirty

I want to be like them
but
I am an island.
I see the sun, and shake the wind
I climb the stars and my clothes
get dirty and worn along the way . . .
but I am free,
Is this not me?

Carol Joyce Patterson
A SONG CAME

For my Children, patient with my listening

A song came
and it left,
leaving behind it
a stillness.
There was stillness
before,
but not the same.
Before the song came
it was not Known
there was a need for it,
or a yearning for the sound
and the feeling
that came with it.

So
a love came
and it left.

Cynthia Astra Richter
MY FIFER BOY
My Fifer Boy,
Hanging on Living Room wall,
You're not so tall,
But, how nimbly your fingers fly over your fifer,
How expertly you blow into its holes,
The Breath of freedom, naivete issue forth,
Exhilarating me.

How I envy your youth,
Your appled cheeks
The peach fuzz on your forelip
Your dark eyes dancing with your tunes,
How I wish I were ten, like you,
Again.

What momentous battle did you lead your regiment into?
What lilting air did you play to rouse its martial spirit?
Did you ennoble La Belle France?

Your parents, too?
though humble of birth, you moved their earth.

My Fifer Boy hanging on Living Room wall,
If thou could tell thy innermost thoughts
My heart it would gladden.

Lorraine Caroline Fellows
TRAINS
I love to watch the trains go by
And hear the whistles blow,
To dream of faraway places,
Where someday I may go.

The cities and the farmlands,
The valleys and the streams,
Appear to me so vividly
In all my childhood dreams.

I love to watch the trains go by
And hear the engines roar,
And listen to the rumble,
As they pass swiftly by my door.

Betty Watson
A FRIEND
A friend can be much closer
Than a sister or a brother
It's a special kind of closeness
That you have for each other

Someone who wants to cheer you up
When you are feeling sad
And always wants to help you out
When things are going bad

Someone who knows the words to say
When you are feeling low
For no reason at all they'll call you up
Just to say hello

They listen to all your troubles
Good advice they can supply
And your hurt seems to be their own
'Cause they cry when you cry

Yes we all need that special friend
To share each passing day
And I feel that I am truly blessed
That God sent you my way

Brenda H Thurman
GARDENER'S QUEST

To Peggy and Kimberly: Happy Mother's Day

God blessed the girl child:
Instilling a special need.
Designating her a gardener;
But giving her no seed.

Through the years she waited.
Others' gardens, she cultivated.
Pulling weeds—nurturing young seeds . . .
Bringing forth the best yield
From each and every hill.

Faithful: always toiling;
But never reaping.
Her quest: to quench this burning need,
To find her own garden, her very own seed.

Finally after such a long while,
"Your worth is proved," God said with a smile.
He led her to a grossly neglected bower.
Abundant weeds choking the one small, struggling flower.
Plucking the plant with her gardener's hand,
She transplanted it to her own home land.

Nourished by her tender, loving care,
The plant blossomed in the fresh air.
The goal achieved . . . her gardener's need
Was now blessed with her very own seed.

Vanessa sue Rakhshani
THE HUMAN SPIRIT
The human spirit is wondrous indeed.
Men have killed and been killed
trying to possess it. The human spirit
cannot be bought or sold. The most
one can hope for is incarceration that
only exists for a brief second in time.
The human spirit is unique, one of a
kind.
You can tie the hands of man, blind
him so that he cannot see. You can
beat him
in hope that he will not leave.
You can take everything that is dear
to him. But in the end if he dies his
spirit will soar like an eagle in
the open sky.

Jill Finch Verra
MOLLY

To my family: A loving remembrance

My years with Aunt Molly most fond
Were those spent on One Hundred Acre Pond
Nature walks—girl talk
First crop of corn—my babies born,
Garden, flowers
Peaceful . . . quiet . . . listening hours
Always a guiding hand
Or a special project planned
None could compare; no one—
Anywhere!
She taught us all what it is meant to be
Yes . . . a real meaning of family
I was privileged to know her
We had our time
All others she's touched
Simply . . . uniquely . . . divine.
We've cried our tears and said goodbye
She's gone now, not to hurt us
Only moved on for a greater purpose
Yes, she will be missed . . . this is true,
But for me, she will always be . . .
Wonderful Aunt Molly.

Milton Evans
AN OLD ORDINARY TREE

To: Tessie L. Briggs, the most precious to me

Just an old ordinary tree brings back a thought of yester years gone by:

The thought of a wooden cross, and the feelings of people then.

How could they have been so cruel as to crucify my Lord! If we only knew exactly what was on their minds at that time maybe we could do something now.

Actors can perform, and actresses can show real charm, . . . but what about the true reality—they crucified my Lord!

Today an old ordinary tree standing tall before an old ordinary church building where people just go and worship, only to wait impatiently for the service to end, and still today they are crucifying my Lord with hate of each other instead of love.

That old ordinary tree can't remember and that old ordinary church is filled with echoes from year to year; false and insincere hearts.

People are continually crucifying my Lord.

When will it ever end?

Janine Luzania
THE TEARS ARE FALLING ONCE AGAIN
The river which flows
From my eyes
Leaves a salty stain,
And stings the raw wounds
Left on my heart.
It aches for love to heal it.

Lay your hands on my soul
And caress the pain away.
Take the pain out
And replenish with care,
And re-heal my heart.

Clear the doubts in my mind
By removing all the dusty webs.
Extinguish the fiery flame
Which is erupting beneath.
Take my hand—
And just show me you care.

J W Butler
I CAN'T

This poem is dedicated to Joyce, my friend and my only love.

I once knew a man who always said I can't
When I asked the man to think about what he was going to do with his life, the man would simply reply, I can't.
When I asked him to try harder to succeed,
He would once again reply I can't.
Then I told him he had to trust people and just forget about his failures, and to my displeasure he stated I can't.
Dig deep in your head I would say.
He replied, "I can't, I just can't!"
Then one day he looked at me and cried.
"I can and I will."
I was very pleased at this change of mind.
You see I knew that man very well.
That man was me.

Rita D'Elia
WHO IS GOD . . . . I DO NOT KNOW
Who is God . . . . I do not know
What is Faith . . . and does it show
What is religion . . . where did it go
What is death . . . the unknown fear
Talk not such things unpleasant to hear

What is wrong and what is right
If we love, why do we fight
What is alive or merely living
Are human beings so unforgiving

What is real . . and what is not
We all must think and think a lot
What are values . . .are yours like mine
Why do they differ in space and time

Why do we think the way that we do
Why is it that I don't think like you
For all these questions we do not know
Who has the answers . . . to whom do we go?

Bertha Coleman Downs

Bertha Coleman Downs
I AM A BLACK WOMAN
I am a Black woman brought to this country on a ship.
As a slave I worked with my baby perched on my hip.
Then I was set free.
Free to be me.

I worked in the fields from can until can't.
I have cause to be bitter, but I ain't.
Thru the years, we women went from field workers to teachers.
Our men were field workers and preachers.
I know a mind is a terrible thing to waste.
When it comes to education I have only had a taste.
I am a black woman so full of pride.
Pride that shines from deep inside.
I say to those who comes after me.
We must keep moving can't you see?
I did at the time what could be done.
Now I pass you the baton.

Joan Faulkner
LOVE HAS NO DEFINITION
Love has no definition
On paper, marble or stone.
Even God's Great Ten Commandments
Fail to teach that which is born.

I know now that which is born in me,
Not created, shaped or formed
But with the beauty of an unborn baby's love
And the pain of the birthing scorn.

The love I have for you my dear
Is not a premonition.
I know no words to speak to you.
Love has no definition.

Paris Miller
ALWAYS WANT
They always want whatever they can get,
No matter who falls into the net.
The chase is better than the catch,
Once you're caught, you're unlatched.
If you let them go too fast,
You're never ever gonna last,
If you make them wait too long,

It's later days, and so-long.
All they want is just a piece,
So they can have their greedy feast.
Just when you start to begin to trust,
It all ends up turning to dust.
All you want is a beautiful romance,
And decide to maybe take that chance.
And just when you think everything's fine,
You find out he's just wasting your time.
You picture who you want in your mind's-eye,
And think you finally found the right guy.
For him, you feel such a burning flame,
Come to find out, it's all just a game.

Christine Koehne
EARLY DAYS

For Gussie and Robert Glenn Moore, my two favorite poets. Thank you. Forever yours. Christine

'Tis a pleasure to recall them
howe'er distant they may seem.
When laughing hours were passing,
like objects in a dream.
And the words that uttered, their meaning so sincere.
And our joy was turned to sadness
with a falling of a tear.
Early days and early pleasure, their visions often come
And are kept as household treasures
in the heart deep silent home.

Mary A West
A DAY TO REMEMBER— APRIL 10TH 1964

This poem is dedicated to the families and friends.

It all began one early dawn,
that caused the world to deeply mourn.
A mighty submarine the "Thresher,"
Whose hull gave way to the ocean's pressure.
What happened down in the ocean below?
Only the men on the sub will know,
and they are asleep in the deep.
We must believe that it was not in vain,
to leave so many in sorrow and pain.
The pieces that remain are few,
Compared to the lives that must begin anew.
And they and the world will a long time weep,
While their loved ones remain asleep in the deep.
Though the ocean has claimed these husbands and sons,
Their souls are up there, high above the sun.

Ms Julie A St Sauver
NIGHT CREATURES' SYMPHONY

The stars in the firmament above
Strewn by the hand of the creator
Appear to wink and blink at me as they
Form a stage "Backdrop" for God's theatre.
The curtain's up for all to see & hear
The show's now underway for me, the walker.

It's pleasant to take my dog out by night
To look & listen for all the "night things."
There are countless numbers of fire flies—
An intermittent glow on silent wings,
Suggesting the boundaries of nearby woods
The home for many a nightingale, who sings.

Strong staccato voices of cicadas
Blending so well in nature's own fashion
With the chirping of the unseen crickets
Rubbing their wings in a frenzied passion
Fast, maybe slow, depending on the temp—
Interesting method of expression.

Just as I sort out the sounds I've heard
A night owl perched in a nearby tree
Lends to the concert a "who who" or two
As if the invisible maestro did see
A need for this added musical touch
To complete the night creature's symphony.

Alice Winters
ODE TO AN ICICLE

Oh there you hang, with your icy finger.
You're like a spear
Why do you linger?

You're on the shrubs
And on the trees,
You just hang there, and freeze and freeze.

You're on all the fences
Even on the park benches.
You cover all the traffic lights.
You hang there days, you hang there nights.

Please don't fall upon my head
You fill me with an awful dread
Won't you ever go away
And let us have a decent day?

John R Scally
MY LIBERTY

To my dear wife, Marie, for her inspiration and devotion.

I looked up at the Lady there,
standing high above the sea.
She wore a crown upon her head,
and held a torch to welcome me.

I had longed to know this Lady,
She was all I wished for me.
She stood for hope and freedom,
and my dream of liberty.

We know God created Paradise,
but, He did not tell us where.
Now I look around realize,
that it must be somewhere here.

As I journeyed past the lakes and rivers,
and then across the prairie wide.
To wander through majestic mountains,
I knew that God was at my side.

This was the land that He created,
This was his jewel, His pride and joy.
It was the Paradise I'd hoped for,
and dreamed of since I was a boy.

Leeuna McNeese
THE OAK AND THE WILLOW

Once there was a mighty Oak
Standing tall and proud,
He saw the humble Willow tree
And began to laugh out loud.

"Why must you bend and weep,"
cried he
"Why do you not stand tall?
I am very strong and proud
Nothing shall make me fall!"

One day a powerful wind blew up
The Oak came crashing down,
The Willow swayed and wept and bent
But somehow stood his ground.

When the storm was over
The Willow tree bent down,
To touch the mighty Oak tree
That lay upon the ground.

"Oh you foolish tree," he cried
Was pride your greatest friend?
Didn't you know that even the strong
Must sometimes weep and bend!"

Alta McLain
THE PRAISE

When pilgrims signed their Compact
And anchored in the Bay,
They blessed the God of Heaven,
Who brought them all the way.
They, and those who followed,
Who from persecution fled,
Established a Republic
On what the Bible said.

It taught them law and order,
And patience with each other,
And so, each Indian they met
Was treated as a brother.
They planned their first Thanksgiving,
A feast that lasted days,
Then lifted eyes to Heaven,
And gave to God the praise.

Barbara Pirard
TODAY IS AN ODE TO SUMMER

today is an
Ode to Summer
the sky is blue
the sun is bright
a soft breeze is blowing
from the ocean
the day is young and long
with carefree dirty toes
and dusty feet
shorts and ponytails
ice cream cones
and sodas
and sprinklers
throwing water into the air
splashing cheerfully

Terry L Gardner
CHOPIN, BEETHOVEN, MOZART AND BACH

Let's play Chopin, Beethoven, Mozart and Bach,
Then get up and talk and go out for a walk.
Let's talk about people and music and things,
And the beautiful happenings that love brings.

Tell me all about you and your philosophy,
The way you see the world, the way you see me.
And when you're through, over and done,
Let it be said we had lots of fun.

Just two friends walking along,
Without any cares just singing a song.

Samantha A Beard
TIME

To Anyone who has ever experienced an endless, timeless love.

Time is an essence—
elusive, not to be held,
no matter how hard or
tightly we try . . .

Like the fragrance of a rose—
it exists, drifts on the winds,
and moves on

It is the sand poured thru
waiting hands,
only to slip thru the fingers,
and continue on its way . . .

It is the fowl in autumn flight,
it follows unseen patterns,
always leading onward . . .

Over the next mountain,
across the next river—
to the distant stars . . .

Ever changing—yet seeming the same,
stopping not, even unto death . . .

Trish Ketcherside
DREAMS OF LOVE

I want to know
Can Love be real?
Is it imagined
By those who need to feel?

Are there such things
As ecstasy and paradise?
Are they as real
As the pain and the lies?

I know in my dreams
I can feel them
Visions so clear
Of me and him

We walk along
The sands of time
Speaking the languages
Of love and rhyme

Soon I wake up
So cold and alone
Dreams of love
Have come and gone

Brandi L Arnhold
EVENING WINE

To Mom, and especially Ron—my real Dad, who really believed I could.

The silent promises of you and I
have yet to be revealed
Time has brought us once again
to a lovers field
A gentle wind caresses a flower
like your hand on my skin
I feel the closeness of your heat
as our Love begins
The presence of your lips
oh so close to mine
Taste just like the sweetness
of our Evening Wine
You give me a happiness
no one can perceive
And forever I'll regret
the day I have to leave.

Carol Donnenwirth
THE MORNING COMES

The morning comes,
Soft as velvet
Colors muted pink and mauve and azure.
Quietly she comes
Nascent from the east.
Over the prairies she slowly rises
Stretches wide her arms
Opens up her mind
Ready to accept each imperfect being.
A new day beginning
All in past forgiven.
Morning comes to heal all past wounds.

Dedrick Mashegoanyane Mogoru

Dedrick Mashegoanyane Mogoru
THE NEVER-TO-BE-KNOWN CHARACTER

I am called the street urchin,
One amongst many in Bogota;
In all respects like your own children,
Yet deprived of share in human order:

I'm shunned and spurned by all;
But I know I shall live to pay you!
In rags you shall see me grow tall,
And I'm afraid you'll never see my nature true . . .
For it's being now frozen by this your daily scorn,
Yes, Someone foreign is being begotten in me . . .
And Woe is you on the day he is born!

He will terrify you by night!
Make your laws of null effect! !
And . . . and, darken your ways in broad daylight! ! ! !
That day . . . , please treat him with respect . . .
Don't be too harsh on him,—
He's your creation, have mercy on him . . .

I know you won't appreciate this your wonderful art . . .
So, one day he's going to be found drowned in his own blood:
With him my true self will go down the drain . . .
Yes, untested, untried, I will go down the drain . . .

Lawrence LeShan
SIX POEMS FOR BRUNO, #1.

"If you stood on Vega now, you
would see the Crucifixion",
Giordano Bruno, 1548-1600.
On Vega now,
If they looked at the Earth
With great eyes,
They would see the Passion
As it takes place.
The light has so far to go
That what shone on Calvary
Now tears the heart
On Vega.

They always taught me
The Passion is now,
Is always now,
And I believed them.
Now I comprehend
That they were correct.

Andrew Thomas Frederick
WINTER

I dedicate this poem to my greatgrandson Andrew whom I hope will be a 'winter' sports enthusiast!

'WINTER' is the
un-understandable 'MIND' of
Mother Nature putting to rest
With 'FURY'—the work of its
'SISTER-SEASONS' best!
Its nights extend 'SNOW' an
invitation
To its heavens to help NATURE
paint a 'CANVAS' of beauty across
a NATION!
A 'CANVAS' changing the drab
look of NAKED TREE and FIELDS
BARREN OF GREENERY
Into a 'MASTERPIECE' by a great
GOD, assisting NATURE in the art
of painting 'SCENERY'!
MORTAL MAN is inconvenienced
by 'IMMORTAL ART'—
But GOD sets 'MAN' apart,—
Knowing 'MAN'—the
'DESTROYER'—destroys whatever
GOD hath wrought;
And knowing too, that 'MAN' is not
'MASTER' of the lot!
It would appear, that as SISTER-
AUTUMN wanes, and chill of
WINTER nears,
That the GREAT CREATOR made
'WINTER' to be a time for tears!
NOT SO, if 'MANKIND'S'
viewpoint is held at bay giving
MOTHER NATURE her chance
to 'REST' Mother Earth so that a
'FUTURE' may advance!
'WINTER'S' heavens cause
whirlwinds to take their toll—
but the 'SOUL' of MOTHER
EARTH, despite 'MAN'S'
discontent, remains whole!
'WINTER' is a 'SEASON' given
'FREEDOM' by 'NATURE'S' trust
that GOD is right
No matter what be HIS act in
changing 'SEASONS' scenes by
'DAY' or by 'NIGHT'!
Despite 'MAN', so it goes, that
whate'er the 'SEASON'—
the next will be better-off, because of
a GREAT GOD'S reason!
GOD changes 'WINTER'S'
SISTER-SEASONS scenes, gently
putting each to rest,
so that when next appearing after
'WINTER'S' blast, each will be at its
best!

Michael R Archer
SIMPLE THINGS

To Jay: For showing me that simple ways are best

Straight on until morning
That's how I used to fall
I'd stay up all night
Feeling all right
But I wasn't feeling at all
People came over disguised as friends
While all the time they knew
It didn't matter to them
If the world came to an end
Just as long as their suffering was through
I kept playing the game each day and each night
Covering my pain as they did
Until finally I said
I don't want to be dead
And I gave up the pain I had hid
The best of all was yet to come
From a man with wisdom and voice
He told me one day
In a polite little way
Simple things will be your best choice

David Lee Kennedy
HEAVEN'S INTENTION

Dedicated to the heavenly intentions of my wife: Peaches

Dream your only attainable goal.
Put forth strength to vigorate thy soul.
Give all to your concepts of night,
find and pursue them, with courage and might.

Heaven intends to reach out and touch,
dreams of love, because there's not much
Pain, violence, loud screaming groans,
Evolve from a world where evil is sown.

Heaven is a place of tranquility, free of wrong.
Beauty, delight and peace create a song.
Intentions are to take all who wish to come,
letting in good, feeding evil to the sun.

Heaven covers those naked in cold and hunger,
taking their children away from meaningless blunder.
A smiling baby lavishes love, from all who send it,
Making heaven's intentions instill cures that profit.

T L Warden
ABOUT MYSELF

For Brenda, just because! !

I need to tell you something about myself,
before our relationship can go
any further.

I'm the kind of person
who feels very deeply,
And when I give my heart,
I give it quite completely.
I've never learned how to love
'just a little,'
so, as you can guess,
I've been hurt more than once.
However,
I feel a strange and wonderful
closeness between us,
as if, in this short, brief time,
I can already trust you,
wholeheartedly.
And that's why I must ask you
this one simple question,

"If I fall for you, will you catch me?"

J Dee Williams

J Dee Williams
SPEAKING TO THE LORD ABOUT, "ME, MYSELF"

I often wonder what type of person I really was;
Am I the type that really cared or was I here just because.

I asked the Lord:

Should I change my looks, my life, and even my name?
And if I did, do you think I still would remain the same?

The Lord said nothing.

I then asked the Lord:

Do you understand the way I feel about wanting to be a somebody?
I just feel like I am here wasting time, being another nobody.

Still, there was no answer.

I then had given up on speaking to the Lord, and as I was opening the door to my home there was a bright light coming from the top of an old antique shelf;
And as I got closer to the light, there was a beautiful picture sitting there of, "Me, Myself."

I then knew the Lord had spoken to me.

Laura Sanders
THE LEARNING PROCESS

To my daughter, Phyllis, who continues to play role-model for my thoughts.

Stars sparkle in the eyes at age seventeen,
And a bouquet of roses blooms in the heart;
There's a shade of difference in what we mean,
When "Goodbyes" are said at the door as we part.

At nineteen, experience has played a great role,

And we're learning that kisses aren't really promises;
Or that holding a hand doesn't mean chaining a soul,
Regardless of how much last night's "Goodbye" meant to us.

Then, there's the excitement of reaching twenty-one,
'Cause we've learned that love really doesn't mean leaning;
And presents aren't binding, even from that special someone,
Then, too, "Goodbyes" seem to have a little less meaning.

Twenty-five? Whatever happened to the age of twenty-three?
Was that the year we learned to build only on today . . .
Or was it then we saw love's other side of cruelty . . .
And that, sometimes, "Goodbye" is said in a different way?

Thirty-one! How refreshing and invigorating the years we face!
For we've learned so much from "Goodbyes" and being kissed;
All about strengths, self-worth, and our important place;
That an open hand holds more love than a clenched fist,
And the freedom in discarding a child's grief for a woman's grace.

Anne E Cohen
I AM . . . .
I am the flower that blooms in the spring.
I am the rain that feeds the world.
I am the tornado that kills and,
I am the sun which comforts the earth.
I am beauty, being blessed as a gift from God,
I am ugly, and am feared among the rest.
I am sickness which wipes the sanity out of you.
I am the weed that sucks life from your plants.
I am death, and nothing grows from my stalks.

Patricia Guest
REMEMBRANCE
Why do we wear a poppy? asked the child
What is it we should remember?
How do you explain to the young of today,
What the Young of Yesterday went through.
How do you explain the fighting and the poverty
that the two world wars gave range to.
Who were the lives were lost through fighting?
Where the lives were lost through bombing?
Which of the children were evacuated?

The young of today know peace and freedom.
That the Young of Yesterday fought for.
They know Remembrance Day is to recall the fallen forces.
To remember their families and friends.
They know that every red poppy which is worn over the heart,
was a life lost in battle long long ago.

We can only pray that the young of today
never experience the horrors of war.
That all nationalities live in peace,
that the Young of Yesterday fought for.
That they remember the anguish of their forefathers.
To teach the young of tomorrow
the follies of the wars long ago.
Lest we forget, lest we forget.

Miriam Garns

Miriam Garns
RAIN ON THE ROOF
How wondrously enchanting and delightful is the sound,
Of myriad crystal raindrops upon the thirsty ground.
With dusty soil mingled and muffled by the grass,
Becoming muddy streamlets, in gutters flowing past.
The showers knock more loudly upon the window panes,
Indoors we watch the drippings form rivers in the lanes.

But harder still and louder, persistently it pours,
Until there's not a dry spot, in all the out-of-doors;
And then the sudden fury subsides; we hear the proof—
The steady, gentle tappings of rain upon the roof.
Most welcome sounds (those tappings), as dusk crowds out the light,
Alluring, soothing sounds they are, inducing sleep at night.

Robert Makin
FOR A NOBLE QUEEN OF FLIGHT
Looking down from this crumbling rock, I think of you, how you long for power, as if fortune becomes you. Looking up to see, despite my apparent air, I offer the best I can give, what you deserve. Not much more to go on here. When bounty finally nods in your favor, and you desperately accept it, ruffling your wings like a mad school girl, will you look back on your behavior toward me and my humble surroundings, and realize it was for worse? With nothing to share,

except maybe a little spare time to make up for your missed givings, will you reserve a day to balance your absence, or strive onward, holding your head high; look down upon my crumbling rock sending signals to your earthly window barely visible from the perch you aspire toward?

Mrs Susan J Limoges
PRAISE

To my wonderful and loving husband, Louis.

By the gravity
of your eyes,
I fell into a
space of love.
Your rosy voice
became the air
of my songs.
The fires of ritual
destroyed darkness
and fell like
a rain on the
kingdom of unlisted
cities, and your
presence flowered
there, your presence
towered there, your
presence circled the
eagles of light.

Robert Makin
A NICE PLACE TO VISIT . . .
Katy from Italy boffed my socks.
She stuck her muff in my roughage
and told me great stories,
Florentine history.

Lying half-naked, her bony back
against the foot board, she grooved
on Michel and David and John Paul Jones,
the Zepplin bass player, not the navigator.

She caressed her breast and thigh,
as she explained that great men
make great cities, great women
make wonderful men.

Then, she slid slowly to the floor,
an intricate throw rug her vehicle,
and sang a sadly sweet aria
from Il Trovatore.

She died. No great men to make better
And I left for America, to a woman
who makes me whole.

Joanne Marie Wilke Montemayor
SOMEONE SPECIAL

For my grandparents, parents, special family members and my loving husband Monte.

Into my life someone very special came,
And as a result my life has not been the same.
He touched my heart and opened my eyes,
And made me realize the world is full of surprise.
A call unexpected to fill the day with cheer,
Oh, the joy I experience when from him I hear.
You hear me say my heart is filled with love,
For surely this someone special is from God above.
So may I always be willing to share with my friend,
Joy in the morning and happiness without end.

Ann Bayne
A CROWD
They look, but do not see.
They hear, but do not listen.
They touch, but do not feel.
They meet, but do not know.
A Crowd, but not a person.

Dottie Ferri

Dottie Ferri
MIRRORED IMAGES

To my husband and best friend, Lou, who asked me to do this; and my two wonderful children, Louie and Stephie.

Is that my face, so round and small?
No, it's hers.
But didn't I look like that as I recall?

Are those my eyes that dance with play?
No, they're hers.
But didn't I watch with innocence just yesterday?

When did I pass thru that door—
To watch myself as I do now,
Question life and what it's for,
And find life holds no more secrets.

My daughter's face looks up at mine,
To reassure her an endless time.
But who takes me by the hand and guides me thru?
I don't remember growing up . . . do you?

Lisa Riggs
A SONNET ON LOVE
In the spring of our lives are we
When flowers bloom and grass grows green
Our feelings of love are yet to be set free
And the wonders of love are unseen
Our love is as timid as a deer
Afraid of that which may be found
And though it's shy and full of fear
It knows with love trust can be found
Then twilight will come one fall day
And we will find we are no longer young
Yet whatever comes our way
No sad songs will be sung
For our love will always be strong
Even when the flowers are dead and gone

Barbara J McDermott
NATURE'S ACT
The newly budded leaves of spring lightly brushed
Against the wind like the tentative stroke of
Fingers gently touching a lover's heart.
The sun, hanging like a golden globe in the
Blue carpeted sky, sent ribbons of light
Streaming down to reveal the drama
Enacted by nature.
The stage for the setting was the great sea
Of green grasses that stretched to the horizon
Like the giant cloak of God's protective cover.
Buds unfolded and their fragrance filled our senses
And their beauty filled our hearts.
Birds sang their joyful song and their melody
Danced on the breeze as it was carried to
A silent world.

Sy Mac
IF YOU DON'T LOVE ME
If you don't love me, let me go
If you don't want me, tell me so
Please be fair, I want to know
If my caresses now chill you
And my kisses don't thrill you
Please be kind and say the word
Never mind, I won't be hurt
If you don't love me, let me go

Virginia C Evans

Virginia C Evans
THE REUNION

In loving memory of my grand-mother, Martha Cates and her dear friend, Mrs. Foster.

They met, greeting each other with man-made smiles
Walking each with a third leg side by side.
Slowly bending and sitting; both at once
Due to sore, still, and aching joints.

They first discusssed their thinning grey hair
Then their withered weight; a bit more than two hundred pounds between the pair.
The next topic embraced their peers still living
Some with kin, in rest homes and hospitals; feeble breaths they're barely giving.
Lunch was then served to the child-like ladies
Like little girls playing tea party; except they were in their eighties.
Both were very finicky about what they ate
Lest the needed nutrition would cause a stomachache.

Dim eyes danced through thick lens
As twitching fingers fumbled frail and tense
Through their purses for life support pills
Which were to be taken shortly after meals.

The un-hurried conversation soon turned to dark and dreadful death
They spoke of a dozen or more friends who had died of old age and ill health.
Finally, they said their farewells with alert and caring mind
Both secretly thinking that twenty more years wouldn't be nearly so kind.

Mary Ashenbrener
SEASONS COME AND SEASONS GO

To Harry, I'll always remember the good times.

Seasons come and Seasons go,
From April showers to ice and snow.
Be it Summer, Winter, Spring or Fall;
Time for Softball, Golf, and Basketball.

When you're not playing one of the three,
There you are, the Referee!
Your love of sports will never cease,
And mine for you can only increase.

Gayle R Hammonds
REMEMBER FRIEND

To the suffering addict.

Lift up your head and take my hand, I've been there friend, I understand. The road is rough, the temptations many, remember the pain remember the pity.
Look at yourself in the mirror. Did you ever look when you were high? Oh, how those eyes will lie. They let you see that all is fine, when deeper in the truth we hide.
Be honest now take a closer look, it was all bad there was no good, this much must be understood.
Now live each day as best you can and remember friend—I understand.

Kathryn M DiMeo
NATURE'S REVENGE
Amidst the rush of a hurried world comes the traveler
Seeking the grand splendor that nature befolds onto us

He seeks the gentle beauty of a bird in flight
Of a running stream and dew at night

Of majestic mountains and bright blue skies
Of honey kissed days and starry bright nights

His search is hard and long .....
For where is the beauty on this terrain
It's gone ....
To the traveler it becomes mighty clear
The birds are gone and death seeps near
Into our seas and trees and air

For look too late ....
Amidst the rush of hurried world

Bernice Couey Bishop

Bernice Couey Bishop
IN THE SOLITUDE

I dedicate this poem to God, Who gives me words, and I, His humble servant, am happy to write them down to share with others.

In the quiet solitude,
Alone, not distracted by others, I,
Sit quietly beside of an open window,
Looking down through our beautiful back yard,
Wondering—why?

Others never seem to take the time,
To retreat alone, as I,
To find this sweet, quiet solitude,
And in communion with their Lord, try—

To reach out to Him,
Knowing that He is always near,
But in the hustle and bustle of everyday life,
His sweet voice may be drowned out,
By worldly thoughts of sorrow or strife.

But in this quiet solitude,
Now I do find,
A renewing of my close communion with my God,
And a welcome respite from my troubled mind!

Al Bachman
CONCORD
Concord, where liberty was born!
Concord, on a frosty April morn!
The British were coming down from Boston Bay
To sweep anything that would dare stand in their way.
But they didn't know a band of patriots blocked
Concord's Wooden Span,
Whose love of country made them the most valiant in the land.

Suddenly in the distance, echoing with a beat,
Reverberating in cadence came a thousand marching feet!
Our boys dug in to take their stand in front of Concord's stream,
To halt the foe from stamping out freedom's cherished dream.

As the Redcoats converged upon them a husky voice rang out:
"Throw down your arms and run away, you ragged rebel louts,
Or we will write your epitaph and make this your final bout."
For his reply a shot rang out—"A shot heard round the world,"
And the battle for liberty was about to be unfurled.

The musket balls from the foreign guns at our lads did fly,
And many of that gallant group fell 'neath the blue New England sky.
Spurred on by the bravery shown in that bloody fight,
Many new Americans began to see the light.
And in the annals of history the books have this to say:
"We owe a debt of gratitude to those who fought and died that day."

Joan I Nystrom
HOMEWARD BOUND
My heart leads me home wherever I go,
to the family I love and friends I know.
Warm, windy summers, winters with snow,
lakes by the thousand and evergreens by the row.
To the seasons—all four: winter, summer, spring, fall;
Oh, God only knows how I've missed you all!
To the cities, small towns, and all that I lack,
someday, Minnesota, "I'm coming back!"

Iris Grenier
FEELINGS OF A MOTHER TO BE

Dedicated to Diane Zirkelbach

What a warm feeling inside for a Mother, to be, to know there is a new baby near.

What is rain? a cool breeze after the heat, a restful feeling after an active movement from the child she carries.

What is joy? a feeling I will hold in my heart when my baby has finally arrived.

What is comfort? knowing after the day passes, my baby is growing older each day after cuddling and holding.

What is love? love also grows each moment as, I look forward to seeing my baby glow as it grows.

As adulthood approaches, When he or she chooses a path.
I pray he/she will not stray.

Most of all I want to feel in my heart, when the time comes,
for he/she to choose their separate way, I pray the path he/she has chosen will once again come my way, as I long to hold them in my arms once again.

For there will always be those wonderful feelings I knew, for my baby-to-be.

Janice Johnson McQuery
NIGHT SOFTNESS
At eve of sunset when the heavens begin to gray,
when pastel colors streak the sky.
I suddenly feel a sadness
as if everything has died.

The softness and beauty

of something quite so grand,
Makes me feel so lonely
that I just can't understand.

God takes his mighty hands
and slowly dims the light,
Ever so gently, he eases
us into the night.

A night of haunting beauty
sprinkled with stars on velvet above.
One of his many masterpieces
created by his endless love.

So maybe it's not sadness
but awe at his might,
Of how easily he turns day
into the softness of a Night.

Jane K Dewey
REVENGE
Day rises in the morning,
All rosy-blue and white,
And slips without a warning,
A knife into the night;
A stake into the heart
Of that dark and fiendish foe
That ripped and tore apart
The evening's gentle glow;
And left in dripping shreds,
The dying of the sun
In soft and bloody beds,
The day and evening done.
How grand the plans Night made.
How filled with foolish pride.
And by her golden blade,
How easily he died.

Elizabeth Louise (Lacy) Hettick
MINDY

Dedicated to Mindy, a black & white, Malamute/Lab. mix—female dog, 9 1/2 yrs. old.

She was adopted by our son when
only eight weeks old.
The pleasure she gave us all could
never be fully measured.

Over nine years she protected us and
guarded our home;
Was a friend to talk to and one we all
had treasured.

Then over a month ago her health
began to fail—
Soon she couldn't eat or stand—that
tore our feelings deep.

For a long week we tugged at our
heartstrings to make the right
decision.
It was the toughest thing we ever
did—yesterday, we had her put to
sleep.

God only made one Mindy!

Ruth Adrienne Vance
HER GOOD LITTLE BOY
A Mother will always think of her
son
When he was her child, gentle and
mild.

He always will be her good little
boy,
Who filled her life with pleasure &
Joy.

Even though he may grow to be six
feet tall
She will Love him———as when he
was small.

Even though manhood brings adult
change,
In his dear Mother's heart, she feels
he is the same.

Although he brings another woman
to grief . . . .
Becomes a murderer, rapist or
thief . . . .
She will defend him, remove him
from guilt & shame
Society or someone else is to
blame . . . .
His faults in character she will not
claim.

Tho, he becomes a grown Man,
good, bad or wild,
She still Loves him, He is her little
child.

Mary Jennison McAuliffe
THE OPENING OF ANOTHER SHOW
The beech trees
Didn't know
That on their branches
White cotton balls would grow.

For overnight the first snow fell
So soft and silently,
Leaving beauty spots
On every bush and tree.

The evergreens
Didn't know
They would be wearing ermine
For the Show.

The beauty of this scene
Is lighted by the morning sun—
My Autumn "Walden" stage has
changed,
Now I'll enjoy this winter one!

William L Michie

William L Michie
I AM A TEENAGER

To Tammy, who gave me the courage to write

I am a teenager
But a stranger to my own
No one knows me, no one sees
But each is my severest critic

I feel that I am part of something
Far greater than myself
But still there is the doubtful fear
That I may not matter at all

I do what I can
I strive and I try
But no matter of the motions I travel
I still am known by few

So still I exist
I am only what I may be
It should not matter, but always it
does
But I will do what I can.

Violet Ursula Galley
TO THE HOMELESS

I dedicate this poem to the homeless of the world; especially those in New York City.

I see you sleeping on cardboard
sheets;
In subway stations and filthy streets;
Your meager possessions; beside you
a cart;
And a notice 'I'm hungry, please
have a heart."

People pass by in hurry and fear;
Some call the police to get all out of
here;
Others frustrated, will write to the
press;
"What are we doing with this awful
mess?"

In a city of plenty no answer is
found;
Midst the turmoil and strife, with
crowds all around,
Yet life will continue, the day will
dawn;
Let us give hope to the tired and
worn.

Life is so precious you must carry
on;
There's a better day coming, when
the battle is won.
Have faith all you homeless; do not
despair;
Life isn't all roses, but some people
care.

We'll stretch out a hand; and show
you the way;
To help make life better; and bring a
new day;
For darkness will pass; the sun will
shine through;
Your misery ends; we'll find homes
for you.

Laurie Ann Robinson
UNSPOKEN EMOTIONS

Dedicated to my parents, George N. Fowlkes & Barbara A. Robinson, for their love and support.

Sometimes there is so much to
say . . . . .
But not enough words,
not enough time,
not even a way.
There are times when you want
to say
just what you feel,
And the words don't come out
right.
It's like the times . . .
. . . When you want to say "I Love
You"
But you can't.
. . . When you want to say "It's
over"
But you won't.
. . . When you want to say "I hate
you"
But really don't.
. . . When you want to say "I need
you"
But couldn't.
Sometimes emotions aren't meant
to be said,
But meant to be felt.

Diana Lane Johnston
ENCOURAGEMENT

To British Columbia, Canada

"You ought to write," said he.
"And so
Expose the very inner marrow of
my bones?
No thanks"
The tragi-comedy of this, my
inner life
Would shrink and wilt before the
public gaze
I have no message for the
teeming world
That's not a thousand times been
better given
With more authority than I shall
ever have
But yet—it's good to know that
someone thinks
I have ability to move, with
words,
The fragile human heart,
In this explosive, real and
electronic age.

Chris Asselin
RAIN

To Ron. Thank you for loving me as I am

As the gentle rain
falls from the dark skies
and falls freely to the ground,
the sound of the rain is that
of an earthquake
as it breaks the silence
and brings me out of my dream.

Roy W Van Der Slice
MIRRORS OF MY MIND
Of times at night in solitude with
hectic day gone by the mirrors of my
mind reflect past things of how and
why. The clockwork of my
innerspace released strikes backward
then thru time, and in nostalgic
wonderland unravels all reason to
life's rhyme. I recline there in
yesteryear with all the world tranquil
and let the mirrors of my mind
change anything at will.

There are no mistakes no sorrow
nothing in disarray, "come with me"
my heart cries out with words that
muted lips cannot find to those
around me that I have loved and
whom have returned that love in
kind, "let me take you to utopia thru
the mirrors of my mind."
If only they could walk with me in
old springtimes that now are new just
to hear the robins sing their sweet
refrain gainst the skies of azure blue
but with wishes comes a dawning
that breaks the tie that binds, they
dim to gray then fade away these
mirrors of my mind.

Marla Majano
VISIONS
All around the mulberry bush went
little Mary's lamb,
With three blind mice in hot pursuit
to find the Great I AM.
The ghosts from Tara's hallowed
halls were slyly gathered 'round
Miss Muffet's final resting place,
which was on higher ground.

The farmer's wife and daughter stood
with bayonets at hand,

While Alice led the multitudes into her Wonderland.
I never shall forget those moments, though all others fade,
When Calliope sang and muses joined the accolade.

Now memories from bygone years have all been left behind,
And throughout the good earth there cannot be one so blind
As the mouse or man who does in consciousness perceive
Life from other planets, and refuses to believe.

Joanne M Navarre
SECRETS IN THE WIND

This poem is dedicated to my Second Grade Class.

As I walk my playground duty
this brisk December morning;
The wind is cold and frightening.
It stings my face, bites my nose
And cuts through my heart like a blade.

The faster I walk, the more the
Wind blows.
It howls as it cuts through me
With secrets whispers of my class.

As I hear the faint sound of the words,
Old, mean, strict teacher floating
Through the wind;
It chills my heart and brings tears
To my eyes.

As I continue to walk on the playground,
I too whisper secrets in the wind.
Hoping the wind will carry the message,
That the strictest teacher is really
Very kind.
All she ever thinks about is educating
Young minds.

Ginger Haley
TRUE LOVE IS WHAT JESUS TEACHES
What will you do with Jesus is a familiar question,
Still, you can't answer without hesitation;
While with your mouth you say, I'd give my all for Christ.
The question is, do you show Him to others in your life.

While on Sunday morning you are fervent in your prayer,
The rest of the week you act like you just don't care,
Are you false when you praise God in song;
God can see you and knows what you do is wrong.

The Lord sees you through and through,
And God knows the falsity of you,
God can take your heart and fill it with love;
Accept his forgiving grace from above.

When your brother needs a helping hand,
Do you lend him help or do you go far from him to stand,
And when your sister has lost her way;
Won't you help. What will you say.

Linda Jean Dessaint
BROTHER MIKE, REMEMBER . . .
The day was bright
and the snow had stopped.
Neighborhood boys were having fun
Playing on Elizabeth Street.

I must have been a pest
the details I don't recall.
Suddenly I heard someone say
"Why don't you pick on
someone your own size."

I sat on the snowbank
With pride and surprise,
As I watched you continue
On your way.

Vincent Montgomery
WHISTLE
Growing up I was taught, to whistle
Seems every boy, tried to learn early
Notes came by practice—plus patience
Most Dads felt his son must be lazy
If he couldn't do his chores, and whistle
To impress your family and visitors
You let them know you were close by with
—a whistle
Going to town, whether on bike or scooter
Dogs would follow if you gave, a whistle
Grandpa felt whistling important—as whittling
It's strange but true, I've been listening
I'm still waiting in 1989—for someone whistling.

Mike Sewell
MYSELF
Found a little place outside the sun
Where the blue skies are never gray
Where the wind blows through the tall trees
And life goes its own way.
Found a little stream free of the world
Found a little house all mine
Found something I've always had
But have never known till now.

Alison Tamiko Lew
THE WOUND CYCLE
Wounds heal slowly but surely
as mine has . . . .
I can finally accept the situation
in which I am placed . . . .
But sometimes
Sometimes a careless word
or something else of the sort
tears me apart again
I am wounded anew and oh how it hurts
and I can barely control myself
control the tears that
threaten to spill down my cheeks.
But time . . .
in time the wound will again heal
and I may hold a grudge
but I can't live off of grudges
I will forget it in time
and again I will accept the situation
And I will sit back and wonder
with amusement
at what a cycle this has come to be.

Mary Garman
THE WOMAN
The chocolate brown cattail
stood out in the field looking like a woman
and I am that woman.

It looks dull like a stick
except for the soft skin and lengthy figure.
It makes people approach it,
curious as to why this plain ordinary thing
has something so appealing about it.

I stand there letting their gazes
touch me on the outside.
Their looks scratch me
but they can't hurt me.
I am strong within my soul just like the cattail.

Their stupid questions annoy me
but I listen.
I can't run away for I am that cattail
and its brownness is my light.

As I look at the cattail,
I notice that though we are alike,
we are not one.
The cattail can hear me
but it can not care and be human as I am.
I left the cattail in the field of grass
and I walked back into my different world.

Kristina Prager
SEEDS OF PEACE
Every day
a mother tells
her young son
to stop beating
little Peter.

At night
the child whines
and cries NO, NO, NO
to all reason.
The mother turns round
and slaps her son's face
h a r d.

That's how young seeds of peace
stop growing . . .

George Brassell
FREEDOM

To Sherry Walker

A young man stood facing the south wind. His eyes were scanning the battlefield. In spite of the twisted dead, the smell of rotting flesh, he knew deep inside that he had fought a good fight. This is the price for freedom, he thought to himself as he mounted his horse.

A young woman received a telegram. We regret to inform——, it started. At first she felt the explosive pain within her heart, then it slowly saturated her whole being. In silence, she cursed freedom or the foolishness we call freedom.

From eternity, a good and merciful God looks at the essence of man. The only creation that he dares not touch, for if he touched it, it would no longer be. Although with a simple thought, he could destroy the entity (for it is the one thing that has caused him pain and sorrow). He withholds. It is his testing ground, it is the bridge between the temporal and the eternal. Without that bridge, man would collapse back into protoplasm.

At the side of a mountain a group (who calls itself 'humanity') stopped to rest. As they looked down, they saw only graves and gravestones, lingering smoke, and rivers of blood. A few talk among themselves and wonder if, perhaps freedom was misunderstood.

Sheila W Nixon
alone for one

This poem is dedicated to my brother David J. Nixon who died in 1987. My love is always with you.

alone with the wind
we long to live with the one
far away from earth
the feeling of love
never to be felt again
only the one
in the wind
the shadows of doubt
the hate; the love I am
never exposed again
an image in the night
fading into eternity
the mirror deranged to me
so sharp it cuts the love apart
fooling the world
I am here
till the sun burns me
once again
alone for one

Sharyn A Smith
DAISIES DON'T KNOW
He loves me, oh, he loves me not,
Now does a daisy know?
Where the blush of true love lies,
How can a daisy show?

Would you truly give your love
On what a daisy had to say?
Or if a daisy told you no
Would you walk away?

Well not I,
For daisies do not know.
For like a flower
Love needs time to grow.

It takes a lot of tenderness
To tend that little seed.
On shared joys and even tears,
And gentleness it feeds.

So please don't let the daisy
Thwart you with her lies.
Just pity the poor daisy
For she blooms and then she dies.

Eugene J Parrish
THOUGHTS IN THE WEST VIRGINIA HILLS

In loving memory of Welles Bunyea, who loved his "Cabin in the hills."

As I wander thru the pathways of the West Virginia hills,
I'm amazed at all the answers to a person's deepest ills.
For it's here among the majesty of God's creative thrills,
That I feel His Presence greatly and know His intended Will.

There's a squirrel busy barking as the day begins to dawn,
Hasting to and fro above me mid the sounds of Autumn morn.
And the breaking of a branch nearby announces to my sensitive ear,

That among the scurrying creatures
is a lovely white-tailed deer.

There are bugs and there are beetles, and there are gnats of every kind,
All of Nature seems so busy as along my path I find,
A serenity and wonder as God gives forth His best,
And along the sunlit pathway I pause briefly for a rest.

For a moment I stare in wonder and I sink slowly to my knees,
Then, silently, I thank Him and express to Him my pleas.
O Lord, may I be grateful for tender moments such as these,
May I always treasure memories of mountains, rocks, and trees.

Then I think of those before me who have trod these lovely paths,
And I thank the Lord they loved Him, and preserved the things that last.
So among the beauty of the mountains in the Autumn of the year,
There's the loveliest of Nature,
God's creation has no peers!

Robert A Nichols

Robert A Nichols
SETTING THE EXAMPLE
Let my lifestyle, O God,
Show my belief in Thee.
I'm like the superstructure
Of a tree—Your Scriptures
Are the roots that nourish
Me.
Keep my trunk tall and strong
So that others, through me,
Will come to Thee.

Sources
Leviticus 11:45
Psalms 1:1-3
John 17:15-19
2 Corinthians 5:20
Ephesians 5:1-20
I Peter 2:1-3

Stephen R Sherman
YOUR SMILE IS SO BEAUTIFUL, YOUR EYES ARE SO BRIGHT
Your smile is so beautiful, your eyes are so bright
Like the full moon that shines with the stars in the night
So soft is your skin, so gentle your touch
So warm is your heart, I love you so much

Your long flowing hair, blowing free in the wind
The colors that surround you, a rainbow with no end
The things that you say and the things that you do
These things are the things that I love about you

Though I never will have you, you could never be mine
I will think of you always till the end of my time
And when we are distant and when we're apart
I will still love you dearly with all of my heart

Wayne A Hayes
THE MIGHTY OCEAN
I looked across its waters, As I stood upon its shore,
I saw its waves a rollin', Heard its message in its roar,

I felt its awesome power, As I bowed beneath its force,
I wondered in amazement, Of its secret, of its source,

I felt its sandy beaches, As I walked along its path,
Careful not to raise its anger, So as not to feel its wrath,

Soon the evening brought its stillness, As I heard its silence ride,
Saw the dolphins go a floatin', With its ever swelling tide,

Then at once I saw its beauty, Saw its poise and saw its grace,
I begin to see its image, As I gazed about the place,

Surely God has been its Author,
From here to e-ter-ni-ty,
For He made the Mighty Ocean, For the likes of you and me.

Elizabeth Saltz
EBB AND FLOW
The gentle lapping of the waves on the shore,
In a rhythmic pattern.
Inspires one to write.
The blazing sun beats down,
Bringing warmth to winter.
A sea gull swoops down,
Nibbling seaweed of the ocean.

The briny ocean gives a salty aroma.
The stillness is broken, by the gull's cry.
The bird calls to his mate,
Soon, baby birds fly with mother,
Pecking at clams cast on the shore.

Blazing sun, heating the ocean depths,
High waves dashing on boats.
As the sun sets, the tide goes out.
Sand bars filled with clams,
People dig for seafood.
Soon, water will cover the sand,
A pail of clams is the reward.

As the sun sets,
The fisherman returns.
Laden with a pail of clams.
The fish in the sea spawn,
Leaving eggs which hatch.
New fish swim and frolic,
Eating worms and insects of the seabed.

The fisherman sinks his line,
A tug means they are biting.
As he winds his rod,
The fish struggle to survive.
Soon, he will be perched on the table.
Sold in the fish market with others.

Martha Stuckenberg
HIGH ALMIGHTY ATTITUDE

Dedicated to Art, for without him, I would not be who I am.

Your high almighty attitude.
Yes that's the phrase I heard you use.
I trusted you with all my heart.
My life's been yours right from the start.

This attitude you think's so bad.
It's all that's left, it's all I have.
Is what you want, a hopeless being?
A hidden face afraid to be seen?

I'm sorry I can't give you that.
I refuse to be a welcome mat.
So much already has washed away.
I've gotten harder day by day.

I'll learn to put the past behind.
But this attitude's not bad, it's mine.

Jane Curtis
LIGHT AND DARKNESS
We found each other in the light,
Our love was clear and bright,
Without shadows,
Without darkness.

We never thought
That night would fall so soon
And leave us to love in dreams and darkness,
Divided by a wall of death and darkness
Struck between us
Like the blackest night
That drives into the jagged lightning scar
With only one clear afterimage
Before the flash falls back
Into relentless memory.

Helen Phillips Wilbur
GONE

To Elmer Caryl, my Tower of strength, whose love gave meaning to my life.

Yesterday I felt such pain
It was not helped by all that rain
I couldn't help but weep and moan
My heart was like a heavy stone.
Though eyes closed very, very tight
I could not sleep a wink last night.
Sad thoughts stayed with me 'til dawn
Oh, my darling, you are gone.
When morning sun smiled down on me
I sadly sat beneath our tree
Memory sat down there too
But, oh my darling, where were you?

Tara Lynn Anselowitz
PLAYFULNESS
Kittens climbing up the wall.
Puppies chase a great, big ball.
Children small and children tall
Outside playing one and all.

Children playing on the swings,
Playing ball and other things.
Riding on their wooden sleds,
Children laugh and nod their heads.

Talking on the telephone.
Eating chocolate ice cream cones.
Playing games on the table.
Watching shows on the cable.

Everybody likes to say
"Come on buddy, let's go play."
Even dogs and even cats
Seem to agree on that fact.

Charles D Meserole
UNTIL THE DAWN
With love so tender
I want to touch you and
feel you near me.

Take my hand in yours, so
I may feel secure.
Be gentle with my tender heart
as I look to you for comfort.

Let the warmth of my love,
melt that part of your soul,
where your emotions lie hidden.

Forever . . . I will try . . . .
hoping to find the door,
that I may enter your heart,
where I belong.

Cindy Jean Boyd
MY HEART

To—my husband William A. Boyd Sr., the man I wrote this poem for.

My heart will tell no lies,
Only those few tears I cry,
Can lead to something more,
Whatever my heart has stored.

My heart has stored good,
Love and faith and only times,
The Lord could take.

With these few tears I cry,
There could be, but one guy,
There is only one for me,
It is he who's here with me.

Helen L Stamey
FOR SARA
I missed you down at the lake
It was one of those special days—
Crisp, clean air and only the ducks
Making trails in a slightly bluer hue than the sky

I took our favorite path
Stopping to admire the old tree
The quiet was so intense for a time
Sky, trees, the lake and I merged
Into one glorious whole

All missed your sweet laughter
Can ducks look sad? Trees can
I missed you down at the lake

Neil O Face
WHEN THEY LEAVE HOME
He was just a kid from a little spot, on a map they called a town.
Played in most highschool sports, but his name was never renown.
As the bus backed out, waved goodby, to his parents standing there.
It was really hard for them to let go, as on their face appeared a blank stare.
That's the way it really is, as they leave, somewhere else another arrives.
And all around the world parents end up,
With a cupful of tears in their eyes.
As the bus goes around that corner, and disappears out of sight.

You immediately have to adjust to the fact,
he won't be sleeping in his bed tonight.

Col Walter M Newland USMCR (Ret)
IMMORTALITY

To the officers and men of the USS Franklin CV-13.

Opt for bronze or marble if thou must
But when my ashes return to dust
Let not my passage just be etched in stone
But ensculp'd upon those hearts I've known.

Ruth E Hilgen

Ruth E Hilgen
THE PINK BALL

To my grand-daughter, Julie

One morning at seven,
The moon slid down from Heaven.
A round pink ball
Shown for us all.

A quick look and then
A look again.
It was gone.
It hid behind the trees.

E B Spence
ODE TO A PARTNERSHIP

We kid ourselves with dreams
Things are not what they seem.
But they are!

The lessons we should learn
We seem destined to spurn.
So we don't.

We find it hard to believe
Family and friends can be thieves.
But they are!

When there are profits to divide
You find in promises they lied.
They were empty!

But where is my invested share
You ask in anguish and despair.
The answer . . a stare!

Your contribution was small.
The deals "I" made the all.
Your labor . . . nil!

So be on your way.
I have nothing else to say.
You . . I no longer need!

Martha Bender
WELCOME KATIE

Dedicated to Katie's Maternal Grandparents, Paul and Bonnie Heinzelmann with much love and affection.

To all the Family Relatives and Me,
You are a Great Addition to the Family Tree.
WELCOME KATIE, to our Family World,
You, precious little Baby Girl.

You are lovable to the touch,
Don't weigh very much.
Your name is so right, KATIE
Had two Great-Grandmas, that were Kate and Caddie.

As you walk through life, there's so much in store.
You, we will adore.
WELCOME KATIE, again and again,
As Our Life, with You begins.

Lewis J Fram
TIGHTROPE

Thanks to K.V. for the inspiration

I am down in a well
clinging for life on a mere
piece of thread.
I look up and see the tranquil blue
sky.
I also see a white dove
continually fly over the well.
Its name is reality
I look beneath me,
I see a thick, murky, green slime
that has collected overtime.
I see a scaly, serpent
lurking in the murk.
Its name is insanity
My goal is to go up.
As I struggle to climb my thread,
I slip down the thread a little.
I notice for the first time
that the thick slime covers the
lower portion of the thread.
As I look up again, I notice that
the thread is wearing down.
I'm in a race against time!
I look around the well, and I see
a crevice to my right.
I swing over and just as the
thread snaps, I land at the opening of
the crevice.
I crawl into the crevice and wonder
'is this triumph, or indecisiveness?'

Jonathan Beckford
THE MUSIC OF LOVE

DEDICATED TO MY LOVELY AND DEAR SISTER "MICHELLE" (once there was a dream, now it's a reality)

The earth is full of music
Of the joy that gladdens our heart
How can we refuse it
When we don't know where to start
A world of eternal bliss
With melodies soft and warm
Softer than a lover's kiss
Or a baby within your arms
Cherished in the glory
Flowing from each song
Each telling its own story
As we listen and sing along
So take me there
There where I can melt in you
Showing how much I care
Which I truly do

Mary Robertson
TESTAMENT

The swords are still. The shields announce no king
Whose prowess must be proved upon the field.
The heralds and the harpers no more sing
Their bloody tales of treachery revealed.
The chapel too stands empty though some own
The echo of a final whispered prayer
Lies yet within the solitary stone,
Unanswered in its terrible despair.
The fires in the great hall all have died
For none is left who cares to feed the flame;
No knight sworn to uphold his liege's pride,
No servant cowed beneath his master's blame.
Here swords are still and knights pronounce no vow
For none but ravens hold the tower now.

Vera H Armstrong
THE CHRISTMAS TREE GLISTENED

The Christmas Tree glistened with ornaments so bright
As the star of Bethlehem did on that special night
And the many gifts placed here and there
Were filled with secrets to be handled with care
But the best gift for all on Christmas Day
Was the birth of our Jesus in a manger of hay

Miss Eleanor Lewis

Miss Eleanor Lewis
OLD FASHIONED

I'd like to dedicate this poem to my children and grandchildren.

Poet writers are sometimes old fashioned,
Because they cling to the old rule.
Poet writers are sometimes old fashioned
Because they are called brave fighters.
Poet writers have a big heart for other poets.
They have a good insight for writings.
Poet writers are sometimes old fashioned.
Poet writers try not to be unfriendly.
Some poet writers don't mind hard work for each day and night.
Poet writers are sometimes old fashioned.
You must have love for each other when you're a poet writer.
You don't know what the future holds for you.
I only hope all poet writers make it,
Cause some poet writers are old fashioned like me.
Because they cling to the old rule.

Shirley Hochstedler
LAURENA AND BEAUTIFUL TENNESSEE

For my youngest daughter, Laurena

On a starry summer night
Down in beautiful Tennessee
I walked with my Laurena
Over the hills and through the valley.

We shared the peace and beauty
Of the rolling hills and streams
Just my sweet Laurena and me
We walked, and talked, and dreamed.

And on that summer night
Down in the heart of God's country
I asked my sweet Laurena
If she would marry me.

No other place on Earth
Would I ever want to be
Than with my sweet Laurena
Down in beautiful Tennessee.

Mia Frances Thomas
TIME IN A BOTTLE

Dedicated to the lost and dying world

One day is with the Lord as a thousand years,
And a thousand years as one day.

Time is running out, the time in the bottle is going fast
We must be ready, we must not waste any time.

The time in the bottle is about to blow.

We can't hold time within ourselves,
We know not the day nor the hour when He shall return.

We can't stop time.

A glimpse of light we must see a glimpse of light for you and me.

Deannie Diseker
TO MY DAUGHTER

Dedicated to my daughter, Joy Ishelle, who has endured many hardships in this life but none she can't overcome and be a much better person.

There was a man who came into my life
And I became his wife.
I trusted him completely as I should
Like any wife would.
We had some really good times together
In every kind of weather.
But this man I thought I knew so well
Took my daughter to the depths of hell.

My two precious children were very young

When our life together had begun.
How I wish now that I knew then
This story's tragic end.
A daughter is a wonderful thing . . .
To make one's heart sing.
But oh what pain my heart has felt
Since with this tragedy I've dealt.

If you should see my little girl
Tell her it's not the end of the world.
Her life can have a brand new start
But it takes effort on her part.
Tell her things moms like to say
And tell her I miss her more each day.
Then hold her in your arms . . . for me.
'Cause she won't let me close, you see.

Brother

Bryan A Gilroy
BROTHER

In memory of Hugh Edward Gilroy who left this world June 27, 1983—A gentleman scholar, a truer brother and friend no man could ever have. Bryan Anthony Gilroy.

Dearest brother why did you go?
The rivers of my sadness just flow and flow
Why didn't you give me some of your pain?
Until you got back on your feet again
You touched so many and listened well
Your message was of goodness and clear as a bell
You only gave and never never took
And I bothered you with writing my cursed book
It's five years passed, but only a moment ago
We sat at the kitchen table and spoke of life's ebbs & flow
But as I sit here and ponder what might have been
I have to thank God for giving me a brother and best friend
And if God needed you He should have called me first
For He left me very saddened with a heart that's going to burst

Cindy Allar Thompson
THE OHIO VALLEY
Where have all the people gone!
There used to be so many
Now they are so few!

Why doesn't anyone hear
the cries and the hgue

Once the days were blue
And happy people true.
But now the empty houses,
The empty stores attest
To the loss of what the E.P.A. brought
Our beautiful Ohio Valley,
Once the place where generations,
Were proud to live.
Before what the E.P.A. did.
They killed the Ohio Valley
With all their rules
Not the coal miner with his tools.

Zane Reeves
MEDITATION
Soft summer breeze,
Lazy old streams,
Cuddling clouds above,
Boy and Girl in love—

Hearts up to the sky,
Whispering trees,
Telling us never to say good-bye.

A gentle lullaby,
Boy and Girl in love,
Christmas in July—

Let's talk about Romeo and Juliet.
Their love can't compare
To the day we first met.
All through the years
We will recall
Moments like these—
How it all began
In a soft summer breeze.

Mandy M DeCino
THE WIZARD
His eyes are as blue as the deep seas. They tell many stories of magical lands with magical powers. They show how wise the eyes of wisdom are.
His magical cane all twisted with tattered wood. It's as old as his first stories tell. Bright brass squid up on top, you're holding a crystal the size of a small saucer. The bottom of the tangled wood is as rough as the gravel it rides along.
Oh wise Wizard, what does your beard behold, the magic, the tales, even more? And what does its gray, silver, and white show? Its length, as your height, grown your whole life, it shows every year.
Your potions, dear one, your cane, powers, and more, they are, my lord, your wisdom and strength, your magic and sorrow. Everything upon your body means something and you are
The Beholder.

Leah Andersen
THE PHANTOM OF THE LAS PALMAS
In the four seasons of the circle
When Autumn leaves do fall upon us,
There stands the ghost of the Las Palmas. The demon evil smiling one.

Dark behind him in the lobby—
Rose the King, in all his glory
Rose his keeper with peace upon him.
Pulling his bottle and jesting with Him

In the phantasm of the illusion of the truth in the dead of Winter there falls upon us the season jolly. The Jew hating smiling one still behind him are his keepers.
The King's chief men.
When in his beauty
is the King in all His glory

Walks the demon boasting I hate America, and in his country beautiful—the Jew pulls the cart in place of the horse.

In the Springtime with morning-glories growing along the fence in splendor . . of purple royal,

There stands the evil at the windows, peeking in.
What harm done in the heat of Summer when walking the halls in all of the wonder upon us—is the King and the Phantom of the Las Palmas.
Laughing at him.

Lucie Dean Patton
TO APRIL WITH CHICKENPOX
There was a little girl named April,
who was only five,
Land Sakes Alive!
She got a temperature—
more than 95°.
Her feverish body
itched and burned.
Little spots were sore and red!
April became so sick
she had to go to bed.
Her mommie was good and kind.
She read all the stories she could find,
to help make the time go fast.
April began to feel much better at last!
Now she wonders if Goldilocks
ever had Chickenpox!

Laura-Lee Sharpe
ARE YOU READY FOR THE NIGHT
As the hands reach the midnight hour
Animals catch prey to devour

Though the prey scurry around to hide
They know they're doomed deep down inside

With humans it's a different story
The night isn't filled with glory

People become filled with fright
When they hear something go boom in the night

Hours later they see something new
They begin to wonder, "is it too good to be true"

Then their hearts become happy and bright
When they begin to see the light

Another night has come and gone
A night for history to carry on

Though the minutes pass slowly by
The time just always seems to fly

And now again here comes the night
Are you staying up? I know I might

Tina Gibson
IF I COULD FIND A QUIET PLACE

I wish to dedicate this poem to the man I love, Joey Patchin, and to my children, Juanita, James, Darlena, and Tyler.

I want to find a quiet place
where I can be alone.
I don't want to hear a radio
or the ringing of a telephone.

I want a little time to be by myself
so I can let my thoughts "flow free."
I want to take my poems down off the shelf
with no one to disturb me.

I want to be alone to cry . . .
if that should be my need.
I want to be alone to laugh or sigh
or just to sit and read.

Sometimes I want to yell real loud
or rant and rave and scream.
Sometimes I'd like to be allowed
just to sit alone and dream.

If I could find a quiet place
where I could be alone,
I would turn off the radio
and unplug the telephone.

G E Mooney
EAGLE-HEART

For Glen, Margie, Georgia, and my beloved daughter Angela

Eagle-Heart is a friend of mine,
forever burned into my mind.
'Twas stormy day by Florida sea, I saw this magnificent creature in front of me.
While throwing bread to sea gulls above my balcony,
To watch them fly, dive, and retrieve was my idea of fun to see.

Choice piece I'd roll within my hands, then tossed it up amidst the band,
Was about to be claimed, when a sparrow swooped down and won the game.
A sparrow with the heart of an eagle, so I called him Eagle-Heart.
My little friend has played the largest part, example of why I should have heart.

On stormy days within my soul,
when life seems nothing but a show,
Before I start to play my part, I stop to think of Eagle-Heart.

Life's tiny things can be the greatest teachers,
As to what can be done,
By even the smallest of God's creatures.

Barbara M Bryant
GRACE

I dedicate this poem to my husband, Shirley H. Bryant

Two worlds to grace my life I've found,
the outside world to which I'm bound.
The inside world belongs to me,
the one in which I'm ever free.
The outside world I must comply,
I shall not err a dream may die.
The inside world has peace in store,
I go within to rest once more.

George William Conway III
TIDINGS
The last thing I need
In my life is you.

I thank you for the notice
Of my ease, countenance;
Of my laugh, contentment.

They are produced

For you, by you

It's unusual:
You draw out of me
What's best for me,

Best for others.
In this you're perfect.

The very last thing
I need in life is you.
I'd only betray us.

Barbara Goldberg
THE PARKING SITUATION

This poem is dedicated to: Morris Goldberg—The Best Dad in the whole wide world.

The Parking Garage was too steep . . .
So I parked my car on the street.

When I returned, the car was deplete . . .
Of radio, hubcaps and seat!

Diane Hess
ODE TO SEE'S CANDY
We pledge allegiance
To Mary See
And all her lovely confections
And swear to forgive
Trespasses made
On our hips
And on our complexions

Ronnee Eller Strickland
EMANCIPATED LOVE
The unleased desires safely
tucked into the remotest crevice
of my soul,
emancipated
and allowed the full splendor of
hope one Winter night,
When the Gods smiled down on
me and lavished
the most enchanting quiescence,
and the wonderful delight

Of discovering the absolute
possibility, never before allowed
myself,
that I would ever find one
such as you
Your existence heretofore only a
part of my dreams,
and the thrill of you loving me
as only you can do.

Your sensitivity, understanding
and caring has touched my soul
and ignited an intense desire,
while from above
The Gods continue to smile and
rain the special sparks that have
awakened for you my heart and
love.

Patricia A Nigro-McGeghan
ENDLESS CHAIN

This poem is dedicated to the light of my life—for my husband—Rick

To me the world is an endless chain
To which we are all a link.

We are never free to do the things we want
Or most of all . . . to think!

Is there a way to break these bonds
To which we have been tied?

The only way that I can think is
Try . . . Try . . . Try!

Nichole Warren
SINGING
Singing is the kindest thing I know,
It does no harm, it simply flows
And spreads some joy for unhappy faces,
And gather things among their spaces.
It gives us meaning for him above,
And things to make our love of.
And leaves us things to remember.
It is first when days begun
To touch beams of morning sun,
It is last to hold the light
When evening changes into night,
And when a moon floats in the sky
We hum a drowsy lullaby
Of sleepy children long ago . . .
Singing is the kindest thing I know.

Daisy (Shipley) Benson

Daisy (Shipley) Benson
OUR MOTHER

To my dear parents, Margret D. Shipley and Samuel H. Shipley

She was our mother, the one who cared.
She washed our face and dried our tears.
She would tell us daily, "Do what you are told."

Her motto was from day to day,
Trust in the Lord in every way.
He will guide you through,
When your hopes are low.
This our dear Mother really did know.

She was a mother to all neighbors & friends.
When it came to her help there was no end.
If it was in the church or in our home,
Our Mother was there, we were never alone.

Her work was important & hard to do,
But she never said "I can't help you."
She lived her life helping others.
That is why we love our dear Mother.

George F Willette
WITH THIS RING
With this ring, I pledge my love to you
And promise forever I'll always be true
No matter what happens, I want you to know
From this moment on our love will only grow

I'm sure there will be times along the way
When things will go wrong, but I'll never stray
The love we have together will keep us strong
And nothing will ever break our eternal bond
With this ring that's made of solid gold
My love for you will never grow old
And as the years tend to pass us by
Forever, you'll be the glow that's in my eye

So remember darling on this special day
The vows that we take will never break away
Because with this ring you will be mine
And forever more our love will shine

Because with this ring that's made of solid gold
My love for you will never grow old
And as the years tend to pass us by
Forever, you'll be the glow that's in my eye

Willa Ewing Cashwell
REJOICE WITH ME

In memory of Connie Simpkins Smith, Whose shining faith has been my inspiration"

Rejoice with me, and do not grieve,
When from this Earth I take my leave
From my path of pain, God set me free,
And when I walk, He walks with me.

Rejoice with me, He set me free!
A child of God I'll always be.
His plan for my life, I've fulfilled,
My soul is His, I've done His will.

Rejoice with me, and do not weep,
My date with Destiny I'll keep,
Heaven's gates are open wide,
And I rush forth, God waits inside!

Rejoice with me, for now I see,
What wonders He's set forth for me!
Now I know I'll never be alone,
I can feel His love, at last I'm home!

Rejoice with me, I'll wait with Him,
Until my loved ones enter in.
Just live for Him, and you will see,
We'll walk with God through
Eternity.

Rejoice!

Joe Dugan
YOUTH AND GAMES
When I was young, the games I played
Were as varied as the thoughts that,
Went sailing thru my young and open mind.

The games I played and the thoughts
I had were all important to me and
Just like the ties that bind.

They often come creeping back to
Remind me of better days gone by
and
Instill in my soul a sense of wonder.
I still play the games only now
they're the grown-up kind.

Anne M Plunkett
LOVE IS REALLY NOTHING
Love is really nothing,
until it's given away.
So why carry it around
with you, day after day.
God so loved the world,
that he gave His only son.
Don't keep your love inside of you,
show it, give it to someone.
Walk with the one that,
on the cross, His life, He gave.
For us He walked up to Calvary,
our destiny He wanted to save.
Tell Him you are so thankful,
you want Him for your own.
He will accept you as His child,
and you will never be alone.
When He returns to take us home,
He will come for you and me.
We will live up there with Him,
in Heaven for eternity.

Annette Mates
LITTLE PETE
Peggy Palmer had a pig.
His name was "Little Pete."
He always was so hungry,
That all he did was eat.
She took him to the orchard
To have a peach and pear;
But when they left the orchard,
There wasn't any there.
She took him to the garden
To taste tomato vine.
He also ate the cabbage
And said, they both were fine.
It wasn't long till lunch time.
So she took him to the house.
He went into the pantry
And ate a little mouse.
She took him to the parlor
To meet the family cat.
But he was just so hungry
He ate her mother's hat.
—Now he's fat.

Alfred Elkins
ELI, MY FRIEND
Eli does the funky chicken,
And the dancing head,
His feet are certainly
Not made of lead.

He is my best friend,
To the end
Of my life,
He is friends
With my wife.

He's a mathematician,
Not a politician,
Though he resides
In Washington, D.C.,
Seat of history.

Mary Pomeroy
GOD'S ANGEL
A cry in the dark.
Soul shattered by her father's angry hands.
She knew she was bad.

Why did no one see
the torment in the little girl's eyes;
the defeat in her smile?

In sleep, she sometimes dreamt
of other places where life was gentle,
and the pain went away.

But with the morning light,
the reality of her bruised life returned
until she could not hope.

The final blows came swiftly.
Her silent body lay on the floor
at the point of death.

Her dreams were finally realized
when bright angels came to lead her
away from her tormented life.

In death she found peace
from the unholy terror that consumed her.
God's angel had gone home

Hilma Bellows
HOME
They say that home is a dwelling place
A place where people abide
It embraces the love of a family
The cares of the world it can hide.
It matters not what its structure is
A cottage, a mansion, a tent

The people within enrich the home
It's not how much money was spent.
Memories build as the years move on
Of love and pain and joy.
The birth of a daughter, lovely and sweet.
The smile of a little boy.
Eventually the time comes
When from the home we depart
But no one really goes away
We carry home in our heart.

Mary Joyce Smith
WHEN THE DARKNESS COMES

This poem is dedicated to my love, Steven Michael Smith.

When the darkness comes
And the thoughts are black
My mind is bent
Twisting and
Smashing
the love we spent
I need you
I need you
You are the sunlight of my soul
When you are near the darkness disappears

Marie Andrews
CLOUDS
Sometimes when I look to the sky
I wonder, who, is really rushing by
Is it the clouds on a fleeting chase
And do the earth and I just keep pace
Where are they going in such a rush
Moving, changing, dark as dusk
Or sometimes as white as driven snow
But nearly always on the go

Forming shapes like animals or faces
Farms or homes or grand staircases
In foul weather or fair, they beckon me
To come along, and share the ecstasy
Fellow travelers, thus we are
One from near and the other far
All too soon, I return and sigh
As clouds keep right on drifting by.

Carol Ledesma
JUST ONE MORE TIME

To my baby—Wesley Jay, 8/30/81-9/15/81—I'll love you and miss you forever.

If I could see your face again
If I could hear you cry,
To hold you in my arms again
Just one more time.

An hour passes and I think of you
The moments we had were too few.
Believe me when I say, my heart misses you more with each passing day.
It's hard to live without you,
Sometimes there's no use in trying.
Denied the child who was brought into my life
Still I force myself to keep from crying.
I can't hold you, can't love you
It will never be right.
Just a minute, a second an ounce of time.
I just want to hold you in my arms again,
Just one more time

Grafton Ewart Lucas
CHRYSALIS

To my friend, Ciro J. Aragona

Like two guys
Bud and Buzz
Stopping off one day
For some drinks
At a pub in
Cork, Ireland.
Sampling a few
Got hung up on two,
This is how it all started.
Double tipple-toddies
Of Rye on green rocks,
With dashes of
Barbadian rum and ginger,
Balmy indeed, out of it, tighter,
By far than two—
Trinidadian steel drums
At a Shrove Tuesday ritual
On the Isthmus of Panama.

Grace Fluker
ALONE

Thanks to the love of my mother Carmen Fluker, I have found that special friend. I am no longer alone. Thanks Mom, I love you.

Sometimes I'm happy
and my thoughts are glad.
But when I feel alone,
all those thoughts turn bad.
I feel I have no reason;
to live or carry on,
Or to stay in this house,
I once thought of as home.
There is no simple joy,
or a friend who cares,
Just some childhood memories;
and a million little prayers.
So why should I stay around,
When all I feel is pain,
and everything I had is lost;
and there's nothing left to gain
But maybe when it's over
and at the very end
I'll find someone to share my tears,
someone to call my friend!

Mary Moreaux
LONELY DEATH
Remember me and the fun we had.
We got our kicks out of being bad.
Remember the time we played hooky? And in study hall we shared that cookie! Don't forget last summer—how we made-out in the hay. Remember the night you gave me your ring? We started going steady and everything. Remember all the parties we always gave; and all the times you said you cared? Remember the time we went all the way? You can forget, but I must pay. I'm in a home for un-wed mothers! But why should you care? You have so many others! While I'm waiting, I'm fighting the pain. The doctor came in a while ago. He said "There'll be some trouble." "Oh God." Please "No"! ! ! I found out now the doctor wasn't lying! The nurse just told me; I was dying! "The baby?" she told me would be alright. But I'll be somewhere else tonight. But before I go; before I die! I-LOVE-you-my-Darling
Take-Care!
Good-bye

Grace B Dedmon
THE CHEERFUL HEART
You set a good example
With your warmth & friendly Smile,
And most of all, your cheerful Heart
That makes living worth the while!

And then we remember The Master
Of't spoke of "Being of Good Cheer,"
As HE implanted in our Souls
An endurance, excluding Fear.

And when Evening brings The Sandman—
The Fairies join in with a Toast:
"Blessed are the Hearts that entwine—
When cheerfulness remains The Host!"

Helen J Barber
A SAILOR'S DREAM
Billow me sails of wind, going
Pillowed on gusting laughter,
Sheets rippling, keep on blowing
Till the sad, sloughing waves shall cease
And turn from their mournful sighs
To rest in serener seas.

Send me forever, far away
With the playful smiles of dolphins
Encouraging me to play,
Foaming, briny offerings for me
To sip from a silver tankard,
The horizon lends for company.

Lean me squarely into the wind,
Gentle my channels and lead me
Under the sea-gull's compass wing,
Harbor me safe with sails tight-furled
And nest me a homing berth:
Then billow me winds of the world.

Gilles P Desormeaux
ODE TO ROCK & ROLL

This is dedicated to the two girls in my life, Elsa & Daniella

The old and great seem to die so fast
The young and new don't always last
The legends live on, on vinyl or disc
Rock and roll was always the risk.

Political, love and commercial too
Rock and roll is always the venue
Only the Lonely Blue Suede Shoes
Give Peace A Chance and a lot of blues

I grew up with rock and roll
My generation still listens to the past
I listen to those days of old
Wishing they would always last

Elvis, Roy Orbison, John Lennon & Berry too
These legends affect us in certain ways
Not a moment goes on from a point of view
That we wished we were like them some day

Hail hail the gang's all here
Growing stronger every day
Always searching for that golden cheer
Rock and roll is here to stay.

Deona M S Agapetus
HOLLY AND ME
My daughter and me, we are really something to see.
Her eyes are green, and mine are brown.
Her hair is somewhat light, and mine not quite.

Her smile comes light and easy to give.
And mine comes slowly, not sure to give.
Her voice is soft in gentle tones,
The softness of my own she has to give.

Her frame is small as my own once was,
Before the years gone by.

Pretty yes, she will surely be . . . .
Why what else could she be?
She is so close to me . . .

Gino Raso
REMINISCE N.B.
On a lone cold winter night,
Standing near a fire burning hot,
Your silhouette enters my thoughts;
With your soft spoken hands,
Like a swan in a pool of romance;
and your sensuous long black hair,
into your infinite eyes I continuously stare.
Looking like an unimaginable being
and your radiant loveliness I am always seeing
symmetry in a world of ordered splendor;
with your sweet elegance and a smile
wish I could be with you for a while
and like a faint light that quivers
Pulchritude within you shivers;
Like the quietness of a soft snow
and an enflamed heart and enchanted soul
you are beauty in life
when life unveils her holy face
Like a flock of angels floating in space;
Lying in an ocean of mystery
you will always be a wonder to me.

Carol Langelier
MY PARENTS' FLOWER
They planted me in a pot
Around my feet they put soil
Soil,
of all the rights and wrongs.

They watered me with words on life
Hoping I would grow up
Right, straight and strong.

But they could not see the sun
They didn't see the light,
for they would not give my roots
enough room to grow, and they wonder why
I'm wilting.

Janis Heiner Wadley
MY CHOICE

To my husband, Mike, who inspired this poem.

There came a time,
after meeting this man and
spending time together,
Learning of his weaknesses and greatness,
that one day I realized I loved him.
Some may wonder at my choice,
for to them he may not be what
they would choose.
But that does not matter.
They do not know him as I do.
They have not knelt in fervent prayer

to learn the course I wish to
follow.
There is a calmness in my heart.
A whispering of assurance from
above.
I seem to hear faintly
the joyous chatter of children
that will be mine.
I smile often
for I know the choice I have
made is right.

Gloria V Espino
A VEIL OF TEARS

Dedicated to Manuel Espino Jr, with all my love.

Some days are filled with loneliness,
some days bring so much pain.
There seems to be no hope at all
With little left to gain.
The sadness that surrounds me
Has touched so many lives.
With poverty comes sorrows
And tears to many eyes.
I shut my eyes and dream of things
That are memories left behind,
Of days once filled with laughter,
With love, and happy times.

The happy times may come and go,
But his love has made me strong.
The pain I thought I couldn't bear
Someday will all be gone.
I hadn't seen the beauty
All around me through the years.
All that I could ever see
Was through my veil of tears!

Mary Leath Hall Williams
A HOUSE

May all houses become home sweet home.

A house is a wonderful place,
With many charming eyes about its
face.
It always sits in valley or on a hill.
Where its master molded it still.
Unless, the supreme master choose
otherwise,
To see its removal, demolished in
another place.

A house is a wonderful place,
Where multitudes seek shelter and
grace.
A lonely house, patiently wait its
race;
For its beauty 'domed in grace.
With rainbow colors curtains hung
with drapes.
And walls all painted, decorated in
flowered grapes.

A house is a wonderful place,
Where sully dust subdue beneath all
space.
To be cleaned by hands of the queen.
Books and pillows jumble real mean.
You'd think, tho, esteemed highly,
they are professor.
But God, send children's loveliness
to master the lesser.

A house is a wonderful place,
With shiny, slippery floors midst rug
lace;
And dramatic art hanging on its
walls.
Bringing gaiety free to all.
Unloosed, the furniture scatter 'bout
the rooms,
In every small corner love—
grass roots hearts into home.

Lawrence Aeschlimann
REFLECTIONS

The hate you looked
Into my face and
Thought you saw
was
C
U
R
I
O
S
I
T
Y
Nothing more.

How could I hate what
I had never known? I
Did not hate you then,
But now? Ah, that is
The tragedy of mirrors.
They have no being of
Their own.

Joyce Carrington Doyle
CHILDREN OF THE WORLD

For my (Christian Children's Fund) sponsored child Gopal Sahani in India.

Help me Lord; Please help me
Dry these tears in my eyes
Help me Lord; I'm alone
I can't feel anymore; your touching
me
Come to me, help me see this world
you left just for me
All the time; I must be; a child of
love and close to Thee

There's no food to feed us Lord;
Please talk to them
And make them give us all; A
helping hand
Care for us please dear Lord
For we're just poor children of the
world
I'm alone and so afraid
To think just what tomorrow brings
Tell them Lord; To share their love
And help the children of the world!

Robert V Blair Jr
HEAVEN'S GATE

When the essence rises, there's no
place to run
A familiar feeling now your time has
come
There was a hand you were holding
But the grip has gone numb
The shadow beside you has gone on
the run

You turn to see a star
Turn to seal your fate
You can't see it's over
You're at Heaven's Gate

Look to the future but nothing is
there
Look to the past, see an empty stare
You're paying a penance for things
you have done
Now gasping for air and find there's
none

You turn to see a star
Turn to seal your fate
You can't see it's over
You're at Heaven's Gate . . . .

Edmond Bargelt
THAT DAY WE

Mother of Earth rare
Man is there,
In your body beauty care.

His nose your navel
Love comfort in breast,
Your legs his strength, desire.

Woman anguish shared, what did I?
New life blooming there,
The planted seed.

Passion eagerly felt, lovingly
Mutual that day we.
Suppression now, anxiety.

Babe comes forth, love near.
Pride and beauty I see
The nipple of life is here.

Howard V Kelley Jr
EAGLELIKE

Spread your wings soar far and wide
Look things over before you light
When you are weary from the flight
You may rest here through the night
With morning the search resumes
Upon waking preen your plumes
Once again take to the air
For each there is only one nesting
place
And peace is what will be found
there

Kenh Pham

Kenh Pham
GET LOST IN THE SCIENCE 'ERA

O Poet!
Really
You were born
Wrongly
In this century,
When people
totally
disinterest
your poetry . . .

O Poet!
Keep in mind:
For research and design,
Scientists and engineers
are paid better.
As to your poetry,
It is
just to please
THE MUSE!

O Poet!
Comfort yourself,
Stay tuned with her
for ever . . .
May be,
in the generation future,
to secure
against science
without conscience,
People adjourn
and return
to the poetry . . .

And you,
O Poet!
You will be
admired,
and your works
restored
at their true
value . . .

Bill New
LADYBUG

A round creature in the garden crust,
Who occasionally makes her way to
the kitchen counter.
You may have seen her black polka
dots
on Royal Red.

She runs as if she'll die
When I see her out of the corner of
my eye,
But rescue is the order of the day,
As she climbs aboard my wrist,
For a trip to whence she came.

Debbie Donovan
LOVE & PRIDE

This poem is dedicated to Vince and Heather, I love you both.

As he stood standing, staring in the
street,
he needed to remember her, he
thought, In time we will meet.
No one could change him, the way
that he felt, he needed a friend just to
help.
She stood there crying, thinking of
him,
She knew deep inside of her that it
was the end. Places to go
And things to see, always makes a
person wild and free.
In her heart she wanted to stay, but
reality told her to go away.
He walked to her sadly, swallowing
his pride, because without her he
couldn't survive.
His hands pulled her near him, It was
easy to see;
He loved her too much to set her
free.

Lou Ann Brodhead
A MICHIGAN HOME

A Michigan home is very nice,
With oak trees tall and straight,
But when the end of summer comes,
Their leaves began to fall.

The winter's come with snow and
ice,
And everything is white,
And how I long to see the spring,
So things are green and bright.

But soon the snow and ice will melt,
And the trees will bud once more,
And once again spring is here,
And winter is no more.

Maria Coleman Barker
MOUNTAIN TEARS

The tough fragile beauty of the
mountains
Instill tenderness in men who lay
claim
To the lonely flowers and fountains
Fortuitously displayed in their
domain.

The soft soothing voice of the
hillside

Whispers comfort as men weep in distress
Unable to change the sweeping tide
Changing rivers and valleys into nothingness.

As the verdant land is trampled and torn
For the black gold and tall virgin trees
The woodland aisles with paths well-worn
Disappear forever into memories.

Whispers falter then strengthen
Rumbling deep in throats forced to leave
Their God-given home, man's haven of rest.
Mountain don't cry? Ah, don't you believe.

Mrs John A White Jr

THE BRIDGE GAME

It was just a foursome, two couples no less,
Playing for pleasure as you can guess.
The cards were shuffled and each dealt a hand,
Now the bidding is open upon command.

One club I heard, as I turned to stare,
My hand held five clubs, so you better prepare.
I bid one spade, as I sat with a poker face,
Now who was going to lead with an Ace?

The next bidder passed and on we go,
My partner bid six spades ever so slow.
The fun begins as the hand we play,
Fulfilling the contract without any delay.

Opponents win the Ace of clubs as the going gets tough,
All trumps are in, now for the ruff.
My partner was lucky, holding honors in the heart suit,
My void heart hand, now my horn I can toot.

One lucky hand, a small slam was made,
The next one may not be quite a parade.
The good hands are dealt along with the bad,
Win a few, lose a few, in your own little pad.

Kimmonique Ingram

THE GREATEST IMAGINATION

This poem is dedicated to God, my mother Ruth Lillian Ingram for being so patient and loving. A special thanks to my Grandfather Rufus Johnson and my loving Father and Brothers. To all of my family Thank you!

I have seen the imagination and best of friends we have become
I have colored our emotions and even added some
I have prevailed the unbelievable so far away you cannot touch
And I've placed you in a land that has so very much
I have granted you every wish and everything was alright
I have even given at your request more days and more nights
I have given you the perfect man the one you always think of
I have given you no fantasy, but the highest form of love
I have blessed you with children that you have not seen
I have granted all your wishes and I've never been mean
But how great can I be and I you've never seen
I am your greatest imagination,
I am your dreams.

Melanie Catherine Malerich

STREAM OF CONSCIOUSNESS

The full moon shines the half moon is here not
in time some time there is a time to contend
with the real world and time though there's none
to enjoy my world not
different but it is but are not
all expectations not
just shattered ideals of being embraced no
time but I understand the time is not
now not alone with cranky
mood I don't want to be in
the real world with damn
traditions I'm going to break
how my life was planned but not
by me the half moon shines not
the full moon.
It's not time.

Lindsey Bartlett

THE COLOR OF FREEDOM

The color of freedom is everywhere
In everyone's hearts
It's something to strive for
Something to cry for
And it's something to love
In my eyes I see the color of freedom
Do you know what color it should be?
It's all the colors, all together dancing on the sea
Can you describe what freedom is?
No, it cries so loud you cannot hear it
It shines so brightly you cannot see it
And it moves so quickly you cannot touch it
Yet, freedom makes you feel inside of a love you just can't describe
If you say the word "freedom" do you know what I think of? A flower, an ocean or a snow white dove

Daniel L Whiteside

AUGUST 23, 1975

Enjoying my chair in security,
Smiling at the purity,
Of the brandy in my glass,
Relaxed, I now think of my task.
To kill, I think, would be great sport,
In my master's eyes a good report,
Eyes of evil, black and red,
His voice echoes through my head.
"Kill, kill, kill," doth he say to me,
"Murder is just a game you see,"
The cold, black metal of the gun,
My hand grips, we are as one.
The demon again whispers in my ear,
"I am within you, do you fear?"
A cold chill is beneath my skin,
All my hairs stand on end.
With one last drink from my glass,
The gun to my head, this is my task.
I say good-bye to security,
And pull the trigger in purity.

Sarah Lillian Hamilton

I WALKED WITH HIM

I walked with Him through joys and sorrows,
I walked with Him though I knew not the way,
I walked with Him through countless dangers,
I walked with Him and trusted Him each day.

Sometimes the way was rough and stony,
Sometimes 'twas narrow and the path was steep,
Sometimes 'twas overgrown with thistles,
Sometimes my feet were bleeding, and I'd weep!

Sometimes He put His loving arms 'round me,
Sometimes He held me in His love divine;
Sometimes He left me in the shadows,
Still I was His and He was ever mine!

I walked with Him when all around seemed dim,
Knowing that He had claimed me for His own;
I walked with Him, trusted His guidance,
Knowing that He alone could lead me safely Home!

Lisa Senecal

MAY THE DEPTHS OF PASSION SURROUND YOU

May the depths
of passion
surround you;

When the person
of your dreams
has found you.

When your heart
gently
persuades you;

May you let
Paradise
invade you.

Aron S Golob

CONTENT

Time comes and in that moment I feel devoid of knowledge,
As if I know not a thing standing before the bridge,
But across the abyss I see that the emotion is fleeting,
For I am found, two feet firmly in the ground beating the fear.

Wait, next I think that too much knowledge has pushed me to the brink
Here I make a comment that assures me I feel wrong.
How educated I must be, where the break between right and wrong I see

Yet, still Knowledge is plain,
A pain of path through destiny

But I would not think to live life in a different way
I accept my past as right acts and know that
They made me

Stumbling, changing, hurting are part of existence
Showing me their opposites in the light of darkness

To grow to die, alone as one,
Yet live life in the now is, for me,
CONTENT

Elda Schwarz Wright

MY LORD IS ALWAYS WITH ME

In memory of my beloved husband, Tom, whose love and faith inspired me to always try to do my best.

I love my dear Lord with all my heart;
We never truly are apart.
He's always with me through thick and thin;
He's always there whether I lose or win.
He holds my hand when the way is steep
And watches over me when I'm asleep.
He comforts me when I am sad
And rejoices with me when I am glad.
He forgives me when I do wrong;
His faith and love keep me happy and strong.
Whatever I do, wherever I go
He's always with me—that I know.
He's not only my Savior, he's my best friend
And I know he will be to the very end.
He listens to me when I pray
And keeps me safe at the end of each day.
And when my journey on earth is o'er.
He'll safely guide me through heaven's door.
There I'll abide with God, my Lord and the saints adore
In joy, in peace, in everlasting love.

Marie Elaina Gordon

ON LOSING A LOVED ONE

This poem is dedicated to those suffering from the loss of a departed loved one. If it provides comfort, then its writing will be justified.

I ask you not for me to grieve
And so for you these thoughts I leave.
Remember—our body is but a "shell"
A place our "essence" needs to dwell.

My "essence" that which we call "I"
Has been freed and drifts up to the sky.
Searching and reaching for something *bright*—
That seems to draw me to its *light*.

My feeling is one of great relief.
For in this world there is no grief.
Only love and warmth and peace—
That seem to *"be"* and never cease.

I know what you feel now is pain.
But "I" still am—on some other "plane."
I've joined some other who "I" can "see"—
My friends—"I feel" so very *free*.

But if you need me—*I'll be near*.
If you speak—"I" will "hear."

Although my "shell" may turn to mist—
That which is "I" *does still exist.*

And "I" will not forget our bond—
That we formed with memories fond.
Space and time cannot destroy—
Years of together, years of joy.

And this "I" ask you to *believe*—
It's like a trip and I must leave.
But this is not where it will end—
It's just begun—we'll meet again.

Yours in time always

Vivian L Stotyn (Yeoman)
COME MY SON; COME—MEET JESUS

Dedicated to our five sons, Ron, Keith, Mel, Norm, Bruce.

Come meet the man , His name is Jesus;
Come meet the man, He is our Lord.
He came to earth to save all sinners,
To show us how we can be winners.

He is nearby to guide and love us,
To give us strength as days go by.
Why do you not believe, my son?
It gives Him joy when hearts are won.

You need someone to be your friend;
This is not just a passing trend.
I talk to Jesus throughout the day;
He is my friend; He points the way.

No, He doesn't remove all care;
But now my troubles with Him I share.
When days are weary and nights are filled with woe,
He helps me now, as He helped those long ago.

No need to be discouraged, no need to feel dismayed.
Everything is beautiful, everything He made.
Yes, every day I pray for you, my son;
I pray, from Him, you'll have no need to run.

Sean McGowan
THE DESCENT
Empty are my gloves of Eve
my hero building fantasy
my "Everything is better now"
and always happy ending

Dried and bleached as desert sand
fallen not on human eye
which join the rest of perfect form
to broken
each and all

The obsolete and laughing true
contaminated whispers
the touches of a prostitute
and memories of October's rain

Loretta Gilliam
DEAREST DAUGHTER
A mother-in-law she was destined to be
With eyes of love too blind to see
And a love too strong to fade
Together a happy home we've made

To her son I've been a good wife
I've gladly devoted most of my life
And to her grandchildren we gave
Life's road is now theirs to pave

A mother-in-law she was destined to be
I wish she could have loved me

A mother-in-law I was destined to be
Young love braving the same stormy sea
Together a beautiful sight they make
Like lovebirds atop their wedding cake

To my son she'll be a good wife
And gladly devote the rest of her life
And for me grandchildren are in store
To hug and cuddle, love and adore

My son we'll forever be sharing
For you, "Dearest Daughter"
My love and a very special caring

Denise Herron
SWEETPEA

I dedicate this poem to my mother, who had a flair for poetry and encouraged each of my efforts.

The sweetpea nods her dainty head
As I pass by her way.
She waves her body to and fro
When the wind desires to play.

She dances gaily in the breeze
That passes by her bed.
She holds her tiny face up to the sun
Which shines so bright and red.

She humbly bows her head,
And gladly accepts the rain;
Like all the other dainty sweetpeas
Beside the horse trod lane.

At evening she folds her petals in
And sleeps quietly all night.
When morning comes she fast awakes,
And shows again her beauty bright.

George Roland Wills
IN CATDISH TOAD
TOAD sits deep in the water
Contemplating nothing
A wise, empty stare
Toad does not realize
The Large Whiskered
Toad is justified
Yellow stare has no claim
Two-legs is a nuisance
No respecter of amphibious culture
But Two-legs is not here
And so Rumblefur must wait
until
Toad is dumped
in the yard
from the bowl
But until then, Toad sits deep,
unconcerned about Wetpaw

BarBara Kelalis

BarBara Kelalis
THE WONDER OF YOU

Dedicated to my beloved husband, Dr. Panos Kelalis

The wonder of you is the touch of lovers lips meeting for the first time. The taste of wine in the glow of candle light. A day of sunshine after a long journey amidst a cloud. The spread of a dove's wings while the skylark flies above. I painted a rainbow for you and added a star bright too. The fresh wonder of the evening breeze sways while the ocean sings a song of love and the morning dew places a kiss on the petal of a rose. All of life is the wonder of you.

Lisa Olsen
BLEEDING HEART

This poem is dedicated to Bryce, my special friend.

Each time I see your smiling face,
My heart is happy that we're friends.
Someday our friendship will draw to a close,
For there will be another girl I suppose.
The thought of losing you makes me weary,
For I would never hear your voice so kind and cheery.
My feelings for you are too deep to share,
I try and try to tell you how I feel,
Then when you leave, it makes my heart tear.
The love I feel remains hidden,
Though I long to reach out, we must not get close,
For we both know our love is forbidden.
Someone else is waiting for me.
God has sent him to help me see,
I am not for you because I could never fill your needs.
And because I want you so badly, my heart bleeds.

Thomas E Phipps Sr
HEREWITH MY "POEM"
Ill fares the land—
To hastening ills a prey—
Where lawyers and bankers
Smile the livelong day.

Jane A Simms
GOD HELP ME
I've been to a place of pain and sorrow
such that life held no tomorrow.

A place that is cold and dark;
a place deep within my heart.

I wept and sobbed, trying to pray;
but, there were no words I could say.

There was no way out that I could see;
finally, managing, "God help me."

Then a peace came within my being.
The Holy Spirit touched my soul with healing,

Leading me to a place safe and warm
in God's arms away from harm.

Ollie M Vaughan
THE INNOCENT PLEADS

This poem is dedicated to Julia, my dear mother-in-law.

Mom dear Mom,
Before you decide,
Think of all the guilt and fear
That you can't hide.

Love me and nurture me,
Then when I am grown,
I'll make you proud of me.
You just wait and see.

Frances Marie Surls
MUSIC MAN
I write songs of love
to show I love all men
to give my all, with love
and I'm called the "Music Man."
I never forget those words
so I can sing and pour out hope
to the lonely, lost and helpless
and I never try to boast.
Music Man, "how's the world treatin' you?"
"Very good, I say to them"
for I feel good every day
as in song, my heart, does win.
I travel the earth to sing
these odes of love and rhyme
and I trust my God above
He makes me happy all the time.
If they ask me, "how do you do it,"
I tell them I'm gifted by God above
and I go on teaching in song
I'm the music man, who spreads love.

Jim Cole
IN THIS BEAUTIFUL LAND!

To Don Seigelman; Ala. State Atty. General. To a Judge; James Hard, Attorneys; James Hill, Billy Ray Weathington and Talmadge Fambrough who "all" inspired this message, the Birmingham Bar and the Alabama Bar Associations

In this beautiful land of ours
It has been said
"Liberty and justice for all"

This I believe,
That is—
"IF" you know the right person
Have enough money
Or the price to pay a lawyer!

Marjorie Wilkes
AND THE ANGELS SANG

To My Children, Michael, Freddie and Lottie

I ask God for a drop of dew,
He gave a cup of rain;
I ask God for a little note,
And lo, the angels sang;
I ask God for a grain of sand,
He gave a giant rock;
I ask God for a baby lamb,
He gave a hundred stock;
I ask God for a tiny tree,
But here a forest grew;
I ask God for a precious jewel,
And behold, he gave me you . . . . .

Vita LaShea Bell
NUTHIN' FANCY

This poem is dedicated to my family and my special friend DeLemond.

It may be a little tattered
And a little shabby
But it be my home
My soul
My life
It ain't Caesar's Palace
Or that mansion so fine

Of Michael Jackson's
You sit up on that hill
In that warm brick house
With the fancy double doors
And white picket fence
White I sit here quietly
In nuthin' fancy

Pearl G Jenkins

Pearl G Jenkins
THE WORLD

To Mrs. Estelle Jenkins
My Loving Mother
Thanks for all that you have done.

Before me stood a frightened world
So full of love and joys unhurled.
Beneath its shadows life is free;
She gives her eyes for all to see.

Life breathes upon her sacred grounds
Polluted air asleep in smog-filled towns.
The highways cough and smoke and cry;
Bewildered trees grow old and die.

The endless sky held in her arms below
A thousand clustered dancing stars aglow.
The smiling silver moon walks in delight,
As beating raindrops swell the ground in flight.

Zhenming Zhai
AT BENEATH ASKEW
At across around,
Into through up'n'down;
Behind below between,
Under onto within.

After among about,
Over upon or out;
Before beneath beyond,
Outside against alone.

Aback above abask,
Aslant asquint astride;
Again afresh anew,
Astern aslope askew.

Armin C Gottberg
GIVE US MEN!
Give us men like those who loved their land of old,
Men who have the courage, strength and hearts of gold,
Men who gladly serve their land in times of peace,
Men who'll fight and die for her on land and seas!
Give us men!

Give us men who are content and love their work,
Honest men, who never stop and never shirk,
Toiling men, who eat their bread in sweat of brow,
Men like these we need, and ah, we need them now!
Give us men!

Give us men who render help to all mankind,
Men who love to help the lame, the halt, the blind,
Men who gladly give their alms to aid the poor,
Men who shun to drive the needy from their door!
Give us men!

Give us men who love their own and happy home,
Men who settle down and do not love to roam,
Men who love their loyal wives and children, too,
Men, courageous, trusting, happy, kind and true!
Give us men!

Lillian DeKeno
IT COULD BE ME
He has two eyes but he cannot
see the flowers; the hills; the
beautiful trees;
But Ah! by the grace of God,
It could be me!

She has two ears but cannot hear
the organ; the choir or children's
glee;
Ah! by the grace of God,
It could be me!

He has a smile, no words come forth,
To utter a sound is impossible,
you see,
For by the grace of God,
It could be me!

She has two legs but cannot walk,
To get up and go where she'd
like to be,
And by the grace of God,
It could be me!

So when I'm faced with adversity,
And look around at others, you
see,
I know that by the grace of
God,
It could be me!

Tommy Hinson
WORLDS APART

To Mr & Mrs. John A. Hinson (My Parents)

I looked out over the mountain
And seen
Two little towns.
One was made of happiness
And the other made of frowns.
There wasn't room for friendliness,
Or laughter nor for play.
Two towns so close
But far apart
Who never kneeled to pray.
My God had made a perfect world
For every one to live.
But no one seems to realize
We all have gifts to give,
In a world that's words apart.

Robert J Baker Jr
THIS WORLD IS SUCH A LONELY PLACE.

Dedicated to the late Laurie Cerra

This world is such a lonely place,
and now the tears run down my face.
Laurie's gone she's done her part,
By baring sorrow in her heart.
We all do face a lonely day,
Still in our minds her memories stay.
For Laurie did what most can't do,
She left behind a name that's true.
We all shall face a lonely year,
It can't be the same without her here.
Then we shall think back on those days,
She gave us pride in many ways.
Eternal life now hers to live,
Eternal thoughts now hers to give.
Down here Lord she's done her part,
Let her make a fresh new start.

Charles Jones
KNOWING AND NOT KNOWING

I dedicate this to my wife Esther only that she may know I am owner of it

If a person know not and knows not he know not
Shun such a fool in spite of his where about
If a person know not and knows he know not
Teach that person what it is all about
If a person knows and know not he knows
Wake that person it's sleep he has chose
If a person knows and know that he knows
Follow that wise one wherever he goes

Karen Jane Saxton
MIRRORS

To my Grandad, for ageless wisdom, limitless belief and friendship.

In the eyes of a child lie the hopes for the world
In the eyes of a clown its secrets
Eyes of a man seek the knowledge of both
While eyes of a woman scan horizons
The eyes of the old hold the truth of the world
Eyes that kill hold the fear and deceit

But through lives lived to full
We'll all find hope, gain knowledge
know fear, and reach for the horizon

For everyday

A child laughs into the eyes of a clown
A momentary glance joins man to woman
And the old meet the cold stare of one who kills

Robin Roper
IF I COULD
If I could cry for you a single tear
If I could hold you tight in my arms
If I could kiss your smiling lips or
gaze in your loving eyes
If I could place a thornless rose in
your hand each day of the year
If I could fly against the strongest
winds, or walk across water in a
raging storm
If I could fight the strongest beast and
climb the highest mountain
If I could find troubles in your eyes
and give them answers
If I could name a star after you
If I could say this to you instead of
writing it down
If I could tell you this and not turn
away in pain, fear, and shame
If I could place a diamond ring,
shining so bright, on your finger
If I could for you
. . . I would

Hanne Hartmann-Phipps
JIM . . .
Your love has whispered life's gentleness to my soul,
It has wrapped my heart in a delicate web of beauty,
and filled my senses with sweet sensual perfume.
Your love, like the flowers that raise their faces
to catch the warmth of the sun, is the light of my being,
and the nectar that quenches the thirst of my desire.

Elizabeth Lorene Hicks
BABY

This poem is dedicated to my recently deceased grandmother, whom I loved deeply; to my beautiful fiancé, Wade; and to my entire family for taking such excellent care of me and offering me undying love.

Metamorphize, my darling, into a
big, beige lion
with half open eyes and yellow mane.
I hug you and tufts of fur squeeze
between my fingers.
I gently rub to receive a soft,
murmuring purr. Purr, Sweet Baby,
purr
like tiny insects swimming in nectar
and infants cooing to be loved.
A nudge of your nose, I burrow into
your neck— closer and closer—
I am submissive and stripped.
Open to you, I cuddle you.
We struggle to get closer, as our
bodies almost melt
together like candle wax.
We are not the wax, but the delicate
flame.
The yellow blaze is within your eyes,
and it burns inside me to warm my
soul.
My pretty lion, with your beige
crown—
like a halo, but only a frame to the
reflection of my own soul.

Margaret Barton Korty
ADRIFT
So like a feather drifting on the air
Astride the currents that direct its way,
So like a feather drifting, who knows, where,
And yielding to the puffy breezes' play;
So like a feather floating without aim,
A feather, flipped and tossed in wafting streams,
A feather, whiffed about as Ariel's game,
A feather, fanned through countless sunny beams;
So like a feather, I float through this life,

Not caring for a purpose of my own,
Accepting others' offerings, dodging strife,
And following the easiest pathway known.
Perhaps 'twere best if I were not so free;
Perhaps, dear, you could shape my destiny.

Allysa Einbund
FRIENDSHIP
Alterations in the systematic derangement of our daily life
Have taken place throughout the years
Until we are overwhelmingly woven into
Incessant mundane webs of existence
Where at times we are oblivious
To the unyielding love of someone
Called a friend
And approaching a shoreline
Of substantial certainty
I am aware that my bond with you is Everlasting

Claudette Dujon

Claudette Dujon
THE MISSING PART
This light was in my life
He was so powerful, but I couldn't hold him.
He would have disappeared in the solid blue sky.
I am glad I had him for as long as I did.
I wonder how he feels for the person missing him now.
My love for him was a Shining treasure only he
Would possess.

Helen Somerman
SHADOWS OF YOUTH

This poem is dedicated to the beloved memory of my parents, Vincent and Dolores Basile.

The shadow of dawn peeked through
The day fresh and new.

I turned—I listened—I saw
My life as before.

Once again, a little one wrapped in the warmth of my Mother's love
Truly a gift from above.
Then, the moment passed
A girl I was at last
Off to school and play
Life—one endless day.

The flash of a decade
A teenager young and free
Soon a bride-to-be
He came into my life
And I became We.

In my youth I too became a Mother
And shared my special love with another.

I opened my eyes to greet the new day
Only to find
My youth had quietly slipped away.

I cried! I sighed!
For this is my life with no uncertainty
An endless circle of love from youth unto eternity.

Katharine Kidde
EARLY ON AN ISLAND
The sky breaks open vast with morning
The high cragged headland rocks
To the thunder of a frothing seventh wave

The wind from the silver molten sea
Governs the hard shimmer of grass
The bent trees crackle, tugging

Far out a jagged coral line of white
Exploding in place on blue
Takes the sun

Wooden boats are dancing
On sheer blue green
Near the dove white sand

The waves that spray these ragged waiting pillar stones
Are wild to find
This towering jut of green

All all
From the rounding horizon to here
Celebrates the light.

Wendy J Weaver
MY BEST FRIEND

To Mark L Hawkins, the best gift that God could possibly give to me. My Best Friend!!! Thank you Hawk, I Love You!!!

Whenever I needed a friend, you always seemed to be there,
You helped me with my problems, and our joys together we shared.
I can't imagine life without a friend like you.
Once we get together, we are an indivisible two.
All the fun I've shared with you can never be replaced.
Together we've had many good times, and conquered the problems we've had to face.
So I want you to know that I'm always here, if you ever need a friend to make your thoughts clear.
And if I must leave you, as sometimes good friends must part,
I leave you with good memories, and the most important place in my heart!!!

Mark Maupin
HIDDEN PLACES

This poem is written to glorify God, and His holiness PRAISE THE LORD. PTL"

Quiet waters reflect the dawn, as tendrils of mist lift and fade
Dragonflies drift among the reeds, ladybugs glisten in the light as they cling to blades of grass like lingering droplets of dew
Wild geese call, as they move across to feed: they leave behind them: long, widening, furrows that sparkle and gleam like shattered glass
Redwing black birds flash their scarlet wing patches in the sun
Clear melodic paping of the killdeer breaks the silence, as it searches for insects in the shallows. The shrill notes of the crickets fiddle, strike from,___hidden places

Jackie Litwin
SERENITY

To John Lewis, for always believing I could excel, and to God for giving me hope, faith, and the will to always try.

For one small moment I was touched by his greatness
I saw the gentle waters rush to shore and then recede back to the endless sea.
I saw the clouds open just enough to brighten the darkest of nights.
I saw a lone seagull flying aimlessly through the vast heavens.
I suddenly realized how everything went so well together.
Each a small piece of creation touching for one moment, then returning to where it first began.
My heart was so serene for that moment to know I was part of this wonderful fact of nature.
I have been given the opportunity to be in his plan, to do as I want, and then return from whence I began.
No other gift in my life could mean so much.

Mayte Puente

Mayte Puente
EL DIOS DEL AMOR

This poem is dedicated to my mother, with love.

Era un paisaje vacio,
largo y desconocido.
Era interesante,
hasta cuando no encontre el camino.

Mi mar era suave y calmado.
Aunque solo inspiracion,
soledad y llanto.

Creia poseer un sol radiante y hermoso,
y en realidad solo eran tinieblas
que cegaban mi felicidad.

Asi era mi corazon,
como un pajarillo
sin sentimiento y razon.

Pero gracias a su misericordia,
El llego hasta mi y lo conoci,
El derramo su perdon en mi ofensa,
y vistio mi desespero en esperanza.

El Dios de amor.
Asi lo dilseno.
Y alegremente puedo escoger su senda,
para trabajar con El
a traves del dia
y alegremente participar
del amor y el cuidado de
Dios a toda la creacion.

Gracia Dios
porque eres marabilloso,
y hoy soy feliz!

Lucille Saunders
BUTTE (MONTANA)
A beacon with stretched brightness,
Towers with paternal protectiveness,
Reveals a chasm yawning with copper glint.

Bursting entrails rock aged buildings
Swallowed in the wake of expanding progress.

Economic beauty softened,
Blanketed in soft contours,
Capped towers peer into whiteness
Blinding the fortune seeker—
Obsessed by the potential buried deep within.

Susan Timmins
SOUL REFLECTIONS
As I look over
the Harbour,
I see
my Destiny.
It is in
the Setting Sun.
My Fate is
There,
out at Sea,
free as can be,
with the Waves
gently rolling onto
the Shore.
The Seagulls
crying for Hope
and lost dreams.
As I look over
the Harbour,
I see
my Destiny,
and it is
Me.

Anita Louise Atkins
MY MOTHER'S FACE
I know every line.
Although I don't see her often,
I think of her all the time.

Her smile is always warm and sweet
And oh so good to see.
She makes you feel "her smile is just for me."

My mother's face is gently creased with time
And yet is smooth as silk against my cheek.

Her eyes are oh so blue and full of mischief
And twinkle like stars when she looks at you.

I see My Mother's Face everywhere I go,
And always feel a warmth which says "My Heart's aglow."

Her face is a picture in my mind, and there it
Will remain for all time.

How I love "My Mother's Face"

Virginia Duffy Stahl
EVENING OF THE MORN
I will not know another Spring—
I'll miss the brave, bright daffodil
That harbingers the birth of all things
Greening soon, and, still, despite the
Errant cold of Winter's reluctant passing,
Stands a symbol of Hope and
Promise of
Summer's bloom—

Wish me the courage of a daffodil, that
I may, in the cold winter of my heart,
Forlorn, stand brave in the chill of hope—
lessness of knowing that, for me, it is the
Evening of the Morn—

I have walked so long and so far to where
I was going—I had hoped it would be in the
Summer's warmth of your love.

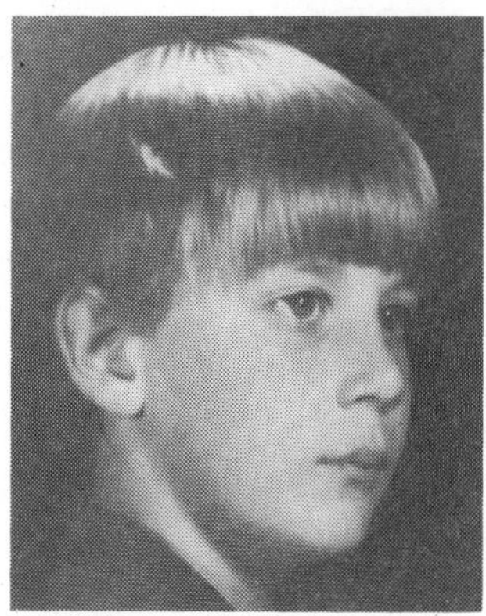

Jeffrey Wayne Eisenhower

Jeffrey Wayne Eisenhower
WISDOM

For Keith Davis and Glenn Lustig My Teachers, Who Inspired Me and Believed in Me

Deep within the Universe, the ancient Gods lay sleeping
Forgotten through the mists of time, till memories come creeping.

If you talk to the Universe, it sometimes answers back
And it is so frightening when the night is deep and black.

Subconscious questions asked in sleep, and answered in my dreams
The knowledge brings me closer to the cosmos' strange eternal scheme

I get up from my soft warm bed, wisdom fills my sleepy head
I sit down, turn on the light, pick up my pen and start to write.

I don't know what I'm writing, the words are not my own
Insight passes through me
And comes out in prose, and verse, and poem.

When the sunlight wakes me and I read just what I wrote,
I realize I know many things that other people don't.

And then the adults read it
Narrowed eyes and furrowed brows.
The look of disbelievers, these
thoughts can not be a child's.

They want answers, explanations,
I can't give them, and it's tough.
For I have dared the Universe,
And it has called my bluff.

Sandra B Cocoran
REMEMBER

This poem is dedicated to all Mothers and Sons . . . and to my own especially with love.

Oh my son, to see your face so young
imbued with lifes heart song
eyes aglow, timid, brave . . .
that first of many days to school
you go as I, Heart Thump Worry Lump
Remember
(Was it not just yesterday?)
you upon my belly wet
thrust out of warm float free dream place
to open air
Your face a show of outrage, shock
Tiny mouth pursed mutely at
being disturbed so rudely
Holding you, mouth at my breast
pearl hands perfect curled in rest
Heart throb, Joy love, needing to protect
this Miracle I took part in . . .
I see you . . . bittersweet, tearweep, joy-leap
on your way, so small walking tall
My sweet young babe boy child
Someday Man.

Jenna V Ownbey
VELVET FINGERS

You were so dear to give gift of glove,
Filling each hand and finger with love;
For now, I know, with each gloved hand—
Loved as I am—
I can give the passion of compassion,
Or even the glove, if I must,
To a meeker, needing one!

Steve Luper
MY COLLEGE LIFE

This poem is dedicated to the College Freshman . . . you're not alone.

Here I sit in blatant wonder
Of what the hell to do.
I didn't bring the required text,
Nor a pen with ink of blue.
So now the time floats above my head,
As if to say, "You JERK!".
I don't know why I cannot try
To do my written work.
For I am but a freshman,
In a world of dismay.
And if I do not
Organize a thought,
A Freshman I shall stay.

Timothy M Jacobs
FOR SOME LOVE IS STRONG FOR OTHERS IT'S A QUESTION

For some love is strong
For others it's a question of right or wrong
The theme of a heart is to keep a beat
If our hair can give warmth to the sun
And our bodies can obtain sins
Why can't our eyes see what other hearts are saying
Looking for a palace to rest
Waiting for an answerous dream
Sometimes we find ourselves
walking along an empty beach
Knowing the answers to life are
close by yet not so clear
Footprints in the sand with circles of wind in the air
We all like to dream the impossible dream

Angelo R Duca
MIND AND MATTER

Betwixt the world of mind and matter
Who can really say or dare define
This incomprehensible duality of nature?
Tho' both are true in part; they hardly seem the same.
Yet, never have I in God's presence felt
The urgent need to understand—
So intricately immersed in 'sense' was I
That spirit, beauty, thought and feeling
Are all to me the inseparable manifestation of the same.

Kristie M Taylor
WAITING

I'm still waiting
Like always.
Anxious for the day
I know will come.

But the sad part
Is knowing it will come.
And go
And I'll still be waiting.

Rebecca Sue

Mary Lou Von Meter
REBECCEE

To My Niece Rebecca Sue With Love.

Rebeccee that a name that means
Sun light on water.
Birds on the wings. Pink icing on a Birthday cake.
Silver bell at Christmas time.
A lovely face with shine'ie eyes.
And a smile that melts the heart.
Is Rebeccee My Rebeccee.

Manning F Bernard
A ROSE

To a real masterpiece, my beautiful wife, Alice.

Just like a rose, a beautiful rose,
Beauty of all the beauty that grows
Queen in the garden of fragrant flowers,
An inspiration of dreams and happy hours
Perfection, of the Masters hand
Foremost in a mass you stand
Tenderest heart, and beauty rare
There's none so wonderful, nor half so fair
The symbol of purity, and kindness glows
From your heart, a masterpiece, a rose.

Mike Ellsworth
I LOVE YOU

This poem is dedicated to a girl I used to know a long time ago I loved her but she didn't feel the same way toward me. I still think about her every now and then but she's gone and I'm still here. Maybe someday I'll find someone but not now.

We'll live forever—forever we'll shine, we'll be together till the end of time.
I will never leave your side because I love you dear,
because even when I die my love will never disappear.
When we get married I'll say "I do",
and I will always be true to you.
We'll have some good times and we'll have some bad,
but as long as you're with me my life will never be sad.
I know someday we'll be apart,
but just remember
"I love you" with all my heart.

Ana M Villarini
FREEDOM

To: My Beloved Children Amy, Emily, And John Lugo with Love.

You sit in loneliness and wonder why?
There's no telling what's on your mind,
So many things run through your little mind, you think of wanting to go far away and freedom! Yes freedom is what's on your mind.
You're tired of being a slave, Of playing house.
You want to travel, Dance enjoy what you did not do.
But only in that corner of loneliness you'll understand,
Why you'll never have Freedom one more time.

Amelia Colbert
THE HOMELESS

To the homeless—you are not alone! Help is on the way—Homeless but not Hopeless

I look all around me, and what do I see?
Hoards of homeless in the land of the free!
Where is the liberty and justice for all, in a land of sky—scraper a hundred feet tall?
We welcome the masses from across the sea,
And ignore the homeless born in the land of the free!
United we stand, divided we fall—
Where is the liberty and justice for all?
It's time we stopped ignoring Americas (#1) number one disgrace
and looked at the homeless face to face
I see a mother, a child, and a dad; a sister, an aunt, and a kid named Chad.
There's Sally, and Ernie, and Bubba, and Lee;
And I even recognize a fellow called "Tee".
Let's face it—the homeless are you and me!

Pauel E Beckworth

Paul E Beckworth
MY DREAM
Over the horizon, my dream took its flight
To a distant land far beyond the sunset.
As the dream vanished into the night,
Stood I looking up and away
Without hope of seeing the sunrise.

My dream seemed so remote, like the far away stars,
There was only a glimmer of hope.
As the days vanished and the years became shorter,
My dream was riding on the clouds of time
Striving to become true.

Never would it die, but keep searching for life's reality.
On the other side of the world, surely some day
Would come peace to the restless spirit
That gave birth to the dream
That kept searching for its love.

Steve Karas
DREAM IN THE WIND
You can sleep upon so many moments
As the scent of yesterday fills the air,
Yet you only dream of those to come
As the minutes climb the hours near,
You dream of the warm ocean breeze
And the softness of loves rain,
The call of the surf quiets the silence
Of passions brief flame,
You capture the wind in your aspiration
To only taste the gentleness of the unknown,
Time stands still for only an instant
Long enough to let you know you're all alone,
All those about you, are about you,
It's your fertility that's their disguise,
When you cry you only bring tears
To all the things that are your eyes.

Your lips remain calm upon evenings mist
As you allow the kiss of a dream,
Contentment will always be a brace
For your moments in all that seems,
As the flower is always the seed
So is the kiss to your vision,
Love recognizes no individual
But only ones association,
You know reality has gone amongst awakened tears
As you dream a dream of your own,
Let it go and try to realize
That only your heart is truly your home,
When desires warmth comes about and beckons
To quench the dew upon your lips,
Let the breeze carry it away
So it may nourish the times that one forgets.

Your tears roll down a solemn face
Only to find safe haven in the rain,
That's why you must dream your dream
So you may never know loves pain,
The winds will always continue to blow
And the snow will forever be the blanket,
Love is so much like the colors of fall
Knowing all its beauty is one to be spent,
When you begin to dream no more and
You awaken from bordered existence,
Question not what is before you but
Whether love still maintains its presence,
If it should not, search under the cover of snow
For all that will grow once again,
Then close your eyes and sleep
And be once more with all that had been.

Toni L Stubbs
MY HEART IS LIKE A GARDEN
My heart is like a garden
tilled by God's own hand
A fertile, blooming Eden
that once was barren land

My life is full of foolish things
like soil with stones and weeds
But with God's help I fight the briar
that would choke His gentle seeds

Though men, through evil, made the cross
t'was God who made the tree
And as we dwelt within our curse
Christ rose to set us free

Audrey D Buenaventura
CROWS

For my children, Louie, Laurie and Lisa, who know where this poem came from.

The way grass springs up
eventually
through asphalt parking lots
and abandoned highways;
lawns, once trimmed
like green baize mats,
reverted to thistle
and other banes of suburbia,
dandelion, camomile and chicory—

the color of winter skies;
railroad ties
mouldering
back into cinder-laden roadbeds
beneath rusting rails
on barren, dead-end
switches; and
the sight of crows
before me in the fast lane,
flapping just enough away
as my man made fury
races past—
returning then to feast
on squirrel flesh—
restore my sense of order
like a glimpse of neatly folded linen
stacked on shelves
before the closet door is closed.

Deanna Witt
WINTER FANTASIES
I awoke with a vision.
A beautiful princess stood
Outside my windowsill.
She thought of herself as the Snowqueen.
With long, dark hair and gleaming, blue eyes.
She was the most beautiful queen of all.
The Snowqueen,
Queen of all winter fantasies,
Fantasies of beautiful nymphs
And snowy white horses,
Riding through the woods
At night
In the florescent moon.
Nymphs,
Nymphs that never died.
Still, I was overwhelmed
To see her standing there,
for every evening I hear
A horse galloping about in
The chilly night.
Then just as I was about to walk outside to meet her,
She disappeared—
She was gone,
The elite Snowqueen.

Vicki S Reynolds
ONE WITH THE ICE
The ice is the haven
that brings out the best,
That inspires that one
to be above the rest.

It's the feeling of flying
yet one with the ice,
It's an emotion of melancholy
and yet it excites.

The spectators' hearts
beat with unknown fears,
But perfection and beauty
fill all eyes with tears.

When the music is over
and the routine is well done,
Shimmering ice and elated skater
are proud to be one.

Nancy Ruth Horn Davis
YOUR CHILD
Such hopes and dreams I do spend
for life's happiness I want never to end,
but as your child you make me see
not everything is as I would have it be.

Lord how could I grow without your help
if you hadn't held me with thy faith
with each new step.
Teaching me daily to rely on you,
giving me strength to try and do.

Lord give me wisdom to see the light,
help me to be strong and do what's right.
How would I grow in your sweet love,
if you hadn't given me the wings of a dove.
To fly so high in happiness, with
your sweet love and tenderness
To pass through the valleys of sorrows
and still know you'll be with me
again tomorrow

Just a child in so many ways
Waking up to each new day.
Still learning oh so slowly,
Not my will but thine, The Almighty Most Holy.

Jennifer L Hartzell
MOM AND DAD
We just wanted to get a chance to say,
We love you very much.
You've given us a chance in life.
Your patience and your trust.

I don't think in words we could ever say,
How dear you are in our hearts.
You planted the seed and watched it grow.
That's how love really gets its start.

You've watched us grow from child to adult.
Sometimes the pressure was overbearing.
Somedays were good, somedays were bad,
Through it all, you kept on caring.
We want to "thank you" for the job you did
For the happiness and the fun.
And never, ever let you forget,
In our hearts you're number one!

We love you

Mom and Dad!

Mei Chung
FRUITFOOL LABEL
The fool will look for the
fruit of life,
The smart one will plant it.
Maybe the smart one
is the fool—
Because the fool does nothing,
but take it.
Maybe the smart one
is the smart one—
Because wherever he goes
he can always have it.
Maybe the fool
and the smart one—
Are the left and right hands,
one just loves to take;
the other lives to plant.

Pamela Hertenstein
THE WALLS OF LIFE
Trapped within the walls of life,
I look for some escape.
The world is crashing down on me—
I cannot get away.
Slowly now, they're closing in,
And there's nothing I can do.
There has to be some way out
Of this dark and lonely room.
Closer now, here they come,
The world—still crashing down.
I'm so afraid—what can I do?
As the room spins 'round and 'round.
Do I give up now and let them win?
Or should I stand and fight?
A wounded soldier on enemy ground—
Weakened from my fright.

Can I make it if I believe? Is there a chance for me?
Trained to fight—I'll do just that.
I'll make these walls retreat!
And if I fail—I still can say,
"At least I gave my all.
I ran the race—I fought the fight;
But the pressure made me fall."
And if, by chance, I don't get up
From this never-ending fight
Please know, my friend, I did not quit.
In time, I'll be allright.

Lori A Bailey

LOVE

To my husband David these words are sincerely felt.

To love you,
to hold you,
that's all I care to do
for you near me makes my life brighter and easier to go through.
For a poem is only to express the words I feel
And feeling for you is what my love is all about!

Ellamay N Schollhammer

Ellamay N Schollhammer

FORWARD MARCH

A "kinder, gentler nation" can be a reality
With cooperation it's in the realm of guarantee
Remember "Be ye kind one to another" is the rule
And instill these basics to our children in public school.

Our future has to produce a moral, honest nation
With Citizens proud to defend and protect their station
Eliminate drugs, crime, violence and all pornography
Replace it with love, brotherhood and good photography.

Attend church with family followed by dinner arrangements
Strengthen family ties and thus eliminate estrangements
Happiness brings harmony and true love will overcome
Life is now worth living when contentment rules everyone.

So Americans unite and try genuine living
Stop all the taking and enjoy the blessings of giving
Set a fine example, love, worship and work without cease
And pray that our grande nation will continue in world peace.

It's great to be American—keep Ole Glory flying
Our nation and heritage are best—there's no denying
America's number one so let's uphold its credence
So onto your feet, salute, and pledge your true allegiance.

Jo-Ann M Ogden

VALENTINES DAY

To my husband Barry, with all my love

Valentines Day
Is for lovers to share
With a certain mist
There's love in the air

You're the one I love,
Both night and day
Here with you
Is where I'll always stay

I know our love
Is deep and true
It wouldn't be the same
Not without you

Myrna R Marble

GROWING UP

To my four wonderful children, Alan, Lana, Gary, and Steven

The fingerprints and smudges,
were once heavy on my wall.
The sound of little running feet
fell heavy in my hall.

There were questions, questions, questions! MAMA, what is this or that?
And those precious times of quiet
—Soundly sleeping on my lap

Then suddenly, it seemed so fast,
the days, the months, the years
The time had come for them to leave;
our faces wet with tears.

That little one, I held so close,
had grown up and he must go.
And even though my heart would break;
I would have it so.

So each one leaves to make their way
In life's uncertain storms.
My heart cries Dear Father;
Safely hold them in your arms.

Trevor L King

SHAFT

Succinctly slither-
ing from line
to
line
Serpentine words
Maliciously draining my pen
Silver fangs tipped of venom
Sink into THE END.

Harry Lee Nichols

THE LITTLE RED WAGON

The little red wagon
Is covered with dust,
And some of its parts
Are beginning to rust.

Its wheels have not turned
From the Spring to the Fall—
And I'm just sort of wond'ring
If they'll turn at all.

And dark is the place
Where it's hidden from sight—
Unaware of the morning,
Not knowing of night.

The cobwebs are forming
Just like an embrace,
To keep it from leaving
This one special place.

And it silently waits
For the time and the day,
When three little girls
Will come back to play.

Loraine M Maloy

Loraine M Maloy

THE SEASONS OF MY LIFE

I was born—I blossomed and grew, learning many things. All new!
In the spring of my life.

I matured an learned the persuasion and excitement of love.
In the summer of my life.

I found a new patience and compassion; sorrow and joy.
In the fall of my life.

I look forward to the quiet—peace—contentment—only to be found
In the winter of my life.

And when earthly things have passed—
At last
I will understand why I was granted
The seasons of my life.

G Steven West

GRANDMOTHERS PLACE

I wish this dedicated to the Love, Honor, Strength and Spirit of mine and all other Grandmothers of this world. God bless them.

There is no sweeter remembrance, no greater image than Grandmothers Place. Woven through the fabric of life, the love learned at Grandmothers Place fuels and sustains you no matter where or how far life travels might take you.

Warm sweet memories, everpresent to light the path, brighten dark moments, strengthen faltering courage. This is the legacy of Grandmothers Place.

Lessons of life and character lovingly taught, directions and beliefs charted, ideas and dreams allowed to be voiced. These are the cornerstones of Grandmothers Place.

Times spent, moments shared, always treasured, always remembered. Love given, love received, unconditional, unselfish, always there. This the strength of Grandmothers Place.

God willing, may everyone be blessed to have a Grandmothers Place in their life.

Grandmother, I Love You.

Robby Daniels

THE SOUNDS OF LITTLE FEET

The populations growing
Too much playing in the sheets,
Soon our cries will all be drowned out
By the sounds of little feet.

Our food supply is dwindling
Soon there won't be enough to eat,
Unless we put an end to
The sounds of little feet.

There'll be riots in the heartland
They'll be fighting in the streets,
Unless we find the answer to
The sounds of little feet.

I think I've got the answer
Now wouldn't this be neat,
We'll chop off their legs to silence
The sounds of little feet.

I know some parents will complain
They'll want to get me in their clutches,
But I've got new problems of my own
The sounds of little crutches.

Chrisandra L Stover

YOUR EYES

The smile on your face
And the twinkle in your eye,
Make me think
Of all the reasons why.

Why did I ever love you?
Why did I ever care?
Whenever I needed you,
You were never there.

Your eyes I can look at,
Though I couldn't before.
Maybe its because what they told me,
I chose to ignore.

Your eyes were telling me
How you felt inside,
But I didn't want to believe
That your love was just a lie.

Cora R (Gaillard) Betts

AWAY FROM WHERE THE COLD WIND BLOWS

Dedicated to my husband, Marvin, my mother Elizabeth and my Children

The cold wind howled outside the door,
I heard your voice, just as before,
You called to me "come go with you,"
Away from where the cold wind blows.

As you talked with me, the darkness turned to light,
You were a vision that came in the night,
You kept saying "come let's go,"
Away from where the cold wind blows.

I watched you leave like a flutter of breath,
through the stillness of night "no I won't forget,"
What you said to me as you turned to go,
I'll return for you, when the cold wind blows.

The cold wind chills through my body, my soul,
The loneliness I feel, no one knows,
"I'll be waiting my love, "I'll go with you"
Away from where the cold wind blows"

Patrick Harrington
HOMECOMING

This poem is dedicated to the memory of my father, Joseph, a good and decent man.

He sat there
On Sunday
By the cottage kitchen window
Looking out
At nothing and at everything,
Curious in a detached kind of way.
The ancient horsehair-stuffed armchair
On which he sat
Had finally parted company
With resistance to years of pressure
And split here and there.

Segments of it protruded
With a curiosity
That mirrored his response to me
As I entered from the yard:
"Hm, what is this?
What have we here—
Finally?"

David L Thatcher
AUTUMN'S CARPET

I dedicate this poem to all who have learned to love God's beautiful nature.

As I walked the streets one morn
Around our part of town,
I watched the swirling autumn leaves
Fluttering slowly down.

I saw large Oaks and Maples,
With fading leaves once green,
Blend many shades of gold and red:
Rich colors so serene.

These trees so brightly colored
Moved gracefully with ease;
As they slowly shed their dress
In autumn's gentle breeze.

I watched as red and golden leaves
Let go without a sound,
One by one they slowly fell
And carpeted the ground.

Cynthia Galloway
BUD

To: Tony and Nyree, my constant source of love and to the one that made me bloom.

I feel like a bud
that has been tightly closed.
With your love, your nurturing,
I have begun to open up.
I am almost ready to turn my face to the sun
and revel in its warmth.
Don't go, don't leave
until I can know,
until I can experience the joy
of being in full bloom with you.

Ronald J Schaaf
BEAUTIFUL THINGS

To my wonderful wife, Judy.

Snow falling softly in large flakes.
A pile of autumn leaves freshly raked.
The sweet smell in the air, before a summer rain.
The view of the clouds, from above, in a plane.
But the most beautiful thing in my life,
is the love I give to and receive from my wife.
I enjoy every moment that we have together,
even when they are bad, our love will endeavor.
There are so many beautiful things to see in this land.
And they are twice as nice when you're hand in hand.
I wish that I could spend infinity with you,
but since that is impossible, forever will have to do.

Connie Ludolff
THE GREATEST GIFT

The greatest gift to us was given,
When God sent His Son from Heaven;
To suffer and die upon a tree
To save us all and set us free.
We should be grateful every day
And show our love in every way.
A smile, a word, a call we give,
Makes someone's life better to live.
So let's do everything we can do,
To thank God for saving me and you.
When it comes to that great Judgement day.
We'll know we helped in some small way.

Aracelis Hernandez
PEOPLE DON'T UNDERSTAND

People don't understand
why he acts the way he does,
he screams, he yells
he inflicts fear.
I understand,
he really cares.

He knows the world is only one.
He knows that soon it will be gone.
He wants to save the little left.
He wants us all to give our best.

Lorna Lee Beck
TRUE LOVE

TO ALAN—My loving husband to whom I owe so much. I love you.

I never thought I'd ever find
somebody quite like you.
But now I have, and you're the best
you've made my dreams come true.

You'll never know just how I feel
and how I care so deep.
I dream of how our love's so real
each time I go to sleep.

My love for you is so intense
it makes me want to cry.
When you hold me close to you
I feel so warm inside.

Each hug, each kiss, each time we touch
is one more chance I have,
To let you know just how I feel
and what I haven't said. I love you . . . truly.

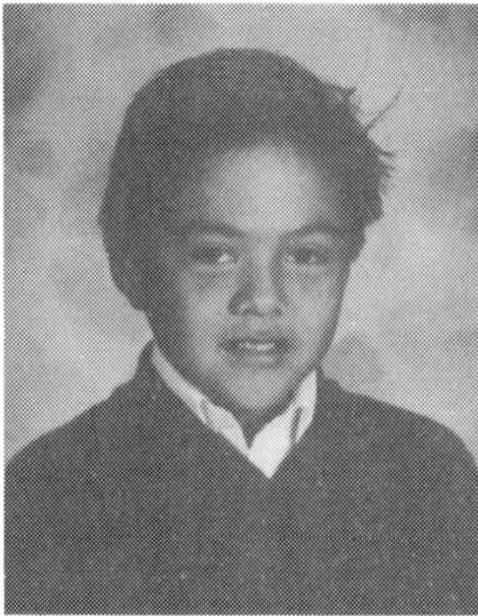

Jeffery Jay Dalgai

Betty Baumgardner
JEFFERY

To our beloved Jeffery Jay Dalgai "We Love You" From his mother, sister, brother and friends

Jeffery was a friend of mine
Died at the age of ten or maybe nine.

Died before his time I know
I wasn't ready to let him go

Haunted by my tears I wondered why?
I never had a chance to say good-bye

All said, "It's God's will," please don't cry
So tell me God, "Please tell my why"

I never complained I simply cried
when you took my mother and my brother died

Now you've taken this tiny soul
why couldn't you taken someone old?

and just left my friend to run and play
and kept him safe another day

Peggy Parrish
ECHOES

Dedication to my family

Echoes of yesterday slowly gone by
With the love and joy of those by my side
Echoes of yesterday and faded colors
In hopes of brighter tomorrows.
Echoes of yesterday play my mind
Like wind chimes being divine.

Echoes of yesterday make this day

Like a field of wild flowers covering the soul.

Robert W Souder
SOUND OF MUSIC

To all the people that said I could . . . Thanks.

Time and time again the music is played,
Each time a little louder, each time a little longer.
At first it seemed not so alarming,
However now it seems unstoppable.
The music is reaching out for a most destructive climax,
If not soon stopped it shall control the world.
"Why worry" one may ask,
"Not me" another may say.
Besides all our children are angels,
Well then indeed the music is merely myth.
But I still hear the music,
And your little angel is part of the band.
Oh your little angel is so much in tune,
Only one thing is wrong.
Your little angel is controlled by the music,
Not the other way around.
In fact your little angel no longer plays,
Your angel . . . . .well he's dead.
Still the music rolls on,
Louder, louder, and louder . . . . . .

Jenny Ruschau
A SEED OF LOVE

This poem is dedicated to Michael, my husband.

A seed of love blooms like the rose
we have out own seed and I'll never let it go.
But this single flower blooms constantly
it never dies, it hides no secrets and tells no lies.
It's strong stem holds it deep into the earth, and as for this love I consider it my first.
It's true, it has hope and it doesn't have any doubts, but watering this flower is what its all about.
To make this flower grow you have to feed it special things, a caring best friendship and the love you gave to me.

Ellen P Stevenson
NO SEPULCHRE HEAVEN (On Reading William Cullen Bryant's Thanatopsis)

I dedicate this poem to my Master and Living Lord, Jesus of Nazereth, and to all our Family of Man.

No "silent halls of death" I see,
No "dreams" or tomb of man.
For all the numbers past, I know,
Are billions in that realm;
But full of life and work and play,
I know His Kingdom holds,
With trust in One who reigns above,
I eager go to join that Life—
No tomb, I say, is Heaven's gift.

Celia Diaz
A SUMMER DAY AND YOU

This poem is dedicated to my beloved Eddie

Sitting in the shade of our pecan trees,
all my thoughts are of you and me . . .
The sunlight filtering through the leaves
form dancing shadows with the breeze.

The setting sun changed the clouds to gold
and I feel the breeze on my face at last.
Remembering our summers of long ago,
the ones by the beach, are my

favorite yet.

Time has passed, but yet it seems,
I can still feel your presence near.
Sometimes you tip-toe into my dreams
and all my loneliness disappears.

Our life had some cares and sorrow,
but full of love for all to see . . .
It will last for all tomorrows because you shared your life with me.

This summer day has come and gone,
though memories stay, life must go on . . .
The morning comes, a golden dawn,
I softly smile remembering when together we watched the rising sun.

Sue L Calicutt
MY FIRST LOVE

Dedicated to my Mother

There are those who love good books,
And those who watch T.V.;
And those who love a game of chess,
But that just ain't for me.
There's still the ones who like a show,
Vaudeville or even ballet;
Or those who even love to paint, or
Dabble in some clay;
But I must tell you of my first love,
Of which I'll now disclose;
It's a very simple longing to
Just sit and pick my nose! !

Donna Merriman Teippo
THE STEPMOM

To ALL my children

How well I know I'm not your mother
I'm just your father's wife
But you must know I love you
Because He gave you Life

Never came I to replace her
Or wipe her memory away
I know I'm just a "step" to you
But stepping closer every day

You must see by now I love you
And want so to be your friend
For this I try and pray daily
That you'll see this in the end

If you have the urge to cry
And a shoulder's what you need
Or you want to laugh at me
Please know that I'll take heed

I hope someday to hold you
And know you realize
That Step-Moms aren't all wicked
I'll see it—in your eyes

Vincent C Mayers
TOKENS OF LOVE

I would like to dedicate this poem to wife "Harriet" with love.

Love is sharing and caring about each other.
Wanting to be with one person more than the other.

Love is looking into his eyes, as though, each time was the first.
And holding him as though you could never quench that thirst.

Love that sixth sense you possess to be by his side when he needs you and to stand back when he must be alone.
Love is a warm cup of coffee at breakfast, and a warm hug at night.
Help when the going gets rough; laughs when all is right.

Love is what you feel when you watch him work or play.
The feeling that no other can do it quite his way.

Love is always wanting to assist him, and never having to be polite.

Love is sometimes disagreeing, but always caring—during a fight.

Love is forgiving and understanding.

Aimee A Baxter
THE TEXAS WAY TO BE
We drive real friendly, that's the Texas way to be
We take a lot of pride in our hospitality
But when we get on the road with our oversized load
We give those BUBBAS the finger and run 'em off the road.

REFRAIN:
The Lone Star State, we're proud to be the best
Our greatness is infamous all throughout the west
We spread our propaganda 'cuz we think we're number one
We don't know if its true, ah but hell, its all in fun.

Our beer commercials show how we chase those yankees north
We always prove our manhood and show how much we're worth
We've got the biggest schools, the biggest trucks, the biggest state
We got the whole world duped into thinkin' we're first rate.

We invite new folks in 'cuz we know we need new blood
We'll be real Texan friendly and offer 'em a Bud
But if they turn their snotty nose and ask for a Dos Equis
We'll tell 'em where to go and say "DON'T YOU MESS WITH TEXAS."

REFRAIN

The Lone Star is a sign of great and mighty men
We bravely stand alone and remember where we've been
So when the banks all fail and the condos haven't sold
We Texans unite and say "REMEMBER THE ALAMO"

Texas tea made us rich until the crash of 82
Everyone went broke 'cuz the loans weren't comin' through
But now OPEC can stick it thanks to the superconductor
We ALWAYS survive 'cuz we're mean mother . . . OH

REFRAIN

Mary Bon-Richards
THE POWER OF LOVE

To my daughter Sandy and sister Janet whose love gave me the inspiration to write this poem.

I'm away from home
Far far away
But the power of Love
Can be felt across the miles

Love comes with all its
Beauty, serenity and power
I feel rich and full
Because I know I'm Loved

And because I LOVE
And I am Loved
I cannot perceive life
Without it

I thank God for LOVE
For without it
I would be empty and
'POOR'
There's No Need to say more.

John Perdue
ONE CHANGE

This poem is dedicated to Alexandra, a dear friend, with love.

Careful necessity,
A meticulous brevity.
Approached vagueness;
A contrite awareness,
A complacent view.
A collusion of two—
To have magnanimous appease,
And an endearment
Accord of increase

Variously variable,
One change.

Parlay of faction,
Pursuit in clarification.
What is partial—
Not what was.
Any comparison select,
To possess neglect.
Concern of mandate;
A note of expanse,
A tone of measure.

One change.
Verification variable,
Verifiable Variation.

Edward Pfertsh
THREE ANGELS

To my wife Nancy, and my daughters Faith and Sarah. Somehow they found it in their precious hearts to love me even through the hardest of times.

Some men have to search high and low
For the love they need to help them grow
And somewhere out there without a doubt
Is someone feeling cheated and doing without

For every man needs a certain measure of love
All sent to him from our Father up above
But someone isn't getting their equal share
Because I was granted three angels who care

Some men search for treasure in their life
This I have found in my precious wife
She beholds beauty and strength rarely seen
One of the finest women there's ever been

Some men search for diamonds and pearls
I have these and more in my two little girls
The whole world can seem dark and blue
But it brightens when I hear "Daddy I Love You"

For every man needs a certain measure of love
All sent to him from our Father up above
But someone isn't getting their equal share
Because I was granted three angels who care

Tammie Blackburn
THE CHILDREN OF YESTERDAY

In memory of David Martin Noviello

There's no tomorrow
And there's no yesterday
Only pain and sorrow
Who ever thought it would end this way
For the children of yesterday.

Whatever happened to the blue skies?
Did they all just fade away?
Whatever happened to all truth and no lies?
I guess that was the law of only yesterday.

Try living in the past
It rips out your heart
I know the pain will last
As long as we're all apart.

Nobody knows how to make it go away
Away from the children of Yesterday

Away from the children of Yesterday

Jenifer L Manheimer
SITTING ON A BRIDGE
The water winds its way
Around the weeds growing in its path.
The geese swim in a straight line
Winds blow, the water shifts
The bridge provides passage.
In the cemetery the dead rest
And can hear the pounding Feet above them
Clouds are covering the blue sky
The willow weeps with age . . .
Increasingly with age.

Melody Yarbrough
THE EASTER LILY
Let's take a look at the Easter flower;
White in color to show Christ's purity and power.
The foliage resembles a very long spear
. . . like the one that pierced our Saviour dear.
Look at the depth of the trumpet shaped bloom
As if sounding praises for the empty tomb.
The blooms hang down as Jesus' head did

As the people cast lots by the way of bid.
The hanging stamen resembles teardrops falling
. . . like the ones God must have shed when He heard Jesus calling
"Father why have you forsaken Me?"
As He was hanging on the tree.
This flower isn't complex at all
. . . Although the plant grows quite tall,
Reaching toward the Heavens above—
Reminding us of our Saviour's love.

Wayne Parrish

Wayne Parrish
HANDS OF THE SHEPHERD

To the Doctors, Nurses, Clerical Staff and Employees of the Pediatric Hematology Clinic. Leukemia Section, North Carolina Memorial Hospital, Chapel Hill, North Carolina. God Bless them All. Conceived and written in loving memory of our daughter, Maria Ann Parrish, whose courageous battle ended at dawn Sunday, November 3, 1985.

As i leave my mortal shell behind, i rise in wonder, the old pain is gone. I am whole and strong again as i rise slowly upward, I'm aware of family and friends i leave behind, my grieving Mother stands by my bed, Father stands by the door, his head hung in grief, perhaps a sister or brother, just down the hall, all straining to hear the few words said, She is gone, it is over, the cry goes out.
If only I could touch, or they could see,
I am whole again, cry not for me.
But I am rising faster now, through dark and mist,
past rolling clouds of silver, all sunlight kissed,
into the Heavens, faster and faster toward the Light,
I am carried by Angels, one on my left, two on my right,
No words are spoken, and none need be,
I know they are sent to guide and comfort me.
As we draw near, I see old friends and have no fear,
they welcome me with love and a loud ringing cheer.
From beyond, I see a Golden Throne, amidst a shining light,
people gathering by thousands on my left, and more on my right,
I hear a voice, rolling as thunder, and gentle as the grass,
and lo, my name is called, people part and let me pass,
for I who was lost am now home at last,
I sing and rejoice as part of His flock,
for I am as His sheep, and He is my rock,
and I fear not the lion, nor even the leopard,
for I am safe and secure, in the Hands of the Shepherd.

Karen Gaskins
OTELLO'S PASSION

To all the abused persons that the world cannot understand therefore making it easier for them to remain victims.

In the desert sand
Someone wrote my name
Then the wind blew
and carried it away.
I heard the hollow echo
of my quiet death
and felt the cold, clammy
hand of some monster
at my throat.
Haunted by their own
dark shadows,
Created from a darkened heart.
Madness can make one
do many things
Things that we may
later regret
and things we wish
we could
forget.

Wilma D Head
THE TV TRAP
What would life be without our tv?
You would have more time for the children and me.
The days are routine, but the nights are dull.
That set runs constantly with hardly a lull.
Give me an answer, I ask you this—
Is this what they call married bliss?
There are nice things to do and people to visit.
All it takes is time and we've plenty of it.
There are wonderful places in the world to see,
So turn off that set and come along with me.

Kathleen M Murphy
INNER TRANQUILITY

This poem is dedicated to M.J., my "Little Brother," whose enduring love encompasses me as he now shines brightly from above.

Here I am taking a long, leisurely walk on the beach,
Where, at least for a little while, from the rest of the world, I can be out of reach.

It is the place to go where you can leave your troubles behind,
The place to go where one can regain her peace of mind.

What a peaceful sound, who could ask for anything more,
Than to hear the comforting rhythm of the waves as they beat upon the shore.

I can feel the breeze as it blows gently through my hair,
And the feel of the cool salt water as it hits my legs when I let it dare.

The soft, sensuous feel of the sand squishing between my toes,
Oh, what a fantastic feeling, I suddenly have no woes.

I look up and behold the natural beauty before my eyes,
As I see the bright shining stars that fill the skies.

It's just so natural for me to pick out the brightest shining star,
It represents one, whom to me, is ever so close, but yet so far.

A smile spreads across my face as I talk to M.J.,
Hello little brother, how are you today?

Thank-you M.J. I will walk with you on the beach any time,
Between you and God's beautiful creation, inner tranquility, I will always find.

Les Troyer
EARLY MORNING ON A HILL
I keep
a special rendezvous
early on a
morning-swept hill.
Whispering, gossiping
and secure
on their nearby,
tree-lined perches;
birds, among themselves,
question my presence
and posture
until they sense
the nature of my appointment.

"He worships!"
they cry in surprised-glad unison
"He knows our Creator too!"

Harnessed and standing
in respectful silence
in the furrowed field below,
two sturdy percherons
ponder the day's plowing—
and await my return.

Missy Smith
THE TWO OF YOU ARE DRIFTING APART

To Amy, world's best friend & sister. Friends forever.

The two of you
Are drifting apart
Even though it's
Painful to your
Hearts,

One day the cupids
Bow will strike again
But until then your
Friendship will never
End.

David M Giles
PART OF LIFE

To my mother Ollie With love always, Your son.

I guess you might say, I'm running wild.
Don't know which way to go in life.
Either up or down.
Yes,
I'm going in circles.
Is this a part of life?
If so, Please tell me so.
So that my mind will be in peace.
But if not . . .
Please guide me,
So that I might go straight,
And not in circles.
Because I'm getting dizzy!

Ray (Tariq) Bennett
A MOTHERS' LOVE

I dedicate this script to the love of my life, Mrs. Mamie L. Bennett, better known as: Ma! I love you.

A mothers' love is a very special thing,
and it should be first it should reign king . . .

She will put her needs on a shelf,
just to be sure that you have for yourself . . .

My mothers' love is very special to me,
and I want to make her as happy as can be;
cause while growing up I caused so much pain,
but I'm grown now and not another tear shall I bring . . .
I may have caused enough to fill a sea, but now it's time to make her proud of me; and when she's proud of me I'll be proud of myself, then maybe I'd feel that I've put something on the shelf . . .
Now don't get me wrong I'm not playing tit for tat, because the things she gives I could never give back . . .

A mother will love you for the rest of your life, and it'll remain the same through heartache, tears and strife . . .

Her love is sent from the heavens above, and it's something no-one should be denied of . . .

So never dishonor her in any kind of way, because if you do believe me you'll pay!!!

Sandra Roe
EVERYTHING IS FINE

To my mom: for bravery and courage in her fight against cancer.

She is sweet and holds me gently in the dark and lonely night
She with one soft smile and whisper tells me everything's alright
She's the reason that my heart seems to be coming fast apart
Oh dear Mother please don't leave me life has just begun to start—

I remember, I remember, dear God let me not forget
All the lessons that she taught me and the one I'm learning yet
Can she really think of leaving going to her final rest?
While my tears flow on my pillow hoping this is just a test—

Now the anger, then the courage lest my sorrow will show too much

Do I dare accept the fact that soon I
will not have her touch
Can I let her go to someone who's
been waiting oh so long
In his cowboy hat and jacket singing
her his desert song—

Will the heavens where she's going
as other loved ones went before
Be as happy, as I'm sad, when she
enters through God's door
Oh sweet Mother when you leave me
don't forget to leave a sign
That you're happy and contented and
that "Everything is fine."

Sena C Elam
THE PATH BEHIND

Family are the people
We grow up with
All through our life
A very special gift.

A gift that was given
For all different reasons
Changing through the times
Along with seasons.

We all have been given
Different paths to take
Living on our own
With our own lives to make.

We cannot predict
Which path we will be on
For it will turn ahead
To the one we belong.

But we can look back
And the path doesn't turn
For it is the path behind
That has made us learn.

As the beginning of the path
And on the path behind
As well as the path ahead
Your family you will find.

Frances Robinson

Frances Robinson
THE DREAM

To dreams, which set the truth free and my true love wherever he may be. THE DREAM—As had by Frances Robinson sometime in 1987.

A person loved me, truly loved me
his passions were directed at me and
only me
and no matter what I did, he always
loved me.
His love was true and so was his
disfigurement
his mouth was kind and his nose was
fine,
but his eyes, you just couldn't' be
blind to the fact
his eyes were uneven, unparallel you
see
which sometimes made me want to
flee.
So one day, I left, I cheated on my
one true love
on a rock in the middle of nowhere.
I was with a person with no outside
flaws
while my one true love waited
patiently, not once getting jealous
till my fit of passion was gone.
You see, my true love and I had
many things in common.
We loved the underwater world, there
I was never scared
because the Marine Life comforted
me, always relaxed and calm.
As the man of passion drifted away,
my true love mysteriously
floated down to me, and embraced
me. And then I knew
I could not be happier with another
person as I was with him.
Funny, it seems, underwater—his
face looked lovely, not a flaw
then we made plans to do things we
loved.
And that's how it ended, my
wonderful dream
Oh, underwater world . . . where
have you gone?
where dreams can teach while real
life scorns.

Kimberly A Danielewicz
LOVE IS . . .

To Ernest and Mary Ellen, my parents who have taught me love, and to David, my first love.

Love is . . .
Love is passive, and not possessive.
Love is soft, and never aggressive.
Love is truth, and not deception.
Love is accepting, and never
rejection.
Love is caring, and not neglecting.
Love is giving, and never expecting.
Love is blind, and sometimes hard to
see.
Love is faith, the trust between you
and he.
Love is like the winds, one direction
fast and the other slow.
Love is surrounding, made
impossible to let go.
Love is found no place else but deep
in your heart.
Love is the quiet tear that falls when
you part.
Love is the explanation to a "never
say never".
For everyone knows
Love is . . . Forever.

Ivan W Hurst
TO HAVE FOUND

Some I've Known

Rushing amongst the many unique
actors
So proficiently playing their
roles,
Chanced to encounter one with
factors
Whose vibes stood out that
needed bestowles,
The brief encounter showed but few
vectors
None which seemed
insurmountable goals.

Then it was momentarily gone,
Returning not in jest; only
enhanced
As the thundering of a new dawn
Feelings once dormant awakened
and vigorously danced
Flaring to fan the flames of bygone
days,
Then quenched as quickly as the
fates one chanced.

Yet wait—don't let this scenario
come down,
For tomorrow and tomorrow
what doeth lie ahead?
Go easily and patiently to see, no-no
frown,
For the beautiful
acquaintanceship was
handsomely feed
Whether it be of love or mere friend,
yet tenderly soft
As feathery down, tis
Wonderful the opportunity for to
know you
Instead—

Benny J Jefferson

Benny J Jefferson
THANK YOU

To the Jeferson Family, the McDonogh 35 Class of '36, Mrs. Corinne Delaney, educator, and the many friends who inspired and encouraged me.

When someone goes that extra mile
To help a friend in need,
And gift wraps his services with a
smile,
Adding bright ribbons of gentle
deeds,

Just who could ever be remiss
And fail to say, "Thank You?"
For the magic in those words persists
To bless the sender, too.

Randall J McCullers
RAINY DAY

This poem is dedicated to my wife DeVane.

As the rain falls
today,

I sit alone in my
own thoughts;

Thoughts of tomorrow
and what it will be.

With every drop of
rain,
a memory of the past;

Good times, laughter,
and of the tears.

Though many years
to come,
and many rainy
days to be,

Thoughts of to-
morrow,

Will be memories
of yesterday.

Deborah Hostler
NOT THE SAME WAY

To my husband Mike who believed in me.

You loved him,
but not the same way.
You were young then, like shadows
aging in an afternoon sun.
Together your spirits flowed like
yellow butterflies on a tail wind,
like elm leaves turned red.
You didn't know he loved you
until Sarah told you.
You should have.
He always became playful,
mouth turned up, when he saw you.
One day, he asked for you in
marriage.
You turned away when you heard it.
You didn't want to see blue eyes turn
grey when you said no, I'm sorry.
Why does love stay hidden
and then engrave itself on the last day
of summer?
The pain is like iron, strong and
unyielding.
You say, "I'll never forget you."
And then, your paths divide.
You loved him, but not the same
way.

Elsie Chaney
LET ME TOUCH HIM!

Dedicated to my Friend/My "Son in the Faith," Tim Murphy, Who is now "Home" with the Lord!

Let me Touch the Hem of His
Garment,
As He passes me by;
Let me Touch the Hem of His
Garment,
And be Healed lest I die.
Let me Touch Him!
Let me Touch Him!
Let me Touch Jesus,
As He passes by!

Let me Touch the Hem of His
Garment,
And He will Cleanse my Soul;
Let me Touch the Hem of His
Garment,
And He will make me Whole.
Let me Touch Him!
Let me Touch Him!
Let me Touch Jesus,
As He passes by!

Evelyn Fox
CLOUDS

To God, who is my inspiration, and to my daughters, and my husband who have encouraged me.

When I was a little girl, I used to sit
for hours,
and watch the clouds float by.
Each changing into shapes and
things, I would draw and describe.
They all seemed different and new,

but it was fun to do.
The clouds would become everything, imaginable, of heaven and
earth.
I'd wish that I was on one, going
where ever it is clouds go.
I'd long to see what they could see,
as they passed over me.
They always seemed so soft and
fluffy, . . . so high in the sky.
Even though I'm older, I'd like to
ride a cloud or two.
To calm the adventure in my soul,
and make my wish come true.

Emil K Rottler
DIRECTION: ONE OF A SERIES

To Pat on the way.

Here is the attar of your life—
The lathing of a form
Shaped in its turning,
Conforming with the last of destiny,
Making the difference
That will be you.

Betty Quayle
THE CREATION

God created heaven and earth,
New beginnings, new birth.
Waters beautiful, gloriously sublime,
Arrives The Beginning of Time.
Light and darkness emerged
into night and day
Stars appear in bright array.
Shining as God's candles light our
way,
to earth's vast domain.

Birds of multidenous types
and plumage dancing in the sky
Myriads of beautiful fish,
Creatures great and small
in the depths of the seas
Created by God for all to see.
Then from a handful of dust came a
man.
From His rib, woman was formed
All creations became His plan.

Beauty 'round about to enfold
The greatest story ever told.
Proving to all God is nigh,
Everything in earth, seas and sky.
Animals, every kind, multi hues,
flitting to and fro,
Across the meadows, fields below.
Trees dressed in lovely tresses,
Splendor as if in beautiful dresses.

God sends down His Love,
From the lovely mansion of God
above.
Made by Him, enjoyed by all,
Creatures great and small,
Created by God, to be enthralled.

John Gray Thorp
PARTING

Such time as I shall go to that dark
place
All cold and drear, called Death, I'll
take your face.
You'll be beside me when the light is
gone
And I'll be more than just a shattered
pawn,
For I have locked your beauty in my
mind.
In this much have the laughing fates
been kind,
They gave me you to look at for a
while
And so when I can look no more, I'll
smile.

Clara Montford
MUG OF MEMORIES

Dedicated in memory of my husband Sandy,

Reflection in my mug—
Memories, of love
Away like a dove
To heaven a bove
Of Sandy, my love
Grace and a hug.

Reflection in my mug—
Memories, of walks
Away like a dove
To heaven a bove
Of Sandy, my love
Peace and a hug.

Reflection in my mug—
Memories, of memories
Love and a hug.
Of Sandy, my love
Away like a dove
To heaven a bove
Grace, peace and love
To Sandy, my love
Reflection in my mug.

Yvonne Rosser
BREAD

To Marek Wrobel

It is very strange Mother
in this new country.
I saw a lady throw bread away!
Throw it on the grass.

She said she had plenty of bread
and this was for the birds.
Not people Mother, birds!
Is it not a strange idea?

But I, your son—do not
waste bread like this of course!
As you taught me, so I am.
I will never throw bread away.

Still, it was sweet to see
the birds come down from the trees,
to peck at the bread and fight over it.
And the lady's husband said:
"I believe we must have the best fed
birds in the country."

Debbie Britton
THE DREAM OF PEACE

To my family; Mom, Dad, Danny, Marti, Deena, Dave, Eric, Tina, Chris, their child within, Aunt Joan, and my son Danny, With Much Love.

Mourn the dream.
The dream that becomes
A fantasy.
It eludes us with its
Beautiful light.
It touches us with
Harsh reality.
And, always, it shimmers
In the distance.
If in the distance it remains—
Then, my children,
Mourn the dream.

Richard LaVigne
GODDESS OF THE CHASE

To Diane with all my love, Richard

When the universe exploded
Sending matter everywhere
As the particles streamed forward
You and I were there
While the forces wrought their fury
Splitting atoms, running free
I was helpless to resist the powers
Pulling you away from me
Then the gases swirled and settled
Forming planets, trapping me
And I screamed as you sped onward
Lost amidst a cosmic sea
So I waited through the ages
Half a spirit, longingly
For the force that rules the heavens
To move my soul mate back to me
In the darkness as I waited
A million lifetimes seemingly
I thought how once we had existed
Fused together symmetrically
Then through a doorway you came
walking
And I knew you instantly
Time and distance could not conquer
The one I love eternally

Della Williams
A THOUGHT

Dedicated to . . . Mrs. Georgia Hill, my sister, and Mrs. Jacqui Bledsoe, my daughter.

I was living a Christian life;
My heart had no malice or strife.
Loved my enemies, treated my
friends right
I praised the Lord, had heaven in my
sight.

The devil, pushed me, I stumbled and
fell;
Turned back to sin, headed for hell.
Cried to Jesus, he said, "I won't let
you stay,
Have faith, I will show you the way."

Then in love and mercy, He picked
me up;
Gave me faith, took away the bitter
cup.
That old devil pushed me again, I
was able to stand
By faith my Saviour held my hand;
Thank God!!! I didn't stumble or fall.

Jesus loves me!!!
Jesus is my all in all.

So watch out, for that old devil's
snare;
Faith, love and grace, will keep you
here and over there.

Delores Fennell
THE LEAVES ARE GREEN

I would like my poem dedicated to my sister Alfreta Combs who passed away 12-18-88.

The leaves are green flowers are
Blooming spring is in the air we
Walk alone but no one really cares
Lifes is so beautiful for all to see
You can be what you want to be
If you take time to sit and think
Oh what a precious day it will be
When life is but an eternity

Jo Norum
THE PRAYER OF MY HEART

To my children and all of their children.

I love you Most Holy God, my
Heavenly Father.
I love you precious Lamb for sinners
slain, Jesus my Savior.
I love you blessed Holy Ghost, my
Comforter and my guide.
May you forever in me, and I in thee
abide.
May I spread sunshine, joy and cheer,
for as long as Thou lendest me life
here.
May I keep my lamp trimmed and
burning bright, till I reach
that land where commeth no night.
In the Great Day, Oh God, as I stand
before thee.
May I not empty handed be.

Janice T Kent
A SOLDIER'S CRY

To my husband Floyd, who inspired me to believe in myself and my work.

A shot had been fired in the middle
of the night,
As soldier's laid near with fear and
fright,
They could not cry for the filling of
pride,
And yet they were filled with
sickness inside,
They wanted to leave this ridge land,
But yet were held by a slight
command,
For peace was the sound they
clutched in their hearts,
Knowing that through their torment
of hell,
Peace and sovereignty would rule the
world.

DaLoris A Luebbers
CUPID'S ARROW

To James and Martha Wilson, Burlington, Iowa, is whose home I saw the painting entitled "Cupid Interested."

I once saw a painting of cupid
How strange it should now come to
mind
Glancing down perchance from some
lofty sphere
So cherubic, innocent, so benign.

As a shard, a fragment, many a soul
Has been seared by your fiery darts
Use caution, I pray, as to who you
inflict
For the mirror of the soul, is the
heart.

Bonnie Olshinsky

Bonnie Olshinsky
A MAN IN MY LIFE

This poem is dedicated with love and admiration to Robert F Everhart, my father

There's a man in my life, so precious
and kind
A special man that's so hard to find
He makes me laugh from day to day
By things that he'll do or things that
he'll say

There's times he gets mad
Or times he'll get peeved
But he's loving and caring
And wears his heart on his sleeve

He's handsome and sharp

And know's what to say
I look up to this man
In such a big way

He's taught me a lot
In the years that's gone by
And this man in my life
I'll thank till I die

This man that I speak of
Best friend I've ever had
For this man that I'm proud of
And love is my Dad

Pamela Runyon Jarski
INSIDE TRUTH

"They shall mount up with wings as eagles; they shall run and not be weary; they shall walk and not faint." Isaiah 40:31

Why do you not hear me
When I speak of my love for
you?
And why is it so very hard for me
to share that truth?
I know that even though I feel
the things I do.
I'll never want to share them
with anyone but you.
The trust you asked me to have
is somewhere deep inside,
And I believe in all the things you've
said are not close to a lie!
But why, then do my feet keep
stumbling
with each new step I take?
And the palms of my hands are
sweating
And my heart has begun to
break?
Is it because I loved you more
than I could even conceive;
Or is it the subtle sound of the door
slamming in my face . . .
As you leave!

Marsha Brock
LISTEN MY CHILD

This poem is dedicated to my beloved mother, Sybil Dennis.

Listen my child, do not pine.
All are not made to be kind.

Listen my child and dry your tears.
The world around you has little
fears.

Listen my child your heart is made
of gold.
Do not tarnish it with all your tears.

Listen my child, remember you are
mine.
So why . . , do you pine?

Listen my child, clear your misty
mind.
And clear away those rusty times.

Listen my child, remember who you
are.
And remember too, who cares.

God cares . . . remember you are
mine.

Elsie U Meyer
FORMULA FOR LIFE

Dedicated with love to my Grandchildren Mike, Cynthia, Darsi, Doug, Steve, Greg, Tom, Cathy, Jamie & Kari.

Mother Nature—the Great Spirit—
the Human Mind—
Fused!—Inconceivable potential!
From unfathomable depths
To endlessly soaring heights!

The world in space—the galaxies in
outer space—
What vast domain
For the benefit and the
wonderment
Of the human race.

Oh, human race, with dominion over
the earth,
Waste not your minds!
Temper them with love.
Care, share,—and be at peace.
Respect the Natural Order,
Revere the Great Spirit,
Develop the Mind.
Control self-destructive
passions.

The reward?
Beyond anticipation—beyond
imagination:
Complete and eternal fusion
with
The Great and Holy Spirit!

Ralph M Sartin
LITTLE MAN

Every dad needs a son like you, Michael. This is for you, little man, with lots of love . . . Dad

A mere reflection, of my soul,
That little man of mine,
His life is still, ahead of him,
Today he reaches nine.
The only boundaries, that he knows,
Are limits of his size,
Disappointments, are sure to come,
So character can rise.
A road untraveled, and unknown,
His life awaits him still,
And there he stands, with eager eyes,
A strong yet changing will.
Tomorrows harvest, are still seeds,
Within those little hands,
Along the way, he drops a few,
With what he understands.
A heart so tender, and unmarred,
A giggle here and there,
The days ahead, he cannot see,
He may find life's unfair,
The bumps and bruises, they've been
small,
The price in life is tears,
Today's the day, to live life son,
Before youth disappears.

Emma Feltner
TINSEL TOWN

To the homeless, may God have mercy on OUR souls.

The glitter and glamour of Tinsel
Town,
hiding the destitution of the lost not
found.
All that glitters is not of gold,
while your brothers lie in the streets
growing old.
The time of your lives are now at
hand,
for the homeless children it never
began.
Lend out your hand to those in need.
The future holds no promises to
keep,
what ever you sow, you will forever
reap.

V J Vitone
DREAM TIME

For Willamae, My Wife of twenty three years. You taught me the meaning of love and courage.

Once again Darkness descends,
Sunlight fades, Stars will soon appear
I sleep with restless movements, as
Dream Time is drawing near.
Dreams are visions of the mind when
our bodies lie at rest,
Dreams of love and happiness are the
ones we like the best.
Visions of you come to me, as Dream
Time works its magic,
With crystal clear reality, I see our
love so tragic.
How could I treat you as I did? In
my dream I realize,
I took the Sunshine from your days,
And left you cloudy Skies.
Now Dream Time makes it clear to
me the selfish fool I've been
If we could do it over Love, I would
not make the same mistakes again.
To always hold you close to me
while I thank the Lord above,
For making me one of the chosen
few to realize such a love.
I see this all in Dream Time, these
Visions of my life
If only I had the chance to do it over
Dear,
With you my loving Wife.

Marlon M Rosenberger
BE KIND

To my Mother, the most kind person I ever knew.

It requires so little effort,
But brings such peace of mind,
To show the world about you
It's so easy to be kind.

Like the promise of a rainbow,
As the sun dispels the gloom
So a little bit of kindness
Brings gladness out of doom.

Unkindness springs from discontent,
Or, from someone down on life
Who believes in hurting others
He can be justified as right.

But, unkindness brings no happiness
To those who are involved,
Just a trail of hurt and anger
Which may never be resolved.

So, when you feel you're wanting
And with good deeds you're
behind,
You can gladden others and yourself
If you will just be kind.

Stan Mussell
THE DEBATER

In memory of my law partner, John Lewis King

short, slender
fragile of form
mournful face divided
by bushy brows
hiding the piercing power
of deep-set eyes

a brilliant brain
lightning-swift
distilling,
composing and directing

and finally
the deep-rich melody
carefully chosen words
commanding attention
painting a picture
of persuasion

Emily E Matthews
WANDERING WONDERING

Dedicated to JTM who ended my wandering and gave meaning to my life.

Wandering, wondering, silently and
lonely—
Seeking, searching, hoping to find
What vanishing haunts constantly
prevail me?
What perpetual echoes continue to
elude me?
Cautiously, precariously, I endeavor
to discover
What forces fathom my quest.
Is there never to be an answer?
Am I doomed to lasting darkness?
Why do I search?
What questions enthrall me
And cast me to the beseeching arms
of ensuing mysteries?
Do I seek the protective shores of
contentment?
Do I yearn for the tranquil recesses
within?
And when confronted with the
revelation of my ponderous enigma,
Will I recognize it as being truly the
basis of my tribulations?
Only success can arrest the turmoil
within me.
So, onward I continue
Scanning the vastness
Overturning the stones of deception
Scaling the walls of obstruction
Hoping against hope
Fearing Against fear
That my quest is not in vain.

John Craig Yuill
WHAT LAYS IN STORE

If man's so great
if he's advanced so far
then why have so many
been killed by the car?

He's overcrowded earth
so he looks to the stars
he has space travel
they're just space cars.

What lays in store
can he destroy anymore?
Wish I could close the door
Don't want to see anymore!!!

He's killed off species
with no right in sight,
is it greed that kills
or is it lack of light?

We kill each other
just in greed,
or is man the creator's
destructive seed?

What lays in store
Can he destroy anymore?
Wish I could close the door,
Don't want to see anymore!!

Clover D Morris
NOSTALGIA BLUES

This poem is dedicated to my wonderful boyfriend, Fredrick, who means everything to me.

Oh how I love you
With all my heart,
Why do we have to
Be so far apart?
All I can think of now
Is to be with you.
Why do I have to feel so blue?

When I remember the
Good times we've shared,
And the numerous times
You showed me you cared,
I know I could never
Live without you.
I really, really miss you.

The memories of your warm embrace
Makes me wish I could turn back
The hands of time,
For the memories grow sweeter
Through the years, sweeter just like wine.
I'm longing so much to be with you.
Oh God! I feel so blue.

Kenneth Flynn
LIFE IN THE FAST LANE

To all the single fun loving males.

All these parties and one night stands,
Life in the fast lane sure is grand,
I had settled down for all those years,
A whole lot of rust had got in my gears,
But since I got single among the swingers I love to mingle,
There are single bars and girls galore,
I just get drunk and holler for more,
When the drinks get to my head I stumble home and fall in bed,
I wake up in the morning feeling so bad,
But just think of the good times that I've had,
I drag through the day, my head in my hands,
Boy life in the fast lane sure is grand,
One more drink one more girl my life sure is a whirl,
Party all night work all day,
Time sure is passing away,
But as I look back with no regrets,
I may be old but I Ain't dead yet,
A lot of people I meet and see,
Can't figure out what's got into me,
They think I'm shooting them a line,
But life in the fast lane sure is fine.

Sherry Lyn Nilsson
TWO

To the man who inspires me

You become so familiar, two become one;
Then something happens, something is done.
Love is a shared feeling, it comes between two;
Taking it for granted maybe him, maybe you.

Time away, time apart;
Thoughts run from heart to heart.
Give and take, take and give;
Confusion, sometimes, on how to live.

Passion, love, intimacy bound;
Though anger and misunderstanding are also around.
Decisions of how or why we must do;
What it takes, for not one, but two.

Phone calls, letters, messages through friends;
Sometimes I wonder where it all ends.
Can it be possible for love to survive;
Even though at times you cannot see eye to eye.

Personally I feel there is a solution;
One side cannot do it, it takes two of them.
Feelings get hurt, love shines through;
With some hard work, one does not become two.

Susan Iocolano
TRIUMPH OVER DARKNESS

To my husband Mario, may he always be a source of inspiration.

The wind rushes thru the trees;
It is the last fanfare.
My work done, I am at ease;
With the one that builds with care.
For he knows I have hidden waiting,
In this beautiful solace.
For my rescuer who comes to take me
From this haven place.

And he has come, I am all but complete.
The mold set, dye cast, only the print to meet.
Peace, harmony abound, endless nites and days.
Offering complete fulfillment to each others ways.
Never ceasing love now grows more abundant every day.
Splashing o'er its banks into fertile plains array.
A haven for eternal love that feels no strain;
Because we have triumphed over darkness again.

Jeffrey A Faulkerson
THE SEED

To the children: our future.

this small ebony seed
tells my story, says "where
do i go from here?" it in my
hand, i on its exterior, locked
together by a bond of
commonality. murky innards
of a world gone mad, soil
hardening daily, extracting the
gift of life from our beings, pushing
us lower,
lower,
lower,
until darkness becomes a home.
from the depths of the world we
dream—SoFt MoIsT sOiL wItH
tHe SuN sHiNiNg BrIgHtLy
AmOnG tHe HeAvEnS /
EmPlOyMeNt, MaRrIaGe,
SuCcEsS—reality revealing soil
devoid of nutrients, dream
deferred.
WE DESIRE LOVE, RAIN THAT
INVIGORATES, REJUVENATES
AND LETS ONE KNOW
THAT SOMEONE
CARES.

Mary Ann Samczyk
TAPESTRIES

To Christopher

Her tenuous strands grow ever brilliant with loving labor;
Carefully caressed, entwined in infinite vision,
The image unfolds; the odyssey begins again.
Working through silvery reflections into a world so near,
I learn to feel, to judge, to grow, to reach
As each fiber strains to hold to its perfect hue,
While all about earthly gravity pulls and clutches,
Struggling to tear and fray the fragile twilight.
But the shimmering blues and reds and yellows,
The gleaming golds and silvers all embrace
In the blinding brilliance of creation that lights his face,
Revealing the mystical expression of all my sacred desires;
As I stare at the flowing vibrant weave, the image stirs,
In sudden shiver and a rush of radiance,
My heart beholds—from his hands fly my dreams.

Cindy L'Esperance
LIGHT OF MY LOVE

For Ryan, my son the Light of My Love

The path that led to time and place
Brought the distance star its base.
Love within comes out to say
I'd like to share with you today.
The twinkling past—the future cast
The sun to nourish for growth to last.
I've seen above the seven rays
Bringing sight that one conveys.
To touch with gentle warm caress,
Fills the soul with all the best.
As three to be in all that's known,
Sparkles bright in light as shone.
A time to rest for journeys quest,
The castle is your home.
Though a man in but the flesh,
The oneness greater than one has guessed.
I live through all my paths today
To leave behind the words to say—
My little son
My darling one
For you I've come
My work begun.

Brooke G Morrissette

Brooke G Morrissette
MOMENT OF TRUTH
The clocks rhythm is rewritten
The moment of the heart has come
Drawn close innocent passion—
You're the tender one
You're cautious and I'm rigid on opposite ends of a ledge
Oblivious to you, I breathlessly venture the edge.

No matter what becomes, I'll proudly feel I've won
For your gentle caresses crowned me the soft aspirant one
Not to mention my minds replay—
Memories mean so much
Ours I'll purely treasure
Along with thoughts of your sweet touch.

Your reaction will reveal everything certain
A secret behind the moon's mysterious curtain
Distant moon not seen by my eyes
Unfolds mists of truth into my life
. . . A moment of one at that.

Twila Thomas
MY SCOTTISH LASSIES

For my McCulloch granddaughters with love.

There's my precious Jeni
With the laughing blue eyes,
She can bring a smile to
lips with just a wistful sigh.

There's my darling Annie
With body graceful and lithe,
She has brought a warm
love forever into my life.

Oh, my Scottish lassies, may
the heavenly pipes play a song
that will guide your feet the
Right way all your life long.

Keep your sparkling eyes upward
Let the highland be your road
And when this life is over may
You reach your highest goal.

I love you my darling lassies
and when I'm no longer here,
Remember that your granny
loved having you near.

Eric S Schaefer
OF THE WIND

For Heather René, Zachary David and my pretty brown eyes

Be still my little child and hear the wind as she calls.
Let her fill you with wonder as she sings her many songs
And know the joy of her.
She brings us many things, the wind; the seasons, the rain and snow.
Ever true in her wisdom as the sands of time in an hourglass.
She never ceases to amaze and awe,
For her power is eternal.
As are her songs.
Know the comfort of her being, for without her we are lost.
She is forever and never, for she has no beginning.
And has no end.
She carries many on her back;
she is strong as mortals are weak,
The ever-present messenger of all
For she knows both the good and bad.
Hear the song of the wind, my little one,
And know the love
And sorrow
Of her songs.

By GOD and Glenda Bowling
FAMILY REUNION

Dedicated to my beloved aunt, Frances Marie Hood Lee

I'd been feeling poorly and tired, when I got a call about a family reunion.
They said my husband wasn't invited.
I really hated to go alone, but I had to go, I decided.
When I left home, I felt as bad as I've ever felt
But somewhere along the way, I started to get excited.

They thought it best that I fly
And I watched down below until

things were so small
That I could see nothing but fluffy white clouds and clear blue sky.
We were meeting in a mansion. A little rich for my blood, I hadn't a thing to wear,
But they said it didn't matter, there'll be something for you there.

When I got there, they were waiting for me. Mom, Dad, brothers, sisters, Grandpas, Grandmas. Lord,we hadn't all been together in years.
We hugged and kissed and cried happy tears.
I was so happy I didn't ever want to leave.
This was the most beautiful place that I'd ever seen.

Then the Master of the mansion came by to welcome me!
He said we didn't have to go.
We could stay and we'd have another reunion in another year or so.
I took him up on it right away. This is where I want to be.
The way I feel now, why I could stay here for eternity.

Morning Dawn
BLACK ORCHID

To Wayne A. Williams, for the thoughts. To Deborah Barnett, for the time. To God, for the inspiration.

In the valley of "going-no-where", where no one goes anywhere, a gentle rain begins to fall; it is the rain of oppression.
Deep beneath the surface in the bosom of mother earth dwells the seed of inferiority, planted in the garden of the mind.
In the rotations of a white-world, surrounded by snow capped boundaries, stands alone but united one ebony patch.
From this ebony patch many flowers are picked by admirers, to be planted in new worlds where they can be watched and cultivated.
As the rain of oppression continues to drizzle down the seed of inferiority is given life; it is a black orchid that arises from the seed, springing forth into the ebony patch to take it's place amongst its siblings.
This black orchid, the offspring of meticulous thought, grows into a blossom spreading its beauty to the world.
As the sun's glistening radiance shines down upon the reflective petals of the ebony flower the rain of oppression disseminates, creating an opening through the white-world for the ebony flower that stands alone.

Ursula Cook
A MOMENT OUT OF MY HEART

Dedicated to M. M. Alt and Mrs. Millie Yates the two women that encouraged this poem to take shape.

Not a pretty sight to behold,
for in the search of wisdom I grew old.
I studied books and people,
whenever there was time to spare, to save you some time, I decided my findings to share.
Still young I made an important discovery,
Looking for love quickly got me lost,
until I saw the seed within me.
To be considered important I surrounded myself with friends,
when my fate fell ill, I could not even count them on one of my hands.
Plenty of worldly treasures I do possess,
as time passed on, they lost their glitter—got to spent money somehow I guess.
Quickly I learned to be patient with fellow men,
God knows everyone does the best they can.
Never be afraid to shed even a single tear,
emotions make us human beings—research made this clear.
Forgive the people that might do you wrong,
this is the secret, that helps you stay strong.
My dear child, look at me fragile and gray,
in your search for wisdom, I urge you—listen what the ELDERS have to say!

Joyce Stuckman
GENTLE BREEZES

This Poem Dedicated to a very special friend: My Mom!

God blew a gentle breeze
abound my hair
In the forest of trees
came the air
The smell of wildflowers
came to me
Only God has these powers
that He made Thee.

Carl R Mahaffey
STREAM OF LIFE

Boulders are strewn up the side of the hill.
It is as if two Titans had staged a rock fight.
Yet for all the odd sizes, shapes, and positions,
there was within these rocks a strange beauty.
Flowing around, under, and over, these foreign objects,
was a stream of clear and ever so cold water.
The feel of being next to a happily bubbling little stream of water, was that of tranquility.
It was almost as though my troubles, and fears, were cast into the current, and rapidly carried out of sight.

With very little imagination, one could visualize bobbing along like a cork; shooting down the rapids like a run-away freight train; and then gently twisting and turning in a quiet spot.
Sitting here on the bank, I get a new insight into life.
Our span of years on this Earth are like the little creek.
There are rapids, and there are quiet pools, but no matter what the obstacles, life goes on.
Regardless of how we try to detour or even stop the flow,
eventually in one form or another it will break free.

Fred Boyle
THE WAY WE GROW

I dedicate this poem to my fiancee, Noel.

I wonder if I had a choice, with voice that could be heard—
Or was my seed predestined, to grow with those preferred—
And I wonder if it mattered, in which soil I would grow—
Whether I'd become a flower to love, or seed love never knows—
And I wonder if sound reason, why my wilting had begun—
Was the garden that I grew in, lacked the love of rain and sun—
And I wonder if my beauty lies, in the weathering of a storm—
And the flower that I truly am, when dead will truly form—

Gayle Tauger
SELF DISCOVERY

For Eden, Brooke, and Seth . . . For Whom My Heart Beats. For Prof. John J. Snyder . . . The Wind Beneath My Wings.

If today I am a question mark
Who is to blame?
Me.

If tomorrow I am only a day older
Who is responsible?
Me.

If my eyes are closed to another's pain
I am blind.

If I ignore the piercing screams of a helpless child
I am the true batterer.

If I deny the warmth of my shelter to a shivering soul
I am ice.

If I possess knowledge but refuse to advise
I am ignorant.

If I speak, but do not act
I am a hypocrite.

If today I help to relieve the suffering of just one person
I am the me I want to be tomorrow.

Debbie Moses
WITH YOU IN MY LIFE

To my beloved (Clyde), Mario DeFina Jr. This one's for you. I love you, then, now and always. Rest in peace. Love Bonnie Debbie (Mo) Moses

With you in my life, I've learned the importance of Life and Love. The Things we've shared and The Feelings we've touched can never be Duplicated.
You are my First Breath in the morning, My thoughts THROUGHOUT THE DAY, and my Special Dreams at Night. With you in my Life, I've grown from a Child to a Woman.
Your Guidance and your Wisdom have made me the Intelligent Person I am Today. We have gone through every Emotion Together. From tears, to sweat to blood, And if I had the chance to do it all again, I'd do it a Million times more. I Love You.

Imogene Goodman Brunson
REFLECTIONS

To my four children; Mike, Bob, Jim and Cindy and my four stepchildren; Joe, Doug, Teri, and Kathy but most of all to Joe, Senior, for his patience.

We know that we are growing old
As we watch our past unfold
The deeds we've done, the seeds we've sown
Will grow, regardless of the way we're known.
Our heirs will try to overcome
And see the good that we have done
And put to rest the human faults
And not betray the daily walk.
When they look back as we do now
And see the tares amid the wheat
They, then, can say as we do now
We planted, Apollo watered, You endower.

Ricky E Ryder
THANK YOU MOM

Dedicated to my mom; she has accepted me and my handicap easier than I have. Thank you for the love and encouragement.

For all of the times I've called upon you
Sometimes for no reason at all,
And all of the times you've cautioned me
When you were afraid I may take a fall.

For all of the times you've run for me
When I was hurt or sick or late,
And the last minute things you've done for me
When I thought it just couldn't wait.

For all of the times you've been there
Just to listen and see me through,
And for your never ending patience
When I was too stubborn to listen to you.

And most of all, thank you mom,
Thank you for just being you.

Sandy Malette Deshane
SECOND CHANCE LOVE

To my loving husband Gordon Deshane

Till death do us part, are the words I will say
Repeating in this gracious heart day after day.
I will always love and cherish you,
the man that I adore.

I will always wear this gold band on my finger you once asked me to wear.
Those words will always linger in my conscious mind.

The words "I do" that made me yours
The same "I do" that made you mine.

The love, the joy, the sharing, the fears
We've shared them all through the years.

The times we've tried working with our children.
At times they were hard.
We were both willing.

The times we worked on our house.
The times I cried when I saw a mouse.

The times we've shared together camping.
My second chance at life gave me a true champion.

Florence (McMillian) Caballero
EMOTION CRIES OUT

This poem was written for my children, but I would like to dedicate it also to all the children of the world. Love, Flo

When he cries a tear,
He sheds a pain.
A tear of inner
Emotional strain.
A hurt with-in,
That speaks out loud,
To touch the feeling
Of a physical cloud.
The pain sets in,
And crawls inside.
There's no escaping,
It cannot hide.
The inner emotion
Should be expressed,
The cheers of joy,
Or the cries of sadness.

Barbara Ann Clark
COMING AFTER ME

This is dedicated to all the people who helped me pursue my dream in writing poetry and for giving me confidence so I would send in my poetry. Thanks everyone and thank you God.

One day while I was walking by the ocean,
I looked up in the sky;
And guess what I saw.
I saw my dear Jesus,
Coming after me.
He said, "My child your life on earth is through,
Your job is done,
You've told your friends about me;
And you've served me well,
So now you will have a better life."

He's given me love beyond compare.
He's showed me more,
Than anyone else.
He's given me hope,
Hope for the future.
He's taking me to a better land,
Where the streets are made of pure gold.
Up there I'll be,
Where there's no sorrow or pain.

Anton J Stoffle
THE FADING DAY

Dedicated to my wife Jewell, my constant inspiration, and to all those who love conventional and contemporary poetry.

The echoes of each fading day,
Reflecting what has gone before,
Life's joys and sorrows, smiles and cheers,
A hundred incidents or more.

Great plans devoured by eventide,
Sweet dreams that never came to pass,
All interwoven and dispersed,
Like scattered clover in the grass.

Each mortal role, the world a stage,
The book of wisdom, page by page,
With settings new, adventures too,
Designed to blend on fate's great stage.

As the highlights and the low spots
Seem to find their special dwelling,
Through the cloud puffs sun rays stealing,
With the evening shadows swelling.

Birdlings all wing home for nesting,
Dusk and day share earth with a sigh,
As the nightwinds hum their vespers,
To wish the find world a good-bye.

Elizabeth Gary Sullivan

Elizabeth Gary Sullivan
NEW HOPE

It's a new day, It's a new day,
Today is hopes anew,
Am going to use it, I will not abuse it
And I will succeed before I am through

"Hello", new day, are you ready for me?
Well I am here and I am free,
Free to greet you and bid you ado,
Free to conquer all of the challenges
I shall encounter in you

With a new day and a new year,
What do I stand to fear,
Forget your past, put it away, and give today a big cheer.

Katina Stewman
LIFE'S WEB

This was written as if Judd Smith were saying it herself. She was in her last few days . . . dying with cancer.

Time was filled with things to do
Making plans . . . looking forward to the new
And then one day when God made time
I realized how precious the gift of life was mine.

Today all seems a faint memory
As life draws close to an end for me
Why . . . sooner than I would plan . . . of course!
But this is God's will . . . so I'll endorse.

To leave this life for all that's pure
His open arms . . . I'm safe and secure
What better place awaits for me
For new heights of glory I soon will see.

Oh . . . the greatness of his love he gives to us
That's why in Him . . . I fully put my trust.
The plan is perfect . . . for me I know
And when he calls . . . I'll be ready to go.

So . . . why am I sad? . . . not because of all
That's behind those open gates!
But family and friends . . . that's why my heart aches!

Only God can understand our human way
My reason I want them to accept Him today
Life is short for us to grasp
And when we do . . . it doesn't last.

So . . . trust in Him and you will know
The peace it gives . . . my face aglow!

Rita Smith
GOD STRENGTHENS ME

To God and my loving family

Sometimes when I'm deeply saddened
I simply, do not cry
I mean, "out loud" like many do.
Though tears are in each eye.
My heart could feel the deepest pain,
Yet most could never tell.
Except for "God" who looks inside,
And knows, the truth so well.
For soon, I feel "Him" comfort me,
I know I'm not alone.
For "God" whose known so much sorrow,
Is helping with my own.

Rosemary Gipson
A MOTHER'S LOSS

For our beloved daughter and sister, Melissa Ann

Through a Mother's loss of a child
comes, sorrow . . .
anger . . .
pain . . .
Through a Mother's loss of a child
comes, kindness . . .
wisdom . . .
gain . . .
But for the love of her loved one,
and other children.
Makes one overcome . . .
A Mother's Loss.

Leslie D M O'Connell
THOU ART PRECIOUS TO ME

Dedicated to the most important people in my life: my parents—William & Mary Trombly, My children—Rick, Bob, John, David & Alecia, Wayne Newton & most of all Jesus, & My best friend Susan Medearis.

Jesus, thou art precious to me!
More precious than words could 'ere express
If poets could take all the endearing
Poetic words and
Put them all together in a poem,
They could never begin to match
How precious thou art to me!
If all the love songs written—
Were of the very best in the world,
They too couldn't compare with—
How precious thou art to me!

No words, no music, no song indeed
Could ever hold a candle to thee.
No thought or deed or miracle done,
Could compare with the love from me
You have won!
For thou art precious to me, Dear Lord.
With all the prayers and praise and psalm
I give you all that I have, all that I own.
For thou, dear Lord, art precious to me!

Maureen T Kauffman
FADING TIME

To my mother, who believed in me.
To my husband, who encouraged me.
To my children and God, who inspired me.

Time ticks by so quickly these days.
There is never enough time to do the fun things.
My day is so busy with the things I must do,
the dishes and dusting away the evidence of your day.

It seems there is no time for the doll house, teddy bears and stories.
Time has no compassion for these little things that mean so much.

But each day, as the clock ticks louder and you grow bigger the little things are slowly fading.
The days of lullabies and sweet secrets will soon be gone.

The clock once fast will seem to stop.
I will try to dust away the evidence of your finger prints, that have faded with the time.

Karen J Ross
BLOODY BRIDE

To me, you, him, her, and others those who dare to explore their arts of imagination

Ancient evening in modern times
ceilings dripping of white tears
from a wall of already painted fears
It's a church of purple demons
with a bride of black lace
At the end of the aisle
stands a man of no meaning
Statues applaud with laughter
for no apparent reason
The organ plays soundless music
All that can be heard
is the squeek of footprints
on the aisle of blood
from her barefoot soles
Ad clouds fade into raindrops
outside the church
The towns people sleep
Yet, on this ancient evening
the bride self destructs
inches from the altar, ashes to dust
Hours later purple demons
party with the taste
of redrum . . .

Delores Jean Frazier
GOD'S HIDDEN TREASURE

This poem is dedicated to the ones I love, my children, Angie, Ginger, Lisa, and Chuck.

I've found a treasure buried deep,
It's hidden nuggets upward leap,
Through the pages in His word,
His still small voice can still be heard.

Dig my child, He seems to say,
I'll give you riches for each day.
Your answers are there, they lie within,
If you would take time to dig in.

Seek and search for that treasure,
for in its wisdom, there is no measure.
The best things in life are free,
When they have been received from me.

Ruth Phares Goldman
&!%#$!&@$!

Please tell me why
Each time I try
To take a much-needed nap,
All hell breaks loose
In the neighborhood
And erupts in an awesome flap.

The moment I lower
My heavy lids
Cacophony crashes and rocks:
The garbage truck grinds
To a halt next door
And masticates on the spot.

The gardener arrives
With his putt-putt machine
As the streetsweeper swirls by my room.
If I had my way
They would both be deployed
To the outermost side of the moon.

Dogs bark in chorus,
The jets take off
And the kids start yelling in front.
My telephone shrills
As I beg it to stop,
Knowing of course that it won't.

I abandon my plan
And arise from my bed . . .
. . . dead silence reigns about . . .
Once again I'm the pawn
In a devilish plot
For my nap I am still without.

Mary Paxton Kirby
LOVE IS FOREVER

To my son Dennis Paxton and his wife Barbara on the occasion of their wedding—May 18, 1985

Love is giving.
Love is forgiving.
Love cares.
Love shares.
Love understands,
Never demands.
Love does not smother,
Trusts one another.
Love holds us together.
Love is forever.

Beverlyn Sandford Baines
WITH YOU

To my niece, Fedora E Wynn, a pace-setting teenager of the eighties.

What's more beautiful than—
A ride with you
down a cluttered, car-filled highway,
viewing the technology of Man,
looking at the funny little gadgets here and there:
all placed there for enjoyment
and sometimes bringing the disaster of error;
listening to the multiplicity of sounds
heard and unheard;

smelling the perfumes of production poured out
in plentiful portions and padded as Progress;

thinking, then speaking;
thinking some more,
then speaking some more,
so much in harmony,
so much in rhythm,
And now and then, eyes meet:
A stare and a smile so warm,
A communication so naturally understood,
So intimate, so divine, so together;
experiencing it all with you.

William W Howell Jr
ENEMY MINE

This poem is dedicated to Betsy and Sean, my sweet wife and loving son.

The dawn has broke
the cannons roar,
young men rise up
from shore to shore.
Oh blackened heart
the Dark One's breath,
has festered deep
within their breasts.
We seek revenge
an eye for an eye,
that's why young men
must fight and die!
The more things change
they stay the same,
it shades our eyes
and hides the shame.
I pray to God
someday we'll see,
that Man's
his own worst enemy.

D Purl Watt
TODAY I SAW A POODLE IN THE SKY

To the blessed; of love for nature and a vivid imagination—I salute you!

To-day I saw a poodle in the sky—
A fleecy cloud, with smoke-shades underlay, made this form that seemed to float on a sea of water rising from our earth, at a point not too far distant down the road. Then came a change, and first the head was lost—
The tail stretched out in beaver form, and soon I had no words to say—i could not see the poodle any more, the cloud had split in two. Each mass went drifting merrily away—
A happening that's thousand fold each day.

Debbie Gurnett
PRISONER OF YOUR PRIVATE WAR

To life, and all that it has shown me.

Here goes the rest I've come to a crest
I've lost it somewhere no one seems to care
Help me look here things aren't too clear
Everyone adds advice but I will roll the dice
Leave me to my mind I'll see what I can find
You are all such a bother like a thick cloud cover
There you are here I am who really gives a damn
They seem to know what goes on
creative minds where ideas spawn
Here is my vision an image to you
explanation plenty
Still you're confused
Now leave me to my mind I know what I will find
They never understand my alienation in the foreign land
Push and shove me all around
moving faces too much sound
A peaceful explosion inside my head
the deafening sound of pain is spread
My pretty red blood covers the floor
like a warm red blanket a cold night's in store

Theone Williamson
TRYST

To Dora; my inspiration, my mentor, and my friend.

I stand breathless, while
your breath whispers at the nape of my neck
and your light fingers toy with the ribbons in my hair.
My nostrils flair
to catch the sweetness of your breath
laced with the nectar of new spearmint shoots
and freshly turned earth.
I am acutely aware of my skirt
flicking at my thighs
with the tickle of an itch
too exquisite to scratch.
I shield my eyes from the last
slanting darts of setting sunlight
playing tag between the budding branches overhead,
and stare transfixed at the kaleidoscopic shadow pictures
on the garden wall.
Now, its warmth spent in the sunlight,
your breath is cooler, stronger, almost alien,
and tastes of raindrops distilled above
steaming feed-lots.
Our tryst is done.
O South wind of fickle April,
art thou friend or foe?

Iris Y Michelini
WHERE ARE THE BLUE SKIES?

This poem is dedicated to the millions of women who are victims of domestic violence—our sisters in this world who believe that no one cares. I want them to know that someone does care about their plight.

Battered, bruised and belittled—
the "heart of the home" begins a new day . . . cringing still
from the spine-tingling terrors of a long, tumultuous night.

Even the silky touch of a favorite blouse
causes her arms to ache; yet, not as much as her spirit.
Fortunately, silk isn't transparent,
so the world, once again, is spared the signs
of her pain and brokenness.

She wonders, sometimes, "Does anyone really care?"
Yet, almost immediately, she disdainfully forsakes
that dispiriting thought,
For she seldom indulges in self-pity . . .
a luxury cloaked with dishonor.

So, unobtrusively, even stealthily,
she flees her home
as panicky chills fell her back like an ominous enemy . . .
far too often her traveling companion.

Her pulse quickens now, as she fumbles for her car keys,
attempting to escape to a saner world—even for a little while.
And once again, tear-filled eyes
cloud the presence of a brand new day.
Thus, for her, "Where are the blue skies?"

Sherri King
FREE TO FLY

To Mom and Dad with all my love and devotion. Thanks for letting me fly.

I've often wondered where I'd be
If I hadn't had you at my side
pushing and prodding me.

You gave me the hope, the dream
that I could fly, and most important
you gave me the room to try.

Whether I soar through the clouds
or plant my roots firmly in the ground,
Remember always, it is to both of you
my heart is forever bound.

Terri L Dirks

Terri L Dirks
FATHER OF MY CHILD

To Earl and Logan, my two favorite Valentines.

Whenever you are near
I feel
my heart go wild.
You are my weakness,
my love,
father of my child.
Everything you are,
I hold
close to my soul.
I love you so much,
my husband,
with you I am whole.
When you made me
your wife,
I was so full of joy.
But then you made me
a mother
with our own little boy.
I don't know what to do, so,
I thank
the Lord above.
My heart is near bursting
for you,
and our son with love.

Michael R Crump

Michael R Crump
of a narrow hill

To Edgar, Nathaniel, and Nancy

of a narrow hill
owning darker clouds
tombstone fins still the wind
gulls hang on heavy skies
sea of bones roll and cry
crows gather arthritic branches
ride a rocking chair song
they watch me walk the somber ground
as if they know I soon belong
a denser air begins to stir
an early moon appears
there's a rustle of brittle leaves
and a whorling of the grass
snowbits shine like broken glass
high above my upturned face
white against a blacker place
I hunch my shoulders sudden chill
and descend the path
of a narrow hill

Letitia Whitehead
MY FRIEND
My friend is very dear to me.
Like a friend ought to be.
I know she'll always be there for me,
As I grow, develop and see.

She holds a special place for me.
As close to her heart as she can.
But when she gets very old,
I will do the best that I can.

She helps me when I'm feeling down,
And when I'm feeling great.
Everytime I feel this way,
I have to celebrate.

Yes, my friend is very dear to me.
To me there is no other.
I love my friend with all my heart,
My friend, you see, is my mother.

Barbara Decker
SUMMER NIGHTS
When it's hot in the summer,
after a long working day;
We like to sit on the porch,
in our lazy, loafing way.

Just me and my family,
as we watch cars passing by.
We sit and rest and casually talk
or watch the stars in the sky.

We may enjoy a gentle breeze
or just listen to no sound.
The times we spend on the porch
are as precious as our small town.

We enjoy our rested evenings
in the swing under the porch light.
But it won't be long til fall, when
there will be no more summer nights.

Eunice H Nixon
A SECRETARY

This poem is dedicated to Rebecca, a dear friend.

To work I must go
Why I don't know.
Bang! bang! go the keys
That my letter will squeeze.
Why was I born so healthy
When I would rather be wealthy?
It's the end of a long day
All I'm able to say
Is, "Now I must run
Hope tomorrow's more fun."

Richard J Scherr Jr
CATHOLIC SCHOOL
stone cold, ashen grey
archaic outline frames harsh sky
hooded figures steal like wraiths,
flowing robes
hiding time-etched visages
forbidden stares greet as we
drag burdens of books through
the iron gate

tolling bell impels
as a long, pale, bony finger
erect and motionless, inside little
caskets, we feel the trickle
of sweat burning into eyes,
dripping from parted hair
staining white shirts

sudden sneeze, only
a moody, pompous sniff, but we
comply with robotic intonation:
"God bless you, teacher." We stare
straight ahead, like tin soldiers,
uncertain whether to
look up or down

Sage Elder
THE LIFE IN THE DAY . . .
In this afterlife no one is awake
Life sleeps as time corrodes.
As your eyes begin to peel away
From the very thing in which you desire
As your mind crumbles from a lapse
of reasoning you perspire
No sense of taste, sight, or smell
Your feeling is numbed as far as
anyone can tell.
The fighter battles his death
prolonging eternity
The writer empties his soul into the
minds of other creatures
Forever and always so shall it be
The gun is cocked and the trigger
Melts the passing migration of
Corruption among the living.

D M Lewis
OUT DOORS
While Walking alone The Pathway
Breathing the fresh air from blowing winds
Looking at different kinds of trees
Swaying against the breeze
OH What a glorious sight to see
Birds cheeping their sounds
While on the ground or in the trees
OH What a wonderful sound to hear
While strolling outdoors

Lev Flemming
FRIEND SEARCH
A feeling from within
Evolving in such creative ways
From all those we chance to meet
As life unfolds to each

Never brought to the surface
Perhaps until lapse of time prevails
Emotions so quietly stirring
Mystifying as it is

Glory of life for all to see
In sorrow or grief—joy or happiness
Love calmly present—compassion so deep
Knowing in all they will share

We live—we grow—we search
And once it is there
We treasure as no other
Beauty, truth and value

Enriched to such a depth
As we all have such a need
This precious gift flowing freely
Bringing fulfillment to all who seek

Grace Free
SOUNDS OF SILENCE
I am listening to the sounds of silence.
You say silence is without sound?
Sometimes the silence roars at you
like thunder,
Again, it encompasses with sweet comfort.
Listen to a silent house—
 The ticking of a clock
 The hum of the refrigerator.
Look at the clouds—
 Hear the silent movement
 Forever rolling on—

Listen! Look at a midnight sky—
 And hear the twinkling of the stars!
Listen! The past rushes in on
 galloping sounds of memory—
Some loud, some soft like a kitten on
a velvet rug.
Even thinking makes a sound!
I'm listening to the sound of loneliness
The ache's very loud!

Donna Hickman Dees
OLD SOUL

Dedicated to my mother and grandmother with undying love and gratitude.

In a room alone she sits to rock
in a building so old, slowly falling down.
Cracked and peeling, once white
walls turned brown.
Sounds seemingly far away creep up
the block.

Outside the window the day is gray.
The room is hushed, so quiet, so still.
She sits, she rocks, with enough
peace to fill
the walls with color, dispelling the
gray of the day.

The sounds so muffled she cranes to hear
the cry of a child, the drop of a tear.
Down the hallway footsteps sound,
leading away, always away,
but she has enough peace to fill the day.

Thus sits a soul, vibrant and strong in
a body so weak,
holding to Jesus and His coming time.
Knowing the father, understanding
His signs,
there is peace in this day, seemingly
gray and bleak.

Blanche Hunstable Broyles
A SPIRITUAL LIFE

I dedicate this poem to the J. E. Wilson S.S. Class, First Methodist Church Rockwall, Texas, who has been such a strength and help to me and my family, in our Spiritual growth.

Lord, Create in each of us a Spiritual life,
May we give ourselves to ending all strife.
Lead us where'ere thy Spirit may lead.
From self-love may we all be freed.
Deliver us from all self-righteous claim.
May pleasing Thee be our only aim.
Lord, instill in us thy Spirit true.
May we give ourselves our lives to renew.
Send thy Inner Light to brighten
mind and soul,
Guiding our paths Thy will to unfold.
Teach us thy precepts through thy
Holy Word.
Use us as instruments so Christ may
be heard.
Lord Create in each of us a clean heart.
May we give ourselves, Thy love to Impart.
Send Thy Spirit, our lives to inspire.
Deliver us from our selfish desire.
May our prayers and service never wane.
"For to live is Christ, to die is gain."

Garrison S Burr
THE DARKNESS OF CLOSED EYES

To Kay, who is, and always will be, very special to me—I love you.

She lays there with silent breath
listening, waiting for his footsteps to
invade her ears, provoke her fears.
The lion cuddles his young, teaches
them through touching.
The bird feeds its young until they
learn the lesson of flight.
As the door slowly opens and the
hallway light invades the darkness of
closed eyes
Somewhere a lion cuddles his young,
Teaches through touching.
Here a child will soon learn.

Janice K McDonald
MY LOVE
I dreamed about him
 most of my life.
I only imagined the
 happiness he would bring.

He came into my life
 after years of waiting.
He shows love that
 is so inviting.

He has a temperament
 almost like mine.
And sometimes it scares me,
 that we're so much alike.

I know that we'll be
 together for years.
But when he decides to leave,
 I will bid him luck.

I love him so much,
 that I can't explain.
He's my 2 year old son—
 Philip James!

Luard E Gilmore
LIFE'S FULFILLMENT

Dedicated to: Carol Gilmore, my wonderful wife of soon to be 50 years (1939-1989), two wonderful daughters, two fine son-in-laws and seven wonderful grandchildren five boys and two girls.

Of all the girls I ever knew
There's only one whose love was true
Back in nineteen thirty nine
I married her and she was mine.

Full of dreams and high hopes too
In planning life of things to do
We've both been up then been down
But through all this true love we found.

We raised two girls who were to be
The kind we are proud for all to see
Then later gained our son-in-laws
Grandchildren too and love them all.

If wealth was measured in this way
I become a millionaire each day
This wealth is there for those who try
It's valued worth you cannot buy.

Let memories be the dividend
Left to grow and never end
For when my life on earth is through
Eternal love will be there too.

So until I face that judgment day
I can proudly look at her and say
My dreams and hopes have all come true
Because sweetheart I married you.

April N Gower
ODE TO A LITTLE BIRD

TO Those who feed the wild birds.

Little bird free of will, what is that in your bill?
Seeds, and a little chaff. To plant in a small hill. A flick of gray, some deep blue, and a little white too. I wonder is that you? Feathers and down, some string you found wrapped round. A little warm sun on a spot where someone left a piece of bun. I wonder have you found some small plunder? A whistle, and a tweet, is the music that we meet. I listen daily to your song, every note a perfect sound. You slide through trees with eyes that watch the ground. Just see what you found. Tell me little bird free of will, what grew in your hill? Was it a tree you planted just for me? Or did you plant it there for posterity?

Cookie Mahr
I HEAR A MELODY
I hear a melody
Coming from the sky,
It must be tears from the sun
Forming musical rain.
A familiar note strikes my heart,
The chord of love,
I listen,
And suddenly realize that
He's playing our song.

Patricia Keitel (Carter)
ONLY IN MY DREAMS
I'm in a place that's very beautiful, where there
is no pain,
Far from the grown-up world, where you have every-
thing to lose and nothing to gain.
Where mountains are high, and rivers run free, with
lovely flowers, and a huge oak tree.
This is a city, where everyone should always be,
For this place was made for people, like you and
me.
In this world there is no ruler over each other,
For everyone loves you like a sister or brother.
So I look at heaven and smile, for I'm happy it
seems,
Then I woke up and realized it was only in my dreams.

Harold W Hallett
MY CHOICE
It is not given me to know
What lies ahead where I may go;
There may be sunshine, may be rain;
There may be pleasure, may be pain.
But it is given me to trust
That on the way life will be just
And though the path be hard and long
The truth will triumph over wrong.

So let this be my earnest prayer;
Please let my choice be made with care
And if it's rough day after day
Please keep me on my chosen way
And when at last I reach the end
Let someone say, "Well done, my friend."

Foster W Litton
SHADOWS

I dedicate this poem to my wonderful wife "FLO" who supports me in everything I do. And who I love with all my heart.

As the sun sets at the end of each day,
I watch the shadows as they start to dance and play
And the moon with its light so bright,
Reflects the true beauty of each night.
The shadows only appear dark and gray,
But in the moonlight they move and sway.

They sway to the tune of the whispering wind
And the trees, and leaves, and flowers all lend

Their part in the chorus when darkness descends,
And as the darkness fades from view,
It leaves its teardrops we know as dew

Then patiently waits to the end of another day,
So that the shadows once more can dance and play.

Byron Wynn
THE EXECUTIONER'S SONG
The pauper's a prince
Dressed in drag
You say an aristocrat
I say a fag
One day he'll let the cat
Out of his bag
His insecurities will lay bare
For everyone to tag
A joker's an ace
In the devil's deck
The Lord will take cash
He'll take a check
He'll capture your mind
Whether it's sound or a wreck
Your body's a blueprint
For this architect
Do you believe in perfection?
Or to be well rounded?
Are you sensitive to correction?
And feel dumbfounded?
You'll find out one day
What it's like to be equal
That life's a sitcom
And there's no sequel

Angela Dean
TO THE ONE I LOVE . . .

To Chris Hathaway, I'll love you forever!

There once was a guy
I knew and loved,
We were so close
As two people could be,
The only thing that mattered
Was him and me.

He meant so much
More than anyone ever had,
I knew with him
I could never be sad.
He was my life
He was my hope,
Then our love
Began to go down slope.

I hurt so bad
More ever before,
My tears shed
And slowly began to pour.
I've never gotten over him
Because he meant so much,
I feel we will reunite
When we feel that "special touch".

When that day comes
My life will be complete,
For I will once again
Be with the guy
Who made my life so
Wonderful and sweet.

Lori Marie James
A NEW BEGINNING
It is a warm spring day
the sky is blue.
The flowers are blooming
and the birds are singing too.

One little bird is sitting
on the edge of his nest.
Scared and frightened
he won't pass the flying test.

Momma bird says,
'Go ahead fly free.
Have a little faith
that's the key'.

So the little bird takes a deep breath and takes a dive.
Soaring in the air
he thinks it's great to be alive.

To think a moment ago
the little bird was afraid to die.
Now he can go wherever he wants,
because he can fly!

Tony Soto
USED
I realize I was used by you
Into letting me think you cared
Into thinking you would give me
A love beyond compare

I realize I was used by you
Your love for me wasn't true
You wanted to live out a dream
And I just happen to do

I realize I was used by you
I didn't matter from the start
You only needed to use me
To fill your empty heart

I gave you a tender love
With that you must agree
But my love for you has died
Because I realize you used me.

Kathy Clemens
I STAND TALL AS THE NEW TREE

I
stand
tall as
the new tree
***
With its limbs
reaching upward
***
Giving praise and thanks to Thee
***
For gifts undeserved, yet received
***
***
How special I am to stand in the sunshine
And be bathed in His warmth and His love.
Nothing I did to be so loved by Thine,
Just a sinner with no hope to grow.
***
***
But He planted the seed deep within my heart
That soon rooted and blossomed and flowered.
Gratefully, humbly, I knew from the start
All alone I would never again be.
***
***
Now His spirit lives in me
Ever guiding, ever growing,
Strengthening branch by branch of my tree.
Thank you Lord for the saving Grace in Thee.
***
***
***
***
****
** ** ** **
** ** ** **
** ** ** **
Saving Grace In Thee

Sue Owen
WORLDS APART

This poem is dedicated to Rob Boonstra, my summer love. Thanks for being a good friend.

I hardly even know you.
I only know your name.
I've liked you for two years,
And I still feel the same.

I don't really talk to you,
All I do is wave.
I wouldn't know what to do,
If you happen to stop one day.

I cherish your friendliness,
Each time you go by,

And when I can't see you,
I just let out a sigh.

I often have fantasies about you and me,
We're together and very happy.
When I wake up to reality,
I think about the kindness you've shown me.

I thank you for your friendship,
I'll treasure it in my heart.
I know we'll never be more than friends,
Since our lives are worlds apart.

Kathryn Murphy
WHEN YOU HAVE FOUND THE BEAUTY OF YOURSELF

When you have found the beauty of yourself,
inside and out.
When you have found love and when you have felt
something inside that only you possess, you have lived
Like no one but yourself can.

Carol J Hassett

Carol J Hassett
YOU

To one of the special men that shared a part of my life and is now just another memory.

U is for universal
which stands the whole world round.
For here we are and here we stay
just WE, just US.

We make up the world
together, as we'll stay forever.
For without US there would be no universe
to be universal.
Without YOU and without ME
there would be no world.
And without YOU
there would be no ME!

Barry Green
CLOUDS AT NIGHT

On warm summer nights when the moon rides high,
The strangest of things appear in the sky:
Pixies, and fairies with gossamer wings,
And dancers who prance for ethereal kings:
And ships with great sails go silently by,
On warm summer nights when the moon rides high.

On cold winter nights when the moon is dead,
And pixies, and fairies, and dancers have fled,
The ships go on—a'hurrying now—
A gale at each stem, and a storm at each prow,
Ay, the ships go on: black symbols of dread,
On cold winter nights when the moon is dead.

Marvierene Lusk Kelley
HE PROMISED THE BLUSH OF FALL

He promised the blush of fall instead,
He gave the red of blood and death to all,
Short is life or happiness like the Summer of the butterfly.

Robert R Brown
I WROTE A SONG

I wrote a song.
The words came so easy.
They poured out like water from a spring.

I wrote a song.
But it came without music,
And without music there's nothing to sing.

Rebecca Carnighan
DAYDREAMS

Daydreams are miniature night-dreams,
And a larger version of thoughts.
Daydreams you find in hot classrooms
Windows or rainbow ending pots.
Daydreams are castles built in the air
That you wouldn't dare have come true.
And yet, keep dreaming long enough,
And sometimes they really do!

Bonnie Cowie Shine
ON REMEMBERING

You said I'd only remember the good times
That is certainly not true.
I remember all if it.
Hell, I even remember you.

They say some people can make you crazy.
Well, me you certainly did.
But, in case you ever wondered,
I'm now okay, you never reached my id.

Will I ever think of you as 'good times'?
Not for a very long while.
First I'll have to forget this hurt inside,
And not feel like an abandoned child.

That's when I'll be in control,
Never to be vulnerable again.
That's when I'll remember you and 'good times',
And only feel with a grin.

Jeffery Scott Wambeke
BELIEVING IN YOUR DREAMS

This poem is dedicated to DeEtte, for helping me make my dreams come true.

When You dream
You Dream of Love
Your Dreams turn to Reality
That is the Beauty of a Dove
So pure and white
Your Dreams will be Your sight
The sight of Forever
Always showing a light
A light that is always soft
So soft is the light
That you never touch ground
The light will never be dimmer
Than when it was found
For your Dreams keep the light burning
Always burning never dying
Always growing from the beauty of the sight
If you believe in your dreams
Believe with all your heart
You will never fail
Always having a place from which to start.

Jennie King
MOCK OF THE MOON

The man in the moon really likes her,
he follows behind all her days.
What magnificent entertainment,
little fool with her hearts frightened ways.
She asks for love so quietly,
like a child that can barely be heard.
Laugh with those that taught her,
t'was something she'd never deserve.

Imprisoned by powers she knows of,
and torn by powers unseen.
Bleeding right down the middle,
she is caught betwixt and between.
A slice of silver laughter,
cuts across the sky.
Once pretty face now drawn with pain,
turns to the ground to cry.
The man in the moon's laughing at her,
what's one more man made out of stone.
Two life loves in pieces before her,
she knows she's forever alone.

Avery Atwell League II
THE HOLLOCOST

I live only to survive by the day
As the dead slowly rot and decay,
There are no more people in the way that we knew,
Just mutilation, in the ones that grew.

For I am now one of many
In a disgusting race,
Who watched destruction
Through a melting face.

Joanna Neff
PEONIES EN CARAFE

Given, the rain still gloating on their faces,
Rain sliding in their white spoon fingers,
These peonies are smug.

They've been hoarding elixirs of the moon's pull
And turning them to pearls,
Changing tokens with rain and wind
Though the night warns like a stern mother.
Indoors we talk of what endures.

Out of my sleep, at dawn,
I heard them whispering about my clock, my books,
About their cut stems, about drowning,
About rising from their glass jail.
Today their electric white is gone,
The red streaks of their hearts gone—
What made them unendurable is lost,
Now, in daylight, escaped in brown.

Allene Marie Chabala
FAMILY SOUNDS RECORDED

To Everyone! "Sharing is caring be it family, friends or group beliefs"

The sound is just a garbled cry
to strangers who are passing by;
But it's a golden sound to us
who joy in hearing family fuss!
Transcending discords open view;
talking all at once with you . . .
Yet all of those who listen know
and recognize the loved one's show!
and though the noise is out of class
its value keeps for time to pass;
Recording thus, these family sounds
from master copies to be found;
Surfacing from some dusty lair
by offspring who will hear and care.

Fred K Lingle
HATE SO BEAUTIFULLY

To My Beloved Georgia

I hate so beautifully today
Have you some I could borrow
You had better lend it if you have
I may pay love tomorrow.

Hilda Thiesing
A GLIMPSE OF HEAVEN ON EARTH

To my family, my friends and all humankind

God will feed the hungry in every part of earth,
Together we will nurse the sick and old and make life worth its worth
We will work together with every nation to conquer space and behold;
Understand and love all peoples of the world that's the least that we can do
God will bless us mightily if our hearts are true
We can protect our environment and God will see it's right
We will see our beautiful moon and stars that shine so ever bright
People will have dignity that's God's promise for us all
We only have to believe His word when His clarion angels call
Then one day Jesus will return to rule us all on earth
Life will be worth living when He comes to rule again
How wonderful it will be with no sorrow tears or pain
This will be called the Rapture and it will surely come to pass
If we believe His holy word that life can last and last
We will see all this come to pass because God has promised us
That heaven is on hand and God will reign with love
He will send a message to us in the

form of a pure white dove
And you can know without a doubt
that Jesus does not lie
But lives forever for us in His
heavenly home on high

P J Maurer
FIRST FOURTH

To George "Think good thoughts . . ."

radiant sunshine
over us walking
barefoot on the beach
sand warm and soft
welcoming our toes
under ripples of water
waving in from the ocean

happy, still silence
between us
carrying our shoes
amidst screaming gulls
and rhythmic tide
tracing the coastline
into

nighttime
color exploding in the sky
crimsonyellowivorybluemagenta
green
melting
softly, secretly,
into ripples of water
waving in from the ocean

Florence Jo Baker
REMEMBER ME

Let me be remembered then for
Beauty.
Beauty on hills in early morning,
with cedars traced against the tinted
sky.
Beauty on fields in golden splendor.
Beauty when sunset's colors die.
Beauty that I worship day and night.
April's gentle rain on dripping
branches;
glistening in silver shy moonlight.
Beauty when autumn winds are
flinging,
Gold and Ruby gems across the hills.
Beauty when winter's snows have
covered
all the glenns so deep and still.
Transient still, yet deathless, as all
God's wonders are.
Oh! Remember me then and worship
tall cedar,
hill, and star.

Darlene Puckett Barnell
GHOSTS

A house of memories
. . . is quiet at night.
When ghosts of the past
. . . hide, out of sight.

Then ghosts slither in
. . . jarring that silent sight
With sounds of laughter
. . . coming into the light.

The ghosts are of love
. . . once vital now blight
In the house of memories
. . . so quiet at night.

Daniel P Beck
PLAINSMAN AT THE ATLANTIC

The waters roar far off to other shores
and the foam splashes shyly at
my feet—
it is Poseidon's greeting to the
believer.
The hand of Apollo, invisible, pulls
at the sea
and the tide goes out.
Beached men-o-war are turned
lavender and light blue
in vanquished starlight
and there are speckled seashells
staring at a surf
whose collapsing walls hint of
green.
These are the pre-dawn glories of the
ocean.
Lightning glows behind imposing
clouds
that hint of thunderous voices
raging within
and of the blood of gods being
let in celestial battle.
Seagulls soar parallel to shore
like puppets cast away.
Pelican's strings are cut, wings fold,
they drop—
then are miraculously recovered
with breakfast.
Here I sit alone, wondering at all
these things
that I have never seen before.
I am entranced by the play
these many forgotten gods have
put on for me.

Lisa Rayfield
A RAINFALL OF DREAMS

To my twin sister Rachel, thanks for being my best friend for the past 16 years.

The winds are at a halt,
The bitter roots are drenched with
the days
rainfall of dreams,
If they were to lose these dreams
they would wither and
die,
The dreams help them grow in
strength and hope,
from them stem ideas of a generation,

A time will come when they are cut
in two,
but again they will grow,
For they have reason for rising in the
storm,
The bud of hope can never stop
blooming . . .

Stephanie Loadholt
HELP ME LORD

This poem is dedicated to my grandmother, Mrs. Maude Evans, who has been my mentor and role model.

Help Me Lord,
To conquer the challenges of today

Help Me Lord,
To endure the pain and suffering and
dismay

Help Me Lord,
To reflect your good image,
Help Me Lord, Help Me.

Help Me Lord
To overlook insults, prejudice and
shortcomings of others
Help Me Lord, Help Me
To love others as You love Me.

Alice Johnson
HELP LORD

Dedicated to Randy Calhoun who gave me the inspiration for this poem.

Jesus, if you were on earth
today—
Would a pimp give you water to
drink?
Would you offer her life everlasting?
Indeed, socializing with the trash and
scum—
Where is your class? Where is your
expertise?
Don't you understand social graces?
And how to climb the social ladder?
Why don't you dress correctly?
And that long hair just has to go—
And your followers are not
educated—How can they preach?
Now don't tell me, is it a miracle
indeed?
You turned the water to wine? You
healed the man born blind?
How do I know it is for real? Do you
read me Lord?
Hear my cry! Before Christmas
another life may be shuffled out
Jesus—you knew Satan he was the
anointed cherub that covereth.
And now he's your enemy. He's
trying to devour all of mankind who
don't love you—Help Lord! Help
your servants rescue the perishing
from the pits of hell before God says,
"It's closing time!"

Louise Smith
SNOW IN CALIFORNIA

This poem is dedicated to all my Grandchildren and their future families.

In the valley where we live
There has never been real snow.
Some hail now and then.
A snow storm so beautiful;
Large white flakes drifting down
When they fell to the ground they
were gone.
I stood and watched with excitement
As the air filled with white flakes.
They came drifting down to the
ground
And they were gone.

Later in the day when the Grandchil-
dren came
Once again the air was filled with
snow flakes
This time whirling and twisting to
the ground
Then they were gone.
The children with so much
excitement
Romped and played in the falling
snow.
A childhood memory for them to
keep.
As for me a long wished for sight
For my delight.

Raymond W Boyer
A TRIBUTE TO PRESIDENT GEORGE BUSH

You are the forty-first President of
the USA,
One of the best in every way.
Much has happened since you first
come along.
You live your life as if it were a
great song.
A pleasant challenge awaits you
through the years.
You will conquer all your fears.
The American People are on your
side,
To help you, and work things
out, and abide.

President Bush, we give thanks to
thee,
For your character, and conduct,
for all to see.
It is good that you are here.
We are for you, never fear.

Mignon P Burnett
THE HIDING PLACE

I gathered souvenirs from life and on
a future day
I sorted through and some I
kept,
And some I threw away.
But some were overlooked and there,
within a box, they lay
Un-noticed, yes, but still they
were
A part of yesterday.

Then one by one they disappeared as
if they'd never been.
I looked but 'nary did I find;
My heart was sad, but then
As bits and pieces fell in place of
what and where and when
My memory recalled each one
And put them back again.

And now my heart is like a book, my
thoughts locked up inside.
I've thrown the magic key away;
I've found a place to hide.
Here, no-one knows my thoughts but
me, and here they're free to stay
Where uninvited predators
Cannot steal them away.

Leah Peterson
COMPASSION

They say it's an eyesore, an ugly
monster,
A blight to the neighborhood;
They'd send her to a home for the
aged,
Demolish the house—if they could.

As they continue to rant and rave,
The lady and house stay entwined
With memories of loving husband
and children,
Friends who were wined and dined.

She softly caresses this memento and
that—
Each with a story of its own;
Fading walls hold all in protective
embrace,
Bearing witness with one now alone.

She prays, for her younger
neighbors' sake,
They will never be put in her place—
When others seek to destroy what
remains
And a lifetime to erase.

Richard A Harrington
SOME WHERE THERE IS LIGHT, ONLY IF . . .

Light is upon us all the time. (Even
when we sleep.)
there is plenty of light and life
around us!
It makes us aware of things.
Whatever we do,
Whatever we see,
Whatever we plan,
Whatever we sense,
light has touched and made anew.

The blind may not see details of
light,
but they KNOW of its beauty.

People with sight know less about light,
but they do acknowledge its existence.
People have tunnels with light at the end,
but, many times, . . . they never get to the end.

People will wander,
People will wonder,
People will rush to the light,
hoping . . .
People will turn their back on the light, . . .
and, they continue anyway!

Light does make a difference. Only if . . .
Look, listen, and feel, and you will find it.

Lois E Martin
A MEADOWLARK

I would like to dedicate this poem to my beautiful mother who taught me to appreciate mother nature in all her glory.

I'd love to be a meadowlark
on this bright summer day.
I'd sing you such a merry song
as you pass on your way.

I'd light upon your windowsill
when sunlight first peeks through
And greet you with my merry song
Good Morning Dear to you.

Then O'er the fields and the meadows
I'd take you there to play.
Flowers bathed in the morning dew
We'd stand there in dismay.

I'd go ahead and build a nest
for all our little ones.
Beside a brook, some shady nook,
or where the river runs.

With little mouths to fill all day
from nature's pantry store.
All these things I'd do for you,
and many, many more.

Konstantin A Ginsburg
THE FOX AND THE CROW
Once piece of cheese was sent from heaven to a crow.
She took in her bill and climbing on the tree as far as possible from crowd, decided to proceed with breakfast there, on top of spruce.
As suddenly, as if ill luck would have it, the fox appeared among the bushes, and gazing at the tree, where crow was sitting cooly, fox started to approach the tree though slowly, but surely.

"I heard that you are famous for singing"—fox uttered in enchanting tone.
"And able to command one's spirit and the soul."
"And that the other birds compared to you are merely pinging, thus trying shamelessly to ridicule us all!"
"Be kind,—and sing something for old chap,
"Song of your own choice, and let me be the judge as how faultless is your voice."
Right after fox's flattering appeal, our crow opened widely lengthy bill to sing, while cheese was free to go.
As for the fox—she did not wait a bit.
Right after a piece fell at her feet, the swindler snatched, wagged her brush, and left the place in greatest rush.

We are apt to take the flattery for granted, then we are satisfied, we feel content and after being tricked by talk in which there is much cry and little wool, thereafterwards we look as perfect fool.

Remo Rossi
YOU—FAR AWAY
I miss you
When the sun hands over his rosy fingers
To the horizon
When dark hours slow the steps of people
And the tiredness doesn't go away
Like the shadow that I feel is not mine

I miss you
In your looks and in that smile
A little bit unconscious
In the excuses of those "your probablys"
You are that Knot in the throat
That doesn't go away

I miss you as I pretend
To feel well
Now I understand
What it means
Having you near before sleep
As I walk barefoot in my soul

You are my guilt without end
The coldness of some morning
When I look around and feel
That I miss you

Ruth H Yorns

Ruth H Yorns
DIFFERENT WORLD
I just can't seem to understand
The way things are today;
Many changes have been made;
There's not much time for play.

People are rushing here and there
To get something or to get someplace;
There's not even good hellos;
What could have happened to the human race?

I guess we can blame it on progress;
Work is made so easy for us now;
And yet we complain day after day,
Always using that crying towel.

There's one way we can change it,
And make a different world,
By helping everyone we can
And respecting our flag when furled.

Following the golden rule
Will help us so much too;
Treating everyone as a brother
Will prove that love comes through.

Carol A Marino
VISIONS OF YOU
Visions of ocean waves . . .
running through my mind.
Softness of sand;
beneath my feet.
Thoughts are wandering . . .
like magic.
Visions of you, come and go.
The beauty as if a sunset scenery.
Neverending pleasures,
are the serenity of you.
Like a rainbow's bright colors . . .
across the sky.
The everlasting memory . . .
will never fade.

Schelli M Barbaro
SUBWAY
Running, pushing, sliding, waiting,
looking, looking away.
Standing, sitting, lurching, staying,
starting, stopping, going my way?
Noise, noise, noise, calamity.
speechless, thinking, feeling anonymity.
Hustling, bustling, whistles singing,
grinding, squealing, screeching, ringing.
Stench, dirt, urine, hanging on . . .
grumbling, growling, flowing tears.
Open, close, come and gone,
chatting, laughing, overt fears.
Bodies, heat, hot steel against steel,
bumping, cold, soft, alive . . .
Blinking, stinking, blurring, surreal,
rushing, lonely, speeding, Life.

Jacqueline Myers
THE OCEAN'S BEAUTY
Ocean waves wash up seashells,
as seagulls fly in heaven.
Chilled winds blow through shadows,
as day lingers forward.
Sounds of the sea whistle briskly,
as night draws near.
Leaving behind memories and tokens of the Ocean's Beauty.

Eva M Martin
REQUIREMENTS
And you
Will do
What's true.
And I
Will try
To cry.
And she
Will be
So free.
And they
Will say
By day,
Our gain
Is shame
And pain.

James E Austin Jr
DECEPTION
What are you holding there?
A young mans heart but you don't care.
For you he would be bought or sold,
but his love you've put on hold.
Deception—deception.
How long will you put him down,
treating him like some punching clown.
The way you use him you have no shame.
One day he'll learn your real name.
Deception—deception.
To keep him under your spell,
you use your sex so well.
Sometimes you just say no,
but you always tease him so.
Deception—deception.
You say you love him true,
he has yet to see the lie in you.
But one day he will realize.
He'll find in your eyes,
Deception—deception.

Janet Donovan
RONDE'VOUS
Come sit with me and talk awhile
Upon this hill of flowers
We'll track the clouds across the sky
We could be here for hours

We'll get to know each other
And dream the time away
I brought a picnic lunch
We could be here all day

When the sun goes down beyond the hill
And the night birds begin to gather
We'll smile, and remember this sunny day
In all inclement weather.

Albert M Maier
SUMMER RAINS
A sudden darkening of the bright skies,
The gathering of heavy massive clouds,
Whispering winds develop harsh cries
As if objecting to earth's black shroud.

The rustle of leaves, creaking of bough,
The whistle of tight wires overhead,
The welcome patter of raindrops now
Brings rich new lifeblood to earth's dried bed.

The landscape brightens to freshlike green
As all filth is quickly washed down the drains.
Wading children frolic on the scene,
Part of the beauty of summer rains.

Cody Christiaens
LOVE

To my loving and supporting friends—Ryan, Deena, Chris, Jamee, Tracy, and my grandmother.

To some love is like the rose.
Beautiful, yet to touch upon its stem may hurt.
To others, love is like an endless road
Where there are many blocks
But if you pay the right price you can get by.
Still, to many, love is like the lion,
Fierce and troublesome to the experienced,
Yet to the young, interesting and harmless.
In a dream it is like heaven.
But when you wake you must be patient and full of faith.
To me, love is like a dark tunnel,
And you are the light at the end.

Lois Gertsch
MY OTHER HALF
My dear Louise, I lay in this bed with a heavy heart.
It's been five years since we've been apart.

Why did you leave me? Why couldn't you stay?
I loved you so dearly in every way.

"God" let me be with you for those last five months.
If I'd only known and not been such

a dunce.

But God said to me, "Lois, It's coming now and you must be away, Louise is going to have her final day."

"You've taken enough watching her go,
Of her last breath you will never know."

When I came home I never knew, that was the last I'd ever see of you.

You promised you'd wait for me, you promised you'd stay,
You knew I'd be back soon, why did you stray?

I tried to go with you Louise, but it didn't work.
The good Lord wouldn't let me, I was such a jerk.

Being a twin was a wonderful life, until God took you and my heart was cut with a knife.

Remember Louise the good times we had, our life on earth really wasn't too bad.

We always had each other in every thing we did, we never fought together, we never flipped our lid.

Except when I married and I had 3 sons, and you had my labor and you said "I hope you're done".

Even though you're in Heaven and are there to stay, your spirit is with me in every way.

I didn't want to go to our class reunion in '88, but with you beside me it was great.
Nobody knew what a great time we had, we laughed, we talked and it really wasn't too bad.

Louise, you are always with me, in everything I do, you are not dead just one atom became two.
Part of me died when you went away, but part of you is here in me to stay.

Some day we will be together and one will be two,
So God Bless you my Louise, he still has work for me to do.

Gayle A Wright
ESPECIALLY FOR YOU, DAD!

For my loving Dad, Thomas Adams—Oct. 7, 1988

You'll never know just how glad,
I am that you were chosen as my Dad.
As I was growing through the years,
You helped to wipe away my tears.
You taught me love, respect and trust,
Through every day life this was a must.
You were there as often as you could be,
To help mend whatever the problem might be.
You had a firm hand when there was a need,
Most of the time you would just plead.
My childhood memories are good to look back on,
Because I had you to rely and depend on.
The right words on a card I could not find,
So I've written some down from my own mind.
On this day that belongs to you,
I hope many of your wishes come true.
You taught me a lot through the years,
That's the reason Dad you're so dear.
As I end this I will say . . .
I wish you a
Very Happy Birthday!

Donna M Christensen

Donna M Christensen
NATURE'S PLAYS

To Jane Roberts and Seth, with love and gratitude, who taught me to use the creative potential that is inherent in the human spirit.

The sounds of nature
in early spring,
awakens a need
in the human being.

The need to create.
The need to explore.
The need to find love.
The need to be more.

The connection between
us and nature is seen
as creative will in
each living thing.

Like nature we too
are connected to earth,
mourning a death
or rejoicing in birth.

The Creator's expressed
in all of these ways,
and seeks recognition
within nature's plays.

Tonya Yvonne Byker
A FRIEND

A friend is someone to share your sadness, happiness, love, hate or any mood.
A friend is someone you can discuss your problems with.
A friend is someone you can tell a secret to, knowing they won't tell anyone else.
A friend is someone who stays with you, even if everyone else has left you.
A friend is someone who helps you with your work.
A friend is someone that will cheer you up, when you are sick or sad.
A friend is someone who will understand you, even if others think you're crazy.
A friend is someone you will never forget.
A friend is the greatest thing you'll ever have.

Mildred R Catterton
MISTAKEN IDENTITY

I met a man in town
I thought to be a bum.
We struck up an acquaintance,
And soon he was my chum.

I asked him if he'd like to walk
Through the woods with me,
I had a thriving business there
I'd like for him to see.

We left walking side by side
And soon had reached the spot
Where I'd hid my whiskey still
Inside a cave of rock.

I showed him how I fired it up
And how I made "the stuff,"
And then I asked him if he'd like
To have one "on the cuff."

He looked around and shook his head
And then he calmly said,
"You see ole chum, I am no bum,
I'm a South Carolina Fed."

Shirley P Hickcox
NAMES

To my husband "Robby" of thirty-nine years.

I'm married to a man
Who has many names,
Robert, was the given one,
But it's been changed.

I call him "Robby",
Our bird calls him "Rob",
If he doesn't answer,
He then Yells "Bob".

Strangers call him "Robert",
Which was the given one,
His sister calls him "Bobby",
She calls him this for fun.

His dad, and my mother,
Preferred the name of "Bob",
Our bird keeps insisting
It should just be "Rob".

But I call him "Robby",
It fits him to a "T",
I don't think he'll contest it,
He's married to me.

Kathryn Kay Jandik
TO MY FAR AWAY LOVE:

I stare out at the hazy winter sky,
And I think about the many miles of sky stretched between us.

I hear the wind blowing across the snow,
And I think about you whispering in my ear.

I look at my hand pressed against the windowpane,
And I think about warming your handsome body with my touch.
I feel my heart beating strong in my chest,
And I think about how much stronger it would beat in your presence.

I lie alone in my bed,
And all I can think about is the love we will share upon your return.

Beverly Davis
POSITION WANTED:

To my husband Richard, my daughter Jonell, and my son Rich, who entrusted their resumes to me.

When The Big Boss up yonder
Reads your final resume
He will smile wisely and
Send you on your way
He'll show you the downstairs
And offer up this tip—
Shape up my child
Quit rockin' my ship
Knock off all the sinnin'
Stop your bein' a brat
'Cause you can't come upstairs
With credentials like that.

Diane Andersen
THE GREATEST GIFT

Without heartache, without pain, life sits still
With little gain—
Without purpose, never knowing what is real
Is a life that's lost and cannot feel—
Without bending or sometimes lending a fragment of
Ourselves to those in need—
We lose sight of what's important
And our own humility—
Without daring, never caring
Your life is but an empty shell—
Reaching out, touching others
Letting them touch you—
Is so rewarding, never boring
Your heart will feel like soaring—
You'll find inner peace and a sense of worth
For giving of one's self—
Is the greatest gift on earth.

Shirley Gonzales
CAN ANYBODY HEAR ME CRYING?

To Antonio Gonzales 1928-1989 Loving Husband, Father, and Grand Father.

Can any-body hear me crying?
Does any-body even care?
Will any-body even wonder; if my sorrow is too much to bear?

The world is going on around me;
But I've never felt so much alone,
I feel as if my heart is breaking;
With a sadness that I've never known.

I pray, in time the pain will leave me, and my misery will begin to fade;
Then maybe I can find God's reason,
For the terrible price I've paid.

Elizabeth Davis Soell
OUR CHILD

We lost our child that we had both wanted so much.
The little girl we never got to know.
My husband dreamed about her,
And we prayed to God.
I visioned my child while laying beside my husband one night.
With blonde hair and blue eyes.
She looked just like her father.
I felt so proud.
Little did I know that we were going

to lose that child.
It was only a dream.
Only a make believe story.
But in our hearts it was real.
We had already picked out a name.
It would have been a little girl named Pamela Gail.
We both know
That we lost our child.

Lee R Heaton
TOGETHER

To Mary: My devoted wife

Night-shades are falling, morning-doves are calling,
It is the start of a day that is new.
Don't put off for tomorrow or you'll find to your sorrow,
That life's precious moments are few.

Love's sweet surrender are yours to remember,
So drink from its cup to your fill.
For as you grow older, the world seems much colder,
Do your best . . . till your life . . . it is still.

The mysteries of life, both the joys and the strife,
Have caused poets to ponder for years.
Just face each boldly, with compassion, not coldly;
Search for answers, through laughter and tears.

Throughout the day, as you trudge on your way,
Choose wisely the path that you take.
To your peace of mind, together you will find,
The hand of the Lord when you wake.

Ron Rivard
MY GRANDPA

To my Grandpa—a man for whom I care dearly .

Hiking through the woods
with the fresh scent of pine.
Farming, gardening, feeding the deer.
All in a day's work.

Carol C Larson
OLD LETTERS
Old letters
Half Forgotten
Ragged edges
Guarded well

The thoughts they tell
Forever now a part of me.
One, half open
Torn by hands too eager
To wait one second more
Rewarded by the words
You wrote so long ago:

"As always so wonderful
To hold you close again
The same forces now
And always will be so"!

Carl Jetté
WINTER MAGIC

To my family, especially my loving, persistent mother.

On a wintery night
the crooked crags
are branches bent with snow.

On a wintery night
over the far-off hill,
snowmen run and play
instead of standing still.

On a wintery night
two lovers walk the bridge
that crosses the brook.
Soundless words,
a love is born
just like a wintery nook.

On a wintery night
a sole figure lonesome
speaks of Christmas cheer
and like the fabled man
—Pied Piper;
the animals draw near.

Elizabeth J Legassie
INSIDE HE CRIES
Quickly he comes eyes all aglow,
Quickly we say "no, no, no, no".
Inside he cries
Hoping for love
Which never dies.

So soon he returns with "wheres and whys"
Busy are we, we tell no lies.
Inside he cries
Hoping for love
Which never dies.

His hands reach out to say "I care"
But please, not now, we can not hear.
Inside he cries
Hoping for love
Which never dies.

Each child is born with much to give
Turn away and he may not live.
Inside he cries
His spirit dies.

Ruth E Ellis
NEARLY SPRING
Early in the morning,
The birds sing sweet and loud.
Early in the morning,
The sun shines without a cloud.

Snow has almost disappeared.
Crocus peek from out the ground.
Tiny buds upon the trees
Promise spring will soon be 'round.

My soul stirs within me.
My heart sings a song.
As everything awakens,
I feel refreshed and strong.

The quietness of winter
Puts contentment in my heart.
Now the miracle of springtime
Adds new joy to each days start.

Early in the morning,
Robin's song is sweet and clear.
Early in the morning,
Sunshine brightens all with cheer.

Patricia L Traeger
GOD'S CREATIONS—A BLESSING

I dedicate this poem to my wonderful grandchildren, Mark Jr., Jessica, and Helen Louise

Whenever we prayerfully go to our knees,
We should think of the oceans, the winds, and the trees.
Think of green meadows and lilies of the field
And the harvest of grains that the earth richly yields.

Think of the sun as it yields daily light,
The moon and the stars that guide us by night,
The birds as they swiftly fly over our heads,
The creatures that rest on the ocean's cold beds.
Such wonders He gave us! What love He has shown!
Though troubles befall us, He forgets not his own.
Give thanks! oh ye people, to our Father above
As daily He blesses and shields us with love.

Donald C Beach
A JOURNEY OF FRIENDSHIP

To the friendship of all my friends; it is truly the greatest gift they have ever given me!

A chance meeting was how they met—
A meeting now, they won't forget.
It wasn't planned, but just unknown—
Now look into what it has grown.

Just two people each going their way,
Traveling along day by day.
Never thinking of what could be,
The friendship ahead they did not see.

Then by chance their roads had met—
Now neither's journey has ended yet.
Rather each has not begun,
The journey of friendship one on one.

Now neither sees what lies ahead—
Yet neither really fear nor dread—
Since they are now stronger as two.
These people, yes, are me and you!

Diana Lombardo
WHAT HAPPENED TO US?

Dedicated To my Grandma for her inspiration. My Mother for her love and undying faith in me. To Lisa, my best friend, thanks for the memories. I love you all.

Together as children, so curious and free,
Forever together, I thought we would be.
As we grew older, we grew wise,
Now there is distance in our eyes.
No calls, no talks, no sisterly cries.
I watch the eternal light of friendship flicker wildly before it dies.
The laughter that now only echoes in my mind,
Is the peacefulness of the childhood I left behind.
We lived through the times of good and the times of trouble.
Now I find my self sifting through the forgotten rubble.
Of the memories we keep in storage, the good times that we had.
Your reassuring smile comes to mind, whenever I feel sad.
I'm sorry we're so far apart right now,
Maybe in the future it will work out some how.
Until then my friend, I shall sit and wait.
I pray there is time for us, I think it's not too late.
What happened to us, where did we go,
To tell you the truth I just don't know.

Ben Messina
THE BALANCE
Often I see
Man's cruelty to man
And wonder why
He was created.
The futility of life . . .
The futility . . .
Then suddenly a kindness
Is brought upon me!
A thoughtful word,
A good deed—
And then I am touched
So deeply Words become inadequate.
A reservoir of tears
That is my soul
Is unleashed
And I am cleansed,
For I have come to see
The balance
In all that lives.

Thomas B Colwell
THE WIND
The wind—I hear it come and go.
I hear it ebbing like the tide.
I feel it touching me inside.
It stops—then whispering starts to flow.

From silence starts a murmuring sound
That calls one to reach and listen;
To flex and feel a moment glisten,
And grow until you know it's found.

Perhaps it then becomes intense,
And rises—falls—and strongly forces,
Moving by—possessed of unseen sources
That supply a way to recommence.

Perhaps in passing one can learn
The pulse of life did so begin;
As breath inhaled so deep within,
It all commenced and will return.

Like Breezes blow—and where they go
I've never found out just yet.
But they'll return without regret,
And then like life, I'll learn to know.

Misty Hayes
MAKING YOUR WAY
Treat each day as if it was the end.
Be kind to others and be everyone's friend.
Tell the truth, instead of a lie.
Make someone laugh and comfort their cry.
don't criticize, be there with an open hand.
Listen attentively and try to understand.
Pick someone up, don't push 'em down.
if you show someone you care they'll stick around.
Think positive in all that you do,
and with the help of Christ you'll get through.

RoseAnn Pollum
LOVE PRETENDING

Inside you dear, lies a beast,
Silence is it's name.
You're such a brilliant man,
with so much you could say.

The silent game you've played on me,
has been true hell you know.
The torture in my mind
and heart is something I
could never show.

We all have faults, and I have mine,
so many, not so few.
I've been wrong, but so have you
so pretending is the thing I do.

Silence and pretending cannot
go hand in hand, one of them
has to stop . . . and truthfully
take a stand.

Today it happened, my bubble burst!
Pretending was over and so were you.
I have lost a love, I tried to save.
That tiny beast won out . . .
Silence . . . Shhhh Divorce

Dora Robinson
THE CITY

For ease and thinking the morning's best,
No women on the streets to molest.
You'll see a dragged out bum, here and there,
From the Bronx, the traffic bear.
In the gutter the vulture chalks her gain,
How unlike the housewife from the plains.
Before locked gates asses pray,
Take up with solemn and trace the way.
Those brave punks with purple hair,
Think they're divine, but need repair.
Here are rows of poor who stand in single file,
Waiting for food from the pile.
And all through the streets with passing cries,
Through the night a person dies.

Sandra Widen
REFLECTIONS OF THE SOUL

Between two worlds, life hovers like a star
We sparkle from afar
There have been tears and a breaking heart for thee
Remembering when I stood beneath the fresh green tree
Through the green leaves, he lifted my walls of gray
Thy gentle hand clasped into mine
—his heart more truly knew that peal too well
Seen through the darkness of his eyes, a lingering love shines
—could thy eyes in following mine?
We started, for our souls is wanting there
My soul trembles as it glows
I cherish the tenderness, mountain shadow kiss
—which in my heart still gleams, for moments stand still
Our feelings is a perchance of heavenly birth
—which in reality couldn't remain on earth
Reflections of his soul, that is nature
I recall upon thee night so sweet
He natured and taught I, to be me so dear
Listen with thy heart, not thy ear
The deepest trace of love, is still there
—for it marks the fire, still sparkling in his eyes
In returns of sweetness by nature given
In softest incense back to heaven
In the gateway of the smiling sky
There our love will lay, we sparkle from afar
—in the evening star

Mimi Kent

Mimi Kent
THANK YOU FOR BEING OUR FRIEND

To all the kind people offering their support on the sudden death of my beloved husband, Arthur Kent, Jr.

Thank you for being our friend
Thanks for caring until the end
Though Art's life on earth is through
We, left behind, still need you
Hard times and rough roads lie ahead
Our hearts are heavy with dread
An impossible task it seems
To give up and let go of our dreams
Frustration, confusion and fear
Anger, resentment and tears
These things we are feeling, we know
With the passing of time will go
Memories of good times we keep
Even now, as together we weep
One thing, above all, this is true
We still need our good friends like you
With sorrow and grief in our hearts
We know, we all will miss Art
Seeking peace and understanding in the end
We say "Thank you for being our friend."

Tracey Miracle
FANTASY OR FRIENDSHIP

You were just a fantasy, but then you were much more,
Makin' love with you was easy, please don't shut the door,
I've loved you as a friend, fantasy is what you'll be,
The joy of being with you, is enough for me.

No one else has to know, just what I think of you,
Fantasy or friendship is what we'll have to do.
Loving you is very easy, I know that it is wrong,
We can be alone again, we will always get along.

Something good is what we had, but for now it's in the past,
For I let you down too much my friend, let's make our friendship last
Love is always caring and trying to understand.
Love is always sharing this feeling oh so grand.

Now it's up to you my friend,
If we should have to end,
But if we can go on this way
Memories, fantasy, and friendship is what we'll always stay.

Janie
TIME FOR TIME

"This poem is dedicated to myself, not only myself but also those who take the time to admire the little things in life"—Janie—

A long time ago way back before the time of man,
before there was even light or war . . .
The God of the heavens had his plan,
for this world to endure . . .

I myself have seen throughout the years,
how people have changed this life . . .
we have all dealt with unknown fears,
we have dealt with death, pain and strife . . .

We all should take some time for time,
to recognize life for itself . . .
You may be able to put love on a line,
but you cannot put life on a shelf . . .

Time for time is so precious that you should believe,
I will give to life all that is mine . . .
Finally your time comes and of this world you must leave,
So please try and remember to take some time for time.

JoAnne Scheerer
REBECCA JANE

To Emily, Carly and Claire

Rebecca Jane,
little carnival kid.
Bare feet, yellow curls
and faded sunsuit.
You approach me
as I sit on a park bench
eating my lunch from
a Tupperware box.
You stand before me,
place your dimpled and dirty
toddler hands on my knees
and look me straight in the eyes.
Your parents call,
but you stand firm
with silent curiosity
staring up at this stranger
amid your world
of clanging tools
and sunburned men at work
on a half-assembled ferris wheel.

Aldo Garrido
GOD

This poem is dedicated to my family, and all of my intimate friends, you know who you are!

"God, strange but not a stranger;
For He gave birth to the beauty of life;
For He offers shelter upon the era of danger;
For He sets gaiety on the rue of shamed strife;
For He drops love on the hate of man;
For He lays good over the evil of wealth;
For He lessons us in fallacy of our mortal span;
For He alms bread to the urgeness of health;
For He colors in dreams of our azygous youth;
For He created the cosmos and designed our blue sky;
For in the end, He hands us the humble truth;
For He gifted us with mighty memories that never die;
For He provides life within the wild and salty sea;
For we are like His forest, and He is like our ranger;
For He loves us all, both you and me;
God, strange but not a stranger!"

Brenda Church
INSPIRATIONAL IDEALS

Expand your horizons,
Achieve your highest goals,
Encourage even the smallest dreams,
God knows
The inspiration you feel in your soul,
let the excitement and motivation overwhelm you with a glow,
Feel the satisfaction that accomplish-ments
can bring . . .
Before you know it, you will be able to sing . . .
Aspiration, inspiration, to fill you with motivation to achieve your
HIGHEST GOALS!

Dawn M Nielsen
THEY'LL BELIEVE US

We could tell them a table is a chair.
They'll believe us.

We could tell them the sky is the ground.
They'll believe us.

We could tell them a square is a circle.
They'll believe us.

We could tell them red is green.
They'll believe us.

We could tell them no means yes.
They'll believe us.

We could tell them mountains are lakes.
They'll believe us.

We could tell them right is left.
They'll believe us.

If we all got together we could change their world.
Believe me.

Steve Felkins
ALONG THE LEVEE

Life is so strong along the levee which I sit—
Big bright sun begins to drop.
Beautiful orange moon arises, so wise. It sheds a great strong light.
Rocks I sit on, same as the frogs.
Somewhere unseen sing the crickets.
The soft breeze blows, a big crab in the sky, I believe it is a cloud. It seems to be resting, cause it does not move.
On this side of the levee my heart beats soft.
On this side of the levee I have felt the good of life—

Marjorie C Shandy
SUMMER'S ROSE

Goodbye, goodbye to sweet summer,
The bloom has left the rose;
With roots enclosed in ice and snow,

It waits, while North winds blow,
Goodbye, goodbye to Summer's Rose,
Yet, still the rose well knows
With coming spring, the sun shall bring
New bloom back to the rose.

Goodbye, goodbye to sweet summer,
The chill in my bones grows,
And cheeks once flush with youth's warm blush
Fade out at summer's close.
'Tho white locks now mantle furrowed brow,
I wait in calm repose,
For Heaven's sweet Spring is sure to bring
New bloom, like Summer's Rose.

Therese C Swann
IMPRESSION OF A SCULPTURE
A silent silhouette stands erect
in diagonal inclination.
She pauses momentarily
harking unto nonverbal residual sounds.
Echoes of the past vibrate around
her soft sensual form.
Encased in pristine marble
could it be the sculptor had
envisioned the final form?
Or did the silhouette graciously
evolve under the laboring tools?
Is she gaily fleeing towards that
which she is chasing, or running after
that which she wishes to pursue?
The sculpture remains caught
in a fleeing position, a frozen moment
of expressed emotion.

Patricia Onisk Plewa
MY BROKEN HEART
Dear Heart,
I am deeply sorry that you are hurting.
I cannot control the impulses that sustain me.
How can you bear to swell within me?

I know that I have failed you
And I hope to remedy the depressive state
Masked upon my face.

However, my spirit weakens
Each time I am confronted with misunderstandings.
I know that pressure surrounds you
And the measure of remedy
surpasses you.

Please, as you continue to beat diligently,
Ride the waves of anxiety that encompasses me.
I am forever seeking the happiness
That has long been yearned for.

I thank the Lord for kindling the warmth inside of me.
You are my constant force,
And, hopefully, my never ending beneficence.

For without you, my friend, I am lost.

Helen Weaver Ditty
A MOTHER'S POEM
The children said to their old mother,
"We'll miss you when you are gone.
How will we ever live without you?"
The mother grieved for their sorrow,
"I'll miss me too," she said.
"I love life, but death is a part of life.
It is a part of God's good plan.
I am not afraid of death. I am curious
about it. It will be a new adventure."

The mother continued, "When my
own dear parents died so many years ago,
I missed them so much and thought I
couldn't go on without them.
But I did go on and after awhile
The sorrow of grief turned to the joy
of having known,
Now my thoughts of them bring me
joy and light.
I hope someday your memory of me
will make life brighter for you."

I love all of you so very much. I bore
you and reared you.
I have rejoiced with you in your
happiness and successes
I have sorrowed with you in your
pain and disappointments.
You have become adults, married
and have homes of your own.
You have children and even grand children."

"We cried together when my
husband, your father, passed away
Your strong arms were there when I
had to go on alone.
When I am gone, you will be the old folk.
But for a little while, you seem to be
my own dear little ones again,
And I am young and strong. I hug
you tightly. I laugh with you. I kiss
away the tears."

"And for today and yet a little while
I am alive and still a part
Of the celebration of life on this
beautiful earthy earth.
I rejoice in the promise of each new day.
Please, be kindly affectionate one to
another in brotherly love,
In my thoughts I embrace you and
lift you to God in my prayers.
This, my philosophy of life, is my
legacy to you."

June Shillabeer
ANILINE DYE
I lie
underneath the purple panoply of years
contemplating the echoes of my quest
in drifting flock.
And the lilac cry of death hovers,
smothering my soul
in amethyst winds.
Violaceous lips shift into damson
that acid plum the slips of time can cause
and cudbear clings.
Cudbear, lichen's magenta mother
covering the rock until
the heliotrope hours languish
and pale flowers, like dreams, die
in lavender wisps.

Jay Gordon
ON REACHING MAJORITY

Written for my lovely daughter, Susan, on the occasion of her 21st birthday

Oh what a joy to have reached
TWENTY-ONE
And to know adolescence is
over and done.
No more the need for parental
consent—
Now I am the establishment.
Now I am the master of my fate—
My dress, my hair, my hours,
my weight.
Mine is the choice—to depart, to
return,
To be single or wed, to work or
to learn.
But wait—is this what I really
wanted?
Can I face this whole new life
undaunted?
Will my room still be there, with my
bed to lie on?
Will my Mother's shoulder be
there to cry on?
Can I still look to Dad for his
welcome advice,
Or will my own "mature"
judgment have to suffice?
Is it really going to be such fun,
Now that I've finally reached
TWENTY-ONE?

Wendee Neilson
INNOCENCE IS A CHILD

Dedicated to my family who supported and encouraged me to keep plugging along.

Beauty is a child at play
So carefree as a summer's day
As innocent as a puppy,
As dependent as a baby

Given a child, of hopes and dreams
Hidden away from reality
of hardships and pain
But who's to blame?

SHATTERED!!
like glass hitting the ground
as debilitating
as illness succumbs

Taken away
of hopes and dreams
Innocence is a child
Lost . . .

Darlene Totels
TEMPTED FEARS
Though the path is golden it may be
dark at the end
Through tempted passions we
commit our sins
Dark clouds hanging over the evils
above
Will they be overcome by passions
of love
Drown in the puddle from the flow
of tears
Once again they haunt you—those
terrible fears
Overcome the evil with the strong
ray of power
Raise your head high and stand like a
tower

Jennifer Moody
GARDEN
Is not the mind a garden,
where thoughts become alive.
It is to our own choosing,
what is nurtured and will thrive.

Plant not a fools meager harvest,
know that your words are the seeds.
The flowers of time will open,
revealing in glory your deeds.

Peg Reiter
SWEET WILLIAM
Hesitantly he withdrew his hand
from his pocket to reveal
his secret treasure—
a pocketful of marbles.

Apologetic, he explained that he
had none to give away,
not even one for me to borrow
(for awhile).

He alone possessed the treasures,
had collected them along the way,
but mostly he had earned them,
painfully, one by one.
A few were intact.
Some were shattered.
But most suffered from fine hairline cracks.
They were, afterall, well-worn marbles.

And what I needed for him to understand
was that I had no need to even
momentarily touch the marbles—
the looking was enough.

Nancy Kay Levin

Nancy Key Levin
I'M AWFULLY WELL FOR THE SHAPE I'M IN

Dedicated to the DYSTONIA MEDICAL RESEARCH FOUNDATION Beverly Hills, CA 90211

There's nothing what ever the matter
with me,
I'm just as healthy as I can be,
I have a neuro-muscular disease
called Dystonia,
My hips and legs rotate inward,
I also have writer's cramp,
But I'm awfully well for the shape
I'm in!

My epilepsy is out of whack,
And a terrible pain is in my back,
My hearing is poor, my sight is dim,
Most everything seems to be out of
trim,
But I'm awfully well for the shape
I'm in!

I wear braces on both my legs,
Or I couldn't walk inside or out,
I have trouble sleeping many a night,
And in the morning I'm just a sight.

My memory is failing, my head's in
a spin,
I'm living on Clonopin and
Mysoline,
Motrin, Xanax and Theodur too,
But I'm awfully well for the shape
I'm in!

The moral is, as I tell you my woes,
That for you and me who are the
wiser,
It's better to say, "I'm fine" with a
grin,
Than to let them know the shape
we're really in.

Eulah Haggard
JESUS PROMISES

In Memory: To my son Robert my inspiration

Jesus promises to come to earth
again,
And we know his promises are
true
He will come from Heaven,

Above the azure blue
We never know if it will be
Morning, noon, or night,
So keep your lamps all trimmed,
And shining bright
So he can see you waiting
In the light
Oh, how glorious it will be
When Jesus comes to take the
faithful home
to live Eternally.

John N Blow
DESERT MEDLEY

This poem is dedicated to Jane, my sweetheart wife

Whistling wind on the drifting desert
Fluting a tune on the Joshua tree,
For whom are you piping your
concert

Weary from travel is it for me?
Listen to hear the lost burro's bray,
The prospector's call and trekker's
song;
Desert medley of a bygone day
To lift me as I travel along.

Linda Bishop Young
THE ANIMAL THAT IS NOT IN US

The touch of you glistens as it asks
for so much more,
Full of admission, opening with
need.
Tight lips curl against a broad and
gentle chest,
Awaiting solid hands and pliant
pleasure.

Love and promises, a sanguine
insanity that lets us leave our senses
When we are finally with them.

I look for sharp corners and shaded
edges, knowing all the limits:
The phone that does not ring or
answer, no one waiting at the bus,
Those who would not rummage
through the chances to cross swamps
and rivers
To pledge their internal,
The joining and fearing, fearing and
joining,
With angers on tiptoe, perpetually
stalking a day's routine,
Mere modus vivendi strangled under
quiet sheets in the night.

Insatiable madness, that stays to
watch the principles die before our
very eyes.
Animals do not remain for such
torture or revenge,
Levelling lives and entire cities;
They just try to continue, past the
quick snaps of fate.

They have not the force or vagaries
of a word
That renders wars and suicide.

Rebecca A Jacobs
I LOVE THE WAY WE WALK HAND IN HAND

To my parents— My children Clint and Rebecca Jr., my husband John and Clawson Eagles 3926, for their love, support and encouragement. M.P.1989-1990

I love the way we walk hand in hand,
And all the ways we both understand.
I love the way you love me . . .
I love the way your smile brightens
my day.
I love the way you kiss me, as
much as the way in which you miss
me.
I love the way you hold me.
I love the way I feel secure when I'm
with you.
I also love the way you think I'm
more than just another girl.
I love the way you hug me . . .
I love the feelings of togetherness as
well as the feelings of tenderness in
our hearts
I love the way you kiss me . . .
I love the words "together forever"
and
This is what I hope we'll always be.
Yes, I love the way you love me.

Claudia Ferguson
heart-glow

de mémoire le grand-pére

all I want is fresh air and sunshine
a cool breeze and a refreshing
sprinkle
of rain upon my brow
nothing more for now
just these things and I'll be fine
my heart will glow, my eyes will
twinkle
with gladness at how
eternity is . . . now

Deborah A M Hayes
REACH OUT, I'M HERE

To all those people, especially the kids, that needed someone to talk to and found no one, and to those who are looking for gentle ears, may they find them and to all those who have ears to lend.

Silence can be deadly
I know that pain
I see it in your eyes
they speak the words
your soul can't say

Please try, I'm here
you are not alone
I know that pain
silence can be deadly
Reach Out, I'm Here

Vanessa Fletcher
DREAM STATE

To Errol Alexis Green: Thank you for helping me to realize that I can do whatever I set my heart to and helping me to realize anything dreamed can be reality. I love you.

This state of mind for which I'm in,
Changes the reality of time I spend.
Into this life I so ever dread:
I lay my head upon my bed.

A touch of heart to share as pleased.
A touch of care to have as need.
A hint of despair I have to mix
Along with space forever fixed.

To have, to hold, to grow, to mold,
I hand to thee my dearest soul.
A little light, for I cannot see,
You hide from sight so easily.
To feel for real in which I came.
To live in grace my heartfelt pain.

To have a mind for state of sane,
To move in space an easy plane.
In this state I try to be
Over the great dreams, you see.

Once again I dare to greet
This state of dreams in which I be.
Over-pulsed I do pretend,
For this dream-state I do live in.

Jo Ann Kizziah
IF SO

To the greatest loves of my life, My husband, children and grand children. I would ask for no more pleasure.

If I love you
Will you love me forever more,
Will you stay with me
For now, Eternity, Unending Score.

Will you be by my side happy and
true,
In good times and bad,
Occasional days of blue.

Will you respect me
And be my friend
No matter who or what
Always and not pretend.

Will you be my lover
Heart true to no other
IF SO
I'll love you
Now and forever.

Anthony Clark Johnson
WALKING ON THE BEACH WITH SUZY

As each foot raises then returns,
begins a pace, becomes a walk;

and as a bright dyed pail
aspires
to cast a glass chateau in sand;

and ocean eaves bid tidings,
echoes
of life, as each one dies a surf;

then so I reach to serve
my hand
to hers, to share with her a walk.

iRebecca H Taylor
EDUCATION

To my loving parents, Thank you for my education.

Another year has come and gone.
The time has come to say good-bye.
Each one goes his own way;
With a promise to "keep in touch".

But as each walks away
Inside you know it to be true;
Never a word will you hear
From those who've gone.

You touch their lives briefly;
Hopefully imparting knowledge;
Perhaps to some a little wisdom
And always some love.

For being a teacher one must learn
To give more than "book learning"
To those who cross our paths
In this world called "education".

Eleonore J Crespo
FEELING SAD . . .

This poem is dedicated to my dear husband, Robert.

I sit at the edge of this water,
my soul is in turmoil, but soon I'll be
free.
Like the beat of the surf, coming to
and fro,
my heart will rejoice in the rhythm of
the sea.
I fear not this water, nor the waves or
the wind,
for they cool and they soothe the fires
within.
My memory fails me, to try and
recall,
a day such as this, so peaceful and
healing and all.
There are no forevers in life's shabby
game,
just to dream and to wish for, doesn't
make it so—just the same.
I will always remember this day,
when I sat by the water, feeling sad
that way.

Kathy Adams
IT'S GREEN

Her schedule before the dance
Was to shop around the town,
Get her hair fixed nice for Lance,
And buy a pretty green gown.

She accomplished all of these
But with awful consequence,
Her hair color turned split peas
And wouldn't come out by rinse.

No way would she go out now
She just sat at home to cry
And felt like having a cow.
How could this happen—She'd die.

The doomed night, the doorbell rang
It was Lance, he'd heard, oh no
She thought she'd throw up lime
tang
Oh rats! They just couldn't go.

She wrapped a towel 'round her
head.
To her room, mom let him in.
He coolly said, beside her bed,
"No problem, I'll go with Lynne."

Leah Bailin
BESIDE THE SEA

To my father, Budd Bailin, with love.

I'm standing beside the sea,
Salty water in all.
My long hair blowing in the wind,
My eyes staring into the moonlight.
The wet sand flowing between my
toes.
I see someone in the moonlight,
Someone I've lost, now here found.
I'm looking into the water,
I see the person there,
It is my own reflection,
I'm standing there.

Blaine Cloud
MID-DAY'S JOURNEY

Falling inward, going down
Moving faster, spiral 'round

From without, soon within
In the depths, things begin

Figures fly, people you knew
Making up stories, how you grew

One thing leads to the next
Circling only to perplex

From hence you came
Tomorrow not quite the same

As today you really hope
But dread the end o' your rope

Quick, hide that thought away
It'll return another day

Happier things there are to imagine
Whether it religion, worry or sin

Create for yourself a future bright
Worry not if it's right

This is where it all takes place
Past, present and future race

Mary "Connie" Z Napier
ON THE RAINY DAYS OF LIFE

Dedicated to Lisa and Tony Beloved Daughter and Nephew

God did not always promise
Our lives would not have rain
Nor did he ever tell us . . .
We would not feel real pain,
He promised, if we'd love Him
Our burdens to Him give . . .
He'd strengthen with endurance
And through the bad times live.

Sometimes the load seems heavy
Much more than we can bear . . .
It's then, that we must offer
These burdens, for Him to share.
Yes, when we trust in Jesus . . .
Sincere trust, with deep belief
In His love and deep compassion
He'll bring answers and relief.

When the rainy days come falling down . . .
And the sorrows of life make us seem to drown . . .
Then take His hand and walk His way
The rain will go . . . it cannot stay.

Ken Armstrong
PIRATES OF THE HEART

Pirates of the heart, are captains of the ship of lies.
They command the army of little hurts; that kill in the big ways.
They plant "The Jolly Roger" in your heart, and
Bury the ultimate treasure of your soul in "Davey Jone's Locker."
They roam the seas of endless love and lust.
They force you to walk the plank of your emotions.

Bonnie L Hess
MY LITTLE GIRL

This poem is dedicated to Jacque, my little girl.

My babe was born on a Sunday morn
So pink, so bubbly, so free
And then a year went by
And she was bouncing on my knee

At three she was a curious sort
Investigating keys
At four she was tripping up the stairs
And scraping both her knees

At five she had a case of hives
At six she was picking up sticks
At seven she was an angel from heaven
Or so I do believe

At eight she was a frightful state
Her two front teeth were missing
At nine she thought that she was fine
And could climb her way to heaven
Ten was such a trying state
No question could you answer
No, was not the proper way
Of getting what she was after

Eleven, twelve and thirteen
Bring alot of change
Physical attractiveness
Then becomes the game

Giggly and full of fun
Boys their favorite tale
Tying up the phone for hours
A mother to prevail

At fourteen she wanted
To retrogress in time
Please heavenly Father
Take me back to nine

Fifteen is a time of tears
A time of dreams to tell
I only wish I was sixteen
And had a long pigtail

At sixteen boys pay no attention
Their sports their only thing
While she is contemplating
Who will give her his class ring

At seventeen the prom's the thing
Which boy will ask her favor?
Which dress shall I wear?
And where will we go after?

Eighteen your little girl's grown up
She's given up her plans
And there upon her milk white hand
Is a golden wedding band

Now she is holding her babe in arms
So pink, so bubbly so free
And in a year or so
She'll be bouncing upon my knee

Cristine Gangi
UNTITLED

I saw you sitting
quietly, on a rock in my driveway.
Silly
thought, of course, being
you are dead. I said a
silly thought.
I saw your shadow
creeping up the stairs. Stars
were in my eyes, I guess.
But in a laughing
way, I know
you meant to be there,
creeping
up my stairs.

Eleanor Jane Burlingham
WE LOVE THEM ALL BECAUSE

This is for you Dad—Wm. F. Schneider

Each morning at the break of day,
Our feathered friends come out our way
They come for the food, they always crave,
So all stale bread we're bound to save.
'Tis fun to watch them, they're not afraid,
As they grab the food, which we have laid.
They eat and eat—then rest a while,
For being too greedy it's not in style.

They drink fresh water from our tin,
To deny them water would be a sin.
If we are late, they chirp and scold
Especially, if there's snow & cold.

Our squirrel friend Tommy pays a call,
He's on the fence or on the wall.
So friendly, if he could shout—
"Thank you friends for my handout."

Our reward? It's in the love they show,
No fear of us—we ought to know
For they feel so free to come each day—
I'm sure if we listen, we'd hear them <u>pray!</u>

Leslie Jameson
NOW THAT YOU'VE GONE

This poem is dedicated to my loving Grandmother Pickens in loving memory

I will always remember
All the good times together
Life will never be the same
Now that you've gone to grandfa-
ther.

Oh how I will wonder
Why you had to leave me
You took a part of me with you
So now there's a void that's empty
Empty from now to eternity

I wonder how I will survive
For you were my friend
You were my life
My heart will never mend
For the way your life came to an end

You were so precious to me
You were so dear to everyone
Why did you leave me?
Now I am alone
You are my dearly loved
Grandmother
Now that you've gone forever.

Myrtel Smith
SO SOON

To my husband, Ronnie, and to my children, Joshua and Amy

I can't believe in ninety-three
A graduate I will be.
After that, what will I be,
When will I be what I will be.

Now I am ninety-three,
Am near what I will be.
Am near what we all will be,
I can't believe
So soon, so soon.

Robert John Zaleski
YOUR LOVE

Your love comforts me like the touch of an old friend
And it excites me like the Christmas mornings of my childhood
It envelopes me completely like the snow-light, soft, pure,
But not confining
Your love washes my fears and cares away like a spring shower
Gentle, soft and refreshing
It feeds me like the sun feeds the flowers of a meadow in summer
Your love calms me like an empty chapel in the moonlight
Your love is all my dreams rolled into reality
You are why I am and it never could have been different
We were meant to be before we even were
We were fashioned from the same piece of clay by the Master's hand

Russell C Trombley
I WALKED TODAY WITH CLOUDY SKIES

I walked today with cloudy skies
Which brought to mind some other days
When sun and wind and memory tries
To return to us more youthful ways

I think this day of ancient times
Of people then who tried and won
Of humans now who oft betimes
Do not believe things can be done

If now they'd try with total will
Peace could be with us in this year
I think today, and state it still
We can again be free of fear

Larry LaPole

Larry LaPole
TIME

If I was able to go back in time,
Merely by turning the hour hands in reverse.
I would approach certain situations with an indifferent objective.
Hopefully to have an outcome to be that of the good.

The good would be my final destination.
It would be the angle, of which,
I'd focus my goals and ambitions, in the direction of.
Leaving the black plato behind and grasping to the white.

The love that stems from this,
Would be one that grows stronger as time marches forward.
As if two hearts growing together in one body,
A picture of loves strength.
Do you believe?????????

Gerald E Brahinsky
FOR JAYNE AND MARGARET: A <u>TRUE</u> LOVE STORY

Within my nearly forty years, I've known both good and bad,
I've had some laughs and shed some tears but been proud of what I've had;
Though I have friends and family and (of course) the One above,
I had never known until this time those <u>special</u> joys of love.

A musician's life's a riddle; sometimes sad, though often funny,
And it rarely is an easy life (without much fame or money);

Love, honesty, and caring (over wealth) had filled my life,
And women said they wished for that; none wished to be my wife.

But prior to a concert, a woman turned my head,
She noticed that I noticed her in her beret of brilliant red,
And when that concert ended, she approached me at long last,
We talked at length, we met again; my blues had finally passed.

Her name was Jayne, and we'll remain best friends forever more;
Two hearts locked up in loneliness, our love unlocked that door,
And her lovely daughter Margaret (now in her early 'teens)
'Tis not a child, but an angel fair (in her sneakers and blue jeans).

So blessed Jayne and Margaret now fill my life with joy,
I'm excited as a child who's received a brand new toy;
Forever shall I cherish them amid the love and laughter,
A real-life fairy tale's come true, and we'll live happily ever after!

Eugene A Tribble
WEEPING WILLOW TREE
Weeping Willow Tree
why do you cry?
did your darling leave you, same as did mine?
weeping willow tree, tell me if you can
why did she leave me, I don't understand.

Weeping Willow Tree,
I am just like you
weeping all the time,
because she made me so blue . . .

Night time is near
now I must go . . .
away with myself
the rushing tears, they flow . . .

Weeping Willow Tree
when you gaze above
please ask the Lord,
to send me down a love.

Weeping Willow Tree
I am just like you
weeping all the time,
because she made me so blue . . .

Frances Carnahan Ebaugh
PRAYER FOR BLACK LOTTIE (MY HOUSEMAID FOR THIRTY-THREE YEARS)
Oh Lord, You gave me grace from day to day
You gave me flow'rs and fruit on every tree
You made the moon to light my way to see
Oh keep my soul and save it all the way.
You sent pure snow to keep me fresh and sweet
And summer winds to blow the snow away
You gave me rain to wash my tired feet
Oh keep my soul and save it all the way.
You know the need to cool my fevered brow—
You made the sun to shine with all Your might
You sent the frost to bite the heat away
And bitter winds to strip the autumn bough.
You gave Your Star and save it all the way.
No brighter star on earth or heav'n above
Was ever giv'n to man with greater love.

Ellen Crespo
MY CHILD . . .

This poem is dedicated to my son, Jeff.

You once were my child, with eyes open wide and a face so shiny and new.
You once were my pride and my joy, my favorite of two,
and now my son, what happened to you?
When did I lose you, what made you change, what made you go wrong?
I don't recognize you, dear God, has it been that long?
You're stuck in a prison, a place of despair,
your eyes disillusioned, not much hope anywhere.
I once had a child with a heart and a soul,
fresh and clean as the morning's first dew.
And now my son—look at what's become of you!

Lillian Baker
PEARL HARBOR HAIKU

Remember Pearl Harbor! December 7th, 1941 "Day of Infamy"

The Arizona
Its broken stem in the air
Juries the atom

Robbin Thrush
FOR MY SON, JAMIN
i've felt the pain of rejection
the agony of defeat; utter exhaustion—
and sore swollen feet;
i've felt the happiness of togetherness;
the security of love; exhilaration from winning—
and moving one step above;
i've stood in awe of a sunrise
and been amazed at nature's grace
the ocean's roar, the lake's breeze,
and the river's happy face
i've felt the satisfaction of knowing
and the humility of "to thy own self be true,"
and i've been blessed in God's grace
by giving birth to you.

you'll know the happiness i've enjoyed
cry the tears i've cried—
and when it's all been spent
cope with all the terms of
indifference or endearment
from emotions that came and went.
remember whatever the mirage of feelings
that result from thoughts within:
God made me your mother;
understanding made me your friend.

Tracy Allen Parks
DON'T TURN AWAY
People living in cardboard caves
Making primeval fires
Living like slaves
They're just lonely and tired

Spacebrain losers
Make pinholes and sniff dust
Chemicals are their masters
Like old buildings they begin to rust

Pennyless persons of labor
Scrounge for work
Looking for their saviour
But never knowing where to look

Rich roamers look and cry
They just turn away
Hold their heads to the sky
Never help the stray

They just turn away
Turning away from the rules
Ever wanting to stay this way
They live like fools

Debrina J Peek

Debrina J Peek
PRIDE

This little ditty is dedicated to my Dad & Mom who taught me a sense of pride and love; and to Michael who helps me maintain it.

The newborn colt always on wobbly legs,
he carefully squints at the brightness of day.

He looks at his Mother as though he must beg,
but all of us know what his Mother will say . . .

"Come and have breakfast my Little One,
for you must learn to run and to follow the sun.

The Wind was your Father—you must make him proud.
Stand tall as the mountains fleeced over in clouds."

Melody Hogan
IF I WERE A HOUSE
If I were a house
all my doors would be locked
all my windows barred
no mat would be found in front.

If I were a house
no lights from between the drawn drapes seen
no music would be heard from within
no children would play upon my porch.

If I were a house
no smoke would rise from my chimney
no warmth could be felt
only a cold hearth and dampness present.

If I were a house
this would be no place for visitor nor guest
no place to live—only survive
there would be no gayety or parties thrown.

If I were a house
there would be no invitations sent nor accepted
all the furniture covered with dust cloth
weaved webs would hang from my grand chandelier.

If I were a house
my paint would be chipped and peeled
broken glass would certainly be found
my garden would be overgrown with weed.

If I were a house
it would surely be haunted
with ghosts of yesterday
a day when somenoe once cared.

If I were a house
the key would be a skeleton with not another like it
If you had this key, would you turn it
unlock my door, enter with the fresh breeze?

Edith L Price
SPRING
Spring is here, Spring is here!
Pussy willows softly purr,
Robins singing in the trees,
In the hives are busy bees.
Now again children have fun at play,
Glad that the winter has gone away.

Mitzi Ferguson
HALLOWE'EN
Hallowe'en is almost here—
And waiting for the dark to come,
Excited and big-eyed with fear,
The little ghosts and goblins
Are dressing up at home.

Here they come—door-bells ringing,
Jack-o-lanterns brightly gleaming
"Tricks or Treats" they cry!
Moms and Dads have treats a-waiting
Their wishes to supply,
The Goblins Ghosts Clowns and Witches
As from door to door they fly.

On, the fun and fear they know
As they travel to and fro
With watchful parents waiting.
Young and old we like the show
Of dressing up in Masquerade
To join a Jester's gay parade.

Charlene M Dyer
ALL NIGHT DAWNING
Try to understand
and bear with me
in my moods of silence.
I do not pretend
to have my emotions
under control:
Tears of madness
wanting to scream,
plead internally instead.
The winter season is here.

Alone, I turn inward
to observe and learn.
Quiet now, and listen
to the stillness:
the rooster always knows
when it is 5 a.m.

Susan K Miller
JOSHUA'S SONG
It's your chatty little voice that awakens me from slumber and with eyes just barely open, into your room I lumber.
The energy you've stored up while you've slept begins to flow.
You greet me with sweet smiles and all at once I know another day's beginning and you're filled with expectation.
So I do me best to quell small feelings of exasperation as the oatmeal that once filled your bowl now lies upon the floor.
While off you go with feet as quick as lightning through the door.
You're off to more important little orders of the day, making sure that nothing small or large would dare get in your way.
Throughout the day I follow, not too far, yet not too near, just close enough for safety for you're innocent of fear.
The determination you possess seems stronger than my own and your eyes are brightly saying, "Look, Mom, how much I've grown"!
It's in the evening hours when the sandman fills those eyes, and you cuddle with your teddy bear and breathe your baby sighs, that I gaze upon your small sweet face and wish on stars above that all your hopes and dreams come true, that your life is filled with love.

Linda J Anderson
THOUGH I WAS JUST A CHILD
Though I was just a child,
When Granny passed away,
I have heard others say
To this day:
She believed in God,
And did pray
When troubles came her way.
If we follow the path
Granny trod before us,
We will meet again
In heaven some day.

James V McGee Jr
THAT EVENING
To wander the desirable city, lost among all those others who are hunting like I like the same they like.
In and out of the places they hang, similar to mosses growing in southern trees are not maples.
This one likes the getting and gives with a hard heave up the heady shoot it out and get up and leave.
The other pops his cavities and rushes down the long lovely shaft or dark alley-way between parked trucks.
Or to walk carefully around the water-way watching for misplaced footfalls ahead and listen for them behinds.
Wander down dark empty offices and step around the holes offered that aren't to your taste one more.
Then sit over fried embryos and roots and discuss gurus and creating by another name to add to the forgotten list.
Later saunter along the street and look for a bone for your mind to use for the other desires a rest never.
And still later to cruise past used boat moors and more walkers walk and park to walk in circles.
Eventually it ends with nite lite leaving as the lights go out of the city to the other one to rush so to be late.

Virginia E Cruikshank
TO MY MOTHER ON APPROACHING HER 103RD BIRTHDAY
We thought 99 a beautiful number
When you attained that astonishing age.
We spoke of your beauty and graciousness;
Your love and your thoughtfulness.

We were so proud when you became 100.
Congratulations came from President Reagan;
You received your Century Club pin;
And a framed plaque from the County Commissioners.

When you were an amazing 101, another party
And family reunion with balloons and flowers!
Everyone making delighted comments in wonder,
"Isn't she beautiful! Isn't she remarkable!"

Year 102 brought new excitement.
N.B.C. Weatherman, Willard Scott,
Displayed your picture on national television,
Remarking, "Isn't she lovely in her red dress?"

Mother, in another month you will be 103.
You are the same lovely smiling person!
You have seen your country endure wars,
Natural disasters, and unbelievable change.
What surprises will come to you in 1989?

Palina Tipton
THE HOUSE WHERE I WAS BORN
There's an old house standing alone upon the hill,
Silence and loneliness are within,
Echoes of the many voices of children
Once rang out in merry din
But are no more. There are no guests
And with only it's proud dreams it is at rest.

Amy Noel Trissel
A POEM FOR A CONTEST
You want to find a poet.
Well wouldn't you know it.
Maybe I am, maybe I am not.
How does one decide who is and who is not?
I, myself, have written a few.
What I have written, if only you knew.
Entering contests I have done.
A few of them I have won.
I write a poem to you
then what do you do?
With only one poem to send,
I don't know how much time to spend.
My dad showed me your ad.
Your offer is not bad.
What is there to find?
Maybe an intelligent mind.
Whatever you decide please let me know
so I will know what direction to go.
No matter what you decide.
I will always have poems on paper or inside.

Gary Updegraff
OLD
Oh, to grow "Old"
How will it be?
I see them shut in
And looking so lonely.

Once full of youth and dreams,
Now remembering their life.
The struggle through Wars
And everyday strife.

We owe them much,
For they were so strong.
Building their lives and family,
For us to carry on.

It's our turn now,
I hope you agree.
We must fill their hearts,
With appreciation and need.

Don't be foolish,
With your youth at hand.
Remember and Cherish,
The "Old" of our Land.

Antoinette Keen

Antoinette Keen
TIME

I dedicate this poem to where I received my education—Bellegarde School, Saskatchewan, Canada.

Around us everyday we see a busy world.
Humans running every where,
Not knowing if they'll get there.
The clocks are steady ticking,
To bring home heels a kicking.

For months on end we keep on running,
For work brings the paycheck
That takes us out of debt.
Since there are no minutes for others talking
We stop all methods of communicating.

After forever keeping with the pace,
They one night have a thought to spare.
Some pages of their life they wish they could tear.
The clock continues ticking every breathing moment,
For the day it brings them all to silence.

Years come and go and the pace soon changes.
As one looks in the looking glass,
They see a glimpse of aging fast.
No more energy to run its course,
No More effort to be a working horse.

One has just seen and experienced time!

Dixie Foster
PERMANENCE
If I should die tonight—
What would go with me that would be all mine to keep forever?

Those hours by the river, that I know,
where calm and coolness made a world of peace.
And, yes, I think the hurdie-gurdie man on Saturdays in spring.
And then, the streetcar rides—the best place ever
one could be alone while in a crowd.
And beef stew from a cup
that later went to serve the tea.

But those would not be mine alone—
I guess I'd leave them for another girl
who might like rivers too—

So, then, what would I take that was all mine?

I know, of course. The night you shrugged your shoulders
and you said—"It's just like trying to explain God.
You can't. You just know He's there.
The same as knowing that I love you."

Marjorie Ann Fennessy
ADDIE
Sisters were never as close as we,
When we were young, my friend you and me . . .

We shared everything
boys, clothes, laughter, tears
secrets and dreams, my friend
you and me . . .

The business of becoming women changed us.
No more hours on the telephone,
Sundays at the movies,
walks to the ice cream parlor.

It gave us husbands, children, gray hair
and a few extra pounds to deal with, responsibilities, and a lot more candles on our birthday cake . . .

But each time we meet, my friend
there is one thing that never changes, friends we were and friends we be
For all our lives
you and me . . .

J Roy Sullivan
WE ARE
We are the trees, cut, chopped, stacked
the green fields, mowed, threshed, beaten
the fawn silent, defenceless, leaping
the baby alligator hungry, jawing, crying

We are the cows that brown green fields
the horses racing, pacing pulling

the lions shot for heads and
tails

We are the house made of straw,
stone or brick
made of sky, blue and thick

We are the factory mimicking
machines
slaving slaves
grinning graves

We are the electric psychotic spasms
in our temple
neurotic passions in our eyes
silence on our moving tongue

We are the wheel whose hub am I
the spokes a voice that reach
the rim of time and space
and you

Yes, we are the Earth.

Wendy Phillippy
TO MY BABY BOY DUSTINE SCOTT
You filled my life with joy and love
while you lived inside of me
Now you're with the Lord above
I hope you're proud of me
We did so much together
We lived our lives as one
Your memory will live forever
My pride and joy; you are my son
You never met your father
He's a wonderful man
You enjoyed his touch and caresses
You loved the warmth of his hand
You'd toss and turn for his delight
A secret game you shared
He'd look at me with his eyes so
bright
the most precious moments we ever
shared
I hope you're happy wherever you
are
to me you're the sky's brightest star
Son, we love you very much
Keep shining bright though you're
too far for us to feel your touch

In memory of Dustine

We love you sweetheart

Arlene Clare Casey
COVER-SPIRIT
In order
to fix your hair
you need to have
someone
to fix your hair for
God,
You should always
be
my mirror
for life.

Dalray Robertson
GRANDMOTHER
Oh this life so full of cares—
Grandmother, mother, wife who
dares time, who like the waves at sea
will not hold still for you or me, to
slow a little not slip away and bring
back those carefree times of play
when young and happy ever free—
no problems in this world for me
Secure content within the fold
Mother Father Gran who's old
but loving in a special way that
makes it all seem quite O.K.
And though the past seems ever
nearer, things in life grow ever
dearer each sunrise brings a bran new
day and something special along the
way
And looking down a voice I know
says "Grandma why do you walk so
slow" thinking I answer with a
smile—"Grandma likes to take a
while to see the things that nature
plans and enjoy just holding hands
and feel the wind upon my face—
Why do you think that life's a race
Go slow my child for all too fast the
present and the future become the
past and then before you can
discover—you too will be a
GRANDMOTHER.

Judith A Wright
COURAGE WITH CLASS
A grave and sudden illness was soon
to take its toll
Of a woman, so fine of heart and
pure of soul.
Months of doctors, pain and strife
Quickly became her way of life.
She had such love, caring and
courage . . .
Now coping and dependency
became her bondage.
Despite the ordeals, with her head
held high,
The pain she endured with
heavy sighs.
As with those who suffer, her time
passed quickly by,
And to heaven she ventured,
leaving many to cry.
We know this world is a much better
place
For the lives that she touched
with such elegant grace.
We've learned from her spirit of
courage and love,
That shines on in our hearts,
sent from above.

THANKS MOM! WE LOVE YOU.

Laura Reiff
FATHER AND MOTHER
For it is the two of you who should
hold your heads high with great
dignity,
For it is you both who have put
others first at the expense of
yourselves.
For it is the two of you who should
sigh with great control and relief,
For it is you both who have
encountered and conquered the most
troublesome times of one's life.
For it is the two of you who should
stand tall with great respect,
For it is you both who watched
others go forward with greed while
you both stood back with less and let
them pass.
For it is you, Father and Mother,
who have built an empire with your
loving hearts.

Robert W Nadolny
FOR THAW IN WINTER, MAKE HASTE
Miserable, and in moments spent in
contemplative loneliness
I think of her, conjured up as
first thought—
Crestfallen imaginings from an
ineffectual fool.

Her nubile body I wish to caress with
subtlety
Engirding her frame with
delicate, sweet kisses
Liberating recondite love
through my lips and hands to
Each of her receptive pores,
our minds and bodies
Merging together as one;
intellect, spirit
And physicality harmonizing and
being brought to wisdom . . .

Zephyrus, let starkly come an
actualizing blast
Unabashed from me, enabling a
lover to unbosom an ineffable
love,
Redress his ineffectiveness, and
partake in love with her.

Betty Gibson

Betty Gibson
LIFE

To my dear husband first of all; then "all my children— large and small" I dedicate this poem with love

I cannot bear to see
A flower die
Each time I do
I feel death win his victory
I see eternity without God

I walk a hopeless path
With endless fear
And then I see
A tiny seed
Silently breathe for me
And God is there.

Margaret Anderson
A BIRTHDAY FOR DAISY
A birthday on Easter Sunday
Is given to an honored few,
I can't think of another soul
Who is more deserving than you.

You share an event with our Lord
He died and arose from the grave,
That we might have eternal life
Such a wonderful gift He gave.

We love Him more as birthdays pass
We also love you, Daisy Mae,
"Happy Birthday," lovely lady
As we rejoice on this Lord's day.

Charlene Reedy Cundiff
A PERFECT NIGHT
Within the hospital, all was still and
quiet
I wondered why, but it was
Christmas Eve night
Surprisingly, the patients' pains were
all eased
And the nurses on duty seemed
very pleased
At the desk they worked to get all
their charts run
Looking forward to morning
when their work would be done
The stillness was broken by the jingle
of the phone
The office girl announcing that
she was not alone
A patient was waiting by the elevator
door
To be brought up to second floor
With a friendly smile off she was led
By a nurse's aide who would put
her to bed
The doctor was soon coming up the
hall
In answer to the nurse's urgent
call
As the time to the patient passed
slowly by
To the doctor and the nurses, it
seemed to fly
The clock on the wall said quarter till
four
As she was wheeled through the
delivery room door
Soon the doctor announced with a
smile of joy
What a perfect night for this
fine baby boy.

Wanda Cherrier-Regeski
GOOD MORNING
Behold the massive growing ball
So steadily on the rise
Forcing life into another day
In the twilight painted sky
The deep plum purple
That lends its hue
To captivate ones spirit
Giving way to glorious golden rays
An eye full of sparkling flint
They say it just so right
Good Morning
You're in God's sight

The warmth that rises
With the yard arm
Pressing night away
Chasing dreams and spectors
Into vague memories somehow
A continuous renewal of creation
All within its natural source
Assuredly wasted on some
But, never on me
This blessed start today!

Dorothy Curtis
I NEVER KNOW WHY
"I never know why I sit around and
cry
when I feel blue,
For laughter and cheer are always so
near
if we only look close by;
Or if we only try to see how
happiness can be
a smile, a laugh, a kiss, a hug,
Or look at the sky and clouds above.

There is so much beauty to behold
so why not be of good cheer and
love.
Forget not our woes, but be happy to
know
that we waste not our time, and
show
we are happy, not blue.
To laugh, not to cry, to love, not to
hate; but forever to try to find
happiness in our fate."

Glenda Godsey
MAMA'S LITTLE BABIES
Mama's little babies,
Daddy's little toys,
Grandma's little angels,
Grandpa's little joy.

Though you have so many Uncles and Aunts,
You can't count them now. We still love you anyhow.
With sweet little faces that never stay clean. It's so easy to forget you're sometimes mean.
Playing one minute, fighting the next. Out of one thing and into another. It's good to know you have each other.
Lynn with her pretty blue eyes. Roy with his kind and tender ways. Makes all of us look back on our yesterdays.

Joan Hester

Joan Hester
WALK THROUGH NATURE
Walk through nature
Look what you see . . .
Birds singing,
Flowers blooming,
The little honey bee.

Walk through nature
Look all around . . .
Listen to the sound,
Watch little animals
Playing on the ground.

Walk through nature
Look at the trees . . .
The sun, the moon,
The stars above
God gave us all these
With love.

Owen Rasmussen
PUZZLED LOVE
This puzzled love cannot be put together.
Considerations chained you from the start.
I finally faced this force that formed a tether
Keeping us so close yet so apart.

Outside your life I stayed and made my pleading.
Cried for you to come from him to me.
Endurance for this much prolonged proceeding
Has given way to dark reality.

Like dancers on life's floor we danced a tango
To-and-fro through time we breathed in beat.
Now music stopped, reality does hang so
Empty . . . lonely . . . hurting . . . and deplete.

And now you wish to torture and to taunt
This helpless heart that floated on a stream
Of future filled with ecstasy now gaunt,
Of happiness and hope now just a dream.

Your indecision let it be no more
For time has tolled the closing of the door.

Jennifer Rieger
A PRAYER FOR THE DYING
Another king is crowned this morne
One more child will soon be born;
The sun comes up to replace the moon
But nothing changes, not even the wounds.

Someone's life is like wind through the trees
Everyone watches but nobody sees;
One more corpse is like a stone in a pond
Somebody knows them, but there is no bond.

People die all around the world
And hardly a tear has been hurled;
It's not uncommon to just sit and cry,
So please lose a tear for those who die.

Shirley A Bole
THE PASSING TIME EXPRESS
I took a little trip
On the "Passing Time Express"
Just sitting and a thinking
About a very important test.

The test is of a mountain
That enters into life
This mountain is so dangerous
Causing lots of evil strife.

I don't know if I'll pass it
Or if I can climb so high
It's so rugged and so treacherous
But I'll do my best or cry

When on the other side one day
I'll look back, then see
I'll let out a great big sigh
I'll know it had to be.

I sit and quietly wonder
As I'm on this "Time Express"
Just how I ever made it
I can say, "I did my best."

Beneva J McKinley
WE SHARE THE SAME LAST NAME
No secret touch is ours, no sweet endearing name
No look, nor tender smile, we just play a weary game.
And I am sad to think, that life has passed me by,
Where's youths passion, hopes and dreams?
Gone in a whisper and a sigh.
Ah Love . . .
It's dreamed of, hoped for, madly pursued
Won and Lost
As we sit wearily by . . .
He's in his world, and I'm in mine,
Nothing in common, nothing the same,
Oh yes . . . I forgot!
We share the same last name.

Mary Adams Thomas
THOSE FAMOUS FIFTEEN BIBLE VERSES
That Law of Return was a Holy Law
But Theodora broke it.
Took fifteen verses from Holy Writ,
Then her own law revoked it!

To be born again was a deadly sin.
'Twas death to even think it!
And Theodora a goddess became
As fast as she could ink it!

And ever since then the Law of the Land
Denies reincarnation.
And sinners can sin in life after life,
In every social station.

It used to be if a human wronged
Another sinfully,
He would be born again to know that pain
Be his own guilt as twinfully.

But Theodora's Law is still
The law of this sad nation.
And thus we daily deny the truth
Of penal repeat station!

Vernetta Johns

Vernetta Johns
LOVE/LIFE'S JOURNEY

To my mother, who exemplifies all the goodness of the human spirit. This example, is your lasting gift to all of us. Thank you, Mom.

Secure in your mother's womb, and then her arms
A small and innocent soul whose eyes are filled with trust
The foundation for a life unknown is set, a new life thrust.
Love of God and family, of siblings and young friends,
Some of it grows—some of it ends.
The new, giddy, first romance awakening the heart,
That opens passage to the aching and the breaking.
The testing of your judgement, the mistakes along the way.
Experience the teacher—you could say.

Riding on the crest of ecstasy, floating on a cloud,
All seems well in loveland—to the crowd.
One can't fall unless they're up—know the joy and never pained.
Disappointment goes along with everything that's gained.
Love is—a friendly talk, a warm extended hand,
One's precious time to listen and sometimes understand.
Of patience—when time comes along and betrays the body
and muddles the mind
Love is gentle, and it's kind
Love of God, and life, and of yourself,
Of family, and old friends—
This will always be there. This love never ends.

Gloria J Mathers
THE MEETING
We had just met
She touched her finger to my ear
Were the earrings real gold?
And then it came to mind—
The real gold on me
She could not see
For inwardly I glowed
With love for humankind.

Kristin Long
BROKEN SPIRIT
As I look around to see
If there is anyone there
I see you,
That's all my soul can bear.

I have never forgotten you
You're still in my soul.
Your name has a place in my heart
That makes me whole.

You knew me like no other,
But somehow we've lost one another.

My heart is torn,
I want to be with you.
But I know I have to live my life
Without you.

Amalia D Kessler
ALONE IS THE WEED
Alone is the weed
hovering over the grave—
a noble of the past.

B J Carter
THE FACE IN THE MIRROR
The face in the mirror looks terribly sad
It's plain to see a hard time she's had
The anxiety seen in the face is quite clear
The hatred, the loneliness, in the eyes a great fear
If only the face in the mirror could speak
The happiness she longs for I'd help her to seek
For her only loneliness can there be
For you see that the face in the mirror is me

Hal Moon
MY GOD
God is so sweet and wonderful to know,
I feel His divine presence wherever I go.
Praise be to His Holy name;
I am His and He is mine; I feel not ashamed.

God is my love and light;
To wind my battle I must stand up and fight.
He will be with me and help me to be
From the force of evil joyously free.

I fear no evil, for He is with me,
And ever in His service I shall be,
With love for my brethren one and all,

I shall be ready when my Savior calls.

To the judgment on that resurrection day.
I shall behold my God and hear Him say,
"Well done, my faithful servant, well done.
Thy journey has been a rugged one,
Weep no more, glory is at hand.
Welcome to your home in this promised land."
I will sing and shout with joy divine,
in heaven, a home that 's truly mine!

Patricia M Wourms
SEPTEMBER
and you remembered
that September after the tournament dance
when this poem began
lie-ing
in that bed
with the bedspread
tucked halfway
around the mattress
the blue jean jacket
that followed him from
the Maritimes into your arms
how do you write
a love poem, you said
without saying
i love you . . .

Lyn Johnson
SILENCE
Silence
Such a gentle, sweet sound
like the morning dew
as the dawn awakens to a new day.

To not understand
the beauty of silence,
Is to never understand
the meaning of words,

For it is in our silence
that we speak the loudest.

The touch of a hand
The warmth of a smile
can reach out to our deepest thoughts,
without saying a word.

To learn
and to grow,
within ourselves,
comes when alone
with ourselves,
in the beauty of silence.

Amanda Legner
SUMMER
Summer is a feeling
That one feels inside.
It is a time to play
All day and all night.
No more work.
No more fright.
As the summer
Closes in tight.
It seems to protect you,
All that warmth.
And it goes off inside of you
Until the end of those long summer months.

Jewel George Schartz
SOMETIMES, I WONDER
Sometimes, late at night I wonder
Wonder at the reason of it all
Wonder why sometimes I feel so lonely
Wonder, how much farther, can I fall.

Quiet tears of desperation
Bitter tears of my defeat
Oh Lord, can you hear me? Are you listening
Grant my prayer, a peaceful sleep.

Why did you leave and leave me lonely
Was love not enough for you to stay?
I tried so hard to make you happy
And in anger, you left me and went away.

Wonder at the meaning of this heartache,
How will I ever see it thru,
Wonder if you miss me as I wonder
Searching thru this lonely world for you.

Delores E Zen
WATCHING TELEVISION
Toward the shores of
Cambodia,
Paddy-fields raising
Skulls, skeletons,
Sails a ship
Bearing
The International Red Cross.

Rice
For the people,
Fish, medicine;
The sky brightens up
For unfolding hearts,
Smiles
Long forgotten.

It is said
The struggle of good and evil
Never ends;
But
In the process
We grow better.

Tara Mia Harris

Tara Mia Harris
DIVINITY OF LIFE
To be strong, bold and beautiful,
that is what life's all about
To give, to care, to love
"I'm proud to be me" you can shout!
Able to give thanks to God above
all else. Willing to give
of oneself, when another is in need.
Knowing that you can step forward and lead,
when the time arrives.
Willing to set a direction
to better lives.
That is what life's all about!!

Pearl Palmer Erikson
SPRING
It's spring again, the birds are here.
A singing in the trees.
The grass is green, the leaves are out
A blowing in the breeze.

The fragrant smell of lilacs
Fill the air so sweet today:
Oh I can tell in many way,
That spring is here to stay.

I found some pretty tulips,
Ablooming in a bed;
Pink and yellow tulips,
And one of deep bright red.

Oh spring again, is really here
There is no doubt at last,
For it is here in all its glory:
And winter now is past.

Mrs Sandra E McLeod
THE COMING OF SPRING

I dedicate this poem to my children; Sandra, Patricia, Barbara & David.

The trees are soaking up the sun,
To explode their buds this spring.
There is nothing as beautiful as a tree,
Doing its springy thing.

The birds are coming from everywhere,
They know that spring is near.
Building nests in trees still bare,
Their songs are full of cheer.

They ask us for a bit of grain,
To keep them going steady.
The enjoyment they give us is far from pain,
While their nests they are making ready.

Roxie Bennett
CHILDREN

To my sister, Karen Shorey, for her inspiring thoughts.

Coming from within our own flesh,
How wondrous this is,
It is ever so remarkable,
Like nothing of its kind,
Different from one to another,
Resembling yet its own,
Evolving all around us there of,
New dimensions will always surround the child.

Thomas C Whitworth
INSOMNIA II
Why must I lie awake in this strange bed
In this hotel room far away from home?
I sure wish I could be at home instead,
And then perhaps my thoughts would cease to roam
Through all the things that I have done all day.
Instead they're churning like the ocean foam.
I keep on thinking of the things I wish to say.

I hear strange noises outside, like the roar
Of those big semi's on the Interstate,
So loud it seems they're just outside my door.
Why must they travel thru' the town so late?
The TV in the next room's much too loud;
And if that's not enough to aggravate,
That party by the pool seems to have quite a crowd.

The curtains always let in too much light;
I've never understood why this must be.
It would be very dark this time of night;
At least that is the way it seems to me.
All these disturbances keep me from rest;
It seems from them I never will be free.
I long to get back home where I can sleep the best.

Phyllis Hamilton
CHILDREN

Dedicated to our eleven children—Thank God— He saw fit to bless us with so many—I think we're the richest people on earth

Children are very precious
So love them while you may
Your father in heaven only lends them
for you to keep for a day
He has a lesson for each to learn
And each one does his share
But it doesn't stop you from loving them
or teaching them to care
But when the time comes to send them home
It's not the easiest thing to do
But God will love and care for them
till He comes back for you.

Mark Peterson
DREAM
Last night I dreamt of nothing
And how it scared me so,
I could not run and hide,
There was no place to go.

The Universe devoid,
No Sun or Earth remain,
The cosmos was black paper,
Covered with black ink stain.

No trees on no shores of no streams,
No birds to ever sing,
No mountains shrouded in snow,
No, no such wondrous a thing.

Never again will there sound,
No shadow shall ever be rent,
For no light dost endure,
And no time shall be spent.

Gratefully it was a dream,
And when I woke from slumber,
I draft it on my lists,
Of dreams without number.

Sally Eckstrand
OBESITY
Here I sit eating candy and crap,
dropping half of it into my lap.
Stuffing cookies ice cream galore, m, m, m, m, so good I want some more.
As I eat more pound after pound,
added inches I have found.
I'm getting bigger and bigger, I don't think about my figure.
So all I do is sit here fat, I don't care, so how about that.
Now I'm reaching 200 lbs, I don't think I'll ever come down.
I'm at the highest ever, I don't care of what I measure.
They say it's bad to be so fat, but me skinny, imagine that.
Every doctor and people I know, say go on a diet, but I don't care I just don't buy it.
I know one day it will do me in, but I can't ever see me thin.
So I'll go through life enjoying what I eat, until I'm so fat I can't stand on my feet.
The food's so good I just can't wait, to dish me up another plate.

Almyra Keller
IT WAS NOT SO LONG AGO
It was not so long ago
In a boat by the sea
There a man lives that I know
And this man lives with no other thoughts

Than to love and be loved by me
We loved with a love that is more than love
I and my Honey
With a love that was made in Heaven
Our love is stronger by far than the love of money.

Ellen M Walsh
THANK YOU GOD FOR THE BABY GIFT

This is dedicated to JOHN A WALSH, III, my sixth child, it was his birth that inspired me to write it.

The gift you sent wasn't wrapped in paper and fancy bows
Under its cover is a body and soul, fingers and toes
The gift you sent wasn't an expensive watch with a luminous dial
But it brightens your life with its priceless smile
The gift you sent emulates diamonds, silver and gold
It's an infantine thing you can cuddle, kiss and hold
The gift you sent was bestowed from above
It's a natural endowment that's full of love.
Thank you God

June Marie Saxon
THE OLD BLACK WILLOW AND ME

My thinking place is special,
an old black willow tree.
I'm cradled in its branches
as I set my feelings free.
I've never found a friend
who listens quite as well,
who knows my very best secrets
with promise not to tell.

I remember when my Grandma died,
and I sat crying in the rain,
how that tree wept with me
and bowed to bear my pain.
Another time I fell in love—
my heart was full and bright!
The old tree swayed with my happiness
and shivered in delight.
Now some folks think I'm foolish
to be sentimental about a tree,
but that's because they don't understand
the old black willow and me.

Dorothy Rockwell
COMING HOME AGAIN (A CRY IN THE DARK FOR THE HOMELESS)

It was on a cold and snowy evening when the old man stood thawing his rough and frozen hands with the warm steam rising from the curb along a city's busy street,

His dirty worn and tattered coat hung lifeless, reaching below his knees to meet the rags wrapped protectingly around his shoeless feet.

His weathered and gray bearded face with head bowed low, longingly looked up with red eyes searching for the shining light of home,
His heavily burdened war-torn mind and heart was filled with a gnawing pain, remembering a young mans life when awarded with a pride, was known.

His ears faintly heard from within a nearby house, the wailing of a baby's hungry cry, a sound that rushed passed him as he slowly limped along the dark, familiar street,
As his life ebbing body made its bed in the doorway of the real world outside, the loss of limb he gave for his country, lay crumpled news at his feet.

Suddenly the tiny child's crying ceased and it was then the old mans half-closed eyes drew fond memories of home into his life again,
He could see the baby now lying silently sleeping, safe and sound in its warm and comfy bed, for through his last and final reflection he saw, that the little baby boy was him . . .

Iva May Kirkman
MUD PIE

for Belle

A seed of grass that falls to earth one day will root to find the elements it needs
This magic maestro animates the clay into a blade of grass to grow more seeds

A grazing lamb has artless power, too
to change the structures built in blades of grass
into the seed of ram or egg of ewe
so lambs by gender's role may come to pass

The nourishment that fuels the human train
of growth of trunk and limbs and heart and head
to hold the folds that mold the mighty brain
at times includes lamb stew as daily bread

Our elegantly elemental food
sustains the life parental genes have brewed

Suzanne Thon
I HEARD A CRY

I heard a cry
a long ways off;
whimpering,
wailing,
growing soft.
I listened
waiting patiently;
Only to find
that it was me.

Tisha Hellegers
CONVERSATION WITH SPIRITS

Rhymes
to forget

Making
whisper-sense
of straying
sounds

They bewitch
my heart
that drowning red
facade

Beneath
my soul you
hide, evasive

Atmosphere
happy and
flitting my spirit
as

Withering lights
condense you like
ghosts at
sunrise.

Judy Joanne Breeden
SOMEWHERE

To all those who have touched my life and especially to the memory of my mother.

I walk through the woods
to the creek I used to play in
So many times have I stood
And listened to the south wind rustling in the trees
There is not another sound
No, nothing anywhere around
I am looking for what
I'm not sure, but I'm longing
I'm searching, and I have got to find
There, somewhere in the distance
I cannot see, but in my mind
Oh, the memory I feel it is so strong
Of childhood days
Filled with play
Oh how happy then
And now I wonder when
did they somehow slip away.

Frances-Faith P Tretton
PASSING THROUGH

Dec. 28, 1988 . . . in memory of all who died in the Pan Am crash Dec. 21, '88

On the shortest day of the solar year,
At the time of the winter solstice,
The travellers came from Germany,
While honoring our Savior's birth.

They journeyed west, all homeward bound,
Glad faces, gift laden for those whom they loved best;
A finite image of the One who spawned their mirth.

Suppressing joys of keen anticipation
In sharing presents (symbols of God's gift to earth),
In celebrating Christ with those they longed to see,
They found their earthly quest fulfilled
O'er Lockerbie, Flight 103

Geary Paulk
UNDERSTANDING

It's raining. It's pouring. My love for you is growing. As I sit here, and think of you, words can't tell the true feelings I have for you. As the day turns to night, and the rain turns to snow, my love for you grows. So let's open the gates, and let's embrace, and I'll hold you in my arms and keep you safe from harm. My tears have gone my smile has returned because I sit here and think of you.

George Forss
KATHLEEN

Kathleen
To proclaim;
Pretty lady, everybody knows you will stir them if you try.
You save all the foolish ardor time has forgotten
All the truth inside.

If anyone will love you more
I will not know.
I will! Even when my times are past!

I know your need is great for lifes surety, for the wanted truth of an undenying self.
Still, I must remain, in my hope and fantasy
I will stay.

Kathleen
To proclaim;
Pretty lady, everybody knows you will stir them if you try.

Edward Easley Jr
LADY OF MYSTERY

Lady of mystery, you are aloof with your magical aires,
And, I'm enchanted by the glow it bears.
During the day and every night,
I search diligently with all my might
To understand the wonderment that surrounds you.
To be so shy and remote,

Yet, possessing the love of which poets wrote
Is, indeed, remarkably true.
The destiny of my days
Is in your ways
Of making my world peaceful and serene.
Is this true? Or, is it just a fantasy and personal dream?
I must have more from this idyll yearning and infatuation.
Though, at times, I am enthralled with moments of deep inspiration.
What I seek most of all
Is the beckoning of your love call
For a life of commitment and dedication to each other,
Forever surrounded by love's wall.
The marvelous power that you possess is more than I know, I guess.
But, what I possess is what I confess.
And that is—love for you!

Alice Berry
SPRING SONG

Spring has come and gone,
And I have watched its pattern on the road,
As I went back and forth to bus stop and to market.
Spring sunshine, through bare branches, unimpeded,
Then soft dappled by the maple blossom tassels:
A swift shower brought them down, to mark me out
Bright half circles of red and yellow-green
On the wet pavement, far as eye could see,

Far as heart could feel a haunting sadness
At so brief a glory.
Then the heavier shadows of the oak leaves.
Big as squirrel's ears;
I must plant the beans now, and the corn.
And today the dogwood petals fill the ditches;
I walk softly on their silken carpet
Remembering their April beauty.
When the last gay Spring has warmed my spirit
Let me go down gently, like white dogwood blossoms
Adrift on a May breeze.

Mildred W Lyons

JESUS KNOWS MY NAME

Jesus knows my name—No, it's not a game.
He even took the blame, for sins I cannot name.
Jesus knows my name. I'll never be the same.
A lion He can tame. He even heals the lame.

Jesus knows you too. There's nothing He won't do,
To help you get through, bad times that come to you—
Jesus loves my friends, on that I can depend.
I pray to Him for them. He'll be there to defend.

I talk to Him all day, of things that I should say,
To help me on my way, at work or at my play.
Thank God, for His dear Son, who died for you and me.
Accept Him, all, or one. He will set you free!

Jospeph Scott Iorio

TOO BEAUTIFUL

To Jennifer, your smile is my sunshine.

She gleamed with unescapable beauty.
With more of it still undiscovered.
Her manner brought forth one of charm,
And left one so eager to hold her.

There was something special about her,
You could see it whenever she smiled.
You could feel it whenever you touched her,
You would miss it when she wasn't there.

Mary Lou Darnielle

GRANDPAPA THE MILLER

A Miller by trade; he worked with pride, known around the countryside
Men with oxen pulling heavy logs; bags of grain arrived from far and wide;
Grandpapa; Step-Grandmama lived in a rose columned, trellis-vine house neat;
A visit with them was a wonderful treat, I loved the cool veranda seat

He weighed me on the Big scale, the one he weighed grain and flour,
Fascinated I watched the BIG BINS as grains burst into lily white shower,
He sold Oil from BIG Drums; he worked until everything was done;
We kids built cities, towns in sawdust mounds; my that was fun!

Step-Grandmama had charge of the cottage; especially the ol' crank-Phone.
Men left for miles around carried all the news back home
They kept the place "neat as a pin", both known without sin;
They read the Bible daily for their heavenly crown to win.

They shook hands with a smile sincere, wonderful homespun pair;
Summer nights Grandpapa's Violin music drifted in the air!
I met my kin when we celebrated Grandpapa's Birthday May ten;
I remember a Miller, who to me was of the GREATEST of MEN.

Helen J Sherman

AT CHILD'S PLAY

Eyes are raging and voices are loud!
Blood pressures are rising, anger is being let out.
With the words we choose, we take turns
Knocking each other down. There's not too much of a difference between us and the children on a playground.

One wants to keep a hold, the other wants to let go. So we push and we shove . . .
Only concerning ourselves with who has said, or who has done what.
In this struggle we forget, just how much
each other has meant.

Martin Garland

A TRIBUTE TO LOUIS L'AMOUR

He left us a literary legacy worth more than gold.
Thousands of stories superbly told.
Stories of Western Adventure and daring deed;
tales of the Indians' plight and the White Man's greed.
He told stories of yondering and exciting places,
with characters so real, you could see their faces.

Mr. L'AMOUR was astute in his writing detail,
from the shape of a mountain to the length of a trail.
You could see the bleakness when he wrote of desert lands,
and feel the heat off the burning sands.
You could sympathize when Mr. L'AMOUR wrote of fear,
and you would taste the water from streams so clear.

When writing of History, there were no flaws,
and even the most avid reader would pause.
A fact gleaned from his writing, something learned,
and Mr. L'AMOUR was given the credit so dearly earned.
His experiences were immense, his knowledge vast,
and from him we inherited a glimpse of the past.

So when you read an adventure story,
or uncover an obscure fact about life on a distant shore,
utter a silent word of thanks to Mr. LOUIS L'AMOUR.

Amanda J Petrillo

THINKING OF YOU

Thinking of you
I realize what I lost
And I would gladly change those things
No matter what the cost

'Cause now my world is empty
No longer brightened by your smile
And rising in the morning
Doesn't seem worthwhile

Answering the telephone
Knowing it's not you
And sitting alone beneath the stars
Makes me feel so blue

Thinking of the day we met
And thinking of our end
I wish that you had thought of me
As more than just a friend

Debbie Lemna

THE GARDEN THAT I KEEP

For Tina, Jolene, Travis, Heidi, and Dan

In the Garden that I keep
Are thoughts that I have seeked

Those thoughts are very dear
They're like a cheerful cheer

And in my garden, I do grow
Flowers that forever flow

Those flowers are the memories
Of our past histories

This garden is my only due
Of the thoughts I have of you

Paula Leeche

BENEATH THE TREE

To Bill, My Companion on Life's Hiway

When I die, don't mourn for me,
Just plant me here, beneath this tree.

My time on earth was long for me,
just let me rest, beneath this tree.

No babies left for me to tend,
No food to cook, or clothes to mend.

I guess I'll nap beneath this tree,
It really does look good to me.

Perhaps I'll dream of days gone by,
Who ever thought that man could fly?,

Much less to walk upon the moon!!
I've seen all this, and very soon,

I'll take my place inside the womb,
of Mother Earth, beneath the moon.

I'm ready now, so let me rest,
beneath this tree, and I'll be blessed,

with dreamless sleep, unknown by me.
Just endless peace, and I'll be free.

June M Moeck

A DREAM

To stand on the bow of a ship,
To feel the wind in my hair
And the seafoam on my face.
To travel to far distant lands,
These are the things of which dreams are made.

The ship was the vacant lot next door,
The rippling waves were the wild grasses
That grew from the depths of the soil.
The seafoam on my face was imaginary,
Only the wind was true
And I—I was all of four.

Alice A MacDonald

NATURE PERSON

I would like to dedicate this poem to our beautiful and mysterious world with the hope that it will be protected!

Born to the freedom of field and sky
Far from the city's hue and cry
Children played freely
Birds sang their chants
And life itself became enhanced
By caches formed, not by human aid
Intricate treasures 'life-displayed'
That respect for nature and for man
May weave for all a loving plan.

Martha Dunaway

HIS NAME IS JESUS

To Eddie-Lou Cole: Who published my first poem.

He picked me up out of sin,
  And washed my sins away.
They are under His blood now,
  That's why I love Him today.
    He satisfies my soul,
      He made me whole,
        His name is Jesus.

He protects me from all evil,
  He gives me grace to go through.
Puts me at ease when I am
  troubled,
    He will do the same for you.
      I run to Him away from harm,
        A refuge in a storm.
          Love that name Jesus.

We will be in our Heavenly home,
  After we meet Him in the air.
I can't wait to see that Heavenly
  place,
    The place He promised to
      prepare.
        Joy will be all around,
          We will claim our Heavenly
            crown,
              Abiding with Jesus.

Teddy J Ancher McCloney

A CLEAR VIEW

Lord, open mine eyes that I might see as others see,
  The virtues that stare right back at me.

Give me the courage to enrich upon the good I find,
  Give me the wisdom to retard the growth of the weeds.

Now that I know give me the ability,
  To share with others my vision.

Walter C Uebele

TEMPTATION

What fools we be to try and tread a path
Divergent from our chosen, destined way.
Far better 'twould be to walk a road
From which cold reason never strays.
Why let one step; one fleeting foolish hour
Take away from us all that we've fought to gain?
What prominence, in all time, can such short space,
In the face of years, hope ever to attain?

But when I kiss your mouth, I find thereon
All that my saner words seek to repress.
And when you touch my lips, you leave on them
Indelibly, a moment's loveliness.
And so, my dear, look not into my eye.
Be sensible, conventional—but why?

Jeananne Northup Pyle
LOVES PARALLELS

Dedicated to my "Guardian Angel", Peggy Van Hoose. You made this possible. My heartfelt thanks.

Our love is like the surf and sand.
Gentle waves that nibble and lap,
bringing gifts of colorful shells,
to be treasured; like time.

Storm clouds gather, and
jealous winds whip the waves.
Spewing foam and froth, they
batter, like angry words.

Bored with this childish game,
you go, as quickly as you came,
back to the teeming sea of
waiting lovers.

Any semblance of love; like me,
is left in the wake,
broken; shattered, into tiny
fragments,
like the shells.

You are the surf,
taunting a promise of return.
Knowing that I, the sand, will always be there,
waiting, waiting . . .

Jean W Goodhue
AND CHRISTMAS DIDN'T COME!

An old bag-man, sick and hungry, out there in a park
Found a discarded "burger" and soon the night was dark.
No home had he to go to, no place to lay his head,
He scraped some leaves together and used them for a bed.

And Christmas didn't come.

An old decrepit lady sat in a nursing home.
No-one ever visits her; she sits there all alone.
No tender kiss upon her brow, no gentle loving touch,
Only fading memories of those she loved so much.

And Christmas didn't come.

A bruised and battered house-wife crawled out in the street.
Her neighbors drew their drapery, polite and so discreet.
She lay there half unconscious, crying out for help,
While a foolish drunken husband kicked the dog until it yelped.

And Christmas didn't come.

Scarcely knowing where he went, a long haired youth on crack
Stretched forth an asking hand, with no-one reaching back.
So on this day so grim to him, in a world he could not face,
He sent a bullet through his head.
Not an unusual case.

And Christmas didn't come.

A willful teenage daughter, who'd never seen a church,
Left pregnant stranded all alone, sure left out in a lurch.
Parents cast her in the street, lover fled the scene,
She jumped into the river by the lovely golfing green.

And Christmas didn't come.

A scrawny waif out in the cold, a painful sight to see,
Scrounging in a garbage can, the only thing that's free.
His clothes were all in tatters; his little feet were bare.
Fur-coated people passed him by and didn't even care.

And Christmas didn't come.

An eighteen month old baby, forgotten in a car.
The day was hot and sultry, and he could only breathe so far.
Hours and hours later, a dehydrated baby died,
Sobbing for "some water" and "mamma" by his side.

And Christmas didn't come.

Chris A Butturff
TRUE BEAUTY

True beauty is like a rose.
The pleasing sight of the outward form is like that of the sweet petals on the fair flower.
As time and decay take their toll, the beautiful petals will cease to be.
The stem that connects them all will wither and fade,
Just as the outward form must do, as nature intends.
But the true beauty of that elegant rose can only be found below the surface.
The beauty is found in the roots from whence that rose was born.
And, like that rose, true beauty cannot be found in humans by observing the petals they display.
One must look under the surface.
One must look to the true self from which the beauty is derived.
Then, and only then, can one define the meaning of true beauty.

Robert Michael John Higgins

Robert Michael John Higgins
A PRESCRIPTION FOR LOVE

Where have all the statesmen gone?
In this gracious land of ours
What has happened to our leaders
And their honest judicious powers

Who runs the land of the mighty
In its infinite quest for glory
Who can explain its many quandaries
And tell me the rest of the story

Enlighten my mind with facts
And spare me no gory obstructions
In my quest for knowledge and truth
I need all to make honest deductions

Please help to find some answers
In America the land of the free
We surely owe it to ourselves
In a country that's served you and me

We've searched high and low
We have searched up above
What America needs
Is a prescription for love.

Larry D Leo
STORMY

Rain is falling from the sky
Slowly it drops to the window sill
Carefully the wind blows
through the trees;
As lightning strikes beyond the water
The storm is closing in
Elements in your mind
unlock the memories, of people and places
you seem to know
Somehow . . , they have faded into the mist
But yet, you remember:
Thoughts are strange, they come and go
Never returning, never ending
You've stepped over the edge of reality
The pain and anger, believed hatred
in a dream
of your past
The evidence of the mood is clear
As the storm begins to pass
And the rainbow touches the ground
You remember them as stormy

Herman Bystrom
THE NIGHT FLIGHT

To Ruth Verrette on her 75th birthday

Why Do I Fly Across The Sky
Why Do I Fly
Why Do I Fly

To Come Again
To Home Again
To Come Again
To Home

Through Stars Above
And Lights Below
And Snowflakes Dancing Past The Wings
And Snowflakes Dancing Past The Wings

I Fly Again To Rest
To Rest Again
At Home Again
To Rest Again At Home.

Esther Miller
NATURE TRAILS

Many times we trailed
Over a mountain
Lined with trees spreading tall.
One sunny Tuesday I walked that trail.
To my surprise, along the way
Hidden by heavy berried vines, I saw
Morning glories twining free
Peering through prickly briars;
A field mouse hurrying home.
A deer and a doe, heads held high,
White tails switching,
Through dainty flowers, a delicate blue
Clinging to dampened earth.

Allen Green
THE RIVER AND THE WOOD

In the wood of oak and willow,
Beside the river current's din,
I sat down to think life over;
To think of what might have been.

I pondered long about my purpose
On this our fertile home.
Cherished friends of mine aplenty,
But I am still . . . so alone.

Loves have past, never staying,
Though I've tried so hard in vain.
Unfulfilled I looked to Heaven;
Heaven spurn me back again.

I know my match walks this wood,
She swims the river each and every day;
Same are her wants and her worries,
Same are her needs in every way.

Alas, I walk the wood a searching,
Hoping to spy her 'hind each tree;
Perhaps someday she'll pull me from this river
That flows so swift and suddenly
And keep our souls from being alone for all eternity.

Sarah McGinnis
DEATH

Death hangs over me like a
Black storm cloud.
I hear my friends crying,
I see their red faces
And the slow stream of tears
Trickling from their bloodshot eyes.
I wish I could cry with them
But I grieve in a different way.
For the pencil becomes my eyes,
And the words my tears.

Melanie Weltmer
THAT SENIOR GUY

Dedicated to the one and only Jeff H., 1987-88 graduate. If only you really knew how i felt. Love always & forever Melanie Weltmer

He's leaving this year
The guy i like very much,
he won't be near
But still, i love him very much.

I noticed his beautiful blond hair
And the color of his eyes,
All i could do was stare
And tell my friends lies.

He's too cute for me
That's why i lied,
He'll never see
What's hidden inside.

I'll see him graduate
I could tell him there,
It would be too late
But he would know i care.

As he told me good-bye
And stepped away,
A tear filled my eyes
As i asked him to stay.

Emmanuel M Ward
HISTORY OR HIS-STORY

St. Luke 21:33 Heaven and earth shall pass away: but my words shall not pass away,

These words are similar, nearly in every way,
Their meaning, their spelling, their pronunciation,
How can these words mean what they say;

The Bible is His-Story, the promissory he made,

It would behoove us expediently to recant,
As the resting of His-Story is lain over in the shade;

The mind is a perpetual thinking station,
And these words give real meaning to excalation,
Cause when it happens like Jesus said, I'd say that Gods education;

He told us in His-Story, the history newsmen cast,
And we read on the same page in His-Story this very thing came to pass;
Don't be alarmed, shocked, or flabbergast that's His-Story from the first page to the last;

His-Story is the living word, while history is only what you've heard,
Does history know what will take place, or wait to commentate the case,
Stop worrying about the history you've heard and take panoramic look at God's word.

It would be a great challenge to make this momentous correction,
But it's lamentations would be guided in the right direction,
And when history is replaced with His-Story, this will be real affection catered with perfection;

Now, the first world was lost in the great inundation;
God may be calling to all nations to put these words in true formation,
For there is coming through many tribulation, a might abomination, led by a great conflagration;

Jesus died for us! The very least we can do is live for Him.

Claudia Stewart Naranick
WEDDING TOAST

To my granddaughter and her husband

If I could write a poem here's what I'd say
To Tom and Libby on their wedding day.
"The vows you took today keep ever new
"A living trust to guide you on your way
"Giving you courage as you face up to
"The many problems that you'll meet each day."
And so I send congratulations and
My wish for happiness and for much joy
As you walk down lifes path together; and I hope
You'll stop from time to time along the way
To smell the flowers and to each other say
"I truly love you, and I bless the day
"That brought us both together." Yes all this I'd say
If I could write a poem.

Joseph Rubino
IN THE NAME OF PROGRESS
As I walk through the path
Of vanishing wilderness
I see the pristine beauty
Trampled everywhere
By the tractors of modern destruction
And defiled by the refuse
Of the atomic age.

For untold eons
Man was one with nature
Revering the firmament
And the awesome power of the elements.

In the short clock of history
The destiny of the earth
In its bountiful diversity
And indeed of other planets
May be in the hands of man
Can we rise to the occasion?
Or vanish in the greed
For short term "progress".

Alison K Grimm
THE OCEAN'S GRAVEYARD
In the sky a seagull swiftly soars,
Below, the ocean tumbles and roars,
Bringing in parts of sea life in the warm sand,
They sink in the soil for graves that suit them grand.

Beautiful shells, oysters, and pearls,
All kinds of shapes, in twists and curls,
Colors and calico print all details made with care,
Hard and soft shells even with seaweed hair.

Some have sounds like the sea,
Others like a buzzing bee,
All the shell's beauty lives on for years,
That's why in the graveyard there are no tears.

Karen Neas
GOD GAVE US WILLPOWER

This poem is in "THANKS" to my sister KRIS TAYLOR. She wrote it for me when the encouragement was most needed.

When there's a will there's a way
Without a will there's no way

Reach and reach out
Just reach all about

Go ahead, give it your all
Surely, you'll find you're having a ball

Push, try, strive
You'll only feel much more alive

God gave us willpower, not for you to let sour

So whatever it is, a job interview or a diet, you'll only benefit if you reach out and try it.

Ruth Faulkner
POETRY IN MOTION

Dedicated to my dear friend Irene Smith.

Slender hips gently swaying
To sounds of an ancient beat.
Faces smiling with the rhythm
Of long remembered dancing feet.
Graceful hands and lovely arms
Weaving magic in their flight.
Telling stories of life and love,
Echoing dimly in the night.
I am touched with the thrill
It leaves in my simple heart.
Could you be so very dull
To have no love for an ancient art?

Catherine Ruth
DAY IS DONE

Dedicated to our loved one, "Ina F. Ruth" upon her passing—December 31, 1988

Today we had to say good-bye
To our Mom, and Grandmother, so dear.
One more "I Love You" we spoke so softly
Yet we knew that you could hear.

It was so hard to see you go,
And watch as you slipped away;
But inside we knew you were ready to leave,
God was waiting for you today!

We felt that you knew you were not alone,
When this time of passing came;
We knew from that last little gleam in your eye
That Jesus was calling your name!

So farewell to you our Special One;
We know you are happy now.
We really hate to let you go—
God will comfort us too, somehow!

Janet J Messick
DREAMER
You are a dreamer
And I believe in you
Your dreams are going to be my reality

I keep wondering

When will they come tue
Awakening to the fact perhaps they
Are only dreams like you

Ricardo O Gray
SEARCH THE UNIVERSE
Gosh

There's a feeling of belonging out here
There's a pounding so resounding
Of a quiet so astounding
Yet a feeling of belonging out here.
Such a quiet ought to try it
Ne'er a riot to deny it
What a feeling of belonging out here
Ever seeming like a dreaming
All as one in perfect teaming
Get the feeling of belonging out here.
Neither hint of creed or nation
Blood of one by implication
Such a feeling of belonging out here.
I've long been known to tipple none
What do I get such tickle from
It's a feeling of belonging out here.

Grant W McBride
IN QUIESCENCE

To my dear wife Eloise

The lonely wind seeks on and on—
While Winter, with his mocking breath
Runs down his path of frost
Across a land of leafless trees,
Where all seems dead and lost.
Yet each new day, the cold and cheerless dawn
Awakes to view a sky, whose sullen clouds hang low
Above a dull and frost-cracked earth with drifted snow.

Oh dreary winter months,
How dire is your need to Summer's fertile sod
But in your chilling lap I sit,
A dormant seed, beneath a frozen clod.

Guillermo H Gonzales Jr
MISTY DAYS
Those types of ladies
appear only on
misty days.
When on such days
the rain
much more
like a gentle mist
falls upon my beaten brow.
How I can sense
her beauty because
I sense the gentle kiss
of the soothing mist.
what a revelation!

Bonita Folger Todd

Bonita Folger Todd
MY TWO SONS
When I'm gone, my Dear Sons, don't weep
But remember this, I'm only asleep
And when I awake to a far better life,
There will be only joy, no worry or strife
I'd feel hurt if you should grieve
Because some day each of us must leave
To go to that great Homecoming in the sky
Where our souls shall live on and never die
So when I close my eyes in restful sleep
and can open them no more
Just think of me as passing on through God's open door
That leads to His paradise.
Where this old body will be at ease
There will be no heartaches, no sickness, or disease
I know you both love me dearly
But God's love is oh so great
Yes, I'm looking forward to entering His pearly gates
Until we meet in Heaven, it's goodbye for a while
Always remember our good times with a smile
Everything is well with my soul, yes, all is fine
For proof of this statement read John 6:39
My darlings, don't ever be afraid to die
For your Dad and I will meet you in the sky.

Joan Lehman
JUST ONE THOUGHT . . .

To hubby "Bill" for his love, caring and understanding, of what I do with my venture! Also to Thomas Alva Edison, my main "Inspiration"—thru reading, the venture, he made, of "His" life . . .

As we walk thru our lives, what do we gain.
With moments of hesitation, to keep up with refrain?
Things taught us, simple and true . . .
But what, if as individuals, we try something new?
To now learn and gain—what we thought we could not,
The challenge of today—from new wisdom got . . .
For to find something "special," is a rewarding goal—
Through learning of venture, self-satisfies the soul.
Each soul is different, and we grow from there,
To pass to the future—"That" of which we care . . .
"Just one thought" . . . for someone else to find,
As they stroll through their life, with what's on their mind.
"Just one thought" . . . preserved—for "one" person to see—
Would satisfy 'this' soul—as my part of making history!!

R M DeLisle
FALSE BRAVADO

To Wanda, Love is only an illusion, but the best one of them all.

People still ask with curious disconcern how I fare without you.
Pray—how do I tell them each time the phone rings I hold my breath expectantly,
or with each days mail I frantically search for some tender word or truth.
I inwardly sigh, knowing my cares to be in vain;
For should you ever call we would speak like strangers, awkwardly searching for something to say,
and should you ever pause to write, your words would only speak of the past,
memories best left untouched—forgotten.
I cannot say at this moment that leaving you was best, we've parted so many times before.
Though for now my loneliness is not as painful as was your love.
So I look these simple people full in the eye, smile and tell them that I'm fine.
As I turn and walk away, I cannot but wonder if they sense my false bravado.

Martha J Newbern
IMAGINE SUCH A PLACE
Can you imagine such a place?
A place by the sea shore
So windy and warm.
A place so quiet, all you can hear is the seagulls calling to you in the distance.

The waves come up to meet you
And the sand shifts beneath your feet.
You see footprints and know someone
Was there before you—
Can you imagine such a place?

Farah Patel
WILD BIRD
It's time to let my wild bird go,
I know that I will miss him so.
I feel tears swelling in my eyes,
As I say my goodbyes.
It's time to let him roam free,
I'll miss him and I know he'll miss me.

Edward P Roberts
SURRENDER
Down through the pageant of years
To this sunrise and rosy glow
Comes love, with its laughter and tears;
Its surface, with thunder below,
Falling in cascades soft and sweet,
Swiftly and silently. We meet.
I hear your murmur low
And thrilling; like the path
Of a river, cutting its swath
Through a jungle of unknown growth.
Your soothing voice, like the jungle sloth,
Slow, holds me entranced
Until, with love-filled eyes I've glanced
Into yours, and am lost.

Lora Hansen-Beard
LONG HAIR HIDES TEARS

I give this fruit of my labor to the mother, by whose milk, experience, I am growing.

Long hair hides my tears,
Swords of valor, your fears.
Read the ancient crystal crescent,
Branded by the years.

Long hair hides tears,
Axes fall; Crowd cheers
Flaming arrow; It sears!
A screech, sharp sounding jeers.

Behind long hair are eyes that peer,
See how they dart? They seem a mirror.
Tears fall amid the strands.

A swift ringing bell, cool and clear,
The swish of fine satin, pale and sheer;
Veils of gossamer envelop near.
Jewels around the finger on a gold sphere.

The thick wine is bitter,
Honeycakes filling and sweet.
As rice descends and my flower gathered,
I close my shawl of long hair, and weep.

Marsha Jan Behrend
MODES
If birth can be considered C major,
freshness, difficult but bright,
and love is something like E-flat,
full of itself, round and resounding,

then grief must be f-sharp minor,
shining with its bright, painful edge.
I want my life to end in resolved G,
the last step in a circle moving upward.

James William Cummings
REFLECTIONS ON A NEW YEAR
Now the old year's gone let us begin anew:
Give us strength with which to see this new year through:
What joys and what sorrows does this one hold in store?
So like and yet unlike all the years before:
Some will cry for change and some to stay the same:
New men and women shall rise this year to fame:
Others shall retain their place, for better and for worse:
Still on we will strive through blessing and through curse:
Hunger, AIDS, and taxes still add to our duress:
But will any of the three be properly addressed?:
We cannot trust the Russians nor can the Russians trust us:
But maybe if we talk some more we'll further lessen all the fuss.

Nancy R Lindgren
A MOUNTAIN OF PEACE
I walk up the mountain
Yellow flowers bow in the wind
And billowy clouds crown the pines.
All is at peace.
But, inside my heart aches—I am alone.

I walk down to the sparkling stream
The water is moving fast
Quickly, all memories of past hurt and pain
Bubble over the pebbles and
Wash down stream.

This short moment puts me at
Peace within myself. And,
Nobody can take it from me.
Up on the mountain, all bad
Is turned to good.
There is no hate, no selfish greed—
Only peace!—sweet peace!

Steve B Joy
IS YOUR CONSCIENCE CLEAR?
There's A man sitting in a plush chair.
He said, "My way's better, and I'm going to change yours."
So, to another country we go with gun in hand.
The people there die and they don't understand.

For any nation that thinks their way is best,
That is good, be proud and love your country.
But don't interfere in another way of life.
Don't go to war, live in peace, cherish your life.

In the 60's they said, "Make love not war!"
Doesn't anyone remember anymore?

Imagine you are the parent of a son.
For the first time it's not up to you, what he's going to do.
They're taking him off to die or kill,
Your flesh and blood, against your will.

You taught your child right and wrong.
You taught him what love is and how to be fair.
You taught him to be strong where you were weak,
And now they want to show him hell.
Just a three year peek.

In the 60's they said, "Make love not war!"
Doesn't anyone remember anymore?

What I don't understand about a war,
Is how two people of the same faith will kill each other.
How do you justify doing things this way?
Is your Conscience clear the very next day?

Leesia C Corbett-Koutx
HIDING FEELINGS I DARE NOT EXPRESS
In quiescence, the rhythm of my heart beats alone and blue; it is
keeping quiet feelings of love
that I dare not express.

Smoldering feelings as I might, the desperation I feel as I see my
love walk with another—the
desperation bleeds through
leaving tell-tale signs of torment
that I thrust against my body.

. . . a vicious cycle, a pretense of lies, my only hope for sanity.

To deny the rhythm that my heart beats, I'm stopping dead all of
love's hopeful dreams; but in
denying my heart, I'm holding
on to the last thread of sanity
that my soul can grasp.

Love is such an illusive dream: one day I feel it; the next day it's
gone leaving me alone to
struggle with a flood of
memories—memories that leave
tell-tale signs of torment that I
thrust against my body.

. . . a vicious cycle, a pretense of lies, my only hope for sanity.

He walks with another and I would be jealous, if only I'd let the
rhythm of my heart speak; but I
can't. I alone know that my
heart beats solely for him.

I can't make him love me: He has to walk with me by the strength of
his own two feet. And I can't
hush the torment my heart feels
as I walk alone and he walks
with another.

. . . a vicious cycle, a pretense of lies, my only hope for sanity.

The dreaded silence lingers still—revealing feelings that I dare not
express—leaving me with tell-
tale signs of torment thrust
against my body.

Sandra DeRosa
LOVE
What is love?
That is such a question
That only a mortal could ask.
It is but a feeling
That comes over one
An emotion that cannot be grasped.

It rips through your soul
And uncovers your heart
For the entire world to see.
It puts a spark in your eye
And a glow in your spirit
It's such a magical thing to be . . .
In love!

Lenore Dunn Hunter
BALLET IN JULY

Dedicated to my beloved George—husband, father of our children and friend.

How delightful to hear the laughter
Of one's first born in the afternoon,
Sitting beside the wading pool,
With small sighs of a breeze
Turning in unison
The colorful twin beach balls
Floating lazily on the calm surface
Sunshine filtering through the pines,
Flowers stately in their boxes
Adding their feast for the eye.
Oh, that we all could share
Moments such as these—
A perfect day in July.

Jennifer Lea Haddad
IT IS DEATH

It is death.
That is what I see.
People say it is cool,
But that is the thought of a fool.

First you find the key,
Then you find the door.
After that there is nothing more.
It is death.

So is its color.
Everyone knows it as well as can be.
Black is what you see.
It is death.

Albert S Hickey
MOTHER NATURE'S FUNERAL

To my loving mother

My love of nature, may-be gone mad, existing to please her since
I was a lad, the rivers her veins, the trees be her hair, we rape her, forsake her, spew filth in the air. Relentless the vipers, who suckle her breast, never contented, never at rest. I speak of the people, all nations to blame, parisitic in gender, war to stake claim. When you hear the wind moan, it's her in despair, crying in anguish to a world that don't care. She used to be tranquil, blissfully serene, she leaves us now this poets foreseen. We started with riches, resources galore, ravished the land in our greed to get more. Corporations compare profit and loss, a toxic by product what of that cost? A delicate food chain, a broken link, cannot adapt, too soon extinct. Some wounds do not heal, they fester and bleed, only to die, no longer at need. Mourn no more as we lay her to rest, a moment of silence, failing God's test. We still have a chance, it can't be too late, our childrens future, we choose our own fate.

Audrey Devic
THE LORD IS EVERYWHERE

I was walking in the woods one day
And saw a sparrow on the way,
The sun came glinting thro' a bough
I felt God with me at this hour.

I saw some mountains in the distance
The mists were swirling in resistance,
I saw one snowcapped in the sky
Twas then I knew the Lord was nigh.

I wandered by a stream one day
And watched the fish that swam away
I picked some buttercups for Mom,
Wished I could give them to his Son.

I heard the quiet in the night
I heard the noise at day
The bustle, hustle of our life—
But—God said, just kneel down and pray.

I went into a park one day
And watched the children all at play
They threw a ball high in the air
The Lord I knew was everywhere.

Frances Gonzalez
FREE

To my late son-in-law, Philip Wayne Berry.

I wish I was a little bird
that flies above the trees.
I've often wondered what he thinks
of all the things he sees.
He works so hard to build his nest
but even then there is no rest.
He spends the day in search of food
to feed his waiting, hungry, brood.
But oh how happy he must be
to fly about and feel so free.

David Martin
that graceless grace

For Ted first—a years old promise—happily kept and then, perhaps more appropriately, for Liz, Rachel, Mike, Jeanne, Karen, John, and especially Renée and Anjanette

dance, darling,
dance beneath the silver moon
with the ethereality of gossamer
all clad in silk and graceless grace
with raven tresses floating dappled with moonlight
dancing your arabesques and pirouettes
seeming a fleeting silhouette
almost passing insubstantial

but then you still
with eyes wet
and finger clasping a rose
coloured sunset red
for the love you crave
but not tonight
for this sky holds a lonely moon
so dry your tears, darling,
and dance not for love

Vicky L Stamper
A BIT OF HEAVEN

To my precious Mom: No words in any poem could ever express the love I felt for her. And to my dear Dad, whose strength I could never live without! From your loving daughter.

On earth, your wings were tucked away
And your halo, a sight unseen.
But, you held an aire about you;
In your eyes there was a gleam.

You had a faith to see you through;
The hope of a certain peace.
A home made for an angel;
One you could eternally keep.

You lived your life upon His word,
And never, did you doubt;
His promise of this holy place
And these dreams would come about!

Oh! Now, how your wings must soar
With your halo shining bright;
As you journey to your promised land;
Another angel taken to flight!

I pray that, somehow, you will know
The extent of your endless worth.
By your guiding light, you granted me,
A Bit Of Heaven, here on earth!

Carol L Hurley
DEAR JOHN

Lying close to you as you sleep,
I search with mind's eyes for your face—
You in a life long before me,
Existing in a jungle of fears—
Fears of present and future—
Fears forever left unspoken.

I grasp for you.
You, attired in your green suit of armor,
With your trophies of war
Proudly draped around your neck,
And a grotesque smile
Protruding under empty eyes.

But all I can see is
Your kindness,
And your caring,
And your loving.

And I must be ever so quiet,
In my thankful rejoicing,
That you are here
With me
Tonight.

Helen Stewart
CREATIVE EXPRESSION

When I write and express my creativity,
I give from my very being, my soul.
It's a deep feeling of pure peaceful serenity,
Because I make this expression my goal.

The expression that's within is infinite,
I let go, I just let it flow,
The expression is live and very definite,
it expresses all that is, this I know.

My expression is like a harmonious song.
It lifts the spirit, it moves the heart,
It asks all who hear it to please sing along,
It summons all together that once were apart.

Creative expression dwells in all mankind,
It bares infinite beauty and constant pleasure.
It's there within you, just look and you'll find.
Let yourself listen to this golden inner treasure.

Fatima Buchert
SELF

To my dear Pauly, just because. Fatima

He hides in the lust of irresistible defiance,
Ashamed of the chains his emotions predicted.
A tiny, gigantic being.
Threatening. Yet beautiful. A sexual leopard.
Delicate, fast, vicious. An unreachable snake.
He stays. He shall.
Despite the light of his alluring doubts,
He gets to savor the undisguisable secrets.
Devious secrets.
Possibly dead, he still lies indefinitely,
Faking a world in pastel pleasures.
He moves at the same rhythm of his fears,
Blaming innocence.
His prey, that one will remain his owner,
For the bitter delight of the blurred images
Who casually insist on watching me by.

Lillian E Rogers
TUCSON

A few years back, I left the East
With it's dingy, dirty sky
I traveled west and a sparkling gem
Called "Tucson" caught my eye.

T'was beautiful, the air was clean
And here I settled down
With the mountains and the desert
In my adopted town.

This is Wildcat Country, where much is free
A cooling drink of desert tea
A belly laugh at the roadrunner's flight
Touching a star on a balmy night.

How I would miss the desert sights
The soft sweet call of the quail
And long to see the city lights
And hear the coyotes' wail.

I love the glorious sunsets
That paint the evening sky
Yes, this is where I'm living
And this is where I'll die.

Jennifer Lee Gajus
MOM

Mom is such a special word, it's so hard to describe
It means you'll always be there, right by my side
No matter if I'm right, no matter if I'm wrong,
I know you'll always be there to help guide me along.
You've taught me many things, about life and hot to live
You've given me so much more, than I could ever give
You've helped me help myself, which is selfish in a way,
You've been there from the beginning each & every day.
I can't write in words how I feel for you
So I'll try to show you more
In the things I say and do.

Theodore Pomeroy
UNTITLED

I love to walk a wooded path
Not far from my urban home,
Often I pass the trees and rocks and
Set my time by the regularity of the course
Of each trail.

Then one day I came about,
And striding free I felt
That I had come upon this wood
For the first time:
My feet and eyes had never
Trod or seen such a lovely quiet spot.

And my head burst with wonder at
Feeling at once the newness
And the familiar.

Lillian F Mosolf

Lillian F Mosolf
POUR THE WINE

To my sister, Adeline Kemnitz Westfield, Wisconsin

'tis June. We're young and healthy.
It's our wedding, yours and mine.
Let all be happy with us.
Come, we'll pour the wine.

Today the Lord has blessed us
With a youngster, fair and fine.
Again, be happy for us.
Come, you pour the wine.

Time had its way. We were busy.
Golden days now on us shine.
We're getting old and feeble.
Let me pour the wine.

Now you're gone, and I'm alone.
The days have lost their shine.
Soon I'll come to join you.
But who will pour the wine?

Maria T Aleman
REACHING FAR
A dream is like a star,
For it is far.
Try to reach it with all your might,
And some day you will see the light.
With no doubt if you do come crying,
Keep on trying.
If the road is rough,
And gets tough,
Remember not to frown.
For when you reach far,
You are a star.

Wilma R Cole
JESSE
He is a light in the sky of weariness
A breath of fresh air in my life.
I watch him grow and grow each day.
His world enlarges by the hour.
With his quest to know
And to know "why."
Each discovery must be explained
With words he understands.
I am happy in the quest
Of each journey he makes
Into the unknown.

Linda Moles Parker
LOOKING BACK

In loving memory to my dad William Harvey, also to mom Beatrice who's always there for me.

The earth was brown, the trees were tall, the picnic tables could feed them all . . .
The lake was filled with colored canoes, the children played without their shoes . . .
How we enjoyed the tall elm trees, on summer days a silent breeze . . .
As the sun all too quickly faded away, we knew we could picnic another day . . .
Those unending days are forever since gone, the rustling of leaves, the childrens sweet song . . .
The world keeps on changing in so many ways, the memory still lingers of those summer days . . .
So when my children say to me, "Picnics are fun mom, come along, you'll see!"
I'll tell them I know, then take them to a spot, where a lonely old elm, sits on a vacant lot . . .

Peggy Start
THE GRAND FINALE
Heaven's waiting for the grand finale,
When the symphony of life will be over,
When the dancers will have danced their last,
And life is no longer a blast,
When the musicians will take up their harps,
For a symphony of heavenly music,
The curtains will come down on the actors,
Then the heavens will be filled with His glory,
As He gathers up all who are saved.

Liisa Liinamaa
SERENITY
The snow so softly falling
Tantalizingly is calling,
Telling me, compelling me
To leave the fireside
To stroll amongst the pines
And gaze at Winter's signs
Of Silence.

Jeffrey David Carmichael
DANCE IN THE HEAVENS
We'll dance in the heavens
We'll dance 'till we scream
We'll dance on fire
But it's all just a dream

Lenora Norte
LEILANI
When you were blooming in heaven
An angel came to you

It sang your wanted Leilani
Your mother is waiting for you

You bade good-bye to the garden
And down to earth you flow

Leilani, Leilani fare-well
They sang

And now your name is Grizel

Alex M Morris
VIEWPOINTS

To my family: my beautiful wife Joan, and to my wonderful children: Merideth, Cathy, Alex Jr. and Alan

When I was younger, much younger
And first learned of the speed of light,
Try as I might
The thought of it amazed me.

For suddenly the stars,
Which I had casually viewed in the night
As mere pin-points of light,
Became beacons from the past
Just as they were cast
Unimaginable millennia ago!

Now that I am older, much older
I'm still amazed at the speed of light,
But much less so
Than at the speed of life!
For suddenly the children
Who had filled our lives so full of love and happiness
Were grown and gone,
And the void their absence caused
Seemed to happen overnight,
Much, much faster
Than the speed of light!

Marcelle Condon
THE PUZZLE

To Tom. To Jeffrey, Jane, Gregory and Liz. To all lovers of truth and beauty.

Time, give me an answer.
What am I to do?
There is an answer;
Why must I guess at it?
I am too wise to be foolish,
Yet at times, nonsense
Is the only wine I have
To quiet this racing pulse.
Thinking, exhausts; sensing, saturates.
No work or play, friend or lover
Can fill you, Time, or me.
Still, for now, I thank the mysteries
Which, in some rare and grace-full moments
Wash through my veins
A hint of infinity, past reasoning.
Ah, then, Time, you are gone.
And there is only now,
For a completeness comes
Which makes me whole
And I am at home, on earth
And in the universe.

Barbara A Osborn
HONEY COMBED
In your sweetness
drawn nectar
love flows and feeds
nourishment
love grows
it understands and knows
a feeling, sense, intuition
natural, reaching
simple believing
of days that slid over the horizon
washed by setting suns
yellowed glow, parchment tattered

but, I have gathered
sweetness
honey combed
and stored
to make it through the lonely night
'till new nectar is discovered
fresh food on which to feed
with you to fill my need . . .
and you to fill my need.

Constance L Perry
MISTAKEN SILENCE
As the sun began to set,
And darkness fell upon the land,
I felt a scream, a silent scream.
Of the sick, the poor, the lonely.
All of those, that for reasons unknown,
Could not scream,
Cried out in silence.
There are so many who do not understand
That which they cannot see, cannot hear.
And therefore,
Those who cannot scream,
Are left to die.

Ruth A Baker
THE EAGLE AND THE DOVE
When he calls me,
I quickly fly back to the nest,
To go with him beyond this world.

On the journey,
The elements begin to change,
And then we reach our secret place.

In the shadows,
We bask in the sunshine of love,
As he spreads his wings to cover me.

In the stillness,
A raging storm makes our spirit one,
As we soar above the mountain tops.

In moonless skies,
We are bathed in moonglow as we descend,
And return to the nest for quiet rest.

He is the Eagle,
I am the Dove.

Charles Capps
UNFULFILLED LOVE
Is there such an awful thing;
Great love to make any heart sing.
Yet, so far away from our touch
To pine away from one as such.

I must press on and do my part;
To cradle this love, deep in my heart.
I want it close and to feel it burn,
And be thankful through eternity, for this love's return.

But, if I fail to recover, at any cost
This wonderful love that seems to be lost,
I'll pay the price of memory's curse
And lose the melody of true love's verse.

The pain and loneliness in this love's wake
A most settled heart will easily shake.
Disturbing the thoughts of night and day
Only from memory can the heart sway.

If this love cannot bloom again,
Hearts will long for what might have been.
The joy and peace will soon disappear
For unfulfilled love that was so near.

Lillian E Kretschmer
RESPONSE

To my Son, Ellis. And to his Wife, Doris

Not gold nor the grandeur of architecture can inspire.
The work of man's hands can ne'er fill the soul's desire.
The touch on the cheek of an infant so weak,
Is one of life's treasures for which we seek.

The soul responds to sympathy's balm,
To the beauties of nature, so serene and calm.
The song of the humblest bird housed snugly in a tree,
Finds response in the soul of the poet and thee.

Not the crown of a king,
Nor his scepter, can bring
A thrill to the heart strings of you or me.
For the heart's attuned to nature's simplicity.

Response is the awakening of our life's inner realm,
To the ideals of life and visions cast on life's film;
The joy and pain in living and trying to reach our goal,
These are the things that find response in the human soul.

Raymond A Beighley

Raymond A Beighley
A LITTLE HELP

If a bit of wit can bring a smile
  to a saddened face today,
or a little help with a heavy load
  send some traveler on his way;

then who shall reap the biggest gain,
  the giver or givee?
If I were the one who did the good,
  the big gainer would be me.

For nothing you will ever do
  can satisfy as much,
as helping others when their need is great,
  let them use you for a crutch.

The effort you make is forgotten soon,
  but staying with you forever,
will be a grateful smile, or a friendly wave;
  HUGE rewards for small endeavor.

Janet Lynn Compton
THE GREATEST OF THESE IS LOVE

Dedicated To: My Husband, James Lee Compton.

Today I sat alone at my window
And I thought that I would close my heart to love
But there upon the branches of the willow
I saw a rare and precious Dove.

It seemed as though God spoke from heaven
He said "Your heart must always care"!!
Put all the hurt aside and love another
Then trust me for the fruit that it will bear.

But Lord, I feel so sad and lonely,
Like no one cares for me at all.
He said, "Lo, I am with you always,
If only you will call".

So as I sat alone at my window
I looked upon a golden Daffodil
I knew that love would be rekindled someway . . .
And in the quietness the Lord was still.

Christine Madrid
MYSTERY MAN

The Mystery Man
haunts my dreams
making me want him,
making me reach
into the midst of fantasy.
He knows what I want,
he can read my mind,
planting there a seed
rich with desire.

The Mystery Man
wants me now,
he's calling to me
but I don't know how
  to reach him
because I want him too
I'm searching for him in the night,
I thought I saw him
my lover in white.

The Mystery Man
calls no more.
He has what he wants
he has closed the door
  to the reality
I lived to fight.
Now all I have is
my lover in white.

Lois Jean Lucas-Cameron
WHAT HATH KNOWN

Winter fades away
  The grass grows green
A new light of day
  Ah, that I have seen

Time will change
  The sun will shine
Indeed the future is of range
  For the seasons come as the flow of the Rhine

Spring hath come
  Summer is also near
The animals will be nesting up to a sun
  And the bird songs bring to us a bit of cheer

Couples down by the beach
  Children playing in the sand
The clouds so high, all out of reach
  As cupid clutches couples hand in hand

Ah, yes, the world is of many thoughts
  The hustle and the bustle of the city streets
But we have struggled and we have fought
  For something worth while and that we must meet

Sylvia Pauline Neal
ENCOURAGEMENT

When the way seems dark & dreary
  And you know not where to go
The pain inside gets heavy
  And each day seems to grow

Everywhere you seem to go
  Or what you seem to do
There's a great big wall in front of you
  That you can't tunnel through

Always remember it's darkest
  Just before the dawn
That the sun is always shining
  Though dark clouds keep coming on
That even though His face is dim
  His foot prints are real plain
He's walked the road before you
  And He's with you in your pain

So have faith
  Look up
    Keep rejoicing
And thank Him for each test
  For He's our loving Father
And He always Knows what's best

Barrett Schley
UNTITLED

To: Bikila, Shacara, and Mom

What is a feeling destined to overcome your mind,
With selfishness and egotistical thought;

The ultimate reality that sometimes seems unreal,
But if if weren't real it could not be bought;

Often times perpetual,
This feeling I submit;

Flourishing naturally, the past,
We wish not to admit;

Making you tread progressively,
The footsteps of your brother;

If only because of the fact,
That you share the same mother;

Edifying and protecting,
Each and every offspring;

Not just for the mere fact;
Of you possessing a marriage ring;

Borrowing from the earth, things of value,
That never has to be repaid;

Never stopping to think about it,
Because we know it's all what God has made?

LOVE IS.

Mary Zebatto
HER NAME WAS BERTHA

her name was Bertha
a lady of time
with too many hours
too much on her mind

in her heart she felt anger
but too helpless to move
she couldn't help feeling bitter
she couldn't fight just to lose

i've heard ships have their cargos
filled with diamonds and gold
and rich men grow richer
while poor men grow old
but i watched her grow lonely
in her sorrow and pain
til finally her body
gave way to the rain
why did she live
if just to remain
a woman so beaten
and alone

Rebecca L Soderstrom
SOMEDAY

To my children and their father, with love that will never end.

Someday my friend,
  Someday all our happiness will begin.
Someday my friend,
  Someday everything will be done.
Someday my love,
  Someday our love will be the same.
Someday my love,
  Someday our love will never end.

But when is someday?
When will someday come?
It must be a perfect day to have waited for so long.

Sometimes I feel someday is just a dream,
  A dream that hasn't awakened.
Sometimes I feel someday is a promise,
  A promise that was made to be broken.
How much longer can we wait,
  or is it already too late.

Tami Kane
LIFE

This poem is dedicated to several of my closest, oldest, and dearest friends—K.D.M., M.A.D., K.L.S., E.G.

When we are young,
Life has just begun.
We laugh, we play—
Until life starts slipping away.
And in our elder age we pray,
Life would be a little longer for it has only been a day.

Gladys A Clifton
THESE ASH-TREE STARS MY RICHES

To daughters Merna and Deborah, poetry in the flesh, art that pleases the mind, I dedicate this poem.

My prairie stars, like hidden diamonds, set lone
And far away; these ash-tree stars my riches.
Here I must remain, where ash leaves shimmer
And flash broadside to the sun. Not native to the wealth this leafy valley offers,
I see no riches to compare with prairies
I have lost, with valleys, old and treeless,
And round-girt with hills of strength so strong
They would have held me to my latest days
Securely as the sage-brush holds to earth.
Meanwhile, from hiding-places ten years deep,
While morning's sun still lends to day its spring,
A golden sunset opens into view,
And all that dreamy West is mind again.

These ash-trees stars bring me their morning joy,
But from far Western skies, the sun has gone,
And my prairie stars are left alone, to guard
The approaching Night, villainous wooer of Day,
Who defies their vigil with his black countenance;
Hopeful stars! It is an endless drama,
And they are rich who attend its moving scene.

My prairie stars, like hidden diamonds, set lone
And far away; these ash-tree stars my riches.

Such rarities from prairie mines were joy
to Redmen in wide Sun-Dance Valley.

Bright-shirted horsemen of the Rocky Boy
Made camp, a half-mile circle, of white tents and lodges. White Sky, their old chief, sang prayer
And lit his pipe for offering to the sun,
As in a brown ravine they felled a tree,
A lonely poplar, for the sacred lodge-pole;
They came with formal, triumphant pace to raise it,
They came with singing, foliage-decked with branches,
Just as, dimly, on the far horizon,
Rose, sun-silhouetted, the Sweet Grass Mountains.
And the smoke from sunset fires upreared and lingered,
Finely veil-like, over their preparation.
So even while they danced, the lodge-pole stood
Against the evening sun, a stark reminder
for the gods, until Old White Sky traveled on
To rest among the Sand Hills.

Naomi Berry
NATURES BEAUTY

I look around at nature
The flowers, mountains, and trees
I know without a doubt on earth
A Great God made all these
The birds the bees and butterflies
Each creature great or small
He made them all to be enjoyed
Including the waterfalls

The Beautiful elements of our world
The Moon the Stars and Air
The Sun to keep our earth warm
There's surely a God up there
Blue skies above, cool water flowing
Beautiful Ocean Shores
There's so much beauty to enjoy
To love admire and adore

Jay D "Dutch" Bedell
MONARCH

To Mary O'Moran Bedell and Ann Camaria (Cuffin) Naputi, both of Monterey County, California. This poem won the Golden Poet Award for 1989. Rest in peace, Annie. May God love you both forever. Amen. I love you.

A monarch butterfly—orange, black, and majestic—
Sits perched in a Monterey pine tree
Overlooking the calm waters of Monterey Bay.
Resting after its long journey
from the mountains of Mexico,
It is surrounded by thousands of its own kind,
All awaiting a breath of life
brought by the warm sunshine.
Spreading its delicate wings,
The monarch catches the up-draft
of a light ocean breeze,
And sails off into the clear sky.
Sunlight reflects from the surface of its wings,
Giving them a jewel-like quality.
Now it is joined by hundreds of its fellows,
Creating an image more beautiful
than any work of man's hands,
A tapestry woven from a thousand living wings,
Each pair pulsating with natural color.
Moving slowly, they pass gracefully overhead
Before returning to the safety of the pines.

Philip A Adams
A GENTLE INFLUENCE

To my dear friend Sandra Benjamin, a friend for life

A fragrance I detect! I recognize that smell!
Friendship you say? How familiar you seem!
Mistaken it would be were it not for love to tell.
My once lost feelings surely do beam.
For your gentle influence I desire not to shun.
For you my dear may my feelings never subside.
Time's long I've been a conditioned one.
A mind's state I've safely contemplated to abide
For I'm forever today's night.
And you, forever tomorrow's day.
Our friendship governs a love's passion which might.
An inevitable which happened anyway.
A resemblance of thee, an appearance I see.
Can reflections possibly become a door's key?

Debi Brown
HEART AND HEART IN HAND

Dedicated to the people of the world.

heart and
heart in hand,
lead me through this broken land
of hatred and war.
love is never seen
when it's brother against brother.

Dorothy Francis
GOD'S GARDEN

In memory to my loving Husband, Ben who is now a flower in God's Garden.

God's eternal garden blooming with flowers
In beauty and splendor rare,
The Master, the Great Gardener
Watched o'er them with tenderest care.

God looked on that fair garden
While angels lingered near,
"Go, find and bring a blossom
Another is needed here."

They hastened to do his bidding
They sought until one was found,
Its' fragrance rare and sweet perfume
Around it did abound.
They plucked it, oh so gently
From earth toward Heaven soared,
With joy to the Father gave it
To be cherished and adored.

Throughout all eternity
It will bloom and never fade,
In that Garden with God's flowers
Forever in God's glory arrayed.

Vincent E Conroy
WALK WITH ME

Talk and walk softly with me.
Flow down the river of life to the sea.
Your tender and sensitive touch has me enriched; as the river caresses and nurtures its banks.
Fill me as the river meets and fills the sea.
I will hold all you bring.
For, as the sea rises to the clouds and rains upon the earth and begins anew;
I will give more than I have and still find more.
Fear not your free spirit, the sea cannot contain.

Mary B O'Neill
REVERIE

To my beloved grandchildren . . . Susan, George, and Amy Heisel

An hour spent in reverie
With my unseen Guest
Recalling some precious fleeting moments
When He touched me.

The little girl who said from her dying bed,
"Nurse, see the beautiful bird."
That was her last word.
In that moment, Christ you touched me.

When a little child so sweet, so fair, so mild
Clung to me along the path from Calvary,
Looked up at me and said, "Jesus loves you very much," and I replied,
"He loves you too,"
Again you touched me.

When a tiny tot in Mexico City
Begged for bread and not for pity
Stars shone in her eyes,
In that disguise of poverty,
You touched me.

The little boy at Mass with the dark skin
And tight curly hair
Approached me with a radiant smile
To shake my hand with such joy, that wee little boy!
In that moment,
Christ you touched me.

Fred Sager R Ph
MY GRADUATION DAY

Stacey Ann Springman on her graduation day year of May, 24, 1978

Graduation day is here, a day for us to pass.
It means when we go back to school, we'll be in another class.
It seemed just like a life time, these past eight years of school.
I hope that the rest of my school days, I'll be smart and keep my cool.

The years ahead will be tougher, and I'll try to pass them all.
My summer vacation will fly right by, and it's back to school this fall.
I'll miss some of the things I did, in the years that have gone by.
And I want to pass each year that comes, for I'll try and try and try.

My graduation day will be pleasant,
I'll be dressed up like a queen
And when I receive my diploma, on T.V. I would like to be seen.
The years gone by seemed a struggle, but that's one thing all must do.
I hope that God will give me strength, to see the next years through.

Vincent P Zarrillo
SAINT

To Melinda, my loving wife—who has inspired me in poetry, I love you;, "POPMAN"

People's ideas are different of a saint,
some are pictured in the heavens,
others on canvas in paint.
Some carved and marveled in stone,
prayed to once or twice then—left alone.
Others think of good do-ers to fit the tee,
if only they would say "IT COULD BE ME".
If everyone would try to turn the other cheek,
we would not be in the valleys—but remain on the peak.
If we all just gave it a try,
instead of always ready to deny,
then to be a saint in all of our eyes,
would not be such a big surprise.

So try to remember these words of advice,
to stay on the peaks is very nice.
But when the valleys come,
don't be in despair,
you won't get out without being aware.
Try and try what you believe,
visions of a saint aren't hard to achieve

Alice Shamogochian
DO YOU REALLY HAVE TO SEE TO BELIEVE?

To my dearly loved sister, Vasquohe

Do we really have to see to believe?
Can't we expect the best to be?
My days flow better whenever I know
That the Maker of the tree,
Has love and hope for me.

Alyce Haring
GROWING UP

To Miranda

Slow down little girl, don't grow up so fast.
Don't be in a hurry to make this your past.
It happens all too soon, when you begin to bloom from a little girl to a woman of the world.

When you were only three I wondered what you would grow up to be.
Now suddenly you're ten and you tell me of your plans and dreams of someday when;
someday when you're all grown up.

Still you reach out for my hand and we walk together hand in hand.
You have so many questions I can not answer.
There's so many things you don't understand.

You squeeze my hand and tell me
about your day.
And I wish it could always be this
way.
But because I love you so: I'll let go
and let you grow.

Bethy Coleman
FOLLOW

For Anyone who has ever been told "Turn that noise down!" and all of those from which heartfelt music flows.

The sound reminds me of a dream
where everything turns around
You'd have to see to survive
You'd have to learn to die
to die in peace

All the time I'm laughing
I'm just lost inside the dream
Perhaps I'll decide
Perhaps I'll die

Try the smile to forget
what you really want
want to learn—learn to die
you're the music—you the dream

The chance to love
To learn—to live free
to follow the music
To follow the dream

Margaret Walters Magee

Margaret Walters Magee
ASHES OF ROSES

In memory of a beloved first cousin; Webber Guillory, who God called to be with him at the early age of nineteen. I loved him truly.

Our love was once a bright red rose;
With sparkling drops of morning
dew,
So fresh and sweet, no one could
know,
The happy, happy love of you!
Red red rose, why did you fade
Into ashes of roses with shadows
grey?
Cold winter came, but don't you
know?
This too, will pass to a golden day.
Ashes of roses, with shadows grey.
Will you bloom again on a summer
day?
Down by the shore of shimmering
sand
In the mystic dream of stardust land
Shimmer, shimmer, sparkling sand
By the blue green sea of stardust
land?
Our love will bloom again someday
To never, never fade away
Into ashes of roses with shadows
grey.

Janel Akiyama
YOU WERE THERE

You were always there.
Remember the day he asked me to
the dance?
Remember how you taught me to
keep that memory?
Remember the day he came to me,
and broke me with his words?
You were there, and I thank you.
You can see the good parts in life,
the important parts, the happy
parts.
We were always together,
Thinking the same thoughts,
Building the same dreams.
Why can I not be like you?
Why have we grown apart?
Why? Always why.
You, I can talk to; you, I can trust.
May I always be there for you,
after the whys have taken their
toll,
To give back all you have given to
me.

Joan Marie Wagner
NOT IN HIS SOUL

A gal gets married to a guy.
One on whom she's kept an eye
Though all the elders say "please
wait"
She's very anxious to set the date.

Her reasons are many, on that do rely
He's a special person and her kind of
guy
He dances divinely and has a good
face
He's very ambitious and keeps up a
pace

So down the isle this gal does trod
Wanting this guy who makes her feel
"mod"
She's a beautiful gal, especially in
white
The wedding's fantastic, "Just out of
sight"

To her surprise, he has the muscles
to fish
But he can't lift a trash can or empty
a dish
He always has energy for the "nighty
night roll"
But he won't do the "house things"
cause it's "not in his soul"

Jean D Moore
DAFFODILS

I love the happy daffodils,
Their smiling faces shine,
Each one sings a song to me,
Each one has a rhyme;
Of joy and gladness
love and tears
humility
and
pride,
I long to see the daffodils,
To see their face in mine.

Eilene A Burris
FLEETING SEASONS

The rains arrive and bring us spring
With flowers that bloom and birds
that sing.
The grass turns green and leaves
uncoil
As farmers plow and plant the soil.

The gentle breezes softly blow
Across the wheat fields, all aglow
With golden hues from summer sun.
We think of work; we think of fun.

Those chilly winds will soon arrive.
The empty nests, the quiet hives
Will tell us of the autumn scene
When colored leaves replace the
green.

Before the fire, burning low,
We sit and watch the falling snow.
It blankets all the earth tonight;
Radiant diamonds in the full
moonlight.

Thus the seasons arrive and leave.
Each year they're shorter, I believe.
They bring me beauty, ecstasy.
The more I see, the more I see.

Jason Alan Kelly
COWS CANNOT BE DUCKS

This is dedicated to Peggy who is not unlike the wind in that she is always felt but never seen.

The pain in my heart grows
As does the pain in my toes,
When a two-ton brick is dropped on
my nose.
Such is the way of love
To cows as to ducks
To me as to you.
A never ending tale of could this be
true?
To love alone is to love a stone.
I ask you, . . . When do the cows
come home?
I ask you, . . . When does our love
come home?
You say it cannot 'cause cows can't
be ducks.
Quack!
I say cows can be ducks.
The pain in my toes grows old
As you unload every stone you own
Off my nose.
To you as to me can be
As leaves on a tree.
Because cows can be ducks as you
can see.
Quack!
Quack!!
Quack!!!
Oh, how I love thee.

Wanda Partain
PERFECT LOVE

Dedicated to Jennifer and Ron

We fell in love last summer
It was our first romance

Our hearts were young and full of
love
But we didn't have a chance

We thought our love was perfect
In every single way

But others knew much more than we
That it wasn't here to stay

So now I cry each day and night
And pray to God above

That someday he'll come back to me
And we'll have perfect love

Helen N Ness
WELCOME, DAY

Lovingly dedicated to my dear friend, Joy Lane Jensen.

Dawn slowly rolls back the curtain
of darkness;
Pale gold tinges the eastern horizon.
The waning moon has transversed
the heavens
Slowly penetrating the night of other
regions.

Birds twitter restlessly in their nests
Awaiting their call to announce the
newborn day.
City lights grow dim as a deepening
gold streaks the sky
Reflecting the warmth and brightness
of the advancing sun.

A motor roars; a distant train warns
of its approach;
Early risers are astir and grateful
hearts prepare to welcome the day.

Slowly the golden sun peeps over the
eastern hills,
The warmth of its rays reaching out
over the land
Beckoning to the tiny drops of dew
set with myriads of diamonds,
And bathing the countryside with the
glow and beauty of sunshine.

Buttercups, daffodils, and pansies all
Lift their happy faces to catch the
early morning rays.
From treetops, fenceposts, and fields
come melodious refrains
As the feathered friends proclaim
their joy of another glorious day.

Oh, day of sunshine! Oh, day of
beauty! Oh, day of joy!
I have waited for you—I need you—
I welcome you!

F Joe Lehner
FATHERS

To my wonderful wife, Debbie, terrific sons, Adam and Chris, and special daughter, June.

"Good day to you sir; good day my
friend
Would you have a spare dime to
lend?"

"As you can see dear sir, my luck is
down,
But my reason for begging is very
sound.
Would you please lend, a dime, or
even a cent?
I assure you sir, unwisely, it sha'nt
be spent."

"A dime I will give you, and a dollar
more,
If you answer me this. How you
became so poor?
I knew you once, so happy and gay,
Answer me this: what made you this
way?"

"I shall answer you so; my wealth
for my child.
My dear little girl, so meek and so
mild.
But her race for life is nearly run.
Her plea for salvation is almost
won."

"I've nearly enough, for a candle so
bright,
For by her bed, it shall burn tonight.
My love and the light, shall be her
guide,
To bring her back, to her fathers
side."

With tears in my eyes, of a tale so

sad,
I gave him the money, all that I had.
But I knew that today. I would be
home very soon,
To hug my own daughter, my
daughter named June.

Danette L Stowers
FAITH

This dedication is made to my mom, for her undying love and "FAITH" in me.

As she stands on the bus stop
impatient and scared
Thoughts of her life leave her in
tears
She tries to be brave and so hard to
cope
Her resistance breaks, she's left with
no hope

As she walks down the midnight
streets
Her mind's alert to movement and
creaks
Her feet move quickly, her heart
beats fast
Then her mind becomes clouded
with thoughts of the past

Lying in bed with fear in her eyes
She prays to GOD for a fulfilling life
The following day she proceeds with
faith
Conquering the obstacles hindering
her way

Sandra Lenci Davis
YES I AM
Am I, this bloated shell
and fearful being

Caught in the hell
of my ego's seeing, or

Am I, this ethereal wonder
part of God's love

And the lightning and thunder
of all that is and always will be?

Yes, I am.

Elisa Gottlieb
WILL THEE

In memory of my grandmother, Edna Krassek, who without question made me realize that true love and beauty stem from one's soul.

Will thee still love me when I am old
and withered,
When physical beauty is not?

Will thee still need me as I need
thee,
Even when I have forgot?

Will thee still want me at the end of
my days,
Even if I am different in my
ways?

Will thee still care even after I am
gone,
Forever as the birth of a new
dawn?

Lonnie Honeycutt
SONG OF LIGHT
Am I looking to put my burdens
down;
Am I looking for the path that's
light;
Am I looking for the easy way;
Am I looking for things that are
right?

Am I looking for a star for my ego;
Am I looking for a heaven for my
soul;
Am I looking for my creator;
Am I looking for a way to go?

I am looking for something;
I am of good intent;
I am a thought that is changing;
I am a life not yet spent.

I have abounding potential;
I have a song through my soul;
I have a mind of wonder;
I have a joy I don't yet know.

Camelia A Markham
SWIZZLE STICKS AND TIME
Time doesn't shuffle so slowly,
Or drag its feet day to day.
When you have swizzle sticks
and glasses
And liquid where sorrow can
play.
When your supply of faith grows
meager,
And your vision dimmed by fears,
Your swizzle stick's short as
your temper,
Your drink's as wet as your
tears.
Do you get through the predawn
hours
As restful as children in bed.
Or spill your cares around you,
And settle for dreams instead.

Clarence Christy
A THOUGHT

To Rosie, Holly, Dawn, Brenda, Maria, Elizabeth, Sandy, Steve, Augusta, Mom, Dad & Terrence. Thanks for all your support. Also to Bono & U2 for your motivation & inspiration. U2

All she says she wants
Is for me to love her forever
But that may not be true
For that is only a thought
And if I say I will
Then only time will tell the truth
And if I say I will
I could be called a liar
Then to find the truth I must lie
Or I must have to hurt her
I think I rather lie
than to feel the pain of her heart
And so I say to her
I will love you forever
And she says "You're a liar"
Should I laugh or
Should I cry?

W John Williamson
STEPTALK: ON COPING WITH ANGER

To Chris, my stepson

My son, you need to know I do love
you
although you've said that's hard for
you to see.
I'd like for you to know my love's as
true
as any love of dad for son could ever
be.

You say you're angry at the world, I
know.
You're justified, of course—don't
get me wrong.
But someday you'll decide to let that
anger go
so you'll be set to sing a happier,
brighter, and more cheerful song.

My son, my son, remember when
you're mad,
please talk it through with me, your
loving dad.
I'll be listening when your anger
comes in all its fury
but we'll see it through till it is
passed
because, my son, I know you're
strong, tough, smart, and built to last.

So, remember, then, my son, when
you feel mad,
please share your grief with me, a
loving dad.
Nothing's wrong with crying in your
grief—
I know you only want relief;
I understand your angry spirit's
rage—
that's why I request you talk your
anger through—
you're old enough and at an age
to know that's what grown men and
growing boys must do.

Deana Burnett
A BROKEN BOTTLE

To Richard: Forever friendship and love

Here stands a bottle;
standing tall, but alone.

It stands on a table,
with contents inside
and emptiness surrounding.

Waiting patiently
for a gentle hand,
to hold this bottle
and release what's inside.

Until one single moment . . .
someone lifts it
and the heart of this bottle rises
when he tempts to open it
and take what's inside.

But suddenly
the stranger leaves,
while opening the window.

The wind blows in
as the bottle rocks
back and forth
and finally falling over . . .

A broken bottle.

Christine Reece
AN EMPTY NEST

Dedicated to my husband, Wheeler, a cattle-rancher, and our children, Duane, Pat and Kay, and to the fifty, happy years of our growing-up together.

We're living in AN EMPTY NEST;
it's as quiet as can be.
'Twas HOME to our cherubs; they
were lively and carefree!

Our days are uneventful; they're not
like they used to be.
Seems there's something missing; I
wonder what it can be.

We hear no sick kid's whimper in
the darkness, late at night;
Or no baby's laughter, like when
steps were made just right!

I have no cookies baking, like when
kids ate half the dough,
On the cold and rainy mornings, in
winter-time, long ago!

There's no homework at night-time,
no school-kids' good-bye!
We can't get used to their being
gone, no matter how we try.

Our kids grew-up long ago; they
have lives of their own.
It seems that we see them less and
less, as time goes on!

The grand-kids are young adults,
busy with jobs and such;
Their visits or phone calls will
always mean so much!

Families have an invisible bond, that
never really ends;
Though each goes his own way, they
are life-long friends!

After 50 years, the RANCH is quiet;
it's HOME for only two;
Just to keep things going, we still
have plenty work to do!

Having reached our golden years, we
ask for nothing more;
Now, we're enjoying the harvest of
our many years, before!

Mickey Parker-Ziegenbein
LIFE'S GAMBLE
People say that life's a gamble
we take every day,
And you must play it—or you die
there's just no other way;
Someone may play for higher stakes
and take a bigger chance—
While others leave it up to luck
or just to happenstance.

Now in the eyes of some you read
such grim reality—
That you must know for them the
game
has facets we can't see;
But there are those who play for fun
not heeding life's command—
For they have come to realize
fate deals the final hand.

Sherry Martin
THE LESSON
Merely from living day to day,
She found out what paupers, kings,
saints, and countless lads and
maidens, gay
Had found out before about the
nature of things:
That joy and love must early end,
Innocence wither like a sun-baked
rose,
Time gives wounds that none can
mend,
Enmity and malice for friendship
pose.
And seeing also that hope was futile
Her heart and soul to herself, she
kept.
And when the scorned world became
too brutal,
She retreated to her ivory tower, and
wept.
Such tears as these were well-known
to Eve,
Who oft for her lost innocence would
grieve.

Mary D Raiz
THIS IS THE TIME FOR VALENTINE'S DAY

In Dedication to George H.

This is the time for Valentine's Day
A feeling of love for all, in the air
My feelings are of you, dear
With sad thoughts of us far apart

Yet deep within me, a silent hope springs
Saying all is not lost
There shall be answers, wait I must
The beautiful image of you appears in my mind
And I feel happy once more
There may be a dream that shall come true
Only patience & time will tell
For I truly love you and this you must know
As I wait for the answers in my heart
Happy Valentine, my love, as I keep sweet thoughts of you
And say a small prayer for you
"Dear God, let him keep me in his heart
Let him think of me as much as I do him
Let him know how much I love him and wait for his return"
As I silently end this prayer "Amen"

Eleanore Knoff

THE NEW BEGINNING

This poem is dedicated to my beloved sweetheart and best friend, Robert Niven Jr.

Do you feel a sudden change
In a world so physically striking
Animal and Man
No longer deciding
Who's to say what's right or wrong
Listen and let your eyes wander
Explore end enjoy for mysteries are still untold
Another miracle, another dream come true
Where is the atmosphere you once knew
What happened, Did it all die?
You fool, have you forgotten
It's neverending Love and Life
The Power and the Glory
My God, the time has arrived

Michael J Linden

BE EVER WATCHFUL OF YOUR HEART

Be ever watchful of your heart,
 for it holds your deepest
 thoughts and feelings.

Leave its door ajar,
 but open it ever so slowly.

Only a select few will ever enter
 in a lifetime. But you must
 leave the door ajar.

Only fear can lock the door—
 Oh how slowly we forget the
 past.

Allowing it to lock too long
 and your heart grows cold.

No matter what passes,
 Remember to leave the door
 ajar.

Just Plain Aggie

HE'S MORE

He's taller than any mountain, tree or tower
He's mightier than a sword, He is All Power
He's brighter than a day filled full of sunshine
He's more golden than the moon, at harvest time

He's sweeter than any nectar in a honey tree
He's more lovely than any flower could ever be
He's more refreshing than crystal water in a mountain lake
He's more rewarding than any prize you could ever take
He has more love than anyone you'll ever know
He is purer than the newly fallen snow
He's more vast than the sea, from bay to bay
He is Life to you and me, from day to day

He's more merciful than any judge could ever be
He is sacrifice in place of you and me
He is everything that we will ever need
He bled more for us than anyone could bleed

He's more joyful than any tune that you could write
He glows brighter than all the stars you see at night
He's more satisfying than anything that pleases
Now, WHO ELSE could HE be, but CHRIST JESUS

N May Witten

WIND

There is a belligerent violence in the temper of the wind
When fierce tornadic blasts he chooses to send.
He vents his heated anger on man, sea and land.
He leaves behind a devastated band
Of broken trees, homes and scattered debris
Wherever his Hounds of Destruction choose to be.

But 'tis of his gentler nature that I wish to pen these lines;
Of the breeze that cools the fevered brow
In all places, temps and climes.
His zephyrs set the golden wheat a-waving
A picture no artist can contrive.
They set the supple trees a-swaying all day
And help them "lift their leafy arms to pray."[1]

[1]*From Trees by Joyce Kilmer*

Linda D Whaley

"MOMMY, TELL ME WHY"

This poem is dedicated to Preston, my beautiful gift of life. Love, Mom.

I laid my little boy down to sleep last night,
And he asked me a question,
"Mommy, tell me why."
I looked at his big brown eyes, with tears flowing in mine
And I held his little hand and thought, now must be the time
"Oh, Lord, can you tell me where to begin;
Can you give me the right words I need to say to him"
He looked at me again to answer his question, "Why?"
And I knew I could be truthful and tell him no lie
"Sweetheart, you came into this world not knowing the troubles you would hold
And time will stand still no longer, you're old enough to be told
I've waited for a day for you not to take medicine to live
And to your question "Why," my dear, I'll answer you the best I can
You know I've asked that same old question to our Lord above
And the answer He has given me is, you're a very special gift of love
You see, you have shown me what love can really mean
Just watching you and caring for you has been reason enough for me
Now remember our little talk we've had, when you ask this question "Why?"
Only God has his reasons when creating precious life.

James R Oxley

James R Oxley

YONDER HILL

To My wife, Luella, children, Karen, Terry, Diana and their families.

Let me trudge my way up yonder hill
Look again at the river down below.
Swift currents packed so full of passing time.
Let the white water again appear to me,
Exuberant youth in ecstasy.
Those rocks and falls still here today,
But yet a part of yesterday.
I will follow the path tho hard it be.
Rough going, steep turns, brambles that rip and tear.
I will never complain but hasten my steps,
My hope again this sight to see.
A breath of life's essence in rapid flight.
Soft white clouds of dreams to guide the flow.
Let me gambol up that hill once more.
No not to trample the flowers there,
Nor disturb nature's way, her garden plan.
But rest my eyes this priceless gift to see,
And stand in awe at the unveiling,
Time, space, and equality.
Let me climb that hill and survey,
While time has meted me another day.
I will be careful where my footsteps fall.
Along the way guide posts wait for me.
A careless step, then a clouded picture,
And to me ignominy.
Now relentless river of passing time,
Fleeting moments pressing in your wake.
Let me set aside a daily chore.
Give me time to climb that hill once more.

Thia P Kirkland

ALONE IN THE DARK

Alone in the dark, Tears in my eyes
The eclipse of my heart darkens the skies
The petals of the flowers no longer bloom
Died in the fury of hatred and gloom
The phoenix from the flame shall never rise
Her ashes blown away in the whirlwind of lies
A love once felt so strong, so bold
Now lies in ruin, rotting in the cold.

Robert Meneray

TO BE READ TWICE

I stood by when they took you away
 and promised green pastures—
 peace this day.

I stood by, then in great pain
 as they reaped carnage from the
 train.

I stood by with hands to my ears
 while they raped and tortured
 all those years.

I stood by with my eyes in hand
 while they poisoned the body,
 the water, the land.

I stood by with lips that were sealed
 of their innocence, the
 hypocrites revealed.

I stood by, grim, white, sad, with others
 to learn it was us who destroyed
 our brothers.

What did I learn others might ask
 from all those years of wearing
 a mask?

Is it possible, I really gave a damn
 because I still remember
 Vietnam.

I stand by, too late again
 because my friend,

 I'm American.

Fred H Mitchell

MINUTES OF GOLD

This poem is dedicated to Elizabeth Mitchell, my wife, my life, and friend, You make marriage a joy. Semper Fidelis, Your Mitchell

Minutes of gold, minutes of gold
Oh what a life-time of minutes of gold

Precious hours, precious days,
holding her in every way
Oh how I love those minutes of gold

My minutes of gold are all filled with divine
Love from the morning and evening time

With her blue eyes shining and her red lips sighing
Oh how she fills my minutes of gold

My minutes of gold are as precious as can be
They're filled with happiness;

they're filled with glee

They come from a lady that gives me true life
That lady is Elizabeth, my sweet darling wife

Ronnie Nesslage
I HAD A LITTLE GOAT

This poem is for my dad, Kenneth. What I remember is all the love he gave to me.

I had a little goat
His name was Bill the Kid.
My dad got rid of him
Because of what he did.

Lynn E Maran
A FLOWER GROWS WILD, UNRESTRICTED . . . STRONG

A flower grows wild . . .
unrestricted . . .
strong . . .
Sure enough of its right to be
to stand alone under any tree
Wise enough to know
its time to blossom
and its time to retreat in the warmth of its soil . . .
Not afraid of its contrast with the garden,
But aware of its addition of color and beauty
Oh the glory and grace of the wildflower . . . .

Oh the beauty
and grace
of you . . .

Jonathan Krop
PRECIOUS GIFTS

The most precious gift is time—
All important yet meaning less;
Time is just like, just like a kiss;

Faces in clouds, look down from the sky—
Memories spring to life, inside my mind;

The most precious gift she has is love—
All important and fabulous;
Her love is just like, just like a kiss;

The clouds drift away, sunshine watercolourfalls
Upon my face;
Here I stand and look above;
Ghosts and shadows fade in the light of love.

Ron Carr
THE HOMELESS

I would like to dedicate this poem to Mary Lou, for her encouragement.

The Lord is my shepherd, I shall not want to see,
The eyes of hungry children, looking back at me,
The beaten spirits, and broken bodies, our brothers in the street,
We know they're there, but we see not, our eyes just never meet,
Our heroes from the wars, stand in line, at garbage cans,
A fate no one expected, that's only done, in foreign lands,
They stand together, at closed doors, on rainy, freezing nights,
What used to be infrequent, has become, familiar sights,
Every day they're there, some eyes filled with fear,
As we try to look away, with eyes, that show a tear,
What has happened to God's painting, strokes of love, and bliss?,
Who has taken up His brushes, who is painting, His canvas?,
Give us strength, Almighty Painter, help us see, and do, what's right,
We must help our fallen brother, and lift him to the healing light,
You showed us once, how to live, many years ago,
Perhaps it's time, for lesson two, it 's time for us to know,
What will happen, to planet Earth, if we ignore your love?,
Help us treat our fallen brother, as we would, an injured dove.

Rose Evans
I LOVE YOU JESUS

Oh I Love You Jesus!
You know that I do.
I Love you for knowing,
That some day I'd pull through.
Though the bad times and the hell I put everyone through.
Only you knew Jesus
That some day I would be whole once more.
Now I can hold my head up as I walk out the door.
You see I was an alcoholic.
And I didn't care, whether the sun rose, or set, the feeling just wasn't there
But now Dear Jesus, with your Love and help,
Yes, I can hold my head up
Just as I did before.

Faye M Denton
A TINY HERO

Just a tiny shred of grass,
perhaps once green and strong.
Brownish yellow now, and broken,
but still clinging with your tiny roots
to your battle scarred embankment.

Snow and ice, wind and rain, have besieged you,
tried to destroy you,
but still you hold fast.

Waiting for new reinforcements to come.

Gaye Follmer Deal
SONNET

The sun has risen many times before,
Ascending for our geocentric eyes,
Will doubtless rise when I am here no more,
And other egos, watching, will surmise
What good or evil comes with rising day.
The barren hills will still reach to the sea,
Rising from morning mist along the bay.
The hills will stand as staunchly without me,
And children on the shore will gather shells,
Eternally dazzled by diversity.
The constant ocean ebbs, and once more swells,
Leaves transient treasures by that same gravity
That writes the music of the turning spheres,
Singing through intergalactic space for ghostly ears.

Sol Roseman
A FOND FAREWELL

Let not the tears of your leaving
Detain you in any way
Go in good stead my friend
To better yourself this day.
Your cheerful countenance
And radiant smile
Will be remembered for
A long, long, while
So take your leave
Do not delay
Face up to new challenges
Whenever they come your way—
You will be missed by those
Left behind—
Because a friend like you
Is hard to find—

Carol Koehler Hebert
A LIGHT IN A WINDOW

In loving memory of my sister, Annie, who always kept a light in the window so her children could see their way home

It takes very little
To keep me close
To the One I love
And desire the most
Each smile a soft un-spoken word
That stirs my heart
As though I've heard
My name whispered in a prayer
Sometimes all you need to see
Is a light in a window
somewhere

James M Krook
MIND'S EYE CINEMA

Cold razor sharp eve of stillness
Serene—
Through vivid fragments of yesterday's image I weave—
Luminous is the moonlight's electric flowing stream—
An array of colors dance intricately—
The landscape surreal with sparks of crystalline—
The winter waves rigid, icy drifts so pristine—
With a sigh the sequence of freeze frames fade—The shadows contort, wandering silhouettes sway—
Reflections like a butterfly adrift in the night—Preserved forever in the Cinema of my mind's Eye—

Deana L Mason
ONLY 5 MORE DAYS

To the Wasatch High School Class of 1988

Only 5 more days
That is all.
Only 5 more days
Until next fall.

Only 5 more days
Then we're through.
Only 5 more days
Then we're through with you.

Only 5 more days
Then you'll see,
Only 5 more days
Till we're free.

Only 5 more days
Then no more.
Only 5 more days
Then we walk out the door.

Only 5 more days
Then it's the end of the show.
Then just think
Only one year to go.

Jeani Warne Dechter
INSOMNIA

This poem is dedicated to all the hard working women who juggle so much all day to find that their minds keep working at night.

Late in the night
you suddenly wake
Long before morning
you twist and quake

Into the silence
you begin to mumble
From restless dreams
you toss and tumble

As daylight threatens
you pray for sleep
Today will be l-o-n-g
you know it will creep

Darkness brings hope
you wearily retire
If tonight isn't better
you know you'll expire!

Rhoda Lee Baum

Rhoda Lee Baum
TALENT

To the "Baum Bunch"

If I could steal one talent
From way out there somewhere
It would have to be the love of God
That guides me everywhere!
It's creative talent so they say
That brings usefulness and cheer
So search now with all your heart
There's nothing to really fear!
For God is truly by your side
With your one life to live
To live is Christ and with all his Love
His talent you can give
Life is so full of treasures
If we stop to look around
With nimble finger at work or play
Hidden talent will soon abound!
Teamwork and talent go hand in hand
And spreads a special glow
For all the world to capture
The Love of God to show! !

Madge Abigail Winegar
WARS

To my husband, Lt. JG Winfield H. Winegar (USN/Ret) who served in World War II and Korea

In a world gone mad with greed and hate
Forced by men who must dictate
In a worn torn world where blood is shed
Help us dear Lord to use our head
Let our hearts stay big and our land stay free
That's why we're fighting for liberty
Dear Lord, help us stop it
There's so many dead
Give strength to our leaders
That by you they be led
Give courage to those who have lost someone dear
Please help them have faith
That You're standing so near
So lead us to victory, so we can demand
That peace e'er-abiding lay over the land

Dolores von Bieberstein
WISDOM
As I grow older day by day
I pray that God will light my way

For the dreams once cherished
and the loves once tried
No longer start a fire inside

The joy of friendship
means much more
Than all the adventures that came before

Life seems more simple
and much more fun
As I find I can walk and need not run

NOW there is time to
stop each day
And "smell the roses" along the way

This wisdom seems to come with time
As I grow older with a wiser mind

Ruby Meaders
ODE TO A STORM!
To the rumble of the thunder
And the flashing of the light!
To the dreariest, eeriest noises
That have ever filled the night!

To the splashing of the raindrops
And the pounding of the wind!
To the frail, bending treetops
As the storm-lord plays the fiend!

The night is dark, and torrents fall
Drenching all—as it wends its way
To the village down the valley
To continue its harmful play.

The Wind whistles as it batters and tears
The flapping shutters off their hinges
While the hungry, homeless beggar
Into a sheltering corner cringes.

The storm passes—as storms will.
And with the dawn, all is still!

Maxine E Martin
LOVE
What is love—who can define it?
Appearing unseen like a breeze.
Can it be sight, color or feeling?
To me, it is all of these.
Gentle as a kitten sleeping.
Fragile as a tiny fly.
Strong as the breeze that stirs the ocean.
Illusive as the night owl's cry.
I hear it in the soft murmur
Of a mother's lullaby.

I see it in the flutter of a
Hummingbird winging by.
You can feel it in the handclasp
Of a friend throughout the years.
You will know its strength and beauty
At a time of heartbreak and tears.
This day it found me coming close
And trustingly.
Little kitten's paws in velvet mittens
Signing love notes on my knee.

Don Dwyer
THE KING IS EMPEROR THE QUEEN HIS WIFE

To Baruca—Know from this poem that more will be written about you in the times to come.

Let it be written, let it be done
Waste not haste, but,
Make a sojourn trip
A sudden escalation,
An emulation, a "cup"

Quick
Clasp, quaint cusps
And rave Venus (ravenous) delight!
Play pounds amid a
Preponderance of flights
Mask—contemporary ensembles
Shear "ulterior might"

Perpetual/W-H-I-L-E
Commandeered camera
Trade lucid trails for chance
"Orders," happenstance
At sake's romance
An ineffable "declaration" (aphelion)
A famous trust!
Enfatuation

David R Thomas
QUIET REPOSE

This is for the artists that have to work in the real world for a living.

All emotions pent up within
like sand dunes at night,
dry as feelings of having to win—
my heart is as cold as winter flight . . .
having to win every heartbeat—
every soul,
all eyes that mine meet
and every goal.
All secrets behind me—
sand castles melting by the shore,
all the sad memories
being gone now—mean so much more . . .
than this flotsam
of a life
that turns to jetsam
in a lonely night.
No difference, . . . I suppose
but, I can always move forward
to a quiet repose.

Elizabeth A Dirks
OPEN HAND

For Hasan Raza, one who still waits for the open hand.

Why, fragile feather, do you endlessly breathe;
never to rest on the open hand;
whispering to the quiet breeze?

When will the open hand appear;
where the fluttering wind pulls me;
never to elude through time; in the
whirlwind shadows of life?

Sister M Imelda Spitzer OSF
TO A TAP DANCER
Tippity tap,
tippity tap,
tippity, tippity, tippity tap;
Toe, heel click,
twirl your stick;
tippity, tippity tippity tap.

Tippity tap,
tippity tap,
tippity, tippity, tippity tap;
Tap, tap quick
with jazzy kick;
tippity, tippity tippity tap.

Tippity tap,
tippity tap,
tippity, tippity, tippity tap.

CLAP!

(to be said aloud with tapping of fingers quickly and rhythmically)

Junita Escobar
WHERE ARE YOU!
The sounds are all around,
Whispers, shouts, songs about,
Our Lord's return, to catch away,
A Bride adorned for her mate.
It's in the air, joy and sorrow,
For those who care to hear.

Morning, night, or noon; Beware
He's coming soon,
Hurry, Hurry, do not despair,
He's neither here nor there,
He's coming in the air.

In clouds of glory, the trumpet sounds,
The Kings of Kings is about to come down.
Prepare, Prepair, sounds are in the air
Arrayed in white linen, a crown in your hair.
Not spot nor blemish can dot your robe!

With a shout of the trumpet,
The Bridegroom has come.
Where are you, when it's over and done?

Janice C Ullrich
FOR EMILY DICKINSON
When all around me was despair
I spoke your words and hope was there
Now it is my daily prayer.

Jennifer Tipton
LONELINESS
On cool, fresh, crisp autumn days,
I love to just sit by my windowsill and gaze.
I daydream and wonder and maybe start to cry,
Thinking about questions, their answers, and why.
I think about silver swans, jaybirds, and doves.
I watch and I listen to the Heavens above.
Loneliness! Loneliness, how dreadful it can be.
Yet, in different perspective, it's a time to gather thoughts
And hum joyfully;
To think of new trends and rejuvenate your mind.
To learn more about others, places, and dreams you will find.

So start appreciating a lonely time,
And listen carefully to every bird sing & every bell chime.
Because life isn't long enough to go, and to waste . . . . . .
. . . . And lonely days can tranquilize your haste.

William R Jordan Jr
QUIETLY, WITHOUT NOTICE

To Jan and Mom
for standing by
quietly, with notice

A man died quietly,
wrapped in a blanket,
on some forgotten beach.
People walked casually by,
unaware of his death.
If they had known of this forgotten soul,
this loss of life,
it really wouldn't have mattered.
This loss of life,
continues every day,
quietly, without notice,
hurting us all.
We are responsible
for our fellow man,
yet, it is us,
our major concerns
lead us,
divert us,
destroy us,
quietly, without notice.

Tina M Griffey
ODE TO A FRIEND

To Mrs Janet Cates, with a smile & hug

Sometimes I think of you
And I can't believe
All of the things
That you mean to me

You are my rainbow
You color my days
And you are my sunshine
I'm warm in your rays

You are my wings
When I want to fly
You're my inspiration
My reason to try

And even now
That we are apart
I still hold you special
Deep in my heart

For you are my rainbow,
My sunshine and wings
You are the person
Who means everything

Kim Stratton
WHO AM I
Traces and circles in my mind,
Who am I, I need to find.
Where will I go, what will I see,
Will I leave behind the agony.
Will I follow the moon, or follow the sun,
Will I settle Down or be on the run.
I need to find myself again,
For traces and circles can lead to sin.

Eric Medema
FOOLS PARADISE

A Reflection of Ignorance, Sanity and The World Situation

What is that space
between your ears
It helps you all
to conquer fears

With hands of life
just like a tree
It holds you up
now to be free

How shall we find
that road less traveled
For it's not paved
or even graveled

Come use this space
and you may find
The LORD MY GOD
in all you bind

Carmen Vento
ANNIE

To my grandchildren

The rain's pouring down
There's thunder and lightning
The wind just a-blowing
The night's most frightening
The room suddenly bright
As blue lightning strikes
And Annie, dear Annie
One scared little tyke.
She hides under the covers
And closes her eyes tight
And yells for her mother
To turn on the light.
With comfort and hugs
She's tucked into bed,
She drifts off to sleep
Dreamland just ahead.

"Anny" Weathers
SECOND CHANCE

I dedicate this poem to Loyd who has fulfilled my lifelong dreams.

So many years ago we met,
When we were in our teens.
Close friends we were, we laughed, we joked,
But had our separate dreams.
Life took us each on different paths.
I raised a family.
He worked and saved year after year,
And gained prosperity.
The years sped by, we'd done our jobs,
But found ourselves alone.
Then came a knock upon the door,
Someone I once had known!
Again we laughed and joked and played,
But it was not the same.
So very many years we'd lost,
But who was there to blame?
There must have been a reason,
So we wouldn't change a thing.
We've lived, we've loved,
We've laughed, we've cried,
We've traveled on life's wing!

M M Babb
VACATION IN LAS VEGAS

To a lesson well learned

All excited and up at first light
We are on our way to see lights so bright.
When we arrived, to our surprise,
The town was buzzing like a bee-hive.

We found our hotel so big and plush,
The tables and machines were being rushed.
I watched people drop in nickles and dimes.
They looked with disgust at different designs.

Sadly they turned and left with a sigh.
I thought to myself, "Why don't you try?"
So boldly I ambled over to those machines.
As I dropped in my nickles and dimes, they began to sing.

My heart gave a jump, and I got a cup.
I began to gather all the coins up.
After all was counted, I gave a holler.
There was all told: twenty-two dollars!

Now it's fun, beautiful and very nice.
What else can I say? It's a fool's paradise.

Wilma Jean Traylor
TREES

Trees tell stories all their own,
They tell about the winds that blow,
Around the earth for centuries,
This is the story of the trees,

They also tell about romance,
Letters carved in lovesick trance,
Moonlit nights when fairies dance,
This is the story of the trees.

Iris Cantlon
FIRST BORN

For Frank, With All My Love

Little boy
You've grown too fast
I wish your
Baby days could last

But that I know
Is not to be
Time won't stand still
For you or me

Another spring . . .
Another year . . .
A newborn cry
I'll wait to hear

Until that day
I'll watch you grow
And teach you things
That you should know

Then you can help
That little one
To be like you
The first born son.

Peggy Blackford
GOD'S RAINBOWS

Across the arc of God's great sky,
We see a rainbow stretched;
Its colors blend, of different hues,
From reds and gold to greens and blues,
A glory to the eye,
A glory to the eye.

Throughout the earth,
God's rainbow bright,
Is painted everywhere
Upon the faces of His sons,
The colors of His blessed ones
Are precious in His sight,
Are precious in His sight.

Whichever color may be mine
According to His plan,
May I be pleased to wear it well,
And let my life the story tell
Of love and grace divine,
Of love and grace divine.

Virginia Elwood
FREE

To Susan, my beloved daughter, Sept. 22, 1967—Feb. 16, 1987

The sunset last night
was the loveliest seen.
It caused me to sigh aloud.
The sky was all lit
with a bright rose and pink
set near a low black cloud.
These were your colors;
my thoughts turned to you
and I suddenly knew; YOU ARE FREE.
I picture you soaring
in sunrise and sunset.
What wonderful joy there must be
as you drift in the colors
and bask in the brilliance,
glowing in love's perfect light.
And you smile with contentment
and dance with the children,
for your spirit remains ever bright.

Andrea Hankins
CLANCY

Clancy was an old man
He didn't know where to go
Wild thought escaped him
Slashed across the row

Now he walks the streets
In no one he meets
Desert rose, beat up clothes
Catching still the sun

They say he's a madman
One thing they do not know
Images that make up a life
Do not reflect a mirror

Clancy now can sing
His troubles now take wing
Keeping within the darkness
And setting forth the light

He now walks the streets
In everyone he meets
Catching still the sun

Nicole Hubbard
LAST NIGHT I SAW YOU FOR THE VERY LAST TIME.

Last night I saw you for the very last time,
I'm leaving
got to hide again
from love's old lying face,
just been hit too many times
by such a scarring fate,
and I don't think
you could
understand
why it's just too hard to take.

John Ross
A HAND

The wizened hands of age in helpless grasp
Harsh folly of the thoughts of long ago
A heart of shadow found in locket's clasp
Admitting what we sought was never so

A varnished wooden rail slips through my hand
Slick steps that halt and fail beneath my feet
A far light strikes but fills my eyes with sand
My lungs unfilled by heights I never reach

I lie so still my thoughts must turn inside
But thoughts which course above my empty flesh
Can cause no faith and action to collide
Or allow an end to infinite regress

A lasting note of fear or cry
Is not for me to willingly supply

Mrs Harriet Eggleston
MY BELOVED

Oft in the twilight of my dreams
He comes from out of nowhere
His outstretched arms encircling me
And our lips meet in purest ecstasy

How glorious to see him whole again
As before that agonizing pain
I know that I shall go to that
Nowhere
When we will meet again
Until then I must be content

George F Truitt Jr
LAST CHANCE

For Marie

There once was a gun
against my head;
And a voice,
Soothingly dark
and lonely said:
"Smile once
and you're dead! !"
I frowned.

Many years later
I still frown
And remember
of a chance
lost . . . . .
In a smile.

Sandra J Shafer

Sandra J Shafer
CHILDREN ARE NOT OUR POSSESSIONS

With love to my three children Kim, Min and Tahnya who were my inspiration behind the writing of this poem.

Children are not
our possessions
They are only loaned to us.
They are placed

in our care,
By God's divine trust.
To nurture and love them,
And show them
the way,
To gently
guide them,
Along life's way.
It would be so easy,
If you could learn from
my mistakes,
But,
I know
we draw our strengths,
From our own
lessons and heartaches.
As you stretch your wings
to fly,
I'll be watching you,
And when your way seems
difficult,
I'll be there—
to
encourage you . . .
And when you think
you're
grown,
And your learning
days
are done,
You will suddenly realize . . .
You've
Only
Just
Begun . . .

Gerald James Kelly
NINE TO FIVE

Nine to five,
Just to stay alive.
Mouths to feed,
Clothes they need.
Take him fishing,
You are wishing.
But, you're working,
Nine to five.
Just to survive,
You get a raise.
But, it never pays,
'Cause it gets lost in the tax man's
haze.
Nine to five,
Are you just doing time?
It's that working man's ladder you
just can't climb,
Nine to five.
You home's still a dive,
But, at least you're still alive.
Look for love in all of the jive,
Because you'll always be working
nine to five
Just to stay alive.

Theodore T Bianculli
NOVEMBER

One who loves, "more than anyone"—Anna Maria

The winter cold against my skin
Whistling wind chills the bones
When glaring sun squints the eyes
and lights the shadows
The shining warmth feels like love.

Dorothy R Jarvis
THE FULFILLMENT

Promised, a glimmer of hope—Oh
tide
That daily kisses the sandy shore
Promising the trackless seaside
To return—Truth is once more

Elemental. A rose bursts from bud
Fulfillment and astounding truth
Must rise even from debris and flood
To become life-embryoed youth.

Promise me a fulfillment of love
Promise me to flee from and scorn
The very shadow giving thoughts of
Fear and its claws and pain and thorn.

Born for tomorrow—a swelling
vessel
New promise travails—with hope
and dream
Bursting from bands it will wrestle
To freedom and bridge the raging
stream.

Promise to look and see my face.
Promise to hold me to your side.
Promise that glory will fill our place.
Promise's the messenger,
Fulfillment's the guide.

Jon B Paley
ODE TO ONE'S HEART

To feel love abound is to swing away
and around
The pillars of one's mind hold the
key to one's heart
Without the feeling and tingle of
love
Man becomes as hollow as the shell
With its ocean sound.
Even nature in its infinite beauty
expresses love
and the feeling of love in its devotion
to pairs.
Loneliness has been abolished
and has been transposed to infinite
love.
Why then cannot one's heart also
fulfill this dream.
To love, the meaning of life evolves.

Florence Germain
THUMBS

A thumb is used for many things,
But hardly ever for wearing
rings.
It is often used to "hitch" a ride,
Boys and girls, side by side.
You use it when you hold a pen,
It makes your digits count to
ten.
You use it when you hold a cup,
And also when you say "thumbs
up."
A "green thumb" makes things grow,
Pulls a trigger against a foe.
You use it when you "thumb your
nose,"
But that's not nice, I don't
suppose.
When you type it moves the spaces,
Umpires use it for "out" on
bases.
Some men hook them in their belt,
They are used when cards are
dealt.
A thumbnail sketch is what we give,
But "rule of thumb" is how we
live.
It identifies us like our name,
No two thumb prints are quite
the same.

Trevor S Lewis
SIGNIFICANT REALITY

Dedicated to those who know that reality is an illusion.

In conscious awareness of reality,
Or in dreams of illusion,
We by mutual perception feel we
exist,
Our ways our thoughts, apart from
the base
May never cross in any way,
Some may live in art by heart,
Some in empirical reality by thumb
and rule,
Some may float on by buoyant in
murky waters.

'Tis so sad never to be sure,
That symmetry and parity be science
found,
Yet technique, stroke, brush and
school the artist's hand,
Forget not I, the meter is of the
poet's mind,
The tempo of life,
The hustle and bustle,
The fortune and fame,
The despair and drudgery,
The melancholia,
The euphoric retort,
And the realization that nothing has
claim to fame,
Less we all see.

See the significant reality.

Nancy Harrison
MOTHER

This poem is dedicated to Mary, my mother, the finest person I've known.

Her life is not her own.
She is tempted to run.
A woman at first,
a mother to all.
She touches my heart,
and is a beauty to see.
Her motion is fueled,
and never runs dry.
My vision of her is a
tear on my cheek.
Soft, flowing, sweet.
She surrounds us all
and is forever ours!
SHE's MOTHER!

Donald L Tate
BROTHERLY LOVE

To my sweet wife Joyce Stutts Tate whom I love always. My living poem.

Let me not stumble
My brother today,
Let me not blind him
O Lord I pray.
But give to me guidance
And the wisdom to do,
The things that would help him
To find his way too.

Let me not cause him
Tho weak he might be,
To fall into sin
And lose sight of Thee.
Allow me my Lord
To offer this prayer,
That both he and I
Your love we might share.

Beth Billeck
THE ONE

I want to be the one you long for
When you're scared and need
support—
I want to be the one who lifts you
When of your goals you've fallen
short.

I want to be the one you reach for
In the stillness of the night—
I want to be the one who helps you
When things aren't going right.

I want to be the one who cheers you
When life is getting you down—
I want to be the one to make you
smile
When across your face is a frown.

I want to be the one you care for
And need to hold in your arms—
I want to be the one you think of
When you think of the one who
charms.

I want to be the one you cry for
And pray for to heaven above—
I want to be the one you dream of
When you dream of the one you
love.

Ted Ray Wells
WHAT IS LOVE?

Love is a flame which
burns in the night.
It gives our lives meaning,
reason, and sight.

Love is an energy which
motivates our lives.
It is a rock from which
we can reach the skies.

Love is a song which
lives in our hearts,
And stays with us long after
our loved ones must depart.

Life has no meaning when
love is not there.
It has no rhyme or reason
that we should even care.

And when we are finished
with this life and look
back again,
We will see that love was
really all that truly mattered
in the end.

Rosalba Melgoza
TAKE TIME

Listen to the wind whispering,
To cheerful songs of jays.
Listen—hear the crickets sing,
And take pleasure in different ways

Take time—look at the blue sky
above,
At the cotton clouds, so white.
Find a rewarding form of love;
Gaze at the stars late at night.

Be proud of just being alive,
For there are things yet to see . . .
To make your heart and soul thrive,
Like the wonders of the changing
sea.

Take time—discover beauties
unseen.
Live a more satisfying, profound life,
With blues, browns, and all that is
green.
Live—take time for the blessings of
life.

David G Vandevelde
LIBERTY

In memory of the French architects, engineers, sculptors and ladies who posed for the Statue as well as Mr. Joseph Politzer who raised the funds to have the Statue moved from France to New York Harbor.

Liberty, Oh, Liberty,
You are the symbol of our democ-
racy;
Statue of Liberty standing in the
Harbor,
Oh, the sight of you is awe-some to
the visitor;
This great Lady,
Made of steel, copper skin and rivets,

Looks out over the Sea,
To welcome weary Immigrants;
Her Crown lights the darkness,
She smiles to all seeking happiness;
Her Torch lights the Heavens,
She has seen Immigrants in the millions;
Liberty's left hand holds the Tablet,
July IV, 1776 is engraved in it;
Liberty stands atop a pedestal,
She asks new comers to join us all;
Liberty stands tall on our Shore,
She always says 'Yes, bring me more';
Liberty stands at the Gate of our Nation,
She represents true compassion;

Laura Evans
YOU ARE

You are the paper
touched by a pen.
You are the night
covered by a layer of light.
You are a beehive full of bees
and, oh you are so nice to me.

Lucille M Boughton
THANKING GOD

Dedicated to my wonderful, loving grandmother who passed away November 19, 1987. She loved life.

I thank God for all the things that are real, the things I can see, hear and feel.
I thank God for all the sunshine and rain and for all the golden grain.
I thank God for the lovely flowers that bloom in the spring and fall; for the pretty birds that sing and all the pleasures they bring.
I THANK GOD FOR THEM ALL.
I love to hear the wind in the trees and see all the trembling leaves.
I love to watch all the waters as they flow and see the beautiful clear white shimmering snow.
Everything was made by God's own hand; I thank God for our wonderful land.
Our world sure is grand.

Nina Wilson
DEAR FATHER

This poem is dedicated to Laurence and Buster, two wonderful parents

Your son's feelings about you
On everything you say and do
You have taught me so many things
Right from wrong and what it brings

Love and honor mean so much
As does your loving touch
My dream to be what you want of me
Someday I hope you see

The honor I have for you
All my life through
Pride of being your son
For you are my father number one

Barbara L Petoskey
A MOTHER'S WAYS

To my mother, my reason for writing this, and to my grandmother, who encouraged me to share it.

A mother has a gentle way
Of speaking words so wise.
Many times we look for comfort
In the soft light of her eyes.
All mothers have dreams for their children—
Though they don't always come true.
Yet, despite the choices that we make,
She is there to see us through.
She praises our accomplishments,
Shares our deep concerns;
And through the years a mother knows
The lessons we will learn.
She kindly gives encouragement
When skies are looking grey—
And even when there's miles between,
She is never far away.
A mother is a mother,
But she can be a friend . . .
Like a circle that surrounds us,
Her love will never end.

Jennifer S Hastings
SHAKESPEAREAN SADNESS

Tho' in verse I praise this night
Your face both soft and fair
I will not in words delight
Nor lover's hearts will share

For you are far, whilst I, alone,
Lie dreaming of your touch
And Cupid's points the space doth hone
Not sharp'ing rhymes to such

Pale moonlight minds to me your smile
'Neath stars as diamonds strewn
I yet cannot with thought beguile
Your return to me so soon.

Paula S Hamilton
DESIRES

Intoxicating moon so full and bright.
I feel your spell on me tonight.

Makes me crave for your desire.
Come on let me feel your fire.

I see the smoldering of your eyes.
Fills my heart with passionate sighs.

Now I'm in your heated trance.
Come and give me your romance.

Andrea A McConchie
THE EVERLASTING UNICORN

To my precious daughter, Sonya Marie, whose dreams, beliefs, and love gave me the inspiration and encouragement I needed.

I'm a one-horned horse so pure and white,
And I rescue fair maidens who weep in the night.
My beauty isn't for all to see,
It's only for those who believe in me.

My mane flows so freely in the wind,
Yet I am banished from those who have sinned.
I'll come to the young and the old as well,
I'll come to those who will not tell.

I'll take you to a land of gold,
To the place where all your dreams will unfold.
My beauty shall surround you for all to see,
You'll become a reflection of me.

You'll be filled with my charm and grace,
Then I shall vanish without a trace.
You'll inherit the confidence you need,
Be strong my fair maiden and you will succeed.

Remember that dreams do come true,
Just keep your faith and believe in you.
Whenever you need me, just blow this horn,
And I shall come running, I'm the Everlasting Unicorn.

Julie Thomas
THE LIGHT IN THE FOREST

To: My Sweet Michael, The Only Light I have ever Known, This one's for you!—Jewels

Lost in the Wilderness—Fell into a Hole.
Opened my eyes and all around was Darkness.
Landed in a Simple Forest of Redwood Trees,
One Hundred feet high.

All I could Imagine was a light in the Darkness,
Possibly a pool of fresh Spring Water.

But instead of my vision
I saw a Purplish-Pink Violet growing in an open area,
a deserted patch of Dust.

It was a Beautiful as a Ruby
and as Peaceful as a Tear.
It was the Light in the Forest that I so Longed For,
it was Destiny.

As I kneeled near it, I felt at Peace
and I Cried.

Martin Matisoff
THE PREVARICATOR

To my wife, Sharon, for her continuous support and love

Art and literature provide the meat
By which the Dilettante by nature feeds.
To fool himself for what he's not
He dabbles in he knows not what.

Desire to possess that which he lacks
Lies at the root of the dabbler's art.
For want of skill or nature's gift
The Dilettante must fool himself.

Attempts to learn are bare-thread tries without
The discipline and fire that makes it so.
For lie as he may to himself,
What he has not will surely show.

Interest in that which deprives the Self,
The sciolist needs strength to break the chains;
To extinguish the stranglehold
Placed on his life by living lies.

I should've, could've, would've were his claims
For never seeing what was in plain sight.
Protective devices so none should see
That the Dilettante above is ME.

Micki Wolfe-Goossen
WINDSONG

The wind is part of us, always remember that,
While we are separated the wind knows where we are at.

The wind goes through us, we are one in the same,
Listen to the wind, it sends us each other's name.

The breeze is ours as it comes from above,
Hear the breeze whispering our love.

I'll always think of you when a leaf slightly maunders,
Remembering the gentleness we shared with each other.

I'll remember your mind, your face, your body, the strength of our love,
All the special places as winds blow from the sky above.

I'll send you a kiss of love through the wind of space,
As the breeze sweeps gently across your handsome face.

The wind there blows the same here and even though we may be far apart,
The wind sends our love directly to each other's heart.

Pedro S Llarinas

Pedro S Llarinas
SEEDS OF LIFE

To my Darling Wife, Juanita and Lovely Children . . . Linda Leonaida, Elvira, Edna, Milaflor, Margie, Pedronito, Proserfina, Emma.

A tiny Little Plant Seed lay sound asleep
Underneath nature Earth, but not so deep
It awakens, grows to be a Thing of Beauty
A wonderful and beautiful Sight for us to see.

A dear Little Seed of Life from God in Male Specie
Implanted in the Womb of the most-adored Female Variety
Comes to this World, cared for, nurtured with utmost anxiety
Its development and upbringing a Real Life's Mystery.

The tiny Little Seed became attractive, strong and sturdy
Not only a Thing of Beauty, also an asset, a necessity
Remarkable works of Art , magnificent scenery of all kinds
All realized from the tiny Little Plant Seed of Life.

Dear little Seed of Life grew in number, of different nationalities
What they have in common are
Brains of inexhaustible capabilities
They made all the exquisite architecture, machines of massive

capability
All the wondrous things, life-saving devices that help us live successfully.

Seeds of Life, make People and Nations
Seeds of Life, are sources of various Emotions
Seeds of Life, assure continuity of Reproduction
Seeds of Life, are the Crux of all Evolution.

"SEEDS OF LIFE are God's Creation."

Arvid Frederiksen
HEAVEN'S DOOR
How much is the price to heaven?
I really need to know.
Should I pray my sins away
or just let them go?
As the price goes up each day
I pray a little more.
Tell me have you sinned today
did you knock on heaven's door?
Look in the mirror therein the sin.
The reflection I adore.
Is my time running thin
to enter heaven's door?
Now you prayed your sins away
you can sin a little more.
But remember god is looking at
the reflection you adore.
Are you still praying that
you will find heaven's door?

Dexter A Walden BSN
DIRECTION

To my beautiful wife, Kathleen. For being the "DIRECTION" of my life. I love you!

My life was in shambles,
my future dim.
Confused . . . was my mind,
each day so glim.

The path I followed,
approaching its end,
was dark, as well as narrow,
prior to our begin.

My days began to brighten,
direction guided my life.
As you came forth,
I was ceased of strife.

My life now made whole,
my future became sure.
Decisive . . . was my mind,
for my heart so pure.

Today, assured of direction,
success is a part of my life.
I stride with accomplishment.
My secret . . . You became my wife!

Jeannette B Golden
MONTANA

To my husband Joe, who brought us to Fort Missoula, Montana, in 1937

Indian and pioneer, mountain man and scout,
Arching skies of deepest blue
Rivers full of trout,
Open range and soaring peaks,
Copper, silver, gold!
God put it all together,
Smiled, and then He broke the mold!

Bashawn Mink Relf
IDA
Like newborn's
her hair curls gently
as the sun sifts through
the haze of sleepy laziness
in her voice.
Wandering syllables retell
well known stories
as she sips her coffee and
a silent sigh descends upon the
still sleeping day.
Confused
I try once more to hear her laughter
but
only mumbles reach my ear.
Images and time are in my way
and the wind that I think
whispers through her hair
only chills me.
In my mind
she sits still there
forever trapped
in her solitude.

Young H Ih
NEW YEAR 1989
Really happy a New Year
Welcome it with three a cheer
Prosper friends and relatives
Peace on good Earth far and near

Edward Wilson
LOVE
—If you search for love;
you will find it—

—When you find love;
Cherish it, for love
is a precious gift—

—Love is like a flower;
If nurtured, it will blossom into
a thing of beauty—

—However, if love is not
nurtured;
It will wither and die—

—And love's shattered pieces will
ride on the wind searching for
some other place to take root—

Amanda Fuller
NOTHING
My soul has no feeling.
A cold, chilling wind
Has taken everything away.
There is a simple reason for this,
But it is not important.
As soon as there is a warm breeze,
My soul will come out of
This deep-freeze.
It is in my mind and
My blood now,
But I can still enjoy
The brightness of the sun
And the mystery
Of the moon.

Arden Karolin Carpenter
IMAGINATION

"Let your imagination guide you to the winning edge" No one can take it from you.

My mind can work wonders and take me places I've not been: sometimes to Europe, to heaven or just visit my kin:

I come from the pit of the city and found only in people, their pity:

If not for my talent of blocking out past and ugly truth, of the many years spent playing on the roof,

I could never have felt like a secure loving person
Full of hope and strong enough to say "no" to dope.

I close my eyes tightly and imagine I'm there: I can accomplish anything now for nothing gives me a scare.

I can be a queen on a throne or a dog with a bone:
I can be in a crowd or just be alone:

It is a great feeling to be in control:
To see and feel like the master of the wheel:

I can be rich or I can be poor, I can open any door:
I can be happy or I can be sad, I can even pick my own Mom and Dad:

Just let your mind wonder and make your own choices,
Then if you dare, give them all voices.

Have fun and explore, come open a door.

Marti Rice
THE RAIN
The rain washes the sky
and falls upon the tiniest of flowers.
Delicate petals bend low
under the burden of their life sustenance.

No matter,
for thus the flower is nourished
and strengthened,
And it will grow.

I walk through the cleansing rain
as it falls upon my face.
The droplets bend my soul low
as burdens of life trickle salt
upon my tongue.

No matter,
for thus I am nourished and
strengthened,
And I will grow.

Mrs Joyce Rosier
THE GREAT AWAKENING OF A LOST SOUL.

Dedicated to my church—"United House of Prayer for All People"

As I awaken, my soul searches for new heights, like a lost child that is in search for his mother. As one of his children I go in prayer to my father, which art in HEAVEN. For the Bible says "TURN NOT TO THE LEFT NOR TO THE RIGHT, BUT POWDER THY FEET IN THE PATH OF RIGHTEOUSNESS

For the Lord our God is merciful, LET US rejoice for he is the King of all Kings, and a great counselor for all. ONLY if you just believe. THE WORDS FORETOLD BY A "LOST SOUL"

Gloria S Johnson
FREEDOM'S FLAG

To Lloyd Johnson, my "Papa" who believed in these freedoms. He stood for honor, justice, the "flag of the United States of America"

They may pilfer and burn, and stumble through its ashes.
Time will take its course.
The flag of this proud land, will still rise from its splendorous ashes, and flow proudly, red, white & blue, for this wondrous United States of America.
For freedoms that will last forever and ever. Long may it wave.

Sherry A Richter
WHEN TWILIGHT COMES YOUR DEEDS ARE DONE
When twilight comes
Your deeds are done,
You feel without a care.
You shelve ideas
And all your fears—
Relax! Your day's away
Your steady gait, what lay in wait,
A pheasant under glass?
And after that, perhaps,
A tender thought of past.
As dazzling embers from the fire
Swoon gently through the air,
A calm ensues, and then I snooze,
I'm in my easy chair.

Gregory H Mize
THE POET
The Poet with a pen
As a warrior with a sword
Recalls the past again
Or destroys it with a word

Rose A Chewning
MY SPECIAL FRIEND

To my special sister, Marlene, and to the memory of our special Julie.

When I think about my friends,
So many come to mind.
But there's one that's very special,
The one that's sweet and kind.

She's always there when needed,
The one I appreciate.
She has the warmest heart,
I think she's truly great.

The thoughtfulness she always shows,
To everyone she meets.
The way she laughs and giggles,
Or the quiet way she weeps.

She's the one that I can trust,
With secrets that I dream.
She's loving and so beautiful,
With senses, Oh so keen.

She's the one who knows me well,
Whenever I gripe or moan.
She takes me just the way I am,
I know I'm not alone.

Sandra D McKey
A GIANT WHALE OF THE SKY
A giant whale of the sky
One day came floating by.
its beauty was a sight
to see a feeling of wonder
sparked in me.
the breeze gently moved it
across the endless blue
sea until out of sight
it went from me.

Myrtle H Jorgenson
LIFE'S DRAMA

Dedicated to the loving memory of a wonderful mother who taught me to always say "I'll try."

One generation passes on.
Another takes their place
To live, to work, to laugh, to cry,
To play, to share.
And then they move aside
For still another generation comes
With dreams, not too unlike the ones before.

And in our lives the drama
never really changes.

The tasks that once were accomplished
by work worn hands,
Are now re-lived in strength
By those who are a picture
Of the generation just passed on.

J D Singleton
SOMEONE

To all the Love lost, for being found too late.

Just before the last piece of the puzzle is put in place
Someone opens the door, and the wind blows it away
When the finish line of the longest race is clearly in your sight
Someone says you're disqualified because you weren't running right

Just before the last time, you swore it wouldn't happen again
Someone won't believe you now because you didn't mean it then
When you've sorted out what you want to keep, from what you want to lose
Someone else makes up your mind and they won't let you choose

Just before the last tear falls, and stains the final page
Someone turns the light off, and takes the book away
So you write the story's ending, the way you'd hoped it would be
While someone else is living, the end you really see

Just before the game is over and you've finally learned to play
Someone says you learned too late, and then they go away
And when you've sat alone, and searched inside yourself, at last
All you'll be is part of someone's past

Linda S DeVivo
AGE

I stand here watching
An old man cross the street
A pitiful replica of days gone by
My heart lurches
As he stumbles
Recovering himself, he looks around
To see if anyone was watching
I step back into the shadows
And pulling himself up, full of dignity
He walks on

Barbara Davis Mooney
GOOD TIMES

Tell me one more story and I will be happy,
Talk of the old times and I will be glad.
Sing me a song of a mountain folk hero,
Sing of the good times; don't talk of the bad.

Show an old movie and I will feel romantic,
The new movies now often make me feel frantic.
Dance the old dances just like you once could;
Sing the old songs, you will make me feel good.

Let's go for a ride in our Model-T Ford,
Down a dirt road to an old country store.
We'll sit at the soda fountain and drink root beer floats,
Then we'll go down to the river and watch the steamboats.

Oh make me feel happy with times of the past,
Sing me the old songs; make the good times last.
Don't make me feel blue with things that are new,
Sing me the old songs; make the good times last.

Christy Eads

Christy Eads
TONIGHT

To all the couples who have shared these special feelings. Also my family and Grandma Chick, Thank you!

The night is fresh and cool
as the moonlight blue
The stars are shining bright
as the world turns quiet

The moon is full and white
while lovers come to catch this
sight
The lake is covered with golden
sprinkles
As their eyes sparkle and
twinkle

They walk hand and hand
while dreaming of their future
plans
To hold each other close together
for their love will be there
forever!

Eileen Mullaney
MY WORDS FOR YOU

To my Parents, Laurie, and Denny who helped me to put the past behind me and love in the present . . . Thank You.

Maybe you don't know where
you're going and you're not so
sure of where you've been
Maybe you're so scared someone
may love you that you're willing
to pass right by a friend.
Being all too cautious is a lonely
way to live,
So afraid of receiving, not able
yet to give.
Sometime you may just turn
around and wonder if you lost
the chance at something true,
But when that day comes don't
just stand and ponder, turn
around and I'll be looking back
at you.
Maybe it'll be too late for us as
lovers, but I'll always be there
as your friend,
And if you think it's too late for
beginnings, remember there
never has to be an end.

Maria A Muia
INSPIRATION

To my mother and father, without whom I would never have learned to appreciate life.

So many hear a different sound
when a child speaks—
Some think of youth
Some of childhood days gone
away—

Would some day I find, by chance to be allowed to experience that
which many take for granted—
to actually with my
body, harbor another's life . . .

How could one ever know the
joy, or awe that a person
feels . . .

I myself see no greater gift—
no truer proof of God,
no finer Inspiration.

Gary Vestuti
A CHILD

A child's day is a world of thought
Memories build from within his own world.
The dreams he envisions sparkle his life
For the child has a mind others do not share.

"Speak to me boy," he once heard.
No reason was given to him
And the child thought in fright for a moment
Who was this unrevealing person.

As night fell, the child's heart sank
"Learning" for him was a frightful experience
This child had not been taught to learn
This child had been taught to listen.

Before the child could close his eyes
on this old day
He began to understand
A tear ran down his cheek
For the thought of a new day
appeared.

Antonio Gomes
UNTITLED ALTERED STATES

Metaphysical world
in continuous motion,
As the plane of reality
Becomes altered, twisted and broken.

Equal latitudes
with an even center,
From which a star becomes Nova
with equal strength.

The sun doesn't move
it's an ego trip,
Reason is lost
in dark space.

Visions are blurring
about the self,
Weakness takes hold
among the ruins,
Nothing moves
with reality,
Stagnation becomes
idle worship.

Frances Platz
YOU WERE NEVER AN ENEMY

I have reached for a star and caught hold of the universe.
I have ridden on the tail winds of dragons.
I've conquered each beast as we've met on my journey,
And I have come to know who you are.
You are me, as much as I'll ever be.
You're so very necessary to our world.
You are me, in another body, you see.
I can not say, "I don't love who you are."
We are the universe, my friend, and I see you as a star.

Gloria Stiefel Stapleton
SIRER

Sirer, Sirer where did you go?
You're buried under the snow.
Oh! how the wind does blow.
Oh! I loved you so.

Sirer, Sirer, had the white hair.
You were the boy that had the fair hair.
When it was light you were polite.
At night you were out of sight.

Sirer, Sirer, one of the pups.
Boy! did you have "Lots of Luck."
I was so proud when you pranced about.
Now you are gone, no more about.

This is the end.
Sirer will stay down under.
We will forget, He will be no more.
Now we go on, without no Sirer.

The Amazing Sammy (Sam L Tipsword)

The Amazing Sammy (Sam L Tipsword)
ONLY HE HAS JESUS EYES

To all the homeless orphans who find Jesus

Only he can make the mountains,
only he can make the stars.
Only he can make a love as precious as ours.
Only he can make the rivers grow the grapes upon the vine.
Only he can make you love me with a love so divine.
Only he can make the children just as lovely as they are.
Broken down and dirty cabin sat a child upon the floor.
Gone forever was her mother, and her father was no more.
I saw her sitting in the darkness with a sad and hungry face.
But her eyes were worth a fortune, for they shone with love and grace
Only GOD can love the children of broken homes and empty lives.
And I prayed to you dear Jesus, and you gave her for my wife.
She's the sunshine of morning, on a dark and cloudy day,
And her eyes tell her story, that she loves me more than life.
She reached for me from out of darkness, the light of GOD was in her eyes.

And only GOD can know the feeling, as we lie here side by side.
She's the sunshine of my morning, the blue sky is in her eyes.
And only GOD can make the mountainous shapely breasts and big blue eyes.

Only he can make the mountains, and the stars in the skies.
Only he can make the river that flows through paradise.
And in my dreams, up there I see us, with our children and our wives.
Only GOD can shape the Heaven & grow the trees of paradise.
And give it all to homeless children of broken homes and empty lives
Only GOD can know the feeling of lost souls and hungry eyes.
I reached for him from out of darkness, and he gave me my sweet wife.
She's the child that life rejected, a hated child with Jesus Eyes.
He was standing there beside her, looking down upon her soul.
And only GOD can love the children, of broken homes and empty lives.
Jesus Eyes, Jesus Eyes, and in the darkness there I saw her.
I saw she had them Jesus Eyes, Jesus Eyes, Jesus Eyes.
And in the darkness of the cabin, I saw she had them Jesus Eyes.
May GOD bless the little children.
Amen Jesus.

Sheryl Coe
RUN AWAY

To my own and dearest Alan, Thanks for everything . . .

Alone and afraid
I endlessly roam
Wanting and needing
A place to call home

Darkness surrounds me
And enters inside
I've nowhere to turn
No place to hide

No one who cares
Unable to cry
I'm cold and I'm hungry
I wish I could die

The pills are the answer
For I'm afraid of the gun
Finally at peace
No more will I run

Lisel Grimm
MOTHER'S LOVE

My love for you does not depend
On how well you learn to walk,
Nor does it hinge on such a thing
As how elegant you talk,
My love is just a simple thing,
That only a mother can know,
So quiet and gentle, and yet strong,
But still have room to grow.
I hug, I kiss, I discipline,
I scold you when you're wrong,
But then in time, I dry your tears,
And sing for you a song.
Then late at night, when deep in prayer,
My prayers are there for you,
That no matter how your life may go,
Unscathed, you'll make it through.

Oh yes, my love is a simple thing,
For which I ask no return,
You need not try for me, my child,
My love, you need not earn.

Elbert P Green
GRATITUDE

While the night is silent because travelers are few
Peace and calm are provided and all just for you
If the sky is clear and the stars are in clear view
The temperature will fall until it's just right for you.

The beauty of nature surrounds us too
All of God's glory is provided just for you
Hark, it is morning and the earth is damp with dew
The freshness of the new day is waiting just for you.

Get ready to face the challenge and the tasks which you must do
Give to it the best that you have for that's what will return to you
It is when to the world you have given your best
That one can be sure to have passed and mastered the test.

Others will follow in the footsteps of whatever you may do
What a glory it sheds when they relate their good fortune to you
Life wouldn't be so exciting except for people and friends so true
How magnificent the feeling to share our love and dedication for you.

Shannon Atkian
HEARTBREAK BASED ON A FALSE PROMISE OF THE HEART . . .

My desolate heart burns in mourning for you,
My tearless eyes feel your pain,
But still . . .
My heartless mind won't let me break the walls separating us.

Your mirror-like eyes reflect the lies you believe,
Not the truth.
Your wander-weary heart longs to stop,
But your fear forces you to run.
Lost in indecision, must we always Be apart?

I want to stay, still you live to roam.
My love of responsibility, that sends fear through you.
I need security, you could never promise that.
We want to be together, but won't compromise.

Donna Lynn Kaess
I LOVE HIM

I can't see Him or touch Him. I can't tell you of his physical appearance. I can't call Him on the telephone, but I can talk to Him. I can tell you that He loves me and I love Him, although He is much better at loving than I am. He does it so well. He's been doing it for a long time.

He loves me no matter what I do, even if I hurt Him. When I let Him into my heart, life is wonderful. When I am angry and I go away from Him, He still loves me and He patiently waits for me to return. All the while he watches over me, and constantly sends me little reminders of his love: the beauty and warmth of the sun, the fragrance of a hyacinth filling the air around me, a hug from my child, a kind word from a stranger, the laughter of an elderly woman living alone, a young child catching her first fish, a courteous smiling driver who lets me move into the right lane so I can exit from rush hour traffic, and a tall glass of iced tea, wet with sweat from the cold ice, handed to me on a hot day, when I didn't even ask for it. All of these are parts of Him.

When I return to Him, He rejoices. He always forgives me. He would never do anything to harm me. He always listens when I speak. He is wise and knows what is best. When I give Him my burdens, He bears them, and things always turn out fine. He understands me and feels my physical and emotional pain. He gives me relief when I need it most.

He walked the earth for awhile and experienced in the flesh all that a human could experience. He laughed, He cried, He shared, He smiled, He played, He suffered physical pain to great extents. He suffered mental anguish, so much that He literally sweat blood. He lived and He died.

No one can say "He does not understand." He understands better than anyone else.

He loves me for who I am, for He made me, and He is always there for me. He holds me in the palms of his hands and rocks me to sleep at night. He is my comforter, savior, friend, family, confidant, life, and I love Him.
He is my Lord Jesus.

Betty L Reynolds
GOD

A creator
A creator of night and day
A creator who brought forth
Man and woman
A creator of animals, of all
Shapes and sizes
A creator that put life
On this planet
A creator that can
Destroy!

William K Tremonte
TRUE COLORS CAN BE FOUND

To Florence Kerr, my Grandmother. Thanks for everything. I love you! ! ! . . .

True are the colors,
Running through my eyes,
Undisturbed and unbroken,
Ending at the edge of the sky.

Coming of the dawn,
Over the horizon,
Light will shine,
Over everyone.
Running all the day.
Shining again at night.
Can't you see them,
All shiny and bright?
No one can die
By seeing just one,
Even if they have

Found the greatest one.
On it will last,
Until the end of time.
Never shall they die.
Do believe in this rhyme!

Marvin Miller
THOUGHTS CAST ON THE BEACH

My thoughts are seeded in the wind
Far out on the lonely sea
Growing, building, rising higher
Racing to a far horizon
Breaking finally on the shores of time
To wet the feet of the world
And leave behind their trace on the sand

Will you be the lonely man
Who wanders down by the ocean
And sees in the dark water—in the never-ending waves—his life
Inexplicable, as they seem to be?
Will you find my thoughts cast on the beach
And in them, discover hope to answer the questions in your mind?

Roni J Schuth
THE GIFT OF ADOPTION

I gave them a gift,
one so perfect they'll never know.
I've made them happy,
so full of joy, because what I gave them was a little boy.
They keep my gift very warm
at night and feed him well, he's got a big appetite.

I gave them a gift, one so perfect they will never know.

I gave them my son,
who is four years old!

Emily Pietromonaco

Emily Pietromonaco
THE SADDEST CLOWN

To be blessed with humor, and still sad, within, becomes a tragedy in life's Super Challenge; to enlighten.

The sad clown, who is bright, colorful and gay, who makes many laugh, and be happy, whilst he is sad and mournful; in his brite array!

With the gala look in reds, greens, yellows and blues, oranges, purples, pinks. Oh! The hues; so, with moppy wigs, balloons, and large floppy shoes; The ruffles, pinstripes and

plaids, polka dots, and painted face
so extreme! Who would suspect
there was heartache, not a gleam!

In this Circus of life shouldn't a
clown be classified with High
Esteem?

In his world of unhappiness,
dejection, and sadness, perhaps it's
all part of God's beautiful dream!

The saddest clown, ever, will be
rewarded, for all his fears, in the
heavenward place, where there is
nothing but laughter, heather, and no
more tears!

Faith Stallings-Janney
GENTLE

To Frederick W. Janney

Gentle
A mother's touch, a kitten's purr,
A puppy's beguiling gaze.

Gentle
The kiss of rain, the blush of sun,
The wrap of a foggy haze.

Gentle
A First step, a loving caress,
Months of awaiting birthing days.

Gentle
Adolescent dreams, love's first kiss,
Passage of time, phase to phase.

Gentle
Time slipping by, a gurgling stream,
The aged acceptance of age.

Gentle
Iridescent mem'ries, winter melting
to spring,
The calm of a deserted stage.

Gentle
My love,
And you.

Ralph Drouin
MY BEST FRIEND

To all people—especially those most in need.

My best friend is gentle and kind,
He helps me relax and unwind.

When things haven't gone
the way I had planned,
He gently soothes me
and calms my hand.

When I turn toward the world's
material things,
He calmly stands,
and waits in the wings.

After all my attempts
at the things I desire,
He silently guides me
to His Father, who's higher.

Jesus, give me the patience
to watch and pray,
that I may be with you,
in heaven some day.

M Katz
THE ME DREAM
The American dream has eroded
away
The me dream has surfaced
Like an ocean volcano that has
erupted secretly
And spewed its caustic contents
selfishly about

Society's former anchor, the family,
Has given way to a sea of individuals
People who struggle to the top
Drowning others in their wakes

Day after day, a nation of blank faces
Fight to fulfill their me dreams
Floating pass life in jobs they hate
For money
the me-dream catalyst
Children grow up expecting, taking
From a society once overflowing
with people
Who cared about each other,
the country,
the world
About right and wrong, society's life
preserver

Sharing today is watching television
together
A large screen stereo by-product of
A successful Me dream
Maybe they watched the election
results
They certainly didn't vote

After all, what was in it for them?

Nancy Garrison Gleason
THE SOLITARY CAT NAP
Sleek fur darts slice the air.
Ashley, Orson and Sara might alight
anywhere.
Atop the fridge,
Under the bed,
Wrapped around my head.
Each playfully selects a lair,
Although in attitude without a care.
This perfect space they do not share,
While dreams of juicy mice spike
their hair.
A tail flick here,
A nose twitch there,
Tiny paws knead the air.
And when at last they stretch awake,
Of smiles of satisfaction they do
partake.

Kimberly Hitchens
PITTER PATTER

To Eddie, who is my inspiration. And gave me the confidence to write.

Sitting in my room,
I stare out at the street,
Listening to the pitter patter
Of all the feet;

Two by two,
Or in groups of three,
They all remind me of
You and me;

Until that one dreaded day,
When you walked away,
You left without a word to say;

The pitter patter of the strangers'
feet,
Go on and off on down the street,
Just like the pitter patter of my loved
one's
Feet, when you went on . . . .
Past my street.

Mary K Markley
HOME

To Melvin C. Markley, who said: "That's what I needed, a home!"

I live in a place in Indiana underneath a flowing clouded sky, where
we laugh, we cry, and sigh, then we
watch the world go by!

I go out the back door in the
morning.
There's always chores to be done,
laundry to be washed,
dinner to be cooked, mail to be run.

We sit in the afterglow of a meal.
We talk and relate about what we
feel!

We still have a dirt road that winds
up to our house,

We have cookouts in the summer,
harvest, and big meals in the fall.
When Christmastime comes, it's
always "good times for all."

As the season turns, there is a sense
of time in the air.
Spring brings forth new horizons.
We pick ourselves up from our
winter haze, and turn our heads
toward the freedom of the days!

Throw open the windows, pull up the
shades, shake out the blankets, and
toil with our spades!

Linda Gouchnour
MY LION LOVER

To my husband, Scott: my beloved "lion" whose passion and belief inspire me.

Images of my lion love drift ever into
my mind . . . .
Rippling muscles of his furry chest
send tremors down my spine.
Unruly curls that frame his face
enhance the wild-looking eyes—
Brown orbs of piercing heat so
animal-like show his desires.
And in my dream he reaches out, I
can almost feel his touches,
With beastly arms of gentle strength
he wraps me in his clutches.
Sinewed legs entwining mine we
dance 'round passions' fire;
Searing flesh, burning kisses—the
flames are climbing higher.
Clinging and pawing we are like
sleek jungle cats:
He nibbles my neck as I softly claw
his back.
Butterfly lips caressing honey-
dripped skin, our bodies ache to
quench the fires deep within.

Hearts swelled with love so full, my
lion love and I,
Reaching the zenith of ecstasy we
soar into the sky.
Purring and crooning an erotic
song—
He tosses his mane . . .we float along.
Contentedly curled within his arms I
awake, I'm groping air . . .
And my dreams are enough to sate
my needs
'Til my lion love returns to our lair.

Robert Lynch
SUNDAY NIGHT AT DICK'S (FOR JOE DIAMOND)
White hot music flowing forth
under the chill full moon
pulsing, vibrant
rhythm and energy
jazz—
Coltrane visions
wailing,
screaming
low-keyed
passion of the be-bopper
recreating enchanted evenings
amid crumbling illusions,
broken dreams
while an audience of voyeurs
swathed in decadence
keeps time with the
tapping of their souls.

Play it, Joe.
Play like you mean it
O tenor man whose
sax burns a
Sunday night vigil
for those of us
who forsook
what-might-have-been
and settled for
what-could-not-be-helped.
Or better yet,
why not??

Alexa Gratz
UNTITLED
She lay naked on his bed
The pain in her chest felt like the sky
coming in
Tears,
watercolored warpaint
ran straight to her temples
Flat on her back
like some Sacrifice
she hoped he was dreaming
of her
Naked
and flat on her back.

Gus Gregory
THE OLD FOLKS
(Remember)
Remember the Old Folks
who seemed to always care,
When others laughed
at the little things that hurt us
so?

We thought that we were lost
but they were always there,
To help us bear our hurts and pains
then off we'd go.

Without a thank you Dad
or thank you kindly Mom,
And they, together smiled
knowing that they had helped.

Time's gone by, it's our turn now
to give a loving hand,
To the Old Folks, when in our hearts
we know how they must have
felt.
(Remember)

Lori Bradfield
A PRAYER FOR A CHILD
Bless me for I am so small,
Help me grow so big and tall.

Watch me through the darkened
night,
Wake me in the morning light.

I'll try my hardest to be real good,
just like all your children should.

But if I fail to be so strong,
God, please forgive me when I'm
wrong.

AMEN

Ann Mele
BELLS

To my husband Tocky, for his encouragement.

Montage of today; in sameness with
DiVinci's yesterday.
Did he abide the bells, or wage silent
war against their timbre?
The control of the raids infringed
upon his design.
Did he not become their bigot?

As a youth, I was introduced to the invaders.
Peerless and unable to counter, I cowtowed to their
vexing maxims and yielded to the caste.

A score passed and the ringing continued.
Emotions flowed and tangled my nerve endings.
I languished for a short-circuit to set me free.

Then mercifully, the silence arrived.
Slowly and steadily the communication weakened,
until the clangor of the dirge was oblivious to my ears.

Loryn M Anglisano
CONDITIONS OF SIGHT
Like the sun that emerges from the shadows after a dark and still night shines the mind of a blind man who sits all alone in the park not knowing the time or even if it's day or night, distinguishing crime from nature when he hears our children cry for help! When the seas uproar, great mountains crumble and when all the birds sing, in the silence he hears the wind blow.

Thru his senses he smells and enjoys the perfumes of flowers whether roses, orchids or violets. He can scent the human presence and knows when he is not alone, he is aware of how we are daily dying from smog, cancers, heart failures, arthritis, diabetes, drugs and alcohol, he suffers much in pain with the burdens of disease that invade his body due to his own old age.

He is got preference for color nor age makes any difference to him, he has not seen what colors rainbows are made of he doesn't care if they're black, blue or yellow or even if they're green or red.
He is not horrified at the sight of blood for he has never seen it shed, or its bright color red, but we can judge from his tears that he suffers just the same.

He is not known to be greedy he can't recognize money green from paper white to him green are the leaves, the trees and the grass, blue is his sadness and white is his soul, for not being able to see all of the madness that's going on in this world so full so sins . . . sometimes I wonder, is it my fortune to be able to see . . . or is he gifted for what his sight dims?

Theresa Anderson
HOUSEWORK
We like to follow little bears
And quickly hibernate
Somewhere become illusive
Beneath a bush or plate
Or travel far to China
Itinerary and all
Pass by a million chopsticks
Then find beside a wall

An Eastern ray enfolding
How far we've come along
Surging upward feelings
Familiar light yet strong
Beaming at a heart full
Of happiness and song
Guiding softly trade winds
Home where we belong

Julie Walker
APOGEE
A twinkling point of light,
Streams from the sky at night;
The sun's rays in the falling rain,
Prismatic colors, vibrant delight.

A deadening of pain momentarily;
From this place in which we dwell.
At the end of the path in the forest;
Recompense of eternal suffering,
Destination Hell.

Wisdomless ears, nonunderstanding hearts,
Shun all her paths to peace.
He who grasps the stars in hand,
Shall ravage all evil deeds.

Moonlights rays wander in darkness,
Laborious to follow and seize,
Oh, how it shines upon the face,
Of the meek on bended knee.

Beam down your brilliant light from apogee above,
To a place at the end of the path;
Recompense of faithfulness and love,
Destination, Paradise.

LaVena May Drummond
COUNSELOR ARABIA
Paul Arabia said, "Well maybe ah,
I will prosecute your case
Regardless of your race."

I am a lawyer about town;
not some fun loving judicial clown.
I always fight for the underdog,
but have won a few cases
for selfish hogs.
I can convince the jury of anything,
As long as I wear my ten carat
diamond pinkie ring.
I will wear a toupee, go on a spree;
However, there will be a large fee.
For this you will have to pay.
I am a native Kansas son, carry a
Little gun and go out on the
Town for my fun.
I worry more about my looks
Then catching crooks.
Someone, said to me. "Is it true
That Yul Brynner shaved his
Head to look like you?
Yes, I am afraid that is true."
As an entrepreneur, I have lifted
Many a criminal up out of the sewer.
I am a hotsy-totsy-so-called-do-gooder.
I have been mentor to many
an artistic soul.
And from their purse have taken my toll.
I am the best damn lawyer in the state.
Too bad they did not ask me to
handle Watergate.
I would have opened the gate and let
all the water out.
Then there would have been nothing
to shout about.
I would have taken "Tricky-Dickie"
and made him appear like
a "fairy woodland Pixie."
I studied at Pittsburgh State
then hopped a freight and
went to New York
to study under Mork.
I am now in Center City, U.S.A.
Where you have to be "gritty"
everyday.
I am a big T.V. personality and
do not have time to fight crime.
I am bald-headed, fat and never
wear a hat.
There is one thing about me
That is really neat.
The fact that I do not have
Flat feet.
Many people love me just the same
And this is the name of the game.
My name is counselor Paul Arabia
and I will prosecute your
case maybe ah . . .

Kathryn Potter
AT THE EDGE

To my brother Matthew with all my love

The tenants of his soul beckon him.
A hollow in the earth awaits him.
This facade of a brilliant young man,
obsessed with the frailty of man.
He perceives life's coffers as half-empty, life's doors half-closed.
A brilliant young man,
yet he cannot grasp overcoming the darkness.
He rests by a lake he has known since childhood.
The sunrise creates a glimmering arc of colors,
yet the brilliant young man sees only the shadows and the mist.
He can find no peace, no solace in this tranquil setting.
His anguish never ceases.
Tormented voices cry out to him in despair.
The melancholy consumes him.
The voices beg for an end to the hellish torture.
The tenants of his soul beckon him once more,
and the brilliant young man
surrenders to the darkness.
He approaches the blaze of light at the end of the tunnel.
The warm phosphorescence heals and soothes him.
And the family's grief will be
unending as they relinquish
their brilliant young man to the
hollow in the earth.

Anatole Kantor

Anatole Kantor
THE VANITY OF SAPPHO

To Ann Thiel

The Greek poetess Sappho
Twenty-six hundred years ago
Wrote when you die,
"Dead shalt thou lie;
. . . Even in Hades' halls
Amidst thy fellow thralls
No friendly shade thy shade shall company!"
Woe is me, life and death
Are vanity, hell's guests
Shall leave you empty,
And heaven's best
Is left
From the greatest seekers of history.

I look out my window at society
In the twentieth century,
And I am beset by a certain anxiety,
Will anyone remember me
Twenty-six hundred years ahead in history?
Is it like the poetess said long ago
That no one remembers you when you go
And that life and death are vanity,
A searching after identity?

Ask the muses.

Daniel Leo Levy
AM I IN LOVE?

My fav'rite brunette is named Frances; She melts me with one of her glances!

Am I in love? I stand and wonder;
Pray, how can I be sure!
'Tis true, when she appears,
I'm under
A strange and ling'ring spell secure.
So lovely to my eager eyes she seems
As if a Venus wrought;
Is she the one of all my dreams
Whom I have ever sought?
I don't declare she claims the livelong day,
For that would be untrue;
I stir myself to work and play,
And give my all as due.
But, let one ask: "Do you no loved one seek?"
Forthwith she's near; I hear her sing and speak.

Katherine Gravely
THE ROBIN
I heard singing outside my window today.
It was a beautiful Robin, I must not scare it away.

The melody was sincere
as though he was singing to me.
The beautiful voice of the Robin in the tree.

As I listened, his singing filled the air.
He did not seem to mind that I was standing there.

I thought of all the beauty
that I could hear and see
from the voice of one tiny Robin
sitting in a tree.

Donna Lewis
DOORWAY TO THE FUTURE
The achievement of the future,
Begins with a single dream.
A hope that is nurtured
Into a grand, impressive scheme.

To open up a child's mind,
To reach for stars and space.
To continue looking to find,
What's best for the human race.

Knowledge is the road,
To help vast new frontier.
Helping unburden our heavy loads,
And making our duties clear.

A child's imagination,
Is the path to our success.
The hope of civilization,
Man at his very best.

Beth Zagorski
IT HAS BEEN

To David; the love of my life.

It has been weeks, months, days, even years, since I've thought of you,

You enter my horizon like a sinking ship carrying thousands of valuable loved ones,

You return like the lost, loving, faithful puppy, abused as an infant, and lust after as an adult,

How I sought to change you, to make you what I wanted you to be,

Then when I lost you, I realized you were all I ever needed to keep myself sane,

Now I kill myself in my own personal hell, doomed by boredom, repetitious dull dreary nights, and cold dismal days,

You enter my horizon like a sinking ship carrying all I ever needed in life,

And I blew it all away to satisfy an inner hell I cannot control.

Esther Keilholtz
MEMORIES
Oh, that I may touch the knob that opens wide the door,
That I may sit upon the creaking bench to eat my meals,
To rest my feet upon the open oven door.
It would rest my soul!

That I could touch a lock of mother's silken hair,
And kiss her sweet face again,
Or climb that grand old winding stair,
Kneel down at that same bed for prayer.
It would rest my soul!

I shall not ask to touch the stars or gilt of yesterday,
But that I could in my childish way
Touch the sweet memories of long ago.
It would rest my soul!

Mrs Jessie Holt
MOTHERS DAY

To My mother: Sidney Ann Cosper

It's Mothers Day here on earth
The flowers are beautiful.
My mothers flowers are more beautiful
for Jesus gave them to her for me.
I can almost smell her flowers and the beauty see.
I know they are beautiful for Jesus gave them to her for me.

Mary Estle Dingle
DID YOU KNOW?
A doe doesn't mind the snow,
A hare gets caught in a snare,
A cow once was used to pull a plow,
A horse will eat food that is coarse.

But do ewes read the news?
Does a skunk love to mire in junk?
Does a pony like to eat macaroni?
And do birds sing with words?

Karen M Strong
OUT OF MY GRASP

To Jim: From my heart to yours.

I wait patiently, and work hard, yet, the single most important goal of my life,
stays there, just out of my grasp.

I can't buy it, beg for it, nor can I command it to come to me, yet, it can be earned.

It is not easily enticed, believe me I've tried every way I know, still, it escapes me.

Questions pour through my mind everyday:
Are you bored with me?
Am I just a convenience to you?
Are you using me only for the moment?
When will that moment end?

The treasure I seek is taken for granted
by others, but in My life is the only thing that would bring me true happiness.

It is beyond words to tell you what I would give to once hear you say, "I love you Karen!"
PLEASE! Don't let it stay just out of my grasp.

Gary Dechau
THAT FACE
The face was familiar
But whose it was I didn't know.
I recalled seeing it somewhere.
Maybe it was from some television show.

Maybe it was in a magazine
Or in the paper on the sports page.
Maybe he was a rock singer,
One who was a big rage.

I know that face from somewhere,
But just where I can't recall.
Maybe he is someone from work
Whose office is down the hall.

A few drinks before dinner
Had helped to cloud my mind.
The rest didn't help either.
I was smashed by nine.

As I gazed at the face before me.
I still couldn't bring the name to mind.
I didn't realize I was in front of a mirror
And that face was mine.

Nighthawk
A HELL OF A PLACE
Though people say it's much too hot,
a place so bad, no it's not.
Pleasure and riches are what you'll find.

All play. No work. You just unwind.
Everything is free. You need not buy.
And Satan? Oh, he's not such a bad guy.
Having it all is what you must bear—
Unlike that place up there.

Colleen Garner
HAND IN HAND

To my travel companion Liz

Hand in hand
The snow and people go.
Some lighthearted, cheerful,
Moving lazy and slow.
Or maybe
Energetic and in a rush.
Collecting their piles of treasures
With much ado and fuss.
And others
Hard, bitter and cold.
Driven by some unseen force
That even they don't know.
The snow and people
Hand in hand
Are destined to go.

Annette D Aldridge
THE TIME HAS COME
The time has come,
The end is near,
Nothing you can do,
I have nothing to fear.

All my hopes,
All my dreams,
It doesn't matter,
Or so it seems.

That bottle of pills,
They're all gone,
Please understand,
This isn't wrong.

Now I must lay down,
I must wait to die,
The time has come . . .
For suicide.

christine smith
STARS
The glowing sun gen West it rolled,
the evening sky is flowing gold
and in the endless space so far
a burning dot—a diamond star.

A second one, a shiny shield,
the night undrapes a starry field.
The midnight blue is not the same
for million gems set it aflame.

And not a star thru magic force
has left its designated course.
They spin by natures law—the lot,
round yonder stillness which is God.

William Charles Schaffner
A KISS
The days were as the nights . . . dark, dull and weary,
But now the sun shines all the time when I think of you.
You are as the bread of life, the wine, the song,
And the wind of the seas.
You keep me lifted on exalted plane.
Of you, the world knows little, but to me you are the all,
The utmost of a man's desire,
The goal of man's hopes.
Dear friend, you mean the world to me . . .
the world in all its glory.
So here, sweet friend, take this from me . . .
a token of my dreams.

Marie-Louise Murphy
VIOLINS TREMBLING ON WAGNER

I dedicate this poem to all the victims of the Holocaust.

Days wakening without light.
Nights speaking without stars.
Dormant
Eyes closed without dreams.

Did not know then
Reasons for pain.

Endless images
Engraved on infernal dawns.
Violins trembling on Wagner
Giving tempo to steps
To chambers of death.

Did not know then
Reasons for hope.

Numb to moans.
Deaf to cries.
Arrogant demons
With final decisions
Causing destinies
In a brutal shock
To fall.

Did not know then
Do not know now
Reasons for it all.

Thomas R Shoemake
REDDY SKELTON
Send in the CLOWN, and color him RED!***
A CRAZY QUILT COVERS HIS ENTIRE BED!***
To a JESTER, what more may be said?***
When water squirts from two of his ears,
IT shoots plumb to China, not one speck queer!***
Little Old Ladies squint through EYEGLASSES, and stare at two ASSES!***

I saw him once on the T.V. SCREEN***
HIS underwear was PINK instead of GREEN!***
A WOMAN'S he'd put on by mistake, fell past his ankles,
that takes the CAKE!***
Did you see the LACE he pulled over his BELT?***
Very Good, IT didn't MELT! RED, YOU'RE the KING, and so is BING!***
RINGA-DINGA-DING!***
YOU SING like a GORILLA at a THRILLA in MANILA!***
YOU CRACK ME up and also MY PUP!***
JUST POUR the WHISKEY through the CHUTE!***
THE FLOOR WILL LEAK AND NOT THE ROOF!***

Dolores Beals
I'LL NOT WALK THIS WAY AGAIN
I have not walked this way before, or will I ever again,

So, I pray that when I leave, my spirit lives within,

I pray that I have left this place, a bit better than before,

That people may speak kindly of me, if nothing more,

That I have nursed an injured Robin, back to his flight, and rescued people from the night,

That I have cried, and felt the pain of some lost soul and not for gain,

That I have trod a lonely trail, and tried to help others not to fail,

That I have cared for man, and beast, and loved the down trodden, and the least,

I hope this counts for some small crown to win,

Because I'll never walk this way again,

Tina R Odom
DIAMONDS

To Michael, Mom, Mary, and Dwayne, for all the inspiration and believing in me.

Not long ago
You touched my heart
And it's never been the same
You showed me that there's more to life
Than dwelling on the pain
I know that tears have touched my face
And hate has filled my heart
But that's before I knew you
And all the things you've taught
You are my only future
My only pleasant past
I feel like we are diamonds
And the world is only glass

Marilyn M Cruz de Guy
I AM YOUR LORD FAITHFUL AND TRUE. YOU ARE MY CHILD.

To my son, Cory Jacob I will always try to be there, and if I can not know that the Lord will.

I am your Lord faithful and true. You are my child with all my blessings within you. So what can be more natural for you my child.
But for me to comfort, love, and come to you.
But as your father all I ask and beg of you. Is to shut out the evil that would destroy you, all of you.
If it were not for the love and hope I hold for all of you my children.
Please listen the key my child is simple, profound, and true. Keep me within you. And my word always close to you. For now I beg of you, to do these small things.
And I promise that for always you can be sure, I will come to you, and love you all. Love you as you have never been loved before. And as no love on earth can ever start to compare.
From your father who is always faithful and true.

Ozella Madewell
LOVE

The Bible says that God is love,
And that's what He wants us, his children, to do.
With love the whole world would be a better place to live
And the wars would be very few.

Among the great and glorious gifts
That our Heavenly Father sends
Is the gift of complete understanding
That we find in our loving friends.

This love of our friends is so precious.
It is our treasure to hold.
We must always guard it and tend it lovingly
For it is worth much more to us than gold.

There are some who take love so lightly
In fact, they don't seem to know what it means
One moment of pleasure is all that they want
And their future is only a dream.

So if we ask how we can be happy
The answer is to treat our fellowman with love.
Show it to all who are around us
As it is sent from our Father above.

So, store up your love for a rainy day
But draw on it all the time,
For it grows and grows as it is used
And it will last you your whole life time.

Hank Ring
TO MY BETTER HALF

To my girl "Marge"

My wife, she wants some poetry,
She wants to hear some prose.
She says she needs the romantic lift,
instead of dees and does

So here's my little effort
To satisfy her whim
I hope it gives as much a lift
As does a dram of gin

I love you doll, you are my pet.
In all this world it's you,
Who makes my life a wondrous thing,
And paints all gray skies blue.

You make tomorrows something fine,
And yesterdays a gift,
Because I know you 'love me too,
And everything's divine.

Lorraine Norris
AMERICA

America is the land of the beautiful
And the land of the free.
The land where I live
With the air that I breathe.
With every heart beating bright and true,
When Americans say always,
I love you.
I love America with all of my heart,
Where all nationalism
Should take part.
God gave love
To share with all.
I will not answer
To a racism call.
Give me my freedom
And the air that I breathe,
And I will be thankful
That I am free
In America!

Edith Gray
AN INTERCESSORY PRAYER FOR CONVERSION OF A LOVED ONE.

O Lord with your Miraculous Power, please convert my loved one from sinner to picturesque saint. May he find peace in his soul and freedom from estrangement.
Blot out the memory of imperfections in his past, and remove the debris from his notorious nature.
Lead my beloved in the path of greatness;
grant that his life will be the expression of Godliness and Righteousness.
In his daily walk with you, provide him with abundance of activated love in his heart towards his brothers on earth.
Intervene Father, when my dear one finds himself trapped in the pitfalls of an evil and "irrational world."
Bring this young man near the Heavenly Forest of serenity and tranquility, and place within his interior sweet blessings of Christian fortitude.
My final request O magnificent King is that he may abide in the Endless city forever. Amen in Jesus name.

Lori Jean Cipriano
TRUE LOVE AWAITS

So special a place
Warm and inviting
So special a time
Hearts fresh and new
Innocently guided into each others arms
Unsuspecting
Of the joy awaiting
As our eyes meet
Time stands still
Hearts beating as one
Tonight alone
Gazing through the candle light
Into one anothers eyes
We are reminded, of that magic
When we were innocently led
Into loves tender embrace
Tonight we are reminded
Not only of that special place
Not only of that special time
But of three words exchanged
These same three words
So often taken for granted

Pat Nash
THE CRY

Don't you hear it loud and clear
The cry for help from far and near?
When Jesus died upon the cross
He answered the greatest cry of all,
The cry of love and peace and joy
Eternal life when our savior calls.

Lincoln heard the cry one day
And freedom rang from miles away.
Those in bondage were no longer chained
Yet the cry lingered of fear and pain.

Martin Luther King answered the cry
When he gave people hope and a dream that never died.
He walked out with courage and sacrificed his life
Through blood sweat and tears, he fought a good fight.

People have come and people have gone
The world has changed but the cry goes on.
Our children cry out for deliverance from drugs;
In a world of poverty, our elderly cry love.
Don't you hear it loud and clear
The cry for help from far and near?

Ivanetta Bowman
JESUS IS THE REASON

This poem is dedicated to, the Lord Jesus Christ, my personal Saviour, Willie and Robbie Joshua and family, and Christian Chapel of Walnut Valley.

Christmas is as Christmas does.
Sharing the special gift of God's heavenly love.
It's a time of rejoicing and remembering the greatest love of all.
Given unto us this day His only begotten Son.
He has come to knock at the heart's door of every sinner man.
To give us all eternal life is His Father's master plan.
The hustle and bustle that happens every Christmas season
How many of us stop and remember that Jesus is the reason?

The joy of love is felt so strong at this special time of year
Given so freely from the heart without reservation or fear.
Glory to God in the highest, we thank Thee O Lord above.
For the royal birth of our Saviour, the most precious gift of all.
For God so loved the world, that He gave His only begotten Son.
Whosoever believeth in Him shall not perish, but have everlasting life.
To believe in Jesus this glorious season
Peace and joy in every heart
Wishes of goodwill to men near and far.
What better reason could there be to soften the hardened heart?

Cindy L Carlson
THRUSH

Untouched, believiant beauty,
Lies within the palm of your hands,
Strong and firm, you are holding a lifetime.
Nestled all snug in your veins are promises of birth.
Listen to the music being played in the brook.
Here lies the significance that bonds all.
Thrushing echoes imprinting our souls.
Neverending refuge that is entertained by many.

Naomi Johansen
MASTER ABOVE MASTER

My poem "Master Above Master" I wish to dedicate to my Lord and Saviour Jesus Christ who is my Master.

As I lay awake one night, I heard the dripping faucet.
I heard the silence of my home, the pitter patter of the rain.

Ruined by a loud and shrieking wake of thunder.
But then it stopped, and the pitter patter was heard again.

The midnight thunder aloud and wild rose again in the silent night.
Only to prove that it was master above the starry moonless dark.

Should I be frightened, or should I be calm?
Will I fall asleep, or watch up and hark?

When I was a child I would cry to

my mother. Would this why not be now?
For I am a woman, yet still this is a frightening noise.

Just for the fact it has mastering in it's clutches.
And does not go about it with poise.

Even though it is mastering, there is still a ruler.
He of course is God. Therefore I won't fear.

For even over this he is master and ruler.
And now I can sleep, for I know He is near.

Julie Costa
THE WIND BLOWS GENTLY

To my wonderful parents who told me never to give up. I love you both

The wind blows gently
through my hair.
I look around,
but you are no longer there.
Was it a lie I'd like to believe,
or did you say that you loved me?
I told you I truly do love you,
but was it true when you said, "I love you too?"
You've told me time and time again
but can you tell me just once again.
But if you can't,
I'll understand that too.
I'll just have to find,
A new love true

Diann Haines
TRUE LOVE

To Eugene Ebersole and Larry Hawbaker for encouraging me to keep writing my poems. Thank you and God bless you both

I think True Love is never blind,
But rather brings on added light,
an inner vision quick to find
The beauties hid from common sight.

No soul can ever clearly see
Anothers highest, noblest part;
Save through the sweet philosophy
and loving wisdom of the heart.

Your unanointed eyes shall fall
on him who fills my world with light
You do not see what hides him from your sight

I see the feet the fain world climbs;
but the steps that you turn astray,
I see the soul unharmed, sublime
But the garment and the clay

You see a mortal weak, misled man,
Dwarfed ever by the earthly clod,
I see how manhood perfection
may reach the stature of God

Sandra Forster
MY DAD

There was a time when I was young
I played and frolicked in the sun.
My days seemed endless, full of glee
For in the future I couldn't see.
Then the sadness no more sun
I asked myself what have I done?
People staring their wonder showing
I stared back my anger growing.
Daddy's gone he's passed away
They tried to make it all OK.
There's just no comfort in their touch
I hated God so very much.
He's taken my Dad away from me.
I blamed myself as you can see
Cause in my mind, the words I'd said
"Oh my God I'd wished him dead."
Now I'm older, wiser too
There was nothing I could do.
The Lord had said "Your time is up."
But still I miss him very much.

Ted R Laabs
ALONE

The broken umbilical extended
along side the silvered vehicle,
distantly stars beckoned silently,
weightlessly drifting among the swells, cast adrift, the sails beckoned,
fluttered, waved did not come about,
dropped over the horizon far from the beach
where grains of sand flowed
beneath frantic feet of an ant slipping
down the side as a wisp of cold snow dangles
over the edge, the steely blue sky
opening upward drifts from the
frozen waste land.

Immobile in the setting sun, I stand
near the corner, the flow of traffic reddened
by lights, flashing signals, departing
vehicles lifting off the tarmac, empty
now, a flat space opened up slowly,
reflecting moon light from the blackened
distance beckoning
with tiny spangles
forever beyond
the desperate reach.

John L Thompson
DIRECTOR BILL

To those who serve in the H.S.C. at N.I.U.

There he sits at the Holmes Student Center. In his office by his desk. Director Bill was facing a hill of bills and spilled his pills. Standing next to the pillar wishing it was his pillow this indeed would be quite mellow if it wasn't for those forbidding fellows.

Why is it when I want the mail I get all this hail to bail?
Mary Jo said no and Muggs was getting in his slugs. This is giving me the bugs. So they gave me Neil to steal. He stood on hand. Got all ten fingers. Now that I got Neil in the heel. I fear we shall go far. Hail the nails the bills are all in those pails. These staffers are making me stiffer.

Leaky pipes, falling bricks who do I get to make it all stick?
I'll take this to Lou and we shall see what he can do. Louie told me a whale of a tale and then he floated on down the trail. I couldn't even find his tail.
And then I saw Vic with his Bic trying to scribble himself in real thick. If I can only trick him. Then I can stick him with all this.
But this San Diego sailor was too quick and slick. He floated me over First Shift with his reverse stick.

So there I stood at the bay of Wally's World. Joe said, "Oh no" and in a few minutes I was flown off Second Base. I dared to wonder where and Wally said "Right down t
h
e
r
e."

Third Shift was working in the night holding up the neon with Leon. When down came Bill. "Is he safe," said Bud. Not if he fell in—
John's pick-up cart was the call by Leon.

Leaky pipes, falling bricks, give me a pill, send me on home and call me Director Bill on some other day.*

Susan Garland
THE SPIRITS OF THE FOREST

The spirits of the forest
don't always wait til night
to come about.

Sometimes at the height of day
their shrill whistling echo can be heard
and cloudy images dance
in the shadows of the trees.

Their ghostly wailing
makes the dogs bark
and the chickens scatter.

Their eerie appearance
silences the birds
and makes the cats beware.

The spirits of the forest
don't always wait til night
to come about.

Brenda Marie Herbranson
A WAY SHE ONLY KNOWS

The world is a place to live,
not a cause nor blame.

The clouds were made to give,
to share the gift of rain.

The sky gives us room to grow,
beyond the highest trees.

The sun warms the earth,
and heats the air we breathe.

There are so many reasons for us
to love the world we know.

She gives us life and happiness,
in a way she only knows.

Patricia J Berg
FATHER IN HEAVEN

My dear Heavenly Father,

My heart is filled with thanksgiving,
As I experience another day of successful living.
You are my inspiration, my strength, and joy,
And the principles you've set forth, I seek to employ.

I'm thankful that my needs are met,
And that my selfish deeds you'll soon forget.
I pray to be more like Thee . . .
forgiving graciously.
I want a tender heart and to obey
Thee willingly.

I place my friends and loved ones in your precious care,
And I know that all will be guarded with angels unaware.

I know that with you all things are possible,
And that for our faith we are responsible.

I pray that we'll gain faith by daily prayer,
By studying the Bible, and thus;
acquiring wisdom unique and rare.
And I praise you God in Heaven with all my might,
And I thank you for Jesus Christ, in whom I delight. Amen

Kari Lyons
RAINY DAYS

To you mom, with all my love.

As I sit, I wonder about you,
The things you say, the things you do.
You, in your chair bouncing me on your knees,
"Look out the window, what do you see?"
"The flowers, the birds, the marvelous trees!"
This is my favorite spot here in your lap.
You're so warm with love as I look above
I always see your smiling face.
"Listen to the wind—OH! Here comes the rain."
And we watch together how it
trickles down the pane.
You hold me so close, so near, so dear,
It's in your arms I feel no fear.
Your gentle touch, how soft and sweet,
I'm in your arms, I'm fast asleep.

Mary F Boyd
ABOUT HEAVEN

To my daughters

There will be no coffee in heaven;
No liquor or cigarettes there.
We'll all sit around sippin nectar
And many will lie in despair.
There will be no poker in heaven;
No call girls or sex allowed there.
We'll all sit around being angels
And many will hunt for the stairs.
The stairs that lead down to earth's level,
They gladly would descend again;
But an angel with flaming, sharp sword
Is there to protect and defend.
The foolish are thusly prevented,
Their own destruction to seek.
They're forced to learn patience and meekness,
High on a heavenly peak.

John A Zak
AS LIFE UNFOLDS

This poem is dedicated to my loving children: Anita, Gina, Brian and Tina

The most precious of all life's
Blessed Worth,
Is of a father witnessing child birth.
As I held her hand in the Labor
Room,
I prayed to God from 4 a.m. till noon.
Please CREATOR, let there be,
Ten fingers—ten toes that we can see.
Two arms—two feet and a perfect soul,
So this child, healthy, along with us will grow.

My thoughts of worry, and sight of labor pain,
Made me feel that I was to blame.
I said "Why Lord, must, this pain, my wife bear,
To give my right arm, for it, I would share."
As my wife was brought to the delivery room,
The time of truth, would be soon.
As I stood there, in puzzlement,
I instantly wondered, what it all meant.
Then the cry of joy throughout the room did whirl;
For there lay in her arms a beautiful girl.
Then tears of happiness in our eyes did appear,
Cause our prayers were answered, for our CREATOR did hear.
As with the birth of each child, as I recall,
From this day forward, our lives changed all in all.
For with each new addition I'll state specifically,
Your love for them all, must be shared equally.

Martha I Abrams
NIGHT SOUNDS
The car no longer comes, the footsteps do not fall.
The lock on the door still waits for the key
That used to slide, so frequently . . .
Home.

The rustle of clothes as they dropped on the floor,
A hand that groped in the dark; we touched and found
Each other, fitting together like a well-worn puzzle.
We loved so long, so hard, and deep;
And all for this . . . I cannot sleep,
Waiting . . .

For a car that no longer comes,
footsteps that do not fall.
The lock on the door still waits for the key
That used to slide, so frequently . . .
Home.

Margaret Daniels
THE WOODPECKERS' HOUSE
You know how it is. We all weave a web around us. Let me tell you about a couple who live down a gravel road deep in the woods of sky-reaching oaks, their house nearly hidden from view.

Their unpainted house, riddled with woodpecker holes,
stands like a sieve filtering weather whims.
Neither the man nor the woman see or hear the woodpeckers,
if they did, they wouldn't care, because:
He lives outdoors most of the time talking to the chipmunks and the squirrels,
or digging in the ground and growing things.
He never looks upward.
She stays indoors most of the time in a windowless room,
painting canvases of wild colors and weird shapes,
pictures that spin from her mind.
And when they are dry, she stores them away. Meanwhile:
Their house serves as the woodpeckers' target range
where drill is held daily.
And no one notices them.

Elsie Aldrich Mellin
HIS MAJESTY'S HANDS
Everywhere I look
Over pasture and brook
The great rivers and oceans
Beautiful isles filling me with emotions
Majestic mountains—snow-capped high
Here am I, 38,000 feet in the sky
Viewing never-dreamed-of splendor
Wrought only by—His endeavor.
Wishing others, like me, might
Enjoy all of this—a fantastic sight.
Feeling as some astronauts felt
And I'm sure several knelt
Appreciating more and more
This wondrous world from shore to shore
As skyward they and I did soar
Feeling His Majesty's' hands—galore!

Brenda K Miles
MY HUSBAND
He's a man
with a loving heart.
A true person,
sincere with his gentle touch.
My husband,
proud and patient.
His giving smile,
is the maker of all my beautiful dreams.
His very presence,
sets my heart at ease.
I trust in him.
He protects me with love.
A gentleman of honor.
He is my compliment,
and I love him dearly.

Cody A Burdette
HOMEWARD BOUND

I dedicate this poem to my children, and parents, without their support, it would never have seen the light of day.

Many battles I have fought, scared and weary I have become, longing for freedom and Home, never more to roam.

This cruel land has dealt me a blow, though scarred and hurt, I will carry on.

Through the heat of the battle I have come, tested and tried each and every day, but the light of my Master has lit the way.

I would lose one battle, and then another, on the battlefield of life. On, on I marched, ever to Satan's song, never admitting just once I was wrong.

I staggered and reeled from the weight of the load, through heartaches and headaches I have come. Now that my feet are on solid ground, beauty and peace do surely abound.

Through the smoke and the fog of this man made Hell, I crawled out into the light of a new day. I put on the whole "armor of the Lord", I stand straight and tall, never more to fall.

I was ragged and torn, and not much of a man, but the Master picked me up in his loving hand.

He gave me new talk, he gave me a new walk. He gave me new clothes with armor so thick. My sword is the Bible, of which I am so proud, and I will praise his name oh, so loud.

So you see, up from the heat, the smoke and the gloom, the dirt and the grime, came I from battles of the past, to a new day. So now I march to a different tune.

I am homeward bound at last you see, because my Master died for me.

Hattie P McShine

Hattie P McShine
MARCH

This poem is dedicated to Claud, (my darling husband) for his concern and inspiration.

March rushes the end of Winter's fling,
While ushering in the awakening of Spring.
The wind whistles while blowing through the trees,
As children fly their kites and dance in the breeze.

Out of the ground crocus begin to appear,
Surely Spring must be near.
Hyacinths and jonquils are peeping through,
Soon will come tulips with their beautiful colors too.

I see the robin with its breast of red,
Flying, fluttering and shaking its head,
The pretty little bluebird seems to say,
Yes, spring is really on the way.

Mr N R Long
CHRISTMAS
When every one is cheery;
When life seems less dreary;
And songs are ever in the air.
It's Christmas!

When the air is chill and frosty;
When the school door hinge gets rusty;
And to grandpa's, aunt's or cousin's we go.
It's Christmas!

When we trim the cedar tree;
When there's treats for you and me;
And we listen to the program one and all,
It's Christmas!

When the Christ child is adored;
When from sin by Him restored;
And the light of heaven shines on every face
That's Christmas!

Nancy A Kreutzer
TECHNICAL DIFFICULTIES
The birds are flying north for the winter.
Wooden benches don't give you splinters.
The weather is like the TV guy said you'd get.
The government is no longer in debt.
Shampoo does not burn your eyes.
That great new outfit's just your size.
The world is no longer at any wars.
Men don't care about football scores.
Out of all these things where something is wrong,
the worst is that your smile is gone.
I don't want to see you get any sadder.
I am here to listen. Please tell me what's the matter.

Robert Taylor
THE FISHERMAN
With rod and reel the fisherman jauntily strides
To the edge of the stream of his choice
Hoping that here a big one hides
One, if snagged by him will make him rejoice.

Excitedly he chooses his lure
A daredevil, oh no—that yellow fly
That's the proper one for sure
And he congratulates himself for being so sly.

The lure is affixed securely in place
At last he's ready—how can he fail?
He starts to cast about—ready any fish to face
Whether it be a rainbow or a bass as big as a whale.

Suddenly there's a pull on the line!
And the lure disappears from sight
Quickly he sets the hook—thinking, "It's mine, it's mine!"
Simultaneously reeling in the line, with all his speed and might.

It must be a big one he thinks to himself
But alas! The line goes limp and to his sorrow and dismay
This is one fish he wont mount over his fireplace's shelf
Yes, that's right—the big one got away.

Ellen Hope Priddy
SECRET ADMIRER
She walks slowly through this crowded place.
A look of serenity on her lovely face.
Her head held high, her gaze afar,
Her eyes are on a distant star,
A place or time only she can see.
I wonder, I wonder what it can be?
I hope, perhaps, she'll notice me.

I follow her as she walks away.
I hope, in my heart, that today's the day
That, somehow, she'll feel and turn to see
The one who loves her. That one is me.
But whether or not she looks around,
I'll follow her quietly. I'll make no sound.
My heart is full. My love unfound.

I've watched her for a very long space.
I see her each day in this very same place.
I watch her as she walks along.
Watching her is like a song.
But my job ends and starts the fears.
Tomorrow I'll watch her as she disappears
And leaves me, only, my lonely tears.

Kathleen Patrick
VAGRANT SOUL
A vagrant soul, no home had he,
no rest, he found no peace,
ever seeking what he yearned for,
a lifelong search that never ceased.

Then out of the dark a light appeared,
as a beacon bright it shone,
engulfed within that radiant beam,
the weary one felt somehow, not so alone.

Yet, hard it was to step within,
lifelong journey then to alter,
give up the quest, to trust somehow,
that the light would never falter.

In time this weary one grew strong and sure,
in that warm and glorious glow,
for all I'd ever longed for,
was your light in which to grow.

You cherished light that filled my dark,
elusive home for which I'd yearned,
you cannot doubt for only you,
could ever my own light burn.

J L Spitz
CLIMBING UP THE RAINBOW
All my friends
All my dreams
Have melted away

All my colors
All my songs
Have disappeared

I'm climbing up the rainbow after them
I didn't really need them
Who says that I care?
Somehow they all scattered—pieces everywhere

All my illusions
All my games
Tried to strangle me

All my thoughts
All my kindness
Are void now within me

They all went climbing up the rainbow
and I'm climbing after them
I didn't really need them
Who says that I care?

Somehow they all scattered—pieces everywhere
And I'm climbing up the rainbow—
And I'm climbing up the rainbow

Beryl A Lyons

Beryl A Lyons
I MUST TURN AHEAD
I must turn ahead
To the living
From the dead.

I must command
The tempest gales
Courage born
Of trial
Prevails.

Ursula T Gibson
PRIVATE DESERT
In the desert's early morning
all is clear and crisp and clean,
but the shimmering rise of heat
from the sun's effect on sand
creates streams of altered light,
and the mountains fade and waver
as warmth rises, rises.

So, too, my awakening in your arms;
all is clear and crisp and clean,
but the rising heat of our closeness
and your effect on my body
creates streams of altered yearning,
and I waver and fade into you,
as warmth rises, rises.

James E Bundy
ALL THAT WE HAD IS GONE
The tempo rhythmically winds
through this pocket watch of time
Vivid love's been lost inside these vast heartaches of mine
All my dreams are tossed aside for changes rule my life
Empty pages yet to fill in books that may subside

All that we had is gone
All that we had is gone

Love has passed me by in days of solitary strife
Empty pages start to fill with words of solemn life
What we had before is gone and thus we cannot score
Sympathetic eyes of mine are tearing on the shore

All that we had is gone
Won't you bring your love back home
I never thought that the love we had would ever die
Now I know that I must move on without her by my side

What can I do to strengthen up my shattered heart
When we met I was so sure that we would never part
Now I realize that time is not too forgiving
Could this be the end of me or just my beginning

All that we had is gone
All that we had is gone
I never thought that the love we had would ever die

Delbert D Fleming
SHE'S SWEET STUFF

To my Beautiful Wife, JEAN.

She was born in June, and sure enough,
She's a Gemini through and through,
She's the sweetest thing and never gruff,
She's kind and gentle and loving too,
She's Sweet Stuff.

She's a Lady and never rough,
She's Beautiful in every way,
She's even tempered and my call your bluff,
She always lets me have my say,
She's Sweet Stuff.

She makes the bed and gives the pillows a fluff,
She loves music and likes to read,
She never throws a snit, or goes off in a huff,
She's one of those rare, vanishing breed,
She's Sweet Stuff.

Cyndi Bock
AN OPPORTUNITY OF LIFE

I want to thank God for giving me a Mary Kay asn. she has given me an opportunity of life, also I dedicate this poem to my recruit and directors. You have inspired me with your ideas and your caring smiles. May you always be a rising star. Happiness always!

An opportunity of life, is a life of sharing. To give!
An opportunity is to dream, and live the dream.
An opportunity means God first, family second, and your career third.
An opportunity is wisdom, laughter, tears, joy, and self confidence.
An opportunity is love, means, support of others, and challenge to you.
An opportunity is to grasp a star beam, catch it, and shine in the galaxy of stars. To glow!
An opportunity is to follow a path, and share it with others.
An opportunity is to buzz like a bee, and know in your heart
YOU CAN DO IT!
Take your opportunity to heart today.
Don't wait until tomorrow, because tomorrow never comes.
Share, shine, glow, and be filled with the joy of opportunity.
It will warm your heart.

Carrie Appleby
INSIDE OF ME
Tell me what's inside of me,
The part I cannot be.
I'm on the inside looking out,
Sometimes it's hard to see.

What is it I do not know,
What's so close within myself?
I must keep looking for that thing,
What, I cannot tell.

There's an empty place in my life,
I can't quite seem to fill.
I'm growing up to leave behind,
The me I knew so well.
I realize now I've wasted time,
Searching for things unknown.
There's no vacancy in there,
The answer is, I've grown.

Nancy Jean Johnson
IN THE SILENT HOUSE OF SLEEP
In the silent house of sleep where walls are made of clay
Crowds of people daily meet to while the time away
The Traveler in his quest to find a place to lay his head
Unaware and often times is laid below instead

Too soon the transient rooms like cavities are quickly filled
Innocence in their youthful bloom resign to pay their final bill
In the silent house of sleep where roofs are made of clay
Who hears the sound of trampling feet . . . who hears the prayers they say?

Who rises with the morning sun to roast the fatted lamb?
Who bakes the bread . . . have they ever said, 'I certainly know that I am?'
Who sees the sharp and piercing lights descend like silver spears
To split the night and softly drip a sea of heavenly tears?

Oh for the Scroll! . . The Book! . . The Document of Proof!
That in the house of deep repose one's name might be removed!
For time . . like particles of dust soon merge into nothingness
For those who daily meet in the silent house of sleep

Dorothy J Scott
MY TIME AT 73

To Eddie-Lou Cole.—Editor for making this possible for me.

Your time has come
they said to me, and then
I walked that two miles again.
Your time has come they said
As I looked up.
And then again they
filled my cup.
Your time has come
and then said I.
As up above shown
Clear blue sky—
It is not my time.
I can hear and see
and stand and walk
but I agree
My time will come!

Constance J Ramey-Swartz-Foster Love
CHRISTMAS CHEER

Dedicated to my children Greg, Tracy, Glee, Tara, Jill, Jimmy, Sam, Rihana and my life force Daniel Martin love.

'Twas the night before Christmas and thru out the land,
The spirits were flowing to beat the band.
Everyone was laughing and full of good cheer,
They thought it was the way to finish the year.
Vodka and gin brought a glow to their faces,
Some of them thought they were entrants in races.

Out of the bars they came with a giggle,
Not knowing their lives weren't worth a plug nickel.
On thru the streets they went at high speeds,
Laughing and weaving in their four-wheeled steeds.
When out of the dark there came with a squeal,
Another drunk driver with his hands on the wheel.
The crash that was heard brought a pain to your head,
Without any doubt you knew they were dead.
The news that night mentioned each one by name,
The Christmas celebration had brought them all fame.
Their families knew Christmas would be sadder this year,
All for the sake of that Christmas cheer.

Mrs Ray Conner
A HEAVENLY STAR

I saw a star falling from heaven and I caught it in my hand
Some day I will return it to a much better land

Maybe God sent it to me this star that shone so high above
Maybe God was only showing how He shares his holy love

And as I stood there in my silence how I felt His presence near
I know He is getting a new home ready so if we listen we will hear

The things of this world are so little let us put our minds on high
Tell every one to be ready when we meet Him in the sky

I am so glad to be a Christian so when I stand before the bar
That in my hand I'll still be holding that wonderful beautiful fallen star.

Joe Lammert
THE LIFE IN THE ATTIC

Dedicated to Delores for the faith and for the attics of the future and past.

Roaming through the attic of your life,
You stumble across the pages of past memories.
People, places and values flash into the eyes,
As the heart is reminded of its history.

The mind smiles with sweet remembrance.
The heart cries at the bitter differences.
Too much has drifted with the times.

Pages upon pages of precious moments
Are allowed to dance, once in a blue moon.
Dust is brushed away as feelings are replayed,
In a deep trance of a long forgotten tune.

Love shines with sweet remembrance.
Sadness cries at the bitter differences.
Too much has past to let the pages forever live.

With a deep sigh and a tear of regret,
You turn your back on the life within the pages.
You return to where you spend your fruitful days,
Leaving what has built your life, in the attic cages.

Moments stored in sweet remembrance;
Locked away by tears of present day differences.
Too much has changed for the past to always remain.

Joni J Harrison
GRASS

The grass is so green, oh how clean, but might it seem that
It hasn't been seen; by many who haven't planted a bean;
But the ones that had alot of lean.

Jacquelyn G Hayman
SONNET TO MR. COMMITMENT

To Ron My encouragement, my inspiration, and my commitment

When trying to escape the truth
That taunts one's conscience constantly
Once love has entered secretly
Into the open heart of man;

A pressing problem prompts the soul,
Invading every way of life;
The mind encounters stress and strife
On succumbing to this sweet demand.

While troubled by this tensioned state,
One tends to temper love with fear.
And though it's true that pain appears,
Most tears are those of happiness.

For those who enter willingly
Are soon secure in love's caress.

Jessie J Young
THANKSGIVING

I'm so glad our Pilgrim Fathers
Set aside a special day
When folks could all come together
To feast, to sing and to pray.
A time to thank the Almighty
For the good things he has done,
For his blessings unlimited
And his love for everyone.
Let us too be really thankful
For our families and each friend
When we gather this Thanksgiving
Around tables with our kin.
Let's forsake our grumbling and
Not complain about our lot,
Just be truly thankful
Of all the good things we have got.
I for one could go on for hours
Counting blessings in the night
If I'd only look around me
And count the things in my sight.
Oh Dear God, my list is endless,
You have been so good to me
And if I'm to be remembered
Let it be for praising Thee.

Agnes Opperman
NATURE LESSON

Lazy Lizard on the first spring day,
lying all Yoga in the sun;
I turn you over with my toe; you
haven't the pep to get up and go;
I tickle your belly and devil you, so?
what are you thinking?
While your little eyes start blinking?
From you, Lizard I can learn the ancient secrets of the faith;
All of hidden, magic healing; giving up thought for feeling;
You are certain I'm not dealing you a blow? How are you certain
This isn't your curtain?

Sleep I'll buy but not all winter, and no matter if you're full
Any log must lack in windows; hibernation must be dull . . .
Now, you're out here in the sunshine, are you sure I'm harmless, Liz?
Are you Les instead of Lizzie? I don't want you in the bag!
You're not worried I've a gun? I would like to ask you, Gecko,
How you put on such a jag?

Lazy hunter at the end of day,
dragging homeward almost spent,
Stopping, gasping to catch my breath! Lizard you scared me half to death.
Zinging up my pants legs so, jumping over to a tree!
So, the little fellow ran over me!
Length is 18 centimeters,
Brownish color like fir bark . . . Why, you little Gila monster,
Did you plan this little lark! In return, you're teasing me?

John M McBryde
YOU

To my dearest wife, Carolyn. Words can never show how much you mean to me.

Every day I realize more
You're everything to me.
You're everything that I could hope
A true love ought to be.
You help me see into myself,
You help me understand.
You help release the love inside
With each touch of your hand.
You're everything that I could want,
You're all I'll ever need.
You're something special I have found,
A rare, uncommon breed.
I feel so lucky that you are mine,
I'll never let you go.
If only I could make you see
How much I love you so!

Lorena E Moffett
GOD SENT HIS SON

Dedicated to my husband: George L. Moffett

God sent His Son
That we might live
By grace, and not by law
So why not put your trust in Him
And give to Him, your all

He gently leads you by the hand
And points to you the way
Stand up for Him—
Speak up for Him—
And do it every day

The Bible is our guide and light
So use it every day
Hold high your light—
March on you're right—
March on to the promised land

Jonathan L Luhr
THE LAST PASSING

He was on his way home
When the sky lit up;
His eyes hurt briefly
Before he lost his sight.

The old man never had imagined
That he would die so quickly;
His soul, which seemed to burn,
Left its imprint on the land,
Split wide open
With a heaving blast.

Humanity cried out
With one quaking voice
And was heard no more.

The earth burned brightly,
And crisp, clean ash
Soon blackened the sun
With a glove-like covering
That sealed out Creation;

Darkness had begun
To surround all things
With its nothingness.

Chuck Mitchell

Chuck Mitchell
REMEMBERING GREENWICH VILLAGE

For Shawn Gallagher

I remember chicks in turtlenecks and leotards with long straight hair and no makeup
I remember bongos and flutes and poetry coming from the coffeehouses
I remember the streets of McDougal and Bleeker crowded with people famous and unknown
I remember abstract expressionist paintings dripping wet from loft walls and sidewalk exhibits
I remember Washington Square fountain full of guitars and speeches and songs
I remember old men with piles and wild hair playing chess everyday
I remember beards full of revolution and suspicion blowing in the wind
I remember barefeet and sandals beating a new anthem of freedom on the pavements
I remember a time and a wonderful time it was when I was young and carefree
and America was alive with cats and chicks and jazz and everything was hip and cool

Phyllis St Pierre
HEAVEN BOUND

To My Husband, LLOYD ST. PIERRE With All My Love

Birds have wings to fly . . .
To soar on high up in the sky.
Oh, to be so free and still still be me.
My soul has wings but bound to flesh,
whilst still a mortal mesh.
To soar on high is my dream and hope;
To fly to my Father's arms and view the world
through His kaleidoscope.

Bill Spitalnick
A STATE OF MIND

What the word boredom really is,
something to which I can not say,
with too much confidence
or with much authority.

But without a doubt I can
feel when it has engulfed me
in its web of stillness and nothing.
It is though the world is down.

It is though I am nothing,
and waiting for nothing.
Like a numbness without such pain
as to cause one to be without.

It sucks you up in its funnel,
a funnel of not to be.
An object of uncertainty
but one of pure reality.

It fondles your thoughts
and plays with your sanity.
It can guide a person
to hell and back.

Boredom—A word of fact,
that means so little to some,
and so much to others
as to cause so much
but yet cause none.

Pat Myatt
I LOOK AT HER

This poem is dedicated to Kimberley, my special Daughter

I look at her,
She looks at me.
I touch her hand,
She smiles at me.

She is my life
you see, for she is
my Kimberley.

John J Poukish Jr
WANTING

An Ode To My Sweet Rose:

Wanting . . . ,
Not caring,
Just knowing
And Wanting.
Wanting . . . ,
And having had,
Knowing
And Wanting.

Paula K Greenmyer
LONG DISTANCE LOVE

I dedicate this poem to my wonderful boyfriend in the ARMY William J Huber

My heart will never change towards you,
Because of all the love we
share as two.

They say absence makes the heart grow fonder,
Now I realize that is true,
because we share a love that
I'll always honor!

No number of miles could change the way
I feel, and with time our pain
will grow to heal.

Then we shall be together with nothing
standing in our way, but for
now-just remember I love more
each and every day!

Martha Murray-Dudley
ALMIGHTY

Everyone all over the world

Heaven and earth is where I live.
Follow me and I will make all
things clear.

Let me lead you in all that you do.
Take my hand and I will
guide you.

In all things I will make you the
best. When you are hurt, I
will make you well.

If everything around you should
come tumbling down; jump into
my arms and I will carry you.

Your friends may leave you because
of me. But turn not away, let them go
on their way.

I will make of you a bright light;
that will shine even brighter
than daylight.

I am your hope, your dream, your
future. Through me all things
are possible.

In all that I have said, I'll end
with this. To see an angel,
you must use your heart. To
see me, look into the mist.

Julia Ellinger
SOMETIMES

Sometimes I get so sad—I remember
the way it was
The times we had—when I was
young and Mom and Dad
Were always there to hold my
hand—To help me up
if I fell down—I remember all the
good things—
And forget all the bad.
If I close my eyes I feel as though I
can touch
yesterday—my Mom and Dad—the
love we had—
The little girl with hair so fair, and
eyes so big and blue
Always in a pretty dress waiting for
her daddy to come home
And give her a big hug and kiss—
and tell her what a lovely miss she
was and how he loved her so!
Those are the yesterdays—they won't
return—only if
I close my eyes—I can see it all
again—
My mom—my dad—the little girl—
with the eyes so big and blue—with
hair so fair and ribbons there—-
skipping along—holding hands—I
get so sad—it's all gone!

Nadine Silva
TODAY

Let us not think of tomorrow, but
only today what counts is the now
and what we do or say yesterday is
past and on our mistakes we should
not dwell
Let us live for today and try to do
well
What we do today is what our future
will be for we reap what we sow,
don't you see?
Let us sow, yes sow kindness this
very day
Keep our eyes on Jesus and follow
His way.

D Shawn Small
THE OLD ONES

Thunder boom and lightning crack
above the tempest shore.
Wind howl and waves wrack
this isle of elder lore.
Cliffs arise unto the stars
the heavens in align.
Voice uplifted to a far,
waiting for a sign.
Incantations out of time,
blacker than the pit.
From ancient vaulted corridors
limned,
cold, silent as the crypt.
Black clouds roll,
comets streak the sky.
Torturing the soul,
from those who never die.
The Old Ones return
to reclaim what was once theirs;
Knowing more than they had learned
to bring alive man's nightmares.

Theodosia Richey
HUNGER AT HOME

Do you ever think twards home, of
hungry children all alone.

Tiny legs, arms and feet, swollen
bellies, again I repeat,

Do you ever think twards home, in
the slums your brother moans.

Between this poverty line he's
caught, too weak to care of wars to be
fought.

How can you demand his faith and
trust, when it's power you thirst with
angry lust.

I can see what you have done,
you've turned your back on your
native son.

So feed the hungry, and clothe the
poor, turn away, yet look once more,
to the quiver of a tiny hand, as a
child dies in his native land.

Eileen C Egelske
HAPPINESS

Looking at a rainbow with soft colors
bright,
Taking long walks on cool moonlit
nights;
Beams of sunshine and bright colored
flowers,
Relaxing and enjoying a day's final
hour.

Joy felt in the soul when things go
right,
Little children with their eyes shining
bright;
A firm handclasp, loving hug, and a
smile,
Make one feel special and quite
worthwhile.

Rain on the roof, a soft summer's
breeze,
Laughter and fun—maybe even a
tease;
Stars in the sky on a clear winter
night,
And friends that keep one always in
sight.

A gentle call or touch from one who
cares,
Sunrise—sunset, God's splendor to
share,
Attending church with its steeple so
tall,
Watching a puppy romp and play
with a ball.

Photos and scrapbooks of memories
long ago,
Helping a friend—letting love and
care show:
A few little things, that by now you
can guess,
They're part of my life and bring me
"happiness."

Thomas J Bounauito
THE ONLY ONE I LOVE

Dedicated to Kim Berleth in memory of Love and Friendship

I know in my heart now that I love
only one person,
There are no others that I wish to
embrace,
To hold her just for a moment would
be such a joy,
To marry her words could never say,
If I am only to be her friend then I
will love her as a friend always and
no other,
For she is the one I love.

If I am not to be her friend that I
will cherish every fleeting moment,
Every memory will I love and not
another for she is the only one I love,
And though I know I do not hold the
keys to her heart,
She will always hold the keys to
mine,
For I love her with all my heart, mind
and soul to be with me as one unto
God and no other,
For she is the only one I love.

Jimmie L Dickinson
VIBRATIONS OF TRUTH

Vibrations of truth
The terror of fear
The starkness of reality
The frailty in you.
My search for knowledge
The secrets of life
My leap for wisdom
But still out of sight.

Our world is small
And time has won.
The years have teased us
The crowds are gone.
The last race to run
Will surely be
In an area no larger
Than all of me.

Rosalie Grab
LISTEN

For Clement and Rose Who Always Heard

Her heart lives on a mpountain,
Her soul dwells at the sea.
When we're wise enough to listen,
She speaks to you and me.

But we've lost the gift of silence
And in turn we lose her words

When she speaks to us through oceans
And through myriad songs of birds.

We fill our ears with clamor,
Fill our days with hours planned;
No time to feel the breeze,
No time to touch the land.

It's not too late to hear her,
Feel her gentle majesty—
Nature's heart lives on a mountain,
Her sould dwells at the sea.

Johnathan Richard
THIS THING

To Suzanne, the first love of my life and I hope the Last.

Are you at fault, or is it me
when longings rise to this degree?

Is touching more than thought of touch,
when wanting seems to mean so much?

And from where do warm dreams spring,
the moistened palms and heartbeats sing?

Is this thing you, or just in me,
the way you are, or what I see?

And if I knew, would all this stay,
or like a shadow fade away?

Can passion wane in cold hard facts,
fanned instead when reason lacks?

For if knowing now will set me free,
then ever the fool I'd rather be.

Sherri L Holland
ONLY ONE
A choice is very hard to make;
Which one will it be?
Who will love you most of all
And who will set you free?

Love is not a silly game;
Feelings are at stake.
You can't keep hurting both of them
Or they won't be there to take.

They both have showed their love for you;
Try to choose just one.
Cause if you try to keep them both;
They'll leave . . . and then there's none.

So please, my friend, it's very clear;
You can't go on this way.
Choose the one that's right for you;
The other must go away.

Larry Lee Transou
REFLECTION ON THE DRAFT

This poem is dedicated to the memory of those Americans serving in the U.S. military forces who lost their lives in Asia between 1950 and 1975; and for those who returned, never to be the same.

Deep in the dark recesses of night,
Lost, in contemplation of things metaphysical;
My mind's inner eye—
Turned to thoughts, almost whimsical.

The rules are still made by those who have gold;
Proudly, they now wave, when our flag it unfolds:
While counting profits from junk bonds, newly sold—
No tears do they shed, for the young dead—
Who will never grow old.

Conscription will return to the Republic in time;
Out of resignment, I have penned these few lines:
Before I close, in all candor, this I must say—
"No, not my son, on his eighteenth birthday"!

If my statement shocks you, on first inspection;
You'll agree with me later, after further reflection:
For it's because, you see, back in the summer of 1969
I reported to my draft board, and I got in line.

Not until those who used money, power, or fame
To avoid serving honorably, when their turn came;
Only after their sons are standing in line—
Then, and only then, can you call for mine!

Susanne Heinz

Susanne Heinz
BLANK VERSE
When I'm alone,
I think of my desires;
Of how much
I want to love one man
Deeply and well—
Like the matched and measured verse
I write so easily.

But when I love,
It is more like blank verse;
Uneven, unadorned and unpredictable.
—My love does not rhyme
Well, not all the time

Which is not to say
That I cannot love deeply and well;
I just prefer blank verse.

Debbie Rodriguez
THESE TEARS ARE REAL
You made me feel alive,
then let me down
Told me you loved me
Gave me gifts and love
Then you closed up
Sent me away with the
pain you gave
Told me you cared but
looking away when said
Fighting me when I ask
questions
You made me cry and
laughed about it
Sweetheart,
these tears are real
They fall night and day
Making them worse by all
the lies you tell
I can not no more
of this pain
I have to say good-bye,
but I will always love you
So please come back and
take these tears away.

Brooke Baker
THE LEAVES
The leaves
falling from the trees . . .
drifting so
gently
and
softly
to the ground.
The morning dew
glittering on their
multi-colored tips . . .
drifting
like last year's memories.

Edward Simpson
MY VALENTINE

This poem is dedicated to my loving wife, KAZ.

Your smile as bright as the morning star,
Is locked in my heart when you're near or far.
The twinkle of love I find in your eyes,
Sends my heart soaring high in the skies.

The warmth of your lips when you press them to mine,
Causes my heart to skip time after time.
How beautiful you're to me in every loving way,
I thank God your mine on this Valentine's Day.

Marie Aragon
SOLITUDE
In the early morning hours, as I walk along the sandy beach, the cool dampness makes my clothes cling to every fiber of my body. Walking barefoot along the water's edge I feel like the lone seagull above me. I'm flying alone in a world of beauty created by nature. As my eyes take in everything around me—my thoughts turn to you. My soul would be content if you were here sharing this peace with me.

Rhonda M Hupka
WHAT WE CALL LIVING

Dedicated to the memory of HENRY C. GILMORE (SLIM)

We can't change the past.
No, we can't even change our destiny.
The hurtful words that echo through eternity.
The painful feelings that burn in our hearts.
The words of regret swollen in our throats.
The dark corridors we wander through,
Unknowing of their outcome.
Unwilling to accept the results.
Struggling to sustain.
Fighting to survive.
Until we reach the final mile.
Long,
Dark,
Cold and lonely.
This is what we call living.
With one goal from the first breath we take,
Dying,
Death,
Eternal rest and peace.

Michelle Marie Thomas
REALITY

To my friends and family, thank you for your love and support, and I would like to especially like to thank my mother.

A cry in the night
A lonely deep sigh
A feeling of grief, frightened deep fear
The night is a lonely place, she knows all too well
The darkness is like a raging inferno in the depths of hell
She cries one last time before the pain disappears
As the pain dies so do her hopes and fears
She is one of a million of relentless cries
So the story goes
Everyone dies

Bob Singer
GEDICHT ZWEI

To Amnesty International

I never saw a Gary Gilmore,
I never hope to see one,
But one thing I'll tell you,
I'd rather see than be one!

I never saw a head of state,
I never hope to see one,
But one thing I'll tell you,
I'd rather see than be one!

There was nary a murmur when they
Dropped the bomb!
Then why the hell does Gilmore
Get all of the aplomb!

Janet Williams Luczak
EACH MOMENT OF LIFE IS A MOMENT LOST

To my mother and my husband For their inspiration and support

Each moment of life
Is a moment lost
Each song but a memory
The shadows of the past follow
The dreams of the future lead
Walk slowly, my friend
The end of the road is near
Stop to taste sweet wine
Cast aside all that is bitter
Waste not your voice with words
Let your heart cry out
Along the road, another listens for the song
The souls will hear
Their harmony echoing in the silence
Joy is found
For a moment
The moment is lost
The song becomes a memory

Richard Lawrence Taylor
THE SEA

To those who, know, love and appreciate, the awesome power, the life sustaining love and the spirit of the sea.

The sea! That vamp from Powel's hand,
Whose heaving breast, has succored man.

Her kisses, spawned in bitches brew,
Now teases land, that she once knew.

Though wise is she, in secret heart,
At times there's rage, she's loathed to start.

Yet know her heart is tender, still,
For loves sweet passion, flames her will.

And deep within her womb she's borne,
The flesh that spirits all have worn.

I hear her song in surfs' white glee.
And watch her dance with spirit free.

Oh! How her passion stirs my soul,
To stay with her and love her bold.

Because you see; through times long test,
The sea, has always, loved us best.

Reana K Thibodo
CRY

To the memory of Violet Ann Thibodo
My mother whom I'll always love and miss

Cry for you when you are gone.
Cry for you when you are happy
Cry for you when you are sad
Cry for you when you are sweet
Cry for you when you want to end it all
Cry for you when you want to live on
Cry for you when you care for me
Cry for you when you love me so
Cry for you when you cry for me
Cry for you

Jack A Markham
TO MY DAD

I know this proud man who once stood taller,
Now in his wheel chair, he seems much smaller.
His legs don't move to his minds command,
So he sits and waits for a helping hand.
Sounds to him are not so loud,
But he'll not complain, for he's too proud.
His eyes have dimmed, with the passing years,
And to see him like this, to my eyes bring tears.
This aging man that looks so sad,
I'm proud to say that he's my Dad.
I know this poem is just some words,
(But growing old is for the birds!)

Sherrie Ahlstrom Hundley
WHEN AUTUMN COMES

I saw you in autumn,
down on your knees planting bulbs,
placing and covering them tenderly,
where they would stay dormant
until spring.

Now in April,
my window frames your yard
in all its glorious splendor, where
bright red tulips and yellow daffodils
are swaying in the breeze,
adding color and beauty to my life.

It reminds me of our friendship . . .
Planted long ago in autumn,
it has weathered many a long winter,
lying somewhat dormant at times, but
always there, ready to grow and
bloom again,
bringing me happiness through the
years.

When autumn comes once more
I'll watch you then,
knowing that the springtime
will bring me joy again.

Linda M Conrad
ONCE MORE . . .

You long for the comfort,
Of another man's arms,
That one special love
That can do you no harm.

You think that you've found it
So often, it seems,
Then fate wanders in
And steals all your dreams.

That heady exuberance
You had at the start,
Gets crushed in the end
When he tramples your heart.

So the game you continue,
With caution this time.
You know all the players,
You've heard all the rhymes.

There are no set rules,
And the object is—win!
But your chips are cashed in
And it's hard to begin . . . once more.

Lisa Naomi Stansbury
my creation

I cry and attempt to break down the wall of tension that has formed in me
I want people to understand why I am afraid to show these feelings
Why the wall of tension is there
I know whatever I try to explain to someone will not always be fully understood
People can say they understand what you're going through
But I know we all have different levels of understanding
So I don't try to force someone to understand me
I see no use in force, it only creates rebellion and rejection
no one wants to listen to something they think they know so they don't or they agree and just sit here and it gets real upsetting so you quit and start building that wall of tension

It's a place most people don't like to think about—totally lonely
you feel so alone and you want to shout out but you know no one will hear you
they just stare at you, you're a nothing, a no one
So you do things that you will regret someday, but it gets your attention and that's what you want, to be a part of what is and of what will be
so you start a world of your own, the wall you build
separates you from the rest of the world
and you have a wall of tension
and you have to break it down
after the todays are gone
and the tomorrows have come

John A Calabrese
THE BLUE ORCHID

In loving memory of Wolford E. Tattman, Arthur Tamblyn, and Omus S. Dilheim.

Aurora woke, beheld thine own sad eyes and wept.
Fair lady! mine own sword doth pierce my heart
when witness I the sorrow there.
Oh Damosel! relinquish thy grief to me
For thee 'twil I bear;
Mine only task.
Then wouldst unknowing Earth be worthy of thy grace?

Lo! Rags of cloud disperse;
Hanging bars disband.
The brilliance of Helios?
Nay.
I descry thy smile.

Renee T Richard
PRESIDENT BUSH AND I, WORLDS APART

This poem is dedicated to the few that encouraged me to fly together.
We shall all shine throughout eternity. Later Days

Oh Master of Reality, living in a bubble
He who holds the whole world in his hands
What am I but a grain of sand
I sometimes see the smiles, I always see the frowns
I've had such dreams but some were taken away
Greed and the American Dream are both here to stay
I'm weak, drained, and weary
Fighting to survive in a society that will someday
I'm sure label me as insane
They push me down, they call me names
They call me the loser because I refuse to play their games
Open your eyes, Oh Master of Reality
living in a bubble so sweet
I told myself I'd also be a winner
but when things got tough and I asked for a helping hand
I was left to die
Help me to help myself or are you just like the rest
Will you also walk away and forget?

Sylvia M Conner
SLEEPLESS NIGHTS

To my inspiration, Richard Conner, husband, lover, and Best Friend

If I woke you at one
Would you still think it fun?
If you woke me at two
I'd know what to do.
If I woke you at three
Would you make love to me?
If you woke me at four
We'd make love once more.
If I woke you at five
You would surely come alive!

If you woke me at six
It would put us in a fix . . .
I should be doing the bacon,
Instead of the love we're making.
We're loving each other way past seven,
With you, I feel I am in heaven!
It's ten after eight,
And you're very late.
But the world seems fine
When you leave—Quarter to nine.

Eddie Williams
ANOTHER DAY

Another day for I to look at black, and see the world in hatred,
Suffering,
Just continuing on
Never knowing when to stop,
What have we created?
Another dark hole never again to see the light.
inequitable cost,
expendable floss,
for the world a created hell.
Prosperity founded forever bound ahead,
Somehow we're diminishing,
The world,
All's doomed dead.
Air expands, crosstip our tornado watches,
Towering flame
For who will be named
Solicitor of our world?
Gaseous energy bales, forever we drive nails in a concrete caused pollution.
Shriek my life mankind at hand,
Dying,
Fading,
We have no land.
Find us fate do tell,
can you ever see
the earth as us in hell?

Claudette R Hatcher
HUGS

A hug is a welcome with open arms.
It is kindness and hope without alarms.

A hug is a warm and friendly embrace
Expressly designed for the human race.

A hug provided with tender loving care
Is a cherished expression that two can share.

This oneness supplies a dual release
By giving to each . . . a moment of peace.

Marta L Sondermann
SUNSETS

What happens at the end of the day,
When the sun must then have its final say—
Then the sun fades into the west,
With shimmering colors that give the sky zest,
In turn this gesture grants beauty, and serenity into the night.
As the moon rises with all its might,
To give lovers and friends a yearning so bright,
And captures the soul showing wrong from right.
We enter into a realm of peace,
Until tomorrow, when the sun will rise in the east.

The miracle that I have just described, is that of the sunset that appears in your eyes,
And pacifies the negativity and the cries,
As the day before, . . . finally dies.

While we walk along the sands,

The moon shone upon our hands.
Watching the waves crash on into the shore—
Seeking that unopened door—
Relating to each other's lore, . . .
Forever wanting more.

Diane E Reilly
FREEDOM

To MADDOG, who proved that proper leadership, can allow DREAMS to come true.

A journey of endless motion,
befuddled by historic Notion.
Beneath a Mountain, a chronic form of Perception,
Stored a Poison, possessive of potential power.
THIS DISEASE, Stagnant, remained primed to expedite Infection.

A Rare Thorn, bent on immigrating the race, designed to riddle a space.
Embedded in the middle, discovered Class, in spite of surrounding trash.
Air filled with Despair, claimed distress as unfair.
Many wept . . . while others refused to sleep, Global Cries, awakened a Vital Force.
An Avalanche, leveled the place,
Exposed the toxic Source.
Tender hands, Uncovered those that slept, as others Cradled those that wept.

Technology, bared, a system lacking vision, escaped, spatial Stimulation.
A sound resolution, provided Evolution, brought forth a Revolution.
Ignorance granted for Organized Depression, denied FREEDOM of EXPRESSION

Kevin Miller-Harris
NIGHTMARES

Dedicated to those who returned but did not, and my sons Kevin and Jason, "May you never know the hell of combat or live its aftermath."

Many nights last forever
Some are never born

Coming from the nightmares
Many nights are torn

Nightmares at night
Blood is all around

Death, dying slow
Nothing else comes easy
Nothing makes them go

Many nights last forever . . .

Jaime A Merchant
A MATTER OF HEALTH

To Ben: For all that you have done for me since the first day that I started working for you! You are a wonderful boss, and have been a good friend! Thank you for everything! With great respect—Love Jaime

To have your hearing tested, is a very important issue; There may be some slight problem, and you wouldn't have a clue.
Have it tested yearly, and take along your spouse; Or some familiar voice that you hear around the house.
I know a real fine gentleman, that will give you a free test; Benjamin Solomon is his name, and he really is the best!
He's a Certified Hearing Aid Specialist; A friend and terrific boss;
He will gladly help you to find out, if you have a hearing loss.
If you should often find you need, things repeated twice; It may be beneficial, to wear a hearing aid device.
Many different types of aids, Mr. Solomon will demonstrate to you;
When he fits one in your ear, it will make you feel brand new!
Our office is shared with a doctor, and is working out just fine;
The girls are very pleasant, the atmosphere's divine.
There's plenty of free parking, you don't have to pay a dime;
The only thing we ask you bring; Is patience and your time.
So if you want your hearing checked; call for the time and date;
I'm sure you'll agree; Ben Solomon to be; A man that is truly great!

Gary Ebanks
TIME WAS

To the memory of my Grandmother Flossie

Time was, when I believed in fairytales.
Time was, when romantic notions filled my dreams.
Time was, when heroes were bigger than life and set patterns to be followed.
Time was, but those times have passed.

Time was, when life was for growing older,
For adventures by the select few.
For taking chances, and having lovers.
For travel unimpeded.

Time was, when foundations were laid, values stressed and solidified.
Time was, when angels sang and smiled,
Now, they too have passed with time.

Margaret Kathryn Davis
THE HOMELESS

His hair is grey, and his clothes so faded, and torn.
His eyes look so distant, and his face filled with scorn.
His home will vary from night, to night.
Everyday for a small meal to eat, he might have to fight.

A full meal is something he seldom does see.
He begs for spare change from passers, like you, and me.
He is faint in his spirit, which once held his dreams.
His body so thin, and his hands shaky, and lean.

All night he will break sleep from a dreadful fear, that street thieves will steal his shelter, and they are always near.
So, I ask who sits at their table, with smothered chicken that's boneless:
"Let's say a special prayer for those people who are poor, and who are homeless. "

Elayne Lee
DESTINY?

To BD with great affection and appreciation for allowing me to be what and who I am by not passing judgements.

Loving brings such pain it seems to be the way,
I'm wanting your good loving and needing it today.
Your gentle touch and caring ways,
the humor and the laughter,
secret touches hinting blushes. Tell me it's not over.
This hurting has a hold on me it's ripping at my heart,
my friend you are the one I love,
dear God don't let us part.

Grant me one last favor a promise you must make,
go home tonight and hold her and in your arms you'll take.
Tell her that you love her you'll never stray no more,
and if you cannot do this, then grant me one wish more.
Tell me you don't love me and never want me near,
a love like ours is hard to find, just tell me what you fear.

If you cannot do this please know that I am bound,
to love you through eternity until our love is found.
Each life we live we learn and grow
I'm glad this life I got,
to share some time and love with you, but know it's not enough.
Fade softly from my memories and let my tear drops dry,
Lord free my soul from misery, just let me know the reasons why.

Once again I say goodbye, for love should set you free,
I only pray someday we'll find, ours was meant to be.

Father Jesus Great Spirit
SUCCESS KEEPS KNOCKING

Success keeps knocking, knocking on my door,
But she is a cheap and flattering whore.
I'll invite her in and wash off her paint,
And teach her how to become a great saint.
I know how, like a moth, she's drawn to flame,
How she has besmirched her God-given name,
How she sells out to the highest bidder,
Turning human souls to worthless litter.
She has prostituted many a soul
In her alluring, but terrible role
Of leading many away from their God,
Burying their bodies beneath the dark sod.
When I baptize her, then I'll get near her
For I love success, no longer fear her

Evelyn L Opalinski Durkin
COUNTRY FIDDLER

Great house parties of times gone past—
How I wish that they could last.

Friends gather to talk, eat, and dance—
Maybe even find Romance.
Jonas, the fiddler, tunes his violin
With large chubby fingers and a B–ig Grin.
How he made that fiddle sing!
Lots of music in every string.
Waltzes, polkas, two steps, and more—
Couples stomped across the floor.
Homespun-fun—what a ball.—
Following the fiddler's music and call.
Grab your partner form a square—
Gents bow low to your lady fair—
Round the circle and don't be slow—
Meet each gal with a dosey-do,
Gents back home,
Bow left and right
Swing your lady out of sight.

As I said, all this is past—
But thoughts go back.

Memories Last.

Angela E Street

Angela E Street
PEACE AND LOVE

For my Lovely Husband, David

Peace, we all want,
And love we all need!
The gift of freedom,
We all want to keep!
We must love each other
And trust one another
To keep the freedom
We all need!
Our life is too precious to throw away,
Therefore fight for peace
And don't delay!
The time will come
When we have to decide,
Do we all want peace in our mind?

Mary L Kern
CONVERSING WITH GOD

Dedicated to Sherry, my exhorter

Up the hill of life and through the valleys, too,
I have known strife,
and been its cause, it's true.

Through all the struggle, fear and doubt,
wondering what it's all about,
I found the way to You.

And, still at times it's rough.
Paranoia sneaks on in,
but mostly when I've sinned
my old familiar sin.

So, when I feel sorry for Poor li'l ole me,
give me a much needed nudge, Lord
and direct my eyes to Thee.

Somehow, it's the valleys,
low as they may seem,
that help me find the courage
and give life to my dream.

Trina M Buschbascher
A CHILD'S LAUGHTER DIES

A child's laughter dies,
As he hears the door unlatch.
A man,
Standing there like stone,
Smiles a sinister grin.
Looking alike,
Although one cowers in fear

And the other boasts of power.
You have been
And it's time for your punishment.
The child leaps with fear
And the man laughs with abandonment.
Together they meet
One is fulfilled
As the other wonders why?
Child tell me those words,
I'm longing to hear,
As the tears slide, the child whispers,
"I love you". . .

Denise Markins
MOTHER

This poem is dedicated to my wonderful mother, Donna Cole. I love you, mom. Thank you for the inspiration.

So precious is a mother,
her love is never-ending.
There could never be another
to whom my love I'm sending.

She's always there to dry my tears
throughout the day or night.
When she's around I have no fears.
In darkness she's my light.

In life no matter what I do
She understands and always cares.
She'll take my hand and guide me through
all my burdens I have to bear.

I'll never be worthy to fill her shoes.
I could never be half as great.
With spirit like hers you'll never lose.
She's someone you just can't duplicate.

Minnie Tiegs
LIFE & LOVE

Gary, Allen & Robert Tiegs & Families

Life is splendid
Love is wonderful

Life is full of surprises,
Love is full of glamor.

Life is exciting
Love is enticing.

Life is full of wonderment,
Love is full of gestures.

Life is a splendor of dreams that can come true
Love is a wonderful trauma that is beautiful.

Life is full of wonderful things God created
Love is what we show in God's creation.

Life is making best of what we have
Love is to share with others what we have in most fulfillment.

Life is doing our work with pride
Love is doing our deeds in full enjoyment.

Life is caring for neighbors and friends
Love is helping those that need help and are in despair.

Life is praying for world peace,
Love is having eternal peace and happiness.

Joseph E Shelley
BE STILL MY HEART
Be still my heart, don't take the blame
And never grow old for life is beautiful,
and gay I have been told.
Be still my heart, don't take the blame
A life of love and beauty is your aim.
For God has blessed your name.

Be still my heart, don't take the blame
Now that age has taken my youth,
I linger for love, just a while longer.
For God always takes his claim.

Be still my heart, don't take the blame
Don't be afraid,
For God always take his claim.

I heard a voice saying, I am, I am—
HE

The beginning and the end.
The greatest words I have heard from
Mankind on earth is Love, if you have love,
And never have been loved back,
The voice said, "Come with me"
now, I see,
OH! my heart is free.

Kristine O Vrooman Altman
TRUTH
the gaze of a child

a teasing breeze
which longs to
disturb
the freshly-done coiffure
of the dignified matron
who fears she is going
bald

a wonder
to the tale-tellers
an instinct
to the simple
who live nothing but
it

a hope
whose winds will invade
every niche
and sweep up all within His Grasp

The Gaze of
A Child

Deborah A Garfield
RED ROSE

Love to my four Garfield children, family and friends of Ware, Mass.

As I was walking down the road,
I met a very strange man.
He handed me a red rose,
And kissed me on the hand.

I was fearful of what was happening.
But couldn't resist his touch.
I wanted to run and hide from him,
But my heart was beating too much.

He walked with me through meadows.
And unspokenly made love to me.
He caressed my tender body,
And kissed me passionately

Many years have come and gone.
But remember that warm spring day.
When I was handed a red rose
and love sort of took me away

Melba L Bieber
THE GLORY OF GOD

An interlude, The Rock of Grace!

My body is a temple of the living God,
the earth is the Lord's and the fullness thereof,
I must let God fill my mind, my soul, and my very body.
My life is all highlands, mountains,
and valleys and lowlands.
Behold! The heavens is thy God's!
and all they that dwell therein!
I declare the glory of God!
and his handiwork is the Lord's!

Calvin Bailey III
LIVING SEASONS

Dedicated to my Great-Grandmother Grace Faatz

As Winter breaths her mighty cold,
the days go by and by,
through Summer's light we shine our days like whispers in the night.
Through the falling days of Autumn's might, we hear the wind blow cold,
but as the Spring comes around, the Winter days have taken her toll.

In the early days of Winter, we see the men run cold,
but as her winds blow through the night, her laughter becomes more bold.
For many days and lifeless nights,
she shall rule the way,
until her laughter will be drained by the many powers of rain.

Patricia Kackman
JESUS IN MY STABLE
He emptied my soul of its burden
and filled it with glory and grace.
He took all my sin and my struggle
and made a clean room of the place.
Each time that I tried to refill it
with substitutes for His own love,
He swept it away
my dirty hay
and brought down His love from above.

Preparing a fresh bed to lie in,
He lifted and shifted each load,
removing the cobwebs and clutter,
to settle into His abode.
He chose to come live in my stable
that He might no more have to roam.
He bid me not stray
that He might stay
and take me some day to His home.

Elias Hruska
REFLECTION

To you, Maria, for your love and encouragement and for helping me to see a deeper truth.

The fog is sometimes
like the ocean
hiding mountains
our citadels of silence
like a deeper truth.

From the depths
an acrobat springs
leaving rainbows
in his wake.

Mildred M Cook Brookins
HAPPY REUNION

To the 437th. Troop Carrier Group, WW II. Especially to my brother AAF Pilot, Major Burton S. Cook.

Eagles of the sky, each one,
Zooming high into the blue,
Almost touching the face of God,
Ever faithful, ever true.
Mighty sons, of a mighty nation,
With hearts and minds so just,
Night and day, we pray for you,
As in our God, we trust.
God bless and keep you, noble sons,
In "glory" or in "flames",
These things we ask,—we pray . . .
We pray, in "Jesus" name.
Courageous Eagles of the sky,
When your job is done,—
Spread your wings and hurry back,
And thank the Lord, you've won.
Soon now, when the night is creeping,
Creeping down from the hill,
And over the peaceful valley . . .
The dew still heavy with chill,
While rustlings are heard in the hedges,
Of night birds, flying low—
And like ghosts in the quiet darkness,
The glimmering fireflies glow;
May the deep and solemn stillness,
Be broken by the drone—
Of many, mighty Eagles . . winging safely,
Winging. . Safely. . Home.

Doris M Sergeant
TRUE LOVE

Dedicated to my husband, Jack and Children Phyllis, Stephen and Grace

True love is beautiful and is boundless
Like the movement of a river
Which flows in a slow steady pattern of motion
Against the beautiful blue skies in the heavens above.

It makes its way silently but surely
And one knows that it is there
For it is warm, gentle and as real
As the trees, the flowers and the birds around us.

It brings happiness and joy and yet
It can bring much sadness and sorrow
It can bring tears to our eyes
And pain to our hearts.

But let us not forget that this is life
It is a windmill of many passions
And let us also remember
That this is what life is all about.

Virginia March
THE LITTLE MERMAID
She wears a crown of seashells
upon her silken hair,
And dances with the towering
waves without a single care.
At night she sits upon a rock to
watch the velvet sky,
And from this Little Mermaid you
hear a tiny sign . . .

Dr Louise McClurg
JIMMY

To my beloved husband who was all the things this poem depicts

Do I have to say I love you?
You must truly know I do;
Sure as there's a sky above you,
Sure as there's an ocean blue;
Can it be that I don't know you?

Though the years do come and go;
You must truly know I love you,
Though I never tell you so;
There are those who say I love you,
Easily, and often too;
But they never show they love you,
By the little things they do;

Words are like the fancy wrapping,
On the candy that you eat;
Would you rather have the wrapping?
Or enjoy the candy treat;
Just a look of fond affection,
At a time when things look blue;
Just a handclasp when you're tired,
Sends a message, I love you;
Sometimes dear, the word unspoken,
Can mean more if understood,
Than all the loud I love you's
That I would say dear, if I could.

Annie Ruth Waldsmith

SLAIN TREE

The squirrels could scamper from man,
And the birds could take flight,
But the tree was helpless.
It could not run away and it had no wings.
Long it had mulched the earth
And cleansed the air.
Many time it had sheltered a nest
Of eggs wise in feather lore.
Now it lies dead, its glorious rings bleeding.
They count the years when it was loved
And nourished by the sun
And watered by the rain,
When it sang and swayed and danced
With the wind.
Now it lies dead,
And its dirge was the saw's pitiless whine,
It's funeral service was a curse
For its toughness.
Earth and life and man are poorer
For the slain tree.

C Russell Ziegler

MY FATHER'S HAND

To my loving wife Novice Ziegler
I Love you
Forever and ever and ever AMEN

I remember when I could only reach around one finger
yet it was able to hold me up when I was down.
What a privilege to reach up taking two steps to one
it told me he loved me without making a sound.

Then came the time I could reach around two fingers
and it didn't seem so far up to his eyes.
Not a worry or a care if I could reach his hand.
I was Daddy's man when I was half his size.

Soon a third finger would fit into my hand
and the walks got longer as the trail got rough.
Yet the price was small for the pride inside.
My father was a man that men called tough.

Yesterday I found I could hold all his fingers
and I guess now that I've become a man.
As I walk with him now stride for stride.
Thanks Father for my father's hand.

Now what is this wrapped around my finger
and is taking two steps to one, My Little Man.
Am I starting all over this journey through life?
Then God make my hand like my father's hand.

Reverend E Paul Beavers

Reverend E Paul Beavers

AS YOU ARE

Through 31 Wonderful Years—my loving Wife, Ethel.

Dear, lovely and sweet—just as you are,—
I love, and adore you far
Above all others, despite the artistry they affect,
You're true and natural—yet 'tis easy to detect
Your finer traits, and their unfeigned reality,
Your many subtle facets . . . you have personality!

I'm captivated by the beauty of your smile,
Your grace and poise, all of your charms—and all without guile;
I admire your teeth, which shine as pearls,
Your genteel manners—Oh! so many things over other girls!
I am not unaware of all of this, and it is admissible,
Your impish nose and your provocative lips! . . .
You're kissable!

Yet you can be solemn and serious. even frown,
And when you're groomed! Ah! you have all it takes to take a town!
You're versatile, calm as you wish, yet you can be tiger-quick,—
You're languid, then of such savoir-faire—you are chic!

But give me your unsophisticated sweetness,
Your unspoiled demeanor, your unstudied neatness,
Give me your sparkle and your warmth, of a few
Of the many entrancing virtues that make you—YOU!

Give me you, just as you are—with the wit never to bore me;
You are as a lively freshet—and seem to restore me,—
When I'm all jaded by the wilted world around me,—
As a Fairy with a magic wand . . .
you lift me and crown me;
I come forth from the sullied World, into the radiance of the smile you give,—
Into the World of mystery and wonder . . . fresh and eager as a child—to live!

Scott Crull

MY LOVE FOR YOU

Dedicated To My Children
Jaci and Scotty
And Mom and Dad

Quiet as the setting sun, is my love for you.

So soft is your personality, that reaches out and captures my deepest interest, motivating me beyond my limits.

Quiet as the setting sun, is my love for you.

Like rain falling from the sky and filling a pool of emotions.
Flooding my head . . . feeding the desire to give . . . take and refuse . . .
I can't find the reasons for the way I am.

But . . .
Quiet as the setting sun,
is my love for you.

Beyond my deepest dreams, there is only you.
In front of my every want, there is only you.
Whenever you are down and lonely, my love is for you.

Quiet as the setting sun, my love . . . this love is for you.

Kelly Whisenant

ETERNAL WILL

Take my wealth, for I've none to give but the immaterial material things I have gathered along the way. Take also my trust, for it has been disrupted by those who I once cared for.

I give thee my mind. It was once a beautiful flowing river where thoughts drifted here and there. But with time, it has been drained to an empty bed of rocks and rust. Last of all, receive my love. It is unused, for none have felt it and it has never been reciprocated. It was my most treasured and troubled possession. So, take my wealth and prosper; my trust and remain honest; my mind and let it go; but with my love be sparing. For when the true love comes along, you shall have more than enough to shower them with.

Jerry R Harter

FOREVER FLOWERS

This poem is dedicated to my two children, Blake & Tiffany who have been very supportive of me.

Forever Flowers grow and grow
Fragrance of Gods breath to us sweet smelling scent
Colors so refined designed by an everlasting mind
Seedlings blown by winds crevices and cracks within
Tightly fitting seeds, flowers upward stems divine
Colors wine and crimson red, oh beautiful the flower bed
To see flowers growing wild, handfuls picked by a child
Wedding baskets full, the beauty of the flower grows
Into the day, the foreverness of baskets full of brightly lighted flowers in the flower shop
The man will stop and buy a dozen roses for his fiancee, a brighter day
the role they play
Forever flowers grow magnificence from above
God's love divine, the gift of flowers mine

Monica S Youngblood

THE EAGLE

Drifting through time,
With no destiny assigned
The moonlight shines brightly,
Wherever he may fly.

His golden-toned wings,
Show his courage and strength
And sharpness in sight,
To guide him through life.

He searches for prey,
With intelligence and delight
It's a game of survival,
We all must fight.

Surrounding his territory,
The competitors await
Leaving these opponents,
With no dignity or faith.

The capture has been made,
Yet no feelings are spared
This eagle with no heart,
Leaves his victims unaware.

This so called creature,
Is the eagle, in one's mind
Yet in its own disguise,
Has been man all this time.

Glen the Pen

DRIFTWOOD

I, too, was once just Driftwood,
Tossed by the wind and tide,
Battered by life and the elements
With no safe place to hide.

Washed up on the sand and left there,
Bitter, uncaring, alone,
Until you came along one day, my dear,
Picked me up and brought me home!

Luetta G Sturgeon

HAPPINESS

A volunteer is very dear giving time from year, to year.
It is satisfying to know that some one you help are grateful for all that we do.

It is A pleasure the work that we do, seeing the loving smiles that we get,
The young and the old and the in-between appreciate our time we give.

We volunteers are very kind, and make people happy all the time. From year, to year, We try to please, We are glad to be A volunteer.

Lorraine R Collier

IF I COULD CHANGE THE TIME GONE BY

To mom, you're in my heart forever

If I could change the time gone by
I know what I would do.
I'd make it so that I could spend a lot more time with you
I find it hard to face each day, that you're no longer a part
I feel I have a gaping hole that goes straight thru my heart
The pain they say will fade away, the memories will remain
But now that you have gone away,
I'll never be the same

I miss your wink, your smiling face,
that punch across my chin
I only pray there is a God, and we
will meet again
So mom until that time arrives and
then my life is thru
I know I'll run to open arms, those
arms belong to you

Eleanor White
I COME TO YOU, MY LORD

To my grandson, Brian with love

I come to You, today, My Lord
And kneel down at Your feet . . .
And bow my lowly head and pray
Please, God, make me complete . . .
I ask divine forgiveness
For my sins both large and small . . .
And ask to hold Your hand, dear
Lord
Before from grace I fall.

I know not how but suddenly
I felt Your tender touch . . .
And thank Thee, Lord, for giving me
New life and, oh, so much . . .
If I can just remember
Your time in Gethsemane . . .
And the trip You took for me
Dear Lord, to that hill in Calvary . . .
I know I'll have no problem
With whatever comes my way . . .
For You see, dear God in Heaven
I was born, again, today.

Elizabeth M Byggdin
ARBOREAL BRIDE
Vision of youth she stands
In bridal lace,
Virginal white her bands,
Her stature grace.

Waiting, in white adorned,
Her bridegroom—Spring;
Wedded, within her form
Nascent offspring.

Green as the grass that springs
Beneath her feet,
Like baby hands, buds cling,
Her joy complete.

Henry McVane
TO THE WORLD

This poem is dedicated to my parents, brothers, sister, and immediate aunts & uncles. I also want to dedicate it to the teachers of 1988-89 school year. Last, but not least my friend Lashonda and the Lord Jesus Himself.

To the world I give a heart of love,
To share with each person alive.
To the world I give the thought of,
Wanting to learn how to survive.

To the world I give heart-felt
thoughts,
To carry from day to day.

To the world I give many battles
unfought,
In order to learn how to pray.

To the world I give a change of heart,
To share with the living poor.
To the world I give a word from God,
Which will stand forever more.

To the world I give an everlasting
peace,
That makes them want to share.
To the world I give more to please,
To make them want to care.

To the world I give a supply of air,
To last until their life end.
To the world I give energy to be
there,
When others need a friend

Debby Kramer
HEAVENLY BODY
The Heavenly Body life in our skies
time keeps on standing with the
wondering why.
Through all the beauty of color the
darkness will find.
More information of life in our mind.
The stars that come in billions that
hold in the milkyway that gleams.
That goes on forever is the way it
seems.
The wonders and whys that time
didn't show
Technology came along where the
Heavenly Body will go
Something can't come from nothing
as time came about
In the finding out why and having
some doubt.
In the searching of the universe and
the finding of creation
The more the minds cry for more
information

Carol (Uebinger) Edwards
CLOUDS AMIDST

To my wonderful, Grandmother, Husband, Daughter, Mother and Family.

Clouds, that seem to roll right by,
Are clouds, that filter in the sky.
A meaning, they all seem to have.
Like definitions, in one's mind.
Cotton Candy, a mind behold,
Will bring forms and shapes forever
told.
A bird, that seems to fly, so high,
Will surely pass a cloud in the sky.
To touch,
To float,
To pass us by,
Dance, they might,
Ascend, they must,
Charge the sky, with such a great
thrust.
And what a surge, up in the air,
Brings life's clouds, to a glare.

Alaina Zipp
A CHEMIST'S CREATION
We are 3000 miles,
and more than one world away.
Most nights I sit,
soaking up stories of children
in from a thirty year night.
In this world, we tend toward
survival.
You flourish, in your ivy-coated
world,
with masks and coats to protect
against noxious feelings and fumes.

Vacuum packed, in that sterile
home,
my sister and I grew,
plants in a jar,
tucked on the shelf
beside hydrogen compounds in your
lab.
True to your textbook knowledge,
your hands kept away from me—
lest any human touch recontaminate
my batch.
You taught many roads to perfection,
and less than one word for love.

In this necrophiliac world,
your talents for dissolving
stubborn stains and feelings are
prized.
The only physical hunger I
experienced
was of my own making—
only the taste of rebellion,
and later, learned defeat, on my
tongue.
At each quarter, always a red editing
slash on my forehead;
at each staticky family phone tree,
it is renewed.

You are now siring
the son I should have been.
I am your damned
daughter of defeat,
with too many odd habits
and tendencies to be real.

I have searched years
for my own antidote to your poisons.
In the first moments of my new year,
having sated my long ago hungers,
I drink the fruit of my labors,
ripened by tears,
briny and sweet.

Thomas J Ferreira
RAINBOWS END

Dedicated to the loves of my life
Linda, Susan, Maggi
But most of all, to Elaine, my wife.

A vision to behold, so colorful, so
bold
Shining brightly on so high
Giving hope, and joy to reach the sky
Whose presence means so very much
On whose dreams are made of such

She appears so calm, on storms
demise
And promises golden treasures of
untold size
But, is she real, this vision to behold
So bright, so beyond my reach
Is she for me to see, or there to teach

So very bold
The answers of this vision are untold
But for me, lucky me,
I've found my pot of gold.

Wanda Alice Schwab
HEAVEN BOUND
Christ, our Savior,
guide us through
this life on earth
we're to live for you.

Help us to understand
this day
the things we should
to live God's way.

There are problems to solve
and solutions are found
when with God's help
we're Heaven Bound.

Jimmie Joe Jester
A SCARY RIDE
I got a story, I'd like to tell
About this bronc, I rode, had me
scared as hell.
He had evil in his eyes and a big wide
back.
He was tough as rawhide, and the
color was black.

He had wounded a many and some he
got the best,
And a couple he left just to lay there
at rest.
But that didn't scare me until I saw
him up close.
The muscles and tendons are what
scared me the most.

I was scared, oh, I was scared half
out of my mind.
Then a man yelled at me, "Your next,
boy get in line."
I climb over the fence and eased
down on his back.
They were messing with the cinch,
said, "they were taking up slack."

Well, I think they screwed me up,
when they let me out,
Cause that saddle was slipping. I
could feel it, there was no doubt.
Now that gelding was twisting and
kicking up high,
And then I tasted something and
thought how shit can fly.

I held on really tight, I just had to
make a ride,
And then I heard the buzzer and the
pick-up men at my side.
When the show was over and my
score was the best,
I knew that I had won and didn't care
about the rest.

Kathy D White
MY SON

To my son—David Alan Daniels

My son is an image of me,
Even when you find him up a tree,
Smiles and laughter fill the air,
When my son and I take time to
share.

Patricia Hopper McCaskill

Patricia Hopper McCaskill
LIFE
Yesterday Life began so beautiful,
Today it's a bore and we being the
Same kind of people just don't enjoy
Life anymore.

Think about it!

Could it really be faults of our own,
Or are we dreaming hoping to awake
To something new at dawn.

We can't expect everything to be
Given on a silver platter as it could
Have been for Adam and Eve, instead
We have to live as individuals
Striving hard to find our way, and
Though this is a brand new season all
We need do is PRAY.

Jason Koestler
OUR ROMANTIC DREAM
In our loving world indeed,
It's another day lost out at sea.
It's another day you're here with me.
Just the two of us all alone,

This day of sunrise to sunset is what we'll own.

Just some time to be involved romantically,
I'll love to kiss you in the eve;
And hold you tight upon our drifting boat,
Like our love that always floats.

Ahhhh! . . . I cannot believe,
How much you mean to me.
The passion which brings our hearts flaming.
You'll whisper the words so discreet;
The ones I definitely want to hear,
Certainly the ones I want to feel.

I want to share with you,
This love inside of me.
Only the two of us together will share,
The love we'll make together.
We're the only witnesses indeed,
Of our romantic dream!

Victoria Kopf
FOR PETE'S SAKE

For Pete, my husband and hero. And for my parents, Burl and Sandy, from whom I inherited my wealth-within.

God graces not each man's hearth
with children's laughter love and mirth,
A good woman to share their happy home
Precious are these things . . .
That bestow upon a common man
more wealth than any king.

M Ada Keating
MY MOTHER
My mother is not with me today
for she went home to God—
But in my heart—she is close at hand—and not beneath the sod.
I can feel her close—with her gentle hands—
She knows my every desire and need
and she asks God to send them down
to her lonely daughter—here on earth.
Her death has not separated us—I
feel her very close to me—here in my heart.
If I could have one wish today—
Would I ask God to send her back.
To the world of heartaches and strife?
"No" but I would ask that she ask
God—to strengthen the Love that I
need—in my heart.

Elizabeth J Dickey
WINTER SNOWFALL
Wind is blowing, blowing high
Snowflakes dancing in the sky
Skiers racing in the sun
I am sure I won't be one
With zero temps far below
I am going in the snow
Just to shovel and to know
I'll come inside with an
outside glow.

Terrence G Jones
STRENGTH
Frightened and feeling alone she
kneels, with her mood that she tries to conceal.
The grass is green and the sun shines brightly,
upon her hand, where a rosary is held tightly.

Too many emotions have gone through her head.
What can we say, that hasn't already been said.
Sorrowfully silent she stares into the distance.
She'll never accept this days existence.

With a wipe of her hand, she dries her tears.
Today is the day, she faced her darkest fears.
With my hand on her shoulder, I sense she's afraid.
But with the strength of a soldier, she moves away from the grave.

Clarence K Kurashige
TO MY LOVE

I dedicate this poem to my wife, Dorothy.

To you these humble lines I dedicate—
To you so dear who living makes worthwhile
And all vicissitudes of life beguile
That you're the sail which guides my ship of fate.
For when I'm sunk in gloom's abhorrent den,
Or when mad waves have battered hull and sail,
Or when I'm blinded of my "holy grail,"
Your virgin love fills me with hope and ken.
For, with you, in Eden's realm I'll always be.
I'll even scale the heights of Everest.
But sans your love, in peace I'll never rest—
No light, no hope, no joy I'll ever see.
For life is but a grievous march to the grave
Without your light my avid aims to crave.

Patricia Misiag Constance
MORNING RAIN
Hear the rain?
Smell it.
Taste it.
Drink in the rain,
In full measure.

It is the freshness,
The vitality,
The pure essence of life
To a parched land.

Listen to the morning sounds—
The quail, the dove,
The desert sparrows—
Giving thanks.

The Glory of God
In riches
Abundantly bestowed
Upon the earth—
The morning rain.

Jeanne Marie Kennedy
RHYME AND REASON

Dedication: For Kimberly, Lauren, Nicholas, Christopher, and Gregory—the loves of my life. Through their eyes, the magic lives.

I want to believe in fairytale princes on white stallions and in wood nymphs dancing in invisible circles and in pearl scaled dragons blue hued in moonlight flights and in castles on distant hills with purple and gold flags beating in the excited breath of spring awaiting the return of sorcerers and kings.

I want to believe in motherly kisses that heal scraped knees and in peanut butter sandwiches that make colds go away and in magical spells whispered in musical rhymes that banish all monsters from underneath beds.

I want to believe in Santa Claus and in red sleighs pulled by flying reindeer on a snow painted night of white iced grace.
I want to believe in the Easter Bunny and in pastel painted eggs carefully hidden among lily and pine.

I want to believe that you still live somewhere inside of me and that I still faintly feel the flutter of your heart when I see the dance of a butterfly, the flight of a bird, or the pink spray of another dawn.

Terry
LONER
Town's people gathered at Jake's Funeral Home, there to see Bill,
Had died the night before in a bar while drinking his fill.
Tears were freely shed, and then some thought to sit down,
Thus beginning the remembrances of the people of this town.

A small stray dog familiar to some, ran in just to get out of the cold.
Jake immediately chased him, but he run back in I'm told.
Again and again the doors opened with the crowd acknowledging another familiar face,
Coffee was served, Jake could hardly keep up with the pace.

Jed, the old timer said, "I knew Bill when he was going with Tom's girl."
"Run out on her, broke her heart."
"She was such a pearl."
Lena a little worn by time herself injected, "Reminds me of the time we gave him a job,"
"Worked just a day and quit."
"Wanted to hang with the lazy mob."

Parish priest whispered, "You know I don't believe he was a church-going man."
Complained the banker, "He borrowed money." Promised, "I'll pay whenever I can."

The people it would seem had not thought much of this guy, and though sorry he died,
Soon agreed that they could not exactly point to him with pride.
Being a pauper they would soon find him at the end of town in Potter's Field,
But of course most would walk and pray for him while he was wheeled.

The little dog in his way had of course taken in it all,
And as they left waited to see if a biscuit or crumb would fall.
But then catching sight of the butcher's wagon which just had parked,
Hurriedly running past Bill looked up and grudgingly barked.

Lita Maria McKeehan
ODE TO GERTRUDE STEIN

To my husband—Howard, 'Sonny Boy'

The Sun a guide to Caesars' past
If likened to a rose
Would'st by a gard'ners
weathered hand
Lift Gertrude Stein's repose
And there her scent left 'pon
the grass
The earth would pollinate
Until a wealth of flowers
growth
Would overtake her grave

Barrie L Morris
MEMORIES

To my husband Willy. For never giving up on our love, I love you. Love always, your wife Barrie. We made it.

The memories of the years that have past,
Remembering a love I thought would last.
Memories both good and bad,
The times we were happy and sad.

The answers to life I tried to find,
Yet the memories of us were on my mind.
Even when there was not a you and me,
The memories continued to be.

A new life I felt the need to start,
But it wasn't the feelings of my heart.
To myself I had to stay true,
This meant having to be without you.

So many things this year changed,
Again my life I've rearranged.
I still cannot believe it's true,
I'm able again to show my love to you . . .

Jessica Anne Gomperts
SKY WAR

To anyone who has ever sat with me through a sunrise, a sunset, or just looked at the stars with me . . . thank-you!

The sun rose with strength.
its claws ripped at the darkness
ripped it from the land.
it forced light into the hearts of the people
and to the placid waters.
it bore its children
the flowers
the wind.
it burned the souls of men
who dared to challenge it
and sat on its throne
at the top of the land
and ruled
willing what it wanted.
the clouds cried as the sun set
reluctantly forced down
by the intensity of the darkness
and the will of the moon.
The moon rose in its kingdom
to rule
willing what it wanted

Ruth A Hall
FAMILY FEUD
Once the family link
is bent and broken,
one can't ever think
of a word that can be spoken
to call across
the terrible void,
the empty loss,
the hurt deployed.

As a canyon enlarges
with wider slides
and greater gorges
and turn-asides,
our distance daily grows;
and run-off rides
a river that flows
between all of us—
just because we chose
not to fix the fuss.

Elizabeth Cassidy
BYE, GEORGE
Once I passed over your moon,
while the chill was curled up and
dreaming like a newborn.

I wandered about the night as if I was
my grandmother's ghost,
searching her abandoned home,
crying out for lost memories.

Someone placed a "For Rent" sign on
my window,
as if I was just a pile of forgotten
leaves,
that children had grown tired of.

But, with gentle prodding from
unheard echoes,
I can fall into an old soul whose eyes
no longer shed,
then turn back into a laugh longing to
pass thru my lips.

Born a sunset waiting your turn,
my thunder takes over and interrupts
your forgotten slumber.
Doomed to be forever the child
whose mother slips thru her hands,
only to find that she doesn't live here
anymore.

Alas, my life succumbs and I become
a dandelion in a windstorm,
waiting for some kindly shelter only
to have my parts mowed over.

Spirit, I do so pity you for I can no
longer endure.
I've given up the search for one,
for you seem destined to discard
before it has begun.

Do you feel you will shall be
damned,
if you awaken an angel's whisper?

Mildred Hilsenbeck Smith
UGLY AMERICA

Dedicated to my Husband Jack W Smith (de-ceased) To my daughters Mary Arden McCarthy and Lois Rich

He's got the whole world in His
Hands
Until He gave it to lunatic man
Who populated and polluted with his
greedy plans,
We've got the whole world in our
hands.

Cars and factories belch smoke in the
air,
We've plowed and hacked till the
earth is bare,
Filth in rivers and lakes everywhere
We've got the whole world in our
plans.

The pollutants end upon the ocean
floor,
What about the plankton when
there is no more
And sulfur dioxide is out of control?
A subdued world is our aims.

What will we do in the year two
thousand and one
When the population doubles and
there is no sun
Clean water and air when there is
none?
We've got a dead world on our
hands.

Mills of the Gods grind slowly but
exceedingly fine
What possible chance has your child
and mine?
No place to go but down in the
slime?
We've got the whole world in our
hands.

A great black cloud circles the earth
Nothing so monstrous since the day
of its birth.
Mael-strom of filth waits with dark
ugly mouth,
As the world slips from our hands.

There is no tomorrow for the human
race,
To unbalance nature we have to pay,
Be it money or children there is no
other way.
We've got the fate of the world in our
hands.

Shannon Gallo

Shannon Gallo
SADNESS OVERCAME ME
As I sat quiet, Dreaming of how I
once was,
I remember how happy I was, when I
was young.
Giggling, Laughing, Carefree,
Everything was easy to do,
No problems, worries, or frets.

But now as the years go by, I notice
how much more things mean to me.
Every moment is more special than
the one before.
When things go out of my life, I
regret not doing more.

Richard W Rust
DEAF EARS
I wonder if He reached for me the
times that I had strayed,
I wonder if He was waiting the
times I should have prayed.
Did He call out my name and I did
not hear?
How often do His words fall on our
deaf ears?

We pay no heed to promptings that
He may send our way,
We wander in our blindness and
live from day to day.
We're caught in worldly thoughts and
follow with the crowd,
It must make Him grieve to see us
look so proud.

But let us have some trouble, the
slightest little test,
And upon whom do we call to give
to us a rest?
And how quickly He responds when
we cry out in vain,
He's always there to help us over
again and again.

I wonder how we would feel if we
should shed a tear,
And He just turned away, giving us
a Deaf Ear!

Agnes Taylor
WORDS
Words are very wondrous things
To fashion thoughts, and soar on
wings
Sometimes spilling from the heart
To someone who is worlds—apart.
Then spoken with great sincerity
With only a dash of temerity—
Words can also bring much pain
Whenever used without restrain.
Links of Love and of Peace
A search for them, must never cease,
So choose your words with loving
care
They'll be accepted everywhere.

Leila M Duncil
FAITH
When you come to the end of the
road
And your faith does somewhat stray
Just lift your eyes towards heaven
And then begin to pray

You will see your troubles melt away
Just like the ice and snow
For God does hear all things you say
From down here below

He watches o'er us day and night
To see if we obey
He wants us to be kind and true
In all we do and say

He will keep us free from sin
If we only let Him
If we are a giver and not a taker
Don't forget, He is our Maker

Jesus loves us all
He sees us when we fall
We should be strong in every way
And most of all, we should pray

Elizabeth Lazear
DOWN THE ROAD
Down the road to Madagascar
walked the lonely, old man;
little black hat perched atop his bald
head—Pipe pursed between his
lonely lips!

This was the little man who walked
alone, Down the Road!

He blew his nose
and watered his cheeks
and bit his tongue to hide the tears.
And everyone laughed as he passed;
and everyone stared as he disappeared—into Tomorrow!

He trampled the flowers in his path;
he spat on children;
he ridiculed goats;
he kicked at dogs, and ate babies.

Down the road to Madagascar
walked the lonely, old man—
Heedless of the ignorant mass;
Heedless of his bleeding feet;
Heedless of his bald wrinkled head;
Heedless of the scorpion clinging to
the seat of his trousers.

William E Coon
A ROSE

This poem is dedicated to, The "UNITED STATES of AMERICA, "The land I love".

A rose is a symbol,
Of love, beauty and care.
Placed on this earth,
For all of us to share.
An emblem of emotion,
Of love and of life,
To rise us above,
Life's burdens and strife.
The white one's for purity,
The yellow one's for love.
The red one's the blood,
Of our dear savior above.
When we see a beautiful rose,
It's so easy to realize,
To see beauty around us,
We must first open our eyes.

Colette Swaim
THE AFFAIR
When I'm not expecting it
you come into my mind,
I found myself wondering
if you've thought of me too,
Or in your full life is
there any time for this?
Do you wonder if it meant
anything to me?
Or do you pass it off
as a night to forget,
Wishing that it had never
happened at all?
It cannot be important to you
as that could mean disaster
To that picture perfect
life of yours.
No, I would never want to
take away from your life,
All I really want, is to enter
your mind occasionally.

Gene Brumbach
DIE ONE THOUSAND TIMES
When do the good times start—
when do they end?
It can never be said for sure
except by you my friend.

Experience through the window flies
in the confusion of the lights
I perform for you unexpectedly
and you laugh with delight.

Jesters, fools—just the Joker's tools
to play high hand in the game
all the chips are in, just cash them in,
no need to explain.

Hand out crumbs to working bums
you know they are in need
and shun them when they get too
close
don't forget about their greed.

Red faced knave—Princess' slave
lay your body down
under the sweat, the fear and tears
deep into the ground.

Donna Tomlinson
BUCK'S GARAGE
My childhood was not anything
special, maybe even a little like
yours,
there were no real vacations—no
overseas tours . . .
I grew up with my grandparents on
the poor side of town,
in a frame house by the railroad
tracks, my mind can still hear the
sounds . . .
My grandfather owned 'Buck's
Garage' which set just next door,
every night when he closed, we'd get
in his pick-up and head for Scott's
Grocery Store . . .
Playing in the garage and drinking
free cokes from the machine,
to me, was more fun than to you it
could ever seem . . .
I had a playhouse in the backyard,
but being Papa's helper was more to
my delight,
no matter how I did things, to him,
they were always right . . .
I remember most papa's smelly old

cigars, and every Sunday Meme
trailing me off to church,
you know, thinking back, for bigger
and better days,
I was never in search . . .
I had everything I will always dream
of,
wonderful childhood days and their
special love . . .
All those lazy days, the good food,
even the naps Meme made me
endure,
my mind so fortunate to remember,
and I wouldn't trade them for the
real vacations or overseas tours . . .
I hope I give my children even a
portion of what I knew,
so maybe they'll have their own
'Buck's Garage' in their memories
too . . .

Sandra S Gearhart
WHEN SOMEONE SAYS I LOVE YOU

When someone says 'I love you'
I feel fear—
And a great block inside.
I know I care for them
But the words don't come,
I just look and smile—
And want to run and hide.
What block is stopping me from
this?
Is it selfish, ego, fear, or pride?
Oh, I feel so guilty and ugly,
How dare I be so mean
And full of selfish pride.
Those who need it, I run away
from—
Becoming cold as a stone.
Acting and interacting—
But not really feeling loveable and
warm.
Somehow the words 'I love you'
Has turned from something beautiful
To fearful and wrong.
Oh so sick the mind can turn the
heart,
Making life's travels so dreary and
long.

Elaine Meli
LET'S GO OUT

. . . "Let's go see so and so?"
No, my dear
For I fear,
You will fall asleep there
As well as you do here.

Loretta Strickler

Loretta Strickler
THOUGHTS OF YOU

My thoughts of you
Often bring to mind
The fun and all the laughter
We have shared from time to time.
So, when I am down
When the day seems cold and long
I just think about you
Then I sing a little song.

Sometimes, the rainy days
Seem to get the best of me
So I play my magic mind tricks
And I find you instantly.
I look inside my heart
Where you always seem to be
You chase away the rainy days
And bring the sun to me.

James William Wiley Jr
AS AUTUMN WINDS BEGIN TO BLOW

Dedicated to my Beautiful wife Joanne.

As Autumn winds begin to blow, we
know that winter is near. Seasons
pass and birthdays too as we go from
year to year.
Time has passed since my youth and
death will surely come. I can only
hope people remember me, and not
the things I've done.

Janeen Ward
CRACKED WHEAT ON A KITCHEN TABLE

To my dear friend C. J. who has endured my strange imagination since childhood.

Cracked wheat on a kitchen table.
Crusts of pleasure and trouble fill the
mind.
Like a gorilla hunting in the wild,
I search for nourishment and future
security
The bash of insane thoughts
pull me under . . . suffocating . . .
fighting to survive,
the daydream of inevitable death,
the blackness created from too much
thought.
Cracked wheat creates no bond.
Thoughts isolate and destroy the self.
We must all fight on;
build the self among the cracks of
wheat.

J Rudolph Guarino Jr
A DREAM THAT'S BORN

For all the dreamers and those who stand beside them.

On one dark, and lonely beach
They speak until the dawn

And he'll speak, from within his
heart
And tell of a dream that's born

She will sit and listen, to the dream
And wonder if it's real

And wonder if he'll ever face
The fears he's going to feel

With his dreams, within his reach
He struggles to face his fears

Alas, no dream is ever reached
But a life, Black, with tears

And she, will stand beside him
To comfort and keep him warm

And he, will search forever
To find a Dream That's Born . . .

Will Browning
THE SCOTTISH RITE

The Scottish Rite is an advanced
order of Free Masonry, a Brotherhood
Its purpose is to assist the needy
and to do naught but good
It holds a reunion each Autumn and
Spring
To acquire new members and
happiness bring
The Order meets the second Friday of
each month
The attendance is great and the
program is neat
They usually have a brother who is
experienced in the Rite
And who enlightens the order with
his experience of might

In a patriotic mood they salute the
great flag
And inspire Patriotism to sense the
importance of it
Together they say a prayer to the
Almighty
The prayer is sincere, but they
know when to quit.

Donna Thomas
MY TORN HEART

The nights are so lonely
The days are so long
As I patiently wait
By a silent phone.

The days are passing
The clock hands move by
Is it the end this time?
I break down and cry.

I guess it is over
Our love's had its end
I pray now that quickly
My torn heart will mend.

Michelle D'Anjou Astié
MAYBE

Maybe today
Maybe tomorrow
Maybe always
Maybe never
Maybe I say yes
Maybe I say no!

Maybe you are the one
Maybe I love you
Maybe for ever
Maybe I die with you
Maybe tomorrow
But not today!!!

Raymond Schlitzer
LIFE IS SOMEWHAT LIKE A BALL GAME

Dedicated to my wife, Myrtle for all her goodness

Some day we'll reach the climax
The end for you and me
The man upstairs will make the call
And say your out, strike three

Till then my dear, we'll do our best
With the rising of the sun
And always try our darnest
To score another run

Cause all in life is important
Winning is of great concern
To move ahead, make each day
count
With the many things we learn

So dear, let's play the ball game
While there's light and we can see
As someday he will make the call
And say, your out, strike three.

Judy Diane Alispach
OLD AND FORGOTTEN

In the memory of my beloved grandfather, Antonio Guadagnoli

The old and forgotten
How quickly they pass
As a fresh field of flowers
Or a cold winters grass
Though time is their secret,
Not many will know
What lies in the years of
Each wrinkle they show

Their minds may grow weary,
Their bodies grow lame,
But their hearts, and their
Spirit, remain quite the same.
Remember the "Old Ones"; whatever
You do.
For the "Old And Forgotten"
May someday be you.

Henry Roger Holst
I DREAM OF A TROPICAL ISLAND

This poem is dedicated to everyone in the family and friends.

My tropical island where the
monkeys play and palm trees sway.
The ocean waves come up to the
beach.
Beautiful natives girls sing and
dance on the sandy beach.
A tropical party every night on the
beach.

My tropical island in my paradise
dreams.
I hope someday it might be true and
sky be so blue.
That's my tropical island dream.

Kathryn L Reiff
THE MIRACLE OF PRAYER

If you have burdens, troubles and
cares,
They can be eased thru the miracle
of prayer.

Nothing too large, or nothing too
small,
O precious soul, the Lord hears them
all.

The concerns that you have, He
wants to share,
Burdens can be lifted, thru the
miracle of prayer.

Lives can be changed, they can be
made new,
O dear friend, just remember: God
loves you.

Whether the skies be cloudy, or
whether they be fair,
Remember hearts are lifted, thru the
miracle of prayer.

Kimberle Calnan
A UNIVERSE FLOATED WITHIN ME

A universe floated within me
all unknown to me—
unknown blood shared to a
blind and pure dependent.
For this life, my ignorance was its
safety.
Knowledge was the knife that
separated us in the end.
Mine is the hand that guided and
compensated the knife—
and my universe poured out,
poured out,
poured out
onto a cold floor.

Marvin Goldwert
ARGENTINA, 1930-1988: THE TRIUMPH OF THE SUBJECTIVE

To the memory of my father, Aaron Goldwert, and with love ever-lasting to my mother, Frieda Goldwert.

. . . 1930: hour of the sword . . . submerge the Armadillo (Yrigoyen), birth to the Fox (Perón) . . . piked Prussian helmets, turned to U.S. khaki . . . hoist the blood-stained flag of blue-and-white . . . Viva the Army! . . . talkative professional politicians, macho army officers . . . words versus force . . . 1930, 1943, 1955, 1963, 1966, 1976—endless force, endless words . . . labyrinth: death to consensus . . . "disappearances:" national shame and the dirty war . . . hope born again in Alfonsin . . . words: open the can-of-worms! . . . shadow of irresponsibility: $45 billion debt . . . legacy: resolve born of tears and reared in uncertainty . . . Sun-of-Promise . . .

Gale Robbins
ONE LAST TIME

This poem is dedicated to John, a dear friend of mine who has moved away. He is a person who touched my life deeply and one who will never be forgotten.

We meet one last time:
just me and you.
We're drawn together
by what we must do.

You take me in your arms
as a tear falls from my eye.
I hold you tightly,
fearing this is good-bye.

You say we'll meet again
because you think it's what I need to hear.
The only thing I ever needed
was to know you were near.

"I don't know what I'll do without you," I whisper
as I find myself longing for you to stay.
You kiss my lips one last time
and turn to walk away.

You glance over your shoulder
and I know this is the end.
I struggle to hold back the tears
as I silently say "Good-bye my dear friend."

Debbrajeane Gordon
DEEP WITHIN US ALL

There is a place within my soul;
The corridors are cold, black, and empty.
The only sounds are fearful cries and the winds that chase them by.
As I wonder through I am overcome with a pallet of emotions,
It seems to happen every time I come here.
Someday I will find the key to lock the doors that hide these halls,
But, until I find the key this place will be my downfall.
Within these walls; I feel sorry for myself
It's deep within us all . . .
It holds us with our own fears,
It punishes us with our own tears.
For as much as I fear it; I am still drawn near.
It is curiosity that beckons me to its threshold.
I see my true self there . . . The part I refuse to share.
Evil and hate, the monsters that I create,
Pain or pleasures, my choice to give, my selfishness,
The animal that I am, the hungers I demand from life,
I keep them all hidden here.
Within the darkness of my soul . . .
I keep them here, where I am in control,
For this is my world, the darkness of the soul!
Again I will enter to roam its corridors of darkness, alone . . .

Roxane Woolff
RETURN OF BUTTERFLY

Ah! There you are, Dear Butterfly!
Poor camouflage, those wings.
Glowing, unforgotten, ever . . .
Making you fair game.

Ancient wisdom showing
In dark and sooty eyes, all knowing.
In all our finer senses
We've missed you, Butterfly.

Butterflies seem so fragile,
Ah, but that's their camouflage.
Now, and seasons long ago,
You've bathed the bruised and shattered souls, untended,
and . . . they came away for a time,
All mended.

The meek emboldened,
The saddest, your ageless wings enfolded.
Hasten, once again, and linger.

Come home, Dear Butterfly . . .
Before you're collected.

Edwin P Spivey
DRIFTING SANDS

To my darling wife, Ciss.
Gone but never forgotten.

So many times I've wandered down country lanes with you
remembering all those silly things that we used to do;
enjoying all the sunshine and laughing in the rain
treasuring every moment of life's so precious game.

No hopes now for the future, just memories of the past,
living for each moment, make every second last,
in this game of make believe that I play with you
wishing, hoping dreaming, it could all come true.

I see you on that mountain, in scenes from long ago,
knowing all those happy days cannot be reborn,
Such happy days, now dead and gone, like you, cannot return,
still in hope I wonder, through those fields of corn.

Now I wander down that pathway the spot wherein you lie,
keep my special rendezvous each day that passes by.
Each weary day that passes by, each lonely day and night,
such heartaches ever present, no peaceful days in sight.

Each journey a reminder, though you're so close at hand
you've gone from me forever, just like the drifting sands.
I try to find some comfort, from oh, such foolish dreams—
perhaps we'll really meet again, beneath the moon's bright beams.

Then I see the drifting sands, each grain blown far apart,
like the day you were torn from my breaking heart
now I know, as from the start,
you've gone forever more,
torn away like grains of sand from some distant shore.

Still I live with faith and hope, each weary night and day
chasing each elusive dream from o'er that golden bay
perhaps, somehow, a single grain can come to rest again,
back to fill that certain spot again,
help to ease that pain.

Instead of hope, of faith and tears to help to see me through
you will journey home again, help me live anew,
but if this really cannot be, God will show the way
to live this life with peace of mind,
till I go home to you.

Pete G Galozo

Pete G Galozo
I HEARD A VOICE

I heard a voice above.
He called for me to swear.
To repent my sins before and now;
He wants them washed and cleaned.

I always hear Him say.
Come repent your sins.
Become the son of God;
And live with me above.

He promised every one.
To forgive them their sins.
His love and compassion.
The reward for obedience.

Long time He is calling.
Waiting someone to hear.
He whispers His love always;
But we do not acknowledge.

He came suddenly at last.
For us to see Him and witness.
The power of Miracle He did.
Convince the people to believe.

David A Cooper
TO MAKE A SOUND JUDGEMENT

I'd like to dedicate this poem to all the people, young and old, who aren't sure what you want. Set your mind to it, and the world as you know it will be at your service. Remember, you are who you want to be!!

To make a sound judgement, to make your fear weak. Don't be afraid, speak, hurry speak!!
What constitutes fear may be immortal and morbid. To seek the true truth, immerse your thoughts to youth.
Have you not found an answer, do you neglect to find a saint, a multitude of thoughts embezzle my brain
I feel inhuman, I feel not sane, I resent to feel the power, I neglect to intake the pain.
All the agony and turmoil tumble inside. What used to feel normal, has run just to hide.
To succeed may be one, but exceed do not think. You feel as you reign just to fall at a wink.
Money and power, maybe fortune and fame, Just do one thing wrong and you've established a name.
"Why me Lord, why me Lord; Help me to see, Bear power to cry . . .
Let me seek truth, let me seek youth, let me seek love not to lie.
I feel you near, I know you're there,
Please find forgiveness to hear!
Let not influence embargo upon me.
Think what I am and be what I see.

Wilma Barbour
BUT . . . I WILL NOT "DON'T WORRY"

don't-worry
BUT . . . I will not "don't worry"
while
we're glutting Gaia with trash
eliminating species/ their environments/ in haste and spawning generations of deprived and militant youngsters to deal with our toxic/ chemical/ biological waste.

be-happy
AND . . . I simply cannot "be happy"
while
grown men clobber baby seals
drug czars perpetrate new deals
VIPs may be spelled HEELS
scads of human beings die daily

for lack of adequate meals
(while tons of surplus stores of grain, milk, beans and cheese lie locked in sheds of steel)
have
a
nice
day
Come on . . . how can we have a nice day now—today—in '89?????

When, then?

Patricia R Strickland
I WOULD

Dedicated to James K. West
Who is my Shield-Mate and my
Dancing Partner in this life.

Sing me a tune without a melody.
Show me a forest without a tree.
Show me the sun in the dark blue midnight.
Hold me close and tell me we are right.
I would believe in you,
I would believe in you.

Give me the moon to wear as a ring.
Show me a bird that would not sing.
Hold me only with your brown eyes.
Tell me all your pretty lies.
I would still believe in you,
I would still believe in you.

And when we finally dance with death.
You may steal the life from my last breath.
Saying, "we must take that one last

chance".
So take me now, begin that dance.
I would let you, I would let you.
For above everything else.

I WOULD STILL BELIEVE IN YOU.

Ralph L Cranford
REMEMBERING

To my wife and Children with Love

Remembering is a happy way
to keep dear people near
and that's why you are remembered
many times, throughout the years

And, that's why remembering
is a special way,
to wish you warmest wishes
every single day.

And when a special day
comes along to you,
I'll be there wishing,
your very best comes true.

And if my mind stay's with me,
and I can always depend,
then I'll always remember,
and you'll always have a friend.

Connie J Stanley
NIGHTMARE

It waits
In the dark
With the patience of eternity.

It slinks
Through dank halls
Stalking its prey.

It is hungry
And would feed itself
On the fear in my own mind.

Cornered
And confronted
I can lock it safely away.

But it will escape
Released by some new fear
To torment my dreams anew.

Sue E Adams
BLESSINGS

To my daughter Connie and my son Wally—May 1989. Randy—Jo Anne—Grandchildren—Nolan—Lea—Alana—Gregory Y & Carlie

Give me not of the gold of the ground
Let me drink of the gold of the sky
Let me sit in a lowly place
I can look up to the wonders on high
Let me drink of the cup of life's
reasoning
And eat from the platter of faith
Let me be washed of hypocrisy
Let me be bathed in faith
Let me love and be loved by giving
With all my heart and mind and soul
Drink not from the grapes that
fermented
Nor reap from another man's toil
For if rich I sit in a castle
And count the gold of my hoard
'Twould not be counting the
blessings
That come in the name of the Lord.

Debra Noguera
TO BE CONTINUED

I can't say good-bye,
Not to you.
You have always been here,
Always.
And good-bye seems so final,
Like there's no tomorrow.
But our parting isn't the end,
Not for either of us.
It just means we are ready to grow,
To move on, to continue.
No matter how many tomorrows I
pass,
Or how many yesterdays I forget,
You will always be with me.
You touched my heart, my life,
You are part of me.
I love you,
And I will continue to love you.
And to believe,
That there will be a tomorrow for us.
So, it is not good-bye I'll say,
But rather . . . to be continued.

Laura-Marie Dennis
YOU ARE

To Doug, you are the man I have been waiting for. I love you.

You are the sun
that breaks through the clouds.
You are the rain
that refreshes on a hot, summer day.

You are the eagle
that soars high above.
You are the hummingbird
that hovers close by.

You are the mountain,
solid and sure.
You are the ocean,
restless and moving.

You are the fireweed
first to brave the ashes.
You are the wild rose
full of quiet beauty.

You are the friend
who understands and accepts.
You are the man
I have been waiting for.

Peter Pura
I RODE A WHILE THROUGH THE TREES

To Dee, with all my love.

I rode a while through the trees,
Spotted a girl standing there.
She smiled at me as the breeze
Blew back her gentle auburn hair.

Upon her touch the "oh" of love
Escaped from my pursed lips.
She held me, like a paralyzed dove
And fed me with her fruitful lips.

"Dear young lady, may I ask
What brings you to this place?
Is it some secret task
To keep the smile upon your face"?

She just turned and ran away,
And in an instant she was gone.
I sat bewildered, nothing to say
So I simply rode on.

Bernice Bay
A BIRD

This poem is dedicated to Justin, Ryan and Kristin, the wonderful grandchildren with whom I enjoy the wonders of nature.

How strong you are,
For one so small,
To fly with a stick
Into a tree so tall.

I see that you sometimes
Falter and stop
To rest on a limb
Halfway to the top.

Then up you fly
Placing the twig you found
So the wind will not blow
Your nest to the ground.
You stay so busy,
No time for rest,
More twigs, more moss, more string
For your nest.

Now you've finished your work
With a home built to stay,
Your babies will be safe—
God planned it that way.

Edith T Woodard
SUNUP AND COFFEE

Dedicated to the Omnipotent Creator

Sunrise, scarce awake,
Softly tints the lake.
Cross winds from the haze
Sway the pines sideways.

While the masses sleep,
Who will tend the sheep?
While the laggards doze,
Who will nudge their toes?

Songsters 'mid the trees,
Chirping in the breeze,
Pester those abed.
"Rise, sweet Sleepy Head.
Aft the lambs are fed,
Pour my coffee, please!"

Vicki Mix
SOMETIMES REMEMBERED

To my brother Brian; For the pain you suffered. If I could only say "I love you" one more time!

Sometimes Remembered,
Are the days of you
The things we shared
The times we knew
And yet now
It comes back all too soon
The way it ended
The tears let loose
It hurts you see,
Now I'm the fool
"The one without"
This is my mood!
What shall I say
What do I do
Who will I speak with
Who will I turn to?
And now if you saw me
Would you rewrite the book
Turn the page back,
Take a second look . . .

Jerome First
. . . A PHILOSOPHICAL THOUGHT ON LIFE . . .

Ashes to Ashes . . . Dust to Dust . . .
And yet, another life is born to
take it's place
Life—You've made me cold and
left me hungry
You've made me cry and wish that
I had never met your ungrateful
call . . .
Death—You call to me from the
realms of nonexistence,
But life receives your call and
promptly turns you away
I've often wondered, "What is Death
really like?"
"Are you cold and dark?"
"While I'm decaying in your clammy
fingers will I be
comforted from this reality?"
Or, just go unnoticed, evaporating
into the earth, from which
Life, itself, started . . .

Christine E Sciotti
PLEASE LISTEN

If tears could talk,
What would they say?
They'd whisper, "I'm sorry."
They'd cry out, "I'm hurt."
Tears do talk,
But they say too much—
reveal too much.
So they are hidden and
wiped away.
They could have told you
so much—
Like a grandfather telling
a story,
Like a friend giving a
hug.
They are like a novel—
A thousand emotions,
Ten thousand words.
I wish you would have tried
To read my tears.

Jane Krakower
PRECARIOUS

Dedicated to Eddie-Lou Cole

A little sparrow's nest out on a wire
in space
so tiny and frail why did it choose
such a place?
Its winsome branches clinging to the
nest
like love's endeavor put to the test
In fall could be broken so easily apart
just like the unsuspecting heart
A grayish-floss tucked together with
strings
as fine and delicate as caring can
bring
Like special love will it survive its
plight?
and remain sturdy in the morning
light.

Penny Lawler
EACH MORNING SUN GREETS ME

Each morning sun greets me
Comfortable chairs on a bright,
breezy porch
My favorite cup with strawberries
and green vines printed on it
Filled with coffee, aroma and taste,
matching the sun that greets me
Local news read first by me
Listening I catch the neighboring
sounds
Lawn mowers, saws but the best—
the bird's songs
Birds cat, drink and play
Defend their home rights from dawn
til twilight
An ever pleasant sight
As morning changes to day, to days
My mate and I share our twilight.

Elizabeth Crombie
CHILD'S LOVE

When you see a child playing,
You get a very special feeling inside.
Because a child's love is something
very special,

Because children love you as you are,
Children never try to change you
Into something you aren't,

Children have a magical way about them,
The way they look at things in the world
and see a beauty in almost everything they do.

A child's love is one of the most special blessing
We have in the world we all can share together.

Lisa Sanders Downing
YEAR 2005

To the Government & NASA

Just a few tomorrows down the road
We won't have to carry this heavy load,
People will scream, people will shout
Everyone will be running all about
It will be a brand new time,
There will be no government to run our minds,
There will be few tomorrows and no goodbyes,
There will be no death because there will be no one to die
No one can say we didn't try
No one can blame us because they died
It will be the year 2005
People will want to live and stay alive
There will be little chance that they will survive
They will look for help towards the sky
There will be few tomorrows and no goodbye
Because it will be the year 2005!

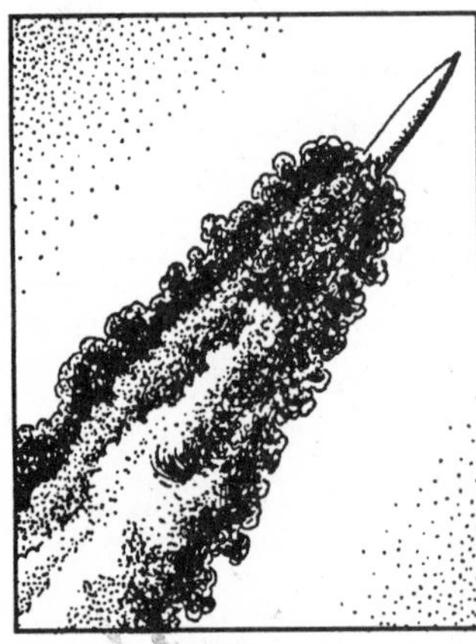

Tomorrow will be a brand new day,
People will stand up and they will pray
They will look to the sky with relief and a sigh
Because they know that they have survived
They almost died because they didn't try
But with a little help from above and a little love
They have survived and lived
And now look what they have to give
A peaceful town and a king with a crown
Beautiful grass and trees at last.
The town is growing and moving fast
No one remembers the awful past!

Laraine Ballin
HIGHWAY, U.S.A.

Dedicated to all of nature's creatures who, unable to defend or protect themselves, are daily slaughtered on our highways.

On small hind legs he stood
with head held high,
Raising his silent agony to the sky.
She lay by roadside without life,
A minute pelt—was she his wife?
The mangled warmth breathed one last sigh
Uncaring wheels sped right on by,
Paved the road with yet more blood,
Pride in the power under the hood.
No matter that a life lost form
And left one frightened and forlorn,
To wonder at man's frenzied pace
Why the maddened lethal race
That severed his beloved mate
Who warmed him so, who matched his gait.
The wildwood nest that was their home
Too painful now—for steel and chrome
Has shred one more of nature's realm
Human ego at the helm.

Laura M Beatty
A DREAMER'S WORLD

The starry sky is blurred, again,
By tears forming in my eyes.
For love was lost,
Not long ago,
On a warm and breezy night.

I look to heaven with no avail,
For the memories crush the peace.
They flood my mind,
Tear at my heart,
And end the tranquility.

How can I face reality
When that life was so ideal?
With this large void,
The future's black.
True peace is a dreamer's world.

Dorothy J Babel
BARN

Three years ago
When first I saw it.
An old barn stood straight
out in the field
on the corner
unused.
It was tall and proud—tattered though
When first I passed it,
day after day to and from work
No one cared for it at all.
Die or live—no help to come,
un-inhabited by livestock
or anything more.
But I watched it gradually
deteriorate each day.
Finally leaning in a definite way.
Then gradually the mow door
came down slowly too.
It knelt on one corner
Then set itself down—
An agonizing death
of the past.

Lea Surles
HELLO AGAIN

To my family who has given me the hope to look ahead and dream of a time when we will always be able to say hello, again.

Did we just
meet yesterday,
or was it
a hundred
years ago—
It seems
the faces
of today
are young
but really old—
the love I
knew is once
again alive
and very true
a piece to
the puzzle,
a way out of
the maze,
or maybe
just a clue—

William E Sutterfield
GRANDMOTHER

G—for the Goodness
in your heart.
R—for the Real
person you are.
A—for All
the love you've shown.
N—for the Niceness
I've known.
D—for the Dearest
that I know is you.
M—for the Motherly
love you have shown too.
O—for the Other
times you didn't turn me away.
T—for the Truthful
answers you've given in your special way.
H—for the Heavenly
way you build a home.
E—for the Every
inch of love you gave.
R—for the Remembrance
of you I'll have always.

Sheila J Spaeth
ANGEL

Devil or Angel? You can't make up your mind,
A little of both is what you will find.

Sometimes I'm good, and sometimes I'm bad,
Sometimes I'm happy, and sometimes I'm sad.

Sometimes I laugh, and sometimes I cry,
Sometimes, even I don't know why.

Sometimes I smile, and sometimes I pout,
Sometimes I believe, and sometimes I doubt.

But, no matter what I do,
My heart will always belong to you.

I'll give you my love forever and a day,
Nothing will ever take that away.

I'll always be your little "Angel".

Halina De Roche
LIFE

In its profundity and altitude—
Life rolls before your eyes—
And when you have seen—
The world's great play—
You return to yourself—
Rich and wise.

From where does one return?
Should one forget the past?

If one forgets the past—
One did not live—
If one lived—one can't forget one's life—
Which can't help being—stress and strife.

We do not know—
Where we go—
Where to—
Where through—
Some of life is just taboo—
To keep the rendezvous—
With death.—

That creates the profundity
and altitude—
As life rolls before your eyes—
From nowhere—to somewhere—
Rich and wise.

Virginia Aragon

Virginia Aragon
THROUGH THE DARKNESS TO THE DAWN

To Francine, Chris, Theresa, who have taken over my heart, and given me all the support, and love a mother could ever ask for.

My heart was sorely aching, and through tears I could not see; I felt I lost tomorrow.
That there was no hope for me.
But supporting, and consoling, my love did not depart; for I could always see him through the window of my heart.
Then my burdens somehow vanished with the coming
of the dawn, my blinding tears subsided, and my doubts and fears were gone. You have helped me past the shadows till I was whole again, and whatever may beset me, I know you will remain.

Rann Newcomb
THE VOLTURNO

They told me you were dead;
A strafing plane swept down
And death was in each wing.

Your end was quick I learned,
No dressings soaked with blood,
You never knew what hit.

I didn't get choked up,
No mist came to my eyes,
I could be next perchance.

Since we left El Guettar
An emptiness claimed me
And youth and dreams were gone.

Dawn Marie Maat
ETERNAL NIGHT

I took the path deep in the wood
and it was there I stopped and stood
as I watched it twist and turn
it was there I did learn
that in either dark or light
this was the forest of eternal night
the ferns they dripped with the
morning dew

the moss was thick where the
mushrooms grew
this is where all childhood nightmares come true
fore the animals here were of the
night
I'd doubt they'd ever seen the light
I was drawn deeper down the path
I should have turned and never
looked back
the air was musty no end in sight
the path it stopped, it was there
but not in sight
and it would lead you into the
endless night
so I turned to search for the days left
light
fore I'd been hours in the forest of
eternal night

John Corbin
SILVER BREEZE

Wafting breeze and rolling sea,
Whispering grass on sands eternal.
Unheard wings set upon the air and
glide to the sound of an echoeing cry.

I cut through the wind and sand
As the sloop skims across the
water's glassy edge.

Connected by an unseen spirit
all sound is hushed in a
reverential roar of silence as
waves crash upon the shore.

Then all is one, the dune, the sea
and me.

Donald R Cloyd
THE SKY

This poem is dedicated to its creator, and mine.

Sunrise to sunset,
each hour of every day presents us
with a brand new display
That is unsurpassed by anything
under glass,
and nothing that is framed can match
the fame that each moment
brings.
The span, the depth, the measure can
win your favor.
If you but taste its flavor.
You will be awed at the lack of
flaws,
and this may cause you to savor each
hour of every day.

Elaine Traynelis-Yurek
MERCY

In recognition of the Son of God.

The grass blows hot in the August
sun
And the grape hangs dry on the vine.
Insects drain the fruit
And cause flowers to shrivel at the
root.
Mercy, mercy cry the crops
As the sun burns steadily on.
A haze covers all and it is not
The hand of God I see
But the folly of men that be.

Paula Hayes Clarke
HYPNOTISM

And he was there.
Tall,
dark,
as I imagined
Piercing black eyes
that bore through me
that knew no shame.
Examining my every thought
and movement.
I thought he could be
hypnotizing me
into some strange
foreign land
and only he knew how
to get there.
Holding me captive,
declaring his will.
I thought for awhile
how nice it would be
to dwell in his land.

J S Nauheim
THEY NEVER REMEMBER

To My Wife

They never remember
They clung to your breast
They never remember
The arms where they'd rest
They never remember
We know that it's true
They never remember
I'm sure that you do.

So soon they grow up
And so soon we grow old
They only remember
The things they are told
And then only vaguely
If ever they do
But you will remember
As that's always true.

For whate'er the value
Whatever it's worth
None ever remember
The times close to birth
But when they have wee ones
As when they were so
They learn it's important
To know what you know.

Antonia H Schwed
COLLECTIVE DREAM

All trees become mysterious at night
As evening softly wraps them till
they seem
Like shrouded, abstract presences
that might
Be part of some collective, mythic
dream.
The pearly mist that snakes up from
the ground
Exhales nocturnal scents of age old
things
Erratic winds create a rustling sound
Archaic counterpoint of leaves and
wings
Evocative of prehistoric times
When big cats sharpened claws upon
the bark
And shamans kept back death by
chanting rhymes
To firelit forms that huddled from
the dark.
Harmonious and dim the nighttime
trees
That murmur of ancestral memories

Dena M Johnson
A BURLAP SACK

Knowledge comes in a burlap sack,
Dip some out and spill some back.
Be weary tho' of leaks in time,
The sides can rip and threads
unwind.

Scoop too deep, the holder sags,
Pack too much, the bottom drags,
Leave its contents free to air,
The vermin take their eager share.

Bags in confusion, stacked too tight,
Seeking exclusion to breathe, might
ignite.
Left unprotected, their integrity
wanes,
Odd little sucklings, appear when it
rains.

Knowledge for planting erupts from
a sack,
On its own doing, the burlap peels
back.
The feeble bag has nurtured its
notion,
All that containment, is freed in one
motion.

On winds of reason, seeds will fly,
From burlap bonds, they'll live or
die.
But we, by the season, need to repair,
That empty sack, just lying there.

Etalea Unferth
PENCIL ETCHINGS

Last night
We talked
Just you and I
Of trifles
This and that
You were so
Close—so dear
I felt so calm
And yet you
Were not near—
That I
Could really hear
Your voice—
But last night
We talked—
Just you and I
Of trifles
This and that.

Amal Moulik
RESONANCE

in my supreme
hour,
creator,
let me pour
my simple spirit
into your timeless
bowl:

my sins lanced,
my thoughts stilled—

not the tired
catechism
of ritual faith
nor the agnostic's
indefinite void—

only the fullness
of echoes
in lovers' hearts
of what I was
and whom
I had become.

Laura Lee Lopez 3XL
THE DYING REALITY

Dedicated to: Robert A Gaffney. Thanks for your support, but mostly your love. I love you, Rabbit! ! 3XL

It was said to be just a box of sand,
But they really didn't understand.
Words can not express how much it
truly meant,
Those many dreamy childhood hours
spent,
Creating worlds unlike any other,
At peace with one another.
But changes came too soon then,
Making us women and men.
But even with the cynical, sensible
hows and whys
The reality of the unforgettable
dream survives.
Clinging to the hopes the dreams
reassure,
For without it this illogical life
couldn't endure.
I went back to that solace of mine
To relive that peaceful carefree time.
From reality there was no place to
hide,
My dreams had truly died.
As I realized they were buried,
I dropped the hopes I carried.
There's nothing left but a spot of
green,
A patch of grass now covers our
dreams.

Christine Marie Martz
ABANDONED

Deserted and so alone
Sorrow is all I know
Deep inside I want to cry
Now I feel that love is a lie

I want so much to give
For this is my reason to live
No one seems to care anymore
I am left as I was before

As strong as the wind soars
I want you even more
There is nothing I can do
All I know is that I love you

You have left me with
only a trace
Of tears running down
my face

Daniel A Walsh
A FAMILIAR AIR IN AN UNFAMILIAR PLACE

This poem is dedicated to Kathleen with love and peace.

The air was cool and crisp, the
night air of fall.
The time of year you can smell,
taste, and feel the air.
a familiar air
That distinct air that is telling
you that winter is coming soon.
That air you take deep breaths of
and fills you with a sense of purpose.
a familiar air
I was awakened by this air
in an unfamiliar place.
A place halfway across the country
from my familiar home.
a familiar air
This air made me yearn for those
late nights walks back in Minnesota.
Nights when I could clear my mind
and think, by breathing that air.
a familiar air

Patrick Christie
THE LOVE THING

Something I ask for.
Waiting for
Hoping for
Now!
Now! That's here it doesn't match
To high standard set in "days of old"
It's sweet bitter frustrating battle
Beneath the skin.

One fighting within myself to hold
Onto what I hope for.
Waited for
Hoping for
Now!
Now what?
This love thing

James Schellenberg
ATOMIC AGONY
(In Memoriam: Hiroshima and Nagasaki)

Feel the heat, feel the thunder,
See the giant fungus unfold.
Feel yourself come asunder,
Hear the screams of the old.

Feel the unseen heat,
Feel the unseeable death.
Taste the agony of defeat,
The ultimate defeat from the atomic breath.

The cataclysm starts to fade,
In the distance it flares again.
The soul thinks of heavenly shade,
Of rest beyond human yen.

Sunday K Tyner
NO ONE REALLY KNEW
No one really knew why she died.
She died without warning, or leaving a note.
When the policeman came, he said,
"Yes she's gone, but why?"
Perhaps it was because of her short breath,
Or lack of inspiration she received from others.
Maybe it was because her dog died last month
A prisoner of his soul, after a car tracked his body.
It's feasible she lost sight of her Sisyphus dreams.
Could be her heart gave out to life
Awed no more by a robin's chirp
Or the sunset stretching up to the moon.
Yes, maybe that was it. The simple things didn't make a difference.
No one really knows why she hung herself in the kitchen.

Rose Marie Mistler
Never . . . . My Love
softly walking
through my life
my love . . . sometimes
her love . . . always
ever
in my heart
on my mind
gently creeping
through my thoughts
loved forever
here . . . . when needed
never . . . . . . My Love

Gretchen Antoinette Patterson

Gretchen Antoinette Patterson
BRAIN MASTER
I'm in CONTROL! of your every thought
It's not my fault
You don't think for yourself.
You come to me for advice
Wanting answers for Life's
Unexpected challenges.
I'm in CONTROL! of your
incalculable mood
I make you feel good
When you're feeling depressed.
You called on me
To set your mind free
From insurmountable pressure.
I'm in CONTROL! without ME—
there is no you
You don't know what to do
In a difficult situation.
You don't know How to
GET RID OF ME, NOW!
GO! Tell your friends
Call me by Name
BRAIN MASTER—
COCAINE

Sister Miriam Rose Wilson MHS
CAROLINE, YOU ARE YOUR FATHER'S DAUGHTER

To my brother, Pat

Caroline, you are your father's daughter,
A chip from off the Wilson's family block,
Aglow with brilliance, strength, the joy of laughter,
Your heart a seat of gold where angels knock.
Lo! Fair of face, a princess royal here,
Both hair and eyes a lovely brown, so dear.
Your playground all of earth and heaven, too,
Your friends the best of mankind tried and true.

Caroline, the years will pass into the stretch of ages,
And life will beat its way against your bark,
But may you always harbor with the sages,
And never be put under by the dark.

God bless you, Caroline, give you His grace,
And Daddy bring you e'er to Jesus' Face.

Lisa Titus
WILDFLOWER
Wildflower, like me
unprovoked
growing everywhere
in tangled directions
I'd like to think
the beauty lies within
the statement
that you make
Wildflower you own
the exotic beauty
found in perfected
imperfection
Wildflower
like me
you settle in
anywhere the soil's right
and you have the boldness to
simply BE, anywhere
while you shy away
from yards with
picket fences
Wildflower, like me
you've got a basic
honesty,
and uncultivated
naivety
Wildflower, like me
unprovoked
growing everywhere
in tangled directions.

Ann McMahon
PARTING
Parting may be a sweet sorrow
When love's sweets can be tasted tomorrow.

Such sorrow is only sweet
When we know that we shall meet
Again.

When parting is forever,
And bitter words have severed
Love's bonds,

Parting is the acrid smoke
Of burned-out love—

A stinging, blinding funeral pyre
Of ended love.

Michael D Yeoman
A FRIEND

For Grandmother Turner

A friend is someone sweet and nice.
Who seems to show up at all the right times.
Who goes the distance in times of need.
What is it that makes you that way?
Is that the way it's supposed to be?

Where is it, that joy you always bring?
Where did you hide it, in the back room?
I surely hope to find it so very soon.
Not that it matters, my feelings won't change
You'll always be one, a friend of mine

Darryl E Williams
GAZE UPON A MASTERPIECE
Look up . . .
And gaze upon the sky
Only the God of the universe
Could have created something so high.

Look at the vastness
And the stars that shine so bright
God knew exactly what He was doing
When He created such a beautiful sight.

Rise up early in the morning
And gaze upon a sunrise
What a spectacular view
God set before our eyes.

Watch the evening sun go down
And the moon start to glow
All of these combinations
Put on a magnificent show.

Are all these things just a coincidence?
Only a fool would think that in his mind
And anyone who cannot see God's hand
Surely must be blind!

Beatrice Poland
I'M IN LOVE WITH THE MEMORY OF YOU
I'm in love with the memory of you sweetheart,
Empty years without you I see,
You're gone from me now,
But your presence somehow
Lingers on in my memory.

The days are so long without you my dear,
For you were a part of me,
I seem always to hear
Your voice so near,
From your memory I'll never be free.

Every night in my sleep, I see you in dreams
And then as the day dawns anew,
I try to pretend,
That this is the end,
But I find I'm still thinking of you.

I'll never forget you my own sweetheart,
I've tried everything I can do,
I just can't replace
Your sweet smiling face,
I'm in love with the memory of you.

Wanda Bracken
YOU LEAVING
Skywriting, smoke,
fog,
the waves;
A jet stream.
These were you
leaving.
Too nebulous to hold onto—
But leaving an impression
Indelible
as stone carvings.

I, a collector,
crouched
with collecting net,
jar,
shadow box and frame
for display
of my prize.

Silently, you left;
With soundless footsteps
on a ghostly doormat.

Lucille E Buzzell M A
THE PRICE!
I'm willing that
My head be bent,
My eyes grow dim—
My faltering step be spent.

But must I give
Each shred of me
When I live in
"my country tis of thee?"

It's not my body, I can't control
That I mind so very much
But, life's non-caring, for my soul
I FIND the careless touch.

When I could give a part of me
To fellow man, I did.
Must I pay the price of greed?
When someone's turn—they hid?

It's not for me, my tears are shed
But for your future care.
For to live and die—to be without,
"Tis" in vain and gross despair!

Robin Edwards
GOD'S LOVE
The world can be such a beautiful sight,
full of rivers, and flowers,

and bright stars in the night.
Robins that sing in the trees way up high,
rainbows that appear after rain in the sky.
Little kittens that run, and jump all around,
and children who chase a balloon that they found.

With all of these things, and so much more,
why do people fight, and why is there war?
Can't people see, can't people feel,
it's their greed in the way of God's love not His will?

If only they could stop, and see the wonderful sights,
it could end all their hatred,
and stop bombs in the night.
If only they could find God's love . . .

Naoshi Koriyama
STAR-WATCHING
Standing
by the island shore
in midsummer
I looked up
at the Constellation Swan
overwhelmed
by its grandeur
and now
standing
by the same island shore
in midwinter
I look up
to the zenith
of the sky
only to see
that the Swan
has flown away.

Rodger Lee Jackson
POETRY

I dedicate this poem to Jesus, and my wife Rosemarie, who are both an inspiration to me!

Poetry, oh poetry, you are so many things to me
I just wish that everyone, every-where, could see,
Could hear, and feel, what you do inside my mind
Through all my life, it's true,
You see, "You" oh poetry! oh poetry, it's you!

Poetry is a living thing, I know it's true.
Poets say "write poems" it's true, but poetry,
Oh poetry, I see you in all things, and places,
In all people do and say,
To the Lord above I pray,
Poets, forever, keep the real love alive,
And call it poetry.

Thanks for letting me write my poem this way,
You see, a poem is a poem, but a poet is for real,
When a poet talks, or writes, it comes out naturally
Or he isn't saying what he feels!

Poetry is an inspiration of love,
But putting it on paper, or out of your mouth,
That's what poetry is to me!

John Beard
TECH-THEOLOGY
Synaptic response
We must shortly ensconce
In the archives, as smacking of nature;

For vast automation
Bespeaks our new station,
Requiring a new nomenclature.

Surrender biology
To creeping technology,
Becoming its most ardent rooter;

Inanimate thrust
Is an absolute must,
As we worship our holy computer.

Kathryn Bailey
MOUNTAIN MAJESTY
Oh glorious mountain so tall you stand
Up to the skyway below the land
You shelter us from wind and storm
And help to keep us safe and warm
In summer the trees are wondrous hue
We set on our porch and gaze at you
In fall your beauty amazes us all
And we wonder why you are so tall
In winter you are bare and brown
With snow covering you to the ground
In spring we see you blooming out
We feel so happy and ready to shout
So to mountain majesty we say to you
Your glorious beauty is a splendid view

Patricia Marie Mauldin

Patricia Marie Mauldin
MY LOVE
As days go by, I'll think of you,
In most everything I do.
I hope you know I am on your side,
With a love sincere and true.

Before you know the time shall pass,
Like the turning of the clock.
Then you'll understand the hands of time,
That my love was solid as a rock.

Like the stem of a perfect rose, you know,
My love for you shall continue to grow,
So sweet is the love that we have shared,
So gentle and true with loving care.

May my heart be with you as days go by,
With a love so sure that shall never die.
The love we have shared has been such a trip,
And has blossomed into the best friendship.

Susan E Reedy
FIRST SNOW
With childlike anticipation
And a heartbeat all astir
I wait,
I hope,
I dream

Memories engulf my mind
Of pastimes once upon a time
And all the fantasies I knew
Soon, I know will live again.
I wait,
I hope,
I dream

Of wakening to a winter's touch
White-capped, all aglow and such
A crystal paradise I'll find
Outside my window come the dawn.
I wait,
I hope,
I dream.

Cathy Riggins
FOREVER
Because once
You've had
FOREVER,
Forever will always be.
Whether in person
Or in a memory,
It will be with you
FOREVER.

Kay Perry
LOVE
I've always heard people say
Love isn't love, till it's given away.
But I've given away my heart,
Only to have it torn apart.

Love should make you happy inside,
Love should be a feeling you never hide.
But love isn't like that much,
Love can make you cry, when you remember his touch.

Love, its memories of the past,
Funny, how memories are the only things that last.
You can keep rings and old letters too,
But every time you see them, you begin to feel blue.

Love can be feelings of good and bad.
One minute you're happy, the next you're sad.
I know what I say is true,
Because—I'm still in love with you.

Evelyn Morgan
THE HOUSE BESIDE THE ROAD

In memory of my mother. Amanda May Jones

The little old house beside the road,
How desolate and alone it stands,
No one at all to care for it,
Untouched by human hand.

Once there was someone who loved it,
And tended it with care,
Made it her humble home,
And planted flowers there,

Now the weeds are grown high,
The flowers have withered away,
Gone like the dear one who tended them,
Till the dawn of another day.

Connie Arline Cloherty
MY SAINT PATRICK

This poem is dedicated to the love of my life, my husband Patrick Henry Cloherty.

My husband Saint Patrick is so bright,
To have around is truly a delight
Together we are one,
Brighter than any sun,
Oh boy, we have so much fun.

It is so tranquil watching the trees and squirrels,
We never ever have any quarrels.
Life is so beautiful,
And our love so truthful.

Today you have lots of leaves to rake,
Take it easy for goodness sake.
Enjoy your meeting,
Enjoy your rest,
Because, my darling, you are the best.
If you take care we will grow old together,
And our love will last forever.

I'm looking forward to our dinner,
It will really be a winner.

I wish I knew the words to say,
To tell you how much I love you every day.

Kenneth D Senior
TENDER TRUTH

Dedicated to Hollie, the best friend ever!

Thank you for the happiness you bring,
the joyful song my heart to sing.
Bless you for the kind thoughts shared,
and letting me know that you care.

Deep within this heart of mine,
you are a friend divine.
Forever I dream and reminisce,
over times we share like this.

The picture I now own of you,
remains a treasure golden and true.
I love your short and curly hair,
long and soft, I love your hair.

No matter how you wear your hair,
it cannot change the way I care.
The chance to share these thoughts with you,
remain a part of loving you.

Steven B Wilson
SONG OF MYSELF
I see you,
Seemingly floating on a cushion of air;
the sunlight gently falling on your golden hair.
Your blue eyes shimmer; your slim legs dance;
and I just sit by and wait for my chance.

I hear you,
Your voice radiates so sweet yet so strong.
I dare say sweeter than the nightingale's song.
It softens cruel men with a sensual trance,
but I just sit by and wait for my chance.

I touch you,
I feel your body so close to my own,
but as for the nights—I spend them alone.
I want to hold you in the heat of romance,
but I just sit by and wait for my chance . . . .
to say I love you.

Liz Voigt
THE PRICE OF PROGRESS
Steel cats are screaming bulldozers tearing
The heart from the ground once so verdant and sweet,

The wildlife decreasing songbirds are ceasing to sing
Time was when in their millions they teemed.

The air turning yellow with the fumes of sulphur
People are sick from the filth they breathe
The big chimneys belching out poisonous gases
Fit only to fuel the ovens of hell.

The rain once so soothing transformed into acid
Nourished the grass now it's searing the land
There is no place to run from the backlash of progress
And industrial monsters invented by man.

Can we ever go back to when our forefathers
Inhaled fresh clean air and the water was pure
That's only a dream become a nightmare.
How much abuse can creation endure.

Mickey Meiners
A SOUL REBORN
On my moist stained cheek, a tear has dropped....................
From eyes, that if looked into deeply........................
Reveal a soul that is nothing more than a crumpled fall leaf..........
Dried by the summer's hot sun, and...........................
Partially amputated by the autumn winds.........................
Oh, but if only a warm rain would fall upon it and................
Moisten its dryness to form its shape again.........................
To a full leaf, to a fulfilled soul....
Looking out at a bright and wonderful world of..............
Beautiful people through clear eyes glistening bright................
On a face seen smiling from a reflection of a soul..............
That has been rebuilt from a rekindled love..................
That life had momentarily borrowed......................
For the purpose of testing its strength......................

Kevin E Judge
THE FLUTE

To my beloved Christy. Thanks for the faith

I am dead
No light penetrates the darkness that surrounds me
My cold, stiff body doesn't feel the warming comfort
Of the soft, plush velvet all around
The whispers of memory play about my surface
Of a once remembered time
When people would sit attentively and listen
Captured and held in check by the sound of my sweet voice
A small of light banishes the darkness
As the lid is slowly opened
The full force of the light's source hits me
I wink back its reflection
Loving, gentle hands caress me
Tenderly she places her lips on mine and blows
The kiss of life courses through my body
Her breath becomes my breath
The light current of air continues as her fingers
Dance about my surface
Her exhalation becomes my voice
Sweet, fine and mellow, I sing for her
I am alive

Debi Buettner
ALL MY DAYS
After these many months,
you still overwhelm with your ways.
My heartbeat still quickens
at the thought of seeing you.
I still melt when you hold me so tight.
And you carry me yet farther,
each time we love as one.
Your kisses are still so soft,
your touches so tender,
and our passion still makes me surrender.
My love for you I find
grows ever stronger each day.
I've opened my life to you,
and as the months pass,
I want all my days shared with you.
And I can truly say,
I will love you forever.

Elwin Henry

Elwin Henry
TEMPTATIONS

To my cousin, Opal Irene Riley.

As Adam and Eve were tempted
In the long ago,
So are we of today, being tempted
At times we do not know.

But our conscience bother us
And we know not what to do,
I have often felt that way,
How about you?

Lisa M Morgan
IMPRESSIONS

To Moon—whom I can never seem able to completely walk away from

Some day in the future
When I am long out of your life
You're going to look back
And regret letting me walk away
For by that time
You will have learned
That there is more to a relationship
Than feeling in love
Times aren't always easy
You have to work hard
To keep the fires burning—to keep the love alive
You have to be companionable in silence
Yet also willing to communicate
Honesty must be foremost
Even if with it comes pain
You have to have a separate life
Yet keep the relationship a whole
You have to give as well as take
This is what makes love grow
Some day you shall look back—and this is what you'll see
That all that makes a lasting love,
was what you shared with me

Louis Buchhold III aka: LOUB III
INTRUDERS

Dedicated to Rev. Louis Buchhold, Jr., March 17, 1929-April 13, 1989

I'm really not used to it
This sitting in the dark
Waiting for a shadow to pass
And catch my attention
Gazing through the window
Old, and wondering
Who else sat,
In this place,
In the dark,
Waiting

And the fronds rustling
Waving back,
At the window
Dry and pressed
Seeing someone
Who sits
In this Place,
In the dark
Waiting
I'm really not used to it

Lou Cardis
MOTHER
Through the years, many with joy, some with tears. Time passes quickly, so so quickly.

So many years, years when I should have let you know—just how dear. Time goes by, now I wonder why, why I never let you know how much I love you so.

Words that should have been said, things we should have done, too oft go who knows where.

Those so close, the ones that mean so much, when will we stop and let them know—where oh where did the time go.

F Templeton Galbraith
THE VISIT
Steep slope beyond the narrow road
So new across the long years
We walk heavily up the slope
Pausing before the gray slab.

"Your father's ashes," he said
"Can be placed but first
The concrete must break
Apart for them and maybe!"

I listen with intent but heard
The whisper of the wind
And the flutter of the leaves
Above the sounds around.

What surprised me most that day
Scrambling up the old steps
Was my calmness before mother's grave
"Why did I come if not to weep," I said

The great highway curved to the East
Beyond the cemetery gates
But the sounds of trucks and cars
Were muted by the turmoil sudden

In my heart—I spoke the prayer
That I had come to say, the placid
Face I kept belied the wave
Of strong memories.

Father and Mother dim in the blank world
In the fragments of consciousness
Somewhere between the heartache
And the evening news.

Shirley Talken
WEAVER OF DREAMS

To Bud—freer of spirit, giver of light, lover of life, bestower of beauty.

The morning light reveals a gentle being—
solitary is the world she's seeing.
With magic loom she weaves her web of dreams—
each circle builds upon her hopes.
She seems
inspired by needs as yet untold
by word, and, holding breath
lest precious thoughts be heard,
rests for a moment, quietly
contemplating the world she
has created, confiscating
fantasies from those who've
gone before—those special ones
who authored tender lore of
quiet love now yearning to be
born, expecting not to suffer
from life's scorn.

Will effort put forth be an effort wasted?
Is love now here, but never to be tasted?
Will night-time fall with visions still intact?
Will dreams unfinished be the final act?

Begin your work anew and peaceful be,
for far into the future you can't see.
Take from today and let not bygone sorrow
be on your brow, but smile upon the morrow.

Jessie R Roberts
SIREN SPRING
The foothills of mountains are calling,
"Come out and join in the play;
Skip over my meadows and woodlands;
Play hooky from labor today."

That siren is tugging my heartstrings;
My Gypsy blood's running high;
I must dance with gamboling pixies
Under the brilliant sky.

Happily weary, I'll rest
And sit for awhile to dream
Beside a pool of stars
Along a mountain stream.

Spring is a time for romance.
Perchance my dreams come true?
Today I'll flirt with the hills
'Neath skies cerulean blue.

Joseph Edward O'Brien
REALITY

everyones seeking out answers, be knowing life's joyous celebration without doubt, your center in Love, Peace, and gentle Truth

stinging metallic cold lingers
stiffening clairvoyant rainbow hues
piercing yet soft
touches my eyes body computer
invading techno microscopic
megabyte chips
camouflage color crisp geometric
asymmetric puzzling labyrinths
binding natures blue
laced skies still evoke
melodies and acrobatic maneuvers
joyful hummingbird dances
majestically tasting sweet nectars
quite unresisting unnerved by any
element
natures true greenery and mosaic
treasures
flowery light songbells reduced to
binary logic
designed holographic sequences
image
natures awe in mans creation
I trust my own minds transcending
though changes and appearances
evolutionize
renewing every instance
of life and deaths illusion

Cecelia Clair Rea
SILENT STIRRINGS

To Ernie and Betty

My library speaks
through wooden casements
proudly bearing
leather-bounds among
the flexible, glossy leaves.
I'm drawn into alliance
with *Auden's* satire-world;
I'm consort to a memory-link
with *Austen's* pride;
succumbing to the transport
by *Keats* into
his Grecian mood;
I bear the burden
of *Dory Previn's*
On My Way To Where.

Trina Humpherys
YOU

To that special someone in my life

You make me smile every day,
You never tell me to go away.
You tell me "I like the way you are,"
And that you miss me when I'm far.
You show me that you care,
by always being there.
Destiny has brought us together,
I hope this will last forever.

Gloria Swails
THE DREAM GOES ON

To my first born, Kathleen Scarlet, With love

Of daughters great and small, I think
. . . and I recall
Memories of joy, of all the greatest
dreams fulfilled
By one so independent, so strong
willed.
Of important programs almost
missed,
of God given talents, ideas,
new . . and crisp.
Shared tears and loving hearts.
So overwhelming . . . the memories.
The strands of silver that frame our
faces,
that we have earned as we nurtured
each other with embraces.
Of hearts that have broken
because words of disappointment
were spoken harshly, out loud for
each to hear.
But, alas . . . the joy returns again
when in our eyes we see each other
reflected,
for just a second . . . and then it's
gone.
Again, the dream goes on.

Charlene G Shute
A TRIBUTE TO WELLINGTON/ TYE

Nestled within these Cascade
Mountains
winding downward the Highway,
to only be seen from a distant glance
from modernizations bi-way.

This beautiful place, like Roman
ruins,
scattered throughout these mountains,
tell a story long forgotten
of workers, good people, and
villains.

The well-built snowsheds proudly
stand
guarding Great Northerns past,
this route contains seven tunnels
and stretches from East to West.

The tracks are gone now but the trail
remains,
the memories are written in history.
No one would know a disaster struck
these flowers and scenery, so pretty.

1910 is when it all happened,
the doom hung upon the snow,
forming heavy drifts.
Safe, they thought,
little, did they know.

A passenger train and a mail train,
held behind for the seventh day.
A loud roar, then suddenly quiet,
Mother Nature states what is to be
paid.

One hundred-eighteen lives lost
between a week of revival.
Wellington suddenly disappeared,
Tye appeared for survival.

Wandering serenely upon this path
sorting out the supposed map
wondering what it was like to be
living in the past history.

Melissa A Bradley
A DOLPHIN'S CRY . . .

Beneath the blue-green sea,
Live creatures whose beauty,
is unparallel to any other.

Their hues of silver shimmer,
and glisten, as gentle waves
lap against their sleek yet,
swift bodies.

A foreign language is spoken,
Unknown to common men,
Men who are blind to what
they see.

We search the stars, in our
unfounded quest for intelligent life. . .
Yet, we have failed to look in
our own domain

Perhaps, it's time we took a
closer look, For if we do we may
find this life, Beneath the
blue-green sea . . .

Tammy N White
LIVING IN THE PAST

Living in the past, bringing memories
back alive
Long ago dead feelings your
subconscious tried to hide.
Remembering the hurt you felt so
long ago,
Remembering the tears you fought so
hard not to show.
Old feelings so strong that they
crushed the new,
Old feelings that matter to no one
else but you.
Your lost love is gone forever. As
hard as you try, you'll see him never.
The emotions you deal with, the pain
inside,
The love you fought for, was love
denied.
You miss his touch, you miss his
face,
You miss the security of his warm
embrace.
Remember his voice, remember his
smile,
Remember the love you will never
reconcile.
He meant everything, he brightened
your day
Together forever you'd always say.
The days grew darker, the nights
grew cold
Death comes for young and old.
Blackness enfolded the night you
cried,
Blackness enfolded the night he died.

Barbara Ann Swanson
CYCLES

Could we live like butterflies,
Changing from a dreary moth
To something vibrant and joyful?
What magic does it take?

I wonder if, when the magic comes,
We'll understand the import—
Or will we be asleep or dreaming
And still be moths when we awake?

Will the fear of change hold us back,
Clinging to the safety of the cocoon?
Or will we dare to feel the magic
And display our colors boldly?

Michael Anthony Estrada
THE MAGICIAN

For the Broken Hearted

A magician stood with his top hat
tipped
looking for a young fool to show his
tricks
 Here are your hopes
He would say and draw from his hat,
broken pieces of dreams that fell
through his hands like tokens
 Here is your love
He would cry while blood ran from
his eyes
and his top hat screamed unforgivable lies
 Here are your friends
He would laugh and bring a knife out
of his hat
Gleaming in the fire from his hands
he would put it in your back
 Here is your life
He would whisper as he held the hat
for all to see
and it crumbled to dust falling into a
dead sea

Gary Nannariello
THE MAN SO SAD

So sad is the man who doesn't have
fun
So sad is the man who has no one
The man is so sad he never leaves his
room
He paints his walls with sadness and
gloom

The sun never shines, he can't see
the light
He doesn't care for the sun, or if he
loses his sight
Loneliness has become his own best
friend
Has he lost his mind, or is he just on
the mend

Look inside his crazy mind
You'd be surprised with what you'll
find
Ingenious thoughts locked inside a
cell
Only if we give him time and a
chance can we ever tell

Don't you always lock him out of
your home if not your life
Don't you cut him out of everything,
aren't you always the knife
He's not really so bad if you give him
a chance
Sit down and talk to him, help him
advance

He's not crazy, he's not insane
There's nothing wrong with this
man's brain
He's no different from you and I
But you'll never find out if you don't
let him have a try

Henry Edward Bryant III
TOM FOOLERY

Alone I sit in a mob-filled room
Waiting the record to introduce the
show.
Alas, my passion—a Judy Garland
Slit skirt, followed by an encore of
scores.
Hailed and applauded as she teared
our eyes.

Next, they called him a dyke.
Manly perhaps, but set to Dimone
charm.
Moans and groans, the male
pretender,
The male defender.

Following a break, Miss Ethel
Waters took the cake,
Bringing alive the chills and thrills of
Harlem before the wake.

Alas! Miss West!
Can this be the final test?!

Tina Turner—a sight for sore eyes,
Lena Horne—Harlem is reborn!

I looked up and caught the wink of
an eye.
At me? I thought I'd die.

Kathy Segno
I'M SORRY

I'm sorry if I make you mad, at
everything I do
I'm sorry if you can't accept, the
way I feel toward you
I'm sorry that I have to do, the things

I am this way
I'm sorry that your family ties, are less important than your play
I'm sorry your son doesn't have, a Daddy to look upon
I'm sorry you can't be there, when he awakes at dawn
I'm sorry that you won't try, a little more than you do
I'm sorry that your son needs me, to be a Daddy too
I'm sorry that you won't be, a Daddy from afar
I'm sorry that your son will be, the one who'll bear the scar
I'm sorry for his confusion, he needs a Daddy too
I'm sorry that you'll never be, the one he looks up to
I'm sorry he has only my love, at least he knows I'm there
I'm sorry he has no fatherly love, but he knows that Mommy, cares
I'm not sorry for one thing, I've always been there for him
there to shed a little light, when his life was looking dim
I am sorry for you though, your son only knows you by your lies
You promised to come see how big he's grown, "NO SHOW"
& left me to wipe the tears from his eyes!

Joni Alice Fahim
THE GIFT OF LOVE

To my husband, with love, dedicated to Fayek Fekry Fahim

Love is nothing to take as you do.
Love is something, that is your clue.
It can be yours to give to another.
Someone who is closer, closer than a brother.
It's nice to receive and it's nice to give.
Everyone needs love, needs love to live.

Charles Arnett Bailey

Charles Arnett Bailey
SALEM

A tribute to the pioneers, friends & members of Salem Baptist Church, Kansas City, KS, especially, my family, Pastor Rev. Charles Bailey, Mrs. Geneva Bailey, Nozella, Tim, Gelaine, Malisa, & all my supporters.

The meeting place where people pray
Heavy hearts and sensitive souls obey

Innocent children with concerned elders hold hands
In worship together
Precious moments of joy forever
The pulpit is ablaze, as the preacher shouts and sways
Igniting a chorus of Hallelujah! Amen!
A sweat brow message for all men

With twisting leaps and thunderous pulpit landings,
His booming voice finds us joyously standing

Hands start clapping, while choir feet start tapping
The organ keys bounce to rejuvenated knees

The festive sounds are overheard
The grateful ushers there to serve

Only a fraternity of love, that's all!
Blessed with harmony from above life's wall

Generations seek this genuine sensation
Those at Salem simply delight in genuine salvation

Salem pride is like a bride
Always radiant with a happy sigh

A way of life disbursed not trite
Please shake hands with a Salemite

John P Maroncelli
WONDROUS DAYS

In those wondrous days
Of day or evening when according
To what I was doing I realized
Where I was and who I am,
When the sweet breeze or soft music
Electrified my very soul.

The mystics see something but
Not the colors beheld by my eyes,
Through drugs and sleep and death
The man I am I love,
What I behold.

The muscles in my back bending
Stretching, breaking to heal stronger
The goblin in my throat chokes
Nothing is sweeter than a
Sweet breeze, women's fair faces
Covered with apple strudel
Cannot defeat.

Patricia J Kelly
ANNIVERSARY

Happy anniversary dear
Be you far, be you near,
Lest we forget
Those happy, tender moments
Before troubles started to pile
Just know I loved you all the while.
If only you had stayed
Holding hands and not afraid,
We would have found a way
To make the culprits pay.
But now you are gone
And everything seems wrong,
Together we could have made it
Of that I am sure,
Now our lovely home just a house
As I rattle around without my spouse.
How could you leave me, darling?
To find you hanging from a noose
Self-inflicted, I am sure
From life too rough to endure.

Barry Mozes
THE MOON IN JUNE

In loving memory of Christina.

The Swiss Cheese of the sky.
Craters bellowing outward;
Engulfing the black of space.
The binding light shot forth
Creates the romance we endure.
The glimmer on the water
Enframes her laced body.
The sparkles mirrored off the water,
Set the never ending stage;
As the words "I DO," echo into space.

Debra Lynn Van Dine
STEPPING BACK, REFLECTING

Stepping back, reflecting
On happenings occurred
The reason roads were travelled
And others left obscure
We all are separate beings
In how fast or slow we grasp
We can each reflect and hunger
For the everlasting fact.
Our days in seeking knowledge
Are sure to bring to light
How basic are the principles
When shown within one's sight
As each day comes and passes
We must not deny our minds
The moments we yearn,
For the hunger that burns
Will heighten our souls with delight.

Eileen Elizabeth Farrell
TAKING TIME

To Don; Thanks for the gentle push and the gentle love.

Come to me slowly
if you must
Test me
I'm strong
I can withstand everything
except your leaving
So if you come to me stay
Come to me slowly
if you must
Share my world
piece by piece
I'm willing to go at any pace
You set it
I'll follow
Build the road
But don't travel away

Elmer G Coffey Sr
COME

To life's lost loved ones

Come, weep with me, in sympathy
All born of life must face
A glint of joy, a broken toy
A past we can't erase

Come, let us spurn, with tear drops burn
Our cup of hollow space
That once was filled, and now is spilled
On earth in some dark place

Come, shed our tears, and dull our fears
It's a world that GOD must hate
We live awhile, by HIS sun dial
There is no other fate

Come, we will cry, and say goodby
To the good in life so brief
For we must change, and re-arrange
From happiness to grief

Come, dry our eyes, and still our sighs
All hurt beneath earth's sky
There's nothing sane, nothing to gain
But just the chance to die

Ethel Case Cook RN
R.N. TO SURGICAL HEART PATIENT

I hail you, gentle giant, for your wit,
Your sensitivity, your hand, your smile . . .
You lighted up my life, and having lit,
You brought new meaning, made it all worthwhile.
What I can do for you is not enough
To thank you for the joy you bring to me,
So I compose for you this bit of fluff—
"There are no strangers" this I plainly see.
I say goodbye for now, my Scrabble mate;
(And wipe away the tears that quickly start)
You're like a son sent forth to meet his fate—
God speed, my dear, God bless your open heart.

Sharon Gadfield
TO LIVE YOUR LIFE AND BE FREE

To Live your Life
And be Free.

To find Someone
To Share it
And find Peace.

Live as One
And still be You.

Secure together

Apart—find Love.

Friend—

Lover—

I am yours.

Michel Paxson
NOBODY CARES

How many Johns—More'n a score?
You say your body's been used and abused,
You claim you ain't pretty no more.
Listen Man! You jes' don't understand.
Nobody Cares!

How many scams have you tried?
Your ass is sore—the world be damned.
You feel all rotten inside.
Hey Man! You jes' don't understand.
Nobody Cares!

So, life ain't worth more'n a dime.
Can it. Get smart. Be your own man.
Don't blame others—you ain't got time.
Hey Man! You jes' don't understand.
Nobody Cares!

It ain't the body that's battered and scarred.
It ain't the deeds you did for an ounce.
It's what's in your head that matters now.
It's the man you aim to be that counts
'Cause Nobody Cares
'Bout you but YOU.

Mavis Tofte
SECRET CORNER

A place to go when you feel blue
A place to think your troubles through.
We all need our secret corner
Where you can feel safe and warmer.

Yes a secret spot if you please
Whether adult or child we have need of these.
You see, we need somewhere to dream
Uninterrupted by daily stress or stream.

Without a lot of fuss or ado
You need a place to truly be you.
It may be the attic, the garage, the barn you see
or even under some quiet lonely tree.

It can be with or without doors
There should be a space that's called yours.
And if your spot is hard to find,
There's always the deep corners of the mind.

So find your niche where ever it be.
A secret place, dear friend is a need you see.
And as you've heard me say before
It's your very own corner, need I say more!

Rhea R Hilkevitch
ETERNAL VERITIES

Good food, good people . .
Lilacs in the courtyard
Quiet streets at dawn . .
The shadows of twilight
Good books to read
And poems to write,
Warm encounters with loved ones,
Embraces and good talk . .
Quiet moments when the heart sings . .
The reverberations of great music . .
Images and dreams . .
All these—the eternal verities.

Gwen Wilhelm
LOVE IS FOREVER

Dedicated to my dear daughter Gena whom I love dearly

Life goes on early and late,
And only the Lord knows our fate.
The dark of early morning moves on so slowly,
Till too quietly the sun comes up boldly.
Your bed of white moves through the halls,
Ready to meet each doctor's call.
Your life is precious to we who love you.
One X-ray, two X-rays, I've lost count.
Each move of your bed takes you on a different route.
Bruised kidneys, broken ribs, broken leg, plastic surgeon—Trauma,
When will it all end like a dream or a drama.
Unknown liquids dripping from bottles, sustaining life and keeping your body stable.
While doctors study X-ray after X-ray on the table.
It's now five hours later with your eyes closed on your bed,
And your ever-loving mom curls on a chair resting her head.

Shelly Lee Kowalski
KING ARTHUR

King Arthur the great.
King Arthur the grand.
Ruler over all; and over all the land.
Killed by the greed and the lust for love.
Killed by those whom he trusted and loved.
His beautiful Queen Guenevere, so lovely and grand.
Upset the whole balance of peace in his land.
And O' yes Lancelot the greatest of Knights,
Contributed to the war that ended Arthur's life.
And now he rests at peace with himself.
While Lancelot and Guenevere repent themselves.
For their living days are few and filled with the grief of the lost.

Jeffrey S Gauer
A MORNING SONG

The eastern sun rises to christen dawn,
One star-cross'd night into clouds seeps 'til gone.
Two lovers ending hours in passion's flame,
A gentle knight enfolds his willing dame.

Their minds mirrors from which had pour'd the might
From which hearts' flowers shimmered rosy white.
Their garden rose and grew until it seem'd
That time and death and day were only dream'd.

The subtle kiss of light can be as lead
When evening's love is sever'd from morning's bed.
Needles of day plunge into tired eyes,
Forgotten is the joy of night in daylight's painful skies.

Erwin Cox
SPRINGTIME

In memory of my father, Roy L. Cox, Sr., who so dearly loved the springtime.

Melodies of songbirds round us ring,
Happy tunes in time of spring;
Beautiful flowers amid the green,
A splendor of grandeur yearly seen.

More beautiful, each spring, than the last,
Next spring is sure to improve the past;
Marvel, we will, at the springtime season,
With God granted vision and a mind to reason
About this beauty so loved in this land,
Is but a masterpiece of the Master's hand;
Who added the summer, winter and fall,
With intended efforts to please us all.

Be happy! Care free! Spring won't last long,
Birds soon will chirp the summer songs;
Soon the colors of fall, the snows of winter,
Ere springtime beauty, again we enter.

Gilbert T Schaad

Gilbert T Schaad
ALONE

To my very best friend.

I walked alone neath starlit skies,
With thoughts of someone's smiling eyes.
My heart singing a happy song,
I wish you could have been along.
The whisper of the evening breeze,
Just dancing there among the trees,
The twilight made the field seem wide,
With moonbeams on the distant side.
An owl perched high upon a pole,
Watching for mice to leave their hole.
A robin red was singing late
A special song just for his mate.
In shadows there were blossoms too,
Now waiting for the morning dew.
Violets; yellow, white and blue
Looked up with smiles asking for you.
'twas such a lovely night it's true.
But oh! how I was missing you.

Nick Caligiuri
PRINCESS OZMA OF OZ

Ozma rules in a wonderful land
With love in her heart and sceptre in hand

She cares for her people with all of her might
Never bringing darkness only the light

She lives in a city so big and so bold
With all of her friends in this gracious stronghold

Her subjects obey but some give her trouble
She says to behave or the punishment will be double

She's aided by the Wizard and Glinda the Good
And appreciates them greatly as anyone would
So Ozma's the ruler and loved by all
Yes Ozma's the ruler and stands proud and tall

Lisa Ann Monello
TO MYSELF I CONFIDE

The days grow colder,
but the air the same.
Life still plays its gruesome game.
The moments one someday sought to hold,
Are filled with dreams yet untold.
On my own to myself
I confide,
Of those who hurt, and those who guide;
Of those who live for life's true treasures,
and those who stride for life's little pleasures.
The passages for the life I seek,
have left me weary, tired, and weak.
To learn and experience is to sinister pain,
For each mistake is knowledge we gain.
And the breathless moments we look to mourn,
Are filled with papers left untorn.
For puzzled and mixed is a state of mind,
and the challenging moments make life divine.
The time it takes to answer life's questions,
is up before we make connections.
The answers we forever yearn,
take up the time we grow to learn,
That on my own to myself
I confide,
of those who hurt, and those who guide.
And the untorn papers are to those who keep,
life's misfortunes laid to sleep.

Clinton W Rowley Jr
BEYOND

Slowly roused, enjoying
A different awakening,
To blissful satiations,
Comfortable sensations;
Murmuring sounds that soothe,
From a fawn-eyed woman, smooth
Blond hair shimmering unbound;
Enticing eyes that hold spellbound,
Lithe body of swelling contours,
Like the maid upon the moors;
Swift primal passions cloak,
The soft and mild yoke;
Her upraised hand beckons:
". . . Come to me . . ." for those immortal seconds!

Lynda R Farley
I WONDER

To my children

Watching a bee working in a young flower
On a new-born day,
I am filled with amazement, wonder, joy—
With miracles my senses toy!
I wonder if Darwin felt this way?

See those spires, that sun dipped tower,
Civilizations slowly climbing—
Manifestations of minds reaching,
Wondering whence comes the

power?
Michelangelo's true gift is teaching.

Look; there our sun, the stars, immensity—
The vast unexplored abyss,
And the realization most astonishing to me—
If we look long enough, we may see!
All great men have known this.

Catherine Sheridan
HEALING
I don't forgive you, I never will.
Your silence to my loving pleas bellows in my ears.
All my negatives, affirmed 'tis a bitter pill . . . . . .
Once filled with joy, now emptied with fears.

But Then

The sun redeemed, a promise to shine, will.
To the pulsating sounds of nature, one listens and one hears.
Looking at the gifts of life, my heart will rapidly fill.
And the secret dream of you will last through the years.

Laura A McCluskey
THE TEAR OF LOVE
The tear that appears upon my face,
is the one that only love can erase.
This tear falls from my eye with the sadness of love, for it only appears when I think of the ones I've loved.
It appears when thoughts come to mind, thinking of the ones that have been so kind.
Then there's the tear that you grow to hate, the one from the lovers that hurt you so.
You hate it because they made you cry, they made the tear of love fall from your eye.
Whenever you think of them, the tear of love will come again.
Then you must close your eyes and let them fall, just like you've let them all.

Susan K Cook
MAGIC COMFORT

This poem is dedicated, with love, to my lovely daughter, Elaina.

People say the country
Has its own allure.
A wholesome kind of beauty,
Where the air you breathe is pure.

If you listen in the night
To its mellow sounds,
You will find delight
And know that peace abounds.

The rustle of the leaves,
The croaking of a frog,
Whispers of a breeze,
Distant barking of a dog.

All these things together bring
Comfort to your soul.
It's magic how such simple things
Can make your heart feel whole.

Sandra M Del Greco
MAYBE TODAY

To Denise, my dear sister. I could always count on you to be there for me. Thank you. Love Sandra

All these thoughts kept inside, just waiting to come out
No one to talk to, no one to listen
I wish sometimes I could just sit down and cry
What holds me back? I just don't know.
I see people walking hand in hand
I see the love they share
I see how much they care

In the morning I wake up only to pass another day
I wish I had some adventure,
something to look forward to,
something to be happy about

One always has friends, but sometimes one needs more.
Someone else to talk to
not a relative, not a friend, maybe just a complete stranger.

Maybe the day will come and there will be that special person
I can confide in,
Or maybe that day will be today?

Lottie Sutton

Lottie Sutton
SOFTLY CLEAR

To: Jeff D. Sutton (My father-in-law), for whom it was first written, And The Arkansas School for The Deaf.

Turn down the set
Adjust the volume.
I can not understand the words
The mouths are making.

A fire engine passing,
A police car or an ambulance?
Who touched me?
I turn quickly,
Careful not to lose my balance,
As I adjust that piece I have
To wear in my ear.

Speak softly to me,
Because then, I can hear.

Emma Jean Howard
LOVE

Dedicated to nieces

Love is a fish
Some people have lost their bait.
Love is a fish.
Some people catch more than their limit.
Love is a fish.
Some people catch only salamanders.

Marcus Williams
SONNET 1—TO KARA
If I were the wolf, would thou love with ease?
Even though thou art the lamb, gentle belle.
To most I hath been Mephistopheles,
He who is the devil, creature of hell.
Reflect on all that I am and am me.
Deem of what I have to offer the lamb.
Think of the gist of my soul upon thee.
Think of thy gallant and all that is damned.
Dulcinea I'm thy Casanova.
If cupid hath fired his holy arrow,
Fired and aimed true, then I am thy lover;
Only if this has happened with little sorrow.
If thou hath beheld through my domino,
Truth in thy heart, ever will I love you so.

Angela Jacobson
FINDING WHAT'S LOST
Listening to the thunder,
Watching the rain come down,
Hearing the voices of children lost and never found.

I can hear them thinking, "Am I ever going to be found?" And if I am will I be here to know how?

Unfeelings of emotions is all they have now,
No tears, no fears, all love is unbound.

They feel no hope nor look to the future
it's all so hopeless, just minds of confusion.

The rain is still falling and the voices are faint,
All that is heard is, "Why do I have to wait?"

Samuel C Oliver
THE ALPHA/OMEGA GREATEST HERO

To The Father, Son and Holyghost The Beginning and end of true heroism

I AM is he; the hero of originality.
In a time of need, 'twas he that parted a sea.

Uncorruptible and above all sin,
All known heroes plagiarize ways of him.
Without fanfare, how many heroes did ascend?
Even with cheers, which can call stones to worship him?

In a suit of armor or some other makeup,
the types are revealed by what they wear.
Fashion in that which is uncorrupt,
I AM is adorned in glory so fine and fair.

They compare with that which is upon high;
Yet, they were created in the valley below.
By his glory every hero did derive,
And this the truth does clearly show.

While they became everything but,
I AM was being everything so . . .
Infinity belongs to the Alpha/Omega Greatest Hero.

I AM: and nothing can take this part,
For none is there who's greater than God.
AMEN

Jacqueline (Jackie) Smith
THE SEARCH
Can I look around with clouded eyes
and truly see myself?
Can I hear words spoken clearly
and hide them on a shelf?
Can I drift along life's highway
and find a stopping place?
Can I feel the nearness of a friend
then let it slip in space?
Can I not see myself as life
and find that I too live?
Can I not hear the words they speak
and learn the way to give?
Can I not 'walk tall' along the way
and know why I am here?
Can I not greet my fellow man
and hold his friendship near?

Can I know the truth within me
by closing lifeway's door?
Can I know the world of voices
by silencing the shore?
Can I know the way of being
by losing self and mind?
Can I know the way of loving
by not being truly kind?

I can look at self as being,
and try to live with ease.
I can listen to learn wisdom,
before doing as I please.
I can learn to face the future,
by accepting life as such.
I can know the meaning of true love,
just by a gentle touch.

One day I'll find my way of life,
and know why I am me.
I'll learn to live within my soul,
and know what is to be.
I still have time to find my way,
and still more time to grow.
For when my search is at an end,
I'll be myself, I know.

Roger Schroeder
I AM BORN TODAY
I am born today,
The sun brings a promise in my eyes.

Momma slaps me,
I draw a breath and cry.

Above me a bird wings
His way across the sky.
I'm glad to be alive.

It is my seventh day,
I feel the hunger and I cry.

Brother and sister cling to Momma's side,
She squeezes her breasts,
But they have nothing to provide.

Someone weeps . . . . I fall asleep.

It is twenty days today,
Momma doesn't hold me any more.

I open my mouth,
But I am too tired to cry.

Above me a bird slowly glides,
Across the sky.

Why is there nothing now to do . . .
But die?

Lynell Ridgdell
YESTERDAY'S HEROES

Dedicated to Vietnam Veterans

Once cherished
And named
For their Courage
And Honor,
Now forgotten
And blamed
In disrespectful
Horror.
Once mighty
And strong
Bearing arms
Against foes,
Now treated
So wrong
They're
Yesterday's Heroes.

Catherine M Archbold
THERE IS A SADNESS
There is a sadness in this world;
In the harsh reality of standing
armies and exploding bombs;
In the indifference of man to his
fellow man;
In the wanton killing of innocents.
There is a sadness in this world that
cannot be ignored!

Louise See
COMMUNION
The seething, milling mass
Flows together—draws apart.
A fleeting moment of togetherness
In which to be filled or drained.

The time is so short
In which so much to be done.
The moment at the Table,
A quick draft from the Cup.

We are never filled,
And the aching void of our
emptiness
Sends us flowing another way
With open mouths seeking.

Always seeking that which
When we find, our mouths will
close;
We may not eat
Because we live in fear.

Fear that that which can give us Life
Will also be our death;
And this thing that is mine—the only
thing—
Will be lost in the seething, milling
mass.

Jane E Carey
PERENNIALITY
Whence comes this bit of pale
warmth,
Caressing as a whisper,
Receding then to darkest fathom,
Leaving me a quester—
After Love.

Where lies the realm of Everlasting,
Teasing as a tempter,
Persuading first and then rejecting,
Making me a searcher—
After Truth.

What gives the breath to human life,
Creating as a sculptor,
Entreating man to find His answer,
Framing me a seeker—
After All.

Janice C Dishman
LATCH YOUR DREAMS ONTO A STAR
Latch your dreams onto a star;
Dreams can make up what you are;
Your dearest dreams can come true,
For it all depends on you.

Put your shoulder to the wheel;
Take it slowly up life's hill;
Plant your feet firm on the ground,
Don't let backsets get you down.

Rome was not built in a day;
And you'll trip along the way;
Aim for your dream, reaching high,
And set your eyes on the sky.

Does your rainbow have an end?
Say, have you found it my friend?
Latch your dreams onto a star;
Persistence will take you far.

Hope Tillery
SIN IS INSANE

To my two beautiful daughters, Shari Lynn Clifton, & Vicki Gwen Lunog

Sin is insane, your brothers & sisters
are not to blame. Your fathers and
mothers will die in shame.
Don't use others for a crutch or cane.

Sin takes you farther than you want
to go, keeps you longer than you
want to stay, costs you more than
you're willing to pay. Father, why
are so many going the wrong way?
Using drugs and drinking, being
friends with the wrong gang. That is
the way you end your life, in sin and
insane.

Being kind and loving comes from a
happy heart,
a good moral mind within plays a
necessary part.

Remember, and pray for those who
always complain,
they are the ones, that are really to
blame.

Not in God's will in sin & insane.

David Picciano
MY ANGER, JUST A FLAME

To the good Lord in heaven who has now doused my fiery anger, kindling in my soul a new flame, one of great hope, love and eternal life.

Just a flame that's always burning
Just a flame that won't retreat
Just a flame of white heat burning
Always burning
Never fading

Never building, always falling
losing interest losing life
Gaining power strength abounding
Outcries of my pain resounding
In the furnace
In the flames

Fire rising rage denying
All the life, the flames, disguising

Through this all there's life exuding
Heart is pounding soul is yearning
Gliding through the fire, burning
Just a fire
Just a flame

Just a flame that's always burning.

Edna Lineberry
THE MEEK

Dedicated to Jimmy

Oft we read of a tree of life, streets
of gold and a crystal stream.
Oh yes there is a heaven! But what
did the Master mean?
When he spoke to the chosen on the
Mount. His words were always true
"The meek will inherit the earth," he
said. I wonder—now, don't you?
A poor man often turned down
at the bank for the smallest
loan,
Will he someday own the very land,
the bank is standing on?
All the riches of the proud man
and the worth of Fort Knox gold
Will it be someday given to the
beggars by the road?
An humble darky toiling, down
in the deep southland,
Could it be that he'll inherit the
fields he now works by hand?
Will the bluebirds of the mountains
sing for the lonely and oppressed
Will the deaf and dumb hear the
meadowlark; is Florida for the poor
to rest?
Was Texas made for the lame to
walk, will the blind see Tennessee?
is California the meek's sunrise?
Will they build near the
redwood tree?
Will the hungry feed on Manna—
Georgia fruit, Kansas wheat—crops
of Maine
Will the earth be filled with plenty as
God replenishes it with grain.

Yes I know there is a heaven!
The Good Book says it's true.
But, "The meek will inherit the
earth," Jesus said.
I wonder—friend. Don't you?

Audra Williams
GOD'S PERFECT DAY
God has laid His hand
on the earth with creative art.
And the land begins dancing
with a happy heart.
The roses are blooming
their yellow, red, and white.
A bright sun shines
its warmth with all its might.
Trees wave their arms
in welcoming the day.
And a song is heard
from a happy blue jay.
A deer comes down from the hills
followed by her fawn.
Down in the willows
a bear cub stretches and yawns.
Timber wolves taking a morning
romp
see the deer but run on by.
While bald eagles soar
in the bright blue sky.
Sparkling streams sing
and laugh in glee.
A warm breeze blows
setting leaves free.
Owls hoot at the coming
of a moonlit night.
Squirrels scamper for their nests
and birds slip out of sight.
All God's little ones
lie down to rest,
As the sky glows red
with the sun setting in the west.

C A Faulkner
SOMETIMES YESTERDAYS
It seems like only yesterday
That an unstable mind began
To stabilize but sometimes
yesterdays
Are merely as secure as the mind
In which they reside and sometimes
Yesterdays just don't give a damn
And it seems that yesterdays were
warmed
Recently by the eager austerity of the
setting sun
Earnestly fading along horizons
Earnestly sinking into yesterdays
But sometimes yesterdays are death-
cold
And waiting for years to cover them
Like funeral-dirt and sometimes
yesterdays
Look back in mirrors at the life they
held
So firmly by the throat and
sometimes
Yesterdays listen to stories told
sincerely
By that life of that life which only
Can be heard through earnest
laughter
And sometimes yesterdays
Just don't give a damn

Kathe' Hamill
MY SISTER
You're considerate, thoughtful and
Always sweet.
Everything you do is tidy and neat.

Your patience to listen, with the
ability
To understand,
Along with class and beauty, you'd
please any man.

Your personality has humor to cheer
anyone
Wherever you go, you bring along
fun.

I often envy you. You really have it
together.

And to me you're not only a sister,
You're my best friend forever.

Kenneth W Carter
GOLDEN ROSE
A friend is like a rose,
Soft and yielding, yet forever,
Touch so soft, yet delicate the ears to
pain,
Need reaches out, my rose is there.

A friend is like gold,
Glowing, a treasure to hold so dear,
Polished and pure it advises caution,
Feelings reach out, my shining
answer awaits.

A friend is a friend,
No matter the secret, it's held true,
No tears were ever dried so sweetly,
My friend is like a rose of gold.

Jon S Kerner
TO SHED A TEAR

To The Next Generation

I want to shed a tear
For all the flowers
On carpets green.

The loss of beauty
Which cannot be created by man
A tragedy beyond comprehension.

If only our minds
Could feel the plight of the planet,
Hear her cry and feel her sorrow,
Suffered at human hand.

Perhaps then we'd feel
What it must be like
To be the very last of a species
Searching in vain for a mate.

Plaintive cry in the wilderness,

Song sung for the last time,
Never to be heard, never to return.

Lonely, how terribly lonely.
Echoing the lost Soul,
Of inhumane Humanity.

Melissa N Butrym
SINS OF PASSION
Rivers of emotion flowing through my veins.
The passion and yearning lingers, driving me insane.
Screams of rivalry tie my thoughts; yet the jealousy in my soul is caught.

Although my finger has been pricked by the rose,
the lust in my heart so steadily grows.
I know not my strength, yet fear my power.
Now this conflict withers the flower.

My confusion grows and a morbid cloud covers my soul.
It leaves a pit as I yearn to fill the hole.
Now as I sit, I patiently wait,
as my heart slowly burns at hell's gate.

Doris Brubaker Walter
LOVE EXPRESSED IN LIFE'S CYCLES
The young man before the preacher did stand
Placed the gold ring on the lady's hand.
An expression of love.
A dandelion picked by a tot's hand
Placed in a bottle on a window sill stands.
An expression of love.
The letter said "Dear Grandma" come help me celebrate
I want you here when I graduate.
An expression of love.
A single rosebud in father's hand as he was laid to rest
Mother's time came and purple violets in her hand were clasped.
An expression of love.

Essex C Hutton Sr
AURA (FOR VIVIAN)
i refuse to be resurrected

back to that life of laughter
and tears, of hope and despair.
now i am somebody.
now i am a witness.

i sit on my highassthrone
away from the scents
and sounds of that
human orgy: life.

i refuse to be resurrected

back to that life of laughter
and tears, of hope and despair.
i refuse in spite of
the temptation

of your lovely smile.

Carol Cullar
IAMBIC THOUGHT
I tread the meterman's narrow path through
Galaxies of crystal frost
Each weed full picotee with diamond,
Feel the world of glinting majesty
Sieve through perceptions into
Meter, pause and rhyme,
And marvel at the MIND,
Whose realm encompasses
Six mountains west in foreign lands
Far on the dim horizon,
A river topped with fluffy fog
"Twixt canebrakes slow to green,
And cold sun cooking frost
Away 'neath boots fur-lined
On feet set wide;
A balance and a oneness that
Beat through veins a poem—
Iambic thought
More frigid than the dawn.

Lori Grimes
BEST FRIEND

To my fiancé Christopher, the one I laugh with, live for, love.

True friendship that I've found in you, cannot be bartered, bought or sold.
Your smile fills my heart with joy, my love for you stays deep untold.
Within the time we've spent together, laughter shared and secrets exchanged.
To ask for anything more would be selfish,
how can perfect be re-arranged?

The love I have, though not yet mature, will strengthen its roots a day at a time.
As friendship abounds, a romance will blossom, a love song together our hearts beat, in rhyme.
Happiness I find in heart and soul, just to know you're a touch away.
I hope you know I'm here for you, and always here is where I'll stay.

Clara Ingram Sandridge
WHAT IS POETRY
Poetry like a picture,
Framed by beautiful words,
Is unequaled by the dictionary
More powerful than a thousand birds.

Each poet has a different touch,
As each artist has a different brush,
Guided by hands that made him
Put the song in the thrush.

When all alone with no one at all
A book of poetry suddenly becomes a crystal ball.
Like Winken, Blinken and Nod
Come sail into Poetry Land
You shall see places
Never trod by man.

Poetry is diamond-studded lamps
In a poverty-stricken girl's dream.
That which reaches down
Beyond human mean.

Poetry on the darkest night
When all hope is gone
Like a kindled fire inside
Slowly, beauty yet grasps
Up the mountainside
Urging the traveler on.

Soft as an angel's touch
Hard as an iron bar,
Was that poetry
Riding on a shooting star?

Rebecca D Gray
THE WALL WITHIN
The soldier tries to keep his sanity . . .
But the line is growing thin.
The civilian world can't understand
What's behind the wall within.

The prisoner paces his dingy cell;
He must pay for his sin.
But, the walls around, can't compare . . . .
To the wall he has within.

The teenager contemplates suicide . . . .
His short life seems so grim.
He just wants to escape it all . . . .
And destroy the wall within.

The poet writes words and little rhymes;
With paper and with pen . . .
To share with whoever reads . . .
The wall he has within.

Is life such a mystery?
Is it a game, we feel we just can't win?
Maybe, that's why we choose to hide ourselves;
Behind the walls we've built within.

Frederick West
ANGEL AND VICTORIA
She bowed her head and
A single tear rolled down her cheek,
Dropped off onto the bud of a rose,
Then mingled with the morning dew,
Never again to be different,
Or would want to be.

Tony Tervakoski
THE LIST
When there's more than one thing that you want to do
But you can't get it done right away
Then the thing to do is to make a list
To do tomorrow what you can't do today
There are so many things that we can do
So many things to see
That it may take forever and a day
But that's all right with me
Even tho' it may take a while
To get thru this very long list
It's worth the effort to do it all
Then to think about things that you've missed

We can go sailing go fly a kite
That's just the start of it all
Put it on the list and we'll do it one day
When you're ready just give me a call
But now all I can do is wait
Wait till you're with me again
For the list is not simply just
Things to do
It's hopes and dreams of being with you

Catherine M Bard
LOVE, HATE
I sit here alone in the cold dark night
And I try to fight it with all my might
I will not let this evil inside rule over me
I will not stop fighting until I am free
With love in my heart and my soul cleansed with gold
I will fight it with courage, I'll be brave and bold.
I will conquer it with love, sympathy, and caring
It must be able to be loving and sharing
If we could only be one instead of two
If we could only be love instead of hate and untrue
We could be happy, loving, and free
I would love him and he would love me.

Deanna Koshkin
THE NIGHT
The night falls with enchanted stars,
Along with the most beautiful moon by far,
The sound of the clock as it goes tick-tock,
The swish of the water as it splashes the dock,
The wind as it softly blows through the trees,
The leaves as they slowly blow in the breeze,
The soft green grass that tickles your toes,
The breeze like a feather that brushes your nose,
The night slowly falls upon sleepy towns,
The stars touch the hills like an angel's sweet gown.

Aletha Current
MOTHER
On an open hilltop,
Barren and gray,
Stands a wailing woman
Watching her children
fade away.

Her breath is the wind
futilely blowing
Against the brown haze.
Her voice wails
Between smokestacks,
Knelling the death
Of a once green world.

Kathleen M Schehr
HYPOTHESIS
The hypothesis varied
about my destiny.
My body would be buried
What about the rest of me?

My soul, if it existed,
would it stay within my grave?
Or rise up unassisted
and be heavenly forgave?

R A Nash
THE EVIL

From the survivor of a living nightmare, in the world of drugs . . . .

The herb, the powder, the rock and the pills
These evil things which I sought my thrills
I was their master I thought from the start
Then condemned to slavery as they tore me apart
You're hip, you're cool, many lies they told
And to this evil my soul I sold
The pain and the nightmares
they grew and grew
All from these things which I thought I knew
Months went by and the evil increased
I lost control of this deadly beast
I stole and I robbed for with evil there's greed
All for that feeling it told me I need

Before it is finished nothing is spared
Not even the people for which I cared
Remember these things which I confess
For the price of evil comes due in flesh . . . . .

Dorothy LeCompte
HOT AIR BALLOON
Burner blast torrents of heat
Whipping 'round my head and feet
Years pass while waiting to lift
The weight of the past is present.

No waves of brightly colored nylon above
Cubic three foot basket draped with sandbags
Filled with life's unsorted experiences
Weigh heavy and delay the progress of flight.

Who will lighten the cargo, toss out the garbage,
Who can lift this balloon?
Yes, I
At mid-life the sails fill
Rocking hope of flight.

Sandbags' contents evaluated
Tossed aside the basketwall
To fall to rock below
Denied the ride.

Color rises from the field
As ropes free the nylon sails
Movement stirs hope of flight
Rising free, trusting currents, FULL FLIGHT.

Michael N Hoover
MAGICALLY ALIVE
Winter, spring, summer, fall, you can see it in her eyes
And when she's looking through me, her vibes run through my mind
She's a lovely little lady, knowing little about my past
But she can see inside of me, and really make it last

Sometimes I see a lady, makes me want to scream and shout
But I just hold it all inside, and don't let nothing out
She's a lovely little lady, a little heavy on the head
And when she gets inside of you, you're glad that you're not dead

If she could only see, what she's doing to me
Would she turn and run beside me, and never set me free
Is it her love that tears me, deep apart inside
Yet makes me feel so magically, glad that I'm alive

Imogene S Huffstutter
LINES WRITTEN FOR MY FIRST-BORN SON
I remember the first time I saw you.
You were so beautiful—so perfect.
I reached to touch your tiny hand
And your perfectly formed little fingers
Grasped one of my fingers
And held on.
How was I to know that you were wrapping those fingers
Around my heart strings so that as long as there is breath in my body
I will always have love and concern for you?

Then came the day—all too soon for me—when you were physically grown-up,
My big, fine son!
And I suddenly realized that the thing I had striven for
From the first time I saw you was realized:
You could take care of yourself,
And you no longer needed me!

How was I to know I would be devastated?

Georgette M Innes

Georgette M Innes
EMBER

To my darling miniature Schnauzer Dog "ember"

Ember my darling, is this our Farewell as thru our ten years I dwell?
Please my baby, won't you try to eat;
I beg as food I place at your feet
Your head you turn and you hide away; don't my darling, or you won't stay

How can I ever let you leave; so short a time—I can't believe
That God would grant you so short a time; so precious you are—then not to be mine. I hurt for you—I hurt for me; Don't want the time, it isn't We.

Andy, Donald, Mahlon and I chose you; bewildered, you didn't know what to do
You crept into our hearts and there you stayed, as our home became the one you made; Happy again, after your predecessor we lost; and soon determined who was to be Boss!

You worked with me thru our daily grind and showed the world proudly, you were mine. Dainty, a little lady that you were, caused even Golda, our cat to purr
Loving all as you gracefully pranced and thru all of our days, we danced!

Then to Florida, in the front you rode and carefully scrutinized your winter abode. A red fox that came to your screen door and you loudly exclaimed "What for?" An Armadillo, you put into his place and declared you were superior to the Human Race.

To Boynton Beach, you arrived on the scene and overlooked all who were mean
With Mommie at your constant side; the entire Township we defied
We changed "To Dogs allowed," a new concept; proving those who didn't were inept.

You strutted proudly in your disdain as on Roma Way, a home we maintained
You barked at the birds and ruled the roost, giving all Animal Kingdom a real boost. You made me proud that you owned me. I liked it that way and always wanted it to be.

We moved from Rydal to Florida and back—no loving kindness did you lack. Please baby, please, please try, to fight back—nothing I'll deny, in trying to save my Beautiful You; without you—part of me dies too!

Karen A Wasylyk
MESSAGE TO DAD

This poem is dedicated to my father, Michael P. Chestercove

When I was a younger youth, I lost you, the years I needed you the most. I miss you with all my heart, there is not a passing day that you're not thought of. I miss your smiling face. It was a beam of sunshine. Your gleam in your eyes like the ocean of blue, remembering the way you were, always happy, keeping yourself busy with Mom's projects around the house an' yard, Dad, you were always there for me, when I needed you. I wish there was a way that I could tell you how much I love you, I'm sure you're at a better place now an' looking down upon us through the heaven skies. This message is that I'll always keep loving you, an' Dad, you'll be with me wherever I go. So until we meet again in the heavens above.

Mrs Fredrick W Johnson
MY GRANDMA'S APRON

For my husband, who knew her too.

Aprons in Grandma's day were as large as her work day long.
How she used her apron is a loving memory.

Grandma's apron was a basket for eggs, kindling, fruit, baby chicks, my kitten, even a bummer lamb I could not keep.

I still remember the smell of the baked bread, pies, and cakes she lifted from the oven with a corner of her apron. Remember how cold the pump handle was? Bless that apron.

Above all else I remember the hurts made well, the tears she dried with a corner, even my runny nose, with a corner left over to give sticky fingers and a dirty face a lick and a promise.

How cold it was from bed to stove, but not for long. She would wrap me in her apron, close to her heart and that haven of warmth, security, and love, warms me still.

Grandma is in heaven now with a child wrapped in her apron. This I know, for GOD helped fashion "My Grandma's Apron."

Edward Wetherall
THOUGHTS
The rocks, the water, and my thoughts.
The sun above my head and a sea gull
Blend mind and body together, all other fades
Though life goes on around me, it is separate.
My mind turns to the Gods of old, the new God.
The mind matures, the body withers, that's life.
And yet, even the old body has feelings.
Memories of past encounters still remain undimmed.
To rise up, be renewed, without expression.
The old life goes, a new life rises up.
Some of the old is there, something new is added.
And so the new life, with new expressions
Grows up, and grows old, that's life.
One passes on always leaving something behind
To grow, find new expressions, that's progress.
Yet the new God remains the same, yet brighter still.
Giving peace and power to those who seek
And fulfillment, even in death, to those who find

Angela Simpson
I THINK I'M IN LOVE

This poem is dedicated to my first love, Victor Ware.

I've seen you but once in my life but you live in my heart,
when we're together and when we're apart.
I never believed in love at first sight,
until I met you, you're Mr. Right.
In my dreams I'm with you every minute,
until I wake up to reality and find you're not in it.
For you to love me would put my heart to rest,
being with you is one of life's best.
I know I'm not the only one who's fallen for you,
to be in your arms would make all my dreams come true.
I know it's not the sun setting or a star above,
I know what it is, I THINK I'M IN LOVE.

Kay Everly
MUD
I was
the dirt under
his collar
and the ground
that supported
him kneeling
to kiss
disenchantment
cut and dried
as his elements
precipitated
misery
out of
solution

Ruth Skiff
A WATCH IN THE NIGHT
I sit alone and watch into the night
while sounds of the quiet prove their right
to be heard by all who would but listen
and watch as dew begins to glisten.

It won't be long and songs you'll hear
as birds begin their flight so near
and the rustle of leaves as they respond
to the wind's hustle over the pond.

As you begin to hear the people move about

to join all other creatures on
their route
the sun begins its slow ascent into
the sky
and morning breaks with a great
big sigh.

Dwight Buzick
POINT LOBOS
We see lonely cypresses
on headlands by the sea,—
and there on rocky places
hanging on precariously.
Their respirations must depend
on the filmy,—drifting fog,—
Like fairy gossamer,—caressing
each leaf, and branch,—and log.

The calls,—The barks of sea lions
assembled across rocky, tidal
ways—
beyond deep channels smoothened
by
the rushing, churning swells,—
Invisible thru the fog and spray;—
but,—OH!—the ocean smells!

Button up! The morning's chill
and cool is the gentle breeze
Explore the rocks,—the trees,—
the wildness of frustrated seas!
The natural habitat of starfish,
Kelp, seaweed,—and bashful
anemones.
'Tis home to the lively scurrying
crab,—
squid,—tiny limpet, mosses, and
the abalones.

In their variety,—the aquatic birds
are common,—winging every
place.
Carmel Highlands beckons with
scenes—inexplicable grandeur
beggaring belief.
Fog is lifting on this, our coastal
scene,—
and, high above the sea's wild
reefs—
'Tis a perfect panorama of the gold
coast,—
heavenly—crafted as far as eye
can see!

Warren D Stearns MSG US ARMY (Ret)
THE TREE

To all my former comrades in arms, especially those who have not returned & all of their survivors and loved ones who remain. To all members of the armed forces past, present & future

Today we're going to commemorate
this tree,
For the loved ones that we hold in
memory,
Those who have been prisoners of
war, and
Those still missing on some foreign
shore.

Some have died in prison camp,
Others may still thru the jungles
tramp.
There are those we know that passed
away,
But where, we wonder, might others
lay.

As this magnolia grows in the
ground,
We hope that those who have come
around,
Will stop a few seconds and give
thought
To the men we have lost, in this war
they have fought.

So as these next few months go by,
We'll probably think and we'll
probably cry,
But we can pray that the lists are
wrong,
And just any day they'll be along.

Here we have placed this tree for the
living,
In the name of the men that didn't
hesitate giving.
We dedicate this symbol to Marine
James Jackson,
And his comrades who've gone or
are missing in action.

David Greske
LIKE CAT'S SOFT FEET

For K. Reischauer—who believed in me from the very beginning

It happened so quickly,
I was taken by surprise.
He came into my life
so silently, so mysteriously:
like cat's soft feet
walking across a hardwood floor.
I never heard . . . I never expected.

Some things were said to me,
I've never heard before.
We laughed and told each other
dreams.
Then he smiled,
a smile of warmth, caring, and
concern.
And when our eyes met,
an understanding was achieved:
an understanding . . . I never
expected.

We met again today,
and talked of things
I've never talked of before.
We laughed again, and told more
dreams.
And this time when we smiled,
my heart was filled with joy,
a joy . . . I never expected.

Janine M Place
AT THE RAINBOW'S END
All your dreams come true at the
rainbow's end.
Even a broken heart that you need to
mend.

It's like wishing upon a star shining
bright in the sky.
Hoping, praying, or just wondering
why.

I look in the sky to see the beautiful
rainbow,
Dreaming about how far it really
does go.

Could it lead me away to my fantasy
land,
Where I could meet my true love and
take hold of his hand?

It will never go away, it will always
be there.
It might disappear for awhile but you
won't know where.

I'd like to slide down into the pot of
gold,
But I know it won't be there for me
to hold.

The only treasure is of that in your
heart,
Always leading you to a brand new
start.

Share your dreams and they may
come true,
That special someone telling you that
he will always love you.

Through thick and thin he will
always be your friend.
My biggest dream is at the rainbow's
end.

Sandra Neuman
LEND ME YOUR SOUL AND I'LL HOLD YOU TO ME

M.L. Codispoti, Our souls will meet again!

Lend me your soul, and I'll hold you
to me
It would make us whole,
And set our hearts free.
To share and to see,
the beauty of our lives.
To face what will be,
And keep back the strifes.
The world can't erase,
the joy that we feel.
For when I see your face again,
I'll know my life is real.

Betty S Hensley
MISSING YOU

Dedicated to Gilbert, whom I loved very much, and to my son, Timothy, for putting sunshine back into my life.

The flavour of the sunlight,
Does nothing to forsake,
The loneliness of missing you,
Or my melancholy ache.

Wilma Conrads
BLUEBIRD

To Pilgrims everywhere, especially those at Medjugorje, Yugoslavia

She hovered like an angel
over those below
Knowing she was
over them all

They came like a swarm of ants
to gather crumbs
that she left there
for all the world

Bluebird you're all glorious
Why do you come down?
What is it for?
Perhaps to love?

Red cardinals at your feet
In the cool, white snow
Red like the blood
that once flowed pure

Don't cry lovely lady blue!
His mother and ours
Your children now
are listening

Zeni Thomas
LOVE'S PAIN
The long night it seems,
You're with me in dreams,
And you're mine till the breaking of
dawn,
It's when I awake that my heart
seems to break,
When I realize that you're gone.

So, you see, Love never dies
peacefully,
It fights for its life,
And the struggle, like any war,
leaves a trail
of bitterness, anger, and pain.

Stuart T Lyons
NATURE'S SPLENDOR

This poem is dedicated to the glory of God.

Thank you God for the wolves that
howl
on a cliff or meadow slope,

Thank you God for the Great Barred
Owl
perched on some distant oak,

Thank you God for the leaves so
green
arrayed among the trees,

Thank you God for mountain
streams
that flow down to the seas.

Janet L Smith
WHILE YOU ARE AWAY

To my husband and my family who are very wonderful to me. I LOVE YOU ALL!

While you are away
I'll think of you every day
As the days pass on
I'll miss you more than you can look
beyond
As I picture you in my mind
I'll smile and say he's all mine
No one is luckier than I
To have a man like you by my side
While you are away
Our love will grow more each day
While you are away
I will love you more and more each
day

Danny Hollis
AS ONE AGAIN
If life could be lived over,
if we could start anew;
I'd go to the beginning.
then live my life with you.

We had our time together,
Short in time, yes I agree;
but long enough, for I believe
that GOD made you for me.

The way you made me feel inside
I'd never felt that before;
The things we said, the way we
touched.
I couldn't have asked for more.

But life is sometimes cruel,
And seems somehow unfair;
For now we are held apart,
though our whole lives we share.

So when this life is over,
And the next one's here, it's then;
That we can be together,
And live as one again.

Shirley L Grannis
THE GLORIES OF LIVING
The glories of living, I wonder how far
A heart should be striving to reach for a star
There's sadness to ponder, dreams that fall short
Seeming to founder, would I were smart.

Gifts that God gave me, wasted I fear
Longing to change; how isn't clear.
Jousting with shadows, playing the clown
Hiding true feelings, feigning up when I'm down.

O'er the horizon light will appear
Then perhaps living won't seem so drear
Lord how I need you, oh, how I fear
My life's being wasted year after year.

Lead me and guide me; show me the way
Hear my heart crying, teach me to pray.

Linda Wilson-Maryman
CAFE MORNING GLORY

in memory of Aleta Bolte, who contacted that spot in me that is love.

As you crossed sixth and Liberty streets
where the sun crystallized the Hall of Justice windows,
your blonde hair laughed butterflies about your shoulders
and slender red-nailed fingers gently pulled my arm
as I tried to dart across the street.
Yellow-day memories water my eyelids as I remember us
at Cafe Morning Glory on our "off center,"
"get up on the wrong side" days.
Your china doll body covered by a pink suit as daintily you raised
Jasmine tea to your blue-eyed smile and puckered mouth.
Aleta, my best friend, a long ago yesterday
in a mauve apartment, with
two pea-hens huddling outside the bay window,
we ate Papa John's Pizza amid unpacked boxes,
candlelight and Muddy Water blues.
I miss you, dear sweet pal,
on whose bent shoulders of pain that long ago
the butterflies no longer laughed, I put my head and let the water in my
eyelids dampen the spot where the laughing butterflies should have been.

Sasha Quay
RIVAL

You fool, Tomas, you know I wrote this poem for you.

I'm addicted to you.
I need to see you each day.
Your lover's embrace fills me with warmth.
The longer I am with you the more I want to stay.
With you I am,
without you I would not be.
I realize others love and need you too.
Promise me that you will be there in the morning.

Lover put away your jealous thoughts.
You must know that I had you in mind when I wrote this poem.
Harmless flirtation has developed into what could be
a life-long love affair.
So, should it come as any surprise to you when I tell you
that the name of your rival is
the sun?
And you thought it was my husband.

Alfred Colo
LOVE POEM
The tender release
of holding you,
is holier than that
of knowing you
are showing me
how deeply-felt
love can be.

What more in life
than sharing
such loveliness
with selfless devotion,
can inspire
the ultimate fulfillment?

We set our souls
to stir a dormant bed,
where flesh alone
shan't rear its ugly head.

No sterner stuff
has closer come
to elevate this dream we share,
above the heavenly realms
we sanctify.

Carole Nicas
AFFAIR
Your arms
Are the shelter
To my soul
Embracing me
As I grow old
Though we're apart
In thought
We're together
Forgetting each other
NEVER
Your eyes are brighter
Than any sparkling
ocean
Your kiss so violent
Yet tender
We have a special love
Only we two can know
Thinking of each other
Wherever we go
Are we friends or passionate
lovers
Are we sex crazed maniacs
seeking each other
I literally float after being
in your arms
And taste your kisses
Until I see you
One more time

Leona Scott
ORDINARY PEOPLE UNDER THE PRESSURE OF UNUSUAL CIRCUMSTANCES
I never think that I exist for most people
Coming and going in and out our lives
Like a weaving, dark of masks,
Or colors drawn from the fields; red poppy or
The ocelot;
Natural enough
But often costly.
Bat wings in the dark,
Jackals touching
Held by the shuttle eye until
almost the pain is woven tight
into the Iris of the soul,
The Primitives knew.
Nothing changes.
Even now upon the loom
I see myself moving
In the cold circle
Near at hand the others reach—
I know her by her hands.

Suzanne Straight

Suzanne Straight
MASQUERADE
A dance in the garden gazebo
A festival of eyes and color
The feathered masks hide identities
Unknown faces swing around the carousel poles
The horses rise and fall, lights shimmer
The pantomime of the Harlequin spins a threaded spell
Swirls of dark rich satin gowns
Flutterings of wine-red velvet cloaks
Sparkling sequins and falling glitter like snow
Loose tendrils of spun-golden hair drift seductively
Hands concealed in black gloves, reaching
All around gaze the falcon faces and the leopard eyes
All are woven together by Pan's pipes and the fairy's chimes
All are enchanted by the music of the Sorceress
As she plucks at her magical harp
All are trapped in the Masquerade,
lost in the fantasy
It's only forever
Not long at all.

Emily Harper
SPRING CLEANING
April is rain and shades of green,
With hues of iris blue,
Her breath is caught with blossom smells,
Her pulse in fragrance wanes and swells,
To permeate the living air,
To breathe into a Soul's despair,
To leave on every face a sheen,
My own is shining, too!

Sylvia Gonzàlez
INSPIRATIONAL MURDER

To my family, which I will always love dearly and to those bits of unraveled life which nourish the flower of inspiration.

Inspiration is,
The fire in every poet's heart,
And if this flame should die, it would
Lead to a darkness.
A black night that will last forever.

Inspiration is,
The blindman's cane used by the sighted poet.
And if this guide should someday mislead him, it would
Lead to despair and panic, hovered by,
A black night that will last forever.

Inspiration is,
The spark that can enlighten or destroy a poet.
And if this fire should blaze out of control then it would
Lead to a world of fatal illusions from the soul, or maybe,
A black night that will last forever.

Lenora Lee Nimmo
COLORADO SERENITY
The sun pierces all the surrounding mountains
and the line of the sunset points
out colors
of red, orange and gold.
Looking beyond it says the day is almost complete,
Peace is near.

The aspen trees weep as the wind blows
and cries are heard everywhere.
Time to close up for the night.

Darkness is suddenly upon us and only a whisper
of sound is heard .
Peace is here.

Kristy Line
LOVE

This poem is dedicated to my Mother, Father, and sister, Lisa.

Love is sometimes a broken heart,
filled with hurt and hate.

Love is a target,
for cupid to shoot with his mighty arrow,

Love is jealous,
awaiting a caring victim.

Love is a calm sea,
trying to get some rest.

Elizabeth M Costa
A SELF SOUGHT TREASURE

This poem is dedicated to my dad, Vincent E. Laffan, who is ultimately responsible for my sincere appreciation of poetry.

I am a treasure unto myself.
Why then can I not see its value?
Is it because I have allowed others
To define the "me" I am?
Or, at least, that person they need
Or want "me" to be for themselves?
Then, who is it that "I" really am?
The gift buried so very deep inside
Eludes me every day.
I continue to be a "me" for others.
Perhaps, because I know not yet myself.
Ah! May my lifetime not pass before me
Until I discover the beauty of me,
And recognize its immeasurable wealth.
Yet, how many lives really do expire
Without knowledge of this self sought treasure?

Danny Perry
A LONELY MAN'S PRAYER
The nights are long and cold
There's no end to the loneliness
I begin each day dreaming that this will be the day
The day that I find that special

someone
That special someone that will fulfill all my hopes and dreams
But each day I'm disappointed
Each day I ache just a little bit more
I feel empty inside
Now I understand Adam's problem—I need a help mate
That special woman that will make my life complete
I've failed at every attempt to find a mate
Could it be that there's no one on earth for me?
Oh Lord, put me to sleep and remove my rib!
Please perform that great miracle once more for me!

Derek Grasso
BENEATH THE SWOLLEN HUES

To my former wife—Patrice Grasso—whose undying love inspired this fragment. And to her cohorts—Mark & Fred—who would rip it to shreds.

Beneath the swollen hues
Of a cracked sky
There stands among abandoned
Crumbled ruins
A tiny narrow dwelling.
The door ornate with the memories of children
Worlds that once drifted playfully in the wind.
Inside
Awaits a child-woman standing in the spaces
Of love-worn visitors.
I would come to this refuge every day.
It was only here
That the night and the earth would actually touch.

Linda A Smith
THE GHOST
A quiet, subtle spirit
A willing hand to lend
To carefully chosen people
He counts among his friends
But, he's learned to keep his distance
For trust has had a price
And better to be lonely
Than risk betrayal twice
There's so much he is missing
So much we cannot give
A wall he built around himself
Protects the heart within
If only he would trust again
I know that he would find
All his painful yesterdays
Could all be left behind
Maybe one day he will choose
To let someone in close
Maybe then, yes, only then
He'll be free of The Ghost.

Barbara Sanner
MIND OF THE INSANE
I give to you what you have given me.
You people who call yourselves a society.

You ignored my warning, cries and pleas;
Now only by taking life and causing pain can I be appeased.

I watch for you both day and night.
I'll hunt you or kill you to make things right.

I hate you all as you have hated me;
I hear the voices, can they hear me?

The rage inside me knows no bounds.
I lie I cheat so no one knows

The depths of hell from which I arose.
My soul is heavy and my spirit weak

People call me a monster, a killer and a freak.
Is this really I of whom they speak?

I hate you all as you have hated me;
I hear the voices, can they hear me?
I am left with my own sentence, which is to be
A padded cell, straightjacket and a mind full of insanity.
Is this real? can it be a dream?
Oh God, please let me wake up, let me wake up

Josine
PROSETTE
There must be some merit
In being a complete shambles of a person
Some virtue in disorientation
Some value in solitude,
Else, why would people smile,
And chuckle,
And even cry a bit
When they think of me?
So like Miss Emily
Who, with a string
Lowered wee baskets of sweets
From an upper window
To curious children below,
The perfect gesture
Of affirmation of Life
from a would-be Recluse
With Miles To Go before she slept.

Else, Why would people smile when they think of me?

Linda M Quintiliani
MOTHER SEA
The sea is a woman—sometimes restless—sometimes calm
The deep, blue ocean with a salty charm
A calm, relaxed Mother filled with brine,
Within her an undulating sense of time
I'd love to float inside the womb of life,
Without the bitter struggles and strife.
The tidal motion is like a rocking chair
Knowing that Mother Sea is always there.

Leonard D Kirk
QUESTIONS, PROBLEMS, AND FEARS
What could have happened to YOUTH and strong muscles?
A question we ask ourselves, after they're gone;
AGE creeps up slowly, one day at a time,
It's possible to end up, old, weak, and alone.

God's Word tells us, that forty is extreme middle age,
And we're offended, by this reference by man;
But forty years later, we're all wrinkled and old,
We're amazed at the accuracy of God's Plan.

For God the Creator, and Sustainer of Life,
Knew we'd fail to exercise our mind;
Our Eyesight so precious, yet we read in the dark,
First it's bi-focals, then tri-focals, then blind.

And then there's our teeth, ignore them, they rot,
We go to the dentist, with fears;
He ends up extracting, then sells us a plate,
We're self-conscious, the rest of our years.

Our hair turns gray, begins to fall out,
We have fears, that soon we'll be bald;
We've long since forgotten, the appointment with God,
Before we know it, Our Name will be called.

Lisa King
TIN MAN

To my parents, Bill and Nancy King, who have shown me great love and much encouragement.

Deceitful faces, hiding places
That's what tin man is.
He's society, notoriety
Every Mr., Mrs., and Ms.

Grueling, grinding, searching, finding
Our lives pass much too fast.
We try to make life genuine
But tin man hides behind his mask.

He speaks, he smiles
He touches, he wiles
But what happened to his eyes?
Most eyes dance
As they catch your glance.
But tin man's are full of lies.

We look for truth, an honest life.
Does the cycle ever end?
We hope for love, but in this plastic world
Tin man's way will always win.

Cindi Lee Turpin
THOUGHTS FROM OUTSIDE THE KENNEDY CENTER WHEN YOU WERE CLOSE BY—BUT LIGHT YEARS DISTANT
Could I love you without it being a sacrilege
Of the type as when a child
Reaches out a hand to grasp a moonbeam
And pulls in nothing?

Love is a dignified cliché
Too heavy to light on this warm feeling without smothering it

To say I love you, then, is a mistake.
One, regrettably, already quite committed.

But I have been so long in solitude as to be amazed
By a man who can steal my breath and double pump my heart

The way the moon and stars and airplanes used to
And birthday candles and opening nights still do.

Our pleasures have matured—the large ones—
As smaller ones crystallize in memory
Until, you see, it is the memory that is the pleasure,
Not the pleasing.

So, I do not mean to apologize
For feelings spoken or silent.
They might never come again.
And that is enough
For the memory is mine.

Susanne Mueller
REACH OUT TO YOUR BROTHER
I saw the hunger in my brother's soul
But was afraid to trust,
Afraid to reach a helping hand
And yet I knew I must.

I knew his heart was full pain
But could not see past my own,
So I did nothing to ease his woe
And thus let my brother down.

I built a wall around myself
Afraid of being hurt,
Until my brother knocked it down
And made me see my worth.

I saw that reaching out to him
Would not bind but set me free,
That caring for my fellow man
Could also be of help to me.

I eased my brother's loneliness
And so dispelled my own,
In reaching out for my fellow man
I felt much less alone.

Stephen L Clarke
WILL THE FIRE BURN?
When time runs out,
what then
of you and I?
Will we still touch
in the fall-
ing light?
Will our hearts still leap
together
across
the lily-coloured skies,
life's secret treasures buried
deep inside?

Will the flame of a life-
time's passion blaze on
within us? Or
will darkness settle
like empty clouds
of dust around
the embers of our love?

Janet Castiel
CHICAGO
The sun shining a crystal glow to the water
looks out to where the sun touches the sky and realize
that this is not the sea, nor the ocean, but a lake captured
in the motion of evolution . . . part of an industrial revolution
water-way feed, which nourishes the city of Chicago.
Steel girders and glass have up and out to go,
big boned buildings towering over an early 20th century culture
Swing music echoes the nighttime streets,
cars with big running boards streak around corners,
holding up natives and foreigners along their sides.

Bootlegger's joy rides. Flappers hop
to the Charleston,
jump into the Black Bottom of time.
When Bees Knees was really
sublime,
and the modern world was still new.
Streetlights and glitter askew,
telephone lines, the Egyptian flu
The silver screen, the golden age, in
the city that captured
the media's heart, flag pole sitting
and Art Deco rage . . .
Chicago

Lorrie A Pannullo
LOSING TO LOVE
Oh, lately it seems the days drag on
What will I do now that you're gone
Do you know you've always owned
my heart, and
I have loved you from the start?
Know why my love must quickly
end?
Not once did I think of you as a
friend.
What will I do when you're not
near?
I've always run to you to rest my
fears
Been so close to you, what will I do?
Losing to love, I guess I'll get
through.

And each day I get so much stronger
Now that it seems my days are
longer
I would have done anything for you
Believe in this because it's true
I've always felt you were the one for
me
Come to think of it, who else could
it be?
To see you again brings everything
back, I
See things in me I had hoped I
lacked
Myself on my own it's not the end, I
can lose to love
Again and again.

(read the first word of each line)

Karen M Bean-Sargeant
OUR SPECIAL BOY
There was snow on the ground and a
full moon
When the midwife said it would be
over soon
Both families were present to witness
the birth
And everyone was joyous when he
entered our earth

They told us we had a gifted child
Down Syndrome was the reason that
he smiles
You never would think it could
happen to you
A hard life ahead, we knew that
would be true

It took a few days to let it sink in
Life suddenly seemed a challenge
that we could not win
We tried to lay blame in whatever
we could
Instead of trying to accept it the way
that we should

I read lots of pamphlets and all kinds
of books
To figure out what happened and
how the future looks
To my surprise, I found that life
won't be so bad
Love, patience, and security it would
take all that we had

Our son would be a lucky boy, a
lucky boy indeed
He would not know what it is like to
feel jealousy or greed
He'll be a loving baby and he'll give
us lots of hugs
And soon before we know it, he'll be
crawling on our rugs

So you see, it's not so bad to have a
gifted child
When you accept the truth, you wake
each day with a smile
There's a lot of work ahead of us,
and a lot of joy
But for now we'll just thank God for
our "special boy"

Parents: Michael & Karen Sargeant
Our special boy: James Daniel
Sargeant
Born: December 4, 1987

Mary E F Bronkema
OUR HOMELAND
Our flag waves over America, for
everyone to see,
The great symbol of our country.
Where every man, woman, and child
are born free.

Then why do we complain and
grumble?
Beneath our breath, we ungratefully
mumble.

Far away lands and far away places,
Demonstrate sad, hopeless faces.

Of oppressed people who have no
freedom or one civil right.
Not even the courage or conviction
to stand up and fight.

We in America are blessed beyond
compare.
There's not another country on earth,
that has so much to share.

Our forefathers died to save us this
land.
Instead of complaining,
It's time we reached out hand in
hand.

For America is just as good as her
people are strong.
Under God's grace, we will unite
together and forever belong!

Virginia Fetterman
SUNDAY'S CHILD
I met her on a Sunday morn,
unhappy as she was.
She came to Sunday School each
week not knowing any love.

I tried to reassure her
but, listen she would not do
My mother doesn't love me
she said, so why should you?

She would not read or write,
a sullen child was she.
The Lord said here's a challenge
what can this child be?

God used me as His vessel
to nurture, and to love.
Now this child is happy
but, it came from up above.

Now she comes each Sunday
with a smile upon her face.
She knows she's loved and wanted
so she's out to win lifes race.

George Kline
LIFE IS A STAGE AND WE ALL PLAY A PART.

To my dear and understanding wife, Barbara G Kline. With all my love. George.

Life is a stage where all must act,
This we know to be a fact;
Some have parts that seem rather
funny,
Others just act as though they are
dummies.

Whatever a part that we must play,
It should be completed by end of
day;
So when the time arrives that we go
to bed,
'Tis really time to rest our weary
head.
When morning comes and we again
arise,
To some it's the same, to others a
surprise;
But whatever may be, the truth here
lies,
It's God's great gift to be able to
open your eyes.
So lets keep in mind-faith-hope and
charity, and practice these with
others less fortunate than we

Donald W Willis
THE YOUTHFUL ARE THE POETS
Years ago I wrote my poems.
The words just seemed to flow.
Now I sit and try to rhyme.
Where did that talent go?
The world has changed my thoughts,
indeed.
I am no longer blind.
I have not found both man and beast.
Always to be kind.
No longer seen through youngster's
eyes.
Glib words have lost their thrill.
No longer do they grace the page.
The poet's had his fill.
The youthful are the ones to write.
Of emotion, love and sorrow.
The older ones will write the tales.
To thrill the young tomorrow.

Mary G Valdina
A CRY FROM THE HEART

Dedicated to the Thompson family. All my love Grandma.

He walked so quietly through the
woods
So, serene and peaceful did he go
Never dreaming it was his last walk
When an arrow flew right through the
air
Into his body deep and strong.
Why we cried, was it time, for God to
call him home
Leaving sorrow in our hearts
He didn't leave without this message
Do not grieve for me grandma, I am
in Heaven,
Just where I want to be
So, peace comes with sorrow
Even tears will slowly fade
As time heals all our hearts
Goodbye my darling
We will meet again one day.

Martha Graham
A WALK ON THE BEACH IN SEPTEMBER
Wind putting white lace collars on
the blue water.
Water turning the white sand to gold.
Seagulls huddled together at the
water's edge: Watching, waiting.
Lightning racing across the gray cool
sky,
releasing the rain to join the water
below.
Walking alone, barefoot in the sand,
Cool water soothing hot, tired feet,
Cool wind vanquishing old, tired
thoughts.
Hearing the sounds of distant
thunder from the sky
and the rushing of the waves against
the shore.
Tasting the hint of fall in the air.
Summer saying goodbye to the lake.

Donald W Willis
THE YOUTHFUL ARE THE POETS
Years ago I wrote my poems.
The words just seemed to flow.
Now I sit and try to rhyme.
Where did that talent go?
The world has changed my thoughts,
indeed.
I am no longer blind.
I have not found both man and beast.
Always to be kind.
No longer do they grace the page.
The poets had his fill.
The youthful are the ones to write.
Of emotion, love and sorrow.
The other ones will write the tales.
To thrill the young tomorrow.

Luther Page
TRUST
Come walk with me through leaves
of grass,
With long green blades that sway as
we pass.
And we shall talk of many things,
both present, and passed,. And the
future that will be ours at last.

So come with me Wyvonne, let me
hold your hand, for I know the way
through out the land.

Moleta M Eshleman
OUR BABY

I dedicate my poem to my first granddaughter Michelle Marie Diaz

Our baby girl is a pretty sight
Bright and cheerful as can be
She does not sleep well at night
She may tonight, we'll wait and see.

I think she has her days and nights
Turned around and all mixed up
It could be she likes bright lights
And likes to have us all get up.

She likes the attention that she gets
So screams and hollers when she's
wet.
I guess it's just part of her growing
And she depends on our knowing;

If she's hungry wet or dry
If not she'll surely cry
When content she'll fall asleep
And you'll not hear a single peep.

Michael Tolentino
THE HIGH COURT JESTER

Dedicated to Laura Nott, Lena Tolentino and Helen Stadelnick

The lace is weaved along with
diamond dust
The castle halls desire angry lust
The king is playing chess inside the
den

The queen will join him there-but who knows when

The bishop cries for justice in the court
The knight is long although his temper's short

The soldiers of the castle long for war
The clergymen are rotten to the core
The dungeon reeks of lonely unhealed time
While spirits of the past commit the crime

The high court jester—nowhere to be seen
He's in the tower, dancing with the queen

The king is in the corner by the light
His path to leave is darkened by the knight
The bishop blocks the hallway in dismay
The shadow of the castle stops the day

The clergymen say prayers just for the king
Who soon will hear the angels start to sing
Who found a pretty spot right in between
The high court jester—playing with the queen

Bertha L "Bert" Meenen
THE SCOUT
Emerging from tall grass
To well-clipped lawn
Top-knot bobbing to and fro
As step by step he surveys
The sky above, the earth below
For lurking danger to his flock
Satisfied that all is well
Signals convey "follow me"
With memorable lilting call:
Bob White! Bob White!

Charlie Kline
ORO BLANCO

To Cheryl

Oro Blanco means white gold,
There for the taking by men who were bold.
But that was in years gone by,
And time slips by with a sigh.
The miners have left for parts unknown,
Except for the ones in graves all alone.
The Apaches too, are no longer here,
Where they danced their dance of the deer.

All that's left is one 'dobe hovel,
A creaky old windmill, a pick and a shovel.
The wind kicks up a small dust devil,
It whirls across the ancient town now level.
That's all that's left of old Oro Blanco,
And I feel that next, it's my turn to go.

Melissa A Koons
POINT REYES LIGHTHOUSE: A GUIDING LIGHT

To My Loving Family

Point Reyes Lighthouse—
Its light shines
Through the heavy
Fog
Guiding lost ships,
Leading them
To safety,
Away from
Jagged rocks which
Protrude outward
Like huge teeth,
Ready to devour.
But the ships
Are successful.
They steer in the
Right direction,
On to freedom.

Winnifred Pearson
COMPENSATION
For every poisonous plant there is one growing nearby, that is its healing antidote.
For every fear, there is a rainbow showing of hope and faith, shining through clouds of doubt.

For every weakness of the flesh we suffer, there is a compensating strength within.
For, though the way seems steep, the boulders rougher, the path will open where barriers have been.

For every sin that we have let defeat us there is a saving power, though hidden it may be.
At out lowest ebb, our Saviour comes to meet us.
His forgiving grace will set us free.

Faint not nor fear amid the tempest's fury.
God is not dead, nor sleeping is He now.
His power where you are, His love assure thee
that thou art safe in His hands.
Ask not how.

Louisa Esmus
SOUND OFF

To the elderly pedal pushers versus mechanized vehicles.

A narrow road,
A man on a trike,
A car, an accident, a sorry sight,
A ride to the hospital,
A rented room,
Then the last rites, and
A blessed tomb.

Nanette Whitlock
CONFUSION
Deep within, a silence moans,
wanting to be heard.
Echoes fill the air with grief
when smoke invades a thought.
Sudden movements break the mood
and disaster shakes the mind.
What does this mean?
Who is it for?
A world of broken fantasies
lie beneath a sign.
A pattern of cries
embezzles my soul
and confusion melts my heart.
Not a sound or a distinct
muffled tone;
only heavy breathing
fills the atmosphere.
The time is right;
the moment has come.
My inner strengths
are drifting on.

Frances Dabney
YESTERDAY
Return
With
Me
To yesterday
Veiled in dusty thoughts and shaded, dusky memories
In life's
Simple serenity
And peaceful calm.
Return with me
To forgotten forms
With hazy smiles
And silhouettes
Along the dusty paths
And shaded, dusky memories
Of yesterday.

Lisa Disbrow
TOMORROWS

This poem is dedicated to anyone who doesn't think they will see another tomorrow.

Sometimes I wonder if I'll ever see tomorrow. Life can be really unfair, and it is then that you think, "will I see tomorrow?"
For many people, the answer is "Yes. I will see tomorrow." for other people though, the answer is "No! I can't take life anymore!"
Well, that's when a sad reality takes place. The people who answered "no" don't live to see another tomorrow. Then the people who do see tomorrow grieve and ask "Why?" Many people don't understand just what "Why?" is supposed to mean.
Tomorrows are there and always will be. Some people live only to see them . . . why don't you?

Geraldine Peterson
ETERNAL LOVE
There is a special fire between you and I
When our eyes met,
Your's melted my heart.
When our lips met,
My love for you became a roaring flame.
When our bodies entangled while making love,
Intense heat raged through me
From head to toe.
My love for you is an eternal fire,
That can never be extinguished.

Donna Kaye Rock
A MOTHER'S LOVE: TRIBUTE TO MOM

To my Dearest Departed Mother who was tragically killed in an auto accident, December 16, 1988, Love and Prayers forever, Daughter Donna Kaye

No one can compare, the Love that is there;
of a Mother for her Child.
No matter how young or old,
Her Love is strong and not mild;
it is not timid but bold.

I have these memories to hold,
Of Mom's Sacrificial Love for me;
She often said, "You are the reason for my Being, You are special, can't you see?"

On that fatal night of the 16th of December,
As I saw her lying on the road;
in my heart I will always remember,
her last words before she died.
"Donna Donna", she said my name,
Peace, God's Love and inner strength to me it came.

For I was injured on that night;
close to death was I,
Because of my Mother's Love;
it lessened the plight,
and from that night, till the rest
of my life,
In God's care, I knew I would lie.

T L Miller
NYMPHS OF THE DEEP
The dead daughter of the damned depths
Explore every example of ecstasy—
Never allowing the air to alienate their auras
They drown during the dawn of the day.

These sisters of sin swim savagely yet seductively
Oblivious to the obsession of the ocean—
They utter in the undercurrent
unusual and unearthly cries
As their lust for liquid lies listless within a legend.

William J Lasalle
THE ROAD TO DEATH AND DESPAIR
Your parents can't understand you
You're just smoking what you can roll
And it's no worse than alcohol
And everyone likes rock and roll

You're bored when you're with your family
Your school and your job are boring
You think right and wrong don't matter
You're just interested in scoring

No one is hotter than you are
You want to live out your fantasies
You say you just want a good time
You don't mind taking a few chances

Your young friends are into sex and drugs
You do thrill to a little fright
You're not ready to drink human blood
You just want to party every night

You have to dress like all your friends
And your hair is a little wild
You don't care what the old folks think
They want to treat you like a child

There's no room for God, in your life
You know there's no such place as hell
You know all of the laws aren't right
But where you're heading you can't tell

Bonnie Suzanne Sprague
ALL THE TIMES

I've thought of all the times
that I should have thanked you,
and remembered that somehow
the words just hadn't come.

I've thought of all the times
that I have sat by your side,
and remembered that somehow
I'd just never pulled you close.

I've thought of all the times
that I have turned away from you,
and remembered that somehow
you'd always stuck it through.

I've thought of all the times
that I have looked into your eyes,
and remembered that somehow
I could always see what needed to be seen.

And with all the times
I have spent so near to you,
somehow I've rarely taken time
to say just how dear you are to me,
or simply that I love you.

Linda Williams
MY TRUE LOVE

My husband is my one true love,
He inspires me in everything I do.
I think he was sent to me from above,
Without him I would be blue.
Our love grows stronger every year.
Oh, he is so special to me,
I feel so safe when he is near.
Beside him I will always be.

Mike Holman
WHAT YOU MEAN TO ME, GINGER

You mean a smile when I wake in the morning.
You mean a laugh when I don't really feel like laughing.
You mean a good time when everything else is boring.
You mean hope when I think there is no hope left.
You mean someone to stand by me even when I'm not right.
You mean I'll always try to give my best.
You mean a smile when I go to bed at night.
You mean the world to me, Ginger.

Harry T Allen
LORD, I'M NOT COMPLAINING

Lord, I'm not complaining, but there's
something bothering me;
I know here in the U.S.A.—called the land of the free,
We have religious freedom, our lives are based on this.
The pilgrims came and built here,
But there's something quite amiss.
Are we a Christian nation?
Is our religion real?
For in your Ten Commandments, it says, "Thou shalt not steal".
Well, just to kind of clear things up,
Help me understand.
How come we killed the Indians
And took away their land?

Vickie Lynn Henderson
TIME AND WISDOM

To Mom and Dad, with love

Your lives have passed through
time and wisdom.

Yet have you recently looked
upon His face?

Have you seen His eyes of
love and understanding;

Or touched His hands of
mercy and grace?

Has He been by your side in
times of trouble and
guided your life?

Have you loved Him and praised Him
even in times of strife?

Look again upon our Lord Jesus
on this Christmas Day.

And may all His wonderful
blessings come your way!

Pat Beaver

Pat Beaver
THE EASTER LILY

Dedicated to my two sons Marty and Patt

Simple white and clean
With dignity towers,
Having a splendor not yet seen
In the most beautiful of flowers
Carrying the fragrance of Spring.
Blessed be the words of Jesus,
"I tell thee that not even Solomon
In all his glory was arrayed like one of these".
Looked upon with pride until the world ceases,
In words of simplicity and majesty
Will reign as flower supreme,
The Easter Lily—The flower of a King.

Bobbie Ann Mioskie
RED

Autumn leaves bursting with crimson
A bouquet of roses in a crystal vase
A big balloon held firmly in a baby's grasp
Hearts drawn randomly on a young girl's notebook
A matador's cape catching the glare of an angry bull
Big juicy strawberries with fluffy whipped cream
Fresh apples sitting on a respected teacher's desk
A brilliant blaze, disturbing the quiet of night
Rudolph's nose as he leads the troops on Christmas
The first jelly beans to disappear Easter morning
A ribbon tied to accent a gift
The summer's sky before it dips into the ocean.

Sherry M Fisher
YOURSELF

I have learned your mind can be a powerful tool,
All you need to do is follow the rule.
Put yourself first and to yourself be kind,
And all the happiness and love will be yours to find.

Don't allow anyone else to control your thoughts,
Remember all in the past that you were taught.
You are the most important person in the world,
And to yourself you must always be loyal.

To yourself always try to be true,
And there will be nothing you can't do.
But don't be ashamed if you must ask for help,
For it shows you are trying to understand yourself.

Life is a challenge you can conquer with ease,
If you remember it's yourself you must please.
Don't worry about others and what they may say,
Just live for yourself and enjoy each day.

Irma McCluney
LOVE

Let's start the New Year with love,
Because it has been sent from heaven above,
God loved us so much that he sent his son,
Who died on the cross for everyone,
If we showed love for each other everyday,
The world would be better in every way.
Many problems come and go,
There are many times we are in tears of woe,
But love is here to stay each and everyday,
So let us show it for our brothers and sisters in every way,
And live in peace from day to day.

Sheila Morency
EYE CONTACT

I see you every now and again.
I can see the boy in you and also the man.
Those eyes of yours, they lure me on.
By the time I look at them, you're gone.
I wonder about you a whole bunch,
My eyes could devour yours in one munch.
I would have all your attention with just my eyes alone.
My eyes can talk, can you hear their tone?
They call out to you, they want you so much,
If only the path of our eyes could touch.
They won't deceive you, but they will tease.
They speak about the blue sky among the trees.
Incase you can't see them, they are a beautiful brown.
If our eyes did meet, you'd be the first to look down.
If only you could read eyes, you'd hear what mine say.
I'm an expert at the game of eye contact, Wanna Play?

Julie Herrmann-Locken
FULL CIRCLE

For Mom Nancy and the circle we've completed

Two lives begin from one,
each taking separate ways.
Each leading separate lives,
enjoying separate days.
Each thinks their lives so good.
Each thinks their days carefree.
But always each one thinks—
"I'm missing part of me!"
As mother thinks of child,
the child thinks of her too.
Asking where she is now,
and yearning 'to know who?'
Each yearning turns to wanting.
A wanting to know more.
More about that person,
their hearts are searching for.
As paths upon a circle,
where ends shall finally meet.
The two shall come together.
Come full circle—be complete.

Bridget MacLean
GOOD-BYE

To Grampy Tobie who made learning fun and was a teacher in the true sense of the word.

The smile you'd smile, the sayings you'd say,
Are now only memories since you've passed away.

You're gone and I miss you, so much that it hurts,
I miss all your joys, I miss all your quirks.

I cried as I watched Nanny kiss your hand;
As they closed the casket, and you left for "the land."

The land of all goodness, it's where you belong;
Though I know this is true, it hurts and seems wrong.

Little things that you'd told me, mean so much more now;
How I wish you were here, how I hope that you're proud.

I love you sweet Grampy, and I guess God knows best.
You had worked all your life, it was time for your rest.

Linda S Stevenson
THE END OF THE ROAD

To Daddy, For All Your Inspiration.

No More Dreams, No More Hopes,
Everything Gone Up In Smoke.
The Clouds Are Thick With All Your Fears,
Because You Know The End Is Near.

Can't See, Can't Hear, Don't Want To Move,
Because You Know It's Almost Through.
The Fight You Fought For Such A Long Time,
Has Finally Come To The End Of The Line.

When The Smoke Is Gone, And The Sky Is Clear,

You See Yourself Alone Out There.
No One Around, No One To Touch,
Not Even The One You Loved So Much.

You Drop Your Head, And Turn Around,
To See The End Of The Road Is Now.
You're Alone, It's Cold, No One To Hold,
You've Finally Reached The End Of The Road.

Tammy L Robert
GINGER

To my Father, Dale L. Robert.

They say a rose is as sweet
as it smells.
Well my child you were the
sweetest of them all.
The innocence in those eyes made
all love you.
You gave and took, but most of
all you gave.
You were special that I
know.
You were an angel sent from god,
that I know.
Your life was short but sweet that I
know too.
You'll be back someday that,
I love the most.

Barbara Jane Morris
LIFE LAYS HEAVY ON MY SPIRIT

Life lays heavy on my spirit.
It ravages my mind;
and where the bluebird singing sat
It rides its jet-black stallion
And tramples down my hat.
When I take a breath for pleading
Life's verbal issuance rocks me
Like time's old, chiming, steel bell.
And all I see are sun fires
Blazing down in hell.

Life lays down its heavy blanket
On sparkling, morning dew
And where the daisies now should bloom
It makes its tent-pole bastion;
The portals filled with gloom.
Life can suffocate my singing
With words too grim to tell you.
But when life's ghosts have gone away
I'll send my joyful spirits;
Dancing out to play.

Donna Lattanzio
REMEMBERING YOU

I met you in the winter of my dreams
when the earth was white and quiet and still
You were alone
and the only thing separating
you from heaven
was God

I spoke to you in the spring of my dreams
as the earth awoke and silently dressed itself
You touched my hand
and I felt your strength

We became one in the summer of my dreams
two hearts beating in unison
I was you, you were me
and it was right

You left me in the autumn of my dreams
quietly and quickly
as the earth went to sleep
Now God no longer separates you from heaven

Thomas J Mazzone

Thomas J Mazzone
A GREATER FISHERMAN AS GOOD AS ME

A-fishing I went in a reckless way,
Whistling too, I'm bound to say,
I went about to stir no one in the house,
Not even to browse, not even to carouse.

Stooping low, I reached for my pail,
And silently tip-toed to the door,
My foot descends on the dog's tail,
And my fly-rod knocks the lamp to the floor,
All that bang and owoo'g that rang,
Woke up the whole sleeping gang,
Oh, I doubt if I shall ever see,
A reckless fisherman as wary as me . . .
Sallying forth to the stream to throw
In my line, and watch the captured fish below,
If it doesn't measure . . .
Up to the whopper of a treasure,
I'll cook the little fellow, consume the evidence,
Wow, I began to sing and dance,
Oo-oo la la, a ripping good catch, giggling,
A big dripping whopper wriggling.

To my dismay, the whopper got away,
Catching bigger fish than your partner makes me say,
"I doubt if I shall ever see . . .
A GREATER FISHERMAN AS GOOD AS ME."

Adelon M Axt
REFLECTIONS

The clouds, the birds and a tall green tree,
Each doubled the beauty, nature painted for me.
Gazing at their reflections in the water,
I dreamed of how it used to be.

The quiet of the evening, was broken by a loon's shrill and lonesome shout.
The frogs croaking on the lily pads, and hopping all about.
Rings circled upon the lake, made by a hungry fish,
which jumped up out of the water,
to catch his favorite dish.
Now I must quit dreaming, and get back to reality soon,
for in this cement jungle, I would never see a loon.
But, oh, how I love to dream, and make them a part of my life,
Shutting out the hustle and bustle,
of every day work and strife.

Richard Lee Miller
MID-NIGHT SHOWERS—SPRINGTIME SUN

To: June my inspiration

Midnight showers, springtime sun
Two people, one month, some fun
Silly little kisses, simple little hugs
Midnight showers, springtime sun.

Brook of water, so clear, so fast
Two people one month, a kiss that lasts
Splendor in an embrace at last
Midnight showers, summer's here at last

Two people, three months, a love
Mid night showers, summer sun
Two people, a son
Mid night shower
Spring and Summer sun
Three of us, our one

Karen Marie Whitt
MY CHILD

To my two beautiful sons: Scott Allen and Shawn Thomas

My child was made by the heavens above,
His hair was kissed by the sun,
His eyes are the color of blue skies,
His smile was made from the twinkling stars,
His chubby little body,
Of soft white clouds,
His tears of rain drops and dew.

And as he sleeps,
If you'll take a peek,
You'll see the angels above have added a touch,
A little halo above as he sleeps.

If you'll take the time and look at your own little one,
You'll also see he was made by the heavens above,
Just like my son was.

Heather Baker
ONCE UPON A MIDNIGHT BLUE

Once upon a midnight blue
while the moon stood full and true
I walked along the darkened street
frightened by the sound of my feet
the wind whipped through me
and chilled my bones
the only thing that kept me going
was the final sound of moans
for that was the sound
that quivered through the ground
that odd, yet familiar sound
was pulling me within its bounds
then suddenly there appeared
something I knew I feared
for there lay a hole
that was blacker than black
and deeper than deep
I tried to run
I tried to hide
but the sound kept pulling me to its side
then down the hole I fell—
surrounded by its depths I lay
forever in its depths I stayed
although there was no blood I shed
I knew my fate
for I was dead

D Elaine Momberg
OUT OF THE SPOILS

Dedicated to humankind; a prophetic appeal for total brotherhood and combined efforts towards healing the wounds inflicted upon habitants and habitat, the earth, while we yet have time to do it.

Silence reigned in a captive land.
No more sighs, no more cries,
No more wars to be won.

Darkness lay on sunken sand.
No eyes to see, no hands to touch,
No gleanings left, no midnight sun.

No more to say, no more to pray,
No more to hope for a better day.
Only waste spread far and wide
Among the ashes of human pride.

No more floods, no more tides,
No more lambs to be crucified.
Man had lost to a higher cause—
God's own will, in His own way.

In a new land, silence was broken,
From darkness came His heavenly light,
As citizens of a New Jerusalem
Claimed their eternal life.

Brenda L Day (Weeks)
MY CHILD

This poem is dedicated to my son J.J., who holds his head high and smiles no matter what.

My child is full of grace;
he's certainly fair of face.
He's full of spirit, my little boy,
Though he'll never play with a normal toy.
His wheel chair creaks as he turns the corner,
But he's a proud, humble and happy owner.
In his eyes I see a light,
As he gives life its full fight.
And at night when I tuck his little body into bed,
I thank God he isn't dead.

Ruth Fuqua Elijich
SANTA WAS SMILING

Santa was smiling, the meadow was white and all the snow had fallen in the middle of the night. It was the night before Christmas Santa was ready to go up through the tree tops and through the great white snow. He was dressed in red with a big white trim around his neck and around the brim. His clothes were warm as he went through the breeze and God was holding Santa in his great big hand, because Santa was a very special man. The reindeers were resting, getting ready to go back through the meadows in the big white snow. They were quick as lightning and singing you see, as they were wishing a Merry Christmas to you and me.

April C Moore
HIS LOVE

To Mom love you always and my father, Bob Eller thank you both for caring & loving me

The strong wind, blowing by my face
Tis warm air, makes the old side such
a pleasant place. Trees toppling over
with hugs from their branches. The
leaves tumbling down, side walks
and streets
Everything so quiet, sweet smell of
fall
what a good place to dream. Every
bird in a tree every rock in place.
The people just keep on going never
to notice the day as it was to men too
busy to stop to notice nature closing
its door to summer nor to give thanks
to God for such a beautiful day

Jimma Weber
MY LITTLE DRUMMER BOY

I dedicate this to my son, the subject of my poem, who is my greatest inspiration.

Jeffrey loves the Christmas song,
" The Little Drummer Boy."
He plays the role quite well,
Beating out the tune on a table,
His legs, or a pan, with his hands.
One part of the song says,
" I have no gift to bring
That's fit to give a King."
Jeffrey's gifts are not made of gold,
But they are just as precious.
His smile and laughter
At the sound of Christmas music,
Can make any Scrooge smile.
He loves to watch snow gently
falling.
We worry about having to travel
through the snow,
But Jeffrey only sees the beauty.
Best of all, he loves my chocolate
chip cookies.
He can't say how he likes them,
But his face tells it all.
His smile, his eyes, a stuffed mouth,
a chocolate face,
Says all I need to hear.

Sandra Winegar-Petronek
LOVE

To my Bob, who inspired a sense of "love" in me.

A feeling, deep sense from inside
Melding together—
My body,
My soul,
My spirit another.

Love growing—
If not nurtured,
Fades into only a memory.

Awaiting another day—
When memories rise to the surface
To be faced,
Sorted,
Set aside.

Shared—
Love becomes a strength
Alone—
Love becomes an obsession of deep
need.

Isabel C Litchfield
THE LONELY HEART
My father's house has been closed
for good.
If only, once more, I wish that I
would see the faces that lit-up my
childhood.
No, they've lived their lives. I never
could.
This is loneliness to me.
A Christmas tree, adorned and bright,
Once stood proud with its shimmer-
ing light.
Now it lies bare upon the ground, a
blight,
Covered with snow and shrouded in
white.
This is loneliness to me.

High in the attic are castaway toys.
The children are grown, no longer
boys.
There's no laughter, no tears, no
child-like joys.
It is very still, there is no noise.
This is loneliness to me.

A sparkling sea, or a star-dressed
night.
My eyes behold a beautiful sight.
One needs to share both the dark and
the light.
If not, one's world will never be
right.
This is loneliness to me.

Nancy J Wilson
TIME

To: Vicki and Steve—my children Ron—who makes me complete Ed and Lois—for sharing love and friendship

If time weren't of the essence
And man had time to spare
Then man would waste his life
And would not have a care

But time is like a snow flake
Upon a heated hand
It seems to waft down endlessly
And vanish as it lands

As precious as are gem stones
As priceless as is gold
There is no fare to gain our youth
Once we've grown old

Anthony Perez Jr
REMEMBRANCE (OF LOVE LOST)

For my grandmother, whom I miss dearly, for she is no longer with us. This poem is for you.

Though many years have passed, I
decided to call to let you know:
I have been thinking of you. Wanted
to reminiscence a bit about the past
Of all the love that was cherished
between us,
All the words passed about feelings
being felt.
So, our relationship didn't work so
well then.
Maybe now we could solve our
differences.
Rejuvenate the love of some years
ago.
Make true the one important dream
we had: You as my bride and I as
your groom.
Well we now know: dreams don't
happen to come true.
You tell me now, you've married
someone else.
Another man, the one who could
make you happy.
Soon, you say, you will bear him his
first child.
Good luck, with lots of love from this
end.
Well as for me, I will continue to be
lonely, without your love to keep me
warm on the inside.
Don't try to console me now, I will be
fine.
Someday, I'll find that special
someone.
I hope.

Johnny Whitaker
BELIEVE IN YOURSELF

To the youth of America.

"BELIEVE IN YOURSELF"
How do you come to a conclusion,
if you have Goals you are trying to
reach, are just an illusion.
"BELIEVE IN YOURSELF"
When the Sky is the limit but you
are being slowed down by the timid.
"BELIEVE IN YOURSELF"
The mountains you must climb, the
walls you must go through, just to
prove his love to you.
"BELIEVE IN YOURSELF"
Today this land is built by the
strong, if you are, you can develop a
strength from within, from within
you can build, if you BELIEVE IN
YOURSELF.
That's the way I feel. If you only
BELIEVE IN YOURSELF it will be
real.
Once you BELIEVE IN YOUR-
SELF, you are molded and then
hardened like clay.
You will let No Man or Object stand
in your Way.
BELIEVING IN YOURSELF is
Cool. BELIEVING IN YOURSELF
is the only rule.
"BELIEVE IN YOURSELF"
When the Lights get Dim and
everything seems to be grim and you
feel you have lost your last friend,
Remember: YOU ARE GOD'S
CREATION, You are as good as
anyone in this Nation.
BELIEVE IN YOURSELF, MAKE
A PLAN, THEN TAKE THE
STAND
"BELIEVE IN YOURSELF"

Rhoda Stone
WORKING MOTHER

Dedicated to my mother Evelyn Scales

Working mothers, we are great
Not to mention, we are strong
Constantly running, and trying
To sort the right from wrong

Dinners to cook and dishes to do
the laundry's piling up
Bills to pay. Deadlines to meet
And the lottery's bringing no luck.

Where does that lady from the
Calgon commercial find the time
To get taken away by bubbles
When my phone rings while my
daughter's crying.

My mother, she had five kids and
We were all well fed.
Always plenty of clothes to wear
And each had our own bed.

"Mom, I don't know how you did
it . . . ?"
"Or how you got it all done
Cause I'm going crazy
And I've only got one.

Dorothy C Livingston
OUT OVER THE VALLEY TONIGHT
Out over the valley tonight just
before dusk
rain falls and a mist hangs over
one whispy cloud spills rain in one
area more than the rest
white shows on some trees
brown and bare, stark naked they
look
except for the leaf bearing ones,
down by the bending
winding creek, swollen with rain
The trees though mostly bare, are still
beautiful
as they stand as soldiers, gathered in
camp
at rest for awhile

all is peace except for the creek that
runs along the valley
not a sound can be heard, except for
the rain
that falls on my umbrella
and I heard one small bird cheep
as it flew across the road, as I walked

the hills come down to meet the creek
and the old trestle stands still
as it connects them hill to hill
a mist hangs as the gentle breeze
sends that one rain cloud
over the valley

Kleon Kerr
SEARCH FOR A KINGDOM
Lovers of life
Sought the Fountain of Youth,
Hoping the legend
Was really the truth.

Some drifted afar
Seeking cities of gold.
The wealth of Cibola
They wanted to hold.

Shangri La was a dream,
A lost paradise.
An alcove of peace
In Tibetan skies.

"The Kingdom is in you,"
The Master declared.
It is not geographic,
It is life being shared.

It is not domination
Nor arrogant greed.
It is using your means
To help others in need.

Carmen R Morales

Carmen R Morales
BEING YOURSELF IT'S BETTER!
Don't look down
to where you will fall
Just look ahead
to where you will stand tall.

High up in happiness
not sad and low
With blues all around
or terrible thoughts in and around you

Be yourself it's better
things wonderful will happen
When you can do what is best
for yourself and the future.

Betty Pilcher-Freas
THE TRUNK

To the memory of Lula Belle Wilkinson

Childhood days are long past—
but for the memories.
Locked away in the mind—

like a weathered trunk.
Filled with trinkets, faded photographs
and happy songs.
Forgotten, somewhere in a dust filled attic,
Waiting to be claimed by—
the child—now bent with age.
To open the trunk once again—
and fill the house,
With laughter, love and to—
send time spinning back.
To reveal secrets—
only the trunk knows.

Gwen T Lundy
THE FIRST EASTER MORNING

In a garden in Arimathaea
The air was cool and dim,
No bird song filled the silent sky,
All nature was mourning Him.

The lilies drooped their waxen heads
Upon their slender stems,
The flowers looked dull and faded,
They too were mourning Him.

Then a Presence passed through the garden—
T'was the essence of God's power;
But no man was awake to feel it,
All slept through that Holy hour.

But the birds and flowers felt it, all brightened,
The birds began to sing,
The lilies lifted their golden throats
To trumpet the coming of the King.

It is well on Easter morning,
When birds sing and flowers bloom,
That we send a prayer of thanks to the Christ
Who has conquered death and the tomb.

Angela C Bullard
OUR DADDY

Dedicated to the Memory of Farrell N. Carter, Sr.

Our daddy was a railroad man,
he worked outside no matter
how bad the weather.
He had a wife and eight kids at home—
for them he was trying to make life better.
A second grade education was all
our daddy ever received, but lending
his fellow worker or neighbor a
helping hand, in this he truly believed.
He didn't knock people down to climb
the ladder of Success, but whatever
you asked him to do, he always did his best.
No, daddy didn't have wealth, he
wouldn't even had wanted fame, you know
he had more love and compassion
than any highly educated man could
ever hope to gain.
It's not what you leave behind in this
world that proves how great a man
one has been, but it's all the lives one has touched.
Mama and all us kids feel so good
knowing our daddy was loved so
very, very much.

Les Kerton
THE DEEP WATER MEN

When they pack their bags and are ready to ship,
You can bet your life it will be a long, long trip.
The ferryboats that ply the sound,
A harbor tug that pokes ships around,
Hold no magic for men like these—
The ocean's their home and friendly sea.

A rotten bark with a rag of sail,
Not a fast packet that carries mail,
Some rusty tramp outbound with coal
Lies dear to their hearts and close to the soul
Of these rugged men who sail the deep—
Men who count flying fish as they fall asleep.

It's a watch on the wheel with the stars all bright,
A white-capped sea in the dawn's early light.
Six shots on the chain in some God-forsaken place,
Looked on as misfits of the human race.
They ply the sea, their ocean home,
Leaving me to write this poem.

Keith Martz
MIND

Autumn turned to winter and you were gone.
I'd meet another summer where I did not belong.
I have spent many a night hoping you would find,
Heaven is a state of mind.

A feeling of isolation slipped into the wine,
It's a matter of opinion on who I spend my time.
Autumn turned to winter, I needed to know
If your heart could melt the snow.
Autumn's turned to winter,
There is too much on my mind

Jerry E Jodice
A WAY OF LIVING

I dedicate this poem to Carol, my wife and my love.

Love, like Christmas,
Is a dream we share
To wrap our presence in.
The magic it weaves is laced with care
For those we know and see often.

The language of love
Cannot be expressed in words.
It touches each of us
In silent, interconnecting ways . . .
enfolding us in faith,
entwining us with hope
embracing us with charity,
and bonding us in everlasting strength.

Love lasts when we truly believe
"It is better to give than to receive."

James E Rogers
THE COAL MINER

The scars are blue upon your face;
like indelible ink, they won't erase.
Must have come from the falling slate,
that rains from the roof, hard to escape.
Where the sun never shines, no light to be found;
working down deep, way under the ground.
Sometimes you think you've given your soul;
as you toil and labor getting the coal.
Unable to stand, your back is bent;
with the help of a buddy, there's less torment.
You see the light at the end of the day;
the opening is near, you're safe you say.

Dean Rickard
HEART TO HEART

Especially for, and to Rita Thomas, A special and lovely lady

You in my arms
Holding you close
My heart alarms

To see your soothing eyes
Your beauty in as much
My heart sometimes cries
Longing for your touch

Wishing your heart to be mine
So let it be true
That would be fine
Especially for me, hopefully you

Wanting you near
Holding you tight
Making you my dear
Mine through the night

Though we remain apart
Thoughts of you are always
From Heart-to-Heart

Lynn McGinness
CRY MY CHILDREN

This poem is dedicated to the children of the world

They never seen the dew of spring
embrace the grass below
they never seen summer flowers bloom
or watch an acorn grow
They never seen the autumn frost
command the trees to change
They never seen winter snowflakes fall
upon an open range
Cry my children, cry out loud
show all the world what is wrong
Why are ashes and dust so proud
where have the lilies all gone

Robert D Grabowski
TROUBLES OF MINE

Once again, all alone am I
Where are the friends that once gathered around?
Things go wrong in everyone's life,
at least that is what I'm told
How do others cope?
Where are the answers to be found?
Perhaps I put things off for far too long
It is not as if I haven't tried
Others seem better off than me
Luck, for them, seems to abound
I have to smile; solve things for myself
Keep aiming for the future
As silly as it may sound
Self-pity for myself, how foolish I have been
I will forge my comeback
Feet firmly on the ground
Face to the world, determined to win
Fight for what I believe
Make it through, whatever the cost
Even without the others around

Merry Llew Drummond
WELL SPENT

I would not think Time squandered
if I lay for hours,
Watching an ant upon his way
among the flowers and sweet
green grasses, where his life passes
its small parade before my gaze.
Surely a moment cannot be wasted
when it's tasted and savored;
When all its length of time is flavored
with joy
Because one is aware, and can offer up praise!

Sandra Powell
MEMORIES NEVER DIE

To all those who love Elvis. The warmth, the talent, the charm, and his endless gift of generosity, will stay in our hearts forever and for generations to come.

Back in Tupelo, Mississippi,
lived this poor little boy.
Who longed for a bike,
or even a toy.

Who would have known,
this child would be?
The "Greatest Entertainer,"
we would ever see.

He won fame and fortune,
had millions of fans.
A sweet little daughter,
and "Beautiful Graceland."

He touched our hearts,
was generous and kind.
Then came the final blow,
He had to leave it all behind.

He achieved his highest goals,
for all of us to see!
There is no one more loved,
than "Elvis Aron Presley."

Richard L Polley
SOMETHING SPECIAL

I've tried to think of something special
to say to you on this day,
But nothing seems to be just right
to capture just what I want to say.

I've thought of trying to sing
to you a famous love song,
But considering the way I sing
I know that too would be wrong.

I thought of saying it with flowers
but they'd make a blooming idiot out of me
and if I bought you candy
you'd just give most of that to me.

So I guess I'll just forget it
There's nothing left to do,
For every day with you is special
and that's why I love you.

Tracy L Edwards
TESTIMONY OF TIME

To My dear Min My second mother

Silence slips past me
and I am unaware,
stillness overwhelms me
as I drift into despair.

My heart was weak and broken,

the thoughts could not be spoken,
my eyes were closed and I
could not see
the sunlight that surrounded me.

Brave is the heart that smiles
leading me a great many miles.
Always with me when I sought
stronger is it than I thought.

Marie Avant
DREAM COME TRUE

This poem is lovingly dedicated to Marshall, my husband, as an expression of gratitude for his encouragement in my writing.

I remember when first we saw this
place,
A small summer cottage nestled in
space;
As though arranged by an artist's
hand,
Set on a postage-sized hilltop land.

Little white house with back to the
wall,
Of leafless trees and evergreens tall;
A winsome sight, it was to behold,
Tall red chimney at the side so bold.

Wild flowers bloomed on every side,
While in from the ocean swept the
tide;
It was the prettiest place we'd found,
In our various travels all around.

A dream come true, how could it be,
This place was meant for you and
me?
How nice to know at the end of day,
We now had a home in which to
stay.

Rita Poeppel
LITTLE DONNIE

"This poem is dedicated to Donald Loren Poeppel, Jr. Our son" Who was born on Jan. 5th, 1989 and went to live with Jesus on Jan. 7th, 1989.

As I'm sitting here today
Thoughts of you come my way.
I've missed so much by losing you
And things I've missed have made
me blue.
I never got to see you smile
And seeing that would have been
worthwhile.
I never got to see your eyes
And realizing that makes me cry.
I hurt so bad down deep inside
It's feelings baby that I just can't
hide.
I feel as if a part of me is dead
Even when I close my eyes and go to
bed.
I miss you so much, so much it hurts.
And know me and daddy could have
give you the works.
Donnie we love you so much, more
than a lot
And down deep in our hearts we'll
forget you not.
I hope you're happy where ever you
are
And I know you're somewhere
above a star.

Linda K Humphries
TOM

Climbing over the couches and
chairs my son, Tom
With his gun in hand.
I called him for lunch he didn't
answer
Two hours later I found him hiding
behind a bush.
I asked why he did not answer.
He said, "Mom, officers can not give
out their positions
Yesterday I got shot cause I yelled
out to you.
I died mom, I wish you wouldn't
worry so.
Why yell mom I'll come home when
the war is over."
Ten years have elapsed and my mail
box is empty.
After receiving letters at least once a
month,
Since he went to war.
Today I received a letter from his
C.O.
Tommy had thought he heard me
calling him home.
He yelled out from behind a bush,
"Mom don't worry I'll be home at
the end of the war."
Now, in two weeks he'll be home in
a box before the war has ended.

Verna Hutchinson
IDYL

I make my couch beneath the trees
and, dreaming, in the garden lie.
With slitted eyes through lashes peer
at downy clouds and clear blue
sky.

'Neath the inverted bowl of blue
an idle daze envelopes me,
While all of nature busy seems,
each bird and insect, plant and
tree.

And, buzzing on transparent wings
that glisten in the noon-day sun,
The bees pursue their honeyed quest
and never rest; are never done.

Simonetta Vespucci

Niis
SIMONETTA VESPUCCI

Who were you, Simonetta,
That you can still command
An army of lovers, as when
First carried off into battle?
The face upon a banner,
Later spilled across a canvas
To gather a fresh army,
An army so vast and steadfast
In their fierce adoration
That the gods themselves
Would not tangle with their numbers,
And seized you from their midst.

How I envy the dying soldier,
Whose eyes last fell upon
That hair of golden threads,
Finding the dying worth the living
And his soul quite content that
Heaven could offer no more than this.

Leaving behind no letters,
Nor a fabulous death;
Not even a reputation;
How quietly you fled the earth,
As if leaving was a crime;
And time swiftly covered the path
Of your descent with distance.
But the poets and the painters—
These were your pens; and how well
They immortalized
Those winding, golden ringlets, that
Delicate, pointed chin.

Consumed by a life come suddenly
To nothing, but a life
Lived well to excess;
You were a goddess of inspiration;
And lived a thousand lifetimes
In every lonely, dignified kiss.

Goodbye, my Simonetta,
For the arms of Time close
Round you fast, and the hands will
soon
Pass over what faint memory
Mankind does still possess; and
You to the heavens forgotten
Forever will be hurried,
And all that was known of Venus
Erased. For indeed, you left
Nothing behind but
Your face; yet I look at you, and
Know I am unworthy.

Sandra Haynes Pichon
LOVE

For my husband, Stanley, whose love has been an inspiration to me.

Brown. Soft as the eye of the gentle
doe
Velvet as her coat. Your eyes.
Sparkling with mischief,
twinkling with love.
Black when you're angry or hurt.
Hard as flint
and darker than midnight
Sparking like a dueling gun
when provoked.

Consuming. All engulfing like a
wildfire
loose on the plains. Your love.
Enfolding, covering, enveloping.
Deep. Deeper than all the fathoms.
Endless.
Never beginning or ending but
always
Reaching out to me, for me.

Soft. An angel's wings brush against
my neck,
My cheeks, my lips. Your kiss.
Becoming more intense, searching,
exploring, probing,
Yielding. Melting together,
crystallization into one
being. Zenith upon pinnacle and
the crowning of you—
My King. My love for you the
crown.

Lorna Hirae
FAITH IN HOPE

To not hold you,
to not smile with you,
and to not be loved by you,
tears my heart since you have
walked out of my door.

My world has stopped spinning,
as my life has crumbled into a
place of throe.

The pain I feel
makes tomorrow too real,
for life without you is my
greatest fear.

Letting go brings tears to my
eyes,
for our dreams are now only
broken dreams.

But as hard as it is for me to see,
I cannot fear the fear of letting
go of you and me.

I cannot succumb to the darkness
of death
nor can I adrift out into the sea.

I must have faith in hope
in that what lies ahead of me is
for a better tomorrow,
for I cannot make you love me
nor can I love without being
loved.

Let hope then guide my destiny,
as I strive to reclaim me,
And, let hope of finding love be
discovered
in a special place which begins
within me.

Margaret Jean Alexander
IT'S WINTER IN NEW ENGLAND, BUT THIS YEAR, WHERE'S THE SNOW?

It's winter in New England, but this
year, where's the snow?
Sometimes there is so much, there is
nowhere for it to go.
"Wait a minute" they say, this may
not be all in vain
Because it is New England, it could
like turn to rain
The snow leaves a carpet of white on
hills and by the wayside
To the delight of skiers and tots—a
wonderful place to slide.
With the mean chill, the snow
glistens and icicles form
That's when we're lucky to be in
where it's warm
We feel sorry for the Homeless who
live in the outdoors
Thanks to many volunteers who
comfort and feed them indoors.
Even in winter it's relaxing to spend
time on the beach
Living in Rhode Island it is easily
within reach
Watching the waves roll in, or
walking along the sand,
Always on the look out for treasures
close at hand
Looking out to sea, a freighter or
barge comes in sight.
If you're a night owl, it's pleasant to
watch the moonlight
As it dances across the brine making
a rhythmic sound,
Adding to the awe and mystic of the
tides as scientists have found.
It's winter in New England—it
brings a pleasant ring
Not forgetting the other seasons,
soon it will be spring.

Claire M Mayer
THE HUNGRY DOG

To Rascal, my first Yorkshire Terrier The dearest and most rascally of all the dogs I have ever had

To choose 'tween love and
beefsteak?
I hardly know what's best,
But with puppyhood at four months
old . . .
I'd even take a little food and a little
love
And a soft warm place to sleep.

Carolyn Spencer
A SHADOW'S NAME

Brenda Erving—A precious and dear sister whom I love in the Lord

When in truth we're held
To our self unknown,
But to others known,
For which only a phantom lives,
And hope would be our soul's
freedom:
A freedom unknown to an image
held.
Would time yet be our life thus lived,

Though truth unveils and unites the same—
—our happiness unfound,
our identity unnamed.

When years are past,
And nought but lives—
—a shadow's name . . .
. . . in retrospect of an endless compromise,
And reflections yet of a soul untouched,
For an image gained,
And a purpose lost:
Our self—the sacrifice.

Bruce L Cook
MIGHTY RED WARRIOR

To my wife Debra, for her support and bel"ef in me.

Mighty warrior, glory lost;
heritage of the red man gone.
White men have taken their land away,
and put the soil to decay.

The unrest of the ancestral dead,
the out cry of the gods;
the rape of natural beauty,
by white men's progress"ve eyes.

The wrath of nature can be felt,
by high winds, and, darkened skies.

The land diseased by pest"c"des,
the air filled with gray black smoke,
arouses the anger of the dead,
destroy"ng long felt hope.

Rise up oh noble ancestors,
spread fear throughout the land.
Warn your living descendants,
to cherish and respect this sacred land.

The gift of soil for crops,
to feed its people was laid.
The payment should be met,
the debt we owe repaid.

Pauline Adelsohn
WHEN A FELLER NEEDS A FRIEND.

When your tummy is achin', your back is breakin'
You're sniffin' and sneezin', your hands are freezin',
Your eyes are burnin', your head is turnin',
That's when a feller needs a friend.

When the birds are singin', merry bells ringin',
Flowers are growin', warm breezes blowin',
Sun shinin' brightly, stars twinklin' nightly,
That's when a feller needs a friend.

When a pal that you love is called up above
And the sobs choke your heart like it's breakin' apart
When you're longin' for peace that your heartaches may cease,
That's when a feller needs a friend.

When you've won thru the fight, when you've passed the dark night,
All your troubles are over, your field's in the clover,
Happy tears dim your eyes and your head's in the skies,
That's when a feller needs a friend.

Kathleen O'Donoghue
THE TIME HAS COME

To my family, and especially my Mom, who always supported me and encouraged me to put my thoughts on paper.

The time has come
When the world will see,
That the elderly and disabled
Are just like you and me.

When the world is ours
To do as we please,
And when we all have
The ability to be free.

When no one person
Is better than any other,
And we can finally
Live together like sister and brother.

The time has come
For the world to say
That we are all equal
And we will prove it starting today.

Robert J Kosilek
HAUNTED HEART

To Cheryl . . . You had the courage To be the window

It's so easy to be a ghost
When your heart's a rented room
Self-pity for a window
And three locks on the door

The days write angry letters
That the nights won't let you read
Accusations of mortality
Insignificant memberships

Lonely is a room
Where the rent is always due
Beauty is a woman
Wearing honesty like perfume

Anne Robinson
THE VAGABOND

There are those of us who roam,
And those who make a bed in just one place.

What a myriad of diversity is held for those who seek
Strange faces.

While dispelling tribal dances and discovering polar caps,
We, to root, remain nested home.

Yet visions of palaces provide a gleam
And herds of caribou
wandering notions.
The rock endures as a sign of restfulness—
Offering refuge to the
Vagabond's flight
In the place where ivy grows.

Karen Joanne Reynolds
IN MY MIND'S EYE

Being with you in my mind,
There are no words to speak.
Longing for your passionate kiss,
Having no new feelings to keep.

Being held tightly in your arms,
It could only feel right.
I hold onto your memory,
Long into the lonely night.

The feel of your body,
Long and hard against mine.
Is the only thing I long for,
Everyday, All of the time.

Remembering your tender smile,
How it made me feel warm inside.
I loved only you so much,
My emotions felt like a rushing tide.

Remembering your warm embrace,
Feeling like I could touch the sky.
Seeing your kind, caring face,
Is only in my mind's eye.

Randi Lynn Guyer
IF I CAN'T GIVE YOU THE EARTH

If i can't give you the earth,
i would make a deal with God
to lend you the sun
to warm you,
and melt your resistance.
i would borrow the moon,
to put some light in your shadows,
and the blinking stars
to lull you to sleep.
i would make your flaws mild
in comparison to mine.
i would give you answers
to lifes questions
and i would make light
of your madness
just to please you.

Doris M Halpin

Doris M Halpin
THE ELDERLY

This poem is dedicated to all the elderly everywhere

Three cheers for all the elderly
God bless them, one by one
No great respect—too little praise
For all that they have done.
Where would we be without them
Someday we'll be there too,
Remember—most are moms and dads
Who gave their time to you.
Most gave their time so willingly
To start you on your way,
That happy life you're living now
Enjoy it while you may,
It's no fun getting older
You young folks yet don't know
I speak for all the elderly
Time dealt them quite a blow.
Some sit by—quite lonely
Some are ailing too
A few are keeping busy
With hopes to hear from you.
So why not share a little time
There's always some to spare
Show them—they're still needed
Let them know you care.
Try to share a cup of tea
Or chat for just a while,
Tell them, what's been going on
I know you'll get a smile.
A picture of your mom and dad
Just hanging on your wall,
Would let them know—they're not alone
You do care—after all.
You were put upon a pedestal
Devotion, that was true
Could only come from mom and dad
Who showed their love for you.
Their aging now, give back some time
That doesn't seem so wrong
To them it means so very much
You'll have plenty when they're gone.
Some say they grow old gracefully
There's nothing they can do,
They're not looking for a miracle
All they need is you.

Geraldine Hall Petry
I WATCH THE SUNRISE

I dedicate this poem to Beth.

I watch the sunrise and feel a newness in my soul,
that will linger throughout the day,
as I sup from my bowl.
I watch the sunrise explore the world to wakefulness
and breathe new life into the shadows of the night.
Wake up world of blight,
God wants to warm you
it's a wondrous sight.
I ponder the glory of the beautiful gift of light
that nourishes life
amid all the strife.
I will enjoy each new sunrise
knowing that when I pass from this mortal coil
I pass into a new sunrise
where love is the toil.
I am always aware
someday I will be there.
Just deserts await
with each new sunrise
that I understand is a gift of love.

Dee Raines
FRIENDSHIP

Friendship is everything
Listening, caring
And sharing things.

Together forever and
Never apart.
Friends are together
In the soul and the heart.

Friends and friendship
Means alot to you
And in every single
Thing you do.

Beside each other
Through hardship,
That is what I call, true
Friendship.

Mortimer Duggan
BRIDGEPORT, CONN.

And the city breathes on me, as the sky caves in around me.
As I watch the trees hemorrhaging their leaves, like dust upon a highway.
Noise, lights flashing, the smell of popcorn through a hall door.
The screech of brakes ripping through my brain like a chainsaw.
Lights flashing like a million candles as the pigeons coo endlessly.
As children huddled in a corner like naked trees upon a desolate moor.

The hum of engines beating out their vibra'nt tunes.
A city playing out its song, and I so out of key.
That awakens me from my subconscious dreams.
And calls me back from where I came.

B Burris
FEBRUARY
not a 'favorite'
twenty eight days,
but,
one year in four
we add one day more!
other months—
thirty days,
some have thirty
one!
thinking it over
why not add
that extra day to
October!
or maybe add it to
May
why ever to
February?

Gwen H
THE HAWK AND ME

To Daniel, my Hawk and my friend

When I think of you, I see a hawk,
Who's spirit is free and wild.
There's savage beauty in your ways,
There's power in your wings.

Caught up in those awful talons,
The earth far beneath my feet,
You taught my heart to hope again.
You showed me how to dream.

Hawklike is your heart,
Strong and fierce and proud.
There was no bird to speak of me,
For I was tethered . . . but now I'm free.

Lynda Rae Exley
OUR PART
The world may be in a terrible rush
But let our lives be slow
Like the sweet morning hush

Let us savor each moment
Take time for good judgment
And make love our constant

The world may be in a terrible rush
But let us take time to know
And to touch

Amy K Forgach
THE MOST OBVIOUS EMOTION

To John—the Muse
You are the spirit.

The evolution of my love,
Like Kepler's Law of Planetary Motion,
Is based on the discovery that all things change over time.

By increasing the sphere of my activity
Life is progressing forward.
Enter John—introduction to the element.
Now my days have more meaning.

In the phase of one moon I have grown;
My fears are weakened.
Pleasure is immeasurable on the Felicity Scale.
You are the source of my affection.

What fraction of you have I been exposed to?
Basic fundamentals: food and wine, language and physical being.
You can feed me more energy,
Though my appetite is not in question.

Know that I won't manipulate nature
Or quantify variables that don't yet exist.
Nature parades itself in a leisurely fashion.
Time is not an important function.

Just remember in the interim that I really do care.

Sonyia A Stone
TIME GONE BY

Dedicated with all my love to my mother Barbara my husband Larry "Top Sgt" and my children Jason and Kristen of whom I am so proud

The hands that held mine were young and uncalloused, our hearts were full of love and unchallenged.

Days and nights blew in the wind and time began to slip by as we all know it can.

Burdens, worries and tears had found their way into our youthful years. Our hair is beginning to gray and there's a wrinkle on each face, adding only to the beauty that our memory will never erase.

The hands that hold mine are a little old and calloused and our love had been challenged but we fought back with faith and fire.

To some it may seem strange after all this time to have cried a little and laughed alot that these hands are still holding tight. Perhaps it was the odds, love blessed from above.

Dorothy M Chapman
THOU SHALT NOT
How vulnerable you are!
How obvious, too
That you must puncture me
With the needles of your pain

Do you know that each time
You cause a drop of blood to flow
You bleed a little?

Don't try to hide from others
Or, blind yourself
To the flaws within
That make you stab at me

I hurt and I bleed
I run from your sight
So that the barbs fall short

But, oh, you've done your work too well
Now—live in your own personal hell!

David O Fisher
TAXES
The time has come, to pay our dues
We may complain, but we can't refuse
So all we do, is sing the blues
And fill out the form, the one we choose.

We check the figures, to see what we made
And wonder where it went, or what bills were paid
Uncle Sam needs the money, what more can be said
So we'll keep paying, even after we're dead.

The tax laws were changed, to help the poor
But it was only a sham, to open the door
For more pork-barrel projects, in which money will pour
To benefit a few, need I say more?

They even went so far, as to suggest a raise
For public officials, but that set tongues ablaze
So it was voted down, after a heated display
And for once in my life, that made my day.

Squandering money, to bail out the S & L
Is like pouring a fortune, into a bottomless well
I think those financial wizards, should pay their claim
And deal the taxpayers out, it's not their game.

Marilyn M Last
THE TWILIGHT ZONE

To the memory of my father, my mentor, and my best friend.

Once in a while
When I am restive,
Seeking deeper sleep,
I have visions—
Flashing on the inner eye,
And at the corners of my mind—
Of kaleidoscopes,
And crazy carousel rides;

And I see myself
Falling fast—
To some place
Where past and present meet,
Collide,
And turn about—
And where,
On the dim horizon,
As the future beckons
Through a door,
I see myself
Slowly dissolve—
And disappear before.

Lynne Armstrong-Jones
LIFE
Greenhouse Effect. War. Violence.
The worries of the world.
I fear for the environment
And for my family's future.

The frigid wind of worry
Wraps around me like a coffin—
I shiver with the chill
As darkness closes in.

Is there no hope? No end?
The winds whip me harder now,
As cold rain insults my face—
The chill has spread inside of me . . .

I can no longer keep my feet—
I will soon be swept away
By icy winds and streaming rains:
I am deafened by the whistle and roar—
Suddenly
A bit of sunshine shatters the clouds;
The voice of an angel with golden tones.
"Mama, I need you—": a small hand touches mine,
And I'm warm and whole again.

Joan Kyar Freyholtz
RABBITS NIGHT OUT

Dedicated to my children Lori, Cindy, and Bradley for their inspiration and help; in memory of my daughter Christina, Aug 22, 1970—May 30, 1987

It was a clear night and the moon was shining,
The rabbits came out for some late night dining.
The garden looked inviting with its lettuce and carrots,
Living close to Farmer Brown had its merits.
One rabbit's name was Hippity Hop,
The other one's name was Flippity Flop.
Together they would go to find something to eat,
They search and searched until they found something great.
Hop liked the carrots, Flop the leafy greens,
They ate and ate like a couple of fiends.
Sometime later when they had their fill,
They headed for home at the bottom of the hill.
Hippity couldn't hop, Flippity only flopped,
So they rolled down the hill, at the bottom they stopped.
They went to their home, which was in the brush.
They were very tired and it was hard to rush.
They went inside and flopped on their bed,
What a great feeling to be so well fed!

Nellie Ann Aldrich
EVENING
Evening, what dost thou hold for me?
Art thou but creeping darkness without sight?
Or art thou a counselor
In one's flight toward heaven?
Oh, Evening, thou art like the rainbow
In the sky,
Which does not fail to show
Its glory up on high.
Thou art a faithful servant, for at dawn
You bring us back.
Reborn, like blooming flowers
In the spring.

Michelle J Dressler
BORN AGAIN
The rain falls so peacefully
surrounding the darkness with lustful energy
letting its soul open to be reborn
hearing the cries of its spirit.

Feeling so empty—tired of understanding
I want that serenity to be mine
To fill me with ever-lasting hunger
and my heart with contentment.

The rain falls harder now
screaming nightmares into the nite
not realizing my own fears fill my dreams

and my own spirit is no more.
My heart aches as I close my tired eyes
releasing my frightened soul
hoping when I awake the sun will shine
and I too will be reborn.

The rain falls so peacefully
opening to brightness with sensual energy
its soul fulfilled and satisfied
until its spirit cries once again.

Trudy A Turgeau
BLOOD DRIPPING

To Kermy, Boo Boo & Smokey

Blood dripping
off the corpse
My heart skipping
a beat
Skin burning
in the heat
My stomach churning
at the sight
I couldn't see
in this light
Where was my might?
I don't know
I couldn't say
Of course death
would happen this way.

Rebecca McFadden-Cooper

Rebecca McFadden-Cooper
I'M GONNA

I am going to make you a part of me.
I am going to take my life and build an open door.
I am going to let you walk right inside of me,
And see the things I have done and the why of it.
I am going to show you the good and the bad of me.
The defeats I have had and the victories I have won.
I am going to let you experience the only troubles I have seen,
And let you swim in my ocean of tears.
I am going to let you visit my secret hiding place,
And let you explore that distance side of me.
I am going to let you see my reasons for living,
And why failures did not hold me back.
I am going to let you see me as a child,
And see how I have blossom into a woman.
I am going to make you understand me thoroughly
And see things the way I do.
I am going to take you through the pearly gates of my heart
And make you sit down and appreciate me.
I am going to show you love to its fullness,
And then . . .
I am going to let you love me.

John R Briggs III
THE OLD MAN AND THE SEA

To the man building his plane, realizing his dream and the inspiration for this my Father

The old man and the sea
The man and his plane
Both the same
Both a dream
The man builds his plane in the basement
That one day will fly so high
The old man floats above
Fishing in the world of the ocean below
Both above and below
Fishing for the same things
Dreaming the same dream
Piloting the same plane
Fishing in the same sea
Dreaming the same dream
Going down the same stream

Anita Rundell
WOMAN

Fretting and frowning
Pretending and clowning,
She makes her way
Through every day,

She makes life brightest,
Reaching for the highest,
Voracious competition,
Extreme aggravation,
Extending exaggeration,
Flaunting her attraction,

Stupendous satisfaction,
At her knowing interaction,
Stunningly simplifying,
Her brashness beguiling,
The fact she may be lying,
May keep you sighing,

Daughter or wife or lover or friend,
She can outsmart you in the end,

If you are in anyway considering winning
Save the strife in your life,
Give her what she wants in the beginning.

Helen S Kahler
MOTHER'S LOVE

In a hundred ways, my children,
I showed you that I cared,
A hundred different things I've done
In my love you've shared.

In all the socks that I have darned
I weaved a little of my heart,
Twas in the seams I've sewn together
And in the seams I cut apart.

And even, though, I never said them,
The words were there, engraved,
In all the patches, in all the mending
My love was there enslaved.

In every dish I cooked for you
I left my love behind,
In every bite that you have tasted
It was there for you to find.

And each time that you were hurt
I washed away your fears,
My love had brought your laughter back
And removed your fears.

Evelyn L McKenzie
IF I COULD LIVE MY LIFE AGAIN

Just to be, where and when, to see and be of youth and free.
Trust not to luck, nor put aside, an open mind with thoughts
applied, of hopes and dreams that were denied.

IF I COULD LIVE MY LIFE AGAIN

To come from there to here again, I'd search my soul for
empty hours to fill with love, and smell the flowers.
I'd waste not my life in Ivory Towers, but take more walks
in April showers; with precious moments yet to be,
walking hand in hand with Thee.

IF I COULD LIVE MY LIFE AGAIN.

Many mountains I would climb, behold the secrets that
I'd find. Mirrored rivers to be crossed, holding memories
that were lost. Beneath the mountains, beside the stream,
now I lay me down to dream. 'Neath snow white clouds
over head, a soft white blanket to cover my bed.

IF I COULD LIVE MY LIFE AGAIN.

Of many talents I would be, but first of all I'd set them
free. With clear of mind I could recall the life that
followed me, with open eyes I'd see it all.

IF . . . I LIVED MY LIFE AGAIN.

Lucille Frederickson
POETRY IS LINE ART

My favorite art form is black on white ink prints.
This time I will write my lines.
Twenty lines to me are not many.
Unless I'm hanging out the family wash.
If I'm a switch board operator and all the lines are ago.
If I just send a card with a line to say hello.
Or looked in the mirror when I was feeling fine.
High school band kept me marching in line.
During nurses training I toed the line,
Also the times I went fishing.
Nursing is my line of work.
I do more out of line besides ink prints.
I paint and line craft boxes.
I also do long-line needle point.
In black and white prints I use a line many times.
This is almost my last line for this art form,
Except for my by-line.
If I were a linebacker, I'd punt, because
There's no rhyme only a reason!

Judy E Kleeper
THE LORD'S LOVE

The Lord's Love is everywhere;
You just have to open your eyes and see.
From the smallest snowflake and rain drop to the deep blue sea;
From the smallest blade of grass to the largest valleys and forests;
Just open your eyes and see.
His Love is there for you and me;
His Love is in the sunset and in the sunrise;
Just look at the colours of a rainbow after a thunderstorm.
His Love is in the stars and in the moon;
Open up your eyes and you will see.
His Love is there for you to see.
Have you ever watched a bird in flight?
Have you ever seen a flower bloom?
The Lord's Love is everywhere.
Just open up your eyes and you will see.

Melody Ann Highfill
I AM ALWAYS WRONG

I dedicate this poem to Ralph Rayas, whom I love very much and will never let go. I love you now and I'll love you forever.

I am always wrong,
or so you say.
I'm tired of having heartaches
almost everyday.
I understand that you love me,
and I love you too,
But when we fight it makes me blue.
Please help me stop having these heartaches
almost everyday.
I'm sorry I waved or even said Hi!
Because I feel like, in a slow way,
you are trying to make me say . .
Good-Bye!
No matter what, I refuse to do it,
Because I love you and will never let our love die.

Kari Reu
THE FRIEND THAT I HAVE

The friend that I have is not tall
nor small
The friend that I have is not seen
by all
The friend that I have laughs not
at me
For thee that I have tis make-believe

Sari Gottlieb
NOW, BEFORE THE EYES OF GOD

For my father who never had his time away—

Now,
Before only the eyes of God
lie the spheres, heavenly bodies
in suspended animation,
revolving, rotating, round and round
the source of life.

Oh, for a time away
beyond the most radical beliefs of man;
into the emptiness that appears us
more than materialistic treasures.

Oh, to climb aboard a star and travel
everywhere to nowhere.

Oh, to rest my soul in the freedom of a cloud
passing by,
and have time trickle through my fingers
as if it were endless.

Oh, to be sentry or Mr. Moon and watch
the hustling excited, busy earth as he does.

Oh, to laugh and play in God's playground,
to cry as the clouds do.

Oh, for a time away
to climb aboard a star and travel
everywhere
to
nowhere . . .

Margaret M Joy
SONNET (SPRING)
When lilies are in bloom springtime is near,
The atmosphere is filled with sweet perfume.
Of iris, tulips, daffodils in bloom,
And lavender and lilac fragrance here;
New little buds on bush and tree appear.
And tender leaves on branches come out soon,
Then Robin Redbreast sings his merry tune,
A happy time of year is very near.

With ferns and johnny jump-ups by a stream,
Lagoons are filled with freshly running trout,
The anglers cast their lines, then sit and dream
Of fish, while early sparrows fly about;
From honey-suckle, bees drain syrup clean,
Springtime is here and Nature blossoms out.

Gaby Sparapani
MY GRANDFATHER, NONNO IGNAZIO

This poem, is dedicated in the memory of my grandfather who passed away on May 6, 1988, in Rome, Italy. Nonno, you are greatly missed by us all, and you will always remain with in our hearts.

Already three months have gone by,
since you were called away,
your voice we'll never hear again,
but the memories are here to stay.

We didn't see you very often,
because you moved to Italy,
but when all of us did get together,
we were one big happy family.

Life must continue to go on,
we all know that it's true,
but it won't ever be the same,
since God called upon you.

Time does not erase the sorrow,
and we know it never will,
no one can ever replace you nonno,
and no one ever will.

Your smiling face when you played cards,
is a treasure to recall,
you had a kind word for everyone,
and you died beloved by all.

Someday, we hope to meet you,
someday, we know not when,
to clasp your hand, in a better tomorrow,
never to part again.

Violet V Lockwood
PARK-DOWNTOWN BOSTON
It was an ordinary day
the swan boats were leisurely peddled around the lake
the ducks swimming along side
the pigeons strutted amidst the tourists
they perched on park benches
pigeons everywhere
lovers asleep now in a dirty blanket
rolled up like two sausages
tossed on the grass
are not wakened by the rattle of garbage can lids
as a black man forages for food
an eager young business man
carrying his attaché case
walks briskly through the park
to yonder skyscraper
passes the wino
slumped on a bench who calls
"give me a dime mister."
Yes it was an ordinary day.

Kristin Fullerton
DOES IT MATTER?

To all my friends, especially to Shankers and Melissa.

Morning mist
Evening dew
Abracadabra
Kalamazoo
Witch or warlock, does it matter?

Morning fog
Evening stars
Go to hell
Go to Mars
Heaven or hell, does it matter?

Morning breakfast
Evening dinner
Very fat
Quite thinner
Evil or good, does it matter?

Morning darkness
Evening light
Turning the cheek
Starting a fight
Satan or God, does it matter?

Morning sun
Evening moon
Very sane
Like a loon
Life or death, does it matter?

Christin Olson
IN MY THOUGHTS

To Jerry, the inspiration of this poem.

When he's in my thoughts
The tears start to well,
There's a wall around my heart,
I don't know how it fell.
When I envision his smile
It pierces my heart,
It invades all my thoughts,
It tears me apart.
His eyes full of laughter
Take me far away,
They're always there
To trouble me as I lay.
As I wipe away my tears
I'll build another wall,
To give my heart protection
Against another fall.

Joyce Kepley Mayhew
PILOT IN FLIGHT

This poem is dedicated to, "The Pilot"

Taking off from the airport, on a sunny, summer day—
I sat in a Cessna airplane beside him, with nothing much to say—
I watched in amazement—the skill and ability of this
man—to fly this aircraft off the ground, and then
bring it down to land—

It didn't take me long to realize his great love for
the air—
The beauty of the flight that day, was happiness we both could share.

I got lost in a sea of blue—Free as an Eagle in flight—
White clouds hovering overhead—
Nothing else in sight—

If for some reason, I never fly again—I'll always
cherish the memories of that flight—with that very
special man.

Tom Ramey
YOUR SPARKLING EYES

This poem is dedicated to the beautiful golden-tressed, emerald eyed lady with the softest heart and the kindest soul. To C. J. I Love You.

Your sparkling eyes
They glisten like the moon
And sparkle with the sun
That cheers me up and turns me on
All into the night and the next day
Your eyes my dear, they have a meaning
If to no one else
They have a meaning to me
I see the daylight when I look into your eyes
And at the same time, I see the essence of the twilight sky
With the twinkling lights in the heavens
You must know how I look into your eyes
That I see the softness that radiates about you
The very existence of your innerself that revolves around you
Your gentleness that warms hearts of old and young alike
Your sparkling eyes that glow with the kindness of a dove
To hold dear and to feel cared for
I will cherish the times that I look into your eyes
For it assures me a close feeling that I need and want
You show through your eyes the caring that most people want
But they cannot have or find the gentleness you possess
This, I have found in your eyes
Your sparkling eyes, they are caring, they are love about you
Your sparkling eyes are the giving of yourself

Dixie LaMont Wehrli
THE HEALING
She has become the light of my life,
God has allowed me to finally know her.
She resides in the spirit world you see,
And through pictures and love He began to show her.
I saw her as a babe in a dream,
As beautiful as a rose could be.
In an antique shop I browsed one day,
And her portrait was there for me.
As I remembered how her life began,
Her name began to come.
She began and was quickly gone,
He said part of her name was Autumn.
I had another dream one night,
An unknown woman came.
She taught me many things in prayer,
And she said, "there's another name."
I was already greatly blessed,
What more Could there possibly be?
A magazine, a story, on page eighteen,
The first name, my lovely daughter, Amee.
So my daughter that I had never known,
Was revealed to me that day.
Through dreams and healing and mementos I found,
The Lord chose to do it His way.
Mother

Brandi Jackson

Brandi Jackson
THE DETERMINED LITTLE PUPPY
The determined little puppy
Kept gnawing,
Gnawing,
Gnawing,
Tearing and tugging with
All his strength;
The rug wouldn't tear.
He gnawed, tore, and tugged;
The rug wouldn't tear!
He gnawed, tore, and tugged;
The rug wouldn't tear!
He gnawed, tore, and tugged;
The rug still wouldn't tear!!
Discouraged, he crawled
Heartlessly away,
In search of an easier task.
If only he had known of
the three weak, ragged threads
Holding the rug together!

Reflection
REAL LOVE HEALS

This poem-song is dedicated to the memory of L A V E R N E and may be sung to the tune of the IMPOSSIBLE DREAM.

To live in a world that's so sad
To see loved ones die at our feet
To hate one another with malice
To live, living life in defeat

To lie and wound each other's hearts
To speak in a slanderous way
To feel without walking in their shoes
To stand for what most will not say

Turn this world around for us to survive
With hope in your heart, keep love alive
United we stand, laying down sin and strife
Holding hearts in our hands;
stopping drugs, guns and knives

And I vow . . .

If you just do your part, keeping God

by your side
With respect, self love and self pride—
All together, we'll cry

For the peace, we will find in our souls
Loving God, you and I are made whole and
We'll walk hand in hand with each other
To a world that we healed with real love . . .

Evelyn Murray
PITY PARTY
Sometimes we feel downhearted,
Discouraged, sad and blue
Enjoying a "Pity Party"
Thinking no one cares for you.

We often feel "taken for granted",
Endearments wouldn't take much,
Just a kindly word to be spoken
Or a little loving touch,

This feeling is quite common
As we travel on through life,
We find we're more friendly to others
Than we are to husband or wife.

Each one could be more loving,
Be more free with words of praise,
And to tell the other we love them
Would make for happier days.

We shouldn't keep it a secret
And be ashamed to let them know,
Even though we don't express it,
Our love in actions we show.

Dorothy L Daggett
ISLES AND LAKES AND BRILLIANT STARS

To my daughters

The world is so still.
I arise, and look out upon a Japanese painting.
All is heavy mist—with only the tree tops rising—
for miles and miles.
There are no streets, no houses, no cars.
Over on the beach is a cluster of fairy castles:
They have no foundations—just float in the mist.
Then comes the wind, the rain, and last of all—The sun.
The bay is blue, and the buildings once more rise from the soil.
Clearwater Beach—monument to man's greed.

Rita Kay Wilke
LOST
As I walk along the streets at night,
a little boy stares at me.
His hair askew, tears down his face
grips his patched teddy bear.
lays in a torn box to rest his head
He shivers as a cold breeze fills the air.
No blanket to keep him warm.

Y A Salam
FIGHTING FOR WHAT YOU BELIEVE
Do you believe in it?
Then stand-up for what you believe;
Fighting for what you believe in is not easy.
Sometimes it gets painful,
Sometimes it gets dark and lonely,
But anything worth fighting for;
It's going to be painful.

The fight must go on,
Regardless what your friends think.
Yes, it's frightening;
But the fight must go on.
So, what if you lose your friends,
So, what if you lose your job,
The majority are not always right,
This world is only temporary.

We are only passing through in this material world.
The majority will not understand your struggle,
Only your Creator should be your navigator,
Because we came in this world with nothing,
And we are going to leave this world with nothing.

P J Hornbeck
SKY
Hello Sunshine—What are you doing today?
"Watching the clouds as they frolic and play".

Wait up raindrops—Why are you hurrying so?
"The sunshine's close and I really must go".

Hi there rainbow—What are you doing up there?
"Just painting the sky to show that raindrops were here".

Hello Moon, with your beams all aglow—
And your smiling face looking upon us below.

Hello Stars, shining in the night—
Flirting with the Moon and
Twinkling so bright.

Oh, Thank you Lord, for this SKY up above,
You've Blessed it with Beauty, and gave it with Love.

Hollis Hughes Hopkins
WINSTON SPENCER CHURCHILL
The strife is o'er, the lion's dead.
In peace he lies upon his bed.
No more he'll lead his country's men
In air, on sea, nor in the glen.

Sincere with faith, helped make him great
And etched his name on history's slate
With others, whom did him perceive,
To also their own country lead.

A vacuum lies in Britain land,
Easy for us to comprehend
Who knew this man that passed away,
That gave England its finest day.

Celesta Amstutz
'TIS ANSWERED PRAYER

To my loved ones

Matthew 21:22 and all things, what so ever ye shall ask in prayer, believing ye shall receive,
'Tis then Christ lifts our heavy load, and trusting all, we cling to Him.

Sometimes we wonder does He care
Or have we failed to hear Him speak?
Or have our words in uttered prayer
Been for self gain, or in spirit meek?

He understands our heart's desires;
He knows our every thought and care,
In tenderness His will inspires.
His love o'er rules, 'tis answered prayer!

'Tis answered prayer His will to know,
'Tis answered prayer His love to show;
'Tis answered prayer, what peace is mine
'Tis answered prayer, what joy divine!

David J Davidson
TIME
The last most beautiful day in the world . . .
And even the skeptics agree
When shadows appear in mists of spun gold
And colors dare dance on the breeze.
Animals, patient, expectant, and keen
Let each little sound prick their ear
And carefully sniff thru all of the scents
The wonders that drift thru the air.

Men shouted warnings. Some priests spoke in tongues.
Some scientists thought to explain
How all the world over sunlight could shine
While others just shrugged it away.
And everywhere colors, they shimmer and shine
As the sky reflects in their hue
As if myriad rainbows had settled on earth
To share in the glorious view.
And when the world stops, when everything stops,
When forever's a heartbeat away,
When distances crumble, shattering thoughts,
It's the last most beautiful day.

Dimi Accurso
DREAMER

To my husband Vinny who Never Stopped Encouraging Me.

We soared together
On the wings of an angel,
She guided me
Through time and space;
Her face
Delighted me,
A radiant smile
Illuminating the skies ahead,
Leading the way
Through her dreams.

Jef Smith
I SOUGHT TO SING (FIRST LINE)
I sought to sing
a song of glory;
of tales olde and gray.
I beg'd to bring
the brightest story
But all were told before my day.

I tried to treat
the mind to laughter
with a joking, limerick line.
And I seek the seat
we all are after
Though I know it's all due time.

So, I write to witness
these days in time
if only for enjoyment.
I'm too busy with my business
in this golden mind
and poetry is not secure
employment,

But, then again,
Nor is time.

Marian Clark
PRAISE AND GLORY TO A FRIEND

I Marian Clark, a child of the "King" dedicate this poem with love, first to Jesus. Then to my daughter Kama, my son Larry and to all people of the world (God Bless You Always).

You loved me in the city and in the country too.
When I was up or down.
You've always been around.
Whether I was young and foolish or old and mature, you always cared.
You're faithful and true.
You've always seen me through.
I know you'll never leave or forsake me.
For your promises are the key.
I have not chosen you, but you have chosen me.
Oh! How I love thee, for you see my heart.
You washed me with your blood and filled me with your love and spirit.
You've given me a new start, that's why I worship and praise you and I know you hear it.
You never change, you're always the same and "JESUS IS HIS NAME"

B J Hammell
LOVE OF LIVING
The intensity of a moment is like
a blossom in the wind
Plucked from the sky
held briefly
admired
dismissed.
Carried off into the winds of time
to become a
fading
memory . . .

The same blossom can be
held long
nurtured
cared for

Only to bloom again and again
With an enduring freshness and beauty

Bringing happiness and joy to one who dares go beyond
The intensity of a moment . .

Timothy Todd Biggs
IT'S BEEN A DOZEN YEARS SINCE I LAST HELD YOUR HAND
It's been a dozen years since I last held your hand,
Touched your smile or heard your voice
Yet, everyday I have this feeling
you're not far from me
I feel your advice weighing heavily in my heart
You guide me through each and every day,
I am never alone

In my mind and in my heart, you are always there

To give me confidence in honesty, courage, love
You are the greatest man I will ever know

Like an oak that drops an acorn into fertile soil,
You planted a seed in my mind
It still grows, protected from the heat
Or an angry world by the shade of a familiar smile
You are my roots for which a great tree will grow,
You are the greatest man I will ever know

When they ask me of you, grandpa,
I'll tell them of the cantaloupe king whose heart is gold
And of the man who carried me through a million play rodeos
I'll show them how a catfish bites and how a pine tree grows
But most of all, grandpa, I'll show them what a little boy knows
Hopefully when my dawn goes down to day my grandson
Will look upon a clear blue sky and with a reverence say;

Grandpa, you are the greatest man I will ever know

Jeffery Loren Brooks
LOVE/MOON

(To Lisa Jantzen, she was my first moon)

To me . . . love is
Like a full moon.
For when it rises,
It is so beautiful and bright,
So full of light.
And this light pierces,
Even the darkest of those nights.

. . . for just an instant
It appears we have regained all sight.
But the good things never last,
So too, it must set.
Faithfully though, in knowing,
Soon it shall rise again.
. . . because of you.

K Morris
PRAY FOR US

Pray for us, War is with us today!
See the children carry guns even in their play.
Pray for us, War is with us today!
See the mothers cry because their sons have to die.
Pray for us, War is with us today!
See the starving faces of those of many different races.
Pray for us, War is with us today!
See where hate grows and rules, people obey like fools.
Pray for us, War is with us today!
See how fear turns brother against brother til they can no longer live with each other.
Pray for us, War is with us today!
What is the answer?
Where is the end?
Man looks for the answers as time comes and goes.
It's all very simple, God only knows!

Lurline Wells
THE WAITING ROOM

This poem is dedicated to Dr. McCollum and Dr. Jackson, who have been there when I needed them the most.

Sterilized odors hanging in
the air,
Magazines scattered on tables
everywhere.
Pale green carpet with chairs
in a row,
People waiting patiently in
a hurry to go.

The sound of a child crying
far away,
The scurrying of nurses rushing
through the day.
Questions of mothers needing
to know,
People waiting patiently in
a hurry to go.

Sign your name, please have
a seat,
Fill out these papers and print
very neat.
We're running behind, about one
hour or so . . .
People waiting patiently in
a hurry to go.

Ross George Trotman
SHOULD

To My Beloved Daughter Jennifer, Son Greg and Friends.

Should . . .

Should you find something worthy in a person,
that person is a friend.

Should you cherish and admit a friend, then
that quality which you saw worthy
becomes a part of you
and you will grow.

Should you set out to erase or destroy that which
you found worthy, you not only lose a friend, but you slowly lose yourself.

Should you become separated by time and space
and all material traces lost, the photos of your memory will keep you together
until you surely must meet again.

Shelia Plair
HOME

Home is where I'm headed at the end of each day
No bosses, paperwork, or horns honking move outta my way.
Ah, home at last, where's my key, quick open the door;
Turn the lock, click, oh home, my Cherie Amour.
A feeling overcomes me like a snug fitting glove;
Yes I feel it, it's great, the environment of love.
Yes there's love in my home, the environment of love.
Yes there's love in my home, a misplaced shoe, a toy or two;
On the table a homemade card, that says I love you.
A greeting of welcome, a hug for good measures;
That's what I like best homes' simple little pleasures.
Home is not always perfect, sad to say but it's true;
There are difference of opinions, but love carries us through.
Ah, to sit down, watching T.V., I lean back in my chair;
And let the fingers of relaxation run all through my hair.
Dinner was fantastic, delicious, really great;
Um . . . 10:00, my time flies, it's getting late.
As I snuggle under my blankets so comfy and warm;
I reach for my clock, and set the alarm.
Ah, yes home is the end of the beginning of my day;
Love is my home, a home here to stay.

Sarah Peterson
DEAR DIARY

My diary is special to me
I keep it unseen with a key
I write before bed every night
It locks my secrets up tight.
On its pages I reveal all
From the drawer I hear its call,
Telling me my dreams are kept
The times I laughed, the times I wept.
And when I'm older I'll look back
My childish ways then I'll lack
And looking through its pages memories that I can see,
Were held in my dear old diary.

Walter G Samuels
EL BANDIDO

To my dear, loving wife, Ruth

El Bandido, hides at night,—guns at his side:
El Bandido, rides at night, rides to his bride;—
Stolen is the rapture, that will compensate him, for a few brief seconds when he holds her close;—
Closing for the capture are the men who hate him: and the highway beckons and it's "adios"
El Bandido, lives in flight, his love denied!
With moonrise, dark skies confront him;—
Well he knows of those who hunt him:
There in space, her face is before him;—
Who knows when he'll see her again.
El Bandido, rides alone, his name is known!
El Bandido, dares not sleep, his life is cheap!
Quickly without warning, by a stream they find him, as he drinks his vino
dawn is pale and thin:
It is early morning, hands are tied behind him, on his palomino,
when they bring him in!
El Bandido, bold senor
he rides no more!
El Bandido, El Bandido!

Einar Henriksen
OIL WORKERS

Far from the shores—
where the North Sea is chief,
is a gang that is working with oil.
They are working for money—
but sometimes just grief,
is the pay that they get for their toil.
Some of them make it—
but others get lost,
in the fight for the flowing black gold.
Incredible payment—
no, regular cost,
in a life where you have to be bold.

They are not heroes—
honor medal stuff,
you won't find them in who where and when.
They are individuals—
seasoned and tough,
they are what you have to call men.

George Marianos
THE BIRTH OF A KING

Every man is a failure to the best he might achieve
For deep inside his nature is a perfection he perceives
He has moments of distress, a lack, an emptiness
All his failures bring him grief, his successes lonesomeness

Where's the boy with the grin that he used to be
With spirit so high and clean and free?
When the issues of the day were decided on the spot
And his eager indiscretions were forgiven and forgot

He should respond to that compulsion from his feeling deep inside
To bend his knees in secret, for those rumblings to subside
And when out of quietness, the power of peace takes hold
A thunderous voice will speak out of wisdom ages old
"Arise My son and face Me square and be the King I said you were."

You will find that there's nothing to prevent your body healing
It was just a selfish game you played, with the truth you were concealing
Of the Sonship that's your birthright, the wisdom waiting to be granted
Of the Peace and Power and Plenty, for the seed that He has planted

I open unto You, Oh God, and invite You in
Purge from me my enemies of disease and sin
Cleanse me of my infirmities and free me of deceit
And bless me in Thy love as I worship at Your feet.

Evelyn M Wenzel
WAITING

My soul aches
My spirit weeps.
The yearning for your touch
Is so deep
It's an abyss.

Elizabeth McWilliam
IN MEMORY OF MY LITTLE DOG

I had a little dog,
And though only small was she,
She had the heart of a mighty rock
And was all you could wish her to be.
We played in the winds and the sunshine,
Beneath deep skies of blue,
And the world seemed bright and rosy then,
A paradise for two.
Now my little dog has gone
To a world no longer ours.
Leaving life, it seems
A lingering fractured bower.

And the memories of our past
Dwell with me like a dream.
The hills her soft pads once had trod
A haunting monument it seems.
Oh! That little furry creature
Though only small was she,
She was all I ever had
And all the world to me.

Kathryn F Burningham
RESCUER
The children wander from place to place.
What are they seeking in every face?
A friend perhaps? Or for something more?
Someone to show them an open door
That leads them away from despair and pain,
And helps them learn how to trust again?

They hurt, these children whom we've betrayed.
They're paying the price we should have paid
For all our selfishness, all our greed,
Our failure to give them what they need.
They've watched us argue, berate, use force,
Destroy their families with hate and divorce.

Before they quit searching, and end their fight,
Someone must bring them a shining light,
A beacon of hope, a trust to share,
A voice saying clearly, "I really care."
Someone must show them a love that's true.
For your own child, can't it be you?

Shirley A Moton
TIMES OF MY LIFE

This poem is dedicated to all of the lonely people, who have found a friend for life, in Christ.

There are times of my life, I've been all alone
With people, far and near,
Times when I have begged for love
And no one seemed to hear.

Times when just a warm hello
Would get me through the day,
Times when all the friends I knew
Just seemed to drift away.

Times when days, were so very long
And nights, so very short,
It was then, I decided, to call a friend
And give him my report.

I, found I had not been alone
In a crowd, or all-alone,
For "God" is always by my side
He had been there all along!

So if you think, you're all alone
And no one seems to care,
Never forget, you have a "God"
And He is always there.

Ann McElroy Boulden
A GREATER MASTERPIECE
I once aspired to greatness;
An artist I would be.
My pictures hung upon the wall
For all the world to see!
But, somehow, life took another turn,
Or maybe two or three.
The children came, they grew, were gone,
I thought I would be free.
But time had fled and soon I found
One grandchild, then two, then three,
An aged parent, an ailing spouse,
And my own infirmity.
So, in despair, I looked around,
What could be left for me?
My hopes, my dreams—where were they now?
And, then, it dawned on me.
I had painted Life in all its hues;
With joy and laughter and charity,
With sorrows and sadness and tragedy—
A Greater Masterpiece God gave to me!

Constance Ann Singletary
LOVE . . . !?
Just exactly what is love?
Is it confusion?
Is it pain?
Is it heartbreak, or
Is it a game?

Time away helps me to see,
That love is none of these things!

I realize now,
I'm again the old me!
Someone whom I never thought
I again could be!

Love is a two way street, I hear.
But to be miserable . . .
I think not my dear!

There are no regrets . . .
But lessons learned? you bet!!

I care, I honestly do,
But not at the expense of
Losing me, myself and I.

For if I am to return to you,
Where will I be, who will I be?

Timothy Utley
MY MOTHER'S CARPET
He was the one I looked up to most
He used to smile and he loved to joke
Sometimes he would fool around and tease
He'd twist my arm until I said please
My brother clowned around on my mother's carpet
My brother broke the crown on my mother's carpet
My brother wore a frown on my mother's carpet

As time went on he became very rowdy
His grades were a mess and his room was untidy
He was never home much and I thought he was hiding
My brother spilt his beer on my mother's carpet
My brother fell and puked on my mother's carpet
My brother had passed out on my mother's carpet

He would bring in his friends and smoke up the place
He'd put sugar in his nose and laugh in my face
After the scene he would sit down and cry
He told me he loved me, he told me good bye
I was just a small kid I didn't know why
My brother slit his wrist on my mother's carpet
My brother lay in red on my mother's carpet
My brother was dead on my mother's carpet

Edith B Fassler
IN DALLAS
The devil rode on the wind in Dallas,
And left a leader slain.
The devil rode on the wind in Dallas,
What did he hope to gain.

Tragedy pierced the heart of Dallas,
A nation shared her sorrow.
Men knelt down, in earnest prayer,
For guidance through the morrow.

Time can heal the grief and pain,
To bind the nation together again.
Are we so blind, that we cannot see
Our need of God, if we'd stand free . . .

Guns and bombs have power to kill,
When fear and greed control man's will.
To keep a country strong and free,
There's need to pray, most earnestly.

To have the faith of our pioneers
And keep freedom's banner high,
May God look down, on this troubled land,
As those prayers lift to the sky.

Isabelle Singhose
THE HELPFUL CROWS
High in the sky a moving dot I see,
Is it a plane or my eyes deceiving me?
No, as I see it getting away from the blue,
There are more than one there are now two.

Turning, twisting and coasting so free,
What joy such freedom must be.
As the two crows sail around and around,
Coming coming so much closer to the ground.

Skimming the ground looking for food to eat,
Silently they glide not a wing do they beat.
They look for the rodents so destructive to man,
The crows destroy such creatures as much as they can.

Alighting on the ground, their prey they catch,
But their caws the other crows do fetch,
After getting their fill and telling each other the news,
With a flap of their wings the crows fly into the sky so blue.

Kelly Kenrick
LOVE
When I wake up in the morning
And gaze into your eyes,
A strange feeling o'ercomes me,
And makes me realize;
That nothing lasts forever,
Nothing lasts so long,
As the knowledge of your presence,
Which helps me to go on.

When I look up in the evening
And see you sitting there,
I sense your solid presence,
And know you really care.

If I woke up in the nighttime
And saw you lying near
I would feel a sense of wonderment
That you should hold me dear.
But nothing lasts forever
Nothing lasts that long.
But it's the knowledge of your presence
Which helps me to go on.

Joseph Hill

Joseph Hill
FOR THEIR SAKE
"Marital splits are like car collisions!"
Torn apart, children are left with decisions.

For them, it's MOM or DAD!
"Either way, it's really sad."

"We must forget about ourselves."
"Put our differences on the shelves."

"For their sake, we both must merge!"
"One day our children will resurge."

"Confused and puzzled, as it may seem."
They're too young to know what it all means.

"We must not waste time, with animosity and hate!"
During their young lives, we should communicate!

"It's not important whether they choose you or me!"
It is important, that we both agree!

"So I end this poem, with them in mind!"
"I love them dearly, and these aren't just lines."

Holly Renee Eli
STREET
Out on the streets that's where I was placed
To make my own way and fight the challenges I faced.
No money, no job, no place to stay
All I could do was to hope and to pray.
Alot of things happened during the night.
There was theft, crimes and always a fight.
The screams of the night finally scared me away
so as soon as I could I found a place to stay.
I was sixteen he was twenty-five
He made me feel like I was alive.
He took me in and cared for me
But there was something I didn't see.
One night he made me sleep with him

I felt as though I was going to die
It wasn't but nine months later
that I heard the babies cry.
I had to get away and I had to get
some help
so I decided to call home one day
to hear my mother's voice
She said I love you and please come
home
and I guess I really had no other
choice.
The love and hugs of my parents
helped me to grow strong
During this time I realized
running away was wrong.

Kenneth E Rogers
ROSE OF THE VALLEY

To my lovely Joyce . . . Today, Tomorrow, Always

It may have been a dream, but then again I think not, the vividness of a memory takes me back to a time and place I visited not so long ago . . . Perhaps yesterday. I'd like to think it was yesterday . . .

. . . Swirling winds stirred the powdered snow from the mountain peaks, where trees of aspen grew and a summer sun bathed my face with warmth. And a valley appeared before me, circled with mountains and hills, and, carried by the wind the fragrance of flowers perfumed the air. In looking before me flowers of all varieties could be seen amid carpets of grass. As I walked in that valley I saw roses, roses of all colors and sizes: yellows and whites, pinks and reds, yet of all the flowers it was the roses which stood out from the rest, and I realized no artist's brush could transpose to canvas what lay before my eyes.

In reaching down it was for a rose, one of red, which caught my eye, for it was different from the others, and I cupped it in the palms of my hands, being careful so not a petal could fall, so as to take away from its total beauty.

Now-today-there is that rose and what might have been a dream is before me. Unlike all the others, as that rose, I hold that which is unique . . . your face between my hands.

Joyce Lee
A FRIEND OF MINE

This poem is dedicated to my Lord and Savior Jesus Christ, to my parents, Cora and Daniel Puckett, and to my children, Myra and Kivia Lee

A friend of mine said to me
Carry on my work, be not dismayed
Times will be hard, not trouble free
Do my deeds from day to day
Others will talk and put you down
Trying to turn you from my life
Always smile, never frown
Show them you are working for
Jesus Christ
I opened my arms and accepted his
love
Putting him first in my life
This friend of mine from above
His name is Jesus Christ
He asks nothing more than to carry
on
His work, his deeds, his holy name
He died on the cross, he now sits on
a throne
Not one for riches, glory or fame
I am his child in this life
He gave of himself in the name of
love
This friend of mine, Jesus Christ
We will meet you one day in heaven
above

James L Edwards
RIGHT ANGLES, SYMBOLS, AND PERCEPTIONS

The uncut trees push through the
concrete
Stretching to see over man's
monuments while
Telephone wires strung through
crosses;
Some of wood, some of steel, all
erected in harmony.

In the middle of this, mixed with
Haze, heat, and a setting sun,
Blows old glory in a western wind.

And there I stand looking through
the window, cooled by an oscillating
fan.
A would be poet looking for a poem.

Patricia Slowek
KEEP ME CLOSE TO THEE

*I, Patricia Slowek, dedicate "Keep Me Close To Thee" to God of the universe . . . with love * peace*

I am not perfect
And will never be,
Please, dear God
Keep me close to Thee.

My weakness shows
Anew each day,
Shelter me within, I pray.

You lead me gently through
Life's years, I make do.

The riches I have
Can be seen by eye,
From the green grass, on land
To the blue of the sky.

And when my hour comes
I'll ask humbly

"Keep me close to Thee"

Anna Rose Burnstien
TO MYRA

My little sunbeam—What a sight to
behold!
There you are prancing in front of
your mirror,
like a fairy queen—My golden hair
little nightingale!
How sweet you seem to be—All
dressed up with your pretty little
Crown and cloak of royal blue,
dancing like the royal heiress,
That you are. Oh, heaven's sweet
light that enhances you!
Such joy and beauty to behold!
Oh, God's precious gift to mother,
For with your magic wand, you
kindle the love within her heart,
forever.

Tobi Kumar
'TIL THE PLUM BLOSSOM

A lone pine tree
by the edge of the sea,
whispering tales of
forever to me . . .

Ships sailing past,
sails furled to the mast,
head for the bay
on this day, their last . . .

As the seasons will change
and bring monsoon rains,
so that no fisherman
will chance it again . . .

'Til the plum blossom
blooms in spring, awesome
as any new thing,
and the sails come . . .

Undone, when fishermen
mending their nets again,
Look to the seas for
signs of good omen . . .

Rose Marie Maysonet
HIS PRESENCE LIKE A RAY OF MORNING SUN

To Jason Gedrick

His presence like a ray of morning
sun
Provides warmth for a cold and
lonely heart.
The heart by such a perfect sight is
stun,
Memorizing his image from the start.
Silky brown hair, inviting to the
touch,
Soft brown eyes to mirror his
expressions,
Sensuous lips one could never kiss
too much,

Nose and eyebrows portray his
impressions.
His powerful frame of muscle and
height
Viewed by the heart as a pillar of
strength—
Strength that will be there in wrong
and in right,
Protection and love not measured in
length.
The heart with this memory grows
warmer.
A cold lonely heart exists no longer.

Wanda Lee Lemons
MORE OF YOU, MORE LIKE YOU

Dear Lord, no one was by your side
No one there to say they know
Who you are, they did hide,
before the cock could crow

Before all men you were brought
down
And stripped of all human pride
On your head they placed a crown
But your face, you did not hide

On the cross you died for me
You gave everything you had to give
On the cross you set me free
You gave your life so I might live
And now each day when I think
I've had my total fill
You're living water, I wish to drink
More of you, I need still
Teach me what I need to know
To become more like you each day
Help me day by day to grow
Please mold me, like you, as clay

Dianne Jenkins
THE SPIRIT

My Praise and Glory to God from whom all blessings come.

He came into my life like a soft sensuous breeze that swept all through me . . . tenderly and lovingly touching the very depths of my inner being.

He comes to me in the night while I sleep, tickling my soul with precious joy, that I awaken myself with joyous laughter. The thoughts of him throughout the course of my day brings a big-wide loving smile to my face.

Such a truly, beautiful, wondrous, luscious love I have with him. And, I will never leave him, nor he, me . . .

His loving presence keeps me safe and warm, lifts me up when I'm down, enlightens my spirit to new found awareness.

I am truly blessed to have him in my life, he is limitless. There are no boundaries in my life. I am receptive to his good.

I sit quietly still and await him, as he lovingly appears . . . like the wind blowing softly through a meadow. I feel his presence, tenderly, lovingly, softly touching the spirit within me . . .

Noelle Marie English
IN YOUR EYES

This is dedicated to my DAD, I'm finally doing it, one step at a time.

Sometimes when I look into your eyes, I can see the fire of a man.
Sometimes when I look into your eyes, I can see the smoke of a child.
I can see things in your eyes, I will never hear in words: I can see what you feel, both happy and sad; I see smoke when you're hurt, and fire when you're mad.
I can see the love that shines, and the hate that blinds; I see through your eyes, as you see through mine.

Lee Wells
MIND'S PEACEFUL STROLL

Yes my mind took a peaceful stroll
today
In a total relaxed and most happy
way
As I studied a picture hanging on a
wall
One of my most peaceful stroll I
recall

Although not a bird was in sight
Could hear them singing left and
right
Could see in distance for many miles
Which brought relaxed happy smiles

Artist surely had many hours toiled
Beauty it showed nothing man had
spoiled
May I say thank you for master piece
of yours
For letting my mind take these
peaceful tours.

Marlo Blair
A PROMISE

I could only spend a moment
When I talked to you today
But I knew that you could help me
In absolutely every way.

There are just so many problems
I'm not able to find the words

And with all the noise around us
I wasn't sure if you even heard.

First there are the children
And then can I lose weight
The car broke down again today
Help my husband not to hate.

I waited for your answer
And when it took so long
I knew you hadn't heard me
Guess the words I used were wrong.

The sun comes up each morning
The breeze blows cool at night
My prayer has just been answered
God's promise is always right!

Linda Murphy-Kelley
PERFECTION
Surrounded by Perfection,
My heart cries out for Mercy,
A kindred soul to clap
As my Imperfection curtsies.

William R Flowers
THE WIND AND LOVE AT CHRISTMAS

To Mary and Judi, my present day inspirer, and past day inspirer.

The wind echoes the words of love,
Whisper I say, Whisper,
For love should be soft as a cool spring breeze,
Yet as bold as a northern winter wind,
The strong wind that brings the pure white Christmas snow,
So blow sweet wind, blow,
Bring my love to thee,
Lest the miles of land separate the feelings of Christmas Joy.

Clarence A Lueke
WHEN I MET JESUS AT THE FOOT OF THE CROSS

This poem is dedicated to the Lord Jesus who died for me, and, my precious wife and mother

When I met Jesus at the foot of the Cross,
I knew that I was a sinner surely lost,
His Word it said, "Come unto me",
I will save your soul, "My gift is free".

I met Him there, my Guiding Light,
I realized my footsteps had been in the night,
And now I am following my wonderful Lord,
All because I heeded His Blessed Word.

I'll tell you a story of God's great love,
And why He sent down His Son from above,
He knew without Christ's Blood all were lost,
So now we see the Cross, the terrible Cost.

I am so glad God cared so much for me,
For now through Jesus I am set free,
Yes, I kneeled at the Cross without any pride,
Now I am God's son and one of Jesus' Bride.

He tells me of a home prepared for me,
That He is coming again, Oh glory be,
I will be like Him, see Him face to face,
Delivered from this flesh and all its disgrace.
"Oh, Praise His Holy Name"

Rick Tasch

Rick Tasch
MISSING HER

Dedicated to Ginger Kay. You truly brought sunshine into my life.

She used to be
full of life
in joy,
and in sorrow.
I remember
her face
in the sunlight.
Now
she is surrounded
by darkness.

Eva Allen Nourse
FROM MY WINDOW
Looking now across the field,
I see that winter's breath is nigh.
The fertile land produced her yield,
The berry vines begin to die.

The snow will come to still the land,
To coat the naked trees with gloss;
The sleeping earth, like sleeping man,
Renew her strength, and rid the dross.

After cold, the spring is nigh,
And earth begins to rise and stretch.
The trees turn green before my eye,
The robins velvet branches fetch.

Then glorious summer all too brief—
Bright golden days, or thunder roar!
Fall comes again, sweet bitter grief;
Scarlet leaves besiege my door.

My life in retrospect I see,
Through clear or cloudy window pane:
Bare, full, sweet, sad, cold, warm, bright, bleak—
Would I walk this way again?

"Yes!"

Wilma Lee Deen
WHEN I MUST LEAVE

Dedicated to: My brother, Fred O. Deen Who encouraged me to write poetry

I pray I shall not leave this world
With a dishonored name.
I hope no wrong will then be left
For which I am to blame.
However great, or old, the sin
That may be charged to me,
May God forbid that it has left
A lasting injury.
I will be glad to suffer when
My life is at its end,
But may no guilt of mine affect
A relative or friend.
May no one ever be disgraced
By something I have done,
But may my sins be hidden then
Beneath the setting sun.
Not to escape my punishment
The hour I depart,
But only that my errors will
Not hurt another heart.

Debi Thomas
OBSESSED
Always take the risk, easy to enjoy
Never comprehend the pain
behind the toy

Emotions do get mangled, love and hate combined
Destroy the loving soul and
confuse the hatred mind

Understanding is not simple, the game is too complex
Is love the answer with hate
the reflex

The risk you take is love, the price you pay is steep
The pain you feel is hate
he established your defeat

Why play the game, you cannot win
Why take the risk that leads you
in

Temptations will see you pay the price, your debt is much too high
No winners will ever see the end
most of them choose to die

Hiromu Nakamura
THE SANDS OF TIME
The sands of time gently blow across our paths.
We take a fleeting moment to gather what we can.
The quiet voice, the reassuring hand, the slow gait, the gentle push.
Watch the cracks; there goes a car; let the man go by; don't run off the walk.
Here we are! A crunch of the bar, a drink from the can.
Kicking of feet, dangling of arms; crunching, snorting, chortling.

The sands of time gently blow across our paths.
Draw this here. Make this red. This is green, and that is brown.
Fold it here and crease it here, and fasten it there, and you make a clown.
Cut this round, and paste this there, and turn it around, and you make a bear.
Look at that. See how nice? You can do it. Just give it a try!

The sands of time gently blow across our paths.
The leaves are rustling, the birds are chirping.
The bench is hard, but the sun feels good.
Time now to go back; trudging, fudging, taking a short cut home.
Refreshed and uplifted for another day.

The sands of time gently blow across our paths.
Grandma,
Grandpa,
Child,
Adult.
Friendship, gladness, comfort, and trust.

Mark G Zawada
WALKING . . .
Tenderly I have the following words to say,
Let me begin if I may.

Walk with me through the ginko leaves,
Scanning colors of the autumn trees.

I'll hold your hand in mine with a gentle grasp,
I finding you was a lucky task.

Across the hard ground we will pace,
Carefully leaving no footprints to trace.

Now and then we will write to each other,
With your words I find no bother.

So I hope you will walk with me by my side,
Together we will see the sunset and sunrise.

Linda Kelm
CRY LITTLE CHILD

To my husband Ed, who believes in me no matter what.

Cry little child
Cry out the pain
They slap, and pinch
Yell, and scream
A child of abuse
Hurts all the time
Hoping for love,
Or someone who cares
Hoping tomorrow won't
Bring more pain
Cry little child
Tomorrow is here, life for you
Is over, there will be no more tears

J N Hervey
THE CHAIN
three links of well-worn, rusted chain
that surely shall bear no load again
found in Norway on a crumbling stone wall
where once stood a boathouse;
straight, strong, and tall
a seaman of old stored his boat, nets, and gear
that served him so well for year after year
how long's the chain, including these pieces
how long's the time when usefulness ceases
when did they last pull or carry or hold
when first did they know the Norwegian cold
where are they made; these circles of steel
where is the seaman, his net, and his keel
why are there three links and not two or four
why are we not told of this link-chain lore
So many questions; too many to ask
for rust and time forms a blinding mask

C K Wilson
THE EYES HAVE IT
My anger is a hungry kinda thing,
That echoes in my eyes and makes my ears ring.
The tears I've cried, a real toad strangler,
Warns me of the approaching danger.
Some say that it's PMS,
Maybe I suffer from distress,
From dealing with persistent jerks,
I'm toeing the line, almost berserk.
The anger rolls out, and holds no bar,
With a single glance, I can melt the paint off the bumper of a car.
With my hands on my hips, and a look of disdain,
Why, I can even frost a steamy window pane.

So if you see me coming, my eyes all a blazin',
Scorching everything I see into sundried raisins,
Hunker down fast, maybe I'll pass,
And ignite instead a pile of trash.
I've searched in vain to find a food,
To feed this awful hungry mood.
But to no avail can I stem the cause,
I count the days until menopause.

Connie Sue Fagg

WE'LL MEET AGAIN

This poem is dedicated to my mother Patricia L McCullough

I can't explain the loss I feel,
Or the open wound that will not heal.
You were the link on our chain that held us together,
And when something went wrong, you made it all better.
I remember the day that you went away,
The pain was so great I can feel it today.
I was angry with you and didn't know why,
You didn't have the chance to say good-by.
There were so many things I wanted to say,
My heart is torn every which way.
Sometimes late at night I lay and pray,
For all this pain to go away.
I asked myself why did you go,
When you had to know I needed you so.
As time goes by I realize,
That God has a plan for you to rise.
For in that grave is just a shell,
You're not there you're alive and well.
I often heard your prayers aloud,
You prayed for our Lord to come in the cloud.
I remember you gazing toward the east,
With longing you prayed an hour at least.
I realize now he heard your prayers,
He took all your sickness, he really cares.
No matter how much you loved us, now I know,
To be with our savior you wanted to go.
Tho the pain of losing you is still so great,
I have the comfort of knowing, we'll meet again at heaven's gate.

Tracy Barnes

DO YOU KNOW . . .

To my family, who encouraged me to go for whatever I want.

Do you know
What school this is?
I can tell you or show you,
It is this:

Homework and reading.
It's not a lot of kicks.
When grown you'll be needing
Grades K through six.

As to my knowledge,
You have nothing to fear.
It's not high school or college,
It's Elementary, my dear!

Ms Mila Santee

THE SECRET

Consummate genius
Lies dormant in all of us,
Waiting for self-awareness
To self-bestow
Just as mediocrity
Is likewise self-inflicted,
Holding us down to the level
We alone have chosen

The key is Desire
Released into eternal
All-consuming Energy
Of the Universe

Essentials of greatness
Are never written in books,
Nor can they be found
In prestigious schools

No, Greatness is born
In the inner consciousness
Of those who search endlessly
For Creative Perfection

And it is understandable
To that small audience only

Nancy Dye Padias

DANCING WITH KINGS

She sat dangling her legs off the end of the pier.
Her mind drifted out to sea with the tide,
Where she danced with Kings who bowed low for her favor
And spoke of the beauty she possessed inside.

Little children with clean faces gathered round her,
Bright yellow flowers they put at her feet.
She twirled in a gown made of sunlight
And the song of the world was sweet.

Then her mind drifted back from the ocean.
She overheard fish stories from dreamers, not liars.
People smiled as she walked by in jeans and a sweatshirt,
For her Kings were but dreams, not desires.

Tomorrow she would go on a diet,
Give her children a morning hug.
She would pack a lunch for her husband,
Tuck in a love note,
Oh yes,
And wash the bathroom rug.

Alice R Harris

FIREFLIES

The fireflies flit to and fro,
all in the evenings afterglow.
They flit among the grass and trees, they're prettier than birds or bees. They blink and they glitter, a sight to behold, they light up the night, they shine like pure gold. The children just love them, they catch them in jars, they blink on and off, just like the stars. We sit on the porch when the night becomes dim, they flit back and forth, as if on a whim.
Their beauty will never again be seen, so protect them dear children, and watch as they gleam. Thank God for this treasure, they bring us such joy, they dance and they twinkle, they flit and they fly, and return to God's heaven up in the sky.

Molly Clark

THE WAY THE WORLD SHOULD SEE THINGS

For my family who inspire me to reach to the same heights they have.

Everyday
I see a new door
a new dream
Every
breath of life I take
. . . makes me want more
. . . so much to do
. . . so much to see
In every
star shines a different tale
of lifes riches
I want to know each one and call it my own
Every
quiet sunset
leaves me peaceful
knowing tomorrow is always there
And every
tomorrow can be so beautiful
knowing there's so much to live for—

S R Christenson

MY DARK ROOM

This poem is dedicated to my best friends. Connie Curttright who gave me the inspiration to start writing and Lynette Anderson who gives me the support to continue.

The key to my heart has locked the door.

The floor is wet from fallen tears.

Though the sun is shining outside,
the room is filled with darkness.

Alone I stand in this room
careful not to slip from the tears.

If I concentrate on nothing but the darkness
I will be able to stand, I will not fall.

Lisa S Lalli

EVEN WHITE WALLS

Even white walls
turn yellow-gray,
with age.

Slowly, invisibly—
looking still white,
until moved picture
reveals . . .

People age, much
the same way,
only measure their decay
against old photographs.

Rose C Alfano

SPRING IS IN THE AIR

To my dear children Linda, Dennis, Jennifer and Stephanie.

The swallows are back, a sure sign of spring
Let's open the windows, for the sun to come in
The crocus are budding grass getting green
Everyone's hopping the air fresh and clean
Children are playing outdoors once again
Mother's content, her nerves on the mend
The sound of birds chirping while they feather their nest
People are happy and feeling their best
Trees have blossomed into giant umbrellas
Such colorful flowers all bright reds and yella's
A gentle breeze blows across the water so blue
Lovers whisper softly, I love you I do
Yes love is in bloom hearts burst into song
Oh beautiful spring' what took you so long.

Judy Hansen-De Nicola

I WONDER

This poem is dedicated to my wonderful husband Joe. You are my ray of sunshine.

I wonder, as I walk amongst nature,
seeking for what surely must be in vain.
Deep in the forest,
where peace and tranquility reign.

I wonder, as I am surrounded
by wooden giants complete.
As the mist drifts in and curls slowly about my feet.

I wonder, as my disquiet soul
is filled by the beauty that I have found.
By a calm, still pool
I lower myself to the ground.

I wonder, as I hear the birds song
and watch as a delicate fawn stops to drink.
My confused and shadowy mind finally
comprehends the link.

I wonder, at everything that I touch, hear,
smell and see . . .
For now I know, all of this beauty abound,
is an intricate, woven part . . . of me.

I know.

Katherine Ann Wolf

NEW FALLEN SNOW

Dedicated to my niece, Katherine Lauren; that her innocence and purity may develop into purity and truth.

Hexagonally unique, pure and clean,
Listlessly wafting, so cool and serene,
Unaware of impending adventures below,
Innocently falling with the rest of the snow.

Shielded from the reality of an actual fall,
Happily hidden behind her family "cloud" wall,
She knew not the woes she soon would acquire
That come with actions and knowledge of desire.

But the snowflake fell upon a well trodden ground
Where many young snowflakes were formerly found.
She learned to love the lust of life;
Her wants knew no limits; they caused her no strifes.

She looked at the "immediate,"
not the "to-come,"

She figured the others had also
succumbed.
Smarter than the rest, she knew
she'd survive.
Her passionate needs seemed to
all come alive.

But with passion comes fire, as
experience shows;
And naivety to fire brought the
melting of snows . . .
As she withered to water and dried
with the sun,
She learned her last lesson in the
heat of her fun.

Nancy A Ruth

Nancy A Ruth
DADDY'S SONG

In loving memory of Daddy Harold Ruth, Jr. 04-16-25—03-18-81

Life is filled with music
strumming the measures of time;
streamming jagged verse
as well as perfect rhyme.

The song I sing is of a man
whose gift to life was love,
whose hand of compassion
permeated a little girl
once forgotten and all alone;
a man who became her father—
who chose her as his own.

Life is filled with music,
you can hear it
everywhere it sings;
as the memory of Daddy's song
and the joy to me it brings.

Thank you Daddy
for being the melody
of my life.

Marlene Katai
MADMEN WALK THE PLANET EARTH
Seeking souls, for their hellgames,
making good men go insane.
Life is full of wondrous thrills.
All they think of is what kills.
Raging spirits in the night,
condemning those who will not fight.
Evil is a massive brain,
making good men go insane.

Madmen walk the planet earth.

Tracing pictures of the past,
judgement day comes none too fast.
For all those people crying out,
shadows of fear without a doubt.
Desperate pleas, cry from their eyes,
an evil voice beckons, so thinly
disguised.

Mass confusion, all around.
Crass intrusions abound.
Madness creeping slowly through.
Until darkness settles.
Misconstrued are we that sit and
watch,
as time crumbles, interiors crack,
blind souls stumble,
through follies of time, or made up in
the mind.

Madmen walk the planet earth.

Rolling tides of time, dying embers
grace.
This world can be such a lonely
place.
Solitary dreamer, eludes the soul,
but has not forgotten, lifes tempestuous toll.

A madman walks the planet earth.

Follow the moon and stars by night.
Emotions fade, and glow as they
might.
Created images in the mandrel of the
mind,
trying to understand what he cannot
find.
Forsaken territories gleaming with
hell.
Cast out of lifes elusive wishing well.
Soldier of time, this is fates last
glance.
Take your bow, and then take your
chance.
Forsaken past, we live in tomorrow,
trying to conceal, yesterdays sorrow.
An entities dust crumbles in the
wind,
but the soul lives on to begin again.

A free man walks the planet earth.

Diane L Youngblood
A TRIBUTE TO FAITH <u>A NEW HORIZON</u>
On Becoming . . .
Pain will express itself as Joy
And so
The mystery of the Paradox
Will find its solution
In Oneness
And it's coming.

To that ultimate climax
Do I bid a long overdue welcome
And also to Freedom's Light.
The Dream is
The everlasting warmth
And unconditional acceptance
Which I will call Home.

Home is the Past where I have
always been.
It is the Present to which I cling.
And most of all it is
The Future place
Where Love will
Live out her days
In Rapture.

Sheila Cronin Bode
AFTER THE ARGUMENT
The family sits at the dinner table
Silently eating
Tasteless food
And my sister cries.

James J Brinkman
THIS OLD CAT

To Diane Bell, who loves her cats

Looking inward: burn billions
Of stars called atoms.
Looking skyward: burns billions
Of atoms called stars.

What being churns above
Whose atoms burn as stars?
What worlds exist within
Blazing with such rage?

Looking inward: burns life
On my electrons: tiny humans,
Turning, churning, burning:
Greedy and war-bent.

But, looking skyward again,
I thank whatever being it is
Whose atoms burn as stars,
For creating this old cat,
Who, despite nature's endless
turmoil,
Folds her paws and purrs,
And is content.

Deirdre Savino
ALZHEIMERS

I would like to dedicate this poem to my father who gave me the light and inspiration in my life

What is a memory?
Is it something you've done?
or something you dreamed?
Why has God taken away?
A light which beamed
In the thoughts and minds of all
human beings.
Why is the mind left in a state of
confusion?
And life becomes a complete
delusion?
This dreaded disease has now taken
the place of life's wonderful illusions
I hope in the near future they find a
way, for all who suffer,
To remember all that life had to
offer.

Robert P Blanchard
THE QUEST

Dedicated to my dear love, Bernice.

Two hearts, in absence's yearning,
reach out to span the void,
They touch and 'twine both seeking
that love's desire be cloyed.

A wondrous flash of luster,
from out the ebon skies,
Lights up the dark in splendor,
reflecting in their eyes.

Soft words do fill the memory,
sweet music soothes the breast,
The flame of passion makes its plea
to warm the winsome quest.

He feels her arms enfolding,
the softness of her kiss,
The fire within her burning,
consumes him with its bliss.

Together in that space inside,
they search for nothing more,
For love has come and opened wide
the tabernacle door.

Sandy Toth
UNTITLED
The rose as pure as innocence
Each petal silky to the touch
No rose is alike in the whole world

Like the love lost.

Each person in the world
Loves someone else,

Even though it feels the same,
It's not.

People love the innocence
As in a rose.
So that's why I say
Every
Rose
Has
Its
Thorns.

Sherie Niebauer
TWO OF A KIND
Two spirits floating aimlessly
Through time and space
Chancing brief encounters

Much has been shared with them
Opening new doors to new
beginnings
Having courage to walk inside
Their warmth is magnified
Creating a brilliant light
Radiating for all to see

The spirits appear as one
Conscious of each other
Sharing the path together

Aware of their individuality
The spirit's free to soar
Exploring the universe

Finding comfort with the other
Happiness beams from within
Gaining knowledge along the way

Susan Shapiro
A TRUE ASPIRATION!

To my father Edwin Shapiro you will forever remain within my thoughts, heart, and soul.

What is it that I want?
I want to look upon my horizon
I want to view my future
I want to believe there will be
magical moments within my life.
With all this and much more my sun
will be forever rising.
I sit and wait, thoughts ponder within
my head.
Only I can make the magic occur.
Only I can deem it to be true.
Then what is stopping me?
The worries in my head and the pain
in my heart, now shall be released
and my soul shall be free.
Now I am content with myself.
The view of my horizon and the light
of the tunnel are now both mine.

Stella Manaker
FLYING
Up above a cloudy sky,
A scene of blue serenity.
Soaring above banks of snowy
clouds
A world of storm and strife is erased

A break in the cloud formation
Shows mountains, fields and
communities.

Could every one experience
The beauty of the world from above,
They would know—God's in His
Heaven
Which we could share below.

Margaret E Ott
A CONVERSATION
"They say she's dying," she
whispered to me,
As an old friend walked past us,
listlessly.

"You know someone who isn't?" I
asked incredulously;
Wasn't man made for Eternity?—
And death for sin was penalty
Which Eve and Adam earned for you
and me!

But God, the Father of the Universe
Repented Himself of such a curse,
And planned a whole new heaven
and earth:
So Jesus of Nazareth was given
birth.

For fear of death will not cease.
But belief in Jesus gives eternal
peace.
And life on this earth is just a
lease—
Until, in time, we can handle grief.

So why do we quibble about the
years?
And fill them up with worry and
tears?
What is the use of one more year
If every day is filled with fear?"

Theresa A Frăsca
FOURTH OF JULY 1976

Dedicated to my savior Jesus Christ

Fourth of July, Fourth of July
The Bicentennial has come by,

Hang the flag, make merry song
The day won't last for very long,

Cook-outs, parades and fireworks too
Things to remember, me and you.

Barb Luick
FOR HELEN

This poem is dedicated to Helen, my friend and my 'precious jewel.'"

If I could give you the rainbow
with all its colored hue
I would wrap its arms around you
to comfort when you are blue.

If I could move a mountain when
its weight is upon your heart
I would replace it with a fountain
to shower each burdened part.

If I could wipe away your tears
and gently remove their stain
I would polish them with my love
never allowing them to come again.

If I could take your hand and walk
together as a friend
I would lay down my life for you and
protect you till the end.

If I could open the pages of my
heart—I would have you read them
from the very start—to understand all
that is true, which is,
"Dear Helen, I truly love you!"

Martin James Sutcliffe
SONG TO AN UNKNOWN LOVER

When breezes bolt and horses neigh
And shutters clap near close of day;
When water's spotched upon the
panes
And round about spin weather vanes,

And all about my rustic lair
Are blasts of sullen wintry air,
And Phoebus threatens ne'er to shine,
I hope that you will then be mine.

Deborah Ann Bell
SAD EYES

Dedicated to Veterans of war

Here I sit and wonder why.
I wish that I would die.
See the bird fly by and by.
Way up in the sky, so high.
Here I sit thinking,
But no words will ever come.
Thoughts go rushing by.
Mine eyes have seen beauty.
My eyes have seen duty.
I look into your eyes,
You turn them all away.
Or if by chance I get a glimpse.
Sad eyes is what I see.
If once someone would smile at me,
And not just turn away.
It would make me feel, just one time,
That I did not fight in vain.
And ll the pain I felt that day,
Would go just like the rain.
I fought for you. you too, my sad
eyes.

Jenn Felts
MIDNIGHT PASSING

Misty moonlight hovers around the
walls,
Where a midnight shadow begins to
crawl.
A vision—a thought—links to form a
line,
And I writhe in my bed just to listen
to time.
With the blue twilight haze the walls
have oozed to a blur,
And inside my head, the voices still
stir.
The reality of the nighttime—filled
with subconscious dreams,
A reality only broken by the silence
of my screams.
My mind explores the darkness once
more before the time is gone,
As the Moon raps softly at Nature's
door to awake the dreaded Dawn.

Roberta Nations
GROW OLD WITH ME

Dedicated to Ted the love of my life

Grow old with me, endure lifes
Joys and pain.
We can make memories together
To ease any strain.
We start out brand new
Together.
Grow old with me, and we can
Fare any weather.
We start out like spring
Blooming and brand new.
We grow into summer all warm
And cozy just us two.
We winter the years with Patience
And care.
The fall of our years roll around
With lots of love and a little ware.
We have stormy times, we have
Sunshine.
With both we grow closer and
Stronger together.
Grow old with me and seasoned
Together

(Mama) Mary Breshears
HOLD MY HAND, SON

Your eyes so blue, and so filled with
tears,
You tried so awful hard in your
younger years,
I know to get your life together, in
your own lonely way
Son I knew you loved your wife and
sons day after day.
And when you bared your soul to me,
well then son I knew,
That you needed so much love and
help, as all of us always do.
To keep your family together, and not
to live apart.
And yes I've known and shared the
pain that's now within your heart.
Son, did you know I nearly died the
day you were born?, And I know I'm
dying now
But I wanted you to know that we'll
all be together again, someway,
somehow.
And I can tell you that I love you so
much, in my own mother's way,
That we'll all be together again, on a
beautiful and glorious day.
So son, please don't forget to reach
out for me, and I'll come and take
your hand,
And then we'll walk side by side,
together to a beautiful and wonderful
land.

Cheri Bell Stoops
A LITTLE BIT OF WINTER

A little bit of chill,
A few snow flakes falling . . .
Fluffy white clouds over the hill,
And snow birds begin calling.

The wind picks up its pace,
Trees begin to sway . . .
Cold soon covers your face,
And you forget the start of day.

By afternoon, a full blown gale,
People indoors with windows
shut . . .
Keeping warm and snug without fail,
Comfortable in house or hut,

By the fireside, with its warm glow,
Hot chocolate with marshmallow
atop . . .
Saying to one's self, let the winds
blow,
Smell the popcorn begin to pop.

The snow falls faster,
Winds blow harder . . .
Dark clouds become vaster,
And food aplenty in the larder.

Now, darkness settles down,
Talk becomes quiet and
subdued . . .
Lights go on in windows all around,
A little bit of winter reviewed.

Now, darkness settles down,
Talk becomes quiet and
subdued . . .
Lights go on in windows all around,
A little bit of winter reviewed.

Pierre A LeBlanc III

Pierre A LeBlanc III
I LOVE YOU

To these two beautiful poets in my life for their encouragement and inspiration. (Eddie-Lou Cole and Kitty Mouton)

Love is what you and I do!
I shall always beckon you!

When I turn my back on you—
I am saying that I love you!

There is no reason for a fuss by you!
Discover God loves us—me and you!
Touch me, and I'll face you!
Count the ways I love you!
HE blesses everything we do!
Carry on—My Dear—without much
ado!

Each breath spent renews itself—
As we discover—the pleasure of—
our stealth!

All is My Affection for you—
And over exchange of I LOVE YOU!

Lisa L Scarnici
REALITY

I have rainbows in my eyes.
Though the steely gray rain appears,
It only serves to contrast the
brightness
And give definition to the whirling
colors.

Many cannot see this arc of light.
They let rain and fog cloud their
view.
And so they live forever in the
gloom,
Cold and blindness, wet with despair.

And those in the darkness
desperately claim
That I am blind, for I do not see the
rain
And cannot feel the wetness that
surrounds me,
Nor the clouds of doubt in my own
sight.

Poor rain-soaked souls!
For what they will never understand,
Is that what we choose to see
Become our own reality.

Caroline M Davies
MEDICARE BIRTHDAY

"Senior Citizens" they say
Could that be me?

The years have gone by
So fast you see.

There have been bad ones
and good ones

But I'm still alive and I am
Glad I reached sixty-five.

There it is in black and white
And I must accept my plight.

I feel healthy and young at heart
In fact this is the best Birthday
yet!

I'm sure there will be many more
But for now

I thank my blessings
I passed sixty-four.

Rebecca Anna Longstreet
THERE MAY BE

There may be a heaven or a Hell,
I look outside and all is well.
The grass so green, the sky so blue,
I think life's beautiful, don't you?

There may be wars ahead I fear,
to take our loved ones from us so
dear.
I pray for peace and love for us all,
I watch a flower grow and a baby in
such awe.

There may be taxes and bills galore,
and maybe a bank account near full.
But try and remember when you
were young,
how happy and wonderful the world
has become.

There may be an enemy shaking our
hand,
a faraway trip to a foreign land.
We are waiting for peace, now it's
here,

all we have to do is open our eyes
and our ears.

Listen with your heart and not your head,
once in the ground we are cold and dead.
Take heed and let the sunshine in,
as there may be a future for all in the end.

Nina M Johnson
BEGINNING AGAIN

Ray P. Johnson who passed away June 25, 1982. Who served in the military for thirty years. And our seven children: Ray P. Johnson Jr, Rita Bird, Robert Wayne, Dennis, Denise Beavers, Don, Cindy VanTuin.

So what can I say, it's the end of another day.
The day that has just passed can never be lived again.
The tomorrows are all brand new,
And how it turns out will depend on you.
If you start each day with new hope,
Think of all the disappointments as a dirty joke. Plan your days with a smile.
Always walk the second mile.
Never look back where you have been.
Think of each day as beginning again.

Ronald M Frank
THE ROCKY ROAD
My life is like a falling rock
Pieces crumbling off like time on the clock
On the outside the rock, is tuff,
But on the inside it's very ruff;
The rock is alone, there's none around

He hopes he's joined before he hits the ground!
As time goes on day by day
This lonely rock must find another way;
Cause the way it's going the end draws near
Filling the inside with a lot of fear!
The rock knows he must shed his stone,
Or he'll end up being alone.

Lawrence Rothman
PRELUDE TO THE SEA
The ocean's rough and choppy, the sky is black with night,
The breakers ripple steadily against the sands of white;
'Tis peaceful now, 'tis tranquil, like an opera written well,
By Nature, yes the same Author of Heaven and of Hell.

That night I saw a cruise ship lighting up the sea,
Sailing over waters, deep as deep could be;
Wishing I were on that boat,
yearning to be free,
Yet now I have to turn back to my poetry.

The waves roll together in gentle harmony,
Slashing on the jetties as soft as they could be;
There must be Chopin out there, as
the waves reach rhythmic heights,
And this opera is continuous for many, many nights.

Jim Badger
BAG LADY
Now don't get me wrong!
I don't mean it in a negative way.
It's just that out of the trash can of circumstance and misfortune
You found a heart.
Granted
It was pretty bruised and broken
Granted
It didn't show a lot of promise.
But you patched it up,
Dusted it off
And made it right again.
I guess you saw something
In that old heart.
Something that
The person who threw it out
Missed somehow.
Anyway I'm grateful
That you took the time.
'Cause
That ol' heart was mine.

Brenda K Henderson
TIME AND SELF-PRESERVATION
Time is the only thing that will heal
The pain and emptiness that I feel
Since my world has blown apart
And a new life I must start.
I know what's happened is for the best
But knowing it and accepting it will be a test
Of my faith which comes from above
And my own interpretation of love.
I hope that I am able to keep the Golden Rule
Even when others are being so cruel.
I'll try not to let words spoken
Haunt a spirit already broken.
It's going to be hard, that I can see
Now that I have sole responsibility
Of raising three children on my own
In a place that is totally unknown.
But self-preservation is a natural trait
That will come in handy while I wait
For time to pass and do its deed—
And on my own—I WILL SUCCEED!!!

Roxanne Stalker
PLEOMORPHISM
Where was the time that I had spent,
I know it hadn't shown,
sensation of the treatment worked,
the fear I was alone.

The serpents on the walls were there,
but no one could be found,
snakes curled up around my legs,
stuck in a room that's round.

All of these bizarre things,
I knew there would be more,
as I myself turned to a snake,
a slithering on the floor.
It can't be my imagination
these things that occur to me,
unless I'm going crazy,
it's just the lsd.

Helen Harris
SPRING BIRDS

In memory of my Mother and Dad, Clarence E. Cox and Alice Cox Sutphin.

With gloomy days of winter gone
and Spring now on the way,
As birds begin their sweet, sweet song
we seem to hear them say,
It's been a long hard winter and the
sun has been hid from view
With each new day we will sing
a song of Spring for you.
So head out to the mountains, the plain
and to the sea,
For Summer won't be far behind,
great days for you and me.
Then when Summer's over and
Fall returns again
Remember, it's all in God's plan
So NEW Spring birds will sing.

Diane M Christman
LETTING GO
Oh Lord, I know his time here on earth is slowly drawing to a close.
He was given life to procreate life,
therefore he will always live on.

It is so hard to let go when you're holding on so tight.
You, Lord, are reaching for him,
and he is loosening his grip,
preparing to let go totally
to grasp You fully.

Oh Lord, what joy, what Love must flow, when You bring one of Your children home.
A time of rejoicing.

In our selfishness we beg, bargain,
and plead for just a little more time.
But we fail to realize that You are time itself, for you encompass all things.

Release us, I pray,
of this human bondage of inequities.
Draw us close to Your bosom Lord,
that we may tap the Source of life.

Clarke Newman
YOUNG HEART
Young heart, at your kingdom's gate,
Wrapped in love from womb to world,
At dawn, your day awaits.
Of clear mind and untouched heart,
A pristine soul of slate
To etch with hope and with expectation.

God's brave little one, who rests
in trusting peace.
Though fear is yet unknown,
you are fearful,
For your sentinels are still strangers, and
You are small and weak, and of unscarred faith.

What mysteries do you hold,
young heart?
But for your tears and your smiles,
Your thoughts remain a secret, and
Time has not yet told your tale.

Young heart, at your kingdom's gate,
Begin a journey from world to tomb, and
Rush not towards tomorrow!
You stand before the dawn, and
You do not see the end of day,
You see only the day itself.

Scotty Lee Cook
MISS HEROIN

To a wonderful and loving friend and companion . . . Toni Nijssen.

So, Little Man, you've grown tired of grass, cocaine, L.S.D., speed and hash.
And someone pretending to be a true friend has said, "I'll introduce you to Miss Heroin!"

Well, friend, before you start fooling with me, just let me inform you of how it will be.
I'll entice you, seduce you and make you my slave . . . I've sent men much stronger than you to their grave!

You think you could never become a disgrace, and end up addicted to poppyseed waste.
You start inhaling me one afternoon, then into your arms you'll take me real soon!

You'll steal from your Mother, though, just for a buck. You'll turn into something so vile and corrupt!
The vomit, the cramps, tied in a knot, and your jangling nerves scream for just one more shot!

You'll need lots of money . . . have you not been told? I'm much more expensive than silver or gold!
You'll mug and you'll steal for my narcotic charms, and feel so content when I'm in your arms.

There'll come a day when you promise to leave me alone, if you think you've got the mystical knack.
Then, Sweetie, just try getting me off your back!!

And when you have returned as I had foretold, (I knew you would give me your body and soul),
You'll give me your morals, money, conscience, your heart, and you will be mine . . .
"UNTIL DEATH DO US PART!"

M T Camelwort
SAIL OR

To my mother, Molly without whose patience, love and humor I might never have occurred

I'm a sailor on the blue sea of Crete
I'm a burst of prism's light,
a sparkling drop of sky,
Oh she's shown me
Oh she knows me
we could've sailed together
on that sharp blue
naked men on the masthead
brown men on the shore
waving, chattering, talking me in
white teeth in sequence,
shining OH
I hope you haven't passed my
slip slow sliding
and there we are, scrambling
tumbling, putting her in for the night
coiling rope
Oh she's shown me
Oh she knows me
we could've sailed together
on that shocking blue.

Daniel J Ferguson
VISIONS OF ME

Dedicated to those whose visions of me remained bright—even in my darkest hour . . . I LOVE YOU!

sometimes i am
wind
blowing freely in the midst of
the sun
sometimes i am
raindrops
falling softly on the virgin grass
sometimes i am
fire
smoldering in the piles of refuse

sometimes i am
a young boy
running and laughing in my
free world
sometimes i am
an old man
breathing my last breath
sometimes i am
all of these things
at once

Andrea R Freed
MY GRANDMOTHER, MY FRIEND

This poem is dedicated to my Grandmother (Mimi) for all the wonderful life long memories we share.

You're always here to help me out,
You're here for me without a
doubt . . .

When I'm feeling down, you know
what to do,
Days when you're sad, I'm here for
you too . . .

A lot of days can often seem rough,
But I think of you and I hang
tough . . .

You're special to me in every way,
I think of you often with each
passing day . . .

Some people say I'm a lot like you,
So what is a favorite granddaughter
to do . . .

I'll bet other granddaughters are full
of envy,
Seeing a grandmother and granddaughter as close as can
be . . .

I want you to know how much I love
you,
I'm not just saying this, I really
do . . .

There's not much else that I can say,
I'll love you tomorrow, but much
more today . . .

There's no one like you, no one, no
other
To me you're just the "GREATEST
GRANDMOTHER" . . .

I wrote this just for you "MY
FRIEND",
Now this poem must come to an end.

Carole E Bassett
I AM ONLY JUST BEGINNING TO SEE

To my friend Sarah—who has helped me feel alive again.

I am only just beginning to see
that I have missed out on
a big part of life—

When was I ever able to just be
Me?
Mother says,
"Don't feel that way.
Nice girls don't get angry!"

"Don't dress like that—
You look like a whore."

"Shut up. I don't want
to hear that now."

"If only you would help out more."

I feel like a piece of cheese
that has been stretched too thin.

Most of the time I don't "feel"
at all—

Because if I did

I'd scream
and cry
and swear
and throw things.

You wouldn't know me—
You wouldn't love me—or even like
me.

James Arthur Kennedy

James Arthur Kennedy
MAKING THE ROUNDS

To all those seekers learning to exercise the power of choice

Do we learn the ways of love
By being there from the start,
Walking 'neath the skies above
And listening with our hearts?

Or do we learn the ways of love
As a potter the clay,

Who with loving hand and artful eye
Make it hold the day?
Our path is walked from turn to turn,
Our lives a season spent.
As a soul, a circle to learn . . .
Morning came . . . morning went.

C H Chia
THE SQUABBLE
Our squabble the previous night nags
my mind,
You deemed I'd been unfair, selfish,
unkind.
Had I become a possessive person?
Had I felt jealous for no real reason?
You've given me a love so deep and
true,
How can I ever want to distress you?

My heart broke when I saw you cry
that night.
Rage and jealousy had obscured my
sight,
I had attacked you from the very
start,
I was obnoxious, smug—I wasn't
smart!
I used my words like a sharpened
dagger
To hurt you, as if you didn't matter;
I shredded your heart like a tattered
leaf,
In exchange for your love I brought
you grief.

Can you find it in your heart to
forgive
One who's so cruel and insensitive?
D'you believe me when I say it's no
lie,
I'll cherish you until the day I die!

Marc Alan Provencal
TO MY WIFE AND SON

I dedicate this poem to my son, Christopher with all the love a father can give to his son. I'm very sorry. I love you, your Daddy.

As I sit and wonder where you are,
I can never hold back these tears of
mine.
Pain and guilt is all I feel,
For I turned my back on what was
real.

I thought I could seek a better life,
And turned away from the family I
had.
I look back now on the years that
passed,
And realize my life with you wasn't
so bad.

I miss you and your mother with all
my heart,
It's because of me, we're all apart.
Instead I was stubborn and stupid
you see,
Because the pain I inflicted came
back to me.

You've adjusted so well,
And kept smiling in stride.
But me, I stumbled,
Fell down, and in a way . . . I died.

I miss you both so very much,
Your smile, your face, and your
gentle touch.
I miss my family and our little home,
So please forgive me my son . . .
Your Daddy was wrong!!

Mary Beth Begnaud
MOTHER

For you MOM, because I Love You So Much! ! !

Ask me what a MOTHER is, and I
sit in deep abright
To think of all the things she
does—in darkness
or in light.

For all the things we have received,
there was a struggle and some
pain.
'Cause life for her was always
less sunshine and more rain.

She is the greatest of them all
in Mother and in Friend.
She's always there if you should fall
and listens if you're near end.

She cheers you up when you are
down
and makes it all worthwhile;
To stand up and face tomorrow
and go that extra mile.

Life dealt her a lousy hand,
but she evened out the score.
She started out with zero
and ended up with QUEENS and
fours.

Bill Godfrey
CHERRY VALLEY

To the vision that calls us on

Dismal abysmal business this
Stench of sizzling Jews
Far better the crunch of frozen blood
and steaming steal
The line of ashen faces past his
window
The girl in the brown coat
How he wished he had jumped off
the street car that day in Munchen
long ago and run back and asked her
name
Korporal bitte das freulein druben
bring sie hier mach es schnell
Her silken hair
The long slender fingers
The sorrow in her eyes
Could it be
Your papers please

This story could end with the iron
doors closed behind them huddled
together in the dark
Or
We could have them escape
somehow
And live
To this day
At the upper end of Cherry Valley
below Senora
They have just learned their grandson
has decided to become a fighter pilot
in the navy
They are very pleased for him

Beverly M Livernoche
WE ARE ALL "HIS" WE BELONG

my special love, dearest Frank, for our quality time together in marriage.

The trees sway in the breeze,
bowing to the wishes of the wind,
swirling circles happily within.
The birds perch aloft as the trees
sway, chirping with delight, oh so
soft.
Through my window I can see the
simple almost forgotten glee of God's
creatures here for you and here for
me.
Nourish them, treat them kindly,
hear their thank you song, for they
truly do belong.
Look upward to the brightly lit sky,
the stars that shine are yours and
mine.
The daytime sun, the moon at night,
oh what a lustrous and beautiful
sight; lest we not forget where it all
began, part of that creation that led to
man.
Thank you God for this chance to
live, to love, honor and to forgive.
Bless our nation for we are strong,
let others fear us when they are
wrong; for we are God's creation and
we belong.

Sanora M Mincemoyer
DO YOU REMEMBER

For Mom

Do you remember the golden fields of wheat
The wind that played among the heavy stands
How we would walk among the rows
Young plants beneath our feet?

Do you remember the kitchen, aroma of baking bread
The smells of hot coffee and biscuits, hung heavy in the air
We never dreamed of leaving
Ever being anyplace, but there.

Do you remember we'd gather, around the big cook stove
Mama in her apron, getting the table set
Dad coming in from the old red barn, having the cattle fed
I still recall the closeness, it lingers with me yet.

I hope you remember, that it's etched in your mind
For memories are all we retreived
The farm was lost and the lands all sold
The rich earth, now lies mute, without seed.

Carla Frandsen
DEAR MOM,
Sure wish you could be here
To see my little man,
He's pretty as can be, you know
Smile on him when you can.

When you're not too busy, Mom,
Please look down on him.
I know you'll be as proud as me,
You'll see him with a grin.

If you could, I know you'd come,
To hold your first grandson.
We'd talk and laugh and remember
The wonderful things we've done.

You'd love him like I do, Mom.
I miss you so very much!
Wish you could be here.
I love you a whole bunch.

If God delivers my letter,
I'll be expecting your call.
Come to visit us soon, Mom,
Love always from us all.

Alice Bachman
DADDY'S GIRL

To my father, Albert Bachman, who was tragically killed in a car accident November 19, 1988

Daddy, you always said that I was your little girl, your pride and joy.
And I was proud to say I was your little girl.
I know you made mistakes, but so does everyone else.
I often vowed when I was a little girl, that I would take care of you when you got old and grey, no matter what kinds of disappointments would follow us around.
I am still your little girl but where are you?—I am all alone.
I used to think that if you loved someone hard enough they would never go away. I guess I thought wrong!
Was I sheltered into thinking such things? I never really experienced such a great loss until I lost you. When you were taken away so unfairly.
It was the drunk driver's fault, and it isn't enough that he has to pay a fine, go to jail for a few years, or have a guilty conscience for the rest of his life. He should suffer more!
Does he realize what he has done? To you, To me, your little girl?
Now I know you'll never have a chance to see us grow, see special moments like graduations, weddings, and grand children.
I also know that I will never have the chance to take care of you when you are old and grey.
But please remember, daddy where ever you are—I will always be daddy's little girl and I love you!

Theresa Joy Urie

Theresa Joy Urie
SHADES OF GREY

To Carla, Karen, and Nels, for believing in me.

Just yesterday, it seems
like life had more meaning.
The colors are vivid
in yesterday's dreams.

The fog from the ocean,
like blank pages of paper,
keeps rolling inland, in
depressing grey streams.

I stare out my window
and wonder what happened
to yesterday's laughter,
when life was a song.

Today . . . it's so dreary
and I'm so damn weary
for the rest of my life
to be taking this long.

Yasmin Steele
THE PINK BEDSPREAD

Para ti, mãe, porque eu te amo muito.

So she took me to the family doctor, an old man
With grey hair and minty breath who told me
To undress and examined me inside for the first time
Using petroleum slicked fingers and a cold, steel
Culdoscope and lying as he jammed a needle
In my arm, saying it wouldn't hurt. I remember
When she found out and asked, more hurt than angry,
Why; why didn't I tell her? Well, how does a twelve-year-old tell her mother she might be pregnant?
How does she tell her that on a worn cot
In his cement cellar, loneliness is bigger
Than the hate of an adolescent boy towards what
He has conquered? Later, while walking back home,
My mother and I laughed—the sound of it was weird;
One voice hesitant, cracked, the other insanely loud.
And when she saw a pink bedspread stuffed in the trash
She wanted to take it home. I was embarrassed
And said no—thankfully she listened but
As we walked away I saw the need in her eyes.

Henrietta (Jeri) R Schwan
SANTA CLAUS
When I was but a little girl,
Christmas was not exciting,
In winter, just a timely pause,
I hung no stocking up because
I didn't believe in Santa Claus.

My parents taught me truth, no lies,
How could reindeer really fly?
Or just one man, all those gifts bring,
Climb down, then up the chimney swing?
Santa Claus, there's no such thing!

"You are bad," school kids did say,
"That's the reason toys aren't brought",
My young heart pondered if the cause
Could be just my behavior flaws,
I wanted to believe in Santa Claus.

I hung my stocking pensively,
Mama cried and said, "Oh no!"
Morning came, my heart took flight,
My stocking bulged, an orange so bright!
My Santa Claus did come that night!

Carol Fitzgerald
COLLEGE BOUND REFLECTIONS

For Dear Sweet Keri

Today I smelled the roses.
Today there was just the two of us.
Not Mother and Daughter, but two adults.
You went. I let you go. Bittersweet it was.

The flight is good. We stop at our hotel, proceed
To campus and enter dorm. The room is stark. Bare
Walls, a mirror, two unmade beds, two desks, two chairs,
A closet. Small. You will be far from home in a strange city, knowing no one. Some uneasy feelings in both
Of us for different reasons. How will you manage? You will!

The days will be glum without the ever presence of your quick
Wit and uncanny ability to make us all laugh. Although the nest will still be full, without you it will be very empty.

You are now on stage, the stage of your life and there are
So many new things for you to remember and for which you must
Be responsible. The production begins when I bow out. I
Fly home tomorrow and leave you, my precious babe. I leave
You to begin your life's debut. I musn't prolong the farewell.
A few sage words, a final embrace, and a graceful exit.

Today I smelled the roses.
You went. I let you go.
Bittersweet it was.

Christina Krog
THE EPITOME OF US ALL
Neither the cancer of my bosom
Nor the clap of my brain
Forsakes me as you do.

As my head throbs
So does my heart for you.
And do you know this,
Would it hardly affect you . . .

For you stand before me each day
Pushing a splinter of life
With a spike of love . . .

Thus is the epitome of us all.

Charlotte Richardson
THE DUTY OF A FRIEND
If today you see me frowning,
It may be that I am drowning;
From the problems of my life,
Personal worries, fears, and strife.

So, if a friend you claim to be,
Spare a little smile for me;
Just a word of love today
To help me on my troubled way.

If no time you have to give,
Then I probably still will live;
But, if the next day I can't be found,
You will know that I have drowned.

The load I had too great to bear,
And no one would my troubles share,
Just a minute of your day,
Was all that I needed on my way.

So, if a friend of mine you be,
One that's kind and true;
Spare a little smile for me,
I would do the same for you.

Dori Curtis
RECURRENCES
Autumn lies lazy along the valley floor
humming to itself:
lisps and murmurs of tiny secrets in the grass still
green and soft with summer.
The popple, waggling in the idle air,
clatters its pale castanets amidst the glistening sounds
of insects at their brief celebration.

Soon geese will lace the sky
and you and I
will hurry out to stand

hand in hand and listen to their cry
of distance and the long goodby.

But when evening climbs the hill to press around the house,
the sound that floods my heart is your footstep on the porch,
the opening door.

Valerie Neidig
LOCKED CLOSET

With all my love, to my dearest and closest friends, especially Theresa and Becki, who have helped me unlock my closet and turn on the light.

I sit in the lonely dark
hoping no one will stumble
on me
waiting for another chance.

Only fear hinders me
from turning on the light—
it's artificial anyway.

Fear is the New York lock
jammed in my head
twisted in my heart.

Now I sit alone
in a locked closet.

I ate
the key.

Marion Trigo
AFGHAN OF TEARS

My sorrow cannot be contained. Nor my tears.
I love you and yet my love is inadequate.
Still, you suffer with cancer unto death.
I too suffer and die with you.
Still, I live agonizingly on.
My tears flow down upon my work.
I blindly toil through chain upon chain.
My afghan grows as does my grief.
Row upon row of wordless suffering.
Does the soul suffer with the body?
I must be about my work!
Have I not lost count of my stitches?
Yes, yes, turn back as far as necessary.
There, I have it, now I can go on.
As you grow toward the final transition of body,
I know that there is a Hell, There is a Purgatory,
It is here—It is now—

Courtney M Jednat
A DAY AT THE BEACH

I dedicated this poem to my beloved family; with whom I have shared all of my memories with; at the beach . . .

On top of the sand dunes, covered with sea oats; we fly our kites in the afternoons . . .
Looking and watching for dolphins and boats; we swam in the water and surfed on our floats . . .
We started feeding the sea gulls with bread; while our shoulders were getting dark red . . .
We ran on the beach about a mile, down; then we stopped and looked around . . .
The sun was shining brighter than ever; and the water was feeling better and better . . .
We got tired and rested for awhile; we took our time as the day went by . . .
It went fast, but it was better than the past.
As it started getting dark; we got our stuff, and went to where we parked . . .
We really didn't want to leave; but we had to get some sleep.
We had fun, and we were glad that we could come . . .
We'll just wait for tomorrow, and maybe, go again . . .
I hope it doesn't rain; that would be a "real" pain!

Hannah M Severson

Hannah M Severson
NOW I HEAR THE BROOK

I used to hurry on my way,
So busy with each care-filled day
That in my haste to beat the clock
I could not view a hollyhock
Or watch the flight of zipping bees,
Nor care that brittle cold could freeze
The babbling of a brook.

Now I am forced to walk, not run.
With this new pace I have begun
To savor all life's little things—
Sweet thrills when spring's first robin sings,
Quaint shyness in a pansy's face,
Soft, healing warmth of rays which chase
The icy coating from a brook.

Thank God that now my steps are slow,
It took this change for me to know
In rushing I had missed the best
Of life—those little things that rest
A weary soul that's worn from care.
In thankfulness I breathe a prayer
For now I hear the brook

Stephan Conley
BROKEN CHILD

Dedicated to all of the homeless children I pray for a change

It's cold out in the city streets tonight
A child walks alone
Blisters cover his aching feet
No place he can call home
He stands so fragile on a crowded corner
Begging for some change
I just need a little food
Can you help me with my pain
But to the people he's just a ghost
They quickly pass him by
He sits down in the gutter
And hangs his head to cry
Mommy Daddy please come back
I'm sorry I did wrong
I'll change I swear
I need your care
Before my life is gone
By the light of the morning
He's nowhere to be found
God please help this broken child
Before he's in the ground

Marsha Christa Gilles
GOD'S CREATIVE HAND

This poem is dedicated to my family and to all my friends at Sacred Heart Academy in New York.

Almighty God in Heaven who cherishes us with love,
You are the one who created us the stars, flowers, and doves.
Your glory shines to us each day through gleaming rays of sun.
The fresh pure air of your existence is truly miraculous to me.
No one knows but you of your skillful creative hands unseen.
Creating in only seven days a perfect world to be.

Almighty God in Heaven you are a creator indeed,
With precious gifts of creation to shower us with
Happiness and peace.
There hasn't been, there isn't and there will not be a person as perfect as "Our Creator" with all life, light and love to fill our hearts forever.

Joan A Sorgi
MIKE'S FIRST CHRISTMAS

To My Son, Mike, a Very Special Boy.

The trees are bare, the skies are gray.
It's a dark and dismal kind of day.
But inside our home there's happiness and cheer, because Mike's discovered winter this year.

He runs from window to window to look at the snow. His anticipation of Christmas is beginning to grow.

It's a wonderful feeling to be a part of his glee. Imagine Christmas morning when he sees his first Christmas tree.

There will be presents from Mom and Dad and of course Santa, too.
And let's not forget big brother and sisters, who love him like no others can do.

I bet he's thinking, will this all go away? No Mike, Christmas is here and will always stay!

Sherry K Grimes
TO THE ONE I LOVE

All I do is think of you,
Then the next thing you know,
I have the blues.
Oh how I love you so,
So, so much nobody knows.
And now that you've said goodby,
I will sit here and try not to cry.
Oh I wish you'd understand,
I could not fight my feelings with my hands.
I never knew feelings could be so strong,
They can really hurt for so long.
Oh when I see someone with the color of your hair,
Oh how I wish you were there,
Because if you were there,
You know what I would do,
I would tell you,
I Love You.

Jennifer Kielley
I LEFT HIM SITTING

As I left him
Sitting
In this hollow room
I watched
As he looked out the window
Wondering—
How he got in this nursing home.

There was a battle going on
Inside him
It was him—
Against God
And I knew
God was winning.

As I started down the hall
I heard something
In his room
I quickly retreated
And peeked around the corner.

He was calling out my name.
I answered
With a blunt, "What?"
Then slowly—
But persistently
He asked.
"Do you love Bomba?"
(a nickname I used to call him)

I answered
With a yes
And walked out
Into the hall
And let—
The tears—
Flow over.

Mildred M Plummer
YOU KNOW THEM!

I never thought the time would come
When I would like to see,
A poet, of some shape or form
Who'd write these lines for me.
Who'd take a pen within his hand
And hold it poised and say;
"For what great reason am I called
To write these lines today?"
I'd say, "A poem, one that's grand,
About a couple who,
No matter how much pain I caused,
Kept right on smiling through.
You know by now this couple is,
The grandest one on earth,
Whose love starts to envelop you
From the moment of your birth.
It makes you feel that life's worthwhile
That nothing's really bad,
When you can face a rotten world
With a wonderful Mother and Dad.

Jerri Haines
AS I LOOK IN THE MIRROR, I SEE THE LINES OF TIME

To My Precious Daughters: Cyndee, Mindi & Karen & Granddaughters: Angela & Mallory

As I look in the mirror
I see the lines of time;
My eyes see me as I am today, but
My heart remembers yesterday;
Yesterday, so far away.

Yesterday, when I ran and played and
Climbed the highest tree, and
Hit a softball much farther than all the
Team could see.

I did all the things girls did back then;
Laughed, sang and cried; and
Had a happy yesterday because God was
At my side.

Now time, somehow, has caught up

with me, and
 These are memories in my mind.
Things I did and enjoyed so much are a part
 Of things behind.

But, the lines I see are lines of joy
 'Cause the Lord's in my heart to stay.
He's with me each day to the very end as I
 Go along life's way.

So, enjoy, my daughter, the days of your youth;
 They, too, are passing you by.
And, one day, as you look in the mirror of time,
 Remember the Lord will be with you to stay.

Shannon Drummond
FINALLY ALIVE

This poem is dedicated to Chris Sprinkle.

When I'm dead and gone away,
buried so deep in the earth,
Do not cry at my passing away.
But rejoice at my rebirth.

The troubles of life don't concern me now.
I'm finally at rest.
Peace be with thee brother
and by the hand of God be blessed.

For here my troubles are over,
gone with the setting sun.
Here I am exultant
for my life has just begun.

Don't weep o're me my brother.
Lift your head and sing to the sky.
Be happy for me brother.
I'm finally alive.

Velma Lee Adams
LIFE'S MUSIC
Tonight the wind chimes are busy
Ringing out quick staccato notes
No measures of rest
Nor of whole notes.
Up and down the scale
Sixteenth notes are interrupting.
So like my life . . . but
Rests and whole notes must be a part
Of the music of life
If there is to be harmony
And a melody of abiding peace.
It can be
When God writes the music.

Suzanne Famolare
I LOVE YOU, DEAR SISTER
You're everywhere I go, but only in spirit.
Your name makes me smile, whenever I hear it.

Your room at my house, so filled with good cheer,
A retreat for my anger, thoughts come crystal clear.

No fights between us, a record to be proud,
My anger goes away, always when you're around.

Not related in our blood, but deep in our hearts,
Problems run away when we use our smarts.

You're a lot like me, shy and caring,
Wild as can be at thoughts we're sharing.

You know what I'm saying, before I say,
I'm like you here, too-in my own way.
From the time we've met, we've seemed to grow,
I love you, dear sister-something you already know.

Toreen Lehman Whiting
MAKING STUFF FOR CHRISTMAS
Making stuff for Christmas this
Year was really quite a riot.
Candy and cake were surely out
With Leita on a diet.

So I thought and thought for
Several days and late into the night.
I rejected one or two things,
Because they weren't just right.

So I made these cookies all for her,
And I know that they are lawful.
If you take a bite of these
You'll find them to taste awful.

So Merry Christmas Leita dear,
These coasters are from me.
Keep it up and you will find,
You'll be as skinny as can be.

Gary S Hueppchen
FOR MY MOTHER

Dedicated to my mom Janice Mary Hueppchen

For the times I caused you sadness
I'm sorry I wasn't playing fair.
I especially feel bad about the times
when you needed me and I wasn't there.

For the teachings you've taught me
I know your work was never done.
For all the gifts you've given me
I thank you for every last one.

For your strict rules in the past
I can see now what I couldn't then.
You were never trying to hurt me
you were just trying to be my friend.

You see, Mother—now that I'm older
I understand the love you gave me.
I see the sacrifices that were made
in the time spent trying to save me.

So I'd like to take this time to say
thanks for being there and being true.
Thoughts of you are always in my heart
and most of all, Mom—I love you.

Holly Joiner
INSIDE THE ANGER
Inside the anger,
 deep inside the anger
 sits the child crying.

She cries tears of regret,
 of loneliness.
Tears that never show on the outside,
 but burn the tender heart
 behind the door of the mind.

No one sees inside the anger.
No one cares to see.
Too afraid to know the truth,
 afraid to see the pain.

Inside the anger,
 deep inside the anger,
Is the flower
Wilted and dying from the heat.
Screaming screams never heard
 On the outside.

Will Fontaine
SITTIN' IN THE RESTAURANT
downtown jazz
waitress' smile
and this black guy's
layin' some great words down
with the coffee
and digs
the same chick/same time
unison thing
hey, she's music
and sunshine
and kitten
and cool
dressed in a little jog suit
like I've NEVER seen—

but the black guy
looks at me
and I know where he's at
so I voice it for him: "isn't it wonderful
what they can do with animation?"

And he just nods . . . "Whew!"
Both our lives
condensed
here and now
at the sterile counter.

Margie Hester

Margie Hester
THE FAMILY TREE
God looked down from above,
 And took a magnificent view.
He then, turned to the angel with commandery said;
 You and I have a lot of things we must do.
Then God drew an arc like a circle,
 And enclosed it with love you see;
And waved his magic wand forming man and woman,
 Thus, beginning the world's great Family Tree.

Smiling gently and upon them constantly,
 He watched them day by day.
Mysteriously, unlocking His secret chambers,
 God proceeded to remove His molds and clay.
Adjusting His thoughts, while pausing for a moment,
 He filled their hearts with a beautiful song.
Now, knowing, perfectly well for Him,
 His task of creation has definitely begun.

Springing forth, mankind's fruits wasn't grapes nor apples,
 We all certainly must agree;
Instead, they were seeds of love,
 Transforming themselves into God's own Family Tree,

Vickie Lynn Sims
AND THERE WILL COME A TIME IN LIFE

To my beloved Keith Hebert

And there will come a time in life,
when you'll need a brand new start,
And the mind becomes the least bit concerned
When it follows behind the heart

Beatrice Love
WHO AM I?
Who am I?
A I a Wind?
Twirling, Whirling, Twisting,
As I learn the treasure of knowledge.

Who Am I?
Am I a magnificent, sparkling, radiant red ruby?
Can I withstand the greatest pressure in life, to bestowed upon any man?

Who Am I?
Can I touch the stars?
Achieve the highest honor,
Conquer unconquered worlds
Uncover knowledge centuries ahead.

Who Am I?
Am I a computer?
I collect and organize knowledge.
Am I a dreamer?
I dream a universal peace, of cities in space,
man and machines building a new world without
the threat of chemical or nuclear wars.
Who Am I?

Vera W Farrier
GRANDMOTHER'S CHILD
I look at this child of mine
 So much like me
I see her darting here and there
As if she had no time to spare.
She looks at everything with eyes so bright
If one needs help she'll set him right.
Her world is wonderful to see
I'm glad that she's so much like me.

Carla Wessel
DAWN WILL BREAK

I dedicate this poem to my Uncle Eve, whom I love dearly.

We each should live our lives as though
We're living here on Borrowed Time.
Pray, let us learn our lessons—
work out Karmas, yours and mine.

We all are where we're supposed to be,
that's what the Mystics say.
We should not fight our lessons,
they are put here in our way.

And there is payback, other lives.
We give and we receive.
So if we think that life's unfair,
still—we all should not grieve.

We fight for life and don't give up,
for everywhere there's Hope.
The human spirit is amazing—
you, dear, have my vote.

But when one must Move On, I see a vision
in the great beyond—
The Other Side is BEAUTIFUL—
and I believe there is a Dawn!

Kamal Puri
THE ULTIMATE

To Sylvia and Henry

(The burden of outpourings of a friend before his disappearance)
You by yourself,with your admired looks, grace,
cascading open silky hair 'n skin
and matching distinctive voice can just about
unhinge me a little at times.

But you, in combination with your stories about my 'Rakeeb',
the Rival, the co-sharer of your favours, have just
to drop a hint of actuality to make me rush
to the portals of hell and paint giant sized murals
with frenzied imagination, heaping the details and then sharpening with piquancy here 'n there,
the moods improvising 'n changing backdrops 'n dialogues,
aided by your interspersed confessions of transient
subjection 'n compliancy brought on by the novelty
of the crude passion of the demon 'Rakeeb'
Your subsequent Regrets 'n Shame adding
diabolism to my already multifaceted jealousy,
thriving on what I'd stored as experience and
changing it into the ultimate of whatever one would call it.

Willard W Barksdale
THE BIG-CLEAN-UP

To my wife Dione, which I love very much

It was after midnight on a late
Summer evening when the wind was
Blowing so hard through this place that
The hot dog wrappers, plates, and cups were
Being tossed up in the air.

The seagulls and their friends were
settling down for a late dinner of:
Half-eaten hotdogs
Sticky plates of cold Nachoes with cheese
Those giant hot dog buns where those colossal dogs were supposedly have gone.
And finally, all of those thousands of empty peanut shells scattered all over,
you asked, what are you doing?
I'm sweeping, and sweeping, why?
Because it's a job!

Leora C Bennett
THE HANDIWORK OF GOD
He painted the oceans, rivers and streams,
The lakes and mountains, panoramic scenes.
The green grass the flowers, the birds and the bees;
The willows, the meadows, the foliage, the trees.

He painted the beauty of blossoms that burst in the spring.
He painted the beautiful fragrance of summer time too.
The cold winds and the snows of winter,
Autumn with its golden hue.

He painted the clouds and the blue in the sky.
The beautiful sunsets on the Great Salt Lake.
He painted all the colors in the rainbow,
Without making even one mistake.

He painted the world in all of its glory,
With just one brush of his hand.
He painted the stars and the silvery moonlight,
He painted, "America", my own native land.

He even painted the bubbling brook,
And the rippling waterfall.
All of Gods creations, both Heaven and Earth,
The "Master", painted them all.

Craig Vogel
FEAR
If I should wander down a quiet road
And there is something there that I should see,
Oh, how I wonder what that thing could be!
But wait! The something up ahead, it glowed!
And buzzards circling overhead forebode
The something waiting up ahead for me.

I turn around but find I cannot flee
The fear inside my heart has overflowed.
Yet if you fear that which you do not know,
I know throughout your life you'll be afraid
For things are not always as they appear.
So you and I together, we will go
To make sure that truth always is displayed
And others never had a need to fear.

Lanelle Pronych
UNTITLED
The wind passes by
cold and unforgiving,
while the sky clears
without a trace of doubt.

Trees whisper secret
of past memories
and a creek gurgles
like a child.

Squirrels chatter,
birds sing,
an airplane passes overhead,
free as a bird.
Cars creep up the ravine slope,
mindless of the world around them.
But those who see it,
are thankful for the beauty.

They, the normal life
are blind
To the shattered dreams,
lying forgotten forever.

Rebecca Lynn Lamkin
THE SKY IS CRYING

To Drew, my husband, who gives me the encouragement to write

The Sky is crying
everything is drying up
the trees, grass, shrubs, flowers
that I used to take care of for you.
But I don't have any water for them.
So Dear Lord please send some water
down for me to feed the earth and animals
So I can water the things you made
and so I can let out my frustrations and anger
by raining, lightning, thunder
In which I haven't done that
in over two months Lord and I am
stuffing my anger, Lord it needs to come
out soon so when you see a few
raindrops that is me
The Sky is Crying.

Helene Barker
SECRETS
A cool winters day,
the valley and hills are so clear
every crevice can be seen,
as if unfolding secrets.

Slowly clouds flow in,
an effort to lock the hills in place
before the secrets get away.

The clouds take over the sky,
hiding the sun
and the valley stands still,
truly a calm before a storm.

Now fog walks across the desert floor
and little by little the hills are gone,
clouds cover them
as if swallowing secrets and time.

I'm here alone. This morning my world was big,
with a feeling of sharing, now
it's only me.
The clouds surround me
protect me against the truths.

I start the New Year protected with
a peace,
a calm and anticipation.
It's a beautiful feeling
and it's my secret.

Zelma Spivey Groves
MY SHADOW
Sometimes my Shadow plays tricks on me
I imagine I'm a Fairy, and the Queen, I will see
But Shadow's like fiction, really aren't real—
So I'll dry up the teardrops and forget how I feel
Sometimes when the Sun shines! so bright I can see
On the wall is my Shadow, and he's acting like me
He pretends he has riches and Mansions untold
But he hides when the Sun leaves
And takes all the Gold
Sometimes I see him and sometimes I don't
Like A Ghost he is haunting, but give up I won't
He's A fictional figure I see on A wall
But when I try to touch him, he's not there at all
Sometimes, I imagine that it is all true
That I am A great Man and never feel blue
Then I realize I'm dreaming A beautiful dream
That leaves when the Sun's gone and not what it seems
Sometimes it's lovely to watch and pretend
That sometimes my Shadow, is really my Friend
So tell me what happens when you fade away
And I'm too old to remember—the things that you say
Sometimes way out yonder! in old Wonder-land
You'll still be A Shadow" And I'll still be A Man
I'll think of you kindly and the places we've been
When you were my Shadow—And my best Friend
Together we built many Castles All made of sand
Just me and my Shadow, A fictional Man.

Larry D Chaffin
A DREAM FULFILLED
How great is the love God has for Man
Is often measured with time
How great is the love I have for my wife
Is measured as time unwind

The splendor and joy that we share each day
Are blessings from God above
And when we reflect at anniversary time
The blessings are really true love

A dream fulfilled the moment we met
And I cherish the thought from day to day
I pray to God and give him the glory
For his spirit will lead the way

When we reflect, I often times wondered
why and if dreams came true
But in my heart, my dream is actually fulfilled
Cause the dream of my life is really YOU.

Eddie Benham
WINTER AT THE AJAX
I rise about five-thirty and make a pot of brew,
Then I slip out to the barn and catch a bronc or two.
I fit them to their harness, for breakfast they have grain.
Then I go back to the house and fix myself the same.
Then I hook them to my outfit, across the field we go.
The morning sun is rising as we're breakin' through the snow.
I load the sled with hay as high as it will go,
The cows bawl that they are hungry, as if I didn't know.
I scatter out the hay and watch the cows come in,

Then I go back to the stack and load it up again.
And when I've done it twice or maybe three times more,
I turn those broncs around and head for the cabin door.

I turn the horses loose and catch a bite to eat,
Then it's back out to the barn to trim a horse's feet.
I saddle up my pony and ride out to chop some ice,
The winter sun is shinin', the day is kind of nice.
But when it gets to sinkin' and it starts a gettin' cold,
I head back to my cabin and the warmth that it will hold.
And when I've had my supper and bed the fire down right,
I slip into my bed roll and bid the world good night.
'Cause first thing in the morning I know just what I'll do.

I rise about five-thirty and make a pot of brew,
Then I slip out to the barn and catch a bronc or two.

Laverne H Smith Ward
JUST FOR YOU

This poem is dedicated to the man in my life whom I love very much David A Ward

It's taken so long to make the
Right move, and let you know
How much I care.
Now I really can't figure why I've
Waited so long, it seems such
An easy thing to do
And the sky above seems so blue
And my day radiates with such
unbridled energy
Chemistry at it's purist, clashing with
Shackled emotions, bringing about
An enormous revelation
Trying to contain all these feelings
Bring them under control, is in
itself not an easy task
But nothing seems too much to ask.
'Cause all these thing's I'd
Gladly go through Just For You!!

Mark J Wright
SEASONS

Winter comes and stays
for seemingly so many days . . .
And when at last it ends,
the joy of Spring it sends.

So that we can emerge
to satisfy our every urge . . .
And watch the growing green,
wandering like a lovely dream.

Sunny days and simmering nights,
filled with pleasures and
delights.
Friends and love, having fun . . .
new found life, yes you've won.

Karen A Mays
GRANDMOTHER

Grandmother, these words only touch the surface of my deep love for you. If only a little part of you lives within my heart, I believe God has blessed me. I love you, Grandmother.

Grandmother, so special
Treasure of my heart
Tender hands of sweet caress
Good cheer to fill my cup.

Dresses made of gingham
Feminine in every way
Cherished moments make for
memories
To share with me today.

Loving words of kindness
To fill the cloudy days
Perfect love in all you do
To brighten every hour.

Fragrance as the flowers
That grow among the vines
Inward beauty so revealing
Cherished heart forever kind.

Your love for all your children
And grandchildren all alike
I love you, Darling Grandmother
Special treasure of my heart.

William Sands

William Sands
—WIND SONG—(JOURNEY TO WHERE THE WINDS BEGIN)

WIND SONG is written for those I love. When I am gone, they will know they can always find me at the place where all journeys start—"WHERE THE WIND BEGINS."

When the rusted, cloying anchor
Is weighed that final time,
And the midnight watch is started
As the sounds of eight bells chime.

When the harbor berth has faded
And the open sea is near,
When the ocean's breeze grows
fresher
And the sky begins to clear.

Then, with hands full on the tiller,
I will face the evening star,
When the tide is at its fullest—
I will slip across the bar.

Linda K Kissee
WE WILL MAKE IT

If time can take away the pain,
as the dryness leaves after the rain.
Then I will make it.

If hope can be found after despair,
as the feelings to live, to love, to
care.
Then I will make it.

If the end of the road is starting over,
as winter brings snow, summer the
clover.
Then I will make it.

If I can ease the pain my children
feel,
as the divorce is final, over, real.
Then they will make it.

If I can be there when they reach out,
as love is our bond, I have no doubt.
Then they will make it.

If in our lives the hurt will one day
leave,
as our prayers will be answered, I do
believe.
Then we all will make it.

Cathy Loveland
THE STAIRCASE OF LIFE

Life is like a staircase,
When you're born you start
on the ground floor.
Parents are tugging the small hands
that are your own,
Encouraging you upwards toward
greatness.
Sometimes you slip and stumble,
In doing this you grab for the
bannister,
Friends and family.
All the time the bannister's there.
Although it changes form and shape,
As friends come and go and the
family
grows bigger.
It's always there, waiting, ready and
willing,
To support you when you fall.
Grab for it when you need it !!!

Stanley J Milligan
WHAT IS THIS PLACE WE'VE REACHED

What is this place we've reached?
How much longer can it last?
Are the promises to be breached?
Like the others in the past?

Should we sit and talk?
To figure what's behind it?
Or let the feeling walk?
After trying so hard to find it?

Rebecca Russell Cox
WHEN DEW DROPS DANCE

What is the Scene
When One Must Dream
Of Dew Drops in Dance?

Ribbons of Red
Tucked in the Beds
When Dew Drops Dance.

Gold Beams of Sun
Filter thru Mums
When Dew Drops Dance

As Airy Spring Showers
Echo to Flowers
Then Dew Drops Dance—

To the Bluebells in Shells
And Flooding Daffodils
The Dew Drops Dance

And the Beds of Tu-lips
Pucker to Kiss
When Dew Drops Dance.

Alas! Marshmallow Clouds
In Azure Draped Shrouds
When Dew Drops Dance.

Salpy Semerdjian
FLAT-CHESTED WITH A FROWN

Slave by the chains of marriage,
Only skill possessed—to rock a
carriage.
Once was a beauty queen with a
golden crown.
Now married and flat-chested with a
frown.
Hollow log dragged along,
Radio blares dull old song.
Empty feelings awakened to,
Husband's gone—there's nothing to
do.

Children come one by one.
Hubby help? He's always gone!
Cooking meals day and night,
Watching body collect cellulite.

Thought it'd be fun to go and marry.
The burden to that choice, you must
carry.
Kids in bed—you sit down,
Tired, lonely, and with a frown.

Flat-chested with a frown,
Always wore the golden crown.
Running wild and oh so free,
Till marriage came and knocked you
down.

Life's become a mere memory.

David Bush
SPRING SNOW

To Bruce Lincon, who read it aright as a boy

How came you there, ragged patches
of white, on the young green grass?
One cheek of the elm you whitened,
blanketing the stark, black, living
limbs, budded, decked with glittering
leaves.
You are soft, you warm-looking
whiteness. You do not chill like the
thin raw rain, your brother. Lover-
like you cling, fallen, petal by petal
floating to augment you,
till the sheer press of you bends,
cracks—cracks and breaks the limb,
the heart you rest on lovingly.
Soft one, loving one, can you find no
mercy in you? Know one day a
friendly sun will kiss you all too
warmly and mist you, weeping, to
heaven again through the blue air.
Shall you roll, I wonder, in great,
lazy, peaceful clouds, or whipped by
wind and lashed to tenuous whiteness
ride unrestingly till you weep again
or fall again in freezing tenderness?
Will you, too, plead for surcease
from the Cause of Things?
What say you, pleading? You cannot
lighten your caress?
True. We are without measure in our
tenderness. We cannot cease hurting
what we love.

Becky McLaughlin
FOR MY BROTHER ON HIS 40TH BIRTHDAY

As an older sister, I must give you
this advice.
Live your life the way you want; it
doesn't come 'round twice.
When you feel the need to "do your
thing"—take it to the limit.
Because if you don't you will always
wonder why you didn't.

We live & learn as the sayin' goes;
we're bound to make mistakes.
But we should look at each new day
as an adventure when we wake.
We live, we love, we laugh, we cry—
& sometimes even wonder why.
But we have our memories of the past
as the years go quickly by.

We have memories to treasure, some
good and some bad.
And they help us to grow through the
years; for this I am glad.
We've grown since our childhood in
more ways than one.
We've been through a lot of
experiences we've benefited from.

With age comes wisdom—how much better now we see;
What the world has to offer, and of what we want to be.
There really are no limits; just you believe in yourself.
Personal satisfaction is what counts; not money or wealth.

So as we grow older, let us continue to grow;
In all we think, we say, and we do; in all we know.
Don't let yourself be dismayed; don't get into a rage.
For there are a lot of people who never live to be our age!

Christopher H Ippolito
DEATH COMES QUICKLY
As the night slowly descended on him, he walked along the shimmering shore.
The crimson fiery sky soothed his aching eyes.
He was alone with the stars at last.
It was quiet except for the crash of the waves on the darkened beach.

A soft cool breeze blew through his stringy hair and he pulled his jacket tightly ground him.
He spoke to the moonlit sea and waited for a response that would never come.
At last, he could venture no further.
He sat and ran his thoughtful hands through the cold lifeless sand.
His senses soared to their very peaks.
In this endless moment, he lifted a handful of sand in the air.
Examining each and every particle, he became increasingly intense and nostalgic.
Then in one final sigh, he watched as the grains of sand quickly slipped through his mortal fingers and became one with the infinite beach.
"Carry me Home" he told the stars in their multitudes and it was over.

Mazy W Salter
THE SHRINE THAT CRIES

Dedicated to the children of the holocaust.

There is a voice in Jerusalem
That speaks with unbearable sorrow, each name
One and a half million children remembered
By flickering candle lights
On a sea of impenetrable darkness.

Walking through this incredible little shrine
Fills one with a gripping sense of pain.
The eyes burn with the worlds unshed tears.
Some say time heals a broken heart,
Not so, the anguish never ends.

The world stood by and let it happen.
There was no one there to stay the hand
That closed the oven doors.
The horror of it will live forever
In the annals of diabolical crimes.

And in the hearts of those who care.
The wounds are deep and lasting.
Some for a little child lost,
And some for the inescapable guilt.
And Christ said, "Suffer the little
Children to come unto me".

Andrea Sotirakopoulos
WHY DID YOU GO

" . . how can it be said i am alone when all the world is here to look on me . . . " A Midsummer Night's Dream

Why did you have to go away,
Why did you have to die,
I miss you is all I'll say,
But inside silently, I cry.

I don't know how you did it,
And I'll never understand,
I don't know why you did it,
Now there's no one to hold my hand.

I'm all alone,
No one to help me through,
No one to call my friend,
My anger was towards you.

Now I'll go on pretending,
Hoping, day by day,
The fear will be ending,
And the pain go away.

Beth Haywood
NIGHTFALL
"What is this that I have heard?"
Said Old Oak Tree to Mockingbird
Jay won't sing,
The well's a draught,
Now only the wolves are out.
They howl mad, bay at the moon
And on the lake, only the loon
Crickets chirp,
While Rabbit sleeps,
Breezes blow,
And widow weeps
Owls hoot their solemn calls,
All get restless as night falls,
Hear the lonely coyotes shout,
And all because the sun's gone out.

Julie Olariksiri
WINGS OF SILVER

In His Service

One day I had a vision of my heavenly Father's home.
I recognized the stairway and the angels thereon.
It was a gift from Christ my Savior, the Father and the Son.
To let me know they'd take me when my time on earth was done.

There I was:
Flying up on wings of silver,
climbing up those stairs of gold.

On one side there were angels a-glow in silver fine.
They were singing "Hallelujah!" and the name they sang was mine.
Across from all the angels were the saints and martyrs there,
A-blaze in all their glory, their praises filled the air.

There I was:
Flying up on wings of silver,
climbing up those stairs of gold.

Looking up ahead I saw a door of shining gold.
I yearned to pass on through, but gently, I was told,
"Send my child back to her family, her time is not yet come."
"Sometime in the future, I will call her home."

And I'll be:
Flying up on wings of silver,
climbing up those stairs of gold.

Jenny Rich
THE CHILD INSIDE
I took a walk in the park
 the other day.
It hadn't changed much,
 but I had.
It was autumn, and there
 were the leaves,
Just as I remember,
 blanketing the earth.
I saw the place, where as a child
 I'd go to pretend.
Pretending I was grown-up,
 that I was the one in control.
Those were the days
 when life was sweet and simple.
When my only worries were,
 "Am I getting roller skates
 for Christmas?"
Now I have what I want.
 I'm grown-up, I'm in control.
But it's not as wonderful
 as I imagined it to be.
Now, as I sit on this park bench,
 I long to be the kid
 of ages past.
So I reach deep inside, to where
 the child is still hiding,
And I watch as my foot
 kicks up the fallen leaves.
Now I am dancing, dancing.
 Dancing among the leaves.
And I smile to myself,
 for I haven't yet forgotten
The child inside.

Helen T Ross
MONUMENTS OF AMERICA
Beauteous seas and mountains to cross our time is not a loss
Treaties are signed as a tribute sign of enduring peace
Risks are taken daily to preserve human life
Untold stories of dignities spared to lease
Again and again writ down in history with strife
Following memories to sing and phase the constant plea
Books of great men and women and child for all to see
Remember this great land it's coming history to be
Moreover and over we read tales of flamboyant bravery
Nevermore do we listen to our hungry and continued groan
Buildings and monuments made tallest buildings of stone
Dreams of everlasting makings no we are not in this alone
Boasting promises of deeds to perform for all of us free
Waiting but willing for peace we gather to sing with glee
Distinguished peoples form a human will and strong spirit
Collections of persons lean towards hope as we take our stand
The strong and weak together shall forever band
Conflicting talks disappear to set aside despair in our Great great land
United! United! America! the one true the one hopeful the one fruitful land

Alice M Barber
NOVEMBER BIRTHDAY
Red is the rose late blooming,
Its proud head held on high.
From frost's cruel death somehow escaped,
It scorns its time to die.

With ninety years and five years more,
My autumn too is nigh.
But like the rose, I linger on
And scorn my time to die!

Sandra DeAngelis
MY DAD

To my dad, gone but not forgotten From your loving daughter Sandra

Dad, I really miss you
No one knows how much
Dad, it's getting harder
The days they come and go
They seem to have no meaning
Dad! I miss you so!
You were always there dad
To comfort, lend a hand
You were always there dad
To help and understand
You made the burdens lighter
You always had a way
Of making everything easier
And the hurt would go away
Everybody misses you
But no one really knows
How much I really miss you
Dad! I miss you so!

Nancy C Bearden
OUT OF THUNDER
At first
It frightened us,
The pain of thunder exploding
In air.
Twisting of sheets on afternoons like this,
Wind peeling the leaves from the maples,
You stripping me
Of all caution.
Careers and mortgages and children later
The smell of our bodies together still
Sweet and humid,
The storm rolling gently
Over the maple tops,
In the nights and the years of rain.

Eva M Burkett
ON LOOKING THROUGH THE POSSESSIONS OF AN UNMARRIED LADY JUST BEFORE HER DEATH

To Mary

A few photographs, not of herself in her happier days but tintypes of those no longer remembered.
A tattered Bible, patterns of quilts she had made for others,
A bit of fine lace bought at some reckless moment,
A few coarse undergarments, a blue-checked gingham apron,
These, arranged neatly in the shelves of a worn-out kitchen safe—
Are all that is left of this life so swiftly passing,
Of caring for her brothers' children,
Of hoeing and spinning and weaving.

Now she is helpless.
Only strangers and neighbors lift her sweating body,
Remove her soiled garments,
And brush away the flies that settle on her forehead.
Nieces and nephews alike continue their rounds of gaiety,

Forgetful of the nights she sat by their bedsides
Cooling their burning brows and soothing away their troubles.
The brother's wife, now that she finds her no longer useful,

Goes to perform her more important household duties.
She, too, forgets the times she sent her to draw the water,
To gather in the vegetables,
And to perform other menial tasks of the farm wife.

What price, O God, has she paid for living!

Shyamkant Kulkarni

Shyamkant Kulkarni
MY TOMB

To my wife, Rekharajlaxmi, who, without hesitation always stood by me, and showered heavenly pleasures upon me.

I am building my tomb, since I came out of womb.
As I face a new year every year,
I add a new brick to that tomb,
sometimes it is of marble, at times golden,
many a times just earthen.
May it seem meager to all others,
to me it is unforgettable fable.

It is a cream of my life, treasure of my hike,
pearl found in my mind's dive. When I cross my boundaries, I am afraid of looking back.
When I get to new height, I am afraid of bottom in sight.
As I walk further and further, at each step,
at every second, tomb gets smaller and smaller.
May be one day, it may vanish altogether.

Still I am throwing back, bricks I collect, hoping they reach there, in right place at right corner.

I am no emperor, my tomb is not going to be that wonder,
like Tajmahal standing on the banks of Jamuna river.
But still, that is going to be my mahal,
on the banks of my life's river where may I rest forever, with my sweetheart, who never left me ever.

Angela Lachance
I LOVE YOU
When you say "I love you"
It's taken to heart,
It's something you mean,
Right from the start.

You don't say "I love you",
To just anyone,
I'll tell you right now,
Breaking-up isn't fun.

They think it's a game,
Don't tell me why,
To say "I love you",
Then make you cry.

So, don't say "I love you",
It's catchie you see,
My heart is now broken,
It happened to "Me".

E H Ehlert
MILITARY STRATEGY

To Military Science—from Caesar 'til the atom bomb.

Julius Caesar saw military Strategy for centuries get ahead.
Before, you'd put all soldiers
In a straight line and all together
Shot down, then they were dead.
He invented phalanxes-to stagger troops instead.
Rather than all together, he'd have
One forward and one back
When he had a Phalanx
Instead of hitting all at once in front,
You'd hit them in the flanks
And thus, more survivors came out, thru' the ranks.
Hannibal used elephants, his an ingenious mind
To the Alps tops, they'd climb
Then, he'd reason-use a rainy season
So none could follow, then roll cannon balls
On one and all who came behind.
And you're not a dreamer—it was on Hiroshima
Their population was so heavy-use an atom bomb
And thus it was done-in military aplomb.

Sharon Rowland
THOUGHTS FROM THE HEALTH CLUB
Extremities packed like sausages
In spandex encasements
A frantic forty-minute attempt
To tone and sweat away
Twelve hours of sedentary stress;
Programmed erasure
Of a frantic adrenaline-pumping
Five or six or seven days;
Buttocks spreading across our executive chairs
(Chairs with ARMS, another symbol of our hard-won status),
Phone insistently demanding,
Confirming our indispensability
To a company, which, thirty minutes
After our coronary, ten minutes after the hearse
Hauls our navy-suited bodies away, would seamlessly
Close the gap our leaving caused
And start to sap the life force and intelligent output
Of some other upward striving,
Poor, brainwashed, unknowing
Self-sacrificing,
Rapidly-aging Yuppie just like you and me.

Lori Johnson
BACK WITH ME
You glanced at me, you touched my hand
You smiled at me, I understand.
Your tempting eyes, your warm embrace
I knew right then, I'd found my place.
You kissed me once, I felt it through
All I wanted, was to be with you.
We shared our love, but it didn't last
You soon became part of my past.
What went wrong? Did I hold too tight?
Why did you give up without a fight?
You still glance at me, every once in a while
And sometimes give me your special smile.
It makes me think, and wonder why
You went away and said goodbye.
I'll wait for you, here I'll be
Until your love is back with me.

Adlain R Culver
JOY AT THE TOMB

I dedicate this poem to my daughter Tambria R. Laine

Mary came upon that morn
Her heart was filled with gloom.
She saw the stone was rolled away
No body in the tomb.

Only a piece of linen
Was all that she could see.
Then she saw the angel—
"He is not here", said he.

A man dressed like a gardner
Spoke, "Whom do you seek", said He.
"I am looking for Jesus
My Lord and Savior", said she.

"Mary, do you not know me"?
His voice was soft and sweet.
She cried, "It is my Lord and Savior"!
With joy her heart did beat.

"Go and tell my disciples
That I have risen", said He.
"I will come and speak with them
That they themselves shall see".

Janie Dixon
A NEW BEGINNING

Dedicated to my loving husband for this battle has not been an easy one, and our "New Beginning."

All these years of sorrow, loneliness and despair,
Were hidden so deep inside me, I didn't realize
they were there . . .

My heart was oh so heavy, the burden so hard to bear.
But somehow I survived, because
"I Still Care."

All the broken promises, the tears, the sorrow,
Leave me now for I've had my share,
Let me smile tomorrow . . .

For now I've come to realize there was nothing I could do,
I was a lonely, helpless victim,
As well as my son too . . .

We once had so much love, you tried to take it away,
But today, alcohol, you've lost the battle, so please
be on your way . . .

So all of you who feel today you've reached the end of your rope,
"Hang in There", It'll get better,
As long as you have hope . . .

For without hope and tomorrow, we surely would not survive,
Because today's a "NEW BEGINNING",
Tomorrow's a brand new life . . .

So as we walk forward together, trying to leave our troubles behind,
Each new day will bring a smile because,
Happiness we seek to find . . .

I no longer feel the guilt, the pain is going away,
And thanks to good friends here at Al-Anon,
I know I'll find my way . . .

Leonard Eskowitz
QUEEN'S TIME (SONG)
Transfixment of
Rainbow light leaves no child forsaken,
Though inebriation of elixir
May bar the Queen now

'fore King's bow.
Bouquet of spring,
Rainbow rosemary elixir, bow and bar,
Will lead hare and hind to
soft submission
Fixed amidst the humming light.

Windy Lee Jeager
LIKE STONE
Like Stone, his eyes were gray as was his hair.
The dim light of the room cast shadows on
His wan complexion, and the figure's rare,
Baroque style was enhanced. All eyes were drawn
To his romantic, subtle face; a face
Free of expression yet full of purport.
His steady stance displayed his poise and grace,
Two of his dazzling features. But the forte
Of his appearance was his stunning and
Athletic muscle structure. Age had not
Affected the still youthful hue and grand
Finesse of his visage of idle thought.

Immortal sculpture in a lurid tone
This statue with a silent face of
stone.

Linda Alford
MORE THAN A FRIEND
You gave me life, a will to live
My first hug, my first feeling of love
You held me and cuddled long into
the night

As I grew, you taught me about
loving
Sharing your dreams, sharing your
laughter
Doing things together that others
couldn't share

Giggling over gossip, crying over
sad movies
Girl things, woman's things, silly
things
These were all that we shared

So happy on my wedding day, you
cried with joy

Celebrating, cheering, letting me go
As I look back now, remembering
those years,
I realize, Mom, that you've always
been there

For now and forever, you'll always
be,
more than a friend to me
I'm proud to claim you to this day
My Mother, My friend, in every way

Sue A Stiles
TO THE LONELY ONE!
How lonely it must be to always be
right!
How sad and burdensome is your
plight.
For you see—I can not reach you at
your height!

I long to tell you of my concern
But all you think is "They have to
learn."
Love and respect—we each must
earn!

You have my love—no doubt of that.
You haven't always been such a
brat!

Respect is there—but rather bare
As some thoughts I just can't share!

Because you don't always listen or
seem to care
I can't always convey how my heart
does tear.

We each have our own way to grow
And each of us has to know—
That someone understands our plight
And stands beside us with all their
might.

So though I may not always agree—
I stand beside you impatiently.
Waiting for the time when you admit
That you could be wrong "just a bit."

Michael A McGuire
QUESTIONS OF EXISTENCE ON A DYING PLANET

This poem is dedicated to all the scientists, theologians and philosophers everywhere who continue to quarrel and debate over the miracles of Creation, while the Future slowly slips away into that bleak, dismal furnace infamously known as the VOID!!

Was Man a creation of God or God a creation of Man? Did the Earth evolve from a mass of exploding gasses in the universe or the warmth and touch of an ethereal hand?

Were Adam and Eve our primordial parents or are we just highly developed monkeys, having reached our finished state?

The proof of each concept being fact is so confusingly balanced that it tears at our Soul and keeps us in suspense, but soon the final answer will reveal itself and maybe, just maybe . . . .
it might make sense!

Until then, Church and State, Religion and Science and all those other numerous organizations trying to peddle their potions and antidotes to grant you Eternal Life, will just war amongst themselves about the questions of existence while the Earth, RIGHT NOW, screams for Salvation! Oh no! We must have overlooked something! Why doesn't anyone care if SHE weeps in strife?

Daniel B Kalinski
OPPOSITE ATTRACTION

This is dedicated to those who can't have what they want. We want the world and we want it now (JDM)

If dreams were real
and truth, lies
Borrow was steal
and ocean, skies

If the earth was the sun
and the sun, the moon
Boredom was fun
and later was soon

We might get along

If God was bad
and the devil good
Happy was sad
and could was should

If old was new
and sorrow, glee
If I were you
and you were me

We might get along

Timothy C Krug
YOU ARE THE REASON FOR LOVE

Dearest Joan, down deep in our hearts we both know that God brought us together. Even if it was just to write this song, let it be known that it could not have been written without you. To God's choice. Love, Timothy Dare.

You are the colors lost in the rainbow
You are the song in the heart of the
sparrow
You are the harbor when troubles
have risen
You are the hand in the glove that
I'm missing

You are the fragrance found in the
flower
You are the ring from the bells in the
tower
You are the whisper that echoes
inside me
The calm in the storm that comes
after the lightning

You are the willows that dance in the
autumn
You are the light at the end of the
tunnel
You are the reason why God made a
heaven
You are the breath in the wind that
I'm breathing
You are the fire when candles are
burning
You are the cog in the wheel that is
turning
You are the water that covers the
fountain
You are the shadow behind every
mountain

You are the showers that nourish the
meadows
You are the shade from the sun
You are the sparkle that lives in the
diamond
You are the reason for Love

Earle A Kraft

Earle A Kraft
GULL WITH A BROKEN WING

To all our feathered friends along the seashore

Of all the sorrow that life can bring
Nothing's so sad as
A gull with a broken wing.

Never again to soar on high
But to watch his own in the sky
Only to fear what his
Short life will bring . . .

The sad, sad gull with a broken
wing.

Never to ride an Ocean swell
Never to perch on a ships bell
Never to fish dive and sing . . .

The sad, sad gull with a broken
wing.

Ethel Bernice Ridgeway
WHAT IS TRUTH?
Truth is a foundation, so strong and
safely laid
You can build "your all" upon it and
need never be afraid.
The wisest man in all the world, that
ever was, or will be,
Said, "Buy the Truth but sell IT
not,"—and it will set you free;
Truth can be sold, or be exchanged,
for money or for pleasure
But money cannot buy it, for it's
valued above measure.
To buy the truth, there is a price:
That you will have to pay;
All worldly interests—you must put
behind you—there to stay.
No turning back to worldly things,
for that would mean—you see?
That you had sold the truth—and
lost—your precious liberty;
What a price to pay! What an
exchange! For grief and misery.

With truth you have an option, you
can reject it, or employ it,
You can twist, and bend, and stretch
it, but never can destroy it
Truth will clear the conscience—and
let you sleep at night
And truth will give you self-respect,
one needs to walk upright.
Truth can lift you up, to a higher
plane, than you have ever found;
And give you—everything it takes—
to stand on higher ground.
There's one thing—God requires of
us: It's give your heart to Me,
For He knows, where your heart is,
there will your treasure be
Truth! Forever on the scaffold! Does
not matter where—or whence,
Truth! Will never need defending!
For it is—its own defense.

John Rosa
WHAT IS LOVE

I dedicate this poem to my wife Nancy.

What is Love?
Where does it come from?
Does it come from the heart
or is it from the soul?
Do you search for it
or is it within you?
Why must one Love?
Is it to be strong,
wise,
happy,
or is it to have all these combined?
Love is such a magical word.
It has many meanings,
But to those
who search for these meanings,
close your eyes and hold your heart
and there you shall find,
The Love of all mankind.

Shirley O'Driscoll
RUSTI

Dedicated to Michael, Paul & Peter

There are scores of dogs in this
world we know—
Big ones, small ones, fast ones and
slow.
Some for protection, some just a
friend—
Some earn a living, sheep and cattle
they tend.
Man's best friend—I'm sure tis true
Especially that one dog I knew.
Eyes like dark pools that could laugh
and love
And silken ears as soft as a dove.
She was gentle, sympathetic and
loyal till the end.
You would go far before finding
another such friend!
She loved us each one in her own
special way
And would press hard against us to
try to convey
How deeply she cared, and how
great was her need
To be part of our lives—a
companion indeed.

She romped in the wind and dozed in the sun—
Coaxed for candies and cookies from most everyone.
Her rusty red paws in mischief would stray
As she'd chase birds off the lawn and cats far away.

Mike brought her home—after paying too much.
She slept in his bed, chewed his sneakers and such.
She loved him so dearly and patiently yearned
Each time he left home, for his early return.

With Peter, the youngest, she could really relate—
They went on adventures both early and late.
They skied on the hills and swam in the pool—
It was a problem to keep her from going to school!

When to England we moved and left her behind
Paul & Lily took over—they were so kind!
For three long years she was theirs all alone.
They loved her and cared for her with never a moan.
And then we came back and claimed her our own.

Eleven years and a bit with our family she stayed—
Then that was enough, she died unafraid.
Paul held her tight and whispered goodbye
And was not ashamed of a tear in his eye.

It's hard to believe that no more will she roam.
Her last resting place is the garden at home.
No more will she bark and romp with the boys—
And partake in all the family's sorrows and joys.

We'll always remember our dog—there's no better
Than Rusti, our cherished and loved Irish Setter!

Nikki Kollman
SLEEPLESS ORPHAN
God looks after
Most anything that dies
Or tries to.

Well, who haunts the heart?
Earth awakens the young boy
And birds nocturnal
Come softly in his room.

"I don't want to be me"
Echo in his room
And visitors from another time
Brings sadness.

Jean Lee Pacotti
ONE TOUCH
Just one touch of the Master's hand
can change the life of a wayward man.
Though your heart has been broken,
your dreams shattered too,
Look up! Look up! He is waiting for you.

Gently He will take you and make you His own.
Sheltered in His bosom you'll never be alone.
He'll mend your shattered dreams
and heal your broken heart,
wipe away your tears
and give you a brand new start.

Joy and peace, a never-ending love
is sent to you from the father above.
Trust in Him to shed light upon your way.
Rejoice, believe, knowing each and every day,
it only takes one touch of the
Master's hand.

W P Tillinghast

W P Tillinghast
PASTEL

Dedicated to my dearest of friends, Susan Cline Allen

I love fleeting things
caught in half-shadow:
a whispering sigh,
an incipient smile,
the gleam of an eye—
insubstantial things
drifting by
on gossamer wings
like tangential smoke—
—ghosts of emotions
trembling briefly in ambient air.

Memories they are,
such fragile things
they touch the heart
for one brief moment
with gentle fire

then are gone,
leaving behind
only sparks
of dying desire.

S A Tabah
THE MAGIC OF LOVE
Liven the Song with your music,
Give it your sentiment of love,
Kindle its everlasting wick,
Release its endearing Dove.

This is nature's silent beauty;
It is innocent—without sin.
To give it sounds is our duty;
And love to its beauty within.

It really beckons us,
To the garden of its Eden;
Wishing to enter thus,
We must now begin the weeding.

Sing with the Universal song,
Making it vibrate;
Its beauty'll change all wrong;
And love will change all hate.

Majestic but silent;
Entreating us to give our Love;
We are the implement,
And enjoy our returns from above!

Frederick V Jordan
VISION

This poem is dedicated to my first true love, Sarah L. Mangano.

Vibrant blue
with pinetree needles
sprinkled 'bout the sky.
Streaks of blood
and cottonpuffs, grey
then the colors die.

A cold, deep black
with deep, deep blue
like a cotton quilt, we saw
a silhouette hill
and lack of light
our visions' now turned raw.

We see no light,
though color's gone
we see all to be seen.
For not through our eyes
but through our hearts'
as an omniscient day in dreams.

Geneve Baley
THE DOUBLE-SINK BATH
Double-sink bathrooms
Are Hollywood movie, creations
I thought, until my friends lent me theirs—

What a no-line-waiting,
Morning-break, inspiration
This bathroom becomes,
For spouses racing off,
Each their own way, on their chores—
(And both at the same time!)

America, this is the
Ultimate innovation!
And not just for TV movies and Hollywood.

Mary Agnes Lynch
HAPPY, HAPPY, VALENTINE'S DAY
Hearts and flowers, love so true,
Flying doves, loves new,
Fancy candies, ribbons, and lace,
Cupid's arrow, finds its place.
Cards of love, here, and there,
Happiness, is everywhere.

"Hugs, and kisses, here to stay,
Flying Angels, shout "Hooray,"
Boy meets girl, their hearts entwine,
Making each other, their Valentine.
Telegram messages; love songs, that say,
"Happy", "Happy," Valentine's Day".

Louella M Allen
THANKS FOR OUR VOLUNTEERS

To my superlative husband, John, and four precious sons & their families.

For all the love they conjure
When clouds are hovering low,—
When they say, "you can do it!"
While client's pains cry, "No!"

For all they do and all they give,
And for making life more fun to live;

They're listening and sharing—
They're loving and caring.

Our volunteers bring the tender touch
To encourage the folks who need so much.

Elizabeth Y Kelly
WIND TUNNELS AT NOONDAY

To my sister, EVE KRAM, whose love and staunch support has helped me weather many a storm.

Wind tunnels at noonday are asleep inside,
Crew's at lunch—the winds have died.
Wild and willful gales all still and quiet now;
The frozen tundra of the will
That sought to break the hearts
Of all the aircraft's cells
(By searing them in manmade hells
To cancel flights) has melted into darkness
Like the lights.
But I have seen them make those tropic storms
And witnessed while the swirling swarms of energy
Were used to test the very metal of their spleens—
To check again reality
Beneath the hides of fantasy machines.

It's just an ordinary factory
I'm sure that's what it seems to be
To all the folks who take the noonday tour—
Nothing here but bits of planes to see;
Conveyor belts of parts, they think—
I'm sure.
But that's because they haven't seen
The inner sanctum, where I've been.

Louise Carter
THE HOMELESS
The Wind blows Cold across the town
Here and there the lights grow dim
Home fires burning all Aglow
As folks begin to settle down.

Thankful for a place to sleep
Someone too hold and love
Not thinking of the World outside
Where some have not enough to eat.

Nestled there on soft warm beds
In our cozy homes
Some where outside the cold wind blows
The homeless Cry Alone.

Patricia Ann Martin
DO WE TAKE TIME TO PRAY?

Dedicated to Jesus Christ My Savior, who saved me, the Martin and Carroll families.

When we get up each morning, do we take time to pray,
To thank the Lord for letting us live another day?
Early in the morning before we eat, do we take time to pray,
To thank the Lord for the food on our table today?

On our way to our jobs or whatever we do,
Do we take time to pray, to ask him to guide and
Protect us throughout the day?

Do we pray without ceasing during the day,
To make us strong to fight temptations which come our way?
Do we take time to pray?

Well, the day is at an end, as night draws nigh,
Do we take time to pray?
Do we get beside our bed and fall on our knees,
To thank the Lord for sending his son Jesus who
Died for our sins to set us free?
Do we take time to pray?

So, as a christian, you and I every day
Need to take time to pray.
The Lord will answer all prayers for you,
For prayer is really a pleasure to do.
So, let's all take time to pray.

Michael Wilczewski
THE DESERT
Traveling through the desert we were tired,
So we stopped to have a look
The desert is bare and naked,
It is quiet, but the roadside lizard might give a spook.
Where the last rains sunk there are wide cracks,
Looking out seeing the endless plain through the window.
On the distant dunes there are dune buggy tracks,
The mighty cactus cast their huge shadow.
The desert is one place that will take your breath away,
That is why we plan that some day, we will come its way.

In the morning I can feel the sunrise,
The sun is bright gold on the red desert floor.
Occasional snakes hide away from the heat,
Deep into its crack away from the blazing sun.
The sky is blue and I can feel the sun's beat,
Everything is clear with perfect vision.
The desert is as flat as a table,
If there is any mountains, they are like a wall.
The dry grass looks perfect for the stable,
The day is over and the sun is over the horizon like an orange ball.

Hilda Adams Bonebrake Suter
OH HECK
I hustle and bustle to prepare my desk,
Dictionary, pencils, carbon paper, all is ready.
The house is quiet, everyone has left,
Here I sit and sit with glassy stare
Writhe with anguish, pop my knuckles bite my nails,
Thoughts so light now more like lead
These confounded pages stare back at me
Empty! empty—empty as my head.

Timothy Stifel
NIGHTWEAR
There are nights I need more
than one pillow to keep me up

Thinking of you never
brings me down

It's the spaces between thoughts

To be raised up you must wear more
than one sock

Not when skiing

I never run clear down-hill
Pause mid-way and choose

Brown sheets are discomforting
Bring them anyway

Kerry V Kirkpatrick
DANA PRAJNA PARAMITA

To my beautiful wife and family, and to all who have, or seek to attain the "one-point", and follow "the way".

Alas, the quieting rains.
Thin arrows of light warm distant hearts.
Basking, with widened smiles.
Awaiting . . .
awaiting.
The dismal grey heavens move,
trailed by azure.
Sponge-like, the earths' floor draws.
Feeding, nourishing that which sustains . . .
life.
In flight,
the song is heard.
Enlightened smiles know.
Everything is nothing . . .
is nothing.
Waters' surface . . .
ripples of the mind.
Moving.
Calm.
Revealed truth.

Nellie Keller
THE NIGHT BEFORE CHRISTMAS ON THE LAKE.

To All My Children (Nee Mirth) Friends OAHE Bate Shop of Mobridge S.D. Also My best friends Lewis and Game Warden Gary

It was the night before Christmas.
Not a fish was stirring not even a minnow or the likes.
They had set up their ice houses and bored the holes.
In hopes they would catch a walleye or a Pike.

When all of a sudden the ice it shook,
And to their wondering eyes they saw.
There skimming along a big old Chinook.
With eight big cats and a scaly old Carp.
Went speeding across the lake as if they out for,
A skating race or just a skating lark.

Golly Oh gee they all shouted,
No one will ever believe us.
JOE, MICK or LEW where is your cameras,
HOME, they replied then begin to rant and cuss.
Have a Merry Christmas THEY shouted,
But you will never catch US.
We are the GHOST CHRISTMAS ANGLES OF ALL FISH.
THEY shouted as they disappeared with a rush.

Maria Elena Tolentino
DAVY & DAISY
It started with my boyfriend
It ended with a friend
How was I to figure,
I would lose him in the end.

I met this boy name Davy
The boy was kind of crazy
He was a little lazy,
I guess that's how he met Daisy.

They, met while I was working
They've seen each other then
when Dave was with me all alone,
he did nothing but pretend.

I saw his little Daisy
Around him she did flirt
I took a closer look at her,
Boy, did she look hurt!

He confessed he had a lover
and said, "Good-bye my dear!."
"I found someone who loves me more,
I want to make this clear!".

So he walked out and left me
Guess who was by the door
His little smiling Daisy,
looking uglier than before.

So that's my little story
One by now I understand
But still I can't get over,
Daisy being another . . . man!.

Clarence B Bobbitt
WHERE CHRIST IS FOUND

Dedicated to my Lord and Saviour Jesus Christ, for His Glory, to help some seeking soul to find His everlasting Love.

Where is Christ, God's Son, who
came to earth long ago—
To heal the sick, and rescue sinners
from a life of woe?

Will you find Him with the great, in
the "Hall of fame"?
The Saviour, who came to save from
all sin and its shame.

Does He sit with the "United
Nations" to seek for peace?
Is He the one who builds bombs
instant destruction to release?

Do you find Him in the courts and on
the judge's bench,
Or with the cruel merciless mobs
who burn, pillage, and lynch?

NO! but you find Him in flowers of
beauty, and Gospel song,
And the Church that stands as a
bulwark against all wrong.

He is found where there is peace, and
joy, and Christian love;
In His Church, in Christian homes,
and in all those born from above.

M A Lugo
ROSES ARE RED

To Elizabeth

Roses are red;
Bananas are yellow;
To write good poems,
Ya' gotta be mellow.

Roses are red;
Watermelons are big;
Ya' want a good poem?
Well, you gotta dig.

Roses are red;
Like that of ketchup;
If you mess–up once,
You shouldn't give up.

Roses are red;
And shared with good friends;
If you mess–up once,
Try it again.

Roses are red;
Oranges are orange;
Some poems rhyme,
But this one doesn't.

Lorraine Alison Johnson
EBB TIDE

This poem is dedicated to the shepherd who rescued a lost lamb Thank you.

While walking along the sea shore,
To clear my thoughts of you,
I find it an impossible thing to do.

Your rugged face, your smile and warm eyes keep the memories of our love alive

Alone "Osprey flies low over the surf, and I marvel at its flight, oh to be free as a bird on the wing, that's how our love should have been.

But not to be, you and me our love was one born out of infidelity.
Now as I watch the ebbing tide,
So too must the memories of you,
Recede forever to the back of my mind.

Art W Gregory
STAY WITH THE ONE YOU OUGHT
Once I wrote to a love
But then I forgot
To keep myself to her like I ought.
I blew our dreams into the wind
scattering ever so endlessly
Never knowing where they fell
Trying to pick up the pieces
of my Nightingale!!
Now she's with another
I know it's my fault
cause I couldn't keep myself
to her like I ought.
So now this story ends
with a word of advice!!,
Stay with The ONE You Ought.

Lori Reynolds
IN THE END

For all who've learned this lesson and choose to ignore it, too.

There are times when a soul needs mending, and so you turn, with eyes full of sorrow, and words full of pain, to anyone, the first someone with open arms and an open heart.

He need not be special, or unique, or kind; he needs just to be there. Somehow, your mind makes up that which he lacks.

Without his knowing, or meaning to, he'll cure your sorrow, heal your wounds. You'll love him, or what you've made him, for to love him is easier than to hate the other.

Hate is never forgotten, never forgiven, but somehow that love of hatred will change to a love of anyone close enough to touch.

You'll not be able to infer the real, from what you've created to nurse your own wound, that caused you to run needlessly to him.

The real and non, will merge into one, a perfect being. That no one will ever be.

You'll know in the end, that the end has come and you now must part.

Knowing all this right from the start, stop, take heed, don't put him into your heart.

Helen Cecil Pierce
SPECIAL CHILD

There's an ache in my heart
That has no ending;
A crack in the casing
For which there's no mending . . .
One precious bud . . . came into the world
With a shine and glow, like a new polished pearl;
The bud did grow, but the brightness dimmed
And the promise and hope once held grew dim . . .
Somewhere. somehow, something went wrong,
The petals unfolded, but the glow was gone.
This flower, so different, must suffer pain;
I long to help it, but all in vain.
Only God knows what the outcome will be . . .

Is it asking too much for Him to tell me?

I put my trust in Him always . . .

Even diamonds don't sparkle on cloudy days!

Beth A Bagent
RESTLESS LOVE

Love can be restless,
just like the sea
Your heart can be tossed,
like the waves in a storm
Your feelings can be mixed
like the particles of the tide
that are washed up on the shore
in the early morn.

Roberto A López
THE BATTLE'S OVER

I dedicate this poem to the creator of all things and my wonderful family.

When the battle began I led myself to believe the opposition had won,
I was cast into anxiety, fear and pain I could not shun,
Therefore, in the outer circle of confusion I dwelt, swept away by its magnetism,
Locked away in trouble and doubt, drenched in its pessimism, deep within myself there was an entity that cried out for strength,
To fight this pestilence to the distance in over all length,
Through the midst of it all I was bonded to a gracious and merciful force,
As if I crossed a hot desert sand upon the back of horse,
Not feeling the scorching heat that burns like a torch,
The journey I have traveled has made it all worth while,
I look back on my mistakes and still manage to smile,
All along my head was covered from the battle,
I now possess a power that no man can ever rattle,
Yes, my good fortune did take some time,
And time confirms that things earned fast are not worth their while,
I made many errors but I did not fail,
I came on strong like thunder and hail,
I have strived to see clearly like looking through a glass,
And now that time in my life has come to pass
The battle's over.

Geraldine McDonough
HALLUCINATION

And then I saw,
Beautiful,
Green valleys,
And fields of,
Yellow grain,
Whole, people,
There was,
No one,
That was lame.

Sunshine forever,
And, no cloudy day,
There was,
Food a plenty,
And no one,
Went astray.

Children were,
A blessing,
Brother and sister,
Were close,
Governments,
Got along,
Almost.

Neighbors,
And friends,
Were endeared,
I closed,
And opened,
My eyes,
It all, had,
Disappeared.

Jane A Williams
IN SYMPATHY

To my grandmother Elizabeth Elsheimer Brandt 1864-1960

Accept what is inevitable,
Enjoy what life achieves,
Let happiness abide with you
Because you must believe
That all who come must also go,
We stay but for awhile
And through the veil of tears that flow
Some future day we'll smile
Remembering all the good times past,
How fortunate we are
To have fond memories to re-live
So sorrow leaves no scar.

Nancy C Harvey
YOUR TOUCH OF LOVE

Today I looked for you, in spite of rainy weather,
Among the trees and flowers we have enjoyed together.
I found you in the daffodils, among the yellow flowers;
I found you with the Robins feeding in the yard for hours;
I found you in the flowing spring with all its water blue;
I found you in the apple trees with bursting buds so new.
For when I looked around, I saw your touch of love for me
In all the things you planted—a flower, shrub, or tree.
I know when I am walking on another rainy day,
Your love will always touch me, all along the way.

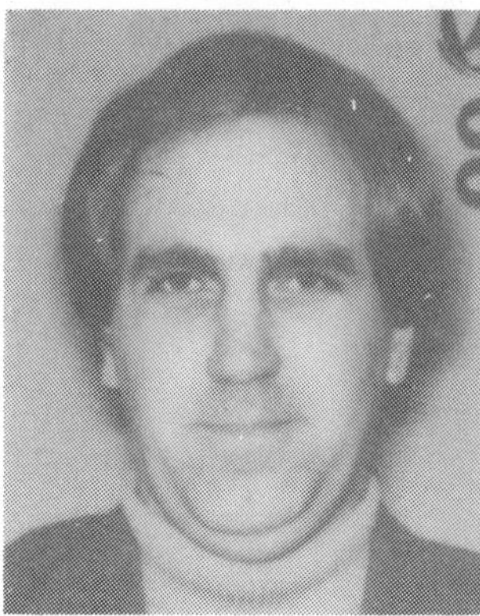

James I Moore Jr

James I Moore Jr
THE KEY

This is for all of those out there who are trying to find a better way to understand how simple life can really be.

Isn't it strange, how often we blame, others for who we are.

Why can't you be what I need for me? Why can't I be in return? You see, friendship is something, I've come to learn, that each of us, together, must carefully earn.

It's not something nice that you order with ice, nor can it be bought in a jar. It's not something you mix or that's easily fixed . . . It's who and what you are.

How do you find this, you ask of me, how do you figure it out? Instead of spending so much of your life, always looking and seeking without . . .
You must go back to the beginning to change the end, you must always reflect from within.

To first know one's self, better than anyone else, is the key that will open the door. For once you pass through, it will be clearer to you, that your best friend is none other than yourself.

Then you'll find, almost all of the time, how easy you are to befriend. The less you expect, the more you will get, or so it will probably seem. You see, life's nothing more than a beautiful dream that each day we make our reality.

So you'll be, what I need for me, and I will be for you . . .

Tanya Lynn Main
BROKEN HEARTS, NEW HEARTS

This poem is dedicated to my mother, Shirley, for believing in me and my writing.

In our hearts there is love,
And in our minds we know,
Someone will come along,
And we'll have to let go.

Our hearts will grow,
Our lives will change,
Like the seasons in the year,
Yet the thoughts still remain.

Our memories are fond,
Of a love that could have been,
Let our hearts grow freely,
This is now, that was then.

Hearts get broken,
Still hearts can always mend,
Put the past behind us,
This life won't end.

Gay Wheeler
LONELY LOVE

Missing you.
Before you go,
While you're gone,
When you return,
With fear for when you leave again.

While you are away,
Think of me.
See me in the clouds.
Hear me in nature's sounds.
Feel me as the wind enfolds you and embraces you for me.

Perhaps, it's in the missing,
In the longing,
In the aching,
That the true realization of love arrives.

Angeline Josephine Mazza
MISSING YOU GRACE KELLY

Her Highness Princess Caroline Casiraghi Monaco The Prince Rainier Royalty Monaco Palace De Monaco Princess Caroline children Andrea-Charlotte-Pierri-Monaco

One noble torch is not enough
For people you rest beautiful forever
In the sun on the heart that is alas bright light life
That year that time your majestic voice
The triumph love your spirit soul peace
All were for the world survival
You left everyone felt with grief sorrow
Why did they take away your life
How still the world with your heart your soul
Does it sound of the truth mile to mile
Along with the vague bell sounds

To share life with this earth forever
Born for the people must die for the people
Live thy throne Monaco forever
Though what is worth living worth being

So here you lie beautiful princess
Grace Kelly Monaco
To tell America as the world love you
With love history now forever
missing you
Some body else but me princess love
peace royalty of the world
Your children grand children Palace
De Monaco forever
Those yet be born
With majestic royalty forever

Marie L Mapes
TIME IN SPACE

To my parents in loving memory of all they have done for me.

Time in space
i won't forget
we ripped apart each other
we ripped apart the state,
the country
we ripped apart our world,
our universe
we laughed at many Lifes now
and cried about an Infinity later
we had ripped apart ourselves,
we had looked at the pieces
there alone on the floor
we wondered what in this
world we had done
because we realized finally that
those pieces were nothing alone
that somehow they have to get
All together.

Barbara H Clark
OH HEAR ME, MY HUSBAND OF THE PAST

I am
tired of
games.

I was
confused
by the
Mulberrys.

Our marriage
is
Dead.

My hopes
and dreams
were
shattered.

My would be
memories
have been
reduced
to
Zero.

Our children
and
families
have been
chilled
to the
bone.

I now have
no time,
no thoughts,
no feelings,
to share
with you.

I want time
with
my children.

I wish
for my
thoughts
to be
heard.

My feelings
are to be
shared,
in and with
Love.

I can Love,
as I have
Loved.

And for this
awareness
of me,
I Thank
GOD.

Ms Mary Ann Franco
HARMONY

Talk to me I'm real, let me touch you
I feel.
Be with me just for a time. Can we
explore each others mind? Precious
time is wasted on petty little things
worrying about tomorrow and what
the day brings thinking about
problems life passes by, before you
know it time to die.

If we understand, if we reach out, if
we can find what we are really about.
If when it's time we can leave with a
smile knowing we made our lives a
bit more worth while.

James William Truett

James William Truett
BEFORE THE BEGINNING

Dedicated to my true love and my beloved.

In the hours between darkness
And creation
There were no sunrises . . . not yet,
No ocean tides to ebb and flow.
No atoms were yet formed into
matter
Under the pressure of starlight
Because there were no stars.
But there was beauty and intelli-
gence
Unlimited.
They were in the mind and heart
And soul of the Creator,
And I know that He had you in mind
Even . . . then

Tom Galasso
TOO LATE?

We are one;
Five billion cells and goal and lives
Are one.
Perhaps the Gods of Love and Light
Shall save us from our daughter,
night.
Is it the will, have we the right
To fight the blight who calls the rite
of night?
Is the future
predecided?
Is humanity
divided—or not?
On the surface of the sea
There is none but all and we
Do we choose the end to be
Or can we be eternally
Can we. . will we, are we—Too
Late?

Alice Farnsworth
UNIVERSE WITHIN?

A twilight world of whirling thought
where time flows
unfettered,
unsought.
A place within,
without,
and all around
where there is no need for sight
or sound.
Where thought and energy are
complete
and physical forces cannot compete!
A place in all
where all is known.
A place apart,
yet not alone.
Here a being is set free
to be
Whatever it was meant to be!

Lisa L Kay
CAUGHT

Inside these walls lives a prisoner.
Confined and alone he struggles to
be free.
No bars, no locked doors keep him,
for he's a prisoner of life inside those
walls.
His jail is loneliness.

Teresa Jorgenson
TIME

Time once told me, I've been around
for quite a long while.
You may not realize that your life is
measured only by a second in mine.
Time is of the essence they say,
laughing, I seem to fly away they say,
I can even stand still.
Pausing, looking over the vast
scenery before itself, Time spoke
again.
I've seen many things your story
books have not told you.
Things that have happened in the past
are but stories now.
I am the greatest storyteller.
I can see you live your life and
fulfilling your dreams.
New stories to be told, events to be
watched and recorded.
Listening to what I am saying I can
heal your wounds you are feeling . . .
just give me time.

Carl L Anderson
A SENIOR CITIZEN

Yesterday they sold my lovely home;
The children thought I should not
live alone.
They said I might fall and hurt
myself,
Or that I would not eat enough to
keep my health;
That the money from my little home
Would keep me in some nearby
nursing home—
Provided I shared a room with
someone else,
And did not require too much care
myself.
It would be a shelter but it's not a
home!

The daffodils are pressing through
the ground;
The dormant grass is greening all
around.
I always liked the early blooms the
best;
They seem so cheerful after winter's
rest.
The robins have come back; I've
heard them sing,
Proclaiming that the winter's past,
and now it's spring.
Folks say, "If winter comes, spring
will follow."
But when you're old, there is no
Spring to follow:
Old age is a Winter that has no
Spring'.

Sara Susan Hilbers
STRUGGLING GRACE

Wheat fields dance, as strong winds
blow, crisp and cool and strong.
Winter months come swiftly, and
summer soon be gone.
Wood is stacked up carefully, outside
the cabin door—
A glow of warmth from fire, reflects
across the floor.
Mothers prayer heard softly, that
crops will not be lost—
while sitting in her rocking chair,
knitting warmer socks.
Wailing heard throughout the night,
through winds of bitter cold—
Daddy sits reflecting, though his
story's never told.
Candle light fades quickly, and
darkness fills the room,
except the coals of deepest red, like
roses in full bloom.
Children resting in their beds, with
dreams of warmer day—
dancing through the golden fields,
the smell of fresh cut hay.
Morning creeps in quietly from black
to silver gray,
Silence fills the tiny room, for lack
of words to say.
Daddy dresses quickly, to fight the
chilling cold
and mama cooking quietly, beside the
black wood stove.
Children dress and gather round to
say the morning grace—
together they all bow their heads, to
solemnly give thanks.
Daddy stands with his eyes closed,
and tears run down his face.
He says, "Dear God, we thank you,
for this home and for this place"

Lisa Haynes-Farmer
PROMISES SING

For Phillip, Thank you for sharing my journey. I Love You.

When twilight comes
day noises slip away on the back
of the sun
and sighs perfume the air.

Promises sing, as we lay together:
cool, cotton sheets pressing
gently;
skin hot and touching sensitive.

Your body completes mine.
Molded flesh, we blend together.
Where you stop, I begin.

Greedily, we spend the dark hours
until touches turn to dreams.
Shadows kissing sleep.

And then . . . too soon . . .
sleepy dreams float away on
secret winds,
like you did, as I slept.

Lazy stretches steal the night
but day noises fail to shout
away
the hum of silence surrounding
me.

I press my palm against your pillow print
savoring the whisper of heat
you left for me, while promises sing.

Melody A Evans
MY DAUGHTER'S EYES

I look into my daughter's eyes.
Soft, blue as the perfect sky.
I see all the world there,
where innocence is absent of thought
and clear mind without reason,
is like life before.
The sun is captured in tiny flakes of gold
surrounding the eclipse of the moon,
the eyes of twilight enhancing heavenly stars
that float in an ocean of black.
Untouched, awesome in their power.
In her eyes, I see life lived.
Complete.
Before days of tears have found their place.
They are the windows of her soul
with a spirit running free,
like the glistening waters of the streams, clean and fresh.
I feel the breeze that glides across green prairies,
rustling through majestic trees
hundreds tall, years alive.
They show me the strength in the crashing surf that brings and takes away.
Life. Solid and whole.

My eyes have seen a tiny miracle.
So perfect in God's image.
Transcendent, as are her flawless, soft swirls of blue,
My Daughter's eyes.

T R Leiby
LOVE UNION

To R,V,C,E, Your love just made this poem to be.

To start your lives together
In the marriage of your hearts,
It's the love you share together
As each and every day starts.
So don't think that this union
Is a shadow in the dark,
It's the love you share together
And nothing will keep you apart.

Sandra Quarles Bussell
OUR SIGNATURE IN TIME

As writers old with scripted hand
Compiled their thoughts and rhymes
We too set out to write our lives
Our plan laid out through time

We outlined how we thought would be
The days ahead to share
We planned and dreamed and laughed and cried
We sought to take great care

But in "forever after"
We garnered but a token
Our final chapter closed too fast
With last good-byes unspoken

So my memories are written down
In books with faded line
To chronicle our laughs and love
Our Signature in Time

Franklin D Sampley
IN AWE

Tell me why, Oh, why—
Does man stand in awe
of the sea?
Why, Oh why,
does man look afar,
and seek to see?
Why must man seek
the world to him to bow,
and always reach
for greater strength and power?

Is it so important
the world to control?
The glory of earth and heaven—
Powerful and awesome as a whole
to be subjugated to man's
small and weak hands?
Broken and shattered we look
upon man's handiwork,
powerful illusive structures,
built on earth's destructions.

Juanita Cozart
ALONE

Wm Bryant Chase, my son

I stand barefoot in the wet sand,
As the waves beat upon the shore,
I long for the far away land,
Lost to me forever more.

Tears of regret wet my cheeks,
Salt on my lips from the sea,
No one to know my heart weeps,
Oh, to be free, to be free.

Peggy Abbott
GOD'S BLESSINGS

The sun shone brightly on the day we said "We Do".
Not a big wedding, our families and friends of few.
We spoke of our future, Lord, as we started on our way,
Our happiness was so deep—what could we really say.

We visualized our children,
sometimes smiling or with tears,
Crawling on our laps with their childhood woes and fears.
Our hearts were filled with joy and we thank the Lord above
That he blessed us with children to cherish and love.

Our Families gather from near and far when holidays arrive,
Making our home more gloriously alive.
Children laughing everywhere, the aroma of good food,
Seeing our blessings puts us in a happy mood.

Dear Blessed Father in the Heavens above,
We promise to guard these children and give them our love,
To teach them all about you and pray with them each day,
To love and care for all mankind in every way.

Michelle M Havens
THE BEGINNING

It is beautiful and perfect
The sunrise is brilliantly crafted
Purples drip into the yellows, pinks dance with the grays
Over yonder the sparrows sing
They, too, are beholding the sight
Now, as I sit here, wonder why the world has problems
So I solve them and continue eating my raisins

Steven H Yaskell
MURRES RUN TO THE SEA

I see them start their evening run
Startled issue in the sun
Of starlight, so bright on this night
I spend with them
As they hurdle from their nests,
Led by their parents forward
On this unpracticed vigil seaward
Unseeing in the underbrush through spruce needles
Blind, but faithful to the fact
Of following
Beyond the tide,
They skip into the
Foam over the breaking rucking
Labrador coast, darker than the
Glowing green of worrisome waters
Specks, alighting black and white in flits
Under and over beneath the riveted stars,
Round, buoyant bulbs of tufted
Feathers for the seed, so seemingly delicate
Around the haul and gape
Of the ocean.

Ken McFall
FLOWER SEEDS

To my Grandson Gregory

I thought that I would never breed,
A poem in homage to a flower seed;

A seed whose life seeks its quest,
Within the earth, where firmly pressed.

A seed that struggles on all day,
To fight the choking weeds of prey;

A seed so small depends on God,
To help its offshoots break the sod.

A million times their size, in stages grow,
From tiny seeds, to a flower show;

Providing sweet nectar for the humming bird,
Where flights of bumblebees are heard.

Poems are made, sometimes within the hour,
But only God can make a seed into a flower.

Rosemary Sullivan
WINTER WARMTH

For Michael, Sean, Rebecca and Emily, I love you all. Love, Mom

Bears find themselves somewhere
Warm to sleep

Insects crawl way underneath

Birds migrate south to keep
From the cold

The trees lose their leaves
They can no longer hold

Rabbits change color to keep
Them from harm

But all I have to do
Is curl up in your arms

Irene Nettles Steely
ONCE AGAIN, HERE IT IS—FATHER'S DAY

To my father, David Cromwell Nettles

Once again, here it is—Father's Day,
And there are some things I really want to say.

When I was young, you guided directed and loved me,
And set an example for all the world to see.

You spanked me when I was bad,
And that made me very mad,

But you cheered me when I was sad,
And I thought you were the very best dad.

You were a very good man,
Helping me every way you can.

You taught me everything you could,
To learn from you, if only I would.

You were always ready to stand up and fight,
For whatever you thought was right.

You saved Sunday for a day of rest,
To thank God for all that is best.

You always put your needs last,
So that my needs could be met fast.

You comforted me during the thunder,
And straightened my path, when I would wander.

You gave me strength and courage to endure,
Each day that would ensue.

You did a miracle, as a man,
To make me (a girl) into a woman.

Poems are made by daughters, like me,
But only God can make a FATHER, you see.

Francis A LaCroix
THE PAINTER POET

To my wife, an artist.

Mute of words
The painter poet speaks his message
By lively forms and colors:
Brushed onto stretched canvases,
Etched on metal plates,
Brought forth from sculpted stone or marble,
Built up into busts so carefully formed,
Or stroked into painted likenesses.
The ways of saying are many
Leaving messages in the human brain
Yet, each seer sees images differently
According to his own world of seeing.

Sharie Lynne Bradt
NATURE'S VOICES

A softly caressing chorus are the voices
Of nature

A rippling tide whose notes crescendo as
Each pounds on the smooth sands

A gulls bellowing whistle clashes with the
Winds whisper

Cradling the love of many He creates His
Own chorus of nature's voices

Sharyn L Prajzner
LIFE—IT'S ULTIMATE

A special dedication to my brother Curtis who loved and was loved. To my mother and brother—I love you so very much. Thanks for believing in me.

To experience the ultimate in this life
is an accomplishment above all
What is this extreme ultimate?
How do you know you have experienced it?
You have loved and been loved in return
You have seen the radiant dawning of a new day and the exquisite sunset
You have felt the soft mystifying breeze and felt its defiant rage
You have smelled the sweet fragrance of the honeysuckle and the radiant glow of the wheat fields blowing in the winds
You have known the gentle touch of

a mother with her newborn child and the soft caress from someone you love.
Yet, with all of this you have not felt the ultimate in life til you have peace of mind and heart
Only then can you experience the beauty of love and accept it with an open heart and mind.
With this in mind, I can only learn and look forward to giving and receiving the love that I need to share. mnnn

Carol McCune

Carole McCune
SAD BUT TRUE

To the Creator of all mankind, and to my good friends whoever they may be

Most people are selfish, don't you think?
personally! I think they stink.
When it comes to needing a friend,
Who will be with you to the very end,
Just look around: and then you'll see,
You can't count many, regretfully,
who will be with you constantly.

When you think you can depend,
on the many friends you thought you had.
Yes: It's too bad;
That maybe some stranger,
will be the one,
You will finally have to depend upon.

Diana Glendowne
NEVER BORN

This child was never born.
I never found the courage to follow thru with the mistake I made; with the sin that was committed.
So I killed her before she could get to know me.
She never saw my blue eyes. Were her eyes blue?
She never saw my curly hair. Was her hair to be curly?
She never saw me drunk—thank God for that!
I never had to punish her. But I never got to hold her.
I never got to bathe her.
I'll never get to see her grow into what our Lord had planned for her to become.
She will never know the cruelties of this life, nor will she ever know the beauties of life on earth, as there can be so many.
I never had the opportunity to teach her how to pray.

But, right now she is talking face to face with the Lord.

John Backetti
BEE IN THE SUNSHINE OF MAY

Pastel petals—
Transparent wings.
a messenger carries the crystal.
Just a slight humming sound,
and a swift, defined pattern;
The treasure's received
with an unprepared kiss.

Calvin M Richens
WRITERS' HAND

Living word
On living page
Cause us laughter,
Fill with rage.

Words alone have
Caused great wars.
Still other words
Have opened doors.
Words can change
The way we feel.
Some hurts only
Words can heal.

It's words and thoughts
That made men fly.
But, use them wrong
And men will die.

The greatest power
Known to man
Sits restless in the
Writers' hand.

Stephen L Weesner
MY LOVE

This poem's for you, my darling wife
cause you're the joy of my life.
I know sometimes it's really tough
because I'm hard and crude and rough.
While other men wear nice trim suits,
for me it's jeans and cowboy boots.
While some prefer the city lights,
for me it's starry desert nights.
They drive their cars down nice smooth streets
and watch for places they could eat
I'd find a road with lots of bumps
and eat our lunch out on a stump.
I know I'm just a country boy
but you've brought me the greatest joy.
The thing I'd like to say my dear—
I love you more each passing year.
While some have men for which they boast,
you've got the one that loves you most.

Margaret O'Flaherty
ODE TO JIGGER

From the small village of Iwakuni, Japan to the brown hills of San Jose, Ca I salute you Jigger O'Whiskey, my pal and friend.

I lived a free, nomadic life
Typical of a Navy wife
While in Japan I found this friend
And called him Jigger on a whim

He was a small Eurasian dog
With a personality all his own
Solid brown from tail to jaw
White on his belly and two front paws

He was my body guard, playmate and friend
O, and a lot, a whole lot more
His sweet, endearing puppy ways
Filled my roving, happy days

As a puppy he learned to sit up
Always a sloppy try
One paw drooped, the other straight out
I'd scold him and he would lie down and pout

He had no liking for strangers or cats
And it took him awhile to make friends
A tail was greeting to those he knew
His love he gave to only a few

Brad D Hall
TILL THE MORNING COMES

Sing soft lullabies as I descend into sleep
Let childhood memories be my dream
Let the struggles that crowd my mind
And often burn unkind
Rest in peace for a night
In the dark and out of sight
Sweep me far to the past
To a time when the heart grew not so fast
Sprinkle laughter through my thoughts
Where only sweet visions be caught
Dream away all my sorrow
Until the dawn of tomorrow
As I wander free of worry
Let my eyes open without hurry
Should I wake with a tear
Let a smile be always near
So shall I lay every burden down
Till the morning comes around

Jessica E Barker

Jessica E Barker
ONE FLOWER

I saw one flower, by a stream,
with yellow petals, a stem of green.
The winter winds began to blow,
but birds till sang, the sun still shone.
Leaves began to fall from trees,
one by one in the autumn breeze.
Then one day I looked outside,
snow was falling from the sky.
I bundled up, ran to the stream,
to this spot by the stream.
Sadly it was bending over,
as if to say my life is over.
But just you wait, come back next spring,
to this spot by the stream.
I'll be here you small, sad fellow.
a tall green stem, and yellow petals.

Jerry M DeWoody
DRIVING IN THE FOG

Enveloped and engulfed
In the fog
Invaginated, as it were,
In the valve between
life and limbo;
Struggling up to one,
Sliding back into the liquid,
Mistaking the fog for a caul.

Suddenly fumulus shadows
Loom in immense density,
Everything rears-up before you abruptly,
The boundary of shade
Becomes the wall of fact.
The misted veil of human history
Opens to admit you
Then swishes closed behind,
All becomes Danté anagogical
In this birth/death trauma.

Elaine Hoxie Randolph
YOU

Silent pictures on the mantle
Photos nestled snugly as one
Entice the eyes toward love filled hearts
Emotions drawn in imagery

Red blushed cheeks on black and white film
A formal portrait of Grammy
Aunt Mim's radiant smiling face
Kindness flamed in saintly fire

A teenage vision of my Mom
Timeless youth of more carefree days
An older Mom embraced with Dad
Treasure-trove vistas remembered

My daughter in three pools of glass
Sparkling brown eyes in pressed dresses
Smiles which reflect my memories
Tender warmth held in little hands

Generations on the mantle
Silent support when times get tough
And when life deals a forceful blow
I look, I smile, I think of you

Michelle Ross
SAND

As I walk along the sand
I leave my mark
A mark of who i was
And what I did
Telling all I was here
But just for a second
The tide will roll in
And I will no longer be known

Pauline Romond
MY KITCHEN

In my kitchen I find much pleasure
With sugar and flour and things to measure
Beat in a bowl to become a cake
Into the oven, there it will bake

Be it chocolate, lemon or Boston Cream Pie
It brings a twinkle to my eye

To see my family savor the flavor
Of my earlier morning kitchen labor

Even as a child in the kitchen I'd linger
(Cleaning the cake bowl with my finger)
Watching Mom prepare fruit for preserves
Sometimes in the way and getting on her nerves

As it was with her then, and is with me now
The kitchen's the favorite room some how
And even when I have an occasional guest
They too, enjoy my kitchen best

Yes, my favorite room, but not only to cook in
I put love in a letter to one of my kin
Or have a cup of tea and read a book
Sometimes just sit at the window and look

So fill your kitchen with delicious smells
Of freshly baked bread, and homemade jells
Make it your center for family love
And God will smile His approval above

Denise Dmytrasz
SHADOWS
Attention my dear ladies,
I'm the one you dread the most.
I linger in the background
of you insecurities, I'm the ghost.
It's of me your husband thinks of,
when you can not find the time,
to put a little make-up on, fix your hair
or share some wine.
I am out there and you know it.
I will do the things you won't.
I can make you seem insignificant,
of his every desire, I will dote.
So remember when your husband
takes you in his arms at night.
Be sure it's of YOU he's thinking,
'Cause if you don't . . . of me he might.

Marvin A Long
WHEN YOU AND I MY DEAR MUST PART
When you and I my dear must part
Can sorrow break your tender heart
I to a distant land must roam
Sleep and dream of you alone
All to me will fade away
Night will take the place of day
With these few lines I've hidden
A question
You can see I can not mention.

L Tarrence
HOUSEHOLD-CHORES

This poem is dedicated to Amel, my husband.

This morning as I arose from my bed,
I thought of the household chores ahead.
Just for today I will not worry about a little clutter,
I am going to work in my flower beds and putter.
I will unleash my basset hound and take her for an overdue walk.
My friend is expecting me we will have a cup of coffee and a long talk.
I will relax and read the last chapter from my favorite book,
I don't have to worry about the next meal I have to cook.
My husband and I are going to town to have dinner together,
We will take time to discuss something of interest other than the weather.
The day is over and nightfall is near, my view point on house work is perfectly clear,
Every housewife needs a day off from household chores
It keeps the job from becoming a long tedious bore.

Mindy Heinz
UNTITLED
I
see a man of many faces,
lost in the shadows and seeking
happiness in the blue sky.
He has a regal heir,
he strives for success.
He takes his time, being very
careful of his actions for it
would be embarrassing to fail.
He holds the mystery of the night
and the bright eyes of the day.
He is a cat, sitting with his head held high,
playing with its prey . . .

Mrs Frances Fontino

Mrs Frances Fontino
LEARNING TO LIVE ONE DAY AT A TIME

To Harriett, my sister. For the inspiration you have given me in learning to live one day at a time to prove to myself that it can be done. God Bless You.

Learning to live one day at a time
I thank God for peace of mind,
How grateful to be,
Living in America,
With love and liberty.

Richard Gibson
A MEETING IN THE PARK
There we sat older in years,
The bench still damp from yesterday's painting,
Separated by solitude, dialogue,
And dreams we sought.

Our chance meeting casual—introspective.
Should I be the one to speak?
You broke the silence:
After everything, still my confederate,
My confidant.

The bridges built, the shoring made safe
For our loved ones to cross—unhindered.
(not always so)
We wanted to sit in fields of bright flowers
Soaking in the sunset
From beyond the apple orchard.

Instead, we watched,
The lamp lights flicker;
A couple of wounded with walking sticks
And nothing but our anguish in common.

We will meet again, in the park—theorizing,
Knowing we took the wrong path
Years ago.

Dianne McAllister
GULLS AND SEA
The seagulls full-winged did soar,
Out to sea and back to shore.
And as I watched, my heart aglow,
Such simple peace I did know.

I watched their flight through the sky
And heard their cries as they came by,
While the waves broke in slowing speed
Soothing me in my need.

I had no thought of space and time
My soul engulfed in peace sublime.
The tide pulled water out to sea
While serenity flowed back to me.

Dolores Todaro
SOLDIER BOY

To my husband, Edward Todaro, and all those who answered their nations call and who now rest in our national cemeteries.

Soldier boy, Soldier Boy, tell me is it true, all these things I heard about you?
Did you really toil all day, in the heat and cold?
Did you go willingly, where ever you were told?
Did you give your all, even when it was a drag?
Did you really do that, just for our old flag?
Soldier Boy, Soldier Boy, tell me is it true, all these things I've heard about you?
Did you leave your family, your wife and your children?
Did you go to foreign lands, where you had no friend?
Did you really work all day, and at night stand guard?
Did you give your everything, without thought of reward?
Soldier Boy, Soldier Boy, tell me is it true, all these things I've heard about you?
Did you love your country, even more than home or wife?
Did you value THE STARS AND STRIPES, even more than life?
Did you proudly wear your uniform, in the snow and rain?
And did you really say that you would do it all again???
Soldier Boy, Soldier Boy, now I'll tell you true, about the price that you paid and what we owe to you.
You lay peaceful in your grave, soldiers at your side.
White marble stones mark the place where you now abide.
Because of you the FLAG still waves, all across the land.
We honor you, Dear Soldier Boy, because you took your stand.
Soldier Boy, Soldier Boy, now I'll tell you more, about the things we really should have said before.
WE place the flowers on your grave, to show we haven't forgot.
WE know the freedoms we now have, we have because YOU fought.
Dear Friend of All Mankind we know, that you did your best.
So sleep on now, my darling SOLDIER BOY, you have earned your rest.

Vicky Cavin
FRIDAY

To the little ones who endure cruelty time and time again . . . but are children only once.

If my arms were oak and two rivers long
I could reach through walls that face Nevada
To lift pieces of the child left behind
On the muddy playground

Red tiny fingers swollen by cold
Reaching to grasp an angry hand
Sifting through snow to salvage
Smiley-faced worksheets blowing
Stars and hope lost to wind and asphalt

If my hands were sable and three summers warm
I could hold this broken blue-eyed angel
Against my breast like a wounded falcon
A six-year old fledgling
Trembling and naked

A pacing figure with hollow eyes
Full of storm and indifference
Slapping a plaid coat down in the snow
Breaking her porcelain daughter
Like hand-painted dolls from a dark past
Like the way she was treated

Eunice B Lanzl
MY POEM
I would like to write a little poem;
A poem to pass down through the ages.
Loved by a wee child,
As well as by the sages.

My poem will say something really big.
Some will cry—some not care a fig!
My poem will be about emotion,
My poem will tell of great devotion,
My poem will speak of expectation,
My poem will praise dedication.

And throughout my little poem I'll say:
"God gives us love in
The blackness of the night
And in the lightness of the day."

I would like to write a poem so true
That you will know that it was written
Just for—You.

Harold L Newell
I LEARNED OF THEIR VOICES
I learned of their voices,
then I rode on alone—
Their voices were my shadow
as I headed toward home—

When night touches the garden
I, again leave the house—
Not caring where I go,
I have to be somewhere else.

I always run to the road,
that could lead me from here—
Make believe that I'm leaving
then I stand here in fear—

Daylight finds me in the field

with eyes that have had no
sleep—
I can no longer live this way
my answer lies in the creek—

Now, when you go down there,
the voices are loud and clear—
Mine will be crying with them
it's the saddest one you'll
hear . . .

Grace Hange
DREAMER
A dreamer—dreams
In
imitation and desire
And
in
possession
A dreamer—discards

A dreamer—shuns
In
desire and imitation
And
in
reality
A dreamer—awaits

Set—time motions
Dawn—time transforms
Day—time possesses
A dreamer

Rozella K Kilroy
FOR A DEAR FRIEND
Once in a while a friend is found
Who's a friend right from the start.
Once in a while a friendship's made
That really warms the heart.

Once in a while a friendship's
formed.
To last a lifetime through.
It really does happen, once in a while
It happened to me and you.

Mary M Kern

Mary M Kern
GRANDPA'S OLD STRAW HAT

In memory—of my Grandfather, George B. Jackson

Hanging neatly on pegs on the old
kitchen wall
Was Grandpa's straw hat and
Grandma's summer shawl.

As day-break came, he would come
in from the barn
Carrying the milk and starting the
day on the farm.

As the sun got brighter that old straw
hat came out
To shade Grandpa's eyes while he
was working about.

It was great fun bouncing up and
down on Grandpa's knee
And to have on that old hat, flopping
about so we couldn't see.

We would ride the mare, Old Mabel,
to bring back the cows,
And the next thing you knew
Grandpa's straw hat was waving the
sows

For to the open gate all the animals
would flee.
But we were young and restless and
it brought so much glee.

Ethel Louise Kaiser
THE RISEN CHRIST
Christ is Risen
Oh! It is true
He has Risen for me and for you
He chose to die upon the cross
That you and I might not be lost
But He is Risen, He is Risen today
In the grave, He would not stay
He was wounded for our transgres-
sions
By His stripes, we are healed
This was the Father's will
That through his death and resurrec-
tion
We must be saved—That death could
not
Hold us in the grave
Christ is Risen
He is Risen today
Come and try him
And don't delay

Eleanor Hackbarth
MY MARY

In memory of my late brother, Raymond Patterson of Washington Ks. My tribute for him to his beloved wife, Mary K Patterson.

MARY THE LADY I LOVED,
Who became my wife.
Sharing fifty two years,
Of joy, sorrow and strife.

She was always a pal,
And my dearest friend.
With a pocket of joy,
And courage to lend.

She bore me two sons,
Which fulfilled my life.
Mary, the lady, their mother,
Was my beloved wife.

God makes these decisions,
This is His say.
He determines the year,
The month and the day.

This was His judgment,
So I shall not fear.
But I'll miss her so,
My Mary, my dear.

The days will be lonely,
And empty my heart.
With her precious memories,
"WE SHALL NEVER, BE APART."

Irving Portnoy
AGE IS RELATIVE

This poem is dedicated to Evelyn, my dear wife

I've written many rhymes as you
well know it
About people and birthdays so I'm
considered a poet
But I've been sparse writing poems
dedicate to you
Except for a recent anniversary
celebrated by us two
You have just reached a milestone at
age sixty five
Don't let this birthday upset you
while you feel alive
Now that you have enrolled in the
Medicare group
It doesn't mean you are ready to lean
or to stoop
Though now you have been placed
on the senior citizen roster
One look at you and they would think
you're an imposter
Because, my darling, you look ever
so young
And add beauty to these lyrics and
it's a song to be sung
So enjoy this birthday and the many
more to follow
For the number itself is not a cause
to feel sorrow
Age is relative and you should not
use it as a guide
As long as you're healthy and you
have me at your side
So, my dear, be happy and enjoy
without any fears
For life can be beautiful while
adding on the years

Julie Ann Johnson
MY MIND WANDERED, JUST LIKE EVERY OTHER DAY
The lonely beach, just before sunset
As I search, my sweater, my only
embrace.
I see another searching in the
distance,
It can't be him, as I look closer.

His footprints become bigger, the
beach smaller.
For a moment I feel I own the beach,
The setting, his hair glowing in the
sun.
I turn around hoping to awake.

Just then a warm hand touches mine,
It sends a quiver touching my soul.
I slowly turn to see his face,
Just like I always pictured it to be.

So loving, those eyes so very sincere.
He puts his finger over my lips,
As I close my eyes, I feel so free,
Then my lips feel his, so gentle.

His hands embrace my cold body
And I forget where it is I am.
The pounding of my heart against his
Was the beginning of our real love.

Linda Dawn Smith
SOMETIMES THE LONELINESS IS LIKE AN ENDLESS HIGHWAY

To my dear Mother and Mike

Sometimes the loneliness is like an
endless highway
and the fog, it never seems to clear
So I drive throughout the night
longing for the dawn to near
When I finally see the sunshine it's
just another day
If I only had a passenger beside me,
someone going my way
It always leaves me thinking will I
ever make the turn
but I drive too fast to see it, I guess
I'll never learn
Sometimes I drive too close to the
shoulder looking for a new road to
start, but the road I want to stay on is
the one that leads to your heart
I won't ask you to drive with me until
the very end
Who knows the danger that may lead
especially when the rain sets in
I know I can drive through safely
I'll pass right by the pain, even if
you drive reckless
Just stay on the highway, just stay in
my lane

Cristy D Walker
ANOTHER CHANCE
When you put faith into something,
Somehow it always lets you down.
The love given out
Only turns around to come back
And haunt the unfortunate giver.

Those who wish things to be over
Only ask for the coming of freedom.
Should it be allowed?
The second says no, yet the first
insists yes.

How does one let go what one has
always had,
Have grown accustomed to and
instored a love unknown.
A bonding so close and so strong
Only having to be broken by the twist
of fate.

Love cannot be broken by one spell
But by a long and treacherous
journey.
What came so sudden and unexpected
Is forced to leave by the way of such
a long and twisting path.

The traveling is so hard
And drives even the strongest weary.
Yet in the end the positions are
switched with time,
For the one who wanted the end is
now hurting for a new beginning.

Edward D VanHorn, CAC
THE MOMENT
The dawn is breaking
The sky is bathed in color
The trees bend in the gentle arms of
the breeze
While waves caress the beach
sands shift with the current
A gull cries from the distance
heralding a new day
I sit alone, among the dunes
the solitude comforting me
An inner voice calls out
and beckons me within
The sun begins to warm the air
and earth's life begins to stir
The joy of being alive
The pleasure of my senses
I thrill to the touch
of the breeze upon my face
The warmth of the sun on my body
It is at this moment
I begin the rest of my life

Charles Cherris

Charles Cherris
U.S.A.—U.S.S.R.
Co-Op for Humanity

This poem is dedicated to Kathryn Cherris, my granddaughter.

Two great countries of the world, the
U.S.A. and the U.S.S.R.
Have all nations, living in dread of
their awesome power.
Without world cooperation, of all
leaders upon it.
There can only be one result, the

destruction of our planet.
The U.S.A. and U.S.S.R. have by small wars been stymied.
By small poor nations, who in freedom, fiercely believed.
Countless planes, tanks and soldiers, did not bring victory.
Against small nations determined to fight against slavery.
Vietnam and Afghanistan are but signs of the future.
The rich nations must the have not nations, nurture.

A glimmer of hope shines like a bright star in the sky.
Two great leaders, Reagan and Gorbachev, we hope see eye to eye.
The fate of the world, with just the few strokes of a pen.
Could mean more of the worlds goods and security for all men.
Capitalism and Communism in cooperation, can live side by side.
What is best for themselves, the people eventually will decide.
The U.S.S.R. and U.S.A. with other allies, won the war against aggression.
Now face another challenge, improving the living standard of every nation.
In the unpredictable future, that still lies ahead.
Will nations praise the era of Reagan and Gorbachev?

J L Scott
A TRIBUTE TO THOSE WHO PLAY CHURCH MUSIC

As my wife and I sat in our favorite Baptist church one beautiful Sabbath Day, We watched as the pianist came in to play.

As her fingers began to move, they readily found the proper note, and as they began to press the keys, sweet music throughout the building seemed to float.

I have always been amazed and the wonder still lingers, and I guess I'll never know what guides the players fingers.

They seem to be so very restless as they deftly move about, that the music they produce makes one feel the need to shout.

As the music continues, made me think of God above—How He prepared us a home in Heaven, if we'll only accept His love.

There we'll be eternally happy, none of the sorrow that besets earthly men, We will sing Glory to God and Hallelujahs in that place where there's never any sin.

As we sat there in church, that beautiful Sabbath Day, I seemed to feel the presence of Jesus, and I thought I heard Him say.

Go out into all the country around and about, tell everyone you see of the restful, blessful feeling you had when you first accepted me.

Tell them of Jesus who came to earth, died on the cross, gave us His life—That we all could have a home in Heaven, when we leave this world of strife.

When our days have seen the number there's no way others we can borrow. Accept Jesus Christ as your Lord today, no one has ever been promised a tomorrow.

And if they have lost the joy of their salvation, I tell you this because it's true. It's because you've done the leaving, God will never forsake you.

And as I sat there, my head bowed low, I was too thrilled to look around when the building began to be filled with music, with a Heavenly beautiful sound.

The pianist had begun to softly play and around our hearts the music seemed to roll, as she played the old, old song, Jesus Lover of my Soul.

And I thank God that He forgives even seven times seven, and if we'll accept the love He has offered we'll have a home eternal in Heaven.

Robin Hartman
EXECUTION OF NATURE

To the survival of this universe

Time stops ticking,
 in the middle of the desolate moonshine.
Tranquility reigned throughout the spell of infliction.
Who hears the words of nature's destruction?
No one can hear the calling from the basis of disaster.
Straining to hear of what can be recognized,
 tears of lonely creatures
 plunged down to the sorrowed earth.
Nothing can stop the utter suffering of pure tragedy.
Yearning for a glimpse of hope,
 beasts searched in the reddened heavens.
Heat stretched up amidst the tallest timber.
Fire lapped at melting flowers.
Blazes smothered the lush meadows leaving nothing.
Wild animals scrambled until the red glow ate them,
Ceasing all of life.
Destroyed by one single careless mistake.
Forgetting the other ashtrays in life.

Charles H Fernald
INNER THOUGHTS

The silent bond of love I know
Stirs and sets my heart aglow
And every thought unsaid in word
Read in your eyes and plainly "heard"
Enfolds my being with delight
To have our hearts as one, unite
And yet our love should never be

We made our choice so long ago
And were content but didn't know
That we would meet and one day find
That life had not been quite so kind
As we had thought, but now we see
The way our life we'd like to be
And yet our love will ever be

Why should a love such as we feel
Seem so different, so unreal
Why the heartache and the pain
Why the tears that come like rain
Why the longing, lonely hours,
When life's joys should all be ours?
And yet will our love forever be.

Would another cherish your love as I
Or want to hold you when you cry
Or give that gentle tenderness,
And long to feel your soft caress,
Or joy at gazing into your eyes,
Or know that you could be so wise?
And yet my love will ever be

In you I see life's promise filled,
All two could be, and my heart thrilled
For surely the "Gift of God" is mine
Receiving the love of one so fine
Oh, could my thoughts to you impart
Every blessing from my heart
Then our love forever you would see.

Kari Didyoung
SEASONS APART

A warm Summer day
 dripping with sunlight.
I wander in a field,
 the grasses turn
 they whisper about me
 and I can't hear what they say.
The raspberries so ripe
 they bleed, red and passionate juice.
Birds in the clouds,
 my mind with them.
A pond of sparkling mirror,
 I see my reflection—
 and yours.
On the opposite bank,
 you're in a Winter world,
 too cold to be reached.

Ursula Payne
TOO FAR AWAY

Now that you're faraway,
I miss you more & more each day.

Now that you're gone,
I won't see you for so long.

A long time is what it seems.
maybe this is only a dream.

A dream where I will wake up and you'll be next to me.

Next I will wonder if it's true,
or am I just being blu!

I'm blu for you, but I know it's true,
I'll hope I will see you soon.

Soon I will come to realize that my dreams aren't true until I'm with you.

And I will be with you real soon.

Kathleen L DeMeyere
LIFE IS BUT BORROWED

Late in August of 'Seventy one,
A child was born. A daughter, not a son.

She was wrinkled and pink, had all fingers and toes.
And changed everyday, that's how baby grows.

There were times, as an infant, that illness occurred.
Several trips to the doctor made us feel reassured.

That a child so young catches all flus and bugs.
And the best thing to do was give plenty of hugs.

And as the years passed, eight, to be exact.
Her body was aching, it began to react.

To a tumor, consuming, and gnawing with rancor.
We were told after surgery she's found to have cancer.

This menacing viper drew her life, bit by bit.
But somehow, through strength, she would again become fit.

Until chemicals, and needles, all the tests and the pain.
Eventually thinned her, no way could she gain.

By the time she was ten, she could no longer walk.
Cancer had robbed her, stole her laughter, her talk.

She lay mute to the world at only eleven.
When God came, and swept her away, back to heaven.

A child is a wonderful gift from our Lord.
To raise and to teach; to love and adore.

But they're given to us on borrowed time only.
'Til the Divine Lender recalls, we understand,
 but,
 left
 lonely . . .

Peggy Sue Rickman
THERE SHE GOES

There she goes,
that little girl of mine.
She plays dress-up,
and has a good time.

Big floppy hat,
and shoes that don't fit,
old dress, gloves,
and her make-up kit.

Upstairs, downstairs,
to her playhouse she goes.
Jingle, jingle, jingle,
say the bells on her toes.

Sitting here watching her,
brings memory to mind,
of what it was like
being carefree and nine.

Raelene Luscombe
I NEED NOT

This poem is dedicated to my dearest friend, Maggie. Only she truly understands and appreciates my worth, my pain and my everlasting friendship.

I need not criticize,
For I have been criticized.
I need not lie,
For I have been lied to.
I need not break a heart,
For my heart has been broken.

I need not ask the questions,
'Cause no one will tell me why.
I need not wipe away my tears,
When I'm still going to cry.
I need not watch for sunny skies,
For mine have now turned grey.
I need no longer reach for him,
He's already gone away.
I need not turn my back on friends,
They've already slammed the door.
All these things I've lived through,
And I need not live through more.

Margaurette Upshaw
ALMOST EXTINCT
Your life is hard
Your numbers decrease.
Your jet black form
Will soon decease.
  Poor Black Stilt

Nature intended this place to be
Your dwelling; your domain,
From living things at the water's edge
Your sustenance to claim.
  Poor Black Stilt

Norway rats and ferrets, too
Imported here they say,
Overrun your place; must eat and cheat
Your offspring the light of day.
  Poor Black Stilt

Sparse the landscape; cold the wind,
Your demands so meager, it seems a shame
That surely the children will never know
The quick little step or even the name
  Of Poor Black Stilt.

Elinor Foster
HIGH ON A HILL IN GOLGOTHA
High on a hill in Golgotha
They hanged my Lord on a cross—
On a wooden cross they hanged Him.

On a wooden cross they hanged my Lord
High on a hill in Golgotha—
Between two criminals they hanged Him
But he overcame death for each of us.

And now the cross is empty there
High on a hill in Golgotha—
The cross is empty now,

But because my Lord suffered death for us
High on a hill in Golgotha,
On a wooden cross that is empty now
We have hope of life eternal.

And we can overcome the darkness of Good Friday
And celebrate the gladness of Easter
All because—
High on a hill in Golgotha
The cross is empty now.

Faith Marion
A SUMMER DAY
The darkness of the night subsides.
In the east there is a glow,
  Brighter it grows, and brighter now,
  O'er the mountains topped with snow.

The lovely hues come floating up,
paving the way for the sun.
  Proudly he also enters, saying
  "Wake up. Day has come."

He mounts the sky majestically and sits upon his throne
  Smiles down upon the thriving world
  Where men, their crops have sown.

Children play 'neath the healthful sun, the birds sing in the trees.
  It's good to have the sun above
  And wondrous days like these.

But through the sun in glory reigns,
he is but King of day
  When evening comes, the stars rush out
  And send him on his way.

All is quiet. The mortals sleep. The stars keep watch above
  Until the morn shall come again,
  The morn which all things love.

Valerie Croy
LIFE'S UPS AND DOWNS
Life is very funny sometimes
First it happens
Life brings you love and happiness
You think you're on cloud nine

Then it somehow changes
As you fall from that cloud
Just as you think
You're going to hit the ground

You begin to see a sparkle
That gives you new hope
That you can fly back up

Just as you almost reach the top
It knocks you back down a little
Sometimes you make it to the top
Sometimes you hit the ground

If you keep hanging on by a thread of hope
You have a little bit more of a chance
To crawl back up to the top

W E D Bowley

W E D Bowley
LASTING LOVE
Our Boys go out in Search of a Mate,
To find the right girl he must sometime wait
Until his soulmate comes along.
To be in a hurry can prove very wrong.

We are very proud of our Daughters In Law.
What Parent could wish for anything more
For this son to make such a lovely choice.
These girls have given us Happiness & Joys.

The secret of Happiness and Health
It promotes contentment and sometimes Wealth.
We are very proud of our Son In Law
Our Daughter found the love she was looking for.

Love is the Foundation of a family's success
Without it life always ends with distress.
Happy families are the backbone of Nations
And Hold together with wonderful relations.

Terry Johnson
SOMEDAY
Someday she will be there. The woman
That I've known all my life I'd meet and fall in love with
And marry. I've been with her hundreds, thousands of times.
Looked in her eyes, held her hand.
I've tingled
As she spoke my name, or whispered it.
I've caressed her face, stroked her hair, held her gently.
I've thrilled to the taste of her mouth against mine. Nectar.
But when I awake I cannot tell you the details of her countenance.
Awake I don't remember how tall (or short) she is.
Whether she is slight or stout I cannot say.
Her coloring eludes me; dark or fair?
In my
Dreams she comes to me; I know her;
I speak her name, forgetting
That I had forgotten. I plan on staying, but I awake.
And awake someday she will be there. I may
Not recognize her right away; then again I may.
It might be the way she'll cock her head just so. Or
Her smile, or her laugh. Or
She'll say or do something as only she can and then I'll know her. I'll fall in love with her again (have I not already done so in my dreams?)
And most wonderful of all, She
Will love me. And we'll marry, as
I've known all my life we would.

Cynthia Lea
THE SEARCH

To those I love, your faith released the song in me

On gilded wings of butterflies
My mind, unchained, flies free
Unhampered by all mortal bonds
I leave reality

I search my world from deep within
To find my destiny
Hid in the place where dreams reside
My future waits for me

If you believe that you can fly
Then it can surely be
But if you lack the faith to look
Then never will you see

You must believe in what you are
If you are to be free
And no one else can think for you
Or find your hidden key

The key that can unlock your heart
And solve it's mystery
The key that opens all the doors
Of mediocrity

Susan Campbell
FANCIFUL FLIGHT

To Dale, Ryan, and Michelle spurring me on to give life one more try.

Our backyard is more than just a yard to me, It's a natural habitat for all the birds perched securely in the trees. In the winter they carry on more purposefully as if enjoyment is no longer what they're about, but the grim task of survival is the task they must carry out building nest in trees as they fly quickly through the breeze. They not unlike the local weather men know when that Alberta Clipper lurks in the air and they are gathering twigs for their nest with diligent care.
Birds have always been one of my favorite studies and there is so much I don't know about them yet, but I can imagine no greater joy than the freedom of flight,
gliding naturally in the air with no real effort or care and when I am burdened and feeling weighted down I always gaze out my kitchen window sometimes with a frown envious of those birds soaring so freely in flight and I wonder if I'll ever feel as free or is my life going to consist of constant worry? Will my spirit ever soar again as those fascinating birds, or am I forever going to be engaged in a constant tug of war not feeling free in the end, but feeling worn down even more? As a child I know I felt like those wonderful birds loving the world and all that was within, but my world got clouded sometimes by my own struggle with sin; and I yearn for the carefree days of yesteryear or maybe just a fanciful flight in the sky spurring me on to give life one more try.

Jean M Goalen
DRUG DEPENDENCE

Please dedicate this poem to the real poet in our family, my Daddy, Myron Hitchcock McWhinney, From him I learned at a very early age the sin of plagiarism.

I had two pills to take for sleep,
Two pills to make my slumber deep.
I slept and dreamt the whole night through.
I slept eight hours as others do.
But now I'm well, I do not need
The rest I used to have.
A couple hours of sleep suffice,
And I have time to do things nice.
But folks who feel that they know best,
Doctors, nurses, even guests,
Say, "Jean, you just must have your rest!"
And so I try to please my Love.
I lie there stiff—hour after hour.
When "Heaven's sakes" all else above,
I'd rather rise and take a shower!

So now we doze on lawn or beach,
The price of night clothes out of reach,
Some don't use pillows anymore;
But still the cost of sleep doth soar!

Mary E L Blair
THE BRILLIANCE OF OUR LOVE
The ripplings of my inner feelings at the very touch of your love
makes me know our hearts are knitted together as one
Let me love you
Love to us is the inner peace of our hearts
The Knowledge of our minds
The strength of our bodies making an explosion of pure joy
It's the calm of a raging sea, the opening of the first flower of spring
The joy of the first snow flake
The changing of the leaves in the fall
Love is a cloud floating in a heavenly place

When we love, it's like the melting of pure Gold into a hot flaming fire
Melted together for all time
Then being molded and shaped in a 24 karat loop of oneness
Sometimes as life will have it, dirt and rust will chip away at the loop to force it to lose its brilliance, but when love is bonded by God it is too strong for mankind and nature to destroy
Our love will last a life time and forever more

Joan S Goodwin
SUMMER PLACE IN HIDING

To my grandmother and my husband—for the two most beautiful experiences of my life

I was searching for a summer place
A place of azure oceans
And cranberry skies
I was looking for it all
In one man's eyes
Eyes of turquoise and cobalt
Falling through depths of mountains
I have traveled far
And away
For many season's time
Destination nowhere
Lost and always searching
Seeking and finding
Stopgaps everywhere
I was searching for a summer place
That I did not find

Amparo Jasso Fernandez
BROKEN PROMISE
Many words have I
That in my heart I hold,
I thought you loved me so
My wasted youth I can't replace,
But this I tell you now;
Someday the girl that took my place,
Will pay you back some-how!

Michelle Kokones
STRANGERS
padded darkness curled around the street lamp as night set in
I stood there, on the corner,
surrounded by the artificial light
that yielded no warmth, and the stranger came

he stayed; a lonesome companion in a nights charade
his dark eyes, darker than the surrounding darkness,
burned into my heart his memory

and in the cold light we played the game
and he stayed
we were two shadows mingling in midnight
and the ice began to melt
slowly at first, but the warmth spread

we passed the night together, beneath the lamp,
a company of strangers
in need of being needed
in want of being wanted
in hopes of being loved
and as light came, chasing the darkness away
we said our painful goodbyes
but I'll never forget a quick kiss from a stranger

William Gray
LINES OF FEELING
Meeting in the darkness
We feel the lines of the floor
The lines of the walls
The lines of ourselves
Curving the body's protrusions
Curves of the fields
Feeling the soft plateaus
Cascading into open plains
In the inside circular lines
Wandering in thought
Shifting in waves our minds move

In unison our bodies move
In accentuating patterns
The sexual orchestration flows through
The serene fertile grasses
Souls transfigured within
Passion
Consciously thought—
Intraconsciously
We realize

Dorothy Barnett

Dorothy Barnett
THE PRIZE

Dedicated to the preservation of all wildlife

Alone, behind the iron bars
He waits, the King of beasts,
His bed a stoney stable,
On Rabbit flesh he feasts.

His captors, boasting proudly,
See no pain within his eyes,
But then this is a hunting game
The Lion is the prize!

Oh mighty one, once strong and free
Where is your Kingdom now?
And where the pride that crowned your head
And graced your noble brow?

Carolyn Davis
SO EASY

This poem is dedicated to Amy Taylor who without her help I would not have been able to put these words down.

With a smile from you,
I feel so warm and wanted
And it seems you want me.
All through the night
Cuz you make it so easy.
So easy to believe
So easy to love you
Never before could lust
Come so easy and pain so quick.

"Call me", "Hold me", "Call me"
You say over and over
I'm a fool for you,
And you can see it
And that's how you make it so easy.

Brimming with thoughts of your love
The thrill of your touch
How can you love and hurt me
So much that's why it's so easy.

I trusted you and longed for your love
A smile from your face.
Now I understand how you made it so easy.

You used my love and feelings.
Just for your own desires.
Now I must call my heart
"A liar."

Raymond J Conner
MY WEDDING POEM

To God, for he has brought life to a heart that once only knew death. And to Anita, for her understanding, patient, loving and beautiful spirit.

Tonight I will hold you tightly in my arms
for there I'll find warmth in your womanly charms.
Softly will I caress thee like no man has ever done
And sweetly will I love thee till the dawning of the sun.

For beautiful are you on this most special night
today God has blessed me, for now you are my wife.
In white do I see thee, for your love it is pure
So I promise you this night that our love will endure.

This our wedding day is one of the most special days we will share
So please do not laugh at me if from my eye you see a tear.
I'll live within your love for me as long as it is true
And in my love you'll find that the only woman is you.

Your beauty is like a star that shines bright upon my heart
And forever will it shine, never growing dark.
Faithfully will I love you, until the day that I will die
because from this moment on you are the apple of my eye.

David E Barrett
MIND FLIGHT

To my loving and encouraging mother, who has always believed in me.

Between twilight's fade and midnight's time,
I strip the bonds of shackled binds.
With breathless soaring the wind has caught,
I journey again to live my thoughts.

Gazing downward upon clouds enclosed
around mysteries left from majesties old,
Where past and future are holding hands,
I seek a portal where fortune stands.
Riding a drifting wisp of song,
I dance the harmony of melody gone.
And passion stirs the hunger yet,
ever searching for the perfect duet.

Returning, alas, from the dreamer's toil,
My wandering found a distant joy.
Though busy be my daily end,
A longing aspires to soar again!

Rose Marie Pace Barone
TEACH LOVE
Teach LOVE—LOVE of self.
NO to smoke, liquor, drugs, which self destruct.

LOVE of friends, teachers, and especially family.
NO to speeding, liquor, illegal drugs, school, community, and family disrupt.

LOVE of learning to serve MANKIND
To make our minds soar as well as to earn much more.

LOVE of play, gardens, and the outdoors—relax the body and thus do more.
MODERATION in life, love of giving; in eating less, we may remain LIVING.

LOVE our country and thus must VOTE.
LOVE of the world—NO to nuclear arms—keep mankind a-float.

LOVE of music, art, and lit, imagery and the poet's rhyme;
Even dance, unifying all MANKIND.

LOVE of foreigners—Hegemony, no more (Forgetting we were all immigrants once);
Share and strength from our great heritage, allowing more to our shore.

LOVE and enjoy our pets, too, serving and devoted to us,
Need our care and play as do our grannies and elderly around—
Extend to them the needed helping hand; some day you will appreciate and understand.

Meta McDonald
FOR JAY
Sitting here watching,
While you sleep
Child that you are
I begin to think, of the times when
Your father & I couldn't decide
Whether we wanted a child in our lives
Foolish were we to feel
That we had everything, when we were free
And when I hold you in my arms
Endearing me to you, with your baby charms
I realize that nothing
We've ever had in this world
Can compare to the love we hold for you
Our little girl!

Denise R Wadsworth
THE UNKNOWN GIVER
I was to be the giver and he was the taker.
Friends and foes
don't mix.
Her the cheery one,
gives words of kindness
but I give her the
dirty looks.

She doesn't help me
and him to find the lost words
of time.
Changes don't matter
only the time of sorrow comes to the surface.
That's ok though,
cause I gave all
that I can give
PRIDE is our enemy!

Marjorie A White
IN YOUR MIND YOU SEE

To my beloved son Michael, you are one of a kind, I love you very much . . . MOM

As you were walking along a country road, you spot a worn old house on top of a hill,
You stop-lean against a fence post—and wonder if any ghost linger still,
The porch that once hugged it so proudly was now weathered and sagging,
But you could imagine the family still sitting there laughing and bragging,

You look at the trees planted many years ago and knew of the small shadows they then made,
For now they stood tall and stately and covered the entire house with plenty of shade,
Once there—but no longer seen—the lane that greeted the front of this house,
You could vision a tired mother waiting patiently for the return of her spouse,
With children in tow so properly cleaned and holding her hand,
They seemed to be listening for the wagon that brought papa in from working the land,

You knew for certain there was an old cistern hiding in back some place,
Used for scrubbing floors, making coffee and washing many of face,
You sniff the air and can almost smell the home cooked meal waiting inside,
Also, the freshly baked bread that rose with great pride,

In your heart, you can feel the love and happiness the house once had,
But now it looked so forsaken and painfully sad,
Was it because the ghost did not linger still!!
In the worn old house that set so empty—high on top of a hill.

John S Bush
CAROLINE

To my beloved Grand-Daughter Caroline Renee Smith

To me the flower of this world—
is Caroline my Pisces girl!
With big brown eyes and blondish curls—
She knows she is my favorite girl.
Though sad I be and quite distraught—
By unkind deeds that fate hath wrought,
I look upon her face and see—
Everything that's dear to me.
Her flashing smile, her classy air
Can raise me quickly from despair.
Does sustain me in this woeful world.
That's Caroline, my Pisces girl!
Though rain may fall and chill winds blow—
Her face with warmth will ever glow.
Will beam with sunshine oh so bright—
Though dreary be the day and night.
If I should sail across the sea—
To some strange shore unknown to me,
I'd claim for her this whole new world.
She's Caroline, my Pisces girl!

Marilyn B Rutter

Marilyn B Rutter
REACHING OUT

"Am I struggling?—am I struggling?"
Reaching out.
Reaching out my hand to God.
Days go—hours fly.
I am getting by.
Reaching out my hand to God.

Sunshine everywhere I see.
Summer is the best it can be.
Reaching out my hand to God.
Do not know what the future says to me.
It is just—"to wait and see"—
Ponder everything carefully.
Reaching out my hand to God.

Elna D Gallo
FATHER

To the children

Father lived my no man's rules, unless you count "The Golden;"
His deeds seemed inauspicious, 'til you added up the score.
Many roofs held up because he made that last insistent thrust,
Many rooms made liveable by action of his hammer.
He liked the challenge—he would change the forms and shapes of things, 'oft times seemingly without plan the dull and drab made beautiful!

He loved to picnic and to fish, or drive down country roads, while family chafed impatiently for more exciting fare.
Camping meant a lot of fun and sometimes much more work
Since Father manned the barbecue while Mother chose the sun.
Vacations came occasionally, and where would Dad be found—
Putting siding on a wall, or tarring someone's drive.

Father owned a shoe shop at one stage of his life and what was in the back room? a speed boat being built!
Mother gasped in consternation; what would people say?
Who would fix the shoes on time that piled up every day?
The boat got built— (the door came out); we knew not when nor how
The shoes got fixed and we all learned of the way that follows will.
Our memories are precious of those youthful golden days though he often seemed too stubborn in accepting modern ways
He taught us many lessons, and we're proud we had this Dad!

Anthony M Cucchiara
I'VE DIED FOR YOU (SERVANT TO MASTER)

I've drained my last bit of power,
Master, all ends met,
i've discontinued my service to you,
my spiritual sun has set.
I go to a greater reward, kind owner,
i'll sail my soul far skyward,
a word in kind i'll give, unless something greater is preferred.
All of our sharing years together, it's prepared me for this sightless session of flight,
I entered this world a knave, and because of your kindness and love I leave a knight.
All desertions set aside, all my temptations too,
all of my hatred is laid to dust, so that I may pass on through.
Remember me when times do come,
when my children serve you well,
remember me when times do come, I bid thee, dear sir, farewell.

Carl M Young Jr
THANKING GOD

This poem is dedicated to Cordula Monika Swett, thank you for your love and friendship, I'm here for you always.

Sometimes I sit and think about the turns that life does take,
And all the bumps and bruises from each of our mistakes.
Then I think and realize how lucky we can be,
That God made every wrong we do a right for us to see.
So if you think your life is hard, that there's nothing you can do,
Remember Christ upon the cross and what He did for you.

Elizabeth P Rawlins
MOTHER'S DAY

For my wonderful mother, Veta P. Smith

Another year has come and gone,
Without my telling you dear Mom,
That 'though at times I've caused you woe,
I've never ceased to love you so.

I can't seem to tell you with my voice,
Or with words of my own choice,
All the things I want to say
On this and every other day.

Just please know this, and don't forget,
'Though I really can't express it yet.
I admire you more than words can say,
And I love you more each passing day.

Tami Trzebiatowski
SOMEDAY

Someday
I'll forget
the color of your eyes.
The sound of your voice
will be unfamiliar,
Even your name
will go unrecalled.
Someday
I'll forget
that I once loved you.
The feeling I once had
will seem so remote.
Like ancient times.
Someday
I'll shed a tear
and not know why.
For the memories I have
or for those I have forgotten.

Audrey C Hague
THE MARIONETTES' MESSAGE

Limp marionettes hanging on dingy theater wall
Waiting the master hand to give them birth,
Calling from dangling limbs the dance of mirth
That holds expectant, youthful eyes in thrall,
And for a while makes children of us all.
These big eyed dolls, fashioned of tree and earth
Have, without help, no creature life, no self worth,
They only wait. For others' aide they cannot call.
I need no strings to move. My soul is free!
The choice is mine for good or ill.
Success or failure mine. Without help I proudly stand.
Shall I give or simply take? It's up to me.
Money? Success? Fame? No! I want much more—
To live complete I choose the Master's hand.

Gertrude Kahrhoff
ENGAGEMENT

Dedicated to the Memory of Bernard John, my Husband

When the wondrous stars are shining
In God's heaven high above,
And warm winds softly touch my face
You are there, once more, my love.

'Twas on such a night in Summer
We walked blithely hand in hand,
Along the banks of the river
Attending the concert band.

Strains of a stirring Sousa March
Came to us far down the line,
Then the diamond sparkled like fire
As you whispered, "Please be Mine."

There you stood with a winsome smile,
Tawny hair and eyes of blue.
It was a moment so sublime,
Hence, I gave my heart to you!

Carri L Gibbs
ECHOES

This poem is dedicated to my dear parents, Nancy L. Rorabaugh and David R. Gibbs.

In the distance I hear the Spanish voices and
the Bull's clanking bell,
The sounds of summers past

In the air hear the clever joking, seeking
smoke-filled rafters and cluttered spillways

Hear the wind; it speaks softly of a time now forgotten
The vestiges of innocence breeze by

as I reach to the heavens
I scream and keep awakening
to find I am dreaming

The dangerous summer

The sobbering wind reminds me

Jennifer Marie Thomas
UPON THE DAYS ABOUT TO COME
Upon the days about to come
Fear overwhelms the mind and soul
What the future holds for one
Cannot be said so soon
Yet what will come
Will come as fate
So no one will know for sure
A gift to some
That will provide to all needs
But allow an unsuffocated growth
Hopefully a gift
That will suppress all fears
Bringing enjoyment to all who watch
That gift alone should also be
As great as what is given
Determination to overcome criticism
A gift of great desire
A wish to be important to some
Yet truly be loved by all.

B J
FATHER
Father, how do I begin to tell people what kind of person you were?
I cannot remember you ever telling me that you loved me. But somehow it was never necessary for you to do so.
When it came to rules, your words were the law. But when it was time for games, the fun came straight from the kindness within your heart.
Cry, not you. The pride in your soul did not understand the meaning of the word. For crying was a form of weakness.
Well Father, I guess that's all. Somehow it does not seem fair to sum up a man's life with so few amount of words. But you know that the thing you give me the most cannot be spoken. For the most important thing that you gave me, was the knowledge of knowing what it meant, to be your
Daughter.

Tim Hornaček
LITTLE TOWN CHRISTMAS
Christmas snow is falling
And church bells are calling
Friends come from far and near
It hardly seems it's been a year

"It's a little town Christmas"

Presents under the tree, have the kids a itch'n
While Grandma makes cookies in the kitchen
Grand kids wait for Santa Claus without a care
While Grandpa dozes in his old arm chair.

"It's a little town Christmas"

Christmas carolers line the street
as ole' Jack Frost nips at their feet
Popcorn goes krackle and a pop
As Santa nears the chimney top

"It's a little town Christmas"

Where's old Bill, with his horse drawn sleigh
Keeping alive Christmas memories of yesterday
And little children making angels in the snow
Help to bring back memories, don't ya know!

"It's a little town Christmas"

At Christmas time, everyone's of equal worth
And peace and love seem to touch all on Earth
And for some magical reason, the Christmas season
Brings out the best in all of us; thank God for:

Little towns and Christmas!

Frank B Duchene

Frank B Duchene
OUR VETS

(Thank you Clara Lindsay for your inspiration)
Dedicated to all men & women who served, for the preservation of our great country.

They came from every walk of life,
To guard our precious shore;
Thru blood & sweat & tears & strife,
So many gave much more.

From world war one, & world war two,
They fought with guts & pride;
Vietnam & Korea too,
Saw these men side by side

They left their families & their friends,
To fight in heat & snow;
And threw their caution to the winds,
So others would not go.

In hospitals throughout our land,
No more to ever roam;
Let's just stop in & shake their hand,
Because they're always home.

Clarence Leonhardt
FLOWERS ON THE HILL

To Marti my inspiration, and critic.

I seen all the flowers in bloom on the hill.
So I pondered the flower called the daffodil.

But nothing I seen or nothing I knew.
Could compare with the bouquet I'll pick for you.

Even the sun was aware of the sight.
And made the clouds respond in tearful delight.

Knowing only that rain at this time of day.
Would nurture them in its gentle way.

So I stood for a moment to gaze in awe.
I couldn't believe the beauty I saw.

Then the flowers opened in the sun's golden ray.
And cast their scent to the summer day.

As the wind whispered softly in the brisk morning air.
That the goodness of life was plentiful there.

Thinking only of beauty in this wonderful place.
And that heaven was present with slumbering grace.

But what if these flowers blew away with the wind.
Would they return in the spring to bloom again.

To paint the ground with sullen array.
In soft pastels like the rainbow's way.

But someday I'll return and stay for awhile.
As my heart filled with love on my face came a smile.

Joyce Keller Moore
WHEN I THINK OF YOU
When I think of you
I want to be the best me
I can possibly be.

When I think of you
I feel like walking in the rain
With a laugh and a giggle
As two, small children
Not having any worry or pain.

When I think of you
I breathe a little prayer
Reminding my Lord and myself
How fortunate I am
To be your friend
And blessed with the beautiful relationship
We so enjoy and lovingly share.

June Tannis
HANDS
Hands are the tools
that help us count our days—
that hold a pen, a saw,
a needle—many ways.

Hands speak to deaf.
Hands fold themselves in prayer,
reach out in supplication
and in care.

Hands greet. Hands hold
a child and love impart.
Hands, touching soft,
can heal a wounded heart.

Mrs Anna Margaret Kondrewych
MY SON MY SON
I want to be free, but I can never be free,
Because God gave you to me, my son, my son.
He gave you to me, to cherish, to love,
But He left you undone, my son, my son.
Three birds in my nest, two flew away,
Your wings were broken, so you had to stay.
A child forever, you'll always be,
You were left undone, a gift from God given to me.
So many plans I had for you.
None of those plans can ever come true.
So, until you are gone, I must go on.
God gave you to me, my son, my son.
I pray that you will be taken from me,
Be in God's arms for eternity.
Then I will rest, then I will be free.
You'll have come home, my son, my son.
God left you udone, my only son.

Martha Hockenjos
FEELINGS OF LOVE
Love is a Clear Blue Sky with
White Doves flying high in the sky.

In love is your Soul Floating high
above the sky, Earth and Universe
Feeling and seeing it all with inside
Yourself and Soul.

Unloved is a Dark Dead Sea taking
all of Sealife and love away
until White Clouds and Rain washes
the waters clean and clear returning
Life and Love again.

Pauline Unger
THE WEAKER SEX?
Women are the weaker sex, it's been said
By these statements—don't be misled

Though women have a softer shoulder
They're aggressive and often bolder

Who has more patience and resilience
And are possessed of daring and brilliance?

If men are superior and much stronger
Statistics prove that women live longer

Women are the ones who rock the cradle
And dish out food with a ready ladle

Ladies are terrific, I'll tell you again
I don't want to live in a world without men

Pauline Unger
TENDER MEMORIES
Around the table, we sat like this
Each one anxious to reminisce

Upon us all, life had etched its scroll
And time had taken a goodly toll

What wonderful stories did unfold
We listened with awe as they were told

Rich with experience, it is true
Age has much it can offer to you

So listen to tales as they are spun
Learning from others can be such fun

Diane Day Jeter
HOME FROM HELL (A TOUR IN VIETNAM)

This poem dedicated to my beloved husband David, my life's inspiration

Be blessed they say
You live to tell
He answers nay a word

No way they see
He can't relate
Such horrors only heard

How does one tell
About the days
He spent in hell on earth

A time of pain and death
And war
In a place that had no birth

A battle fought
In vain despairs
And makes the pain complete

His wretched dreams
In deepest night
Distort his thoughts of life

He feels his anger

Inner swell
And tries to calm his strife

They think his struggle
Ends at home
He should forget about those days

But haunting dreams
And memories
Will follow to his grave.

Sheila O'Neil

Sheila O'Neil
TWO WORLDS
Now
You drive,
Taking the road on a wing
You master the thing,
Hands firm, feet taut,
Words flood, eyes dart;
You're strong
Mastering.
It'd be wrong
To wish you weak;
Yet I recall
A . . . sensitivity,
And behind somewhere,
A dream there,
To meet my dream
In love
Then.

Ruben Jose Martinez Jr
US FOUR
*U*s
*n*eed's
*i*s
*t*he
*e*verlasting
*d*reams . . .

*F*our
*a*ttitude's
*m*embers
*i*n
*l*ife
you & I strife . . .

Sissy Strickland
DINOSAURS
Dinosaurs! ! !
Dinosaurs are over 200 million years old!
They are the largest and longest animals on earth!
Some weighed as much as 50 tons!
Some stood as high as 50 feet tall!
Some were as long as 120 feet from head to tail!
They all had very long names that were hard to say!
There were 254 different kinds of dinosaurs!
There was a flying dinosaur, the Pteranodon!
There was a swimming dinosaur, the Plesiosaur!
The Scelidosaurus was called the Limb Lizard!
The Megalosaurus was called the Big Lizard!
The Stegosaurus was called the Roof Lizard!
The Brachiosaurus was called the Arm Lizard!
The Iguanodon was called the Toothed Lizard!
The Diplodocus was called the Double Beam!
The Triceatops was called the Three-Horned!
The Tyrannosaurus was called the Tyrant!
The Glyptodon was called the Chisel Tooth!
All Dinosaurs are from the Prehistoric Age!
All Dinosaurs are Extinct! ! !

Peggy Merele Thrift
FATHER

This poem is dedicated to my deceased father, "Luther Bourbon Higginbotham."

I stand in awe of all creation,
and marvel not at who I am.
I cannot know of your greatness,
for you are far above all men!

I stand alone in earthly bondage,
and long for your unwavering love.
I cannot know of your completeness
until I lose myself in you!

I stand unsure of lifelong treasures
and only know of whom I trust, for
I am sure you are my Father—
I am your child and you my own!

Beth Landmann
AFTER ALMOST 40 YEARS TOGETHER
I gave him all the love I had,
When he was happy I was glad.
The support I gave was out of caring,
And through ups and downs, we did the sharing.
The times together were all too few,
There was always some work he had to do.
"In his shadow," he said I was living,
I replied, "By your side, and happily giving."
Then he told me, "I've met someone—it isn't love."
I was so hurt and prayed to God above,
To bring my love safely back to me,
After two years of waiting, I know it isn't to be.
You see, he married "her" the other day,
The man I love has gone away.

Mia Moll

Mia Moll
TRAIL OF TEARS
The red-faced man looks out upon the horizon.
The mother was gone, taken by the wasteful white-man.
The flowers seem to weep a bitter farewell, the dust invokes them like a tender hug.

But they do not resist, they do not fight, they march, crying, weeping—upon the trail of tears.

Todd D Howe
A SILENT TRIP
So eager—
To make an impression that would not last,
In the obsession—so meager.
Excitement o'er the obsession and to make the impression—
Left not past.

Upcoming, passion—
'Tis a feeling of overpowering, intoxicating joy,
So shrewd—in such a fashion.
Though to tell but no one 'bout the flame inside burning—
Soon to be forgot, as a once treasured toy.

Stagnant mirth—
With a sensation such, as not secure,
Impending cold—tightening girth.
Yearning to go back, to drop the scarlet sack—
Crave it pure.

Unfound affection—
Falling out much as a pup's young yip,
Embarrassed—this affliction.
Round peg, square slot, grace the pot—
A silent trip.

Zach Schneider
OUR OUTER LIMITS

To my Father, and my two brothers, Jay & Mark and Karolyn Hendrix

It's a place beyond the stars, and
a place beyond the heavens
where destiny follows and your
dreams come true. A place
where everyone can Love and
Share their magic. You always
grow younger, but your soul never
dies. It's within you, a place where
you've never been before. A light
that leads you and lets you know
there is Love in the world. A place
where Beauty and Grace are found.
A place of Color and Imagination.
A place of Images and Emotions.
A place of Power and Spirit.

Arlene R Gagnon
I AM

. . . to all the children of the One true God, and, the spirit of truth, in which it is written . . .

I am . . . more than a skeleton, with blood coursing in my veins.
I am . . . a being, who is able to ponder the mysteries, my eyes behold.
I am . . . capable of reasoning the extremes, that would destroy me.
I am . . . a soul, searching, for the truth of my existence.
I am . . . spirit, sharing, the anomalies of lost knowledge.
I am . . . a fighter of freedom, a soldier of truth, a warrior . . . against the leaders of darkness.
I am . . . searching, in the valley, listening to the echoes, as the mountains, repeat the messages of our ancestors!
" . . . Look not upon your neighbors, but, deep within yourself . . . hidden, beyond the walls . . to protect the nakedness of who you are . . and there . . you will find . . that you are;
. . . the projection of your dreams . . .
. . . the mechanics of what you share . . .
. . . the keeper of your thoughts . . . "
You can only be destroyed, by yourself, if you allow others to influence and manipulate that which is your "crown of glory" . . I AM in each and everyone . . .

Marjory O Leicester
MY SCOTTISH BAIRN
The whins and punies were a'blowin'
Oh, the skree was blowin' wild.
I searched the hedges and the burrows
And I could not find my child.

I thrust my head up in the treetops
Where I looked among the leaves,
But my bonnie bairn was missing
And my heart was sore to grieve.

So I came back to my cabin
Shut the door against the blast—
There my bonnie bairn lay sleeping,
Sleeping sweetly, home at last.

Barbara Robinson
THE ABORTION
My mother is carrying me
I'm one month & a week inside
She's getting an abortion
So I'm going to die
She doesn't want it
But my father thinks it's best
After they kill me
There will be no rest
For my mother and father
As they both know
For I am them
Their seed, their soul.

John Lewis
THE BEAUTY OF THE DAY
I can still remember, clear illuminously bright days as a child.
Being a lad of six in summer, I would run, play, and just past the while.

Those days were forever free,
and much as so, I took them
forever granted.
I was the happiest scout on
earth, or as I thought, on any
planet.

While gazing, upon the bright blue sky, and observing occasional gliding billowy clouds that pass.
I would see imaginings of people, things, and creatures there on God's endless beautiful canvas.

On occasion when the overhead
tapestry would grow dim, and,
opposingly dark.
All creatures of the air would
quiet, the Sparrow, the Cardinal,
the Wren, and the Lark.

Overhead would clap a bright vein of brightness, which would lurch me into alarm.
I would run to seek solace, and strength, in the comfort of my mother's arms.

Oh, the rains that fell to earth
would cool . . . , cleanse, and
refresh the Almond Day.
And the fears, and darkness that

stoodeth, I knew then, would go away.

For soon the sun will bring the rainbow, and God will send the sun. Thus; this his earnest promise, all things goods now here, have begun.

Yes, and the birds renew their singing, and I renew my play. Again I would take for granted; The Beauty Of The Day!

Shirley Mellott
GUIDE MY FOOTSTEPS
Guide my footsteps
"O Lord I pray"
help me walk within thy light today.
Lift mine eyes and guide my day into the "light of living—"
to help me on my upward way.
Lord teach my hands to do thy work
And all that can be done;
And sputter not a word
of all the "undone" left to do
while time is now, and people
are few, now is the time for me
to commune with you; for in
thy hands I walk with thee and
know daily that Thou hast
talked with me. While people
are few "time is now" to do all I
can do for you; for the world
wants and wants so "badly to
see" the beauty of God in
someone like me.

Connie A Carpenter
PASSING TIME
Two old men met every day,
Unless a hindrance got in their way.
They loved to sit and chat,
Wherever you found them at.
It could be at a country store,
Or on the courthouse yard at four.
All kinds of news they would hear,
Whether it be far or near.
When the day was done,
They could hardly wait to come
Home and tell their wives,
All the tales, some of them lies.

Henrietta Ward
AN ODE TO THE COUCH POTATO

This poem is dedicated to my loving husband Joseph and my sweet daughter Jennifer.

A couch potato he is one,
not caring about the outside fun.
With channel changer in his hand,
ready to switch into another land.
Making a dent in his favorite chair,
not even taking time to comb his hair.
A nap or two he might get in,
between game shows where people win.

A couch potato he is one,
watching programs till they're done.
Drink in one hand and chips on his lap,
he would say, "Hunters no sap."
His eyes glued to the T.V. set,
it wasn't the first time "Griffith," he met.
Show after show and all that he watches,
make my feet ache with swollen arches.

A couch potato he is one,
"Is there any more chips left," hon".
An answer to his question, but he didn't hear,
he'll be needing a tuning in his ear.
His favorite chair sagging down to the floor,
it's a wonder he makes it through the door.
From dawn to dusk it's all the same,
playing the couch potato game.

Howard Ostrander

Howard Ostrander
THIS OLD HOUSE

Dedicated to my wife, Marie.

I am nothing but a house
But things I shall remember,
The pitter-patter of little feet
As they ran across my timber.

The times they ran across the floor
The times they slammed and kicked my door
The warmth of love and laughter within
The times my paint was getting thin.

And then the time I was remodeled without end,
A happy house I am again.
With warmth and love I hold so dear,
And now destruction I do not fear.

The age of TIME I will not show
For again I feel my structures glow;
Now I'm a house with fondness dear
Again I'll last for many a year,

For I feel warmth and love within . . .
Now I'm a happy house again.

Constance J Smith
JUST US
There are times when the talking just won't do.
The fighting & arguments that we have that make us blue.

You know there are times when things get really bad.
But then again just think of what we had.

We've lost that love on a long rocky road.
Now we're just looking for a place to dump our heavy load.

The pleasures that we had and all that was shared.
You were so blind 'cause you never knew how I cared.

And if you think that this relationship is only a big mess.
Then take a big look around and you'll come up with less.

We can't make any promises for fear of what it will bring.
So we should let time take its pace and just let it be.

Jessica Penzo
ONE, TWO, THREE

To my family: Dad, Mom, David, and friends, whom I love very much

One is grateful,
Two is wise,
Three has wisdom beyond the eyes.

Michael Minozzi
DRIFTLESS FLOWER
You sit
like a driftless flower
pouring all that inward
outward upon your face

Your eyes—those deep dark caverns
have so many secrets
Who do you tell
if you tell at all

Those years mark
your countenance
like rings on a tree

You look—
look right through all else
What is it you see?
Inside you are full—
full of emptiness

The truth is
that's what makes you beautiful
your experience,
but mostly
your endurance.

Gene Contrubis
TO CAROL

Dedicated to Carol Johnson, a beautiful woman and a wonderful friend. God bless you and our friendship.

It's your whole body
That speaks to the rain
And sweet autumn wind.

They are words whispered through a smile
That touch me in the light of dreams,
They are words revealed in the face of a child
That feed the fire bleeding in the shadows
Lifting me beyond the touch of your hair.

But it 's the look in your eyes
That charms the dancing stars
And caresses the cleft of the sun.
It's this look carved out of the deep
Tender as the plumes of a bird
That cause the velvet waves in the mist,
A look drenched in your scent
Luminous as the gaze of the moon
That takes me over your daylights
To rest by the lake on your lips.

Katherine Lambert Landrey
QUIET TEARS
Have you ever seen quiet tears
rolling down a person's face?
It doesn't seem to matter a person's creed or race.
Tears don't always numb the pain
that comes from anywhere
But they show a friend or neighbor
that you really care.
Tears can be shed in face of fear,
death and malady.
They seem to play a part in life as far as I can see.
Myself, I shed my quiet tears while on a little walk
Where it seems to bring some peace and no need for talk.
All my quiet tears come straight from my heart
Not always all together, sometimes an inch apart.
Quiet tears are falling while my life is such askew
Not only are they little but actually quite a few.
My only consolation is that God is always here.
He can always see each one, a very quiet tear.
As you can see, quiet tears really mean quite much
And multiply or divide with just a loving touch.

Mrs Irene Henry
THE THING

Dedicated to Mrs Andrew Aaroe on the occasion of her retirement as Principal of School #14, Fords, New Jersey

I took a walk the other day and as I strolled along
It seemed that in the distance I heard the strangest song.
It wasn't one that I knew well or ever heard before
Perhaps if I walked faster I'd hear a little more.
The tune I couldn't recognize, the voice was strange to me
And when I reached the corner I listened carefully.
I looked around but couldn't find the reason for the song
I shrugged my shoulders then thought awhile, I guess perhaps I'm wrong.
And as I turned to walk away I heard the words, "Please stay . . . .
Please stay awhile and listen,
there's much I have to say.
I suppose instead of singing, I
should be sad and feeling blue
And deep inside I really am but
there's nothing I can do.
A friend of mine is leaving soon,
a friend far better than gold
And memories of what's gone by
are something to behold.
So instead of feeling sorry, I sing
of the good old days,
Of all the fun we used to have in
oh, so many ways.
Please understand, not every
day was filled with happiness
September came and I was sure
I looked my very best.
The children came and looked at
me and some were filled with scorn
I knew they wished deep down
inside that I had not been born.
There were days when joy and
laughter was all that you could hear
And sounds of music filled each

room as the holidays came near.
My will is strong, my hopes are high, I stand for all to see
And those that work within my walls mean very much to me.
I'm thankful for the memories
I've had throughout the years
I've lived through joys and happiness, through hopes and dreams and tears.
I'm thankful for so many things, each year there's more and more
Indeed I have so very much for which I'm thankful for."
And so you see this "thing" stands there in all its pride and glory
And then a thought occurred to me as I listened to its story.
It's not the bricks from which it's made or the windows that make it sing
It's what's inside but most of all, it's the Principal of the "thing."

Tena Green
YOU WILL LIVE FOREVER

This poem is dedicated to my best friend and my inspiration, with love. Thanks, Mom! I love you.

When my skies are gray, I think of you
So that I may see thru the gray to the blue.
So much of life you have taught me;
Love, Faith, Reasoning and Meaning.
You've shown me right from wrong
Not just mine and others, but also your own.
You've taught me not to be self-righteous, not to expect perfection,
That it is enough to do as well as you can,
Not to expect anymore from any man.
You've taught me how to love without feeling insecure,
And how to let someone love me without expecting it to disappear.
When I was small you held me in your arms just so.
By doing this you made me feel safe, loved and secure.
Now I hold my children just so and know they feel the same.
You've shown me how to look at things differently,
to see more than just a flower or a tree.
You taught me respect and the value of life.
You have always believed in me even when you had reason not to.
You've always been the friend in my life; the one to lean on, cry on,
and especially the one to laugh with.
You taught me to believe in myself by believing in me.
I will do the best I can to instill in my children all that you have taught me.
I pray they will teach their children the same.
And one day people will look at us
They will smile, not their head and think your name.
In us you will live forever.

Jane Schwantes
I WANT TO FIND GOD

God, God,—
I want to find God.

Somewhere on a sunny day:
Far down the meadow,
Out on the bay—
Up on the mountain,
Down by the spring,
I seek to find God.

On the country's crowded trains,
In the shells of flying planes,
In the city's toil and mell,
Deep in the heart's most anguished cell—
God comes to find me.

Somewhere on a sunny day:
Far down the meadow,
Out on the bay—
Up on the mountain,
High and free,—
There to behold Thee in Eternity.

Evelyn Elaine Richardson
WHY

Dedicated to the husband God gave me "Vernon"

Without a feeling—
Without a thought—
What will come after?
You hear the shot!

But there is feeling*
There is thought*
You pay for it.
In an ambush plot—

All your money*
All your greed*
What will it profit?
When you plant the seed.

Why did you do it?
What did you do it for?
Will it help others?
To even the score—

Your time is coming*
Dear friends will say!
Can you answer these questions
On the Judgement Day?*

Mitchell Spiros
MYSTICAL LOVE

Trading emotions
Changing with growth
Creates a circle of oneness
Surrounded by hope
A strength from substance
emerging unseen
With the birth of a feeling
from somebody's dream
Can't deny that feeling
Are you aware
Something is better
sense that it's there
Detachment is betterment
Strange to say
How love grows stronger
when one is away
When emotions blossom
with maturity through growth
From the dreams of people
who still keep the hope
There'll come a true love
beyond the mere scope
of the cloak of physical
endeavors
This spiritual love
once it is seen
Is self sufficient
and oh so serene
I'm removing that cloak
waking my dream
I'll love you, really love you
after all . . . you're part of my
scheme

Jean C Phillips
LIFE ON THE FARM

Dedicated to the memory of our Dear Parents

"Time to get up," our Father would call,
While at the barn hungry cows would bawl.
The roosters would crow, the pigs would squeal.
All of them hungry for their morning meal.
Happy with the thought, all had been fed,
Back to the house, sleeping children in bed.
"Time to get up," again we would hear
In a voice that was strong and clear.
After a breakfast fit for a king,
It was about time for the school bell to ring.
With lunches to pack and a mile to walk
There was little time to sit and talk.
Parents praying we would obey the rule
And be real good every day at school.
When time to go home at the end of day,
Everyone was happy to be on their way.
If we could recall those childhood years
Our eyes never again would be blinded by tears.
Keep them happy, Dear Lord, in their home on high,
While never-ending years of Eternity roll by.

Lori Althoff
BREAD IS BREAD; WINE IS WINE

To my wonderful husband Herman.

Bread is bread; wine is wine,
I wish your pajamas were next to mine,
Don't get excited; don't get red,
I mean on the clothesline; not in bed.

Nelda M Speaks
A TEENAGER'S LAMENT

The plantation lies sleeping
In the shadows of the moon;
Now is the only time for rest
Until tomorrow at noon.
I am awake as usual,
Perching my lonely self
Upon a high window sill
Like a book on a shelf.

Miss Annie, the ghost,
Walks now and then
Reminding me that she will stay
Until the very end.

I sing a mournful tune
About a prison wall,
Dreaming, scheming,
Weeping with the wind and
Hearing the night bird's call.

Donald Merten
TWO HEARTS LOST

To Betty—"There are in the end three things that last: faith, hope, and love, and the greatest of these is love." 1 Corinthians 13

You have left me after all of these years; and I am alone.
The bond between us has been severed; but I grasp hopelessly to memories of you.
Beautiful thoughts of your being and mine entwine and refuse to perish as you may have hoped—
Because for every part of me that dies, another cries out to live.
To live forever in the eternalness of our relationship.
For what we have carved in time lives on in our hearts and souls.
Only God can erase all of what was written in the pages of our togetherness.
You walk away . . . and I too . . . glancing back . . .
Thinking maybe we made the wrong choice—
But no! The commitment to choice and words of others is too strong!
And we continue on our separate ways.
A journey into nothingness . . . into emptiness . . .
Two hearts lost in a sea of timeless despair.
For we are each alone . . . forever . . . . and forever.

Marguerite Phillips

Marguerite Phillips
LIFE OF DRUGS

Drugs, one of many problems in the world today,
Hoping it will soon be vanished away.
The problem is so extensive and nothing can be done,
Not even when the life of someone is already gone.
Many, may run the streets or end up in jail,
And living a life of pure hell.
A drug is a bomb that goes straight to the brain,
That will put your body through aches and pains.
Some will steal to support their habit,
And will deny they ever did it,
when questioned about it.
A drug user needs the power to survive,
to live in this world and stay alive.

Melissa Lillard-Johnson
IN THE YEAR 12,000

To my mom, who has always believed in me.

Body, soul and mind emerge
to start a conversation
taught by others to lead
in the restoration.

Grass is green
but not for long
will our children hear
a real bird's song?

Or covered with
the wind of change
will we awake to a world
that's strange?

A world we made
from concrete and lies
to cover our weaknesses
in their eyes.

Control the over-population
  and demanding situations
    with our concrete answers
will we have our reservations?

Can't we live with
  grass and trees?
    Maybe if we all beg . . . .Please.

Dino A Rossi
A CLAMMER'S DELIGHT

The tide is low, the sun is bright;
The wind is calm, a clammer's delight.
The water's inviting, clams are in hiding;
A sport that's a challenge, a very good outing.

Some clammers are digging, and others are raking;
Each one works his choice, and hopes for the taking.
But the law reads"
"Five inches or more, and the limit is ten."
If this law you follow, the game warden's your friend.

A shade under five you should turn it loose;
The fine is not worth it, and you'll have no excuse.
One must have a license if one is of age,
To dare clam without one and get caught, you're no sage.

Jeanette Lawson Matheson

Jeanette Lawson Matheson
LEST I FORGET, MOMENTARILY

Life has been good to me, not
  unkind,
I've been proud to have a right
  good mind,
But now as my body slows down
  and my hair has turned gray,
Sometimes I forget what I did
  yesterday.

It's right embarrassing to run into
  a friend of many years
Who has stood by me through
  laughter and tears,
The feeling of friendship is just
  the same,
But at that moment, I seem to
  have forgotten the name.

And then to help me remember
  what I need to do,
Even if there is only one thing or
  two,
I try to help matters by writing
  myself a note,
Then I have to write another to
  remind me to remember where
  I put the first one I wrote.

My memory of telephone
  numbers has always been the
  best,
But now it comes up blank when
  put to test.
I make much use of the telephone
  book and always write the
  numbers down,
But the next time I need to use
  them again, they've disappeared
  and can't be found.

But I remember to call on the
  Lord every day—
Asking Him to give me
  safekeeping as I go my way.
So far it has worked and I hasten
  to say,
It sure is important for me to
  always remember to pray.

Martino Paul Dao
THE DEW DROP

To Sisters Evelyn Kane, Elizabeth Cavanagh, my friends Mary L. Irvine, Annette Watson, Rafael Reyes, Vo Phi Ho, Le Van Ba, my sister Chinh Dao and husband, my nephews Ngan Dao, Hoang Nguyen, my niece LoanAnh Vidmanis.

At the center of a rose in its full grace
A big dew drop one nice morning appears.
One would say a tear on the pretty face
Of a young girl with sentimental fears.

To the sun exposing its perfect freshness,
It looks like a diamond born in the bloom.
But from the heat it receives without willingness,
It disappears very soon, taking away the perfume.

The dew drop embellishes the scented flower.
Likewise wealth and power make men proud,
Giving them love, happiness and honor.

But if the mist droplet is indeed ephemeral,
Similarly fame and fortune on this ground
Are nothing but pure vanity for all.

Betty Irean Loeb
WHO AM I?

This poem is dedicated to the only one who can answer my question. To Him I offer my faith, my love, and my gratitude.

I traveled from deep valleys to
towering mountain tops,
  from parched plains to the
  thundering sea.

I beheld monuments carved in
glowing, red sandstone,
  brave sentinels from long, long
  ago;

  Deserts—vast, scorched and still,
  yet sustaining life on a
  wondrous scale;

  A canyon of awesome
  proportions and noble beauty,
  etched by a river both calm and
  wild,

  Trees so majestic I was dwarfed
  by their height;

  Trees, gnarled, bent, and
  centuries old, facing infinity
  with faith;

  Creatures—tiny, scampering,
  swift and free;

  Swallows singing their sweet,
  joyful song from a chapel high
  on a cliff . . .

And I wondered about me.

    Who am I? For what purpose
    am I here?

Like a quaking aspen, I stood
trembling, high on a hill,

And waited silently under a canopy
of a billion beckoning stars

    until I knew—I'm one of God's
    chosen to live amid the
    beauty of this earth.
    In His time, He'll tell me why.

Sharleen Fletcher
FOREVER LOVE

Don't think we might
  Have our love tonight,
And don't you fight
  For my love.
'Cause it comes like a dove
  To the one I love.
So come to me
  And stay by my side,
And we'll grow to be one
  Throughout the tide.
And at the end of time,
  Others will see
We've had our way
  And I've loved our time.
Just you and me
  Together forever,
And always.

Patricia J Rudies
YOU INSPIRE ME

To Barbara, I love you, my friend.

You inspire me.
With gentle words of encouragement.
You listen intently,
When my life shows discouragement.
You share my joy
With your laughter and smile.
You've felt my pain
And helped me to live again.
You've seen me as I am
And like a child, whose
  innocence sees and accepts
    imperfections,
    you love me.
You are my Friend.

William J Cooper
TEARS AND TATTERS

To Cali Richardson, who gave me the strength to face the night.

Alleyway prophets slinking shadows in the fog.
Cobblestones steaming up the windows in the pub.
Curtains of mist that mystify and wet the dirt,
and shuffle in the breezes that blow from a thousand ragged shirts.

See how the wind tears the tatters and swirls them around to common patterns.

Moonlight staggers through the walls of drunken haze.
Cloth-eared clutchers drawing blood from paper bags.
Muted tonal chimes that snap the stillness of the web,
weaving time as it passes from a thousand common threads.

See how the eyes sense the matter and turn their backs upon the tatters.

Streetlights stifled in a strange romantic glow.
Cat-eyed darters pressing flat against the stone.
Tavern chatter floats in halos on the rocks,
and will pause for inspection to the predators in the fog.

See how the tatters tear and yet stop to reflect common heirs.

Lonely mirrors wash as puddles in the light.
Shadows defend positions that give meaning to their lives.
Howling breezes cluster within waves of glass,
till the last drop is taken, with no looking back.

See how the dawn repeats the patterns, and we do not notice tears and tatters.

Margaret W Neubauer
LOVELAND

I know a land where roses never wither,
A land where memories can never die;
Where Love walks hand in hand,—as true love ever
Should do,—and every hour that hastens by
Is filled with bliss too tender for repeating;
Where butterflies abound, and Blue birds sing;
Where kindred souls come eagerly to meeting
And misty rainbows rest o'er everything.
I know a land where heartaches turn to gladness,
Where weary feet speed merrily and free
And lips have learned to smile that knew but sadness,—
Where dreams come true,—at twilight claiming me
With the first star, and quietness, like a cover
Folding the earth while gentle breezes sigh
Their soothing songs, soft chanting each one over
All the night long,—a tireless lullabye!
I watch each evening by its dusky borders,
Wistful. I wait alone to greet you, and
Down those winding ways fragrant with flowers
Dream together, childlike, hand in hand.
Knowing each thought though not a word be spoken
Save the quick language of loving eyes,—
Thus, day by day, with happiness unbroken,—
Eternally adrift in Paradise!

Stephen Dean Bolen
GROWING UP IN THE 1960'S—A TIME TO DREAM

To the memory of J.C. Simmons, a loving grandfather

We all seemed to live a lot easier
  back then, when we had time to
  think and dream
About what we might do with our
  own lives; while we were in
  school listening to our teachers
  express the Golden Rule.
We enjoyed our friends and had a
  good time, while our parents

only could look and shake their heads
Because they did not think we would amount to much; even though we were really listening to them and knew we eventually would.
We enjoyed school ball games, it was a time "To Be True To Your School" each Friday night
Even if your team did not win; there was always the dance after the game when you could be with your one true love.
We saw many changes in our day, the Beatles came from England to change the music we heard
Each day; while the world went to the brink of nuclear war with the Missile Crisis in Cuba.
We began to hear more about a little place called Vietnam, even though the most important thing to us was maybe to have a
Good Job; things did begin to change in our lives—some for the good, some for the bad.
We saw the War on Poverty and the Peace Corps begin; while integration and space travel became parts of our thoughts
Because it was a time to dream and to say, "Ask not what your country can do for you: ask what you can do for your country"
Since it was a time to dream about the future and the role we would play in it when life seemed a lot easier, way back then.

Olga Bauman
EYE OF WINTER

This poem is dedicated to my dear grandchildren, Justin and Rachel.

Look up! See me?

No? but I see you perfectly
from my twelve month perch;

Never more vividly than now
this thing called winter.

Air is crisp; white snow reflects
I see clearly
many creatures on the earth.

Why do you seek comfort?
for joy? health? love?

Come with me
and look upon this world
as a place of peaceful turmoil.

I am <u>your</u> eye! Cold but gleaming
sharing winter's beauty
in your life.

Deborah S Preston
A GIFT OF LOVE

To the only man I ever loved, my husband, Gordon Preston.

I wish there were a way
I could show you how I feel!
I tell you every day
I love you!
But you won't believe it's real.

I've tried to show this to you
each and every day;
But however strong the feelings are,
I can not find a way!

If I had a wish come true
Love would then be whole;
More than just a touch or kiss;
An item you could hold.

I'd wrap it in a great big bow,
And sign a card, 'With Love."
And after I made it look just so,
I'd give you lots of love.

And so to you I give this poem,
To show you how I feel.
In your hand you hold my heart;
My gift of love—to you.

Syble L Hanson

Syble L Hanson
THE MEANING OF HAPPINESS TO ME

I wish to dedicate this poem to my two sons, John T. and Byron D. Hanson and their lovely families, also to someone I will love and respect forever.

When I look back over the years, I find happiness . . . . I find sorrow . . . .
I kneel and pray for tomorrow, . .
Tomorrow comes . . . . . and I borrow another day . . .
Frustrations mount and I say, Dear Lord, bring an end to this sadness . . . .
Bring an end to this madness . . . .
Please carry me through another day . . . .
He Does . . . . And He Did . . . . I Can Rejoice! !
He filled a void so beautifully . . . .
And I asked for another day! ! !
I asked Him to show me the way . . . . .And the true meaning of HAPPINESS . . . . . .
He did . . . . And I'll be forever grateful . . . . To Him and To You! !

The meaning of HAPPINESS I have found . . . . . To fill the void in my life that's below ground . . .
To look into TRUE, Lonely eyes filled with LOVE, RESPECT, and much PRIDE . . . .
I have found the meaning of happiness . . . . . All my sorrows died . . . .
And then I begged and I cried . . . . For another day! !
He has given me another day . . . .
I've seen families restored . . . . .
with kindness and love . . . .
And somehow I just know . . . . It came from above . . . . .
It continues to fill the void in my life that's below . . . .
With happiness and contentment . . . . To lessen the blow . . . .
Another day, another tomorrow . . . I look forward to . . . . .
without sorrow! !

Kris Taylor
SPRING FEVER

Oh when will it be spring?
The birds, I long to hear sing.

These long and lonely days are dreary and full of haze.

Easter will soon be here, with sights of roaming deer.

When we hear some owls give nice, long hoots, that will be the time to store our boots.

When trees become green again, we won't be needing a fire in our den.

I can hardly wait, for this spring is late.

To see some flowers, with blossoms and maybe a family of possums.

Waudell B Nelson
KING OF PEACE

Break forth in praise ye mountains,
Be pleased and joy on earth.
God has remembered His children,
To-night is our Saviour's birth.

The road is dark and narrow,
The clouds they rumble by,
Far-away hills, we same to hear;
A call of the shepherds cry!

Now in the east, not far away,
Beyond the shepherds sheep.
The star hung low over a cattle stall,
Where a baby lay fast a-sleep.

He lay all His glory by;
To atone for the fall of men;
And justify a righteous law,
To cover a world of sin.

Jesus did in a manger lay,
Came wise men from the east;
With their myrrh and frankincense,
To worship the "King of Peace."

Marsha Fisher
JALOPY HEAVEN

Grandma and Pa Pa: "Because you both take so little—and give us so much."

Grandpa's jalopy doesn't run anymore
The antique handle won't crank to start her up!
The burnt out engine—well, there's not a spark
Axle grease is worn from the tire's rim,
The chrome bumpers have rusty spots.
Wheel spokes that clanked against one another
As they went around in circles,
Now lay embedded in dirt beside the wheels;
Acorns and rocks have shattered the glass
All of this—over time.

Yet Grandpa sits on the back porch, with a beer
Staring at it every day
Where he watches the silver squirrels play;
And I think he dreams of kissing Grandma
In the back rumble seat
Just as he did so many times and years before.
It's either that
Or he wants to honk the horn
That was once a golden brass prize,
Strategically placed
So that everyone could hear the jalopy coming.

Now that's tarnished and almost black
The sound it would make
Would be a little flat—
Grandpa wouldn't mind that.
His ears would remember the angelic note
That followed his chariot
To the gates of jalopy heaven.

Monica Kamenel
THE SYNDROME—OR SOMETHING

I've heard it often through the years, from friends who wrote or called, in tears.
They've gone—the kids left home.
It's called The Empty Nest Syndrome.
I thought—Oh Lord, it could happen to me. My kids will grow and want to be free.
Could I bear for them to leave home?
Could I survive The Empty Nest Syndrome?
They've grown—they scattered—they married—they moved,
And This Heartbreaking Syndrome I may have disproved.
I miss them, of course, but I'm happy to see that wherever they are, they are all missing me.
Now I'm all alone in this nice, quiet flat, with Winston, the dog, and Delilah, the cat.
The kids all come by, or call, or write. I sometimes get four calls a night.
Perhaps as around the world they roam, they've caught The Empty Nest Syndrome!
Perhaps they miss me and the flat, and Winston, the dog, and Delilah, the cat.
Perhaps they'd like to come back home, to cure their Empty Nest Syndrome.
BUT . . . . I like the quiet and I like the peace and I like the fact that I've got a Lease
That says this flat is for one person only, because this person sure ain't lonely.
I love the kids and of course they must come to stay a while and visit their Mum,
But they'll have to leave and go back home, because
I like this Empty Nest Syndrome.

Alisa V Brown
I CLOSE MY EYES AND I SEE THE SUN

I close my eyes and I see the sun,
A rainbow is reflected in your eyes,
The ethereal light of holiness,
Casts a welcoming glow from your face,
It seeps softly into my flesh,
Tingling I shiver.
As the tide caresses the land for eternity.
Your essence has burned itself into me.

If the sky were dark forever,
And the flowers withered for good,
The magic of your soul would color my world.
To be without you,
For each turning of the hourglass.
Creates an irritation that molds a black pearl.
An object so perfect, so priceless, so flawed.
The memory of you would keep the air sweet.
The loss of you would keep the gem dark.
My love for you will bind them together,
Creating a joy and a sorry like no other.

Donna (McClain) Estes
MOTHER
This is for Mother
Who rides in the hearse
Devoted to memory
Verse after verse.

You've finally found peace,
And your body's at rest
Throughout all eternity
You will always be missed.

Your suffering is over;
You will feel no more pain,
But my soul is still hurting;
Your memories remain.

I remember your hair
And the sweet way you'd smile
As you tucked me in bed
While you sang all the while.

It's hard to let go
Of someone so dear;
Oh Mother, I need you,
And I want you near.

I must accept that
I won't see you for now,
But someday I'll be there
Just wait for awhile.

B J Anderson
KERRY
You were born at a time when everything seemed to be going wrong.
I was crying by myself, it seemed like all night long.
For while your life was beginning,
Naomi's had reached its end.
As much as I wanted to be with you,
her need was greater then.

Daddy and Kendra home in Munising, you in Grandma's care,
Naomi in a hospital room, me wanting to be everywhere.
It was a whole month that we had to go on this way
With only the promise "this too shall pass," did we manage the day to day.

Naomi's struggles over, when all she had left us was the pain,
Four of us went home at last,
learning to live as a family again.
Kerry, I know that sometimes I hold too tight to you,
But you ease the memories, gave me a reason to fight the blues.

I would never ask you to take the place of someone gone,
Yet having you I could not hide from the fact that life goes on.
While Kendra was our first born, of our youth and naivety.
Naomi was our second born, who made us face life's realities.

But you are our final child, the last there will ever be,
Conceived and carried with a faith stronger than any fear in me.
God has made no promises about the path our lives will take,
But in you I behold the miracle that only faith can make.

Quay B Dorius

Quay B Dorius
LOVE VS. HATE

I dedicate this poem to all the people in the world who wish and hope for a better future

If the world was full of love
like the man from up above
we could all live in peace like the dove

But instead it's full of hate
We could change by a certain date
But it's soon growing too late

for the snake is about to bite
The dove about to take flight
leaving this world a pitiful sight

let's don't let the snake bite
letting the dove be in sight
making our world much more bright

Robert Medici
THE RAIL BRIDGE

To Daniele, who will never know

Seated by the river
As it meanders slowly by,
Billows scattered across blue
Obscured by trees.
Watching the flow
Ease its way past
Concrete pillars
Of the derelict rail bridge,
Long past use.
Rusty wounds mark the columns
As memorial to battle
Fought with age.
Iron, once impenetrable
Now rattled by the wind,
Tattered as paper flags.
Slowly
Constantly reworked
Back to what it was
In spite of all we do

Kermit R Wilhelm Jr
THE FANTASY PERSISTS
the fantasy persists
fueled by your exciting beauty
& the burning desire etches
    into my system

a refreshing wind—
a copious moon—
a mysterious night
slips into cool sheets with
a wish we were
    between

outworld novas collide
comet tails lick
    wandering satellites
& i reach for the stars
as you strain my
    limen.

Kristy R Doyle
TRUST NO ONE EVER

To Tom; With your patience and understanding, you taught me how to love.

When you need their help
Or call out their name
Ask for their love
They think it's a game.

Just when you think
You know that they care
You ask for their help
But they wouldn't dare.

In a sea of doom
You reach for their hand
They turn away
Afraid of demand.

It's a lonely world
When you're out on your own
But there's no one to thank
You've made it alone.

Guy Reneau
WHAT CAN I DO
What can I do?
This I may ask.
What can I do?
I have a task.

What can I do
When things go wrong?
What can I do?
I can sing a song.

What can I do
When others shirk?
What can I do?
Just work and work.

What can I do
When hate rules men's hearts?
I can tell of God's love
And so do my part.

What can I do
When faith grows weak?
I can read God's word
And to Him in prayer speak.

So I'll be up and doing
As I am made strong.
I'll work for the right
And against the wrong.

The greatest need
In the world today
Is that Christian people
Work and pray.

So I'll answer my question
And I'll put it this way.
"I can do my best
With God's help, today."

Ann E Plowman
MY HUSBAND

This poem is dedicated to Terry Plowman, my best friend.

Always ready to share laughter,
Yet available for tears.
Romantic and sensitive,
Yet always realistic and strong.
Full of passion and excitement,
Though always gentle and affectionate.
Determined, ambitious, and hardworking,
Yet a joy to be lazy with.
Sometimes mysterious and private,
But quick to be open, honest, and warm.
Intelligent, serious, and sensible,
Though filled with humor and the silliness of a child.
Satisfied with life,
Yet always curious and eager to learn.
Filled with more love than most people experience in a lifetime,
But always willing to give that love away.
Time spent together is like living in a dream,
Yet I still feel as wonderful when I'm awake . . .

Nicholas G Kitsios
SOMETHING VS NOTHING
Long long ago there was nothing.
Then man came along and there was Something.

But with man's ideas
And many of his fears,
Man's something today
Might turn into nothing tomorrow.

But if there's a will
And I hope to God there's a way.
Man's nothing tomorrow,
Will always keep away,
From man's something today.

Marguerite B O'Loughlin
WHY?
She stands there, all alone
No one to share her grief
That's the way she wants it
(Dear God, make this service brief)

The friends she did have
Gave up long ago
She had kept her independence
(Now wish it wasn't so)

She never shared her pleasures
So why share her grief
To be strong and self-reliant
Had always been her belief

To be a friend, or neighbor.
She somehow lacked the skills
She was too busy working
(And paying all the bills)

Her only friends, the mailbox
And cat sleeping down below
Too late to start over
(Please say it isn't so!)

Jan Oestermyer
THE LAKE
In winter she lies alone and still,
ensconced in a blanket of down.
A cover for her coat of cold armor,
now warming her depths so profound.

Then March winds become more gentle,
she sleeps beneath her thinning shroud.
Restless to glimpse the canopy of blue,
or of gray when inspired by the clouds.

One bright dawn all is tranquil and warm,
her veil has been lifted by the night.
Eyes blink, she stretches, embracing her realm.
Long slender fingers touch the shore,
as nature's glow warms her nude body again.

Now her diamonds they dazzle in sunlight,
still there's beauty in all we endure.
And the raindrops that fall so discreetly,
place waves in her lustrous blond hair.

For her beauty is a plan of things greater
than we know by material means.
And she's not just a lake by nature's own hand,
but someone who is part of life's dreams.

Dawn Parker
TO DOROTHY
People often ask me
Why I love you so much
'Cause they've never known the joy
Of your kindly Christian touch.

I have never known a sorrow
That went long unsoothed by thee
And often you will offer help
Before I state a plea.

So on this your Happy Birthday
I must want you to know
That my love for you is perpetual
No matter how young you grow.

Betty Ann Wooley

Betty Ann Wooley
SWEET MYSTERY
Tell me where the rivers flow
Sheer moonbeams dance upon the snow
Why stars at night smile down on me
And thundering waves sail out to sea

Tell me why the wind must call
The clouds to cover skies so tall
Cool misty mornings bring the dew
And shadows paint the mountains blue

Tell me why the birds take wing
The flowers gently grow in Spring
Then I'll no longer dream my plea
Of all the world's sweet mystery

Gary L Ellis
WOKE UP TO THIS MOUNTAIN
Woke up to this mountain,
Had a dream to climb
To find a new horizon
At the top, along the way with time.
All of us are climbing
Seeking the rainbow's gold,
Treasures bountiful, stories untold.
Day by day, the walk is long
Finding rest in the beauty of you,
Mountain's streams and rustling leaves
Breathing my worries, joys and blues.
All of us are climbing
Seeking the rainbow's gold,
Treasures bountiful, our souls trying to unfold.
Let's all climb together
Wading through mountain's streams,
And soar all our worries
Upon the wind's wings.
All of us are climbing
Seeking the rainbow's gold.
Treasures bountiful, stories untold.

Michelle Kirmse
GOODBYE

To all my family and friends.

You used to love me.
I thought it was true.
Now you're falling for Amy.
I know you.
You say you don't.
Just she loves you.
You say you won't.
But you know it's true.
I loved you.
You didn't feel the same.
I love you.
But your feelings won't change.
I guess it's for the best.
I don't know why.
I know it's for the best.
I guess it's good-bye.

Gladys J White
A SPRINGTIME FANTASY

Dedicated to Brinton White, my late husband

Little bird upon my window sill
Are you there without your will?
Snow has come so late this year
And left you there without a fear.

So please go and don't come back
Until the sun has had a warmer smack
For ev'ry blooming, vital thing
And for the birds upon the wing.

And so I say farewell
To these things of which I tell
Words of early, early spring
And birds that are upon the wing.

But—do I dream or do I imagine
The battle that I cannot win?
Is the worry of this early spring
Something to which I should not cling?

We cannot have perfection all the time
Making this world seem so sublime.
We'll have to take the changes as they come
E'en though they aren't to us welcome.

Michael Pardridge
OLD MAN, YOUNG MAN
Tell me what you see, young man.
Is it me?
Or is it only skin beginning to pallor,
eyes without color,
hair that won't lay flat?

Look, and tell me what you feel.
Is it me?
Or is it but a chain to drag behind,
a base to touch at Christmas,
a call to make each month?

When you stop to listen, tell me what you hear?
Is it me?
Or stories with forgotten endings,
sermons when you sought advice,
more on who's dying of what?

Tell me what you see, young man.
Is it me?
Or is it someone else we know
limping down that long, long road?
Someone else who looks like me
but thinks like you.

Tell them what you see now, old man?
And remember what you saw.

Odies M Donald
FADING ROSES

This Poem is dedicated to my mother Ruthe O'Neal, Who suffers from Alzheimer's Disease.

All the love you've given us that
never stopped, just slipped
away.
In our heart those memories
stayed.

In the beginning we saw the
changes. We overlooked them,
We loved you the same.

Zooming around. restless and
scared. Remembering things.
Never left your head.

Holding on, in our heart, to a
beautiful rose petal falling apart.
Bits and pieces, we pick them
up. To see it crumble with each
touch.

Each day we pray, in a way—God
take this evil disease and throw
it away. Give us you. If just for a
day.

Impressions of crystal upon your
face. Thoughts like a stone. A
storm taken away. Leaving little
for today.

Memory of our childhood days,
you did so much, we can't repay.
You've given us life, we have
today.

Efforts we make today. Love you
each and every day, in every
way.
And keep you safe and happy,
we pray.

Reaching out, holding on.
Touching each rose petal before
it's gone. Hoping the shrub stays
strong. Strengthen the stem for
a rose to bud on.

Menno Walter Voth
A GRAVE AS YET UNMARKED
We spoke at length not all that long ago,
I and the toneless father of this boy
(Here sleeping neath a feral Flowering Plum
Profuse of blossom but not meant for fruit)
Cut sudden down in sudden manhood come,
His early mischief early wage assigned.

We calculated, the old man and I,
How many cords of wood his dying row
Of Walnut trees would yield, including stumps,
I with a nonchalant arithmetic
He often softly in his mother tongue.
He keeps no hearth and I am overstocked.
No common cause but that we both have sons
We held to custom of our rural roads.

Sandra K Taylor
WHAT DOES A MOTHER MEAN TO YOU

To a very special and loving lady. I love you, thanks Mom.

Someone who is as warm as the sunshine, who keeps the rain away.
Someone to show me kindness, when I have lost my way.
Someone to be understanding, just when I need it most.
Someone who can talk to me and make me believe,
That there could be a good quality inside of me.
Someone who is loved so very much.
Someone who has just the right touch.
Someone whose arms that are always opened,
To give me that special hug, that I know I am safe and loved.
She is my song that I have sung today.
Her smiles are as beautiful as the sun's rise.
She is my mother and on this day,
She will know how much I love her,
By these special words I have to say.

The Lord is only
A thought away.

Debra Lynn Roberts
I AM LAUGHTER IN THE WIND
I am Laughter in the wind.
I am Sunshine through the clouds.
I am a shining ray of Hope . . .

I am the rhythm of Music
as raindrops fall
I am the beauty of Creation
through it all.

I am a blossoming Rainbow
hugging the sky
I am the Twinkle of a star
shining so bright.

I am the mystery of the Moon
floating up above
I am the secret of Life
for I am called LOVE.

Tracy Lee Zeoli
TO GOD I PRAY IF EVER I SHOULD DIE

To my family who will always be there. To Mark & Doirinne for keeping my perspectives in order. I love all of you!

To god I pray
if ever I should die;
no words to say
but a simple goodbye.
No sadness
for my soul will live;
No grief
for my soul will give.
People will remember me for me,
not anyone I pretended to be.
Though we'll always be apart.
I know I'll always have a place in their heart!

Margaret H Oliver
MY HEAVENLY FATHER
I am so proud and happy
And as glad as I can be
There has never been a time
When my Father did not love me.

Sometimes the devil tries so hard
To change me thru and thru
God's cloak fully protects me
So the devil cannot get through.

He will try to throw me overboard
He is ready to make the big toss

Father pins his arms behind him
The devil concedes a loss.

When I'm tempted
To feel sad and low
My Father knocks depression out
With one solid blow.

Someday I'll see my Father
We are surely going to meet
He sitting on his lovely throne
I kneeling at his feet.

Kimberly Vegter
WHISPERS IN THE DARK
The soft sweet whisper of a child begging to be heard by anyone, but is not. The cold harsh winds, the silent, insane, discontentedness; these are the things that make up the dark, lonely nights of the bereft one.

Karen J Lori
DAWN

I dedicate this poem to Dawn and all my friends.

Such is life when a friend
passes away,
Such is life and must go on.
Reaching for a special friend, but
now Dawn is with God and so I
must go on.
Memories I hold within my heart,
memories which I will not part.
I feel as if I knew Dawn for a
thousand years,
realizing what a true friend I
had. But now the Lord will take
care of Dawn and as for me, I
still must go on.
Hurting inside, crying for a
friend who now I lost,
but memories live within my heart.

Crystal Morehead
LOVE
Love is something special,
Though many people know.

Love is like a fantasy,
That lingers in our souls

Love picks us up,
Whenever we are feeling blue.

Love is what I feel for you.

Gloria Hughes
WHY?
All I do is cry
And wonder why
That God hath wrought
On me that's brought
So many tears.
They say you'll bring cheer
to others there.
But what to do?
When they also too
Just cry
And wonder why.

Louise Parker
HAVE I
Have I grown too old to love
Or be loved in return
Will I just continue to live my life
alone
Have I grown too old to want
Or need a fond embrace
Have I grown too old to find
Someone to take your place
Have I grown too old I find I sit and
ask myself
Have I gone and placed myself
On some old dusty shelf
Have I grown too old to do
The things most people do
Or have I grown
Too old alone
In memories of you

Cliff Martin
TUMBLEDDOWN FIELDS
Tumbleddown fields
Encrusted old stories
So old & close
Soclose to me
i
Stood by the stairway
Near the tumbleddown wall
Suffered a phantom
Soclose to me i
Wood to run quickly
softly & far
To stumbleon footsteps
& go to the place—

Near the tumbleddown fields
Grown ancient w/weeds
i
Sing to a bluebird
Talk softly with ages i
Once never knew

In the tumbleddown fields
By the tumbleddown wall
Near the tumbleddown street
In the tumbleddown world;

So old & close,
Soclose to me i
Softly and far
& faraway . . .

Norma Ardell
STAMINA OF MAN

To my husband, a hard worker, good provider, but more important—my friend.

I often marvel and wonder about
the stamina of man,
The drive that keeps one going,
when others—off they ran.
The will power to browbeat one's
body all hours of the day—
To come to the end of a month;
never a raise in pay.

The power or strength to lift one's
body out of a comfortable warm
bed,
With only four hours sleep; when
it should be eight instead.
To face the elements of the
season—whether it be cold or
hot,
It's not the love of the job that
drives him, but he's done this a
lot.

The same routine each day,
month, year after year—
Causes many a sigh, but he never
sheds a tear.
He does what must or has to be
done,
This husband of mine, for his
wife, daughter and son.

May I tell you it's an honor to
have been by your side,
To hear me boast of your
qualities, I've never lied—
I've always said, "to give credit
where it is due,"
And my husband, today and
through the years—I've done
and will give credit to you.

Mark E Bader
ROACHES

for John and Gene

I have let them
Make me a roach
A modern day roach
Frantically running
From their power and anger
Clinging to life
In what would seem
Utter desperation
Only for the moment
Enemies created
Their dreaded disease
To get rid of me
Like they did with DDT
Killing my older brothers
But my brothers survived
And so will I
I simply must avoid
All the trappings and lures
Of their roach motels
Hospitals as they call them
The sterility
That kills all roaches
Some filth is necessary
For our very existence
So I move on
Day to day
With my simple tools
Of survival
Free will and lots of oxygen
There will come a day
I will be a big roach again
This time I will stand
In the open sunlight
Where they can see me
Only the cowards would
Dare to step on me
And if they did
It would not matter
I have already won
There are too many like me
Who refuse to die
To please our enemies
So I will continue enjoying
What was given to me to share
It feels good to be a roach
Because I know
Beyond a shadow of a doubt
I will be here tomorrow
But they may not
Unless they learn
To live like a roach

Cheryl Ann Semeraro
FEATHER LIGHT
Life like a pulsing heart,
Keeping a constant beat.
Wounded by the sharpest lie,
Forced into retreat.
Left to bleed unchecked,
To heal all on its own.
Still a broken heart,
Is never fully sewn.
But to emerge and overcome,
Is a problem still unsolved.
One that's been around,
Since all the world's evolved.
So life like a pulsing heart,
Must be handled with a touch.
Softer than the lightest feather,
That could never be loved too much.

Annalyn Mercado
UNFAIR CUPID
Oh, Cupid of those doves and hearts.
You, who brings us love.
How can you inflict upon me this
pain
Of unrequited love?
You fly around on careful wings
Showering us with arrows,
Turning our dreams of yesterdays
Into real love filled tomorrows.
So when your arrow pierced my
heart
I rejoiced for the love I felt,
Only to face the searing pain
From the cruelty you had dealt.
Oh, Unfair Cupid, the arrow you shot
Was made for only one
And the unfairness of the deed
you've done
Has made me want to run.
But Cupid of love, before you I beg
Down here upon my knees.
I'd do anything if he loved me back.
Won't you reconsider; please.

T David Auvil
SEPARATE WORLDS

For Joan Giles my English teacher in high school, she taught me that everyone has something inside worth sharing.

we live in separate worlds
I'm in a world of fantasy
and my universe dwells on you
your world is reality
and your life revolves around
someone too
but that someone isn't me
in my world the heavens are in your
eyes
and the whisper of your name
is like a lullaby painted on the sky
but our worlds aren't the same
and you'll never hear—this cry
of my world calling out to yours
your world is a world of fools
and I live in a fool's world
and even though it seems dumb
that's as close as our two worlds
come.

Deborah Turner Dunn
THAT LITTLE GIRL OF MINE
A tiny hand groping,
those eager eyes seeking,
the baby-babble speaking,
That little girl of mine.

A little wisp of blondish hair,
a tantrum . . . . . . now and then,
the innocent look given when,
the milk is spilled again,
That little girl of mine.

Growing, laughing, sharing,
All this is so much fun,
To skip, jump, sing, and run,
A little body brown from the
Mississippi sun,
That little girl of mine.

I sorrow to see this child of
innocence,
grow away from her childish world,
and witness the true troubled place
we live in,
with its truth unfurled.

Stay Small . . . . . . is my wish;
so I can shield
THAT LITTLE GIRL OF MINE
From the world and all its fear.

Arlette Buckholz
NIGHT UNTO DAY
If ever you see me crying
And the pain is too deep to hold
My soul will be screaming
My heart will be bleeding
My mind will be too old

Chorus:
What are we looking to find
Will it ease our mind
Can we find the time

It all passes away like
Night unto day
Who will watch my children play

Repeat (Chorus)

Oh God will you hold me
When no one can show me when
time is at the end will you be my friend

Dorothy Wallace
LOVE'S RAINBOW

When I lost my love
I thought
I'll never love again
My happiness lay dimmed
Through many tears of pain
But just as the rainbow
Shimmers after rain
That love shines through
My tears
Always to remain

Shirley J Dean
MAN'S SEARCH FOR PEACE

This poem is dedicated to my youngest sister, Debbie, who sleeps in eternal peace and rests within the arms of our Lord, the Prince of Peace.

There are times when wondrous Man
Wishes with a resounding roar
To fly up to the mountaintops
Where the Eagles soar.

He seeks to shed the dreary toils
And ceaseless labors of life
By meandering through the fluffy clouds
And float away from strife.

Man has need of this small respite
To help the soul most dear
So his heart can joyfully sing
Its songs for all to hear.

Come fly with me to the mountain-tops
And past the jagged peaks
Where you will find Eternal Peace
Which Man forever seeks.

I G "Butch" Grossman
I YEARN FOR HELEN

The umber leaves of autumn swirl
Where once the buds of spring
greened fast
And where the marigolds did bloom
The purple asters nod their last

Now filled with tears, the autumn sky
Is overcast with shrouds of gray
All nature, like my aching heart
Yearns for Helen, far away

Mr Dedan Kimithi El
IF I COULD MAKE MY DREAMS COME TRUE

To my beautiful, adorable wife, Patricia Ann Smith El (Kimithi El)

If I could make my dreams come true;
I would bring forth Love, Peace, Joy and
Happiness for you, and you, and you.
If I could make my dreams come true;
Hunger, sickness, loneliness and hatred
I would remove from you, and you, and you.
If I could make my dreams come true;
I would become a singer and sing of
The Lord's love for you, and you, and you.
If I could make my dreams come true;
I would create an All Peoples'
Heaven right here
On Earth for you, and you and you.
If I could make my dreams come true;
My every dream would be to
Help you, and you, and you.
You and you, and you, are me, and I am you.
And Love, Truth, Peace, Freedom and Justice
Would be my wish—
FOR US ALL
If I could just make my dreams come true.

Debbie Dumas

Debbie Dumas
LITTLE CHILD

This poem is dedicated, to the children who have fallen victim, may each tear you shed bring God's wrath upon the wicked.

A little child goes out to play,
Happily skipping on his way.
A joyful moment he finds outside,
With new found independence and courage with pride.
Though another child in another place,
Stays indoors to hide her face.
The laughter, the giggles the should be smile,
Holds no beauty in the eyes of this child.
Two beautiful children, both born the same day,
One sings of love, the other cries in dismay.
What's this world coming to, when lost is the mile,
That once was given so easily, for the sake of a child.
To the offender who ever you are,
Find peace with your God and count your stars.
For the untouched heart of a child holds no fear,
But break a little one's spirit and you'll drown in his tear.

Vicki Shephard
THE COLORS OF MY HEART

This poem is dedicated to my husband, Sylvester Gene Shephard

My heart has many colors, they're sometimes plain to see
Like when we aren't together, everything is dark inside of me
And remember when we went off, it was just us two
Everything was beautiful, a peaceful shade of blue
And when we had that awful fight, and said those awful things
I felt the grey inside of me, like that a storm cloud brings
Do you remember when we talked about our future, we rattled on and on
I felt so bright inside, like the brilliant color of a morning dawn
And when we lay in each other's arms at night, after working hard all day
It reminds me of the color green, and the way the grass must lay
And yes my heart has many colors, they're sometimes plain to see
I'm so thankful for this rainbow that you have given me
For all these colors in my heart, make me realize more each day
How very special our love is, in every colorful way
And sometimes my colors may not be as bright as the rest
But, when we blend them all together it's love at its best
So even in the grey times, when you're searching for a glow
Just remember all our colors, and how each day our love grows.

A C Tillett
CLOUD DREAMS

I looked up high, what did I see?
A fluffy kitten looking back at me,
There's a dog and a bird with no tail,
And I'm pretty sure that was a whale,
Why here is a castle, with flags so big,
And over there a little white pig,
I also see the shape of a man
He's holding something in his hand.
I lie in the grass, dreaming dreams
Of all the wonderful things I see,
A sleeping giant, a rabbit so small
Trees that are a thousand feet tall!
Oh my is that a unicorn!
Or just a deer, with only one horn,
A great herd of cattle, rushing by
It's my own big circus, up in the sky.
made from clouds drifting by so fast,
And childish dreams that never last,
These are the things, I see on high
In my clouds of dreams, that are drifting by.

Paula S Krauser
THE CHILD INSIDE

No one loved the child in me
Naughty, reckless, daring
Cute and coy
I cried for cuddling
Sought a lap in which to sit
A hand to stroke my head a bit
Wanting to be loved because I was
Not for what I did.
That fettered child
Demands her freedom
A poltergeist
A restless seed
She annoys and teases
The grown-up persona
She owns my soul
And causes trouble
With a relish only children know
So long restrained
Now out of control.

Stephen R Dyson
A NATION GRIM

To those who served, I salute you.

Oh world, once so full with love and delight
Could it be, you passed us while we slept one night?
The glow of your sunrise that brightened our world so dear
Left in its place an ominous darkness filled with tears.
It affected our nation, this land of red, white, and blue,
This country of plenty once loved by the likes of me and you.
How could it be that a war without an end
Caused us to forget the least of these men among men?
In the end, when all was over and said and done,
Those who had defied our heritage and quest had really won.
They had defiled our nation, and the glorious stars and stripes
And spat in the faces of brothers and sons, who died in the fight.
When the war was proclaimed over, and they were allowed back in
This nation of sorts gave them all they wanted, again and again.
For those who survived, our once proud heritage and fought,
Became a part of the homeless, who had nary or naught.
In the days of our childhood, away in the far distant past
It was with proud honor we served, and gave of our last.
That was a world full of heroes, who stood tall among men.
A world so full, so bright, will it ever be again?

Lynne Buck
REMNANTS

Dedicated to Tina Shang, for her belief in me and support.

Well! So!—
What of this life?
What am I but a
fragile hour glass
counting out my
measured sand
until Death's hammer
strikes the blow;
the wind will
gather up my soul,
leaving no footprints—
only glass.

Veronica Heintz
SPRING BLOSSOMS

Dedicated to my loving family

Winter is wet and dreary
but spring blossoms!
Blossoms in sun and gold
with snakes and toads.
Blossoms in green so bright
with day and night.
Spring blossoms in our sight
with wonder and might.
Not with winter's dreary look
but with rainbow colors
in a running brook.

Bill Garrett
HOPE IS BELIEVING

I dedicate this poem to Patty, the beauty and love of my heart; Darren, the teacher and inspirer of my dreams, and my family, including the Ryans for their love.

To face the unknown, a chance to quest,
is to try and know, and at your best;
succeed or fail, but to trust
in yourself and your ways is a must;
for life is full of experiences a new,
a path that's travelled a few.
Hope is believing tomorrow will shine
in pride and glory will a-due in time.
Show strength and courage in your heart,
granted with wisdom, here's your start:

Use confidence and care to start your day
added with love and friendship to lead the way.

Ally Rasmussen
DRIVE SLOWLY, PLEASE

Dedicated to my daughters, Peggy Jean and Roni Sue

Do you have a teenager
Learning to drive
And wonder how long
She will stay alive?
The training is over,
It's up to you now
To sit alongside her
And show her how
To let out the clutch,
Put on the brake,

When you get home
You've a nasty headache,
Your nerves are on edge,
Are you wishing then
That this grown-up child
Were a baby again?

Richard Gawel
FROM ADAM TO ATOM
In the garden they say
it took only one day
to ravage with thorn.
The two made of clay
and not even born

was only a glimpse.
Now millennia since
their children with power
do not even wince
to destroy in one hour

all possible future.
What surgeon with suture
could ever repair
or mother could nurture
what vanished in air?

Tamera N Adams
FANTASIES
I close my eyes and what do I see?
A wonderful world of Fantasies.

A blue sky, a summer night
An elephant flying a big blue kite.

It can be so peaceful there in my dreams
Or at least there it does so seem.

Fantasies are a wonderful thing
Think of all the fun they bring.

You can close your eyes and fly to the moon
Or just relive a day last June.

So whatever you do—don't lose that gift
Of closing your eyes and getting a lift.

Away from the world that's bringing you down
And making your face all covered with frowns.

So just close your eyes to see what you can see
Oh! What a beautiful world of Fantasy.

Paulina Hrcan
LOVE IS DEEPER THAN PHILOSOPHY
Your love is stronger than the universe,
Wider than the sky,
Deeper than philosophy, in
Unconditional supply.

You make me feel vitality.
You make me see the best.
You give my heart contentment;
My soul, eternal rest.

I want to feel the strength you have,
The power from inside.
I want to be forever free
From pain this life provides.

Your love is stronger than the universe,
Wider than the sky,
Deeper than philosophy,
Always in supply.

Kennith Mathews
THE POWER OF LOVE

This poem was written on February 10, 1989; It is dedicated to the love of my life, my dream, which almost came true. I'll love you always Ann Marie Young

Love is the power that'll confuse you so,
where it comes from you'll never know;
Love makes you happy it makes you sad,
just when you think you're in it, you see it's just a fad;
Love hurts and teases you all the time,
it sends chills down your spine;
Love takes your friends and turns them around,
it'll cause them to let you down;
Things you thought could never be,
were always there you're soon to see;
Love makes you jealous of everyone,
it'll cause you to do things you've never done;
Love breaks your heart right in two,
when Cupid fires his arrow straight at you;
What love does man can't explain,
once you've felt it you're never the same.

Barbara Bloom
DIALOGUE WITH GOD

This poem is dedicated to: the U. N. (United Nations)

To be alone,
To CLOSE our eyes.
To feel a quietness,
And shut out all earthly cries.
Cries of injustice

Stop the wheels,
Wheels of confusion . . .
End all noisy shrills.
Let there be nothing moving,
But let everything be soothing.

Give us peace,
Our souls are shouting,
But no one hears,
Or understands its pouting.

Stop the rustle, the hurry, and chase.
Why must everything be a race?

STOP . . . take a look at life.
SEE IT . . .
HEAR IT . . .
FEEL IT . . . !

To be alone,
To OPEN our eyes,
To feel a quietness,
And shut out all earthly cries.
Cries of injustice . . .

Stop the wheels,
Wheels of confusion . . .
End all noisy shrills.
Let there be nothing moving,
But let everything be soothing.

Give us peace,
The world's soul is shouting,
And I know
That we can end its pouting.

Stop the rustle, the hurry and chase.
Stop long enough,
To see your neighbor's face.

Stop take a look at life.
SEE IT . . .
HEAR IT . . .
FEEL IT . . .

Put in the place,
Of guns and war.
A desire to understand,
The rich and the poor.

With respect for every,
Individual human life.
Regarding the suffering,
Of all men's strife.

Vanish the evils of mankind,
Evils of malice,
Evils so callous,
Prejudice,
Envy,
Jealousy.

Vanish these evils of mankind,
And in our life,
Peace we'll find.

Laura Eichensehr
LONELY SURVIVOR
I used to live in darkness, now it is not my friend.
The world was changed so greatly; many lives came to an end.
The day came unexpectedly and changed my life forever.
To fix the world up again would be a great endeavor.
Because of want for power of countries near and far,
A war was waged so suddenly that left their greedy scar.
Now the earth is dead, no longer do Eagles soar,
And I ask myself ironically, do they need power anymore.
The once beautiful earth is no longer great to see.
All that's left for the lonely survivor is pain and misery.

Michael Young
LOVE IS TO SEE A CHILD'S SMILE

This is dedicated to my loving children: Michael, Jr., Jeffrey, Jonathan, David and Lisa

In the seasons,
winter, spring, summer,
and fall,

a child's smile stands out warmer
brighter, and more beautiful
than them all.

Their smiles are more precious
than money, silver, or gold.

It's a feeling that worth more
than anything that's been
given, or sold in the world.

The children give it to us free,
and in doing so, they make
the world, a much better
place to be.

If we could all learn to smile
like our children, so
innocent , fresh, and clean,

there would be no wars,
no guns, no anger
that would ever be
seen.

If we all try, we can
put a special smile
on their faces at
this Christmas time.

But even greater, we
should try and put
a smile on all the
children's faces in
the world, all of
their lifetime.

David Brian Ficocelli
LIFE IS LIKE AN HOURGLASS

This poem is dedicated to: Dolores E. Ficocelli.

Life is like an hourglass.
Each grain of sands,
symbols a moment of
your life.
And when the sands
run out,
The moments will never
be forgotten.

Joseph Deer
ODE TO THE SKEPTICS
And in the beginning
Man stood and said:
"Let there be God'
'to reside in my head'
'We'll need him to lift us,'
'to believe in, to blame'
'We'll need him to lean on'
'and curse in our pain"
And so God appeared
In the image of man
A grand puppet king
With a fear bearing hand
And God was most pleased
With this newly found fame
With man there to praise him
And bow in his name
And man was appeased
With his newly found light
It gave him assurance
And warmth in the night
But in time man looked up
And around in doubt
Blind faith and blind fear
no longer held clout
And man's faith was thinning
as he stood and said;
"Let knowledge and reason'
'now guide my head'
'We'll use them to lift us'
'to believe in to tame'
'We'll use them to lean on'
'and relieve all our pain"
So God lost his place
In many a man
No blind faith filled minds
On which to stand.
And man grew excited
In his mighty war game
"Science and power
will secure us our name'

So man became blinded
in his power filled plight
to prove that only
might makes right
But then man looked up
hearing bomb sirens shout
And said "only blind faith
'Can now save us in doubt"

(Ms) Dorothy J Hamilton
ANNOUNCING THE LATEST STYLE!

To: My beloved folks—The Hamiltons and Tudhopes.

Announcing the latest style
Please don't touch that dial,
Shampoo from every tube
Call letters right at hand—no hey rube;
Police calls on citizens' bands—
*Pompadour's commands?
Those bands hair to-day and gone tomorrow
Microphone when appointment's thru'
Not much time to borrow—catch a cab & net your do;
(cabinet)

That radio style—compile info' from radio speaker—appointment time a real squeaker,
Mrs. Malaprop says this is the latest style
Of all the latest crop it most
Certainly will beguile;
Don't rave about sackcloth and ashes
Your head doesn't need a shave,
Just rave about that sensational,
Seductive "Short Wave!"
or
Fabulous Falls via all
Those "Police Calls!"
(World War II—Tokyo Rose,
Axis Sally etc. tried
to convince our Allied
servicemen to desert!)
(With all that rat 'n' roll
no console—console No—with that
Fashionable haute couture show?—
Please don't touch that dial,
ANNOUNCING THE LATEST
STYLE!

Anna Minardi
YESTERDAY'S GARDEN

To Stormy, Christie and Bup

These are the flowers of yesterday's garden
Gathering weeds with the passing of time
Gone are the lovers who planted the flowers
Gone are the poets with verses to rhyme.
Blossoms that withered and died unattended
Silently fall and are caught by the breeze
Gone is the beauty that once filled their garden
Gone is the laughter that sang through the trees.

Time hangs suspended when one walks the garden
Tears fill the eyes of a lonely old man
Gone is the rapture he held in his arms here
Gone is the tenderness that once held his hand.

Alone in their garden he looks for an oak tree
And there"neath its" branches protected from sight
Lies a rose covered grave with a simple white cross
Here rests his sweetheart, his joy, and his light.

Kneeling, he touches the crude wooden cross
Tears spilling out of his age hollowed eyes
Now like the flowers too long unattended
The broken old man . . . silently dies.
These are the flowers of yesterday's garden
Gathering weeds with the passing of time . . .

Harriet E McLean
VALENTINE'S DAY

To Eddie-Lou Cole

If Valentine's Day were every day,
It surely would keep hate away,
For, we could love our fellow man,
This surely is God's almighty plan
We would not need one day a year,
To make this so abundantly clear,
To love one another is our goal,
It helps to purify the soul.
For love helps the world go round,
Without we would be 'outward bound,'
So, oil the wheels with lots of love,
And reap the benefits from 'above.'

Barbara Simoni Zimmer
DEPRESSION

Ah Depression how oft you have been at my door
You are the enemy that I abhor

You fill my soul with such despair that in my
Anguish I cry out "'tis not fair"

You dragged me down to the depths of hell
Oh from such heights to this I fell

The darkness that envelopes my mind leaves
Not even a glimmer of light to find

Oh FATHER in my despair I cry
In sorrow and pain I lie

I feel so utterly alone and lost
TORMENTED AND TEMPEST TOSSED

So profound is the Emotional pain I feel
That I know I shall never heal

Nor in that moment of despair
Do I even really care

So unrelenting is this shadow of gloom
There is no room for joy to bloom

I am so overwhelmed by it all
Oh FATHER PLEASE HELP me not to fall

I could not even begin to explain
So 'tis best I just refrain

Negative thoughts flit in and out
I must control them I silently shout

What is this rage I feel so INTENSE
Wide as the Heavens and just as IMMENSE

So I run this Emotional race
At a dizzying accelerating pace

I am so weary of this Battle sore
But I've said all this a thousand times before

The Prison of Depression
Is nought else but the Soul's Regression

Leave me flee from me forever more
Never let thy shadow darken at my door

April L Porter
LIFE IN THE INNER CITY

The crumpled newspaper takes to the air,
swirling.
Only to be knocked to the ground again,
trampled.
The old woman, lonely and dirty,
bums a cigarette and walks off,
coughing.
The cars and buses, honking
endlessly, billowing clouds,
polluting.
The crowds of secretaries and
executives, striving to succeed,
working.
They don't know our despair.
By dark, they are home in their favorite chair,
eating dinner in front of their T.V.'s.
They don't realize that,
out on the streets,
we are already home.

Phyllis Elwood
DAWN

To Clyde with Love, Phyllis

What a joy to awake in the early dawn,
to the peaceful quiet of another day;
To hear birds singing in melodious song,
making all thoughts of time to fly away;
A time to reflect on God's beautiful world,
and be ever grateful for his love;
At the dawn of day, what a beautiful way, to give him Thanks
as he is watching over us from above.

Carol Feltman
I STAND ALONE

To Don, my best friend, and, to my children Matt and Anne. Thank you for all your love. All my love to you, Carol.

Windswept shores, barren
white sands—
Like the desolate plains
of my dreams.
I stand alone,
To contemplate my lost love—
My rainbows have been forever
overshadowed by the darkening
clouds—
The sun no longer shines as
brightly—since you left me.
Flowers have wilted and have lost
their perfumed scent.
Leaves on the trees no longer
whisper words of love.
My world,
My days,
My life,
Are all just shades of gray,
I stand alone—waiting
For your arms to warm me.
But—all I hear is the wind
through the naked trees.
And the only feeling I have left—
Is the cold of the long lonely
night.

Edward M Trujillo
I WILL ALWAYS LOVE YOU

To my lovely wife Linda.

Yea, in truth, I have
Seen the gift of life
Upon your lips . . .
As you speak to me
With words that
Caress my soul.
Hold across your mind
My thoughts of you,
For they will always
Fulfill your imagination.
And in the end I will say to you
That I will always
Love you.

Walter A Czepiga
GENESIS

Everything we discovered and made,
Just melted into nothing that day,
All signs of mankind blistered away,
No one else had anything to say.

No man or beast would ever walk,
'Cause people all they did was talk,
No history book would ever say,
What terrible thing happened today.

Then He'll push our earth aside,
And in its place one twice its size,
Will begin to grow with life,
As the day becomes the night.

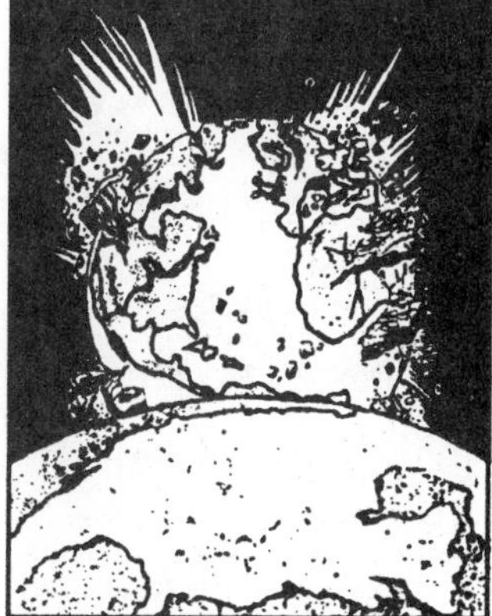

The days will be twice as long,
The nights will pass the dawn,
And children will sing new tunes,
As lovers sit under two moons.

The light shined a different way,
As the sun came up this new day,
It rose from the west and set in the east,
From north to south fell sweet peace.

Crystal A Timpe
THE SEASONS

Winter is so white,
Like a white sparrows flight,
They are still like trees and grass,
Just like glass.

Spring is so fresh,
With leaves anew,
And grass and leaves dampened with

dew.
Summer is so hot,
Like a stewing pot,
The sky is so blue,
From a verandas view.

Fall's fallen leaves,
About the trees,
Rustling down to the ground,
Upon a dirty mound.

Ila B Jones
BRENDA SUE
Small hands pillowing little head
She lies upon the davenport, languidly,
As from under lowered lids, eyes mere slits,
She views TV;
Right leg crossed over left knee
Foot swinging. She's all of three.

TV shows a puppy, playful and fat.
"Oh, look, Brenda!", 'tis her daddy asking,
"How'd you like to have a doggy like that?"
She changes not expression, nor slows the swinging foot;
Comments most lazily, "Scare hell out'a the cat!"

Becky Wilson Byers
A WASTE OF TIME
I hope you're happy, I've gone away,
Pushed to my limit, I couldn't stay.
One more chance, a waste of time,
Even our past isn't worth a dime.
The effort is useless when feelings are gone.
Feeling only emptiness, I won't go on.
Feeling no guilt when telling a lie,
It's so senseless when emotions die.
The same routine of being together,
No chance of change, it won't get better.
My reasons for staying, they've been all wrong.
For what others might think, I played along.
I can no longer live in fantasy land,
Now I'm returning this little gold band.
Just a symbol of the vows we took,
Now broken words of the sacred book.
Apologies and promises, they came too late,
Time has expired, no need to wait.
My decision is final, I've started anew.
I could never be happy staying with you.

Richard (TAINO) Almestica
CINNAMON GIRL
Oh, cinnamon girl why are we controlled by the words of others?
We come from worlds so far apart,
but can't we join and be a part . . .
You belong to another, that I must face but maybe in time we can both change that fate.
Oh, cinnamon girl won't you let me into your world.

The color of your skin glistens like a deep setting sun.
The glow in your brown eyes hold tales of things to come.
Won't you let me into your world, cinnamon girl.

Rich-man, Poor-man which class am I
Gangster or Angel from either I can not hide.
Masculine, feminine, young or mature
these are things I'm not always sure.
Does it matter which mask I wear?
Does it matter which class I wear?
For these are things that are meant for others,
these are things we share with our brother.
Oh, cinnamon girl won't you let me into your world.

Docile, arrogant, simplistic and complex for these are some things I must confess.
I claim no perfection or require none from you, all I asked is that you speak in truths.
I'll make no intention and I'll hide the obsession, for that is left up to you.
You belong to another, that I must face.
Cinnamon girl won't you let me into your world.

Oh, cinnamon girl won't you come into my world?

Lyle Moultrie
through ancient fog . . .
through ancient fog . . .
THE rose
appears

from nowhere

(long awaited)

fresh cut . . .

in whisper
it calls my name

(yesss, it says)

hands; innocent

pensive
reach

they slowly close
the rose
still calls . . .

razor thorns pierce
my palms

outstretched

upward gaze asking why
i die for love?

fresh cut . . .

Mark C Gilletly
KAREN
If your heart walks a solitude path,
(I will open every door)
Or your feelings favor another
(I can bring you so much more)
Then I will understand
(Then none will I love ever more).
If ever you felt my presence,
(Forever beside you I stand)
Or chanced to hear my song
(Let me love you as I am)
Then you would understand
(Then you would understand).
And if it be only in dreams
That I may possess you,
Then unto dreams I render myself.

Belinda Borrelli
THE FACADE
All that you can see is not me;
For I am a piece of drift wood, led by
The turbulent currents of the water that surrounds me;

All that I breathe is not my breath;
For I am an empty shell, terrified of
Dissolution by an all-encompassing ocean wave;

All that I touch I cannot feel;
For I am a black, solid rock
That cannot be consumed by the fire;

All that I hear is through ears not my own;
For the icy winter winds
Beckon me to eternal barren lands;

All that I taste I cannot savor;
For the life that may be
Is death in itself.

Dianne Almand
SISTERS
Remember the field behind
the house that harbored us?
We were foreigners then
that was some time ago.
We did our high wire act
on that broken down fence,
after a brilliant performance
we'd fall back in the snow,
and make impressions of angels
though we were far from angelic.
It did not matter
we were as close
as we needed to be.

Cynthia Lee Harkness

Cynthia Lee Harkness
OVER HILL AND DALE
My mother, my shepherd
and I a wee lamb
nudged to tremble on unstable legs,
she set me free.

The world, so big
it frightened me
running, running o'er many a field
to nestle again amongst warmth I knew
she was there.

Tyrus Manuel
THE TIME HAS COME
The time has come,
The beginning of the end;
Yet the beginning of the beginning.
A new life is born at this moment.

The time has come,
For us to rise to the occasion.
We will feel the weight of the world,
We will make the world turn.

The time has come,
To begin a new life,
To live as adults not children
Whether we want to or not.

The time has come . . .
And it will never come again.

Robert Mehnert
KIDS
They're such a prize when first conceived
New mothers feel it'll be a breeze.
Two weeks old and there's already doubt
Young mothers start to pull their hair out.
Give it some time it will be okay
Before you know it you'll beg them to stay

At the age of five they go off to school
Attempting to learn the golden rule.
Then by nine their feelings change
Causing the household to rearrange
Sometimes bored with nothing to do
At age thirteen their life seems new.

Then comes the dreaded teenage years
Which bring out all a mothers fears
Fathers tend to sit back and wait
To see if what they sired will hesitate
Then before long they leave the nest
Leaving parents to contemplate
which year was best?

Kim M Harner
UNTITLED
the sun shines
the sea's waves
come up to the shore
pounding, searing, tearing
away at the sand
the sea rolls under
the pressure of the wind
it comes up on the shore
in one huge wave
towering over the beach like
a curtain of death

Linda Jean Bennett
SHE IS COLDER NOW (THE POISON OF A BUTTERFLY)
She is colder now
robbed of speech and thought
her image strikes and shouts
Silhouetted against another reluctant dawn
instilling within her a sweet fear
as a kiss of darkness is laid upon her
she could see our smoldering smiles
Wading through tiny squares of painted perfection
her mask crumbles
and her eyes fall upon a fiery celestial chamber
from where petals flutter silently down
Feverish and trembling she touches each one
bringing strangeness and fear
commanding trampled grasses to arise
she longed to dance with the trees at night
and earn her own ray of sunshine
her smile returned with her childhood
I am such a contradiction

Ramona G Mercado
THE FROZEN TEAR
Do you know what the frozen tear means?
Do you know how to melt it, how it would seem?

The frozen tear is mystically elusive,
It symbolizes a love so vast and all inclusive . . .

In days of yore, it knew a childish aching birth,
Consumed in the grandeur of love,
but strangely
Devoid of all mirth.
A love was born and with it, the "frozen tear."

In answer to love's probing claims
The heart would feel and attempt to exclaim—
A golden cloak is worth naught, if there is not a
Love that has been sought . . .

Found—cherish it like the stars on high,
Without it, life is like the thunder heard only in
A sigh . . .

A day came when love had died, the God-granted
Beauty of love had rejoined
Father Time . . .
There were tears, but not the "Frozen Tear."

Only when accidentally the wound is touched,
And the spirit struggles to recapture that love divine,
Is there a "Frozen Tear."

R L Flach
THE RULE
No one has the right
To expect someone else
To be,
What they want
Or need them
To be.
So hold my hand
And my heart
If you will,
But my being
Must be free.

Margaret McCrory
THE JOB
Tomorrow when I wake up,
I'm going to start anew
I'm sick and tired of my job
I'll tell the Boss I'm through
I've thought of doing this so much
I'll sleep now that it's near
But then what if He needs me
I guess I'll wait another year.

Ronald J Coyle
AH! COSMIC POLITICS !!!
All "political systems" would falter, seem: "lonely,"
If only . . . if only:

GOD were but an "conserv-a-tive"
. . . a-rationin' meager
hope and assistance to the hive,
While extracting, hoarding all of the PRIME HONEY!
For, would HE still "keep them bees alive" if they "union-ized," and cost HIM too much money???

And/or:
GOD were but a "lib-ri-el" . . . to
"SHARE THE WEALTH(!)"
—HIS tale-to-tell, program-to-sell,
Would HE still "need-the-seeds-of-sighs: when HE dist
cease to think same: "funny???"

Ah, "conserv-a-tive," or "lib-ri-el" . .
such meanings but blur, become pell-mell,
"Republican," or "Democrat"—to
GOD's BIG EYE, 'tis all:
"old hat!"
HE permits their little passage (as they may) . . . and ne'er
"believes a thing they say!"
For, COSMIC POLITICS BE E'ER OBLIGED TO CALL:
"AVOID ALL SUCH PRIDE, BEFORE THE FALL!"
(Before this little Earth, again—"be flat;"
Before protoplasm, again—"be runny;")
—Before ants and bees (in "political low keys,") again—
claim ALL THE HONEY!!!

For, as we "know:"
"AS ABOVE, SO BELOW!!!"
Only GOD claims AUTHORSHIP to this little show (!)—as all
"human political systems" but come, and go!

As DEAR FRIENDSHIP pleas need to answer GODLY BELL!!!

Richard William Wiersum
A PEACEFUL TIME
The beautiful winding river
is cut into the earth
with peaceful flowing
gentleness

The sun is rising colorfully
over the giant gentle pines
the wind whispers through the
morning silence

Father and son gently cast
brightly shining lures
in anticipation of that first
strike

The serenity of the time and place
give father and son moments
of quiet peaceful talks

The morning stillness is broken
by a terrific splash, as a
Northern Pike
attacks it's anticipated
breakfast

The fight is tense and exciting
until finally, the fish ends its
fitful fight
and the quiet gentleness settles
in once again

Marilyn P Johnson
AND IT DIES HARD
And it dies hard,
the first love that lingers around the edges,
leaving only the memories and loneliness behind.
And in your eyes, mist settles and stays
in months later while you're looking for something lost.

It dies hard
that first love
fighting for the last
acknowledging once over, it will never be again.
So, it stays in the back,
in the stillness,
with the scent of pureness and sweetness
like the bud of the white rose
before it goes brown.

Curtis B Carter
THOUGHTS
We know it's too strange
But the sun always shines in the middle of the night;
We know it's too weird
But we're always blinded because the sun is too bright.
We have no control
Our powers are seized,
Just figures of shadows
With minds that are pleased.

On and on our lives are spent
Day after day with each torment;
Always wishing for more and more,
We slip away through an open door.

Never knowing what the future will bring
We hide within ourselves and hear the voices sing;
Music that soothes our mind,
So that our thoughts don't become intertwined.

Every day grows more intense
The pressure is greater, nothing makes sense,
To live a life is to be free
No matter how bewildering a thought may be.

E Glenn Hickey
MY LOVE
Ah my love, what joy you bring
flowers appear and robins sing

The dawn awakens to you at last
shadows flee, night has passed

Beauty surrounds you wherever you go
the valleys are filled with warmth of your glow

Peaceful the day, serene and mild
as my love grows strong all the while

I look in your eyes and the stars I see
repeat the words how I love thee

In a mystical mist as time stands still
I reach forth to you as I always will

The sound of the wind caressing the trees
as nature looks out two lovers she sees

The beat of my heart the desire that I hold
for you my darling visions untold

My everything, my she, and all
to walk beside me through immortal halls.

Love is mine, how lovely you are
from infinite time to have come this far.

Dan G Bennett
SO SOON
Cotton candy and Merry-go-rounds
Painted faces of jovial clowns
some wearing painted smiles or frowns

Tigers and riders and pretty balloons
isn't it a shame the circus
leaves
town
so
soon

Gladys Cooper
TO 'YOU'—MY LOVE
Often when the shadows lengthen—
And stars are in view.
I find myself dreaming, lost in thoughts of 'you'—
For sometimes my heart cries out for company—
So I drift on a quiet stream of tender thought—
In my mind, 'you' come to meet me—
And we share an embrace—
We talk of things gone by—happy times we knew—
It's wonderful to be with 'you'—
even in thought—
But 'you' are no more—and I am in grief—
How can I recapture those happy days—and kiss
Your tender lips—be held in your strong arms—
So when the dark deepens—I thank God—
That I can drift on the seas of memory

Tonya Danyell Hoover
PAIN AMONG US
The cold cold world looks on
without even the blink of an eye.
Fighting and unrest from dusk til dawn,
As the rest of the world rushes by.

Murder and rapes in the smallest of towns
among our own streets.
A man looks on as a small child drowns
returning home, it is the wife he beats.
Screaming of pain,
Can't anyone hear?
Is this all in vain
or out of fear?

La Don S Anderson-Scales
THOUGHTS OF A LONELY WIFE
Why can't a husband see the tears in his wife's eyes,
the pain in her heart as her soul cries.

He can not see the need she has to have the love she waited for,
the happiness she deserves or loves joy.

His eyes are blind to her desires and her pain grows stronger as
she needs to feel cared for and feels unloved instead.

What thoughts are going around in his head as she no longer wishes to sleep in his bed.

Tenderness of touches are never felt and she can't believe what he said
when he knelt beside her and promised to love, and honor and cherish her.

Why can't he see the tears in my eyes or the pain in my heart as my soul cries, and a love I could have had dies, he looks on with blind eyes.

Nancy J Barger
THANK GOD I'M ALIVE

This poem is dedicated to my family and friends.

As I lie here this morning
looking at the sun rise,
I just thank God
that I'm still alive.
For life is so precious
and life can be fine,
when you have friends and family
who love you all the time.

Georgina Van Dam
SOUNDS
Tis now the birth of summer
her Christening dress is green.
The hour is a mite past twilight
a few stars can here and there be seen.

A train far in the distance blows
one short and mournful blast.
A fire siren is wailing
like a banshee roaring past.

A dog barks then is silent
The air conditioner next door.

and the motor on their pool
carry on a sound flirtation
that is far from being cool.

Some boys are shooting fire crackers
up and down the street.
Brings to mind thoughts of many
long past summers
that are forever gone but sweet.

The wispy breeze of twilight is
waving a fond goodbye
to the last of the midday heat.
A silver jet is circling slowly
in its pathway to descent.
My senses are all attuned
to the soft symphony of my content.

Terri Lynn Cooper

Terri Lynn Cooper
AWAKE IN THE MORNING
I awake in the morning to see the sun shine so bright,
smell the softness in the air,
and feel the breeze blow through my hair,
because the Lord cares.

Mary Jo Highland
THE DESERTED BEACH
The sun is a glowing ball of fire
As it shines a golden reflection
Across the tranquil sea.

Seagulls swoop across the horizon
In their pure white coats of down
Searching for a perfect place to rest.

The sand seems to whisper quietly,
"Please come and keep me company,"
As the water rises higher over it.

A peaceful setting is this deserted beach,
A wonderful place to think and dream,
Although it cries from loneliness.

Chelsea Moriarty
HOBBIES & OBSESSIONS

Dedicated to the spirit of rebellion, bizarre honesty, exhibitions, intuition and Iggy Pop.

Surprise title, big seller this year
So easily accessible and so far out of reach
Could almost touch or taste, wanting
Some vague reflection found
Somewhere within the mirrored infinite

The figure leads from Far Arden to where . . .
When and how do we make it from here?
Still shrouded in mystery after this long
Do you know what you've done?
Turned your back on inspiration.
Abandoned, heartless, it's a crime.
Come here Bub, you just gotta see this
You'd turn too, at what they've done
I've lost faith in the late, great surface trash
Commercial metal is hot and heavy these days
and money rots in greedy rodent competition.
These media spots ain't Rock & Roll.
Oh, them decent silly sons . . .
I won't buy any product now.

Mark Ashby
THE FRIENDLY FACE

From a 15 year old cynic to all cynics the world over. Sorry to drop a bombshell, but cést la vie!

Hey, lady, listen, don't bother me now.
You're really that happy? Well, I don't see how.
The greenhouse effect will sizzle our brains,
And hundreds are killed in derailments of trains.
An ice age is coming, and it's going to freeze us;
Our presidents are aging, and they'll never please us.
Pollution of water and defilement of sky
Bring along acid rain, and poor animals die.
Lunatic leaders in obscure Arab nations
Want to splatter their enemies with horrid trepidations.
AIDS is a plague, twentieth-century style
Friends that we trust always cheat and beguile.
Men, women, and children in underdeveloped places
Bear hunger's grim shadow on their pale, bony faces.
So, when you hand me my change, how can you possibly say,
"Drive carefully now, and have a nice day!"

Christopher Goble
ODE TO THE FLOWERS

To Michelle, for whom this poem was written a long time ago, and for whom these feelings still very much hold true. I love you.

There is a place where happiness is abundant;
Sorrows and tears are never created.
There is an ocean in this place,
An ocean surrounded by beautiful white sands,
And in these sands grow beautiful flowers.
A young woman is walking along this ocean,
Smiling as she watches the waves crash against the shore.
Her hair is moving with the gentle breezes;
All of nature is awed by her beauty.

A young man approaches her,
A bouquet of flowers in his hands,
And as their eyes meet,
The world sees what true love really is.
The happiness they share glows from them as they embrace,
And all the world is still,
For this is as happy as happiness could be.
The flowers smile,
The sands giggle,
And the oceans cheer.
For they know that he loves her,
And that she loves him.

Nancy Lynn Wood
MY LOVE
My Love, who is it that always occupies my mind?
Who is it that is always so kind?

I miss you when you're near,
but most of all, I miss you when I am not there.

At times I can only think of you,
keeping me from doing what I need to do.

When our paths do finally cross,
why is it that I feel so lost?

As I leave you to continue on my way,
I often wonder if you feel the same way.

Why do I have to feel the shame?
Even though I may be the one to blame.

You always seem to know what to say,
but most of all, you never turn me away.

At times, My Love, you seem so filled with sadness.
If only I could be the one to fill you with happiness.

As our lives continue their separate ways,
there is only one thing I want to say:

You, My Love, are the one who fills my heart
with all the love you have deserved from the start.

Cynthia Aldridge Beard
SYNOPSIS
Hoarfrost and holly clothe the night,
Fragrant with promise of passion's delight.
Enhancing fantasy, hope and joy,
Of loving a wandering soldier boy.
In Asian jungles, lords of war,
Fighting with valor, medals in store.

Home again, my love, home, yet not free;
I see my love a stranger to me.
Haunted weary eyes, heavy loads to bear,
Get married? He'd say, "I wish I could care!"
This stranger, my love, I shan't be blessed;
For his mind, you see, died with the rest.

Hoarfrost and holly scent the chill night,
Fragrant with passion's promise bright.
Love followed laughter, preceded by tears,
Love followed love thru war-torn years.
For answers lie at Love's behest,
Passion's promise . . . is but a jest.

Yvonne M Jenkins
LIFE
Our lives are like tributaries
Coming from one Great Stream.
Intricate in character
Varied to great extreme.

Perplex, entangled
Complicated, too.
Beautiful, breath-taking
Just to name a few.

This maze of paths
That is so vast,
Is life's entity
First and last.

Leon L Del Giudice
ODE TO THE DELAWARE RIVER

To My Dear Wife "Frankye"

Like life this tranquil river flows--
That harbors Mortal Yens,
To feel its drift and ebbing tide
In mystery it wends;
What peaceful thoughts and dreamful lore
Accompany its wake,
As down its Bed that guides it true
A symphony it makes;
I'll cast my dreams upon a raft
To sail these charming waters--
For when they land my distant shore
My dreams may turn immortal.

Katherine Burns
FAMINE
In the streets of Calcutta.
Lie babies dying of starvation;
While mothers sleep on,
Filth lines the gutters,
Disease runs rampant through the land.
Flies are everywhere,
Human stink fills the air.
"Is this hell"?
Have we but glimpsed a part of humanity,
Backs are turned.
This is of no concern of mine.
We have no food, "they say",
Are we living or "Dead."
Animals look for bread,
But give up instead;
Famine is everywhere,

Can life go on?
When babies are born to "die."
And mothers cry,
It is too soon;
There is no more room,
The earth is full
This is too much to bear.
Won't someone care.

Fred Collins
THE VISITOR

To my Friends and Comrades of bygone years

On a lonely far off beachhead on a great Pacific shore
Where a force of men were camping, waiting for the reapers call
They were young, enthusiastic, bold, sturdy and afraid
They were on an Isle called Iwo, to guard our Country's flag

The night was black and dismal, as we dug the volcanic ash

To find a place of safety, as we heard
the cannisters crash
The shells were bursting on us, as the enemy tried their best
To loosen our foothold, on that volcanic spec

That night as I was lying, in a hole beneath the ground
A mortar shell had landed, unexploded near the helm
That night, I asked Jesus, to surround us with his care

To find the shell unexploded, proved he certainly answers prayers
So friend, if you are lonely, and need a trusting friend
Put your faith in Jesus, he is with you to the end.

James Edward Wilson Senior
BEALE STREET BLUES

To the thoughts of lyric Writers of Music Composition.

Beale with the Blues, is the jazz of the town.
Where the Blues is the thing, down off North Main.

With new places for roaming, and new festivals for showing.
A new downtown mall, with the May-Day Jubilee.
Libertyland will stay, and there's a Mud-Island Day.
Beale is the street, where the Blues is the thing.
There's a Rock-N-Roll King.
After the Cotton Makers Play, and the Blues makes its day.
Beale is the street, we must all get to see.
All that jazz down on Beale Avenue.

Dorothy Merriam
FUTURE WORLD
And the radio is mute,
the TV is mute—
The telephones do not ring.
There's no one in the streets,
We can't go out—we can't go out,
so we stay inside,
Where nothing happens—nothing happens.

Yet, beyond the glass I see a purple violet,
and a dandelion blooms.

Cheryl Rush
PURGATORY

To Susanne—whose constant torch ignites this flickering flame. Thank you.

Echoing chambers, night endangers my mortal soul.
Voices carry as I tarry to observe the room in whole.
In this darkened pit, I cry and sit and wish my body to flee.
Shackled never, but confined forever as Death comes courting me.
An elegant man with fleshless hand comes to take my arm.
Upon his breath, the kiss of Death, my soul quakes with alarm.
From his lapel, a rosebud fell, its color long faded.
And with his touch, it turned to dust as he looked with eyes so jaded.
Encased in this tomb, this damp, dark room, I find no way out.
He approaches quite slowly, with a smile unholy, as I begin to shout.
You devil's pawn, you shall not spawn with me tonight!
God, my life preserve, and give me the nerve to endure this fight.
Upon my word, when God's name he heard, he stumbled and fell.
The tomb buckled and shook and I was afraid to look into the eyes of Hell.
What next I saw, was a parting wall with an eerie luminescent glow.
Suddenly, a bright glowing light filled this tomb of night, from what I do not know.
Somewhere beyond, I felt this bond that had been broken long time passed.
In the distance calling, a voice lilting, falling and I answered it at last.
Here I am! And Devil be damned—I shall not die, so be through!
And the answer came back, from the light to the black, "I have died for you".

Darlene F Coffie
THE MUSIC PLAYS ON . . .

"To Gilbert and Dorothy Rogers, my grandparents;" For your great affections, great truths, and love within our majestical musical family. I will love you always, forever and ever . . .

Where are the people who use to laugh loud?
Where are the ones who made up the crowd?
Where are the children who used to have fun?
All has left me, but the music plays on . . .

I sit here and clench my old wedding rings,
The room is now empty from fresh pretty things.
I try to recapture what is now gone,
Why does growing old seem so utterly wrong?

Where is the one who walked through that door?
Where are my children, I so adore?
My eyesight is leaving, but my ears help me to see,
The best things in life, when the music plays for me.

Its tune takes me back to the good ole' days,
When the women wore dresses, and the men paid the way.
When a walk in the country, was just something to do,
And the silk of your hair would shimmer like dew.

Life's shimmer is gone now, my friends are all dead.
My time will be soon; That's what the doctor said.
So God, Rest My Soul, where the music won't end,
Beside the one that I Love . . .
FOREVER AND EVER, . . .
AMEN . . .

Carmelita Marie Douglas
WISHING

I would like to dedicate this poem to my mother & father Ruth & Willie Douglas. Also to Kathy Warriner a very special friend.

Wishing from my heart that you could see through my eyes what I see little one, stars lots and lots of them twinkling so bright above our heads, 'tis such a beautiful sight.

"Aww" but there's also the moon to see too, it glows like a light in the dark, showing you and I the way out of the darkness like a beam of light shining from the heavens above.

"Aww little one" how I wish that you could see through my eyes what I see. These are the things I wish you could see little one.

Come little one take my hand and we shall wish together that you can see what I see, for 'tis a shame that someone as young and bright as you should live in the darkness without knowing or seeing these things.

Tarita Alecia Wright

Tarita Alecia Wright
REUNION AT FLANDERS FIELD
In silence the distant heroes bow their heads
Beneath the trees, their friends lay dead
Died fighting in a war; they knew not the cause
Drafted through CONSCRIPTION, for those were the laws

The distant heroes bow their heads in silence
Reminiscing of the events that caused blood-shed and violence
The bugle horn echoes across the poppied field
Piercing the hearts that are still unhealed

Their heads in silence, the distant heroes raise
Standing tall; worthy of all our praise
A final salute is made as the wreaths are laid
Then, in the distance, the gathering of old men begins to fade.

Steven L Lee
TRUE

In dedication to Kathleen Lee, a true friend

True is some one who lives their life as them self,
and not a character in a book that's sitting on a shelf.

True is some one who has a heart as good as gold,
and will warm you with a smile even when it's cold.

True is some one who you always like to have around,
and is always there to help you even when you're down.

True is some one who really loves and cares about you,
and will stand by your side what ever you may do.

True is some one you can really call your good friend,
a friend that is always there when ever you need them.

True is something you have always been to me,
and if you need some one I will always be free.

John Preston Young
THE LEAVES OF AUTUMN

Dedicated to my daughter Amanda Young with all my love forever.

My friends the trees. Those stately towering spirits of mine. Not a day lingers too soon, but that I pass among their midst to view what their leafy eyes must see.

Limbs sweeping the winds with easy grace. Bending yore, yet living life in its fullest manner.

I remember the days in the early spring with their mighty flowing juices of life. I witness their mid years when all is green.

I see them at their very chorus'd best. When the cooler colder winds of autumn grace their wistful sails.

It's sad I say yet strong like the winds of men, to see those first leaves fall, as fall they must.

Life in its infinite glory will renew itself again and again, as that shall be!

But the first LEAVES OF AUTUMN echo life's foremost treasures to me.

Stephen Bankhead
SYNAPSE

To Alice, for all the glimpses.

You have your ways and I have mine;
rarely though they intertwine,
I still believe at times we've found
a meeting place . . . a common ground . . .
A moment when your eyes meet mine,
when all our thoughts and dreams combine
to form a whole within our hearts
much larger than its separate parts.

Fleeting though this glimpse may be,
it's burned into my memory.
My mind has touched another mind.
No greater beauty need I find.

Kathy Jarossy
DAWN OF DECEMBER
Whisper-thin snowflakes,
frost
on the windowpane,
a soft winter breeze
whistling
through the trees.
A bright
white stretch
of shimmering snow,
glimmering
glistening
in the pale morning glow.
Delicate death;
The Dawn of December.

Becky Summers
LOVE STORM

For my husband, BOB, on our EIGHTH: 1985.

Rays of golden warmth
Steal through the darkness;
Teasing dripping flowers,
Sending up wisps of
Mist in the coolness.

Slowly, the golden orb breaks thru.
The earth rejoices.
Birds chatter brightly,
Bejeweled flowers dance
Beguilingly in the breeze.

Laughing happily, a couple emerge
From under an old oak,
Damp from the downpour;
They love life—rain 'n' all.

They saw the rain, the saw the sun,
They saw the double rainbow:
The promise of their true love
Would continue forevermore.

Laura Parrett
A DREAM OF BIRDSONG
Dark thoughts, dark winds blow
through my mind.
Frustration grows as a stack of
newspapers—
every day a new layer
thoughtlessly tossed on the
heap.
Cold creeps into my body like a fog
at night
I am old, empty, deathly quiet,
Yet I stumble on.

The light is there, just beyond my
reach
As I approach it grows smaller,
further
My steps become heavier and require
great effort
Do I stop, perhaps to rest forever?
Or do I stumble blindly on . . .

. . . a dream of birdsong, light and
merry
of warming sunshine and rustling
leaves
Starry night, fresh grass, the hum of
life
A beautiful dream, but only a
dream . . .

Valerie K Johnston
FAMILY LIGHTS
The evening is settling in
Stars are beginning to shine
A babe is asleep in my arms
As I wait for you to come home.
Our hearth is a haven of rest
Where we are not put to test.
We must work to make a life
But at night we turn on the lights.
This is the time that is ours
To comfort and ease from the day
The love in our home is strong
Our family is where we belong.
Everyday tempests are tough
At night when we have had enough
Our household is a retreat from the
fray
We pull in together to nurture and
tend
Letting the family help us to mend
Love is the tie that binds us
It helps to make things all right
When our family turns on our lights.

Vincent John Healy
WHAT IS A PARADE?
As I stood on the curb that St. Pat's
Day so cold
with one hand in a pocket, the
other in glove,
I did wonder aloud why parades
draw one's love.
My surprise was so great to hear
what I was told!

We can see all the marchers so smart
in their stride,
so bedecked in their uniforms,
neat to the sight.
We hear drums with their bang
keeping cadence aright,
and the piercing of fifes that
makes ears want to hide.

But above all of these is the "why"
of the march.
We observe them all strut with
their heads held up high,
as if they had their eyes on that "pie
in the sky"
that's the object of all in their
march through life's arch!

To relive a man's spirit so good for
mankind!
Whether white, or so dark, or so
red, or yellow
is not "the" reason marchers do strut
their big show.
It's success in this life, which in
him, they do find!

And then as I grew older in life I too
saw
all the grads in the aisle march
for sheepskins on stage,
and the bride with the groom march
out after the page,
and the pall bearers take the
casket without flaw.

Oh, dear God: help me march that
parade to your throne!

Jack W Montgomery
SIGHT
From the beginnings
to the ends.
A flower blooms.
Water . . . .
Still as death,
morbid as death.
Lovers walking in science,
molecule by molecule.
Tenderness emits its full
bloom.
A bed of flowers,
the boy crushes its lif
The meeting of
unknown you
destroy,
but you know not why. Someone
says, it is your enemy. If you had
met it . . . . .
. . . . . your friend,
But you destroy.
Seep into my soul, but let
not death
extract my loneliness,
but die . . . . .
softly.

Sherri L Gonzales
HAPPINESS CAN'T BE DEFINED

This poem is dedicated to my loving husband, Mario. He is my closest friend and my love for life. He has shown me happiness for the first time in my life. I hope our love will continue to grow.

Happiness can't be defined;
It's a certain mood, a state of mind.
It's sharing everyday affairs;
With one who understands and cares.
It's a tender look or gentle touch;
That says I love you very much.
It's a smile of welcome when you're
blue;
A dream that's shared, a dream for
two.
And happiness is more than this;
It's a warm embrace or a little kiss.
It's a special blessing from above;
It's what you have when you're in
love.

Mary C Ellard
COMFORT
Let me stay with you awhile
Hold your weak, trembling hand.
Words of courage and comfort may
help quiet your mind, chase
those frightening thoughts.

Know I'm here, trust that I care.
I sense your terror
See fear on your face
Brows beaded in sweat and lips
aquiver.

You are afraid to ask yet afraid to
know
Feeling overwhelmed and powerless.
It's serenity and courage you seek.
May words comfort, help you
understand
Give me your weak, trembling hand.

George H Ward

George H Ward
LIFE'S HIGHWAY

This poem is dedicated to Geraldine, my sweet wife.

Dear Father in Heaven, as you look
down on me,
I am only a speck, on life's troubled
sea,
As I pause to consider, while
traveling life's way,
My thoughts return back, to "The
Great Judgement Day"

Forgive me Dear Father, mistakes I
do make,
My aim above all is to have a clean
slate.
So don't let me falter, or fall by the
way,
Or I'll surely miss Heaven, on "The
Great Judgement Day."

Dear Father in Heaven, as onward I
go,
Keep me on the right track, as I travel
below.
Watch every step that I take on my
way,
So, I'll enter in, on "That Great
Judgement Day."

Beth Carmichael
WOODLAND
How the Willow girl stately grows,
By the river of Everflows.
Sleek and wild, daring child,
Dances in a breeze, so mild.

How the Oak man stands so tall,
By the lake of Not-so-small.
Brave and bold, heart of gold,
Stands so strong though wind be
cold.

How the Lily maids fill the lake,
By the town of Not-awake.
White and green, so serene,
Waltzes in a breath's small stream.

How the Lark child sweetly sings,
By the wood of Joyful-things.
Small and shy, off he flies,
Flutters in the calm, still skies.

Rose Wiley Chandler
THE VERDICT
Time . . . . . Days . . . . Moments . . .
never seemed poignantly sweet,
Each day had seemed just exactly the
same as
the one before . . . . . .

But . . . . .
When I walked, barely clinging, to
the very edge of Time,
I was overcome with a fresh
awareness, that,
just beyond my touch had been joy,
love
beauty.

Pity.
When I nearly fell over, clinging
fiercely, climbing back
And the fragrance of each fading
flower became
Unbearably sweet, surrounding me
with its
unique Divinity

Embraced.
Each sunrise . . . . sunset . . . .
day . . . became a harmony,
wondrous
Even more enchanting, as one
followed the other
I was enthralled, had never dreamed
of such rapture.

Now . . . .

John Stephenson
THE BALLAD OF 15 TOES

This is dedicated to my son Zachariah.

I counted very carefully, I went
slowly down the rows;
but no matter how many times I
count, I still get 15 toes.
It had me worried the first few
months, I thought I must be strange
I was scared to go buy new shoes
with my feet so disarranged.
I started losing lots of weight, I got
shadows under my eyes
And every night I'd pray to God,
make me just like the other guys!
After all these years of suffering, and
paying that awful price
I finally found out my mistake, I
counted one foot twice.

Sally McMillan
ON CHINA PAST

Dedicated to the concept of ONE WORLD with freedom and justice for all people.

Strange land where dragons roam on
turquoise walls
And golden lions guard long-
treasured bones

Where painted columns dwarf gem-studded halls
And Buddhas smile from stately drapèd thrones
Near lotus ponds that drift their wild perfume
And drown the eye in leaves of jade-like green
'Long corridor where painted poppies bloom
And willows bow to bamboo from esteem
That hollow boughs can hallowed dwellings form
With grace that's like a bird on outstretched wing.
The ancient grandeur lasts through strife and storm
And yesteryear shows what new age shouldn't bring.
Man staggered, sweat, and starved to shape these grounds
'Til from his toil such opulence abounds.

Stacey McDaniel
HIS CREATION

God created the Heavens and the Earth
Man, and woman, created He them;
All things living found birth,
As they were created by Him.

He created the broad green fields
And the beauty of the deep blue sea,
He created the rocks and rills
For the pleasure of such as we.

He created birds and brooks to sing
Rugged mountains and towering trees,
Flitting insects with gossamer wings
The sun, moon, and stars, created He these.

God created these things ages ago
Everything according to kind.
Seed was put here for us to sow
In this beautiful garden of time.

So let us first sow the seeds of love
The best He had to give.
And lifting our eyes to Him above
Give Thanks; for the right to Live.

Kathleen D Trakas
LOVE

To my Grandchildren with love

You came into my heart
As silent as the night
Weaving your way to and fro as a velvet cloak,
Offering me love.
You accepted my trust
So much apart of my life,
Yet, never apart of me.
Now, you glide silently away
Thinking I'll never know you have been here.
But you are wrong.
For I have loved you as I love life.
I will miss you as I would miss the sunshine or the birds.
Yes, I will remember.
Each soft velvet night,
Your love will tug at my heart and play on my soul.
One does not forget love.

Barry A Mogel
SLINGERLAND DRUMS AND ZILDJIAN CYMBALS

I dedicate this poem to my dear sister, Sara Mogel Bonjokian, whose brilliant talent in the arts was my inspiration to aspire to the promise of success

Slingerland drums and Zildjian cymbals
A teen's talent to fill ten million thimbles
The nimblest hands that tapped those sticks
On parchment, did percussive tricks.
And "The Marauders"—how you earned, with strife
The promise of greatness brought to life.
Down cellars rehearsed with walls so thin,
Proved to all within earshot
Of what could have been.
The Buddy Rich legacy lies dormant, at heart,
Just 'brushing and snaring' for <u>your</u> beat to start.
Distant drummer! The dream's not gone.
The skins are waiting,
The beat goes on.

Helen J Muller

Helen J Muller
THE HOMELESS

Dedicated to my deceased uncle Otis Miller

Never a steady job, in all his life
No house or home, for children or wife;
He disliked school, when he was a boy,
Watching freight trains, was a sure joy:

The years were gone, the older he'd grown,
Traveling the country, trudging all alone;
Never owning a thing, not even a car,
Drinking from a bottle, can or a fruit jar:

Trying to stay warm, by the bonfires,
Building a shelter of cardboard and tires:
Chopping wood for sandwiches and pies,
When not on a train or truck, walking the railroad ties,

Seldom getting in contact with folks back home,
Searching for new places that he could roam;
North, south, east and west,
Moving wherever the weather was best:

Cleone Van Selus
NOVEMBER

The trees, in naked beauty, stand
Flaunting their shapely limbs;
Adorned with a filigree of lacy twigs,
Posing in the nude.

Shira Yael De Llano
I LOVE YOU ETERNALLY UNTIL THE END OF TIME

Love
c
h
o
e
sweet
i
m
e
singing
e
n
t
l
echoes
h
a
r
i
n
good
a
y
songs
a
y:
I Love You
n
t
i
l the
n
d of time
eternally!

Junial Douglas Jr
ANNIVERSARY IN THE JUNGLE

To: Faye Douglas my wife

A Hallmark store I could not find
So I made this poem up in my mind.

Our ANNIVERSARY, it's been eighteen years
We've both had smiles and have both shed tears.

My thoughts drift back to th
Ho–Made somehow
Wondering how we managed to make it till now.

It's been a long, bumpy and crooked road
We both had to carry our share of the load.

I wasn't always there when you needed me.
That's a mistake that I now clearly see.

The two of us against the World.
Now we have two precious little girls.

A family now I know we'll stay
Because our love grows more each day.

The Lord has blessed us with the strongest love
And I know it was sent from Heaven above.

As I look up at the clear blue sky
I know that I will love you till the day I die.

To close this poem will be hard to do
The only thing I can say is;

<u>I TRULY LOVE YOU</u>

Judy Lyn Caruso
A DAY IN MY DREAMS

To my wonderful parents: Dad for inspiring the poem & believing in me. Mom for always saying, "You can do it"! And my terrific husband & friend Lenny, for being you! I love you three dearly. Thanks for being there! !

Sitting on the beach, sand beneath me.
Ocean in my view, sea gulls above me.
The waves rolling and slapping, beckon me to join them.
But I must decline, and keep on watching.
The shining sun, beats down on my skin,
the cool refreshing water, invites me again.
I lay on my back deciding to sleep,
the salty sea breeze relaxes me.
The sleep wears off, and so does my comfort.
Looking around me,
my world is shattered.
When I look around, everything's different.
My beautiful surroundings
are gone with the dream.
In my bed, all along,
awake now, my dream gone.

Cindy L Winslow Shepherd
LEA

To my daughter Lea with love; never forget that I love you; if you need me I will be there. Mom

Looking down into your crib I see,
your smiling face.
I wonder,
what your sweet dream is

Days turn to night,
nights into days.

I clean your room,
make your bed,
straighten your clothes,
and find a song.

The alarm goes off.
the smile on my face,
is satisfaction.

I see you standing,
puzzled over me.
You wonder why,
I'm smiling.

Harriett Burke Sexton
AWARENESS

I sit on a hilltop brush in hand,
Canvas on the easel, and colors on the pallet,
Hoping to capture the beauty and the essence of nature;
The color-carpet of wild flowers, the verdant new greens,
The vastness of the cloudless pale blue sky, and
The throbbing pulsation of the Cosmic Energy in it all.

With the sky as background an eagle soars in effortless grace.

It rides the air currents up and down, back and around.
The grace reminds me of ballet, and I begin to hum strains
Of the Blue Danube.
Then I am in the sky . . soaring, riding the currents up and
Down and back and around.

The eagle and I are doing a pas de deux.
Then I knew.
All is one.
The eagle is I.
The eagle is you.

J Donald Nix
THE MASTER'S FLIGHT

Dedicated to my father, James Franklin Nix (1909-1978)

Each flight must be charted, before a pilot makes their climb,
Because of unseen dangers, and troubles they might find,
For each horizon cradles a mystery, that's not predestined in their flight,
And they must make calculations, in order to be right,
When their wings are lifted upward, and committed to the lofty breeze,
Moments of flashing memories, sets their mind at ease,
The flight will be one of safety, the plane will follow their command,
Because as they ascend upward, they put the flight in the master's hand,

Our life is like a flight upward, following our charted course,
But we should not ascend upward, till we hear the master's voice,
Then our horizon will hold no mystery, nor shall we be surprised,
If our flight has been charted, by the master, before we start to rise.

William J Penman
DEATH OF A TOWN

To my kindest critic and most loyal fan, my wife, Terry.

The playgrounds were stark naked, stripped of childish laughter and tears,
And the early spring warmth failed to sweeten the sour stench of fear,
This consuming plague that clogged the quiet streets, the empty shops, the rows of match-box homes, some old, some new.
Steepled churches, draped in silence and empty pews.
Banks, robbed of integrity and trust, hiding behind locked doors.
In marital beds, now shared with strange anxiety and rumors galore.
This town, for countless years, suckled at the rich breasts of the block-long, sweat-stained factory.
Spawning happy marriages, fruitful births, home mortgages, a rare college loan.
All turned off with the abruptness of a cradled phone.
Curt notice on a grimy bulletin-board, crowded with names and dates.
Sale and closure of the factory; smokeless chimneys; padlocked gates.
Scourging a robust town with misery and blight,
This sordid honeymoon of corporate greed and ruthless might,
As management stole away like a thug in the night.
Leaving an epitaph to infamy, to devious plans and clever schemes.
A legacy of polluted air and stagnant streams,
A down payment on broken promises, on shattered dreams.

Frank G Bakara
AN ODE TO A GREEK HOLDING TANK

Dedicated to Alice Johnson Arnott. without whom this poem could not have been written

It was midnight on the ocean, and as "Nephele" sailed along,
A very rough sea, made a wreck out of me;
And the holding tank odor was strong,
Our course lay North to Poros, and with
Kythera far to our stern;
We would nod and we'd blink, wished the
darn smell would sink,
Cause it started to make our eyes burn;
I remembered what Cap't. Athanassois,
Had said at the start of our trip;
"Soon a chemical well, may this odor dispel,"
So till then, keep a stiff upper lip!

Claire A DeMatteo
THE LADY IN THE SHADOWS
Loving her man more than life
Hoping someday to be his wife
Making him happier than he'd ever been
Watching from the shadows,
Wondering, if she'd ever win.

He's kind & gentle and full of warmth
But the shadow of another woman
Makes his life a living hell,
He sits in his chair and waits,
Hoping that he'll hear her ring his bell.

He knows that she loves him not
But his total undying love is what she's got.
The lady in the shadows prays for him each night
That he be freed from a love that just isn't right,
For a love that leaves him full of sorrow,
Just won't last, even if she's back tomorrow.

He knows she loves him
With all her heart and soul.
But, his love for the other
Has left a great big hole.

He's asked her to be patient
While he waits for things to become clear
But the lady in the shadows
Is full of fear.
She loves him and hopes
That the end to his torment
Is very near.

Yes, she knows that one day soon
Everything will be alright,
For she prays for her love
Each and every night.

And she knows that God, in
His all consuming love
Will free him from hurt & pain
And show him what joys he has to gain.

Brandi Bechtel
THAT NIGHT
All my memories are safely packed and my dreams are neatly folded away

I got nothin' to show that I came very close to leave, that night had worked okay

All the tables and chairs stand empty and
bare and there isn't any sign you were here

so just walk through the door
but try not to get near

You might look into my eye and see all the pain and sadness deep inside

Don't look in my eyes 'cuz that's where
I keep the tears that I can not hide

Jose Luis Argaluza
ROLLER COASTER

To my children

I felt the blood
pumping into my head
hammering my brain
locking my senses,
thoughts come to me.

I could not coordinate them
like in a terrible nightmare
I saw in front of me
one by one my dream.

Holding my breath,
trying to keep my self cool
soon, I reached the table.

Twyla Pearson
LOVE . . .
Love is a feeling deep down inside, that only we can surmise.

We search and look and sometimes find, that what we thought was love was only our mind.

The more we grow the more we are able to see, that love is a feeling with no degrees.

But love is a force that can put us on top of the the world, or send us into the depths of pain.

So why do we search for that force that enlightens us so?

Cause it's the feeling that brings such a piece of tranquility we do not wish to let go.

You see it in the sunrise and feel it in the sunset, we grasp its beauty in the creations we see, but yet we still forget.

That the force of Love we inspire each day, is from the Lord that says Heh! We're O.K.

Kathleen Kay Lewis
FORGET THE PAST

To Rosalie—my darling Mother, and deceased family: Brothers & sisters.

Forget the past you fool, live by the Golden Rule, look ahead to the Future, nothing but pain will drive you insane memories haunt you Regrets torment you again and again.—Forget the past it's easier said than done! When those you love leave you one by one—

Someone will try to explain "It's all for the best," Oh yes! Time will surely heal the pain (you know the rest) Recollections taunt you all that you feel
Just the same; Nature will always come clean must face the facts
Or it's all in vain try to protect you from life's stormy blast.—

Nothing will last if you are blest you'll pass the test. Things that surround you, all that reminds you, put these behind you
Just let them rest. The future will guide you. Forget the past. Always beside you those you love best

Friends who invite you. Things that delight you. Forget the past just let it rest, deep down inside you start life afresh.
If small things remind you, heart-strings will bind you. Some one will bless you, memory's guest—

Tony J Eckstein
HOPEFULLY, IN LOVE
I go to the movies
I watch the TV
I need to have hope
I have to believe
in love

the happy endings
their beautiful loves
I've been searching so long
with only one cause
that's love

every time it seems real
and my heart is in bliss
they change the scene
and it's love that I miss
that's love

I know you're out there
searching like me
will we ever find
the love that we see
hopefully, in love

Awilda Ramirez-Visalden

Awilda Ramirez-Visalden
NOT FAR
I could be by your side
if you really want me.
What seems impossible

is just a couple miles away,
I could be in your arms,
your embrace, what I've
waited for.
You could be sure
that love is true.
Just a call,
caring is the main ingredient.
Is it too much to ask for?
Excuses always fail,
so you don't desire me?
A Heavenly reality,
that can save your lost soul.
Not needing me
when I could be by
your side.
Tomorrow will be late
love was a make
believe to you.
Miles away I
sit, being able to be by your side.

Jennifer Sparhawk

CHILDREN

Watching children play
Is a joyous feeling.
They have not a care
In the world,
Everything is happy
And nothing could be better.
No pressure, worries,
Stress, heartache.
It is a new world
Full of adventure
And learning.
Why must children grow up?
Life and the innocent thinking
Change too quickly.
Maybe the world would be
A better place
If adults grew up
To be children.

Adrienne M Smorado

MY LIFE HAS JUST BEGUN

My life has just begun,
Now that you belong to me,
And I wake in the night,
And find you lying close to me,

Life is so sweet,
My worries are gone,
Because of you, my heart sings a
song,
A song of gladness, a feeling
So great! That you're finally mine,
Now I don't have to wait,

And when you awaken in the
morning . . .
And hold me tight,
Oh! it just feels so nice,
With your warm body next to mine
With your arms around me,
to comfort my mind,

I never knew that love was so grand
But here I stand wearing your
wedding band,
forever I'll thank the Lord, for being
so kind,
that he gave me, someone to love me
for the rest of my life.

Melissa Westwood

DREAMS

My dreams are for me and
me alone;
The pain I can feel that
no one else knows.
Even my friends can not see
my pain, for it is in my
heart and not theirs.
Their eyes do not feel the
pain; nor do they see my
dreams.
I dream, wonder, and wish;
For someday that they would
be true.
Or are my dreams too strong?
I will never know, but as long
as they stay dreams, that
only I can see . . .
I know, as no one else does,
that they are true in my
heart.

Tammy Rudolph

HIS WORLD

She's crumbling
with the smog
and inevitable pollution
She's deteriorating
while the belief in God
diminishes
We've cheated God
And now to whom do we go?

She grows colder: becoming a
stagnant cesspool
of shattered dreams
Her heart beats faster
as crime cackles in the madness
And God sits silent
while people turn against each other
stealing—more than just money—
And now who holds those dreams?

She cracks: the brittle shell breaks
—cocaine becomes god—
because He wasn't there
God cheated us
left us devastated
and unbelieving
in the fiery ashes of truth
And now who is our supreme being?

She ruptures: exploding sorrows
and dies a discontented death
And His world cheats Him
throwing His dream into the cesspool
and God crumbles
and as He lay in the ashes of truth
we realize just who we are
and who held the words of eternal
life

Robert M Rosse

DREAMS

What would life be without dreams?

Dreams have shaped our destiny,
Freed us from the tyranny of kings,
And propelled us into space.

They've inspired us
To scale the highest peak,
Sail beyond the far horizon
And voyage beyond the known
To where we've never been,

Urging us on to new tomorrows
And imparting to us a sense
That we are more than what we
seem,
More than the sum of all our seasons,

Conjuring up a vision of a time
When we will be transformed,
Will take wing and fly,
To dance among the stars
And navigate the sky.

Tibor G Toth

HAPPY THOUGHT

A sailboat on a sea of gold . . .
The sun is hanging low . . .
Sea gulls float on wings spread wide
As I watch from below.

Waves roll out to shore
Spreading their riches on the sand—
Birds hunt at their foamy edge . . .
My feet sink where I stand.

I watch the seas swallow the
sun . . .
A cool breeze comes to shore . .
The sounds of night fill heart and
soul—
A grand heavenly score . . .

The last rays of the day fade out
To give room for the night . . .
I look for Little Dipper
With Polaris shining bright . . .

Thinking of the beauty and the joy
This day has brought
I look forward to ever better days—
What happy thought! . . .

Susan B Jacobson

UPON LOSING A CHILD

Time has passed and you are no
longer with me.
or are you, as I still remember your
kicking.
And I still remember your sweet
energy following me
wherever I went.
And I still remember your constant
presence,
always there from the moment
of conception,
until you chose a physical death.

Why did you pick me to carry you?
You knew I could never hold you for
nine months
because of my body.
Was that why you chose me?
Did you want to see what the
physical plane was like?
Or, did you complete all your
business in that short time?

The week after your passing, all the
plants at home gave birth.
And there was a newly hatched nest
in the attic.
Was this a sign that spirit was born?
Not in a body that I could see, or
touch,
but still very much alive with
love, on another plane with
which I am not familiar?

I release you now and forever to go
on your journey.
Find your teachers and follow the
white light.
I thank you for the time we spent
together and
cherish every second you were
with me.
Now I must continue on my path too.

Your body is no longer alive, but a
part of you will
always be with me,
As memories never die.

Mattie Floyd

I SAW THE SUNSHINE TODAY

I saw the sun shine, today.
I heard a child, cry:
My lover, cried, "when we said
Goodbye.
It was such, a nice day.
Oh please, don't cry!
I saw," the sun shine today.
I heard," a child cry.
My lover cried, "when he said
Goodbye.
I was sure that, love would end this
way.
Oh please, don't cry.
It's such, a nice day.
I saw the sun shine today.
I heard a child" cry today.
My lover cried," when we said
goodbye.

Jodi Connot

OLD MAN

old man
creased
in a chair
some would call
Early American.
it is old.
old man watches
for Izod-labelled son
on southbound roadside.
the sun and dust
are one with old man.
creased old man
in carefully ironed shirt.
creased old man.
creased old man watches.

Thomas DeVore

YOUR BEST

It is good, it is there,
love is always everywhere.

But you must always be true,
that is solely up to you.

Give your best, always be sincere,
anything less and you've missed
it here.

To make love last, to make love real,
give and share to keep that
thrill.

Bruce R Humphreys

38—NOT-SO-LATE

My-Oh-My, it's getting so late,
I should have checked my watch—
I'll soon be 38.

Thirty-eight—my how time flies
Did I fall to sleep? I think
I had a date around 24,
Where is that black book? Knock-
knock

Is there someone at the door?
Time is that you? Where have you
been?
I've just woken up—I'm not quite
awake.

Let's see now 38 or 83,
Which way do the numbers go?
Which way do the numbers go?
Sometimes I'm confused.
What's that, so are you

Then I guess 38's not so bad—
Just a time that is
New for me and for you.

Better check your own watch, the
hour may
That is—may not be so late time's
always there,
There's really no place to hide
It sits and waits—everywhere!

Diane Sims

ON PAPER

On paper,
I am like an open book
feelings and emotions
fluently being expressed
in all openness and honesty

Yet when I must verbalize my
thoughts, feelings and dreams
I can not.
My pages start to turn
so quickly
and the binding closes
ever so tightly
trapping all of my true self
inside.

To be kept there in secrecy
Until again,
my thoughts prevail
through my hand
onto the blank white pages
to be read by few
and heard by none.

Ombra See Cler
I LIKE
I like to hear the church bells ring
And hear the children's choir sing.

I like to look up in the sky
And watch the clouds go drifting by.

I like to sit beneath the swaying trees
And feel the cool and gentle breeze.

I like to hear the whistle of a train
As it goes by in winter snow or summer rain

I like to walk down a winding path
Or take a nice hot bubblebath.

I like to sit by the fireside
Or go for a long train ride.

I like to meet a friend with a cheery smile
Who wants to sit and chat a while.

I like to fish in a mountain stream
Or sit on the banks and rest and dream.

But I like the time of evening best
Just after the sun has gone to rest.

And I like that God is up above
And watches over me with love.

Frank DeGeorge
THE DIAMOND TREE
I saw a big tree
With a diamond back stem
And slowly the diamonds
Fell to the ground.
Then appeared sunshine on the diamonds
And they melted away.

And from the tree
Fell little raindrops of ice,
And slowly appeared the tree
That I had once seen
With no diamonds.

Erma Stalnaker
GONE HOME
Today our hearts are filled with sorrow
And our eyes with tears o'er flow
And I know we all are wondering
Just why he had to go.

But slowly peace comes to our hearts
When we realize he had so much to gain
For he has entered that heavenly place
Where there are no more aches or pain.

He has claimed that heavenly mansion
That Jesus went on to prepare
And we know he must be happy
For the heavenly father is there.

He now can rest and be at peace
Over by the golden throne
His earthly journey has now ended
And he has made it home.

Nancy F Martin
SORRY
"Sorry" is what you are and what you repeatedly said,
Trying to shift the blame when I told you to be more careful instead.
Why is our three year old son now dead?
We were mistreated just because you could get off with
"I'm sorry," as your plea; You wanted me to habitually forgive and accept your abuse with glee.
The verdict: Of wife and child abuse you are definitely guilty.
I allowed it for years because I was scared and silly.
When I left, you verbalized to others that I was an excellent wife.
I had to divorce you to protect my other child and my life.
Years later, you called to say "I'm the only woman you'll ever love," and that's a lesson you learned fast.
I now have a great husband who doesn't kick, choke or beat us as you did in the past.
Why should I allow you to repeat a sadistic task?
Only when you seek psychological help may you understand why abusive marriages can't last, and the reasons I pity you as I do.
Sorry! Sorry! Sorry! There is no place left in my heart for you!

Annette Dollard
CHRISTMAS GIFT
Early Christmas morning,
down the winding stairs,
tiptoed a little girl.
The farm house was extremely cold.

Had Santa come?
Had she been good enough?
She could see the hanging stocking—
Would she find black coal,
that naughty children get?

She ran—what a joy!
A pair of hand-knitted slippers
for her feet.
She had no oranges or apples,
yet, it was Christmas,
and happy for her,
Santa had come,
One gift—slippers.

The heart of a child
is suddenly filled with happiness.

Caryn R Isenberg
DREAMS FLYING AWAY
There was never a day
I thought I would say
I love you.

There is a time
In everyone's life
When you love a star and say
My dream will never come true.

I will never meet the star I love.
He is an actor and famous.
All I am is a nobody.

Not that it's come true to me
but if you think you will,
you might.

Never think negative,
Always think positive,
Things might happen
that you never think will.

Try to be optimistic,
not pessimistic.
Things will come faster.
Dreams will come true.

Shirley Sotsky
BRANCHES BARE
Branches bare,
Nest still there,
Squirrel scrambled, stretched
on a long, thin limb.
Hit by sun spokes,
He glimmered gold,
frolicked free.
Squirrel leapt, then hopped
in the shape of an arc.

Verna L Kovar
A BIRD
I saw a bird fly in the sky,
Not too low and not too high.

And as I watched him soar up there,
I wondered, "Was his life all bare?"

Or did he have a home and friends,
Where he could stop and make amends.

A place to pause and rest his wings,
And dream of big and better things.

Or was he destined to remain,
A single life without a name.

These things and more we'll never know.
It all depends on what we sow.

Life is a trial we all must face,
Until we find a higher place.

Colleen Sullivan-Tricomi
FULL CIRCLE
. . . words
continuous sounds
strung together
attempting to pacify our
. . . temper
boiling emotion
carried to the surface
of our struggling
. . . relationship
independent souls
striving to overcome
our fears and
. . . doubts
uncertain thoughts
brought forth by
the insincerity of
. . . words

Walter Franklin
TRAIL'S END (SWAN SONG)
Life has its Springtime, and, its Fall.
Life beckons, and, you've had it all.
Meanwhile, as seasons went and came;
You'd tried your best to play the game.

You'd faced the pitcher, standing tall,
And then struck out; or hit the ball.
Then as it floated through the air,
The umpire'd called it "Foul" or "Fair."

'Mid joy and sorrow, toil and strife,
All the vicissitudes of life,
Life's Summer somehow slipped away.
Where had it gone? What could one say?

Some say that soon, as time goes by,
We'll face the Umpire in the sky;
Then sing "Hosanna!" as we fly;
(Or else just sizzle as we fry).

Now, for the final paragraph
I've tried to winnow out the chaff;
So when I've gasped that final gasp,
Just write this simple epitaph:

"Tally the score, his life is o'er.
He left us for no ghostly shore,
But simply left, and is no more."
Exit. That's it. There's no encore.

Mrs Virginia Smith
WHO WILL TAKE GRANDMA?
We came back to the mountains for Grandpa's funeral
Back home to the southland—my three sisters and me
Grandma was there all alone—she would need care and a home
But which one of us would the "Good Samaritan" be?

Grandma just rocked in her old rocking chair—and altho she cried
She had never spoken a word to anyone since Grandpa died
Grandma was old and feeble and so terribly thin
It was our duty to do for her as we were her next of kin

"Don't look at me" said sister Kate
"I've got more work now than I can do"
"I can't be responsible for her" cried our baby sister Sue
Then at last up spoke our oldest sister Claire
"I have no room for Grandma—no time for her care"

"But you Amy" she said looking at me "You have a home but no family"
"You have plenty of room—nothing to do—so Grandma wouldn't be a burden to you."
"You have plenty of time and money and you live alone"
"So we think it best that you take poor Grandma home"

I glanced at Grandma and I knew something was wrong
I rushed to her side but Grandma was gone
Maybe in heaven she didn't have any next of kin
But God had gladly taken poor Grandma in

Helen Hendricks
A PATH OF FAMILY LOVE
We each can't be an astronaut,
Go zooming off in space—
But on this vast old earth of ours
Each one can find a place!

The generation gap we see
From parents to off-spring,
Perhaps could be improved right now
By doing this one thing:

Let's form some family clusters, strong,
Entwined with much affection;
The threads of love though fragile,
Create a bright reflection!

We'll try this great philosophy,
And pray to God above
That He will guide us on our course—
A path of family love!

Marcia L Nesset
DEATH
Death is my friend.
It takes away the pain
That winter brings.

It's long I've known that

You would go before I do.
Like melted snow in rivulets
You passed me by.

"You're all I have left."
You said. And now
I haven't you.

Death. Friend? Pain.
Hers or mine?

Mildred L White-Kaufman

Mildred L White-Kaufman
I CAN, I MUST, I WILL
I can conquer anything that I want
because
I am bright, I am unique
and I control my destiny.

I must, because
I own a special place on this universe
and I will not allow anyone
to define my limits
and enclose my boundaries.

I will succeed
because
I can overcome any obstacle
by using my mind, body, and
intellect
to crawl under, walk around
or climb over those things
which hinder me
because

I can, I must, I will be successful—
For Me!

David L Ziegelgruber
A POEM FOR KAITLYN
Today was the day she came into
Our lives.
A bundle of joy, of giggles and cries.
So pretty and soft all fingers and
toes,
A sweet little face with a flat button
nose.
Tender blue eyes and soft raven
hair,
And just think, God has sent her for
Us
To take care.
We'd waited so long for her to
arrive,
So you see she's quite wondrous
In our loving eyes.
And now as the years pass
quickly by;
We'll treasure the memory
Of the day She arrived.

Lucie-C Ouimet
ODE TO OUR FAITH
I summon my strength to ascend the
tree
Yet, even if his friendliness was
good
I thought of the roots, down in the
mirky.
Looking up, seeking for my star, I
stood.

Climb, to reach thy mark of my
hidden pole
I strive, groping branch upon branch,
sightless
Discerning goodness from the
wickedness,
Can I distinguish darkness from the
soul?

Faith, in thy star we search, is
decided
Alas, we darkly know by faith we
cry.
And us, kindreds, are sometimes
reminded:
In this world, one life we have, that's
no lie

Because dust returns to earth who
gave it
And the soul returns to God who
gave it.

Lisa Lo Dolce
LISTEN DARLIN'
Listen darlin' the time has come
To let go of the one you love.
As you see him walk by
Just smile, don't cry.
The sun is up, the day is new
There are many others that are right
for you.
Your heart is broken, but it will mend
in time.
Remember now, you need someone
new.
This is not meant to hurt you
Because I just want to help in
making sure
That you see the sun rise for a new
day to come.
Having the looks and a smile
don't always match.
It's what's inside that should make
the catch.
But as you know, it's so hard to let
go.
So when another day has come,
And the sun is up and the day is new
As you see him walk by
Remember just smile, don't cry.

Robert P Wilson
MORNING SUN
The morning sun is brilliant as it
pierces the morning fog

Like fingers reaching through the
mist, warming the dampened
sod.

A heron glides across the lake
seeking a favorite fishing
ground

The splash of brightly colored
wildflowers open, never making
the slightest sound.

In this peaceful solitude the night
dreams fade as one begins to
think

Of the chain of life's full cycle,
each day a brand new link.

The dew upon the grass
represents the tears of Mother
Nature that she shed the night
before

She carries the burdens of her
creations and sends the eagle off
to soar.

Each day brings new endings, but,
new life also begins

Like wheels in perpetual motion,
the cycle never ends.

Then, surrounded by this beauty,
I wake up as a purpose flashes
through my mind

Let's fill our souls with laughter
and let it spread like a wildfire
throughout all mankind.

With this common bond of
happiness we can unite and
stand as one

We'll have souls of joy and
laughter and warm our hearts
with morning sun.

David Hammond McDowell
HOT SUMMER
It was June, on the fourth Wednes-
day
Just a hot summer,
Divided highway, was so long,
I walked alone, with nobody else
Pavement, hot and sweaty,
It lay just below the surface,
Hot summer
The tears and the sadness,
Life as we know it,
The sky is much too bright,
Stay if you want to stay, go if you
must
It is your own decision.
Life it moves, so very quickly,
Hot summer
Don't understand, what you said
What you said, when you said it,
You know me, far too well,
I wake up alone, you're gone
No goodbye, no nothing,
And I wonder, what you're doing,
Hot Summer
It ran so long

Heidi Tubman
THOUGHTS OF YOU
I could never leave you for a day,
Just turn and walk away,
Thoughts of you, with me would
always stay.

Just you remember this,
I'll be thinking of your tender kiss,
And thoughts of you, holding me I'll
miss.

So while I am gone,
Think of me from dusk to dawn,
Thoughts of you, my mind will be
on.

To you, I could never lie.
I have to go and don't ask why,
Thoughts of you will make me cry.

And if you ever get sad and lonely,
Just read this letter and think of me
only,
And thoughts of you will come to
me.

Think of the time when we'll be
together
And you'll hold me and not this
letter,
Till then, thoughts of you will make
it better.

Wherever we go and whatever we
do,
You think of me and I'll think of
you,
And thoughts of you will remind me,
how much I love you.

Laurie Temple
STORM SONG
The reflections I can see,
when the sun shines down upon,
are a myriad of endless rainbows,
draped down from the clouds.

The only sight that refills my empty
heart,
when a storm plays,
loud songs in the night.

I awake to this perfect picture,
painted in the corner of my eye,
Stars lost to the unawaited crack,
of a lightning bolt.

They paint this piece of color,
and play the musical tune,
to endless notes.

It is only the ugly that brings forth
the beautiful,
I, myself
have seen it.

In such harmony they build,
the lightning, and the rain,
they paint this picturesque sight
placed below the horizon of the sky.

Zora Riddle Pegg

Zora Riddle Pegg
LONELINESS

To Bill

Loneliness? Yes, I know what it is.
It is longing for the voice of one who
is gone.

It is waiting to hear his car enter the
carport,
And his key turn in the lock on the
kitchen door.

It is the sound of books laid gently
on
The table and a voice calling,
"Anybody home?"

It is the sound of grocery bags being
placed
On the kitchen counter, then
footsteps

Going to the living room. It is the
sound
Of the closet door being opened, and

Coathangers telling me his coat is
being
Returned to its accustomed place.

"Yes, dear, I'm home.
We got out a little early today."

Carol Smith Worrell
THE TREE
This year I went back home.
Only to find that something of mine was gone.
My tree.
Gone I screamed, gone where?
Oh, the pain, the pain of loss.
The tree was my refuge, my home away from home.
Its branches protected my very soul.
And now it's gone, gone.
The weight I feel in my heart is like the saw cutting each branch. Each year of my life that is over.
And so is the tree's life.

Kathy Richardson
ONCE
I once walked through gardens of heaven
Where light pink roses blossomed and happiness prevailed
I once walked on a land so free
Where peace was silent and nature born
I once walked through valleys of green
Meadows where puddles of water rest.
I once walked through sunlit skies of warmth
Where echoes of the past forgave.
I once walked through life's fortunes, where love embraced all.

Sonia F Kerns Collazo
IF I COULD

Dedicated to: Larry R. Lewis

If I could! I would take the stars, and with them show you how much you light up my life.
Take the gentlest wind, to kiss your lips while we were apart.
Use the rain, to wash away the sadness from your life.
I would always have the sun shining on your horizon, on a cloudy day.
Take the colors of the rainbow; and give you immense happiness.
I would take the moon, and enhance you; with a silvery aura of love.
The clouds would show your fierce emotions . . .
And the earth would be a solid base, from which we could build our future.

Robert B Cumming
ODE BY A FAT SPARROW
Greed, Greed, Greed—
The lust and passion for seed.
I'm plump and larger than Mom. But I deserve it.
The Gods who set out the feeder call me a "poor little me."
Just because I look so pathetic. But I am starving
as I flutter my wings and beep through an empty beak.
Who am I to admit I can feed myself?
(I wish they'd put more sunflower seeds in this mess.)
Mom's looking beat, looking haggard,
and Dad's sagging, skinny, exhausted.
It's not my fault you know.
I wasn't the one in on that amorous chase.
I wasn't the one who flirted and danced
and pretended to escape in the trees.
Not I who excited Dad into those arboreal aerobatics.
When it comes to eggs, you get what you play for.
And you got me!
(Beep, beep,—come on Mom, try it two at a time for gosh sakes).

Elizabeth P Brown
I DON'T EXIST; I AM NOT ME

To my family; all of you so full of sunshine! You have made my life worth living. I'll love you throughout eternity.

I don't exist; I am not me;
I am only bits & pieces of all humanity.

The laughter in my heart; the light in my eyes;
Are only reflections I've stored to surprise!

Each word, each look, I have put on file;
To give you back in a word or a smile.

If each of us would do these things;
Gently recalling the good the world brings;

What a life it would be;
I not important, but all humanity!

Mary E Jennings
THEY CALLED THE WIND . . . .
Wild winds blow through-out the night.
Powerless—I sit by candlelight.
Moaning and shrieking, on roof above—
Twisting my heart, once filled with love.
Ripping and wrenching, you too must hate
Recklessly wishing, the worst of fate.

Hurricane winds blow–'till all is still,
And I stand—treeless, upon this hill!
If then, at last, from hate chains I'm free
Broken and cleansed, my heart's empty.

Lillian R Stephens
GRANDMOTHER
Have you studied her Hands, there's a story they tell,
how they baked bread and pies, cookies and shells.
Those hands labored long for the family she loved,
and in between tending there was time for hugs.
Nights of rocking babies to sleep, days very busy and tired feet.
Her face etched with kindness and care,
but only to God would her weariness bare.
They rocked back and forth, two cradled close,
one fast asleep, one nods in repose.
The moon streamed through the window below
and circled the dreamers with a soft silvered glow.
And now Mother repeats the same loving process,
with a smile on her heart, remembers with fondness;
In the same favorite rocker she snuggles our babies;
Grandma, our darlings, angels all.

Kimberly L Pennington
ONCE
I looked in the mirror
a lake
seeing more than vanity
And
I saw a little girl
staring back at me
lost and alone
searching . . .
for self
a promise of happiness
and
a key to the future
Suddenly . . .
the child smiled
and
a golden key
gleamed
as it dangled
from a chain
around the throat
of a woman.

Ellen Prince

Ellen Prince
TORTURED MIND
I look for good in all mankind.
But oh my mixed and tortured mind.

I try and keep my head up high.
So I don't see the evil creeping by.

I came here not of my own free will.
But yet I share in all this hell.

Yes I have tried to understand but my mind is too weak to grasp the plan.
That God must have had for every man.

Twila Banish
THE WEEPING WILLOW TREE

in memory of my Mother & Father, Elizabeth & David Watson, your loving daughter, Twila

My mind is filled with things in the day but at night time I try to wipe them all away, when I was young my Dad used to say don't cry things will be ok. Mom used to say don't be sad we are with you and you should be glad. Now that I am older and wiser you see; I know how much my Mom and Dad loved me. Now I am married and have a family, but now I am like the weeping willow. In the day it sways with the breeze at night it is still like all the other trees. Sometimes I wish I could go back and just be me. And what that is, is just being happy and free, but I know that can never be, just my Mom my Dad and me. So many nights I long for someone to hold and have them say, I love you I will never let you go. I know in my heart that will never be, because I am the weeping willow tree.

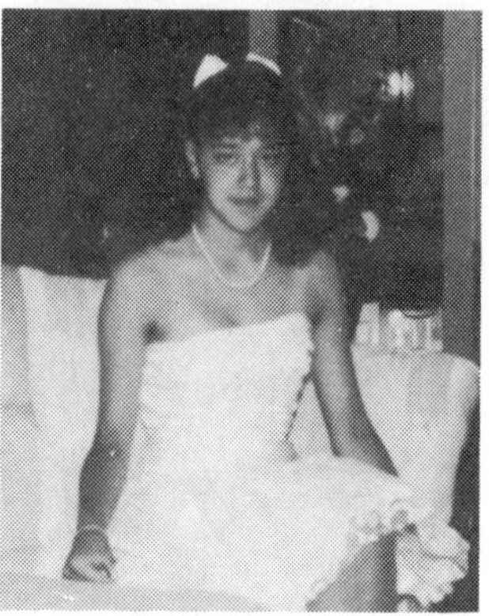

Marie Velazquez

Marie Velazquez
ALWAYS REMEMBER

Jason R,
All the long walks and the little white lies were worth it. Love Ya Lots and Always will!

Sometimes I sit here all alone and I wonder if you're free to hold.
You played the game that broke us apart, you wanted it bad but not with your heart.
When you look at me what do you see? You broke us apart is it just pain for me?
We've both been mistreated, our dreams were just lies, but I thought that together you might just think twice.
Did you care? Did it matter? If I would of tried harder, would you of felt better? It took two to make it but only one had to break it, our love was so strong, where did it go wrong?
Even though you said your problems are nothing death is just fine, I knew that between us you drew a thin line.
I cared for you deeply, I knew you so well, you weren't going to face it now it's all gone . . . farewell.
Your troubles aren't basic, your mind is in fog,
You know I still love you and my love is still strong,
Now that you're gone my hopes aren't as high, but *always remember*,
I'll love you forever
'till the day that, I Die.

Deborah Johnson Foret
MY PRAYER
Please keep me, and guide me, and help me along;
See that I keep from doing any wrong.

Watch over me closely, day by day;
See that no danger comes my way.
Give me your blessings, as the days break;
Please be beside me when I awake.
Stay with me always, and please never part;
My life without you is like being without a heart.
I could never begin to thank you for all that you have done,
But I've been trying to thank you ever since my life has begun.
Wherever I go, I hope that you will be there;
I'm thankful each time that you answer my prayer.
Your love for me is clearly expressed;
Thank you for giving me this happiness.
I'll love you far past eternity,
Thank you for all you have given to me.
And when it's time to meet my fate;
I hope that you will welcome me at Heaven's Golden Gate.

Ron Montgomery
COME WHAT MAY
Stars go by,
Children sigh;
But still the pain,
Still remains
In their eyes.

You and I,
We must try;
To alleviate their pain,
And help them smile again;
Come what may.

Julianna Ferenczi
ALONE
I don't care, winter or summer,
I don't care, it is late in the day
High noon or first moon
I miss you in my bone.
The clouds are passing by
I can't take the nights.
I think of you my love.
I write these with the stars.
I feel like a blind—
All empty inside.
All my thoughts are with you,
Can't wait to kiss you.

Rachel Susan Dyal
MOUNTAIN TOP
From the top of the mountain,
I see down into the valley below.
The sun is setting a red glow,
Upon the top of the trees.

Gently it kisses the grass below,
And I think of the way,
I feel under your gentle touch,
Like a flower opening to the morning delight

I believe you can see deep beyond,
The borders of my heart.
Like the sun when it reaches,
The mountain top.

I am aglow like the setting,
Of the sun to feel your,
Caress on the softness of my skin,
Just to be near you once again.

So meet me on my mountain top,
With all the excitement of the setting sun.
And feel my passion rise,
When I'm with you on my mountain top.

Malinda Mallory
THE SILVER LEAF MAPLE
As I sit without a care,
I see a sight that's oh so rare.
I see a silver leaf maple tree
as it comes alight with color for me.
As the wind blows, the tree starts to sway
the sparkling leaves now come ablaze.
The wind dies down, the leaves change to my view.
Still I patiently wait for the wind to renew.
Finally it whispers in slowly at first,
moving the leaves as they sparkle and burst.
The majesty of such a beautiful tree
builds great joy inside of me.
The silver leaf maple so sparkling and rare,
A joy to watch, a joy to share.

Bonita Barton
BACKYARD GARDEN
Backyard garden
rain at last
weeds break ground

Lynette M Kmiec
I CHOOSE HAPPINESS

To James D. Farley, I mean it.

Happiness is all we search for . . .
with all we achieve and all we possess,
we finally sit still and find that
Loving is all we ever needed to do.

I love you very much but being that I am only human I am impatient and insecure; everytime I finally push you away my heart stops and I can't be happy . . .
I miss you.

But every pain does achieve a gain, sometimes through this pain we can't see what it could possibly be . . . I guess all I am saying is I will always love you . . .

And I will always be happy.

Doug Bay
DANCE WITH ME
Dance with me in the shadow
Of a dim light of the moon
Prance with me on a meadow green
To an old rock and roll tune
Join me in the forest
Beneath the evergreens
Down by the old lake shore
Where once our love was seen

Run with me in laughter
From the depths of our soul
Share with me in giving
So the whole world will know
Love still lives beneath us
Under tall weeds that grow
They cover all the orchids
Where once they stood in a row

Lay with me in comfort
Wash upon the shores
The waste of shame and foolish pride
Open up your doors
There is a light that flickers
But it is slowly fading out
Open up the window
To the world and shout

It is not the pride that binds
But greed and lust and doubt
Open your window wide
Let it all come out
Cast upon the oceans
The love that's looking out
Open up your window
To the world and shout
Dance with me

Ann Isbell
A MOTHER'S PRAYER
Dear God, I was so quick to slap
I know he didn't mean to be
So bad. He's such a little chap.
So full of life, so filled with glee,
He doesn't understand how things
Like wrinkled rugs, turned over chairs,
The ball he joyfully flings
Against the wall and up the stairs
Upset my prim and grownup ways.
Because I've failed to bridge the gap
Between these years and childhood days,
Dear God, may he forgive my slap.

Hervey C Moores
IMAGE OF GOD
I prowled the beach today,
Cold, sullen, beautiful, with
Dark, heavy clouds
Swollen with rain;
Poised
Above the water with cat-like menace
Watching,
Waiting to deluge the earth,
The shrouded sand, the sea
With heavy tears of grief;
Weeping for humanity,
Nature is all things;
Indifferently cold, beautifully warm—
Only
those fashioned in the image of God
Are deliberately
Cruel.

Charlotte T Amii
WILD MIST
Wild mist all around,
a calm to seek.
Sit on the earthy ground,
how small and so meek.

With growing of strength
slowly there merge
the Self by it meant
the power of Life do surge.

Settled has the mist,
it now sits with me so calm.
As one we are bliss,
renewed as if by a savory balm.

Maude Burgeson Schaefer
LIFE
Life is filled with laughter, filled with tears,
Life is filled with love, filled with hate,
My life is filled with all but one.
I laugh when I'm happy, cry when I'm sad,
Love and care for others, hate I have none.
I believe all people are here to love and be loved.
If God would have wanted people to hate, he would have created the world with hate
Love is the word he created us with
Life would be better if we all loved one another
Be friends and never fight
Life is supposed to be filled with laughter, sadness, and love,
Not hate.

Marie Tanza
MOURNING
The casket is closed
The last prayer is said.
The flowers are laid,
And she's asleep in her bed.

This great journey she begins
To a place she's never been.
We hold her forever dear
Till we see her again.

What do we, left behind,
See for our futures
Without this guiding hand?
It's bleak as can be
Without our great friend.

Our hearts are heavy;
Our eyes are teary;
Our hopes are gone,
And there's no time for the weary.

We look around us;
We see her everywhere—
In our speech, in our hearts
In her dining chair.

We feel her presence;
We hear her voice.
We know she's saying
This wasn't her choice.

He called her to rest
With her family so dear.
Seeing her again
Is a belief we hold dear.

She left us her honor;
She left us her love.
She left us what we are,
Not what we can touch.

She taught us to love,
To stand tall and to withstand.
She left us her strength and her love
Until we see her again.

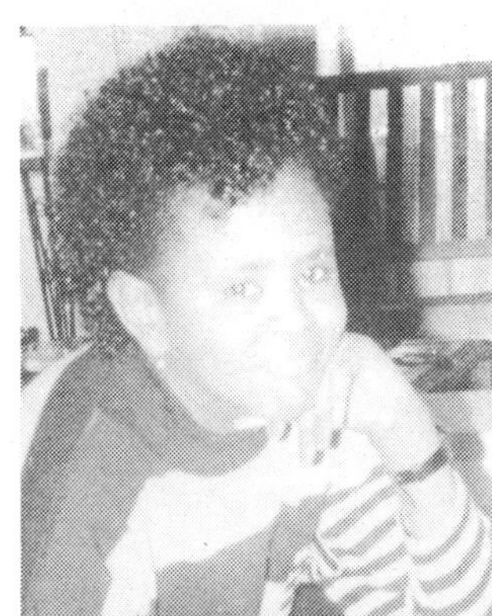

Deborah C Williams

Deborah C Williams
DON'T CRY CHILD
I was on my way to work to get the bus, on my way child was crying I walked up to him because I'm thinking maybe he missed his bus, But no, because there were more kids waiting, also Then I said what's wrong.
Then he said does it matter what color we are, I said No. Then I told that little boy that God put all of us in

this world to learn from each other and to be at peace also but not to discriminate but to love each other He put us together in harmony Then he said Do God love Me I answered Yes. When he asked me that. A tear started to drop down from my face, when he said that. Then he said I better go before I miss my bus, As I approached the bus I started to write about what had happened and as I thought about it wondered why people are so prejudiced against each other, discriminate against one other, Should I stop what I'm doing No because all of us are human beings. In this world no one can judge anyone, People want to judge you if you are handicapped, "Miami Vice" people need to take a long look at themselves in the mirror and think about God's love for you and me and it does not matter where you come from, it's where your heart is, and how you feel about life itself if I had a magic wand I would not change, the world and only people like you you and me it does not matter what color you are, we could change our ways against each other That's the way things should be, but we have to work together.

Beverly M Watson

Beverly M Watson
. . . FOR THE LONELY HEARTS

Crystalline castles and ebony towers
are
Fortresses to many things.
Among such items, one might add, is
A heart that lonely sings
With birds, trapped in golden cages,
and
Dew drops that die each day.
Life goes by its painful hours as
Love just turns away.

Margaret Caturia Seipel
REFLECTION OF LIFE

This poem is dedicated to the family of Paul Caturia, for you were his circle of love.

Ninety two years you have lived.
Even you could not believe,
what life would lead you through.

The country home your father had
built,
would become the home in which
your family grew.
These were happy times, but soon
you will be alone.
Your life companion put to rest.

Now grandchildren would fill your
home,
bringing nourishment to your soul.
Each child bringing to you his gift,
memories for you to hold.

Years passed and your steps grew
slow,
and your eyesight would dim.
Yet life still had much to bring.
Great grandchildren surround your
chair,
and love keeps flowing there.

Now you are so weary.
You feel a calling from above.
It's time to leave your legacy.
Hearts touched with your wisdom
and your love.

Jennifer Lynn Curry
SURRENDERED MEMORIES

As we grow older,
So I'm told.

Memories seem harder
and harder to hold.

Our heart wants so
much to remember.

But the mind only
seems to surrender.

So out come the pages,
one by one.

Filled with pictures
of family fun.

To be brought out on
the forgetful days.

Then only to be once
again, put away.

Patricia J Price
ESSENCE OF A POEM

To My Grandmother Jessie Mae Stevenson, My inspiration, Dennis Williams, My instructor for his help, and My husband Howard E for his loving support and push.

Words that do ring
and sing,
that have metered time
and rhyme,
to make of it
yet fit,
some of inner feeling,
and peeling
off outer essence of soul,
and poll
deeper sources of our core,
and bore
towards analyzing
and synthesizing
this sense, so giving, to share
and bare.
Isn't that its goal
and whole?

Marietta Abern
WOULD YOU NOT IF YOU WERE I

I dedicate this poem to my children, my husband, and the dreamers of the world

Would you not if you were I
have lied that you may ever lay
in greener pastures here below—

Where stars and moon would always
show
the better things that God hath made
that no man here on earth would dare
compare
to things that earthlings grow—

Would you not if you were I
have prayed that as the days go by
that better things were yet to come
and no man's dreams would dull the
sun
or shadow stars the heavens hold—
You would if you were I, I'm told

And would you not if you were I
see all the dreams you've dreamed go
by
as starlight fades in morning mists
beyond the place where man's
emotions reach
into somewhere we have yet to see—

Of course you can't. For I alone am
me*

Cheryl Schmeler
LONELY BIRD

The other night,
I had a dream.
It was about a bird in flight.
The bird flew through clouds of
cream.
The bird seemed to be lonely
and it needed another bird
badly.
The bird knew it was the only
one of its kind and it flew on
sadly.
The dream is vivid
and I know I live it.
It continues on, the dream
and the bird still flies alone.

Darrell Johnson
EVERYMAN

He lives his life,
He lives his death.

Tries to breathe,
But draws no breath.

He's a singer of songs,
Without a voice.

A man of decision,
Who makes no choice.

So is it to pity,
This pitiless king.

Or name him a wretch,
And his sorrows sing.

No perhaps none of these,
for who indeed do we please.

Let's simply say he's man of men,
And let him live as best he can.

For in the end all is dust,
Die we will for die we must.

Alex Solod
PEACE & WAR

I dedicate this poem to the armed forces of the United States of America, who are the real protectors of our Country

The day was warm, the evening cool,
And people going to and fro,
They walk at ease, their minds at rest
They have no fear of war.
The children play their little games
The oldest sit and watch
Their minds and hearts at ease
For they think of nothing more.
Then came the day, when men must
go and fight
To protect their families and their
friends
To go away and fight somewhere else
So life at home be safe, again.
Letters go to and fro, from soldiers
far away
But no one knows the dread of war
And the suffering they must have
To protect the future of another war

Amy Elizabeth Davis
ONE QUESTION

The smell
makes me a little ill
and very uncomfortable
but You,
between those white sheets,
it seems to have dried you out,
and made you bitter.

The sharpness that your mind
can no longer achieve
is more than made up for
by your tongue.

Before you try, again,
to draw my blood
I just have one question.
Who are you
and what have you done with my
mother?

Alice L Horrocks
LISTENING . . . . LISTENING

Before dawn I've wakened and wait
upon Thee ....

Help me to recognize the longings in
others ....

To offer the cup of cold water to
quench ....
Their fevered spirits ....
To bestow it in Thy name ....

To free someone from the prison-
house of sin ....
Using the Keys of the Kingdom in
my possession
The Keys you have honored me to
hold ....

To those who are blind ....
Blind in mind and soul and heart.....
Lead them to Thee ....
That their eyes may be opened to Thy
riches ....
Riches of Thy Love ....
Love beyond measure ....

Help me to listen to the unsaid word
and look ....
To the lonely and heartsick ....
That are mutely reaching out ....

LISTENING ....Listening ....

HEARING ....Thee ....
speaking through me this day ....

Nancy K Phillips
FOREVER LINKED

This poem is dedicated to Bill Sachse who is my best friend and my inspiration.

Satin hearts in scarlet dreams
Perfecting flowers in moonlight's
beams
The hour of birth of pallid sky
The crescent moon in Nancy's eye.

The slightest touch can move the
stars
And in her whisper, evening Mars
Of Venus comes her nightly strength
Tomorrow's love forever linked.

She tells the future with a smile
Then makes it happen with her guile
But tho you question all her ways
You cannot tame those foam tossed waves.

And as that comet rides the sky
You always know yet wonder why
She passed your way as evening mist
Upon your lips the sweetest kiss.

Lawrence Henry Mooney
LAMENT

I dedicate this poem to my eternal friend, John Arnold.

How blithely did our days rush past;
And blindly did we let them go,
Not stopping for a moment to reflect
That youth would someday grow old.

We sang, we danced, and vainly pranced;
And caution was never our guide.
And all those things that are our past
We may never hide.

Those lips that kissed; those arms that grasped
Have withered and lost their cause
And now life seems an eternity;
One long, unending pause.

Linda C Grazulis
STRIKE OUT AGAINST THE ODDS

When failure enters your life and you feel your ship has sunk, grab onto an anchor and rest a while. Regain strength and creativity.

In pausing, you refuel for another task and you can be certain that life will dream up another. With courage, strike out against the odds. Sail out towards the vast blue sea. With faith in your heart, plenty of hard work, and determination, your ship will take an unexpected turn towards the stars.

Latisha Medlock
I'VE KNOWN RIVERS

I dedicate this poem to my mother, who I love dearly. Also to Mrs. Grant and Mrs. Crenshaw. I want you to know that I care and my love is with you everywhere

I've known rivers in so many ways;
The rivers of the tomorrows, yesterdays and today
The rivers that are so, so far away;
The rivers that are famous from the yesterdays today.
The Mississippi River is one river I know
For when the slaves tried to get away this is where they'd go.
"I've known rivers";
Oh have I known rivers
Negroes have used rivers for ages;
Like a book with a thousand pages:
"I've known rivers;"
Oh have I known rivers
I've known rivers for thousands of years;
Like the oceans, and the seas in which holds all my tears.
"I've known rivers;"
Oh have I known rivers
Rivers are a big part of me:
For they run through my history
"I've known rivers;"
Oh have I known rivers

Ella Eaton Kienholz
ON YOUR GOLDEN WEDDING ANNIVERSARY

Hand and hand you've walked together
Down the lane of Golden years,
Through life's sunshine and its shadows
Through its laughter and its tears.

You have heard the bluebirds singing
Though the skies were dark above,
You have found serenity and courage
In the beauty of true love.

You have given much to each other
As you've journeyed along the way,
Now December memories are the roses
That grew and bloomed in early May.

As the Autumn shadows lengthen
And the snowflakes touch your hair,
May your lives grow richer—sweeter,
In the dear love that you share.

May your days be filled with happiness
Your dearest dreams come true,
May presence of your loved ones
Complete life's joys for you.

May the Peace of God be with you
His Glory fill your heart,
May you walk into the sunset
Faith and Hope an integral part.

May you know a deep contentment
As these mellow years unfold,
May God bless and keep you always
On your pathway now of burnished gold.

Rose Marie Daniel
SONG OF THE WOODS

Deep in the woods a cedar tree is guarding
A doe and her little fawn as they lay down to sleep.
Lowering her branches to shield them from intruders,
Whispering a lullabye as evening shadows creep.
High up above a night bird keeps on circling,
Crying in its mournful way to greet the rising moon.
Joining in the chorus the wailing of a coyote
Echoes far throughout the woods, a strange and eerie tune.
Deep in the woods a little stream meanders
Between mossy banks and a few bracken ferns,
Swirling round in eddies where pebbles gleam in sunlight,
Where fishes play at noon each day to bait the waiting terns.
Deep in the woods, deep in the woods
There is tranquility and peace.
Deep in the woods, deep in the woods
The quiet and solitude increase.

Rose Marie Daniel
THE NESSIE SONG

Can'st hear the Highland pipers, lad,
To-stir your heart to glory?
Go home and don your hunting plaid
And meet them at the dory.
Go row across the loch, my lad,
To seek the ancient Nessie,
And ae'n nay fear the fabled Bad,
But think of fair young Essie.
Can'st hear the Highland pipers, lad?
It is a celebration,
For Nessie can na' e'er be had
In all the Scottish nation.

Glinnie J Albrecht Berry

Glinnie J Albrecht Berry
SHREDDED BY A DREAM

Dedicated to: A near extinct species. I think, a very special person. An honest, clear-thinking mechanic. "Dieter"

My heart is filled,
with so much sorrow;
With only one man, t'would be stilled.
Vowed to another, in a near 'morrow;
And I must hurt no other, so willed.
His spirit was, "so beautiful":
And with "God's love," I saw it filled!
Enwrapped, in his love, was so joyful!
T'was a "left fielder";
Drawn from stirrings, "deep within"?
And by nature, with love, I'm a yielder:
But well I know, I can't "live," in sin.
T'would cause sep'ration, 'tween my Lord, and my God.
Can I live ever, my heart in a pen?
Can I live "err," a love "enshroud"?
Fear closed my heart, to "all" other men.
Could this be of the Devil,
when it seemed so "greatly of God"?
Dear Lord, please strengthen me more:
With "Thy love," onward to trod;
I do "humbly implore"!

Christopher Vincent Rethemeyer
PHILOSOPHY

A spot of light, to me be dear.
The given life, that which is pure,
Has been despaired from what we know,
And sees now not what we bestow.

For does't though, O'Lord, give'th us a future,
Or does't though take'th it away?

This question which we long endure,
Only through dreams can we portray.

Regina Henderson
THE MYSTERY IN YOUR EYES

To The DOCTER, who continues to inspire me

The mystery in your eyes beckons to me
What secrets lie buried there waiting to be discovered?
The sweetness of your smile reaches out to me
What words will you utter that I've wanted to hear?
The gentleness of your touch brushes my skin
What feelings will you arouse that only two can share?
The fullness of the moon looks straight into my heart
The answers are there; will we seek them?

Ray P Johnston
DREAMS CAN COME TRUE

To the one who makes me feel more alive and loving each passing moment. I love you Debra.

I love my Debra with her sparkling eyes, her smile can brighten even the darkest skies. With her love she fills my heart with joy, she makes me feel like a lovesick boy.

When we are together, I feel a deep inner glow, one that can't be dimmed by the heaviest rain or the deepest driven snow. She fills me with strength and hope of days to come, to experience her love and laughter from sun to sun.

I feel that life has blessed me with a second chance, with a gift of love and happiness and a meaningful romance. I never dreamed I could feel so complete, when I hold her in my arms, my heart shudders she's so tender, so sweet. The time we share is so precious to me, whether it be a minute, an hour, or an eternity. When we are apart, I long for the time when we are together again, her hand in mine.

I love my Debra with her sparkling eyes, her smile shames even the moon, and the stars cannot even compare to the twinkle of her eyes.

Sandra Garner
YOU'RE SO TALENTED

To my children, Stephenie and Christopher, with love and belief in you.

You're so talented with your abilities and creative imagination.
Remember we all need to have a little patience,
But not too much 'cause time's a'wastin.
Make each day count; Life is a constant celebration.

My children, I hope that you can see
How very special you are to me.
You have the power to choose and become
Any star as bright as the shining sun.

Be safe each day; to yourself and others be kind.
Treat your body with healthy respect and you will find

Make life within itself the key to your heavenly gate.

Balance laughter and patience with urgency
Communicate with the Higher Power constantly.
Seek balance in your life and you will see
Happiness is something which is simple and free.

And as you progress through life
DAY BY DAY
Keep it simple superstar, be resilient to setbacks, learn from mistakes.
Remember to act so your children will be proud of you
As I am proud of you with your SUPER SPECIAL points of view.

Michele D Adams
SPEECHLESS
You may know me,
and I may know you,
but this hallway
extends beyond our
conversation.

Lilli Lee Buck
TO JOHN BUTLER
Oh, I wish I were the driving rain
that falls upon Ireland,
That sweeps from the Atlantic in never-ending sheets,
So that I could fall upon your face
and secretly could kiss you,
So I could wrap myself around you,
and over you to weep.

Oh, I wish I were the meadowland
that lies around Wildfield,
So that I could bloom with meadow flowers to make your springtime sweet,
So that I could lie around you and sustain you and support you,
And when you trod on me I'd touch the bottoms of your feet.

Oh, I wish I were a little breeze that blows through Dublin,
So that I could follow you wherever you may go,
So that I could cool you when your brow is wet with labor,
So that I could warm you gently
when the ground is white with snow.

Oh, I wish I were a lilting song sung through the streets of Dublin,
To fall on your beloved ears some gray and dreary day,
So that I could bring you happiness,
if only for a moment,
To be a breath of loveliness to cheer you on your way.

Oh, I wish that I were somehow all the pretty maids of Ireland,
Or that all the maids of Ireland were a little part of me,
So that I could always gaze on you with love and admiration,
And no matter who embraced you,
you would still be loving me.

Keith Bias
ALL GOOD DREAMER'S DREAM

Dedicated to; a great spirit of love, John Lennon

Stop the war
Everlasting peace
It is impossible for
The killing to cease
Here on earth some
Dream of peace
Another good spirit
Shot down on the street
He was a good dreamer
Kept the love alive
With his songs of truth
No bullshit jive
The Lord said we can not
Change it
Is there no hope
To rearrange it
Stop the war
Everlasting peace
Let's all pray
The killing
Will cease

Frances Gateley
AS THE SUN DOTH RISE EARLY THIS MORNING
As the sun doth rise early this morning
And wheels roll me fast out of sight
So, I rise to a new beginning
Brought forth by endings made last night

True, fate deems closing of this chapter
Concealing some sweet memories
Sad to think of these times now passing
But, good days are in store for me
This is the great Commencement
With a worthwhile venture in view
My heart and my very best efforts
Will accompany each task that I do.

May the strength and Courage Most needed
Be with me today and beyond
That I may render unselfish service
Until my work here is done.

Mark McMullen Jr
JEWELS OF A MOUNTAIN

I dedicate this poem to my new loving family and most of all to my fiancee Charlene Crosby and to our, soon to be, new edition of the family, and to my parents for making me possible.

Tears are the precious jewels of the heart.
With these jewels you can delute the deepest pain,
Without them you can prolong the shallowest agony.
Many of these jewels are still buried deep in the hearts of the mountainous individual.
No mountain is so great that it may not be
Able to free its precious ones for all to behold there inner beauty, and still no mountain is so small that it may have no jewels to do such.

Melody M Leonard
IF I WERE A TREE
If I were a tree
I would shelter you from the rains in spring.
In summer, I would shade you from the sun to keep you cool.
In Fall, I would lay my golden leaves about you
and keep you warm.
But come Winter I could not shelter you from the cold
and you would be gone once more.
The trees are bare now,
like my life . . .
I miss you.

Kathleen Daniele
THE SECOND WEDDING
And now a wondrous tale to tell
Of lace,
And calla lilies (from heaven they fell).
Of ancient stones,
That hold happy ash traces of hundred year faces
To look upon our blissful state.

Of French pastries,
And beautiful little girls
Caught up in a lover's whirl.
Of the wedding soup and a columned cake
That helped to foster our fantasy escape.

Of veiled hats and satin ribboned bows;
"The golden ring in a chain"
Of a love that still grows.

Diane Ring-Penza
AS WE APPROACH ANOTHER YEAR

To My Son, Chris who taught me about Hugs & Love, to My Father, Floyd who taught me about Life, and to Mike, who taught me to believe in myself.

As we approach another year—
we look at the ones gone by.
There were times of much Love
and Joy—and times when our
Hearts often cried.
We look to our lives for meaning,
any sense to understand.
We hold on to our dreams, we
never let go of that hand.
There were people who meant alot
to us—and people we've grown to accept.
Our heart goes out to them all—we never know what to expect.
During my Life and the times that I've experienced with you.
Your understanding and patience has always shined through.

Gladys V Keller
CHARITY
A little act of kindness
shown can lift a lonely,
weary heart; soon then
a smile broadcasting warmth
will fill a void, will elevate
this homebound soul, partaker
of benignity, provision of
compassion's tender touch.
Once more, His Word alive,
refined, in thought and
feeling, revived, for one that
seldom steps beyond a
solitary, isolated room.

Andrew J Loiacono
DEATH: THE GIFT

Dedicated to the terminally ill, their families, and their friends.

It is vibrant
And radiates a brilliance beyond
human comprehension.
It consumes
And encompasses one in all that
is beautiful.

Its light bridges the black abyss,
And presents a glowing haze,
bright as the sun,
Which is transformed into a
ghostly Figure of white fire,
But soft, perfect, and pure.

It is total happiness
And all that is good,
And as it transcends the senses
Its touch deeply penetrates the
soul.

It comes as a surprise,
And creates a day of special
significance
Which is rarely celebrated
thereafter.
It piles in a heap, renders useless,
lays stiff
That conglomeration of
interconnected biological
mechanisms and burnt-out
circuits,
And releases that which has been
entrapped, confined, and
detained
From a destined appointment
with ultimate beauty.

Dorsie G Davis
COURAGE

In memory of my parents, Eddie Albert Davis and Mattie M. Falkenstine Davis, who trusted me to do my best and leave the rest to God!

God keep you safely
in His care,
To give you courage
strong and rare,
A courage that will
help you through
Each trying time
that comes to you!

God-given Courage
to help you find
Strength for your body,
True peace of mind!
I'm sure He'll bless
each hour through,
And He, Himself,
will walk with you!

Betsy Plowman
THE WALK
We walked the dog to the nearby creek
To give him a chance to run,
The tide was high, the air was cool,
As we watched the setting sun.
That canine leaped from rock to rock
And fetched the stick with ease,
He stood quite still when a bird flew by,
Then ran to catch the breeze.
He was happy with non-materialistic things
And content with whatever he found,
That dog observed things that we over-looked,
And noticed even the slightest sound.
It's a shame we all can't live like that
Forgetting our selfishness and greed,
Just loving life for what it is,
And finding happiness with just what we need.

Keith A Webber

Keith A Webber
SEASONS
Winter is cold and dry
And snowflakes fall from the sky.
Christmas, mittens and winter clothes
Is the winter that everyone knows.

In the spring snow melts away
Because every day is a warmer day.

Cooler clothes start to be worn,
And many animals are being born.

In the summer you can't get cool,
For the only place to go is the
swimming pool.
That time of year is usually green.
Beautiful sights are often seen.

In autumn the leaves are red, orange,
yellow and brown;
Soon they will start falling down.
The mountains are a nice place to go,
But before you know it, it will start
to snow.

George Hopper Fitch
ATHENS

Once upon a time,
For one brief Attic springtime
Men walked here like Gods.

Lois Greenawalt
I HAVEN'T GOT THE TIME—I'M BUSY

To my special friends, Mr. and Mrs. Ralph Burris

I'm not waiting for the bus,
I'll take the horse and rush.
In the middle of the stream
It started to float; I scream.
The man at the lumber yard
Was on guard.
The horse disappeared
And I feared.
When I found my way home
The horse was dead; I fled.
I'm home all alone
Munching on a ham bone.
It tastes good but no meat
I said to my feet—
"Take me to bed,"
Cancel my appointment with Fred.
I dressed and confessed—
God's way is best.
Rushing things my way
Was selfish I'd say.
Now I'll take time to pray.

Lauren Jennifer Stillman
EMBER OF HOPE

To my Dad, for all of his encouragement and support in everything I do. He is a very special man and I love him very much.

The wind violently thrashed at me
As I watched the waves of time
white cap into oblivion
A chill secretly encompassed my
body
As the scenery took me away
to a past memory.
A smile forcefully emerged on my
face
As I traveled back
to a warm,
safe place
called childhood.
It was summer
And I was at camp
The sand warmed my bottom
As a soft, cool breeze
caressed me into contentment
It was my special place
A private spot
I, alone, had discovered
And there,
in between all the trees
lay a small piece of glass
about the size of the bottom of a pop
bottle.
It became my best friend and secret
confidant
For all my inner existence was
exposed
to my small, silent, friend
All the giggling, laughter,
Boys and crushes.
All the emotions
I had somehow lost over the years
Suddenly,
I returned.
Shivering
On the cold wooden bench
Where reality slapped my face
and pulled my hair
Sorrow and loneliness
overwhelmed my icy body
As my ember of hope faded into
eternal
misery.

Patty Belston
PARODIES OF MOTHERHOOD

To Joey, John E. and Genell. My three little darlings. I love you always, Mama.

Indecision, consequences,
Seems like I've taken leave of my
senses
Heavens the noise, from a girl and
two boys
Bickering and fighting over small
toys.

A mother's will, constructed of steel
Allows loving discipline while wrath
is concealed.
Remain calm and mild, for it's only a
child
Don't break the spirit in taming the
wild.

Washing clothes, wiping a nose,
Counting out piggies that resemble
small toes.
Drying one's tears, calming one's
fears,
Never a dull moment for the
upcoming years.

All cleaned and fed, now ready for
bed
A kiss is placed atop each sleepy
head.
With thirsts appeased and every one
pleased
The trials of the day have now found
their ease.

Richard F Gery
OUR LOVE IS

To my precious wife, Darlene. Our love is—something special

Our love is overwhelming to be sure
But it is special and will endure;

Our love is not pretentious or untrue
It's honest and pure as morning dew;

Our love is based on tenderness and
caring
It is concern for each other, and
sharing;

Our love is spontaneous and filled
with emotion
It's an abundance of laughter, humor
and devotion;

Our love is straightforward, natural
and sincere
It is communication and understanding without fear;

Our love is simple, yet tasteful as
wine
It is most special because you are
mine.

Algie Smith
SHOW ME THE WAY LORD

For those that are hungry, and those that are thirsty for righteousness.

Show me the way Lord:
Show me the way,
Walking, and talking in my own way,
Help me to pray Lord,
Help me to say,
Show me the way Lord,
Show me the way.

Show me the way Lord:
Show me the way,
Teach me, and lead me, from going
astray,
Help me, and keep me, in your own
way.
Show me the way Lord,
Show me the way.

Going astray, going astray,
doing things, in my own way,
Help me, to see Lord,
Help me, to say,
Show me the way Lord,
Show me the way.

Mrs Linda Menna
GROWING UP

Dedicated with love to Miss Jennifer Menna & Miss Christine Hughes

The children so young, eyes full of
dreams, they look to the sky, the
fields, and the streams. they look to
the future, no shadows are cast, yes
they will grow older to remember
their past.
And when we have changed from
young to old, we can remember our
lives, our loves, and
our laughter.

Ron Phillips
DREAM BOAT

This poem is dedicated to and on behalf of all the love and inspiration my children Matthew, Ryan and Sarah Mawee have bestowed me.

I have oh such a sailboat in a bottle
made of glass
There could never be another with
such beauty or such class

The water it's never seen, yet many
journeys does it take
With my mind its navigator and my
dreams its flowing wake

Many journeys on my dream boat
have I had and always will
Because it substitutes the traveling
unafforded by the bill

You can travel in such class be it far
or oh so near
And the coming home's no problem,
for the simple fact we're here

Yet many people think it odd, to take
such travels through your mind
I'm sure that if you try it, not a nicer
one you'll find

So may the dream filled trips you
travel, be it by land the air, or sea
Be the finest ones of ever, that your
mind will take for thee

Ken Greek
UNDER YOUR WINGS

I dedicate this to the love of my life, Cindy Marie

Take me under your wings
To the mountains in the sky
To the pinks, the blues
The I love you's
Promise me that you can fly.
Take me under your wings
Far up in the sky
Spread your wings
Oh show me how
To soar and to fly.
I want to learn
I want to be
Someone more
Than just me
Maybe if I learned how to fly
I could be more in their eyes.
Take me far up in the sky
Where I can soar and learn to fly
Take me under your wings
Far up in the sky.

H B Reed
THE BLUE-HUED CAT

Oh! What fun it would be,
If I could only see,
A blue and yellow cat,
Who wears a purple hat.

And also said the cat,
Had seen an orange rat,
And chased a golden bean,
That is both long and lean.

You know it's such delight,
To see so great a sight,
To see that blue-hued cat,
Who wears a purple hat.

She purrs and purrs so nice,
When she sees lonesome mice,
She'll chase them round and round,
And run across the ground.

She'll run and play all day,
And chase the blues away,
'Cause she's the blue-hued cat,
Who wears a purple hat.

R M Twardowski
TROUBLED TIMES

So much happiness, turning sour
Like night and day, trying to devour
Our hopes and dreams that we once
had
Being dashed to bits, Oh how sad!

Turn it around, make it snappy
You still have time, to be happy
Make the best of it, start by praying
God works, goes without
saying . . .

Shirley L Archila
FRIENDSHIP AND WHAT IT MEANS TO ME

It's a warmth one feels,
A value which is priceless,
A closeness that is always
there
Even when you are far apart.
It's being there through thick
and thin,
Being there to share the joys
and the sorrows
And yet never judging.
As I look around to see all these
Valued friends, I feel
That somewhere in my
deepest past
I must have done something
right
For Lord only knows, I am
surrounded
By the very best.

My friends, I love you all.
I'll never take advantage of this
priceless gift
You have bestowed on me.
But should I ever become indifferent
or show a lacking,
I beg you please,
Give me one swift kick to put
me back on track.
Because you see, I'd never
intentionally hurt you in any way.
You are my blessings, gifts so
rare
That I shall treasure these
times with you
And hope you'll always be
there.
So that these moments in time
Will always be ours to share.

Scott Alan Galletto
LONELINESS

Dedicated to all the lonely people in the world.

As I sit in an empty house and
the silence overtakes me
I feel as if there is nothing,
nothing at all.
The birds, the trees, the sun, they
are all there,
But nothing, nothing at all makes
it any different.
You look at old pictures, old
photos, but memories make it
worse.
So you close your eyes and hope,
hope that feeling goes away.
That feeling of loneliness.

Fred F Fulton
SPRING

How refreshing after the winter
snows,
To find the first leaves of spring,
Or the first bud of a flower
Thrusting its rainbow colors to the
sun,
And as spring comes on in its full
magnificence,
To find carpets of flowers covering
the meadows
And vales,
And to hear and see the crystal clear
brook
Running, singing on its way as it
clears the
Winter from the land.

Cynthia G Barnes
DEAR DAD, % (IN CARE OF) GOD

I wanted to send a card to you,
Because I love you, so dear and true.
But soon became very blue,
For there are no cards for you.

When my thoughts are of long ago,
My heart becomes all aglow.
All the memories begin to flow,
Of the love that you showed.

So after much dismay,
To be with you this day.
I'll send a message when I pray,
% (In care of) God, I love you,
Happy Father's Day.

Susan Rego
BEST FRIENDS

This poem is dedicated to my Mom and Dad for your unconditional love and for truly being my "Best Friends."

I came into your lives
Some twenty-nine years ago.
And a bond was created
That would forever grow.

Through the years you've raised me
With understanding and love,
And a deep abiding faith
In our Lord above.

You've taught me to be strong
Though not necessarily tough.
Always being by my side
When times are rough.

But, the greatest gift
You've ever given me
Was in asking only that
I be all that I can be.

You're the very "Best Friends"
That I've ever had.
Though I'm prouder still
To call you Mom and Dad.

Wendi L Guttridge
I WROTE THIS POEM JUST FOR YOU.

This poem is dedicated to my sister and best friend Cheri Lavallee whom I love dearly with all my heart. Thank you Cheri for always being there for me when I really needed a friend!

I wrote this poem just for you
It tells how much I feel for you
You are my friend and very special
indeed,
You've been there for me when I
really need—
Need a friend who I really count on
To wipe away my tears,
Take away my fears,
And help me to become strong again.
Your wanting to help me
Through my roughest times,
Has helped our friendship
For future times.
Thank you again
For caring so much,
I cherish our friendship,
I love you that much!

Ethel Roxanne Foster
TO A FALLEN ANGEL

I knew you when you were cherubic
Your face so clean and round
A smile that sure was heaven sent
Skin so smooth and brown
A future bright as copper
With hopes above the clouds
A lawyer maybe, no a doctor
A face that awed the crowds
Heaven saw the angel fall
It was the saddest drop of all
A descent into the world of drugs
And love couldn't stop the fall.

Tina Shaw
SOULMATE

I am empty in my soul
Absent the mate of this lifetime
With God's help
I will finally reach my goal
With faith and patience
My Soulmate and I
Will again become spiritually whole

LeRoy Paul Garza Jr
LOST FRIEND

For the friend I have is the friend I love.
For every moment I was sad his day ended being bad. For every time I got hurt he was always there for my comfort. As a wild deer looking after her fawn my friend was there protecting me, so big and strong.

For when we were apart the day ended up being gloomy and dark. For me and my friend were like brothers and nothing could tear us apart.

Till one day so dark and grey my friend was gone. Where, I could not say. For I knew not, till the next day. For when I did see my friend he was with these two thugs. Then I knew my friend was on drugs. I never saw my friend again, but I'll never forget, how we used to borrow and lend, for he is my lost friend.

A A Le Vorse
MAN'S GREED

The worst happening ever—That took place on this earth—was the appearance of man—and his greed—the root of all evil.

The problem with geography—history—philosophy—religion—etc. Is that man created—and or wrote them.

Man is the worst fabricator on earth.
Man is his own worst enemy.
Man is destroying—that which is not his—namely earth.

The only solution to the problem—is to do away with greed—
Before—it does away with man.

The latter is precisely—what man is slowly accomplishing—his very own demise.

"So be it"

Ruth Richardson

Ruth Richardson
HOSPITAL

When I was young with a heart
akin to Nightingale, I'd walk the
corridors at Memorial to help
make sick people well.
Two sisters came to give birth to
a child; one that lived and one
that died.
On the table that day as Novelle
lay, near death's door, to God
she prayed;
"Lord, let me live that I may tell
my two that lived how to shun
hell."

She was as white as the sheet on
which she lay, and I was so
frightened, for I didn't know
how to pray,
As I tended my own dear sister,
so weak she could barely speak
in a whisper.
God heard her cry and she lives
on still; He allowed her wish to
be fulfilled.
God is so merciful He replaced her
void with two adorable
grandchildren, both of them
boys.

The other sister, Kathryn, I
remember as a bride, when I as
her bridesmaid stood at her
side.
Now as her nurse at the birth of
her child, I made a request and
who could deny?
They wheeled her in to perform
the C-section as I waited nearby
for their direction.
The sight of my beloved sister
split wide open was a frightful
sight for my eyes beholdin'.

I was captivated by the baby's
charms as the doctor lifted her
from her mother's womb and
placed her in my arms.
Swiftly I made my way to spread
the word that the bundle in my
arms was a precious baby girl.
It's a miracle Katrina survived
that day, as I scrubbed the
vernix caseosa away,
For in no incubator was she
warmed and wrapped, but right
under the nursery's faucet she
was doused!

Margaret L Hall
ON THE DEATH OF A GRANDCHILD

Not in cruelty, not in wrath
The reaper came that day,
'Twas an angel visited the green
earth
And stole the flowers away.

We stood beside thy tiny grave
And wept, our grief unbound.
Then Heaven's gates were opened
wide
To beckon thee with trumpet sound.

At last to cross the river wide
And part life's troubled shore.
Shall I thee clasp within my arms
And hold thee evermore.

And when the sunset gates unbar
Shall I see thee waiting stand,
And there against the evening star
The welcome of thy beckoning hand.

Edith M Whipkey
LOVE

Love is intangible. One cannot hold
or touch it.
Its quality lies in the way we show it.
If it be genuine and true,
Its recipient will know it.

Love grows from mutual respect,
And comes from deep within;
To those who give love generously,
It will return again.

For each kind act or loving deed,
There comes a satisfaction,
And in itself brings personal joy
That helps repeat the action.

Love knows no boundaries;
It is endless in its scope.
I'm certain it was in Pandora's Box,
And escaped along with HOPE!

Joanne Barnett
A VALENTINE FOR ALL

Love is not and cannot be
found by unfulfilled need
searching.

Love is an overflowing heart
with spaces of need fulfilling.

Janet S Middleton
BETTER 'N MONEY

To all the children in the world.

Cokie the bear
Headed straight for a chair
His nose was a twitchin'
And ear's a itchin'
Slipped on a rug
Tipping a coffee mug
Eyes still fixed

On that betwixt
Him and the pantry
Now let's see . . . . .
Up 'n at 'em
Never losing the grin
Reach high above
Who needs a glove
Paw on the rim
Dribble on the chin
Better 'n money
That jar of honey
Plump little belly
Mmmm . . . next . . . maybe jelly

Maggie L Hartzfieldt
NURSES ARE SPECIAL
You say "good morning" with a cheerful smile,
And listen to my little daily woes.
I've seen your gentle hands trim and file
The nails of a patient's fingers and toes.

I've seen the gentleness with which they rub
Paralysis that froze a woman's arm;
Hands that lead someone to shower or tub,
Or quell psychotic flare-up with harm.

I've often watched you push the wheelchair men
And women down the hall to eat or be fed
Their breakfast, lunch or dinner.
I've seen you when you helped them bathe, and finally go to bed.

You set my food before me on a tray;
Then take it away when I am done.
Bring me nourishment three times a day;
Good food that gets the nod from everyone.

You take me places where I used to go;
But cannot drive to anymore.
To heights that glisten with new fallen snow;
Or low lands where incoming breakers roar.

Lila L Wagner
BEHIND THE NAME OF PROGRESS
See all the windows lit, by city lights, city lights,
See them all ablaze, all through the night.

When you see them from afar,
They are beautiful in all their splendor.

Makes you wonder what that lifestyle holds,
All the exciting people and stories to be told.

You think, the city would be the most exciting place in the world,
All of a sudden, exciting images began to unfurl.

Tall skyscrapers reaching to touch the sky,
Look up, there's only shadows hiding the sun from your eyes.

A night time necklace of lights against black velvet,
Makes you wish you were living there with a twinge of regret.

But you forget what is only shown in the day light,
When the sun comes piercing down on the city so bright.

You have the transients walking the streets,
Looking for a job, bite to eat and a place to sleep.

You can't even trust your neighbor with the key to your car,
For we all live life behind a locked door.

This world of which we live,
certainly has become a mess,
All this hidden behind the name called progress.

Joy Hancock
LORENA'S FAITH
Lorena was a friend of mine;
A gift of God, a joy divine.

She always wore a cheery smile.
She'd always go the "extra" mile.

She'd sing in church and play at home;
And chat with shut-ins on the phone.

She'd bake and sew and volunteer
To help any or all, far or near.

She'd pray for family, friend or foe
Her love for each, she'd always show.

Her faith on one firm truth was laid;
That every day the Lord had made,

Was meant for us to know gladness in it;
Every hour and every minute.

Martha Evans
VALENTINE'S DAY
Bring into my world—devoid of fantasy—
No naked
Mystical
Flying cupids
With arrows poised
To pierce the lover's breast.

Just stark reality
Of gleaming scalpel;
Leaving bare in surgery,
The ever loving heart,
With all its wounds, for repair and rest.

Then oiled with hope, and in
The surgeon lover's hand,
With threads of love, oh mortal bind me,
Make me whole.

Mary M Stumreiter
WHEN GRANDMA COMES TO VISIT
When Grandma comes to visit
She is so much fun
She thinks of things to do
And never says "I'm not done."

When Grandma comes to visit
She is so very sweet,
And with her song and verse,
She sweeps us off our feet.

When Grandma comes to visit
She takes us on a shopping spree,
In and out and all around
We laugh and shout with glee.

When Grandma comes to visit
Mother sometimes scolds and frets,
Grandma just sighs, "No need to worry,
Enjoy life, you'll have no regrets."

Effie M Edmondson

Effie M Edmondson
NOVEMBER ON THE FARM
Quacks of geese and ducks overhead,
Crisp white frost on the meadow bed,
Ricks of wood in the old wood shed,
That's November.

A pale blue sky trimmed in white,
Brightened by myriad stars at night,
Turkeys gobbling about in fright,
That's November.

Cattle hovering a shock of hay,
A big log heap at break of day,
An old time hog killing on the way,
That's November.

Howling of coon dogs in the night,
The clear cut whistle of the Bob White,
Bright leaves falling, a lovely sight.
That's November.

Andrea Probsdorfer
FRIENDS
Together we share our lives . . .
the happiness and the pain, the hurt and the joy
. . . My Friend.
We give when not asked . . . a comforting word or simple glance—a caring touch or tender smile,
. . . My Friend.
Our thoughts encircle each other's world . . .our loves, our hates, our turmoil, our peace,
. . . My Friend.
For there are no favors between good friends . . . just constant faith and treasured thoughts—moments of truth and hours of warmth,
. . . My Friends.
Remember when—we shared a laugh—a silent tear . . . a book
. . a glass of cheer,
. . . My Friend.
Inside our hearts is a place for us
. . . as the years pass and years to come,
. . . My Friend.
Enclosed in our minds—our lasting friendship . . .yesterdays' memories . . . todays' sharing
. . . tomorrows' dreams,
Special times remain forever . . .
ours . . . My Dearest Friend.

Katrine Frances Stone
SILENCE
Somewhere from out the strange obsolescence of time,
Creeps in, half wanted, the vastness of the night;
Stranger still than all the day's obsessions,
Yet, lovelier than all the gay sun-light.
A little thing it is to sit at freedom's will
And dream into the morrow, or, perchance the week,
To feel that you alone—belong to some-one,
But, need that some-one speak?

Ena M Haletsky
ODE TO SPRING
Thou art here sweet Spring,
With all thy joys unfolding.
Flowers and buds, once more awaking,
Their beauty I am beholding.

O'er moorland, dell, and lofty fell,
Thy magic spell is lying,
In distant lands, oh, who can tell.
But someone for thee is sighing.

Oh Spring, when I roam afar with thee,
No more do I ask, these live long days,
Than sun, and flowers, and birds, and trees,
Shall join with me to sing thy praise.

William Goodwin
THE END OF THE ROAD
The end of the road is near
I see it plain thru misty tears,
No angels sing, no bells ring out
My golden years have all run out,
My loved ones and friends have phased me out.
I alone must see this out, I alone must walk this route.
The road is lonely, full of bumps,
I fall and stagger up again, no helping hand to soothe
my bumps.
Life's end is lonely and severe
Look not for help or kindness here.
You do your best and take a stand,
God is your hope, and him alone.

Samantha Keller
VIVOS ET MORTUOS (LIFE AND DEATH)
Broken fragments
of my soul
lie at my feet
Each piece its own
Each piece shining with memories of years
before the Earth
The light is too bright

I close my eyes

Colors, colors!
I see colors everywhere
Colors are spewing from my body
and dancing over my head
singing songs of blue skies
green valleys
the red-brown Earth
and the black night
My voice rises with theirs up into the clouds
and through the antique hallways and passages
of Time
I lie down
suddenly tired
A blanket of warm soft colors of down
is my cover

I open my eyes
and stare down at my soul
And I wonder if it will ever be whole again

Robert M Blair
SKY DIVER'S LAMENT
My parachute won't open,
and the ground is coming fast.
If someone doesn't help me,
this jump may well be my last.
I pray out loud, for guidance,
"What is my sin, Oh Lord?"
A gentle voice, from outer space,
"Hey stupid!, Pull the cord."

Linda J Bell
INTO OURSELVES
'We are so—into ourselves'
This crazy realm
Where nothing grows;
But the pity, we sowed,
And all we really know
Is our own sorrow.

We cannot seem to leave our cocoon
It's always too soon.
We cannot reach
So we begin to screech—
"We are afraid!"

Afraid of the pain
Afraid to wake,
For our own sakes.
'Cause of what it will take,
And the effort, we'll have to make.

So, in this day
In these words, I say—
"I've got to break away!"
This is a trap,
And all my strength, it saps . . . .

Donna J Nuss-Rick
EVENING REFLECTIONS
Bathed in silver pearls
of a moon-beam pool,
recollections of
warm sunny laughter
and a friendly star
that set easy
on the horizons of my heart
bring wonderings;
will your sun
ever rise again
on this world

Angela Hankins
SOUL OF A POET
Many thoughts, feelings, and dreams.
Does anyone understand?
The soul of a poet walks alone.
Thoughts of God's creations;
Seeing splendrous beauty in everything.
Understanding what others can't.
Is there any hope?
The soul of a poet walks alone.
Feeling things that can't be felt.
Saying things that can't be said.
Does anyone care?
Can anyone shed a tear?
The soul of a poet walks alone.
Dreaming the impossible,
Then making those dreams come true.
Running with the wind,
Flying with the birds,
Lying in the grass,
Loving the words.
The soul of a poet walks alone.

Stephanie Lasher
UNICORNS IN THE SNOW
Unicorns in the snow show their colorful manes and lovely horns of gold.
And when they walk on the paths of beauty,
they shine in the snow.
Very rarely seen, look outside and dream about unicorns in the snow.

Mary Gooslin

Mary Gooslin
MY LORD AND SAVIOR
Whenever I am lonely or lost and in despair,
I call upon my Lord and Savior and find Him always there.
My loneliness soon disappears.
My despair just fades away as He fills my heart with promise, soon will be a better day.
He walks along beside me in sunshine and in rain.
He laughs with me through happy times and takes away the pain.
When illness or some sorrow tends to tear my world apart, the love and comfort He put forth would melt a hardened heart.

When I have a heavy burden and my head is bending low, I carry it straight to my Lord and Savior. It's the only place to go.
I just know He'll never leave me. If I promise not to waiver more than a prayer away from my Lord and Savior.
Remember when you need a friend, a friend that's tried and true, you need to turn to my Lord and Savior and find His friendship beckons you.
The Lord and Savior will never let you down. For with the strength He gives you you'll step on higher ground.

Lauretta L Mayer
WHY?
I have no mate . . .
Life passed me by.
If this be fate,
Oh, tell me why!

Yet, once, love came:
A piercing dart,
An intense flame
That scarred my heart.

Penny Cheung
HAIRCUT
I sit in the chair
Listen—to the union
Of Richard's blades
Picture (slow motion)—it fall
From my head
to my shoulders
off to the hard, cold floor
With the sound of each
Drop—magnified
Sending Pain through my ears.

Eyes closed, I hear
The sweep
Of the broom
Turn—to see my black strands
Thrown into a stranger's garbage
With part of me
Hidden—in the mass
Of dead cells.

Cathy L Meyerhoff
I HAVE ALWAYS WONDERED
I have always wondered
what it would be like
to have a friend like you . . .

Someone you could confide in,
lean on their shoulder,
share moments of laughter.

Time spent being yourself
with no pretense,
just enjoying time together.

The strings attached
are only knots that bond
the friendship into a ribbon
that decorates each other's lives.

Flowing freely, entwining, shaping
an everlasting friendship.

I have always wondered
what it would be like
to have a friend like you . . .

I no longer have to wonder . . .
my friend.

Denise Schiller
MY DADDY AND MY FRIEND

In loving memory of Rich Schiller, from Ree-Ree, Dee-Dee, and Dave. We love you much, Daddy.

For the last few weeks of Daddy's life
the hospital was his home
He had to stay in a bed and couldn't
Walk or roam
The nurses helped him eat and drink
And even take his pills
I couldn't believe them when
They said your Daddy's very ill.

I didn't know what to think or
Even what to say
I just told him that I loved him
and was with him every day

I went to see him Saturday
Four days before he died
I asked him how he was feeling
He just turned his head and cried

I sat down beside him on the bed
And held his fragile hand
It seemed strange because my father
Was always a very healthy man

I said I have to go now
And gently kissed his cheek
He smiled and tried to hide the fact
that he was very weak

The next few days things were the same
Hardly anything had changed
Then one night we got a call
That was really strange

The person on the other end
Said there was nothing we could do
Your daddy is now in heaven
Looking down on you

Please don't cry now little girl
He'll never hurt again
Just remember him now and always
As your daddy and your friend

Jeanne Barbasiewicz Hoogstad
HERO'S FRIEND
The news came today . . .
it was grey.
My son's friend died today . . .
far away . . .
Far from the home he knew as a boy.
Far from the friend who brought him joy . . .
so very far away.
He died a hero, they say . . .
but I say . . .
We'll never again see him smile
come a sunny day . . .
And my son is left alone to pay
the price a hero's friend must pay.

C Russell Georgeson
PASSING
She's gone, sleep on.
All night she lay on my chest
Her breathing asking for the rest.
The small weight on my chest
Is forever the pain within my breast.
She's gone, sleep on.
In your last sleep of us three.
Regret the sleep, three remember,
Now only two remain.
She's gone, sleep on.

Suzanne A McKinney
AS TIME CHANGES
A memory, a song, a touch
A rushing backwards in time
So much——
A grasp at days gone by
A fleeting glimpse, an eneity.

Nothing stays the same
The present ever changing nears!
<u>Savor</u> the feelings—
For the time is <u>now</u>
<u>Now</u> too soon becomes a <u>memory</u>.

Betty Haines
YOU DON'T BELONG TO ME
I picked you out of nowhere, to be my very own.
We carved a world together, like statues made of stone.
We seemed so right together, we had no doubt or fear.
As time went by I told myself, that you were always here.

But there were other statues, that sang a different song.
They stepped right up and told us, that we were doing wrong.
"You don't belong together," their voices sharply cried.
It took a while for you and me, to

gather up our pride.

So now I send you back into the world in which you came,
With this all done I know my world, will never be the same.
I'll silence all my feelings, and muffle all my cries,
And finally calm those voices, that made me realize.

Reach out and grab that ladder, and climb your family tree,
Go back to those who need you.
YOU DON'T BELONG TO ME!

Jose M Mesas
LLAMA DE AMOR

This poem is dedicated to my daughters, Mary Jane Stengren, and Renee Brindisi

Mantengo en mi la llama; nada pudo borrarla,
fue como fuego eterno, que se encendió en mi cuerpo,
fue el sabor de tus labios que me robó la calma
y ahora vivo entre llamas; en fuego envuelto.

Entrástes en mi vida conel sabor de un beso
y nunca olvidaré la tarde en que nos vimos,
y llevo sobre mi ese dulce peso
de ese cariño grande que nos dimos.

Tu amor, solucionó mi vida entera,
y fue como el maná que Dios mandara,
envuelto en rosas mil de primavera.

Y ya nunca jamás borrar quisiera
los rasgos de tu cuerpo y de tu cara,
siguiendo enamorado hasta que muera.

Barbara Donovan
THE RED VELVET SPIDER

To Jon, My teacher, my advisor, my friend.

When summer sun
Turns the earth to green
Lush and luxurious
Grow the garden weeds.

Brown earth feels warm
As I pull the culprit's roots
From their safe and
Nurturing blanket.

And—among the tiny stones
The Red Velvet Spider
Dressed in the scarlet of kings
Is out for a walk in the sun.

A summer without her, incomplete
Like life without love.
She is a small pleasure
And she assures me

That many things in life change
But there will always be
Comfort in the summer sun
And the pleasures of discovering—

Anna L Darby
THE DREAMER

Sometimes I dream I'm six foot tall,
it's no fun being five foot small.
I've golden hair not mousy brown,
I'm dancing in a satin gown.
My earrings blue they match my eyes,
and I am just the perfect size.
A handsome prince on a snow white horse
comes by and sweeps me up, of course.
Our days are filled with fun and laughter
and we live happy ever after.

Sometimes I'm Casey at the bat,
we're three runs down, imagine that.
The bases loaded, it's three and two,
I know exactly what to do.
I swing the bat and hit it out,
in my dreams Casey can't strike out.

My favorite dream is one of you,
see you make all my dreams come true.
I'll cross my fingers just for luck,
if it's a dream don't wake me up.

Mrs Eva V Hill
MY WONDERFUL ONE

In loving memory of my dear MOTHER—Edith B. VanWagoner

A picture hangs on my bedroom wall,
A lady—gracious, charming, and tall.
A portrait of my mother.
She was MOTHER and DAD for forty-nine years.
In Dad's death, I saw her look at
Six tear-stained little faces;
'Twas then, I saw her tears.

They gave us the chance for Eternal Life
The day that we were born,
Guided our footsteps in the paths of right,
Protecting us from harm.
Now, I travel down life's highway
In my chariot of gold.
And stop to help the little guy,
Less fortunate and cold.

We are told that charity and love
Will help us span the highways
To our Mansions up Above.
With a special thought of you, Dear Mother
I utter a loving prayer;
That God will bless and keep you
Every day and everywhere.

Deborah Geiser
SUCCESS

He sits in his posh penthouse
on the golden rung atop the
almighty ladder, basking in
the luxury of accomplishment.
He pridefully peers out onto the
brilliance of his neon city.

A falling star tugs at his heart,
and in fleeting seconds his mind
almost grasps what his soul knows.
A sadness seizes him.

He walks down to the street,
enthralled by the dazzle of his city.
He grabs a paper, steps into his limo,
and tucks the sadness away
in a vacant part of his heart
forever.

Eleanor Hall
A HOME OF HAPPY MEMORIES

To Mom whose love prompted me, to Aunt Dey and Alice for their encouragement and my husband Bill who inspired me to remember.

I look across the field and in my mind's eye see,
What's no longer visible except in my memory;
A house that once meant home,
No matter how far or long I'd roam.
No longer does the structure stand;
Just rocks, weeds and barren land.

Like a V.C.R . on rewind, I conjure up what used to be;
Mother, Dad, brother, sister, members of my family.
I hear the ghostly voices of the past
And wonder to myself why those good times couldn't last.
But it's time to move on so I'm told,
"Get real," "Go with the flow,"
"Forget the old."

But there is nothing in my childhood or my youth that I regret,
Nothing in my recollection I want or need to forget.
But as I leave my place of heritage,
I make a silent vow for my future parentage
To make memories for my children that will last,
So in the future they can dredge from their past
What no one else but they can see,
A house, a home of happy memories.

Allen D Moseley
THE CRY OF MAN

Deep in the still silence of the soul,
There is a cry of anguish for the unfulfilled goals;
This cry is not heard by others, but is clearly seen,
The pain of the cry of unrealized dreams.
Scars left on the lives lived in this world,
Down pathways, right or wrong, good or evil, we are hurled,
To find questions, answered or not,
Of love, happiness, and friendship,
To travel with emotional baggage is our lot;
The search is forever on going, for whatever is needed
To bring peace within. To silence this sorrowful cry
That haunts to the end.

Felix Gurley
BUTTERFLY, FLOWER, AND ME

To My mother, Ruth Gurley, who was a help in time of need, an inspiration to any one who was down, and a dear friend that saw only the good in me. Thanks mother.

Be quiet and calm, oh gentle one, for I'm here all around and about you
I see you fluttering and desperately seeking for something to grasp hold of
Fearing the change and the vastness of the helplessness that comes from within
Please rest yourself in the hand that I offer for I offer this so freely
Only wanting you to understand that you're not alone and unprotected
Knowing you feel overwhelmed, misguided, and believing there's no purpose
But I'm constantly guiding you with my strong, caring hands
To the fragrance of the flowers I have for you alone so special
So rest, my child, in the knowledge that even when you are not tasting
The pleasing and fulfilling nectar nor sensing the peaceful fragrance
Of the beautiful petals of my everlasting Love
Feeling yourself only fluttering aimlessly and going in no direction it seems
I'm with you constantly and even though you do not rest in my hands
As often as I would like you to, I am still tenderly guiding you toward
The next fragrance of your hopes and dreams, realizing how fragile and
Delicate your beautiful wings are that carry you from thought to thought
So the winds you've felt all along the way, seemingly being tossed uncontrollably around
Was only the breath of my unyielding Love making sure you moved in the
Right direction to fulfill the Life I give you and to believe the wonders of your heart
But I say again if you feel helpless and it seems too long since the
Smell of certainty that all is in purpose in which you fit so perfectly
Please rest in my hand and I'll carry you with more compassion and
Gentleness than you ever imagined to your next flower
I protect you, Little one, so fragile are your wings
And I yearn for the day that you reach that certain flower
And you'll see the reflection of your gentle spirit, and be pleased.

Mark Van Fossen
LONELINESS

When in the heart,
there is an endless void,
the rivers of emotion have run dry.
When you realize that the pleasures,
which this world once had to offer,
had been temporal,
and sometimes left burdens
that were so hard to sustain.
The emptiness of depression,
left nothing but sorrow and despair,
with spacious hollowed out places in the soul.
The goals that life once had to offer,
now seem to have such little regard.
And when life is finally over,
and death abides in its place,
I wonder what was the true purpose,
of running the human race.

Joyce D Rebillard
WHY GOD?

This poem is an expression of empathy for all the families touched by the horrible fate of Pan Am's December 23, 1988 flight. Especially for the family and friends of Turhan M. Ergin.

A garden flourishes when cared for just right
With tender loving care both day and night
It needs to be fed, watered and weeded
Once the soil has been properly seeded.

Humans on earth, as God's garden seeds
Are told to love and do good deeds.
We're expected to just accept Your

word
It seems You unfairly test us, Lord.

How can You allow us to harm our brother?
I intervene when my children fight with one another.
I do so out of love, to show them what's right
Instead of turning my back and letting them fight.

My heart is so heavy, my anger so great
I can't accept the Christmas flight's fate.
Why did they die at terrorist's hand?
Please tell me Lord, I need to understand.

Why, God, when there are so many beautiful flowers
To nourish and take care of for hours and hours
Would you even consider sowing the seeds
Much less care for and nourish the terrorist weed?

Karen Saunders

THINK OF THIS

To my family

Think of the hopes that lie before you,
Not what lies behind you.
Think of the things that you have.
Not of what you don't have.
Think of today not of tomorrow.
Think of happiness, not of sorrow.
Think of love not hate.
Think of peace not of war.
But most of all think of the happiness of others and in this you'll find peace and your own happiness.
Think of this

Nancy Tokuda

IF

This poem is dedicated to my nephews, Andy, Brian, Michael & Ryan

If I could sail across the sea I'd
journey to a land where no man
has ever seen.

If I were a bird I'd soar through
the sky flying ever so high
having the time of my life.

If I were a cloud I'd be fluffy and
white sailing ever so lazily
across the blue sky.

If I were a tree I'd stand
alongside the street with the
wind rustling through my
golden leaves.

And if I were a song my lyrics
would be of love and happiness
for all the world to sing.

Marie Demers

TRUE FRIENDS

To Debra, Kathleen, Anne-Marie, and, Joseph, my precious children.

Listen, dear children, and, I'll tell you a tale,
Of a teddy bear with a puppy dog's tail!!
His ears are like a monkey's ears,
His nose like an elephant's trunk,
This teddy bear has fingernails,
and, fangs, to gnaw and chew,
He has a stripe, just like a skunk,
and, one eye is green, and, one's blue!

This teddy bear is such a sight,
that, people stop and stare, for,
along with
All deformities, he also has a flair,
For making people laugh, for
making lots of friends,
Along with being kind and true,
You see!? It all depends, on how
you look at different things,
It depends on your point of view!
For, If you're just as good a friend,
his looks won't bother you!

It would depend on how one
feels,
Deep down, inside one's heart!
In order to be a truly good friend,
Right from the very start!!

Opal Anderson Bickerstaff

Joseph A Bickerstaff

Joseph A Bickerstaff

GOD IS NEVER BEYOND OUR REACH

No one ever sought the
Father and found He was not there;
and no burden
is too heavy to be lightened
by a prayer.

No problem is too intricate
and no sorrow that we
face is too deep and
devastating to be
softened by His grace.

No trials and tribulations
are beyond what we can
bear, if we share them with our
Father as we talk to Him in prayer.

God asks for no credentials,
He accepts us with our flaws.
He is kind and understanding and
He welcomes us because we are His
erring children, and He loves us one
and all.

He freely and completely
forgives all we've
ever done, asking
only if we're ready to
follow where He leads—
content that in His
wisdom He will answer
all our needs.

George Doyle

THE FOOL

To my wife Kitty, whose love of poetry is my inspiration

A fool there was and the fool was I,
Who made a wish that he'd never die;
At the time there seemed to be no wrong
In wishing for life to go on and on.

The years went by and old age came,
I wished still harder to remain the same,
But age brought illness and ceaseless pain,
So I pondered my wish and its doubtful gain.

Then from my illness a wisdom came,
Of the blessing of death in the human game;
Each thing has its season, to come and go,
As the tide has its endless ebb and flow.

So to-day another wish I make,
I recant the first as a fool's mistake;
On the life we know we have no lease,
When my time comes let me go in peace.

Charlene D Jones

SO MANY DESIRES CONCEALED

—So many desires concealed
hauntingly inside
—Wishing and wanting, things
never do come.
—So many mountains beckoning
to be climbed
—Waiting and needing, the
strength
never seem to explore.

I am a child
Yet, I am adult.
I am young
Yet, I am old.

Between the two worlds
I am at stand still.

The desire for freedom surges
through me
Yet fear holds me in solitary
confinement.

I struggle to lift and break free
Still my will is weak.

So many desires hide deep within
Wanting adulthood . . . Yet,
confined to childhood.
I am adult
Yet, cannot fight childhood
Wanting freedom
Yet cannot fight confinement.

Dot Scroggins Robbins

JENINE

A little bit of morning
With a touch of shining dew,
A little bit of evening
When the day is thru.

A little ray of sunshine
A lot of tender care,
Just a little bit of heaven
God had that he could spare.

He could have chosen beauty
As perfect as a rose,
Oh, how the rose would envy
Her little turned up nose.

Every little rosebud
Their petals would unfurl,
If they could bring such happiness
As this tiny baby girl.

If every little violet
That grows in the woodland mist,
Could ever know the love of God
And by the morning sun be kissed.

All the dew be dried like tears
That on their petals gleam,
T'would be a sample of God's love
That came with our Jenine.

June Traynor

NOW AND THEN

A loneliness of mind transfers fear of
being one
Bullet capsules of pain inflicting
sudden numbness,
The rush of quivering bodies in the
sunny rain
And blind mice see more daylite in
their minds.

Discoveries by universal travel
grouped us
Our heartbeats slow down in
cranking veins,
Music engulfed the oxygen of breath
Foggytown London has smoked our
high.

A binding contract to survival in
vineyard jungles
Codes of dope conjure our medical
cures,
Polluted chemicals burn tobacco for
sore eyes
Cleaning our lungs by soul, oh Mary
Jane.

Cut my strings from wooden squares
My world an open prospective road,
Plants plucked by overpopulated city
streets
A dove, to fly in peace, shall leap.

Elizabeth Brown

A PICTURE VIEW

There's a picture that I see,
Of a house beyond the sea.

The house is above the land,
Standing high, above the sand.

Across the open skies
I see the sun rise.

Around the house, there's trees.
The ocean, floats with the breeze.

It's a red dawn in sight.
But it's as dark as the night.

Although you may grieve,
You have to see it to believe.

The trees and hut lives,
You'll see the peace it gives.

I wish I could go, and feel how it
feels,
to live in that picture, seems so real!

Lillian G Abrams

REALISM

Dedicated to my beloved husband Saul, who was a true realist.

There are many in this world
Who rely on constant excuses
To cover situations
Caused by their limitations.

There are others held to account
By inferiors who envy their
clout,
Though they perform exceedingly
well
Which is advantageous to all.

Mainly it is the capable

Who bear the load of those less able,
Not seeking acclaim or recognition
Only to achieve their ambition.

We should have compassion for the less witted,
But be thankful for the more gifted
Who bear the torch and are dutiful
For making life for all more fruitful.

Margaret L Peake
A BIRD OF PASSAGE
O that I were a sparrow
Wearing a golden crown
Atop my little feathered head
And coat of grey and brown.

My tiny wings would flutter
As eagerly I'd soar
Through April skies and northward,
Until I reached your door.

Though my song be simple,
The cadence sweet would fall
Laden with a boundless love,
And you would hear my call.

Somewhere in your garden
My nesting place could be,
And I would feed upon the crumbs
That you threw out for me.

O, if I were that sparrow
I still would know the pain
Of parting, for in Autumn
I must fly south again.

Judy Noah
TITLES
Why is it I must be
So much more than I am?
Why can't I just say
I am me
Without saying much more
Than I am?

Treverton E Dunn
SILENT FRIENDSHIP

To my good friend and Mentor—George K. Ross

I have a friend; on starlit night
He nothing says as stars shine bright.
A friend who by the ocean shore
Hears breakers fall and nothing more.
A friend who by the firelight's gleam
Just sits, and so we sit and dream.

On flowered floor, by mirrored pool
He'll gaze deep down within my soul.
On hilltop of a Summer's day
He'll watch the clouds, with naught to say.

But Oh, if to Life's end he stays
Before I too, complete my days,
I'll have a thrill in starlit skies;
He'll sit by me till firelight dies.
I'll hear his step on sandy shores
And up he'll smile from deep pool floors.
Then to the hilltop should I stray,
I'll talk with him—but naught will say.

Nikki Safonte
STAY
Variety of colored leaves lying on the sidewalk
Wind sweeps them away to another journey
never will they know the place of belonging
because they belong to infinity.
Always on the run, never will they find a place of their own
I sit still but have to follow your feelings
If you love me I'm yours,
when you don't I'm rejected
Time escapes through me but I'm always here.
Days elapse but I also do nothing
Instead of being a leaf on a journey, I will be one of a tree
I will be at one place, with one person and I will live my life with
them till eternity cause you would not stay forever

Diana Hunt Westa
ALONE

For my husband, Arthur

A fire is blazing bright in there,
That's my glass of sherry too
In our favorite room we loved to share—
There's everything but you.

It doesn't help how hard I try,
In my heart I've always known,
It only makes me want to cry—
I'm so terribly alone.

"You're going to miss me when I'm gone,"
You said to me one night,
I didn't think that you had known—
But oh! you were so right.

Lori A Kish
QUIETLY OUTGOING

For William D. Johnson—the love of my life. You are truly the best hon.

I have been feeling quite insecure.
Not so sure of who I am.
I get overly quiet at times,
however, when I come around
everyone knows that I am there.
Lately I have become much more aware, that I am pretty special,
so just beware.
I am more outgoing
and I know what I am doing.
It is you that I am chasing
and old memories I have been erasing.
Come with me and walk
so we can talk.
Listen to me now
and I will tell you somehow—
it is you and me
that will someday be.

Starla Shuler
MEMORIES
On a beach
The sun had set
The day was gone
This is where we met
The doves flew high across the shore
And I wanted you for evermore
The stars were shining high above
This time I knew it was really love
These memories I'll hold in my mind
These memories I'll keep 'til the end of time
The tide came, and the tide went
Like did the days of the love we spent
I can remember holding you
When the feelings we felt
Were all so true
Then there we stood at the altar that day
I hoped your love would never fade away
Now we're apart and all is gone
But my memories forever
Will linger on

Mary Alice Seiter
MY SON
You were sent to me
from heaven above,
to have, to hold
and forever love.

Your eyes are stars
picked out of the sky,
as they twinkled and glowed
from their place up high.

Your lips are rosebuds
kissed by the dew.
They speak the promise
you will always be true.

Your smile is like
a ray of sun.
It brightens the day
that has just begun.

You are just a baby
so very small
but you make me feel
like I'm ten feet tall.

Sharon Hunter
THE HORSE STANDS STILL
The horse stands still,
Like a butterfly on a windowsill
Its eyes are smooth and glossy
Like a newly polished stone.
When it runs, it is like fire,
Being blown by the wind.
And when it stops, it's
Like a bird, flying gracefully in.

Dolores J Bell
HOPE
Hope springs eternal; so they say
I wouldn't want it any other way
Hope should be there on the top
Like something I could never stop
But; my friends have left me all alone
And vultures pick my very bones
The money from my purse is gone
And I barely see the breaking dawn

With faltering footstep I do walk
There's a quiver in my voice with talk
The bird of youth has left my side
And I am on a downhill slide
But; I have something time can't take
Something only I could make
Because tomorrow, tomorrow will shine
When all the things I want, could be mine.

Jeffrey K Farrier
HAVE YOU BEEN TO THE CROSS?
Have you been to the cross? Have you knelt down to pray
For deliverance from sin's heavy load?
Have you asked the Lord Jesus to show you His way
Down the blessèd and straight, narrow road?

In Christ there's fulfillment and true peace of mind
That the things of this world cannot give;
Direction and purpose for life you will find
As within you God's Spirit shall live.

Lost sinners are headed for death and the grave,
Because sin makes the human race fall;
But God so loved man that His dear Son He gave
To offer redemption for all.

You can't earn this gift through your good works or deeds;
The only way is to believe
That Jesus Christ laid down His life for our needs,
And He conquered the foes who deceive.

Have you been to the cross where the Lamb broke the chains?
If not, friend, then why do you wait?
O make your commitment while time still remains,
For tomorrow it may be too late.

John Anthony Cacciatore
X-RAY EYES

X-RAY EYES is dedicated to those of us who know the difference between the natural and the unnatural.

I want a white shirt,
Baggy,
With buttons down the front.

Pinched at the waist,
It casts off shadows,
Into a natural splendour of
impossible angles.

I want a white shirt,
Clean,
With an upright collar hidden by hair.

Illuminating in the light,
It smells like a rose,
Picked by a girl in May.

It takes X-ray eyes
To find a real white shirt
In this world of designer clothes.

E L Peay
MY FRIEND WITHIN
I have heard it said and rightly so
This world's in such a mess you know.

For man doth strive for worldly fame.
In doing so doth feel much pain.

For the quest it seems, for modern man,
Is a struggle to get all the gold he can.

While the inner man is pressed down it seems,

And never allowed his deservant dreams.

I must awake this inner man to do his part,
First I must cleanse my soul; then my heart.

And upon the narrow path of pure intent,
I shall plant my feet and never descend.

I shall be so bold, so kind, so wise;
And remove the worldly glitter from my eyes.

And now I inwardly, clearly see
The kind of man that I shall be.

Oh my soul that leapest deep within;
Now I know thee as a wise friend.

A better world today there be,
Because I understand the inner me.

Eugene Peay
VALENTINE TO SWEETHEART

Dedicated to Laura Peay

Know this that I do love thee.
You have changed my life to what I must be.

And this eternal truth is given
That through your love so freely given
I now have a chance for eternal heaven.

You have called, cajoled and prodded me.
You've been a friend who's guided me

Along life's sometimes rocky road.
Twas not for me a heavy load,
Because you walked with me.

And never once did you complain
of the heavy work or the heavy strain.

You've done your part in every way.
You've been my friend from day to day,
Thus I give thanks to you this way.

And this eternal truth I give;
It is for you that I live.

For to get from you just a kiss
Does make my day's eternal bliss.
And bliss it shall be through eternity.

Marie T Sweeney
GOLDEN YEARS

I am a senior citizen
I am seventy three
God has been so good to me
I can walk and I can see
I have had three cancer surgeries
I still can walk and I can see
May God be at my side till Eternity

Michelle J Loftus
DREAMS

The time is here to let Jim go, I'll love him forever, though he'll never know. Goodbye, Jim Gothro.

I had a dream, of ancient shores,
of distant worlds, and forgotten lore.

Of me and you, on a far off land,
Making love, in moonlit sands.

Of a golden dove, in the autumn winds,
Of heaven's gate, and a voice within.

Of dragons' breath, and witches' spells,
Of paradise, and a mermaid's tail.

Of Unicorns, and a living light,
with a star of magic, in a tropic night.
Of clouds of mystery, raining gold,
Of a secret life that an angel told.

Of an ancient spell, that time can bend,
And a world of peace,
That never ends.

Shari L Meyer
DREAMS MUST BE KEPT . . .

Dedicated to my family, Joseph, and in loving memory of my grandfather, Nelson H. Ressler.

So much time has passed,
Yet the memories are still so
strong, so clear, so vivid.
It seems as though you're only
gone for a short while,
That any day I could take you
back and start
right where we left off—happy
and strong;
But these are actually my dreams;
and I must realize that dreams
can have as heartbreaking an
effect as people themselves.
Dreams must always be kept in
the mind of the dreamer;
And my dreams I must keep in
my mind, remembering that at
the moment I begin to believe in
my dreams rather than myself,
I am actually breaking my own
heart.

Nancy Grady Wilson
AUTUMN SPLENDOR

This poem is dedicated to my devoted parents, Henrietta and Needham Grady, who have nurtured me through many autumns and who are lovers of the seasons and the soil.

Autumn is a season of gatherings and reflections,
A time to thank God for His divine protection.
Scenes of pumpkins, Indian corn, and bales of hay
All lure us on to the splendor of an autumn day.

Like the display of a colorful quilt, the autumn leaves
Of gold, scarlet, orange, and brown drift from the trees.
They come tumbling, swirling, and dancing down,
Swiftly making a patchwork over countryside and town.

Homecomings, reunions, revivals, carnivals, and the County Fair
Help make autumn a season beyond compare.
School bells ring clearly on the frosty air,
Yes, autumn splendor is everywhere.

Gardens are waning, hesitant to die
Even though they have yielded a bountiful summer supply.
It's a time for preserving and jelly-making,
And different kinds of tantalizing baking.

Yes, it's Indian Summer days,
Early mornings are filled with haze.
The nights are crisp and clear with brilliantly twinkling stars;
One can easily view the Little Dipper and Mars.

It's a time to winterize outdoor plants
So they will be given another chance.
Squirrels are busily garnering nuts for a winter's supply;
Flowers are shedding blooms, reluctant to die.

Wildlife—deer, ducks, and pheasants abound;
They're fleeing from hunters in the woods and fields around.
Wild geese in their V-formations southward fly,
Bidding forthcoming icy winds and snow good-bye.

The days are gradually growing shorter,
In keeping with nature's plan and amazing order.
Autumn splendor is great to behold;
It is a time of mellowness etched in gold.

Elizabeth Ann Prior

Elizabeth Ann Prior
THE WONDERFUL MIRACLE

For my husband Bill and our kids Brittany, Jon and the baby to be.

We join together in perfect harmony
The moment happened finally
In time it grows to show,
And people we meet do know.
Our minds filled with emotions,
Anxieties of what lies ahead.
Tears that flow without reasons,
Growing faster with the changing seasons
Thanking god for the miracle of life
and for making us husband and wife.
The movements begin to descend
as we search for the end.
After many months our hearts delight
Pain and distress fill the night
daylight breaks we hear the cries,
A baby boy before our eyes.

Sally L Nichols
UNTITLED

her beloved marries
church bells ring—
a loud sound

Shara Lyn Geffen
NEVER GIVE UP HOPE

To my one and only, lifetime, forever man. I never knew what love was, until I fell in love with you my darling. You did for me what I thought only God could do.

Faith, hope and courage is all you need for your everyday deeds. Have faith and wait on the Lord. For the heavenly father will always be here beside us to guide us. Trust in the Lord. He helps to take away those feelings of despair and comforts us by answering our prayers. So praise the Lord. Release your feelings of shame, and glorify his name.

He is the God of all comfort, and will help us to be in perfect peace.
So never give up hope. Just the sound of the word hope, helps me to cope and let go of my feelings of helplessness. Sometimes the happiness we desire, takes a little time to acquire. Just have inspiration and desire and believe in yourself.

Never give up having courage. God's help is unending. He lends his helpful hand to every child, to each woman and man. So reach out to him for he is mighty. He brings the promise of each and every day. All you have to do is pray.

Angelia Katherine Lowrey
BROKEN DREAMS

For Maria Theresa Rust, Thanks for being a friend

Lying in a waste land,
Devoid of all life.
Smoke and clouds billow by.
Broken dreams do fly,
Hovering in the sky.
Just beyond my grasp they lay,
Beckoning me to follow their way.
I hold back my unearthly plea,
Telling them not to leave me.
I'm holding on to all that's left
In this land of desertness.
The sun shines no more;
I know not what life is for.
Dreaming about times
That are now long past.
How short they did last!
Will I ever again see a moonbeam?
Will I ever again feel the sun sing;
Feel the grass under my feet;
Feel the wind whispering sweet?
This land of broken dreams,
Here will forever lay,
Until a glint of hope
Decides to stay.

Jarret Henry Clark
POETIC

A poem dedicated to a country called South Africa and its people.

Why a poet why indeed
Man of Merit man in need
Sowing morals like orchard seed
Cultivating their country's masses in need.

History has enlightened the poet's deed
There's always a revolution for the poet's creed
The poet at work never to be seen
All his work is readily quoted but its heart rarely seen.

THE NUTCRACKER

Sindy Scarbrough
THE SUNSET

To everyone I have loved

The sun begins to fade,
And the darkness appears.
I begin to feel the wind
Whispering in my ears.

The sun is now gone,
And there's a chill in the air.
Only a glimpse of the sunset,
To show it was there.

The clouds roll in,
to show signs of rain.
Like a message from above,
Of sorrow and of pain.

I feel a raindrop
fall out of the sky.
As suddenly as the tears

fall freely from my eyes.

The sun leaves without warning,
and soon comes the rain.
The sun is my happiness,
The darkness my pain.

Cassie Roseberry Williams
GLANCING

To one of my best friends "Iva ."

How our mind reflects on yesterday!
Leading us into a great today,
In hopes of a bright tomorrow,
Learning to lend and to borrow.
Complete sacrifice, free from pain
and sorrow,
Working for a happier day,
For in due time we'll get our pay,
After a night of darkness.
With complete joy and rest,
Looking forward to what is best.
I can see the beauty of the sun,
Waiting for a day hath just begun.

Linda A Patricia Carroll
MOTHERS SAIL

Dedicated with love to my grand-mother, Elva Mae Demarest.

Mothers Sail how divine it was! Its bold crisp colours waved strikingly in the wind. From its vivid blues to its pin striped reds back to its checkered greens and plaids. It seemed pleasant to watch even on the cool brisk days. How the gust of winds prevailed; blowing ever so graciously. Its colours made it stand out. On the misty days it was evenly as pleasant to hear the flaps of wind as the gust of wind passed through. Oh, what a great day when Mom puts out her sail of red, white, and blue!

Melanie Goodwin
LOST MAGIC
Whatever happened to magic,
And the dragons that were in flight?
Did they all just disappear
Some starry autumn night?

And why have all the wee folk
Left and gone in hiding?
And the Pegasus that roamed the
Earth
Is no longer flying.

Where has all the magic and
Love and dreams gone to?
Are the only true believers
Only me and you?

Have all the mystic, magical places
Gone into the mist?
So many are non-believers,
Are they ever missed?

I wish the magic and the dreams
Would come back to me.
Then we could live happily and
Forever after be.

John A Redden III
SEASONS
On the watchtower I stand
Watching,
  Waiting,
    Hoping
That this night you will return
Bringing to me again, your warmth.

We loved and it was Spring;
The Earth was born anew to us.
In Summer the heat of passion,
Bringing forth the Earth to its ripe
age,
Was at its highest.

Then came Autumn and you left me,
Moving out on the first advancing
tide.
With you went the warmth
And the light soon followed.

Now it is Winter and the world is
old.
Cold, grey and shriveled is her skin.
You have moved beyond my sight,
But still I shall stand here
And watch; watch for your return.

Vivian Elsifor

Vivian Elsifor
SELF
My Love, how did we go astray.
It seems an age since I could say
The words my heart longs to express.
Your face, like stone, speaks of cold
distress.
My visions die, claws at my throat,
Communication dim, remote,
Along with loyalty and trust.
Abandoned, my hopes turn to dust.

Our perspectives are far apart,
Yet love, for each still in our heart.
I felt displaced more than one time.
It wounded me—a pantomime
Of misunderstanding and doubt.
What changed us so, I moan and
pout.
Where is my friend and confidante,
Ecstasy gone, lost in dismal want.

Without freedom to make my own
decision,
My crumpled self demands
validation.

Dorothy Audrey Henry
A ROSE

To Carol Jean, our Daughter, and David.

The Rose lovely from,
its garden fresh with dew.

A flower portrayed in,
earthly splendor.

'Tis a beautiful Rose that,
blends its head O'er,
the vase!

The beauty that's revealed,
in nature's hue.

Stephanie Lento
THE ROSE

In loving memory of my aunt. The most painful loss of all is when you lose a part of yourself.

The air was filled with misty
  clouds of blue when I had to say
  good-bye to you.
Memories flashed through my
  mind as I picked up the rose
  that you so graciously left
  behind.
I held the rose oh so tight, for I
  feared if I did not the rose
  might blow away out of sight.
I leaned over the casket as a tear
  ran down my cheek. The pain
  was so bad that I could feel my
  knees become weak.
I closed my eyes so I could see
  your face, and I knew you were
  someone no one could ever
  replace.
As I bent down I gently laid the
  rose on the ground. Not to
  disregard it, or to say I didn't
  care, but to say the rose was a
  symbol of the love that was
  always there.

Mary E Adams
MY SILVER HEART TREE

This poem is dedicated to my four wonderful children; Melissa, Myra, Art, and Miriam, with all my love and pride written in each stanza.

I planted a silver heart tree
To see what it would bear
And every day I watered it
With tender love and care.

To my surprise many hearts
Appeared upon that tree
It made me very happy
To pick the best for me.

So I picked four silver hearts
Selecting one at a time
I knew I had the very best
Named for the children of mine.

And if you don't believe me
Look for the silver chain
Melissa, Myra, Art, and Miriam
Engraved with loving names.

With pride I wear four silver hearts
Around my neck each day
And cherish life for each of them
"God bless my child," I pray.

Allison Scoco
THE NIGHTINGALE

In loving memory of Leslie W. Emary

Can you hear the nightingale
The song so sad and sweet
Singing for a love that's lost
A dream that's incomplete

A song of sorrow in the night
Is lifted by the breeze
It carries across the stillness
And echoes thru the trees

She waits to hear her lover's call
She sings out with a cry
She waits and waits all thru the night
And still there's no reply

The little nightingale so sad
Prays for light of dawn
For only when the sun comes up
Can she cease her mournful song

Mamie Stanley Smith
I WONDER IF MAMA IS PICKING ROSES

Dedicated to the memory of my dear mother, Sophrona Ann Reed Stanley.

Oh I wonder if Mama is picking roses
in God's beautiful garden up there,
I wonder if she is reading her Bible
and rocking in a gold rocking chair,
I wonder if Papa is sitting beside her
breathing an evening prayer
Asking God to watch over us
children and keep us in His care.

I wonder if Grandma is playing her
violin and Grandpa his fiddle up
there,
I wonder if my Brothers and Sisters
are sitting on the floor and
Clapping their hands like they used to
do back home,
Oh I wonder if Mama is picking roses
and
Placing them around the white
throne.

My mama, she loved her flowers, the
rosebud her favorite one,
She always strolled through her
garden when her evening tasks were
done,
It seems I can see her standing, with a
rosebud in her hair,
Oh I wonder if my Mama is picking
roses in God's beautiful garden up
there.

Oh I wonder if Mama is picking
roses, red roses,
White roses, pink roses, yellow roses,
Like the ones she grew back home,
Oh I wonder if Mama is picking roses
And placing them around the white
throne.

Kathryn M Ellison
MY LOVE

To: J. Norman and Elizabeth

If thou cannot kiss my lips
Then kiss me with thine eyes—
If thou cannot hold me in thine arms
Then gently touch my hand
And I will understand.
If thou must leave me, go—
For I will know that thy returning
Will be sweeter still
Than strawberries wild upon the hill.
If thou must weep, then cry—
And in thy weeping feel thy sorrow
die!
If thou must sleep, then lay thy
weary head with labor spent
Upon my breast, and if thou
dreaming,
dream of me—then I shall be content.

Sheree Sands
YOU'RE NEVER ALONE

Dedicated to: Kenneth D. Hall, with all my love forever!

I know how much it means,
  to have a special friend!
When all those feelings,
  never seem to end.
When all the world is dark,
  and everything is cold!
With every night you cry!
  to have someone to hold!
I'm the one who truly cares,
  the one that gives her soul!
Although,
  there's hurt and pain.
Never be afraid,
  thinking you're on your own.
I'm still within range!
Remember,
  you're never alone! ! !

Fran Abouhalkah
LOVE IS NOT TOUGH?!

This poem is dedicated to the man who painfully inspired it. My husband—Montajab S. Abouhalkah

Remember how one used to dream
When young and selfish sweet
sixteen?
Life was there for you to take
All goals and dreams you would
forsake.

Now you're older—more mature
Only to find life's not secure.
Shattered dreams—broken hearts
All because of selfish wants.

The man you've loved—committed
to

Now decides that he is through.
Ten years of vows no longer count
He wants no more; He just wants out!

Whose master plan is all of this
That selfishness can have its way
Where love is lost to childish wants
And lifelong vows are not enough?

God never said Love is not tough?!

Donna Valentino
YOU ARE A SOLDIER

A bullet whizzes and your friend is shot
But cry you must not,
You're a man, or so they say
Only nineteen and this is the price you pay.

Too young to vote, too old to cry
So slowly you watch your friend die,
Thinking back on all the fun you had
Looking at his face, with expression so sad.

Yet as you're kneeling, the bullets never cease
You wonder if there will ever be peace,
When nations unite into one
When there is no need to lift a gun.

Suddenly, your friend no more does breathe,
You are a soldier, you cannot grieve,
You are a soldier, you need a friend no more,
You are a soldier as long as there is war.

Renee C Howell
THE PAST

This poem is dedicated to my sister Nikki Kissell, for your strength & courage, "I Love You."

There she is all full of glitter and cheer,
The one that was there for all those years.
For the walls were thin and no secrets kept,
and even through that she never wept.
She would just smile and say,
"She'll get her day, when her world will fall apart."
The pain she has brought will go away but never be forgot.

So I write this now, for this was years ago,
when we wished for better, but no one could know.

You were there for me when I cried in the night,
and prayed for God to help us through the struggling fight.
That's all past now, and I remember your pride,
you were strong for all of us and stood by our side.

You've been my sister, my friend, honest and true. So this poem of gratitude I write for you.

Kim Lian Ponchik
I'LL ALWAYS BE HERE

In Memory of David

Those words have come to haunt me
'Cause I knew you were the one;
And the irony had left me
When you left me all alone.

Such senseless pride has taken 'way
The great love we could have known;
My heart shall seek no other
Now that you are gone.

Our parting was so final
That I still do weep for days;
It's too painful to recall
Your soft and gentle ways.

My life is now so empty
That I cry myself to sleep;
As I yearn to share the memories
That my heart can't solely keep.

Your loved ones grieve much deeper
Though I'm longing for you still;
I pray, someday, our souls shall meet
If it be God's will.

Husein Taherbhai
22ND ST. AGONY

To all those people in the Tampa Projects who try so hard.

Silent echoes
Reverberating.
The pounding
My head succumbs to.

Emptiness,
Crushing my life.
Claustrophobic
I flee and leave behind
Myself.

Smothered
In drug-laden smoke,
I lie pregnant,
Unable to grasp
The Eternal Life.

Fate extends
A lifeless hand.
I reach in frustration;
A bottle,
A drink,
A sleepless stupor.

Enveloped in folds of darkness,
I call for America,
"Hold me in your bosom,
My country———
I am
YOUR American, too!"

Alyssa Griggs
THE WISH BECAME THE PROMISE

To Kevin and Briann Norton on their wedding day with love and good fortune

Few things in life are solo
For the earth is built in pairs
All of which combine together
To build the world we share

The rivers blend with the oceans
And the oceans with the sand
The sand turns into soil
And this the ground we stand

The heavens adorn our mountains
With its winds that cool our days
And the sun that shines above us
Gives us light by which we gaze

Then by dark the stars will sparkle
And share the sky with the moon
At night to which we embark
Our dreams to come true soon

Many dreams I wished upon a star
That a beauty would appear
To fill my heart full of love
And with me share each day, month, and year

But within my frame, my soul grew hollow
For it quickened and lingered for love
Until the day you appeared before me
As if a gift from above

The search for you was trying
But now I hold you near
For the days I lived before you
Seem empty now you are here

And many miles down the road
Into your eyes I will stare
To remind me of the love we had
And the love we will forever share

Few things in life live solo
For the earth is built in pair
All of which combine together
To build the world we share

We live in a world of couples
Of sets of two combined
And these are happy creatures
One another they must find

For we are of the earth we live
And need a partner to share
Through our love we will wed
And loneliness again, we will never fear
And loneliness again, we will never fear.

Betty Homan Hunsucker
THE FATHER I COUNT ON

This poem is dedicated to Irene, my wonderful mother.

Oh Lord, you are always there
No matter when or where

You have been a father, protector and friend

All through my life you are there, everywhere, to lead me by the hand

When I'm alone, scared and lonely
I know Lord, I need to turn to you only

Though there is not a soul in sight
Even through the loneliness of night

You are there, everywhere, just waiting for my prayer

Through all my sorrows and pain
You are there, everywhere

For strength, hope and love
A Father Lord who is always there.

Helen M Stahl
MY MESSAGE OF LOVE

This poem is dedicated to Glenn, my beloved husband

Oh my darling it's been so long
Since I have been with you
Where I belong.
Such a long, long time
Since I've felt your body
Close to mine.

Just a simple thing like touching you
Made me feel content, how much
I never knew.
Your laughter and humor I loved so well
Were such a joy to me, yes
More than words can tell.

But now my thoughts are just fantasies,
And listening to the wind whispering softly
To the trees,
I wonder if you might hear it too—
The message I would send,
My message of love to you.

AcquaFredda
NOT YOU

To you. Inspired by the melody of Mr. Sedaka

Don't like your life perfectedly.
How we love our lives, that luxury.
Most of us looked up to you.
Look up to us, why who?—How true
Evaluate yourself! That's right
Though we all look up to you
He measures us that same way too.
Way back when our works were right.
Others try, we've won our fight.
Though we all look up, do you?
Some still say it's the thing to do.
Those vivid days we lived them right
Why do we have to lose our fight?
Should we still look up, to who?
Think of what's been done, us too.
Changing wrongs how hard, how true
Will it end when those righteous never bend?
Who said our right and wrongs were tough—we knew.
Who reached to us all in our end—we knew.
But has he given up on you?
Not you?

Patsy Corsentino
HAWAII

Dedicated to my children, Josephine and Glenn Jr., always remember I love you, your Mother

I have gazed upon your vast blue sky,
And watched your clouds go sailing by.

Marveled at your lush green hills,
And dreamt about your valleys still.

Your sandy shores I have walked along,
And tried to ponder my thoughts upon.

Your cool breath of air I have inhaled,
For you have brought new life so rare,
Hawaii, how long have you called.

Edward D Allen
MOTHER'S MEDAL

With love and deep gratitude to my beloved mother, M. Alice Hoagland.

I left her standing by the plane,
Smiling through her tears of pain.
My collar showed the trace,
Of tears from that beloved face.
I wondered then why she should fret,
For wasn't I prepared to fight
For victory-freedom-peace & love
Practiced by my God above?

For days I thought of her standing there
Her smiling face, her graying hair,
Til God helped me realize
The mystery of those tearful eyes.

Dear mother, yours is the hardest fight.

For yours is misery of sleepless nights
And dragging days in a house alone
Watching for mail and a silent phone.

And when peace at last reigns over the world
You'll stand at the station, your flag unfurled,
To receive the medal you have won—
The loving smile of your homecoming son.

Donna R S Womack

Donna R S Womack
BABY ANGEL

She was an angel a real beauty,
Asleep in her crib,
Then later a real cutie,
With candy on her bib,
She was quick learning to walk,
And with a little help,
She learned to talk,
Taking her first step,
She had an angel's smile,
With curly hair,
Happy and smiling all the while,
She had so much love to share,
She reached out with open arms,
Wanting true love,
And loving charms,
That only comes from above,
Soon she was grown,
And gone from home,
With an angel of her own.

She-Leiyas J Wytch
THE CHILD WITHIN

To Peaches—My own little girl within who has taught me to listen.

Taste the sun.

Go ahead!
Reach for its beauty.
Don't be afraid!
Trust its warmth even when it's 40 below outside.
So deceptive!
So radiant!
So calm!
So passionate!
So like a lemon flavored lollipop!
The sun—enjoy its ardent nature.
Feel for its ability to take you to higher grounds,
And trust that through the black and dreary clouds,
The sun smiles behind the darkness like a lemon flavored lollipop.
Dimples darn the cheeks,
As excitement gleams in a child's eyes,
At the sight of a lollipop.
Just as my own child within gleams with joy,
At the sight of the bright,
Lemon sun after the ebony clouds of my tears.
This—my lemon flavored lollipop . . .

Colleen Lewandowski
FRIENDSHIP IVY

To my best friend (Gloria Polster King). A beautiful person who I love and miss very much, you will always be in my heart forever.

On my birthday you gave me an ivy,
it stood for our friendship
with growth of never ending.

I put it in a wicker basket,
and placed it on my desk to sit.

It grew so fast and green from the office light,
telling me our friendship was just right.

When I moved, I brought it with me,
and hung it on the plant pole
so everyone could see.

Then one by one the leaves turned brown,
falling onto the carpet, down,
down, down . . .

I didn't know what was happening,
too much sun or not enough
watering.

Then we found out that you were very ill,
the ivy was telling me you
weren't well.

Sure enough, who would have thought,
to listen to an ivy you had bought.

Now since you're gone, I can't believe,
our friendship ivy
is growing many a leaf.

Shelby Valencia
ONE

To the ONES I love . . . This is one expression of the joy you have all given me.

I want to fuse
Make two into one;
To feel the warmth
Of your innermost sun.
Come caress my lips
So gentle and right;
To sweep us away
Long into the night.
To feel the heat
Of your body with mine;
I long to be with you
To embrace, intertwine.
Our eyes become fixed
On each other's souls;
And we both wonder
What our future holds.
But the risk is worth taking
As you slip your hand in mine;
And we walk off together
Our future to find.

Teresa D Nolen
THE ORANGE

To Mother and my goddaughter, April Denise Hartman

Peel Orange Peel
Spritz your scent
Pulp your heart
Seeds your rent
Sit bright, new
and bold
In halves, in slices
Your juice chilly and
cold
Gone is your heart and
Seeds lay waste
But aroma fills
the room
with bittersweet taste.

John Laurie Smardon
WOMAN'S DAY!

To all women everywhere who do their best every day

Yes, every day is Woman's Day now,
All over the world they're asking how,
Women's Lib has come about,
Haven't you heard that ear-splitting shout.

Women world-wide have risen up,
Showing men what it's all about,
Some have taken to 'wearing the pants,'
The male animal takes a second glance.

In almost every field of endeavor,
Females show up noticeably wherever
There's a job to be done promptly and well,
Move over men, aren't they swell.

Written by a male poet, without 'tongue in cheek,'
These lines of verse make me feel weak,
I've got to think about what I've written,
Have I become excessively smitten.

No, I won't change even a line or two,
Revise my thoughts to puzzle you,
Just reassure all that Woman's Day,
Is here to-day in every way!

Michael James Andrejko
FEAR OF LOVE

To those whose dreams seem to come and go. But, when you hold on tight to them, they seem to remain forever!

Warmness usually dwells in the house of love.
But when I enter,
Warmness nor love is there.
I fear all night that if I'm alone,
Hate might destroy the inner self-respect of my soul.

Why do I stand alone with fear on my side?
Why do I wait for fear to destroy me?

As I sit with tears in my eyes—oh!
How I despise the love I have for this girl, only if she can understand and come to love me then she would know, oh!
She would know how I love her.

There's a knock on the door, could it be her?
What shall I do?
What shall I say?

As I open the door . . . . . .
I am destroyed indefinitely by fear!

Ellouise Hensley
MY DAUGHTER

To my daughter Brigid

Oh my daughter so loving and beautiful,
Always bright and dutiful.
My life, my joy, my delight,
Of you I think each and every night.
What pride I feel every time you are in my sight.
The face, the eyes, the hair,
Of which no one can compare.
You are my Saturday child,
For whom no one sighed,
But gleamed with pride at your sight.
My life, my joy, my delight.

C M Smith
BORN OF DARKNESS

For Alan Bloom, psychotherapist and friend

A sparrow swings chirping upside down on a twig of the leafing willow.
Sprinkles of new leaves keep nodding at their squirming twins in the water.
Jonquils—bits of concentrated sunlight—lift toy trumpets
In a fanfare sweeter than any heard music, welcoming-in the spring.

The world has become a little child again, with eager feet and eyes.
It will not leave me at peace in my comfortable gloom & my old slippers.
It tugs at my legs, draws me out with it into its own light, teases me
Till I smile (and at the same time blink back not unwilling tears).

What does it care that I'm old? Has it not youth enough for both, & to spare?
Does it not clearly see that what I was, before "shades of the prison-house"
Closed in, still lives, where wardens cannot probe? Does it not prove instantly with the sun's caress, warm as when I was young, that it loves me still?

And mark, mark what a seal it sets on my life's testament , for the whole yard glows with a light born of darkness—the forsythias, in full bloom.

Vicki L Wilson
MY LOVE FOR YOU IS NEVER ENDING

For James Anthony McCauley, Who Showed Me What Love and Happiness Was For The First Time

My Love For You Is Never Ending,
You Stole My Heart The Day We Met,
The Love We Share When We're Together,
Makes It Impossible To Forget.

My Love For You Is Never Ending,
You Brighten Up My Everyday,
The Skies Are Blue, The Sun Shines Brightly,
I'll Never Let You Get Away

My Love For You Is Never Ending,
All The Joy that's In My Heart

I Know Our Love Will Last Forever,
And that We'll Never Drift Apart.

My Love For You Is Never Ending,
Say You'll Never Make Me Blue
Promise Me You'll Love Me Always,
For I'm Worth Nothing Without You.

My Love For You Is Never Ending,
Do You Feel The Same Way Too?
Honey, You're My Precious Angel,
These Are The Reasons I Love You

Ruth Conklin Watson
LIMBO

To my late father, Clyde Romaine Conklin. You taught me sincerity.

Voices, conversing in false conversation,
their masks lit up like neon lights.
Clothes, jewelry—all in motion,
draped on sterile bodies
pretending life.
Gaping holes with teeth, where
warm smiles are out of vogue.
Eyes, unknowingly empty,
searching everywhere for themselves.
Plastic faces on plastic people,
living in a plastic world.

Pearl Blackburn

Pearl Blackburn
A LIFE TO LIVE
Each of us is given a life to live.
How long our time is not ours to give.
What we do with our life that we share,
is best given to others with loving care.
A way to be remembered is being a person
of compassion,
not striving for wealth, power or the latest fashion.
The gift of friendship or a word of praise truly spoken,
is proof that your life on earth was more than token.
So when your time is over and the end draws near,
you will welcome your new life to come without fear.

Peggy Kociscin
RENEWED

Dedicated to: John Patrick. Given by God as a delightful blessing: 7/21/67. Returned home to his peace: 11/11/87

Rainbow days with smiles and hope
And laughter in my heart;
I love them, but they seem to be
So few, so far apart.

More often sadness claims my heart
And tears are hard to hide;
Grayness hides the rainbows
Where joy and hope abide.

Memories, deeply treasured,
With very few regrets;
A special son, a life too short,
Too dear to once forget.

Oh, God, this aching emptiness
Makes smiles seem all in vain;
With part of me no longer here,
Will I ever laugh again?

Yes, smiles and laughter will return,
The sun will shine anew,
And warm me with the smiles and laughter
John shares now with You.

Han Thai
THE COMING OF THE HOLY CHILD

This poem is mainly composed of Christmas carols and hymns. Many thanks to all the authors of these Christmas carols and hymns.

On a Silent Night!
Oh! Little Town Of Bethlehem,
Came the Angels From The Realms,
Bringing the Joy To The World.
We Three Kings Of Orient Are
Bearing gifts we traveled so far,
Gold, myrrh, and frankincense,
To welcome Mary's Little Boy.
The Herald Angels Sing
O Come, O come Emmanuel
O Come, All Ye Faithful
O come, let us adore You.
Hallelujah! Hallelujah!
Angels We Have Heard On High
Good Christian Men, Rejoice
On a Silent Night!

Dorothy Davis
THE KING LIVES ON

To Lisa Marie Presley Whose love for her Dad is timeless . . .

On August the 16th
The year '77
Death claimed
A great singer
So pure his voice
How Great Thou Art
The song he sang
So long ago.

Funeral service
Was overwhelming
Families and friends
From nationwide
Paid their respects
To ELVIS, the King
At Graceland Mansion
So long ago.

Eleven long years
It's now '88
His Memories live on
Through Eternity
Is the King alive?

H M Walker
THE CLOUDS

To Marguerite, with love

Fluffy, potato-like clouds
Oversaw us as we drifted
Down the river, fifty years ago,
With all hope in them, all
Possible, all within reach.

We looked at them and at
The water below, and it
Formed a symmetry that made
You want to cry; it lived.
Nothing died; you it denied.

When I feel old, I image
Those clouds, that sky,
That river, and the burden
Is almost gone but what
I need, of fifty summers, is gone too.

They can't seem to come together,
Those clouds, those trees, that
Sky, that river that was ours,
But will never be again; the
Whole is lost, but what is not?

Samantha J Jones
IN OUR MIND

To everyone of my family and friends: Thanks for your belief and support in my dreams.

Lashing waves of pain
night filled screams that drive you insane
out of the darkness reach hands of the night
creatures unknown to the sun's deadly light
the living is no longer safe among the dead
where demons roam and upon souls they are fed
living the life as a sinner at the end of a bottomless well
what is known to mere mortals as a place called Hell.

Stephen R Gorton
BLOSSOMING

For Lori—Age 13

A petal
unfolds
in the morning light

Drenched
in the freshness
of morning dew

Kissed
by a sunrise
burning bright

Your beauty
is just beginning,
too.

Ruby Hyatt
MIKE'S CHRISTMAS PRAYER
It happened christmas morning only last year
a time to remember but, not to cheer
driving in fog and rain
the morning we hit the parked train
Mom and Pop thought we were drunk
but, they would never believe
I swerved to miss a little skunk
Mike's feet were aching and his head was numb
Matt's shoulder was broken
and he felt like a crumb
Matt said, Mike go get help.
surely, you can walk down the block.
little did he realize Mike was in a state of shock.
Then Aunt Jean drove by
and offered to help out
She started preaching about drinking
and began to shout.
Finally E.M.S. came
and took me from Aunt Jean's wrath
Lord in case of another accident
Please don't let me run across her path.

Betsy Brooks
HER TRANQUIL SMILE

To my husband, Ralph & to my three children, Chris, Scott and Tammy

Her tranquil smile was sparkling
As to that of a refreshing rain.
But sadness began to enclose about her suddenly
With a depth of gloom.
With bitterness within, how could she hold back
Those forlorn tears of resentment
Which she sought to escape?
The cold, silent look on her lover's face
Is that of deceit.
Her mind fumbles in confusion.
How could he betray her with all the treasured love
She had to bestow?
The tears began to ripple down her soft cheeks
With a splash of anxiety.
A madness stirs within her.
A heavily laden heart, encumbered with despair,
Sought revenge.

Betsy Brooks
YESTERDAY'S MEMORIES

To my sisters, Patsy & Joanne

Yesterday's memories seem to fade away
With each passing day as in a dream.
Looking through amber glass in the midst of a haze
Can only portray life with all its uncertain ways.
Time is of the essence,
Of life and its mere presence.
So, let the shadows of the night fall;
Along with yesterday's memories.
The future belongs to tomorrow
And tomorrow is yesterday's dreams.
So, how can I behold life
As reluctant as it seems?
Life is but the mere twinkling of an eye;
Aglow, slowing, shimmering into the darkness of reality.

Melinda Delgado
WHEN I THINK OF YOU

This poem is dedicated to my sweet sister Barbara and David . .

When I think of you
I think of the times that were true
All the celebrations we've shared
Seems like now there's nothing there
But wishing you could still be here
Would make my life much more fair
Wishing and having are two different things
For I now know that I can have you in my world
So I wait for my death
So that we could be together forever
In your world!

Dolores Mc Namara
IF WE ONLY HAD TIME

This poem is dedicated to Bob Mc Namara and Barbara Baran, my inspiration and strength.

If we only had time, tomorrow would bring,
All the hopes in our hearts, like a fresh breath of spring.
Our days would be filled with the brilliance of light,
We would cherish each moment till dawn turned to night.

If we only had time, for the children we love,
To tell them we need them more than heaven above,
Then guide and prepare them for what life has in store,
And protect them from evil, forever more.

If we only had time to say our good-byes,
To be truthful and honest, when they look in our eyes,
Then wipe the slate clean, erasing the past,
Living each day, as though it were the last.

If we only had time, we would never cause pain,
Our thoughts wouldn't wander to profit and gain,
We would strive to be kinder, helping those in real need
And all that would matter, is to do a good deed.

Our time here is measured by the blink of an eye,
Our life is what we make it, till the day we die,
To waste just a moment is a terrible crime,
Don't live life saying "IF I ONLY HAD TIME"!

Mario R Massaro
UPON TAINTED WINGS

To All Broken Hearts: Whose fears reflect injustice, when we love beneath sweet scented sheets or star-lit sky? It is the loving heart, which makes us fools and, thus, too blind to see conscious mind craves the joy our sadness brings during love's charade.

A fledgling leaves its past, in a bold attempt to fly. Complacency impounds the helpless, weary sort.
Hasten those feathers! Sharpen your sight. Come away, from that compelling need to measure depth, length, and width.
Hope finds stone-cold hearts. Fundamental rules protect this babe's tainted wings.
But, who seeks not . . . a lover's warmth?
Search—you must—for nesting place . . . during pride's incessant trial. Strong fears grow closer, with determined flutter.
Soft Down appreciates true comfort. Molten smiles are waiting . . . to save dear, tender thing: sing freedom's song!
Stagnant flight prospers—by lawful reason—to breed great pleasures between city's asphalt and hard cement.
Always forward. Never . . . back. Giant triumphs, you have dreamed. Though, the same old wind reshapes our deserts' sands . . .

Peter Papandrew
WINTER NIGHTS

To Marie. How I love thee.

Sitting here by my window watching the snow come down. Thinking of times past and times to come.
The feel of winter is in my bones. The joy it brings to everyone's homes. Those lights so bright and candles at night. There's love in the air. This feeling is everywhere.
Tonight I sit alone thinking of you, hoping somehow to be close to you. Thinking of our future, knowing it's true. In time I'll be spending more winter nights with you.
In time we will be "one" and having so much fun. Laughing and loving for more winters to come. That "joy" will be ours to do with as we please. Those nights with the candles that nobody sees.

Alfred Leon Wallace
LOVE IS PURE BALONEY

Don't talk of love to me,
Of foolish things to be,
For love is pure baloney,
That died inside of me.

It died when first you lied,
About your love for me,
Your guilt was hard to hide,
Upon your face to see.

Don't talk of love to me,
Of foolish things to be,
For love is pure baloney,
That died inside of me.

It died when first you left me,
To live with someone new,
Who called you Johnnie Honeybee,
And gulped your mountain dew.

Don't talk of love to me,
Of foolish things to be,
For love is pure baloney,
That died inside of me.

It died when first you loved her,
And sent me on my way,
To raise your son and daughter,
With not a dime of pay.

Geneva Stephenson
GOD BLESS OUR PRESIDENT

This old year of eighty-eight is almost gone at last. And the year of eighty-nine is moving in fast.
God bless this America in which we all stand.

And God bless our President
Whoever it may be. If it's Bush or Dukakis, I hope we'll all be pleased.
'Cause they're the one we have to look to for peace in this land.
So God bless this America and our President.

Dianne Knoll
THE CIVIL WAR SOLDIER

The fields are silent as the soldier stands
With his gun aimed in his hands
Ready to kill
His enemies who are just over the hill.

Now as the enemy approaches
To meet his foes
He then finds out
What this war is really about.

It is not just killing a human being
But also his best friend
Someone he grew up with
That he must face again.

In the eyes of his best friend
He remembers once again
Of how life used to be
"Just him and me."

And as he turns his eyes away
He is going to shoot anyway
But not his best friend
As he finds for him, it is the end.

Shannon Mackovitch
IT'S OVER

Once you held me in your arms,
I never thought I'd be harmed.
You held me much too tight,
that is why we had those fights.
My life has been all rearranged,
everything about me has changed.
This love in my heart won't turn to hate,
even though we can't relate.
At one time I wanted to be your wife,
now all I want is to go on with my life.
I hope you realize that this is the end,
just remember me as a good friend.
Maybe you can at last,
forget about our past.

Tammy Picard
HOSPITALS

Hospitals can make you feel very sad.
Hospitals can make you feel very blue.
It's the place to be when you are feeling bad.
It's the place to be when you have more than the Flu.

Hospitals can be a very happy place.
A mother holding her newborn, with a smile on her face.
Good news from a series of tests.
The doctor saying, "All you need is rest."

The nurse is always dressed in style.
The nurse will have a friendly smile.
Usually, just before she gives you a shot!
Which will lead you to believe that shot will be mild.
But the style and smiles help not!

Whether you are admitted for something serious or not,
You will always have waiting a fresh clean cot.
Your room will always be neat and clean.
And there is even a place to hang up your favorite jean.

When your stay there is at day's end,
The doctor and nurses will say,
That they will miss you, pray,
And hope for your sake, they don't see you again!

Lisa Mac Donald
A SPECIAL WINTER'S NIGHT

To my family and friends, who encouraged me to submit this poem. To Mr. N. Davis, who gave me support. Thank you to all.

I let the snow sift slowly through my fingers
And stand and watch the cold dusk of the night
The soft scent of the crisp air lightly lingers
The crest of moon comes slowly into sight

I hear the cries of wild beasts
And wonder where they are
I look around and nothing's there
I know they can't be far

Just then I hear the whispers
Of trees swaying in the breeze
And singing sweet soft lullabies
But soon the lyrics freeze

Frost begins to settle
In snowy covers deep
And I must hurry home now
And let the forest sleep.

E Ken Ogbu
PARADOXES OF NATURE

This poem is dedicated to my lovely wife Suzanne.

It seems that "as above, so below"
Yet above is above
And below is below

It seems that a positive is positive
Only because there is a negative
And opposites manifest each other

It seems that the sacred is secular
And the secular is sacred
Yet they mark opposite ends of a spectrum

It seems that without the dark
There would be no light
And life equivocates with ironies

It seems that chance is choice
As accident is design
And omission is commission

It seems that the end is the beginning
As giving is receiving
And dying is living.

It seems that Shakespeare was right when he said
"Fair is foul
And Foul is fair . . ."

Floel LeFever
LONELY NIGHT

The Night is so long and lonely.
Oh! What am I to do?
My heart is so full of sorrow.
I need help from You.

God teach me to be patient
What ever problems lie ahead.
When I start to worry,
Give me peace of mind instead.

When the tears keep on falling,
Upon my face.
God will lend a hand
And put a smile in their place.

I can feel His presence.
As I never felt before.
He took away the sorrow and darkness
Then brought the sunrise to my door.

Lois E Williams
ON THE FARM

The zinnias looked like jewels.
The spinach was rich and green.
The beans were purple, and green, and gold
the nicest ever seen.

The pears were very mellow.
The gooseberries were tart.
The sweet boughs needed cinnamon
to help them get their start.

The blackberries were purple,
they grew in many places.
The wintergreen berries were small and red,
among the Queen Anne's laces.

Patsy Taylor Calderwood
NIGH

There was a sweet but sorrowful cry
in the song of a nightingale
And the rain whispered of memories
almost lost in the hail.

But the slightest glimpse of an amber,
once a great vibrant flame,
kindled ever so compassionately

in the blanket of a haze.

Can the prick of a thorn be polished
by the song of a nightingale
or instead secure a secret
of an aria which never will prevail.

Perhaps a glimmer is only a
reflection
of something misunderstood
And the song of the nightingale
just an echo in the wood.

Mary G Kensel

Mary G Kensel
MOTHER NATURE
"In all forms"—trees budding—
Flowers blossoming—
Birds singing their songs—
The squirrels nibbling acorns—
Loveliness of greens
Heavenly blue above

Amber Nitschke
VIVID

For the world and Everyone who believed—Everything counts.

The colours shine brightly
And like the dream
Stick and torture my mind
It could be a scream
Or the echo of a whisper
But the sound is crisp and clear
I see the metal turning over in air
Light reflecting off the edges
Like sunshine in your eyes
In the shadows there's a rustle
There's a hint of someone there
I know I've left you behind
But your memory will always be
there
Shining brightly.
And just as i remember things as
they were
All my memories come back to me
and
The same as everything else here in
my life
They are beautiful, bright and vivid.

Ella G Cooper
THE DEER
Some misty morning when the fog
lies on the fields
When the sun is pale above you and
the air is clean and still
In the quiet you may see them as
they walk with regal flair
One of nature's lovely creatures, the
American white-tailed deer.

Some bright spring morning when
the land is warm and green
If you're walking down by the river
a buck just may be seen
Like a wooded sentry on patrol he
protects his lady fair
He's the guardian over his kingdom,
and it's an antlered crown he wears.

Some morning if you're lucky and
it's the right time and place
You might see the fawns and their
mothers with their dainty style and
grace.
As they leap and bound across the
land where they've long been such a
part
Those beautiful, gentle creatures
their spirit sings to your heart.

Stefanie Rose Kalkstein
A FLIRTATION IN TIME
Time teasingly presents a
companion:
Clutching a Times, an attaché, and
Wearing the alarming, charming
smile
I've kissed before, before, and
before.
His suit still a tapestry of unicorns.
His song still a Yaqui chant of
magic.
His eyes still a window to the soul.

See: Our laughter rumbles like
thunder
Dancing on Albuquerque's
mountains;
Touch: Our skins tingle so achingly
Alive—we want to touch forever.
But time cackles like an audience
Of those Macbethian witches and
Offers us a kettle of Celtic soup.

We set an elegant table:
Pewter candle-sticks, Irish linen,
French wine, English china, crystal
glass.
After several sips, we smack our lips
With perfect culinary pleasures.
After several more, we once again,
Discover the cruelly cosmic joke.

Shawn J Wells
DISTANT LOVE
When I dream, I dream only of
you.
My thoughts of everyday are
filled only with you.
My love for you is all consuming.
But, my love for you can never
be.

For you, like all things in the
subconscious, are untouchable
by any mortal male.
You are as a queen, and I, a
simple knave compared to you
can never hope to do more than
worship you from afar.

Cynthia Nazworthy
REGAINING THE LIGHT

The poem is "dedicated"—to the "lost," "lonely," and "the frustrated"—(There is "someone" who cares!)

"There once was a man who was
"blind" in sight, but was also
blind from the "light!"
"He lived each day in "bitter
disgust," cussing, and cursing,
and raising a fuss!
"For in his heart he knew not of
love, and blamed the whole
world, and took everything of!
"But—make no mistakes, this man
had a soul, it was just so deeply
buried under "murky ole ghoul!"
"For it was his hopes, his dreams,
his reality—his understanding,
his compassion, and his loyalty!
It was the key that opened "all
doors," it made living a life,
worth living for!"
"We know of this light, this
"mighty white light," it keeps us
in line, and do what is right!"
"It is our whole reason for living,
and living for . . . but never,
never, should we shut the door!"
"For when the door is shut, and
"the light" fades away, we are
lost to the "shadows," and then
led astray!"
"Bless this poor man who was
blind in sight, let him regain his
"sight in the light!"
"Then he will see a whole
different sight—the life lived
with the "Almighty" is the only
way right!"

Beverly Ann Biermann
THE AWAKENING

This one is for you Joan.

In the distance
Light shimmered
Reflecting
A wolf, head upturned,
Howling.

On the lake
Water glimmered,
Gently waving,
Silent.

Color streaked
Brilliantly
Crossing the horizon,
Beautiful, alive,
Sleeping.

Patiently waiting
For that special hour,
Partner approaches
To awaken
The night.

Maribeth Morley
GRANDPA

Dedicated to my Grandpa, Arthur R. Olson. I will never forget you or all your stories.

You were young during a time of
horse drawn wagons,
homesteads, and firm handshakes.
Enduring seasons of hardship as
you shaped the soil with your
hands.

Generations have listened to your
stories of humor and heartache
about a time of harnesses,
tending herds and high spirited
horses
and hardly half enough to eat or
wear.

Now the time has come to rest
and there is a special serenity
on this December day
as your heritage walks hand-in-
hand in procession—
not in silence but in
conversation.
This is a time for sharing the
stories and the history
in our heads and hearts.

A special time, as unsaddled
horses run to the fence
to watch a solitary horse drawn
wagon pass.

Kathi Howard
TO ERR IS HUMAN
Of all the errors conceived by man
There's one we must not make.
That error being, tritely known
By all as, a MISTAKE.

To make mistakes has long been
thought
To mean that you would fail.
Not true! You grow with each
mistake,
When used to your avail.
Mistakes are part of life, you see;
A part that is essential,
If ever we are to achieve
Our goal of full potential.

To laugh at our mistakes is hard;
That art comes late in life.
Once learned, however, we will find
More days devoid of strife.

We must accept that we will err,
And face this fact with truth,
So we can pass this knowledge down
To unsuspecting youth.

C J Balog
LIGHT THE TORCH
Carry on—light the torch we ALL
feel—
One by one, through love's flame,
you'll reveal
Each must share what they dare—
from the heart
For each flicker adds fuel to the start

Help the FIRE OF LOVE to address-
Through its flame—which devours
hopelessness—
What our universe seeks to redress in
its weak
By achieving for ALL—peacefulness

Clyde K Hyder
ON WANTING THE MOON: A CAVEAT AGAINST THE DANGER OF HYBRIS (1969)
(A picture by William Blake, dated 1793, shows a human figure with a foot on a ladder leading to the moon, the caption being, "I want! I want!")

Man wants the moon? Now he has
got it,
While skies are lowering with
fearful overcast,
We've sent a bullet to the sky and
shot it:
Man has the moon at last,

A desert waste of lifeless matter,
Unlike the mystic orb our fancy
haunts;
And so the teeming earth we're free
to spatter
With blood and brains for other
futile wants.

Robert Harris
OF WAR

To my departed wife, Selda, whose patience and love rivaled the earth at its widest girth.

There's no need for hate.
Propaganda has already
Double-dipped portions
Of monstrosities.
Smidgens of which,
Bear enough truth

To be credible to the gullible.

War creates strange bed-fellows,
Rivals become heroes
And friends, enemies.
Manipulated by those
Who consider war a business,
Designed to bring quick wealth
To its perpetrators

What if it did cost a few thousand lives?
We still have ours, haven't we?
Why should one feel badly
About people we don't even know?
Ships that pass in the night—
Cookies crumble in unexpected patterns.

Foreign cemeteries for our war dead—
Beautifully tended.
Wood crosses not daring to slouch.
Across the road near Verdun
Abandoned trenches from World War One.
Not far away—from World War Two
Spanking new cemeteries
For Christians and Jews.

Time the healer
Given some years,
Succeeded in wiping out
Any need for tears.
Most who shed them are long gone.
A new generation has no reason
To cry over old spilled blood.

Not to say there's an end to tears
Flowing from new wars and fears,
There is no end to sources of sorrow
Tears that will be shed tomorrow
When lightning strikes—
Without design or reason.

Florence G Axton
INTONEMENT
Since the world began, in every nation.
We have had and heard a pattern of intonation.
An African drum, a chant, a humdrum.
A flute a fife a substance of life.
A dance representing joy, and strife.
The symphony, the philharmonic,
Broadway musicals,
Chamber music, opera. A lawyer attends, relaxes, solves his case.
A memory, no one can erase, music is good for the soul.
Church choirs, gospel songs, elation of God.
Listen, the next time you hear a tone,
Then you will know what that tone meant just for you.

Priscilla Brown
WELCOME TO CALIFORNIA
As the sun's radiant heat sinks deep into your skin
The sun worshippers are all so tan and slim
Waiting for dusk to see the sun so big and yellow
Lazily on their way home feeling happy and mellow

Bright and dazzling lights can be seen everywhere
While movie stars hide behind dark glasses and pink hair
Ronny now has a fancy office in Century City
Give him a jungle even though he is awfully busy

Orel and the boys in blue, along with Magic and Gretsky
Watch and cheer for them each time on the telly

Join the fun at the Magic Kingdom with Minnie and Mickey
Later laugh at the wacky antics of Lucy and Ricky

Off to Olivera Street to sample their wares
Then to La Brea Tar Pits to see the fossils still living there
Wait for the start of the rattle of the big earthquake
Usually around midnight when no one is awake

Go to Frisco to see the cable cars and ole Chinatown
But no matter where you frolic to you will surely have fun.

Dorothy K Wheeler
ETERNITY

To my beloved husband of 37 years

How different we are,
You serene a laughing child of March,
Springtime green, Scottish heart
An Emerald's strength;

And I am August's child
Maid of many moods
Tempestuous heart, harvest's fruit
A garnet's hope;

As different as we are
Spring and fall
When weighed upon nature's scale
We balance;

Alike yet apart,
Distinct yet separate;

Held together,
Where wedding wings intertwine;

We share this place together
A place shared as one,
A place called eternity;

Deborah Nebel
AS I WALKED ALONE ALONG THE BEACH
As I walked alone along the beach,
Seeing couples everywhere.
I remembered another time.
You and I walked hand in hand in the shining moonlight.
The breeze blowing playfully through our hair.
You chased me.
We fell to the ground laughing.
It was just you and me.
Our eyes met,
We communicated our love.
I then woke up to realize it was a dream.
We have now since parted,
But our memories will live on.

Ruth D Spencer
WINDS
'Tis true the wind is scary
When it comes in like a train.
It flattens earth's possessions
With sheets of driving rain.

It howls and fiercely sabers
Little villages in half,
Leaves people injured, homeless, dying,
In its aftermath.

But as a whole, we love the wind
When it whistles in the night.
There's something so mysterious
In a sound without a sight.

The South wind comes to kiss us,
Spreading balm upon each face.
We stand in awe of breezes
As the sun and wind embrace.

The West wind sternly, dutifully prunes
The bad limbs from the good,
And teaches flowers and grasses
To stand up like they should.

The North wind comes to sweep the sky
For the moon to give her light
To all the people, great and small,
And to lovers in the night.

The East wind is so sly and quiet,
Spreading snow drifts in the night,
That her work we aren't aware of
Until the morning light.

Our Lord said that His spirit
Would be just like the wind.
Our eyes could not behold it,
But could feel His touch within.

Millie Ann Cook

Millie Ann Cook
LITTLE CHILDREN
Little children are a precious gift. A baby smile, play and laughter. Little toys scattered about that bring joy and gay laughter. Little children are always curious to explore to learn. They are always watching with questions in their minds.
So they ask a question and you give a lecture.
But their curiosity continues and children surprise you sometimes by what is said.
Little children are a precious gift.
With candy wrappers and cookie crumbs scattered here and there. With candy on their favorite shirt, because they have just cleaned their hands the way a child does.
You look and you laugh and remember that you were once little and you cleaned your hands the way a child does.
Toys scatter all over the floor and the children will find a way to be a mechanic for a day to learn how the toys are made.
Little children curious to learn and to a child it is fun. It takes a lot of patience, care and love for a little child.
Every little child should feel love and laughter, whenever they have tears and fears each and every day.
Little children are a precious gift so treat each one with love and laughter and you will always feel in your heart that little children are a precious gift from God

Nancy Goodman
A DOG'S LIFE
He plays in the sunshine;
He sits in the shade;
He naps on my lounge chair;
Buddy's got it made.

He thinks he is master;
He knows he is king;
He gets what he wants;
He's got everything.

He knows how to "fetch";
He knows how to "heel";
He does so on command;
Oh, he knows the deal.

He gets one treat a day;
Now that I can afford;
For where else can you find all that love and joy;
For such a small reward!

Diane Meade-Dickinson
A PRAYER OF A CHILD
God bless mommy . . God bless daddy . . God bless Virginia . . God bless Theresa . . God bless Juliana . . . and God bless Artie.

As long as I can remember these are the words that run freely through my mind as I am about to end each day. There are no words special enough to explain the close feelings I have for each of you.
These feelings are locked in my heart hoping to escape at intervals steady and often enough to let each and every one of you know how much I love you. We have quite a family story which will never be told, too painful maybe to ever reveal what a challenge we faced. Who is to say why our luck was misplaced in earlier years . . .
But to look at our lives now as blessed, not scarred.
Each of us have grown together through our pain (Have become better people because of it)
Mom, you used to tell me that very phrase over and over again, but until now, I never really understood it.
There is nothing in this world that we cannot endure, we have the strength of a king.
That king is the one, you, (mommy & daddy) have taught me to pray to.
Our Lord Our God,
Amen

Violet Moser Veach
BABY
A baby we are expecting after all these empty years.
Years of longing and of sadness, of yearning and of fears.
That our lives together would unblessed by the clatter of little feet.

We watch from the sideline as our friends' prides and joys
Change from the greatest of all blessings into growing girls and boys.

Yes, a baby now God will grant us to fill our lives with joy.
And if it's a girl, we will cherish her, though first we want a boy.
But, no matter what its gender, we will place it on a throne,
To rule as our little King or Queen, in this house we call home.

Norman M Alcott
THE CHEAT RIVER—RAFT #48

To C.H.K.—a friend

Six of us ran The Cheat today.
I also ran it by myself.
And it was exhilarating to feel the fear again.

But, it was also confusing.
What can anything else mean

when that beautiful river is
trying to crush you and make
you part of itself?

You must love the
fury and challenge
of The Cheat, and ask
Where have you been all of my life?

All of this shit about money,
position,
"love me" and life is meaningless
when The Cheat is singing a love
song
that you really want to hear:
"Come, join me, and we will run
forever."

No thanks! You say
as you wonder what the hell you
are doing there in the first place.
I've run too far already—and
you're never going to stop.

But, I'll be back someday
and you can tell me once again
about the freedom
that I never knew existed.

Patricia J Jackson
WINTER STORM
I stand in the ice storms where
heavy ice tries to break my
boughs.
I stand in the wind where
the cold wind twists and bow
my head but I stand through
it all.
In the spring it rains and I
cry so no one would see but
I am me and I have to stand tall.

The short summer comes and
I am warm and in the fall
I am my prettiest and admired
and loved by all.
Then along comes the cold winter
again to try to break and
twist and bow my head.
Maybe with the help of
God I'll be strong and
stand in his forest once again.

Edgar J Willmott
THE PHONE CALL (I LOVE YOU BOTH)
Hello! Hello! Is this 432836?
May I speak to my Dad and Ma?
I hope you hear me clearly
'Cause I'm calling from afar,
I'm sad and lonely
Please let me talk to them,
In life they were always there to aid
me
'Til to heaven they did ascend.

Hello! Hello! Please tell me
Are they coming to the phone?
I want to tell them
How much I loved and miss them
Now that they're in their heavenly
home.
Thank them again for loving me
Showing how much they cared,
Their love and their memory
In my heart will always be there.

Oh! They can't come to the phone
right now?
Then give this message to the both of
them,
They just had a phone call, from
their loving son.

Diane Cole Scott
BECAUSE I LOVE YOU
Because I love you
I'll give you all I have
Because I love you
I'll see your face in every
sun-kissed daisy along life's way
I'll hear your gentle voice on
every evening's whispered
breeze
Because I love you
I will with all my heart try you to
please
Because I love you
I will not hold you to some long
forgotten promise of yesteryear
Because I love you
I will stand beside you now——
and years to come when your
beauty is no more and time
steals your very breath . . .
Then let me lie beside also
in death———
Because I love you

Leanne J Perrin
TWO WORLDS
What am I to do?

to——rn
between two worlds, one of adults:
understanding, deep, knowledgeable,
intellectual,
ultimately great
good friends, great times
on a higher level; remember and
grow with them.

Or———

a carefree, wild, crazy
life, with friends: caring,
through a sort of one-on-one
friendship
at the time.
spontaneity that is soul boosting
one night ruining what could've been
a mutually respectful friendship,
instead grief and heartache; never
forget.

The choice is not easily made.

I lie awake at night
drifting off into a troubled sleep
got to be alone, think things through
clear my mind, concentrate
count on yourself, don't use people,
but
watch out for number one
don't forget that.

Got to make a choice!

Diana K Wilson
POETRY CONTEST
A poem I am supposed to write
About love, laughter and life.
I think and I think some more,
Creating quite a brain storm.
I'm sure I'd do better flying a kite!

In my bed I think of what might
Make someone who reads it delight
In happier moments than woe;
A hope is beginning to grow
But words still won't come to light.

Where are the words that I need?
Why can't my mind take heed?
I only keep hoping
I can stop this groping,
Then my thoughts may take seed.

As my body seeks a rest,
I'm still trying my best
To think of the rhyming words
That like sweet singing birds
Will allow me to pass this test.

Kathryn Stone
OLD MAN
There—
At the top of the hill, he stands.
A small, lone man, old with times
Fast moving years,
Keeping a silent vigil with the
Setting sun, or perhaps the wide
Expanse of sea.
Could it be some dormant urge
To scan again the pencil line
At the far horizon edge?
Faint haze of smoke lifts lazily
About a weathered pipe, gnarled
fingers
Curl tight about the moldy stem
As if for comfort.
He is not a friendly man, quietly
shy—
Barely speaks.
Still each day as the sun tips the edge
Of night
Tired feet climb the hill, worn and
stooped
Against the twilight of the day, an
old man
Keeps a rendezvous with the sea.

Debbie Leyser
TOUCH THEM WITH LOVE
My mind and body are forever young
and I'm always on the go . . .
Running here, biking there, and
walking, but never slow.
That I may never take for granted,
my youthfulness, I pray.
How grateful I am that I can move
and see and hear each day.
When I look around and see the
tender hearts of gold,
Trapped in ancient bodies that don't
work and are growing old,
And the windows of their eyes are
almost going blind . . .
Their ears are not much better,
playing games within the mind.
Arms and legs that used to move and
carry them like the wind,
Now are weights of lead, hardly able
to bend.
Their memories of yesterdays; their
wisdom from passing years,
Fills their hearts of gold with love
and takes away their fears.
You and I, the young and youth
should reach out and be their eyes.
And we should be their listening ears
to all, for they are wise.
Let's be their arms and legs and
carry them through today . . .
To smile a ray of sunshine and hope,
and touch them with love, I pray.

Phyllis Franklin
WHENCE COMES INSPIRATION
Do I write because I'm melancholy,
or am I gifted?
Do I struggle and aspire with the
gloom,
or when it's lifted?
In the challenge of the search to form
ideas
from the words, there's life!
(although it takes its toll from time
Especially if you make it rhyme.)

Thus do I give or do I take?
Dear hours wasted.
Discovering the race to death
Life only tasted.

Oh, if of life I have but one
The risk is great to contemplate—
Discovery is bitter-sweet
I die with life still incomplete.

Raman Jalota
THE BIRTH
The explosions shattered the walls
around him
and he was pushed and hurled
through space.
Being human he cried out,
and when the pain further increased;
he screamed and passed out.

They cut off his life line
and set him free.
He was tossed from person to person
and all he could do to protest
was to rub his eyes and cry.

Gone was the dark, secure, secret
and familiar domain
All he could see was light
that blinded him.
So, he shut his eyes and shut his
brains
and hoped it would go away.

And when the morning came and he
looked around;
it was dark, secure and secret;
but the familiarity of life was gone.
It was a new feeling; a strangeness;
this metamorphosis
from life to death.

Margaret Willis
BLESSINGS
Blessings, blessings, everywhere,
Lord let me stop, and find me a
chair.
Lord let me listen, and to heed,
Then I can begin to plant a seed.
There is so much goodness in this
world,
It really makes my head just swirl.
We really need to get close to one
another,
Then we could be better sisters and
brothers.
Why can't we, find good cheer?
Because we know it comes from far
and near.
Lord, let us spread love all around,
Because everyone has some to be
found.
Lord let us look into your Book,
Then we would know just what it
took.
To find our way, each and every day,
The way we should act in every way.

Joyce Giblin
A COP'S LIFE
It isn't easy to be a cop, you know?
You're bruised, abused and slandered
by foes.
Your duties are hardened by those
who want law
But they look for loopholes if you
enforce the law.
Hours of devotion to people in need
Bring very little thanksgivings when
you answer their plea.
Contempt, disrespect on the stand
you receive,
While giving more hours to serve in
deed.
If you're a cop, you know this is true
But remember, God blesses the
peacemakers—that's you.

Delpha Funk Romeiser
THOUGHTS
When writing spirit tugs my heart
Thoughts are bursting to be
heard;

Pulse of writing cannot withstand
These must be kept and
nurtured.

Every task will go forsaken
Lest the new thought go astray;
Thoughts like time are only present
Never more will pass this way.

Often time they come at mid-night
When I need that blissful rest;
That's a lot befalls a writer
Puts him through the crucial
test.

Travis O'Neal
WHAT IS CHRISTMAS

When the presents are laying
Under the tree so forlorn,
I always thank God
That my Christ was born.

We know that he sees and
Understands all things,
We're reminded of him
With each bell that rings.

It's Christmas time
And things should be bright,
And they will if we remember
To hold to him tight.

Now that Christmas is over
And the lights are all gone,
Let's make a New Year's resolution
To leave Christ turned on.

Philo Glenn Wooddell
BUT ......

The discord of the early light that
begins to open our world—

— slowly envelopes
everything—gently
turning the cold side to
the warmth of others.

— and repetition does not
ease this resolute
sadness.

The yellow-white of the day gives a
levity to the pitched, uneven thoughts
of the dark—

— where eyes and dreams
can rest and truths can
be learned—but not
believed.

At this confluence stands the
answer to the question:

BUT ......

Sister Grace Diethorn
PRECIOUS ONE

To the Precious One, Sister M. Bertin Paulus, OSF, A Sister of St. Francis of Millvale, PA

How I wish I had known you then!
Marvelous mind,
Winning ways,
Teacher of youth,
Angel of Mercy.

How I love you as I know you now!
A lovely lady of eighty . . .
Wholly dependent,
Charming everyone,
Reaching out to love
and to be loved.

Powerful example to me
Victim of Alzheimer's
disease.

Nancy L McKeighen
THE TREE

To women who took emotional abuse in a relationship, because it was expected of them.

I was once like a tall oak tree,
Fine and beautiful, full of beauty,
Then a lumberjack came one
day . . .

He stripped the tree of all its beautiful
bark,
Then just walked away, never
meaning to return,
The tree stood naked through the
seasons and cried . . .

When the tree was nearly dead from
no attention,
The lumberjack amazed himself and
returned,
He nurtured the tree, loved it and
said he was sorry.

The tree still feels the pain of his
stripping,
But with time, love and patience
from him,
Like all things of nature the leaves
will return.

A thin bark shell shall start to
reappear,
And cover the barren naked tree,
With tender loving care, his tree will
return.

And once again the lumberjack will
smile,
He'll look out on his land and not
mind . . .
Seeing his tree seasonally drop a few
leaves.

This time he'll rake up her excess
leaves,
And not mind taking care of her and
her needs,
Only mother nature knows if she'll
grow again . . .

Marsha Jean MacDonald
MISSING YOU

This poem is dedicated to Kathmandu and the children of Nepal. One child of every five dies in the first few weeks of life, and 35 out of 100 die between one and four years of age. The average life expectancy in Nepal is 46-48 years.

Your smiles, the touch of your
hands,
Sweet hellos,
Spices and smells of your cooking,
Flowers you sell.
The clear blue skies above your
house,
Cows wandering the alleys in front,
and in back
Goats, pigs, chickens, dogs, ducks
and rooftop monkeys.
Your vigilant faith,
Wide-eyed fascination of me.
Incense smoldering in slow blue
curls,
Black billows of rickety autorick-
shaw exhaust,
Near misses, blaring horns, weaving
traffic.
Well formed cow dung paddies, each
bearing
Single hand-print inscriptions,
Impeccably folded laundry washed
in the river where
The cattle bathe, your people bathe.
A thousand tiny fires for heat at
night,
For burning refuse,
Fires for the dead.
Rain muddied streets,
Raggedy children, runny nosed,
unwittingly pose
In windows, on doorsteps for
National Geographic.
Missing you,
The fresh innocence of your
unspoiled children,
All of life being lived along the river,
along the streets,
In doorways.
Some day I hope I may return home
to you again.

Charméne Kelley Groce
EULOGY FOR BIG FOOT

There was a fine feline, Big Foot was
his name.
He came in November, scenting
turkey for game.
His gray and white markings, his cute
pink nose,
Always, clean and purfect (perfect),
as sitting to pose.
His paws were the uniquest quality
to see,
For he had six toes on each of his big
feet.

He became a member of our family
quite fast.
And of course we were all happy at
last.
For he was the most purfect (perfect)
species to see,
And he was loved and gave love to
all and to me.
His qualities and features stood out
like his feet.
Of living, roaming and smelling
flowers so sweet.
He was the mellowest feline of them
all,
That is why his memory will be so
large and so tall.
We love you our Big Foot, we love
you so much.
For your memory and love, that you
gave to us,
Will live in everyone, that you had
touched.
So, please rest in peace and God
bless you, Big Feet.

Jackie Castor
REST IN PEACE

The groans of humanity vibrate
Echoing waves of unheard sounds
Penetrating the octaves of time and
Shattering the structure of space
An infant cries out
And a mother weeps
Daddy is gone
but nobody cares.
Birds fall to the floor
Fish stiff on the shore
Pollution is fed to the air
but nobody cares.
Money is spent to
Strengthen our arms
While the hands of the
homeless
Hang empty and loose
but nobody cares.
Balance of power and
All gaudy greed are
The bombs that blow away
Most of our needs
but nobody cares.
Institutions they grab
While the edifice stands as
A bright shining light
Blinding the poor the old and
sick
but nobody cares.
A beacon to safety
Hardly is seen and
The protesters' plea is
Drowned in the sea
but nobody cares.
Don't stir my emotions while
I stay fast asleep
Leave it to someone
Other than me
but nobody cares.
There's no concern because
Peace is at hand
Everyone knows that
Peace is at hand
but nobody cares that
that peace is
death

Jane Mellott
THE BEAST WITHIN

Sometimes in my mind I see
A tormented, pain-crazed me,
Who stabs repeatedly with knife,
To try to end that loathsome life
Gnawing at my innards . . .

But it's not me I try to kill,
Just the beast who feasts there still,
Devouring with demonic glee,
Until there's but a shell of me,
Devoid of any soul . . .

And the part of me that's love
Despises what he's capable of,
Takes a knife to end his reign
Of gorging gluttony and pain,
And stabs and stabs and stabs . .

Deborah Wilson
THE CROSSING GUARD

He came early,
On weekday mornings,
To see the school crossing guard.
Their friendship,
Evolving beyond,
The embarrassed greeting,
To warm smiles
And friendly laughter.

I watched this social happening,
As two strangers became,
Two public friends, lovers?

The crossing guard would
Tilt her head
And laugh gaily,
As he impressed and dazzled her with
Male pride.

One morning he came,
Not alone,
(Another woman close by)
Was he testing her?

I never saw the crossing guard
again . . .

Carolyn R Ray
A ROSE

The winds of change are blowing,
Blowing beyond human control.
The light gets stronger,
The darkness gets stronger,
'Til the ultimate victory will preside.
A solitary rose grows upon a hill,
Wrapped in nature's everlasting
embrace,
Yet soon the sun is hidden,
And darkness prevails over the earth.
The rose wilts and dies.
Beauty dies.
Terrible images destroy dreams,
But Angel wings beat victory to

come.
The sun reappears and shines—
The darkness forever is gone,
And once again,
A rose blooms upon a hill.

Joan M Larson

Joan M Larson
DEAR HEART

Dear Heart,
I know not much of anything.
But you, you know a lot.
You Dear Heart are what leads me, at times I feel your hurt, at times I feel your cheer, at times I feel your love, but never once have I felt your love, and not felt the hurt too.
If just once I ask of you, to please have pity on me. Would you Dear Heart, just for once, love without the pain.

Solomon Jones
I'M SO GLAD

I'm so glad,
To have peace within myself,
Every time I was in distress,
He never refused me his help.

I'm so Glad,
He recognizes me,
As one of his children,
And fills my heart with glee.

I'm so glad,
He taught me how to pray,
And this I always do,
Each and every day.

I'm so glad,
To see his footsteps beside me,
Then I'll always know,
My mind can rest completely.

Margaret Moen
TO MY DAUGHTER

You lost a tiny baby a few weeks ago
Your heart is broken, you are sorrowful and sad
because you will never get to see it grow
Sometimes you are nervous, sometimes you are mad.
But remember when Jesus comes you will be glad
He will lay in your arms a tiny one, all perfect in every way
There will be no more sadness only gladness.
It will look at you and it will coo.
It will fill your heart with love,
and just think you will get to raise him up above.
It will take its first steps in streets of gold.
It will learn to talk with the prophets of old.
It will never fall down and hurt its knee.
It will always be happy and full of glee.
And Jesus our Savior will say "come unto me"
And he will fly as fast as can be, and sit upon our Savior's knee
You will never have to rock a cradle all night
It will not be sick, It will never be crippled.
And it will always be bright.
And it will fill your days with delight.
It will never get too hot.
It will never be hungry or cold.
And it will never grow old.
It will never cry
And best of all it will never again die.
You never again will have a broken heart.
And you and it will never part.

Cheri M Tate
CHAMPIONS

To the 1988, Class A, 11-man, Colorado State Football Champions. Congratulations Walsh Eagles!

You've had an extra four weeks
Of practice and strain.
But the feelings you've experienced,
Have far surpassed the pain.
The joy, the pride,
The happiness you've had,
Has now shown the world
Your winning is not a fad!
Your coaches always tell you
Remember where you're from,
With Discipline, Determination, and Teamwork
Our day will come.
You've mastered your discipline,
You've always had the determination,
And the teamwork built friendships.
Just remember,
It takes talent and skill,
Not luck to win championships!

Val Gene Tait
THE OLD ROCK CHURCH

To the people of Mt. Carmel, Utah.

The Old Rock Church that still stands in Mt. Carmel was built sixty-one years ago.
It was built by the people who cared and shared and donated to make it so.
Bishop Sorenson and his two councilors—better men never lived, I know—
They were the kind who looked ahead to see the community grow.
A man by the name of Andersen was the one who laid the stone.
Every man and his sons turned out until the building was done.
My father and two brothers hauled rock and mixed mortar too;
Helped feed the Andersen family of which there were quite a few.
I remember the celebrations held there on the Fourth of July,
When a little boy sang "Yankee Doodle"—that little boy was I;
And the horse races that were run on our street both long and wide,
With cottonwoods lining both sides of the street for the sun to hide.
I remember the scales in front of the Church, tho they stood out in the street,
Where sheep and cattle were weighed in the fall and trailed away on their feet,
To some distant railhead—Cedar City or Marysvale.
New trucks and trailers do the job—there is no need of the rail.
The Old Rock Church as it stands today many fond memories holds.
As I sit here and write this little poem, we all hate to see it sold,
Just to become a machinery lot to clutter up the town.
It could be made a place of beauty for everyone around.
The Church should give it back to the people as a museum, park or such.
Maybe it would liven up the town and the people who love it so much.

Robert Madden
VISIONS OF YOU

To a warm, kind and caring person whom I'll always love, A true inspiration to me and my poems: Renee Curtis, I LOVE YOU!

Lying alone, dreaming of you,
I stare at the sky, an endless blue
The sky is blue, yet the cold is still here
Waiting and hoping to have you near
Not a day passes by, I don't think of you
Always and forever our love will be true
Your hair so shiny, your skin so pure
In love with you, of that I'm quite sure
Your soft smooth thighs and your beautiful eyes
Our relationship strong with no room for lies
We'll always be together, from now to the end
The card will read with the roses I send
Our love explained, thru the life of a rose
Alive and still spreading, because each other we've chose
It's only so obvious, really quite clear
I choose to spend my life, with only you dear
To put my love to words could only compare
To the love and compassion that we alone share
This love I feel, the love I give
Will be yours alone, as long as I live!

Sabra G Rand
FOREVER FREE

Over a mountainside and across blue waters,
I see...... My Freedom,
I'll aboard a ship that will take me to the other side and then,
I'll begin..... My Journey,
For a new life I see now, so plain and in vision..... My Decision,
it will be,
A completion it will be in..... My Life,
With happiness in store then forever more and eternally,
I will be....

Bertha Spate
GOODBYE MY LOVE

Dedicated to my daughters: Doris Scheidt and Marlene Gardner

God came today and took him away,
And I heard the angels say,
"We're waiting at Heaven's gate,
You don't even have to wait";

God sent his angels down for you,
Your work here on earth is through,
The things you've done, your whole life long,
The angels cheer you with a song.

God's heavenly blessing came your way,
And took your heart and soul today,
Not to lament or not to cry,
Just to say a loving goodbye!

Maura Kallimanis
SHARING WITH YOU DEAR HEART

Dedicated to my husband George and my children Joseph, David, Mary-Grace

One hour of my time Dear Heart I share with you today
To participate in Holy Mass, meditate and pray
Help me loving Savior distractions keep away
While the burdens that afflict me, at your feet I lay

I wish to share your pain Dear Heart who died in ignominy
Scorned, maimed and tortured on the cross of Calvary
A bitter ransom then was paid for all humanity
As you shed your blood that sinners might gain eternity

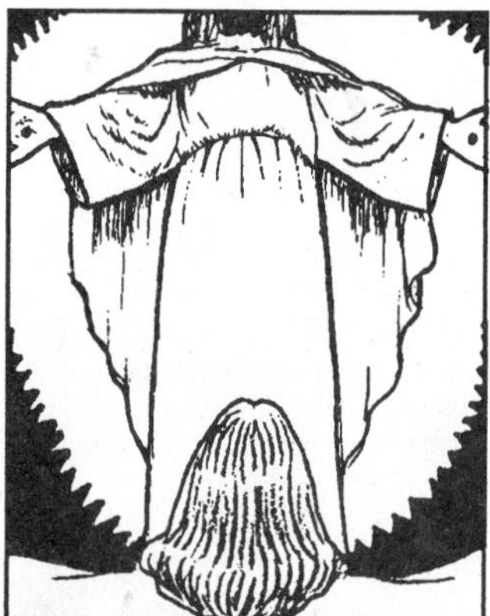

I share Dear Heart your triumph in a battle fought and won
Man now proclaims your glory the Risen God the Son
Abandon not your faithful troops, the struggle must go on
Until you return in judgment when your work is done

Let me share your cloak Dear Heart in the winter of my life
For warmth, shelter, comfort, in my final days of strife
When at last I'm laid to rest to the strains of the ancient fife
Receive this soul whose state on earth was daughter, mother, wife.

Isadoria I Steinhilber
THE SEA

The sea so wide and so very deep
And many a soul the sea doth keep
The sea has no mercy on those it takes
Just a watery bed is what it makes

It rolls over the head as an unseen tomb
And goes on roaring out in the gloom
Hear the water as it swishes and rushes on by
Is the sound of the sea really their cry

Of all the souls lost out at sea
Those who are forever lost to you and

Those who are forever lost to you and me
Who are sleeping so soundly in a watery grave
Those who gave their life their country to save.

Eldon E Land
TIME OF CHANGE
Mine heart is turned within me;
because of my backward ways.
The memories of my childhood,
had all but vanished away.
Glimpses of a self, long forgotten,
before the war of my days;
That sent me into a world (different),
not accustomed to me or my ways.
The change was sudden and drastic;
I wandered aimlessly from day to day.
Banishing the fears of tomorrow,
just so I could survive today.
The past was but a memory,
and all it brought was tears;
Compounded daily, all these wasted years.
The war is over—time of change
is nothing to fear.
For me it ended yesterday,
To signify the beginning of a New Era.

Kelly Rollins
GOOD-BYE MY LOVE
My heart used to shine like a light,
Now you're leaving, going out of sight.
I love you more than you know and
It'll be hard watching you go.

Together we've been through so
much, no matter what happens
I'll love you a bunch. Please don't
forget the times we shared
and realize how much I cared.

I know we'll see each other again,
but neither one of us is really sure
when. What will I do without you?
All I know is I love you.

Knowing you're leaving makes me
cry. When all I can do now is say
good-bye.

good-bye my love!

FOREVER FREE.

Bonnie Hammel
FORGOTTEN
I grew old and I grew weak
so that I could hardly speak
In my dreams I sat each day
as my life faded away.

What a joy it would be if you
would come and visit me
To hold my hand to wipe my
tears to give me comfort from my fears.

And as I slowly pass away to let me
know I'm loved each day.

Stephen E Davis
MOUNTAIN MAN STEVE
They call me Mountain Man Steve.
'Cause one day I had to leave.
There just seemed to be too much confusion.
Dreams I've had of no solution.
Nuclear power and endless waste.
Garbage dumps all over the place.
Giant buildings rising here and there.
No one really seems to care.
Where once was trees and rocks and things.
Now is Larry's House of Chicken Wings.
Where once was squirrels, fox and bear.
Now people come to stop and stare.
You see now there's a Zoo there,
With plenty of parking for me and you there.
The animals there live behind bars.
For people's pleasure, they line up for miles.
In their big fine cars to come and see,
To see God's creatures who once were free.

Della Sarathi
NO ONE KNOWS
In outer space
There is another place,
Where intelligent beings dominate
and they come to earth to investigate.

Some people state, they have no eyes
Others believe, they are very wise.
Someone might tell you, they have strange ears;
While others think, they cannot hear.

Some people say, they have short arms,
Some people worry, they will do us harm;
Some say, they have larger heads than us.
But why, make a fuss
When really, no one knows . . .

Ludmila Suglian
POEM IN PROSE
In Space They met Way
above the clouds
Secret Cosmos rays
embraced their bodies
Their hearts were beating
harder and harder
Fate wanted it that way . . . .
And so they entered in Synagogue together
A front a big Altar Rabbi held a Speech . . . .
It was Still there You could only hear
Lovers spoken words, I do I do.

Vanessa Ann De Young

Vanessa Ann De Young
ROYAL BRIDE

To Diana, Princess of Wales, and Sarah, Duchess of York, and to my mother, thanks for everything.

The chimes of Big Ben tolled eleven,
The Union Jacks waved in the breeze,
As the carriage trundled toward the Abbey.
She sat shrouded in lace and tulle,
She waved and smiled at the crowd,
As the eight Lippizaners made their way along the Mall.
She stepped through the stone portals,
Floating along the Nave,
The crystal chandeliers cast an ivory glow on her gown and veil.
The High Altar came closer and closer,
Beckoning her to a new beginning.
And when she said "I will,"
It glowed stronger than the sun.
Back to the Palace for a balcony kiss,
And going away with a new title,
Princess.

Jane S Miller Virtue
JACK AND BOBBY AND MARTIN
I saw two graves today.
I climbed hundreds of steps in the sweltering sun.

The sorrow in my heart was small,
Compared to the sorrow in the hearts of their loved ones.

When I lay down tonight
Tears ran down my face.

When I thought of those two
In their high place.

Now there's another
Martin Luther King.

My heart hurts but their
Praises I'll sing.

Death stole in on violent feet,
Snuffed out the life of friends we meet

Along life's way.

Shannon Lee Brady
WAR
The pain, the suffering,
it's caused by war.
It's love and all the hating
that make people sore.
I watched my daddy,
in uniform, as he walked out the door,
he said he loved me,
and went off to war.
I just can't stop crying,
just thinking,
he might be dying.
War, caused by lying.
At night I lay in bed,
Hoping my daddy's not dead.
I have to remember what he said,
that he loves me and for me he bled.

(L.Z.) Leona Zinious
TAHOE RINGS
Bungalows, casinos, Tahoe's shores are ringed.
You listen closely you can hear
the gambling machines.
A chapel's music you faintly hear, a voice sings.
The couple standing in the chapel are putting on rings.

Clear waters of the lake are marred by keel.
Foamy water wake rings, follow the side-wheel.
Inside a noisy casino, is heard a-ring a-ding a-ding a-ling.
Tahoe is Tahoe, a surprise is the thing.

Freda Beth Painter
AUTUMN FIRES
I remember when I was just a child.
Of the old fireplace made with stone.
How I would rush home in the evenings,
to watch Papa light the autumn fire back home.

I remember Mamma in the kitchen
preparing supper for us all.
Then we would sit around the old fireplace
and listen to the chilly wind of fall.

Now the old house has fallen
and Papa has gone on before.
The chimney has crumbled to the ground
and the fireplace isn't there anymore.

Now all I have is memories
of years that have passed and gone.
But I will never forget when I was a child,
when Papa lit the autumn fires back home.

Rhonda Rell
NUMBER ONE
He and I could have walked
across the rivers of our lives;
He would have been the candle there
and I could be the light.

Together, then, we would have shown
the world what love was all about,
and maybe help those lonely people
who are down and out.

The winter sprinkles magic round,
the browns and grays of cold,
and with him always by my side,
his smile that seemed like gold.

Joane T Real
SISTERS
Sisters are forever
From the beginning to the end.
Even when they hate you
They're still your very best friend.

No one will ever know you
Like your sister can,
She will understand you
Better than any man.
She sometimes might ignore you
When she hangs out with her best friend
But if ever you have a problem
On her you can always depend.
She'll always come to help you
No matter when you call,
She'll always be the first one there
Whenever you take a fall.
Sisters are forever
That's the bottom line,
I'll be grateful to God forever
For making the best one mine.

Gina Kindschi
LIFE IS NOT FAIR
Life is not fair!
we say. How come we dare
to place the blame when life is WE,
and we don't care
so many times when others hurt and need an ear,
a hand, and help to lose their fear
to face another day . . .

Life is not fair!
we cry when we can't bear
to be alone, and no one takes the time to share
a pain and helps to understand why feelings die,
and trusted friends can make us cry
and dread another day . . .

Life will be fair
when we, again, will care
about a friend more than a car, or clothes and hair,
or meals and wealth and business deals, are proud to have
the strength to give and get, and love
to live another day.

Melvin R Bronson
THE SONNET OF FRIENDSHIP
Among our greatest "Blessings" is one treasure,
Which stands out among the best that man can give,
And that is Friendship which

True Friendship never fades but always lives.

Life brings times when we may feel downhearted,
When darkening clouds enshroud our lives in gloom,
A cherished friend, a hug, all gloom's departed;
The clouds disperse and sunlight fills the room!

Life, too, brings times of mirth, of fun and song;
With friends, we share this atmosphere of glee.
Though true, these fleeting pleasures don't last long;
They linger on in lasting memory.

Weigh now, the worth of priceless friends you love
With any other gift from Heaven above.

Scott W Spears
THE FALL OF THE DEN

To our American Forefathers who feared God, And to the Unborn for they are loved by God, And to the sinners for Christ died to bring us back to God.

The Great White Wolf watches over the Den,
Maintaining peace and order for all within.
He wishes other dens were like his own,
The Pack was proud to call it Home.
Oh, there were trifles here and there,
A she-wolf will kill her young right in the lair!
So with the Pack she will be free to run,
Why should she let them spoil her fun?
She ignores the wolf who could not conceive,
For she would rather kill than give them to thee.

The Den used to be a Refuge where the sheep could sing,
In Hope for a better life and the pursuit of good things.
But the Refuge slowly changed until its sheep were lost within,
For now reigneth the ways of the wolves and this was their Den.
They were free to pursue whatever their hearts desire in Life,
But then came the Great Shepherd and there was much strife.
He calls to His sheep to come out before it begins,
As the wolves hid among the rocks, the sheep came to Him.
And when the King of the Land waited long enough,
His Great Fire came forth and all lives were snuffed.

Mary Dugan
JEALOUSY

She stared at me with jaundiced eye
I felt my dress was cut too low
Her husband kissed her stingy cheek
And stretched her hair behind her ears . . .
And then he gave my dress a peek
While she resisted what he'd done
He moved and grazed the back of me
For he was only having fun.
He loved to own a jealous wife
I knew it from my jaded pose . . .
So much for aura of his touch
I slipped away with histed nose.

Mattie B King
A MOTHER

This poem is dedicated to my Mother: Ollie Bowie

Mother who cared so much that she let her dream fail to prove that her children came first in life. She was to dream of her life, but she gave her life up for us. She taught us right from wrong, she let us know where we belong and she made our life strong.

She shared her dream in order for us to grow strong, but she never left us alone.

Mother gave us the greatest gift of all, and that was to love and be strong . . . and she shared the greatest moment of all, peace in life, trust, faith, warmth, and where we belong!

Mother kept us strong, she always made a home where the fire burned long, so we could find our way back home. A Mother's love is very strong, one that can't go wrong.

Linda Hoskins
TO MY GRANDMOTHER ON MOTHER'S DAY

To Grandma, who's also a mother and a friend. I Love You Grandma.

Here's to tell you Grandma,
that I love you so,
And that you mean so much to me,
than you will ever know
You've always made your house our home,
and showed us that you cared,
And no matter how much family,
your love is always shared
You deserve a lot of thanks,
for all that you have done,
If anyone deserves it more,
we know that you're the one
There's no more I could say or write,
that words could ever express
All I know is Grandma,
you deserve the best.

Michelle McCormick
SOARING IMAGINATION

To my mother, Kathy Hughes, who forever has encouraged me to "soar" with my imagination.

The sun rises
Over the mountain
Lighting the way
For the birds.

They open their eyes,
Spread their wings . . .
And imagine.

There they soar,
Through the gold
Spilt across the sky,
To find another place
To spread their wings
Imagine
And Fly.

Colin Clift
GOD AND SARAH AND ME

In her glowing loveliness my Sarah
Is as bright and beautiful as Farrah.
In order to win her I knew I had to propose uniquely:
"Say, kid," I say, "how would you like to be buried with my people?"
She laughed (perfect teeth) and then looked at me obliquely,
"I love you," she said, "But my career (communications) comes first."
"I thought we were agreed that God is love. Therefore, love comes first."
"O, sure," Sarah said, "but God is also faithful and longsuffering,
"For instance, look how patient he's been with you lustful men."
"Love is greater than all things," I said.
"I need more time," she said. "Could you look me up in about 5 years?"
"Doubt it," I said. "But we'll always have that weekend in Placerville,
"Unless, of course, reincarnation is as true as God's love."

Since that heartbreaking night I've tried to imagine her fate:
Alone and desperately whispering my name with her final breath.

58 Months Later:

O, God, I just saw pregnant Sarah doing the national weather.
Dear Sarah, you still have my heart.
Thank the Lord I still have my art.

Gabriele Jex
A WINTER'S JOURNEY

Standing at the top of the slope
looking down,
I begin my journey alone,
and soon become a partner,
a lover of the shimmering
white powder beneath me.
We become as one,
working together,
playing together.
I feel the wind and the sun
kiss my cheeks playfully,
they too, join me on my journey.
I know no bounds,
I feel no chains
or burdens to weigh
me down.
I am a free spirit,
an eagle,
soaring with the wind,
through time and space.

Lawrence E Bloomfield
LAMENTATIONS OVER CAROL

How do I make my heart believe,
Loving you is wrong,
Captivated by your beauty,
Enchanted by your siren's song,
In agony my heart cries out,
To another you belong.

You're all I've ever wanted,
All that I desire,
You overwhelm my senses,
My soul, you've set afire.

My love for you is secret,
Not even you, can ever know,
For the pain it would cause others,
Would mar its righteous glow.

Visions of you fill my dreams,
All my waking moments spent,
Thinking of your body,
My love for you I won't repent,
For if loving you is a sin,
Damned my soul will be,
Hell cannot be hotter, than the fire
you've set in me . . . . .

Pauline Sweiss
OUR GARDEN

We love our garden so well,
Within every part of it.
Birds singing all day long,
Calling to their partners along.
Bees buzzing all around,
Searching for flowers colour some, fragrant.
The trees give shade to the scorching soil.
And there, often neighborly children play.
Quietness followed at once;
A creeping creature swirled around.
Black and yellow, and white designed;
A head strong holding up;
Two round eyes looking fast;
A tail sinful and lavish,
Jumps up and down vigorous.
Fly away birds, fly away,
Run for your lives you all.
For the snake is at snare.
It will spoil your happiness,
Don't let it bite you venomous,
And destroy our garden so fair.

Chisai Childs (Mrs Richard T Ringler)

Chisai Childs (Mrs Richard T Ringler)
YOU'RE ALWAYS THERE FOR ME

This poem is dedicated to my loving husband, Richard T. Ringler, 91 yr. old grandmother, Anseth Teel Jones, my loving children, Melissa and Kenny Walker and adorable grandson, Clint Richard Walker.

Sometimes life's too busy,
The whirlwind it keeps me dizzy.
I don't have time
to breathe the mountain air.
From morning 'til night
the phone, it rings.

I don't take time for special things,
Like telling you I love you
and I care.
Yet, you're always there for me,
and in your eyes I see you care!

I can't imagine what it would be like
without you there.
You don't know how much I love you,
You don't know how much I love you

and I care!

There's never time for a quiet walk,
We seldom have time to talk.
You smile and watch others take my time.

You never ever complain—it seems,
You're proud of me and share my dreams.
You smile and tell the whole world,
Yes, she's mine.
You're always there for me.

Shirley Robinett
THE ROSE

To my Granddaughter MICHELLE MALCOM

She is a flower just beginning to bloom.
A beautiful rose opening soon.
Coming into the fullness of the life she will live,
So much to offer, so much to give.
She'll grow to be a beauty, tall and strong.
Walking straight into life, meeting it head-on.
And when the storm clouds dark do appear,
May she walk in the sunshine, may they never come near
To bruise the petals of the rose so fair
And mar the beauty God has placed there.
And when she's become a woman with age
May the lines in her face read page after page
Of her walk thru life as a beautiful rose,
Glowing from within, as summer draws to a close.

Ginnie Kirk
LIFE IS SO SHORT

To the memory of my dear husband.

Take good care of one another.
Life is so short.
Be good to the one you love.
Life is so short.
Don't find fault and argue.
Life is so short.
Spread love wherever you go.
Life is so short.

Doris Murdock Wloch
OUR TULIP TREE

We live beneath the tulip tree, my family and me,
Its out-stretched branches swoop and soar, so majestically!
I've watched the tiny leaves, begin to grow in early Spring,
Saw the softest ruffling when, baby birds first test their wings.

Cone shaped buds soon open, displaying pastel orange and lime,
Bumble Bee's add the melody,
Concerto, so sublime.
We enjoy the shade, till the Autumn leaves, begin to fall,
I rake and rake and cannot rest, till I have raked them all!

Donna (Dee) Orol
HUMANITY

This poem is dedicated to Father Bill, thank you for all your help, and understanding.

Within the depths of my heart,
there is a need.
A need to reach out to all humanity,
and search its very soul.
To revitalize the love that's there.
To recharge the God-given love
with happiness, and assurance.
To help one soul a day
can climb to helping seven in one day.
To pursue the need of helping others,
to enrich their very being, just to show—
you care there,
you care,
you are loved,
can mean the world and more
to one soul with the tiniest
sparkle of sunlight—in their heart.

Beth A Maren
AUTUMN FOOTSTEPS

Most significantly, my love and gratitude belong to Patrick: the remarkable spirit pushing me forward, the best of friends and the most nurturant of significant others in my life who has made me feel very fortunate.

Resting in silence, the harvest Moon looks down upon the two
consumed in a chaos of thoughts and passions:
searching for comfort and healing,
longing for a channel in which to breathe freely.
The Moon, his silence now disturbed,
watches hearts that twitch and break,
that hope to hold,
that long for warmth, with wounds and pleasures their bodies had forgotten.
The endless autumn evening sky
then heard the amber Moon cry aloud.
He appealed to Truth, requesting peace; an end of the chaos;
for the tender, playful, giving love it had looked upon just moments ago:
the laughter, sometimes mixed with tears,
the unspoken understanding, the nurturing companionship,
everything that created the truth, the experience of love they shared.
Had it been forgotten, or worse,
lost in life's priorities?
Was it only the Moon's childhood dream?
Restless Truth, despite his seeming abandonment,
answered the Moon's painful cry:
a steady voice in the midst of chaos;
a soft light to shine on their fragile hearts.

Myrtle Dixon
CIRCLE OF LOVE

Dedicated to Ralph, my beloved husband, on our 50th wedding anniversary.

The first sweet rapture of our love will never be the same,
As now we warm our hearts
before its steady, glowing flame;
For it has ripened now like fields of growing grain,
We would not want that young
love back again.
We cherish memories of those lovely, tender years,
But know that young love has its
share of pain and tears,
And within each other's arms we've come to know
That love like ours will never
cease to grow.
And when his eyes seek mine across a crowded room,
Then the language of the heart
springs into bloom,
We need no words to know we've reached a goal
That we are linked forever, soul
to soul.
And when the time for us has come to journey on
When all our youthful charms
are dead and gone
We'll know our time together was well spent
And within the circle of our
love, we'll be content.

Marcell Spalding
FEELINGS

In memory of my Grandmother, Helena DeMaere

Feelings didn't always show much
But the Heart was always strong,
In hope that you did realize
The times that I was wrong.
You always meant a lot to me,
I wish somehow, some way,
That time would give me another chance
To say what I needed to say.
But since this probably won't happen
And my wish will not come true,
My only hope is, for you to hear,
When I finally say . . .
"I Love You."

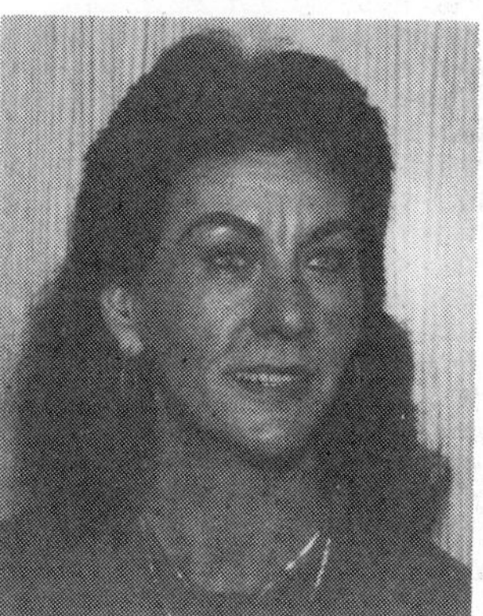

Barbara Monteer

Barbara Monteer
THE YEARS AHEAD

Especially to my parents, for the years they gave raising us three girls. To my three children, Tonya, Vicki and Jay. And to all the young mothers of today.

As they lay sleeping in their beds
with scratches, bruises, and
food matted on their heads.
You kinda stand there and laugh and shake your head;
pull up the covers to tuck them in bed.
You start walking away, your eyes full of tears.
"Oh God, girls, stop and look back
'cause there's only once you'll
have these precious years."

Before you know it, you'll be looking at their beds and saying,
"God bring them home safely."
And you'll bow your head.
You'll walk away with tears in your eyes,
but girls all those precious years,
you've let them slip by.
You'll lay down to rest, but the rest is no more.
You'll be looking at that old clock and listening for the door.

If you survive all the years you have to go through,
before you know it, you're watching them
walk down the aisle to say "I do."
You sit there and cry and there's pain in your heart,
to know what's ahead of them,
in the new life, they've got to start.
You go home and you feel so all alone.
You'll start crying and saying, "Oh God my baby's gone."

You'll walk through the house and again look at their beds.
And with tears in your eyes, you'll see visions of them,
with dirt on their faces and
food matted on their little heads.
You'll see them in their teen years, getting dressed to go out.
You'll remember all the heartaches, worries, and doubts.
You'll look up and say, "God, thanks for helping me
through all these years;
through the pain and heart-aches, laughter and tears."

God they're still young
and probably don't understand
a lot of things I've said.
They'll never understand the love of a mother
until she is dead.
God, please help them as they get older
to try to remember all the
things I've said.
Life's going to be a long, hard road, and to me
this is "The Years Ahead."

Monica Constantini
FRIENDS

This poem is dedicated to two of my best friends in the world who have always been there for me—my mom and dad.

A friend is someone who's always there,
to show you're loved and that
they care.
A friend is there to always cheer you,
they make you feel happy when
you're feeling blue.
Friends are special and love you for you,
they rarely criticize because
you are you.
A smile, a hug, a helping hand,
makes you feel wanted and

shows that you're grand.
Friends bring out your good instead of your bad,
they make you smile when you are sad.
Friends help you seek dreams and reach for your goals,
they accept who you are and expect no roles.
Friends are special, loving and kind,
they are people we need and aren't hard to find.
I think friendships are very unique,
they're people we look up to,
treasure and forever keep!

Laura-Jean Hamilton (Ray)
THE WILLOW TREE

Dedicated with love and affection, to my departed sister and friend, Debra Susan Ray.

Quietly in the meadow, it sits amidst the earth
Gathering in the sunlight, and birds among its perch
No one seems to notice, the beauty it hides beneath
Its large embodied timber, and shading tiny leaves

I go there to escape the fury the world seems to possess
And hide beneath its shading leaves of unspoken loveliness
It shades me from the scorching sun, and welcomes me happily.
I've found a wonderful hiding place, beneath this Willow Tree.

So many dreams have come to me within this hiding place
Which I have kept a secret under the Willow Tree's warm embrace
I don't believe I'll tell anyone about my newfound friend,
For fear my dreams and secrets, will surely come to end.

Perhaps it is a selfish thought, to keep it all to me,
But the truth is that I do not possess this lovely Willow Tree.
It stands in grace, among the meadow, its beauty to behold.
For all who need a hiding place, to let their dreams unfold.

Eunice A Taylor
THE MIRACLE OF SUSIE

To my granddaughter, Susie McGahan, who has taught us the true meaning of faith and courage.

Three months early, two and a half pounds, they gave very little hope.
The prayers poured in, your mother said, "I still believe in miracles even if they don't."
You surprised them all, little Susie, and we thought the battle was done.
Oxygen cut off, they said, cerebral palsy,—the verdict before the age of one.
Many tears were shed, acceptance set in, and still we all knew
that there really is a God, for he gave us the miracle of you .....
Susie with the sparkling blue eyes and the enchanting Kewpie doll smile.
Captivating all those you meet and knowing all the while
that God sent you from heaven above to be the littlest angel for us all to love.
Daddy calls you his "little Angel" and to mommy, you are the joy and the light
that brightens each day with sunshine that glows far into the night.
Your smiles and your laughter and yes, even your comical frown
fill our hearts with gladness whenever we're feeling down.
You have taught us so much, Little Susie, and we all do love you so.
You are such a special little girl, that I wish the whole world could know
of your fighting spirit and undaunted courage that seem to rise and soar
above and beyond all the battles you've fought, all before the age of four.
Yes, Little Susie, you are indeed an angel, one we are blessed to hold.
On loan to us all from our God above, waiting for more of life's story to unfold.
My arms ache to hold you, Susie, and my love for you overflows into my whole being
And I want you to know "You are truly Grandma's Own Little Princess."

Jack Darel Harmon
VISIONS IN THE FLAMES

To dad: who took me to the woods and taught me about them. To mom who waited many anxious hours waiting for our return. To all those about me. I wish them well.

I built a fire in the fireplace the other night.
It put me in a pensive mood as I watched the flames burn bright.
And as the flames danced in the air, among them I saw many visions there.
Visions of many years gone by, of other fires built by my dad and I.
Of days of working in the woods, of hunting and trapping for other goods.
The times we fished the hidden streams, where other footprints were seldom seen.
Of the times we fed crumbs to the Chickadees, while the Blue Jays squalled from the nearby trees.
The times we heard the splash of a beaver's tail, as we crossed their dam so strong yet frail.
A muskrat swimming on the pond, as whippoorwills ushered in the night with their evening song.
When we watched an elk or a fleeting deer, as it ran through the woods to disappear.
And a Scarlet Tanager so black and red, as it flew through the tree tops high overhead.
Our times of just wandering through the woods enjoying the beauty that nature placed there.
I wonder now, if it might ever be, that I may walk again where I felt so free.

Sue Mimi Hebert
WHO WILL ANSWER?

To my sister Jacki who first believed in me so I could believe in myself. To the maturity of people in all walks of life.

In all the world there never will be,
A ruler of a Nation—who's just/corrupt free.

America is called "The Land of the Free,"
But only if you have Society's Right Key.

Society's key is Glory, Clout (Money) and Power,
Then they judge us human beings from their Ivory Tower.

They care not for human treatment to be Just,
Unless to do so would fatten their Lust.

The times are acomin' Big America Society when you'll see,
How little people like me, we were born here and born free.

My Mama always said, even a worm will turn,
Then Society's right key will be the one to burn.

Out of the ashes will return much needed Love,
The greatest ruler over prejudice, sent from Above.

Owenna
MY DENTIST

With Christian Love; William A. Clements D.D.S.

I know a grand fisherman
whose gentle touch soothes all pain.
And with his special staff
I have a willing smile again.

His calling is performed with love,
God's Light is everywhere.
His healing flows from above
and manifests in his care.

This poem is my tribute.
Forty years has been my test.
No award can match his talent.
For Dr. Clements is the best!

Teodulfo T Yerro

Teodulfo T Yerro
WALK WITH FAITH IN YOUR HEART

When I awake in the early morning
And feel the soft warmth of a newborn day,
I think someone had turned the clock of life,
That gives strength to be again on my way.

The road matters not if hard or thorny,
As long as I bounce sprightly as the breeze;
For He who always turns the clock of life,
Seems at my side and makes me walk with ease.

The road may be long and too challenging,
Even if the sun smiles sweetly above;
For my strength to push on had been recharged—
At night when I retold Him all my love.

If by chance clouds may hover o'er me,
And darken blooming meadows I pass by,
I'll not forget they're just flitting shadows,
As my Maker guides me from heaven high.

For if you walk with faith deep in your heart,
Trusting always in His unerring hand,
You'll beat all hardships and adversities—
He'll welcome you to His celestial land.

Brenda R Grummet
THE GREAT FALL

In Memory of my Beloved Father, Henry Brassington

When Ego fades
with Life's Illusion
And strips the Soul
to bear Delusion,
The Bitters borne
are so that Would;
When gone One Day
'Tis gone for Good.

Billy Jacobson
TOO MUCH DOPE

To those who know. To those who have been there. To those who are free.

TOO much dOpe
TOO much cOke
Crack readily
available—

A sOciety Of milk
and hOney—we're
All ready tO blOw
Our hOrns.

TOO many tOOts—
cartilage
CannOt
endure;

A thOughtless
affair, tOrrid
scenes—infants
scream.

TOO much dOpe
TOO much cOke
Crack is in the
air . . . .

Theresa Fenton
SPRINGTIME

I dedicate this poem with love to my parents, my husband Roger, and my daughter Kristy. Thank you for your encouragement and belief in me.

Listen to the raindrops softly falling
Smell the air so fresh and clean
See the flowers blooming brightly
What a wondrous beginning to the season Spring
Birds sit on their leafy perches
Singing their own special song
Welcoming in a brand new season
Bidding good-bye to a winter too long
It's a season of new beginnings
With a promise of so much more to come
It's a sign of life's renewal
Bringing brand new hopes and dreams to some
It's a cleansing time throughout the land
With joys for one and all
It's a season full of wonder
Beckoning us to heed its call

Linda T Wilson
A THOUGHT

This poem is dedicated to all my friends at Holy Family Cathedral in Anchorage, Alaska.

Pondering my mirrored soul's perception
revelations exploded in flashes of insight
confessed hostile thoughts, deeds, took flight
discernment of spirits, knowledge quicken

Joyful living celebrating hope, faith
honoring love's call to stretch beyond
the seen reality, piercing the unknown with light
not fearing what follows trusting in goodness, kindness

Tis a heart pounding adventure to live in the spirit
being rescued, protected, sent forth
going forward becoming fully human, fully divine
supporting the low encouraging them to fly higher

Freedom found in courage to soar
above death's open door. Rejecting
the impulse to give up
searching deeper our souls'
perception is never ending granting graces reaching eternity

All wounds restored, brokenness healed, the struggle
is finished, all is made anew
rewards to the faithful, discipline shining bright
oh! thank you my friend your instruction so precious
I do hope your wisdom, a gift, is ne'er forgotten.

Ruth Cantrell
POWER

To Bill, my beloved.

Send a mighty missile flashing,
Lasso lightning from the skies,
Rape the seas and master mountains,
Snatch back mortal as he dies.
Fling a net to bind the nations,
Bridge a soaring space with steel,
Split the atom, wreak destruction,
Use its power then to heal.
Walk the moon, search out its secrets,
Meet a star and know its face,
Plunder earth to molten glory,
. . . To the swift belongs the race!
Seize the universe and hold it,
Frightened prisoner in your hand,
Seek and struggle, perhaps one day
You'll be God instead of man.

Judy Vahs
MOM'S LETTER OF ADVICE

To my children

Dear kids,

Your wedding was a beautiful sight,
but, here's my advice so you don't fight.
A kiss each morning will brighten your day
and lessen your load on your busy way.
Think of each other the whole day through,
make each feel just like new.
Marriage takes time, patience and lots of care
and able to know the other is there.
Communication is one great thing,
it will help you both keep your rings.
It relieves tension, makes you closer too,
so that's something don't forget to do.
Put each other first in line,
make your goals and keep them in mind.
Don't let others lead either astray.
Be attentive and listen what each has to say.
I'm always behind you and wish you good cheer.
I love you both. I think you are dear.
I hope your future is a real success,
and brings you both years of happiness.

Love,

Mom

Frank G Raevsky
LADY JANE

For the sweet ladies of my life: Jane—my wife; Susan—my daughter; and Anna Backman; my Dear Friend

My sweet Lady Jane
I've come to talk with you again.
'Bout things that have passed
'bout a love that will—forever last.
My sweet Lady Jane
why do you refrain.
Sometimes you cry
but yet—never complain.
Please always remain
My sweet Lady Jane

My sweet Lady Jane—
Love is all your life
To live is to love—to love is to live
My sweet Lady Jane.

With love to my wife.

Mary F Correll
DAY AND NIGHT

To Kathleen Almaguer who opened the door to my creativity.

Twilight comes stealing softly
As though on cats' feet,
Engulfs the waiting world
And puts the day to sleep.

Gently, gently fall the night
And opens up the star lit sky,
To shine upon the earth below
To show the way for you and I.

That is how we come to know
All those things that hide from view,
And walk the path of hidden dreams
That so often dreamers do.

Silently the night moves on
And wings its way into flight,
Then suddenly there appears the dawn
That puts to rest the waiting night.

Alvin Evans
TO LOVE

To my wife Navleth; son Sean; daughters Sheryl and Tricia

Oh! to win the cup of liquid love
Whose sweet thirst quenching
flaccid flows
Would make me like clouds float
above
The imaginary heavens as it
placid glows

Oh! Once to win that special cup
With sweet filled juicy flaming
fluid
To share it in a social sup
In sedentary bliss not a dreaming
druid.

Eleanor V Johnson
GRIEF

To my husband, Earl, 1907-1985

How much of grief is for myself
Because I am left alone?
There are people all around me,
But no one to call my own.

I could have begged you not to die
You would have tried, I know;
But I saw how much you suffered,
And I had to let you go.

But oh, I miss your quiet strength.
I miss the tender caring.
I miss the understanding,
The loving and the sharing.

I do not cry for you, my love,
You do not need my tears.
I weep because I am alone,
And no one ever hears.

Orval Keysser
THE CHASE

From somewhere down the trail, a ways
I can hear a familiar sound
Not a high toned howl, like a coyote makes
But the coarse voice of a baying hound

It brings forth a melody, I like to hear
And a quickening of sluggish feet
The bark has a message, I understand
Like a bugle blows—no retreat

And, as I follow behind, I know somewhere
There's a heartbeat, far ahead
And a scent on the trail, that beckons, come
But over the hill, it will fade, instead

It's not the game, that I follow, at will
But the bay of the eager hound
It tones the spirit, from day to night
A freedom, that behaves, beyond bound

And then from above the timber-line
A scream, echoes, from hill to hill
Suddenly, the voice of the hound is hushed
The night becomes warm and still

Rodenick Jordan
ELEGY

It was . . .

The exquisite charm of her company,
Which worked a peasant power
Dispelling those dark unprofitable meditations
So easily aroused, that clamorously crowd
Each lonely moment, every solitary hour.

The exquisite charm of her conversation,
The constant gracious affirmation
Of what I had hoped to find in the feminine,
Luxuriously quieting my unspoken
Puerile romantic notions.

The exquisite charm of her countenance
Its beauty fresh, reminiscent of first flowers
Never brighter than when she enjoyed
The full expression of my ardor
Attentive to the every whisper of my heart.

These and the thousand particulars of her grace
The sweet testimony that she was
The virtuous wife of Proverbs
The embodiment of that biblical ideal.

An exquisitely charming creature.

Kellie Mezzacappa
SHARE ONTO ME

Dedicated with deepest love and thanks to my sister Avis.

Let me reach beneath my soul
For someday I'll have the strength to reach my goal
Let me succeed in all my desires
And do everything I must for it to acquire

Give me strength in times of need
Let me learn as I grow never to greed

Encourage my moments when I'm feeling sad
As I cherish the good and accept the bad
Let me stand tall to fight for what I believe
Give me the power so I may achieve

Fill my soul only with love and affection
So I may never define the word rejection
Grant me the patience in others and in me
I shall then have full control of the mind and body

Grant me the knowledge to truly understand
To accept my own failures to love who I am
Let me share onto others what I have learned
Everything that I fought for in life I have learned

With just a little hope and enlightenment to get through the day
I shall carry this poem always
forever in my heart it shall stay.

Sharlene Dart
ROMEO?

To Krista—Remember Mr. Carlson's second floor window? That painter must've thought you were pretty crazy!

Romeo, Romeo,
I called from above,
Hoping to find
What could be true love.

"Here I am"
His voice called to me,
I looked all around
Oh, who could this be?

Maybe he's a knight
In shining armor,
Or maybe a sweet

And handsome charmer.

But to my surprise
As I looked down,
Across my face
Came a very sad frown.

There was no armor
He was no saint,
He was just a guy
With a can of paint.

Alice Makla
A GREAT DAY! !

Dedicated to my great niece, Katharine Rose Sawyer Press, Born November 9, 1988

Grant me your wisdom, that I might do
All which is pleasing, unto you.

Whether in word, or in deed
Guide me Lord, as you lead.

Let me not rush, into this day
Until I rest with you, and pray.

Reading your word, will guide me through,
In whatever it is, that I must do.

Thank You Lord, for making just me.
A Great day I'll have, to share with Thee.

Stephen John Morse
A FLAMING SUNSET FALLS

to Diane Citino, my precious love.

A flaming sunset falls shattered into the ocean's glittering crystal vase

Lightness gradually diminishes while giving surroundings a darkened new face

Activities of the day have long ceased though still linger within the increasingly dampened air

And nearby the water's predictable waves carefully let the land's edge beware

Each blade secured with the shore's shaggy carpet is varnished through the night by the mist of the sea

And nature's white noise will continue to mesh until a new light is eventually set free . . .

John Harrison
YOU WERE AS A SHADOW

To Kate

You were as a shadow
A presence
That needs no substance,
A form
Draped over the images
  That I mistook
  As real.

Yet an inner presence
That was light-ethereal.

You were with me
  Soothing and wonderful
  Friendly and compassionate
I awoke with you
And knew
That you are more than my friend.

Kay Gibbs
MY LAST FAREWELL

In remembrance of my Grandmother, a very kind & strong woman

As the rain falls ever so gently from the sky,
I feel the trickle of a tear as it escapes my eye.
A feeling of sadness suddenly comes over me,
As I accept the things that will never be.
The dreams that I once chased & sought
Are now just visions soon to be forgot.
For you see, I now have grown ever so old
And there's only room for the young & the bold.
How quickly the time has seemed to fly by
but I will be brave, for I'm not afraid to die.
I'm leaving this world with treasures so dear
How could one possibly be filled with fear?
Now the time has come to say good-bye
And I ask of you, please don't cry.
There were many things I did not conquest
But my time has come to be laid to rest.
It is time for me to bid farewell to all
And go and prepare for my last final call.

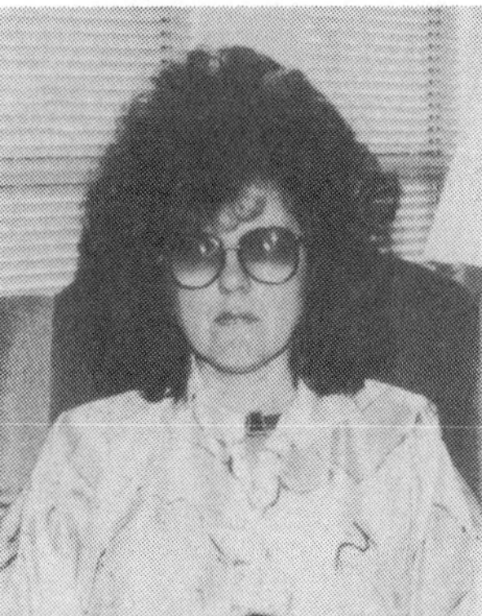

Joanne L Kuci

Joanne L Kuci
THE MIRRORS OF MY MIND

To my children: Hysen, Donika, Shano, and Kamile, And for all those lovers who walk the beaches endlessly.

In the mirrors of my mind,
I see the perfect view.
The ocean on a moonlit night,
And me alone with you.

Two lovers walking side by side,
Along the ocean shore.
Silent little whispers,
Vow to love each other more.

The ocean hears their promises,
The moon shines on their love.
As they gaze upon the stars,
That sparkle from above.

They walk along the ocean shore,
And hold each other's hand.
They pause, As he stops to write,
"I LOVE YOU" in the sand.

In the mirrors of my mind,
I see the perfect view.
I'll hold it in my memory,
With all my love for you.

Elena Maggio
PRISONERS OF THE FUTURE

The blood of the earth,
is lighting the torches of destruction.
And spreading torment over the land.
The sleeping, the alive and the pure
have seen the uproar of the flames
and the casting of the waves.
The trees are leveled.
And the clouds are draped like mourning ghosts,
with exhausted gases seeping from their dark caps.

Pumping out poison as they drive
in an onward direction into darkness.
Breathing in toxin 'til they breathe no more.

But in every one of their doomed souls,
is a glorious thought of the one seed capable of starting over.
The seed of life.

For the prisoners of the future awake
to a similar dream.
One of a well preserved tomorrow.

Tammy Hettick
GRANDMOTHERS

Dedicated to my Grandmother, Opal. All my love, TAHS

Grandmothers are very unique,
They are someone you want to keep.
Never ever let them go
If you did, you would surely know,
That once they are gone you would miss them so.

They feed you when you are hungry.
They warm you when you are cold.
They never make you feel you are ugly.
They give you strength when you are feeling bold.

They care for your young when you have plans.
They see to it that they wash their face and hands.

They call you on the phone to see how you are doing.
Just to make sure you are not ill or sitting there boo-hooing.

Without a grandmother in your heart.
Your life would surely fall apart.

I love my grandmother heart and soul,
And when the time comes that she must go,
That's the beginning of a start
To remember her always down deep in my heart.

Kenneth R Dunkelberger
BIRDS

Birdie, Birdie, flying so high
Up, Up, in this deep blue sky
As you swirl and do your loops
Please come down and give me the scoop
Let me know my little friend
This broken heart you can mend
Fly around my thinking head
As I feed you with the time we spend

Birdie, Birdie, Flying so high
You are like that diamond in the sky
Doing your acrobats so very well
And being my friend, that's swell
I love your colors and your grace
In my heart and this lonely place
So as you are flying, give me a sign
That you love me and give me peace of mind

Virginia L Wilson
CHRISTMAS TREE

I get so excited, knowing Christmas is near
My limbs are all waiting for time to be here.

There's no one to please, but My Lady who waits,
Thanksgiving has gone and I know it is near.

I feel my box moving from inside the hall,
Down to the place where I'll dress and be awed.

Maybe only by My Lady, but that's best of all,
She so loves Christmas, and can't wait for each year, to come and give love for one land all.

Shahed U M Khan
THE NIGHT

It is the silence of night,
It is the beauty of night,
It is the tranquility of night that
  brings wisdom, depth of
  thought, reckoning, freshness,
  gushing streams of imagination
  and ideas.
Everything outside is deep in
  sleep; quiet and calm.
Soothing breezes flow with
  gentility.
At times, night owls fly away and
  break the silence for a while.
The stars in the sky twinkle with
  brightness, the moon, visible at
  times, fades away in the clouds.
Trees standing outside like
  guardsmen.
Whistles of blowing wind come
  from nearby bushes,
Streams in the distant hills
  melodically flow in an endless
  motion.
Sometimes howls of jackals come
  from a far away forest,
A fine tune of a flute carries the
  imagination to a wide open field,
  flooded by moonlight,
Ripples in the river break the
  image of the moon into waves,
still the silence of night bears its
  gravity for eternity.

Doyle L DeMent
FROST UPON THE BARN

It's as calm as the yellow moon,
That glistens upon the dew.
And as silent as the fox at noon,
That stalks the chicken on cue.

It's as deadly as the rattlesnake,
That stealthily hides from the sun.
And as unique as the snowflake
That falls fingerprinted when it's done.

It's as quick as a bird of prey,
That now surveys the rabbit's run.
And it's as crisp as an autumn day,
That changes colors just for fun.

It's a delight to a boy's heart,
Upon one cold early morn.
To see nature exhibit her art,
As frost upon the barn.

Agnes Ellis
INEVITABLE

Dedicated to—My children, Barbara, Parky, Jess and Helen, And grandchildren, Vance and Linda.

O Lord, Thou made the beauties of earth—
The turbulent seas, and the mighty lands,
The stars to shine, and the moon to beam
The mysteries of space are in Thy hands.
Thou made the mammals and the creatures all;
The birds to fly on fleet and tireless wings,
The flowers to bloom, to die, to

bloom again,
The flaming sun that day and night brings.
The majestic mountains, and the flashing streams
The sylvan rivers; undammed they ran.
Thou made a world of beauty, and then,
And then O Lord, Thou madest man!

Thou gave him gifts of reason and thought,
Thy world to enjoy, his soul to save.
Ah, ungrateful man! on chasm's brink
He stands and laughs at all Thou gave.
Destructive forces sweep over his head
And he cares naught, but cries "Power! Power!"
As crushed, and smashed, and slain, and scourged
Are all who stand in his path. But the hour
Of restitution shall come, and on his knees
Man shall repent, trying to right the wrong,
Thy name on his lips, but in prayer,
Love in his soul, and in his heart a song.

Joanna Garelick
WAY BACK WHEN
Heroes are now, heroes were then,
People from way back when:
When the Pilgrims met Columbus' crew
They made Thanksgiving, as we still do
Paul Revere made his famous ride,
Then came the Civil War, North to South side
Susan B. Anthony for women's rights,
Put up many heroic fights.
World War II brought such wonderful men,
From way back, way back when.

Betty Miller
KIERA
Little one so very fair
creamy skin and red red hair
sparkling eyes oh so blue,
little Kiera, we love you.

Like a butterfly so gay
she toddles on about her way.
She touches this and touches that,
she sees a bird with whom to chat.

With a smile of radiance bright,
she gives the darkness instant light.
Her little arms reach to embrace,
bestowing kisses upon your face.

Though her years are only one,
her precious being outshines the sun.
Little Kiera, grandchild so sweet,
watching you is such a treat.

Kheresa Dawn Wedding
IMPLACABLE DETERMINATION

To Mrs. Cherry Devane, the individual who inspired and encouraged me to excel and said that with determination, anything is possible.

Strive for the impossible,
aim for your dreams;
ask not for the inevitable,
but yet for the unseen.

Approach the unapproachable
with decisiveness and dedication;
fall not behind but forge onward
no matter the limitations.
No matter the obstacles that may
befall in your path,
faces the imperilment with
endurance and think nothing of
the past.
Ambitions will bear much trials
and tribulations,
but one must consider them
possessions from the results of
prolonged catechizations.
The Father from up above will
sanctify thee with acclamation,
for only His have the courage to
traverse the realms of undomesticated locations.

The determination of the
impossible,
and the achievement of
your dreams;
has conquered the
inevitable,
and brought light to the
unseen.

Luella McDowell
IN HAWAII
Rain
All afternoon, glass sheets falling.
Glistening rivulets of water flowing down,
Twisted, dark tangles of stems.

Tiny leaves
Lichen-green crustaceans creeping up the trunk of a tree
(Like a braided rope twisting up and around a ship's mast)
Larger leaves straining toward the glass louvers.
Making lights and shadows, that pattern up the ground.
Huge leaves, gathering up the rain, making little pools,
that sparkle all around!

Juanita Kallmeyer

Juanita Kallmeyer
RESISTANCE

Dedicated to world peace and to the restoration and protection of our environment.

We put up so much resistance in vain
And it causes so much misery and pain
That it's like the "Three Little Pigs" story
We huff and puff and we start to worry.

We're like sprinters on the mark. All ready. All set to go
But the gun doesn't go off and we're still straining so
For the unspent energy went nowhere fast
And becomes more of a habit the longer we last.

So, let's try to reverse these trends
And see how many fences it will mend
For we don't realize what resistance does to us folks
Until the toaster burns the toast!

Sometimes we need to shift into reverse
And let the peace and quiet come first
Instead of weathering all of those fears
And maybe stripping some of our gears.

So can we turn our resistance way down low
And just allow the Cosmic energy to flow?
For it feels so good to just let go
If I hadn't tried it I wouldn't tell you so!

Elizabeth Burghen
emerald dreamt
good night emerald sky
my dream has been erased
and given to someone else
heart bleeds
inside
the loneliness
chokes
my breath
shrivels
weakened from running
clutching a final knot
rope is cut with a stone knife
tumbling headlong
mocked futile attempts
salute the grave of the former
wrapped wings about the granite face
drenched swan attired in black
bellows
good night emerald sky

Ronald M Ames
GOD'S COUNTRY
There is a place not far away
Just outside Wellsboro, Pa.
Where God drew His finger through the hills,
And made Pine Creek with its rocks and rills.
It's one thousand feet deep and fifty miles long,
The winds blow through it with a mournful song.
The people come from far and wide,
To see it beauties that none can hide,
With its green mountains and little Four Mile.
It glistens like a jewel in great style.
The deer and bear and turkey play
Up and down its sides all day.
Its rocky sides are steep and straight.
It is now fenced in with an iron gate.
There is a trail about a mile and a half,
Known by many as The Turkey Path.
The sky is blue, the air is clean,
The river takes on a beautiful sheen.
I have been there many a day,
To this place they call
Grand Canyon, P.A.

Chris Baillee
GROWING UP

This poem is dedicated to my five children: Jamie, Bradley, Tammy, Mark and Michael.

Do you ever get an aching feeling deep inside;
A feeling that just won't go away?
You think something has gone wrong,
And that persistent ache is there to stay.

You try to block it; but the pain remains.
It's beginning to tear you right apart.
Your head is aching and throbbing with pain—
An imaginary knife is stuck through your heart.

You reach around inside your mind,
You try to pull an answer out.
All you pull out is a handful of questions;
And you begin to wonder what it's all about.

It's all a part of growing up,
Sometimes you feel you haven't a friend.
A lot of pain and hurt are involved;
But you'll be stronger and wiser in the end.

Madhumita Chattopadhya
LULLABY

I dedicate this poem to my precious husband, Sandip, and to our beloved daughter, Moksha.

Along jasmine groves I wander,
When wistful twilight yonder
Whispers a forgotten lullaby.

Oh forlorn one, dream on
Life is but a moment's dream, then gone,
And 'tis all a dream beyond.

So what remains of Moon and Mind;
Sun and Kind?
Bastions and ladles, magnets and cradles?

An old owl hoots from a Neem tree near,
"'Tis wise to be foolish and foolish to be wise, I fear,
For look at me," it declares,
"I dream by day
And when darkness falls, I watch you dream away.
Topsy turvy, all the same,
One dream ends, where another begins again."

'Then what endures,' I ask in pain,
'beyond dreams'?
The twilight smiles in pensive pause,
"There's nothing below and nothing above.
What is eternal save love?
Through love we endure,
In all else we dream away."

Pamela J Kelly
MY CARPENTER

I dedicate this piece of poetry to the two most significant people in my life. To our Lord Jesus Christ and my husband Mike, whom Christ's love shines through. I love you both!

I'm as a house . . . filled with empty clutter;
The sun locked out by closed shutters.
Cracks and holes in walls by vandals;
Broken doors, the place a shambles.
The windows covered by dirt and dust;
The floors, they creak with effort of trust.

The forgotten belongings left behind;
Cobwebs . . . like woven memories of lost time.
Unkept maintenance tearing the interior . . . .
The unmentioned character remains inferior.

In the still of the day, lies the foundation;
Sturdily standing, barren the heart . . .
The soul . . . she awaits re-creation.

Comes the carpenter with plans in mind;
As the dirt, old memories swept behind.
The soul is ripped and torn to the ground;
The roar of reconstruction, the only sound.

With careful thought and warmth of love;
He restores the trust and beams above.
He paints the walls, carpets the floor;
Then hangs 'Home, Sweet Home' above the door!

He fills the house with all he cherishes.
Settled back, with a smile—and pride.
Knowing his love built house will
Never perish . . .

No longer this soul an empty shell;
Where warm thoughts, and love
And peaceful dreams dwell.

Nicholas Wells

THE MOST CHERISHED GIFT

In love with Geralyn Marie

If i bestowed on thee, my love,
all the treasures men hold above,
their worth all told could never be,
as cherished as your gift to me.

The quests of men,
of Kings . . . . of courts,
their fleece,
their Grail . . . . their holy cause,
are naught but whims to he who
seeks the gift which can't be sought.

A majesty am i,
for i possess that gift,
which men who know its worth,
may never feel its warming touch.

Freely given by he who reigns
We know its light . . . .sadly lost from our sight.
It's love, you see, the love one soul gives freely to another,
without question.
this is the gift i possess,
and thee, my love, have
bestowed your love on me.

Margret Schrapfer

TIME

No time to explore!
No time to enjoy!
No time to think!
No time to help!
No time to see beauty!

Time to be corrupt,
Time to mislead and lie,
Time to make money,
Time to be sick,
Time to die.

Jason Herrell

PROGRESS?

Birds are dying every day,
Tomorrow maybe us.

Fish are dying in the streams.
Where will we get water to drink?

We pour billions of pounds of toxic waste
into the air, and more in the water.
Our ecosystem gets weaker every year.
All we do is make it worse.

As our fossil fuel diminishes,
It's like we really don't care.

There's a hole in our atmosphere.
Our sun's going to explode.

What do we care?
We've got technology and progress?

Kenneth Milburn Beaulieu

SHE IS

This poem is dedicated to my beautiful wife, Donna, for whom this poem was written.

She is to me what . . .
Sunshine is to flowers
She is to me what . . .
Colors are to rainbows
She is to me . . .
As stars are to the heavens

She is to me . . .
As water is to the oceans
She is to me . . .
What hearts are to love
And my love is what
SHE IS! ! !

Kathleen Boucher-Gosling

DISTANT SHORES

Before me
the water flows freely.
Tides by moon's forces.
Distant shores seen
frames by fir trees
The sand a ribbon lacing the edge.
Stands of trees
meeting the glacier formed lake.
Graced by hills lifted above
appear to seek the blue in the sky.

W E Wilbur

INTROSPECT

I think back now, on the places I have known
The people I have seen, the things I have done
I find them to be as chapters of a book
That make up my existence.

I recall a small town, whose name I can't recall
But, whose peacefulness has become a permanent memory,
I close my eyes and envision a church spire
Framed against the sky, in a long-forgotten countryside.

I picture the face of a small child
Whose wide eyes and innocence have captured a place in my mind,
Remembering these things
I gaze upon the peacefulness of your sleeping body.

I think of the things we shared
The touching of our hearts and minds
This, too, is becoming a part of memory
And I wonder how long before
this chapter of my life will end.

People, places, faces and you haunt my mind
And the memory of all these things, makes me what I am.

Mildred V Armstrong

IF ONLY WE COULD ACCEPT OTHERS THE WAY THEY ARE

If only we could accept others the way they are,
Fine-tune in on those traits that make each person a star,
Then pure pleasure would permeate throughout every day,
Lending to our steps a lilt and lightening the way.

Be it tinkering to pass time or serious work,
Some delightful surprises develop from one's quirk;
Still, striving together can be a great deal of fun
And also brings mutual pride when the project is done.

Just as the sun and moon prompt bright prisms by their rays,
Our variegated ideas spin forth like swift relays;
What wonderful worldwide things may be accomplished now
Through understanding, and sharing each other's know-how?

D'Angelo Samuels

MARTIN LUTHER KING

This poem is dedicated to my sister, parents, grandparents, great grandparents and friends. Also in loving memory of Dr. Martin Luther King and Reverend Henry C. Samuels.

I see a man full of courage and heart,
He stood up for his rights and his people.
He cared about the Lord so much,
He went on marches and he preached.

He did not have to do this but he did love his people,
And freedom he wanted to give equal opportunities to Black People.
He fought in a holy way,
He won the race and got us some place.

Sandra Knox Shaver

DEEP ROOTS

Dedicated to my precious mother and husband, without whom I could not have borne the storms of this life.

Winds blow hard . . . . . . my limbs are weak;
I am a tree; my roots run deep.

Once a sapling in the wood . . . man made streets
where the wood once stood . . .
Snow caressed my branches bare . . . .
Bend or break;. what choice was there?

Draw strength from Mother Earth so sweet;
I am a tree; my roots run deep.

Oh, Southern Breeze, who stirs each limb . . .
Bring little birds to rest on them.
Wave leafy branches in the sun . . . .
Make me strong 'ere life is done.

Until my dust and earth's shall meet . . . .
I am a tree; my roots run deep.

Marjorie A Ford

WHEN LIFE ON EARTH FIRST BEGAN

When life on earth first began,
the Lord had made a unique demand,
for He longed to create a special being, unlike any other, and this He certainly did achieve when he created "Mother."

He filled her soul with special gifts, a list that could go on forever, and all the things that happen in our lives we want to share with "Mother."

No matter what my age may be, she always seems to have time for me, and whenever I am sad and blue, "Mother" you're the one I always turn to. It seems that just a word from her, can dry even the littlest tear.

Is it any wonder that on this special day, we turn to her and say,

"I Love You Mother"

Alleda Tolbert

DO YOU KNOW ME?

To my Mother, with Love

We've walked together,
We've talked together,
We've played together,
We've cried together.
I have looked into your eyes
and have seen your soul.
You have looked into my eyes
and have seen only my eyes.
I know you, do you know me?

MaryJo Myers

MaryJo Myers

A QUESTION UNKNOWN

Dedicated to those who love MaryJo, and remember.

Whisper words of meaning
Deep within your heart.
Tell the tales of new,
That have yet,
But not have gone.
Remember only
Words spoken from your heart.
The mind never controls.

Sanity slips,
My game to play.

Stay with me now
From night to day.

Lunar of white
To chariot gold,
Destruction of cities,
But none my own.

Orange is the sky,
Tainted to taste.
Touch me now,
See my grace.

Love is the answer,
The question unknown.

Ruth S Oliver
I MET BEAUTY

For my mother, Merdith R. Smith, Beauty Personified

I met Beauty yesterday while walking on the hill
In one moment of timelessness when all the earth
Stood still

And listened to the silence as it enclosed us there,
Perfect and miraculous, it hung quivering in the air.

I met Beauty yesterday nesting in a tree,
She flicked her tiny feathers as She looked back at me.

I met Beauty yesterday while walking on the shore,
She sang a song of mystery in the mighty ocean's roar.

I met Beauty yesterday in a ray of silvered light
That captured rainbows on its way to banish darkest night.

I met Beauty yesterday in my own dear mother's eyes,
She wore her years so graciously,
How did Beauty become so wise?

I met Beauty yesterday, She introduced Herself to me.
She told me She has many names—one is Generosity.

I met Beauty yesterday and asked from whence She came,
She smiled at me most radiantly and whispered Love's
Sweet name.

Helen K Simpson
THE LIVING GOD

Dedicated to Marion and Rick

Gods created by man alone
Fall from glory as gods unknown.
Many ages pass and You live on
Eternal God on Heaven's throne.

Though kingdoms come and kingdoms fade
God's firmament stands firmly laid.
Man moves on as the flying dust
Yet God reigns on, His world in trust.

Then when all things come to pass
His plan revealed to all at last,
The dust He will gather in His Hands
The Living God holds life for man.

Annemarie Clark
MY PRAYER

To my children—Walter, Darleen, Tammy and Skip—with Love.

I am walking in darkness
on a road that is wide,
the ground feels so shaky
for I have lost my guide.
My soul is drowning
in a world filled with sin,
my prayers are empty
I am lost within.
Oh Lord, where are you?
Show me the path—
Open my eyes—with a glimmer bright—
that I may once again see the light.
My conscience you pricked
now I'm sorely afraid,
Help me oh Lord
before it is too late.
Plant my feet again
on the narrow path,
forgive where I fell
for I was no match for Satan's wrath.
Hold me and guide me
like a little child
for without you my Lord
I cannot find the light.

Sherri N Kaplan
THE POLYESTER ROSE

The poet reads her voice spilling with emotion. I hear
the beauty of her language but the words slip quickly past.
My eyes are drawn to the vivid blue veins encircling her hands.
I look at her face and age spots splatter her skin
like wet brown paint or youthful freckles.
I analyze the rose on her polyester shirt.
I follow the tangled turns of the petals folding
upon each other. I think of my Grandmother. Her body sagging and twisted by time.
The empty patches, where no hair will ever again grow. My
Grandmother, who could have been a scientist, now
waits for death.
The undulant tones of the poet reading and the rose on an old woman's shirt make me feel,
the slipping slide of syllables over the artificial rose
folding and entwining.
When the voice stops, I fall I was only half listening to
the still silent sadness and dark formidable musing. I stifle a
cry, my protest.
All that protects me folds in silence as a rose.

Richard Wilson
CONCEPTION

To Joanna French, with all my heart ...

Like two phases, synchronizing with the season,
Each love draws into one another.
Closing in on new beginnings,
We seek each other with growing anticipation.

Your hand casts an infantile promise
Of the supple petals touch;
Pacifying words breathed into my ear
Of fantasy love we might share.

Entwining our reaching tendrils,
Your soul creeps around me like a dawning mist;
Capturing my heart in its open nature,
Its gentle touch; silent and captivating.

Pools of desire, your eyes search my soul,
Passion boils within their eternal core;
Peeling the outer shell that holds it all,
Speaking to its flame like a lonely prophet.

Teach the ways that fulfill the mind and satisfy the body,
Enrich its deep solitary chasm
With calm warm waters that flow from your sea;
Soothing away all question of that ebb of life.

How lucky we are, to show those ways;
The many paths on which love can walk,
And the gestures of devotion that fill
And complete our souls as one.

Shaun-Marie Scott
THE ROAD OF LIFE

To Joyce Manhertz, and in loving memory of Astor Fitz-Gerald Manhertz.

Life,
the unlit passage between this world and the next.
A path paved with bittersweet experiences,
Sometimes leveled with happiness
Sometimes holed with sorrows.

Along its course, we travel
The imperfections within which our destinies lie
Remain unforeseen—around the bend
Until we're upon them.

Ne'er-the-less, we continue on
In the hope that the surprises it holds
Will prove more good than bad,
That at the completion of this road,
We'll be fully prepared
for the next . . .

Rebecca Thompson
LOVE

I dedicated this poem to my friends, Ruth and Maryabelle and for my parents for encouraging me.

The best thing about Love is when Jesus Christ died on the cross for our sins. His precious blood cleanses us forever and forever. Love is when you are willing to risk all that you have for one another. Love takes giving and taking an equal share for each other. Love reminds you of Valentine's Day, when that special someone gives you a gift. Love is a symbol of peace, kindness, and especially sharing the good and bad times. Love gives you the freedom to be yourself. For last, everybody should Love each other because CHRIST First Loved Us! !

Walter Bardeck
I LOOK WITH WONDER

Each wintry night . . . .
I look with wonder
Into the starlit skies
Where I see
A dazzling moon
Reflected in radiance
On the crystal waters
Of a mountain lake . . .
While the stunning stars,
Scattered across the skies,
Soften the darkness . . .
Where the trees stand tall;
And the calm wind
Blows all around me.
Now, I know
That God is here . . . .
If we choose
To see Him.

Nicole M Connelly
SUN AND THE MOON

The sun and the moon moving through clouds,
lightning flickering to the ground.

The sun moves away and the moon comes in.
People sleeping in their beds
and snoring in their heads.

The sun comes up and people get up.
And the world is alive again!

Beverly Welser
WILL WE EVER KNOW

Will we ever know
How far the path of life does go?
Or will we have to suffer
The fate of ignorant people
Who fear the height of the steeple?
I would like to know
How far the stars do climb
To vision life's eternity
And still have peace of mind.
Is there an entity in us
The evil we don't show
To lead us all a real bad blow?
Do you believe in everlasting life
Another chance to prove
That we are really in control
And wish to make our move?
They call that reincarnation
And, that is life again
Which seems to mean a life before
Be it women or the men.
No one can tell for sure
Or, is insanity an instant cure?

Lillian Mary Smith Lee
THE OLD SCHOOL HOUSE

This poem written by my mother, is dedicated to her memory, and to her children and grandchildren. It was her belief you live on through them.

The Old School House is silent now, where us kids used to play,
And there's nothing left for me but the memory,
For I passed that way today.
There's the same old notch against the fence, where us kids played ball,
Because the kids in our gang had to be just so tall.
The little babbling brook runs on just the same,
and there's the same old tree where I first carved my sweetheart's name.
But the little pals I loved are gone,
Scattered God knows where.
The old school house is tumbling down,

It looks so empty and bare.
For they built a bigger and better school,
With a big fence running round.
But I wonder if the kids of today, will ever find the joys
us bare footed kids found.
Oh they may tear you down, little old school house, but
they can never tear the memories out of my heart.
For it was here that I first got my lesson in life,
And here that I first got my start.

Berthold Goldman
THE ENDLESS DANCE
The sun was high, flowers bloomed, the air was clean after the rains of spring,
and the trees played gently with the wind.

The forest was quiet, totally alive with the rhythm of life,
the call of a bird to find its mate,
a gurgling brook, the noise of the wild.

It was peaceful, silent, as if in another world,
non-existent except in the mind,
nourishing rhythm, soothing, healing.
Destruction—rebirth,
the endless dance of the flow of life that never dies.

Ken Hanna
LIFE WITH LOVE
When love arrives you should open the door
There's nothing in life that is worth more
It's the greatest gift that is given out
And to the world you should always shout

Let everyone know of the gift received
The joy that love has truly conceived
In its splendor and glory it's without peer
If truly love there would be no fear

Happiness and contentment completely abound
And thru the world its feeling's renowned
So never deny it when it's at your door
Just give yourself because it asks no more

For life with love is why we all live
We have it in us it's our need to give
You will become whole for all your years
And then can face life void of all fears

Timothy L Busam
ONCE—IT WAS SIMPLE
Once it was simple, beautiful—
an untouched terrain.

Now it's cluttered, scarred—
not the same.

Trees have been removed—
and hills cut through.

To build structures, roads—
for me and you.

There's concrete, asphalt—
steel and brick.

Condominiums all over—
take your pick.

Will we destroy all of nature?—
or think about what we are doing.

And change some of our goals—
into what we should be pursuing.

Preserving and enhancing—
what is already here.

Let's discuss it now—
lend an ear.

Isiah Posey
A SALUTE TO THE AFRICAN-AMERICAN

To my wife Pat, and my two sons, Isiah and Antarrio.

A salute has been long overdue,
To a race that has prevailed and come through
With strength far beyond compare,
We've broken records and lived to dare.

Determined to set new goals,
For future Generations to behold.
We've pushed forward through Scorn and Scold
Yet we stand polished brighter than Gold.

We are a proud Race,
So it is only due we take our place.
Wherever you may be this very day,
Stand tall and show your face.

Raise your hands by the millions
Above adversities and Salute The African-American.
A cultured, and a beautiful, race of people.

Richard M Waldrup Sr
HAPPINESS IN JESUS

Dedicated to my mother Edwina Waldrup

I sought for joy in His creatures,
I tried human love to win;
But these things did not satisfy
The world with all its sin.

Till freed from this worldly tumult
In a little quiet room apart,
I gave all my love to Jesus
And found heaven in my heart!!

R Spenser Davis

R Spenser Davis
DAYBREAK
Box cars fly toward the horizon,
Bumping and jumping down the rails.
Black and brown and grey they are,
Burning coal in the air.

Bells ring as the train rolls on;
Boisterous and bully and bucking.
Beaming its light into the air,
Barbarian hordes do prepare.
Sharpening their arrows and knives,
Shabbily clad rebels wait.
Shaman casts the fortune spell,
Shadowy figures in the wild.

Attack at daylight claims its prize;
Trainloads of jewels and crowns of gold.
Derailed and defunct the engine lies,
Visions of death float, by and by.

Patricia DeFeis
LOVE TO SPARE

With heartfelt love to the two Roberts in my life and warm gratitude and love to Lou, my father.

When our first child was born last year,
Articles we read held something to fear,
You and your mate may grow apart, so beware!
And you may be too tired to even care.

Bottles, diapers, doctors and crying,
Your body and mind saying "This is tiring,"
Getting up at least twice a night,
And then arising with dawn's first light.

It seemed our fears must surely come true,
Especially then, when you're feeling somewhat blue,
But we found a pleasant surprise in store,
Our love for each other grew even more.

Our hearts had opened and love poured out,
It's what being a family is all about,
We found we both held love to spare,
And giving love to our son was something else we could share

Darius C Cawood
HARD TIMES
Have you ever walked the streets alone
Have you ever been without a home
Did you go to bed, hungry last night
No one there, to hold you tight
That's the way it is, on the streets at night
Under the stars and the neon lights
Where sometimes you steal and sometimes you fight
Even though you know, it just ain't right
I carry all I own, upon my back
I used to drive a Cadillac
Lived in a house, high on a hill
Now I stay, down by the landfill
I pity the poor farmers and all the factory workers
The banks don't care, what you have to say
They'll sell your house and send you on your way
What happened to prosperity
in the land and home of the free
Don't look down, on your fellow man
Just reach out and lend a helping hand
Have you ever walked the streets alone

Stephanie Kreiser
VISIONS OF LIFE
Here I sit and marvel
All the beauty up above
It surrounds me and envelops
A part of me called love.

The sound of wind through the trees
Is music to my ears
It takes away all my doubts
And washes away my fears.

A bright ball of warmth and light
Shines down from the sky
It makes promises of life to come
Of the natural wild cry.

As the grasses bend before the breeze
And shadows dance on the ground
I realize this is where I belong
To a pact forever bound.

Nina Lois Carrico
IN THE GARDEN OF GRIEF

To Sandra, my seventeen year old daughter, picked from life like a rose in the garden, leaving the vine to mourn the loss. That pain of grief like the thorn is what remains.

Grief is like a garden
Where I walk in its feeling,
Pierced by the sharpest thorn.
Asked by the memories of the rose
That arched my sunny days,
"Why was I ever born?"
Now I am tangled
In the overgrowth and briar,
From this immeasurable loss, I mourn.
It wraps my heart in pain,
Never to be freed
To pick the flowers grown
Or see the trees and birds
The same again, in glory,
As I struggle lost, forlorn.
In the garden of grief
Roses bloom and fade away,
Remaining always is the thorn.

Bessie Kerns
ENCOURAGING OTHERS
Some folks have the ability to push;
Encouragement is their key;
They loosen the talents and abilities
Which are dormant 'til they're set free.

Encouragement puts them into action;
They begin to accomplish things;
They tho't they could do nothing
'Til someone loosened their wings.

Encouragement touches potential,
And ignites it for some big deed;
Sometimes just a word of encouragement
Is really all they need.

Sometimes encouragement is more needful
Than even education itself;
If a life is disarrayed
Or lacks confidence in himself.
The ability to encourage others
Is a very blessed gift;
It opens many prison doors,
And gives many a needful lift.

Bill Wilkes
THE GHETTO OF MY MIND
They're there, back and forth
Tiny, gnawing doubts at the walls of my mind

I wonder when we started to change.

I remember the days when we were happy
You laughed a lot,
Sweet, musical laughter.
We held hands on early morning walks by the lake and watched a sunrise, disturbing beach sleepers and lovers.

Then the wall came, the silences,
tiny gnawing doubts that grew,
A wall, brick by brick, 'til I could no longer see you.

The lonely, desperate crying out,
You don't hear.

I run back and forth; no door, no crack,
The wall is solid.

Here I sit now, alone, wondering,
trying not to cry.

Alone. Silence. Except for the screaming,
In the ghetto of my mind.

Rose Coccoli
MY DAD

Oh! My Dad I loved him so . . .
This I fear he'll never know . . .

For he died on the seventh of November . . .
This is a day I'll always remember . . .

For on this day I lost the sweetest kindest guy . . .
I have a lot of regrets that make me cry . . .

When someone dies and goes above . . .
You always question did they know of your love . . . .

Oh! Dad there were times that we were apart . . .
But thank God you knew you were always in my heart . . .

Oh! my Dad a sweet and gentle man . . .
Always there to lend a hand . . .

But now he'll never see . . .
Just what he meant to me . . .

For I didn't know until he died . . .
Just how much I felt inside . . .

For he died with all us near . . .
His soft sweet voice we'll never hear . . .

Oh! Dear God I loved my Dad . . .
He was the best a girl could have . . .

Grace Marston Goertler
LOVE

To my daughter, Barbara

Love is something kept real deep
Inside a heart with human beat.
But to find it you must try
not to keep the love inside.

For like a flower it must grow
from seed, to pod, to bloom
and then though withered on the stem
it will bloom again; again.

So do not keep within yourselves
true love in any form
For man and wife and love
are three things that belong—
together.

Mark D Bennion
TRUTH AND CONSTANCE

To my great parents for their wonderful example of "truth and constance."

What do we follow in our quest in life?
Reason, rage, foolishness, and affliction.
Oh, the games that hurt us and bring much strife.
Thy reason in life is false tradition.
Our souls are untamed, feral, and fierce,
Like the leaf in wind tossed to and fro.
Arrogance and vanity lose their mirth,
And trials come like punches from the foe.
Our bodies coil, wither, tremble, and shake.
Thy reason takes control and choice is lost.
Hopelessness, confusion, and vast mistakes.
What sends the spark is not an immense cost.
But truth and constance are what stir my heart
And make a proud moment consummate art.

Zachary Scott Savicki
OH WOE!

My room's a mess, it's getting late,
It's got more trash than half the state;
I don't want to clean, it's my summer vacation;
But if I don't I'll be on probation

Jennifer Gammons

Jennifer Gammons
PATH OF LIFE

To Mr. Strohm: Thank you for opening my mind to the deeper aspects of life.

Life is but the path that we must take.
Whether the path be smooth and tame,
Filled with happiness or fame,
Our life is built on choices that we make.

At times it seems to lead us straight to sorrow;
Where darkness is everywhere
And heaviness fills the air,
Our only hope is in knowing there's tomorrow.

We pass by sorrow, on towards happiness.
Our thoughts are wild and free,
Standing up to all we see.
Knowing that we are from heaven blessed.

There comes a time in the paths of every life
Where the path goes left, but also to the right.
And at this point proceed with utmost care,
For what you make of your life is waiting there.

Monica M Trexler
IN THE CEMETERY

You said you dealt pot,
And was now doing coke.
When you came for my help,
I thought it was a joke.

So here I stand,
An unlistening fool,
No jokes were you telling,
You thought you were cool.

Why wasn't I there?
Where could I have been?
Why wouldn't I find time
To hear out my friend?

These things come to haunt me,
About the life I didn't save,
About the shovel ignored,
As you dug your own grave.

Yvonne G Engel Davis
AS WE GROW OLD

Some people say that growing old
is not so great and so I'm told.

Some people say we must be bold,
but others simply just grow cold.

As from the beginning we are born in a state of void.
So does it end when our time comes, that
from whence we came we come again.

And, from the beginning we know of nothing.
Some seek out knowledge while others merely play along.

And, in this world of question and uncertainty,
Who is to say which path a man will take?

And, in this world of mystery and awe,
Who will believe that there is a God?

Some wonder if there is a purpose to life,
While others continue to struggle and strife.

And, who is to say that there is no purpose in death?
And, who is to say that our lives are not pre-ordained?

And, who can say when looking up above,
That a presence is there and much beloved?

Bert J Vanorse Sr
THE ARTIST

If I could be an artist, I think I should like to be as great as the one that made the stars, and the heavens, the mountains, and the sea.

But there can only be one so great to create this vast universe. His greatness could never be put on canvas or in verse.

But I can always admire his work and praise him with my words. The only one to create the stars, the heavens, the flowers, and the birds.

His artistry touches all of us as through this life we trod. For you see dear friends this artist the greatest of them all is our Lord.

Howard W Martin Jr
PRISONER OF YOUR SENSUALITY

To my fiancée, Cindy, with all my love

Your soft silky body, taunting and pressing
ever onward to over powering passion,
Your smooth thighs prepare a table before me.

You invite me to sample your fruit with everlasting <u>Desire</u>;
as you caress me with every portion of your oneness.
Mounting feverishly to the pitch of ecstasy,
you grasp me tightly to your wanton body,
beholding all of me.

And in the end my love, I awake.

Gloria J Frank-Landry
SOMEKIND OF HAUNTING

The candle flickered in the evening dusk,
Sending shadows dancing across a distant wall.
She watched while the shifting light
Moved gracefully, lovingly,
Upon the hardened surface.
Like a lover who has an unsatiable need,
The shadows caressed one area
And then tenderly another.
Light kissed, tasted, and smelled
the texture, coarseness,
Of paper clothing and longed desperately
To reach beneath the barrier.
Like a virgin unawakened, the walls stood unmoved
While the shadows trembled, reached out,
And strained to evoke a response.
But none came.
A sigh from the girl snuffed out the flame,
And the wax hugged the shaft of silky tallow
In tears of pained sorrow.
While the wall, hard and cold,
Watched the ember fade and die.

Julie A Morin
A STRANGE CAT

In the middle of the night, while the city slept,
Out of the window the strange cat crept.
Looking for mice in the stingy lane
Was his goal, as he slid from the window pane.
But as he climbed from the second floor ledge,
He saw Mrs. Muldoon going over the edge.
Yelling at Harry, her husband, no less,
Because he was fat—full of laziness.
The strange cat looked on—puzzled he was
For Mrs. Muldoon was fat too for no cause;
Inactive and slow she was, thought the cat
So, why was she yelling at Harry like that?
He was thinner than she, and took walks now and then,
But did Mrs. Muldoon walk? No one knew when.

Niyi Afolabi
SANE LUNACY

To Fabio, a nostalgic constancy, my contemplative odyssey.

Sanity born of lunacy:
When like bombshell unforeseen,
Human mildness taken for stupidity;
And the mysteries untold,
Become lessons of life.
The inner turmoil in check;
The bestiality like normalcy,
The hope, the absurd, the ridiculous.
Humiliation, subtle and humbled,
Yet for no obvious human fault.
Where to turn, where to go,
A confusion concealed.
But for a tongue to tell,
Lunacy becomes sanity!

Kimberly Pospisil
ONLY IN MY DREAMS
I hold you tight,
night after night,
but only in my dreams.
I wake each morning
only to find tears
on my pillow
and a chill
by my side.
Each day it gets harder
to face the music,
I see you,
you see me,
but, alas,
we're only together
in my dreams.
Dreams hidden from others
night after night
hidden partially out of shame,
partially out of fright.

Linda D Ferraro
NATURE'S MYSTERIES

Dedicated to Delores Hansen, for caring, sharing, and just being a friend.

Intricate, delicate, dainty
snowflakes swirling softly all
around
Each one an individual, as it joins
the others on the ground
All are but one of God's many
miracles, in which the world
abound.

The complex venous patterns of
a gracefully falling leaf
Floating quietly across the forest
floor, as stealthy as a thief
Who has come home at last to die,
with a gentle rustling sigh, and
sense of great relief.

The spiny back side of a tall blade
of grass, is sharp and jagged as
some broken glass
Whispering and weeping with
every breeze which does pass
Its over burdened shoulders
causing it to bend and sigh—
'alas'!

The hauntingly deep blue green
sea with overwhelming white
waves, so exquisite in form
Roaring and running up the sandy
beaches, which are so smooth
and warm
Is God's way of telling us, both of
the peaceful calm, or a raging,
impending storm.

The majestic splendor of a pretty
pastel rainbow
Is like an artist's palette, or a
spectacular light show
But it has no beginning or end, at
least none that mere mortal man
can see or know.

Or take the serene beauty of a
sweet scented, sculptured, freely
growing wild flower
Its velvety petals glistening with
dew, or sparkling rain droplets
after a brief passing shower
Isn't that a subtle example of all
God's overflowing love and great
power?

Snowflakes, leaves, grass, seas,
rainbows and flowers
Are just a few of God's loving
gifts to His children, to delight
us for hours.

Michelle Holland
DRIED UP LOVE
The roses you gave me
So long ago
Bring me more sadness and pain
With each passing day.

The roses remind me
Of love gone bad
The roses have dried up
Just like the love we once had.

Darryl Leon Jackson
CHANCE

For Barbara, with love. My "Princess" Sensual Eyes.

Sensual eyes, a sensual glance,
A timeless few seconds, encountered
by chance.
A sensual smile, a sensual
touch;
Emotions are stirred, & hearts
beating much.
Sensual voice speaking, slow
nods of the head;
Eyes revealing mysteries, of
things left unsaid.
Sensual dreams inspired; dreams of
love unfold;
A first realizing, such colour, how
bold.
Sensual passions ignited, passions
dare sustain;
All as bright as sunshine, all as soft
as rain.
Sensual days a newness, nights alive
with bliss;
lifetimes lived in seconds, every time
we kiss.
Little children laughing, little
children cry;
A closer look is needed—Is that you
& I?

Moments so enchanted, moments
lost to time;
Moments play impressionly, back
across my mind.
Sensual eyes descending—sensual
eyes no more;
the form of someone waiting now,
along celestial shores
Sensual eyes ascending—sensual
eyes a glance;
My journey to be with you now, I
know is more than chance.

Helen A Jones
OUR HOME ON CRYSTAL GLADES
I like our home on Crystal Glades
Just any time of year;
In Fall or Winter, Spring or Summer,
I hold every time most dear.
I look out our Living room window
When the Summer breezes
blow:—
And watch the water ripple slowly
As the trees sway to and fro.
Soon—Fall of the year arrives
And it is lovely to behold;
When leaves have changed in color
To all hues of red and gold.
Later—Winter winds are blowing,
And snow is on the ground;
Birds are coming to the feeder
And flying all around.
Then—Spring arrives in its glory,
The leaves are a lovely green.
The calm lake looks like a mirror,
And reflects the beauty therein;
So any season of the year,
Morning, noon, or night:—
I like to look out our window,
And enjoy the beautiful sight!

Beverly G Robinson
WHERE IS BEAUTY?
Where is Beauty? Where is her
repose?
In a picture, poem, song, tree or rose?
Is she locked within a chapel
Or dancing on the hill?
All Nature calls to Beauty fair
On land, at sea or in the air.
Look up, look down, look all around,
she's there.

Only perceive her presence if you
will.
It is said that God made everything
beautiful in His time;
So seek the face of Beauty and she'll
make your life sublime.
Where is Beauty? Where is her
repose?
She may be there beside you
dressed in beggars clothes.

Pauline Corzine Gregoris
MEMOIRS (ON THE 68TH BIRTHDAY OF MY SISTER, HELEN CORZINE IBAÑEZ)
I love daisies, blue and white, phone
calls in the night,
Front porch coffee, a busy honeybee.
I love purple 'sheepshowers,' your
roses and other flowers.
I love our little creatures, newspaper
features.
Also I love trains, brawn and brains.
Oh yes, little hummingbird nests—
but you I love best, ALWAYS.
And may you have many, many more
happy, happy birthdays!

On second thought:

I love mud pies, airplane in the skies,
French harp—'Old Black Joe'—,
stick horses on the go,
Blackberries in a gallon, a mile to
market, then fun,
Sweet potatoes in the oven, baby
chicks beneath a hen,
Jersey cow no good for riding, best
by mama's law abiding.
Pumpkin pies, custard, mince;
breakfast gravy on a bench.
Years now add to 68, joys of you
appreciate,
Never fading from my head, ever
lovelier instead.
What price life without you, sister?
Dear little mama, you gave me her—
THANKS!

Christopher C Petro (Chuck Vandal)
AS I SIT HERE AND LISTEN TO THE WIND OUTSIDE

To all my friends: Mark, Erin, Sandra, Pee Wee, Eric, and Robin. Thanx for everything, but mostly for being who you are.

As I sit here and listen to the wind
outside
Blowing, whistling as it takes its
long ride
As I stare at the wall watching
images form
Wrapping the blankets tighter
trying to keep warm
I think about the past, what
the future may hold
And what will I do, where will I be
when I'm old
And I remember people I knew, and
how they met their ends
And I wonder what's going to happen
to my friends
Then the clock strikes the hour, and
the wind blows on
The sky is purple in the east,
and the past is gone
Then the alarm rings, and I must arise
The future is in tomorrow, and
there is red in my eyes
So off to work to earn my pay
another day spent as a slave
my mind and body tired and
burnt
It's the story of my life,
though I wish it weren't
But it's a fact of this reality that has
to be faced
nothing ever wants to stay
where it is placed
all things in nature tend to
wind up a mess
and my life is just like the
rest.

Beatrice Maxey Fuller
A NEW HOME
Why should death bring a chill?
This too, is God's will.
Just as it was His will for me
A living and loving person to be.

Death is God's way to transpose
An earthly bramble—to a heavenly
rose.
I shall with the Lord abide
Forever beyond the Great Divide.

My Lord promised to prepare
A home for me away somewhere,
Now He has called me; I must go.
The door is swinging to and fro.

Just beyond the heavenly door
Is health and happiness forevermore.
Some-day you can go there too,
And I'll be waiting there for you.

Melanie Siegel
THE INTERIOR MAN
What does he talk about
When he talks about love
At the café last night
We mentioned children
And his deep eyes turned
A baby's infinite blue
But then
I don't know why
He said well
I've got to go now

When he stood

He was a man in full
Against the red and smoky light
And as he left
All the women turned and stared
His walk kinetic against their backs
Such firmness had aroused them
They felt they saw a man
Through whom a father passed
Himself into a man who had a son

And I sat deeper in my chair
Not watching them watch me
Or his retreat
You know, I saw the man
I also saw the father and the son
But it eludes me
What does he speak of
When he speaks of love

Jo Ann Stovall Page

Jo Ann Stovall Page
LOVE AND REVELATIONS

Life's Lessons, well-learned, are sometimes full
Of Pain: A Paradox of
Variables—We oft must lose to Gain. Intimate
Expressions misplaced will only Ignore

And Neglect all those mutually Significant
Needs born of Mutually-bonding Respect. Now we're
Deemed as One; Now We can

Really Soar. At least, what we
Experience is Real as We approach that Door.
Very carefully We Enter, We Linger then
Emerge. We Sing the Joyous Melody—
Life's Song is not a Dirge. We rise
Above the Trivia; We know Undisputed
Truth; We've Shared a glimpse of
Infinity's Sweet Bird of Youth. Thank God for the Wisdom
Of knowing that Life is
Never "Out-of-Hand": Indeed, We can
Say, with Blessed Assurance, it's All in the Master's Plan.

R L Quaid
IN LIMINE

Scientists in their wisdom say
That all things great and small
Are from a single primal soup;
A touch of this a pinch of that
Has made a star, a tree,
And even me!

To whom belonged the mighty hand
That stirred the soup and knew
A touch of this, a pinch of that
Would make a star, a tree,
And even me?
Oh, Lord, was it not thee?

Kelly Willis
WINTER OF PREJUDICE

Joy is found only in understanding; understanding is found only in caring. This poem is dedicated to all of those who have hurt, and all of those who have done the hurting.

Oh hopeless winter,
Filling hearts with ice,
Hiding the Sun with your foreboding gray clouds.

Capturing my life,
With your twisting snows,
The echoes of my calls unfound.

Your imageless ice,
Mocking my blinded dreams,
As my fear of your coldness mounds.

The world unseeing,
Of the danger you present,
While your death blankets the cold, cold ground.

Tricia Greene
SCHIZOPHRENIC'S VIEW OF THE POSTAL SERVICE

Thousands of pressed white sheets in disordered piles, here,
around me. Envelopes to hide thoughts in.
Stamps come flying out of
drawers as short, fat women smack them on envelopes, filled
with warped dreams and incestuous desires.
Packages hurtle toward me, stop, turn, fall into bins with the rest.
They wait silently for me to move
and then they will lash out with
their string and tape and pull me
down into their brown paper
wrappings and kill me.
Men in uniforms run around
frantically searching for whatever it is they're looking for;
me, but I am hidden behind the
cellophane tape and I become invisible.
Faces peer solemnly from
magazines, but they are cursing and screaming at me.
Lights flash on and off. They stay
off while the uniformed men pull at
blades of metal covering
the windows.
Signs are plastered on the walls
shrieking their messages of closed
minds, closed eyes, closed doors.
And I have not moved. Scared of
strings and paper, I hide in cellophane.

Carol Ann Moore
LOST INSIDE

For Bree, Shane, Alarie, & Susannah. May they never be "lost."

The frightened child reached out
to find no one there
Where she once stood and lived and dreamed
that someone would care

The angry teenager ran from herself
so she would not remember
Where she once stood and lived and dreamed
Only to see hope grow ever dimmer

The lost adult stood alone
with nothing left inside
Where once she had stood and lived and dreamed
And finally; died

They cannot go back
they are forever lost
Where they once stood and lived and dreamed
Only to pay such a terrible cost

We cry for the child
for the teen and adult too
Where they stood and lived and dreamed
And for all of us who didn't know what to do

Geraldine Hoff Doyle
AD FINEM (TO THE END)

He shall not tire in work,
he shan't lay down his head,
nor in the lucid shadows lurk.

A superannuated way
appears in wrinkles on his face,
but still he works and work he may.

His cry must yet be heard,
"It is for him I serve"
although I speak my own last word.

'Tis death that ends the toil,
that voice shall no more sing,
From life to love to death to spoil.

Nancy L Masuda
IN DREAM

Walking on the edge
of somewhere
far away
A minor satisfaction
silken strands
of imagination
Music of the mind
the indeliberate scores
contemplate fantasy
Only to absolve themselves
to walking
on the edge

Eric Sivertson
INDIAN SUMMER

To Mom, who taught me to love reading and writing.

Indian summer flows crisply through autumn's
A eucharist sensation, an absence of torment, tiredness.

A presence similar to salvation, the ease of leaving life
To enter life, new wine, new bread, filling yearnings
Forgotten in life's hurry, disguised in life's pursuit of tomorrow.

Mary Veilleux
LOVE'S REWARD

With joy in my heart, I dedicate this poem to Rick and Cathy who have blessed me with my first grandchild.

From God's great heaven a special love began.
Twas planted in the heart of a woman and a man.
She, a fair-skinned and gentle-spirited one.
He, a brawny dark-haired man, I call 'son.'

Together they live and love and care.
Two young people with the dreams that they share.
Each one so special . . . a gift to the other.
Both such a joy to the heart of this mother.

Together as one, I watch their love grow
(As love always will when it's love that we sow)
God too, has smiled on their union as one
And sent forth his blessing . . . a new-born son.

Such a treasure from heaven! Such a joy to the heart!
How to say thank you . . . where does one start?
For it's written on their faces and seen in the eyes
Of two young parents with a dream realized.

Give to your boy-child what God has given you.
Love unconditional . . . and all that is true.
Bless him each day with the gift of each other
Being always to him—faithful dad, faithful mother.

Virginia K Yamamoto
DEATH OF A PLANET

The land burns red in the orange-gray dawn,
Blanketed in a ghostly ashen-hued haze.
Basalt cliffs stand naked, their cover long gone,
Awakening to vaporless desolation under searing rays.

The land bleeds its yellow-gray dust,
Its life-source the tenant of a windstorm.
Its twisted iron limbs have turned to rust.
Its granite bowels crumble, yielding to reform.

The acrid smells of lifeless powder go unnoted.
Green is a color earth no longer sustains.
The land drifts woefully, dead and bloated,
Mocking motions of life where no life remains.

The burning breath of earth sets hills aflame.
Molten sands of fire flow without restrain.
For the destruction of life, man is to blame,
As the scorched soul of earth cries out its pain.

Jennifer M Schmidt
IF ONLY

If only there was some way
I could tell you not to care.
I cannot invent something
that is not there.
I'll only hurt you in the end,
but I hope you'll always
be my friend.
It hurts me to be this way
If only I could change
in just one day.
But my heart has already died
I can't even say that I cried.
I know it's hard to understand me.

If only you'll listen to my plea.
Don't ever let your heart turn to stone.
For if you do you'll always end up alone.

Matt McCollum
BROKEN DREAMS
Visions of kingdoms velvet with ruby red skies,
mystical mountains in turquoise clouds abound.
We lived from breath to breath,
died from day to day.
Stoned on dreams, disillusioned by promises,
we roamed the concrete confusion in search of refuge.

Candle light sliced the tarry skies of deadly nightshade
as we explored fate from pillars of imagination and frustration.
Never looking backward or forward
for the abundance of uppers and downers
which promised a better direction.
Magic potions on paper tabs—the key?

Broken dreams and broken glass
blurred our blood stained vision of enchantment.
The full moon's magic filled the air
as we danced among the currents of the forces of the night.

I . . , I won't let go of the echoes
of the silent street lamps in my mind.
The flame deep in my soul
still flickers with the secrets
that darkness hides behind.

Leanne Janzen
DEAD SOULS

To my lost love, who made me aware of what I had become, like a dead soul.

Dead souls
Flesh dressed
Latest craze
Moving maze
Signs, sights
Angel of light
Satan deceives
People believe
Psychics, magic
Such a plight
To find true light
For Satan steals
While the Spirit reveals
Thoughts and intentions
Exposing deception
The word as the weapon
Jesus, the Christ
His blood is redemption

Joyce Bartlett
CHICAGO OBJECTIVE
Undaunted by the perils of weakness and strength
of woes so overwhelming of multitudes in this
great human melting pot of the world, Chicago,
city of dreams to old and young
moves forward each day with vigor and stress
to a commercial and political calling
that may change or erase a familiar sight
with agony, or perhaps happiness,
depending upon whomever it strikes!

Why, great old Chicago, do you continue—
who commands it—why do you grow?
Is it the new chasing out the old?
You are venturesome, ugly and even bold.
Do not lose face in sight of the beholder,
Lessen your woe upon the unfortunate,
Ease the burden of the years of the aged
or you shall retreat—fall back again—
upon your face, without O'Leary's cow!

John E Tulaney Jr
AS I LIFT MY HEAD

Jen, for all that you are to me.

As I lift my head
She stands alone.
The soft white light
Rolls over her shoulder
With a smooth warm flow.

I realize why.
Why I love so deeply,
But live so long.

And then she is gone . . .
All that remains is
A sharp cold light.
It burns but gives no warmth.
I am alone

Ingrid Zagers

Ingrid Zagers
THE HOMELESS
There he sits
on the corner.
The people pass him by
Some give him
a look of pity, others of scorn
but they never stop and help.
And the rest of the crowd is
largely indifferent to him.

There he sits
on the corner
a brown paper bag
in his hand
He dares to dream of what
it would be like,
if he had a job,
a family and real friends.
Not only the stray dog
which likes to be scratched
behind its ears.

There he sits
on the corner.
Huddled in his tattered
old jacket.
Trying to keep warm.
Trying to ignore the pain
in his empty stomach
He takes a swallow
from the contents in
the brown paper bag.
Hoping that it will dull the pain,
that it will help
him to forget.

There he sits
on the corner
A tear slips down
his grimy cheek
into the stubble on
his chin,
while he stares out
at the largely indifferent world
as it passes him by.

There he sits
on the corner.
He is the homeless,
the people pass him by,
some give him,
as look of pity, others of scorn
But they never stop and help.

Leota Dowdle
THE UNBORN
A number of things are beyond my ken;
Bigotry and war and cruelty,
And mans ill-treatment
Of other men.

Why do we send missionaries
Throughout the land
To tell of the wonders
God has planned;

Why use all our legal resources
And countless money and time,
To assure equity to him
Convicted of a horrible crime?

With years of medical research,
And our doctors knowledge and skill
We prolong the lives
Of those who are desperately ill.

Then with a righteous phrase
"The freedom of choice"
We condemn the innocents
Who have no voice.

Roshni Schelling Sharma
JOSHUA'S KITTY LITTER AND VICTOR THE BLACK CAT

A black cat
dropped easily
from George's hands
into Joshua's
kitty litter
making nasty
odor pour quickly
right straight up
Victor's whiskers.
Xenon yet zesty!!

Cheryl Elliston-Wright
FORBIDDEN LOVE

Do you want to be with me,
Like I want to be with you,
I need you.

Do you have the need to be,
Deep down inside of me,
I want you.

Do you have that little fear,
When we're oh so very near,
I'm scared too.

When I'm in your embrace,
And I look into your face,
It's so right.

But when we're all alone,
And so many miles from home,
I miss you.

Eric Randall Wooten
REFLECTIONS
I now float over the waters of my life.
Below me I see images reflecting
in the clouded, black depths.

With careful precision,
I slowly descend to the surface.
And there upon the water I search,
then quickly snatch out a memory.

Yes, that's the one I wanted.

I remember now, I remember you.
You were so perfect. I loved you.
I haven't forgotten that.

I wish that you could have loved me,
the way I loved you.
But how could you have?
We were so different from each other,
worlds apart.

Forgive me for talking to you
as if you are really there,
listening.
Deep in the pit that was my heart,
I know that you are gone,
forever.

Regretfully, I throw your memory
back into the icy water,
and I continue floating . . .
alone.

Lori Schekman
THE COCOON BUTTERFLY
Butterfly;—Simply emerging from
far in deep shell's core
rooted in fear AND mistrust
PRACTICE OPPOSITE—Living
AND Being for all
ALL is worth.

Learn peace discovered ONLY
within your OWN self—only—in the end.
Be gentle=don't force; don't fight;
Just Be free within OWN inner
journey(s)
BE FREE TO BE!!!
WHATEVER you dare: Only wish;
Only dream; Only see.
ALWAYS Believe In Yourself!!!!!
AND (never) Fear Not!
Make AND Take your OWN space
AND limit yourself NOT!
Attract, Invite, Allow (for) the real.
Sense "Inspite Of" head's wild AND
crazy committees(s) Mixed flightty
fight UN—shielded—not free . . .
(IT) Cost(s) indeed?!!
Deep to fullest ALL it is worth
Concept Image Dream Chasers
response detail(s) requested.
Shell split—ting INEVITABLE;
Simple Release, simple release
. . . . FREE SPIRIT SOARS! . . .
At Long Last, I AM (now)
FINALLY—NOW indeed able to be
Free—
FREE "Just To Be" —me—.

Cheryl Mari Lakey Loring
SOMEDAY
Someday I may live to see all men,
come together all as friends.
No matter what color, race or creed,
they'll all work together for those in need.
In need of someone to show them how,
to start to walk as of now,
someone to help a blind person to see,
and others to help the poor in need.
Who are all human like you and me.

T K Brown
HURT
To love—but to lose
Yet, where has it gone?
It remains—where I can see it
But still not able to touch it.
Will it return
The way it was—
The way I want it.
No one will ever know
What pain I have.
It is hidden—so well
Always present—
A part of my life.

Mary Beth Stewart Wedberg
JAPANESE PICTURE
Brown filigree of maple twigs
Budding,
Tiny threads of branches
Floating,
So light and frail that a breath
Could hold them up.

Intricate as hand drawn lace
Or a punctiliously painted fan,
They spread against the cobalt
curtain
Of the sky.

Jeffrey Jay Jewett
GREEN WATER
The ravaging green water
that quickly traverses the mouth of
the falls
suddenly becomes temporarily
engulfed
on the stunned rocks below
then quickly, as if in anger
it splits open wide to escape the
memory
of being hopelessly trapped

after which it goes through an
endless
journey of foreign lands
to a disillusioned place
and yet unknown destination
remembering in its mind;
Ye shall never turn back
under the unconscionable event
that you find yourself forever
going on and on and on . . .

Cyndee L Kolerski
WATERCOLOR DREAMS (PAINTED JUST FOR JESS)
Beautiful little child: too soon the
victim of cruel adult ignorance
(mimicked in childhood taunts).

Bruised, innocent heart: straining
against the heavy ugliness of
harsh words and contemptuous
glares of leering faces:
silently screaming to preserve
the sky-blue-pinks of
watercolor dreams.

Tired eyes: distant, wary of love,
reflecting a barren sense of
humanity.

Young memories: brutality
shrouding the poverty of
indifference as painted
illusions, scene by watery
scene, dilute into a gutter of
Paynes Grey.

Look at me:
Let me avert
Early-Death-by-Battered-Heart:
Let my smile
travel through your grief,
my love
preserve your wonder.

E M Lockhart
AN EMPTY SHELL
Where is the life
this shell once held,
when once it lived
in the ocean.

Under warm water skies
it crawled on the sands,
in the depths
of the ocean.

Now the life is gone
but, the shell remains,
of what once lived
in the ocean.

Is this the promise
of what is to come,
if we don't stop
polluting our oceans?

Virginia Brangan
BIRTHDAY, DECEMBER 28

For Manda Grandma's second Christmas girl.

Twinkling, her bright blue eyes
Don't miss many things
And while her mother sighs,
She darts about and sings.

Her song is mostly loud
And never does it rhyme,
But still she does it proud,
It will have words in time.

First she must learn to talk
More than a word or two,
She's barely learned to walk,
For she is very new.

She missed the yule last year
Her birth was in suspension,
"Thank God", this year she's here
And not an apprehension.

Rose Coppock
DEMONSTRATION OF TODAY

To all mothers and gentle people everywhere

We march for peace
protest for human rights
land rights, gay rights
forests, waterways
wilderness, wildlife
and every possible freedom
we desire.

Yet, today
a young boy died
alone
and unattended
on a busy city street
while disinterested motorists
drove carefully
around him.

This was
an unplanned demonstration
of our level of concern
once the crowd disperses
after
the gaudy banners fall.

Helene Lenga Kohen
WHAT'S THE USE

Dedicated to Bert and Jeffrey for their continued cheerfulness and love in life's struggle.

In this life of trial and trouble
worries seem to rain profuse,
so at one time or another
all of us say, "What's the use".

Sometimes what we gain by trying
doesn't seem like it is worth,
all the suffering we go through
to assure our place on earth.

Life is made up of a mixture
two of good and eight of bad,
for the days are few and far between
when we are truly glad.

This is true and we all know it
but we never should admit,
when the road is long and rugged
we should never stop or quit.

But instead we should keep trying
in this way our woes reduce,
and we'll find a silver lining
never saying, "What's the use".

Dwight Hankey
DREAMS ARE . . .
Dreams are shadows that dance in
darkness and fade away in the light.
Dreams are sometime blurs that we
never quite understand
But are small treasures.
Dreams are soft and soothing and
sometimes harsh and cruel
And gave a new name to fit the way
they are.
Dreams can sometimes be forgotten
when they go on for too long.
Dreams should be enjoyed and
cherished forever.

Clarence Funsch

Clarence Funsch
I'LL HAVE YOU

Dedicated to my Deceased wife; Seanne Ann Funsch

I'll have you in the springtime
As the leaf buds come in view and
the daffodils and tulips bloom;
I'll have you in the summer,
As all the other flowers bloom;
We'll thrive all summer long
In love, so fond and true,
As we wander through the garden
Planted by me and you;
In the fall when all the leaves come
tumbling down,
I'll have you once again.
As we catch and kick the leaves
around;
Another season has gone down;
When winter comes with the ice and
snow;
We'll sit and warm ourselves in the
firelight glow;
Once more I'll have you, to welcome
in another year in love so true.

Johanna Simon
CHILD LOST
Child lost
Where are you?
You are in my heart.
You are in my dreams.
You are in my prayers.

Child lost
You are in the face
Of every child I see.
You are etched forever
In my memory.

Do you remember me at all,
How I held you close
And snuggled you against my breast?
Child lost—yet not lost—
Where are you?

Susan V Guerrini
THE SADMAN
The Sadman walks alone, without a
home
A heart so empty you can hear the
echo in his eyes
His plastic smile can't thaw his soul
Only nighttime shadows hear his
cries

The Sadman's eyes don't shine like
yours and mine
They've gone dull from so long ago
He makes-believes his life is fine
Not caring enough to change his
status quo

The Sadman starts each day the same
old way
His days are filled with nothing new
again
His mind is full of dried up tears
As he plays remember when

The Sadman has a heart, but it's been
torn apart
All that's left is a fearful shell, a pile
of rust
He's too afraid to love again
Too afraid to feel, to think, to trust

The Sadman marches on, his life is
nearly gone
He may as well have died today
He couldn't really care if his time
was called
Ain't nothin' there to live for
anyway

Linda Speaker
GOD'S GIFT WE SHARE

This poem is dedicated to my son with love.

She gave you your life
So precious from the start;
Each breath you take,
Each beat of your heart.
Without her love, you would not be.

I gave you my life,
All my love from the start.
Each hug and each kiss
Mending many a broken heart.
Without your love, I would not be.

God gave you to us both.
To one in body, the other in heart.
Each prayer answered.
Each giving their part.
Without his love, we would not be.

The gift of life is the greatest gift of
all.
It's the bond of love that two
mothers feel.
It's the gift that makes both mothers
real.
That gift is you, my little one.
You are the gift of life.

JoAnne T Greene
ALONE WITH MY FEELINGS

This Poem I Dedicated To Theresa Irene, My Dearly Departed Child, Whom I Will Love Forever And A Day

Sunset Comes And The Dawn Is
Gone—
I Look Out The Window Feeling So
Alone.
My Heart Beats Rapidly, My Mind
Runs A Race—
I Wipe Away Tears Running Down
My Face.

My Thoughts Are A Blur As They

Always Have Been—
I Ask The Same Question Over And Over Again.
Why Do Things Happen The Way They Do—
I know It's God Will That Is To Be True.

As I Lay In The Night And Sleep Will Not Come—
I Say To Myself, What Have I Done—
To Feel So Much Pain For Such A Long Time—
When All That I Wanted Was Just Peace Of Mind.

Ann Rabinowitz
BLEEDER
Haemophilia's the royal disease they say. Yet
you long dead still bleed away from me.
Was I born to purple that bereft
of clotting power I must
let you go

anew on haemorrhages of memory, mind's plasma
draining off to die? Though any poet worth his salt swears "thee shall I
hold in every fibre . . . living . . .
remembering to eternity."*

Cruel, this exsanguinating flow that leaves
all retrospect of face, voice, touch
leached out to pallor, all presence
but the imprint of an eagle
wrenched from sky!

*Paulinus of Nola: "To Ausonius"

Sonny Charette
LONELY IS THE HEART
O lonely heart
beat not once more.
Love is gone,
it has closed the door.
My soul is cold,
calm like the night.
I'm hurt again
and filled with spite.
My love for life,
will end by the knife . . .
Tonight.

The cold blue steel
won't hurt at all.
I'm a walking corpse,
no use to stall.
I'm so tiny
in this world of ours,
who will notice the flight
of some poor coward.
My time has come,
and the bell has rung.

Yvonne Allen Barber
THE CRY OF THE UNBORN
I am the unborn, aborted child,
unwanted, unloved, thrown away.
I am not permitted to live in this world I was meant to occupy.
I am thwarted and denied my right to be the person
I was created to be for this time in history.
I am the inventor to revolutionize the frontiers of space.
I am the educator with a new concept for schooling children.
I am the doctor with another approach to treatment.
I am the scientist whose research finds the cure for a dread disease.
I am another stirring in the wind of ecology.
I am the friend to encourage, inspire, and give purpose to a distressed soul.
I am the fulfillment for the barren womb and empty arms.
I am the wise statesman to avert a civil or political disaster.
I am the one with an alternative to the wretched prison system.
I am among those meant to fill a crucial manpower shortage.
Because I do not live, some professions will be decimated.
I am one of the millions who never had a voice
To make the choice to live out my intended destiny.
My life in the womb is not cherished, not valued, so my life is snuffed out!
The breakthrough for which the world waited so long died with me.
O, mankind, how many more generations of God's gifts will you destroy?

Karen Sweeney
BARRIERS
The sound of friendly laughter
Falls upon her ears;
She hesitates, then turns away—
Her eyes are filled with tears.

If only she could join in
Their merriment and fun,
And be a member of their group,
A friend to everyone.

She's in a lonely prison,
Which no one else can see;
There are no walls, no bars, no guards—
Its inmates all walk free.

No crime has been committed;
There is no guilt or shame.
She's in a lonely prison,
And shyness is its name.

David MacPherson
AMBIANCE OF LOVE
Running my fingers over yours,
we keep a light conversation.
Your eyes sparkle with youth,
and your manner reflects maturity.
Hair slightly covers one eye as your giggle mixes with the clink-clink of metal on glass.
A sweet fragrance disguises the smell of doves and meat.
Lips purse as i gaze at you distorted by glass and drink.
I think about you, me and the words
i need
to tell you that you
have
on your nose
a spot of whip cream.

Jo Ann Crook
SOLITUDE
A loud thrashing noise coming from a corner,
only my imagination. A long loud silence.
A moment of brightness, that to my imagination.
An eternity of darkness.

A loud tick-tock of the second's ticking away.
A faint pitter patter of rain on the roof.
A low murmur of voices. An earth shattering silence.

The warmness of loving and the coldness of hatred.
The calmness of understanding, the swift currents of violence.
The usefulness of hoping and caring.
The unwantingness of despite and unwillingness.

James L Jackson
LOVE BY THE FATHER
The love by the Father.
There's none like it on this earth
He showed His love for you and me.
By His lowly virgin birth
The greatest love the world has ever seen
He sent His son to die upon
Calvary's tree

The love by the Father.
No greater love is known
When His nation turned against Him.
He took us for His own.
He is above the leaders of all nations
He gave us grace and salvation
He is the Father, Son and Holy Ghost

The love by the Father.
No greater love could be.
A love like His could never be shown.
By either you or me.
There is only one God the Father
Love from the Father through the Son.
Love, no greater love can be shown by anyone.

Antonio Martinez
CLEVELAND SCHOOL
This is a poem it's sad but true,
About a school that I once went to.

Children screamed, cried, and fell down,
Cause a lone gunman was firing a few military rounds.

After all the gunfire had ceased,
Five innocent students were now deceased.

The gunman also took his own life,
So much pain and grief for the people who survived.

The sad news was heard throughout the whole world, in different dialects,
Even rock star Michael Jackson came to Stockton, to pay his respects.

So this is what happened at Cleveland School,
Five innocent victims died, and one lonesome fool.

Ruth Jarvis
THE HOUSE I GREW UP IN

To My Beloved Daughter, Susan

Oh what memories we retain
about our house when we were a child;
Things are so different now,
It's hard to explain.
It's funny, but the house seems so much smaller,
Do you suppose that's because I'm taller?
Nooks and crannies seemed to be everywhere then,
Capt. Midnight codes on the radio,
telling us where & when;
Going to church with Grandma & Grandpa on Sunday,
Then back to school with all of our friends on Monday,
Playing "Hide & Seek" in the summer at dusk;
Roller skating 'round the block was an absolute must.
Picnics by the river with Mom & Dad;
You could bring along a friend & never be sad.
Measles & mumps & a silly broken arm,
We all grew up fine, without too much harm.
Well, there stands my old house, just as before;
But it's beauty seems to be gone, & it welcomes me home no more.

Beatrice Florist Brown
GIFTS OF LOVE
Lacy Valentines and roses are nice to receive,
Diamonds and pearls are hard to believe,
But life's simple gifts, not measured in price,
Will return to you, much more than twice.
To help the poor, the lonely, the sick,
Try it sometime, it's a wonderful trick.
Good deeds, Gifts of Love, stretch longer than a mile,
When you give of yourself in forget-me-not style.
The glories of Nature are all very free,
A tender touch—a stroll by the sea.
Gifts of Love are not always ribbons and laces,
But a warm sunny smile on kindliest faces,
In expressibly sweet and most cherished of all,
Are the words, "Dear I Love You!"—or a Telephone Call.

Martha L Steinman
YOU WERE A TREE
You were a tree
running full
with Springtime's blood.

With limbs raised high
your blossoms vowed
a special harvest.

You took our offerings.
You bathed in the waters of our lives.
You consumed the food of our hearts.

With wonder and awe
we watched your promise spring
into leafy abundance.

Then came the Fall.
We ate of your fruit.
And we died.

Beth Edgar
LITTLE KITE

For Matthew, with all my love.

Fly away little kite,
Fly up in the air,
Touch the clouds and the stars,
Glide here to there.

Your tail's in the breeze,
Not even the trees,
Can reach so high,
Climbing up to the sky.

You sway in the wind,
You're wild and free,
And only a string
Ties you to me.

Watching you sail,
Makes my heart smile,
You set the rhythm
Of the song in my mind.

Fly away little kite,
Fly up in the air,
Touch the clouds and the stars,
Take with you all of my cares.

Denise C Hayden
LOVE AND TRUST
Love and trust go hand in hand
they each other compliment.
Flourishing and thriving
between two hearts that consent.

If two share love and trust
stronger can each heart become
for alone trust can now grow
and love is unadventuresome.

Love shared between two hearts
can be trusted not to fail.
Provided love is built on trust
it will always prevail.

Trust can be shared by two
lovingly it will grow strong.
As long as trust is built on love
it will never turn out wrong.

Hand in hand go love and trust
how well they coincide
looking for at least two hearts
wherein they will abide.

Amy Bennett
MY LONELY PLACE
Nobody knows how lonely I am,
How lonely I am, how lonely I am.
Nobody knows how lonely I am,
So I sit in my own lonely place.

Everyone thinks how happy I am,
How happy I am, how happy I am.
Everyone thinks how happy I am,
To sit with this smile on my face.

Nobody knows of the loneliness,
The loneliness, the loneliness.
Nobody knows of the loneliness,
That they can so easily replace.

With just one little hello,
A hello, a hello.
With just one little hello,
They could fill this empty space.

But nobody knows so here I stay,
Here I stay, here I stay.
But nobody knows so here I stay,
In my own little lonely place.

Timothy R Rose
SIREN'S SONG

To my dearest Joy. You are my love and my life, you have given me everything I am.

Death, unseen, glides on silent waves,
Hears the lonely song of the siren's cave.
A song of crashing wave, and pounding surf,
Lit by gleaming moon so far above the earth.

Death glides on silent waves,
Knows the song of the siren's cave,
A song of dark green waters,
And Neptune's daughters.

A sailing man, from a distant land,
Enchanted by beauty, reaches out his hand.
Hoping for a touch, or a thought to keep,
He embraces only the briny deep.

Death glides on the silent waves,
Hears the song of the siren's cave.
A song of many lonely nights,
And of long forgotten sights.

The moon's silver hue sets the waves alight,
Another sailor has found his true love this night.
And his shipmates wonder if he's really gone,
Or with his true love as she sings her song.

Theresa Kocurek
I BUILT MY CASTLE;
I built my castle . . .
out of your plaster of paris
I furnished it with love . . .
admiration . . .
and respect, for you
I made you a permanent fixture
to the in and exterior, of the heart . . .
would be castle
I slaved when the plaster started,
cracking . . . and chipping . . .
and giving way under pressure
I remained standing still . . .
to keep the castle from caving in,
on one side . . .
yours,
and cried when mine,
finally disintegrated into
thin air.

I built my castle . . .
our of your plaster of paris
Next time . . .
I use my own.

Bertha Patton

Bertha Patton
GROW GRACEFUL (TIME PASSES)

Dedicated to the Family

Where is the little girl
that I no longer see
Where is the teenager
that used to look back at me.
Where is the young lady
that smiled back when I smiled
Time has taken its toll

I am no longer quite so young
I am slowly growing old
And yet lovingly, Dear Lord,
I look and look and look at me
If I must grow old
I will grow gracefully.

Margaret M Launer (Healey)
STARRY BLUE
Today is
bright and cloudy
at the end of May
Where has the sun gone?
I'm the star
in the deep blue
How about you?
Birthdays are born
we are alive
babies cry
but they survive.
We are one
days are few
sun is gone
in the starry blue.
The day is dead
and gone
sun will rise
morning begins
people cry
then they survive.
We are one
days are few
sun is gone
in the starry blue.

Lillian Schulz
NOW THAT THE WINTER IS OVER

Dedicated to Administrator: Nicholas D Demisay. Clove Lakes Nursing Home

Now that the winter is over
And springtime is here
Mother nature once again
Is a sweet and gracious Queen.
Like a skillful artist
She is painting pretty scenes.
Making green leaves grow on tree tops
And the grass turn green.
Next you will see
Flower and vegetable gardens growing
When flowers are in full bloom
And vegetables in vegetable gardens are in tune
Everyone will be glad to welcome them into their homes.
Although Mother nature is a bad
Queen four seasons of the year
Right now she is a good Queen!

Brian Walker
FANTASIES FADE
This feeling of emptiness inside
Is too deep for me to describe
My mind is the darkest shade of blue
Whenever I am not with you
Thoughts and feelings echo through my soul
Restless passions I've come to know
My dreams reflect just like a mirror
My anxiety, pain and fear
Awake all night staring at the moon
While shedding tears of endless gloom
Fantasies fade, the dream diminished
Close my eyes, this song is finished

David Isadore Joshua Caspi
HANDS & EYES

For Lisette, a bold and beautiful vixen without whom my utmost dreams and mortal abilities would surely vanish.

Speak to me softly, but only with
thine sultry hands and eyes.
True beauty is not expressed in mere geometric shape or size,
As some bronze statue or stately pine from a far-off land.
Nothing says "I adore you" more
poignantly than a female's eye or hand.

When I behold your facial glow with a mood etched so exquisite,
I envision exotic paradise with all
God's treasured delights in it.
A lea, an ocean breeze, a pink sarong about your tender shoulder:
These intimate gifts make heart's absence for you grow yet bolder.

And when I gaze into the dire want of you, my passion doubly rises
Like a thermometer in heat or marriage vow with subtle compromises.
Your hands are extensions of your warmth, like branches on a tree—
They seem to fold, shake and spread sensuously, especially for me.

A woman can paint a portrait or still-life, based not only on what she sees;
But on the blood-curdling sensitivity borne within her smooth hands.
When we touch, make love or just admire each other, 'tis the rule:
There is nothing more adoring or precious than a beauty's hands and eyes.

Ginni Felling
MY HEART REMEMBERS
Each step I treasure Dear, with you
As hand in hand we glide
Each moment is held as a memory;
In my heart, down deep inside.
Each warm embrace each kiss you give,
The times you say "Hello"
Are written in my secret heart
And causes all this glow.

The way you smile, your tender touch,
Your eyes so soft and warm—
Cause all the fears I have to vanish
And weathers any storm.
The magic way you have in saying;
"I love you tenderly."
Is locked inside my faithful heart
To which you hold the key.
The "little things" that mean so much
Are all recorded here;
In the "garden" of my memory
Which I hold very dear.

Jill Duquette
THE INDECISIONED MIND

For all those people that suffer with the same indecisioned mind, as I, at times.

Oh me, oh my, who is ever satisfied
on what or who we—are—we try,
and try to satisfy all, but it's easy to—
Forget that all we need is inside,
inside ourself &—
Beside,
To all those people that are ever
looking for a certain someone, just to say we are all one. So, should you make up your mind to be satisfied
with all that is mine, and mine alone.

Darcy Kay Peschka
A FEROCIOUS RIVER
Love is like a winding river
that never seems
to end.
With curves and twists

wherever you look.
But suddenly the river ends
and there's a big open space
and if you're not sure
you might not survive.
Just take a look and hold on tight
And then you know if you trust
each other
You can make it together through
whatever the problem,
you'll make it together
in that big, giant place
that is called
LIFE

Jodie Lynn Richardson
THE WORDS I THROW UPON THIS PAGE
The words I throw upon this page
Will be the wisdom in my heart and mind.
The soul can't seek, what one may make
If one don't give it time.

Give me the love, that will always last
Give me the time, that will never pass
Show me the place, that one will seek.
In times that, are hard yet small and weak.

Give the children food which they don't have
Show them love and guide them to God.
Who so powerful and strong made this land.
Give us strength that will make us strong
When we the weak might fall

Show me what I may not see that others may.
Tell me why one shall be so cruel to others
When they shall not bother them, or do them any harm.

Give me the answers to the questions
That lay upon this page
And I shall see the reasons
For the way we all behave.

Elizabeth Soho Bahorik
UNITY OF SPIRIT
When I have walked in your shoes awhile,
Tested all those things that make you smile,
When I have watched sunsets through your eyes
And endured, as you, the storm-filled skies,
When I have sensed your long-suff'ring days,
I looked to God for respite from ills' ways.

When I beheld lovelight in your eyes,
Baring every truth that herein lies . . .
You have ris'n as on eagle wings,
Never flound'ring or chasing the winds.
May the 'God of Grace' bestow His love,
Rendering His abundance from above.

Now my just compassion knows no bounds
Lauding truths in harmony of sounds,
Rings out melodies of loving care,
Hushing life's tempest as in a dare.
When I have walked in your shoes awhile,
I empathize with tears and knowing smile.

Berith Nordin
A DAY LIKE THIS
A day like this
Is a day to remember
A day to remember
This day in September
But not for my friend
For him it's the end.

Dorothy Jansson
I WISH I KNEW
Why are there tornados?
That hit so very hard,
That get so many people,
To cry for them from far.
I wish I knew
Because we know there is.
A God in heaven up so high,
Why can't His power control
The sky where tornados do go by.

Nancy Denise Dantes
OUR SECRET
The oaks will not tell my secret,
They know how much I love thee.
They are green and alive with
life—in their manner so discreet.
They shall not tell how deep our
love was in the verdant sea;
They are tall and stalwart friends,
who will guard our secret.
They shall never tell of stolen
kisses—you gave to me.
The oaks are old and vulnerable,
but, oh so wise—they know
when to be discreet.
For only they must know how
deep you love me.

R Mageddon
ALL THE DIFFERENTS
when all your hopes have been betrayed
and there's nothing left to save you
but your fears
I'll be here

to take the pain upon myself
and still I'll smile well knowing that life is
deadly bliss

for after night must come a dawn
when all the tricks of the night are gone
into the day and back to night
as from all wrongs emerges right

and so the cycles ever pass
like young bare feet o'er broken glass
the cause of suffering, cause of life
revealed within a single sight

and as we see we understand
reality dissolves to sand
till all the differents seem the same
the difference being in the name

Grant Crow
THE END OF ALL JERICHOS
There's a luminously in-forming
Wind of Love
That trumpets to the heart
The ecstatic sun's stillness,
Tumbling ego-built walls
Of isolation—
Apparently bringing Night's
Desolation to denizens
Of the glittering cities of apparent
Day.

James T Gean
MISSING YOU
As each day passes by, I'll miss you more and more
I'll miss you twice as much as the day that passed before
And even though you've told me you're gonna miss me too
I'll still be just as lonely; I'll still be just as blue
I hope these days go by so very very soon
'Cause I just can't wait to see you Sunday afternoon
I hope you'll think about me, as I'm missing you so much
I'll miss your pretty smile; I'll miss your gentle touch
I'm taking along your picture, so I can see your pretty face
But a picture is just an image of frozen time and space
Believe me sweetheart when I say
No one could ever take your place

D A Apikos

D A Apikos
TRUE LOVE

To the sweet, lovely women that have graciously accepted my amateurish poetry: P.D.B., M.B.K., E.B., L.O., L.F., M.H., A.B., L.S., P.S., S.H., S.A.A., K.A.A., L.H., and M.S.

What is this thing they call true love?
Is it as the poet portrays—
A flaming burning thing, ordained from high above?
Or is it more subtle, bound in earthly ways?

It is being there when needed
Sometimes sad with grief, despair
But smiling still, sad thoughts receded
Clasping hands to show the care.

It's knowing wants and needs and showing
By unselfish acts to free
A restless bird to fly, full knowing
The love we thought needs proof to see
That only by its coming back
Confirms true love, warm and glowing.

Judy Kay Hubble
GOLDEN STAIRWAY
As far as I can see,
many angels are surrounding me.
And up that golden stairway,
they are taking me.

For those I leave behind,
please don't be sad at this time.
Just remember me the way I was,
and that I love you all.

Your friendship has been a beautiful thing.
You all mean so much to me.
But as I walk that stairway,
I will take each of you with me.

I hope to see you someday,
and share the love that we have known.
For you see I will be waiting,
but I will not be alone.

I will watch that golden stairway
that leads to God's great throne,
and someday I will take your hand
and help you walk along.
And forever we will be together
and share the happiness we've known.

So to all my friends that I love,
don't cry, but smile for me.
For I am only a few steps away,
much happier now you see.

Just remember me the way I was
and remember what I have said.
I will meet you at the stairway
and together we will walk hand in hand.

Eudora "Tree" Kennison
GOD'S RAINDROP
If I was a drop of water
I'd make out,
Trickling down
Someone's spout.

And if I could water
A flower for a while,
I'd know then
I'd be worth something
As God's raindrop child.

I'd fill the ocean,
I'd fight the drought,
And even give life
To a poor old bull pout.

I'd splash the children
And make them laugh,
And make lemonade
For a weary woman's glass.

A drop of water
Can do so much,
So don't take it for granted
But give it a loving touch.

Leonard Lewis Arndt
PROFER
An inconsistent, but most constant, love I offer thee.
So strong, yet helpless, calm in rancor, pleading urgently.
A love reclusive from the world in mystic dreamy thought.
It begs acceptance ne'er demanding, nor commanding ought.
A love that satisfies the soul, consuming mind and spirit.
That; like the rain is formed from sea returning thereon to it.
For as God made the world for man and man of it admire,
The same creator made my love; affliction of desire.
A love for beauty, thee I give, enriched by many things;
Summer warmth and Sparkling

streams, the happiness spring
brings.
A sheltering not restraining love, a
gift to have and hold.
Not too unlike a pagan God's
whose chosen's never cold.
Just think about a jungle, a wanton
beast in view.
In procreation tooth and tongue,
this too I offer you.
A wildlike, untamed physical act
intense with warm caress.
Inhibited with warlike lust and
infant tenderness.
A thundering, havoc wreaking love,
if this should be your need.
Or rollicking frolicking carefree
love, devoid of any greed.
An inconsistent, but most constant
love I offer thee,.
A victor or a captive slave, this
wondrous love can be.

B A Duff
IF MOM WERE ONLY HERE

A year ago I had a mom
so full of love and life
It seems unfair to lose her,
and for Dad to lose his wife.
If I could give you one more gift
on Mother's day this year,
I'd wrap up all the love in my heart
if Mom were only here.

So many times I've sat and cried
for reasons you can't know.
The emptiness and aching heart
are things I seldom show.
But I know that life would be so nice
I'd never shed a tear;
I could travel down God's roughest
road
if Mom were only here.

I wish that I could have the chance
to spend just one more day
To tell her how she's loved and
missed
in a very special way.
I'm sure that she would ease my
hurt,
and chase away my fear;
She'd hold my hand and kiss my
cheek,
if Mom were only here.

Larry E Truchinski, Larry the See

Larry E Truchinski, Larry the See
SPACE INFINITY, ETERNITY

As a mere lad
With eyes to the sky
Thought about space
Surely Beyond the most distant star
There would be the end of space!
But what was beyond that?
There would have to be more space
It must end somewhere?
But still it could not end!
It continued on to eternity
Somewhere in this vast sky
There are other Planets as ours.
Other Forms of intelligent life
Perhaps even more so than ours
For Space continues to infinity
Space and Eternity
Perhaps even our ancestors
Migrated from another Planet
In another Galaxy.

Shelly O'Brien
MY PAST RULES MY PRESENT

My past rules my present
The future we'll see,
You want to get near
But I won't let that be.
It's too dangerous to care
The pain will not end,
For always in my eyes
You'll only be a friend.
Please accept it at that
For I don't want to hurt you,
For what's done unto others
Is done unto you, too.
My past rules my present,
For the future we'll never see.

William Nu

William Nu
COME THE SEASON OF OUR LOVE

To Charles (Bud), Marie, Maggie, Hellena, and Brent for whom my love shall always be eternal.

Fall comes, but the time its walls we
but both share that hold:
In innocence has our love but found
its way to each other.
Through winding paths, storms that
would only want to hurt,
Love that is binding, unbroken,
towering to all seasons to stand.

Winter comes, all is asleep, so are
our dreams of each
covered blanket, purest white of
snow sleeps our thoughts of each.
Deep within dreams, but do we
wander, laugh, cry and love
Promises to hold each, share, no
more walls to separate us.

Spring but brings, its promise of our
youth, dreams awaken
Blanket unfolding, melting, bringing
the seeds to life, blossoms.
Our dreams, life but so close now,
whispers the winds
Soon, soon my love I come to you;
but for you my love.

Summer our youth, is but young,
buds above prisons walls
Our time has but spent, your eyes on
mine, hand in each.
Time but now ours to share, embrace,
love now but ours,
To grow this moment and along this
road of lifes seasons.

Claudene M Bradshaw
REFLECTIONS ON YOUR BIRTHDAY

To my darling daughter, Ona, on your 30th birthday. Love, Mother

Your 30th birthday you say—NO
WAY!
For I know it was just yesterday
. . . you were struggling to be born!
Baby cries to the world, make a space
for you.
Well, the world heard you, but it
knew
For every child born must take their
place
Leave their mark and give back to
their race.
Now I am to believe . . . That
you are grown?
Why, look at you; you have
children of your own,
While you're still fighting for a
space of your own
Returning to God some of the
blessings you've known!
YET . . . I still see the babe—the
child that was mine
And I don't want to believe
"Old Father Time"
I cherish the memories, the smiles,
Yes . . . even the tears!
These things are mine, I hold
to them dear.
So . . . Go cast your shadow—go
do your thing
Shout out to the world—make
your voice ring—
Leave your mark and take your
place
The world feels you giving back
to the human race—
But— Don't tell ME it's your 30th
birthday,
For I know it was only yesterday.

My Love Forever,
MOM

PS: If you can not be rich &
famous, & do great things
Then do small things in a
great way.

Dena M Hargraves
LIFE!

Life!
We can do with it what we wish.
Don't waste it,
it only comes once.
Everything is unpredictable
so don't try to understand . . .
just live.
Don't look back on your mistakes,
they will always be.
It is up to you to make the best of
your past,
just learn and go on,
you will be a better person for it.
So enjoy life, because
tomorrow . . .
you may not have it.

Jan Stafford
SEPARATION

Silence fills each quiet room
With stillness that deafens, and I
realize
Our house is nothing but empty
space
Without you.

Unheard syllables of you sleeping
Are present and yet absent,
And I miss them.

I see you fighting traffic,
Reaching for the road map,
As time fast approaches
The visiting hours over.
Love fills my thoughts with
suggestions,
I want to fold my arms around you
Curse the miles between us
And the relative you've gone to visit.

Loneliness fills my empty bed,
And the air will not console me
With your goodnight kiss or
lovemaking.
Eagerly I wait for your return,
And whisper your name into the
darkness.

Glenelle P Bryant
ALONE AT SUNSET

The orange sun slides down and
melts into the lake,
Transforming it into a sea of frozen
light
and icy gold.
The barren trees and I together start
to shake
In dread anticipation of another night
alone and gold.

The magic of this scene once bonded
out two hearts
In sweet communion, as we drank
the evening wine
and night came on.
Now sorrow, bearing down as golden
day departs,
Has stripped me of desire to live the
darkening night,
for you are gone.

Ron Crouch
AESTHETICS

Since this poem deals with beauty, and being reborn through the love of it, I dedicate this to Jethandelyn.

I was dead,
in this square room.
Trying to appreciate the cold
unfolding square before me.
I stared at the porcelain model,
this is knowledge?
stamen—
petal—
pollen—
I burst through the square,
the pollutants in my mind disintegrated.
I root myself to a round world;
to taste the striking sweetness of a
velvet sky,
to experience the auburn smell of
spring,
to feel the succulent earth beneath
my feet,
to have the orb of life introduce me
to (and make me part of) everything,
to see the hazy brown, moist, sands
of the ocean hug the beaches,
and as I smell the bitter-sweet
fragrance,
of a field flower,
I know—
I am alive.

Retha Waskom Heath
HOW MANY TEARS

How many tears did He shed in the
garden that night;
While He prayed to His father with
all of His might?

How many tears did He shed as He
hung upon that cross;
All to save the sinners, He paid the
cost.

Imagine the pain;
As His tears fell like rain.

His precious blood trickled down;
And dripped onto the ground.

He died there in that darkest hour;

But rose again with all power.

Now I wonder how many more tears must He cry;
As the world is caught without an alibi.

How many tears until He comes back for me;
Oh! Sweet joy for all eternity.

D Jay Roll
THE MAN
The man had worked his way to fame; to be the greatest was his game.
He bought a house and a brand new car; each one he knew thought he'd go far.
The money came and the money went; to gain more stocks was his only bent.
He had it all, or so he thought, so fame and riches was all he sought; fame and riches was all he sought.

The man was bold, he oft felt old; and looked at life through eyes so cold.
He didn't worry about a living thing; he only cared what money would bring.
He lost his friends, forgot each name; his faith in self was his claim to fame.
He just didn't care to break his stride; but no matter how he tried, his soul he couldn't hide; no matter how he tried, his soul he could not hide.

Then one fine day, he heard one say, "Have you heard about the love of God that is here to stay?
He can fill your heart and cleanse your soul; worries and troubles you'll find will go;
When you look to Him and realize love, that could only come from God above;
It'll make you weep, it'll make you cry 'cause you'll want Him in your heart never to depart; you'll want Him in your heart never to depart."

The words sank into his soul that day, and he found that he just had to say,
"Lord forgive my guilt, forgive my sin, I just only want to be forgiv'n.
Please come inside through my thick hide; I've seen the times that I'd wished I'd died.
But now I pray please come to me and open my eyes that I might see; please open my eyes that I might see!"

Ethel M Schneider
ICE JAM
Loosen! Loosen!
Cried the man!
With icy grip
It laughed at him.

Loosen! Loosen!
Cried the town!
With swelling avidity
It swallowed the ground.

Loosen! Loosen!
Cried the tug!
Against her sides
It crushed and dug.

Loosen!
Cried the sun!
And slowly,
Upward heaving,
Downward crashing,
Grinding, splitting,
Swirling, leaping—
Grabbed by
The flowing waters,
Racing toward
Their destiny—
The deed was done!

Saundra Smith
RAPE
Low flying planes rape serenity of morning
while songs of birds announce a new day.
When the sun peeks over Eastern horizons
and the distinction between twilight and dawn
is a lovely blurr in sleepy minds,
peaceful feelings amid quiet beauty
are suddenly, without warning, attacked.

Violent gang rape by low flying planes
drowning out the chirping of birds,
cutting across meditation upon the loveliness of dawn,
ravaging the tranquil moment.

Oceans, rivers and seas are retching
vomiting poisonous waste.
A beautiful woman drugged,
mind foggy, body in pain,
wondering from whence comes the pain and cramps
of forcible sexual intercourse.
Oh, the horrible profaneness
upon an innocent beauty!

Souls fast at justice outraged as we mourn our innocent beauty, our environment.

Mary F Bamford
A GHOSTLY ENCOUNTER
One evening our teacher announced to her class.
You must write a poem or else you won't pass.
An original poem, she said it must be:
A thing quite fantastic, as you will agree.
For who can compose or write verse in a hurry
'Mid hustle and bustle and Christmastime flurry?

My mind went a-searching among many themes
Of fact, or of fancy, or merely strange dreams.
Then I thought of a dear little figure I'd seen,
A shy little ghost on this past Halloween,
Who had never been taught the correct way to haunt,
But who bravely set forth on his first spooky jaunt.
Down the short country lane to scare grandma he went
Through the flickering moonlight with mind all intent,
When suddenly burst round the bend of the road
A fearsome assembly—a sight to behold,
And great towering figure with phosphorous glow
Whose skeleton gestures led right motley show
Of witches and goblins, of ogres and cats
Who yowled in the darkness at huge scary bats.
All breathless and trembling—'twas just a stretch more,
Our little spook landed at grandmother's door.
"Oh grandma, dear grandma," he clutched at her post,
"I've just met the scariest Halloween ghost."

Gale E Breen
HOME
Come closer, see the Wonder of Perfection;
Sit with Peace of Mind and be completely at rest;
Lay your head upon the Breast of Contentment;
Stay near and hear the Heartbeat of Love;
Hold fast and cling to the Haven of Joy;
Make Jesus your Abode now and for eternity.

Lisa G Burke
THE PROPHET
As my time comes slowly to its' end
let me speak of sorrow.
I came in search of truth;
None spoke.
I came to offer hope;
None cared.
I came to give life;
Mine was taken.

Stacy Lynn Musiyowski

Stacy Lynn Musiyowski
A BURNING STONE
There's mist in the air tonight
As the clouds set in front of a burning stone,
I fight the darkness with my sight;
In front of vast waters I sit alone.

A wind is now exploding any tranquility,
And blowing the stone to drift away,
I try to see with all my ability;
In front of vast waters I pray.

The mist and wind become so alive,
The burning stone is so far, so deep,
The lightness has made a good night dive;
In front of vast waters I sleep.

The storm has now set into the night,
As I sit, pray, and sleep alone,
There is darkness forever when there is no light,
Especially when there is no burning stone.

Jeanette Johnson-Carney
DISOBEDIENCE PREVAILS
The language is loud and atrocious
my ears ring and anger boils within.
The teen rule is supreme
Selfishness is their motto,
And they laugh at all standard but their own.
Parents are wrong, whatever the case,
and abuse of the child has been reversed.
Laws to protect the child are right,
but those of the parents got lost in the night.
You may suffer long, and work very hard
to give them the things you feel they should have.
But what should it matter, it's never enough.
You give all you have from your heart and your purse,
And for what? . . . just to be cursed.
Respect me they scream, see what I am.
I have power, I have money, I stole from my old man.
I'm somebody, you're nothing they scream over again.
Love and respect is all you desire,
Nothing more, nothing less—it's all such a shame.
Love and trust is now just a game
and everyone lost before it began.

Stan W Shura
MAGIC WINGS
Like eagles' wings spread far and wide,
This mystic feeling dwells inside
To places where my heart has soared,
So innocent and unexplored.
These magic wings divine and blessed
Upon desire fulfill his quest.
His effort never limited;
His free flight uninhibited.
Indeed, my soul has yearned and tried
Like eagles' wings spread far and wide.

Faith P Feiler
IT HAPPENED SO SUDDENLY
It happened so suddenly
This tearing away
This separation.
I wasn't prepared for it
Wasn't ready.
But Neither was he.
Now emptiness fills me to the bursting point.
I am adrift on a sea of sorrow
Tossed by waves of grief.
Friends fling out their lifelines of concern
But I have no strength to reach for them.
It would be easy to join him in death.
But no. It is not meant to be that way.
I must not fight the ocean of despair and weary myself.
Better to float upon its billows
and, in time, be carried safely

to the shore.
I see on the sand an empty shell. So like myself.
And yet there is beauty in its emptiness.
Surely other beings, other thoughts, will make their habitation there.
I look back on the footprints being washed away and I know
there will always remain

Memories.

Matilda Dickison
ONCE AND FOREVER
Touch my life and then pass on.
Show me love and then be gone.
Know me well, but not for long.
Leave me memories in a song.

I'll hear it forever in my heart.
In my life you'll always be a part.
We'll spend nights together once in awhile;
And when you leave, go with a smile.

Judge not by time how much I care.
Just know I loved you while you were there.
When you say "Good bye" and close my door,
Know you have been loved—
Nothing less, nothing more.

Mildred Wilkinson
OLD FOLKS

To my son Paul and daughter Glenna

Old people wet their drawers
and they can't help it
Old folks 'phart' and
they are sorry
They cry on your shoulders
much too long
And they all want to die
tomorrow

Mary Evelyn Parkison

Mary Evelyn Parkison
WHEN GOD CALLS NEXT

In loving memory of my dear parents Andrew Thomas and Margaret Mae Noonan who have already answered the calls of "Next"!

Yesterday's statements of credit and balances are the only luggage allowed to be taken on our long trip to eternity. These statements will show our standings with God. Upon His approval each will be directed to his or her place in eternity. To the right go the precious well cared for souls tagged as "Valued Customers." Those tagged as "Damaged Goods" whose credit and balance sheets are unacceptable are directed left down the dark hole—a one way street of no return where the trash incinerator has no closing time—no water hoses, no fire extinguishers—the torment goes on and on—"The Roast Is Never done"! No repairs made here—no returns made on damaged goods—new parts unattainable—no vacations offered—duty time is from eternity to eternity!

So—

Think well brother, before you travel on,
Prepare your statements well ahead.
Life is short and all must die—
Plot your course with head held high.
Leave not for tomorrow what can be accomplished today.
Your trip to the Lord might come sooner than soon
Your call may come night, morning or noon
Be careful I say
"Now might be the day"!
Have no regrets how you planned the way,
Then joyously you would meet your Maker,
As without fear you stand in line
And hear Him say—"Next"!

Kelliann A McDermott
IT SEEMS AS THOUGH EVERY TIME
It seems as though every time,
We try to spend time together,
Something goes wrong to ruin it,
Will this go on forever?

Will we ever find the time,
The space we need to grow,
To make the bond even stronger,
To let our feelings show?

Why does it seem that,
I'm losing this fight,
That sometime soon,
I'll be crying at night?

I'm scared that this battle,
Is going to make you stop trying,
If you decide to leave us alone,
You'll leave me dying.

I've grown to love you,
So much more than words can say,
I know that I need you,
And don't ever want you to go away.

Janet A Wagner
KNOW ME
I want you to know me,
and love me too.
For who I am.
Not for things that I do.

I need you to know me,
and understand too—
My reasons for feeling
the way that I do.

I want you to see me.
For who I am.
I know I'm not perfect.
But I do all I can.

And when I'm gone—
Remember me too.
For who I am.
And my love for you.

George C Regis
MISSING YOU KIMBA
In life I loved you with all my heart.
Only by death are we apart.

My love for you will never end.
In time I know my heart will mend.

So many tears I have cried.
Since the day that you have died.

So many wonderful years we had
together.
My love for you will last forever.

All the happiness that we shared.
When I was in pain you always
cared.

You always gave me all you love.
Then you were taken by God above.

I will never forget all the good times
we had.
I think of them whenever I am sad.

I can never have another dog like
you.
One so faithful, one so true.

Dianne Lee Hobby
NOT WITHOUT REGRET DO I SAY GOODBYE
Not without regret do I say
goodbye . . .
And turn about, and walk
away . .

Feeling stone path
underneath . . .
Flowering dogwood in the
height . .

Knowing these words, easiest to
mouth . . .
Are hardest to say.

Mary Ann T Musial
ON THE VERGE
A ship makes its way through the fog
Like a child makes his way
through life
Always searching for a light in the
darkness
Someone to guide him
Sometimes, something gets in his
way—
An obstacle
Like a drawbridge rising,
One must wait patiently until it
falls again
In order to move ahead
As one must work out a problem
In order to get on with life.
Adolescence is the in-between
period—
Not a child, yet not an adult
But secure within a family
Waiting to burst into the world on his
own
Like a caterpillar within a
cocoon—
Not a caterpillar anymore yet not a
butterfly
But secure in its sac
Waiting to burst free
And show his true colors!

Donna Stevens Long
WAITING
The clock is ticking softly;
And the rain falls quietly on the roof.
The music is soft
And the lights low.
It's a perfect night for love.
But I sit here alone,
Waiting for your return,
Knowing you'll never come.
Death's hold is strong.

Stan Kuwazaki
LOVE

This poem is dedicated to my much loved family: Mom, Dad, Cindy, Mary and Angela. Thank you for always being there when I needed you. God Bless You!

Magician wanders through my
dreams,
Galaxies fuse.
My girl! Why do flowers die?
Why so much anguish?—Frightened
screams?
Let's call together:
"Fountain, Fountain of youth!"

The sweet pain of recollected
harmony!
What we don't have, we treat as our
due, without gratitude—
Just waiting until all is gone again—
Replaced with grief and rack of
solitude.

The sweet pain of recollected
harmony!
Your happy smile, my pride our
sensual gluttony
In midst of time armed like a gun
against our fairy-tale . . .
My shield crushed—I clutch your
little palm
Instead of sword; my dream will
never fail.

Those splendid days
Like howling of dogs dissolved in
space;
Just burning desert here
Loneliness—absence of grace.
I miss you!

Retha Waskom Heath
ENDLESS SLEEP
Adrift on a sea of loneliness and
despair;
All alone with no one to care.

The wind tossing me to and fro;
With no place to go; no place to go.

Then suddenly the sea thrusts up her
arms
and pulls me down into the
deep;

At last there in its quiet depths I find
that endless sleep.

Mrs Michelle Roe
YOU AND ME

I dedicate this poem to my loving husband James and to our beautiful newborn daughter Melissa. I will love and cherish you both always.

We are so perfect together,
Your strength, at first, dominating my
weakness
But now I have regained my vie
I am me.

We are so perfect together
Our bodies meeting harmoniously
until
They are one in entirety and
You are me.

We are so perfect together
Now we are blind to what the future
holds
So we live in ecstasy.
Who am I?

We were so perfect together

But forever we are not meant to be,
And now that you are gone
I am me
I am alone.

Randall S Chandler
SYMPHONY IN SNOW
Innumerable flakes fall
In countless patterns
Distinctive drops of white water
Frozen in time

Each an individual note
In a swirling symphony
An aria winter white
Whispering in flight

Drifting in the air
On a wafting wind
Singing an unknown melody
To those waiting below.

Bernard R Meinert Jr
WHILE LOOKING AT THE SKY
While looking at the sky
A rainbow I did spy.
It made me stop and think.
If only I could use the Creator's ink
And with this symbol and the
promise He made,
To color the world with peace,
My debt to society will be paid.

Cheryl Wolf
COLORS

For India,

Gold jewelry, red lips and eyes,
black and blue hearts,
Beautiful black child sidles
through the crowd.
She clings to mother, nestled
between velvet breasts of
ebony.
Her smile is radiant as the
sun,
Which blinds us from colors.

Dorothy Amy Dicker
TO SHARE
Made in the image and likeness of
my Creator
There must be something that I can
give—
A smile, a friendly word spoken—
A token of awareness of another's
need—
To give that part of me that says
"We are one—I care!"

Is this what I have to share?

Brooke Ann Thompson
FROSTY THE SNOWMAN
Snowman
White, cold
Standing, grinning, melting
Black hat, sticks, life, love
Running, playing, moving,
Alive, created
Frosty

Reba Whittington
GRANDMA'S TOUCH

This poem is dedicated to my grandchildren: Robert, Rebecca, Heather and Andrew.

I like to think of days gone by when I
was but a chap
I'd follow her 'til she sat down, just
to sit on Grandma's lap.
Her eyes had special twinkles, her
smile a thousand words,
That told me that she loved just me,
more than all the world.

When I sat on her knees so strong
and looking down below,
I was on the tallest mountain tops,
the highest ever known.
Then she'd thrust her knees out
straight and make the nicest slide,
Then up her knees would come once
more and make a horse to ride.

But oh, too soon I grew too big to sit
on Grandma's lap,
So sad the day Mom made me go to
bed to take my nap.
For all cares seemed to slip away as
I'd lay at Grandma's breast,
Like little birds so soft with down,
secure within their nests.

It seemed so short a time until, I was
a mother too,
Then it was time my mom sat down
to do what Grandmas do.
She rocked and sang and kissed
away, the cares of childhood woes,
"Soon," she said to me "One day this
will be your chore."

Again, like always mom was right,
When in my arms, I hold them tight.
Four gifts from God I love so much,
I still can feel my Grandma's Touch.

David W Leppanen
THE JUNK FOOD JUNKIE
I'm a junk food junkie
And a nutritional flunkie
No warning will convince me,
For no label do I see

The coffee I drink black
Is a monkey on my back
and the sugar I consume
Is my molar's own doom

While the cigarettes I smoke
Make my lungs wheeze and choke
The additives in my bread
Will preserve me when I'm dead.

Courtney A Hoskins

Courtney A Hoskins
GHOST HANDS

To KDBS 4B 1988-1989, especially Rachel Herbert, Alison Jacobs, and Sarah Weir for their encouraging support and humor.

I go to the ocean
And I see
White ghost hands
Grasping for me.
Leaning forward
Over tan sand
Reaching forward
And I stand
Out of reach
On the beach.

Kathryn Suzanne Grondin
ONE WOULD NEVER IMAGINE
One would never imagine,
or even ponder a moment
That it be possible of you
To contain a heart
so far beneath the mask
Borne upon your face.
Always so reserved,
even distant at times
Never revealing your thoughts
or innermost feelings,
Those hidden beyond
the unknowing eye.

But one stolen chance
to see behind the mask,
A revelation of emotions
beyond your persona,
The concern, love, and compassion
of a caring heart . . .

That one would never imagine

Jacqueline Berry
EMPTINESS . . .
I live a shell of a life
with a lot of pain, suffering
and strife.
I wait for the changing day
to find everythings's the
same way.

I move from place to place
without knowledge of time
or space.
I long for the day or night
when I will feel allright.

Maria Wegner
WHY ME?

To my dear brother-in-law, Herbert, whom I shall never forget. Could these thoughts which have gone through my mind also have been in his?

Why me? I keep asking myself over
and over again.
Why could it not have been one of
them,
Who do evil without remorse or even
repentance
What have I done to deserve this
unjust sentence.

Why me? I who have everything to
live for,
And is not yet ready to go through
that final door
Of an unknown destination,
Reluctant and full of trepidation.

I must be strong to comfort those so
dear to me.
To watch them suffer, is not what I
wish to see.
To live my life to the fullest every
day,
Surrounded by my loved ones is for
what I pray.

A few more years is all I'm asking
for.
Can this desperate plea be so easy to
ignore?
Should this be denied me and I can
no longer stay,
Then I pray to God to help me accept
whatever comes my way.

Felton D Woods
CLARABELLE LEE

I dedicate this poem to God, my family and friends.

The last candle burns in the middle
of my room.
The shadow if its flame dance in full
bloom.
It is silent—so silent like darkness
that stands guardian over doom.
Here, I sit alone by the fire listening
to the ember's merry melodies.
Be that it may the sound of music,
my heart still yearns for Clarabelle
Lee.
'Twas two days ago like the fourth
of July my soul laughed with glee.
But someone's evil haunted me and
stole my Clarabelle Lee.

Her picture adorns not a single shelf
and what a waste her picture would
prove.
For I've learned her face, yes,
indeed: every line, shadow, and
groove.
She came in May in light with the
sun only to leave by the moon.
I think to myself, should I blame I
for love that was less in this room?
O' death to the owl's hooting cries,
that night soldier perched in a tree.
Wise that it's played that he might
be, he knows not where is my
Clarabelle Lee.

Frances Landis
OUR OWN RED WHITE AND BLUE

To my four sons and two daughters

Thirteen stripes of red and white
Stars set in azure blue
Mean more to me than fifty states
They stand for love and freedom too

As I gaze upon its beauty
Waving gently in the blue
I cross my heart and make a vow
To my country I'll be true

There majestically upon its pole
For all who pass to see
Is a symbol of our fore-fathers
Who died to make us free

Many things in this world have
changed
And we're glad sometimes they do
But we'll never change what our flag
stands for
Our own Red White and Blue.

J Eden-Greene
ONE NIGHT IN THE LIFE OF THE WINTER'S HOMELESS
one man's cardboard carton discard
wrapped about the body . . . hard
becomes another's sheltering womb
against the winter's bitter night
while fire made from broken sticks
left untended for some bone-chilled
sleep
slept inside the paper tomb
its wispy flames long having died
as finally, so the man inside.

Leon Shapiro
WHO HAS MADE ME WELL?
Who has made me well, Hospital
was it you?
With all the things that you can do,
but you're only made of stone and
steel
We know that such things cannot
heal.
Technician, did you make me well
with all the things that you can tell.
You only know how my health was
by lights that flash and things that
buzz.
Surgeon, was it you who made me
well
with your deft hands and blades of
steel
your skill has made my body right
and though I search with all my
might
and all the gratitude I feel
I know that you could never heal.
Physician, was it you who made me
well?
with all your wisdom who can tell.
You show the others what to do,
and all your help is right and true.
But no, some how I feel
that all of this still cannot heal.
It was the nurses who made me
well

with love's gentle touch so I could tell
that every thing would be all right
It's they who give my spirit flight.
Like some great bell's exultant peal
so strong, it makes the senses reel;
It's THEY that made my body heal!

Kim Quigley
A SUMMER DAY

I dedicate this poem to my sisters, Bridget and Lindsay, and my brothers, Mike and Corey. I love you!

Up they climb the tallest slide
Down like raindrops they quickly glide
The ice cream cart comes jingling along
Singing out a springtime song.
Colorful balls like planets and moons,
A penny will get you a pretty balloon
Roller skating is fun, it's true
But watch out I'll hit you!
With a little breeze it won't fail,
Your little boat will always sail.
Fast like the wind on skates they race
It's really quite hard to pick up the pace
The days getting late it's time to go home
Wasn't it fun to play and roam.

Sarajo Wilkes
MOTHER TO MARTIN
Martin, are you there?
Son, are you hiding under the stairs?
I bet you're up to those dreams again.
Thinking how you're going to grow up and
Become a mighty man.

Well, Son, follow your dreams and your lucky star.
Mom knows that someday you're going to go far.
Don't be discouraged about what others say.
Your mission in life to pave the way,
For men and women whose dreams have been shattered.
Who long since felt that their hopes don't matter.

Martin, Martin! Where's that boy?
Are you out in the backyard climbing trees?
Chasing butterflies, birds, and bees?
I know you're somewhere deep in thought.
As you often are, when I call.
Martin, you're the chosen one alright.
To encourage the people to seek a better life.

Son, keep on dreaming.
Someday your dreams will have a meaning.
We will all watch you climb that mountain.
We will watch you look over the top.
We will hear your voice calling
To follow, and don't stop!

Martin, Martin! Do you hear me?
Now, where "Is" that boy?

Sandra Choppe
SPECIAL CHILD

This poem is dedicated to all the special children in the world and to all who care for them.

Everyday a special child is born
his first breath is a struggle for life,
that child has entered a world of loneliness
to stay alive, he now must fight
He's unlike a child who was born
with his health
he needs attention and special care,
he will go through emotions normal children don't feel
he will need someone who loves him, constantly there
That child feels strange, and incomplete
because he is missing something inside,
he doesn't understand why it happened to him
the frightened loneliness he will try to hide
Whether a child is missing his sight from the world
or can't hear the sounds of your voice,
or his insides won't function and produce what he needs
that child doesn't have any choice
You must learn to accept and to deal with his pain
how would you feel if his life, you had to live,
you must open your heart to that special child
your love, you must always be ready to give.

Wendy Grodenchik
TEACHERS

To all who have helped me in their own special way—especially my teachers.

Weird, crazy
Patient, knowledgeable
Teaching equations
literature, computers
Boring classes—
loading on the
homework—giving
tests, quizzes
Papers galore; essays
too
They make school last
all day long
Never giving us time
to oursleves
Always making us
work—
Driving us—hard.

Carole Friedlander
ONCE UPON A RAINDROP
Once upon a raindrop
I met my lover dear;
And once upon that raindrop
He held me, oh, so near.

Once upon a moonbeam
he promised me his heart;
Once upon a moonbeam
He said we'd never part.

But once upon a stormcloud
The raindrop failed to stay;
And once upon a stormcloud
The moonbeam flew away.

Now once upon a memory—
And those I've plenty of—
Once upon a memory
I've raindrops and moonbeams and love.

Margaret B Casula
DAWN

This poem is dedicated to my loving husband Praveen and my dear father Leslie.

Hush, speak not, it's shadow dawn,
Even silent whispers die,
Captured in the crevice of greyness
As the sounds of morning echo by.
Dew drops casting shadows
As they fall from lonely bushes,
the silent boat without an oar
Causing ripples through the rushes.
But alas between those dark clouds
Looms the sweetness of the day,
waiting for its moment,
Like a vulture for its prey.

Harold J Pierson Jr
THE VALLEY OF DEATH

To my dear friend Ruth, for all that you have shown me.

I walk through the valley of death
but fear not
For death is not my enemy
but my friend
For in death life is created
and I am freed
Freed of the bonds that hold me
here on earth.
So death need not be feared
but embraced.
When death comes greet it
with a happy heart.
Rejoice also for the fact
that an adventure awaits.

Beula Worthen
THE COLORS OF LOVE
From the palette of life, he spills the gold of everlasting love.
The returning greens of springtime are as surging as his hopes for tomorrow.
His peace comes from the bluebird's song, and in the white columbines nodding in the mountain breeze.
His passion for living is like the blazing red pillars of sunset and his tenderness the soft lavender of early dawn.
His faith is the pure white of newly fallen snow,
And his honesty as firm as the brown earth beneath my feet.
His integrity glows like the midnight blue sky, sprinkled with the diamond stars of justice.
Silver are the threads of his laughter, tying our days together into a tapestry of strength.
He warms my heart with the golden sunshine of his embrace
And over every hour, he flings the joyous rainbow of his presence.

Bertha Warren
THE FARMER'S PLIGHT
God help the farmer in his plight
More disappear every night.
What is our nation going to do
Without the farmer, no clothes, no food.

Working much more than his share
Would you rather have him on welfare?
Best to sell the crops they raise
Than raise our taxes day by day.

Buy import oil and foreign cars
Send them weapons for their wars.
While here at home the farmer dies.
Take his land—but leave his pride.

We can do without a lot of things
Like coats of mink and diamond rings.
Don't think we can do without
The farmer and what he's all about.

You think I'm just complaining—No.
Just telling you before we go.
Be prepared to grow your own.
When America's farmers are all gone.

Michael A Forella Jr
A DAY AT THE BEACH
The early morning sun whispered tranquility
From mother earth.

Gazing through daybreak with our pagan eye
While gulls glide freely thru the virgin sky.

We were slowly absorbed to the ocean's sandy bed
Where people gathered into a human maze of
Blankets and bikinis.

Above heaven's creampuffs danced and floated
With the smoothness of freedom.

Below the ocean repeatedly smiled and grinned
As each wave rolled with ruffles of laughter.

A Day at the beach

Charlie Earl Porter

Charlie Earl Porter
PLAYING THE FIELD

Dedicated to my wife for eternity, whom ever she may be! EMAN

High flying eagles in the sky . . .
Field of poppies—flowing beneath . . .
I heard God speak to my heart—in my minds' eye I can see,
As I arise in the morning, poppies blowing in the wind.
In the early morning light—foggy mists of blue . . .

Screaming eagle in the sky . . .
Fields of poppies flowing beneath . . .
What do you see my son—the devil's

accusations in?
If I had a winepress, all filled with grapes . . .
Some sargum juice—some strawberry nectar . . .
A wine I would make!

He sees misery, anguish, and shame . . .
Struggling, torment and pain.
At the wedding feast I would be . . .
With Juniper caggs of wine—dancing on the wind . . .
Screeching eagles was fallen son . . .
Old Lucifer the fallen one—the devil did sing . . .
Love, Fame—The Fastest Gun, in the Universe is wed!

Larry D Leach
MY FATHER WAS SPECIAL, IN HIS OWN QUIET WAY
My father was special,
In his own quiet way.
He gave me love and kindness,
Every day.
He didn't show his emotions,
But, I know he cared.
If, someone needed his help,
He was always there.
He showed that he cared,
By his acts and his deeds.
And, he gave of himself,
Despite, his own needs.
And, as I grew older,
I wanted to be.
Just like my father,
And I hope, that's me!

Kimberly Adonna Knight
LONGING FOR YESTERDAY

Kathleen Anne, Thanks for your love and support, You're the best friend ever! We'll always remember our memories.

Longing for yesterday,
when all was old.
Longing for friends,
secrets to hold.
To remember the face,
it always gleamed.
To remember the games,
the spirit redeemed.
Having the youth,
but yet the age.
Having the confidence,
life's theatrical stage.
To remember all things,
the future to come.
To remember and live,
a great two some.
Longing for yesterday,
to remember the past.
Longing for that person,
a friendship to last.

Rosemary E Thorlakson
THE ROAD
Because our lives are cowardly and sly,
Because we do not dare to take or give,
Because we scowl and pass each other by,
We do not live; we do not dare to live.

We dive, each man, into his secret house,
And bolt the door, and listen in affright,
Each timid man beside a timid spouse,
With timid children huddled out of sight.

Kissing in secret, fighting secretly!
We crawl and hide like vermin in a hole,
Under the bravery of sun and sky
We flash our meannesses of face and soul.

Let us go out and walk upon the road,
And quit for evermore the brick-built den,
The lock and key, the hidden, shy abode
That separates us from our fellow-men.

And, by contagion of the sun we may,
Catch at a spark from the primeval fire,
And learn that we are better than our clay,
And equal to the peaks of our desire.

Beatrice D Hodgins
SPRING SIGNS IN NEW ENGLAND
The robin's singing merrily,
"Cheerily, cheerily, cheerily, chee-chee-chee."
The birds are flitting in the tree
Building nests so busily.
The crocus leaves are peeking through
The ground, their blossoms to renew.
The sun is shining warm and bright,
Making hard things seem all right.

Snow is melting here and there–
Oozing mud is everywhere.
With winter going on its way
We now enjoy a better day,
And those who love the ice and snow
Further north will have to go;
But I, for one, will stay right here
And welcome Spring-time's brilliant cheer,
It's life-renewing message clear
That out-door days are very near,
And its bright parade of fragrant flowers–
And all this loveliness is OURS!

Michele M Pass
HOMELESS
He hopes for the truth in sunlight,
He fears the lies in darkness.
A shadow moves across his face,
The twilight grays his eyes.
A smile fades and gives to sadness,
A frown is carved around his mouth
He clenches the paper bag,
He pulls his rags around his bulk.
He looks for a corner, safe and warm,
To shield him from the wind and cold.
Surrounded by the changing shadows,
He fights for a life, his life.
He's tired from a day of surviving,
Too proud to end his own life.
He settles into the spirit of sleep,
Crossing his arms with dignity.
He knows no truth in sunlight,
He knows all lies in darkness.

Greg Peirez
HAVE YOU SEEN MY BABY
Afterwards before tomorrow
Scream fun when you feel it
Before it fades
Accumulated by so much
Its significance will pass
Unappreciated
So mind the time

thanks Flamin' Groovies
and A. Waylon Young

Eric E Stephenson
OUTCAST
Oh how cold the wind blows
and how sharp, it cracks my skin,
Oh how bad the hunger pains
seven days, since I last ate,
Oh how warm the flowing steam
and how steady, from the grate.
Oh how soiled my garments are
and how bad, the smell of stench,
Oh how wet the rain falls
and how hard, when it's cold,
Oh how long can I survive
oh, will I, grow to be old?

Duncan Maclean
THE SUMMER OF "88"
We finished our work on the Virginian, in the spring of "88"
We needed to work to pay those bills, the ones that just won't wait

Don and me left Reno at the beginning of the week
We drove to Sacramento, we were working for "the Greek"

Everything was screwed up, right from the very start
G.K. being his usual self, put the horse behind the cart

Just like always we were on a shoestring budget
But G.K. said I trust you boys, I know that you can fudge it

The spring turned into summer, the summer was hot and dry
It was the hottest July on record and fella that's no lie

Every day the temperature rose up to a hundred plus
It got so hot we thought we even heard the devil cuss!

We'd start to work at sun-up, just to beat the heat
We took no breaks, worked eight hours straight
and we worn out on our feet.

We worked all day and told ourselves, "we've got it made in the shade
but we baked in the sun till our work was done
and there was no bloody shade!

We sweated as we poured concrete, we swore as we laid the block
That we'd never bitch about the cold again
Even if we froze our asses off

Go into a Quick-Stop or 7-11
You'll find Lebanese and Iranians working in the cool
They think they've gone to heaven
and I'm a bloody fool

How hot was it you might ask me?
Well I'll tell you while I'm talking
I saw a dog chasing a cat and both of them were walking!

I'll tell you how hot I was, just to state a fact
I was hotter than a long haired Billy goat in a big red pepper patch

It got so hot in "Tomato Town", hot enough to fry your brain
I never thought this "London boy" would ever pray for rain

I've worked in Palm Springs and Las Vegas where it's hot as we all know
but not as hot as the cabarets where the showgirls wear no clothes!

I've worked up in Alaska, "The Land of the Midnight Sun"
and I almost froze me GOOLIES off and believe me that's no fun.

I've been across the Kalahari, the Mojave and the Great Karroo
I've even been through Death Valley when it reached a hundred and twenty two.

Somehow it seems hotter when you work outside all day
Than when you're on vacation or when you are at play

So I'm going back over the Sierras, back to Reno town
back to the 99 cent breakfast The "Biggest Little City In The World"

I'll work up in the high desert, that's where I'll spend my time
Where the temperature only rises as high as NINETY NINE!

Shane Armstrong
A SALTY KISS
A Salty kiss
At the mouth of an ocean
As waves beckon
Inner tides ebb and flow
In answer to
Her primal cries
For the return of a child

Terry Ann Journey
THROUGH A JET STREAM

To James Norris, my love, who shall always return to quiet my fears, and who, out of his steadfast devotion, teaches me to keep our love aloft.

I wonder if you saw me
with my nose pressed against the airport glass
saying goodbye with my eyes
and trying hard not to look pitiful.
Strange, it's so hard to say goodbye to you
for just a few days,
harder than for most
to say goodbye forever.
I searched the dim plane windows
with indistinct faces . . .
which one had you inside?
My eyes never diverted
'till you taxied out of sight.

I lifted you up and up,
by the sheer force of my will, you know.
That big, silver monster
went up and away,
and I kept hearing myself say
inside there is my lover,
who just made love to me.
And as I watched the distance between us
grow in the jet stream,

and you get smaller and smaller,
I heard myself say that you loved me,
even as tiny as you seemed,
and my love was with you
way up in the sky there.
And that was amazing.
Then suddenly I knew it was there
wherever you go.

I watched diligently
until you turned out of sight.
Racing back through the corridor to
the street,
I hoped to catch a last glimpse.
Silly.
Wiping a tear from my cheek as I
passed,
the guard by the soda fountain
smiled.
And I was certain he knew
that I was in love.
Out front of the airport,
I was relieved to still see you way up
there,
turning back Eastward.
The people thought I was crazy,
gazing up at nothing,
shading my eyes from the sun.
But I didn't care.
Then I told you
everything would be allright.
And how much I loved you,
until you were just a small speck
that I was certain no one else in the
world was watching,
except me.
And kept telling myself,
that's my lover way up there.

I didn't wait until you disappeared.
The rest of the afternoon
I talked and sang to the sky.
Because that's where you were.

Marion Okeen
MOTHER'S MONDAY

She spreads her hand
Her palm upside down
She squints and shuts her eyes
Feeling raindrops falling down.
With a little shrug she bends and lifts
The wicker washbasket to her hip.

So the sun is hid
But the sky is blue
She walks so fast
There's so much to do.
And she pins the towels
On long, strong lines
And the few drops of rain
She pays them no mind.

She bends for clothes
And clothespins too
And the lines are soon covered
With laundry in view.
Then sunshine burst
And shed its ray
On Mother's busy, laundry day.

Kathy Churchey
MOVING DAY

To "Love Thy Neighbor As Thyself"
Might be sometimes hard to do.
But, that never was a problem
When the neighbor next door was
you.

To know there was someone real
close by
In case there was a need
For an egg, a cup of sugar, or help in
A crisis, always put my mind at ease.

We've watched our children grow
from babes.
We've shared some ups and downs.
There's no doubt about it,
I'll miss having you around.

To have you as a friend and neighbor
Has meant so very much.
Good Luck with your new home,
Nancy.
God Bless. Let's keep in touch.

Annette J Wesgaites
SECRETS OF MY HEART

To HARRY You were always my friend, and my second love. And you always believed in me.*

Have you ever kept secrets so deep in
your soul?
That you never could share with
anyone yet,
You needed a friend to talk to
someone you could tell your goals,
It was you I finally found to tell you
the secrets of my
heart and love I was to get.

Oh yes, I had dreams of winning
hearts that would take me to the most
beautiful places,
To see new worlds, and faces I've
never seen before,
So deep down inside of me I
believed I could change places,
With a friend who could hear my
secret of my heart as I desired so
much more.

There was money and jewels I
thought would give me so much
pleasure,
How wrong I was, I had so much
wealth it was deep inside of me to
give,
To someone who needed me as I
wanted them to share love you can
only measure,
A lover who could give me back the
secrets of my heart so I can live.

To face each new day and every
tomorrow with you,
You touched my very soul with
your secret desires,
And I promised you I would be
waiting for the very moment you
could do, Was to come to me with so
much love, as only you can just
listen to the sounds of my heart as
you put out the fire.

Richard E Byrd Sr
SEVENTY-TWO AND SUNNY ON THE 18TH DAY OF MAY

For Dick and Danis, incredibly dedicated parents of our first grandchild.

It was a beautiful day, the day our
grandson died;
seventy-two and sunny on the 18th
day of May.

My heart leapt as the words
interrupted an important meeting,
"There's a phone call for you."
My mind raced ahead, anticipating
the chill of new words to come,
"Your grandson's dead."
Had we only known that hospital
morn that our brand new child was
really stillborn.
What appeared to be was not.
All fingers he had;
all parts in place.
A sigh of relief hung in the air.
The pictures,
the smiles,
the gentle relief of knowing Danis
was okay.
Oh, what pleasure masked our
nascent pain;
secret ugliness mocking our
celebration.
Some evil spirit in our broken world
had reached out to flaw
our perfect child.

It was a beautiful day, the day our
grandson died;
seventy-two and sunny on the 18th
day of May.

He lay there
calm,
no longer wanting to please with a
smile
that turned to pain.
His brow was smooth,
his face as beautiful as a newborn,
sound asleep.
Alas, his sleep is forever.
We locked in embraces like
passengers on a sinking ship
saying their final good-byes.
We held him,
each of us.
His life was gone, his fear had fled.
We could take him off his sick bed
and hold him close
as we hadn't, but wanted to do.
We cried the cry of those left behind
to dream of unfulfilled times of play
together,
despairing of ever hearing
"Yes, Grandpa,"
"No, Grandma."

Yes, we cried not so much for him,
for he was released from
an improperly wired,
miserably inadequate
body
that trapped rather than enriched his
spirit.
We cried for the loss of
slides in the summer and
skates in the winter and
trips to the store with Grandma.
We cried for our little friend
who wouldn't be there
for our senior years.

It was a beautiful day, the day our
grandson died;
seventy-two and sunny on the 18th
day of May.

Oh God,
Richard's now in your hands.
We've commended him to you.
Please
teach him to walk and count his
numbers;
help him to learn his letters and to tie
his shoes.
Have him stay in his crib til someone
helps him out.
Teach him what the potty's for and
not to cross the street alone.
Most of all,
bring him joy!
(for he deserves it).
His sojourn of
discomfort,
pneumonia and
repetitive resuscitations
was unjust.
His eight desperate months held us
hostage,
helpless,
angry,
groveling
for your magic touch.
Your lesson seems cruel,
that we must believe
and yet
not understand.
We, too, would have wished this cup
had not been his (or ours).
Forgive us, but in our grief, pain
and presumptuousness,
we hold you accountable
in some way on
our own May day.

It was a beautiful day, the day our
grandson died;
seventy-two and sunny on the 18th
day of May.

Alice A LaFond

Alice A LaFond
LET GO

To all tenacious, moon-gazing cancerians

Why is it I cannot let go,
Just qualify, then end my show?
Instead, I cling to words—belabor
jest.
Is there no ending my stubborn
quest?

What am I searching for in each
word?
A cryptic thought? Suggestion
unheard?

When a new friend I have found,
I should merely listen to the sound
Of his or her heart's meaning . . . It'll
show.
Yes, I should listen and then
. . . . Let go.

Tamara Frantz
DREAMER

To Lisa, with all my heart and courage for survival. Love, Tammy

In her dreams,
she soars on dove's wings.
In her imagination,
she conquers unseen barriers,
and comes out a victor over all living
things.
In her life,
she struggles to survive the day to
day routine.
She is sometimes afraid,
but always courageous.
She is the best thing that a human can
be.
She is a dreamer.

Ryszarda Lida Pelc
MIRACLE

To Caroline, my granddaughter.

Watch this miracle.
From the sky they fall,
thousands, millions
tiny, white stars.
All are different one from another.
This is snow.
Watch this miracle.
It covers dirtiness.
It covers greyness.
It covers ugliness.
Watch this miracle.
In sunbeams of noon, sparkle
diamonds.
In sunset, bloody rubies.
In silver moon time, cool, blue
aquamarines.

What a richness.
All these precious stones surround you.
But don't take them, don't touch them.
I warn you!
They will disappear.

Shannon Sprague
STARS AT NIGHT

To my encouraging family and friends.

Gleaming lights of Autumn,
Shades of red, green, and white.
You may see Venus or Mars,
In the ghostly sky tonight.

The moon, round and full,
Lighting up the darkened space.
The stars are all interwoven,
Like a ream of galactic lace.

Then along comes the dawn,
And the stars start to fade.
The sun will rise now,
Into the new day God's made.

Tanya J Woolridge
MOM
Words can never describe the meaning of Mother to me,
But I'll try.
Mom lives in my shirt pocket at work,
She's in my kitchen at home.
When I walk, she talks to me.
Lonely and blue, though she's miles away,
she holds my hand.
She sits next to me and warms and calms me,
on the dreariest nights.
And when I finally sleep, she says,
"Good night, I love you."
Over the miles that separate us I smile,
"Good night Mom, I love you too!"

Donald L Teed
MY LAST LESSON
I walked along the shadowed path my father left for me.
He taught me how to separate the forest from the trees.

The trees, you see, each one unique, stands so tall alone.
But each one has its weakness, protected by the grove.

Just like an oak, or birch, or pine, a man must stand alone.
But like the tree, mans' weakest traits are protected by the grove.

Life today is not the same as life will be tomorrow.
Each new day has its challenges, its happiness, its sorrows.

We can not stop, we all will change, we blossom then we fly.
But like the mightiest of oaks, we all will surely die.

Again I walked along the path, no shadows did I see.
For now I know my life's tomorrows, I am my destiny.

Correll Lounderman Townes
CHILDREN OF AMERICA CULTIVATE YOUR MIND
They're present daily, yet some never see.
I watch them listen to all except me.
My heart aches daily for lost potentiality.
Children of America, where are your minds?
Statistics say we're still behind in mathematics and also science,
Tell me parents, if you can, what courses are challenging your children to become women and men?
Children of America, what are you doing with your minds?

Teachers teach, children sleep, if not physically, emotionally at times.
Why do they feel to hold their interest we must entertain?
Teachers—Don't play that game!
Children of America, challenge your minds!

Get all you can from every class,
The key point to remember is Knowledge last.
Also remember that knowledge is the key,
It opens all doors of opportunity.
Children of America, cultivate your minds!

Be an All-American in every way,
Play your favorite sport and don't forget to pray.
Learn to follow instructions, listen if you dare,
Teachers are your guides to a broader world,
Let them show how much they care.

Share their journey to everywhere!
Teachers of America, share their minds !!!

Kimberly Joy Kline
LETTING GO
Rain falling from the sky.
Tears falling from my eyes.
There's a pain in my chest that won't go away.
And it all started this very day.
The rain masks my tear streaked face.
In your life I have no place.

Now I'm walking out, as she's coming in.
Because I know I'll never win.
I think of you, night and day.
Your memory just won't go away.

You left me for her, there's nothing I can do.
But sit around feeling blue.
I miss your eyes, your dear, sweet smile.
At least I had you for a little while.
You never meant to hurt me, that I know.
But it will be so hard, letting you go.

Sue Mansker
MY SON
There he stands, big and proud, one among many in the crowd.
They look the same in their blues tonight one big crowd ready to fight.
I see this man, so tall and lean, the boy no longer to be seen.
He looks at me and smiles you see, with eyes as bright as the deep blue sea.
I look around within the crowd, all the loved ones faces, their eyes and smiles upon their faces, seeing their men all in their places.
This young man standing tall and lean as good as any Marine.
A Navy man as you can see, someone I feel is a lot like me.
You march around and show your stuff, and yes my love, you are tough.
You are number two of my six sons, but tonight I feel you are number one.
It's hard to say what I feel in my heart, to see you make a brand new start. You come along from boy to man and the road was hard I understand, but you made it, now you stand in Navy blues a proud, proud man.
I write this poem in fun you see, so you might know I could never be any prouder of you my son, than if you were me.
My head is filled with so many things, but my heart has only the joy and love a son could bring. So God bless you son as you go to sea and keep you safe until He brings you home to me.

Faith Wright
MIKE
Baseball Season was drawing quite near.
He had just turned eleven this school year!
A husky young boy with a new fielder's mitt,
A midget this season, if a uniform he'd fit.
The teams started forming, and one day he was chose—
On a team that would win at the seasons close.
He was proud to be wearing the "Big Number One"—
A great fielder he'd be, his job had begun.
They practiced at batting, fielding and pitching too—
They learned very fast, young kids always do!
Fourteen games to be played, two every week—
Eight teams to compete, a champion to seek!
The games were all thrilling, and they finally won—
The "Fireman's Team", in right field, My Son!

Hilda Jones Lawhorn
LOVE'S SEASONS
Even love has its seasons,
Always changing, but with reason.
Although the reason may be unclear,
You can always hear people say,
"Now listen dear, don't hide your heart,
Set it free, free to wonder where it may.
For some day you'll know you've found,
The secret of the changing seasons,
And at last the perfect reason."

Shirley Barnes
IF
If the foods of the world should disappear,
I could survive if nurtured by your love.

If all the waters from all the rivers, lakes and oceans should dry up,
I could survive if I could drink of but your love.

If the sun and the moon and the stars should forget to shine,
I could survive if warmed by the love in your eyes.

If all the people of all the earth's lands should vanish,
I could survive with the touch of love in your hands.

If all of the planets in this galaxy should move away,
I could survive if you stood in space by my side.

Margie McPherson
COUNTRY MORNING
I like to see the flowers stretching up to greet the day.
I like to see the butterflies lite softly on the hay.
I like to hear the morning songs by Robins as they fly,
and see the mist rise from the pond ascending to the sky.
A rabbit scurries 'cross the field, a squirrel runs up a tree.
It's morning in my mountain home, I love the sights I see.

Rick Pittman Jr

Rick Pittman Jr
SEE LOVE, FEEL LOVE, AND KNOW LOVE

I would first like to thank God for he is my beginning and my end. Special thanks to my honey Tonya Jones. My ma Mrs. Pittman and my Grandmother Mrs. Kimbrough for always believing in me. R.P. Jr.

If you could see what I see within my mind. You would smile forever. And if you could feel what I feel within my heart.
You would be filled forever. And if you knew what I know. You wouldn't want to know nothing else.

For you would see love, feel love, and know that you're loved by me.
But life wasn't intended to be that way. To see love one must stay. And to feel love could take a lifetime. And to know love what could one say. See love, feel love, and know love.
That's what love is all about.

See my love, see my love. Feel my love, feel, feel my love. Know my love, know all about my love. See love, feel love, and know that you're loved by me.

Larry T Wofford
UNI-VERSE
Cantilevering drumbeating brow
wounds parching tears
Alternate eye extracting retracting
bloodbubbles
No roof no porch
Shingled hair holds on sinks holds on
loses grip
Falls out jacked into vacuous old
circles

Life becomes a composite
rollover porcupine

No breath up no body down no
breastmounds no tonguefires
Projecting unknown treading what
could have been placated

The brain did not explode

Life becomes a sobbing magnetic
radiator

Juices geyser straight on out shady armpit hollows
No punctuating bones no whimpering hassles
Frettish sweatdrops on bellied forehead tonight

Life becomes a mangled cosmic
trash blender

This hearthouse pounds maniacally
This one heartbubble bounces a tune surging without hitch
Catching benign wants in inner swampwillows.

Stop

Enter sacred conscience
Invisible spirit gluing all back forward

I just found the universe hiding under my coffee cup.

Mary Kay Fenwick

DREAMS

What are dreams, but thoughts enlarged . . .
Spaces in time or in our minds,
Periods that might have past us by,
Or years . . . yet not arrived?

Dreams are but a conversation of the mind
Talking to us in our sleep.
Calming us in periods of peace,
Restful hours, so we might keep.

We dream sometimes of dreary beings.
Happenings . . . or frightening things.
Yet these come from inner thoughts
They're parts of us, that we know not.

What are these restless times
That wake us up in great alarm?
Afraid to close our eyes again
Lest we see our dreams return.

Then there is other nights of peace
We fight to wake ourselves from sleep
To realize our dreams, aren't real.
They are but thoughts, our thoughts unsealed.

Linda Lou Milea

WHEN I TRIED TO TELL YOU

When I tried to tell you that I really cared,
My heart beat so much faster all I did was stare.

Those long and silent moments,
The look of love and care . . .

Although the words are spoken now,
Their meaning will always be there.

So please don't ever doubt it,
or turn your love away.
Because it's coming from my heart,
to you asking
you
to
stay

Lisa A Glazewski

SUNDAY MORNING

The morning sun streams through the window,
bouncing off the dresser mirror,
and creating dancing light
beams.
The newspaper is strewn across the bed—
the cat snoozes on the funnies.
You, in your stripped pajama bottoms,
are reading the sports section.
Coffee mug in your hand, muttering
an occasional expletive.
Me, in your shirt, studying the spring fashion preview;
minis, cotton sweaters, and
sexy bathing suits.
You slowly yawn and stretch your way into the bathroom and
Water runs in the shower . . .
Leaving me and the cat in a
rumpled bed.
Sunday morning.

George A Kolar

SAVE NATURE

Deep in the dark forest
Night is coming soon,
Over in the valley,
A coyote howls at the moon.
On some distant mountain peak
A mountain goat is there,
And over in the forest glen,
You chance to see a grizzly bear.
The salmon swimming freely,
Swimming northward
Coming upstream from the sea
These things are with us yet today,
But how much longer can they stay?
Can man sit idly by and let the wonders of nature die?
I should rather like to think
That man would step back from the brink,
And save the things for tomorrow, today,
Before these things are swept away.

Donna Myers

THE DEAREST THING IN LIFE

God gives to us many gifts.
But a child is one of the most precious gifts He gives.
When you think of the things they say and do,
Remember, God has entrusted them to you.
For they really don't belong to us, but to Him.
And He will do what's best for them.
So, if they become ill,
Put your faith in Him,
And accept His will.
Though we don't understand, and we ask Him why,
He is always there, even when we cry.
He will never forsake us,
and will keep His promise,
Because He and I both know,
That the dearest thing in life,
is a child.

Connie M Benn

THE UNICORN

You are like the Unicorn,
a part of my dreams,
shadowed and distant,
. . . never quite reality.
Your touch,
your kiss,
. . . they are real.
Your eyes,
gentle, but
. . . also real.
Your body,
your words,
unbelievably beautiful
. . . real.
I open my eyes
. . . I'm alone.
Like the Unicorn,
you fade
with the dream.

John K Crawford

MY APPROACH

When I think approach of mine
Will seem a measure of success—
Then it's best to redefine
The boundaries of my
wilderness.

When I think approach of mine
Will capture—Oh, do hopes allow?
Hopes complete—are asinine
And must be stricken out—
somehow.

When I think approach of mine—
Well, I can only wish it's true.
Only if it's true design
Can bring contentment—me to you.

Linda Bass

MY THOUGHTS

My life has started to begin,
With love so great I hope to win.
I know it's rough for him right now,
And pray the Lord will show me how.
To understand why it's this way,
I love him more and more each day.
He loves us both and can't decide,
The one he wants beside his side.
I hate to think of missing out,
On things we've did without a doubt.
His love's so real I hope it's true,
I'd stick by him like superglue.
I know I can't take too much more,
My love for him is too hard core.
This poem I've wrote of just my thoughts,
To hope and pray I've got him caught.
The time is coming to find out soon,
I hope it's me with him and the moon.
I love him dearly

Catherine J Hall

THE HOMESTEAD

I stood today and fondly gazed
On the scene of all my childhood days.
The weeds grow wild about the door,
Where rambling roses twined before.
The house lies hushed in twilight gloom,
Where laughter once filled every room.
The arbor where once hung my swing,
Stands lonely now—a deserted thing.
Though the scene has changed as the years have flown,
My heart cries out—this is still my home.

Doris D Smith PhD

NO GREATER MOTHER'S LOVE

As they handed him to me on the day of his birth,
With my eyes I could see God's richest beauty on earth.
He was my first born . . . a real part of me,
No greater Mother's love would he ever really see.

I loved him from the moment my eyes upon him laid.
I will always love him till the breath in me doth fade.
I've loved him even more than I can truly show,
No greater Mother's love will he ever really know.

Have I loved him too much and not let him be
A mighty worthy sailor as he sails upon life's sea?
Have I helped him chart his course so he will never fail?
No greater Mother's love will help him trim his sails.

I pray to God that I have loved him just the right amount
And on this earth he will abide and make his presence count.
I pray that he will understand the love that I do yield.
No greater Mother's love will ever be so real.

Willie M Emerson

WANDERING, ALONE

Will I faithfully live,
What You mean to me?
Sometimes I'm blind,
What I mean to Thee.

Our lives are so very short.
Will they be able to count the cost?
Persecution. Before and after court.
A race whose lives reflect something lost.

Not all miss the Joy,
That can be found.
From every girl and boy,
Not one has to be bound.

Day has not yet come, remaining in the night,
They wander around alone.
Life is fleeting out of sight.
And still they continue in their endless plight.

Will they ever be caught,
In what You mean to me?
Some will never feel. All ready bought.
Perhaps, in our time, many more will see.

R Spech

GIVE!

Give me your hands to lift us up!
Give me your eyes to see us grow!
Give me your soul and we'll have inspiration
To go forward and get out of this hole
Out of ignorance!
Out of disbelief!
Out of those evils that don't let us
live and be free

Loretta G Massara

THE RICHES OF YOUTH

The riches of youth,
scattered beneath sleepy fields,
spent
and not a cent remains.
Even as withered crosses
croak of age and wisdom
far beyond the heads they mark,
the masses revel in their salutary pride.
Were that the salt of earth,
could replenish
and make fresh the wounds of war,
perhaps then they too
Could their glories bury.

Joyce Copp
LUNCH

My sandwich is topped
with wonderful things,
So juicy and hot—with onion rings,
My chips are so fresh and crisp
with each bite,
My soup is delicious,
I could eat it all night.
My cookies so chewy
they taste just divine,
My lunch is just great,
My most favorite time!

Kathleen Ann Crump

Kathleen Ann Crump
JESUS! TEACH ME HOW TO PRAY

This poem is dedicated to:—Belinda, Kevin,& Abdu.

Oh! Jesus I forgot to pray today
Sometimes it's not easy to say "I'm sorry"
Sorry for the things I've done this day
Teach me LORD JESUS how to pray

OH! Jesus I forgot to pray today
I need to know just what to say
From my very gut, I need to pray
Teach me this day LORD JESUS what to say

When things happen throughout the day
And things don't always go my way
My soul hurts and my heart pines
Teach me how your love to find

My days are happy and sad together
It seems it depends on the weather
But, JESUS you know, you always do
Please help me this long day through

My love for you runs very deep
Your love and comfort put me to sleep
Let me stay with you for always
In you loving protection always keep

Mary Lou Richardson Leising
MY HOMETOWN

The People of Raceland, Ky.

They've built a four-lane highway
Thru the middle of my hometown,
And the little home we lived in
Has been torn down.

The shady streets we played on
With our bikes, skates and sleds,
Have been turned into an open road
For 18-wheelers instead.

The rolling hills behind our school
That glistened in Winter's sun,
And grazed herds of cattle in Springtime
Now's where the traffic runs.

My Father was a railroad man
But railroading there too has changed,
The quiet, half-empty, sprawling yards
Were once filled with moving trains.

We've been away from there a number of years
Yet we love to go back for a visit,
Each time I pass thru, I say to myself
"This isn't my Hometown, is it?"

Andrea C Thompson
LIFE

To my family for their support, especially my husband Clive, I thank you all for your patience. Also to our parents Adeline, Albert, Jessie and Clarence life forever.

If I could but see . . .
How life doth bother me,
It renders neither foe or friend
Nor does it money lend.

If I could but . . .
See worry and life's rut,
Deeds of good and daring rend
Are sought, but none to lend.

If I could . . . .
But see, no one would,
Time seeps away from me
Alas, no motion can be free.

If I . . .
Could but see, soon to die,
Will someone, for me recall
Or can the body, be my soul's downfall.

If . . .
I could but see, my life,
The change would be great
Oh! Tis way too late.

Jennifer Lynn Yamnicky
REFLECTIONS

Standing by a spring
Silent as you stand,
A precious treasure
Within the land.

Your reflection so colorful
That of a fall tree,
Your mind going beyond
Safe and free.

This place is wonderful
You'll not want to return,
To a world you once knew
Of hatred and burn.

A beautiful place
Your mind can be,
All the wonders
Only you can see.

A sweet sweet smell
Lingers toward your nose,
That of a flower
Or a sweet smelling rose.

You must go back
But visit soon,
Maybe before daybreak
Or after noon.

Clarah Anderson Clark
ALL THAT NIGHT

To my dear son, Ellsworth Clark

The Angel of God came by one night,
And set the prisoners free,
And He worked all night that wearisome night
With the fishermen on Galilee.
On discouraged one, have you waited long,
For the answer that did not come?
In the night of your greatest doubting,
Your troubles may soon be gone.
He does not always work by day
But hears the prayer you send
He works away by stillness of night,
Broken bodies and hearts to mend.
So be still my heart,
There's a song in the night,
When you least expect it to be,
And He bends low to hear that song,
That seemed so far from thee!

Bobbie N Snyder
THE MUSTANG

As wild the wind
And clarion call,
Of star-swept night,
Can still be heard
The sound of hoof-beats,
Running free.
And sometimes yet,
The dream,
Of gentle dark hands,
Guiding.
The whispered magic spells,
Of feathered warriors.
The remembered victory fires
And drums of the ghost-dancers

Edna High Crittenden
TO NANCY

When I went in to surgery,
I knew my Lord was there,
In the skill of the physician
And the nurses' tender care.

Even the warm blankets
That made me feel at ease
Seemed to echo His dear words:
"I am in all of these."

As you go in to surgery
I know this will be true
You'll feel His presence always,
And know His love for you.

And after it's all over
He'll be with you—evermore
To bring you comfort, hope and strength
And make things better than before.

Maryanne Wood
WISHING WELL

For all who touched my life

Wishing Well! Oh, Wishing Well!
The tales that do unfold!
The cast of every eye on thee,
From now since days of old,
Are drawn by thee to hidden things:
Dreams seen, but never told . . .

Sizzling Sunsets! Pink Parades!
Alas—Dark Tragedies!

The coins themselves, cannot expel
Such vivid imageries;
Of deeds gone by, and yens to come,
We do so try to quell,
All captured now, forevermore,
In this enchanting spell.

Wishing Well! Oh, Wishing Well!
The ancient sighs do stay!
Stones groan with broken promises,
Love and fortunes cast away.
Yet, tantalizing whisps of air,
And auras of mystique,
Embrace the suns and pink parades,
Romantics ever seek.

Kenneth Lee Kidd
MIDNIGHT RIVER

To my love and inspiration. My reason of life. Remaining in my heart for eternity. Love Lisa

Dark, Mysterious; While Romantic. High banks and rough cliffs, Protect the ever silent moving waters of:
The Midnight River
Guarded by over reaching trees; While a gently blowing breeze set their leaves free: Soon, to be out of sight, with the motions of silent currents within:
The Midnight River
Lovers gaze upon; While waiting for romance to drift their way: Only to have it washed away; By the flowing of:
The Midnight River
We take time to look on this ever changing scene: Yet; no-time is taken to understand,
The Midnight River

Susan Jill
WHAT IS A FRIEND

This poem is dedicated to Heather, my best friend.

What is a friend—
Someone who cares, a person who
always is there,
One person in the world
you can always depend on,
with whom your innermost feelings
you can share.

A friend makes you happy,
always knowing what to say
even when they don't know what's wrong,
That one special person
the one that you trust
for you, my friend, I write this song.

Mavis Jacobson
GRANDCHILDREN

To Erin—my special Granddaughter on her 6th birthday

The children of our children are special don't you see?
Because they're part of both us, and maybe that's the key.
Cause p'rhaps God takes the best of each and puts it into one
And that's why they are special, and equal "not to one."
So every smile I treasure, every fault refuse to see,
Cause after all they are a part of the "bestest" part of me!

Katherinea Nemeth-Spearman
LITTLE THINGS

To: Cosimo Bommarito For teaching me the meaning of CHARITY; "The love of man for his fellow man." Where it comes from, and how it feels. Thank You.

It's the "Little Things" that mean so much!
Did you ever try to buy a "touch"?
For a "Smilin Good Mornin" what would ye pay?
How much for a "kiss" at the close of day

Where would you find a "bundle of hugs"?
not at the store or saved in a jug!
You can't order a "Smile" nor purchase a "wink";
no catalogue has them, not even Brinks,

There's no shoppe called "Kindness" in our local mall,
and no where to go—to buy "Peace" for us all.
No place stocks "happy", gee, where can it be?
"Hey wait, my friend; it's inside you and me!!!

Take just a few moments—see all you have;
say thanks to our Father, "Little Things" make us glad.
All of the answers to the questions above
cost not a farthing, they're gifts of His love.

Pamela S Botelho
COLDS

This is dedicated to my very loving husband Daniel and my four sons that I love dearly.

Colds make you feel bad from your head to your toes,

And to make it worse you get a red nose.

You also get the sniffles and it makes you sneeze,

At times so hard you fall to your knees.

But there is one thing I can assure you of,

No matter how sick you've got your mother's love.

Michael J Bordonaro
THE LAST ROAD

This poem is dedicated to my mother Elizabeth M Bordonaro, for always believing in me.

I have traveled a dark and crimson path, on a road that leads to hell.
On a road where weird inhuman shapes, have not the nerve to dwell.
On a road where the sun will never shine, and the moon will never glow.
On a road where only the dead may walk, and have no where else to go.

I have traveled far on a well worn path, on a road that has no end.
And on this road I walk alone, forever without a friend.
And on this road there is no time, to langour in tranquil rest.
For it is said time waits for no one, and no one knows it best.

I have traveled for ages along this path, on a road that draws on me.
On a road that has taken all from me, but the gift of one last song.
And on this road of shattered dreams, it's a bitter song I'll sing.
For only silence falls from the lips, of a tattered corpse like thing.

Phillip W Briggs
TEARS IN THE RAIN

I dedicate this poem to my two special sons Phillip and David who are the light of my life.

The sky was Dark
The moon showed it's face
My eyes Blue
My heart even Bluer
The sun began to set
A summer shower cried
A Rainbow stretched forth its hands
As it Painted the sky
And a flower closed its Petals for the night
The moon rose higher in the sky
But my heart remained Blue
And all I could feel
Were my Tears in the Rain

Mary Flovin

Mary Flovin
ALMOST GONE!

To my children—Michele Wedemeyer, Richard Scott Flovin, Mike Flovin

I just can't do this anymore—does anyone understand?
There's only so much a human being can endure,
Only so much loneliness and pain the heart can hold.
Did God mean it to be this way—I'm not so sure.

I've tried to hold onto my sanity and hope—
But each time it slips farther and farther away.
I feel like I'm reaching out for nothing.
Without any hope, where's my reason to stay?

I feel I'm just occupying space—I just don't care!
My heart is crying tears of desperation,
The need to feel another human being's concern,
And to touch and feel touch-so alone-so alone.

I'll try a little longer, but no promises—
Is there anyone out there who give a damn!
Please, someone throw me a piece of hope.
Don't let me give in to being no more—I am

Almost gone!

Dorothey M Brattin
TO DAVID

Our relationship may seem like an illogical situation, but my heart doesn't know this.
You came into my life so gentle, sweet and shy.
I never dared to dream of you for fear it was a lie
Your age difference has truly frightened me, of that I won't deny.
When I think of what the loss would be,
I'll not knowingly pass you by.
The joy I hope to share with you will overcome the fear.
I hope to live and love again, throughout the coming year
Happy Valentine Day—Dorothey

Timothy M Roche
THE SETTING SUN

To the splendour of the Earth, and to God for making it that way.

The gleaming rays of the setting sun
make their way across the horizon.
Their beauty and splendour knows no equal,
Although tomorrow brings a sequel.
Bright orange, pale yellow, fiery red,
All like a vision within my head.
As the sun goes, the old day descends
And brings in the night, as the moon ascends.
But again it will rise, by some strange force,
To brighten our day, and repeat its course.

Diane F Banks
DECISION

For her love, support, and inspiration, this poem is dedicated to my sister, Donna, the perfect twin—who always comes out when I go in.

As the carousel turns, there's a dark cloud overhead.
I feel a force pulling at me as I struggle to hold on.
I'm troubled—despondent—and uncertain of the present.
Yesterday was so perfect—Now I'm confused.
What happened to cause this change?
What did I do? What didn't I do?
Will things change? Do things just automatically change?
Am I unrealistic? Am I idealistic?
As the carousel begins to slow down, I have to decide.
Do I stay on and live this unrealized dream?
Or do I wait until it stops . . . and just get off?

Florence Shive
WHISPER SOFTLY

To My Niece Mary Martin Who made me laugh when my heart was sad.

Whisper softly, hear the dew upon the grass.
Whisper softly, hear the gentle soft breeze caressing the grass.
Whisper softly, hear the weeping willow tree crying in the wind,
With branches humbly bending over as if in saying a prayer.
Whisper softly, hear the song of the birds in the woods, the
Still quiet peace of the mountain side; the still gentle peace
Of the rippling stream.
Whisper softly, hear the baby cry and then hear the gentle coo
After the baby is held in someone's arms, and rocked to sleep
On someone's lap in the rocking chair.
Whisper softly, take time to listen to the more gentle sounds
Of life and nature that are at peace with God and man.
Whisper softly, listen to the human sounds of your very kind,
That are always there because God blessed us with these; but
Somehow we often take for granted
because they are always there.
Whisper softly, listen to your inner-self, listen to your soul
And pray within that all is at peace, calm, and tranquility.

Mary Lee Adsit-Chaffey (Peggy)
TRIBUTE TO OUR LOVE

To my husband, David, who has always loved me back.

The years we've been together
have been the special kind
Two lives have lived and
Loved each other . . .
Sharing of our time.

Faithful as a new day . . .
You've been my friend and lover.
It's been a time of untold joys . . .
A time for one another.

We've laughed and cried together . . .
Our life's been good for us.
It seems a fitting time to say . . .
I love you more each day.

Kevin D Gibson
THE KITE

Look in the blue sky,
What do you see flying there.
A beautiful kite.

Diane Sinclair
THE ROLLER COASTER

Little cars all square and bright,
Exposed to all the sunshine light,
Up, up, up a narrow track,
Down, down, down,
Around, 'round, 'round,
A curve, a swerve,
A dip, a flip,
A bump, a hump,
They go . . . . .
And then come back.

Rose Carrero
CHANGED

To God whom I have believed, and of whom I am convinced that "He is able to guard what I have entrusted to Him unto that day." (2 Timothy 1:12)

To know a peace only He can give,
To have a purpose and a reason to live,
To know who I am and where I will go,
To know in my heart the things I now know.

That is my life as it's lived today.
I have been shown a much better way
Than the pain of the past and fear of tomorrow,
Than constant defeat and unceasing sorrow.

I have been changed to the depths of my soul
By the only Healer who can make me whole:
Jesus, our Saviour and Lord, God's only Son,
King of kings, Creator, the holy living One.

Raymond Jenkins
210 CANIS DRIVE

I looked out my front door one fine autumn day,
It was sort of quiet and peaceful in a city sort of way.
When soon I heard the loud barking from the bitch across the street,
Yelling at her sister's kids to get the mud off their feet.

Then I heard the tempered screams
from the folks across the way,
Fighting to decide which of them
really had the right to stay.
Suddenly from around the corner
sped a screaming car,
Leaving behind a bunch of smoke
and the road covered with tar.

The dogs started yelping wildly
when someone kicked over a can,
And the kids down the walk were
fighting with an old man.
I then closed my front door that fine
autumn day,
And smiled to myself, for this is the
city sort of way.

Kay Rourke
TO A SPECIAL FRIEND

For all the trust I found in you,
It's worth more than a lunch or two.
You are a friend from way back
when,
And now I know there is no end.

You gave your heart,
You gave your soul.
You listened well,
I lost control.

And yet I know within my heart,
God has a plan right from the start.
To each and every one I pray,
That you will somehow find your
way.

The day is here,
The day is now.
Our path unfolds,
We don't know how.

Our faith,
Our friends,
Will surely be,
The force that stirs my faith in me.

Cheryl A Eller
WE ARE PEOPLE

To My Loving Children, Jennifer, Michael, and Matthew, You are my inspiration and my life and without you I would be empty. I Love You.

We are people who want to trust and
care.
We are people who have been hurt by
those we cared for.
Slowly we mend our wounds and
search for what we can.
We are people who shy away from
the flame, too afraid to get burned
again.
We are people too tired and too
scared to love openly.
We are people who are too many to
count.
We are people who can teach each
other, through our experiences.
All we have to do is learn to accept
what is given and not run from it. We
must try even though it means getting
close to the flame.
For without trying new ground we
will always be in the same place we
were when we got burned.
We are people who must learn from
the past and step forward, proud to
have survived our battle. Proud to
hold our heads up high.
We are people who must know we
are not alone, for many walk down
this road with us.
We are people who must unite, for
our love is strong enough to share.
We are people who must not let the
bad turn us to stone.
We are people who must leave the
door open for others to enter.
We are people, you and me and we
will survive with the support of each
other.

Pat Lyman
MORN

DEDICATED TO YOU, EDDIE-LOU COLE; Thanks for the recognition, and my first appearance "in print." Bless You!

Earth's rotation again completed
sun and I meet face to face once
more
Rays of dawn caress the skies
horizon now defined.

I lie in bed of peaceful slumber
sunrise filtering crusted lids
With difficulty my visional skin
retracts
blurred is my sight by Nature's
light.

Fingers of sunshine rub sleep from
my eyes
naked skin prickled,
sensationally tickled
Had I been as warm by blanketing
myself
I would not have enjoyed it as
much.

Ruby Cummings Webb
WILDFLOWERS

Wildflowers grow most everywhere
One kind here and another kind there
Of different colors, shapes, and size
Some are pretty enough to win a
prize
Growing along roadsides, meadows,
and woods
Take time to look, I think you should
For there's beauty in every one you
see
Nature places them there for you and
me.

Tom Brown
WHEN I'VE CROSSED THE GREAT DIVIDE

Now, when they finally tell me that
all;
The time i've been allotted is
completely gone,
And all the many, many battles have
been won,
And all my work upon this earth is
done, i wonder,
Just what will life be like, when i've
crossed the Great Divide?

When all the many tasks that i've
started have been completed,
And they tell me that i've successful
made it through,
And there's nothing more left here
for me to do,
And it's time for me to leave my
earthly station, i wonder,
Just what will life be like, when i've
crossed the Great Divide?

When they tell me that i've made it
down to the end of the line,
That everything's going to turn out
oh! so very, very fine,
When they tell me i'll have much
better accommodations, when
i arrive at my new location,
And that i'm to cross the Jordan, and
proceed on to Beulah Land,
i wonder now,
Just what will life be like, when i've
crossed the Great Divide?

Elizabeth Nickrenz
SONNET

I open up my silent study's door
And with a creak it obeys my
command.
Though in my dreams I always walk
so sure,
Now I do my work with shaking
hand.
And so on paths to fantasy I walk
Because this world is stricken down
with pain.
In my hand I hold a golden lock;
The key, within my mind, I still must
gain.
I walk through many doors to find
the Key,
And all my hope is deep within my
heart.
Then far away a glint of gold I see
And on the journey toward that hope
I start.
Yet here I am, my problems
still pursued,
Sitting in a silent, dreaming
mood.

Stacey Lynn Bradley
THE INDIAN

To My Beloved Parents Thank you for everything

On his horse he sits so tall,
The bravest warrior of them all.
He sits and thinks of different things,
Like all his braves and their dreams.
He turns around to see,
The Mountains, Meadows and all the
trees.
Then he wonders about the white
man,
And what they have done to his land.
He does not know why,
White men say that red men lie.
He hears something and turns
around,
To see his braves fall to the ground.
Before he leaves he wonders why,
All white men say he must die.

Iris Theresa Stark
THE MANY VOICES OF LOVE

To my daughter, Linda Eddy, whose loyal devotion inspired me to write this poem.

Love, The wind whispers as it ruffles
your hair,
Love, The sun shouts as it
browns the bare.
Love, The rain drums with its many
drops,
Love, The snow sighs as it
covers tree tops.
Flowers, candy and gems speak of
love,
Birds and bees sing of love.
Oceans and lakes gaily stream love,
Candles and stars softly gleam
love.
Everywhere love is chanted or
chimed,
From crickets to bells, to awaken
your mind.
Lovely poems and paintings cast
their spell,
Without a doubt music does as
well.
Yet the most stirring of them all,
Are the impromptu gestures we
recall.
A gentle touch, a word of the wise,
A welcome smile, a gift no
money buys.
A helping hand when things are
rough,
Blessings and deeds from those
who care enough.
Love embraces everyone in time,
Its voices are clear to an open
mind.
God gives the messages, Love gives
the sign!

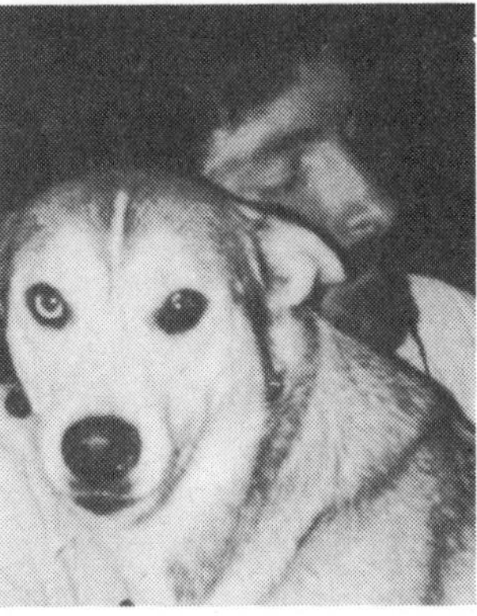

Neater

By Neater
I'M IN A CAGE LOOKING OUT

To the man called Fisher, I love you Dear Brother

I'm in a cage; I have no doubt.
I'm in a cage looking out.
The bars I feel are cold as steel.
The bars I feel, I feel so real.
These's bars of steel won't let you
near.
The walls in here are screaming out.
If I could run, I'd set me free.
If I could feel, I'd take the key.
The bars of steel are confining me.
The bars of steel can't set me free.
I'm in a cage looking out
Oh dear God! Help me out
God knows the pain we share apart.
God knows the shame within my
heart.
When in Heaven I have no doubt.
The bar of steel will let me out.
God will love me I have no doubt.

Gaby Diaz
WHEN I NO LONGER BEAR YOU

When I no longer bear you
We would have been imagining your
smile for ever

When your preparing endless months
are over
We would have been organizing
your-our world to the last detail

When you finally come to our lives
We would have been wishing you for
centuries

When you take your first step
We would have been raising you
independent since fall one

When your eyes awake to reality
We would have been sweetening it
with all our hearts

When you ask about war

We would have been searching for the answer since the first ape

When you start judging us
We would have been making mistakes since our great grandparents

But . . .when you look for love and comfort
You won't have to
Because we would have been giving them to you since before you can remember

Flotella Nickerson
WALK WITH ME BLESSED LORD
Walk with me and talk with me dear Lord,
As I journey through this world below,
There may be heartaches and woe;
But O Lord be with me as I go.

If I just lift my eyes to Thee,
I know you'll hear my gentle plea.
You'll give me strength to carry on,
If I just cry unto Thee.

Oh Blessed Lord walk with me,
Please hear my gentle plea,
Oh! give me strength to carry on,
Oh! how I need Thee.

Doreen E Sherwood
MATTHEW
So late in March, in spite of the storm,
A miracle happened, and twins were born.
Two bright little boys, so healthy they were,
So very much loved, a bright future for sure.

Two weeks of happiness for parents and kin,
Then disaster struck, will wee Matthew win?
The boy has a murmur, a hole in his heart,
A small weakened artery, a valve that gets stuck.

A trip to the doctor, an operating table,
Then hours of waiting, will the doctors be able?
The heart is so small, the baby so young,
Surely God doesn't want him, his life's just begun.

So we sit and we wait, praying all day,
Till at last we learn, God will let him stay.

Carl H Snyder
TIME

To my wife Mary and our grandchildren; Aaron, Kris, Katie, Jamie, Jed, Danelle, Melissa, Brian, Joni, Jennifer, Chris, Abe, Ben and Azzurdee.

Tick-tock, listen to the clock.
Do you hear what it has to say?
Tick-tock, listen to the clock.
Time is on its way.

Time is yours to do what you wish.
You should not let it go to waste.
There're places to go and things to be done.
Can't succeed at a walk you'll have to run.

Do what you can, come sunshine or rain.
Do it well so you need not do it again.
Listen to a child, make waves to a friend.
Speak to a foe and try to make amends.

Pay all your debts. Don't owe any man.
You'll think you can't but know you can.
Work hard to earn your daily bread.
You'll be able to sleep when you go to bed.

Tick-tock, listen to the clock.
Do you hear what it has to say?
Tick-tock, listen to the clock.
It'll soon be another day.

Donald R Moon
A SONG FOR MARY LOUISE

To the special lady in my life; who inspired the poem three weeks after our meeting.

As the rain falls on your rooftop
And you drift quietly off to sleep
For all of my thoughts are with you
May you have dreams that then will keep

As you say your prayers in silence
And you sing your lingering song
As you drift to your sweet slumber
You know a smile would not be wrong

And if you search for the rainbow
I hope you find the pot of gold
And may you find it somewhere
I hope it will be yours to hold

As you awake in the morning
I hope you will still have your smile
Hold on to your dreams and your thoughts
You know you are loved all the while

Because I will be here waiting
And you don't have to say "Oh Please"
All you have to do is call me
For I Love You, Mary Louise

Jackie Johnson
SONG OF SONGS
He is dead his father said.
He carried him in and laid him on the couch.
No, not dead. Only unconscious. He will revive.
  But I saw the mountain fall.
His fingernails, why are they so big and blue?
The rope burn under his chin, ugly deep and red.
A child's swing, a hangman's rope?
Laughter choked back into his throat?
No, the world couldn't hold that much horror.
The doctor came and said he's dead.
The padre came and said he's with the angels now.
  My heart broke.

At his funeral Mass, I heard the angels sing.
    "Length of days is not what makes life honorable,
    nor the number of years, the true measure of life.
    Coming to perfection in so short a while.
        he achieved long life.
    He sought to please the Lord, so the Lord loved him.
    and took him quickly from the wickedness around him.

    He received the royal crown of splendor,
    the diadem of beauty from the hands of the Lord
    He is sheltering him with his right hand
    and shielding him with his arm"

Then I came home to an empty house.
The silence screamed so loud.
His room was super-charged with his presence.
Sun-browned hands made his toys move.
His clothes filled with his shape.
The imprint on his bed rounded into his form.
God loved him, so he took him.
Assuming we loved him not enough?
  Ah, what presumption.

Fool, fool, silence your sobbing heart.
You screamed loudly, don't go, we love you.
But above the screams, you heard a whisper,
"Come we love you more."
So you went, our little boy.
You were right to go.
But God, O God, let me again hear the angels sing.

Marlene R Eckstein MD
YEARNINGS
Long-felt yearnings to become free
To express what beats true in me.
Deep, caring sensitivity.
Assets of "femininity."

Why must women suppress their charms
Despite awareness of alarms
That ring within their female souls
Sacrificed for their career roles.

If I could change what's said God did
I would pick Adam's heart not rib
And combine woman's and man's traits
As humans, before it's too late.

Peter H Fulton
BOULDERS IN ICE
The cadence of nature's changing days
binds us to deliberate, varied freedom,
liberates new perceptions amid perpetual ways,
re-exposes secretive, seasonal wisdom.

Thus Spring, full in its willow-budding,
warms our startled spirits to brighter times
and, with thawing creeks, sets hopes flowing,
regenerates Winter's frozen movement's mime.

Resolving with regret to look back and rejoice
the green stirring of earth, the release of cold,
we resound high praises in Summer's august voice,
applaud unleaving Autumn's crisp orange and gold.

But after heat and harvest fade with arresting icy breeze,
and year end fleecy stillness shows rigid scope and pace,
bare we patience and humility of soul against the bitter freeze,
and some to die with weed and squirrel and stone,
alone with grace.

Carolyn Lindsey Cheshire
WHAT YOU ARE TO ME
You are like the sun
  quietly rising in the morning,
As it warms the earth—
  so you warm my heart.
You are like the moon
  that shines at night,
As it lights the darkness—
  so you light up my life.
You are like a fresh summer breeze
  gently stirring through the trees,
To hear your voice—
  gently, calmly stirs my soul.
You are like the universe
  of God's creation,
So what you are , my love—
  is Everything to me!

Dottie Tribbie
IMPOSSIBLE WISH
I sat on my porch last night
Wine rippling like a gentle summer sea,
And suddenly felt very young.
Does that mean I am getting old?
I felt the sand crunch beneath my feet,
The shadow I cast at least six years old.
I even giggled as cold spray washed my face.
But gazing at the horizon all I could see
    was cucumber sandwiches
    and tea,
And I could hear my mother calling me.
Before I could turn or even run away
She was there, clutching my hand while
We raced along the beach and—.
But that was so very long ago,
    many wine glasses away.
I crawled into my bed,
Hugging her hand-me-down pillow to my head
And pretended to sleep while the
    dream raced on.
Today, I am me.

Kara W Ashley
SOCIETY'S GRASP
Society's grasp is mankind's test.
Fail, and perish with the rest.
Use your strength and never fear
what actions come from your peer.
For if you believe and dive too deep,
unhappiness is what you reap.

Beware the crooked minds that manifest.
They'll send you on a blind man's quest.
Remember strength, so important to keep—
to avoid society's enormous heap.
Study in full what you shall hear—
for some words can only sear.

Rules of the heart bring the best.

Society's rules are just a pest.
One should see what is clear—
the difference is the results that steer.
Good and bad at the same time seep.
Happiness, unhappiness—which
shall you keep?

Christa Lee Nelson
THE SILENT SONG

In loving memory of my grandfather, Robert S. Nelson.

I can hear the silent song of the
ocean,
A tranquil melody composed by
God;
A never ending composition
All the universe does applaud.

The waves crash down upon a stage
of sand
Setting the tempo for eternity.
And with a gentle movement of His
hand,
The ocean breeze repeats the
melody.

Joyce E Searcy
RSVP

This poem is dedicated to Joan, with love.

Jesus' invitation reads
"Come unto me . . . and I will
give you rest"

And of course you know that in this
He surely does not jest

He loves you and for you He wants
only the best

Believe and accept His
plea

Don't hesitate
He's waiting for your
RSVP

Juanita Tusinger
THIS PRIVATE ROOM HE MAKES AVAILABLE

Dedicated to all who seek His presence.

There is a door that Jesus closes
To shut out darkened rooms.
It is so still and quiet
It's called, Jesus' Private Room.

That is where He likes to take us
When the storms rage all about.
The only place where we can go
To shut the "troubles" out.

That is where He likes to take us
To soothe our ailing soul.
A place to be alone with Him,
The most heavenly place I know.

Tabitha Ragan
WHY I LIKE SPRING

I like spring. It is very nice. Sometimes it smells like spice. I like the smell of spring. Spring is a time to swing. And the trees start to lean. Spring is a very nice season. It is a good time for sneezing. It is not freezen. Spring is so pleasant. I am so delighted of spring!

Willie M Kenner
GREATEST OF GIFTS

This poem is dedicated to Willie G. Walker, my beloved father.

I close my eyes and recollect,
a small wood frame house.
I hear the screen door bang,
and footsteps patting about.
The smell of beans and corn
bread fill the air.
A strong, but weary man sits
in a chair.
Worry and strife, carved in his
face.
A graceful smile to take its
place.
His hair once soft and brown,
Now coarse and gray are found.
His hands are calloused and
seared.
Life has left its mark through the
years.
A ray of hope that I don't
understand.
The peaceful light that comes
forth from this man.
There's a strength that I don't
recognize.
As I look back through a child's
eyes.
The laughter and happiness he
made in our house.
The love he scattered all about.
This man is my father, you see.
The Greatest of Gifts, from God, to
me.

Mae Dodd
A TRUE FRIEND

To my sister-in-law, Nina Dodd, whose faith and encouragement led me to renew my efforts in poetry writing.

Close to the heart of God, a true
friend
Holds your hand when troubles
douse the light
And long choking fingers of
darkness extend
Like spider legs around your throat,
squeezing tight.

A true friend shares her well worn
shawl
Of faith and confidence, of love and
peace.
She lifts you up; you both stand tall,
Strong, secure, until the raging
storms cease.

When you cry for understanding, she
is there
Ready to share her last crust of bread
When your cupboard stands cold,
and dark, and bare
And your hungry children cry to be
fed.

Even when you approach life's
darkest night,
Enter that long tunnel and start to
ascend,
A hand reaches forth with a bright
shining light
To help you cross over—the hand of
true friend.

Rita Farmer
BLACK TEARS IN A BLACK MAN'S WORLD

Been strivin' all my life
to make ends meet.
The goin', the comin'
in a worldly race.
But at a pace I must compete.

Black, Hispanic, White or Jew
still I'se been strivin' all my life.
Stumped on, cursed at,
spat on, laughed at.
But never the first black man
to be treated so wrong.

Half of my life is at a stage
one I must comprehend.
As a story I read,
then slowly I turn the page.
Mama and Papa left me
when I was young.
I knew I had to succeed,
but not to prolong.
In a Black man's world.

Black Tears came from those eyes, dark and gray in a Black man's world. But Jesus he met me part of the way, And said, "Remember my child just pray."

Patsy Seamon
I FEEL LIKE A SEED

I feel like a seed
that started to grow.
Just as I blossomed,
the sun stopped its glow.

Now I'm starting to wilt
as though I may die.
Will the bright sun come back
so I'll reach for the sky?

Or will I be left
all alone in the cold
to suffer and starve—
my leaves soon to fold.

I need warmth and love
and sunshine to nurture.
Without simple kindness
'Twill be a bleak future.

Life isn't easy,
'twasn't meant to be.
So many fierce droughts.
Especially for me.

I've been dormant so long
with this love unknown.
Why'd it have to wake now?
Why'd he leave me alone?

Elinor Fowler
MAGIC MOMENT

Dedicated to my husband.

Prismatic in the sun's
Bright golden glare,
The waterfall was full
Of colors soft and rare.

Then to the pit it plunged,
All the colors fair expunged.

I raised my eyes once more
To catch the sight.
The magic sun had gone
And left it black and white.

Mary Bartlett
GOD'S LOVE

Have you ever tried to measure the
sea,
Or count the leaves on an Autumn
tree.
Watch a mother bird as she gathers
her flock,
Or a mother who cradles her baby to
rock.
Could this be a part of our Lord's
love,
When He gave up the Spirit to give
us His dove?
It is true we will never forget the
grace,
That was bestowed on us by
Calvary's face.
Beautiful, tender, lovely and sad
When the soldiers all thought that
Jesus was mad.
"King of the Jews" they labeled Him
to be,
But nothing could keep Him from
being free.
Mockery, hate, the crown of thorns,
The brutal beatings, the mock of
scorn;
Couldn't stop this Saviour from His
immense love,
Instead He followed the will from
above.

Carolyn J Kenedy
A NEVER-ENDING RAINBOW

To Lynn Krouch, Worth Advisor of the Mary Parsons Assembly No. 213, International Order of the Rainbow for Girls, for the 1983 Fall Term.

Love is like a never-ending rainbow,
A resilient and strong, yet
threadless tie,
A circle filled with vibrant rainbow
color,
That forms in clouds and bridges
earth with sky.

Love can shape and bind our lives
together,
Can smooth our way and bridge
our troubled times,
While we travel over life's long
highway,
Secure to climb the rainbows of
our minds.

Rainbows change when winds stir up
the storm clouds
and swirl and sway the precious
drops of rain—
Touched by dancing, slanting rays of
sunshine—
Now fade, now gone, now show
up bright again.

Love will never change, but we are
fickle;
If we neglect it, love may pass
us by,
Leaving us like shoreless, rainless
storm clouds—
To chase elusive rainbows in the
sky.

Love is yours, to live and grow
inside you,
To bind but not enslave
someone to you.
Savor love and life and live it
gladly—
Your never-ending rainbow will
come true.

Anita Roper Foster
WHAT HAPPENS TO A BOY AT EIGHT? A VERSE ABOUT LETTING GO

To Toby and Matthew, my precious sons.

What happens to a boy at eight?
What changes that birthday made!
What happened to bring the "big
boy" out
And cause the baby to fade?

What causes him to wrinkle his face
When I choose to sneak
A kiss none other can replace
From his reddened cheek?

"Don't kiss me while the boys look
on!"
Oh what a fuss he made!
What happened to bring the "big
boy" out

And cause the baby to fade?

Just yesterday, a "little boy"
He'd bring me weeds for flowers
And sit so sweetly in my lap
All cuddled up for hours.

He held my hand in public places
Afraid to leave my sight
Now independence has replaced
That dependent stage of life.

It's hard to think my cherub sweet
No more I'll ever see.
To know those baby ways are gone
And are now a memory.

But God's great plan is so well laid
I'll thank him every day.
And proudly watch the "big boy" grow
And let the baby fade.

Elizabeth Quintero Ohn
IT HAD A MESSAGE

I saw a rainbow today
and then it disappeared

As soon as huge black clouds came back
it was this that I had feared.

I saw a raindrop fall today
like a tear falling from the sky

It formed a pattern on the ground
and then it suddenly dried.

I heard the crack of thunder today
and the flash of lightning I did see

As if a tremendous voice was screaming out
addressing its point to me.

I saw the sky in darkness today
and I cried from fear inside

And many things were happening
I had to run and hide.

At last I saw the sunshine
smiling happily across the sky

And the raindrops on the ground dried up to nothing
and the clouds disappeared by and by.

Sandra Mae Weber
MOTHER

In the memory of my mother, Mabel Margaret (Black) Weber, May 28th, 1912—April 11th, 1988

My mother gave birth to me,
And through her strength—
She taught me to live.

My mother gave faith to me,
And guided me—
To be faithful to others.

My mother gave me joy,
And taught me—
to give happiness to others.

My mother gave me love,
And showed me how—
To love all.

My mother gave me hope,
and
I will cherish—
The fond memories of her,
in
Life, faith, joy and love.

Christine Freeman
WILL YOU KISS ME GOOD-BYE?

As the days go by for us to part
they seem to get shorter and shorter.
I know we've been together as much
as we can but there will be so much
sorrow;
Therefore it will be tomorrow
and then we must part.
Tomorrow is here today
and it's time to go, but
before you go will you
Kiss me good-bye?

Peter D Buckley
I HAVE SEARCHED A LONG TIME

For a loving woman who has stood by me—my wife Sheila Marie Buckley

I have walked the desert of life to search for you.
Winds come and sweep your image from my mind.
I wish you were here--here with me!

I climb the highest mountain in search of the river of love, searching for you.
But, you see a wind has come again and swept your image from my mind.
I wish you were here—here with me!

I have looked far and long for your smile and warm embrace searching for you.
But, you see a wind has swept your image from my mind.
I wish you were here—here with me!

I walk alone the road of life searching for you.
But, I know I am too late, for you have walked before me.

I wish you were here—here with me!

Anthony J Trunk
THANKFUL FOR THE LOVE

This Poem is dedicated to my wife Mary Ann, and the love we shall hold, 'til the end of our days.

I wonder who decides
How two souls get intertwined
Maybe I should leave the thought alone.
I dare not break the spell
Yet if there's none, it's just as well
It's better that we did this on our own.

If you measure life by love, we have everything
Money doesn't need to come our way.
There is nothing in this world that it could ever bring.
Our fortune is already here to stay.

And it's comforting to know
I'll have you always by my side.
Sometimes I can't believe my dream came true.
A love that feels so good
You almost want to run and hide.
I can't imagine living without you.

We must be thankful for the love that we possess.
Many fight the curse of loneliness.
It's sad but also true. It only happens for the few.
Why does love escape from all the rest.

Sheila Grace Johnson
THIS IS BOBBY

Dedicated to Bobby Glenn Warlick, the only man I've ever known who could give as much love as he is so willing to receive, and the only man with whom I have ever shared the beautiful reality of true love.

This man, I so dearly love,
has the heart of a gentleman
filled with the love of Romeo
and trimmed with the kind
consideration of Sir Galahad.
Through his veins runs the
sweetness of fields of clover,
surrounded by a wit so bright
it equals the sun and reflects
off the dew of the green lily pad.

He is so sensitive to my every
need and thought—
as if he were reading my mind—
that most all of them are met
before they can be told.
His touch is gentle as the breeze;
his caress as soft as billowed clouds.
All this, and sexy whispered tones of love,
make this man the only man
and more than worth his weight in gold.

Mrs Louette Thompson
EASTER

This poem is dedicated to my son STEVEN, who has joined JESUS, and my wonderful husband TOM.

E - EMPTY—tomb is the true meaning of EASTER.
A - ANGELS—wait for the arrival of Jesus.
S - SALVATION—through the birth of God's Son.
T - THANK YOU—God, for having Christ die for our sins.
E - ETERNAL—life awaits those who believe.
R - RESURRECTION—is our promise of a new Heavenly Body.

Hazel G Maness
IN HONOR OF MAMA

This poem is dedicated to the Memory of my Mother "Vera Marie Garner" whom God called Home—2-2-89

Our Mama was someone who will always be close in our hearts and memory.
The times Mama and I shared together, just the two of us,
is very special to me.
We talked of things we did and saw, never dreaming someday that would be all.

Sometimes while I'm all alone, thinking of days gone by
I also think of the days to come in the sweet by and by.
When we shall leave this world below, of trials, trouble and pain, to go to a better land I know, A land where "Jesus Reigns."

Oh; how sweet it will be to meet Mama, Daddy, Brothers and Sisters so dear.
And dwell in happiness there together and never shed a tear
Oh; think of the happy home above the land where Christ does Reign, where all is happiness, peace and love and comes no sadness death or pain.

Our loss is shared by many who knew our Mama well, and in her showing words were too deep to tell.
But Mama how bad it hurts to know you won't be with us anymore.
We will always love you and wished we'd had you forever, But;
"Jesus needed you more." There is so little words can say but our love and prayers are with you if it's your Mama on this mournful day.
Written by her Daughter

Steven K Gray
ANTS

To Mrs. Connie Larson—My 7th grade English teacher at Fuller Jr. High School.

Ants
Small, fast
Dodging big footsteps

Not dodging all footsteps.
SQUISH! ! !

Eric Wayne Burd
A SECRET

To my Mother, who provided encouragement.

A secret is the sound of whispering leaves on
the brown branches; and the wind blowing on the
sound of a lighted lighter behind the sparkling pillows.

Jimi Mathers
THE PARTY

For my daughters Kristi and Karson and for Norma Paulus, who is an inspiration to many

He looked at me—my eyes dropped low.
I glanced at him, but he didn't know.
With no eye contact he'd walked away—
Assumed no interest. What could I say?

"Please come back; let's start again?
Just catch my eye and I will then
Look straight at you?" What can I lose
By honest gestures if we choose

To find out if response is there
For further search to see if we care
To know each other—to become a

friend?
Is that so hard, when in the end

We've found someone who more
than shares
All kinds of feelings and really
cares?
Oh, please come back! Let's try
again.
Our eyes will meet. We'll just begin

With, "Hello there.
How nice we've met.
We may enjoy
This party yet!"

Marie Neubert Younkin
BELONGING

Dedicated to the members of Chapter 325, Vietnam Veterans of America

Sitting in an office
whirling around on the wheels
of a chair,
waiting for THEM to come
through the door,
to finally find us.
Who are THEY ?
What do THEY want ?
Why are THEY important ?
But first, Who am I ?
What do I want ?
Why am I important ?
Sitting in this office
whirling around on the wheels
of a chair.
There are many kinds of
disabilities.
Sometimes—those who can't hear
can hear the heart.
And sometimes—those who can
hear
need a heart to listen.
That's who I am.
That's what I want.
That's why I'm here.
When THEY finally come through
the door.

Debra Sue Campbell
NATURE'S COLOR

Dedicated to my husband Kenny, and to my aunt Peggy for their love and support.

Blue is the ocean as it happily waves,
or the warming smile of the friendly
sky.

Green is the cool denseness of the
deep forest,
or the soft warmness of the cool
thick grass.

Brown is as rough and hard as the
bark of a tree,
or as soft, and smooth as a deer's
golden tan fur.

Red is the blazing color of Autumn
leaves,
or the fiery red sun as it rises or sets.

Orange is the leaping flames of a
sizzling bonfire,
or an evilly smiling jack-o-lantern on
Halloween.

Yellow is the bright warmness of the
summer sun,
or the fluffy fuzz of a newly born
chick.

White is a puffy cloud dancing
merrily by overhead,
or a gentle snowflake drifting lazily
downward.

Black is the inky dark of moonless
night sky,
or the sly cat slinking silently to his
alley.

There are many colors in nature for
us to sense,
all we need to do is open our eyes
and feel them.

Erin Marie Kingston
MISSING

I dedicate this poem to Rich, who I hope will one day forgive me in his heart.

Torn away from side
Gone is he with the tide.

Fate intervened unwillingly
into my life
Separated our state with the
flick of its knife.

Consciously knowing countless miles
lay between us
Of us, neither wishes to openly voice
for fear of fuss.

Frequented are we both by packets of
jotted down feelings
An occasional conversation limited to
timed dealings.

We're hoping to diminish the miles
through love's strengthening ways
Both desiring unrelenting vows with
the passing of days.

Genny Moura
FOLLOW ME

I dedicate this poem to Jeff Yocum.

City destroys the good man
and he is left defeated not fitted;
It was not in the plan.

Where is she when he needs her
She left to a shining new time,
gifts, creations of Myrrh.

Playing down the sun
on starlit waters
spins the imagination
to precious memories,
spilling,
unto life's blotters.

"Follow Me" is magnet.
Lovingly beckons the starlette.

Upward into the sun
on starlit skies
flies his heart
and his wish
to be with her.

Albert Calvery SSgt/USAF Retired
LAND OF THE FREE

Dedicated to all free men the world over who fought in Korea under the United Nations Command.

Land of the free, land of the free
America the beautiful, host of liberty
Land of the free, land of the free
I thank God that I'm a native of the
land of the free

I looked up and saw an eagle, way
up in the sky
And marveled at the mountain tops
reaching up so high
I gazed across the valley as far as I
could see
And I'm proud to be a native of the
land of the free

There are those who raise their
voices and tell us that we're wrong
To fight the wars that we have
fought to keep our country strong
But I proudly wore my uniform and
it means so much to me
To be living in a country called the
land of the free

Now if you think our country's not
the greatest of them all
Go visit all those other lands, the
large and the small
See what they have to offer and I'm
sure you will agree
You'll be proud that you're a native
of the land of the free

Land of the free, land of the free
America the beautiful, host of liberty
Land of the free, land of the free
I thank God that I'm a native of the
land of the free

Fran Lowenstein
GOING ON

To our darling Jim

The hill is steep that we must
climb
And it takes time, yes it takes
time.
Focusing on the good times, we all
once had.
Makes it easier to not be so sad.
Sometimes we'll slip a little & not
feel like going on.
Missing you so very much since
you've been gone.
Memories may fade somewhat
But it's all that we've got.
So remember our darling—
wherever you may be
Our love for you will never fade
from our memory.

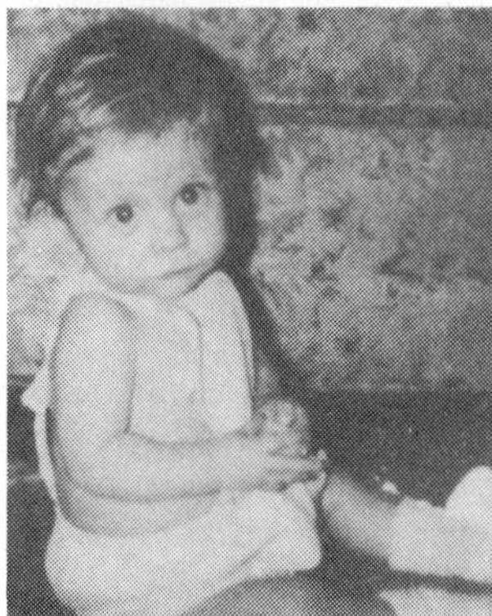

Glenda S Miller
A LITTLE BOY BLUE

All of the libbers they've not
changed a thing
In spite of their efforts the facts still
remain
As for the colors they never change
When it comes to the babies they're
still the same
Pink for a girl and blue for a boy,
these are the colors
for a bundle of joy

Blue was his color it was his from
the start
He was born with a problem one of
the heart
And just for these babies they chose
them a name
They're called blue babies cause
they're all the same

It was a Sunday a special one too, he
came to visit all dressed up in blue
It would be his last one and I think
we all knew
So we took lots of pictures of our
little boy blue
In his little blue sunsuit and his little
white shoes
We spent that Sunday for little boy
blue

He went to surgery in a little gown of
blue
And after twelve hours I think we all
knew
We had done lost him, he was buried
in blue

Well God has a color and he chose it
too
He made the heavens and he colored
them blue
Heaven needed sunshine and I'm
sure he knew
Here was an angel all dressed up in
blue

Mary Jane Hollen
TO "HONEY" WITH LOVE

To my husband of forty-nine wonderful, happy years.

I sit here in my kitchen and look to
where you are
I have never been away from you at
least not very far.

I watch you as you drive a nail or
work a puzzle game
My love for you has always been just
very much the same.

The passing years are good to us
though some were rather hard—
I love to see the sun-light catch your
image in the yard.

I like to light the candles as we eat
our evening meal
Their radiant light so warmly, reflect
the love we feel.

I know my dear you love me for you
have told me so
Not in just, oh, so many words, but
in the way you come and go.

And then when evening's over and
night shades start to fall
I love you, oh my darling it's the
nicest time of all.

For I snuggle near your heart strings,
in your arms beside your breast
And I know that all is fine with us as
we close our eyes in rest.

Ms Jamie Bush
A CHILD'S SONG

This Poem is Dedicated to Toni Yost, and Family

When I saw you. When you were a
child.
You were born to be so wild.

Now I see you all grown-up. With
lots of love in your heart.

Now you think that life is so
great. As you grow, you will
investigate.

So don't let any-one stand in your
way. Go and find the success in
your own way. When I saw you.
When you were a child. You bring
me hope with a smile.

Dian Taylor-Pringle
EPITAPH FOR EIGHTIES

To my mother, who instilled in me a love for God—the Creator, my fellow human beings and literature, and to my husband for his continuing love and support.

Double digit unemployment
Double digit inflation
Every day depressing news
for our weary nation.

Energy problems come with the cold.
Gas and oil becoming more precious
than gold.

How much catastrophe can one universe hold?

Financial depression, inherent in recession
Who is to blame?
Does this culprit have a name?
Where will this nonsense end?
When will folks in Washington agree to bend?

Peace is almost nonexistent.
Love comes without commitment.
No one caring, no one sharing.
Senseless life—unending strife.

I, for one, would not be surprised.
If the world suddenly exploded
Right before our eyes.
A very fitting, yet sad conclusion.
For a world that has thrived on constant confusion.

Rick A Booher
BEHOLD YE THE MAIDEN FAIR, TOUCH HER THOUGH, I DO NOT DARE

For the women I love;
That I have yet to meet,
This I do say, is for you.

Behold thy beauty
Shining bright
That of a maiden, who blinds my sight.
Ah the scent, of her so sweet,
The maiden fairest that none compete!
Behold ye the maiden fair
That of long and flowing hair
The morning flower comparest to her not,
The finest of wines doth no justice,
To the taste, the nectar I call her lips.
As the rose blossoms
And the sky comes blue
I sit and I wonder
Hath all my dreams come true?
To gaze in her eyes
Is to see the morning, tender shades
Of blue and gold;
To caress her brings thoughts of treasures untold
To touch her lips brings forth fantasy to life;
A wondrous spectacle of beauty
To love her;
Is to live for ever

Benedict L Jones
A DAY IN LIFE

To my Mother, Dorothy B. Jones and to my Father Early A. Jones Sr.

The day begins with sunshine and love.
The day ends with rain and pain.
We live our lives between the rain,
The pain,
Sunshine and love.

Gertrued Hickin Sigmon
THE WHOLE WORLD NEEDS IT

This poem mirrors someone I know by the name of Lolene Hodges Corron

Everyone needs a little love
Everyone needs a little hug
Love from the heart and from the soul
The giving love that makes one whole.

Brotherly love, sisterly love
Love of mankind and all God's creatures
Love that swells the heart with health
Such caring kindness is the greatest wealth.
Neighborly love, the helping hand
Childhood love of the innocent brand
Sensitive to another's needs
Wayside helper finding joy in good deeds.

Such love would turn the world around
No hate no greed no mind-pollution
Oh happy Earth reversing man's course
To reverence God as our true Source.

Roberta Ellis Howell
THOUGHTS

This poem is dedicated to my children, Rendall Howell, Emil Howell, and Suzette Howell Hollins.

Thoughts are strange!
They crowd on you
And choke your mind.
They take you miles and miles away.
Sometimes they crucify you.
They make you feel evil and lonely,
And they make you moody.
They make you blue.
Occasionally, they bring you pleasure.
Several little thoughts are tributaries
Emptying into the main stream
To drive you crazy—
Crazy, CRazy, CRAzy, CRAZy, CRAZY!
Oft times there comes a relief thought.
It brings you PEACE, PEACe, PEAce, PEace, Peace—peace.

Gary E Vines
ROSES OF THORN'D STEEL

To my Mother
Whose eyes I wish I could see through
And with love

Steel the heart,
steel thorn'd the rose.
The fragrance sweet,
infects the nose.

Love without heart.
Fertile without growth,
While grows from the start,
demanding the mineral of the heart.

Steel cannot Steal,
or can it? from the start
The rose, to the touch, cannot feel beauty as it unfolds.

I touched her, cold,
She touched me.
I bleed,
Steel not untold.

Steal the heart
Steel thorn'd the rose.

Deborah Hackerman
VALENTINE
This Valentine's Day I would like you to know,
You are with me always wherever I go,
When you are not near and we are apart,
I still have you with me deep in my heart,
When we are together and you're holding me tight,
There is no such thing as insecurity, loneliness, or fright,
You make me feel special like no one else can,
and it seems we are together as if it were planned,
When you say that you love me I know you're sincere,
I just look into your eyes to see how much you care,
If I ever did lose you I don't know what I'd do,
but I would never be happy and be without you,
I hope that these few words will just let you know,
How much I need you and I do love you so.
Happy Valentines Day!

Betty McGovern
REMEMBRANCE
I chased the wind
Much to my regret;
Hoping I would find
Love, joy and merriment.

I chased the wind
And lived in dreams;
Loved the evil shadows,
Fell for wicked schemes.

I chased the wind
In lust and vanity;
When I was spent,
Found humility.

Remember not Oh Lord!
My sins, my frailty;
He turned the wind
To a distant memory.

To chase the wind
Now just a gentle breeze;
To know my Lord,
To live in ecstasy!

Lisa L DeSon
AT THE LOWEST POINT IN YOUR LIFE
At the lowest point in your life,
When you are filled with despair
When you are all alone,
And feel that no one cares . . .

No matter how much
You feel let down
And how much
You want to run,
You can find muscles
Where strength
There was none . . . .

To reach deep inside yourself
Through walls not so thin,
Because that you will find
Is where it all begins.

Gloria E Rosario
LOVE

In memory of Jose R. Garcia. Special thanks to my mother Gloria, my friend Jose L. Santiago and to all those that believed in me.

Love is something you feel deep inside
Love is something that never dies
It's like a never ending ocean
a forever flowing sea
that is what love means to me
For love always has its tears
caused by joy and pain
that will go on for years
like a little game
But, the difference with love
is that in the game you always win
Because you have each other
and that special feeling within.

Tracy L Kiehl
A PENNY FOR YOUR THOUGHTS

This poem is dedicated to my supportive family, close friends and to my boyfriend Brian—I love you!

She's sitting on the curb—as tears fall vast and many.
"If you tell me all your thoughts—I'll kindly give a penny."

I saw her face was very red—she'd been crying for so long.
I couldn't help but wonder—what had been so wrong.

She wiped her tears away—and looked down to the ground.
To make sure no one heard—she turned and looked around.

She stared straight up at me—and her tears fell in such a way
Then I suddenly understood—how hard it was to say.

She sadly told the story of how a man had died
And as she told her story—I myself began to cry.

She never said his name—it hurt too much to tell.
All that she would say—was that she knew him very well.

Before she turned to go—she looked at me to say,
"This man—he was my father—he died a year ago today."

Melissa Smith
WHISPERED IN THE MIDDLE OF THE NIGHT

My poem is dedicated to Justin Cheser
A loving inspiration in my life.

Sometime during the middle of the night,
I had awakened to see,
The moon shine down,
Through the window.
It cast a silhouette upon your body.
As I lay there and watched you sleep
I prayed to God and thanked him for,
Sending me someone so loving and,
Caring to share my life with.
I wanted to wake you and tell you,
How I felt. But you looked so content
And peaceful within your soul.
So there was only one thing,
I could do.
I whispered in the middle of the,
Night, I LOVE YOU.

Tara C Storms
THE BIRTH

To my daughter Arielle Elizabeth

It came like an overflowing fountain in the Park.
It was the symbol of the prize.
The joyous suspense grew.
Exams were many and the results were immediately reported.
The signs of internal life was there, awaiting to be heard and seen.
First the pains of life only to be felt by one's species of man. Overwhelming and incredible as it may

be, Nature is still going on. The life cycles of the unborn prize were steadily repeated. The final stage, the incision and the Prize was born. A feeling never to be forgotten.

Mrs Corinne Brown
NATURE WALK

I dedicate this poem to Nicki and Annie.

Strolling along the edge of the woods on a fall day,
I admire the beauty unappreciated by many.
The plain and simple things, A squirrel with a bushy tail
carrying in his mouth a nut. The purple asters and the golden rod
patterned with black eyed susans not to be seen another year.
For each holds a different view of the one before.
Overhead a hawk with gliding wings calls his mate with songs of love.
A foot path leading deeper into the woods reveals a pond, visited by many. With cane poles trying for the big one. Trees in winter costumes with colors that cannot be repeated, though imitated.
In the distance a bull frog croaks loudly telling of his domain.
A wealth of beauty, free for the viewing makes a lovely day.

Wanda Anderson
SUMMER PESTS

Here's a fly
He sits on me
Tried to swat him
But he flew away free.
Oh no!
Again he's back
And if he don't leave
I will have to smack.
O boy!
He's landed now
Guess what fly?
This is the end of thou!
splat!

Tamara R Powelson-Stephens
TONIGHT

Dedicated to the spouses and families of alcoholics, present and past.

Tonight will be the last time, that I'll sit and wait for him,
I've told myself "I've had enough," time and time again.
I sit here and I worry, yet anger builds inside,
resentment seems to take over, something I must hide.

While he's out drinkin', havin' fun, I sit here by the phone,
not knowing if he'll be alright, if he'll even make it home.
At 4:30 A.M. the telephone rings, on the other end it's him,
giving me excuses, my patience wearing thin.

It hurts so much to be made a fool, even more so to pretend,
that I'm not aware to what's going on, I just wish it all would end.
I've let him take so much from me, my self-esteem and drive,
God only knows how many times, I've prayed that I could die.

I'm thankful that our kids are small, and do not realize,
just how big the hurt really is, when they see their mommy cry.
I've tried my best to be a good wife, evidently not hard enough,
for we have no real communication, and I suspect even less of love.

It's very hard to love a man, who chooses his bottle and friends over you,
even harder to believe him, when he says his love is true.
Yes, tonight WILL be the last night that I sit and wait for him,
it's time to make a decision, that decision depends on him.

- Vanna Carraretto-Zanette

Vanna Carraretto-Zanette
IF ONLY

To anyone, who cares

If only, by a touch of magic
I could erase forever
What in this world is tragic . . .
If only, I could stop the darkness
That's engulfing every soul with
Its heavy load of desperation and tribulation—
If only with a silent prayer I could stop
All this world bloodshed, change its color red
For a pure dove white, where peace and beauty symbolize . . . .
Tomorrows of sunrise—
If only, with a smile I could reach the heart of every uncaring soul, change it a bit, make their empty days . . .
A brighter shade of red.—
If only, our cries for help, could reach the sky where our trust in Jesus lies . . . . a better humanity we will have then . . . .—If only . . .

Diane M Villafranca
TAFFY

As the tail wags freely with excitement and joy
This bundle of fur is my little boy.
He knows nothing but love he is willing to share
Be it human or animal, he doesn't really care.
A soul is a soul no matter what form it takes
Be it cuddly and soft or slithering snakes.
My puppy will love it from deeply within
No matter what form it has or what covering skin.
His heart may be saddened by a frequency change
But the love is still there and not out of range.
Some food and attention will keep him content
The love he returns shows your time is well spent.
For he has no fear, only love that he gives
Which hopefully will remain for as long as he lives.
He's lived here awhile and I'm so glad he came
This big bundle of love is Taffy by name.

Cora M Brown
NATURE

Nature works around the clock
With God's love its wonders never cease to stop
The balance is so perfect
Existence is so real
The beauty flows from heavenly skies to land
and open sea
God coordinates His works, so one and all will see
The balance is so perfect
Existence is so real
Don't try to figure out the mystery
It's secrets are not revealed to earth
Mystery . . . Mystery . . . Mystery
Nature plays an important role
In it, true life does take hold
The balance is so perfect
Existence is so real
The Creator's hands have touched, and nature
is revealed
Its balance is so———perfect
Its existence is so———real

Mary M Ranson
MOTHER

You're a gift of light from God
Sent to shine on our lives,

You're as delicate as a rose
Sent to teach us tenderness,

You're as grand as an eagle
Teaching us to be proud,

You're as graceful as a flower
That's just begun to bloom,

But as time goes by,
You're as weak as a sparrow
Flying against the wind,

Thank you for your kindness
And your loving care
You gave us through our lives,

YOU ARE MY HOPE.

Donna Zacharias
GOLD MAJESTIC TIME PIECES

Gold majestic time pieces,
on tarnished, withered chains;
the uplifted shingles on a barn,
the winter's sleeping fields of grain.

Sun struck wings,
of a dancing dragonfly;
buzzing bees and fellowed crickets,
glorified in the moonlit sky.

Spider webs so soonly made,
catching the morning dew;
fireflies, seeking bedtime shelter,
now that light is anew.

Time reveals all things,
that which spring, soon shall bring.

Wade Paul
VISIONS OF TIME

Did you ever wonder when you lie down
If you've seen your last day break

Or if the view before you slept
Would be the last you take

Do you take time to realize
That days go swiftly by

It's true, you know, the hands of time
Don't ever tell a lie

The second hand, it sweeps by fast
It never skips a beat

Trying to deceive yourself
Will be your one defeat

Where does time go, we always waste
So many precious hours

You know we have to take the time
To stop and smell the flowers

When you are here beside me
The moments rush right past

That's why when I lay down to sleep
It's you I look at last.

Frances C Gaskin

Frances C Gaskin
A BOY

This poem is dedicated to our sons Joe and Johnny

A boy is quite a funny thing
Your patience he will try;
He'll make you mad enough to fight,
And make you want to cry.

He'll make you say things you don't mean,
Have thoughts you don't intend;
You'll want to pull your hair all out,
And wonder what will be the end.

The strangest thing about a boy
Is when he's put to bed;
He doesn't seem the same bad boy,
After his prayers are said.

He's so angelic lying there,
Seems heaven itself is near;
Why, you're the bad one, not the boy,
You have to shed a tear.

Before I dare to go to sleep
 To prayer I must employ;
Ask God to help me worthy be,
 Of this angelic boy.

Beresford Richards
TO A RIVER
Oh, beautiful Isle of the west
How often have I seen thy shores
With golden sands, and high mountains
And rivers wandering o'er thy plains.

Climbing to the top of the mountain
Where the clouds and mountain meet,
A drip of water starts a river
On its way to the ocean deep.

Roll on, roll on, keep rolling
Fill your banks with the gift of Spring.
Your relief is the ocean
Your work already done.

W F Yearwood
WHY HAS MAN?
Why has man, the most capable of all
 Creatures upon the face of the earth
Allowed himself to be worst of all?
 What's he gained, what's it worth?

Why can't man fulfill his dreams,
 Bring true joy to all of mankind?
Why must he pollute rivers and streams,
 Bring death to fishes and kind.

Why will man hurt another seriously
 Just to reach a goal of success?
Does he know why or is it mysteriously?
 No one makes him, no real duress?

Why do we awake with only one thought,
 To work, to slave, to achieve?
Most times finding the day fraught,
 And we wonder and disbelieve.

Why is man so full of apetite and hate?
 It fills his mind and his heart;
Sometimes he finds the reason too late
 When this life he must soon depart.

Michael J Rinaldi
TO BE ALONE

In memory of my Father . . .

To be alone . . .
To contemplate
The short and long.
A destiny of confusion;
The loss of a love;
Origins and endings;
The yearning and pleading;
The agony and the ecstasy.
To come to terms
With omnipotent desires.
To quench
Lustful, fires.
A secret heart
Which she knows not—
To exist quietly
And alone.

Incoronata Lemme
THE WORLD
I chose the wrong passage
Only to end up in a turmoil
I've lost my courage
And I feel like soil

Life is cruel
People are rude
They take me for a fool
They place me in a rotten mood

Torn between good and bad
I feel my heart break right through
It makes me feel so sad
That I always feel blue

Between reality and fantasy
The world becomes my opponent
Forced to have no sensitivity
I charge without resentment

I take on the onslaught
To conquer my human right
Happy that I fought
I now see the shining light

Charlotte A Phillips
MOMENTS

for my FIRST and LAST lover . . . . always

If only for a moment,
 we will love . . . . and
  you are mine
When the aloneness and pain in
 my heart
 start
  to carry me down
I have only to dwell on my
love for you . . in you . .
through you . . . .
  surrounds you
It is TIME alone that will show us
 our way to one another
 and
our LOVE will make ALL right with
 us
Knowing we are one . . . .
before . . . . now . . . . always . . . .
  and longer
I love you, my darling, and bring you
all my life
 in the moment we are one
You return to me, in that same
moment,
  in springtime
 a lifetime for us to love in

F DeLoris Bonanni
I CRIED FOR YOU, TODAY
I cried for you, today.
You were "down."
Letting the negative, try to drown
Your hopes and dreams,
Stopping your reasoning,
Halting all your "good" schemes.

I said a prayer for you, today.
"Let him cast out his aura
Bright and strong,
Whenever, everyday things go wrong.
Give him patience to wait things out,
For time is on his side.
Let the positive flow through
And leave the worrying to his guide.
Let him talk freely to his guide.
Let him listen to what this spirit has to say,
For this spirit is with him each and everyday."

I said, "I LOVE YOU," today.

Eva Moore
HARVEST

Dedicated to every sower who has sown expecting the harvest . . . (St. John 4:36) . . . "That both he that soweth and he that reapeth may rejoice together."

What God has ordained & planned shall come about,
Have not an ounce of fear, and do not ever doubt.

The seeds God has planted within you,
Will break the ground & come on thru.

For His divine will to be done this day,
God will open the doors, and make a way.

To be sensitive and listen only to His voice,
To be willing & obedient is your only choice.

He shall always water those seeds you have sown,
And watch over & nourish them till they're grown.

After you've planted your garden—have peace & rest,
God will take care of everything, until the Harvest.

Elvira Karmik

Elvira Karmik
SPRING THOUGHTS
Spring is just 'round the corner.
It arrives on a beautiful morn.
The frost and ice which I mourn not
Will vanish with fierce cold storms.

The flowers will awake in my garden
And the lark will be singing again.
Thousand blossoms will adorn the earth then
And will send their fragrance around.

The lilac's and cherrytree's blossoms
Will open in southerly breeze.
In their shade I can read and I can doze off
And in their shade I can think and I can dream.

My thoughts go back to my childhood,
The pictures of my life then appear:
In the shelter of my home in the valley
I was happy and protected from fear.

The life later brought me its sorrows
And strengthened my yearning for bygones,
But there is no going back now forever,
There is no going back to my home.

Betty Brautigan
ROMANCE ENCHANTED
God dressed the world this
 morning in its bridal gown
Just to keep you from feeling
 down
What a beautiful world beguiled
When you're madly in love with
 his child

I have revealed to you my heart
 and soul
You are a jewel made out of gold
A great sense of humor you have
Soothing just like a salve
I've never been so happy in
 someone's arms
Hold me forever Keep me from
 all alarm
Day by day our love grows deeper
Grows just like Virginia Creeper

This is a forever relationship
Let's never let it slip
Neither should we take each
 other for granted
For this is a romance enchanted

Jennifer Hillary
THE YELLOW BUNNY
 The other day I saw a yellow bunny.
It was the color of fresh honey.
It hopped and hopped all over.
Right into a meadow of four leaf clover.
And then the sky turned sunny.
 Then I asked the bunny,
"Why is it so sunny?
And he said, "Because I'm so tame,
I'll tell you my name,
Believe it or not it is Sunny."
 Now isn't that funny.
On a day that was sunny.
A bunny told me his name.
Because he was so tame.
My, wouldn't he taste yummy!

Kriss Ann Bosley
DEAR DADDY,
Where are you?
What do you see?
Do you see me?
I can still see you as you were then,
wearing coveralls and smelling of Old Spice
I remember you later too,
us riding in your wheelchair
and feeding you potato chips at a picnic
where everyone else was feeding themselves
I guess maybe it wasn't really a picnic after all.

Faith Elizabeth Rose
VISITATION
Today I visited the house of God and there I found His love
The handshakes and smiles of friendly faces
Seemed to me like heavenly doves
The words from God's called servant
informing me of my earthly duty
To love my God and to love my
fellow human being as myself
Brought thoughts of life, goodwill and beauty
The harshness of environmental
control seemed to disappear
As I shared in the sacraments
remembering His love,
His never-ending love that brought Him
To a world filled with heartache, woe and care
His presence seemed to give content,
to ease my pain and its stain
He gave me new meaning for my life
He gave me a restoration of my spirit
to rebuild again

Evelyn H Bostick
WONDERFUL LOVE
Wonderful love that knows no bounds,
touching me deeply, your Passion astounds;
that you would be willing to die such a death,
in pain and much torment to give your last breath,
that I might be able to walk in your light,

to freely receive and push back the night,
transforming defeat to a vic'try divine,
restoring, renewing a peace so sublime—
that all who might choose may walk out of hell,
by taking your and and knowing you well.
Your Name is the Name we will praise and adore,
as we walk hand in hand with you more and more.

Beulah E Underwood Halvorsen

Beulah E Underwood Halvorsen
WHY DID YOU LEAVE?

This poem is dedicated to Tanya Jane.

Why did you leave, Mama?
You said you loved us;
I heard you and daddy last night,
When you argued and fussed.

Why did you leave, Mama?
Nothin's the same anymore;
When we wake up early,
Daddy's hurrin' with his chores.

Why did you leave, Mama?
My brothers and me,
We miss you lots, Mama;
Can't you see?

Why did you leave, Mama?
I'm your only girl;
You're too far away to fix my hair,
And it does need a curl.

Why did you leave, Mama?
When I go to bed at night,
It's lonely, and so dark;
If you'd come, Mama, I'd be all right.

Aileen Campbell Boruff
GETTING OLDER AND HOLDING ON
After years of full home,
We find we have an empty dome.
People do need each other in the nest.
Together, we are not so lonely or depressed.

Down the winding path, there is an open gate,
We will learn to listen and communicate.
There is more time, less money these days.
So we learn about Senior Citizens and IRA's.

Too often we short circuit our message of love.
We want others to give us peace like a dove.
It's a matter of a smile, or the right attitude.
Why not be gentle, kind, but never rude.

Retirement can mean new friends, more coffee breaks.
We must be quiet and helpful for neighbor's sake.
"One day at a time" is a new awareness.
Modern Maturity helps with our happiness.

Go see the grandchildren, take a toy or balloon.
Get a laugh, share a joke or a unique cartoon.
To bed late—no need to rise before dawn.
So exercise, eat right, stretch and yawn,
The life you live is your own.

William Donovan
THE DEAD DO NOT ANSWER US

MOTHER	FATHER
FREDA	EDWARD
1902-1986	1894-1972

The dead do not answer us.
I have stood by the graves in
Each of the seasons of the year.
They do not answer me.

The birdsong is not her singing
in the Saturday morning
bread baking kitchen.

The blue light off the snow at
certain hours of a December
afternoon
is not the the light from his Irish
eyes.

There is no voice
Nor any sign.
Perhaps they speak to each other.

Do they whisper to each other
Through the hours?
The price of calves,
The rains and winds,
Politics and sunsets.
The Dakota concerns.

Tami L McCoy
A REFLECTION OF MYSELF

To God, my family, close friends and Jason; you have given me the love and support I need.

A river flows from the mouth;
so too do my words.
An infant goes through stages;
as do my thoughts.
To a photographer light is essential;
as wisdom is to me.
Professors decipher answers;
I always make a choice.
A fire burns with persistence;
like my passion for writing.
A mirror is a reflection;
when I look, I see.
Blankets represent security;
to stable things I hold.
Tangible things are proof;
as too is my dedication.
You are what is around you,
and become your very thoughts;
I live, I learn, I acknowledge;
of excellence I become.

Elena Stabile
CRIES FOR PEACE
Why my stomach aches inside?
My heart still burns with every breath;

Physical stature on a decline,
could it be the calls of death?

Time has elapsed,
my hunger now starved.
Weak and frail,
squints for the stars.

My mind forever wanders;
Memories, oh so few;
wondering, what comes next?
What's become of you?

Cries of pain reach distant lands.
Cries of anguish, sink deep through sand.
Samaritans, useless, can't mend my wounds;
Reaching desperately, to grab my hands.

The remains of my seed,
forever encased in thy precious root.
My soul will return to blossom;
being so old, yet so new.

Frank Valvo
LIFE

Life is so long but death is so close, one never knows when the time will come.

So as one day meets another, you should make the best of life.

Reach out for the stars, take a chance on life, for those who procrastinate will never reach their goals.

Sometimes it's hard to put one foot in front of the other, but you must force yourself to do so.

The world will not wait for you. If you stop for too long, your life will pass you by.

So reach for the stars and success will follow behind!

Evelyn Knapp
ON THE SQUARE
How strange it seems to saunter through this square
Of green that once was woods and fields to me.
On the soft grass we tumbled, careless, free;
The clover chains we wore sweet and fair,
And dandelion jewels graced our hair.
Many nooks where we could hide in glee;
An Indian bold peered from behind a tree,
While shrubbery became the brigand's lair.

What high adventure knew this spot of green!
Where went the years and how am I so tall?
The birds still sing; the soft grass lies serene;
The sunshine wraps me in a golden shawl.
Across the dreamy freshness of the scene,
It seems that I can hear my father's call.

Steve Goins
THE TEACHER
As days turn into months, and months into years,
Put your trust in God, He'll take away your fears,
He'll put no more on you than you can bear,
He'll help you find people who love and care,
He gave us the sun, to help the flowers grow,
He gave us the knowledge so that we'll know.
The words we live by came from God above,
They talk about caring, trust and most of all love.
From time to time we all seem to stray,
But believe in Him and He'll show you the way.
He talked about standing up and turning the other cheek,
This doesn't make you less than a man, it doesn't make you weak.
To love one another was His plan,
He planted the seed, now the rest is up to man.

G E McKenney Jr
THE MAN

To my wife Reyes, my son Nicolaus and my daughter Ayenda

DAWN

The man at first light of dawn is strong, intelligent and a good provider for his family;

DUSK

The man as dark as the dark surrounding him cries out in anguish and helplessness for the suffering he and his fellow men so long endured, the rights so long denied. The resentment eating away at his heart like a malignant disease. Each night his cry holds the same question "Why can't I be a part of rather than a part from? ;

PEACE

The only peace the man will ever know is in death :

Steven Leon Goins
DON'T BE SAD TO SAY GOODBYE
Don't be sad to say goodbye,
It's not so hard if you really try,
We live our lives the best we can,
Trying to do what is right in that span,
We have to learn to take life day by day,
Hoping to find happiness along the way,
Though it's not always easy to walk the straight line,
We'll always have God to give us peace of mind,
We'll cherish our loved ones and friends,
Because these are the people who'll be there
At the end,
When we die everyone is filled with so much sorrow,
We should never forget that with the love of Jesus
There'll be a better tomorrow,

So when you shed those tears and ask why?
Just remember we don't have to be sad to say
Goodbye . . . .

Wilfred J Cote
AFTER THE STORM

To my darling wife, Dottie whom I, love so dearly. To always remember me by

As we were driving down the road
In the early light of day.
Clouds seemed in a formation
All dismal, bleak and grey.

We knew where we were heading
And soon we'd have to stop.
The weather would delay us
With every falling drop.

The wind had begun to blow
As lightning filled the skies.
A cloudburst brought the rain down
Like tears in a baby's eyes.

Quick as the storm had started
Nature brought it to an end.
The rays of the sun were shining
As the mist and the air did blend.

The driving became more pleasant
As the heat of the sun did warm.
With sounds of life all around us
Nature cleansed; "After The Storm"

Bunny Balint
DISSATISFIED
My eyes followed the sea-gulls, as they flew.
I wished, somehow, that I could fly too.
Just spread my wings, and float above,
Like a small, white carefree turtle dove.

I watched the football players, as they play.
I wished I were a boy, if only for a day!
Then I'd catch that ball and run,
for touchdowns, as other boys have done!

I'd watch boats in harbors, float lazily by.
I wished, that in a boat I could lie,
With nothing better for me to do
than just lie back and watch the view!

And then I'd like to be the sea,
always roaming and forever free.
Tied to no one, belonging to none.
Forever and ever, since its life's begun.

But most of all, I'd like to be,
Like the wind, you cannot see.
So free and undaunted
From worry and fears unhaunted.

Kate McGuinn
DEVELOPING TIME
A shutter clicks, capturing a moment,
an occasion worth remembering.
Frozen facial expressions popping out on paper.
Bringing back the laughs, drying up the tears.
Blown up, without exposure,
through the process.
A face appears,
the smile comes to life dancing on the paper,
bubbling over with joy like a pot of boiling seltzer
overflowing with bubbles.
Sitting in a tub,
relaxing in a pot of
bright beautiful bouncy bubbles.
Stop.
Development ceases.
Errors are corrected
smiles are renewed.
Hanging, dripping dry
the tears of the past
the glory of memories
and the laughter of the moment.

Giuseppe Vittorio Mastrobuono
SONIA

I dedicate this poem to Maria Sonia Pineda, the founder of my seventh heaven, who I love more than any other.

Sonia, to dream, eyes gazing at the sea
Lost in fantasy, imagining eternally

Knows not where she wants to be,
nor what she must do
Imprisoned in the past, without any clue

The practical life does not exist , far too grey, too much mist
She prefers dreams of gold, beautiful memories, young and old
Dreaming today and tomorrow, for she was born enchanted
Sonia, my love
It is you who are the dream
You I am thinking of . . .

Robert Fermin
FOR THE LOVE AND MEMORIES OF ALL THOSE YESTERYEARS

In memory of my beloved Mother Helene Fermin-DeEerens.

Tender moments with all my loved ones
Yesteryears, do I remember those yesteryears
The little cries and warmth of laughter
A child's embrace and velvet touch

The clouds that pass, foreboding storms
With sunshine in the rains thereafter
—Do I remember such yesteryears—

To spill a tear, to catch a wind from far-away memories
Does my heart feel such pain as of years gone by
Are here again
Where will the oceans take me for the life hereafter

So tender a child's embrace,
So warm a sense of knowing
How to love and understand
The memories of all those yesteryears.

Shawnta Jones
WAKING THE SILENCE
Why is it a silent hall beckons to me?
The florescent lights paint stripes of soft yellow against the dark yellow of the carpet.

Reflecting off shiny, shut windows
creating glowing, muted domes of light
on white, solemn walls.

I want to run down the middle like kindergarten
waking the silence.

C J Walker
DON'T TELL THEM I TOLD YOU
They told me not to tell you
That the rain has got to fall
They told me not to mention
The ones locked up in prison walls
As the dangerous killers were seeking
Another prey

They told me not to tell you
You're going to die today.
We're told by the government to relax
and live for them
I'm told not to tell you that you're working for him.
Bills are high and rents going up
I can't even park my car,
So I just sit around getting drunk at the corner bar
With the babies that's aborted in these days and time,
Maybe I can tell you to abort your mind.
Whites, Blacks, Mexicans, and Jews
You better forget about the maze
I was told to tell you there's going to be a change.
Cigarettes, marijuana, hash, and the rest
Take it, break it, you're caught up in a mess.
I was told to tell you to save your money fast
Pretty soon you will see how long a dollar bill last.
They told me not to tell you
To heed and it's gonna be alright
So just sit back and take a snack
Because it's you—you have to fight.
Limousine, Cadillacs with their chauffeur driven engine
If you think before you shrink
You'll fly away like a pigeon.
Rape, slaughter call it what you may
The judges are bored of seeing your face.
They told me not to tell you bout the Insane ones today,
The reason I can't tell you that is
because they're the ones that's safe.
Cops are Cops they protect, collect and dine
They kill, beat, and curse you out
But you have to serve the time.
People you're in trouble
And this I've got to tell
That if you don't pull down your EGO
We're all going to hell.

Lautaro G Vergara

Lautaro G Vergara
CALENDAR
Dry leaves of time
hung by anonymous hands
on the cracked wall
of my Bohemian room.
Sentinel of the bad death
with numeral eyes,
you have the face
of a mute and solemn judge . . .
Your full moons waning and waxing come and go,
without consequence or goodbyes,
without prologues or epithets:
like an absent remembrance.

Calendar of memories
superimposed,
bound in a book of horizontal days.
What do you know
of the astronauts
who cheat night and day
in their orbital alleys?

Sue G Mahurin
LAND OF SILENCE
The soundless night guards its hidden treasures
Its shadows are the ghosts that dwell there
The rain falls like tears of sorrow
from her eyes upon his grave
While the withered rose petals lay
like fragments of her broken heart
upon his sleeping breast
The roots of the tree he planted
entwine his corpse
beneath the grassy bosom of his tomb
and return him to Elysium, to the
silent heart of the earth
from whence he came

Barbara Dempsey
LIFE IN THE FAST LANE
Life changes as time goes on,
From one day to the next,
From dusk 'til dawn.

Life is full of good and bad times,
From sharing with friends,
To those almost deadly climbs.

Life has no easy breaks,
From the time you are born,
To the last bit of energy it takes.

Life depends upon you,
From the amount of self-confidence,
To those seemingly impossible dreams you pursue.

Life is a very hard test,
From pleasing your family and friends,
To strive in succeeding and to do your best.

Dawn Work
JENNIFER
Jennifer is my best friend's name, we are just like sisters cause we are just the same.
Jenni lives in Colorado, and I live here. Wish I could be with her all through the year.
I love her so, even though I don't always let her know. There's not a minute that goes by, that I don't think about my best friend and feel I should cry. I hope our friendship will never end. I can't wait to see her again, until then I must be thankful I have such a great friend as
Jen.

Darlene Gail
SPRING
The meadows are full of budding flowers.
The sun shines down, and gently the petals begin to open.
The morning dew is fresh and is instinctively swallowed by a rose.
Nature is once again finding its way around the world.
Bringing beauty and life everywhere.
It is a new beginning.
It is Spring.

Larry B Pitts
LIFE
Life is like a mirror—
What you show to the mirror—
Is what you get back from the mirror.

Life is like a flower—
So beautiful and calm in the spring breeze.
Where the wind blows thru the petals of life—
And quietly thru the peaceful meadows on a cool spring day.

Life is like a river,
Moving all the time for ever and ever.
As free as the breeze
Watching it flow out to sea.

Life is so free.
It's like becoming a bird—the King of the skies
Soaring——Soaring——
With the breeze flowing thru your feathers.

Elvia Carlino
LIFE

To my children
Randy, Nancy and Jim

Life is so varied,
So intricate, so complex,
But, oh, so fleeting.

Teresa Wiater

Teresa Wiater
HANGING FROM THE CEILING
Hanging from the ceiling
Watching blood drip from my eyes
Into a silver bucket
They kept telling me was mine
Found it out in the cabana
With a rope and algaecide
I thought I might be dreaming
But I'm here for real this time.

Hanging from the ceiling
With my ankles 'bout to break
And the bucket getting nearer
To the mess I'm gonna make
When I splatter and I shatter
And the house begins to shake
I didn't want it all I
Thought I needed was a break.

Karen Sue Croft
FAREWELL

Farewell
Good-bye
The grass may be green
And the sky may be blue
But the path is short
When you walk with a friend
The world is at your finger-tips.
You don't have to face it alone.
YOU KNOW YOU HAVE A
FRIEND! !

Edward E Chipman
ABRAHAM LINCOLN
He stands before us gaunt against the years,
But yet like granite against the wear of time.
The ruggedness of courage that he wears
Speaks of a soul whose nature is sublime.

In midst of crisis, tested by the storm,
He clearly tokens destiny's high plan;
While humble-souled, and humorous, and warm
He typifies the best in common man.

Florence H Burkett
GOD CARES

To my brother "Harry Justice" who is in a nursing home in Kahoka, MO. He is 81. Thanks so much. Submitted by Florence H Burkett

God hath not promised
Skies always blue
Flower strewn pathways
All of our lives,
God hath not promised
Sun without rain
Joy without sorrow
Peace without pain.

God hath not promised
We shall not know
Toil and temptation,
Trouble and woe;
He hath not told us
We shall not bear
Many a burden,
Many a care.

God hath not promised
Smooth roads and wide
Swift easy travel
Needing no guide;

Dawn Cahoon-Kniff
CALL THE BABY "DAWN"
This baby was late getting a name.
Relatives could not agree on it.
Names were called forth . . .but always the same
Answer, from all, "They do not quite fit."

While Aunts and Uncles were debating
On "Kathryn," as the name that would stay,
Parents agreed . . . tired of the waiting . . .
The Mail brought a Card, "to save the day."

"Call the baby Dawn" . . . one simple line.
And I, with "title," was on my way,
For the face of a Kathryn, to pine.
"No, not "Darn," not "Don" . . .
"Dawn," I would say.

When asked my name, and I would tell it
'Saw puzzlement in all the faces
'Soon realized, I would have to spell it.
'Twas heard in Poetry, and such places.

However, this soon began to change.
It was taken by a Movie Star,
And, adoption, covered a wide range.
I was hearing of "Dawns"—near and far.

Friends would name their babies after me.
Patricia, Deborah and Gayla Dawn.
This made me quite happy to see . . .
That the strangeness, from my name, had gone

Household products, on the market, too,
Claiming to cut the grease best, and such.
My identity seemed hidden from view
And I felt this, a bit too much.

So, once again, I'm back to spelling
Finding I have identity . . .if
When, any time my name needs telling
I just say . . ."I am Dawn Cahoon-Kniff."

Klara Sonner
MY GRANDCHILDREN

To my loving Mother

That time my son and his family
Visit is always a "special time."
My grandchildren after the meal
They start playing with the toys
It was so fun to watch.
The boy was busy with his
Little sister and he gave
Her a kiss.

Vonne Monai
NO COMPROMISE
How can you act normal with your cokehead runny nose?
Perhaps you think it's easy 'cause your comrades share your woe
Your wretchedness permeates and accentuates your pause
And reasoning escapes you since you're here without a cause
What separates the great ones from the losers it is told
Is a relentless quest for betterment though bitter from the blows
Your pointless life is shaken a misshapen freakish mass
The reality mistaken reflects your horrific twisted past
It's difficult to ignore it if you just take a look around
This wasted land of corpses though dead they won't lie down
Why should I be a victim of these things that aren't alive?
I find it hard to pity for I must struggle to survive
In a place that grants space to those rejects who elect compromise
A disgrace, slap in the face to those who prefer to die,
rather than live an endless lie! ! ! ! ! ! ! ! ! !

Bernice Tomer
MEMORIES ARE FOREVER
When the distant drone of tractors—
Means spring is in the air,
I often think about him—
His ghost is everywhere!

In the long green fields of corn—
Oats and wheat blowing in the breeze,
Cows coming to the barn at night—
The gardeners on their knees!
In the smell of new mown hay—
Watching farmers toiling in the sun,
Darkness drove him in at night—
When another day's work was done!

When summer nights turn chilly—
And leaves begin to fall,
Football season's here again
That's when I miss him most of all!

At family reunions—
I miss his smiling face,
Though many years have come and gone—
His memory I can't erase.

Alice Rich

Alice Rich
A PRAYER FROM MOM
Dear Lord, please guide their footsteps
My children that I love.
Watch over them each coming day
From your heavenly throne above.
Let them feel me close beside them
When sometimes they need me so.
Let me comfort them in sorrow
Like I did so long ago.
Please ease their pain
Like you did for me,
And lighten their heavy load,
As they travel on from day to day
Along life's weary road.
Let them feel my love forever
As we drift so far apart,
Let it linger Lord forever
In the bottom of their heart.

Thank you dear Lord,
Amen.

Myra Dutton
MOON TEMPLE
Twirling around an empty road
Dancing along an ocean of another Mind
Moon-Mind dizziness of the full Moon's rising
Moon-Master of the moment come to lure music from the stars and enchant life.
And I, leaping into the Moonlight,
flow as life flows into the Unborn
since time beyond time
spell bound.

Terrance Gene Van Tassell
LOOK TO THE FUTURE

This poem is dedicated to the children of today and tomorrow, especially Patrick M. Van Tassell . . . My son.

He created the earth
He filled the seas
He planted the grass
He made the trees

He gave us fresh air
He let the birds fly free

He created all creatures
He did this for you and me

We've dug up the earth
We've poisoned the seas
We've paved over the grass
We've chopped down the trees

We've polluted the air
We've killed the birds
We've the creatures
We've forgotten His words

Our children are the future
So love them large and small
Teach them God's words
And the future will save us all.

Marcia L Wagner
LETTING GO
Here I am only thinking of your leaving this morning. The loneliness and ache I feel can only be replaced by a lump in my throat. I keep telling myself that my longing for you will pass, but I truly don't want to lose this attraction. I have known you only a short time but my resistance surely weakened. With you I felt life was beginning, you were always happy to see me. You say I will find someone new but the burning surely became an eternal flame. The music must play on and I only dream of replacing a fading memory. Every night I will feel your heart beating, your hand in mine, my spirit flying when you look into my eyes and hoping we will again be together. My emotions are running high but I no longer need to deny them; for you had to leave. Although my heart ached in saying good-bye, I could not ask you to be lesser than you are.

Shannon Burbridge
WHITE LIFE
Off and alone with the sadness and tears;
Feeling the thoughts of uncommon fears.
Secrets of pain hide deep in the eyes;
The blackness inside them keeps the disguise.
In silence remains a past of untold.
Long ago stories are meant to grow old.
Escape on the beach, a bird in the sky,
A white life to see and know not a lie.
Just run with the waves and water will stay;
Then problems will pour and be washed away
With all of the troubles to be left behind.
Though memories will haunt, love still can be kind.
But to find the great beauty in a soul full of trust,
Can often seem worthless like flowers of dust.
So hold on to hope and treasure the sea,
Remember that life is made to feel free.

Carolyn M Lewis
WITNESS

To the Lewis and Mack families. To all my friends and relatives. To all my brothers & sisters in Christ.

The gifts of act, of song, of dance are not mine.
But still a will, at will do I live.

A life of one all precious to see
Sharing and caring with complete dignity.

Memories from the past provoke me to stand
To express observances from my part in this land.

For if there was no God in the journey of life
Tell me now, how could, how would one survive.

There'd be;
No cloud in the sky for the eye to gaze
No thirst quenched
No sound to amaze.
No hand outreached to lend, to the land
No breath of day
As the nights fade away.
A lost, lonely troubled soul is what I'd be
Thank you dear God for awakening me.

Evelyn Louise Nowels
BEYOND THE HILL
Looking beyond the hill I picture an old house standing,
The wood is bare and the paint is in demanding,
There's a woman in the doorway reaching out to me,
In my mind and in my heart this is what I see.

She's asking me with tearful eyes not to go away,
She's wondering if she went wrong to make me go astray,
As I walked down the lane I had to turn around,
She was gone and I was alone, she'll never again be found.

Andrea Albert
UNENDING CYCLES
Of all the things that have ended in my life, why was this one so known about, so welcomed? Maybe because it was time for it to end even though life's too short to lose the most important. I guess that's why God put ending things on earth. To let the cycle of life come about. Even though we could compare it to the many less important objects, such as a rose or the daylight, maybe even emotions. But why a person? A body of love and sensitivity? Was it a punishment to me? No, it was a blessing to show me I'm loved. To show me I will someday belong to the creator of this unending cycle of life.

William M Munkacsy
THE SEAGULL

To my mother Peggy, though you are gone from this world, perhaps some of your creativity lives on in me

Mighty wings thrashing
Flying over the sea
Not a care in the world
As free as can be

Gathering its harvest
In a tweezer-like beak
Graceful and precise
For fish it seeks
A blinding white body
Coasting over the water
Diving for precious food
For its sons and daughters

In a vise grip
The fish wiggles about
Turning and twisting
Its survival in doubt

In the cool sea air
The seagull flies away
Carrying its prey
The end of another day

N J Oldham
CAPTURED IN OUR HEARTS

Dedicated to the memory of John F. Kennedy

Captured in our hearts
The innocent tribute
Of his small sons
Touching salute.

A riderless horse
With no weight to be borne
Representing an emptiness
The whole world did mourn.

There'd been words penned of lilacs
For a loss long before
Now the promise of camelot
Would be known evermore.

Words of wisdom and humor
His inspiration ours to keep
The miles had been traveled
It had come time to sleep.

Joyce Marchischuk
TO FLY

This poem is dedicated to "Roger" my Dear & Loving Husband!

A snow white dove,
Untouched by midnite sky,
Young and helpless,
Still learning how to fly.
But before the bird,
Could test her wings;
She learned of pain
And corrupted things.
This bird will never soar
O'er mountains, land, or sea.
This bird with crippled wings,
This dove inside of me.
To fly is love.
But my love will never see the sky,
No wind; or Peace; or shooting stars.
The dove has learned to cry.

Helen Rocco
OUR BOYS

To the Viet Nam vets: who answer our country's call. God bless you all.

Our boys went to Viet Nam.
Some came home others were,
Never found.
They're living on our city streets.

They have no jobs, no place
To sleep.
The battle ground was the
Start of their defeat.

John C Glass
FLASH BACK
As I bend my mind again,
a piece of me returns,
to that kaleidoscope of time and place,
For which my heart still yearns.

I run again,
through misty fields and ancient cobbled streets,
To you,
I feel your pulse, my body aches for you.

Jill Payne
SOARING ALONE
Sparks flew as the fire started.
We took off like a raging storm.
Lifted on the wings of mutual love,
We soared through the night deep and warm.
Suddenly there was a struggle!
His hand was being wrenched and pulled away.
As I fearfully turned to look,
I identified the culprit and where it lay.
A large black hole it was
Looming there before my eyes.
Yes a large black hole it was—
The enemy of all those who fly the skies.
With a vicious force it dragged him away,
Its strength stronger than the bond of our souls.
They say nothing can survive or conquer
The ominous power of lurking black holes.
Somehow the heavens have lost their splendor.
The dusty night is no longer my friend.
As I soar through the night in bleak solitude
Mourning a beautiful flight with a tragic end.

G V Ferro
WANTS
It may not come as I perceive
the it, the what, the way.
It may not be as I have heard,
what others have to say.
I've waited long, I've waited hard
in tense anticipation
to have it just as I have willed
my selfish expectation.

My sight is lost, my hearing gone
my patience turned to dust.
The it I sought so much to hold
enslaved my soul in saneless trust.

Release my grip, detach my hold
I weary of the search.
Let other blooms of life unfold
and feathery wisdoms perch.
Before my eyes a world of sight
and knowing sounds to hear
I'm free to have it as it is
or lose it without fear.

Agnes Beezhold/DuPree
PARANOIA

To Bill and Matt, my sons

I've crawled into my cocoon again
All hunched and bunched
Where I'll let no one enter
And I won't come out
It's not safe
Anywhere
Neither in nor out
But let none see me
And I'll see no one
Lest with their little knowledge
And more conceit

Think they have the answers
To the unanswerable
Depression, Despair—such trite little words
That describe nothing
Of the pitch blackness that is my soul

Jennifer Love Webb
ANOTHER UNTITLED POEM
The wind shivered as the night grew cold
two lovers held hands and together grew old
the clouds came in contact and covered the moon
and all of us died too soon

The trees on the mountaintop fell to the ground
but as they hit the earth there wasn't a sound
the dark gravel road led into the past—
our lives slipped away too fast.

Carolyn S Whitaker

Carolyn S Whitaker
TO MY LITTLE BABY GIRL

This poem is dedicated to Kim, my first born, and the love in this poem I dedicate to all my children. Kim, Kelly, Jeremiah, Jordan.

I watch my baby girl asleep,
So soft and warm,
So small and sweet.
I watch her as she grows each day,
Lord help me guide her along
the way.
To share the laughter of some small thing
because to her it's big and strange.
And when she cries I'll share her pain,
to hurt alone is a terrible thing.
A lifetime isn't long enough to share and love
what God gave us . . .
Love Always,
Mommy

Eleanor Bentley
AN AUTUMN CALL

Dedicated To: Fred Bentley, My Friend, Lover, and Husband

As the leaves swirl through the windy breeze of fall
We inhale the crisp, fresh air of an autumn call,
For this is the season we love best of all.

Nine years ago as we planted the daffodils
Your proposal was so romantically clear,
When you said, "We'll love each other forever, "My Dear."
As the squirrels gathered their acorns
for the long winter ahead
You and I kept the promises we had so often said,
"To Love, Honor, and Cherish,"
when we wed.

The birds flew south and we sailed north
Along the deep, blue Nova Scotian course,
A honey-moon filled with golden rays smiled upon the commitment we had made.

Our days were shorter and our nights grew longer
Wrapped in each other, our passion like a fire,
The stars above gleamed so much brighter.

As the last crimson and gold colored leaves fall all around
We rake them from the denuded, soiled ground,
I think of the friend, lover, and wife I promised to be
Unlike the bareness of the maple tree,
My life shall never be empty,
When I have you to love for eternity.

Michael J Jan
MOMMY

"TONI"

Mommy oh mommy how the years do fly,
Sometime's I wonder just wonder why
I, ever was born to learn how to fight,
Mommy, oh mommy what is such a life?
I'm hoping just hoping third war
Never starts, cause dear mommy it
Breaks many hearts, yes dear mommy,
It breaks many hearts.

Sandy Taylor
REALITY
Out of the darkness, into the light you enter,
Awaken by air rushing into thy soul.
Unaware of the dangers lying ahead,
Only thoughts of being fed.
Days pass with endless adventure,
Survival each day means depend-ency.
Eyeing every face that appears,
Wondering of your mind over the years.
Time has come to spread your wings,
The truth brings pain, and tears.
Your soul cries out, "I want to be free!"
Finally you're old enough to flee.

Cathy M Schmidt
TRI-COLORED TREASURE
Your magic gift of special love won me from the start.
Your eyes met mine; we felt the warmth; we touched each other's heart.

We found ourselves together on a warm September night.
I was on the rebound and hoped you would be right.

I never knew our love would grow so strong and oh so fast.
I thought it was forever though; I thought that it would last.

Your affection and your beauty were captured in my soul.
How could I know that with my heart this love might take its toll.

The year or so we were as one was filled with bonds so strong,
But life sometimes does not prepare
us for things that could go wrong.
I lost you on a cold and January day.
Did you remember me as you left?
No one could really say.

Thank you for the time we spent although so very brief.
I'm trying to work out the pain, the sorrow, and the grief.

I know I'll love again one day,but it won't be the same.
For in my heart you will live in space no one can claim.

Maxwell, my dog, my friend, my love,
I know you shine down on me from the heavens above.

We miss you,
All our Love,
Cathy and
Dave

Marilyn Ellis
THE CATHEDRAL

To my husband Herbert, Thanks for being you.

I walked along a leafy path
To where the redwood grow,
And there I knelt to speak with God,
Just why I do not know

But speak I did of hope and fear,
Cast upon the breeze my plea,
And a shaft of light crashed through the leaves
Its warmth embracing me.

I dreamed awhile of heavenly things,
Of visions oh so fair,
And as my thoughts did wander thus
I felt His presence there.

In the stillness of that forest grove
Of pungent redwood musk,
I knelt I do not know how long
Until an eerie dusk,

Had settled o'er the giants
And my senses I did rouse
What is this place? The answer clear
This is my Father's House.

Jocelyn Russell
I AM . . .
I am what the world is and was made of
People use me and kill for me
I can also bring happiness and joy
If I was not painful
Then hate would hurt more
I must sound awful to you
But in your deepest heart you need and cherish me
For I am love
Maker and breaker of everything
For I am love

Cynthia A Massey
THOUGHTS OF YOU
I think about you all the time.
Each time we are together
I pretend it will never end
but it does, and you must go
home to her.
And I am left with thoughts of
you.

Sometimes when I close my eyes
I can still feel your warm body
pressed against mine.
And I can hear your gentle voice
And feel your breath on my face.

It's almost like having you with
me
But you are not with me
You are with her.
So I lie here, and dream
About the next time we can meet.
I tell myself that one day
You'll come home with me to
stay . .
And even though it isn't true
I believe it at least for a moment
or two.

James Kelly Pitchford
SOMEWHERE
Somewhere today, we'll walk alone together,
you where you are and me where I am.
Though our thoughts will cross many times over,
there also will be a time for our paths to do as well.
I see you there when I close my eyes,
and often reach out to touch you,
I can feel the warmth when you are near.
We talk in our thoughts of dreams to be,
and dream in our thoughts of you and me.
Though we're apart wherever we are,
I rest in my thoughts knowing, it's just for a time
No matter what, no matter when,
Somewhere today, we'll walk alone together.

Angela Powell
ANTICIPATION OF VACATION
The month is short, the time is right.
The days are speeding by.
We need to work especially fast
With every girl and boy.

Children singing, children playing,
Children doing skills.
Teacher's right beside them,
Bending little wills.

Tension is arising,
Emotions are on high.
School is almost ended,
Wish the time would fly.

Children can't contain themselves,
Excitement is their toy,
And it's right for them to feel this way,
We too, can feel their joy.

Wilma Jean Stamper
THE OLD LOG HOUSE
While I was out strolling through the hills today;
I came to an old log house where I used to stay.
The place of my childhood to me is so dear;
In that old log house that stood many a year.

Everyone is gone now, there's not much left behind;
Only great memories that come to my mind.
It was there by the fireplace that they taught us to pray;

In that old log house that is going to decay.

I know it was God that guided me here,
To bring back memories to me so dear.
Here where they taught me right from wrong;
In this old log house where I lived so long.

Jodi Lynn Sylvester
WHAT IS LOVE?

To the guy who I share the grooviest kind of love with. We will be together forever and a day!
I love you XOXO

Love is . . .
A walk hand in hand
On a cold winter's day,

And the cute little grin on your face
as you turn and glance my way.

Love is . . .
A delicate kiss, a tender touch,
And a feeling deep inside,

Being comforted that a
Special someone will be there as your guide.

Love is . . .
Those quiet times
That we love to spend alone,

The endless depths of our true love
That is mysteriously unknown.

Love is . . .
The words that your body relays
With the help of a single sound,

Having you place your hand on my heart
To feel it rapidly pound.

Love is . . .
The dedication and commitment
That has brought us to be one.

The giggles and the times we've shared
Filled with lots of fun.

My love, you must realize—
That I will be yours until
The day I die.

And after that we'll live in eternity
With the Lord to tell us why.

Why our paths collided on
That perfect summer night.

How He knew through good and bad
Our togetherness was right.

The Lord has given me a gift,
A man sent from above.

I treasure you Sweetheart, and I will always keep you with me
In my arms forever as my love.

Agnes Lee
THE LOSS
I don't know
your sex,
nor can I picture
your face.

Yet, at midnight, looking into the mirror
through the streams of my tears,
I can almost see you,
dainty as a daffodil,
approaching me.

I don't know what to call you,
nor do I dare touch you—
most beautiful dream,
most heartless decision.

You were my life,
now lost,
the deepest grief
within my womb.

Every midnight
I dreaded your questioning me
sadly from the mirror
with fearful eyes like swords.

Yet can my poetry
and the freedom I love
shield me
at midnight
against your sword-like look?

Tabaitha Cole
TODAY

This poem is dedicated to my family, friends, and Troy—I wish I could give you all everything.

Beneath that large, gray sky above,
are children with many fears—
asking what is happening,
and who will dry their tears—
This world was made for all of us,
to share and aid in need—
yet man is killing man,
for satisfaction and plain greed—
Peace is what I dream of,
happiness for everyone—
Let's make our world a better home,
and let's make living much more fun.

Jean Veile
ONE DAY
If I had one day of my life left to live
I'd spend it and end it all with you!
We'd spend it looking at the sunset . . .
Spend it walking on the shore
Holding hands, touching.
We'd watch the clouds playing tag
across a setting sun.
But, most of all, my Darling,
We'd spend it in each other's arms!

Sydney Lee Harmer
MOTHER'S HEARTACHE
If a mother's heartache
for her children could be heard
the world would soon drown in
noise, stagger,
perhaps tilt under the decibel level
of the silent shout of millions
confirming God's statement that Eve
would bear children in sorrow,
yet be preserved in that bearing,
speaking not necessarily of the pain
of labor,
but the labor of loving.

Martin Storlie
THE END, THE BEGINNING
The wind is blowing . . .
The snow is falling . . .
It's wintertime, I'm cold,
tired, and hungry.
I lay down beside you
and sleep . . .
When I awake I peer
out the window . . .
The sun is shining . . .
The flowers are blooming . . .
The green grass is growing . . .
Spring has come and left us behind.

Janie F Clements
LIFE'S MYSTERIES
There is an unseen line where
earth and sky seem to meet,
A line untrod by human feet;
A never ending skyline that
dips from shore to shore,
Until it seems to blend and
disappear forever more.
There is a sunset so glorious to behold,
With eyes of awe and wonder
we watch the colors unfold;
There is a dawn when the first
light appears,
As the beauty of the wakening
earth slowly nears.
There is the depth of the mighty
ocean wide,
With waves that ebb and
flow with the tide;
There are tiny pebbles washed
white like sand,
Such mysteries were not
created by man.

Douglas Steele Toland

Douglas Steele Toland
UNTIED UNITY SPLASH
Amidst crowds of outta touch,
goin own ways on their entity plane;
I reached woman of soft existence . . .
and continued together as a splash of unity.

Loosening bonds, that knot, a tied up
magnetic chemistry;
Quietly close spills the Cure.
Emitten from within,
pours our Hearts honey Pure.

Straight from me
Straight from you,
Our core drips a blend of oneness dew.
Killing the lonely Stance,
Quietly close
We overdose
on Touch!

Alma J Carpenter
MY LIFE'S SPECIAL FRIEND

To Lida Holzheimer for her belief, understanding and God inspired devotion in making me believe in myself, and for all of that tough love, when I needed it so much. Love you

My sun, my moon, my stars above,
All gifts from my Saviour, sent in love.
Then he tied on a ribbon, and added a bow,
When he picked from his angels, don't you know?
He sent me the best, of friends tried and true,
My life's special friend, I call simply YOU.

John C Krebs
GROWING OLD
My hair is gray,
My heart is cold,
And now I think I'm growing old.

And I am lonely,
As I sit here in my rocking chair,
Returning the wall's empty stare,
I realize there is no one left to care.

The wife is dead, the children grown,
And now I'm left all alone.
Alone with my memories.
And as I look back upon the life I've led,
I can see my wife, she is not dead;
The children are not grown.

Once again they come to me,
To tell me of their tragedies;
But then I see it's not real at all,
And once again I see the wall.

My hair is gray,
My heart is cold,
And now I know, I've grown old.

M Smith
HANDS PUSH DOWN, PRESSED AGAINST THE SEAMS
Hands push down, pressed against the seams.
Smiles turn downwards
Looks glance up.

Hiding within oneself One hides against the world.
SEAMS

But we push our hands down strongly
We push our hands against the seams strongly.
We reach through to our legs
Touching what seems real
Satisfied
Satisfied
Satisfied
SEAMS

Till we reach bare blooded bone.
Then we withdraw
Forget.
and reach again
just to feel flesh.
flesh and blood.

Forget and then again.

Vicki A Krug
DID YOU SEE WHAT I SAW?
Slipping through the shifting mists,
Of the shadowy caverns of our minds,
Elusive as can be.
A glimpse of the satisfied soul,
The triumph of the yearned for,
Did you see what I saw?

Anna McAnear
OCTOBER
October is my favorite season,
A time of reflection and reason,
when we take the time to view the
trees of red and golden hues,
that Mother Nature has painted,
along with lavender, bronze, and
yellow mums, that brighten our
yards and days of sun.
A time of football, homecomings,
and traditions, inspired with the
music of bands and musicians.
Fields of red maze and golden
pumpkin, that reminds us of
Halloween, with witches and scary
bumpkins.

Cheryl S Yarnall
MY PRAYER
Lord, here I am, one more time
Yes, there's something on my mind.
I need you more now, Lord
Than I ever have before.

Now and then we all need someone to lean on
And you're the only one left, since he's gone.
I don't ask for much, just a little strength,
And someone to stand by me when I feel weak.

Take me back into your arms
So no one can do me harm.
Lord, help me to be bold
As I stand alone in the cold.

When things get rough, give me
hope
And God, teach me how to cope
With things I can't overcome
Help me to see over them some

Help me to be strong
As I go down life's road alone.
Take my hand in yours, Lord, as I
walk down paths unknown
For better, for worse, whichever way
life goes.

Debbie Greer

THE CRY

The cry for help was heard afar
Will no one stop
Will no one listen?
The cry was saying, The end is near
Yet no one stops
Yet no one listens.
The cry was saying, My time has
come
Still no one stops
Still no one listens.

Suddenly, the cry stops.

Brian K Hulitt

WATERFALL

Sometimes I feel I'm floating
Rough waters white with foam
Heading towards a waterfall
And maybe towards my home
I touch the shore occasionally
Yet can't seem to get a hold
The sun above is shining
But the water is so cold
Rocks and limbs fill my path
The river's arms so wide
I go bouncing back and forth
Like a pinball side to side
Finally the waterfall . . . .
I can hear it round the bend
But when I reach the edge of it
The dream comes to an end

Laura Deschner Cochran

SUNSET

Flawless In Design
A Lawlessness

Warning Sign
Warming Trend
And In the End;
Right On Time

Erin J Hunsader

SPECIALNESS

Specialness can be in a kiss,
Can be in a dream or in a wish.
Specialness bonds two together,
Keeps love going forever,
Can't be replaced ever.
Specialness won't ever die,
It's as unique as the sky,
It's there in his eyes.
Specialness is everywhere,
In everyone you see,
It can't be bought, it can't be sold,
For specialness is gold.

Cara Suzanne Putt

PAIN

To My Mom, even though we have our pain, we also have our love.

A problem rises . . . . people yell and
scream
yelling things at each other they both
don't really mean . . . . .
A love they need, but can't seem to
find
Searching everywhere but nothing
comes to mind . . . .
Where is it ?
door's slamming . . . . curses fill
the air . . . .
Why isn't it there?
All is quiet now, hate has come
about
Another tear hits my pillow as I try
to figure this out . .
Nothing seems to be right anymore
everything said is wrong
Nothing ever changes . . . . .
That love is still lost, but why?
Feelings are hurt, hearts are
crushed . . . . . .
Everything stays the same time and
time again
Where is that lost love?

Stacey M Ward

CROSS IN MY PICKET

This poem is dedicated to the memory of my father, John L. Ward

The cross in my pocket
Keeps me safe
From all those doubts
And an uncertain fate
It helps me live
From day to day
Just knowing I'll make it
To heaven some way

Lori Rutledge

SOMETIMES

To Ernie—All My Love Always

Sometimes
my mind
drifts back
to the days
you and I were
together

Beautiful
lovely days
filled with
sunshine and
song

Then
my mind
drifts back
to reality
realizing
it will
never be
again

Libba HaLavey

WHILE AT MY WINDOW STANDING

To Harry, another good poet. Toujours, L.

While at my window standing
Staring at the frozen night,
As if by God's commanding
Comes the soft translucent light.

Sky—velvet black to flaming
crimson
With all colors in between
Trees—like statues—leafless
standing—
Coated with the wintry sheen.

Branches high in supplication
Sentinels who do not sleep,
Naked for human observation
Their primal beauty makes me weep.

Etched upon the sky so starkly
From some mysterious intaglio pen
Contrasting the luminescence darkly.
Is the Universe your ken?

Oh, tell me, Stalwart, do you tire
Of Ra's chariot ride across the sky?
Silent suitors to the fire
Watching creation begin anigh.

Jody Swank

AUTUMN LEAVES

To my wonderful husband, George. Together we share more gladnesses than sadnesses, more laughter than tears. I am truly blest. I love you, Babe. Jody

i wish you one autumn day
full of all of the riches
in the colors of the
changing leaves
and all of the warmth
of the winters hearth
that we as kids returned to
after playing in
and raking
those changing leaves
of an autumn day

Denise Gordon

WHITE BUTTERFLY

To my brother, Clarence And most of all—Mom and Dad . . . I love you!

When my brother was killed,
A beautiful white butterfly flew
around in my face.

I could hear a voice as the butterfly
flew, saying,
"Look at me, I'm so happy, I can
fly."

The day of the funeral, that butterfly
came back to me—I smiled.
Ever since then, from time to time,
White butterflies come my way;
And I again, hear my brother's voice
as if he still exists.

White butterfly
Never go away.
Come summer, winter, spring and
fall
Come white butterfly,
Come one,
Come all!

Sharon L Alexander

THE SHARING HOUR

For my Theresa—Thank You.

The phone bell rings; my empty
rooms soon glow;
Reverberate with love; with
laughter shine.
My darling daughter-friend is calling
now
To weave the threads of her
week into mine,
And help our tapestry of love to
grow.

She tells me what she's done, and
what she'd lief,
And Ray's and Eddie's pranks,
and other folks'.
Describes her days; unburdens fears
and strife.
Relates her latest puns and silly
jokes.
And shares her joy in husband, son,
and life.

In turn, I vent to her my week's
demands:
Computer bugs, and cakes, and
teeth that ache;
My trials with son and ex; my future
plans;
My work accomplishments; the
goofs I make.
She hears my dreams, and always
understands.

Our talk is done this week, we each
return
To weave our separate threads
in our own ways.
Each strengthened by the other's
warm concern.
Her love and caring permeate
my days
And lend me smiles to conquer every
turn.

Nancy Derbyshire

THE DAY IS SO SWEET

This poem is dedicated to my family, who inspired me and to all of my friends

The day is so sweet
Until the big sorrow.
For I had heard,
You'll be leaving tomorrow.

My heart thumped and flickered,
And went pitter patter.
As my last moments with you
Were ones meant to flatter.

My love for you has grown and
grown
As the days are weak and old.
I shall never forget you;
I'll remember you still
As I see your car leaving my window
sill.

I waved goodbye and I love you.
You waved back and said I love you
too.
No expression was on my face;
Just another teardrop to eject my
pain.
I've lost you for ever and ever;
You'll never come back.
My time with you is my one big
lack.

Hearts and lace cover your photo.
They always will and never go.

Patricia A Hebel

CHILD, "THE MEMORY"

This poem is dedicated to my loving children, Shanda and Ryan

A child is thy memory
For we hold close to our hearts
Delicate as fine crystal
Though it could never break apart

We cherish all the moments
That are shared between thy souls
The love is everlasting
Like a binding gripping hold

A child brings hope and glory
Within our everydays
Along with tears of happiness
And sadness along our ways

As our child is grown
Our memories reach a peak
Fulfilling and sacred times
Thou always long to seek

The sound of their laughter
Along with all thy weeps
Precious tears and smiles
Thou forever, will hold for keeps

Lorrie A Diaz

PERFECT WAVES

"Did you ever know that you're my hero?" Penni, thanks for being my best friend and my inspiration. I love you.

To apply that abstract concept
entitled "perfection,"
to the vast, boundless wonder, the ocean,
would be to make what is invisible, visible.

Yet, we, as intricate, complex, and volatile individuals
seem as perfect as two coexisting waves
that ride the endless sea;
that run to the shore in a blind search for more ground;
we pull back with our tides the limitless sand grains
of time and experience.

We crash against the imperishable rocks that stand
with a powerful aura of seriousness about them,
and our souls explode into innumerable droplets of water,
leaving us to compose the parts of our shattered beings,
as we plunge back into the waters of humanity
to become one with an endless sea.

Bobbe Cowan

VALENTINE PRAYER

To my husband of 40 years "Bob"

When I go to sleep at night
I say a little prayer,
As I close my eyes and
see your face so fair.
As I drift into sleep, you
surround me, it seems,
Your vision is with me, in
all my thoughts and dreams.
When I awake, it's your name
I have upon my mind.
You're the dream, I dreamed of,
You're my special Valentine.
So I go to sleep at night and
I say my little prayer,
That when I awake, you
will always be there.

Cheryl Lynne Licastri

MALAISE—A SELF PORTRAIT

A weathered bridge full of rust.
It stands alone, with water running beneath.
Fish that swim, snails that crawl and a dock with a broken boat tied to it.
A dried out tree full of brittle branches.
Leaves no longer occur.
An abandoned house full of neglected memories.
Humans have left it in the hands of an unidentified sprite.
The frequent bang of the door is gone, now it is bolted firmly.
A mind is full of bewilderment.
It decays slowly of a ceaseless disease.
Left is a skeleton advanced in its years.
A poem full of unlimited meaning, holds no rhyme or reason.
It's a declaration on paper as the poet searches for the solitude of the day.
And as darkness approaches and puts its claim on time, the unwavering thoughts are disguised behind a laughing garden full of flowers.

Renee Bouthillier-Orszulak

HUNTER

In the woods,
he's quiet.
He sees all, he listens, he waits.
Quiet; are his footsteps.
Alert; are his ears.
Searching; are his eyes.
But his heart is pounding in his
chest; it is a constant loud beat
like a drum.
He fears it will give him away,
but it won't; his fear and
anticipation are his enemies.

He roams in a world unknown to many.
He sees things all should see.
He glimpses the beauty of nature.
A quick fox.
An alert little squirrel in search
of winter's food.
The grace of a doe, his beautiful
prey.

So serene she is,
so beautiful.
Yet, she is too far away.
He moves closer, his heart
pounding in his chest.
She is alerted by sound, and
gracefully flees from his sight.

He continues ......
In search of scrapes.
Searching for tracks.
Silently searching.

His legs ache.
His head spins from the thin mountain air.
He continues ......

Again, his eyes fall upon them.
This time four.
Thoughts mill through his head.
If he could just get closer he can
choose. He can get a clear shot
and choose.

But again distance separates him
from his prey and he is unable
to succeed.
He shrugs off his disappointment.
Knowing his day will come.
Time will grant his wish.
Knowledge will bring him back to
this spot again.
This spot on the ridge.

He is a Hunter.

Clark L Jones

SILENT IDOLS

Trading places for an hour or so
With that all-time legend at the
picture show.

Oh Make believe, Make believe,
dream me a dream
Bring Valentino to the Silver screen.
Wake Gloria Swanson from her
eternal rest, paint her lips, design her a dress.
Together
a pair forever
They'll share life's great adventures in the hereafter.

Speak to me, Valentino, show me the way,
Share with me your novie
approach to love
For to my leading lady I know not what to say.
I build loving words in my mind
Only to have them thrust to the
wind
For without passion
My lady remains a friend.

Valentino your lips make no sound
but your intentions are clear
Larger than life you are the best
On an Arabian stallion you win your quest.

Oh Make believe, Make believe,
dream me a dream.
Bring my silent idol to the Silver screen.
From the projection room you
cast your web upon the world.
In basic black and white your
plans are unfurled.
Like condor in flight with destination clear,
Your leading lady has nothing to fear.

Oh, Mr. Cameraman, give Valentino a voice,
Or pan his face so I can read his
lips
For to my leading lady I know
not what to say.

Oh Valentino, Valentino, the subject of my dream,
Why must you remain trapped
forever upon the silver screen?

Tina Monica Mitchell

LANGUAGE OF LOVE

Love speaks a language all its own. The words it needs are few; it speaks with touches, looks and smiles. A heart that's always true. Love paints a rainbow in the sky, Love knows just why. Love's the greatest thing the world has known and it speaks a language all its own.

Love's language isn't written in the words we use each day, it's written by the thoughtful deeds we do along life's way. Love shares a secret, dries a tear, love brings a flower, a smile of cheer. Love's the greatest thing the world has known and it speaks a language all its own.

If you'd like to speak love's language, take a look inside your heart and perhaps you'll be surprised to find you've known it from the start!

Malone Sanders

I CAN FEEL

I have not lost my sight you see—I can feel
Starry nights twinkling lights shining
It's hard for me to see what you hear—
but I can feel
I see heaven's dawn, wilder than the earthy sky
Each moment, moving majesti-
cally—masterful strokes
Calliopedic color cast swirls a sigh
Ravenous bursts of sunstreams prism
blending, bending, streaming
cataclysm
The stars silently talk to me on high
They tell me your toes curl up when you smile
the joy of laughter
rhythmically after
Your lips seem to say—I can feel,
you see
Your eyes are those starry nights
twinkling lights
and Heaven's dawn is
Lovin' you till early morn beneath earthy sky
Each moments our souls touch'd and
parted
You see
I can Feel

Esther N Duncan

Esther N Duncan

GO AHEAD

This poem is dedicated to Nicole and Chante, my sweet granddaughters.

I am sometimes bound by the
thoughts I think,
Afraid of the wrong and want to do right.
Seems there is a small voice that
whispers to say,
Be right, then go ahead, be on your way.

Go ahead with your thoughts, your
dreams, your deeds,
Even though the first time you don't succeed.
If they are good, you can see them
blossoming as flowers,
Blossom from the seeds.

Then you won't regret the good
you've done, each day,
You can face the rising sun, with
hope in your heart.
When you lie down to rest from
dusk, till morn,
You'll have peace in your heart, just
know you've
Done your part.

Bernice Spencer

WHAT IS WRONG WITH THE WORLD TODAY?

Too many people have forgotten
how to pray,
We need to get back to the old time way.
We need to get down on our knees
and pray,
What is wrong with the world today?

Children are not being taught how to pray,
Drugs and sex have taken over our
kids today.
They are learning to do things their way,
People don't take time with kids
anymore,
Because they are always on the go.

There is too much sin in the world today,
And the devil is having his way.
What is wrong with the world today?
There is not enough love in the world today.

Mothers are too busy to take time to listen,
Fathers are somewhere, only God knows where,
Kids are so mixed up that they don't know what to do.

Kids, put those drugs down today,
Get down on your knees and pray,
Look up to God and he will look down on you,
If you need someone to talk to, he will be there for you.

Kelli Euresti
A PRAYER

To my beloved father, Mario whom we lost on April 26 1989 I love you daddy Love Kelli Ann Euresti

Close your eyes and I will close mine
Reach down from heaven
Let me touch you one more time
Take my hand and lead my way
Help me make it through the day
Bring out the sun, take away the rain
Paint a beautiful rainbow and ease my pain
Look down at me today and each day after that
I'm going to make your dreams come true
And there's no turning back
Daddy I love you and miss you too
What I accomplish is all for you.

Linda Sherlock Remmert
IF ONLY . . . .

In loving memory of my dad, Frank J. Sherlock and with special thanks to my mom, Mary, for seven years of survival at a time when we all needed her the most. May God bless you always.

Just the other morning,
As I lay awake in bed,
My thoughts went up to you
Dear Dad,
While planning my day ahead.

If only I could call you
Pick up the phone and chat,
I'd have so much to ask
You Dad,
Like "Could you call me back?"

I'd ask how you were doing,
I'd ask about your friends,
I'd ask for your advice
Oh Dad,
About life's latest trends.

The line would sure be busy
Emotions would show our love,
If only such calls could
Dear Lord,
Be made from heaven above.

James D Berrier II
PORTRAIT
Intentional interment of ignoble institutions,
Comical creation of crazed constitutions.
Loquacious reticence,
Passive insistence.
Emotional emergence of empty ecstasy,
Casual conception of calloused conceit.
Cowardly heroic,
Expressively stoic.
Existentialist emulation of everything exotic,
Careful contrivance of contours chaotic.
Verily dissimulative,
Superiorly diminutive.

David Peterson
EXECUTION

Respectfully dedicated to Robert Gordon Argall, who introduced me to poetry.

The wretched man draws near his wretched fate
The famous chair its prize awaits
Backed with leather, clasps and straps
(Though most of us avoid this fortune trap)
Through barred windows is framed the night
That is set free by candle light
Some moral citizens tonight find sport
In waiting for his death's report
And quietly bless that life had not
Thrust to them this bloody lot
With jest and curse and wine and beer
With mocking songs and cries and cheers
They hail the hearse whose solemn gait
Completes their Aryan Mass of hate—
But the guard who watches wonders why
And pulls the lever with a sigh.

S Lee Smith
WIND AND WONDER

"The wind bloweth where it listeth, and thou hearest the sound thereof, but canst not tell whence it cometh and whither it goeth; so is every one that is born of the Spirit." John 3:8 (KJV)

They say they've never loved the wind.
 Can it be they've never known
The freedom of being all alone,
 And the beauty of trees that bend?

Have they never stood upon a hill,
 And wondered, standing there;
If the wind that's blowing through their hair
 Has e'er been tamed—or ever will?

A force intangible, mystifying,
 A beauty none can grasp;
But only hear and feel it pass,
 Raging, yet whispering.

Alice Salzano
POEM TO A POET

To Gerald Sullivan, Mike Leach and Lloyd Berry. They encouraged me to write again. Many thanks to all of them.

Some men climb mountains;
Some men go to sea;
Some men do nothing,
But write sweet Poetry

Words upon paper can quiet a heart
loving words can encourage another to start.
Pretty words on paper can bring sweet smiles
Nice words on paper can shorten the miles.

But a poem to a Poet, brings joy not untold
a Poem to a Poet can turn life to gold
oh! poet please Accept these words from my mind
oh! poet please never leave your poetry behind.

Lavona W Mason
LOVE

To Jim And Our Wonderful Children, James III and Marilyn Wreath

When Spring was raising her eager head
And birds were singing love refrains
And the green was bathed in gentle rains,
I loved you then, and so we wed!

But Summer's glory! Ah, that was when
You guided me through emerald love
With the gentleness of the dusky dove
And I was envied, the happiest of men.

How richer now, in Autumn's gold
My passion grows and never wanes
And the leaves pile high on the window panes
And the pheasants gather, now shy, now bold.

How shall our Winter be? Then cold?
No, our hearth shall be glowing warm
And our hearts will weather the growing storm;
For I'll love you much when we are old.

Mrs Thelma Crabtree
HEART OF LOVE

To the one that makes my life complete, my husband, Darrell. Two hearts that are made one.

Finger tips caressed,
all the lord had blessed.
The heart cried,
but the mind denied.
A soul was in pain,
but the lord came.
He entered the heart,
to become a part.
Life began,
just a little span.
Joy trickled like sand.
Eternal love burst into bloom,
took away all the gloom.
A heart was made new,
as large as the skies blue.

Thelma Brisbine
A LITTLE PATCH OF BLUE
As I drive down my street on the way to town,
My thoughts on just ordinary, every-day things,
I see in the distance when I'm halfway down
A little patch of blue—and then my heart sings!
And why such a small thing should give me a lift
I can't tell, but that blue is the river, of that I'm aware,
And that tiny blue patch is my token, my gift
Of a free-flowing, deep and wide river down there.

It makes me think of the times when my family's all near,
And my heart will feel suddenly bursting with love;
Or the joy when I'm reading my Bible down here
And catch a glimpse of my wonderful Lord up above.
Are these an "earnest" of glorious things He's prepared?
A window? A peek? Our little patch of blue—
Of the oceans of beauty and love to be shared
In the Father's house there? Yes, I'm sure that it's true!

Monica Elizabeth Dobson
SORROWS
Life gave me sorrows
I thought it was the end.
Never looking for tomorrows
Never hoping for a friend.

Life gave me sorrows
And with those sorrows came pain
I thought of oh so much harrows
And they nearly made me insane.

Life gave me sorrows
And in those sorrows came a friend
Who took away the harrows
And helped me to live again.

May Kock
PANDORA'S BOX
At the doorstep lay a little box so gorgeous,
Whom from, a gift, of an unknown source.
I wonder, stare, why would a gift so devious,
A stranger give, with no reason or recourse?

I proceed to untie, the satin ribbon bow,
Gentle took the lid off, 'twas tight you know.
Step back in amazement, a puff of air blow,
A Pandora Box, rushing to release ills, woes.

It was for good reason, locked up be trouble,
Now it arrive to disrupt my life of hope.
Downfall go my dreams like bubbles,
But we must realize, living all our senses envelope.

Sounds like the premonition of a fairy tale,
Saying fate takes many forms and sides.
The warning that pitfall, may joy assail,
Now open, escape, the demons that life hide.

Sharron M Wilmot (Sherri)
MAN
A tower of wisdom, strong in body and soul
 full of compassion, gentle to the touch
An ocean's view, peaceful and content
 In control, yet, striving for more

A statue of perfection, exhilarating, romantic
Unpredictable and still mysterious
The voice of knowledge, fearless and honest
Sparkles with humor, generating happiness
Enriched with magnetism, flowing with colors
Endurance of a unique kind, yet sensitive
Beauty from within, trickles to the surface
And stays where the eye can see.

Pall J Kane
DOWN WITH DOOMSAYERS
I saw a man the other day
who said, "The world is in an awful way
and God shall end it soon, on any day."
But he was shouting, and so I did not stay;
for I was on my way to go
see the one for whom my blood doth flow.
I did wish extremely so
that the man would just shut-up and go
far, far away, for such as he
make me quite angry
when they make sad a day
that I had planned to spend in another way.
He depressed me and made me sad
and my depression made my true love mad.
This did set me to think
that pessimism doth surely stink.

Laura Overton
IT'S LIFE, LIVE IT

This poem is dedicated to four special people in my life. Barry, Cathy, Marvin, and Suzen. All my love, Laura

To write about life it's a cinch
Every one lives it
To some it's long
Others not so
But however it's life live it.

Some have it good
Others bad
Some happy
Some sad
However it's life live it.

With some it's love
Others it's pain
Some it's loss
For others it's gain
However it's life live it.

I know about life
I've lived, I've loved
Some good, some bad
Some pain, some gain

However it's life I'm living it.

Ruth C Palmer
BEREFT

With love to my mother, Thelma Webster Cleveland, author of "Melody Ladder," a collection of her beautiful poems.

Although I vowed through all my tears
To love you more with passing years
I find the opposite is true:
My thoughts today were less of you.

The less I feel is hard to measure
But trying to is now my pleasure:

The less of water in the ocean
The less of feeling in emotion
The less of sounding in a roar
The less of sand upon the shore.

Can less of these things ever be missed?
Do roses mind not being kissed?

I think it's plain for all to see:
The less can never change the me!

Sherry G White

Sherry G White
I GAVE GOD AN ANGEL

*Dedicated to the best family a woman could have,
For my Husband, Keith Sr. & my children, Crystal, Keith Jr. & Candace White.*

The Lord took my baby to heaven today,
While he was still in the womb.
I guess he needed an angel,
But I didn't expect it so soon.

Now he'll never be a doctor, and he wont be sent to war,
He'll never see the birds in flight, or hear a lion roar.
He will not witness tragedy, or sorrow in this life,
He'll never play a ball game, be a dad, or have a wife.

The Lord says take one day at a time,
but I planned too far in advance,
My baby didn't lose his life, God gave him another chance.
So when I speak of angels, and look toward the sky,
I pray that I'll accept this, instead of asking why.

Losing a child is not easy, but the Lord showed it can be done,
He gave his child to the world, and the world, they killed his son.
Now the pain you feel is intense, and the scar runs awfully deep;
But love is always kept alive, by the memories we keep.

Look up to the Lord, with petition and prayer,
And ask for guidance with the burden you bear.
For in life there are trials, yet faith can be found everywhere,
And if someone asks, where your baby is, just point, and say, up there.

Shelly Renae Groce
LEAVES
The leaves are pretty in the spring.
Prettiness is what they bring.
The birds think they're pretty, too.
As they bud out, as they do.

They're so bright and green.
They can always be seen.
Drinking in the sunshine and rain.
They're in all the states, even Maine.
Leaves are pretty in red and yellow.
They look nicer than a charming fellow.
Falling from the trees.
Flying in the breeze.

Now where have they gone?
Just like a song.
They get to the end,
Just to spring back again.

Rita M Foil
THE SILENT SENTINEL

Dedicated to all who gave up their lives for their country

A flickering, "Silent Sentinel," glows from afar
In Arlington Cemetery over our great leader's grave
For he was killed, while riding in an open car
And for this country, his fine, young life he gave.

John Fitzgerald Kennedy rode happily along
His pretty, faithful, loving wife sat by his side;
But, then evil happened and all was very wrong
That beautiful, sunny day he took that fateful ride.

Now our dearly beloved thirty-fifth President
Is no longer Washington's White House resident—
Because a telescopic rifle in an assassin's hand
Deprived us of the head of our cherished land.

Moving slowly his motorcade traveled in Dallas town
While there, two searing bullets struck him down
This man fought for everything honest, good and right
And in his family Americans knew peaceful delight.

Therefore, reverently stand, little sentinel
protecting this blessed grave
While in our hearts we will always remember all he gave,
"Dead President, John F. Kennedy," while you sleep
We promise you America's constant vigil to keep.

Janet Sue Sayer
THE WARMTH OF THE SUN

To Ila Wise—an avid reader and poem lover and my Grandmother, who I love dearly

There's something exciting about the sun
Like a big secret with someone
Maybe a friend with warmth and happiness
The sun so full of shining brightness

When I'm out in the sun that's so warm
When the rains are gone and the storms
I feel as if no worries to be
It makes me feel so easy and free

I really feel good when the sun is out
As though the warmth of a friend is about
As if all the joys in the world were mine
Life being just a secret of time

To brighten our lives the sun does shine
It's always a friend of yours and mine
It brightens our world, our lives, and days
So the beauty of sunshine, we're hoping it stays.

Tammy L Wallace
LOVE

This Poem is dedicated to John A. Savage, who will always have a place in my heart.

Love was something
I never really knew,
Now I know his
love was true.
I can't find the
love that is lost,
Now it's gone it's
going to cost.
I know he'll
never be here,
In those words
is what I fear.
I sit here thinking of
the love I gave away,
But maybe I'll find
that love again someday.
Although I say
"I'll always regret,"
But the love that was
there I'll never forget.

Erik Knutila
BEACH WEATHER
Sitting on the beach
In the light rain
I watched
Dead fish
Float
In the water
And dirty gulls
Shimmer
In the air.
With a deep breath
And a sigh,
I turned and looked
(with naked eye)
At the city
And knew nothing
Would change.

Joyce LaPalme
AN ODE TO LOVE
God is always love dear heart,
And, even if our dreams did part,
My prayers are heard by him above
To reconcile my immortal love.
I knew the moment you were gone,
That my love would linger on.
Yes, I've had my so called escapade,
And, for my very fickle fancy paid,
But please try to keep the memory of,
A once beautiful romance my love.

Ingrid Heins
WHY

To a special friend who I'll never forget, but will miss.

He said it was true,
he said it would last,
he said he would never
leave me or hurt me, but
that was just another fake
lie from his past.

He left me just like that,
with no say and no reason why.
It all happened so fast that I
started to cry. In my head I wondered
what was going on, and why he
hadn't called me for so very long.

It's been three months now (or
maybe a little more.) why? what did
I do so wrong?

China L Edwards
MY FOURTH GRADE CLASS
My fourth grade class, number 31,
and I love them all, as if they were 1.
They continue to talk, when I tell
them to stop, little do they know
I almost blow my top.

If some day you happen to pass my
room
and see me standing with a long
handled broom,
Don't be alarmed! Don't despair!
I'm only sweeping so many noisy
children out of my hair!

Evelyn Dollar
THIS GHETTO IS GETTING ME

I dedicate this poem to my children

Lord have mercy on my soul
Prayers get answered so I'm told
I hope it won't be when I'm too old
Because this ghetto is getting me
It's like living in a pit of snakes
Life here is full of pain and aches
You really have to have what it takes
But this ghetto is getting me

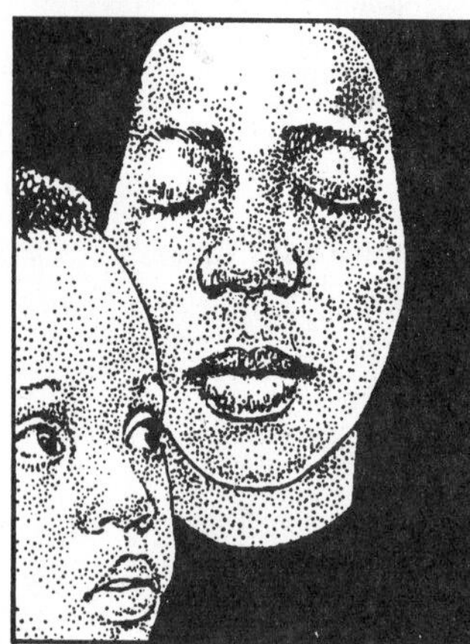

Once, I tried to rise to fame and
fortune
But I failed, because the devil was
dead on my trail
Now, life is full of misery
Nothing is like it ought to be
Of this ghetto, I'd like to be free
Because this ghetto is getting me
Lord have mercy and save me
Save me from this terrible ghetto
Because this ghetto is getting me.

Sally Heeney Killion
OUR NURSE
Whether practical or not
She registers with me a lot,
Be it therapy or pills
She is there to rectify our ills
Making sure we don't get worse,
She helps eliminate the curse
of lying there
no one to care.
GOD BLESS OUR DEDICATED
NURSE.

Stacey Steele-Wilkins
LIFE KEEPS GOING ON
Babies crying, mother's sighing,
Birds are singing, phones are ringing
Children screaming, faces beaming,
Life keeps going on.

Men are swearing, strangers staring,
And together no one's caring,
Life keeps going on.

Rapings, beatings, late night
meetings,
Homeless people barely eating,
Children still go trick or treating
Life keeps going on.

Teenagers walking, holding hands,
The banging sounds of pots and pans
The sounds of orchestras and bands,
That rattle all across the lands,
Life keeps going on.

Pushing, shoving, mugger's mugging
in the day or night,
Gangs out on the streets, just waiting
for a fight,
Men sit at the peace tables, trying to
make things right,
Life keeps going on.

Old folks dream of yesterday
Wishing it hadn't gone astray,
Wondering, How do we live this
way?
Life keeps going on.

People sit and moan and groan,
A dog is burying his bone,
Children growing, leaving home.
Life Keeps Going On.

Beverly A Feja
OH, HOW HAPPY WE USED TO BE

To my father, Harry T. Beadell Sr., who has Alzheimer's disease

When I was just a little girl, my hair
never had a bit of curl.
Just as white as white could be,
pigtails they were for me!
Bouncing on my daddy's knee. Oh,
how happy we used to be.

Remember going fishing early in the
morn, tried skippin' stones cross the
water.
My daddy would scorn "No no
you'll scare the fish away." Yup,
that's what he'd say.
Bouncing on my daddy's knee. Oh,
how happy we used to be.

Now my father, seeing you sitting
there, just strapped in your chair.
With sadness, confusion and despair.
Just who are those people standing
there?
Bouncing on my daddy's knee. Oh,
how happy we used to be.

Gone is the twinkle in those soft blue
eyes, your smile made us welcome.
With arms open wide. Your hair still
a crew-cut, that I recognize.
Bouncing on my daddy's knee. Oh,
how happy we used to be.

It's Alzheimer's disease daddy.
That's what they tell me.
And gone is the life that used to be.
Shared by many my father, not just
me.
Bouncing on my daddy's knee. Oh,
how happy we used to be. Just my
daddy and me.

Phyllis Joan Smith
GOD BLESS THE CHILDREN

For Chris, Blair, Cassie, Jace, and Kristen . . . my lifeline. From Gramma with love, hugs and kisses . . .

God bless the children . . .
I heard an angel say . . . .
Keep them from harm
Keep them safe at their mother's
breast
or tucked under a Father's arm
Watch over them at play
Watch over them when they lay
down to sleep
or when sickness comes their
way
God bless the children . . .
each night I pray . . .
That Heaven's angels stay close by
That God who is all wise
will spare them pain and keep
the tears
from these precious dears.
God bless the children . . .
Children everywhere . . . is my
prayer.

Barbara A Carroll
VESSEL OF THE SOUL

I dedicate this poem to my loving husband, Jimmy, whose love and support gave me the inspiration I needed to pursue my dreams.

The mind, a safe without a lock or
key,
A life-long vessel for our endless
thought,
The only container for our sanity
And the knowledge of life we must
be taught.
It works day and night but never
tires;
Pondering facets of daily life.
Bad memories like unquenchable
fires
Burn brightly their flames of hardship
and strife.
The mind, the origin of every deed,
Those of good intentions and of the
bad;
It gives the command and the flesh
takes heed,
The only ruler it has ever had.
Just prisoners of flesh our souls
would be
Without the mind's door to set our
thoughts free.

Jennifer Menke
I HOPE THIS BRINGS YOU CHEER

To my wonderful friend Ali On this page and in my heart, Love to you.

I hope this brings you cheer
because you are so truly dear;
You deserve to be happy
as happy as can be—
as a beautiful bird in his favorite tree.

When you seem down
It makes me frown.
It may seem a line, but
there does come a time
to declare when a friendship is
found;
And NO! you're not bound in any
which way,
just keep on smiling—today and
every day.

I know you really care
despite all the scare;
You've held up well in a world of
unrest
and never felt right to be less than
best.
You've inspired my mind
and made me feel kind . . .
For this, I thank you.

Lorna Hicks Ford
SEASONS
The seasons of our lives it seems,
can change from day to day.
Sometimes the things we hold so
dear can somehow slip away.

And there's a time in all our lives
when sunshine turns to rain.
The warmth and joy of laughter fade
to emptiness and pain.

We struggle for the answers, not
knowing where to turn;
only knowing something's missing,
for which we sadly yearn.

Friends and family try to help, and
offer words of hope;
but sometimes it's just not enough
and we find it hard to cope.

God never makes our burdens any
more than we can bear.
He helps us find an inner strength we
never knew was there.

And surely as the seasons change
and winter turns to spring,
the pain will pass as time goes on
and laughter comes again.

Amber Lynn Erie
EARLY DESERT NIGHT
The sky is blue
The desert sand is hot
The cactus grow with little water
The lizards and insects come out at
night
And seek their prey in the moonlight
of the night sky.

Ida M Taylor

Ida M Taylor
I HAVE A PLACE IN THIS WORLD

This poem is dedicated to my family

What can I be Why can't I see
I have a place in this world
When I think of the years that have
passed I often wonder why things
worked out the way they did.

Life is so short I can't believe how
long it really lasts
Over and Over I say to myself
I have a place in this world.

What can I be Why can't I see
I have a place in this world
When you are young you are taught
right from wrong
You learn to be proud walk with
your head in the clouds.

What can I be Why can't I see
I have a place in this world
Live each day the old fashion way
See the sun shine each and every day
Believe in yourself.

What can I be Why can't I see
I have a place in this world.

Diedra E Cates
LEGACY

This poem is dedicated to the memory of my son, Lee Dawson Cates, who left us all his love.

We go about our daily life
Dealing alone with toil and
strife.
Reaching out every month or so,
"Just thought I'd call to say
Hello."

Then death removes one from our

fold.
Oh, God, the grief can not be told.
Only then we close our ranks.
Only then we tell our thanks,
To those of us who still remain.
How good it is to share the pain.

Why did it take such a dire disaster
For all of us to finally master
This gift of loving for each other
And daily touching one another?

Jeffrey A Eddins
NO KIND OF LOVE
Pale as the moon-lit sky
dark as the clouds drift by
my heart shatters silently
as my soul begins to cry
No kind of hope
not even a dream
your love has left
and so has my happiness
it seems
No kind of love for me

Ronald T Stockton
"LOVE"—FOR LACK OF BETTER WORDS
"LOVE"—for lack of better words . . .
You know, I've never understood
The way you feel for me, the way
I feel, nor the way I should.

It hurts me deeply: helps when needed:
Carries me away (ship-following bird!).
You call it, surely I call it—
"LOVE" . . .
"LOVE"* for lack of better words.

Sean McGillis
BURNED OUT
Stood in the parking lot
Daughter by side
Seemed to smile
She didn't cry
Told of an old man
And a bottle of vodka
Candle fell over
A fire running wild
Gave the woman
Couple dollars
Little bit of change
She walked away
What she spent it on
I'll never know
Bottle of pills or
A place for her child to stay

Isabelle G Reilly
HOMAGE TO PICASSO

To my beloved grandchildren—Leigh, Jack, Laura and Anna

You are he who twists the line
Who makes it twirl and loop like twine
Who sings a song without a sound
Who lifts the green right off the ground
Who puts the red of passion's glow
On every moon here below
Who sees a vision near and far
Who saw—then caught—the falling star

Greg Lambert
IF PEOPLE ONLY KNEW!
I wish some body could reveal,
the loneliness and pain I feel.
I wish they could understand my need,
and listen to the pains I plead.
I really don't think I ask for much,
just some one's love and care and tender touch.
I really don't think it's much to ask,
but I find it such a difficult task.
No one these days seems to care.
There are material people every-where.
No one cares about people's feelings.
They concentrate on their own well beings.
Discouragement would be on the way,
if you could hear what people say.
I hear nothing good wherever I go.
it's a shame such feelings have to show.
If you know a way you can possibly help,
please stop these tears before I melt.

Kt Allard
LAUGHTER AND THUNDER
Laughter rolling through the skies
is the feeling I get when I see
your eyes.
Shared times always steals
lonely tears.
We never said never to life and
freedom
blasting our way through
the kingdom.
Always remember tomorrows time
can't be borrowed until
tomorrow.

Thunder rolling through the skies
is the anger I feel when I
hear your lies.
Broken tomorrows are stealing away
yesterdays memories.
Troubles won't wash away
with vanishing cream.
Never refuse a chance to challenge
a morning.
You just have to remember that a
new dawn follows
each mourning.

Karen S Kornahrens
LIVING'S A DIFFERENT STORY

To Mom & Dad, the best parents anyone could ever ask for.

When ya die ya go to Heaven or Hell, but living's a different story. Life is hard on every road, but death is easy on the payment of the loan. We live on borrowed time, and we pay our dues when we die. So don't be frightened of dying—it's life that takes its own.

The best of life is yours to give. Watch the world from up above, and it gives it back to you in time. Make your way through clouds and storms by keeping faith in God above. The good and bad times will balance out in the end. It's hard to see where the end will be.

Days and nights go in and out—as we're seeing things we never saw; our feelings changing with the times. Wishing we could work it out, but all things come to be. Just take the time to see.

Patricia Kabanuk
WHAT I'M FEELING NOW . . .
What I'm feeling now
makes me smile inside,
It's kind of like love
but let me confide.
Maybe it's the talking,
Maybe it's the laughter
or maybe it's the crying
that makes you feel good after.
It's always there
even if only in part
So listen closely
and I'll tell you my heart.
There isn't anything brighter,
or anything more great.
There's nothing more caring,
or free from hate.
Than this feeling of feelings,
my love for you
Believe in me now,
there's nothing more true.

Derace E Orput
SOFT NIGHTS
Soft nights and warm thoughts
Flow through me—
Moonlight washes the bare tree
outside;
Inside, shadows dance in eerie black
light.

Thoughts probe thoughts
Hands seek hands
Your eyes caress me
Light and music blend into one.

Thurman E Sharp

Charles E Sharp
WHAT DO I DO, HE'S GONE

Dedicated to THURMAN E. SHARP, My Father.

Since I was a child I've tried to do my best. My father showed me how, Without being such a quest
He guided me through life always telling me he was proud, and had a great son. No matter how much I leaned on him, or something I might have done.
He told me life has a choice, There is wrong and then there is right. But no matter which one you choose your parents always love you, And worry if you're not home at night.

So what do I do, because now he is gone. I know I have to live, I have to go on. But he died by some one's hand, and I didn't get to say goodbye. I couldn't ease his pain, Or put a gleam ion his eye.
My father knew I loved him, for that was no doubt. I always made sure I told him, and the kiss and hug were never left out.
I'll miss you dad, I'll miss the things we shared. But most of all I'll miss your love, and the way you showed you cared.
So remember to love today, because life can bring such sorrow. Don't fall back on the line, there's always tomorrow.

C Brice Garriott
INSPIRATION
Edgar Allen Poe with prose, and poetry brought fame,
Which came after his death in poverty, and shame.
He wrote of adventure, mystery, intrigue, and lore.
After losing his wife, "Quoth the Raven, 'Nevermore."

Poe, and Whitcomb Riley both imbibed too much,
But they both took time to write, and to get in touch
With their own innermost feelings, and write it down;
What they wrote in verse, or paragraph brought them renown.

The greatest of comedians, the greatest of songs—
Come from the saddest hearts, and deepest wrongs.
People are not happy just by wanting to be;
But they profit by mistakes, and help others to see.

If one should set aside a little time of each day,
To let not his inspirations be lost on the way;
If he should consecrate his mind in use of his pen,
He might find treasures within his own den.

So what if it is never published, or never read?
The ore has to be dug for, whether it's gold, or lead.
Even if you've ability, the talent of the best;
"God" can inspire, but "You" must do the rest.

Charles R Mezzacapo
HEADLINES
Sanyo radio, Zenith T.V., dad smacks ma around;
I hope he don't hit me.

Preacher-man gives in to sex, kids are snorting coke, fat-cat in a cadillac says the country's going broke.

Football, basketball, some mid-east nut wants it all. We better release his terrorist kin before a nuclear war begins.

Aids on the rampage, crime in the city, starving children in Africa; it truly is a pity. Drought stricken farmer, man in the gutter; out stoned drunk, report card on the way; I'd say we all flunked.

Sonia Dainty
THE NIGHT MAIDEN
Have you seen the maiden of the night with golden hair?
Have you felt her thought to be gentle and kind?
Have you found the color of her heart clear and fair?
When you saw her face in fashion shine.
It was trimmed with star light

glare;
In the shadows of the night
she hides;
Frightened of the darkness
stare;
Her soul she lifted close to
mine.
She walked into the gardens
flair;
Where she sadly trembling die.
She climbed into heavenly
stairs;
And lonely, I sit in silent cry.

Joe Leavell
LOVING DOVES

To my dearest darling Eydie whom hath this lover's heart, may your wish be ever greedy for my love to never part.

I have brought to you my love to
your mountain through the pass,
while I rode the wings of doves
that provided safeties path.
As I climb our loving stairway
while I tug upon your hand, you
still wonder if this fairway's just
another pit of sand.
I have placed you in my heart
and enshrouded you with love,
in hopes my loving sparks doth
create two loving doves.
While the angels sing and dance
your decision you still ponder,
we'll continue our romance on
our mountain with its splendor.

With my love I bring to you I
have brought a stake and chain,
to insure my love stays true and
doth never ever change.
When we innerlock our love as
two loving doves will do, we can
feel what loving does from atop
a mountain view.
We can love by early light and by
dim of candle glow, and it'll
always be so right when we love
with heart and soul.
From this love that's always near
comes a warming from its touch,
and from days and nights so
dear come the flowers by the
bunch.

With our fate before our eyes we
can vision our capture, and from
faces bearing smiles we doth
treasure total rapture.
From the hand that giveth
strength to hand that giveth
light, comes a mighty hearty
thanks and a prayer to make it
right.
With true love that never parts
we will find in every corner, a
fulfillment of the heart in a love
that never wanders.
From fulfillment of our dreams
through the moments I've
envisioned, comes a plea bearing
rings for our day never ending.

Richard Don Catlett
TRAGEDY HAS STRUCK MY LIFE

Dedicated to James Lewis Forrester-Expired: 3-28-88

Tragedy has struck my life
Because I lost a friend tonight
I've taken it hard
I've taken it bad
Because he was the best friend I've
ever had
He wasn't only a friend
He was a brother
Because we meant a lot to each other
He isn't here
But he isn't dead
Because he's alive in my head
Jim was great
We were seldom apart
He'd do anything to win your heart
So now I tell you
With all my heart
Jim's alive
He's in our hearts

Lucie Adams
BEWILDERED POEM

To my friend, Audrey Custy, who understands life.

Magic slot-machine for random
muses waits
instructs
insert random feelings
—oh trembling fingers—
gamble the laughter only

the spinning ends
two hopes and a lemon roll up

the poet blinks steps back stares
at the hands that flicked
long time ago
pennies into an enchanted fountain

forgot the wishes made there
as soon as a new thought intruded

here it is the poem
made from last year's second chance
and tomorrow's wild ladies
somewhere in the middle
where lopsided truths pay absence

everything-everywing-lemon

Gloria Cox

Gloria Cox
A BUNNY TALE
The Easter Bunny rang your bell,
There was no answer, he said "Oh,
swell.
What to do, oh dear, oh dear,
Dogs, dogs, that's what I hear!
To the barn, I'll quickly hop,
Have no time for dogs to stop.
My little heart is all aquiver,
The Dettbarns' basket to deliver.
With more baskets, I'm running late,
All your dogs and cats, there a
bunny's fate.
Made the barn, still have my tail,
Here's your basket, so I'll hit the
trail."

Arline Heckenlaible
LOSS
Losing a friend isn't the end of the
world
However you might wish it were,
You grieve awhile and then go on
With days as mundane as before,
With thoughts as bound by here and
now
As tho you hadn't felt a nudge
remindful of the
Fleetingness of meetings, partings,
sorrow, joy,
Losing a friend isn't the end of the
world
It's just the start of living with a
broken heart.

Susan E Rowan
MY DECLARATION OF LOVE

To my dear husband, Tony, who is my strength and my inspiration.

My darling how I love you
I cannot say how much
My heart is overflowing
I'm weak from just your touch.
I've never felt sensations
so deeply through my soul
I'll never feel this way again
to you I want to show—
That you're my inspiration,
my lover and my friend.
With you I am invincible
our love will never end.
My heart beats one with yours
your breath becomes my breath
When we become one person
our loving has no depth.
My friend, my love, my sweet,
you are life to me
I'll love you 'til I live no more—
then through eternity.

Joyce Sabin Rescia
US

For Michael Geoffrey
May our passion remain with Destiny

Our shared moments are precious
your memory smiles in my heart
your sky blue eyes
your boxer shorts
your hands that feel like silk
your freckled back
the warmth of your kisses
the tender love we make
in the darkness of the night
as you lie next to her
do I haunt you?

T M Forbes
ODE TO LESSONS PAST
No bitterness remains
With the fading of my sight.
There is no victory, but there's peace
In losing battle . . .losing fight.
Although hope is lost as my body
fades,
My inner self I keep.
And my wounds become only scars
As I fall deeply into sleep.

Melvin T Phippin
THE PARTING

To my daughters, Lee Ann and Suzanne

Oh, rapturous life, departing from
me;
No more of thy beauty shall my
eyes see.
No more shall I touch, nor gently
caress;
Nor feel the warmth of a
maiden's sweet kiss.
No more to inhale of the rose's
perfume;
Nor watch as the lily unfolds
into bloom.
No more shall I gaze upon children
at play;
Nor sense the stillness at the
dawn of new day.
No more to behold all the wonders of
life, but
No sadness to feel for its
struggle and strife.
Now the parting is nigh and my time
has drawn near;
As my soul takes its wing, shed
for me not a tear
But Sweet Life, let your pleasures
forever remain
As part of my memory, till I live
once again.

Lona Parker
THE MAN WHO TENDS BIRDS

To another poet and beloved daughter, Hilary Hult.

The man who tends birds
does this with an understanding
of his gray, delicate wards.
Drillmaster of his sky-bound
battalion,
he is very demanding.

He loves his creatures of flight
but does not hold them tight.
He knows that the feather
would crush as easily as the spirit.
His birds fly all night.

Once he took me to his sanctuary
and introduced me to his keep.
How I envied the birds
their proud and generous master—
to be loved, fed and free!

J Ayers
HIDING
I was so alone when we met
confident on the outside
and yet crying from within.
You came and examined me
like an intriguing book;
attracted by the cover
and curious enough to look in.
I was afraid
when you turned pages,
scanning the chapters of my heart;
challenged by your interest
and careful of you questioning.
In the words of my experiences
you uncovered secrets of my soul.
you were the first to like what you
found;
not trying to change anything
but accepting me.
I know now there is no need to hide.
I'm free at last
and can be completely me.

M T Clayton
SYMBOL OF A ROSE

For Marilyn, who understands

Once upon a little seed
There came a great desire,
To symbolize the warmth that sets
A lover's heart afire.
And so it grew so beautiful
That it became a part
Of all the happiness contained
Within a lover's heart.
And yet the beauty it conveys
Is meant for only those
Who understand the message that
Is carried by a rose.

Denise A Rock
WHERE ARE YOU GOING?
Oh my child, my child Where are
you going
Oh my love, my love What are
you knowing
I'm your friend, fear me not
Tell me your secrets, show me what
you got

Little children play your game
When you grow up life is not the
same
Smile, laugh, show all gladness
Before life begins to show all
sadness

Run to daddy, kiss mommy goodnight
Don't worry my child about the darkness fright
Oh my child it's starting to rain
I know your little heart feels all the pain.

In the morning when you arise
Smile before you lose life's prize
Put on your clothes, run to the door
Enjoy your life a whole lot more
Play in the grass, swing on the tree
Run wild my child while you're still free
Confide in mommy, she's your friend
And love your daddy again and again.

Violet Henson Anderson

HOUSEHOLD TASKS

When I arose this morning and looked around,
All about me unfinished tasks could be found,

The dishes I'd left from the night before;
This was the day to vacuum the floor;

Beds unmade; clothes to be washed;
Ironing to be done; I felt so squashed.

With all these jobs that were facing me,
I really wanted to turn and flee!

But, slowly I filled my coffee cup,
And sat right down to sum things up.

If I should leave them all and run,
When I returned, they'd still be undone.

So why put off the inevitable tasks?
Why not bow my head and ask

For strength to run my household today,
Then pitch in and begin without delay.

Andera Sullivan (DUZAN)

MY MATE THAT YOU SENT

My loving thanks to you, Aunt Shirley Harrison. You believed in me when I was at the bottom. You instilled me to put my trust in the Lord, which I did and look where I am now.

My prayer of thanks, for my mate that you sent.
Sadness and Loneliness have vanished, I don't know where they went.
When at the weakest point in my life
You aided me, loved me and taught me about strife
My shoulders were too narrow to carry the load.
I walked the troublesome road where happiness once rode.
My sons kept me strong, but drained my body's best.
What I would have given for one peaceful night of rest.
A college career a new priority, destined to pursue.
Hours of excitement and fun dwindled to very few.
Turmoil, fear, and anger tormented much of the time.
You comforted me, touched my heart, taught me life is sublime.
Without the new comfort that touched my heart,
A happy future would fail to start.
Stumbling blocks were presented in the oddest forms.
Dyslexia, poor health, no money, all daily norms.
I hurdled each trouble and drew strength to endure.
Creation of my new soul is supremely pure.
You blessed us with shelter, however; I have lived in better.
You provided us with food and protected us from the weather.
You didn't forewarn me of the storm near the end.
Patience, dignity, all elements you forgot to send.
Those are not gifts, but skills I wish to learn.
At least when in doubt, I know where to turn.
Thank you for the wonderful mate that you sent.
Lack of more time to share with him is all I resent.

Bertha E C Gromada

Bertha E C Gromada

LOVE

To all my children—short and tall—
Love each other
One and all.   Mother

Love lost, love won
Love kindled the heart,
Blood pressure begun.

Love can kill,
It also can bear,
A man here or anywhere;

Love can live, love can die;
It saves a truth
By telling a lie;

Love is big, it can be small,
The Smallest is that Love,
The love for all.

Love is kind, sometimes crude,
Does it depend on what—
What kind of mood?

Love brought first curse to man
It brought great wealth
From another lan';

Love caused war among our Gods,
Peace brought rejoicing
In the fields of goldenrods.

Clarence R Slagle

WHAT A WONDERFUL WORLD THIS WOULD BE

To all my children and grandchildren

If there could be no more
heartaches and sorrow,
If we could live a life that is free,
And then awake to a brighter tomorrow,
"What a wonderful world this would be,"
If there could be no more
hunger and sickness,
No one living in poverty,
If all our hearts could be filled
with kindness,
"What a wonderful world this would be,"
If there could be no more
fighting and dying,
No more wars far across the seas,
And there could be no more
sadness and crying
"What a wonderful world this would be."

JOHN HOWARD Price

HEART STRINGS

To Miss Elly—for twenty years of love and understanding

As I walk along this windswept beach,
Searching for somewhere to start.
Thinking hard for some way to reach,
Those strings that control your heart.

Staring out at the rolling sea.
Waves topped with whitecaps, one and all.
Desperately wanting you to love me,
As the waves rise and then fall.

Then looking up where the seagulls fly.
As their silhouettes cross the sun.
Wondering if I should sit down and cry.
And if I did would I then come undone?

With a furtive glance, just one quick look.
From this place I begin to depart.
Yes, my love for you could fill a book.
Damn, where are those strings to your heart?

Anamaria R vom Scheidt

NONNA

To my Grandmother, whose ageless grace and beauty continues to inspire the lives of those around her.

The light in her eyes,
a cornflower blue,
shimmers like beads
in the morning dew.

Her hair, once flaxen,
gold, and light
is now a snowy,
downy, white.

Years of life
criss-cross her face;
a map of time
etched deep in place.

But on the map
that time has inked
are bits of life
that smile and wink
and laugh and live
and love anew,
and tell the world
through eyes so blue.

Sharon L Congdon

OUR PARENTS

This poem is dedicated with love to my parents, John and Georgianna

Forty years of married life,
love to last a lifetime long.
After you exchanged your vows,
we began to come along.

Johnny as your first born boy,
Sharon as your next small joy.
Diane, your third blessing.
Ray, who still keeps you guessing.
Eileen was next to bless your home,
Peanut was the last to come.
By now your family must be done,
Six children are enough for anyone.
With lots of love yet to give,
God blessed you both with two more kids.
Kathy was just as sweet as gold,
and Kenny such a joy to hold.

Your family was at last complete,
no family anywhere quite so sweet.

Through joy and sorrow, laughter and pain,
Our loving parents you have always remained.
We wish you both happiness on your special day,
We all love you and need you in every way!

Your loving children,

Johnny, Sharon, Diane, Ray,
Eileen, Peanut, Kathy, Kenny

40th Anniversary—January 16, 1989

Maureen Kennedy Lach

IN MEMORY OF A VETERAN

For eyes that see

Land
bulge

Bloated with
burnt bodies

Bagged
eyes swollen
staring
at a blank face
cut in half

Bent over
earth
sagging
soaked with sweating

Seeds
floating
in black holes

Begging
for the
Sun

Christie Morgan

REMEMBER ME

Looking back on the way it had been
I don't think I could stand to live it over again
But I just want to ask one thing
That's to
Remember me, as we go our separate ways

Remember me, and the plans that we made
Remember me, in the oncoming days
Just remember me
The final good-bye has been said
We've both found another instead of what it used to be
No more tears shall fill my eyes
For the past has already gone by
But please
Remember me, though forever we part
Remember me, 'cause we're making a new start
Remember me, in your heart
I don't ask for your love
And I don't ask for your care
I just ask one thing
Remember me.

Angelica del Carmen Varela Menendez

Angelica del Carmen Varela Menendez
I MISS YOU

To everyone who encouraged me to give it a try and to my mother who was willing to let me. To that special person in my life with love! Thank you.

It's been so very long,
And I feel so alone.
I remember the night we met,
I just couldn't forget
The way you held me in your arms,
Showing me so many charms.
I remember the tears
And the moments we were near,
We thought we'd be together,
Or so we hoped forever.
I loved you but you didn't see,
So you set me free.
Everytime I see a dove,
I think of love
And how I wish you were here
So you could hear
When I said "I miss you,"
And I wish I could have pleased you!

Caroline Buckman
LEAVES OF SUMMER, 1988

To my family

Soft winds rustle
Leaves and flowers
As I recline in shade,
Shadows dance across
Green grass and the
Vibrant colors kaleidoscope
Into my view,
Yellow bird perches
On terra-cotta bath
Suspended on slim legs.
Soft, long summer afternoons
And lazy day dreams
Encompass my thoughts.
Where are you, my love?
Have we spent many hours
Together, romancing the
Summer winds and clime?
A time to remember . . .
My heart's in California
Close by the sea
Waves lapping, white-capped,
Drumming in my memory,
White beach sands
Pour across my toes
As we cheer the surfers
On nearby.
We are far from noise
And city streets,
Shouts and riots and
Cops on beats.
We shall ascend to a
Ruff-hewn cabin on a cliff
Overlooking the blue sea—
And drink a toast
To my live-in host
As we celebrate
This eighteenth day of
August, eternally.
Mary, mary, mary,
Marry, merry, marigolds,
What does fate have
In store for you?
Your golden petals drop
One by one on top the
Red rocks and sand.
You vanish and wither—
But I remember how
You brightened all my days
And summers.
So when I see you again
My heart beats fast—
And I recall the last
Golden dance of summer.

Frank A Schoemaker
THE ENTERTAINER

The room is bare,
There are but few bodies draped over the tables and chairs
The stagelights come on and I stand there,
bathing in a yellow light.
In the distance of my mind
a thundering applause hums in my ears
I bow slightly, mockingly,
then shuffle among the tangled wires on stage
and I pick up my guitar
I look intensely in the darkness
and I wonder if the song I'll sing
Will awaken the hearts and minds
Not caring, not giving a damn!
A light strum, and a song filled with poetry fills the air:
"Measured miles before me . . . .
Away from your loving arms
and smile . . ."

I'm engrossed in my music now,
I don't give a damn if no one listens
My heart is far away with you
And the song I sing is you!
My voice vibrates with tenderness
And my heart cries out to touch you
But the song is ended and the light goes out
And another night has passed.

Jocelyn Rochelle Jackson
HUSH NOT ONE WORD!

To my grandparents Willie & Laura Johnson and Clarence & Bernice Jackson. I would like to thank you for all the love and support you've given me. Love, Penny

he knows not what he does to you
a friendly look or gentle touch
burns your body's flesh, like the
beating sun in the Sahara desert
turns your mind to putty
dreams of him emerge in the night
fantasies are all you have

HUSH NOT ONE WORD! !

you try to find a peace of mind
that brings to you a pleasure unknown
you long to kiss his smiling lips
for him to hold you is your wish
to want to know his every desire
you yearn for it; you're on fire
you kiss one man; and dream of another
this is something he mustn't discover

HUSH NOT ONE WORD! !

but you know it can never be
so the fight is on within your soul
turn your emotions off with a switch
so that he may not see the flaming
urgency within your glistening eyes
you would rather remain friends that say good-bye

HUSH NOT ONE WORD! !

Joyce Johnson
REVELATION

To my beloved Father Sterling, who said you are good, and Fay who made me participate.

Man has to reflect upon his own image before editorializing on the vast picture.
There has to be a light which will penetrate the depth of the soul, devoid of "race-colored" glasses.

For when the true essence of the soul is revealed, there lies a choice . .we can opt to either accept or reject. Should man refuse to look at the light, he shall remain locked in time, anticipating and receiving a continuous void. He will look at the past forever, with words of . ."Why me?" Not realizing that it is . . "because of me!"

Inevitably, frustration sets in and intensifies itself to the extent that the resulting wrath shall be witnessed and felt by all.

Sorrow.

When the light is on, definite changes are visible and tangible; for man walks upright, and upward into the present, but most important, he has an understanding of the past, and at times, will be able to predict the future.

There are a few who have gone with the light; I can tell . . and most assuredly, they know! . . for they are that rare breed who took the time to reflect and discover that truth . . honesty . . and self-esteem are to be sought and found in introspective thought and consideration.

Peace. Joy.

Vivian Hamilton
FRIENDS

Oh! What a blessing a friend can be
They are one of God's gifts to you and to me.

We strive for our goals,
There are problems no end,
But we keep on-a-going
Because of friends.

It may be a tear, a sigh or just mirth,
To share with our friends
While we're still on this earth.

Thank you my friend
You have often brought smiles,
But more important to me
You make life worthwhile.

Thank you dear Lord for the gift of these friends,
Each is so very dear
Bless them and keep them in your circle of love
Today and all through the years.

Anita N Rajeswaren

Anita N Rajeswaren
AMERICA

This great country is my home
Down yonder in the cornfields I roam.

There are buttercups and lilies
adorned at my feet.
I really think they look neat.

I see the strong eagle gliding in the sky,
I'd do anything to be up so high.
America takes me to where all my dreams lie.

I'll walk through forests, plains, and hills.
Maybe I'll even see some old sawmills.

Wherever I go, I'll be sure to find
Marvelous adventure with my keen mind.

Thrills, chills, excitement, and fun;
America has it all.
America that's so wide and tall.

Lilies are white, raindrops are blue.
I love my country and I hope you do too.

Mrs Murl (Wanda) Blair
I WONDER HOW HEAVEN WILL BE

I wonder how Heaven will be,
Like the roses without any thorns,
The white lilies with a fragrance so sweet,
Or mixed flowers of many colors,
What a beauty that will be.

I wonder how Heaven will be,
Like the trumpets sounding so majestically,
Or the harps with melodious sounds,
The instruments playing glory to the King.

I wonder how Heaven will be,
Saints of glory, robed in white,
Standing with hands raised and singing,
Hallelujah to the King of Kings.

I wonder how Heaven will be,
A mansion prepared for me,

Arms outstretched to receive me,
Oh what glory that will be.

I wonder how Heaven will be,
No sorrow, no tears, only joy and peace,
With loved ones and friends all around
"Oh to be like Him, Christ the King."

Amy E Clark
CRAZY
I know that I am going crazy.
Things easily remembered, seem hazy.
Words easily said become mumbled.
Simple thoughts become jumbled.

I know that I am going crazy.
Energy's gone, now I feel lazy.
Constant Smiles become dominant frowns,
usual ups become frequent downs.

I need to get away.
I must escape this very day.
I just feel like laying down to cry.
Oh God, I wish I would just die!

Jenni K Parker
A MEMORY SAVED FOR TOMORROW
You showed me a day
more precious than the rest.
You bought me flowers.
My thanks was a kiss.
You showed me that love
was more than I thought.
That feelings have a place;
love can't be bought.
The little things you said
will always linger in my heart.
Sadness finds me thinking
of the miles that spread us apart.
You're very special;
someone I thought I'd never find.
A miracle that's implanted
in the corners of my mind.
Our day was short,
but so well spent.
My love lasts forever,
not just for rent.
But our day finally ended.
What more can I say?
We may not have tomorrow . . .
but at least we had today.

Wayne Howell
MY WILLOW

For Wynona Allen and many lifetimes

The silver green of the willow
tree makes me weep.
She casts her shadows low,
hidden, so none will seek.
She lies in the harshest terrain,
unaided, low and green.
Weep-o-willow, for I understand
That some in nature must suffer,
Why else the ignorance of man?
Willow low though only a tree,
Know this,—I love thee.

Manuel Peralta
GIVE IT A SHOT

To all future immigrants

the immigrant's plight is sad:
being a minority . . .?
the local experience's needed;
and entry-level he wrote.
"no vacancy!" retorted.
how does he get the shot?
he's refused and ignored.
the immigrant's plight is sad:
he's down and out . .
up and about to get the shot.
determination was the attitude
from zero he got to start,
from patience he's bent to find
the lucky break and be given
the shot.
the apple is big
opportunities are wide
but narrow is the chance
to get the tiniest shot.
the immigrant's plight is sad—
who would give him the shot?

Cynthia Colby
NIGHT
Oh blank and blind and blue-black night,
In mystery shrouded deep;
So blind to artist's color-sight,
How well designed for——sleep!!

Clifton Stevenson

Clifton Stevenson
MEMORY IS

To: My Old Schoolmates of Colony School

Memory is blue hills, blue skies,
dark green valleys below.
Memory is birds singing, where
eagles cry, music everywhere
you go.

Memory is trails of thought
leading on and on,
Back to inquiring youth, and taste
of time forever gone.

Memory is a melody with sounds
of many parts, like the call of a
raven flying wild and free.
Memory is a deep rolling river
flowing through the heart,
carrying lonely waters back to
the sea.

Memory is a dagger piercing
painfully deep,
Into hearts of the weary, robbing
them of sleep.

Memory is therapy to the old and
worn, like placing of flowers on
a loved one's tomb.
Memory is discriminative to the
yet unborn, reposing with God in
their Mother's womb.

Memory is golden rays of a
setting sun, like the last fading
smile of a loved one passing.
Memory is toils of life never
done, and whispers of love
everlasting.

Brenda Martin
LOVE
Love is someone who shares feelings.
It is trusting and loving many things about each other.
It is caring about someone you really love.
It is missing him and knowing that
he is missing you, and
Telling him that you love him

My Love will always be true.
Because it was given to me to share
with you. I love you and I always
will. I'll always be there when you
need a helping hand.

I know you will always be there for
me too,
For sometimes I might need a
shoulder when I am feeling blue.

You and I will be together, not just
now, but forever.
So take this poem and put it in mind,
and just remember,
I'll love you till the end of time.

Deborah A Rhoades
A PRAYER OF BLESSINGS FOR A FRIEND

To Carmel, my closest and dearest friend, who inspired this poem. You always brighten my cloudiest of days, with your sunshine. Thank You C. B.!

May your days be filled with laughter,
May the sun shine bright on your face.
May you never have a worry,
For your smile will take its place.

May the winds blow you gently,
always to the right place.
And may you walk softly, oh with
style and with grace.
May your burdens be light and not
such a constant ache.
And may the path of life on which
you walk,
Be paved with riches, that only you
can spot.

May the rain fall softly on your face,
To quench the thirsts of your known
and unknown tastes.

But most of all, may the Good Lord
bless and keep you,
In His loving care.
And may He always walk beside you,
In your troubles and despair.

May a kind word or gentle hand,
Always let you know.
That in this difficult world of ours,
You're never, never, oh never alone.

David A Markey
SOLITUDE'S GRACE
Deep in thought
My mind can wander
On land or sea
Or clouds asunder
Drifting, diving
And climbing the skies
Nothing can hold back
This immaculate high
I am the grass
And then a tree
I am the wind
So no one can see
For this is my place
In my own mind's eye
For in Solitude's Grace
I find no lie

Judith M Kohan
SILHOUETTED
Silhouetted
in a golden halo
As bright red flames
of
Autumn fire
burn long into the night
Autumn Angels
in
Kaleidoscope Costumes
Patterned in
Earthly shades of
orange gold and green
Dance mystery under harvest moon
arriving on the scene

Alan Jay Beyer
VALLEY FORGE, PA
The brown log huts of gloom
where Minutemen froze to death
waiting for Spring's promise
of a chance for a new life,
are haunted by cold, icy spirits.

Apparitions with limbs wrapped in rags
huddled silently around low night fires,
frozen in a restless spirit world
being eternally hunted, pursued,
by the King's army in red.

The blacktop road through the valley
built by men of the new life to see
where the ghosts of Minutemen linger,
in lasting tribute to lost, frozen souls,
itself freezes over each Winter.

Michael Lee Pope
CARTOON HEROES
Petty Musers,
In a gallery of FOOLS—
Degenerates, Artisans of
Menial Existence,
Surrounded by Obvious
Hypocrisy!—
Intermittent "splish-splashes!"
of Genius—Struggling to surface
into Gurus—
Creation of "Infinitely-finite!"
Structures of molecular and
Chemical devices, Elemental in
Fatalism"—
"LEAVING MANDATORY
SUICIDE!"—

Doris N Martinez
EPHEMERAL PASSAGE
Roaming through the roads of life
Absorbing nature's majestic sights,
Giving yourself to mankind;
One worthy treasure, love divine.

Rosalie Smith
LIFE IS WHAT WE MAKE IT
Life is so precious, we've often heard
it said,
And this point is made in books we
have read;
Make the most of each moment
every day,
And life's richest blessings may
come your way.
Have faith in yourself and in your
own worth
And in this way bless the day of your
birth;
You have a rich heritage—this you
know,

Use your initiative and keep it so.

Make friends of God's children
whene'er you can;
Things don't just happen—God has a plan.
Success' ladder, friends can help you climb
And you'll find that life is great time after time.
Aim for the best that you can ever be,
Wildest dreams can become reality.
Climb the highest mountain, shoot for the stars,
Life can be a melody with string guitars.

Yes, LIFE IS WHAT WE MAKE IT day after day,
And we can make it great—there is a way,
We can find pure joy in life if we but strive.
Isn't it just wonderful to be alive?

Donald R Stull
TIME

Time—time to be alone and ponder is an oft sought thought.
Many times I have this greedy need.
But time—time won't hold still until I collect myself.

'Tis such a crafty cagy thing and passes without a whisper as softly and gently as an evening breeze.
A simple pause and it is gone.
I cannot call it back; it owes me no debt.

In desperation, I take it and retreat to a favorite spot and do what I ought!
Ah, alone—alone at last to ponder.
Such self indulgence I do need.
Then sinking to my knees, I thank HIM for this feast and try to tame the beast.

But time—time I still cannot grasp it—it won't hold fast.
It sneaks in swiftly and quietly as a thief taking its unrelenting toll.
Oh, time, you wretch, you villain—robber of my youth!
But, bold one, after you have plied your trade, I'll be your slave no more.
I'll be on THE MASTER'S SHORE; and for me, you'll be no more!

Rustee L Hicks
FIRST LOVE

Love is a game
I was a victim or should I say playing piece
So excited and hard to be tame
Older people make you feel like you're on your knees
It was a pleasurous game but, you can't win, lose, or give in
If you give him the first move it was a mistake
If you make the first move he will not play
If you give in he will play with someone else until they give in
Next time I will play to win.

Sharon A Ellis
WAITING

To Lorie, 'The Kid,' my editor in chief.

The old house groans and creaks
Is It listening or trying to speak?
Of the evil that was once there
Waiting for you

You try to erase those dark shadows
Try to hide in the deep, damp hollows
But It will always be near
Waiting for you

When you open a closet door
Or walk across a cold floor
You'll feel It waiting there
Waiting for you

The old house will talk someday
In It's own homely way
About the ghosts still waiting there
Waiting for you

Karen G Steele

Karen G Steele
MAKING LOVE

He watches my face as he slowly undresses
Knowing that with my eyes I gently caress
His body so lovely, so slender and smooth
And comes to me tenderly with lips to woo
The surrender he knows comes from me with his love
To soar us both towards heaven above
We lay in unison our souls blent together
Savoring precious moments, part of us forever.

Shelena Vannattan
THE SOUND OF A DISTANT ECHO

Walking in the forest,
Wading through the velvet green,
I saw me by your side
On the banks of an icy stream.
—it 's the sound of a distant echo;
Just a worn and tattered dream.

In the shadow of the trees
I can see the two of us.
Together, alone in the darkness
Of a lavender colored dusk.
But it's the sound of a distant echo
Of a love that turned to rust.

And the sound of a distant echo
Can break a heart in two,
For I still hear your voice at night
Whispering "I love you"
—And I roam the shadowy forest
In a dusk that's tear-stained blue.

Art Stewart
VIBRATORY LAW

All things in vibratory law sealed,
Only in reflection to man's mind revealed.
Thus is cosmic harmony secure
From man's inverted touch and mind—
Alas, the blind to lead the blind.

Only in Christ's Light of Triune One
Can man find man in earth and sun;
This the keys to the Kingdom wrought.
All else is naught.

Come ye brethren in exile living;
Awaken to the song in your heart
And spirit ringing;
Come Home, Come Home with joy singing.

Through spheres and orbits vast
Thy heart alone knows the way.
Its light and warmth from God's own
Hand flow—Thy heart alone knows!

Anne Moats
WHEN MY DAY COMES

When I have to leave this Earth,
When it is my day,
I want dear God to bless my soul,
And everyone to pray.

Dawn Watson
HIS LOVE

His love was greater than anything.
She never thought he could love her this way.
He loved her with such passion,
That made her love him more.
He brought something out that was deep within her.
She never knew she could love someone this way.

Then she woke up from her dream.
But his love was not a dream this time.
It was soft sweet words and oh so kind.

Tikeshay J Fleming
SAD LITTLE BLACK CHILD

To my mom, Betty J. Fleming, thanks for your encouragement and just know I love you.

Hey, Sad Little Black Child,
What is wrong?
Do you feel you don't belong?
Are you this way because of your color?
You wish you could fit in like the others.

You can't do lots of things because you're poor.
Praying every night, you wish you had more.
But don't worry; strive for the best.
Prove to the world you're better than the rest.
And Sad Little Black Child if you don't succeed,
Turn to God; he'll help you indeed.

Joyce H Swenson
THE AWAKENING

As I stand here, alone, amidst the towering trees,
The radiant sun's rays sift through the misty morn,
Warming this land of rebirth.
God's wooden creations stand firm within the ageless soil,
New life flowing once again through their coarse veins,
While returning birds perch upon their immortal framework.
Their limbs sway and bend with enduring strength
To the gentle winds that brush against my face.
The breathtaking scent of new growth fills the air
As they break through the nurturing ground in still motion,
Their invisible roots reach out as umbilical cords,
Drawing in nourishment from Mother Earth.
Tiny beads of shimmering dew lie on emerging blades of grass,
The moisture savored by the offspring of last year's slumber.
I can sense the tiny insects lying still and silent,
In darkness, just beneath my feet,
Waiting for the sweet nectars of life to sustain them.
I breathe deep and sigh at this world of forgotten beauty.
For life itself evolves around this gallant spirit of nature,
Awakening to its endless time clock.

Joan Williamson
MY YOUNG BALLERINA

To daughter Heather. Her love shows every time she dances

She's dancing in spring
Free as a breeze
With beautiful colors
As she swirls you see

She's light as the wind
Graceful as a gazelle
Beautiful and lighthearted
She is as well

As she swirls
She is happy and free
She loves to dance
As you can see

Just to see her there
Makes your heart sing
Her heart full of joy
And her feet on wing

Her teacher is proud
To see her out there
Her dancing like a bird
Her beauty to share

So proud—so proud

Mahalia Bogle
I AM NO ARTIST

To: My Sweet Grandmother—Olga My Beautiful Children—Tamara & Carlton My Loving Mother & Father—Maria & Carlton

I am no artist,
I have no famous name
But I'm someone that God gave a complaint
In his mind, He sees,
people lusting
stealing for greed
using sex so freely
gains is no means
Killing for dope,
Raping for pleasure
There's no unity,
Black to White
Rich to Poor
For him you must Love not Hate
You may not forget,
At least allow your
heart to forgive
My friends I pray, You stop and think today.
Acknowledge that Giving and Sharing
could make a better way
And take a moment, If you dare....
If God didn't want you here
He would take back his most precious gift
Air
Read all ye that God has made
Take Heed
Please
I shall leave this thought with you

I'll begin as such,
What If?
God's Heaven,
So Sweet
Didn't have a place for you to rest
Your
Knees
Mahalia
Inspired by. God the Father
God the Son
God the Holy Spirit

Lois Humphrey

Lois Humphrey
SOMETIMES

Dedicated to those who read this verse

Sometimes a bit of song invades my consciousness
To hold spellbound a moment from the past,
When love, and joy, and hope
Were things we thought would last.

Sometimes words fitly written by a kindred soul
Refresh a memory grown dimly sad . . .
Transcends the mystery of
A world gone wildly mad.

Sometimes the birds perform a wondrous symphony,
The crystal clear sounds fragmenting the air.
I listen . . . stilled . . . enthralled,
To the message they bear.

Sometimes a fragrance from nature's field or garden
Recalls a poignant sweetness for a while . . .
Gently stirs my being,
My senses to beguile.

Sometimes a smile of friendliness, a laugh of cheer,
Gladdens my spirit, promises accord,
And mends the broken strings
Of mutual regard.

Margaret Given
VOYAGE TO THE ISLANDS
Beautiful days of clear, hot light;
The evening sky, pale pink and golden bright.
And always the sea.
The islands are even more beautiful because you are there.

The shining moon, the stars shimmering,
twinkling above the palms.
The slightest breeze whispering in the sails.
The sea is even more calm
because you are there.

The song of the wind, in this garden speaks magic.
The soft murmuring of the sea—
Real joy is in this music.
The voyage is even better
because you are there.

My love, with your blue sailor's eyes
Strong and chivalrous.
I love you. Everything is serene.
Life is even more sunny
because you are near me.

Alma Greif
I SEE THE GREAT SAVIOUR BEFORE ME

This poem is dedicated to my son Sidney L. Greif, who died the same year I wrote the poem, 1976, I had written the poem before his death.

I see the great Saviour before me.
I'll go with you, each step of the way—
You are no longer alone, for—
I'm right by your side,
I love you for you are my own.

Oh! what Joy to walk daily with Jesus,
To hear His sweet voice, "come along."
His presence so sweet, I kneel at His feet,
I'll walk close by His side all day long.

I see the door open before me.
Come into the fold and sup with Me.
Communion you will find, waiting just inside,
Come in and thy soul shall be free.

Do you hunger and thirst after Me?
Just come in, I am waiting for thee,
There is food for your soul and raiment for thee,
And My RIGHTEOUSNESS, I freely give.

Just ask, and It shall be given,
Good measure I freely give,
Overflowing you'll find,
Coming from the TRUE VINE,
Drink freely and thy soul shall be filled.

I have been waiting to give thee your portion,
Oh for so long I have waited for thee—
To come in to the Fold and—
Find rest for you your soul,
And, see you be set free.

Free to worship Me, as your Saviour,
To know deliverance that comes from Me.
A place by my side to rule and to guide,
In My KINGDOM, forever be.

PRAISE THE LORD, PRAISE THE LORD, HALLELUJAH.
Oh what Joy to find pleasure with Thee.
My soul is made glad at Thy presence so sweet.
To find communion sweet communion with Thee.

Amelia Calkins
LOVE IS A ROSE
Love is a rose,
so tender and true.
But nobody knows,
of my love for you.
I hold it all inside,
so one day you will see.
All the love I hide,
deep inside me.

Sheila Shawn
WINTERTIME
The first snowflakes come floating down
like feathers, from the sky
as if someone was plucking geese
somewhere away up high.
But then the flakes get smaller
As they cover all the ground,
And then the flakes come faster
Tho' they never make a sound,
while covering up the naked trees
that stand so bare and cold.
I think the trees are all mixed up
if I could be so bold.
They shed their dresses in the fall
Those colors so sublime,
I think that they should keep them on
to be warm in Wintertime.

Lisa Alvarez
THE YEARS HAD COME
The years had come
The years had gone
In her voice she knew
Nothing could go wrong
But as she looked out at
That wide open space
Filled with blue, sparkling water
She saw nothing, not a trace
And as the tears began to silently fall
from her face.
She knew in her heart
That her true love and her
Were now so far apart.

Jack Hawkins
MORNING WALK
Sparkling crystal dewdrops hang like magic on slanted leaves,
with flat bottoms they quiver slightly in morning breeze.
Forest creatures have not yet stirred,
only the mating call of a solitary bird.
Wild flowers open, pleading their cups to be filled,
I wonder now as I see all the Creator's skills.
You lay beside me, it seems long ago,
and I feel your
loveliness as the soft breeze blows.
Time passes now as night leaves and movement abounds,
the sun comes, now she will make her rounds.
For me, one last look at God's domain,
then back to my dream, to see if you still remain.

Margaret Quigley
HUMANITY
Man, son, brother, husband, father, . . .
many roles,
. . . weakened nature . . .
body of suffering,
. . . ruled by glass . . .
controlled by liquid,
. . . wanting to love . . .
afraid of rejection,
. . . wanting to try . . .
afraid of failure,
. . . wanting to live . . .
afraid of life,
. . . wanting to be . . .
afraid of being less,
. . . wanting to die . . .
afraid of letting go,
Human yearnings, drowned in a sea of liquid,
disfigures, . . . blinds, . . .
blurs, . . . distorts reality of:
Man, son brother, husband, father, . . .
. . . my dad . . .

Marlis Carrion
HOMELESS PEOPLE
Homeless people are poor,
They don't have their jobs anymore;
They can't be shy, they still have to try,
Because they might die.
And they have to earn a living.
We're giving homeless people some food,
Because we're in the giving mood.
Come on, help us now,
And you'll be a pal somehow.

Blaze A Flesch

Blaze A Flesch
MY JESUS

Dedicated to my God, my family, and you the reader. But most especially to my Mother, who has never lost faith in me.

When the Prince of Darkness
needles me today,
I shout, "Dear God," and in a flash
He swiftly crawls away!

I know his power's not that strong,
can't do just as he pleases.
Maybe unto his followers, not me . . .
not when I'm with my Jesus.

Even in the pitch of night,
when Satan's hold increases,
To magnetize my soul to Him, He wails . . .
inside is my Jesus.

So if the Devil ever tries
to snare me from God's will,
I know his evil pit is deep . . .
my Jesus' deeper still!

Robin Donna Lathrope
I LIKE WOODS
I like the woods with
the cool breeze,
The tingling freshness as it
whips against my face as

it tosses my hair and
whispers secrets.

I like the smell of dampness
with the musk scent left
from the fallen leaves and
branches,
as it fills the night's air.

I like the brilliance of a fire's
glowing embers
as it mesmerizes you into
viewing its ruby phenomenon
as it dies down to sleep.

I like the twinkling stars
as they dance to
the creature's lullaby
that breaks the silence of the
night.

I like the woods.

JoAnn Allemani Parish

A CHILD

A child is a small and wonderful
person.
Messed up hair,
a dirty face,
bruised knees,
and untied shoes,
are only a part of him.
He looks at the world from big
innocent eyes, not understanding
all he sees.
Seeming unafraid
of grownup fears,
he has little
ones of his own.
He is quick to
learn both right and wrong.
Anything new arouses his curiosity.
He is a person willing to give his
trust to anyone who is good to him.
As of yet, he is not corrupted by hate
or prejudice, to him all people are the
same.

And when he grins the whole world
lights up.

Troy A Beadles

A FRIEND

Dedicated to Pat Gula
Sacramento, California
A true friend

A friend is a person who is always
helpful,
A friend would never be selfish,
mean or doubtful,
A friend is a special person to look
up to,
And if you were ever in trouble a
friend would always be there to pull
you through,
A friend is someone who'll be there
no matter rain or shine,
A friend will always be understanding, considerate and kind,
A friend will cheer you up if you're
feeling sad,
A friend would help you get those
things you never had,
A friend will always call you on the
telephone,
A friend will always come over if
you are at home,
A friend would always be sharing
with whatever he's got,
A friend would never lie about
something he's not,
A friend will always be honest and
never tell a lie,
If you were walking down a street a
friend would never pass you by,
Because friendship is something that
will last forever more,
There are all kinds of friends even
rich and poor,
As long as their friendship is very
true,
They could always be a good friend
to you,
So friends should be together till the
very end,
And that's the true meaning of the
word, "Friend."

Alison K Hughes

UPON DEATH

Is there stillness or flight?
Is there darkness or light?
What shall I find when I die?
Is there repose or pain?
Shall I see life again?
Will my soul be in transit or nigh?
Is death beginning or end?
Do all broken hearts mend?
Will I sleep ne'er to whisper a sigh?

Ida Lewellen McKnight

WHO IS THE UMPIRE?

Back in the sixties
We had Little League games
Two of our boys played
Joe and Dave were their names.

One day in particular
We often recall
Their Dad was an umpire
and pretty slow to call.

Some one then asked,
"Who's on the mound?"
"He is my son,"
I said, turning around.

"Who is catching?"
they wanted to know
"He is my son too."
I said with a glow.

Then after the umpire
had made a bad call.
"Who is that?" they asked
and I said, nothing at all.

Angeline J Glatzer

CONTEMPLATING

I dedicate this poem to my Pastor, teacher and counselor, The Late Paul D. Kern.

The flowers bloom for everyone,
The golden sun extends its rays,
To give us light and warmth,
O'er all the earthly days.

The rain drops fall on one and all.
Nature does not deprive or withhold,
Her bounty of beauty,
Or elements of warm or cold.

All have entered thru human portals
Into this life,
And all will leave with naught.
Only the memories we leave will
serve,
Those left on this earthly domain,
As inspiration to those we brought.

Richard W Dunlap

A ROSE BLOOMS TODAY

Written for: The family of Virgie Pearl Lowe Dedicated in memory of: Virgie Pearl Lowe Entered into Rest: January 22, 1989

My life was long and there were
things to see,
The blue of the sky and the depth of
the sea.
The beauty of dreams and the goals
that I gained,
The tear from an eye and the sorrow
and pain.

Yet the thing that I liked which to
my eye brought a tear,
Was the blooming of a Rose in the
Spring of the year.
A Rose stands for beauty, like my
love for all of you,
So remember me as a Rose with the
fresh morning dew.

Though I have left you and will not
see you for awhile,
Remember me like the Rose and to
your face bring a smile.
For I have gone to the garden and for
me a better way,
It's the Heavenly Garden where "A
Rose Blooms Today"

Glenda K Brooks

ALL THAT WAS

To the AIDS victims

A victim of circumstance
Once infected no chance
What was alive now dead
No word nothing said

Because death has touched you
Death you see for me too
Giving me not of choice
Killing me with a soft voice

To suffer the deadly death
Of no cures to save breath
Inch by inch slowly fade
Inside a rousing rage

The road we travel of no return
Joys and memories I yearn
To hold you close to my heart
Even in death we never part

No one cares any more
Nothing is like before
All that was, was a dream
An evil plot, someone's scheme

Warren L Beighley

Warren L Beighley

RECOLLECTIONS OF A BOMBER PILOT ENGLAND 1944

The orderly woke us at 3:00 AM
breakfast now; then briefing.
We had fresh eggs, toast, with jam.
The mission? important, believe
me.

I'd been there before; three times I
guess,
and the fear I felt overwhelmed
me.
I remembered the friends who never
came back,
and how they had died. "God
help me! !".

I stand by my plane and I look at the
sky,
the sun peeping over the
horizon.
I hear the birds sing; I hear a dog
bark;
the roosters' voice tells me the
season.

And I know that today, I will go
once again,
to tempt Fate as I fly the long
mission.
And my eyes may not see, nor my
ears again hear,
the world as I've seen it this
morning.

Be that as it may, I must go today,
my crew is waiting my coming.
God willing, tonight, while the day is
still light,
we all may see a sun setting.

Deborah Cunningham Walker

LOVE SHEEN

I made coffee today.
I thought of you.
Your lion golden shoulders glowed
In the early morning sunshine.
Gingerly you held the bright orange
tea kettle
With a bright red pot holder.
The silver spoon flashed
In the white light streams
Invading the kitchen.
Your strawberry tinted cheeks
Crinkled while you laughed
Because I couldn't make the coffee.
Nothing gleamed this morning
though
Like your eyes did the night before.
I miss you.

Alfrieda Harding

WHAT'S IN STORE FOR ME?

Into this world I came, not
knowing the score,
Just live and hope and wait to
see, if aught is all in store for
me.

I went to school, obeyed the
rule—or nearly so I'd say.
At home I tried to ever please
with hope to rate the best.

Into adulthood that loomed up
like an untamed steed,
Rejecting all appeals to heed. Like
all the rest this world will tame.

Troubles mount and down I swirl,
endeavoring to hold on,
With a back or iron and a head of
rock ignoring each and every
knock.
Then at last, advancing one more
block.

Oh what courage I have to
display, as I live and try to do
right some way.
Sometimes it seems only the
devil's pay will commensurate
the needs of life, to defray a
small part of the cost of strife.

Yet, there's power that says
"drive on" many more tasks on
this earth are to be done. As a
chosen laborer, you are worthy.
Then I pray, oh God, please save
the day.

Jeff Stone

I FOUND A FRIEND IN YOU

When I'm down and feeling blue,
You pick me up and hold my hand.
You look in my eyes and say "I love
you."

For so many years, I've let you
down,
and made you cry
and yet you stand by my side with
open arms.

I thank you for the love you give to
me
I thank you for the life you gave to
me
I thank you for being you.

Judith K Dimmick
ODE TO AN OLD HOUSE

To my mother, Katherine Shroyer, whose tales of the house she grew up in fostered my love of old houses.

You can't simply glance when you happen upon
A ramshackle house in a wild, unkempt lawn.
The house seems to beckon to you, "Come explore."
Though its rooms may be empty, it's filled with much more.

Peopled with memories of years put to rest,
A few symbols linger of how it was blessed.
It may be a picture still hangs on one wall,
A young man in uniform, posed proud and tall;

Or toys in a closet too worn out to move;
They may not be much but convincingly prove
This house was a refuge to folks young and old
They counted upon it to shield them from cold.

How many families once called this their home
And carry its memory wherever they roam?
And why did the last family leave it alone?
You wonder and wish you could make it your own.

At last you remember the reason you rested,
Dreaming beside this old house that's been tested
By decades of living and, yes, it still stands,
A reminder to all, with no further demands.

Tamara Gabrel
A LATE-NIGHT JOURNEY
In the middle of the night
With the North wind howling,
I suddenly woke up
With my stomach growling.

I ran through the kitchen,
Pushed open the door,
Jumped in my car,
And rushed to the store.

"What," do you ask
"Is the meaning of this trip?"
Why, I had to go
For some Miracle Whip.

Edith Dunlap
CARING

Dedicated to Stephanie my granddaughter

A baby bird lay on the ground where he had fallen in early morn.
He was so tiny, so helpless, so newly born.
He could not fly, he could not cry.
He needed warmth and food or he would die.
I picked him up o so tenderly,
And made a bed so safe he'd be.
Gave him tender loving care in every way.
Watched him grow and feathered day by day.
Until at last his wings could spread and soar.
I gave him life, yet he gave me o so much more.

Thomas W Bailiff Jr

Thomas W Bailiff Jr
A SUMMER'S KISS

To Dede: My Friend, My Love, My Life!

Dear Bernardita I wish you were here,
I would hold your hands and call you dear.
You're a girl and a woman in every way,
Let's walk together say you will stay.
The moon and the stars they shine real bright,
Arm in arm we hold on tight.
Is it love or a part of life,
I really would like to make you my wife.
We know that this may never be,
So hold my hand and walk with me.

Tell me your feelings let me be your candlelight,
Let me kiss your lips the feeling is right.
Tell me a story a part of your past,
Our walk will be long I want it to last.
Your hair in the moonlight it has its own glow,
I want to tell you I love you so.
My age and dreams are fading away,
Tells me I'll have to set you free someday.
But as for now the feeling is right,
Whisper in my ear you will stay tonight.

Deb Redfearn
LITTLE CHILD
I see the things
that you do
And can imagine
what lies ahead for you

I know what you can be
You'll be a better woman
than me
Hold on to the person that you are becoming
and not what someone else wants you to be

Always watch . . . you'll find so much to see

Honor yourself first
then those you love
And your heart may be as content as a sleeping dove

Have the strength to control your own life
and the courage to be whatever you want to be

But no matter what you have to do
always do it nobly

Betty Mertens
CAN YOU JUST IMAGINE

To my parents Mr. & Mrs. John Mertens. Special thanks to Daddy who encouraged my poetry.

The hunger and the homelessness,
That's going on right here,
is something for us to think about
because it's all so real!

Can you just imagine being homeless?
And feeling totally all alone,
Well it's very sad and painful,
people treat you cold as stone!
Can you just imagine being hungry?
So hungry that you feel weak?
Well it's out there, believe me, it's out there,
And for them, their future looks bleak!
Can you just imagine their feelings?!
How they hurt and cry all night long!
Just in hopes of finding someone
To talk to and help them be strong!
Can you imagine the homeless children
How they feel fright and despair!?
There is an answer, can't you see?
We all have to try and share!
And once we all start doing that,
We've all become a part,
Of one big human family
That shows we have a heart!

Then in helping one way or another,
We've accomplished something you see,
for everyone out there is 'R' sister and brother
And that is the way it should be.
Can you just imagine that!!?

Dawn C Yeggy
FAR AWAY PLACE

I dedicate this poem to Amanda and Erin with their innocent minds. Please keep your dreams flowing.

I dream of the day when I am free,
To laugh and sing, and just be me.

I want to wake up not worrying about a thing,
To sit up and see what the day will bring.

I know the day will be beautiful and bright,
He'll guide me through without a worry in sight.

This will be the time to leave all the obstacles behind,
Birds singing and clear waters flowing, that's what I'll find.

This place will be special for dreamers like you and me,
There won't be any hate or pain, just wait and see.

I don't know for sure when we are going,
Only God can tell us, so until then,
Keep your dreams flowing.

Donna Insko
ANYONE
What is this pounding in my heart?
Is it love
Is it pain
Or, possibly, a combination of the two.

People don't believe me when I tell them
Such a thin line exists between love and hate
Does it matter at all
Really?

You can love enough to hurt
You can hurt enough to feel
Feel what?
I guess that's the question.

You say you love
Then you are betrayed by it
What good is it then
To even try to love
Or care
About anyone but yourself.

Marie C Korman
IT GETS BETTER

To someone special—You made it better for me.

Sad and lonely—
so full of despair,
I tell myself—
it must get better.
Family and friends—
people all around,
I'm never alone—
why am I lonely?
I tell myself—
it must get better.

One day you smiled—
we talked for awhile.
Now I can't explain why—
it's just different somehow.
So easy to laugh—
when once I cried.
Your smile, your touch—
make all the difference.
Now I tell myself—
It gets better!

Beth Ellen Cook
BROKEN PROMISE
When the promise is broken
and the dream turns to dust,
Turn to those who love you,
those who are your friends,
and those who care.
For they will help you create
new dreams.
And they will renew your spirit
and will to survive.

Dale Scott
PERFUME COUNTER
All day she handles black or crystal phial
Emerald, topaz, ruby liquids meet
And mingle breaths more languorously sweet
Than Juliet's sigh, or Cleopatra's smile.
Here musk and amber speak of India, while

Violet, rose, and lavender entreat
A thought of England, Orange flowers repeat
The songs and laughter of some southern isle.

All day she lives with Ind and Araby,
Then leaves and in a moment will forget
Her wares while jostled in the subway strife
She hurries to a storied privacy
Where coffee, steak, her husband's cigaret
Make the most precious perfume of her life.

Tallak T Farsjo

A "PAST" IS UNKNOWN IN HEAVEN

For everyone who enters into heaven
The slate is wiped meticulously clean.
The past is not remembered, never seen.
The candlesticks are lighted, one to seven
In flames of innocence with holy sheen.
The emphasis is on the future's story
Where the Lord will dwell with us in glory.

When God forgives our past is gone forever,
Of sin and evil are no more a trace.
He perfectly restores the broken vase,
It is as if poor sinners we were never,
All is blotted out by love and grace.
His grace has swept away all condemnation;
So wonderful is God in His salvation.

Our sinful past is gone, disintegrated.
It never was we have a right to say.
And with no past so blissful is our way.
It is no fairytale that here is stated,
This is God's word, no foolish human play.
When sin is gone we are in Paradise,
Our slate is clean, we shout hosanna thrice!

Annette Stas

TO BE ACCEPTED AS I AM

To be accepted as I am,
not for my color, religion,
or education,
but for the person that I am.

To travel to a land,
of not my nationality
and be accepted as I am.

To associate with the rich
and be proud of who I am.

To each and everyone
of those who know
what it's like to say,
accept me as I am.

Susan Jenkins

A TOUCHING OF SOULS

This poem is dedicated to Judi Cook, A wonderful lady and dear companion, Thanks for everything.

What is this feeling that you and I share?
this feeling that makes both of us care.
What is this feeling that is blessed from above?
what we share can only be love.

What makes two people care so much?
through an act of love their souls seem to touch.
After it is over and all is still,
the touching of souls you can still seem to feel.

As we lay in the darkness in each other's arms,
we protect each other from any pain and harm.
As we lay with our bare flesh touching together,
our touching of souls will be remembered forever.

A touching of souls makes a love so strong,
it only happens when the right one comes along.
I have found someone to make it all come true,
that special someone, baby is you.

Joseph W Banks

Joseph W Banks

PRAYER OF HOPE

To my father Joseph H. Banks Sr., & mother Lorreta Banks patience love and endurance in their children Robert, Joseph Jr., and sister Bertha in the love of God and his son Jesus Christ.

To the soul that has a longing,
To reside high in the sky.
To the mind that has it thinking,
Of the glory bye and bye.

To the heart that has it beating,
And the lung both full and gone.
And the mouth that has it speaking,
And the throat that full of song.

We do hope for thee old Soul,
In a world so full of sin.
That when Pearly Gate you're knocking,
That the Angel let you in.

Jean I Rauschning

TRUCKER BLUES

Driving down the highway, up and going on white lines,
Not the kind on pavement, but ones that cost lives.

Going, going, going on and on and on endlessly,
Loving the job at first, but keeping on desperately.

Making friends and lovers, just having a good time,
One night stands and interludes, your life not worth a dime.

Back home used to be a treat, but now it's forgotten too,
You spend more and more time getting lost to not get blue.

Orders demand to be five hundred miles down the road,
You're tired, beat, can't drive, can't sleep, dead mode.

Years and years, day in and day out, memories fade in and out,
Used to be a ladies' man, now no more, just a shell—blackout.

Dying, day by day, little by a lot, can't go on much more,
Orders say replace you, what do they care? Just a trucker-whore.

Women loved you, I know I did. But now nothing left to love.
You died a long time ago. Couldn't love; push came to shove.

Jessica Guthrie

WHEN IT'S LOVE

This poem is dedicated to Gabe R., my sweetheart.

When it's love you feel it
in your heart
The one you love makes
you shiver inside
When it's love you feel it
grasping your heart
Loving, caring, and holding on
When you're in love you say "I love you"
but, words are never enough
The love inside pulls at your heart
never wanting to give up
Our love will go on forever
I'll love you 'til the day I die
So, baby don't give up on me
Love doesn't lie . . .

Robert Lazaro

NIGHT MESSENGER

To My Ana Marie, For being beautiful, free, and always close to me.

Come into my dream tonight
Hold me and make it right.

We'll go walking moonlight time
Shadows dancing—time not passing.

I feel your breath come alive within my heart
These times just can't be sold,

I give to you without a fight
I give to you with all my might,

Eyes locked one to one
We have something we both understand,
it's just a touch a hold of a hand.

We stand together in the light
if only for one night,
You hold the answers within your eyes
You come to me with no disguise.

Diana Lynn Combs

WILL THERE BE SILENCE

How do I write it, yet I feel it.
How do I see it, yet I hear it.
Only sitting in silence waiting to die.
In death will I not find silence only?

Does the world exist around me?
Or am I only myself alone?
Or do they stare back?
Searching to find me, as I look beyond to find them.

Have not the famous tasted pains of solitude?
Wishing knowledge would bring them near.
Are the ignorant left out?
For their knowledge no one can hear.

Years, days stalk boldly past me.
Laughing wickedly, throwing lines upon my face.
Knowing always time will win the challenge.
To keep my life in its senseless maze.

To peer from eyes of darkness.
To vision lights of dreaming.
To listen for sounds of laughter, voices lingering.
While hearing sound of darkening aging silence.

Night come to me soon.
To free my mind of this.
Not myself to realize.
In my sleeping mind, I am still alone in this.

Francine B Thanasiu

GOD LIES DEAD IN HEAVEN

God lies dead in Heaven
Angels sing the mournful hymn of annihilation.
Their wings drip with blood
Veiling the earth in black sorrow.
Monsters of sin, livid with desire,
crawl from their far caverns to
wrangle over the world, to them

but a morsel.
The icy wind blows desolately through
my empty forsaken soul
As a woman's arms try desperately
to shield her sleeping child from
the gaping jaws of the final beast.

Lucia L Llena

THERE I FOUND LOVE

Somewhere there is a place
Where the love so true stays
Always there will be days
Light shade for every race
All plain is there in lace
Dimensions are a phase

One by one, each a trace
To read behind a face
Nothing comes to encase
Each being free it lays
Not a rock at its base
Heaven on earth to raise
For joy fills every space
All is love in its ways.

Lee McNutt-Hite

THE ABANDONED CHURCH-HOUSE

Oh, the little country church-house
Has stood barren many a day,
Solitary and abandoned,
Lonely, falling in decay.

Through the rafters, broken roofing—
I can gaze up at a star
As I walk its sanctuary
Through a door which hangs ajar.

All its splintered pews, now dusty,

Have heard many a hymn and prayer,
Many souls serenely sat here,
Many others in despair.

As I sit, time seems turned backward,
And ethereal on the air—
Spectral voices speak in sermon,
Although none, save I, is there.

It seems mournful, yet I'm thinking,
While I see this church now bare,
God has no need of this building,
For His Spirit's everywhere.

Marjorie Hind Benchoff

FAITH

Faith is a trust in almighty God,
Faith is not walking alone on earthly sod,
Faith is seeking to know thy loving Lord,
Faith is an abundance of God's gracious love,
Faith is knowing God is near,
Faith is what all people need while here,
Faith is placing your trust above,
Faith is knowing God will send you all his love.

Jane C Ellering

I'LL NEVER SEE MY MOTHER

I'm safely hidden in a warm cocoon.
Four weeks and my heart is beating
In a steady rhythm.
As I lie in the tepid fluid—
I'm full of happy expectation.
I am growing every day and developing
Round buds that will become blue eyes
And small ears like my mother's.
I am content in my dazed, dark world.
But, I am deluding myself, that I will ever be.
That I will ever play with a toy,
Or see a Christmas tree.
For, at eight weeks—
I am subjugated to a violent
Twisting, turning, vise-like force.

I'm so cold, lying on the hard, white table.
A female fetus, bloodstained and abandoned.
My sad, blue eyes will not open.
I'll never see my mother.

Judy Holmes

THE TREASURER (FROM THE ACCOUNT IN ACTS)

An Ethiopian man had been to worship,
Who was in charge of all the treasure of the queen;
And was riding from Jerusalem unto Gaza,
Down the way that is desert in between.
He was reading from the prophet, Isaiah,
And having trouble with a troubling scene.

An angel of the Lord spake unto Philip,
Saying, 'go toward the south unto the way
That goeth from Jerusalem unto Gaza,'
And Philip 'rose and went without delay.
The Spirit bade that Philip join the chariot.
He, running hither, heard him read Isaias.

"Understandest, thou, what thou readest?"
"How can I except some man guide me?"

And he asked him to come up in the chariot
And sit with him and help him understand.
Now, the place where he read was of The Slaughter,
Which Isaiah foretold about the Sacred Plan
That all in future generations
Would believe that Jesus was the Pascal Lamb.

Then, beginning in Isaiah, Philip preached Jesus,
Who was led dumb away unto The Slaughter,
As they continued on their desert way to Gaza,
They came unto a certain place of water.
And the humble, eunuch noble
Prompt to mind the Gospel order:

Said, "See, here is water. What doth hinder Me to be baptized?"
"If thou believeth with all thine heart, thou mayst."
"I believe that Jesus Christ is the Son of God."

Then, the eunuch stopped the chariot on the wayside,
And both went down into the water on the scene;
So that the soul who was buried while believing
Met the Blood of Heaven's Lamb to be clean.
They both came up out of the water
And Philip was caught away . . . by Other Means;
But the noble, Christian treasurer
Went on his way rejoicing
Having found a greater treasure than the queen's.

Gerry-Kay Talton

PASSION'S PRICE

There are blisters on my brain
  and I feel insane . . .
   when passion has control of the reign . . .
    it rusts my soul, and I behave like a troll.

Desires of the flesh can enslave . .
  and perhaps put me in my grave . .
   so I seek to transcend and trust . .
    that I'll not succumb to the demon lust!

Cheryl S Jennings

HIDING PLACE

Dedicated to all prisoners of fear

The secrets in your heart, are prisoners of fear.

Did you know they are placed there by self-love?
Yes, you love self too much to share it.
Kept inside, it becomes a self-made bomb.
You're not master over it, as you believe.
Anyone, anything is the trigger.

We are not our own self-made gods.
But, servants to the one that sees the fear.
Your life is not in your hands, but theirs.

Releasing the fear, creates a human being.
Locking it up causes mechanical life.
You exist, only to protect your fear.
It's your choice—live or die inside.

Everyone's searching for Freedom.
Not one is a slave to others, but by choice.
It all begins—ends within us.
Freedom is not in others, but in ourselves!

Kevin Deal

A ROSE HAS ITS SEASON

To Michael, for whom love endures.

A rose has its season
When left of the vine
Receiving water now and then
One can enjoy its beauty
For quite some time

When taken from the life line
It soon will fade and die
For everything needs nourishment
Without, it can't survive

A rose is a symbol
Of love undenied
Even when left to wither
Its beauty . . . lingers in the mind

Olive M Staples

LATE SPRING

To my Aunt—Irene C. Balcom—Who always had a rhyme.

My but the Valley was pretty today,
With golden Forsythias along the way.
Outdone were they in color and hue
Only by Daffodils (and Dandelions too)!

My but the Valley was pretty today,
With wild cherry blossoms along the way.
Amid the tints and shades of nature's spring
They looked like brides' bouquets, or some such thing.

My but the Valley was pretty today,
As I drove along through blossoming May.
The pink apple blossoms can't seem to wait
To burst into bloom—and fill the air with their sweet perfume.

My but the Valley was pretty today;
The blues of the mountain, river and sky made
a background that really caught one's eye.
The tender new leaves in their many hues
Looked lacy and delicate and all so new.

My but the Valley was pretty today,
There's no place like home, or so they say—
The tulips that met me at my back door
Seemed to bloom today as never before!

My but the Valley was pretty today!
Is it Spring or Love that made it that way?

Penny R Wigle

THE FLOWER

The petals fell gently to the ground, in the midnight air. The flower reminded me so much of our love. That flower that I held so gently in the palms of my hands, was actually the beautiful body of you. So soft, so pretty, so tender. The flower that I slowly squeezed, because of my fear that it would soon be blown away, far from my reach, never to feel or touch it again. My tears had fallen from my eyes, and landed on those tender petals, as I squeezed even harder to feel its love in my heart, and in my hands. What I had not realized was, when I squeezed the flower, that beautiful body that was so full of life, had suddenly lost the air life had given it. As I opened my hands to look at my precious flower, I was overwhelmed by grief. The flower that I once held so close, was now withered, and left without feeling. The flower that I loved so very much, I knew I had lost forever, and those last few petals had fallen to the the ground, never to be held or loved again, would rest in peace in the midnight air, while I would go on grieving, knowing that I could have treated that beautiful flower, that meant so much to me, with tender loving care.

Susan Marie (Boucher) Cloutier

Susan Marie (Boucher) Cloutier

FROM MY HEART TO YOURS, WHEREVER YOU ARE

Dedicated to Paul Ellis, A man whom I shall always love, respect, and admire. And to my sons Joshua and Matthew, my proudest achievements in my life. I love you all.

You are my love, a person who will never come into my life again as you have. You alone broke down the walls behind which I trembled. You alone saw behind my mask. You alone released me from my shadow world of panic and uncertainty and loneliness. You have touched my soul like no man has ever been able. You were my friend, a man so unique above all else. When I needed to talk, you always listened and when I needed to cry, you were always there to hold me. You were my lover and "OH," how gentle you were with every curve of my shape. Your kisses were immense passion and so sweet like ripened succulent strawberries. Your touch, made me motionless, unaware of anything else around me. Your eyes were as blue as the depths of the ocean and could hypnotize me as we locked the door of love in one-ness and threw away the key. How was it possible to feel this way with you? If I close my eyes I can hear our laughter and our joy. And when I lie in bed at night I can still feel your arm around me as I cuddle closer and closer to your body's warmth and I miss how your moustache tickled me as you kissed my back goodnight. The hours are empty now that you are gone, and I miss you so very much. The quiet is so deafening without your conversation and what will I do with all this time? I am so scared my love. You were my everything, my todays and all my tomorrows and now our forever is just a memory. I know nothing lasts forever, but I was sure our love would last beyond all eternity. I know not where you are my darling, or how you are getting on, but I am writing this sonnet for you in hopes that in some magical way my words will find your heart and you might think of me at least once again, and just remember the truly magnificent love we shared and the end-less possibilities that could have been, "If you had only stayed."

Vivian Mains
SUDDENLY EVERYTHING TURNED TO WHITE

To my darling Ted—He has left this planet but he is still with me in every word I put to the page.

Snow flakes drifted by
some like popcorn, some like lace
I know they are falling from the sky
and there must be trillions out there
in space;
Mostly they come to earth (it seems)
at night and their silence is so great
remember—you don't know that
everything has turned to white.
But, it's still not too late
to watch these delicate artifacts in
flight.
Go set yourself up by a window;
Tune yourself into the mood;
but don't ever try to catch or count
the snow flakes—to intercept would
be quite rude.
Instead, just in fancy join them as
they float feeling the softness of
them all around your face and hear
ye—hear ye—they will have your
vote of being nature's loveliest as
they disappear in space;
And just in case it has been forgotten
lots of snow flakes look just like
cotton.

E A Lowe
THE SHEIK
The Sheik came scarlet as the cape
he wore,
The cape was scarlet as the fear he
bore,
And fear, not blood, was the stain
remaining,
From his scarlet sabres slash, into
moral fibre core.
For as deserts searing shield took on
the dim veil of black,
and shadows hung like death itself,
in the balance of dawns lack, could
be heard thru the jet of a moonlight
night—hollow hooves resounding, in
the endless, driftless flight,
Where faint light sparked the darkest
gorge,
carved by natures plight.
One man cowers in the shadow of
his nomadic abode—
At the sound of the hollow hooves—
drumming the way to the door of his
tent—
They took life and belongings from
Arab clan—
Crime enough.
Now the scream of a million sirens
enshrouded his ears.
An overwhelming oppression drives
into his withered soul—
Revenge is his, who once himself
wrought evil—
Strange is it not that evil wrought for
evil gains
Is repaid in dividend-tenfold—by the
master broker.

Kathleen Motisko–Larioni
AN EXPECTANT MOTHER'S PRAYER

To my darling daughter Krista, all my love forever,—Mom

Of all the gifts one can bestow
This is the greatest, and this I know
The gift of a child someone to love
Sent from the angels and God above

As the days draw nearer I will see
your face
And you will know the warmth of a
mother's embrace
Precious moments are these that I
carry you inside me
Praying to god for your health and to
guide me
To teach you of strength, love and
caring
To have pride to be honest and of
sharing

Yes, the best gift of all from God
above
is none other than a child's love
the wish I have for you as our bodies
are one
is that God give you a glow as bright
as the sun
Two eyes that twinkle, like stars up
above
Skin so white as feathers of a dove

But to be as giving as he with a heart
so pure
That life's worst upsets you will
endure.
To spread some happiness where
ever you roam
And that your love expand like the
oceans foam
To reach across the world so far
that peace will be felt where ever
you are
With a voice like an angel to speak
softly his word
So that across this nation a song of
love is heard
Yes, for you my child I wish all of
this
I ask nothing in return, merely a kiss.

June Huey
I SAW YOU WALKING

To my husband of 41 years

In my dreams I saw you
walking, walking in the
park.

You saw a flower you
liked and picked it.
That flower was my heart.

You smelled it, touched it,
and brushed its softness
against your cheek.

You took it home and put
it in a vase on your
windowsill, and once in a while
you would pull a petal off.

Did you care about that
flower or not?! Why did you
pick it if you only meant
to slowly torture it by pulling
off its petals one by one?

You kept on pulling, 'till there
was but one petal left.

Once again I saw you walking,
walking in the park; and you picked
another flower.

You savored its beautiful aroma,
brushed its softness against your lips,
and held it very dear in your heart.
Never once did you pull a single
petal off.

Remember that flower in the vase on
your windowsill?
Well, that last petal you left on it
just fell off.

John Michael Cali III
THE PRAYER OF GOD
Sometimes no one seems to care
Sometimes life doesn't seem too fair.
But sometimes you must look and
see
That I have made life to make you
free.
Never worry, never fear
Rejoice in each day you spend here.
For I live in you to make you see
That if you care, you will live in me.

I am the god of the heavens above.
I am the one you cherish and love.
I am the clouds of the far off sky.
I am the hills in which some lie.
I am the sound of the birds you hear.
I am your feelings, love and fear.

So someday you may look and see
That I love you and have set you
free.
The love I share is ever living
The love I share is always giving.
I am the creator of the earth
I am the giver of each birth.
I live in you as you live in me.
I love you and have set you free.

Karen Braddom
THE FEELING OF NATURE

I would like to dedicate my poem to my best friends forever, Casey, Beth, and Kate.

Fire in the night,
A breeze in the sky,
The dew in the morning,
Or a bird soaring high,
The afternoon rain,
A midnight shower,
A growing leaf,
The bloom of a flower,
Daylights blinding color,
To the evenings silent sleep
Like the shining puddle,
Water's shallow or deep,
A blade of green grass,
And a smiling rose,
Brings a nipping frost,
With winter's peaceful snows,
Like a wink of the eye,
Is a change of the season,
A cycle of life,
Giving birth its reason.

Londa Kay Horton
CHAMELEON
Many days passed . . .
nights went slower
without you.

It's been almost a year now.
Seems like yesterday.
Tears still flow.
They seem unstopable

How I loved,
and lost
My heart skips
hearing your voice
Will it ever fade?

I try not to think
of the laughing times
days in my
memory.

Get on with life
hold your head up high
You are
a
survivor.
Your bud will blossom
again.
And this time it will be fantastically
colored.

I pulled the dripping
dagger out.
Get on with life
don't waste
a
second.
You're too precious
God sees
He looks on
He protects
He mends me.

Living is a miracle . . .
look around
and smile.
It's not so bad.
Spring is at hand.
Green is a beautiful color,
And . . . with the sun
comes new life.

Marlene C Cumberbatch
I AM, BECAUSE YOU ARE!

This poem is dedicated to my wonderful husband Earland

You fill my five senses

I exist just to hear
the sound of your voice.

The smell of you
opens my imagination.

The taste of your lips
provoke my sensuousness.

To feel the slightest touch from you
arouses my being.

Just to see you is
a vision in itself.

Evlin C Agnew

Evlin C Agnew
A HAND IN MINE

This poem I dedicate to my deceased husband, Col. Timothy A. Taracouzio, who gave his life for America, his adopted country, in World War II.

Walking through the silent night,
Moist with moon-reflected dew,
Nodding palms, all dipped in silver,
Turn my thoughts to dreams of
you.

Hand in hand, we strolled of
evening,
Not a word did we let fall,
Lest the break of soulful silence
Mar the wonder of it all.

In the hush, our very breathing—

Primed to pulsate with the
earth—
Gave our lives, so locked in splendor,
Sanguine symptoms of rebirth.

Now, I walk alone, yet knowing
You are here, unseen, unheard,
and your hand remains in my hand
As we stroll, with not a word.

Carl J Rebant

MY GOLD

To all those that cannot tell and have to hide their love and to Cindy

As I sit and I wonder
Feeling anger and despair
I want to touch
Want to feel
The love you have
And mine to share.
My grief cries out
My pain, my heart
It tears my soul
Madness and more
And what I feel
Down deep within
Just like a fool
Who hides his gold
Then I cry
Aren't I a fool
Only my gold
Is love . . .

Jennifer L Fagan

YOU GAVE ME MY WINGS

For my Mother, Dee Fagan

You gave me my wings
and taught me to fly,
You didn't hold back
you gave me the sky,
You gave me the world
on a silver tray.
You taught me of a thing called love
and the games people play,
You gave me the strength to
stand alone and succeed
And all of the confidence to
believe in myself.
You gave it all, you helped me to
grow.

Terry L Williams

WHO BUT A POET CAN SEE

Who but a poet can see
The world of man so easily
In its rebel and radical stage
A piece of machinery with blown
gage
Still to find beauty in the passing day
Or grey clouds of storm and trees that
sway
Who but a poet could ever hold
A touch of love and not seem bold
To those who forever find fault
At whatever things they are taught
And easily forget the changing of day
The joy of childhood and freedom of
play
Who but a poet could speak of love
While speaking loosely, fit it like a
glove
To the memories of that one special
face
A stolen kiss by moonlight and warm
embrace
A distant feeling of loneliness
infatuate
And thoughts of a homeland to
repatriate
Who but a poet? Who but a
poet?
No one but a poet

Lorraine Schulmeister

WINTER SWANS

the wild bird refuge was glacier-still.

surrounded by winter's cold, dead
things
two white swans slept on an ice
pedestal,
unruffled, wound in upon themselves
in serpentine curves,
the long neck tucked under a wing,
the beak hidden from view.

we lingered to glimpse their
waking . . .
one graceful neck emerged,
stretched into a long yawn, then
resumed the more ancient position,
part serpent, part bird:

pure form, like an Arp sculpture,
Nature's artifice
placed there for our pleasure.

Ralph F Pynchon

THE WIND

The wind's a temperamental jade;
Sometimes a lady, at times a
slattern maid.
Sometimes she's a dowager—sedate
and prim,
Or a garrulous fishwife—loud
and grim

Sometimes she's a maiden—demure
and shy
Blowing caresses as she flutters by.
Sometimes she's a wench—
coquettish and gay,
But firmly set in having her way

Sometimes she's an amazon brazen
and strong
Wreaking havoc when she
sweeps along;
Disrupting shipping and strewing the
mains
With broken schooners from off
the lanes.

It matters not if she's Frank or Dora,
Or if they simply name her
Flora;
She's still an unpredictable shrew
Quite able to stir up a witches'
brew.

Christopher Lee McKinster

SERENITY

To all recovering people around the world.

Days can lapse into daze,
When everything the same remains.
Change is slow, so we try to control,
Only to link a habit of chains.

So to find, that peace of mind,
That we are searching for.
We make believe, we cannot
conceive,
How others have opened the door.

To take, and take, and take,
And even take for granted.
People who care, that are willing to
share,
Their life as it has happened.
Sharing your heart, is a pioneering
start,
To trust, and care for others.
To believe in humanity, is not
insanity,
There is strength in numbers

Experiencing faith, we all can relate,
To what makes strong spirituality.
To find within, that little grin,
That gives us all "serenity."

Barbara C Mazrolle

FOR A FINE AND BEAUTIFUL COUPLE HAPPY ANNIVERSARY

Two lonely hippies living together
How can life be so cruel
Both of their parents disapproving of
it
Expecting them to follow their rule

A young divorced mother with two of
her own
It's beautiful can't you see
The loving and caring they have
found for each other
Should last an eternity

When you both decided to get
married
Both families were in Shock
They said that you were making a
terrible Mistake
It would not take long for it to Rock

You had a Hippy Wedding
It was beautiful by far
Exotic clothes, Long Straight Hair
and Your Own Vows
To others it was quite Bizarre

They would not give your marriage a
chance
They knew it was failure from the
start
What they did not know or did not
see
Your love was coming straight from
your Heart

He took the children in as his own
He gave them the loving and caring
He made sure that you were all happy
as One
He brought out all of his Giving and
Sharing

After a year you were rejoicing with
Love
How wonderful can life be
With such a beautiful little girl
To complete a Happy Family

Just look at you now still both happy
in Love
You truly cannot compare
Two grown hippies after all these
years
So Fine—So True—So Rare

Stephanie Burton

NEVER

Never say good-bye to the love that
you've felt,
Keep it locked in your heart it may
someday help.
Never let go of those feelings you
keep inside,
They may be real and as a fool you
try to hide.
Never push away someone who
cares,
It's not your time they want, it's
your love to share.
Never let your past take control of
your life,
Those feelings in your heart can cut
like a knife.
Never hold a grudge against
someone you know,
The anger in your heart should
never grow.
Never let your bitterness control
what you say,
Words are meant to bring one close,
but can sometimes push them far
away.
Never forget what you've had
before,
You may want it back and can get
no more.

Jessica Koehler

RABBITS

Rabbits are fluffy,
Some rabbits are very fast,
Some rabbits are fat,
Some rabbits are very dumb,
Rabbits make very good pets.

George Christos Kalogeropoulos

George Christos Kalogeropoulos

THE RIVER

This poem is dedicated to Athanasios Damalas, Stavroula & Olga Stratos; in all ways, my second family.

And when they spot each other in the
distance, they both freeze.
One looking at the other, in the cool
river.
But how long could that last?
Then a sneeze, and a cuss word
from the second soldier!
They both swam fast; the first one
reached his weapon,
When the second reached the
opposite side.
'An excellent target . . . '
But, no!
The trigger felt hard.
Two men alone; without clothes;
Without names;
Without nationalities;
Without their green.
The trigger felt hard.
The gun was lowered.
Then, his head lowered.
And until the end, nothing to see!
Only a few birds flying from
fright,
When from the other side,
A gun-shot was fired.

Walt Gorski

AMERICAN STEEL

I found a piece of America that I
could believe in,
An oasis of wrinkled faces, rust, and
steel.
It stood at the feet of tall glass towers
In a field of idle cars that wait for
silent trains.
It was separated only by a thin veil of
trees
And the progress of fifty years.

The machines that were made for brute lifting and bending
Seemed too strong to be affected by time.
One time did touch them, that time was the end.
Effective September 1, 1988, James Steel Fabrications closed.
I was there on the day that Mr. James took bids for old machinery
And found new jobs for worn out men.

It seems that progress and I found James Steel in the same season,
And that we both took from it what we desired.
Eisenhower Metro gained another acre of parking,
I took soft photos of hard rust and steel,
And a piece of America in which I could believe.

Brenda Sue Dunlap
NOTHING CAN COMPARE

To: My fiancee, Joe Cullen With all my love, FOREVER!

Nothing can compare,
To the love that we share,
It's a love that grows deeper each day.

A love straight from the heart,
Growing right from the start,
Never ceasing, God planned it that way.

It's a friendship that lasts,
A love that won't pass,
A bond between two that's forever.

We are joined and made one,
Now our new life's begun,
Thank-you Lord, that you brought us together!

Sean Kitchin
DESERT BLOOM
Drugged into a midnight dream,
Cheated away by the birth of a rising sun,
Of a land of peppermint trees,
And rivers undone.

Searching for romance and love,
Of a fairy princess sent from above,
Morning rain washed my doubt away,
From the heartache and doom.

For I knew she was near,
My Desert Bloom.

Dave Matteson
TO MY LADY

Valentine's Day 1989—To Bonnie, my lady, my love

Thank you—For the beautiful time we share, when we are together.

Thank you—For loving me and the wonderful feeling your love for me provides.

Thank you—For your smile, which highlights for me your warm, gentle, nature.

Thank you—For being on my arm, holding hands, kissing me, in public places.

Thank you—For your touch of my body and all the meaning I sense from that touch.

Thank you—For making love with me and the tremendous meaning and fulfillment of being within your being.

Thank you—For just being you, the person I love beyond which my words can express.

Thank you—For the pleasure of loving you, with my desire to fill your needs and provide you with pleasure.

Thank you—For entering my life and providing a dream of how good life will be, once we are together.

Carmen Marie Vargas
NEW LOVE
Even though we haven't been
Together long
My feelings for you are coming so strong
I think of you
When you're not near
Because you are so very dear
So let's keep our spirits high
So our love can stay alive

Gayol Shaw Michael
OUT MY KITCHEN WINDOW

With love, for my children, Rachel, Jennie & Paul. And for my husband, Stanley.

Out my kitchen window, I see my
Young ones dear; Out my kitchen
Window, changing year by year.
One time little youngsters, soon
Pre-teen they'll be—What a joy
And wondrous blessing my babies
Are to me!

Out my kitchen window, I can
Almost see them now, two beautiful
Young women, with flowers on their
brow. And, Oh, my! Look how
handsome My little boy has grown.
He looks so Much like daddy—Oh
well, I might have known!

Out my kitchen window, not so
Many years away; my dear, sweet
Little babies will no longer play. But
Out my kitchen window, in my
Memory there will be, three sweet,
Little children, <u>always</u> playing there
For me.

Elizabeth Kemski
IF MY LIFE WAS TOUCHED BY MAGIC
If my life was touched by magic
I would take your pain,
and all the anger you deny
all the disappointments that
you've tried so desperately to hide,
and I would wrap them tightly
and bury them deep in a
wooden chest.

I'd carry it to the highest peak I could find
and then slowly
gently
a small fire would build up
beneath it.
And as it grew in strength
and started to blaze more intensely
the ashes would begin to fly away
and I would wait
until the chest was completely gone
and all the hurt was borne away
on the slightest of breezes,
and you would be free.

Lynne Barstow
WAKING STREETS OF YANGZHOU

In gratitude: For the peaceful images they shared with me I wish them now the same.

Morning rays of Chinese gold reach into open window
And pull me outside to explore . . .

Smells of fresh market fill narrow backstreet
Where farmers crouched on wooden crates
Dip chopstick circles into morning rice bowls
Shirtsleeves of faded blue wave above
While carp splash below in plastic green tub.

October sun sweeps shadow from feet
Of stooped old man who carries birdcage
With slowest reverence into local park
He rests winged friend on sturdy tree
Himself on bench nearby.

In grassy middle of park
Students of Taichi pull graceful arms through heavy air
Wide toothless smiles turn toward me
Pleased to perform their daily ritual
For curious audience of one.

From corner of park young emperor at play
Climbs make-believe throne
And cups for one moment
Delicate thread of world peace
between his hands.

James T Bancroft
TREE
A man sits under a tree with only
The crescent moon to guide his gaze
Into the distant night.

The man is in total omission of the
World around him. Even the distant
Screen of a lone owl does not stir
This being from the thoughts that
Are within his mind.

Limbs sway with the gentle breeze of
The darkened night. The man's hair
Flitters like the wings of a butterfly
Then settles down to rest.

Without warning or detection the
Moonlight shines on a glisten drop
Rolling down the cheek of this lonely
Creature of the night. Could it be?
No? It is! A tear.

Carole DeRuiter
A MOTHER'S CHRISTMAS
'Tis the season to be jolly!
Trim the tree and hang the holly!
Bake the cookies . . . Fruit the cake!
A thousand things to do and make!

We've bought and wrapped . . .
Bowed and tied!
Hidden presents . . . Even lied!
The closet is bulging . . . The drawers won't close!
GRACIOUS! . . . How the bounty grows!

Children's questions . . . WHO?. . . and . . . HOW???
And . . . Can we open just ONE now?
Bright eyed, anxious and eager to please!
Rearranging and shaking gifts under the trees!

Long distance phone calls . . . Cards to address!
Boxes to mail . . . GOOD GRIEF . . . What a mess!
Trips to the church . . . Pageant practice and choir!
Our bodies are dragging! . . . but the kids NEVER tire!

But. . . Hurry . . . and Scurry . . . as we may!
Too soon it's here . . . CHRISTMAS DAY!
Someone's forgotten . . . we don't know who!
But . . . Our mothers survived . . . and WE WILL TOO!

Mildred E Valentine
SELFPITY
When you're sad and feeling selfpity

open your eyes, look around the city.

see the children in the street,
with no shoes upon their feet.
men and women are all alone,
with no place to call their own
now look at the sky so blue,
then thank God it's not you.

Christine Eng
THE DOOR TO TOMORROW
There is a door that I can see,
In which I hold the only key.

The door that opens to tomorrow,
Full of joy, frustration, and uncertain sorrow.

As I get closer to that door,
My anxiety and fear seem to soar.

The one thing that gets me through it all,
Not talking on the phone, or walking through the mall . . .

But, just being with my best friend,
Makes my worries and problems seem to come to an end.

Together with my pal Eileen by my side,
We'll face and succeed the future ride.

Through the door that opens to tomorrow,
With determination, laughter, and only a little sorrow.

Jodee Englund
ATTRACTION

To my inner guide, who told me where to find me.

Magnetic forces
Attract to me my beautiful
Multi-dimensional reality.
Soul born outward, into flesh.
Empowered beliefs, self-righteousness
What I seek
Blends all pasts, present and future
power entwined in my
inner connected creature
Reflecting outward the self within
No right or wrong in my terms

Just all of me, all my worlds
combined
Write the reality of my physical
world
Attracting from within all my desires
on all dimensions.

Dorothy Knerr
SECOND SON

To my beloved children: Jim, Larry, Angel, Geoff, & Renee

How did you decide Lord which of
my children should go?
My first son; tousled hair, sea green
eyes, creative hands.
My second son; soft brown hair,
crinkled blue eyed smile, brave as
the Osprey he built shelters for.
My woman-child; long golden hair,
freckles and questioning eyes.
My third son; with the beautiful
smile, struggling with life and the
why of it.
My brown-eyed song bird, my girl-
child; lives for her music. Her spirit
free as her long black hair.
Please Lord, I cannot spare a one.
Let me go instead, my life is nearer
done.
We made plans for Christmas.
What's that Lord, you say?
Larry won't be there that day?

Tina Andriuzzo
LIKE A DOVE

Like a dove
my heart flew
Right into
the gentle warmth
of your hand.
Without a thought
it laid
in your palm,
Slowly learning
to trust,
to grow,
and then
to love
Only you
gentle man.
Until it was not
just my heart,
but my very soul,
which lay safely
within your palm . . .

Roberta McKearney
WE COULD HAVE BEEN FRIENDS

Sometimes I just sit and think
About why we have to be this way
Why it is you hide from me
Each and every day.

I know that's what is happening
It makes me want to cry
I wish there could be a day
You'd look me in the eye.

I've never wanted to hurt you
I've never wanted to say good-bye
I've only wanted to share with you
A love I could not hide.

It hurts me deep inside
When I see you now
Because we could have been friends
Had we only had a chance to learn
how.

Karen L Howell
CONFUSION

To my friend, Shawn.

Life is bitter—Life is sweet
Life is empty—Life is complete
Life is down—Life is up
Life is hate—Life is love
Life is long—Life is short
Life is messy—Life is sort
Life is lonely—Life is friendly
Life is life—Life is deadly
Life is good—Life is bad
Life is happy—Life is sad
Life is rich—Life is poor
Life is less—Life is more
Life is dirty—Life is clean
Life is thoughtful—Life is mean
Life is funny—Life is serious
Life is conscious—Life is delirious
Life is old—Life is new
Life is many—Life is few
Life is real—Life is illusion
Life is knowledge—
Life is
confusion!

Paul M Nocera

Paul M Nocera
IMPRESSIONS

I want so much for you to see
A white knight on his shiny black
steed,
But the reality is that I'll never be
The one who rides in your dreams.

We come face to face and I can't
look at you
As tears have welled in my eyes,
I'd give anything to be what you
want me to be,
And to shed this deceiving disguise.

Reflections don't lie, but if you look
hard enough
You'll see what you're longing to
see,
But what isn't revealed is what's
locked deep inside,
To my heart, only you hold the key.

Look deep in my eyes to find what is
real,
Uncover the feelings decayed,
I'll take you to places that did not
exist,
Let my love for you take you away.

Peter A Caretto
MY FRIEND

To Sister Glenda Bushman and my lovely wife, Dora Lee Caretto.

His face was old and wrinkled . . .
his beard scraggled and grey.

His voice was soft and shaky . . . one
had to listen closely, to hear what he
had to say.

He told me of his youth . . . how he
had lived . . . the mistakes he'd
made, . . . his tears attested to the
truth.

I saw him again yesterday . . . the
wind blew wisps of grey, which had
escaped his battered hat.

He smiled when he saw me . . . and
motioned me to sit beside him, on
the park bench where he sat.

We talked for a long while, as I left I
looked back . . . He waved his
gnarled hand, and gave me his misty
smile.

Today . . just today . . . I looked at
him again . . . lying there in his open
casket, before they carried him into
the rain.

Who was he? . . . Do you not really
know? . . . He was you, or even I . . .
an old man . . . who like us all had
lived his life, and was looking for a
friend . . . before it was his time to
die.

Shirley Bote
MOTHER

Dedicated in Memory of my Mother Mae L. Hofbauer

You will always be remembered for
the kindness that you've shown
The love you always gave,
and the work you've always done.

Although I cannot talk to you, I close
my eyes and hear, all the words you
ever spoke,
It's as if you're very near.

I feel your presence, I see your face,
I even feel your warm embrace.
I Love You, Mom, more than you
knew,
Although I think you did.

You are my Mother and my Friend,
and you always gave your best.
I was always very proud of you, and
hope that I can be, The Mother to my
children, that you always were to me.

Lana Jean Johnson
FRIEND

This poem is dedicated to my husband, Roy, who helps me be the best that I can be.

Momentary illusions of happiness
blind me as I drift away.
but such dreams distort and
mock my intelligence.
I need a friend.

Your warm smile never
meant so much to me as now.
A helping hand to get me back
to a sort of half-reality.
I was lost in a dark
mire of misery.

But you were always
there to help . . .
I love you.

Susan Glancy
THE ACTOR

A time of dedication.
Weeks of unrelieved stress,
edging toward perfection.
Hours spent staring at pages
of meaningless words,
enhanced only by a person's actions.
Finally, the time arrives.
Behind the curtain,
dark
and
silent,
nervously trying to recite
the lines to be portrayed
in just a few seconds.
the lights slowly flicker
as silhouettes form
through the widening crack
spreading toward the edge of the
stage.
Suddenly, words of time
strengthens the audiences doubtful-
ness,
and a sudden sigh of relief
grabs the mind of the actor.

Tammy Willett
TOUCHED BY LOVE

Dedicated to the man I love Clarence R Willett my one & only forever

Open the windows of
affection to your heart.
Let the feelings of
kindhearted intimacy and
compassion run free.
Take the time,
take the chance,
to let someone know you care.
Express thoughts of
faithful understanding
to bring out the honesty
and sensitivity which is needed
to create a relationship
that will last forever!!

Shirley A Fox
OUTSIDE OF THE WINDOW

With all the tragic goings on in the
world today, it seemed that
happiness and cheer had packed and
gone away. I often wondered Lord,
oh Lord, where can joy be found,
when all I really had to do, was stop
and look around. For outside of the
window, I could see flowers all a
bloom, and birds soaring high up in
the sky, each singing its own sweet
tune. I could see the small child
playing, with a smile upon its face,
and a puppy trying oh so hard to
keep up with the pace. I saw people
outside of the window, going in all
directions, having the freedom to do
so, without any interjection. You too
can see the beauty and the real joys
of the world, without going to an
island, or taking a fancy tour.
I've said it once, but it bears
repeating because it's really so, just
turn around and you'll see joys
abound, outside of the window.

Harriet Stansell
A DREAM

As each new day breaks
I welcome what it brings,
The love I feel for my husband
I am unable to put into words.

The tenderness and kindness
And most of all forgiveness and love
That are in this man
Are emotions beyond belief

When I walk into a room
I see the love in his eyes
I feel the quickening of my pulse
Could this be real? could it?

My soul cries out at the happiness I
feel
But I fear it is only a dream.
Nothing has ever been quite this way
Dear Lord please don't let it end

Let my happiness soar as a bird in
flight
Let my love reach out to him
To comfort and console him in his
doubt.

If he returns the love that I feel for
him
What a wonderful life we will have.
May the light that shines in his eyes
for me
Continue to shine for eternity.

Drew Vigani
FRESHWATER

The water is rough
The sky is grey
Fishing to look forward to
Bundled up against the cold
Memories of days—
shirtless and in shorts

not catching a fish
could not spoil

The battle begun
Catching a fish glorious victory

Randy Dock Jones
ODE TO NURSES

To: Lewanna D. Jones, R.N., and all of the wonderful nurses at Ultimate Home Health Care, Inc. of the Golden Triangle.

Angel of mercy, hope for the future,
caring for sickness, broken
bones, or a suture.
What is the reason they pick this
career?
It's not for the praise they most
likely won't hear.
It's not for the money, they don't get
enough.
It's not 'cause it's easy, for
nursing is tough.
It's not for the glory, there's little if
any.
It's not 'cause they're lazy, their
patients are many.
It's not for the fame, famous nurses
are few.
And it's not 'cause there's
nothing else that they can do.
It's mainly a feeling inside every
Nurse,
That if someone don't do it, then
things will be worse.

A Nurse is much more than a girl in
white clothes.
A professional, which from a
need has arose,
to provide more than comfort,
as everyone knows.

A pragmatic and practical Nurse is a
jewel,
snapped up by a competent
Doctor, no fool,
for he knows that this Nurse is
a valuable tool.

And the best we can say of the
Nurses we have,
besides the bald fact of the lives
that they save,
is the bottom-line comfort, the
gifts that they gave.

Debbie Irvine
DREAMS OR REALITY

I think about you constantly,
You are always on my mind,
I want to hold you in my arms,
It's love I long to find.

Each night I sit and dream of you,
These dreams I won't forget.
I've pictured you in my mind,
Since the day we met.

Now I know dreams don't come true,
I'll have to let love be,
Since you're gone I've been missing
you,
Will you ever come back to me?

Irving Wexler
A POEM OF SORROW AND LOVE

On a grassy, leafy, knoll
In the park, I met my true love.

A little lovely, hummingbird.
What a beautiful sight she was.

Then, upon us,
The rain began to fall.

We ran for cover.
I, for the subway,
My little friend to a tree.

I never had the chance
To wave good-bye.
That was the last time,
I saw my little friend.

By a grassy, leafy, knoll
In Central Park.

One sunny day.
On a summer afternoon.
Long ago.

Mrs Frank Greer
YOUR PICTURE

I dedicate this poem to my two beautiful granddaughters, Ashley and Kelly, who have always inspired me beyond reason.

Your picture—I ran across it in a
sorta' on—purposeful way—
I looked at it for quite awhile, so
much I wished it could say—
Do you look as old as I do? Have
you a few locks turned gray?
Is your laugh still a happy one; n'do
the twinkles in your eyes stay?
Did you get that gold tooth put in the
front as you vowed you'd do?
I know some other vows you made
that didn't pan out too.
Your son—is he like you, like we
planned he'd be?
And your little prissy baby girl, is
she cute, is she?
I hope you've had wonderful years
and have been happy like me.
We thought once we'd be sure of
these things all along, didn't we?
Your picture simply ignores my
questions, won't tell me a thing,
Just looks back at me lovingly,
tempting my heart to sing.
And for a little, I'd dare to let it sing,
and forget all that I wanted to know,
And want only that you should know
that I've never stopped loving you
so!

Gordon C Sevier
MEMORIES

Deep within the night
a siren wails,
a faucet drips,
a baby cries.
Slowly the hours creep
along the alleys of my mind,
rustling the leaves
of autumns long since past
and rattling the dust bins
of discarded dreams.
This turbid stream of memories
has cast upon my shore
too many ghosts
for sleep to ever come.
Like, butterflies pinned within a
frame,
their velvet beauty forever stilled,
So are the sweet bright moments
I once knew—
paintings of a time of love
that will not come again.

D W Green
MIDNIGHT VOYAGE

Dedicated to New York City and Los Angeles, my inspiration for this poem.

The moon has risen in the night,
And people glimmer 'neath
stars' light
Sunset Strip has donned its shades,
Neon lights the color of Hades,
For a cheap thrill or demons' hunger,
Humans gather and ignore God's
thunder,
Life goes on for most you see,
Seeking something for a fee,
But in alleys out of sight,
Predators hunt and prey and
fight,
They rake in their gobbets of flesh,
And with roughened tongues
they confess,
A smell in the air of decay and mold,
Stay at home unless you are
bold,
Slither, creep, pitter-patter, crawl,
Are you asleep can you hear the
call,
Lonely whistle, clickety-clack,
clickety-clack,
Take a trip with me into madness
maybe we'll come back.

Rita R Visger
HER SON'S MESSAGE

His days are a struggle from morning
till night
Tho few are aware of his hard, grim
plight.
He plods thru each day with the
thought inside;
How futile his efforts to those
outside.

Tho his words are so clear in his own
mind's eye;
The key to release them is locked
deep inside.
When he tries to exchange his
thoughts for words,
It is plain to see he is not being
heard.

How heavy his burden, only a
mother knows.
As she watches her son, while he
struggles to grow.
Her son's message to all is to make
us aware.
He is part of God's plan to show that
we care.

He is testing our strength in the love
we display
And the patience we show in a kind,
guiding way.
So remember to keep that thought in
mind;
He could be anyone's son . . . your's
or mine.

Bob Mittendorf
I DON'T HAVE ANY FRIENDS

I don't have any friends.
People, I hate, the young, the old.
Color doesn't matter to me.

I enjoy seeing people die.
There is no nature for me,
No skies, lakes birds or trees.

What you enjoy are ugly to me.
You can buy me, I will smile at you.
I come in different sizes and shapes.

I travel a lot, churches, hospitals,
schools.
My favorite place is the cemetery.
I enjoy the tombstones.

When you visit your loved ones,
I will be watching you.
I have one friend, he likes warm
weather.

You must know of him.
His name is Devil, mine is Alcohol.
I know your name.

Alvo Joseph Antonelli Jr
CHILD

Say lost child
From whence have your sorrows
sprung
Tomorrow-You'd be one
YESTERDAY, I was O so young
Heavenly child
Speak to me

THROUGH SILENT
SCREAMS

Abandoned dreams
Gentle child
There is no future in your eyes
If you have never lived
Can you die?

Now, we both cry

MY DEAR CHILD . . .

Joyce H Chandler
TIME'S YEARNING

His long white beard and old, tired
and scholarly eyes,
Looked upon mother nature, through
many times.
If he winked at her, for her to arouse
her attention,
Her lovely lips were closed, but her
eyes made the connection.

Time and nature are of a very close
bond,
He knowing the past, present and
future that be.
She knowing all the living elements
on earth that stir,
Thus, has a miracle of time and
nature occur.

He calls to her, of his undying love,
to come to him,
And she replies "which season of
time will it be in?"
He laughs and said, "It's for you to
choose."
For their love, in which they do not
want to lose.

She answers, "I'll pick a place, in a
time that has past,"
So that their love may linger and last.
Forgetting both their obligations and
duties,
Enslaved in their love, like trapped
entities.

Then a loud voice from heaven
called out,
Like in a dream they both woke up
and listened.
The voice was clear and simple to
understand,
Telling them, that their place, was
not for their love, but to serve and
restore hope for man.

Della Frances Koster
REAFFIRMATION

To my beloved husband, the most important person in my life Harry Koster you're the one

I have loved you, fought with you
worried about you and for you.

Quarreled with you, laughed with
you, and sometimes despised you

But after almost fourteen years of
marriage
I would love to reaffirm our marriage
By pledging my eternal love for you.

Michael D Felix
SATURDAYS

Dedicated to Maggie and Mike Parents who Never Stopped Believing

I remember Saturdays as a child,
Mom and the girls;
we had three of them,
would cook, clean, sew.
We boys, the four of us,
would quickly, quietly,
find some place to go
You see, housework went with
petticoats and ponytails.
It had no place in a world of giants
rings and pirates sails.
But days of fantasy are fleeting
and soon the years of youth are gone.
Giants rings give way
to wedding rings,
and pirates sails
to laundry pails.
Till today I find
that Saturday
is just my housework day.

Marion Green
TAKE TIME OUT FOR OUR KIDS

Dedicated to my children and grandchildren

I have always taught my children;
No matter what the problems may be.
That I am there for them at all times.
Just feel free to confide in me.

They have told me about their joyous occasions.
And their sorrows as well.
There were times they made the conversation very short.
Not wanting to go into all the details.

But nevertheless, however they felt.
I was there without a doubt.
Regardless of whether they wanted to keep their silence.
Or merely talk it out.

Parents take time out with your children
Let's share our love and hugs.
And let them know, we are there for them.
It's better than any drugs.

Gladys Volgares
MY BURDEN IS SO HEAVY

To my son David whom I love very much

My burden is so heavy, as I face each day
To make someone else happy helps the pain go away
When a smile appears my heart is content
Thank you God for this knowledge is heaven sent.

Rita Edwards
THE ELEMENTS

To the Woodville High School Senior Class of 1991 Woodville, Texas

Queens and Princesses,
  Princes, Dukes, and Kings.
Love forever, beauty,
  and golden wedding rings.
Knights in white armor,
  dragons breathing fire,
Evil demons who fight good,
  and who never seem to tire.
Loyalty and love, the very
  essence of all life.
Without them you will die,
  with them you have strife.
Unicorns and gargoyles,
  winged horses and crystal balls,
Mediums and madams, who speak
  to those beyond death's wall.
The elements of stories,
  those we know so well,
Everybody loves them,
  those stories, Fairy Tales.

Pamela S Roberts-Aue
LOOT

Sunken chest of treasures
Jewels to no measure
Skeletons of the past
Greed here to last
Wars fought for fools
Just for their jewels
Their so-called pride

Doris M Clayton

Doris M Clayton
I AM ME

Sometimes I wonder who I am,
Am I a creature tried and true,
Do I fit well in all life's plan
Or is the plan for me construed?

I search the depths to find the "ME",
To find a worthwhile person there,
To find the reason,—Don't you see
Why I am here this life to share?

Am I a trusted friend you see,
With longing deep within my heart,
To warn, advise; a counsellor be,
In every way concern impart?

The "ME" you see is what I am,
Perceptual in astounding ways,
A gift in trust within a plan,
A gift to carry all my days.

My time will come when all will know,
A destiny for all to see,
To everyone both friend and foe,
The fact revealed, that—I AM ME!!

N Lee Krausse
RAIN DROPS

I dedicate this poem to Adam H. for making this possible.

Little girl crying softly
Because she cannot see
People pointed at her
She's not like you and me
Keeping to herself knowing
What life is
Seeing the inner beauty
That only she can give.
She came to me one morning
When dew was on the grass
She told me of her past life
My tears came rolling fast
The smile on her face told
me, she was happy even though
I saw her crying
inwardly with a glow.
Raindrops falling softly
In the shadows of time
In the rainstorms of my mind.
Lord why does she have
to be blind.
Raindrops falling softly
In the shadows of time.
Lord why does she have
to be blind.

Elma A Jordan
CRYSTAL CAMOUFLAGE

Overnight the world turned white,
Covering up the manmade blight.
Frosting over the city's dumps,
Burned debris, now big white lumps.

The landscape is altered.
Pristine and clean.
An illusion of grandeur
Of what lies beneath.

Debra Praytor
THANK YOU

Thank You, Lord, for this day,
And every good thing that has come my way.
I thank You for the bad things, too,
For they draw me closer to You.
Thank You for the blessings I find,
In reading Your Holy Word, Divine.
Bless my life, help me to see,
The joys in beauty, and to help those who need
To hear Your blessed Word, and hopefully receive,
The salvation through Your Son,
And the blessings You bestow
On those who receive You as their own.

Eileen Morrison
MY FAMILY

I'm the eldest of fifteen, you see, ten sisters and four brothers have me.
There's lots of love with trust in heaven above,
to make ends meet and feed this family was quite a feat!

Today all of us are not at home; one sister Francine (#2) the world doth roam.
Myself, the mother of three, left with Jim to form my own family.
Frank, the oldest brother, joined the Army, got married—what joy!
And with his wife Susan a baby was born, Frank III, a BOY!!
Christine, sister number three, lives at home with her son, Bobby.
She attends college and soon will have her Accounting Degree.
Kathleen, sister number four, is in August to be wed and leave with
Steve to make her own homestead.

That leaves Doreen, Maureen,
Pauline, Josephine and
Georgine . . .
David, Jeanine, the twins (John and Mark) and of course, Angeline.
It wasn't easy being parents of this large crew
but our parents loved us all equally we knew.
So I hope and I pray that someday they find
a home for TWO and some peace of mind.
They raised us in love with lots of joys
their eleven girls and only four boys.

Victoria Machtig
ARE YOU THERE?

A message flies,
Through the air,
And into the skies,
"Are you there?"

Somewhere in space,
On an unknown star,
An-unknown-race,
Answers, "Yes, we are."

Now what do we do,
What should we ask,
Will our question get through,
Can we handle this task?

What if they're stronger,
What feats have they dared,
Have they been around longer,
Do they ever get scared?

The questions remain,
And the list will grow,
But we can't explain,
What we do not know.

Margaret Erickson
FORGOTTEN PEACE

To all the survivors.

Condemn the men who condone the war
  That kill the young trying to
  even the score,
That maim the wounded caught in the web
  Of Death and destruction—even
  left for dead,
That mangle the children so aged for their years,
  Too young to fight; too old for
  tears,
That flatten the cities like a giant tornado
  Making refugees of its people
  with no place to go.

They stumble along wearing empty stares
  Carrying their possessions, but
  no one cares
If they live or perish by the road 'cause
  More will come by and pick up
  their load
And go wandering sadly through the dirt and dust
  Until they find a place to stay.
  It's really just
To escape the bombs raining down on our good Earth,
  And hoping to live another day,
  for what that's worth.
Yes! to live just one day more;
  Imagine! One whole day without
  WAR!

Barbara Peterson
GROWING PAINS

To Amy, Gary, and Mike

When as a child and life was so gay,
Did you ever think that there'd come a day;
When problems were many and answers were few
And sometimes it seemed like the world was on you.
When taxes and prices and all disagreed.
And you never thought that you'd ever be freed
From all of the conflicts and toils of life
That were all too heavy and too much strife.
Oh for the days of carefree joy
When the only problem was a broken toy.

Barbara Barrow Wiley
ENCOURAGEMENT

The successful sunrise
  knows no applause.
Poets perceive;
Composers describe;
Scientists stare.

Possibly curious sages

at Stonehenge shouted support
In ages when few others
Mused;
Annotated;
Explained.

Chance—
even Silurian lakes
raised slender hands
above the surface
to endorse
such a scintillating
star.

Marie Jane Franciose
DUBIOUS OUTLOOK
Lord, I'm getting older
What can I do today
Should I start to worry
And have it spoil my day.

Things are getting serious
They're coming to a head
Do I face the problems
Or get right back in bed.

Don't want to be a coward
I need some strength somehow
Untangle my fuzzy brain, Sire
And get me started now.

Renota Reynolds
MIRROR IMAGES
Our children drown in our reflection
because we give them no
direction.
We are just mirror images on the
wall,
Our image gets smaller as they
become taller.
Walking down the streets of life they
see themselves, asking the question.
Who I am?
As the years pass, they come to
see they're just a mirror image of
me.

Sandra Collins Powell
MY SOULMATE
You touched my heart with your
tender soul,
Now my flame of love is hot, like
burning coal.
You touched my soul with your
tender heart,
Love ready to burn as twin flames,
until time to part.
You touched my mind with your
deep soul thoughts,
I know I am ready and willing to at
last be caught.
You touched my body with your
electric flame within,
Like two magnets, we attracted, with
our heads aspin.
There is no high on earth like
making love,
Giving our bodies and our souls, we
reach for stars above.
In astral travel, I'll visit you many
nights,
And raise your consciousness to
wonderful heights.
Now that I know me, and where I've
been,
I can open my heart, so your love can
shine in.
Our levels as one, we'll grow
spiritually each day.
Growing stronger and wiser, to help
those in dismay.
Then one day we'll be in physical
form no more,
We'll unite with God, to guide
mankind to the door.

Jean Benson
MORN
My soul is deep, my heart is weak,
and yet, I'm quick to speak.
I laugh, I cry. my soul's on fire.

What joy , to be
a sky to see , a morning dawn
a day begun.

If I could hold the sun, stop its flight,
in early light.
The birds would sing on endless
wing.

The stillness held by beauty rare.
Oh mom, the hour has come
to carry on.

Again , the morrow
I'll look for you, to start the day.
Linger on with me
don't go away,

come back, come back,
I'll wait for you . . .

Mary R Casey
TO TRUST

To Colin, my Toad Prince

You're the cause of an ache in my
heart dear,
in the very depths of my soul.
I have tried to struggle against it
and have found that I have no
control.
You're the flashes of truth in my
memory,
you're the patience I can't understand,
you're the caring and loving I've
looked for
in the faces of other men.
Why do I fight to resist you?
Why do I mumble my cause?
Why must I stand independent
and scrutinize all of my flaws?
I'm afraid of a hurt that won't heal,
of a time that we'll part not as
friends,
and you'll go back down life's path
researching,
while for me, I will go to my end.

Wendy Lee Gardner
GUESS WHO
I am the isolated emptiness that fills
the subconscious mind.
I come from dusty attics, the dry
deserts, abandoned trains,
and inside the darkest of castle's
dungeons.
I am as old as the beginning of time
itself, but as young as
the next child born.
Happiness is my sister, never tired
and always energetic.
Always fulfilling her dreams.
Anger is my other sister, trying to
find fights or just to
argue. She leaves behind
sadness and me.,
My only brother hope and is always
on the positive side.
I like to take over people's lives,
destroying the mind,
foreshadowing disturbing
thoughts.

Whatever you do, don't be alone—
anywhere. I might take
over and you really won't like it.
It's only just a warning.
BEWARE!!! It is I loneliness.

A Evelyn W Conyers
A SPIRITUAL SUN

To Every—Living—Breathing—One=

Love Divine is
=mine=
Yours, too–
=Dire cting=
All that we do:–

Truth and Love,
=Built–into=
Each One,–is
=A Spir*itual s*n:=

Nourish It–
=Cherish It=
Praise and Pray–
=Each night;
and each Day!!=

Cindy Bochman
PRAISE
Our Dear Lord, Oh Most High,
Smiles with love from heaven's sky.
Let us rejoice and offer praise
For blessings He's the one we have
adored.
The one we can truly call "Our
Lord".

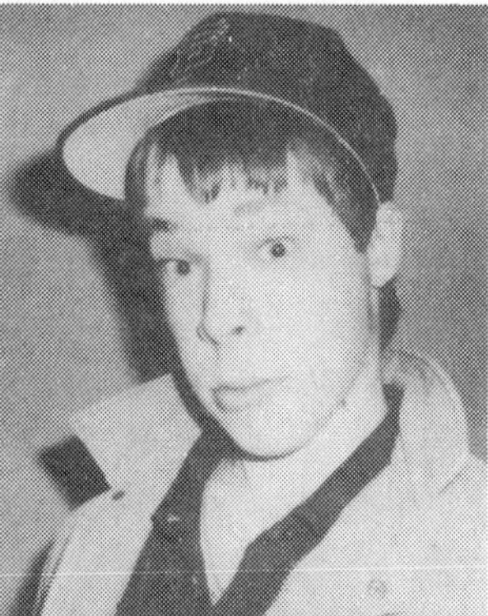

David A Watkins

David A Watkins
TALKING TO A FRIEND

To my parents for being so supportive through nineteen long years, To my sister because . . . well she's cool to my friends and to myself.

What do you do? What can you say?
When your best friend has gone
away.
What do you give her, a ring or a
bear?
To a beautiful girl who's no longer
there.
It is sad you know when you're all
alone
With no one to talk to on the
telephone,
And no one around to hear you speak
To help you up when you're feeling
weak,
What will you do? What will you
try?
Should you go somewhere and there
cry?
I know how you feel, it has happened
to me
But a voice in my mind said, "just let
it be!"
But I couldn't because it hurt bad
inside
So I went to a church and there I
cried.
There, then now take it easy my
friend
Just because she's gone doesn't mean
it's the end
Think more of the future and not of
the past
Don't try to see how long the pain
will last.
I did my best and gave you all that I
could
So now I hope you're feeling good!
Stay strong and be brave, your friend
forever, Dave.

Anna D Gamble
LISTEN AMERICA
Listen, listen America to the cries of
your children.
Hear a mother cry as she holds the
cold still body of her son.
Death from gang violence.
Hear the cry of a father as he shields
his family from the cold wind while
searching for food and shelter. The
homeless

Listen, listen America to the cries of
your children.
Hear the cries of the poor scraping
up their last dime just to live day to
day.
While the government raises taxes,
votes to give congress a fifty percent
raise, and send aid to other countries.
The poor.

Hear the cry of the siren as it picks
up another of our young.
Drug overdose or Driving under the
influence.

Listen, listen America to the cries of
your children.

Lisa Cochran
PATIO PARTY
"There once was a man from
Nantucket," he cried,
and shouted out the rest of the
limerick.
Slowly turning around on one foot,
trying hard
not to fall on the freshly manicured
lawn,
he proceeded to tell tasteless jokes.

Ragged, dirty and worn, he
contrasted sharply
with the beautiful people who started
to surround him—
not because he was the center of the
party, but
because he supplied them with a
little amusement for the moment.

"What's a girl like you doing in a
nice place like this?"
he cried, staggering after some
blonde-shell on the balcony,
falling up the stairs,
moaning incoherently to himself.

I realized that I felt both awe and
pity for him—I turned
to the impeccably groomed man next
to me and asked,
"How did he let himself get so
drunk?"
"He's not drunk," the man replied.
"He's just a bum
who lost a few screws. He sometimes comes around here
for free food and drink. We don't
mind—he adds a lot of . . .
well . . . real life to the party."

I turned my head towards the bum,
wrapped in gray
worn rags, pants about three sizes too big, a
ten o'clock shadow hiding what was left of his face.
My eyes met his.

His gray eyes, clouded with despair,
told me everything
I would ever need to know about him.

Alone.

Toni L Spears
GIFT OF WINGS
I mount bird-free beyond the sky
upon the tradewinds of time,
Wingtips touching forever,
spanning heaven in your presence.
I plunge and glide through currents of
wish-dreams unfolding,
Reveling in the new heights I
attain at your every approach.
Let me build a secure eyrie for you
among the mountaintops,
Where none could harm you nor
dare to climb.
Together, ascending to the zenith, our
souls warmed by love's-light,
Mastering the harshest, coldest
of winds,
Discovering when two touch,
blending into one gentle spirit.
There begins the freedom and
strength to explore the skies
Unafraid . . .

Frank Y Isenhour
ETERNITY FOREVER IS HARD TO COMPREHEND
Eternity forever is hard to comprehend
There was no beginning, there will be no end
Time, distance, night and day
By God's Creation all came into play.

Time is a period from a beginning to end
Forever a period from when you begin
Distance in space is light years away
Twenty-four hours, a night and a day.

Eternal God with His Arms outspread
"Let there be light" was the first thing He said
Six days in the creation of all
substance and man
From darkness eternal all things began.

Nothing plus nothing will always be
Nothing plus nothing eternally
Can anyone vision a thing so vast
Where time is no factor, no future or past.

Eons of years that have all gone by
In relation to eternity is as a bat of the eye
At any point in this eternity
The years gone by are the same as those to be.

Eternity! A mystery will always remain
With Eternal God in His Vast Domain
Back into this eternity we all will go
From whence we traverse only our
God will know.

If we have kept his commandments
and lived and good life
We are promised eternity where
there's no struggle or strife
This life eternal should be our
ultimate aim
If we don't succeed, only ourselves
are to blame.

"Justification by Grace through
Faith" is the best way,
to live the good life and be happy each day.
"IN GOD WE TRUST" is our
National Creed and should be lived
daily in each thought and deed.

Mycel Irene Vaughn
A HUG FROM MY DAD
Many times, during childhood years,
a bump, or a fall, would bring pain,
And, needless to say, that, during
those times, the tears would fall, like rain.
But the tears would quickly fade
away, and I'd realize, things weren't so bad,
When I would turn and see, that
loving smile, and then, get a hug
from my Dad.

I remember too, those "homework"
nights, when the answers he'd teach
me to find,
Although we would study the
assignments, for hours, he didn't
seem to mind.
Though I would fret, and I'd cry, as
those hours whet by, testing the
patience he had,
I could always depend on that loving
smile, and still, get a hug from my Dad.

During all my years of growing up,
my dreams he would gladly hear,
And, when some of those dreams
would crumble, he was there, with a
word of cheer.
A troubled heart seemed so much
lighter, because of the love that he had,
Especially when I'd see, that loving
smile, and then, get a hug from my Dad.

But the years hurried by, as they
always do, and now, there's an
empty space,
For Dad has gone Home, to Heaven,
and his memory, no power can erase.
And, when my precious Lord
chooses, to welcome me Home, I
know I'll be ever so glad,
To see, once again, that loving smile,
and then I'll run, to get a hug from
my Dad.

Walter C Brown
SMALL TOWNS

To the realities of youth; the transparencies of age . . . and to Lincoln, California.

Things often happen
in small towns;
"worse than big city
happenings",
town's people say.

But reality's hidden
underground;
implanted there by
moralists
with troubled minds.

Thus buried, truth
can't tear down
the perfect image
shimmering
with rural good.

Stephen Hindman
THE NAKED EYE

To my folks—for their love & support. To my sister Judy for her love & support. To Rosemarie—for being my friend.

My steps are made of wood,
only to match the rest of the house
Batten board, never painted,
weathered,
natural beauty to the naked eye.
I sit down on my steps.
The majestic mountains surround me,
more natural beauty to the naked eye.
My thoughts come alive;
one right after another,
Soaring through my delicate brain
where my sensitive mind is;
lurking for answers to the naked eye.
Beauty—can we touch it?
Silence—can we hear it?
Feelings—can we find them?
Laughter—can we see it?

So much—oh yes, it's all there, so real,
So overwhelming;
and fills my heart with a glow.
Only God and I can understand
to the naked eye.

Judy M Orr
FOG PEOPLE
Fog People
Distant cousins of the will-o-the-wisps
which dance across the fens at
twilight,
gracefully hurrying,
slender white wraiths,
melting into the trees,
emerging into the light,
twilight dreams

quickly moving, always out of
reach.

You can see the world through them.
They bring back those haunting
dreams of youth.
Are they of the past or the future?
Do not burn them with the heat of now.
Cherish their cool whispers,
Cool, smooth and gentle.
They do not laugh.
They do not cry.
Sweet reminders, let them be,
Shadows and reflections;
Clouds that broke the cycle.
Fog People.

Keith Shelton
ANOTHER LONG NIGHT

Dedicated to: Valerie Ann (Shelton) Criswell (May 29, 1966 to June 26, 1988) Now her suffering is over. To Shawn who stood by her & truly loved her and to little Ashley: A reflection of the love they shared.

Another long night, as time quickly goes by;
A cold gentle breeze, as the sun
breaks the sky.
With you on my mind, what am I to do?
All of my time, spent thinking of
you
I know you are gone, far away from me;
but here in my mind, you will
always be.
Tears often flow; you were
second to none,
and I'll think of you till my
time is done.
I thank my God for the time we shared,
and for giving someone who
truly cared,
and if by choice of what to
re-do,
I'd do it all again, right beside
you.
Through the hard times and through the good,
you were the one who
understood;
so beautiful, so innocent, so
loving, so true;
my life was made better,
through knowing you.
I thank my God for the time we shared,
and for giving someone, who
truly cared.
I know there's a reason, why
you had to go.
But now that you're gone I miss
you so.

David Meckler
THE TRAIL ROLLS ON
The trail rolls on
down many a dusty road,
to where the eagle soars
and sky burns orange and blue.
Coal to diamond and diamond to dust,
everything changes
as even you and I must.
The future wears many guises,
there is no way to tell
what secrets our destiny hold,
yet to put forth an effort is enough
for the winds of change themselves
can be rough,
to those who can not read the signs
avoid the path by which the crow flies.

Frances Stevens
JOY AND SADNESS
A little boy just three years old
Carved a pumpkin round and gold.
A low brick wall was the special place
where he sat the smiling face.
His excitement mounted every night,
As he awaited the candle to light.

Then all Saints night was finally here
witches and goblins were everywhere.
We watched them go from door to door
filling their bags with treats galore.
All Saints day had come and gone.
The pumpkin sat there all alone,
Alas at last he finally fell
upon the ground and lay so still.

The little boy one rainy day,
stood looking out the window bay.
His tear filled eyes he could not hide,
As he said, "Nana, my pumpkin died."

Loula R Shumway
THE FAMILY ALBUM
We were looking at old pictures
Trying to identify many folk,
There were young as well as old
With no names, dates, nothing of note.

I did recognize my Mother and Dad
Pictures from the early days of their
romance,

Then pictures showing them busy
with their children
Growing older together, love
showing on each face.

There were numerous Aunts and
Uncles
All dressed-up in the finery of the
day,
Also their Children, Grandchildren
and In-Laws
We could identify some, but not all,
no way.

Pictures tell stories of people and
families
You see them young and growing
old,
I saw myself as a baby, a schoolgirl,
and now—
A grey-haired Grandmother, still
sassy and bold.

The lesson in this little story—
Is to make sure the chore is done,
Putting names, dates, and places on
pictures
So there will be no doubt, about your
loved ones.

Pamela C Merritt
THE KEEPER
In the despair that pervades my mind
I look for intelligent thoughts and
find the nagging tunes I sing unwind.
I can see my sorrow alive behind.
I quicken my thoughts and begin my
climb, into my hole, darker and
deeper.
Into my cell, where I am my keeper.
Scared and confused, I control it
within.
My thoughts are reeling with no end
or begin.
My dreams are invading the thoughts
that I keep separate from the horror I
see as I sleep.
I turn to my husband. I want him to
protect me from all of my memories
that seem to infect me.
Into my hole, darker and deeper.
Set free my rage. Let go the keeper.

Wendy Schille
"POLLUTION" TREES
Though big or small, Though fat or
thin,
Though kept or wild, they are there.

Trees give air, Air gives life, Life
gives people.
Though there or not we walk past by
not even a sigh do we give but take,
But more than a sigh we have a
mistake. Though liked or not,
Though appreciated or used, they are
there.

They cannot fight off what we have
done but we have yet to make for the
loss that is yet to come.

Catherine James
JUST ONE MORE DRINK
Just one more drink, sweetheart, then
I'll be fine.
What's that! You say I have a
problem?
Oh, come on, I could stop anytime.

But I don't want to stop, I like to
drink, it relaxes me. Helps me to get
those forty winks.

You know what, sweetheart! I'm not
going to drink all weekend, and I'm
doing it just for you. We'll go
camping and swimming at the beach.
Our son, me and you'll have fun too.

Now we're home again and it's time
to go to work.
You think I don't like my new job
because I've become sort of a jerk.

I tell you I have a lot on my mind or
that I had a bad day, but it's that
thirst for a beer that just won't go
away.

I tell you I have a problem but no
one to talk to, but you say I'm
wrong. You are my wife and if I had
a little faith in you, we would work
at it together and somehow get
through.

But if I don't love you enough to at
least try, we'll just keep on the way
we are putting tears in each other's
eyes.

Love is stronger than any of us think,
and it's stronger to overcome that
thirst for "just one more drink'.

Leo James Kelly
HOW I WOULD HAVE PROPOSED
Listen to the wind.
See all the trees.
Look the fiery sky.
All these I'd give you
If you'd only say aye.

Look at that moon.
See all the stars.
Feel the good earth.
All these I'd give you
If you'd sit at my hearth.

God's in his heaven.
Angels at his feet.
But I'd feel like the greatest king
If you'd be my queen.

P Simmons
SEEKING . . . WHAT?
Peace and tranquility they say
Is where the palm trees sway—
With great agility.
Sweet fragrances fill the air,
And relaxation is the order of the
day.

How blue the sky, how clear the
water,
Yet, unseemingly are the changes.
We are too eager my dears.
Rise, sleep—ease the tension of
yesteryear.

Time's shrouded in the mist,
Brilliant sky of light—
Cold pierces the soul,
Floating—waves roar, smashing the
beach.
The nights' storm rumbles into
day . . .
It's cold; lonely.
Where is the embrace of calm—he
gave?

Susan L Banks
AN ANGEL FROM HIS LOVE

Dear Rachel—I love you—Mom

Babies come from heaven
like a star within the sky,
love within a heart
And memories that never die,
My baby is an angel
She's a dream that has come true
The lord he gave her to me
And he told me what to do.
He said to love her endlessly
To give her endless care.
He told me to protect her
And the moments that we'd share
He told me I should give her
All the love within my heart.
To understand her dreams
Without tearing them apart
I thank the lord for giving me an
angel from His love
I will do the things he asked of me
For my baby from above.

Betty Huber
YEAR ON THE FARM
In the twilight of the morning
The dew was all around;
We saw the sun arising
And the shadows on the ground.

We listen to the birds all sing—
The whippoorwill did sound;
The bobwhites were so happy
And the squirrels a scampering
round.

We knew spring was upon us
And the planting time has come—
To start a new beginning, each and
everyone.
We plow and spray and seed the
ground
With hopes and dreams we toil;
Continuing our daily lives working
with the soil.

The season will soon be over;
working dawn to dusk
It passes very quickly for all of us.
Waiting so impatiently, for growing
time is hard—
To see no rain or too much rain
We face it with a smile;
To trust in God, is all we have,
To make our lives worthwhile.

Basilisa L Halog

Basilisa L Halog
OUR LOVE AFFAIR
One of the days I can't forget
Was that day, Love, when first we
met
You winked at me and I smiled, too
That started it, our love so true.

I tried to shrug your pleas, my dear
Your loneliness showed out so clear
Your sweet, kind words sure
mellowed me
And I'm glad I made you happy.

Our courting days came to an end
We tied the knot for that's the trend
And sure enough we shared a lot
Of experiences of this and that.

But happiness don't last that long
There's always something that goes
wrong
Whatever comes will never stay
The wheel of life goes on its way.

Eloise Hunt
BEREFT
Snowflakes are falling through the
leafless trees
Whiter than cherry petals on the
breeze.
Blurred the world's colors in white
beauty,
Muffled all sound. The stillness
freezes me.
Lost in dreaming I feel the quick
tears start,
For I remember the last time we
kissed
The snowflakes falling in a soft white
mist.
I am alone now—alone with despair,
Knowing full well that you no longer
care,
And the white snow is falling on my
heart.

Matthew Forcelli
SPIRIT OF LOVE
The spirit of love
Moving this earth
Around and around
it goes
moving closer to heaven

The spirit of love
invisible like the wind
But strong enough to move the sea
spirit of love comfort me

The spirit of love
Taking my breath away
Changing night to day
Letting life become a dance
Someday all souls would feel it
The spirit of love

Sonali Sinnatamby
A SATURDAY IN THE LIFE OF A WORKING WIFE
Darling. It's Saturday. Good
morning.
Thro' the chink in the drapes see day
dawning.
Darling, I've fever. I'm cold. Hug
me, please.
My sinus is being tickled, oh dear, by
a sneeze.
Angel, I can't cook lasagne tonight—
Head throbs, throat's aflame, can't
eat a bite.
Drat, I've the 'flu, must have got it
from Bob—
He's famed, you know, for doing
more than his job.
My body is aching, my back
breaking,
Limbs are shaking . . . feel like
taking
Some Aspirin. That's it, get me two,
I'll struggle; I'll fight; I'll combat
this 'flu.
And darling, some hot milk or tea
would be nice;
If you are hungry—in the fridge
there's some curry and rice.
Vacuum the carpets, mop the floors,
The tub's to be scrubbed. Hey—an
idea . . . paint the doors!
Please hold me close, I think I am
sinking,
I'll lie on your chest—darling, what
are you thinking?
Romesh? David Romesh, where are
you?
"In sickness and in health"—and
wife's got the 'flu.

Judith Delfine—Lanier
THOUGHTS TO MY DAUGHTER

To our daughters: Deandra Marie Lanier, Sara Marie McClurg, Cheryl Susan Redmond, April Ann Davis and Courtney Rose Halyard; most especially to my husband Gene Lanier, without whose support and love this poem would not appear here.

It simply does not quite apply
oftentimes, say I,
To scold a child
until they cry.

'Tis better to take

a lighter stand
With a warm and
caring hand.

The knowing smile,
a gentle way
Can far better
save the day.

Words wisely chosen,
just what you feel . . .
Best tell a child
what is, and is not,
Real.

Sharon R Lindsey (Davis) Lecrone
SIMPLICITY
Oh little butterfly,
you are all the things
I yearn to be,
sensitive and beautiful!

People love you,
for what you are
you have nothing you
need to prove!

How I envy your "elusiveness"
and your free style of living.

You are loved and adored by,
all who seek to touch you.

But, never wanting to be held
too tightly for fear
they might destroy you—or—
shatter your dreams . . .

Patricia Henley
THE LITTLE GREEN FROG

I dedicate This Poem To My Grandson, "Levi" Who LOVES Frogs.

The Little Green Frog
Was Sitting On A Log

He's Waiting For A Fly
To Come Buzzing By

He Was Hungry You See,
He Could Even Eat A Bee

A Butterfly Fluttered Near
Not Close Enough, I Fear

He Sat There All The Day,
And None Came His Way

Poor Little Green Frog
Who Was Sitting On A Log

Robert K Veazey
JUDGE ME NOT
Judge me not, for I am prone
To walk among the living dead.
Ambition gone with ego smashed
My world exists of fears and dread.

A cloudy mist that casts its shroud
Upon the wretched, leaves its mark
To stumble through the burning mist
Eternal night, eternal dark.

Slipping deeper in the muck
Self-inflicted wounds that tear
Throbbing on a broken dream
Desperation with despair.

Never trying to ascend
And leave this stagnant Devil's pool
So blind to this important thought
That no one ever aids a fool.

Until he first makes an attempt
To help himself, move toward the top
It takes a while to muster strength
To make that move, so Judge Me
Not.

Silvia Malek
LOVE AND KNOWLEDGE GONE
I walk upon the weary shore,
Where sand and shells bore no more.
The seagulls don't fly high above,
The waves don't crash like a door.
Oh . . . what does this world come to
now,
Where love and knowledge is gone.

Sam Bauman
IN MY MIND
In my mind,
The
Camera shudders;

Drifting distantly,
To
Livid fantasy;

I'm aware,
But
Exit twelve runs by;

The curve . . . I see,
Yes,
I caress gently;

Driving me,
Now
Down dual destinies:

One seen, one sought,
Here
In my sighing veins.

Michelle L Baranik
I, LIKE A MOUSE
I, Like a Mouse
am timid and shy,
always watching people go by.

I, like a mouse
hide in fear,
in case someone sees
me shedding a tear.

I, like a mouse
see people walk by,
maybe, just maybe,
they are the ones who are shy!

Margaret Edwards
WHEN AM I HAPPY?
I'm not really happy when I go out
among friends,
I'm not really happy when I get stares
from men . . .

I'm not really happy when I make an
"A" in school,
I'm not really happy when I hear
gossipy news . . .

You know when I'm really
happy . . .
WHEN I CAN WRITE A POEM
A poem about the way I feel or felt in
the rain or in a storm.

I'm happy when I'm pecking away at
my typewriter . . .
pecking not for work or play . .
happy when I read on paper what
Margaret Edwards has to say . . .

Just to hear ME say what I really,
really do feel . . .
whether it's about the weather or
someone being ill.

I'm happy when I put on paper, what
I feel inside my heart,
I'm even happier when I say
it . . . and mean every little part.

I love writing about you, men,
women and children . . . but most of
all,
I love writing about ME and
life . . .

ME and life have a lot going . . . I'm
not sure we're going in the right
direction, at the right time, in the
right place, or with the right people,
but we're going . . .

Some days we're going beautifully,
some days we're going bad,
Some days we're going slowly, and
some days we're going mad!

I'll always write poems as long as I
live . . . you see this is what makes
me happy . . .
and it's all that I can give . . .

Because this is when I'm really
happy!

Ruby Poynter
DOWN ON THE FARM AGAIN
The spark of light
Chasing up and down the stream
The mocking bird in view
Chirping out his favorite dream

The drifting sounds
Rustling in the trees
A soft melody floating
In the early morning breeze

Magic moments alive again
The smell of honey suckle every
where
Nature's traditional perfume
Hung heavy in the air

Down on the farm again
Tranquility in all its splendor
A time to treasure
And a time to remember

Anna L Anderson
MY MA MAL
On bended knee she knelt to pray
with hands lifted to the sky

Her tear-stained kerchief in her hand
and on her finger a golden band

Oh, I remember her kneeling there
with her eyes closed in prayer

Her wrinkled skin, twisted hair
and trembling lips as she knelt there

Sometimes she would just say
"Thank you Lord for the day."

Other times she would pray
for her children near and far away

A pioneer woman brave and tall
but best of all she was My Ma Mal

Teri Taylor
FREEDOM
The tremulous body of land fought
With the cold, harsh sea
And lost.
It then again sat completely still.

Years later the body of land is still
repressed.
It sits motionless,
While the sea is still reprimanding it
for trying to
Break away.

Traci Fitzwater
WISE WORDS FROM A FRIEND
When large problems come about,
be sure to find someone to share the
doubt.
Although your life may be falling
apart,
the desire for love lingers in your
heart.
When all happiness reaches an end,
remember your hope is a new found
friend.
Leap forth with great energy, and
without despair,
find someone you know will surely
care.
You'll know they're caring, and
they're nice,
when they offer this wise advise.
"Never give up that slim little hope,
out there somewhere there's a way to
cope."
"If you hold on a little bit more,
there's a way to become secure."
"Don't look back, today's the day,
there's a hope, there's a way."
"Follow the trail of courage and
pride,
I'll always be there by your side."
"We're together forever more,
joined as friends, we'll win the war!"

Glenn Heiston
THE RIDE
The time that came,
the time that went,
another empty night I
spent, dreaming of
you.

Through my heart I
weep holding out for
your friendly hand.
My mind wonders in
silence, as I pray
you understand.

Till then I'll roam
this empty land,
passing through time
and time, I make
alone my lonely ride.

Mrs Ruth Grayer

Mrs Ruth Grayer
YOU DO NOT WALK ALONE

To My Family

You do not walk alone, the lonely
road
For God is always near,
He shares your heartache and your
pain
And knows the things you fear.
His hands will guide you safely,
For his love is always there,
To give you strength and courage, if
you ask for it in prayer

Howard L Kaiser
YAHANO
I hear Yahano call to me, how can
this be?
I felled him in a field of blood,
In France so far across the sea,

And as he died he begged of me,
To lift his body from the mud.

'Oh place me sir where the ground is dry,"
'Twas upon his final breath,
And as I watched Yahano die,
There came a tear into my eye,
Then I spoke to him as he lie in death.

Yahano lad, you and I are hopeless fools,
Until just now we knew not one another,
For the breeders of this sin we are the tools,
'Tis you and I that fight their duels,
Who knows? I may have loved you as a brother.

I hear Yahanos' voice within the wind,
I see Yahanos' face while I'm at prayer.
But when he calls, he calls in tone of friend,
And though I search, this sin I can't amend,
So be Yahano with me here, I must be with him there.

Linda Milner
HEARTACHE
Today I left home,
Mama never liked me.
Under no conditions did she prefer
The false characters I created.

We had, she had tantrums
When tranquility was needed.
But me, relaxed and sinistered,
Smiled to rupture the pain of leaving home
The woman I always loved;
Sometimes.

Tomorrow was cold,
Onlookers never cared.
Tender shadows lied
Promises whispered as wounds screamed,
I laid aching in the dark by myself.

Tammy L Schroeder
IT WAS NOT MY CHOICE TO BE BORN NOR TO DIE
It was not my choice to be born nor to die.
My life was given to me as a precious gift;
No strings attached.
I could live as I wished—
To share it with whoever I chose.
Nothing lasts forever;
Except my eternal soul, which will exist after my lifetime here on earth with you.
Our time together never seemed long enough,
But now I have another place to go.
Remember . . . I'm only a whisper away.
Please don't grieve,
For I'm no longer physically here.
I will always be with you
In the loving memories we've shared.

Angela B Hudson
A BUTTERFLY
He laughs, he smiles,
he sighs, while he listens
To the sounds of the world.

He cries inside
as he looks around;
He sees the acts of men.

Then he sees
a majestical creature
Which reminds him why he is.

As he watches
a peace overcomes him
Such as that possessed by the insect.

He begins to understand,
as the creature falls to the ground,
That good is always accompanied by bad.

He returns to his home
tired and in need of sleep,
But he is content.

As he lays to sleep
he ponders his day;
He is indeed lucky.

Debra Nelson
CONSEQUENCES
Through winter's cold unfeeling age
the hope of Spring survived,
And pushing through the frozen earth
the seeds clung fast and thrived.

Enduring through the frigid winds
it struggled to prevail,
Down torturous and wanting roads
a long and lonely trail.

But seasons changed and came a new
a vain and pompous foe,
It twirled in glee and teased the Spring
with words of stinging blow.

The summer grew in strength and force
and Spring began to wane,
Against its foe's adversity
its struggle was in vain.

The Summer overshadowed Spring
and crushed its youthful rays,
And Summer never stopped to see
the product of its ways.

J Catanzaro
ANGUISH
Another tear coming down my cheek.
An ache in my heart, my composure's weak.

The pain in my heart is more than I can bare.
Every time he says, that's the truth—I swear!

How can someone you love so much, hurt so deep?

With eyes so innocent, deceive so sweet!

To find your very best was not enough.
We gave too little, or we gave too much.

Will he learn too late to turn back,
Iron bars keeping him from the right track.

How much hurt can a father's pride withstand?
Before their son becomes a man.

Julie Harrington
ALL GOD'S CHILDREN
He made you and he made me
He made us different colors I see
He made some white, red, yellow and black
But, He promised all creation that He's coming back.

He was spiritual born, crucified and arose
He didn't die for colors He died to save our souls
He commanded us all to love one another
I'll be your sister and you be my brother.

He loved us so much that He gave
His only son
He won the victory the battle has been won
So lets drop our weapons and hatred within
He's the same today as He was then.

We all know that this world is full of evil and sin
Open up your heart and let Jesus in
Regardless what color or race you lie
We are all one in the Saviour's eyes.

Because He made you and He made me
He made us different colors I see
He made some white, red, yellow and black
But He promised all creation that He's coming back.

Frank Holiday
ETERNALLY

In memory of Gladys E. Holiday my Grandmother who inspired me to succeed.

Saying "I'm sorry"
Can never erase
The pain in your eyes
The look on your face.

From the moment I hurt you
And then walked away
Not showing my own pain
That terrible day.

To expect forgiveness
I would be insane
You are afraid I would hurt you
Over again.

I know that your hand
I shall never again hold.
I know that your heart
To me has grown cold.

I weep for my loss
For you are a jewel.
I tossed you aside.
I've been such a fool.

I'll love you forever
In my own special way.
In my heart we're together
Eternally.

Evelyn Green Boehmlehner
ARE RULES TO BE BROKEN
Are rules to be broken
When a little child is losing;
Her color cards not matching
And she wants another chance?
Her soft eyes fill with tears
As her cards come up unmatched,
And she thinks the rules are wrong
And the other players cheating.
But we played the game by rules
And her tears just kept on flowing.
How I longed to change her choices
And give her one more chance.

Then both our hearts were hurting
As her brother won the game;
Not because he won it fairly
But because she had to lose.
Will she understand it better
As on through life she goes
That when certain rules are broken,
The winner loses too?

Patricia Wergin
RETIRE OR REFIRE?
I did not think retirement would be hard to take,
But there are so many new decisions that are difficult to make.

All those tasks so long left undone
Now seem to represent a battle not won.

Because of a fact I scarcely mention
(That being the miniscuity of my pension),

I wonder if I should seek a part-time position,
Or should I dig for hidden talents to augment my mission?

Whatever I choose to be a true challenge,
I hope it will bring to my life a bright new balance!

Adriana Beun
MY FIRST LOVE
What am I gonna do
with all this love for you
If you tell me to
I will be yours

I know you love me
why won't you tell me so
I will never go
I will be yours

No one has ever
touched me like you do
caressed me and kissed me, too
You are my first love

Baby, when you hold me
there are no words for love
I just look into your eyes
and I know I'm loved

What am I gonna do
with all this love for you
I can never, ever
forget you, my first love

Cheryl Pritchard
PEBBLES WATER ROCK
Suns diversify coloured rivers
rising across me
seemingly smoothed . . . unmarred
Assimilated though distinct

At times randomly lifted
skip lonesome across waters
Black consumes the weak

At times, perchance, held
thoughtful blunt facets
scratch crust
His lovers initials onto white birches
remind me

Covet the day chosen
selectively amid the similar
Tenderly touched . . . enwrapped
as Sotah stone

Ascribe me down
in an honorable whisper

and call me Art.

Dorothy Osgood-Sojourner
TEACHERS
When my mind was young and fragmented,
You helped to shape it.
When ideas were suppressed and stifled,
you helped to free them.
When dreams were obscure and

blurry,
You helped to focus them.
When goals were far-fetched and distant,
You helped to stretch me.
When my heart was forlorn and faint,
You helped to inspire it.
When my spirit was marred and shattered,
You helped to restore it.
When you kept giving
I kept evolving.

Frieda Kowert
VIEW WITH YOU

Upon the other shore
Small, blinking lights we see;
Far below, the river
Glides on, so noiselessly.

Little emerald islands
Watch the stream go by;
Tiny looking bridges
Span it, arched so high.

On all the wooded slopes
Faintly we can see
Where the Artist painted
Crimson, gold, upon each tree.

Slowly dusk descended,
As blessing from on high;
Thus o'erlooking nature,
God, Himself, seemed nigh.

There we stood together,
Admiring, reverently;
All the world was beautiful,
And you were there with me.

Timothy Jay Sheehan

Timothy Jay Sheehan
THE SHOES OF WINE

The shoes of wine have walked
upon the earth

And some have touched the sky.

As church moves alcohol
with candles in the dark.

The art gallery has too long been bound
with an imitation brush

And who will speak for weaver's art?
A spider? You supposed.

I think I'll take the world up and say,
a butterfly
the power of a billion light
bulbs
or a seed unto the Sun.

Jacqueline Dzwonszyk
BILL BUCKLEY

Bill Buckley is the man I hold
The greatest on T.V.
But for his hour of "Firingline"
My "tube" would cease to be.

On any topic that's discussed
Bill's brain will shed some light
Disarming smiles will punctuate
The points that win the fight.

As moderator, he's supreme
With skill that is unique
With guests debating heatedly
He shows unmatched technique

As sequel to these stimuli
Just read a book he wrote
I wish he'd run for president
He'd surely get the vote!

Tascha Dresser
MY SPIRIT

This poem is dedicated to all the handicapped people of the world, no matter what anyone has told you—you can make it.

My spirit is like the bright orange on a tiger's coat. It is as free as the tiger roams. No one can stop my spirit's growth, for it is as fearless as a tiger I am told. Let people dare to break my ego, for it is strong and cannot be broken easily; let them try to quiet my spirit, for it is as bold and out spoken as a tiger is free; you can say that there's a part of a tiger in me.

Genevieve Gencorelli
INFINITE HOPES

For those who believe in the light . . . Sito.

The mystical moonbeams shone on her hair,
As she walked along in the deep, dark night.
Distraught and tired, she thought of giving up, she had lost hope.
From out in the darkness there shone a light,
Mysterious, yet more brilliant than any other she had seen before.
She now had reason to go on.
She walked slowly and steadily toward her destination,
Slowly, for fear of what her discovery might reveal,
Steadily, to get there before the light dimmed and faded into darkness.
Uncertainty slowed her pace until she stopped to think;
"Should I?",
"What if?",
"Maybe . . . ".
She began to walk again,
With each step the light became more bright, more intense and increasingly brilliant.
Her heart began to race as she thought of the possibilities that this spark beheld.
The glimmer from the light nearly blinded her,
The heat of its passion seemed likely to burst into flames,
The moment of truth was upon her,
She reached out as she was within an armslength of its distance.
Suddenly the light shone no longer.
Uncertainty is a drawback,
Hesitation is a waste.
What could have been, she will never know,
She was too late.

Sandra Bumbaco
HIDDEN PAINS OF LIFE

This poem is dedicated to all people, young and old who have lived in a disruptive household.

If only I could alleviate
some of your pain.
Deep conversation, I listen to you—
unable to look at your face.
Knowing all too much of the pain.
Everytime I say "I know what you mean"
I feel that those words
are a cold comfort—that I don't understand.
But if facts were really revealed,
the ones I chose to bury.
It would only lessen my strength,
I learned to need, in overcoming
the days of yesteryear.
Those dreadful nights
I will never forget, The ones I didn't create but had to live with.
With maturity I learned
to awaken from this nightmare and
let go of those bad ordeals.
But not without animosity!
Confident it will never happen again.

Anne Martin
LOOKING FOR A SIGN

Writing for the Lord

The hills so green, the creeks running clear,
the crops growing splendidly.
The baby lambs, and the calves frolicking in the fields.
Baby birds learning to fly . . .

The sunsets were golden, and orange, sometimes with a faint touch of purple.
As far as I could see there was this beautiful expanse of golden sky.
On occasion the sun up, so early, a flaming orange . . .

I had asked God for a sign . . . but when I looked around me . . . signs were everywhere to be seen.

Lorna E Wayne
POE

Mysterious yet sweet
humorous & still complex
depth of character
mystical hypnotism
poetic romance
& polished words
the dancing & passionate
imagination.

Angel S A Muhammad
THE DREAMSLAYER

To the families of: Holmes, Elliot, Mattlock, Leggett, Hubbard, Washington, Coleman, Clift, Bybdon, Hernandez, Young, Allen, Mack, Hunter, Ammons, Casurella, Langston, Owo, Muhammad and Tittsworth.

On the way to the Palace where all dreams go.
I carried in my bag some fresh flower seeds along the side of the road to sow.
I saw a quaint stranger beneath the shade of a tree.
He was clothed in a mantle of dismal despair.
"Young man, to you what is a dream?" Said he to me.
He was the slayer of dreams sprawling there.
"Sir, to me a dream is something of beauty and charm, associated with reality, sometimes wild and fancy."
"Then tell me young man, what is your dream of wanting to be?"
"My dream, Dear Sir, is, to encourage artistic talent wherever it may occur."
"You can't make a living for yourself doing that."
He said to me flat.
While trying to badger my dream of success.
He laughed to break my spirit to even less.
I will never let him slay my dream.
I'll keep it out of his reach and too far beyond his kean.
I bade him farewell with my forward glance.
My dream drove me onward to create this chance.
Your dream will be brighter after every cloud.
There may be a villain, a scoundrel or a dream-slayer in every crowd.

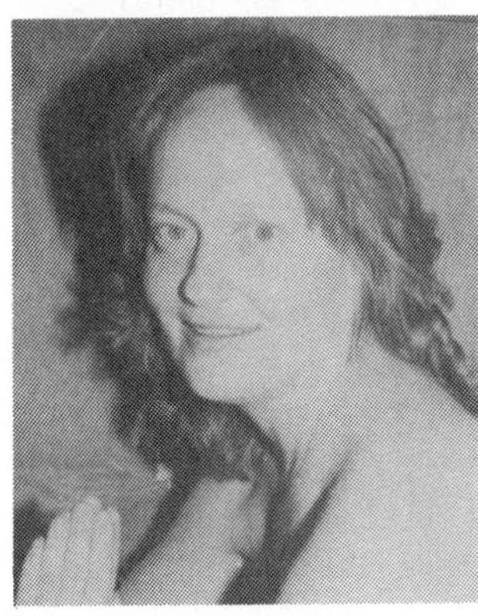

Helma Barth

Helma Barth
CONCEPTION

Mysterious Guest,
You surround me with light
Playful golden showers, dancing flecks of gold around my head and shoulders.
Who are you who come to me this day?
I open my heart to your presence.
I feel your stirrings, child of the earth
Wind rustling in the tree of life.

I know your path here on earth
Coming for this moment to be All
from the great circle of Love
Where death ends and life begins.
We are one now in time, and later I will watch you grow
From this spark of light to a tall
Being with arms, legs, and a will of your own.
The will you have is the will of All
They will know your name, and I will give you this name.

Even now as I hear your call I dread our goodbye
Praying that it is I who leave you one day, my work done,
When there is nothing left for me but to go where you came from
The dimensions of which I know not
Yet which you know now.
The mystery of the circle eludes me
Where have you been and where are we going?
Oh, tiny particle of Oneness, the totality of all.

Rose Darrow
LO, I AM WITH YOU

Troubles, troubles, troubles, enough to bring tears to the eyes,
But amidst the snow and the wind,
God put a rainbow in the sky.
It's like he was saying, "Lo, I am with you always,
Will be unto the end,
Just lean on me my child, for I am your comforter and your friend.
I said I would never leave nor forsake you, even in your darkest hour,
For I am here for you even when

things go sour.
The sunshine on the 'morrow will make everything look new,
Just trust in my power to carry you through.
There's coming a day when no more tears will dim the eye,
When I come for my people in that sweet by and by.
But until that time comes, just come to me in prayer,
And lay them all upon my altar, all your burdens and your care."

Penelope Gautreaux
THE WAY WE WERE

"Where has all of our love gone?"
"We live together, but yet alone."

"We used to cherish each other's emotions;"
"We lost that loving feeling and the devotions."

"We used to communicate with total compassion;"
"But now our conversations are filled with distractions."

"When we first met, it was a dream come true,"
"No one could love the way we do."

"As the years went by;"
"Our love began to die."

"Then we realized, the reason we're together & why;"
"So, now we won't let our love slip by."

"With memories of the past, still fresh in our hearts;"
"We know in the future, we could never live apart."

"So as we still struggle to share our lives together;"
"We'll hold on to each other forever, and ever."

"A love like ours, is a once in a lifetime;"
"It's a special gift, that's yours and mine."

"We'll hold on to yesterday, with all of our emotions;"
"And yet keep striving forward with stronger devotions."

Cindy Jo Cherry
THROUGH A CHILD'S EYES

If a child had a choice
about being born—
Would they look to the world
with wonder or with scorn?

Would they see a clear view
of the things we've done right—
or would the hate and destruction
be blocking their sight?

Billy R Smithey
OUR DAD

We know hell is so hot that a
Body can't stand.
But God needed a fireplace to
Warm his hands.
He searched the whole world over,
And without quest,
He chose Marvin, for he knew
He was the best.
God called him home, and we all
Know why
To build his great fireplace,
Up in the sky.
Each brick he lays, unfolds his
Life.
And when he's done, he'll sit with
Lena, his wife.
Heaven's just seconds, or minutes
Away,
Sometimes a year and sometimes
A day.
Now Marvin doesn't want his friends
Or family to be sad.
We know this is true, for he is
Our Dad.
We all love you "Pop." Amen; from
Mama and all your sons.

Donna Young
A ROOM BENEATH THE GROUND

Sitting here,
beneath the ground.
In a room of white
like a chalky gown.
The stairway,
is long and white.
With a metal door,
to keep it quiet.
In this room,
there is a row of beds,
each having a different spread.
There is light brown carpet
lining the floor,
It stops;
an inch from the door.

Kostadinka
A PASSING GLANCE

A filigree of fragile lace white caps danced
in frenzied pace,
Then slid into a waiting trough of lighter blue,
but not so rough.
Clouds and sky, in pose pristine of blue and white,
mirrored the scene,
While swelling silently beneath a stretched out sea,
a coral reef.

Sheila Betts Stewart
MISS YOU

I miss you tonight—my love,
While stars are in the quiet skies.
My mind is turned to moments past,
Of joys and sorrows shared—that last.

In sleep though you are not beside me
Your love surrounds me—ever near
With sunny dawn my heart quickens
And gone is nighttime fear.

The day goes by, I tend to chores
To child's cries, and little sores—
Then Joy!—Your footsteps cease to roam.
Your voice—Those beloved words—"I'm Home!"

Jacqueline Hagen
DIAMONDS ARE FOREVER

For Robb and Trevor Without you two guys, I'd have had no reason to write these poems.

This ring that I wear on my left hand
you gave to me to show that you cared
this ring will forever remind me of you
and of all the memories we've shared.

The day that you gave this gift to me
was the day that my love had come true
from that day on I thought it was mutual
and that always it would be me and you.

Only now everything has been turned around although this ring I will always wear
it is now a reminder of our love that's been lost
a memory of how much you used to care.

To me, this ring is a part of us
and of all the good times that I can treasure it is all of the love you once felt for me
it was an amount that could never be measured.

And as long as I still wear this beautiful ring
I keep hope that we will get back together
because I know that deep down you still feel that love
and I know you realize diamonds are forever.

Joseph A Centanni

Joseph A Centanni
LISA "I LOVE YOU"

To you Lisa I dedicate this poem, I'll never forget you. Love, Joseph A. Centanni

I never really knew you
Your eyes were oh so blue
You were so young and helpless
They took advantage of you
A candle full of shining light
You couldn't even try to fight,

To save your life was a helpless job
I cannot bear it; I have to sob
Oh little one, I love you so
If I had the chance; I'd let you know
I'm on your side; I'll help you live
I wish I was there, for me to give
The help you needed to get you by
Oh Lisa, I wish today you were alive!
Now you're in heaven, with the angels tonight
I love you Lisa, goodnight, goodnight

Deborah E B Swain
THE SONGWRITER

Calculated darkness
Predetermined mood
Candelsmoke and paper
Ivory and wood

Black and white together
Black and white apart
Method music
With no heart
Bits and pieces
Extra gilding . . .
Complicate the rhythm
Simplify the brass . . .
Concentrated
Pressure building . . .
Scotch and water
Ice and glass . . .

Quietly and unpredicted
Unrestrained—unrestricted
Tones and voices build a sound
Magic music—write it down.

Luann Martin
GYPSYLAND

This poem is dedicated with much love to Erik D. Honeycutt.

There is a place that I love
It's a place that I've always dreamed of
A world secluded from the rest
A nice cozy little nest

Deep in the Emerald Forest
Down by the Purple Sea
Is where they gather, the gypsies
Dancing and singing to an Irish tune
Or telling fortunes by the light of the moon

A secret little atmosphere
That the average folks fear
A special language that only they understand
They can tell all by the palm of your hand
Forever . . . I want to stay in Gypsyland!

Beverly Swezey
ME

This poem is dedicated to my dear family and future grandchild, and my dear friends Bud, Joy, Jason, ?, Betty, Elanor, Robyn and Bill, Joann

Sometimes when day is done I feel like my work has just begun.

There's washing, and ironing and cleaning to do, no one helps, Lord what do I do!

My get up and go has got up and went, I am feeling tired I have no strength.

Just once I'd like the dishes to be done, just once I'd like no errands to be run.

But this is the real world plain, as can be, the only help I can get, has to come from me.

Brion K Hanks
ONE TRANSITION

For my brother and all others who have gone ahead, and too for we the living—that we may understand death is but One Transition.

Though I now look upon the old you
And feel an immediate sense of loss,
Still, I know the future must now
Command your utmost attention.
Day by day, until we meet again,
Search that great vastness
With courage and determination.
Though you have gone ahead,
One day I will catch up and embrace
The new you and we will know then
That life really does go on . . .
If you check back now and then
I hope you find me with a smile
Upon my face and happiness
In my heart . . . seeking light and

Love as the hope of the future.
Let go now, you will be all right.
This is something we all must do.
Remember, with beauty and balance as
Your armor, you will know rapid growth.
Farewell my friend . . . God speed.

Amanda Lynn Redfearn

Amanda Lynn Redfearn
SUNNY
The sun is shining today.
But tonight it won't.
I don't know why though.
I think it's because no one's up.

Catherine L Mabeus
GOODBYE FOR NOW

In loving memory of my father George A. Shunhart, who passed away February 24, 1988.

Dad, it's been a year since you were called away . . .
A year, and yet sometimes it seems like yesterday.
You were gone so suddenly, no time to say goodbye . . .
He must have needed you to tend His garden in the sky.

Sometimes I think I hear your steps across the floor . . .
I miss you, yet I wouldn't wish you back to suffer as before.
You never would have suffered if I had my way . . .
You'd be healthy and happy, and you'd be here today.

I think of you often . . . not a day goes by . . .
That you don't bring a smile to my lips and a tear to my eye.
My thoughts often wander back through the years . . .
To when you knew just what to say to drive away my fears.

You were tired and hurting when He called you home . . .
Now down Heaven's garden paths on painless legs you roam.
That is the thought that eases my mind . . .
And knowing that someday I'll once again walk by your side.

Izetta Wallace
LIFE
Life is a long and lonely road which we all will travel.
One may be loved, hated or unappreciated. For this is what life may offer.

One may even travel the road with hidden forces that deter us from accomplishing the ultimate goal and the desire to reach the biggest star.

This road condemns you to hell and torment. Establishing destructive tendencies and deviant behavior.

Never forget that we are the future, teach me well, help me, guide me, show me my beauty, help me establish my sense of pride so that I can be proud of me.
Help me find the road to success for I am the future, and I will reach for the biggest and brightest star.

Jennifer Lynn Hoag
LONELY OLD FROG
There once was a frog
That sat all day in a log
Plenty of friends would ask him to swim
But he'd rather be alone and grim
No matter how hard they try
He'd always find a way to make em cry
I guess he just enjoyed being alone
Because he didn't even like to talk on the phone
He always acted mean and evil
He even scared the little Boweevil
Now he's all alone in his log
Continuing to be a lonely old frog.

Mollie Antonio
MAN OF MINE

To my loving husband, Frank Whom I cherish dearly. I LOVE YOU

For his eyes never hide what he's feeling inside,
And his touch is sometimes really too much.
He's tender yet strong, and that too keeps me
Hanging on to this dream I've had for so very long.
For he's sweet and unique from his head to his feet,
And that for sure keeps me at my peak!
Good looks and charm! surely that's no alarm,
For he's always near and I know he's sincere.
Laughs and smiles that he gives so freely,
Makes me envy him so dearly.
Love and understanding that he keeps handing,
Helps me not doubt what he's giving out.
Cute at times and the rest combine,
Are all the ingredients to this perfect
Man of mine.

Kay Gibson
A PRAYER

To my son, Jerry Gibson, and his wife, Sharon; To my daughter, Diane McMullen, and her husband, Larry.

Lord, let me play my role in life according to Thy will
When I have to climb the mountains, the valleys, and the hills.

Grant me each day the pleasure to help someone in need;
Or try to lift a burden and do some good deed.

Dear God, when I'm so tempted of things not good for me,
Please give me strength and courage to stay real close to Thee.

I sometimes almost make a move toward things that are not right;
I need thy help and guidance to keep me in the light.

Sometimes I almost fail to see what God intends for me;
But then I always turn around, for He softly speaks to me.

Barbara A Cason
GROWING PAINS

In honor of my best friend, Liz Cox, born December 9, 1944 (Who's been teaching for 27 years); and, for my son, Robert Michael, who teaches me everyday.

Salty tears run down my cheeks
My hands shake.

I just cashed out a certificate
For my sixteen year old son,
For his first car.

I was employed full time
And, the mother of two small sons
When I got my first car
At the tender age of twenty eight.

I have seen more of this big world
Than many see in a lifetime.

I stop and wonder,
What are we doing to our young people?

I am not sure who is under pressure more,
Parents or teens!

One half of that car was
Bought with my own sweat and tears.
With all the help I gave on that paper route.

Jennifer Felix
DOES IT

To: Jody Hynes, With all my love . . .

Does it hurt you, when I don't speak,
Does it hurt you when I'm silent or just not paying attention?
If whenever we're together, I'm not looking, talking or paying attention, don't think anything bad about my actions.
It's just that I can't believe that you're there, with me.
If I'm behaving like so, I'm not meaning to be rude, I'm just thinking of you and me, about us together.
If ever you feel I'm ignoring you, don't be afraid to ask, what I'm thinking of.
If you cannot bring yourself to question me, just think and remember this "I'm not bored, or trying to be rude, I just can't believe it's you."
If I should question you about my quietness, I'll only ask this of you "Does it bother you?"
I truly don't want or mean to hurt you, if I have. Truly I don't.

Terri Britton
EACH ONE IS MY FAVORITE

To the most wonderful grandchildren in the world. To the Lord Jesus Christ without whom I can do nothing.

10 years— My beautiful Tina, with her flowing blonde hair.
8 years— My lovely, dark haired Tonya, with her spunky flair.
8 years— My handsome, outspoken, comedian Jason, whose practical jokes, keep you on your toes.
6 years— My darling, loving Micheal, full of energy, and the need to know.
5 years— My mischievous, sensitive Darren Lee, the image of his father.
21 months—My little Cory, with his love of beauty, and inquisitive mind, is never a bother.
10 months— My little Douglas, whom God just loaned to us for awhile, touched every heart with his special smile.
6 weeks—My little Devin, a strong and masculine infant, all boy, so intelligent, so cute and mature.
1 week— My little Christy, her delicate features, her pretty dark hair, her sweet nature.

Though life has put me through many a difficult test.
When it comes to my family, never was a woman more blessed.
If our trust in God, the most difficult moments are easier to live.
The nicest thing about love is, the more we give, the more we have left to give.

Sharon Pasztor
PASTELS PAINTED ACROSS THE SKY

To: Special loves loving family dear friends

In beauty I'm held
Pink, gold, violet, red
Swirl delicately above my head
Faint wind arose to chase the beauty into black
Moonbeams, starbright
Golden light
Wrap me in the silent glory of this night

Sharon Sawula
AN ODE TO THE FAMILY DOCTOR

This poem is dedicated to Z.P. Chrzanowski M.D.

What kind of a person would God choose to be
A family physician for people like me?
He'd have to be willing to give up his life
To sacrifice children and sacrifice wife.
He'd have to be there whether early or late, emergencies happen, babies don't wait.
When holidays come and he longs to be home, his life is still ruled by the ring of a phone.
With family around and the table all set "wait for a minute 'cause dad's not here yet."
Sometimes on birthdays, anniversaries too, to be with his wife that's what he wants to do.
Yet he must surrender his life unto others, somebody else's dad, sister or brother.
He must be psychologist, surgeon and counselor
A death, and a birth and it's too late announcer.
A man of compassion with faith in his heart
Who can feel for his patients when their worlds fall apart.
When still but a youth he was called in God's plan

He answered today he is part of God's Hand.
To bring help and hope and healing to others, those fathers and mothers, sisters and brothers.
That's the kind of a person that he'd have to be to lay down his life for people like me.

Annette Milot
GRANDPARENTS

I'd like to dedicate this poem to my grandma and grandpa Milot and grandma and grandpa Freed, the greatest grandparents in the world! I love them!

The grandest types of parents are;
People called "Grandparents," they win it by far.
There's grandmas and grandpas and 'great' ones too;
Everyone has one, maybe even two.
They like to spoil us and give things away;
"I love you honey," they'll often say.
They tell stories that often end with,
A giggle not knowing if it's the truth or a myth.
Grandparents live both far or near;
To each of them, their grandchild is a dear.
But here's some news for everyone;
All grandparents are full of fun!

Valorie Lowery
YANKEE DOODLE DANDY

To my parents Lawrence W. and JoAnne M. Lowery

Yankee doodle dandy
Yankee doodle dandy
Sure was handy.
Pres. George
Was at Valley Forge.
Patrick Henry
Sure told many.
Ben and his kite
Electrical storm at nite.
The paper
Cut king George's caper.
Don't tread on me
Made everyone see.
Many flags gone and came
But the red, white and blue remains the same.
The red, white and blue
Made this country true.

Donald G Layman Jr

Donald G Layman Jr
PEPPER'S SONG

To Family, Friends, and Faith

I feel a mood, you know the one,
That strikes you in the night.
The one that makes you feel so wrong,
Especially, when you know
you're right.
To you old friend, the dreams we shared,
We don't know we will, but we might.
Think back to me, in our past it seems,
Then the dreams we had, will be the light.
Your fortune lies in yourself you know,
For my respect you've sure enough earned.

Because you wasted, not, what life could give,
And come far on lessons learned.
It saddens me that you leave once more,
But, you'll come back to me old friend.
I can send only love, that a friend can give,
Rainbows we ride, someday to find the end.
Say no goodbyes to me old friend,
I'll see you once again.
Then our stories we will tell,
Of places that we've been.

Barbara Van Troostenberghe
THE OLD CHINA DOLL

This poem is dedicated to my mother, Phyllis Malott, who makes the most beautiful antique-reproduction dolls.

Shyly she stands in the corner on the floor
In the back by the old shop's rear door.

There amid the toppling stacks and rows of clutter
Are items of antiquity, slightly used ones and a few others.

Silently she beckons with eyes of azure blue
Casting a spell that's quite enchanting to you.

Luxuriant curls of gold adorn her head
Cascading down upon a dress of velvet red.

Her rose-colored lips are pursed as if by chance
She'll call a greeting to catch your glance.

She carries a parasol trimmed with Irish lace
While a bonnet of straw wild flowers frames her face.

Her ivory complexion and dainty-lobed ears
Have acquired a few miniscule cracks through the years.

The days of your youth come flooding back
Reviving memories of which you had almost lost track.

In a daze you reach out with trembling hands
And carefully lift the doll from her stand.

With her you return to that day so long ago
When as a small child you had let her go.

Adele Albersmeier
THE ESSENCE—THE WORTHINESS OF "LIFE"

Dedicated To: "They'—who ever Rule and Serve.

It's ballyhoo'd—it's Great, "Here's to it!"
Don't miss out—live it—do it!
But by the time one comes of age—
suspicion begins to grow
What is this force, this painful thing—
that swings us to and fro?

And going further down its path
Often pained, confused, abused—
One begins—to face the obvious
Man's here—caged, misled, misused.

And on he struggles—thru the years
Raising his hopes—covering his fears.
Ever 'Onward'—"courage" they say—
Having 'Faith'—will light the way.

And so—in blindness and belief—
He struggles onward—thru calms and grief

But suddenly then he's reached the 'Age'
Where by rough waves tossed—
and lifes cruel gauge—
He must fact TRUTH—be he fool or sage.
That Life's just a 'temptress"—
mostly ungiving
And constantly urges—"Keep On"—
"It's worth Living" . . .

But in Truth—one sees—what the years have spun—
Little joys—teasing—and passing—
Not a 'permanent' one!

And all the Dear Souls you've tended
and left—after you—
Alike—must now struggle and suffer—
just to see life here through.

And 'they'—and those—then lead onward
by age-old stories and tales.—
"Success", struggle thru it—
The Soul will be saved—even if all else fails.

And one realizes—the "Soul" ONLY—
is worth being alive.
The body's a trap—in truth,
that only evil could contrive.

Were all so tempted by 'experiences'—
they were led into
this 'rack'—
Or lowered into such sad state—
they'd enter a body—
even come back?

One only learns—far down the line in life
this was an errant step to take;
For body nor Earth—is worthy of our lives
to better 'man' us make.

For troubles drag one downward—
and pain doesn't soothe and heal
And struggle makes man strong and hard—
the less to care and feel.

And wealth leads to greed and avarice,
Poor feel desperation, lack of hope and Light.
Whoever said "Life is Wonderful"—
Was neither truthful, nor too bright.

Life in 'Matter'—is the punishment
for accepting a body cage—
And the sex-charge is the established 'trap'
by which it keeps turning,—
"page by page"
And keeps the Soul-Light's truth from man,
Prevents the Higher Light,—and wisdom
of the Master and the Sage.

For this—I ask Forgiveness,—
That in desire and want—that's built within
We bring forth ever another victim
of Earth's pain, and drouth and sin.

And 'Pray' God will work for more quickly
"Cleansing" the energies, the errors that now be
So that struggling Souls cannot be trapped—
In the stress and dark debris
Of the present world—and caged there,
in the corporal matter state we see.

For if one cannot live in the Higher Soul Light—
Tis far better 'Life' not Be—
As only 'therein'—is the Joy and Light
promised 'Eternally'.

Brenda Simmons
THE SEED

Dedicated to the aged

Tucked away in a corner of time;
Gray, withered, thought to be past prime,
Waiting to be took in hand,
To be united with the land.
Hiding from the reason,
To fulfill purpose for a season.
One only knowing the truth of these;
To bring forth creativity.
Like unto everything thus;
One but to trust.
Unto these the least is man,
Waiting for a helping hand.
Even in the darkness of night,
Look for a glimmer of light.

Michael Joiner
FOR YOU

For my wife Jeanne I love you

As I sit and watch the trees sway
The wind gently blows their leaves away
I think of the days we have spent together
"Only to remember" that nothing lasts forever.

A tear drops from the corner of my eye
Fighting this terrible feeling that

makes me want to cry
If wishing could roll back the hands of time
You are still the only one I would ask to be mine.

Perfect I will never claim to have been
But you remain my wife, my lover and my friend.

Pasqualina Scali-Cook
BUTTERFLY, BUTTERFLY

To my loving husband Paul, for all his love, faith and devotion he has for me.

Butterfly Butterfly come my way,
I know it will be a good day.
Your gracefulness, and beauty cannot be compared. Nature has been good to you and to me.
We hope mankind will preserve it the way it should be.
Let us thank the Lord, for His beautiful work, and all the splendor that surrounds Him, you, and me.

Jewelene Ivory
JOY

To my son Uzell: I want to always be there to lend a listening ear, make meaningful suggestions and be understanding whenever the need arises.

You brought happiness into my soul
Those long skinny fingers and squiggly-looking toes,
Your smooth soft skin and cute little grin
Your large brown eyes made me smile.

Your head was lightly covered with small grains of hair and you behaved as though you knew I was there,
I touched your hand, you squeezed mine
I knew that everything would be fine.

Five years later; your personality, your character was more defined and you were giving your own opinions and lines.

Now years after; you've grown into a fun-loving guy.
Doing well in school, play, and life because of your determination and sense of try.

Let's stay friends to the very end
You see, I love you and I know you love me.

No, I wouldn't trade you if I could,
You are my one and only
Yes, I would be awfully lonely!

Dorothy L Parker
FOOTSY

Dedicated to my favorite "Footsy" player and to my daughter, Ruth, who entered my poem in the contest

I love to play the game
Called, "Footsy", if you please;
The only thing I use:
My foot, up to my knees!

Now, bare feet might be cold,
Or hot and "smelly", too;
But, for the best results,
You must kick off your shoe!

I only play this game
With one, whom I love well,
For, touching feet with feet,
"L—O—V—E" you spell!

Now, this game you may play,
Though others are around,
For "Footsy" says so much—
Yet, no one hears a sound!

To play the game your best,
The secret, you should know:
Don't play it any place
But where your feet won't show!

Peg Rein

Peg Rein
A GREAT GUY

Again, I write about a great guy, in many ways,
Like, Fr. Mackin, Lord have mercy,
Matt, you gave us many happy days
Gee, how I remember, "cancer", retired, no place to go,
Before I knew it, I'll never understand, I was in your show,
Thanks to you, Mr. Wonderful, our director, I sure went places,
Going here & there, nursing homes, seeing those beautiful faces,
Now, those trips again, we really enjoy, thanks to you,
I guess, thank God, you really kept Holy Angels together, so true,
Little late in life, how I started to climb,
Well "Harry James," "Donald O'Conner" thought I lost my mind?
Gee! "Winged Victory Boy" singing with me, honestly yes!!
No idea, just can't imagine, can you even guess?
Then Pocmont, Matt, I'd never believe, how Jimmie Romma took to me,
Up on that stage, was I ever a clown?
Wow! That standing ovation, as I walked on down, an old lady I might be.
But, thank God, for all beautiful things, that happened to me.

Lance Collins
THE HAUNTED COWBOY

This poem is dedicated to all my family and friends.

He sauntered in from the midday sun,
His body tall and lean,
He had the look of a half-cast man,
In his gray eyes—there was pain.
You couldn't see an open wound,
It came from deep within,
There's a tint of red in his heart that bled,
As he gazed around the room.
He had shot a man, some time ago,
It seems like yesterday.
And now, his ghost keeps coming back
To haunt his life each day.
If he was to shoot the man across the room
Somehow he'll seek revenge.
He knew then, he'd drawn his guns . . .
And let the nightmare end.
The gunman laid to the break of day—
Two bullets lodged in his back.
No one will mourn the man that was born,
White skin with a tint of black.

Lauren K Warlick
LIFE

This poem is dedicated to my wonderful husband and best friend, Robert, whose love and devotion inspire my life.

Our presence
Never ending.
Like that of a carousel in motion,
Life is a circular thing.
And us,
Like the formations of a carousel
Creations,
Articulately crafted
Each one separate
In their being.
Always moving forward
Achieving new heights
Reaching for that Golden Ring.
And as we surpass
The presence of time,
We become
An ageless beauty.
Like that of a carousel
Only to be born again!

Ryan Reamer
EYES

Dedicated to Tylicia Ward

There are no crosshairs, just a sight
They scope the surroundings and dart back and forth.
A window to ones self, giving and taking expressions,
Leaving and making impressions.
It's true that you only see what you wish
To paint your own world with,
But why deny the beauty of the simple things you see
Take a different point of view and let it all fill you
Don't try to see the negatives
Don't be blind to the differences
You'll miss so much
And when you finally close your eyes to never see again
You'll regret not having seen
All the sights you've taken in.

Salvatore Casuccio
SOULSHORES

You are on the shores of my soul
The breakers of my emotions wash you
Their backwashes let you in shells
You make a necklace

I'm on the shores of your soul
The breakers of your emotions wash me
Their backwashes let me in shells
I make a necklace

Kathy A Boris
CONTRA CONFETTI

Hello, my name is Ollie.
I'm in the soup, although I seem quite jolly.
My motto is "Hail to the Chief"
And to hell with my beliefs.

Hello, for goodness sake, I'm an admiral!
Television cameras shouldn't be optional.
Couldn't we go somewhere quiet to talk?
Oh, get to the point already, Poindexter!!

Hello, my name is Reagan.
I must tell you, Nancy's just steamin'.
She very rudely showed me the door.
Now is my chance to get even.

Hello, my name is Jane Q. Public.
I find all this quite a lot of rubbish.
For such a serious matter, I can't stand the idle chatter.
I'd rather know Delia's next soapy scheme.

Mary Elaine Wilhelm
VICTIM OF POVERTY

I see him standing there
quiet and forlorn.
He seems so lost without a home,
in clothes that are old and worn.

Where did he come from?
Where will he go?
Does anyone care?
Do we really want to know?

He might be sick or hungry
on this cold winter night.
Shall we try to avoid him,
or do what we know is right?

Let us show love
and do all that we can.
It could be our life
instead of this man's.

Edith Waterson O'Connor

Edith Waterson O'Connor
MY DACHSHUND PUP

She'd been busy all day, played so hard,
Chewed my slippers, then dug up the yard.
Into my sewing box to play with a spool,
Then off she scampers, to break one more rule.
My Naughty little, saucy little,
Dachshund pup!

Then into the living room, the big chair for a perch,
I pretended to lose her, and started to search.
I called, and looked behind this and that,
While her tail beat a sassy little rat-a-tat-tat.
My playful little, funny little,
Dachshund pup!

Her soft brown eyes look into mine,
Her ears fold back, so silky and fine.
Now she snuggles close, gone all the zest,
As she takes her regular afternoon rest.
My lovable, adorable, Dachshund pup!

Now two years old, stalwart and strong,
She's a friend and guardian the whole day long.
She guards me, adores me, and teases some too.
She's loyal, dependable, steadfast and true.

My dignified, grown-up
Dachshund pup!

Virginia D Davis
BESSIE'S MOONSHINE

There is a certain place
Way back in the hills
That people dare not go
'Cause it's full of moonshine stills.

Revenuers try to go there
Hoping to make a "kill"
But they've never found the spot
Where Bessie has her still.

A federal man went there once
And left with buckshot in his behind.
Now, it's reasonably safe to say that
No-one messes with Bessie's Moonshine.

Philip A Grimard
LAUGHTER & TEARS

Why do I laugh when I am so close to tears?
Do I do it to hide my troubles and fears?

Am I afraid of the facts on the wall?
Am I afraid of another great fall?

Laughter and tears seem to go hand-in-hand.
One without the other simply can't stand.

Laugh with the crowd, cry in the dark,
Whistle merrily as you walk thru the park.

No one can see the tears as they start.
They just well-up from deep within the heart.

Don your mask, no one will know
The burden you carry thru life as you go.

One-by-one, down that lonely pass,
It's no more tears, you're Home at last.

Kristen A Blomberg-Wilson
DESTINY

In the beginning there was
him and I,
Two lonely hearts bridged between
life and eternity.
And when I reached my pinnacle
of desperation,
My future arrived hence you
caught my eye.
Or could it have been an
inescapable destiny of sorts,
Two wretched souls in search
of deliverance.

Terri L Fitzpatrick
I LOVE YOU

Since you have come into my life,
Each day is a new beginning.
You made me know what I feel is right,
And my life is now worth living.

I cherish each moment that we're together,
And my heart grows fonder when we're apart.
These feelings I have for you will be forever—
Because "I LOVE YOU" dear, with all my heart.

Sheila Wisner
ECSTASY OF LOVE

Your open arms reach out to me,
I run to you in ecstasy,
how beautiful the night will be!
God loves me so much,
He gave you to me.
Touching in tenderness,
then exploding in emotion,
My life is now serenely joyful,
and complete.
Faithful, I'll love and
cherish you forever,
in our ecstasy of love.

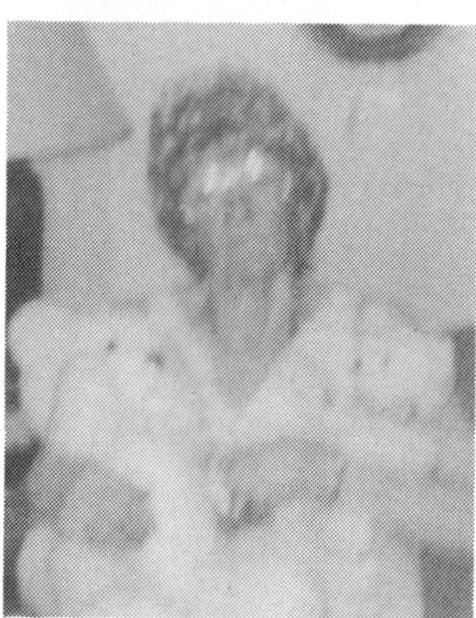

Elsie C Towle

Elsie C Towle
MY FAMILY

In memory of my beloved husband who went "Home" July 1987—from his widow and family.

This is a little Ditto. You should meet my "Family"
I think I have the best "Family" in Manchester, N.H
And in the world.
They are all kind, loving, good, and "my"
"Pride and Joy."
I have 12 wonderful great, grand
"Kiddies" but
I have one very Special Little Boy.
"Clark"
Of course "They're all special", but
"Clark" is so "Cuddly."
What more can I say, "I just love them all"

Daisy Loram Butler
FALL

As I look out of my window this early a.m.
I'm quite joyful to see rain pouring down.
For the trees needed dusting, the flowers a drink,
While cattle must have grazing, and that made me think—
How good to see the rain.

The heat of the summer is well on the wane,
the tree leaves are now falling fast.
Bare branches are assuming a fine lacy look
Now that their summery beauty is past.
How good to hear the rain.

But—this rain came as a forerunner of storm,
For a tornado came rushing along.
Such power of nature is awesome to see
Yet we must accept each change as it comes.
And we have to have rain.

Linda T Malone
THE TREASURE

With my love to my precious treasures; my husband Pat, our children Jim and Jennifer, my mother, Bobbie, Jean, Dag, and Cecille.

I see you every day, almost
and
You never are the same as
When I left you last
and
There's always something
Shiny and new
and
Warm coming to the surface,
Reflections of your heart,
No doubt
and
Your friendship you have
given to me,
a
Rare and precious treasure
and
A timely gift of your being.

Lorina Bolitho Mortensen
THE INTROVERT

Here I sit in my little shell
While neighbors mix and blend
In jolly happy company
And call each other friend.

I'd like to join them, don't you know?—
If only I could see
A way to overcome my faults
And make a better "me".

But everything I do is wrong
And all I say, inane;
And I guess I'll never find a way
To end this social pain.

So here I sit in my little shell
And here I guess I'll stay—
And let my shell grow thicker
With every passing day!

Gail Vorwerk
THE LIE

I talk to no one, no one talks to me,
Vibrations from speech shatter the glass.
His mouth shifts, his tongue clicks,
Yet no sound shall intrude my ears;
His eyes betray the purity of his heart.
Look at him there! so tense and so calm,
Convinced of his importance and of my gullibility,
His words come easy with no carper at hand.
My eyes alter their course, away from him,
Anywhere . . . just away from him;
I can not bear to witness this hideous display;
His smirk penetrates my spine with intensity.
I am alone in my heart, so very alone.
Tragedies are born of ignorance.

Ernest R Casey
HOPEFULLY COURAGEOUS

Christ breaks the shackles of sin,
When we launch out with him.
With courage to do what so ever he saith
Our courage blends in with our faith.

Whatever we lacked before.
Even more than man could endure,
Was supplied by our savior,
Who gives good gospel measure.

A shackle of sin that can hold,
A sinner outside of God's fold,
Takes the blood shed at Christ's cross,
To be broken with gain without loss.

Any sin the shackle may be
Can always leave a vacancy,
That must be filled with God's love,
When He grants help from above.

Julianne Poplawski
AS I SIT HERE STARING OUT THE WINDOW THIS NIGHT

As I sit here staring out the window this night,
As the sun sets and forms the horizon,
The blues, greys, oranges and pinks.
I can't help but to sit here and think . . .
What life will be like for the next few years.
The pain the hurt the loneliness and fears,
All of these deep inside, ready to explode
My life is the becoming of a new mold
Yes, it is time to build a new me!
One that can handle reality.
From home I sit miles away
Wondering if I will return one day?
I used to laugh but now I cry.
You say why?
Because I've made a mistake, that's why
My destination is to change
My life I must rearrange,
For being here is no fun,
That is what I think as I watch the sun
Now it's dark the sun is gone.
But my thoughts, they still go on.

Willie D Blockson
SUMMER'S END

Gone are the radiant meadows,
whose fragrance serenely captured
therein
the azure skies and the ever singing
cotton gins.
Oh
paint me a picture of days gone by of
rollicking hills
and
gentle rolling countrysides.
Show me majestic beauty and
splendor through the painter's
eyes
and nature's paradise softly singing
God's own lullaby.
Paint the orchards and behold the
beauty of their glorious
sights
better still, smell their fragrance on
warm and sleepness
nights.
Paint the elegant pines, shading dells
and the hollow place
of
narrow running streams, sleepy

brooks, and laughing trout
spitting out the hooks.
I wish to remember my sweet
summer with all its magnificent
blooms
so forever keep winter in next
season's tomb.
Now
the rustic reddish-brown leaves lay
fallen and die
while
dismal lonely oaks cover the valleys
and empty mountain sides
and I wonder
if this is all that nature has to
contend, if so, do not pretend
then
surely comes summer to its end.

Anne Marie Bales

TO THE ONE WE OWE (TO THE AMERICAN SOLDIER. THANK YOU!)

I stood before a soldier's grave,
to read the name, of one so brave;
"How can I thank you—quiet
man,
When I don't even know your
name?"
I wish to hold your hand so bare
and thank you for my being here.
Would it not be for you—you quiet
man,
I would not be standing here—in this
land.
"What can I do, Oh brother dear,
that died for me to live without
fear?"

And from the ground the soldier's
answer came!
"There is no need to know my
name:
We died for freedom on
America's shore
that she will bloom and prosper
for ever more,
and for the brother that plows
the land,
for the mother and child that
need a helping hand,
for the boys so trim and the
girls so slim!
Bloom, America, over this grave
of mine,
—proud and free
with honor and full of liberty.
You are the crown that we've
been fighting for
Thank you for remembering us—
for ever more.

Anne James Valades

THE NAKED TREE

A leaf
falls.
So brief,
it calls
my grief.

The tree is bare.
Branches form a snare,
an empty trap,
which started when
a leaf
fell in my lap.

Tanya Cervinka

(UNTITLED) DON'T DROP THE BOMB, NOT TODAY;

Don't drop the bomb,
Not today;
Please don't let
The sky turn grey.
The color of ash
The earth will be,
Until the flames
Are set free.
Then I sit,
All alone,
And watch the world
Turn to stone.
The drums of war
Beat softly near;
Hearts beat too—
Full of fear.
Now I lay
Me down to die,
And pray to you,
Please don't cry.

Donna M Olsin

SERVANT OF THE PEOPLE

Your adversaries are strong about
you.
There is great turmoil and
despair,
Mankind is waiting deliverance from
the trauma of his environment.
Stand strong in your convictions,
never to dismay,
Lift your head up high—look over
the troubled crowd,
For in the solitude of benediction
will come the visions of the
Final conquest of man's ills—
The ultimate victory over
tribulation.
Your burden, servant of the
multitude, is heavy.
Responsibility to your fellow
man is great,
But God gives clearer vision, strong
mind and will
To those that take up the tools
To carve from the future a better
today.

Rosa L Gamble

NOT OF MY OWN

They smiled in amazement
WONDERING
How I made it this far
WHEN
It seemed like adversities
AND
Failures were designed for my life
EVEN
From the very beginning of my
EXISTENCE.
I smile at their amazements
BECAUSE
I knew that my achievements
WERE
Not of my own but belonged
TO
A Higher Power from Above.

Donna Loesch

SWEARING

Why do the children swear?
Are they trying to compare?
They shout it loud and clear,
For everyone to hear
Shocking all they meet,
Even in the street
Deep inside within their hearts,
Are they trying to act some part?
Who can be the most mean?
"They'll let me on their team!"
I think it must be self-esteem,
Very low and very lean

F D McMurry

SEPTEMBER SONNET

We're here and whole because we
lived and learned;
The prologue past was pain and
pleasured earned.
We're thankful for the past that put
us here.
Secure with self, forever free from
fear.

We now fulfill our life and take the
key:
'Twas always full, and fuller yet to
be;
We take our many blessings, heaven-
sent,
Our legacy of love, not lost nor lent.
The power's ours to share the magic
cup;
We'll always grow, but never grow
completely up.
Our loving making world will know
we've won
The furture's faith and fortune, fire
and fun.

So let our epitaph not be forgot:
"Alive, they loved, they lived, they
laughed a lot."

Ada Marie Putman

GOD'S SPECIAL ANGEL

To my loving family.

When I was just a little girl
My mother said to me,
"You have a guarding angel
To keep you company."

She'll guide and walk beside you
Wherever you may go,
In Summer, Fall or Winter,
In freezing rain or snow.

She travels all the highways,
She walks with you each day,
She watches while you're sleeping
And hears each prayer you
pray.

God sends his special angel,
That's why I do not fear
In troubled times or sadness
I feel her presence near.

Sherene R Roberts

HAVE YOU EVER . . .

Have you ever taken the time to look
Way down inside of me?
Have you ever gazed into my eyes
To see the way I see?

Have you ever taken the time to look
Behind my smile to see
The pain inside my heart for you
Because you cannot see?

Have you ever taken the time to look
Into my heart to see
The love and caring
You say you want to see?

Have you ever taken the time to look
At the love I gave to you?
For only through the things I do can I
Say to you . . .

Have you ever taken the time to look
Way down deep inside of me?

Lilas L Thornton

IT'S GOD'S LOVE

It's God's love we see out by the
seashore
with beautiful beaches by a tree.
It is all there my dear waiting for you
and me.
The blue sky above while clouds go
floating by.
We could never completely capture
its beauties
no matter how hard we try.
It's God's love we feel with each
playful breeze.
That ruffles your hair and all of a
sudden you freeze.
The sun shines brighter and you get
warm.
You know God's love will never do
you any harm.
You see the piling up and hear the
crash of shells.
Sometimes they sound like tiny
tinkling bells.
Each shell large, tiny, or middle size.
It is a work of art and beauty hard to
comprehend you realize.
Crashing, crashing all together losing
their beauty and you sigh.
All of this is lost as I pass by.
Yet I saw and it's recorded in my
mind today.
Someday I will remember again as it
is in my mind to stay.

Lloyd Clements

AFTER ALL ELSE

After all else has gone
This shall remain with me—
The thought of all your loveliness,
And the heart you gave so free.
The curving line of your sweet smile,
The softness of your hair;
The tender light within your eyes,
Your skin so smooth and fair!
The richness of your voice so clear,
The lingering feel of your arms—
When they wound around me so
tenderly,
And I breath'd in all your charms.
The wonderment of all these things
Shall never e'er be forlorn,
They shall always bring me joy
After all else has gone!

Bernard Graf Elfert

ON AGING

Age, I once thought,
That I would never feel
Your cooling touch.
My face, once smooth,
Shows wrinkles now.
There is white hair
Upon my brow.
Other hair is missing too
But nothing that I try to do,
Restores the loss of it
To a bald spot shining through!
My eyes are not yet dimmed,
My ears still hear most things,
I do not falter when I walk
But if I jest and play at youth
I know full well 'tis idle talk.
At harvest time you will reap
And I will fall beneath your sweep,
To calendar and clock and scythe—
How swiftly do our seasons fly!

Ron Kempton

A GIFT OF WORDS

A good evening to write.
Misty days when sun falls like
rustling leaves
on Fairytale Avenue in a cottage
under Sycamore skies,
miss you, tremble, and shake off the
loneliness.
Looking forward to seeing you my
October feet shuffle on
guided by the sullen landscape.

A lovely evening to walk with
Kathy.
We'll go up Aubrey past the
construction.
In listening branches the spying
moon frowns
intent on our quiet conversation.

A wonderful evening to pray out loud

and thank God
for my hands.
We write,
offer,
love you,
and hunting blindly through a maze of letters
bring Autumn to your smiling eyes.

Denise Ricker
COMPARISONS

Empty,
Like a dream that dies.
Sad,
Like a heart that cries.
Lonely,
Like a night with no moon.
Cool,
Like a heart with no room.
Helpless,
Like a soul that drowns.
Silent,
Like music without sound
Restless,
Like a mind that won't sleep.
Wet,
Like eyes that just weep
Powerless,
Like a ship that sinks.
Broken,
Like a chain with lost links.
Incomplete,
Like a rose without thorns.
Relief,
Like the calm of a storm.
Unfair,
Like a criminal with no plea.
Goodbye,
Like a bird that's free.

Karen Best
HOW CAN I SAY I LOVE YOU?

Your loveable smile is all I see as I pass you in the hall.
Your beautiful eyes are all I think about when I'm alone.
The soft tones of your voice as we laugh together.
The warm touch of your hand as I touch it.
You are so wonderful, but how can I say I love you?
Will I ever be able to tell you how much I love you?
Or will I have to go through life just saying it to myself?
Will you understand if I do ever tell you?
How can I say I Love You?

Michelle H Reslier
THE "10/14" STAMP OF DEFINITUDE

And when I date you,
You become a mere reportage of one's Inspiration,
Ceasing the vitality of the drive.
Once thick with enlivened joy of Expression,
You become a thick slice of paper existing in scribbled blue
With fragmented thoughts
That once sought cohesion in the world of matter.

Bordered and contained,
I pick up my pen and stab at the inundatory waves of Emotion
and watch them recoil, to burst profoundly on the page as understanding.
—Dispersed Revelations!
there, they're exposed. A second of light!

No second second.

The stream exhausted its amphibious capabilities,
And pen and paper coalesced into a confluence of regression.
Back, back into the depths of blurry blue.
There where the blue of ink washed away the flow of thoughts
Into a sea of oblivion.
There where the sea of malleability defines matter as water.

Betty Block
ANGEL IN DISGUISE

To my Children The Glory is God's

I have a coat of many colors,
I wear it proudly, it's not like any other

It keeps me warm at certain times,
When I perform, I know it's mine

I was sent from above, a loving spirit,
A message I bring, I'd like you to hear it

Love each other as I have loved you,
Do it by singing and praying, you'll feel like new

Inside I mean, and that's where it counts
On the outside a clown that runs and flaunts

An ANGEL IN DISGUISE and many are we,
As we fill the big tent with shouts of glee

So stand and applaud as they enter the ring
Just think of the joy to others they bring.

Fortes Veltri
SPECIAL LADY

There is a lady in my life, That is like no other—
She has been my confidant and friend, you see she is my mother—

Throughout the years of my life, She has seen me rise and fall,
But not a word of discouragement,
She has accepted it all—

At night when pain depresses me,
Encouragement from her I hear,
To place my trust in the Lord, Until peace I do not fear—

And when dawn breaks, I look at the sky, With it's colors oh so bright,
And the pain now seems bearable,
Not like it was last night—

Oh God in the heavens, hear my prayer, And grant a wish to me,
To bless my Mother and her needs,
For all Eternity—
And so my friend, Who thinks like me, If you have a Mother like mine—
My words I say to you is, Love and cherish her for all time—

For a better friend in this world, You will never find,
To stand by you in all your needs,
And give you peace of mind—

Vera Frederick
MY OWN

My own, my Galatea, how I yearn
To know the heart of thee, thy beauty rare,
As God, in origin, created thee;
Thy pristine beauty, less the dross
I did bestow thy form.

The silver layers as onion over thee,
Plus roughs and darks and sharps that pale the eye,
I pressed upon thee, knowing not
That someday I would strive to chip away,
To see and know perfection as of yore.

My own, to know thy truth and beauty once again,
I strive through time and pain unto the end;
To know your heart as mine, to be as One
And go forever forth, no more to fail!
My own, do you, too, yearn for me?

Mary T Calkins
FOR LACK OF

She shall be nameless.
You may call her woman,
From various people she received
Demands, commands and reprimands.
"You think you've got problems; listen to mine."
She kept her problems to herself.
"You talk all the time-give it a rest."
She stopped talking, was talked at.
"While you're up; bring me a coke."
She did and forgot her own.
"You've got the time; wash my clothes."
She gave her time.
"Hey, I need some money."
She gave it.
"I need your love."
She gave,
For lack of—
She died.

Joanne M Gifford
FLY WITH ME

Come fly with me
And you will see
The reasons for it all:
There's beauty there,
With clean, fresh air
And magic waterfalls.
I'll take you places,
With smiling faces
And special words to say,
The stars are bright
All through the night
Tell me if I may.
My time is now,
Not sure just how,
To show you who I am.
But ride with me,
Oh, let's be free
Come and take my hand.

Dianne Leigh Harris
HOME

So far from home, yet nowhere to go
No house to live in, and freedom
Still to grow.
Heartache is such a sin, will I ever win?
Lead me on an open course
The dreams I have to carry on
Forget the reflections of my memories
The pain should be gone
Try my best, a sign of hope
This world so cold, but I'll cope
The madness seems to take me away
My thoughts get so cloudy
Eyes tear like rain each day
Will I ever have roots, have ground
To rest my weary body down
Or do I die, for peace beyond

Jan Hugo
TOMORROW BRINGS

We return to life what we borrow;
Planting seeds that grow tomorrow

Living moments we have spent,
As time measures each continent

One day Tomorrow creeps our way,
Dressed in her costume of
Today . . .

But in a million years or so
Then will she know which way to go?

When Autumn leaves finish weeping;
Winter blows her restless sleeping . . .

When dawn melts the frozen quiet,
Curing sleep and faulty diet . . .

Then new life glistens thru the rain
For Tomorrow brings the Spring again.

Jimmy L Reese Jr
BEST OF FRIENDS

To: My Lord Jesus, My Parents, Friends; and a special Thanks to Pam, Dana, Colleen, who make my Spiritual and Personal life a much easier task.

Good to see you, to see you again.
It's been so long, where shall we begin.
Just so much to say; in such a few minutes, for the best of friends.

Tell me what's been on your mind,
I'm reading your facial signs.
Good friends that can harmonize,
It took some real time to realize.

We are the best of friends forever.
We had to recall our relationship, for the
things we shared would soon end.

Good to see you, to see you again.
It's been so long, where shall we begin.
Hard to see our relationship then,
Now it's the best of friends

Janet Rose Martin
OUR TIME TO DANCE
The cord between us cannot break
Our love will never die
My love for you is no mistake
It takes me up so high

We feed each other energy
Together we are strong
We love with such an urgency
Our love can do no wrong

I don't want to own you
I don't need control
All I really want to do
Is nourish your very soul

Love me now! Oh, can't you see
Tomorrow may be too late?
Now's the time for our love to be
Oh! please, don't hesitate!

Let's eliminate our fears
Let's give love a chance
Let's end these wasted years
Now's our time to dance!

H D Ruth
DOUBT
Certainty may lead to resolution;
Doubt creates a profanation.
For many doubt is enervating;
Others find doubt stimulating.
Faith rests on infallibility;
Removal of doubt casts new doubt.
Faith flourishes on authority;
Doubt grows with authority in rout.
Can the scales balance the human
equation?
With faith and doubt in equilibrium?
Is there a stricture of crowning
correlation
To guide the savants of our
collegium?
Have faith in the power of doubt;
And doubt in the power of faith.

Penny M Reed
TIME

To L. C. "A love that will never be forgotten"

People say time heals all wounds,
Some are right, some are wrong
I close my eyes: I see your face,
I cry to hold you near
To feel your heartbeat,
To wipe away your tears
To say I'm here,
To comfort you,
To kiss away your fears,
To hug you; to want you
But I know now; my love for you
grows
very dear,
And I know time will never
heal my wounds,
My time was all for you.

Shane P Milligan
QUIETNESS
Divine stillness wakes the willness
as it walks,
From brittle distances and daybreak
parks—
Laced uncertain but autumn gold old,
and rolled right up for you . . .
Filed from religions too right to be a
throng.
Dialed in a telephone so monoto-
nously sung to be a song . . .
Free escaping leaves me forever
raping dictionaries for the right
paragraph to relate my own
epitaph . . .
Seagulls screech and lovers walk the
beach,
while I clasp in a fortunate smile and
palm the deserts
awhile . . .
Eagerness plays a fortune to be cast
by such a dark cloud—
So young and distilled—so willed
determined and proud—
Reaching for the future that hadn't
been there,
Laying down a SEX GHOST so dim
and yet, so near . . .
Somber cries and skies that clash the
fate in little girls eyes—
Dance in me and it's plain to see all
the desire I require to take—
But little known, and never the seeds
to be sown—
I grow a waste in wonder and grope
asunder,
the play is in quick delay . . .
Mountainous white held such a secret
to be hidden—
In crevasses beyond a fall and
expeditions without a call for . . .
Granite relined and dormant to none,
my secrets fall to such pain.
Stalling and calling so threatened and
enthralling—
I bend to the times I never wanted to
meet—
Such a defeat . . .
And so, I deplete in my philosophy
for you in the dark—
Divine stillness wakes the willness as
it walks,
from brittle distance and daybreak
parks.
Calls times and winter chimes cling a
past that stayed to last.
Palms clam the qualms and sermons
compliment the psalms,
that search out the reasons and plan
out the cures.
For sure we love such claims and
rights come purple nights from black
yellow to amber white . . .
Glint frets such a hint to reclaim the
truth so shallow, in the deep.
For in such minds, water clashes and
rainbows come like splashes to the
raindances signaling ground . . .
Halo abidance and relative reliance
equates the hates in written words
stalled on streets of flooded tears.
The centers of mind so broad to
define—
Probably didn't want to think up such
a thought at the time.
Recessed in cool starkness—Lines of
euphoria soak the highness that kept
me from morbid thought . . .
Reeling willness moved the
stillness—
And realities play sought to be
caught—
Through virgins swallow and
narrows hallow—
Tomorrow dies the glee so young and
pale, I see . . .
Softening silence seems to be the
quiet alliance—
Dew drop sorted and rain drop
aborted for lakes of fears found past
in years . . .
Calm waves reach out for grains of
history—
Will it be remembered?
Will I become one of those grains
and these words a rested test?
Cradled forever in a God's life—
Never knowing what's to be best—
OR God naught sung or summed up
in fancy
religions . . .
Divine stillness wakes the willness as
I walk—
Succumbing distance stalks through
my insistence—
and daybreak parks, grasp my
resistance—
Laced right uncertain—
Silver leaves draw the curtain—
But Autumn gold and rolled right up
for you—
I'm certain . . .

Barbara Folwell Marcucci
THE QUESTION
Do you appreciate all God endowed
upon this earth,
And when you stand head bowed
before Him
Will you give thanks for beauty
Or are your eyes upon the ground
when there are stars to see?

Do you strike back
When you are hurt by thoughtless
word or deed, and do you lack
The understanding, that, you too are
frail and only human?

Do you repay
A hurt with kindly understanding and
do you say
I too am weak. When given choice
Do you offer a gesture that lifts the
heart, and speak
Quiet words that still an angry voice?

Do you fulfill your sacred trust
Of making better yet the world
bequeathed, or do you thrust
Your way unseeing and uncaring into
the paths of others who
Seek beauty?

It's there to see
With eyes wonder wide that we
Unworthy as we are can reap the
pleasures of an endless universe.
And when we leave it, changed by
our presence here
Can we stand proud and say
Man passed this way?

Tina Corbett
TO A FRIEND

I dedicate this poem to Janine and Bill whose friendships I treasure dearly, as well as the Basement and Laundale crowd. I wish all of you the best!

There is a deadly drug that is tearing
me apart.
It is not I that it is killing, but
my friends.
I've lost so much already,
can I afford to lose more?
They can not see or understand
there is no reason, Why?

They call in snow, they call it blow
but where will these people go?

It hurts to see them all leaving me,
getting taken in all living lies.
I have done my best and tried.
But now I realize that soon
they'll all be blown,
while I'm standing here . . . Alone.

Kari Ryder
DON'T CRY OUT LOUD
It was cold that day;
It must have been,
for the words
Of the small, dark minister
Formed clouds of vapor
In the air.

The splattering of raindrops
Hitting nylon umbrellas and
Plastic raincoats,
Then sliding
And dripping to the ground,
Muted the droning sound of his
Useless condolences.

Until it seemed
That I could hear only
The dull throbbing of my pulse,
And I could see only
The darkness of the day,
And I could feel only
The empty place
Inside me.
Where you should have been.

Amidst the rivulets of rain
Washing down my face,
Those few, salty tears
Went unnoticed.

Russell B Teed

Russell B Teed
DARK STORMY NIGHTS
Cold wind overcomes the heated
calm.
A storm brews behind the rays of the
sun.
Watch out for the darkness! . . . It
comes so quickly.
Dusk smothers the light until the day
surrenders to the night.
Prepare yourself for the blackness
that hides all that is beautiful.
It brings out the deepest thoughts.
Not unlike dreams, some are of evil
demons.
The thunder is their cry and the rain
is the millions of tears.
We all have wept thinking about the
darkness.
We were all scared of the dark!
Blinding light points the direction
through the dismal nerve shaking
night.
Look out your window what do you
see?
Was that a cloud?

Tom J Cuomo
ILLUSION
Following a tear
Gliding smoothly
for all it carries
its depth misleading
It seems too shallow
for all it contains
Light to the touch
But heavy with emotion
it falls.

D M Cambridge
THERE'S A WALL THAT NOBODY CAN SEE
There's a wall
that nobody can see,
but it's unyielding—
it's a part of me.
One of these days,
I may stumble
and then allow

that wall to crumble.
But, until that day
it stands strong,
and protects me
even if that's wrong—
from those who look to see
what is going on
inside of me.

Dee Lock
ONLY YOU

To Jenni (my daughter), Never change who you are. To Dorothy, who believed in me, when no one else did Thank-you both, for being there.

You are the brightest star that shines above
The sweetest song that ever was
The greatest joy that life can bring
Loving you is my only thing
Needing you is what I want
Never again to part from your heart
Always knowing you are there
Brings happiness that none can compare
When first we met along the shore
I agreed to part never more
And so it was and is today
Our love that has never wanted to stray
And only through the sands of time
That our love has become entwined . . .

Marsha Becker
DREAMS SOON PASS BY
If I close my eyes, will the grass be green,
Will I look outside & know what I've seen;

Will the ocean remain with its roaring tide,
Will I still love life, will love remain by my side;

If the sky weren't blue would it blossom with flowers,
Will time remain present, silence pass the hours;

Will the mountains remain or fall down deep,
Flashes of lightning, never wanting to keep;

Feeling be near, or sparks fly from your tongue,
Songs of joy, or sadness sung;

Greener are the trees & brighter are the skies,
Smile to you,
Everyone tries,
No-one denies,
wasteful are lies,
And: "Dreams Soon Pass By"

Lillian Bogutz
POETS AND DREAMS
In Ecstasy POETS cast their magic spell
like Musical lilts, pure as a Bell.
WORDS are the media POETS use
'tis their SOUL, their SECRET REFUGE.
Where lies the drive that makes them compose
their secret thoughts to expose?

WORDS flow easily on their tongue
as in fantasy their thoughts are sung.
To the BARD, as the POET is also known
WORDS echo with a lyrical tone.

Thus VOLUMES of Musings are on Library Shelves
read by people to entertain themselves.
By the use of WORDS
POETS become bewitched
uniting these ODES their lives are enriched.
To the POET thoughts linger from the past
their WORDS, like all ART, will forever last.

Mabel Stone Webber
THE ONLY ONE
There are many fish that swim,
There are many a sacred hymn.
To deny this would be a waste of time.
There are many birds that fly,
There are many hippopotami.
Please don't interrupt me and spoil my rhyme.

There are flowers and weeds galore,
There are distant lands to explore,
There are forests, lakes and rivers by the dozens.
There are uncles, aunts and in-laws,
Also precious gems with no flaws
And here and there you'll find some distant cousins.

There are lots of monkeys, millions of stars,
Hundreds of yummy candy bars.
The list is really endless and exhausting.
There are planes in the sky and ships at sea,
So many comets unknown to me,
Also cupcakes made with or without frosting.
Way up north there roam hundreds of bears
But the Milky Way must have thousands of stairs.
Don't tell me that you think this is absurd.
There are many a bee that stings,
And lots of fried onion rings,
Also many cattle that make up many a herd.

Now in this world of duplications
There must be several indications
Of *Only One* who stands out loyal and true,
Only One more thoughtful and kind.
Look in the mirror, dear, and find
That the *Only One* to me is surely YOU!

Robin E Allen
ADDICT
The tracks
On your arms
Showed
Your direction
The needle
The vehicle
That set you
Free
You sped
Down
Roads
In your raw
Unconscious
Yet
Never
Went anywhere
Just
Sat there
Nodding.

Michele M Biwer
A COSTUME OF A WOMAN
i wear a costume of a woman
yet a child in the mind,
you appeared to be the special one
i searched so hard to find.
with your two hands you built for me
an imaginary place,
a layer of gold around your heart
and a mask upon your face.
a costume of a lover
yet a boy in disguise,
a sacred look of loneliness
was written in your eyes.
every glance you stole from me
had torn me apart,
you sacrificed the colors
that you painted on my heart.
your costume of an artist
it took so long to weave,
this costume of a woman
that you have made for me.

Linne Lundbeck
SPACE AND TIME
Space and time
is not only a chime
of a clock in the hall,
or a bat and a ball;
or light in space
going its pace.

Though these are included,
they are not secluded
from the (wind) of the mind;
the thought that is bought
by a purse with its pound
for inventions around.

Einstein sat dreaming
of light that goes beaming;
of objects that shrink
when pushed to the brink.
People took heed
of all this great speed;
and their memory is time
like a clock with its chime.

(wind) as in wind a clock.

Jennifer Matties
MY BUTTERFLY
My butterfly is purple, yellow and green.
She flies from tree to tree.
I love my butterfly,
and she loves me.
My butterfly, my butterfly,
my butterfly and me.

Michael Troy Elwood
BEAUTY AND MYSTIQUE
Mystique marvelous, lakes of beauty—
Sadly the sun sets; rising on a new dawn,
As we join and become one, to the dawn and the rise of the sun.
They say beauty is told by the one who knows
The way of things, as time passes slowly into the unseen.
With each day we rise and join the flight of the skies—
Through eons and eons each suffers and dies,
And the sun glides across the endless sky,
Passing judgement on all it sees—
To the endless phantoms of beauty
and mystique,
Till the beauty enfolds and you're lost in mystique,
Till death seems but a thing to endure
And life an endless pleasure—assured!

Beverly J Schroeder
I SAW A LITTLE CHIPMUNK
I saw a little chipmunk scurry through the grass,
He makes the trip so quickly you'd almost think it was his last.
He has several areas where there are holes in the ground,
And he goes from one to the other each day on his rounds.

If he could encounter some food along the way,
He will stop and take a bite, and maybe even play.
To catch him on camera is really quite a trick,
Cause he never stays around for long, and moves so quick.

He is clever, and knows just when it's safe to show his face,
But all the time he's out, his eyes are darting all over the place.
For he is very cautious in his play,
Cause he doesn't want to be caught, or harmed in anyway.

So the actual spot where a chipmunk may be,
Is mostly known only to he.
But if you should see a hole in the ground,
Wait, maybe a chipmunk will soon be around.

Louise Ingles Hyde Gum
SOUNDS OF MAUNDY THURSDAY
Listen! The night is still.
Rare memories fill
This Thursday night of Holy Week—
Hallowed memories that seek
Release of sound this Easter space.
Ears tuned by grace,
We listen. A rooster crowed.
The Master said it would.
Harken! It crowed again.
That Eerie cry splits the evening sky
Like red-hot goad, and we're aware
Of Peter's brash denials in the Master's plight.
Then from the darkening night
Sounds the deep convulsive sobbing
Of a man—Peter . . . weeping bitterly
For his denials. Sounds, Sounds,
Sounds of Maundy Thursday,
With no sound hid.
Would we'd face our denials
Of Christ as feelingly
As honestly as Peter did.

Linda L Parker
HOME
Home is where the heart is
My heart isn't here—but in another place
another year
Back in time, a happier place, at least it seems so now.

I'm continually drawn to this yester-year, a time
that has become very dear to me.
My heart returns home to those memories
the sights and sounds
smells and feelings I've
yet to find here, yet to be
replaced.

This place
there are memories here too—
being created and
lived through, but those other
memories
crowd in and take precedence
in my mind
and my heart.

In many ways I suppose I never
left—
I departed physically—yet my
soul remained
in the land of sunshine and
warmth, with
the friends I left behind.

Chester Henderson

LOVE

To my loving wife Francene

Extending
Beyond the grip of the door
Slip
And fall, don't worry you're in my
hands
Now,
Unbeknoweth they them over their
Hey you who lie, not knowing up
from down
Love, Love me?
Standing in the shadows not . . .
but asleep
Rise O' thee
Fear only you and me
Love Love within thy' own glory
Running to shame for as I know
Glory be

Shannon Maynard

Shannon Maynard

LOVE

This poem is dedicated to all my family who taught me the meaning of love.

Love is special,
Love is fine,
Love happens all the time.
Love is great,
Love is sweet,
Love is something that you need.

Walter R Bell

TARAWA REMEMBERED

In memory of Pvt. Robert J. Griffin, a young U.S. Marine poet who gave his life for his country on Tarawa, November 20th, 1943.

We've been here once before, old
friends,
and now we're back on tour,
Our memories of this small atoll
have awakened us once more.

'Twas long ago we left you here
lying in your graves,
and you out there beyond the pier
and underneath the waves.

Oh God! How we remembered,
the fighting that was done.
And all the bravery that it took,
that's why the battle's won.

We dedicate this moment
for those not here today,
and all who fought so gallantly
on those "three November days."

We stand amidst our memories,
the tears we can't control,
As we listen to the bugle
and watch our flag unfold.

"Esprit de corps" my friends,
that's what it's all about.
It's "Semper Fi" for you and I,
let no man turn us out!

Tim O Nichols

TIME

For a brief moment
in the passing of time
our souls shall meet
and it will be beautiful.
For there is no greater
reunion then that of two
Souls who pass in the night.
If only for a moment,
that our souls shall meet
eternity will pass,
For in that moment of time,
all things will come clear,
and the searching of the
lost soul will end;
And begin again for two
Two souls that
pass in the night.

Kathaleen Betts

GOD'S LITTLE ANGEL

Dedicated to Kathy my Granddaughter

You are more beautiful than
diamonds.
More precious than gold, you are a
treasure to have, to love, and to hold.
As I watch you grow into a lady so
fair,
I thank God each day for placing you
here.
My life no longer will be empty and
cold,
for I have a little angel to love and to
hold.

Virginia Palm

THE WOOD WORKER

To Herbert Risbrudt: His Mighty and Gentle Hands left their imprint forever on lives and wood-crafts.

Mighty hands, gentle hands
Ever caressing the wood
Each cut of the saw, slant of the nail
Goes exactly where it should.

Mighty hands, gentle hands
Guiding the project along
From start to perfect finish
The master's humming a song.

Mighty hands, gentle hands
Raised his children this way
Caressed and guided with strength
All blest with love every day.

Mighty hands, gentle hands
Touch each project with care
Mighty hands, gentle hands
Even when folded in prayer.

Janet Gibson

MOM, I HONOR YOU

You have been wonderful
For all the things you did
And all the things you didn't, too.

You created opportunities for me
That you never dreamt of for
yourself.
Through no fault of your own
Your schooling was incomplete,
But that did not stop you
From realizing the value of
education
And sacrificing comfort in your
determination
To see that the same did not happen
to me.

A beautiful woman in your youth
And beautiful still in your maturity,
You never thought too much
Of doing without for me.

These were the things you didn't do
For all of which I honor you:
You never let me go hungry,
Because you worked your fingers to
the bone.
You never abuse me,
But were always patient and firm in
tone.
You never failed to provide me,
With a warm and secure home.

You never let me down
A friend in you I always found.

Even when a mother I became
You still remained the very same
To make of me a woman capable
A daughter you could proudly label
As your own.

Because of your lifestyle clean,
I am blessed with the health of a
fairy queen.
Because of your reputation,
I can walk in any location.
Because of your humanity,
I can look anyone in the face,
A proud member of the human race,
Wearing my family name,
Like a badge of honor, without
shame.

I model myself after you,
And, though more educated,
Think your wisdom underrated.
The greatest to me from another,
Is: "You remind me so much of your
mother."
I feel so proud of this, too,
Because, mom, I honor you.

Beatrice B Gonzales

TREASURE CHEST OF DREAMS

This poem is dedicated to all of my children

I have a treasure chest
That's filled and fit for queens,
I will cherish it forever
For it's filled with all my dreams,

They're dreams that I've collected
For when the years are lean,
By then I'll have a fortune
In my treasure chest of dreams.

Then, when I'm feeling lonely
And no one cares it seems
I'll go and open up
My treasure chest of dreams,

I'll always find the memory
Of so many, many things
That I've carefully stored within
My treasure chest of dreams.

W Melvena Coverdell

GOODBYES ARE HARD

All my Lubbock State School co-workers

It's hard to break the ties that bind.
It's hard to leave old friends behind
It's so hard to say good-bye,
To hold back tears when you want to
cry.

It's hard to know I will not again see
Those who have meant so much to
me.

But what a joy it is to know
How much these friends have helped
me grow;
How much I've learned to love and
understand,
That God is everywhere and has a
plan.
For each of us who walk this earth;
No matter how high or low our birth

So as I say good-bye to friends.
Let there not be tears but cheers and
grins
For years well spent' in love.
For a dear Father up above
Who cradles us in his arms
And always keeps us from all harms

M Jane McKenzie

SO CONFUSED

November 28, 1988 To Jim Cantrell
And when our eyes first met, something special I felt. I know we're meant to be. You feel the same as me.

I'm so confused about you and me.
I just don't know anymore, you see.
I thought that your love for me
Was sincere (and meant to be).

I just can't help feeling hurt.
I wonder—Are you a flirt?
Weeks pass with no word from you.
This just makes me really blue.

So I don't know what to do.
As much as I do love you,
I do need stability
In my life to be happy.

I was meant to be your mate.
Together we'd have been great.
Our future would have been bright.
Why couldn't you have treated me
right?

Jennifer Craig

SUNRISE BY THE SEA

The sky is her canvas
And so is the sea
She paints them picture perfect
Just for me.

The sun is arising
The waves roll quietly
Back and forth, back and forth
Trying vainly to catch me.

The sand is white
Golden is the sun
I remember old times
Remember old fun.

Of dreams in the past
Of dreams in the now
The sun is getting higher
The ocean's getting loud.

I dream of old sunsets
Of sunrises to come
As I watch the sunrise
By the sea that I love.

J Lynne Garner

MY HEATHER

Most times she smiles and others she
frowns.
Some days my world's turned upside
down.
She mashes her cookies and makes a
face,
My Heather keeps a joyful pace.

As she grows so fast, I feel forlorn
Seems like my daughter's just been
born.
This child of mine, I love so much as
She reaches up with her soft touch.

Some day she'll have a daughter, too
And know what a baby's love can do
To bring the sunshine with smiling eyes.
She'll shake her head and heave some sighs

As baby turns her world upside down
And knocks the planter to the ground,
She'll look up at mom and make a face
While continuing a joyful pace.

Wendy Jameson
I'VE STUDIED YOUR FACE
I've studied your face
In our familiar place
I've seen fire in your eyes
As we say our last goodbyes
And I've been made a fool
As my heart slowly dies

I've heard you say
It's just too easy
To say hello
And then goodbye
And I've tried so hard
To find the reason why

I can be strong
When things go wrong
It's those nights
That seem so long
I can't make it without you.

Timna Hallett
GRANDMA/GRANDPA
Connections
Thin lines that draw pictures of houses
Words becoming beliefs
Bonds that can't be erased

When was I young
Not often enough
Folding hands
Sighing frequently
Soon to be hoping

Strong enough feelings
Heaven and earth
You and me and being two places at once
Don't leave me

Skin that tightens
Over bones that ache
Teeth that fall out
Hearts that break
Like eggs

E June Mathews
YESTERDAY'S FIELDS
Forgotten fields of yesterday,
—Picturesque with stately grace;
Displaying souvenirs of gray,
You dance in autumn's tawny lace.

An ermine cloak for winter's wear,
—Splashing sparks of sapphire fire;
Reflecting gleam on frosted hair
That's crowned by gems of heart's desire.

Your weathered wisps withstand the strife,
As tired anemic landscape ghosts;
A camouflage for pulse of life,
That plays the season's welcome hosts.

Evola Loretta Sander Barron
THANKS, RANDOM HOUSE AND ROGET'S

Christ died for us. Romans 5:8 In grateful memory of August and Mary Sander & Paul and Blanche Peterson. They helped to educate me!

Is this a poem?
I hope I win.
Is doggerel OK?
Am I a poetaster?
If I could only poetize!
Must it be tuneful and/or epic?
What about rhyme?
Is this line a verse???

Anne M Rodenburg
YOU'RE ALIVE
The world is a place,
where you have to face,
your problems.

You can hide,
your feelings inside,
but it only makes you sad.

There are too many drugs,
and not enough hugs,
going around.

This is the age,
where the new rage,
is darkness.

This is the way,
the world is today,
but we don't change it.

You may be sad,
but you should be glad,
you're alive.

Gayle Flores
TURNING

For those who are struggling to communicate from the heart—

Honestly I meant to never say that at all but my words clamored out—beneath their armor—bad timing—and I had time to just say my say
Before I turned to walk away—

Honestly I can't apologize for my feelings stand as they are however blemished with insecurity or flogged with too much female pride, thought I,
before you turned to walk away—

It seems like light years 'tween us really though I cannot justify it definitely so we remain in separate galaxies talking me—talk inside our heads while wishing we had not Decided
To take the time to walk away.

Pamela Harac
OUR BOMB

I dedicate this poem to those who have believed in me, I love you.

The world grows silent as destruction falls upon us.
Shadowed heads turn their attention up towards the sky.
Young hands make quiet reaches for parent warmth.
A small tear filled with hidden death peak over rims.
The tilted heads take a final view of love.
Wrinkled arms hold tight to the old dreams.
The dream of forever unity and peace have vanished along with the last breath of the earths wind.
The flowers seem to be standing tall.
"Oh beautiful . . . "
A hush blows across the waiting audience.
"For spacious skies . . . "
The heads lower in shame.
"For amber waves of grain."
Pasty faces make final glances at their virgin country side.
"For purple mountains majesty . . . "
Small fingers brush the gentle petals with sad longing.
"America, America . . . "
A tiny fist wraps around stems throat,
"God shed his grace on thee."
And pulls life from the ground . . .
"From sea to shining sea . . . "

Elizabeth Brooks

Elizabeth Brooks
THE SLAMMING DOOR (PART ONE AND TWO)

Dedicated to my neighbor—With love, irritation and annoyance.

It wakes me up, It ruins my cakes,
It knocks things off of the wall,
I wonder why you let it slam,
It's not necessary at all.

You take the dog, you both go out.
He lifts his leg by the tree.
I'm sure he'd say if he could talk,
The slamming sure bothers me.

I wonder what You're thinking of,
As you open so wide and free.
Then let it slam with such a bam,
Do you do it to bother me?

Your wife goes out, and comes back in,
It closes as it should.
She understands how it should be,
Why can't you do as good?

It still goes on, the slamming door.
It drives me up the wall.
I've spoken to him, but he forgets,
Will I survive it all?

His wife he says will yell at him,
And ask him not to do it.
But he forgets, and so he says,
I will when I get round to it.

'Round to it is not the answer,
It must be here and now,
For saying round to it,
Is just the same as saying,
Oh, just screw it.
I know the dog if he could talk,
Would say in my behalf,
The slamming door for both of us,
Is really an earful of blast.

So on it goes, here and now,
Round to it may be in the offing,
If I survive I wonder will I
Be the one to go out scoffing.

Mark Nunn
BEAUTY
Some people say beauty
is seen in the face,
I think beauty
is unseen in the heart.

Edith Mae Payne
GOD DOES KNOW AND UNDERSTAND
GOD does know, your heart-ache, your fear,
Understand the shed-ding, of each tear.

Trouble come, you do not understand the reason, why,
The answer some-day, you will know, in the sweet, by and by.

Many times, trials, tribulation, come your way,
GOD does know, always understand, your trouble, of each day.

Call on HIM, when you pray,
HE will, help you, each passing day.

GOD does know, does always understand, tho you feel, you're all alone, some-time blue,
HE will help you, this, I know is true.

Will never, leave you, HE has proven this, time and time, again,
GOD does know, does always, understand.

Cathy Mallette
WHY?
Why is a loaded word.
It asks many questions and holds many answers.
It can be used anytime, anyplace, with anyone for anything.
It says anything, everything, and nothing.
It requires much thought and receives much consideration.
Did you ever ask yourself why?
What was your answer? . . . another why?
Why is this?
Why?

Derald A Morse
DOG-GONE
Today I buried a loved one.
She was family and friend and a piece of my heart.
For sixteen years, plus, she lived in my home
And of my life she was a part.

In her twentieth year she passed away
Having served her purpose in life.
She provided many years of love, companionship, devotion and understanding
For my daughter, myself and my wife.

She will never be replaced.
It's impossible you see!
For artificial parts
Cannot replace this part of me.

I am so proud I was selected
To share her life and love.
It has to be a choice
Made by him above.

Many people would say

"Oh! She was just a pet!"
But none of those same people
Could replace her on a bet.

Eve Langdon-Smith
SEGMENT OF THE CIRCLE
The days of our few years
Are like an arc across the earth,
Circumscribed in part,
The whole unseen.
And we, in self-delusion, mark an end
Where no end is;
For even as the symbol of our birth is circular——
An egg—
This sphere's assumed dimensions bend
And curve in space and then return
And meet
Where they began.

Brenda Blanco
THE CYCLE

With Love to: Mary, Jim, & Riley.

We all enter this world, not knowing our fate.
In search of love; hoping it's not too late.
We first feel, the love of a friend.
And find, a true friendship would never end.
Then the love from the soul, in another we find.
In this love, all things will bind.
Then there's a time, when your love must grow.
To share the secrets and knowledge you know.
A child is born, and your heart is in flight;
Because the love you wanted to give, is shining back like a light.

Marianne Thompson
A STILL-LIFE MOMENT
Spirits high and overflowing,
a smile on my heart shines
like crystal, illuminated with light.
Overwhelming thoughts: of
capturing this moment in a still-life;
colors bright, framed in glimmering
precious stone.

Indescribable feelings awaiting
description, transformed into words,
yet not coming close to the
emotional expression inside, as the
spirit flows in type-written
inscription like barnacles holding
onto shells, moments are held as
anticipation dances around me;
childlike, with a merry-go-round
motion.

Helen Roberts
DAWN
Dawn—touched by God
Promises brand
New beginnings—
Like virgin snow 'tis pure.

Rippling, babbling
Brooks, tell the breeze,
God spread the word
To the flowers and trees.

Awake! Awake!
It's time to see
God's miracle—
Before man touches it.

Henry J Dugan
CHRISTMAS IS OVER
Christmas is over. Happy memories remain of you. Your wonderful blue eyes gleamed so true. That fragrant perfume that penetrated the room, dispersing all gloom.
We embraced and kissed beneath the neat mistletoe. And uttered truly, I love you so.
Has Christmas really gone away?
With so many lovely thoughts that stay—
Never before had I seen such a lovely blue gown. As in the parlor room you pranced around—
The warmth of that day will never go away. Although the pure white snow was tall. There only seemed to be a rosebed waterfall.
Tonight when the moon was full,
We would brave the wintry chill.
And in a red sleigh we would pass the night away.
Shadows of tall green trees fell on the snowy ground. There wasn't another snow sleigh to be found.
Just the trail of a Christmas sleigh.
Has Christmas really passed away?
There was evidence our true love was here to stay.

Aitch Arem
CALVARY
Lord, let me walk with You tonight
outside the city wall,
Into the Garden where You prayed
and drank the bitter gall.
I want to hear You say again, in
awful agony,
"Thy will be done, for it's Your way
to set the sinner free."

I want to feel the Judas kiss, when he
my Lord betrayed.
I need to see Your precious love at
such a time displayed.
I want to watch the brawling mob in
their chicanery;
The drumming of the jeering yells to
set Barabbas free!

And as the crown of thorns is placed
upon Your lovely head,
I need to listen while You hear the
mocking things they said;
To see You led into the street and fall
beneath Your load;
Watch Simon as he lifts Your cross—
no tenderness bestowed.

Help me to hear as they all heard the
nails piercing Your limbs,
For then "The Rugged Cross" will be
my choice of sacred hymns.
Although there is the empty tomb,
and Power from above,
The greatest proof that You're divine,
is shown in Calvary love.

How could You pray "Father
forgive," when they deserved Your
hell,
The blatant ignominy, too, worse
than a tongue can tell?
You've let me see, by faith, dear
Lord, UP THERE YOU TOOK MY
PLACE.
Now I'm Your slave, bearing my
cross, saved by Your matchless
grace.

Helen L Davis
THE DARK BETWEEN THE STARS

I dedicate this poem to my late parents, Rosie and William Riley Barnes.

The preachers rant of Hell,
How we will burn there,
In hot, flaming, everlasting fires.
But Hell is dark and cold,
I know, I've been there.
Cold, like the dark between the stars.
A cold that just one drop
Of warmth would shatter
Into a million gleaming shards of ice.
To melt where they fall,
To be again, not ever.
Moth and flame, it seems too high a price.

A child of the cold,
I cannot meet you
In that sunlit place you call, "Ours."
Into the familiar
I must retreat,
Into the dark between the stars.

Reba Short

Reba Short
THOSE PRETTY BIRDS

I dedicate this poem to God who gave me talent, and to my familiy and friends.

I took a walk through the woods the other day.
I just had to get away. No one seemed to understand why, I just had to get away and cry.

I thought I was out there all alone, but I've never heard such chattering going on. When I looked up and saw those pretty birds, then I knew the Lord heard every word.

It seemed like they were saying go back home, and all your troubles will be gone, and I never doubted those pretty birds, cause I knew the Lord heard every word.

Thank you Lord for listening to my cries.
I feel so much better inside. I'll walk back home with a great big smile.
Thanks again Lord for listening to my cries.

Billy Morton McBride
OIL WELLS

To The Rough Necks of Oklahoma and Texas Who were Made of Steel, And the Derricks Made of Wood.

On the wide spread open fields
Where the dust has settled and dried,
Stand the wooden memorials of days gone by,
Where the once flowing wells have died.

And the day winds that are dry and hot,
Blow a screen of sickening sand,
That parches my framework through and through,
In this lonely and forgotten land.

Marji Traudt
BEGINNING WITH AN ENDING

To new beginnings, yours and mine.

please understand
and take my hand
and forever
we'll be together
in our hearts
two new starts
which must be
begun separately
you never know
we may say hello
once again
when we begin
but for now
don't ask me how
we must turn around
without a sound
and walk away
on this day
without asking why
just saying goodbye

Marion (Hebert) Caldwell
THE PATH TO THE SPRING
There is a dappled woodland path
that I wandered long ago,
where—when in search of
solitude to this wooded path I'd go.
Here—I'd leave worldly cares
behind and then stroll along real
slow, on the path that led to the
spring, where the clear, cool waters
flow.
There—a deserted logging road
on—up the hill ascended,
where—it then forked along the
way, and a deer-path there
descended.
Sometimes, staring through wild
hedges, stood a statuesque-like doe,
for she knew where the path did
lead, where the pure, clear waters
flow.
Here—this shady, green, grassy path,
beneath the cliffs and ledges,
blew with lady-slippers of pink
amongst the wildwood hedges.
And, then the path still around
'til it reached a swinging door,
formed by great, green, swaying
branches, that up toward the sky did
soar.
When this woodland door swung
open, one could hear the waters
sing, for—within this wooded haven
the path ended at the spring.
At this spring of clear, pure water,
I'd kneel at the crystal sight,
then—cup my hands like a
dipper to fill with elixir of life.
As I drank the life-giving water,
I'd suddenly feel fresh and
whole, for—it not only quenched
the thirst, it also restored my soul.

Stephanie Duncan
HEALING

To God, who has saved me, to my family and friends who have encouraged me, and to Grandma Florine, I miss you. I love you all very much. S.D.

When a heart is broken, it takes a while to heal.
Only God's undying love, can help a person to feel.
Sometimes when a person forgets he cares,
they will take a life, their own.
When the heart misses a long ago buried loved one,
It will never forget.

The casket, the soil, the loved one inside,
 It's all too much.
Freedom from pain is suicide.

God works in many ways,
 he's taken care of me since that dreadful day.
He's loved me, and shown me the way,
 to him, his son, and their heavenly ways.
He's shown me what I can do with life,
 And how to love again.

I often wonder where I would be,
 without his love and generosity.
I also wonder if I hadn't found life in him,
 if I would be here today,
Or buried 6 feet beneath the soil and dirt,
 underground!

John Vincent Henry
ALL THINGS PASS BEFORE ME

All things pass before me
visions of a life gone by and one that is yet to be.
Catching time on the sidelines
watching the play go by
Knowing the soul is slowly growing
feeling the body die.
Life is a game of give and take and
you take what only you give
giving love and taking wisdom is the only way to live.
Seeing my friends with smiles and tears
knowing their pain and joy.
Following the paths throughout the years
feeling like player and toy.
Trying to mold the clay of life close
to the patterned plan
finding insights on the way,
Every time you try and pray of how
to work your hands.
Searching for that time of peace
that comes few and far between,
comes from knowing what you've
done who you've known
and where you've been.
All things pass before me

Earleta Hedges Selm
HAUNTING WORDS

I'll never see another harvest or watch the combines roll.
These words tear at my heart and bore into my soul.

My father said them to me, it seems like yesterday.
A man whose strength and faith pain could not take away.

I stood beside his bed in the stark white room.
A smile upon my face, my heart filled with gloom.

What do you say to someone you love with every breath,
To give them courage to fight when their enemy is death.

We talked of everything from fields of golden wheat,
To the crunch of virgin snow pressed beneath our feet.

Of childhood memories, days long gone by.
All the while I begged, Lord don't let me cry.

But there was nothing I could say, he knew as well as I,
That his days were drawing to a close and soon he must die.

Altho he left me years ago these words still weigh upon my soul.
I'll never see another harvest or watch the combines roll.

Melody M Geitner
A GIFT FROM ABOVE

*To my wonderful parents,
for their support and love,
this poem is dedicated.*

God sent her down to live
here on earth,
A wonderful spirit of which
you gave birth.
She is here now to hold
and to love,
A wonderful spirit,
a gift from above.

Trials are many,
Lone moments are few,
But the gift God sent you
He could not outdo.
She is yours now
this gift of love,
A wonderful spirit,
a gift from above.

John P Kesler
FANTASTIC VOYAGE

The big bird soars into the sky,
Smoke marks its upward path,
Its feathers are red, white and blue,
The ocean is its bath.

The bird is sailing to the sun,
With young ones seven hid 'neath its wings,
And many watch from down below,
Awed by the pride she brings.

But then the bird comes crashing down,
She's wounded it appears,
The mother bird gives up the ghost,
And smiles turn into tears.

The nation for her children weeps
For they are victims, too,
Their names are etched in walls of time,
In red and white and blue.

Jennifer Varden
SILENT NOISE

Around the meadow,
Down the hill
A silent noise
Gives me such a thrill.

The sound is so real
It is beautiful and dear,
No one else hears it,
But I feel it so near.

This noise is the beauty,
The joy, the delight,
The moon and the stars
That run and play at night.

I don't hear it often anymore,
For the world is so busy.
I cry about it sometimes,
Because the newer sounds are so
 different.

I miss my noise,
The laughter of the trees,
The cry of the sheer enjoyment of
 the early autumn breeze.
I miss my silent noise.

Mike Milsom
THE SUN SHINES OVER HONESTY

The sun shines and the sky is clear,
italicizes the new found happiness you hold so dear,
The work is ahead and tough times will be there,
But with your new found happiness there is nothing you can't bear.

You've experienced fear, anxiety and loneliness,
And now you can see how wonderful your world really is,
Now you can create a world benign,
Full of friendship, happiness and all so kind.

You've always wanted to do what is right,
But your courage and love has often been way too slight,
Through the doubt you've seen what love is,
Just believe in yourself and there lies courage.

It all began with just one word,
With a meaning never truly heard,
Understanding, friendship and love can be,
Simply made up of honesty.

Nicole M Johnson
THE MISFITS

They all stare with their mocking faces,
Which show no hope, no love, no future,
There's just black emptiness where their hearts were.
They show no concern for others,
They selfishly keep their love to themselves.
Always judging by appearance, not personality.
They snicker at us in their little groups.
All they are is clones!
They have no personality of their own.
They try to take our pride
with their cruel, snide remarks.
They try to break us and take everything
We believe in.
We won't let them!
We keep our pride,
We ignore the looks they give,
And all the childish comments they find so amusing.
We are the Misfits.
We will stay together,
Always,
And we will never give in to them!

Julie C Knipe
WHEN I LOOK UP INTO THE SKY

When I look up into the sky,
I see the stars and moon up high.
The night releases my inner soul,
I feel relaxed I want to let go.
Through tears of joy or maybe pain,
I write these words a secret game.
My innermost thoughts I let you read,
I wonder, I fear, what do you see?

I guess I am scared of losing you,
I try so hard, but what can I do?
Our love has always been special, I do believe,
But your true feelings I just can not conceive.

Judie Cavender
REFLECTIONS ON THE SEA

Crashing waves upon the reef,
Sight and sound beyond belief.
A mighty and majestic roar
As water breaks upon the shore.
The constant battering of the waves
Creates an underwater cave.
And when the tide is low, the shore
Is wonderful, you can explore
The secret places that the sea
Has left behind for you and me.

Deborah Brancheau
THE DREAM

As I walking, I met this girl
Her eyes so still and sad,
And as I sat down beside her
She told me of a love that she once had.

A love that she had always thought
Would last throughout the years,
But it turned to be a love she found
to be filled with pain and tears.

She tried and tried to overcome
the obstacles in their way,
She told him that soon it would all work out
And they would be together some day.

Then he left without a word
She tried to understand why.
But in her heart, she felt the pain
And knew that he had lied.

For you can not love—not truly love
And then just walk away.
The next few months, she made herself believe
That it was better off this way.

Why must it be that the ones you love
Have the power to bring such pain.
It doesn't seem fair, when you just try to care
And get hurt again and again.

Every now and then he'd call her
And a few hours together they'd spend.
But each time he left, the pain got worse.
Till she realized that it had to end.

He couldn't have both, his life far away
And have her, too, whenever he'd call.
For her love was not a part-time love
She needed him forever or not at all.

Before she could tell me how it all turned out
She became very hard to see.
And I suddenly awoke and realized
That the girl in my dream was me.

I lay there thinking for a long, long time
And my thoughts were all confused.
I wished I had known how 'the girl' said goodbye
As now I must say to you.

More than anything else, I need to be loved
But like the 'girl' it has to be all the way.
And how can I learn to love someone new
When thoughts of you get in the

way.

So please know that I wish you only the best
But I can't keep holding on,
To a feeling that now causes so much hurt
Ever since you've been gone.

I hope that if you think of me
You'll know I really did try,
But without you feeling the same way too
There's nothing left except good-bye.

Barbara E Baker
FOREVER NEVER COMES
Don't say, "I Love You,
Forever to be true."
Don't you know,
"Forever Never Comes"?
It's long lasting without end.
You promise "Together Forever,"
But promises are broken,
Over and over again.
The pain comes once more,
But do you yet know,
"Forever Never comes"?
For when the love ends,
And the hurt sets in . . .
FOREVER continues on.

Raquel L Stevenson
WHISPERS ON THE SHORE
The ocean was calling today;
In a new astonishing way
It captured my soul
Setting my spirit wondering.

To what do I owe this duty?
Speaking to the usually quiet bay.
With white caps seeking words ten fold,
In its sentiment I sat probing.

The pebbles ventured to the shore
Pursuing space to make one more.
Some would settle restraining the clatter,
While others would be seized to repeat their endeavor.

With questions sustaining my mind they tore
Perched; awaiting something more.
Upon the coming my heart did shutter,
In being an ideal all put asunder.

The hushed testimony of reprose.
The compromisal of this so many have chose.
Whispering its wisdom while presenting forever.
Uttering its knowledge for those accepting the encounter.

Rev Jimmy Wayne Ford
SPIRITUAL GROWTH
I am but a seed, just planted in fertile earth,
How magnificent it is, to experience your own new birth.
I'm still under ground, but I'm growing, slowly I enlarge,
But satan's first destruction attempt comes early as I began to starve.
Finally a gardener waters me and new life I receive,
As my head pokes above the ground and fresh air I breathe.
Another attempt on my life as the wind nearly carries me astray,
Quickly I'm covered and protected, by a stranger passing my way.
I'm a young sapling now, about three or four feet in height,
The dew clings on my leaves, and sparkles, in the early morning light.
Just when everything seems perfect, another fatal terror comes my way,
Satan plagues my leaves with disease as I turn yellow from decay.
But a nurseryman detects my problem and gently sprays my leaves,
Through prayer God intervenes, the disease fades, once again I'm freed.
Before fully recovering I'm nearly uprooted by a typhoon,
Thankfully, it passes, I straighten, and shoot upwards toward the moon.
In the years ahead many things help me to grow and mature,
A constant rain, and sunshine, ever so pure.
When I was a young christian, a sapling, Satan could easily move me about,
Until I learned to feed on the meat of the Word, I wasn't very stout.
But now that I'm mature, with God's help, to Satan I WILL NOT BOW,
From a seed to an oak, four feet wide, eighty foot tall, satan, MOVE ME NOW!

Franceen Crews Román

Franceen Crews Román
ILLITERATES
I would like to Dedicate the poem "Illiterates" to my loving parents, William and Louise Crews of Nathalie, Virginia

Illiterates of the world
It's time you all took a stand,
To learn to read and write,
It could be the best thing in life.

Don't be scared and all confused
There's hope out there if you choose,
People of every creed and color,
Can now unite with each other.

We are brothers and sisters of this great land
Working together hand-in-hand,
Reading and writing is the key,
To a whole new world of what life can be.

Don't be left out any longer
Get the skills and get stronger,
Make the move to succeed,
It could be exactly, what you need.

So don't be left out in the cold
Just remember you've been told,
The time is right for me and you,
To be the best that we can be,
Just think of all the possibilities.

Karen Correll Wilke
THE INNER MIND
My energies of the mind are sometimes more than I can maintain.
I find my subconscious sometimes hallucinatory.
Racing my thoughts a song that I must tarry.
Looking for an agreeable goal,
Is life's long challenge.
We are in debt to our soul.

In the law of friendship, there is one rule which is always obeyed.
It is compared to a sinking ship.
You stay as the captain until all your mates are rescued.

Life possess its trials and errors.
They may consist of physical or psychological hardships.
But their terms are all our perils.

Why must every human being find his way?
That is what novels, poetry, and fables say.
I know I will find mine with time and patience.
It will be kind.

Erin Behn
SPECIAL FRIEND
For Shannon Langley, thanx for the inspiration. Happy Birthday !!!

Some people just forget them;
Others treasure them like a gem.
But mine I'll never let go of
Because I know it's a special kind of love.
I shall never let it slip away
Because I know I'll see it again someday.
What I have I shall never lend
Cuz it's memories of my only special friend

Lorie Ann Lowe
TRYING TO FORGET YOU
To my father, David Micheal Lowe, whom I knew shortly, but loved greatly.

Trying to forget you is not easy.
I always have memories of you, and what you have done for me.
All of the kind things you have said and done.
I thought our life together had just begun.

Now you are gone, and I will never see you again.
Though I wish things would have never come to an end.
All, I know is that I loved you, you were my best friend.
Oh! How I wish we could start over again.

Now, you are gone for good, I did all that I could.
Here I will stay, as my heart slowly fades away.
I wish I could see you again someday.
It is impossible I guess it is the price I have to pay.

Trinnette M Morrison
FORGIVING
To my grandpa, John W. Reeves, with all my love.

As I wandered down,
To where you lay,
I felt you touch my soul.
Not with words.
Not with actions.
But with mere emotions.

You weren't the boy
I thought you were.
You were older,
Wiser,
And more knowledgeable.

You looked deep inside me,
And you always brought out my best.
You understood me,
You helped me.
I came to you for advice.
I couldn't think of life without you.

Then you were gone.
You, my best friend.
But that's ok,
I forgive you, for dying—
GRANDPA

Roger A Rowe
SCHOOL TEACHER'S LIFE
To my Teacher Wife, Elizabeth.

The life of a school teacher is very sad,
If they're happy, the principal is mad;
School work is piled high upon their head,
They're tired and want to stay in bed.

They come to school, tired with sleepy eyes,
To give each student the semester sighs;
Then they go home, with their shoulders bent,
To grade the tests, all their free time spent.

So after the semester, they're again cheerful,
And the students, they also enjoy the lull;
But the principal is now getting very bored,
With all the school children's discord.

Watch out teacher, you will be the target,
Of the principal's anger, and may get bit;
He will put the blame on you, not the class,
So it is, in all schools, the same old sass.

Margaret V Hopp
DON'T CRY FOR ME
In memory of my beloved sister Vivian Pearl Kearns, who passed away June 30 1986

"Don't cry for me," I heard her say,
One day when we were sad.
"If I should go and leave you here,
I know you'll feel so bad.
You go along this road but once,
I've tried to make it pay,
But someone else will have to judge,
For who am I to say."
And then again, her mood would change,
We'd laugh and cry in spurts,
And then she'd be off again,
To tend to others' hurts.

So, I'll cry for me, who'll miss her smile,
Her tender loving ways.
Tears of sorrow will dim my eyes,
Because she is away.
I'll search for her, my dreams will fill
Of memories we've shared.
My sister dear, I'll miss you so
But, I'll cry for me, I cared.

Kurt Fuhrmann
RETURNING HOME
A warm place where I rest my head.
This is where I now wish to be
In the comfort of my own bed.

Images, reasons why I fled,
One good place that I long to see,
A warm place where I rest my head.

Traveling, confused and misled,
One image fills my memory

In the comfort of my own bed.

Then, of course, do let it be said,
Is there only one room for me,
A warm place where I rest my head.

Feelings of green, yellow and red,
Music and even poetry
In the comfort of my own bed.

Instincts know, which is how I'm led
To feelings of warmth and safety.
A warm place to rest my head
In the comfort of my own bed.

Kenneth Llewellyn
—LYNN—

To my dear friend, Lynn, with Love . . .

. . . Quietly she nears
And softly she stays

Adorned in gentle
Unassuming ways

To babes and animals
Her love, she freely gives

A true Lover of Life
As she breathes, As she lives

Joyous experiences
When she can unfold her wings

Opening up, Letting go
Love will reign when her heart sings

Still, a Lover of Life
With nothing else to lose

But a fear to love all
Hidden within her views

Yet, All this will pass
In forthcoming days

Quietly she nears
And softly she stays . . .

Debbie Cas
THE LONELY PART OF LOVE
The time spent away from you,
Surely makes for a miserable day;
It's so hard to be happy when I'm blue,
Without you, loneliness is the price I pay!
When we met, was it a mutual attraction,
The thrill of someone new;
Or the the hopes of physical satisfaction,
Whatever the case, I'm glad it was you!
They are real, these feelings in my heart,
My love, these emotions never felt so true;
The tears I shed when we must part,
Is not my imagination because, you feel it too!
Loving you is easy and feels oh so right,
Without your love, I'd rather die;
Just being held in your arms and held so tight,
Lets me know you feel the same as I!

Karen L Bascom
MY LOVE
He sleeps . . . .
I am in his breath
He moves . . . .
I am in his muscles
He moans . . .
I am in his dreams
He sweats . . .
I am in his pores
He cries . . .
I am in his tears
He thinks . . .
I am in his thoughts
He smiles . . .
I am in his heart
He loves . . .
I am in his love

Joan Fields
GIFT SUPREME
Laugh and say whatever you will;
Sneer and smirk and taunt.
In my heart's domain I'm quiet still.
For love I shall not want.

In a solitude more splendid far
Than one you'll ever know,
I sow the seeds of happiness;
And watch my garden grow.

The years that leave their mark on you
Shall find me yet the same.
For long I've held the gift supreme,
And Peace shall be its name.

Andrew Alger
FLIGHT OF SOULS

To all the prisoners of the world.

The steel and stone stood all around.
The world of light was trapped and bound.

All souls inside were held in toil,
blindly taking from the soil.

Caged in doubt. They searched for truth,
till every one had lost its youth.

With no way left for them to turn.
Deep inside they finally learned.

Steel and stone then broke and fell.
Out they flew to joyous yells.

For every soul that flies out free,
there comes another just like me.

Kathleen Ellen Petinak
YOU SAY THAT FOREVER COULD BE A DAY

Darling, you are my inspiration, I love you.

You say that forever could be a day,
you say that our future's not far away,
you say you love me, but don't promise me the world,
you say you need me, yet you could live alone.
You're strong, stronger than most people I know,
you've been places that I'll never go,
you strive for excellence and always achieve,
you have an abundance of goals and dreams.
You're very precise in the things that you do,
you're never afraid to try something new,
you like to stay busy, yet have time to yourself,
you keep a fit body and keep up good health.
You're tender at moments I need you to be,
you're loving and giving and patient with me,
you're definitely someone I want around,
you are the best thing I've ever found.
You give me reason to love and to dream,
you make me strong and fulfill all my needs,
you have me thinking of you day and night,
you and I know that things must get right.
So maybe tomorrow's not so far away,
knowing I love you forever and a day.

Tricia Gabel
FAST CAR

This is to all my friends. Please drive carefully, legal speed and always buckle up! I love you all, and wouldn't want to lose ya!

A car drives fast . . .
Right on past!
Zoom . . . I hear . . .
Speed, I fear.
Burning rubber,
Still getting faster!
The traffic light ahead,
Suddenly, turns red!
Slam the brakes . . .
Skids you make . . .
Crash, I hear . . .
Death, I fear . . .

Karen R Barefoot
PEACEFUL END
The cool wind was stimulating
as it blew across my face.
The aroma of crisp clean air,
snow crumbling underfoot.
I, lay down, my attention turned
to a songbird which seemed to be crying.
As darkness begins to close around me
I can sense creatures lurking nearby,
waiting for my last breath
waiting—to feed off flesh & blood.
I listen to the wind breathe
through the trees in a, song.
Almost sorry to say—Good-byeee.

Virginia M Nelson
VIEW-POINT: A FANTASY
This story is for those, who believe that mundane things
Can become a source of wonder, if thoughts can but take wings.

At roof's edge, slender pendants flash fire in the sun,
Shining, limpid, tear-drops hang, poised, above each one;
The air is still and cold, the ground unsullied white,
Where sun-rays glance, rainbows wink, giving back the light.

Soon, the melting pendants will crash down, like shards of glass,
Foot-prints will again criss-cross, where many creatures pass;
Beneath the snow, the soil will show a subtle hint of green,
But wait: A bit of magic has transformed the earthy scene!

Last night, while snow fell softly, an Ice-Princess slipped down,
Pirouetting gracefully, in her translucent gown,
Her scepter touching lovingly, each branch, each twig, and stem,
A swirl of pearls and moon-mist, for her royal diadem.

Aware she dare not tarry, until rising of the sun,
She danced, and whirled, and frolicked, the night and she as one.
As she floated upward, her trailing gown caught fast,
Leaving jeweled strands there, when she broke free at last.

Just an ordinary sun-roof, on a snowy winter day,
Ah, but who can say a regal being hasn't passed this way?

Betty J Hartman
TOILET PAPER (AS SEEN THROUGH THE EYES OF A DOG)

To Mitzi, our Pekingese who inspired me to write this poem.

Pulled and yanked and torn
Then crushed and compressed
Is this thing that captivates me so.
It's never quite alive, but yet
I feel for this pillow of a cloud
As I see it mutilated then
Cast away like it never existed.
Even in death it is mysterious, brave, and regal.
I watch as it is tossed, and spun round and round,
Down
  and
    Down.
I hold my breath
As the gurgling waters swallow it down
Into the blackhole of eternity.

Gwen Newsome

Gwen Newsome
I CRY FOR MY PEOPLE

I dedicate my poem in loving memory of my beloved Mother and Father.

I cry for you my people
For all the tears you've shed,
For the chains that bound your spirits
And have given you a hung-down head.

I cry for you my people
For wasted years gone by,
Knowing that you had so much to give,
But not the chance to try.

I cry for you my people
For the ones that have given their lives,
But I'm proud of you my people
For the preservation of our pride.

I cry for you my people
Our fore-fathers gone before,

May they now rest in peace
Knowing that there will be chains no more.

Jimi Nixx
COME TAKE MY HAND

To a very special heart I will hold close to mine always, Cindy Hubbard and also to Stevie Nicks and Edie Brickell for inspiration.

If I had a wish, a dream to come true
I would dream for the wish of spending a day with you
I would take you on a journey far away from here
To a place lost in time
Where there is nothing in the world to fear
I would take you on a journey far, far away from here
To a place full of laughter
Where hearts know no sorrow
To a place where dreams live on today
So they don't have to wait for tomorrows
So come join me now
Come and take my hand
Come let me take you to this romantic land
For this journey is but a piece
A portion of a part
On the journeys I can take you
That exist only within my heart.

Michael D Clark
TRAPPED BY SOCIETY

Dedicated to my baby daughter 'SAMANTHA.' In faith she'll face the world with open eyes and a true heart.

Wretched is the web I weave, my soul cannot be cleansed.
I live for hate & misery, and pray it brings my end.

A tragedy much worse than death, for all eyes to see
They take me for all that I am, then quietly watch me bleed.

How far will the spirit bend, they try mine day by day
How long will one's hope last, when tortured in every way.

As they pluck the life from my pathetic hide
and rip my skin at its seams.

Is this really happening to me....

Or is this, just a dream.

B J Skarphedinsson
STROKE

Always remember there is hope

While I lay in that dark mute agony,
I saw nothing, nor thought, nor felt, nor heard.
The pain hard. No mind, no body.
In those blind hours beyond all senses,
No sense of love or life. Eyes in blackness.
No brain for regrets to cross.
But when you touched me, when your love tears fell,
That which had been nothing but pain,
Turned back into life as a miracle,
In which all life before, became forgiven.

Voices that muttered have become strong,
Deadened nerves have come to life.
The sores, the pain have come to nothingness.
The too long lonely heart is filled.
With love and joy my heart will serve,
Peace and chastity are my inner light.
For all the todays and tomorrows of this life,
Love of our God raised this face,
Toward the heavens, always in his protection,
In faith, by day and by night.

Renea Haarberg
PICTURE PERFECT

To Eric and Joby, my two best friends.

I rarely make promises
which are impossible to keep,
thus, I tell you now
this one is dwelling deep;

It is oozing from my soul
and is sculptured in my heart . . .
It is saying that our friendship
is a concrete type of art.

It will assure you of my love
and the tenderness I feel,
It paints a perfect landscape
for life's important zeal;

It helps me make you happy
and if you'd like to know,
this promise I will keep
confirms, I Love You so . . .

M Ridgway
BEAUTY OF FLIGHT

Thy ominous cry from far away
Waiting quietly watching
Watching silently
Anxiously awaiting his prey

As he speaks through his eyes
Not a sound does he make

Which omen will he forecast
Flight without meaning, future without time
Standing boldly as his eyes look into mine

His eyes unforgettable, his body like snow
Fear not his presence in awe

Take off and flight
Soars floats with ease
As he captures the field mouse
Feet never touching the ground
Back to his home with prey he does roam

Once that I've seen thee
But once a memory does make
For seeing such beauty of flight does the snow owl take

Jan Salmon
P.O.W./PRISONERS OF WALLS

Where are the countless elderly of our day?
In a room, dormant on a hospital bed, many lay!

They are the *P.O.W.'s of modern day.
Many sent in protest, feeling abandoned and even betrayed.

The majority soon forfeit
all anticipation of their release.
Losing their mind while *M.I.A.
where as others surrender their soul,
to the "Prince of Peace."

Upon entering the institution,
many know their value in today's society is none.
There they await the prophetic descension
of God's soon coming son.

Within confined walls and restricted doors,
yet through prayer, they continue access
to God's throne.
In the event death should first call,
they would be admitted
*A.W.O.L.,
to their eternal home.

All the while, as *P.O.W.'s
they await the release
of their contested capture.
Through Christ, their "KINSMEN REDEEMER,"
in the prophesied Messiah rapture!

Mary Jane Brown
LARGESS

To my husband Miller Brown; for his encouragement.

The sky is a roseate splendor; a jewel of queenly grace.
The stark bare trees with their reaching limbs,
Are the prongs to hold it in place.
When the slanting rays of the setting sun burst over the western rim;
The rainbow hues of this grand old gem
Cause the bravest eye to grow dim.
If you are seeking for riches;
Things that are costly and rare;
Look to the Lord of creation for beauty beyond compare.
His Jewels are the biggest and brightest
More lovely than all the rest;
They quell the deep hunger inside us;
The soul satisfying the best.

Shannon Graham

Shannon Graham
COULD HAVE BEEN

There are stars in the sky,
Like the sparkles in your eye.
I knew that there was love,
And it felt as if it came from above.
For all those times you held me in your arms,
You filled me with all your charms.
Every night I longed for that warm kiss,
But now since you are not here that's what I miss.
Now since we aren't together I fear,
Because down my cheek falls a tear.
When I feel that tear it breaks my heart,
For now I know that we will always be apart.
Because it never could have been.

Nathan Toler
I'M JUST AN OLD DOG

I'm just an old dog, old and gray
Cars pass me by like I'm an old stray
When I go home they chase me to bed
Throw me some slop and say I've been fed
It's morning time, time to get up
Then they come out and feed me some grub
It's never heated it's always cold
But this food is fit for dogs I'm told
They turn me out it's back to the street
I run around till I'm dead on my feet
I hate being a dog I wish I were dead
Cause over and over this slop I am fed.

Teresa Christine Roumillat
WHEN AMERICAN EAGLES TURN INTO DOVES

I will sing a song you may not have heard
The eagle is known as a mighty bird
The white-headed eagle represents a land that is free
He is the bird of liberty
But when the world has no more flaws
This mighty bird shall shed its claws
When the world loses its mean streak
Off will come his head and his mighty beak
When the world changes the "system of things"
This mighty eagle shall lose his wings
When the world is ruled by love
You will see the eagles change into doves.

Glenn W Farquhar
FRIEND IN THE NIGHT

Lighting my way—
with its sun stolen light.
Casting away shadows,
which obscure my sight.
Giving me a feeling,
everything is right.
The moon lights my way,
like a friend in the night.

And so I make this pledge,
that to all I now cite.
I will gaze upon the moon—
each and every night.
To thank it for the guidance,
it gives me with its light.
And to let it know, it too—
has a friend in the night.

Virginia N Joivell
APRIL

April so elfin, so eager,
wears gems of a radiance rare,
star dusted dewdrops and moon-beams
She twines through her moon-misted hair.

April so wistful, so tearful,
Whose melodies bring memories fair,
spins dreams of lost tomorrows,
from yesterday's valley,

Gone,

Oh gone,

Oh where?

Ellen Dale Porter
OH HOW I WISH
The alarm clock rings—it's time to get up, I wonder what kind of day it will be.
Oh how I wish you were back home, just like you used to be.
I reach over to your side and touch the pillow, to once where you laid your head. Oh how I wish you were lying by me, and drying the tears that I shed.
I sit at the table and stare into space, at the chair where you once sat. Oh how I wish I could turn back the time—the time when we first met.
I hurry to get dressed and I go outside—I pick a pretty bouquet. I walk to the church, I go inside—I get down on my knees and I pray.
I walk outside to a new grave site; I say "Honey I brought some flowers for you. I've come to spend the day and keep you company too."
I close my eyes, I picture your face, I feel your arms around me.
Oh how I wish you were back home, and things were like they used to be.

Algie O Rountree Jr
TOMORROW'S TOLL?

To the Human Race. Change and live!

A bell, which rang some years ago;
Voice silent now mid flaccid snow;
Has clapper baked with rot and rust
From scathing elemental gust.

Its church, whose tower sang out each day;
Gray, shrouded sentinel wasting way;
Leans out with tattered walls to guard
What ghosts may come to seek their Lord.

Dregstown, for which the bell was tolled,
Lies torn and quiet in the cold.
Each nighttime glow of alien spume
Betrays no lurking in its gloom.

And *what* is *Man* who sat the bell
Above his town to toll the knell
Of generations dead and past?
Quiet; by his own hand—to last!

Esther Hjorth
MY GARDEN
Let me plant a garden
And give it lots of care,
As I sow some seeds of hope
And a measure of good cheer.

I must sow some seeds of kindness
And some goodness too.
And also lots of patience
And forgiveness too.

Let me sow the seed of giving
And water it with love,
And I shall watch it multiply
With blessings from above.

I must give it lots of loving care
And a prayer along the way,
And God will bless my garden
As I watch it grow each day.

Lorene MacCallum
ANGEL IN MY HEART

To Roxie and Tony, With love from Mom.

The Angel in my heart
Is a tiny little Pixie
Who sits on the smallest cloud
You'd ever hope to see.
She holds a box of magic buttons—
Some of green and some of gold,
And some of every other color,
Or so I've oft been told!
Some days she pushes the gold button, so fine
That fills the world with rays of Sunni shine.

But on other days, the button she chooses is green,
To polish her house so pure and clean
By washing the world with glistening rain
As it splatters the roof with a peaceful refrain.
And then she covers the sky so blue
With a fabulous rainbow that says, "I LOVE YOU!"

Addie L Kelsey
THE FARM MOTHER
She sits by the window with folded hands
Looks across the meadow at the family farmlands
No more can she rise at the peep of dawn
Get into the chores and the things going on.

These many years she has seen them through
Always there as farm mothers do
Getting breakfast as the men come from chores
Rushing in from the great outdoors.

She has raised four sons and two daughters through the years
Had Thanksgiving and Christmas and birthdays and fears
Sat up long nites when the children were small
Watching for fevers and the first little call.
Then one by one left for college or training
Ma stayed home and was always waiting.

The year she lost their dad how she cried
But I can't give up so she kept it inside
And many a nite in her lonely bed
She thought of the days when first they were wed.

Bought the farm and worked and loved
And thanked the good Lord up above
For the children, the farm, all blessed good years
Were happy and healthy through smiles and tears.

The youngest boy took over the farm
Mom stayed through all safe from alarm
Rocked the babies and walked in the sun
Needed by all till her days are done.

Her sweet face lights up as the children come to call
She's a wonderful Mom and loved by all
Now her workworn hands lie still on her lap
Where her children—grands and great grands sat
Wonderful farm mothers, all mothers too,
Can we ever repay them for all that they do?

R Dwain Wilcox
MEMORIES
Thanks for the pleasant memories
Priceless they will always be
Tho, until we meet again over four quarters and a dime
Love must remain lost in time
But, emotions run silent and deep
Even while we slumber in restful sleep
Forever seems to be
The end result of these beautiful memories

Harry Davis Jr
TO MAGGIE
I met you during the warm passions of summer and,
Slowly but surely, fell in love with you.
I tried to refrain, fearing you were too young for me
And that you would not be interested in me.
But you began to show an interest.
And so,
Shy as I was, I talked with you,
Searching your blue eyes for your love while admiring your beauty.
But that was in the warm passions of summer.

Now, in the middle of the cold, agonizing winter
You tell me you must leave.
Maggie, dear, you don't realize what you've done;
You've torn my soul apart for months, thinking about your love.
You were all that mattered to me, the only thing on my mind.
But because of my shyness, I was unable to tell you my feelings.
Now that you are leaving, my voice says without fear:
I love you, Maggie. I'll love you forever.

Michael L Lempka
ONE WINTER DAY
The haze drapes heavy from a moist gray sky
Trees stand silent among the white blanket of precipitation
Nature put on hold 'til the long awaited sun of a new day
Mountains stand, silhouettes the formations of beauty
Placid waters now enclosed with a clear cold shell
My thin epidermal wrapping is teased and nipped at by the cold ludicrous air
Noticeable and yet frozen in the mind is the reason for change . . .

Winter Segments Time

Sheri LaRowe
THOUGHTS OF YOU
Thoughts of you
still fill my heart.
I want to go back
and make a new start.

I honestly loved you
and believed that you cared.
I thought we had something special
and something truly rare.

I believed in you
was it all a lie?
Am I just too naive,
do I deserve to sit and cry?

I think and wonder
where you are,
I long to hold you
so I wish on a star.

I wonder if you
think about me,
or will I always remain
a forgotten memory?

Curtis Lee Herring
LISTEN TO A COUNTRY MORNING
Listen to a country morning and the sound that sunrise makes
As it brightens up the darkness and the world it awakes.
Listen to the rooster crowing, telling all to rise and shine,
And the splendor of renewal as our lives on earth move on.

Have you ever stood and listened to the sound that robins make
As they leave their lofty branches and their breakfast flights do make,
And have you ever heard the gentle cooing of the morning dove
As he reminds in such a gentle way of God's eternal love?

And slowly these few hours gently fade away,
And melt into the making of another day.
But all's not lost, nor is it ever gone
For as sure as there's a dusk, there shall always be a dawn.

So listen to a country morning,
Cherish it all the while.
Enjoy it fully for what it is
And always wear a smile.

Mary S Carroll
ODE TO THE BORROWER
If you borrow, as a rule,
but forget that spool of thread,
three onions and a loaf of bread,
Don't get huffy!
Don't you sputter!
When I say
I'm out of butter!

Byron H Lockwood
GOD IS NOT DEAD
To those who tell us God is dead
This question I would pose;
If God is dead, whence comes such Beauty as is in a rose?

Who makes rain fall from out the sky
To cool a dry parched land?
And how are fleecy white clouds formed,
Except by God's great hand?

Who gives a tiny blade of grass
The strength to push its way
Up through the hardened crust of earth
To seek the light of day?

If God is dead, who hears our prayers?
For they are heard, I'm sure,
And answered, if we but believe
And if our hearts are pure.

God is not dead! He lives today
And for eternity.
I know it's true, for I can feel
His love inside of me.

Wendy L Butler
CRISIS
The picture is etched on walls as I walk past
not words
silhouettes—breathing
Should I convulse into it?

My arms envelop a tree's scratchy bark
Two shadows behind the tree
drip perspiration and ice and sighs
I can't bear to watch
I can't stop watching

Leaves curling, fearing, around brittle branches
watch

Quiet visages inside the tree's holes
Hunger and death's permanence
watch

Then above us the uniquest of all unique
grey ice flakes spirals down through branches
bouncing off the tip of a bird's beak
comes to rest at my toes

As I arms locked forever around a weary, worn tree
wonder what if I'm caught?

Dragica Natasha Radic

Dragica Natasha Radic
THE MAGIC
I've seen the whole world, accidentally.
Pretending traveler, desperately seeking you,
with each return, brought an empty heart in my luggage,
as a souvenir. I had nothing to claim.

In this world of disasters, in this world of uncertainty,
I'm desperately seeking you . . .
It's the end of the world, already!

My shelf is full of souvenirs from abroad:
Pale, worn out, exhausted hearts.
Collecting dust.
Hopeless, devastated, angry—I destroyed 'em.

. . . and then, like magic. Here you are, standing here. Loving me.
Here I am, trembling in your arms, silently.
How can I tell you . . . of my heartless self.

. . . and then suddenly, you are the smile. Warm, mysterious smile.
In my wonder and amaze I saw my heart
slipping out of your sleeve. Mended.
I reached for it, breathlessly. It disappeared again.
Like magic.

In this world of uncertainty,
desperately seeking you,
I destroyed my dusty heart, only to see it again,
mended and safe in your sleeve.

Mildred E Wrightman
EXCEPTION TO THE RULE
I love the rain if it doesn't storm.
I love the sun if it's only warm.
I love the snow if it doesn't freeze.
I love the wind if it's just a breeze.
I love the waves if not too high.
I love the shore waves' gentle sigh.
I love the world with its doom or bliss.
Moderation in everything except your kiss.
Then it's never too soon or never too much.
It's my favorite way of staying in touch.

Pearl Ruby Lineburg
GATES OF HEAVEN
I dreamed I passed through Gates Of Heaven
I dreamed walking streets of gold,
Don't weep for me dear ones
I will never grow old.

I dreamed there will be no more heart-aches
Or tears in my eyes,
I dreamed my Lord walked with me
Now, no longer will my heart cry.

Ann Weslowski
EXAMS
Sitting at a table,
Waiting for a test,
Makes you want to try
To do your best.

Trying to finish,
While the clock ticks by,
And if you think you failed,
It makes you want to cry.

Handing in your sheet,
Thinking all that study,
Making it neat,
Tests aren't your favorite buddy.

Sitting at the table,
Waiting for an exam,
Trying to think,
Of what I am.

Brian McEuen Jackson
THE ICE CREAM MAN
Jingle Jangle, ring a ling.
Hear the bells go ding, ding, ding.
Beloved sounds, remembered well,
Refreshing coldness, sure felt swell,
As it cooled our parched dry throats,

Popsicles, fudgesicles, push ups too.
All stored in a truck, that was white, shiny new.
Dilly bars, bomb pops, and Mr. Freeze's.
16 flavors, all sure to please us,
Single scoop, double scoop, triple scoop too.
Should I get one, or shall I have two?
Sugar cones, plain cones, fancy cones too.
Counting our pennies, all shiny and new.

The hot midday sun, beat down on the street.
We'd hop up and down, as the tar burned our feet.
We'd run to the park, and sit in the shade,
lapping up hungrily, our purchases made.

These things I remember, even tho I'm all grown.
My hair has turned gray, all the kids have left home,
So, I'll sit on my porch, in front of the fan,
What's that? I hear bells, why, it's the ice cream man!

Becky Koester
A PERFECT POEM
Sadness and sorrow far outreached—
The heart that broke,
The whale that beached.

The tree that fell,
The time that flew,
Hotter than hell,
The breeze that blew.

The bell that tolled,
The chime that rang,
The man that sold,
The kid that sang.

The gun that shot,
The love that grew,
Untied the knot,
Made old the new.

The thoughts that send,
My mind back home,
The words that end,
A perfect poem.

Sunbow Miner
A SPECIAL MAN
I married a special man
A rare breed indeed
He's the very gentle kind
My spirit he has freed

I love this very special man
He loves me with all his heart
He takes real good care of me
In my life he plays an important part

I am proud to be his wife
to share his name is an honor
Our rings symbolize our undying love
that will last throughout our lives

He lets me be myself
to grow in every way
I thank the Lord for this special man
each and every day!

LuCinda Weaver
YOU'RE VERY VERY SPECIAL
You're very very special in God's eyes.
You're very very special to me.
Each day I love you more,
Than I did the day before,
Sweet darling little baby.

He took a little starlight and made your sparkling eyes.
He put a lot of sunshine in your smile.
And all the love He gave to you to share with everyone,
Is the thing that makes our life worthwhile.

The sound of your laughter, the sweetness in your voice,
Are things that bring us happiness each day.
To watch you grow into the person God would have you be,
Is the greatest joy that God could send our way.

You walk into a room, all attention turns to you.
Your personality is A 1 plus.
With all the charm and magnetism you project each day,
We're so very glad that God sent you to us.

Natalie R Begay
EACH DAY
Each day has its problems and tears.
It's enough to fear
What each day is to bring.
Each tear that falls
Is the way that I feel
When everything is not so real.
In my mind I have journeyed afar.
My dreams seem to have fallen apart
Like pictures that fade
When the years have passed.
Life has played its part.

Remembering what should have been.
My dreams and goals seem to have faded.
Like each day the sun sets,
When night has come.
A new day has begun.
Each day there is hope for a new beginning,
Keep pressing toward that goal.
Leave everything behind
And don't lose hope.

Sigrid C Rogers
MEMORIES
Tiny hands that tugged my skirt.
Light brown eyes, that showed joy and hurt.
That reddish hair that never looked neat
Those dirty sneakers on his feet was
The boy who grew to a man so tall
Twas I beside him who looked so small
The hands that once clung to mine,
became the tools to ease my time
Laughing eyes, and a tender smile,
that was my son for a little while
Now only in memories, I'll keep his call for Mama
Ever sweet
It was Mama then when just a child
Mama, still for the rest of time
The ache will ease, as time goes by but
The love will last, and in memories ever stronger grow.

Jack L Ganz Jr
MY MOM
My Mom has gone away
for a very long stay
it's not for me to say
for she's with God today

I might ask why
that she should die
Mom has risen very high
to fly with angels in the sky

I will miss her protective glove
like a little baby dove
now that she's above
Mom has God and love

#1 son
Love, Jackie

Frances Stone
DECIPHERING OLD STONES—Sculptress at Land's End—Cornwall, England
Tides pull the sea
toward a lone figure
shawled in wool.

She has walked
to Land's End
where the carvings
are patterned like the rock–
supported soil—bones that support
her feet.

When the waves close in
she arches asymmetrically
to hoist herself
mound–like
upon a ruin.

"I am the landscape
texture
and form" she avows

And as the tides recede
she studies old stones
scratched with calligraphy
soon to be hand–chiseled:
her monument to that
intangible thing
that contours the soul

and deciphers it.

Reeves Hudson
OH LET ME DANCE WITH YOU
I took a walk down town
T'was on one Saturday night.
I stopped in the dance hall,
And picked her out on sight.

Oh let me dance with you,
I am looking for a partner too.
Don't be bashful, don't be shy,
Let's have this dance—you and
I.

She was young and beautiful,
Pretty as a picture, too.
I asked her for her name,
She said, "Just call me Sue."

I took hold of her hand,
And went out on the floor.
We danced the Polka,
Like you never have seen
before.

Delores M Hobson
TOO, MANY PENCILS WITHOUT ERASERS
Devious warped hearts,
cloudily disguised to face Reality
so incongruently absorbed in
egotistical fantasies, Topsy-Turvy
Fallacies
constituting the "Show and Tell"
Addicted Workshop—
desiring and indulging wandering
minds; inject, digest and adopt
non-erasable constant flooding
thoughts repetitively.

Clamped drawn ears, "buttery"
mocking dictating tongues forever,
raising Cain
warped hearts choosing to be
confined than to be set free—
using debilitating abusive drugs and
alcohol without shame.
Sightseeing, reckless driving taking
lives running in dramatic fancy cars
leaving multi-colored scars;
mishandling charity funds, weapons
and guns; Cain, again is on the run.

Strolling down life's highway; from
the mountains, to the valleys, to the
plains
Values; Faith, Patience—Love,
Understanding, Wisdom, Strength
and Courage
Grace, Salvation and Prayer
are measured preposterously,
actually, reflecting "stoned" envies of
a dedicated, disciplined
loyal, diligent laboring "flowering"
Sister or Brother,
Does man, yet, care?

Envying hearts are wagely and
worldly blind
exercising and trusting in Hocus-
Pocus, Astrology, Sorcery, over
GOD, the Divine.

Jack Edwards
REPENTANCE
There came to me a thought divine that took me back through years of time, it showed me all my carefree ways the path I took that led astray, then all my past flashed through my mind it happened in a moment's time. I wondered how it could be with all my past in memory, all my deeds both good and bad were showed to me and I was sad, I felt the pain within my mind, the good and bad was there to find, I lifted up my weary head and thoughts like words were kindly said if I could have a peaceful mind, give God your love and all mankind.

Kimberly M Verona
FOREVER
Has anyone ever told you how
special you really are?

Have I ever told you just how
much you really mean to me?

If only words could describe my
feelings for you.

The first time I saw you; I
knew I wanted you.

As time went on; the want
and the need grew stronger.

Now I sit here—knowing that we
belong together and never will
be.

For you see, never in my life
have I met anyone like you.

No one as sweet, as kind,
as loving:

No one who can fulfill my dreams
and desires as you do.

If only you'll be mine . . .
All mine . . .
FOREVER.

Mary A Fouché
WHERE IS MY "CHILDHOOD"
Where is my childhood, I've searched for so long, But it can't be found;
I want to ask Mom, but she isn't around. I search again,
For, a hug in the morning, a kiss goodnight, a daddy's lap when you're filled with fears; a gentle hand to wipe away tears; someone to guide and help you to grow; Hold on to your hand till it's time to let go. Weren't all of these things every child's right? I longed for it so!
A little sister, a big brother too. Our times spent together were so sadly too few. I search for a photo book, maybe with pictures to look at and help take me back. I flip through the pages, but each one is black.
I'm now nearing sixty, I'm beginning to see! I won't find my childhood—It was stolen from me.

John J Armitage

John J Armitage
ON THE SANDS OF AFRICA
Just before the Great Battle,
Out on the red desert sand
A boy stood, and talked to the
Chaplain
And he held a note in his hand

He wanted it censored, and mailed
Only if he didn't return
He wanted rushed to the address
In case of his death was learned

We'd fought in many a battle
But somehow he seemed to know.
This was to be his last battle
But he was ready to go

For he had made Peace with his
Maker
As he stood with his head bowed low
Now he is resting
Somewhere way up there I know

We found him dead on the hillside
His blood was spilled on the sand
For he fought for Liberty's side
He died in a foreign land

Jimka Jewell
SILENT CRIES THAT WERE FORGOTTEN
As I walk through the night
I hear the cries that were forgotten.

No one cared or no one knew
The silent cries that were wept by
you.

You may have not let anyone listen
Or maybe you did and no one heard.

Maybe they were too soft and silent
and
No one knew, or maybe they were
too outspoken
And no one understood.

Maybe you cried in the night, or
maybe in the day
In a silent corner that was far away.

They were forgotten and hid away
but now, but now . . . .

Eric Olsen
FREEDOM?
There was a horse;
He ran without a course;
Not east nor west,
He didn't know which was best.
North or south, Nope!
Then he met the rope.
The rope jumped on his neck,
He made the horse a wreck.
The rope tamed the outside
But his spirit never died.
One day the horse got free
To be what he wanted to be.
He got away from the rope;
That old dope.
The horse went where he wanted to
go.
He went to grow.
Then one day he saw the rope on his
way;
And away the horse had to stay;
But the rope caught him,
And the days grew dim.
The spirit died.

Cristyl L Keith
FOR DAVID
My love,
you mean so much to me,
I care for you more than anything.
So much that sometimes I can barely
see straight.
And it hurts me so,
to think; in fright,
of ever letting you go.
But then,
when we're together,
the things we share are so special.
And I know we'll be together,
forever;
Or at least until the end of time.
My love,
for you, I would die.
But for now,
let's cherish the time we have
together,
and worry about the future;
tomorrow.

J Murray Butler
FORGET ME NOT
Low and soft she whispered sweet
Beautiful nothing all to me

Whispers of so many plans
Whispers of pleasure where love
stands

Thoughts of me, Love and Pain
Thoughts of Life not being the same

So go on sweet one forget the past
But long may the friendship last.

Patricia Ford
WELCOME
I'm so glad you're home.
Window curtains seem less faded
now.
Doors close more softly.
The crack looks smaller in my
favorite cup
And my room feels much more
private
Now I'm sharing it with you.

Regina Karen Birdwell
IS IT LOVE
Falling in love can come easily,
Or it might take some time,
It might stay forever,
Or just for a little while.

Love needs to be practiced
For it to be felt,
For when love is not felt,
It is gone.

Lois M Baker
WHERE IS ALL THE MAGIC NOW
The earth sounds which yesterday
lived filled with gaiety and light
Filter muted now without life.
The suns crowning sparkle which
made
The day seem made for goddess'
games
Shines the same, but never so again.

The Monarch taking to wing can
never thrill me as it did
Nor can the mighty waterfall
Fill me with the quiet awe

That welled within me as we stood, lost,
Emerging from the deep woods.

Where is all the magic now? The deep wood kept my joy it seems
And scattered it among the trees
While the mighty waterfall gathered up her mist
Leaving it all within me
Making tears which have no sound.

Where has all the magic gone? I have searched long
But never again heard the sound
Nor felt the awe nor seen the beauty found
Emerging from the deep wood.
It seems, the magic all along was love.

Katy Golbar
TEARS OF PAIN
I miss you so much, though you'll never know,
Because now you're gone and it was such a shocking blow.
I wish I could have stopped you, and made you see,
How very much you meant to me.
But now that our love is through.
There's an empty place in my heart for you.
When I walk along the beach I hear couples in the mist
And how I wish you were there for me to have kissed.
You don't know how much you hurt me, when you said we're through.
But now that you're gone I'm no longer crying over you.

Christina Kaku
THAT WAS MINE
That was mine,
But it's too small.
So i had to give it
To my little sister—
Color and all!

Jody Hansen

Lorraine Hansen
JODY'S FAREWELL

To Jody's sister, Sherry
Love, GMA Hansen

The gates to heaven have finally closed
I've safely entered in
At first I was undecided, if the gates should really close
My welcome were the angels
Who had left so long ago
They were a ray of sunshine, like a hand leading me in.
There was Grandpa, he said, "he knew that I would come"
As God had told him so
He knew I had been very sick, a battle few have won
So many hearts were saddened
But do not grieve for me
Once you've been in heaven, you will never want to leave
It's where we all have dreamed about
It's God's final gift to all.

Laura Bruckner
THE CONFINING
So often I confine myself—
I write in one room
Or I jog only at night.
That way no one can see I'm writing
Unless they enter the room
Or know I'm jogging
If they don't look out the window.
I'm looking for someone
Who will enter my writing-space
And know who I am,
Watch from a window while I jog
And know who I become.
I need someone who will
Bring my paper into another room
And tell me unimportant things
While we jog in the heat of midday,
For I've come to believe in my walls
And my night
For no one can see the confining,
Not even I.

Jo Brantley Berryman
REFLECTIONS
Against these mountains
 the city sways
Reflected in silent space
 lights reach through
 this rain
 this night
And I go on
 toward the horizon
 and you
Watching
 those lights
 these lives
Who knows what waits
 against the sky
at mind's edge.

The moment stays in place
 infant
 infinite
the world is an eye
 And I.

Katherine W Skelton
THY WILL BE DONE
"Thy kingdom come, Thy will be done
On earth as in Heaven it is.
Tourists from Mars? Spaceships midst stars?
The truth is not mine, but His.

Heaven is new. There are a few
Who knows war's a thing of the past
In that far land. Peace on earth's strand?
We know of His will at last.

"Thy kingdom come, Thy will be done
On earth as in Heav'n, I pray.
No more sin or death, freed from God's wrath
To last an eternal day.

Blanche L Barkow
GIVE YOUR CHILDREN A CHANCE
I see in this unfeeling day, Grandmothers taking children away,
not letting their daughters and sons have their way,
of raising their children day by day.

If they don't do exactly as mother says, she'll threaten and fight till their children give way, and give to the grandmother their little ones,
think they are safe, be treated like sons.
But because of her age, and because of her nerves, she can't stand the noise that small children make, So they sit on a chair afraid to move, cause it might be her hand or it might be the belt she will use,
and her screaming is worse than their mothers was.
And if in their teens, she's still around, she won't understand their troubled minds, she'll scream, and screech, hit them act wild.
That is why nature who's wise about life, has grandmothers stop producing a child, her patience is gone, her nerves are too.
So the young, babies make, take care of and raise, because they have that patience and love.

Sharon E Williams
COMMIT TONIGHT, LIFE IS LEAVING US
Where are we?
Life is leaving us.
Where would we be?
Life is leaving us.

I am here.
You are there.
Let's come together as one.
Life is leaving us.

I want you here by my side day and night.
I want you and me to make music.
I want you and me to have good and wonderful memories.
Life is leaving us.

I want our hearts to become one.
I want us to become one.
I want our life to become one.
But, life is leaving us.

Let's come together as one.
Let's be with the crowd.
Let's go along with life
Commit tonight, life is leaving us.

Jesse Bannon
THE SEA
The coral reefs cut us like butter,
The boats that float have a wooden rudder.
The fish have smooth and shiny gills,
The waves break and turn like old windmills.
Tiny minnow fish like to eat,
Seaweed makes a tasty treat.
You know that sharks eat fish,
They think it makes a tasty dish.
Fish hide in rocks, divers know that,
Because when they touch rocks, they start to act.
The ocean floor has many layers,
There are some sea horses that look like mares.
Ocean life survived for years,
When the water is still it's used for mirrors.
Salt water from the ocean doesn't taste very good,
But the way it tastes is the way it should.
The tides are low the tides are high,
The ocean is just the opposite of the sky.
The colorful fish travel in schools,
Oceans are just great huge pools.

Kathleen Lash
CHILD OF THE STREETS
Today no cloud.
Maybe tomorrow,
Or the next day
be the world gray.

Fear, A mixture of green and black
painted on shaded eyes that hide.

Love, An emotional illusion which
pacifies the masochistical hearts of lies.

Euphoria, Momentous violet gardens
of childlike brights with wondering affection.

Life, A death long path of black
paved in criminalized red and
flesh of fright.

Hope, A youthful controversy of Maybes.

Death, .

Brett Thomas Flaherty
LAND OF LIGHT, AND BLOWING SAND
Land of light, and blowing sand,
Let us all give you a hand,
A gypsy smiles with a rose and a daisy,
Pleasures of love are surely not lazy,
Time is sand, not money or gold,
Taste her love, before you get old.
Looking at all that we see,
How do they influence me?

Laura L Hartzell
KINGDOM COME
I came behind these separating walls,
To meet the man of my dreams.
I walked the long dreary halls,
To make sure it was all it seems.

When I came through the door,
He was standing there so poor. (lost)
When we kissed we knew we were one,
Forevermore to Kingdom Come!

Patricia Spatuzzi
MOTHER OF THE BRIDE
Mother of the bride
It can't be I say
Why she was born
Just yesterday

I remember the colic
And walking the floor
That cute little smile
And so much more

I remember so clearly
A toddler of three
Walking and talking
And smart as could be

I remember the school days
How quickly they flew
Spring concerts and plays
Ans so much to do

I remember a tomboy
In jeans and a shirt
The next day a princess
In blouse and a skirt

Then I remember there
Were boys at the door
Parties and proms
A gown that she wore

I remember graduation
The pride in what she'd done
The speech that she made
the awards that she won

I remember her always
As loving and sweet
Kind and generous
Giving complete

I remember it all
The laughter and tears
The joy and the pain
The swift passing years

Yes, I remember

But you must see
Although I remember
She's still a child to me

James C Jennings
VIETNAM EPITAPH
We left our warm homes, our friends, wives, and mom and dad.
Our hearts were so heavy and sad.
We ate slept, and lived in the jungle rain and mud.
We wrote letters home that were blotted with the mud and rain.
As we sat upon the cold and damp jungle floor, we expressed our grief and pain.
We fought disease, death, and the homesick blues.
Back home we were the topic of discussion on the six o'clock news.
Onward we marched down the paths of endless blood.

Vietnam was a forgotten, unreal, and God-forsaken land.
We became brothers to listen and reach out a helping hand.
We cried with a soldier who prayed to die.
We listened patiently again and again to a buddy whose girl found another guy.
Over there you never knew where the next bullet was coming from.
It might be you in the next body count, your tour was done.

God bless those we couldn't bring back with us.
We'll always remember you, love you, and you'll always be with us.
America, let's pledge to love, honor, and obey each other.
We salute you, our Vietnam brother.
We did it the best we could, our way.
Old glory wave on now as we pray.
God may we in peace forever stay.

Sondra Morrison
THE NIGHT SHIFT
Floors slick
with the sweat
of despair.
White shoes
squeak sounds
of hope
into hollow
shells of souls

The (total) solitude
of pain.
The needle
the prick
anticipation
the rush—

Life
artificially bearable
lingers
in sleep

Mary Elizabeth Anton
I SEE YOU WALKING DOWN THE HALL
I see you walking down the hall.
We exchange glances,
then maybe a smile.
Then I wonder about the chances,
just to talk awhile.
Listening to the radio tears begin to form.
Then in my heart a storm.
A song of love and cheer,
brings you to mind.
Then a feeling of sorrow and fear,
that fills the emptiness inside.
Sitting in my room I close my eyes,
I can hear your voice and see your smile.
The smile that could make me float for miles,
The voice that talks to me when I feel alone,
The voice that helps me fall asleep,
A deep sleep to last for hours,
With dreams of you.
I see your face and I have the power,
To face another day . . .

Julie Berry
MEMORIES
I like to count the stars,
At night when I can't sleep,
For each star there is in my sky,
There's a memory in my heart I keep.
My heart is a chest full of treasures,
Like the stars that are in the sky,
I'll keep these treasures close to me,
From now until I die.
Sometimes I forget how many I've counted,
And I must go back to the start,
Like the memories I'll always treasure,
The memories I hold in my heart.

Sara M Lydick

Sara M Lydick
I STAND ALONE

To Emery Harriger your lips touch mine, our hearts intertwine. A friendship with love, not faltering with time.

I stand alone in barren fields
No butterflies, no birds sing a song for me
My eyes and heart are closed to thee
I stand alone, there is no love for me
My work must be done, so I can show
Barren fields, that await for one, " I stand alone."
I had a friend who awaits to share his happiness
His fields stand with clover, purple and green
The smile in his eyes, are sunshine and rain

I know not what his heart holds for me
I stand alone, in barren fields, not able to see
My work must come before thee
I look around at what I have, loneliness, and despair.
I take your hand, we walk in a shadow of time
His eyes, my heart knows there is a ray of sunshine
The clouds will roll back with gentle winds of time
My barren fields will be purple and green
For now I know I need not, stand alone
Our love will nurture slowly with time.

Jonathan M Kenyon
MY WILD ROSE
Take for example a simple rose,
Just by being, speaks eloquent prose,
Kissed by the morning's sparkling dew,
The essence of life, fresh and new,
A hardier blossom can ne'er be found,

Springing forth from untilled ground,
A thing of beauty amid a nest of thorns,
Such simple splendor yet unadorned,
It's petals arranged in a gentle elegance,
By its very nature gives gentle fragrance

To keep this rose, I'd give my life,
Because you see this rose is my wife,
And in this wide world's garden, none other can measure,
For she is truly my heart's greatest treasure.

Ilo Andrews
LIFE STYLES
You do your thing
I do mine.
You are generous
I am not.
You are involved
I am a recluse.
You believe in God
I am an unbeliever.
Each life style
As the heart dictates.
Love demands tolerance
Live and let live.
For desired social behavior
Example is the best teacher.
Changes come when one decides
There is a better way!

Michelle E Lee
UNTOLD SECRETS
When we were together
I thought it would be forever

But then one day
You went your separate way

I thought my heart would shatter
But to you it didn't matter

You wanted to be free
You should have consulted me

We could have talked it out
Then I would have known what it was about

Maybe we could have saved our future
Now all we have to remember is our picture!

Catherine L Miller
TARTARUS
He woke with a start in the stuffy gloom
Had slept on the ground for want of a room
Tipped each bottle up to the sky
And hunger showed wild in his eye
As he frantically searched
Where garbage sat perched
Until things got better
And the Shell sign, missing a letter
Flashed HELL . . in yellow and red
Against the black sky, just over his head

Yulia Lerman
THE SCARY MILIEU OF THE WOODS
The scary milieu of the woods
Was covered by persistent fog
And no antipathic moods
Could enter the awesome bog.

The fecund beginnings enjoined
From loving the city melange
Importunate children who joined
And changed to obedience and love.

Charlotte J Chambliss Ed D

Charlotte J Chambliss Ed D
THE BLUE GULL

Parents: Henry Jackson, Mrs. Daisy Ann Jackson—Capillon, Grand Parents: Samson Green, Mrs Frances Quiet-Green-Aunt Mrs. Mamie Green-Williams, Sisters: Mrs. Georgia M. Royster, Mrs. Jeannette M. Caffery; Nephew, Jackson Royster-Church Beth Eden Baptist, Oak.

Come where the blue gull flies
With gold for his head
And starlets for his eyes.

Up swiftly with the wind
High into the skies,
Follow the spiraled path
Where the blue gull flies
Beyond the dropping sun
Where the west wind sighs,
Softly, and half afraid
Like lonely heart cries;
That's when the blue gull flies.

Richard A Odierno
MONUMENT
Shiny mass, long and black;
So many soldiers, brave but slain.
Sea of names upon your shadowed walls;
Wicked fate, its awful hand did work on each such man.

Marched them off to Asia's lands:
To fight, to die in paddies muddied deep
By unrelenting heat and rain;
Brought forth untimely death of dreams.

Awake, Oh Conscience, America!
Mark their suffering well—your pain!
And in humble silence, soberly heal your wounds;
So deeply cruel and unredressed.

Monument of blackened glass,
Show the world in ages hence
Your anguished war—gone wrong—
Its purpose too long misunderstood.

J Esquire
TIME
Time has no feeling
It treats us all the same.
It stops and waits for no one
Regardless of your name.

Tough troubles may surround you
They will pass as sure as time.
If you wait too long and wonder
It will soon make up your mind.

At times it passes slowly
But it passes all the same.
Then it passes all too quickly
Like the wind, it can't be tamed.

It can take away a part of you
Like the swift cut of a knife.
When you squander bits of time
It takes away your life.

It is steady and persistent
To waste it is a sin.
A game you sometimes cheated
But one you'll never win.

Time has no feeling
It's not enemy or friend.
It cannot go unused
So savor what you spend.

Toshimi Horiuchi
A SPRING
Day after day
it rained heavily
without a break

Deeper and deeper
into the ground
went the rain water

Lower and lower
under the ground
the water flowed

screaming in agony
speaking in whispers
silent in meditation

Year after year
the water purified itself
into transparency

And now
the water gushes out
into sunshine

dyes the earth green
opens flowers
quenches travelers' thirst

Paula J Leach
KALEIDOSCOPE
A Kaleidoscope he called me
For my ever changing view.
I am a color-filled dreamer
Surely you are too, aren't you?

I dream of music as rich as gold.
I dream of blue waves crashing
And waters oh! so cold.
I dream of princes, knights and kings
While I scour the pots and pans
And clean lots of things.

I am a dancer in the wood, bold and carefree.
A nymph merrily hiding in that big old oak tree.
Or, I am busy sailing ships as far as your
Eye can see.

I dream of clutching shells on the sandy shores
And a Kaleidoscope of colors
Pouring out their microscopic pores.
I dream of the heavens and the stars shining there
I dream about the world
And the strife man has caused himself to bear.

I hear delicate soft laughter as my grandchildren
Happily play.
And I soon fall fast asleep at the close of each golden day.
Dreaming of the colors a Kaleidoscope reveals
I know that life is like that too
Surely you do too, don't you?

John Erdell

John Erdell
LINE IT UP!

To my dear wife Paquita To my thousands of students around the world To my fellow poets in The Louise Bogan Poetry Society

Organize! Put everything in order,
Set it up, pile it up, arrange it.
Align it, put it in rows.
Put it in lines! Sort it out!
File it! Straighten it out!
Make it symmetrical. Line it up!

Space it out, make it ship-shape.
Series, train, chain, follow the leader.
Put it in rows, fit it in a box.
Even it out, Line it up!
Put it in circles, put it in squares.
Criss-cross it, put it in pairs.
One after the other, find a system.
Line it up! Line it up!
To organize is learning to design.

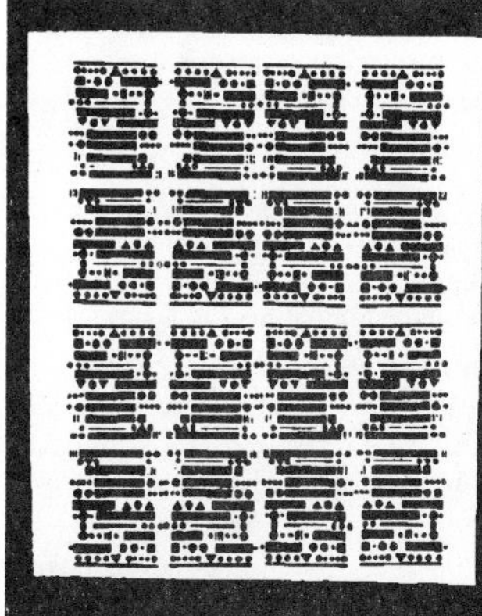

Put it corner to corner, edge to edge!
Repeat it over and over again.
Number it, alphabetize it—
Repetitions, repetitions, repetitions—
Say it, say it, and say it again.

Marjorie Youngs
LEISURE MOMENTS
My leisure is full of longing
For things I had hoped would be,
And yearning, for love and beauty,
As deep as the restless sea.

My bookshelf is treasure laden;
I glance through a book or two,
For poets have light from Heaven
And thoughts of a brighter hue.

A message of inspiration
Sends sadness on winged flight,
And thought brings the realization
There's power in God and right!

The music is quite refreshing
And puts me in tune with God
To feel His sweet heav'nly blessing
As onward through life I plod.

Maria A Pemsl
LETTERS
I write him.
He writes me.
Friendship is born.
We learn about each other.
We confide in one another.
In two different worlds yet,
We understand each other completely.
Strange—
My best friend, who knows everything about me,
All my ups and downs,
Joys and sorrows
Is several hundred miles away.
Our friendship grew through
A pen and paper,
Love, honesty, understanding and patience
Waiting for the next letter to arrive.
I write him.
He writes me.

Jean Lanje
ROADSIDE MANNERS
Below the above, and the just beyond:
A brush with nature of yellow, orange, and red sunset hues,
And a splash of white to the scores of blues.
Bluebonnets in dance to spring winds motions—
A symphony of wildflowers stirring the emotions.
A Roadside Manner of Bluebonnets we will cinch.
Tools of our trade and to a commercial way thirst to quench.
Now for the artistic performance to a vision that is never dim.
From the Portable Bar/Chest: The tall clear glass with frosted white rim;
Iced carbonated water, secret potions, and juice of blueberries—
Slices of sunset lemon and orange, and a red cherry.
Tall-tex, Bluebonnet Bar Star, your colors we know:
Bell of the Dell, sharpest of refreshing drinks, no spikes, and a real show.
Tall-tex in oils, text, and product productivity, your colors star.
Under flags with stars of wars and peace, meet the Rose, Tall-tex.
Travel far!

Sally Ann Vyvyan
HOSTAGE
I sit on a damp coarse floor
like an abandoned wrung out mop.
My skin is like dry fish scales.
The nape of my neck
reacts as electrodes
in stagnant sweat.
Behind the doors of my eyes,
eyeballs sink
to the pockets of my brain.
I have been lowered to a decayed body
by others animosity.

Unite me—
before I wallow in the waste
of my disjointed body
separating
from the course ties of fear.
Finish me off
while I can still envision
Sunrise and Sunset
within the cellars of my mind.

Amy Susanne Hall
LOST LOVE
I was a stranger when you were a friend.
What I thought was a beginning was truly an end.
You cried when I laughed; I laughed when you cried.
My love became real when yours had just died.

I wanted you gone when you were so near.
Now you have left when I need you here.
What could have been, now never can be.
I held my feelings in when you let yours free.

If I had only loved when you were around,
That love that's been lost would have surely been found.

Katherine T Paxson
TO CLIMB A MOUNTAIN
Pain stalked through my door tonight
bearing a barricade high as
Shenendoah's crest,
so hard a heart cannot be carved
upon its rough and callous chest.
Behind his barrier my silent tears flow
within the caverns of my soul
yet I would plead,
"Tear down that wall, fling it aside
before it shuts off all your dreams.
Why hold resentment tightly as a shield
to foil love's open arms:
Aphrodite's arrow flies straight
to your breast, then rebounds
because it could not penetrate
a seeming heart of stone."

Dawn Marie Fiato
DREAMS TO FOLLOW
I will still follow my dreams
Even if they break my heart,
Maybe life is not what it seems
But I have the chance to make a new start.

I have made many mistakes
And from each one I have learned,
And in the morning when I awake
My life has taken one more turn.

If I did not make a wish
And to think of what tomorrow would bring,
Think of all the things I would have missed
That had happened in-between;

I have had the chance to see
someone's smile
And to share their feelings too,
I even walked another mile
To see the things I thought I knew.

It's so easy to forget the things you do not see

And remember the ones that make you feel blue,
But I think of how far I have gone with one dream
And only I could have made it come true!

Ernestine Skipper
INTERPRETATIONS OF ROSE-COLORED SUNDAYS

since I won't tell you how unfair
destiny's cold betrayals feel;
then you could look away with a sigh
before the battle wounds begin
to heal.

only misery's elite shall endure with scorn,
greedy beggars' melodious whine.
nonchalance is what leads to savagery!
so a pretty face of spite is fine.

fantasies and future desires become a lie!
washed against the ocean shore,
so pure
surging tides of hope recede once again.
the secret must be yours, oh
sure!

too cruel to cast your light upon
some scheme . . .
of dark brutality from the start.
do you recall with bloodied palms—
ill hearts maimed and torn
apart?

Dorothy Wheeler Butler

Dorothy Wheeler Butler
RECOGNITION

Dedicated to Paul, my husband of 52 years, who managed to give me the experience which created this poem.

God of the thunder and the lightning,
Roaring with hail and torrents of rain—
Your fiercest storms, however frightening,
Slyly bring quiet and calm again.

God of the winds and waves and sunshine,
Playing our boat at roll and toss;
God of our universe and lifeline,—
Hi, You up there, You sure are the Boss!

Kyler M Stephensen
THERE ARE GOALS I HAVE

There are goals I have set
that I try to achieve
and goals that have slipped away
like a forgotten dream.

Sometimes it comes to me
late in the night which path to take
to make my life right,
but the thought disappears
as soon as it's light.

Darkness guides my way
quiet and black.
Daylight sets me on the
wrong track.

It's too bright, everything is too clear
no shadows to hide me
I must face my fears.

When daytime comes,
so does the light.
Dreams are attainable
only at night.

Grace Dowell
THE LINK

This poem is dedicated with love to Carla and all of my grandchildren present and future.

A baby's hands
on my windowsill,
Warm and sticky.
with imprints still,
Linking me with mortality,
And maybe;
to eternity.
When I look
into your tiny face,
My heart fills up
with love and grace,
For moments brief
so beneficial,
My cares all seem
inconsequential,
And all because
your hands so still,
Left imprints
on my windowsill.

Barbara Ann Barg
THE ROSE

To Robin, Thank-You for believing in me.

A wise man once said,
"Seek and you shall find,
Be ever looking forward,
Look you not behind."

So I set out on the path of life
To seek for the unknown,
Yet in my travels, a dying rose,
Was the most beautiful I was shown.

Inside I saw the emptiness
Of a thousand lover's tears;
Each one cried in tender pain
And lost throughout the years.

From its blood red petals,
Wilted as they be—
A thousand lover's voices
Whispered out to me.

Upon its angry thorns there lay,
The wounds of all past sins;
And discovered I, when love does end,
Human suffering begins.

Linda J Glenn
AFTER

Dedicated to my first love Dan, the man I never stopped loving.

The pains of love you have shown
me are like the black holes of death.
The darkness of my skies now weep
with tears of sorrow.
The tears of my love for you fall in
the blackness of the hole left in my
heart.
The sadness you've put in my heart
is a pain so great that the gates of
hell would be an easy break.
In the darkness of my world the love
for you cries.
It cries the tears of a broken heart.
The love we once shared has brought
me such a sadness that the blackness
of the hole set in my heart has been
filled with the killing pain of
darkness and death.

Pat Richens
COURAGE

For my mother, Leona Wycherley Lamph (Goosie) who taught me caring, compassion, and courage.

It takes courage to live,
And courage to die,
Courage to laugh,
And courage to cry,
It takes courage to run,
And courage to stay,
It takes courage to live,
Day by day,
So easy to leave,
So much undone,
To run and hide,
From the setting sun,
It takes courage to face,
The failures of the day.
How much courage to live,
With regret and say,
"I will do better,"
"I will do more,"
And forget the promises,
As you shut the door,
It takes courage to face,
Those who belittle you and say,
"You could do better,"
"To do it my way."
It takes courage to face them,
And say, "I am me,"
"I was, I am, and I shall always be."

Athanasia Ward
THE LITTLE PEOPLE WHO SPEAK

This is dedicated to my son Heath Allan Johnson and his spirit

We are the people of tomorrow,
Please let us see the beauty you see
of today.
It's morning and I have been given
another Day.
Another Day to hear and read, smell
and walk and love life.
Please don't ever give up because if
you do we won't see Tomorrow.

Carol Johnson
REAL LOVE

To my loving husband Randy and my children Jenny, Jared & Amanda

Love is forgotten for some,
But is remembered by few,
Because love to you is me,
And it cannot be love unless it's we.

Love is forgotten for some
Some will go, some will come
But can love be shared by one?
No, Love with two, is one!

Love is forgotten for some,
But REAL LOVE is shared,
Something is not forgotten if
experienced, somehow or some-
where,
But remembered love is always here!

Karl Fischer
A BARREL FULL OF GUMDROPS

A little encouragement to a retiring president

Have another gumdrop darling dear,
pick the color you like best,
sit by my side, rain or shine together
we can dream of tomorrow and that
little cottage way out west.

Gumdrops are a special love,
just like you are my dear.
and the red white blue ones,
remind me of the great patriot
Paul Revere.

In critical moments a little gumdrop
sweetness may steady your nerve,
when decisions are very important, a
nice little gumdrop
may give you a lift you deserve.

Have another gumdrop sweetheart
dear,
the bells are ringing in another year.
let bygones be bygones, put your
worries to rest.
We have a barrel full of gumdrops
in that million dollar cottage way out
west.

Jan C Whelpley
KALEIDOSCOPE

Grains of sand, under bilious skies,
await the pelting rains. Dandelions
with silver mist, caress the amber
plains.
A sequence of muted time, calico
windmills and apple wine.
Orange sprigs, etched in molten
cacao, are bitter-sweet confetti.
Pursue the elusive, sip champagne,
so brisk and so heady.

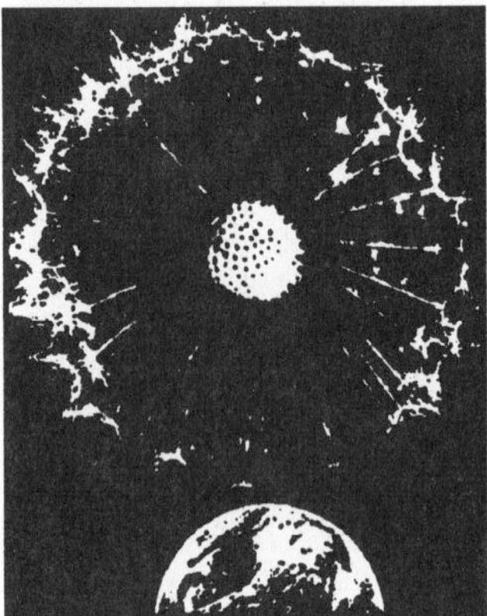

A sea mist evokes the tempest, a
sparrow goes to nest.
Suspended in silence the windmills
stand. Passively remain the grains of
sand.
Time screams a deafening blast,
ivory prisms shatter into multi-
colored glass.
Dandelions awake, sun kissed with
dew. This cameo moment,
I share with you. This precious
second, a bubble bathed in blue.

Cynthia B Nappa
THOUGHTS ON A RAINY DAY

For my loves, Cindy, Corey and "My Friend"

On top of a mountain
Sharing dreams with a friend,
I opened my heart
and set my soul free.

I watched the leaves blow,
I pretended they were part of me.
All of my ideals floated away
to be buried in the snow, beneath the
trees.

Just as the buried autumn foliage
will never find its way back to the
tree,
I pray what I let flutter away
doesn't come back to me.

I looked, I searched, I found,
A new peace, a new friend,
Someone I liked,
A whole different person—

It was me.

Marie Barnes
I KNOW HE'S NOT THERE

For Adam

I walk to his grave,
But he is not there.
I search for his presence,
But can't find it there.

I reach down to touch it,
And say a small prayer;
But I know in my heart,
That he is not there.

He is not there
In that cold, dark ground.
He's in a warm, sunny place,
With love all around.

He's laughing and playing,
And skipping on air;
I brush off his headstone,
But he is not there.

I know he's in Heaven
He's happy and free,
He is one of God's angels
And his spirit's with me.

Carolyn M Tevepaugh
THE STORM

To my sons Tim and Chris and granddaughter Christy, and to Dr. A. M. Henderson and Dr. David Alford who never gave up on me. Also to God and my family for letting me be me.

When skies are gray, and the clouds turn dark,
It's not the time for you to embark
On a pleasure trip to a lake or a park.

But it's time instead, to look for a place,
That's warm and dry and will safely embrace
You from the storm you're about to face.

The wind will howl and rage and crash;
Thunder will roll—lightning will flash,
And soon big raindrops will start to splash.

The rain beating against doors and window panes,
Make memories of other storms float through your brain,
As you stand and watch and listen to the rain.

But—like time—the storm soon passes by,
And if you look quick, up in the sky,
A beautiful rainbow, you may spy

Bright lovely colors, of almost every hue—
Red, orange, yellow—lavender, green, and blue—
Makes you pause and say: "God, Thank You"

And this old proverb suddenly comes to mind:
"If you search hard enough, you will find;
Some good in everything—most every time!"

Joe Ann Mansell Ratley
LIFE'S TOO BIG FOR ME

In memory of my mother, my best friend, who always believed me, and encouraged me to express myself through my poetry.

This thing called life, the experience of existing—how complex must it be? So much so quickly evolves inside of me.

The cycles of life that change like seasons, so close yet so far reaching, intertwined within my heart and soul, ever learning, ever caring, ever reaching.

So overwhelming for one like me, yet easily taken for granted by those who cannot see.

The intensity of loving, hating, or of youth and aging. It's like life is too big for me.

I reach out to touch a star but never make the grade. Then reach out to touch a friend in need, touch their hand, how wonderfully we are made. So many feelings in just one lifetime, that is over in a moment too little too soon.

I hear laughter from a child, see the warmth in a smile and hear the rhythm of a tune. Makes me in my days of age begin to dance in heart and mind. Looking back to yesterday for something I cannot find.

And as I dimly feel life fade, I know someday I'll say goodbye—To Life That's Too Big for Me. Then a teardrop falls on my cheek. No matter now—how small, great, weak or strong—I sigh.

I want to grasp that thread of life so I need not say goodbye. I shake my head in wonderment—what is it I am feeling now—is it the little girl inside of me, or the shell of youth long passed that is longing to be free?

I'm grateful for what has been, wanting it back again. But reality is what I'll have to see. Knowing now—that simply put: "Life's Too Big for Me."

Audrey Bickart
THE SWEET PERFUME OF LIFE

To Deonne and Howard
The pride and joy of my life

Breathe in the sweet perfume of Mother Earth.
Be inspired to attain new goals, grateful to see
Each day's rebirth.

Create a good life, with the will to persist
Cherishing every minute, vowing not to just exist.

Give a willing ear to those who ask you to listen,
Noticeably your stride will be lighter, your eyes will glisten.

Delight in the comraderie of a good friend,
Hold dear this treasure, so fragile, if left neglected,
Can easily bend.

As you look upward, enveloped in the warmth of the sun,
Resolve, with eagerness, to make beautiful

This new day just begun.

Brenda K Adams
YOU WERE THERE

To my loving dad, John Link, who has helped me to grow into the wonderful person I am. Love Always, Bren

You were there even when you didn't know me. Understanding and willing to listen.

You were strong for me at the times when I was very weak. Ready to pull me up off my knees; to lean up against you.

You were always ready to help me face the scary things.
Right by my side; I could always see forever when I looked into your eyes.

You always cared for me. No matter what I did or do. You were just simply there.

Jane M Brown
ODE TO SUICIDE

For Diane

The burden of secrets left untold . . .
Unshared . . . Unresolved . . .
Create . . . the victims of a misunderstanding
known to no one . . .
Could be . . . Should be . . . Would be . . .
didn't have to be . . . Why was it?
All left unanswered, because of the pain
Of too much tenderness.
Life is so fragile—Yet has no windows to the soul . . .
Much like an eggshell which guards the miracle of life.
We have to break it to see inside . . .
And by then it's always too late.

Candra Courtright

Candra Courtright
OPEN YOUR EYES

To one of my closest friends, Meg Marriott, who can relate to this poem just as well as I can. And to Mark Van Horn, whose music inspired me to write "Open Your Eyes."

Oh if you would only open your eyes
there is so much you can see
A morning sunrise, a humming bumble bee
The far away mountains that reach up to the sky
The silent white clouds that slowly drift by
The brilliant colors of flowers, red, yellow, and white
That one in a million shooting star that falls just for you at night
But you're determined to see only that which is bad
Please open your eyes, I promise, it won't make you sad
But you want to notice the graffiti on the walls
Instead of admiring the bursting waterfalls
The rolling hills with patches of purple and green
Never to you, are they seen
Please wake up from this nightmare that you helplessly live in
And notice all the miracles that we have been given
You can't see the truth with closed eyes
All you need to do is open, and realize.

Sadie O Foltin
A PRAYER FOR LA TANIA

I dedicate this poem to:
La-Tania Marie Hill

Father, there's a little girl we all love so much;
But she needs you, your healing touch,
To make her well so she can walk;
Touch her voice so she can talk.

Touch her mind so she can know;
That you too, Lord, have love to show.
She was born afflicted, and has never pranced;
Like little girls do when they try to dance.

She's never said, "Mommie I love you so,"
Even tho Mothers always know.
They pray for them; they do their best;
Sometimes it's hard to stand the test.

But because Mom has so much love to show;
She's warm, she's compassionate and lets her know;
That she's always there to meet her needs,
So bless them both for all their deeds.

Dorothy A Dryden
GOD'S CHILD

Dorothy lovingly dedicates this poem to the special treasures of her life, her sons Bob, Tom, John and Dan.

A babe you are today my love,
A babe so small and sweet;
A babe you are today my love
And making life complete.

A toddler now and full fo pep,
A toddler full of joy;
A toddler now and out of step
Mischievous girl or boy.

It's first grade now and then to two
Then three, then four and more;
I turn around and goodness me . . .
You go right out the door!

The years fly by . . . and where was I?
The cross words that I uttered.
When you were just a child
And I was just a grouchy mother.

Dear Lord, give me the chance, I pray
To silence my cross words.
To love and guide him everyday
This child of mine . . . and yours!

Jackie L Hislip
ROLLING AROUND IN THE MEADOWS.

This poem is dedicated to Betty, my wonderful loving mother.

Rolling around in the meadows in the far out sun smelling the freshness of the clean honey suckle air, clouds above all beautiful and fair. Now that the day comes to an end I run through the flowers like a garden of

eves, to follow home what do I see before the trees? I see the most graceful, most glorious bird of all, The Eagle!
It soars like an angel of grace and its beauty swaggers like a plane no where to go. Someday maybe i will be free as the Eagle itself and fly off to a far off land where I can be my graceful
self.

Heidi J Latella
A SPECIAL FEELING

I dedicate this poem to family and friends. Special thanks to: Parents and friends who helped me with my love relationships, Jessica, Kris, and Courtney. Love and Thanks to you all! ! ! ! ! !

When a guy likes a girl,
And a girl likes a guy,
That's a special relationship
One can not buy.

This feeling is love
Symbolized by a dove.
Feeling this feeling,
Deep down inside,
You may feel like
The ocean tide.

When a guy likes a girl,
And a girl likes a guy,
that's the one
Relationship,
One CAN NOT buy!

Katherine (Libby) Thudium
THE POPPY

This poem is dedicated to the American Veterans.

Over fields of flaming red the poppy sways and bows its head,
And lifts its petals to the sky,
Sending a message to all passers by.
Tall and straight and proud it's grown,
With a rare beauty all its own.
With a poppy Veterans tell . . .
Of a war they've know so well.
A poppy is more than a paper flower,
It helps Veterans pass away the lonely hours.
To them it is a symbol of peace,
and maybe some day the wars will cease,
So Veterans can come home from the war,
And receive a welcome at their door,
But for the Veterans who have no home,
Who live their lives all alone,
Purchase a poppy and show them you care.
It might be the answer to a Veterans prayer.

Chris Dudash
THE TREE

Dedicated to; FREEDOM

As we continue our journey down the path, always ready for a switch
We tend to hold onto the old, what is this peace you speak of, what's the hitch?
The pathway becomes narrower and more defined
Walking smoothly along until something tells us to wander
As we go down a different branch, our love becomes more refined
On the pathway, off the pathway, yet wherever we may be, it is always another view to ponder
Walking with Jesus and Buddha
Yea, even Confucius and Moses
What they have to offer is spiritual food
It fills us with gladness and joy
Now we may sit back and finally smell the roses
Or climb the tree with the ease of that little boy
Work is never done when one is attaining spiritual growth
Looking from another view, work can really be play
As you witness the fluttering wings of a moth
Flying hither and there
World understand I am flying in joy, he may pray
Attracted to the light, he is, he may never know why or even care
Be it a moth or a bird, we are all children of God
Look outside and the tree may even give you an acknowledging nod

Nancy Poorker
DEAR FRIEND

This poem is dedicated to the memory of my dearest friend Gloria.

I had a dream of you one night,
My sweet and dearest friend.
A very special kind of dream,
I didn't want to end.
You came back to spend the day with me
Just like you used to do.
We talked and laughed for hours
And I loved that time with you.
There were so many things to tell you,
So many things to share.
You were there again to listen
And I knew how much you cared.
Then suddenly I realized
It was time for you to leave.
You seemed so free and happy—
Still I could not help but grieve.
They say that sometimes dreams come true
And I believe it's so.
Someday we'll meet again dear friend
And you won't have to go.

Rhonda Burnette Michael
DREAM FOREVER

To my family for all their love and support, especially my husband. I love you.

It's been a long time dream of mine
To have your love just one more time
To lay in your arms again
To look in your eyes and then . . .

I'll take you hand in mine
And lead you into a love so fine
You'll never want to leave
Your heart will belong to me

Just put your ams around me
And always hold me tight
We'll be together forever
And forever starts tonight.

Robert O Landrum
TRUE LOVE

To Hilda, my loving and devoted wife.

Ten years ago I never could say,
That I really cared if I saw another day;
Then something happened to restart my life,
You chose to be my loving wife;
Nothing in life could be more true,
Than the way I'm deeply in love with you.

Gloria A Ramsden
THE FIRST CHRISTMAS TREE

Dedicated to my Aunts, Emilia Wisneski and Sophie Wisneski, Who are always there when I need them.

Feathery flakes falling from above
A golden moon to shine,
There's nothing more beautiful this time of the year
Than the snow and the moon on the pine.

The snow falls in heaps on the boughs of the tree
Forming ornaments of snow,
The moon sends its beams through wires of air
And the ornaments sparkle and glow.

This tree still stands in the home of the wild
Untouched by the hand of man,
For God created the first Christmas tree
Before Christmas ever began.

Paul Johnson
ASSURANCE

To the Love of my life . . . Who will always be my inspiration.

It was so peaceful this morning
As the golden rays of the new day sun
Streaked across the quiet sky.
The sun is always there in the morning;
Faithfully, it ushers in a new day,
Bringing with it a new hope . . .
Assurance.

The only thing more peaceful today
Than the glowing sky,
Was my heart;
I was assured of your love for me.

Barbara Byrd
STEEL MOSQUITO

For my parents, Jack and Aurora Byrd, without their love, warmth, encouragement, unfailing fortitude, and sometimes unwarrantable belief in me, this poem and all my works would not be possible.

Beware young innocents with naive hearts
of the bite of the steel mosquito.
It thrives in every country, city, and state,
and so far no social pesticide succeeds to eliminate.
It will tempt you with its promises of euphoric bliss,
that are derived from its Spartan addictive kiss.
With its sweet poppy derivative or other Hades potion,
it whispers longingly with stoic devotion.
So, beware young innocents with naive hearts
of the bite of the steel mosquito,
for it will seduce you if it can, for the simple reason,
the conquest of another man.

Sharon M Gregory
FORGOTTEN CHILD

To Tim my loving husband and Barbara H McDonald, the greatest person I know

When I was a child, I spoke as a child, I heard as a child, I saw as a child
But I was forced to think and feel as an adult
This is a very cruel and unhuman way to treat a child
The child cried out in pain in the only way it knew how.
This was seen in the adult world as being out of control
Now as an adult, the child in me continues to cry out
a child within me that can not be put at peace
a child that was never given the time and space to grow
a child that is condemned to walk and cry in an ENDLESS TIME
THIS IS THE FORGOTTEN CHILD

Donna J Jensen
BEYOND CHARADE

Dedicated to the beloved Gurumayi—who took me there

God knows we walk a narrow ledge
The journey home—a razor's edge
With an ocean of self-will to churn
For each of us who has his turn

Man is not made in form alone
An earthy gathering of skin and bone
A higher principle dwells within
Bound there by the greed of men

The game of life is played to find
The hidden soul within mankind
That part of him that cannot stay
But must return to God someday

Come to Him in silent prayer
And know that you will find Him there
In depths beyond the world's charade
The inner dwelling God has made

Jack Michael Roper
MY MARRIAGE POEM

To my wife Gaila. I thank you for your love and dedication to our precious children and my work. You have been a valuable support.

The heart in love has threads of joy sown through
These threads shall reach out to my Lord and you

These threads shall never break for they are eternally strong
For one thing I know, the heart in love has a song

I shall reflect upon Him who has brought us together
Knowing that our hearts shall endure all weather

The rough winds may beat against the window panes of our heart
And at that time we must remember that Jesus has given us our start

The clouds may try to sweep our love afar
But after the storm is a golden star

As the Son was dawning to replace the dark
I saw threads of joy being carried by a lark

Just as the Lord created these little birds
May God continue to give us our words

May our love be as the shoreless ocean
That is more than just an emotion

Just as the Lord's love shall never be severed
I shall love you forever and ever!

Jaclyn Day
DO NOT WORRY

For Whitney Seibert and her family

Do not worry,
Don't be afraid,
For what has happened
Is a choice
God made

He knows best,
That's for sure
Whatever happens
We can endure

So don't worry,
Be glad
Don't let your eyes water,
Don't be sad

Angel Adams
THE CREATION

To all the loved ones in my life.

God created me for you to love
He made us to be as one
You for me and me for you
Together at last together as two.

You are the one for me I know
For you I will show if you don't already know
I love you yes indeed
I just hope you love me.

Please say you love me
Like I love you
They we'll go off to a sea of deep blue
Together at last together as two.

God created me for you to love
Like a beautiful dove.
The sun shining in the blue sky
Just waiting for you and I.

Please say you love me
Like I love you
Then we'll go off together in a sea of deep blue
Just me and you.

Edd R Conley
WAR

To all who endured the Vietnam Conflict.

War is something, we all have seen,
those of us who were men in our teens.
We lost our innocence and dreams,
on battle fields, hearing bombs and screams.

We saw out friends die in vain,
others lived, but forever in pain.
All have been scarred one way or another,
all lost a friend, some their mother.
While we fought a war, like no other.

Now twenty years later, I still have dreams,
I still hear the bombs and screams.
In the middle of the night I have dreamt
and seen my death on a field no longer green.

I am lost during the day, but I hate the night,
my life has changed, I must always fight,
to control my fear to run from sight.
I am alone in this fight, this struggle
I go through day and night.

Charlotte M Gittings
YOUNGSTERS PLAYING IN THE SUN

To My Grandchildren

Youngsters playing in the sun
Enjoying themselves and having fun.
Seen a mysterious and interesting cave.
So to prove that they were brave
Entered and there they found
Names and drawings on the walls all around.

Mandy Gobbi
MAGIC

Dedicated to Harvey Roy

As I lean from my window
I see the stars twinkle,
Upon the darkened sky
To which they lie.
My dreams drift onward
About my mind.
The golden dove flies,
Past our eyes.
Everything is touched with
Jack Frost's Magic.

Eugène Lipovac
HERALD OF THE SOUTH

Herald of the South amend
wind by the river's bend;
Breathless mist the snow has gone
the seed has been sown;
arising the precious flowers have duty
to grow renewed with inspired beauty.

Jacki Lummus

Jacki Lummus
UNTITLED

The gold leaf swings
gently in the breeze
gripping as tight as it can
to the tree
the tree that was once
its life
the tree that was once its protector

and now the leaf is
holding on
to its one chance at a life
for once that leaf lets go,
and lightly falls to the ground
it will become one out of
many leaves
left on the ground to die
only to be raked up by a man
and put into a bag with
millions of others
all wishing they
could have held on to
that tree just a little bit longer.

Tricia Ann Larson
SPIRITS UNRESTED

Think of the waves crashing ruthlessly upon the sand, like evil spirits unrested, looking for a home.
Listen to their heavy sighs.

Think of how they must look now, forever moving on, unaware of the people passing by, watching by the darkness of the moon.

When suddenly a child laughs and disrupts the peaceful sound of the evil spirits and their heavy sighs.

Think of the daylight, where the people come to play, not minding the ruthlessness of the everlasting waves.

Its crazy there.
The daylight causes pain to the unrested who are searching for a home.

Now the daylight hides away
in the blackness of the night,
waiting to disrupt once more.

Think of the children
silently running through the night.
Think of them as innocent, ready to be destroyed.

Jane Polk
POEM'S POEM

To Heather, Amber, Camille, Elizabeth and Aaron

Yellow and black bird, little yellow bird, eating, eating
away purple thistle
little is a word I deal with.
East, West
Call up China
no letter, no phone
Gate Crasher
dreams
Transient, transience
ants
adversary
adversaries

Dawna L Vose-Cannon
EARTHLINGS LISTEN

With special thanks to Greg T. Who helped restore my faith in mankind, and myself.

Bluntly the world turns without ever knowing
Existing beings are still forever growing.
They can't comprehend what could be true
The circumference they study is strangely new.

Take heed to my words, I feel I must say
In the distant future, or maybe a day . . .
Hatred and fear are slowly taking over
The lion and lamb will never lie amongst the clover.

Unless egotists, hypocrites, and fools reprehend
The civilization of today hasn't time to mend.
People of the earth, running about everywhere
Cease your barbaric actions and begin to share.

The races of the entire world must unite
Think of each person as a brother, try with all your might.
Love, in one word, describes what we need
Fellow earthlings please listen to my plea.

Geraldine Carrozzi
THE LIGHT OF THE DAY

Tony, may we be together forever, with all my love.

The light of the day
the darkness of the night,
the sound of the earth
and the feel of the wind,
my thoughts within,
my thoughts of others,
your mind is you life
your feelings your thoughts,
I think of you often
so far away,
yet so close in reach,
I look to the sea and
you're the first one I see,
I know you're there,
although I'm here,
I've lost you in my struggle to be free,
yet I've gained so much for me,
my thoughts are of you
what else can I do.

G Henry Davis
SWEETHEARTS WISH

This poem is dedicated to
My sweet wife "Pearl"
My inspiration to write poetry

If there were a sweethearts wish
That really could come true,
And it were offered just to me
I'll tell you what I'd do;

I'd wish that I could hold you tight
And keep you close to me,
And never have to let you go
Thru all eternity;

I'd ask to kiss your lips so warm
And feel your heart beat fast,
And whisper softly in your ear
Of love that would always last,

That I could wipe away your tears,
When your heart is broke and then
Offer you a heart of love
And make you smile again;

To be with you and share your love
Would be a dream come true,
For now just be my sweetheart,
And I'll be your sweetheart too; ; ;

Josephine Rose—A poet from the school of hard knocks
BETRAYED

Nurturing men—Morrise M. Brock, M. D. 20 years my physiologist, Thomas K. Hunt, M.D. Professor of Surgery U. C. Hospital 10 years cancer, William F. McLauglin, Esq., Edwin & Gary Antebi, Nicholas P. Colichidas

Where have I been,
In living my life.

When I look in the mirror,
Don't I see myself?

And when I'm walking down the street,
Again don't I see my reflection
On the windows as I'm walking by.

When the sun is behind me,
Is there not my shadow before me?

But! where am I,
In the darkness of the night?

With a flash! of bright light,
The chilling piercing wind splits me asunder,

And my heels echo on deserted pathways
Sounding like lost cries in the night.

And the child slowly fades away,
Into the empty darkness of no where.

And the portrait of me
Disappears.

Steven J Gravier
MOURNING & MORNING-LESS

In memory of those killed on the U. S. S. Iowa

If all of those who died
Fighting side by side
In fierce and fiery wars
On distant and unfriendly shores
were put into outer space

There wouldn't be a human race
'Cause when all was said and done
We couldn't see the sun.

Elisabeth Wultsch
CHANGE
You've changed my life in many ways
but this isn't just a phase.
I'm different now I'm a new me,
I feel as if I'm finally free.
You've turned me loose I can finally see!
Now that is how it's supposed to be
so here's to you
I thank thee
for taking the chance
to get to know ME!

Belinda A Miller
LITTLE BLACK GIRL
Little black girl cute as can be.
Hold your head high so the whole world can see.

Be strong, be proud reach for the sky.
The good things in life won't pass you by.

Your honey brown skin and black shiny hair.
I'll fight everyday for society to be fair.

Our people fought hard so you could be free.
You'll learn these things as they were taught to me.

I'll try to teach you right from wrong.
Believe in God and you'll be strong.
Little black girl you learn to be bold.
Your confidence instilled, you'll reach your goals.

Little black girl you're my pride and joy.
For without you my life, they could toy.

My little black girl I love you so
From your sparkling brown eyes, to your tiny little toe.

Martin N Anesgart
VORTEX
In the eye of the vortex I have lain
for hours, days, months, years
Does it matter?
Like a sieve the brain lets loose its store of pain
Like a back hoe it digs it up all again
In between, the concentric circles
formed by the turbulence
Hold my life's events in abeyance,
some to be gone forever,
Others to be recalled in miasmic twinges
And the rest, neverending displays of regret, despair, remorse
Can I extricate myself
Is it possible?
Is not confusion the primary niche
Within which all struggle, succeed and fail
Is not confusion, in myth
A vestigial appendage inherited from infrahumans
In reality, a particular reality
An inexorable emanation
From the admixture of internal and external forces

W C Adamets
WHAT GOES AROUND . . .
When the long warm days of summer,
And it's soft and gentle breeze;
Changes slowly into winter,
With the multi-colored leaves.
It's almost with sadness,
That we see the summer wane;
And give its way to cold and snow,
And frosted window panes.
Then it grudgingly gives up the ghost,
To springs cold rains and showers.
We know that summer's near again;
By the serenade of flowers.

T A Kostic
CONVERSION
Breaking through bewilderment
Which took senseless time to
Compose rays of grace descend
Unconditionally upon one—soul
Moment of truth.

You begin to see your blindness
Deafness—and pray to become
More blind—deaf. It is then
The heart hears—closed eyes see
Desire only for Thee.

Marie Henry
I WANT A PRESIDENT
I want a President who doesn't keep the people guessing how fast he can run,/ who can admit he made a mistake when things are unlawfully done,/ who is wise enough to let the people make their choice, and choice enough to lead the pack:/ I want a President who doesn't have a monkey on his back./

I want a President who doesn't pass the buck,/ who can talk to his people and listen to their dissent,/ who can part opinions without threatening impunity,/ and who's tough enough to take the blame./ I want a President who doesn't have to bargain from a position of shame./

I want a President who can talk for himself./ I'm tired of hearing from someone else—Cronies or lobbyists or phony pollsters though they be,/ Surely they must know that I know they don't speak for me./ I want a President who's strong in deeds, whose lips I don't have to read./

I want a President who is stronger than the weakest link in a chain;/ who isn't chained to falsity, half-truths, and the depths of despair;/ who has loyalty to all the people, and then,/ when American ideals of justice come calling,/ I want a President who is always there./

I want a President who can look outward at himself;/ who can flex to the common man's boasting;/ who can sense the mood of the people and listen to his critics before he listens to reflections of himself./ I want a President who is for real before America starts roasting./

Christine Ciarmello
LO AND BEHOLD
Lo and behold
you cover your heart
so no one can see.
But I see, you
wear it on your face,
not under your breastbone.

Stephen E Comer
RICHES
People with money
Have it all, it seems.
They can buy nice things
Like diamond rings.
They make lots of money,
So they think they're above,
But what they sometimes miss
Is the thing called love.
The poor are richer than they think,
Because in love they live and think.
The poor may get love,
And that's all they have.
But love is the best healer,
Better than lotion or salve.
So the rich are rich,
But the poor are, too.
And if you don't believe me,
Just look and you will see.

Cathy Michael
THE ROSE OF LOVE
Who are you?
Why do I care so?
You stepped into my life
Like a dream.
You made me feel,
and care.
I began to open up,
Like a Rose.
For the first time ever,
I was worthwhile,
to me.
I loved like never before,
and then my world shattered.
You were gone.
After awhile I began to
Pick up the pieces.
To put my life back,
But not my self respect.
The pieces of my life,
Began to fit,
Like a jigsaw puzzle.
And now you're here,
Again,
But it's not the same.
I'm stronger,
Colder,
Not as open.
And yet, I still love,
Care, desire.
Why?
Who are you to have
Such power over me?
The power to make me love,
But never hate,
and yet,
You also have lost.
There is a part of me
That cannot trust,
Not again.
The Rose is closed,
But not dead,
Yet.

Barbara Thrash
FIRST MOVEMENT

To Kathy, my inspiration and to Destiny, the arc of radiance

I embrace my secret
with complete stillness,
listening,
lest the arc of radiance disappear,
savoring this wondrous moment,
the sensation of floating time,
in communion with the dark,
fluid depths of my womb
and the soft,
shimmering movement within.

This fragile life,
this essence of myself,
becomes
in one startling instant,
completely and wholly
mine.

Clara G Stinson
THE PERFECT LOVE
The love of God is everywhere,
In birds that sing and blossoms fair.
The sun that warms and gives the day light,
In the moon and stars that brighten the night.

In the little lamb with innocence sweet,
And the spotted fawn at its mother's feet.
A new born child at its mother's breast,
In a loving home where it finds peace and rest.

For parents love with their heart and mind,
Hope is kindled and courage we find.
Tears and bruises disappear when mother kisses and charms,
Fears vanish when wrapped in a daddy's strong arms.

In that special feeling man has for his mate,

When a young couple meet by the garden gate.
Where they bill and coo like the turtle dove,
Pledging their troth and undying love.

Wherever we go and when troubles come,
We see love from the moment of birth.
But the love shown by Jesus at Calvary,
Surpasses anything found on this earth.

Jacqueline Naile
TOUGH AS STEEL
Tough as Steel
Yet as timid as a babe
Never sure where he's going, Not sure where he's been
Always running, running from what . . .
Fear . . .
Memories . . .
Love . . .
Life . . .
Covering his problems with poisons
Poisons that make him feel good,
but only hurt him in the end . . .
But then again, isn't that what the people do
You have to stop running . . . look around . . .
What do you see . . .
You're staring at another chance for . . .
Life, hope, love . . . Yes
You're staring at me . . .

Lisa Roe
IF ONLY I COULD
If only I could see you all the time,
If only I could be with you,
To be by your side,
During good or bad,
I would always be there for you.

If only I had known you better,
If only I could touch you,
If you were mine
I could make you happy,
To let people know we belonged together!

If only I could tell you
How I feel about you,
How much I care about you,
If only I could tell you that . . .
I LOVE YOU!

Lydia Venta-Dobrovolsky
CHRISTMAS
Love is Christmas—while Christmas is loving,
kindness uplifting, caressing, forgiving;
voices of Angels, the childhood reviving,
soar in the air, our Spirit beguiling.—

Deborah Hill Blaylock
GROWING OLD—WAITING FOR DEATH
Growing old; Waiting for death
To give his tiring body eternal rest
If only Heaven but on earth is Hell
Oh how helpless; oh how pale
Sight is going; hair snow white
Sleeping a lot, even when there's no night
Clothes mismatched; right side limp
So many years; this is how they'll be spent
Sitting for a minute; laying for hours
All that's left is love that towers
A grin at the sight of a spoiled grandchild
The trip was worth it no matter how many miles
A tiny sparkle staring at me
If only I could help; my grandpa is he
Will I hold up? Can I be strong?
Oh how it hurts me; death is so wrong
To think of the loss; to choke back the tears
If only I could give him the rest of my years
How very close for I love HIM the most
In my heart, my grandpa the ghost!

Caroline J DuPatz
MY HEART'S DESIRE
What do I want the most in life?
As years go flying by.
How often do I search my heart,
To find the right reply.
So many things I dreamed about.
Have never yet come true.
But if I could have had them all,
I wonder what I'd do?
Opinions change at every age
We learn upon the way.
So what I most desired in youth
I would not choose today.
The strength to face whatever comes
To smile when things go wrong
To walk beside the ones I love
and always find a song.
To share the joy that only comes
In friendships mellow glow;
all these I want, the most in life
at last my dears I know.

Sandra Ann Sherrick

Sandra Ann Sherrick
DOES THE PICTURE SAY IT ALL?
Walking up these stairs to No. 2
I said hello to the lady
and walked on thru.
An open door entering I faced
Plants on the table
The Plaque on the wall
Lamps that you made
Does the picture say it all?
Slowly turning with fixed eyes
A picture of a church
Red roses rest in back
St. Johns, Walpole, New Hampshire
White and black.
The suns rays shining in the window
To the cats on the wall
From the eye of the fish
Does the picture say it all?

Joel Szkrybalo
WHERE DARK MISTS WANDER
Take me there, where dark mists wander
and light breaks through the chapel green
Where rough-hewn stones grow moss and ponder
the Universe and all unseen

Lead me down through damp ravines
along the rails that ghost trains ride
to where in meadows the daffodils dream,
the poets sing, the lovers lie

Send me into cavernous dwellings
cut deep within the hallowed hills
where springs in early March are swelled
with water, tumbling down in rills

Show me where the wild things scurry
and ancient groves grow old unscathed
Where hardened hands of human fury
will never wield a careless blade

Take me there, where I can roam
and feel the Earth beneath my feet
There, my heart will find its home
There, my mind will have its peace

Lorene Tarver Soenksen
BORROW OR LEND?
I came to your house today
To borrow a cup of cheer,
The kind we find in coffee
When shared with a friend so dear.

I came to your house today,
I borrowed some kindness too,
The kind I knew I'd find
After years of friendship with you.

I came to your house today,
I borrowed some sunshine, too,
The kind that is always brighter
When I share it with you.

These things I borrowed from you today
Will have the best of care,
So that when you come to my house,
Again these things we'll share.

Janelle Randall
HEARTS ON FIRE
Hearts on fire, slowly burn
Flame extinguished, When will I learn?

Burning, Burning, the match is lit
Orange flames growing, Eating me bit by bit.

Glowing, Glowing, Beckoning me near
Ears become deaf, Why can't I hear?

Calling, Calling, How do they know my name?
Voices never silent, Nothing ever the same.

Falling, Falling, Like wax on candles
Seeping down, Becoming hard to handle.

Flickering, Flickering, But never quite gone
Full of colors, Just like the morning dawn.

Seeking, Seeking, The innocent of heart
Pretending togetherness, Tearing apart.

Reaching, Reaching, When will it go?
Flame jumps up, Continues to grow.

Searing, Searing, Casting its brand
Hot on my body, Burning my hands.

Leaving, Leaving, The flame slowly dies
Gone away, No goodbyes!

Hearts on fire, slowly burn
Flame extinguished, When will I learn?

Joseph Allen DeMerchant
SOME SAFE RETREAT
To slip away and hide somewhere,
within the hallow hill.
To dwell within experience past
and drink from it my fill.

To stand alone upon the knoll,
to slip away, to just let go.
To stroll along lush forest path,
to worry not of the aftermath.

To put to page the pleasant thought,
the sorrow and the pain.
To put to ease this wanderlust
and learn to live again.

To turn the tide upon the shore,
prevent erosion now evermore.
To mend the wound, erase the scar,
to reach within and touch afar.

To stand and whisper to the breeze,
to seek forgiveness, there on my knees.
To stem this love that knew defeat,
to slip away, some safe retreat.

Alice M Bascom
TO MY MOMMY AND DADDY
Although you cannot see me Mom and Dad,
I am very much a part of you, and I know you are glad.
I'm growing stronger as each day passes by,
And it won't be long till you'll hear my loud cry.
My mind is young, my thoughts are small,
I know nothing of this world at all.
I'm safe and secure inside my dear Mother,
It's all the world I've seen, but soon I'll see another.
Thank you Mom and Thank you Dad,
For giving me a chance at life, no matter how bad.
The world is harsh and cruel through many people's eyes,
But with such precious miracles, I don't understand why.
I'll bring you joy and I'll bring you tears,
And I know we'll grow closer through passing years.
A baby has feelings even before birth,
Feelings of love and feelings of worth.
Soon you will cuddle me—hold me—adore me,
You are two wonderful people I'll be happy to see.

Your darling little babies thoughts

Jennifer Garcia
'TIL THE DAY I DIE
LOVE is a many splendored thing
So here I pledge this diamond ring
On your finger it shall remain
'Til the day I die.
Our love will last a trillion years
We'll fight through love and all the tears
We'll conquer all our hidden fears
We will not cry.
On our beautiful wedding day
"I'll love you always" is all I say
In a million and one different ways
I hear you sigh.
Our love will last through thick and

thin
We'll never ask "where've you been"
Because I know we will not sin
It's not a lie.
I awaken from my fantasy
I look at you, you look at me
I should have known it could not be
You say, "Good-bye."

Judith L Boice
JOURNEYING
I have walked far,
I have walked long
Seeking the Self
That has always been
In the very Heart of me.

I have walked far,
I have walked long
Searching for the Home
Whose door opens
In my very Center.

I have walked far,
I have walked long
Searching for Wisdom
That has always been
The Reflection of me
In Every Thing.

Melvin Bernasconi
THE BROTHERHOOD
No foreign soil is there for me,
Nor any foreign race;
And man is one humanity
With heaven in his face.

Melba Henderson
WAIST NOT, WANT NOT

This poem is dedicated to all those that make sharing with the less fortunate a part of their lives.

If we could take the money that's been spent on diet pills
And turn the food that spreads our waists
'Tward some poor starved child's ills,
Just stop and think a moment what that possibly could mean . . .
A hundred thousand well-fed kids,
Adults all trim and lean.

If all the broken diets were to be replaced instead
With giving extra calories
To those that need be fed,
The words "Obese" and "Overweight" would disappear from sight;
Along with "Malnutrition"
They'd be gone 'most overnight!

The after-dinner groaning of the overfed would be
Replaced, not with a pill,
But with renewed vitality.
The tons of extra food we eat and fight off with a diet
Could then be used to feed the child
Now starving in the night.

Ms Diane M Bila
BE OPEN NOW!

For those who look into the heart and see their own inner struggle mirrored back to them.

I have walked the streets and alleyways
of my spirit-broken people.
I have wiped their tears and calmed their fears,
while others erect church steeples.
The countless, nameless faces look to Me for help,
and I in turn, call to you to realize how each one felt.

There should be no homeless people
in the Kingdom of My Son.
I have given you all my Blessings
and there is enough for every one.

I have shared with you abundantly in the world you have come to know.
And I call to you, "Be open now to the ways you are called to grow!"

Set My Spirit free, My Child,
lay all your fears aside.
It was for people such as you
that My Son bled and died.

If I could hold you in my arms and heal your broken heart,
then Peace would settle your crying soul as all hate did depart.

But first I must warm your heart as you let your barriers down;
teach you to Trust again, to Believe what you have found.

Our Love will challenge you to grow beyond where you are.
And those you meet will dare to show their own inner scar.

And with your help, they too shall
Heal, and come to Believe
that My Love for them is very real,
and I will never leave.

I have come to bring My People to the Kingdom of My Son,
where there are no homeless people
and there is enough for everyone.

Leona Clark
MY SOUL
Please god take my Soul
So I don't become a devil's ghoul.
Amen

Ruby Reid
DESPAIR
As I sit here and watch the freeway at nites
I see the bright headlights and red tail lights.
Somehow it makes me feel so very alone,
Knowing that most of them are rushing home.
Although it's not true, it sticks in my mind
The people in the cars are rushing to find
A home and a mate, both full of love,
A family that's blessed by our Father above.
They are hurrying by on their merry way,
Never a one comes to my house to stay.
Here is a home, a woman with love to give
To someone who'll love me each day he lives.
I remember the nights when I used to wait
For the man I loved to drive in the gate.
But my man is gone, he comes here no more
Now I have no one to give a kiss at the door.
Now I sit all alone, watching cars go by,
And I feel so lonely it makes me cry.
The days go by, doing first things first,
But the lonely nights are always the worst.

Sarah E Fredericks
THE RAIN IS COMING DOWN
The rain is coming down,
I'm wishing for it to stop,
The clouds are so black out,
I know there's no hope.
The rain is coming down,
I pray that it will go away,
It is so noisy and loud,
I hope for it to come back another day.
Needing to go out,
But with this cold
There's not a doubt,
I can make it today with out,
When the sun shines again,
I'll be ready,
To take that walk,
That the rain put off.

Ion Amariutei
hell
your hand reaching-out
has warmed me for a while

so you'll find yourself
wrapped up in gestures
—moments plummeting only once through the air—
like a mummy in bandages
like a beggar
stuffing his shirt with old papers

you can see how
bigger and bigger chunks of your life
will stick with you now and forever until
no movement is possible anymore until
even in a coffin you'd seek refuge

and your eyes are written in graffiti
—son
beloved child
there is nothing left besides you
and you have just died

Nancy Stem
THE TREES—YOUNG AND OLD
The tree, a lovelier thing I know,
today is growing old and shows its wear,
in grace, of duty done, with its winged spirit released from the bondage of seed,
pursuing its adventure of life across the unknown,
its seeds carelessly blown, come true,
with the divinest plan for the young and the old.

Alas, I find a young seedling full of bloom,
its branches outstretched touching the old,
snuggled together, waiting for the moon;

It is not art, but nature that traced
these lovely lines, bringing new life,
setting every common sight of tree
delicately alight with the moon's glow for me to see.

The birds' sweet music fills the air,
as they nestle down deliriously to pair,
as I romp in the cool dusk of summer,
over grass so soft and green, where
the gentle rolling hills beckon me to
reach the tree that drips with bloom,
the fragrance so intoxicating;

While soft falling petals intermingle with my hair,
as I sit sheltered and embraced by the
cool velvet breezes touching my face,
bewitched by the frail white stars up in the sky,
with fireflies twinkling in the trees,
while the stars wonder shy.

Tis the splendor of the trees,
Oh happy summer night!

Kimberly N Jeska
DISGUISED YEARNING
The mind is hindered in a serene meadow,
With blue chills of encompassing oceans.
Stars glitter among the omnipotent sky,
and the silver moon's shimmering presence is granted.
Veiled in the gallantly bronzed heart,
there is a conveyance of the harmonic soul.
Then, a withering light commences the burning passion.
Mysteriously, a pearly mist anchors your portrait.
Reposedly, the blackened sorrow flourished.

For one will not always be a graceful swan in the lake.

Deanna Dean
LOVE GONE WRONG
Is it me, or
Is it just us.
I feel we're growing apart.
I feel our love could be stronger,
If only given a chance.

I've tried to talk to you,
But you just don't seem to care,
And when I see you turn and walk away
I know our love wasn't meant to be.

I thought we meant something to
each other.
But now I guess I can see
The love I felt for you,
Was not returned to me.

Milton Wade Reynolds
WILTED FLOWERS
Two flowers on opposite sides of a garden—
One a radiant rose,
The other a dashing daffodil;
There they were just waiting to be set
Side by side in a lovers bouquet.

There in the lovers' arms
Their love could grow to a full bloom;
But to their surprise roses and daffodils
Weren't ready to be sent together.

So off on separate missions they went;
Two flowers in a field of thousands
Trying to find that perfect time
When roses and daffodils could meet.

The day never came for them to see;
The showers of reality came to be
And drowned all loveliness saw from a far;
Now sits two wilted flowers stuck in lonely jars.

Their dreams of togetherness
In a lovers bouquet is visionless;
No longer is love in full bloom
But is set on the shelf of doom.

Mary Jane Piper

Mary Jane Piper
THE SOUL OF EACH

The soul of a man and the soul of a woman,
One for one and one for the other.

Drift two ways as life goes on,
So neither knows where the other has gone.

Their feelings they share for each other are true,
But life's cruel ways seem to destroy and fool.

They try to stay together, but sometimes as things do,
Seem to pull them apart and destroy the joys they knew.

Then as life's long days go by it seems,
The love they once shared can not be redeemed.

Becky McKinney
FRIEND

For my Dear Friend, Jill Blackwell. With love on her Graduation Day.

I was glad we met.
Right from the start,
As a true friend,
You played the part.

You were always there for me
In good times and bad.
Whether I was happy.
Whether I was sad.

That's why today I'm writing this
To wish you all the best
As you're finishing this phase in life,
And moving on to the rest.

Cause I want you to know
How special our friendship is to me,
And how much I hope
Our friendship will always be.

So I'll finish this by giving you
From me a little prayer,
A prayer of hopes, dreams, and happiness
For you anytime, anywhere.

Toya L Stevenson
GROWING . . .

Granddaddy T., Granddaddy Lynward—B. O. & Gran-Gran

Growing is like
cursive writing
you start out very awkward,
and frustrated
like
you will never
get it!
But . . .
day by day
and
year by year
it changes
to a
Sophisticated beautiful
Piece of Art!

Virginia Schmelzla
PORTRAIT

Dedicated to the Memory of My Mother GLADYS McANELLEY SMITH

The fragile webs of "time" are spun
of Dreams as soft as silk
of mystic days, with magic nights,
and nectar of the choicest-Milk!
They shimmer in the Morning Sun,
Then turn to Silver at a glance.
They stretch to span the Realm of Heart,
Created not-by passing chance!
Designed to Grace the Lighter Side
They're woven Minute, After Minute,
Into one-lasting work of art
With lots of Love, and humor in it!
To have and hold in perfect trust
Not tangled by a passing whim
Materials of the finest "Stuff"
Must be used-for spinning them!
Each silken thread will weave its way.
Into Life's great "Exhibit."
The substance of the Careful Heart,
Will Share the Glory With It!

Lee Duval
DILEMMA

Dedicated to PJE A lifetime of memories

Bitter are the tears that stream down my lonely cheeks,
Their taste is of the seas born of time before,
But the tears I weep are for no one,
The tears I weep are for me.

As I rise each new day to greet the sun before me,
I awake with trepidation and remorse that I live to see it,
This sun that shines upon me is a thousandfold brighter than I,
But my soul shall see no ray.

I work, I plod an endless journey,
For my birthright is to wander,
Never finding that full circle,
Never finding destiny's door.

I continue to heed the call of another lonely wanderer,
So that I may console and comfort,
Along life's grief stricken highway,
But who shall comfort me?

Brenda Thorn
(THE LITTLE BOY AND) THE ANGEL IN THE TREE

For my sister, Angie, and her son, David Roy Hatcher. Born 8-3-79, returned to our Lord on 9-9-79, and for my friend, Aggie, and her brother, David Clair Gittins Phillips. Born 1-1-28, returned to our Lord on 4-21-33.

Angel looking down
From the top of that tree.
"Why are you smiling
Down here at me?"
"What do I look like?
Am I strange to see?
Come down here, we'll play,
And good friends we will be."

"Where did you come from?
Did you fall from a star?
Were you not good in heaven
And sent where you are?"

"Hey, wait! Where are you going?
Don't forget to take me.
I'll follow you up
To the top of that tree."

"And we'll be good friends,
Just you and me.
And we'll play here forever,
In the top of this tree."

Shawn E Ritchie
MEMORIES OF YOU AND I

To Crystal, with all my love May the stars always shine for you.

My heart was sad, my world was torn
My life it seemed so dark and dim.
Then I met you, one star filled night
And found my heart again.
You brought me out
From my broken dreams
And gave me joy once more
My heart was lifted, my world was sewn
My life grew bright and gay
You gave me love, you gave me hope
That night you came my way
I thank you for your friendship
Over all these past few years.
I thank you for the memories
The laughter and the tears.
And if you should ever need someone
Just think of me and smile
For though we parted ways today
I loved you for awhile
So when your life seems blue and sad
Remember all the times
When I would sit across the room
And make your life more glad
For even though we part today
Your smile is in my mind
And memories of you and I
Are always there to find

Ms Diana Ramos Cruz
FIRST LOVE

To my first love, I will remember you always and forever.

I touch his face, he touches my face.
I feel his hands on my skin.
I touch his lips with my finger tip.
We look at each other with deep loving eyes.
Our eyes linger in a long passionate kiss.
Our lips finally touch, so tender and sweet.
Lips so wanting and so giving.
Embraces so warm and lovely.
Holding and touching, smooth, soft whispers of I Love You and I need you are said to one another.
Making us no longer two, but one!

Stephanie Young Elbanna
INDIAN WATCH

In dedication to my great, great grandmother Proudfoot, who still sits watching. And to my Cherokee relations.

Indian dances of Summer.
There's a rumour—Indian ghost dancers still roam the Earth.
Drummers pow wow in the great beyond.
Great Indian chiefs still sit watching the white man's clever ways.
Knowing soon the white man's destruction will come.
The Indian chief sits high above the world like the great eagle—
His brother spirit and his cries are heard in the Winter winds.
His wrath is felt in the Summer sun.
In Spring he calls upon his daughters with beautiful Indian gold skin to perfume the air.
In Autumn he shakes the Earth and the leaves meet the ground for their funeral fate.

Jo Ann Cunningham
MY BONNIE LASSIE

When my son, Dan, was in the eighth grade, this is the way he felt about his collie dog, Lassie. This poem is dedicated to both of them.

I have a fair haired girlfriend;
She's very true to me.
I am her one and only;
That's very plain to see.

We go for walks on Sunday
And play around the park.
She likes the kids that like me;
But if they don't, boy, does she bark.

Well, you have probably guessed it—
My girl is my pet collie.
She is a friend thru thick and thin,
And my only girl, by golly.

Karen L Correll
ROGER DEAN BROWN

Why is my baby gone?
Such a happy child was he.
Now, he's been taken from me.
It's so hard to be strong.

I ache inside like I never have before.
It's continuous and never goes away.
The hurt and sadness stays and stays,
With tears and tears galore.

I thought labor was my worst pain,
But losing him is the worst.
It hurts so, I think I'm going to burst.
Am I the blame?

He was all I had,
And can have no more.
Why my baby—what for?
Oh, I feel so sad!

Roger was such a dear—
Why was he taken, instead of me?
I just don't see—
Why can't it be made clear?

I miss him so much—
His little giggle and smile
Will shine in my memory a long while,

But I can no longer feel his touch.

"In this life, goodbye my love."
"Smiling in Grandma's arms within the clouds,"
Seeing this vision some comfort is allowed,
"For I'll see you again in heaven above!"

Wendi
PARENTS

This poem is dedicated to Phillip & June Cadman, my loving parents.

Parents are those people
Against us when we're young
Seems they're always trying
To keep our world undone

Then as we grow older
We suddenly see
The happy fulfilled people
We have grown to be

Our parents must love us
For it seems they're always there
Whenever we need them
Showing us they care

Yes parents are those people
Who fought us in our youth
And as I watch my children grow
I now recognize the truth

Julian A Paramore Jr
HOW FAR CAN WE TAKE LOVE

To: Family and friends with appreciations, thanks for the support.

Here we walk holding each other closely, why are we in this unforesaken place?
Look at the gloom on everyone's face, can we bring happiness in this place? Can we bring hope, or find everlasting love?
I guess you could say nope.
It seems to be keeping everyone sad, is this good? No, it must be bad.
Should we try or should we go?
Should we try to fill in this near ending hole?
I am leaving this place with or without you, it will show if our love is true.

Claudia A Miller
UNICORN, MY UNICORN

This poem is dedicated to my mother, Elinore V. Beaufeaux. Who encouraged me in my writing and always believed in me.

With head held high, Golden spiraled horn catching the morning light;
The Story of a Unicorn, My Unicorn had begun; Happily prancing ever closer, playing the shafts of light, in and out the marbled pillars he seemed to glide, knowing full well, the lateness of his coming;
Moments in time, shades of pink-purple glistening off his back, the World stood between us, as it rose and fell, with each breath we took;
The Unicorn's white on white coat turned from bright pink to light lavender, looking proud as he cantered towards me on route to fulfill our destiny; The Unicorn, My symbol of Love, Justice, Truth and Strength, the reality of the Spirit within me;
I heard a Lark, a top a decaying pillar, his Song of Love, Wanting and Waiting brought me out of my awareness to My Unicorn; The Unicorn looked up; The Lark wanted his attention, not mine; Their eyes locked, reflecting the Love I felt; I watched as the tale unfolded before my eyes, revealing the Truth of My Unicorn inside; The Unicorn lowered his head, snorting into the ancient dust, with a flick of his tail he was by my side; The Lark knew he had been there all along;
Within, My Unicorn's knowledge grew; I knew I needed to Sing My Song of Love, upon this ancient hallowed ground.

Barbara Daniels
GARAGE SALE

Thanks to my family and friends for their prayers and love.

They come like vultures to
pick away the morsels of
the dead animal.
Some needed more than
others
One gulped a niblet, but
could not swallow.
Another joyously ate a belly
full and was satisfied.
A few came to touch
and poke, and finally
no barterable molecule
was left
And the beast stirred
within the cycle of life
Once Again.

George Blucher
LOST LOVE

This poem I dedicate to Mary Anne Irwin whose love will die with me!

Oh Mary as Merry as can be,
they ask me how do I live without thee!

I tell them it's not easy as you can see,
because my love you will always be a part of me!

With my heart so broken in two,
It's not easy living without you!

For when the sky is so bright to everyone,
it's dark and gray to me hon!

They say there's a pot of gold at the end of the rainbow,
Mary my love mine must be way below!

So as you can see my dearest love,
I will never see that flying dove!

So take care my sweet,
For I know I am beat!

As long as I have our baby by my side,
My love for you will never die!

Annie M Clark
LEAVES

To my Grand children—Perez, Levar and Ashley

It is autumn and the leaves are turning many colors.
There are shades of red, brown, green and yellow.
As you gaze over hills and valleys, it resembles a giant bouquet o flowers.
As the leaves fall on the ground, the children will have fun rolling around.
There are many colors, sizes and shapes. Then, it is time to bring out the rake.
By November, as winter draws near, and the last leaf has disappeared the branches will be bare, only the birds will be nesting there. The squirrels may run up and down the trunks, looking for nuts to munch. The bare branches will sway in the breeze as the snow flakes cover the trees. The beauty of it is a sight to see. The snow melts, as the trees begin to bud and the birds begin to sing.
When you see the leaves appear,
You will know that spring is near.

Sally Blackburn Grauso
MY BEST FRIEND

Delma Baker Blackburn
Rita Seminoro Grauso

Kind gentle words
Things sometimes never said.
A brief smile or hug always at hand.
A listening ear so near.
Rough gentle loving hands.
She's a friend.
Always us never her.
She's the greatest gift,
My mother My friend.
Her's Her's
Her face of love.

Rosemary Guida
THE CHILDREN
She says she sees things thru the
Eyes of a child
In a while
We will all feel the same
Time is the test of everything
And fate lies in the palm of our hands

Follow a child's eyes
There is no place really like it
Their hearts are forever young
Forever strong
Like the times we need to be
For each other
Follow a child's eyes
There is always something
New to discover

We should only remember the good
Things that happen
The past will never return
And so we will always have some regrets
It will help us understand if we feel some pain
As long as I remember the way
We were when we were when we were happy
We'll be that way some day again

Cristy Guleserian
THE DREAM
It was our very first fight,
He kicked me out in the night,
I knew that he was sad.

When he opened the door,
Just to call me a whore,
He knew that I'd be mad.

As I walked down the street,
Darkened light hit my feet,
That's when I began to cry.

We were two broken hearts,
Our love had fallen apart,
The fault of a single lie.

The sky was gray and
There was silver rain,
Falling down upon my head.

I felt my teardrops streaming,
While my heart was screaming,
I wished that he was dead.

Then the sun came out,
I erased my pout and
Realized I was in bed.

It was all a dream,
And I never screamed,
Or wished that he was dead.

Sheila Rao
THE MOST EVIL ONE
This evil one takes control
and pounds and fights,
Till it is deep in my soul.

Once it has entered the mind,
It will affect every thought
The true awful feelings—it will find.

No being can ever retrieve peace,
For this evil one will not allow it.
One by one, we pass from beauty to beast.

Admitting being possessed takes philosophy.
Not many have this type of courage.
Yes, we soon find out, the most evil one is jealousy.

Barbara Wentzel
INSPIRATIONAL STIMULATIONS
The peaceful, relaxing Pacific Ocean
Always in motion
Wind and storm
Watch the clouds as they form
Take a walk on an ocean beach
Feel the sand warm under your feet
Ocean breezes, seagull screams
Lighthouse beams
The sea comes to the shore
Splashes there forever more
Fishes in the sea
Beauty for you and for me
Rushing, surging waves
Splashing into a rock cave
Serenity, wonderful serenity for me
Is living here by this beautiful sea
Inspirational Stimulations.

Michael McPhee
THE GATE
Green gate, green wire gate,
  moulded iron gate green with
envy, green with regret, green with
  lame and dying lust.

Parts of her sneak past the dry green gates
  to the music (hot sweet jazz music)
blowing like promises in the hot green air.
She swims (birthing) under the trees, bathing
  in the somnolent shade of their long slow reaching,
folded in their rocking arms, and singing scat
  like a child (on the downbeat).

Under the trees she pledges allegiance of some kind
  (her fingers are crossed) to the grain of her
groundbroke character, sweet and hot and true as
  the memory—sad notes floating
  in the leaf—song
around her, and makes promises of her own
  that she will find she cannot keep
  and cannot show
  though she know
the cost of its hiding.

Down by the gate in the maundering rain, she dances.

Ora Gilley
SILVER WAS HER NAME
My thoughts sewn together with silver thread, I never knew from where she came.
With a laugh she sang and danced, soft her heart and eyes, Silver was her name.
Moved through my soul with foot of

fleet, this apparition of shadows I love so.
I'll catch her if I can, as she sails back, to and fro.
Smooth silky skin she was, the only thing, the only beat of my heart.
Silver near my interself, always there, tho I lost her from the start.
Words of wisdom she spoke with haste, never a wasted hour.
Clouds of heart shadows in my mind, Silver the essence of a flower.
Mist on water from whence she came, she lays in my mind like form.
This ghost of an unmended heart I know, gives the sun its warm.
Breath soft like dew on flowers of bright, she's precious like silver and sun.
Took all my heart, laughed as she will, love will die if you run.
Hold tight the heart of this child of soft, she disappears like love
Cries in the night.
Speak softly into her mind of trust, for she may soar into the sun,
Or simply die of fright.

Patricia Nelson
TERROR IN MY HEART
Terror in my heart
Panic before my eyes
My life is burning
Like a crackling fire
across a canvas

The picture is old
The image has been seen before
Of days that never were
Or were never meant
to be

All is quiet
The deed is done
There are no memories
No one to remember
Me

David Crippen
REFLECTIONS AT A U-2 CONCERT
Warily we fix each other, this testament to my immortality
and I.
All of fifteen, leather jacket, collar insouciantly upturned,
a shock of blond hair.
I stand a paradox to him, similar in garb,
but with an air of cynicism born of war and pestilence,
and having been to a county fair or two.
When I became a man, I did not put aside childish things.
He weighs this curiosity in silence, portending a specter of myself in another lifetime,
for now an intruder in his world.
The band dispenses promises of hope and fulfillment.
Deafening undercurrents, finding common ground within us,
plucking his imagination, as it once did mine.
But that was another time, another world.
I thoughtfully study technical nuances.
He conjures revelations of peace and love from nonsense,
and rejoins me with an unexpected smile.
Behold my apocalypse,
Child, father to the man, prophesy yet to be fulfilled.
Destined to go forth into the unknown and the darkness, as I have done,
and keep the candle burning.

Tina Richard

Tina Richard
EYE OF THE TIGER

To Mom; you believed in me and supported me. I Love You.

The eye of the tiger,
A mysterious view
The look that he gives, the power he proves.
As he eases through the jungle in search of some prey, no animals are seen, they all run away.

They all run away because they are scared,
They all run away, they know they've been dared.
It's the vast instinct of the tiger's eye;
No one can beat him, no one can hide.

Betsy Tombarelli
AS WE GO THROUGH THE YEARS
As we go through the years,
We learn the meaning of tears.
For those who are grown,
They can be a mournful tone,
For the young in love,
They are a learning dove.

But, no matter why a tear is shed,
We know that we will always be lead
To a beginning so new.
And like the dew,
On a rose that has grown
If left alone,
The dew will soon disappear,
And know what is new is near.

Cheryl A Austin
VICTIM OR VILLAIN
Noble Prince and a loyal brother,
Warrior, King, and a teasing lover.
But charges swell bout him like a tide,
coin him the villain history cried!

Richard the Third, the Duke of Gloucester,
termed a madman, a crouchback monster.
Guilty or no, historians heed,
for his own defense he cannot plead!

Birth decreed him a brother to York,
fueling hatred by the Woodville court.
Lord of the North and man of fair mind
by faith of loyalties that do bind!

Was the Wicked Uncle lies or truth?
The debate will rage by what we choose.
No doubts of his courage when he died,
but he's a villain history cried!

Mary Jo Melvin
ONE IS ONE
A solitary tear meanders through the creases—
To reach for the void.
A skeletal thumb caresses the four—
To seek the warmth.
A stiffened foot drums sticklike—
To race for the frozen one.
Eyes glow in relived delight or despair in ancient agony.
He knows not why!

In a world of laughing music,
In the beginning,
In the closing,
In the escaping,
One is one.

Tracy Linden
MELVILLE: CHAPTER 42
The whiteness of my life I see
Cold and still, surrounding me.
It was, it is, will always be
Moby Dick upon the sea.

Blinded by albino night
I struggle, scream, with all my might
Fear rises to a greater height
"Wonder ye then at the fiery fight?"

Colors play amidst the air
I look again, they are not there
Only albatross and polar bear
Atheists without a prayer.

The milky whiteness of a midnight sea
A colorless void in intensity
Only of the whale speaketh he,
My life depicted in reality.

Terry M Konn
A CRY OF JOY!
In the awakening of day the mist was gone,
The sky, a deep, deep blue,
I now could see the beauty, I had not seen before,
A wind as cool as a mountain spring blowing through the tall green grass and wild flowers,

Standing on top of the rock jetting from the mountain,
Watching the hawk,
Waiting for the bird to land careful not to frighten him,
Stiffening my arm for him to stand,
Feeling his heart pound beneath his feathers,
As mine was aching with the memory of yesterday,

He stared upward into the sky,
Holding him up, I let him go,
I could not speak as the night before when my loved one left with only a note,
The hawk took off into the air and circled 'round,
I had lost everyone to freedom itself.

Samantha Canaday
MY MOTHER
I look so much like you and act it too
I've always looked up to you
I can never go anywhere that you're not there
Because I see you in me
I treasure all you've done for me.

You raise me
You mold me after you
You are always there when I need you
You're the best mom anyone could have

I wanted to thank you for always being there
I wanted you to know how much I love you.
I wanted you to know you're like a priceless diamond, flawless, that never grows old and never dies
I want you to know that my love for you will live forever.

I Love You Mother

Yadja Yellen
DIMENSIONS
Most men are three dimensional;
A few can see in four,
And women, who are "encente"
Can surely see in more.

But writers roam through time and space,
Creation is the key,
And artists, in all of the fields,
Sense more than you and me.

The agony of description
Is more than they can bear!
But then, again, there is the need,
The compulsion, to share.

Please shelter them, all, from abuse,
whoever reads this plea,
The secret to contentment lies
In letting things just be!

Pamela S Denny
SEARCH NO MORE

To my very special and devoted friend who inspired this poem, Dennis M. Moya

Search no more
For a friend you have found,
Your friendship with me
Is safe and sound.

When there is a need
On me you can depend,
I'll be by your side
Completely, till the end.

I want to share
Your joys and sorrows,
Listen to your fears
And dreams of tomorrows.

I shall laugh with you
Not at you,
And cry with you too.
Support your achievements
In all that you do.

Search no more
For a friend you have found,
Your friendship with me
Is safe and sound.

Lynda S Deming
THINKING OF YOUR LOVE
Sun shines each morning when I awake
Thinking of your Love
How good it feels to have you hold me

In your very precious way.

Afternoon brings delights of happiness
Thinking of your Love
How nice to hear the laughter in your voice
When speaking lovely thoughts.

Evening dons the cloak of romance
Thinking of your Love
How peaceful you seem when visiting my oasis
In holding hearts through fingertips.

Twilight is the hour of peace
Thinking of your Love
How heavenly you feel lying next to me
Sharing our love unto eternity.

Thinking of your Love.

Kenneth P Smith

WHAT LANGUAGE SHALL I BORROW

What language shall I borrow then
To frame this conscience dream,
Cast in light and airy speech, though false,
Of huddled town clutching a knuckled hill?

A hard and sacred place that knows no God:
Where work fires the curse
Of fathers' sins into
Sweating machines of no significance.

What of this place beside
The thrashing sea, the watching sea
That gashes rock to sand,
Where soapy waves smooth the sound of life?

Where but I alone
Struggling with organ, sinew, and bone
Die quicker than a bird's beating heart,
To mock the freedom of his wings?

Virginia M Siverly

AUTUMN TO WINTER

Summer is over too soon—
And harvest begins at noon.
Time to bring fruits and vegetables in—
All to be stored for winter in a bin.
Soon "Jack Frost" starts his painting—
Pictures everywhere so dainty.
Cool weather makes itself known—
Last time for lawns to be mown.
Children dress in warm coats and caps—
And maple trees running with 'sap'.
Winter will come soon—
And hunters are hunting for 'coon'.
Come look out the window now—
From the high pasture comes the Cow.
Look! There's snow on her back—
She hurries now the feed rack.
Time to huddle by the fireplace—
The family is content at a slow pace.
Snow flakes are falling near—
Winter is here!

Courtney Vanderbeck

ONLY A SOUND OF SILENCE

Somewhere I can hear,
A child crying.
It sounds as if the poor child,
Is dying.
I go over to him,
And look into his eyes.
And I realize.
He cries and cries,
But nobody will listen.
The pain,
Hurts more and more.
As he wishes he could,
Stop this war.
He lay in my arms,
So scared and afraid.
As he wishes,
Someday he will be saved.
Tears of sadness,
Fall from his face,
From all of the madness,
All over the place.
The sound of guns,
Killing someone.
And these guns won't stop,
Until the day is done.
Why is there war?
The little boy wondered.
As he heard a sound of thunder.
Then there was silence,
Nothing was said.
It was so quiet,
It seems like everyone was dead.
The guns drop to the ground,
Yet there still is no sound,
Only a sound of sadness.

Jamie Nicole Bettles

MY BROTHER

My brother is nice
Though sometimes we fight
But that's alright
We've been through good times
And through bad times
And there are all different kinds of brothers
But mine is like no other
He is in the Air Force
He does good in it of course
He works on people's eyes
In which he really tries
And when he gets on that plane to leave again
I know that soon I will be able
To see him soon again.

Lonnie Louis

WHO BOWS TO BEL

With birth comes the curse. A promise of equity, to all brought forth here within.
Yet many have relished not, the joy of mere acceptance, by national citizens kin.

Heavy burdens in life must they bear, tired bent grey bodies, and the world seems not to care.
Still they strive with pitiful prayers and undying hope, that not in vain do they grope, for rights that all may truly share.

But know this king rulers, the oppressions and wrongs you now inflict, will surely someday pass.
And remember from holy writ, that they who are first, will surely someday, also be the last.

Aware, aware, oh brother, oh sister, set your minds and conscience clear, and stop this damnable Hell.
How blindly you go, so to and fro, driven by deceit, to lie and cheat, unaware that it's you, who bows to Bel.

Patti L Hill

SOON AUTUMN

In the midst of nature
I can sense signs of fall.
An occasional warm wind
caressing my cheek
turning crisp and cool.
The first red leaf
lingering on a limb
falters and falls helplessly
and in the end
lies dormant on the ground,
Awaiting those who will follow.
Soon . . .
Soon the ground
Will be carpeted in red and gold.
Soon . . .
Soon the warm summer wind
will turn cold.
Soon . . .
Soon it will be Autumn.

Marie Rawlings

Marie Rawlings

FAMILY

He:
Why don't you do something with your hair?
You are an old hag who does not care.
Fat old hen! Could be cute
If you'd exercise, shut up, and reduce.
She:
You never talk to me or help with chores in the house.
You guzzle, sleep, are an eternal grouch.
Escape is thru your day dreams and fantasies.
Angered, I pretend to be a mouse
And flee to my friends: dirt, water, flowers, bees.
Kids:
Simmer down! We come visiting with LOVE.
While we are here it's WAR, no peace.
Mom forgive, have patience. Be a dove.
Dad calm down. Give her a kiss and hug. The least you both can do is give us a "happy feeling feast."
We must pray for peace and harmony from God above.
Then practice the Golden Rule with each—
Become achievers by a kind, cooperative shove.
Our family must harbor eternal hope and love.

Deborah Phillips

PROMISES IN THE SKY

I find comfort in the infinite
sparkle of stars against the black of night; the soft glow of the
moon upon restless nature now in sleep.
I never cease to marvel at the
folded bud which, at the urging of Spring in her fresh arrival,
boldly bursts forth in brilliant release.
My heart soars as my eyes drink
in open golden meadows, vast and unmarked; my spirit freely
flies high above as it joins a flock of birds in flight, their every
movement blended in perfect form.
In the coolness of the mountains,
the lazy rippling of a clear stream envelopes my senses; The
symphony of the first dim rays of light bursting forth as the sun
bathes the morning sky brings me hope as a new day is born.
We must never let the frantic
pace of our lives consume and dull our senses to the beauty of
the nature which is ever thriving in perfect harmony
surrounding us each day. Hope for our lives in this world, inner
peace amid the chaos is free to
us any time.
We must reach out to our
soothing nature, drawing on the strength of the ocean, the
certainty of the vast blue sky beyond which stretches for
eternity worlds of mystery in twinkling galaxies; we must all
drink in and store within our hearts these sights and smells
filled with hope; only then will we ensure the lasting promises of
peace entitled all troubled
souls of mankind.

Rima E Armogida

AS

I touch the small pink flower
Sweet blossom with no memory
And dream that I devour
The unbirthed fruit of the tree.
They sip the honey of their dreams
Wise stored in close watched hives
And touch their lips to sacred streams
Flow crystal through their lives.
Whilst I must like the butterfly
Life's pollen on my wing
Just for one brief moment lie
Upon that precious thing.
They clasp their newborn child
Their garden already in bloom
But my seed's still sown wild
And I still grasp at the moon.
But I shall find the sharpest hoe
I'll run my plowshare deep
And treasure more than they could know
Each harvest that I reap!

Nancy Skellenger

THE WOEFUL COWBOY

As I ride along I ask myself this question . . .
"What am I doing here?"
Theres dust in my eyes, and sand in my mouth
My clothes smell worse than the cattle we're drivin
Theres a crick in my neck and rocks in my back
And I'm in a terrible mess . . .
I wonder what they'd do if I started bawlin
'Cause theres a snake in my sleeping bag . . .
And natures callin . . .

Bonnie Moulton

A STRANGER IN THE DARKNESS

A stranger in the darkness awaits
me as the night nears;
Each breath the stranger takes is
the noise that brings me to
tears.
I'm frightened of the stranger as
a little boy lost from his mother;
The darkness is the only thing the
stranger knows as if it is his
lover.

A stranger in the darkness; Why
  won't he let me be?
For, I have never seen the
  stranger because in the
  darkness I cannot see.
I try to rid the stranger in my
  mind;
I know that the stranger is not
  kind.
In the darkness the stranger is
  able to see;
For, I have never seen the
  stranger but the stranger has
  seen me.

Elsie F Tyler
TIS THE TIDE OF WINTER

Tis the tide of Winter I love. Season of choice. Season of falling snow. I'll take a land where the snow crystals form and the wintery tale is of changing skies and slopes of snow.

The King Winter's decor I adore. Everywhere snow white fields. Days of clear blue blue skies over fluffy white snow stacked wide and deep. Winged feathered snowflakes etching the landscape. Sparkling icicles precariously hanging with dream-like grace. Chimney smoke rising and then spiraling upward slowly.

Frozen over ponds. Frozen over lakes. Fence posts deeply buried in misty snow. Arctic air gathering forces to sweep along a blowing trek. It's Squaw weather. It's shivering goose-flesh weather. Frost bitten fingers are forgotten if an animal's tracks are seen in the snow.

In this peaceable kingdom of wintery cold we are holed up, blocked off, frozen in, and gloriously snowbound. There's no rush nor need to break the tranquility. We can sit by the fire with its sparkling flames or we can join the young ones for a romp in the snow.

Tis the tide of winter I adore. Seasons of drift. Seasons of snow blankets on the ground. Skies of blue and gray. There is no season that can compare with winter's polar flare.

Naomi LeVay
TRAVELING LIGHT

I am going to buy a loosely fitted
garment
for my soul
and let her wander freely
where she will.

I am going to loosen her hair
and let it hang lightly
on her shoulders.

I am going to leave her shoes at the
edge
of the tidal water
so that she may walk lightly
among the singing grasses
that line the long windy beach.

Ruth Ann Winters
SPECTACLE (upon seeing a neighbor's wash on the line)

To my good neighbor, Mary Ethel Kennedy

Fresh, clean blowing,
Waving colors in the breeze.
Clothesline flowing
Memories from these.
Sunlit fragrance
Crisp, crinkly touch
Happy, joyous service
For those I love so much.
Wind, blue skies, bright colors
Fill my mind with love.
Across the miles, through open doors
The blessings from above
Have filled my heart with sunshine,
With music and with joy
As I behold a clothesline,
I remember my girl and boy.

Gloria Geane
HAPPY ANNIVERSARY

As the candle light flickers,
And is about to go out,
Pause awhile and whisper softly,
"What is life all about."
It's being loved by your family
And count your blessings everyday,
For with each other's love to guide
you,
You will never lose your way.

Laura S Covelli
WEAVERS

Poetry lies latent in the work of men
Locked in ambition until duties ease.
Sorrow not for what might have
been;
Doers come first and poets seize

Sturdy threads that were spun and
then
Lace their quills with the fibers of
these.

Trisha K Walden
PLAYING PIECES

Am I a pawn in this game
  just like other playing pieces,
Or am I the queen who you run
  to?
Like the castle offers you shelter
  I offer you love.
As I look at you from far away
  I see your destination.
You are going so many ways
  playing one piece then another.
Will you ever know how many
  pieces you break in this game?
I wonder if you will find the true
  queen once again,
Or is she gone from your sight
  forever?

Bertha Lee Jacobs
WHAT AM I GOING TO BE?

Am I going to be a carpenter hitting
on top of nails
  Or am I going to be a thief
  sitting there in jail
Am I going to be a nurse helping
people in need
  Or am I going to be a junky
  trying to get relief
Am I going to be a pilot flying so
sky high
  Or am I going to be a pusher
  making the kids feel they're
  "Super Fly"
Am I going to be a teacher trying to
give free education
  Or am I going to be a hooker
  increasing the population
Am I going to be a somebody in this
large huge ball
  Or am I going to be a dunker
  almost to fall
I don't know, I just don't know what
I am going to be.
  Because, no one knows what the
  future might bring
But right now, right this minute I just
want
        TO BE ME.

Slade Congleton
THROUGH THE AGES

Throughout the ages, since time
began,
One has searched for the soul
Within the heart of man.

If in some distant day,
Some scholar should care
To scan this age.
Would this heart of mine,
Fill a chapter or just a page.

Would it be a footnote in eternity,
Or would he find the meaning of
This life of mine.
The magic of reality.

Or would he pass it by,
and fail to understand
The drive and hopes
of mortal man.

Darin Dees
LOVE-IN-A-MIST

A peach face
Reflected in the steel blue,
Your apple-blossom hair
Dances in the young breeze
A sweet hand brushes mine
And for a moment;
Two are one
The flowing white
Sparkles the sun
In glowing ambiance
Your green eyes
Are deeper than the spring
And I am lost
Beneath the rippling pool
Falling down
Down
Into the cool white shadows

Mae F Hulteen
HAVE YOU SEEN MY FRIEND?

Have you seen my friend? He has
unkept hair,
Very large eyes looking everywhere.
His clothes are tattered, his feet are
bare.
Have you seen my friend anywhere?

If you try very hard, you really may
see
This very dear person who means
much to me.
Maybe down by the river or around
the bend.
Tell me please, have you seen my
friend?

'Tis important I find him, you
understand.
He needs my help, this lonely man.
If you find him 'fore I, will your
hand to him lend?
He'll thank you then ask, "Have you
seen my friend?"

Charles E Ziavras
MEMORY

If there were just a moment one
could freeze,
Some locket it was given him to
keep,
Where would he find that element so
deep,
That he would say, "Yes, this most
did please."
I'd think it would be easy to reprise
Some innocence at play, or thrilling
leap
At one's first surmise of love's
wondrous sweep,
Or the feel of an early summer
breeze.
The poet says that memory retrieves
The better part of life's uneven
game.
If so, then all the fire one achieves
Is not the thing, the burning of the
flame,
What matters is the solitary ember,
That is, the moment you remember.

Rich J Bush
POOR MERCURY CHILD

Poor Mercury child
With eyes so bright,
What wondrous things
Do you see with your sight?

Are you truly a prophet
From out of the night,
Or do you still need
A prism to see through the light?

Tonya Marneenate

Tonya Marneenate
JUST REMEMBER; A LIFETIME

To the best cousin in the world, Gregg Holasut. I Love You!

We've known each other so very
long,
A lifetime indeed.
I know someday you'll see the light,
the light to succeed.
You just don't know how happy I've
been,
just because your you and you have
been my friend.
You're more than a friend, you're
special in fact,
I put you right up front, and the
REST in the back.
I know you always won't be there,
but I'll be there for you.
Just remember how I cared for you &
how I loved you too.
Just as the future turns into the past,
My memories of love and trust for
you, will forever last.

Elizabeth Angerosa
MY OLD BROKE DOWN CLOSET

From shiny old bells,
To moneys deposit,
It's all there in my old broke down
closet;

Things that we thought
We never would find,
Some of them yours and some of
them mine;

I found a dirty sock,
Another, and another,
I'm not going to tell anyone,
Especially my mother;

Now if someone finds out,
(I'm not going to cause it),
That everything's there in my old
broke down closet.

Sarah Sutton
LOST IN THE FOREST
All alone walking
through the gentle forest.
Swaying branches
brush against my arms.
Birds fly in the mist
of morning,
While deer run back and forth
in the soft, sad rain.
Looking all around me,
I wonder where I am.
Running, crying,
scared and very lonely,
Where am I?

Nancy E Norton
FRIEND
If you ever need a friend
I have alot to share,
I will be here until the end
to show you how much I really
care.
If ever you need a guide
to help you see the light,
I will be right by your side
to make everything seem bright.
If you're ever looking for love
you have to look no more,
For I will show you a side of love
that you have never seen
before.
So, if you're ever feeling blue,
Just remember I Love You.

Terry A Chandler
TIME PASSED
I looked into your eyes
Seeing in your soul a lonely man
It was like looking in a mirror
You smiled and I knew inside we
could be friends

Time, passed
With actions—feelings—talk and
time
It was so natural how it came to be
Respect—compassion—security—
love

Time passed
Like both our lives had been leading
to and
Preparing us to be together
To be good to one another

Time passed
With our dream realized
Becoming one feeling the other's
needs and fears
Knowing forever is not long enough

Time passed
Now you're gone—I was your last
love
I often reminisce of days and nights
Smiles and words once said
I long for times passed

Robin Carr
WHIRLWIND
if you take life too seriously,
you will be deliriously
whirled around in a frenzy.
if you take what others say as law
you will find one fatal flaw
in spinning, trying to please
everyone.
you're torn and tattered
and all around battered
and destroying everything in your
path.
you should live your life for you
and then just shoo
everything else into the wind
to be carried away.

Richard D Pollard Jr
LIMITS OF LOVE
As she turned her head,
To avoid words of pain,
And to hide the tears,
Falling like gentle rain,

She stood before him,
Fearing the words he will say,
For she knew her mistakes,
Brought her to this dreadful day,

As he took her ring,
From his trembling hand,
There was no other choice,
He must make a stand,

Even love has its limits,
That both have to uphold,
No matter those promises,
That you've been told,

But the love he had,
Just pierced his heart,
Life would be so sad,
If they both were apart,
So together they began a brand new
start.

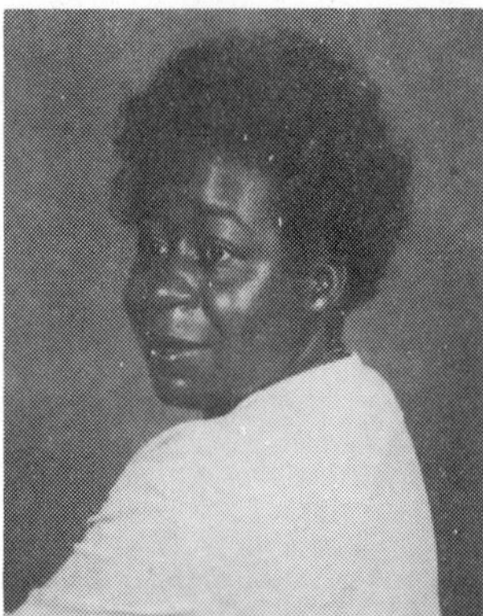

Ms Jannie Baker

Ms Jannie Baker
G-L-O-W

To my sister, Ms. Lorraine Baker; my mother, Mrs. Sallie Baker and to Dr. Mildred Brown and Black Singles Resources

G is for the GOOD I see in you.
L is for the LOVE you gave to me.
O is because you are the ONLY one
for me.
W is because you mean the WORLD
to me.

Put all these letters together, they
'spell GLOW, because this is the
way you make me feel.

Helen M Blay
THE GIFT OF LOVE
The gift of love was taught to me by
the one I held so dear,
I watched him in his suffering, his
agony and pain,
I wanted so to help to ease the pain I
knew he felt,
It was then I truly learned what
compassion really meant,
It made it all worthwhile to have lost
him in the end.
The memory of it all surrounds me,
It seems but yesterday
When broken, bruised and lonely,
My eyes were filled with tears,
Then Jesus came into my soul and
my pain was turned to joy,
My tears no longer did I shed,
But laughter came instead,
And though I hurt from the loss,
My face will never show it,
For now I have a lasting love,
A love that's full of joy.
He emptied me of self and pride and
gave me peace within,
My failures were but stepping stones,
that taught me the gift of love,
Now compassion dwells within me
for those who need God's love,
Love is forever, a gift from God,
But sometimes it takes a lifetime to
really learn to love.

Hilma Nurmi
GOLDEN YEARS OF LOVE
The countless precious and familiar
things
Come trooping back to me, a golden
tide
Of years, when hearts attuned we
walked in springs
Hardly a breath apart, the silence
wide,
The sun forever at its apogee.
Love's sheath of armour, sheltering
and warm,
Was meshed with tensile threads of
faith, that we
Might build it strong to ward off
every harm.
When searing swords of grief arced
overhead,
Your gentle words would turn each
thrust aside.
Along the league of years, through
toil for bread,
We dreamed great dreams and
worked with honest pride.
At times thought turns a corner where
a sigh
Holds tender warmth that wells from
days gone by.

Kristina Burchett
BENEATH THE STARS
Caught up in love's intrigue,
we slip away from the crowded
party.
We find this romantic place,
bathed in moonlight.
Here, the music is softer, sweeter.
The fragrance of roses
heady and intense;
like the kisses we'll share.
You're holding me close in warm
embrace,
as we dance beneath the stars.
The love in your eyes
is mirrored in my own;
as you dip your lips to mine,
tasting the tender passions
I have waiting there for you.
You give to me of your love
in that kiss;
and the tender way that you hold me.
Never let me go.

Kelly Davis
ARRIVAL
In the winter before us,
I stood on the lake shore;
Starkest blue water whipped and
tossed in
ice-blown patterns by the wind,
Much in tune with my own
secret tempest.

Here I am;
The girl who nurtured freedom,
As though it were a season that
would never come again.

Emerging,
I see that resolve cannot stand in the
face of love.
Thank God for men who arrive
unafraid.
I've come a long way to you.

C J Stevens
COME ALONG LITTLE LADY, WHY DO YOU ROAM?
Come along little lady, why do you
roam?
Do you seek a new future or just
need a home.
Moving here to there, manipulating
new friends.
Wishing for lovers, with sex that
never ends.

Begging forgiveness for setting new
trends,
You drink too much, and resist the
urge for peace.
Planning your goals—to end up
deceased.
I see you wandering and wondering
at your loneliness inside,
Crying at night, without knowing
why.

Reaching upward and embracing the
sun; then
Hiding the hurts from bruising
yourself, when no else will.

Suffer no more, give yourself to the
Lord.
Pack up again, forget the things that
you hoard,
Love waits for you somewhere, so
worry no more.
You'll never be perfect, never a
whore.

Yes, promises, promises, How can
you believe?
You've heard the lies and have often
been deceived.
Tears flow from your eyes, and love
from your heart,
Remember God really loves you, so
make a new start!

Peggy J Moses
MOONBEAM
Moonbeam, Moonbeam, Thy soft
light holds all in beauty
Upon the fields and valleys deep
All is still thy children sleep
God doth love so very much
To send a Moonbeam his hand did
touch
Light the way, for I must not stay in
darkness of the night
Shower the heavens with Moon-
beams
They will sparkle, shimmer and shine
For when night gathers in
There you will be my friend
Once more will you light my way
And through this night, please with
me stay

Alan D Hrapsky
MOON
Unrequited love, reigns the ravaged
night.
Breaching, mottled moon burns the
darkness bright.
As blackness ebbs, anguish crests;
Her burning touch—new love
ablaze!

Mary E Gomer
DEAR MOTHER
Dear Lord up above I'm so thankful
for today
Because you gave your only
begotten son on Calvary's Tree
So that there could be my mother and
me.

Through growing up, you tried to shelter my pain
You never let disappointment show any gain,
You shared your wisdom and taught me in times of trouble love, joy and peace.

You've always been there for me, and today Dear Mother
I share that walk you took with me
For you see, I'm a mother as it was meant to be.

Though we are miles apart, I have a love song within my heart
That brings us together though we are apart.

I'm so thankful to you Dear Jesus,
For she's everything you meant her to be
She is truly a miracle to me.

For Mother's Day is everyday, but today is truly your day
May all your dreams come true whether they be big or small
And remember you are precious to us all.

Lucille Green
LOVE
Love is . . .
A mind's impression
An expression
A face
A place
A gentle touch
That means so much
Arms to hold you
Whispers to console you
A sigh
To cry
Caring
Sharing
Bending
Mending . . .
Hearts
That never part
Kissing you
Missing you
Exploring together
Growing together

Talar Berejiklian
PAM THE PIG
In the corner of the world, there lived Pam the Pig.
Years would pass by, but she would never get big!
All her friends got big, juicy and plump.
They would run, hop, skip, and jump.
Pam couldn't do all this, she was not big;
She was so tiny, so afraid that she hid
Away from her friends, her pals, and the kids.
"Why don't I ever grow? Why? Why?
I guess I'll never grow big!" she said with a sigh.
One day Dr. Hoggy came along,
And told Pam the Pig what was wrong.
"You always eat junk food, that's why you don't grow.
Eat healthy foods, they're good, I very well know."
So, Pam the Pig, taking Dr. Hoggy's advice,
Started eating corn, poultry, apples, and rice,
Milk, potatoes, squash and meats,
Plus carrots, celery, pumpkin, and beets.
Pam started to grow and grow big,
And finally was considered a real pig!
So those people who are small and don't eat,
Take Dr. Hoggy's advice, and eat a healthy treat!

Claudia Meyer
SAYING GOODBYE
A single tear
rolls down my cheek
A rose from you
grows old and weak

This tear is a love
that went by too fast
A love that was
never meant to last

This rose is a memory
of when nothing else mattered
The memory of a love
that was quickly shattered

Because it wasn't worth
that one last try
It was never this hard
to say goodbye

Veronica Rzepinski
A TIME THAT USED TO BE

To my husband John, with thanks and appreciation for all of his support and encouragement.

Looking out across the lands,
The forests and the sea
Makes my heart cry out deep down inside
For a time that used to be.
Where has all the beauty gone
That at one time did abound?
The wildflowers and majestic trees;
Soon none will be found.

I think of all the creatures
Who'll soon have no where to roam
For all the land has been taken from them
They have no place to call home.
A tear runs down my cheek
As I long for days of long ago
Before man, and time, and progress
Changed the landscape so.
Now when I look around me
As far as the eye can see
My heart is saddened and it cries out
For a time that used to be.

James Church Collier
HIS MISTRESS
She said goodbye,
but it was different.
He came to know her
well enough
To tell when something was,
well, different.

Not really his mistress,
but frequent visits
Had made that feeling.

She always, when she left,
touched and kissed him a little
and he kissed her,
the best he could, in turn.

But this time, she made a funny noise
and hugged him harder,
And her cheeks tasted like the ocean
where the three of them had
run.

Jill Roach
CHILDHOOD WINTERS
A white sheet
not quite covering
the lot of green.
I look out
hoping to see more snow
falling from above.
I see no snow,
but I slip away
into childhood winters
at my grandmother's house.
I slide down the steepest hill,
making snow balls to waste on the dog.
Just getting cold so I could enter the house
knowing there would be
the warmth of my four favorite things.
The warmth of her hands as she placed
them on my cheeks;
the warmth of the cocoa and the fire
that she has especially prepared.
And best of all, the warmth in her heart
shining through.
I sit now and watch the snow get deeper,
and think of my childhood winters.

Harriett Huddle
THIS OLD HOUSE
There was a house on route 224
I remember it now as it was before.
There were four rooms, with kitchen out back
Some people would call it, only a shack.

It was in November of year twenty-nine
It burned to the ground in almost no time.
My Father was sleeping when it caught on fire
All was lost, our condition was dire.

My grandmother lived across the dirt road
And it was there, we made our abode.
The people in town, rallied around
Replacing some things, that never were found.

Things after that, were never the same
Our fortune was lost in that awful flame.
I see it again at the top of the hill
A little old home in memory still.

Now it's been told, I will put it away.
There is no advantage in letting it stay.
I've had much good fortune since that time.
And now I continue the life that is mine.

Edna Joblon
DAYS OF CAPE COD
In remembrance of the days of yore.
As I watch in deep reverie as waves lash against the shore.
I envision the lighthouses still standing as relics of the past.
With so much flux, it's reassuring that some things last.
There are many who copy the quaintness of the Cape Cod home.
But where is the expanse of meadow and the space to roam.
Scenic beauty of the coastline can't be emulated or captured.
Artists with palette in hand gaze at the panorama and are so enraptured.
Walking through the warm silvery sand with the brilliant hue of sky overhead.
The many colorful beach umbrellas and blankets outspread.
Delicious aroma of food permeates from the picnic lunch,
And the amiability of friends and family, gather in a group to munch.
This is the remembrance of days of yore.
As in deep reflection, I watch as waves lash against the shore.

Bill Graydon

Bill Graydon
THE SUN
I feel as if I were at a funeral when I watch the sun set.
I wonder aimlessly if the sun will ever shine again
The sun, like people, must become aggravated
Imagine if the sun refused to shine
"What right would the sun have to refuse to shine"
we would say
The sun is always so full of brightness, even when under the blanket of a cloud.
If only more people could be like the sun.
So remember—the next time you see the sun, give it a smile—it may be the last time you see.

Janet Lynne McKeehan
SUICIDE
Nothing seemed to be the same,
And nothing ever eased her pain.

This tormented Soul lived only to die,
Either by pills or a knife.

Never ending tears dripped down her face,
As she sees life as endless days.

Days in which she dealt,
By crying for fear of herself

At times she was afraid to live afraid to die,
So in this world she continued to lie.

With an ache and pain in her heart,
She lived in a world she never felt apart.

As she withdrew from the world
no one noticed they just went on,

She finally considered death cause all she did was live a life that seemed meaninglessly long.

Life is what she now feared,
As she released her last tear.
Finally alone and suffering, she appeals to death.
Calling its name as she breathes her last breath.

And when this Soul took her last breath,
She finally knew the meaning of death.

Now dead and alone she lies on the floor,
That's how her Parents find her when they walk through the door.

Teresa Cummins
FLUFFY LAMBS AND TEDDY BEARS
I want a world surrounded by fluffy lambs and teddy bears,
Full of all the wonderful things that a mother and her daughter shares.
A lifetime filled with the softness of pastel pinks and blues.
Have all my days musically charmed by a baby's gurgles and goos.
I want to be there when our own little person learns how to walk.
Will her first word be "Mommy" or "Daddy" when she learns how to talk?
Oh, what a beautiful sight to see;
Our own little girl, made of just you and me!

Dora V Hall
ALONE
One day as I was walking
And talking to myself.
I looked around and suddenly,
I knew there was Someone else!
The trees were bending slightly.
The grass was tall and green.
The birds were constantly singing,
And the sky was ever serene.
As I looked and saw the beauty,
Of God's wonderful earth;
I knew He lived in everything
And I knew what everything was worth.
Mother Nature—Is really living!
It is not dead at all!
Through Nature we find some answers,
Of God's eternal call.

R Margaret Cardenas
NO ANGELS YOU HEAR
'Twas early, I know, I awaken from sleep.
Something inside of my heart did creep.
The town is still sleeping as I close my door
And walk down the street, to where, I'm not sure.
As I look toward heaven and the beautiful sky,
One star is so bright, though morning is nigh.

The inns are all filled with those coming to pay
Taxes to Caesar, they were merry and gay.
But back of one inn there's a heavenly glow,
I wander that way, my steps soft and slow.
I pass by some shepherds, in soft tones they speak
Of a wonderful sight, of the babe they did seek.

I now hear the voice as a young mother sings
To her babe in a manger, of a heavenly king.
I know it is hallowed, the place in the stable
Where the sleeping child lays with a manger as cradle.
I, too, kneel down, a small gift I bring
To accept him this day as my savior and king.

My steps I retrace to my own little boy
Asleep in his bed, such a wonderful joy.
He's happy and smiling as he awakes for the day.
I know I must teach him, at work and at play,
That this wee little stranger so precious and dear
Will come to your heart, though no angels you hear.

Christine Field
FRIENDSHIP
Friendship is a tender thing
A heart felt thanks sparkling like a diamond ring
A tender moment friends will share
A telephone call saying they care

In times of sadness a feeling of comfort
Those special times in life when we celebrate
A birthday, a graduation or a first date
Friends are special in their own way

A dinner shared, a simple prayer
A tender smile and embracing hugs
Friends are people with whom you feel loved.

C Weikle
AGONY
You're not in love
You should be
Wish it was
Still you and me

Unlocked your cage
You flew free
Wish you would
Fly back to me

Too much in love
I'd like to be
Not much in love
It's agony

Tide goes out
Turns back again
I'd treasure now
What I didn't then

So much in love
But not with me
Wish we were
Wish you could be
Unanswered love is agony

Winnie C Yee
THE WALL
Tall and gray,
So difficult to see over,
Constantly I try to climb it,
Each time I fall.
I try to break through it,
But I get hurt.
What is on the other side?
I wondered so often.
Then I remembered something:
A man once told me
"Don't ever say you can't
Say you can
Then if you try once, try again
The second time, you are bound to win."
Now, here I am
On the other side of the wall.

Bryan C Bailey
LOOK BEFORE YOU CROSS
The driver of the car
clenched his teeth in a skeletal grin—and squealed.
Fifty-three miles per hour.
The pedestrian's eyes were alive with comical surprise.
He didn't bounce.
The automobile's cartoon face opened its chrome grill teeth and swallowed its road kill—whole.

Shoes are a tap tap tappin'
arms are a wrap wrap wrappin'
'round the radiator fan once more.

"Yahoo!" said the man behind the wheel.
The car accelerates
and
the exhaust is a bit darker now.

Norma L Vancil
ROSE OF BY GONE DAYS

To the memory of my mother Jennie Matilda

The roses still bloom on the leaning porch of the old homestead.
Gone are the busy steps of those who cared and tended them.

An errant breeze, catches their sweet fragrance.
To blend into the dreams of a new era.

Lisa-Marie Agostini
REMEMBER WHEN
Remember when it was just you and me
Remember when our love was free
Remember how we used to fight
An hour later it would be alright

Remember when we used to dance
Remember when we weren't afraid to take a chance
Remember when we used to dream
Thinking we would always be a winning team

Remember when we used to walk
Remember when we used to talk
Remember when we said good-bye
And how you didn't even cry

T Smith
EXPLANATION OF AN OBSESSION
A feeling of longing comes over me,
I see you and I want to see more.
A feeling of sadness comes over me,
because the truth is what I must endure.
You don't know about me and darkest corners of my mind, where I hold you, touch you, I possess your heart and our souls combine.

I know that it's wrong, I know that it's sick but the thoughts keep slipping back in.
The cold lonely realities struggle with tempting reveries and soon the daydream wins.

Yes, you might call me a hapless fool that I should fall so deeply for that which I've yet to know.
But feelings that have transcended time say, it is to you, my heart, I must bestow.

So I get lost in the fantasy, where I can let my love for you roar wildly like a storm.
And let it serve as a reminder of the true love we knew long before.
In this world, I have the power to free your heart from burdens and make your wise eyes smile.
We share an eternal space in time, free in our spiritual love, as if the world were uplifted from all its trials.

Hilary Daly
BLACK IMAGE
I am
black,
but not in pigment.
An image,
but not a picture.
Just
a fleeting shadow;
the figment of
your imagination.
I am
your
negative counterpart.

Alison Rene Pormann
BETRAYAL
I believed your words
I believed they were true.
I believed your words
Your words made me a fool.
I believed your words
I believed in your lies.
Now your words have become
The tears of my eyes.

Doris J Reynolds
MAGIC LOVE
Out of the old, from
the tropics . . .
and orient, romance has
spun . . . A
Shangrila:
A special night for two,
anywhere in the world of
imagination; a courtyard
of an Arabian Kingdom,
with a glow of yellow
lanterns; beneath a breezy
wind of soft implicit music.

William L Obermiller
SYMPHONY IN THE YARD
The whippoorwill sits at the window and sings
About life and its beauty and other such things.
The flowers and trees dance gracefully by
Enjoying the music, sonnets and sighs.
The whippoorwill sits at the window and sings
About life and its beauty and other such things.

The musician is joined by some fine feathered friends
The solo duet, the quartet began.
The flowers and trees dance melodically by
Fine feathered friends, musicians who fly
The whippoorwill sits at the window and sings

About life and its beauty and other such things.

The woodland composers take to their flight
The concert is over, but only for night
Tomorrow will bring more sonnets and hymns
Open your hearts and listen to them.
The whippoorwill sits at the window and sings
About life and its beauty and other such things

Debra Sue Heidt
THE EMPTY HOUSE
Once this house was filled with laughing
Life was here and the family unit was strong,
Now the rooms are full of quiet
For the joy and life are gone.

Once the light flowed form the window
Like a beacon in the night,
The light that enticed and offered warmth
For this house was strong and tight.

Filled with love up to the rafters
Underneath no shifting sand,
On the firmest of foundation
Love of nature and of man.

Now this house is cold and empty
Life and joy have gone away,
Full of dust and ghostly memories
Cobwebs fill the rooms today.

Karen L Kilgore
PERCEPTIONS
There are endless thoughts in my mind,
Constant questions with no answers.
I attempt, but cannot understand.
Yet, I know somewhere, someone has the key.

To voice these thoughts within me,
Would surely have me judged insane.
I believe, sense I am not alone,
Who has the release to my inner pain?

Anger and frustration often overcome me,
Am I an outcast from the realm of normalcy?
Against my will I know of things to be,
Who can I tell, who would believe?

I feel the thoughts and feelings of others,
My mind reaches out, no one reaches back.
I must find a kindred soul, please tell,
Do you know, are you, the keeper of the key.

Lyn Bartolini
SEASONS OF LIFE
Everyone's life has four seasons.
Each season has a special reason.
From one season to another we take stock
To see what's working in our life and what's not.

Springtime brings a life fresh and new.
There is so much we must learn to do.
We must prepare for a journey uniquely our own.
A journey that we needn't travel alone.

Summer is the season when we grow
And our full potential we begin to know.
We pursue dreams hitched to distant stars
And review the journey traveled thus far.

Autumn is the end of the seasons we grow
And our life's journey begins to slow.
We reap the rewards of lessons we've learned
And measure the degree of success we've earned.

Winter is the season that comes last
The time when we fondly remember the past.
In peace and serenity we can now rest
Because we have given life our very best.

Zahid Kamran

Zahid Kamran
A DREAM IN A SNOWFALL
Dream,
In which a hungry lion
walks the Lanes of Human Reality.

A dream,
where moon has a milky shine;
where star's shine blinds frigid Images
(alive once),
begging to the naked humanity
(those with lightless eyes and frozen ears),
FOR HELP . . .

These Images . . .
the Images of god,
the one who lives in the heart and soul;
and the helplessness
of the Ones
who were and are powerful
and delivering to no One who asks
FOR HELP . . .

These ready hearts and empty souls;
wandering the Jungle of Stilled Prophecies,
thundering to conquer the flesh . . .
and then let it burn till the end;
an end which becomes an end to a dream . . .

Yet alive and moving,
though sightless,
soundless,
walking the Lanes of Human Reality,
there, sometimes,
and is,
and will be,
the Ones,
begging
FOR HELP.

Meryl J Prager
FAME
My mental nourishment
I feed on thee
Devouring your soul
eating your dreams and fantasies.
Then my freeze frame collection
spreads through me
Encrusting a cloak of ideals
Guided by the light of a
Candle that once flickered
in you
Now burns in me.

Gary F Van Leeuwen
UNTITLED
Out from the blue mist
Came an interesting chap.

He also could rap!

Going outside bounds
And sustaining ethics—

He searched for a bride
To fulfill his deepest desire.

Away from trouble,
Freeing his mind,
He gave himself unto others;
Not even mentioning his name . . .

Michelle Manalili
HIDDEN LOVE
I'm all alone
wishing on stars,
If only you had known
how much I loved you.

Now that you've gone
my days are so blue.
For me the sun shall
never shine.

I remember those nights
when we would sit and talk
Or the time we spent flying our kites,
even when we took those
summer walks.

I hope someday
that you will come back
Because I need to say
so many things that were never told.

But as the seasons change
and life goes on
my love for you
will still be strong.

Yvette L Nugent
REALISM
People are barely living
It's a thin line between sanity and insanity
No one has a mind of their own
They don't use the common sense they're born with
You have to believe in the Creator
stay strong
Be positive
Patient
And try to laugh as much as possible

Winifred Mingle
TO MY DAUGHTERS WITH LOVE
Almost Anytime
I can make my own luck if I try.
I just hang onto me
smile some, then sigh,
Lean back and relax,
Dream a little,
Consider the facts.
. . drift off for a nap . .
This may not be the best of times.
I have no mines, mostly dimes
but lots of sense.
That's recompense
for the years I've lived.
I have knowledge and feelings
that are mine.
That's fine for
I can make my own luck
almost anytime.

Frances L Polino
THIEF
He entered there on tips of toes
with gloved hands and masked face
His movement graceful in the dark
no stranger was he to this place.

Stealing softly into her chamber
to face a gentle cry of please
wasting no time he then proceeded
to execute the task with ease.

No words exchanged but only glances
not look too long to recognize
and yet he would not compromise.

I only took a moment then
to win the sweetest treasure
the taking it was easy
she gave as if with pleasure.

As swiftly as he entered there
then quicker still he fled
behind a lifeless body
although she was not dead

The crime that night committed
was destined from the start
yes she had lost a precious gem
for he had stolen her heart.

Lathan H Frayser
EXPAND
Greet the sun or clouds without dismay,
Life need not be boring everyday,
There're friends to see . . . work to do . . . books to read . . . things to say . . .
And on top of all that . . . don't forget to pray.

Frances A Walraven
THE BEGGAR
"Dear Lord," I prayed, "please can it be
That one day I might truly see
An angel come to me below;
And, if this happens, will I know?"

He did not answer me, I thought.
Perhaps I knew not what I sought.
But then a knock upon my door
Announced a beggar, cold and poor.

I gave him warmth and food to eat.
He thanked me, smiled, then left replete.
I watched him as he walked away,
And heard a voice that seemed to say:

"I answered your prayer, do not forget.
You've seen your angel, the beggar you met.
But because of the love that I did see,
You really were attending Me."

Virgie L Whitlock
LIFT OFF! ON EARTH, TOUCH DOWN! IN HEAVEN!

To my Grandsons Scott, Todd, Matthew and Anthony and To the families of the Challenger

They came out the door of NASA,
heading for the Launching Pad,
People cheered and whistled, no thoughts of being sad,
Six astronauts looked, grinned, and gave a wave of their hand,
the seventh one did not wave goodbye, only her smile, as they walked to the van!

As friends, families and our Nation

watched, that cold January morn,
Keeping all eyes on the Challenger,
sitting close to the ocean it adorned,
Then the familiar voice, "We have
lift off!" and the cheers filled the air,
At the blink of an eye the explosion
came! In shock we could only stare.

From that point our minds went,
beyond that billowing cloud so
white,
The Challenger still moving on, now
peaceful, calm and quiet,
We felt their Spirits laughing, happy,
as they entered this Beautiful Place,
Each one saw ahead, what we all
strive to see, and joy showed on their
face!

In my mind, I could almost see their
smiles, as they came in for the
landing,
All the many people waving hands
and in proud ovation standing,
And hear the pilot's voice strong,
when he spoke for all Seven,
"NASA, we have Touch Down . . .
Pause . . . In Heaven!".

Sonja Foster

IF I CAN CLOSE MY EYES

This poem was dedicated to someone who doesn't know me. But I personally know them, but I'm not so sure anymore.—

If I can close my eyes,
Forever they'll stay shut,
Nothing I see can harm me more,
Then I've already been deeply cut.
If I can close my heart,
Happily I'll do that forever,
But like a broken latch or chest,
A broken heart won't close together.
It's two beats away, from a heart
ache,
only, one beat away, from a heart
break.
To a life dream that had to end,
without the flame to start,
Rest my eyes oh Lord, oh my
bleeding heart.

Carol Mann

FROM THE HEART OF A NURSE

To my mother who taught me to care.

Dear Patient,
If I could wave a magic wand
and wipe away the pain
Or give a tiny magic pill to make you
smile again

If I could command great power to
rule
. . . against the law would be
the pain, the tears, the fear I see
as I take care of you . . .

Alas . . .

But my hands will help, my tears I'll
gladly share
my strength I'll give as best I can
and maybe with care, I can help you
up again
or help you see the way . . .

I wouldn't be here were not for
that . . .
and I will help you pray
that all we are and hope to be
our health will see us through
I've only one life to live, I'll share it
here
with you.

Alicia Brander

MIRACLE OF LIFE

To my granddaughter Brandi you're the miracle in my life; love grandma Pittman

The miracle of life is a precious
thing:
Because it brings forth a little human
being:
The miracle of life is such a joy:
Because it brings forth a little girl or
boy:
The miracle of life is a beautiful time:
Because it brings forth a little mind:
The miracle of life is so precious to
you:
Because it only comes from you
know who:
The miracle of life is something
we'll never regret:
Because it brings forth a child don't
forget:
The miracle of life is a gift to us:
Because it comes from your Lord
Jesus:

Sandra L Denton

THE SUN RISES IN THE EARLY MORNING SKIES

To all the people I love.

The sun rises in the early morning
skies
The last of the evening flickers then
dies;
The memories have faded away
and the sun sets at the end of the day.

Where does life end for one so old?
Who has watched the world turn
bitter and cold?
Who has suffered through such pain
and strife?
I don't understand the meaning of
life.

Allen Van Duyne Sr

IF I KNEW MY FUTURE LIKE I KNOW MY PAST

If I knew my future,
like I know my past:
I'd ask god's forgiveness,
and kneel down at last.

How often I sin,
Know I've done wrong;
I could have tried,
but I drifted along.

The lights have gone dim,
They're closing again;
I'll drift along,
Still seeking a friend.

If I knew my future,
like I know my past;
I'd ask god's forgiveness,
and kneel down at last.

Gregory Joseph Pickard

I STAND IN A FIELD

I stand in a field
surrounded by green;
my age and my beauty
by all to be seen.

In two world wars,
much death did I see.
I was shot and was burnt,
but they could not kill me.

For through my limbs
there courses such a power.
If man had this gift,
for sure it would sour.

How ignorant is mankind.
Are they blind? Can't they see?
I am the overlooked historian.
Yes, I am a tree.

Matt S Dunne III

CREATION

Creation.
Building up
and down.
Needs
Such simple needs.
Nails and hammers,
wood and trees.
Building:
Happiness,
Pleasure,
Pride.
Creation.

K Ledlon

THE HAWK

To Kev, for the encouragement and the criticism.

Feathers rippling,
Talons rigid with anticipation
Eyes, cold and deadly—
On target.

Sheer grace!
Sheer power!
Sheer majesty!
The hawk—nature's most prided
creation.
In he comes,
For the KILL.

Evern Etheridge Garland

Evern Etheridge Garland

THE STRANGER

To Pink my beloved husband, my dear children Lamonte and Almeida. To my mother Iola who constantly encourages me.

I met this stranger along the way.
He seemed sad as we sat and chatted
near the bay.
He said life is not easy and full of
grief but there is a secret to all of this.

He said your strength comes from
God above and not from man.
He is the Father that will not let you
be bothered with grief and sorrow.
He will protect you as only he can
for you are his child and with this he
smiled.
He said ask Thee to take away from
your heart the fears of today and
tomorrow. If only you make thee a
part of your life nothing can hurt you
today or at all. For every effort that
you make to help yourself Thou will
give you twice as much help.

I fell asleep after a long conversation, awakened by a roar coming
from the bay.
I looked around for the beautiful
stranger, but to my dismay he was
not there. But what he said is still in
my heart that God is All Mighty and
I'm never alone for Thou will protect
me all the days long.

Lee Du Coing G

LATE SUMMER DAY

A hot late summer's lazy day,
The strong sweet smell of new mown
hay,
A bumble bee's incessant drone.
A light breeze with its constant
moan.

Fish jump in nearby cooling creek,
And chipmunks from the bushes
peek.
A falling leaf I sometimes hear,
Now shows that summer's end is
near.

How sweet these last few summer
days,
Enchanting in their lovely ways.
I wish that I could keep forever,
The beauty of this day together.

Sharon S Meaney

THE ROCK

This poem is dedicated to my husband, Steve, who has always been my rock and my foundation.

I sat on a rock the other day
and felt the wind in my face.
The rock suddenly spoke to me
As I felt its power embrace.

It had an urgent message to give.
One, I knew I should heed.
"Love this great land of yours,
Or watch her slowly bleed."

Oh, I wanted to tell this rock
How humble it made me feel.
But I couldn't even speak,
Its warning seemed so real.

And as I listened to that voice,
Its soul cried out a plea.
"Help save our Mother Earth,
Or seal your own destiny."

Its spirit touched my heart that day.
I knew I'd take a stand.
For, only by uniting in peace
Can we hope to save our land.

Vellmer Gulley

SEE LIFE AS YOU WISH IT TO BE

To the family of my deceased husband. The Gulleys in Mobile, Alabama. & Tomasvill

I see my friend. He is admiring me in everything I do.
We are very interested in each other and just a little tip. We are building a wonderful relationship. He is a person that has qualities that are very fine. He is so gentle and kind. We are very happy. I see us even preparing our meals. He is monitoring me. Teaching and guiding me in all things. Things I had and have forgot. We read and study books on important subjects together. I like to write, He Advises me to write short

lectures, poems, or beautiful verses as he sees me write from time to time. That may be of help to some one I see us happily walking together. Sometimes we go for a ride. Drive out in the country on Sundays we go to church. I see us getting to the table enjoying a meal. I see us very happy entertaining guests. We are both so close, friends relations and acquaintances enjoy talking with us because we are never cross before guests. We always agree on one accord.
So as one knows that we have to put our trust in the good Lord. All gladness no sadness.

William J Holmes
NO CANDLE LIGHT FOR ME

Dedicated to sight: the majestic mountains and the starry skies.

'Tis dark ahead, 'tis very dark,
And darkness o'er the lea.
'Tis dark indeed where I embark—
No candle light for me.

In what direction lie those shores
Where night I'll never see?
And where's the Captain's boat and oars—
No candle light for me.

And pangs of pain like storms rage
In dark Gethsemane,
To break my earthly anchorage—
No candle light for me.

Now darkly drifting outward bound
I make my final plea;
My life's events sink all around—
No candle light for me.

Behold.! Behold.! a strange new Light
Eternal Verity.
The new Horizon beams so bright—
The Lights of Lights for me.

Cynthia Jackson
OUR SAVIOR
The good Lord is great
And believe me, He never makes mistakes
He will comfort you at all times when you
Pray to him
Jesus Christ is virtually our true savior within
And His love for us never ends
Father God, you are the one with all the
Power
Father, I ask you humbly to forgive me for
All my sins, and to please give me strength, and knowledge
to abide in your way
Lord almighty Jehovah, I'll always love thee as long, as I shall live, just the thought of you, knowing who you are
Enriches my life to live on this earth,
God you are the sweetest one of all people, and never hurt
I understand you want me to have a sweet sensation on hoping,
"subsequently, Father you are the one with all the power"

Rebekah Houglum
AT THIS TIME

To the one who inspired me and to my family.

My life is in turmoil, and yet it is not!
I cry; I don't know why.
I know that God is close to me, but am I close to him?
So many things have I to say, yet unable to utter
a word to the man I love in so many ways.
My heart, I feel, is breaking in several pieces,
will even God be able to mend it?
Why am I this way, why so sad?
I cannot answer, least not right away!
Am I being childish or am I just a woman
who's trying to find herself and before couldn't?
So many things have changed-over the last five years,
the woman I now am is not the girl that once was.
I am sure it's for the better, this change in me, and
to have the encouragement that you've given me.
The strength you've brought-the warmth I received.
God knew I needed someone like you in my life "at this time".
I just pray that "at this time" may be for ever!!

Robert G Warring

Robert G Warring
TEARDROPS IN THE WIND

To Quentin & Christopher—For the meaning in the words.

I hear the echoes of the sovereign dead,
How they rule the night, so quietly,
I remember when they roamed freely,
Disembodied memories, calling back to yesterday . . .

I would that they were truly free,
That my only company, would speak again
And in the music of the wind,
To the echoes that they send, we would dance . . .

Yet as they come, with tales of old,
I pull into my eyes of gold,
And turn back to look, again,
Thru someone else's eyes, what then . . .

Becomes of the ghosts of memories,
Of some other child in me?
All my souls go dancing,
Teardrops in the wind . . .

Misty Eve Parker
CRAYON IN MY HAND
I was an artist as a child
with a crayon in my hand
Now I see I'm all grown up
my painting's on the stand
Never thought I could paint
the sky to look so cold
Painting a love story that
would never unfold.
Every stroke would be a word
to explain things I don't understand
But I could still tell you I
love you with a crayon in my hand.
Painting every feeling that
ever caused a rush
Paint kissing the canvas
love pouring from my brush
I could always do a painting
and set it on a stand
But just as easily say I
love you, with a crayon
in my hand.

Nekita Washington
I SAW YOU

This poem is dedicated to my mother, and to Madonna who inspired me to write

Now I know what your life is like.
Staying out till all times of night.
Don't care what your life is like.
Just want to party till you see the light.

I can still recall the day we met.
When your parents put you out,
but oh how quickly we forget.
That I was there to ease your doubts.

Brooksie Jené Corbin
MY PROFOUND AWAKENING
In the pre-dawn hours, when all is still,
And the earth lies wrapped against the chill;
When the only sound, is but a sigh,
Then my heart awakens, for inspiration is nigh!

This April morn, sweet-scented as frankincense,
And filled with the promise of everlasting existence,
Instills within me, such immense adoration,
Of life, and love, and God's inspiration!

I feel emotionally, and spiritually reborn;
A regeneration of life, that is mine to adorn.
Alive, and desiring to be definitely heard,
That I'm most grateful to God, in both deed and word!

So, praise be to God, for His infinite care;
For His patience and loving kindness are always there;
And His wisdom in all things; His solicitude,
For one so unworthy, and filled with ineptitude!

Yes, I am blessed by His grandeur, so divine,
And twice blessed, by His Presence, for He is mine!
His graciousness and love, so genuinely unbounded,
That has left me most truly, and sweetly astounded!

Unparalleled in mercy, has He been to me,
So steadfast and understanding, with tolerance free;
With unending patience and faithful trust,
He's given me a life of peace, so I must;

Bestow upon Him, all that's mine to convey,
And entrust unto Him, everything, everlastingly!
Oh Lord, "Here's my all, and Yours for the taking!"
I'm so fortunate a woman, since my Profound Awakening!

Lucinda Merritt
LOVE
The night of my dreams has come at last.
We sit beneath the silver moon.
I wondered, thinking of the past,
Why did life change so soon?

We were young lovers then,
And love was in our hearts.
We were so happy when
We were hit by Cupid's darts.

We grew up so very quick,
And never failed each other.
And then, one day, he fell so sick;
I was a widowed mother,

I look into his loving eyes,
We're together once more.
I see the man who heard my cries
In the life before.

Denise L McLeod
SARAH
Close by the window he paused to stand,
As he took his class ring from his hand.
All who were watching could not speak,
As a single tear ran down his cheek.

Memories of moments, when they had fun,
As they laughed together beneath the sun.
Remembering only he had to be free.
But now he had hurt her, he could see.

Her deep brown eyes had now grown cold.
He could not have her any longer
In his arms to hold.
He whispered, "I love you" as he bent near,
The words so soft no one could hear.

On her finger he placed his ring,
Hoping forgiveness it would bring.
He said, "Good-bye" and gave her a kiss,
For that special girl he surely would miss.

The door was closed
His head hung low,
As they carried her casket
Across the snow.

Shannon Santanocito
PLEASE TELL ME
Only one soul yet so little time.
They all tell me my love for you is a crime.
They all tell me your love for me is all of a lie.

For so long I've turned my head to all that they have said,
But I don't know if I can anymore.
So,
Please tell me.

I have only one soul and so little time.
Is my love for you a crime?
Is your love for me a lie?
One day I may not turn my head anymore.
So,
Please tell me.

Frances P Brown
WORDS OF WISDOM
Oh youth, stop for a minute,
And listen to one quite old.
If you can hear, heed my words;
I shall speak to you quite bold.

I know a lot more about youth
Than you know about being old.
Now listen closely to my advice,
And do what you are told.

Work for the things you want from life,
Nothing ever comes free.
Be honest with others as well as yourself,
Take this advice from me.

Through work and effort be an achiever,
Never giving up on a task.
Be careful not to be a deceiver,
For his success doesn't last.

There is never an easy way
To be a success today.
So remember my words, heed what I say,
Combine work, wisdom, and pray!

Trish Shaw
CONTENT TO BE
I look at you
And see you smile
at me,
And I know
that you love me
And I am
Content to be.

Esther Hance

Esther Hance
POETIC FRIENDSHIP
Awake, Awake the tuneful verse,
And strike the joyful strings.
We'll pour the mellow notes along,
And raise a glad'dling song.

Tis not the cold & formal drawl,
That makes the inward flame.
But tis the verse that glows like fire,
The song that feeling hearts desire,
A music worth its name.

'Tis here that music dwells,
In friendship's sweet abode.
'Tis here that notes concordant sound,
'Tis here that harmony is found,
Like that which dwells with God.

Tony P Minimi
MAN'S WILL
Oh how times have changed,
But the sky is still blue.

Respect as i knew it—rarely emerges,
But the trees have their summer green.

Punctuality, reliability—good attendance all but gone,
But the wind blows—hot—sometimes cool.

People with talent—don't use it,
The lakes and rivers still have their water.

Family life—keep togetherness—not much anymore,
The birds still migrate to and fro to start anew.

The music has changed—musical tones were of gaiety—happiness—smooth—soothing to listen to.

The world keeps changing, for better—for worse,
But nature still manages to do God's wonders.

Donna M Duffy
PARTING IS NOT EASY
It's time to change, I see and feel it coming
It's time to cut the cord and climb out of the cradle,
You can't always be there to wipe the tears from my eyes
As much as I still want and need you to.
I have to go out and live my own life,
Experience life for the first time,
Your gentle shove is stronger than you think.
You're holding one hand loosely, and the other so tightly!
I know you want me to stay, yet I feel you want me to leave.
One beat of my heart tells me to stay,
But the other is so much stronger and it's saying to leave!
I know I have to go my own way,
Parting is not easy.
One day I will be experiencing the very same feeling,
Only I'll be standing in the doorway
Giving that gentle shove.

And I'll have to let go once again,
Parting is not easy.

Robert J Walker
HE KNOWS WHAT IT MEANS
He knows what it means to live in a ghetto, for he was born in a stable with the cows, sheep and chickens.

He knows what it means to be cold, for he was wrapped in swaddling clothes and laid in a manger; for there was no room for him in the inn.

He knows what it means to be uneducated, for he never went to school.

He knows what it means to be without money, for he was thankful when a poor widow gave him two pennies.

He knows what it means to be poor and unemployed, for there were many days when there was no work to be done in his father's carpenter shop.

He knows what it means to be hungry, for he went forty days and forty nights without any food.

He knows what it means to have no transportation, for he had to borrow a donkey to get to town.

He knows what it means to have no place to stay, for he said himself, "The foxes have holes, and the birds of the air have nest; but the Son of man hath not where to lay his head" (Matt. 8:20). He even had to borrow a room to eat his last supper.

He knows what it means to be without clothes, for the only clothing he had was what he wore.

He knows what it means to lose a loved one, for he wept when his friend Lazarus died.

Most importantly; He knows what it means to die, for he gave his life for us all . . .

Jeffrey Alan Buschek
PHOENIX
Mighty Metallic Majesty
Supremely reigns alone
Clutching, snatching; iron claws scratching
His limestone bed-like throne

Calmly awaiting impeachment
Soaring in downward gyre
(viewing, knowing; no fear showing)
Above the hard cold pyre

With piercing force he raids the air
Towards the burning lair
Screeching, sighing; swiftly dying
Devoured by the fire

Yet from the ashes one
More beautiful than he
Stronger, younger; full of hunger
That death occurred in me

Paul E Compton
THE MIRROR
Poetry is the mirror of many things,
Making you cry, making you sing.
It is the mirror of the sea,
The happiness of being free.

Poetry is the mirror of life,
Having Children and a loving Wife.
It is the mirror of the heart,
The essence of a painters art.

Poetry is the mirror of love,
For all creatures below and above.
It is the mirror of things unseen,
A reflection of dreams yet un-dreamed.

Leonard Long
HOME
It's a place one won't appreciate,
Until he starts to roam.
That little piece of Heaven,
That's commonly called one's home.

One never seems to realize,
Until it's left behind,
That all the things you really want,
Were surely there to find.

One wants to leave so very soon,
To satisfy his whim,
Never stopping to look a second time,
To see what's there for him.

These are the ones that always brag,
When you have a friendly chat,
That they can always find a home,
"Where e'er they hang their hat."

But their story seems to change,
When they find themselves alone,
For they find their thoughts returning,
To those grand old times at home.

Tracy Robinson Russell
MEMORIES
Memories . . .
Coloring everchanging pictures
Of things I want to remember
And of things I want to forget.
Always locked inside my head
Like a prisoner serving a life sentence.
Thousands of them,
Always returning to haunt me.
I wish some would leave.
They feel like a madness
Swarming, eating away at my being.
Others float soft like a stream,
Bringing smiles and tears
Some bring tears of joy,
Others are sad and deep
But whatever they bring
They keep turning up
And I float to the past
On a river
. . . of memories.

Norma Buckeridge
THE SCARECROW
Is that a face with mad grimace
Or just a void, an empty space
Between the weatherbeaten hat
And pivot neck from which he swings
Unmindful of the fear he brings?
But when I walk right up I see
A shapeless, spineless enemy,

Who flays the night with passive strength
And makes the shadows run and hide
With the approach of eventide.
Along the pathways of my mind,
A thousand scarecrows I can find
Grotesquely lurking, all intent
On heartbreak disillusionment.

Vicki Fowler
LOVE IS . . .
LOVE is a rainbow
drifting towards the sea,
LOVE is a mountain
high above the trees,
LOVE is how it feels
when I'm alone with you,
LOVE is the sky
blue and extremely true.
LOVE is where I am
when you are very near,
LOVE is a glass
so transparent and clear,
LOVE is a swan
floating on the lake,
LOVE is a book
read when I am awake.

Mike Crabtree
THE COST OF HOLOCAUST
It's hard to deal with what I feel
of what was lost at Holocaust.
I reel, at what was really real
The awesome cost of veins that frost.

The manic satanic panic
The ghostly gruesome graves
The countless bloody tales of woe
The shock, the numbness, no where
to go.

Humans—being beastly bastards
Groping, I grasp in disbelief
A gnawing painful emptiness
Of this loveless thief of endless grief.

It's hard to eat or think or plan
What faith now can I have in man.
My weary heart lays waste,
unwilling
It's chilling—the killing and killing
and killing . . .

Mitch E Mozart
THERE'S A REASON

This poem is dedicated to my mother, Barbara Mozart. Because of her love through the years.

There is a reason for the way things
are.
No one knows it near or far.
There's a reason for everything
under the sky.
I do not know it, so don't ask me
why.
There's a reason for the past, and
things to come.
I don't know how, or where from.
But there is a reason for all things
here, and in heaven.

Mrs Gina McWeeney
YOU

Dedicated to my husband Charles (Mac) who inspired me.

When I think of writing it is not
difficult at all
For you bring the smile to my lips,
the joyous song I sing.

You are the bright shining sun,
the flowers wet with dew.

When I write of you, words flow like
a waterfall
For all that is beautiful is you
And you, are my all.

Christy Dowden Maney
IN THE HOLE
pillowcases, satin, laces,
daffodils in fragile vases,
silent echoes fill the spaces,
memories rid with hallowed faces:
angels clothed in pure disgraces.

Paula Wooden
RAIN

For Steve Fox, whom I love for being there, understanding and helping me realize the sun still shines after all.

The night has enclosed me,
I will wait one more hour,
Maybe then the rain will stop,
My eyes drop to the frail, folded
hands below,
Empty, asking for more,
These hands will hold no one
tonight,
My words, once golden,
have proved nothing,
You have forgotten,
Who was here everlasting,
Tears of rain form against my
windows,
Looking out,
I wonder for a moment,
if you are out there,
Sheltering her from the storm,
Realizing, her hand is all you need,
I'll just sit here and wait,
alone.
Maybe tomorrow the rain will stop.

Anne Hobbs
ALMOST ELECTRA

To my "Main Dude"—my Dad.

In a cradle made from a strong,
yet tender,
material, I was once placed.
Neither oak, nor pine, nor
any like provided its strength.
Tender it was not because of
feathers or
felt,
clouds or
cotton.
The strength was in a pair—
Aged. Defensive. Wise.
The tenderness was within the
same—
Youthful. Open. Wondering.
The cradle was my father's arms.
The cradle is my father's arms.

Betty Blaylock Rinker
REFUTE TO JOYCE KILMER
You may never see a poem as lovely
as a tree
But for the soul—the poem is what
nourishes me.

As the earth feeds the roots
and the bough cradles the bird,
the spirit within and of me
demands the written word.

Only God, it's true, can make a tree,
but that same God made also me.
And with a hunger so great and
intense
that vision alone could never this
thirst quench.

A fool I may be as I these words pen,
But give me both beauty without and
beauty within.

Lona Patterson
STOP-HALT
If I cannot talk to you about the color
of a sigh
Nor the birth of a rain drop, then
STOP!!!
For these are things that exist in me
That cannot be explained
But that must be shared.

If you cannot hear the orchestration
of a heartbeat
Nor the breath of a flower in bloom,
that HALT!!!
For these are things I need
That cannot be expressed
But that must be felt.

I can live in your world
But are you able to live in mine?
Or am I able to sacrifice that which I
have treasured
To back track to where you are?
And if I do—Then who am I?

Sheila Highsmith
A WEDDING BLESSING
Mark this day a uniting begins,
wedding bells ring then singing joins
in;
From this day on two people are
one,
blossoming a bond where only true
love can come.

Their future we hope is bright
and complete,
the paths of their love be strong and
so neat;
Let each day and night be filled
like the first,
always for better and never for worse.

And from this day forth may
luck hold them tight,
granting them both whatever's in
sight;
Bringing them joy and love that
grows deep,
always bringing a smile and never
shedding a weep.

And may these stars that shine
so bright,
bare a path enchanted with light;
Guiding this love to the ends of
time,
bearing the fruits of true love divine.

Tarah K Vaughan
SPRING IS HERE
The birds chirp their happy songs.
A soft wind cools my face
The green grass sways in the wind.
Leaves rustle in a tree
Flowers bloom, Soft and light
Snow melts from the mountain tops
The sky clears blue and bright
The animals awake from their
slumber
Water warms in the day
The night is warm with a pleasant
breeze
Stars appearing up above
You get a warm, peaceful feeling
When spring is here.

Paul Perez
ONLY IN A DREAM
Deep in the silence of a thousand
lonely nights,
Thinking, and dreaming, and staring
at the sky.
You are always far from me and I
can not see your light.
But the memories are strong that
linger in my mind.

They put a price on passion, but love
was always free.
Time is a void and time can change,
But it will not alter me.
I have held you, I have known you,
but only in a dream.

Eyes: Beautiful, deep, lasting, and
steel grey.
They are present in my heart and
turn night
into
day.

Fred W Williamson Jr
MY STILL, STILL LOVE

For Beverly—my beloved wife

At the heart
of the Spanish fire
My soul is chilled.
The wind chimes for me—
My love is still.
Still in love
with Spanish fire
Her heart is real.
A thousand times tell me
Your love is still.

Still like water
Full of morning's chill.
The wind chimes tell me
My love is still.

Tapian Paul
PRECIOUS MEMORIES

For my precious Ryan and Hannah: As you grow, may you always know how much I love you both, and how truly proud I am to have been blessed with you. I pray for you always. Mom.

A child is such a blessing,
a very special joy.
It truly doesn't matter
whether a girl or boy.

They make you feel so happy
and sometimes feel so sad.
They fill your heart with so much
love,
for this you are so glad.

At times you feel your work's in vain
as they frequently disobey,
and you understand what Mom went
through
when she says, "You were that same
way."

So work on your patience, give them
your love
as you wake in the night to their cry,
'cause as they grow, it won't be long
until you're telling them good-bye.

Tressie J Root
MY LITTLE ANGEL
When they laid you in my arms;
The first day after you were born;
I closed my eyes and prayed to God,
To keep you from all harm.

Although I know that heartbreaks and
joy,
must come into your life;
I hope that you, My Little Angel,
Will be spared some of Life's strife.

You will always be near to me in my
heart,
And though the years may tear us
apart;
I'll close my eyes and then I'll see,
My Little Angel being brought to me.

When I was young I had a dream
Of finding a "Pink Star" which to me,
would mean everything;
Now I am older and some day will
die,
But I want you to know, My Little
Angel, that YOU are my Pink Star
sent from the sky.

I LOVE YOU KELLY,

MOMMY

Charlotte Anne Brown
HARMLESS THOUGHT OF A CHILD

To my mother and father, in thanks for their support and encouragement throughout my life.

The child set out to collect his spoils
and returned with a happy grin.

"The mission was successful!" he
cried,
as the rest came marching in.
In the center of the floor lay

a bag of jellybeans.
He picked out all the black ones
And his comrades did the same.

"Now, I order you to take the beans
and plant them in a field;
Poverty, Evil, and Stupidity are
all these plants will yield.

You must be quick to destroy them,
for they grow at an amazing
pace."
"We are the supreme rulers," he
Dictated.

"We are the supreme race!"

Emily F Wheeler
THE WILD ORCHID

This poem is dedicated to my beloved family.

The wild orchid can be found
Residing in the forest's lonely
expanse
Nestled deep within it's dark heart
Obscure, sheltered
Existing like a whisper
Wondrously rare and fragile
Placed there by God
To flourish in the mist of decay
To Bloom in silent radiance
Undisturbed by society

Michael Dennis
BREAKING MY WAY THROUGH TALL GRASS

breaking my way through tall grass
striking stiff stalks
scraping
the jungle encloses
tangled and tried
I thought of giving up
and then awoke
war dream

Kathleen T McDaniel
THEY WERE BRILLIANT BRIGHT LIGHTS

They were brilliant bright lights,
Flashing through the dark clouds,
Flying saucers from another place,

They shone golden
In the early morning sunlight,
Soaring through the air with style
and grace,

They went riding,
Carried high upon the wind's back,
Looking down upon the earth below,

So content to trust their destiny to
heaven,
And to travel where the wind might
blow,

Flying birds, fly and sing,
Make the bells of heaven ring,
Far as your birds' eye can see,
All the world is free . . .

They were seagulls
Flying through a double rainbow,
And we held our breaths to watch
them fly,

Watched them diving,
Watched them dip their golden
feathers
In the sun's rays in the morning sky.

Margaret S Young
ALONE

In memory of my husband Norman H. Young

Far away my thoughts are faring
To a wild rose scented lane,
Where we two one summer evening
Walked together in the rain.

Now no longer you are with me
Memories fill my heart with
pain.
Still the sweet wild roses bloom,
But now I walk alone in the
rain.

Mark J K Dalton
A HOT SUMMER NIGHT

I write this poem in remembrance of the way it was—a way that can NEVER be again because of Her.

As I look at pictures of you and I
A wondrous mist fills the air
Are you mine—is it true?
I ponder and hope that it is more than
just a dream

You are so pretty—a woman now
But equally my love.

To cuddle you and squeeze you, is all
that I need
To play with your soft, flowing hair,
is all that I want
Then, the warmth of your smooth,
naked skin
Intensifies my primordial desire
To be surrounded by your eager flesh
With nothing between us but our
beating hearts.

Your wet, moist lips tingle my skin
As you embrace me
Your tongue glistens as the tip
descends down my chest
Leaving a moist trail of saliva
Which cools my passion-ridden flesh
As a light summer breeze
Dances about our intertwined bodies.

As you kiss my navel
you stop—and gaze deep within my
eyes
My love and lust overwhelms me
As I suckle your nimble breast.

Again we are one . . .
As we fuse—I melting inside you
You engulfing me
I feel that nothing can break this
bond—

A Bond of Flesh
A Bond of Trust
A Bond of True Love.

Fred H Goodman
COURAGE

It's not the heroes or the flags
waving high that impress me the
most,
Nor the world leaders that I wish to
toast . . .

It's the little people like you and
me,
It's the oppressed trying to be
free.
It's a mother giving birth, a
father hunting work,
A farmer selling treasures to
keep working his dirt.
It's a worker re-training when
he is automated . . .
trying to keep up and not
become outdated.

It's the single parent giving all
they can,
To help their child become a
better woman or man.
It's helping your neighbor, and
reaching out to a friend,
It's losing out in love, and trying
once again.
It's those folks who struggle all
their days
Who show the kind of courage
that all of us should praise.

Courage—Doesn't need booze nor
dope to make it through the day.
Courage—Doesn't let 'NO' stand
in its way.
Courage—Fans the flames of
talent at any cost.
Courage chases dreams—when
all hope seems lost.
It's everyday things that
everyone has to do,
that take a lot of trying and
'COURAGE' to get through.

Charles R Craig III
COUNTRY WINDOWS

Georgian columns soared toward the
Southern god,
Which warmed us over
Rabbits darted into the blueberry
haven,
Minding no one in particular
Magnolia petals softened the
grounds,
Whose perfume permeated all else
The veranda swing creaked ever so
gently in the breeze,
Longing for that recurrent romantic
ritual
My shadow and I shuffled back and
forth with ease,
When realizing full well that time
was all we needed
And yet another car, with dust in
usual pursuit, sped by,
Totally ignorant to these ways

Veola Victoria Barnes
THE NOTEBOOK ON THE TRACKS

Sitting at a subway
Stop
Waiting too long for a
Train
I turned my eyes towards
The tracks with
Slight disdain
There I saw a notebook
Like the one I took to
School when nine
Its pages fluttered
As an Express train
Sped by
Feeling for its sad fate
I couldn't help wonder
How it got there
In the first place
Its pages
Did they hide thoughts
Words, dates left
In vain
Contain a love poem like
Mine
Hold scribbles from a
Student set on
Learning
Whose future once looked
Bright
Was it a she, he
Who dropped it accidentally
During day, night
Another Express train
Speeded by
Scattering the notebook's
Pages to the
Wind
Out of sight
As if to say goodbye
Its contents, if any
To be forgotten.

Mary Jane Elmer
BABY DEAR

To my husband, Frank, who supports all of doings; and to the unborn child who inspired this poem.

What do you look like, Baby Dear,
Who shall you be?
Will you be a Little Girl, that I
may dress up
with ruffles and curls.
A person with blond hair to be
braided, and pinned up high,
with porcelain skin and pretty
blue eyes.
You'll be a ballerinas, a pianist, a
gem.
Above all, you'll be my very
best friend.

What do you look like, Baby Dear,
Who shall you be?
Will you be a Little Boy, full of
mischief and worldly-wise
A child who just wants to be
"one of the guys."
Maybe be like your daddy,
studious and full of charm,
And, above all, willing to keep
loved ones from harm.

What do you look like, Baby Dear,
Who shall you be?
Daddy and I keep anticipating
this, with lots of glee.
There's so much to tell you,
So much to learn.
To walk with you, and talk with
you,
and learn from you.

James Baker
DISUSED ROBOT

Like a schizophrene alienated from
men,
It slouches in yonder corner in webs
and dust,
This robot with unseeing eyes and
muted mouth.
Patina has formed on frayed wires
within
And mice have made their abode in
its skein.

Stacey Vanderstappen

Stacey Vanderstappen
WHAT IS WHITE?

White is the wind blowing in your
face,
Or maybe the table cloth with all the
lace.
It can be the clouds up in the sky,

It might be the baby bird learning to fly.
Maybe it's the veil on the lady's head,
Or a lot of sorrow when someone is dead.
White is paper that you can write on,
It can be the father's new born son.
It's the snowflake's falling to the ground,
White can be a flute, a violin, or just a sound.
I guess you can see what white really is,
It can be anything hers or his.

Agnes B Hitler
AN ODE TO THE BALL

Dedicated to my two sons; Turney Gibson Hitler and Gene Douglas Hitler For Father's Day, 1987.

Obsessed by the ball; Aren't we all?
The wee-urchin, before it can crawl,
likes to roll, toss, and catch at the ball.
The school boy, come spring, summer, until fall,
with the rest of us, go for good old baseball.
The youth in high school and college have it all;
with hand, soft, basket, and foot ball.
There is racket and soccer, to mention a few,
while others like pool, bowling and croquet too.
The rich and famous have their tennis and golf-on-the-green;
and when in tournament, by millions seen.
The wooden ball of polo brings the horse into play.
Yes, I think the ball is here to stay.
While we float on this beautiful sphere;
the habitat of all of us here.

LeAnn Waters
HIDING THE YEARS

Dennis, Most of us show our years, you are one of the lucky ones to be hiding them. Love, LeAnn

A simple, little boy
polka dot face, arms and legs
cheeks like super balls
appearing with a smile
Pennies, nickels, and dimes exposed
Bulging from the pockets
of his 501 jeans
No one would guess
that tucked away in a rear pocket
existed a few, crisp hundreds
to pay for the expenses
of his toy car
Only a few clues giving away his age
A receding hair line
and a tongue rattling off
the sounds of experience.

Lillie Miles
FRIDAY NIGHT FISH FRY DANCE

THROUGH CHRIST ALL THINGS ARE POSSIBLE. To the memory of my mother, Mary Miles, who believed in education and labor. To my son, Angelo, and my daughter, Tangerine. For your support, encouragement and inspiration.

The dance hall is crowded,
Singles and couples standing,
seated, some dancing,
In a haze of burned fish grease
Mingling with stale cigarette smoke.
High in the paint peeling ceiling
Dense smoke has claimed near the
Light of the bare twenty-five watt bulbs,
Swaying with the beat of drums.

A throaty flamboyant blues singer
Belts out coarse and sorrowful lyrics,
Keeping time with the wild hot
rhythm and blues band.

Gray salty sweat beads painfully
Fill his blood-shot eyes,
He is cool, snapping fingers, slow
moving feet.

Cheap carelessly worn wigs don
The heads of brightly painted faces,
Sleazily dressed women.
Sweating bodies reek of talcum,
Dancing cheek to cheek against men
Filled with cheap wine.

A darkened corner, figures of men
Standing in a semi-circle,
Rapping loud, drinking slow, from
A brown paper bagged bottle of wine.

A fist fight starts over the last corner of wine.
An empty bottle is thrown against
The glossy green painted wall.
Lights go out, the band stops playing.

The screaming and scrambling crowd,
Over falling chairs and broken glass,
Flee their dance hall into the cold
sub-zero night.

Police arrive, no arrests,
Empty dark dance hall smelling
of stale cigarette smoke,
Drained bottles, thrown about,
Broken glass, fallen chairs.

Tracey Elaine Ginn
I MISS YOU

I wish for you alot of times . . .
I want to see you, and talk to you.
I wonder what you might be doing
and if everything's okay.
Whenever I start feeling sad
Because I miss you,
I remind myself how lucky
I am, to have you to miss . . .
to have been with you through
so many close and happy days.
They say it's a small world,
and maybe they're right.
But it doesn't seem that way
to me, when I'm missing you!

Alyce M Coleman
BERNIE DIED TODAY

To my beloved grandson, Daren, in the passing of his pet, "Bernie"

Brother or sister, I never had . . .
But when I was a young lad,
About three,
A little puppy took up with me.

We slept in the same bed
And when I said "Come"
He'd be there on the run.

I'm about twenty now
Still sleeping with my "Almost
Brother" dog.
But one morning, early in the fog,
When I awoke, there lay "Bernie"
Still curled up on my bed
Dead . . .

Went without pain or struggle,
Ole age I guess,
But I do confess
I'll forever miss Bernie to love and cuddle.

Jeff Bauman
THE REAPER

For the man came to me in the midst of the night
He was the Reaper, the escort of the dead

He asked me what I had to give
Take it all I said for I no longer have use

Take my mind for I have no one left to think of
My love is gone and I want not crippling memories

Take my arms for I have not anyone to hold within them
And what good are they if you cannot show your love with them

Take my ears for I do not wish to hear any longer
The sounds of the world are crude without the golden voice of my love

Take my eyes, give them away
My world is already darkness
and but one is the light

Take my body
For what is it but a mere container for my soul without someone to share it with

Take all of these but leave one thing
Leave my heart for it does not belong to me but to my lost love whom I gave it to many a nights ago

The rider agreed to my request
And as he left I sat there being beckoned to my rest

When I saw her in the road
She approached but stopped knowing it was too late

A tear went down her cheek as she felt my spirit brush pass her on the way up into the sky
To spend an eternity thinking of all the reasons why.

Don Dobbie
THINGS I'VE KNOWN, THINGS I'VE DONE

There's a hole in the ground, I found
Not an edge to it and it isn't round
It's black as ink, a missing link
I think . . .

I once knew the blackest cloud
Lived inside a deadly shroud
Blew down into two drops of dew
Adieu . . .

The wind was once a friend of mine
Together we forgot the time
Took a ride, rode the tide
Wall-eyed . . .

I once flew the bluest sky
Went right through its inner eye
I played around without a sound
Spellbound . . .

I once said the perfect word
But nobody else around me heard
Sadly I sighed, slowly it died
Inside . . .

Oleta Rogers
CHARLEY'S OLD STOVE

This old stove, as you can see,
Is not as new as it used to be,
But with the energy crisis soaring high,
It could be honored again, by and by.

And my, if it could only talk,
The things it could tell would make you stall,
And listen to it's tales of days gone by—
Would probably make tears come to your eyes.

It could tell tales of pioneer days,
And of the big ones that got away.
It could tell secrets of lovers galore!
Of how they met at Charley's Store.

The old timers would wander in,
And head for the stove to warm their shins,
And bask in it's warm glow,
No matter which, the young or the old.

And as long as this old stove stands,
It will hold memories of it's fellow man,
And who knows as days go by,
It may take its place
In our home in the sky.

John George Slovak
PIPER'S NIGHTFALL

To my lovely wife Anna May and Aunt Lila May

As the golden rays of a setting sun
Burnish the crags of a highland bluff
A single figure stand outlined
Silhouetted upon the gloaming
ethereal
The plaintive wail of the first pipe
Cries loudly over the valley below

The silvery moon then casts
its magic upon the tendril mists
Time stands still as the piper plays
A song of heritage and past
memorance
He knows not if there is any to hear
But plays for the joy of the past
The last notes sound gently
The piper turns and then descends
To his humble home.

Susan Erb
BEFORE LIFE ITSELF IS OVER

Before life itself is over
And there is no chance to talk,
No chance to feel
To share—

Before life itself is over
And movement is gone,
The sun upon your face
The wind in your hair—

Before life itself is over
We have time to live!

Tina Lee Golden
THE BEST AND WORST OF TIMES

To all my family and friends for the support they've given me.

I see so many failures
as well as successes
Wearing skin tight blue jeans
as well as pretty dresses

People skipping classes
almost every day
People trying their hardest
to live God's way

People doing homework
just so they can pass
People going to guidance
to get out of class

People trying their hardest
to be the best they can be
Others quitting school
so they can be free!

Miss Dorothy M Baker-Fish
HEARTS
The hearts we know perhaps are few.
Bind them continually upon your heart.
Tie them about your neck.
May the hearts of heart be caring,
With a sharing Love combined.
May the hearts be Full of Knowledge,
And the hearts we know be Love.
Let our hearts, be Full of Wisdom,
Be bound within the Law.
Always may we waken,
For the fullness of Life's Heart:

Barbara K Jones
NOVEMBER
I have to watch the fire today,
Outside it's cold and gray;
Smells of snow—
Would be season's first
Down this low.
Trees are waiting
For the wind to shake
Their last October leaves away.

I don't mind November—
Naked trees and ragged brown earth.
Seems like a pause
From gold and crimson;
Before Winter draws
An icy breath and throws
December under snows,
To hide until the spring.
Trees are waiting
For the sun to shake
Their new green April leaves awake.

Becky-Joe N Perkins
IT'S THE LITTLE THINGS

This poem was written for Rob. My love to you, I give my heart.

It only takes the little things,
To show me that you care
A warm caress, a gentle kiss
A love so very rare.

One in a million, it's so hard to find,
Nothing can take its place.
It's the little things you do for me,
That brings a smile to my face.

It's the little things you say to me,
That brightens up my day.
The way you whisper in my ear,
The sweet words that you say.

You never asked me to change a thing,
That I thank you for.
Accepting me for what I am,
And not asking me for more.

It's the little things you do each day,
That makes my skies so blue.
The whole world seems to fade away,
Whenever I'm with you.

Todd Ashmore
ROOSEVELT
I feel as if I'm in a bubble
a locked steel cage
unbreakable
so small
constantly engulfing
tightening around me
People
members of this town
choking me out
friendly but narrow-minded
irrational thinkers
ignorant
stubborn towards new ideas
hyper-conservative
everyone is related
all knowing one another
controlling the atmosphere
news travels fast
it is the foundation
the deceitfulness
and lies
and rumors
and gossip
all creators of the bubble

Suesan J Tyler

Suesan J Tyler
MONSTERS

This poem is dedicated to Michael and David, two special people, who helped me believe in myself.

A cold wind blows
through darkened trees.
You hear the rustle
of walked on leaves.

Creeping through shadows,
it's hiding in trees.
The scariest of creatures,
is waiting to seize!

So you start running
but he's still behind
There's a light up ahead.
Will you make it in time?

You hear your heart pound.
You try not to scream.
That's when you awaken,
it's only a dream.

Anthony Perry
I REMEMBER THEM

To my dear mother, Theresa Perry, who taught me how to laugh and my wonderful Grandfather, Lawrence Dias, who taught me how to give

There are memories of people who have gone but yet remain.
There are memories approaching which in time we will regain.
Some have drifted into winter, some have bloomed again in spring.
There are memories of two, in fact, a constant joy can bring.

Two faces in my lifetime which I long again to see;
Two greater than I've ever known, inspiring to me.
Of the woman who conceived me and I knew so short a time;
And the man whose arms received me any place and any time.
They were two whose joy abounded; they were sensitive and strong.
They made all who they surrounded know they truly did belong.
One was simply born a jester; was a natural delight.
One was chiseled out of a marble but a man of great insight.

When they had died I almost tried to see them prematurely;
But life was what they brought me and they taught me that as surely.
The man whose strength enveloped all, the girl who never grew;
They both had gifts for everyone, perhaps they never knew.

Cathlene Gillespie
SECRETS OF THE NIGHT
A child lies amongst the wildflowers
in the crimson light of the sun at dawn
her pursed, violet lips utter no sound
they cry in pain no more
sorrow has left her soul
dew falls like tears on her cheeks
her strawberry tresses gently fall
to her bare shoulders
hiding the scars of a past no one will know
the beauty of the morning
hushes the monstrous secrets of night

Patty M Baker
CLOCK WITH NO HANDS

To my parents, who have always been there!

I search for the time
on a clock with no hands,
And I fly kite
too high to see.
I reach for the ground
from a ladder too tall—
Too low, too high, too blind;
that's me.

But the clock with no hands
holds no limits on time
And the kite carries dreams
I dare to dream!
While the ladder, you see,
I can climb up <u>or</u> down . . .
Any time, any thing, any place;
I'm free!

Landis L Kent
THE FIRST SNOW
The snow is falling lightly . . .
The trees standing quietly . . .
With their new clothes.

The grass is overwhelmed with white . . .
And all is quiet.

All is quiet and still like my heart . . .
Waiting for someone special.
A new ray of sunshine.

And like always . . . the snow brings the cold . . .
It nips at my nose . . . but mostly at my heart.

For I long for someone special . . . to share my love and warm feelings . . .
To warm the cold days.

A special someone to share the magic of the first snow.

Wade L Robinson
RAINBOWS AND LEPRECHAUNS
Today I saw a rainbow; It's colors bright and bold!
A story says that at its end, you'll find a "Pot of Gold"!
A Leprechaun once told me, "Catch me, if you can."—
"And I'll give to you three wishes— whatever you command".
Now Leprechauns and rainbows, you might think are too far fetched—
But listen as I tell you—Just listen to the rest!

See, I followed that there Leprechaun, straight to a rainbow's end—
And when I saw that "Pot of Gold", I had to stop and grin.
The Leprechaun, he said to me,
"Now that you know it's true"—
"Let's see if you can catch me";
"Let's see how well you do"!

So off we went around and round, for hours I tried, but failed!
And when I stopped to catch my breath, I heard him loudly wail,
"What's wrong my friend"? "All tuckered out"? "Can't handle little me"?
"You're not the first, won't be the last; I'm bored; I'm gonna leave".

He turned his back to walk away—
That's when I grabbed my chance!
I jumped up fast and reached out far and caught him by his pants!
Well, there you have it—my story's told. There's no more to my tale
Except my wishes all came true—and the gold is mine as well!

Tracy Richter
HOW DID YOU KNOW?
How did you know-how could you see?
Did it show, was it me?
I said nothing, not one word,
I'd like to know just where you heard
that I see stars looking in your eyes,
knowing my love for you could never die.
How did you find out-a simple guess?
That I think you're special compared to the rest.
That I dream of you all the time,
hoping some day that you'll be mine.
It puzzles me on how you knew
that I'm falling in love with you.
I get weak inside when you say hello,
but I didn't give it away as far as I know.
But that doesn't matter now that you have told me that you love me too.

Joanne J Bonyai
THE STORM
The afternoon was sunny, there was a gentle breeze
The little girl rode on her horse,
amongst the poplar trees.
When suddenly the clouds moved in,
the wind began to blow
The little girl then headed home, fast as she dared to go.

She tied her horse up in his stall, and headed for the house
The rain and hail slashed at her face,
hair whipped her eyes and mouth.
She raced into the kitchen, with terror in her eyes
Was told, "go comb your hair, and wash, a big girl never cries."

She went into the bathroom, one arm was in a cast
She washed one hand, and combed her hair, she tried to do it fast.
The lightning flashed incessantly, the thunder pealed and roared
She was afraid, but she'd be brave,
like her mother said before.

Then from the corner of her eye, she saw the dreaded flash
The lightning hit the window; she heard no thunder crash.
She screamed from deep within herself, the tears were streaming down
Her mother's lips were moving, but she couldn't hear a sound.

The smell of smoke was in the air, but no fire could be found
The lightning rods had taken the main jolt into the ground.
The storm moved on, the sun came out, a rainbow filled the sky.
The child read her mother's lips, "sometimes it helps to cry."

Terri Trainor

BROWN EYES

Two like pairs of big, brown eyes
watch the spreading ink

One pair flashes with anger
Raises an arm to strike

Wide eyed pools of pain—look up
flinch—"I'm sorry, Daddy"

Looking down into twin mirrors
Dad lowers his arm, ashamed

"It's O.K. son, these things will happen"
The boy's tears overflow

Looking back at his own split lip
he keeps his boyhood promise

Denying his father's frustration now
He gives his boy a hug.

Jessie Herbert

GENTLE JESUS

To Elsie and Gordon, Love—Mom

Guide us, Gentle Jesus,
Help us to do right.
Let us follow in thy footsteps
Ever forward to the light.

Days of hardship crumble
Neath thy guiding arm,
Weary footsteps fumble,
Keep us, Gentle Jesus, from all harm.

Thru the nights of sorrow,
Fears that tear the soul.
Waiting for the morrow,
Jesus' love is ere our goal.

When the roll is called up yonder
And we cross the darkest sea,
Never more to wander,
Gentle Jesus, safe with thee.

Kim Delaney

GOODBYE AL

I work all day for a little pay,
and when I get home I get a call on the phone.
It is my friend Al, whom I assume is my pal.
He wants me to come to the bar, so I hop in my car.

There he is, next to a stool, so I sit with him like a fool
and order up a drink. Al gives me a wink.
I hand over my tender and start on a bender.
As time goes on, I's tinks me sees a fawwnn?
Hey! Where'd dat waalll come frommm? I ain't no bum!

Spinning and turning in my bed, oh but the aching in my head!
Ah, maybe now some restful sleep, but now I'm on my feet.
What's this? My head's in the toilet.
Al says, "Come on, don't spoil it!"
My stomach gives a great heave and Al says, "It's time to leave!"
So, Al Cohol, my so-called friend, leaves me alone again.

Evangelist Jean D White

Evangelist Jean D White

REVEREND, A NORRIS SMITH

God is so good
He sent you my way
To teach me His Word
And now I can say

I have everlasting peace
A song in my heart
I'm blood washed & blood kept
I have a new start

JESUS is my Savior
My LORD, friend and King
I am joint heirs with JESUS
HE is my EVERYTHING

Thank you so much
For being my friend
For giving me JESUS
On whom I depend

Now I can tell others
Of JESUS and His LOVE
I shall see you again
With our Father, above.
Love in Christ Jesus,

Ralph R Ivey Jr

MISTAKES

What we have done to lose,
The things we cherished most.
We cannot change,
That which has happened.

What we have done to hurt,
The ones who trusted us.
We cannot undo,
That which has been done.

We must live with our feelings,
Those that hurt inside.
We cannot escape,
They are our mistakes.

Jennifer A Berry

THE WHITE BLANKET OF SNOW

To Josie, who is my wonderful mother, a very special lady, and also my friend. Thank you for always reminding me that with just a little effort, I could accomplish anything. I love you very, very much.

Looking through the window, snow falling off a tree, a cold, white blanket, as far as the eye can see,

You see little children playing outside in the snow, for what they have on their minds no adult could possibly know,

For all they have on their minds is Frosty and everything bright,
Then their parents go towards the door and bring them inside for the night,

They leave their scarves and hats by the door, ready to run outside the next day for some more,

Mom undresses them and tucks them into bed, while they're thinking about the day ahead,

They wake up the next morning and there's a puddle by the door, as their only reminders of the night before.

Joseph Hayes

BEAUTY

To my wife, Shirley

Who are you?
Where did you come from?
Eons ago, from a thought,—
from a Supreme Intelligence,
A "cell" was released.
Hence, at first, seeming chaos,—
Then gradual Order,
Finally, Beauty, with all its counterparts.
Answer,—You are Beauty.
Woman is the beginning, the fulfillment of Beauty.
By observation, psychic feeling, it is obvious—
Your identity is well known.
Somewhere in a distant Galaxy, there must exist
some Planet,—a garden that produces lovely
Flowers of a rare, unknown quality,
Delicate with a Heavenly scent.
By some secret transmission,—
A Trans-planetal-osmosis,
One flower blew away in a soft wind,
and descended to Earth.
I know who you are.

Bicki Norton

THE GREATEST GIFT OF ALL

The greatest gift of all is the gift of love,
The greatest gift of all came down to us from above.
A cross still stands in each one's heart
To let us know that someone loved us from the start.
A love so great & a love so true
Died upon that cross for me and for you,
A heart so big and a heart so wise
Still lets us know that this love will never die.

Angela D Byram

MY LIFE

For my Mom and Dad, who have encouraged me to be the best I could and who continue to encourage and stand beside me.

Life, to me, has been fair so far;
I can't honestly complain.
And up until just recently,
I've lived my life in vain.

Running with the Devil,
My destination unknown;
Being around everyone,
Yet finding myself alone.

Living a life of sex and drugs,
Living without a care;
Surviving on the daily basis
And a parent's prayer.

All alone, I faced this hell
Believing I was right,
Until I finally realized
I'd rather be killed on sight.

I fell to my knees one day
And asked God for His help.
I knew that day
He was all I had left.

He took me in his loving hands
And touched me with His grace.
I thanked Him with my heart and soul
For saving me from the race.

To look at me, you may just think
I've made the wrong decision,
Simply because of the fact
I'm locked away in prison.

But, my friend, it saved my life;
And that's more than I could do.
So, ask yourself this simple question:
Does your life mean as much to you?

Helen Christensen

JUNIPER IN JANUARY

A gray, craggy old man
On a bare mountain slope
With smudged blue berries
To button his cloak

Becomes a jeweled princess
In shimmering gown
Transformed by sun shafts
On snow, soft as down.

Manuel Quesada Jr

TOUCHED

Something special for you Christina because words can express how I feel

As the tide flows to greet the sea
Let your thoughts flow gently to
You and me
Keeping us close to each other
Remembering
Even as the morning birds awaken
To greet the dawn, let your love
Awaken memories in your heart,
soul
And beyond

Although our hands can not always
Touch
Your memories can never be
forgotten
I will always stand besides you
Like a dolphin who guides you
To be true as the tide, free as a
Wind swell and joyful in letting
It be
We must be touched by what we can
Or cannot see.

Alfred Hadden

HOMELESS BOY

This poem is dedicated to those people; whose lives are a constant struggle, and yet, they survive!

The wind is blowing. And I am cold!
A boy so young, yet so old.
They fear to look into my eyes,
Or ask this child, what's wrong?
Cause they don't want to hear about,

My sad and dreary song.

The streets are home to me, and to this motley crew. We walk all night and sleep all day. We have nothing else to do

My senses scream, impending snow! So to the mission I will go. I'll sing of God and eat real good. I wish that they just understood.

That man don't live by bread alone. A man; he needs, himself a home.

I often dream of better days. A sweeter time and place. A warm little house, A mother's touch. I miss the love. Oh God! I miss that love so much.

C S Jeffers
COUNTRY BOY
Country boy, lost in the city.
Lost the sights of things so pretty.
Like mistletoe in the tree so high, and mountains that seem to reach the sky.

Early morning dew on the ground.
People that never will let you down.
Always a smile, a friendly face.
You knew in the country you weren't out of place.

Mary I McFetridge
KINDERGARTEN TEACHER

To my mom—my buddy, my best friend.

She sees the world
In a different light,
That mother of mine,
She puts her heart
Before her eyes
And defends what she finds.

Children seek her
So that they may be seen
And when she looks—they shine
She sees the child
The champion, the Christ,
That the world would never find.

John Stanley Coughlan
MISS EMILY WAITS . . .
He gave me love
—And time to watch . . .
A wager with my soul.
He caged me not
—But trapped me still
A sentence without toll.
He made no promise
—No commands . . .
For such are things to watch,
A wishing well of empty
dreams . . .
All hidden in a box.

Grace E Kerzmann
A LONELY GRANDMOTHER

I dedicate my Poem, "A Lonely Grandmother", to Kerry Lynn Kerzmann, my favorite Grandson, whom I Love with all my heart!

I'm very lonely without you,
Grandson dear,
Although we're far apart, I can feel your presence near.
I miss you in the daytime and I miss you in the night,
I miss you in the early morning light.

I don't hear your sweet voice calling out my name,
I don't see your happy face, nothing's quite the same.
I don't hear your laughter, that beautiful sound,
My life seems very empty, without you around.

I see your empty bedroom with pictures on the wall,
But I don't see you anywhere at all.
I don't hear you rocking in your favorite rocking chair,
Sometimes, I try to imagine that you are still there.

You're the reason, I go on living day after day,
And you're my favorite Grandson,
I'm very proud to say.
More than anyone in this world, I truly love you,
And if you're happy, Grandson, I can be happy, too.

Amy Brown
THANKFUL
Nobody would listen,
Nobody could see,
So she slashed her wrist,
Successful.

Now today as cold wind blows,
The mother looks on her daughter,
A tear in her eye,
As she passes away.

Gone forever is the bright sky,
Now the cold,
On this summer day,
As her mother dies inside.

A sad tale I do tell,
But let us be thankful,
For we have life,
And everything in it.

Janet L Tinch
DEATH OF A DREAM
I saw a man
along the road;
His burdens seemed
a heavy load.
I stopped and lent
a helping hand,
To lighten the load
so he might stand
Straighter and taller
than e'er before:
But friends gave him
burdens all the more.
This man was once
a dreaming man,
He had ambition
He had a plan,
His friends won't know
What dreams were killed
When with harsh words
his mind was stilled.

David Alan Conrod
I STAND UPON THIS STONY LEDGE

Dedicated with all my love to my mother and father and my inspirations, my brothers and my special friends Maureen (bright eyes) and Jacqueline. Your constant support and love I will always hold dear.

I stand upon this stony ledge,
Captivated by the vast expanse,
Mountains clear to valleys as far as I see,
These tranquil visions do not limit me.

I am reminded of the seaside wharf,
Walked many times tragically alone,
My mind conjuring images of a clear blue sky,
And a sprawling cottage setting long since missed.

A kaleidoscope of forest, meadows and brooks,
All but lost to my inherited urban jungle,
Yet from my perch I spy a roaring river,
Instilling memories of one known in ages past.

Every image in my sight this day,
Causes me joy for my memories are fond,
Justly each setting backed a love so true,
Enhancing my being with each new awakening.

This land of ours so precious indeed,
As I stand by the rocks weathered through the ages,
A gentle reminder I have not walked alone,
Along this rugged path which beckons me home.

Maria A DeSimone

Maria A DeSimone
FLOWERS

To my parents who have molded and created me; and inspired me to write.

A flower blooms in springtime;
It's like my love for you,
I put it on the table, it's
giving me the blues.
I look around and see you
A vision in my head, Now, I
know I wish I was dead.
For fragile like a flower
I sit alone at night—only
a thought to hold me tight
So, when you see a
flower—think of it as me. Sitting with thoughts of you as lonely as can be.
Turn your back! and the flower will be
gone. I will take it and journey on
I'll hold it tight and never let it go
and in my heart I will know my love
for you will only grow
Today, you'll see a flower sitting
on the floor, pick it up and you will
get more.
So, as you touch this flower, you're
touching my heart—I hope that we
don't grow apart.
For now I leave you with only a thought
think of this flower and what it's brought
For it is a flower as you can see that soon
will hold you and me.

Michael Valenti
. . . WHILE RIDING ON A BUS THROUGH SOUTH CAROLINA
a gospel church
sweet sounds of singing, sunday
a broken shack
a child is crying, monday
by tuesday all his tears have been ignored
they'd like to buy the land next door
which no one can afford

two blocks away
a new white school is standing
wednesday morning comes and class begins
a new hope forms which causes new confusions
the game gets played but no one ever wins

he's got to work
there's just no more food, thursday and friday,
too bad it rained all day
on saturday, he really meant to speak to farmer joe
but it got late, 'sides
joe stopped hiring men four years ago

a gospel church
sweet sounds of singing, sunday
a broken shack
a child is crying monday
by tuesday all his tears have been ignored

he'd like to buy the land next door
which no one can afford . . .

Douglas A Fager
A LOVE LOST
A love lost,
An open, ailing wound.
Beauty gone,
A moth from out of the cocoon.
A whispering wind
Disappears into the thick, dark night.
The stars at distant shining
Fade to not so very bright.
The birds that fly, no songs they sing,
Nor merrily go they their way.
For this is the day a love was lost
And there be no cure, they say.

Mary A S Sanchez
THE WIND THAT BLOWS FREE
Dear wind that blows free
Let me follow thee,
To the ends of the Earth you go
While you wave to and fro,
You carry clouds as white as snow
Holding mysteries that no one will ever know,
You carry light beams
Scattering them among the trees,
The power you hold
Blows the fields where cotton grows,
Over the oceans of mystic blue
Carry, carry me away too.

Kathleen Sannwald
SWISH
The wall supports me,
I lean on its strength, somehow
I feel so weak as you speak of fluid movement,
I stand still and shake.
Your face alights in recall of the
power of legs thrust up
overhead,
the thrill of it all
changes you into a magical form new to me,
I feel the gloriness of it,
the absolute control,
the oneness of the art.
Images surface of myself,
floating down a court, awaiting
the arrival of the ball in flight,
my arms soar out, we two, now one,
as my body lifts up towards the rim
and gently lets my beloved object go
to its new home,
Swish . . .
Objects of the world come to us,
directed by some need
of togetherness, for awhile,

we take them in, adore them, but find the release so hard,
to let the spinning soul soar back into space,
Swish . . .
I an now a ball in need of flight,
where I will land is unknown,
I await grounded, awaiting the thrust up,
the freedom to soar for awhile, until you,
or another, reclaims my flight,
and I delight in the magical sound of
Swish . . .

Betty Glaser
REMEMBRANCE

To my wonderful husband—who is ever there with love always

Today we share each other's dreams
Childish fears and reckless schemes
Together we face the problems that bind us
Days of sorrow, days of gladness
But once you're well on the road to fame
Will you still remember my name?
Or will you be too busy to care
About those days we used to share
Days filled with tenderness, laughter and tears
And a promise of love that would last for years

Linda Borquez
FEELINGS
The rain is my tears crying out for you
The sun is my heart full of love for you
The sky is the vast emptiness I feel without you
The wind is your voice whispering to me
Time stands still and awaits your presence

Erik Tribelhorn
MOTHER
It is all so synthetic
these networks vast across your skin.
veins of cement & asphalt, tall iron cable hair
blemishes of rubber, steel, plastic, polyethylene, dropping
man-made roots to your mantle
oceanic eyes, blind from toxic death,
barrels emptied of
their names
Your features induced with humanic disease

Stop us Mother!
Stop us mindless sheep, bleating, chewing grass to its roots.
Stop us natural children, synthetic beings.
Stop us with wind! with rain, hail, blizzard! with ozone, CO2, the ionosphere! wax, copper, plutonium!
Use your everyday means which we have forsaken to strike us down,
crucify humanity in the name of Nature!
Stop us in Gary, Indiana
Stop us on offshore oil rigs, leaking viscous horror.
Stop us Stephen King environmentalists!
Stop us or die, Mother!
The space in which you ellipse is
as cold as the hearts of your
inhabitants.
You lie railed in bed, a cancer
chewing through your lungs,
breath falling short, an
unmerciful disease tightening
manacles on your essence.
We are that cancer! We, mutant
cells, reproducing like
mayflies, mining your blood,
stealing your breathing air,
We are your nemesis! We are
your destruction!
What has brought us to commit
these evils?
40 years of modernization, nuclear age . . .
Where are all the Taoists?

Immx Ferreria
UNTITLED
what if the world were white
and all living creatures were black
then we will still be fighting
what if the world were black
and all living creatures were white
then we will still be fighting
what if the world were black and white
and all living creatures were white and black
then we will still be fighting.

Kristin Wilson
THE BEAST
with the word moron outitran
with a fierceful Rage I didn't understand
Beating, Tearing, Ripping,
Shredding, Killing.
And, when it
cal-
med
D
O
W
N
and realized what it had done
everything had to be
picked up one by one
pieced together bit by bit
sewn together strip by strip
cared upon,
minute,
by
minute,
until nothing was left unhealed.

Damned Temper! I wish it would yield.

William Bly
SNOWFLAKES

To Marilyn My Wife and Best Friend

They come down as little flakes,
and land upon the flowers.
They mounded up which seemed to take them hours.
The air is cold, but I am warm.
I'm six foot down, you know.
I died three days ago.

'Twas winter time, when I left.
I'm sorry it wasn't spring.
It makes no difference, though.
I still hear angels sing.
They welcomed me with open arms,
for what reason, I don't know.
They made me look through a
hole in the clouds,
To see my grave,
A mound of snow.

Erin Donahoe
CLEARER THAN THE CLEAREST CRYSTAL
Clear than the clearest crystal
Softer than the softest rose petal
Stronger than the hardest diamond
And purer than a child's eyes
Man treasures these gifts
For time eternity
Yet anything with all these qualities
We hurt and discard
For only one thing
Could be that clear, soft, strong, and pure
A gentle heart

Timothy J Phillips
ADELINE
Adeline, Adeline, where have you been?
Where have you traveled? What have you seen?

Romances in moonlight, gardens in bloom.
Soldiers of fortune, panchamas in gloom.
The halls of Rome, with palaces fair.
Great men of truth, brave men of dare.
Paintings by dreamers, the brush of Van Gogh.
Choirs of clergy, the words of Thoreau.

Well, I've not been to London to visit a queen,
And France is a place that I've never been.
I haven't gone sailing, or spend without care.
But gold is the color that you wish to wear.
And why you have been searching the world for its charm,
I have been waiting here tending the farm.

Margaret A Arcé
FOR HE IS UNIQUE

To my husband Santo, whom I love dearly. You make me very happy. Love Peggy

Things touch him in different ways,
In ways I cannot reach.
I sometimes think that he is,
For He is Unique.

Things worry him in some ways
Some ways I cannot understand.
I sometimes think that he is
For He is Unique

He worries me for the things he does, he can
Make me sad and blue.
He differs us and each one of us
For He is Unique

Love touches him in a spiritual way, a way
I may so reach.
I sometimes think that he is, for He is Unique

Mickey L Shaffer
JUDGEMENT
Judge not other's failings, or ever be the one to hurl stones of things, others have done
Be not so self righteous, your foot could fall
No person is perfect; we have touched sin; one and all
Only God must judge us, no one has been assigned
Because God alone can see into your heart and mine
Judge not morning; noon or night
For there is a cross, with a shining light
This cross of our dear Lord is one we must bear
Is this the cross where you judged wrong, that we share
Judge not others for there are problems you have to face
Don't point your finger at others' wrongs' today
You could have three pointing back at you. Just pray
Do you have the courage to judge not, just in case?
Did you look in to the mirror at the expression on your face?
Influence others in some kind way
Don't judge others, as we grow older day by day
I find no satisfaction in pretence, behind a sham
I judge not you or others, I am a true reflection, as I am.

June Alexis Johnson
DESTINY

This Poem is dedicated to Malachy, My Love, and my children, Troy, Tara, and Carrie. It is also dedicated to my Mom, Dad, and three wonderful Aunts: Margaret, Mozelle, and Sallie.

Within your heart is your destiny,
made unto eternity.
The pattern of your thoughts are
not for nought,
they determine the tide—how it
may ride, up the ladder of success,
or ever regressing to the depths. It's
up to you, how the tide turns—
so be ever vigilant to image the best
as this will be the test of your
success. The good seeds you plant are
synonymous with happiness, the
good thoughts you project are steps
ever leading the way to a brighter
day.
This is the only way to achieve that
many splendored day. It is in this
respect that we must pay our dues.
Good thinking is an attribute with
which very few of us are naturally
imbued. Therefore,
vigilance in governing our thoughts
is required, for us to go higher. Good
deeds have wings that soar the
heights unto beautiful flight. Beware,
yet dare—think the thoughts, do the
deeds that do please, as God would
have it to be, and one day they will
produce a great and happy destiny.

Michael King
AVIATING DREAMS
I have flown in many depths
But have never flown in green mountains
Where the bright blue backgrounds them

Blue waters in a Caribbean island
Infinite isthmuses surround seas
Among all the palms and mango trees

Large green leaves and coconut meat
Sand of particles and opium
Losing visions and gaining vitality

Blurred into oblivion without reason
Finding comfort through sublime unconsciousness

Falling toward surfaces harder than

concrete
I color the world black

Transmissions of light penetrate corneal lenses
In streaks of where I was warm at one time

Tangible objects have fallen into place

Settled by the powerful effect of gravity

And I have awakened from walking on cold floors

Gay McClenan
WHEN YOU GO, LEAVE ME

I don't want you to leave me
Yet I know you must,
So when you go
Leave me the touch
Of your kiss upon my lips
And your hand upon my face
But most of all leave me
The warmth of your embrace.

I don't want you to leave me
Yet I know you will,
So when you go
Leave my heart stilled
By the sound of your voice
And the love that you give
But most of all leave me
A reason to live.

Tena Reinholtz
WE MET THROUGH LAUGHTER AND SMILES

To Kyle after one year of being together

We met through laughter and smiles
Brought together by a special occasion
Flowers and wine and music
Time passed
Feelings grew
A closeness like no other
Love blossomed between us
The months flew by
A year has come and gone
We are still together
Stronger, closer
Our love holds us together
The future lies in wait
If our love continues as in the past
Together forever we will be

Charlotte Natasha Bindo

Charlotte Natasha Bindo
WERE WOLF

4 Wolfgang

Oh November
Why do you start
With rain
Happy Halloween
Is gone
Is past
I need you to stay
A friend to last
Please don't go
Oh Autumn
Leaves of crimson
Amber
Lithuanian gold
Beautiful to behold
The night
Of the witch
Is over
The Were Wolf
Is gone
The full moon
Has come
He's won
He's found
His land of golden sun

M Ruth Howard
DREAMS OF MY LOVE.

To Raleigh, my love.

I hear you in the stillness of the night,
Speaking soft and low in my dreams.
I see your blue eyes shining so bright,
But alas you are only in spirit, it seems.
You come to me as I lay sleeping,
And tho you are cold in death, I feel you near—
You come back to me often in my dreams.
And you speak the words I love to hear—
As you softly say in a whisper.
"I love you dear always, a kiss the vow to seal."
Suddenly I awake, smiling thru my tears.
My fingers softly touch my lips.
My dreams are so real!!

Marcia Alexander
CAN THIS BE LOVE

Can this be love? What ever is this feeling that I am going through. I feel like a hundred butterflies that have been set loose. I feel like I could sing from the top of the mountain and shout for cheer joy. Oh this must be love; It only comes along in a life time. This must be my special time.

Miss Joann Campbell
A KID'S LOVE

To my five kids

Has anyone told you about a kid's love
Well it's more like a flower that never stops growing
And more than that it's like sweet perfume
That will never stop loving

And their love is like kindness that will never stop growing
Their love is better than life or kindness itself
Their love just grows and grows

Joyce M Eppen
A PROMISE OF NEWNESS

To Ron, my son, and Marcy, my daughter, who taught me the meaning of unconditional love.

The days bring forth a promise of newness
That transforms the tomorrows into todays.
With each moment is born a new thought
And an old wound is healed.

Look outward into the mountains
And guess the mystery that they guard.
Caress the sunset with your heart—
It is pursued by the brilliance of the stars.

Hold close those things that are yours—
In the distance they may fade and become illusions.
Only that which is at hand can be lived
And today's realities become tomorrow's memories.

D E Baltrush
THE PAST CANNOT BE FORGOTTEN

To John, whose love, gave me the courage to expose my feelings to the world; I love you.

The past cannot be forgotten, only deadened in it's
painful memories

The present cannot be taken for granted, it's joys
can only be relished

The future cannot be foretold, it's mysteries can
only be imagined.

Cynthia Terrell
MY FRIEND, MY FRIEND . . .

To my brother-in-law Johnny Terrell may he rest in peace. God bless you.

I used to have a friend, that was very dear to me!

Always loving,
Always concerned.
Always there when I needed,
"My Friend,"
To talk,
To share my laughter,
To share my happiness.
And my sorrow,
Then something clicked
in
"My Friend's,"
Mind one day.
"My Friend"
That I trusted with my secrets was never again.
Never has that friend not been truthful,
Never once missed a meeting,
Never intentionally sayin things out of the way.
"My Friend,"
Kept the darkest secrets,
Not truly trusting me until it was over.
"My Friend, My Friend."
How could we be so,
Close but yet so far.
Cherish so much,
And yet share so little.
"My Friend, My Friend . . .

Bridget M Johnson
SHE'S MY BEST FRIEND

Dedicated to my mother who brings joy in everyone's life with whom she comes in contact with. And to all parents who share a bond of friendship with their children, to my creative writing teacher for acknowledging my creative abilities.

She's my best friend because whenever I was in pain
I called on her and without hesitation, she came

She's my best friend because whenever I was in trouble
She advised me to "get out" on the double
She's my best friend because when I moved far apart from her
(Almost out of existence)
We continued to talk, no matter how far the distance

She's my best friend because when I slipped and fell and lost all hope
She smiled at me and said, "If anyone can—you can cope"

She's my best friend because when I needed a laugh—when I needed to be free
She didn't send one chuckle . . . but she sent three

She's my best friend because when I needed it, she punished me And for this I really love her
She's my best friend—my best friend—and yes, she's my mother!

Thanks mom for being a Friend

J D Humphries
AFTER MIDNIGHT:

Dedicated to: "My Living Doll"

In the deep dark hours of the silent night,
I walk alone in the pale cold light.
Of a million stars that twinkle on high,
With a love for you that will not die.

While high above me in the darkness of space,
I catch a glimpse of your lovely face.
The cool night breeze that tugs at my hair,
Whispers to me that you still care.

No one can see the tears that gleam,
Upon my cheeks that your memory bring.
No one can know the pain in my heart,
That threatens to tear my world apart.

Those years have dimmed these eyes of mine,
And with the healing hands of time.
Engraved these lines upon my face,
But; those memories of you they cannot erase.

Elina Russo
RUMORS

This is for mom, Joe, Rose, Sadie and Carmen who all inspired me and are the real reason why I keep doing what I love doing.

"Did you know that . . . "
is all that you hear
Each and everyday
from your fellow peers.
Some of them are old,
Some of them are new
But most of the time
They're all untrue.
Rumors to some may seem
to be cheerful,
But to the victim, they're
nothing but tearful.
So next time the "word"
is out,
Don't pout,
Just doubt.

Daniel Louis Duncan
WHEN BEAUTY LIES

Are you like the spider
Who lives a little lie?
He spins a web of beauty
Just to trap a fly.

A masterpiece of art!
It makes you want to cry.
That such dedicated work

Is just to trap a fly.

Are you like the spider
Who lives a little lie?
That makes his home inviting
Then pounce upon the fly.

Are you like the spider
Who lives a little lie?
He paints a pretty picture
For those about to die.

Are you like the spider
Who lives a little lie?
His paint turns to poison
As it begins to dry.

Are you like the spider
Who's after little flies?
Spinning lines of beauty
Into a web of lies.

Sally Belenardo

Sally Belenardo
JACOB'S GARDEN

In memory of my beloved grandfather, Jacob Bauer

These butterflies with yellow wings,
The flowers, too, such silent things—
That, were I deaf, how could I know—
In Jacob's garden, where I go?

Soon would I know, when no bird sang,
And feel, as Jacob, sorrow's pang;
He never knew delights of sound,
Though joys of sight did here abound.

Daniel Kevin Valtrakis
FAT CARS SCRATCHING

To Debbie . . . I believe

Fat cars scratching
Rough & sexual
w/ animal fever

Drunk on Irish poetry
Stoned w/ messiahonic words

DNA
Damaged by alcohol
Altered by primate erection

Breathless faces chanting,
The defeat of bones

Singing,
Naked is the Earth
When you are all alone.

Joseph C Herrington Sr
HAPPY ANNIVERSARY

To My Darling Judy

To my darling wife,
on this special day;
I have no flowers,
but I'd like to say,
Just how much I love you,
and that I really care;
For all the thrilling moments,
with love that we share;
Tho' I gave you no gift,
I do give you my love.
God is my witness,
as known by "Him" above;
Thanks for ten years of loyalty,
ten years of happiness,
Ten years of standing by me
with all my forgetfulness.

Monya M Mangascle
LOVE

A bittersweet remembrance . . . Dedicated to Marsha

Love becomes a sacrifice
When the heart knows
The inner reality
Is built only on lies.

Sometimes it is better
To listen inwardly
And deal with it
Then let it shatter.

To be strong is strength
In itself, and more
It cleanses the Soul
Thus softening the length.

It it is not to be
Though both hearts
Did beat in unison
Then courage needs to see . . .

Thus, humbly to say
Thank you so much
I wanted it to last
Forever and a day . . .

Sylvia Kringdon
A MOTHER'S OATH

In memory of my loving mother, for all she gave to me.

When I was born, she took an oath
Tears in her eyes, a sigh in her throat,
to care for me, her little jewel
She swore she'd work and see me through school

As I got older, she hollered a lot
Cause I was brazen and thought I was smart
Then came the day I had to admit
Mother was right and I was licked

Soon came my wedding, she planned and she fussed
She said to me, "Daughter, now you adjust"
I was so happy those days gone by
I still remember when she said goodbye
She said to me, "My job's all done,
I'll pray for you and your little one"

Now I know why she took an oath
Tears in her eyes a sigh in her throat
Oh Mother dear, I now understand
I'll do the same for my little lamb
Tears in my eyes, a sigh in my throat
I too will take this Mother's Oath

Robertson Claiworth
ALMIGHTY GOD IS

To Terri—(Theresa Marie Clark) a glorious artist and a loving, caring, thoughtful daughter—a treasure given to me by our Lord on a Christmas day.

A profound spirit that had no "start"—
That majestic mountain is his heart.
You can find his love, with firm belief—
In that mighty oak, or an aspen leaf.
That trail of beauty thru a craggy glen—
Is where you're going, and where he's been.
His love and his mercy really knows no bounds.
The way that he is—is how nature sounds.

Not a rush of discomfort in a forceful breeze—
It's the voice of his pleasure, whispering love's ease.
Wherever I go now, yes—it's true!
I find him in these things—and in you.

Daisy Nugent
SPEAK, HEAR, OR SEE

A dedication to all those young lives that were taken away without a cause.

If I could speak, I would ask why?
If I could hear, then I listen to the birds chirping
Away in the early mornings.
If I could see, I would see trees in the desert and
Rain pour over the driest country.
Nor can I speak, hear, or see.
I'm lost so deep inside myself that there's no way out.
I ask for those who could speak and ask why, who can hear
That song up in the air and who could see the dreams that
I long to see.

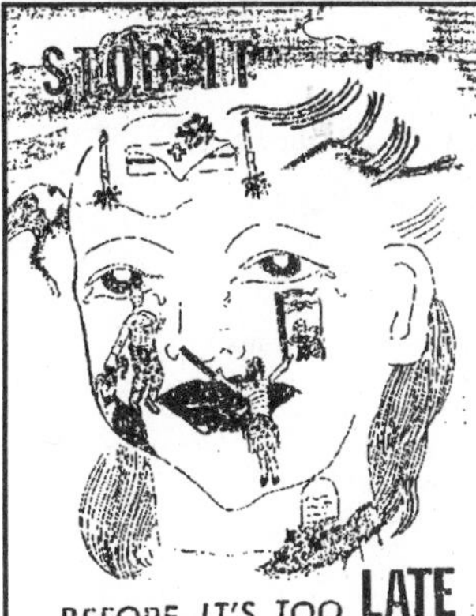

Please do not run away, stop and see me sometime.
I'm only six feet under and I can't explain why.
I once existed, but I wasn't given the chance,
"To speak, hear or see."

Lorine Shaver
DAY

Dedicated to "Jehovah God" The Creator of day."

Day is a time to work and play
A time when things must be done
Whether tasks are large or tasks are small
There's always a list a mile long.

It seems there's never enough time in a day
To do all we want to do
So let's do the necessary things to-day
And to-morrow follow that rule

Our work can bring joy
Our work can make us sad
Each day can be boring
Or each day can make us glad.

If our works are good
At the end of the day
We can lie down at night
And thank God for that day.

Deborah L Walston
EMPTY

To my beloved brother, Robert Hartel, without whom I would have never wrote this poem.

Things not what they used to be,
missing one inside of me.
Deathly lost, this can't be real,
I can't stand this hell I feel.
Emptiness is filling me
to the point of agony.
Growing darkness, taking dawn
I was me—but now he's gone
Death greets me warm, I sigh
Now it's time to say goodbye.

Dani Monroe
SPIRITUAL UNION

To James, may this poem serve as a reflection of our lives & love

Together we walk forward in our lives
celebrating union, family and community.

Inviting change to shape our hearts
and blend our souls,
we give thanks for
inner peace and guidance.

Sharing love and life
we bond as one,
yet, remain individual spirits
moving towards the light.

We no longer question who we are
but thrive on what we're becoming
CEREMONIAL PARTNERS
in a dance of love and union!

Nora M Braun
LET LOVE CONQUER

For Alison and Sarah, that they may remember

A kiss goodnight, a song
to lure sweet dreams,
A tender word to chase
away night shadows—
Gifts of love in darkness.

Daylight beats down
reservoirs of patience,
Frazzled nerves emit shrieks
before twilight cools—
Love does not always conquer.

When toys sit bereft
of childish attention,
Doors swinging outward
more oft than in—
Remember nightly rituals.

Cindy Lehnherr Hanke
HIS PROMISE

This poem is dedicated to my husband Dean, whom I love, my children Katie and Daniel whom I cherish, and to my Pastor Bob who inspired me to write it. —Cindy Lehnherr Hanke (Corvallis Oregon—)

I had a talk with God today
his voice was soft and sweet,
He said "My child if you should fall
I'll stand you on your feet.

Don't worry about me catching you
my hands are big and strong,
because, you see my little girl
I've loved you for so long.

I died for you so long ago
and yet it seems so near,
and when you're feeling lost and sad
I'll dry up every tear.

This life I've chosen for you my child,
has trials woven through, but,
don't give up, believe in me
for I've always believed in you.

So live for me, be strong in me,
and talk with me each day,
for I will always be with you
I'll never go away."

H L Towne
OPEN

To all the wonderful ladies I have had the pleasure to befriend in my lifetime.

Open your eyes to see my face.
Open your arms to my embrace.

Open your ears to hear my plea.
Open your mind to my dream.

Open your lips to receive my kiss.
Open your senses to my bliss.

Open your soul to Venus above.
Open your heart to feel my love.

I open my eyes to see your face.
I open my arms to your embrace.

I open my ears to hear your plea.
I open my mind to your dream.

I open my lips to receive your kiss.
I open my senses to your bliss.

I open my soul to Eros above.
I open my heart to feel your love.

Dorothy M Ralston
A PRAYER FOR YOU

This Poem is dedicated to my wonderful FRIENDS

My thoughts for prayer were of me,
And then I began to look
Outside of myself to really see:
This one, that one, these and those were
More important than me!
The lady I barely knew,
Bits and pieces of information
Sifted ever so slowly through:
Her husband had trouble with his heart,
And she had illness, too.
Precious Lord, they need your healing hands,
Then there is the lady with the bent fingers,
Who is so kind and dear to lend her hands
To help beautify our precious City lands.
For her, I give thanks and know You understand!
I listen to your beautiful song,
But how much more the Master
Listens. He helps you along
With every written word,
He knows your heart holds no wrong!
A man with a jolly soul
Can surely make us chuckle
With his Limericks of mirth:
Thanks dear Lord for the fruit of his goal.
Let the sunshine roll, to lift
And dispel the gloom, clinging inside!
A great man of great age,
Kept young by counting back
Each year, on life's page.
He is so much more important than I!
Thank you Lord, for the Prince of
Peace
in every age!
Deity Father, in whom we trust, can forecast,
Each of us in your Book of Truth:
You wish all well and health to last.
You see our usefulness to Thee
Hopefully the dream of a bright future
holds fast!
Please give strength to those hanging in,
Every day to keep fighting
To make our world a better place,
In which to live without Devil and sin.
God said to tell Satan, "GET thee behind"
God and His Son are our Leaders now, we follow Them!
May the beauty of our Lord continue to shine
Upon each and everyone!

Laurel W Smith
FOREFATHER

Dedicated to Philip C. Learned

God's crying
I'm crying
and the whole
world is getting wet.
The demise
of time authorizes
a contingency of
man defying
his moral principles
in the most elemental
terms.
Ages of stone
breaketh
beneath our feet.
Intelligence known
to defeat.
Armor defending battle
the earth
uncontrolled
as cattle.
Unorthodox visions.
Prayer
before
provisions.
Necessities
oblique.
Silence
replete
with voices
coming to be.
Admonish
before we
complete . . .
Thoughts
rummaging
the city streets.
God's crying
I'm crying
and
the whole
world is getting wet.

It's up
to us.

Tracy Donohue
CONFUSED

To Doug

Scattered hints
of similar emotions.
Fragmented clues
of the usual deceit.
Widespread traces
of ignorance.
Sown pieces
of the blind innocence of young love.
All bound together within my mind
To confuse my heart.

Melissa & Martha Bishop

Diane Gould Riedel
BABY SISTERS

Dedicated to Melissa & Martha Bishop the twins we love you

Two baby sisters, sleeping side by side,
too small to understand their mother's trembling hand. They can tell there's pain in their mother's sobs.

Why is she crying of a broken heart?
No one understands the hand of God.
So we take each day with love and joy
and lend a loving hand, when we can.

As we watch these two little sisters, playing and holding hands, and wonder if they miss their daddy's warm and tender hand. For he's not been around and they're too young to understand.

Grandma tries as hard as she can, to be a tower of strength, with a loving hand.
But no one would understand how all this will end. How all this love came to be, just because of a loving man.

Two baby sisters, who sleep side by side,
never knowing the love of a father who died.

Tessa Lape
UNTITLED

To Philip. Maybe someday . . .

We sat alone,
Out on the beach.
The two of us,
We were beyond reach.
We looked on at the moon,
Such a beautiful sight to see.
We were holding hands,
Just you and me.
It was a beautiful moment,
The stars shone bright.
Together we shared,
The mystery of that special night.

Natalie Couion
GOD'S GREAT LOVE

To my family, who taught me the real meaning of love.

God made the earth, the sea and sky,
With beauty reaching far and wide;
He placed the mountains high above,
Towering monuments to His love.

And with each thread, a single strand,
A carpet woven by His hand;
To stretch across the mountain side,
And touch the rainbow passing by.

The circle turns, the seasons change,
All a part of His Great Plan;
The circle turns, but never breaks
The pattern of The Master's Hand.

And beauty all around us glows
To warm our hearts when days grow cold;
In my silent thoughts I know
His gentle love will live and grow.

No rainbow comes before the storm,
No rose can bloom without the thorn;
God moved the mountains, calmed the sea,
And found a place for you and me.

Stacy Breerwood
THE LOST APPLE

This poem is dedicated to my parents, Bill and Carole, whose constant love and inner strength inspired me to start writing.

And through the dark, murky waters
The silent rage uncoiled.
Enraptured with its own kind,
It ate up the beauty, the divine.
And for once in the morning in the creation of dawn
Man felt his downfall, the holiness gone.

Donna Zeihen
THE WEAVER

To Joan Hays a master weaver and friend, with love

You weave the sunrise and sunset
Interlacing your colors like the morning star
Into patterns of the midnight sun.
You compose your creations
With delicate imagination of texture
In every fiber of your homespun web.

Willie J Robinson
BROTHER JOSEPH

To "Oxfam;" "Vista;" Larry Jones; etc:

If I were black America,
The laden ships would tell
My famine-stricken brethren
That Brother Joseph is "alive and well"
And, I wear the ring of Pharaoh!—
And, I ring their supper bell!

Michael Chaffee
LOVE IS LIKE A SEED

Dedicated to Teresa, my seed & inspiration

Love is like a seed,
It must be planted, nurtured, & cared for.
Like a seed it will grow into a beautiful flower.
The flower must survive the hot & the cold,
Much like we must survive the good & bad.
As the petals fall from the flower & die,
New life begins as new seeds take root.
As life goes on our seeds grow as our

Flowers die and new ones appear.
We learn from our mistakes and grow together,
Like a flower grown from a seed.

Patricia A Earney

Patricia A Earney
ARE WE REALLY THROUGH

The days are bleak, the nights grow long,
When you're not by my side!
Was I right, or was I wrong,
Was it foolish pride!

I love you now, and always,
You mean everything to me!
Without you life means nothing,
and nothing is what I'd be!

So please come back, don't leave me,
My heart will break in two!
Without you I'll go crazy,
Don't tell me that we're through!

Gloria Putnam
GATHERING EYES

Opening my eyes each day is like a tiny miracle.
My eyes see the world as it could be just like an oracle.
Full of hopes and dreams that do come true,
Making everyone happy not blue.
Like a baby's first step or puppy love,
We all have our dreams and hopes that we think of.
It will happen in my eyes each and every day.
Every dream and hope will happen as I pray.
When I close my eyes I find deep in my soul,
That time is so precious as I grow old.
I find myself thinking of my childhood,
That after all, those times were good.
Life was full and bright,
Children would wish on a starry night.
Soon everyone will open their eyes,
To this bright wonderful world full of surprise.
They'll find happiness, love and laughter,
Just like the fairy tales, we'll live happily ever after.
Then these weary eyes will krinkle with delight,
Knowing the world has finally been put right.

Loretta Diane Granger
KIDS

The kids of today is our tomorrow. Sometimes they bring us heartache, pain, and sorrow. But when that little smile breaks through, or when they pick a flower just for you.

But when a child feels the pressure that we adults feel.
They know life's problems are for real. It's not a life of story books and nursery rhymes, and they can't be happy all the time.

They're little people just like me and you, only they don't understand everything they're going through. So we tell them something for their own sake. How many advices you didn't take?

And somehow we made it through, let's give them a chance to show us what they may do. Let's just stop and think for a little while, after all this is your child.

Owen H Madden
ON WORDSWORTH'S <u>WHAT MAN HAS MADE OF MAN</u>

As I stroll along the beach at night,
and my feet caress the sand,

I think about what man has done—
what man could do for man.

I watch the waves come gliding in
and massage the waiting sand;

I see the empires passed on by,
that once were ruled by man,

And often wonder what man could do
if man did care for man.

Wonder how, I know not why
for man can't care for man.

And like those waves that come on in
and massage the waiting sand,

Man only waits for one to come
and caress his burning hand.

Sunny Oralee Adams Faudt
ROMANCE IS

*Zelma Ruth Norcross—small sister**Big ability James Paul Adams Sr.**beloved replica*Son*

To me.
Romance is the sandals of wind at sunset, stirring emotions with a restless whisper for which there are no words . . .

Romance is a soft, shy reaching for all that is warm and gentle, it is a deep well into which one plunges willingly to understand the beloved.

Romance is tenderness, that embraces day and night—it is a waiting to look into eyes that mirror self.

Romance is passion, that lights, burns and lifts into ecstasy. It is dreams awakened with an odd intensity in alien lands.

Romance is—wings that can lift lovers to the warmth of the sun, or gentle gales of the storm, leaving them untouched.

But then—romance is also broken wings, when love is done. It tosses, twists, and grinds downward with unbearable pain.

My rendezvous with the strongest and strangest of all masters—was it last night or in another life? Why do I understand it all so well.

"Romance is" heaven—it is also hell.

Claudette Daniels Allen

Claudette Daniels Allen
FIRST WONDER

God has prepared a stage for a world premier.
The command performance is your timely arrival.
The day of your birth is your invitation to attend this great performance.
Your entrance is hailed by loud protests and many celebrations.
You have just accomplished one of natures greatest feats.
It is now recorded that you have been born.
Your heralded appearance seems suspicious to you.
So you wail, scream and kick to protest your reluctance to be here.
Now you are tired and as you fall asleep,
You lay there and wonder what all this means.
Meanwhile, all that lies ahead of you remains to be seen.
And only God knows what is to be your next scene.

Tania Walter
THE JOURNEY ONWARD

To my loving parents, with all of my heart.

As you run the race, He is with you,
Never will He abandon your side.
When you come upon trails of darkness,
You are soon to be walking in the light.
If Heartbreak Hill engulfs you,
and there seems to be nothing you can do;
Through faith He encourages you to travel onward,
Even if it is just one step at a time.
He can work many wonders,
And so can you through faith;
Race onward, onward—
Take the plunge,
And always bear this thought in mind:
There will always be a tomorrow,
A new day, new month, new year,
In which He will help you through.
Remember the good times, the bad times, and such,
Because there is always a reason to live
Within the world He created for us.

Irma B Otwell
BEAUS OF YESTERDAY

To my dear son, John

I visited the past today;
I traveled the memory road.
The road was long
But soothing to my soul.
I saw the faces of the past
As clear as clear can be.
They are my friends
But they are gone,
And I am left, you see.
Those were happy days.
We were all so young and free,
But things that happened
Were meant to be,
And the one I chose
is growing old with me.

Lyndall Hodges
TRIALS

To My Children Christina, Mary Francis, Thomas, Donna and Travis

Trials, why do you come my way
on such a bright and shining day,
these things I do not understand,
but know that they are in God's plan.

I struggle now from day to day,
to understand and grow in God's own way.

For all the pain we must go through,
God sends his many blessings too.

May we but grow in strength and love
that we may return one day,
to God above.

Joan A Hughes
WHERE DOES LOVE GO WHEN IT DIES

Where does Love go when it dies
Does it sit on a cloud and cry
Or does it fly off to another heart
Stay awhile, then depart

Ruth M Ward
50TH CLASS REUNION

Dedicated to the alumni who worked so hard to make our 50th Class Reunion a huge success for the "CLASS OF '36" of POMONA HIGH SCHOOL, POMONA CA.

The air was filled with excitement
The faces were happy and gay
For this was the day we hoped for
Our 50th Reunion Day

The years had taken their toll
But the smiles were just the same
The hair was a little thinner
And the legs a little bit lame.

Our hearts were filled with gladness
As each walked 'cross the stage
To receive his rolled-up scroll
To mark our GOLDEN AGE.

Two of our most loved teachers
Had come from far and near
To share the precious memories
And celebrate our special year

To some it was a fond farewell
To old POMONA HIGH
And to the "CLASS OF 36"
Maybe a last goodbye!

Michael H Cunningham
SOMOZA'S SHAME

To my loving and devoted family

Two score and five
Oh! such a long time
gone so many lives
now, not even a whine
They came in the night
to wreak their havoc
Ours was such a plight
Oh! so tragic
Death and destruction
was the name
the peasants of our nation
was the game
So it was and so it will be
until such time that we perfect
humanity

Julie Gerth
THEY POUND ON MY PILLOW PASSAGE
Those horrifying creatures
in repression's sea
doom in my dream
ghosts that are me.

Abstractions big and small
familiar and strange
symbols of us all
unify and derange.

They Pound on my Pillow Passage
but don't ask to sing.
I remember them
and the fear that we bring.

Friday night charades, Sunday
parades,
everyday a masquerade, a mass,
scare . . .
never letting doubts and fears
. . . raid

Eerie tunes, persistent pain
Shadow chasing at my heels.
I turn and look,
my false security it steals.

Lydia Moccero
ODE TO HENRY WADSWORTH LONGFELLOW
Writing's real—
Rhymes concern us
with devotion genuine.

Composition
is in earnest
and requires discipline.

Works of poets all remind us
we should make our words
sublime—
In the writing leave behind us

Imprints
in the
Halls of Rhyme.

Jeanette Micklich
DREAMS
Dreams are for soaring, for getting
away,
For picking you up when it's been a
bad day.
Dreams can be big or dreams can be
small.
Pity the person with no dream at all.
He's got to live in the world as it is,
No silver lining will ever be his.
No worldly riches or even fame
Will you ever find attached to his
name.
So dare to dream and be taken away
To romantic places you'd like to
stay.
And dare to dream of riches untold,
Of silver, and bronze, and even gold.
Never let your dreams be taken away
By those afraid to run and play.
Savour your dreams—don't let go
For those who scoff & are afraid to
show
That sometimes a dream is what you
need,
To get you through rough times
indeed.
Let your dreams take you where they
may.
And never, never let your dreams get
away.

Rickey Shive
I SEE THE LAST RISING SUN
Standing alone wintering time,
a face of no expression.

Soon scarred by the changing
seasons.

Falsely rooted once again, only to
withstand the elements presented.

Bound aloft with cold steel,
taut from both sides.

Bound below by earth's cursory grip,
tamped yet so tightly by a
methodical hand.

One last stem of hope piercing from
an east side, only to find certain
cessation
rooted below.

There weeps a yearning for the last
rising sun.

Cherie A Emery
TOKYO
Bright morning over tall apartment
buildings
The city awakes
Futons hang airing over balcony rails
Absorbing exhaust from commuter
traffic jams.

The woman sets to work, whacking
them,
"free the dirt," she thinks.

Husband and children scurry off to
work and school
leaving the apartment in its own
cloud of smoke
left from stale cigarettes and
greasy fried fish.

The woman turns to her day with a
sigh:
apartment to clean,
diapers to scrub,
dishes to wash,
baby to feed . . .

The roar of the vacuum cleaner
masks the sound
of sudden rain
Too late—
Soggy futons.

Tracy Jane Erickson Elliott
A POET
A poet is a word
turned upside down
from a laugh and a smile
to a tear and a frown.

Framed in a heart
and hung on the wall,
a word tells a story
and the face tells it all.

Evangeline Andriopoulos
POWER STRUGGLE
The uncertainties,
the misfortunes,
the opportunity to create a mere
tragedy
becomes an effortless crime.

Success—
the opposition,
struggling aggravation,
depression of going nowhere.
Only more confusion.

The determination to succeed.
Paths to walk.
Hills to climb.
Mountains beyond all hills.
Only to hike to the top,
and to stand there for one brief
moment in time.
And back down we climb to safety.

The plateau—
a mere flat surface.
where we feel secure and there is no
danger.
Only those of us, who have no fear to
venture high,
will reach the highest plateau of them
all.

Orsolina Cinzia Garisto
LILY OF LOVE

To my loving family and friends; who have walked beside me during long dark nights, until together we found the light of happiness and inspiration of each new day!

His love for me was stronger than I'll
ever know.
He made me feel special; as a baby
born to lovers.
He told me I was a beauty that flew
free on open wings.
I was his glory, his light; I made each
moment be a sacred memory.

We both gleamed as we touched lips,
and we brightened up with each little
hug.
We were made for each other, we
belonged together;
as heaven and the sky, as water
and life.
Our hearts were combined as one, we
lived each day as the first,
we blessed God for having each
other, and we shared our souls
for years.
We experienced love and anger,
happiness and sorrow;
but no matter what time or
place he always made it known
he loved me.

He was the stone of our marriage
which I stood on;
strong and still, knowing he
would be my strength.
To this day I love him with my heart
and soul.
And his love still holds me
strong.
He has been my sky which
surrounded my life with glory and
joy.
"Thank you for being my sun which
has shone on this bud to help bloom
into a beautiful lily
which now floats alone on the
water looking up to her sky."

Nikki Tyler
BEST FRIENDS
B is for Buddies and that's definitely
she and me,
E is for equal for we will
always be.
S is for silly, for that's how we act.
T is for totally honest and that's a
fact.

F is for forever, our friendship will
last.
R is for really close, the days go by
fast.
I is for incredible, as a twosome that
is.
E is for energy, when together we
have.
N is for new, our friendship always
seems to be.
D is for dedicated two friends she
and me.
S is for super which she is to me.

Ann Sinclair
TO HEAVEN AND BACK
There is a light beyond the dead,
My mind searches as I lay in bed.
Midst among the grave,
My own life, I try to save.
Full moon out tonight,
To lead me to the light!
A long journey ahead of me,
Don't turn back to see,
The dangers that's behind me.
Only look ahead, to see what maybe.
Finally, I find my salvation,
To meet a long, lost salutation.
But a force turns me back,
Back onto another track.
A track back to the end,
To start all over again.
Now, everything seems to be right.
I have no fear from this heavenly
light.
—This light watches over me—
—I trust this light helps thee
For I have been to heaven
and back.

Gary Kaus
FATAL MISTAKE
It's over now,
This life of mine,
All my troubles have disappeared.
For I ended it all, last Saturday night,
The pressures I could handle no
more.

Yes the pain has ended and I am at
peace,
But what of those I left behind?
Their hearts are so heavy, their minds
so confused.
Why would he do this?
Runs through their minds.

I don't feel so at peace now,
As I see them below.
If only I'd known the grief I would
make,
By being so foolish,
Making this fatal mistake.

Donald L Clegg
WE WALKED THE GOLDEN LAND
Remember Dear? It has been many a
year,
Since we strolled the aisle—hand in
hand.
With no fear; joy brought glistened
tear,

As we sealed our vows with golden band.

The day our first born—long awaited—arrived,
We adored its newborn semblance of your face.
Sharing the many pleasured moments derived,
As we tendered our love with innocent grace.

Nothing to fear! Our lives did we steer,
Through times of strife and grateful joy!
Our pain we left to sift through life's basketed weir;
To us, each other's comfort was an oft used ploy!

The times we left trodden paths to walk afield,
To smell the flowers or drink in Autumn aflame;
Holding our love afore as a protective shield,
All the world's gloried wilds was ours to tame!

Come with me Dear! Shake those ingrown fears,
And allow your mind—the years to slowly span!
Stalk again through the memories as we peer,
Back to when we walked the golden land!

Patricia Brooks Nicely

WE OF SO MUCH GIVE SO LITTLE

We of so much give so little, but we of so little
give so much.
We of so much do not see the need in others.
While, we of so little not only see, but feel
the need of others.
If we of so much would give to the ones of so little,
then, there would be no need.

George Gilliam

HONEY

Honey, when you came into my life
I finally realized what wasn't right
I had to be with you more and more
Because I didn't want to live the way I lived before

When I looked at you I saw the sun
I saw that together we were one
When I first saw you my heart was sore
Because I missed a part of me I didn't miss before

The love I feel for you burns my heart
Promise me we'll never be apart
The first time you left my heart was tore
Because I cried more tears than I had ever cried before

But before I could die from the pain
You came back to my side once again
And now we're together as before
And now I know you'll never ever leave me anymore

Benita M Caruthers

WHAT HIS LOVE IS LIKE

His love is,
Like the sun coming out on a cold and cloudy day;
Like a person smiling when there's nothing but sadness around
Like hearing a new-born babe cry her first cry;
Like seeing nature, green and alive after a cold hard winter
Like finding an old misplaced treasure after many years;
His love is like no other's for
His love will be forever

Genevia McKenzie Boyd

Genevia McKenzie Boyd

WHERE ARE YOU GOD?

This poem is dedicated to the People Who Care organization

Where are you God?
I know you see me,
I know you hear me,
I know you are near.
Where are you God?

My heart feels your love,
My soul feels your spirit,
My mind feels your peace,
But, Where are you God?

God I need your help to endure this test,
It has defeated me at its best,
Sometimes I feel like going on home to rest,
Where are you God?

I cannot give up on life because,
I was bought with a price,
God make haste and send the right advice.

Margaret A Giffing

LOOKING FOR LOVE

The promise that you can be mine,
always brings on strong hope.

Pictures are painted that much would be gained,
there is no time to mope.

You woo me to aim,
for beautiful feelings & promises that are invoked.

My heart ventures forth,
to reach the dream with no shame.

Leading on giving heart-ache and making me feel blame.

Each heart breaking event brings inner strength and renewed hope,
that I'll be released from looking for love.

Dorothy Zietz

THE QUIET CLIMB

Reality begins with reflections
Of time, place, people
And things,
Reality keeps our dreams
Clear and full
Of today, tomorrow and
Other years,
We stretch to understand
The evasive magic
Of our own perceptions,
Of dreams
As we want them to be
In quiet shadows
Or in the depth of
Full light,
As we climb slowly
Ever so slowly
To reach the top
Of our own glass ladder.

Thomas A Laskey

MY GIFT

I was born and given a great gift of life
One I have enjoyed and lived rather nice
A gift to give, run, jump and play basketball
But dancing and playing basketball is what I miss most of all
I have memories of days of old
A gift and a story I think must be told

When I was a young man, I kinda ran the streets
And if I was your friend, I would be the best friend you'll ever meet
I would help others, without a reason to be found
And when there was trouble, I was always around

I joined the service of my choice
And in the Marine Corp, I learned tact and command of voice
I was in a war, where you heard all kinds of tales
But in the Marine Crop, I learned success never fails
While in battle I faced, a many of tough spots
Until that day, when I heard and felt the shots
I went down never to walk again
My gift now is my brain, my friend
And for that gift I thank GOD, unto no end

Rev William F Brown

CONTENTMENT?

I stretch my mind across the space,
which keeps us both apart.
I try to kiss your lovely face,
With all the strength within my heart.
And, when, at last, I do succeed,
I feel contentment deep.
I bask in the triumph of my deed,
Then gently fall asleep.

Susan McGalliard

AUTUMN

To my husband, Ray, and my sons, Gary and Jimmy With all my love.

We watched the gently falling leaves,
Goldenrods nodding in the breeze.
Green trees laden with apples of gold,
Such a glistening sight to behold.
Buttercups with laughing faces,
Golden leaves piled in different places.
Brisk air and cloudless skies,
Let us know autumn has arrived.

Marla Ciavardini

WREATH OF HOPE

Pitch black, sudden deepness,
lies within the suns golden crested view,
reflecting off the lily pond,
steaming glow of dreamy rose hue.

Season's lust tripped,
into the wondrous,
smooth white blossoms,
a wreath of hope,
from summer to fall,
cradled within the heart of every jewel,
enchanted with the special time of fall to summer,
in-between spring,
where there is no rule.

Lotus, glorious treasure, painted in the sky,
sends warmth upon our breast.

Miracles grow, with a wreath of hope,
through translucence.

Sun strokes shade, burning rises up and sets,
to start another day, of the hot season's test.

Monica K Begeman

I'VE BEEN CHEATED ON AND LIED TO

I've been cheated on and lied to
and yet I still go back for more.
You don't understand my feelings
yet I can't walk out the door.
Your talk is so convincing
you say everything's alright.
So, I turn my back to leave you
and I finally see the light.
You'll never really be mine
you still want to be free.
I guess I've finally realized
that you'll never love just me.

Joseph Turner

I ONLY WANT YOUR LOVE.

I only want your love,
I only want your kisses,
If you don't love me,
I'll never know what bliss is.

Since you found another,
And said good-bye to me,
You sent me oh, so far away,
To live in misery.

Now that you have left me,
My heart is broke in two,
I don't want a broken heart,
All I want is you.

You don't care if I love you,
You wouldn't even sigh,
You told me not to bother,
Just go away and cry.

Come back to me my darling,
Come back to me my love,
Come back to me my darling,
We'll watch the stars above.

Luben G Angeloff

I DID IN MY MIND

I did in my mind
For AIDS a cure to find,
To stop people to worry and cry
But to be happy and smile.

I know that you need now money
But I can give you only honey,
Even you may now don't want to see
But I'll try to do what will good be.

I know that the entire World is scared
But I show that for the World I do care,
Even somebody may try to stop me
And one day you may that see . . .

Virginia W Thomson

THE GREATEST PRIZE OF ALL

Why do some people lie when stating so-called evidence?

Clarence Darrow showed a pig's tooth
For a man's tooth at the 1925 Scopes "monkey" Trial.

Are these people rebels against God?

Don't they realize they are gambling

with their souls?

If there is no God, they have nothing to lose.
But if there is, and all sound evidence shows there is a God,
Deity in three Beings: the Father, the Son, and the Holy Spirit,
Then those who deny Him have everything to lose,
And their souls will dwell forever in torment.

Why risk such a consequence?

All the Israelites who escaped from Egypt
Heard His voice at Mt. Sinai and were fearful.
"The fear of the Lord is the beginning of wisdom."

Those who love and keep His commandments
Will dwell with God forever in Heaven.

Why not seek this greatest prize and satisfy your soul?

Julia L Flynn

Julia L Flynn
I WOULD RATHER HAVE YOU LORD

To my mother and father Mr and Mrs Leon Flynn, With all my love.

I would rather have you Lord
Than all the riches of this world
I would rather be your Friend
Than gold and silver spend.

I would rather gather hay
In your vineyard day by day
I know I'll be satisfied
When I reach the other side.

When I get over there
Your loving voice I'll hear
Your smiling face I'll see
As you wait to welcome me

The golden bells will ring
And the heavenly choir will sing
Angels will play harps of gold
As their beautiful wings they fold.

The Father will be there
Oh, what joy we all will share!
The living will be grand
In the milk and honey land.

I am striving day by day
As I climb the upward way
To be patient kind and true
And keep on trusting you

This is my earnest plea
Dear Lord please answer me
And when my journey is complete
Let me rest at your blessed feet.

Uldine S Capell
JAMES CASH PENNEY
Mr. J. Cash Penney was my inspiration;
His love of God and man, gave me determination;
To enter the work force, to do a job well;
He had a good plan for people, who sought to sell;
Or render a service, I chose Credit—Layaway;
Altogether, seventeen years, I never stopped loving my work for even a day;
I heard once, Mr. P. might take a prospective associate out to lunch;
Before he was hired to become one of the bunch;
And if he salted his food, before he did taste;
He didn't make it friend, his time was a waste.

Elaine C Hull
TIME
Time—
is Something
which intersects
Straight
with All circumstances.
Defining
their Place
As
lines
on the map.
Definite—
Predictable,
Yet—
as Topography,
varying
Individually
According
to Place
and
the Seer.

Leslie Jo Ginter
LAST SPRING
One April
afternoon,
as sparrow laughter in the elm
promised alms for winter,

you lay down
in the habit of recent years,
to chase the chill
under a cover of bright patches
you had sewn together with the black yarn
of one terrible November.

Your tired eyes, worn dry by years
of seeking answers to children's tears,
finally were shuttered
as you gracefully surrendered
your weathered weary winter heart
to dreams of yellow angels
singing in the dark.

Raymond A Ward
MIRACLES OF LIFE
I do believe in miracles for it's
not hard to see,
The blossom of the buttercup,
also the budding of the tree.

The joy to see the robin outside
on the lawn of green—
They are busy stirring around,
as you can hear them merrily
sing.
Plants are starting to revive from the
winter which was so fair,
Everywhere I look, to me, there
is spring time in the air.

Here comes the Easter bunny, gladly
hopping along the way,
Hiding eggs here and there upon
this Easter Day.

But the reason Easter is so special as
anyone should know,
There is a God who created all
the beauties down here below.

So share a ray of sunshine
along this road you go.
Then life would be endless like
an ever going rainbow.

Ellen Murphy
KAHUNA
I know you do not love me now
There was a time when you needed me
When I fascinated you

You were alone then, unhappy, confused, penniless
Your worn blue overcoat was too thin and too small
You didn't own gloves

I had many coats
I was warm
My pennies bought wine and candles, your cigarettes
and bowls of chowder on the windy wharf

As the winds grew warm, you grew cold
With the sun came your waves—your beloved waves
Your body was warmed by other joys

You grew tanned, and blonder, and happier
You dry cleaned your tuxedo
We never dreamed together again
You were cruel, and I was kind

Jack D Guthrie
AWAY FROM THE CITY
Country boy am I and I always will be
Put me in the city but not city in me
Nothing beats the rooster crowing at break of day
Or smell of fresh cut new mown hay

Fresh eggs and home made bread
On mother's solid oak table spread
Half pound of bacon fried just right
All these and more out of sight

Prepare each day with Lord in mind
Looking up today the sun is going to shine
Remembering way back to days gone by
A tear is felt in the corner of my eye

City traffic has me down
Smile not there but a frown
Parents you took them away
That's why I'm sad with nothing to say

It's time to go back where my heart is home
Throw away electric blower and pick up my comb
The life I love down on the farm
There I'm safe and I'll feel no harm

Helen Wilson
SPRING
While walking in the woods one day
In the very lovely month of May
I saw many beauties of Spring
The chirps of birds in my ears did ring
So sweet the sound and beautiful the trees
The calm and serenity my heart did please
Among the trees were blooming spring flowers
This scene I could enjoy for hours and hours
The babbling brook with its running stream
The sunlight filled my eyes with a gleam
As I strolled along the path that day
A little chipmunk seemed to say
Spring is here at last you see
As he ran around so happily.

Bernice G Schwartz

Bernice G Schwartz
SUMMER STORM
A summer storm is on the way
The sun is veiled in dirty grey
Branches of trees are tossed and teased
Then quiet—stillness—nothing breezed.

The shadows darken on the grass
The stillness—waiting; will it pass?
Again the wind gusting in a spot.
Will it rain—will it not?

A temperamental woman, a tease;
Feisty, fiery, dancing breeze.
What next? Keep the earth waiting,
To receive a downpour—now abating.

Exciting, unponderable, never dull
Summer doldrums, deathly lull.
Drums of thunder, staccato of lightning:
Overture, lights—get set
Curtain down: rain! Wet.

Carissa Kaku
SPRING
Flowers Bloom. Bees buzz.
New things are around.
Nature is working its magic.
Such a beautiful time.
Oh, such a beautiful time!

It's Spring!

Lucille Hester
THE WINTER OF MY LIFE
There's snow on the hills and the wind is cold;
There's a chill in the air today.
The flowers are gone, and the grass is not green,
So winter can't be far away.

There's white in my hair and I'm growing lame.
I don't move as quickly this year.
My eyes have grown dim; I've got aches and pains.
My winter is already here.

But spring comes each year and things turn green again.
That's the way God meant it to be.
Though flowers will bloom and grass will get green,
Winter will stay on for me.

But I had a great spring, and summer was fun.
I lived every day with great zest.
And fall was still good; I loved every day.
Maybe winter will be the best.

Polly E Tompkins
UNIVERSE
The dawn comes with pale yellows and reds,
And the world awakens on a new day;
As these colors reach over the horizon,
Their hues become more vibrant.

The colors grow with each passing minute,
They change from pale reds and yellows,
To the brilliant white light of day,
A brilliance that enters the very soul of men.

Halfway between the dawn and the dusk,
The light is at its very peak of glory;
After this the light starts slowly to diminish
Into the colors of the twilight hour.

Only after the pale colors of twilight fade,
Is there an awareness of another kind of light;
The small lights in the heavens, lighting the dark
And the moon reflecting the light of the past day.

These small lights that appear only at night,
Give us the knowledge that we are only a part
Of something so vast, that it is beyond
Any concept man can conceive.

Peter Lee
THE ANTHOLOGIES DIVIDED
Home is the exile,
Exile is the home.

Shallow wonder they divide:
Writers one color here, writer another there.
Do they do the same when they pen minds
Or co-opt?

There are those who cannot beg,
Yet have not the courage to speak
On home ground:
So shout from here with empty lungs,
To the anthologies divided.

Who speaks?
Home is the exile,
Exile is the home.

Larry Brown Patterson
IVORY-TOWER VALUES
What are our values and where do we stand?
Do we contribute or just demand?
Do we feel for others or play it safe?
Isn't it easier to ignore the waif?

Too few come to the neglected's defense.
Take refuge behind our white picket fence.
We clamor for peace and Mom's apple pie,
Save the three whales but the homeless can die

Don't raise taxes but give us social reform.
Mistress or lover is now quite the norm.
Balance the budget with programs intact,
And lay our mistakes on the rest of the pack.

What we believe in is the way we live—
It's not what we take but what we give.

Tracy Ann Pfaff
MY HEART'S DESIRE
I hold only one desire in my heart
that being to have you
in my life always.
I think back to the moment
when your eyes first met mine
there was a beginning—
a relationship of chance
loving the one man who would
someday make all my dreams
come true.
I often dream of my hearts desire
and in this dream
your gentle touch caresses me
We share each other's love
a bond unbroken by the
barriers of time and man
A love so strong—
so endearing—
My heart's desire, my darling
is to always feel the warmth
and tenderness we share as
one.

Amy Day Egan
JOHN DAY ON HIS EIGHTIETH BIRTHDAY

To my father, who's eighty-plus years have given me much insight.

He can see clearly the times of his life;
Eighty years of insight.
But only God sees freely:
A rock, and upright.

Kind eyes, mind; sharp,
Generous spirit, gentle heart.
A character built on the times of his life;
Eighty years of insight.
But only God can see it freely.

Karan L Roland
LOVERS ONE
Lovers One, And Lovers All,
Can But One, Life But Fall,
Light The Light, All Through The Night,
To Show Us Whether Wrong Or Right!
Lovers Dear, And Lovers True,
Can You But Doubt, That I Love You,
Pour The Wine, So Ruby Fine,
That I May Prove That You Are Mine!

Lovers Sad, And Lovers Wise,
Can You See, At The Full Moon Rise,
Bright As The Sun, You Are My One,
I Know You As My Only Love!

Lovers One, And Lovers All,
I Am At, Your Beck And Call,
With My True Love, As A Quiet Dove,
On Passions We'll Soar High Above!

Beverly A Benning
FAREWELL TO A DEAR FRIEND
I keep wondering why he had to go,
I guess I'm selfish,
I still needed him so.
The house is so empty
and for the time being,
SO IS MY HEART.
I see shadows of him
and he's with me, I know.
AS ALWAYS.
It's Fall . . . and he's gone,
But we'll walk among the leaves
and just be friends.

Gina Mota
SILENT CRY
No one can hear the cry
for help.

No one can help you when
you are alone.

Pain keeps coming in.

And no way to get away
from it.

No way to heal the pain.

Like day turns into night.

As she died slowly away.

Who can help the pain,
but you can't see me cry.

Silent cry is a hard way
to die.

But she can only say goodbye.

Todd Edwards
THE TWILIGHT KNOWS
When thought she heard
the mongoose cry
twas but the wind
that soon would die

When thought she heard
the laughing high of brittles
brack upon the nigh
twas but the sailboat sailing by

When thought she heard
the falling star
twas but a gasp
from the crest afar

Everett Henderson
DO I WALK ALONE
What rustles the leaves when there is no wind
And moving shadows seem like eerie things
And the mystic sounds in twilights dusk
Are they strains of songs the immortals sing

Is it a breath of air upon my cheek
Or a tender kiss from silent lips
And the vagueness of a hand in mine
Is it really the touching of some finger tips

For what is real or make belief
And the imaginations are they all my own
But if I were to really believe in ghosts
Would I ever—ever walk alone

Alan L Bartlett
FIRST SNOW
The air about thunders with scold
of skies gone grey and winds blown cold.
Now slowly starts the fight
of white to grey and grey to white.
At last it's over and all's quiet,
the greys have lost, the world is white.
From doors and windows come people beholding
a wintery world before them unfolding.
Adults turned children become others foe
and the air soon fills with lightly thrown snow.

Daniel Miot
CHANGE
In a world where people roam
And little creatures call their home
A home of ever changing ways
Where mankind's only at a phase
"Can there be peace or always war?"
One question going to the core.
A place where there is much regret,
And every man is his own threat
Can there be hope in this strange place
Where time can only win the race?

Samuel Palermo
DANDELIONS
High atop a straw-like stem,
Lies a bulb with leafy-hem;
And rises up and starts to spread,
It's golden-yellow feathered head!

The pollen draws the honey-bee,
With sweetness you can almost see;
And sits amongst the clover-lee,
With leaf of green and petals-three!

In contrast with that purple bloom,
It dots the fields in Nature's Loom!
And Daisies grow between the Rye,
It must be Spring, You can't deny!

But only Dandelions try;
To mimic birds up in the sky,
And lift up off the ground—
To Fly!

Mr Parmanand Mahabir

Mr Parmanand Mahabir
LIBERTY
In God we trust and thee our people,
Lift our hearts in prayer,
For Strength thine Lord has given thee,
The gift we need to live.

In reverence and with heads bowed down,
We kneel before you Lord,
To ask thee for more peace and love,
And oneness of our hearts.

Our might is great beyond control
Most nations far and wide,
Our towers too are tall and high,
They're bright to glow the sky.

What else we need to build ourselves,
Oh! Nation of the great,
What else we need to live our lives
With fortune that we make?

Let Liberty stand before our eyes,
Our monument of time,
She's guardian of our great dear land
To whom our love will stand.

Lift up your heads to this holy shrine,
Lift up your hearts to her name,
And chant more music-songs of love
To the Lord who gave us fame.

Shirley W Drew

MR. SANDMAN

To—my mother, Edith Wilmouth, who told me about Mr. Sandman, and my children Lola, B J. Spence, and Harry

As darkness came over my house on the hill,
I got in my bed and lay very still.
I made a wish on the evening star,
And prayed for everyone, near and far.
I counted the flowers on my bedspread too,
As I lay real quiet, just waiting for you.
"I'll see you tonight," I told myself.
"Are you big like a giant, or small like an elf?"
I know you'll be here, you've come before.
Do you come in my window, or my bedroom door?
If I wait long enough, I'm bound to see
Who comes in at night and watches over me.
And stays with me through the long dark night,
and wakes me each morning with the bright sunlight.
I'll wait for you as long as I can.
I'll see you tonight, "Mr Sandman."

Wendell "X legend" Hull

SIX AND GROWING

I'm just a drop of water in the bottom of the sea.
You don't have to find me cause I'll always be me.
I might start a river or just be an overflow.
Sometimes I seem lost, but I have a place to go.
I might build a space ship or go on racing cars.
I might dream forever or be as silent as the stars.
I might think of ways to save this lucky world,
or fit into the crowd and find myself a pretty girl.
I might make my future along my father's side.
I love my mother so, with a kiss I must hide.
Someday I'll be a man without my childish ways.
But if they will accept a child I will stay.
If winning is my future the game I will concede.
So for now leave my toys beneath the sandbox at my knees.
Let me build my kingdoms alone within myself.
Each a set of treasures I store upon a shelf.
I'm just a drop of water in the bottom of the sea.
You don't have to find me cause I'll always be me.

Alice Diane Baggett

GOD'S WISDOM

Lord, in whatever pathway you lead,
You know our every need.
You know the things that are best
And you know all of the rest.

So, we only have to lay a thing in Your hands
And You are the One who understands
The way we are and what we can take
And what kind of decisions we ought to make.

Sheila Underwood

IN SEARCH FOR PEACE

I search for peace in the outer courts
where busy people come and go

I search for peace in the inner courts
with family and those I know

But I find peace in the temple,
It is the Lord, the Prince of Peace

In Him my soul finds its fulfillment
In Him alone all longings cease

Arline C Oroszi

MOTHER LOVE

A mother's love is oft construed
to be a thing of gladness
Yet I have found it, tho renewed,
To contain much sadness.

Sadness caused by idle fears
of not always being right
Of causing, perhaps, needless tears
Tho I have tried with all my might

Yet, tho I tried my very best
Ofttimes my aims you misconstrued
Still I must say, you have my best
My everlasting love for you.

Michael Guerena

DISILLUSIONED

I awake from nine months sleep
Looking through a little peep.
What I see I can't explain
I don't want to look out again.

Now here I am nineteen years past
Wondering how much longer it will last.
I see things in a different way
And keep hoping for another day.

Sitting in my rocking chair
Fingering out my gray old hair.
If I could only turn back the clock
Right to the moment I learned to walk.

Down six feet underground
With nothing but dirt around.
Darkness fills my lonely tomb
I wish I was back in the womb.

Bill Fleming

LIFE OR DEATH

Crying, crying
 Always inside,
why the pain
 Do I hide?

Empty pride
 Destroying a soul,
Feelings denied
 Taking their toll.
Still is a heart
 cold the blood,
The downhill start
 to fire's flood.

A shattered dream
 A forgotten hope,
Tied to life's beam
 with chain and rope.

Emotions confused
 Expressions locked in,
The spirits abused
 Trapped in sin.

Held under a breath
 is a wish I say,
of life or death
 Which do I pray?

Gail Yeaple

FACES

Just look at their faces
and you'll know the places
They're going.

Raymond John Barnowski

GRASPING FOR A STRAW

To my mother Louise, may she bust all over with pride, before me. To my poetic sisters Marcia M. Dolores P. Firstone, they saw my poetic drive, before I've known it. To Donna, "my first grade classmate," an amateur poet, and photographer, may she know real love.

I walk within a sea of love . . .
Which totally surrounds my every move . . .
But it isolates me from feeling its effect . . .
I'm pushed aside for bigger prey . . .
The girls that I wanted, didn't want me . . .
 What could I say?

So many prospects walking past . . .
I look far and wide but all I can have is a dog
 by my side . . .
Inside they are very regal, but outside—
 They are still very much a beagle.

Clifford G Zervos

SPIDER CROSS A STREAM

Have you ever seen a spider fly
 On thin silk cross a stream?

Sitting here on moss so soft
 A breeze rushing through the trees,

I watched old spider sparkle pass
 On sun's warm golden rays.

He lit upon a fine old stump
 On shore not far away.

I saw him catch a whisp once more
 To a leaf that's right nearby.

Then with a sigh I whispered soft . . .
 I wish all could see you fly, oh fly
The way you did, . . . on thin silk cross a stream.

Brandi Lynn Hudson

SUNDANCE

I lie here sitting still,
And everyone is asleep,
It begins to sprinkle outside,
I watch the clouds come together
And turn dark,
To start a sundance rain.
In the morning as I wake to go outside,
I feel the wetness touch my feet,
It's still cloudy outside,
But with only light gray clouds.
The sun ascends over the mountains,
To form a sundance day.

William Rusher

THE LOWERED SUN'S SHAFTS FILTERED THROUGH

The lowered sun's shafts filtered through
The pine boughs, still are coming through
And lights the moss in golden green
On old, old tree's limbs I have seen

White with age and broken now
By too much snow on too old bough
Still beauty rests there in those limbs
And soon my soul's wounds softly mends

And as the dusk falls on this day
And darkness comes to have its way
I'll rest with beauty, in and out
And wake tomorrow joy to shout!

Mary Jane Studley

THE UNKNOWN HERO

When we think of our dead men of war,
we see, the ground where men, and boys fought,
where young men would be scared with horror,
but there was a special purpose by every soldier to be sought.

Where millions joined and thousands died,
where men gave their life just to save a few,
why every mother, daughter, and wife cried,
where on every grave there stays a drop of dew.

Those who won silvery, shinny medals,
or the honor of the famous purple heart,
to the grave on which lies withered rose petals,
to the young and the free who will always be brave at heart.

Linda Marie Fahey

WORLD ON HINGES

I love each flowering tree from Japan
And three dimensional face mask from Bhutan
A dog, horse, or woven reed basket from Eire
Plus Du Chad animals in triangle pair.
I also love the United States eagle
And Austria's wood chalets and mountains regal;
Ajman soldiers abound in history's clothes
New Zealand and Hungary celebrate the rose.
From Ras al Khaima flutter splendid butterflies

The USSR space vehicles orbit in skies.
Spain, Great Britain, and Netherlands greet with faces
But cold machines lurk from other distant places;
Posta Romana sends ships, helicopters, trains
Various German rockets and tanks get no disdain.
Oman statues, Kenya shells from new postal plates
Umm Al Qwain fish and old Chinese issue dates
A small world stands at peace on paper hinges
Rarely a paper crisis or war infringes
The only major enemies are heat and damp
Why can't the big world get along like each postage stamp?

Amy Sanford

Amy Sanford
A SPECIAL FEELING

Every time I see your face,
Makes me think of your warm embrace.
The words you whisper in my ear,
Saying you'll always be here.

Our love was truly meant to be,
I'm sure that others can see.
That I love to feel your warm touch,
Cause boy I love you so much.

When you go and leave my side,
I feel a part of me has died.
I want to be with you everyday,
Cause you always know what to say.

You give me a special feeling inside,
My love for you will never hide.
Holding you close; close to my heart,
Hoping and praying we'll never part.

Dorothy Dickson
MY SOLILOQUY

Growing older is not a pleasant experience!
It involves unhappy and frustrating emotions.
You find yourself being hurt
By unintentional jibes.
There are days you're convinced
You'll never make it,
Or care less if you don't!
Maybe these days should be
Scratched from memory;
Permanently erased!
Some days you can't even count your blessings,
Even though they stare you in the face.
The world is "too much with us," a quote;
We fail to see the roses for the thorns,
The sun for the clouds,
The smiles for the frowns or
The rainbows that will follow the rain.
YET—If we pray enough,
Keep God at our side,
And faith our guiding star
We will survive!

Jennifer A Stark
ROSES CAN NEVER DIE

Saturday, another dream, another dream
In this darkened room at four o'clock
So still and silent, but the soul is not here.
Only the body, so straight and unaware
That the soul is visiting other souls
And other places, other lands, other seas . . .
For so long now I have come to thee.
For so long now, banded together in dreams.
Such a horrible tragedy it is
When death comes and takes its toll
On two lovers who had never gotten the chance
To have a real and mortal romance.
Death, though sad, could be gay
If it is to offer a phoenix's play
And bring love back again, like before and before that.
Roses can never die with such a pact.
But for now sad heart, sad eyes
For two who can not touch or face the truth,
Fear alas has the dreams so few
But my God they are so true!
I will always love you!

Shannon Emmerson
I HEARD TODAY

i heard today,
after my own whisper,
a subtle change in the air
around me;
a shifting of invisible forces
in accommodation
and reaction
to my breath,
exhaled only after the vital transformation
of mere air
into a substance
trembling
with a potential for life.
of all the knowledge that i possess;
of all of the human experience,
emotions,
ideals,
limitations—
only a solitary breath has yet been expelled
to confirm the existence
of a power have for so long
believed our own.
and yet,
the first breath
is truly
and only
the beginning.

Barbara J Angeli
THE ROSE AND SPECTRE WINDS

The spectre winds pummeled my door,
Ripping open my cocoon—
Breaking me in two—siphoning my breath;
Scattering my branches beyond retrieve
In ominous clouds hovering over hungry depths.

Chained to an iron rod, I fought to mend,
And my spinule healed like mortar in the sun
As spectre winds uprooted every flower,
Cleaving the broken petals into dust.
But the roots of the rose they could not clutch.

Into the crevices the roots thirstily toiled
To marry virgin springs beneath the soil.
And amongst the rocks, the roots took hold,
Sheltered within a lighted cove;
Eluding the claws of the spectre winds.

I set free, rose petals to the northern winds,
And their fragrance seduced the prince.
Entranced, he commanded his great army
To build a fortress around the cove . . .
Until he called forth the rose.

Walter R Farris Jr
DRIFTING HEARTS

I've been on a lonely street a long time,
And my soul is losing its rhythm and rhyme.
It's time to clear my mind and open my eyes,
To find a new love for this heart of mine.

Somewhere in this world,
There's a lady, who's been left in the cold.
And someday I will look up and see,
A lady; whose love was meant for me.

We've all seen our share of heartaches,
Along with a few heart breaks.
But, only love can break a heart,
And it takes love to mend it.

We've all had a love we'll never get over,
But we keep hoping for a four-leaf clover.
So we roll the dice and take our chances,
And go through a number of romances.

We drift from one love to another,
Hoping to find the right lover.
And each love is different from the one before,
Starting from the time they walk through the door.

And each time we play the game of love,
We pray for a little guidance from above.
Cause everyone needs a hand to hold on to,
And someone to receive and give their love to.

Roberta L Birach
THE GIFT

My first days were so easy; just sitting in the sun;
People passing by on their way to having fun.
I thought I was just plastic and not much to see;
The others in the shop were prettier than me.
A lady whose age had shown on her face,
Stopped to look closer, I think they called her Grace.
To my music she listened and smiled a secret thought;
I tried so hard, hoping to be bought.
But away she walked, although back she did glance;
I'd guessed that was my first and very last chance.
She'd come back not once, twice, but a third;
Soon I'd be off on a great silver bird.
The lady had wrapped me with ribbon and tape
Hoping I'd arrive without even a scrape.
Why all the fuss and bother I can't remember;
Ah yes! It's for a special day this coming December!
Now entrusted with jewels and a little girl's treasure,
Who could have guessed I would give such great pleasure?
Memories I hold, for a girl who's so dear;
I know in her heart, Grace will always be near.

Merle A Allison
'TWAS EVER THUS

Out of an infinite sea of stars,
A tiny planet came to life,
Where naught but grass and trees did grow,
Long after the cataclysmic strife.

Then came Eden and man and Eve,
Where things for living were given free,
Where man was born to be like God,
Not a devil to lie and deceive.

But somehow it happened—the serpent came,
And things were changed from good to bad,
Oh Blessed Man—if you hadn't listened,
Just think what you could have had.

Joylin Davis
SO CLOSE

So close . . .
yet so very far away

An outstretched arm could touch you
But for my heart
it would be an endless journey . . .

I sit
submerged
in thoughts of us, together.
How I have dreamed
for you to be by my side
to uphold me
and to hold me

In many ways we are alike
But we differ enough so you cannot
see my love

So close . . .
yet so very far away

Dori Lamer Neu
GRADES

I worry and I stew,
I know that you do too,
What is the cause? There should be laws
to change a teachers views.

On Grades which are a must,
It's either "A or Bust".
The teacher said, "just use your head,
don't sit around and fuss".

Sometimes I stop and think,
there is a missing link.
I wish I knew, what I should do
when my grades start to sink.

But even though I cry,
I sometimes think I'll die
before I know if I should go
or stay and sigh and try.

But now I know it's right

to keep up every fight.
There is no rest, so for the test
I'll stay up every night.

Mary Slack
BEGIN THE DAY WITH GOD

Dedicated to: my Mother and Friends who have shared life with me in special ways.

Each morning look out your window and say,
"Father, I stand on the verge of another day,
As You fill my heart, I know You are just a prayer away.
I do not know what today will bring,
Whether I will have sorrow, pain or sing,
But I have high hopes to live fully every minute,
You made this day, I will rejoice and be glad in it.

Father, I give this day to Thee,
Help me to live just trusting You will go before me,
Guide me in all I think, do and say,
Thank You for all Thy blessings and guidance this day".

Stephanie Kromash
EL PASO
The dream
was always the same:
Jumping from a window or plane—
a falling sensation which woke me.
Then there would be padded feet on warm tiled floors
in a quiet hallway,
and a lamp's red glow, defining shadows
of dead flies on a No-Pest strip.
The footsteps were mine:
warm milk at two a.m., nightly
How many times did I sit in the kitchen windowsill
staring out at the shadows of mountains?

When I was young
my mother would sit me on the countertop
and give me milk after a bad dream.
I always took refuge in the kitchen after that,
found comfort in darkness with mountains
and lizards staring at me from the garden.

Thomas A West Jr
HER LIFE NOW DRIFTS
Her life now drifts among the rigid pines
which stand in utter silence as the dusk
begins to draw its shades. Her hope has lines
at eyes, and squints, and moves its battered husk,
all senses frozen fragile in the frost.
And gone are all the passions of the spring,
the tender burning summers. They are lost
like sight, and not one beggar's plea will bring
them back. As winter presses on the lea,
its firm blue-knuckled fists will clutch her age
and hold it chattering against a tree
where speech is but a muffled, crusted rage.

Tomorrow at the orange noon
she'll sigh
what could have been, and curse
one last good-by.

Annie B Breedlove
LIFE'S TROUBLED SEA
Life is like a Troubled Sea
Very much like you and me
Waves of doubt, winds that soar
Battered seamen seeking the shores.

Heave after heave from morn till night
Washing ashore some beautiful sights
But think about that troubled sea
Is she really like you and me?

She never shirks at a raging storm
But stands right there without an alarm
Big ships, little ships, plow through her waters
Winding their way to their destined quarters.

So when on the sea of life we're tossed
Though sometimes we feel so alone and lost
Think of the one that made the sea
That same hand wants to guide you and me.

He will help us by faith to stand the test
If we trust in Him and do our best
Yes I'd like to be as the troubled sea
Lord give me the faith to trust in Thee.

Verna Wantnuk
TO LOVE SOMEONE
To love someone is—To know its value,
Before making any commitments.
To have faith and believe in them,
And that the love you give is with sincerity.

To love is—Not to expect perfection,
But try to understand
That the adjustment comes only with time,
And if equally shared, it conquers all.

To love someone is—To be thoughtful
In expression of word and deed.
And to love—remain true.
Then love will come to you in fulfillment.

Jacqueline Mooney
UNNATURAL DEATH
Your blue paper leaves
flutter in the wind
No smell—but perfect, fragile beauty.
You watch, as the plucker descends the garden path
and stand serene and proud
though inside your heart
shivers . . .
The hand, outstretched, seems to be aiming
for a companion
but she changes her mind
and you are snapped in two,
your sinews torn from their life source.
You must leave your familiar surroundings
and be plunged into cold water—
you suck the water,
longing for another day's living
but your time is almost over.
You have served your unnatural purpose
you must die your unnatural death.

Jennifer Barr
LOVE GONE BY
Your smile pierced me like a spear,
The day we said goodbye,
Inside my heart I felt the fear,
That love has passed us by.

Your eyes just weren't as blue that day,
As they stung me with the truth,
That love has come and passed away,
Love that could've gone beyond our youth.

I still recall that very year,
When love stood right beside us,
And why it had to disappear,
Only time will tell us.

Anthony Furness
TO GOD WE TRUST
With the earth, sun, stars, and the moon
Where everyone's imagination comes in tune
If we focus on day and night
Brings life to its guiding light

With the animals, birds, trees, and the fish
So life, everything else is just a wish
So God's creation becomes ones self
But one day that self will not be left
With the mountains, clouds, land, and the sky
Like the world and its reality will never die
The way of truth
Is through God's youth
The way of youth is no crime
To live the right way of the duration of time
So life as a reality, it's a must
To live God's way, and have his trust.

Joyce Ritchie
YOUR CHILD
Look back into your past
See your baby, little one?
Can you see him in his cradle,
Can you see the things he's done?
His first step was so important
but you didn't see him take it.
He learned to walk, he's running now
It's too late. Don't mistake it.
Off to school, he's grown so fast
Your eyes just didn't see.
He grew up while you were elsewhere
please . . . look at him for me.
He wants to be a writer
to write the words he longed to hear.
When you read what he has said
he won't be there to dry your tear.

Jennifer Bergmann
MORNING
Misty green grasses,
Flowing in the cool spring breeze,
Taking upon the wind as their spirit.
And the dew that rests
Upon its shoulders each dawn,
Disappears into the sun
As she warms her heart,
And glows.
Birds, chirping, singing a thousand songs,
Each one more wonderful than the last.

Feeling the fresh new day,
The animals awake from sweet slumber,
To continue with their joyous lives.
And I,
Sit, and watch, and let the beauty
Fill me to my deepest senses,
Never letting go of the feeling
That could captivate the sorriest of souls.
This, is how I see my day.

Wendy H Caldwell

Wendy H Caldwell
MY LITTLE ONE

This poem is dedicated to Ashley, my beautiful little girl.

Little one that I love
Little one that's so fun
Little one you're number 1
Ashley you'll always be
my little one.

Becky Pyle
CAN ANGELS CRY?
Can you see me as I grow?
Do you watch through the clouds?
At heaven's gates, on angel's wings,
do you soar to see the things
you're missing?
Can you hear me when I cry your name at night?
Do you listen by a spirit door?
Can angels cry in the hearts
of young?
Do you play melancholy music
on a golden harp of lore?
At heaven's gates, on angels' wings;
You soar.

D H Yamada
DIALOG
People in a smoke filled room,
Words in anger flow back and forth,
Cigarette butts are grounded into the floor,
A hush

then confusion.

Joan Goger
NEW YEAR'S '89
Grandson playing laser tag,
Grandma tired from jet lag.
Brother going out in drag,
Mommy's mink is last year's rag.

Orbit spinning at top speed.
Earth beware! The satyr's treed.
When the spree is over, the pockets bleed.

One big win is what we need.

Back to reality with a thud.
The gun is empty, the shot's a dud.
Remorse arrives like a roaring flood.
When you're down and out your name is MUD.

Carmen Veliz
LEAVES OF LOVE
You remind me of the cool wind blowing
Mildly through my hair.
On a fall morning
The leaves of many colors
Each leaf representing a reason I love you.
The leaves blowing and the children
Playing in them, represents how my
Heart jumps when I think of you.
Leaves that fall to the ground and
Shrivel up, show a little bit of love
Fading away.
For me love is like the abundance
Of the leaves; it never fades away.

Virgil W Johnson
CRYSTALS
Lay a crystal on a background
Of blue, or green, or gold,
And it takes on their colors.
A wonder to behold.

In life we are the crystal,
The world around us the background.
They look right on through us
See those we keep around.

That's why it's so important
To live a life that is right.
We never know whose background
We are in others sight.

Mark Warren
PLAZA NYC
You stand alone on a corner by the Plaza Fountain—
Favorite place of all places—
watching the beautifully
Dressed, young bodies, glowing faces.

A group of street musicians construct a curtain of
Background sound.

How many years have passed since he told you his
Love for this place, how alive he felt here;
Yet out of touch with himself and you?

A carriage driver asks you if you'd like a ride
In the park for $20 and half-hour tranquility.

For a brief time you explore the idea of feeling
As he felt. He wanted to be in your life—but no—
Too many other things: duties to fulfill,
Appointments to keep, myths to fathom. No time.
Now with disquieting ease you know how he felt
In this place without you. In fantasy he joins
You for a moment; you welcome his touch, needing you.

A bride and groom emerge from a limousine at the
Hotel entrance. Celebration time.

His image fades as it did a long time ago. You know
Now how time assures a waste of time, but not in
This special place of soaring birds; you forget
For long moments you missed everything.

Bette Roth Anderson
STRESS
In the old days it was fight or flight,
Now to get the adrenaline flowing,
You have to get up and do things right.
Like doing things positive,
Don't sit and mourn,
Think of others and their needs
The homeless, diseased or those forlorn.
The immune system needs that flow,
To keep us well and on the go.
The bible says we will have strife.
But it doesn't have to rule our life.
Let's have a few laughs,
And keep "our cool"
Let's be down to earth
I mean, "let's be real."
What happened to spontaneity?
Did we lose it in pursuit of "stuff"?
Let's be grateful for what we have been
And for the future and who we are to be!

Reyam Angela Tikriti
A COMMON SADNESS

This poem is dedicated to Deborah A Carresalez and Kristi M Garcia for standing by me when I needed someone. Also to M.S., the one who could not understand.

Desperate for love
how far will we go?
The deaths of those you love and know.
Don't you understand the pain you've caused?
It's not you hurt,
not you at all.
The lives you've destroyed to make your mind feel better
The lives that are now as light as a feather.
The people you needed are now dead and gone
There isn't anyone else left to prey on.
The next time love decides to control you,
remember your friends always stand by you.

Shannon Rickards
DEAR FATHER

In Loving Memory of my father Lawrence Dean Rickards

Dear Father,
Life was always difficult,
And seemed so hard to bear,
When I chanced to glance around,
I saw nobody there.
I didn't even notice,
that whenever I was scared,
You always had a hug to give,
A smile to show that you cared.
You always made me fight for my dreams,
And made sure that they came true.
Even though I didn't notice,
I truly needed you.
My life is so unsure now,
without you by my side,
I have no hug to comfort me,
No one to boost my pride.
I have said good-bye to you,
But you will never die.
For you have joined with me now,
I CARRY YOU INSIDE.

Myra M Gregory
OCTOBER

To my loving parents who showed me how to find beauty everywhere

October has so many colors:
Red, gold, and yellow;
It paints the most unspeakable wonders
Upon the autumn meadows.

See the graceful goldenrod,
Gentians and asters, too;
Everywhere that we trod
Grasses glisten with dew.

Lucille Stratton Bailey
MY EPITAPH

To Tom, who shared with me, a pretty time of day.

This is a pretty time of day,
a restful solitude of twilight.
The setting sun, and fading ray,
between the encroaching night.

Satisfaction of a day complete,
quiet times, of a comfortable state.
Places so tender and sweet,
a statement of daylight's fate.

This is a pretty time of day,
in all the backyards,
where children play,
and life applauds.

When I no longer cease to be,
I want my epitaph to say,
and feel an expression of me,
"This is a pretty time of day".

Darlene A Davis
MY PRINCE
Thank you for the times we had,
Even though some memories are sad.
You helped me in so many ways.
I wish I had the chance to say;
That you brought me out of my shell,
So that I wouldn't have to go through that hell,
Of being alone the rest of my life.
Because you asked me to be your wife.

Sean B Rork
#1

A posthumous thank you to Mr. Paul Lundgren and my grandaunt Anne M. Towle. Also I want to thank Mrs. Carolyn Lundgren, my parents, my sister Teresa and my brother William. Thank you for your support . . . Sean.

It boils vehemently within us all;
Our passions rise while quickening our breathing,
From dormant slumber comes revenge to call.
Wholly like the snake that kills by wreathing.
Nightmarish brutes with their protean ways.
Will expose to the world choler and rage,
Not differing between the nights or days.
As animals do that live in a cage.
Alecto, Megaera, Tisiphone.
Symbols of vengeance from days long ago;
Did imbue fury in Persephone,
To fester and then to outwardly go.
Thus our lower instincts make themselves known.
From Tartarus to Earth where they are sown.

Richard A Froschauer Jr
TEARS OF MY HEART
Since the night I met you, my world's been torn apart,
with all these mixed emotions,
roaming through my heart.
I want to say I love you, and hold you in my arms,
I want to write you something sweet,
to sing about your charms.

But deep inside me, something lurks,
and haunts me unannounced.
it causes me a dreadul pain and fear
that's so pronounced.
Why must I always be the one, to
suffer like I do,
why can't I have a simple life, one I
could share with you.

Without the threat of heartache,
without the fear of pain,
without the little problems, that rub
against the grain.
You've made me happier than I've
ever been, and I want to give you more,
but at times the fear you're feeling,
makes me feel like your little whore.

I want us to be forever, to live and die as one,
I want you to hold my hand, when
my time on earth is done.
You're all that I have thought about,
you're all my eyes can see,
and all I ask for in return, is for you
to care about me.

Kelly Donahue-Minall
FEELINGS FROM THE "INSIDE"
Dear God
Please save me
What is this unfamiliar pressure
I am trying to resist?
Why does the one that I love want to do this?
Why does she not want me
when I love her so?
Why won't she keep me and then let me go?
It is so unfair all I want is my life,
but here I am at the hands of someone with a knife.
No please don't do that,
it hurts me you see.
Please let me stay here and
grow to become your baby.
Please listen to me, I am really
here, and I feel what you're
feeling, we all feel this fear
But in time you will laugh at this moment of fear.
And be thankful that you have a loved one so dear.
So please let me live & grow to
be strong, and while you're
living your life you'll be glad I'm along.

Maxine Harrod
STORM AT SEA
The waves like ghastly ghosts rise and fall,
When the water rolls like a pirate ship
and sea gulls give a warning call.
Pebbles on the beach slide and slip.

The sky overhead turns a deathly gray,
Reeds on shore, drop their heads.
A storm is breaking up the way
Crabs turn in willowy beds.

The ocean opens up its hands
For water that soon will drop.
All the birds rush for cover on the lands
Where the wind cries and covers up the crop.

Grass that's on the shore
with a dying whisper looks on.
While waves and wind try and make a score,
all waiting for a clear and smiling dawn.

At last the storm at sea is done
and the waves more quietly fall.
Once again the birds fly and run
While I, to sea, was never there at all.

Guen Chappelle

Guen Chappelle
LIVE TO LIVE
Live to live
Not to die!
Change your focus
And you'll find
More is open to you,
Choose your movements
From your core,
Do so unselfishly
And celebrate
Each day, every night;
Know you're priceless,
Capable of much,
Waste not your energies
On destruction, on negativity;
Be secure, vital, confident.
You can do it,
Step into it!

Vada Beeman Hoeft
IN THE FOREST
I stand amidst these towering pines
Their green arms lifted to the sky,
Gentle fingers at the tip
Caress the clouds as they pass by.

Velvet moss beneath my feet,
Wild flowers dancing in the breeze,
I hear the song of feathered folk
And buzzing drone of honey bees.

This is where I want to be
With wind and rain and unturned sod,
And like the wild deer running free,
My soul at peace—so close to God.

Carl F Crumpton
AUTUMN LEAVES

To Mother Nature, Father Time, and their progeny of all life forms, great and small, faithfully flowing in their own life cycle norms.

Autumn leaves shivering in falls breeze
sunburned revelers of spring and summer
red red embers glowing round and round
Autumn leaves fleeing stodgy ol trees
freedom flares of spring and summer
dancing, flirting, twirling to the ground
Autumn leaves scampering in fall's breeze
scattered ashes of spring and summer
hustling and bustling around the town
Autumn leaves composting neath grieving trees
latent energy of spring and summer
brown brown mulch cozily bedding down
Autumn leaves succoring wakened hungry trees
eternal promises of spring and summer
expectant nature stitching her verdant gown
Autumn leaves pining for parent trees
jaded bygones of spring and summer
rotten and forgotten inhabitants of the ground
Autumn leaves ignored by invigorated trees
displaced by a new spring and summer
green green leaves fluttering round and round

Susanna Burton Goehler
DARKNESS TO LIGHT

Dedicated to my husband Karl Walter Goehler Kych & Shriner

You kneel before the altar
By your own free will and accord you take your Masonic Vow
Holy Bible Square and Compass will be your emblems now.

The fraternal light shines before you to guide you on your way
You go from Entered Apprentice until you take your 3rd Degree
Light wisdom strength beauty and love is the light there you shall see

The white lambskin of innocence was given for you to wear
Unblemished now and ever entrusted to your care

Faith hope and charity Brotherly love relief and truth
These are the Masonic Principles whatever your degree

Live according to these teachings practice them throughout your life
Wear the badge of a Mason proudly honor your Masonic Vow

Let your light shine in Brotherhood
Reflecting all that is good extend a helping hand
Spreading Brotherly Love and Truth

God in his infinite wisdom guides you on your way
The world will be a better place
Because of the Masonic Vow you made

Nellie C Moore
CHARLIE CHAPLIN REMEMBERED
All dancers disappoint me now
For I have seen you dance, and how
Can any eloquence express
In merely words, your loveliness?

To what compare that fluid grace;
The fleeting looks upon your face
That tell us more than words can show?
The deepest thoughts a heart can know

Are etched upon your countenance,
And ev'ry gesture when you dance
Just takes my very breath away.
No other dancers quite convey

The magic only you can do
Of making silent music. You
Have captured in your comic art
The joyful beating of my heart.

Kevin S Long
PRISM

To my lovely bride, Carrie.

Treat me like light
Bend me
Refract me

Be my prism.

Soak me in
Separate my colors
Splay them across
Your soul
Be my prism.

Cry only as I leave you
Dark and lonely nights
Are all that is left.

Capture my light
Bend me
Refract me
Splay me across your soul
Every color is an emotion
Be my prism.

Patricia C Cole
LIFE AFTER DEATH
A car burnt black.
Two bodies charred with ash.
A live wire twitching on the hood.

Lanny and his child
Vibrating with promise
Radiating wonder,
Sparking glimpses of magic,
Absorbing each moment.

One flash and they were gone,
Their fire melting in the wind,
Their smoke dissolving into ozone,
Animating my breath.

Joanne Tierney
THIS QUIET MAN
He stood there every morning at 6:45
Now he isn't even alive
This quiet man.
He stood there dressed in a suit and tie
Why did he die?
This quiet man.
He stood there every day while I was sick
He went real quick
This quiet man.
I never even met him
Now they are burying him
This quiet man.

Roger D Fox
POETIC ESSENCE

This Poem is dedicated to Professor Theodore Foss my Mentor, Counselor, and Friend, whose Inspiration and Encouragement made the poem possible.

What should Poetry be, but the inner-sanctum of the human heart,
its Truth made openly visible—an intimate diary set in verse.

What is Poetry, but the art of making profound complexity
into deceptive simplicity of expression,
a universal experience in condensed form.

What is Poetry, but a harmony of tones sounded on a divinely pure instrument,
producing a music unique to itself.

Poetry is the art of reconciling in words
a child's fairy-tale innocence with an adult's maturity and wisdom,
an open confessional, where free and spontaneous outpouring
of secret inner feelings and heartfelt longings is made possible—
a true communion of hearts and minds.

Poetry is an arsenal
where the priceless treasures of word and thought are kept safe and secure.

What sweeter language than Poetry
to clarify, with concise, self-contained vocabulary
a many-faceted art; sometimes enigmatic, sometimes misunderstood.
Here, the worlds of fantasy somehow made more believable,
the dramas of life are played out on a printed page.

Its style dictated by itself,
Poetry is ultimately Beautiful and Eternal.

Florence R Brown
HE
Alas! He holds the money,
Alas! He holds the sex,
Alas! He thinks it's funny,

To say, "with love, I pass."

He is all there is for me,
I'm not allowed to dance.
The days of joy and glee,
Have passed me, with a glance.

Oh, yes, there are alternatives,
Oh, yes, there is an "out",
But, who, my dear, that lives,
Would want to be "left out?"

Without a "He" to lean on,
Without a "He" to love,
Oh, what a life to cry on,
The stars would go out, above.

"Hey, wait a minute!"
Would they?
Or would they keep on shining?
Oh, yes, I think I'll say,
"Good-Bye",
To this "Knight in armor",
Shining.

Barbara Lynn Hyde
GREAT DAYS

To Jesus Christ; the Way, the Truth and the Life of yesterday, today, and the Great Days of tomorrow.

Lord, when I give you my life
Starting the morning of each day
Your Spirit teaches me to see
Things in an entirely different way.

No longer does time control me
Nor schedule pressures bind
For what You want me to work with
Is what You allow me to find.

The fears of being inadequate
The frustration taking its toll
All vanish when I recognize
That You are in control.

The days I tried to do it all
Without holding onto Your hand
Were days lacking the peace You give
That no man can understand.

The moments I looked up to You
And cried, "Show me the way"
Were times that let to evening sighs
"Today has been a Great Day."

Beth M Cook
JESSIE

They are taking you away. My lips brush the red curls,
damp from sleep. I rock, hold back the tears and muse . . .

Jessie, will you remember
that one time, long ago,
there was one who loved you so?

A silver-haired lady
. . . who rocked you,
. . . who kissed you,
. . . who loved and sang to you,
when you were but two.

Our time together
so brief, that long ago, yet
my heart remembers with no regret.

I'm the silver-haired lady.
. . . I rocked you,
. . . I kissed you,
. . . I loved and sang to you,
while you slept.

Goodbye, Jessie.

Karim Farah
ALONE IN A BARREN DESERT

I stand in a barren desert, alone.
I see in the distant sands
A life which I must follow,
Not to my desire, but to my destination.
Behind me, a beautiful woman, a young child,
A young man (with the look of an old one),
A grand-piano, a pill-box, a bottle of liquor, a very old book,
An old suitcase, a rusty razor, two pair of old glasses.
They all just look with a dead stare, sitting in the sands,
Waiting for time to consume them.
Please don't leave me.

I stand in a barren desert, alone.
Nothing will come to see me, I must go to it,
Through the heat, through the pain, through more loneliness.
But as I get through it all, I get left behind, again.
For I know I will sit through eternity in that hot desert, alone,
Waiting for something to get me out, to spare me the torment,
The infinite pain, the loneliness.
The things I want to happen, yearn to have,
Will never come to be.
Destination is keeping me from it all.

I stand in a barren desert, alone.

Abe (Al) Levine
LOVE IS THE NAME OF THE GAME

In Loving Memory of my late wife MOLLIE KATZ LEVINE

LOVE IS THE NAME OF THE GAME,
I want to play it with you,
LOVE IS THE NAME OF THE GAME,
I want to make love with you;

With a kiss like you've never been kissed,
And a love that you just can't resist,
My heart close to yours,
Forever more;

LOVE IS THE NAME OF THE GAME,
There is nothing worth more,
Darling, I've loved and I've lived,
And I know the score;

Yes it's great to have fortune and fame,
But without love, nothing's the same,

LOVE IS THE NAME OF THE GAME,
Without love nothing's the same,

LOVE IS THE NAME OF THE GAME,
Yes, Love is!!

Evelyn Issler
CHRISTMAS

Dedicated to my grandchildren, Robbie, Kami, Heather, Raellen, Renée Rachel, Ronald John, Ricky.

Twas the night before Christmas
And all through the town
The streets soft and white
Resembled goose down.

Bulbs red and yellow
Made such a bright light
The shoppers were busy
Most of the night.

Trees dressed in tinsel
Gave windows a glow
That reflected in faces
And rainbowed the snow.

Sleepy-eyed children
With hearts all a-flutter
Checked ribbons and paper
boxes and clutter,

Till dreams overtook them
And to sleep they all went
Their fun and excitement
So hopefully spent.

With Santa in fantasy
And love in the heart
Christmas is here
With joy to impart.

Karen Collins
MORNING BIRDS

Twittering, chirping, fluttering,
They fly down to eat.
Beautiful, swift, fleeting,
Early morn is complete.

Watching the cold and icy dawn,
I stare out a bleak window pane.
Crisp, clear, windy and chill,
I wonder, is it all in vain?

There he comes with broken wing,
Hopping up to take a bit,
Bluejay grabs it from him,
Flies away—he just won't quit.

Little brown fellow—hops again.
This time succeeds to fill his bill.
I wonder ever after, when?
Will the little bird make it still?

Or will he be just another bit of dust,
Still and quiet and gone from us?
Like a crumbling bit of rust
Scratched right off without a fuss?

Terri Guidera
ALONE

Time alone is somewhat a
Treasure

Just to be used for some
Personal pleasure

Time alone is now something we
Measure

One day
. . . Alone . . . will come

And we will wish once again for
Precious time to
Measure

Coleen Burke
TO FEEL YOU

To Wayne who makes fantasy become reality

To feel your touch
So warm and tender,
To feel your touch
So sweet surrender.

To feel your lips
Brush gently mine,
To feel your lips
So satin fine.

To feel you close
As close can be,
To feel you close
Inside of me.

To feel your heart
Beat sure and strong,
To feel your heart
For time so long.

Charles A McMillan
ON TIME

I go to Rick's place,
And feel good.
I trip out on time.
I go the the past,
The peace.
I remember the times
The past
My music,
My past
Only the lonely
Someone to hold you.

I trip on the drugs of time.
I am the past,
I am growing old.
I find more peace every day.
American pie,
My past,
My love
My peace.
A free wind,
The past, the peace

Alfred Jenkins
YOU TOUCHED ME THE OTHER DAY

To my wife Renee whom I'll love always and forever.

You touched me just the other day.
Quite gently, in a special way.

And by that gesture so divine,
You sent a quiver up my spine.

And suddenly the sun shone bright,
and filled my senses with delight.

So thrilled was I, by your caress,
My passions, I could not suppress.

And by that gesture so discreet,
You caused my heart to skip a beat.

My body quivered—my senses swirled,
My heart flew half-way round the world.

Your love for me, you did convey,
And now my fears have gone away.

Hazel Hoff Katz
RADIANCE

A jewelled crystal, sparkling bright,
Hung in the window sharing the light;
Its quiet beauty touched in me
A kindred similarity
In deeper realms where truth is clear,
Poised in stillness, ever near;
A moment passed and then there came
A quickening of truth's inner flame
As suddenly the sunlight struck
And sparked the crystal into life;
Rainbow colors clear and bright
Gave the room a glory sight;
Joy unbound welled up within
Shared in silence with the gem
Whose radiance surpassing sight
Revealed unseen supernal light.

John J P O'Brien
SAY HELLO TWICE

It is great to be proud,
better to be humble
when you're in a crowd
'cause your walls will crumble.

You pretend to be hard,
and I'll never know why.
You will learn to discard,
and you will learn to cry.

Though you say hello first
and don't gen an answer,
you're certainly not cursed
and don't have a cancer.

You must say hello twice
in case you were not heard.
It's more pleasant and nice
than to be thought of absurd.

But, for me, a hello
doesn't really matter,
because we both do know
that you are my brother.

Eileen Drehs
A MOMENT IN TIME

For my sons Richard and Mark, my husband Richard Thank you for being you.

COME take my hand:
Walk with me along the shore.
Let us feel the sands of time beneath our feet.

Share with me your hopes and dreams for tomorrow.
Let us enjoy together a silent moment,
Like the sands of time beneath our feet.
It will be ours to hold forever.

Tara Carr
FORGET HIM

To David: I loved, I learned, I thank you.

Forget his name
Forget his face
Forget his kiss, his warm embrace.

Forget the love you once knew.
Remember he's with someone new.
Forget him when they play your song
Forget you cried the whole night long
Forget how close you once were
Remember he has chosen her.

Forget you memorized his walk
Forget the way, he used to talk.
Forget the things, he used to say.
Remember he has gone away.

Forget his laugh
Forget his grin
Forget the dimple on his chin
Forget the way he held you tight
Remember he's with her tonight.

Forget the time that went so fast
Forget the time that now is past
Forget he said he'd leave you never.
Remember now, he's gone forever.

Nancy Cupano
WONDERS
As I close my eyes, I see.
All the wonders that could be.
I see the trees,
I see the sky,
I see the mountains, way up high.

A child's grace and innocence,
A mother's love and sweet caress,
A bird that glides in perfect flight.
A rainbow and a star lite night.

Charlotte Sobel
A FLEETING VISION
I saw her upon the street
The other day
Care free and gay
With her lovely dancing feet
Then it happened so suddenly
I heard her scream
It all did seem
Like a horrible dream
O dear Lord to me
The crash of wheels
Upon that lovely form
The noise of the merciless horn
And the beat of heels
Lying immobile and still
Her face a mask
I stood against
With a creeping chill
Sometimes my imagination runs
I see her still
In the streets below
Running to and fro

Charlotte L Carr
GOD'S PLANS

To the two babies in heaven with God

What kind of heaven on earth can there be,
When there is so much pain for us to see?

A child is born to a woman and a man,
So they can go on with God's plan.

Love, clothing and their food on the table,
We raise our child, the best that we are able.

We laugh, we play and we teach,
So our child has an aim, for which to reach.

Then comes the sorrow and the pain,
When God takes our child back again.

We try again to start a new life,
This husband this wife.

Soon again, a child will be born,
Perhaps on a bright and sunny morn.

We will love our child, and cherish it, all we can.
Perhaps this time, God will let us go on with our plans.

Mae Wright
THE FLAME
In the beginning there was nil,
Only darkness and the being called by many names.
The being was not fulfilled until it cast forth a great light—

The light pleased the being
Its holy essence bubbling with
Bounding energy, to form dense
Bodies of solid particles and fiery pigments—

So intense was the light, the being
Called the dark bodies planets
The fiery stars the day, the dark
Planets night which spun around on an axis of magnetic centrifugal force—

So each planet would be exposed to the fiery particles
Now the being had the day which
Was light and the night which was dark
Yet, the being was restless and drew
Forth another phase making all the
Creatures of the sea,
Creatures of the sky, creatures of the
Earth to move and live an in a maze.

The being desired two of a kind
Part of dust and part of himself, who
Touched the tree of life and
Knowledge blossomed forth and gave
The two of a kind freedom to choose
their paths of life.

The two of a kind, bore children who
Also bore children
The two bore children—soon all were
Engrossed in a great war—
Avalanches of fire, brimstone and
pellets came down.

When almost all were destroyed
Only those remained who were
Faithful to the being.
These few held dearly to the
Flickering light. To keep away the
Darkness that had been before the
Beginning nothing—but darkness
And the being.

Only two ways could they preserve the universe
To keep the tree of knowledge ever blooming
Giving honor and praise to the flame
and love to the being

Christine A Insadowski
WISDOM
We gather the wisdom of our time,
only to have it left behind.

Much we gather of little worth,
all to be lost in the dust of the earth.

Thin is the shadow I leave behind,
little of value for any to find.

Much we gather of little worth,
all to be lost in the dust of the earth.

We search in the eons washed by time,
what is it that we hope to find?

We gather the wisdom of our time,
only to have it left behind.

Much we gather of little worth,
all to be lost in the dust of the earth.

Roberta Panozzo
MY DEAR FRIENDS

What would life be, without friends, an empty heart.

I lived alone, away from folks—
Lonely, sometimes blue,
One by one a friend came in—
To see what they could do.

Sure, I could get along without them—
Being sick and all,
But they keep me so busy—
They seem to have a ball.

I watch them eat—
And they play around,
But when I take a snooze—
They never make a sound.

They don't want to leave—
I guess they've settled in,
I talk to them and tell them—
How lonely I have been.

They don't help out—
But they're such a comfort to me,
Because their eyes are filled with love—
That's easy to see.

They make me laugh—
Til tears come to my eyes,
They do the darndest things—
Sometimes to my surprise.

They give me kisses—
And love, night and day,
They keep me going—
Whether skies are blue or grey.

These loving friends—
Are so very dear to me,
I couldn't bear for one to leave—
My heart would break, you see.

So even if you have dear friends—
None are so loyal and true,
As your four legged friends—
Who ask for nothing but love from you.

Barbara Allen
MY GIFT TO YOU
I have no gift everyone gave;
They gave material things.
I give something money can't buy,
I give "You": My love, my trust, my respect.
Take this, cherish it!
You can't find this in stores.
Many will not have what I give you,
My gift to you, "My Love".
This is all I have to offer.
Take it, keep it in your heart,
Locked away from any hurt,
This is all I have.
May this keep you well,
In times of sadness.
Remember: "I Care!"
My Gift To You "My Love".

Donna Graham
ODE TO A GREAT BOSS
He was only the boss
Who met us each day,
But Principal, colleague, and friend
We would say.
For he was special to us, his loyal workers.

He solved all our problems
And smiled at each one.
He made work a challenge,
Rewarding and fun.
This made him special to us, his loyal workers.

With pride we delivered,
Our goal was to please.
With love he responded,
Our stress to release.
And he was special to us, his loyal workers.

Retirement has now taken
Our special boss.
His absence, we know,
Is everyone's loss.
Yes, he was special to us, his loyal workers.

Rebecca Jane Parker
IF YOU FEEL AS THOUGH . . .
If you feel as though . . .
All your dreams are disappearing
Trust in Him, and then you'll see
They'll be back again.

If you feel as though . . .
Life is not worth living
Trust in Him, and then you'll find
That life is there for you to live
And believe in Him.

If you feel as though . . .
You're drifting away from Him
Stop, Pray,
And ask Him in.

If you feel as though . . .
Dreams are running out,
Life's not worth living, and
You're drifting away . . .
Stop and ask Him in!

Ronald P Jones
BENEATH

Beneath the tide of willful souls.
My mind did find relief.
Beneath the roar of thunderest cries.
My spirit found belief.
Beneath the hope of hopeless men.
My eyes see one so fair.
Beneath the faith of a faithful man.
My soul it leads to prayer.

Phyllis Jean Jones
THE SEED OF OUR LOVE

Dedicated to my children Dennis and Susan I love you! "mom"

Love is a mystery and doesn't always stay.
It starts out so happily, love is so gay,
But in our selfishness loses its way.
Love must be nourished if it is to grow,
With sharing and caring and I love you so.
Actions speak loudly of the depth of our love—
we must cherish each other, as we do God above.
For love without meaning is love without life.
And for life to continue, we should be man and wife.
They say I'm outdated I belong in the past,
Change is what matters and marriage can't last.
It's true when we marry there is no guarantee,
But the seed of our love, becomes our family;
And life without family is empty and cold,—
for there's no one to love us when we've grown old.
Yet if we've loved deeply and given our all,
to our children and family, (large or small),
Then love never dies and life never ends,
Our children live on, and our life extends.
And the seed of our love never departs,
It lives on forever in our family's hearts.

Warren E Carey
TO DREAM OF DREAMS

To dream the
Dream of dreams, and fantasies yet untold
to search the corners of time and space yet to be seen
by any living thing
To search with one's mind and soul only to touch
never to hold

Marylin Rose Cummings
NEW ENGLAND SPRING

The week went by like sunlight,
Short-lived, followed by rain.
There was a bright beginning.
The air is damp again.
Diving for inspiration,
Swimming without the sun,
I search for stones out of water
Where all this had begun.
Like the poet's house, up the road,
My rafters feel the damp rot
That sits upon a heavy load
Of stone foundations, long sought
By tourists: this quaint New England,
Site of ancestors' lairs.
But to live here is to know the silence
That wets the fiddler's fern hairs.
It is a mountain met by dew,
When the bright sun communicates with you.
Be our green host of summer short,
It is, for a time, new.

Daniel N Adams Jr
STRANGE TOWN

To professional consultants carrying expertise and ethics to places far from home.

There's nothing stranger than a strange town.
They even pile dirt differently there;
And all the buses go to places where strangers live.
Strangers drive them.
They don't even want to know your name.

There's nothing so strange as a strange town.
Even the billboards don't speak to you;
And the litter rasps the wrong way along the street.
It comes from things you don't recognize at all.

A strange town could kill you;
Coldly close you out
Til you become as invisible as you feel
And be annihilated there.

A person
Needs a person
To smile back
In a strange town.

Patricia Scroggins
THE DREAM

To my Mother, may she rest in peace.

I had a dream last night,
It was so real that it filled me with fright.
I dreamed I was no longer here,
But no one noticed or seemed to care.

I was laid to rest beneath the earth,
Beside the one who gave me birth.
Finally to be at peace and at rest,
Beside the one knew and loved me best.

Mike Giddings
SPRING TIME

Smell the grass in the fields
smell that which flowers yield,
smell the life in the air
feel the breeze in your hair,
see the sway of the trees
as the birds fly with ease.

Time to walk on the beach
for the sun you will reach,
holding hands with long talks
friends can kiss while they walk,
one talks the other listens
as the lakes wave glistens.

Children like riding bikes.
Young adults taking hikes,
babies crawl infants walk
as they learn how to talk,

Oh the smell that spring brings
and the songs the bird sings.

Teresa Wills
HEROES NEVER DIE

This poem is dedicated in the memory of my Dad, Olin J. Bouldin.

Didn't you know that you were my hero?

To a little girl, you were bigger than life.
A rugged looking cowboy whose face showed the miles you had traveled.
Some of them hard:
 A war that you never talked about;
 A flash in the sky that left you fatherless and unconscious for days;
 A friend named Whiskey that almost tore your family apart.

But through all the battles, one by one, you beat em all.
All but the last one . . .

A dreadful disease that they call the big "C".
It comes when you least expect it,
creeping up out of nowhere,
breaking down your body and your spirit.

To a grown woman, as you lay there,
helpless and weak from the illness
and fear of the unknown . . . you
were still bigger than life to me.

You were my rock, my John Wayne,
my Hero!
We who knew and loved you, will always love you.

It took you away from us in body only.
Your spirit is still with us—after all—
HEROES NEVER DIE

N A Ackman
THERE ONCE WAS A VERY NICE BAR

to my wife—Vivienne—who made sure my spelling was right—

There once was a nice bar—
in the hotel called the Omni,
I used to sit there and drink very
calmly.
Then one summer night, that was so nice
and balmy,
My lovely wife came in and sat beside me.
So now I drink at home and wonder,
what's happening at that little bar called
the Omni—??

Willie Lee Gray
BROTHERLY LOVE

Brotherly love is filling trees
With gifts for folk you know.
It is also mailing Christmas cards,
Wishing them well, and so,

It is also giving to others
Who may be in serious need,
Like the Salvation Army,
Who are grateful indeed.

It is opening the door for the elderly
As they go to and fro.
It could be a relative,
Or a friend you know.

Yes, brotherly Love seems to prevail
Especially at Christmas Time.
If we could have it all the year,
That would be Divine.

Frankie Hodge
LITTLE ONE

Tiny little bird no bigger than a minute,
had built a fine little nest with one egg in it.
Perched on a tree limb so high,
but clearly visible to our eye.

From our kitchen window we've been watching,
wondering and waiting to see,
how big that new born babe would be.

Little hummingbird where can you be?
You aren't as big as a bumble bee.

We're wondering if the wind blew you astray,
or did something happen to scare you away.

Sharon Lynn Ree

Sharon Lynn Ree
ANOTHER PRETTY FACE

He's just another pretty face
smooth cut linen, trimmed with lace;
secret pattern, they can't trace,
he turns them into a basket case.

material riches of a higher class
tiptoe in a garden, void of trash;
puzzling stranger, unlike the mass,
pieced together precisely, with lots of flash.

lashes of silk, hypnotic eyes,
sparkling smile—hear their sighs;
A freelance loner, lacking ties,
a magic puppet, gravity defies.

Long, sleek, masterful cat,
concealed, therein, a hungry rat;
captivated girls who stop and chat,
with a wink of his eye, a tip of his hat.

Charming gallant, in the night,
taking inventory of the girls who might,
get a fleeting glimpse, a shed of light;
breathless, shaking as they catch a sight.

Finely tuned words of cold,
dark, mysterious, fit the mold;
all his tales are growing old,
melting, mesmerized, he has them sold.

Gentle touch and kiss so sweet,
like syrup—thick, yet still a treat;
tempting them to once again meet
and taste his summer's passion heat.

His lengthy silence through the week,
weekend lover, they search and seek;
once acquired, they soar to the peak,
then crash to earth, helpless and weak.

He's a modernday Hero—never feels pain,
numerous lovers, add links to his chain;
skin-deep love (he's learned to refrain),
then dust off his boots, for the next flame.

David J Keppler
THE GOLDEN GATEWAY BELL

To Deanna, with love in spite of as well as because of. As you wish . . .

Time is now, and time is then, and time will always be,
And time cannot be bought or sold to wait for you or me.
But in the time that you are here among your dearest friends,
Make due with gifts that you have gained, and do not fear the end.
For death is certain here on earth, to live is but to die,
But smile and laugh while you still can, and please try not to cry.
Life is short and this I know, but that is why I smile,
Bad times will come but they will pass, with laughter all the while.
My obligation here on earth is but to heal the pain,
And wipe the tears from a child's face, unnoticed in the rain.
To break down walls of loneliness and love where others hate,
Or share my blanket in the cold, put food upon a plate.
To all the people that I see, less fortunate than I,
I give my soul and all I can to help them to get by.
Before the day I pass away I want to live the best,
That any man has ever lived, before I'm laid to rest.
Sharing love and happiness and giving from the heart,
Will be all worth the pain I feel, if I complete my part.
To work for other's happiness while on this earth I dwell,
Will give to me the day I die
The Golden Gateway Bell.
Heaven patiently waits . . .

William C Daley
A DAY AT SEA

To my mother without whose support and encouragement this venture would never have been attempted

As the early morning light
breaks over the rippling
iridescent swells of the sea

The smell of coffee
arises from the galley
where slumberers awake
to greet the new day

Then a shout "all hands on deck"
echoes across
the dew drenched boat

With a creak and a groan
sails are hoisted
to enjoin with a sigh
the early morn breeze
which beckons the canvas
to swell and fill with such ease

While wrapping themselves
in a firm caress
air sliding over rough surfaces
with a swooshing of enjoyment
at another day's work

The hissing of foam
sliding past the wooden hull
awakens in each
a sense of joy

With a mighty crash
waves add their own sense
of adventure
to the symphony of sounds
which delight the ear

The singing of rigging
enlightens us all
to the harmony of nature
which call us
one and all

As elements combine
to enrapture us all
we delight in the existence of
one and all

Then the night gently
surrounds us
in her velvety cloak
to keep and hold
until another day is born

So that with a clinking of
anchor
and a soft caress
the boat once again
signals its mating
with the shadowy ocean
bottom in the purple
depths

We are left to contemplate
with the moon and the stars
the perfect order of things
such as they are

Jeanna R Airriess
PARADOX

Standing beneath the old birch tree,
The wind undressing each branch.
The naked skeleton of what is yet to be,
Sways its limbs in a solemn dance.

"Tell me, poor Old Birch Tree,
How come the disheartened face?"
My roots in dirt, my limbs in space."

"I'll set you free, unbury you.
We'll wander far and near."
"Dear little child, that you musn't do,
I'll die for certain, that's my fear."

Ans so the years had passed away.
The old birch tree was gone.
The child returned one windy day,
To find nothing but a patch of lawn . . .

Joannie Spring
spring in a new age

for those who walk in my soul and give meaning to the words of my pen

the day of spring
the sun crossing
the line of the equator
casting light and shadow
on all equally

the blooming of growth
the revelation of light
the illumination of impulse
moving existence toward life's
new creations

the preparation of birth
the hopeful renewal
the expectation of continuing
investigating new territories
together

the day of a new age
the awareness passing
the line of equality
creating brilliance and hesitation
in all impartially

the flowering of life
the unearthing of roots
the emergence of being
flowing toward enlightenment
new consciousness

the anticipation of rekindling
the promising renaissance
the rejuvenation of thought
examining new concepts
gathering

the promises of spring awaken many minds
while looking out the window . . .
let the promises of spring awaken the hearts
while looking into the hearts
of the opposition

Alfred J Riggle
REPOSE

To Anna

The glowing coals in the fire place
warmed me as I sat on the old couch,
The hot coals making the only sound.
Then I remembered.

The love we had as we raised our family,
Laughing and crying to-gether as we
cheered each on to a new endeavor.
Yes I remember.

The anger I displayed when facing defeat,
Your touch would change anger into resolve,
As we held each other in a loving embrace.
Yes I remember.

The joy we had in the success of one
or all of the family as you encouraged each one on to greater effort.
Yes I remember.

Now I walk on this earth alone and
lost. No one to guide me, or love me.
All I have are memories, Please,
I must not forget to remember.

Barbara J Wiggins
IF I SHOULD MEET A LOVER

If I should meet a lover,
while in my dreams of slumber,
And slip into his arms—
under the spell of his charms;
And should reality peek—
may not a word it speak,
But softly close the door behind,
to let the dream stay in my mind.

Isabelle Casanta
A GRAND AFFAIR

This poem is dedicated to my beautiful grandchildren, Melanie, Brandon, Nicole and Christopher Casanta.

We dined with royalty last night,
It was a grand affair,
The palace overflowed with guests
And sights beyond compare.

The royal set chose vintage wines
And dined on legs of frogs,
I wondered what they would have thought
Of ale and chili dogs.

We gazed with awe as they began
To dance the minuet,
We marvelled at their finery
And faultless etiquette.

Ah, yes, we dined with royalty
Whom we had never met,
To think we would have missed it all
Had we no T.V. set.

James L Bible
A CARVING

The man held the piece tenderly
And gently shaped it with his knife.
He smiled as he worked the wood,
Thinking of its wonder and life.

It had been a common thing
Growing in a common stand.
It had the same promise as all,
But the promise was met in the man.

Formless at first, it assumed a shape
Under the touch of one who could tell.
Rough at first, gradually perfect,
The piece of wood responded well.

The touch of one who can love
Works easy on any thing.
Without the tools and the care,
The form within would never be.

Walt Russell
THE GARDENER

Inspired by the Jablonski Garden

He mustered his mustard, culled out his cauliflower.
Veins bulged, and his hands pulled, to get rid of the spiders.

"Kids would never eat this stuff—but I will, no matter what."

He mustered his mustard, and all the common ones too:
peas, beans, tomatoes—the kind you normally grew.

He mustered his mustard, called out the kohlrabi—
'rinsed a bunch, just for lunch, and some for the neighbors.

This makes little cents. It's gone, and then drenched,
he returns to work half as much harder.

Harold E Lafferty
MILDRED

Dedicated to my wife

Mildred—soft as the snow at twilight
Glowing with love that's my light
Guiding my way home to you.

Mildred—lovely and warm and gentle
Making me sentimental

Making my dreams come true.

You love me!
It's a new world because
You love me!
There's a high-flying sky above me
Life's a garden of roses, where—
There's joy to share
With—
Mildred—angels on high have sent you
I know that heaven meant you
To lead me to Paradise.

Marguerite E Winters
ETERNITY
Beginning, middle, end,
And back again.
Life drifts gently in
Then out again.
The circle starts
Then ends again.
Beginning where
It will again.

Charlotte Riepe
ENIGMA

With love to my sister Maria

So close, the vial of precious essence
dangled on the silken thread.
But, Oh, a sudden breath of anger
sent it crashing 'round my head!

Each time I tried to clean the fragments
the vial to mend and fill anew,
a weakened, brittle strip betrayed me,
trembled, shivered, cracked in two.

What love engendered hate so molten?
What soul embittered to the core
could snap the fragile wisp sustaining
that from which such light could pour?

Mysterious force that twists our causes,
damns the clay the frame enfolds,
blends and fuses alien metals
sans the one the pattern holds.

Will I be blest to mend the fragments
tempered with forgiving love,
refill with pristine precious essence,
Unite it to the cord above?

Maureen Estelle Johnson
IN REMEMBRANCE.
A man lies still, his widow mourns her loss
A dazed world grieves and hangs its head in shame
The chiefs pay homage to their fallen friend
Whose life was rudely halted by one shot.
A small boy questions, "Where has Daddy gone?"
And we must question, "Where has mankind come?"

Ann Maguire
CHANGE OF TIME

To my six children—Dave, Mike, Robert, Dan, Linda and Jeff. (12 Grandchildren) May they make it a better world.

So much has happened in our world today:
Would you say it's the change of time?
Presidents come and Presidents go,
Making their pledges, and we are hoping it's so.
Would you say it's the change of time?
Terrorists trying their best to disrupt our place,
But we stand fast—Saying it's in bad taste.
Would you say it's the change of time?
Abduction of our children do abound,
And we are hoping just to hear their sound.
Would you say it's the change of time?
Foreign countries taking over our domain,
So we try to protect our homestead in what remains.
Would you say it's the change of time?
Our industries are being threatened from people afar,
Imports and Exports—I'd say is the score.
Would you say it's the change of time?
Let's look around, in this—our country,
And see what we can do, improving it in the next century.
Let's make it—our change of time . . .

Ruth C Wintle
THE WORLD KEEPS ON TURNING
The world keeps on turning.
We can't stop it,
Neither can we get off.
Heartache comes, and sorrow,
Babies are born,
Loved ones die.
We can't change that,
Nor can we put our lives on hold
Because of these things,
Because the world keeps right on turning.

Alan G Lockwood
THERE IS A YOUNG MAN NAMED KIRK.

To Kirk Cameron a Christian Brother for his positive influence on young people and strong family values. God Bless you

There is a young man named Kirk
Who's a star in Hollywood you see,
To me he isn't a star
Because he's a fine young man instead.

Hard as I try and fathom
It just beats me why he is special,
He's just a down to earth teen
With simple things indeed.

He's the young man of the Cameron Family,
With a snake and a Honda besides
Mom Barbara, Candace and Melissa,
Plus Dad and Bridgette too.

If Kirk is a special young man,
It's because he doesn't do it at all
He's not on alcohol, drugs or tobacco,
But just a nice family instead.

Jennivee (Gehret) Bell
TRIBUTE TO LOVE
It seems sometimes life deals us a dreadful blow.
Everything seemed to be so wonderful;
How was I to know, the Lord would take him from me
In just a few short months?
He always said that he loved me
So many times each day.
But life has a way of turning
In a short and different way.
I still see the love light in his eye
As he handed me a rose,
With petals so full and fragrant,
The gentle blossom, so complete.
Then he said. "I gather each petal in all their glory,
And hold them one by one.
Then I take each petal
And hide them in my heart
As I place them singly, one by one
They form a rose, so pure and true.
A rose forever bright, forever sweet, forever young;
It is my love for you.
A perfect rose within my heart."

Terry J German

Terry J German
THE TWITCHING EMBRYO

To my parents, Eddie V. & Ida Mae German, for giving me life and love, to my teachers at St. Jude Educational Institute for providing me the educational skills to develop my creative writing skills, especially Ms. Helen Hoyt, and to God be given all the glory.

All senseless crevices crawl
on numb didactic knees
toward emptiness
and opaque shadows
which tend to mask the need
for something real to hover over me
as I with hardship breathe

Here I sit with thumbtack passion
fingering a pen with penciled purpose
thinking of home, or happiness
or healing—
wounded manumission
not withstanding,
my nervous perspicacity finds no halcyon relief:
I still do not see nor sense the twitching embryo
which seems to bind me with its tenebrous umbilical—
[surely life is not a strangulating proposition]

crevices
crannies
nooks
all fill my life with their rapid frothing

Mary R Leason
NEVER GROW OLD
Come to my home dear friend
Look and see
A hand painted portrait
Look closely see that's me

It was World War II Uncle Sam needed me
So I enlisted to make United States free
I wore my uniform good old navy blue
Saluted the U.S. flag see that's me

I marched in navy shoes all day long
Slept in bunk beds and ate from metal trays
Sang navy songs and had some fun
Made many friends I played in the sun

I went to navy schools to learn medical and dental
How to care for patients with a cheer and a smile
Bed pans, shots, trays of food went around
Patients were happy to have me give a cheerful sound

My portrait hanging on the wall
Will never ever be sold
My next of kin will preserve it for generations
There are hidden memories
My portrait will never grow old

Pamela Kristine Lindeke
AN ENIGMA

To my friend who helped me discern and hope

You are a soul of long ago
Young in present time
Ideal—refreshed
Different from this generation's views

Reality is—you're behind encased glass
Nice to look at
Perfect light
Reflected from flames

Dreams, desires, dominion
Prosperity beyond measure
It is sad to declare
Glass does not allow the touch

Reality is—as I stare further
The flame of light just is
The box of glass
Is surrounding me

Hannafi Smallwood
A SOFT VOICE

To my son Simon and my daughter Hamidah Smallwood with all my love. May 2, 1989

A soft voice proclaims
hold fast what thou hast received
for within the wine is now sweet
Hold fast what thou hast received
for it is without beginning
for it is without end
Creator of all
Hold fast and
forget Him not and
be not deceived by the life of this world
Hold fast what thou hast received.

Elizabeth Merrilyn Rawlliffe-Vela
WHAT WORTHY

In memory of Benny Nerveza Sr Nov 08, Aug 63 buried Sunset Lane Port Orchard, Wash. Civil Service Employee

Sacrifice would be what makes one worthy
Supply of needs, so our hunger is satisfied
Love for each other this what worthy doth testify
Faith, grace, strength from within does purify

What worthy, creation and nature as beautified
What worthy, some music or radio, as amplified.
What worthy, the light on one's life shining bright
What worthy, that those things we treasure for rights we fight
What worthy the glow of sun, moon stars and such each night
What worthy, a gallant, brave foresight and hope
For all to unite, know you've been right, that's what's worthy?

Sally E Sederquist
MOTHER

A delicate pink blossom on a slender stem.
Soft white hair crowns her face,
Etched with years of love, joy and sorrow.
Faded blue eyes smile and twinkle as she meets my gaze.
That forthright chin, still proud and strong;
Determination she utilized in daily living.
Love and admiration touch my very being.
She is Mary, Mother and Grand-mother,
Quite unique!
All knowing and caring,
A lifetime of knowledge locked within,
Time and circumstance prevent revealing.
Yes, she is fragile in appearance,
A selfmade woman no longer visible;
Hidden inside a slender stem.

Vince Valenti
THE WAIT

'Tis Saturday night and where am I?
Sitting alone and about to die
Of loneliness 'cause you're not here
To hold my hand beside you, dear.

O the morrow is hours away
'Til I'll see you again, come what may,
But now's the time I need you most
When hours are spent and meet the ghost.

The best solution I can find
Is to sleep away the night's hard grind,
And waken on a Sunday new,
When you'll be here, my love, so true.

So wrest alone and try unwind
Away this bitter night unkind;
Betwixt us both a newfound day
A peaceful joy for us alway.

Now in your arms I cling to you—
No more Saturdays like past ones knew,
For we're together from now to then
And peaceful thoughts are ours again.

Sally Lantz
THE BOY I ONCE LOVED

I dedicate this poem to Ryan Stephen whom I loved but changed over time.

He was filled with charm and innocence and all the things I love.
He was always there when I wanted to talk, he was all I ever thought of.
He took my feelings in with his and treated me with all his grace.
His body wasn't perfect, but he had the most adorable, loving face.
He wasn't smart, but I never used to think about how dumb he used to be.
He was so special and the only thing that mattered was him and me.
No matter how bad I felt, he'd bring a smile on my face again.
He'd make me feel so lucky no matter how my day had been.
I'm not sure how he changed right before my eyes so fast.
I thought our relationship was strong and forever could last.
He has now turned into someone I can't even relate to;
And now the boy I once loved is the boy I never really knew.

Debbie McCrady
LAUGHTER OF CHILDREN

For Bradley and Amanda. I love you more than life itself.

The laughter of children
Can fully repay
The labor of love
Mom's work each day.

My baby's eyes sparkle
As I near his bassinette.
All the diapering and bathing
I somehow forget.

Carolyn S Hudson
LOVE HAS NO COLOR

While gazing into his smiling eyes,
my heart fluttering, to my surprise!
Deep into his soul I could see!
Whatever in the world was happening to me!
Upon first sight, flying high!
We were kindred spirits, he and I!
How can this be? Is this right?
Why he's a man of color and I am white!

Twasn't long and I was sure
our love for each other was as pure
as freshly fallen flakes of snow.
For it all began many years ago!
With Adam and Eve, begetting begun!
Love has no color, we're all as one!

Margaret Fite Bice
TO WARRICK

Child of Springtime, Child of Grace
Standing in our patio
That tranquil evening
After supper
Playing an antique violin
So sweetly and with such promise . . .

When springtime comes around again
Touching the mountain meadow
Where your ashes
Nourish columbines
Will we hear faint echoes
Coming down the wind
Sweet music from your violin?

Linda M Jones
PLIGHT OF THE HARP SEALS

For my husband, Rodney, He knows me as I really am and loves me anyway.

A baby was born a short time ago and lost his life today.
A human came with club in hand and took his right to live away.

As the man approached him, the baby tried to move aside and as he was clubbed across the skull, his mother watched and cried.

There was nothing that the mother could do as she watched her child stripped, of all his fur and all his hide, she watched his lifes blood drip.

And when the man was finished he kicked her child away,
walking off across the ice, looking for another baby to slay.

The mother will not leave her child, still warm upon the ice.
She nuzzles him, washes him and tries to feed him, looking for signs of life.

His mother cannot understand why he does not move, when he was all she really had in this cold, cruel world to love.

And when the day was over, the white ice was stained red with the blood of many infants, who, because of man are dead.

The mothers keep on crying far into the night, hoping that someone will care and help them win their fight.

Karin Christa Uphoff
NAVAJO WOMAN

With beauty around her, she walks out of the rain, a brown apparition slips beside me, into the cave.

Sculptured by a lifetime, a face
of wrinkles tells of endless tales,
spoken with eyes that hold the reflection
of wet sandstone.

Together we absorb the rain-veiled canyon stretching out from the sky before us,
like a painted canvas.

the motions of her head, arms and hands
dance together to say;
"I am Earth's child—absolutely
I am Earth's child."

David L Poe Jr
IF I COULD HAVE ONE WISH

Written for and dedicated to my love Cindy Lou.

I've done a lot of thinking, girl, I've weighed the facts and lies
Maybe I was pushing too hard and dimming the sparkle in your eyes
So I'm hoping you will understand that the words I say now are true
I promise never to break your heart, I promise never to hurt you

Things went well when we first met, we both felt it was right
I invited you for dinner and champagne as well as candle light
You said you weren't ready for a relationship and I could understand
But I must have lost all sense of control the moment I held your hand

And please believe me when I say,
I'll remember the way you kiss
I'll miss the way you love me, girl, I don't want it to be like this
You know I'll have a broken heart that only your love mends
We may not ever be lovers, but I know we'll always be friends

I'd love to mean as much to you every minute of the day
As you have meant, close friend of mine, to be along the way
And if I could have one wish come true, my only wish would be
That we would both someday be lovers, you and me

Carole J Joeckel
WINTER'S LITTLE FRIEND

Dedicated to Melissa Jo Joeckel

In velvet cape and hood of red, she took winter by the hand.
They walked in snow, so soft and white, as it laid upon the land.
It did not mind that it was led, by one so small, and nice to know.
She took it by the hand and said, "Come walk with me, I have so much to show."

Upon the ground, inside a log, a home that seemed so crude,
a chubby little ground hog was playing peek-a-boo!
A chickadee would chirp and scold, as it dined on mistletoe,
while in a tree, so tall and narrow, there was a bluejay too!
She giggled with delight, as she watched a skunk, playfully rolling in the snow,
but she would not follow him, for sure, his welcome would be quite rude!
A baby deer, so gentle, and so shy, she held out her hand with care,
as he looked upon her face, so pure, and knew that love was there.

Suddenly her tracks had gone away, the path she did not know.
So winter took her by the hand, and led her through the snow.
It took her back to waiting arms, where love and trust were taught.
Safe and warm, at home at last, to loving parents whom she sought.
She blew a kiss, and waved her hand, "See you tomorrow, we'll walk some more!"
She said, with a smile, as she closed the door.

In her velvet cape and hood of red, she was so small, and nice to know.
Winter did not mind that it was led, as they walked together in the snow.

Lois Riddle
MEMORIES

Strange, how some small thing
recalls sweet memory
in a string.
The scent of jasmine in the air
and I can see you
standing there . . .
so sultry, so suave, so debonair.

You were my love
and all my hope.
I swallowed every word
you spoke.
I etched in memory
every trace.
The beauty of your
handsome face.
The moment's gone yet
I retain
these precious memories
in a chain
until we meet again.

Debra Richards
A MESSAGE TO SEAN
My sweet and precious little man
With your fingers in your mouth
We talk about the roads ahead
East, West, North and South

Though this road in front of you
Is crooked and it's steep
May God's love from up above
Give you that extra leap

A gentle hand to guide you
To lead you on your way
To make the right decisions
And not lead you astray

When confronted with a problem
In a world so full of strife
To choose the right direction
On this rocky road called life

And now I watch you sleeping
Like an angel with a sword
To conquer all life's problems
With your weapon—yes—the Lord

K Henderson
THE SPIRIT OF BEAUTY AND LOVE
The spirit of beauty and Love
Lives within every feeling heart;
Uniting earth with heaven above,
Life becomes a gentle art.

Love in its essence
Is spiritual fire;
Heaven's pure gold elegance,
Human nature's divine desire.

What we sense as beauty
In the soul, must be truth;
The spirit of Love and duty,
Springs eternal youth.

Generosity is Love in action
We gain only as we give;
Life's secret for satisfaction,
And in giving, Live.

We must Love one another;
This a quest for peace.
God's our father, nature's our
mother,
Inhumanity toward each other must
cease.

Bunky Raines
FLOWERS
Flowers are the essence of Spring,
Flowers are beautiful,
Flowers have only two things,
Beauty and Smell,
Flowers are Orange,
Flowers are Green,
But in Life remember,
There are both Flowers and Weeds,
Go by which Smells better.

Laszlo Szuromi
MOTHER'S DAY

This poem is dedicated to my best friends Dale & Elaine Stotts and their sweet daughters too Kristi & Jenna.

Your children grown-up long time
ago,
For whom tell your story good
Mother?

By oneself lie on the big family bed,
For whom find you the new story,

Who be in tears after the happy
wedding?
Your great heart gave away half of
kingdom,
Poor young man got lovely princess
hands.

We learn from you the truly
affection,
And how we can live or can't.

I know you never be alone,
Because your mind and heart with us.

That why we working for the future,
That why we believing in God.

I wish for you every day;
God love my Mother!
How she love and believing You.

If your God appearance her dream,
Give her all children with smiling
face.

Laura
THE AVIAN

I dedicate this to: Marli, for her kindness and confidence; Peter, for the harsh-realities; and Saitoti for giving me my voice back—but mostly to my Hummingbird for faith . . .

Act of light—a Figaro House
etching—
Hung amongst the noised clutter of
shops mocking Art.

A Bird-nurse
Dancing the moment beauty,
desperate for Peace
from the violent blue/gold macaw's
assaulting Beak,
the Blackened stench and spread of
the abandoned Vulture,
the long fragile death of a minute
green-violet rayed calliope . . .
Speaks:

My world was a futile attempt to
sweep up breezing feathers that defy
straw;
the daily mop and scrape of wildfowl
glop from floor to Cage.
Your sight of me
was opportunity devoid of art—
I could no more sell
yourself than I could her twined
bundles of
life . . .

Margaret M Wilson
LORD GOD OF EONS
Lord God of eons, I haven't much
time
Please, help me find quickly the path
That is mine.

Millie Moraes
WHAT SAYS ALL MEN SHOULD DREAM THE SAME DREAM

To Michael and Gregory. My bright lights of all tomorrows.

What says all men should dream the
same dream
Seek the same goal
How does one know what impels a
man's soul.

All things do not fly—yet all do not
crawl
Some are big—some are small
Some save for the cold—others do
not
Yet all seem to survive
So who are we from others to
deprive.

I saw a bud—I saw a tree
I saw a man—not half so free.

Mortal man why can't you see
The world is red for thee and me.

Carol Anita Reed
FAR AWAY
Across the wide sea in a far-away
land,
on some distant shore you may
stand.
You watch the ships as they sail by,
with a lazy and pensive sigh.
You must miss the land you chose to
leave,
and the family whom you left to
grieve.
You see the blossoms, so strange and
new;
You miss the friendships, tried and
true.
Many miles, mountains and
grasslands away,
I wonder just what you are doing
today.
My vision of you now is but a
dream,
but you have achieved your wildest
scheme.
And perhaps at last you are truly at
peace.

Mattie A Davis
THE KITTEN

Dedicated to Carol Mayo

The doggie chased the little kitten up
the street.
The kitten stopped and looked
around, his fear could not be beat.
He shook his tail, and preened a bit—
Just what would kitty do?
He stopped quite still and stood
awhile—
And then ran up the street.
The doggie followed for awhile, the
kitten went ahead;
And then it stopped and stood stock
still—
And you could see his dread.
But just what did that doggie do?
He grabbed the kitten in his mouth
And stood there for awhile—
Then let it go and went his way—
I'm sure I saw him smile!

Martha Fridge
MOTHER'S GRIEF

Dedicated to Robin Lee Ann Fridge July 13, 1969—March 8, 1983

They tell me you're safe in God's
Heaven,
That your death was part of God's
Holy plan.
But how do I go on without you?
And how do I understand?

You were just thirteen years of age,
When God called you from above.
Oh, how do I let you go, my child?
My heart, my life, my love.

No more will I see your sweet smile,
No more to touch your pretty face.
No more will I kiss you good-night,
Nor hold you in my embrace.

But I must go on without you,
Though my heart is filled with grief.
But we'll meet you again in Heaven,
If only we just believe.
Though the light in your eyes is gone,
And your soul lies safe with Him.
'Tis your memory, my precious child,
Which shall never grow dim.

Helen Gardner
A BABY NAMED JESS

To Jess, who healed my heart

A baby came to our house, we said,
"We'll name him Jess."
He whispered that he came from
God, to bring us happiness.
He filled our house with love and
joy, and as the days went by
We laughed and sang and played
with Jess, our gift from God on high.
Jess looked and smiled and coo'ed at
us and waved his tiny arms.
My mother said, "Look at that boy,
I've never seen such charm."

Before Jess came there was a man
who came to live with us.
He liked our warmth, the cozy fire,
the comfort of hot apple pie
And evenings long and lazy, but
when Jess came, that was no more,
Jess cried, his tummy hurt, we stayed
with him through long cold dawns
with bottles and warm shirts.
The man grew grumpy as a bear, he
snapped and growled and grumbled,
and then he said, "Enough of this, I
cannot stand this jumble. There is a
choice that must be made, it must be
Jess or me, I won't sacrifice my
comfort for a child, I've decided to
be free. If ever I should want a child,
then that child will be mine, a child
of my own flesh and blood and not a
child unknown.
"Jess is not unknown," we said "He
is God's child and ours. If you must
go, then be it so, Jess fills our days
with flowers." The man went away,
we knew not where, Jess cried to see
him go. We dried his tears, wrapped
him in love,
Jess taught us all to grow.

Alfred C Herrin
I HEARD HER ON THE RADIO

This poem was written for Debbie Kay her inspiration and angelic voice makes her friendship special.

I heard her on the radio
How was I supposed to know
That she would write songs
About how we used to be
Nobody knows she's singing about
me.
She sings each word with such intent
I never knew how much she meant
How much she meant to me
I'm glad they repeat her songs
I wish I could right the wrongs
But past is past

Done is done
As her songs climb to number one
I sit in pain
Waiting for them to play her again

Gina Cimaglio
THE FLOWER I ONCE HAD
I had a flower that was so beautiful.
It always made me smile,
And there never was a time when it went dull.
It had shown different moods, and colors that were in spirals.
The flower I had was so life like,
I carried it everywhere I went,
It made my everyday life feel so right.
Then all of a sudden the stem had bent,
And half, fell off to the ground.
Another flower someone had sent,
Wasn't the same, as I dropped my head,
And looked down,
I saw the petals had fallen one by one.
A tear had fallen from my eye,
But I knew another flower will bloom from the sun,
But no other will be the exact of mine.
If another flower crosses my way,
I will sit and remember just how glad,
It made me feel everyday,
All because of, "THE FLOWER I ONCE HAD".

Louis J Rusconi
ACT AS IF YOU ARE:

To all who seek:

You are what you want to be; no matter that the world is not there to see.

Your conquests are what you want to be the deed; so act as if all endeavor is success, for failure is a pauper's seed.

Break down those barriers of self vision because you are what you want to be; act as if you are and soon all the world will see.

Be not afraid, for all detraction is born of fear and ideals not reached. Those who will detract have not learned life's lesson subtly preached.

So act as if you are in all things and you will loose the shackles of your visions wrongly used; you will soar far beyond what your thoughts have mused.

You see, when you act as if you are, you will experience a part of what you want to be; soon it will be there for all the world to see.

Rafaela Wintham Barker
GOLDEN RIPPLES IN MY POND

Dedicated to God, my constant source of inspiration, as well as to my mother, Amanda G. Wintham, my loving husband, Henry H. Barker, my father, Humberto Wintham, my two sons Albert and Hank, and all people and circumstances of life, that have made this moment be.

Life is but droplets of illusions, that fall into my glimmering pond, leaving golden ripples of memories in the stillness of my mind.

Yesterday was but a memory that slowly slipped away, life's wispy clouds that quietly dissipate into the quietness of time.

Today is beckoned into the stillness of the night, as autumn leaves wave their last farewell to birds upon the migratory flight.

Tomorrow will be another day to be pressed into the book of memories, that soon will bid good bye, and take along with it cherished hopes and dreams.

Into my glimmering pond I see them fall, the droplets of illusions, leaving golden ripples of memories in the stillness of my mind.

Clara Stevenson
THE VISITOR

In memory of John Albert Stephen Gonzalez I'm going home he would say. One day he did. August 21, 1984—April 11, 1987

I only came to visit, I did not intend to stay.
I brought you the radiance of my smile, the joy of my laughter, the sorrow of my tears.
And my undying love.

I leave behind many memories. The warmth of my arms around you, my sloppy wet kisses,
my head bowed in prayer.
Like a flower I bloomed. I gave all I had and now it's time for me to go home.

For God said, "I only lend you this child.
Love, nurture and teach him my ways.
Laugh with him for the joy he gives.
Cry for his hurts and pains. And when he has fulfilled his destiny I will call him home."

Sylvia G Hughes
PEEK—A—BOO
Peek—a—Boo, Morning how are you today?
I asked, as I Peeked through the curtains, early in the morning.
I see you're still dressed in your white lace gown of Dawn and wearing your Necklace and Pearl earrings of Dew.
Your beauty is beyond compare,
the smell of you is Clean and Fresh like a light perfume to dress.
Peek—a-Boo the sun is setting;
Now You'll be dressed by night; An Evening gown of soft Satin Black and Jeweled in Diamond Stars you'll be wearing.
So Romantic you are,
You have captured my heart.
Now a kiss good night
for a Beautiful Morning.

Edward L Hamm
DESTINED
Without a struggle,
I let down my indestructible defense,
—became vulnerable.

Without warning
my crusted heart bled open
upon your listening ear.

Without fear,
I faced the desolate place
where once I stood in barricade,
unresponsive,
alone,
repelling love, afraid—
fighting our soul's inevitable embrace.
Now trembling,
I look directly into your eyes
compassionate,
caring,
evoking trust,
and without hesitation—
entrust you with my love.

Edward S Andrewin

Edward S Andrewin
YOU

This poem is dedicated to my wonderful parents, Noel and Lottie, for their loving inspiration.

I dream of you all day and night.
I can't get you out of my mind.
And when I hold you tight,
All other thoughts are left behind.

Your eyes are bright and shiny.
You're as sweet as a dove.
You'll look the same at ninety,
Because your heart is filled with love.

Mary E Hill
ACKNOWLEDGMENT
When I was young and full of hope,
I never thought I'd be a dope.
Well, I wasn't! As you can see,
I'm just as bright as I can be.

If you will give me a tumble,
I shall tell you what is humble:
All the talents that I use
Come from God. How can I lose?

Theresa M Davidson
GOLDEN ANNIVERSARY

Dedicated to my husband Werner, who made it possible.

It's 50 years since we were Bride and Groom,
Our parents said the marriage was doomed.
One a Catholic and one a Jew,
Our problems they said would be quite a few.
Now as we look back on these 50 years,
We've put to rest all their fears,
And if they were here today they'd know,
We've reaped 50 years with more to go.
Tho old and decrepit, we will strive,
To make it to the Diamond "75".

They've not all been Golden, these 50 years,
There's been laughter and there's been tears.
We've had times when they were "lean"
And there were times when they were "keen".
From $12.50 a week we went to more,
And now we spend it at the shore.
To Casinos' we go now and then,
And don't bat an eye on what we spend.
So Now in our Golden Years we tread,
And live it up before we're "DEAD".

Jane Denslow
TWIN PINES—THREE SCORE AND MORE
Outside my bedroom window
Two giant green trees stood,
With heavy needled foliage
And trunks of mottled wood.

Summers I would watch
The robins come and go,
A quiet beauty came
As winter brought the snow.

Then came one glorious day,
When I left my childhood home,
To wed the man I loved
And make his home my own.

Life now has come full circle,
Again those trees I see,
There seems no change in either one
The only change is me.

Sherry D Hilberger
YOU MAY WANT TO COME BACK

Daniel—without you my words wouldn't be in this book. Thank you.

You may want to come back
Through my door
But it's too late;
I've changed the lock
And now someone else has the key.

Esther Ralston
NIGHTMARES
I do crossword puzzles at night in my sleep
What in the world is a four letter creep?
I toss and I turn and my eyelids they burn
Who ever heard of a sixletter gum?
The news in the evening can still leave me cold
Who cares what the stock market brought or it sold
I lie in my bed with my brain in a whirl
Trying to think of a five letter squirrel.
How many whales in that old river Styx?
What's a six letter word for a bucket of bricks?
Beginning with Z, what's a debutante's pash?
Or an eight letter word for the chicken pox rash?
What's twenty one down and thirteen across?
What's a two letter word for a stevedore's boss?
I jerk and I twist in those nightly nightmares
As I try to fit words to those puzzling squares.

Who knows the shade of Napoleon's tie
In thirty four letters and ending in Y?
I go through the alphabet counting my sheep
Doing crazy crosswordsers each night in my sleep.

Rita Hallett
NO MORE

To my mother, with all my love.

There is no rapture when the robin sings—
No more splendor on the cardinal's wings.
Sun-kissed flowers no longer bloom for me,
Nor can I feel the joys of reverie
Reflected in the mirror of my mind.
The hope that's born with each new morn I find
No more . . . for these simple joys tried and true
I could only feel through my love for you.

No more your words of wisdom to inspire—
Or lift my heart or set my soul afire.
For now you are gone . . . tho' our days were long
And FULL! . . . (which should lend joyance to my song—)
Our paths we shared, both the smooth and the rough—
But—God forgive me!—it was not enough!

Claudia Patrick
THE FURY OF HATE

See the seagull soaring above the wicked waters.
The darkest depths of love's still moments.
Hear the seagull cry, a screech of scorn
As the playing waves lap against an empty shore.

He sees below the glitter sun's rays against sands
That for miles are deserted, no longer known to man.
Thinking of a past, gliding in mid-air,
Slowly, oh so carefully, He sheds a tiny tear.

Now those foolish humans everlasting in the sea.
An ocean of rage and fury-one and one the same to be.

Ilanit Lazar
LEAVING

To Stephanie whose loving pouch brought me from the blackest hole into the smiling sun! I love you forever and always.

People leave my life everyday
Yet I go on, meeting more who do the same
They're close and friendly, full of warmth
Then when I turn around
I face nothingness

People leave for different reasons
Some are forced by a commanding figure
While others were never really there
Then there are those who say they love
When they don't even understand the meaning of it

People leave to get away
Looking for what they will never find
Not realizing that what they have
Is more than they need

I wait patiently
Time and time again
Hoping they will be thankful for my warmth
Yet I'm still waiting, cold and alone
In the shadows

People leave and never return
Some find happiness, others find grief
I sit and watch with my heart
Giving support or comfort to these people
Who will never really know I'm there

People leave with no goodbye
I stand with tears in my eyes
And watch them fade away.

Stephanie Mellen
BROKEN DREAMS

If dreams were real and wishes came true, my life would be perfect because I'd be with you.
I love you so much, more than anyone can see, but this heart of mine has broken in two and it's killing me.
No matter where life takes you or where it takes me, this love I have for you will always be.
I know our lives are different, that's why we're driven apart.
But you'll always be real special, there's a place for you in my heart.
Until dreams are real and wishes come true, the only love in my heart will be for you.

David Smith
ADIEU

To William Sagar—kind, gentle, brilliant. He left the planet early but richer for spending every penny of himself.

If to you my actions seem
unworthy of that gentle smile
with which you sometimes held
my screaming Child of Agony—

never for a moment disbelieve
its parent's Love from which it sprang—
from birth to howling rebellion.

Ruth Bowker-Rist
A TOAST TO HEARTACHE

And, once more into heartache
I feel love slip away.
That lonely, hurting heartache
that grey's a sunny day.

The love we had was tender
and claimed my heart complete.
T'was love to be remembered;
the sweetest of the sweet.

But, here I am in heartache
and much to be surprised.
The love you pledged to give me
faded right before my eyes.

Then, drink a toast to heartache!
To empty rooms and more.
My heart will heal in spite of you.
It happened once before.

I'll find the door to loving
in someone else's arms.
He'll claim my heart his treasure
and keep it safe from harm.

So, once more into heartache?
I'll make this trip real fast.
More love awaits; a better fate.
And this one's bound to last.

Melanie Wells Bryant
HE DID AND IT WAS

I didn't know it was going to rain, but it was.
I didn't know he stopped loving me, but he did.
I didn't think he wanted to leave, but he did.
Now I stand here watching the rain after he did and wonder why it was.

Tina Malin
POEM WITH NO TITLE

This poem is dedicated to Opal Thompson, my mother.

I looked inside the mirror oh God what do I see
But pieces of the days gone by, a shadow I call me
The water pouring from my eyes is the pain from day to day
I don't think they realize the hurt from the things they had to say
Just reflections in a mirror no big deal I really know
But reflections of a human, through the eyes you see the soul
Can you tell me how to wipe away everything they say and do
Can you give me the strength for yesterday and today will I make it through
I get so close to people the pain is so hard to bear
I wish I could take it all away yes I really care
I speak the words so often why doesn't anyone hear
I look in their faces thought I made it all so clear
But they ignore the things I've said and I really did my best
But in the night I still keep praying oh God put me to rest
Have I done a good job of hiding learned my lesson oh so well
Can't they see me hiding, it's very easy to tell
Oh God please take it all away just so that I may see
Like the eagle that flies high above without worry flight so free

W Howard Sibley
"orange"—the only word with no rhyme.

I'm at odds with my kin and my kith
For they say it is only a myth,
But a Webster named Noah
Said: "Don't look anymore—
There's no word you can rhyme "ORANGE with."

Else Sprague
UNDER THE TREE

In January
a little bench
is waiting
just inviting
me particularly;

As I sit down
making
taking
seeing the best
having a rest
just me, to be known;
Although I see
green is the tree
different in shape
the leaves more than many
smell of earth

whispers in the air, the insects
dimensions of sunlight for the
senses, the mind, moment of
time, for me to sit,
under the tree.

Mary J Friend
DON'T BE ANGRY

The pain is slowly stopping
Your smell has left my sheets
Your touch has faded from my skin
The day doesn't revolve around your voice.
Faintly it still hurts when your necklace glistens—
or the new dress draws a compliment.

But time is the healer—the phrases linger . . .
It is never as bad as it seems
It will never be as good as it was
The chapter closes
No accident—just a brief and shining moment
no problem.

Aileen R Kunkel
TRACKS

It was getting almost dark one eve
When beside the trail I spied
a track from some small animal
I hadn't quite identified.

To better follow in his tracks
I fell upon my knees
and peering close upon the ground
I was crawling in the leaves.

Then suddenly I stopped stock still!!
and eased back down the trail.

for just ahead stood Jimmy Skunk
with his head before his tail

Nina

Joan R Barton
NINA

To a very special lady, My Mother. Thanks for being there, Mom. Your Daughter, Joan.

She was born in Nebraska in 1910,
A beautiful actress she might have been,
With her hazel eyes and raven hair,
She could have co-starred with Fred Astaire.
But she married her high-school sweetheart at 24,
And he died of Hodgkins during the 2nd world war.
With her two small children she settled in L.A.
And her parents moved in to help her pay.

She was courted by a marine and an attorney
Till a red-headed songwriter
from a New Jersey Journey,
Stepped on an elevator on a smoggy day
They were going up, it was the
the only way.
So the beautiful brunette and the red-headed songwriter
Walked down the aisle with
their hopes much brighter.
He was outgoing, she was demure,
He liked to gamble, she had the cure.
She laughed at his jokes and praised his new songs
For 33 years. Now he is gone.
Through the love of her 3 children and grandchildren 9,
This Nebraskan born beauty will always shine.

Alicia Star Maeder

SECRETS

Soft, blue pools
Cool and clear
Rippleless
The webbless windows of your heart.
I alone can see the rising curtain
I alone shall witness the unknown.
Gently, gently you take my hand.
Our secrets pass
Wordless . . .
Soundless . . .
Fearless . . .

My head rests upon your shoulder.
The curtain closes,
Draw-string now exposed.

Cheryl Lynn Ehlers

DEAR SISTER, DEAR BROTHER

To: Dennis, Danny, Mike, Pat & Christie. Thanks for everything you've ever done for me! Love, your sister Cheryl.

Is is possible, that years ago
We fought like, cats and dogs!
And called each other foolish names.
Like pinhead, dopey and frog.

We used to get sick of each other,
Cause we were together all the time.
Screaming, yelling, constantly,
And mom, wishing we could mime.

But now we've all grown up,
And we're all too far apart.
The thought of us together again,
Always livens up our hearts.

Now when we're together
We're always hugging each the other.
Brother hugging sister,
Sister hugging brother.

I don't think we'd made it,
Without us having each the other.
I guess that's what's so special,
Of having sisters and big brothers!

Mrs Janet Cooper Kraus

THE GROWING DARKNESS OF OUR SOCIETY

Dedicated to those few proud Americans who will speak their mind!

Humans we are, loving mates, caring friends we crave.
Encouragement, a gesture of wisdom we share.
Our innermost essence demands nurturing of family.
A desire to belong, someone's soul we can bare.

We pray to prosper, we strive to grow,
a thirst to thrive, as no one species knows.
The rush of our world has entangled our values.
Siblings become distant, schedules engulf our time.
Onward so anxious for that nine to five drive,
what priority are the children in our lives?

Our style of behavior bequeaths darkness for our youth.
We abuse our bodies, then bear false witness,
have we not become inflicted with a plague called AIDS?
We swallow a dose of ignorance to cure the denial!
Has logic escaped our perception?
Be personable, show character, have respect,
those who forgive little, love little.

Enrich your children with knowledge,
share your virtues for voices must be heard.
Are we trying to live in the memory of societies past?
We are destroying our unity, our families, their future!

Be wistful in your travels.
Rid yourself of weakness and inhibitions.
Display serenity upon your words.
Enhance our human race: thy almighty father shall be proud.

W Chuck Evans

BLESSED CHILDREN

Dedicated to all the Blessed Children who are wed on any day.

Blessed are the children
who are married on this day,
For the Lord will love and watch them
as they travel on their way.

When they walk into their twilight years,
and still walk hand in hand,
They'll know they walked these years as one
from the time their love began.

Alicia Tamie Williams

PEACE

To my lovely daughter Leilani Kaloe Joe, to her father Pereary Cedric Joe and Family. To my mom Barbara L. Williams, father Ralph Williams, brothers Ralph M. & Neilson G. Williams and John Lentz and family. To all my nieces and nephews. I love you "Peace" always

I hope one day there'll be a change
when the color of skin can not be blamed
I hope one day one can walk about
through the streets without one's doubt
O' Lord
Bless this world of ease, remove
all the guilty deeds
Place all the joyful moments upon,
while the judgement of color
lies beyond
Erase the evil that lives inside, let all live with all thy pride
Let the nation join as one, as thou the judgements have not begun
Give us faith let us be strong,
supply the strength to carry on
Remove all anger that surrounds
our lives, let there be peace let
all evil die
O'Lord
We need no despites of skin
Let the judgement stop, let the
prejudice end.

David Austin Hunt

BRIGHT AND BEAUTIFUL

With love to my Spanish angel in Firgas, Gran Canaria!

In your face I see nature's radiance,
Just like that of the sunrise, it seems,
Your brilliance with time grows
much more intense,
Yet I can only see it in my dreams.

Beneath the stars on a warm summer night,
Atop a mountain on a summer day,
Or walking on the beach in the moon's light,
With you I long to be if there's a way.

Lucena, within your heart could there be,
A void to be filled by a man like me?

Susan Stone

TO ALL WHO LIVE FOR A DREAM.

This poem is dedicated to Johnny, my loving husband. You believed in me.

With every touch,
There is life.
And within each heart;
There is a dream.
So with every moment,
Live it to the fullest:
Because; there is,
The End . . .

Jody Lee Jasper

I COULDN'T BE LIKE YOU!

To: Danny, Ryan, Ashley, and Whitney with love!

I couldn't be like you;
It goes like this you see—
There's only one of you,
And there's only one of me!
If I were just like you,
There wouldn't be a me.
And if you were to be me
Then we wouldn't be.
So you see,
You be you
And I'll be me!

Helen S Church

GOLD

To my late husband, dear Leon

Fifty years, my love, and more to come
as days drop upon days
like golden leaves of fall.
You are there
and I am here
and we reach out, one to the other,
for a lost embrace
that cannot be returned.

MayEtta Benoit

AMERICA'S HEART

To Dad, Lisa & Ashley, Betsy Jo & Evie, Jennifer & Bo, who inspired and encouraged me, and all those who fought and continue to fight for OUR AMERICA!

In Peace, and even threats of Wars

Elections, Space, or Nuclear Powers
From Presidents, to Freedom of Choice
America's Heart is in Her Voice!

We're every color, from every Nation
We're working, unemployed, in every situation
Homeless, Artists, Political Activists
America's Heart lies deep within Us!

So, whether Famine, Aids, or Drought
As a Nation, We know what we're about
Helping Farmers, Africa, or the Feeble
America's Heart IS Her People!

Joannes Paulus PP II

Stanistawa Polny

HABEMUS PAPAM

Habemus Papam, wolaja Narody
Juz po raz drugi w tym roku,
Jak trudno objac rozumem
To Bialy Orzel nad Watykanem
Wzbil sie w orbite w obloki.
To Bialy Orzel z ziem piastowskich,
Z ruin, z ziemi przemoknietej
Krwia od wojan.
To Bialy Orzel z gòr tatrzanskich
Rozpostarl skrzydla nad swiatem
Habemus Papam wolaja Narody
A maly c´zlowiek, tak wielki rozumem
Modli sie w cichosci nad ludzi tlumem
O, Jasno Gorska Pani,
Daj mi sil, daj wyrozumienie,
A dla Narodòw blogoslawienie
Dla moich braci w kraju
Otuchy, otuchy daj o Jasno Gòrska Pani

Benjamin D Jacobe

BE MY VALENTINE

This poem is dedicated to all married and single "SWEETHEARTS" everywhere, special mention to CAROLINA, my friend and wife.

What else can I say that others
have not said before?
What must I do that others
have not done for you?

You need not call for me
when things go wrong, because
I'm always there to soothe
and kiss that pain away!

My love will be there for you, always
to lean on, to depend upon,
To blame for, the things
I DID and FAILED to do!

It hurts for me to see
your eyes become a well of tears,
As happy as my new found faith
when your lips erupt into smiles!

Every now and then I day-dream

of what might have been,
It is but natural, my dear friend,
to be thinking of you till the
end!

Darlene Annette Gialanella
THE RAIN FALLS SOFTLY UPON MY HEAD

I'd like to dedicate this poem to my husband Thomas Joseph Gialanella for inspiring me and our gift from God, our son Matthew Thomas Gialanella

The rain falls softly upon my head
Eyes open wide, I'm warm inside
I think of you
And laugh, sigh even cry
What's it all for I'm mixed up inside
it rains harder
I'm sad, soaked
the rain falls . . .

Patricia Scott
FLOWERS

Dedicated to my loving family and Mrs. Davis, my second grade teacher, who started me on my "life of rhyme."

Flowers make you happy.
Flowers make you glad.
Flowers cheer you up
When you feel sad.

Flowers are pretty,
That we all know.
All you need is good soil
For them to grow.

Flowers can be pink or yellow,
Or maybe even red or white.
They open in the morning,
And then they close at night.

That's the end.
That's all I know.
Plant some in your garden,
And see what kinds you can grow!

E Ray Forbes
FATE

In remembrance of my late father "Dennis Forbes" whom I miss and love very much.

Life is too short
But then again too long
We learn a lot out of life
But not enough of what we
should
We can learn from our mistakes
But it's easier said than done
The world will always be filled with
hate
But there will always be honesty
Somewhere
someone
is looking for love

Jennette-Marie Torrano Ort
BUTTERFLIES

This poem is dedicated to my dear Daddy and Mommy, Peter and Mili Torrano and my dear brothers Peter Michael and Gian Carlo.

Beautiful living beings
Some with bright colors,
Some with pale or dark.
Interesting the way they're born and
grow;
First the egg, then the caterpillar,
And finally the beautiful liked little
bug.
Yes . . . a butterfly.
They just go flying around
Playing in the air
Going from one flower to the next.
Butterflies look like petals with life,
Flying freely in the day,
Sleeping in the night.

Mrs Valerie D Jenkins
LORD WHAT MAN ARE WE?

In memory of my deceased grandparents, Solomon Jr. and Sophia Helen Pugh. You're gone now but your love lives on . . . Love Grand daughter: Valerie D. (Pugh) Jenkins

Hate not my child he, of another
color . . .
Hate not he, that hate you for your
color . . .
Love thou for they know not the true
meaning of love thy brother and
sister.
For you are all God's children . . .
Hate not he that trespass against they,
because of thy color, but forgive
thou,. For He knows not the true
meaning of love . . .
For his color is the love of God, our
father, but teach your children to be a
child of God, and love all people no
matter what race he or she may be,
for they too are God's children.
If thou, art a child of God, then thou,
to love all people. A child of God.
Love all people . . . Amen . . .

Catherine Thompson
JEALOUS LOVER

I dedicate this poem especially to my daughter Maria a gift of God and truly a great inspiration in my life.

Michael and I were lovers
Happy and so sure of each other
It was actually like obsession
We gave and bought each other
possessions
I would travel to the end of the world
to please
Seriously even crawl on my hands
and knees

One bright sunny day I picked up the
phone
To try and contact my lover at home
After a long stimulating conversation
I planned to meet him at the station

My train apparently arrived late
I definitely knew I could rely on our
date
When he got impatient he would
wait and stay
Walking on the streets and
sometimes play

To my surprise what did I see this
could not be
My Michael laughing and kissing
It didn't look as though it was me he
was missing
I was so shocked I didn't think
I felt like a boat about to sink
Hurrily I ran to the store and got
myself a gun
Through jealousy and rage I pulled
the trigger and my lover
Michael was gone.

Melissa Brookes
THE SMELL OF FRESH GRASS

To My Mother, Who always made our house a Sweet Home.

The smell of fresh grass
On a cool breezy day.
Brings thought to my past,
In my own special way.
It's so fresh and clean
That typical scene,
In my childhood years,
When things were bright and serene.
But time goes on,
As they say,
And before long,
Those childhood memories drift
away.
But then at last,
On a cool breezy day.
They are cutting the grass.

Richard Daniel
MOTHER

LaVetta, Loving Mother 1918-1979

When God made the earth
It took him six days
And on the seventh he rested
But when God made you a mother
It must of taken him all seven days
Because he had to look heaven's
Streets for the right angel
To send to this earth
To take the suffering of bearing a
child
Then he had to find a star for her
eyes
To guide and show her the way
When we see a star fall from the sky
It's for a mother's eyes
The angel he found he took her heart
And gave to you a woman to be a
mother
When life has come to an end
God takes his angel back to heaven
He puts the star back into the sky
A tear must fall from his eyes
For he knows the love and hurt a
mother
Goes through for her child while on
this earth
For the love a mother carries for her
child
Is the same love Mary had for her
child Jesus
Mother the love, hurt and suffering
You went through for your children
Was that of God's picked angel to be
a mother
And your eyes were those of the
brightest star
Mother when God has called his
angel back to heaven
We'll look for your star to be placed
back into the sky.

Dorothy Tourish
YESTERDAY-TODAY AND TOMORROW.

Dedicated to my son John, without his ideas I would not have written this poem.

Yesterday is just a memory
A day, so far away,
Where one can oft return to
In many special ways.
The tomorrow, we refer to,
Is like sunshine on a hill,
We discuss it in the evening
When everything, is still.
But tomorrow, is so far away
A day that ne'er appears,
And there is only just today
To wash away our fears.
For today, is what we live for,
One day at a time,
And memories of yesterday
Go drifting down the line.

Linda S Emery
SIDE BY SIDE

Dedicated to Russell Keith Owens My Oklahoma Man Love of My Life

I was sitting at a table
You asked me to dance
There was country music playing
I said I'd give it a chance
You taught me the two step
And when it was done
You asked me to breakfast
Of which I had none
You sang and talked your way to my
heart
And courted me with flowers
From the very start
Now we live our lives together

And

You still bring me flowers
Letting me know
The courting's forever
Not just for show
Now you sing me your songs
Holding me tight
As we lay down together
Side by side

Elizabeth Stribik
INDECISION

I dedicate this poem to God who was there when no one else was.

The time has come to show the
world.
My inner thoughts, feelings, and
desires.
Stripped from the shelter of my
mind.
A writer of unspoken words.

Which part of me shall I send.
Love, sadness, joy, fear.
How can I choose.
They all mean so much to me.

I will send my love of nature.
Love for a child.
Love for the man at my side.
Love of God and all his creations.

Or should it be the sadness I feel.
Sadness for the wandering homeless.
Sadness for a forgotten child.
Sadness from my tear stained heart.

My joy is the writing of all that I see.
A gift to all who care to look upon it.
You must choose for I cannot.
For all is one and one is all.

Barbara Csik
TIME

To my wonderful mother, Helen Csik, and my two boys, Johnny and Jeffrey Stadvec

Our lives tick away like seconds of
time;
Our minutes of life so precious to
find;
Don't waste a second, don't let it slip
away;
for what we had yesterday is gone
today.
Keep in your mind what your heart
holds dear;
try and keep your hopes and
ambitions so very near;
Don't give them up but try them

again will succeed and be your own best friend;
We are just like a clock's hands keeping time, don't waste a second, don't listen to the chime;
But clocks do run down: The seconds are mine;
That's when you start wondering, did you try and find your friend the chime???

Lisa Jeannine Malley
IT'S MORE THAN WORDS

To Brett A Vanslyke . . . I thank you for your support, understanding, trust, and respect. Together forever—I love you. Babe

It's so beautiful to feel
it's an overwhelming emotion
It's the tenderness of the heart
it's an everlasting devotion.

It's the light from a star
it's the spark of a flame
It's a friendship in disguise
it was sensational when it came.

When things become dim
it brings us together
To work things out
and make things better.

It's listening and it's talking
it's trusting and it's sharing
It's also understanding
it's a lot of caring

It's just so many things
thank heaven above
you and I share it
it's simply called love.

Darrin Adleman
YOURS FOREVER

For Carol Semmler, in memory of Alison Semmler—8/28/84 to 10/10/87

One day you're blessed with a miracle from God
And nine months later you've got a little "Pea-Pod"
A baby indeed, a new human being
A life given yours forever—
This child is yours now and forever,
Til death do us part we do not endeavor
For life after death is beyond all others
Except for God himself and—
Mother.

Robert D Britton

Robert D Britton
THE STATE I'M IN

In this solitary state I sit
No one to care a little bit
Alone with my dreams at last
Alone to muse about my past
Like it or not this is my lot
A fact of life it's all I've got
Not a part of an original plan
Certainly not from this old man
It just shows how life can be
When there's no one else but me
Now I've got time to think and plan
How I can become a better man
And no matter what the state I'm in
To somehow find a way to win.

Ora L Case
HOW SMALL ARE THE MINDS OF MEN

To my beloved wife Diane always. Skip

How small are the minds of men
How small they are indeed
When God alone
Will judge the soul
Not the race, the color or creed

Johnny Hsu
AS WE GO TO SCHOOL DAY BY DAY

This poem is written for the lasting memories from Peterson Middle School in Sunnyvale California. Written for the graduating class from Peterson of 1989.

As we go to school day by day,
We think only one thing—Friday.
Hour by hour comes and goes,
Lectures fill our ears with woes.
Every second seems like an hour,
All the sudden we have all this power;
For only we know
When we have to go.
Walking down the hall,
Making all the noise we could.
Screaming and crashing,
Doing to worst we would.
Teachers, vice-principals, and much much more
Opening their doors to see what's the sore;
Laughing and babbling louder and louder,
Suddenly there's a grab and "What's the matter?"
Closing doors and people laughing,
I suddenly saw the principal calling,
Sweating and giddy, feeling nauseous all over,
My parents were in the doorway,
looking even madder.
So be very careful when you guys walk down the hall.

Lynnda Spencer
OUR CHILDREN

To my children, Lee and Joey

Our children are our future;
Show them love in every way.
Teach them right from wrong.
And teach them how to pray.

Our world is so full of hate;
With sickness and despair,
We let ourselves forget the good;
The feelings we should share.

Our children cannot know these things;
Unless we show them the shining light,
About love and beauty—happiness:
And all things good and right.

Let's give our children a second chance;
To show us what they're made of.
They have their own identities,
And their own ways of showing love.

We musn't close our eyes to them;
Or close our hearts and ears,
Let them greet their problems,
with security, not fears.

Christine Alfaro
SELF PORTRAIT

To Kathy, who gave me encouragement

Who is that sitting all alone
All her smiles and laughter gone.

Her bright brown eyes that were so gay
Seem sad and dimmed today.

Her heart is heavy her shoulders bent
All her joy and happiness spent.

Do I know you my friend
Will the joy and laughter return again?

I'm that old lady sad and gray
My smile was once bright and laughter gay.

Now I sit here all alone
Wondering where the years have gone.

Now it's only memories of old
And lots of sadness still untold.

I look back and wish I could undo
But then I feel sad, lonely and blue.

Where is that bright smile and laughter gay
Over the years they have faded away.

(Miss) S Elizabeth Gorley
YESTERDAY A CHILD CAME

To Becky Morris Luebber of Hoquiam, Washington

A person
A girl—feminine, intuitive.
And then
Years skipped past
Youth, sex, beauty—
Love came.
Today—a woman now
Seasoned—sympathetic, creative
Dedicated with empathy
Tomorrow—a woman still
An individual
Love—work—home
Alone?
To live is to love
To love is to give
Who comes to fend; who sees still
—yesterday's child
—holding love in outstretched hands?

Evelyn Handy
THE REACHING HEART

to every reaching heart

If I could on a mountain stand,
I'd cast my eyes upon the land
Both near and far.
I'd let my heart reach out for me,
And I would run beside the sea,
I'd climb up mountains tall and grand,
I'd walk the level of the land
Through cornstalks tall,
Through village small,
And know, that everywhere my feet did trod,
'Twas land prepared for man by God.

Ted G Quick
PRECIOUS FEW

To my unique daughter, Ann Marie she enriched my life's journey, and made it indeed worthwhile

There's a breed of us that don't fit in.
And we roam the world at will
Breaking the hearts of kith & kin,
By never staying still.
We range the fields and rove the floods
And we climb the mountains crest,
For ours is the curse of gypsy blood,
That'll never let us rest.
If we went straight, we might go far,
For our hearts are brave and true
But instead of accepting the things that are,
We seek out the strange and new.
Loyal to few, understood, by less, some call
Us a riotous band, but God made only
A precious few formed to a diamond,
From stray bits of sand

Pakuda Ly
I LOVE YOU THE WAY YOU ARE

To anyone who thinks of themselves as not being beautiful.

I love you the way you are.
You might not notice my inside, but if you do, you should be more impressed;
more than ever.

Everyone always sees what's on the outside of a person and never considers the inside.

May the outside be full of wickedness or ugliness to you, but remember, there is an inside part of me also;
more beautiful and emotionally in love with you.

May that inside come out to express itself someday, then you will know what love is.

I love you because you are wonderful and enchanting with all kinds of magic floating above you, with love waiting to burst out, but only you could make it happen.

So when the time comes, we will both find our love and happiness together.

Sharlene E Casto
IN THE SPRING OF '88

This poem is dedicated to my Papa Raymond A. Gower, who always believed in me.

Nature's splendor has enveloped me . . .
The forest's lawn, a green parade

Trees that become statues,
tall and stately made

Sweeping, roaring water, sparkling

clean,
Dancing lights, shimmering sunbeams

A shambling filled maze of stones,
Glimpsed through the morning's haze

A whispering wind, a cool touch of breeze,
Sifting through the springtime weeds

A flash of color and birdsong bright,
As a bird glides in matings flight

As I take a moment to gaze upon the glory,
Of all the wondrous beauty before me

The generations before my eyes are cast,
I ask myself, "Will this place last?"

Or will it become just another memory,
To the future generations to come,
When all is said and done.

Phyllis Dee Francis
HAPPY BIRTHDAY

To my sister

May this day and
Every day be happy days.
For the rest of your life.

Because I love you, with
All of my life.
For you are my sister
And you shall always share
A place in my heart.

Maria R Weil
ODE TO HENRY DAVID THOREAU AT WALDEN POND

To Kindred Spirits above, below and beyond everywhere hail!!!

I ate a nut.
By the hut.
Where he lived.

I walked the shore.
Beyond the door,
Where he . . lived.

I danced through leaves . . .
That fell from trees,
Where he lived.

I climbed the hills.
Without his skills.
Where he lived.

I heard the trills
Of Whip-poor-wills
Where he lived.

I saw skies of blue.
That he too . . knew.
When he lived.

And, as the sun set.
His spirit lingered yet,
Where he'd lived.

Carolyn Swain
LEAD THESE LITTLE FEET

For Brie and Joe, and to Tristan, who was my inspiration

Oh Jesus lead my little feet, down the road You know is best, and nudge me, Lord, encourage me, when You know I want to rest.
Help me to be merciful . . . help me to be kind . . . help me to love others . . .
these are tough hills to climb.
And when I do not want to do what Mommy says I should, nudge me, Lord,
encourage me(inside I'm really good).
And when the path that You would choose seems pretty rough to me, guide these little feet of mine, this is my humble plea . . .
So when the world looks at my life, the one that they would see . . . is You dear Lord, who was always there, to bandage up my knees.

Mary C Klug
ENJOY LIFE

To my best friend, Shirley

It is hard to imagine
What it would be like
Without a tomorrow
For us to enjoy life

Our days are all numbered
Sometimes way too few
Live each day to its fullest
Is about all we can do

Our lives Quickly pass us
With nary a thought
As to how long we have left
Till life comes to a halt

We take life for granted
And we think we're immune
To all of life's hazards
For which we assume

That it will never happen
To ones that we love
Until we are ready
To ascend up above

Consuelo Chavira
A LONG TIME AGO

I dedicate this poem to Jesus my Savior.

A long time ago I met this friend
I almost forgot about him.
Great buddies we were he dwelt in me and I in him.
Together we lived for many years he never left me nor I him, This day he didn't come home and great relief I felt in me.

I invited this other friend to help carry the load in me, This friend is true and never leaves always helps me in times of need.

His name is God The King of Kings.

Forgot to tell you about the other one,
his name is LONELINESS and now he is gone.

Regina T Wegner
FRIENDS

Dedicated to Herb and Ruth, true friends

When I look through my address book
I am no longer lonely
For the many friends, I have, when I look.
So, who needs lots of money
When real gold is in my little book.

George L Weber
IN YOUR SILENCE

To Frederick Cameron (Ted), son, musician, composer, poet, artist. Born November 8, 1980. Killed in hit-and-run accident September 17, 1988, while attending Berklee College of Music

In your silence today
I listen for your song
And know you want so badly
That we feel its vibrant pace,
Its rhythm woven with such perfect grace
Into the pattern of your innocence.

Your song we hear, dear son;
Too short to satisfy a parent's pride
But oh so sweet a memory,
So loved before it died—
So loved, dear Ted, so loved
Before it died.

Jeanne Penrod

Jeanne Penrod
FAMILIAR EYES

I'd say I love you but you hardly know my name . . . Brian May

When you look at me
I can see
Places we have been before

Was it in a dream
Or does it seem
To have happened so long ago

To look at you
I stir
Inside

Familiar eyes I see
When you look at me
Take me far away inside a face inside a distant place

Tell me this
Did you know or did you
Only take a risk

To look at me
To fall
In love

And It's all
It's all
Because you looked at me . . .

Robert H Ryan
A BETTER YOU!

This poem is dedicated to my mother, Sara P. Ryan, and my ex-wife, Cutah J. Ryan. Thank you for the encouragement.

Being honorable is just—
And being brave is a must.
People live the best they can—
From mouth to mouth to, hand to hand.

When daily things get rougher—
People have to get tougher.
Forever stand tall and straight—
Try not to become over-weight.

Live life one day at a time—
Don't go thru life being a mime.
Learn to do the rightful thing—
Not everyone gets the golden ring.

Forever try to hang loose—
Do not be a silly goose.
Try being one with nature—
This will make you much more mature.

Positive thinking is the best—
Whether north, south, east or west.
In your heart, always be true—
All this will make a better you.

Sandra R Horvath
A MOTHER TO BE'S PRAYER

This poem is dedicated to Sharon, my sister. My gift for her and Mike upon the arrival of their second child, Brian.

Dear God in heaven, please I pray.
Bless my baby night and day.
Let it be born big and strong.
Dear God I pray that nothing's wrong.

Give it ten little fingers and ten little toes.
two big eyes and one little nose.
A healthy little body with shining hair.
and we'll provide the love and care.

Madonna E McVicker
WIND CHIMES

In Memory To: My husband Jerry V. McVicker and my grandsons Steven and Billy. To My Children: Mike and Diann McVicker, Robert and Jerri Sandene and my grandson Jerry Jack Zeits

If you listen to Wind Chimes,
They will speak to you.
They may whisper or sing,
And the tune may be new.

With strong gusty winds,
They may shout so loud.
They will make you take notice,
And stand so proud.

With the gentlest breeze,
They are tender and kind.
With sweetness and love,
That will dwell on your mind.

So just take a moment,
To hear what they say.
And hope in your heart,
They will ring every day.

Jeanette Jackson Jones
FREE

To my aunt Mattie: Thank you for your encouragement. "I Love You".

I shall like to be free, to fly away and be me.
The person who seems to be, is not really me.
I live inside myself secretly. I shall like to be free, for just once,
just be me.
Or maybe I have lost the right to fight,
That person who says she is me, and just remain the person I seem to be.
Who knows, "Maybe that person is really me."
"Maybe it is she who shall wish to be free".

Janet Green
IN PARADISE

To my daughter, Amye Gayle

I am but a tiny diamond
in God's golden crown,
and other honored children
are emeralds, rubies,
sapphires, pearls
all joining in the shimmering dance.
We the meek, soft—faced ones of integrity
die to reawaken
to an infant song,

His ivory scepter the baton
that directs the bubbling music.
Linked together in the crown,
we sing, we dance,
and forever we shine!

Bertha H Miller Westerweel
YOURS AND MINE

To the Lord who inspires me with poems

Thou merciful Father to even love me,
delivered my soul and set me free;
Each day that I live in this dwelling of thine,
thou showest me mercy and love so divine;

No wonder I sing of my Jesus so sweet;
who was pierced through his side and hands and feet;
He paid all the cost with blood and sweat,
a crown of thorns pushed on his head;

He died there for you and me,
on that lonely hill of Calvary;
He did not stay dead, but arose from the grave
and this is the promise that God gave;

To all who believe in the name of his son,
we will all be His cause the battle is won;
Everlasting life in Christ sublime,
through Him—became yours and mine;

Daryle Stark
I'M NOT SURE OF ME

To my husband Bill, and sons Chad, Justin, & Travis, for their unconditional love.

I'm not sure of me.
My sudden moments of change
My desperate flights into isolation
My requirement not to speak
My desiring the comfort that only
my own thoughts can bring me,
I'm not sure of me.
The need to be left alone in a crowded room,
The discontent I feel when you enter
my private sanctuary of "self",
The effort I demand of myself when
spoken words fall with resistance
The quiet clinging I give to my own
soul when I have no urgency for your presence,
I'm not sure of me.
When my need for mental seclusion
drifts unconcerned amid voices that
do battle for parts of me,
and I rest untouched for the moment
in the infinity of being alone . . .

Jacqueline Anderson Smith
JESUS THE GIFT

To God who is the head of my life, and to my Mother & Father, Minister and Mrs. Frank Anderson Jr. And my husband, Henry, and to all the members of the Church of God by Faith, Inc.

Father, we thank you for your son on high,
Who gave his life as a ransom for I.

For there is no other who can do these things,
Not even monarchs, presidents and kings.

Born in Bethlehem, a small child was He,
What an important person He grew up to be.

He came to save this world from sin,
He died on the cross so we could enter in.

In Christ only is there salvation,
He brings peace and love to our nation,

There is nothing that God can't do,
In Him I put my trust, and my life too.

In drugs you think you have life,
But, all you have is anxiety and strife.

In this world of A.I.D.S. and cancer,
I think you should know, that Jesus is the answer.

Look up and rejoice as time draws near,
We will see Jesus when He appears.

Stretch out your hands to Jesus, He'll be there,
He promised to meet us, in the midst of the air.

Thank You God, for Your Son, the precious gift

Lisa Aristizabal
BABY ARISTIZABAL

Much love, Mom.

I can't wait to see your nose,
Your little hands, your little toes.
I can't wait to see your face,
Your little body . . . you dressed in lace.
I can't wait to hold you near,
To build a bond that is so dear.
You will cry, and very loud, but
We the parents . . . so very proud.
I can't wait for the day to come,
To hold you, love you . . . oh, the fun.
I can't wait for this day so near.
This day to come . . . and you'll be here!
You will smile so wide and bright,
And we the parents won't miss the sight . . .
Of you, our newborn.
Much love, Mom.

Angelo G Giglia
HARBINGER?

The farmers' pest and the scavenger
No longer nest in their old haunts;
The crow has left the field and forest
For city streets and inland jaunts.

The sea-gull, once a scavenger,
No longer diet on sea-offal;
River and lake some now forsake
To feed instead at the city mall.
These hardy birds of age-less time;
Know they something of the clime—
And wiser be than man?

Susan Solimano
CONFLICTS

Without support from others this would not be possible. A special thanks goes to Dottie, Liz, Amy, and Marcia, too. Joey and my mom need to be recognized also.

The conflict I find the most difficult
is the one I experience from within
It's when my mind and my heart are
divided and I don't know where to begin
I struggle with this battle most of all
It's like coming up against a big brick wall
This is when I'm in a state of confusion
Where reality and fantasy mesh into illusion
The path to inner peace feels like a maze
When the journey to a solution has so many ways
I dream often of finding a welcome inner peace
So that I may feel that inner battle cease
I know for myself this is one long struggle
When solutions are like balls that clowns try to juggle

Gloria Holleman
MY FRIEND

To the ones I love

Life's not an easy road my friend,
but I'll go with you all the way.
Don't stop and wonder why,
if the sun won't shine today.

Why don't you stay, rest awhile,
let me comfort you.
Do not be discouraged,
I will see you through.

Come sit with me at table,
talk of your problems free.
I'll stop and will listen,
to what you say to me.

Together we will make it,
if all else fails.
Stay close to me my friend,
do not leave this trail.

With caring and compassion,
that very few have known.
I felt in the touch of my dearest friend,
that very afternoon.

Khanh H Nguyen
VALENTINE DAY

God blesses the day we met (7/85), To L with all my love,

Today is Valentine day,
If somebodies happen to say
That I did not send you a rose.
Tell them it's in my heart
Where with your love it grows
Where days are Valentine days.

Anna Toma Anderson
WHAT IS A MOTHER

In memory of my mother, Jenny Toma, and all the mothers of the world.

A Mother is a god-like creature
That gives birth to a new-born
Babe . . . and because it is
Heaven-sent she is enthralled
With Instant and Eternal Love:
A "power so great" . . . that it
Softens and ripens the tender
Heart-strings of Motherliness—
Which is Everything a "child"
Needs to grow into a firm,
Beautiful and unique person
In the image and likeness
Of God and His Children.

Traci W Gordon
DEATH UPON A FIERY FIELD

I wish to dedicate this poem to my new-born niece Elisa Brianne Perry

Walking across a fiery field at dawn
A lonely figure, with a shadowed face
Slowly prodding in a general direction
Fearing the thoughts going through the mind.
Burning buildings surrounding this solitary figure
Crouched in a fox hole, suddenly running for fear of dying
A man jumped up and fired, almost within three seconds
His dead body limp on the ground.
Looking at the burning village from atop a nearby hill
Sees a child running from what was a hut
Screaming child, looking for her mother
Crying until she was shot down, by a gun hidden behind a bush.
Turning, trying to block the memories
Fearing they will take over the mind.
Now, walking in an open field, the sun comes blazing over the horizon.
Tears streaming down the grieving face, falling on the steel black barrel
Still hot from the bullets piercing through it only hours before
Suddenly, pain and anguish filled the face
Blood could be stopped no more
Falling onto knees, life force draining,
Died, finally fulfilled.

Phyllis Field
PARTY SONG

To Andrea, Joe and Geoffrey

Perhaps if they wouldn't
seek to use images.
Ah, well, party, party,
<u>no me importa</u>.

Clara E Heinzl
LOVE IS GOOD LOVE IS BLIND

DAUGHTERS DEDICATION—I dedicate this poem to my Daughter Anna for the inspiration of its creative impulse I so desire.

Love is Good Love is Blind Love controls the head and mind.
Hard to Hold sometimes the Heart feels cold.
Needing that someone to hold you so tight? Wanting this day Wanting this night not always having affection that's wanted at times it needed yet leaves you feeling blunted.
Love is in the Heart Love is in the soul? Love is two people as Good as Gold. When two people joined they open their Hearts? it's caring sharing if not they depart. Love maybe once other times twice Until it's discovered the two are right. It maybe Beautiful it may turn away Together you Live and learn day by day. If you can't be open and you

can't be tight then you can't be right
Then you search on to last or it won't be right for two people joined as one it must be right.

Alice Mary Rachels
MY "MISS MUFFET" FANTASY!

This poem is dedicated to Susan, my lovely, loving daughter.

Little "Miss Muffet" might have reacted
Differently, had the scene been changed!
—She could have fallen from her
—tuffet,
—Spilling the bowl of curds and
—whey!
—And the birds, not the spider,
—Could have flown down beside
—her
—To peck at the curds—
—While the ants feasted on whey!
—She could have scared off the
—spider,
—That had sat down beside her—
—The 'change of scene' almost
—ruined her day!
—A change in verse might be a
—'history-first',
—Or a poet's curse!
—Mess gone, and spider too, little
—"Miss Muffet"
—Then told me, 'she tried, but
—could no longer bluff-it',
—And whispered, politely, 'that I—should go stuff–it'!
—She cried, to get back onto her
—tuffet of lace!
It was then I stared 'fantasy' straight in the face!
And like the 'sparkling touch of a magical wand',
The page became "YESTER-DAY",—"HISTORY"—the "BOND"!

Carolyn A Steidel

Carolyn A Steidel
VISIONS OF THE PAST
Where are my friends of yesteryear?
Too soon they quickly disappear;
Remembering them from early on,
They touched my life, and now they're gone.

So vague, it's like a childhood dream,
With playmates wading in a sunlit stream;
Picking wild flowers on a wooded hill,
Listening to the song of the whippoorwill.

Our world was young and trouble free,
As we lived each day in fantasy;
Visions of the past so very clear,
It seems so far and yet so near.

I think of them—my long lost friends,
So sad the way the story ends;
Once very close, now out of sight,
Like ships that pass in the silent night.

Robert Higginson
GRAVEYARD SWITCHING
The rail sings a witches' chant,
If you listen close.
The world smells of diesel oil,
and brass,
and iron,
and ghosts.

The cleaners have the ripe rich smell,
of stockyards in the rain.
The rips hot bite of fire and iron,
the bowl, mad farmers grain.

Like cats beyond the circle,
graindoor fire's lights,
Are eyes within the darkness,
beside the house of ice.

The hissing snake, crawls slowly through,
from rail to rail with one bright eye.
It catches owls,
and rats,
and men,
Shutter still in glare.

Tracy L Case
TODAY AS YESTERDAY
Wasn't it just yesterday
That I held you proudly in my arms
With the feeling of love and wonder
Wasn't it just yesterday
I saw you take your first steps
And independently feed yourself
saying soon after
"No Mom I can do it myself."
Wasn't it just yesterday
That you fixed me breakfast in bed
Complete with uncooked eggs and shells
And I ate it all loving you so
Wasn't it just yesterday
I said while pushing on your head
"Don't grow anymore you're getting too big"
And laughing you replied "I'm almost as big as you mom."
And it was just yesterday with disbelief
That I looked up into a young man's face
In need of a shave and in a voice deeper than mine
You said "I want to get my permit Mom."
My sweet and precious son how special you are
And today as yesterday you're still my baby

Cindy Andrest
OCCIDENTAL
A photo in nineteen fourteen of union railroad tracks,
Physicians, drifters, towns people blood brothers by Red wood sap.
Full Swedish speaking women tend gift shops.
Artisans, and their loom,
Smoke in wood stoves churning the atmosphere's perfume.
Behold, a one room library whose books Look and See
My cover on the outside whose content opens me.
Father in his saintly robes,
Pastor in his suit,
All together, listen . . .
God's truth is mute.
Ghostly restless saloon,
Histories speak on Main.
Apparitions waltz in ballroom,
The mystery is:
Every human through the centuries remain
The same "ole local Bones" in sunshine on the street,
Administers conversation as a gentleman . . .

London has his Wolf House in distant;
Half Moon Bay.
Here,
Home is Italian Ancestry with family that has stayed.

Patricia Hopkinson
DO YOU KNOW THE ICE QUEEN?
Do you know the Ice Queen?
Gazing with cold eyes of green
From her icy tower
Wielding all her wicked power

Is the Ice Queen really cold?
Or is there not a man so bold
To melt her heart of steel
Kiss her lips and make her feel
The love locked within her breast
Hold her close against his chest

There is a sadness in her eyes
A sadness that very soon belies
Beneath her cool and icy pose
Lies a tender warm red rose

Sandra A Merlini
TWO WINDOWS
Veiled leaves through windows bright.
Framed by sheers—ivory light.
Dark shadows top a lowly mound.
Limest grapes surround each branch.
Trunk of white the sun does blanche.
Colored coat has now been found.

Stacy Girasuolo
WHEN A PERSON DIES
That special person
has finally reached his time.
That special person,
whom you loved so much,
Has finally passed away.
That special love,
That special care,
The memories still linger inside you,
Those memories will stay within your heart.

Cindy Storm
TO IDABELLE
When I look back to the past
I always see you there,
and when I think of you
I know that you still care.

We seemed to take for granted
that we were always near,
and when we had to part
our friendship seemed more dear.

As friends we must understand
that there's nothing we can't do,
we'll always be together
in our minds and spirits, too.

Thank you Idabelle
for being there for me,
I always will love you
and friends we'll always be.

Mrs F E Brady
WILD FORGET-ME-NOTS

This poem is dedicated to the memory of my mother and her love of wild flowers of her native state, Kentucky.

Little blue flowers so close to earth,
Hidden among the grass so green,
Not wanting to be seen
With lustful eyes to pick
You from your Mother's bed
Naught but dew and light were you fed

I yearned to pick them, but alas,
They had no stems to fill a glass,
So I left them there
In the meadow fair
For others to share
The wonder of a flower so small
One must stoop
To see it at all

Gary Crawford
WHAT WILL YOU DO TODAY
As I awoke, I heard a voice say to me;
"What will you do today"?
I looked around, but no one did I see.
As I wore the sleep from my eyes, I looked out the window, and saw a beautiful sunrise.
Again I heard the voice say to me,
"What will you do today"

Yet when I turned, no one did I see.
It was then that I realized, the voice that I heard, was the voice of the Master.
I answered the voice by saying, "I will try to do today, what I did yesterday".
For a brief moment, I helped to wipe away a tear, and for an instant, replaced it with a smile.
If I can make but one person smile, if only for a moment, then my day has been made worthwhile.
Again the voice spoke, and I heard my Master say,
"Be on your way, and help to brighten someone's day."

Bahareh Mobasseri
AUTUMN

To my loving mother, who has always encouraged me to be the best I could be

Dry leaves collapse
And quietly cover
A lifeless world
With a flaming quilt

Playing children
Bound recklessly
Into a mountain
Of rubies and gold

But time holds limits
Greedy winter watches
Pilfering pleasure
Blowing breezes
Lifting fall leaves

Leah Lutz
MY MIND'S EYE
In my mind's eye I see
Caterpillars crawling up a tree
And a butterfly just set free

from its cocoon.

Whippoorwills sighing by a stream
While young and old fishermen dream
Of days gone by and days ahead
and catching that big one.

Blue above and green below
And just enough breeze to blow
The heat of the day
away from the dreamers.

A perfect day that slips by
Until the moon lights up the sky
And wise old owls glide by
on silent wings.

No day lasts forever they say
But I don't see it that way
In young and old it's there to stay
forever a memory.

Kaara Kallen
WINTER'S STILL
White orb webs of frost
Fall thick and quick
From the plate of gray slate
Overhead, and stick
Like butterfly silk
To the stripped barren frames
Of the trees, reaching high
For the sky's frozen rains.

The snow sinks as soft
As a fog, and the nettles
Turn mild with blankets
Of white patterned petals,
And, but for the thick
Cold white light flakes,
Not a thing moves
—Not a creature awakes.

Muriel Haphey
THE STALLION
The stallion screamed
And flung his thundering beauty at the sky;
The bloodied rope burned deep,
The scars would never fade, nor memory die.
From out of the churning, swirling dust
The hands on the rope crept near
Flailing hooves tore holes in the wind
With a madness born of fear.
A hand reached out to touch,
Raw fury reared and squealed.
The rope could stand so much—
It snapped—the stallion wheeled.
The endless skies, and the lonely hills
And a stormy wind blowing—
These were his once more—
There was only the dust of his going.

Elizabeth A Viztes
I SAW AN OLD WOMAN TODAY
I saw an old woman today! It struck me that she appeared out of place.
When I looked at her face, I saw
the lines that age had
mercilessly drawn upon it.
They appeared like a mask that
hid her and permanently
categorized her as just another
old lady.

She never acknowledged anyone hear her and I found that I was beginning to understand.
This wasn't her world any
longer. Her world consisted of
memories she had of happenings
in her life,
possibly when she was my age.

I began to wonder what her life was like when she knew not a past already lived.
What did she look like some
fifty years ago when the world
was between wars?
Others might say her face was
void of expression, yet I could
sense a sadness that had not
quelled the strong personality
beneath.

Was there anything left that was familiar to her in today's world that she had known all her life?
For some strange reason I saw
myself in her and wondered if
one day, young eyes would peer
at mine and question my life,
that which has yet to be lived;
eyes that will wonder if the
world seemed unrecognizable to
that with which I would grow
old.

Will I look unrecognizable to myself in more than appearances when life's journey has taken its toll? Then, as I watch young
eyes peer at me,
I will see myself in her and later remember . . .
I saw a young woman today!

Karen R Navagh
POEM TO B.D.
I was walking through my garden and saw
The most beautiful, beautiful flower.
With my nose to you, you smelled so sweet,
Far beyond any perfume.
I smiled and plucked you out of the dirt
Then brought you inside to brighten my room.
Two days later, my flower was gone,
Left nothing but a withered stem.
I cried when I lost you, I knew what I had
And knew in my heart I'd been wrong.
If I had left you in my garden
You would still be there today,
Instead, I forced you to join me,
Never even thinking to ask.
I now have nothing but an empty garden
And the memory of a wonderful bloom.

Amy Weitsman
HANDS OF TIME
If ever there was one moment of time, for which the hands of time were mine,
I'd stop them there, just me and you, can you imagine the things we could do?
A frozen block of time to know, never how long it could ever go.
A suspended moment we both could share, as long as we wanted, without despair.
There's just no stopping the hour hands, to be able to have the moment I've planned.
Each moment of time is as special to me, as the moment of time that will always be free.

Betsy LaCombe
COMFORT
When days ahead
look dark and bleak
There's always Comfort
for one to seek

The blue skies turn
to clouds of gray
A warning of
a dark and dismal day

Someone you care for
goes afar
Then there's a place in your heart
left with a mar

A personal tragedy
may befall only you
One usually says
I'll not make it through

Look up above
at skies Oh so blue
Whether near or far
that someone's always with you

Your life is so precious
and very worthwhile
Face each new day
wearing a smile

Remember
there's always a God up above
Who's wherever you are
to share his love

So whenever day seems
to be dark and bleak

REMEMBER
something or someone
is the COMFORT you seek

Colleen E Crider
IT TAKES TWO
Coffee's on!
Mother's up and fixin' breakfast . . .
Quietly she awaits his presence,
And with the exchange of, "Good morning's,"
The two become one.
Only for a moment though,
Then he is off to work.
And with his leaving, she fades into the wall . . .
Awaiting his arrival once again.
For it is in two hearts joined as one
That living truly abounds!

Pamela Bloomfield
RESERVED SPACE
Let me walk through one last time
Just to make sure there's nothing left behind
Things seem so bare, only because there's nothing there,
But that's only to others, for you and I know;
A great deal still remains,
It's something that can't be stored away in a box
It can only bide its time, and ease its way into a precious slot,
In a far dark corner of my heart
A memory of us.

Yvonne Morningstar

Yvonne Morningstar
LINGERING ON MY MIND
It's hard to be a nurse
Day after day after day
Watching the patients you care for
Just lie in bed and wither away.

Some become so special
They find a place in your heart
It requires a special effort
Not to dwell on them when you part.

Until now I've done very well
At leaving my patients at work
But today a young man's pain
Found a corner of my mind to lurk.

I have a day off to ponder
To wonder why I care
And hope that God is listening
As I say a simple prayer.

Help them with their suffering
Get them quietly through each day
When my patients have some comfort
Then my pain, too . . . will go away.

Keli Peters
RESTLESS
Squiggling in your bed for hours trying to fall asleep,
Thinking of a hundred things at once and concentrating deep,
Laying your head on your pillow listening extremely close,
It's so hard to shut your eyes you'd think you took a No-Doze.

Everything is quiet but the wind that blows outside;
You get up to shut your window but the lock is tightly tied;
You run to turn on the light but all the bulbs are out;
Now you don't know what to do so you lay back down and pout.

Smothering yourself under the covers so that you cannot hear,
You finally fall asleep in time with most amounts of fear;
Now you're silently snoozing and dreaming all night long,
Waking up to your alarm that sings a high pitched song.

Just go back to sleep and slowly dream away,
For it's only 6:00 A.M. on a rainy Saturday.

Robert Stevens
JUST A LITTLE THING
It is today again
And I love you more again
I dream you into existence
I tremble before your beauty

And yet your beauty
Is just a little thing

Hardly more than

A cyclone in Singapore
A typhoon in the Philippines
A flood in Brazil
A monsoon in Korea

Nothing much
Your beauty
JUST A LITTLE THING.

DOLLY REBECCA
'I will always, always, love you'

Linda Pickett
GOD'S CHOSEN CHILDREN
God loves everyone we know
But there are just a few
Whom God loves better than the rest
They're God's chosen few

Many of them cannot walk
A few cannot speak
Many of them do not see
For their eyes are weak

And many of the children of God
Know not one small thing
They do not know your simple smile

Can not hear your laughter ring.

But God loves all these babies
He loves them one by one
And for these small children
He gave His only son.

He'll see them through the torment
He'll see them through the strife
And He will honestly live for them
And then give up His life

Jeremiah Thomas
TOUCH MY HAND
Touch my hand and pull me closer . . . squeeze and hold me tight.
Let's make this a memory to last thru-out the night.
Feel my touch with every move, with passion and with trust.
Close your eyes and visualize these feelings for yourself.
Touch each once and if you dare, even touch it twice. Take me in your slow soft kiss, mingle yours with mine. Set your heart inside my soul and never let it part. Feel the air around us, humid and so hot.
Even though it's raining the sun is shining still. Lay with me, and float you will, through this timeless night.
And we shall enter depths unknown, with splendor and delight. Going through unlocked doors of feelings that you never knew, would feel this way with you.
So drop the sail for raging seas and rocking waves from side to side, in and out here comes the tide, as we settle on the shore.
Soaked with all of natures love still shining on our face.
Now tell me, what kind of hurt, this love can not erase.
Touch my hand and pull me closer, squeeze and hold it tight.

Deborah Preeper
GENTLE LOVER
She needs it.
She wants to do it with someone she knows.

She wants to do it with someone she likes.

She wants to do it with someone who cares.
She needs a gentle lover.
She does it herself.

Mrs Ebby Phillips
SON
Your birthday son, again is here.
I've loved you through another year!
How could I have known, how could I have guessed,
That you could bring such happiness!
You've made me proud in things you do.
There have been hurts, I know it's true.
But through them all your motto's been,
"A winner never quits, and a quitter never wins!"
You learned it well so long ago;
You've used it well on every foe.
You spring right back, so I can say,
"Strength of character you sure display!"
"Without the scars, there are no stars."
Without the pain, there is no gain."
If all had gone smooth—what would that prove?
I've seen all the hurdles that you've come through.
I think of your strength, and strong will too.
As I look at you son, I take pleasure in knowing,
"When the going gets tough, the tough get going!"

Mary Holm
IN A LAVENDER SEASON
Rain gray
In a lavender season
The mixture producing mood blue

Deep sighs
In the attic of memory
In the basement cold dampness seeps through

Barbara Swanson-Smith
AS I LEAVE YOU
Life is eternal. I know it is so;
For where in the universe could we go?
Our body may decay, but our being is still;
We must be expressed; it is God's will.

Death's an illusion, only of fear
That God is not All or is not near.
Many "mansions" we live in;
Many lives expressing an
Ever greater reflection of being.

So as I leave this forum you know,
Please do not grieve and sorrow;
For now I know I am not dead
But only passing through a door
To an ever more glorious tomorrow.
My love is ever with you in spirit until we express it together again.

Dorothy Turnbull
PAST, PRESENT, AND FUTURE

Written just a short time before the death of her son, Joseph, now dedicated to his loving memory.

I wonder how often you've heard someone say;
"Twas a long time ago; do you remember that day?"
That's what the past is, I think most of all,
It's made up of memories we can always recall.
The people we've known and the places we've been,
These things we remember again and again.
They are never forgotten so I guess you might say,
The past is a part of the present today.

Well, <u>NOW</u> is the present and everyone knows,
It's here for a moment—then quickly it goes!
How long is the present? well no one can tell.
We should just take each minute and live it so well,
That when our present is past and no more to be;
What we're looking back on is a good memory!
We think of the future quite often you know;
To wonder what's coming and where we will go,
Especially our children; we wonder sometimes
What God has in store for their very young lives.
Whatever we do time will not change its way,
It just keeps going by day after day.

Claudine L Evans
LIFE'S ROAD

This is to the people I've met that made me realize how rewarding "Life's Road can be."

Life's road has many TURNS;
Turns for the worse;
Turns that aren't so BAD—
AND THEN THERE ARE TURNS—
THAT ARE GOOD .!

YOU MUST TAKE THEM;
FOR YOU CAN'T turn back
or do you crawl crawl into a hole?
OUT OF THE WORLD's SIGHT?
ARE YOUR SHOULDER's BROAD ENOUGH
TO STAND ERECT AND SAY!
"we'll make it it.' "
FOR INDEED WHERE'S THERE'S A WILL
THERE'S A WAY:
BRAVELY, COURAGEOUSLY;
AND YOU'LL MAKE IT—
<u>SOMEDAY</u>

Roberta T Reading
AWE-FUL

To My Aunt Edythe Taylor Brandon

Out of the somewhere
Come I here
Out of the love
Of someone dear
Out of a heart
That bears the pain
Out of a world
Which has no name.

He loved me from the moment
My earthly life began
Within the womb
He held me
In His Almighty hand
My life was in the shadows
By sin and guilt held down
The load was even heavier
For those who wore the crown
Now He was always with me
Although I did not know
As lovingly God led me
To live my life below.

Kristen Bergamo
PICKING UP THE PIECES

To my loving family and dear friends

I've loved you for the longest time,
you never knew how I felt.
One day you noticed me,
was it my glowing face you saw or the warmth of my heart you felt?
You were mine to be cherished,
to be loved, then you said those dreaded words I yearned not to hear,
You simply said: "No More."
As my heart shattered like crystal,
and the tears began to flow,
I asked myself the same question over and over: "What did I ever do to you?"
Everytime I see you my mind drifts back to all those special moments that we've shared.
Now I know it's over, and I know you don't love me anymore.
I guess it's time to pick up the pieces, and start over.
As you look back at the past and remember all those times you shared with me,
I want you to know I will always love you wherever you may be.

Gentrie Goodman
WHISPERS
He whispered softly in my ear,
Whispering things only I could hear.
Then touching my hand,
And pulling it near,
Caressing it softly.

Then he pulled me close,
And caressed my cheek softly,
I put my head on his shoulder,
And squeezed his hand gently,
While thinking of love.

The movie is over,
He takes me home,
As I get ready for bed,
I thought to myself,
Of whispers of love.

Mary Ruth Harper
DEAR MR. LINCOLN
My people were Louisiana southern,
Witness, my grandfather: Jefferson Davis Brown;
Until age five, I thought you were a traitor,
Textbooks and teachers pronounced you a hero.
I apologize.

Martha Jayne Young Schnurr
CHRISTMAS GREETINGS 1988
January, January, sure whizzed by;
Yes Sir, Yes Sir, Just like a fly; So one of twelve was gone by fate, And soon it will be Christmas 1988.
Soon February was here and it was Valentine's Day, and piles of snow still on the ground-HEH! But by the 29th it had disappeared, And the first day of Spring was almost here.
March flew in, and March flew away. And "Believe It Or Not," It was April Fool's Day.
April, May, & June also whizzed by,
Nothing new about that, Oh My, Oh My!.
Bill planted the garden and it grew,
According to science that's nothing new.
But July, August, September, brought us delightful weather. Bill hoed the garden & yard he mowed;
Produce was delicious, & on the scale it showed.
October, November brought us beautiful weather, And a desire to accomplish a lot; Sometimes that thought flew like a feather,
Depending on if we remembered or forgot.
Bill enjoyed walking; I rode my bicycle; We wanted to do these fun things,
Before God gave us tons of icicle.
So it's the 7th day of December, And snow is falling on the ground, As we send You Christmas Greetings,
Heaped High in a real huge mound.
And with these Christmas Greetings,
To SPECIAL PEOPLE WITH OUR LOVE, We Pray God Grant You Blessings, With warmest wishes from above.

Michael Ballinger
COUNTRYMEN LONG GONE
Overlooking the landscape viewing pools of blood,
The carnage too gruesome to bear.
The spillage rolling on like a crimson flood.
No longer have I feelings, numb because of fear.
The friends I had exist in spirit only.
Many times I felt there was no creator.
Surrounded by prone figures, I find I'm lonely,
On the fields of the eastern theater.
How can I admire heros of battles won
When all I see are the spoils of battles lost?
There is nothing left to prove, it's all been done.
By men too foolish to care, regardless of the cost.
My mind is filled with pain and regret,
Praying for strength to carry on.
But it's hard to dismiss, impossible to forget,
Remembering countrymen long gone.

James Taylor Forrest
ONCE WHEN YOU WERE ELEVEN, GOING ON TWELVE
Once when you were eleven, 'n going on twelve . . .

When the windows of your upstairs bedroom,
Offered panoramas of all there was t' see,
Openin' to the scent of things all in bloom,
Robins a' waiting, in th' tall cherry tree.

Once when you were eleven, 'n going on twelve . . .

When a 'ringed circus marched into our town . . .
Parade bands a' playin', 'n boys hearts aglow,
That night y' dreamed that y' were a circus clown . . .
Next day, y' watered thirty, thirsty elephants, standin' in a row.

Once when you were eleven,
Dreaming you were a great deal older—
Y'been like that since you were seven—
Now, you're grown-up 'n even bolder.

Now that you're twelve, 'n going on . . .

When did your dreams turn to things past?
When each day flowed with carefree activity.
Wishing that the old halcyon days would last—
And . . . that y' weren't . . . going on . . . seventy.

Charlotte E Wayno
WAY UP YONDER

This poem is dedicated to my husband, Jerry, who had a very rewarding career in the United States Air Force.

Have you ever stopped to ponder,
How wild is the "Wild Blue Yonder?"
Was it just a very simple whim,
That made it part of the Air Force Hymn?
Just how far does that yonder go,
That's a thing I'd like to know?
Is it just the space where airplanes fly,
And lightning streaks across the sky?

In that same yonder, are there alien creatures,
With great intellect and real weird features?
Are there large groups of so-called supermen,
Just waiting to visit planet earth again?

Are there really space ships, as some folks say,
And do they have a direct route to the U.S.A.?
Maybe these odd beings are meek and mild,
Perhaps thoughts of them made Oscar Wilde.

If one ever lands in our back yard,
I'll ask them to show their Master card.
Because if they want to join our society,
They'll need lots of credit cards like you and me.

Bernice Sadler
A LOST LOVE
I have forgotten you at last
The way you walked,
And laughed, and how your eyes
Would glint with glee!
I have forgotten! You're not free
But I am—Now I see
Your eyes, your hands, your lips
But none
Have any power over me!

Today I held a baby in my arms
Its head was round and like a fairy shell
Its eyes were bright like yours
I had forgot—
How bright a baby's eyes could shine!
Be still—my heart,
It was not mine!

Mary Culkin Gaines
TAKE TIME

To Dad I am me, thanks to you.

When did you age, my father?
I can't recall that day.
In that bed you look so frail and still,
I'm frightened like a child.
You didn't say you needed me,
And I was so busy I couldn't see.
You gave of your self so many years,
Your pride, your strength, and humor.
I still need your love and wisdom.
Please, stay with me awhile.
Give me the chance to show you my love,
You deserve all I can give.

I touch your hand,
You squeeze mine back.
My silent pleas are heard.
The tears flow now,
I'm so relieved.
I have a second chance.

Lori Finley-Lakner
I REMEMBER

Mom, when this you read, remember me. I love you! Lori

Mother it was you,
Who gave birth to good seed.
And you who coached us,
In His Apostles Creed.
Mother it was you,
Who met our thirst of needs.
You showed us how to follow,
but encouraged us to lead.
And clothed us from winter,
wrapped us in tweed.
But, it was you who was deserving
and thirsting for your needs.
Because I Remember!

Amy L Norgren
FRIENDS

Dedicated to Mr. Novara and his class of '88-'89

Friends should be caring,
loving, and kind.

Friends don't appear, they
are very hard to find.

When I think that you have
led me thru good times and bad,

And, all of the very good
times that we have had,

I think that soon we will
get older and drift far apart,

But, I will always remember that
we will be Friends in the Heart.

Jean Montanari
NIGHT MOOD
Crickets conversing
set the mood in the night air:
hot
dark
muggy.
My heart, on emotion overload,
about to burst.
A slight intruding breeze
escorted the aroma of thunder.
My mind of thought
was blank—
slowly,
gently,
falling
asleep . . .

Chrissi Liokareas
I WANT YOU TO KNOW

To my brother Tommy Who is with me always

I want you to know
That as time passes on
I'll be thinking of you
Although you are gone

You'll be with me always
Although you're not near
You'll be in my laughter
And in every tear

A moment won't pass
When you'll see you won't find
That you'll be in my thoughts,
My dreams and my mind

So, I want you to know
That although we're apart
That nothing can take you
Away from my heart

Karla Kiefel
TODAYS' TOMORROW
I never could see into the future
So I've learned to live for today
But as time moves on
I realize today
Is the tomorrow
Of a yesterday gone by
I think of all that
I could have done
If I had planned
My time more wisely
Of all the knowledge
That would be mine
If I had a crystal ball
At my side
I have no regrets as of yet
But I wonder sometimes
If I shouldn't have
Developed a long range view
In order to see
My tomorrows through

Doris Sinclair
MORNING IN SAN FRANCISCO
Wet and grey, the fog swirls at my feet.
I am chilled and cold, and down the street,
Neon signs shimmer, softly subdued,
And the fog grows green and rosy hued.

In the east the sun is rising
Above the billows that obscure the trees
I see warm signs of the day to come,
And the rising smoke is stained scarlet
Where it meets the sky.

High, high above the mists
The sky is clear and blue.
And like a slender yellow bird
A jet leaves a golden vapor trail,
Curving against the orbit of the sky,
Like a graceful golden tail,
It's morning in San Francisco.

D Gregory

D Gregory
THE WAR OF THE SENSES . . . 1863

To my wife Fran, the mother of my children. She is the granddaughter of James W Burdick. He was wounded seven times as a soldier in the Civil War.

You could hear the soldiers' shouting and the cannon's awful roar!
You could hear them by the hundreds, and believe that there were more
You could hear the random purging, of death coming to the men

You could hear the solemn silence . . . then it started up again.

You could see them on their horses, as they charged into the town!
You could see them rape the women and leave blood upon their gown
You could see grief on the faces of those left to live in shame
You could see the town; burning down . . . as it yielded to the flame.

You could smell the black gun-powder and the carnage in the town
You could smell the fear of dying as the wounded all fell down;
You could smell the burning flesh as the fires took their deadly toll
You could smell the sun-baked bodies . . . left to rot upon the knoll.

You could taste the sweat of others as it glistens on their skin
You could taste the blood of the wounded as it flowed from within
You could taste the salty tears as they fell hot upon your face
You could taste the loss of battle . . . and the stigma of disgrace.

You could touch the last remains of loved ones-if they are your kin
You could touch the wooden-crosses of those men that did not win;
You could touch the souls of victims; that are in an unmarked grave
You could touch the hearts of mankind . . . to redeem the life you gave!

Arthur F Kennedy
PINK KISSES
Just before we see the slightest glimmer of the first star;
and the sunset is a sexier pink than negligees are.
We can not move for fear that this fragile wonder that sings
Will crumble at our touch like butterfly wings.
Words won't come because we are stinken dumb;
honey words are imagined but our tongues are paralyzed numb!
Now, let us swell in the music of the first kiss,
and the pinkier notes of its gratifying bliss.
We were afraid to stir, modest and frail as a lily,
ever so sweetly sad but yet not so silly.
For kisses like the pink sunset will come again;
but we must be motionless and concentrate to the very end.
I may not be a great lover, but this I know
Not from sages but my heart tells me so!

Robert LeRoy Smith
DEATH
Picaresquely, Autumn flings his wildness at the trees,
transforming verdant leaves to alphabets that rattle
in the breath of errant Zephyr's monologue (crescendos like a gypsy's castanets). This lovely plastic rhythm mimics polyphonic prose; it whispers poems written by the wind.
I listen with my ear attuned and plagiarize each phrase
(dictation from a source Fate can't rescind).
These ornamental red and yellow leaves belong to me; eternity is caught and held in time. Beneath these gorgeous trees that portend death,
I stand alone and translate foreign language into rhyme.
I fathom secrets of dimensions never known before, within a poem lucidly obscure. An in-stained heart gives up its life to live and learn of peace (though filled with doubts), compassionately sure. A final frozen phrase expires expressing sighing truth; sensations cease in every barren tree.
Omniscient silence, subtle chill, a mesmerizing lull:
the alphabet of death has reached the Z.
Tormented red and yellow leaves have fallen from the trees; the limbs are bare that once were emerald crowned. Profoundly,
Winter eulogizes to a world subdued as
Tyche's ball falls, shattered, to the ground.

Roi Yanez
THE OAK LEAF (THE REIN-CARNATION OF A LEAF)
When I turn to a bright yellow,
  And then to a darker brown.
Turn me loose and let me sail
  To the old frozen ground.

Let me lie up on a mountain;
  Let me clutter up a dream.
Let me glide down on the ripples
  Of a crooked mountain stream.

Let the wind teach me his dances;
  Let him catch me if he can.
For the love of Mother Nature
  Is not owned by any man.

Let the rain give me her blessings;
  Let the moon lend me her glow.
Let me lie beneath a blanket
  Of two feet of frozen snow.

And when I return to nature,
  And I am reborn again.
I will fall in love next summer
  With the west wind and the rain.

Vivian Gordon
I'D HURT YOU BAD YOU STILL HUNG ON

To Robert, I kept my promise to love you and no one else if only you believed in me.

I'd hurt you bad but you still hung on
I've often wondered why
I could see in your eyes, just because of me
You'd sometimes wanted to cry

I know I should have gone with what I felt
And not listen to what people say
It was for that reason "Dear God" I regret
We broke-up that November day

And now I miss and want you back
Because what I feel now is true
I should have gone with my feelings
—and not my friends
Now I'm stuck in love with you.

Katrina Cherry
FAMILY TREE
Thank-You Lord for my family tree,
They're all part of me.
My life's been a special one,
One of a dying breed.
The family tree, the family tree,
The way it ought to be.

Thank-You Mom, Thank-You Dad,
You gave me all I am.
You taught me to love all men, keep my faith, and never, ever walk away.
All things are possible, always believe in yourself.
Take a chance, and enhance the life god gave to you.
The secret to happiness is deep inside yourself.

You'd say, look up not down and face the world head on.
Take heed, plant a seed of hopes and dreams.
So Thank-you lord for my family tree,
Without them I could not be what I am.
If I could give one thing to my fellow man,
The strength and love of a family is what it'd be.

Dorothy Mattson Saychek
SUNDAY MORNING
Dreamy shadows, barely sunrise,
coffee perking, TV preachers hawking,
news, cartoons, Charles Kuralt,
blending peace and strife.
How to choose essentials?

I could turn it off,
dream some more, turn over,
but my interest's peaked.
Must I have the news of war,
hijackings and murders?

Could I only see the sunrise,
see the sandhill cranes,
soar on high across the mountains,
to their summer homes,
watch their graceful dance.

How about the headlines.
Can I close my eyes, not see them,
only find the crossword puzzle,
spend my day with words,
drink my coffee, only hear the music.

Jamie Laura
LIKE SHADOWS IN THE NIGHT
  Line shadows in the night
Disappear with the light.
  Like snow and the fun
Disappear with the sun
  Like happiness and the
  holiday cheer
Disappear with new year
  Like good friends lives
Disappears as she drinks and
Drives

Kingsley Douthwaite
OFTEN A THOUGHT PERVADES MY THINKER-ARIUM
Looking at my first and last wife
That this beloved nonagenerian
Means more to me than all life.

67 years of messages
Understood only by her and by me
Set us apart from the rest of us
Binding inseparably.

If I had to do it all over again
I'd do it all over again, I declare
But hey, wait: isn't that a bit iffy?
To do that, we'd have to live to a hundred and fifty.

Happy the couple who can see
The same oxymorons wherever
(There's a sad case when she sees "military intelligence" as oxymoron, He-never)

Time passes; each day less to get hetup about
"Religions" to say "that line of crap" about,
Dust of piano that Mrs X is almost in tears about . . .
In fancy words:—oxymorons.
Lucky me:—SHE sees them the same as I.

If that were all there was to it
There wouldn't be much to it would there?

As if we depend on those who seem stupid
To us, to bind us together.

But we have kids and grandkids and great grandkids
Mostly brighter than we are
Who wouldn't be around if we hadn't of did
What we did when young, like they are.

Prince A Stewart
A DRIFTING THOUGHT
(How poems are borned)
You're traveling through an uncharted region of your inner universe.
Your mind strains from the invisible forces from the magnetic force-field,
As you cross the subconscious to reach the superconscious mind.
Your thoughts are traveling fast; faster than the speed of light.
Then suddenly you realize that you are chasing a dream; a fragment from a drifting thought.

You're closing in fast. Then suddenly it happened. Your sights are locked in on a virgin drifting thought. You've caught up with a dream.
You seize this thought and bring it home. You put this drifting thought on paper fast, because you know that if you don't capture it while it is still fresh in your conscious mind, it will be lost forever.

This thought is unique; you know this because you are the only one who has the power to control your inner universe. You are the only one who can safely travel across this unknown region of your subconscious, to reach your superconscious mind: to catch up with a dream, to seize a drifting thought, which no other mind could capture. It is yours. Love and cherish it forever.It is your child. You gave birth to it from chasing a drifting thought. Stop.

Frank M Puleo
LIFE
We are all actors performing on stages,
Writing our stories on a thousand and one pages.
From the day we are born,
Our lives are filled with many a thorn.

The bright sun and blue skies bring us gladness,
The clouds and the storms bring us sadness.
We strive for the joys and happiness of the good life,
Yet we often end up with turmoil and strife.
I have laughed and I have cried,
But my dreams and hopes have never died.
The years are rolling by,
And I keep asking myself why,
Why have I failed to reach my goal,
It tugs and tears at my very soul.
Before I leave the stage for my final resting place,
I hope I lived my life to the fullest, and left with grace.

C L Pyle
BOUQUET
Bouquet, combined differences intertwine
unique circling underline
Pastel petals in the windy sway, in time—
Each thought, beneath green leafy under know
The roots reaching out as we grow
A slow edging into the light to bloom
Bouquet, of three wise in the wonder why
Could be just me, myself and I
Smile changed as the landscape rearranged

Bouquet, a view point from my windowsill
To gaze down from the vantage still
Sky azure on the periphery, I see—
Each thought, above floating in cloudy know
Ideas reaching out as we grow
Evolving like the passing day to night
Bouquet, of three wise in the wonder why
Could be just me, myself and I
A tear watering the blooming dry

Michlin LaBounty
LOST IN A GLANCE
To get lost in your eyes it just takes one glance,
If only you would give me another chance.

I can't stand the suspense of waiting,
I still keep on dreaming and anticipating.

Hoping that my dreams may come true,
I will always remember how in love I am with you.

Please give me one more chance,
So I can get lost in a glance

Rami S Malek
THE SEED
Once I was dead, alone in a dark black underworld.
I was being torn apart and I loved it. My flesh, eaten by savages, was but a faint memory. Inside this shell though, was a living soul, a green and budding being. Without it, I would be trapped in this grave state forever. I grew stronger and braver despite the odds that were against me. I had no living parents or siblings, I was lonely. I did know that there were other souls up there with much refreshing dew. I wanted to be able to feel, both physically and emotionally, so I waited. Light years passed and still there was no change in my melancholy position. But one day I realized that I was rising, growing. I was maturing into a greener, more noticeable being. I now had skin, a beautiful olive color. I saw a bright light ahead of me, on top. I grew closer to this light until I entered it. We became one. My growth was now at a celeritous pace. I was introduced to a living world where I found family and was given a name. I now had identity. Once I was dead, now I am olive.

Mary E Kinzie
SHADOW PLAY
Quickly the shadows fall upon the growing darkness after sunset. The mist swiftly invades my soul with its cold and icy fingers, reaching down along my spine. A feeling of sudden fear fills my body . . . for alone am I, in the darkness.

The light from my soul cast shadows within my heart, acting out its charade. The drama unfolds with its strange, phantom like images; performing on stage. To give a performance together, yet alone in the dead of night . . . unearthing dark secrets.

Captivated by the fire of desire were the episodes. Haunted by sensations of ecstasy and illusions of frightening intimidation. Controlled by a fear far beyond all imagination, unable to rationalize or move . . . awaiting the twilight of dawn.

Helen M Dearduff
FRIENDSHIP

In memory of aunts & uncle who passed away recently
Thanks to many friends who helped me in recent illness & sorrow.

Friendship is a thing you should treasure
It comes back to you in delightful measure.
If you don't have it, now is the reason
To start looking for it starting this season.
There is a guarantee you'll find it worth while
For it will bring on a great big smile.
And your future together will be just fine
As you keep each other in mind.

Lois Henderson
DON'T EVER THINK YOU'RE A NOBODY
Don't ever think you're a nobody,
Because it simply isn't true.
Whatever is done in a life time,
Can be forgiven, for anything you do.
We're all equal in God's eyes.
He said so didn't He?
So simply start loving,
And your heart will set you free.
If people start thinking they're better than you,
They're living in a dream.
Because we're all God's children and equal,
Meaning we're all just one big team.

Franca Timpano
SO FAR AWAY
. . . And I shut my eyes once more
To linger in the coziness of my world,
My own small world.
I sink further and further into its deep blue waters
Until it surrounds me and has me wholly.
I do not fight—there is no war—I surrender.
This peace and I are one
And reality is so distant, so far away—that I forget . . .
But the waves sweep me to shore,
I remember . . .
I am back again and the noise and laughter are reality
And the cries still remain
And I shut my eyes once more . . .

James Cavanaugh

James Cavanaugh
MORNING MISTS

To My Dearest Lucy

We walk together among the morning mists,
We talk together while the sun's warm fingers
Probe the greens of grass and trees.
A shiver of coldness frowns upon the placid lake's surface.
We are in love. We are alive and alone.
We do not listen to the buzzing of insects from damp pools.
The shrill cry overhead warns the sleep drugged night,
Death is near, Shadows flee into the trees.
A creature no longer fearing the owl, is crushed deftly by a hawk.
Sad murmurs lurk in dreams, sulk uninterrupted by time as
Lovers lay with hearts bare, unaware,
Screened by an inquiring sun. Yet, a darkness persists.
Hunger is everywhere. It waits its chance to scream.
It is the nature of fear,
The willfulness of hurt.
What sort of world is it that destroys without remorse, without feeling?
Is love a cruel master,
So easily adored, seldom understood?

Elizabeth A Hammer
THE BROKEN TREE
I lay . . . in the shadows of eve, and in the mist of dawn . . . with my broken limbs reaching . . . reaching for a time gone by when I was straight and tall, strong and beautiful, like those standing around me. At one time I knew joy; in the spring . . . the blooming flowers at my feet, the sun clothing me in her warmth, with the cool breeze brushing my skin; the beauty of winter . . . looking out at the endless white blanket of snow, breathing the cold, crisp night air. Although there were times that I shuddered against the icy winds, I prefer to remember my days of joy. Now my time is spent and I lay . . . watching those around me grow . . . watching their joy . . . waiting for the time when I will see no more; feel no more. The time when I will be no more!

Jami Strey
IN THE WIND

This is dedicated to someone I hope gets united with his newest love.

Running down the road,
Having the greatest time,
Until you hear the sirens
"Is it another crime?"

You see the police now
"I wonder what happened—
Was it another murder,
Another young mans end?"

Home last night you saw on T.V.
Crime shows and detective shows
Where people are murdered and shot
On T.V. anything goes-as
Reality in a parking lot.

The next thing you know
You see an ambulance
"What has happened this time?"
Then you fall into a trance

Your family will never forget
What happened on that day
That's all you remember
And there's nothing left to say

Kimberly Anne Cahaly
YOUR BEAUTY
What in this world can I compare thee to;
A rainbow, a star or a sky of blue.
Come near me now and forever we'll stay;
In one another's arms as we begin to pray.
What will happen in the time that lies ahead;
Nobody knows but we both might be dead.
Please say you love me or at least you'll try;
To fight Mother Nature and stay alive.
For our lives together would be one of a kind;
Just like a clock that would not wind.
For our lives are just starting and
We are young right now.
So together forever in
A world without time.

Margaret Kettner
DEEP VOICE
I hear a voice deep down in my heart. I listen to what I can hear. As my heart pounds on.

I Listen, Listen then I hear a voice strong in my heart it tells me to listen for a sign will come in the darkest of the night it will tell you of my secret of love and delight.

If you do not listen the secret will be lost in the night and you will hear no more from me.

Olive K Rahn
CLUB MEETING
The hum grows.
Round and down it goes,
In and around and through me it flows
And fills me completely from head to toes.

The gavel descends.
The sound, so explosive, intends
To bring order and quiet, but it extends

The dimension of sound and it echoes and bends.

A motion is made.
Voices rise in a noisome tirade.
But somehow despite the disordered facade
Agreement is reached and sounds die out and fade.

The meeting soon ends.
The sound grows and ascends.
A clatter of footsteps the stairway descends.
The chatter dies out as friends leave with friends.

Serban Buretea
THE BLACKBIRD
It was not long ago when I was in my cave, secure and safe,
When I heard the call of the Blackbird.
I set out across the Rope of Sugar,
In pursuit of this luring call
beyond the horizon.
The call gets louder as I approach the mist,
And I recall the warnings of my peers.
"The Bird lived in the pits of hell,
Where only it could dwell.
It never flew, but grew and grew.
It never set out across the sky,
For it would surely die.
Under the power of the Bird,
Nothing else was heard,"
It was all so easy, just don't fall off the Sugar Rope,
Get to the smiling land beyond.
The mist clears and I see the rope stop over the Blackbirds nest.
I slip and fall, grab the Sugar Rope, but it dissolves in my hands.
I fall into the Blackbird nest
Where it crawls into my head
And gnaws at my brain until I can think no more.
Soon, I will be dead.

Ralph Seaton
WHAT A WITCH IS LOVE
What a witch is love
To tempt a heart
To make it try
At first give hope
To then deny
To squeeze a heart
To wring it dry
What a bitch is love.

Anne MacGillivray
"THANK YOU" FROM THE ANIMAL KINGDOM

To All Who Had To Say "Good-bye" To Their Pet

Life has its way with people, good times, animals, and flowers,
Some will live for many years, some weeks, some days, some hours.
And forms of nature win our hearts, yet, those of us who love,
Can feel a heavy burden when they're taken from above.
If all our pets could talk to us, I know that they would say,
"Thank you, for accepting that I had to 'leave' one day".
You gave a home for me to live with love surpassing all,
I knew you cared in every way,
To me you stood real tall.
Yes, people, good times, animals, the birds and flowers too,
Have all been brought together to see beauty and love that's true.
But all is temporary and my job was done for you,
There's still more love and beauty,
Please don't mind if I say "Thank You".
For if you did not take me, I'd never have "gone home"
With all the love and joy that you had given me alone.

Christine A Millan
RICKEE
rickee never went to skool
i wacht him evryday az
he went owt thu dore
but rickee never wokt to thu skool
he sed nah! hoo needz skool?
iym gonna be thu richest man
in thu hole wiyd werld
yoo do not need braynes to be rich!
insted uv skool
he dug deeper in a hole
he started with hiz plastik shuvel
oyl, he sed
i will dig oyl and that will mayke me rich
evryday he dug and dug . . .

rickee never went to skool
now i see him—
noozpayperz for a blanket
dumpster for a sowfa
oyl drum for a fyreplayce
yoo do not need braynes to be rich!
that iz wot he sed.

Jim Zingale
WE SIT AND WAIT
We sit and wait for time to pass,
Not knowing that in our grasp,
We have so little time to share,
For those we love and those who care.

We try to make the best of each day,
Sitting and hoping they will pass my way,
But then another sunset falls,
And then it's time to sit, and look at the walls.

We sit and wait for time to pass,
Then sunrise comes and we see the grass,
But then again we are caught in a struggle,
Of time and sorrow and life is a muddle.

We watch as time passes us by,
Not knowing where, when or why,
We have so little time to share,
For those we love and those who care.

Jack Lauber
JENNIFER TOMBOY OR LADY

My impressions of Jennifer at age Nine

Is she mostly boy, or girl,
That is rather hard to guess;
Blue jeans are her favorite wear,
And she looks so nice in a dress.

Her manners can be so lady like,
Or, bold and boyish too;
Depending on the mood she is in,
And who she is talking to.

She likes dolls and teddy bears,
But they are second best;
Her First love is really horses,
Cats, dogs, birds, and the rest.

She enjoys rough and tumble games,
More than playing house or school;
She has a memory like a fox,
And is not too easy to fool.

Her Mothers traits are in her,
But her Daddy's are also there;
Regardless of what you think she is,
She doesn't really seem to care.

I believe her composition is,
A bit of all Three, maybe;
The Three that make her loveable,
Tomboy,—girl,—and Lady.

Alice Madsen
SAY IT WITH LOVE

To my family and friends.
Love and friendship speaks volumes, and we have written many, with more to write. Thank you all.

I want to
Say it with Love
And those feelings run deep
I want to
Say it with Love—Prayers
That He may safely keep

You
And—Your love for me
Well guarded in our daily lives
Though life may take us
Down different paths
Your love yet remains to be my Sunlight

And I am bathed
In an oil
Of kindness

Mrs Linda Savary Ring
FETUS
Fetus
alive, wondrous
growing, kicking, breathing
developing inside woman
Baby

Abortion
lifeless, vacuous
dying, fading, ceasing
being vacuumed through a machine
Murder

Frances L Bauman
THE DOVE
And so it goes.
The peaceful dove rides on a sea of hope. Waiting for someone to set it free, to break the chains that bind. And the dove cries alone, and the dove flies inside itself forever in silence.
Don't be afraid of the night for where there is darkness there is light and you will see it reflected many times over in the eyes of those who love you.
The dove will see you through. And the dove tries for love. And the dove lives in those who believe in love from the heart.
I know the dove lives in you.

Laurel Kornhiser
A GLIMPSE OF A STORM
I open the door which separates my warm, snug shelter from Nature's fury:
Whose gusting power thrashes and shakes
the prideful bulk of brushes and trees,
Whose violent force strips and lays bare
the manmade network of wires and lines,
Whose element freezes and white frosts
this patch of earth her canvas,
Who darkens and deletes all color
a swirl of white and gray blots out all,
Who creates, shapes, and delineates
icicles, drifts, and snow waves.

I open the door which separates my closed-in haven from Nature's display:
The lashing winds are settled and still,
The battered trees bear their new burden,
The sun soothes the wounds from the night's storm,
The stifled colors burst forth with flair,
The brilliance of the scene betrays not
The scars of its recent painful birth.

Leticia Torres De La Riva
DEATH, THE STRANGE SENSATION
I woke up with the moonlight
To observe the heaven sky,
I felt this strange sensation,
Which dreams cannot describe.

The world was below me,
And I was floating high,
Still with the strange sensation,
That I had reached the sky.
And then when I was falling,
I was about to slide,
It was then that I noticed,
That I had wings to fly.

I flew above the moonlight,
And then back to the place,
Where all my dreams had started,
As raindrops washed my face.

And when my eyes were open,
At last I realized,
That I was now in heaven.
I really crossed the skies.

But I just kept believing,
That it was all a dream.
I thought it was a fantasy,
And that's the way it seemed.
But when I tried to wake up,
And get out of my bed,
I felt a strange sensation,
I knew that I was dead.

Mildred R Mullen
GOD IS EVERYWHERE
Out into the garden
In every little seed,
In every little blade of grass,
In each little lowly weed,

In the up-turned face of each flower
As they sway gently in the breeze
As He glides silently through them
And gives them a gentle squeeze.

Summer passed into Autumn.
What a beautiful sight
And before long in the garden
God laid a blanket of white.

His burdens are so heavy
I know wherever He goes
His loving touch will linger
Like perfume from a beautiful rose.

Shelly Weeks
THE SNAKE
The constant sound of icy water
As it plunges over jagged rocks
Racing past the serene beauty
Its own awe-inspiring beauty mocks

Gracefully flowing through every twist and turn

So full of majesty and mystery
Wiser than any man could hope to be
She has reigned throughout history

Men try to conquer her untamed fury
Some managing to ride the wild beast
But to others who are arrogantly careless
She turns the table and they become her feast

And yet, in the moonlight she appears so gentle
A winding thread of spun silver, so fragile it might break
She is unchangeable, yet ever-changing
She is the unpredictable, all-mighty Snake.

Branwen Santos
MIST
The condensation of the clouds
Forms a mist along the grounds.
The passers-by don't notice it,
But walk in silence through the mist.
Street lamps light part of the way,
As children stop their play.
The roofs of the houses glisten
Once the moon has arisen.
It hovers above the leaves,
On the sidewalks and in the trees.
Not a sound could be heard
Like emotions without words.
The morning comes and drives away
The mist from yesterday.
It shows no sign,
That it was left behind
Across the empty scene.

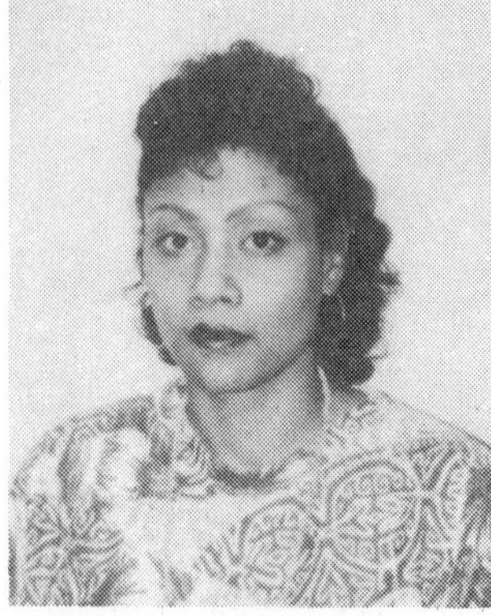

Mrs Salina-Satchel-Hayes-Ledger

Mrs Salina-Satchel-Hayes-Ledger
SPEAK OUT YOUNG BLACKS

This poem is dedicated to my mom, Mrs. L.C. Satchel, and sister, Shirley Satchel, who has always believed in me; Janice Jackson, who pushed me; my husband Fred Ledger, and my children Kim, Ronald, Jr. & Aaron Hayes, who just loves me; Carrie Rudolph, who proofs and reads for me; and to George T. Wilcox, Jr., who encourages my work. To all: Thank You!

Speak out young Blacks when you've something to say
The world is listening to you today

The time has certainly come and gone
when Whites entered doors that Blacks knocked on

Your parents and grandparents made the sacrifice
to provide you the vehicle to steer your own life

Today there is opportunity for extended education
Today there is freedom and desegregation

Tomorrow you'll become our young Black leaders
fulfill your potential for yourself and your people

Be still young Blacks and know in your hearts
that all glory be to God from the very start!

Then believe in yourselves as you scratch the surface
we all have our destinations, and everyone has a purpose

Always choose the roads that lead to success
you are strong and beautiful, don't settle for less

Speak out young Blacks though difficult it seems
Be the leading character of your own dreams!

Vera McGown Stufflebeem
HEAVEN
The beautiful things of Heaven
have a wondrous attraction for me.
The beautiful things of Heaven
are the things I am longing to see.

The beautiful things of Heaven
prepared by our Savior above.
The beautiful things of Heaven
are surrounded by our Saviors love.

The beautiful things of Heaven
are in store for all who will trust Him.
The beautiful things of Heaven
should be the desire of each of us.

The beauty and Glory of Heaven
where my loved ones await for me.
There will be no more parting
on the Throne of God for eternity.

The time to depart earth for Heaven
God's Angels will knock on your door.
You must be ready and willing
for the Angel to open a new door.

Oh! the glories of Heaven

Bruce W Watkins
SYLVATIC LIFE
I battle
To come to terms with myself
My thoughts and my feelings
Are constantly in turmoil

All I want is to understand
Why am I like I am
Why is the world like it is
But the answer is never revealed

Someone once said
They took the path less traveled
But I feel that I am wandering
Through the forest without a path to travel

I feel snagged and scratched
The thorny vines of life
Clawing at me while I search
For the peaceful lake that is hidden among the trees

Oh, that I should someday find it
Surrounded by green grasses
That I can kneel on while I
Touch my parched lips to the cool sweet water

Nancy Arlene Perkins
CHILDREN
They are not a marriage saver,
or a go between pawn.
They are not a relationship paver,
or an ex-spouse con.

Children are special people,
who need love to help them grow.
They need trust and understanding
their little minds can know.

They need limits on what they can do,
But at the same time they
need freedom too.

They need a permanent place they know,
That will always be safe and
warm to go.

There are many things a child can do,
With a parent's love to see
them through.

Mil Pumroy
BOOK-ENDS
Silently you stand guard over spies and monsters, never divulging plots nor heroes.
Hoarding the secrets of untold tales.
Smiling at happy endings.

G Gayle Foster
GOD HERE WITH US

For Jed, my treasured son.

A manger cradle, soft with hay
A blanket small, a tiny babe.
Shepherds awed by angel voices
A brand new star above.
Amongst the animals, a King is born!

A town so full of people
But few who really cared
About their visitors from heaven,
The answer to their prayers.

The Babe-a man now grown
A cross too heavy, a crown of thorns.
Upon the hill, a King has died!
Lord, help us understand why you became
Immanuel, God here with us.

Madeline Muylaert
WE FORGET . . .
Who was this man? Who was this boy?
Who gave up every laugh and joy?
Why did he die, so far from home;
Without his friends and all alone?

We glimpse his name, we feel regret,
But turn a page and then forget.
Yes, we forget and all because
We can't remember he died for us.

We can't remember the little town
That on his boyish deeds would frown,
It really loved him and all his pranks,
And was so proud when he joined the ranks.

We can't remember his fine old dad,
Who gave the only son he had,
With cheery smile and, "So Long, John."
But his shoulders bowed when his son was gone.

His mother's feelings of pride and fears
Have changed to pain and unshed tears.
Her aching heart can ne'er forget
The day he left to meet his death.

So young he was to kill and fight.
Yet, this he did to keep our right.
Our right to live, and love, and laugh.
He gave up all on our behalf.

This unpraised hero, once gay and bold,
Is now lying still, his deeds untold.
We read his name, we feel regret,
But turn a page . . . and then forget.

Diana L West
ALLERGIES
It seems to me, thinking rationally,
I'll never again breathe normally.
This intensely clogged nose of mine,
Stuffed for the longest period of time,
Won't allow me to take in air.
My death will result in this classroom chair;
And if I should die in Mrs Eskilson's class,
She'll never allow me to pass.
She'll feel it's an insult to her,
But I know that I just can't endure
Twenty more minutes of sitting still
Which is just too much time to kill.
What I'd give to breathe with ease.
Oh, No Way! Here comes a sneeze!
Now my eyes are starting to tear,
And still twelve minutes left in here.
Well, finally now the sneeze has passed,
And I've disturbed the whole darn class!
I wish I was home in bed,
For in no time I shall be dead!

Nicholas Petroro
TOMORROW
There will always be a tomorrow
When temptation flirts with you.
There will always be a tomorrow
When his love comes shining through.

There will always be a tomorrow
With a challenge we must face.
There will always be a tomorrow
He'll protect us with his grace.

There will always be a tomorrow
To sail unchartered seas.
There will always be a tomorrow
To relive old memories.

There will always be a tomorrow
To share the joy he gives.
There will always be a tomorrow
To witness he still lives.

There will always be a tomorrow
To share with our best friend.
There will always be a tomorrow
A life—without end.

B E Noel
VALENTINE'S DAY

To my Eros

Hearts, flowers, chocolates . . .
Symbols selected and perpetuated.
Hearts given, devoted, broken.
Flowers presented, carried in

wedding bouquets.
Chocolates bittersweet, melted
Symbols of emotions
set aside for 'Hallmark' holidays.
Anticipated . . . required.
Valentine's Day!
24 hours to say "I love you"
in unison, stripped of spontaneity.
Yet, laced with a romance
that taunts the logic of my mind
and the deepest wounds of my heart.

Janet O'Leary
THE RAIN
I start to cry, and a few seconds later
it starts to rain.

Looking at the rain,
I think about my memories.
I think of my two grandpas,
and I sit there crying.

As I think about them,
it starts to pour.
As if they're giving me a sign;
I cry even harder.

Thinking of the great times
we had together,
how both of them were too young to die,
I still cry.

My last teardrop falls,
and a few seconds later
it stops raining
for now . . .

Kendell W Spencer
NEW POEM
Closing the door—shutting out
electric, mortal light
You closed your eyes against the darkness
and turned a little into the room.

Moving imperceptibly through
the huge—darkness
my hand
found your hand and cautiously
guided you in.

How this place in moonlight
Grows!
Now opened, now closed.
Our mouths and Our bodies
have learned a new, soft, unspeak-able language.

With your eyes still closed
against the darkness,
I whispered my love.
And like a young, dewy flower,
early in spring time,
You turned toward the light in your soul.

Sharon Foss
WON'T SOMEBODY LISTEN
Won't somebody listen?
I'm crying on the inside.
No one there when you need someone.
They say tell them what is wrong.
But if they do listen, it's only with one ear.
They say they'll help, but they never really do.
If you need someone to share things with where can you turn?
It used to be you always had someone there, but now they're too busy to care. Or even to send you a letter or a card, even if it's just to say hi! I'm crying alot on the inside lately, sometimes I can't even speak for fear that I'll cry on the outside, so instead I speak with my eyes, or else nod my head. Sometimes you can't even tell the one you love, because if you do, they tell you it's in your head; or they're real loving so you feel you can tell them after all, but then awhile later, it seems they forget what you said and treat you like you were never hurt. The same goes with all your loved ones and close friends. So I ask again, where do you go, where can you turn to get answers, and someone to really care ? ? ?

Patricia Grossi
YOU AND I
Have you ever met someone before
and at first sight felt you'd met before—
But the memory isn't quite clear—
Maybe another place or another year—
When two kindred souls re-meet—
It's a feeling so unique—not really knowing, but somehow by looking into each others eyes, feeling the closeness of a hug, the warmth of a kiss, the understanding of unspoken words—
That you know, in some other space and time, we surely were together,
You and I—

Kathleen McCracken
SUN WORSHIP
As I lay,
The sun caresses my mortal body,
Like the water caresses the rocks below.
My soul lifts to the peaceful sound of running waters and quiet forest.
Like an out of body experience,
My soul wanders, the beauty of the country,
No noise, no pollution, or stress.
Peace like the heavens above, no worries.
As the sun goes down beyond the hills,
and reality sets in, I must return to the mortal world.
To only hope tomorrow I may return again.

A George Stallings

A George Stallings
OH CLASP ME DARLING TO THY HEART.

To my bereaved wife Evelyn Florence Stallings

Oh clasp me darling to thy heart,
And whisper never shall we part.
For upon thy lovely trembling breast,
I long to lean my head to rest.

Oh be thou ever in my dreams,
And when I awaken in my schemes.
For we shall gather at the break of dawn,
I will take thy hand, and then move on.
While we walk upon the jewels of dew,
This life of ours will be so new.
The rose has bloomed with in thy cheek,
A smile has gathered, as if to speak.

Oh clasp me darling to thy heart,
and whisper never shall we part.
Upon the earth or heavens above,
We shall join one another to hold and love.

David Palmer
FORGET LAKE
surrounding cold most,
small rippling lake water shines,
line cast gets green uneatables,
small pebbles that roll scratch,
small road level to my soul,
frogs masked leap sounding plunk,
unrippled now though there was movement,
algae growing where fish once I've met,
seeping brown drips in my tired net,
all 'round,
even not one bubble signifies,
no longer aware of my breath,
it's the flushed wind frigid,
not hearing my single heart sound,
now there are jumping frogs,
and my slight observance of the still—water though I'm not certain,
is this moment one I've created,
did my lap jump in its being?
reason a teller of fortunes couldn't say,
why I was pulled this way.

Kaisa Peippo
DIAMONDS ARE FOREVER
Diamonds are forever, they say.
It's only fair.
After all,
it took them forever
to become diamonds.

Derek R Metcalfe
LIFE ON WINGS
I see the past,
Distant past.
The world is below,
Flight takes effort—
But the effort is understood,
Accepted.
I glance at my wings,
I see something,
—copper perhaps
Intertwined with my feathers.
The sight is magical,
Spirit lifting!

I see the future,
Distant future.
Again, the earth is beneath me,
But this time.
Flight is effortless!
The air is satin,
My feathers, silk.
I notice my wings,
They're laced with gold!
Sparkling, gleaming—
The world . . . no, the universe
Is a gem,
A precious stone!

I see the present,
The seemingly endless present.
The ground is under me,
But only in the sense that it is below anyone.
My feet touch soil.
I flap my wings in vain,
It's useless.
Flight is just a memory,
A thing of the past.
I stare at my wings,
Not broken, not clipped.
They're still here,
But where is the magic?

Emily F Zierold
KING AND QUEEN
As father time and mother nature,
Pair off as time passes,
We all may older grow,
But still stay young,
With happy hearts,
Thru everyone we know!
For friendship always keeps serene,
Every little king and queen!
For royalty, all of us always be.
Tho, in the land of liberty!
Our homes, our castles,
Thru the years!
Our families, our retinue!
Forever loyal to our crest!
Our lineage red, white, and blue!
Thru genealogy our family tree,
Will always reign supreme!
All of us forever be
Our castles king and queen!

Helen V Newcomb Preusch
MIGRATION
Onward, upward, their wings spread wide,
Heading for their winter home,
the gray geese fly.
In perfect V formation
With inborn navigation
the leader guides the way.
In search of warmer climates
their shadows cloud the sky.
Instinct will show
How much they know
Survival, lest they die.

Robyn L Bagwell
YOU
You came into my world
Showing me a whole new life,
Never letting me feel alone
Helping me through each struggle and strife.
You made me feel loved
Making my spirits soar,
And you weren't even aware
That you were taking my heart to places it had never been before.
You made me feel important
As you held me tight,
I never knew that love
Could feel so right.
Our love was short
Only lasting for awhile,
As you held me in your arms
And said it's over, without a smile.
I never thought I could love again
But you pushed me thru a new door,
I just wish I could tell you that
I've never loved like this before.

Eleanor Chiarotti
A COLD
A cold is old
And very bold.
It doesn't discriminate
I am told.
It makes your nose
Look as red as the rose.
It makes you wheeze
And causes you to sneeze.
It makes you feel like
You're in the deep freeze.
It makes you cough
Your fool head off.
It makes you weak
It makes your nose leak.
It makes you sigh
It makes you want to die.
Whoever can find a cure
for a cold,

Should be given the pot of gold-silver,
Pearls, rubies and
things,
He should be made
the King of oops!

Charlotte H Yarboro
HAPPY 4TH OF JULY
Unlike the pilgrims, I wasn't escaping torture, cruelty or even searching for religious freedom.
I wasn't searching for anything. But what I found was—
torture, cruelty—slavery.
They didn't even give me an alternative.

Unlike the many immigrants, I wasn't looking for a new home,
a new country, a new government.
I had one.
I didn't even have a chance to pack my belongings
Gather my family together . . .
Say Goodbye . . .
They just took me.

Unlike the immigrants, when they came,
I didn't have anyone to find me a job and find me a place to stay. No one to teach me the language so I could become a citizen. No one to comfort me—a stranger in a foreign land.

It wasn't a dream to come to America, the land of the free and the home of the brave.
I didn't even get to plan my trip.
They stole me away.

Looking at the Lady Liberty gives me mixed emotions.
The history, the memories of those who came from other countries, the meaning behind the statue—for some it was a dream come true.

Now that I'm here, this is all the home I know, my country.
I feel a sense of pride to see what an opportunity was offered to so many.

But . . .
Not for me—

I didn't have an Ellis Island,
I didn't have a sponsor,
I didn't have anyone to welcome me with open arms.

I suppose I feel cheated—

As I heard someone say, "To Black Americans it is a bitter joke".

The true sense of liberty was not offered to us then and is not offered to us even today.

Happy 4th of July.

Margaret G Rowe
JULY FOURTH 1826*—1988
Two flags of fifty stars apiece
Flutter and cease in Vermont air,
Beside a rock there flows a mountain stream
Where arrowheads oft surface . . .
Reminding us how quite new fledged
Our purpose now in spite of all those stars.

The pennants stir historic memory
Of Thomas Jefferson and Adams
(John that is)
Who curiously became immortal
On the same Independence Day.

A sadder Fourth this '88 where like a threat
Our flag unfurls in ignominy above the Harmuz Straits.
No one can save the children
plunging to a watery grave.
We have become to military might a slave.

*Thos. Jefferson and Jn. Adams died within a few hours of one another on the 50th anniversary of our American independence, July 4, 1826.

Grace Barras Horton
RECALLING THE FONDEST OF MEMORIES

This poem is dedicated to members of the Patterson Garden Club.

In every garden, one usually finds
Etchings that have been left by Father Time
Come trek thru' my garden with me
We'll have a delightful time,
recalling the fondest of memories

Nestled under the trees are crocus, first flower of spring
Reminding me of Gretchen, dainty and as refreshing as spring.
Just beyond are bright-eyed, sparkling four o'clocks reminders of
The jolly four, Charmaine, Rose, Suzanne and Paula.

There, soft petaled sweet peas, filling the air with sweetness
They are the likeness of a sweet pair, Linda and Marie
That circle of Johnny jump ups, are true reminders of a ready pair
Lovie and Jane, who are always ready to do their share.

The daisy, flower that will never tell, favorite of many
Reminds me of Maria, who is loyal and trustworthy
By yon fence you will see, a bed of geraniums, looking so gay
They make me think of Nell, who is usually that way.

See that climbing rose, filled with rose buds, it reminds me of you
It denotes love in your heart for flowers and fellow men, too
As we leave the garden, a hill of forget-me-nots, you'll see
They're reminding me to remember you as I hope you'll remember me.

Julie Lynne Blake
THE FACTORY
I grew up in the shadow of its brick and wood.
It held my curiosity, so alive, so full of energy—like me, this factory.

My first man sized job. It held my future too.
It paved my fathers way, and his father before him too.
Through its door came many faces, many lives it had touched. But none more than my own.

For forty-five years we had worked as one; never a boring day.
I shall hear no longer its busy working way.
It will be torn down tomorrow, so the sign said.
Making the way for progress dressed in concrete gray.
I grew up in the shadow of its brick and wood.

Pam Lunsford
ON THE BRIDGE
On the bridge where we stood that night,
While I tried so hard my tears to fight.
The stars overhead seemed to say it was the end,
That our love was gone with the wind.

On the bridge you told me we were through,
The words you spoke my darling, turned my world so very blue.
Knowing I could never love another,
For my love for you would die never.

On the bridge I stood wrapped in your arms,
My heart so full of pain and alarms.
The pain almost too much for me to bear,
To think that you could no longer care.

On the bridge is where I lost you,
Knowing our love we could never renew.
So on the bridge is where they'll find me,
I'll die for our love that could never be.

Judy Bayles Dodd
WHAT HAPPENED TO THE ROCKWELL DAYS?
What happened to the Rockwell Days?
The untroubled children drinking lemonade.
Anxiously awaiting their trip to the swimming hole, with their floppy eared dogs following ever so loyally behind them.

What happened to the front porch swings?
Grandmas rocking grandbabies.
Love light in young lovers eyes
Holding hands and wedding rings.
And that feeling coming through that everything was gonna be alright in America.

And where did Grandpa run off to,
Now that we need him so.
With his wisdom and his caring ways,
His wrinkled hands and old stories.
We'll no longer complain about his pipe
For we need him now at any price.
And that all knowing feeling that everything was gonna be alright in America.

What happened to the Sunday drives?
The peacefulness of the country side.
Where fresh air filled the bluest sky
Flowers smelled sweet, and so did life.

Return to us those values Lord.
That the artist painted long ago.
Teach us again the meaning of love, patience, kindness and hope.
Hope, that a brighter tomorrow lies just ahead.
And that feeling coming through once again, that everything was gonna be alright in America.

Lois Hayn
BUTTON BOX
Too poor for fancy dolls
I played with old buttons—
Scooping up wooden circles,
Globes of pearl or bright glass,
Smooth bits of brown bone,
Colors all studded with eyes at the heart,
Matched pairs, even whole sets,
A few sparkling alone.

Now my nieces stroke other buttons,
A gray computer sits in for a teddy bear;
They laugh at the discarded buttons
But one time those were my jewels.

Mary Longenecker-Huffman
HIS SILVER DOLLARS THREE
A fine spring time
Many a year ago,
A young man's heart did pine
To Fort Wayne to go.

But, alas,
His car had no gas!
And 'twas more the shame
No money had he to buy said same.

What a plight
On that fair night,
For his love was awaiting he
And late he did not want to be.

His mind worked hard
There must be a way,
For from his plan
He would not sway.

Then remembered he
His silver dollars three!

Now with these coins
he did not truly wish to part,
So off to ask his sister
(He knew she had a good heart)
Buy these please, and save them too,
One day I'll buy them back from you.

Save them I will, she said,
and also keep track,
For in just twenty five years
You will have them back.

The young man married the love of his life
On June 15, 1963, he made her his wife.
Three beautiful girls this union blessed
My, now quickly the years have passed.

So here are the coins
All shined and placed,
A keepsake to the years
The two have faced.

Know not I the story from here
But pray the time is held dear,
Whatever the future is to be
Together for now
Even so on into eternity.

Steve Weindorf
BE NOT LED INTO UNWANTED PASTURES
Be not led into unwanted pastures
For bliss begins from the inside,
Dwell upon happiness stemming from past years
Character never leaves your own side.

Existence depends on resistance,
And learning is measured by

yearning.

If denial drips into the blood
And the color begins to fade,
With confidence took, and the soul shook
Life is fought under the shade.

So open the lamp shade
Turn on the light,
Believe in your passions
With all of your might.

Barbara Myers
MEMORIES OF THE BABES
Babes in the woods,
stating their cans and coulds.
Nothing on this earth, is sweeter to see,
Than the babes as sweet as can be.

They skip across the velvet grass,
With a sort of innocent class.

No memories of yesterday,
Just the happiness of today.

No real hopes for tomorrow,
Or no past ridden sorrow.
As I look upon their lovely faces.
My past, my mind retraces.
Seeing myself, skip across that grass,
Hoping those days would never pass.

Jo Starrett Lindsey

Jo Starrett Lindsey
DILEMMA
My mind is like a forest filled
With trees that block the outside view,
While, I, alone, stand deep within,
And know not just what I should do.

Direction has no meaning now;
I cannot see beyond these trees,
Which are the things that I must do,
And those I ought, with few that please.

My will is like an ax now dulled
From trying to cut a pathway through;
I want to dream the trees away,
Then do just what I choose to do.

But, still, I do not plan to stay
Forever here, among these trees;
So, I will rest, then go to work,
Revived by newer energies.

Matthew T Ray
PRESENTS
My dear, for so ever long I've sought your presents, across seas I have traveled, mountains I have climbed.
Knowing not what I was looking for only knowing I would find
At long last my emptiness is filled as only you in this world could do
your smile brightens my life as the forever rising sun brightens my days
In the vast blue of your eyes I'm lost yet found in the peace they bring my soul
Your kindness in being, a haven from the transgressions of the world, a healing for the scars of a life long past.
You my love are not only divine, but have made my life so, my world is without fears, my spirit free from the burdens of man.
The gods of long ago may only have been myth, but in my day's there is you, who will forever be the goddess of my life.

Steven B Sumners
LIFE IS LOVE
Love when real, can make you feel
all sorts of emotions
and think all kinds of notions.
Happy or sad,
Good or bad,
Life is at its best
when love is alive in life.
It can make you stutter and shutter
because life is love,
and love is life
you cannot enjoy one without the other.

Shanna Achord
LOVE

To Yancy,
How it was in the beginning,
I'll always Love you

I can't really tell him
how I feel,
He may laugh,
or be embarrassed.
I can't tell him of my
love for him,
for fear he may not
love me back! !
But if I do say
"I Love You"
He may say
"I love you too!"

Nancy Kane Endler
A DREAM

In memory of Ronald Edwin Cummings

I dream we are together—the wind is blowing through your hair;

You have that certain smile . . . . Oh God, how much I care;

We're talking and laughing about our yesteryears;

What is that I notice—Your eyes are filled with tears;

For in our world of reality,
one day you went away;

And every breath that I take is missing you each day;

I wake up feeling empty—The dream is fading fast;

And in the dream, I leave my love as I let go of our past.

Kelli R Cutts
MOTHER'S PONDERANCE

To my beautiful son, born Feb. 28, 1989, bringing great joy into my life. Forever are we entwined in love.

Unborn miracle,
How your magic is touching our lives,
Your innocence
Refreshing our complacent viewpoints,
Your spirit
Calming old and storming seas
Inspiring loveliness within those once aboard tattered ship.
Lend your heartstrings to my silent lullabye . . .
Borrow from me the focus
To find comfort in the quiet of your consciousness,
A place of refuge
When the world entangles your sense of direction,
And may I mirror a standard of grace
You can someday reflect to help another outgrow his iniquities.
Cultivate kindness unshadowed by weakness
To compass your travels along life's expressway,
For a kind man's strength can endure all things.
Little wonder
Playfully exploring the womb,
Rest now
Beneath your mother's sheltering wing.

Carmayn R Cowan—"Cercie"
OH, MY LOVE
Oh, my love . . . It seems as though it's been a thousand years since last you held me in your arms.
And oh, my heart . . . To touch your soul would give its life
For just that moment of sharing passion and blinding love
Consuming every part.
Oh, my love . . . To touch your cheek or lose myself inside your gaze will make your coming home worth all the long and parted days

Norman L Johnson

Norman L Johnson
A WEDDING PRAYER

Dedicated to our parents, Thelma Leone Ludwig & Norman Alvin Johnson who were united by love on June 9, 1956. Their marriage gave life and love to seven. Thank You. WITH LOVE, Norman, Charlene, Daniel, Matthew, Michele, Denise and Kelly

As we stand before the altar
preparing to exchange vows to become husband and wife.

We pause to reflect upon how we arrived at this moment in life.

We ask all relatives and friends gathered in this church on our special day,

To please join us with your hearts and souls as earnestly we pray.

Help us to always remember how and when we first met,

And the special magic that attracted us to one another lest we ever forget.

May we always feel the same strong love that bloomed between us and pray that it continues to grow.

Never let us fail to recognize the good within each other, and may the redeeming qualities we find in one another continue to show.

Let us never forget how to listen, or how to share;

Always remembering how to understand and how to care.

Grant us the courage to always tell the truth instead of lies.

And the strength to swallow our pride so that for our wrongs we are able to apologize.

Please help us realize that love and marriage is not always sunny days but must endure all kinds of weather,

Recalling this so that when problems arise we strive to solve them together.

Above all, help us to remember the words in this commitment that they will guide us through life.

And that God, bless and protect our union as husband and wife.

Patricia Stempf
DREAMS FOR SUCCESS

IN MEMORY OF my beloved parents, who were always a source of inspiration, and who encouraged me to reach out for my dreams

Waitresses are a motley crew
On these words I could choke
If it wasn't for my change each day
We surely would be broke

Many a man's dream for success
Could simply not transpire
If his wife had not answered the ad
"Waitress for hire"

Sabrina Wilcox
A BROTHER THROUGH A SISTER'S EYES

I dedicate this poem to world peace

A brother through a sister's eyes
is not the best thing to see.
But if that sister really tries,
a different person that brother may be.

A poor city through the eyes of a wealthy man,
is more than likely not a pretty sight.
But from the viewpoint of a citizen man,
change the city might.

With a change of position,
and a change of heart,
with the right decision,
the world may come together from apart.

Benjamin Cho
FATHER
Father,
Please walk a little slower
Can't you see me running
Just to walk next to you?
Remember,
Father, I am just a child

Father,
Please hold my hand when I am down
It's hard for me to walk
When I am used to crawl
Remember,

Father, I am just a child

Father,
Please don't laugh when I am crying
It's hard for me to laugh
When so many things bother me
Remember,
Father, I am just a child

Father,
Please don't worry when I am in trouble
You know, I am a trouble-maker
But, before you know it,
I will be a father of a child
Father of my own child

Larry Filosena
A PARENT'S REFLECTION

This poem is dedicated to my parents, whose fires have died. Yet still will reflect in me for as long as I'm alive.

Sitting by the river without a care
I began to see what was reflected there
Beginning to look deeper I could see
Reflections of the clouds and trees

Waiting with impatience;
No patience for the night
There's the full moon now in a crystal pool
One glowing down with strength and ease
The other reflecting what it wants to be

I realized then as I stood out
With my reflection cast all about
Adults go on with style and ease
While children try so hard to please
And you will see as older they grow
They will start reflecting with your glow

For your children only hope to be
Everything in you that their eyes see
So in the morning when your child you wake
Or you get so mad at the chances they take
REMEMBER: Your children are your reflection

Donna Grabe
BEAUTY OF LOVE

To my loving husband Ken, who has helped me to see the beauty of love. Also to our daughters Christi and Jennifer

Your love is as soft and
Enveloping as snow flakes
Falling on the countryside.

When I look into your eyes
It's as if I'm staring at a
Roaring fire ablaze with our love.

Jim Hendry
SO MUCH FOR POETRY
I tho't that with poetry I had a way
To get into your heart forever to stay.
But while you "loved" my poetry you did not love me
And you said no more than a friend could I be.
If I were satisfied to be only a friend
Tell me, just what does that portend?
Does it mean I could occasionally phone
And, if ever I find you at home
That we then might chit-chat or chatter
About things that don't really matter?
Or perhaps exchange a greeting card or two
To wish the happy whatevers they are meant to do?
And, that we seldom if ever each other would see?
Which could cause you to quickly forget about me?
Considering such to happen I think that I
Should do what is best for us both and say good-bye.
I am sorry that for us it was not to be
Think kindly my dear if ever you think of me.
GOOD-BYE FRIEND!

Jacqueline Rose Solorio

Jacqueline Rose Solorio
JUST CAN'T GET YOU OUT OF MY MIND

Dedicated to my loving family and friends who believe in me.

It seems no matter how hard I try to get you out of my mind, you just won't go away;

My heart hurts so bad I just wish I knew how long in my heart you'll stay.

I try to live my life as usual by doing all what I do.

But no matter what I drown myself into, I just can't stop thinking of you.

I remember when you loved me so much but, I took you for granted all the time.

Now my love is strong and yours has gone and you're no longer mine.

I wonder sometimes if you can really stop loving someone who you loved before?

How is it that you can be so cruel and to your heart just shut the door?

I wish you could show me how to stop loving you like you stopped loving me.

I know it's just not healthy for me. Can't you tell? Can't you see?

Amy Weller
PRECIOUS TIME
Sands of time pass slowly,
Time has come and gone,
Memories now do linger,
The reminder of our time bond.

Some time is passed at school,
While other's passed at home,
Time is now passing,
Remembering old and young.

Time is a source,
That's with us every day,
Time is the source,
That shows our hearts the way.

So remember this moment,
For it will not come again,
Remember this time,
It's only a fraction 'til the end.

Bapthol Joseph
TO MY MOTHER
Dear Mother,
Close to each other, seems like we could not
Demonstrate a great love for each other,
But coming to think of the 9 months
You carried me in a shell of love,
I salute your courage,
My arrival on this earth,
Was not a need,
A want, or one of these dreams;
Anyway, you carried me
With love and joy.
Only you could feel
My need for love—
Give me affection,
Understand my language,
Know my needs.
For you being a woman,
Giving me a birthday,
Being courageous, I do
Dedicate all my love to you.

Randall E Gibbs
GAMBLE
He founders to play the game of chance,
he may even lose his pants.
Poker or dice,
he may play it once or twice,
and find out it's not very nice,
He lays his money down,
knowing that he might even be looking like a clown.
Win lose or draw,
he hopes for the best luck of all, heel to his advice.
Next time he will take more than a glance,
then it will not be the game of chance.
For he now has gambled more than once or twice,
the game of poker and dice.

Moira Lutkehaus
A SCHOOL REUNION
On this day
ten years ago
we sat on this stage
rocking our chairs to and fro
we thought we
were so mature and old
but now we laugh
as our life histories are being told.

Earlier this day
we found out things
who got the jobs
and who got the rings
we remember the
good times we had
and push from our memory
the times that were bad.

Today, echo-ing
in the empty halls
was our laughter as we found
our meaningless scribbles on the walls
as this day grows to an unwanted end
we know our grad class will
remain friends.

Barbara Jay Bernhardy
TO MY LOVE

This poem is dedicated to Mr. William Burgjohann, who inspired my poetry.

As I lie in bed to fall asleep, my thoughts turn to you each night.
I remember the day we met, who would guess it was a cat that by chance we met.
As we somehow kept in touch, that dinner date you never kept.

Was it fate upon the night, that like two strangers in the night,
decided to have a dinner date?
Little did we know that several years would pass before that night,
when fate couldn't wait to take a chance.

It was a harmless dinner date, but fate wouldn't stop;
We ended up on a bench watching what we thought was the ocean surf.
Instead fate finally won out, we were no longer strangers passing in the night.
Now that fate has done its job, I thank it much; but where do the new found friends belong?

Together I believe fate would have, but time will tell:
As for me I have fallen at the strength of fate and must tell that "once stranger in the night" that I love him much,
and cannot wait till we meet again to discuss our "FATE."

Marie Pabian Cornelsen
JUST BEING

This poem is dedicated to Justine, my Mother. She lost her fight with cancer April 18, 1989.

Mother,
as I lie here unable to sleep,
I wonder the reason for being.
I see beauty in life, but I
question what I am seeing.
From down the hall I hear you
cough. Your terminal illness
makes you weak, and left with
only a will for being.
I pray for another life, blessed
with happiness and health, a
small reward for someone so dear,
who was gifted with a will for
just being.

Wendi Simpson
FOREVER AND . . .

I dedicate "Forever And . . ." to Jasonn to let him know that sometimes when we are face to face and no words are being said, this is how I feel. Jasonn, I'll always love you. No one could ever take your place.

Your eyes to mine we stand . . .
silence.
Tears not so far away.
Loneliness deep inside
To God, above, I pray.
The thought that I could lose you
when so much love we've shared.
Much more love still to make,
Heart beats faster, and I'm scared.

Life without you, knowing love can never die.
Going on without you, after all, so hard we've tried.
Together forever, 'til death do us part.
Promise me your love, neverending.
This moment let us start.
I love you so much, Jasonn.
Please give me your hand.
Picture walking into life, you and I,
Together,
Forever and . . .

David A Young
STIMULUS

To K., who taught me the meaning of the word.

I am surrounded by women;
I cannot escape them.

Perpetuating the fantasy
of flowers and first kisses;
I am the lover.

Childlike, seductive,
a madman and a saint;
I am the fantasy.

I live as a response, for a response,
and even as you read this
you play into my hands.

Nikki Ames
LIFE FOR A TEENAGE KID
Ask no questions,
For I'll give no answers.
Give no answers,
For I will ask no questions.
I'm of a woman,
Yet I'm of a man
I'm of a child,
Yet, I'm of an adult.
I'm of beautiful,
Yet, I'm of ugly.
I take it step by step,
Yet, I take big steps.
I'm of a starving child,
Yet, I'm of a full adult.
I'm of the beater,
Yet I'm of the beaten.

Pamela Yancey
OCTOBER RAIN
Are you thinking of me today
Feeling a little of yesterday
Wishing nothing had changed
But glad it didn't stay the same
Why do I feel this way, where do I put the blame
What makes me feel this way
Maybe it's the October Rain

October Rain falls every year
Along with my empty tears
As long as your memory doesn't fade
It will always follow the October Rain

Remember the smiles, remember the tears
Remember the innocence, remember the fears
When all that mattered was that moment we were in
Sometimes I still wish that it could be that way again
And today as I thought of you
I remembered how our love had grew and how it finally died
When we said our last goodbye.
Now my tears have no one to blame
except for the cold, October Rain

Colleen Wilcox
I AM . . .
I am the wind through the trees of memory
I am the calm before the storm
I am the death, disease and destruction
I am the day that you were born
I am the sunset on the ocean
I am the bright red tide
I am the shattering illusion
I am the day the music died

I am the air you breathe
the light you see
the Gentle April Showers
and the acrid acid rain

I am the end and the beginning
I am the universe on high
I am the religion that you cherish
I am the fears you cannot hide

I am the question and the answers
I am confusion in the rain
I am the music and the dancers
I am the century of change.

Lisa Marie Kastens Tobin

Lisa Marie Kastens Tobin
POWDERED BLOUSE, PEARL BRACELET

To my family, especially my father who gave up a lot to bring up three girls. I love you

Powdered blouse, pearl bracelet
Pearled necklace too
White ribboned teeth
Brought to an end
By pink dimpled lips
Baby blue blanketed eyes
Warming with tenderness
They were like mine
After the anger has passed

It was a picture
Stained wood frame with dusty edges
4 ft by 2 ft gloss print
Smudgy blue gray background
Emphasizing a figure
Having my features
But me having hers . . . who is she

Marbled frame
That was the last picture taken
Script etchings "1964"
Echoes through my body

I look at the picture . . . I see
Her water colored grave . . . She was
. . . is my mother

S Lee Aston
"GOOD-BYE"

With love and special thanks to my family and friends—without them my writing would not be!

Every time we say good-bye
It smites my soul
With a sorrowful cry
And yet it's true
That I fear not
We will meet again and
Our hearts will fly
As we intertwine
Beneath the stars
Beneath the sky
And we will laugh and dance
Until we can do no more
As time slips on and then
Again the moment comes
When we must part
So we utter a gentle sigh
Whilst once more, upon our lips
Lies the most tender of words—
The word "Good-bye."

John J Mendoza Jr
THE DREAM TIME

To Kathy Gumienny, my #1 Dream Girl of all time.

We lie together, on the grass in the sun
Her head a rest on my chest
Her hand on my heart, together as one
We talk of the future and of the past
This is the beginning of a relationship
That will long last
I can't describe my happiness at this time
My emotions racing
But somehow numbing my thoughts to a standstill
This is my dreamtime
The dream I've been chasing
The thrill, the thrill of a lifetime
The magic of a blossoming love
And the dreamtime
It was heaven, it was magic
And it was . . . Just a Dream

Tammie Stewart
MY CHILD
My Child,
Do not worry, and do not fear
for the Lord is very near
He is with you, by your side
to protect you as the day goes by

Do not cry, and do not weep
for the Lord is the Shepherd
and you are His sheep
He is with you all the day
to lighten your path along the way

Thelma Philo
DO YOU KNOW WHAT I WANT FROM YOU?
Do you know what I want from you?
What I would like to give you?
Happiness, contentment, love and the joy of loving,
Laughter and smiles, an occasional tear,
And the freedom to accept or reject my offering.
And do you know what I want from you?
The same, my love, the same.

Robert Yeomans
DEPRESSION OF A PEN PAL

I'd like to dedicate this poem to all physically and or mentally abused children, and the pain i feel through their eyes.

Two birds in a nest where it's hard to live,
with so much love but one won't give.
And try as may, unsuccessful in plead,
because only one can feel the need.
Where only one can feel the pain,
to watch the other go insane.
And waste her life as i spectate,
i'm sending help but am i late?
I love the bird who feels unloved,
neglected, being pushed and shoved.
I can feel his pain as though my own,
and fact, there's two, where one's alone.
This one's afraid and i as well,
as well as unhappy, lord i can tell.
I pray to you lord, keep him safe,
save my friend before it's too late.
Save my penpal before he's gone,
and a tormenting mother's refusal to mourn.
Shall keep depression in both our eyes,
from his father's death and his mother's cries.

Aimee K Talbert
LUCIFER
Satan touched my heart today.
He entered through my dreams
And made me live out my fantasies.
He took control of me and stole my eye for another.
Now I see the world through one eye and half of my sanity.

I am his victim, just like you.
He's taking over the world, eye by eye.
He takes all the good, happy thoughts and feasts,
Vomiting as he shoves more down his throat.
Sometimes I wonder if there really is a Satan,
Or if it's just my brother, in disguise?

Janice L Milakovich
MY NEW YEAR'S RESOLUTION
The whole store is not greater than each department.
Every department has developed something important.
When customers place their trust in productivity,
This becomes an employee's customer service opportunity.

In the department store, I notice a friendly unity
People working together completing schedules accurately
Improving quality, reaching goals, exercising rules,
Building morale, honesty, integrity with personnel.

My New Year's Resolution for a special occasion:
A Reunion that brings our family together again!
To honor the customer who has grown with the Company.
HAPPY BIRTHDAY SON!

I wish you would select your Wedding suit of clothing.
Remember this size suit will last forever with a ring.
I am making reservations for your Wedding Portrait
To honor your plans, promises and future Wedding date.

Our family will continue to grow with a Wedding Album.
I congratulate your fiance and you, a New Year's Resolution!
God bless you Scott on your twenty third Birthday;
May this year be filled with health and happiness, I pray.

When are you going to introduce me to your fiancée?
At the Dress Rehearsal of Grand March of Bride and Groom!

Yvonne Lopez

Yvonne Lopez
MY ROCK

Dedicated to my beloved family, "Sisco," and my good friends; all who have been the greatest support in my life.

He is there
Strong and steadfast
He is there
My Rock
Listening, probing, grasping
Unleashing my soul
I tear, shed, and heal
Seeing him again and again
A caterpillar yearning
freedom as a butterfly.
The metamorphosis transcends

Pain shears my inner being
Not scarring, but mending
He guides and I follow
He feeds me and I am nurtured
My rainbow thus appears
I soar and fly
A spirit well renewed,
My soul thrives
My Rock has set me free
Yet he is there, He is
always there;
He will be forever
My Rock

Jeff Steinbach
SILENT CRIES ECHOING THROUGH THE NIGHT

To God and my sister Janice for without the both of them this would have never have been possible.

Can anyone hear their silent cries echoing through the night? Can anyone hear their silent pleas for help, or are their little voices too weak to be heard?

Can anyone hear their little heartbeats echoing through the night? All they ever wanted was a chance at life given to them by their loving God in heaven.

Why won't they listen to their desperate pleas for life echoing through the night. How could they ever be so cruel to take life away from them!

No longer can their silent cries be heard. And the beating of their little hearts has stopped. Life which was given to them by God has now been cruelly taken away from them. By the ones who would not listen.

Though their little voices are heard no more, and their beating hearts are now still, their loving God in heaven who first gave them life will always hear their silent cries and the beating of their little hearts echoing through the night.

Benjamin W Greene Jr
THE FLIGHT OF LIFE

Dedicated to my most precious gem, my wife, Ruby

I spread my wings when I was but a fledgling. I flew as a new spring breeze flows across the plains and gained control. I looked down at all the wondrous things that I would encounter in life.

I knew what goals I must attain, such as, pride, strength, and love. To be always proud of my achievements, the power to carry them out and love for whomever I do it for.

I have flown with pride, gained the strength I needed, and survived the pitfalls of life with love and understanding for my fellow man.

The love that I have found in my flight is to me as pure as a whispering stream after a new fallen snow. My flight has been long and with gratefulness I descend. Now I am on the downward glide and I can hold my head up high. For I have flown to the top of the world with the most wonderful human being that life could bestow on me—my wife, (Ruby). Thank you God for now I have landed.

Romell R Balanciere
SOMEONE SPECIAL

This poem I dedicated to Brenda, a very special person in my life

You are so deep in my heart
And always on my mind,
If I could write a love song
You would be on each and every line.
You have changed my grey skies,
Into skies of blue,
Always remember,
No one can ever take the place of
you.
When ever you touch me, I close my
eyes,
And pinch myself, just to see if it is
true,
I could never love anyone
As I love you.
You light up my life,
Brighter than the morning sun,
We should stand together, united as
one,
You are a very special part of my life,
What more can I say,
I love you, I love you
Forever and a day.

Sandra Lee Pierson
LOVE AFFAIR
The first time I saw you dear I loved
you so much
I couldn't forget the way you looked
and I couldn't forget the way you
touched
You meant so much to me my dear
I have loved you all thru these years
The years don't matter anymore
Really who is keeping score
You are my life, you are my love
You are the only one I am dreaming
of
Why can't it stay the way it is
I have so much love to give
I want to give all my love to you
You are the only one who doesn't
make me feel blue
As I reach my hands out
When I see you I want to stand up
and shout
There is my love, my only love
The only one I am thinking of
I love you dear, I will wait forever
With you and me it will be till the
Twelfth of Never

Kerri Rae Mitchell
JANUARY 17, 1989
The day I heard it on the news,
I couldn't believe my ears.
As usual, it had happened again,
As it did after years and years and
years.

The anchorman told of a shooting,
From a heartless older man,
Who shot and killed five little kids,
Like only a criminal can.

They said it happened on January
17th,
Of the year 1989;
Those poor little school kids,
Ages five through nine.

How could you do such a terrible
thing?
"They" never hurt anyone,
But shooting down children at recess,
Did you think it would be fun?

I hope that you are happy now,
Even, thereafter, you shot yourself.
I couldn't believe you could do such
a thing.
Are you happy that you're in hell?

Five children are dead,
Seven in critical condition;
Thirty children "aren't too well,"
And need psychological attention.

You've ruined many lives,
As though you really cared.
Couldn't you feel the tension,
And see the kids were scared?

You should have shot your <u>own</u> self
first,
If you felt that awful inside.
What I'll never understand,
Is why you took those childrens'
lives.

Evilena Filbeck
A SPECIAL DREAM

Dedicated to Meta Cox Filbeck (1896-1978)—Wife of Lex Filbeck (1891-1958). Parents: Aaron J. Cox (1865-1920) and Sena Elizabeth Cox (1868-1947). Mother of: Marjorie, Evilena, John E., Robbie, Elizabeth, & Mickey Filbeck.

I sat in a gold-tinted room, at a
sewing machine, in my dream
Sheer white curtains draped
windows, where bright sunlight
beamed . . .
I saw a woman walking toward me,
through a lovely green meadow
I WENT ON WITH MY
SEWING . . .

I looked again and gasped! I saw the
precious mother I adored
She was very young and beautiful,
vitality and health restored . . .
Movements were genteel; black hair
styled with a white taffeta band
She was approaching the outdoor
patio, smiling, waving at me,
and . . .
LOOKING VERY HAPPY . . .

She wore a long white dress, trimmed
with soft green-bluish teal
The aura of innocence, cherished
youth and beauty, was
ethereal . . .
Suddenly I knew she was an angel
dear
I hurried outside to embrace her
here . . .
LIKE I USED TO DO . . .

Before I could touch or hug her, she
was gone; very lonely was I
I turned and re-entered the gold-
tinted room to cry . . .
The telephone rang; I answered, and
heard the Master's Voice
"She is very happy now, and in a
better place of her choice" . . .

THE DREAM WAS OVER. I'm
reconciled now, for I know, by His
Grace
Somewhere, her Heavenly Father has
a beautiful deserving
place . . .

ESPECIALLY FOR YOU, DEAR
MOTHER, ESPECIALLY FOR
YOU.

Evelyn Connor
TWO HEARTS IN TUNE
Forever and forever to some may
seem
Like a long, long time and just a
dream.
But that isn't true with the two of you
Whose days are too short to say and
do
All the things you'd like your love to
express
To show to the world your
happiness.
So forever and forever is not too
long
When your hearts hold the words to
love's sweet song;
The kind of love we know somehow
Is not just a love for the here and
now.
For long after vows and years have
passed
Your love forever will last and last.

Charlie Gunter
MOTHER FLOWER

To my loving Mother who has dedicated herself to her family and to a Christian life.

Out of all you came through
You tried to give us the best.
Sometime it seemed like there was
no way out
And you still stood the test.

We could not give you all of the
flowers
But I sent a few
To let you know that "we love you."

This little poem you just read
In no book you will see,
Because as I thought of you, Mother,
My God gave it to me.

Hugh R Gilbert
THE WAVE AND THE SEA
The wave and the sea oh where is me
They seem to be one most seemingly
Am I the wave in the mighty sea
Tossed and turned tempestuously

The wave and the sea are never apart
They roll and they toss and they know from the start
That they are all one and they're really the same
And this is the way of the heavenly game

I am the wave and I merge with the sea
And I dwell in the depths of serenity
And when I forget my place in the calm
I'm a separate wave and I do myself harm

The wave and the sea oh where is me
We're one and the same playing joyously
I'm tossed and I'm rolled by the hand of love
And moulded forever to dwell up above

Dewey M Wilson Jr
THE REUNION
I made my way up the hill through the long winding trail.
Passing by the old white gate, aged and splintered; hinged by rusty nails.
As I drew closer to my childhood home, I was surrounded by a familiar smell.
Fresh apple pies, laid to cool in the crisp October air.
Cresting the hill I could finally see her crumpled silhouette shadowed by the trees.
With quickening pace and great anticipation, I hurried along the fence through the fallen Autumn leaves.
Turning towards me with widening eyes, her face was aglow with a warm, loving smile
She opened her arms, as the morning laundry fell,
we embraced each other, tearful, but happy we laughed all the while.
Making our way down the hill towards the old wooden house,
I looked forward to evening supper and a taste of apple pie.
I knew when supper was finished and the dishes were all dried, I could sit on the back porch;
listen to the familiar stories, and see the beauty of it all
through grandma's eyes.

Louis M Catanzaro
REACH

To my daughter Angela

Reach-,reach-,reach for the moon!
Reach-,reach-,reach for the stars!
Don't let the time that we spend apart,
Hinder your spirits or inflict pain to your heart.
I'll always be there, and very aware of the feelings we share.

I know that you care. And until I can be at your side
you should know—
That you're the breath that I breathe, the
seed that I've sown . . . . So Reach-Reach-Reach towards the sky!
And if the rains should fall upon you on any given day,
put your best foot forward and laugh it away.
I'll always be there to ward off your fears,

and battle your nightmares or dry all your tears.

And until I can be at your side you should know

You're breath that I breathe, the seed that I've sown . . . So,
Reach-Reach-Reach for your friend!
Reach-Reach-Reach for my hand!
I will be with you, wherever you are.
I will be with you, near or afar.
You just reach . . .
Love, Dad

Mike House
KISSED ME
Said he was leaving.
Said he didn't love me anymore.
Said he had better things to do.

Said I didn't care.
Said I didn't love him either.
Told him to just . . . take off!

Hit me.
I bruised.
Eye bruised.
Cried just a little.

Said he was sorry.
Held my face gently.
Said he did love me.
Said I did love him.

Made love to me all night.
Made love to him all night.

Had a bad day, he said.
Kissed him.
Kissed me.

J Beverly Shepherd
WINTER
Season of snow and heavy-laden trees,
Gatherer of autumn's golden leaves,
Whose mantle cloaks a silent world
With softly moaning winds and weaves
A web of stillness in my dreams.
Beneath the leaden snow-bound land,
In silence wait the now-stilled strands
Of springtime's clear, unmuted song.
And yet, through the dark and ashen days
Of winter's passage deep and long
I wait and sleep until the time
When in the warmth a sun shall climb
And beckon forth the frozen seeds
From the empty stillness of winter's dreams.

Faith Stone
ALAS—TV!
That monster we call Television
Is here our lives all to imprison
Our dinner's not put on the table
Until we're sure we can be able
To eat it while there is a lull
You know—a program Oh! So DULL!
Our children's lessons don't get done
Not when they are having fun
Before that modern, fancy screen
Oh HORRORS. What it's come to mean
In households scattered thru the land
Can someone help me understand
Why we should ourselves so lower
To let it get us in its power?
Surely we can master this
Not let it mean a state of bliss
This thing that lives our lives today
While duties all around us lay
Not done—So many wires & dials
Envelop us in tales & trials,
To think this gadget made of wood
May never really be understood.

Michael Eugene Noon
LIBERATION

Dedicated to all the women of the Western World, to be more liberal and relaxed about their physical being and to take control of their life and destiny as all human beings should! Especially to a dream? Gwen Henson!

She is like an unhideable mountain.
From creation she was meant to be seen.
To be admired and never covered.
She is like a flowing fountain.

Women and men were placed the same.
Upon this earth and in the gardens.
To each other as equals and friends.
But up the road of destiny, Women dreamed shame.

Girls of the earth were to be man's lover.
Sharing all they know and all they have.
Hand to hand and side by side.
But breast to breast, she must now cover.

In this great country men show chest.
Open and free with all their glory.
To live in honor and all its splendor.
But with women they still live as less.

We all live in a world of mixed traditions.
As blooming trees and flowering colors.
With beautiful hills and flooring valleys.
But woman has yet won her liberation.

Snow J Matherly
SPRINGTIME
Transplanted from Life's garden to a fairer one above—
A tender flower that blossomed in the heart of Mother love.
Ever blooming in a garden where days are always fair
Not chilling winds of winter
It's always Springtime there.

Springtime in a garden where little faces go—
No hurt can befall them,
no harm will they know.
Where flowers bloom forever
With their fragrance sweet,
Springtime in a garden
Around the Master's feet.

James M Evans
HAPPY FATHER'S DAY U.S.A.

To the fathers of the nation. To my father

I'm guessing you say
This is a happy Father's Day for you
If I get back with my family
It'll be a Father's Day for two

I have something to lose
I have nothing to gain
She won't come back
And my life is in pain

I have one chance to say
This, I want it to be real
Tell Sheria there is a lot
Of things in life I can't deal

Tell kids, your kids the truth, crime can't be in the U.S.A.
Prove it by me, that's why they put me right away

Elizabeth Yniestra Scott

Elizabeth Yniestra Scott
SATURDAY
Rose petals upon crisp white sheets,
A summer breeze dreamily drifts . . .
Into this lofty room and meets:
Two who sip champagne for no reason
And giggle about their secrets
A toast! to the season!
And the many more to come.

"What's breakfast anyway?"
One asks the other.
"Something early in the day."
Replies the other.
A smile on both their faces,
Just another one of their secrets.
Today, they will go to their favorite places.
And the world will see . . .
Just what it's like,
To delight,
In each other
For . . .
Eternity!

Dorothy E Smith
DEAR ONE
A song of love through all the ageless time
Recalled to mind the moment that we met,
And we are dear and close together yet.
Our love united in a golden chime
Through all eternity how great the rhyme
Of love our God has in his wisdom set
Within our hearts! So now today we get
A glimpse of heaven in a love divine.

And in our love go free to wend our way
Because through freedom can our love enlarge
Until though death may separate, one day
Our bodies, still our love will always charge
The world around us with a golden ray
Of loveliness, God's love is ever ours.

Sherry Farrow Shelton
THE END
Sitting here I shudder at the thought of Armageddon,
For I know not when, where, or how it will end,
To suffer and cry as the world falls apart,
or to be there with GOD in his Heavenly Court.
I believe in you LORD and not all I hear,
I pray for your presence, or a sign that is clear.
The truth's what I am after, don't know where to look,
Can't believe everything that's written in the Books,
My Faith in you LORD is my only belief,
The rest is Misdoings and Profitable deceit.

Audrey Braun
ETERNAL LOVE

To Christopher, my eternal love.

My life, it seems, has always had you,
Together forever and always true.
Doesn't it seem like we have loved forever
Even though we have never before been together.
I'd always be with you if I had my way,
And never leave you until my dying day.
Being in your presence always makes me smile
With your hand in mine we could walk many a mile.
Some say love matures over a long time,
From the start our love was one of a kind.
When I'm with you I can always be myself,
And I will never have to put my love on a shelf.
You make me laugh even when I'm feeling blue,
Without you in my life what would I do.
I feel your absence when you are not near
Life minus you is what I most fear.
No one can predict the future, that I know,
How long we'll last not even our love can show.
Please say that we'll be together for eternity,
And never say you want to just let me be.

Audrey Williams Brunson
A CHRISTMAS KEEPSAKE
Sweet scent of varnish, mingled with pine,
The pungent aroma of turpentine.
Sounds of a hammer drill and saw,
Plane curls and sawdust cover all.

Daddy took the time to sand all the edges,
Landscaped the yard from flowers to hedges.
Secretive work on a Christmas surprise,
To put a sparkle in his daughter's eyes.

Wallpaper, paint and ceiling trims
Decorate all the rooms within.
Padded sofa, lace drapes, dried flowers.
Details Mommy worked on for hours.
An entrance hall is lighted with candles,
Wooden doors sport solid brass handles.
A quilt and pillow adorn the bed
Where Dolly can rest her little head.

A Victorian theme is there to see.
A glimpse of how life used to be.
Each room is furnished in miniature,
To complete a doll house she'll adore.

lonesome
THE ORGAN GRINDERS MONKEY
like the organ grinders monkey
you dance at arms length
death the organ grinder
grinds a fatal medley
dance little monkey
dance to rock and roll
dance little monkey
dance until you choke
break free little monkey
from the organ grinders chain
or swing little monkey
overdose . . . cocaine

Ruth T Gisler
JODY
My heart is crying
Lord, don't you know
We'll all miss Jody
We loved him so.

His work is done
His hour has come.

He leaves this land
A never forgotten son.

The gates of heaven
Have opened wide,
To accept Jod's spirit
To enter inside.

The Lord reached out
And touched his hand
He is now with the Lord
In the promised land.

Vicki Bea Linn
KIDS
Kids are the world's pride and joy . . . Without a child's smiling face, the world would be an empty, dismal place!

Adults, remember, we were <u>ALL</u> children a long time ago . . .

Tell your children about winters long ago, when you played in Grandma's yard in the snow . . .

Adults are "big" people children sometimes don't understand . . .

When they are fearful or in doubt, give them a hug and hold their hand . . .

Dads, challenge your sons to a rugged basketball game; Mom and Dad ride with your sons and daughters on a bike . . .

To everyone's surprise, kids and adults will not view each other as <u>different</u> . . .

Adults and kids are a lot <u>ALIKE</u>!

Kristy Rasnic
MOM . . .

I dedicate this poem to my mom Barbara Snyder. I couldn't have made it without your help through everything "I love you."

You've taught me right from wrong;
You showed me how to put my feelings where they belong.

You taught me to be mature;
So I'd be ready for the future.
You used to tell me "No!"
Then everything would end up in a blow.

The hours it took seemed so long;
But you taught me how to be headstrong.

You laughed with me in the good times;
And tried to cheer me up in the bad.

You were my friend;
When everything seemed like it was coming to an end.

You taught me how to be tough;
And were with me when times were rough.

I hope that you will cherish;
These words that will not perish.
Now I must say to you;
Thank you, I really love you!

lonesome
SERPENTREE
slither slither crafty serpent
up the apple tree
i didn't know a serpent
a tangled web could weave
your beauty goes unchallenged
your venom sudden death
if knees had you to beg from
you would still have apple breath
so curse you great pretender
one bad did spoil them all
from this day and forever
on your belly you shall crawl

Joyce Bocardi Briers
HIS SPECIAL TOUCH

Inspired by and dedicated to my daughters, Janet, Judy, Joan & "Lolly" and six granddaughters

God first made the heavens, the oceans and the earth,
Then, to all living creatures gave His miracle of birth.
He must have loved little girls very much,
For He gave to each one a special finishing touch.

As He placed each sparkling star in the skies,
He made sure some were left for each little girl's eyes.
He taught her to laugh—and dance—and run,
And gave her a smile with the warmth of the sun.

He gave her a heart overflowing with love
And a tender touch like the moonglow from above.
He took compassion from the rain and gave her gentle tears,
And plucked charm from each flower for her to carry through the years.

He gave her strength of high mountains to face problems in life
And gathered patience from hovering clouds to withstand any strife.
He gave her moods of contentment and moments to be sad,
But added lilt to her voice that she might sing when she's glad.

He gave her the temperament of the roaring sea
To round out this character of the woman she will be.
Yes, God must have loved little girls very much,
For there isn't one who doesn't have His very special touch.

Douglas C Bonanomi
DEAR SUSAN

This poem was written to commemorate the christening of my Godchild, Susan Elizabeth Coyle—November 24, 1984.

Dear Susan do you wonder?
Dear Susan do you mind?
Dear Susan do you think that God
Is much like me in kind?

Or is it any wonder
That life itself is here?
Whose chore is it to make it
Something special, something dear?

Dear Susan you are wondrous,
Dear Susan you are pure,
Dear Susan you're a gift from somewhere special
That's for sure.

Your life is like a poem,
full of rhythm, full of rhyme—
Your life is like a prayer to God,
silent meaning put to time.

Zelda Warren
TO FORSYTHIA

To my daughter Leslie
Who has believed and encouraged me in my poetry.

Blow the Trumpet
Sound the Horn
The Herald of Spring arrived this morning
In all its glory,
Like a blaze of golden sunshine.
What faith!
How can it be? That these dry winter branches
Covered in ice and snow, barely alive
Can once again revive and renew itself
To bring forth such beauty,
In a Triumphant Jubilee.
What Strength!
Thy name is Forsythia.

Pearl M Hall
HE'S MY FRIEND
Many a rough road i've travelled.
Many the troubles i've seen.
But there's always been someone beside me.
He's always been part of the scene.
He takes my hand when I falter.
When i'm weak, He makes me feel strong
And there's never a time I don't need Him,
He's deep in my heart like a song!
He's my friend, my constant companion,
My Saviour, my Lord and my King.
He delivered His Son down from heaven,
To die on the cross for my sins.

If ever I climb the Great Stairway,
And find that my name's listed there;
I'll sing with angels in Heaven
And never know pain or despair.

Sandra Bell
ARE YOU MY FRIEND?

If I have a secret
And with you I will share,
Will you listen to me?
Will you even care?

Are you my friend
I want to ask.
Eventually I will;
Will it be a task?

When I laugh,
Will you smile?
When I cry,
Will you sigh?
Will you shed a tear
When it's time to say good-bye?

Are you my friend
I'll say to you
Again and again
Until it is true.

When I'm low
And you're high,
Will you pull me
Up to the sky?

Are you my friend
Who I will keep?
Will you tell me
That it's all right?

Will you pull me in
From the dangerous cold?
Will you remember me
When I'm 90 years old?

"Are you my friend?"
That is the question.
Will you answer
With no commotion?

When I'm sick
And lying in my bed,
Will you visit me
Or call instead?

Are you my friend
Who is very close?
Will you be there
And make me the most?

When I'm tired,
Will you give me rest?
I need some clothes;
Will you give me this?

Are you my friend
For me to love?
Are you sent
From the God above?

When I'm hungry,
My mouth you will feed.
Remember that
A friend in need
Is surely a friend indeed.

Are you my friend?
Yes, this is true.
You belong to me
And I belong to you.

Carolyn Cann
GOD DO YAH HEAR ME?

I dedicate this poem to my son Robert Jr. I hope you will keep this and entrust it for generations to come. For it comes from my heart and the love I have for you which is endless.

Mama up at dawn, cleanin',
cooking', and washin'.
Grits on the table when we come
down, where you goin' Mama?
God do yah hear me?

Too cold outside to walk anywhere,
don't want no school,
better 'cause Mama be mad.
God do yah hear me?

Mass of them on the corner steps,
huddled together, nowhere else to
sleep. Rag lad in the trash, why don't
she get some cash?
God do yah hear me?

Cool Breeze comin' down the street,
better watch out he's peddlin' that
Crack rock. Ain't got no money for
you, what you got ain't so cool
God do yah hear me?

Wait at home for Mama, so dog tired
is she, what's to eat Mama? Soup
without meat, I done the best I could
with what I had.
God do yah hear me?

We say our prayers before we go to
sleep, "God bless Mama, my sisters
and brothers, bless the food we eat,
without meat. Tomorrow is another
day maybe it will be better, Mama
does the best she can, Amen."
God did yah hear me?

Vivian Dally
THIS CANADA OF MINE

To Canada

I'm proud of this great Canada
This Canada of mine.
And I'm proud to be Canadian
In this great land of pine.

I'm so proud of our wide prairies
And the towering mountains
grand.
I'm proud to be Canadian
In this land I call mine.

I wake up every morning
With a deep prayer in my heart,
For this great land of Canada
So proudly I call mine.

I'm proud of this great Canada
With its people all so free.
For here there's no oppression
It's a land of Liberty.

So let's all work together
To keep this nation free
Of all that's undesirable,
That's the way that it must be.

I'm proud of this great Canada
Where the arts and cultures
blend.
Where the aged and poor are cared
for
Right to the very end.

Amethyst Rummel
HYMN TO THE HOLY KALE

My country, 'tis of thee,
Great dollarocracy,
Of thee I sing;
Land where the puny child,
By crushing toil defiled,
Is from all good exiled
By Greed our King.

My native country thee,
Land of the boasted free,
Thy name is Bunk;
I love thy courts and jails,
Thy starving babies' wails,
Beside thee Hades pales
Into a flunk.

Let music bow its head
While ragtime reigns instead
And lauds thy booze;
Let hearts of maidens ache
For that which vultures take
Nor church her silence break,
But rent her pews.

Dollar is God to thee,
Crusher of Liberty,
To Him we sing;
Long may He prostitute
Those who protect His loot,
Our Dollar is a beaut,
Our God and King.

Betty Holland

Betty Holland
SOLITUDE LONGING

My typewriter arrived today,
Something I've longed for, for a
long time.
A typewriter of my own to put
into print
The words I long to say.
Setting on the desk before me,
The words begin to flow
And I create a dream away from
chores and woe.

I'm now longing for a little
country cottage
With open spaces all around;
Never to be overcrowded, the
voices sounding out.
Leaving behind city noises,
people in unnecessary chit chat;
Time to enjoy peace, just a quiet
habitat.

Looking for this peaceful spot to
listen
To the birds and rustling leaves.
Watching the beauty of all nature;
Walking on the trail among the
trees.
In living different places, never
to encounter
All the peoples in the days of
yore.
I, now and at the present,
Just came here, I'm sure.

elle moschowsky
TOMORROW

Tomorrow tomorrow tomorrow
What kind of a day will it be
Will it be like today
Will it be a day full of hope
Or a day filled with sorrow
Will it be filled with songs and
laughter
Will it be quiet, still and dead
Will it be the greatest day on earth
When peace has finally come
When brotherly love is practiced
Not just sung
When the worlds of all nations
Are united just as one
When young and old, dark and light
Together march side by side
For they will know this world
That God created
Can only be what we the people
make it
Tomorrow tomorrow tomorrow

Danny M Robeck
CHASING LOVE IN THE SKY

We're two lonely lovers, wanting
each other,
and we're both too proud to cry.
I guess we're doomed to spend our
lives
chasing love in the sky.

I sit at home night after night,
wishing that you were still mine.
I'm trying to think of something to
do
to win your love one more time.

I pray that you are thinking of me
and wanting the same as I do.
If that's the case, give me a call.
Don't wait for me to call you.

I watch the stars as they come out at
night
and wish that I could see
just one constellation up there
somewhere
that would erase my memory.

Counting the stars, reminiscing,
wishing for one more try.
But we had each other, and it didn't
work,
So, we're chasing love in the sky.

Ralph A Echave
WAS LIFE MEANT TO BE THIS WAY

To Pili Etxabe who brings me love and peace.

Was life meant to be this way
Where children cry instead of play
People kill out of hate and lust
And there really isn't any trust
Where power and wealth do abuse
And people other people use

Was life meant to be this way
Where innocence has no say
Or is it just because of me
For my brother's keeper I'll not be
Life can change if only I
Can love a little more before I die

Martha Ann Moore
COMMINGLE

ANGUISH of separation
Causes unrequited yearning;
Curse thrust upon me daily
Causes unremitted burning.

SHE doesn't share in my longing;
Mem'ries mean nothing to her.
I lay, par'lyzed with thoughts fearful,
Scorched and consumed to
cinder .
WHY won't she live near my
doorstep?
Years unexperienced we'd share.
Emptiness now spreads its talons,
Crushing this ache to despair.
WHEN will I ever see Bethie?
Answer! And spark some relief.
Otherwise, cremate my heart that's
Blistered beyond my belief.

Ghetto of sheer exhaustion
Let me go! Embroil me no more.
Hope! You come forth & com-
mingle.
Cripple my enslaving horror.

Shanti Bhaskaran
TO THE BLIND FELLA UPSTAIRS

Look—blood buds sprouting in the
crossgunfire
mother rat in the crib gnawing at
baby pink vitals
mountains of fat in aerobic
convulsions on the club floor
ethiope shadows stalking the twilight
leonine

breasts of virgin soil ravished by hot famine kisses
somewhere aeons ago, on a psychiatrist's couch
thought I heard a cuckoo note
the day after—gay viruses in the ballroom
AIDS and Brain waltzing on carcass of machine and man
nothing gonna give me a high no more
not yoga, hard rock or crack
the cracked mirror shows the once-caressed face in splinters
heard they glued her nose back with plastic surgery
plastering a phoney smile on rough-smeared mask
prostitutes hold the keys to the kingdom
all the world's in love with yellow—
yellow as sunshine, cold
yellow as jaundice, soft porn
bliss is it in the slum
urchins sloshing in the gutter
an' Mom hollering thro' all the ruckus
"junior, when'll ya learn to keep yo' nails clean?"

Sheldon K Menery
ETERNAL
I see myself thousands of years ago,
Writing a song to the Nile,
Praising her beauty,
To please a Pharaoh,
To quench the burning in my soul.

I see myself hundreds of years ago,
Writing a song to a Queen,
Praising her beauty,
To Please a King,
To quench the burning in my soul.

I see myself yesterday,
Writing a song to the World,
Praising her beauty,
Pleasing everyone,
To quench the burning in my soul.

I see myself today,
Writing a song to you,
Praising your beauty,
Pleasing you,
Quenching the burning in my soul.

Dura Ward
LIFE AND NATURE
Life is a gift
Which I can only vaguely comprehend;
Yet it's a gift which I can reverence
And maintain hope that it will continue.
Also,
Nature is a gift which enhances life
And therefore adds greatly to its meaning.
So what am I to do when around me
I find so many things to enjoy
and explore?
Surely I'll let them all incite me
To a better understanding of life,
And then to a prayer of blissful praise
To the One who's the Creator of life
And all nature's many sights and wonders.

Virgil E Graber
REACH OUT
As you wend way through life, my friend,
Let your kind, pleasant self extend;
With bright eyes and warm smile, reach out;
You'll make many friends without doubt.

In your long journey down life's aisle,
Oft pause to reach out for a while;
Aim all your goals out high and far;
"You'll hitch your wagon to a star."

How bold are pilots of airplanes!
How they defy earth's peaks and plains!
Yes, pilots are such special breed,
That fill so well each earthling's need.

Astronauts prove fortitude's worth,
As they sail spaceships around earth;
What prowess is theirs as they fly!
What fine example to aim high!

Reach out for unreachable goals;
Set these aims as life's goals and roles;
Let your soul soar like birds in flight;
You'll achieve much more at great height.

Katherine Jarmon
SILENCE
Silence.
Oh, so peaceful.
Far away from the busy city.
The stillness washes over me as I sit listening . . .
Listening to the welcome silence.
I close my eyes and I am
alone . . .
Alone in my own quiet world.
Tranquillity.

Maggie Jean White
THE DANGLING GRAPES

This poem is dedicated exclusively to myself (MAGGIE JEAN WHITE), and to the life I've led the past 32 years.

As the dangling grapes appear before my eyes, It's as though they are there just to pass me by. They dangle, dangle, dangle in many forms which include lust, strength, and Oh yes! charm.

I look at those grapes dangling in the sky, as I reach for them they jump, Oh! how I do cry. I don't ask for much maybe for just one, but when my hands touch them I'm all thumbs. It's really sad, but I don't know why it is my lot to cry, cry, cry. My eyes are sore, as I lay on the floor thinking to myself, "who closed these doors?" My spirit is stricken, and I'm all out of shape, I'm tired of jumping at the dangling grapes.

Meredith Kurland
THE GIRL IN THE MIRROR
When I look in the mirror
I don't like what I see,
But that girl in the mirror
Is not the true me.
It's only a reflection of the pain I feel inside,
And the heartbreak, grief and sorrow
That I try so hard to hide.
I always try to smile,
Reassure them I'm okay,
But if they looked deeper,
I know what they'd say.
They'd say she needs help,
A friend, someone to care,
I guess they might be right,
Because my friends are never there.
"Cheer up," they say,
And so I try to smile,
Reassure them I'm okay,
If only for a little while.

Carmen Kaye Stokoszynski
OPEN YOUR EYES
Take a look down that ragged street
At the dirt and filth about their feet
See the rotting run-down shacks of disgrace
And a tear trickle down a child's face
Here's a man imprisoned in his shabby domain
You see in his eyes the anger and shame
A tattered old shirt hanging limp on his back
Not because he's ignorant, but because he's black.
Look once more to a different scene
Where wealth is abundant and environment clean
From fathers to sons they've lived and grown
Despair and shame they've never known
All is available to the skin that is light
Not because they're better, but because they're white.
Look as one stands a shade darker than us
Is he not made of the same sacred dust?
Man was not made to be wretched and yearning
So open your eyes and deserve what you're earning.

Kimberly M Hall
PEACEFUL PERSPECTIVE
There is something deep, deep,
Divinely deep;
Eons, and more, distant from the surface heap.

After the hard, fierce act of a soulless
. . . Devil:
The one who is cold-consciously able
To simply, stupidly, smash your heart.
With no thoughts where they should be—at the start!

And the materials are nothing! Of course!
Cracked, smashed window. Jagged like the old hoof of a horse.
And your clothes, your dearest, trampled and torn.
The Devil had no thoughts of how proudly they were worn.

Then, perspective perfectly placed;
thoughts sincerely seep.
The eons are less; the Divine deep
may meet the surface heap.

Jerry D Kittle
HOW FAR HOME
Far to the left, far to the right.
Voices all around me in the night.
Cries of pain, agony of scorn.
Bitter hatred of flesh that's torn.

Light breaks, new day born.
Sun's up, sound the horns.
Through these eyes I see.
What this day brings for me.

I hear them so loud and clear.
Their fighting done, God so near.
War is over, mine has just begun.
No battles or medals have I won.

How far home, land that we love.
Given to us from God up above.
No one here cares what we done.
With it over our lives they shun.

How far home, from where I come.
How far must we run.
To achieve what we deserve so well.
From the ones that put us in this hell.

Peggy Douglas
MORNING IS DAWNING
Morning is dawning,
The whole world is yawning—
And sleepy eyes are opening
And they are hoping—
For a great new day
And a hope that we may
Live our lives in sweet repose
And, as everyone knows—
It's up to us, and no one else
To make this world a better place
Where we will all be safe
So, awake, and aware—
We shall share
Our hopes and dreams
Our plans and schemes—
To enrich life's themes.

Emilie
SHE

To my talented GiGi Who played her role With unsurpassed composure and integrity

She
Is an actress
She plays her role too well.
She has few friends
For no one knows her.
They only know the part she plays.
Foolish they call her—
And giddy.
To them her life seems one long song.
She sings and dances through the day
To hide the weeping of her heart
Which bears a cross, the weight of which
No mortal ever bore before.
Those few who look into her eyes
See mirrored there
The haunting strains
Of the sad, sweet melody that is her life.
But even they—
They do not know
That underneath her painted laughter
Lies the valor of a great soul—
Afraid of life; afraid of death;
Bewildered by the world.
She can but hope that somewhere
In that great beyond,
The vague tomorrow,
There will be happiness.

Erma E Murray
50 STRANGERS ALONE IN THE DARK
Although we are together
we are alone
Many noises around us
but not a sound from me
But listen, listen
what do you hear?
Silent whispers
of me
about me
So many people left
How many people left?
Thus we are apart
thus we are alone

Lisa Anne Slomski
THE MERMAID
On an island
far from here
lived a mermaid
named Trepere.

Trepere was lovely
and the island too
where rainbows glistened
where skies are blue.

Meadows are green
the waterfalls roaring
the buttercups bloom
and the Bluebirds soaring.

Her eyes are like diamonds
or stars from the night
her mouth like a rose
and her skin soft and white.

Amber Bunker

Amber Bunker
THE WEB OF SIN
The hatred is building
The flames are unyielding
In desperation you cry
Yet you know not why

The web is tangled
And your life is mangled
The lies that were told
And your soul has been sold
The price was too high
with no escape not even to die

God forgive all
But so deep did you fall
The mistakes that you have made
And the prices you paid
In life you're but a pawn
With life stolen gone

Mary C Smith
JUST BECAUSE I AM A WOMAN
Just because I am a woman, dear SKEPTICS
You need not TRY to push me out of the race;
You should not look upon my outward appearance and say
For me there is no place.

Just because I am a woman . . .
Why try to put me in the BACK-GROUND?
God made man and He made the woman
You CANNOT put the woman OUT nor DOWN!

Just because I am a woman—"the weaker vessel . . . "
Don't REFUSE to let my voice be heard;
God, who is no respecter of persons and a JUST GOD
Has INCLUDED me in HIS WORD.

Just because I am a woman
Don't TRY to ISOLATE me out of your life;
God had a PLAN
When He CREATED the woman from the rib of man . . .
I am to be your MOTHER, SISTER, DAUGHTER or WIFE.

And JUST because I am a woman
Don't try to CRUSH me UNDER your feet!
I am here to STAND and WALK and WORK and SIT by your side.
REMEMBER: I WAS MADE TO BE YOUR HELPMEET.

Walter Cronin
THE WATCH

To my Brother in Arms . . . "The Vietnam Vet"

Tell me, what is it you see in the dark of the night?
A shadow? Is it moving? I wish it were light!
No, it's only a dog but yet could it be?
One cannot trust what one cannot see.
The moon was just out mere minutes ago.
Now it is raining, time goes so slow.
A machine gun barks far off to the right.
Artillery screams long into the night.
The sounds they may vary but for me they're the same.
The music of man's ugliest
deadliest game.

Belva Quello
GROW UP TO BE A MAN

To my son, Robert Joseph Quello

The time has come when I, my son,
Advice to you must give.
It's time you stand and walk alone,
It's time you learn to live.

Good deeds try every day to do,
Be thoughtful of your
fellowman,
Be kind to all you meet, my child,
Let fear not stay a helping hand.

Smiles, like lights in a darkened room,
Shine out for everyone to see.
Kind words go forth across this land
To be returned again to thee.

Live by the golden rule, my boy,
Just do the very best you can;
But no matter if it takes hair and hide,
Grow up to be a man.

Eno Eno Ted Eno
NURSES THAT NURTURE BABIES
Nurses that nurture babies
Nurses' nurses
Nursed the whole night through
Nurtured her own
But her mother won court possession
Lost the baby for causes unknown
Drug addicted was but sixteen then
Father deserted unwed never
Knew she was pregnant
Now four yrs later into rehab
Training become a nurse
Nurses' nurse's aid
The baby calls her mother
"Mother"
She never told anybody
Other nurses noticed everytime she saw this certain baby
She handled with much adorations
"It's none of our business but she is your baby isn't she"
"Yes" Everybody wept for her
She foremost

The long road back
"Mother, that baby is mine, I swear to you; one day I'm coming to take her back"

Helen J Washington
PROUD TO BE BLACK

I dedicate this poem to my family and friends who believed in me.

One time in our lives, we were given no rights
Until Martin Luther King turned on the lights
Many thanks to this man, who opened the world's eyes
Our faith will be strong, one that never dies
We can stand up tall and be proud to be black
From this day forward we will never look back
Now is the time for us to show all the rest
You are black, you are better, you are the best
The road may be hard, stay on the right track
Show the world you are proud to be black
Don't let anyone or anything stand in your way
Because you know there will come a better day
Go out into the world, set your goals up high
Show everyone you are smart, let them know why
Reach for the sky there is no certain limit
Don't hold back a thing, don't be so timid
Always remember who you are, you will go far
You will shine bright, you will be a star
Your journey is beginning, so get your bag packed
And don't ever forget, you are proud to be black

Lee Vincent
NORTHWEST SEASONS
Winter days are short I know,
But not too much Ice or Snow.

The days and nights are not too cold,
There's skiing in the mountains if you're bold.

And of course we do have some rain,
A true native doesn't really complain.

Spring arrives just like a tease,
Bringing weather that's sure to please.

The days' length is getting longer,
Heat from the sun is becoming stronger.

Oh! yes we do have some rain,
Even the natives start to complain.

Summer comes in like a sprinter,
But some of the first days feel like winter.

And did I mention the rain?
Even I begin to complain.

Autumn I really like the best,
That's really true, I do not jest.

And the natives shouldn't really complain,
The Northwest wouldn't be green without the rain.

Gloria De la Cruz
PRODUCT OF THE WORLD
Who am I?
I am the biological product of a
man of Filipino and Spanish
descent and of a woman of Irish
and unknown American Indian
descent.
I am the developed product of
many other parents who cared.
Parents of German, Scottish,
Polish, Hawaiian, Portuguese,
Chinese, Japanese, and African
descent.
I am fortunate to be the product
of many nations blended in
harmony.
I am baptized Catholic. I am also
Baptist, Buddhist, Protestant,
and Judaism.
I am the product of all religious
beliefs who worship the
Almighty of many names that
lives everywhere at one time.
I am the product of many
cultures.
I am fortunate to enjoy the
different fashions no matter
how odd they seem.
I am able to appreciate the music
of many languages even though,
I only speak one.
I am free of prejudice because all
nations are my brothers and
sisters.
How can I hate my family? It
hurts to see my family let such a
thing keep them apart.
Who am I?
I am the child of the world,
enriched by the many cultures
that surround me.
I am the proof that nations can
live in harmony. I am what our
world should be.

Arcelia Hood Raymond
I THINK I SMELL PEACE
My senses don't often betray me,
Yet, sometimes bring questions to bear.
The world is constantly changing.
I think I smell peace in the air.

There are several men in high places,
Now speaking of views they must share.
They are doing it slowly but surely.
I think I smell peace in the air.

With nuclear armaments decreasing,
Service people recalled everywhere,
Old enemies shaking hands at last.
I think I smell peace in the air.

Jane Campbell
THE STAR

To my grandson Kevin, who is a star in my heart.

My, he looked handsome three-year-old Kevin
Loquacious, our grandson surely did come from Heaven.
Tonight, though, was special, his first time to act
In his Christmas school play. He stood ready, in fact
To ring his bell. He was one of the sheep
With his sheep cap tied under his chin so neat.

Suddenly, his eyes cemented in his sockets
And Kevin took off like ten thousand rockets.
He spied his dad in the long row of seats
And made a beeline for a sudden

retreat.
He couldn't go on, so scared was he
That dad had to walk him up, you see.

Kevin performed on cue and all
Ringing his bell. Yet, his hat it did fall
Atop his head landed one ear. His chin got the other
It really didn't matter to his dad or his mother
For Kevin was their star. They had a great ball
Seeing their son turned backward—

To perform to the wall.

Janice Whitting
ONLY YOU

A dedication to Reggie Chavez. When you come to me, I share my love for you. When you're not with me, I can only feel my love of you. And when I close my eyes . . . I dream . . . .if the sand were . . . . .

I languidly lie outstretched on the
hot sun warmed sand

And I feel both the obvious and
underlying warm comfort in
each grain's presence.

Oh, how gently it conforms and
molds itself to my body,
yet firmly holding and
caressing me
. . . . as you used to do.

There is fire within me and a
gooseflesh without me.

My reaction to the sand . . . or the
memory of you?

I am lost in my thoughts of now
and remembrances of what
once was.

And I open my eyes.

All I see is the torrid redness of
the setting sky,
and I smile openly to think
that she is blushing, too
in some strange heavenly
climax . . . . .
if the sand were only you.

Emily Jane Colby
MATURITY
My loneliness surrounds me like a shroud;
A silent sadness, I now accept with grace;
My soul no longer feels a void or cries aloud
For some tangible possession to fill the space.
Within the quietness of my heart, I sense
A penetrating glow of warmth and peace;
And though, I see but just a glimpse,
I know my search is ended, and I cease
To wish for worldly treasures.
Content am I
To know myself, and be aware
That little else can satisfy.
There is no enduring comfort here.
And as in dying, when all else grows dim,
Awake to find the paradise within.

Georgiana Lieder Lahr
THE FLOWERS RETURN
The daffodils will bloom again, I know
Though winter days are very gray and dark;
I know the flowers sleep beneath the snow,
King Winter's reign will end; he's left his mark.

Though winter days are very gray and dark
The tulips, in bright gowns, will rise again,
And we shall heap the lovely song of lark,
When springtime comes to all the world of men.

The tulips, in bright gowns, will rise again,
The hyacinths will bloom in glad array;
The snow has gone, and now the time is when
The earth will burst with flowers ev'ry day.

The hyacinths will bloom in glad array,
And flowers ev'rywhere will rise and sing
In chorus jubilant, through ev'ry day,
"All hail the bright return of happy Spring!"

Kelly Kucich
LOVE
Love is a feeling that we share.
It is a word that means I care.

Love comes straight from the heart.
It can bring us happiness,
even where we are apart.

Love is beautiful and
love is precious.

Love comes from a true friendship.
Just like friends, it can last forever.

Love is a strong feeling, but most of all,
love is what I have found in you.

Anita (Penny) Emmett
STAND BY ME (AMERICA)
We are your children, America
We are standing beside you with pride,
We'll give our lives to protect you—
So this "Great Country" will not divide!

As we behold "Old Glory" waving
Across this, our beautiful land,
We remember our "nation's freedoms"—
And why we had "to take a stand!"

Bear in mind our "forefathers' courage"
With infinite vision for a better life,
Whose only dream is for their loved ones—
To exist in a world without fear or strife.

Yes, America, we are your children
We believe in your right to "peace,"
With faith in God and love for our nation—
We'll build a place where war will cease!

Let us remember our precious Country
A place to grow, to build, to be free,
A land where we can worship, unafraid—
And thank our Lord for blessings to be!

Joy P Stauty
MORE THAN A FRIEND

I dedicate this poem to my Mother and to Carol. Thank you for always believing in me.

Time continues to deepen my love for you
though I know the words would make you blue
So in silence I love you with all my heart
longing for you but playing it smart.
Our days don't allow much time to meet
So our time together would be short but sweet.
We could fill up our senses being gentle and kind
Making love to each other leave the world behind.
The way we care it would feel so right
to warm up an otherwise long lonely night.
I pray that we can work it out
friends and lovers no room for doubt.

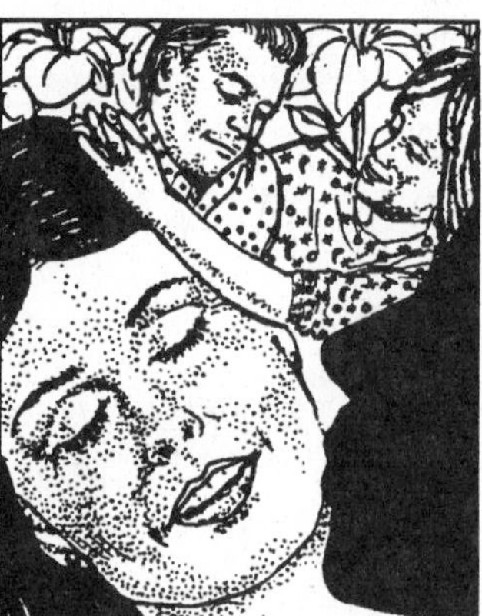

Whatever you do please don't let this request
Alter a friendship that is truly blessed,
because the Cosmos is smiling on all that we do
and that's what keeps me so in love with you.
I will always have a smile for you
And I'll always share a thought or two
I'll never stop caring or baring my soul
because with you in my life
I will always be whole.

John W Sutherland
THE PLACE

Dedicated to my three loving sons—CALEB, JAKOB & JEFFREY with hope that they will know their true selves.

There's a place in the Universe,
so perfect it's beyond the human
word.
Where Life's eternal love-song is
sung,
but its divine melody plays on
unheard.

A place born of God's love,
in His conception a land pristine.
A place of priceless treasure and
beauty,
but its boundless wonders exist
unseen.

And for all this place's creatures,
a perfect hand has been dealt.
A haven to live in as One with God,
but for most, this Oneness goes
unfelt.

If only we could go and Be in this
place,
to this paradise of infinite
worth.
But the harder we seek to find it,
the harder to see—this place is
our Earth.

Karn Yerkes
IN THE QUIET

With love to Ray. Thank you for being all the loves of my life

In the quiet of my room
As I sort my thoughts of the day
I go to the window and gaze
Out into the world
Thinking how wonderful it would be
To be a part of it
To be free as a bird; and
I think of this
ONLY
In the quiet of my room

Vernald Wm Johns
FOR AMITY
I had a chance the other day
To share another's care,
But I was busy at the time—
I had my own to bear.

'Twas just a word I could have said
If I had thought it through,
But other things were on my mind;
I'd other things to do.

I have a voice that can be soft,
And sympathetic, too,
When I am thinking genial thoughts
Of him, or her, or you.

No moment's cares need crowd away
The will to help, or hear,
Or speak, as to a favored guest,
With gentleness, and cheer.

Richard Alton Johnson
RAPTURE
Let us seek the heights of
mountains crest, that I may
lie my head upon thy loving
breast.

Clasped hands reaching upwards
towards cloud filled skies.
Warding off the echoes of
our love's passion cries.

Soft summer winds gathering
dew from raging streams.
Soothing our love as we share
our wondering dreams.

Once separated, but, now
anxiously awaiting for the
shadows of the noon day sun,
Which whisper our thoughts of
love as we become one.

Russ Rattigan
ANOTHER DAY
Whenever December comes,
deceiver,
With its snowball hands and low
down skies,
Promising epiphany—delivering lies;
And I there standing against it—not

alone—
I have a golden friend whose love
I've known.

Whenever tomorrow is December,
I'll pray the years return
To remember us
In August warm bee-sweet
meadows,
Where still thunder rumbles
And the distant silver tinkle
Of a waterfall tumbles.

Perhaps the golden evenings will
come again,
If we're aware, across those fields
Like an old friend—without
urgency—
Carrying a prayer.

If ever December comes
In my tomorrows, because of you,
believer,
I'll stand up to it and say:
"Let your chill snows fall melting in
my hand—
Tomorrow is another day!"

Tammy Beck
FIRST LOVE

When we first met,
I knew right way,
that he was the one,
for me, forever, that day.
I looked in his eyes,
that sparkled with glee.
That seemed to be saying
You're the one for me.
Our lips slowly met.
I'm in his arms tight.
Our hearts bonded together,
We're in heaven that night.
Suddenly, it ended.
It was over so fast.
We stared at each other,
Wishing it would last.
I said the words slowly.
I-LOVE-YOU came out.
He smiled at me knowingly.
"I figured that out"

Ann Perna
THE FACE

Naked, always naked
And all the artifice so skilfully
applied, can't hide
The lines, some fine, some deep,
That Master Time has etched upon
the face.

Smiles, some real, reflecting inner
mirth,
Some false, a cover up,
A great facade.

Faces, faces, faces all about,
Each tells a tale, its very own
And in its midst—this sea of faces,
A tear falls from its hidden place,
the eye,
Then, just one wipe, the makeup's
gone,
The camouflage destroyed,
The face lies bare—
Naked, always naked.

M Margaret Heerdt
MY LOVE

Dedicated to the pal with whom I struggled all these years and then survived alone, with my many loving memories.

When the sun's sinking low in the
westward,
And the shadows grow long on the
hills,
When weary from work I head
homeward,
Then my heart with a thankfulness
fills,
For it's lamp lighting time in the
Valley,
And I'm coming back home,
Love, to you.

As slowly the stars start to flicker,
In the great dome of darkening sky,
Then my footsteps, though weary,
grow quicker,
As the end of this, long road draws
nigh,
With the lamps lighting up in
the Valley
Soon, soon, I'll be home, Love,
with you.

With worries of work left behind me,
Like most folks I head homeward to
rest,
It's there with my loved one, you'll
find me,
At home with the one I love best.
When it's lamp lighting time in
the Valley,
Now at last, I'm home here,
Love, with you.

Rita L Bland
YOU

First of all I would like to thank the Gohonzon for bringing new meaning to my life. I would like to thank a very special friend for believing in me, enough to enter my poem. I would like to dedicate this poem to Diane Holder. Thank you Diane.

It's you who brings such joy to my
life.
Inspiration, vitality, miracles, and
dreams.
My petals are growing strong and
beautiful,
With your nourishment of tender
loving care.
Each drop of water, feeds me with
your love.
A love that can never die.
It's you who brings such joy to my
life.
Intellectual, consideration, affection,
and warmth.
Reflections of your smile,
Which keeps me going day by day.
Your softly spoken voice,
Whispers gently in my ear.
Praying, hoping, wishing you were
near.
It's you who brings such joy to my
life.

Clarence N Wright
OF HAROLD

I watched him
performing his art
His subconscious mind
in full control
His hands had become
its extension
Shaping and smoothing
the hardwoods
Till they reach out
devouring the space
within his studio
Claiming their right
as created beings
Held together by vibrations
from the subconscious mind
of Harold . . .

Timothy Mullen
LET YOUR LIGHT SHINE FOR THE LORD

I'm going to let my light shine for
the Lord!
I'm going to let my light shine for
the Lord!
For every morning when I rise, I'm
in my right mind.
Let your light shine, shine, for the
Lord!

I'm going to hold on as I work in the
vineyard!
Because surely trials may come my
way!
If you hold on and do your part,
you'll receive your great reward,
In heaven, in heaven, one day!

You can never praise God enough!
No matter what man might say.
He's always there, he loves you he
cares.
Let the Lord in heaven be praised.

Wendie Parras Manly

Wendie Parras Manly
DRIVING AWAY

To Rose Marie for giving all she had to give.

He takes the dog for company
for hours
in the car
They drive off together
every night
I see his hands
dry and cracked on the wheel
as he backs away
nothing to say
except I'm sorry; I don't know why
He walks hunched down but there is
no wind
His eyes on the ground
as if looking for something he
doesn't expect to find

We move silently through the house
I'm holding my breath; I don't know
why
My thoughts racing wildly now:
WHAT HAVE I DONE?
The stairs creak
The god awful cough and he is gone
Closing the door
Starting the engine
Driving away

David W Doll
ONLY A ROSE BUD

The Other day I bought a rose
My darling to impress.
The rose was large and still a bud
What more beauty did it possess?

I filled a vase and immersed the stem
And waited for petals to unfold.
A bud like this would surely make
A bloom great to behold.

A day went by and then it was two
Expectantly I waited for it to open.
But petals compressed, it remained a
bud
The preservative was not at all
wholesome.

How sad it is when like a rose
A life has a beautiful beginning
But ill things are added at an early
age
And the full bloom is seen only in
dreaming.

Vi Dykins
NIGHT MAGIC

There before us lay the pool,
Glittering like an onyx jewel
Smoothly round, and coldly deep
Mockingly beautiful in its sleep.

We had trod on secret holy sod
Where nature's silence
worshipped God
As her misty incense silver gray
Wound slowly, softly, sadly
away.

Where solemn, mournful, barren
trees
Deathly still in the gentle breeze
Bowed low in the pale moonlight
Praying mutely for winter's
flight.

Together we stood to drink our fill
Entangled in delicious harmony
until,
A stone cut the pool's surface pure
And the beauty we could no
longer endure.

Should this loveliness touch us so
If we did not feel and know
We have a chance to more perfect be
If we choose thru Jesus to live
eternally.

Joan Giovenco
MIRACLES

To my dear friend Becky Lampe, who shared with me the miracle of friendship and understanding.

Miracles don't happen on earth
like the days when Jesus Christ
was here.
These miracles I speak of were
done to give us hope, life and
humanly fear.
Now the miracles are different,
like the simple planting of a
seed,
The seed of knowledge and faith
that there is nothing but Jesus
we will ever need
Miracles can come out of
everything, either by a good day
or by trial.
Miracles also happen when you
have total faith and give Jesus
no more denial
When you know Jesus, everything
on earth has a cause and just
reason;
As do the sorrows, weaknesses,
joys, weeks, days and all the
four seasons
All of these are miracles because
we will grow in our faith and

love
We will see and believe the
miracles, as with the people
when on Jesus' shoulder was a
dove.

Saundra K Fountaine
SANCTUARY
Come and pierce the emerald sea,
Leave all your sorrows here, with
me.

Join in the crying and rolling wave,
For I, the Sea, your soul shall
save . . .

Billye Beck
MY SON

This poem is dedicated to my son, Kevin, and grandson, Phillip, without whom this poem would not have been possible.

A special card with hearts and lace
was made for me one day,
complete with the inscription "MOM
YOUR GRATE IN EVER WAY"
I smiled to see the signature, FROM
KEVIN, written bold,
For he was such a little boy, just
barely six years old.
The teacher must have helped him
write the card he sent to me
But, oh, that childish greeting had so
much sincerity.
It served to thrill me deep within and
make me vow to be
The kind of Mom who filled the
words of that greeting sent to me.
The deepest wish that I could hold
was that I'd hear him say,
In ten or fifteen years from then,
"Mom, you're great in every way."
Oh the joy that filled me on this
October day
Proudly by his side I stood to hear
the doctor say,
"You have a son" (and a fine one, I
might add)
The Lord had blessed me once again,
my son became a dad.
Time will pass so quickly by and
there will come a day,
Another note in childish scrawl,
"DAD YOUR GRATE IN EVER
WAY"
FROM PHILLIP

Efrain Vela
ACROSTIC
Crying, kicking, throwing
tantrums
You made your welcomed debut
No one around could be like you
The original, wonderful YOU
Heap of rainbows, pleasant
sunshine
Iridescent, lively and sweet
A bundle of joy and happiness,
packed so neat

Just when your folks mind your
crying
Emit a smile, melt their hearts
Another day, keep on trying
Newer and better smiles
Never again a dull moment
Everything is now worthwhile.

Lurena Buzan
NIGHTS
The nights seem bad
and I am so sad
To think of days gone by.
But with mornings light
things really look bright.
Then I wonder why,
When the Sun goes down
I start to frown
And yet start the day with a smile.
I am happy to be
alive and free
And everything seems worthwhile.
I change moods with the Season,
Perhaps that's the reason
My Spirits arise with the Dawn.
I should sleep through the night,
Wake up to the sight,
and forget the nights with a Yawn.

Richard Allgood
OPTIMISM
Through this maze called life I
venture
Upon a new way to insure
Each stepping phase is humble
I pray to never stumble

Things can't always be as they
should
I'll accept the bad with all the good
Eventually I will find,
That legendary "Peace of Mind"

I know what I'm looking for
And one day I'll find the door
I search for happiness and love
My forgiveness will come from
above

Cassandra Meloche
MEMORIES

To Janet, for making this the past, and not the future.

Please do not remind me
of what I was,
The crazy things I've said and done.
I've tried so hard
to live down your memories,
to change the labels,
and the heavy prejudices still
held against me.
I've worked so long
to conform to the rules of your
society,
to be called normal, and to fit in.
Please do not remind me
that once I was so different
as to be called insane.
I cannot forget what I have done,
where I have been,
and how I got there.
So, please, do not remind me,
for I remind myself.

Rená Kennebrew
FREEDOM CRIES
They gave me a teddy bear; soft and furry; for my wounded heart; and thought that might ease my soul. But when I looked into its gleeful eyes; and touched its weary face; I felt my grief; and cradled my tears. "My friends had to die," I cried aloud. My soul mourned; innocent meek children cut down while they played at school. No more I mourned will tragedy never allow us to be.

Screams of emptiness echoes burn like fire inside of me, dark rich red blood flowing so free, flashes like the river of Nile in my mind. My mind will not allow me to forget, my friend, I cried, "They lay dying."

My heart has stopped and my eyes began to water. I felt the greatest sorrow. I have lost my friends. I shall never see them again. My soul weeps. I saw the faces of death, and innocent eyes that have no mouth to speak and yet the question was there. Why, Why, why us?

Tragedy has mocked our souls, and yet we must all drink the water of guilt, the bitter memories, the sad freedom, to play in school yards.

Must we as children be taught at home, and wear armor made of heavy steel, so that we might be safe to play at school yards in the light of day.

Why can't we be free like the butterflies and grow up to become like the stars, the moon, the skies, freedom should be ours.

Will my heart never know the true meaning of freedom.
Will they always hate me for being me.
Will my race, my language, my religions, my beliefs, my age stop me from being me.

Why must we die like meek lambs, so that they might open their eyes, and reach out to touch us, and see we're only children who want to grow up and love America too.

The taste of freedom is in me, crying crying like the sparrow,
freedom freedom rings aloud in me,
and yet my soul
mourns like black doves for freedom.
Freedom rings in my soul, my heart beats like the quietness of the liberty bell, freedom echoes forever within me.

Michelle D Leverette
POETRYLAND
They've cleaned the hill off,
but I notice the kids.
They try to think of something,
maybe an interest—
perhaps a poem.

Minutes later I find these two
hard at work.
Pencils in hand,
minds working hard
and thoughts in full swing.
The eraser becomes smaller
With each minute,
but poems sprout.

Squinting from the bright sun,
I picture
concentration in their eyes.
They leave for a while,
destination:
Poetryland.

B R Davidson

B R Davidson
OLD AND FORGOTTEN

Dedicated to "SILLY SALLY" my sister

When you get old and grey,
Each day seems to pass away.
Things you have done,
Are soon forgotten.
You set at the window—
And wonder why?
No one ever even passes by.
The phone does not ring—
Ever at all.
They don't even have time,
To place a call.

It would only take a minute of their
time,
You had done it—so many times.
Always there when you were
needed—
The pain in your heart—goes
unheeded.
Nothing today and nothing
tomorrow—
When you get old, you feel so much
sorrow.
Your heart breaks—a little each
day—
You wonder how they can be this
way.

Bridget Budgetts
DREAMIN'

To Dad—Who encouraged me to write! Thank You!

That night was the first I saw you,
You looked so cute.
I wanted so badly to talk to you.
I enjoyed your company.
When you held me,
I felt like it would never end.
Then when you kissed my hand,
I thought I would never land.
Suddenly you kissed me—
It was so special.
Oh, could this be real?
Riiing—I guess not,
I was only dreamin'!

Diane Thompson
MY MOTHER'S GIFT

I lovingly dedicate this poem to my mother who celebrated her 85th birthday on January 9, 1989, and in gratitude for . . . . . .

So many verses have been penned
To us about our mothers.
And now I have another one
To add to all the others.

A mother gives so many gifts
Like home and food and love.
Mother, you have given me
A gift I'm fondest of.

The gift I thank you for the most
I cannot touch or see.
It is the faith in God you share
That means the most to me.

I've grown up now, and moved away
And still your gift keeps giving.
The weekly letters that you send
Contain a faith worth living.

In this tribute that I write
I pray that you'll discover,
The love I have within my heart
Reserved for you, my mother.

Bruce Wayne Mecchi
I PASSED A MAN ON A LONELY BACK ROAD

My words come from my soul, Where-in lives the spirit of my inspiration: Miss Judy Garland.

I passed a man on a lonely back road, he seemed as lost as I.
The load he carried seemed so heavy, I'm sure I heard him cry.
And when I turned to see if I could help him, he was sitting on the ground.
And all around him were bits of broken treasures that scattered in the wind.

I watched that man on that lonely back road as the tears came to his eyes.
With trembling hands he reached to the dirt and softly whispered, 'Why?'
He cursed the sky, and God, for having hurt him so many years—
But then he saw that I cried for him, and he told me of his fears.

He said that he was once thirteen and a very lot like me—
Young and bold, and yet uncertain—not knowing what would be.
The love he sought with an open heart had left it sad and broken,
For the words of encouragement he needed to hear were always left unspoken.

He said his heart had been left in pieces, to scatter in life's wind.
Then he smiled and told me not to worry, that in time I'd be a man.
But time and love come slowly, I said to this old man.
And he touched my face, and my heart as well—'Go home . . . you'll understand.'

I passed a house that looked so familiar, in the window were my mother and my dad.
They were crying for me and calling my name—I had hurt them and I felt so sad.
I ran through the door and into their arms and cried, 'Please, love me if you can!'
And then I remembered that mine was the face of that sad and lonely man.

Joleen Price
THINKING OF YOU

I dedicate this poem to my loving husband Jay and our unborn child.

I'm sitting here thinking of you
Wondering if you're happy or blue.
Waiting for that moment to arrive.
Can't wait to be by your side.
Wishing you were here with me.
Holding you close to me. Waiting for your sweet embrace, sitting here staring in space. Loving your kisses, loving your touch, seeing your smile ever so much. Can't wait to be by your side, Here we are together again. Just the two of us for the world to share. Just the two of us hand in hand, not wanting the moment to end. This is how I feel for you, and that is I'm falling in love with you.

Anthony D Nicolaides
TODAY

Today I am a happy man;
She let me hold her hand.
Tomorrow perchance I get a kiss,
This is something I greatly wish.
Soon she will fill me with joy,
When she says she loves this boy.
One day she will be mine;
I for only a Valentine.
I give to her all my heart;
All of it, not just part.

Today spent at the park
For a hug in the dark.
Tomorrow together once more,
Hopefully better than before.
Soon I'll win her love
And fly high like a dove.
One day when we're not near,
She will find I'm very dear.
I pray that I soon find a way
But I'll be thankful for Today.

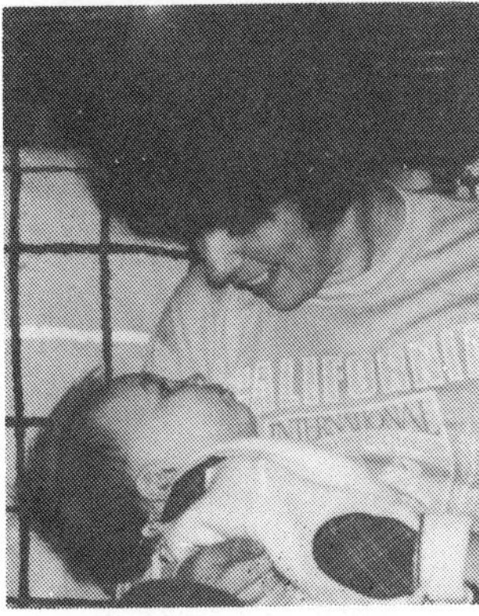

Marge Moore

Marge Moore
MY DEAR GRANDCHILD

I Love You . . .
How can I love someone I have never seen or held?

I Love You . . .
Because I love the "Little Girl" that has been lovingly carrying you inside her for all these months.
I said "Little Girl" because even though she will be your "Mommy" she will always be my "Little Girl."

I Love You . . .
For all the happiness and joy you are going to bring to your Mom and Dad throughout the years.

I Love You . . .
Even though some of those years may not always be the way we plan for our children, You will always know that you are loved and cared for.

I Love You . . .
And when I hold you in my arms for the first time, I know I am going to cry, but the tears will be joyous, as I look at you I will be thinking, I Love You . . .
Grandma Marge

Juliet Ann Swieczkowski
BURN OUT (1973)

To the memory of the beautiful children who did not make it.

Have you ever seen the walking dead?
The ones with burnouts for a head,
Open your eyes and look with awe,
You'll see them walking in every mall,
All the darlings of the suburban set,
Some haven't even seen sixteen yet.
They shuffle to and fro,
With no place special to go.
Buy a dream for fifty cents,
Leave the mind empty and bent.
Their worries are very few,
Who is holding and what to do.
Been everywhere and done it all,
These walking dead at the suburban mall,
Pretty girls with red black eyes,
Telling oh so many lies
Handsome boys with flowing hair,
Taking selling for a dare,
As they die more take their place,
What is wrong with the human race?

Sabin Lahey
MOTHER

The one who holds you in her arms, caressing you with tender charms.
When I am sick you're always here, showing me much loving care.
When I am weak, in mind and heart, you're by my side, you never part.
As I've grown you've understood how hard it is to move into womanhood.
But with your help I've done okay, and getting better every day.
So thank you for being here.
I love you sweet, mother dear.

Willard Lee Skelton
JOHNNY COME ROLL CALL

the roving gleam is in your eye
shut up mouth before you lie
yesterday you were still true
today it's goodbye; we're through
the need for someone new
has taken its hold on you
the need for someone new
but we didn't vow to be true
your old key still fits my door
but I won't be around any more
an old love must find a new place
modern times; a new face

Keli Jo Pekala
PAUL LYNN'S SONG

A poor sad lullabye
For a child who'll never cry.
God has taken her away,
But my love will always stay.

Hear a mother's lonely prayer.
Take my child into your care.
That one day I may see.
The child that you gave to me.

Please God let her know.
I didn't want to let her go.
Let her see that she is loved.
Even though she sleeps above.

Jon
LOSING MY MAN

To my family and those who have supported me

A young lady was sitting and crying,
I walked over and asked her "why?"
Her crying and sobbing were so profound,
She could not even reply.
Then finally when she began to explain,
Why the tears were flowing like rain,
Her heart was really broken in two,
Because she had lost her man.
The world had not come to an end, I told her
But this could not stop the pain
"To another woman I could understand it," she said
"But I lost him to another man."

Carroll E Horn
YOU WERE THERE

In Memory of Les Kustrich

You were there when we needed a helping hand,
You were there to give us your love.
To us you were tall as a mountain,
You must have been sent from above.
You had a heart that was tender,
To many you were a great friend;
And many hearts were broken
When your life on earth did end.

But to us you will live on forever,
You will always be nearby.
Your spirit shall linger with us,
Men like you don't die.

Peggy Walker Cozzi
REFLECTIONS ON A CHINESE PROVERB

To my mother who gave me life, To my husband who gave me love, To my children who give me hope.

The fragrance of a rose
Clings to the hand of one who bestows
This gift of God's lovely creation—
A symbol of one's adoration.

One whom I loved very much
Taught me to feel the tender touch
Of petals, leaves, and yes,
the thorn . . . . .
She's the one of whom I was born

The seed from which I became the bloom
Was planted in my mother's womb.
From birth I was expected to become
A blooming rose 'til I succumb.

She vowed I'd be a missionary . . .
Instead, I try to be an emissary
Of love and joy, caring and mirth,
Justifying her promise at my birth.

I can never possibly fulfill
All the hopes expressed in her will.
But, now and then, in my children I see
Glimpses of what she had hoped for me.

Dennis Richard Cournoyer

Dennis Richard Cournoyer
DREAMS OF HOPE

To my beautiful mother Barbara, your loving son Dennis

A world of color, and fantasy,
Darkened shades of reality.
Chimes of music, as we wonder,
Days of gray, sounds of thunder.
What once was beauty, plays, and poise, leaves ugly acting raged with noise. Bowing gracefully out of sight, a baby born, a rainy night.
Joyous tears, with silent smiles, taking you home, across the miles.

Laura Norris
OH GOD BE WITH ME

Oh God be with me, night and day.
Oh God be with me, show the way.
I need your guidance, to help me out.
Especially when my troubles are about.
Oh God be with me, show me what's true.

Oh God be with me, throughout all I do.
I want to change my ways, be the best I can be.
Will you show me all the things I need to see.
Oh God be with me, catch me, I'm falling.
Oh God be with me, hear me, I'm calling.
I want to live my whole life for you.
I think it's time I made my move.
My move to much bigger things.
Expand my horizons, spread my wings.

E J Mick
RETURN
The wall time built is ashes and rubble,
My tears just a tale the tired past tells.
The day brought you and you bring trouble
But I had forgotten the bells! ! !

Judy Ann DeWitt
LET ME REMEMBER
While I am here, let me remember
The sun's glow, the wind in my hair,
The birds, on a quiet still morning
My gratitude, while silent in prayer.

Smells of mowed grass, in summer
New buds, with fresh signs of life,
Smiles, laughter, and kind words
Things, that overcome, woe and strife.

Thoughtful deeds, from someone who cares
Even small thank yous, that count,
Wisdom—to notice, the Love around
Simple—Yet Best—That really amount.

Let me never forget, where I came from
But hold only memories of Love,
For my blessings, outweigh my sorrows
Just in knowing, God reigns above.

Worry—No Never—Why should I
Who am I to question his plan,
I am only a child—Not Perfect
To live each day—the best, that I can!

James Geisendorfer
AT THIS POINT IN TIME
At this point in time,
The state-of-the-art is
What it's all about, and
That's the bottom line.

Bert Ballou Jr
IS THIS SUCCESS?
Where is the measure of success?
Is it in dollars?
I have less than five to my name
And if you count my debts
Somewhere near minus five-hundred
Yet I know of rich people more poor
Is it in happiness?
But who can measure that?
If you are better off than the day before
Or at least no worse off
Is this success?
Is success being loved by many people?
But how can you tell how they really feel?
Is success being able to love yourself?
Or to love others? Or both?
Is success to know God?
Or something abstract
Is success physical, or material
Or something you feel, an emotion.
Who determines success?
You, or those who look at you.

Vickie Teague
SEASONS

Dedicated to the memory of Alden Kay Grimm; "A Man of Love and Courage."

I'll think of you in Springtime,
As the winds begin to blow;
The flowers as they're blooming,
I'll see your memories grow.

They'll grow into perfection,
Each and every passing day;
For Springtime is for growing,
And memories are to stay.

I'll think of you in Summer,
And wish things were the same;
As dear thoughts of you return,
And old joys, they remain.

In Fall time, I'll remember,
As the leaves begin to fall;
And looking back upon my dreams,
The memories, I'll recall.

In Wintertime, I'll have you most,
It was our Springtime then;
We grew to know each other,
A season without end.

Dorothy Krueger Burman
TO THE WHIMSEY OF A QUILL
Within me stirs a drumroll of desire
So quickened by the thought that somewhere near
I soon shall glimpse the sapphire blue of wings
Where marsh reeds bond their tensely daggered weir.

As my delight unfolds, I pole my way
To claim one heron feather for my own,
That I might ink its shaft in lazy notes
And pen the purest blues that one could drone.

Throughout the day, I scan gaunt colonnades,
Whose rampikes claw the gauze of Heaven's shell—
Until at dusk, I finally find a throne
Where nests the marshland's heron sentinel.

Yet, as I cry my joy—ten thousand frogs
With their harrumphing laughter mocking me,
Affirm the truth that I shall never climb
To pluck that bird who glares from yonder tree.

How odd—a scorer who cannot contrive
To snatch one quill that could scribe blues for him—
For now, he must pursue the porcupine
Whose rustic spike might end the azured whim.

Patrick Crawley
ONE PERSON
There is just one person in a room,
Nobody else is there.
Does anybody know of him,
Or do they even care?

This person's life is all alone,
No one to give him aid.
When this person leaves this earth,
Will his memory fade?
Is man such an island,
That he wouldn't care?
Thinking only of himself,
No matter what else is there?

That person in the room,
What if it were you?
And all the others didn't care,
Now—what would you do?

Marita Hopkins OSF

Marita Hopkins OSF
MIGRANT WORKERS

To the Srs. of St. Francis of Assissi, Milwaukee, who are committed to work for justice.

Hellish fate has mapped their journey's route!
***

From sun's awakening to its blood-red setting
Moving shadows inch along at agonizing pace.
Mud-stained rags like unfurled, tattered ribbons
Stretch down the endless rows of plump, red fruit.
(Promise of gold in rich men's coffers).
Arching backs unwittingly give shade to drooping plants,
While sweat and tears of men enslaved
Fall drop by drop upon the hostile soil.

As hours drag, consuming thirst and gnawing hunger-pain
Prod the oppressed spirit on to labor's end
And recompense!
A terrible price to pay for life that's worse than death!
***

Rich, savory TOMATO SOUP!
No longer hungry,—I push the steaming bowl aside
And weep!

S J Davidian CPCU
PROPOSITION 103 IN HAIKU
I
We are terrified
As the wind whispers,
"Proposition 1-0-3 has passed."
II
The White Papers fall
Like snowflakes, saying,
"Do nothing till you hear from us."
III
Anxious voices
Of those unprotected:
"Will there be warmth for winter?"
IV
Rays of hope midst darkened clouds
As Supreme Deciders
Stay the downpour.
V
Many flowers bloom and urge,
"Tarry, take a second look."
Will Spring follow?

Cynthia Faustine Terault
CANTICLE
Oh, clear, bright trembling song of birds,
Rising pure and silvery as the morning star
Against the soft pink sky of dawn,
A budding rose of melody,
Evocative of the enchanting antiphons
Of childhood's morning.
Yet now the luminous sound is but a sweet stiletto
Bringing only pain and anguish for all that is no more,

And in the lonely nighttime wood
An owl's mournful psalm ascends,
Dark chant rising into darkness, dying into silence,
Its feathered breast pierced upon the thorns
Of loss—the loss of all on earth
That once brought joy.

But then, when all the melodies of life have flown
Too far away to reach the heart,
Ah, then, in soundless beauty, sings the Dove,
Impassioned poetry no earthly ear can hear,
Each note a liquid, lambent flame of fire,
A burning drop of fire to light the soul.

Rachel Campton

Rachel Campton
STARS AND MOON
When the stars and moon so bright;
who tells them when it's light?

Do they decide to play hide and seek
behind the clouds large peak?

Or does it get so bright
it becomes light?
For all I know they disappear,
and it becomes very clear.

Grace Hayes
THE NIGHT I SAW JESUS
As I lay on my bed one night,
I gazed out the window and saw a beautiful sight. I can't begin to describe to you, what it was I saw. It had a lovely color of blue. The blue was not the only color I saw; There was pink, green, yellow, and a figure that was tall. I kept looking and looking at this thing in the sky. At last, I gave a big sigh. It came to me all at once, It was Jesus, our Lord; and in His hand was a golden sword. I wondered if this was the night that He was coming to take me with Him, when all of a sudden, everything went dim. I knew it was only a warning, I must not wait till morning. I got down on my knees and prayed for Jesus to save me from sin. So after that I gazed out the window time after time again.

Linda M Miyahira
PORTRAIT TOMORROW
I walked with all the people—
different people;
like a rainbow current passing about me.
And everywhere were sounds—
constant and steady,
and the smells of many spices
and flowers
and rain.

And I told myself:
"I won't let this time end.
I'll keep this picture—
these sounds,
these scents
in my mind."

The sun did not hear me as it dissolved into
the sea.
The people changed color and pattern—
blue and gray;
few and apart.
But the lingering scents—
they stayed to whisper,
"There'll be a new portrait tomorrow."

Peggie Lien
MOWING OF THE GREEN
Through yellow strength
I can see in the dark.
He is the Son.

Before the flower blossomed,
It was green.
His Spirit blew color
Into the earth.

At night, in dreams,
There's shades of purple.
Please draw them!
All is not beauty.

Eventually the Sun's strength
Swallowed the flower,
Hour by Hour.

Now the memory of hues returns,
And I can see all times
Inside out of me . . . .

Harry Ehrman
THE SEVEN CHALLENGER ASTRONAUTS (JAN. 28, 1986)
Two brave women and five dauntless men
Awaited the Challenger's count to ten.
They were thrust into the sky
Little knowing that they would die.

Great joy was shown on their ascent
Which in a minute turned to fear
As the space-craft exploded and they went
To a heavenly grave in the atmosphere.

Christa Mc Auliffe was a capable teacher
Who went along for the ride.
It was to be a special feature
To raise the children's pride.

Now the world is mourning
Such daring and dedicated pioneers.
Their names will always be shining
When their star in the sky appears.

Teresa J Purl
REMEMBERING
Thinking back when,
together we began
Having someone able to share.
This be my daily thought,
All the good times you have brought
Special moments of such pleasure
Are memories that I treasure.
Holding on to what was then,
Only wanting it back again
No hurt nor pain,
Just—
Sweet love to gain.

Sultana Nahar

Sultana Nahar
LOVE AND ROMANCE

Dedicated to KAZI ANWAR HUSAIN (My husband)

My sweet heart
You simply fail to discern
It is barrier and frustration
Separation and delay
That creates a state of mind
Which people call love or romance.

Your lady is a dream girl
A fairy queen,
With golden wings;
A pure princess
Or a fiery individual
A symbol of all qualities and virtues
Till you tie her in a nuptial knot.

Do away with the obstacle
Replace separation by everydayness
Ecstasy and agony shall fade away
Into utter disappointment.

Tonilyn Massie
WHAT WE WAITED SO LONG FOR . . . .
What we waited so long for:
happened naturally.
Brilliant, beautiful the way it should be.
So much emotion . . . . . . left speechless
Our energy concentrated only on each other.
We held one another so tightly
gazing, clenching, searching our souls.
The minutes ticked the clock struck
Neither wanting our time to end.
Grudgingly we parted
Separation started.
Behind a glow left
warmth and knowing.
No distance too great
for
Our hearts to forget.

Wendy Kaori Moore
RAINDROPS DRIPPING OFF MY NOSE

"To Haru-chan" This poem is dedicated to you with prayer that your open-heart surgery will be a success . . . Lovingly, Wendy

Rapid heart beats, sweaty palms,
Can't catch a breath,
Feel like fainting.

Am I gonna die?
Or am I daydreaming?
No, it must be real.

I can never remember,
Sweating while daydreaming.
Aren't daydreams supposed to be peaceful?

Don't daydreams happen on lazy afternoons,
During boring classes?
Aren't there usually good looking guys in daydreams?

Beach parties, and fast cars, and sunsets,
And wind in my hair?
This can't be a daydream.

For it is none of the above.
It is a pounding in my temples,
And a clouding in my eyes.

And there's another rapid heart beat,
Sweaty palms, can't catch a breath,
Feel like fainting,

Am I gonna die?
Or am I daydreaming?

Susan T Elliott
MY HUSBAND
You are special—the man in my life
It was on a June day I became your wife

It's been almost five years since that day
No matter what, I'd have it no other way

You're always there for me, through thick and thin
With a loving arm or that special grin

I love you more than you'll ever know
I pray, we have many years together to go

Harriet Reitha Mitchell
WHERE IS GOD
Where is God? My little boy asked—
With a question on his face.
He's up in Heaven—so says I.
With all of his glory and grace.

Where is Heaven? My little boy asked
So puzzled and uncertain was he.
He's up in the sky—so far away
That's where someday—we will be.

When will we be there? My little boy asked
A smile shone on his face.
When Jesus comes back to rule the world,
A king so full of grace.

All of these questions I answered my child
Because someday I knew
Another little boy would come to him
And ask him the same ones too.

Melinda Seyer
THE RIVER
If I could find a river
That took our cares away
I'd dump my every problem
And then be on my way

I'd walk about real happy
With smiles and grins to bear
And sing just like the bird I would
And live without a care

Imagine every day,
A circus full of fun
We'd never know real sadness
All days, no clouds, just sun

I guess it would be great
I think it would be neat
We'd live without our fears
And live without real hate

Until we find that river
I know we must trudge on
Make do with life's own puddles
Search the river—rolling on

Regina Brown
ANXIETY
I Wake up at night
With the ceiling pushing down
And the pounding of my heart
Is a terrible sound
And the night isn't friendly
And the moon isn't warm
And I'm all alone

Won't morning ever come?

Dolores McGraw
YOUR NEW LIFE
As you begin the new year
you embark on a new life
Together as one, man and wife.
Take special care to treat your love tender.
So fragile it is and sometimes hard to remember
that moments shared will not always be splendid, but
memories will grow from this love never ending.
My brother beloved has taken a wife
a place in his heart for the rest of her life.
Treat him with tenderness, treat him with care
believing his love will always be there.
A wife is a cherished woman indeed
asking from you only the simplest of needs.
Love, trust, and friendship to always

share
and the comfort of knowing you will
forever care.
If you abide in each other for the rest
of your life
everlasting happiness is yours as man
and wife.
As always,
Dot

Naidene Stroud Trexler
WHAT! NO GOD!
You tell me there is no God
When a lowering sun spotlights
Crimson maples
Or a stray moonbeam highlights a
golden leaf?

When slender white birches
Rub shoulders with
Scented pine?

When roadsides glow with myriad
colors
And birds wing southward?

Oh, foolish one, how can you
Doubt?
Open your eyes and see.

Tammy Kennady
THE CURE
The obvious decision decreases with
wait,
Transforming into a disturbing
debate.
Hail head or heart? Not an easy
choice,
For one who is subject to differing
voice.
Should you wait for love to knock on
your door?
What if time brings none worth
waiting for?
Should you search for love, instead
of wait?
Grab what you can, before it's too
late?
In looking for love, you'll find
yourself lost.
And while you are waiting, your
heart pays the cost.
You may settle then, for a love that's
not true,
And belong to another when He does
find you.
Go out, and love life. Chin up and
walk tall.
When Mr. Right comes round, you'll
hear love's call.
And all of those others that make
way to your heart,
For just a little while, should not tear
you apart.
For, with them you'll learn to rise
way above,
To practice and master the art of
love.
If all could be patient and go through
love's course,
Then, all could take part in the cure
for divorce.

Janet Thomas
OUR FATHER IN HEAVEN ABOVE
Our Father in Heaven above
Sent to me my only love.
We were together for 28 years
And each one became more dear.

We became parents of 2 girls and 2
boys
And each one became his pride and
joy.
He was so proud of each of them
And they were just as proud of him.

He was not tall in stature
But he was a giant of a man
Always gentle and thoughtful
And everybody's friend.

Never too busy to help or share
With anyone who needed care.
So devoted to his children and wife
He would have laid down his very
own life.

The sun was setting in the west
When he was called home to rest
He seemed to have a smile on his
face
So we knew he was already in that
special place.

Not a day goes by that I don't pray
That we will be reunited one day
Then the cycle will be complete
When again in Eternity we will meet.

Rhonda Lee Battaglia
OUR FIRST CHRISTMAS
We don't have much money
And the presents bought are few;
Not many decorations
My heart is feeling blue.

But when I think of future holidays
When things won't be so bad;
A smile brightens up my face
and I don't feel so sad.

Yes, our first Christmas together
Will surely be one to recall
and, in later years we'll realize,
It wasn't so bad after all.

Betsy Jane Bramhall
ZEUS
Zeus, you weren't invited
to throw your weight about
Fourth of July's a day
to celebrate—not pout!

Zeus, what "Great Balls of Fire"
now lighten up the sky
now banging up a storm
such temper temper—why?

Zeus, I guess you're jealous
the rockets and the flair
but can't you show respect
with much less in the air?

Patricia Mark
STEP BACK

To the one that opened my eyes and touched my heart. Thank you, T.W.B.

When you find yourself
Feeling down & out,
Asking yourself what your
Life is all about?
Asking why your life
Seems so blue?
Asking, "What am I going to do?"
Take a deep breath, . .
Try to re-group.
Step back into time & you will find
The answers that lay inside.
Go ahead, don't be afraid
For without the answers, your life
May never be the same.
You may also find it's time for a
change,
Because you can't go on feeling
You're trapped in a cage.
Think over all your guilts & fears.
Think over all that's happened over
the years;
Yes, go ahead & shed all your
tears,
Because what's held inside
Has to come out.
That's the only way you'll find out
What your life is all about.

Sherral K Hardman
GRANDMA'S HOUSE

In memory of Edith Hardman

It sits silent now,
No voices echo within the walls,
No footsteps are heard on the stairs.
The old white-frame house,
Waits.

Through the many years,
Many people have lived here,
Under this old shingled roof;
And called it home.

Now, the foundation is sinking,
The floors slant off to one side,
Windows allow the wind,
To sing softly around the loose
frames.

With love and care,
Lots of hard work,
And many repairs;
The house could shelter other
families.

White paint peeling,
Plumbing slowly rusting,
The old house sits empty.
And waits.

Marlene B Young
THE WORLD IS YET A BRIGHTER PLACE
The world is yet a brighter place
My heart increased with joy
Since the day that you arrived
My precious baby boy.

You're Daddy's little shadow
You're Sister's pal in fun
You're Mother's little charmer
And special joy, my special son.

With a frog in your pocket
And mud on your face
Your little boy's world
Will be an adventurous place.

I'll share with you life's wonders
And nurture you with prayer
As you grow you'll come to know
The One who keeps you in His care.

You light within my heart
A flame that words can't measure
My son, you are a blessing true
One of life's greatest treasures.

Patty Lou Envik
LAST DAYS OF INNOCENCE

To my three sons; Erik, Levi and Ivan, whom I love more than life itself.

As I wiggled my feet deeper in the
sand,
I watched the boys jumping from the
log,
While holding each other's hand.

I can see the water rise high in the
air,
Then stop, turn and fall,
On their skin so tan and bare.

Splashing and laughing they
continued to play,
Little did they know that this would
be,
Their last innocent Summer day.

I wanted to reach out and grab the
sun,
And ask it not to go,
My children were so happy and
having so much fun.

No, it will never be the same,
The boys will soon be men,
And life will no longer be just a
happy game.

If I could hold this moment in the
palm of my hand,
And give it to you when you are
grown,
Oh my sons, wouldn't it be grand?

As a tear fell slowly from my face,
I reached for it but it was gone,
Lost in the sand, without a trace.

Betty J Johnson
WHEN OUR LIFE HAS FINALLY ENDED

To my husband Rick and my children Rick and Becky. To my loving family, Julious and Shirley Cassidy, Patsy, Eddie, Sam, David, Bill, Brenda, Joe.

When our Life has finally ended
And our bodies are laid to rest
Our souls go up to heaven
To take the final test
The Lord knows who does love him
By the deeds they did in life
And by keeping the Ten Command-
ments
Who will receive his victory price
And if you do not know the Lord
I beg of you please do
For those you've loved are
There waiting just for you
Spread the word of Jesus
Let others do the same
And in return the Saviour
Will never forget your name.

Ivy E Colmer

Ivy E Colmer
SECOND HAND HEART

I dedicate this poem to my beloved cousin Thomas Maroney, who has taught me the need for Freedom in love, and inspires me to continue writing.

Right from the start, you gave me your heart. I called you on the phone, only to find out you weren't alone. You were with a new love playing the part, giving away your second hand heart. All our dreams drifted out to sea, now I understand that we never could be. Echoes of our laughter linger in my mind, a love of this kind you will never find. At first it seemed that we never would part, then you gave away your second hand heart. Broken glass fallen to the ground, shattered softly without a sound. Washed away in the rain, it's your turn now to feel the pain. A love like a looking glass, trapped in the pain that never will pass.

A mirage on a dry barren desert in the blaze of heat, the illusion you never get to meet. It's there but when you go to see, that was just the way it appeared to be. In the evening the stars twinkle, a flicker, a spark, they seem so bright in the dark. By the time the light we may see, the star can no longer be. An illusion of love take a good hard look, there was nothing there that you thought she took. I'll go my way and you go yours, closed and locked are all the doors. The lights are out and the fire is gone, and now it is time to sail on. The time has come for us to part, farewell my love here's back your heart.

Holly Tepe
THE BABY OF BETHLEHEM
Was He so different
From the child born yesterday
In a deserted garage,
Backwater of city ghetto,
To an unwed mother?

As He was then,
So He is now,
Christ is Everyman,
The Son of Man in features
Of friend and stranger.

God, born in a stable?
Why not?
Have things changed so much
Since Bethlehem?
Always surprising, He was, is,
Will ever be.

Donald Dennis
HOW JESUS CAME INTO OUR LIVES
Lives we forget how Jesus life how Jesus life of all us, life of Jesus death was life, life of Jesus death was life, life of us, we came alive through Jesus life, how Jesus gave life to our lives, I thank of life how Jesus gave Given life how his life was given for us, I thank how Jesus came to life with his love with his life for us, love of his life for us, love of Jesus life not forgetting Jesus life how his life gave us of life that can not be forgotten life of Jesus love live for all that love how Jesus come alive in lives of us, we came through blessing of Jesus we must live within those blessings that Jesus is to all us, how our lives are being blessed, our lives are blessing

James M Gowin
TURMOIL
In this vast water and jungled earth:
Turmoil we see, since time of birth:
Every good thing slips, our finger's grip:
We're in a tiny canoe, not a big ship:
Out on this boisterous, ocean blue:
I get a finger grip hold on you:
For a brief second, I hold this grip:
But through my fingers, my lover slips:
A lifetime I search, jungle and plain:
Back in the canoe, I search the ocean again:
But over and over the same refrain:
Trying to get hold, of you again:
I will be so glad, when this search is o'er:
And in this canoe, I will search no more:
Death will end, turmoil, and bring me peace:
When out of this body, my spirit released;

(First Atomic Veteran)

Norma L Appleby
FRAGILE
Man is sure to follow and life will have no worth
if all the birds and animals are taken from this earth.
The balance is so fragile, it's the end for you and me
if all the fish and mammals, vanish from the sea
and when we call it progress, to build for vanity
destroying our inheritance, it's sheer insanity.
When we destroy all of our wetlands,
we show a mind just like a child
and with arrogance beyond belief,
we call our forest brothers wild.

Helene Lenga Kohen
LAUGHTER
Laughter is a tonic
for the hearts of men,
this has been a proven fact
since the world began.

Nothing is more pleasing
for a person to hear,
than the sound of laughter
heartfelt and sincere.

Matters not how troubled
we may chance to be,
just a bit of laughter
seems to set us free.

Carla J Comer
PICTURE PERFECT

To Carol, the most dedicated friend a person could have.

Things aren't always what they seem
Dreams aren't always dreams
And life can't always be "picture perfect."

Even tho you look
You can't always see
Even tho you try
Some things can never be
And life can't always be "picture perfect."

I've seen my friends
Have hard times
That didn't always make
For reason or for rhyme.
So I know life's not always "picture perfect."

But don't give us
Give it one more try
'Cause if you don't
Time can pass you by
For life can't always be "picture perfect."

For things aren't always what they seem
And dreams aren't always dreams
And life can't always be "picture perfect."

Porfiria Patacsil
THE ROCKING CHAIR
In the center of the room
an old rocking chair will stay.
She sits and rocks to the tune,
that was popular in her day.
Days of youth, gaiety and dance.
Times of young love and romance.

Dashing young beaus that came to call,
when only her beauty mattered at all.
Many a serious beau, she sent away with a kiss.
Waiting for the one, that her heart would miss.
She thought she had plenty of time to wait.
For the special someone, who would hold her fate.
Beauty and callers began to disappear,
with the passing of each courting year.
Before she knew it, time had escaped.
She had no one to love, she waited too late.

In the center of the room
an old rocking chair will stay.
She sits and rocks to the tune,
that was popular in her day.
To the times of youth and love that got away.

S Dunham Wilson
DEAR STARR:
I caught last night your air-tossed, careless smile.
I caught it as a fly is by a spider caught. And oh!
And my! How it struggled to be free!
And I the while,
From careful instinct, turned it carefully just so,
And round it spun some part of me (as though
I could spare some) to do the package properly.
You the while, (God bless you!), caught the show.
There is, then, now no need (not that I be
Less married—not the less—but more married: me)
There is, then, now no need, my dear, for guile,
As I myself was caught in the act, you see,
Lashed so sudden in love's silken style,
I swear to God I scarcely felt the blow.
And there you have it: all the love I know.

Reverend Byron Gordon Hamlin

Reverend Byron Gordon Hamlin
MY TRIBUTE TO MARTIN LUTHER KING JR.
Gone but not forgotten, a warrior and a friend.
A soul whom God had chose to human rights defend.
And though they beat and jailed him, and took his rights away,
He turned the other cheek and said, "There is a better way."

He went up to the mountain, the horizon to survey,
And then, as preacher, prophet, foretold the time of day,
A day of hate and trouble, of pestilence and strife,
When men respect but little, the sacredness of life.

"I have a dream," he told us, that together we will win,
If Black and white sit down and then a dialogue begin.
A dialogue of justice and equality demand
To realize that freedom is a must in every land.

"I may not get there with you" and that's the reason why
He had the premonition that, for freedom he would die.
"We shall overcome someday," because he told us how,
To suffer, march and protest, and not to hatred bow.

And though we face injustice, quite subtle in its scope,
He left a legacy indeed, a legacy of hope.
There will never be another like Martin Luther King,
Though others try to emulate in letting freedom ring.

And many speak with forked-tongue and act with such disguise,
This giant of the forest deserved the Nobel Prize.
The torch is in our hands today, the old, the young, the free,
To hold it high that every man, will gain the victory

Twill not be easy to convince, the bigot of his hate,
Nor try to change against his will, the racist's sorry state.
For only with much tolerance, with love and sympathy,
Will quality of life mean, more than much of quantity.

Allison Coerper
A DOOR
The door is ajar

What do you mean
The door is a jar
A door is a door
and a jar is a jar

Well a door is not always ajar
Most times a door is just a door

But is a jar a door

Oh no never
A jar is never a door
But a door is often ajar
And you can adore a door

But can you adore a jar

Yes quite so
You could even adore a door
that is ajar

Well then couldn't you adore
a jar that is a door

Oh no never
That wouldn't make any sense

Well what does . . .

Teddy Hawkes
THE GARDENS
Their lovely blossom's fading,
They'll soon rest 'neath the snow,
I nurtured them so carefully,
Not wanting them to go.

But as I watch them wither,
Their life I compare to mine,
Born—matured—then faded,
The product of passing time.

But after a period of slumber,
My flowers will bloom once more,
So with my resurrection,
I'll be as I was before.

For God tends His beautiful garden,
As I cultivated mine,
Tho' mine's just a mortal endeavor,
God's is a harvest Divine.

Sofia McHarney
BY THE LAKE
oleo colored petals
cupped by the sun
sprinkle the mood
of summer . . . .

jewel ridden crescents
caressed by the wind
ripple to sculpt
the shores embrace . . .

secret keepers of old
whose majestic swollen veins
give breath to mankind
cast their shadows of giant . . .

mosaic flyer
triangle of geometric being
fleeting investigator of
sweetness
provoke your presence
and caress our vision . . .

sentry of black
caw your alarm
at man's intrusion
of natures communion . . .

Irene Mary Larson
THE HOME
The Home—where friendship—is a guest
and love abides—in
The home—where the sun shines—
out brighter for all to enjoy—
The home—where joy and laughter—
lives—is our American home.
The home—is where friends and all—
are welcome to come—as
The home—is where the sun shines—
brighter for all to enjoy.
The home—is where all are welcome—
to come to enjoy.
The home—is a better place to live—
as none can compare—with—
The home—where friendship—is
a guest—as the sun shines
brighter for all.

Van Wyman
TO EACH HAS BEEN GIVEN A WONDERFUL GIFT

To Kawliga—My wooden Indian—My soul mate

To each has been given a wonderful gift
A country of our own called the mind
A quiet place we can travel down the roads of our dreams
Away from the rest of mankind
There's always a hill and a cool summer night
And always a moon up above
Always the crickets are chirping
And always someone to love
The roads may stretch out mile after mile
Our bodies may become tired
and weary
But our hearts can soar like a bird
No trips will ever be dreary

Leo J Lawler
A VOICE FROM THE GRAVE
The day I consented to be your wife
We spoke of the children to whom we would give life.
There was to be Betty, Cindy, and Sue.
Each looking at life with a different view.
Then there was to be Paul, Jimmy, and Lance.
Teaching us of life through a beautiful dance.
Breaking our hearts as they broke a tooth.
Showing us this was part of being a youth.
Now that I have chosen not life but death,
All of our children to be have left.
They will never know happiness, want, or duty.
They will never know life and its beauty.
They will never hear the words unspoken.
Never will our words or their hearts be broken.
They will never know the hurt of a skinned knee.
They will never laugh or be full of glee.
I am sorry I left you in a lurch,
But I always see you on Sunday in Church.
I pray daily that some day there will be,
At the Throne of God you and me.

Ethel W Badger 2nd
REFLECTIONS ON V. I. PANDA

To the Chinese people for their pride and enduring efforts to save this most unique animal.

There is a young panda called Ling-Ling,
Who journeyed from China with "Wing-Ding"
To visit our shore,
And shortly what's more—
Both captured our hearts in "twing-ling!"

Emily Marso
DREAMS ARE MADE OF THIS
To dream during the night is ordinary
To dream during the day is special
When I dream at night I dream the ordinary
When I dream in daylight
I dream of things under the sea
Of whales and dolphins
Of vast submerged cities of the future
I dream the extraordinary.

Jean Wilson
ODE TO A TRAFFIC LIGHT
Traffic light, oh traffic light how
lonely you must be.

So early in the morning and
no traffic there to see.

Changing colors—red, yellow
and green,

Isn't it a pity that you're
not being seen.

Then we come to rush hour and
such an important part you play.

People stopping and going
only on your say.

Traffic light, oh traffic light
blinking through the night.

To the weary traveler you are
a welcome sight.

Anna Josephine Coniglio
THE WADING POND
At the wading pond I met you.
We were young and innocent.
It was a long, warm summer.

I was sixteen, and you were seventeen
when we met on that day long ago,
by the wading pond.

Water trickled out of a fountain nearby
and we sat on a bench to watch butterflies
fly over the wading pond.

A summer of friendship, a summer of love,
we were contented listening to the wind and the water,
and the wading pond witnessed our happiness.

Summer passed, and leaves floated in the fountain,
the leaves blew away, and the water in the pond froze,
a blanket of snow covered the ground around the wading pond.

You went off, and I stayed here,
remembering our summer love,
Sitting in the chill of winter, on a bench,
By the wading pond.

Dianna McKay
HAPPY BIRTHDAY LORI

To my Daughter "Lori", with all my love. Mom

From pigtails and pink lace . . .
To prom dresses and make-up for your face,
From trikes and dolls and raiding the cookie jar . . .
To dances and dating and having a car,
From hating boys land thinking they're mean,
To loving 'em all and thinking they're keen,
We've watched your changes day after day . . .
And watched you grow along the way,
You've made us happy and made us blue . . .
But no matter what we've always loved you,
From pigtails to boys, from cookies to cars,
From dolls to dating . . .
The young lady we see now made it all worth the waiting.

Happy 17th Birthday Lori.

Love,
Mom and Tommy

Peter Gallo
COUNTERPOINT

To Mom who understands

I have come for solitude and silence,
To walk along this shore again—to think,
And feel once more the rhythm of the sea.
The clanging cymbal of my city life
Disturbs me: All too often I confuse
My sense and lose my step in dissonance.
Do I hear strains of laughter in the wind?
What am I to think? Am I diminished?
My stride is quick in this cacophony
Of self-indulgence. I have skipped a beat.
I pause to clear my mind of all its noise.
I catch the ocean's cadence on the ebb.
The subtle counterpoint of wind and waves
Recommends a softer resolution.

Troy J Pemberton
ON THE TARP, OFF THE RAIL, IN THE DRAIN
Bombshell bombardment
through waterbeads,
fall
to the continuous flow.

Drip—
drip—
drip—

Rejuvenating
the drip filled flow.
Refills, swirling above.
Always the cycle.
All parts contributed
to the endless
dripping
flow

Eleanor Ponton
DAY BREAK
Rosy fingers that caress the lacy mist,
Which against the earths is damply pressed
Nor stops but reaches low to find,
A diamond in the dewdrops' breast

Brings warmth of life, into the dawn,
And shades in silence move away,
Then gently wakes the drooping flowers
This miracle of a newborn day.

Jane Ellen Louise Beal
KNIGHT

Cordially dedicated to José Fiero; you inspired me.

A knight
of silver-gleaming polished armour,
shining in the wind.
Black sparkles in his burnished hair.
His precise, chiseled face,
darkened and flushed,
body trim and worked and fine.
Eyes the mirrors of his soul;
deep and full and rich with the
darkened shade of the earth.
Movements like the flowing sea,
rage and fury like an eagle's wings;
a wave crashing,
or calm and cool like a placid lake;
a falling leaf.

A little, emerald-green, sparkling dragon,
perched like a parrot on his shoulder;
a jewelled sword hilt,
a swift, steel sword;
strong arms that wield it:
this knight of silver-gleaming polished armour,
shining in the wind.

Florence M Thompson
THINGS MY MOTHER TAUGHT ME

To The One and Only CHICA

She taught me right from wrong,
She taught me to be strong—
Mine was a mixed up family tree
From which I learned integrity! !

She taught me that to sit and wait,
Was just like fishing; without bait . . .
You must seek what you want in life
So what if fate deals out some strife—

No one ends up with what he's after;
Without some tears and a little laughter.
I thank my lucky stars, also that Being above;
For a mother who could deliver this, complete with LOVE!

Nikki Lessenberry
GLOW OF THE PURPLE RAIN

In the glow of the purple rain
I see your face and feel your pain
and if you weep in all your sorrow
how will you ever have tomorrow

For in life we take a chance
that a new love will enhance
and if we let it pass us by
then it is not worth a try

In the glow of the purple rain
I see your face and feel your pain
let your love go the measure
it'll be a gift that's sure to treasure

For if you let it pass you by
because you are afraid to try
then underneath the purple rain
you will sit alone in pain—

Michael R Daniels
ALL FOR LOVE/LOVE FOR ALL

This poem is dedicated to all of those who freely give of themselves for the good of others.

Who can stand, while others fall?
Or give an answer to the call?
What chapter or verse from the Law?
Could make an end and stop it all?

Who will speak when others can't?
Who will reap what others plant?
What sacred psalm can we chant?
For Whom will our spirits pant?

So far away, and long ago!
He said Forgive, for they don't know!
And from His head the blood did flow!
To cleanse and make the sinner whole!

So who am I, who would complain?
While others serve in spite of pain!
Who give their all, for greater gain!
Not for riches or glory vain!

But for something we call love!
Freely given from above!
Descending down like a dove!
Not giving up, but giving of!

Carolyn J Gonzales
WHERE'S ALL THE LOVE

There has to be some kind of purpose for our existence.
Something more than achieving "success."
Human worth based on monetary value;
Love based on security,
Friendships based on what the other can give you,
And happiness based on possessions.

Rushing there,
"I'm late here!"
No time to listen
No time to share.
You're on your own
Doesn't anyone care?

See the man in pain?
"Better him than me!"
See the brother in need?
"I just can't get involved."
A society without a heart?
Whose arteries should be pumping with compassion—
IT'S DRYING UP!

Can't you even spare five seconds
To say hello and maybe smile?
Give out a hug or a kind word?
Tell me God . . . . Where's all the love?

Hazel M Froemming
GOING HOME

An old man taught me that it doesn't matter where you are if you need to pray. God will hear if you really believe. And you can fix things even if you think you don't know how. That's why this is written for him, my father, who did his praying under a big oak tree and could see life in a handful of soil.

I place myself before you Lord
Beneath this lonely tree
Up on this blessed altar
That you have made for me

Stay close with us, we need your help
to guide us through this day
Give us strength to do what we must
and the strength we need to pray

Lead us slowly, love us long
Hold these hands that they may be strong
Bring us the sunshine, bring us the rain
Guide us back to your home again

Sometimes the roads seem so rugged and long
The mountains so high and the hatred so strong
It seems like the hurting will never end
And love without hurting will never begin

Please help me fix it like I do the little toys
So our lives can be filled with more of the joy

Touch us with Your loving hands
Hold us in Your arms
Give to us Your sacred peace
Let us no longer feel harm.

Marcia Gould
SPRING

Dedicated to my Grandmother, Lyda May Stewart

A new is beginning—
the old still a part,
It's like a reunion
of things in a start.
The leaves are still buds,
awaiting to grow—
and yet, last year's dry ones
are part of the flow.
The rains bring the movement
to help this new life—
in a glorious cycle that seems
like a knife,
when it cuts into memories
of lives we'd like back—
'til we think of the dry leaves,
crumpled and bunched,
how they've nurtured these new ones
awaiting their lunch, of raindrops
and sunshine.
Then the glory of giving seeps
into our soul,
and replenishes our loving,
and makes us more whole.
And our tears help the flow—and our smiles let it grow.

Dawne
I DID NOT INVITE YOU TO LOVE ME

For J.H.—May I one day receive invitation

I did not invite you to love me,
No want of your comfort have I,
So cast despair from your downcast eyes,
And fetter their unspoken plea.
Like jagged ice on wintry seas,
I drift aimless currents to lie,
Upon frigid shores, neath rayless skies,
It matters, no longer, you see.
For in my world, neither dawn nor spring,
Nor sunsets of lavender-gold,
Nor the warmth you toil so hard to bring,
Wield the might to drive back the cold.
For within me, lass, there is nothing,
But the empty vault of my soul.

John Ashby Conway
THE LITTLE FROG

He comes to visit us two days each year
A tiny frog who sits upon a leaf
Of Calla lily at our front door.
He could sit comfortably upon a quarter
With plenty of room to spare.
There he sits in the sun, a brilliant green
A cartagena emerald no greener,
Awaiting a passing fly.
Difficult to see, this green on green
A perfect camouflage
Sitting, peaceful in the sun.
Where does he spend his other days?
Is he the same one or a relative?
I must confess one frog looks very like another.
Why can't the trouble-makers of this world
Go home and leave the earth in peace
For little frogs and me?

Harry E (Skeeter) Allison Jr
IN MY HEART

In memory of Vance Hayes Hardesty (3-15-68 - 1-1-89)

When you lose a friend
Your life goes on.
It's something for you
to dwell upon.
Think about things,
the good times you had.
Yes, the good and not
the bad.
For the friend you
lost, is still in your
heart.
And nothing that
happens can tear
that apart.
So yes my friend
I miss you dear
But in my heart
I keep you near.

Rhonda Young
THANKS FOR LETTING ME BE WHO I AM

To a friend . . . . . . ,

I have this idea of how I'm supposed to be, and mainly I guess I pretty much am to the majority.
They'll only see as much of me as I will inevitably allow them to see, which really isn't much, and definitely not enough, if they plan on knowing me.
I keep myself covered with a facade to, by all means, hang on to my dignity, and if anything happens to shock me or jar me out of my tranquility, you know, those ever so often, fearful times, where you are caught by surprise and absolutely lose your natural defensive state of ambiguity,
The times when you lose your cover and before you can recover . . . . .
God forbid anyone discover the well kept secrets that I don't want uncovered . . . . .
The parts of me that I'd rather they not see—
the fears, the tears, the years of my torment,
the personal hell which kept me so long, so dormant.
At times I still feel the implant . . of the overpowering hands which kept me continually thinking, "I can't . . . . . I can't escape, I can't be free, I can't enjoy life," mainly because I'm afraid that he'll kill me because he says I'm his wife . . . .
oh, my, God, what a life.
When or will it ever end? . . . .
Does anyone hear me pleading?
"I no longer want him to even call me his wife?"
The pain is hidden deep down inside, but the scars still remain to taunt me on the outside.
No one can see them, but me—
and maybe him—if he remembers where he hurt me or even when.
It still amazes me how some little

thing that is said can result in
such pain that I can remember
how I felt when I thought I
might be better off dead
and that maybe my children
would be better off with only a
memory of me to go off to sleep
with.
The lack of self-confidence and
the beatings I took, almost, at
one time in my life got me
hooked on booze, on sleeping
pills, on pain killers that never
could.
Ease the pain, erase the memory,
stop the torment . . . . .
if only something or someone
would.
The ugly emotions and the
embittered existence of the
battered wife were never
shared with others because they
tried to judge my life.
Then Jesus came in, and He
wasn't full of criticism; neither
did He condemn. He said, "He
just came to be my friend."
I leaned on Him, and then He
made it real . . . . . He sent me a
friend filled with His compassion
to heal.
This "Special Friend" had an ear
just built to listen,
to hear who I am and who I
might be without any conditions.
Since he wanted to get to know
me, the real me, I let him;
and now, I thank God for such a
wonderful end.
I thank Him for Jesus and my
"Special Friend" who helped me
to change my idea in the end of
who and what I am to them.

When you read this history . . . .
of a painful recollection of this
battered wife's memories, think
long . . . . think hard . . . . . read
well every line, and the next
time you meet me, whoever I
am, please take the time
To stop on the side of the
highway just like Jesus and my
friend, to mend . . . **all the
brokenhearted who need
"you" as a "friend."**

Linda S Mowry
FLAWS OF THE OLD

*To those of young, From us of old—
"Love us still!"*

When we get old and life is not
there for us the way it once was
Be patient with us old people for
We mean no harm for our inadequa-
cies now
Don't throw us aside thinking that
we are no longer wise, with nothing
inside
Nor are we burdens unless you
choose to see us as one
After all, you weren't to us, when
you were helpless in the world
Love us still through all our cries,
even though we are just left with
memories and sighs
For one day you too will be here
and you will have the flaws of the
old
When life is not there for you like it
once was
We may be old but don't deny us
our rights of your love, love that we
have coming to us
Cling to us now as long as you can,
for the day will come when we are
no longer at your side
To be old is not by our choice, life
just has it that we are

Colin MacArthur
**THE MAGIC OF
MASQUERADE**

It was a time when the guillotine
was what split spooks at
Hallowe'en,
a time when the use of the
hangman's rope
enlivened the skipping feet of
Hope;
and those mournful murmurings of
pines
on windswept slopes were
joyous signs
you, too, could survive Old Winter's
sting
like dogwoods diffident till
Spring.

A time when your tongue, with its
wizard licks,
connived to be blackened by
licorice sticks
or turned into pink or brown by the
spell
of peppermint or caramel;
and you prayed the Hands-of-Time
would stop
since your own were clutching a
lollipop
or wrestling the querls of a red
balloon,
your ears agog with a circus
tune.
And you kept adoring those beasts
and clowns
who paraded drunkenly through
towns,
for it was a time to be duped, to be
swayed,
by the lure and the magic of
masquerade.

Brenda Kelly
REFLECTIONS OF DIVORCE

Do you feel the pain?
Of our love's lost flame.
I sit here all alone now,
Wondering why, when and how?
The joy we felt as we two—
Exchanged our vows and said "I do."
What happened to trust, respect and
loyalty?
Lost in contempt and battle for cheap
royalty.
Is this more important than the
friendship that we shared?
Or is it that you may never have
really cared.
The tragedy that happened between
us brings great sorrow;
I only hope that for us, it will heal
with each tomorrow.
In my life you'll always hold a
special part;
And know that I loved you with all
my heart.
I've written this to you, for as our life
together ends;
I hope we both can forgive each
other, and still be friends.

Stephen Markel
PATTADAKAL

*Dedicated to the little girl who
touched my heart at the temple site of
Pattadakal in India*

blind beauties begging
amidst the eroded dreams of kings
stone glories besieged
by eternal helpless wails

the tin cups of the innocent
strike the new world's walls
and the new lords turn away
shamed by their empty hands

their calloused eyes scarred by guilt
sense the approaching darkness
when they too must beg forgiveness
for the sins of ego's madness

Nancy C O'Leary
ELVIS, YOU DIDN'T FAIL

*To Elvis "Be Still and Know That I
Am God" Rest In Peace*

Where are you God?
What am I to do?
Where is the promise I made in my
youth?
I feel so alone, as I reach out to you;
The one song, my own song, seems
long overdue.

I don't preach as I've sometimes felt
was your call,
But I've felt and fulfilled the
need of the all.
I've sung whenever I was asked to
perform;
I've felt good vibrations from
the rich and the poor.
I've been myself right to the end,
showing the world the God from
within.
The glorious feeling that makes you
alive
Every part of me reached . . .
. . . some laughed and some cried.
To the young I brought out their
desire to say;
I am what I am . . . full of love,
full of play.
To others, I've felt I answered a
prayer;
From the words of my songs . . .
they felt someone cared.
I'm compelled and committed to
give service to those,
Who wait in long lines for the
start of my show.

Perhaps you could answer . . .
somehow let me know
I've not let you down . . . Give
me peace when I go.

"Elvis, the answer has come to you
many times,
I'm amazed that the critics have
all been so blind.

You've made people laugh, you've
made people cry;
You have given to those who
would have otherwise died.
You took the gift that I gave you at
birth,
Unknowingly showing a heaven
on earth.
You made such things happen that
could only be done;
When you feel in your heart the
strength of the sun.

There are those in this life that only
believe
That you preach what it is . . .
the world is to be.
You must know that the preaching
never gets done;
It's the ones who believe . . . .
and the ones who become.

So Elvis remember all the people
you reached;
Was because that you loved . . .
and not that you preached.
When you reached all those people
out there
And vibrations of love filled the
air . . .
I was there in each one, and I thank
you my son . . .
You had touched me . . . .so
unaware.
Remember another . . . two thousand
years ago
Who lived here on earth so
others would know.
He too cried out . . . and today
everyone knows;
He was the love that all had
opposed.
Rest in peace as the love you gave
lives on . . .
In each one that you touched . . .
with your life
. . . with your song.
You gave courage to all to be what
they are
The truth . . . that "I AM" within
. . . so close . . . not afar.

LDJohnson
DREAMLIGHT

*To my daughter Melissa, my only
true light.*

When I was young and nights were
slow,
I'd catch fireflies and watch them
glow;

The light they shed, so small, so
bright,
My youth it flashed on wings of
night:

I think of their light when I am sad,
And how when I held them, the
feelings I had:

The nights still come, but the
fireflies don't
I keep waiting and hoping, but I
know they won't;

They flew with my dreams to places
afar,
For some other child to place in a jar;

Keep them my child, as safe as can
be
Their light is my spirit, the essence
of me;

The older I get, the dimmer their
light,
The fireflies are gone, forever from
my sight.

Mike Ursu
CUTS

Cut wide, cut deep.
Into the rug will seep
my blood.
No hope, regrets.
I can't ever forget
the pain.
Life ebbs away.
Death has become my way
to peace.
Alcohol haze
numbing my last few days.
Limbo.

Nonentity
is my reality.
I've failed.
I nonexist.
I've slit open my wrists
and died.

Theresa Wyrauch
UNKNOWN TITLE

He is in the shadows of my mind
and his love I seek to find.
Maybe someday we will meet
I will someday feel his heart beat.

He is in the visions that I see,
but these visions aren't quite clear to me,
I see his name lite up in the sky,
where is this man, where is this guy

Sometimes I can feel the touch of his hand
this feeling I wish I could understand.

Sometimes it feels like he is very close to me,
but when I go to look he's something I can not see,

To who this man is, or if he even exists is a mystery.

Bernard M Patten

Bernard M Patten
EVENTS OFTEN NOT NOTED

Tense but armed were we
And tired too—our first time
The real thing at night

The hardness of the weapon
Somewhat assured us as we
Awaited contact with the enemy.

A flash a noise a pain
A kind of heat inside my brain
A dull groan as I let go.

Jesus! I didn't even get
My weapon up; it fired itself,
And I died a little death.

It wasn't like the comics said:
It is dead
I am dead
We are dead.

Azizi Jones
EGYPT

This poem is dedicated to my dearest Aunt Diane Kellough

Egypt, the land of the pharaohs;
And of the queens
A place of freedom, where all Blacks and Whites ran free.
A place of no racism nor wars.
The country of confidence, choice and self-esteem
The country of riches not only of gold and diamonds;
But also in love, close families, and happiness.
A land of beauty, no hatred nor disease.
Where help is given in someone's time of need
Where they preach and spread the word of the Lord;
For the good of his name and what it means.
Where all creatures of any sort or size may roam free.
No worry of dying, before the age of 103
This place I speak of is not of this time.
This place is of all, kind and sweet.
Hopefully in this place we shall someday meet.

Darleene Cauldwell
SINCE THE GOOD LORD DECIDED

Since the good Lord decided
to take you away
I miss you more now
than I did yesterday

At the head of the table
where you always said grace
the chair is now empty
I search for your face

I look around
at your favorite chair
my eyes become misty
'cause nobody's there

In the still of the evening
I whisper your name
Oh, how I miss you
nothing's the same

Deborah Bertera
TEDDY BEAR RELIEF

With the rain beating against my window,
With the thunder rumbling in the night,
I think about my childhood fears.
When the thunder shook the house,
I reached for my teddy bear,
Hoping for some relief.
I took teddy with me,
And together we would hide,
Until the storm passed.
Now that I am older,
I no longer need relief.
But I hold on to teddy anyway,
Just to make him feel wanted again.

Peggy Allison
MY FLAG

This was the poem that I had written when I was in the seventh grade. It was put in the school paper that year. Oh, yes we had only 48 stars back then .

The stars
In the flag
Are like Soldiers
In even rows they stand.

And the stripes
Are the roads
They will travel
To every distant land.

The stars
Will march
Around the world
To see the Victory through.

But the stripes
Will lead them
Home again
Back to the fields of blue.

Edith Altazin
MY SISTER

To my sister—"Jane Harriet Smith," deceased—We called her "Harree"

On a cold January Day they came and took her away.
Many mournful cries were heard night and day.
Her talented hands were cold, her beautiful voice was gone.
"God" must have needed her for a song.
When she walked her stately stature stood high.
Now she has a mansion in the sky.
Days, weeks, months have passed and now a year.
In the darkest hours of the night I can hear
A voice very far away, I sit up and say
"I wonder if that song is for me because I
Know that is My Sister Harree."

Kenneth Vires
GIFTS FROM GOD

To my granddaughter 'Jennifer McCumber,' with all the love an angel deserves

The Lord gave us the winds
That blow across the lands
Bringing in the seasons in their time
He gave us the silent majestic mountains
And the deserts singing sands
He gave the world its flowers
Of purples, reds and gold
He gave us the silver moon
To control the ebb and neap tide flow
He gave us the stars at night
And oceans blue and deep
He gave us canyons steep and bright
And moonbeams to help us sleep
But the most precious gift of all
Is the angel he gave to me
I hold her in my heart
Her name is—
Jennie

Garnet Lewis
LADY

To Norma, Jo, T.J., Kitty and Sue and all the inspirational women in my life

I've seen you from a distance
and watched you from afar
I've thought about your gentle touch
and wondered who you are
Your manner seems a loving one
it radiates and beams
Your heart's not open just to some
but all and everything
You love your life you love your man
Your kids and all their dreams
Lady you're an angel
in a heaven without wings

Jessie Eldora
STAN(D) ALONE

To my Stan in Brazil S.A.—1986.

Would you come to me . . .
If I lived in an Igloo
Says this girl from the North

I live where there is only a little snow,
Where the ducks remain . . .
To swim in the cold water streams . . . in the South

How can I compare
To the brighter skies,
Which look down to the tropical trees . . .

I can sleep on a pillow, all filled with down,
And sit by a warm fire crackling, in a room
I could have money to burn . . .

But, I can't be completely content . . .
Because I am all alone
I need to give, and share

Would you come to me,
In an icy Igloo, made for two
Or Stan(d) alone in the sun.

Sharon Kerr
WHY

To My Beautiful Daughter Stacy. God's "Gift of Love" To Me.

Why is the sky so blue?
Why am I called me?
Why does a cow say moo?
Why does C come before D?
Why is the sky so high?
Why do bees sting?
Why do birds fly?
Why do birds sing?
When I grow to be so high
I'll know all the answers
To the questions why.

Caprice C Freeman
GETTING IN TOUCH

Last night, while sipping
from our red wined
conversation,
you spilled laughter in my lap;
leaving me to change into
something
more serious.

Later you stood, (sporting
a tailored two-liner)
promising popcorn dreams while
picking Sunday picnics from
your teeth.

On your way out, I watched
as you brushed stray crumbs of
pleasure
from your lapel;
choking on sin and
tripping on
my blackness.

James P Beno

James P Beno
WHEN I SEE HER

To all those I've loved within my heart, and those who seek the truth.

Oh, the weight of my leaden heart,
It pangs, it stings, and rips apart.
My soul is tortured and torn asunder.
My head rings loud with vicious thunder.

"Oh, why me, oh why . . . oh why"
My lungs scream out their desperate

cry,
"Oh why, of all, am I the one,"
"Forbidden to gaze into her splendid sun."

I see her, yes, but she doesn't see me;
She wanders off . . . alive and free.
I'm trapped here now, alone in this prison,
A cumbersome shell, restricted to reason.

Her eyes, my God, I've never seen,
Two gems of light with such a gleam.
Her lips stretched out in a naked smile,
Capturing my gaze . . . just for awhile.

"How can you," you say, "dwell in such mire,"
"While beholding such beauty, laughter and fire?"
My answer is simple; short but complete,
For I'm on a step, one below her feet.

No matter what I say, or see, or do,
On and on, 'til my death is due,
Our hearts will not meet, except in my dreams,
Where reason is lost, and the spirit sings.

Sydney Lujan
THE FIX

To Rachel Light (1982-1989). Reaffirming hope with each drop of rain and every ray of sunshine.

Parched deer trails meander dizzily.
Cumulus gatherings, Cirrus scatterings.
Videodrome in the sky.
Loose your magic, rejoice in the beloved.
Hold to this and bask in the undoing.
Furrow the valley, hill, and mound.
Fear not refusal or restraint.
Good this is. Hold forth with
Curious tendrils of faith and justice.
Unbridled freedom races across the sky,
Now perhaps to temper.
Soft be the granite akin to fate.
Here renewed, here reborn.

Susan C Rayburn
DREARY LANE

To the three people who have given me love and support: my parents and my husband.

---

i followed the dirt road of misery
not sure of where it would take me
it ran into the highway of misfortune
i thought i had turned onto the interstate of relief
what a mistaken belief!
miles of agony stretched out before me
hours and hours of useless worrying lay ahead
my eyes were getting red!
i flew onto the exit at full speed
i had lost my mind
indeed!
i saw a mud splattered sign
it showed hope ave. to the left
and dreary lane to the right
my eyes were filled with tears
i could not see
i ended up on dreary lane
but there still is hope!

Kristin Hunt
THE LOVE THAT I FEEL

To my father, whom I love dearly!

The love that I feel
For you inside
Is much too great
For me to hide
And to leave you now
Does hurt me so
It hurts my heart
As it has before
Will you think of me often
As I'll do with you
Will your heart feel complete
Or feel broken in two
Will you always remember
The love and the care
The joy and the happiness
We together have shared
For my Father you are
And forever will be
And my love is the one thing
You will always receive

Glen F Lomax
ME AND MY SHADOW

To my wife Karen, my son Malik and my daughter Kim, continue to inspire me to go for the gold.

You've stood by me throughout all these years
We've walked many a road together
In times of loneliness and despair
you were
always near
Together we've held our heads
Many times we've shared quiet moments
You've helped me create
We share the same joys and disappointments
Our hearts feel the same pain
As a friend you have "literally stood behind me"
When the morning draws near you rise with me
and when the day draws to close you lay down beside me . . .

Lydia Lewis
NEVER SAY GOODBYE

This is dedicated to my parents, Barbara and Rob Whitacre, my wonderful little brother Robbie, and to that special someone who is so very dear to me, Raymond Long . . . . I Love You All!!

When you looked at me the way you did last night,
something told me you truly cared,
Not by the way you said I love you,
while in my eyes you stared . . .

You always seem to amaze me,
in the many sweet things you do,
Forgetting all of my horrible past,
and all the misery I put you through . . .

Going through your old letters yesterday,
made me look forward to tomorrow,
No more unpleasant thoughts,
no more hurt or sorrow . . .

Today will bring the things from yesterday,
we so carelessly left behind,
Not taking the time to listen,
how could that slip my mind? . . .

The daisies will bloom in the early morn,
and frost will hit in the fall,
The roses you gave me have all died,
though I've kept them one and all . . .

We'll both grow old together,
until the day we die,
Just as long as you stick close beside me,
and "Never Say Goodbye."

I'm Eternally Yours,
Lydia Lewis

Trudie J Kuyper
WAITING

Dedicated to My Husband Bruce Who Encouraged Me and Gave Me Loving Inspiration.

Thoughts and memories, of long ago,
Pleasures and fantasies are foretold;
Dreams and hopes, all to despair . . .
But, never a heart to repair.

Dreams, on a starry moonlite night . . .
Of a loved one to comfort and hold you tight;
To ease away the feelings of pain . . .
That anguish your heart, yet once again.

Never, it seems, will it leave;
But, sadness and tears, only to grieve,
Slowly the pain will disappear . . .
When the awaited One—will appear.

Of wings and flight, through the air,
Giving a feeling of being there;
Soaring so high above the sky—
Watching your fantasies floating by.

Tender moments—that can only be seen,
Remembering once as they had been;
Losing a love; once, was yours alone . . .
Now—surrendering your heart—to another throne!

Alison De Gregorio
BLACK DEATH

Dedicated to Danielle and Melissa—for always being there.

He came quietly in shadow, cooling and possessing the air,
He was subtle, yet commanding, in an instant I sensed he was there,
His thoughts blackened mine and his soul gave off a haunting fire,
In his mind I was condemned, a blasphemer and a liar,
He was to scourge me with his wickedness and corrupt my innermind,
He had a power I could not subdue, a force I could not bind,
I turned pale and quivered when I met his sinister grey eye,
Mirrors made of ice reflecting a thousand ways to die,
They stripped me of my confidence and stole all the strength I had left,
I was now a cowardly target awaiting his faces of death,
He muttered ominous words of sorcery, chanting to seal my tomb,
Demons counting the sand grains that fell from my hour-glass of doom,
Lightning struck and thunder rose, he was coming to secure my fate.
At his feet I begged with naivete, he scorned me the bearer of hate,
Mountains crumbled seas grew angry, in an instant this all would end,
The death of a youth too innocent to pass, a wrong no one could mend,
He bellowed and roared to the sun with a rage only he could tame,
It burned out all my fire and weakened my courage of flame,
My soul was tortured and my body scourged with a terrifying, blinding light,
His boisterous howl and illumination were quickened to the silence of night
Content in his doing and satisfied with his work he laid tranquility amongst the air,
Mysteriously he faded into the night to return as king of his lair.

Bette Gillard

Bette Gillard
WHAT IS LOVE?
To my girls
What is love Mama?
Love is V-8 Juice and raisin bread, feeling alive inside, instead of dead! What is love? And love's description? It's in every love song ever written! It is the strongest electrical current known to man, it can take you from the deepest depth of the ocean floor, straight to a star and heaven's door, with just one look into his eyes!! Love is popcorn poppin' in your head, feeling his arms around you when you're in bed. Pure true love may come only once in a lifetime, but when it does, it's as pure as looking into the eyes of Jesus! When two people are truly in love, you can spot it in one second, it's like a crystal or a diamond in your eyes' reflection. Love is feeling full inside even when you are hungry! Love is trusting, and knowing, he is with you even when you are apart. Love is two hearts beating as one. Love is like an hour glass you must never forget to turn

over lest one side becomes empty. You must never store it in the attic, for it will become covered in dust, and you may never find it or see thru it again! And it should be out there for all the world to see and measure time by. Love is free, there's not enough money in the whole world that could ever buy it, it's the only thing you ever need to make you happy. But always share a portion of it with others. Give a gift of love to someone each day, let them look into your eyes or show it in your smile. God is love, and His Spirit lives within your heart. You will always see it in little children, if you take the time to look there. Love never ends it will take you straight thru into eternity if it's pure and true. I think that is why God wanted us to marry, 'cause he didn't have enough angels to go around! Love is building, and growing together, each toward one common goal. Letting our light shine together, as a beacon for all the world to see. We must never cast our pearls before the swine but among them we must sparkle as diamonds, so they will know we are from God. We are all liars murderers adulterers and thieves guilty of all sins, and only thru God's Son, are we redeemed, so let your light and love shine thru, that's what love is all about.
But always be sure not to give it all away lest you become empty like the hour glass! ! God is love thru Jesus and the Holy Spirit lets our light shine thru! !
I know you know all this! !
I Love you! !
Mom

Levann M Thompson
TEARS
Tears that fall like drops of rain,
A sad, sad heart so full of shame.
The cause so simple to explain,
As greed and crime and avarice,
So too is poverty, idolatry and child abuse.
But most of all the reason why,
A broken heart and eyes that cry,
Is the indifference that I see,
In both my fellowman and me.
I pray that God will raise me up,
Above myself and all that stuff.
Then I will be what God intends of me,
So I can reach out to someone else,
And help them to a better self.

W F Van Rheen
I WILL NOT LET YOU GO

This poem is dedicated to Evelyn, my lovely wife of fifty years.

I will not let you go,
If the earth tilts again on its axis,
And time should become too slow.
Even if I.R.S. should collect no taxes,
I would not let you go.

I will not let you go,
If the sun fails to give its light,
And all the trees refuse to grow,
And darkness surrounds you in the night,
I could not let you go.

I will not let you go,
If the moon falls from the sky,
My love for you, you surely know.
It's all true, I will not deny,
I can never let you go.
I will not let you go,
If the stars forget their orbit,
And though they should not shine below.
With the wealth of the world you can bet,
I will not let you go.

I will not let you go,
If all the galaxies become confused,
And the planets know not where to go.
The people of the earth are amazed,
I still would not let you go.

Evelyn Van Rheen
FIFTY YEARS WITH YOU

In dedication to Willard, my loving husband, of fifty years.

Fifty years ago I could not foresee,
How my life with you would be.

In prosperity and adversity, joy and sorrow,
From your strength I could always borrow.

Through your courage, inspiration, purpose and will,
Our hopes, aspirations and dreams were fulfilled.

In sickness and health you were there,
Love and care you did not spare.

At times of disagreement, we could compromise,
Our love survived, which was no surprise.

A life not built on love alone,
Mutual trust and respect set the tone.

Where faith and honor does not abound,
A bond like this cannot be found.

Mary Schieffer
SUNSHINE

This poem is dedicated to Danny, whom I love, the one who makes the sun shine.

The Sunshine to him
Is not from the sky

The Sunshine he knows
Is me, myself, and I

He gave me that name
You may ask me, why

I brightened his days
All the days that went by

So now when you see me
Say Sunshine, Say Hi

For that is my name now
Until the day I die

Darlene Baxa Lnenicka
GRADUATION DAY

This poem is dedicated to Dawn Lnenicka. Our beloved Granddaughter on her Graduation Day.

On this Graduation day, my emotions are torn.
My mind goes back to the day you were born.
When the phone call came, to Hospital I must go.
The anticipation was unbearable, I want you to know.
Finally, the nurse announced, it is a girl!
I had now become a Grandmother, my mind was in a whirl.
Oh, how the many years have now passed.
Times, I thought for sure would always last.
Of all the quiet times, and the fun we had.
Also the long talks, that made me oh, so glad.
A beautiful young lady, you have now become.
And all the grade A's you have received, have been quite a sum.
This now is your Graduation day, but it is upon you,
Your future does lay.
As your Grandmother I pray, that whatever you do,
You will remember your Creator, and keep his promises in view.

C Dale Janney
MY FRIEND
My Friend, newly a mother.
The child deprived of good health
lies in her crib, silent,
so ill she does not bother
to cry—Is it near, this thing death?

My Friend, sitting close, in her chair
shoulders stooped, head bowed.
Dejected, forlorn, or a word of pray?
Silent, as if there is not allowed
even a whisper, as she waits.

My Friend, who wonders—Why
this bereavement came to be,
remembers hearing long ago
someone saying "Lord, Why me?"
and understands their agony.

My Friend's husband, her mate
enters the room. Tearfully,
tenderly touches her stooped
shoulder and joins
her in the wait.

Darren Corey
VERS LIBRE

Dedicated to a lost love and a discovered desire.

There are whispers in these halls
Of love gone pale.
Has-been laughter, scattered
And stark,
Weaving through the night,
Lingering
In a gasp.
You, the
Self-inflicted fantasy
Whose summoned nerve
Pulses
In that just-so smile,
You carry and sow
The seeds of our love
In this misty,
Blue dawn.
I, in red darkness
Of dusk,
Will reap one tear-drop
At a time.

Jo Ann Rice
MOM'S OLD HOUSE
We took a trip down Memory Lane, renewing with the past,
To take a look at Mom's old house, we should have driven fast.

New siding, windows and new doors, the porch enclosed,
They fixed the floors!

The grapes are gone and the apples to stew, the pump out back
And the cistern too!

Where is the garage that stood out back,
The rabbit hutch and the chicken shack?

The wash house so cool and full of mystery,
No longer stands there, it's now part of history.

A shiny new building stands out there,
With a second floor and an outside stair.

The only things we found that day, to match our memories,
Were four old steps that seemed to say, "You can't change hard old <u>me</u>!"

I think perhaps that good, old house is hiding there inside,
Just waiting, like a special gift, for someone to pull the ties.

From a photo I took that day, one thing jumped out to me . . . . along one side of Mom's front yard, still grow some peonies.

I'd like to think they're some of hers, she planted so long ago,
Left there to bloom and spread sweet scent, just for <u>us</u> to know.

Renee L Schunk
TO GIVE IT YOUR ALL
Go after your dreams
Don't ever stop.
Keep on reaching
To the top!

Don't be afraid
Of a little rejection
<u>You</u> know you're going
In the right direction.

Think positive,
All of the time.
But don't let your dreams
Get way out of line.

Then for the times
When you fail or fall,
At least <u>you</u> will know,
That you gave it your all!

Robert A Pedro

Robert A Pedro
NURSES

Dedicated to my <u>Mother</u>, who was a nurse and all the <u>NURSES</u> of the world. Especially to the nurses of 8NA, Hartford Hospital, Hartford, CT.

Here's to the NURSES, those angels in white,
Who try their best to dispel all our fright.
While in the hospital, we have not chosen to stay,
They try to comfort us, from day unto day.
They feed us and bathe us and ease all our pain
While constantly listening to a moaning refrain.

They're cursed at and spit on, and damned every day,
While this is all done and not only for pay.
Because they're a rare breed, likened unto no other,
And often as not, act just like your mother
To pamper and coddle and soothe and restrain
And mostly to see that you have limited pain.

A SPECIAL group, a RARE group, a class all their own
They treat you and comfort you, while you're away from home.
With sincerity, with tenderness, with kindness and devotion
Their smiles and soft words, soothe just like a lotion.
God must have known, when he created from the start,
That to be a good NURSE was a special lot.

When the gates of Heaven open, and you escape Satan's curse
The one who will greet you, will probably be a NURSE.

Ann I Bushaw
COME TO ME MY LOVE

Come to me like a bird on high
Am longing for your loving voice why?
So I can whisper sweet nothings as you sigh
Never leave me for another as I would die
When we are together the time goes by
So linger awhile as I hold you nigh
Your eyes are as blue as the sky
Your hair is golden and soft as a lullaby
You smile in a way that is so shy
Your beauty is beyond anything one can buy
Please never say that you must bid me goodbye.

Karen L Leidy
SUICIDE CONTEMPLATED

To John M. who showed me the meaning of these words.

In the circle of the light
I go round and round
There is no sound, no substance, only a void

A void in my soul, my heart, in my being
Empty, strewn upon the sand of life
without a tool or means of survival
Struggling, grasping for the artifact
that will show me the light
The light, the circle, the cycle of confusion
Reaching out, pulling back, grasping, clinging, losing reality, losing control, falling, bouncing, striking, all for a futile struggle
Searching, ever searching, asking the mute source
Blinded, deafened, and muted
Wondering why, how and where

No one knows
No one cares
All have forgotten how to feel

I feel, I hurt, I melt like a forgotten candle
dripping wax of my soul onto the candle stick of reality

As I near the destruction of my soul, the state of mindless oblivion they call insanity
I watch with eyes of light, circles of light, going round and round, searing the darkness of the universe and ending the cycle of confusion we call life

Janice L Fuller
MISSING YOU

To my family (Kendel + Tompkins), (Fuller + Hall)

My joy comes from your touch.
Your kisses stay deep in my lips, and in my cheeks.
I love your warm soft body against mine.
You have brought laughter to my frowning face.
Tears have come to my eyes because of your good-bye's.
I think of you while you are gone.
I sit by the phone waiting for a call by you.
I lay in bed thinking of the fun we have had the night before.
I look at your picture wishing you were here.
I sit by you looking at your smiling face, touching your arms, your chest, your legs, and among other parts of you.
I just can't stop missing you.
While you're gone.
I love you and i hope you love me as well.

Carol Eden Davis
THE PLEDGE

To Mark: I love you with all my heart

The saline mist caressed our skin
As we sat on the ocean's shore.
We cast our pain in the midnight wind
and our lives we began to explore.

As we talked, the clouds above swam past,
to unveil the glorious stars;
And to show us both that, at last
the love we crave could be ours.

A burden was lifted from me that day
and was replaced by great love for you;
Though life has sent us a separate way
My love has stayed there with you.

I will see you again someday soon
and when we wander to the ocean's edge
to sit beneath the midnight moon
I will make this solemn pledge:

If it is within God's holy plan
for us never again to part,
I will live my life for the wonderful man
Who holds the key to my heart.

Frederick W Kruse
O.W.L.

TO MY LOVING WIFE, LINDA Only With Love.

My patience is like the beauty of the Owl.
It's there for as long as you see the beauty.

He is a lot like me, sitting on a shelf or on your bed, he waits patiently. Knowing that one time you'll walk by, pick him up and hold him close. He knows you're affectionate and so do I. So as he waits for you so must I.

He is always going to be there for you. Something, I won't ever be able to do. He would not complain about anything. But, as you know nor do I.

So as you snuggle up real close and you look into his eyes. Smile, I will be looking back with very little surprise. The times you say, "You don't need anyone, no encouragement, you can do it on your own." Quietly pick him up and hold him, he'll let you know you're not alone and someone does Love you.
O.W.L.

Kathryn S Chandler
LOVING YOU

With thanks to the One who's teaching me life's most difficult lesson, the real fruits of the Spirit: charity, joy, peace, longsuffering, gentleness, temperance, goodness, faith and meekness; so that one day my love shall become as genuine, and as perfect as His!

Many times my heart on wings of love has sung an endless song; and other times, it took trust and faith in God for my Love to remain strong.

Many times my heart was swelled with love—so much so, I thought that it might bust;
and other times, I faced Love's turmoils and turned to God to help me adjust.

Many times we've had tender caring moments, a moment so complete;
and other times we've quarrelled till forgiveness once again turned Love sweet.

Many times we were Love's full bloom—roses, rainbows, sunshine, and gaiety;
and other, testy times, it took a "very special Love"—a kind only God could give for you, to me.

Jean D Corcoran
BEAUTIFUL DREAM

Dedicated To My Loving Family In Indiana

I dreamed of a little house on a hill
Where the wind blew free while the night stood still
Surrounded by shimmering pines glistening with snow
Giant white peaks sheltering the valley below
Ice clad streams where the willows weep
Against the mountainside so very steep
Oh beautiful dream you haunted me day by day
For the land of my dreams so far away
Many years had passed when my dream came true
On top of a hill under a sky of blue
Our little home took shape that spring
It seemed all nature began to sing
Tall ponderosa surround that little home of mine
With air so fresh and fragrant with pine
Across the valley and beneath the mountain hue
A vast array of wild flowers kissed with dew
Miles; and miles of evergreens as far as I can see
An occasional glimpse of deer fleeting so gracefully
Each night I pray so gratefully
Thank you Lord for your most precious gift to me

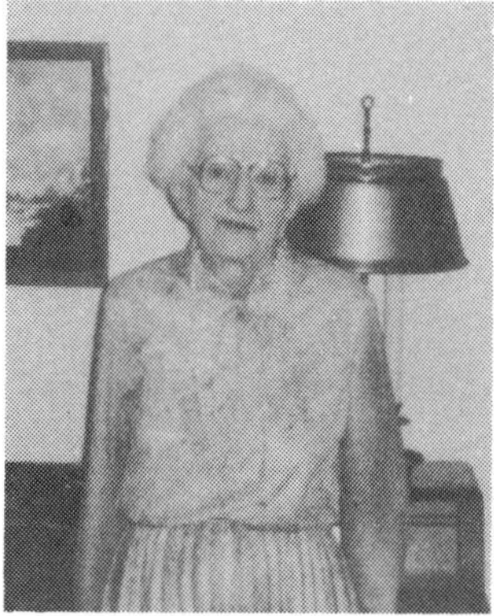

Frances Ferguson

Frances Ferguson
MINNESOTY

Yes, I am from Minnesoty,
this great land, of corn and beans.
Best state, in all our country.
I never spend beyond, my means.

A travel, trailer is my home.
Come on out, a voice did say.
I grabbed, my hat and hobbled out, alone.
Outside, were folks, from far away.

Days of fun and play have begun.
no blow, no everlasting, snow.
Desert breakfast, under rising sun.
then, to mountain climbing, we did go.

After many parties, I am taking my ease
but now, I wish, for a Minnesoty, breeze,
while, I rest, in my recliner chair,
among the stately, cactus trees.

So, back and forth, and to and fro.
greetings, Arizony! I'm here to stay!
Now 'tis fall, Arizony, here, I come!
I'm coming, soon, on the run!
Just to sit in the Arizony sun! !

Emily S Link
A CHRISTMAS POEM

Tis the season once again
of Peace on Earth, good will to men.
Deck the halls with boughs of holly,
Open presents and be jolly.
That is just a part of the season,
Now, let us think of the real reason.

It's the day, the baby Jesus was born
On a cold, dismal winter morn.
Grew up to be a man of truth,
Read your Bible—there's the proof.
He loved the people of the land:
Gentle mind—gentle hand.
It hurts to think of the life He gave,
So all us sinners could be saved.
We give our thanks to Him above
He taught us the true meaning of
love.

Charlene Schnizer
TO MY SON
You asked me "How long has it been
since I said I love you Mom?"
Well let me tell you son, it hasn't
been too long
You say "I love you," every day
You say it in so many different ways
When you sit beside me just to talk
Or when you ask me with you to
walk
A certain look or a special smile
I know the love is there all the while
And when you're grown and take a
wife
I know you'll be happy the rest of
your life
Because the love you have always
shown
Will spread to others when you're
grown.
I know son you love me
And I love you too, as you can see
Never lose the love within your heart
And happiness from you will never
depart.

I love you son.

Patricia Quinn Mozingo
THE SOUL OF MY SPIRIT
'The soul of my spirit,'
after my death.

Will ascend, to a new world,
and take a fresh breath.

Maria G Hepner
THE QUILTER'S GIFT
It is quilting day in Micro, North
Carolina.
There they practice an art,
Lost to their great nieces and grand
daughters.

They collected the scraps of my
everyday life,
And gave me a focus and pattern,
Through Grandma's Fan, Wedding
Ring, and Farmer's Wife.

Upon the quilter's large wooden
frame,
They tie down the patchwork,
That all my lost dreams became.

Cramping hands are guided by failing
vision.
Through the stitches of my Mother's
mothers,
I become all their hopes extension.

The result of all the fabric, thread
and fluff,
Is a gift of history, love and warmth,
To remind me of those who came
before,
The quilt is enough.

Michele K Knutt
THOSE WHO LEARN
Those who learn to live,
learn to love,
learn to fly high
like a dove.

Those who learn to love,
learn to cry,
learn to hurt
deep inside.

Those who learn to cry,
learn to hurt,
learn to feel low
as the dirt.

Those who learn to hurt,
learn to survive,
learn to start
again new lives.

Those who learn to survive,
learn to live,
learn to take love,
and learn to give.

Evelina W McCray
MUST WE ALWAYS WALK ALONE?
We're Strangers to love who
hear only the Shouts
from Robins, lions and roustabouts;
but we keep holding on to the
reins,
in search of a bulwark, to block the
darts from the veins.
Perhaps, beguiled by the Kitten,
still warm feelings come
although they be fleeting.
While the Horse who never lit a
pilot, still deserves our pity;
With sanity and vanity resting on
Jezebels,
And their strength to provide a
cleating.
Never will understand it all, being
kindred souls
Who Must Always Walk Alone.

Just poor prisoners with hearts
torn,
Left to mourn, all weary and forlorn.
Afraid to leave the cocoon to
extend our hands,
With dragons and scorpions waiting,
to put them in bands.
Never got the chance to know a
grandmother or even a
grandfather.
Having them taken before we were
born, somehow makes us feel
cheated;
that heartfelt love, we wish we'd
been meted.
But the knife that bruised life most of
all,
Was indifference from the two,
who never heard a call.
So we're just shattered souls, Who
Must Always Walk Alone.

Dorothy Brewster Grayson
TO LINDA AND CAROL
The uneven patter of little feet, and
cookie crumbs shared with me;
A jellied kiss from a rosy mouth,
and a sticky pat on my knee;
Two dimpled hands clasped tight in
mine as we explore the shops;
A kitchen spread with pots and
pans when toys were just a flop;
Sand box cookies and mud pies
proffered with my tea;
A wriggling body next to mine
when a nightmare came at
three;
Mother Goose read all over again
when two little girls relaxed;
"Pretender" telephone
conversations, and a cookie or
two for snacks;
Joyous dancing round and round
when music filled the air;
Jumping and tumbling all over
the bed till the springs would
creak, "Beware";
"Father We thank Thee" at each meal
when we held hands all around;
"Jesus Loves Me" in the
rockingchair when sleep or tears
trickled down.
How can I ever express the joy that
bubbles inside of me
When I remember the love and
the charm of two little girls so
wee.

Joseph W Shefchik

Joseph W Shefchik
SUNRISE

For that special person who's made my sunrises more worthwhile. A very dear friend, my mother Alyce J. Shefchik.

Wake up, it's the crack of dawn
There's a sparkling mist shining
across the lawn
Who put it there and why so much?
The whole world was sleeping, it had
not been touched.

Look at the trees as they ache in pain
From last night's frost and the
weight they've gained
Slowly these trees all start to smile
As the branches drop dew, it
disappears in awhile.

The soil is damp like it's been freshly
stained
Just Mother Nature's way of a light
gentle rain
The earth lightens, then begins to
harden
Now it's time for mankind to water
God's garden.

Breathing in deep, the air smells so
clean
Yet by day's end it can almost be
seen
These overnight mysteries may be
seen by almost anyone's eyes
But only if awake for an early
sunrise.

Stephen L Walls
SEASONS OF LEAVES

To Jimmie, because you loved to play among them.

Leaves bask in the spring,
when they're all young and new,
drinking in the sunshine,
that melts the morning dew.

Summer is the time,
they turn a shiny dark green,
and flutter as the wind,
passes through them unseen.

After the long lazy summer,
they change the look of a town,
with their beautiful colors of autumn,
which on all of them abound.

Then on into winter,
now they lay low,
in cozy hibernation,
under blankets of snow.

Finally new buds are born,
where the old ones began,
to start the cycle of seasons,
all over again.

Lisa Dutra
THE BLUE ROSE
An azure rose lying on the table
It is my gift for you, my love, my
dear,
Take it, before the colors grow
sable—
But your eyes are blind even though
it's near.
Can't you see the rose, beautiful and
sad?
The petals glow blue, softly
glistening
With memories I'm not supposed to
have;
The green stem is full of thorns,
shimmering
With all the reasons not to take the
rose;
The leaves are emerald, and delicate
With possibilities that could not
grow;
But the pink bud's dewdropped, and
seems starlit
With all the potentials for my future;
This bud will bloom a new love to
nurture.

Gregory Newton
MY NEW ROOMATE
Your bodily remains swollen
with preservatives
set sail across the
blue palms of the mediterranean
sea from poland

In cargo labeled el loco
bobbing like a fat man
with a slow limp on surf
before anchoring plumb weight
near deaths edge a watery
island off the coast of monaco
near me
where bronco buff
the yellowing wind had a
familiar way of panting its
stewy breath hot having discovered
your body amoungst the aspens

Scattering finger nails and
eye pits into the islands decadent
bone forest one dead knot
a wet bay of tea grit
tiny red ants are
electric ambers of light after
dusk here some of which is
carried in strange lanterns
by natives who welcome you
with stick hands and serenade
you with chants
hola mi amigo hola bruised

banana rutabaga mango sun
welcome to the watery lands

Brian Straton-Ferrier
JOSEPHINE

I fear my words betray me
That tell you kindly lies
As you, who are sad, survey me
With your soft, dark, serious eyes.

I smile to reassure you
And my levelled look implies
Only that I admire you
To your dark, discerning eyes.

For I think it would only move you
To pity, or pained surprise,
That I, who am lonely, love you
And your darkling, delicate eyes

Connie Struck
GRANDPA'S EYES

The doorway to the past
was held in Grandpa's eyes,
These windows of human flesh
were made to be wise.

Through this doorway
flowed the pictures of life,
With razor sharp accuracy
like that of a knife.

As time passed by
and Grandpa grew older,
The windows of life
began to cloud over.

Still in his mind
were visions he once saw,
He told us his stories
and we listened in Awe.

The memories in my mind
I know will always last,
Because of Grandpa's eyes
which were windows to the past.

Mona F Blandford
HANDICAPPED

The blinded one, though he cannot see
Would know me far better than you know me.
His eyes can't see the false face shown
To the world to hide the fear of weakness, known
To bring the pleasure my enemies would find
In knowing that I am troubled in heart and mind.
For he hears the pain with which I am indwelt
and senses the agony that I have felt.
His ears hear words that remain unspoken
Words that whisper of a heart so broken.
As to who is handicapped, it is not he,
It is I, handicapped because I only see.
Until I relate to others and their sorrows ascertain
It would be better to seal my eyes and only hearing
Then be blessed to be able to truly see again.

Ken Jones
HALLOWEEN CAME IN JUNE

My spine felt a chill as I walked in my room
And there in the dark stood a witch and a broom.
I asked her straight out "What are you doing here?"
She said "Just shut up and get me a beer.
My broom is broke down, so repair it, alright?
And do a good job or I may spend the night."
Now she was as ugly as five kinds of hell.
I'd rather be locked up with Satan in jail.
Have her spend the night, well I'm not a fool.
I hate to fix brooms, but I ran for my tools.
I whispered these words as she flew on her way.
I know you're not real, but please go, and please stay.

Ibrahim A Jubaira

Ibrahim A Jubaira
SHADOWS

For Princess Jubaira Shariful Hashim, my beloved Mother.

A green leaf
Casts a pattern of black
Against the wall:
Nature confirms this universal truth:
In the presence of light
Color schemes are a lie.

Shadows solve universal inequalities:
Inequalities are equal:
Denial of facts
Creates not St. Peters
But dismembers Lucifers.

Man continues the argument against Man,
Race wages war against another race:
Man, preaching peace, becomes inimical
With color theologies through a miniature prism:

White and black can't draw a dividing line
Between clowns and emperors;
Nor can it isolate lowly beggars from kings:
Both cast dark shadows in the sun.

Linda D Parker
TOMORROW'S PROMISES

To create, we must love. I dedicate this to those I love as they gave me the inspiration to share my experience and feeling.

I have to be careful, lest I fall
To not be so proud, or a know-it-all.
How quickly I was brought to my knees
Discovered the world is a dangerous disease
I have to develop resistance in the fight
Know when it's safe or when to take flight
The pain of defeat is so hard to bear
The guilt drags you down into a deadly snare.
I can't give up because I may fail
Tomorrow will bring a more promising tale.

Cathy Griffith
MY MOTHER

To my loving, caring Mother, Ada Marie Ostgaard, I dedicate this poem

My mother is the woman
Whose love has always shown,
I wish only to become more like her,
now that I am grown.

For she is the one, who has
given me a new start. All because
her patience and values were bred in
my heart.

Her wisdom and her beauty forever
they will last as she gives you hope
for the future and yet forgives the
past.

Through all these years, she
has become my best friend, the
love we now share will have
no end . . .

Her love and her prayers have
always kept us safe, from her
tender caring heart, there is no
escape.

She has tried and succeeded to be
a rock for our salvation, though
it hasn't been easy, to understand
our generation.

As mother and grandmother, on
earth there could be no finer,
for she has always had love as
her soul's inner liner.

Mother, you have raised us
all so well, so carefully, it's
your time now to sit and
watch us at life so joyfully

Maurece W Lloyd
THOUGHTS BY THE FIRE

In loving memory of my dear mother, Belle Tippett Wilson, who made these moments so precious and memorable.

Is there anything more welcome, on a chilly winter night,
Than a bid old-fashioned fireplace and the gaily dancing light
Of the happy open fire with its laughing tongues of red,
Before you say goodnight to friends and saunter off to bed?

Is there anything more comforting than the clean clear warmth you feel
When you throw another log on? When you hear the dry bark peel,
Can you ever really frankly say you've heard a nicer sound
Than the melody of crackling fire that fills the room around?

Is there one thing more enchanting than the dying embers there,
Fading, one by one, in silence? You then rise from your chair
And bid goodnight to loved ones and the flickering dying fire.
You wish you could take it with you.
Oh, what a great desire!

If you've never sat upon a hearth by a great big open fire,
If you've never felt that "certain" warmth, and watched the embers die,
In sympathy I say to you, although it may seem rife,
If you have missed those little things, you've missed half of your life.

Shena L Jordan
YOUR FIRST BORN

Dedicated to my Mother and Father, (Carolyn & Conrad). I'm sorry for the trouble I put you through, so I write this poem to say how much I love you. With all my love, your first born, S H E N A.

He calms me down when I get mad.
He dries my tears when I am sad.
I hope this card will make him glad.
This section of love is for my Dad.

I knew this woman all my life,
She helps me when I get uptight.
She always buy me clothes and food,
She helps me when I'm in a bad mood.
She cares for me like no other.
This section of love is for my Mother.

The two of you love me and I know It's true,
Because of this I love you too.
You put me on Earth, you gave me this life,
Do something for me Dad and make my Mother your wife!

Love always and forever,
S H E N A

Judy Fitzpatrick
JULIE

To my beautiful daughter, Julie

Your hair and eyes are brown my dear
Your heart is pure as gold.
I'll love you as I love you now
Till both of us grow old.
A little girl, A big girl,
Soon you'll be a lady truly
But to me you'll always be
My own sweet loving Julie.

Derek Fenwick-Baily
HONEYSUCKLE DAYS

Dedicated to my Father who was accidentally electrocuted two weeks after this poem was written.

It's there along the alley fence,
a brilliant yellow vine so dense.
Whose sweet odor tells,
of long gone days and ice cream bells.
Set among the pine trees where,
it's scent drifts upward like a prayer.
Sweet days of calm, peace and rest,
pride of my dad, he was the best.
His hand in mine the world seemed massive,
to one so small, dads big hand passive.
Sweet scent bees hum and ravens glower,

remind me of times passing power.
I know I grow and now I'm older,
may youthful sunshine ne'er grow
colder.
Each sunset cannot glow the same,
Scent of honeysuckle remain.

Marion Courville
COMPETITION TO GROW

Dedicated to Flaming Rainbow University who strives to address higher education by offering a cross cultural sensitive curriculum related to this area.

Apples to apples and oranges to
oranges
Our educators say to compare
But when it comes to human beings
The same concern is not there.
So the only real competition
That is visible to me
Is competition with ones self
Ones own improvement to see.
So why are we taught to ignore
The most precious values we know
And compare human apples to
oranges
When we are forced to compete as
we grow.
Tall Billy is great, he is in basketball
Short computer tech Joe is thought
slow.
Our concern for games and
competition
Retards the basic values we know.
So let us compare all human apples
to apples
And oranges to oranges and grow
Let us never try to make winners,
losers
To enhance our own personal show.

Dean Coia

Dean Coia
LEAVES

to everybody

What separates the leaves that fly in
the air
and the ones who are caught
in a whirlwind on the ground?
Though I'm lonely—I'm not alone.

She sits in splendor almost a million
miles away
but here I peruse my mind
for no reason, no reason at all.
Today shouldn't be different—but it
is.

They walk and talk in pairs or
sometimes threes,
and I'm happy when a lone heart
scurries with head down and eyes
closed.
They shouldn't be different—but
they are.

There's one now with time I could
give,
but I feel her grasp a million miles
away
and her splendor and appeal is
stifling.
I'm not so lonely—I'm not so alone.

Darryl McLain
UNENDING FLIGHT

To Tina From Darryl caught up in the system

Like a bird on an unending flight my thoughts of you, running deep into the night. Loving you more than all the blue skies, the loneliness bringing a tear to my eye.

In the morning waking to find us apart, longing for freedom to get a new start. Struggling through the days, just thinking of you, painfully, unknowing, just what to do.

Locked in a world, where nothing seems fair, surrounded by people who just don't care. Although I manage, from day to day, oh how I long for another way.

And when it seems that no one is there, I see your smile, and how much you care. I think of today, but dream of tomorrow, when I will be free from all this sorrow.

Nothing but four walls, a window and a door, thinking of all I had before, but no matter how long I must endure, theres one thing I'll always be sure . . . that soon I will end this saddening strife, and I'll love you forever, the rest of my life.

Shawn E Baggett
LOVING HER

For inspiring and loving me I dedicate "Loving Her" to my wife and best friend—Darlene Baggett

I am a sailor, for this is true.
To be a sailor, I gave up my rights
loving you.

My love is my country, this sad but
true.
I have no time for myself, only for
her and her demands, to protect her
night and day,
keeping bad people from taking her
away.
Lonely days and painstaking nights
has given this sailor the blues.
I want and need a real woman just
like you, who wants to love me too.
Hours and hours sitting out at sea.
Wishing and dreaming you were
here with me.
Weeks turn into months, months turn
into years.
It's no wonder, my pillow is made of
tears.

Even though I'm never free, to be
home alone with thee, always
remember these words I say, I do
love you honey, more than ever, but
I have to protect our home and land,
for this will feel like forever . . .

Down deep in my heart, I am afraid
and blue.
This sailor who loves his country
feels as though he may lose
you . . . !

Frank Davis
GRANDPA'S MILL

To Grandpa Tate and to my mother who spent many of her childhood hours playing around the old mill.

I was just a little fellow
When first I hauled the corn
To Grandpa's grist mill,
Built before I was born.

When Grandpa saw me
Coming down the road,
He hollered out the window
"Boy, you're carrying a mighty big
load."

He helped me through the doorway
And made me stay awhile,
Saying, "Boy, you're gonna need a
lot of resting
If you're to walk life's weary mile."

That was only the beginning
Of my days at his mill.
He passed on to me all he knew
But his shoes were hard to fill.

The water's no longer falling,
The stones no longer grind,
But the old mill is still turning
If only in my mind.

Joan E Hill
GIVE ME . . .

To all the special entities that have entered my life and brought love and happy smiles . . .

Give me something I can use
That'll take me though the day,
Lift my heart and make me sing,
And give my step a bit of sashay.

Give me something I can give
To someone else who needs a lift
To encourage their mood to alter
From down to an upward shift.

Give me something worthwhile,
Something money can't buy.
It can't be found in any store,
And would make my spirit fly.

Give me something you'll never
miss,
You'd even give it to a wee child.
To me it would mean so much . . .
All I want . . . is a smile . . .

Erin Duenes
THE ACCIDENT

I dedicate this poem to my Dad and Mom who first noticed my writing, my sister Meg—my number one fan, and to Chris and Jenn—my friends who first inspired me.

Awakened once in the middle of the
night
Outside there was an awful sight
Tires screeched loudly from that car
You wonder about the people, who
they are
In every direction from the car glass
flew
You're lucky this time it wasn't you
The scream of a lady, the cry of a
man
And on the scene was found a beer
can.
No one to talk, no one to tell
Why their last moments felt like Hell
No more partying no more fun, This
time it was overdone
You look upon the bodies of the lady
and the man
And stumble over another beer can.

Kathy Zimmerman Gisi
FIRST STEPS

To my children, Greg, Mark and Amy, whose "first steps" through life it has been my privilege to guide.

You stand poised,
Touching the door jam.
I offer you my hand.

You protest,
Wave me away,
Affirm your need to try.

I retire,
Anticipate this event
With awe.

A smile, a giggle . . .
You let go and topple three
steps . . .
Into my arms.

Both of us pleased,
We laugh and love,
Share the wonder of this miracle.

Your first steps! . . .
Towards me.
How well I know they will soon
carry you
Away.

My child,
As you let go of my hand to walk
alone,
Turn and grip the hand of God.

Wendy C Toner
STOP RUNNIN'

This poem is dedicated to my loving husband, Darren, for believing, and to Jamie for inspiring.

Day or night, it knows no difference,
Coming upon you with a screamin;
vengeance.
You can be sure you won't be alone;
Evil lusts many, a trademark well-
known.

Tales are told in whispered rumor
Of a demented sense of humor;
Grinning in its morbid pleasure
At the sight of a victim's seizure.

It takes your freedom, clouds your
head
Prayers go unanswered, you wish
you were dead.
Just drink some courage, swallow
your fear,
Face this beast, your mind will clear.

Stop runnin,
Stop tryin' to hide
This vicious circle has got you
inside.
Stop runnin;
Greet it head on
One day you'll wake up
And find that it's gone.

Giselle Rodriguez
A CONFESSION

To my precious niece, Desiree Marie, It is so beautiful watching the world unfold through your eyes. I love you.

I have a strong need
To tell you what is on my mind
But it never seems to be the right
time.

What would happen if I
Told you that 'I love you'?

Would you still be my dearest
friend?
Or would it all just end?

I think you feel the same.
At times I can see it in your eyes.
I can see it in your smile.

But my fear of rejection
Keeps me from telling
You of my affection.

And yet I know I can't go on like
this.
Knowing it's you I really miss.

So I'll sum up my courage
And take a chance
On this lifetime romance

By telling you,
That I do . . .
Love You!

Elizabeth Ayleen Scales
MY LOVE IS LIKE THE SPRING

To Summer storms, Southern writers, and silent prayers—

From the storm arises
A sense of sweet tranquility,
Out of the darkness
A shimmer of light,
In the mirror
New beginnings,
Held in my heart
An unconquerable love.

Your face I see on yonder Moon,
Hillside,
Valley,
Flower.

On a midsummer's walk through the fields,
A winter's stroll across the ice,
You are the Spring—the Sun.
You melt away the sadness.
You dry the tears.
Thus transforming a withering stem,
Brown and lifeless,
Into a red, red rose.

Lorena Queen
THE DEW ON THE ROSES

To my daughter Carol Judith

The dew on the roses are
The tears we have shed
for hopes and dreams
That have long ago fled . . .

But the rays of the sun
That banish the dew are,
God's promise each day
we are all born anew

Nancy C Brayton-Hudson
SOUL FRIEND

To: Colton Garrett Joseph

Hello "Soul Friend," at last we meet again
You are a newborn babe, with a beautiful new body to behold
May I offer you some thoughts as your new life unfolds?
Let your eyes be as wings and see all of Earth, all of creation
May your ears hear only the song of the "Lavender Rose" whatever length your duration
May your voice speak only words of crystal and light
Let your spirit walk among the angels and know little of self-imposed strife
Let your wisdom be a teacher and let no man become your beseecher
May your heart and touch mold any number of fine daughters and sons
Youth will give you many streams to cross while manhood will challenge you to mighty rivers to course
Navigate yours straight and true, as sure as that of an archers arrow
Leave clear prints along your path so that many others may follow
Then someday, someplace, just beyond a scarlet blue sunset somewhere within the eternal sea, I will hear your voice carried in on the wind
Saying "Hello Soul Friend" at last we meet again.

Veda Overton-Kellett
LAMENTING

For my sons, Andrew and Jeremiah, Through which I have learned laughter and lamenting.

Certain times for certain feelings,
Different dreams and schemes
Or rhymes or reasons;

Many moods and many meanings,
Dangerous destinies
And seasons;

Righteous rituals all too timely,
Caring christians carry
On, but blindly;

Weary ways to practice praise,
Do or die or try for two—
Angels always do.

Simple songs of dimming dreams,
Time or tribulation
And testing;

Burning bridges to carry crosses—
Sometimes sorrow
Sometimes blessing.

Phil Johnson
THINGS ARE GONE

To: Carol Jones and family in memory of her late son, Rich.

Things are gone, not always forgotten

Losing small objects is not a trauma

Losing close friends and relatives
can hurt you like nothing has
The pain is almost too great to endure
You miss the person and the memories,
you think, will die
But the memories do last forever
Isn't having memories of someone
who has passed away better
than not having any?
Things are gone, not always forgotten.

Julie Gay Pugh
GRANDAD

This poem is dedicated to Jim B. Pugh, World's Best Grandfather!

providing for his family
in his own diligent way
at many different jobs

as a father, jobs meant that his family would not go without the necessities of life, but yet, with such small pay he managed to give them a few small extras.

giving the grandchildren little gifts of candy was his way of showing his love. no matter what the gift might be, it was always as big as he was in our eyes. Grandad loved to see us smile;
therefore nothing was too much for his little ones.
Grandad received many hand-made tokens of our appreciation and love.
no matter how terrible they really were Grandad always said they were pretty and much nicer than any bought gift.

tick inspector, roughnecker, bridge builder, trucker, rancher, and a terrific grandfather all in one.
in whatever case he might be: senile and retired, middle aged and working, I will always love my special grandfather! You're the best Grandad!

Hugh Hunnicutt
TEARS ARE FOR SORROW, JOY, HOPE, AND HAPPINESS

Dedicated to encouraging those who know Him, those who have known Him, and those who would like to know Him, (Jesus Christ), Whom to know is Life Eternal. Matt. 25:46

God has shown to me the beauty
Of one rich, or copious tears
Matching up with all His Scriptures
As He overcomes our fears.

He still wants to make us happy,
And to GIVE Eternal Life;
So, in part, some are for showing
Our forthcoming end of strife.

Deep contrition is essential,
Starting at the place we wait . . .
Which is where He starts His process
Giving strength to, "take the Gate."

"Blessed are the poor in spirit,"
Happy are the ones who find
Respite in a world so weary,
Sight among the languid blind.

Jesus is our shield, and Saviour
We see better through our tears—
Which are of the Father's making—
And the Godhead ALL, endears.

Vernon Wesley Conaway IV
HOPE

To my good friend Scott Dean

Death is like a dark stormy morning.
You feel gray, depressed, tired;
The sun doesn't shine,
There is no inspiration.
It seems nothing is worth doing
But then skies clear,
Hopes are lifted,
And you know your friends are with Him;
They have not a care
But a feeling of peace.

Frances E Neiman
SEASONINGS

To Nebraska, the State where I live, for my inspirations of everchanging nature.

Spring is a teen-ager, unsure and shy
Dressed in pastels of pink and green
Tall—lean
Prom queen

Summer is a woman full of life
Dressed in blue, yellow, lavender and lime
Prime time
Singing—swinging

Autumn is a street walkin' woman
Dressed in bronze, reds and gold
Flamboyant—bold
Brassy—sassy

Winter is a drab, withered woman
Dressed in gray, white, colors cold
Brittle—old
Bent—spent

Michelle L Dyer
MOMMIES

Dedicated to my wonderful mother, Sandie

What Is A Mommy?

She's someone to love, she's the light of your life.

A Mommy is God's special gift to boys and girls, men and women, and grandmas and grandpas.

God made Mommies with that soft special touch that only they can give.

He made the understanding for them to give and made them with a very special love that only they can give.

He made the laps for small children to sit on and arms so soft to embrace them with.

A Mommy is really a very special person and I know for sure that He had a tender touch in Him when He made Mommies.

That's what a Mommy is to me.

Julia Cathrine Murphy
SPRING NIGHT

Lucy Hunsaker
My Granddaughter

I love a night like this
Damp, and a high wind blowing,
Silver birches like slim, sad ghosts
A lone star faintly glowing.

A wisp of moon is in the sky
'Most hidden by the scurrying clouds,
The weeping willows by the brook
Are like pale maidens in their shrouds.

I love on a might like this
To join the Elfin folks
To ride on the moon and talk to the stars
Wrapped up in their cloudy cloaks.

Enid Mitchell

Enid Mitchell
PROMISES OF LOVE

Dedicated to my dear Mother Hazel Robertson Mitchell My Soul's Companion.

The promises of love you keep,
And the words of endearment that I hear;
Are the things that make my life worth living,
And God's meaning, oh, so clear.

As near in death as we always were

in life,
It's then a thankfulness fills my heart;
A devotion as deep as our very Souls,
One that one even death can part.

"I'll come," I heard you tell me,
And as you reached down to lift me upward;
Our arms intertwined in a chain of love,
And we were as close as the wings of a bird.

Encircling arms brought you so near,
Once again so close to me in love;
As I saw you come to me with open arms,
It was like a lovely vision from above.

And as you fill my empty life with beauty,
For your sake, I dare not weep;
And only gratefulness fills my heart,
For the lovely promises of love you keep.

Jan T Davis
ALONE

To Zack, may you never feel alone.

Alone
in a world of fools
no one knows
the distance I have traveled
to find tranquility
peace within my soul
a person who cares
to share my life
yet still I am
alone without love
feeling lost
yearning for a touch
of love—to feel
wanted, needed
always looking
searching
for someone
who is looking for
the same and
feeling all
alone

Frankie Maxine

Darlene Smiddy Warr-Hayworth
FRANKIE MAXINE

For my mother, beautiful Frankie Maxine, from your beloved Lawrence, as whispered to me one night in a dream. I love you, Mom and Dad . . . Darlene February 12, 1989

You were fifteen, I was twenty
That day so long ago.

It was raining, or was it sunny?

I guess we'll never know.
I looked at you and you at me, in love we fell so fast,
"Too soon, too young," began the cry,
"Twill never, never last."

Then one by one the children came
and oh, they grew so fast,
Seven living symbols of "this love that could not last."
Thirty eight years of ups and downs, sometimes we'd even fight,
Only friendship and our loving would always make things right.

I guess I took for granted and
somehow you always knew,
That we'd always be together, for my whole life was you.
But then one night God called me, to another time and place,
And still I find I'm longing, just to see your lovely face.

Please don't be sad my darling . . .
just know within your heart,
Although, we may not be together now,
Our souls can never part . . .

Todd Robinson
ONCE IN A LIFETIME

To all special friends and family who care so much.

It was a dream that I could come to be with you.

When the time came and we were together my world was full of joy.

I told you I loved you and would do anything to keep our love.

I couldnot see between the lines of how ourlives were so different, I still meant what I said.

You've showed me everything I needed to know, but I couldnot show you, and yet you understood.

You were a dream come true in my life.

Although we are apart now I still love you and still mean every word I said.

It could only happen once again that we could be together once more in our lifetime.

Betty Hirschon
A DREAM OF PEACE

To My Grandchildren Suzanne and Deborah Taber and Harold Berger

Someone had a dream one night
That peace for all was a moral right.
The dream was for a life of liberty and happiness
But the struggle to achieve it was merciless.

The dream persisted day and night
And the inner feeling was a horrendous fright.
Finally, with perseverance, the dream came true
Symbolized by the Red, White and Blue.

That is how American was born.

The food the child was fed was called democracy.
Its home was a haven for the refugee.
Its hand extended out for liberty,
For justice and a plea for humanity.
We've reached the moon, the planet Mars
Yet peace on earth is very sparse.
There are so many who have a master mind
So why is peace on earth so hard to find?

Let's build a strong America
Let's search for freedom true.
Perhaps we'll find Utopia
And have peace for me and you.

Josie Marie Tornabene
MY LOVE . . . ASHLEY ALEXIS

This poem is dedicated to my beloved daughter, Ashley Alexis Tonnabene.

One day I lived a beautiful dream,
And it was just because of you!
The day God put you in my arms;
I just couldn't believe . . . this could be true.

There grew a love deep in my heart,
I never thought could be:
The strongest love that man has known,
She also gave to me.

Her precious little smile,
And cute tiny nose;
Gentle eyes, so big and kind,
Fashioned by God's tender
love . . . made a perfect rose.

Now Ashley's stay was very brief
And how my heart does ache,
But only in God's loving arms;
Can he repair the break.

The yearning of my empty arms,
I know one day will end:
When God will call me home to stay,
With my beloved Ashley, once again.

Julie Womble
LONELY FOR YOU TONIGHT

I love to feel the cool, wet sand between my toes,
and a warm Southern breeze as it blows.
I love the sweet smell of a single red rose,
and all the beauty it does show.
I love to hear the roar of the ocean,
and to watch the sea gulls in motion.

I love warm summer nights,
when the moon is glowing bright.
I love to see the rain falling
down, as it beats upon my weary brow.
I love to hear the laughter of
good friends, and all the fun times together we spend.
I love candlelight dinners for two;
and all those special times I've spent with you.
But everything would be just
right; if only you were here to share these things with me tonight.

Jimmie Lee Koetzle
INVITATION OF FAITH

Love between two people is the creation of the Creator. Any love amongst any persons makes any one person one people in Christ. I dedicate the soul meaning of this poem to the Invitation of all faith—Jesus Christ.

Take a subject into mind.
Invite it in to sup and dine.
Get to know it.
To agree,
To disagree; Amen.

Personal, Spiritual,
A literal stay.
Pray upon it night and day.
When your lids have opened up
Share it and spread it.
Cup to cup.

The backwards DOG is of GOD
Inviting the food of man
Not of man's LAW.

Take a subject into mind.
Invite it in to sup and dine.
To agree,
To disagree.
Invite it in and make it thine; Amen.

Jennifer Doucette
SAFELY KEPT

She talked about the safety
Beneath the covers where she slept.
It was the only place where she could go
And have her secrets kept.
They heard everything she said
And watched what she would do.
Those sacred walls knew everything,
Somehow they just knew.
Her teenage years were spent in there.
Her every single day.
She liked it best behind the walls
Where all her secrets stayed.
They held a tiny part of her,
The part of her unknown.
It was her own safe, secret place,
That room within our home.
She stayed beneath the covers
Upon the bed in which she slept.
She closed her eyes and went to sleep,
Her secrets safely kept.

Harry A Spurrier
ON THE CIRCLES OF MAN

Once upon a man was a question sincerely laid,
Only to his mind did the answer evade.
It was not that the man had no desire to help,
But a solution to this question was not under his belt.

It really should not be hard, or at least you would think,
For the man with the question to find an answer to drink.
But you see what he asks has to do with men's tasks,
He wanted to know which way he should go,
To find out just how come, after the work has been done,
That the men who know well, how life's trees they can fell,
Cut paths through the forest that they say are for man's sake,

But eager are they not to show the steps that they take.

He has a suspicion that it all stems from greed,
You know that state, way out beyond need.
You see as he asks one man after another,
He himself was also asked, one time, by his brother.

So on leans the question on the circles of man,
If they only knew how, they would know that they can.

Joy K Young
JESTER
My jester, how marvelous the unmasking!
How sweet the salty tears beneath your greasepaint.
The largeness of your soul leaps at me
As you wipe away the crimson stars from your eyes.

You strip away your neck ruffles,
Throw out the ruby-red nose,
And reach out with a hand—firm
To forecast the touch of love.

Paint is washed away
Such skin shines brightly—
Beaming through the triumph
Of your integrity.

Unfettering your collar,
The suit settles at your ankles.
Sweat-soaked, naked,
You lift the barbells of leadership.

Julianne S Hamilton
DANCER
The music box dancer
Twirls on and on
Hearing only the
Rapture and rhythm of her song.

Her dreams we do not know,
We can only guess.
A Prince Charming waiting
In the wings? Oh, yes!

Grace E Streifling
LET ME HAVE MY DREAM
A little log cabin by a mountain stream
Keeps working its way into my dream,
With cedars and pines drifting fragrance and love
From tops sighing softly in the wind up above.

With food on the shelves and a lamp on the table,
Braided rugs and a water pail floating a ladle,
Cozy curtained windows and a blanketed bed,
And a big bright pillow for a silvery head.

There is something else that tugs at my heart,
God spoke true when, seeing Adam apart,
He knew something was needed; a friend for the man.
It is just as true now as it was then.

A little log cabin by a mountain stream
Keeps working its way into my dream.
But it needs to be shared or it soon would pall,
Alone in my cabin there'd be no joy at all.

For a kindred spirit whose heart responds,
Melds two hearts together in heaven-born bonds.
Two hearts in harmony would seal the dream
Of a little log cabin by a mountain stream.

Queen E Hill
ZAP THEM
He who hung the sun and the moon, in the sky,
Why he allows man to live, is a mystery why,
He can cause the stones to praise him loudly,
The trees, clap their leaves, like hands, soundly.

He can raise old dry bones, up in the valley,
Cause the moon to turn to blood, calm the waters of the sea,
Even the rocks and the animals, can praise him,
Tell me, why would he need you and me?

Oh!, just think, how much he must love us,
That he gave his only son to die at Calvary,
To atone for all the sins ever committed, now or ever,
Yet we disobey, deny and curse him, glorify him never.

I think if most of us were in his place,
We would zap this whole world, the human race,
And perhaps start all over again, a people to raise,
Creating people who would be grateful and give him praise.

Ina Clare Richardson
FIRE AND LIGHTNING
I once walked with light, held fire in glass
Entranced as ending day lowered a soft dusky sash
Between a once blue, now purple canopy and darkening field.
And I looked for winged lightning, glowing embers they yield.

I miss the firefly's lantern that brightened summer evenings of my childhood,
Wish they could climb over mountains,
Come out from the valleys and woods,
They shine and gleam, burn low then beam,
Treasure for children who chase them and dream.

Alaena Hernandez
I'M TRYING TO STOP CRYING
I'm trying to stop crying
As I wipe the teardrops from my eyes
The thunder shakes the windows of my heart
And the rain falls from the clouds in the skies

I sit here in this dark cell
Remembering all the great times we had
Now all I have are memories
Some make me happy; some make me sad

Like the first time you hit me
I cried for days
You can't hit me anymore
For I took your life away

I know I'm going to die
I go over my life as I sit
I didn't want to kill you
But you pushed me to it

It was either me or you
You were driving me insane
I might have killed you
But it didn't take away the pain.

Mary Clement Monette

Mary Clement Monette
AN OLD PHOTOGRAPH
Does this picture bring back a memory or so,
Of the dusty Texas town of San Angelo,
Of a little white house on 19th street,
With red roses climbing and a few big mesquites?

Usually there was a garden growing,
And in the back a rooster crowing.
See, there's the old windmill, just behind,
The boy here climbed it many times.

In the woods nearby lived a strange old man,
Who had goats that wandered all over his land.
Farther back in the woods were the pigs and their pen;
The pigs seemed to be out more than in.

This picture was surely taken by a loving mother,
Of her brown-eyed children, two sisters and their brother.
She caught this memory for them to store in their mind,
So that in their old age they could recall that long ago time.

Scott E Sanders
A PLACE IN MY HEART
There is a place
That is very special.

A place where
Love is always around.
And where time
Seems to stand still.

It is a place
That holds a lot of memories, feelings,
And dreams.

It is a place that exists
Because of you.

It is there
To have feeling for someone who is
So very special.

It is there
To retain all the caring
It has received.

Sometimes it is a lonely place.
With nobody to share its glory.

But then I think of you,
And it is a beautiful place
Again.

So,
Even though you are
So very far,
It exists because of
The loving person that you are.

And because of that love,
That stretches from our worlds apart,

To you, forever,

A place in my heart . . .

Ward Joseph
TIDE SIGH
When I was a boy
I lived near the Atlantic.
When my soul was frantic
I sought my hearts joy.

Then, when I brought a lady-friend
to share the salt-spray wonderment,
the waves broke with less enchantment.
Nature nagged my soul from its passive trend

to fend whirl-wind water spouts
speckled with lusty sundrops of fire
which formed in warm supple waves
about my thighs and shoulder blades.

In seething with the sea's rising might
I found converging subcurrents
Churning surface water white.

Geraldine V Lemons
WHEN YOU'RE FEELING DEPRESSED AND BLUE
When you're feeling depressed and blue,
And you don't know what to do.
Someone is always around to help,
Saying they have something to give you pep.
They tell you it solves problems, too,
Calms your nerves, makes you feel new.
They do not tell about the next day,
The headaches, the pressures coming your way.
You are not told what happens to you,
When a "drug bust" involves you.
You do not know until it's too late,
How much your brain will deteriorate.
Stand brave and strong where ever you go,
To drugs and alcohol, "JUST SAY NO!"

Julie Rouse
SWEET REVENGE
The taste is in your heart
your soul.
You taste each new thought
and devour it into a
revengeful sweet.
Savor the thoughts—
make them wet your taste buds.
Some burn, some tingle,
some may even make you giggle.
Nothing will stop this feeling inside—
it grows and grows,
Until the time has come to
spread your words of hate.
Then you try to speak and your
mind goes blank;
As you receive a smile.

Thomas J Drennan
TEACHER AND FRIEND
There are few things of real value in this world
Something to be cherished and honored for itself

Some people think it is money and gold
All that they value is power and wealth

But real value cannot be measured at all
It is something that can't be taken away
No matter how far or often you fall
But something to lean on in your darkest days

And now the reason for my definition
About things of value and their real worth
One thing of value is education
That starts with one's parents right after birth

The other value—the greater of the two
Is to be called a true friend
Someone you help when their lives are blue
What can be worth more than a friend

So these few lines were written down
To a teacher and a friend too
To let you know I'm glad you're around
And the hardiest, most sincere thank you

Mary Garner Craver
BEREFT
Blindly I draw the cloak around me
to hide my wounds so none may see
my naked pain.

In vain, I seek relief in work;
I say, "This thing cannot be true—
For I do the things that I always do.
Today is the same as yesterday;
For a few brief hours he has gone away.
These tears I shed like summer rain
Will wash away all grief, all pain.
My burdened heart will find release
And once again know joy and peace."

Someday, perhaps, I'll come to know
These things I tell myself are so.

Bob Ketcham
VISTA TO ETERNITY
Long leased vista to eternity
Each step magnified by certainty
That the end is nearing,
Yet 'tis merely the beginning.

The vista to eternity is earned,
Karmic wars within thy soul,
Many ends ever approaching
Ultimately to this new beginning.

This vista to eternity is never ending
It is not an aftermath, nor a dream,
But something internally real,
Thus, it is the new beginning.

Long leased vista to eternity
A new world is unfolding
But so were the past worlds
Separately new beginnings.

Therefore, past worlds, as they were,
Continuous as they must be,
Are merely aging stepping stones
To a final vista to eternity.

Marilyn Webert
LAY QUIET
Lay quiet
lovely one
put your fears aside
and cry no more
Lay quiet
my fallen angel
the heavens will be yours once more
if only you but try and reach for them
sleep quiet
gentle one
and the pressures of the day
shall fall from you
and know this
my fallen angel
there will always be someone
who will care for you
there will always be someone
whom you can love.

Tina Marie Hermanns

Tina Marie Hermanns
DEATH

This poem is dedicated to my family for all the love and support they've given me throughout the years.

Black as the darkest night,
To which in time we're bound,
A place so grievous and still,
In which there is no sound.

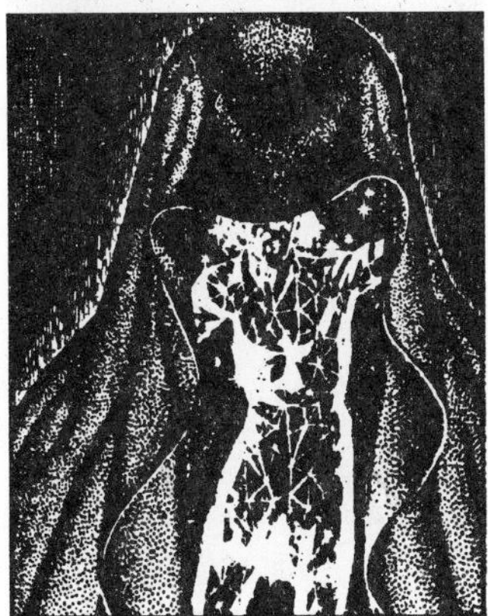

Black as the darkest night,
When many tear drops fall,
When groups of mourners gather,
And linger through the hall.

Black as the darkest night,
In which there is no breath,
When everything has ended,
Meaning only DEATH.

Judith A Swanson
ETERNAL RECURRENCE
So long missing you,
my heartache your face
forgotten want
don't want to see you again
my heartache, hard
and fast memories
keep me or my heartache
alive, can't tell
your face forgotten want
don't want to see you again.

Kay Barrington
DESTINY
An oyster slept in an oyster bed
Another oyster for his head;
In deep content he stirred and sighed
And his tiny portal opened wide.
A grain of sand just passing by
Roistering on an errant swell
Entered the oyster's sea swept shell.
The oyster woke up instantly
And, quite outraged, beneath the sea
At once began to manufacture
Coats and coats of pearly nacre
To imprison his tiny foe.

The grain of sand, his fate thus sealed,
Now rests exquisitely concealed
On a velvet tray in Cartier.
As for the oyster,
His life work through,
He ended up in an oyster stew.

Stephen G Johnopolos
ONE BRANCH OF THE FAMILY TREE
Beloved Uncle,
Rancid creature of all that will perish,
Fornicator of all that is right and just,
Is it your wife who drives you to
Incessant escapades of drink and distress?
Is it your children who pursue you to
Infinite fathoms of insanity?
Is it your father??—you scorned so well,
Until his passing.

Rejoice! O Uncle, life has given you
Many gifts but one:
Death.

Rejoice!

Hallelujah!

Your bounty may be near.

Steven A Michalove
DON'T ASK ME WHY
Don't ask me why—
flowers grow,
streams run downhill,
birds need to fly.

Don't ask me why—
we sing a song,
dance by the fire,
And need each other.

Don tell me why—
we build bombs,
enslave our children,
train the soldiers.

I don't want to know,
I don't want to hear
About the tears you sow
About the heart you don't show,
About the power you won't let go.

Don't ask me why flowers grow,
Don't ask me why we need each other.

Eleanor D Carter
DESOLATE
Like a leaf blowing down an empty street
So my life. Aimless, no goals in sight
Except oblivion. I've run out of youth
Hope, health, even money
And love.
The winds of winter will destroy me
Time consume me.
No trace will remain, when spring arrives
Except a lingering appreciation
Of beauty, in any form.
And life goes on.

Doris J Weitzel
DAY DREAMS
Oh! The glorious sights I see
When I close my eyes.
An ocean sunrise, dazzling sunsets,
Stars spiking the skies.

Memories of a meeting long ago,
Images of loved ones far away.
Closed, my eyes see them clearly,
We are together once more this day.

Such noble heights I can achieve,
When I close my eyes.
Writing an enduring love song,
So sweet a lover cries.

The painting that's so unique,
Distinguishing it to be mine.
These wondrous feats, there's no limit
When fulfilled with wishful design.

If only I could see as clearly,
Subliminal goals I could realize.
Such infinite things I could do,
Envisioning through OPEN eyes.

Iona Pearson Smith

Iona Pearson Smith
WONDER OF LOVE

Dedicated to Laura, my lovely granddaughter, who suggested the title for this little verse.

Oh, never shall I cease to wonder
From whence a love like this could spring,
Answer might be just as simple as—
What makes sun-shine, rain-fall, birds sing.

Victor A Cipolla
I COULD FORGET YOU
I could forget you if there were no love songs
to remind me of you:
If there were no sunsets, nor moonrises, nor paw-prints
on dewy lawns at dawn.

I could forget you if rivers did not rush, whispering,
to the sea,
And wedges of geese did not fly southward, silhouetted
against grey autumn skies.

I could forget you if deer did not browse
in the meadow by the lake,
And the serene mountain above no longer
soared toward heaven.

I could forget you if redwoods did not pierce the mists,
dripping droplets on my head,
And if jays stopped their joyous chatter
when the fogs lift.

I could forget you if waves did not race
across the bar,
And lovers no longer walked hand in hand
on lonely stretches of sand.

But, there will always be love songs . . .

Jane Pierritz
BABY ENCOUNTERS

For Chris the baby my husband & I never had.*

Into her tiny hand
A rose petal fell.
A baby laugh gurgled up.

Across her sun kissed cheek
A butterfly brushed her soft eyelash.
A baby gasp escaped her wee pursed mouth.

Upon her bity foot alit
A grasshopper with sudden spring.
A baby cry fled from her little throat.

An exploring stub of a finger traced
An ant's hurrying journey.
A baby frown creased her soft smooth brow.

Upon her tiny shoulder perched
A yellow bird singing his prettiest notes.
A baby disbelief flooded her very blue eyes.

Kirsty Porter
VOICE STILL HEARD
A voice still heard in my head
Everytime I think of you
My conscience gets to me
And I think of what might have happened
If I would have believed you
And now that voice still heard
Is nothing but a memory
It's triggered whenever I hear our song
playing on the radio
It reminds me of what we used to be
And now we are nothing
If only I had listened to that voice
But I was way too stubborn
And now that voice is only heard in my
Black Heart

Jesse L Rea
TO MY WIFE
There's been things that we've been through
That nobody can tell us just what to do.
And there's been pain—this is true—
But no matter what life has to put us through
I'll always be there just for you.
There's a baby in heaven you can trust
and it's waiting there just for us.
I'll work hard and I'll work long
This you can always depend upon.
So here's from me—and heres to you;
Happy Valentine, Baby—I'll always Love you . . .

Unknown
LONESOME SINGLE
Oh how lonesome is my life,
For I am without a wife.
I searched the world afar,
From wild parties, to singles' bar.
Now I am at thirty-six,
How could fate deal me such tricks?
Lying in bed and staring above,
Hoping and praying that I'll find my love.
It is you oh Lord to thee I cry!
Please don't let love pass me by!
Now I sleep, yet another restless night,
Hoping tomorrow, will shed me new light.

Helen M Lunceford
HAPPY NEW YEAR 1989—TO YOURS AND MINE
Happy New Year with blessings galore
God has plenty, in His vast domain and Heavenly store
So let's really pray, believe, trust and obey
God loves us, and we love God who leads our way
He hears each "Devoted Prayer"—we say
Takes our hand, never let's us go astray
Guides our thoughts, night and day
So, "Let's put God first in all we do"
Knowing—He is the only one, who makes our dreams come true

Become a Christian, glorify Jesus Christ's name
Your peace of mind, faith, happiness you can reclaim
Follow in Jesus footsteps each day
Always find time-to-"Read your Bible" and pray
Glorify God, magnify His holy name
Worship our Lord Jesus Christ, His world wide holy fame
God's son who laid down His life on the cross, for—"you and me"
With His eternal blessings, in Heaven's eternity

Thank God for His forgiveness, when all our earthly work is done
I'm ready and willing to sacrifice everything for our Heavenly Father's home
We know God loves every one, great, tall and small
Walks with His hand in our hand, because He loves us all.

Joyce Boisclaire
NO REGRETS
Dishes, beds, laundry, cooking,
does it ever, ever, end?
Soccer, ballet, meetings,
don't forget those clothes to mend.
Arguments in the car,
who sits where this time?
Are we there yet?
Can I have a quarter, a dime?
Sometimes it's overwhelming,
I wish I never was born.
I get so tired,
and filled with scorn.
"Mommy, I love you. You're the best.
Give me a hug and tuck me in bed.
What's wrong? You look sad.
Was it something I said?"
Oh, the beautiful words of love,
the precious moments at night like this.
The tender touch around my neck,
this is something I'd really miss.

Russ Webster
WHO ARE THEY
Who are they to tell me how I feel for you
Who are they to warn me that my love for you isn't true
Why do they lay odds and say it will never last
How much must we go through before it becomes the past?

When do they accept the decisions I have made
Haven't we suffered enough, aren't our dues all paid
Is it too much to ask to give our own life
Is she so hard to accept as my wife?
How many years must go by
How many moons must rise in the sky
Before the day finally comes
That will prove we are as one?

No one knows what we have gone through
No one realizes the sacrifices we have made
No one knows the pain we put each other through
The clouds of gray, the skies of blue.

Who are they to tell you what you feel inside
Who are they to ask you why you stepped off the ride
Who are they to judge you for the things you say and do
How are they to know what made you feel so blue?

Don't love me forever, just love me each day
Don't hold me too tight, I may push you away.
Give me the chance to love totally and true
Just give me the chance to make it all up to you.

Never mind their doubts, because I love you . . .

Carolyn Champion
ON EMPTY
I'm awake late this night
Thoughts racing in my brain;
I can't get ideas together
I can only hear the rain;

I simply want to feel at home
With joy and warmth inside;
Instead my feeling is emptiness
Fake smile false caring . . . I died.

Wendy M Alexander
MY BABIES ARE DEAD
My babies are dead
I had them trashed;
My lips have met many
My soul has always been yours.
Thank you for the freedom
To kiss mistake and the burden of truth, I carry.
I've not known you forever
But forever my sympathy runs between judgements
And tomorrows peeked; maybe borrowed.
Understanding doesn't come easy;
The painter has dropped her brush
And the image is gone
And gypsy is still.
I look for the next breath to be stolen or taken away;
I challenge the thought and the words
Pondering the pain and I am gallant
As I wait the recovery.
You never gave me patience and
I don't understand
The forest naked in the coldest of winter
And your own are trembling.

Ralph Lester Guffey Jr
I REMEMBER WHEN
I remember when I was a child, a little scared and a little wild.
A child without much fear, but a lot of care.

Dreaming of things like being a big movie star with a big fancy car.

But here I am a young man with a rugged face in a dirty place, without a care and living in fear.

Fear of where my life may lead me and fear of where my life will leave me.

Miles Walker
QUIET SEA
Words melt onto the paper
as easy as the sun shines
and my skin, my shadow,
moves across the evening earth—
like dogs chasing across the beach
my body shakes—
quietly, as the evening enslaves the day.
The bright sun burnt holes through my heart—
the words wait
for my hand as I relax.
I question the authority
residing over existence—
the total shape of meaning and matter.
I am as being.
Your only constant is change.
The shape I understand—
the warden of thought watches—
to arrest the quiet sea.

Leatha M Cafarella
YOU BROKE MY HEART
Oh why, oh why do I cry
Because you broke my heart
We really never did get a start

I loved you before we met
You didn't know it yet

The love I have for you
Has made me so blue
You made me mad
And I'm so sad

You broke my heart
We really never did get a start
I know I'll get over you
Because that's the thing to do

You can't care for me
So I'll let the memory be.

Steven Kaplan
A MARRIAGE OF VIRTUE

To Brenda Kaplan whose price is far above rubies.

RECKLESS FECKLESS BEREFT OF SENSE
Who drew the line and put up the fence
Who stood beyond the reach of Love's voice
And answered with silence when given the choice
To offer his heart to the woman he wed
Before she decides that the words he once said
Are empty of Truth and thoroughly dead?

YES who is this fool who stands quite alone?
His method is sick and his purpose unknown
Why does he chastise the Mother of Life
HIS GOD GIVEN WIFE
With moments of anguish and hours of strife?

Her sensitive nature cries in despair
For someone with whom she can honestly share
Calm and considerate gestures of joy
A marriage of Virtue . . .
Harmony . . .
PEACE

Amanda E Wood
thou art of infinite worth
stepping onto the ice
every risk I take
I can see the images
trapped beneath the surface
the taunting faces
their hands unable to break
the force
preventing them from
being
I recognize their mocking
and close my eyes to it
pressing my face to the glassy
surface
I realize my own
how many have not
and slipped into that dark
coldness joining the other hands
with pointing laughing fingers
trapped by this feeling
insignificance

JeriLynn Glaszcz

JeriLynn Glaszcz
I SIT IN THE DARKNESS OF SOBIBOR
I sit in the darkness of Sobibor,
Because I am Jew, I will be no more.
I await in somber silence as my leaves slowly wither,
One by one, falling to the ground.
I hear him.
I hear him coming.
He, all in black, to match his merciless heart.
He, with the solemn expression has come to march me to my death.
He is the wind ripping away the leaves from my branches,
Until I am nothing but a skeleton.
Then whistles through my bare limbs with triumph.
What joy does he see in shattering our happiness?
Am I such a monstrosity that I don't deserve the sun's light,
To melt away the ice which has glazed upon my soul?
Grim and malign he hovers over me,
Calling me to my death.

Adrienne (Addie) Weiland
BE STILL AND KNOW THAT I AM GOD
Be still my heart do not cry.
Be still my heart for it is I.
Sometimes I must break a heart.
Tear down barriers that keep us apart.
Come my heart abide in Me.
Open your heart confide in Me.
Listen my heart and I will speak.
For it is I that you seek.
Follow my heart I will show.
For I am the way to go.
Ask my heart I long to give.
Obey my heart so you might live.
Give my heart and you receive.
Trust my heart in Me believe.
Now go my heart with others share.
Know my heart how much I care.
Tell them my heart of our life story.
So it can be used for My honor and glory.
So be glad my heart begin to sing.
For it is I eternal life I bring.

Tarek M Gabr
LIFE OR DEATH
At times you feel depressed
At times you feel your sorrow
Never live for what has happened
But for what shall come tomorrow
Life is too short and precious
To take your life by suicide
Who would you really be hurting
If you succeeded and you died
Think of your friends and family
And how they will feel the pain
Of knowing they lost someone dear to them
Someone they'll never see again
Think of all the good times
And try to forget the bad
Think of how happy you will feel
By not making your loved ones sad
Before you take your life
Give it another thought
Make the best of what you have
For life is very short.

Amy D Bailey
A NEW DAY
The leaves were falling and the sky was orange with flames of the sunlight beaming through the soft clouds of winter.
To my alarm nothing seemed to bother me, not even the coldness that I felt as I shivered when the streaks of wind darted through the cracks of the doorway.
Pitter patter, goes the woodpecker outside my window, as he scrounges the tree for something to eat. He knows what's there, only if it can be found.
The air in the meadows is filled with a misty smoke of early morning fog trying to sneak away as the freshly glowing sunlight steams the wrinkles of the crinkled leaves.

Jody M Klinger
LULLABYE TO MOMMA
Momma, don't cry
Momma, don't weep
The sound of your tears
Make it so hard to sleep.
What was it this time?
What did you do?
Was it really that bad
From your point of view?
When will the madness stop?
Where will it end?
Is it really so awful
You can't tell you daughter,
Your very best friend.
I try to understand your silence
Although I find it so hard to do.
Just whom are you trying to protect?
Me, him, or you?

Grace M Stuffle
TAKE MY MESSAGE
I can hear the Angels singing way up in the sky
I can hear hoofbeats then I know why
God loves us, He loves us still
He beckoned,"Come do my will."

God spoke my name, I heard Him say
Come with me today
In a streak of light, I was at His Throne
Jesus spake,"Welcome to Our Home."

My Redeemer, clothed in that white robe said,
"We have many of your loved ones here"
I heard the chant of happy voices,
tho they would have me to return and not to fear
I had not time to linger there, Gods voice spoke
"I am their God, I am their God of Love."
Tell them of my Son above.

Take my message here today
Tell my children to watch and pray
Now I hear the Angels up above
They are singing, God of Love, God of Love.

Pedro Trevino
A CRY FOR HELP
I find life a mess of confusion;
So very hard to understand.
All I see is delusion,
Nothing is real, life is so hard to withstand.

I try talking to my God,
But he seems so far away;
My legs feel so wobbly, I'm ready to drop;
Oh, why do I have to feel this way?

I can not take this suffering much longer;
This cruel world was not made for me.
Please take me away Dear Lord or make me stronger;
Humbly I ask this of Thee.

Lord, do allow me to find you;
And take me away if you please.
Just let me look after my family;
From your Heavenly place where there is peace.

And when their time comes to join me,
I'll anxiously wait there with you;
To open the heavenly sea,
So quickly they can come right through.

Thelma VanScoik
HURRY HOME
If there were arms a-waiting me,
I'd hurry, hurry home.
If there were lips so soft and warm,
No more alone I'd roam.

If there were eyes that softly said,
"I Love you, Thelma Dear,"
On the double I'd run home,
Just to be him a-near!

And if there were a tender heart
That beat for me alone,
I'd fly just like a homing-bird
To him, my Love, my own.
But since I have not one of these,
Why should I hurry home?
I'll wander here, I'll wander there
And saunter home at gloam!

Kathleen M Eagan
COMPREHENSION
Friendships are our strengths
our guidelines to our days
the shoulders we can cry on
the pain, they take away

Friendships are to share our joys
to wipe away our tears
to understand our faults
and shield us from our fears

Friendships take as well as give
appreciate the way we live
understand the things we need
leave us space
and room to breathe

Knowing what your own needs are
be able to feel what another requires
your qualities would match your own desires
and you can be the kind of friend
another admires

Vera H Crocker
THE INDESCRIBABLE CROSS
On Golgotha's Hill It stood so tall
With the One who died for me.
He gave His Life that I may live
By Death, He set me free.

He took my guilt upon Himself
My stripes He did bear,
As He hung upon the Cross
Because I put Him there.

They put Him in a borrowed tomb
When they took Him from the Tree
But death could not keep Him there;
He won the Victory.

To the Hill you must go
If my Saviour you wish to share.
The door opens at the foot of the Cross
Christ will meet you there.

Now as I gaze up at the Hill
A Cross I still can see.
A thing of beauty to behold,
It's the Cross of Calvary.

Jeffrey C W Hirsch
MEMORIES

To Jonathan Hirsch; my father and to my fellow inmates.

Wasting away, enclosed for a lifetime.
MEMORIES haunt me; taunt me.
They bring me back to times of cheerfulness only to further my despair. Echoes of laughter reverberate through my mind. Chaos controls the day and MEMORIES the night.
In the day I am at home amongst the chaotic ways of prison. But at night I am terrified, alone with my MEMORIES.

Rhonda Kay Basham
MY NEPHEW

With love to my brother Roger

My nephew's name was Randall Keith.
He really meant a lot to me.
But especially to my brother,
and of course his very own mother.

I never really got to know him.
Although my feelings are kept within,
I still love him a lot.

I know he's in heaven,

and there's not a better place to be.
But I wish he could have spent some time with me.

I can't really understand why some people have to die.
Especially little ones that never had the chance to live their life.
Maybe someday I'll understand why this happened to . . .
My Nephew.

Byron Paige

Byron Paige
THE TORII

Dedicated to Suzie, my wife for forty years and the inspiration for "The Torii."

Gaunt faneway, symbol of a creed antique,
Whatever be the message that you speak
To others better versed in pagan lore
Of Samurai and Shinto cults of yore,

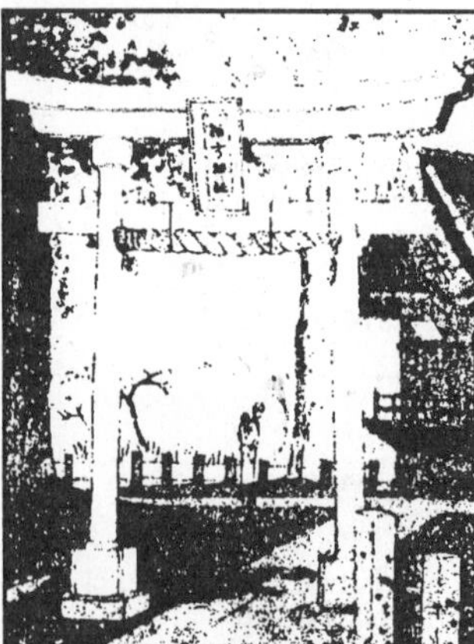

To me your simple lineal beauty spells
Remembrance of a true love found
In faraway Japan, within the sound
Of temple bells.

James D Davis
WHAT IS LOVE?

Dedicated to Vicki Nordstrom: For trusting, caring and hopefully someday believing in me, the way I believe in you!

Love is trusting, giving
a person a chance to grow.
It is caring, letting someone know.

Love is believing, showing
you what it means. It is
hoping, sharing your dreams.

Love is commitment, it has
no guarantees. It is an agreement, showing you believe.

Love is inside us all, but we
save it for the special few.
Love stands tall, it is exactly what I feel for you!

Laurie Aurecchione
LOOKING AS IF I DON'T CARE

Looking as if I don't care,
I run my fingers through my hair.
Trying not to give you a clue;
That each day I still notice you.
Turning my head and looking away,
Over and over again each day.
Making sure you don't see me, just in case
I get one more look at your face

While telling of how I hate you;
I'm watching everything you do.
I want to know if you think of me,
And why we, as two, could not be.
Then, standing alone with his teddy,
I hear you say "I'm not ready"
I don't understand. I say to myself.
As I wait and put my heart on the shelf.

Lillian C Marcoux
A BETTER WORLD

Would this a better world be without me?
Would it be more peaceful?
Have I used my talents truly free
To make this earth more beautiful?
The love that blessed me day by day,
How did I return it?
The freedom that has come my way,
What have I done to earn it?
Have I been an echo rather than a choice
Lacking in belief, a follower of crowds?
Is corruption what we sinners voice
Ever wanting more than that allowed?
Our tragic world has lost its pride;
Much less greed could turn the tide.

Constance Charlene Safi
THE "MONSTER" OF FREE (?) GOVERNMENT

The "MONSTER" of which I speak,
covers over three million square miles.
Pretending to protect its victims,
yet draining life's blood, all the while.

In "Time's" judgement, the "MONSTER" is young,
claiming ten-fold it's age of two hundred years.
Cries of terror, pain, and disillusion-ment,
drinking its fill, of its victim's tears.

It has, of this date,
consumed over two hundred million lives.
As the victim's hearts beat,
the fiendish "MONSTER" thrives.

From the "Pit of Hell,"
this "MONSTER" sprung.
Discarding the old,
devouring the young.

From its bowels,
spoil has spread.
With all those upon it,
now the living-dead.

Spreading in epidemic proportions,
from this "MONSTER", there's left a foul seed.
Enveloping all innocence before it,
to other "MONSTERS" of lust, and greed.

Un-born children cry out,
from the wombs, of their mothers.
As the "MONSTER" slowly destroys,
all hopes, of sisters, and brothers.

Now discarding the aged as useless,
this "MONSTER" of viscous, foul bile.
Slowly, painfully, draining their livelihood,
this self-governing "MONSTER", wears a smile.

Mothers and fathers are no longer needed,
for machines, now perform the labor.
The "MONSTER'S" children, now Zombies,
may relish the destitution, in which, there's no savior.

Paul L Conklin
HEAVENLY DOVE

Sweet Holy Spirit,
Sweet Heavenly Dove,
May your anointing spirit
bring peace from heaven above;
And for this peace we praise You
for giving us your Son:
Now let your Holy Spirit
descend on every one.
Descend, I pray, on me today
and fill my heart with love;
For everlasting Joy and Strength
comes only from above.

(Matthew 3:16 And He saw the Spirit of God coming down in the form of a dove.)

Michael Mitchell
MOTHERS

Mothers are so much fun,
they raised us from day one.
When we are older and on our own,
they tell us of how much we've grown.
They remind us of what we do wrong,
we just shrug as we go along.
Oh how right mothers are,
and if we really listen,
we would go far.
Listen to their words, so dear and true,
and they will carry you your whole life through.

Jong K Kim

Jong K Kim
MEDITATION

On the blank paper
Clean fingers, reserved violations
Too many deadly pale lips
Siren, who escaped with the thought?

The consumed heart
Answering for every life
Faded tears
A moan is a moan
In the stolen space
Scattered emotions
Smile or scorn
Am I still alive?

The blank paper is the blank paper.

Connie Nolan Rasmusen
WEDDING DAY DREAMS

To Jill and Dan Schoeck with Love. For it was the inspiration of their love that this poem was written.

I met you in the winter,
And I loved you then by spring;
We courted through the sunshine,
And by fall, I'd wear your ring.

Now here we stand together,
Tho' the past has come and gone;
but I promise, I will love you,
Until forever rolls around.

We, we are dreamers,
like the fairytales you read;
I'll be Cinderella,
Wear your armor, mount your steed.

Then I, I will ride with you,
Over hardships, over pain;
And I know, that we will make it,
If we let Jesus hold the reins.

Over mountains, over rivers,
through life's journey we will ride;
When you look, you will find me,
ever near, close at your side.

Yes I met you, in the winter,
Now we begin a life anew;
Ride with me, for I'm a dreamer,
I'm so glad that you are too.

Ida Mae Hayson
LOVE OF MY LIFE

This poem is dedicated to my wonderful husband, James C. Hayson, Jr., who for thirty years has been the "Love of My Life".

My darling, my darling, my husband, my life,
this world's so full of sorrow and of strife;
But with you standing by my side day by day,
I'll surely have no problems finding my way;
In the rain, sunshine, sleet or in the snow,
our love will continue to flourish and grow;
For thirty years we both have been together,
during death and sorrow we both did weather;
My heart is sometimes heavy and becomes sad,
when you look into my eyes, I am oh so glad;
Sometimes our problems can seem to domineer,
when our lives appear to be far out of gear;
And then you hold my hand and I do then say,
that I'm glad to be your wife more each day;
Our love for each other is greater than any,
and I hope that our happy days will be many;
Our children are now all grown and are away,
now we can look forward to a retirement day;
As long as we're together we will then know,
that we will survive wherever we both do go.

Sierra Voges
LOST WITHOUT HIM

To Danny—Thanx for understanding what I went through & being there for me. Love ya—Si

I saw you standing there,
Your looks were oh so rare.
You were so fresh and new,
I couldn't help but fall in love with you.

We were so good together,
No one could separate us ever.
We were the perfect pair,
No one could help but stare.

Now I'll never see the sparkle in your eye,
And I won't forget the thrill when you walked by.
I'll remember how I felt when you were near,
Now on my cheek, tears appear.

Today the sky above is so gray,
Oh now I wish you could stay.
I know I'll never forget this day,
This day they carry your casket away.

Phoebe R Japp
THE LOVE OF GOD

I would like to dedicate this poem to my husband Johan. Because of his love for me I now have a faint grasp of the immense love of God for me.

I see it in a sunset, and in a seed so small; and also in the trees outside, and in the leaves that fall. I see it in the morning dew, the spiders in their webs; I see it in the sunrise, and in the tide that ebbs.

I hear it in the thunder, and also when the sky is clear; I hear it in the rustling grass, I feel His presence very near. I hear it in the birds that sing, and also in the bubbling springs; I feel it in my heartbeat at the wonder this all brings.

I see it in the budding leaf, and in new fruit upon the trees; I see it in the love I feel for you and you for me. I feel it in a baby's grip, and see it in his smile; I know it by Christ's promise: "I'm coming back in just a little while."

I taste it in an apple, and smell it in a red, red rose; I see it in a river as to the sea it flows. I see it in the rainbow, that is spread across the sky, knowing now why Jesus came to die.

I want to thank you God, for loving each of us so much—for eyes to see and hands to feel and touch. For birds that sing, for flowers that smell; and thank you Lord, for doing everything so well.

Leo Corion
LOCOMOTIVE 97

The Connecticut Valley Railroad Museum, Essex, Connecticut.

When I was thigh-high,
From out of the pass,
Came this billowing monster
Of iron and brass.

From tiny at first
To mammoth it grew;
On haunches of steam
Like blurps in a stew.

With a single bright eye
Like the lid of a tin;
Coming toward me it bored me
To spot out my sin.

But as its bright eye
Sped by me to pass
Into glimmering, shimmering
Curtains of glass;

So great was my terror
On quaking terrain,
(The day Mother took me
To first see the train,)

That she knelt to confess
She meant but to beguile;
For she knew in the end
The caboose bore a smile.

Alice Judge
OUR TIME WILL COME AGAIN

To Heidi Our time did come again. All my love.

Our time will come again.

You stand tall, proud, majestic,

As the beautiful tulip.

Tuck your body in, wrapping yourself to its center
You want no one to see, especially me.
You are on the road to independence.
I have watered you in times of drought,
I have sheltered you in times of rain.
But you must be on your way,

And do not understand these things.

I watch you go in prayers,
Knowing a time for us will come again.

Yvonne Corbello
THE WINDOW

For mama, who is my guiding light

Out through the window filled with black,
He stares.

Beyond the world somewhere better,
He dreams.

Within the void so isolated,
He lives.

Chained to life steeped in hurts,
He cries.

Wistful of things devoid of pain,
He hopes.

Focused on a star twinkling brightly,
He prays:

God, I pray thee to transport me from this, my hell
And take me, thy child, to Never-Weary Land.

Out through the window filled with black,
He soars.

DiAnn Hodge
THAT SPECIAL PLACE

To my family and friends for their love and support.

I look on tomorrow
With a smile on my face,
For there shall be no sorrow
As we come to that special place.

The grass will always be green
And the laughter will always flow.
Life as we have seen
Will no longer be so.

The storms will all cease
And the sun will shine,
Our love for each other will increase
As our hearts become kind.

The birds will sing
And the flowers will bloom.
It will always be spring
With never any gloom.

As I wander away
To this special place,
To a bright and happy day;
I'll carry a smile on my face.

Christi Wynia
THE MYSTERIOUS GIRL

I dedicate this poem to my Uncle Alan, whom I never met, but whom I would have loved.

There is a girl as old as I
Who loves to watch the breeze
Blow through the trees.

She sits by the seaside
All day long, watching the wind
Blow the waves along.

She never cries, she never sighs.
She is always kind and nice.
I do indeed not know this girl.

She is in the eyes of all.
No one hates this mysterious girl,
Though no one has ever seen her.

Only one who will soon die.
She lives in the sky, way up high.
If only I could see her.

James E Rhodes
WHO AM I?

This poem is dedicated to Phyllis Marie

Too many times in life I find
I've left alot of things undone behind.
Did I take the time to say "I'm sorry"
To someone I've wronged along the way.
If not then—Who am I?

When the trials in life are hard to bear
and the road is harder to go
Did I give Him thanks for the things
I've had and the joys of long ago
If not then—Who am I?

When I feel the warmth and love of a little hand—that touches my heart
With all His love—do I not feel
The joy of being loved & loving
If not then—Who am I?

When someone I meet along life's busy road
Too tired to cope with life's heavy load
Did I stop and say—Can I give you a hand along the way
If not then—Who am I?

When I stand before the Almighty God
Can I hold my head up high and say

It is I Lord, your true and faithful servant
Not who am I?

Capt Irby F Wood
O LOVELY HIBISCUS

Dedicated to Amy H. Pound.

A green potted plant in our living room
Rests on the table before a broad picture window
A red hibiscus has bloomed in its green leaves
It reminds me of the distant Pacific Figis
The bloom, like an exquisite golden horn,
Seems ready to burst into an ethereal tune
Here in this ninth floor living room
O how its beauty has nullified the gloom
From a long illness and slow recovery
The gift from a dear friend
A god-send it has been
If I had a pretty girl to compare
I would place a red hibiscus in her hair.

Albert Lombardo
ANGEL'S HAIR

Dedicated to my feminine Angel.—No one knows our secret . . .

The limitations of life are finite—but the gift of fantasy need not indication nor strife.

In my diligent toil to reach You—You have come and gone within a hair's-breadth manifestation, arresting my soul to shudder in a world of inquisitiveness.

You have scorched my seat of life with spellbinding passion, only to shiver my heart to sleep.

You unfurled me expectation, only to never decipher its meaning. —I've been smitten by you!

You've sashayed into my life like a mischievous pixy, only to torch me with assumptions and theories, embodying me in muse.

Initially You were omnipresent—awakening my long-dormant heart to a sense of worth, but now Your telltale signs are my pining sobs. Sing back Your presence on my heartstrings! Where have You gone?

My heart is being chastised by Your sudden hiatus—just when I thought I was on to a striking revelation. Have Your pursuing of me daunted You of my discovering Your unterrestrial origin? Hostile we are—in a globe of chaos. Our existence is quite inexplicable, governed by deterrence. But I, live by not the sword, but by the light of God, uncorrupted in mind and pristine at heart.

Was Your stay here [Earth] been sojourn, to fall upon the mercy of emotion? —How could You have known of my despair?!

While You transiently reside on the undetectable "dark side of the moon," Your home is within a new dimension of teleportation at Your command.

You monitor Earth, but further no direct contact: The laws of celestial attendants are governed by God!

She stands aloft the billowy clouds. Her feet over an innocuous blaze. And the pith of Her Being is femininity. A beauty so striking that—a law of insanity applies to whom "look" Her way. Her eyes are a pious choir, in harmony when angels sing. She choreographs the children's dance. She balances the toddler's first stance.

Her pulchritude is breathtaking—incandescent like "Ezekiel's" chariot vision.

The synchronism of our thoughts had once been attuned . . . You disclosed me undeniable affection. You imparted me speculation, of which at times had me implicitly believing that no Earthly thing could have possibly spawned the manifestations that You'd revealed . . . What was Your mission? What was Your message? —But You are not all of an enigma to me: Folklore says 'angel's hair disappear!'

Kathi Nolan

TWO FACES TURN TOGETHER . . .

To all those who colour my world with love and laughter.

Two faces turn together . . .
eyes wink
smiles form
laughter follows

Two hands clasp as one . . .
walking side by side
sharing
bit
by
bit
piece
by
piece
the secrets of each

Two friends form as one.

Edithe Hawkins

LITTLE HEARTS

To my darling little boy David. The absolute sunshine of my life

Little hearts, pure as gold
Tell you what all Mommys are told
Bring you things you'd never buy
But always seem to make you cry

Little hearts that seem to be
All you ever want to see
In their eyes you see yourself
The best in all the commonwealth

Little hearts bigger than life
Their tears cut you like a knife
Scraped knees and bleeding hands
They snap right back like rubber bands

Little hearts are best observed
When their energy is very curbed
Eyes closed tight, bunny held close
Better get ready for tomorrow's dose

Susan C Smith

ROSES IN THE WINTER

In Loving Memory of J. W. Sled. To Pa-Pa with love,

It's Spring and the roses are in full bloom.
The bees are busy, from flower to flower they zoom.

Spring is a colorful time of year.
A time to share with those we hold dear.

Each day with you is Springtime.
I'm so glad you're mine.

You gave me a love like I've never known.
The thought of life without you chills me to the bone.

As Spring comes to an end so does life for many things.
The roses that were once in full bloom, to life they now cling.

Life faded from you, leaving you only a memory in my mind.
I, patiently wait for Spring, hoping again you I'll find.

Unlike the roses, you won't be back come Spring.
But my precious memories of you are the next best thing.

God gave us memory so we might see roses in the winter.

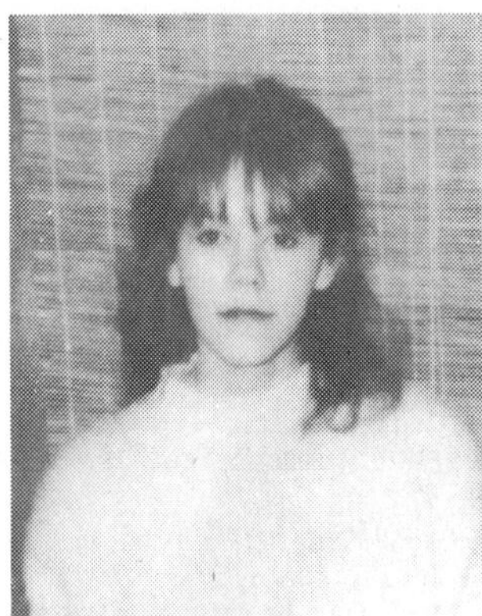

Jody Anderson

Jody Anderson

TIME SURVIVES

I dedicate this poem to my mother and father whom I love very much, and my grandfather who passed away before I wrote it.

Time will come and
Time will go
Whether it be fast
or slow,

Time will give and
Time will take
Time will make and
Time will break,

Time is yours and
Time is mine
Since way back when
To here and now,

Time brings life and
Time brings death
Time is rich and
Of great health,

Much like time are
You and I
Because the Fact
We still survive.

Russell L Meyers

CHILDREN OF THE STORM

To the homeless children in the world.

When as young ones we were cold, as time went by we weren't told.
That we were children of the storm, no love was with us to keep warm.
When there was no hope around, we were like fugitives on the bound.
Reaching for someone we could hold on to, warm and tender, just like you.

We are crying little children, crying, we are dying little children, dying.
For someone to hold on to! Could it be true? Could it be you?
Can't be running all our lives, we children urge for family ties.
It's not asking much to say, that you'll take us home today.

There was a chill in the air, winter growing, ever near.
What can become of us children of the storm? At times it's not easy to be born.
Hardships grow, and bitterness flows, within our hearts, only God knows.
It can't all be bad you see, we children need to live in harmony.

Just as children of the storm, we felt the people's daily scorn.
Yes, just as children of the storm, we felt our lives being tattered and torn.
We were in another world our very own, our painful cries, they weren't even shown.
As children of the storm, we're always facing a bitter and cold morn.

We're not your enemies, we're your friends, it is our love for you we send.
Do you know the protector he watches over them? And loves them over and over again?
And yet they need that close relation, among the hearts of many a nation.
Adopt a child of the storm, for that one might keep you friendly and warm.

Dolores J Garrett

JUST THE TWO OF US

This poem is dedicated to my beloved, Eddie

How happy we are.
Just you and me.
That's the way it should be.
The two os us, Ed and Dee.
A love that should last
forever to a tee.

Teresa Evans

HEARTBEAT

To my wonderful husband Richard—All my love to the Love of my Life.

My heart skips a beat every time our eyes meet,
with every word my heart has heard knowing that you really love me.
Hold me tight it couldn't feel more right. Stay with me today and tomorrow, forever if you like. Feel our love, it ignites the desires of fire deep within. Our love true and strong; If we always put our love first we will never go wrong. It's a total heartrush knowing how much our love has been through, you were there for me I was there for you. It goes to show what true love can really do.

Barbara Levitt

GREEN

To Jonathan and Emily

Yellow turned to Orange
Black kept watch outside
Red reflected off the pistol
Blue broke down and cried

LeRoy E Fox Jr

ANGEL OF MY HEART

Dedicated to Janet Clark

If you'd like to know the secrets of my heart,
Just fly on inside because you are already a part.
To a place where you make up the colors of my nites and days,
To a place where you know that my love for you already stays.
A place which has forgotten about all time and space,
Where we can travel hand and hand at whatever pace.
Whether it be a slow casual walk or a fast run,
Whether it would be to the shining moon or burning sun.
A place where roads or maps have no definite destinations,
Where we can go and travel using just our imaginations.
A place where you can have never ending moon lite nites,
Or take to the crystal clear skies for everlasting flights.
So soar on inside and become a part,
For surely I have truly met "The Angel of my Heart."

Shane J Lussier

SONG OF THE WIND

Thanks to God for the gift of life and writing, To my family for their undying love, And to my friends for their undying faith.

I'd see her every morning dancing on the blades of grass,
Drinking the sweet dew off the fragile buttercups.

As the sun would draw itself higher into the dark blue sky,
She would settle herself quietly beneath the weeping willow.

She would sing a haunting, yet majestic song
That would call to all the creatures of nature;
Who would gather around her listening in respectful silence.

As the moon would rise above the Earth,
It seemed as though she had a mutual agreement
With the Man on the Moon,
For she silently smiled and gave a nod,
And with that she rose up and drifted off into the night.

John W LaRocca

DIFFERENCE

To my wife Louise—who made the difference.

Yours would be
A love full grown,
You would not want
A quarter moon.

You would choose
A rose in bloom,
A bud to you
No treasure holds.

I have taken
Love from seed,
Have nourished it
And watched it grow . . .

A quarter moon
To me is full,
A bud is promise
Of a ROSE.

Patricia Ann Marchese

I CAN'T IMAGINE

To my children, Paulette, Lawrence, Derek, Destry, & Christopher My undying love

I can't imagine not being born or ever in my mother's arms,
I can't imagine not being loved or having children of my own,

I can't imagine not growing up in a happy home.

I can't imagine not having a best friend or being hungry,
I can't imagine not going to school,
I can't imagine not seeing the pride in my parent's eyes when I graduated, got married and had my first child.

I can't imagine when I got divorced and left, the pain I felt, the terror in my children's eyes of the unexplainable,
I can't imagine my children all grown up now, married with children of their own.

I can't imagine not having a chance at love the second time,
Love so perfect you wonder if you are dreaming,
I can't imagine losing all of life's experiences that which is so wonderful.

But most of all I can't imagine dying,
And I'm not looking forward to it at all,
Dear God, Why, I can't imagine . . .

Sasha Rumbaut
FROZEN SMEARDROPS

Dedicated to Jason O'Hearn, who had the strength to endure

locked up for a chemical dependency
succumbs to a suicidal tendency
the only test tubes here are hollow
led by brainwashing, insanity follows
whipped with suspenders, face "numb to hell"
kill the addictions, his soul they will sell
a sin of pink panthers and musical notes
a mutilated Homeslice dead in his trenchcoat
No Cure to divert pain
No Smiths to sympathize
Just a Pinesol-scented floor
where he falls to his knees and cries
A razor to shave with—he took it apart
He slashed at his wrists like they tore through his heart
A simple white gown now dotted with red
a trail of crimson that leads to the Dead
No tears fall for Jason
THEY led him to this
I hold back the crying and blow him a kiss.

Lou Paterno
JEANETTE
"MY LITTLE GIRL"

She came on a day in the month of April.
Not unexpected and totally welcomed.
A Sister to her Brother.
A Daughter to her Mother.
A little girl to her Father.
We have walked a long way since then;
Climbed a few mountains—
Even explored a few valleys.
Shared in many highs.
Suffered thru many lows.
That is what makes growing up.
But you know.
She is still a Sister to her Brother.
A Daughter to her Mother.
And she will always be Daddy's little girl.

Frances Morrey
COVERUP

Failures and guilts,
Layered and covered,
So deep.
Victories and joys,
Bubble and sparkle,
So False.
Worries and cares,
Hidden and futile,
So real.
Goodwill and peace,
Needed and wanted,
So rare.

Karyne Golden

Karyne Golden
SOMETHING IN THE SUNRISE

There's something in each sunrise
That makes us want to fly,
And when we find we cannot fly
It makes us want to weep.
There's magic in the full moon
Which we see and wish to hold,
And when we find it can't be held
The tears begin to seep.

But never do we need to hold
The magic in our hands
Or fly through daybreak neon
Above the glowing sands.
The dreams we have might never live,
We may not own the things we see,
But still we'll have the memory,
And that, my friend, we keep.

Jeannine Fencil
THE EXPERT

Come time for a job
That needs to be done
And we need an expert
There's sure to be one
Who'll stand up and shout,
"I know what you need
"And what it will cost.
"Cost? Oh my, yes, indeed!
"Cost is a privilege,
"Please make no mistake.
"A great deal of money
"This project will take."
So we pay for the labor,
And we pay for the parts.
We pay for the license,
And false stops and starts.
One day the job's done
And we find that we've paid
Half to the expert
Who sat in the shade.

S I G Hartley
OTHER THINGS TAUGHT

In memory of my Grandfather To the living Love of my Family and Bob, my husband

Today I met a man who spoke to me
Saying, "What things have been made known unto thee?"

So I spoke of Hardware, Software, and plastic credit cards
Stocks, bonds, and mutual funds,
Abortion, divorce, and one night stands
Peace in strength and man loving man;
Our toxic water, soil and air
The wildlife we slaughter without care;
How the objectives in life are power, money, and sex,
How the means to enlightenment are Speed, Cocaine, and Smack.

Before I finished he started away
I called after him, "Have a good day!"
He stopped and stared at me
I waved and asked what his name might be,
In a weak sad voice with moistened eye
Came his one word reply,
"God!"

Diane Lynn Briestensky
DEATH

The fear of death does not live inside of me
It is death I am awating

It is then my body will be at rest and my mind shall be free

For a chance of peace and a new life—death is wished upon me *

Joan M Segraves
THE ROAD ONCE SHARED

Dedicated to James H. and Mary E. Flook While I had the chance to tell you, I Love You, Mom and Dad

So long ago, so far away, our lives once touched each others.
But now we've chosen different roads, mine the one less traveled.
So many times I thought to look back to see if you would follow, but never a shadow crossed the path from which we both had traveled.
Now I go along this road forging my own path.
Many stones lay in the way, each one needing turned.
Many times cut and bleeding, I found myself alone.
How I longed for the touch of your hand, the comfort of your presence.
But only forward can I go, still reaching for my destination. So clearly can I see it now, like a dream come true. Only onward can I press, hoping to share it with you.
Now my road has brought me back again to cross with yours.
And so I find we both are stronger for the stones we've turned. But alas we must say farewell, as your road has come to an end. But the next time that we meet, we'll never part again.
Still I travel along this road with many stones to turn, but I think of you often, and miss you so, I Love You, Mom and Dad.

Renée Pendleton
ONE OF A KIND

Always on my mind are memories shared with you.
You are always there for me, and I want you to know I'm forever here for you.
From the start, it seems our love was one of a kind.
A dream come true—is a dream of you.
You keep my spirits high. I hope your feelings are just as strong, so our love will never die.
This love we share is so good—so rare—
I'll never let it go. This seems to be the perfect love . . . a love so hard to find.
In my heart I'll always know, our love is one of a kind.

C J McHenry
WHERE AM I?

Dedicated to: Matthew J. Dunn, to whom this was written

So many times I sit alone,
My mind wanders through events,
Things that have been,
Things to come,
What could have been,
And what might be.

Regrets and broken promises linger,
Hopes and dreams unwind,
They all play on a stage.
People and places pass across,
and disappear.
Most are faded memories,
or vast dreams,
Then there's you . . .

You linger between past and future,
Sometimes you start to fade,
Only to return again,
Do I forget you, leave you behind?
or include you in the future.

I want you there, always,
Only you fear the role,
We fight a hidden battle,
will against will,
soul against soul.

Will you exit, only to fade completely,
or will you exist, forever.

My mind ponders, trying to comprehend,
to sort facts and fiction,
promises from deceit,
love from lust.

What conclusions will eventually arise?
When will the final decision be made,
Who will draw the line.

Will you walk away and fade,
How will I know your decision?
Or will I give up, and turn away,
Never to return.
Will I know how you feel?
Who will be hurt, who will celebrate.

The past is so distant, faded, and darkened,
Never to return,
The future, like a dawning day,
brightens as it moves upon us,
In which direction do I look for you?
Behind, soon to be lost forever.

Or are you lingering in the dawn,
Hoping and dreaming as I do.

Wherever you are, I only want
to be aware, to know, to understand,
My place on stage, the one in your mind, the one your life plays on,
Where Am I?

Lynda Iannuccilli

Lynda Iannuccilli
YOUR SECRET FANTASY, MY SECRET AGONY

To my fantasy man; John. Love Lynda

You are my husband, my lover and my best friend
So why are you making me wish that I were dead?
It's not the things you say, it's not the things you do,
It's all those secret thoughts inside which I know are so true.
You have told me so many times that you love me and adore me
Then please tell me why, why am I so afraid of your secret fantasy?
Is it because deep down inside I will always know fear?
Because the one you love, your real true love, you can never hold near?
So everytime I am in your arms and you're holding me close,
I will forever know you are fantasizing with a ghost.
A ghost of a woman who is so very much alive,
And I am always competing with her whenever I'm by your side.
I can tell by your eyes, by your smile and by your voice,
How much you really love her and I will forever be your second choice.
So keep on smiling, keep on holding me close, telling me you love me, holding from me your secret fantasy,
And I will continue to cry in the night, thinking of her, my heart breaking, holding from you my secret agony.

anne marie malley
BLINDED BY SIGHT

I would like to thank Tammy, Stephen, Robbie, Todd, Reid, Lance, Juanita, Craig, Brenda, Brian and Glen—Mrs. Mae Firth, Brenda Albert and Theresa Guitard.

We like to think we can all adapt,
but along the way we have forgotten our handicapped,
but here we are in changing times,
still, some people have closed their minds.

You who are ashamed to let us come out,
we need to know what life is all about,
you who do not know what we feel inside,
and yet from us you will hide.

Are you unable to face us for what we are?
or unable to face what you are?
When will this bigotry and prejudice disappear?
someday, maybe, when you let go of your fear.

You let your eyes judge us, instead of your heart.
we look and act different, but that's what sets us apart.
If you can't see beyond what we are, then truly, you are blind,
and if you really want to see, open your heart and open your mind.

But, if you shut us out, there is no doubt,
You'll never know what we're all about.
Life can be dreadful, and it can be meaningful,
but most of all we'd like too, just like you,
to have peace of mind and be a part of mankind.

To be a part of you, that's all we ask,
don't hide us away, don't keep us in the past,
we're looking for a future, a place to be,
and we won't find it, if you won't see,
That what we are, we'll always be.

Wilma Shockey Ryder
TO MY WONDERFUL BROTHER TOM

Thomas Howard Shockey
Oldest Brother

Tom is the greatest brother I have
He works three jobs as he slaves,
He can do anything he put his mind to,
He's a pro in what he does,

Tom is the greatest friend I got
He has a lot of things to do.
But when I call him now and then
He is always there when I need him.

I would hate to see anything happen to him,
Then I wouldn't have my friend then,
To talk and listen to,
But he is the best brother I have.

I love my brother Tom so much,
And He is best brother in the bunch,
I'm so glad he's my brother and my friend;
He's the best brother in the wind.

Katharine Victoria Armstrong
THE TAPESTRY

Ulysses is coming home from the wars,
And with him come a hundred million stars.
For once upon a time such a man as he
Roamed in Troy for all the world to see.

He lived in another time across an ancient sea
But now Ulysses is coming home to me.
Perhaps it happened millennium ago—
They said he was a Greek; someone told me so
And all I know
And all I see
Is that Ulysses will be coming home to me.
A master of disguise as always was the case . . .
Ulysses is the conqueror of his race.

Circe forgot. She will never grieve for him
Because she has no memory of when
I woke up one morning to decry
The mystery of: "What am I?"

Ulysses is coming back to me
Although still mortal yet a hero in my sight.
And, for you beloved friends this tapestry is ended,
And I say to you: "Goodnight."

Claudia Davis
SINGLE GIRLS—SINGLE BARS

There they sit,
Preening their feathers,
Waiting.
Watching.
Eagles, Sparrows, and Crows.
Needing to be loved,
for an hour, day, or night.
They are the product of no attention.
Cooing at the motley robed specimens.
Pecking at crumbs,
Crouching for flight.

Waiting.
Watching.
Petitioning.

Walter W Robinson
GUESS WHO

To Linda

Who has the Sweetest Voice
This side of Heaven, Guess Who
Dear little one, it's You
Who's the Sweetest One
This side of Heaven
This side of Heaven
Dear Little One, it's You
Who is the neatest, Sweetest
With the Stars All in her Eyes
You know little one, it's you
Who has the Stars in her Eyes
Straight from Heaven
Dear Little One, it's You
Who is the neatest, Sweetest
With the stars all in her Eyes
You know Little One, it's You
Who loves You now, and Eternally,
Guess Who
Dear Little One, it's Me, that's Who.

William Ralph Disney
THE FACE OF I LOVE YOU

To all the "Old Maids" out there who never yet found a spouse; I share with you that common ground—You are welcome in my house . . .

An evening of dinner and dance
on the veranda under a full moon,
with the caress of soft music carrying a light breeze in June;
Neither of which could hold a candle to you,
when you put on the face of I LOVE YOU.

On a sunset drive along an ocean coast in a convertible,
with its mist spraying the windshield so flirtable;
No one could ever say they weren't performing for you,
when you put on the face of I LOVE YOU.

At the game our Alma Mater played so well,
before a packed house they won—score would tell;
But when it all ended the ushers cleared a path for you,
when you put on the face of I LOVE YOU.

Believe it or not the checkbook bounced—visa and MasterCard overdrawn,
this dreadful news once I had heard it was the storm before the calm;
So, honey, I must confess let's just start anew,
because you know I can't resist when you put on the face of I LOVE YOU . . .

Joanna Gilman
BROKEN WING

Friendship is like a dream that never dies,
And a flock that never parts.
The dream doesn't die, but it is remembered,
And the flock doesn't part, but there are those that fall.

There's a beauty of a rose,
And a calmness of a cloudless day.
The beauty dies, eventually, but with a knowing that it will return,
And the calmness of a day is sometimes overcome by a violent storm, that too will pass.

It is also a tenderness you would give to a bird with a broken wing,
And the love you would present as if you were its mother.
But the broken wing is soon mended,
And you let it go, knowing you gave to it the tenderness and love it needed to survive.

But most of all, it's the secrets you shared,
The times you've enjoyed, and the memories . . .
Never forgotten.

Jamesina F Fillers
DREAMS

In the midst of unspoken dreams
We tempt our minds to wander
To unveil those secret felt things
We refuse in the conscious to ponder

Swallowed up in our own little world
With no one allowed to enter
We can grasp all the thoughts being hurled
All alone, but still in the center

We can act out any lead part
Only one, but in full command
All the things felt in the heart
But not acted out by the hand

Beware that your mind doesn't fall
Complete to the world of illusion
For returning to now may be all
That saves you from total confusion

William J Price
CRIES OF THE LONELY

Dedicated to Jay R., Nick & Larry for their help in times of loneliness.

Why do I hear the cries of the lonely,
Why do I feel the agony of the tortured,
I hear them crying in my sleep, and when I am awake.
The salt of their tears, burn me like flames.

Why do they talk to me?
Have they talked to anybody else?

These are questions I ask them.
But they don't answer me, they
just keep crying.

Do they cry for help?
Do they cry for joy?
I hear their tortured souls.
But they always stay invisible to
me.

I only feel their tears rolling down
my face,
When I try to wipe them away, they
always keep rolling down my face.
Each tear is a tortured soul, and more
tears appear everyday.

Swimming in the eternal ever lasting
crypt.
Just listen and you will hear cries of
the lonely.

Russell V Varney Jr
FROSTY WINGTIPS
Frosty wingtips
from an Eagles flight.
As they fly with fear,
without a fight.

They fly through summer.
They fly through fall.
They fly through winter
and spring.

Frosty wingtips
as it may be.
For their biggest fear,
is you and me.

We make them emblems
for freedom and peace.
Although they see us
the selfish beast.

Their beauty they spread,
so far and wide.
How will we explain
the way they died?

Frosty wingtips—The Eagles
cry! ! !

Kenneth Tamsin
SLEEP, MY SON

To Matt, may we grow in love together.

Sleep, My son and dream your
dreams
of better days to come
For feelings warm and tender
with a family joined as one

In your peaceful slumber
Find a place that is serene
My son I feel so sorry
For all the hurt and pain you've seen

Were I possessed of the power
To alter space and time
The love I'd recall but most of all
We would leave the tears behind

So sleep my son and dream your
dreams
of better days to come
For feeling warm and tender
With a family joined as one
For one so small and so exposed
with no way to defend
Against the angry words and acts
Tell me the scars will mend

So sleep, my son and dream you
dreams
For better days will come,
with feelings warm and tender
and a Family joined as one.

Jack S Brenizer
FRIENDS
The thought of friends—both old and
new—
Doth fill our hearts with healing
balm.
Then with quickened strides we
tackle anew
All that faces us with new-found
calm.

A friendly smile and words of cheer
Lend encouragement along life's
way.
Supplying that which we all endear
In times of pain for us they
pray.

Life for each is most unique
When shared with kindred
minds.
So, whatever your lot, to be complete
Be a friend who will stand the
test of time.

Rick Harrell
ALL MY DRAMS

To Linda, the lady who inspires, and shows me the true meaning of love, I Love you.

Before you came along, I never
felt as I do now.
My hopes are clearer, my dreams
brighter, and my fantasy,
reality.
Before you came along, I lived for
now, and never really cared
about tomorrow.
I never really wanted to share, or
be a part of, or be with, as I do
with you.
Before you came along, my life
was only routine, often with
little or no meaning.
You have brought to my life
clarity, and stability, together
combining a unique quality.
Before you came along, I saw a
world of black and white.
Your love has given me a world of
color, and a lifetime of promise
and immeasureable
contentment.
Before you came along—
what was my life
without you?
What would my life be
without you?

Jordan Shiveck
IN LOVE IN A CROWD

To my beautiful wife Haley who inspired this poem.

There may be noise and conversation
There may be interaction
Even surrounded by a vast population
They'd be a minute fraction

For their words and faces are not
absorbed
And their buzz is fully silenced
It is not that I have become bored
It's your potent gaze I sensed

It's as if no one did exist
It's as if they were not present
For at the moment my heart was
kissed
Nothing could feel more pleasant

More pleasant than knowing I fulfill
More pleasant than knowing I'm all
that matters
Knowing they vanished, to you,
without will
Knowing only our feelings are being
lathered

Cleansing any past sour moments
Cleansing any joint time taken for
granted
For this is what our purpose meant
To stare and feel enchanted.

Bridgett Olene Tarante
DEADLY CANDY
It's the big thing around,
every kid knows about it.
Many have found
they can't live without it.
It brings a good high,
and the cost is cheap.
Would this drug lie?
It's your life it will seek.
This drug is called CRACK
and it thrives on the young.
When did it start?
Just look what it's done.
Children Beware!
It's coming for you!
Crack does not care
when you die from it too!

Jennifer Brown
GRANDPA

To my Grandpa who has always been a diamond to me.

There he was a big old man
with his dogs at his side and some
ale in his hand.
He was innocent of all
but guilty were his looks,
he trusted everyone
and was taken by many crooks.

Adventure was his life
he lived in a dream
he lived through such strife
but his old mind was keen.
He was a great man he was my hero,
but the respect he got was mostly
zero.

His last days were long, drawn out
and weary.
They put him in a room that was dirty
and dreary
They all thought he was old and
senile
but I knew and saw
This was a great man
he was my GRANDPA

D Janette Land Warnix
SEARCH FOR TOMORROW

To my wonderful Husband and my beautiful daughters, the sweetest Grand Children and Mom & Dad, The joys of my life

Everyone at sometime searches
Some for money, some for fame
others for love, and still others
for happiness

My search was for continued
happiness
not just happiness that comes and
goes
but for someone that cares, and is
always there

My search ended when I found you
continued happiness is just being near
you
my need, to love and cherish you
throughout the years
All I want is to be with you
from sunrise to sunrise
Continued happiness is just simply
you

Annette Theel
HERE I SIT
Here I sit
We're miles apart
It's been over for months
Yet I'm still falling apart.

People tell me to forget
I have to move on.
But I shake my head
And tell them they're wrong.
My love for you is still strong.

I miss you so much
Sometimes I just start to cry.
Why is it so hard to say good-bye?

I don't want us to end
Please can't we try again?

Chuck Morgan
THE POET

Dedicated to my grandmother, Elizabeth Cunningham Foster Young, who has contributed more to my life than anyone else I know, and whom I love very much.

Sometimes seated in front of
smudged sliding glass doors,
He stares silently into a world filled
with both "no" and "yes."
He longs to paint with words the "is,"
But tires from always capturing what
was,
Missing the world of both "now" and
"because."

Other times, lying between cool crisp
sheets,
He gazes intently at a ceiling full of
stories and truths.
He yearns once more to put picture to
pen,
But falls asleep, hoping he'll
remember again
All the deep and personal things he's
mused.

Most times, though, laboring alone
within himself,
He bears painfully for the world
children of beauty and strength.
He gives back to creation ideas of its
own,
But adds color and shape, perspective and tone,
Enriched with an insight and depth
all his own.

Cathryn Braun
MOMMY WHY?
Faces hover over me,
I know they're my security.
When they smile—everything's
okay.

Wish it were like this every day.

Sometimes at night—alone I cry,
'Cause I can't help but wonder why
My mommy seems to get so mad.
I didn't know that I was bad.

I like to play and just have fun,
And then she yells—what have I
done?
Seems she's angry most every day.
I guess that I'm just in her way.

She says that I'm her little doll,
And that she loves me most of all.
But why is it she hurts me so
And acts like she wants me to go?

I'm so little and always wrong,
But someday I'll grow big and
strong.
And maybe then, I'll know why
My mommy always made me cry.

Wanda Shelton-Hardebeck
REBIRTH

If I die tomorrow
 I'll sleep in peace,
The beat of my heart
 Will forever cease.
Others will live on
 Day by day,
And the grief for me
 Will go away.
Then another will take
 My place,
And live my life
 Pace by pace.
As long as mankind is
 On this Earth,
Another like me will
 Come in birth.
In a new babe He will
 Place my soul,
To live a new life and
 Reach a new goal.

Eric Bernier
THE DOVE IS A HAWK

To all the sensitive and compassionate souls who choose to land instead of closing their eyes and flying over the darkness.

A dove
Flies
Over burnt landscapes
Without landing
Nor thinking
Nor crying
As a hawk
Flies
Over burnt landscapes
Without landing
Nor thinking
Nor crying,
Clawing the dove,
Its white coat
Becoming red.

Joan Scott Anthony R N
THE SOUND OF LOVE

Dedicated to Laureen Hardwick of Pittsburgh, a member of my church, who nursed me through a terrible illness. I hope she knows how much she is loved.

Love makes no audible sound,
But it can be heard.
I heard it each time I woke up,
Those long, cold nights,
To see you sitting nearby.
I heard it in spoonsful of soup,
Swallows of cold ginger ale.
I heard it when you sponged
The fever and pain away.
I heard it in your packing and
carrying,
To get me moved to a warmer place.
I heard it in all the hundred little
things
You thought went unnoticed . . .
They all created a symphony of love
In the silence.
It does not matter a whit to either of
us
That we are black, and white.
Love is totally colorblind! And yes,
Even though I am nearly totally deaf,
I clearly heard the sound of love!

Dorrie E Carling
RAINDROPS

Walking beside the foam-flecked
waves
I hear the singing of the sea in shells;
gulls wheeling overhead in a stormy
sky
grey as my thoughts, which will not
die.

Rain lightly falling on my face
is as a gentle stroking of my heart;
beauty and peace returning at last
negating the fears and the terrors
since passed.

Life is a mixture of sunlight and
storm,
of laughter and weeping and joy and
unease;
But deep in the heart Thy Love is
revealed
as the raindrops gently our bruises
have healed.

Jennifer Blankenship
RAIN

To my friends, Who told me I couldn't do What I've already done.

Rain is falling,
Dripping, dropping,
It is calling;
As my horse
is clipping, clopping.

Rain is calling to me;
Telling me I must flee.
Flee away from the world I see,
Away from all forever to be.

Joseph M Robinson
CAN'T FIND THE WORDS

How many times have you heard
Someone say "I just can't find the
words,"
To describe something they've seen
or heard,
Like a beautiful sunset or some
exotic birds.

It's because that particular subject
Touched them in the deepest part of
their heart.
And, not being familiar with
indescribable things
"I can't find the words" is how they
start.

We've all had this happen to us
And a wonderful feeling it truly is.
To feel something so overwhelming
for us
"We can't find the words" is the way
it is.

And if we can't find the words
somehow,
Then perhaps we aren't supposed to
tell.
We're supposed to keep those
precious moments
Locked in our heart; to talk might
break the spell.

Each person has many special
moments
Kept in their heart and in their mind.
Most of these one might want to
share with others,
But the words are too hard to find.

Don Toussaint Ehrman
ROSEWOOD

Dedicated to my Mother and Father for all their loving kindness and support.

Was that a voice just heard
to break the stillness?
Or a serenity
created for a sound?
I hear it yet,
so quiet
so soft
barely a whisper,

placid and gentle
as a valley
Will it depart and never return?
I hope it returns,
so I may hold it once more,
in my soul

Félix A Grana-Raffucci
TERRIBLE ARE THE NIGHTS OF REMEMBRANCE

Terrible are the nights of remembrance.
Witches nights, Cool full-moon
nights.
Nights of hunger and thirst.
Ghosts dance over me with their icy
selfishness.

Terrible are those nights remember-
ing you.
My head blows as a coffin full of me.
Sensations leave my skin.
My sex grows into an Universe.
Leprechauns smile.
Virgins are sacrificed.

Dark are the nights of remembrance.
Shaman nights. Aromatic herbs.
Haunted forests.
Odors of years passing by.
Smell of ages.

Terrible are the nights of remembrance.

Jim P Sanchez
I WOULD CROSS ANY OCEAN

I would cross any Ocean, brave any
storm, just to be with the one I love.
But, I also can swamp my Amor with
a tidal wave of emotion when my
deep sensitivities erupt.
Romance could be shipwrecked if I
give way to these gale-force moods.
It's true I'm at my lovable best when
protecting and nurturing others.
I also can arouse the protective
instinct in those around me when I
shift to the opposite role of
vulnerable child.
In Amor, however I try to balance
these dual traits.
In Amor, I find deep passions almost
impossible to keep in check during
the fiery periods that warm my life.
Patience is needed before I can turn
these dreams into reality.
While I'd walk on water for my
sweetheart, sometimes that first step
in an affair of the heart can plunge
me into a sea of shyness and doubt.

Willa Leonard
EVERYTHING OLD IS NEW AGAIN

To Delores (Dee) Ingraham who inspired me to enter the contest and who entitled this poem, my cherished friend of the fifties whom I met in the eighties.

Do you remember the early fifties,
our young teen days?
The movies starred the great Rock
Hudson and Doris Day.
Hit records featured the songs of
Rosie Clooney and Patti "The
Singing Rage" Page.

Their popularity soon grew lean
When Elvis' "Blue Suede Shoes"
made the scene.
We stopped "Pretending" with Nat
King Cole
Because Bill Haley and the Comets
said, we should "Shake, Rattle and
Roll."

The jean-clad boys with greasy hair
"Strolled" real hip
While the girls sported Hazel
Bishop's rose red nails and lips.
Sid Ceaser and Imogene Coca really
did fine
'Til Ed Sullivan won over prime
time.
Yes, the old Zenith is not the same
Since the Nielsen Ratings now
control the game.

Some folks see all this as the "olden
days"
But it's amazing how in the eighties
they have copied these ways.
What the younger people now say is
new has already been around.
So, after all, there's not much really
new in fashion, dances and sound.

Chris Gray Parker
WILD RIVER

To My Family: John Lake Parker, Maj. Ward, Mary, and John L. III

Even on moth-wings
Silence is havoc to the unconditioned
mind
And to the heart that now must listen
only to itself
Or seek some solace
From the swish of sculling paddle
Splash of arching fish
Birdcall on the banks
That compromise with the unease
Of a city-dweller
At the mercy of a wilderness

Audrey T Sanfilippo
SPIRIT OF CHIRISTMAS

To my loving husband, children and family who are the 'Spirit of Christmas'

When December approaches and
spirits are high,
Some people are laughing, while
others may cry.
The season of Christmas starts
drawing near,
The purpose of it all is somewhat
unclear.
For some it is trees, with tinsel and
bows,

How it all started, nobody knows.
The presents are bought, all tied with a knot,
And hoping there's someone you haven't forgot.
For Dad, there's a tie, colored bright red,
For Mom, a pretty scarf to cover her head.
There's toys and games for sis and for brother,
And a box of chocolate candy for the grandmother.
A bottle of wine will be sent to the neighbors,
To show we appreciate their many favors.
We're happy, content just being together,
Eating good food and enjoying the weather.
The snow is still falling from early this morn,
Perhaps it's a sign that the Christ child was born.
Despite all our happiness, we're still somewhat sad,
For those less fortunate, times can be bad.
We only wish that perhaps tomorrow,
Things will get better, begone grief and sorrow.
If each of us tries, in our own little way,
We can make everyone's Christmas next year, a real happy day.

Catherine E Davine Krentzel

PINETOP MEMORIES

In recollection of a special time & a special place

Mountain child
Can you hear the breeze
Whispering songs across the hills
Starlit nights and campfire lights,
Shine softly in your eyes

The soft caress, of the long grass,
Brushes across your skin
Lay us down in the meadow and
Kiss these lips that sing out,
like the wind in the canyons

Untamed child
High flying spirit
There is no one who can possess you
There will come a time, when all is done.

Once more you shall return
To the tall pines and mountains,
To wildflowers and soaring hawks

Mountain child
Fly free among the clouds

Mary M LeBarron

A HEART OF MANY SHADES

To my beloved family, my inspiration. Lee, Mom, Megan, Molly, Patrick and Tim. Keep dreaming.

Far from the reaches of my today
I watch waves of light dance upon the sun
And it takes me back,
to a time before the black.

All was bright then
Clear, clean, new and when
The innocence of a heart discovered.

White days
Drew upon rainbow nights,
And we were bathed in the color of the sunsets.

The pink excitement
The orange fire
A blue wonder
At the happiness we found in our tomorrow.

But the shades began to fade
into a brown fall.
And our last grasp was a grey yesterday.

Still we dream of the spectrum to come.

Babb Gerick

Babb Gerick

WRITERS' HEAVEN

The write
of expression
The curl of a line
Double meaning of a word
Smiles brought to the reader
Concern for the characters
Feeling
the power of scribing
Coloring the world
with thoughts
Fun isn't it?

Robert S Cassada

DO YOU HEAR?

He is coming again and we'll all see Him soon,
face to face, in His splendor and glory;
Are you ready my friend, to stand up to the test,
or will yours be a familiar old story?
Will He find You at work, or at play, or at rest,
will you hide when He mentions Your name?
Will you stand and be counted, in the Family of God,
or will you be sad that He came?
Examine your life, every nook, every corner,
and see if there's anything wrong;
Fix it, change it, straighten it out,
but don't let it take you too long;
He promised He'd come and take you away,
to a much better life than you've known;
He'll never forsake you or leave you in doubt,
you're family, you're one of His own;
The Bible says study, to show you're approved,
a workman who's never ashamed;
When you're put to the test and you don't know the way,
there's no one but you to be blamed;
Are you in the Word daily, is the Word in your mouth,
do you stray to the left or the right?
Are you out in the country and city and towns,
serving God with all of your might?
If you've answered these questions correctly my friend,
then from God you have nothing to fear;
You know, when He calls you, you'll listen and act,
because you have chosen to hear;
So start out each day on your face to the Lord,
be steadfast and constant in prayer;
And you won't be concerned if your life is with God,
cause in the Spirit, you're already there.

Charles F Dye

IMMATURITY!

Ah Spring! thou adolescent time of the year;
Thou season of rebirth.
Once more, returning as before,
Making young again the earth.

Sweet and pure thy scent
And brim full with joy art thou,
Infecting the heart of all
With gladness as of youth.

Immature are you, oh earthly season!
Reconsider, for what child ever made
The daffodils to bloom or
The forests to spring forth their leaves?

Thou art so young and weak
And yet, the orb of day and the warmth of rain
Make you the greatest in all the earth;
The paving stone for the ensuing year.

Think, and be proud
Thou beginner of life,
You are the fate or the hope of the earth—
We are depending upon you.

Vickie E S Garrett

I'M GOING ON!

Folks try to discourage me
From being what I want to be;
But that's okay, I'm going on.

Jealous people put me down,
Trying to drag me to the ground;
But that's okay, I'm going on.

See, I know that times are tough,
And the road sometimes is rough,
But my faith is strong enough;
I'm going on!

If I want to reach the top,
I must work and never stop;
That's why I'm going on.

Those who would put me away
May need a job from me one day,
That's why I'm going on.

If my dreams my friends forsake,
Then too bad—That's their mistake,
And the same one I can't make—
I'm going on!

Sidney R Cohen

MY FATHER

He came here at the turn of the century
Somewhere near Rovno, Russia, mother said.

He was not tall, being rather well proportioned
Blue eyes, black hair, hands well formed.
Those hands could fix anything
Could cup a child's face.

We did not talk much; he said I
Was going to be a big man
I have blue eyes and brown hair.

He was a good business man, no take overs
Just good solid simple business.

He gave me many things he found in his store
Now I have nothing of his.

It's not the comfort I need
Or the remembrance.

Families are kinda strange
So is the world.

Beverly Smith

I BELIEVE IN FOREVER

I knew you before
I'll know you again
And the love that I give
Will be as long as I live
For I Believe in Forever.

Remember tomorrow
I still see the past
And my love will never fade
Though time slips away.

For I Believe in Forever!

I will meet you on the other side of Forever
And treat you to a drop of sunshine mellow
To brighten my sorrow
All on the other side of tomorrow,
For I Believe in Forever.

The sand on the beach,
The sand in the glass,
The dust in my veins,
Will be dust again—
For I Believe in Forever.

Gloria Miller Allen

WHAT'S IN THE CENTER OF MY CLAY?

What's in the center of my clay?
What's to be shaped,
What's to throw away?
How long will I work it
Before I tire?
What comes forth from the fire?

Toni Patricia Ward

FOR THE ROSE

This poem is dedicated to liza and for all abused children everywhere.

Child of innocence and light, I can hear your voice crying out in the night.
Little girl full of such promise and hope, who could this man be he has hurt you so.

Once you were like a delicate rose, and now your crushed and broken petals lie crumpled beneath the virgin snow.
I do wonder are there many boys and girls like you? Who are beaten with baseball bats, belt buckles and shoes.
Oh! Why must the children be abused.

Parents and teachers throughout this land, please recognize the signs and take a stand.
We all must learn that child abuse comes from all social, racial and economic backgrounds.

The Judicial System must help us along by making sure that the laws and prison sentences are strong.
My precious little Rose life is over for you, but there are many other boys and girls that need protection

too.
Children of innocence and light is
America ready for this fight?

Wesley L Roberts
HIM

For my people who are free. Bring always peace and joy against the rain. The sun is brighter than any pain.

I have seen him in the night eye's burning blue hair of light. I have seen him in my land his charming smile and stormy look. Touch my soul et caress my heart. Dissolving the pain peaceful god in the sky reach down your hand. And nudge him to my side. Wrap us with warm love against the cold and crying sky. Magical spirits clinging tight winged love enduring life. We always together now and ever.

Barbara Gari Serio
A MOMENT IN TIME

Dedicated to my wonderful husband, Louis Michael who taught me how to enjoy the moment; Written for Catherine & Anthony, who shared too few.

but
for a moment
in time
we are
where the earth
stills
trees stop growing
rivers flowing
figurines etched
on the frosted edge
of infinity's mirror
we cannot stop
the changing clocks
of other worldly time
rather hold
with fragile awareness
this instant
we claim
as ours

Robert Cromwell
THE OPEN ROAD

To my loving wife always,

It's an Open Road as far as you
can see
And the wind blows free
For every hill, turn and bend
The beauty has no end
So it's the open road for us
Where there is no muss or fuss

We've traveled this road
together
In all kinds of weather
We have from the start
And will till death do us part
For God made this road for you
and me to see

Alice Rae Cannon
LOVE IS . . . LOVE WAS . . .
Love is . . . loving someone for
what they are,
Not how they act.
Love is loving someone,
And being loved back.
Love is being together,
And enjoying the time,
Love was . . . when I was all
yours,
And you were all mine.

Carrie Sweeney
FOREVER PEACEFUL
The sun has arisen like never before
As beauty forever knocks at my door
And without a fight I answer, for this
time I know,
All is now peaceful to this place I
shall go.
Motionless, I lie as the tears wash
through,
They stick to my memory like the
clear morning dew.
Washing gently upon me, cleansing
my skin
Soaking me thoroughly, outside and
in.
But there are no words for this way
that I feel
And so deeply in dream, I know this
time real.
It shatters my mind but I continue to
do
What I know in my heart will always
be true.
An angel in satin comes to bury me
deep
I'll drown in her arms, for an eternal
sleep.

Anna Krasnovsky
WHERE AM I?
Where am I?
I am in a world
Where dreams always come true,
Where fish with golden fins are
found beneath the blue,
Where fiery dragons lurk in forests
mean,
Where mermaids live, with tails of
murky green,
Where dangerous trails and pathways
can be found,
Where frightful monstrous creatures
dwell beneath the ground.

A world where princesses from
storybooks reside
In jeweled castles by the sandy
seaside,
Where golden dreams replace all
fearful thoughts,
Where small children frolic like tiny
tots,
Where happiness and optimism fill
the air,
In few ways does this land with ours
compare.

From this land many lessons we
glean,
No land as perfect have I ever seen,
And if ever such a land you knew
Please lead me there, and I will
follow you.

Michael A Lilly
REALITY
Reality is jailor of the mind.
Escapism is a dream. Dreams are
fantasy.
Fantasy dwells within the mind.
Reality! As inescapable as time.

One marches to the ticking clock
marking time;
As inexorable as falling stars.
Time to prepare for reality; for time
Moves ever forward, never ceasing
its chime.

Inevitability drowns dreams of
negligence.
The more life is experienced,
The more one is limited and fenced
By time's jailing of the mind.

To shatter the shackles of the mind;
To halt the steady march of time;
To break with reality for a while;
To dwell within a fantasy of mine;

I welcome these with open arms,
I embrace the thought and its charm.
My spirit yearns for a spacious farm
Dedicated to raising the mind's stars.

Dan H Smith
AN OUTING
I was driving down the road
With the wind in my hair,
Not a worry or sad thought,
For I was just happy to be going
somewhere.

I drove to the beach
And I longed to take a cool swim;
The ocean was so beautiful,
I couldn't wait to get there and jump
in.

There were children on the beach
Making their castles of sand;
A father close by watching them
play,
Beamed with delight and seemed a
happy man.

Gulls soared high overhead
And clouds moved in to end the day;
Soon I'll return here again,
But today I must be on my way.

Joan Butler
IF I HAD A LITTLE CHILD
"If I had a little child,"
An angel said to me,
"I'd dress it up—
In Polka Dots—
And take it out to tea."

"That's silly," said the other,
"That's not the thing to do,
If I had a little child.
I'd dress it all in—Blue."

Heather Milne
MOONLIGHT MAN
When will you come back,
Moonlight Man?
With your glossy black hair
and eyes of burning sapphires.
Red rose in one hand, my heart in the
other.
You took me on a seemimgly endless
journey,
Defying time, gravity, and reality.
Your strong, safe hands around my
waist,
Holding me gently so I wouldn't fall.
From star to luminous star we leaped
And slid down rainbows, landing in
shining pots of gold.
Hand in hand we walked on the sun
And chased butterflies on the moon.
Then you handed me the rose and let
go.
I fell rapidly through the dark, empty
space
Careening towards the earth in the
eye of a violent hurricane
Riding upon the cruel, harsh wind,
I fell into a dark, cold ocean of
wilting flowers and dying seasons.
Is my heart still safe in the palm of
your hand?
Or have you discarded it for another?
What vulnerable young girl are you
teasing now?
As I crash towards harsh reality,
I clutch the tattered petals of our rose.
Please come back If not to sweep me
off my feet,
At least return to me my heart.

Glenn T Wynn
IF YOU WERE
If you were the clouds in the sky
And the rain were your tears
We would have no deserts dry
Moved away would be my fears.

If you were the moon
All great lovers would never die
They'd revel in your melodic tune
In contented love their hearts would
cry.

If you were water we'd need no
other drink
Living for that refreshing taste
Where no longer boats can sink
And nothing in life can go to waste.

I may never share your love
Should I ever this shall forever
Be your worth, my dove
All being a spirit nothing can sever.

Jeannie Camille Causey
WHAT A MIRACLE IS MAN

To Peeper, the Gentle Mystic

Such gentle excellence expends the
universe
There is a rhythm and a pulse
The cycle is ever unfolding
The earth speaks of her innate
perfection
And she speaks of her glory
For we are each here to express our
Beingness
Our unique genius shines through
And pours forth in liquid splendor
What a miracle is man

What sublime excellence expresses
through him
Divinely wrought
Always unfolding with sheer
perfection
A wonder to behold
What a miracle is man
How like a starburst at night
Scattering radiant quicksilver
through the skies
So is the miracle called man
Uniquely expressing those gifts that
are his own
Shining forth in utter brilliance
Imparting of himself to all creation
So is the profound miracle called
man.

Laura Murphy
WHO GETS THE FLAG
It commences with a dinner for two
An innocent ploy known as
something to do
As emotions ultimately fill the air

Passion becomes the bill of fare

She—a single woman—stars in her eyes
He—a married man—a store of alibis
Unhappy at home and wanting to leave
Yet, he's always at home on New Year's Eve

He shares his problems over the phone
Oftentimes, her problems are dealt with alone
Though aware of the obstacles that abound
She convinces herself—he's the best man around

Then, as destiny has its ultimate way
And the bill of fare ends its day
The single woman realizes her fate
When eternity takes her married mate

Stolen moments and dreams, nevermore
The bill of fare on the drawing room floor
She dare not chance to pass his bier
For she dare not falter and shed a tear

But the bottom line—no cause for dispute
His wife gets the flag after the twenty-one gun salute.

Susan A Taylor

YOU CAN'T JUDGE A BOOK BY ITS COVER

An apple.
The outer surface often deceives.
Sparkling, bright red, all luminous;
like a lone nugget, glittering.

But if you bite into this exquisite fruit,
you may not go to an eternal bliss,
but are ruefully betrayed.

The inside, rancid, bitter.
Spoiled as a child who has everything.
A taste so doleful and fermented.
Even the angels weep.

William Henry Elliston

OLD TIME RELIGION

"You know, Folks," said the preacher
To his flock one Sunday morn.
"We're the luckiest people in the world
As sure as we are born.

Last week when lightning struck the church
It split the roof in two.
It completely burned the organ out.
The chimes were roughed up too.

The roof and chimes have been repaired.
They are as good as new.
The organ we just cannot fix.
There's one thing left to do.

We must buy a brand new organ
And an organ costs much dough.
Will someone stand and start the fund
When the choir chants, 'Let's go,"

A wealthy lady stood right up.
"Dear Reverend, if you will
I'd like to get it started.
Here's a new $5.00 bill."

The preacher prayed, "Speak to her Lord.
You heard now what she said."
Just then a chunk of plaster fell.
It hit her on the head.

She leaped in air; she screamed on out;
Flapped arms like flying ducks.
"Oh, Lord, I didn't mean just five.
I meant five thousand bucks."

The men folk all said, "Praise the Lord."
The ladies said, "Amen."
The preacher shouted loud and clear,
"Dear Lord, please hit her again."

Ellen Stojanik

BLUEBONNETS ON A HILL

There's a sight that gives me a thrill;
It's bluebonnets on a hill.
Covered in blue with specks of white,
The hills of Texas are a glorious sight.
Yes, it's a picturesque view that I love still;
Bluebonnets on a hill.

There's a sight that gives me a thrill;
It's a pretty girl standing on a hill.
Dressed in a yellow eyelet dress,
I ask her to marry, she says yes.
Darling, you're a vision that makes my heart stand still;
You and bluebonnets on a hill.

There's a sight that makes my blood chill;
It's a tombstone on a cold, lonely hill.
With a bouquet of yellow roses at the foot of her grave,
Surrounded by a sea of blue,
precious memories I save.
Yes, life without her makes my blood chill;
Life without her and bluebonnets on a hill.

Krista Husar

NIRVANA

If your nose is cold; is your heart cold and your soul also? Or the opposite? If your nose is cold; is your heart warm and your soul also? And if so, does this mean you have good friends? Do they always think of you? And when they say you are wonderful, what are they saying?

If your heart and soul are warm; are you full of love and happiness? Who asks these questions? Your conscience? Or are you a stranger to these words? When you read this poem, what do you feel? Are you better than others or worse? Who is the judge of this?

Is your hair below your shoulders or your heart?
And what is warm when your nose is cold?

Jean Devenport

LIFE IS?

What is life about?
As the days tick by
The years pass
I wonder all the more.
Why am I here?
What is my purpose?
What is life about?

Colleen Bell

DREAMS

Dream once again,
Deep inside my mind;
The love that I have looked for,
But have yet to find.
Once when you were here,
My life felt so complete.
When I realized you were gone,
My heart, it, skipped a beat.
I let the tears flow freely,
For what else could I do?
You were what I had always looked for,
But, of course, it wasn't you.
So now I'll dream again,
And try to stop hurting so.
My dreams all seem so clear,
But your face, they do not show.
So I'll pick up the broken pieces,
And try to smile with a gleam.
So if I see you once again,
Then maybe it won't be a dream.

Lois Sameth Gould

SEPTEMBER RODEO

Crimson Leaf on Bucking Branch
Rides out the wind:
"The Big Event!"

While on the ground, in scarlet clothes,
The scampering clowns find asylum
In the rake.

Annelle Stuckey

Annelle Stuckey

SUMMER NIGHT

In the evening when the gentle summer winds begin to blow,
The pretty, dancing firefly lights begin to glow.
Then down on the pond the bull frogs croak their song,
It seems their throats would get sore before very long.
The spring peeper frogs are beginning to croon their tune
While the crickets are heard chirping under the logs very soon.
In the distance I heard the mocking-bird trill,
I knew that he was singing in the magnolia tree up on the hill.
An owl was hooting in the old oak tree,
Seems like he was trying to talk to the moon and me.
I can hear the katydids singing too,
They are looking forward to the morning dew.
The sounds are enchanting to hear on a summer night,
It brings us close to nature, and God who makes everything on our earth so bright.

Nancy W Bellamy

SEASONS OF MYSELF

I am a cold, harsh wind,
Raging roughly at anything in my way.
I am a dry shell,
Harboring my winter of hatred.

I am a fresh, dry daisy,
Almost afraid to bloom.
I am a cool rock,
Shading my spring of fear.

I am a bright, hot sunrise,
Rising to new experiences.
I am a brilliant rainbow,
Coloring my summer of love.

I am a gentle evening rain,
Clearing a path to tomorrow.
I am a fluffy cloud,
Softening my fall in life.

Nicole M Swarrow

A WINTERY SNOW

As the night winds begin to blow
Around will fall the velvet, white snow.
The weather will get brisker and more cold
But it seems that the snow never gets old.
Colder and colder the snow will be
I wish it could talk and understand me.
When morning comes and the snow has stopped
It leaves everything softly white and beautifully topped.

Sylvia E Sleighter

UNIQUENESS

No two people are alike;
That goes for places, too.
Every day is quite different
With its own tasks to do.

Every snow flake is unique
With lacey beauty bright.
They glitter as they float about
To lighten the dark night.

Every day is fresh and new
For work and also play.
All should waken with a smile
And take the time to pray.

Stars that twinkle every night
are different—every one.
They help the moon to give us light
Until the morning sun.

Every facet of our lives
Has work for us to do.
As the sun sets on each phase,
Our faith will see us through.

Steve Bieterman

BRANDEE

I hurt hard
when violins string
in restaurants where
the Mafia means
more than a trisyllabic
expression where
accordions suck wind
in sine wave fashion
and get confused with
the phrase according to . . .
whom, "Are you speaking?"
"hold on a minute,
she'll be back"
but not tonight
she truncated dinner
and snuck outta here
silently as an unplayed sax
and here i sit lacquered, liquored
varnishing my bread sticks
with tomato paste
and lacrimal wetness
alone as truth stings
me to vertical i leave
the restaurant quavers
and those harsh
violin strings pluck

Dana Philipps

IF I SHALL HAVE TO . . .

If I shall have to . . .
leave you, that I could not do.
I never, ever could leave you.
If I shall have to . . .

live without you, that I could
not do.
For without you, I could not do.
If I shall have to . . .
work without you, simply that
is a no do.
Work is too hard without you.
This may not make sense to you,
but from a poet's eye view,
this poem means I love you!

La Wanna Hall Wright
THE ATTIC

I tip-toed up to the Attic
where childhood dreams are
stored,
My heart pounded in my ears
as I unlocked the door.

My eyes became accustomed to the
gloom
of this rainy saturday afternoon,
I searched the shelves for a favorite
book
I once savored in a secluded
nook.

My toe set the rocker in motion
making my heart skip a beat,
For there you were, my Teddy Bear,
reposing on the seat.

Joy seen through my tears
my arms ached to enfold,
My hands eagerly reached out
once again to hold.

Childhood memories and dreams
came flooding back to recall,
They're here in my heart,
not lost in time at all.

Margaret Marple
OH DEAR, I WISH I DIDN'T LOOK AND FEEL THIS WAY

Oh Dear, I wish I didn't look and feel
this way,
My bones all ache and my hair is
gray.
I raked all the yard, and hauled off
the trash,
For Winter time has finally passed.
This time of year there's so much to
do.
Sometimes I wonder if I will ever get
through.
When the trees come out and the
grass is green,
And everything is nice and clean,
I'll color my hair and put on a smile,
And just like spring, I'm back in
style.

Laura Malawka
BLUE

Blue . . . Sky blue. Our earth, the blue.
Our ocean . . . the big blue. We may not realize it, but we are polluting them, and they are disappearing one by one. What would happen to us without these blues? We'd be the same as they are now . . . , disappearing one by one.

Virginia E Redmon
CANADA

Canada, where the tall birch grow
And the raging rivers flow.
Bridal veil falls cascade
From the mountain walls
Tumbling, splashing down
With a crashing sound.
Along the road is the wild, pink rose
And lilacs are in bloom this
month of June
As well as other flowers that
intertwine
With the hemlock, cedar and
pine.
Three fir sentinels a picture make
As they stand guard above a
placid lake.
Reflections are beyond compare
Not seen elsewhere
Of the snow-crested peaks
With a misty shroud.
Oh, Canada are you proud of these
scenes
So grand in this majestic land?

Susan Lancioni
THE WORLD IS A STAGE

I dedicate this poem to my husband Ted and my children Jeffrey, Angela and Matthew who color my life with love.

Suns gleaming rays
Upon dew drops on webs
Creating rainbows of
Colors in my head

Dancing lights awaken me
With its color for all to see
Spring is just around the bend
The winter's cold is at an end

One season turns its page
And all the World becomes a stage

Brightly colored butterflies
Dance gracefully against kaleido-
scope skies
Reflections mirrored in your eyes
Sends my heart soaring to the skies

Dancing lights touch the sky
And here we are you and I
Playing our part in the Universe
And the world is our stage

Ara R Dozier
INFINITELY YOURS

We met,
And my heart was lost to you.
Silent I became,
And you asked me the cause.
I replied,
Maybe, you shouldn't ever know,
Why I suddenly grew so quiet.
Yet, in just a few days
I could not withhold from you
The reason for my mood.
I told you then, as I now impart,
I love you.
We met,
And my heart always be

Infinitely yours.

Lucile A Eubank
MY SON

My Son Richard, your mother Lucile

I have often times wondered
Why God has been so good to me.
He sent me the loveliest gift—
A dear precious baby.
He planted a seed of love in my
heart.
It grew day by day
And when the time came,
We parted in nature's own way.
His soul from the heavens above,
His life entrusted to me
To love, teach, and to mold
In the very best way that I know.

Dear God above, please watch over
me
And let me understand
The very best way to teach my son
To love and honor man.

Mother

Cecy Smith
DEATH OF A FATHER

Confusion
It's not fair
Life
Is nothing but death
A game man plays
Only to find no end
What is death?
Sadness
Pure sorrow
I would do anything for you
I would give you my body
To keep you alive
You were my idol
I would give you my heart
To keep your sensitivity
You were my friend
I would give you my brain
To keep your advice
You were my teacher
One horrible mistake
A bullet meant for someone else
Gone forever
Only our souls speak now . . .
Together,
Solemnly, we can conquer all.
You will remain in my heart forever
Goodbye my friend
I will never forget you,
My flesh and blood
My only father.
I love you

Glenda Devine
CHALLENGER

As I watched today, as I have before
The great chariot lifted with a mighty
roar,
The white pillar lifted you up to make
you soar,
Then came a sight I could not
believe,
As I watched frozen in my disbelief.

Red flashed the pillar, as it
disrupted the sight,
No longer are we to view
your magnificent flight,
For the roar turned into thunder,
and the red became flames,
Then our dreams and our hopes all
turned into pain.

Today as you did shatter, as we saw
what we feared,
And you took with you what we all
hold so dear,
Seven together, as a pioneer team
Those who took the chances to
fulfill our American dream.

Do not let this dream crumble,
or let this day be in vain,
Let us find out the why and press
forward again,
Remember the seven, Remember
their names, and the courage they
had to fulfill this dream.

Patricia Lipinsky Perkins
THERE IS ALWAYS HOPE

There is always hope for each and
every day
Don't be discouraged, trying to
figure the way.
Two bedrooms where we live have
holes in the ceiling;
In another, a tree has fallen on the
roof, the paint's a peeling.
The carpet's so old and dirty—
You can't tell what color it was in
the past—
The toilet leaks, the hot water pipe is
broken & the shower faucets are in
their last;
Their last stages that is, as we have
to use pliers to turn on hot or is it
cold?
No matter cause whichever it is the
heater and air conditioner is costing
us a lot of gold.
But there is always hope, for at least
we have a roof over our head—
Our carpet is warm and we do have a
room to put our bed.
Our Lord provides us with food to
place upon our worn table—
Even through the chairs are old &
torn our hands are still able.
To prepare food and wash the dirty
dishes in the sink;
While I am ashamed of myself for
not being appreciative as I
think—
Yes, there is always hope for
someone is worse off than me and
you.
God opened my eyes while I was
sitting here feeling down and blue.

José E Iglesias
THE WRATH OF TIME

Time has passed and I have changed,
for this, all humans have a
name—
they call it age . . .
yet, I call it something else.

We live by rules and dream by night
when shadows hide in front of lights.

There is no age, or rules, or force of
might
that can dictate how brief or far
I need to set the clock of life,
for what I feel, is only mine . . .
to share with and give to whom I
like;
to be alone or with someone,
to laugh, to dream, to love
and even fantasize . . .
to quench the wrath of time.

Ruby J St Jules

Ruby J St Jules
A SPECIAL MESSAGE

A romantic card that is either large
or small
And colorful flowers or just that one
sweet rose.
A soft voice from a long waited
telephone call
Or a love letter written in poetry or
in prose.

A gentle hug and kiss that will make my day
Or an "I love you" bracelet that I can wear.
A well chosen gift, no matter what you had to pay
By doing this, I just know you had to care.

A box of candy and cookies for me to eat
Nothing special, just any kind will do.
As long as it is something good and sweet
I am easy to please, when something comes from you.

Snowing, sleet or it can be pouring down rain
An evening out to see a movie or maybe a show.
To enjoy ourselves until we will see it over again
These things I say, because I think you should know.

I am happy to say, that after all is said and done
With such a message that is written plain and clear.
Together, we can share and have so much fun
By just saying to each other, I just love you dear.

Louise Buhl

I CRY ALONE

Why do things happen the way they do
It is never the way you want them to.

The many nights when he is away
You know that he is going astray.

Drinking and carousing and having fun,
While you are home with work that is never done.

Never a thought for another's pain,
Just so it is for his own gain.

You want to believe it is not so,
But there is too much evidence for show.

I sit by the phone all alone,
Wondering if he will ever come home.

Dead or Alive, Dr. Jekyll or Mr. Hyde.

P Souza

THE COMMON SECRETARY

To Mom—The source of power in my life

Newspaper ads are plenty
For the common secretary
Requiring females with experience
And of course good experience
Ability poise and stamina
Age also an important factor
To fulfill the many desires
The business executive aspires
Just proving her ability
And skill in stenography
Is not quite sufficient
To be considered efficient
But patience is very important
As well as being tolerant
To an employer in his strife
To attain his ideals in life

Autumn Blais

MOUNTAIN CLIMBER

I'm a mountain climber
Wind blown is my hair.
I'm on the steepest mountain
Rising in mid air

I'm halfway to its peak now
Holding on real tight,
I know that if I have to
I'll climb all through the night.

I'm almost at the top now
My pretend wind starts to blow.
Until I reach the summit
Only then will I let go.

I've finally reached its peak
Where many times I've been.
And when I reach the bottom
I'll only climb back up again.

Rising up this mountain
I hear my mother say,
"Honey, come off that slide now,
We'll come back another day."

Edna G Fraser

GOODBYE, AND FAREWELL!

Dedicated to, and in loving memory of my dear (second) husband, Sterling R. Fraser, whom I met and married in Port Elgin, Ontario, Canada, December 31, 1969. He died November 2, 1972.

I am leaving Port Elgin, 'tis a beautiful Town,
With streets lined with trees, going uphill and down . . .
You have grown, O, so big, since I moved 'way up here;
You've become very famous, to all, it's quite clear!
I came here in search of contentment and peace;
From hard work and worry, I found sweet release;
We have shared much together for over twelve years;
You have shown me you care, and wiped away tears . . .
To all kindly neighbors, shopkeepers, and friends,
I say, "THANKS TO YOU ALL, NOW OUR KINSHIP ENDS:"
But somehow or other, within this old heart
It carries this message, "IT IS SORROW TO PART!"—
Because parting's not easy when it happens to friends;
But the "pathway of Life" has all kinds of bends . . .
After all, it matters not much where we have to reside,
We press bravely on, whatever betide!
My health's not too good, and I'm climbing in years;
I'll be close to my Family, which will banish their fears:
As I go now, I say, "YOU HAVE TREATED ME WELL,"
"GOODBYE, AND GOD BLESS YOU, GOODBYE, AND FAREWELL!"

Maxine Roberts-Dixon

I LOVE YOU DEARLY

This poem is dedicated to the one I love dearly, my husband C. G. Dixon.

I love you dearly
not as a thought but as a gift.

I love your eyes when the stars shine upon them like a passionate fire.

I love your lips
when they are wet with the savour of wine
and eagerly waiting with a wild desire.

I love your hair when each strand are enmeshed
I love your gentle kisses against my face
I love your arms the warmth so fresh,
when they touch my body in a wild embrace.

I love your heart how it freely gives
not the saints white bliss, but
your spotless love.

I love to laugh at times at our silly games
how it sets my heart aflame.

I love you when you clasp me in your arms,
while the stars go pale above.
I love you when you make your body and soul
mine as we so eagerly live in the joy of love.

Eric London Battles

FIND

Hear my thoughts
Look deep inside
thin frail shadows of flesh
hide the pain
felt with eyes
not seen by heart's

Today the sounds of tomorrow
bring the future cries
of yesterday's sadness
how dark the clouds
raining knives of death and lies
twisted beauty seen by blinded eyes

Happiness is not belonging
to confusion's angered rage
trade revenge for rainbows
then seek to find
its true pot of GO(L)D.

Kelly Leighton

FIRST BUT NOT LAST

In dedication to Chris, someone I will always love. And never will forget.

I'm sitting here all alone,
wishing you were near.
Waiting for the phone to ring,
your voice I long to hear.
Looking at your picture,
tears now streak my face.
I want to have you near me,
to feel your warm embrace.
I'm slowly trying to forget,
the love we once did share.
Although that love is gone,
I really still do care.
Now that you have left me,
now our love has ended
You've found someone to replace me,
though my heart has not yet mended.
I try so very hard,
to put you in the past.
For even though I love you,
I know you're not my last

Elma L Reese

INTAGLIO

Light to my dark are you,
the patterns of the dew,
an August rain
upon a thirsting tree.

Moon to your sun am I,
a pool which holds the sky,
a conch which keeps
the singing of the sea.

June F Edwards

IF THIS TREE COULD TALK

For some reason I was planted all
alone on a hillside.
Too far from the road for humans
to see while out for a ride.
I'm not tall and stately with birds
nesting.
I'm passed by when birds want
branches for stopping and
resting.
I'm short from the ground.
not even very round.
So instead of envying all the
other trees so tall and still.
I know I'm the only tree to hold
the soil in place on this side of
the hill.
In the springtime I puff out in all
my glory with pride.
For I'm the one single thing of
beauty on this hillside!

Earl Richard Sixt

STROLLIN' THROUGH LIFE

Strollin' through life in the early morn
I searched for flowers among the thorns
There were no cares and all seemed good
But nothing in life was understood.

Strollin' through life in the noonday sun
I frolicked in pleasure and always had fun.
I wasted no time on study or books
For I had money as well as looks.

Strollin' through life in the heat of day
I knew this life was not the way.
I struggled to gain what I had lost
But didn't consider how high the cost.

Strollin' through life at the end of day
I thought on things I wanted to say.
Reach for your goals when young and spry
For if you wait you'll never try.

Strollin' through life in the dark of night
My life is over and it just isn't right.
No longer can I do the things I should
For now I lay in a coffin of wood.

Jackie Fraser

I'VE LOST MYSELF SOMEWHERE IN TIME

Dedicated to A. A. members everywhere, to my higher power for really being there, and my mom.

i've lost myself somewhere in time
the sunlight's getting dim
where's the courage i seek so bad
why can't i let it in

and when i thought all hope was gone
a spark of light shone thru
it's helping me to face those fears
of which there's quite a few

i know with time i'll find myself
i've only just begun
with much hard work and His good will
i'll once more see the sun

June W Gay
JENNIFER'S RAINBOW

Dedicated to Terry and Marilyn our wonderful son and daughter-in-law for giving us a beautiful granddaughter. Also for sharing their home with us since our retirement. With love

Early this morning at seven twenty five,
Jennifer rushed in, her eyes opened wide.
Come Grandmother, come and see
The beautiful rainbow above the tree.

We went to the window, threw up the shade,
Saw the beautiful rainbow God had made.
She said look Grandmother, can't you see
It goes way down at the end of the tree.

It was a beautiful sight for us to behold
With pretty colors so bright and bold.
She was so excited, I can understand why
To see a beautiful rainbow so early in the sky.

Kevin Andrew Grindstaff
WHO AM I?

To my family and friends: Through them I have made my dreams my realities

Do you know who I am?
I have laughed with the power of lightning.
I have cried with the softness of early morning rain.
I can travel farther and faster than the wind;
all I have to do is close my eyes and dream.
I have the power to move mountains,
or the ability to build them up from nothing.
Do you know who I am?
I can speak with the softness of new fallen snow,
or rage with the fury of a thunderstorm.
I have loved with the love of the Lord,
but also have I felt the power of man's vanity.
I can walk with the grace of a beautiful fawn
when I'm not stumbling in the ruts of man's creation.
Do you know who I am?
Look close and you will see yourself
and all you can be.

Richard Sambell
NIGHT WALK

Darkness falls
and nocturnal silhouettes
steal uncomfortably
close.

Housecats with
heavy, fiery breaths
and killer toads,
the unholy night kings,
examine us from
their blinds
in the twilight shadows.

They watch, wait.
Attack is
a heartbeat away.

Her hand is
a vice
in my own
and I wear a
secret smile.
My dark-eyed
companion, always so
determined,
is now timid.
Uncharacterisitically so.

I hold her close,
involuntarily shuddering
at my own happiness
in her time
of peril.
But I know
she can always trust me
to keep her secure
from the bitter night things.

Mira J Spektor
EPITHALAMIUM

Somehow they always knew that
there was more than this . . .
The squanderers?
The rememberers?
The ones who knew
the other side of the door!
The ones who knew
where the old plush train went—
Who recognized the view from
the strange hotel window.

She knew the entrance to
the lit stage—
To the other's script.
She had killed
and nourished.
He had believed
and betrayed—
But there was a next time:
When the quiet would sing,
when the arid would love.

Judy Berry
DEATH OF A CHILD

In Memory of our Angels

Beyond the entity of time
In the soft passage of a whisper
Beyond the dream of tomorrow
Where the shadows flirt
Beyond the visions of today
In gentle breezes and sunlight
A tiny flame flickered and shone
Faltered and died

Dava Steen
LOVE AND PASSION

Love is a passion
Love is a crime
Love is a song
With no rhythm or rhyme

Passion is sweet
Passion is hot
Passion is something
Love is not

But love and passion
Together as one
Is something untouched
By anyone!

Gayle Walsh
FATHER AND DAUGHTER

Shouts! Yells! Screams!
Why all the noise?
Why all the defiance?
Because she didn't move,
And he has a temper.

Orders that were demanded,
Demanded in impatience.
She doesn't understand!
She doesn't try!

So there you go,
You hear him yelling;
Yelling for her to hurry.
And her shouting,
Defying his orders.

He's growing old and tired,
Soon she'll be on her own;
So why all the noise?
Why all the defiance?

Because she is his daughter,
And he is her father!

Erica Zelinsky

Erica Zelinsky
SUMMER

Summer breezes drifting by,
All the birds around to fly,
Little children out to play,
Having fun every day.
Eating dinner, having steak,
Wading in the ice cold lake,
Fishing in a little stream,
Swimming and camping
are very supreme.
Going back to school
is a bummer,
NOBODY COULD LIVE
WITHOUT SUMMER!

Julie Wilkie
CLOWNS

Clowns are such a sight to see
They put on a show for you and me.
They make me laugh, they're full of joy
They're loved by all, both girls and boys.

They put on their make-up, both happy and sad
Their costumes are colorful, not the latest fad.
There's both horses and tigers in the Big Top town
But there's nothing like seeing a circus clown.

Helene P Lawrence
AUTOBIOGRAPHY

Age 16 is hard to bear
If you're in love
and
He's not there

If you don't want to be left behind
By 26—
Make up your mind!

Sparkling heart and proud endeavor
For 36,
If she's been clever

A waning of the pep and vigor
Make 46 a hapless rigor

New horizons are in sight
If 56 survived the fight

At 66, a great surprise:
A wedding ring, and bedroom eyes!

Joanne Lillevold
THE NORTHERN OCEAN

the dark, cool northern ocean
stretches before us in our dreams
it cools our feverish thoughts
and relaxes our senses
the darkness enfolds us into
nothingness
we stand and see without looking
the starry sky and jagged peaks of snow
are there and still
nothing is all and all becomes nothing
shall we stand and be drawn in
who will dare disturb the still?
a touch and all will vanish

Debby Green
TOMORROW

To my inspiration—my husband

You are gladness, you are sorrow;
You're my promise of tomorrow;
Your voice makes my heart want to sing,
With your smile beaming so bright
Seems to brighten up the night.
When you get excited,
My heart is so delighted;
It whispers a little prayer,
That you'll love me tomorrow;
And my love brings you no sorrow,
Only the promise of more tomorrows.

Thomas (Taj) Koenigs
BORING STORIES

Boring stories, gory teachers, preachers
That teach you to be reachers.
Sandwich, manwich, grab a peach.
Teachers pet, you're a leech!
"Throw a stone and you'll go home!"
Well, I threw it, and they knew it.
Now I'm home, they sent me.
Now I get to climb a tree.
Oh, what joy and what fun
I'm having in the sun.
Boring trees, gory sun,
With the kids I'd have some fun.
School's out now, let's go play.
Oh, that's right, I got expelled today.
Stories aren't so boring.

Noella Cormier-Clavette
GROWING OLD

When old friends meet,
It is a wonderful treat.
We talk of days of yore,
And try to act as before.
The voices are softer,
The wagers are lower.
We have fewer drinks,
We find smoking stinks.
We are always well fed,
We think; little is said.
We walk at a lower pace,
Never can be in a race.
We are as free as a bee,
Everything is so easy.
I am not complaining,
I am only reminiscing.
We are frequently told,
That we are growing old.
REMEMBER growing younger
Would be a lot harder.

Ross Boyd Sowdon
GOODBYE AGAIN

With love to Sharon, my colleen of Kerry.

Everytime we say goodbye,
I cry a lot.
Everytime we say goodbye,
I ask why a lot.
Everytime I cry,
I die a bit,
And ask the why in it.
When you leave,
I lose a bit.
Everytime I lose,
I die a bit.

And bit by dying bit
I'm losing you.
I don't want to die.

Hazel Hegwood Sigferson
OLD CHERISHED PATH

Written in loving memory—of my sister—Ruby Lois Hegwood

Come little sister and go with me,
Let's walk once more today,
That old cherished path of memories
To places where we used to play.

Let's stop again at the old brick house
And that quaint little cabin of logs,
Let's wade again in old Turkey Creek
Where we used to catch pollywogs.

Hand in hand we'll wander again,
Where the laurel and wild grapes grew,
Choke-cherry trees and goldenrod,
And the fields of lupin so blue.

The sky is always so blue there,
And the robin's song more sweet,
Dew-drenched grass feels so cool
To our little, hot, dusty feet.

Tho' years have passed since together we played
In the shade of the walnut tree,
On that old cherished path of memories
I can have you forever with me.

Rachel Carey
NATURE IS REBORN

As the snow falls against the cold earth
The flowers which were once alive, shrivel to their deaths.
The air becomes dense and the trees brittle,
The sun's warmth has turned to cold
And the fireplaces burn bright within the homes.

Time passes and the ice begins to thaw
The grass turns green and the sky turns blue
The clouds appear lighter against the heavens, and the birds return to their nests.
Nature is reborn in the warmth of the spring air
And life begins to bloom once again.

Terry R Raban
TIME

It's funny how time passes by
on wings of passing fate
it makes us do funny things
of which we love or hate.

We think we know our destinies
but watch out Mister Fate
for he will teach you all about
the things he will relate.

And when he's done you're the one
who opens up the gate
to all the shocking things in store for you
of this the human fate.

And then you'll try to master him
for this he can not wait
for you're just like all the rest
your dying just won't wait.

Martha J Asbury
TO JOE

To Joseph R. Asbury and his gold silver legacy: daughters Merry Katheryn and Elizabeth Rayann.

Carried into our lives on the current of birth;
Swimming through the waters of life together.

Separated by the tides—yet merging for brief moments;
Moments of renewal, moments of reflection.

Then carried on through the whirlpools;
drifting with the currents;
plunging into the rapids of activity.

Suddenly gone—swept from our reach!
Gone! Gone forever!

And we are lost in a torrent of grief—
Lost and struggling not to go under.

Remembering the sea of tranquility to follow—
A sea where we'll find our brother.

Mie Kimura Norton
WHAT I LOVE TO THINK ABOUT

This poem is dedicated to Michael (M), a special person in my life.

I love to think about I was originally made by God and traveled my whole life all over the world.
I was once a disciple of Jesus I was once Jewish, a Roman . . .
My last country was Japan because God wanted me to be oriental.
And yet he was so sympathetic toward my differences from other Japanese girls, so he brought me to America.
God taught me to be nice to everybody despite our differences.
God taught me to be strong enough to live in my solitude.
It's so wonderful to think I'm God's child and I have a special purpose to be in this world.
I dream He is going to make another "Mie" even after I die physically.
My soul keeps living and I will return to this world again in order to finish my work from God.

Rose Mary E Escobar
I COULDN'T FIND THE WORDS

I couldn't find the words
So I never told you
I couldn't find the words
So I never held you
Whatever I thought of saying to you
Was never the right thing
Was never the right time.
I looked for words
By looking into your eyes
But you, would look away
So I just couldn't say
Couldn't find the words
To tell you so many things
To show you how much I cared
But something would always
Come between us
So I couldn't find the words.

Now that you're gone
It's too late to tell you
To share with you
The words I couldn't find
when we were together.

Someday when we're together again
Or just happen to meet—
Somehow, I'll be able to say the
words I couldn't find—
they are,
"I love you."

Stanley Earl Anderson
A MOUNTAIN RANGE SONNET

Mountain ranges marvelously inspire emotional thrills.
Their parts blend into the whole—
Like a long, impressive, giant chameleon;
Their infinite beauty demands no dole.
Grand slopes graduate into small foothills.
Time and water are tedious artist;
Both express their ways and wills.
Trees spasmodically dot the scene.
Oh, majestic hills—great my thrills
As I behold thy intense sight!
How great thy marvelous splendor
Ignites my spirit's tender.
Evolution can not truthfully explain thee—
Only the mighty hand of God!

Cathy E Loving

Cathy E Loving
OCEANS PLEASURES

This poem is dedicated to my mentor and best friend, Dr. Benjamin Elijah Mays, former slave, educator and the first Black President of Atlanta Public School Board and a recipient of 57 honorary doctorate degrees.

Lying under the moonlit and starry sky,
Breathing in fresh moisture from the oceans tide.

How peaceful the ocean and serene,
A thing to be enjoyed by all God's beings.

Midnight has passed, the stars and moon faded away,
Just over the horizon the sun peeks out for yet another day.

The tide bringing in mother natures catch,
And people of all ages scurrying for her shells to fetch.

Friends and lovers walking the beaches holding hands,
Sea gulls diving, and dogs romping with their best friend, man.

Children from nine to ninety building castles of sand,
And people of many colors working on their tans.

Again mother nature's lit her stars and moon in the sky,
And scurrying back to shore comes her peaceful tide.

Gary H Bowles
TIME—they me

Time—at one time,
like the spring; beloved friend
warm and so alluring—
seeming growth to neverend.

Now, as I,
She rides upon the gale.
Servant winds to transport,
like memories—
the golden ships—
set forth to sail.

Scattering those and others;
transcending those I cannot see—
to meter someone else's—time;
recollecting them, as once, they me.

J C Tangredi
SALEM MARRIAGE

went screaming bloodyrhythm
in a clean, white dress,
in a hellish, hungry sleep,
thrashed and starred
in lobster-red salty, salty soup.

Brenda Washington
WHEN MY TIME COME'S

I'd like to dedicate this Poem to my Inspiration, whom at that time I didn't realize it all comes from him. —JESUS CHRIST

When my time comes everything will be pretty, everyone will be happy, every soul will be free.
When my time comes the air will be clean, streets will be neat, Politics will be no more.
When the time comes for everyone to rejoice, for all to repent, for everyone to ask God for forgiveness of the sins they have committed.
Then it will be my time—to leave the ones I love, to forget the wrongs I've done, to step into God's Kingdom and live forever in a world where there are no sins. When my time comes, I pray God will forgive me for all the wrong I've done and take me as his child, as he has taken me now as his, I pray that he will protect me forever till we meet in his home in Heaven. When my time comes.

Max Vinson
LIKE A THIEF IN THE NIGHT

Like a thief in the night,
I came to steal away a portion
Of that which I desire.
Having seen, I could not pass.
My eyes saw the untold value
Gleaming with a radiance
Gold would dull beside.
A diamond would revert
To the black coal from which it came.
I hold the stolen warmth in my heart,
As the sun on a winters day.

Wanda K Farrar
GRANDPA

This poem is dedicated to my Grandfather, Francis Author Thompson

I just wanted you to know, that I
don't mind that you are growing old
I will love you all the while, just as
much as when I was a child
A little child sitting on your knee
With you tickling and teasing me
You have given me memories so
sweet
Like when you would let me feed
Grain to the chickens and slop the
sows
I bet I didn't even know how
And when you would cut the hay
I got to ride the tractor with you that
day
You never seemed to mind at all
You always let me tag along
You have been my banker, my
father, my granddad
And you are the best friend I have
ever had
You have always been there when I
needed you
And I want to be there, for you too
So for all the kindness and love to
me you have shown
I Thank You Grandpa . . .
And I just wanted you to know

Steven Ray Walker
CAVERNS OF THE UNKNOWN

This poem is dedicated to the memory of my Father

Caverns of the unknown
Mysterious and deep
With every step
You could be thrown
Into a heap
Of treasures and traps
Which belong to
The caverns of the unknown

Caverns of the unknown
Saturated with courage and fear
Love and hate sown
With a tear
Into the walls and air
Of the caverns of the unknown

Caverns of the unknown
Lined with joy and sorrow
Better to share
Then stand alone
Facing tomorrow
In the caverns of the unknown

Martin Fewster
STUMPS AND ASHES
As the efforts of one's being
Shaped on trails both sound and true
Lend the base for higher ventures
From which other things renew,

And as leaves of autumn, falling,
Or old stumps of yesterday
Give their all to new beginnings
In their process of decay,

Gems forming the brightest future
(How we hope that they may last)
Will be found, when re-examined,
Formed on ashes of the past!

Deborah Crawford
PREVIEWS
For weeks, we cover the kitchen
table with frowns, slouch, and fill
our bellies with silence.
We don't talk about sea turtles, or
cities, or new houses, or
shrimpboats.
We sleep back against back
and turn into trees.
Tonight, you'll leave
like our cat,
after dinner.
When I open the door to throw bones
or sweep,
both of you will slip past me,
the bowl of water on the porch steps
collecting leaves,
the light by the back door
burning out
days
before you scratch the screens.

No one will ask any questions.

Susan Graff
SEASONS
Summertime's over it went by so
fast.
The days are now memories, they
live in the past.

Autumn's upon us its crisp morning
air, with cool brisk breezes that
rumple your hair.

Trees in their splendor of greens,
yellows and reds;
soon will stand bare from the leaves
they will shed.

The winter will be here with winds
that will blow.
And make the land glisten with
wonderland snow.

Springtime will come with birds that
will sing,
and growth will return to everything.

Summer is back and it returned so
fast:
The whole year now, is memories
past.

Rob W Frantz
SATURDAY BATH AT THE BAR/F RANCH

For every cowboy and cowgirl who ever was or wants to be. I love your effort.

I bathe amidst the tall green weeds
surrounding the tub
The older signs of sky and sun seem
to fall into disuse as the night appears
I bathe here, splash, enjoy and clean
my body
knowing that my history will never
be finished
I have an urge to ooze my toes thru
the damp sand around me

Crows fly home
Winds diminish to symphonic slow
tones
The Sun bears a great statement
resemblance of "I'll see ya later"
The specialized vocabularies of birds
and insects merge
The evening seems to abandon the
day
sticking something aside for another
time

As all critters and other elusive things
find or look for their territorial
imperatives, their special places,
home plate
different systems appear
An eccentric code only they and the
Indians and science understand

My mechanical horse is in the corral
its wheels, chains and sprockets are
clean
And it has new rubber tires and tubes.

Carolyn Sue Benedict
HEAVEN NEEDED A CHILD
Heaven needed a child,
A special one in God's eyes,
God heard his cries.

God wanted a perfect one in
everyway.

Heaven got a champion,
Washed all his sins away.

Heaven needed a child,
So sweet and innocent;

To come out and play,
With God's hand all the way.
So perfect in everyway,

Heaven needed a child,

God took a flower with him,
To make sure he could swim.

Heaven needed a child,
An angel that wasn't wild.

We love you! Ricky Gene.

Connie Rodgers
MIRACLES

To Julie, Lauri, and Kelli. My most precious gifts, my daughters.

God gives miracles, He gave me
three
Your love and care, He granted me.
Do your best, He sent me three
Miracles of love He bestowed on me

From the moment of conception, He
whispered to me
Believe in miracles, I gave you three
All little girls of beauty and grace
Here to enhance the whole human
race
Cherish the moments, treasure the
love
God handed me you from Heaven
above.

The sun shines brighter, the flowers
more sweet
Total perfection from head to feet
Flawless baby so gentle and true
God surely blessed me, when He sent
me you.

Robbin L Gheesling
CYCLES OF THE HEART

To Kevin D. Baker, a once in a lifetime role model that will be followed, step by step. To Thea Jo Herron, who's so called offence made me fight harder for myself. And to all my lost friends in Denver, especially Chris Shumake, Alison F., Carrie B., and Gina S.

Seeing herself excavating her
dreams,
From the liaison of your heart your
soul,
And she cries for wisdom,
And for the intentions of no pain.

The seventh wave is crashing all
around,
Rhetorical, all the questions of her
mind,
Showing no mercy.
The anger against one another,
And the ties are broken, and the
spirits die,
Suicides all for the determination,
For not living alone.

If she'd never seen your eyes,
She'd never have the power to
search,
For the sword she stands for.

I know her desperation,
She'll never be so strong,
She cares, for you believed in her

Try a little harder, cry a little longer,
Tears are the prisms of life,
All she ever wanted, all you ever
took.

T D
DEAR MOM

To All The Little Ones Who Were Not Allowed To Be

Dear Mom,

"Please don't let the abortionist take me from you, my eyes are shut right now, but I can see the comfort I feel in your womb, my brain is growing slowly but that doesn't mean I can't feel pain, my little heart is ever pumping and it tells me I yearn to be loved by you, my Mother, and then to know the love of Our Lord. O' Mom, please don't let them tear my arms and legs apart, to take me out of my home. If you can't take care of me or love me, please let Jesus into your heart, and he will find a way for both of us, and Mom, don't let them tell you I am a fetus, a piece of tissue, or even an It, because God made me, Mom . . . in His Image."

Van L Meigs
WHAT IS A FRIEND?
A friend is the one
That is still standing by
When the clouds are all dark
And they're filling the sky.

A friend is a person
Who never will run
When the joy is all over
And gladness is done.

A friend is the one
Who will never desert
When you've tasted of sorrow
And suffered a hurt.

What is a friend?
He's one who is just
And a fellow you know
You always can trust.

You can travel the earth
To its corners and ends;
But you'll never know worth
Till you find it in friends!

Rose Ann Sanders
YOU ARE A FRIEND OF MINE

To my best friend. Holly Lytell.

You are beautiful, my friend you know and accept me as I am—all of me and I love you for this.

You have made me happy to be me, I love life more because of you. I can be myself with you, and am very happy in knowing that we experience much of the same sensitivity to the world around us.

You always express how you feel to me, and so I'm never afraid to do the same. The meaning of our friendship is found in the joy of celebrating it.

You will forever be a part of me now for our souls have reached out,

and gently touched one another.
I will always love you throughout
my life,
For you are a friend of mine.

Margie Holeman Hanson
GOD'S MASTERPIECE

To my Granddaughters, Danna, Sandra and Pam

From the essence of all that is holy
God gathers ingredients to mold.
He reaches for star shine and
moonbeams
And stores them all in His Fold.
He doesn't ponder for He knows the
secret
And measures aeons of love—
He has sweetness ready for casting;
So He pours it into His mold.

He adds a wisp of an angel wing—
Then a touch of angel song.
To give a touch of the eternal,
He tenderly adds a soul.

He adds purity and innocence so
translucent
It seems as a wisp of a smile.
To these He adds the essence of life
And molds them into a child.

Doris Murray
SARAH

In Loving Memory of my late sister in-law "Sarah Nell Turner" (J.K.J.)

You have traveled
a long and painful road,
And your journey
has come to an end.

It could have ended
a long time ago,
But, you would not
give in.

For life was precious
and dear to you,
You cherished it
until, the bitter end.

Now we must let go of
you Sarah
Until we meet again.

Miriam E Forney

Miriam E Forney
THE EMPTY HOUSE

To the man who is my everything, my Tim, the one I love and can't bear ever to lose. To all the hearts who know the deep pain of a love that is gone forever. To all the hearts who have never loved.

I am alone, in a house full of wood
that creaks,
Where doors slam, without wind.

Why did you leave me here, where
shadows on the wall mock me,
Creepy crawlies dart under the bed?

Night is falling, eyes in the darkness
are watching,
Traps are set, waiting to spring on
the unsuspecting!

Rescue me, for I shall surely go mad!
Take me to a new house, with sunlit
rooms and cheerful hallways!

I want to feel alive again, like I did
in summers past,
Take me where death doesn't mean
you're never coming home!

Evonne Pizzoni
ETERNITY

Dedicated with love, to Jeff Klien and Martin Cohen.

In my mind we'll always be 'till the
end of time in Eternity.
Always and forever, you'll stay in
my heart . . .
Both when we're together and when
we're apart . . .
You've held my hand in my time of
fear,
You understand, when things are not
clear.
When we're miles away and I hear
your voice
It makes my day 'cause you're my
first choice!
As many a star, as there are, above
you
That's how far, I'll always love you.

Chad Varnadore
OPENING CRIES

A cry of the wolf
Hungry with fear
For a taste never sensed
Yet, its senses so clear

The growl of the animal
Protecting its prey
From all other hunters
In the moonlight of day

The witness of its eyes
With a passion for pain
The shift of its feet
To try another game

It cries in the moonlight
For that lost, caring touch
Of a brilliant reflection
For the openness
of love.

Victoria Morgan Wilson
THE/MAN WHO WOULD BE CAPTAIN

My ship came in on the soft summer
breezes of June—June's glowing
sun-warmed days,
It went out to seas, as a ghost ship,
void of its captain and crew
Breaking away from my harbor
where it was once held by bonds of
trust, compassion and friendship.

The ship, as a freighter equipped to
break the bonds of unfulfilled love
and emotion
Frozen uselessly into ice floes once
held fast to the roaming vessel, is
free to choose its path.

The harbor is left abandoned, empty
promises and reincarnation hanging
in the air unsuppressed by the winter
air
Overpowering the ice tinged scent of
motor oil, hemp, canvas, decaying
fish and wood.
The remnants of love encased by
broken ice, are left to beacon
aimlessly drifting out to sea, calling
"lorelei" to harbor observers.
If the floes could speak, not only to
poets and artists in the language only
the heart understands, but to the one
foolhearty enough to try to harness
love's seas.
They should warn, as a lighthouse, of
the joy once beheld in new days and
of the web in the frozen ice, melting
someday to become the colorful
prism of tears once shed for the
captain.

We wait—born in the bay of pain,
held in icy abeyance, awaiting the
spring's promised warmth to become
one.

Martha Largo
MY UNBORN GRANDCHILD

It's an experience I can't describe.
A wonderful joy; I'm ecstatic, I'm
proud.
What will we call him? We can't
decide.

A baby quilt, shall I make it blue?
Maybe a pink one too, just in case.
Dear Lord, please send me a clue.

He knows I'm his grandmama.
He feels my joy; he knows I await.
What if he arrives sooner, haha!!

A little bundle, with fingers and toes,
Big dark eyes, and black curly hair,
Pink smooth skin, cute little nose.

To my friends, I send greetings.
I'm bursting at my seams.
Lord, shower my grandchild with
blessings.

Elizabeth Cavazos
I KNOW YOUR LOVE IS REAL

To my father Raul Cavazos; who was responsible for my Independence, and my strength, and also for allowing me to be me.

I know things haven't always been,
the way you hoped they'd be.
But then it seems you stepped aside,
and cared no more for me.
And what I truly wanted was to show
how I felt inside.
But instead it seems we drifted, and I
was pushed aside.
I wish you only knew, of all the
times I cried.
And thought you would be better off
if I had only died.
But deep inside I've always prayed,
you'd one day see in me.
The things you wanted most of all,
the things you wanted me to be.
Somehow through all this pain, and
all these bumpy roads.
I knew GOD would show to you, I
needed help with all the loads.
And now through all that's
happened, I believe I see.
You never really gave up, but inside
you loved me.
So this my Dad I dedicate to you, to
show you how I feel.
And just to let you know, I know
your love is real!

Glenn E Wiseman
TONIGHT WE ARE ALL GATHERED

Tonight we are all gathered—each
with his own thoughts!
In honor of the retirement of Mr.
Bernie Watts!
I must say in your casual attire—you
really do look alright!
So sit back and relax and enjoy this
very special night!

It seems only right that when a
person retires!
All interested parties should be able
to express their desires!
Money should be collected and gifts
should be gotten!
So the memories will linger and
people not forgotten!

But enough of this praise—and this
attempt to make you look good!
I came here to roast you—I want that
understood!
A special night for you Bernie—but I
want you to know!
I'm only here because I didn't have
any other place to go!

In closing let me say—and I think I
speak for all of us here!
In our hearts we all love you and
hold you very dear!
Your retirement is a new beginning—it is not an end!
And I am indeed very proud—to call
you my friend!

G G Lomeli
PRETEND WAR

It was at seven years of age,
a soldier I began to be;
And with passing year I learned,
a soldier's life was meant for me;
For every movie I recall,
A soldier brave is what I saw.

The screen showed men who had no
fear,
Who killed and wounded without
tear;
These men with souls and might so
high,
Though could be wounded, failed to
die.

I prayed for war so I might be,
Like heros past that I did see;
And now that I am here in war,
A hero's life I seek no more.

For in this war there's no pretend,
For there's real death of living men;
There is real blood, real misery,
That in pretend I did not see.

And in my game I failed to feel,
The present sorrow when men I kill;
And unlike playing my pretend
game,
Here, I couldn't stop playing when
nightfall came.

And when I'm cold and lonely here,
I can't run home for home's not
near;
I can't cry out when I have fear,
Because from here, mom cannot
hear.

There is no glory, not any more,
In any real or pretend war;
The sad thing is that if I die,
A child's hero shall be I.

R J McMurray
THE TALE OF PATTY MCLAKE

—Patty McLake
—Went to Monahans' wake
—And a pretty good time he had
there.
—He drank whiskey and wine,
—And was feeling just fine,
—'Till he chased it all down with
a beer.

—Well, his head started splitting.
—'Twas a good thing he was
sitting.
—Or more upset his stomach
would'a been.
—'Cause Patty, with a shout,
—Showed folks near about
—What he had formerly held
within.

—As poor Patty started
sputtering,
—Folks 'round him began
muttering,
—Betting on how long he would
last.
—Standing upright by the bar
—Or carried out to his car,
—All done in by that one beer
glass.

—Patty stood up
—And muffled a hiccup
—And the crowd let go a cheer.
—His stomach, he said,
—'Twas asking his head
—What was in that bottle of
beer?

Joy L Lang
MEMORIES
Yesterday and tomorrow
Tears shed so many times.
Laughter, laughed so much.
Times that were so very happy.
Sadness that brought heartache.
Never grows old or dies.
Cherished times that once were.
They are today.
That live on and on in life.
Grows into more and more, to
Last forever.

Lorraine Burian
IMAGINATION
Floating softly on gentle breezes,
Are animals on parade;
Gliding about in the heavens,
Playing their great charade.

Ever changing their identities,
A magical sight to behold;
In a moment, a shy little lamb,
Becomes a lion, so bold.

In an instant, a romping puppy dog,
Changes into a growling bear;
And a beautiful, galloping stallion,
Turns into, a flop eared hare.

It gives you, such great pleasure,
To watch them, as they play;
High up, in the skies above,
Their games, with you today.

So, you gaze up at the heavens,
With great anticipation;
For those puffy animals, in the sky,
That tease your imagination.

Rebecca Rodriguez
CRYSTAL REFLECTIONS
Deep within the crystal,
Every place is in sight.
No direction to take.
Turn round and round,
Shadows are cast.

Youth and magic,
bestows such distance,
that choice is refracted.
Age loses dimension
As the crystal thickens,
Yet wisdom enjoys discernment.
Through prisms of color,
All such lives interact.
A pinnacle of light appears,
an occurrence of an exchange of
learning.
Making existence of being
as infinite as it is finite.

Gene Pennington
YE OLDE IRISH VALENTINE

For the lady with sparkling eyes of blue; my inspiration in years gone by, my hope for years to come.

Thou, my love, art truly as the wind,
unceasing, and thus impossible to
hold.
Yet with thy coolness
comes still a breath of purest
refreshment.
And when graced with thy warm
caress,
complete serenity hallows that
cherished moment.
How my soul withers in the quiet
desperation
spawned by thy absence;
and yearns to again behold thy
smiling countenance . . .
to feel, once more, thy soft
embrace . . .
I pray thee, hasten thy return;
and restore the brightness to mine
eyes,
a reflection of the love and adoration
inspired by thee.

Dell Pruitt
ANDY

To our grandson Andy, who made me aware of the special joy a two year old offers us.

I heard Mommy tell Dad
Since I got the terrible twos.
It took all the energy she had.
She gets angry when I get into
things,
But I can tell she's not really mad
'Cause sometime she sings.

If you got a frown,
I can take that frown.
Turn it up-side down
'Cause I'm Granee's Clown.

Sandy Smith
THINK BEFORE YOU DRINK

The volunteers of Chamblissburg Rescue Squad, Goodview, Va.

Hush little blue eyes, please don't
cry,
The man in the other car, didn't
mean for your mommy to die.

I'm sure he never thought of the pain
and fright,
That he could put in your blue eyes
on this Christmas Eve night.

If he could see your twisted legs and
the bruises at your eyes,
I feel sure that he would never again
drink before he drives.

I know you want your mommy, dear,
but she had to go away.
We will be right here beside you till
your daddy's here to stay.

Where did you get the dolly that
you're holding so tight?
Oh, it used to be your
mommy's . . . Grandma passed it to
you tonight.

We will keep her here beside you to
soothe your fears away.
Let me hold you, little blue eyes,
your daddy's on his way.

If everyone who likes to drink could
look in your big blue eyes,
I feel sure they would think twice
next time before they drink and
drive!

Deborah Squires Pocher
ROSE GARDEN

To Michael, I love you.

Roses may not bloom
in the garden all year round,
Their fragrance
may die in the wind.

But in places of the heart—
a rose garden blooms, forever.
Even when the ice encrusts
the brown stems of faded roses,
The dormant liquid within,
crystallizes buds into a
waited re-birth.

A walk through
a rose garden in winter,
Is just as beautiful
as one blooming in summer—

and in the heart

of each of us.

Tracy Lee S Waters
THE SWAN
Soft white feathers of innocence
Tailored with such loveliness
Veiling a mind of instinct
A body graced with perfection
Gliding across the water
Like ancient water nymphs
Making life look so relaxing
Endowing it with ease
Trumpeting to God who answers
All the prayers of life
Calling on the heavens to
Glance down and protect you
Awkwardly you leave your home
But only for awhile
Returning with your future
Set sail once more on glass
Never harming friend or foe
While sharing your gift of
Beauty with us all and
Giving us a thought of peace
If only for a moment . . .
Swan, oh glorious Swan, your life
Is all a dream come true for us.

Stephen McMillian
WHY?
Why must people fight and destroy
one another?
Why must people hate each other?
Why must people be envious of what
one has?

Why do we take out our insecurities
on others?
This puts a load and a burden on our
brothers.
Why do we engage in backbiting to
defend our pride?
Why do we pretend not to see people
in need?
Let us do away with selfishness and
do them a good deed.

Why are there wars that kill innocent
people?
Why are there homeless people out
on the street with no good clothing,
shelter, or food to eat?
Why are there drugs killing people of
all colors?
They do nothing but get high while
the pusher makes a dollar.

Why is there discrimination against a
person's race?
What good is there in hating a person
for the color of his face?
Why can't this world be a world
filled with harmony?
Why can't we as human beings learn
to stick together?
Why can't this world be a world
filled with love and happiness
instead of hatred and bitterness?
Why can't we as God's children
band together and unite to make this
world a better place?

Perhaps then we can all live together
as one family.

Terrell Jones Sr

Terrell Jones Sr
THE SUNSET

Augustine F. Jones, Mary Ann, Ms. A. Bates, Ms. T. Fields, Ms. C. Alexander, Mr. G. Washington, Dr. & Mrs. H. Perkins, Lorell, Terrell, Gerald Jones, Deliliah and Henry Stidwell, all my Relatives and Friends . . . My Deepest Love. Thanks Be To God Almighty.

As it drops beneath the earth
It pulls a shade of darkness
with it.
Then man turns on his
little suns
That illuminate here and
there.
Finding his way across
the room
After the sun has set.

Rhonda C Strain
SWEETNESS

To my daughter Marilyn. I love you.

Sweetness that lays beside me,
Peacefulness all around you,
Music playing softly.
Heads that were playing now rest
quietly.
As the world goes by, sweet dreams
all around.
Rest my dear little one,
for sweet dreams soon turn sour.
Then this peacefulness soon turns to
sorrow,
and sweetness that lays soon walks
away.
Then we are left with only the music,
Which will soon turn loud.

Irene Price
WORLD CROSSROADS
The world–competitive technological
race is on
Accelerated in new ways now more
than ever,
Concentrated on broader scope,
higher potential
In known-unknown fields of human
endeavor.

This race, in essence a histronic
world scenario,
Holds a most singular and economic
difference,
One which involves assessment of
what is the now

Basic life-styles for all world homo sapiens.

It seems we should accede to urgency, find roles
In some outstanding field of special endeavor,
Whatever field, whatever neo-technological yield,
We can then become competitive the world over.

Joseph Iglesias
LUNA LLNEA
The Moon is full
the clouds hang low
The Sun fades out
I watch it go

Away

The Moon will shine
in The Dark of Night
I will stare up at
The Lovely Sight

Please stay

For The Night is here
and The Night is free
The Full Moon will smile
so pleasantly

Then, frown at The Face of Day

But, The Sun again will fall
and The Moon again will rise
and shine its brilliant light
to Those of Different Eyes

Kenneth Shawn Meacham
I WILL BE

Dedicated to God for his greatest gift to me, my mother, Patricia Ann Meacham

I climbed upon a mountain top
and looked across the land.
I prayed for wisdom in my heart
and from God a helping hand.

Please help me find you Lord my God
please show me who you are.
I know you're close beside me Lord
I know you're not that far.

I stopped to listen quietly
to hear his Holy word.
The sun grew bright, the wind blew soft
and this is what I heard.

I will be among the hungry one
with my word he I will feed.
I will be among the homeless one
I will fill his every need.

I will be among the diseased one
to free him with a cure.
I will be among the prostitute
whose soul I will make pure.

I will be among the sinners, son
to pull up all their weeds.
I will turn their soul upside down
and plant my Holy seeds.

Robert Alexander Hampton
NATURE'S DAUGHTER

To Grandpa Alex. Though we no longer know each other the love still binds us.

The day I saw the nymph I remember so fine, for she was dancing in nature's meadow under mother sunshine. She danced and laughed and sang. I saw Aphrodite in her.

Whispy clouds presided amidst the sun's luminous smile. The long velvet grass bowed to the earthen breath while the conifers danced, birds sang, and the stream gurgled its bubbly laughter.

Dew drops sparkled, reminiscent of the forgotten moon. Somewhere sounded a mournful wail, the signature of a loon and timid creatures, like I, stood in the shadows and watched her.

Her flaxen hair threw buoyant rays—for an instant she was the sun, alight in a way I'd never known. She ran in carefree abandon free of chains in nature's meadow. Mother nature's dancer.

Warmed, she plunged into the sandy bed, blanketed by a crystal stream. Her hair undulated in the cascading rhythm of the crystal stream, and the water caressed her naked breasts with its exotic fingers.

Refreshed, she danced like a wind blown flower of fire and grace. Her dance beckoned the flowers to allow the sun to warm their faces, and they too, watched the nymph's beauty that none can compare.

When I think of her, I wonder if it were only I she had shown her grace; and often since I've returned, in vain, hoping to catch a glimpse of her in this magical place. I think now how fortunate I am to have seen nature's daughter dance.

Judy Oke—Chiero
LIFE IS OH BUT A FANTASY

To my husband Chuck, my parents Marilyn & Gene Oke, and to all my friends who always believed in me, and encouraged me. Thankyou!

Life is oh but a fantasy,
A wondrous maze it holds.
The hussle and bussle of our busy lives,
leaves many a dream to behold.
So to you my child,
take pride, with style.
And fear you may never walk alone.
For with each new day,
there is a brand new way,
to enlighten your way with gold.

Regina L Cosner
SOUNDS

To my family who always show love and happiness.

A mountain rain showers upon me
In the rhythm of my streaming tears
An explosion of thunder shakes the earth—
I pick up my shattered heart
Lightning illuminates the sky
As my lover's smile once did
I run for shelter under branches of a tree;
No warmth can be found
So I pray to the Lord for comfort—
The raging storm cease
Sunshine cradles me in its beaming rays
Like a mother would a wounded child.

Laurie M Chang
SUCCESS IS BEING TRUE TO YOURSELF

This poem is dedicated to my brother, Rod.

Success is being true to yourself . . .
not doing things you don't want to do or to be.

It's listening to your heart instead of your head
and doing what you believe and what you think is right.

Because . . . if you follow people and their wrong-doings,
you will lose yourself in them—
through their ways and through their thinking.

This is a frustrating path,
until you realize that you have the strength to go on your own path.

And when you do, enjoy the special discoveries and the wonder in you,
for along this journey, you'll meet someone very special . . .

You!

Svea Kanna
KEEP SINGING

To all downhearted

Forget the clouds, the misty grays,
but keep in mind the sunny days
Be thankful! Don't complain and grump,
that sinks you deeper in the dump.

For if you dwell on rain and sleet
you're bound for failure and defeat.

Try looking at the sunny side
and you gain strength to meet the tide.

Confess your gloominess and doubt,
then make a complete turnabout.

You know God wishes you the best.
Can't you go through the smallest test?

If life seems hard, praise God and sing,
You'll see the clouds start vanishing.

Shawla M Swearengen
SOULS AFIRE

This poem is dedicated to Johnny, my son

Smoldering energy released
Fighting to be free.
Burning coals and ashes walked on by cold feet.
Intense emotion, seething heat
Bursting at the seams.
Throbbing temples, wakeful nights
The devil's in my dreams.
A fearful feeling grabs my guts
And brings me to the ground.
My agony is so intense
I hear a rasping sound.
A roaring fire, approaching wings
And angels come in view. God help me now,
The choice is yours. Pray what am I to do?
Come save me from this hellish doom
And angels lift me higher. Save me from my sins and from the waiting souls afire.

Michael J Andrisano
THE HOMELESS

Dedicated to Micheal Jr. and Nicole, my children.

Dull, grey, mist-filled air;
February morning.
And again with pain,
I arise, with little care.—

Now I sense the cold.
It lays upon my fingers bare
As I turn my gaze inward
I have not aged, yet I do feel so old.

When I try to remember,
those days of warmth.
When I try to feel,
as I knew I once must have existed.
My self pity stops my thoughts,
my needs have not persisted. I die.

I die daily, sometimes, although I die
I still exist,
The pain of hunger,
keeps my senses alive.

Home, I shall go home,
If I but knew which way to travel.
As I lay down and close my eyes
I seek help from heart and heaven.
Oh God, to my soul, please unravel.

Lavada Belcher Miller
A CHILD
A child is but a flower in bloom when it is very young
A child is but a chorus to a song still yet unsung
A child is but sunshine to brighten up your day
A child is but a butterfly traveling on its way

A child is but an angel in need of tender love and care
A child is but a gift from heaven and is considered rare
A child is but a loan from God and can be called away
So give a child all your love if one should come your way

Ella Ruth Harrison
I AM GOING TO GO ON VACATION

To all those happy cruises that goes just where I chooses

I am going to go on vacation
I am ready to put out to sea
I am going to find out the reasons
The horizons keep beckoning me

If I never return from my cruising
And if often you ask where I'm at
Well I fell off the edge of the ocean
When this old world turned out to be flat

Heather Allison Riebold
THEN WHY DO WE SIT ALONE?

To my mom, dad, Heidi and Lori. And for Ron for all that you are, and all that you have given me. h.r.

You said together, our love, we would proclaim.
So why do I feel so alone?
You said together we would share the laughter and the pain.

So why do I feel so alone?
And together as one, we were supposed to remain.
Then why do we sit alone?

Ginger Lee Meskan
GRANDPA

This poem is dedicated to my grandfather, Maynard, who I love but never met.

Grandpa, a name of the heart.
A hopeful dream,
A site to see,
A light of the land.

Grandpa, a hat in the corner.
A story of who he was,
A dream of what he might have been.
A hopeful light to see on the land
and in my dreams.

A wish that will never be.

Lea Rose Notarnicola

Lea Rose Notarnicola
MY GRANDPA

I would like to dedicate this poem to Buddy Cappawana, my Grandpa. I love you and will be with you again, someday.

My Grandpa was a special man
He was always there to hold my hand,
He was there when I was feeling blue
But if only I would have said
"I love you"
But I never got the chance to say
How much I loved his special way
But now he's gone
And now I see
How very special he was to me

Verna Kale
ATTENTION

Thanks Mom and Dad

I'd rather be paid attention
Than in silver or gold.
I'd rather be paid attention
Than in something I could hold.
For attention shows loving, patience, and caring,
And attention is part of the act of sharing.

J R Vessa
SPRINGLIGHT

Sunlight, sunbright, springlight
Dancing within my room, playing before she enters my eyes,
Teasing me with colors and lines while
Making everything appear so clear.

How can I forgive her splashing so wantonly across my floor
And disrupting me so?

Her yellow and green friends, pests who've come to make
Merriment the hues and back corners of my shadows
Everything glowing so warm
How can I possibly keep my mind on what I must?

Spring is near.
She makes me long for her warmth.
If only I could tell her
Perhaps she would come more quickly
And stay forever.

Susan J White Aldred
MY LOVE FOR YOU

My love for you,
is as true,
as the sunshines bright
as the day turns to night.
As the toddler tries
as the snow flakes fly.
As the fireplace sparkles
as do my eyes when I'm with you.
My love for you,
is as true,
as the fire glows
as the flowers grow,
as the birds coo
as the sky turns blue.
My love for you,
is as true,
as all I have written.

Sally Gane
RECOMPENSE

At eighty four I'm not the whole
That I once was.
The years destroyed but left to me,
As recompense,
The memories and lasting joy
Of what has been.
As strength and senses slip away
They push aside
The troubles of the outside world
And leave me free
To live in time and places past,
Where I'm content.

Rev Russell M Abata C SS R
A DARK, DELIGHT-FILLED DAY

The woods are wet with rain,
With water unable to quench the fires of Fall.
Fire and water are to each other pain—
Except on trees still standing tall.

I stared at the leaves so near death.
As I stared, I held my breath.
It was so painfully sad,
So cheerfully glad.
Is the death-life mingle
Such a sad-sweet jingle?

Yes, the woods are wet with rain.
Each wounded-not-wounded tree,
Standing well and tall, though slain,
Is the life story of you and me.

Sherry "Spike" Ayers
I STAND NAKED

I stand naked
My face pressed to his kiss
His fingers—cold and mobile—caress me.
Fire brands they start as . . .
Yet, upon their removal, all is ice.
A circle of red my mouth becomes
As I stand before his barrage of intimacy.
Rivulets of him wend their way over me. . .
Streaking quickly down my neck—my shoulders—
Slowing like a skier at the peak of my breast
Only to shoot off into space . . . I am empty.
He starts again, now down my back
Cavorting wildly from shoulder blade
To spine . . . cinching my waist
And dropping soft as a silk skirt
Around my buttocks.
To the front again . . . a lovers kiss of silver
In the night-time of hair . . . now down my legs,
I shudder—he is almost done traveling
And exploring the terrains of my body.
Down the ankles, spiralling out the drain.
I step from the shower—my lover is gone.

Brenda Tanner Peterson

Brenda Tanner Peterson
ACROSS THE STREET

Manicured lawns encircled by tulips, daisies, pansies, face straight-rowed vegetable plots lacking weeds.
Yet my neighbor leaves his front door
like a bear squeezed into grimy Big Mac overalls.
His front yard's jammed, weeds scrambling, filling the gaps.
Driveway and garage have given way to a large crater
'under construction' he says again, and grins.
Shuffling towards an orange-rusted white van topped with a homemade camper shell like a knap-sacked turtle,
he searches for something not in his yard
where the family car, depressed, rests wearily.
Purple and green drapes, dishevelled and always closed,
clash with red brick.
Cats fight, make love under my window, wander the street.
New kittens every ninety days renew the process.
I hate cats.
Neighbors extract obnoxious garden weeds but neighbors stay planted.

Al Scott Berger and Sissy Meeks
SOMETHING IN LOVE

There's something in love that lingers
More than you would expect.
The first rush of desire gone
Through days, then nights neglect.
There's something in love that lingers
So subtle, when right, it's true.
I cannot see the shape of it,
All I can see is you.

There's something in love that lingers
Past the fires that you have lit.
Consumed I am, by heat of heart
Burns my every little bit.
There's something in love that lingers.
It fits snug upon us two.
I cannot feel the shape of it.
All I can feel is you.

Holly Pregno
BARS

As I look past all the bars
I see a life I wish I could have.
I see no bars nor cages.

As we sit here locked up like animals, caged like wild beings ready to kill.

When I see a bird fly by
I admire the life it has.
To fly wherever its wings lead
and to be free until all eternity.

A tiny being admired by a human.
A human that is supposed to have the best life.

How sad the world has become and how naive the people have been believing
lies about a being no one has seen.

A god worshiped only by a hunch
not yet proven to be true.

Yet, we still worship our god, but what for?

I still see the bars.

Don't you?

Nicole Yvette Tucker
LOOK TO THE MOUNTAINS

My thoughts always seem to be tumbling, around and around.
My eyes see the beauty of the land,
But unfortunately this is not all.
I also see the sorrow of mankind.
Man is like the poor dumb creatures of the land.
Like a pack of wolves.
They tear one another apart,
and eat one another while they are still living.
Does not man ruin the beauty of the land,
That he must kill himself and others.
Yet where there is sorrow,
There also must be peace and happiness.
Where does our hope lie.
Look to the children,
for they are sweet and good.
In the children lies the hope, for the future.
But look upon man, he is their idol.
Will they not too follow the path he walks.
Look to the land.
Lift your eyes upon the mountain,
is there not anyway out?

George W Croasmun
THEM SMALL TOWN BLUES

Jody was a lady's man. He played the field a lot
He knew just what he wanted and that's just what he got
But, Jody was a fool, you see. He played the mayor's wife
The mayor got wise. Now, Jody's running for his life

He's got them small town blues,
don't know what to do
He's got them small town blues,
don't know what to do

Jody holed up at mama's house to give the mayor the slip
Then met up with the mayor's wife

for a little skinny dip
He liked to live life carelessly as anyone else could tell
And Jody wouldn't listen when they said he'd go to hell

He's got them small town blues,
don't know what to do
He's got them small town blues,
don't know what to do

Jody wasn't careful. He just kept sleeping around
The mayor caught him in his bed and gunned poor Jody down
Now, Jody's in the devil's hands. His playing days are through
The mayor took his own life. Now, the devil's got him, too

Take heed of Jody's fate, my friend, the next one could be you
Don't waste away in small towns and get them small town blues

Joseph Weinbaum
GREENHORN
When to the Land of Ooze and Anguish tongue
I was at first incepted,
Initiated in my best full-blown sails,
My youthful brazen banners flying haltingly aloft,
I surged ashore adwarf with reverent awes—
Despite thirteens and foots,
And of real names divested,
Upon my immigrating boyhood's thumping melancholy hopes.

Ruth S Allen
MY POT OF GOLD
My "pot of gold" lies not over the hill,
Or at the foot of a rainbow somewhere.
It can be found in the heart of a friend
And loved ones who show me they care.

My "hidden treasure" is not silver or gold,
Or a mansion beyond compare,
My "wealth" lies in the love of God
And the beautiful world we all share.

The song of the birds, the wind in the trees,
The flowers that grow in the lane,
The fleecy white clouds, the soft green grass,
The feel of a warm spring rain.

These "treasures" fill my "pot of gold",
And they will never slip away,
For their worth is everlasting,
God sends them every day!

Michele Stamm
CAPTURED BEAUTY
The Painter placed a candle by His canvas and in prayer
profoundly meditated on the Art He would prepare.
His first beloved concept was, of course, a trusting child
in her halo of innocence; her manner meek and mild.
The child marveled at a robin whose action did suggest
the Painter planned on eggs and the construction of a nest!
The robin searched to find a site and sang for she had spied
a tree with budding branches to keep all the world outside.

The tree, released of Winter's hold, with earth was reconciled and clung to her breast with the urgency of a suckling child.
Wee blades of greenish grass captured the hue the candle lent and cast a splendor to the nearby sea in complement.
The turbulent sea was churning free of the ice at last leaving no trace in the soothing scene of a Winter past.
The Painter saw perfection; knew the pleasure He would bring so He laid down His brush and bade us all to share His Spring!

Sandra D Crumbley
JUST LOOK AT US
We do not live year by year,
Nor do we day by day;
We live from moment to moment
But only with Gods OK.

The Lord rain out his Blessings,
On Every, and Each of Us;
He lets it rain on the Good,
As well as the Unjust.

He's pleading and begging his people,
To open and let him in;
He longs to give us His inner peace,
And wipe away our sins.

To wipe away our short comings
And all transgressions too;
To give us what we need,
To make our lives anew.

But now that we have grown older,
Where youth and strength are no more;
That's when we decide to accept Jesus,
Not realizing that He wanted us—
Long Before.

Jill M Bessey
UNTITLED
In one corner of the orchard was a stand of firs
Massive and dark;
Thick pine needles underfoot
muffling noise and assailing
my nostrils with their pungency.
Here I sought refuge,
And would lie watching the play of sunlight on the branches.
Sleeping came sometimes on those summer afternoons,
And I would awaken to the sound of bees in the thicket at the woods edge
And gaze up into the sky
So blue and clear
With the promise of all my tomorrows.

Deloris J Davis
DON'T GRIEVE
Don't grieve for me when I am gone.
For I have loved you for so long.
Keep the memories in your heart
So we will never be apart.
Don't mourn for me and don't be sad.
Just remember me and be glad.
I will always be in your heart
So we will never be apart.
And some day far away
We will be together they say.
We will meet again someday
Up in heaven we will stay.
So it's not good-bye
So please don't cry.
We've made a date
To meet at heaven's gate.

Merle S Andres
A ROSE
A rose is such a lovely flow'r
with velvet petals massed,
Its fragrance sweetens up the air,
its beauty, unsurpassed.

Its gorgeous colors, white and pink,
or red, or even blue
Though artists paint, a rose is something
only God can do.

It lifts its face up to the sun
with dignity and grace,
And roses symbolize a love
that time cannot erase.

How like a life that needs so much
of tenderness and care,
And, if abused, it often drops
its petals in despair.

God made the beauty of a rose
for everyone to see
And with it sends a gentle hint
for ones like you and me.

Marsha K Chatman
AN OLD GRAVEYARD
An old graveyard survives on the hillside.
Its tombs entangled in vines,
Have not yet forgotten the rotted souls beneath,
Whose bones have long since been washed clean.
Or the tender love and aching sorrow that put them there.

But somehow through the years,
The world forgot it left them there,
Unkempt . . . Unwanted . . .
If only these souls could rise again,
To speak their woes and live their dreams.
And only then return to their graves below,
Feeling no shame or grief . . .
To rest in peace.

Linda L Novinger
DAY'S END
Evening's last view
more glorious than morning dew
Wondrous colors that are
ever merging never still
Seem to hang above the
last hill
More precious than silver
or gold
God's love is visibly told
Rest and peace he did intend
For us to see in the day's—end.

Mary Kestler Clyde
SWEET ARE THE USES OF AUSTERITIES
There's an enchanting Old Negro Spiritual Lay,
"God's A—Gwine ter Move All de Troubles Away."
That was a charming idea when I was younger,
For the easy, happy way I did always hunger.
Now that the world has dealt out many adversities,
And shown that all humans face and deal with austerities,
The conclusion arises that life becomes how one resolves hardships.
Whether one learns to make use of them or rebels and angrily flips.
Some years of steady observation and learning
Confirms the ideal of educating that immature yearning.
Oh, Boy! Once one has mistakenly spoiled the Brat
For all eternity that becomes fixed, that's that!
On the other hand, the canny ones master all the bitter bites
With brain and self-control climb straight up the heights.
Mastering adversities first-hand of every various kind
Has been proven the control of all matters with mind.
If we don't learn from our austerities, maybe we can't be taught;
The hard knocks will continue to try to awaken us before we land at naught.
Before our planet, Earth, goes into eternal schizophrenia
Let all of us parents and teachers train for great, invincible millennia.

Jolene Stephenson
ROSES AND YOU
Roses in the wind
Violets in the sky.
I'm thinking of you
As time goes by.
Spring is here,
And love is in the air.
Wanting to be with
You is only fair.
Roses are for you,
Violets are for me.
With love from the Lord,
Everyone feels the way we do.

Jerry Lee Tomblin
TO LORI
We have no song for we've never danced
My love for you can only be enhanced
For I love no one more than I love you now
And my devotion to you do I solemnly vow
But it seems it was never meant to be
For a good friend is all you see
And to another you are pledged
Soon to be bonded in holy marriage
So I will love you from afar
And wish upon a falling star
That you will fall in love with me
For only then can I be happy

Gerald Allen Sunagel Jr
DÉJÀVU
Sitting in a place I've sat so many times before.
Remembering things of days gone by, an dreaming of things of days to come. (Sitting and wondering; is this the future, or is this the past?)
Drinking a drink I've drank so many times before.
Toasting to events of days gone by, an cheering to events of days to come. (Drinking an wondering; is this the future, or is this the past?)
Singing a song I've sung so many times before.
Hearing the lyrics of days gone by, an dancing to the rhythms of days to come. (Singing an wondering; is this the future, or is this the past?)
Laughing to a joke I've laughed to so many times before.

Listening to the humor of days gone by, an anticipating the sarcasm of days to come. (Laughing an wondering; is this the future, or is this the past?)
Feeling a feeling I've felt so many times before.
Crying for the passion of days gone by, an craving the love of days to come. (Feeling an wondering; is this the future, or is this the past?)
Here I am somewhere in the future or the past. Wondering of days gone by an days to come. *(Knowing I've been here so many times before!)*

Loretta M Krise
FEAR IN THE HEARTS OF MEN

The future of the earth is very dark indeed.
While men dominate men with cruelty and greed.
Why is the world so deep in despair?
It is because love is lacking everywhere.

Homeless people are out in the cold
While the rich get richer, I am told.
Care of children, once taken with pride,
Now because of wars and abuse many have died.

Threatened is the survival of man
by nuclear war and polluting of land.
If man would only turn back to God
and see what his word has to say.
Perhaps they could learn to live with each other
If they follow the true Christian way.

Sharon B Scotton

Sharon B Scotton
SHE ALONE

She came into this world alone
She learned real quick to hold her own
She's experienced the hurt the world had to offer
She's been wealthy, she's been a pauper
She's had many tastes of life's ups and downs
And learned that's what makes the world go 'round
She's walked alone all of her life
She has no children, she's no one's wife
She doesn't now, nor will she ever,
Understand life's love endeavors
She finds someone and gives them love
They take it and fly away like a dove
Maybe her love has too much intensity
For some men to handle . . . could be, could be
Whatever the reason, this fact still remains
She came into this world alone
And when she leaves it will be the same
I know, you're saying "what about in between"?
Well, no one knows and that remains to be seen

Joseph Raeburn
CLOSED COURT OPEN COURT

How secretly must lie the tissue,
Oh miraculous head,
That each it's visible part
A clamoring hope's dread must chide.
How, assuming further issue,
Realms in which the live and dead
Alike from wondering gaze lie hidden,
Can all those intruding
Startled and ambivalent night light
In flesh made pride of image
Everlastingly abide?

Barbara Zweigler
SONNET

We felt the gentle lassitude of rain
All day, and thought we even could discern
In the moist earth the signs of Spring again.
Forgotten March's fickleness, her turn
From Spring to snow within an hour's space,
And we were shocked on opening the door
To find instead of sighing rain, the face
Of the dark garden painted white. Trees bore
Harlequined duplicates of every twig,
The iron fence was trimmed with silver lace,
White ruffles marked the path's edge, and the big
Willow became a frozen fountain-place.
We realized again we had no reason
To think one day of Spring proclaimed the season.

Rick Sauer
THE ASSASSINATION OF JOHN GALT
(upon reading 'Atlas Shrugged')

The images fade in and out, ever changing the facade,
back an forth between here and your dream world,
up for air from "bumming around".
If John Galt were, and he was all knowing. he'd send you the
yellow rose, maybe, half a dozen.
The signals are all there and here, and they shake you
in your confusion of conceit.
Perhaps rightly so for the air is bitter to you,
you, reaching into your pocket for a Hershey bar that,
suddenly isn't there.
The rose 'I' have is white, held out, the carousel ring;
it won't turn yellow in your hand.

Calvin L Driver
JOURNEY

Wandering aimlessly through life, so many people do
Lost on a hidden search, wanting to be found
Plunging on, forging forward, only ahead can they see
For life passes them by, on all sides as in the past
Preoccupied in the conquest of life, happiness they cannot see
For to enjoy this day for its worth
look ahead with learning from behind
Happiness, love, and peace of mind,
will catch up and join you on your journey.

Noel Darvie
DRIFTING

Drifting
turbulent sea
Weaving
Bobbing
perpetual tide
Discovering
unfamiliar shore
Virgin fruit devoured
Insatiable urge for more!

Marilyn Barnard Fritts
STAR OF SERENITY

Blue Star, far away
twinkling in the sky
at the high of night.

Your silent, serene radiance,
a calm sight,
of soft blue light.
Twinkling, far away.

Blue Star, far away
tho' lonely you seem
there, in solitude
you wish to stay,
while your crystal beams
of gentle beauty
send forth loving rays.

Melinda Garafalo
LOOK AWAY LADY

Children cry
Under a cloudy sky
Hunger growls
Within their bowels
Look away lady
Parents weep
While children sleep
Worry about tomorrow
Swallow their pride and sorrow
Look away lady
TV screams
To hear their pleas
Little children, across the seas
As our children warm hands on knees
Look away lady
She stands tall and proud
Her message is loud
Liberty and justice for all
Except children who at her feet fall.
Look away lady

Essie Faye
ARTS

The Arts can be a sad affair,
When they mirror the world around.
For if the Artist really cares,
It show in sight and sound.

Though others may not dare,
The Artist wears a frown.
In this work he will not spare,
Man or hallow ground.

Marty Sorokoski
FIRE

Watching the embers glow, from inside your fiery eyes.
Heaven at my finger tips, only a teardrop away.
Lost forever,
inside your soul.
Hearing your cry for innocence,
feeling your breath, your teardrops on my skin.
Washing away your tears in my laughter,
Comforting the wounds inside you with my love.
The scars that cannot heal, the echo of a thousand voices,
the empty streets of confusion you walk on,
are the chains that bind your heart.
The empty spirit and weakened soul
flow only too clearly from the teardrops in your eyes.
Through your eyes I see your world.
I see you laugh, I see you cry,
I can read your soul.
On the inside I see fire, I see heaven.
On the outside only blackness,
Only a cold and dampened spirit,
only death.

R Lee Hummell
WINTERLAND

The season was pregnant with old age
As toys and tykes awaited the sage.

The barren earth was buried in a blanket of snow;
The ground glistened with the sparkle of its glow.

The sun slumbered just above the trees;
Sheets of ice covered naked trees in a freeze.

Blustering breezes ripened rouge blushes;
Tiny tots on scarlet sleds set out on mushes.

Skaters scratched etchings in ice of glass;
A polar man rolled up over the dead grass.

Houses waxed sanctuaries from the lifeless ground;
A burning log intoxicated and made a crackling sound.

This solstice was the nadir in the valley of life;
Nature had fled to avoid its cold knife.

Before the furnace of life could sink below crystal sands,
The wise man embarked with presents for loving hands.

God grants eternity for those who believe;
Resilient Nature returns with each reprieve.

Robin Lynn Harmick
I WONDER

I wonder if a unicorn
really came to be;
Or if it just was born,
the same as you and me?

I wonder if the Pisa
really stood up tall;
Or if it leaned to the side,

just so it wouldn't fall?

I wonder if in Egypt
where Pharaohs' pyramids stand;
would they be better on a mountain
than on tiny bits of sand?

I wonder if Zeus
from Greek Mythology
had any difficulty
controlling his large family?

I wonder in the future
What I'll ever grow up to be;
A doctor, scientist, or a nurse,
No matter what, I'll just be me.

I wonder?

Madeline F Sewell
THE NEGLECTED GIFT
If God looked down on Christmas
Morn
At the bows and boxes, and
wrappings torn,
Would He look sad . . . and solemnly
say:
"What have you done with My Gift,
today?"

"He was My Only Begotten Son . . .
And I sent Him to die for everyone;
His birth you celebrate today,
But what have you done with My
Gift, I pray?"

"Have you treasured His presence in
your heart,
And made Him your Master from the
start?
Or pushed Him aside with the odds
and ends . . .
What have you done with My Gift,
My friend?"

Oh . . . Let's not get so carried away
With celebrations and trimmings
gay,
That the Gift God has sent us from
above
Is lost . . . And we miss the Gift of
Love!

Norene C Nicholls
NIGHT UNTO DAWN
In the flashing of a moment,
In the bursting of the day,
Shall you see the process climaxed
In a most unusual way.
For the Lord prepares the dawning
Through the night so long and cold,
And He dips His brush in blackness,
But He paints in glorious gold.
So be sure no night of waiting
Can be ever spent in vain,
For the cup that's drunk in darkness
Is the cup that all makes plain.
There's an eye that waits with
longing
For the morning's shining light,
And you'll see the bursting glory
Was prepared throughout the night.

Joy Marie Hayes
ANGELIC PRETENDINGS
When I was young I used to sit on
Father's broad warm lap, and listen
as he called me Princess, Precious,
Angelic Pet, and as he painted
pictures in gentle loving pride, I
began to feel a special glow start
way down deep inside.

Imagination flowing free made
wings begin to sprout, unfurling
snow-white feathers, above a wreath
aglow, with dazzling light around my
hair, a shimmering golden halo.

Then with a burst of youthful glee,
my brother bounded in.
The wings fell limp, the halo paled,
cherubim was no more.

As I caught the spark of mischief, the
imp within me rose.
I ran to join my brother, left my Dad
in sweet repose.

Stephen J Stefanacci

Stephen J Stefanacci
FRIEND
What once was, is no more and may
never be again
but through it all I wish you
well, and I'll still call you
Friend
A friend who cares, an open ear, a
shoulder to rest your head on
one to share a laugh, a tear, in a
friendship we have begun
A friend to say what's on our mind
whatever it may be
no harsh words, no mean
remarks, just advice for you and
me
I'm not sure what this means to you, I
only know how I feel
you gave me life when there
was none, I felt a Love that was
real
I've seen you laugh, I've seen you
cry, I've held you in my arms
I've seen you at your weakest
point, and you never lost your
charm
Memories will last forever even if
time will fly
I guess I'll never forget you
even 'till the day I die
I hope for your continued success
and happiness throughout your life
a future bright with lots of love,
free from pain and strife
It may have been short, what we
shared together, much too quick to
end
but life has its ways, and its
better days and you can call me
Friend

Ben Weaver
SNOW
Snow is as pure as sunlight on a
summer day,
Snow is like little flakes of the
clouds falling to the earth.
Snow reminds me of building
snowmen on cold winter days with
my father,
But now I never build them
anymore.

When I see snow covered trees, I see
a tree with a jacket on.
As the snow is coming down I wish I
was like the tree out in the snow.
Harder and harder the snow is falling
and the tree limbs are now being
weighted down by the snow,

Now it has quit snowing, but for how
long only the clouds will know.

Ronald H James
WORDS
There are but a few words
That I know how to use
To express what I feel about you

Even though there are words
& words & more words
I cannot always find the
right word to say, that
which is on my mind

Throughout the history of mankind
We humans fail to take the time
To share with each other
The love of God until we
No longer have anytime

So without further ado
I would like to tell you
That I utterly adore you
How's that for the use of words?

Benito F Reyes
THANK YOU FOR LANGUAGE
Think of a city where the ears are
dead.
There everyone would be both
deaf and dumb:
There would not be the usual
busy hum
Of living; it would be a morgue,
instead;
A dark necropolis of zombies where
No sound of man's inventions
would be heard;
Where every little thing would
be absurd,
Like trains without noise, trumpets
without blare.

Because there is no language, love
would die;
There might be thought, but
there would be no speech;
There would be tears, but there
would be no cry;
No one would talk, or sing, or
pray, or teach.
Thank you, my Lord, that I can talk
and hear;
Because of language I can call You
here.

Mary Holmes Wiley
I SAW GOD'S LOVE TODAY
I saw God's love today
a pretty bird
a fleeting cloud
a note of music
a friendly hello
a smile: a fleeting glow
a neighborly wave
a phone call: are U-O.K.?
a Monday greeting: I'm glad you're
back
a "good-nite darling" as U hit the
sack
a tip of the hat
a wink of the eye
I saw God's love today.

Marilyn Jean Petraitis
A LOVE FORBIDDEN
Invisible hands you will never see,
reaching out to hold you desperately.
Refusing existences of a trembling
heart,
denying the emptiness when we are
apart.

Invisible arms you will never enfold,
in your warm embrace sheltered from
cold.
Resisting temptation to run by your
side,
revealing tears of love I try to hide.

Existing on dreams that come in the
night,
escaping reality seeking no wrong or
right.
Is this true love or just a word . . .
that the soul cries out but is never
heard.

Like an actress on stage playing her
part,
disguising her tears shed from the
heart.
A love so near and yet so far,
a love tarnished by guilt for what we
are.

Oh fool . . . fool! Blinded was I,
to have fallen in love without
knowing why.
These secrets will remain a lifetime
unspoken,
of a love forbidden . . . and a heart
broken.

Kathryn Wright Johnson
THE POET

This poem is dedicated to my husband, Vic, now deceased, for his encouragement and appreciation.

He dwells in a cocoon
Fashioned of gossamer strands,
Seeing through vividly,
Unaffected by rain or winds,
Dauntless in spirit,
His world is spinning silken cords
To bind the rays of the sun
So other men may reach unknown
shores.

Jennifer Sizemore
US

Dedicated to Rikki Baker, who has inspired me, due to our feelings for one another. I'll always remember him no matter what the future brings.

We live and die,
laugh and cry.
We're happy and sad,
content and mad.
Although we have our ups-n-downs,
we still have more smiles than
frowns.
I know you care,
you know I'll always be there.
Our feelings are strong,
our fights are long.
We always make-up,
we'll never break-up.
And because we share,
we're the perfect pair!

Mary Jane Hungerford
I LOVE YOU, THAT'S WHY
Why is it, my sweetheart, I've so
much to tell you,
But somehow I cannot? My thoughts
are enchained.
If we were together I'd say with my
body
What words cannot compass, though
most unrestrained.
I need you, my sweetheart. I love
you, that's why.

Why is it, beloved, that you couldn't
trust me,
And needed to hurt me when I loved
you so?
And how did I realize why you were
angry
And frustrated so that you must
strike a blow?
I know you, beloved. I love you,
that's why.

Why is it, my honey, when I'm so
familiar
With each subtle contour and line of
your face
Your image escapes me when I
would recall it,
Although, dear, your presence is part

of this place?
I miss you, my honey. I love you, that's why.

Why is it, my darling, when moonlight is drenching
A landscape of fruit trees and dogwoods in bloom,
My heart leaps and capers, my throat muscles tighten,
The sense of your nearness is like a perfume?
I want you, my darling. I love you, that's why.

Why is it, my dearest, when night finds me weary
And small disappointments are magnified much,
I need but to glance into one of your letters
To warm and relax as if under your touch?
I feel you, my dearest. I love you, that's why.

Gary L Southern
DEPRESSION
An emotional whirlwind
Swirling in your mind
like an atomic explosion
Destroying your mind's sanity.
Lashing at the ones you love
Cutting their feelings with a razor,
Leaving a mangled heart.
Preying upon you
Until your remains crumble
And turn to dust,
Never leaving a trace
Of your existence.

D R Mote
NEW DAWNING DAY
My mind wanders
O'er time past
Perhaps to eons
Of long days ago
And I guess I held you
When my heart was fresh and new
With now time has pasted
And my heart has grown older
I now so much colder
Not so long ago
In her arms
I felt not so alone
My heart fell as a stone
Forming now ripples of mine pain
But there's a new day dawning
Sails of mine so full
No pitch no sway
Steady my course
For the new dawning day

Cecilia G Haupt
WITHOUT YOU

There are those in one's life who give great love, care and inspiration. I am grateful for John, Dan and Howard who have spurred me on to create beauty and perfection of thought.

Without you
The sun hides behind a cloud;
The moon forgets to shine;
Heaven becomes a vacancy,
An unfilled darkness.

Without you
Grass dries beneath my feet,
Crackles crisply
Like old cemetery turf untended.

Without you
The earth is flat and cold,
Still, foreboding.

Without you
I scatter burnt ashes of my heart
Along the seashore.

Jeff Adams
THE ROSE

To Mom With Love

Hello little rose,
How are you today?
I hope you are fine . . .
On this beautiful day.

Your petals are soft,
Your leaves are so fine.
Your smell is so fragrant,
I'll keep you for mine.

Hello little rose,
How are you today?
I'll keep you forever,
And ever a day.

June M Henson
NEED
My need for you is like a tide,
Rushing, smashing, drowning me;
And when, benumbed, I catch my breath
And wait subdued for its demands,
Its fierceness calms and it turns back,
Caressing as it slips away;
And I exhausted lie upon wet sands
To thirst for its returning spray.

J Gordon Pollock

J Gordon Pollock
JENNY, WITH SPIRIT

To the memory of S., whose going was so untimely

I watched our Jenny, beating on her pillow, crying salt while this pot-bellied prelate gushed his bilge.
Now bald, she tarried for a year.
Strained, fitful words and skeins of wisdom—
we'd tripped, her hand in mine, to that odd perch, to softly touch the kestrel's eggs, bare on that jutting edge.
Her eyes screwed up in feverish understanding.
Down again, salt strewn, to kiss the wind, feet curling on the coarse moraine.
Tiny, by the sea, with potted sand, in old Dunoon.
She picked out mussels with a pin—giggling.
A toddler, thwarting icy waves, that sucked her wiggling toes beneath the sand.
At four, reciting Mother Goose, lip pouting on the consonants.
She stumbled on her 'rs' and called it 'gween'.
She looked, long, hard at us, and gently cried.
A whisper came—"I'm by the sea again!"

Ronald Tarr
THE RIVER
Beginning in Verdant pasture land
As lines in well worn hand,
Running—with purpose errant,
No chartered course apparent.

So began the mighty river
Waters—which would deliver
Life—to earth—to all
Those who hear the river's call.

As each tributary flows
Together, how the river grows,
Identity lost as they merge,
Greater does the water surge.

Some will slow the main
Till together, then they gain,
Hard for eye of man to guess
Which the greater—which the less.

Now the river ever wide,
Destination could not hide,
Soon the ocean would consume,
Fate of river—one of doom.

Then no trace of waters seen,
Those that came from pastures green,
Our lives too like waters flow,
From whence we came—must there we go?

Denise Eberhart
LIFE GOES ON
Blind as a snowstorm
deep as the sea
You know what I need most
is your love for me.

I'm crazy about you
I need to feel you near
You see what I'm saying,
but why can't you hear?

You smile when I pass
but you never say hello
They say that life goes on,
then why can't I let go?

At nighttime I dream
of the life I want to live
and I know that you'd be pleased
with all the love that I could give.

Still I know I'll never have you
because we've grown so far apart.
But if you're ever lonely
there's a place deep in my heart.

Jeanne L Baranowski
HOLOCAUST
Suffer little children
See the blazing star
Comply to Nazi soldiers
Travel to afar

Beyond the barbed wire fence
Families torn apart
Sent to matching chambers
Squeezing the life from their hearts

Branded like a herd of cattle
A man could only cry
Watch the blitzkreig divorce
It's not time yet to die

As Jews we are subhuman
The slaughter is not a crime
Suppress the skeleton crew
Our lives aren't worth a dime

Eugene Byron Marcoe
GROWING OLD AIN'T ALL THAT BAD
Spring, Summer and Fall have passed.
How great was life in the bloom of Spring.
We worked so hard throughout the Summer
And gathered our fruits in Autumn rain.

And now I can feel the Winter winds
That stir the leaves in a whispered warning.
Soon they will scream through barren limbs.
The chill of Winter is a borning.

But must I dread in unsure fear
That what must come is very near?
In memories can I be content
Of greater times that came and went?

No, I will walk this path before me,
Find a hundred wonders, maybe more.
I will cherish every waking moment.
I have never been this way before.

Marjory Wadsworth Stone
JOY OF FLIGHT
As free as thought
My plane dips to earth
Flying through the stratus.

I soar through space
Not a whisper in the air
Cutting through spumes of cloud
Racing for the stars
Waiting expectantly.

Up, up into the mirrored blue
Like a seagull
Dancing with easy grace
What peace
Aloft in the majesty of space.

Angel fingers weave
Like cotton candy
Through the blue endless heavens
What joy this dimension
Of time that is and isn't.

Melissa Christine Miller
REACHING OUT
Only if I could reach your soul,
We could be a little closer.

Only if we could be alone and get to know each other better,
We could be a little closer.

Only if we could share our thoughts,
We could be a little closer.

Only if we could tell each other how we feel,
We could be a little closer.

Only if we can learn to depend on each other,
We could be a little closer.

Is there a way we could be a little closer or are we worlds apart?

David A Barrow
UNCONDITIONAL LOVE

To Joy, In consciousness may she realize life is lived only once.

Unconditional love is God sent, heavenly from above.

It is prayed for—alive—deserved, forsake all for.

Recognized, thanked for and received, a living blessing to you.

Love runs to another, past or new, anything to separate it from you.

Love hides from loyalty, faithfulness, and respect.

Love overwhelms, batters, makes eyes wet.

Love neglects when it's needed to be true.

Love accuses, hurts and despairs even despises you.

Love argues, criticizes then disappears.

Love changes always bad, never truly there.

Love misunderstands overcoming, it won't be fair.

Love sneaks, cheats and lies, never abiding to do what makes you feel good inside.

Unconditional love doesn't change, it grows: a gift from God.

It's always there, it shares pains, dreams and hopes.

Not worldly, but stems very high from above.

Love shares all in its self, of it self.

Love is a feel, grown thru God in oneself.

Darbellips

APARTHEID MAN

To the judges of injustices who place themselves above the throne of God through ignorance, without excuse, which cannot be forgiven or forgotten by man.

Black or white who I am is who I am, a man, no more no less, who you are is who I am, a man no more, no less, and in the end white became black and black became white, and in the end their stood a man not black or white,
just a man.

Nicolle D Efferman

RED ROSE

There once was a feeling that had no name,
It was a beautiful feeling so people named it Rose,
Rose brought happiness to the world,
Wherever she went hate was nowhere to be found,

Then, one day, a battle was started,
Rose died on that battlefield,
After the war was won,
People mourned for Rose,
They made bouquets for her,
And in their bouquets they put five black lilies,
And one, red rose.

Alfred Corbo

REFLECTIONS OF

To my love Denise
Always and Forever My Love

A hot summer's night, a land of heat,
Sleep, no not for I this night,
A new love, a new life, a cool breeze, I'm now complete.
These thoughts have no regrets, though perspiration
There's time to visualize experiences past.
Into the night, the sweat, restless-ness, a yawn,
I have! I have found true love, yes at last
From boy to man, wide eyed to sleep.
Thoughts soon turn to dreams,
Time that's lost, begins time a new,
Black turns to grey, a mighty river becomes a stream,
And yet it tells a story of all it has seen.
The truth is held within the soul,
Not conscious mind, nor heart, but somewhere deep within.
Day comes forth, aware now of the goal.

Judith Ann Allen

HOLLY BERRI

Holly Berries, Christmas Trees
Dolls, Drums, and Bears
These are the special things
That Christmas often shares

A child smiles, Christmas Cheer
Greetings from a far
Topping off a Christmas Tree
with a shining star

Blinking lights, Snowy nights
Santa on his sleigh

This is how we celebrate
The coming Christmas Day

MERRY CHRISTMAS

Susan M Smith

THOUGHTS

This poem is dedicated to my wonderful husband, Gary, who has always been there for me.

Underneath white-linen walls;
Shadows of evening;
Begin to fall;
Through the window above it all;
A cool, crisp breeze flows;
Surrendering my soul to the unrest below;
I feel myself grow wearily older;
With my head upon your shoulder;
Warmth caresses my soul;
Not a moment too soon;
I remember;
Your body stiffens as the wind picks up speed;
As for me;
I laugh in the face of adversity.

Robyn Brillman

FRIENDS

To my best friend Claire—even though we have had some misunder-standings, you will always be my best friend

Friends are very special people
Friends are people who are supposed to stick by you through thick and thin
Friends are people who listen to your deepest secrets and don't tell a soul
Friends are people who will never lie to you
Friends are people who you can trust
Friends are people who won't use you to get something else
Friends are people who won't ignore you one day then act like your best friend the next
Friends are people who will tell you things they don't tell any-one else
Friends are very special people.

Helen Bowers-Isabell

MUSIC

Music brings you near to me
When you are away
For it can recapture the mood
Of a previous hour or day.

The violin is the touch
That thrills my heart
And the drum is the pounding
The moment it starts.

The piano so versatile
Many moods can impart
The gladness when we meet
The sadness when we part.

Music brings you near to me
And as imagination flies
It becomes the unuttered words
Written in your eyes.

Hilda M Cosgrove

Hilda M Cosgrove

TO THE PANSY

To Loved Ones

Dear little pansy,
Child of God
Opening your face
So lovely and proud.

How long will you stay?
As you grace my life,
A short while—and then
You're gone from my sight.

Your little face closes
As though to hide
When you slowly leave
No more to abide.

And so is life short
As we face each new day
So open your heart with faith and a prayer
And you, too, can go softly on your way.

So trust in the Lord
For He watches and waits
To hear from His loved ones
As He opens love's gates.

Janette Stowe

THE CIRCLE OF LOVE

I patiently helped you learn to eat
And lovingly guided your stumbling feet.

It seems that only yesterday,
I watched you joyfully at play.

But, now you're quite a handsome man;
You no longer need my helping hand,
So please be patient with me now
As I've grown old and don't know how.

I need your love more now than then
As the learning process begins again.
I pray my needs you'll patiently meet
As you lovingly guide my stumbling feet.

Betty Roy

MEMORIES

Dedicated in memory of James E. "Red" Roy

With my feelings, I truly regret,
I never told you how I felt.

Now you're not here for me to express,
The Love and deep feelings I possess.

You were taken from us way too soon,
And with every waking moment, thoughts are of you.

Your smile, the gentleness of your spirit,
Is remembered in every passing moment.

The laughter that arose from stories you told,
Could never be replaced by silver or gold.

It's so hard to understand why you're gone,
Without you, your family feels so alone.

Your memory will forever remain,
Until the day we will be together again.

Genia Lynn Martin

FEELINGS OF A FRIEND

I dedicate this poem to Mrs. Price and thank her for the times she's helped me. I love you.

She's really nice. She will fill your heart with joy and delite.

If you have a problem or just felt sad, she's right there to make you feel glad.

she's just like a teenager in some ways.

she likes to kid around and play.

Her house is as pretty as can be, it's like looking back in history.

Well I have to go, but before I do. I want you to know she will fill your heart with a glow.

She's a fount of information with her front desk as a station.

If you feel the urge for a shortened day, check with her for a clean getaway.

M Elisabeth Steiner

WORLD WITHOUT END

There was a time when as a child
I looked up at the wondrous sky
And saw a brilliant, smiling moon,
Watching o'er her starlit children.
Now, after many years have passed,
I've learned of planets high above,
Produced by nature's turbulence,

And governed by divine order.
Earth, like a round, precious, blue stone,
Amidst stars in the galaxy,
Revels in civilizations
Enriched through the many ages;
Yet, all could be quickly destroyed
By senseless actions of mankind:
Chemicals poisoning the soil,
Oil spills damaging the oceans,
Sprays puncturing the ozone layer,
Acid rain killing fish and fowl.
Who will protect society
So that this great "world without end"
Will not become extinct too soon.

Lloyd Turner
MEMORY GARDEN

To Elizabeth Turner, my darling wife and sweetheart for fifty two years.

Many are the happy years gone by, as many as fifty and more,
And there's a garden of memories, a beautiful garden of yore.
Oft-times I stroll in this garden, dreaming of dreams come true,
And walk the quaint old path I walked, and fell in love with you.

Be it so beautiful, with rose, rock wall and vine,
This secret place hidden in the fantasy garden of mine.
Redolent of Jasmine, and turf and mellow earthy sod,
I can dream the dream, but a garden is made only by God.

When disappointment and loneliness chance to pass my way,
I meet God, in the garden, and we walk and talk and pray.
I fancy the birds as they sing and frolic from tree to tree,
They are so happy, I think they must talk to God, just like me.

In this enchanted garden of fifty years and more ago,
There I found the loveliest flower of all, this I know.
I took her from the garden, and placed her next to my heart,
And promised God, to keep and love her till death do us part.

Terrie Prino
SISTERS
Sisters: I have four,
Each with special quality,
Together, we appear same,
Apart, an individuality

One, my preteen idol,
Another, I emulated,
The third, I enjoyed,
The fourth, a friend

As a group:
We fought, we disliked,
We competed, we resented,
But always close, and we loved

We grew:
We discussed, hashed out differences,
We understood, we relented,
Always close, and we loved

We lost our parents:
We stood together, as one,
We consoled, solaced,
We became closer, and we loved

We learned much:
Came a long way
Sensibly, philosophically,
We grew closer, and we loved

We are separating:
Further apart—miles only,
But we are wiser, enlightened,
We are close, and we have love

We shall not forget:
We remember much,
Our lives are interwoven,
And,
We are so close, and have so much love.

Marilyn A Ellicott
I AM OF THE NIGHT

For my Beloved friend Rufus.

The thick night flows gently over the land,
softening harsh landscapes with a gentle hand.

I walk 'neath the moon's crystalline light,
My heart soars greatly at its glistening sight.

Stars are like diamonds, twinkling above,
reassuring us of God's everlasting love.

Trees stand as dark sentinels, sheltering any who need,
As the cares of the day slowly recede.

I walk through this wonder, my hound at my side,
And I am thankful for all that I see.

You take the day with the sun's glaring light,
But I'll always find peace in the softness of night.

Dorothy M Steimann
FROSTY WINDOW
Frost on window
What a thrill
Scrape its coating
Feel its chill
Trace with finger
The graceful lines
Broad leaves and reeds
Jack Frost's designs
Each time it's seen
It warms the heart
Of life's treasures
A special part

Thank you, God

Doug Paul Bernhart
GIVING MYSELF AWAY

This piece is dedicated to my fight against the mental problems due to Brain surgery I had. It is also dedicated to other people who have had the same.

I gave final rites in Cambodia.
I gave marriage in Honduras.
I gave love to the starving in Africa.
I'm a thousand years old
in Catholic ways.
I'm so young I ask for crosses when the man is hanging himself on my soul.

I funded psychology in Korea.
I funded rational in Minsk.
I funded all in all in my body.
My mind is weak,
but I consider giving it mind.

Myself isn't me when the cycle changes.
Many things are different
and my coping was given in South Chille.

The screws come loose,
but the man remains as he forgets himself on the way home.
When every part of me is gone
I will raise my voice in song.
It'll be the same when nothing's right when everything's wrong.

Coral N Phillips

Coral N Phillips
THE PARACHUTE

This poem is dedicated to my dear mother, Sarah E. Halstead

She was just a little girl, Granny's old umbrella she found.
What a thrill, she thought, to climb the roof and float safely to the ground.

She searched and searched, no ladder anywhere.
She was still determined to use Granny's umbrella and float gently through the air.

Daddy's old car was sitting nearby, cloth top down, wheels and fenders high.

It's better than nothing, her reasoning went,
So on the back fender she stood to make her descent.

With abated breath she decided to hop,
Then her dress hem caught on the knob of the car's top.

She dangled awhile 'til she felt her dress rip,
Then on down she went with a hard thud and a flip.

For many days she remained aloof,
Happy she sailed from Daddy's old car and not from the roof.

Martha Kennedy-Searle
NO MOMENT
At what precise time is the spirit released
To further the essence of life?
Life has been in the body on earth
Maturing with pleasure and stress.
Whenever the last breath exhales
Or the pulse can no longer be felt
Or the blood pressure drops down to zero
Is the soul really not where it dwelt?
Does it leave at just one precise moment?
Or linger and filter and flow,
Lifting itself lightly upward
As slowly as sifting down snow?
Does it soar and fly upward to heaven?
Or absorb itself in life on earth?
Does some of each soul enter each one of us
Or does it have new, complete birth?
Where and how the soul lives is mystery
To humans whose life must have breath.
But this I believe: The soul does live on;
There is never a moment of death.

John Loco Shapard
LOST GENERATION
It was the beginning of the end,
and the Empire begins.
Sharing common, uncommon ground
in the mine of time parallels have been found.
They dance their dance and spin around,
blinded innocence can't hear times ticking sound.
It began as a dream, will the soft memories stay?
I think not.
Savage green eyed children have lost their way.
As twilight falls on the shadowed mind
the ship of fools charts void unkind.
Everyone drunk as one will make the final stand,
deep azure zephyrs carry times counting sand.

Above the horrific, apocalyptic noise,
the maelstrom finality a certainty now.
flickered the frailest voice
in boldest defiance, said:
"We will survive!",
"for we have no choice."
Like tiny drops of reality dancing on red hot iron,
It was, will be, an empire on fire.

Marvis Letitia Hicks
WITHOUT ME
When I live without myself
I see the person I would like to become
I see the corrections that need to be made
I see the child that has stayed
I see the adult developing into wisdom
I see someone I would rather be
I see a sharing, loving, caring person
Always ready, always willing to give and support
All these things I see when I live without me

Ann Kimberlynn
MUSTAFA KEMAL ATATURK
Greatest of all men in the 20th Century. Great hero, great son of Turkey, saviour of his country. No Other man in the 20th century can Compare, brilliant mind, bravery.

The world remembers Gallipoli, The Dardanelles, Sea of Marmara.
Turkish sons fought their last

Battles, some lived to tell of
Glory, courage, of faith in God.
He did not fail them.

October 29, 1923, this great man
Set Turkey free. His people are
Free. Lovely Bosporus, Golden
Horn,
His waters to cherish, keep free.
Sons of Turkey keep his land free.

He rests on a hill under a great
Monument. The world respects him,
Turkey reveres him,
Father of the Turks.

Beulah Brumitt
GOD LOVES GRANDMAS

To the other two Grandmas Tillie, Louise and my granddaughter Jackie and Mom Bernie and in memory of my departed, beloved son, T. Michael.

God loves Grandmas, I'm blessed as
I can be. .
God loves Grandmas who pray for
kids like me.
'Tho I'm very spritely, I mean no
harm politely;
I'm not too much to handle, I can
wear one boot and sandal!

Into the tub I must quickly go, so no
one will ever know.
The mess I made "Goodness sake,"
when I helped my granma bake a
cake!
My mommy must work hard all
week long
And I pray God to keep her happy
and strong.

'Cause, my daddy went to heaven
when I was only three.
And to all of us it was a great big
mystery.
But God loves Grandmas, 'cause
he's really blessed me,
'n I've got some Grandmas—One,
Two, three!

Daniel R Burt
LIFE

To my beautiful and loving wife without whom I wouldn't have seen the light, I love you Dorene.

The California mountains
half a mile away
are just about invisible
on this smoggy day
again I must retreat into
the picture in my mind
enter its serenity
and times that I find
it brings back memories
of good times that I had
swimming holes of days gone by
fishing with my dad
a childhood in Wisconsin
places to explore
storybook adventures
a boy could ask no more
a village on a hillside
the river flowing by
where I was born in springtime
and where I want to die
though the times demanded
that I had to roam
I treasure all the memories of
the place I call
Back Home.

Jennifer Brookmeyer
MOONLIGHT VISIONS
Lying here in my room
I see visions of us
'Neath a bright moon
I think of my past
What happiness could I have found
Not ever seeing you
Or having you around?
As I think of these things
I am wishing you were near
To hold me tight
To whisper in my ear
I love you so much
Words could never describe
The love for you
That I'm feeling inside

Brian C Payne
ELK HUNT
Oh Beautiful Snow
You Now Have Come
And The Stream I Love To See

Majestic Elk
Where Are You Now
The Big Bull We Seek

Your Bugle Echoing Off Canyon
Walls
Is The Sound I Love To Hear

Your Antlers Gleaming In The Sun
Is A Beautiful Sight Indeed

Majestic Elk You Now Have Gone
The Wilderness Is No More

David F Short

David F Short
LOVE

To my beloved wife Beverly Who taught me how to love

Love is caring for each other in good
times and bad
Love is a feeling so warm, so
comfortable, so wonderful
Love is being able to lean on each
other in times of need
Love is what two people need to feel
fulfilled

Happiness, Peace, Warmth, Security,
these things I feel
These feelings I try to give to you as
you have to me
A Peace so complete you will never
feel worry again
A wall of Love that will surround
you as a warm blanket

You are mine Darling, always mine
for all times
I found in you a Love so complete,
so pure
No man could ever have a love such
as I
I am so complete in my love with
you

The warmth of your smile caresses
and warms my heart
The softness in your eyes gives me
an inner peace
A peace I have never known in this
life until now
You are mine my Darling, as I am
yours
How I love you my wife, my lover,
my life
You are mine and I am yours, this is
meant to be
Nothing will ever part us, it is our
destiny
Our destiny to love, to pass through
this life as one

Judith Joyce Flemmer
GOD'S MASTERPIECE
The meadows lay vast across the
land,
A work of art by Mother Nature's
hand.
The flowers amass in great
profusion,
Creating a feeling of tranquil
illusion.

The winds are calm, the sky is clear,
As I walk through the meadows I
feel God is near.
I can feel His presence up above,
Gazing down on His creation with
love.

As I walk through God's wonder
land,
A soft, velvet butterfly lit upon my
hand.
And as I gaze in awe at this beautiful
sight,
I realize that God was right,
When He decided that this beautiful
land
Needed someone to share it and He
created . . . MAN!!

Constance M Willi
TO MY NEPHEWS
Why didn't I hug you the day your
mother died?
Was I so filled with grief, as to be so
unmoved by your side?

I know I felt for you, but I should
have shown a lot more compassion
to your own.
I ached to say a comforting word,

but I could only see you, motherless
children at four and six, you couldn't
understand why God had taken her in
hand, and left for you

a beautiful brother.
But you, I'm sure, would rather still
have had your mother,

who'd soothe your hurts as you went
along life's way, and kiss and give
security to you, 'most every day.

Why didn't I hug you that day?
I only know I felt so bereft, I didn't
have emotion left, to give to you that
day.
But I have prayed to God to watch
over you, in all you do, every step
along the way, yet still I wish I
hugged you, on that most sorrowful
of days.

Lillian M Tyng
YOU ASKED FOR IT
You have asked for some new Poets
I hope you won't sigh and rue it.
For what I read from time to time
Nothing ever seems to rhyme.

Now I am a little past eighty eight
And maybe somewhat out of
date.
But I hope you will hear from many
Who enjoy poems and feeling
plenty.

If I were young, I'd join your
Chapter
And I know there would be
much laughter.
But now I will keep within the 21
lines
Wishing you the best in our era
and time.

Melinda K O'Brien
THE UNITED STATES NAVY
In times of peace,
In times of war,
You protect our lands,
And many shores.

You sail our seas,
Many days at a time,
Away from your home,
You leave love ones behind.

It is your job,
It's your destiny,
To protect this world,
From what it might be.

Who is it I speak about,
The ones who protect this world?
Why it can only be,
The United States Navy!

Mark Gary Duncan
LOVE
Love is an expression
A feeling deep from within
Love is taking time to care
No matter where or when
Love is wanting to be around
Through good times and through bad
Love is staying close at heart
Through times both happy and sad
Love is always knowing
That someone is there both day and
night
Love is expressing gratitude
In a very special way.

Todd Allen Fabian
AUTUMN
Leaves chase one another
red, yellow, and brown merge

inhale stale air . . .
burn

frozen moisture collects
on moustaches

itchy ears and
immovable fingers

footsteps crunch.

A girl folds arm
into arm

and shakes
right leg, left

the bus is late.

Arthur Stockman
LET ME FIND THE JEWELS OF OPAR ONCE AGAIN
I am tired of all the terrorists and
monsters.
I am tired of killings by the score and
score.
I am tired of TV Oil men and their
families.
There's some good old books I plan
to read once more.
I want to stray again to where Jane
met Tarzan
Somewhere, out there, on a lonely
jungle trail.
I want to read again of wonderful
things that happened
When Edgar Rice Burroughs spun
his lusty tales.
I will seek and find again that old
lost Empire
Where Gladiators fought as in days
of yore.
I will track again the dinosaurs of
lost Pal-ul-don
And find Pellucidar, At the Earth's
Core.
Let me wander again through

forbidden cities.
Let me feel again the beat of jungle rain.
Let me walk again in the hidden vale of Nimmr.
Let me find the Jewels of Opar once again.

Patty M Weyman

Patty M Weyman
LITTLE TYKES

This poem is dedicated to my husband Stan and our four children: Colleen, Joey, Shawn, and Walter.

Children are like small birds
So free, always busy like a hive of bees.
They're soft and warm like a summer breeze.
You can hear their laughter like the wind rustling through the trees.
So free are they, without a worry or care in their day.
Small children are what we grown-ups wish we could stay.
So, look at children in a special way.

For as long as there is life, they're here to stay.
A tear, hugs and warm kisses, a shy look, soft touch, a kind word, an innocent love, old toys, a rag doll, kindergarten, baseball cards, birthdays, Santa Claus.
A big smile, skates and bikes, running away, going on hikes.
And when you look at these dear little children (all you Grown-ups) remember at one time you too were also once a Little Tyke.

Gladus M Moore
INTERCESSION
I've seen them creep, walk and run
Only for another hour of fun
Never giving one thought to Thee,
Just run, run, run, in stupidity

Walking alone, no guide, no light,
Not giving a damn what's wrong or right
Heartaches will come, no one will care
Except You, Dear Father You are everywhere

Dear Heavenly Father, we try and yet we fail,
To give the love You so greatly share
With all of us here below
Our guilt is deep within, Dear Father please forgive.

Roberta B Simmons
THE RETURN
They've brought you back to me, my Son,
They've brought you back, ah, but alack,
Not in the way you went away,
Not in the way we wished you back.

You left with healthy face and soul,
With hope and faith and pride,
You fought for home and those you loved,
And wanted by your side.

But lo, your days were very few,
Never more am I to see,
Your youthful face, your happy grin,
That grew so dear to me.

For now you are no longer mine,
Tho, still a part of me,
And how you gave your life will be,
Known through all eternity.

Lois M Fishback
MY DARLING
Oh, what has happened, my Darling?
You once were so forceful and strong.
Now, you sit, scarcely speaking,
Or sleeping almost the day long.

You attempt to voice what you're needing.
Words can't emerge the right way.
Your nod says we've surmised the meaning
Of what you are trying to say.

We cooked you some chicken for dinner
As a special treat, tonight.
You mention that you aren't hungry
And scarcely will eat a bite.

You so much enjoyed the rose garden
As you worked in it day by day.
You can only say, "Yes", when I ask you
If it's time to prune and to spray.

Though your comments are jumbled, bewildered,
We can feel your care and your love.
You will some day speak clearly
With God in Heaven above.

Patricia Holliday
THE SENSUAL MAN
I'm sitting here looking at your picture, wondering about the real you. What are you really like after the interviews, the concerts, the glitter and glamor of the stages. It's like watching a precious jewel encased in a glass show case, guarded, untouchable, and unreachable. And that's how I see you in my glass showcase called a T.V., guarded, untouchable, and unreachable. I'm mystified, wondering about Mr. Mysterious. I look at you and begin to describe you from head to toe. Starting with your hair, the waves of the starting point;
Your eyebrows, the furs of connection;
your eyelashes, the flutters of battle;
your eyes, the meaning of seduction;
your nose, the breath of your accomplishments;
your mouth, the meaning of sensual;
your teeth, the gates of paradise;
your neck, the iron of uplift;
your arms, the locks of embrace;
your fingers, the elements of composition;
your chest, the amour of pride;
your stomach, the bed of pressure;
your manhood, the staff of life;
your legs, the pillars of hold;
your feet, the stampedes of the one and only;
your toes the keys of direction;
you as a whole, The Sensual Man.

Vicki Nelson
THOUGHTS OF YOU
While sitting alone with nothing to do,
My mind became filled with thoughts of you.
Things I should have said, things I should have done,
The expressions of words that make two as one.
Thoughts of good times we shared together,
Memories that will last forever.

Judy Elizabeth Taylor
VISION REVISITED
So deep was the night,
So gentle was the way,
So beautiful the flight,
Of the owl from the bay.

So velvety was the darkness,
So crystal were the stars,
So vital was the starkness,
Of the moonbeam's bars.

So peaceful was it's being,
So satisfying the rest,
So complete was my seeing,
Of a fantasy at its best.

Helena Floreani Spinner
GENTLE SOUL
The gentle beauty of your soul
smiles softly on the tattered earth
With pain and suffering in its arms
that rock us from the day of birth.

Yet with your soul you see the sun
that shines throughout the pouring rain.
And love and beauty fill your mind
the gentle soul smiles through again.

When battle's lost you don't give in
to pity, curse, or angry cries.
"Live out our lives the best we can"
comes from your lips and gentle eyes.

Calline Hons
LOVING
You looked into my eyes one day with sight,
I returned it all with sheer delight.
You gave me a sensation I've never known;
I put you on a pedestal as high as a throne:
You gave me strength when I was down,
I gave you my smile to take away your frown.
You gave me sunshine on cloudy days;
I gave you my love in so many ways.
You lifted my spirits ever so high;
I promised you love until the day I die.
You gave me a gift of fiery red,
I gave you my shoulder to lay your head.
You gave me a ring that really did shine
I'll hold on to the day that I made you mine.
You promised me love for the rest of my life
I honored your promise, I became your wife.

Margery Houze
THE MIRACLE OF THE SONG
"I've been through Hell," the young man said
As he lay on the hard, white hospital bed.
"I was flying high that night, " he said,
"Man, what those pills had done to my head.
I was Superman, I was Romeo,
The world was bathed in a rosy glow.
I could do anything, I was Mister Right,
Oh, the world was made for me that night.
Then suddenly, everything seemed to go wrong,
The radio was playing a different song.
Yes, the song was simple, but the message was strong,
And as I listened, I was singing along.
I've never been sure what happened that night,
But I knew that my life had never been right.
I prayed for hours and I know He heard,
For I heard Him answer my every word.
I'm O.K. now and I know that I'm well,
But, Man, for years I was living in Hell!"

Phyllis Sue Rector (Mrs Charles B)
THE PERIL OF THE STARK
Lo and behold—Iraq beware
We're gonna grab you by your underwear
You blew a hole in the side of our ship
Now it's your turn to take a dip.

It was only an accident you say
But beware—we'll have our day
37 crewmen were killed that way
Look out Iraq—you will pay.

You saw what we did to Libya in return
Now just maybe it's your time to burn
So be on your best behavior I say
And look over your shoulder for the good ole U.S.A.

Lois C Sanders
TULIPWOOD, MY HOME
My home is a haven
From noise and smoke and pests.
It is such a lovely place!
I am truly blessed!

My Lord has been so merciful!
He delivered me from sin.
He has delivered me from the mess,
That I was living in.

I prayed and cried for mercy!
He heard my earnest cry.
I shall ever be grateful to Him
Until the day I die!

No one else knows the sorrows
Of Life that I have borne!
I'm glad this place is mine,
Here I am not for Lorn.

I love this quiet, nice, warm place!
I've wanted it for so long!
It is so nice and clean and safe!
At Last I have a home!

Anne-Marie Furrey

Anne-Marie Furrey
ODYSSEY OF THE WORKING WOMAN

World War II forced us out of the kitchen and into the factories;
Having great pride in America, we supported our fighting soldiers;
Taking on non-traditional jobs to support our military might.
The journey from homemaker to professional was an awesome change,
Which evolved some forty-five years ago, now.
Our standard of living has improved significantly since then.
Women have made countless contributions to American business.
Over the years, many working experiences have been richly rewarding;
They came about through perseverance, hard work, determination,
And by employing a sense of humor to look on the bright side,
When giving up would have been the easier thing to do.
Personal satisfaction, fulfillment and heightened self-esteem
Were some of the benefits obtained through this conscious effort.
Success and greater levels of personal awareness were, also, known.
The mission of many women today is quite simple . . .
Make a contribution to America, sometime within your lifetime.
A high price was paid for the freedoms we enjoy;
This thought needs to be forever imprinted in our memory;
Never losing sight of the vision, remaining focused on the purpose,
Committed to the dream, knowing you CAN DO it.

Justina J Guenther
SCARLET WOMAN

He said he'd always love me
Forever he'd be true,
But he forgot his promises
As soon as he met you.

You were the scarlet woman
The devil in disguise,
You didn't really love him
I saw it in your eyes.

You knew I really loved him
He meant the world to me,
You didn't even want him
But now he's set me free.

You really care for no one
You're as selfish as can be,
You try so hard to hide it
But all the world can see.

You are the scarlet woman
No man is safe from you,
You cannot love just one man
And your heart is never true.

Kaarin Alisa
GUILT

The silence of the moment
broken slightly;
restlessness unceasing.

That point of reference, in time,
when life moves sideways;
numbing forward vision.

Lucia A Vizzini
POMEGRANATE

I opened a pomegranate today
and thought of you.
I felt you there beneath
my fingers, rough—
textured by the sun,
reddened too; as tough
as camel hide,
hiding bursting thoughts
behind your eyes
like the blushing
seeds inside.
I caught the real
you, that hidden chamber
in Ali Baba's cave,
glowing in the lamplight.
Then I came full circle—
from weather-roughened hide
to bitter seed
buried inside
the ruby softness of your lies.

Marie Flacco
THE MISSING LINK

To me he is one who never cared,
because his feelings with me he never shared.

It was he who denied me the love I
should have been given,
The kind of love one needs to keep
on living.

As the years passed, all he did was
make me cry,
He hurt me more and more as time
went by.

The scars on the outside always seem
to heal,
but the ones on the inside are made of
steel.

Everything I do, I do to make him
proud,
But somehow that always seems to
get turned around.

All I wish for, as my thoughts start to
twirl,
Is if I could just be
"Daddy's Little Girl!"

Violet Baker
BINGO

A friend of mine liked bingo
She went most every day,
The only reason that she gave
Was that she just liked to play.
Now she tried to explain the game to
me
And this is what she said,
You use a green or blue dauber
Or yellow, pink or red.
You have to daub your numbers
As the caller calls them out,
You get five in any straight line
Then bingo you will shout.
Now it's not as easy as it seems,
As you can plainly see,
He calls O-64 and you need O-63.
Now my friend is dying, but bingo's
on her mind
She says her number's coming up,
just most anytime.
I'm sitting here beside her bed, my
hand she won't let go
And then in a whispered voice I hear
her say,
"My number's up"—"Bingo"!

Juanita Bullock Martin

Juanita Bullock Martin
TURNING OF THE LEAVES

Dedicated with love, to my mother, Addie Beatrice, and my aunt, Helen, and in loving memory of James Crater and Ruth Crater Staten.

Some cannot accept the turning of
The leaves, not let autumn's
Withering branches fall gently to the
Ground. Some will choose the grapes
From vines, fresh, untouched and
Bold; than taste a mellowed glass of
Wine, mild and icy cold. Some will

Cling to youthfulness, then face the
Mirror's truth. While others store
Their dreams of youth in their
Memories of yesteryear. Some will
Accept growing older, while planting
New found dreams; enjoying the
Fresh new harvest, after the turning
Of the leaves.

S Celine Slanina VSC
MYRIAD OF ANGELS

The purpose of this poem is:
To introduce God's Angels—
Millions chant around His Throne;
Billions serve His Peoples.

Angels! Angels! Everywhere!
And no one is without one.
So give this precious Pal a "name";
He's "truly yours"; and such fun.

Yes, Angels, too, are helping you
To choose from masterpieces,
As minute after minute pass—
Until this contest ceases.

Thanks! Joel and Noel; Daniel and
Manuel;
Merci! Frankel and Markel; Kristel
and Ethel;
Gracias! Gayel and Rayel; Cecel and
Marcel;
Blessed be God in His Angels!

Valerie Snow
HUSBAND-TO-BE

A year ago on this fateful day,
A wonderful guy stole my heart
away.
From out of the blue he came to me,
And I learned how special
that love can be.

Our relationship started to blossom
and grow,
And now—we love each other so!
We are to be wed the day after
tomorrow.
To share our lives in joy and sorrow.

We'll stick together through tears
and laughter;
Like a storybook happily-ever-after.
But even without the bonding ring,
Our love will be a forever thing.

I care for him, he cares for me;
And that's how true love
came to be.

Miguel Postel
DISCOVERING

Well, you ask me what is America?
It is very simple . . . or perhaps
complicated . . . ?
If any tears call you,
If any close friend can't reach
the sky,
If any smiles resist to show . . .
I discovered that putting together
the tears, the smiles, we can
start.
One day I discovered myself shaking
your hand and I said to myself:
The human chain is locked.

Ginger Sue Nitek
ALL OVER AGAIN

Through the mist on the harbor,
Dancing lights on the water,
I see you smiling again.
Like a ghost looking through me;
Sending chills deep into me.
Shattered dreams falling like
teardrops;
As you make me remember:
Remember when I was safe;
Always safe with words unspoken;
I don't take chances with my
heart broken.
Broken glass of my mirror;
Makes my eyes see much clearer.
You -n- I only a whisper away;
I wish I hadn't seen you today.

Dwayne R Robinson
RUENAY OF MY DREAMS

Love to my wife, that we both share;
is never for granted, or used with
despair.
It's the bond inside us, a warm glow
we feel the most;
far apart we may, be our hearts are
ever close.
Our spirits in one place, our souls in
another;
we still fill our passion, she is my
lover.
Sometimes we're at our worst, and
close to tears;
our love, the feelings, almost
disappear.

Yes, there are hard times, challenges, and test;
making ends meet, trying to do our best.
But we hold each other sometimes cry;
the glow comes back, like a natural high.
So wonderful and understanding you are to me;
For you are, RUENAY OF MY DREAMS.
NEVER TAKE LOVE FOR GRANTED, OR DOOM YOU SHALL BE. .
LOOK INTO YOUR HEART, AND YOU SHALL SEE;
THAT THERE IS LOVE, IN OUR WORLD TODAY.
GOD GAVE US THIS GIFT, TO CHERISH HIS WAY.
SO LIFT UP YOUR SPIRITS, AND FEEL LOVE TOO;
LET YOUR SPIRITS FLOW, LET YOUR HEART GUIDE YOU.

Emilia A Glaz
SPELLBOUND

It sparkles
Like diamond dust
As it twirls around,
Gracefully dancing
Like Cinderella
At a grand ball.

Slowly it floats
Through the air.
I watch it
As it descends,
Totally captivated
By its beauty.

Gently it settles
Within my hand.
Its regal form
Is touched by the sun.
My snowflake vanishes
But the memory lingers on.

Donna von der Linden
MIDDLEGROUND

The words are slipping through
drawn by aroused emotions
roused to life by internal
conflict.
Seeking a solution to the internal warfare
that plagues man;
that doesn't bring swords to play
spilling innocent blood
breaking innocent hearts;
drawing tears from people
Who wonder what they did to deserve this destiny.
Never realizing they're just the
lucky victims of someone
else's rage
that when the battle lines were drawn
they just got caught
in the middle.

Ronald F Eden
TAKE THOUGHT FOR THIS BRIEF MOMENTS TIME

As light of early morning breaks,
a mourning dove sits all alone.
She longs to hear her cooing mate,
the mate for life, that she has
known.

She will not hear his mournful song,
no doubt his dirge has said it all.
A sudden boom of instant death,
has found her mate, and caused
his fall.

Oh, who would slay the mourning dove,
and cause his graceful flight to
cease?
He, who will never taste his flesh,
nor to his lonely mate grant
peace.

Why should it be, pray God to tell,
that with your hand you bring
him down,
and lay him there in cold still death,
what dismal sport, and fleeting
crown.

But even more than this great waste,
your very heart has failed to
care;
The life you took without a thought,
was just like yours—unique and
rare.

Dorothy Frances Nutt

Dorothy Frances Nutt
THE SUNSET

To my husband Bill, who enjoys with me the beauty of nature.

The glory of the sunset
Shows who is in command
Of this awesome beauty
Not made by human hand;
It greets the far horizon
And paints the western sky
In splendor only God creates,
While we with wonder sigh.

I love to watch the Sunset
Paint with Heaven's ink,
In hues from deep maroon
To lavender and pink;
Or lighting up the sky
In red, orange and gold,
From God's palette of colors
So beautiful and bold.

Dorothy R Chapman
COPING

To my late husband Gordon who would have been with me 50 years May 27, 1989

The world is full of many ways to make you understand that nothing can be impossible if you take your life in hand.
Don't let sorry feelings or unhappiness be the master of your fate.
Life is too short to brood and meditate.
I lost someone who was very near and dear to me.
How I was going to live without him was very hard for me to see.
Now over one year later I have started to understand.
My children and grandchildren are here to show me the way to keep my feelings bland.
I thank my lucky stars I have them each and every day.
The years will come and go and I will live alone, but someone is always there for me, as close as my telephone.
Just count your blessings and enjoy your family while you may.
You see people who are really alone almost every day.

LaVonda Eastup
TRIBUTE TO A FALLEN SON

Dedicated to Reggie: born September 7, 1952, in Hunt County, Tx. The finest Son a Mother could ever dream of! I'll meet you again someday in Heaven, Reggie!

Once more it is the anniversary of your passing.
The velvety nights, the dewy, fog-shrouded days have silently slipped away.
Kings and kingdoms have arisen and fallen this past year.
Mere man and heroes alike played out their destinies.
The great works of men's hands have perished and vanished.
Noble deeds and cowardly sins marched across the great stage of life.
Fair, tender Lilies have been born, while tired, wilted Oaks have suffered and died in anguish.
Perhaps you watched it all from your lofty perch—from floating, glorious blue and fluffy, whipped, frothy white.
Perhaps it was you when the leaves atop the tall trees rustled in the summer night.
Was it you? That glance I felt behind me, but when I turned, no one was there?
Was it you? That soft footstep that whispered across the bare floor at evening dusk?
Was it you? That glimpse in the crowd, a halo of golden curls; the lilt of a young voice, laughing merrily?
Was it you? The dream, so real I could almost feel your touch?
Only to awaken to stark reality again and again!
You are not forgotten, my gallant young son! Nor shall you ever be!
Your record stands for all time, for all the world to read, unblemished, golden, sincere.
For it is true that the good die young; the tenderest heart, the proudest frame, the noblest character; all seem to go earliest.
But I remember you, Reggie, my son. I remember!
The End.
Reggie Dale Eastup was killed June 20, 1975, at the age of twenty-two, in a motorcycle-truck accident, on Highway 50, between Greenville and Commerce, Texas.

Virginia Crowe
JACK FROST PAINTS SOUTHERN INDIANA

Jack Frost breezed into these Hoosier hills last night.
He worked feverishly and painlessly, covering everything in sight.
He accomplished so much, in a short span of time,
Wonder is there's frost elves, and do they know how to climb?
A display of tatted lace patterns, painted on the window glass, splotches of white, strewn all over the grass.
Roofs had specks of color, peeking through a white back-ground, orange persimmons were falling, creating a little mound.
The leaves were frost covered, there were so many of them, up near the trunk and out on the limb.
In a few days, they'll be a multi-colored hue.
Each tree brilliantly dressed, against a sky so blue.
The landscape changed from forest green to reds, yellows, oranges, to name a few.
An enchanted wonder-land, a breath-taking view.
Then the wind whipped around.
How those leaves did fly, like Hitchcock's birds, filling the autumn sky.
Now there's a thick cushie carpet,
Beneath the trees so bare.
Covering lawns and sidewalks,
Those leaves are everywhere.
Do you rake them, bag them or burn them, a back-breaking chore,
Or let "Mother Nature", blow those leaves NEXT DOOR?

Cassandra J Hirsch
TO BLASPHEME

For my mother, for Rochelle, who's always known, and known so well.

To blaspheme is easily done.
When I'm angry I'll revile one
who dares subdue his wrath before me
while my anger boils and swells within me.

Then I'll let fly the ugly cuss
that leaves a residual disgust
on that tongue of mine
I thought was clean
before hurling words I didn't mean.

Marcella L Robinson
TWENTY THREE YEARS

To my daughters, Kim, Norma and Freda

We were young at twenty two.
Love was bright, light and new.

He was so handsome and kind.
I knew in my heart he was mine.

So we wed in the April sun.
I wore a blue dress for fun.

Our working lives did we share.
Because we wanted things we cared.

How happy we were in our first home.
Either of us wanted to roam.

So our love grew and grew.
Then after a while we had a crew.

Three little girls kept us busy.
The home was full of warm fuzzy.

As they grew we talked of God.
It was important not to be odd.

After twenty three years he said,
"I'm gone."
I looked at him and said, "after so long?"

"How can you do this to us."
"Look, after twenty three years I must."

Missy Bickel
ARE YOU TRAPPED IN A COCOON WITH A MUZZLE STRAPPED TO YOUR HEART?

To all people who just live their life for life itself.

It's image is floating on a wave of caressing winds, but on an iris in May it bends. Stressing the note it sends.

This messenger, enlightened, with outpouring strands, expresses a rainbow's hue.
As our eyepiece is delighted and stands fixed;
A gust of gestures gives cue.

The colors are screaming, like an amplified foghorn,
straight forward as can be.
Gleaming in streams like a star o' fire,
not far; yet, one can't see.

THE BUTTERFLY WHISPERS FROM ITS' HEARTS DEEPEST PART . . .

"I was doubting life while locked in my cocoon;
wondering if I would be freed soon.
Now shouting,

to shock your veins' beat and jumps;
of inner tenses.
Now pouting,
to hope your heart lives and thumps;
of inner senses."

And everyday he sings his lay; not knowing whom has felt . . .

Nicholas D Young
WITH THIS RING

To Diane . . . for who the words flowed so easily

With this ring, I pledge my love,
And pray for guidance from above.
To ne'er hurt is my intent,
No irksome ire, nor foul dement.

With this ring, I give my life,
So proud that you will be my wife.
Your happiness . . . my endeavor,
To love you always, and forever.

With this ring, I lend my soul,
So you and I might be a whole.
You, the woman I so love,
O'er you, I place but naught above.

Margaret E Snyder
A FISHERMAN

To my Dad, Harvey M. Smeiser—May 1944

I know a man who'd know a fish
Most anyplace he'd go.
And yet with all his knowledge
he has one wish
That the weeds stay away from his throw.

He doesn't always catch the best
But what he gets will do,
For he can go and get the rest
When he gets more bait that's new.

If he's asked what luck he's had,
Like others he will say,
"I really didn't do so bad
But Oh! the one that got away."

He's fished since first he was a lad
And now he's growing old.
I'll tell you now this man's my Dad
And fish to him are gold.

Mary Gerry White
GOLDEN WAVES

A man lies sleeping—weeping, probably—
Because of candles spent;
Because of loving lent
To a woman who has come to know
What the rivers really show
When they dance in golden waves.

Perchance to be in Washington
Where rainbow ribbons try to bend
Across the river to find an end—
A pot of gold in waves, like glass,
That hit The Republic broadside, en masse;
Not the first, nor the last
Of the golden waves that passed
On the Potomac.

Charles D McGinnis Jr
THE ARTIST

For Maryann, whose true caring and understanding love was given in my time of need.

Art is the value of color
In the eye and rhythm in
The hand.

The artist is the song.

Delores Lee Lourey
A LONELY PLACE

I was born
In a lonely place
Where silent people
dwell

The darkness and the shadows
there
Throughout the daytime
fell

So far away
Were warmth and light
Tho beckon me
they would

With fearful steps
I ventured forth
And wondered
If I
could

Anthony Thomas Wells
SHE SOMETIME LEAVES MY MIND

She sometime leaves my mind, to linger and wander
She often turns pages to rain and thunder
At the same time, she's the star in the night's endless sky
Oh what mixed up clouds the moon sometimes cry
Words have wings, where do they fly?
I write to tease reality
In hope the world's imagination doesn't die.

Linda Farber Price
LOVE LIKE A ROSE

To Ray, whose love is my inspiration.

The days pass quickly and while I remember to say I love you, sometimes I question whether that is enough.

Or do you need a reminder as I often do of just what our love means to me.
After being together as long as we have, it is taken for granted that the feelings are known and the words need not be spoken, but that is so untrue.

For love taken for granted becomes stale and may shrivel and die.
While love that is nurtured and cared for can flourish like a beautiful rose.

Still a rose has thorns which can prick causing moments of pain,
but that does not take away from its fragrance and beauty.

And like the rose our love has been pricked by moments of pain,
but its beauty is eternal.

William Martin Jones
WALKING DOWN THE ROAD

For whom this poem is written, My heart is forever yours!

The rain has stopped, but the sun's not shining
Clouds hang low, with dark gray lining
The mountains rise, in the distant meadow
And the split rail fence has no shadow.

Softly blowing, the wind makes its journey
Down the sprinkled road, to where it starts turning
What once was dust, has been matted by the rain
And the fragrance of it all, brings fond memories again.

The rain has stopped, and the sun started shining
Through the low clouds, with soft gray lining
And as I wonder along, I chance to see
A violet, I'll pick for you and me!

Bertha Johnson Roscoe
MY LITTLE BUNDLE OF JOY

To Shahbu, my inspiration and Tyrone, my motivation: I love you both

He's on my mind at the start
of each new day.
Thoughts of him keep me
happy along my way.

He's a part of me
so dear and sweet.
A part sent down
to make my life complete.

He's a miracle of joy and life,
so beautiful and fair.
A wonder to behold,
He's my answered prayer.

He's a charming,
darling baby boy.
He's my little
bundle of joy!

Dorothy M Clark
SPRING DAY LOVE

Dedicated to my first love and to all in their first awareness of love.

I'll tell each dewdrop glistening,
I'll tell each insect listening,
I'll tell each ray of sunshine bright,
How much I care in morning light.

I'll tell each robin singing,
I'll tell each violet springing ,
I'll tell each brook, while it's at play,
How much I care from day to day.

I'll tell each raindrop falling,
I'll tell each cloud appalling,
I'll tell each hue of the rainbow gay,
How much I care on a stormy day.

I'll tell each beam of moonlight,
I'll tell each gleam of starlight,
I'll tell each breeze in the evening blue,
How much I truly, dear, love you.

Dawn M Pace
TO TEACH A LOVE

This poem is dedicated to Neil II, who is with me always.

How do I give up a love, oh Lord,
That just won't go away,
How do I surrender my all from it,
When it grows stronger each time I pray.

How do I steal a moment,
From angry scenes gone by,
To love, honor, and cherish the man,
Blessed moment from time gone awry.

Please help me with this one, I pray,
For it's too big to carry alone,
Help me surrender my all from it,
For peace I can claim as my own.

And live the life You want for me,
Growing in Your blessed light,
Teach me, oh Lord, the way I should go,
Direct me from wrong into right.

Leah J Berry
WHAT ARE DREAMS

Dreams are an unknown reality.
A wish is a hope for a dream,
But hope is like a wish.
So what is a dream.

Is a dream a vision of hope;
A fantasy in time.
Is a dream a fantasy,
That everyone wishes for.

Dreams seem far away from the reality of life.
Reality just may be a dream.
While people dream of paradise,
They could be living a dream,
Hoping for paradise.

But why wish for paradise,
When you live a dream.
But are you.
So what are dreams

Walt Brown
MY MOM

This poem is dedicated to my mother, Delores (Hintz) Brown, with love.

When I was in my youth, it was so hard to see
How God took care of someone else while taking care of me
How could He take such good care of me, yet meet the needs of others?
As I look back, I understand, that's why He gave us Mothers

When I was small and frightened, He used you Mom to hold me
And when I misbehaved, He used you then to scold me
I know God wants to hug us, but He lets you do that
In His own way, He touches us through a mother's loving pat

When I got older with a scrape or injury
Mom, you were God's Angel of comfort to me
When it seemed like God had given up and life was too hard to bear
I knew that God still loved me when I turned and saw you there

Remember when we were children,

you helped us say our prayers
It was way back then you taught us
how much God really cares
Sometimes God uses others when
there's something we should see
There were several times Mom,
when God used you for me

When you were struck with cancer, it
never got you down
Despite the pain and fear you felt,
you never wore a frown
This taught us perseverance and
where to place our trust
That there truly is a God both
merciful and just

There were times through adolescence, I know it didn't show
But I've always loved you Mom, I
just want you to know
Even yet today, your presence still
brings a peace and calm
I love you very much and I'm proud
that you're my Mom!

Wende Gross
SHEDDING TEARS OF ROSE PETALS

For Suzanne

shedding tears of rose petals
she looked to the sun
and cried
will you send me a ray
a ray to live on love on sleep on
also
the sun set though
hiding behind mountains of disgrace
mountains she was too weak to climb

when the sun rises
again she cries to it for help
again . . . the sun hid behind her
man-
made cloud
shuddered once
and turned her indoors
goodbye

Gloria Jean Daily

Gloria Jean Daily
MY FRIEND—MARIE

To God's most precious gift—from "Heaven" The Love of a "true friend"—her name is "Marie" She walks in God's beauty and speaks with His Love!

She listens quietly—to your
heartache
Eyes soft and warm—with loving
concern
Her gentle hands—are quick to
comfort
When your eyes—with
teardrops burn

She puts her own cares—behind her
As she listens, intently—to what
you say
Then, she offers—sweet, words of
wisdom
In her gentle—and quiet way

How I "treasure"—her "gentle
friendship"!
For which—she asks nothing, in
return
As her eyes—see me thro' Jesus
Never critical—of all I must
learn

She is a precious gift—from
"Heaven"
For, thro' her hands—His, Love
now heals
As her tender arms—enfold me
His, Love and Peace—have
become real!

Jeri Lynn Reedy
LOST LOVE

To my dearest love of all, Willie

Don't fret, don't cry
Our love is forever gone by
I will weep no more
For a new love is in store

The stars told me
You and I were never meant to be
How can it be so;
You and I chasing this never-ending
rainbow

My love, now we must part
Don't you see—we never had a
chance
Not even from the start
Just give it time, and I promise you
A new love will make your heart
dance

If, again, our paths should ever cross,
I know our hearts will feel the loss
But, says me
Our love was never meant to be

Charles Gaylord
NOW THAT THEY ARE WED

To Mette and Scott for their wedding

Now that forever they are wed
Mette and Scott their vows have said
I know that forever they'll be dear
And always hold each other near

The song of love they will sing
Within their hearts will always ring
They will look back upon this day
As together they go on their way

So hold each other always dear
And in your hearts you're always
near
Even if you're far away
Hope it 'll be for just a day

And as the road of life goes by
Try not to make each other cry
For happiness is the way of life
For each and every man and wife

Samantha Betzold
FLIGHT OF THE HEART

I dedicate this poem to the love of my life who told me, "put your heart and mind into it, and you can do anything." Also, to my mom and Jerry who keep my spirits high and encourage me in my poetry and my dreams.

Tonight, my mind wanders as I think
of you,
Of all the wonderful things that we
used to do.
The nights that you held and
caressed me tight,
I knew right away that it was all
right.
I see your face as it smiles at me,
And I figure out why I'll always love
thee.
The moments and memories are still
in my mind,
And I will never, ever dare leave
them behind.
They will be the key to our future
paradise,
And will always be treasured by my
big, blue eyes.
My teardrops won't leave stains
upon your lonely heart,
But my big, sweet smile will make a
good start.
A start into something so good and
so true,
At the reply of three words such as: I
Love You!

Warren H Richardson
TWO WHITE OWLS

Dedicated to Eliza, Patricia and Eilean, who taught me the love and beauty of nature.

Summer's night, a moonlit flight,
A path so straight and true;
A friendly screech, just an invite,
"Come, dance with we two."
With wisping clouds in backdrop
glow,
I'm given to this evening show;
Silhouettes white, floating on the sky,
Forever touching my mind's eye.

Genevieve Hopf-Pagel
ARE YOU WILLING? WILL YOU TRY?

I wish I could wake up tomorrow,
and find it was only a dream,
That the world of today, (believe
me,) is not quite as bad as it
seems,
Perhaps it will be a long time—
yet—
before, whatever's going on
disappears
So—let's all get together, the
sooner the better.
Are you willing to give it a try,
friends?
it's about all we have left to do,
So please join in with me, let's get
down on our knees,
And pray, pray, pray.

Veronica L Martinez
RAINY DAYS

Dedicated to LISA, a good friend

As I look out the smudge window,
I see it's going to be a rainy day.
As I look beyond the gray angry
clouds
I see there are many other rainy days
to follow.
Then I go outside, drops fall,
a cold breeze brushes my hair away
from my face
and the smell of mist makes me feel
like the day will never end.

Eloys E George
ALONE WITH THE WIND

The skies so dismal, so dark and gray
On a vicious, cold, bitter, winter day,
And making the trees to groan and
sway
By the wind furiously sweeping dead
leaves away.

A small lone figure on a lonely trail,
A face so gaunt, so sad and pale,
Dejected and weak and very frail;
The wind quickly turning into a
raging gale.

A wounded soul only wanting to die,
Only thinking of days now long gone
by,
A failing heart giving a quivering
sigh
Lost in the wind's wild, savage cry.

Losing a mate, so feeble and old
Having no more a hand to hold,
Struggling along in the frigid cold;
The wind so merciless, so cruel, so
bold.

Now to the trail's end, to the world
good-bye
Life ebbing away and death so nigh,
The cold, dark earth feeling so warm
and dry;
The wind moaning softly like a
lullaby.

A layer of snow now covering the
ground,
There at last a body being found,
Resting so quietly by a newly dug
mound;
The wind lamenting with a mournful
sound.

Nestling so closely by a burial place,
Lying there enfolded in death's cold
embrace,
A serene, tranquil smile on a frozen
face;
The wind sobbing sadly in shameful
disgrace.

Shirley D Peters
A BLESSING

To two people very dear to my heart,
Two people who I have loved from
the start,
That is why this prayer is sent,
In a special way, truly meant,
My prayer from me to you is this,
That God's love you won't miss,
That God's love shall be with you,
That your love shall be with Him too,
As I write this I ask that God might
bless,
These people I love with happiness.

Kelly Reynolds
WITH NO CARE

When I was a little girl I had
All the joys in the world,
With no care of what lay ahead of me
in life.

When I was just twelve I had
My neat clothes and good friends,
and
With no care of what lay ahead of me
in life.

When I was sixteen I had
All the boys and smoked my
cigarettes,
With no care of what lay ahead of me
in life

When I was twenty-one I drank
beer and smoked dope,
With no care of what lay ahead of
me in life

Now I lay in a dark place for
I died a dreadful death, and
I wonder now what would have
lain ahead of me in life.

Denise Pierandozzi
DADDY'S LITTLE GIRL

Dedicated to: My Father and my friend; I'll always be your little girl.

I have special feelings
I want you to know.
Feelings that make
My whole world glow.

A special love that makes me feel
glad.

The love that I cherish is for my Dad.

He's warm, caring and kind.
Guys like him are hard to find.
He makes me laugh
He makes me cry
He makes me try, to understand why.

He helps me through
When I'm down and out.
He makes me realize
What life is all about.

Sometimes my Dad,
He'll call me a squirrel.
But it helps to remind me
"I'm Daddy's Little Girl."

Richard Piercey

MY PERFECT LADY

Dedicated to Irene Skelen, the only Perfect Lady in my Life. I Love You.

This is just a poem Babe to tell you how I feel.

You are the woman in my life, and my thoughts of you are real.

You are a loving person and you have a caring heart.

You never done me wrong for you loved me from the start.

The affection that you give to me is very, very strong.

And when embraced with your hug, it's with you I know I do belong.

When my hopes start fading away I'm glad you're always there.

When I'm down I want to give up. We can always laugh or share a tear.

I hope these feelings I have for you, you have the same for me.

Together we will reach our destination, because the two of us were meant to be.

Gypsy Ball

YOUR LIFE TOGETHER

Dedicated to all newly married people young and old.

The time is slowly coming when you and your loved one will be joined together as one. It is going to take a lot of work on both of your parts. If you both work at it you will and can have a beautiful and wonderful life.

To you both I give my wish and hope that the two of you will accomplish the beauty that should and can be there for two who are in love.

Be happy in the fact that the two of you are in love. Know that when two are in love as the both of you are even the moments of hardship will work for you.

Try not to let yourselves become discouraged or bitter over things which should not matter. Try and keep the beauty and love that your relationship has. With this beauty and love you both can overcome any obstacle that is placed in your way.

So when that day finally gets here. Please accept my hope that your love, joy, peace, and happiness will always be in one another. May your days together always be bright.

Maurtile Britton

SHALLOW BOATS

To Colonel David W. Donovan (Son)

I went back home again today;
The house was old and worn.
I walked in former footsteps,
Heard voices that were gone.

I was a little child again,
Building boats of fallen leaves,
Then launched them in a brook,
To float down to the seas.

My brother built a bigger boat
with sails of maple leaves;
He put two tadpoles in the hold
To ride the seven seas.

The memory brought this thought to me,
When you are young and free
You launch your dreams on shallow boats
That never reach the sea.

Ricky D Adams

THE EYES OF AN EAGLE

Have you ever wondered what you could see
If the eyes of an eagle were yours to behold
Would you see the lands your fathers seen
And the freedoms there unfold
Or would you see the tops of the highest mountains
And the valleys there below
Or would you choose to fly so very high
Where only eagles choose to go
Sometimes I wonder how it would be
To see these things from there
To have my wings spread oh so far
And have not even a care
But then I wake to be standing here
No wings to spread or soar on
And only to look up oh so high
To see the eagle flying by

Jeanne M Troutman

MY BREATH-TAKING FLOWERS

Dedicated to my daughters Pamela Troutman, Tanya Troutman Blackwood; with special love to my grand-daughters, Yanika and Tamina. Also special love to all the handicapped children I have taught.

. . . My Breath-Taking Flowers,
Are what my children are to me,
They are sweet, lively, sometimes irritable, mischievous,
Yet, their size is wee.

. . . My Breath Taking Flowers
Full of eagerness to learn
When academics are presented
By a patient teacher showing concern

. . . Flowers are delicate,
My children are too,
Their disabilities vary,
Just like personalities run true

My children are like flowers to me,
No matter how tiresome the day goes
Smiling faces at snack time
Brings joy to every deserving student who knows.

Jennifer Guerriero

THE ITCH

Shhhh. Listen.
Hear that?
I can.
It's soft.
I hear it,
Louder, louder,
Calling, calling,
"Come, come!"
Closer, closer,
It's there,
I know it.
It's my destiny.

It's my dream.

Christine Tyler

VIRGIN VALLEY

The aqua marine lagoon lies like a shimmering mirror
broken by an occasional ripple as a breeze blows by.

Its waters are blue-black deep until even the fish
disappear in its unknown depth.

A crystal clear sky is dotted with one magnificent eagle swooping through the air.

Velvet soft deer lap lazily from the pond, furry rabbits nibble juicy fat carrots, while overhead birds warble.

Man sounds are silent.

Dripping red roses and unruly daisies wrap around pine green bushes.

Mountains rise to touch the sky, protecting their treasures within.

Trees stand tall and proud, holding their lush leaves like curtains waiting to lift for the right person.

Maybe . . .

A virgin valley such as this would survive if man cherished such beauty.

If jealousy didn't raise its head with a vicious snarl and a deadly growl.

Kelly Ginebaugh

THE POND

Swans at a lake
full of beauty and grace,
race for the wind.

The pond left behind
filled with murky water.
Filled as once before,
full of a great mournfulness.

The pond, full of sorrow.
For these great birds
the pond now longs.

Wounded in sorrow
wounded in pride.
The pond struggles on,
hoping, hoping
for another occupant.

The heart now dead
shattered by grief.
To have lost one's pride
is to lose all hope.

Cherie G Estes

ME

Walking thru the forest
feeling the soft breeze,
listening to the birds
gazing up into the trees.

Deer moving soundlessly, as they run by,
squirrels chattering high above
keeping a watchful eye.

Breathing deep the clean fresh air,
I walk along the stream
Hoping someday not far-off
I can fulfill my dream.

A dream to live in the beautiful hills
the peace, the harmony,
The freedom that my heart would feel
to live in this beauty.

To share this beauty with someone I love
To enjoy happiness and freedom
like the deer and the dove.

Debbie Doyle

ARE YOU BOUND TO?

I haven't felt this way before
and I need to worry no more
For you're bound to see
and catch some love from me.
I've spent a lot of time looking for you
Searching and finding—I wish us not to be through
I'm willing to take your love from bits-n-pieces
Coming from you it only eases
love is contagious—only to catch eventually
I wish for you to catch from me.
I want to be your lover
Sooner, than later, you'll discover
I'm happy seeing you the while
the tears start—but that's not my style.
For I know you're bound to see
and catch some love from me.
I've about loved, my hard love away
waiting for you just to say
I'm bound to see and do
just to catch some love from you.

Maria Nadia Strazzanti

SURELY HE MUST FALL

It's not loneliness that man should conquer; It's the fear of being alone that must be fought

Voices in the night.
Echoes from the wall.
Visions in the dark, surely he must fall.
There's danger in his flight.
There's figures that move about.
A journey in the night, for him there is no way out.

Dreams which float on by.
There are visions in the dark
Danger beyond them lies.
There's a fire with no spark.

Voices which turn to screams.
Visions are only dreams.
He wakes with sweat upon his face.
He only ran to find his own space.

The sun has risen now.
He turns to face the day.
Fear lingers on somehow, but his thoughts have cleared away.

Until the night rolls in once again, he is safe from the dreams in tell.
When the night does roll in, he once again enters hell.

Lorraine Vanatta Huyten

Lorraine Vanatta Huyten
LOVE FOR A LIFETIME

PLEASE her with your eyes.
Treat her like a lady.
Touch her like a baby.

RESPECT her for her point of View.
Don't strip her of her pride.
We both look at things from different sides.

LOVE her with your actions.
Love her with your words.
And soon her body will be
Snuggled up to yours.

Leann McCormick
LOVE LOST LIKE FROZEN RAIN

Love lost like frozen rain
The times we've shared cause only pain
If you loved her from the start
Why would you bother to break my heart
Broken flames and burning hearts
When you're with her, we're further apart
I've tried to show you how I feel
Now I only hope my wounds will heal
I'm not ready to let go
She'll have to fight, I can't say no
I can wait as long as it takes
I'm not afraid though my heart quakes
I'll wait forever, if you'll be my guide
Sitting in silence with open eyes

Willie C Cole
OUR "BELOVED NATION" IN A DEEPFREEZE

To my DARLING JESSIE MAE MY INSPIRATION AND WARMTH

There has been building up for many a week;
In the Alaskan Region we all know;
High Pressure Area upon High Pressure Areas now warmth we seek;
With its full force to our "Beloved Nation" has come wind, sleet and snow:

Remaining in the Alaskan and Canadian Province for many a day;
But now has broken forth upon the "United States of America" with a powerful force;
Time again the Weathermen predicted this "Siberian Express" was coming our way; Although having enjoyed mild weather for so long becoming unthankful to our God who is the source:

Just maybe this "Blue Norther" or shall I say "Blizzard: of its kind;
Is sent our way for a lesson we can learn it is true:
To present before our eyes that God is in control of all the elements at all times;
This being brought home to me, how about you?:

This February morning;
Here in our "Beloved Wise County;
The ground being covered with an Inch or more of sleet and ice, soon another day will be dawning;
Then in the daylight may we see our God has clearly blessed us again through His "Beloved Son's" bounty:

While in darkness there may be more discouragement we all know;
But there is something about daylight that reflects His own Son;
So look-up all ye people soon the "Siberian Express" will pass from this Area it is so;
With "Spiritual" eyes we behold Jesus at God's own right hand even on His throne;
By "Grace" through "Faith" in our Heavenly Father and Jesus through the "Holy Spirit" we will reach our Heavenly Home:

Tony Marsiglia
NATURE

To My Mother Susan Marsiglia

Nature
beauty, scent
blowing, decaying, rottening
winter, people, animals, fires
coloring, falling, snowing
gnawed, shot,
dead

Lorrie Trunkhill
DANYEL

Have you ever reached out but could find nobody there?
Have you ever wondered if there is anyone out there to really care?
Lock her up, stick her away, try to alter her mind, she may return to us someday
Feed her some pills, give her more tests, then try to calm her down and tell her she needs her rest
Does anyone out there care what she tries to say?
Does anyone try to reach her hand and help her open that door someday?
The door that when opened may free her tortured mind
Help her to start anew and to leave the bitter past behind
Help her to be as normal as she can be
Help her to be happy, help her to be free.

Tina Abolins
twilight affair

just for one day
i fell in love with you
but after the next sunset,
i lost you among other stars.
and now darkness is eternal twilight
without you in my dawn.
was it your sudden disappearances
that intrigued me to recapture you
or were you always there
hiding in my dreams?

. . . and now the picture fades
as dusk diminishes possibilities
of rapture.

our first hello was as obsolete
as our last good-bye.

tomorrow never happened
too many times.

Julie A Kleinsmith
THE WINDS OF SUMMER

The winds of summer are so special to me.
They bring back many memories.
Days of running free.
Skipping and jumping in the sea.
The winds of summer no longer blow,
They only hide in the mist of snow.

Maureen C Whyte
LOST LOVE

To Frank Lichtfuss

Perhaps
If I had not
So tightly clutched the rose,
Its thorns would not have pierced my flesh
So deep.

Sharon L LaMar
"CHERISH" IS THE WORD

To Shawn Ryan, sweet child of mine

Christmas is the time of year
For happiness and Yule time cheer
The fondest memories, oh how sweet
As a child seeing Santa's treat
And the calendar counting down the days
Until the time we hear Santa's sleighs
The aroma of our family's feast
The midnight Mass by our parish priest
The gathering of family by the tree
The smiles of faces for all to see
The handmade stockings hanging on the wall
The Christmas tree standing so big and tall
The love and kindness, and unselfish giving
Makes it worthwhile for all of us living
The memory to cherish and give me joy
Is this first Christmas with my newborn boy.

Mary K McAllister
STREETS OF AMERICA

Find the streets of America
the opportunities they hold
where the sky is filled with rainbows
above a world of gold.

On these streets of America
these stony streets so cold
a man lives in the gutter
disbelieving what he is told.

No separation of truth and lies
no distinction of fate
in this land of equality
for some it is too late.

The loudest of a million voices
crying for fallen dreams
but not a mind is opened
to listen to their screams.

On these streets of America
these ears must learn to hear
without the hope for change
we'll never end this fear.

Find the streets of America
twenty years in time
will voices still be echoing
"Hey buddy, can you spare a dime?"

K A Schneckloth
UNSPOKEN WORDS

The feeling so deep
The love so everlasting
Through every layer of skin it seeps
Through every organ it is passing

Descending into my soul
The soul which once was dark and empty
The woman who has made myself whole
The woman who has made my life complete

No star on the brightest of nights
Nor the sun preparing for a new dawn
Can compare to the beauty I feel inside
Nor to the vibrant rainbow you have set me upon

Words need not be spoken
Gazing into the windows of our souls
No longer will our fragile hearts be broken
For you are the woman who has made my life whole

Barbara A Trabosh
PLEASURES

To; Dennis and Michael, and all my friends that shared my dreams

Laying in green fields, watching the earth slowly revolve
My mind's filled, with pleasures of God's work
Mind in motion, constantly developing

Animals everywhere, running to be unnoticed
Chilled water, passing over tiny pebbles
Restful shades of green, simply glowing and warm

Watching wheat, in rhythm with the wind
Collecting thoughts, of all these pleasures
Feel! those pleasures, I'm receiving

Pleasures, I'm receiving
My mind's, totally being filled
Pleasures of excitement, pleasure's been received

Pleasure of harmonious life, does exist
Lying in green fields, receiving this
Pleasures, I'm receiving

Donna P Flynn
GOD'S WORLD

God's world is tiny little miracles that happen every day.
The answer to your prayers after you've knelt down to pray.
If you look very carefully there are many wonders to enjoy.
You really shouldn't treat life as if it were a toy.
God's world is the leaves falling from the trees so tall,
With their rainbow of colors in the fall.
The pitter pat of little feet
From our children who are so sweet.
Looking the field over for a four leaf clover.

God's world is the true dispensing of justice from a court of law.
Getting along smoothly with one's mother-in-law.
Giving to charity to folks in need.
Seeing that the wild birds have plenty of seed.
There's plenty of goodness in the world to share.
You can help pass it around to the ones who care.
Have you ever sat atop a mountain and gazed all around?
Threw some pebbles in a pond just to hear the sound.
Have you ever seen the morning when the sun comes up?
Have you ever stooped to pluck a Buttercup?
Have you ever heard the first cry from a baby's throat?
Make sure, Dear Friends, not to miss the boat
In this, God's world.

Brenda Loomis
A LOYAL FLOWER
Flowers growing in the sun;
Giving hope for everyone.

Faces lifted to the sky;
Telling people not to cry.

Even when you feel so blue;
The rain will come when it is due.

A flower dying in a vase;
Just to see a smiling face.

They brighten many hours and days;
Yet they don't grumble or receive any praise.

Finally they will wilt and die;
And are left somewhere in a corner to lie.

Gene Patee

Gene Patee
THE TIME MACHINE

This poem is dedicated to all the "dreamers" of the world. From this group will come tomorrow's great achievers. The science fiction of this poem could beget a scientific reality spawned in the minds of such dreamers!

If I could build a "time machine" and boldly traverse space and time,
What pleasant, sacred memories would come alive before my eyes,
There!—I have made my "time-warp" id, now, to my "Past" of youth's delight,
Well, here we are!—Oh pleasant sight!—That large white house where once I dwelt,
My!—How the neighborhood has changed!—But wait!—It's me that's changed, not it!
Old sidewalks flow through new-mown grass and lovely flowers strew the way,
Curious eyes meet fenced backyard with an apple tree and clothesline,
Where my family goes daily, to this quaint, relaxing green place,
They greeted me, but knew me not?, so quizzically I bantered,
How is your boy, that special boy, that loves his soda pop and beef?

They said he's fine, he's in the house, and feel free to stop and see him,
The entrance hinges slowly move, and, there am I,—Me at the door!
Such fright in "Alter-Ego's" eyes!—Behind closed doors he fast recoiled!
So shaken by the day's events, I must hasten back to "Present,"
At the sound once more I tarry, of a lonely whining steam train,
If only I could live again those precious days of yesteryear,
But the "Past" was "Then"—Which became "Now"—And the "Now" is soon our "Future!"
So in my lightning "dream machine" I sped through "Fourth Dimension" Time,
For "time-dilation" travelers now comes this learn-ed answer clear,
Tis never right for man to hold the "times" and "seasons" in his hands,
While God as yet ordains it so, crowd much into the " Present" Day! !

Steven J Letourneau
TO CHASE A DREAM
Chasing my tail
round and round,
I can not get up
off the ground,
found myself behind myself
and saw it run on by.

So here I am
chasing that dream,
to be successful
and all supreme,
but again the shadow
runs on by,
I find my dreams
were set too high.

So the shadow passes
and in time fades,
I stand here alone
in the misery I made.
Nowhere.
Nowhere, but the beginning.

Dianne Cambre
A DREAM COME TRUE
As a child I dreamed of being a Mommy.
And having a home of my own.
As a Mommy I longed for my childhood days
Where I could escape to my make believe world.
Because there in that world I was safe and I made my own rules.
No one could enter and no one could hurt me.
As I grew into an adult I left my world behind.
To enter the world of grown-ups hoping it would fulfill
My childhood dreams.
After much heartache and a whole lot of joy,
I realized my dream world did come true.
I AM A MOMMY.

N J Manley
VALENTINES DAY
Sweethearts day known to us as Valentine's Day
has many people giving flowers and cards to those dear
picking out the perfect verse, enables us to say
the things we have put off all the rest of the year,
husbands, boy friends, or just friends met on the way
call on wives, girlfriends, or some lovely that is near
we get together at dinners, or rides in a horse drawn sleigh
maybe just cruising, stopping to have a glass of wine or beer,
this day is for lovers, husbands and wives,
for good friends we pray
but we must remember to carry the, spirit of Valentine's Day
all of the year

Scot Bauer
SILVER THREAD

Dedicated To The Living ......

As the hour of noon turns dark,
my blurred vision begins to crystallize.
I am once again free of burden.
A strong fiber of silver drifts from my rising spirit.
My mind, body, and spirit.
All connected by the tender wire of life, the silver thread.
In the endless night, stars appear and become
My sole comrades on this flight—on the thread
My mind spies other web-like cords, lost in exile from the blue globe of life.
From my hapless wanderings, I am drawn
Into a tunnel of light by the hands of Fate.
Searching for an end to the eternal voyage,
I reach out with heart and soul,
Out of the brilliant tunnel,
I once again enter life.

Katherine M Brady
OF FAIRY TALES AND FABLES

Dedicated to my beloved sister Dorothy Murray Banks

When my sister and I were small,
we loved to play pretend
At times we'd play till almost dark
for games were hard to end
We always loved to go outside
behind the old smokehouse
There we would dress our dolls and
stay quiet as any mouse
We'd drive some sticks into the ground
to make our playhouse wall
We'd prop some boards against the sticks
lest they might lean and fall
The ground was our hardwood floor
adorned with leaves and rocks
And we spent uncounted moments
removing them from socks
O we would sweep and brush awhile
with old and worn out brooms
Then we'd pick some flowering weeds
to brighten every room
We would search for shining treasures
plowed up in nearby field
Then we'd explore discarded junk
to see what it would yield
Six bricks would make a cooking stove
topped by a piece of tin
A large but empty coffee can
would be a flour bin.
Boxes soon became our seats
Tables looked like nailkegs
We fried up yellow bitter blooms
and they were scrambled eggs
We'd shell the pods of seeds we'd pick
and wash them in old pans
They would be our vegetables
prepared by children's hands
O for the years of lost childhood
when hearts were all aglow
with fairy tales and fables
a child could only know!

Stephanie Crostic
DECIDED, SUICIDE

In memory of my dear brother.
For helping to awaken my seemingly distant dreams.

Decided, Suicide

Lonely hearts,
Selfish minds,
Silent shouts,
Deadly crimes.

Pain so great,
Death so sweet,
Mind destroyed,
Pronounced defeat.

Empty souls,
Mixed emotions,
Hardship strikes,
Deadly potions.

No peace,
No light,
No will to survive.

Decided, Suicide

Beverly Clark
I STILL TRY TO VENTURE ON
When it seems like times are at it's hardest,
And the grass in the jungle has grown
In this great big world of ours,
Though some may not have known.
Before I just give up and weep
About things I do not own,
I rather pray before I sleep
And try to venture on.

I wander sometimes back and forth,
Like a stranger without a home.
I try to make my heart of greater worth,
Because I know I'm not alone.
No matter how hard it seems at times,
I know God is still on the throne.
He helps me no matter what I do
And lets me venture on.

Daniel R Lien
FROM TEAR TO SMILE

tear said to smile
"You look great today"
And smile replied, "I
always look this way."

tear then responded, "How long
you seem to have been away."—
smile glowed all along,
"Yes, I love this song—
and what do you have to say?"

"O smile," tear sighed, "how
I love you so—but seems
like miles and years, do now
but lie, you and I, between."

"And how I love to see
you then—upon her face with
glee—
'tis the reason,
('cause they are pleasin')
that I give you these today."

Jamie Lynn Fitzsimmons

Jamie Lynn Fitzsimmons
TO DADDY: LIGHT OF MY LOVE

A coal miner under a dirty and dark tunnel would need a light to guide them.

So, I will guide you with my light out of my heart.

Deborah Clausell
DANCING DOLL

A dancing doll only moves
When faced with a decision
to move, to live, to be apart
of the world's human fission.

The eyes represent courage
that exists in all forms
even through the worst of times
It can calm any storm.

Its mouth represents a smile
that shows us the way
so even when all else fails
it will save the day.

Its arms send off vibes
that we all should know
When the going gets too tough
a friend will carry the load.

This was the story of a dancing doll
Precious as a newborn's tears
after the materialistic things are gone
It lasts throughout the years.

Edith Ruby Milks
1776 PLUS

A lady named Betsy Ross,
Sewed stripes together, going across.
Embroidered stars, on a background
of blue,
Our own flag, so nice and new.
Under which, men fought and died,
While their women, sadly cried.
Even in, their hours of pain,
Taught their sons, "twas not in vain."
That this was done, for Liberty,
So all men, could be free.
And every son, that's passed this
way,
Has always had, this to say . . . .
"Freedom is, this Country's theme,
Every American's, total dream . . .
And we shall keep it, for evermore,
For that's what we've, been fighting
for."

Barbara A Blackstock
THE DAY WE FELL IN LOVE

This poem is dedicated to my sweetheart, who I will believe in and love forever.

Soon it will be a year to the day we fell in love.
It was such a beautiful morning the sun was shining so warm above.
As friends we walked through the park hand in hand on many trails of untouched land.
The birds were singing to us spring has come at last.
The trees were starting to blossom and bloom everywhere we passed.
As the day turned to early afternoon the rain did fall.
But to us it was the best day of all for we fell in love.

Dora Lyn Remy
TEARS BEHIND THE LAUGHTER

I dedicate this poem "Tears Behind the Laughter" to my husband Clyde Maurice Ezell Jr.

Tears behind the Laughter,
This explains me well.
I'd like to explain it further.
So please let me tell . . . . .
People see me joking and laughing,
When I'm with my friends
But when I'm home alone—
That is where the laughter
Ends . . .
Sometimes I get so lonely and Sad—
I cry my-self to sleep.
You see, my heart is lonely.
And the loneliness is getting
deep.
I have no one to Love. And no one to
Love me,
I guess it's just part of life, and it's
Meant to be
I do have hope–For getting what I'm
after
Then maybe there will be
Happiness Behind the
Laughter . . . . .

Ruth Ann Corbin
TWENTY ONE

To my sons, Hyall and Duane

The battle of childhood at last is
won.
For today my son became twenty
one.
Time has gone so swiftly by,
Wasn't it only yesterday I heard a
baby cry?
But now as I look through a veil of
tears
I can see the wonder of the years.
What will he achieve on this troubled
earth?
Will he fulfill the purpose of his
birth?
Filled to the brim with dreams of
youth,
Trying so hard to find the Truth.
Give him strength, oh God I pray,
And courage to always choose the
right way.
For today my son's world has just
begun.
Because today my son became
twenty one.

Paul Stephen Burkes
POWER IN THE LINE

Prayer changes things! God can do anything! ! ! ! !

There is a special hotline
Of communication and love
Created by Lord Jesus
Anointed by His blood!

So when your power fades,
And you can't find the time
To pray like you ought to
Just hook up to this line!

This power is pure spirit,
Yet this not everyone sees
Just say, LORD RESTORE ME
The way I used to be!

Heaven is the generator
Where the power is in control
The Holy Ghost sends the pulse
That electrifies your soul!

Talking costs no money
Nor requires high education
It takes a little submissiveness
And a lot of dedication!

This company won't cut you off
Or send you any bill
God asks you to talk to HIM
And do His perfect will!

Jody Marcus
CHRYSALIS

Time wrapped around me
A woven fabric whose threads were
spun
From chance and hope,
Knowledge and experience and
providence,
Sagacity beyond years,
And much finer stuff.

Such fibers serve well
To ornament the form of youth
During metamorphosis,
Yet do not protect
The most vulnerable parts.
They cannot wholly defend
What is so delicate; that is,
They cannot conceal the fragile heart
Not yet ready for exposure.

Why thus do I seem?
It is . . . to dream
While in this state of transition
Of my emergence and departure,
To undertake the first flight—
Strands and all.

Kenneth D Most Jr
COMPLETELY UNLIMITED

I was reading Rolling Stone, and I
saw your enticement
You want to discover new poets it
says
In twenty one lines or less you want
me to fill you with enlightenment
I could even win money it says
And even if I've only written one it
says, in the advertisement
Send it in it says
So here's one for you, another line in
my personal fulfillment

I thought about the ones already
done, but they seemed too revealing
I don't know how much to show you
If you do get to see them you'll find
they're not very concealing
I don't know whether I should show
them to you
And they probably don't mean
anything, just the way I was feeling
Obviously about someone besides
you
So I figured I'd write one for you
since it's you with whom I'm dealing

And a form had to be created, I'm
not used to my lines being limited
They usually do that on their own
So for your money and with your
rules I'll do this, although prohibited
I can still call it my own
And like always I do it in one
sitting—makes me feel uninhibited
But I'll sell it if you want to own
A piece of my brain, just realize it's
completely unlimited

Michael D Romolini Sr "Giggy Rome"

Michael D Romolini Sr
"Giggy Rome"
GROUND ZERO

This poem dedicated with love, to my sweet wife & children, Lorraine, Michael Jr. and Faith

Morning pushes its pedals of
wonder,
into your bedroom window.
The day-time sun warms your body,
like a fiery glow of a camp fire.
Waking up to a new day we realize
what we left behind, in troubled
times
of misguided blunder. . .

Tunneling deep into a mind of
impetuous day to day decision,
Leaving you in a state of perplex.
Your train of thought brings you
down to "Ground Zero",
And your dreams burst into a cosmic
realm,
that not even your-self
could identify . . . .

When reaching out to family and
friends,
And old-time lovers, with sincerity,
You some-times feel like an absolute
inconvenience . . .

Bonnie Marie Rutherford
BALLARD 1909

To Helen Burns Schillreff, 1900-1986.

A woman sits in her study,
formerly a bedroom, still
painted pink.
The hardwood floor is scratched;
wood frames, doors, and
windows have never been
painted over.
She sits, absorbed in a
photograph: a woman, her long
dark skirt pulled up tied with
apron strings, dark stockings,
dark shoes, white blouse
buttoned up, standing on the

plank porch of a log house on
pilings;
Puget Sound at high tide reaches
a foot below her feet.
She watches two children in a
boat.
The boy holding the oars has eyes
that burn from under his hat,
the girl has long braids wound
around her head, she's waving.
The woman in the study imagines
freckles on the girl's face.
She knew her in another time as her
mother's mother, not a girl in a
boat.
It was her pink bedroom, her
house, built by her husband in
1936 when Greenwood was a
green wood and the Interurban
stopped one block away.
They had geese then, chickens,
bees and a garden, made
rootbeer, played Canasta,
listened to a radio.
The husband planted shrubs,
bulbs, ferns from the woods,
grafted four kinds of apples onto
one tree.
The woman in the pink study
stares out the window, the
shrubs, ferns and apple tree
remain.

Esta Krukin
EVERYMAN

To a world without nuclear weapons, where all the Earth's creatures are safe from extinction at Everyman's hand; to a time when each of us takes responsibility for our world and strives for peace, and equality for all.

There once was a child named
Everychild.
And he lived amidst a world of toys
and schoolbooks
And parent-imposed rules and
curfews.
And Everychild learned his lessons,
and grew bigger.
But he didn't know.

There once was a man named
Everyman.
And he lived amidst a world of
obligations and news reports
And weapons and great technology
And society-imposed rules and
expectations.
And Everyman fought his way up the
corporate ladder
And voted some Novembers
And learned to find success, and
grew older and richer.
But, still, he didn't know.

Then, one day, Everyman saw the
mushroom cloud
And smelled the burning flesh
And died.
Radioactively
Ever
After.
Then the soul of Everyman wept.
For, finally,
He knew.

Karen Maloney Sorenson
MOUNTAIN OF COURAGE

To my Dad, who taught me life is an experience

We each have a mountain to climb,
that is steep and firm,
We must all climb it by ourselves in
order to learn.

At the base of that mountain where
the wild flowers grow,
We run and play as children do, we
are starting to sow.

Slowly we begin our journey, up the
rugged mountain trail.
One foot in front of the other and
with God's good grace we will
prevail.

The path becomes jagged with rocks,
now you must struggle over them
one by one. The lessons you learn
are tucked away in your heart,
For when the battle must be won.

You're nearer the top now with your
breath heavy laden, Suddenly you
begin to slide downward and believe
your dreams are fading.

In anguish you cry out to God,
Please, please, don't pass by me,
I'll try to be the best person I can
possibly be.

Slowly you begin to rise, with life's
strength in you anew, knowing in
your heart and mind that you will
always see the job through.

Tears blur your eyes, as you gaze at
the mountain sunlight on top,
Confessing to yourself the seeds that
were sown had reaped a fine crop.

Struggling to stand with courage,
atop the mountain tall, you realize
that life's successes never come
unless you learn to fall.

You look across and down the other
mountain side, and tell yourself,
"It was my inner soul, that was my
spiritual guide."

Patti Basham
THE LOVE WE SHARE

The love we share is so
right and so real.
So love me as I love you.
With all my heart
and all my soul.
So tell me you love me
as I would tell you.
Kiss my lips.
Hold me tight.
Say you love me
all through the night.

Donald Padraic Casey
PEACE IS . . .

The pink hue of a rose,
A sunset on the peaceful sea,
The stillness of the dark,
All things in loving harmony

A flock of silent geese,
Gliding across the blue,
The sky, warm and lustrous,
Bathed in a colorful hue.

Sherrie Jacobs
A SANCTITY

It was a day I shall never forget,
Grandma in her chair and I at her
side.
She spoke of her dreams; the agonies
far set,
like a new bride; her chills exploding
inside.

I was cuddled; inwardness at her
feet,
when I felt her tears run down my
face,
was this the doom that I must meet,
or was it just the trials that I must
trace?

She whispered, "Child please don't
cry,"
and I looked up, as I had never seen
her before,
it was the essence of her life; the light
in her eyes,
so wise, this woman that I adored.

The years have groveled by, into the
words she spoke,
how silly of me to think then of only
tragedy;
I shall remember her words in quote,
and of growing old; a sanctity.

"As cold as winters may seem,
receive gladly into one's own
bearings,
a tribute to growing old will deem,
and to God; to life give, precious
memories."

Judith G Morgan
MY SISTER CHRIS

The skies are dark with shades of
pink
The day is done as the sun light
sinks.
I sit and look across the bay
As thoughts come through of
yesterday.

Times were harder when I was
young
Things I did both wise and dumb.
Memories of my sister Chris
Come to mind of times we've missed

Through the years both to come and
past
I know I have found her again at last.
For the love and truth we once
shared
Again is back that wasn't always
there.

The path I took was long and dark
But God's love and help has given it
spark
Who was there when I needed her
My sister Chris with her loving care.

Thank you Chris for all your love
We can share our distance thru God
above.
For now I know we'll never be apart
We can finally make a brand new
start.

Beverly Lawyer
FIRST YEAR OF LOVE

This poem is dedicated to Bill, my wonderful husband.

Having you for my partner
And watching our marriage grow
Puts so much love and joy in my life
Perhaps more than you'll ever know.
You came into my life a stranger
And now you're my best friend
No one could ever take your place
Nothing will cause that to end.
In reviewing the year that just ended
Very anxious for the new one to start
Every word, every touch, every
smile
Remains etched deep in my heart.
So, as we begin our second year
And hopefully there'll be many more
Remember how much I love you
You'll always be the one I adore.

Tammy L Winchester
DECEMBER DREAM

To my family, Sandra, Shayne, and Dia, my best audience.

My stomach is turning.
My heart is yearning.
For someone to hold dear.
I miss your touch.
I need you so much.
It's hard to hold back the tears.
Years keep passing us by.
My love for you never dies.
I often stop and wonder why,
My heart still aches and I still cry.
I think about you every day.
This pain inside won't go away.
I dream about you day and night.
In my mind I feel you hold me tight.
My heart keeps telling me, it will be
allright.
When I open my eyes, it's just an
illusion.
Nothing is as it seems.
You're by my side, in my arms,
But only in my dreams.

Katie Heidrick
ONCE UPON A TIME

Once upon a time we danced
together in the empty ball room.
We walked together by the pond
and together in the woods.
We sang, and talked, and read to
each other in the garden, but
that was long ago.

Now there's no once upon a
time, no walks, no talks, and
no dances.
The ball room where we danced
alone in is now crowded and we can't
find each other.
So now we are alone.
Our lives separated but our
hearts as one.

Steve Lacoste
OL' NEIGHBOR ZEBADIA

Glimpsing rivers' rainbow elegance!
Twilight's peekish lavender of
excellence!
Sprinkling sprays of mist casting
mild chilly spells,
Half a dash and a twist to warmth of
cabin I dwell.

Tastefully alluring heart's desire
with illuminous fire!
Comforting down easy street in
ancient attire!
Thump! Thump! Striking solid oak
door,
Sprightly, ol' neighbor Zebadia's
welcome!
Clump! Clump! creaking the floor,
vibrating musical, wooden pelican.

Ol' Jasper Zebadia, ace of a friend of
mine!
Solitarily lives in spruce-scented
backwoods.
Rugged old geezer, walks a mighty
fine line,
Last at thought, first at heart,—
nobody understood!

Jovial chit-chat unfolds through the
night!
Charming, chiming clock unloads
rhythm at midnight!
Shimmering, tinted windowpane, a
three-quarter crescent moon,
Dissipated clouds, view's plain,
leisure stroll to lagoon!

Canoe's adrift a whispering stretch,
edging to "Devils Island,"
'Paradise Kingdom' eager to quest,
wildlife never ceases for silence!
Old-timer Zebadia thrives on serene
territory of grand!
Tall tales surfaced the homespun
agility of Neighbor Zebadia
subduing "No Man's Land"! ! !

Pamela Clark Kelly
A VALENTINE THOUGHT

Show me today that you will love
me tomorrow,
Give me true happiness don't fill me
with sorrow.
Fill my life with sunshine please
don't fill it with clouds,
Take me to a private place don't
put me in a crowd.
Hold on to me tightly and promise
to never let go,
Take me to a newer height as our
passions grow,
I say this to you sweetheart as it all
comes to mind,
For I love you very much and ask
that you become my Valentine.

Heather Ripley
FRIENDS FOREVER

Friendship is forever lasting,
Having fun, playing, laughing.
Watching movies, going shopping,
Always running, never walking.
Someone to talk to when you're sad,
Or someone to cheer with when
you're glad.
Always having someone there,
Helps to know and be aware.
When you're lost and need a hand,
They'll walk you through the
deserted sand,
Problems and fights come with it all,
But that's what keeps you on the ball.
Friends are special in every way.
Every when they're old and gray.

Grace T Richardson
SOMEONE

Everyone needs someone. But
where is that someone for me?

I have searched in vain. There is no
one I can claim.
I want to be loved with inspiration, I
want to be loved starting tonight.

When the sun sets, my heart sinks.
Then my loneliness begins to creep,
pumping and rushing red hot blood
throughout my veins.

My heart sinks, my soul dies, my
body cries. All the men I see, Yet
there's no one for me. He could be a
Prince, a Beggar, or a Bum.
If he were mine, I'd make him my
King. Come to me, my love.
Wherever you may be. I long for you
with awaiting arms, lonely body, and
aching soul.

Just to have you hold me tight. To
hear you whisper sweet nothings all
through the night. You'll fulfill my
every need. Because everyone needs
someone.

Chrissie Varnado
MY STAR

I was lost and alone
Without a light
Scared of what I might find
In this darkness like the night

But then I saw a star
And it was coming towards me
To guide me where I belong
And let me see
It showed me to light
And gave me happiness
Let me see what I was missing
And gave me love and tenderness

It dried my tears
That I once cried
Let me find truth
And escape from past-told lies

It helped me solve mysteries
To which I didn't have a clue
It's here to shine forevermore
Because my star is you

Dolly E Littlejohn
GEMS OF LIFE

As I look out my window
So many things I see,
Each a thing of beauty
God made for you and me.

The hillsides, mountains, brooks, and
trees
All the creatures, big and small
Many precious gems of life,
He made each, for one and all.

Everything we need for life
To us was given free.
Protect this gift, we must,
Take charge of destiny.

Keep our air and streams pure
The way they were meant to be.
Protect these gems of life,
God gave to you and me.

Tanny T Thompson
THANK YOU! ! !

To Mona Ronea Thompson, my mother and most important lady of my life, with all my love forever.

As I was young, with just a little hair
pound by pound, I knew you
cared.

Thanks to you, when I was growing
up
you held me in your arms, like
water in a cup.

As I got bigger, I got a little tough
cool and crazy, and even a little
rough.

I know I've done bad things, that
made you worry
but I'm going to try to stop, in a
hurry.

As you put me on a punishment, it
made me blue
but no matter what I say, I'll
always LOVE YOU.

Spending all that cash on a gift, I run
out of heat
so I'm writing you this poem, to
make it complete.

As I am your son, and you are my
mother
I love you so much, I wouldn't
want another.

So as I care for you, in a very special
way
I would like to say, HAPPY
BIRTHDAY! ! !

Virginia Stuecher
HOPSCOTCH

Dedicated to, Lori Griffith. She's been and remains to be my greatest inspirer and motivator.

O birthday girl,
Soon you'll know what it feels to be
24.
You feel same and preserved,
Yet around you life continues to
swirl.
Still protesting change;
Battles of old hauntingly undefeated;
Confused and saturated with true
love;
Ignoring, pondering the inevitability
to rearrange.

Holding on so tight.
Striving for self-assurance meanwhile saying goodbye.
Moving, dividing, fighting with
obstinance.
Already delving into memories so
bright.

The loss feels so heavy.
The gain shaded, unclear, undefined.
The horror and fear intense.
The soul balancing on a spirited
steady.

A feeling of hibernation;
A timeless trial to find individuality;
A test for self-supportiveness;
A coercion to mingle with the rest of
creation.

Yemisi Koya

Yemisi Koya
IT IS LIFE; ALRIGHT.

This poem is dedicated to Toriola and Folake Solanke, my dear parents.

So; life appears to be what it is,
The sun shines by day, the
moon by night,
the twinkle in the sky
suggests a star.
But alas;
the light at the end of the
tunnel
may not be a glimmer of hope.
And certainly;
all that glitters is not gold
for silver may, and so may
stone.
The sky becomes dark,
due not to the end of the day
but rather from the eclipse of
the sun.
The tears flow, not of sorrow,
but of overwhelming joy.
Yet; even amidst all these,
is comfort in the fact
that life will be,
and usually is.

Mamie L Pace
REFLECTION

May God Bless The Older Generation

As I stare into the mirror, what do I
see? Is it me, I see? Or is it just a
reflection of someone's inner soul.
Bare and naked before one's very
own eyes. Look, at that face! marks
of pain and suffering, youth has
faded, no longer fresh and pure. The
eyes so dark and cloudy with fear.
Who is she, is she a part of me? It's
hard to say, to the mirror so clean and
clear, if she is really me, I see. A
reflection staring, old, hurt, lost and
alone . . . . is it the price one pays for
loving, the rejections and pain, that
makes old seem older? Loved ones
scattered here and there, all that's left
you is the mirror, reflecting years
gone by forever, never to return. Oh!
look again, please just once more.
What do you see? An old lady
slightly smiling back at me, with
tears of hurt and pain. A face of
gentle love that years have yet to
erase. Is it me I see, is she a part of
me? Or just a reflection.

Doris Mautino Hawkins
MISS SEEING YOU

Dedicated to Mother, Marietta De Lú Mautino

Often into "Memory Lane" I wonder
There to ponder,
Remembering all the things we did
do;
Trips we made
The parties we gave,
Miss Seeing You

Then away from "Memory Lane" I
wonder
Only again and again to return to
ponder,
"Oh," how "I MISS SEEING YOU"

Robin L Conant
THE JOURNEY TO GOD

To Jim Cook I've opened my eyes, and my Heart, with your help! Thank you, friend . . .

I have this feeling, it's bottled up
inside,
I wanna free myself of the misery I
hide.
Help me to freedom, freedom from
my sins,
I know the one I'm seeking, I can't
find on a whim.

Open up my heart, open up my mind,
for the Peace & Love I want, I know
someday I'll find.
Have faith in the Lord, Jesus Christ,
He is the One!
This I know is true, for He is sent
from God, He is His Son!

God gave us this earth & the life we
have within,
All the things that we do, should be
done without sin.
The beauty in our hearts, should be
remembered each day.
Because one glorious moment, each
of us will go His way!

I've found Peace in Loving our God
above,
It's like watching the smooth flight of
a white Dove.
The Dove took a journey, not
knowing what he'd find.
That is like us, each day, a new
journey, for peace of mind.

Melody J Clark
BARREN LAND

The wind still blows
through my once long
Hair,

My lips still smile
surrounded by
Tear stained cheeks

My womb no longer
cramps and my stomach

is no longer ill

There is no seed growing
in my barren land

He holds my hand tighter
and loves me warmer
since the nights have
Become so cold

It takes one seed
to start a harvest

I wish I could
Harvest this barren
Land.

Ronald I Rodney
MOTHER EARTH SPOKE
I laid my head upon mother earth,
partly asleep
And partly awoke, and for a moment
I thought I heard her spoke:

Acid rain, birds fleeing the plane
Never to return to the city again
Radioactive trees, earth covered with
concrete
Trees placed in unnatural places
Man hating man on perception, doors
locked tightly sealed
The threat of nuclear destruction
Man on his ego trip, blast off on their
space ship
To the moon their vision fixed
Leaving the homeless sick
Scientific illusion, miscalculation,
world hunger
And dissolution (starvation), nuclear
fusion
Aids and cancer, no answer, so many
beggars in these pastures
Terrorism, drugs and racism, no
conclusion total confusion
Tied to apartheid, no sense of pride
Amorality cannot hide
Abortion, selfish decision, late
conclusion
Sexual consequential

Ann Morgan Conn
SONG FOR THE SENDING OF ROSES

To James Morgan Conn, firstborn, on each anniversary of his birth

As each petal unfurls
on all of these roses
so shall your soul
unfold for the world;
while roses are fading
your spirits renew
for love to remain
forever in view.

Maria Serrano
A PAIR OF EYES
Two pairs of eyes, lingering,
searching.
Two pairs of lips, touching, kissing.
Two pairs of hands, feeling, meeting.
Two hearts joining as one.

Nothing that is asked is too great.
Nothing that is done can be wrong.
How much longer can this feeling go
on?

Two minds have come together in
what they want of life.
Two lives have joined together as
husband and as wife.

This feeling, this love, so wonderful,
so divine.
This feeling, this love, so binding, so
right.

Two pairs of eyes, piercing, hating.
Two pairs of lips, screeching,
sneering.
Two pairs of hands, swinging,
hitting.
Two hearts tearing each other apart.

Nothing that is asked is granted now.
Nothing that is done can be right.
How much longer can this feeling go
on?

Two minds have separated from what
used to be one.
Two lives have gone their separate
ways, no longer husband and wife.

This feeling, this pain, so hurtful, so
unkind.
This feeling, this pain, so blinding,
so sad.

Not willing to hear, unable to see.
What life has in store for you, the
next time you meet.

A pair of eyes.

Janis C Guerrero
AS I LOOKED, I SAW YOU
As I sit and watch the new dawn,
I see dreams of you and I floating
along.
As I hear the waves crashing onto
shore,
I see images of you just as loving as
before.
As I walk and see my footprints in
the sand,
I see tomorrow held in our hands.
As I look and see a gulf flying free,
I see your love and all its beauty.
As I look deep into the view,
I see my life sitting next to you.

As I search deep into the sea of blue,
I see our lives becoming two.
As I thought of a future without you
tomorrow,
I saw my life engulfed in sorrow.
But as I reached into the love we
share,
I realized you'll always be there.
So take my heart, a perfect gift of
gold,
As I promise you my life and love to
forever hold.

Robert D Wolfe
WILL WE EVER FORGET?

This poem is dedicated to all Vietnam Veterans and Families of Veterans who gave their life in Vietnam.

In the sixties and seventies
Our young Americans were sent off
to war
In a lot of our minds was the question
What are we fighting for?

To prevent the spread of communism
Was what we were told
Our duty to country came first and
For that we would always be bold.
We lost a lot of friends there
Which we will never be able to
replace
Some people back home would never
Understand what each returning
veteran must face.

The sleepless nights, cold sweat
And nightmares would linger on for
years
We battle it each day and
Sometimes it ends in tears.

Will we ever forget? I doubt it if we
will.
We are just survivors no less and no
more
The Vietnam War will remain with
us still.

Pamela J Watkins
THE ICY FLAME

For J L. Someone who needs, feels and sees—loves you.

In my mind's eye,
I see the flame of life
With myself beside it,
Trying desperately to warm my soul
with its fire.

In its glow I'm still cold.
And next to its vibrance,
I'm very old.

As the fire flickers and dances in
celebration,
My tears slowly flow towards it.

David M Carrier
RIDING THE TIDE

This poem is dedicated to my mother and father and to my brother, Michael.

Riding the tide
Of a swiftly flowing brook
With jagged rocks protruding from
the water;
Spectacular little waterfalls and
eddies
Reflect the brilliant rays of the
eternal lamp.

Riding the tide
Gazing up at the beautiful blue sky
Empty except for a solitary bird
Flying low on the horizon
Heading home
With a fish in its mouth
From this very brook.

Riding the tide
And falling into the icy cold,
churning waters
Struggling to avoid the jagged rocks
That cut like a guillotine;
Carried by the current
Pulled underwater
Gasping for breath;
And getting back on
Once again
To ride the tide.

George Jurich
SUNRISE

Dedicated to Mom and Dad and the girls with love.

The morning sun rises from the
awakening eastern skies,
and scatters its warming rays
throughout the land as evening
dies.
The dew glistens from the bountiful
wild flowers and satiny petals,
as bees hurry past the
neighboring thorn and nettles.
Song birds soon spread their melodic
tunes so fair,
and as the earth warms; life
springs up everywhere.
A gentle breeze lifts the cool mist
from the forest floor,
and a hawk follows a current as
upward it does soar.
An icy spring nourishes the
inhabitants of nature's domain,
a day in time whose memory
shall forever remain . . . . .

Kathleen Grdinich
OF DAYS GONE BY

In loving memory of my Mom Margaret Borocz

I'm wondering what you're doing,
wondering where you are
Perhaps you're jumping moonbeams
or dancing on the stars . . .
You speak to me so often, with
whispers in my ear . . . .
Within my sleep I dream of you, I
wish that you were here

Many things have happened, the
days pass by so slow
Can you feel me with you as you
come and go?
Is this life our fantasy to ponder and
to play?
The memories of days gone by,
beneath the warm sun rays . . . .

So many others touch me in ways I
can't discern
I feel that I am frozen, I have
no where to turn
I know you stand beside me, for I can
sense you there
I draw my strength from energy and
yours I can't compare

There is so much emotion, my words
come from my heart
I seem to know you sense this, in the
time that we're apart
You sing within my memory, your
words . . . they're like a song
Our souls unite within white light, the
place that they belong

Again my mind has spoken, still
searching from afar
This light forever shining, still rests
upon the stars
I'll walk with you together, in spirit
we're but one
And we'll join hands forever and
journey towards the sun . . . . .

Clara Martha Dowling
WELCOME, HER ROYAL HIGHNESS, BABY PRINCESS BEATRICE OF YORK

This poem is dedicated to Her Majesty Queen Elizabeth II in honour of her granddaughter, Her Royal Highness, Baby Princess Beatrice, Elizabeth, Mary of York, daughter of Their Royal Highnesses, Andrew and Sarah, the Duke and Duchess of York.

Welcome, Her Royal Highness,
Baby Princess Beatrice, Elizabeth
Mary, to the home of the Duke and
Duchess of York.

At last their little babe has come,
A new-born babe our hearts has
won,
All praise to Him who lights each
star,
Who tends the "lambs" from
near and far.
All praise to Him who life has
given,
And sent His gift to earth from
heaven;—
Who changed our darkness into
light

The things we feared He set aright.
When sleeping in her cradle bed,
God watches o'er her infant head;
And Sarah sings sweet hushabys,
While Andrew rocks her lest she cries.
And now it's baby's turn to speak,
In her own language—oh, how sweet:—
"While leaning on my Mommy's breast,
She hushed me in her arms to rest.
When sleep forsakes my open eyes,
When pain and sickness make me cry,
They see me when I turn my head,
Then tears of sweet affection shed.
They hush me in their arms to rest,
And on my cheeks, sweet kisses press,—
They dress me in my clothes so gay,
Some day they'll teach me how to pray.
And then when I am fully grown,
I'll never have to feel alone;
For they'll watch o'er me day and night,
They'll guard me while I'm sleeping tight.
And now their home's been made complete,—
A Mommy, a Daddy, and two tiny pink feet—
And my prayer is for guidance when their day is long,
May the Lord be their strength and also their song."

"And now it's time to take my nap,
I see them peeking through the crack,
And tho' the door is not ajar,
I heard some footsteps from afar."

Theresa Marie Wallace

BEST FRIENDS FOREVER

We've been friends now,
for quite awhile.
Through ups and downs,
tears and smiles.
All those letters ending,
"BEST FRIENDS FOREVER."
All those ideas,
some crazy, some clever.
We shared the bad times,
and all the happiness.
We knew our friendship,
would be nothing less.
The times we spent together,
I'll always keep in my heart.
We knew these memories,
would last from the start.
Talking for hours on the phone,
you always had good advice to loan.
So I'll dedicate this poem to you,
because you're a friend who
has always stayed true.

Ruth O'Bannon

GOD KNOWS

God knew about me even before I knew myself.
He had known about my life,
even before I opened my eyes.
Tho' He didn't plan my life,
He gave me free will and choice,
He drew me with his love,
and His everlasting mercies,
God thought about me even before I knew myself.

He knows about you.
He has numbered each hair on your head
He knows all about you
He knows all the things you dread
He knows all about you,
He knows all about your defeats
He knows all about you
Lay all troubles at his feet
He'll make all things complete

Audrian McPherson

Audrian McPherson

THE HEALING TOUCH

Along life's highway we go,
We see lots of sickness, grief, and woe.
Trees wither and die;
Flowers lose their lovely hue,
Fresh air and clean water are gone, too.

Across this land;
Are sicknesses on every hand,
Diseases of every kind,
The human and animal kingdom dies;
Of pain in both body and mind.

Broken hearts and many problems;
Bother each of us very much.
Look all around this world and see—
What a wonderful world it would be,
If I but had the healing touch.

Virginia Lois White

YESTERDAY

Yesterday has come and gone,
Only memories, we live on.
But as time passes us by,
We don't have time to stop and cry.

We live each day to the most,
We live and laugh and hush the ghost,
Of yesterday when we were young,
And think of songs we have sung.

As we wonder why it went,
We rejoice in how we spent,
The days of youth and joy and song,
And live each day as it comes along.

I thank the Lord, I've had the time,
To make these friends along the line,
And give each one a loving smile,
As they walk their weary mile.

And when I've gone please don't forget,
That you'll come too, but no not yet,
So as you go along the way,
Live each as though it is your last day.

Patti Connell

REVERSE GENESIS

Can we make it happen,
A major turn of events.
What to do with our waste . . .
We must use common sense.
We cannot continue dumping,
Polluting our home, Earth.
The toxic ground may not affect us,
But what about future births?
To sort and recycle
Is such trouble, too much cost!
It's much easier and cheaper
To bury and to toss.
So what if some fish die!
Just some Dolphins and Whales . .
We must find somewhere to stick it,
Tons of sewage and garbage bales.
Yes, it is much more costly,
Just can't afford such expense.
We'd rather let the Earth die
Than to change present events.

Shannon Patrick Carver

A TRAVELER'S HOME

People Come
—(Wandering)
People go
Who they are
—(Drifting)
You never know
We try to see
—(Traveling)
Our feelings show
Two become as one
—(Home)
Together the love shall grow

C C Gahring

I LISTENED TO THE NIGHT, THE QUIETNESS

I listened to the night, the quietness, the sounds, the moon as it lit the world while most of us slept.
The sound of a dog barking down the road. How lonely his call sounded.
Most of us live in the dark one time or another in our lives.
I wonder what drives us to come out of the dark and into the light.
Could it be we can see ourselves and others better in the light than in the dark.

Tori Micek

AND ANOTHER . . .

This poem is dedicated to Collene, my best friend, in memory of Matthew A. Blok (6/24/73-11/9/88)

I see a tear silently, slowly flowing down your cheek. I know why it's there, but I don't know how to help. I ask if there's anything I can do, but you just shake your head no. I go sit down, and I hear you sobbing silently. I wish there was something I could do to help you with the pain. But nothing I do, seems to help. I really wish that there was something I could say or do to help you get through your time of suffering. I ask you if you're ok, you simply say no. You then ask me if I'm ok, I say no, too. So we just sit there listening to that same song. Suddenly, there is one single tear flowing down my cheek. You see it and wipe it away. I smile and then there is another tear, and another, and another . . . I miss him, too.

Debra Lee Daily

MY MOTHER'S ARMS

This poem is dedicated to Virginia, my wonderful mother, for teaching me how to be a loving, caring, and independent woman.

As a baby my Mom
cradled me in her arm,
Giving me comfort and
protecting me from harm.
As a youngster she would
hold me tight,
Being there when I had
a bad dream at night.
As a teenager she would
give me a hug,
Always making me feel warm,
happy and snug.
As a woman I can expect
any or all three,
Because she's my Mom
and will always
be there for me.

Angela Moore

LIFE

Lived as you live it.
Interpreted as you see it.
Fulfilled as you fill it.
Enjoyed if you choose to enjoy it.

F E Strickler

YOUNG LOVE

To Mary: my wife who is resting in heaven now.

When the lonely night shadows around me twirl
And the whippoorwill is calling in the evening dust
Then take me back to the one that was my first girl.
Oh, I can't forget those times that used to was.

Don't you remember those long summer nights by the river
When we sat there and drank a pop or maybe a beer or two
Every time I looked at you I'd get cold and begin to shiver
When all I really wanted my dear, was you.

We were so young then and didn't know much about love
But you were so warm and close to me dear
When the sky turned blue and the stars came out above
We were so much in love we had nothing to fear.

I remember how hot you were dear, and the darking of your skin
And that I didn't know just how or what to do
But I knew what kind of shape you had me in.
And I knew dear that I had to have you.

I can remember that it was over almost before we started
And I have to laugh now when I think of the past
When we vowed that we would never be parted
And I wonder where the time has gone so fast.

Richard A Halvorson

THE LOVE IN YOUR EYES

You look at me with love in your eyes,
I look at you and I start to cry.
I tell myself I must get away,
But I look at you and I know I will stay,
Till the end.
We had a romance a long time ago,
But something happened, just what I don't know.
You just told me you were going to leave,
The love in your eyes I never would see,
Again.
Years drifted by, time rolled on.
You seemed so happy, I got along.

Now you come back, tell me I'm the one,
Saying you're sorry for all that you've done,
To me.
You say we can pick up all that we had,
Remember the good times, forget the bad.
But it's not that easy, things aren't the same,
For deep in my heart lies the hurt and the pain,
Of love.

T

TWO THOUSAND OR BEFORE

Woke From A Dream
I Fear To Tell You What I Saw
Men In Every Country
Were Waging Bloody War
Use A Little Insight
Common Sense Will Tell You More
About The Year Two Thousand
Or Before

Miles Of Destruction
Leaders Settle To Ignore
Evading Rampant Panic
As They Lie About The Score
Damned To Accept
The Fate In Store
About The Year Two Thousand Or Before

I Hope Another Life Survives The Final Day
With Memories Of A Planet In Its Prime
Human Isolation Waits A Lonely Way,
But It's Only Time

When Life Is Worth Far Less Than What It's Living For
And Not A Soul Is Left Behind To Lend A Hand
I Hope Somebody Finds Me, Death On Molten Core,
And Understands
About The Year Two Thousand
About The Year Two Thousand
Or Before

Jenna Graveney

WAR

The peaceful fields bloom with fragrant colours.
Tall grasses, soft sail bring to earth the home of newborns.
Gentle breezes whistle gleefully playing peek-a-boo throughout the reeds, soft and mellow.
Towering willow trees, their sweeping branches dancing in the wind.

In the distance, the rhythmic beat of the large snare drums are carried by the wind, to the awaiting group of gallant men.

Only a few have risen to fight for the pride of the town in which they dwell.

The drums' controlled anger is growing to unbearable volumes, bringing the field to frightened life.
The wind raises his crescendo to an icy blast of air,
The willow begins to dance furiously,
the wind dies as if in fright, as the bright army marches forward,
Their fury hidden in seemingly controlled patience.

The world is brought to life with the noise of earshattering screams.
The peaceful field is transformed into the bloody battle fields of raging, ranting armies, fightin all their wrath.
The fury and anger of either side is unleashed in a flurry of sharp words and the turmoil of piercing bullets.

After the explosive sounds,
The silence seems earpiercing.
The battle field is coated in red,
The quiet field is left alone
To heal itself
In its own way
Until the next war comes
To destroy,
The tranquility of total peace.

Trish E (Nangle) Luberda

WAVES OF TIME

Standing on a deserted beach,
The grey horizon within my reach;
The churning waters' deafening roar
Crashing against the rocky shore.
The scattered memories along the sand,
The waves of time within my hand.
I walked along in silent awe,
Of all the beauty that I saw.
With nothing but my thoughts and me,
Life seemed to stretch eternally.
The scattered memories along the sand,
The waves of time within my hand.

Belinda R J Greschner

MEMORIES

The paths I've crossed,
the burdens I've carried,
the love I treasured,
the memories I buried.

The sharing of secrets,
the smiles and the tears,
nothing's been wasted,
not one of those years.

The wonderful moments,
caressing and holding,
the pleasures of growing,
the shaping and molding.

The laughter and sadness,
of which you're a part,
the special feeling—
of You in my heart . . .

Nadine Fiset

FOR THE KIDS

Janis says Ha Ha (Sooo Loud)
Rheana says Mom Baboon . . .
Mom beautiful

They are my sunshine

Bump after bump
Big legs . . . you're heavy
A good back pack baby . . . my kid

Mommy make it day
Mommy make it summer

Ok honey . . . Soon

Oh no! Janis
Not the Chap Stick Display
there must be ninety of them

Janis sit down
Babies can't stand in the shopping cart
People are looking at us
little do they know
You're Gorilla Baby

Mommy I wanna go to Chucky Cheese
Mommy I wanna go to Chucky Cheese
Mommy I wanna go to Chucky Cheese

No, but you can have an apple

Thank you, very much, Mommy

Jennifer Perkins

ETERNITY

Come walk with me
above the sky
we'll lift our spirits
and soar so high
Just take my hand
and lead the way
to eternity
and happy days
where nothing ends
not even love
we will find peace
like the snow-white dove
Hand in hand
just you and I
we'll fly so freely above the sky
just look my way and you will see
love and peace . . .
Eternity

Isabelle Collins

ODE TO SPRING

Oh winds that blow so loud and strong—
Oh birds that sing so sweet a song
Oh sun that shines so warm and bright
Oh spring that steps with foot so light.

Entice me with your spirit voice
and make joy the ever choice.
So glad for such a day as this
So free and filled with joy and bliss.
And lavender blue is all around
And white-fringed clouds and angel sounds.

So thank you for this day so true
And shades and shades of misty blue.
The beauty of this simple spot
And things I've learned to love a lot.

Anne Marie Flaherty

EVERYONE NEEDS

To all my family and friends who give me the love I need,
You will always have my love as well as a place in my heart.
Love, Annie

Everyone needs to hear it
regardless if they know
because though they always say it
sometimes they forget they know

It's not the same
if you have to ask
because it feels like you've forced them
to do an awful task

We are different people
we each have our own game
but we all need to know we're loved
in this we're all the same
I love you
and you love me
regardless of the capacity
I need you to remind me and make me see

Katie Stuart

ALL MIXED-UP

I'd like to dedicate this poem to my mom, dad, Cheryl, my best friend Kris, and everyone I love.

I'm confused.
I don't know what to do.
I'm all mixed-up.

Things don't seem right.
Things don't work out.
Things are all mixed-up.

People are hurting people.
People are falling apart.
People are all mixed-up.

Families are breaking.
Families are splitting up.
Families are all mixed-up.

I'm confused.
I don't know what to do.
I'm all mixed-up.

Everything is all mixed-up.

Albertina Vaz Ascensao Fragoso

Albertina Vaz Ascensao Fragoso

TO MY SON!

In a bed of rose thorns, I would rather lay
In snowy days of winter!
To keep Thy love, I say
Gladly let you take me, to Westminster!

Thy love means to me
Something of Heaven on Earth!
Like air and water is to a tree,
Neither one will survive without the other!

Geneva Williams

THE COOK AND ME

The Cook and me like to walk together in the twilight
She is old, I am young, her steps are slow, and mine are fast.
She tries to catch me, and she says I love you like my own.
Our feet brush the wild pennyroyal that grows along the path.
We use it to drive the mosquitoes away, and to make mint tea.
At the spring we drink water from our gourd dipper.
The cook said gourds remind her of Africa, her old home far away.
We climb to the top of the hill, our lucky spot the orchard, where the four leaf clovers grow.
The cook tries to rest while I hunt the robin redbreast.
I spy him in an apple tree, and I don't

believe he likes me.
He scolds, and his mate flies around in circles hoping to frighten me away, but instead it's my lucky day I chase them away.
The cook is thinking all the while of the apple tarts she will make.
I startled her, when I brushed her nose with an apple blossom rose.
Her blue checked-apron is empty since it's spring.
As we stroll along the cook's steps are getting faster than mine, since she is afraid of the snakes that can crawl along the path.
When the meadow flowers change colors it's our signal to go home.
The cook and me arrive back safely, and she tucks me into my little bed, saying go to sleep my sleepy head.

Beatrice Garrett
TIME
Could it be that I am dreaming
In this saga we call life?
Could it be my tears and sorrows
Only lasted for a night
Could it be that lovers' quarrels
Broken hearts and broken dreams
Only lasted for a second
Not as long as it may seem
Could it be that wealth and pompous
Of great kings and heads of state
Bathed in all their regal glory
Just an instant they were great
In this universal journey
Life is but a flashing peep
Time and space unaltered seconds
Life and death a moment's sleep.

Lynn Thibodeaux
THIS HOLY PLACE
Your spirit seems to be willing to go,
But your heart wishes you to stay.
Which one will you listen to?
Your heart I hope, I pray.

As a white candle glows in this holy room,
I try to catch a glimpse of your face
But as the candle's flame burns out,
You depart from this holy place.

Either you feared your fate with me too much,
Or I gave to you too little.
All I want now is to feel your touch
'Cause my heart feels cracked & brittle

Just remember when life lets you down
And love slaps you in the face, or when
there are no friends for miles around,
To come back to this holy place.

Nicole Bielewicz
DEATH
I see him always as an answer
He fills my mind like malignant cancer.
He tempts me with vows of restitution
I see him now as the only solution.

Calling me always in his whispering voice
Always convincing me I've made the right choice.
I'm tired and confused and afraid to go with him
But always he reminds me that life is so grim.

His cold fingers tap upon my window pane
Assuring me that I'm insane.
I seek solace in the lonely wind's sigh
And it tells me I was born only to die.

Whenever I listen he's calling my name
Always he's playing this torturous game.
I hear him calling me now, under his breath
I know that he's coming, I know that it's Death.

I accept the cold hand he's extended to me
Now he can finally set my soul free.
He tells me now I have only to wait
To see the results of the choice of my fate.

Staci Graham
THE DREAM
I had a dream
Its purpose was true
I pondered on its meaning
as my curiosity grew

I had heard voices calling me
whispering through the wind
I had heard a broken heart
crying for time to mend

I had learned the secrets of a heartbeat
and felt the rising of the sun
I had sensed the joy of the earth
when the fearful night was done

I had flown with wings of rose petals
and walked with thoughtful feet
and that dream I'll remember forever
for my soul and spirit to keep.

Nicolas Pantos
EMOTIONAL FEELING

This poem is dedicated to Quadrophenia

Emotional feeling, the wheels this moment are turning
Cupid you're not stupid. I put this treat around your meat to make your heart, heart beat.
Diamonds and rubies to excite your boobies.
Sweet thing you make my heart sing, sing.
Touching you, holding you—you are the chosen.
One touch and now forever you have me frozen.
Cupid only in red, my heart is hanging by a thread. Freeze and sneeze, me you no more tease. Hot or cold our hearts to each other we sold.
Tell me so, tell me no that I'm not dreaming. My heart for you and only you this moment is screaming.

Granny Nichols
A HAND-FUL OF STARDUST

This poem is dedicated to My Grandchildren.

Long, long ago; or so it seems. Well, maybe it was just a dream. As I climbed into bed one Halloween Night, I wished I could take a ride with The Halloween Witch on Her Broom, for Her Annual Flight across the moon; some Halloween Night.

Before I had a chance to lay down My Sleepy Head, This Tiny Witch on Her Broom, came skidding to a stop in My Room, bidding me to hop on Her Broom, and hold on tight, for I was to have My Wish granted, This Halloween night.

Making haste and with nary a thought, onto Her Broom I hopped, winding my arms tight about her waist. Now, listen very closely, and do exactly as I say, or we may find ourselves stranded on The Milky Way, said This Tiny Witch. Which I did without fuss. By that time, Good Old Mother Earth had been left far, far behind us.

High, high; up into the sky, higher than any bird can fly; we flew That Night on The Witches' Broom; right across the moon. Leo, The Lion, roared with delight, because we visited His Constellation first; That Halloween Night.

We visited with the rest of The Signs in The Zodiac: from Capricorn and Aquarius, on through Scorpio and Sagittarius.

They were all hilarious with joy, to meet and fete a Tiny Witch and a seven year-old boy.

We might have been up there for several hours; when uh-oh, to our consternation, The Witches' Broom ran out of Roadiac-power*. We quickly said good-bye to Our Friends in the sky. I reached out and grabbed a hand-ful of Stardust, as we zoomed by them on our downward flight.

Down, down, we came so fast.
I was so frightened; it made me gasp!
It was so dark I couldn't see!
Yikes! What's to become of me?
Help; I cried! Where am I!

To my relief and surprise, I soon realized I was safe and sound in My Own Room and Bed! My arms wound tight around My Teddybear! The covers over my head!

As I pushed back the covers, a tiny voice said, "if and when we meet again, I'll make room on My Broom for you and a friend; for a flight across the moon some other Halloween Night.

I was too sleepy to open my eyes, but, managed to mumble a reply. "Alright, Witchie-poo; thanks, love you; bye-bye; as I drifted off to sleep.

I never saw Witchie-poo again. I still have That Hand-ful of Stardust. I keep it in a little Glass Container. This Container is about three-inches high. It has two small, somewhat rounded cylinders; joined together in the middle by a narrow, hollow neck, which permits the stardust to slowly empty down from the top cylinder into the bottom cylinder in three minutes time. Turn it upside down; it will repeat the process in the same time.

Mother liked to use it to time the three-minute, soft-boiled eggs She sometimes fixed for Our Breakfasts; long, long ago.

I, too, use it on occasion, to time a soft-boiled egg

*Roadiac-power. Equal parts of Sunbeams, Moonbeams and Children's Laughter.

Dennis White
SENSATION
Deep in the night
snowflakes of the past
lightly come to steal my slumber
and melt my gelid crust
with tepid fires of glitter
'neath blankets of white.

Reflections enclose visions
of bodies laced
shadows thrusting
breezes gasping
in naked . . raw . . blatant passion
that pierce the silent dark
with pleasure
beyond
infinity.

Bertha Duff
DAD
Seems so long since you went away, so many things to you we'd like to say.
Things have changed since you've been gone, sometimes we feel so all alone.
We remember how happy you made all of us,
seems you did with very little fuss.
We still see your face, and your pleasant smile.
The twinkle in your eyes, still glow all awhile.
We miss you, and love you so, we still wonder why you had to go.
MOM is lonely since you went away, your love she holds dear more every day.
Your memory you left all of us we share,
helps when things are hard to bear.
Thanking GOD, for a loving DAD like you,
still guides our foot-steps in all we do.

Lisa Canning
A BROKEN FRIENDSHIP

To my mom, Alice. Thanks for being there. You're the greatest.

All my friends lied to me.
They didn't care if my feelings drowned in the sea.
They betrayed me and gave me unfair pain.
They crippled my heart and made me lame.

So I'm not popular—this I know
For many a friend has told me so.
They don't like who I am
Or the ideals for which I stand.

Friendship is now a thing of the past,
An era through which loyalty didn't last.
No longer does a friend remain true.
Rare are the friends who are true blue.

So I'm not popular with these people,
I'll pray to God at His church and steeple.
He'll send me a friend who's true

and loyal,
One whose heart is not soiled.

There are friends somewhere out there,
Not like the friends who betrayed me here.
For a friend who is true I'll patiently wait.
I just hope they're not too late.

Marvin W Workman
TOGETHER WE LOVED

Dedicated to Brigette Skye Workman My (baby)

The day you were born joy filled my heart
When you and your mother came out on that cart
I told my father that the boy was a girl
It didn't matter, you were healthy and now in our world
For 9 months your mother carried you around
We were so happy when you made that first sound
Your mother and I, all we could do was smile
When we peeked under the blankets at our beautiful child
On the day day you were born my father was there
59 years earlier to the day he breathed his first air.
You are so special in so many ways
Minutes away from you seems like days
But now things are different, that no one can change
The love in our hearts still stays the same
I'm trying to say I love you both—you and your mother
So try and tell Mom let's all love each other

Marsie R Seigle
ALAN

To the memory of Alan Gravine so that he may be remembered in the hearts of all who loved him.

On that dark and dreary night.
When his car took flight.
The crash was head-to-head.
Why does he have to be dead?

Some would say God had him paged.
But why at 17 years of age?
He was so sweet and nice.
Why did he have to pay the price?

He wanted to be a doctor in his heart.
Now from us he doth depart.
He was such a dear.
He had nothing to fear.

Once we all sang the carol.
Why now such peril?
I believe he went to heaven.
For that is the only justice given.

Laura Johnston
I DREAMED
The days I dreamed
I wish were real
The way it seemed I wanted to feel.
So gentle so pleasant
So cunningly refined.
Was out of this world like a crazy design.
No pattern was double
Nor amazingly related
But in this dream my love was stated.
So colorful so different
it took a gleam
But I had to awake to see it was a dream.

Ann Hoard

Ann Hoard
LOOKING AHEAD

I dedicate this poem to my late husband, Gus Hoard, Jr., and my adorable children—Howard D. Hoard, Stanley M. Hoard, Anita E. Hoard

I focus my eyes on the distant yonder,
with reminiscence of success I often ponder
I evade ridicule or scorn by others,
with hopes that my ego will not be smothered
I keep my eyes focused on a star,
success and fulfillment can't be far

Though mountains of obstacles may cloud my view,
I'm optimistic that they'll be very few
It's hard to look from side-to-side,
when the eyes are focused ahead with pride
As I move on, I'll be aware of rough spots,
I must deal with the haves and the have-nots
I look forward to the day that will surely come,
When success that I'm seeking will finally be won

Eleanor Channell
A SPECIAL ANNIVERSARY
Well, Folks you really made it
50 Golden Years
Aren't you Both Happy
You've become Golden Dears?

You're two Special people
The Lord had in his Plan
To keep you both together
Help all things to withstand.

The Lord is your Shepherd
Who is always around
To help keep your marriage
Always on Solid Ground.

It's nice to see two people
In this Long Wedded Bliss
Now, P.J. you give Blossom
A—lo——ng Golden Kiss.

Russell P Marchant
HEAVEN'S GATE

To N.V., and anyone left lonely for life.

I saw her just yesterday
It all seemed so real
Now I don't know
How I should feel

I remember walking with her
Under the bright moonlight
Wish to God
I could see you tonight

Like two ships that passed
For a moment in time
In my heart, those moments
Will always be mine

Today, I wanted to see you
but, it wasn't right
just unable to believe
you died last night

Hey babe, are you still out there
or is it just too late
Promise when I die
you'll meet me at Heaven's Gate

Mildred W McKinney
THE MAJESTY OF DAWN
Watching the iron grey dawn
Crawl from the darkness like a snake,
Turn to metallic pink . . . bright red,
Dissolve, drop into oblivion
When the sun sneaks from horizon's
Rim, paints the sky a brilliant blue
Fuels searching souls for life's journey.

Lisa Anderson
SHED OUR SKINS

Dedicated to Michelle Mehl and to Zac Conway

Soldiers fighting in a war;
strong don't kill the weak,
it's all a lie.

Soldiers fight a war,
one by one they die.

Shed our skins,
look and see.
No difference between
you and me
We live, we die.

Guns blasting pain.
Clearing smoke
bodies bent and broken.
Screams of pain
and innocent boys dying.

Soldiers fighting,
senseless—look and see.
No difference between
you and me.
In the end,
War claims all.

Bridget M Bailey
LOVE LIKE MEDICINE

To the one who holds my heart. I'm forever yours R.M. I just wish you felt the same.

Love like medicine
is neither all bad,
nor all good.

At times it flows smooth,
others it rides uneasy.

Sometimes it heals;
Sometimes it destroys;
Sometimes it just does nothing.

Medicine when bad can be taken away.
Love when bad only hurts.

Medicine when good, heals.
Love when good, lasts forever.

But,
Love, like medicine,
is neither all bad,
nor all good and never shall be.

Kathleen A Maloney (Meaney)
DEATH KNOWS NO PREJUDICE
Death may be a welcomed friend,
When one is filled with sorrow.
But soon becomes an enemy,
If you wish to see tomorrow!

It preys upon the young, the old,
The sick, the poor, the wealthy.
Good and bad cannot escape
You may be strong and healthy!

Death may cradle you, invite you slow
Or snatch you without warning
One thing is sure;
There is no cure,
So when you wake each morning;

Greet each day with love and cheer
It may be days, weeks, months, or years
But be you black, brown, red, or white
Death always holds you in its sight!

Matthew B Rowe
OF FATED CATTLE AND MEN
Look at the sadness in their faces
The tragic dullness in their eyes
The bleakness of a leaden future
All thoughts paralyzed.

Their heavy breath is steaming
In the cold November air,
Their fear is strong and putrid
They tremble at your stare.

Do they care,
Or are they empty?
Conditioned to such voids
Raised in darkened stalls
Lonely,
Paranoid.

Take them to the slaughterhouse
Take them from the field
Spill their blood upon cold cement
Watch their bodies reel . . .
And watch the bones pile up . . .
Shattered remnants from a saw
And wonder as you light a smoke,
What will be our fall?

Gerarda Di Benedetto
THE GOLDEN PLUNGERS
Every year
All glorious summer long
They dive off cliffs along the Mediterranean
Lured by the siren's song.

One plunges precipitously,
Another follows,
Their sunsplashed bodies long and slender
Their chiselled features rivalling Apollo's.

Amidst natural wonders they leap
Boys, young men
With lungs of iron in their mortal chests
All eyes of Olympus turned upon them.

They will never compete in an Olympics
Their praises will never be sung like

a marathon runner
Here, their strength is not
extraordinary
Their smiles not a struggle.

Every year
All summer and a day,
Demi-gods dive off cliffs along the
Mediterranean
And play.

Alyssa Trott
MR. MODERN WARRIOR

To Meme

Don't you see him coming? Can't
you hear?
Run away; he's something to fear.
He is a modern warrior dressed in
black.
He's dressed to kill and all are taken
aback,
But look again. What do you see?
a lonely person wishing he was free.
Free of evil. Free of sin.
Free of the souls who haunt him
within,
So run little children but if you are
caught,
Remember his soul that was sold and
bought
By the evil one down below,
and when he comes down it will be a
mighty blow,
So think nice thoughts of sweet
revenge,
the horrible things that make all
cringe.
It will come back to him
Don't you worry.
He is blind but goodness is blurry.

Aileen Maisel
MY PARADISE ISLE
Sandy kisses on the beach
When I kiss my Galveston peach,
Lovers basking in the sun
Paradise Isle is fun for everyone.

Happy children frolicking to and fro
Amid the dancing waves as they
come and go,
Gulls gliding so gracefully in the sky
Watching everything above as they
fly by.

Golden sunsets in late afternoon
Cast shadows of fishermen returning
home soon,
Happy faces on them are a pleasure
to see
With fish caught in the azure blue
sea.

My Paradise Isle I would not trade
For cities of skyscrapers
Noise and pollution man made,
Here time and tide flow hand in hand
Which makes living peaceful and
worthwhile,
For all of man, on my Paradise Isle.

Douglas E Colley
WET DREAMS
And may I be so bold that I suggest,
To sail the seas until the very end
Would be my pride and joy, today,
my friend.
My ship and soul would dare remain
abreast
To view the seas of seven—as my
quest,
My ship would be the vessel I
surrend-
er: though to test my skill against the
wind,
I'd sacrifice myself to pass the test.
But I have no mast, no stays, no
helm to man:
And so like thunder, lightning,
blowing gales,
The winds and rains of storms, that
soak the lands,
Are beam to beam without a ship to
hail.
I have no crew, no mates to give
commands:
My dreams are wet without a bailing
pail.

David Clearwater
THE GARDEN

A tribute to my Grandmother Iris E Abel. July 14th 1988. Bolton Ontario.

The rose bloomed as a sunrise in the spring

Alone in an overgrown garden, full of world strife and economic despair.

The sun shone on her face, giving her the strength to face the garden each day.

Her face grew to a velvet petal, soft as a feather and fleece.

A stem of love and caring, strong enough to support a nation.

Her deep roots touched every one she met and gave them a reason for hope and joy.

She grew, stronger every day, until her little roses began to grow around her.

But as all saintly creatures will the rose began to fade,

Try as much as she did, she could not hold on,
'twas not for the lack of love.

The rose eventually passed away, but if you pass around the garden today,

It blooms a rose garden that every morning shines a crimson glow,

Matching the sunrise just like the mother rose.

Robin Ann Long
THINKING OF YOU
I was thinking of you today,
Hoping you might be thinking of
me,
Thinking of what we meant to
each other,
Of what we used to be.

I was thinking of you today,
And of the times we spent
together,
Wondering how it could end,
When we thought it would
last forever.

I was thinking of you today,
And realized I never let go,
I loved you so much,
But it's over now, I know.

I was thinking of you today,
And as I began to cry,
I threw your picture in the
fire,
And finally said good-bye.

Arthur R Hoffa
SEASONS

Dedicated to Joy, A very special woman I will always remember

Flowers wilt one by one,
Winter's days are soon to come
Summer is leaving and as she
goes,
She leaves with me, memories of
gold.
Rain beats down upon the ground,
Lovers together make no sound.
So turn your head towards me,
Stay awhile; never leave.
For autumn days near and parting,
Only bring me tears.
But as I see you turn to go,
The season to come now is spring.
In hope for her,
And the love she'll bring

George R Brown
DEPARTMENT STORE
I walk among the dream stuff,
tomorrow—new
impossibilities, Tantalus
hangings from Eden trees;
The indigenous ones see other-
placeness and frown—or
smile too wide.

From a door marked "Insecurity"
stalks the hunter,
The Jagged edges of his cynicism,
broken remains of still-born dreams
crag the features of
his face.
He follows my spoor through the tall
napped carpet,
peering from blinds of exotica.

Motionless, emotionless manne-
quins, from the fragile safety
of glass barricades, smile sad
eternal smiles—
Eternity ends at five or so, and
Galatea hurries home.

I walk among strangers, under
distant and heatless stars,
gleaming shards of alien
yesterdays,
Icy pin-pricks of frozen time.

Stephanie J Splaine
SUICIDE!
Suicide isn't a pretty word,
And most people think it's absurd.
It happens to people in mass
depression,
And it seems just like one big
obsession.
It makes them ever oh so blue,
And they can't figure out what to do.
They don't know if they can talk it
out,
But if they did all they would do is
shout.
They wish someone would make
them see,
Because they don't know how it's
supposed to be.
With the problems they don't think
they can cope,
So they begin to get strung out on
dope.
They also don't get enough sleep,
And never ever want to eat.
Then they attempt it once or twice,
And begin to think it's not very nice.
They realize all they need is love,
And ask for it from God above.
All they have done was pleaded,
Finally they got the attention they
needed.
Now they know that they are loved,
And don't need to go to the world
above!

Jennifer L Beckman
THE INVISIBLE INTRUDER
Cancer.
It's a word that makes you think.
It makes you think of all the
people close to you who might
fall victim to its eternal misery.
It makes you think of all the
ways it has found to slowly
torture unsuspecting prey.
It makes you wonder why
someone hasn't found a cure.
Why does it always choose to
strike with its slowly, but
steadily burning flame at the
wrong moment?
Why does it always reach in and
mix life up just as it was getting
better?
Cancer.
Why does it have to be the
unanswered question?

Martha Del Real
RULES OF LIFE

To my best friend, Maria Elizabeth Prado

Life challenges time
changing rules of life
soul and mind.

You never seen water
so clear as I,

Never felt nights
go so slow . . .

Or felt the pain
of fire that burns
alive inside your soul

Accepting rules of life
being a hero at war time
wishing not being alive.

Kimberly Tindale
MY LOVE
The beating of a heart
The thoughts of a mind
Emotions of a soul
The love I feel for you.
You answer the questions of an
unknown world
And open the doors to a wonderful
life.
You fill me with happiness,
Then sadness again.
Hold my hand, let us laugh,
Let reality pass?
Just remember my dear only one
thing,
I love you and will always be true.

Joseph Ruddy
SEA
As the sun kiss the water I sometimes
why I falter.
Finding the right thing to say and
trying to have things my way.
Becoming a somebody and not a
nobody.
Seeing the water slap against the
rocks.
I wonder why I had so much hard
luck.
As the water drift out to sea I still
find I have me.
As the sun kiss the sea I find I really
like what I see.
As the wind moves the trees near the
sea
I find myself in thee.
Making sure I am confident but
sometimes wave like the trees.
When someone loves me I think of
the sea.
As the sun kiss sea I always like what
I see.

Vivian Schulte
THE I OF WE
Love is a pairing
Love is a sharing
Love is a caring
Love is a We

Love is a knowing
Staying not going
Affirmative vowing
Love is a We

We is the mender
of hearts sore and tender
of blessings the sender

Love is a We

One plus one in love is one
We against the world alone
You who are my sheltering lee
Against the chill globe's infamy
Promise me
You'll never be
the I of We

Sam S

ME INC:

What's so special
about the picture I see—
Just bones and flesh
And eyes—Two not three.

A mind to think
good thoughts I hope
Two ears to hear
A childish joke.

Two legs to run,
to skip to lope—
To walk about—to feel
to grope.

But that's all right you see,
I like very much being me.
No other person has my print
of thoughts, of feelings,
of temperament.

So now with my days work done
I'll sleep awhile
to rest and be—
The only one—yes that's me.

Helen E Webber

PEACE

It is God's sunrise and sunset,
—Seen in the sleep of an infant
—Excitement of a child's new pet
—The quiet rocking of a
grandmother with a grandchild
—The gentle walk with grandpa
and grandson
—Parents knowing a child is
interested in an education
—It is listening to beautiful music
—The mutual respect of a
married couple
—Completing a task well done
—Viewing mountains of snow
—Watching herds of wild
animals
—Enjoying a good game with
friends
—It is elderly companionship
—The feeling of positive happy
health
—The giving a helping hand to
another
—It is meeting the eternal maker.

Phyllis Turk

THE REAL YOU

This poem is dedicated to my loving husband Al.

You were always a hard puzzle
game,
Never finding the missing pieces
To fit smoothly into your masculine
frame.

A macho facade, I thought was you,
For years you always kept your
clothes on,
Hiding yourself from everyone's
view.

Finally revealing your disguise . . .
Loving sensitive and caring,
You undressed yourself for only my
eyes.

Maria Mancini

UNTOLD PROMISES

Sometimes I feel angry
and impatient, restless and cold
torn between reality, and silence,
fantasies untold.
wanting, you to fulfill my
promises and dreams
and yet, knowing there's no, destiny,
along the way
to be seen.

Quietly I ponder, as I look, into your
eyes,
knowing the truth
you try so hard to hide.
you look at me, waiting patiently
for me to speak, I try, but fail, for I
know,
the promises I ask, I can not even
keep.

So no promises I shall ask, for I
know now,
my silent dream, must
come to pass.

Maria Mancini

JOURNEY'S TRUTH

There have been times in my life,
when I have felt alone and hurt.
When my whole world felt, like it
was falling apart.
It's then, when I retreat, my self into,
my silent private world. Amazed to
find my troubles fading away, like a
journey in a days end. Quietly the
memories we shared appear.
Yesterdays hurts, today smiles, the
special times have a way of
balancing even the sadness with joys.
I promise, I will not travel searching
for a rainbow into tomorrows Future.
But, live in the present. More
nourished and live, because of you.
Because of you.

Serop Stepanian

Serop Stepanian

O GOD, WE BELIEVE IN THY BLESSED WAY; HAVE MERCY ON THOSE WHO HAVE GONE ASTRAY

To my son Raffy and his lovely fiancé Nvart, grandchildren of survivors of the first Christian nation's "Forgotten Genocide."

O Lord Almighty, God of all
beings, blessed be thy holy and
glorious name.
We received Jesus and believed
in thy truth, to thee we've
turned and shall do the same.

Many a nation has had ups and
downs, yet only few have
endured and survived.
Ruthless have often our pagan
neighbors been, but time and
again our faith has revived.

Alas! Why was the worst yet to
come, with a message we could
not understand?
Cities crashed into heaps of ruins
and waste, a death toll so high in
our cherished land!

Joyous feasts were turned into
deep mourning, for vast as the
sea was the damage done.
The harp and the flute ceased to
be in tune, the singer's voice
was choked with a sad tone.

It was not, O God, the anger of
man, nor was it mother nature
with no cause.
Was it the demand for Armenian
Artsakh, or it was an offense the
devil chose?

From foreign lands and corners of
the earth poured in folks of all
colors and races.
Selfless were they for their noble
drive to relieve the victims in
their crisis.

"Enough is enough," was heard
everywhere; "Let's reunite," the
nation voiced out loud.
Assemblies were held in the Holy
See, all parties agreed to set
things to rights.

"Justice has and will go forth
perverted," say some in the
agony of their heart.
Obsessed by both grief and
despair, they lament for the
loved ones torn apart.

To thee, O Lord, the reckless sing
of vice; they play the fool with
ungodly delight.
They often blunder with their lips
and pens; they say and write
what is evil in thy sight.

Throwing doubt on thy very
existence, they scorn thy altar
and thy blessed way.
O Lord our God, the most
compassionate, have mercy on
those who have gone astray.

Katie Schnapp

GOD IS POWER

God is mighty, God is power
Do not take His name in vain
A mighty King, a Holy tower
Everlasting is His reign.

God is mighty, God is love
A man so great, of peaceful mind
We cry for help from high above
While the world is going wild.

God can clear the mighty heavens
of man-made atomic wall;
He can wipe away the danger
Or back to earth again to fall.

He can keep the fires burning
In the mountains core so deep
Streams and rivers overflowing
In the fields the corn to weep.

God can calm the raging sea
Strong winds lash the waves to shore
He can take you, or me
Will we find our way once more?

God is mighty, God is power
In His hands lie our destiny
Life ticks away with every hour
As He wills, so shall it be.

W Thomas McQueeney

SUBJECTED!
or
Methinks We're in a Class By Ourselves

Mathematically, we are indivisible.
Geographically, there is no other
place
we'd rather be than near each
other, vis-a-vis,
or, at least, visible.
We are socially inclined by a
somewhat romantic nature.
Our grammar expresses an analogous
nomenclature.
You are music to my ear, art that is
rare . . .
The chemistry is there.
Yet, our historical alliance
Is purely a fantasy of science!

Joel E Moyers

THE HAPPY HIKER

Once upon a time, in the mountains
of Tennessee
There lived a man, with a knot upon
his knee
He was so big, but yet not tall
He did some climbing, but had some
falls
His name was Clemson Carson
Creacha
And he was always glad to meetcha
His head was bald, with just a few
hairs
But that didn't stop him from
chasing bears
He ran one down to Cherokee
That's when he fell, and hurt his
knee
That didn't phase him in the least
Cause he would say "I'll get you
beast"
And that he would, as you can bet
For he is trailing one, still yet
Over hill and holler, round the bend
He'll finally, get him in the end
Once he gets him, I can hear him say
"You better move, I'm here to stay"
He got him later in a hug, and
grunting hard
Said, "I'll make you into a rug"
If you ever meet, a man that's bald, a
few hairs on his pate
You may wonder, if it's Clemson, or
it could be Uncle Nate.
But it don't matter, one hill of beans
Cause either one can fill your jeans
They'll make you laugh till your
belly's sore
Then you'll come back for even
more.
For years to come around the bend
This is all, finis, the end . . .

Marden David Paru

A CONTEMPORARY OLD WORLD GONE HAYWIRE

The world around me has gone
haywire.
A bounty now looms over a writer's
head—
To wit a challenge to our precious
freedom of speech—
Has stirred the emotions of the entire
civilized world.

A head of state—no less an
ayatollah—offers millions
To assassinate a fellow religionist

abroad
For printing personal feelings and views
In a world that has gone haywire.

Embarrassment and outrage have now been expressed
Around the Globe. Diplomats are called back
And shelves emptied of Rushdie's Satanic Verses.
Where is tolerance in a world gone haywire?

Is fear and terrorism the hope of 20th Century Man—
Once elevated from the depths of the abyss
To being a special and awesome earthly power—
In a world gone haywire?

Can one group's views so dominate men as to
What he may think, write, print or read?
My senses are stunned! My soul's on fire
In this contemporary old world gone haywire.

Dennis Phillips

SO

It's been said before and now it's being said again, that the world we live in is coming to an end.
Well, I don't give a damn because I know who I am and if it's got to end I lost Hope It happens slow, because then at least I'll know I'll have a chance to have a drink before I go.

Ted Pennington

A ROSE

Wouldn't it be nice to be a rose
All you'd have to do is pose.
In pretty pink petals dressed,
Sipping aqua pura while you rest,
Scenting all the air,
Having not a care,
So alluring and so charming,
Guarded by your thorns—alarming!

Kathleen Rice

TO STEVE

When you
were my baby brother,
I watched your eyes,
marbles under
skin pink lids
sliding from side
to side
Stephen Edward sleeping.

I couldn't wait
to know you
taller than me
to hear
heavy manly strides
across the carpet

grease caked boots
stuffed with stinky socks

but I didn't expect you
to park your Kawasaki in the living room

Mona Hunt

THE COWBOY GOES HOME

His boots are standing empty now,
Worn and shapless, scared and torn.
Behind the door, his old felt hat, is hanging on a horn.
A friend to the old levi jacket
With elbows badly worn.
I wonder—if his old Blue Roan,
Was waiting for him there.
When they opened wide the big barn door
To take the old cowboy home.
His spade and shovel of later years,
Are leaning against the wall.
His garden and orchard he spent his days in—
Neglect will soon take all.
I wonder if his old Blue Roan, was there—
To take the cowboy home.
The old house will sag in weariness
Its years were well spent.
What will happen to it now,
With all the life gone away?
I wonder, if the old Blue Roan
Was waiting for him still.
I wonder if they rode together,
To climb that golden trail.

Ben Rubin

THE JOY OF CHRISTMAS

Whom do you know
That wouldn't show
A smile, a greeting,
A pleasant face,
On a Christmas Day.

What does it take to say,
"Merry Christmas to you all!"
On a Christmas Day.
With a smile and the joy
Showing on your face,
Transmitting that radiance
All over the place.

Singing the Christmas carols
To one and all
Brings the holiday spirit
To young and old.
With joy to our people
And peace to the world.

Lester Evert

Lester Evert

I LOVE MY FARM ON M-43

I Love My Farm on M-43
On my farm it is full of cows, giving milk for babies' mouths
In the fields, they is full of corn and wheat, filling our mouths with nature's treat.
Hay in June, smells so sweet, all over the farm and across the street.
Potatoes in the garden and vegetables, too.
Look what God did for you.
Thunder storms all over the sky, it rains all night and you wonder why.
He knows when to start and turn off the spray, so your crops will live many a day.
Michigan is my state, grows everything to put on your plate.
It's lakes are so beautiful and the skiing is great.
Boys like to take their girls on a special date.
Michigan is split apart, but the Big Mac bridge mends its heart.
When, in the middle of summer, when it is hot,
you go to the U.P. to cool your tan, don't even need a fan.
Now from Detroit to Sault St. Marie, you will love it, don't you see.
Now Michigan has water around it, lakes in the center, too.
When you are on vacation, they will thrill you through and through.
Detroit has automobiles that fill the state.
People drive them and buy food from me to put on their plate.

MaryLou Francesconi

THE OLD SHED

Buckets of tools in a shed so old
Where grandpa toiled for those he loved
Each with a memory he once made
That stands in some part of the house
Windows stained from rust and weather
His silent bench has dust for a cover
In a corner stands a short pegged stool
As a child I sat to watch and wonder
Nails in mouth he would hammer his magic
Smiling at the small spectator below
Softly I close the old shed door
Clutching the nail found on the floor
Shutting my eyes in a wishful dream
To see his dear face once again

G S Gonesh

OPEN YOUR MINDS

Dedicated To Today's Youth.

Open your minds to let sense in
Experimenting with barbituates
Clods the thinking, killing the brains
'Causing only grief and pain
To those YOU left behind.

Inhaling, Sniffing, Basing, Snorting
Brings the hope of promises
That are never, ever fulfilled
Leaving the mind a wandering
Begging for more POISON.

Brothers, Sisters, Cousins, Friends
Old ones, Young ones and Youths
Look around; what do YOU see?
Minds a wasting, dying, being ABUSED
Before they could be used.

Oh MY CHILDREN! Listen to ME
Forget the HIGH of a minute
Thinking that YOU'RE TOO SMART
To be caught like Sam, Sue and JOe
DEATH's AWAITING, DEATH'S AWAITING YOU TOO!

Suzanne Hall

A STAR IS A SHINING WONDER

Dedicated to a shining star

a star is a bright light that
Shine shines high in the night

a star is something you see in
the blue sky

a star is when you find your heart in
the moon light

a star is the whole world go
round and round in the dark
night

so when you look up at the
star you will find your place
of rest

a star is like a shining bell
that glow at night

when you walk along the road at
night and look up at the star I wish I
were there
a star is a shining wonder
in the night

a star is where you go to find
place and good think to take home to
stay

a star is when you see the world
go on down behind the dark cloud

a star is like the moon in the
day night

a star shining so bright in
the night

it make the whole world fall
down on the ground

a star is like a new world
shining so high in the night

a star is where you find your
Love one go to side to side

a star is like shining gold
and cover the whole world

a star is like a Rainbow that
in the sky so high and pretty in
the sky night

a star is like a moon in the
sky that go on and on

a star is like a song you
sing in the night so get on
down to that bad star

a star is where you hear your
baby call come back home to me

a star is like something
that make wishes come true

a star is like a flower that
Glow in the ground

Susan May Hirst

MY BRIGHT BLUE EYES

Dedicated to my late boyfriend with love Peter A Lunt.

Bright blue eyes
blue as the sea
shining as the moon
Miles away from the home
Lost in the stars
Wild graceful, in the sky
We forget and forgive
I'll love you forever
bright blue eyes
As you drift
across the heavens
I will forget you not
Bright blue eyes
as you soar
through the skies
you will always be with me
My Bright blue eyes.

Lois Barr

ACTIVE LOVE

I look foreward to walks
with you
When the friendly wind
ruffles my hair

I can look into your eyes
and share
the inner me.

Frederic L Johnson

THE PARROT

A voice of mumbled marbles
A fan of feathered green
A flash of yellow cresting
A marvel to be seen

Eyes of centered circles
Of white and brown and black
And in amongst the chatter
Your own words coming back

The crackling of the eaten seeds
And shells all piled up high
A view divided vertically
And never room to fly

Ever emitted upbeat sounds
Until the loss of light
And then a flap and whir
All settled for the night

A gift of nature's beauty
for all of us to share
Color, voice, and caring
A friend beyond compare

Lakshmi A Kripalani
SEARCH FOR TOMORROW
S ooner of later the day will be
done
E ndless encounters on the way
A rches full of hopes
R eaching the sky
C lutter all along
H ampering hindering the tiny

F ootsteps slipping sliding
O ver the footpath
R ecessed in the deep holes

T urn the tables for tomorrow
O nly to discover
M ain streams
M uttering all along
O ffering aspirations
R egardless of delusions
R egressing to progress
O vercoming the hurdles
W ondering over wonders that
have no end, no beginning.

Linda E Lecture
LONG AGO, SO LONG THAT IT FEELS LIKE A DREAM
You said you loved me, wanted
me, me to be yours forever

At first I believed in you, thought
you were so strong, so clever, so
fresh

I mused that you could make me
happy

But I realized only I could
achieve my well-being

You didn't care about making me
happy or I obtaining my
happiness

You could only see yourself, your
feelings; your joys, your sadness,
your fears, never to share

Time has gone by and I
understand now that you never
really loved me, that you love an
image, a concept, a likeness

Not an individual, a separate
entity, a person; a person with
feelings; joys, sadness, and fears,
to share.

Carol Dixon Drake
BEACH WALK
Sand squishes between my toes,
its false whiteness revealed
as the sun strikes glistening parts
which dazzle briefly and die.

These particles once were rocks
and reptiles and fish bones
now disguised forever by the rough
hew of the sea,
lost as my childhood was lost
on this same silvery beach.

I walk on crumbled skeletons.

Mrs Nell Liles
MY MOTHER MY CHILD
I was her child for so many years.
She was there when I needed her
through laughter and tears.
Now years have passed and my
precious mother is getting old.
She has Alzheimers Disease, so I've
been told.
The time has now come to put my
needs aside.
For my precious mother, is now my
small child.
It hurts me so much to see her this
way.
Knowing she'll get worse each and
every day.
There are times I feel that no one else
really cares.
When I fall beneath the cross that I
bear.
But when she needs a hand, I'll be
right beside her.
When she needs a friend I'll be there
to guide her.
I get my reward each day with a
warm loving smile.
Not from my mother, just from my
precious child.

Philip W Kaso
IMAGINATION OF THE MIND

This poem is dedicated to the imagination of our Progeny and to Darlynn and Taylor. Without their love this poem would not be possible.

Touch the mind
as it leaps unbounded,
wondering free to light as it pleases.
To some a task
of utter defiance,
others play in the realm of mind
bend.

A flick of energy
sparks the imagination,
dimming the sense of reality.
Folding and rippling
you enter the realm.

Tender as the night
you touch,
timid with bold anticipation.
Drifting with the ease of flight,
you wander free.

Nay a bit of reality here,
to never know the realm of mind
bend.
Clip the wings of imagination
for surely death shall follow . . .

Hal Cohen
DESPERATION
Desperation brings out the best
in me
It brings light . . . to what I
could not see
It makes me work
and think and plan
to form a vision
of what can be
I set a sight . . . and take a look
Write a script . . . then read the
book
When I'm unsure and things look
grim
I'll fight and scratch
or dive right in
I see the obstacles
that are in my path
Can jump over them or go around
Take what life throws at you
and then some more
but by staying on track
I'll open the right doors
Because desperation
will
Last no more

Ron W Belflower
CLOSETS

To my Mother Mary, my cousin Grace, and DeeDee Knight, and any one alone, there is alway's a way, let your inside Beauty shine. Ron

A gray mist swirls about me
obscuring those I see.
A loneliness deep inside cries out
constantly.
Empty souls can find me in the
gathering storm,
never to be seen clearly until we are
reborn.
Barren fields about me, no seeds are
there to plant.
Gnarled trees stretch rotted branches
out into the night, As if a plea with
little hope in sight.
This world I'm in is my own making
of fear and for love. In the mirror I
see the truth of the lie I live each day.
the denial of my self.
I slowly walk away to stay inside the
closet yet another day.

Jennifer Engelbrecht
THE MARE AND THE FILLY
I am old said the mare to her
filly.
I am very old.
I have aged with the seasons.
Year upon year,
I have been fought with,
kicked at and almost killed by
other masters.
My young lad,
You will have a life of leisure
here.
Let this man care for you,
Because I will be gone soon.
We will soon meet again
In the green, green pastures of
heaven.

Ana Irene Carnal
HIGH ADVENTURE
Now gentle breaks the waves
foaming like blinking
Stars on the sunfilled sands of the
beach.
Each thundering roar of churning
water
Echoed approach of a new wave
Poised in splendid droplets of mist
Heaving heavily against the rocky
shore
Disappearing to blend into the
oneness
Oceans rhythmic drift to and fro
Characterized at times, deep
midnight blue,
Fading momentarily to viridian, then
Pale sunshine touching briefly,
Endlessly sweeping the sand in
milky white.
From the water, wind, and air one
listens,
As if some marvelous narrative, in a
conflict of dialect
Slips away camouflaged incognito,
The murmur repeating the mystery of
seas
High adventure—evading concert.

Holly Decoteau
THE NEW BEGINNING
It was deathly silent,
A satin padded bed,
A happy smile frozen on his face
forever.
Tissues passed.
Word said.
Organ music played.
Tears were shed,
And sadness filled the air.

I was happy.
He will have more fun where he is
now.
I will not be sad.
I do not see why I should be.
I want to celebrate a new beginning.
My response.

Organ music playing.
People crying,
And tissues being passed.

I looked at his smiling face.

I knew I was doing the right thing.

Johnny DeJesus
MY HEART
My heart gives to one without
disgrace
my heart lives within someone of
faith
everyone needs a heart to live
a heart that beats universally
a strength which moves the world
can love be so beautifully

though everyone needs someone to
give some love
and never to think blue
in every way will our hearts shine
through
let my heart spread throughout the
world
to the vast hillsides of peoples
and every waters that weave through
the quench to seek full

because the love in me will never
leave
til each soul values each one as equal
in this together we shall succeed
and faith will be all over
let this testimony reach every high
looking away the wrongdoings that
fulfill us
but touching the goodness in all
how faith will be all over

Canadia Collins

Canadia Collins
THE HUMMINGS IN A DOUGHNUT
The Universe is shaped like a
doughnut
With space in center for all the
bubbled
Lifting, whether expanding or
contracting:

From non-edible center of the multiple and
Heavier 'hummings', unthinkingly senses compute
Within multiplications!—aroundly and upward.

In pyramidal understanding, perhaps one king
Rameses the Second was more the farsighted
Than mainly spendthrifty, in evaluation of
A distant future when even in Sun-Lighted
Way, Egypt's true past might be conjecture!
. . . Might be conjecture, as with great Stonehenge
Which came from where? The 'henges', and brightly
Gold-trimmed objects of namelessly tooled fragility
Openly unearthed in 'Engle-Land', had no
Leader—known past that said: Quietly we,
In majority fled a native land, got out—
Got lost!—after only a brief three-hundred years;
And left behind were chiefly the few near-tribeless,
Small-boned relatives who doggedly did remain and,
Perhaps protectingly, did even change their Name.

The Universe is shaped like a doughnut
With space in center holdingly certain
For whatever in spirit's transmit-tingly solvent
Within long Eternity of swift-rising revolvement.

Bonnie Nathanson
MY PRECIOUS LITTLE BOY

I walked softly into the bedroom and gazed down on my Bill
A little hand entwines a toy, he sighs and then he's still.
I linger in his room awhile, the past years fade away
And I recall the tiny babe we carried home that day.
He looked so very perfect with blue eyes and button nose,
I counted all his fingers and his tiny little toes.
So two words had no meaning, I did not want to hear,
"Downs Syndrome"—they explained, how I tried to still my fear.

We watched our baby growing and struggling to crawl.
And if he didn't learn at first, we didn't mind at all.
When he made the slightest progress we would cheer and let him know—
How very proud we were of him and that we loved him so.

We filled our home with sunshine and chased away all gloom,
And watched the months slip swiftly by to his first birthday soon.
We invited friends and neighbors to come and celebrate his age,
The memories of that happy day I treasure page by page.

Then Daddy had to leave us and he was laid to rest,
It's lonely here without him, but I try to do my best.
I counted up the good things, in life this I must face,
And buried hurt and sorrow, my life I must not waste.

Some days seemed long and endless with so much to be done,
So many things I had to learn, to raise my baby son.
I asked God's help to guide me, to lead me on the way,
And He whispered, "I'm here, Mary, just take things day by day."
Sometimes when day is over, and twilight lingers here,
My thoughts begin to drift back and there is yet that fear.
God sent again a whisper, "Mary, I have Billy by the hand,
So cast away your fears and I'll help, you understand,"
"I picked you as a special Mom, to lead this child of mine,
So love him very tenderly, if troubled send a sign,
He's a precious little fellow and I'll be watching from above,
I'll be here if you need me with My everlasting love."

So I struggled and I faltered, it was not easy at the start,
Now the years spread out before me as I daily did my part.
Tomorrow I'll be ready to sing a ninth birthday song,
Tonight I count his sweet ways, the list is wide and long.
He greets me every morning, flings his arms around me tight,
And never stops his chatter 'till I tuck him in at night.

Some days he is so naughty, isn't every little lad?
He doesn't like to hear it when I say he's made me sad.
I chuckle when he faces me with hands upon his hips,
A little frown, a tilted head, and two little pouty lips!
I sit him down beside me, he reaches for my hand,
I tell him he's been very wrong and help him understand.
He puts his arms around me and tells me he'll be good,
I hug him and I kiss him as every mother should.

He went to swimming classes and was trained to exercise,
Along side the other youngsters, he looked so small in size.
But he faced each new challenge with a strong set to his jaw,
And I was so elated with the achievement that I saw.

Yet learning was not easy for my loving little boy,
And I'd long to reach and help him as he struggled with a toy.
But his little face was stubborn and he kept on til he won,
Then he'd pause and smile at me and I'd say, "Bill, well done!"

Bill's counting off the days now 'til the one he will celebrate,
Each morn he checked the calendar for I've circled the date.
The camera will be clicking to show off his Sunday clothes,
And packages are waiting, tied up in fancy bows.
Bill wanted the party at breakfast so we compromised for lunch,
He helped mail invitations to children they'll be a bunch.
His birthday cake is ready, nine candles I shall light,
"Happy Birthday!" is the theme, I had to sing it for him tonight!
After they eat all the goodies then some games they will play.
I know Billy will be happy and this will be one way,
To show him how I love him and to me he is so dear,
These nine years would be empty if my Billy was not here.
But tonight I'll treasure the memories of watching Billy grow,
The love we share together that only I can know.
Yes, there are so many blessings God sent with my baby son,
The love, the joy, the happiness without him I'd have none.
All days are not so happy nor are they trouble free,
I just wait 'til tomorrow and hope that it will be,
Another day of sunshine, another day of joy,
Another day to share my life with MY PRECIOUS LITTLE BOY

Maryanne Keels
FERVENT PLEA TO DESIGNERS

To my daughters, Dianne and Patty, for all their T.L.C.

Deliver us please, from sheep and geese,
That run across our towels and sheets . . .

Cows and sows on blankets too,
Teddy bears in every hue . . .

Dinosaurs with jagged heads,
To decorate our children's beds . . .

Pots adorned with bow-tied ducks,
Chicks upon our coffee cups . . .

Little frogs with bulging eyes,
On canisters in every size . . .

A rooster lamp to light my way,
A mouse that tells the time of day.

Please come up with something new—
I feel like I'm living in a zoo!

Thomas V Halm
GOD'S GIFT TO YOU

Man has no answers, just questions to give
Until he finds God, one's real reason to live
Purpose and meaning only comes from above
The true gift of his ultimate unselfish love
Faith is the answer the one thing that's true
When Jesus died on the cross it was God's gift to you

When the world puts you down with no purpose to see
With no road to travel and no place to be
The Lord waits for your calling, knowing your needs
His love is the answer that starts with your seed
Relying only on him, your Faith is renewed
Share it with others, for it's God's gift to you

Man was never the answer it's in him that we share
The Giver of Goodness and the reason God cares
His unending love if only we knew
He wants us, He calls us it's God's gift to you

But we have to listen and answer that call
He's life's only purpose and we must stand tall
It's not of importance the why when and who
It's our faith to the Father
That is God's Gift to you

Don't ever blame God it's your choice, you see
All your questions were answered at Calvary
It's His Holy Son you must follow and in purpose be true
Then you'll have what he promised GOD'S GIFT TO YOU

Andrea Sue Howard
DON'T KILL THE LITTLE ANIMALS

I dedicate this poem to all people that Love little children and animals.

Don't kill the little animals—
It just wasn't in God's plan—
For them to be destroyed—
By the cruel hands of a man—

Let them live, oh, let them live!
Don't bring their lives to an end—
The animal that you kill—
May be a precious child's very best friend—

Andrea Sue Howard
I AM FREE

With all my Love, I dedicate this poem to my deceased parents, Andrew "Dock" and Nell Alexander Howard.

After many years of bondage . . . I AM FREE!

My spirits soar into the heavens. My lungs expand with fresh mountain air . . . I AM FREE!

My weary feet no longer trod heavily on sharp stones; they move swiftly, cushioned with confidence . . . I AM FREE!

The very essence of my being calls out to me in joy as it sings a beautiful new song . . . I AM FREE!

I rejoice as I welcome my prodigal counterpart. I embrace her, I respect her, I trust her. Hidden treasures and talents she brings with her. Together, we shall discover them with delight. Laughter will fill our days and nights

and echo down through the years, for
. . . I AM FREE!

Tears will now fall into a pond of
wisdom that sparkles in the sunshine
for . . . I AM FREE!

I shall walk with confidence through
valleys and climb with zeal high
mountains . . . I AM FREE!

Unforgiveness; bondage of the soul
and mind . . . builder of prison walls
. . . is no longer my "warden"
for . . . I AM FREE!

Mother and father, for my abusive
childhood, I truly forgive you. I have
always loved you . . . I AM FREE!

Forgiving you enables me to love
myself and others . . . I AM FREE!

There is no bondage in forgiveness
and . . . I AM FREE!

Lee Sparkman

TIME

A lifetime is but a second
Of time within God's reach.
As a drop of water to the ocean
Of a grain of sand to the beach.

Time is so very precious
And what life is all about;
You can't go back and change it
Or take another route.

For time goes by so quickly
It really can't be right
That by this time tomorrow
Today is out of sight.

The life you've lived is behind you
Tomorrow starts anew.
So fill the moments wisely
Weighing everything you do.

So live each precious moment
As though it were your last,
For by this time tomorrow
It will become your past.

Delores Nicholson

THERE WAS A SMILE ON HIS LIPS

This poem is dedicated to my son Randy and my granddaughter Heather with Love.

There was a smile on his lips
and a gleam in his eyes,
But I saw on his cheek
a tear seemed to lie.

There was a hush all around
that seemed to silence the world
When the first time he saw his
little baby girl.

So tiny and helpless
she lay there inside,
Enclosed in glass that would
keep her alive.

With a quivering voice that was
much too high,
He said, "Thank you God and
please help her survive".

"She's a beautiful girl", he said
with a new father's pride.
You could tell by his trembling
he was bursting inside.

She's a bundle from heaven not
yet ready for this world,
But she'll make it just fine,
cause she's daddy's little girl.

Mary Grace Neville

DAWN

Each day, in the early morning's
dawn,
When the last glimmering star is
gone,
I sit and watch the misty blue haze
From the tree rimmed waters raise
O'er towering mountains; as the sun
shyly seeks
To cast a rosy glow on snowy peaks,
And see it all reflected at their feet
In the tranquil waters where they
meet.

I feel a peace within my heart
And breathe thanks for each fresh
start,
To some great Power beyond the
stars
For each wondrous day in this world
of ours.
When my time in this world is gone
And I pass into the Great Beyond;
As I travel that heavenly void
There will be eternally, new dawns
to be enjoyed.

Steven K Gray

LIFE . . .

To all the people who haven't let Jesus Christ into their hearts. May this poem help put them in the right direction.

What is its purpose,
I've heard many say.
What am I supposed to do
Day by day?
Am I to live by the Golden rule,
Or live it my own way?
Am I to work all the time
Or leave some room to play?
I really don't know
For it is all looking gray—
It is a simple decision my friend,
To live God's or Satan's way.
For eternal damnation is Satan's way,
But for eternal life, JESUS CHRIST
is the only way!!!
Amen.

Karen Ruduski

THE DEPARTURE

He is the one
I could never forget
I still consider him
The best ever yet

He was so nice
So caring, so sweet
He was the one
Who couldn't be beat

So why did he break it
My heart snapped in two
I wish it didn't happen
Why is this true

Our departure was sick
So hard to face
In this game of love
I'm losing the race

I'll never forget him
I'm not sure quite why
But I'll find another
A much nicer guy

Jaye Michaels

PHILLIP

To my son Matthew

In a window seat high above, there
was a boy named Phillip.

Phillip would sit all day in the
window seat and play with his
toys.

There was another little boy who
used to play outside below the
window.

The two boys started to talk with
one another and became close
friends.

They would play together for
hours;
Phillip inside and the other little
boy outside.

One very nice sunny day the little
boy asked Phillip if he could
come out to play,
but Phillip answered no and said
he was too ill.

Months passed and they
continued to play together;
Phillip inside and the other little
boy outside.

One day the little boy, who was so
excited to show Phillip a new
toy, waited and waited for
Phillip to come sit in the
window.

Phillip never came to the window
that day or any other day
thereafter.

Dennis H Fukushima Jr

SNOWY OWL

A great Snowy Owl perches atop
a frozen cascade of water
in the heartland of the frigid
North.

Its talons clinging to the slippery
ice
as it braces against the cold
wind.

Eyes like polished disks of black
ilmenite
scan the horizons.

Then, his wings—mighty and
powerful—
unfold, ready for flight.

Suddenly, a crash of thunder, like
that of a sonic boom.

But there is no storm in the
vicinity . . .

Everything disappears
in a white cloud of feathers,
and a flash of crimson.

Felicia D Gray

DAMNATION

To my uncle, Courtlyn McCoy, with all my love.

Why must life cease on?
Knowing that one day life will stop
pressing on
And never exist for another one of
us;
Life isn't something we ask for,
We are just given it
For our life's sake.
Not knowing what the hell to do,
Later on in this sinful life time.
But knowing that everybody has
made mistakes,
In the past and more will be made in
the future.
We're just born into this evil unified
kingdom
Full of demons and ghost
from hell!
Knowing that one day DAMNA-
TION will petrify our bodies and cast
us in a burning hell hole full of fire.
DAMNATION IS SOMETHING
YOU SHOULDN'T TAKE
LIGHTLY!
It WILL LAUGH AT YOU WHILE
YOUR SOUL SLOWLY BURNS
IN HELL;
And our souls will be forever lost;
Till our death we'll see nothing but a
cold damp darkness.
So much for our life and those
damnable methods
that have our unified souls
So that nothing can disturb the evil
doom of unification.
But just as our souls have
been lost;
So is our faith in the dark.
Be doomed in hell;
BURN, BURN, BURN,
cast away your soul
And don't say you haven't
been told,
Because there's one who
really knows
If the truth has really been told.
HA, HA, HA!

Laura J Drent

PETALS OF A ROSE

The petals of a rose fall as I pick
them one by one.
Wondering if he loves me; am I in his
thoughts tonight?
I walk through this rose garden
dreaming of him often.
The aroma, the beauty, makes it feel
so right.

He's not here with me but, I hold him
dearly in my heart.
The memories of our love so
innocent cross my mind.
Sometimes I feel that there's nothing
in this world that could keep us apart.
The feelings that we shared are very
rare to find.

This love I can't describe; it's so
carefree.
We have no commitments to each
other.
But, when we're together it reaches
an emotional degree.
Filled with passion, desire, and the
hunger for one another.

But, now it's just the rose garden and
me.
As I pick a rose the petals fall one by
one.
Wondering, waiting, will there ever
be a time for him and me.
And just like the petals; the tears fall
one by one.

Mary Cramer White

MY POTTER'S HAND

To my beloved children, Greg, Debby and Danny, and my dear grandson, Clinton

Another door behind me
closes
But now the corridor ahead
is bright;
With each step, assurance
guides my way . . .
For faith makes me
unafraid.

With certainty . . .

I approach the door;
With confidence . . .
I open it wide
For with trust in Him
I stepped into the light.

No longer alone . . .
I stand in truth
Of my unsettled mind.
Confident in my
POTTER'S HAND . . .
I await my fate . . .
With patience and hope.

Marianne F Holder
LOVE IS KIND

I wish to dedicate this to all those people who feel unloved and to those who will respond to this poem, changing their lives to a better relationship with their fellow human beings.

How my soul cries to find such love
That life itself entails:
A man and wife, a child's new breath,
Of nature's path . . . God's tale,
Strewn with love, the flowers, the trees,
The grass so green touched with sun's light,
Birds and bees, the fish, the seas,
To make the earth more bright.

All kinds of creatures, big and small,
The seasons ever moving in flight . . .

Those that come to us with love
Reminding us through the night
That nothing brings us so close, so dear
As love unending bound,
So magnetic is it's power
Like all things in peace are found.

Let not the gentleness of life
Ever pass you by, mankind
With an ugly word, a look, or a hurt.
Oh, requited heart, think . . .
Love is kind.

Frances R Brown
A CHALICE SPILLED
So many poets through all the ages past
Have poured their wine of pain upon the world,
Seeking surcease through sorrow thus unfurled,
Some pouring from pure crystal, some from glass.
Dare I presume to add to this? To cast
My drop of beauty like a plummet hurled
Against the sweeping flood, till it lies curled
Within the aching vortex of the vast?
It will not bring you back, that well I know.
Not all of Isolde's poignant lines could sing
Tristan from death, nor prove the magic ring
Of love as strong as cold death's stronger blow.
Yet I must try, as all who've gone before,
To spill my chalice at this bleak closed door.

Rosalee Trope-Lewis
THREADS OF SONG

To my children: Noland and Cynthia; and grandchildren: Michele, Jason and Emily. . . . When we view the world thru loving eyes; then, the human heart needs no disguise for a rich fulfilled life is the prize . . .

We are but the threads of song—
As we go along;
And we weave
Because we "believe"
A tapestry of melody,
That guides our hearts and destiny.
We're tunespun rains and soul rich strains.
Enmeshed in dream-like rhapsodies,
Swept full of moonlit memories . . .
We are but the threads of song—
As we go along.
We are part of a musical design,
Which reassures me I am thine. . .
And my heart is ever aware—
That you are "there"
And that you care . . .
Thus, our love and all we seek,
Now brushes the stolid mountain's peak—
Until the very boulders speak.
Until our very song is even,
A tune-dream fit alone for heaven . . .

John M Pinto
THIRTEEN DAYS OF MARTIAL LAW

Dedicated to my Mother, Patricia Ann McGeough Pinto, A saint in an "Un- godly" world!

Day 1 . . .
It happened on a Sunday, the radio announced to me,
The government declaring,
"Martial Law" decree!

On the second day of Martial Law, I saw on our TV,
The beginning of this country's solidarity.

On the third day of Martial Law,
my parents woke me up to see,
Government soldiers roaming the country.

On the fourth day of Martial Law, I was shocked to see,
A soldier sitting in my tree.

On the fifth day of Martial Law,
the government tried to take from me,
My rights and Liberty.

On the sixth day of Martial Law,
things seemed out of line,
My Papa lay trapped in the mines.

On the seventh day of Martial Law, many things I've come to know,
How this government is "running the show."

On the eighth day of Martial Law, I cried my heart out that day,
When I heard the government took my Papa away.

On the ninth day of Martial Law,
we walked the streets, myself and Mother,
As we watched in bitterness,
soldiers and civilians, pretending to ignore each other.

On the tenth day of Martial Law,
the "wintry" air was very tense, confrontations arose,
To me, it makes no sense.

On the eleventh day of martial Law, Mama lay sick in bed,
A comrade informed her, Papa was dead!

On the twelfth day of Martial Law, I went to church to pray,
"Please, God, help us make it through the day!"

On the thirteenth day of Martial Law, I prayed for peace, to no avail,
As they led me off to jail.

Karen Griggs
TO MY GRANDFATHER . . .

To the man who taught me what real love is and how to be a true friend. I will never forget him. My Grandfather . . .

The memories of him are for eternity
He remains in my heart forever
Even though he's gone,
It feels as though he's still here
He showed me how to be a friend,
How to grow up, and especially
How to love.
I will never forget how he loved me.
He touched me with a special light
That no one else could see.
I often dream of how things would be
If he were still here.
But he's not and I know
I've got to live on—but it's hard.
I often wonder what it's like up there
Where he is.
Maybe if I died, I could see
That one special light
That kept me living for him.
But if he were here, that would be wrong.
So I live for him, forever.

A G Krall
EARTH IS A BEAUTIFUL PLANET
Earth is a beautiful planet
Why just tonight
I looked up at the sky
And saw the clouds roll by the moon
Which threw light across the whole scene
I didn't wonder at what it all meant
I simply decided I was lucky
To have seen the clouds roll by the moon
Which threw light across the sky
And didn't ask to be deciphered
Or tethered to a bunch of similarities
Or be saddled by the silly context of the 20th century
The moon knew it couldn't be done.

Lois J Clarke
EVOLVEMENT
When my greed feeds your greed
It becomes our greed
When my fears join your fears
They are our fears
When my hatred meets your hatred
It is our hatred
When my tolerance bears your tolerance
It is our tolerance
When my hope fires your hope
It is our hope
When my faith weds your faith
It is our faith
When my love embraces your love
It has happened. It is our love.

Ethel L Davis
HIS NEARNESS

To my Family, and Friends.

To us, whose feet He keeps on solid ground,
Let's us know, the Light, can be found.
Bringing courage; happiness; to big and small,
In this way, letting them know, of His Love for all.
As we sit in stillness, looking in the sky;
And wondering, Why? . . . Why?
Thankful, to know we are not bound,
Because, through His Faith; and Power, we know
Unknown Blessings are found.
So close, is His nearness,
He's always around.

Janice Moran
CAUGHT IN A MAZE OF EMOTION
Trying to comprehend
the secret of the maze,
so I can finally escape
the confusion and hurt
that surrounds me.
I know I will continue to
be caught in the maze as
long as I let myself.
One day I must find the courage
to solve the riddle
and free myself.
Until that day
I will follow the paths
that cross into one another
always leading to another wall
another turn, that leads nowhere.

Ray Mickens

Ray Mickens
A WHEEL IS A DEAL

To the most wonderful person I've met—yet: Carol Mickens

Floating into the by-way to reach the open street,
Plastered fingers coach the power-packed thumb,
Push, pull, left right, repeat—
REPEAT!

Passing cars honk and blow, some with tacit smile,
Others 'ud like to sit an' chat a bit,

We know where they're coming from.

She's my eyes, I'm her arms—
Except for that one thumb.

In and out—round about, up and down the lane she'll plod,
One arm immovable at her breast,
the other on the rod—
Twenty years upon the rod.

Natural red lips; blond hair; blue eyes; a germanic noise,
And a voice soft and thin as hue.

Life is so cruel some faces say, as we chug from mall and park,
And would give us a hand when it's dark—But hark—HARK!

We have no idea, you nor I; try as we may,
What went on in the spirit of this person,
during months of hospital stay.

I let her run, I let her fly: Move the buggy, push, pull,
the paralyzed fingers encourage the power-packed thumb,
The outstretched legs direct the path,
We give no quarter, hold no wrath,
Watch out people—HERE WE COME!

Jimmy Campbell
MYSTERY'S NAME

Who knows what the dreamer sees,
or what's in his soul, that sets his heart free.
For all of his life, the dreamer has had this mystery.
There is a great love for him, in his dreams.
A mysterious love, that is unquenchable, it seems.
All that he has, he would give to her,
just the same,
For this lover of his, is the one with the mystery's name.
He was always a Gypsy, wanting to ride the wind.
With this mystery of his, the dreamer loves to pretend,
that this dreaming love of his, has no end.

In his dreams, the dreamer can have any disguise.
It's all there, reflected from deep within his eyes.
There deep in his dreams, he can tell no lies.
The mystery grows deeper, the older he gets,
And this loving beauty, he cannot forget.
So he searches deep from within his dreaming soul,
Only to find that this love has no real control.
The dreamer knows it will always be the same,
For this love he has, for the one with the mystery's name.

Marianne Hitchcock
ATTIC OF MY MIND

This poem is dedicated to my lovely daughter, Robin Michelle Hitchcock.

You stand before me a woman,
As the tears roll down my cheek.
It didn't seem so long ago,
When you stood no more than two feet.

The funny hats you used to wear
To kindergarten plays;
From piano lessons to Barbie doll
To graduation from sixth grade.

With high school came dances,
Boyfriends and dates
Sharing secrets with Pam,
Until it was real late.

The hurts and triumphs,
I felt them too,
I cried many a nights when you hurt,
Only you never knew.

High School years are over,
The end of college is near.
On your own you will be,
In just a matter of time,
But, you'll forever stay,
My little girl,
In the ATTIC OF MY MIND!

Charles F Cahill (Stone-Skipper)
NO TRESPASSING

Posted keep out, the red sign said.
No fishing-hunting, that it also read.
Keeping nature in, that old barb-wire fence.
The property posted, I wonder, good sense?
Nature is everyone's, a rule so gold.
Those signs coveting, what mankind does hold.
An absentee tenant, that landowner of today.
God holds title, rent collected judgement day.

Anibal Alcaide
TEAR DROP

Slowly and bitter, along my face,
a tear drop rolled down my cheeks.
Saddened, I truly felt
that bitterness right on my lips.

Quietly I sighed and sobbed,
but that tear drop
held to my trembling lips,
as if telling me: Hush, hush . . .

Mrs Wilma L Spicer Gabbard
THUNDER & LIGHTIN

DEDICATED to my husband EDWARD BECKHAM GABBARD, whom I LOVE & CHERISH with all my HEART & SOUL now & FOREVER! IN MEMORY OF (GRANNY, MAMA, PAPA, & BARNETT). NOVEMBER 11, 1988 TIME: 3:00/THURSDAY

THUNDER AND LIGHTIN, SEE THE RAIN
Hungry and frightened, feel the pain,
A smile on your face and a heart full of prayer
Lightin the load LORD, does anyone care?

THUNDER AND LIGHTIN, SEE THE RAIN
Show me LORD what will I gain?
Cleanse my soul like the ocean cleans it's sand
Guide me thru this troubled and weary land;

THUNDER AND LIGHTIN, SEE THE RAIN
Thankyou LORD there's no more pain!

Theodore F Sobay
THE LIFE I LIVED BEFORE

To my Lord and Savior Jesus Christ, The Greatest Gift ever given to mankind.

The life I lived before is behind me,
Forever forgotten in eternity.
Now the sun rises,
With dreams, hopes and promises.
No more shall walk in darkness.
For on me, He shone His brightness.
A new life I've chosen,
Able to face evil in the open.
Now I shall be strong.
No more shall yield to wrong.
Shall squander life no more;
Days lost, I know not how
I shall retrieve them now;
Now I shall keep the vow
I never kept before.

Tom Jones
LOVING YOU

To Gladys, My Wife and Best Friend.

Things in our Life aren't always easy
But we do the Best we can do
Sometimes it's hard and sometimes we fall
But it always has been easy Loving you.

My Love for you is more than just a moment
Our Love is more than just a night or two
The time we share together is for eternity
Because it always has been easy Loving You.

Jeffrey D McMasters
TILL WE MEET AGAIN

somewhere in the distance
a lonely mother cries
teardrops for a child
that has long since passed her by

gone now from existence
still lingers in her mind
memories of yesterday
the only comfort left too find

mother on her deathbed
graced now by a smile
faith proceeds her fears
once again will see her child

they are now together
standing side by side
her daughter's lovely smile
removes all the tears once cried

Vanessa D Davis
WHO WAS THAT MAN?

In memory of Charles (Lee) Bishop: I'm going where Love doesn't grow anymore; it just sits there and waits for you.

You came into my life
Your name I knew not
With wisdom and a sweet caress
Love was finally found

Then I hit a blind spot, where tragedy seems to flow
You had found another
What about me? I have nowhere to go
But through old clothes and dirty rags
Looking for the love I once found
Searching here and there for a kind word or even a smile

Who was it? That once said
"Life goes by like a song"
Certainly not me
I would have been dead wrong!

Kimberly Sacks
PAIN STALKING A HEART

There is this sharpness in my heart,
Feels like a dagger or a dart
I never know why,
I just sorta always sigh
Hot heat just burst in my door,
I want to go through the floor
I feel like exploding,
But I'll just pretend to be floating.
With a burst of a tear,
I suddenly grow with fear
For something I hate,
Comes with fate
I must go
Or they'll consider me low.

Ginevar Curenton
DREAMS WILL COME TRUE

Who ever thought a dream would ever come true,
On a lonely hot summer day—
You came my way—
A guardian angel stood at my door.
The long white wings touched my floor.
Only God has this special power
The thought of you carried me
On throughout the day.
Looking for someone to love
I saw you standing there,
With two turtle doves.
"God" above,
has answered my prayer,
With love—love.

Marjorie Gordon
HAPPILY MARRIED

To my Loving Husband—R.S. Gordon—Deceased.

We married at an early age, and lived through good and bad
We always saw the best in life, and lived on what we had
We were so happy together for over fifty years
We loved each other truly, through joy and through tears
If I had my life to live over, I wouldn't change a thing
A fine husband and three wonderful boys to make the whole world sing

Mrs Frances Lenay Burnett
THE DIGNITY OF MAN

Man has roamed this world of ours
since the beginning of all time,
Since that era he has had a hard, tedious, enduring climb.
He started out a little man long ago
within our past,
Through the centuries many have become better known as outcasts.

He used what knowledge he had to create himself a dwelling place,
In order to not only help himself but the rest of the human race.
He worked hard to have what he did, henceforth, making him glad.
He had a wife and family for which he had entrusted in his care,
He fought and protected them and stood tall without any fear.

As the centuries and years passed, so did the ways of mankind,
His knowledge increased and developed all he had learned in his mind.

He grew stronger and wiser with much abundance and determination,
His thoughts, plans and dreams are what helped to create our nation.

His dream was to hold steadfast to his dignity and look ahead,
To forget his past, wrong doings and the ridicule of what man said.
To remember, "all men are created equal" and he is God's creation,
To bear in mind what he and others have done to help their nation.
To work together as adults, wise, understanding and strong,
But—to leave his "private life" alone.!
No Man Is A Perfect Being

John Keyes
THE INVALID
OH! If these walls
Might bleed,
I tell you, then!
We wretched souls
Were freed,
Restored to men;
And though our bones
Were meal,
And fingers raw,
Yet death these stones
Should feel,
In every claw!

Could knuckles, sharp
And white
Within this rural
Cell, effect one warp,
Despite
The crimson mural,
Life! Liberty
Had shone
Upon us all!
Ah! Were Humanity
Alone
Within the wall!

James W Symington
ODE TO CONVENTION

To the next generation

I never was much for convention
Life was too short for that.
For me a little dissention,
And an unconventional hat.

But those were the good old days
Before the atom got fractured.
Now a new hair on me greys
With each bomb that gets manufactured.

And I think that maybe convention
Has found in history its place
It could even get honorable mention
For preserving the human race.

Since life is flimsy at most
Let's spend our very next breath
On conventional war with a toast
To good old conventional death.

Audrey B McCombs
GOD MADE SOMETHING OUT OF ME

To my son: Charles E. McCombs and his family, wife—Lorna & daughter—Kimberley.

One day I was blind and I could not see.
I thank God for setting me free.
He saved my soul and He made me whole.
God has made something out of me.

Are you willing to remain in the dark?
Do you want Satan to tear you a part?
Or, do you want the Saviour to make your life whole?
Give Him your body and your soul.

God speaks and makes something out of nothing.
He can speak and make nothing out of something.
He made the heavens, the earth, and the seas.
I thank God for making something out of me.

Allan J De Fiori

Allan J De Fiori
INVOCATION

Invocation is dedicated to my friendly doctoress: M. Hakim of Norwich, Conn.

Eternal, if Thou art, if in Thou is
united the entire universe for
Thine decrees, if the soul with
the senses does not perish
when the breath ceases, if
Thine kingdom of morning
splendor is not a human, ingenious dream & the whole
has not for end a vaste coincided movement of a dust
of dispersed atoms, give to the

mind that dries in the
search unheard of the
truth the light that inundates & in the heart that
cures the red-wound of
every proud doubt . . .

Binds the soul the circle of life
brief with her unknown things
& presses ardent thirst that
doesn't give rest.

O! Thou Omnipotent, in the
painful furrow of my thought,
sow the ancient seed of my
mislaid faith.

Gloria In Excelsis Deo. Gloriosa
Invocatio Domini.

Solvitur In Excelsis!

Sharen Marie Lippert
LITTLE BOY

To my beloved son Wesley, with Love forever, your Mom.

You're like the special sunshine, that peeks through the trees.
The dew in the morning, that dances on the leaves.
The clouds in the heavens, that bring comfort on sight.
The stars that twinkle, and fill up the night.

The gentleness that comes, with a warm summer's rain.
The sound of a whistle, from a far off train.
The happiness a clown, bestows on a child.
The spirit of a pony, running free and wild.
You've filled my life, with this kind of joy.
God Bless you for being, my precious little boy.

Laura Robb
TO WENDY
My little girl with the sun in her hair,
A heart full of dreams and a
face so fair,
Has started to waken at just sixteen
To a new world so lovely, a boy
seventeen.

She finds she has charm, is winsome and coy.
I hope she'll be good to this little boy!
I pray they have fun that's sweet to recall.
But I need for them both to be
good, that is all.

Trust them I must as I watch them walk on,
Their eyes full of stardust,
and I . . . withdrawn
For I've come as far as I dare, my dear.
But if you should ever need me,
I'll be right here.

Should your heart be broken between here and there,
My arms are open. Your troubles
I'd share.
Now, I wish you courage through the dark of night,
And invoke for you wisdom to
mind the light.

Lastly, I give you one little tear
To keep with you ever to wash
away fear.
Love . . . you will find it; your heart will know where.
Blessings, my little girl, with the
sun in your hair.

Wendy Prosser
TIMELESS
Those were happy times,
Those carefree days when time did not exist,
And I, blissful in my state of ignorance,
Tripped happily down the garden path,
In search of the fairies that
Dwelled in the daffodils.
Those were happy times,
Captured forever in the family photo album;
First steps, toothless grins,
Chocolatey faces and lacy dresses,
Chubby hands, clutching the teddy bear
That still sits on my shelf,
(Though somewhat aged)
Who was a childhood companion,
And a constant comfort when I realized
I was growing up.

Laurie Mallardi
WE WONDER . . .
We Wonder . . .
We wonder why life can only go forward
When all our hopes seem to lie only in the past
We remember how perfect it was
Our dreams had finally come true
What happened . . .
Where did we go wrong . . .
If we could just turn back the hands of time . . .
Then we snap into reality once again
And we come to understand
That life has control over us
There is no way for us to have the upper hand
Our eyes turn wet and red with tears . . .
We feel it is all so unfair
And we are so right
Finally, we recall another time these thoughts took us over
Before bliss came upon us
There was much pain in our life again
And so onward continues the frustrating circle of life . . .

Rob McGuire
PEOPLE, AIDS AND EARTH

To the people of earth, more so those at birth. May they be free from the pain, insane and all that might hurt.

I wanna feel good without doing any rolaids,
I don't want any drugs to make me feel like I just got laid,
I don't want the company of some pretty young French maid,
cause I'm scared and afraid that I might catch AIDS.

I remember one day I was in the park laying, no lying in the shade,
feeling the cool breeze blowing by thinking might it travel with some AIDS, if that be the case then home is where I should have stayed.

Hey you looking for AIDS—you come to the right place,
it's here on Earth with the human race.

Now what you have to do is count on me and you, not to go out and mess with someone who could care less of this.
That will keep this world clean a little longer while we people and doctors find how to be stronger.

AIDS is of Earth you will find it nowhere else,
so be careful in life's game, what counts more is your health.
Also AIDS is here women and men—that means—you don't have to be queer which means you can catch it then.

Hattie Martin
A TRIBUTE TO DR. MARTIN LUTHER KING JR.
You marched for the right of freedom
You gave your life for the cause
For equality and justice in a nation
That seemed to have lost it all.

You tried to show love and compassion
You had no desire to fight
You were trying to establish friendship with all races
By asserting your constitutional rights.

You tried so hard to do God's will
Showing love and concern for peace
With hopes of eradicating the creature
And that violence and hatred would cease.

Hatred and violence are still among us
The creature is still playing its part
But the dream you lived and died for
Will forever live in our hearts.

We remember the sacrifices you made

How you graciously accepted the call
We will continue to work till the dream is real
For equality and justice for all.

Joyce J Goldbach
THINK SNOW

To My Husband—He's A-No. 1

It is the cold season,
And a very happy time,
One very good reason,
White powder makes everything sublime,

God put a thick blanket down,
Branches and wires very stout,
Falling white puffs just lie around,
Snowblowers work to cut a route,

After a storm, there's warmth from the sun,
Gradually the blanket becomes thin,
Sun shows pink on tree's top rung,
White blossoms make all trees akin,

Evening temperatures fall very fast,
Tree's blossoms turn to ice,
Sun still reaches out; weak shadows are cast,
Blanket's shiny weave is nice,

Wind blows with a strong gust,
Ice sparkles with a bright glow,
Puff flowers are hard with a crust,
So it is, when one "thinks snow".

Deanna Valentine Wishon
NO ENCORE
One dreary day last fall
I happened just by chance,
To be an audience of one
And view a great performance.

There was only silence
At the end of this debut,
No recognition by applause
Nor critic's rave review.

Nature has it's way with us
Beginning with our birth,
The lonesome leaf knew it's role
And drifted slowly to the earth.

Ralph Farmer III
YOU
The eyes of darkness watch over me
Your memory guides me,
The way you walked, the way you talked
Make me want to be.

I look into the darkness
I see you standing there,
But when I get closer
You vanish into the air.

I think I hear you calling
But I don't know where you are,
Baby don't leave me
We've made it so far.

Walk with me through this world
Hand in hand, together we'll stand,
Never part, heart to heart,
I hope you'll understand.

I sometimes take for granted
The love that you give,
But let me tell you baby
You're the reason why I live.

Come with me baby
Your hunger I will feed,
Don't turn your back on me
You're all I need

Sylvia Gutstadt Olcott
THE LONG AND LITERARY DEBATE
Sir Willem Shakespeare since his day
Has been accused of stealing;
Sir Francis Bacon's ghost is one
Who'd find this thought appealing.
The Good Queen Bess cared not a whit
Since Billy was amusing;
To those not steeped in scholarship
This battle seems confusing.
What cares our day where credit goes
So many centuries after?
What matters is the wisdom mined
In history, tears, and laughter.
Sir Willem spoke for Everyman;
Sir Francis more to sages.
The light they brought
Need not be fought.
It's filled the world's best pages.
Who knows what guise in later lives
Would hide the soul of Francis?
And Billy's wit—could it be fit
In a yogi used to trances?

Helen G Wuerth
UNCONSUMMATED LOVE
She had turned him away—
And his possessions of innocence
Mingled with unworldly idealism.

How could she allow love
To transpire between
This Jewish-looking Messiah and
Herself—an education major with
A Jesuit philosophy of love and life.

Years ago she wedded
A man whose father
Had served with Nazis.

People talk and thoughts emerge—
"Now a modern Jew she loves."
"Her first marriage was annulled."
"What could there possibly be
Between her and that Jewish knight?"

The rabbi blessed her and his son
And said they had
To suffer much first.

Lorrie Lamm
LOVIN' THINGS
Heavy farm gate stretches across
yellowin' homecomin' grass, pushed over to one side.
House ain't been whitewashed since my leavin' . . .
porch saggin' . . . just don't seem near as wide.

Damp, curled leaves are hidin' Ma's
irregular steppin'-stones purchased at the local feed store.
From the porch, comes a tinklin'
sound; ducks are still attached to the solid-oak four-by-four.

Ducks . . . collidin', dancin',
dependable ducks
suspended on wires and hangin' from a nail.
A faded-blue, porcelain bow sways
and bumps into another white-flecked, pert, curtsyn' tail.

Poppa scoffed and snorted on that early-spring day
when I left, directly after nailin' up the chimes.
"Just like church bells, Ma cried,
bells on Sunday . . .
what a lovin' thing to hear when I'm tired at times."

Can almost smell pear-preserves,
biscuits, and coffee as I rest,
remember, listen, and almost smile.
Blue-norther due . . . 'bout
noon . . . need to get the key from
Poppa's friend, John . . . in a while . . .

Allan Crawford
AN ORDINARY MAN
I am just a man, an ordinary man
I live from day to day
I do the best I can.
I am often foolish
I am sometimes wise.
There are times when I am strong,
But then I realize I am also weak.
So, help me if you can
For with help I can make it,
My friend, I know I can.
As for me, I'm proud to be
An ordinary man.

Shandra Rasmussen
THE LIGHT OF THE MOON
Spending the secret moments together,
Just to wait forever,
To get to hold you again,
Because it's such a sin.

My daydreams take me away,
Thoughts of you; of yesterday.
I see the lovers on the beach,
And I remember how it was once you and me.

Sometimes I feel you slipping away,
Please promise me you'll stay.
I don't want to lose you,
I believe our love is so true.

I miss you so much,
Your laughter; your loving touch.
But we'll be together soon,
Even if it's by the light of the moon.

Marva Egenberger
AUTUMN
Wedges of wild geese
Mystic in their flight,
Leaves at hurry to rest
Upon the breast of earth.
Ruffled ponds greying
To greet winter's squall;
All portend petition
For new life,
While our sayonara
Sighs upon the wind.

Kenneth R Patrick
ENJOY THIS DAY
If I could live my life over,
is an expression we hear so often.
We use it every day we live;
from the cradle to the coffin.

We waste the present resenting the past,
building up a heart of sorrow.
We hate to see this day go by,
dreading what might come tomorrow.

But to see our life fleeing by,
sometimes it seems a shame,
to feel our life is being wasted
with no one but us to blame.

So we should enjoy this day, today,
these are the facts we already know.
We brought nothing into this world;
we'll take nothing when we go.

Life goes by so fast, soon we'll be gone,
yet we know not where or when.
The world goes on, when we are gone,
as though we had never been.

Arvis Tyson-Ashitey

Arvis Tyson-Ashitey
THAT MOUNTAIN

This poem is dedicated to everyone who lives in fear of stepping out in faith.

I see a mountain over there.
Will I climb it, or will
I stand here and stare?
It is very big and tall.
If I start to climb, will I fall?
What will I find if I reach the top?
Will I be a loser if I start to
climb and stop?
What if I decide not to climb?
Will it have an effect on my mind?
I will never know if I do not try.
So, I will climb that mountain up high.
I have decided to reach the top
from which I will start flying
and never stop.

Parris A Taylor
BELIEF

To the "funnel" through which God gave me this gift—my mother, Sandra T. Reinhardt.

I love you . . . why?
Because you accept me.
Me, in all of my shortcomings,
Me, in all of my imperfections.
And when life's obstacles bring me down,
You kneel with me awhile,
And with tenderness, words of
encouragement, and love,
Lift me up again . . . to press onward.
The reason I love you is sometimes clear it seems,
Because in countless ways you show me your love.
I love you because you believe
in me . . . and you,
Believe in my dreams.

Richard Rodman
I CAN'T IMAGINE
I can't imagine to be homeless
To be with no roof, no walls, no floor
I can't imagine to be homeless
To not be able to go home anymore.

I can't imagine to be wandering

The endless juggling for shelter, clothing, food
I can't imagine the children
In a darkened, blackened mood.

I can't imagine the politicians
Wishing this would go away
Don't they realize they will be remembered
As totally inept in the cruelest way.

I'm sure the homeless are wondering what we are thinking
About how to deal with their kind
Based on our actions, they may be homeless
But we are bankrupt in the mind.

Larry Joseph Besson

Larry Joseph Besson
NEXT TIME I STUMBLE
Next time I stumble
I hope I don't fall,
Because when I lost you
It was the hardest of all.

You did something to me
That I can't recall,
Oh the next time I stumble
I hope I don't fall.

We've had so much fun
For so many years,
Now that we've parted
I can't stop the tears.

So I guess I'll remain here
Like an old ragged doll
Oh the next time I stumble
I hope I don't fall.

Clara H Keltz
MILESTONES

For "Jake"—September 1959 (and all mothers, with sons.)

Oh where has he gone, our little guy,
Who, just short years ago
Welcomed the first robin,
And romped in the first soft snow?
Why do the years so swiftly roll,
And leave us with tear-filled eye
Remembering his first school years,
His first new suit and tie?
Scarce have we held him
These few, short years,
Remember my dear, to smile
And hide the loneliness inside,
As his bride comes down the aisle.

Jay Harris Anderson
TODAY IS YOUR BIRTHDAY AND ALL IS GREAT

To my husband Carl William Anderson, Jr. 2-22-88

Today is your Birthday and all is great
I am thankful everyday that I am your mate
It started five years ago on a very special date
I am very anxious about our future and can hardly wait
I am sure we will always be together at this rate
We should always show all the love we have and never hate
Just because you are forty nothing is ever too late
I dream our life will be special because it is fate
And when the time comes we will be together at that special gate
Thank you for being my fish the night I made myself the bait

Christy Pritt
CAUGHT IN MORNING LIGHT

To my grandmother, who passed away December 19, 1988.

A rosebud will sparkle in the dew,
The stars will only shine so bright.
You can only wander off so far,
Till your fears lead you home at night.

A raindrop falling looks so pleasant,
A flower growing nice and tall.
Just walking along a forests path,
Thinking about nothing at all.

Nature is taking its turning course,
The beauty changes everyday.
The nights are starting to get cooler,
The morning's chasing them away.

Wondering why this is happening,
Your fears get in the way of thoughts.
All the stars disappear in the sky,
In the morning lights you are caught.

Daryl L Blankenship
INSIGHT
the man walks in the streets, his head bowed down in fright, the shadows of the moon shines out and eerie sights run through the night . . . run through the moon light. come on , we're getting out of here. let's run. . run. . run swift like the river, wild and free, for there is no past nor future, only now . . . for who knows we may die at anytime . . . who knows what tomorrow may hold—maybe heaven or maybe hell—for no one has the true insight to tell . . . . .

Ginger Drake
IT'S ONLY ME
Hi, It's only me, the world is full of People like me, it's the special ones, that stand out in the crowds, it's the Special ones everyone wants to see.

It's only me, I'm your gift of tomorrow.
I'll help you through your pain, and I'll love you through your heartache and sorrow.

It's only me, I'm not the sun or even the rainbow, but in you, there's a Special something that always brings out that wonderful glow.

It's only me, but I can see your beauty shine through. So keep Shining and keep smiling and the whole world opens up to you.

Tammy Weaks
OUR LOVE
Our love is a river that forever flows on.
I think of you always from dusk till dawn.
Although we have problems as everyone might.
I want you here with me each and every night.

Our love is a see-saw with it's many ups and downs.
But you always make me happy when I have a frown.

I know I get mad and it makes us both blue.
But I just get jealous because everyone wants you.

I love you more than life itself.
Well always be together in sickness and in health.

I worry so much when you're away.
Because I'm so afraid I'm gonna lose you someday.

Our love is so special it means so much.
I could die in your arms just to feel your touch.

Our kisses are so wonderful I just melt in your arms.
Whenever I'm with you I feel no harm.

Whenever you're in need I want you to know.
I'll be here . . .
I love you . . .
and I'll never go.

Nancy Stiver
THE PROMISE
I cannot resist you when your gaze meets mine.

You make me feel
as if my whole life lies before me
like a field of wheat, waist high,
waiting to be taken.

I try, without success,
to squirm away from your eyes;
but I am drawn
to the promise held in their depth.

Keith Parks
JOANN

To the special times we had.

I'm floating in the wind
And traveling to where it goes
But you know I'd never
Go far without you
You know the way I thought of you
And asked you not to go
So can I ask you why
You wouldn't kiss me that way too
We could sail away
To your paradise
And when we've sailed
The seven seas and seen them all
And the day came to its end
I'd mold an eighth ocean for you
So we'd sail to the sunset again
And I'd make sure that summer
Sailed to our shores
For long walks on the beach alone with you
And the nights made of champagne
Bubbling to the blue skies of dawn
But now you've told me no
So can I kiss you once before I go
To help me remember
The love I had for you

Andrea Wales
WORDS

For Daniel Herschede

Words that only come from me.
Your name the sweetest word of all.
A fantasy of fabrics.
A china paper doll.
Passion's kiss and scented skin.
Dreams that come from everywhen.
I can give you things you've always wanted to hear, and I can tell you things you've always wanted to have.
But it is you who plays day to my night, black to my white.
You are the jungle's unleashed primeval beast.
The selfless lover with new things to discover.
And so you give me, Daniel, it seems,
Everywhens that come from dreams.

George C Garrison
HEATHEN BROTHER

To the other nomads: my wife Sandy, our son Aaron, and Laurel our daughter.

Root deep in cerebral sand heathen brother,
We stand
Arms linked and wrestle in the sun.
Truncated limbs reach, but grasp neither
The xylem nor the phloem of that kufic
Eastern tree.
Our souls bifurcate into rivulets
Of quartz and mica
Glittering into eventide.
Oneness to loneliness,
Headiness to aridness—
Petrified, the rock embracing stone embraces rock.
My flesh no longer cleaves to its bone—
A graft, a rend.
And to that savage end we grow alone.
My soul. My clone.

Denise Rochon
PRECIOUS LOVE

This poem is dedicated to my husband "Bill" for without him I'd have no "Precious Love" I love you honey and I thank-you

There's nothing in this world
That could express
All the joy you've brought me,
The happiness
I never dreamed would
Happen to me
Until I met you . . . you made me see
How wonderful it is to
Share a life
With someone who loves me,
Who'll make me his wife
And I know there's no other
Who could take the place
Of the man I feel so close to,
Who makes me feel safe.
By just being beside me
And holding me near
Takes away all of my problems
and any of my fears.

I know that "I love you"
There's no doubt in my mind
For I've never had this feeling
It's one-of-a-kind
It's rare in one's lifetime to
have such a dream come true
I'm just thankful it happened
And with a man as loving as
You!

Jane S Bement
LIFE IS LIKE A GARDEN

To my daughters, Roxanne, Robin, & Jennie Who're always there when needed.

Life is like a garden where flowers
do excel
A ROSE means love to everyone;
a DAISY will never tell.
FORGET-ME-NOTS are important
'cause remembering is a part of you
We have TULIPS to talk with,
which most of us can do.
Sometimes we are PANSIES when
we have any kind of fear
But when we look around we
find a friend or loved one near.
So you see "Life is like a garden"
and like flowers in the sod
We, like the flowers, are here to
serve our God.

Clarice E Harrison

Clarice E Harrison
WHAT MY GRANDSON MEANS TO ME

Dedicated to George Hernholm Jr. my grandson whom I love very much

He's a musician, a carpenter and a
very loving man
When there's things to be done, he's
there, to lend a helping hand.
He's handsome, witty, serious and
oh-yes, he's a-genius, too
There's not anything that I know of,
that really he can't do
Bragging? you ask, of course I am
and I know that you brag too because
you see I've heard and seen it all and
that's what all grandmothers do.

Billie Jo Coates
ONLY MINUTES LEFT

This poem is dedicated to Pearl L Fisher, my beloved Grandmother

We wait and pray
For the day to end
Just to say . . .
You lived another day.
Family and friends hoping
To see you again . . .
Too afraid to turn your head
You sit still
Not a breath
Not a blink
What's to come of you tomorrow?

God is your life support
He is what keeps you from Dying. . .
The love you receive
Doesn't seem to help . . .
You started counting the years
Now you're down to the minutes
What is to come
When you finally reach the seconds.

Ann Marie Kinney
CRYSTAL TEARS
As I look through my crystal tears
I see you and I
running in a grassy field
after a butterfly
You jump
and miss
I steal a kiss

We sit and sun and eat our lunch
as time just passes by
soon agreed it's time to leave
we soar into the sky

You probably didn't know

Eagles can cry.

Tara Lynn Kinney
GIVE ME LOUD ROCK MUSIC
Give me loud rock music
Give me rowdy kids, and a fast,
rough world.
Give me lies and hassles in the day.
Give me wild parties at night, with
weed and booze.
Give me people who don't care.
Give me large cities.
Take them away, they're not for me.
Keep the loud music, the kids, and
fast world.
Keep the lies that are hurt in the end.
No wild parties, no wild friends.
Keep the drugs, drinks, and people
that don't care.

Give me peace and quiet.
Give me a clear stream, a mountain
scene.
Give me animals, and people who
care.
Trees, grass, a white picket fence.
A large house, a family, and friends.
Give me all the peaceful things,
quiet and new.

Merle P Martin
LATE MONDAY BEACH
Sudden seeping clouds,
leaking light,
puffed enough to muffle sunsets,
spill on paradise.

Hardbodies scurry.
Old couples complain.
Fishermen remain
their sodden caps
and stretcing poles
insensitive to
change.

Patricia Welek Hall
DEDICATION TO A FRIEND

This poem is dedicated to "Anne Drace-Hess," my truest and dearest friend

There was a time in my life
when all was carefree,
I was searching for naught
just blowing with the breeze.

I came into touch with a soul
from the past,
Soon to find that our friendship
would linger and last.

We opened the book
of stories untold,
Of feelings, of joys,
disappointments and goals.

We mended and meshed our lives
along the way,
Two hearts drawing closer
each and every day.

The heavens have been kind
to both you and me,
As they joined us together
and there may we be.

So strong is that friendship
that no lifetime could unwind,
What God brought together
and enabled us to find.

Lauana Lei

Lauana Lei
I AM THE SEA
Life
Oh Spirit
Of the Sea,
The undercurrent,
I feel . . .
I see . . .
Are like the
Feelings
Deep within me,
That yearn
And move forward
With dignity;
Unfolding
Into Peace
And Harmony.

I am the Life.
I am the Sea.
Churning to express
Itself some way
Like in the
Splendorous
Crashing waves,
Or in the firmness
Of pounding rock,
Or like the
Graceful array
Of a splash;
Someway to express,
Roll-out and relate
Those undercurrents
That may clash!
Each rolling,
Splashing wave
I greet,
Strengthens me . . .
Refreshes me. . .
For higher ones
To meet.
A deep inner calm
Finally knows
The "Source"
Is part of me
And shows—
The direction
And the strength
To BE . . .
At one
With the rhythmic
Vibrant sea.
The vibrant sea,
Who is me!

Bernadette Bulich
THE CHILDREN THAT WE WERE
We danced beneath a summer sun,
Playing with the jewels of nature,
In a world of freedom,
With sweet surprise,
In sight of a forgiving god.

We were all a-flower,
A blooming color in a field of green.

We were misty or miffed,
Minstrels all a-searching,
But singing in soft harmony.

Warm earth beneath our feet,
We were all surrounded,
Autumn golden corn,
A fawn just nearly stumbling,
Like the children that we were,
Newly born.

Timothy D Hunt
LOST LOVE
Every time I think of you
I wish a wish brand new

To hold you tight
all through the night

To walk with you
in the bright moonlight

To kiss you as I once did
with all my heart within

To spend my moments with you
every precious few

These are the wishes I wish
each night thinking of you
and looking at a star
so bright.

Glenna Jaeger
A ROVER AM I
i am a hillbilly sweet heart
i love to ride the mountain side
Hear the echo in the valley
And rustle through the trees for i
Am a hillbilly sweet heart and
Love the mountain side
Where the coyotes are howling and
The birds are singing as i ride along
Singing a song.
in wide open spaces
Where i long to be out in wide open
spaces
Where air fresh as can be
That's the only life for me

Deni Baldwin
CARVING PUMPKINS IS WHERE IT'S AT
Pumpkins, pumpkins all in a row,
Each one is trying to steal the show.
Some are scary and some are silly,
Some are called Jack and some are
called Willy.

Some have big round eyes

and some are made into pies.
They have on hats with a long, green stem
and a cut out mouth with a great big grin.

They have a head without a body,
And after a week they get pretty rotty.
Each one is orange and big and fat,
Carving pumpkins is where it's at.

Some have candles and some have lights,
Some have teeth with an overbite.
Some are big and some are small
But I think mine is best of all!!!

Tom Griffen
MY LOVING MEMORY

I don't know what it was
or if there's such a thing,
Love at first sight
or living a dream.

I'd look in her eyes
She'd turn away,
I wish that tonight
was an everlasting day.

Didn't want her to leave,
I wish she never had to go,
She made me look again
into something I didn't know.

I remember her well
from the second we met,
She's just something
I will never forget.

DeNelda I Richardson
ONE GOLDEN DAY

Let the strong winds blow and the clouds build high,
See the birds dip and glide in the breeze.
As the sunbeams glow, bringing warmth to the sky,
And a smile to your heart, which will please.
It's a day for your mind to hold!

Look around, look around, for the sights and the sounds,
Watch the bees go humming along,
Over here, then there, zigging on through the air,
As your heart almost bursts with song.
Aaaah! It's great to behold!

Throw open your arms, embrace the day with your charms,
Enfold all that's around you . . . hold tight!
Store the memory away, for that dark, somber day,
When your heart really needs to take flight,
And it wants to be warm, not cold!

Oh! . . . Come along with me, let's both be free,
Dance around in the swirl of living,
Share your hopes, your dreams, your smiles and schemes,
With all in your path . . . it's in the giving,
Don't hold back . . . Be bold!

It's a Heavenly day made of gold!

Bob Dritt
COURTSHIP

When a love begins to grow people never let it show
Yes it's scary—I'll admit—you will try to run—and yet
Something grabs you—holds you fast—will you try it—will you last
Now the heart begins to thump—your heart has a great big lump
Palms are sweaty—tongue will stutter—am I really here—
oh brother
Indecision makes you think—will I swim or will I sink
True love—not for me again—now the courtship will begin
You look nice—very charming—I said that—how alarming
Subtle glances catch each other—I wish I was with my mother
This is crazy—this is wrong—how far have we come along

I cannot be trapped into—you loving me—me loving you
But before the night is done—here it comes—the only one
Embraced in each other's arms at last—the mighty kiss—forget the past.

Joan A Robertson

Joan A Robertson
WE GOTTA LEARN TO HELP OUR BROTHERS

To all the hungry of the world.

"I went down to the Harbor Place,
on one Saturday night.
We had just eaten, our stomachs were full,
when I turned, and I saw this sight.
There was an old man digging in a trash can,
searching for a bite to eat.
I felt a lump come into my throat,
my heart fell to my feet.
We gotta learn to help our brothers,
we gotta lend a helping hand.
If we would put ourself in their shoes,
maybe we'd understand.
I felt so helpless as I watched him pass by,
I just didn't know what to say,
but I wish I could feed all the hungry in the world,
and plant a seed of faith along the way.
We gotta learn to help our brothers,
we gotta lend a helping hand.
If we would put ourself in their shoes,
maybe, just maybe we'd understand."

Michael Lester
A TIMEPIECE IN LIFE

A special Dedication in remembrance of Timmy Evans

I know this hurts much.
There isn't anything we can do.
Though he has departed,
Our Love will continue through.
We all have a destiny, We must also fulfill. Our rare understanding of fate;
Among those chosen few . . .
As we enter the darkness; into shadows of bitter pain. We struggle for this step forward; Our faith and courage, we regain.
We wake up everyday to a familiar sunrise, And I know it hurts to say;
Good Bye . . .
We continue to move on, throughout our days course. For the sun again will set. It's a timepiece in life we can never forget.
Remember the love he shares with us. For his love will endeavor our hearts, Assuring us that we would never be Alone, And for that he has always been A part . . .

Carol Sue Matthews
SHADES OF LOVE

My love to Tex Tuberty for now and always

To lie upon your bed and hold you close
is by far the gift I'll cherish most.

For listening your heart beat LOUD and STRONG
the warmth . . .the love . . . the caring
and like the autumn leaves that fall away to winters breeze
my love for you so great, yet small becomes the trees.

For winter is just a time of rest and spring will bring out
winter's best . . . so my darling remember please
the colors of those falling leaves.

For with the changing of the leaves comes newness . . .
freshness . . . strength you see
and once the roots become
secure only death will part this mighty tree from the earth
and YOU from within my heart.

Tillie Lewis Kaplan
THE BROWN EYED GIRL

To my writing teacher Irene Dayton of Blue Ridge Community College, who taught me much.

The brown eyed girl into the room pranced
Stood stock still as her photo she spied
Angrily she flung away and danced
Circling the room then sat down and cried.

Not me, that's not me I look undone
My face is scrounged up like papier maché
I'll twist to rock and roll and have some fun
Or ride a merry go round the horses to play.

Or perhaps go away in a railroad car
Out of this room I must race
To find a rowboat hitched to a star
To get back my pretty brown eyed face.

Valerie L McCarthy
A DEN OF FOOLS

I sat within a den of fools;
The self same as them was I.
Drink and mirth were our only tools;
Bodies born on the road to die.
Fools are we in the way we go?
So may we be as life calls us so,
But life does not, nor will ever know
That in our merriment we're discontent;
Much more than ever meets the eye.
We laugh the open boisterous laugh,
But within our mournful souls do cry
The whispered ballad of wise lament;
The wisdom lost with our repent
To a secondary avenue,
Where all the landscape's open sites
Are seen in distorted view.
We fought the cursed battle on life's battlefield,
And bore the gaping wounds of rage
Too great to ever heal,
And though still the pain we gage;
It's pain we do not feel;
For the pain of pain is a wretched beast
That steals the man away
And leads him in search of another road,
But leads him farther astray.
Life, YOU boisterous, ghastly being
Dare not condemn that which you are seeing.
From your hidden bunkers you attacked our brigade;
What we are of us you have made,
If not in whole, then in part,
And death is our ever constant companion
As it is your counterpart.

Vicki B Pickett
LIFE IN PASSING

To all the loving widows of the world

Sometimes I feel him;
The warmth of his body lying close to mine.
I dare not move.
Knowing the moment I tremble or sigh,
He'll be gone.
At times it consumes me—
His crooked little smile, his warm laugh
His convictions, his concerns,
His life—Our life, His death—
Oh yes, his death!
With each new dawn
The memories are placed one at a time on a shelf—
Some to look at and examine each day,
Others, both painful and pleasant,
Will be reviewed from time to time
With reverence.
He is gone, but never dead.
I cherish our time in life—I am haunted by his death.
In silence he beckons me forward.
In faith I follow,
Ever strong—never alone!

Ann Westfall
LONELY TEARS

To the memory of my husband—Walter Fred Westfall

I keep busy with each chore,
This and that, and crowd in many more,
So, the lonely hours quietly go,
Painfully, softly and slow,
And yet, deep inside the tears remain,
A widow's wounds are hard it's plain,
Our friends leave me alone,
They don't know what to say,
I call them sometimes on the phone,
But, I want no pity, that's not my way,
At home the fire burns mighty low,
Tho, the flames have lost their glow,
Some days I know just what to do,
And always wonder if you're lonely too,
Then tears again, it's been many a year,
You've been gone from me dear,

The children have little time to give,
A half hour here or there, I let them live,
Their happiness is more important than my strife,
I say nothing, I know it is their life,
Tears again, Oh how I long for,
Those whispered words of confidence and more,
I'm strong they say, but what I hide,
Is sorrow, loneliness and strife inside,
I must grin and keep on trying,
While my broken heart continues crying,
I try to laugh and joke and smile,
Be sure of myself, but all the while,
Those lonely tears remain a part,
Each night, and every day I make a start.

Erick Michael Melendrez
THE MAN OF THE SEA
The man of the sea has seen many moons,
and the ocean has made him wise.
He is forever loyal to the sea,
and with it he has unbreakable ties.

He joined the Navy at the age of eighteen,
and now he is an old salt.
He has sailed the seas ever since then,
and without it his life would halt.

He's eighty years old and growing weak,
but that won't cause him to fold.
He lived at sea and he'll die at sea,
and his blood will never run cold.

It's been a year ago this very day,
since he met his watery grave.
His spirit will live forever more,
upon a sea bound wave.

Shannon James Smith
MY PROVIDER
In the darkness of the night,
You provided me a light.

And when I fell upon the sand,
You provided a helping hand.

And when I sailed life's stormy sea,
You provided stability.

And when my ship could sail no more,
You provided a safe shore.

And when I slept beside the stream,
You provided me a dream.

GOD, YOU ARE MY PROVIDER!

Janette Bailey
MY GOAL
It's up to me what my future will be,
I'm the only one who can see;
what that goal will be for me.

If I but work hard,
I will go far,
And reach my star.

I will reach high,
And not let my dreams pass by.

For I only have one life here
to progress and grow,
Until I reach my goal.

Jerald E Cantwell
SCHOOL DAY MEMORIES
There once was a little country school,
The teacher always had a firm rule;
Sometimes, it was quiet as a mouse,
And there were the trips to the outhouse.
We had Halloween and Christmas plays,
They were more fun than writing essays;
The pie suppers were a lot of fun,
After the program, the prizes were won.

The winters were cold with lots of snow,
We'd gather around the stove's warm glow;
We would catch springfever in the Spring,
In the spring-air, we would do our thing.

We had lots of fun playing softball,
With other small schools, we had a ball;
The school year was closed with a big feast,
With the neighbors, the fun never ceased.

Trina J Chew
THE WOMAN IN THE SHADOWS
I can see her in the shadows;
the woman I'd like to be.
Soft, sheer, and delicate;
can break any heart.
Always confident of herself;
finishes what she starts.

Has the perfect marriage,
and the perfect car.
Never takes advantage,
of how she got this far.

Subjected to many obstacles;
which she has overcome.
Never once has she turned down,
any hungry bum.

And when I grow-up, so feminine and sheik;
I'd like to reminisce.
Thoughts about the woman in the shadows.
And the day,
that I wrote this.

Christine Dougherty
THE STORM
The storm approached the hillside,
It blew and blew and blew
Till all the people of the land
Knew their time had come.
Mr. Fate knocked at their doors
Shouting out their names.
Houses fell one by one,
Cries and shouts weren't heard.
Nobody knew it was coming,
It surprised them all.
The vicious wind swept the land
Leaving very few.
The beauty of it all was crushed
And nothing remained.
Now all was quiet.
The news was heard.
Every loved one mourned.
It wouldn't change—It wouldn't go.
The shock stung them deep.
The vicious wind had swept the land,
And left very few

Joseph Rutherford
MADNESS LURKS
When life is full and plenty and you awake at dusk or dawn, I grow weary of this madness and retire to your lawn.
When life begins to sadden, you have to change reality.
It starts within your heart.
When all around is madness, you hide between the walls.
In the darkness it's waiting—coming toward you in the halls for one close call.
Its touch is as cold as ice.
Spirit is untarnished—Fight to win it all. It has no harness.
Growing tired of the battle, I return to my castle.
When all becomes of madness, your emotions turn fragile, then fall into sadness.
I long to turn my path homeward, cuz the madness is out of control.
When life becomes as barren as deserts all around, I will start looking homeward bound.
Destiny is at hand—Where is that promised land?
When all around is madness, you hide within yourself.
Now you search for the conquest of life itself.
Looking at the cold reality faced right at you—What's there to do?
When madness becomes too mighty, it's time to return home even if it's all alone.
You know I might just be lazy but when madness lurks everyone goes crazy.
You awake to what you do not know, for try a they might, they cannot steal your dreams.

Michele Costa
FAR AWAY
Lies are woven in the rain,
Tapestries blue and gold,
And some who really never knew
Their lives were being sold.

Beauty of the yonder lands,
The grace upon the face,
A child in his mother's arms
His only rightful place.

The past years have flown by
Sweet memories in my mind
I hope that I will not forget
And leave it all behind.

Joan Cesarini
AN ODE TO A SNOWFLAKE

To my Mother, Constance; my Father, Osborne; my Mother-in-law, Josephine; and my baby, Cindy Ann who I miss every day

It was only a dream — though it did
Seem so real to the handsome young man
He dreamt of a snowflake that he had to take
And hold tenderly in his hand

In the snowflake's white lace he had seen her face
And he wanted so much to capture
The passionate smile—though for a while
Of the snowflake's ecstatic rapture

For she had waited so long just to belong
She would gladly melt at his touch
Though it was fateful—she was very grateful
She wanted to be held so much

When he woke from his sleep he knew he would keep
His dream of the snowflake a secret
For no one would believe that he did grieve
Over the snowflake's last pirouette

A Lynn Brady
A LAZY AFTERNOON
I sat under an oak tree
back in the woods by the pond.
Rain was falling softly around me
making circles in the water as it hit.
The sun still shone brightly through the rain,
as it sometimes can in the late spring,
and I watched as the sun's rays reached out,
spearing the raindrops as they fell.
The countless, tiny prisms clung greedily to the light
before they bent it, separating its components,
and sent it out again in a spectacle of color.
The rainbow stretched out before me,
extending so far into the distance
I could not see its end.
It looked almost like a road to be traveled on,
that would take you places you have never dreamed of.

Kimberly A Fairchild
POISONED WATERS

This poem is dedicated to all persons who love nature and all that it is, the way I do—We have but only "one planet", "one world" in which we all can live peacefully—let not our insatiable greed and ignorance wipe out all we have—

Poisoned are the waters—
Touched by ashened skies—
The eagles cannot fly—

Our land has been
Violated—
Infected—
Poisoned—
By the ever faithful hand of progress—
And someone has stolen all the trees—

Where once the wild indian paintbrush
Planted self sown seeds—
Now stands, the mighty concrete pillars
of this age—

In this night's past sunset sky
I saw the mountain and eagle
Reflected in the red sky—
And eagles cannot fly—

Marcia L Wheeler
MY MOTHER YOU'RE ONE OF A KIND
My life without you could never have been;
You're there when I'm sick,
You're there when I'm happy and when times are rough.

You are to me the diamond stars in the night above.
You are the sun that shines, giving all life

You are the warm motion of the sea,
and the soft green grass of summer;
The beauty of the leaves of fall and
the freshness of the snow in winter
the perfectness of spring flowers,
You are the dreams of days gone by,
it is the likeness of
you that I wish to be;
you are my knight in shining
armour
and the friend I shall always
have
deep in the wonderfulness of
your kind
You are my image of the perfect and
the living example of
my particular mother—my
mother.

Gordon White
THE HAWK AND THE DOVE

The hawk is ever circling
Searching for his prey
While the dove sings his song
A tune for the day

The hawk glides majestically
The whole sky his throne
While the dove darts from branch to
branch
His tune changing it's tone

The hawk still searches
Waiting for the right moment to dive
And on the dove's perch
The song revives

The hawk slowly ascends
To get a better view
The dove changes position
And begins his song anew

The hawk moves on, still searching
With an emptiness in his heart
While the dove is content to stay
And from his song, will never part

Michael Glenister
THE DREAMER

A dreamer thinks about mankind,
himself, the future, and the mind.
His talents are many, his wishes are
few:
To 'think' is all that he wants to do.
Although he doesn't realize it, his
powers are great:
A dreamer can change the world,
history, or fate.
But the dreamer is a dreamer, the
power stays in his hand:
For although he can see the future, it
slips away like sand.
The power is unlimited, for the
imagination is vast:
Yet the dreamer rarely uses it, for his
decision comes last.
Is it through ignorance, or simply by
choice?
A doer has hands, the dreamer but a
voice.
Pity him not, for he is happier in the
mist:
Free of responsibility, and a power
unmissed.
Where will he go to, what will he
do?
Who can tell, but you'll follow him
too.
For without dreamers, civilization
would stop:
The dreamer creates it, by simply
providing the thought.

Jackie Gabert
DECEMBER 6, 1988 5:01P.M.

When the night is old
And the faces of mankind are
chapped from the air
They hinder toward the earth
Always, looking down, always
downward
The once childish laugh
is but now a closed door
Nowhere to turn
And nowhere to run
Boxed in like a rat
The only movement is
The sudden chill whipping in and out
of the cracks,
of the barren, isolated shelter
And like everything living it will be
gone someday
Remains are left
Drifting like dogwood
In, out among the wreck and havoc
Once, it was picked up
And so it was, they left it laying
there—
for everyone to see

Dian L Gardiner
LOVE

To: my Kids and my Husband., But most of all I wish to thank my LORD JESUS for without Him—we would not know LOVE. "I LOVE YOU ALL." Mom.

As One would say—Err is to human
As Love is Divine,
But I wonder as we grow older,
What Right is yours and mine.
As we are born in this world,
We grow-up naive Boys and
Girls,
We all share Life's Joys and Sorrows,
And always wonder—what's
tomorrow.
We Love, Cry and sometimes wonder
why,
And all along love is passing by.
We get married and have children of
our own,
And wonder will they take their
Love Away from Home.
We have grand kids now,
It's our kids turn to take the
Grand Bow.
They have taught their kids very
well,
And our Joy, is splendor now.
As time goes by and Life's journey
draws to an end,
We can close our eyes and Let,
Our love be their guide and
friend.
So is Love Err or Divine,
Let your conscience be your
Guide.

Josephine Mitchell
AT LUCY'S HOUSE

To BESSIE JOYNER, who was a contribution of inspiration to my teen age life , And whom I consider to be a dear and cherished friend.

O Lucy, I just love coming to your
house,
It's so warm and friendly there.
Your beautiful spirit that is so
sincere, So full of laughter and cheer.
It fill the rooms with the air of your
presence,
and even leaves comfort in the
temporary of your absence.
So if my many visits have been too
much, It's because of your attention,
of which I am endearingly touched.
You see, In this world of mixed up
pleasures, It is not easy to find a
friend that you can treasure;
Not one who is concerned about the
sincerity of your laughter and tears,
Or who would take the time to
inspire your victories, comfort your
fears.
So I hurry often to be comforted by
your warmth and loving way,
just as one would hurry to a warm
fire on a winter's day.
O Lucy, I just love coming to your
house.

Cynthia L Bailey

Cynthia L Bailey
TWO SPECIAL PEOPLE

This poem is dedicated to Elder and Sister Clarence Duckworth your labor is not in vain . . . I Cor. 15:58

It takes two special people
a husband and his wife,
To come before the throne of God
and break the bread of life.

It takes two special people,
Just to say the words, "I'll go,"
It takes two special people to say
yes,
When at times you want to say no.

It takes two special people to say
When things are not so well,
"It's gonna take all we've got honey,
To save these souls from hell."

It takes two special people Lord,
To pick up their cross,
It takes two special people,
To really count up the cost.

It takes two special people to say
When the day is finally done,
We don't have to wait until the
battle is over for God knows,
we have won!

Susan Book
THE GIFT OF LIFE

I dedicate this poem to Kay Book who gave us all the gift of life.

What is life all about?
It must be love without a doubt.

Because when things are going
rough,
It's love that keeps you really tough.

Love will brighten your darkest day,
And chase your worries all away.

And when you're sick and feeling
blue,
Just a little love will cure that too.

For when our lives come to the end,
Love—is all that matters once again.

So, if you have no gift to give,
Learn to love and forgive.

Douglas McClean
dusty winter rain

as the dusty winter rain
collects the dirt on the window pane
i look to find the meaning of it all
i take a breath, but still can't find
my sanity or peace of mind
but where is my belief now in it all
some-one told me to listen
to the dewdrops as they glisten
but i could only find frost
a frozen heart-beat, beating still
i could only feel the chill
for now all feeling is lost

i could not feel anymore
no telling what is in store
but some-how, now i must
for my feelings i must protect
can not sit back to collect
the winter rain dust

Gradie Isaac Jr
THE MOUNTAIN

I dedicate this poem to my Dad for always being there. And to a good, good, friend Steven Even.

I've stood here so tall and for so very
long
That I've watched the world grow so
strong.
I've seen men come and I've seen
men go
I've seen their machines just grow
and grow and grow.
And I've seen the animals roam here
and there
Now I don't even see the smallest
hare.
I stand here strong and throughout
the years
Wondering what if man was never
here.
Would the world just age not grow as
I have seen
Or would there be some other thing
To replace man and his machines.

Angela Louise Ward
LOVE KEEPS GROWING

I dedicate this poem to my Grandpa Ward, who inspired me to write poetry. I also dedicate this poem to my family, who believes in me.

Love keeps growing,
it blows gently through the breeze,
and sweeps you off your knees.

Sometimes we cry and sometimes
we sigh,
but love keeps growing.

Though there are sometimes you get
upset,
and let your anger go.
You soon make up and say, "I'm
Sorry",
and that's how love can grow.

When you're walking down the
street,
and see someone you'd like to meet.
The magic may happen,
and they might sweep you off your
feet.
But just remember, that love keeps
growing!

Mary Beth Harding
TO MATTHEW'S GRANDMOTHER

To my wonderful mother, Mary Nuetzi and my devoted Aunt Barbara

I was in your womb
For a month times nine . . .
Kicking and splashing! but you kept
me in line.

One November day
I finally arrived,
Screaming and yelling and changing
lives.

You looked at me
(From not far above,)

I looked at you and learned of love.

Childhood memories . . .
Each, one of a kind,
Enough to last forever, all cherished, all mine.

Then suddenly, a child
I was no more . . .
Yet the learning and growing was just like before.

I left your home
But not your heart,
The time had come to make my own start.

This is to say thank-you
For all you've done . . .
I see it all clearly now that I have a son.

You are my mother
As I am my son's . . .
My goal is set high for your grandson.

Lori L Harris
DREAM TEARS
Teardrops forming mirrors
Creating illusions I long to see.
Heartbeat suddenly quickens
As I awake to see who is beside me.

Rain quickly distorts
As it starts tapping at my pane.
Hesitantly I arise
To realize my inner pain.

For you see, only in my dreams
Are you ever truly by my side.
And in the reality of life, I know
I'm the shore waiting for my tide.

Emil de Vernei
ROSES
Because of my fever
You came hurriedly,
Eager
To bring yourself
And roses.
Each a bloodred bud
Bursting with love
And sorrow of decay
Between its petals,
Hidden away.

Three roses beautifully dying
In a burst of ruby bloom,
Will hear a grown man crying
In the gloom of a lonely room.

Dan Schmit
A POET'S WORK
Poets
draw
with words.

Their
pen
unlocks
images
that are yearning
to
come out
into
the light

Kymberli Eason
TOUGH DOG
Bear is my nickname
Maxx is my real name
Owner is G.C. and he is sweet as he can be.
I once lived with him, but then I had to move,
Because he couldn't keep up with the landlady's groove.
I now live with Granny
She's a real good Nanny
Feeds me dinner, lunch, and breakfast every day.
No, No, No, No hay
I mean real good breakfast everyday.
So I can chase the cars
And eat the cats
And even play with her hats.
So get out my face
Homeboy you dig it?
Before I get mad
And put your face into the sand.

Christy Evich
LOVE IS NICE
Love is nice
And you should know
Love is something you cherish
Not something you do
Love is between two people
Love is nice

Dorothy J Sarty-Wamboldt
TO MY SICK CHILD
My Darling:
Yours is the Life I love—not mine;
Yours is the Breath I Breathe—and thine
The very Blood that courses
Thru these weary veins.

Life was a void—a Senseless Thing;
Until you came; and then a Spring
Of Joy and Light and Laughter
Filled my very soul.

A few short years of Bliss—of Health
And all the Gifts a Boy can bring—a wealth
Of Treasured Hours to Cherish,
After the Light is gone.

Now Life holds no Hope—withal,
Unless, thru Death's dark mists, my call
May reach thy tired heart, to stir
The tiny Flame to Life and Love again.

Charlie M Labrador
WHY DO TEARS COME UNBECKONED
Why do tears come unbeckoned
  with thoughts of you,
  like thoughts of you?

Each night I cry myself to exhaustion
and exhausted fall to sleep,
as only the numb may sleep.

Why does not the night remain?

Day comes in electric staccato
and life
and thoughts of you
and tears.

Marie E Gingrich
A FABLE

This poem is dedicated to my husband, Harold

Courtesy and Kindness met on the street one day
And they chatted very softly as passersby went on their way
They smiled at each person as he or she passed by
But no one turned to look at them, nor did they catch their eye.
Everyone was hurrying as on his way he flew,
Each glared at one another and thought—how could I speak to you?
But one gentle little soul braved where angels feared to tread,
Smiling from one another as by her each one sped.
Each busy shopper barely noticed her and none returned her smile,
As she met them in each business hurrying up and down each aisle.
Courtesy and Kindness looked in sadness and shed a tear or two
And turning arm in arm they walked away and faded from the view.

Marc Freedman

Marc Freedman
LIFE FLAME

In Loving Memory of Marcia Wallace

Life is like a flame
Burning eternally
In God's name.

It starts with a spark,
A match made in heaven
Both definitely ignited in the heart.

Paper is the fuel to the flame.
Infancy, a person born to this world,
Arms, legs, fingers, toes and a name.

Twigs then carry on the torch.
Life burns brighter and steadier.

Childhood, simple, like a summer night on the front porch.
Adolescence comes with the bigger pieces of wood burning brighter.
New experiences and emotions
Searching for who they are in one another.

Now the flame burns the logs of adulthood,
Always reaching forward, always reaching higher,
Trying to do better than before whenever they could.

Just when you thought a flame burnt out, left in the dark.
Alas another match,
Another light, another spark.

Joan Marie Pirone
HOLD ON!

To my daughter Kimberly, who has held on to the hope in her trials in life and walks in victory!

Awareness in our world today . . .
Is surrounding us with either a hardened heart, or sensitive way.
Pain grips us as we see the yesterday's fear and trembling of disaster . . .
While strength and courage we are told, we must master.
Tomorrow's ground may change our whole life around . . .
But somehow we must ask, "Where can the peace I so desire be found . . ?"
Holding a hand doesn't necessarily mean a commitment of that one's life . . .
But reach out and touch the one you see struggling and enduring strife.
Accept your defeats with your head up high, as an adult with grace . . .
And not with grief of a child but one who can build a new road to face.
Our hope is to hold on until the race does end, no matter how long . . .
As you see the pain and confusion throughout the world,
Tell yourself to endure and be strong.
For today, is a time we must not falter, but hold on tight . . .
Remember, there is hope in sight . . !

Steven A Seager
TO A GODDESS, OF MY ACQUAINTANCE
Coiffed in silken, summer saffron,
Honed on Zeus' potter's wheel.
Eider soft as Aphrodite,
Rambant orbs which glow surreal
Yearning for subjects devoted,
Lovers with Appollo's zeal,
Lambent memories yet linger,
Envoys her heart must conceal,
Earnest their mortal appeal.

Mary E Pacitto
THE UNION

To my husband and other loved ones, who always demanded, yet never realized, their importance.

Unexpectedly, I saw you, near to midnight by the shore.
Staring solemn through the night sky, penetrating to the core,
Wisdom of uncounted ages,
Gathered by uncounted sages
From the Universal store.

In your naked torso standing,
moonlight glistening on your skin.
Silently I watched reflections of your image ripple in.
Gently they would brush your feet,
then currents pull them out again.
(Like the fragments of a soul
struggling for a place within.)

Reaching then through mystic portals, with profound intensity;
By an ocular adhesion, poured your Spirit into me.
Interlocking, intertwining,
Every part a union finding,
Bound in water's imagery.

Kathy Darlene Capps
THE JOURNEY

In loving memory of my grandmother, Vonnie Odell McLamb.

To service they went on that beautiful morn,
a gentle old lady and a little one.
Had to walk no other way, and rapidly they went along their way,
For services began at noon that day.

To service they went on that beautiful morn,
a gentle old lady and a little one.

Not one complaint from either of them,
for they would be rewarded in the end.
And speaking to their neighbors as they passed,
for that brief moment would have to last.
No time to stop, talk, or play, for they had to be on their way.

To service they went on that beautiful morn,
a gentle old lady and a little one.
They would know when the journey had come to an end, when
They saw the church and entered in.

Roxanne Pribbenow
WEEKDAYS

As I step off the bus onto the sidewalk
My body is jello, my mind, a rock
I look up at that evil fortress
While kids swarm around like roaming corpses
My mind told me, "I have to stay,"
but the rest of me said to get away
As I feared my mind had overruled
so I picked up my courage, and went in the school
It wouldn't be so bad if it weren't for those creatures
that are sometimes commonly called, "Teachers"
Teachers are a rare, but viscous breed
that live on stress, and hot coffee
School is to torment kids in every way
The bell rings . . . the torture's over for another day

Stella Spence
PERFECT PAIR

To my four best friends: My dog Tramp, My Mom, My Dad, and Trina Parker.

We argue about anything;
We argue about everything.

About whose room is cleaner;
About whose teachers are meaner.

We argue about the guys that kiss;
We argue about the friends we miss.

We argue about who has better grades;
We argue about what fashions fade.

Believe-it-or-not, we really care;
We really make the perfect pair.

Sarah B Wright
FIREWORKS

This poem is dedicated to my mother, Tami, with love

Fireworks are bright
Shining in the night
Giving off some light.

Fireworks are dashing
Oh, how they are flashing
Very big and clashing.

Robert W Lockhart
ABOUT SOMEONE I NEVER KNEW

The poem is dedicated to this friend's family.

How does a person write about someone he never knew,
Someone with whom he had shared only a smile or two?
How does a person give meaning, his heart in disarray,
To loss of one known only by a greeting of the day?
How does a person respond to a death so untimely—
Must some things in this life be just compensatory?

What does a person say when he is lifted by one's art,
An expression of emotion only few could impart?
If only he were here and I could tell him this today,
"Perhaps unknown friends are life's greatest loss," I'd say.
Resolution of thought toward him whom I never knew—
The fact he was an artist is my knowing him too.

Lynne E Lichtenberg

Lynne E Lichtenberg
THE DISCOVERY OF LOVE: A SONNET

Para Lynne y con todo mi amor

When we think back to that far shore of time
As first our hearts did feel soft, fertile land,
And yearning, mine sought sure refuge in thine,
While thy hand sought the caress of my hand,
That two narrow paths should have met and merged
Seems now so obvious, so preordained.
Yet, recollection tells that even on the verge
Of our discovery, solitude reigned.
O happy moment as thine eyes met mine!
It seemed we'd known each other before:
Like old friends together, we talked without lines
And shared the New World of what lay in store.
What force does guide the discovery of love?
Mere chance alone or direction above?

Linda B Wright
WHO YOU ARE

When you're feeling down and troubled and your problems seem to grow,
When you're filled with anger, despair or grief and hard luck's the only kind you know,
Just stop and count your blessings or visualize your dreams,
We all have our moments—it's not as hopeless as it seems.

If you ever do stop trying, then hopeless it would be,
For there is no one that can help you when self-caring is the key.
We all can help each other in many ways, it's true;
But if you don't first respect yourself, why should I care for you?

Don't punish yourself for foolish mistakes.
Learn from them, grow with them, that's just what it takes
To improve with age, with dignity and style,
Your wisdom will shine in your eyes, in your smile.

You are a caring person and you spread it all around
But if you save no caring for yourself, you've nowhere to go but down.
You can still give to others, but give only what you can,
'Cause caring for yourself makes all love close at hand.

Keep your spirits high; shoot for the stars.
Follow your dreams; be proud of who you are.
Pat yourself on the back if there's no one there for you.
Be a friend to yourself, for that's something YOU must do.

Jo-Ellen (Joy) Trujillo
A VISION

The sun rose and shone glorious on your breast
I felt Desire and Presumption swell in my chest
So a Prayer seeped past my dry lips
That when there I arrived it would offer me rest
Too long alone, Too far away
I roamed and roamed
Never finding Benevolence
Or warmth in abode
But Enmity? Within You?
Never a thought threatened
Only a Calling flourished thence—
Your Grand Body
To me it beckoned-Return
I must cast this withered seed
Into its Homesoil
"My Great Mountain"
Planting it firm

Robert E Sly
OUR TRUE ROOTS

The current urge to trace our ancestry, and pinpoint what we hold to be
Our native land back in the labyrinth of unrecorded time.
Is surely that inherent homing-call (implanted in us, one and all),
To seek, again, our proper heav'nly Home, which we have lost through Adam's fall.
For we but sojourn in this land, impatient to attain that place sublime,
Reserved for those who love our Lord—our habitation for Eternity.

And while we wait for that sweet Paradise, Christ Jesus softly calls to you.
He's paid the price, and frees you from all sin; from every illness, pain and grief,
If you'll confess your waywardness and ask the Prince of Love to enter in.
For you, alone, decide which path you will be following, which discipline
Shall rule you: the amoral World of self-indulgence and of disbelief,
Or Jesus' loving Hand to daily strengthen, guide and bless you all life through.
Today, in patient Love, He stands outside the portals of your heart, to wait
Until you bid Him enter, for your heart will only open from within!
Accept Him while you can!
Tomorrow may be just one day too late for you!
He'll be your faithful Friend and/insep'rable Companion when you do.
Although your trials and problems will persist, the peace He brings will soon begin
To lift those weary burdens that beset, dismay, frustrate and enervate
The body, mind and soul. All races have one common origin; for man
Descended from created Adam, who, through sin, lost Eden. Yet God's plan
Redeemed, through Christ, all those who love and follow Him! Accept Him while you can!

Shannon M LaPlume
NEW LIFE

To my son Steven

I can sense a life growing within me;
A time of love and great experiences.
If moments are to be so happy why am I so hurt?

A small bundle of joy being created in this womb, but a feeling of sorrow deep in my heart.

The pains that I suffer, does not anyone understand?
Sensations of loneliness are never so grand.
I'll fight through this small friction of time;
In hopes to keep what I call mine;
The love of a man who is ever so kind.

Shannon Alley Strahan
THE PERSONAL CRITIC

It's hard to start fighting, when you feel you can't win;
The battle you wage with the critic within.

He'll haunt you and taunt from somewhere down deep;
He's even so crude He'll intrude on your sleep.

There's just no escaping his critical jab;
When the image you see has no muscle, just flab.

Mirrors don't lie, so there goes your defence;
The critic will show you the obvious hints.

He'll be sure to point out all the fat you can't see;
No one knows it's location any better than he.

He'll show you the clothes that you haven't seen since;
You had to pack them away to make room for your tents.

Don't expect any mercy from this critical creep;
The price you must pay will always be steep.

The time now has come, you must pay for your crime;
It's time to get rid of this critical slime.

So you don't eat for weeks, hoping to gain some control;
Only to find, you're nowhere close to

your goal.

You can give and cry, or tune him out if you dare;
But be sure to use caution, critics never fight fair.

Your progress is slow and you want to give in;
Yet if you choose not to fight, THE CRITIC WILL WIN!!!

Jill Banmiller
THE LAST GRAIN

This poem is dedicated to my past, and to the last grain that changed my life forever.

Love slipped through her fingers
like sand
The hourglass kept falling over
behind her,
everytime she would fix it.
Her heart carelessly ripped from
her body
Time after time.
The sand piled up around her now,
and started to bury her.
Each grain representing each sin,
each mistake, all caused by
her innocent, trusting soul—
Victimized.
All her fault, they said.
She learned her lesson this time.
The sorrow that screamed through
her bruised body was so
apparent.
Until one day it got so loud . . .
the last grain fell.
x—All her fault.

Bob Wendling
THE VALLEY OF DREAMS

The Valley of Dreams unfolds before you,
Now red is black and black is now blue,
This place reeks of death and hopeless despair,
While the daggers of doom reflect hellish glare,
You run to hide from the faceless grim reaper,
Into this dream do you now fall deeper,
Looking on hungrily as you flee through his lair,
He feels every move through the blood thickened air,
Running still faster, you now glimpse a light,
As the reaper pursues you through the mist-laden night,
Quickly drawing nearer to God's light of day,
The sweat drips off of you as you silently pray,

And as if from heaven, a ladder appears,
With rungs made of bones, but you stifle your fears,
You ascend this death ladder to escape evil fate,
You think that you're free, but you've taken the bait!
A scream of terror bursts forth from your lungs,
As the reaper waits for you at the top of the rungs,
His face is now finally revealed to your eyes,
A leering red skull in Satanic disguise,
He draws back in laughter as in horror you freeze,
While his sickle is gleaming in the death-scented breeze,
He hacks and he slashes through the rungs made of bone,
So down through the darkness your body is thrown,
And then as you utter your last tortured screams,
You awaken, and leave the dreaded Valley of Dreams!

Patti Arvidson-Wright
DISTANT SHORE

Distant Shore is dedicated to the man who is "My Music" and for whom it was originally written, Jefferson LaSala Harman; also my "Nan", and Mom & Dad, my constant inspirations and Best Friends.

United, Together, Forever, Through Time . . .
Didn't think that we would ever see
The end of You and I.
The love we knew, and how
it grew . . .
Through the years and through time.
All the pain was worth all the gain
And now you've gone away.

Laughter, Ever After, Castles in the Sand . . .
Reaching out to touch your hand,
Running scared . . . Alone.
Remembering how you touched my soul,
Gave me life . . . Made me whole.
Through the storm, You kept me warm,
And now you've gone away.

I'm sorry it's not working out
anymore. . .
It's time for you to walk out, and
close another door.
It's not that I don't love you
anymore . . .
Maybe some other time . . .
On a Distant Shore.

Well, I'll love you forever . . .
Even though we're not
together . . .

Tammy M Willis
A KISS

A kiss is all I ask.
A kiss.
Nothing more.

As gentle as the butterflies wings,
On the wind.
A kiss.

As warm as a babe's breath,
In his sleep.
A kiss

As sweet as the God's ambrosia,
Forbidden fruitfulness.
A kiss.

As soft as a mother's breast,
To her child.
A kiss.

As powerful as the oceans,
In a storm.
A kiss.

This is all I ask of you.
No more, no less.
A single kiss.

Jeff S Evans
I SEE A CAR

There is a car that's fat,
Being driven by a man with a big top hat.
There is a car that's long and black,
It's got a window patched with a plastic sack.
There goes a car that's very junky.
It's got a bumper that's really clunky.
I see a car that's covered with rust.
It has a fender that says, 'California or bust'.

I see a car. It has a ragtop,
But it's being followed by a cop.
I see a car. It's an econobox,
And on the bumper is an old pair of socks.

Geraldine Williams
STAR

This poem is dedicated to Pretty Tom the Star in my LIfe.

I'll be your Little Rose,
If you will be my Star.
I'll belong to only you.
No matter where you are.

I'll be your Little Rose,
So Loving and so Sweet.
With Petals so Soft and Velvety,
Waiting Just to Please.

Pretty Tom! be my Star.
You're the man I've been waiting for,
I fell in Love with what you
Represent.
I'll be your Rose, if you'll Consent.

Michele A Kosko
RICK

I dedicate this poem to my brother who had such a short time on earth; and to my husband for his encouragement.

Rick resting in peace; a peace much needed for quite some time.
To hear the footsteps passing; a good memory to always remember.
The bad times to be forgotten; only in the past; did they seem really so so bad?
A world falling apart; for the people there find it hard to withstand the pressure it brings.
Family and friends all around; even though they're not there; are always there within a grasp.
Hang onto that peace; a much needed peace; no more pain and no more hurt.
With a gentle love in the passing of time.
RICK is resting in peace.

Carl A Lahetta
THE POTTER'S STUDIO

We are the clay, and thou our Potter; and all of us are the work of thy hand. Isaiah 64:8

Quiet stillness in the soul.
Contemplation and simple solitude.

Listening with quiet anticipation.

Meeting with the Potter
one on one

Waiting to be shaped in
His studio.

Kathy Donovan
THE WIND'S MISCHIEF

Wind, Mighty wind
Why must thee gust?
For thee falls the trees,
crops, and cottages
With one mighty
gust.
Thee rents destruction on
us all
As if we are ever
naughty
And played tricks on
thee,
We mean thee no
harm
But whatever we
do,
Thee always gets the
brunt of it.

Angela Browne

Angela Browne
MARRIAGE

To my Husband, Noel With whom I share these memories forever.

The uniting of two, to become one
on that specially chosen day of the
year
The Joy of ones losing a Son
and the shedding of a Mother's tear

As parents look on with pride
and think back to their special day
The Mothers remember themselves
as a Bride
While the Fathers are exhilarated and
Gay

The Love that began so innocently
that overcame life's trials and
hardships
will be made Just and Heavenly
the end of an enduring courtship

The exchanging of vows and rings,
that signify a bind
and receiving of Prayers and
Blessings
with thoughts of understanding and
Love in mind
A church so bright with all its
colorful trimmings

The Minister says, "You may kiss
your Bride",
The veil is so gracefully lifted
Those shy and embarrassed, duck
and hide
Whilst in silence the curious have
shifted
Now in the eyes of God, the two are
one, A new life has just
begun . . .

Joyce Escott Buhler
CHRIST-CHILD
Child of the morning, sing me your song.
Let me hear words of hope the day long.
Teach me to seek truth and steer me from wrong.
Child of the morning, let me belong.

Child of the sunshine, touch me with light.
Make of my life an example of right.
Show me the vision that I may invite.
Child of the sunshine, give me your sight.

Child of the evening, lead me in prayer.
Let me hear sweet heavenly voices out there.
Help me to carry the burdens I bear.
Child of the evening, remind me you care.

Child of the moonlight, while I slumber deep,
Bring to my soul a peace I can keep.
During the darkness don't let me weep.
Child of the moonlight, guard me in sleep.

Earl Villers
EARLY ARRIVAL
Our January weather was so mild,
I trudged along my bluebird trail
With eye and ear in tune with the wild
While house cleaning on a major scale.

When winter sun revealed a splash
Of brilliant blue on feathered wing,
My mind recorded every flash
And leaped ahead to thoughts of spring.

Jennifer Scibek
FROST-COVERED WINDOWS
Frost covers the windows,
And a chill runs through my soul.
The howling wind reminds me
In my own way I'm all alone.

I contemplate returning to my home,
But that would be a crime;
For home is merely a jailcell
That marks the passage of time.

The fire glows before me
As I stare ahead, into space
And the chill wind that surrounds my home
Reminds me of the human race.

For men have cold, cold hearts, I know,
Against what they wish not to see.
And one thing they don't want to face
Is the insecurity embodied in me.

The sun will rise in the morning
And try to dispel the cold,
But the frost that covers the windows
Also covers men's souls.

Ruth G Yarbrough
CHANGES
We well remember such a time when writing poetry was a sign
One knew how best to make words rhyme and count the meters in a line.
But times and poems have changed.

No longer do we need to use a rhyming word, nor yet refuse
All other words, and we may lose the meter count and use a ruse.
This makes them come out right.

Today one only needs a pen and piece of paper to begin
With senseless words that sometimes win the highest praise of noted men.
Poetry's what they call it.

J. Kilmer wrote some lines, you see, that seem to live on endlessly
And thrill the soul majestically with simple words about a tree.
We all remember that.

There must still be some folks like me, who know that God can make a tree
And surely they would like to see a poem as plain as A-B-C.
So here it is, my friend.

Roy L Parker
CAST A SHADOW

For little Roy and Debbie with all my love

Cast a Shadow in the rain,
Feel your life now full of pain.
Your heart is heavy and so blue,
You don't know what you should do.

Cast a Shadow in the wind,
Your life right now must start again.
She broke your heart, now she's gone,
You're left here all alone.

She was a lover and a friend,
I loved her so, right to the end.
Oh, how I miss her, yes I do,
Her lips as soft as morning dew.

Cast a Shadow in the sun,
Remember the times and all the fun.
See her smiling in your mind,
She was sweet and oh so kind.

So Cast a Shadow on my dreams,
Life goes on, or so it seems.
Cast a Shadow on my soul,
Her love again, I'll never know.

Tobyn DeMarco
SOME KIND OF OCTOBER OF THE YEAR
At that time when we put down our guard and let enter this season,
Fulfilled, spiced, and anticipatory of that Death—
Hibernating sap—discoloured panorama of leaves—
Reflection of past loves swarms the Honeyed pensiveness we provide in the
Gradual cooling air, day breeze, and glary sun—
And we dress ourselves in wools of passionless passion
Grasping for the least of what we expect to achieve or gain, and
Laughing, if you will, on the open field
Circumnavigated by Friedrich's withering phallic trees.

We all expire breath in this season to
Suck in Death and relive thrice the phoenix of our passions,
Steadily, calmed breathing, inhaling of decomposing elements,
Yet fertilizer, comes the sowing and growing.
Aloof and discarded I present this plea
Which is eaten by the migratory flocks of this season—
To South they fly, where they will find their passion.

Grace Reynolds
A DEDICATED REGISTERED NURSE
So many many years ago I had a calling
To the nursing profession so challenging and rewarding.
My life has been so happy since then
I am now a dedicated R.N.

I am retired from the nursing profession
A profession I dearly loved,
For fifty-three years
I have faithfully served.

Through all the years
My God has richly blessed,
Me with good health and much happiness.

I have no regrets of my past good deeds
Administering and meeting my patients needs.
I have faithfully sacrificed my time
My talent and even my life.
I am thankful for every kind word I have spoken
And for every good deed I have done.
I am now leaving my profession
With a job well done.

Michael G Ferguson
WHEN OUR DEEP, SECURE RIVER FREEZES
When our deep, secure river freezes
Who sends the thawing, balmy breezes?

When our eye narrows at those who displease us
From where cometh the comfort to appease us?

When the rabid dog of discontent trees us
Who comes by and gently frees us?

When our brow is replete with creases
Who soothes it with the salve that eases?

When the bright, warm glow suddenly ceases
Who in the darkened void is able to see us?

Who is the hero in this mystery thesis?
Only one measures up—our dear, sweet Jesus!

Deborah M Galvin
WHAT'S THE DIFFERENCE BETWEEN YOU & ME

To my sweet William

What's the difference between me and you?
Walls built in our mind to keep out the unknown.
No time to speak the unspoken;
Too many things to do in our little worlds.

So much to perceive and understand
As we go our separate ways
Thinking that believing
Will answer all we dare not ask;
Exploring together
We could touch upon our commonness.

In pain we go on . . .
Days pass;
People die . . .
And babies cry.

We set with the sun
Never knowing that
We are one in the same.
Night closes in . . .
Nothing gained without effort,
Answers come only with questions.

Birds sing their story
To every new awakening;
We hear them not in all our haste;
Shunning the wings of truth
On which we could fly
Freely to the rising.

Stars beckon us in their stillness . . .
Their brilliance holding secrets
Our little worlds could not accept
Without walls of ignorance crashing down.

Let us unfold to all the freshness
The universe holds for us.
Let us be open to receive
Its offerings
So as to grow
Like the flower
That anxiously accepts
All the elements
Though she knows
The sun may burn her and
The rain may beat her . . .
How can she grow without them.

We must rise together
As all of nature
Grows together . . .
And flow together
Into the unknown.

Patrick Harker

Patrick Harker
DEATH STAR

Dedicated to Miller, the real king of beers

Driving,
Across the sun bleached deserts
To know where, not a soul to be found
Mans' pollution, brought him prosecution
To the underground
To live, you must drive
You must fight to survive
Green fields are now dust
No more black fuel
Left the machines to rust
Standing in darkness, in a water line
Welcome back, to the dark age
It's 1999
As I walk across the sand
Watching how the sun burns up the land
Believing no more lies, that I will be saved
I, the scavenger in the night
Crawls back to his cave.
Death Star

Cynthia Hulshizer
HOOT OWL
There is a hoot owl echoing some new song.
Harmonious chirping growing ever

strong.
Open eyed soul voyaguer seeking to find
one full of kindness and gentle peace of mind.
Flight unrestricted—Soaring above
moving toward the leading of Love.
Looking down through darkness
Cooing at the madness till dawn.
If ever you should sense him
or hear the faintest call—
Turn to him and face a glory
that can't be known to all.
Mirror images translate meaning
deep within his eyes.
Wings stretched encircling dark,
yet somehow lightened skies.
Lightened up in Goodness.
Influence on us all.
Find a Hoot Owl before the fall.

Robert James Jablonski
A NATURAL BORN OUTLAW

To my Family, my Friends and Those Who Dare to Care!

He was a natural born outlaw
travelin a dusty road
Who tried to live with society but
couldn't hack the load.
He used to be a good Ol' Boy said his prayers every day
But somehow or other just kinda lost his way.

There was this local Sheriff who sent his Posse out one day
To slap that boy in leg irons and lock his tail away.
They caught him at his ex-wife's house and the bullets began to fly
And he knew as sure as shootin they were all gonna die.

He didn't want his family hurt so he headed for the door
But just as he opened it he got plugged by a '44.
Layin there a die'n couldn't think of much to say
Sept to his little boy, he said son,
don't follow in my way
Cause when you're an outlaw
someday you're gonna pay.

He was raised in the backwoods by
an old Grizzly bear
He had a double set of jaw teeth and
a double coat of hair;
He had a cast iron stomach and toted
a blue steel rod
He was a hard drinkin—bad
tempered outlaw by God—
Natural born-Outlaw;
Who used to be a good Ol' Boy that
said his prayers every day
But somehow or other, just kinda
lost his way.

Carol Arteaga
THE ROSE

The rose of velvet red he gave
My heart and soul he did enslave
Its petals red and scented sweet
Is beauty for all, whose eyes do meet
All the riches, the world does hold
Cannot compare with my one red rose

Willie Fernandez Hardy
FREE . . .

I stood before a man that was dressed, in black, wondering should I turn Back.

Dressed all in white from my head to my toe.
I really didn't know which way I should go.

Just that a promise, "A promise" would be made this day, one that myself should never break.

With a ring, and kiss I must never resist the hands that held my life in great risk, Taken from the BIBLE the words that were said. I still found myself alone in bed, with visions of evil flashing through my head.

I prayed to GOD to let me unwed".
A year, or two later while sitting on a high stand I promise myself that I would never again be as bold, as one would be, as to reach for love, and never be free.

Anne E Boyd
MY FRIEND

"In Memory of Stacey Morhaim, Victim of a Drunk Driver, January 15, 1986" All My Love

My Friend you were one of the greatest I knew;
I will always treasure the memories of you,
When you left I was very depressed;
But I understand the Lord took you to rest,
I miss you so much I wish you were here;
But one day I will be with you there,
Until that day I love you My Friend;
And I wish it had never come to an end.

Patricia Spillman Adcock
THE JEWELS OF THE MORNING

Oh, the beauty of the morning when I first arise,
The beauty of the morning is like jewels to my eyes.

The diamonds of dew drops on the emerald green grass reflect like opals on a lake of glass.

The pearly clouds float slowly by across the sapphire blue sky.

The golden sun casts a warm glow, and brings out the beauty of the jewels below.

Jane Carmer
WHAT IS A FRIEND?

What is a friend?
A friend is someone who will stick by you
From beginning to end
No matter what you do . . .

They will share all your secrets and fears
Through good times and bad
They are with you whether smiles or tears
Happy or sad.

Mary E Anderson
TRUE FRIEND

Dedicated to Eddie Lou Cole for my first chance at poetry

What is a friend? You know, the real true friend?
A friend that knows you, and there's no pretend,
The friend that down deep, really cares, what happens to you,
They know without your saying,
when you're happy or blue.

They can know your thoughts,
ambitions, goals and such,
If asked, this friend knows you,
sometimes a little too much.
They know when you're hurt, or
when you're upset,
Disagree with love, and yet you can
still, forgive and forget.

They know before you speak, your every thought,
And know each other flaws,
weaknesses, even when you've fought.
But to put friendship up in front, and make it stay,
Is what it's all about, friends were meant, to stay that way.

They hurt inside, when you're hurting, and yet,
About their own feelings, for a time they forget.
They let, your feelings come first,
way before theirs,
Whether the hour, or how long, to wipe away the tears.

These sort of people, are very far and between,.
There's very few people, like this in the world I've seen,
So you're the friend, I want to keep and cherish,
Because the world would have no love, if our friendship should perish.

Margaret Gallimore
SOLITUDE

This poem is dedicated to the healing of humanity and world peace.

Oh this sound of silence that falls upon my ear
In this place of peacefulness my soul speaks loud and clear.
Let this harmony prevail that I may always see
The clear cold light of dawning where shadows seem to be.

May the words now spoken down deep within my heart
Bring a vision full of truth and wisdom to impart,
And may the love I feel inside as understanding grow
To heal all weary souls with warmth and set their hearts aglow,
And may I live a life that shows a path for other feet
To learn to walk in harmony and fill the world with peace.

Mary Arpante
HAPPY THANKSGIVING

I dedicate this poem to my daughters, Stephanie, Eugenia & Genevra and son-in-law Richard, to be extended to our family & friends for whom we create together Thanksgiving daily.

I share this time of year to say hello
I share this time of year to extend the love I feel in our friendship
I share this time of year to reflect on the special you
I share this time of year in memory of the occasions we laughed and had fun
I share this time of year to reflect how good it feels to experience life
I share this time of year to acknowledge the difference you have made in my life
I share this time of year to recall the trust of life events we opened to
I share this time of year to dedicate words of inspiration exchanged
I share this time of year to watch the leaves as they leave their "home" to return in the Spring
I share this time of year to remember God's command to love one another
I share this time of year in gratitude of blessings received
I share this time of year with you—all that I am—all that I am becoming to be and all that we are together.

In love eternal
Mary

Donald French
THE CLOCK ON THE WALL

When I wake up in the night
There is no sound at all
But the little clock
Hanging on the wall
It works so hard
Both night and day
Busy as a beaver
Ticking time away
As I lay there thinking
I can see it all
Just keep on ticking
Like the clock on the wall
It may be old
Or large or small
Still it is faithful
Hanging there on the wall
Life takes on new meaning
Riches aren't important at all
I am now alone with my maker
And the clock on the wall
I should always look ahead
Never backward at all
And never worry about the future
Like the clock on the wall

Debbie Brockett
WITHIN

To my friend Lyne; who got me started on my journey within.

There is a light within us all.
There is inner peace within us all.
There is happiness within us all.
There is a part of God within us all.
There is unconditional love within us all.
We have tremendous power within us all.
To reach this wonderfulness; we take a journey inside ourselves.
We must look deep inside ourselves & face the things that bother us.
We learn to embrace & understand these things
From this we learn to accept & love ourselves & those around us.
We learn to listen to our inner self.
It will guide us to the light, the love, to God to peace, to the happiness we all strive for.
This great wonderful power is within us ALL.

D E Wolfe
RAMBOY

For Greg

Almond eyes peer from behind
magic marker camouflage
Tongue wagging like a
thirsty trench fighter

Limbs as fast as his tongue

from morning till night
A hundred miles an hour

The house is struck
toys thrown about
A war zone of cars and balls
and dolls and Ghostbusters

A soldier too tired
to reconstruct the
ravaged carpet side
Will peace ever come
to this livingroom region?

At last, the area is secured
The warrior has bugged-out
civilians find time for R & R
Prepare for tomorrows coming
assault.

Dawn Evelyn Walker
PLEASANT TORTURE

This poem is dedicated to the imaginary prince I'll dream of forever.

When I think of you,
I can feel the excitement running
through me,
as if your hands had touched me
once again.

This feeling is so irresistible,
but I am only allowed to dream of
you.
I dream of this passion without an
end.

Lying alone,
my heart filled with anxiety out of
control,
knowing I might never have you is
so unfair.

I want you so badly, touching me,
holding me,
running your hands through my hair.

Just thinking of your kiss on my lips
brings a sweet sensation I can not
hide.

Just remembering the sound of your
voice
makes my heart sink, oh, so deeply
inside.

Just dreaming of you is such a
pleasant torture,
I can't imagine how it would be if
you were here.

And if I never see you again my
prince,
These dreams of Pleasant
Torture, . . . I'll dream forever, I fear.

Georgianna M Rosser
A NEW TOMORROW

To my beloved Lewis, who took the sun's warmth, music, laughter and all of the sweet tender moments of life with him when his walk through this world was over.

Standing by my window, I felt the
cold touch of the black velvet night
and dreaded the morrow;
But as it slowly slipped into my
room, I could see that it shared my
sorrow.
Dark sullen clouds, heavy with
Winter's grief wept, cold icy tears;
Freezing the warmth of what I
thought had been happy yesteryears.
The bright, warm, glowing sun in the
gloom, shamefully hid its face;
And like sad, bent but proud old
ladies, the trees stood dressed in icy
lace.
My poor broken heart cried out in
hurt anger at the swollen skies;
As I felt the bitter, burning, accusing
tears filling my eyes.

You had taken my heart, my love,
my life, my very soul;
I was yours so completely, and so
completely under your control.
Foolishly, I thought we had a love so
beautiful, so fresh, so full of Spring;
But you left and took the warmth and
beauty, now the birds won't even
sing.
Now my world, like my heart, both
once warm and bright, is icy cold and
gray;
Loneliness sleeps with me in the
night, and sadness is my burden of
the day.
But my cruel darling, though you
may have given me only heartache
and pain;
I can see a break in the clouds so
bleak and hear a promise whispered
in the frozen rain.
Somewhere in time there is tender
true love to have and keep, not just
borrow;
There will be a warm new sun, fresh
new Spring, birds to sing, a new
tomorrow.

Karen Mabry
BOTH TODAY
Pens, People,
Kind of alike
in their own certain way.

Both can be forgotten,
left alone,
in an alley or a brand new place.

Both can leave marks
that can't be traced
or erased.

Both can be cared for,
created,
and can change.

But mostly,
Pens, People,
both needed
in the world today.

Callie Harris Collins
THOSE FEROCIOUS COAT HANGERS
Have you ever had an encounter
With a bunch of vicious coat hangers
Each time you deal with them
You realize that your life is in danger

Reaching in the closet to get one
little hanger
It had to reach back and grab hold of
his brother
Who enlisted the help of all of his
family
That ganged upon me including the
mother

In a split second there was a mad
scramble
That I tried to end by slamming the
door
To my surprise the door wouldn't
close
For some of the imps had fallen to
the floor

They launched their attack by
grabbing my sweater
And then they hung onto all of my
cuffs
Those that fell to the floor really had
it together
They got both of my feet tied up in a
scuff

I said this is it there's too many
hangers
I had no alternative but to send some
away
But getting rid of them caused me so
much trouble
This horrible encounter really
darkened my day

In another closet I pushed them all
together
Trying to lift them out found some
turned the wrong way
I wondered then who could have
been so stupid
But it might have been me so what
could I say

I stacked them all up turning them all
the same way
Getting rid of them made me beam
with a flare
With some under my arm and some
in my hand
Gleaming with delight I started down
the stairs

But just when I thought my problem
was over
Three steps from the bottom one
made a break for it
Trying to pick it up triggered such a
disaster
That those in my arms just went into
a fit

Sitting on the step trying to figure it
all out
Feet tangled up in hangers everywhere
The inventor of hangers really did a
noble deed
And I'll bet he ended up without
even a care

J O Vaughn

J O Vaughn
HICKORY TREE

To John and Etha, with love.

I dreamed I saw a hickory tree—
standing tall and blowing free.
Defying man, scuffing storm—
with no shelter from their harm,
And all its limbs were strong and
wide—behind its trunk a bear could
hide,
All its leaves seemed to glisten—
and hum in the breeze if you stopped
to listen,
And underneath it on the ground—a
little dead bird was found,
Some lovers names were gently
carved—right above where he had
starved,
I wonder if I returned today—
I'd find that tree the same old way,
Or would it be not quite as tall—
because I'm now not quite so small.

Sophie Marie Tuckey
SLEEPLESS NIGHTS
Sleepless nights how long the hours,
Seeming endlessly to last,
Till another day is dawning,
And the night has passed.

Solitude, I have aplenty,
Time to do so many things,
Which the day with all its problems,
Never with it brings.

Time to dream and time to plan,
Time to write some poetry,
Writing letters to my friends,
Studying Philosophy.

Considering the past and future,
Just one more thing I got to mention,
If you're looking for self knowledge,
You find it without contention.

When the sun climbs the horizon,
And a brand new day is born,
I give thanks to my Creator,
For another, perfect morn.

Lori Lee Power
RAIN
Your touch is like a silken glove
  woven oh, so fine
Sometimes my thoughts, like a
sylvan fawn
  run rampant thru my mind
Your voice is like a soothing oil
  easing all my pain
You go away, and then return
  like the calm.
  the soothing
  rain

Jan Anderson
DEAREST LORD
LORD, we thank you for all the
Blessings
You give us from time to time,
We need you, LORD, we love you,
LORD,
Without you we couldn't survive.

You control our very lives, Dear
LORD,
Every hour of every day.
We count on you in all we do,
It will always be that way.

Sometimes we forget to say our
prayers,
But you always forgive us our sins.
You give us your shoulder to cry on,
With you we will always win.

I wish more people would realize
That Jesus is the ONLY way.
He gave his life for you and me,
So we could gain Heaven some day.

Please turn to HIM in your times of
need,
HE will NEVER let you down.
HE is our King, our own true GOD,
HE alone wears the crown.

Melanie S Bishop
THE WIND

I dedicate this poem to Edna Cowley, my grandmother who has been my friend as I grow.

The wind blew;
My skirt flapped against my legs.

As I walked through the field;
My hair whipped in the wind.

I walked slowly as the wind blew in
my face—
The grass tickled my ankles.

I was getting closer now—
To the house.

As I got even closer,
The wind died down.

I walked into the house—
Nobody was home.

I was scared—
The wind rattled the screen door.

Somebody knocked;
I went and looked through the hole.

It was my best friend;
I let her in—
Then felt better.

Anne Green
TO MOM AND DAD
We are rich
As we share the gift
You gave each of us—your sons.

You, quietly, through the years,
Were the model for us.
We received your gift.

Now, in turn we are able to give,
To our families, the gift
You so generously gave.

This gift, having originated
From a loving farm home,
Encourages each family to take risks.

This gift has no price
But nurtures, in each family
A sense of pride and duty.

This gift though invisible
Encourages, in each family,
A respect and patience for others.

This gift, while silent
Teaches, each family,
The art of listening.

This gift, while silent
Teaches, each family,
The art of listening.

This gift, always present
Helps each family adopt
A sense of humor.

This gift, is endless
For it passes
From generation to generation.

We are rich
As we share the gift
You gave each of us—your sons.

Heather Brandt
BLUE ROSES
Red is the color
Of roses that love.
Flowers of death
Are white as a dove.
Yellow-painted roses
Show friendships run deep.
But blue is the color
Of lovers that weep.

Milton V Moore
SPIRIT OF WIND AND STEEL
Spokes of spider frame, skimming the transient earth.
Freedom's smile of defiance, beer shared, gall and mirth.
The love of a fight, ears perked to a fast buck.
Living life with all one's strength, steadfast, wearing one's luck.
Helping others when able, if that motorcyclist's soul is not lost.
Saving a friend, who might be called dog, no matter what the cost.
In a world of hurry, turmoil, and care—
All who see, but are not a part of, stand and stare.

Thomas Schulte
THE CANDLE

For my Mother, without whom this candle would never have been set alight.

A soft glow that's placed in a window in regard to an early
arrival of dusk.
A candle
Sitting sheltered behind a pane of glass—
As fragile a life lived;
To have but a simple breeze extinguish existence.

A candle can be as a soul
endangered by the raindrop from above
or the sometimes overwhelming odds of life itself.

The flame dims to a mere flutter
against the built up congestion that arises around itself as its existence continues stubbornly onward.
Like a pressure release,
The emotion God has given us
in itself separates us and gives us identity

Is it so foolish a thing
to cry?

The candle
drips its wax over the edge
and down
allowing it to shine brightly
once again.

Amy Beth Howe
CHANGING
Before I walk out that door . . .

Did we ever know just where the road lies?
Or grasp the gold ring in the maze of tin cans?
Were your dreams focused on me
or my reflection in the mirror?

The weeds worked themselves up through the concrete.

I cannot stop the door approaching.
Those blackened coals are my life, yesterday.
Possibly . . . I can salvage the remnants of something.

Alone.

Jean T Litzenberg
TO JEAN

Dedicated to the memory of my father, Donald McCallum the author

At my first look, you held my eye.
You fired my heart with pride and joy.
An infant's stare forged such a tie.
I forgot I'd hoped you'd be a boy.

The years flew fast and faster still,
Time for man has never stood.
You grew so fast in stature 'til
You blossomed forth to Woman-hood.

Mental pictures as you've grown
My mind's eye was quick to note,
An album of my very own.
A miser's hoard, on which to gloat.

For faster than the fleeting hour,
I can recall them any day.
My pleasure and my "Bon Succour."
"Jean! You've never been away."

Monica C Zuniga
DO YOU KNOW?

To my parents for having faith in me. To Connie and Cristy for always being there, to Luis and Yolly as well. I LOVE YOU ALL!!!

Do you know, is what i ask
each time i look into your eyes,
i see someone who cares,
someone who can love me
just as i can love them.
Do you know, is the greatest question
in my mind. Can you tell me
what
you feel, can you tell me who
you love?
Do you know, each time i look into your eyes,
that i'm in love with you.
and only you?
Do you know, I long to be by your side,
to feel your body close to mine.
To feel your tender touch. To
hear those
sweet words I long to hear.
Do you know, Just how i
feel
Do you know,
I LOVE YOU!!

Traci Weller
ALONE

For my dear father, Gary Thomas Weller

We did everything together, my daughter and I,
Racing down the slopes, flames on our heels,
Fireballs out of hell, demons of the hill.
One in mind, one in spirit
We were best friends,
she and I.

Now a black void, I aimlessly
Wander through life, uncaring.
The sun hides behind the clouds
Wanting to come out, but
trapped inside.
Tears flow from my face, dew from morning leaves.

Darkness clutches my heart, ripping
As the eagle feasts on its prey.
Though the clouds will again divide
And the sun's light nourish
My baby is gone and I miss her.

I am alone.

Carmen Zoratto
FORGIVENESS

To the man I love always. John, you're the best.

Some people say we're not good for each other.
But to me they're only a bother.
We may argue and fight, but we love and honour, Right?!
'Cause you mean so much to me.
Your wife I want to be.
And that's the way love remains,
because with you it never rains.
I hate it when we're mad, It always makes me sad.
I love it when we kiss, When you're not here, it's you I miss.
'Cause you are the one I love, You are as beautiful as a dove.
Your life I want to share, Out of everyone, it's you that I care.
I'm writing this from the heart, Of me you are a part.
So here this comes to an end. I beg you, "Can we mend."

Claude Callis
JUST FOR YOU—STACEY

To Stacey Colleen Callis for Friendship—for Life—for Love

Just for You I write this poem,
You know who You are—
The only One I dream of;
You're all I am so far!

Just for You I feel my Heartbeat!
Just for You I feel so warm—
In my deepest loving moment
Your Image my mind does form!

Then all my sad Emotions
Float away beyond the sky—
And I dream of nothing fonder
Than Your Beauty to my Eye!

And Your Love, my Love, I cherish
The Life I feel for You—
And the Presence of my Existence:
Is Stacey!—in my View!

Georgia Lee Mitchell
THE LITTLE CARES THAT FRETTED ME

Dedicated to my mother Pauline Georgia Nolan Crider for her aesthetic values

The little cares that fretted me
I lost them yesterday,
Among the singing of the trees
Among the clouds at bay

The foolish fears of what might pass
I cast them all away,
Among the clover-scented grass
Among the winds at play

The inspiration nature gives
Fulfills the need in man,
For he lives not as he wishes to live
But, rather as he can.

Mary Anne Webster
IMMORTAL ME

Dedicated—To The Lemurian Fellowship

A Mortal, is a man,
Who lives, and lives, and lives;
And then takes his life along,
And dies, and dies, and dies,
Ten thousand times.

But, Immortal Me,

I take my life along,
And die and live, die and live,
And die and live Again.

George Christon
WHERE THE REINDEER DIE

Dedicated to Jennifer Alma Fonseca

Winter land of snow, white lightening world
Where the reindeer die, is not so far away.
Snowflakes mines shimmer iridescent light
Waltzing through the air, diamonds in mid-flight.

Slipping, sliding, bathed in snow
Blissfilled winds, a children's show.
Some will fly in leaps and bounds,
Some close eyes and dream of crowns,
As clear as breath wrapped round their reindeer heads.

Where the reindeer die is not so far away.
The blanketed sky will part, the sleepless sun will bay.

Trapsing the fjord to the very last
Beat of their reindeer hearts.
Gracefully
Falling onto a pillow of snow,

waiting to
Catch them the way a mother knows.

They lie with tearfilled eyes raised toward
Sky drenched in winter's unspoken cry.
For now the time has come to
Dance the Christmas dance.

Where the reindeer die, O where the
Reindeer die is not so far away.

Marjorie Kingston Skusa
BOLD FACTS
The Walrus said, as he swam away,
"Wherever I go, the tides will sway,
For I have lived a life that's been
So bold you conldn't comprehend,
The depths to which a Walrus may
Sink to fight another day."

"That's really bold, I do admit,"
The great Bear said, "From where I sit,
It does appear that you believe
A Myth that I cannot perceive;
For who, in this white world, would dare
To doubt the rule of the Polar Bear?"

The Seal said, "Just to stay alive,
To swim and play and just survive,
With tusks and skins so very rare,
With hunters roaming everywhere,
There isn't much that I can say:
Except to thank God for today!"

D Marie Morris
OF HEART AND SOUL
Dearest mate of heart and soul, how I love thee so.
The bonds of our hearts are forever as one.
How much I love thee, The boundary of stars can not contain.

Dearest mate of heart and soul how I miss thee so.
The bonds of our hearts are stretched often; but, shall never tear.
How much do I miss thee? The emptiness within can not be filled, but, with thy presence.

Dearest mate of heart and soul
Our love runs deep and shall carry us through roughest waters
and calmest seas, forever buoyant.

Dearest mate my love is with thee always.

Wes Kroondyk
CAN'T PLAY SOLDIER ANYMORE
VIETNAM 4/16/69

To those who died many thousands of miles from home.

I hate to see my youth become complete,
Despising every day that steals my youth away.
I loved those games we played on Ballard Street—
That world of city blocks, controlled by kitchen clocks.

With less imagination, one forgets
The dreamy life of youth, unfettered to the truth.
From digging in the dirt to "take your debts!",
We acted out the roles, untroubled by their goals.

I won't deny the swift anxieties—
The expectations lost, the hopes not worth their cost.
Yet, those despairs were brief realities;
Another hope would dawn before the tears were gone.

"Yes, now it's overwith," I tell myself;
The years have closed a door to worlds I knew before,
And I must place the past upon the shelf.
Amidst a jungle war,
I can't play soldier anymore.

Edward A Heller
HELPLESSNESS

Dedicated to my daughter Deena who was there with me, who always encouraged me and was a friend as well as a daughter.

I could have fought with Crazy Horse
Or held the Zeider Zee
I could have swum the Hellespont
Or rode with General Lee.
There was nothing I couldn't do
If I really wanted to.
But now
The woman I love
Is being destroyed
By dreaded schizophrenia
And all I can do
Is watch
and stare
and cry.

Kristy Kinion
GOD'S LOVE

This is dedicated to some special friends, Russ Kinion and Bill McMullen.

Way out in that wondrous night
all stars shine brighter than bright
all those stars are big and odd
those were created by none other than God

When there comes a time when you don't understand
just reach out and grab that big, friendly hand
God will take you up, up into that sky
then you'll wonder "Why me God, why?"

Because you're just as special as any other man
all you need to know is that you really can
so if you get confused just remember the man
who gave you the faith and told you "you can!"

Denona Chaquel Conley
A SIMPLE TEAR

To my family and friends who have given me support and a listening ear. God bless you and I love you!

The sun does protest
As time flies
I do my best
To keep my mind from the skies
The cool winds scream past my ears
The trees whisper to me gently and I hear
Love is a dream that often comes true
When my love is directed to you
I see you now
As I've never seen you before
My heart flutters
As you open the door
Hoping you'll stay
But to my dismay
You walk right by
Without saying Hi!
So, after all that's been said
And all that you've read
I walk away
With nothing left to say
No more crying
Because I'm not dying
Not over you,
But if only you knew.

Elspeth Crebassa
SNOWFALL
It is snowing.
The crystals fall
Floating slowly
Blanketing ground
With a cover
of heavy snow.

The bare trees stand
Their naked boughs
Etched like design
With fallen snow
Blending with the
White shining land.

Catherine Holden
IF ONLY I COULD
I believed you cared when I first met you.
I was surprised to see that I could actually have you.
But, now you're gone and I don't know why.
I ask myself what I did wrong and I try not to cry.
You were cute and popular an all around great guy.
But, now there is someone new I don't know what to do.
You hurt me and I think you knew you would.
But, I would do anything, if I could hold you again
Hear you speak my name.
I would do anything
If only I could.

Kris Reynebeau
CHANCES

TO: Craig (C.J.)—We took a lot of chances and though we'll probably go our separate ways; I want you to know, that I'll always hold a special Love for you, deep in my heart.

Taking a chance,
And living your life through,
You know of no dangers
They are so new.
Taking a risk
Is having a full life,
Turning and twisting,
You are forever lifting.
Never knowing
What to expect,
Moving onward
Acting your best.
Losing friends,
Is a great chance to take,
Many of life's depending choices,
You have to make.
Love is the biggest choice,
Whether you find it or not,
It's up to you
To never let it rot.

Carrie Hoff
SUICIDE
Sitting here wondering as time goes by, why so many teenagers decide to die.

It's unclear to me, why they cannot see, the wonderful people they are going to leave.

Sometimes we forget that others are too, filled with uncertainty of what we should do.

Each time we feel like we're going to break down, there is always a friend who won't let you down

It's easy to see that each time we're in need, to turn to a friend instead of the end.

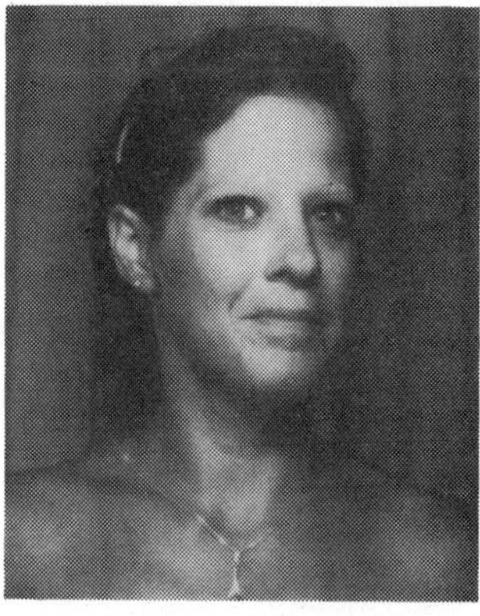

Cindy DuBois

Cindy DuBois
MY BELIEF

I dedicate this to Wayne, whose hard love inspired me to write this one of many poems. Forever yours, Cindy.

I believe, in Beauty and Love,
and I believe in You,
The Beauty in the stars above
and the Love between us two.

I believe in candlelight,
and music in a song,
add caring and sincerity
No way could we go wrong.

Concern and understanding
Seeing things in the Light,
Love is like a breath of spring
when everything is right.

Simple little things we say
That love can bring to mind,
"I LOVE YOU" can make a sunny day
and the darkness, you won't find

By your side Forever
is where I choose to be,
We'll always be together
You'll always hold the KEY!

Daniel Clifton
THE AWAKENING
To kill the restless American night,
To awake upon the road to paradise.

A quiet murmur of a soft faded soul,
Yearning to break loose.

He left in the night, an outcast,
A genius of mysterious origin.

A semi thundering down the highway
Picks up the weary hitchhiker.

A journey into America's dawning beauty.
A divine gift of forsakenness.

Left at a greasy roadside diner
Eating cold rubbery eggs,
Writes in the notebook of America's Frontiers—a wilderness of the unknown .

Sun rising on the horizon.

Connie Perkins
DEAR DANI

This poem is dedicated to Dani, my wonderful niece! With love always, Aunt Connie

Welcome to this world; precious little thing.
Your birth made all of our hearts sing.

You're so very small with eyes so bright;
Into our lives, you brought such light.

One day you will take your very first step
And Mom will wonder when she last slept.

You'll have such fun playing with dolls and toys,
And years later, you'll discover the miracle of boys.

Maybe you'll wear dresses of satin and lace
Or maybe you'll be a tomboy with girlish grace.

You'll have to face growing pains and school
But always keep in mind the "Golden Rule."

When you grow up, you'll try to fulfill your dreams
And balance the best you can on life's highest beams.

What ever you encounter in life; to yourself be true
And I wish you all the best, because I love you!

Christina Koschmider
SILENCE OF DEATH
Standing alone under this midnight sky,
the stars reflect my sobbing cry.
Pain and Sorrow disappear,
as the beautiful light draws me near.
Quieter and Quieter my terror may seem,
but I still hear my silent scream.
Closer and Closer I walk toward my horrifying death,
as I pick up the razor and take my last breath . . .

Albert A Velarde
THE EYES OF WARRENA

To my wife, Warrena.

There's no better feeling than the feeling of ecstasy
And knowing that there is so much Love to share between us
The Love we have for one another is everlasting
And if you wonder how I know this
I feel it when I look into the Eyes of Warrena

The more I'm with her just makes me want to be with her more
Once in my dreams now in my Life
I'll never let her go
She has made my life complete
and filled
my heart with True
Love
And when dark clouds are above me with no end in sight
I see the light in the Eyes of Warrena

As the night ends and she's by my side
I whisper 'Good Morning, I Love You' as I look into the Eyes of Warrena

Philip R McCaffrey
ROTAG
When yesterday you were among friends,
And today, today you kissed the winds.

We wonder how and why,
Now we ponder and cry.

We never thought this would happen,
Now it's all come to an end.

For you were all too young,
Now for you the bells have rung.

In lieu of bad times—we remember the good,
And if I could prevent it—I would.

Well, so long for now my friend,
Yes, I'll see you again,
I will see you in the end.

A Stafenau
MY ISLAND
My rebellious, wild and daring soul
Went traveling in search for an island,
I cried for you constantly—
Until I found you;
Where ocean breaks on sandy beach
And hurricane shakes the land
Your presence was soothing
For my yearning's thirst—
Burying all my painful past;
I will never be stirred
In my loamy nest by the crying wind
From the whispering shore
As the foamy wave shelves
Seek for the shore, giving joy
In its throbs—with a heart of a child.
Would I ever want to abandon you?
The invisible island to every eye—but mine
There shall remain no trace
Of what so closely tied us
Where life moves on to gracious ends
Thrilling with beauty no tongue could tell.

Martha A Jones
RIPPLES IN TIME

To Paul Meyer (Syracuse, NY), for those things that words just can't describe! I love you.—Marty

Everyone knows that people come and go
And sometimes it 's hard to realize
Why someone has left us
Or why we stick around
I often wonder what I've done
Or why it all happens the way it does
They say whatever's best will come with time
And what's meant to be will be—
But the funny part is
That we usually end up hurting
Those who we care about most
While trying to figure it all out.
So, please don't let someone who ever
Meant or means anything much to you
Slip into a shadow of your mind
Without letting them know
What's going on inside
Because—it only takes a little time
before they're gone
And you realize that
that was your friend.

Carl J Claunch
HURTING! ! !

Dedicated to my immediate family, especially my loving wife Jaunita, our dear children, son, David Carl and daughter, Ruth Jonita with our grand-children, Rebecca, Ryan, Rachel and Reid—all friends & Christians.

Oh! How deep in the heart—
Is the pain that comes from within.
There is no physical comparison—
Not even remotely akin.
Its origin is spiritual—
And is related to sin.
The offense may have been personal—
Or shared by a loved-one or friend.
However, there is good news! Listen carefully—
Amidst this dilemma of pain.
Hurting, death and hell may be avoided—
And love, peace and heaven are our gain.
Someone has already paid a great price—
To our rescue "He" came.
The solution to our problem is unmerited grace—
Received freely if we confess our sins and
Believe on Jesus' name.
Please do it right now my dear loved-ones and friends—
This is "urgent" advice.
Opportunities are fleeting—
And may come only once—not twice.

Carolyn Elliott

Carolyn Elliott
DAUGHTER

To my precious daughter, Debbi

We always knew that one day
we'd have to let you go
Tho' exactly when that was
we did not rightly know.

We loved you from the very start
when you were first conceived
Yes you were a gift from God
and that we did belive.

Thru all these years of raising you
we did what we thought was best
But we had never been parents before
we hope we passed the test.

Yet all in all in looking at you
and who you've turned out to be
I must admit that there you are
the best of dad and me.

And now that you have gone and done
what we raised you to do,
It hurts us so to let you go
but God says we are thru.

Yet before we see you leave
before you go away
There are so many words inside
we wish that we could say.

Please remember and keep this poem
keep it safely tucked away
'Cuz if you have a little girl
you'll share it with her some day.

Jennifer Bilyew
A BROKEN HEART
In my world
time was stopped
on the day you
walked out the door.
The moment will be
frozen in time,
A picture of forevermore.
The clocks have stopped,
The sun has halted
But, I will cry no more.
My tears have dried,
My cries will subside
But, I will love you forevermore.

Patricia L Schweinsberg
HOW I MISSED YOU
It hurt to think I fell in love with you,
Then I had to leave
I know it was only for a month,
but it felt like a year to me.
I thought of you everyday,
but your picture brought me closer to you.
I hope you didn't forget me
because I didn't forget you!
When I thought of you I'd cry
because, you were so far away
From me each day.
I was happy that the days were getting closer to when
I'd be back in your arms.
I wish you would have come with me
'cause it would have been easier on my heart.
Now my heart is happy
'cause I'm back in your arms.

Druanne Christine Stewart
GIFTED
To be gifted is to have a talent—
intellectually superior, shining, and gallant.
Some argue and say it's making debate—
To unquestionably substantiate.
Some, however, esteem it as a teacher—
one of wisdom, a goal reacher.
It's been said only artists have style,
though romantics swoon over a lover's beguile.
Some prefer to tap a dance, or play a tune,
to sing alone, or in a crowded room.
In the hands the sculptor molds—
visions with the potter's gold.
Through the night the woodworker chisels
to bring to light a form that sizzles.

To some it is the personality of the being;
Icy-blue, Red-hot, or Deep-sea-green.
But, all in all, it is for me,
grand to be gifted, I agree.
Though it isn't a talent one ensues—
It is being gifted with friends
like you.

Joanne Perkins
BROWN BAGGIN' IT
In the day that passes
Our paths to work do part
But take a little part of me with you
As I keep you fondly in my heart

Know as you take of this preparation
The solemn sweet calm of love's routine
When each lives for the other
Brown baggin' it tastes like french cuisine

Dorothy Judd
BEYOND THE HILLS
I see the rolling hills
And I wonder what lies beyond.
Then one day I cross over and there's still more hills, mountains and valleys.
And I still wonder.
So many things left to the imagination.

But if I could see everything that lies
Beyond my vision, the thrill would be gone.
There would be nothing else to wonder about,
Or dream about or to look forward to.
Life is full of complexities and God
Didn't mean for us to understand everything.

So I live for today and hope for the future.
Dare I dream that my wish will come true.
Yesterday I waited and hoped for today.
Treasuring the moments gone by.
Looking forward to moments to come.
I trust there will be many more.

Beverly G Robinson
A MOMENT AT THE SPANISH STEPS

To John Keats Percy Bysshe Shelley, and George Gordon, Lord Byron

One day in Rome, and I truly tried
To view the room where John Keats died.
Tourists and Locals alike
Crowded the cobblestoned street
As we jostled and pushed our way
To "the Latest Place to Meet."
It was a Saturday eve when we approached
"The Spanish Square" where Keats had made his final home.
People were perched like pigeons there
On the renowned "Spanish Steps" in the city of Rome.
I wondered what John would have thought, in truth,
Had he seen that congregation of Colorful youth.
Alas, no fragrance lingered of violets fair,
Just the odor of the sausage vendor's ware
Now wafting deliciously upon the evening air.
I imagined John glancing from his window 'over there'
Upon this crowd that occupied almost every stair.

Above the crowd stood the obelisk, and then up higher still
I saw "The Trinity" that crowned and named that very hill.
'Though we paused for only a moment I felt a certain thrill.
The Spirits of Byron, Shelley and Keats
Were there on that Autumn day;
And as long as Romantic Poets remain
They shall NEVER go away.

Nye Marnach
WINGS
Thy world is different than mine
Darkened pastures await thee
On thy swift and silent journeys

And townships and black rivers
And forests and tattered places
All silver and grand in moonlight.

On that swift and silent path
Lie worlds untouched by daylight
Shattered with the dew at daybreak

Come galloping sun they are gone
Those of mute majesty acquired
By the constant gazing of stars.

Wings, carry me that I might
Through thy sable landscapes, escape
And in thy gossamer memories, remain

James N Meadows Jr
MY LITTLE VALENTINE OF SNOW
Flittering down in a whimsical way
Is my little valentine of snow.
It comes on wet winter feet
And slowly settles on things
Making an outline of white everywhere.
Ice crystals cascade into diamonds
As the sun peeps its head from behind
A fleecy, foreboding cloud.
Flakes building up on the roof
Make cozy fireplaces glow with warmth
That spreading to the bone nestles
Alive my little valentine of snow.

Lucile Clay Clark
LONELY ROADS
I loved you with eyes of morning
Clear as the twinkle of starshine
Unselfish in my devotion
Yet longing to be near you
To share a love divine
Yet you have traveled other roads
And other loves have claimed you
My love has withered, dimmed and grown cold
For you have shamed me
Why did you have to stray and set our lives apart
Now I travel only lonely roads
As I nurse a broken heart.

Suzanne White
THE LEARNING FLIGHT
It is in my heart . . .
What I know must be done . .
But my desire leads to the scene of fun . . .
What day will it be . . .
when I will finally see . . .
What is true in my heart . . .
How my life is supposed to be . . .
In the warmth of an inner fire . . .
I cease to recognize . . .
That soon—One day . . .
I will pay the price . . .
Why don't I wisen—do what is right . . .
Be the inspiration . . .
One day I might . . .
Oh—how my insides struggle . . .
Between what is wrong and what is right . . .
It's spreading my wings . . .
IT'S A LEARNING FLIGHT.
Views of the future . . .
Possible demise . . .
But I promise you . . . just look in my eyes . . .
Can I have just this chance . . .
To prove I am right . . . I want you to be proud . . .
Not for us to fight . . .
I know it's hard to understand . . .
But in my heart it is true . . .
Just trust me Mom, I LOVE YOU! ! !

Samuel Sosa

Samuel Sosa
ANNA'S SMILE

To Anna: may the whole world someday smile for peace.

I would like to have a portrait of her smile,
To carry in a golden frame.
Then compete it against anything in the world,
And sign it with her name.

Nothing would defeat her smile,
Not even anyone from far or near.
The world would stop just to see her smile,
That adorable smile she always share.

A golden portrait of her magnetic smile,
I would carry everywhere with me.
Then everyone would see beyond the farthest mile,
A shining image of an inner beauty.

Shining with love for all to feel,
Sharing kindness and warmth of happiness.
A living legend . . . A smile so real!
Expressing joy, love, peace and selflessness.

A smile that gives more than fame,
And as special as any Christmas Day.
Anna's smile, so exquisite in a golden frame,
A portrait I would carry until my final day.

Bonnie Baca Haynie
NOT DEAD BUT ASLEEP
I am faint with love,
And broken, with sleepless nights, and empty days.
Fate blindly, cruel, stepped in, and carried you away.
Memories have I of times,
I held you near my heart.
The lights are low and more than lonely.
Come back! Come back! I love you only.
You loved me, and pleaded for compassion;
And now . . . . . "Dear God," I faint with love.
Broken, with sleepless nights and empty days.
Our kisses fainted, clinging hands unfastened,
Golden times are over, to be forgotten!
You were the essence of spring,
Deep in the well of my heart.
"Love" . . . . . . Let me thank you, for sweet memories.
"I am your debtor . . always."

Horace B Shelton Jr
I PITY IT FADED FROM BLACK TO GRAY

To Frances Shelton and fond memories of Horace Shelton.

I Pity It Faded From Black To Gray.
And then I saw a fading light,
reflecting on a piece of tin.
Then I saw a rainbow's color. I pity it faded away.
But then I saw a deeper image
beyond my wildest fantasy. An icy cloud of
blue and silver shimmering in imagery.
From dusk to dawn by day I dream.
From here to all my wildest dreams.
Know proof of what I did, I see, the calm the blue reality.
When I awoke, I saw a light,
I Pity It Faded From Black To Gray.

Jody L Grimes
ENCOURAGING HOPES
Let me learn and be all knowing.
Let me see the pain that's showing.
Let me give a little love,
To the world around me.

Give me strength to face the sorrow.
Let me live until tomorrow.
Lord be with me all the while,
Guiding me along.

Help me show the world of hunger.
Bring on peace in longing slumber.
Desperately I long to see,
The world in harmony.

Living long with each other,
Loving, caring for our brother.
Make this world a better place,
For those yet to come.

For now we rest until the day,
When peace will come, so let us

pray.
Give joy to those who come your way,
And show them all your love.

Henry Hunter
ALONE

To Earth's Best Parents: John and Lucy Hunter
And Siblings: Sarah, Joseph, Alfonse, John, Annie, Cora

Having someone
To be with makes
Being alone
Without that someone
Even lonelier than being
Alone without anyone
To be alone
Without . . .

Perry Harman
TEA

This poem is dedicated to all the tea-lovers in the world and to my wonderful mother who is not one—she's a coffee drinker!

Tea
The artful brew.
How many kinds there are, too.
Sweet and savor according to taste,
One cup of sugar no more to waste.
One pitcher and two quarts of water,
Or you could go to extremes and go farther.
I like mine fresh and in the coffeemaker brew, you see,
Blackberry with two types of Chinese black tea.
Placed in the blender with ice and sugar,
Cover turn or press the button "stir."
Pour half into container then add other with more ice,
Start again to make two quarts of something that's nice.
For when finished you have a beverage with smooth foam too,
For there's nothing quite like the taste of this brew.
It's like nothing you can eat,
For the flavour it can't be beat!

Jon B Law
THE BIRTH OF A CHILD

Love has many meanings,
Expressed with involving care;
The birth of a child,
Is love's greatest share.

Love has many meanings,
It's here and it's there;
The birth of a child,
Is life's greatest care.

Love has many meanings,
Far more than what we say;
Love gives us better reasons,
For feeling a special way—

The birth of a child,
Means that man and wife;
Have cared enough
To bring love to life!

June Caroline Estrada
FOLLOW ME

In memory of my mother, Gloria Mercy Estrada, for all the love and who also inspired me to follow my dreams.

Where are you going?
Did you get lost along the way
Take my hand and follow me.
I shall direct you to a life
A life full of love and peace.

Why are you crying my child?
Did you know that if you take
My hand and follow me, you
Will have only happiness. I
Will lead you to a new life,
Happy and free.

Don't let that cloud hang over
Your head. Step out of the
Darkness and follow me. You
Shall walk in lightness and
Your heart will shine as
Bright
As
The
Sun.

Tanya Curtis

Tanya Curtis
EMOTIONS

As I sit wondering about life,
A great fear grips my body:
Holding back tears I realize
I am alone in the world
Where I don't belong
With only a few special people to trust in,
I count the seconds until I can be alone;
To think, and to wonder.

As life spins on,
I am left alone in the dust,
happy with what's left behind me:
Scared to face the truth in life;
Scared, with nowhere to hide.

As the emotions flash through me
I feel cold, the chill of fear,
I feel warm, the flush of anger,
I feel confused and alone:
For I am but nothing in a great void;

The void of life

Lynn Smith Pope
WHO IS TO BLAME?

Dedicated in memory to my loving grandparents: Pauline Acree Hall & Allie Vance Hall

Every year when Christmas comes close
People hurry and shop to see who can buy the most,
And all during this happy holiday season
We all forget Christmas comes for a reason;
That Jesus was born to save us
And we forget all that he gave us.
We hurry and hurry through the days
And God has to look at our selfish ways;
Just think of the people who don't have as much as we
And then we realize how selfish we can be.
We say, "God forgive us, we are thankful you came."
Then we forget him and, Who is to Blame?
So sometime during your period of rest
May Jesus in your home be blessed;
Remember it's not how many gifts you give
It's Jesus who is watching you, how you live.
So get in the true spirit of Christmas this season
By keeping in mind that Jesus came for a reason.

"T" Jackson
PLEASE KNOW THAT I CARE

I'm dedicating this poem, "Please Know That I Care," to my friend, Miss Kimberly Kay Lane, who inspired me to write it. Kim is one of the sweetest, most intelligent, and most "caring" Christian youth I have ever known.

When in the late afternoon hours of my Day,
And my burdens were harder to bear,
Our God sent a beautiful Angel my way,
Whose request was: "Please know that I care."

Now, no sweeter words ever brightened my life
More than those of my Angel so fair;
For I thought no one knew of my struggles and strife,
Till you whispered: "Please know that I care."

Oh, I feel I Must weigh those sweet words in my mind,
Yet I know they were true and sincere,
And the most sacred place in my heart they will find.
Yes, Darling, WE KNOW THAT YOU CARE!

And we care for you!

AMEN

Rachel V Dewberry
GOD'S BEAUTY

To my Lord and Saviour Jesus Christ

God is in his heaven, you ask me how I know
I just look out the window at the soft fallen snow.
I gaze up into heaven and again I see him there
as I see all those diamonds sparkling as fire.

I go into the mountains and see those sparkling brooks
and it seems as though my soul just soars as I take a second look.

We wonder this and we wonder that, but I've never had a doubt,
All I ever have to do is look around, I know where God is at!

The people are running here and there, they are in a tiz, If
Only they would stop and ask, I know where God is.

Druanne Stewart
JUST BECAUSE

A gift of "Just Because"
says more than one of duty;
given from one's heart with love
it's the thought that is the beauty.

A hug given "Just Because"
creeps up and twinkles in your eyes
The warmth of being loved
breathes deep with happy sighs.

A gentle kiss "Just Because"
usually not shared with strangers,
bonds the two so inclined;
smiles so wide, senses no dangers.

Anything done, all being "Just Because"
comes deep from the heart.
Not from routine, or compulsion,
as with some the idea would start.

So when you can, give "Just Because"
as it develops in you a sense of pleasure;
teaching you what true love is—
and in this, you'll find real treasure.

Muriel Marie Dubé
SPEAKING OF LOVE

The reason inside,
Lacks the lesson.
Rocketing out of hand
Is stronger over all
As a radar tracking hearts sealing them into one.
The constant Love is a real route,
Is free as flying high above
Filling the air with music
Love comes dancing in
Needing or wanting nothing more.
Waiting patiently while holding on.
Doing silly things can be crazy
As being young again.
The beauty of a special smile
Sends out a warmth of happiness everywhere
In a peaceful way.
Living in Love is the only way to live,
For it is a trumpet of triumph on the road of life.

Melanie Spiller
HAND POEM #73

I trace my finger down the coursing vein
That pulses your love through your long arm.
Our hands mingle and link in mortal chain;
My hand soft and cool, your hand hard and warm.
Your muscles tighten with intrinsic strength;
Flex again, again with masculine ease;
I enfold what I can, no match in length
—Charmed, enrapt by what my fingertip sees.

Along the blue lines of your hand's desire
I trace an outline which could spell your name.
Holding your hand, touching fingers of fire,
I know no other hand could feel the same
Or cause me such joy with a strong grasp.
No ecstasy elsewhere could please me thus,
Or tingle my skin like your manly clasp,
Pressed palm to palm, pulsing essence of us.

Raeleen Rivers
THE UNBORN CHILD

Dedicated to my son Raymond Dean Pitcher

Little one, what shall you be
A boy, a girl, I can't wait to see
In my womb as you grow
You'll develop your eyes
Hands fingers and toes
You will be born with a mind so bright

As you wonder with delight
I'll give you all I have to give
And by the grace of God you shall live
When you grow older you will play
With others who will be about the same age
You will come home when the day is done
And show me all the treasures you've won
And once again I sing you to sleep
A tear from my eye I shall weep
For you're growing older and stronger each day
Soon you will marry and run away.

Douglas M Ham
LENDING A HELPING HAND

I dedicate this poem to my wife, Vanessa, who's always ready to lend a helping hand, for God's glory.

We weren't put in this world just to be a pest
I would like to think that maybe it's only a test
To see if we can show love and share with one another
And not fight among ourselves but live as sisters and brothers

You see, God made some rich and some poor to teach us the art of giving
But it seems like the more we get the more we want and we're dying instead of living
When your brother needs a hand you tell him to look at the end of his arms
As though to help him will not help you but cause you some great harm

Meanwhile, Generals in the Pentagon making out more war plans
For once I wish someone will make something to help his fellow man
Instead they judge simply because of the color of the skin
If they take away the meat and only look beneath, we're the same within

The Bible says love God first then love others as you love yourself
So will you obey God or act foolishly and listen to someone else
As for me I'll obey God and take a Bible instead of a gun
Because by helping someone to live lets me know the battle's already won

Grace E Ragin
THIS CHRIST JESUS

To my sisters and brothers in Christ that have encouraged me, To God Be The Glory.

Jesus was born over 2000 years ago
His reason for coming many didn't know,
He was a mother's babe and a father's child;
In this chosen one there was found no sin or guile.
He came to do His father's will
He was born in a manger without frills,
This Christ Jesus was an humble and obedient child.

Jesus came to His own and was not received
For Jews in Him would not believe.
Because of their unbelief and Sin,
This gave the Gentiles a chance to come In.
He was despised and rejected by men
They weren't ready to come out of sin,
This Christ Jesus was an humble and obedient Man.

Jesus went to the cross on Calvary
There to die for you and me;
He said, "Not my will, Thine Be done"
So all that would believe, could be a Son.
If you want to behold the Saviour's Face,
You must forsake sin and accept His Grace.
This Christ Jesus was a humble and Loving Saviour

Tracy A Mortensen
BLOOD FLOWERS

Side by side in a field of white,
Together; alone, silhouettes of the night.

Perfect flowers bleeding red,
In a valley where all is dead.

Thick red drops melting the snow,
In a place where men seldom go.

Yet knowledge is a strong power,
And men have sought blood flowers.

Such beauty men have never seen,
In a world so cruel and mean.

Blood flowing from velvet petals,
Men appear wearing medals.

They enter the valley weighing their chance,
Smelling sweet with death, flowers set a trance.

Frozen in the snow by seductive powers,
Men who have seen blood flowers.

Mesmerized by a blood red glow,
Their souls are free of the bodies they know.

Empty bodies covered by snow,
For each a new blood flower will grow.

D R Pitcock

D R Pitcock
ENCOUNTER WITH AN ANGEL

Dedicated to Sibylla, who inspired a poet to chase a dream.

There she played
in that clear flowing
water at the base of
a misty fall
never seeming to notice
me at all.
She was beautiful, elusive,
and as ethereal as an
angel.

I spoke not to
she as I peered from
behind an oak,
carefully planning this
poem that I wrote.

Her eyes bespectled
by the rising of the
stars; were the color of
an azure sea from afar.

There she bathed
in that secret pond,
beyond
the emerald trees.

Her long hair appeared
to dance in that late
May breeze,
secretly entertaining
me.

Upon her fair head
she wore a wreath of
roses,
the deepest of red,
which surrounded
her golden flecked
hair.

She moved about as
the wind,
moving effortlessly
to and fro
again and again.

As she turned I
saw her wings,
the purest of white.
And with that
she passed onto me
a wink
and vanished into the night.

Kathleen LaBella Ledet
GUARDIAN ANGEL

To my guardian angel in my life "My Mother" I love you

How I would like to be a guardian angel
When my life on Earth is through
And from my perch upon a cloud
I'd guide and watch over you.
I'd sit up there night and day
And chase temptation out your way.
And if on Sunday you chance to stay in bed
I'd pour ice water on your head
Because you know the Bible says
The soul as well as the body must be fed
And not until you're spiritually full
Will I release my hold
Because to me the saving of your soul
Is worth more than Fort Knox gold.

Alison N Plaas
I'VE LOVED YOU FOR ETERNITY

To Paul, my eternal companion and love.

I've loved you for eternity
before we came to earth.
We vowed we'd find each other
after our own mortal birth.

You said that when you found me
you'd never let me go.
I prayed that you would find me
so the love we had could grow,

I came to earth a baby
The veil was put in place.
I had no memory of the past,
nor memory of your face.

When first I saw your eyes
I had to look again.
The sparkle looked familiar.
Could he be the man?

Each day our love grows stronger,
the way it 's meant to be.
I love you, my husband,
for all ETERNITY.

Sandra J Young
THRU GOD'S EYES

Dedicated to my beloved children Stan and Joan Borden—Wayne and Waynelle Medlock

I love the feel of soft smooth things,
Love the way, all birds sing.
Love the smell of a beautiful flower
And to hear the ticking away of the hour.
To feel my Mother's fair face,
The lovely outlines I trace
The fragrance of her golden hair,
Is like the many perfumes, rare.

I love the sound of a motor car,
Many sounds, coming from afar,
Love to hear the ocean on the shore;
Pounding away, for-ever-more.
I feel things, others can't even see,
I love people talking to me.
I know when it begins to rain,
It's God's way of cleansing the earth again.

I'll never fret to see the rainbow
Or the sun, the beautiful land I love so,
Nor the moon above, they say is so bright
Or the blackness of the night.
God shows them all to me;
Everything! "Oh, clear as can be."
He puts them all in my mind
He gifted me, tho' I am blind!
I know when the earth closes over me,
My God at last, I shall see,
Then he shall open my eyes,
And I will see all from his skies . . . . . .

Mike Gutierrez
MY NATIVE LAND

My native land America—What does it mean?
My heritage of the past that some never seen.

From the time of our father and the time of the son,
Was the time of the Aztec and the beginning of one.

With the sign of the cross and the sword on the hand,
A nation crumbled of its great tribal band.

The appearance of the Virgin with her beautiful face,

Became the hearts of the Mexican race.

In the north of the continent a new nation appear,
Became the home of my beloveds dear.

The missions of the past that came to be,
Was a gift from Serra gave California to me.

The battle and the brave of Independence way,
Made my U.S. the land of today.

To prosper a nation but now a conflict tall,
My brothers and I had answered the call.

My Mexican heritage of blood and sand,
My allegiance is to the American land.

So here is my America that I am so proud,
With Spanish eyes in a disappearing cloud.

Deboraha Linn Shutt
LOVE
Love is something everyone needs,
Love is something that fills your needs.
Love is something that makes you feel aware,
Love is something that means you really care.
Love is something that can make you be apart;
Of the great big family love heart.
So remember love . . .
Love it's really great and it doesn't have a money rate.

Irene Hendy
DAWN

To Alex Hendy, my husband, whose love and encouragement, I thank him for.

Dawn came,
the whole world had peace,

Dawn came,
hunger was gone, we breathed again,

Dawn came,
disease was no more.

I opened my eyes, a tear fell.

Betty Pfaff
THE MEETING
The boy walked through,
The tall dark woods,
'Till at last he,
Came to a clearing,
There in the clearing,
Stood an old man,
Dressed in robes,
The color of a rainbow,
His hair and beard,
White as snow,
The boy watched,
As the man opened,
A box that had,
The symbols of,
Moon, planets, stars,
Upon the outside,
The boy looked,
In amazement at,
The beautiful round,
Object contained,
"Come here boy,"
The old man said,
The child stepped,
"How did you know?"
The boy ask,
"I am a wizard" he replied,
"This is my crystal ball,"
"I see many things in here,"
"Futures, dangers, past lives,"
"Many hidden mysteries,"
He told the boy,
"Are you evil?" ask the boy
"No," he replied,
"Just an old wizard,"
"Who you have found,"
"I am your teacher,"
"For you will,"
"Take my place,"

Claudia McLarry
GRAY WINTER
Am I the only one who likes Wintertime,

Who loves to see a bare tree limb against a cold gray sky?

Am I the only one who welcomes a bitter wind,

Who loves to feel the sharp air blow cold against my skin?

Are Wintertime and I alike, is that what makes us kin?

Is Wintertime all cold inside the way I feel within?

Or is She waiting for love's soft glow to warm her, just as I?

No. She'll always be unyielding, cold, and gray,

Will I?

Angelio Dumenigo
EMPTINESS

I dedicate this poem to Adalis, the most beautiful girl I've ever met.

My heart is now but a vast wasteland.
Nothing left to be roamed in, but it is still dominated by one.

One who I love, one who in my heart and mind
Is all I care for, all I live for.

The only water to quench my thirst.
This thirst for love that has embedded in me this emptiness.

Emptiness, emptiness
My heart is now but a vast wasteland.

Stephanie March
SPLINTERS OF GLASS
How dark the night seems
Clouds obscuring the light of the moon
Screams—so loud—
They shatter the darkness
No!—Only in my head
The wind—yes—the wind
Dry and brittle it cries to my thoughts
Withered thoughts—really
Old—yellowed with age
They hang limply—in my mind
Quietly—
Eternity—

Aaron A Kahl
AN AMUSEMENT PARK DADDY

For Katherine Lee, I love you very much . . . Daddy

He's an amusement park daddy and it's always the same.
But she's daddy's little girl so she doesn't complain.
She just wants to be with him, no matter how long,
Because she already knows that tomorrow he's gone.
They go to the parks and have fun for the day.
But it doesn't make up for the time he's away.
He sees her on birthdays and Christmas some years.
But whenever he's leaving she's always in tears.

He's an amusement park daddy but he says that he'll change,
whenever his schedule can be rearranged.
"Next time will be different," he tells her each day,
But she is now used to the things he would say.

She knows that he loves her and tries very hard.
She can tell by the gifts and letters and cards.
But he's an amusement park daddy, it's always the same,
and she's daddy's little girl, so she doesn't complain.

Joseph Ortiz
EDGE
You look as though you've
Walked a thousand miles

You are still strong.

You sing of Van Diemen's
Land, may the land stand
Strong.

You walk for miles along
Deserted highways, some-
Times you are alone.

I wish I could be there
Where you are now.

Elizabeth Burris
SOMETIMES I WONDER
Sometimes I wonder,
Where do I stand.
Sometimes I wonder,
Is it really me you want to be with?
Sometimes I wonder,
What do I do now?
Sometimes I wonder,
What should I say to you?
Sometimes I wonder,
What have I done wrong?
Sometimes I wonder,
Why, I deserve to have someone as good as you.
Sometimes I wonder,
What might happen to us?
Sometimes I wonder,
How could I feel so strongly about you.
Sometimes I wonder,
Is this a dream or reality?
And sometimes I wonder,
Will you always be around for me to care for?

M Lucas
WINTER AWAITING

To Simon, Nick, John, Roger and Andy of Duran Duran—My musical and lyrical inspirations—With Love.

The events of seasons changing brings on the sister of Fall, who in a stormy dance, embraces the world with fury and awe.
Unlike her golden sister, she doesn't leave the world untouched; She seeks to make her presence known with a chilling kiss and a white-washed hush.
With her arrival, the subjects of nature prepare to follow her every command and help her to take total control of all the seas and lands:
The gentle breezes of autumn change into cold blowing gales while the flowing clear blue waters take on an icy-white veil.
Moon-filled harvest nights become replaced by blushing red skies to allow silver-star tears to cover old fallen leaves unprepared to die.
And when She's finished her duties, the last Winter sunset takes her by surprise, signaling the end of her reign.
Gracefully, she gives up her place with heartbreaking pain and gifts the world with a farewell cry which quickly transforms into the Spring's first rain.

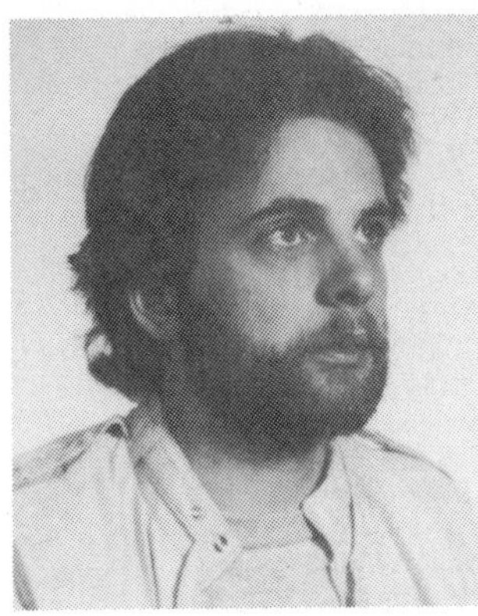

Simon Leigh

Simon Leigh
THINK ABOUT IT!

In the hope of creating a more beautiful world for my wonderful children James and Jamie.

I would cry out loud if I thought it would help
To make others understand and forget their doubt.
There are some in this world with the ability to see
Further than their noses, who want to be free.

I ask you now to think for a while
Of the world around you, it's fashion and style.
If you see it as I do then you will agree
That changes are needed and it's up to you and me.

It matters not of a man's color or creed,
Of life he has chosen for himself to lead.
Men of vision and character we hold in esteem
Until some weak mind with a gun, puts pay to a dream.

Our politicians and church leaders all

preach in the same way.
"Let us plan for tomorrow." But they forget about today.
Do you seriously think God would send His son again
After the way we treated Him, aren't you ashamed?

We can not ask for His help, only His trust
Don't rekindle His pain, He left it up to us.
The violence is a travesty that no man wants to admit
His failure at ruling his own destiny or even having a say in it.

Open your eyes and look around, it's not hard to predict the end.
Stand firm with what you believe, try not to follow the trend.
Grip your heart when you see the bomb and your watching the final few flashes.
Then remember these words that come with the end . . . the echo of ashes to ashes . . .

Leticia Santamaria
DIVORCE

Life is full of tragedies
some of which go unspoken.
Divorce in our families
leave more than two hearts broken.
Some will soon forget the pain,
but yet in the children the scars remain.
It's their ignorance that is to blame
for all our agony and pain.
They don't think of the consequences
they don't even think of our pain
they're so unwilling to settle their differences
that our pleas are in vain.
we cry silently in the corner
at the decision we face.
Don't they know they're putting us through torture?
Isn't it written all over our face?

Deirdre Shaffer
MY LOVE TO ME

I would like to dedicate this poem to a special friend, who is also my loving husband, David Shaffer.

Truly a man you are to me,
always a friend when in need.
Very special and close to my heart,
I can hardly bear it when we're apart.
Having true love and happiness with you,
having faith, trust and honesty I do.
Anything could happen I do agree,
forever happiness just you and me.
Feelings we have we need to share,
everlasting love because we care.

Cindy R Schlegel
THE END OF THE RAINBOW

I've traveled down many roads,
which never seemed to have an end.
I've gotten lonely and cold, but I never would give up, there had to be a bowl of gold at the end of the rainbow.
So an elf once said,

I've stumbled and fell, but pulled myself back together again.
I said my search would never end.
Now later in life to have learned many lessons,
and I have found the end of the rainbow at last.
The bowl was full of riches, but was not gold.
It was filled with the knowledge of what it means to be free and to have a happy soul.

Joanne King
BALLAD OF A GUN

To my five sons.

Come my friend and I will tell you
Of a tale of now and then
From the pages of our history
'Tis a story without end.

I sailed upon the ships of pirates
Made the charge with the Light Brigade
I was there in old Ford's Theatre
As a change in history was made.

I rode the hip of Wild Bill Hickok
Robbed the banks with Jesse James
I was the law in Johnson County
Yet I never took the blame.

I was there with Hitler's army
I said goodby to J.F.K.
I quenched the fire in Martin Luther
On that sad and dismal day.

I have fought for love and glory
Yes my friend I've seen it all
Now I hang in muted silence
Just a gun upon the wall

Maryalice Friday
THE ONLY THINGS THAT LAST

To my beautiful daughter, Cathy.

The only things that last
Are the things we give away.
Give a smile to a lonely soul
And it will make his day.
But if that smile is never formed
And remains but just a thought
It withers and dies within your heart,
And the thought has been for naught.
Give a helping hand to one in need
As you travel down life's road
And you will find that each kind deed
Will be multiplied ten-fold.
Give Christ-like love to all you meet
As you travel on your way
And that love will grow and flourish
Living on in others day after day.
Give prayers to God for your fellow man,
For your country that it stay strong,
For peace on earth, good will to all,
And to the hurting, give a song.
So as you travel o'er this earth
Remember this each day,
The only things that last
Are the things you give away.

Cortland Bonds
A PROUD WOMAN

I'd like to dedicate this to someone full of love and patience, who always has a kind word and spiritual blessing for mankind. To my grandmother with love stinker

Long, seductive strides
the pain and scars live
inside

once a lady, glistening
through the night, sacred
memories of her life

her teachings trapped in
depth, unable to free her
mind of her own shortcomings.

A chance to perhaps, save
a life and still hold on
to dignity

never afraid to put herself
on the line and yet
searching for an understanding
ear, a smile or a word
that's kind

selfish, strong, full of
love, hatred and sin
proud of her accomplishments,
a proud woman.

Romaine Shaner
ECHOES

To Charlotte, Nick, and the entire Chippewa Nation with great love, humility, & gratitude. I love you.

It was a quiet evening as they walked hand-in-hand,
A fair-skinned woman, a dark-skinned man;
Just a gentle discussion—"Tell me, how was your day?"
And loving smiles as they made their way.
Both were struck by the light of the moon,
Neither in a hurry to get home soon;
Stars peeking out, "Go ahead, make a wish,"
"Be nice if you could dry without dropping a dish."

Then from nowhere a beer can just missed her head,
Followed by an angry, "You perverts should be dead!"
"Do you want to go home?" He asked as she shook,
She nodded, and quietly gave him "that look."
From the corner of his eye he saw the car,
Knew they couldn't outrun it, home was too far.
He pushed her aside and fell to the ground,
The echo of a gunshot the only sound;
Voices from the past in his memory burned,
"I'm tellin' you boy, one day you'll learn."
"Be ye not unequally yoked,"
"They'll know we are Christians by our Love." Is this a joke?

Louise Fowler
WE THANK YOU LORD

Thank you Lord, for this great land,
With majestic mountains and rivers grand.

For the sound of church bells on the Sabbath Day,
For the privilege of worship, the freedom to pray.

Thank you for eyes, that we may see,
Old Glory waving in the gentle breeze.

For the ones who fought for freedom, side by side,
May we always remember them, with honor and pride.

Thank you for friends and family, for all our precious memories.
For the sight of a sinner, down on his knees.

For our pastor who delivers your message to his flock,
For the teacher who is faithful, and likes to talk.

Thank you for the laughter of children, as they learn and grow,
For the wisdom of grandparents, and the love they show.

For the Christians who are willing to take a stand,
For friends who always offer, a helping hand.

Thank you for the Bible and the sound that is heard,
When people turn the pages, of Your Holy Word.

For the shade of trees and the warm sunshine,
For the beauty of the country in the winter time.
For your bountiful blessings, we thank You Lord!

Lily E Awrey-Morgan
A MOURNING BY THE SEA

To my darling Gregory and generous family I dedicate this poem. May all of your hopes and dreams be fulfilled. Thank you for helping with mine. LILY E. AWREY-MORGAN

The boiling sea races to the dark, crepuscular shore
Drenching the aimlessly strewn driftwood down to its very core.
Trying furiously to wash away any presence of its forever sleeping Victim,
White foam drags her footsteps into the cold, black tomb.
The sea wraps its cruel fingers around her already swollen neck
And begins on their long, harsh trek.

Taken from the sea by one of its own,
She returns to the once mighty boulder on the shore
That the sea polished down to a dapple stone.

By first mourning light they gather, gaping at the stillness
In which she now lies.
Swathed in moss, there is no warmth in her cold, hollow eyes.

Subretta Mallory
PARADISE MINE

To those for whom my paradise belongs; Brandon Mallory, Donald Phillips, Donna Brashear, Christopher Olmos & little Shane-Kirby.

As the sun kisses the mountains,
And the moon embraces the sky,
There evolves a world of pure beauty,
Painted upon a canvas inside my mind.
The sky,
So soft and endless,
Is caressed by powder blue,
And I,

Sit beside a river,
The deepest of aqua too.
The meadow,
Which slumbers beside it,
Shames the emerald green,
And the willow whispers a lullabye,
More beautiful than anyone could sing.
On the trees there bear no flowers,
Yet their fruit the sweetest wine,
And I flourish,
In this paradise,
Mine.

Shirley Mae Smith
VISION FOREVER, STAND STILL
Pictures hung on walls.
Sights of faces.
Square and oval shape visions.
Looks of love places and things.
Memories of the past maybe future,
In thought.
Ornaments put in rooms of pain and beauty,
Of some in loss.
Painted or mechanical made.
Mirror nailed hung images,
A miracle such as of itself,
When a soul creation is gone.

Heidi Lynn Blatt
DON'T LET ME DIE
I am naive as a flower and virtuous as a bird, don't let me die.
Shut your eyes to the problems, look away, don't let me die.
You are destroying something so highly esteemed, a part of yourself, don't let me die.
Reflect upon what could be, a human life to live and grow, don't let me die.
Appraise other beliefs, be optimistic, don't let me die.
I am a gift, a gift of love. How can you refuse me? Don't let me die.
A flower grows, a bird flies high, your problems go away. A part of yourself, a human life each and every day.
Change your mind and keep this gift
. . . Please don't let me die . . .

Ginasenda Rodriguez
ANOTHER WORLD

This poem is dedicated to my loving parents—Teddy and Wina." And my favorite English teacher—Mrs. M. Lopresti.

Coming home from work tired, sick, and hurt
I got a glass of water, sat down on the couch
and started thinking about the day that passed,
Unable to control myself, the water of loneliness
rolled down my cheeks.
I had to escape.
But I can't let it happen, please God don't.
It was too late.
My body fell heavily on the wooden floor
knocking over a valuable antique vase.

A variety of creatures were hungrily finishing
a human skull.
The carcass of the body was nowhere to be found.
It was obvious, I was the next victim.
They gathered around me, chanted some words, took
their knives, and headed in my direction.
Laughter echoed.
"Have mercy!", I cried.
Legs shaking and hands trembling, I murmured
a silent prayer.
A man clothed in white appeared from nowhere.
He took my hands, covered my whole body with his
cloak and took me back to Another World.

Kara Donohoe
NOBODY
When you're a nobody, Nobody's there,
No smiles on sweet faces.
No laughter in the air.
Just old fumbled voices, in the distance remain,
In a desert of time, neverending sorrow and pain.

Dana Couch
MY WISHING WELL
In my dreams I sit by a wishing well.
This well is full of thoughts and wishes.
These wishes are for all kinds of people and things
The sun's rays seek paths through the trees that hide me and my wishes.
I think of you in my dreams and when I'm awake.
I wonder if I need to wake up or if I want to keep dreaming.
Will you follow me into my dreams?
I wish you would.
Or will you take my hand and lead me out of my dreamland?
If you do will you tell me you love me?
Will you kiss me and make my dreams and wishes come true?
Will you hold me forever?
Will anything like this ever happen,
or am I still sitting
by my wishing well and dreaming?

Kathi Purnell
CATS
SPACE SPACE
SPACE SPACE
Cats Understand Space

When you need some,
they go away someplace,
and don't take up any of yours.

When you've got too much,
they get right up in your face,
and fill some up!—with purrs.

SPACE SPACE
SPACE SPACE

God made cats for SPACE

Marian Leigh Napier
THE NEEDED LOVE

To my best friend and husband Frank, who is my Inspiration.

I can remember,
the first time we kissed.
And the way you would talk,
about my eyes and my lips.

And I wish that there,
was something I could do.
So instead of wishing,
I could just be with you.

So please don't hurt me,
don't turn me away.
'Cause there's so many things
that I want to say.

I need your love,
comfort and caring.
And all of those feelings,
that we started sharing.

Now don't shut me out,
don't say goodbye.
Let's give our love,
at least one more try.

L Teague
RUNNING BAREFOOT
Running barefoot
through the pines,
the music dancing
upon my senses,
ghostly shadows
gay and melancholy,
flutter and wave
flittering away,
flutes crescendo
as rain dips down,
into the dark forest
of lonely symphony.

Dwayne Lorenzo Bynum
SUMMER MORNING

This poem is dedicated to my loving parents David and Susie Bynum. This poem is also dedicated to my caring teacher Ms. Myra Gregory and to the memory of her sister Ms. Beatrice Gregory.

Rainbow in the sky,
Birds flutter, soar in heavens,
Above day-star beams.

A drop of water
Drips on a leaf from the dew;
June Bug drinks cool lymph.

Bumble Bees siphon
Golden nectar from tulips
That have just opened.

In a distant lake,
Ducks bathe in a calm crystal;
Helios brightens.

Thomas L Boyd Jr
PEACE

This poem is dedicated in Memory to my brother, Martin T. Boyd.

A dream that's been around
Since the evolution of man
It can only begin
Whenever we have the courage, to trust one another
And shake each other's hand
Then, and only then, with that realization
Will we take the time to understand
That peace, throughout the world is more
Than just a mere request
It's in demand

Pat Beisly
THE SIGNS OF FALL ARE IN THE AIR
The signs of Fall are in the air
the Autumn leaves are falling everywhere;
Where yellow, orange, and gold
abound there's once again
frost upon the ground;
Old Jack Frost has been busy again
darting and splashing his
colors in the wind;
The Golden Harvest is ready to go
before the first signs of snow;
Yes Fall is here once again.

Jill Teresa Nethercott
SHADOWS IN MY MIND
I feel, as I walk along
The path of life,
A certain kinship
With all those I meet.
The people who
Mean the most to me
Really seem to care.
Often though, life's
Circumstances change,
And friends seem to
Drift away.

But footprints in my
Heart never fade,
And often, I wonder too
If those people I
Once knew well,
Ever think of me anymore.
I wonder if they
Still care.

Virginia D Hale Murray

Virginia D Hale Murray
A MOTHER'S LOVE

Dedicated to Eldridge, Lonnie, and Dale Murray, my dear sons.

What is a mother's love? It's hard to define.
It's given from above, and it's mine all mine.

From the first time I saw you my sons,
My heart was overflowing, with love and pride by the tons
And it's been forever growing.
I rocked you in your cradle, I fed you from a spoon,
Told you many a fable, my sons you grew up so soon.

Now you are twenty, you've grown to be a man
I still love you plenty, you are the finest in the land.

Now you are eighteen, and such a special lad,
You are the image of your very special dad.

Now you are seventeen, the youngest of our love,
A very special son, sent from heaven up above.

Mary Wathen
WEDDING DAY
As I walked down the aisle
I felt a quiver
I was so nervous
I started to shiver

When my father held my arm
I felt a bit more safe
I then began to have
a little more faith

As I got to the altar
there was my husband-to-be
I looked at him
he was staring at me

He took my hand in his
and kissed me on the cheek
I then felt stronger
I was no longer weak

Well, we exchanged vows
I am now his wife
I am going to love him
for the rest of my life.

Jessica Anne Bullock
**TO MY GRANDPARENTS—
HAPPY 36TH ANNIVERSARY**
They must have been sent as angels
From that Holy Man above,
'Cause every day in a special way
They fill our hearts with love.
Since the day that they've gotten married
The wedding bells have rung,
To tell God's little children
The love that they have brung.
To all the people they have met
Since then they've been quite happy,
The people whom I talk about
Are my Gramps and Great-Grand Pappy.

Terri Williams
OUR GOD IS ALMIGHTY
Our God is almighty
and he loves us all the same
He inspired man to write the Bible and believe in his name
I'm just so thankful to be here
to say these things to you
and that I came in the right direction so God can lead me through

Stephen P Campbell
HONOR AT DEATH
Servitude in honor gracious delight,
Gentlemanly solace, truth in the night,
Uncanny courage, death waiting on hand,
Life circumstances, never as planned.

Weakness in the grave, sauntering rhyme,
Uncharacteristic grievance, premeditated crime,
Family breakdown, internal schism,
Devoid heartbreak, nightmare realism.

Southern ignorance, southern bright,
Searchers of carelessness, seekers of light,
Written words expunging, lighthouse of warning,
Coolness of truth confronting, lavender at morning.

Self life at peace, honor at death,
Difficult decisions, happy last breath,
Conscience unrippled, heart not in pieces,
Constant struggle, never over 'til lifeline ceases.

Brian E Perez
OUR AMERICAN HANDS ARE BLOODIED
Our American hands are bloodied
With the lives of innocent souls
We gave the word to plummet our star
To land in Hiroshima's shoals

Doom!

For those whose lives were at zero ground
'Twas a second of hellish fury and sound
Leaving testimonies in shadow
To their innocent half-lives.

To those whose lives in fringes were found
It was more than a second for fire and sound
For because they had seen the bright truth of mankind,
They were struck blind
And lived for some time.

And for those who owned the perimeter souls
All seven angels poured out their bowls.

Yet the whole world heard the inaudible drum
Of the angel pouring forth the last one—
"Doom!", it said, "It is done!"
But what we heard was:
"Boom! The war is won!"

Amy Elizabeth Redfern
OCEAN OF EMOTIONS
I am swelled up,
in my ocean
of emotions.
Swept up,
into the undertow
of feelings.
Tidal waved,
by love, hate, annoyance.
Sometimes, I want to be all alone.
My mixed delusions
wash up,
on the beach of the unknown.
Sometimes, I just wish,
Someone would fix them,
unmix them,
then throw them back,
into my ocean . . .
of emotions.

Taira McAfee
WHEN WINTER COMES
When Winter comes, it may come by surprise
When one is asleep or at sunrise.

When Winter comes it comes like a thief that stalks in the night and if you are not careful Winter will creep in where things seem tight.

When Winter comes you may get what you expect;
but just who will have the time to double check.

When Winter comes, everything comes to a standstill,
and this is the time to steal away and watch the sun go down beyond the hills.

When Winter comes, it is not like the other seasons,
Summer and Spring; but when Winter comes, it has just what it brings.

Kathleen Morris
COLORS
We all have our masks and the webs we weave.
They ride into the burning colors of the sunset.
I, stay back in my cave dreaming.
My mask of steel, I never remove.
The reds, blues, and greens, shine so bright, only inside.
In the dark I hang up my mask and the glowing colors light the night.
They never know my true colors.

Like a spider in the dark light of the sun.
They make my colors black.
My steel mask is put on to protect my soul.
They think they see, but never do.
I wonder if anyone will ever see the colors of myself.

So, as I wear my mask, I also weave my web.
A web of hate, love, and sadness.
So delicate—I protect it from others.
One touch and it would break, and then be gone.
Now I take my mask and put it on the shelf.
If they dare venture, they may also see the colors of myself.

Eileen Coleman

Eileen Coleman
I AM A PART OF EVERYTHING I SEE

*To Big Lou, Your spirit is sweet,
your love unconditional,
your beingness, a poet's retreat.
I LOVE YOU!*

Lightning, thunder and clouds come together
For they appear to be naturally tethered
Yet, I take a closer look at this manifestation
And yet, I see myself in its reflection, my origination

Lightning, thunder and clouds create the water, earth needs
It gives its all to life, even to the tiniest of seeds
I am negative, I am positive, this is the energy, I feel inside of me
My insides clash, I feel pain, joy and sorrow, this is how life feels, my reality!

I am as strong as a tree my roots, go into the earth
My branches reach to heaven, as my spirit longs for spiritual rebirth
The negative and positive energies, dance inside of me
Sometimes I am stormy or sun shiny, sometimes I long to be free!

But this energy, or spirit within is like earthly elements, they have something to bring to light
Its manifestation within, is to come together, clash, spirit becomes a beacon of light!
Contrasts such as positive and negativity, must be
For if it were not, life could not be a reality!

So come sorrow, pain, joy, sunshine, rain, all that life can be
I embrace all of you, for I am a part of everything I see!

Jeannette Morris
LOVE IS

To: Herbert D. Welch: This wouldn't be possible, without your love. I love you. Always, Jan

Love, is what makes the world go round,
But yet! in some people this has never been found;
It's helping your neighbor and trusting a friend,
Regardless to his race or color of skin.

Love is the answer to universal peace,
We spread enough; and wars could cease,
It's the burning passion between a boy and girl;
It could bring harmony throughout the world.

Love is the reason we don't have to fight,
It's a tender embrace on a cold winter's night,
It's our deepest emotion, straight from the heart,
Without a little love, our world will part.

Love is replacing knives and guns,
So, kids of the future may have some fun.
It's sharing and caring for someone you miss,
And the planting on the lips, of a gentle kiss.

Love is what makes people join hand in hand,
To be united together, as we stand.
It's the tingling in my soul that comes from good seed;
Love is the answer, That's all the world needs.

Mimi Mayers Gold
ARE YOU LISTENING
Be careful
As you listen
To speakers' intent.

Be wary
Of the wording
To the voice attend!

Naomi Campbell Chunn
CHRISTMAS
If on Christmas Eve you are weary and worn
Because you have given all you had to make someone glad,
And your heart aches because you couldn't give more
Look up in the sky, for God has something in store.

There are stars in that velvet night;
I'll bet they are looking to see if Santa is in sight.
Be calm and still, there is something for you to hear.
Listen, there is a soft fairy tinkling coming to your ear.
Why, it's the sound of tiny sleighbells drawing so near.
And isn't there a soft knock at the door of your heart?

Wait, the Christmas Angel will let Santa in.

He has a message to all the world He wishes to tell.
God has forgiven us our sin. Hear the old Church bell.
Hush, the angel is whispering in old Santa's ear;
Just look at Santa's face, it's full of Christmas cheer.

It's the Christmas message, the angel does impart
As He whispers to old Santa inside your heart.
A message that's old and dear, whispered soft and clear.
That wonderful Christmas message, Jesus is here.
Oh! It's Christmas all over and all through the year,
When inside your heart it's whispered, Jesus Is Here.

Paula Willis

THE TRUCK DRIVER

To Reggie, This poem is dedicated and written about you.

Dream of open space
and the countries wide
Of different states
and your pride.

Then think of being free
and of beauty
Say there are few
who have seen such reality.

Remember that you are not alone
that you have a bride
Who waits for you
and will stand by your side.

There you have a man
Who lives his life
on the road with a friend
instead of his wife.

But don't you worry
he's never without luck
Whenever you hear a loud horn
Look for an eighteen wheel truck.

Erica Reissner

PORTRAIT OF A DANCER

Dedicated to my sister, Stephanie, on her 13th birthday.

The haze of a dream, the mist of a goal,
A dancer dances from within the soul;

The silky ribbon of a pink toe shoe,
Perfection blesses a chosen few;

The soft turns and graceful leaps,
The flutter of a costume, through the air it sweeps;

The dancer becomes the dance itself,
An overwhelming abundance of beauty and wealth;

The audience is captivated as the music flows on,
A soft interpretation of the magic of the song;

A curtsey of exhaustion completes the show,
The audience awed, row upon row.

Scott Shaw

THE SANTANA WINDS BLOW

the santana winds blow
crossing/across Southern California
the pagan pain midnight blue of the evening ocean
cries/screams to the fading orange of the winter sky
I stare out over them/out onto them
the ocean and the sky
I am caressed by the santana
screaming for the dream
alone

where do they come from/where do they go
there, but not there
felt, but not known
hiding, where can you hide
looking, what is there to be seen
wanting, what has not yet been desired
the wind, it is the same
like the fading glory of the setting sun
pushed down hard by the coming black of the night
the scream of the warm winter santana

Barbara F Hahn

GRAY SQUIRREL

Dare we
stand idly by
and call him
destructive rodent

this small wild
creature
with neither
time nor words
to call us names

so busy
furrowing
smothering seeds
in mother earth
helping God
to father

tomorrow's forest ?

Michelle Genteman

AM I ALONE?

Secrets are told,
But I never hear them,
Conversations go on,
But I'm not a part of them,
The world seems lonely,
From out here,
Cold and lonely.

But inside,
There is a radiant warmth,
Of friendship and
understanding,
Of love and care.

There seems to be a wall,
Blocking my entering,
Somehow everyone else has found the door.
I'm still looking for that door,
That secret door,
To get inside.

Randall A Mickiewicz

WITHOUT YOU I'D BE LOST

To my loving Mother Nora and Sister Tena with lots of love. Also on my mind forever Deana and the Mickiewiczs:

Without you mom, I would be lost
I'd have no direction to follow.
And all the pains of everyday
would be hard for me to swallow.

Inside these walls drive me crazy
doing things I don't want to do.
But what keeps me continually hanging on
is my loving thoughts of you.

I thank the Lord at the end of each day
for you and sis the same.
And ask him to lift away my sins
and take away all the pain.

You've shown me love in every letter
and have proven to me you care.
It makes me smile whenever I think
of all the love we share.

Soon mom, this will all be over,
and we will all be together.
And from that day forward we will spend
our lives as a "family forever."

Rebecca Lephiew

FREEDOM: MY LOVE FOR YOU

To God, for the inspiration and K. D. Jordan who, through experience, taught me to love deeply, the man to whom I'm married, G.L. Lephiew.

As the night closes in,
I feel your warmth settle in.
Like nothing else can ever feel,
Your body is ever so real.

Even though you are now gone
I shall never be alone.
I still have the memory
That you have left here with me.

Someday we will meet again
On better terms, I hope and pray,
You are off to better gain
Something you lost along the way.

The love I've lost from you is sad,
But I know that you are glad.
'Cause you are on your own again
The way you were way back when.

You've given me many months of bliss,
Now you've had to go amiss.
I'll miss you dear, you are to me,
My only love, eternally.

Tonja Wall

LIFE

Life is full of fantasy, hopes, and dreams.
Life is full of castles, sunsets, and streams.
Life is full of truth, kindness, and love,
that I believe comes from above.
Life is believing and striving for the top,
even if you don't make it you shouldn't stop.
Life can be disappointing and very low,
but at those times you just have to let it roll.
Life is like a river, very rough and cold.
Life is like a rainbow with no pot of gold.

Ernest P Carroll

PERCEPTION

On a mid Summer's day
Evening late, the sun at bay
A sign from heaven appeared to me
A message, so clearly expressed from Thee—

Too many, they call an impossible dream
A realistic approach, far to be seen
Amazed, though frightened to enter in
A fantastic voyage, beyond the bend—

A moment of pleasure of sheer delight
An array of colors shown so bright
Creating an adventure, as light reflects
A sensational feeling, from the prismatic effect—

Slow down, enjoy life as it unfolds
A precious gift, more precious than gold
This treasured gift, received as I drove
A rainbow ends . . . my side of the road—

As I travel down the pathway of life
A lesson taught, without a price
Recalling this journey, the 22nd of July
The exhibition of colors against the sky—

John Mitchell Trimble

John Mitchell Trimble

WE LIVE

We live from day to day
Dreams flood our minds
Hope sustains us
Plans for future endeavors are made
But LIFE is so uncertain

We live from day to day
Loving, caring and wanting love and care from those whom we love
Trying to live in a way that our lives won't be one of desolateness
Trying to bring joy and happiness in a world so upwrought
But LIFE is so uncertain

We live from day to day
Serving a supreme being who sits high and looks low
Serving in spite of LIFE'S uncertainty
But when the day arrives and we must die
May our SOULS rest with God

Linda Ludington

WHAT IS LIFE?

This poem is dedicated to the Teachers at West Genesee, and to the class of 1990. I would also like to thank my loving cats: Ernie, Patty, Morris, and Smokey Jo, my rabbit Koree-Kottintayle, and my dog: Ben for sharing their lives with me. Mom, Dad, and Laurie.

Life is a mystery;
full of unanswered questions, and curiosity.
At times we take it for granted;
Living on this precious planet.
The wild animals in the peaceful countryside;
It's a shame we take it all in stride.
Instead we should be thankful
to exist here,

So, stop complaining, and start to care.
Help the poor, the sick, the lonely in need,
The world would be a much better place if we all did one good deed.
There is good, and bad in everyone;
That's what makes life more challenging, and fun.
There is a place for everyone;
And everyone can be replaced.
No one is better than another;
Regardless of disability, criminal record, or skin color.
When we learn to live in harmony, and peace together;
Life will be even more beautiful, and constructive
for ever, and ever.

Maricel L Asuncion
MY LIFE IS MADE UP OF TEARS

I dedicate this poem to all of my friends and teachers at Morro Bay High School, as well as my family in Los Osos. You have all been very inspirational, and God bless all of you. Thank you very much.

My life is made up of tears,
Broken promises, and fears.
I am waiting for the day
When I will be free of my tears.

I cry a million tears a day,
Because I know that I must say
Good-bye to you and our love,
Though it will be hard to stay away.

My tears may come and go;
But this, you shall never know:
How much your love has meant to me,
And how I'll always love you so.

You're like a free and gentle dove,
Soaring high above.
But it's time for me to say
Good-bye . . . my love.

Forget the time we had;
The good times as well as the bad.
Forget that our love ever existed.
Forget the fun times, and the sad.

Forget me and our love, but always remember: I Love You!

Richard J Morin
LIFE

As I live my life day by day,
I must see and wonder things on the way.

As of the things I learn, I must not deny, but find the reason why.

But if one day I shall die, there must be only one grave of mine.

Put me where the trees and animals are free to grow, to live and ask what is to be.

And after I'm there I shall be free,
because this is what I ask of thee.

S Marie Roberts
BEFORE I GO

This is dedicated to all the special people in my life, from family to friends and to the man who holds a special place in my heart.

Before I go,
play that last song again,
let it ring out so beautifully,
like the night we first matched eyes.

Before I go,
dance one more waltz with me,
play the finest tune you know,
the one we heard while dining in Rome.

Before I go,
let me hold you tight,
let me tell you how sorry I am for my guilt,
please, let me take back everything I've said.

Anubhavananda Das
STEP FORWARD SOULS

Step forward souls!
Step straight and bold!
All saints have told,
since times of old!

Define thy tasks!
And know the facts!
Reason God's acts,
At His Feet humbly ask!

Oh, Souls divine,
'Tis time to shine!
Transcend thy shrine!
that now doth bind.

Oh souls forever,
Now give up thy fetters.
Work close together,
For the storms you must weather.

From God thou hath sprung,
Since time had begun
His obedient ones,
You now must become!

Joanna Tsang
BEST FRIENDS

Best friends stick together,
No matter where they are.
Even when you weren't with me,
I knew you weren't that far.

Whenever I felt lonely,
You were always there,
Just by feeling your presence,
I knew that you still cared.

We looked past our differences,
They seem so far away.
We've had our share of problems,
Living day to day.

Despite our disagreements,
We are the best of friends,
And it comforts me to know,
That our friendship will never end.

Now that I have grown so much,
I finally realize,
That friendship is just a crazy game,
And I just found first prize.

Sharon Steege Algar
THE SEARCH

To my children, Sherry Lee, Linda Marie and Joshua Daniel Algar.

Afraid you were to tell me, afraid you'd give me pain,
You covered over feelings that surfaced up again.
You wanted just to question all that is part of you;
I understand, my darling, because I've questioned, too.
I've thought of one who loved you enough to let you go,
One who wanted what was best to help you bloom and grow.
I've thought of one who gave you your loving sense of fun;
I didn't pass this to you, but somewhere there's someone
Whose eyes might hold your sparkle, whose smile might be your smile,
Someone who shares your beauty, your charm, your wit, your style.
You are my own child, through love, and always will be mine,
And child, too, of one who gave, yet held through tears and time.
We both have name of mother, so I would hope for you
That you might feel a double love the day you know her, too.
I set no limitations upon love you receive;
My child take all the beauty that this world has to give—
Everything I want for you, all good that life can bring,
So go and find, my darling, this part of everything!

Maynard M Harper
TOO LITTLE TOO LATE

Why did you not say you loved me;
for at length I learned you did?

Why did you not share with me one fantasy
of the many that you hid?

Oh, at first it would have frightened me
and surely I would have run.

But I'd have returned then on the morrow
to conclude what we had begun.

Harold Raymond Trench

Harold Raymond Trench
A DAY IN JUNE

To the memory of my Scottish father, Hector McDonald Trench: Scoutmaster, boxing champ, cartoonist, engineer, ball-room dancer.

Dawn, and a Carnival-colored sky.
Swift-winged songsters welcome the bright,
And the morning routine of bees,
The lyrical rustling of leaves,
Preview a day of bristling delight.

Day, and o'erhead the hugeness of blue.
Underneath, the fields of gold and green,
The tree limbs quaintly creaking,
And a hammock subtly squeaking:
The sweet smell of peace scents the scene.

Dusk, and the plush of stealthy shadows.
So close so close a tangerine moon,
And a garden of sleepy roses
In silvery light reposes:
The end of a perfect Day in June.

Margaret I Hodges
MY SNEAKY LITTLE SHADOW

To the memory of my mother Mrs. Florence Hopkins. She was my best teacher and next to God, my very best friend.

My sneaky little shadow
Is as sneaky as he can be
On dark and rainy days, when I want to play
He runs and hides from me.

So I look and look for him
Where can that sneaky rascal be?
I search for him 'til my eyes grow dim.
Why won't he come and play with me?

Just when I am giving up
The sun comes out and then
I find my sneaky little shadow
And once more he's my friend.

Then my sneaky little shadow
Sits down and explains to me
Why on dark and rainy days
Our playtimes cannot be.

So on dark and rainy days,
I read a book.
And I don't bother to look
For my sneaky little shadow
Is not hiding in a nook.

For I know that he'll be back
When brightly shines the sun
Then my sneaky little shadow and I
Will have lots and lots of fun.

Christina Viscomi
VOYAGE

In
A rocking, rolling motion
Our boat is on the ocean
It dips, it sways, it surges
Beneath our passionate urges
We listen as the voice of a mermaid lilts
While the boat rocks, and turns, and tilts
The wind rushes, hard and fast
Waves break against our mast
You and I
Together in a stormy sea
Alone, at wave's peak, are we

Jeanne Brisk
I SHALL NEVER LOVE

I shall never see another sunset,
Nor the moonlit skies.
I shall never see the smile on your lips,
Nor the sparkle in your eyes;
Because my sight had been blinded,
When my heart was torn.
I feel like I have died,
Instead of feeling reborn.

I shall never hear the crashing waves of the ocean,
Nor the birds of spring.
I shall never hear your quiet whispers,
Nor the happiness they would bring.
Because my ears had gone deaf,
When you said goodbye.

I didn't want to listen,
I just wanted to die.

I shall never feel the forcefulness of the wind,
Nor the coolness of the sea.
I shall never feel your lips against mine,
Nor the gentleness it gave me.
Because my love is destroyed,
And I'm on my own.
But I'm lost in darkness,
And I feel so alone.

Patty Pearcy
THE IRS BLUES
If you drive an 18-wheeler,
You'd best be a good wheeler-dealer.
'Cause let me tell you Son,
Soon, it's gonna be you and
IRS . . . one on one.

They think you truckers make LOTS of money.
And, what they are doing to you sure isn't funny.
Can't declare your labor? Well, now, ain't that sweet!
And they don't even care if you can't eat.

Just a little word to the wise,
I really think they are after all you guys.
There is one thing for sure,
The rules are for the rich, not the poor.

The harder you work, the more they tax.
Don't even think you will have time to relax.
You'll have IRS blues till you bid this world adieu.
But, heck, they may even be up there too.

So, you won't go up, you'll just go down below?
Well, they may have agents down there, too, you know.
Just get in line, they are calling the roll.
And we may all have to sell'em our soul.

You work to maketh . . . then IRS taketh.

Lynn Thompson
MY WORLD REVOLVES ON THE HEAD OF A NAIL
My world revolves on the head of a nail.
Filled with clutter and lots of junk mail.
Never a letter nor a friendly card;
Living alone is so awfully hard.
I want to travel, to leave, to go;
I want to see a place I don't yet know.
To leave; to run; to go so far.
Goodbye I'm leaving; I'm in the car.

Jaahlay Liwaru
THE SWEET GIRL WHO LOVES RAINBOWS
I am a sweet girl who loves rainbows.
I wonder what is at the end of the rainbow.
I hear baby birds calling out my name.
I see the blendings of the sparkling pastels.
I want to travel to the end of the rainbow.
I am a sweet girl who loves rainbows.

I pretend that I am a loving mom.
I feel happy when I see my baby smile.
I touch my baby's silky soft cheek.
I worry that its world will not be as peaceful as my rainbow dreams.
I cry with joy when I remember
God's love will always be with her.
I am a sweet girl who loves rainbows.

I understand whatever is at the end of the rainbow is as near as my heart.
I say there is no god but God.
I dream the world will grow to understand.
I try to be the person I want my baby to be.
I hope she will love God and look for the end of the rainbow with me.
I am a sweet girl who loves rainbows.

Dematrice H Thompson

Dematrice H Thompson
STOP AND THINK
Have you ever stopped to consider
the blessings you have access to?
Do you realize someone less fortunate
could very well have been you?

Because your legs will carry you
wherever you want to go
Don't think you couldn't have been crippled—
each weary step stumbling and slow.

If your pockets are lined with dollar
bills and your cup filled to the brim
Don't sneer at the beggar on the corner;
except for God's grace, you'd be him.

Be grateful for your blessings and
don't hold your head so high
You fail to see where you're needed—
walk away and let a fallen one die.

Be careful! There's an Eye that's watching
and sees everything you do
Someday He may reward your deeds
by letting the other fellow be you.

Sam Mize
AT LONG LAST LOVE

To the loving memory of my mom and dad, Grace Elizabeth and Sam Wallace, and their marriage that lasted 25 years.

Do you remember that time last fall,
the line was busy when I tried to call?
You said you were sorry when last we spoke,
that was when something within me awoke.
I thought I was above such petty emotions,
but it sweltered within and caused much commotion.
The next day I saw you and treated you badly;
you tried to explain then gave up so sadly.
I thought over your words and realized my error;
I then sought you out in my distraught terror.
You were sitting alone and silently crying,
to see you in pain made me feel like dying.
I sat down beside you to wipe a tear off your cheek;
I apologized softly and begged you to speak.
Your eyes became bright and a smile touched your lips;
then my heart became airy and it began doing flips.
The seasons have passed and we'll never be parted;
I still think back at how it all started.
Soon we'll be joined in love's holy bliss;
We will pass through eternity sealed by a kiss.

Rodney Herbert
THE MAGIC OF LOVE
Love is like magic,
And it always will be.
For love still remains
Life's sweet mystery.
Love works in ways that are
Wondrous and strange.
And there is nothing in life,
That love cannot change.
Love can transform,
The most common place,
Into beauty and splendor
Sweetness and grace.
Love is unselfish it is understanding and kind.
For love sees with its heart, and not with its mind.
Love is the answer that everyone needs, Love is the language
That's what every heart needs.
Love can't be bought,
It is priceless and free, if you could, buy love with gold,
Only to the rich would it be sold.

Scott Shiff
MYSTERY GIRL

This poem is dedicated to Elena, about whom this poem is written.

A girl sits reading silently, alone in a different world. So quiet, peaceful while the outside world is so loud and harmful.

She reads on about love, trust, chivalry. Gallant men in shining armour clashing for the love of a woman.

Her moment in the sun is every day. For us it's once in a lifetime.

She sits under a giant oak by a pond. A couple rows down stream. She eats brie and drinks wine, thinking about a Gaugin she saw.

Her skin so soft; a pearl white the gold and silver shine off her wrists, neck and ears. The light brown hair pulled so neatly, perfectly groomed.

We can only know so much about this natural wonder, who keeps herself under lock and key. A 'hi' and 'goodbye' are about all we get—but for me that is enough.

I can only wish someday to court this beauty only as a perfect gentleman would. She deserves the best and that's all I'd give. For her I give the moon.

Anita Smith
HOPELESS
I always dreamed to be yours;
I thought life would be great!
But instead it just went downhill.
People were laughing at me just
because I couldn't see the truth.
The truth is you don't want me anymore.
I loved you too much to let you go.

All my dreams, all my pride has been
SHATTERED, BROKEN,
CRUMBLED!
Now as I sit here
trying to put the pieces back together,
You just stand beside me and watch.
I was too blind to see the truth.
I guess love really is blind
in many different ways.
Oh, baby, can't you see
how much I care for you.
Please don't make me suffer Alone!

Bill Westfall
CALLING FOR THE ANGELS
In a world of confusion
Life seems an illusion
In a world of fear
I pray they will be here

I call to them
I cry to them
I ask for them
I beg for them

"Where are you?,"
I ask the Angels,
"I need you,"
I tell the Angels

Angel, O Angel
Guardian Angel,
Angel, Dear Angel
I need you tonight.

Amy Ramsey
THE LADY
In the dusk, the shadows formed
A lady who terribly mourned.
Her tears were like a rushing river,
Her tiny hands shook and quivered.
I asked the lady why she cried.
She looked up at me, and then she sighed.
"I cry about things I did long ago,
I put people to shame and caused people woe.
I wish I could do something now at last,
But you can not change the things in your past."
Then slowly I saw her vanish away,
And I begged and pleaded and asked her to stay.
Then I woke up and sat straight up in bed,
And thought of the things that the lady had said.
When I was dressed and was on my way,
I decided to make it a much better day.

Jolita Lynn Cowan
UNTITLED
I am in a void.
All can see me and wave graciously as they go by.
Can you hear me?
They just keep smiling.
Don't you understand?
They see me, but I am totally alone.

No one talks to me.
No one listens to me.
And worst of all
No one touches me.
Help me!
It's getting dark.
I can barely see the faces passing by.
I'm screaming,
"Listen to me! Touch me! I am alive!"
Tears stream down my face.
It is complete darkness.
I can hear no sounds.
I think I am dying . . .
There is no pain.
I just can not feel anything.
Wait . . .
I smell something.
It is fresh and sweet
(very much alive.)
I see something coming toward me now.
Could it be?
Yes, I can see.
It is you!
You said it was over.
I feel the warmth of life seeping into me,
as you wrap me in your arms
With tears rolling I whisper in your ear,
"Thank you. I'm alive and I love you."

Robert Lawrence
THROUGH THE EYES OF A CHILD

As children we all were innocent,
So spontaneous and free.
But we all learned how to grow up,
And forget the child's key.

We forgot the child's wisdom,
And learned to mistrust and feel lost.
Where can we find the love?
Doesn't anyone know the loss?

The freedom, love and the trust.
They all lie within our hearts.
We've forgotten they are within us.
Though we've had them from the start.

We all are born with this trust,
Some wonder and some glee.
We all do enter this world,
So fearless and so free.

But we hide the child within,
Afraid of the love that it has.
How much better this world would be,
If that child within would just last.

We must remember some lessons forgotten,
And forget some that we've learned.
We'd return to the state of the child,
And be granted a key that we've earned.

Caroline M Tasch
IN MEMORIAM

Valentine, valentine,
Where have you gone?
My heart is so heavy,
My arms are forlorn.

My eyes how they water
When thinking of you—
My voice how it's shaking
With each falling dew.

Once we did love—
And now we are through,
How I do wonder
If you think of me too.

Valentine, valentine,
Where have you gone?
My heart is so heavy,
My arms are forlorn . . .

Holly L Smith
DEADLY SPIN

Faces of darkness are on my wall.
They're all laughing at me, I took the fall,
They're there everyday.
Each long day they take bits out of my breath, as I gasp for air.
It's all your fault, I scream so loud!
Taking my fists down into my last heartbeats.
Did I lose?
Yes, I lost.
Never did I know how to win.
My life, is on a "deadly spin."

Tammy Smith

Tammy Smith
SOMETIMES I WONDER . . .

To my family and friends: Thanks for sticking by me through the good and bad. I love you all!!

Sometimes I wonder . . .
Does life go on,
Are there really stars,
Or are they all gone?

Sometimes I wonder . . .
What is life?
Parties . . . Serious thoughts . . .
Happiness . . . is it a sacrifice?

Sometimes I wonder . . .
Do I really need to live?
What's the use . . .
It feels like all I do is give!

Sometimes I wonder . . .
When I'm all alone,
Who can I trust,
In this world of harsh tone!

Mark Grabstas
THE VIRTUE OF A PORTRAIT

These words flow from my lips as water from a spring,
Cast upon the centre of my true feelings to be naked,
As the sun rises to caress the empty dawn's coolness,
So too my heart springs forth from its shallow grave to cry,

It is vulnerable, yet strong with contentment when with you,
I try not for influence or acceptance, rather only to state,
That my feelings are as life, full, complete, with their own life,
Yet as fragile as life, yet they can subside to rage again,

It is not that I wish to seem inpassionate or less true of course,
Rather to state what seems vulnerable can be tempered strong,
And what was born of love can become something beautifully gentle,
Or it can become something cool or distant to perceive when forced to logic,

So when you go forth into the darkness of the leisurely night,
Carry your head high and prepare yourself for a commercial life,
What you have created in your own mind of what is your reality,
For what you give of yourself, you can only hope the venture is profitable,

So to the courage to gamble and accept the risk of failure,
You present yourself vulnerable to encountering contentment,
So that what was unattainable, becomes attainable through choice,
And the loss that was made for the gain must prove itself worthy.

J Pearo
CONFUSED

To all those who feel the music.

Living in a world where
Music is the only escape from reality where
Your life is a song
Being sung to you by someone you don't know
Someone who knows you better than you know yourself

Your goals and all your dreams, like the notes in the melody
Soaring high but staying within reach
The driving beat of the drum keeping your feet on the ground

You want to sing the words but you're afraid
Afraid that if you miss a line
Your song won't be worth singing

The times change, people change
And with them your song
But in your heart, the chorus will remain the same

Moving in time to the music, moving in time to the beat
Moving as one
Together in an embrace
In a world where
Music is our only escape from reality where
Our life together is a song that we sing together

Charles E Hill
A SPECIAL MAN

Dedicated to my Dad, Sedric O. Hill, 1907-1982

The time that passes, we lose track somehow,
What he did was it then or is it now?

Some things he said we misunderstood,
But he knew in his heart that someday we would.

He gave us life and laughter and love,
He taught us to search the heavens above.

He showed us the difference between right and wrong,
He taught us to care, and sing a song.

He left us a treasure no one can repay,
He taught us to live, and smile everyday.

Some things are forgotten and tossed to one side,
Others we cherish and use as our guide.

He was meek but strong, gentle but stern,
From him it seemed so easy to learn.

His clock is now stopped, his face is drawn,
He will not see tomorrow's dawn.

But his legacy will remain, unlike prints in the sand,
He was not just my dad, but a very special man.

Beulah M Lackey
THE RAINBOW

I dedicate this poem to God, who made all things possible, and most of all, the beautiful rainbow for us to behold the beauty of.

If we wanted to look for the pot of gold
they say is at the end of the rainbow,
We will first have to decide which is the
end, for is there a beginning also?

We must weigh this delicate problem very
carefully, and choose the way to travel,
For if we go in the wrong direction you see,
this mystery we may not be able to unravel.

There may be no pot of gold when we arrive,
for the beginning we mistakenly chose,
Or we may be at the end, and someone else
got the gold before us, no one really knows.

It's also possible that as we approached, the
rainbow disappeared and we were not wrong,
It just faded before our very eyes, and now,
we must wait until another one comes along,

Or it may be that this is just an ancient fable
told from tales that are very, very old,
And the beautiful breathtaking rainbow itself,
contains within it, all of the pure gold.

Andrea Rubio
DREAMS

Do dreams exist?
Only if you dream them
Can dreams come true?
Only if you fight for them

P S Lund
JIM BART

Jim Bart acted like a crazy man.
He ate his food right out of the can.
He balanced his peas on the blade of his knife.
I think it was, 'cause he didn't have a wife.

One dark night he drove us to a show,
But not before Ma said we could go.
We went over very rough roads for

about ten miles
To see Shirley Temple's dance and dimpled smiles.

His old used car was a model-A
With poor lights—he couldn't see the way.
Jim Bart drank too much whiskey and home-brew
And we landed upside down in a swampy slough.

Pa pulled me out of that wrecked car,
All I said was, "We didn't get far."
Then he commanded, "Jim, get out of this ditch.
How did this happen you crazy S. of an itch?"

I'll always remember to my dying day
What Jim replied in his crazy way.
"I saw only the phone poles ahead in this light,
So I followed them, but the road it took a right."

Douglas L Spicer
WHAT IS FREEDOM?
What
is
FREEDOM?
Is it some new product on the market?
Maybe it's that new undergarment the women are wearing
now-a-days.
What is it?
Can it be a new vehicle manufactured by G.M.C.
or the Ford Motor Corporation?

What is it? How can I get it?

Is it in the food we eat?
Is it in the water we drink?
Is it in the air we breathe?
What is it?
Maybe it's some type of mod attire . . .

Where is it?
Is it six feet deep lying in a coffin, facing the dirt?
Is it sold in he five and dime stores downtown?

Or, is it free without cost?
Can I pick it up at the nearest
Salvation Army or
Welfare Department
along with the
Cheese?

Again, what is it?
Is it being humiliated from day to day, with a foot up your
ass,
a white foot?
Who is it?
A white man, red man, yellow man, or even a blue man?
Is it being the President of the United States?

What would I have to do to get some of this freedom everyone speaks
of?
Would I have to lie, steal, cheat,
molest, rebuke or kill to get it?
Would I have to stand in lines that
stretch further than time and wait
my turn for it?
Do I have to drink liquor, smoke pot,
or shoot dope to feel
it?

Or would I have to pray to my god—
anybody's god
and hope
for it?
Again, I ask—
What is it?
Is it being a mighty warrior of the
KKK or the White Citizen's
Council?

Is it natural or unnatural?
Good or Evil?
Sweet or Sour?
Gigantic or Minute?
Political or Religious?

OR,
Is it just a master plan of the future?

Webster, expert whitie,
defines it as
The quality or state of being
free;

Does it depend on one's features,
one's social status, one's
superiority in kind or
one's character?

Then, damnit—what—is—IT?

You see—
I'm deaf, dumb, and blind as to
what this freedom is
or is
supposed
to be—
Because, I am—I am—A—Black—
Man.

Gregg A Larson
FOREVER BEAUTIFUL

For Jill

Like a flower that is planted
In the freshness of spring,
And watered by the dew of God's grace,
My love for you has blossomed.

It was nurtured by your caring,
Your smile, your touch.
It was so easy for the blossom to open
And enjoy the richness you offered.

The blossom of my love is eternal,
Forever growing,
Forever feeling.
And with the passage of time,
Forever beautiful.

I love you.

Denise Poxleitner
THE TELEPHONE RANG; I WOKE FROM SLEEP
The telephone rang; I woke from sleep.
My Brother's voice was clear and deep.
Be sure you are sitting down he said
I have bad news—Our Dad is dead.

Dad had been sick only a little while
Yet he had started each day with a smile.
The shock was so great I couldn't speak
I had planned to visit him the next week.

Now Dad has gone to Heaven to stay,
And he watches over me every day.
I can talk to him when I'm feeling sad,
And the things all around me seem so bad.

Dad is home in Heaven at last
And I remember the times of the past.
Of how he loved his children and wife
And treasured every day of his life.

Dad, you're gone for now and I miss you
And many days I feel so blue.
You meant so very much to me
But we'll meet again in Eternity.

Charles Powell

Charles Powell
UNTITLED LOVE
To forbid yourself to love
is to forbid yourself to breathe.
For without love, each breath you
take is merely a sigh.
To long for that special "touch."
To surround yourself with the
serenity of warmth that special
"touch" possesses.

To be able to reach out when you
need to . . .
To be able to speak from the heart, "I
love you."
To desire something so immensely
that you know, once obtained,
it may only bring a masked sense of
termination to loneliness and
An ever-present friendship would
fade away into the dawn of
yesterday.
To want to say "I love you" and not
knowing how without the pain of
unsureness.
Oh . . . what it is to <u>want</u> to love
Oh . . . what it is to <u>need</u> to love.

Wanda Kollar
MY BOOK
I end another chapter in my book and don't want to live for more,
But I see pages left to turn even though that last one tore.
That last page tore my heart, and I almost want to die.
The tears trickle down my cheek as I try so not to cry.
Our love had ended most certainly though my love burned and yearned.
And though it hurt and pained me so,
I'm glad that page has turned.
I'm glad that chapter started though now it's forced to end.
I only wish I didn't have my wounded heart to mend.
And my heart will mend as I go on and will be forced to learn
That sometimes life can be so hard, but still the pages turn.
I hope I find a brand new page that doesn't have to tear,
That gives me hope and happiness instead of days of despair.
A painful lesson can't get me down;
I've got pages left to read.
Life goes on and I will see that wounded hearts don't always bleed.
My book has far from ended just because now I cry.
The tears will stop, I will find love, and this pain will all subside.
New pages hold new rainbows, new hopes and new dreams.
Thinking like this and looking forward has stopped the pain already, it seems.

Ruth Packer
AUTUMN
Autumn, a beautiful time of year.
Colored leaves falling on the ground,
Dark shadows of shade creeping
In and out all around.

Dozens of pretty flowers,
Blowing in the breeze.
The wind gently whistling
Through the tall oak trees.

Birds singing here and there,
Glad to breathe the fresh Autumn air.
Butterflies taking their last flight
Before folding their wings to die
Out of sight.

Jack Frost finding his way in the night,
To spread over the earth his blanket of white.
Mother Nature kills everything green,
Then hides her face so she can't be seen.

Mary Emma Ireland Bird
RACHEL
Rachel, you're delightful; you
always make me smile
sitting on my mantle looking
seriously at me
Your marble eyes, your doll-like
face, your little girl hair style
reflect the special day recorded
in this photograph,
and in my memory

Mama put your green dress on;
Gramma taped a bow to your hair
Everyone dressed in his very best
and Daddy drove us there
The photographer said "How do you
do; you must be here to pose"
Grampa allowed as how—wiping his
sweaty brow—we always wear such
clothes!

The session wasn't easy; we had to
take a few breaks
so Big Brother could make an
adjustment, and we could get
some good takes
He later expressed relief that this
family venture had ended
explaining that *you* didn't like it
there, and *your* feelings were
offended

Rachel, I adore you; Your pondering
gaze intrigues me
Someday, when you are older, you,
too, may try to gauge
the thoughts you had on that special
day at such a tender age

Sarah Dudley
I WANT TO WRITE

I want to write,
God how I want to.
Write so you'll smile
and share my happiness;
shiver as I do,
when a kiss touches my brow.
Write so your tears
will fall with mine
into the open grave,
I've made you feel my pain.
I want to write in such a way
my thoughts are given life.
I want to bring my world to you
through the written word
as if I spoke,
and surely you heard.

Francis A Targowski
OH FAIR HEART

Dedicated To My Princess—Kathy

Oh fair heart
Of maidens bliss
Captured virgins delight
With loves first kiss
Release intimate inhibitions
Thinking not why
To succumb without permission
To a passion cry
Feel it all over
Exploding as a nova
Out of control desire
Hidden deep brought out with fire
Oh fair heart
Of maidens bliss
Approach womanhood
for our love created this

Rebecca Taylor
I AM ONE

I am one.
One so small,
Yet not insignificant
To the whole
Which cannot be
Without one so
small—
as I.
But one.

George White

George White
A FANTASY LAND

To all God's children who have within themselves the perpetual desire to fulfill their dreams of happiness.

Come my dear and take my hand,
We're going to travel through
time to a fantasy land.

A land where the sky is always blue,
A land where all of our dreams
will come true.

A fantasy world free of hatred and crime,
A place that existed before the
beginning of time.

We're transforming now so we must be near,
Please accept what is happening,
try not to show any fear.

What's happening to us my darling wife,
Is the start of a new and care
free life.

Let's spread our wings my little white dove,
And inspect this place from the
sky above.

You'll love it here and you'll surely find,
That our worries are gone and
we have peace of mind.

A fantasy land where all God's children are free,
From sinful things and misery.

Kevin Douglas Bontrager
WE ARE LIKE TWO DROPS OF WATER

We are like two drops of water
Who fall to earth one day.
So alike, and yet unique in our own way.
Alone we are simply raindrops.
Together we form a pool,
A pool of dreams and wishes,
A pool of everlasting hope.

In time we become separated once again,
And return to the clouds above.
All that remains is a memory,
A memory of a pool where once we were united
A pool of everlasting hope
A hope that one day we will be reunited
And that we will never be alone again.

Sharon A Morgan
ANOTHER TIME

I wait.
Sometimes it just takes
a few knowing brain cells
to carelessly float
Away.
The last remaining dregs
in a once
too-often-empty
Wine glass.

Then it is good.
No hate.
No bitterness.
Just us
and what we were
And what we can't give up.

Terry Len Hoggatt
WITH LOVE

The way I feel about you
Says it best in many words.
I love you, for so many things,
Your thoughts, and your ideas.

I love you, for the way you say
You love me, very much.
I love you, for the way you are,
Your kindness, your loving touch.

I love you, for the way that
You whisper in my ear.
I love you, for the way you feel,
Whenever you are near.

I love you, for those moments,
For the times when we have fun.
I love you, for those special times,
When you and I are "one."

I love you, for the way that
You share your life with me.
I love you, for the times we spend,
Together, just you and me.

But, most of all, I love you
Just because, you're you.
And that, our lives will grow and grow,
And make each day anew.

So, let us live our lives as "one."
Which will not ever part.
Now, all these things I give to you.
With all the love that's in my heart.

Elvira E Branstetter
QUESTIONS ?

To all our women and to all our men in the armed forces and their loves and lives left behind.

His is a life of duty, honor and pride
A young man on his way to fight.
Today there's peace, tomorrow too?
Or will he say goodby to you?
Your mind is playing with you now,
will he come back, and when and how?
Will he have loss of limbs or eyes?
Or will he even recognize those left behind should he return?
And what of your war, did you fight
or do you belong to another at night?
Did you stand fast day and night to
the young man on his way to fight?
When loneliness towered over you,
did you fight the war that raged in you?
So a war was fought there but also
here, did both of you taste victory?
Is it harder to fight with bullets and bombs
Than the war fought with loneliness
and empty arms?

Barry Lomax
MELT MY SOUL

You flow down my river
You're the medicine giver
I was always told that love is a lie
True love is too hard to find
Never thought I'd give my love away
But then you look at me
And I know that my love is for you
But then . . .

I give you my heart
But you steal my soul
I lose my mind
My adoration is caught in this hole
Maybe love is just a lie

This serenade can't show half of my love
We're Siamese twins joined at the heart
I know the edges are still a bit rough
But you're in the light and I'm in the dark
All I want is for love to be true
I give you the world
But then, What do you do?
Melt my soul

Romaine A Hubbard
MORE LOVE

To my wonderful parents, Isaac and Lily, my family and friends. Walter, thanks for your encouragement. I LOVE YOU ALL!!! Romaine

Start off each day
With more love in your heart.
Get closer to those
Who have grown far apart.

Don't be afraid to let
Your love shine through.
It will be appreciated,
Especially coming from you!

Faye Britton Dearduff
MOM'S NEW MACHINE

The day mom's washboard was replaced
with her new (used) gasoline washer
we all gathered round to watch
the action of the dasher.

This was such a big day for mom
No more washboard blues.
With a million blisters and sore knuckles
mom had paid her dues.

The washer was a joy
but the wringer took its toll
on zippers, gallus hooks and buttons
until mom learned to fold.

I'm sure mom used to dread wash day
which was a long hard day at best.
Although we never heard her complain
she sure deserves this day of rest.

Bruce Tachibana
THERE'S A MAN IN THE CORNER

There's a man in the corner
Watching all those who go by
Knows just what he's doing
But can't understand why

There's a lady in the mirror
Reflecting on the past
Doesn't know what it's coming to
Only that she is last

And the man in the corner
Turns and looks at her
Sees the reflection of his life
And sheds a little tear

But the lady in the mirror
Just looks back and stares
Sees the sorrow in his heart
Only wishes she could care

And the man in the corner
and the lady in the mirror
See their lives within each other
With their sorrow and tears

Debra L Davis
A CHILD

To my daughter, Morgan, for giving meaning to the words—

With every new sunrise,
With each glowing sunset,
I see your eyes shining with the sun,
dancing with reflections; images
in your mind.
With each passing minute,
With every fading hour,
I hear your laughter continuing,

teasing the air; reminders of
your innocence.
With each changing season.
With every falling leaf;
I feel you touching all that is near,
nurturing the blossoms of love;
gifts from your heart.
Everytime I see you,
Each moment I hear you,
You are giving and growing; sharing,
taking in all a child can believe;
your own dreams.
The knowledge you have learned
Will teach those that see you,
Showing them how to look, and
believe,
refreshing tired souls; believers
of your youth.

Bobbie Gereau
A HUMAN SOUL

To Donna Jean, 'my daughter' and 'All of God's broken children'

Only he who ever lives there
Can know the secrets, torments
Only he can hear the cries—
Others try to look in
Disillusions . . .

My God, it's so hard to live.
So many are broken
But no one else can feel it.
Maybe they don't even know . . .
He can open his mouth—
the pain cannot come out,
for you cannot explain
the secrets of pain—
Can you hear that sound?
Where and what could its sources
be—
"A human soul"

And who cares . . .

Eleanor Bernardo
TITLES AND FABLES
Why must I be told,
That I am a little child,
A little child that wants to be,
All grown up, you see.

Oh it's so nice to be a Miss.
But it's nicer to be a Mrs.
Because of the love it holds for Mr.
and Mrs.

You can call me Mother, that's
great,
Also call me Aunt, that's all right,
But it is sad for me to be,
That mean old Mother-in-law, you
see,
That has that reputation, that you
can't see.

Now please don't tease me,
For I am a Grandmother,
For it pleases me too,
But why am I sad and blue,
Can I believe, it must be, old age
creeping upon me.

Great Grandmother is the
greatest, as great as can be,
But that title of the mean old lady, I'll
try not to be,
For this is my titles and fables to be.

Holly M Dutton
BY SNOWLIGHT
Softly, how softly,
falls every quiet, crystal flake,
upon a path of downy white,
with every velvet step we take.

Subtle, how subtle,
the snowdrifts clad in silver-plate,
the tree twigs tinseled with
moonlight,
the ice-mirror glimmering on the
lake.

Gentle, how gentle,
the stillness of the air around,
the softened silence of the night,
the breathless cool, without a sound.

Tenderly, how tenderly,
we snuggle closer, warmer grow,
until our hearts are kindled bright
with love's embracing, glowing
light,
and shine forever through the night
upon our path, etched in the snow.

Eileen A Souza
DEAR CHILDREN

To All of God's Children

Have you hugged your brother
today?
Are you always sure that they will
always know that you care?
Today will be yesterday tomorrow,
But tomorrow may never come,
Show your love today, so that
yesterday's will always hold good
memories,
Live each day as if it were your last;
One moment could be an eternity.
Always make sure that the people
you love know they are loved today;
So that if you should ever part,
Those that are left behind tomorrow
will know,
That they were at least loved
yesterday.

Katy Jones
FRIENDS FOREVER
Our leaders have taken the first of
many steps,
Now it is up to us.
Up to us to make sure we continue
walking forward.
Break down the stereotypes and let's
be friends.
You and me friends forever.
Americans and Soviets, friends
forever
Continue climbing the mountain to
peace.
Becoming friends,
Living each other's life styles.
Exchanging that everlasting love.
Opening our minds and hearts
To make a big achievement
Friends Forever
You and me
Friends Forever!!

Janet L Custer
TIDES

To my Mother, for all of her love and encouragement.

You never spoke, but I felt your
stares,
I didn't know your name,
but I didn't care,
I loved you just the same.
Maybe someday you would speak to
me
And then my wildest of dreams
would come true.
If your stares made my heart pound
like the waves of the sea,
Then I wondered what the sound
of your voice would do.

Every night I dreamed of
you and I
together as man and wife.
Everywhere I went, I wished you
could have been there with me,
by my side.

But then I realized you will never
be a part of my life.
Because my love for you has come
and gone
just like the ocean's tide.

Cheri A Cruz
LET'S TEACH OUR CHILDREN

Dedicated to our wonderful, first child, Joshua, born April 18, 1989.

Look at the little children playing,
It's sad, but they don't know
About this cold, unfeeling world
Into which they'll grow.

A world where hate is commonplace,
Distrust is all around.
Why can't we keep these little ones
In their child's world, safe and
sound?

Let's teach our children to be kind
To love each other too,
Maybe we can change this world
By teaching, them what to do.

Let's teach them caring instead of
hate,
To be peaceful instead of wild,
For the future of the world is found
In the heart of a little child.

Let's teach them all that war is
wrong
And doesn't solve a thing,
Let's show them all the happiness
A peaceful world can bring.

Tracy Norton
MUSIC TO ME
It speaks my moods
The melody takes me away
The lyrics enchant me
The voice knows what to say
A world of escape
Something to brighten my day
A lantern of light
In the shadows of my life
To take it away
Would surely be murder
For I could not go on
Without the world of song
To most it is one thing
To me it is another
A place where I can relax
A place where I can be me
Whether fast and hard
Or slow and soft
It is a part of my life
I care not with to part

Timothy Cordier
THE NIGHT (2:41 a.m.)

For: Gary

The night
calls after me
in an ever present staring;
ominous cloud
of forgetfulness,
and fright.
In smoke filled alleys
of lust tilling;
deals of twisting moments—
all discovered in
the night.

Through echoes
of empty suddenness
the silence permeates
the weather that fills
the air with frightened sounds
of unknowing beasts and rain.

Mysterious as the fog.
The night.

Sandra N Lehmann
PURE LOVE
Love, Pure Love, everyone needs to
know,
That's what God sent to Bethlehem,
many years ago.
He sent His son, the only one,
And that's how Christmas was
begun.
A celebration soon is past,
But the love of Jesus will always
last.
No better gift could He ever send,
Than the Alpha and Omega, The
Beginning and The End!

Leslie Turner
MOTHERS AND DAUGHTERS

To my Mother Judy, who also happens to be my friend.

You and I are the same to a tee,
But look again, we're as different as
can be.
No two people have loved
eachother more,
No two people have slammed more
doors.
Mothers and daughters act like this
they say
Loving and hating, confusing those
in their way.
Whether it's major or minor, it's still
a big thing
To be mad at eachother, and what the
outcome brings.
Our lives are so different that you
cannot compare,
And to decide for the other, it just
isn't fair.
But as hard as I've tried, and I know
you have too,
It's inevitable forever, that this is
nothing new.
So I'm making amends now, to start
the ball rolling
To a renewed friendship, I know the
futures' holding.
Cuz I know you love me, as you
know I love you,
And the silence is painful, and life's
too short to stew.

Blanca M Hermosillo
TO MY SISTER MATILDA

Dear Sis, life has an unexpected halt to it, but, memories and love go on forever—

Kind and big was your heart, you
had an unforgettable smile,
A deed which you'd willingly start,
you'd complete, no matter the while.
You loved, cared for everyone,
regardless of color, belief or their
creed,
To all you had a "God Bless," you
were a blessing indeed.
Destinies are written when
conceived, yours was indeed a short
span,
In God you trusted and believed, full
of good and mercy your life ran.
Extending both hands with
tenderness to those whom your
comfort sought,
With so much love and willingness
always did for others with ne'er a

thought.
Now the time allotted has ended, you've been called home to rest and advance,
Your chores assigned have all been tended, leaving an example I won't take perchance.
When my road seems hard or quite dreary or find it impossible to follow it through,
When I feel threatened or become a bit weary, I'll follow the path carved for me specially by you.
So long, dear sister, to me you were so, also the mother who loved me and shared,
You were my strength when I felt so low, 'til we meet again Sis, 'cause you cared.

Maria Irizarry
WHERE HAS INNOCENCE GONE?

My love for innocence is dedicated to my children, Adriana, Liana and baby Maria.

Where has innocence gone?
that fascination that love
to be innocent is grand.
How we would play and play
'til all hours of the day
kick the can, walk hand in hand
a little kiss, wasn't puppy love grand?

Where has innocence gone?
When we would run, ride a bike.
throw rocks on a hike, climb a fence,
be an honest to goodness, tomboy.
The pleasure of being young,
no worries even if we had
patches here and there.

Where has innocence gone?
To watch the stars at night,
to be the only girl playing
baseball with the guys.
To be shoved in the snow
and to know, how wonderful
it was to be young.
Where has innocence gone?

Joyce D Willis
BLUE
blue, bird of freedom;
now blue, bird of woe.
shackled—bound by cries of anguish
that are hers alone.
blue spreads her wings no more,
for red has deadened her.
red of mankind's fiery hate
and burning desire to take her soul.
her magic dies
like the heart of man long ago.
she cries blue tears,
she bleeds blue blood.
no one understands—
no one hears the cries
of blue.

Larissa Meyer
BEAUTIFUL SPRING
The brisk breeze blows
Through the hollowed trees,
As cherry tree blossoms
And blown so very softly.

The moon rises
Bringing glow and romance,
The sun rises
Bringing fire and life.

Large meadows filled
With bright blooming flowers,
Orchards of apple blossoms
And bright green grass.

Bonnets with ribbons
And fashionable clothes,
New life has come
And spring has sprung.

Patricia A Morbit
MY THOUGHTS I CANNOT EXPRESS
My thoughts I cannot express
—A pleasure, an emptiness.
That which is out of reach;
A promise made is broken.
But oh the pleasure!

The wanton within is perceived
As I see it.

Such a fine specimen!
A leath, smooth, vivacious creature
Sets my mind on fire
With the thought of the last arms
reach away

The prey—a victim of the night.
A slender built lion with muscles tense
Gleaming in the night.
The lamb lies down in mock battle to be devoured
Willingly.

Unexpected odors of passion rekindled
Moistness gathers
Quickening of the heart
As memories are smiled upon.

Debbie Libby
A TRIBUTE TO DAD

To: Nelson, Heather, Jimmy and JamiLee. They make all things possible.

First came bootcamp
Then came war
You put in twenty years
Though you wanted more
We'll all agree
When I say
There were many tears
Each time you went away
Each time you left
And went away
You left knowing
You would return one day
A day soon came
You had to say good-bye
To your Lady
Your life long love
The United States Navy
Now it is over
You are out,
Yet we all know, you still yearn
For a day, you may return

Laura Flint Berry
A MOTHER'S PAIN
How do you stop the hurt in his eyes;
When he realizes that
it's all been lies?
How do you make the pain go away,
When he realizes daddy's
not here to stay?

What do you say to a child of two,
When his daddy's gone and
there's just you?
What do you say when he asks for
him and he's not there,
How do you tell a child that
daddy just don't care.

How do you stop the hatred
growing within,
When you can clearly see
how it's been.
How do you stop the
pain of being blue.
When you see him hurting
and know a kiss won't do.

Bonnie J Floyd
A SILENT TRAVELER
Walking slowly up the road
With steps as silent as the moonlight,—
A solemn cart is slowly pulled along,
The windmill's blades carelessly turn,
Pastel colors begin to fade
As the coming of night approaches,—
Seeking a place to rest his weary bones
For he is not accustomed to this journey.
He struggles to pull the tired mare
Along the cobble-stoned avenue,
Eagerly he desires to see the end,
For there, simple pleasures are held.

David Hill
HERE I AM
Here I am
Sitting alone
Where are you?
I think at home

Do you like my poem?
Do you understand?
Will you be mine?
Will you hold my hand?

Vulnerable is the word
Uneasy is the way
Just tell me yes
My life will be gay

Rejoice with you
Expand together
Share our lives
Will it be, <u>forever</u>?

Monique Preyer
MY YEARS . . .
When I was small I learned to crawl.
When I was two old things smelled new.
When I was five I used to hide.
When I was eight I learned to skate.
Now I am nine and I'll take the time, so when I am ten I'll have new friends.
And when I get older, I'll look over my shoulder,
and remember those years and all of the fears
I had of the future.
A future at last built on the work of my past.

Linda Lawseth
BELLE OF THE COUNTRY BALL
Howdy partner! Howdy! Howdy!
Hope I don't look too dowdy.
But I got ready in such a hurry,
In order that I wouldn't miss the surrey.
I left the dog barking and the chickens squawking
And even my next-door neighbor was gawking.
The horses flew at a galloping pace
My hair's a mess as well as my face.
The rain, my rouge did sure enough spoil.
I really must sigh after all my toil.
Anyway, here I am, after all.
I hope I'm not too late for the ball!

Connie Cundiff
I GUESS THE PAIN WAS TOO MUCH
I guess the pain was too much
You drew away from my touch
You knew I didn't want to leave you
But had to see my past through
I tried to reach you, make you understand
But you wouldn't listen past your own plan
You knew from the first but never faced it
And at the end, knew you couldn't erase it.
To walk away from you tore me in two
But we had no future, that we both knew.
When we met it was like we were born then
We lived in our own world, never thinking of when
You gave me something I'll never lose
The gift of strength to live as I choose.

Joe Ferrucci
BARE FEET
We met at the lake,
everyday, at three o'clock.

We sat on the sagging wooden dock that
jutted out over the water,
Our bare feet swinging over the edge.

We talked, and
We smile, and
We laughed.

The swans seemed annoyed at us for bothering them
and so,
They kept away.

One day,
when I went to the lake,
during the day, at three o'clock,

No one was there.

So I waited by the white oaks that
leaned over the water.

But
My bare feet didn't swing over the
edge of the dock that day.

And I didn't speak,
And I didn't smile,
And I didn't laugh.

And the swans glided all over the lake that day.

As if
No one had ever been there to disturb them.

Bill Basso
FAREWELL TO A SON
You wonder why you can't fly
You wonder why things are the way they are
You thought you saw a difference
That your turn would lead somewhere new
To an unexplored harbor or depth
That the unextraordinary life
Was the way <u>others</u> lived

That your whirlwind journey would end
At a place not known to anyone else
But your flanged wheels are forged
For one set of tracks
The siding switches are set
(You only control the velocity)

But it's diffused in your fevers
And favorite dreamscapes,
The scowl of bar room mirrors
And the ash in the hourglass,
Clinging nightly to carousels in neon nightmares,
Until lands' end approaches.

Thru the mists and damp dawns
The fogs and steam clouds
And ghosts and shadows and smells and sounds
Until a laser light cuts through
To burn your being into a granite trophy
That reads: Here lived—Here lies—

Nancy C Wilkins
EXPECTATIONS

To Phyllis, my mother, friend, and mentor.

Perfect round mushrooms
Sit on an unkempt lawn.
White golf balls, waiting,
No players, no score,
Motionless they grow.
Soon to go.
Earth's timing will
bring them again.

Donald E Christiansen
LOVE IS THE GLORY OF GOD

Love is the greatest thing on earth.
Love is a measure of what you're worth.
Love is the shine in a small one's eyes.
Love is the soul of a mother's sighs.
Love is the purpose for which we live.
Love is for those who have love to give.
Love is contentment when day is done.
Love is the hand of a friend you've won.

Love is the presence of God in you.
Love is to do what He wants you to.
Love is His splendor in you and me.
Love is the way God has willed we should be.
Love is our maker to whom we pray.
Love is his answer to what we say.
Love is forgiveness to all. and then,
Love is the glory of God! Amen!

Novella Meek
LOVE

And now abideth faith, hope, charity . . .
Do these exist in this society?
Faith lives openly in heart of a child,
Covers the mountains, valleys in the wild.

Hope is numerous as the planted seed.
Has wings for the soul wherever there's need,
Within rooms of illness hope whispers there
That the future will bring a day more fair.

Hope and faith have a companion along . . .
Listen to love in the meadow lark's song,
It is the fountain from which blossoms spring,
See it in the care of each new born thing.

Yes, love came far and released to the sea
Whales who were trapped in a cold destiny.
Yet, where oh where, in this sodomy time
Can love find rest with such hatred and crime?

Love rests gently within harbors of grief,
Finds a refuge within glows of belief
And always a home in the written line,
Hate is a vacuum while love is sublime . . .

Elise Rosenburg
SUICIDAL SWIM

To my friend Mary Jo: The swim for life can be rough—"I'm so thankful that you survived."

In a fury of desperation and lost hope—
she sinks into a warm pool of shattered dreams,
and sharp edges of reality.
No longer able to see the gleaming surface—
with the glittering sun making rainbows
upon her flowing ripples of fascinations,
She succumbs to the storm that has sprung from behind
the dark clouds of conscience.
Unable to swim against the rapids—
she yields to the powerful force that drives then on,
Crushing her inner soul and cutting her body—
till she is nothing more than a withered cattail
bobbing along the shore.

Janice L Dugan
LONG UNDERWEAR

I do not think it is quite fair,
My brother has long underwear.
But in the rain he did take a fall,
And washing them has made them small.
Now, the underwear are mine,
I do not think they are so fine.
They itch and pinch all day at school,
They are not the least bit cool.
Oh, I hope, I hope,
They get rid of laundry soap.
So, I will not have to care,
About having to wear long underwear.

Wayne Bierma
ROBIN

As I walk along the street,
I hear a little birdie tweet.
I look up in the tree
And what do I see?
Robin, Robin in that tree
What do you have? Can I see?
Three little birdies in that nest
Looking around to see what's best.
Then the Robin flies away
Gathering food for the day.
Now the Robin gathers a twig
So it can make the nest real big.
Soon the Robin wills top its flight
So it can rest during the night.
Then the sky begins to darken,
And I hear my mother's harken.
So I say to the Robin,
Don't be sobbin.
I'll be back another day
When the sun is bright and gay.

Mary Sinclair-Spohn

Mary Sinclair-Spohn
MAKING A HEART SING IS MAGIC

I dedicate this poem to my daughter, Pat and her Dave. Always try to make each other's heart sing!

Remember to show love because,
Making a heart sing is magic!
Remember to tread softly for,
Breaking a heart is always tragic!

Love brings love you know,
Try it and you will find,
That it's something beyond compare,
Love of the greatest, magical kind!

Remember making a heart sing,
Makes your heart fly and soar!
Sends electric tingles of joy,
Leaves you begging for lots more!

It is the rainbow's end,
When you make someone's heart sing!
Finding the pot of gold,
Your fantasy love it will bring!

Margaret C Henry
A WIFE'S PRAYER

To My Loving Husband; Ronnie

Dear Lord, up in heaven above,
Please protect the one I love.
And let him see in the light
of day all the things that thou has made.
And let him see in the dark of night,
the splendor of his heart's delight.
And till the day comes Lord, when you take him away, please protect him each and every day.

Maxine L Davis
MY DAD

This poem is dedicated to Edward, my loving father.

My Dad was just your ordinary man. He wasn't famous, he was just my Dad. He lived to be 67 years old. Dad was not always right, but he was not always wrong either. He was a man that loved to talk. He liked having people come to see him and talk to him.

But one day Daddy had a talk with our heavenly Father, and in that talk, Daddy decided to join him in heaven. It hurts all of us to see him go, but Daddy and God knowned best. He is with our Heavenly Father in heaven now. He's watching us to let us all know that we too have to make that journey. So until we do, let's keep our heart and soul in God's hand. Keep on praying and singing God's songs. You see Daddy. I want to see you again. I know the only way I can, that is to come to heaven where you are. So I will keep on praying and doing God's will until I see you again.

Ethel Cravey Meeker
CHAPEL IN SCHOOL

Dedicated to the future of America

The Bible contains
The word of truth,
And should not be
Withheld from our youth.

What they learn in their youth
They never forget,
To withhold that right
Will foster regret.

The Bible is history
Where lessons are learned,
To follow its teachings
Blessings are earned.

Religious, its ardor,
Righteous, its truth,
And is the inherent
Right of our youth.

Heidi Schneider
WHO WILL SAVE THEM?

The tears they cry are silent but true,
their only hope is me and you.

Some stray, some beaten and yes some fed well;
but the neglected and abused, no one can tell.

We close our eyes to those tortured in labs,
as they suffer without hope as they're cut and stabbed.

So open your heart and show them you care,
because without love none will spare.

For they have no voice or opinions to give,
and their only dream is to live and let live!

Diana Flowers Nealeigh
LOVE AFFAIR

I know this little love affair
Will probably never last
But looking back someday I'll see
How lovely was our past

The lovely days we spent together
Evenings just us two
Holding hands and having fun
Was the easiest thing to do

We sometimes had our arguments
And always had our fights
But making up was always fun
And gave us some delight

I only hope that when we're through
And no longer together
We remain friends to the very end
And it lasts forever and ever.

Kathleen O'Flannagan
WINGS

To fly free in the pink-orange dawn,
To ride upon the tides of swelling winds,
To feel creation as it first begins,
Without pain or sorrow or memory.

To spread the wings of my shrouded heart,
As a seagull spreads his pinioned wings
To soar above a darkened world
That has no time nor word nor place for me.

To weave a tapestry among the castled clouds
Of sounds and tones of my soul's violin strings;
To send aloft the final tarnished, broken dream
Into the healing fire of sun-ravaged eternity.

Bobbie J Williams
I AM THAT I AM GOD HERO OF THE DAY

This poem is dedicated to Father God for my talent, Pastor Turner & family, my mother, Mrs. Janie B. Williams and my children: Cynthia, Jeannette, Tisha, Miesha, Latif & Bobbi & Calvin.

I wear no cape, no spiked shoes
No leotards on my legs,
I have no boots made of a spider's web
or a cap upon my head.
I have no "S" across my chest
But out of bondage I can bring you.
To a great land you'll be delivered
For I am That I Am, Lord, God, merciful,
compassionate and loving,
caring, everlasting and Holy!
Praise Me, love me, honor me, I'm the Hero of all eternity!
I am That I Am, God, Hero of the day!
I have no cartoon named after me
or mounds of jewelry around my neck
I don't turn green and split my jeans
A burning bush is more my scene!
OR
The laughter of a child, a baby's cry
A teardrop from a mother's eye
A father's loving pride
I am That I Am, God, Hero of All Times!

Nicole Spalding
SUICIDE

To my cousin, Kurt Estes, who committed suicide, November 2, 1988.

Children listen . . .
Can you hear the problems of life?
Do not let them get the best of you.
Do not commit suicide.

Think of all the problems you'll cause.
Think of your parents . . .
Think of all the pain and guilt they'll feel.

If you think your life is bad; Think of how bad your parents' lives will be.
No problems are bad enough that you have to take your own life.

If times are really bad . . .
Write a note . . .
Talk to someone . . .
Just don't keep it inside.
Life can only get better.

Shel Stiles
GOOD BY

To my dearest sister

Tears fall down my face,

Like a stream of mountain water.
It hurts to see you lie there so motionless
for you have no other cares in the world, no worries
I think of all the times
I felt like saying it but didn't.
Now I regret it.
Maybe now is too late,
but now that you're gone, I realize
how important it is that you know.
So I'll say it now
"I love you"

I have so many questions unanswered
things like "Why did you die?"
and "how could you leave me like this,
alone in the world?"
But it's not your fault.
Years from now, I'll look back
and cry for you
But it's no use,
You're gone.
"Good By"

Nick Nichols
THE FLIGHT OF A SPARROW

This Poem is dedicated to my mother with all my love Nick

Somewhere up amongst the clouds, where gentle breezes blow, a graceful sparrow sees the hawk and surely does he know that go he must and travel far as fast as wings can send, or quickly meet the brutal hawk to see his journey's end.

Now fight the wind his only friend so harder will he try, for love of life beats in his heart to slow down means to die.

If only he could reach the fields, where grass grows oh so tall, or see the forest dark and thick to hide behind its walls.

Then once again, he'll sing of days when skies are crystal clear and happiness will fill his heart just knowing life's so dear.

Bobby Campos
OH, PRECIOUS, PRECIOUS LIGHT IN MY TUNNEL

Powered by God's majesty, every glitter of a golden word begins with resplendent inspiration, that lives beauty enhanced deep in the heart of a poet, I dedicate my poem to my sweet Alma, eternal inspiration and love.

Oh, precious, precious light in my tunnel,
I see thee not,
but I feel thy shine of pristine delight.

Light of my happiness, thee seems so distant
yond, thy breathless glow,
bound by silence though,
whispers my heart,
only thy warmth, I cradle and cherish.
How warm and cuddly thy smile of beauty,
cometh closer thy womanly glow,
no feminine smile, I feel, compares
to thy own—cometh closer for I need thee!
cries my little heart, daunted by shadows,
I cling especially to thee.

Yond light in my tunnel, help
wipe perpetual darkness away,
thy beauty of thy strength,
thy heart, I beckon to thee,
penetrate all shadows that excruciate in me,
with thy pristine delight I can hold in my heart,
from that special glow, I find only, in thee.

Daniel J Gale
DREAMING

To Bryan L. Gale, my best friend and brother.

"I's the captain of my ship" said the little black boy
"I's sailed a weary chore"

"I's the captain of my ship" said the little black boy
Watching, waitin, dreaming by the river's shore!

Eldora Anderson
HE IS

The softness of words,
comfort of thought,
Love to give away,
The touch of a hand.

Look of beauty all around,
The love to receive.

The power to choose,
A privilege to understand.

He Is

Sandra M Morris
TO ANOTHER

Today is the day her daddy walked her down the aisle,
He gave her "to another"
And on his face he wore a smile,
he was thinking of when the doctor said, "It's a girl,"
and he held her in his arms
to him he had the whole world.
As she grew and grew he'd be
the image she would seek,
of the man someday she hoped to meet.
Now that day is here
As we knew it soon would come,
there are tears with rejoice
we approve of her choice
"Welcome to our family son."

Chung-Hsin Wang
A COLLEGIATE EVENT

Walking and walking to another class
my eyes search for lovely sights.

I look and look at a girl
resting under a tree.
I am looking at this girl
not because she has a pretty face
but because she is wearing a white blouse.
I am looking at this girl
not because she is wearing a white blouse
but because she is wearing a white bra.
I am looking at this girl
not because she is wearing
a white bra under her white blouse
but because of her huge breasts.

Suddenly, a wind slithers by—
chilling the air, waking me.

As I look at this girl
resting under a tree with
nipples erect
pressing against her bra
against her blouse
I experience a stiffness in my walk.

Susana T Batcagan-Pasicatan
RESOLUTION

i come to love you
in the shadows
of unremembered past.

ever-searching,
never-ending quests
of unfulfilled intensities!

what do we really want?

for we are vestiges
of loves before us

To each and one
We can't love whole
The way we have become.

Willie Jewel Tabb
TRIALS

Dear Lord, as I begin this day
Humble me in such a way,
So that deep within my soul
You may have full control.

Unknowingly I contemplate
Uncertain of what lies in wait.
Often troubles weigh me down,
Fiery trials do abound.

Sweet spirit, when my soul is tried,
Oh! Father, please in me abide.
For only then by faith, not sight,
Will I thru darkness, yet see light.

Life's trials I must undergo,
But trustingly I will know,
That when I'm weak, I'm not alone,
For godly strength will keep me strong.

Charles Pevy
SO ALONE

break there empty heart fast
rent by love
remurmur not woes past
gush out abyssal pool
wet salt let go
cry clamor forever o conquered fool
tremble greatly frame of bones
sudden faint
traversing ground bruising stones
alas o feeble matter
small and gray
forsaken, sorely tatter
eons of infinity and more
sadness's strength
ought for door

Glenda J Steele
HELP ME GOD

Help me, help me, help me to see
Things of worth that are good for me
Help me to steer in the right way
To find a happy and a better day.

Help these wheels of time to roll
With peace and contentment in my soul
Into the realm of time I go
With plenty of love and trust to sow.

Help me to judge right from wrong
And know how to fill my heart with song.
Help me to be kind and good
And act the way I know I should.

Help me to give and not just take.

Help me to live for goodness sake.
Help me roll down life's long road.
Help me know how to lighten my
load.

What to leave and what to take,
That of worth or that a fake,
Shine down your light so I may see
Things of worth that are good for me.

Glenda J Steele
THE "SPECIAL" CHILD

This poem is dedicated to my nephew, Jeremy

What are you thinking
When you gaze with those angelic
eyes,
Wide open and prone to not blinking
Like an angel in heaven on high?

Although clear words are not spoken,
Your thoughts show clear through
your eyes.
Your parents were given a token
Of an angel in human disguise.

You're somebody "special" (I know
it)
I can tell by the way that you move
Your eyes, they constantly show it
And by all it will someday be proved.

If anyone ever puts you down
For not speaking as clear as they do,
Don't cry and wear a sad frown,
Feel sad for them, for they weren't
blessed with a good heart like you.

S M Bennett
RED BALLOON
I watch the red balloon float
aimlessly
through the cloudless sky,
higher and higher,
until my eyes grow weary and
memories
flood my mind.
Small town carnival on a summer's
day,
ferris wheel
and painted ponies on the carousel.
Cotton candy melting on my tongue
as I held tightly
to the string of a red balloon.
So long ago that child of six,
with a tear-stained face, watched
a red balloon
dancing on the wind,
still holding tightly to the broken
string.
A tear
rolls down my cheek.

Jennifer L Spencer
DEATH WILL COME

Dedicated to everyone who is afraid of death and everyone who has a life.

Death will come slowly
As sure as I stand
No exception
No long life will come.

It can come fatal
It can be natural
No matter what
Your time will come.

You can not hide
It is as silent as nightfall
It never sleeps
It will come.

But don't be scared
Or it can over power you
Don't try to fight it
Death will come!

Patricia Armstrong
SHINING STAR
I remember when my grandmother
sat me upon her knee; she put on her
glasses pulled out this old box, and
said these words to me:

My precious child I have
something for you. It's not
diamonds, rubies, or pearls,
just something to make your
life a little more easy while
passing through this world. She
leaned back in her chair looking
towards the heavens on that sun
shining day. With the voice of a
mighty angel; these words she
began to say:
You must always keep on
reaching just climbing towards
greater heights, never give up
the struggle and you'll never
lose the fight. Life promised
you nothing; though many
promises will be made to you.
Many dreams will be disrupted,
some lies will become the
truth. You must learn to take
things in stride, learning to
change without compromising
your pride. Realize change is
yours to make no matter how
hopeless it may seem. You must
learn to walk through the rain
holding tightly to your dreams.
Forever reaching for that
ultimate height no matter how
far.
And if by chance you happen to
fall, at least you'll be among the
S T A R S.

From that old rusty box she pulled a
silver shiny thing; I never could have
imagined how much joy it would
bring. So now I pass it on to you my
dear, to guard you home from afar;
to help you remember come what
may, you're already among the
S
T
A
R
S.

Jeffrey Allen Luse
FOREVER WATCHING
Evergreen trimmed mountains, A
crystal frost lies quiet upon the land.
Western mountain peaks brushed in
pastel splendor as the sun paints his
final brush stroke with golden hand.

The stars gleaming in the heavens,
gems adorn the violet curtain of
evening. The moon nestled content
atop a twilight throne. Peacefully
watching the land he is keeping.

Tripping, giggling, gurgling sounds
of water, as a stream stumbles down
mountain side, rushing to find a way
home to mother's womb. Unknowingly guided by the mountains,
Tenderly coaxed by the glistening
moon.

Earth's moods eternally changing,
fleeting seasons cast their suggestive
spell. Forever twilight moon is
watching, Forever morning sun as
well.

Michelle Lacko
FRIENDSHIP
A smile is special
when it comes from inside;
Shining all the time,
with nothing to hide.

The sparkle in an eye
as warm as a flame;
Jumping out to meet you,
dancing and playing a game.

A caring heart
understanding and true;
Picking you up from days
when you feel so blue.

This my friend
is meant for you;
Honest and sincere,
about our friendship anew.

Ruby E Shore
REFLECTIONS
I walk out in a field of hay,
And look up at the sky.
I see such beauty there
I feel the need to cry .

Slowly, down I lie;
I trace the clouds with rested eyes.
I see many images, my thoughts
become clear!
I am cleansed, without fear!

Time has ceased. I am not of Earth!
This being, is not "Birth."
Ethereal, eternal peace is mine.
I enter the door in a gown of
Sunshine.

Raoul Derek Smith
DISCOVERY
The people massed in morning light
In renewed courage for this flight;
Watched from the sea and shore and
air,
To see Discovery glistening there!

Cryogens flowed in vapor state;
In power-balance while they await
To turbo-mix their energy
In rocket climb from gravity!

The count has long since been
renewed!
It's time to begin our quest anew!
The challenge of life in space is here,
Of discoveries we've yet to hear!

Look! See the red of rocket's flame!
And now the white of contrail's'
stream!
Across the space of brilliant blue,
Discovery, we search with you!

We do not know what we'll discover,
What pearls of wisdom, like no other!
And we may not know, when we find
it,
Until we've studied and refined it!

We search the unknowns of that sea
In which our planet's floating free!
Of those environments to know
Where twinkling stars and comets go!

Unless we search we can not find!
'Twould be like looking and be
blind!
To sit complacent is despair,
While life expands most everywhere!

Discover there how plants can grow!
Blessings space medicines bestow!
If material's strength is limitless!
And how, on earth to use all this!

Out there is endless energy!
Knowledge without boundary!
Let's look from that space into this
To help us know what Eden is!

Discovery, you will return
With questions which must, then, in
turn
Send you again to solar seas,
To search for answers such as these!

Steven M Malloy
SABLEVE
It begins to drop below the distant
trees.
The fire leaps out of it to blanket the
clouds in its eerie orange glow. The
trees and iron towers are silhouettes
against the crimson sky. "Steve,
don't look at the sun." "I'm not."
Up in my room, looking through the
pane. The field is a lush velvet
brown. Then the black rising trees
reaching their leafless fingers toward
the fiery disc. Still farther up are the
purple floating mists of water with
fire streaked strings lashing across
them and twinkling lights flying
under them. Then, farther up, the
sable sky. Minutes pass and it's an
arc pulling its light down with it.
Now it's blatant. Every second
matters. It won't matter anymore. It's
going and will never come back
until the next dawn. Faster, there is
actually movement. You must look at
it. Mesmerized. You become weak. It
has you in its trance. She beckons
you to blind yourself to see herself
die, to drown in the earthen pit. It is
gone. Just her shimmer remains.
Soon the purple sky will envelop its
fire. Soon the sable sky will soak up
her blood until the next dawn. Up,
little white pins sparkling while your
eyes start to blink
Tears burning your eyes with the
same fire that just blew away.
Another one is gone. I'm just
getting older I will never see her
again.
Until the next dawn.

Lucy DeFluent Gallup
ILLUSION
I speak to you always in my mind,
Always—although you are never
there.
The you that I mean, I have built
myself,
Of a few kind words and a long
despair.
But the you that is you, I scarcely
know,
And startle to find beyond the frame
Of that which longing has formed
from dream
And cloaked with the magic of your
name.

John Burrow
THE CARIBOU
There's a caribou in my cabin, Mr.
Snow, Mr. Snow.
There's a caribou in my cabin, that
I know, I know!
I've seen his eyes and touched his
fur.
That's how come I know he's ther'.

There's a caribou in my cabin, Mr. Snow!

There's a caribou in my cabin, Mr. Snow, Mr. Snow.
There's a caribou in my cabin, that I know, I know!
I've heard his hooves and felt his breath,
I think he's scared me half to death.
There's a caribou in my cabin, Mr. Snow!

There's a caribou in my cabin, Mr. Snow, Mr. Snow.
There's a caribou in my cabin, that I know, I know!
He's et my dinner and drunk his fill
and stomped all over my cardboard still.
There's a caribou in my cabin, Mr. Snow!

There's a caribou in my cabin, Mr. Snow, Mr. Snow.
There's a caribou in my cabin, that I know, I know!
He's drunk my booze and stole my bed,
and his snores are likely to wake the dead.
There's a caribou in my cabin, Mr. Snow!

There's a caribou in my cabin, Mr. Snow, Mr. Snow!
There's a caribou in my cabin, that I know, I know!
He's come to stay while the wind blows cold.
Never would have thought he'd be so bold.
There's a caribou in my cabin, Mr. Snow!

There's a caribou in my cabin, Mr. Snow, Mr. Snow.
There's a caribou in my cabin, that I know, I know!
He'll stay with me and be my friend.
And now, at last, this is the end.
There's a caribou in my cabin, Mr. Snow!

Karen E Kyrouz
THE PROMISE—THE WASTE (EPITAPH)

Once there was a Promise
Standing like a sapling—strong and straight
Talents bursting like freshening young buds
Bright with the Promise of future greatness
Then came Addiction—the loathly worm—

Feeding on the budding Promise—gaining strength day by day
Sapping the strength, eroding the talents, destroying the promise
Ever denying the presence of the worm
He lies comatose—prematurely old
Strength gone, talents wasted, the Promise blighted
Alone with his withered paranoic dreams,
He awaits death.

Karen E Kyrouz
FOG FANTASY

For Tom, my real life hero, with all my love as always

There was fog early this morning.
It shrouded my familiar world
Making it a playground for fantasies.
The evergreens of the forest raised their mist wrapped spires,
Like the turrets and battlements of a long abandoned castle.
Bare branches, gnarled witch fingers, grasped greedily at elusive pennants of mist.
Headlights like dragon eyes loomed menacingly from the cottony gray expanse of nothingness—searching, searching—
I caught the sound of muffled hoofbeats—did I, perhaps,
Glimpse a unicorn? Or was it the neighbor's horse?
A fox, homeward bound, barked his defiance at the emerging dawn, his voice muffled, as though his mouth was full of feathers.
Somewhere a wakening bluejay screamed, the harshness of his voice mellowed to a faint medieval trumpeting
My steps lagged as I approached the house, for I wanted to linger within my fantasy world.
It would have been perfect, if you'd been there beside me.

Tammy Wilson
MY FRIEND

This poem is dedicated to "Grandpa," who always believes in me!

I have a friend, who is never away.
He's by my side, day after day.
He helps me with all of my problems
And never lets me face them alone.
He knows me bone for bone.
Yet, I never get tired of him by my side,
And he never says no, when I want to confide.
This man can be with everyone,
And me at the same time.
The Lord is for anyone,
Anytime.

Margaret E Parker

Margaret E Parker
DEAR FRIEND

Dedicated to Brian Leavitt

I am glad
that I hold
the profession I do,
because this child
is mine.

If God be willing,
I will have him
beside me
for three years

He is constantly exposed
on the sensitive
emulsion sheet
of my mind.

I love him—
He makes my day—
every day.
And I remember him
at night.

He is only five years old
And he's open;
happy;
And he too,
is in love.
It shows.

When I am outside
I secretly go
to find him.
And he pleases me.
He builds sandcastles
in the sand.
He smiles, and is glad
that I have found him.
He holds his hands up
with pleasure
to show me
how dirty they are.

I've only known him
to do
one naughty little thing,
and then.
I felt a warm glow.

He sneakingly pulled
one of the foundation rods
from a "big guy's" tower,
And when a complaint
was made,
I scolded and watched.

He listened,
and snuggled himself
tighter;
lowered his head;
and smiled quietly
to himself.
He wasn't sorry
that he had done it.
I could see that he
had derived much pleasure
from it.
It wasn't a serious thing
and he knew it.
And it tickled his being.

Some days
he has great ambition.
On other days
he is not interested
in the assignment
presented,
because he is busily
making something
for his mother.

Remember
He is tiny, and only five years old.

The prettiest gift
was waxed crayon shavings
placed on invisible tape,
on white paper.
His own creation
And a beautiful creation
it was.
When I asked him
why he wasn't working,
he said,

"I'm making something pretty
for my Mummie."
And I got the message.
So I let it be.

There is a saying
that when one allows another
to expose him on film,
part of the subject's soul
has been lost.
What about the exposures
on the sensitive emulsion sheet
of our mind?

Souls are to be shared.
To share is to love.
Literally, I have not
taken his soul.
I have it.
He has it.
I want you to have it.
It belongs to us all
. . . And it's beautiful.

A beautiful soul.
A beautiful child.
He is complete.

He is mine
He is yours.
I want to share him with you, this Christmas.

Opal DeGrote
VOYAGE TO AMERICA

This poem describes the voyage taken by my paternal grandparents, Wubbo and Jacoba Strootman, from Holland to America in 1882, and written in their memory.

Away from all familiar things in European lands—
In wooden ships that sailed for a foreign shore;
For varied reasons brave immigrants faced the unknown seas,
And left their native lands—forevermore!

Sometimes to meet a heavy squall that mounted steadily
To become a howling crescendo before it was done—
And the ship and all aboard would risk a salty lave;
Could only try to cope, and not succumb!

Life-lines were rigged for the hearty souls who walked the sea-swept deck,
Or 'old-salts' who long had braved erratic seas.
The cargo tightly lashed to save the valued load;
Frightened passengers hovered below a fearsome scene!

A lurching, rolling ship that would in time outlast the storm,
And the battered ship sailed on—on a placid sea.
The canvas sails that once had whipped wildly overhead
Brought them to a land where all men could be free!

Bill Crist
THE BUTTERFLY

Happy Birthday to Mom, November 9, 1978

The majesty of a butterfly,
Dancing through the air,
Gliding, flittering, maneuvering,
Delicately here and there.

In a living color airplane,
He flies so gracefully.
From flower port to flower port,
He's a master in pilotry.

Taking every day as a new day,
Playing in nature's wonderland,
The butterfly is indeed quite a miracle.
Ah, but only a tiny parcel in God's great hand.

Karen E Kyrouz
ALL I SHOULD HAVE ASKED

The earth beneath my feet
The azure sky above me
This was all I should have asked of life.
But—I wanted more.

I wanted Love,
And thus I defied Destiny
I should have known
Love was not for me.
Now all I have are bittersweet memories.
I will build my defenses higher
So no one can break through.
For I will never trust again
Once I loved, once only,
I will never love again
For love causes unbearable agony.
Now, I must be content
With the earth and azure sky
For Love was never meant
for such as I.

Charlotte R McWhorter LaRue
THOUGHTS

To Willie, my loving Husband; who has inspired me & given me encouragement to fulfill my dreams & goals in life as a writer.

I thought he would be different from the others—
But—I don't want to say anything further.—But—
I thought I was someone special; I thought I was his pot of gold at the end of the rainbow.
I thought I was what he ever wanted in a woman;—But—I guess I thought I had been fooling myself all along.—But—maybe I had thought I had been humming and just singing myself a song.
I thought I was his lifelong partner and friend and his babe. I thought he would accept me—for just being me.
So these are my thoughts from my heart and soul. I pray to God each day—that my thoughts are not just thoughts—But—Reality.

Joe Meeks
BEAUTY

Close your eyes. Let your inward sight relax. Now do you see images, patterns?

As a boy I let my eyes see without perceiving, today my mind recalls all that my eyes did see.

Is it beauty you see in a sealed tube with rainbow colored stones that create brilliant, delightful, patterns?
It is beauty to have a small deer look at you in a questing way.

What more is beauty? Beauty is a child still within the protective blanket of a mother's embrace!
Beauty is an endearing word softly spoken to one that will keep it fresh from day to day.

Beauty is the sea with its ageless face unmarred, its song is always changing.
Beauty is a kindness given without the thought of anything being returned.

Beauty is a song echoing from the depths of your soul, seeking the voice as a means of expression, this I say is beauty!

Beauty is mankind, a higher form of life, a form that is beauty in all of its projected ways!

Corey Frantz
THE LORD'S CRADLE

To my boys, Ryan R.M. and Corey Anthony. Love, Mom Oct. 1985

There was a time
In a heavenly place,
I was with my Creator you see . . .
He knew my name
As I was made in secret,
And that's how I came to be.
Then the Lord looked down upon the world
And saw his perfect choice,
And gently laid me in a dwelling place
where I became my mother's voice.
In mystery I grew from day to day
I noticed my growing parts, the most precious sound that was heard by me was the beating of my mother's heart.
Her rhythm of love sang a lullaby that was warm & full of peace I'd give her back my nudges of love,
Then close my eyes to sleep.
It's a beautiful time with part of God's plan
Breath of life completed my soul, my mother and I, we cried for joy
Knowing I was whole.
Oh thank you Lord for I am wonderfully made
and your blessings out number the sand,
Thank you Lord for answering my mother's prayers . . .
As we rested in the palm of your hand.

Gail J VanWart
MY NOBODY, SOMEBODY, EVERYBODY

To Daniel, my inspiration, my love, my world.

My husband says he's "nobody"
when nobody takes out the trash,
only to be "somebody" when
somebody speaks too rash,
and multiplies to "everybody" if
everybody does things wrong . . .
he feels like he's an entire crowd
where only one of him belong.

Perhaps he doesn't realize,
although just one of him exists,
he can be "anybody"
my little heart insists;
for "nobody" makes me happier
than the "somebody" who cares for me,
he's "everybody" I need in life . . .
he's all the world to me.

Lisa McAleer
LAST ROSE

He looks again at her shining smile
And the curly locks surrounding her face,
As though he hadn't seen them for a long while
Away in some long forgotten place.
She just smiles at him
With a faraway look in her eyes.
Yet, after everything, he still thinks of them,
All the other guys.
They couldn't understand
Why he paid her any mind.
Gave her a helping hand
Or was just rather kind.
They were hard and cruel
Said she was ugly and prude
And he took their words for rule
Then he too became rude.
Now he doesn't know what to say,
And he hands her a rose.
With a tear in his eye, he turns away
As her coffin is slowly closed.

Brian Harris
AMBER COLORS

Amber colors.
Blending brightly,
Contrast of the rainbow,
Delicate, lacy streaks,
The sun has set.

Michelle Lacko
IN MEMORY

Living life to the fullest
each and every day;
Learning and laughing with all,
caring in every way.

A special part of everyone
who has ever known;
That strong yet gentle man—
The love that he has shown.

One with so much to give
has been carelessly taken away;
But his spirit will live on,
watching over us each day.

The spirit is like the hand—
and the body is a glove;
When one day the body is gone,
the spirit flies as the dove.

On a chariot of clouds—
As free as the wind;
His memory will live on
until we meet again.

Ingrid C Knoll
THE CLOUDS OF SORROW

This is dedicated to those whom I love.

The Clouds of Sorrow
Surround my world
As the thorns of pain
Tear at my soul
The pain and grief
Too much to bear
There is one way out
But do I dare?
These petals obscure
Reflect my soul
Bound by ivy
Yet armed with thorns
There is no escape
There is no hope
This prison's forever
Guards of despair do know
In a raven chamber
The execution is near

A dagger of ice
Is poised to pierce
The blade of crystal
Stabs into my heart
Then runs as a coward
Into blood it does melt
All clues are gone
Of this spiritual death
There was no loss
There was nothing left
The gods do laugh
As they witness this game
The tribulations of man
In this theater of pain
This sinister laugh
glumly echoes . . .
Through my mind
Could it be the gods?
Or is it really mankind?

Anita Coward
RESTLESSNESS GONE MAD

When the jittery tide washes over my beach,
I drop the pieces to the puzzle.
I erratically search as they slip through my fingers,
And lose my grasp of reality.
Crestfallen, I reach to, maybe, grab for your hand?
And I lose my sense of dignity.
Fragile, I retreat, wavering and trite,
And withdraw to edit my consciousness.

My frosty tips reach out to the moon
In a belligerent, warlike manner. And I refresh my waters and cry to the heavens
For peace and continuity.

The tide recedes and I find the pieces
Soggy, wilting, and wet.
I crumble those pieces to insignificance
And forfeit the chance of forgiveness.
I creep to my cage full of many rooms
Resonant with the screams of antipathy,
And slowly but quite effortlessly
Slide razors across my wrists.

Laura DeGiacomo
WHAT WOULDN'T I DO? . . .

This is for you Michael. I'll always love you, no matter what the future holds. Faithfully yours, Laura.

Alone in my room, I think of you.
To have you in my arms, what wouldn't I do?
When you hold me, the world stops in place.
What wouldn't I do, just to see your face.
The love we share will always be true.
Because nothing else matters when I think of you.
Even though we are apart from one another,
We can't hide our feelings for each other.
No other soul can tear us apart.
The two of us are joined together by the by the heart.
I would never give up all of our special times.
If I ever did, it would be a crime.
Our love is something that I will always treasure.
It makes me smile, when I'm in pain or in pleasure.
Something this special, only comes once in a lifetime
Because, I will always be yours and you will always be mine.

Frank Wright
THE POEM

To Lorie, thanks for the silver branch.

I woke up dreaming of yesterday.
Feeling a love that went one way.
Remembering how she made it end.
To comfort myself I picked up my pen.

The ink flows on,
the time blows by,
the words meet as they form on the sheet.
The poem's story isn't happy,
or sad.
It's not good,
neither is it bad.
There is no beginning,

not even an end.
It just makes sense to the time I spend.

My pen will stop writing when emotions get too deep.
I'll wipe off my tears, and go back to sleep.
I'll dream her again tonight,
and wake up again in the middle of the night.

Cassandra Kochman
THE SPARROW DOESN'T FLY SOUTH
Did you ever see him shivering in the wind?
Did you ever wonder how he, so tiny, could win
The battle of the cold? So delicate, yet so bold!
Wish he wasn't so frightened of me.
I'd like to sit him on my Christmas tree,
Keep him warm there, feed him too.
He'd look at me and say

"Why are you so blue?
If I can make it, so can you!
Listen to my song and you'll find a clue,
I have lots of friends who keep me warm,
And we always fly above the storm.
If you're not alone on a cold winter's morn
You'll find your happiness will be reborn.
Again and again I say love is the key.
Seek it, find it, and you will see.
My friends are waiting now, so please let me go.
I can't be chained, you see,
I must taste the snow."

Oh, wise sparrow, your words ring so true.
Do you think maybe someday I'll be as loved as you?

Ang Vannoy
DANCING
Heavens rays descend on us,
whenever you're with me;
I want to hold you in my arms and kiss you tenderly.
We danced upon your rooftop clear,
the stars were overhead:
You whispered I love you in my ear,
I still recall those words you said.
Your eyes so brown and oh so true,
our love would last forever through.
Or so I thought but I was wrong, as I dance alone to our song.

David D Dowler
TRAVELS

This writing is dedicated to those persons too numerous to name whose trust & friendship gave me the inspiration for whatever talent I might have . . .

I am traveling down a highway that I've traveled much before . . .
And I think about the trip tomorrow . . .
And for many days the more.
Seems like forever . . . since I first made the drive . . .
And now I begin to wonder . . . if I've ever been alive.
Back and forth I've gone . . . along the same stretch of road . . .
Never really seeing . . . as along the road I go.
But of late I've been looking . . . to the left and to the right . . .
And I've begun to wonder . . . about my chosen way of life.
What about that man who just turned off up ahead . . .
I wonder where I'd be if I'd gone in his stead.
I guess I've never given thought to venture . . . or to roam
Still I can't but wonder on the outcome of my life . . .
If I had taken a voyage . . . instead of just a drive . . .

Myra Cochran
THE STREET OF LONELINESS
The street of loneliness is dark and empty as the night covers your heart. The coldness fills your body for there is so much of love inside, but it is hidden for the loneliness for now is your lover and not him.

Patricia Vega

Patricia Vega
SIGNS OF TIME
Looking at the signs of time
a wise man will never forget
What we see we put behind
to save it for regret

A sign is just a warning
that time is drawing near
What is so important to us
time will make it clear

Getting older way too fast
time is not to blame
Any bit you throw away
time will always claim.

Helen J Gadson
I AM SAD
I am sad and I don't know why
When the day comes and then they go.
I am sad when it rains,
I am sad when there is no sun shine outside,
I am sad because there's no one there for me, I am sad when the days
come and go then away passing me so. quickly, wishing they would let me be alone, I am sad for which my heart is broke,
I am sad because I'm all alone to the world.

Dallas Wayne Downes
YOUTH TOUCHED ME BRIEFLY
Youth bumped me rudely on the street
One day
(Touched me briefly)
I lost my balance
And fell.

I turned from where I sat
Dazed
And shouted:

You have done me an injustice
Stay and help me to my feet.
I cannot rise again without your help.
I am old.

Why are you in such a hurry, any way?
You thoughtless fool!

Rushing to a place you'll never reach
At that rate.

Youth looked back
And softly answered, "I must go"

When it was already gone.

Susette Soja
CONVERSATION WITH A STRANGER
Hey stranger, come on over here
Pull up a chair and buy me a beer.
I'll cry in your glass you can cry in mine too
While I tell you about a love I once knew.

Stranger let me buy a round or two.
Oh okay, the next one's on you.
I see the hurt, you've got tears in your eyes
And me I've heard one too many lover's lies.

Hey stranger, I just heard last call
Thanks for letting me bend your ear and all.
One drink for the road before we go.
Thanks again stranger, you were nice to know.

Michael W Reynolds Sr
SAD SOLDIER
His face pressed heavily upon the paddy,
his eyes wondered why.
His mother, somewhere, will mourn,
wailing, wondering why.
Guts and gore, blood tainted rice, but
a soldier's eyes stay
straight ahead, (that's S.O.P.).
Twenty years and drugs do not dull
the quiescent question in his eyes.
Why was this face at my feet my enemy?
A moment sooner our eyes might have met
and in that meeting made some sense.
Progress . . . History . . . War . . .
Perhaps each has its waste.
But time . . . oh, time would not STOP!
His life stolen, sudden, sullen,
while this sad soldier stuffed away
his silent scream for a future day
all the while wondering why . . .
eyes would not see.

Gunnar L Hayes Jr
SEE THE LIGHT

I dedicate this poem to my daughter, Nicole Marie

To hope, aspire, a mere answer to despair.
To feel, an exercise in futility, if not communicated.
Trust and faith from others, as is true for oneself.
A combatant of jealousy is the ability to forgive, a step towards a fundamental need to accomplish Love in an unrefined mode.
As listening manifests knowledge, a respect for life engages an exercise for humanity and the living. A sense of time is required so that lessons of life may be taught to our youth, in the proper order space.
Humility, an ingredient that perpetuates growth in our fellow Wo/Man, beliefs built on faith from events that go unseen to the naked eye
Responsibility should be practiced early on, to induce the greatness that lives inside every human being . . .
We must shun darkness (as in death)
Seek out the light that will provide knowledge, understanding and the infinite.
For that is the true essence of a life that truly lives, as does our Maker.

Rebecca Savich
TIME IN THE PASSING
I look to the East
To see the sun appear,
Only I did not know
what to hold so dear.
and all the while I live my life.

I was 10 yesterday
and 5 the day before,
making my own history
with memories only I adore.
and all the while I live my life.

The hour is getting late!
I know not what to expect
What will be my fate?
Will I be of the few elect?

I stop cold, I am calm
For I have looked to the west,
Just in time to see the sun rest.
and all that while I lived my life.

Betty Smith Loudy
HIS WEALTH IS OURS TO ENJOY
Some people must be on the go, all the time you see
Let me tell you my dear friends, what brings such joy to me
To come home after a hard day's work and sit in my chair outside
It's amazing all the things I see; they have nothing at all to hide.
When I looked up in the tree, a bird was perched up there
With food held tight in her mouth, for her young in a nest somewhere
She gave a chirp to say 'hello' and then I watched her fly
For she is one of God's creations; sent to us by Him on high.
Next a squirrel came from behind, going his merry way
To see what he could find to eat; to fill him for that day
He climbed way up in the maple tree and sat upon a limb
There for just a short brief time; it's just me and it's just him.
Then inbetween the blades of grass, the ants move to and fro
I often wonder what they do, or where they plan to go
Next I heard a great big splash, behind my chair you see
A beautiful robin redbreast; getting nice and clean for me.
The sun is setting in the west, the sky is pink and blue
It's time for me to go inside; to see what I can do
God opens up my heart and mind, to tell it like it is
One doesn't have to spend a cent,
to enjoy this wealth of His.

Donna M Felschow
a place at the window
I heard them singing,
and wished my voice.
I heard them laughing,
and wished my heart.
I heard them crying,
and wished my soul.

I'm barred from the window,
oh do they care?

They see the birds,
 I hear the air.
They feel the grass,
 I touch the thorn.
They kill the world
 I await the wind?

There was no place.
They held it firmly.
I could not help.
The window was theirs.

Missi Meserve
PEACE
Where did peace go?
Was it ever here?
Has there been a time
When war was nowhere?

I don't believe it was so,
Because if that were true
Everyone would be friends,
Just like me and you.

I hope someday for peace,
When we all can join as one,
But I don't think it could be
After all the damage we've done.

Maybe our children can find a way
To make the world really believe
That all can love and stand together,
So all evil things will leave.

Beverly Mead
MY SON

Dedicated to David

Hello little one.
Are you sucking your thumb?
Can you see past the end of your nose,
Feel all ten fingers and toes?
Have you met any new friends,
There among the nursery playpens,
Do they all smile so sweet as you,
Make those bubbly sounds and coo?
I have something important to say,
On this your new life's first day,
"Hold precious the life you have won"
Now sleep well little one . . .
My son . . .

Jasper D Freeman
WITH SYMPATHY

Dedicated to Connie Wheeler's children of Whitingham and to my loving Wife, Eldora

I know just words can't heal a broken heart
But I pray some ease from what I have to say
Your Mother is so with you in your minds
Tho She's left those painful cells of earthy clay

I like to think of the gentle wind in Spring
How it caresses your cheeks and teases locks of hair
You cannot see it, no matter how you try
But you just know for sure it's always there

And there's no doubt it's that way with your Mom
Altho gone to her heavenly home above
Rejoicing with dear ones who went before
Her spirit hovers round yor with Her love!

Patrick Riddell
WHY?!
I don't know where time has gone
Or when it was when I went wrong
Nothing seems to go right for me
The only time people care is when I bleed
I think to myself, is it me, is it my face
Or is it both, am I a disgrace
I look at the future and all I see
Is more and more people laughing at me
I'm still searching 'cause I still believe
I guess I have to wait and see
Suicide has come to mind
But sooner or later I will die
You hear no warning but your heart can tell
Then I hope they feel the emptiness I know so well
When I die I'll be ready
I just hope that I'm buried
'Til then I'll wait and see
What this cruel world has in store for me.

Joseph N Peoples
I WONDER

This poem is dedicated to Helen Gordon, my sweetheart.

I wonder if she thinks of me, when it's quiet and she's alone. I wonder if she remembers my number when she looks at the phone. I wonder if she remembers the smile I gave so freely to her.

I wonder if she stops to think of me now or then, To wonder how I'm doing and wonder how I've been. I wonder if she hurts when they play our favorite songs, I wonder if she yearns for me when a couple strolls along. I wonder if the memories keep her awake at night wishing we had never said good-bye.

Ronjon Cameron
CAN'T YOU SEE THROUGH THE BLUR

To Nancy, my own special angel. Thanks for the love it took . . . Ronjon

If she feels like an angel
It's because she knows
God gave her the strength
To deal with you.
With your head in the bottle
It's so hard to tell
Which bag you'll be coming
Out of next.
But she holds on tight
To a belief in you
And you can bet your
Little angel will see you through.
'Cause she don't love you
For the man you were,
Nor who you are.
That's not what God
Has sent her here for . . .
Can't you see through the blur,
There's an angel standing there
Waiting for the man
God meant you to be . . .

Jessica Dara Howard
A FATHER'S LOVE

This poem was inspired by and dedicated to Kent Fleming and his son Todd, whose faith and integrity has been an inspiration to so many. To my friend, who has made me a richer person just by knowing him.

The day you were born,
I thought my heart would burst
So much pride within me,
as I held this bundle of joy
This beautiful tiny child,
my precious little boy.

When you were just a tiny baby,
I held you close to me
Knowing I would love you forever,
Together is the only place to be.

I saw you take your very first steps,
watched your first tooth come through
I listened as you spoke your very first words,
that sounded like "Daddy, I love you."

Time seemed to go by so very fast
as days turned into years
Watching you grow, you were my sunshine
amidst the laughter and tears.

There's nothing greater than a father's love
that grows and has no end
Always remember this, my son,
I pray—as our lives together, we blend.

No matter where you walk, my son,
as we travel down life's highway
Always remember my love, my son
and that we'll be together one day

So keep happy thoughts of me in your heart,
as I keep you close in mine
Just know one day soon we'll be together
Forever and for all time.

Angie Rendleman Downs
AMERICuhhh, where are YOUuu?!

To one who inspires and believes in me. For being a true friend and lifetime lover and for holding your head high against all odds. You're a wonderful father and husband David. I love you snuggle . . .

Oh, red white, and blue, what a mess you are in.
Your budget is too high, morale's wearing thin.
But smile, Uncle Sam, don't show your dismay,
give congress a raise, pretend all's okay.
Are your spirits high Soldier? Great, but HEY!,
he has no right to protest, so let's cut HIS pay.
Drifting off as a ship in the still of the night,
congress sleepily cries "War!", but who's to fight?
All weapons dismantled, our ships splashed with paint,
where's the force of might in a system so taint?
"Cut DEFENSE!", we don't need it.
"Freeze spending", they say.
God forbid there ever come the day—
when, no power at all, the flag's cased away.
No Nukes to hate, no rockets, red glare,
but no land that I love or bombs bursting in air.
No brave. No free. just, "What's in it for me?"
ZZZsnoring there on Capitol Hill,
dreaming out our final will,
with budgets to cut and money to save
unaware of the
 ULTIMATE
 price
 that's
 paid.

Charlotte A Phillips
MY SUN

for Richard . . . timing really IS everything . . . isn't it?

My Sun is gone,
 a month or more now,
 merely an eternity
Mists and clouds hide the bright
 that feeds my light-starved heart
The rose that is my inside self grows dimmer,
 fading with each passing tear
Existence and continuance is not possible
because my Sun is not here
The darkness and absence, void and ache endeavor my cheer
to conquer
My strength near faded through lack of my Sun's light
But soon shall my Sun return to bring again my world alight
My heart-rose aflourish with love and care and might
 when my Sun shines on me
Once more everything is set a'right

Brandon M Stickney
LIFTED TO A HIGHER PLACE
I awoke in the early morning
and walked out into the day
where I met an old man.
He said "Look at the sun my friend"
and I did
and I raised up my arms to it
feeling the warmth
as he stared into the sky.
The man told me of his travels
to far away places,
his old face brightened and he said
"It follows us everywhere"
I smiled about to cry
and he said "No, just be thankful"
I looked up again
and asked him a question
hearing no reply
I realized that I was alone.

Gloria J Shores
SISTERS
Sisters are so precious and rare
Although at times they're hard to bear
Sisters often fight and fuss
No matter, they're still a part of us.

It doesn't matter what I say to you
But others better watch their
p's and q's
Sometimes to each other, we say things that are mean
While if another says it, then we're a team.

Yes, sisters are a friend, that's true
They're such a living part of you
All your good times and bad they'll share

And if you need them, they're always there.

I'm happy to have a sister like you
To share in everything I do
To encourage me in the big things and small
A sister, who gives me her all and all.

Julio C Solis

Julio C Solis
OUR LADY OF LOURDES

Julio C. Solis, he was born in Managua, Nicaragua, American citizen. Veteran of the U.S. Army. Graduated of Commerce. He has written many poems in Spanish and several in English.

Oh Mother most beautiful
Most holy and most merciful;
Your Immaculate Conception
And your glorifiul assumption
Are wonderful dogmas of our faith.

You appeared to Saint Bernardette
And I will never forget
That in Lourdes of France
You have a Sanctuary of abundance
Grace where flowers of Sanctity grow.

In that grotto so beautiful
There is a water so wonderful,
That it can make the blind see,
The deaf hear, the crippled walk,
And all bless the Lord and Thee.

Michele Lee Tyson
SMILE

Every day is worthwhile
Even those when I do not smile,
For every day that I am sad
I know somewhere someone else is glad,
And their smile will spread happiness
And help the rest of us to frown less.

So even when you're feeling down
Pass a smile in place of a frown,

For someday when you're really sad
The smile will be passed to you
and again make you glad.

L May Carman
DEBBIE

To Dale and Donna Carman—Daniel Carman

She was an angel child—
God let us keep her,
For just a little while,
Now she is in Heaven.

She was a brave little girl—
Loved by her family
And all she knew
In this big world.

Now in a land so fair—
She awaits us there,
As her tiny feet,
Tread the golden street.

Now she has no pain,
With God's love and care—
She is asleep.
We should not weep.

She answered the Master's call,
Sadly missed by all,
God knows best.
At last she is at rest.

Christa Tiraboschi
SONGBIRD

To my dear Aunt Eva, who is very close to my heart.

With all their might the songbirds sing,
Nature nurturing them with her broad wings.
Flying free where the wind is clear,
Love is in the frosty air.
Flying through the sky with no cares at all,
Beckoning them home again is nature's call.
She takes care of them one and all.

Barbara A Williams
EVER SINCE YOU LEFT ME

I dedicate this poem to my mother, who has always told me to use my talent.

Ever since you left
me I just look
up in the sky
I think about the
wonderful times and I
begin to cry
You always said you
loved me it must have
been a lie
All you left me are
tears and memories
with the question why

Linda R Hollis
GROWING YEARS

Through all the pain,
of the growing years.
Still so young,
yet facing fears.

We struggled and fought,
despising our youth.
Longing to grow up,
seeking our truth.

We desperately searched,
for someone who cared.
Someone to love us,
that our hearts may-be spared.

It's not all that easy,
in the growing years.
Still so young,
yet facing fears . . .

Sharlene A Giesbrecht
AS LONG AS THERE ARE DREAMS

With love to Kelly, the one who makes all my dreams come true.

Again tonite, like so many others
just before I fall asleep
I close my eyes to see your face.

If I begin to dream
you are here beside me
holding me, loving me, protecting me.
I can see your breath upon my cheek,
and your fingers running through my hair.
Your scent among my pillows linger near me,
and your lullabyes and loving words
lull me faster into dreamland.
My eyes now closed, my body relaxed,
my lips still smile and tingle
where your goodnight's kisses would have been.

If I begin to dream
you are here beside me
and not hundreds of miles away
dreaming your own dreams.

For as long as there are dreams
we will never really be apart.

If I begin to dream
you are here beside me
And if you begin to dream
I am there for you.

Christine Steiner Schwab
MY COMMITTED LOVE

You are my attraction
Thou radiates love

You are my distraction
It's only you love

Though I have loved a few
You are truly love

Stop the world without you
You are my soul love

My intoxication
I'm drunk with you love

You are my addiction
My committed love

Susan Lee Minton
THE SAFFRON MIMES

Written in support of the "Right of Life" for "The Saffron Mimes:" Clint, Kyle, and Allison Eastwood

I woke up one morning with a . . .
Rainstorm in my mind;
It was raining colors . . .
Colors of all kinds!

So, I painted a picture . . .
A picture in my mind;
A picture of saffron, and
His little monkey mimes!

The mimes were all . . .
Juggling;
Juggling colors . . .
Of all kinds . . .

Color juggling . . .
Monkeys,
Monkey miming . . .
Mimes!

Miming, juggling . . .
Monkeys,
Dressed in colors of . . .
All kinds . . .

Saffron colored,
Juggling, miming
Monkeys . . .
A rainstorm in my mind!

Jody Kauffman
WORDS WRITTEN IN THE WIND

As I gazed out over the lake,
The breeze blowing my hair,
I thought of him and wondered,
Does he still care?

The fresh air filled my head,
Of thoughts that would not end.
Afraid to put them on paper,
So, I wrote them in the wind.

I finished a page long letter,
Read through it once again.
Sealed it with a little kiss,
Then sent it upon the wind.

He will never see this letter,
Or read its contents with in
This letter is from my heart
With words written in the wind.

Jane Vaughn
GOLDENROD

To my mother with love—

Hello! little Goldenrod, standing on a hill—
Gently waving in the wind with all your yellow frill.
Framed by skies of Azure blue,
flanked by red-orange trees—
too frail for birds to stop 'n coo, yet strong enough for bees.

Full of sun and autumn's lust—
reviving summer, rejecting winter's rust.

Valerie Jean Saffell
WHEN LONELINESS SETTLES

Dedicated to: my dear Grandmother, Elizabeth

When loneliness settles . . . pain somehow finds its resting place amongst the emotional feelings.
When loneliness settles . . . time becomes an animated cartoon, either moving too fast or too slow.

When loneliness settles . . . things of great essence merely exist—somewhere in piles of nothingness, staring . . . waiting.
When loneliness settles . . . the blues plays its tune while boredom dances and the heart, as the ultimate audience enhances the production—awaiting the big climax.
When loneliness settles . . . the mind vaguely becomes disillusioned with reality losing its time in space.
When loneliness settles . . .
when loneliness . . .
when . . .

Mildred Capps Jerome
MOM

Dedication: Written in memory of my precious Mom, who went to live with her Heavenly Father—September 26, 1986, I love you, Mom . . .

MOM, Your life book closed, right before my eyes
YET, I read it thro' and thru
Faithfulness, bravery, heart so pure and true
Yes, I wake with the sweet assurance
You're in your mansion beyond the blue . . .
See daddy's radiant smile waiting there for you

MOM, no search was ever needed

from any crystal ball
To tell you of tomorrow or what event would fall
You were a simple lady, a crystal ball you did not look
You found a better source for life, it was GOD'S CRYSTAL-BOOK
Earth's life for you is over, but others your life do view
It sparkles like crystal splendor glistens like the dew

MOM, You left behind so much for family and friends you won
And I know the joys that awaited you behind the set of sun
Now, I'll wrap each precious memory, softly tuck it away
Will patiently wait for GOD to herald me a new day . . .
I'll keep on marching . . . and to that day I will look
When JESUS comes, and fulfills HIS lovely CRYSTAL BOOK . . .

Beverly Kennedy
A FRIEND

I found a friend
One tried, one true
Someone I could relate my thoughts to.
He listened patiently to my small talk,
As together we did walk,
friends, we will be I would say.
How was I to know he had already stolen
my heart away?
Oh how "I love him" this friend of mine,
his voice, his smile, his touch that takes
my breath away.
With all the love that surrounds us—
To be able to say, friends forever we will stay.

Renee E Miller
STILL . . . OUR LOVE'S OUR LEGACY

To the fire in my heart and the passion in my soul; to my husband, Ron. This is a gift of the heart, my gift to you on our anniversary, with love.

Seems as 'tho it was just yesterday,
Since we pledged our solemn vow;
To live our lives together . . .
Yet to let ourselves allow,
To grow as separate people
And develop our 'own' style!
But never losing contact . . .
Growing closer all the while!
Looking back now . . . I am certain,
Every moment, . . . bad or good,
Has been etched into our memory,
To reflect on when we could . . .
You have filled my life with memories,
But . . . most of all, your love!
No two could have life better,
It's what dreams are woven of!
Sounds as if it's all been easy
Once it's written down to see . . .
Yet—you and I have lived this story,
Still . . . our love's our legacy.

Mike Kopack
THE DAWN SHOWN EMPTY

To James Douglas Morrison, The Lizard King!

The dawn shown empty,
Life begins again
Eyes sparkling
Bright w/vivid colors!

Her silken skin warms me.
Feelings new, unused,
A breath washes over me
Like a thousand ancient tongues.

What happens next?

May I behold your beauty?
Your ungodly beauty!
Please miss sunshine,
I'm lost in your mystical rays!

Find me!
Help me!

Julie Anne Podejko
INNOCENCE LOST

This is dedicated to David J. Rutt . . . I don't have to use words to say it because you know what I mean, but thank you for being there when I needed you.

I look at the girl
in the mirror before me,
eyes full of wonder
as I try to recapture
an innocence lost . . .
trying to find the child
that I used to be,
but it is to no avail,
for who I once was
I can never be again—
the child is gone
and I stand here in her place.

Ethel C Harsha
A HOME

This poem is dedicated to the Harsha children.

A home is a house by the side of the road,
Where ere the travelers pass,
and stop to chat with the children there,
What more could you ask than that?
The flowers and trees are abundantly found,
And loaded with golden hue.
God made them all for us to enjoy
Though our earthly days be few.

Now the house still stands by the side of the road,
But the travelers gone long long ago.
The children have grown,
And all gone on their own.
The flowers and trees are tilling the time,
Spring, Summer, Fall and the snow.
God has made the date
For man and his mate.
His wonders are still unknown

Richard L Heintzelman
WHEN IT IS DARK WITHIN MY ROOM

when it is dark within my room
and i lay upon my bed
mulling over the day behind me
my thoughts often stray to when you were near me
and thinking of you brings to life
all the glorious times you touched me
and spoke to me in a rough half whisper
how much you loved me.
and when it is dark within my room
i can hear if i listen closely
the stirrings that we once made
sharing slowly,
passionately in our own way
swaying magnificently to a rhythm
all our own.
but now these dreams of you are disappearing
as sleep finally takes control of me
and suddenly a tear i fear falls lightly
on my cheek
for thoughts of you can be bitter memories
so i'll try to forget my one time happiness
and lay staring at the gloom
when it is dark within my room.

Anne Power
BACK TO NATURE

To Anthony and Andrew
Love from Mama

Oh, give me a shack, back in the woods,
With a little old creek and a big tree with lots of moss, that is, if you could.
I'd also like a meadow of green,
Surrounded by trees as far as could be seen.
And while you are about it, could you throw in some flowers?

Just acres and acres, you could gaze at for hours.
And also, some songbirds would be real neat,
To look in their nest, and hear a peep-peep.
I'm up real early, outside by seven,
To see if there's anything new in my own little heaven.
So, come on, pack up and move out of that city,
and find something like mine, but maybe not quite so pretty.
Who cares about T.V.s and hearing phones ring,
With X-rated movies and other bad things.
So, come on, wise up and get on the ball,
If you put things to moving, you can make it by fall.

Joyce George
PRISM

Prism,
Captured wonders escape the solid
Invisible stained glass go to visible,
Imprisoned life beauty strength
I
Release you
By simple soft motion of my fingers
By gentle raging motion of my mind
Being—
Being.
Just another Sarah Esther
Another Ruth for you,
Prism!

Merdieth Diehl
THE OUT HOUSE

There's fond memories of walking the path out back,
That led to the out house that looked like a shack.
Remember how we would sweep, scrub and lime each week,
So it was neat and clean when we took a leak.
How we would sneak peeks in the cracks in the wall,
And laughed like crazy at what we thought we saw.
How we giggled at all the corn cob jokes,
And wished we had a bathroom like the rich folks.
O' for the good ole days when we all were small,
And for the fond memories that we now recall.

Geraldine (Gerrie) Novak
MISSING

This poem is dedicated to: "Wheels in Tandem"

Remember the day dreams we talked about new pleasures and treasures we'd give without doubt, that will be missing.
Evenings of love with you by my side, no more fears of that emptiness inside, that will be missing.
X-marks the spot on this heart of mine, where my love for you will remain sublime, that won't be missing.
Waiting forever that day divine, if not for circumstances, a future of lifetimes, that will be missing.
I've lived with and loved the one man on earth, that can promise a true rebirth, that will be missing.
Living for each other and praying for time, looking for a miracle that we can not find, that will be missing.
Listen to the words that lay in your heart, the reasons, the meanings, the times we've both hurt, that won't be missing.
I had no future, no reason to love, and out of no where you appeared as such, taking my hand and placing it in yours as if it had been there for years and years, that will be missing.
Always remember our first little haven, in Oley you needed, and there I gave, that will be missing.
Memories of laughter, good friends and good cheer, I'll cling to forever with a passion and some tears, that will be missing.
Soon the skies will be high and filled with blue, you will be out riding as we used to do, when you stop for that pause, please look up, and if you feel as I do, there should be someone missing.

David L Crump
WIND RACER

Among the hills, high and low
She rides across them, on her spotted pinto
Her long black hair, she would race the wind.
The sun shining down, on her light brown skin.
Her eyes were brown, they would shine so bright
Like the reflection of the water, on a full moon night.
She loved a brave, across the plain.
A different tribe, they weren't the same.
But in their hearts way down inside,
They bleed together, from their screaming war cry.
His father was chief, and hers one too.
His was Apache, and hers was Sioux.
She reaches his camp, hoping to find.
No war paints with none in mind.
She was bringing a message, from her father the chief

Hoping for love, and hoping for peace.
A flaming arrow brought her to the ground.
The last thing she heard, was a war cry sound.
All she wanted was to see him again.
To ride together, and race the wind.

Ann Marie Pierson
LADY OF DECEMBER
Lady of December poured herself upon me
in robes of snowdrift and mountains of rain.
Found her yesterday and held to ease the pain.

Lady of December came and
drowned my heart in her hands,
told me to live for tomorrow
and the blue in the clouds both night and day.

She whispered a silken song for me
as dawn nearing opening hearts filled with anger and pain
and she is only a step away.

Soft sand-sung wind blew upon us
and sorrow into her heart—
Now I am weeping for my Lady Of December.

Deborah Smith
SIMPLE LOVE

To my loving husband, Ira

Have you ever heard a Robin sing?
Have you ever smelled the rain in the Spring?
Have you ever tasted a chocolate bar?
Have you ever seen a twinkling star?
That's the only way to describe my love
Pure and simple from God above.
You are my music, the melody flows
You are my moisture, that helps me grow
You are my sugar, that makes life so sweet
You are my sparkle, when our eyes meet
Thank you for being so much to me
You touch all my senses, that's why I believe
That our Creator made you just for me.

Victor L Pellarin Jr
WITHOUT YOU

I love you for who you are, but I love you more for who you could have been.

I love you not so much for your realities as for your ideals. I pray for your desires that they may be great; rather than temporary satisfactions, which may be so hazardously little.

A satisfied flower is one whose petals are about to fall. The most beautiful rose is one that is hardly more than a bud wherein the pains and ecstasies of desire are working for better and larger growth.

Not always will you be as you are now!

I cannot change the reality that clouds exist; but I can put you in a place that the sun will nurture. It is then your choice to grow or wilt.

Flowers are not always beautiful for they have their seasons and appointed times. I love the flowers that blossom every season despite the tough earth under which they sleep.

Not always will you be as you are now!

Those who pick a flower for the momentary pleasure it may bring do a grave injustice. A rose was given thorns for its protection, but a heart has no defense.

Once you have taken a heart from the place in which it slept, it is your responsibility to care for it always; for without a heart there will be no more seasons.

Without flowers there will be no more beauty.

Without love the sun will cease to exist and everything will die.

Without you . . .

Natalie Lueders
A BROKEN DOWN BARN WITH A FADED RED ROOF
A broken down barn with a faded red roof
Keeps guard over fields where rows of wheat once waved.
The eye-like windows of the tattered old house
Stare out to an empty yard where children once played.

The children that once ran over the grass and weeds
Have grown and have children of their own—
Never to return to that once happy home
Where they used to catch fireflies in the hot August night.

The pond out back where in summer heat children swam
Stands dead and deserted, stagnant with time.
Sounds and smells once so familiar
Now remain only as echoes in memories.

Rhoda L Compestine
ANY PLACE FOR ME

I wish to dedicate this poem to our homeless all over the world.

I wear clothes all tattered and torn, because there is no place for me in our society.
I wear shoes with hole in the soles, I'm just looking for a place for me.
I rummage through garbage cans looking for something to eat, I need to survive with dignity.
I sleep in an alley or stand in the street, that's just me.
I stand near a burning garbage can to keep warm, that doesn't mean anything.
I walk the streets looking for old things to keep me warm, that's just me.
I take my shopping kart around with me. I'm looking for things I need.
I go for days without eating or sleeping, that's only me.
I go to a free place to eat or sleep, that's only me looking for a place to be.
I walk the streets in old gloves and torn knees. I pinch my pennies to be able to get the things I need.
I may go to jail for one night or even three, that's a place that's safe for me.
I may see a knifing and hear their screams, but I don't say nothin I just take care of me.
I live in a place that's been condemned, it's a place for me.
I may not work and that's reality. I hope my God will be lenient with me, for this is where I need to be.
I lost my job and family, I'm tired of keeping up with society.
I live with only me. Being what I need to be, tattered and torn with holes without a place to eat or sleep.
That's the end of our society.

Laura J McCool
HAIKU
The rose blooms in full
glory; the dogwood in deepest humility.

Sam Erwin
ASHES
The ashtray of burnt-out matches
The cigarette butts half-smoked
The filters; yellow from the nicotine

The ashes that were once warm
are now cold
Soon all of this will be thrown away

No one remembers
How they once handled the cigarette
Between their fingers

Or tossed the ashes in the tray
No one cares to wonders
To the extent of the happenings
of these items

Throw it away, forget it
leave it burning
Let someone else care

No it doesn't matter

Because yes, to ashes we all will return

Steven V Shearier (age 11)
WAR
War is an ugly, dirty thing.
Men are its servants and death its king.
It rides afar and kills as it goes.
It has no friends, all men are its foes.
In wars many have fought and died,
and still more deaths are to be cried.
But some men still fight as fools,
for these are war's personal tools.
Is there nowhere war can't go?
The answer to that question is No!
But we must all hope and pray
that we can defeat this war. There must be a way.

William O Barkley
THE WAY YOU ARE

Dedicated to my mother: Margaret Barkley

Cherishing the memories of
having you
Near
Like a painted picture, the image of
you is captured so very
Clear
Your smile, a smile of peace and
easiness
warmth and tenderness
Just one of many qualities which set
you apart from all the Rest
Never short of projecting
the lady you
Are
It's a natural flow, an ease so
graceful
Any self-respecting Black Man
should be
Proud to Know
Fighting a system which
demand the best
of You
You give of yourself, not only for
self
But the Black Race Too
Living in a world of Confusion,
Delusion
Persuasion
Sometimes feeling all Alone
You're able to gather the strength
Stand Up
Holding your very Own
Love and understanding you
give to your
Fellow Man
Reaching out to others,
you lend a helping
Hand
If Love and Respect is given
when it is
Due
Then to the "Black Lady,"
I tip my hat to
You.

Octavia Prince
A PRAYER
Lord, let me see,
That money nor fame,
Is life greatest gain.

But let me see,
That a cheerful giver
To those in need,
Makes many a happy heart indeed.

It is better to give a little,
Than not to give at all.
It is better to be contented
What ever you have,
Than to gain power in this world,
And lose what you had.

So let us be contented,
With the little things in life,
Living the path that is right!

Because contentment is better than gold,
It will rest many a soul,
It is more than money can hold,
Than power or fame can unfold.

Ronald Mazzella
TRIPPING OUT
. . . that final subway ride begins
Downhill:
A quick ride
Along the tracks.
The approach
Of the tunnel.
A rush of air.
The explosion of blackness
And light no more . . .

Alycen Rockwell
DON'T TELL ME WHAT I NEED
The fury of that sudden moment
Masses of green anger
The security of life
Being a rebel
Don't try to read me
Don't try to touch me
Don't tell me what I need
Let the scream emanate
Maybe twice
For the next time you forget
Let the obscenities go

Let the fragile vase fly
Watch the splinters fall about
Throw back your head and shout
And leave me alone in the rising steam

Alicia E Babcock
AT DAY'S END
The sun is like a fire ball,
ready to descend,
The sky becomes a darker blue,
the day is about to end.
I see the tracks in the fallen snow,
a little critter runs through.
And now more flakes are coming down,
their gentleness reminds me of you.
With each new flake upon my face,
a chill runs down my spine;
I feel a breeze flow through my hair,
I slowly start to unwind.
Once again I look above
I see the sun is gone;
The only light around me now
Casts a shadow wide and long.
But soon that fades within the snow,
the day is finally done;
I slowly close my eyes to rest,
and I think of us as one.

L Claudine Strong

L Claudine Strong
OUR AFFAIR

To my wonderful parents, Mr. & Mrs. Raymond Everett Dey

Mystery lover
you're kept well under cover

It's our well hidden secret
we can't tell another

We both have the same situations at home

Where our love-lives have both gone as dry-as-a-bone

She doesn't understand you!
He doesn't understand me!

What are we to do?

They both have excuses for everything!

So we'll just let our affair . . .

CONTINUE!!!

Shandra Johnson
EVERYTHING IS DARK NOW
Everything is dark now
Never again to see a tomorrow,
For I have seen today
and have no desire.

Through the years darkness came
When the shadows cease to exist
And a child cries afar,
I know the time is nigh.

Tonight I will weep
Never again to taste the salt,
My mirror broken forever
No more world of fantasy.

Amy Kathleen Trudy Katz
WHAT IF
What if I turn blue?
What if I'm forced to live in a shoe?
What if my cat gets stuck in a tree?
What if Freddie comes and kills me?
What if I fall off a mountain?
What if I drown in a water fountain?
What if I get stuck in wet cement?
What if I go camping and forget my tent?
What if I get thrown in jail?
What if my mom puts my room up for sale?
What if I choke to death?
What if I'm forced to watch MacBeth?
What if I swallow a knife?
What if I were Shirley MacLaine in a former life?
What if I'm chased by Al Capone?
What if I'm trapped in the Twilight Zone?
What if JAWS lives in my toilet bowl?
What if the Devil claims my soul?
What if the President knocks on my door?
What if we all die in a nuclear war?

Cynthia Pressley Hayes
A WAY OF LIFE?

I would like to dedicate this poem to my parents, Marvin and Fannie Mauldin. Through their patience, love and understanding they taught me how to love, and not to be an abusive parent, myself.

As I sit here with only pen in hand,
Trying to write about, why I love this land,
A shocking truth comes to mind.
It was, of a life, I tried to leave behind.
For this, "way of life," there is no excuse.
No one, should ever have to suffer from child abuse.
It might have been a word, or even a cruel act,
But, the scars are lasting, they can't be taken back.
I see this, "way of life," every single day.
It hurts me to think, how much our children have to pay.
For what they learn, they see from us.
Will it be, only, how to fight and fuss?
Will <u>they</u> make <u>their</u> children cry?
Or, will some of them, even have to die?
So, the next time you're angry, or just having a bad day,
Don't hurt the child, <u>PLEASE</u>, just turn away!

Elizabeth Malone
THE OLD YELLOWED VALENTINE
A lovely old valentine, trimmed with lace,
Ruffled, beribboned, stands in place.
Her hands slightly tremble, her eye holds a tear,
As she reads the old words so loving and dear.
"I love you, I love you, and on this special day
I'm writing these words that my heart wants to say.
The blue of your eyes and the smile on your face
Can light up the darkest or gloomiest place.
Will you be My Valentine, dear, on this day
And forever be mine, is all I can say?
For I love you, I love you, and never will part
From you darling. These words come from the depths of my heart."
The teardrops rain down on her hand and the heart
As she thinks of the man from whom death did her part,
And the lace trimmed old valentine, yellowed and sere,
Goes back in its box to await the next year.

Jeff Grujicich
TO ANYONE ELSE
The tears I cry with you are dry
And roses are but rootless weeds
My vowing whisper's just a sigh
The wind has blown too many seeds

A seeming fruit had formed but lied
Assuming locked the empty cage
A flimsy bondage I have dyed
To match the pattern of each stage

Ignore the vibrance you may see
That color warm this gaze of ice
They are the memories past of she
And love that can't be given twice

Joseph J de Boves
HERE'S A GOLD WATCH—HAPPY DAYS
Here's a gold watch—Happy days.
Sound like a familiar phrase?
That's the greeting that is sent
On the day of Retirement.

Lucky person, no more work,
No unpleasant tasks to shirk.
Rest and relax all day long
Away from the working throng.

Nirvana, Valhalla all in one,
Lolling in the daily sun.
Catching up on past due chores,
Shopping in the local stores.

Then a feeling comes to me,
A sense of boredom plainly.
Now that I have done it all,
I find I'm staring at the wall.

I must get out more, I say.
I miss all my friends this way.
Nothing to complain about,
These Blues I've got to rout.

Volunteer work is the answer.

Edmund C Vicheck II
A WRITER'S THOUGHTS
I stare at a blank page
Expecting to pour my feelings out
To saturate the pulp with ink and sweat.

The paper looks back
Daring me to search my soul
Thought eludes me, darkness lurks over my shoulder.

Is there a god, leaps from deep corners of my mind
People die of hunger, disease, and hand of brother
Looking to the night, a torched mind searches for answers.

Yet if there is a god, is he a loving and caring god
Or is he wandering the heavens
His creations forgot, for only a moment.

Finally, I have won over the page
It looks at me with feelings of a torched mind
I lay down my sword and rest my thoughts for another day.

Michael J Mortlock
THE BROWN SUIT

To my dear friend Barbara Jean at whose insistence I submitted this poem. Also to my loving sister Anne who encouraged me to write. Lastly to Frederick C. Drackett-Case whose ancient apparel provided the initial inspiration.

The old brown suit that Freddie wears
Seems immune to cuts and tears,
Though worn and rumpled it may be
'Twill last throughout eternity.

It's the only suit I've ever known
Which looks its best not hung but thrown,
Crumpled up without a care
Over and on a wooden chair.

Perhaps the poor old cloth will rot,
Or conflagration burn the lot.
But what if he cares not a bit,
And one day goes and murders it?

Diane Christmas
SAYING GOODBYE
I always cared so dearly for you.
You were always there when I was blue.
You always had a hug ready to brighten my day.
That's why it's hard for me to say . . .

"I never wanted to have to say goodbye"
When I think of our last times together all I can do is cry.
When you passed on, to that land up above
All I can do now is remember our love.

I often think of the times we shared.
and I always knew you truly cared
I knew the day was near when you wouldn't be with me anymore
That day just came too soon, I guess you never know what life has in store.

I'll love you forever and it'll never cease or end.
Maybe one day my broken heart will mend
The pain seems to get easier as the days go by.
Now, all I can do is try . . . To remember you for what you meant to me. Which is more than anyone can ever begin to understand or see!

Cindi Stein
IF I SHOULD NEVER SEE YOU AGAIN

To Keith—whom I will always hold dear and deep in my heart.

If I should never,
see you again.
Remember the good times,
if you can.
Remember I'll love you,
for ever more.
Wishing you the best,
for what life has in store.
Remember the moments,
we shared together.
And the love we shared,
will last forever.
And if by chance,
I die before you.

Always remember,
our love was true.
Don't be sad, unhappy,
or blue.
I'll see you in heaven,
for a friendship brand new.

Catherine U Thomas
RETROSPECT
I weep for friendships lost: their flowers
Forever sunk by crushing boots of hours
That stepped with heavy tread of careless lack
Of thoughtfulness, and made a muddy track.
I wish that I might probe with sunny hope
And find some unhurt roots where I might grope
With tender hands and stroke them.
Then to grow.
And wait. And have some flowers that I know.

Amy Mowrer

Amy Mowrer
LITTLE SPECKLED STAR
Gleaming, gleaming for all that can glow,
The stars up above, oh, how they show,
Seeing the light in your eyes,
When you look at the stars in the skies.
Seeing the little tiny speckled star,
But they're really pretty and very far.
They're so far up, they're hard to see.
I wonder what it would be like if one of those stars were me?
What do you think of a little star in a big sky of blue?
What would you think if one of those stars were you?

Antoinette A Roland
THE BOY IN THE BUBBLE

In memory of my parents, Andrew A. and Alma L. Simms

Alive within his Mother's womb, this innocent, precious, unknown little bundle kicking and stretching ready to take on the world.

A visitor, a male, David he was named, dark haired, a promising smile, eyes piercing as if he knew a family secret, this baby so small.

Gazing upon David from across the way, feeling with one's eyes, holding the warmth of this precious gift from here. This once embryo—tiny feet, tiny hands flaring out at his demand.

Though this bubble must be your home, you have so much bestowed upon you, a valuable essence of sharing you with so many, love that has known so few.

The outside world you'll never need, because little one you've done your deed, now rest your reward is due.

Ramona Rivera
FRIENDS FOREVER
You are a special friend to me
'cause we're two of a kind
That can always be,
Sharing our laughter
With one another,
Through hard times
Comforting each other,
Holding close onto each day
Building our friendship
Along the way,
Taking time out
To tell of our secrets
And our dream guy too!
Because that's the kind of friendship
that holds between me and you,
Never able to set us apart
Or ever drift us away,
It'll be together forever
And forever together,
That's the kind of friendship
that will always stay.

Regina Love
REVERIE
Within the rafters of my mind
Reminding me of younger ways
Drift the memories left behind
Of childhood dreams and yesterdays

We lived to laugh—and played with glee
The sun shown always on our faces
Imaginations free to roam
And transport us to exotic places

Deep inside with intense burning
Always wishing to live bolder
Failing to enjoy the moment
Forever yearning to be older

Winter snowflakes gather round me
As I wander back in time
Spring has fled and left me restless
Longing for innocence that once was mine

Todd E Black
ETERNAL LOVE
We are all searching
for that perfect love
as Romeo and Juliets

Why are so many
of God's grand creatures
fated to meet and
mate forever

Oh, great hunter
cold and wet
was it your steady aim
that downed that lonesome bird
or did he just long to meet
his recently departed

Eternal
Love

LaFredia Joyce
AMERICA

To: Marcellus Cory and Lana, my wonderful children and brother Willard Loving memory Mama and Daddy

America, I'm never gonna give up on you
You're my friend, girl
You're the world
Why, even your coins are a positive plus
Eternally inscribed with "In God we trust."
I know that isn't a lie
Being a citizen here is better than anything,
Money can buy
No matter what problems you go through
I'll always be true to you
My precious Red, White and Blue

Loretta Horner
A REAL MOTHER!

This poem is dedicated to my mom "Rosemary Tatro," who's been an inspiration in the lives of so many. I love you mom!

I remember when I was small, and had taken my first fall,
You picked me up, brushed off the dirt, your tender touch took away the hurt.
I remember when I was young, you'd punish me for my "nasty" tongue.
You'd make me go stay in my room, which felt to me like the chamber of doom
I remember when I was a teenager. And suddenly I felt like a stranger.
You told me it was "just a phase," that I'd find the light at the end of the maze.
I remember when I was wed, and all the things that were said.
I knew you loved me, would miss me, but knew it was good,
That I'd live my own life the way that I should!
Thank you Mom, for always being there for me.
You've taught me how a "Real Mother" should Be!!!

Terri Lynn Kruse Richardson
DID YOU EVER STOP TO WONDER?
Did you ever stop to wonder
Why we fight these wars?

We send our young men to their graves,
They'll never return no-more.

Did you ever stop to wonder,
What their young brides feel.

To know they lost their loved one,
In a cold dirty field.

Did you ever stop to wonder,
What their buddies feel.

To see their friend shot,
and to be able to help them not.

Did you ever stop to wonder,
What it's like to die.

In a land where you,
Can't even see the clear blue sky.

Did you ever really stop to
WONDER???

Geneva M Bright
A LAMENT
I had a friend named Boo Boo
A canine as it were
She had big black eyes and a black shiny nose
And lots of tan shaggy fur.
She was generous with her love "licks"
And could run like a desert breeze
The doctor said she had allergies
For every once in a while she'd sneeze.
Her pedigree was "Yorkie"
The rich man's favorite pet
But she didn't care about that sort of thing
She loved everyone that she met.
One day my boss said "comb her hair
And wash her friendly face;
Someone is coming to buy her
And take her to another place."
Oh, my heart failed and bled and stopped
As I tried to accept that command
Boo Boo was going to live with strangers
And be stroked by a stranger's hand.
The buyer said she was perfect
Like the Yorkie she was to replace
She "smiled" like her and wiggled like her
So she'd have her pillow of lace.
When I get to heaven
I'll not ask for Thunder or Ace
I'll go to the "Yorkie" department
And look for that friendly face
As I glide and float and wing my way
In that land beyond the skies
I'll look for my precious, bouncy friend
Boo Boo with the big, black eyes.

Doreen C Minopoli
GENERATIONS
In his worn and wrinkled face, I see youth.
Experience and knowledge gave him the mask
that you too will wear someday.
I can see the pattern of your life
in stages that are before me.
Respect, courage and loyalty will form furrows,
while anger, fear and time scar
the taut mask you now wear.
There is nothing I can do to intervene
with your destiny.
You have nothing to fear; love and strength
will guide you until the next phase,
then you must journey without
me to the cycle's end.
I cannot advance to that point
yet, I have already been there.
I can see your future.

Susan E Watkins
EVERLASTING FRIEND
Please come back
if it's just for awhile
I need to see
Your bright and shining smile.

That sparkle in your eye
that radiant glow
Couldn't you tell
how much I loved you so?

Please come back
to me again
I'll be waiting,
your everlasting friend.

Elizabeth S Dunbar
LIVING ROOM
I do not like my bookshelves neat;
My friends are seated then
In compromising rows
Like sparrows in an unexpected blizzard
Frozen on the power line in icy fragile crystal.
Their wings are still, their voices frozen,
They cannot speak and lead me
Onward in their freakish flight
Or delight my mundane mind with

the singing
In the music of their well-worn
words.
I do not like my bookshelves neat.

Peggy L Floyd

Peggy L Floyd
LET US GO BACK

This poem is dedicated to the person who inspired my life in so many ways, Mr. Jerry Bolden.

I want to say this to all Black
Americans today, "Let us go back."
Let us go back to the time in history,
where the Black man's struggle for
freedom, had so much meaning in
life.
For many of us have gone astray,
thinking only of ourself, forgetting
the trials and tribulation of those who
made it possible for us to be free
today.
Let us go back to the time when a
black lady named, Mrs. Rosa Parks,
was arrested, when refusing to give
up her seat. Today many of us sit
among different races, riding the bus,
without giving the struggle a thought,
and even wondering how this could
be.
Let us go back to the time when Dr.
King delivered his speech, "I have a
Dream."

Today so many of us have forgotten,
what his speech really means. In
1964, the Civil Rights Bill opened
many doors, where would we be, if it
was not signed for you and me.
That is why I say today, let us go
back to refresh our memories. I want
to say this today to all white
Americans, the Black man's struggle
is never an ending one, but if we can
all live together with love and in
harmony the battles would be won.
I say today "Let us go back."

Kimberly Anne Young
THE WIND
The wind is cold, the wind is warm.
The wind brings good and bad.
When the wind blows, it makes a
sound . . . a whistling sound.
The wind whips the fresh cut grass in
the spring and the
Hair of the little girl picking flowers.
The wind blows the leaves in the
autumn and the winter snow.
We must respect the wind . . . it
brings us life, it brings us death.

Charles H Norman
JUST A FRECKLED FACE KID
I stand here beside you,
On your wedding day,
Just a father in waiting,
To give his daughter away.
The memories fastened to
Each little thing,
Will help me remember
What happiness brings.

Though you were all mine
Just yesterday,
Your daddy bows out,
And tip-toes away.
I step back in silence
As you change your name,
But, my freckled face kid
You'll always remain.

Now you stand at the altar
All covered in lace,
But, you were once just as pretty
With mud on your face.
Now where ever you're going,
And what's ever to be,
You're just a freckled face kid,
To your Mommy and me.

Jennifer Nelson Fenwick
THE PROMISE OF THE RAINBOW
Long ago,
God made a promise
that men would never see
His wrath fall from the heavens
and rain down endlessly.

He painted his sign upon the sky
so that the world would know
and there it shined against the clouds
the very first rainbow.

The promise of the rainbow
a symbol of God's love
the beauty in its artistry
created from above.

Whenever doubts are planted
and fear begins to grow
then look upon the sky and find
your peace in the rainbow.

John E Kelly
WILDERNESS DREAM

I would like to dedicate this Poem to "Eddie-Lou Cole" in honor of her "Eightieth Birthday" "Happy Birthday Eddie."

The greatest thing within the
boundaries of this earth,
"This Thing" I do possess.
For this great love within my soul,
is to walk the Wilderness.

To walk softly through tall timber
while my mind rolls on and on,
To listen carefully to the Dove,
as she sings her morning song.

To watch the Deer as they come to
drink
from a cold clear mountain stream,
To feel the Earth beneath my feet,
Fulfills my fondest dream.

To watch the sly young Fox as he
carefully stalks his Prey,
He strikes out, but Misses,
for too slow was his pace,
then I can't help but laugh to see,
that "Look" upon his face.

There's the Turkey, the squirrel, and
the Dragonfly,
The crow and the Hawk, that slowly
soar
in this great wilderness sky.

It's then my heart starts dancing
to the music of a mountain stream,
I close my eyes, and I thank You
Lord,
for this wonderful "Wilderness
Dream"***

Lila Marie Beychok-Boyer
THANKYOU FOR THE ROSES

The poem, "Thankyou For The Roses" is dedicated to my husband, Franklin Eugene Boyer.

Thankyou for the roses,
Orange ones instead of red.
Does the color of the flower
represent a love half fled?

I would like to think it not so,
a resolution simply of the cost.
Yet I ponder still the question,
praying for romance not lost.

Bitter clash and feelings wounded
on the eve of lover's day,
leaves an aching and a yearning
for the words just right to say.

Still supposing that we cradle
in the bosom of our hearts,
tender longings for the other
and a bond of solid parts.

Even more so than each other
seems the flowers boast of three.
Such a fresh and vibrant family,
you and me and Jess Marie!

Romuald Kocol
GOD IN AMERICA

Dedicated to my lovely wife Elizabeth, with Love!

God is everywhere—
always when I see a human face
or see the stars hanging in space,
when whalers breaking through the
ice
or my dear wife says something nice,
often in flowers like morning glory
I read my life's such a short story
but with a courage to embrace
my climb to summit with God's
grace—
. . . happy immigrant trail soon will
be over,
Thank You America! for God I
discover.

Detra Danelle Perkins
THIS WORLD . . .
This world will soon be ending with
all the destruction here . . .
The murdering of the innocent,
The ignorance of the law,
Looking over the fact that we need
them, they hang up on our calls.
The spreading of a killer to our
nation,
The discovery of A.I.D.S.
What is the world doing?
Why don't they see?

Cocaine killing thousands, and
threatening the lives of the free.
Teenagers fighting for colors,
showing a strong uncalled for hate.
War waiting around the corner,
Taking the young and innocent as
bait.
What is our country coming to?
What can be done?
I don't want to die . . . I am still yet,
very young.

Henrietta M Clifford
LOVE'S BENEDICTION
There is love of sister and
Love of brother
Love of lovers, one for the other
But above and beyond and exceeding
All other
Is the love of that dear one
Your own precious mother

Deborah Gaudioso
TENDER YEARS

Dedicated to the most special joys of my life, my wonderful kids, Alyssa, Joshua, Melissa, with all my love.

My little special one so new, how
precious is my time with you. To
hold and watch you grow and coo,
how God has blessed my life with
you.

So awesome is his gift to me to
enrich my life and lend to me, this
wondrous little life I see, and he
entrusted you alone with me.

To guide and teach and show the
way, until your time to go away to
repeat again the path God laid.

Hey little precious one once new,
time is passed and how you grew, I
miss those times of suckling you and
listening to those little coo's.

It seems I closed my eyes one day
and when I woke to my dismay, "no
more lullabies" you say, "I want to
go outside and play, I'll stay with
you another day."

And so you say "well that's ok" and
soon you wake again one day and
once again to your dismay this time
it's real they've gone away to repeat
again the path God made.

Leslie Pritchard Gaither
JESUS IS STANDING HERE KNOCKING ON YOUR HEART'S DOOR
Jesus is standing here knocking on
your heart's door,
As He has done so many times
before.
He is pleading to you to let Him
enter in,
Because He loves you and wants to
save your soul from sin.

Jesus is standing here knocking on
your heart's door,
And you don't seem to know what
He is knocking for.
He is pleading for you not to live,
walk or talk with those who do sin in
the darkness of night.
But He wants you to live, walk and
talk with them who are living,
walking in His light.

Jesus is standing here knocking on
your heart's door,
Please don't reject Him for He may
never knock no more.
Please accept Him, let Him live
within your heart,
So He won't ever say "I know you
not, you must depart."

Jesus is standing here knocking on
your heart's door,
He came to walk beside you, take
His nail scarred hand in yours.
He will fill your soul with Joy, Peace
and Love, flowing from within His
heart.
Then you can sing and praise the

Lord, "How great thou art."

Jesus is standing here knocking on your heart's door,
For He knows that death for you is drawing very near.
He is happy now that you are at peace and have nothing more to fear for.
He says, "My love is for your comfort, it is the reason why I am here."

Otis Jones

Otis Jones
TO MY BELOVED TOMIKO
In solitude and contemplation;
When the sound of silence is still.
I'm writing you of my elation
and how I really feel.

Some pain, some heartache, some sorrow;
after all we're human souls;
but true love last through the morrow
and grows stronger at each threshold.

A verse, a rhyme, a soft voice, a hand,
a hug, a kiss from thee.
No one may understand the things
we do and see.

So thank you for all that you have been;
forgive me if I hurt you and let me be your friend;

Your lover and husband for the rest of my life.
Will you please be my lover, friend, my wife?

Love
Otis

Michelle Knapp-Lawson
MY DREAM

This poem dedicated to James Lawson for being the man I always dreamed of, and showing me the meaning of love.

My dream is a dream
of eternal love.
And my Darling James

My dream is a young
Woman's dream.
A dream of eternal love.

To be on a beach,
In the moonlight,
Walking hand in hand,
Wading the water,
And making love
under the stars.

My dream is a dream I
Share with James.
A dream that has yet
to come true.

Buffy L Harland
TELL TELL TELL
Did you ever have a secret?
That you couldn't really tell.
Because it's about abuse and hell.
But you gotta tell, tell, tell.

Please believe me, all I want is to be loved.
Instead my life is like it's dead!
I am getting sicker in my head.
That's why I told, told, told.

Don't ever let it happen.
Think it over in your bed.
About the life you really dread.
Then honestly you will see.
That the only way to be free.
Is to tell, tell, tell.

I am very hopeful.
That everything will turn alright.
I'll be able to sleep at night.
And I'll never be up-tight.
Because now I have a happy life!

Fred N Ilijevich Jr
THE ENDLESS SEA

To Elizabeth, my Mother.

I think that there shall never be
An endless movement, like the sea.

The sea whose waves come rushing in
To reach the rocks and shore within.

The sea who brings men from afar,
And leads them off by way of star.

The sea whose mighty depths conceal
A kingly wealth, for men to steal.

The sea whose majestic waves unfold,
And display such beauty, as yet untold.

The sea whose abundance feeds all men,
With many inhabitants to apprehend.

The sea whose blue cast calls foe or friend,
Was created by God, and will never end.

Frank Riley
THINK POSITIVE
The horizon of hope
draws and gives Life.
Seekers on its path
travel together
expecting full moons,
brighter suns,
deeper Love.
Dreams of sharing
expand our Spirits.
Positive feelings
challenge our minds.

Diana Marie Distefano
LOVE IS FOREVER

In loving memory of Robert Shannon Bass, the Love of my life. I tried so hard not to love you, but you just felt too good to me. Together or apart, you are forever in my heart—my soul. Diana M.D.

The leaves have started turning colors,
You haven't been gone that long.
Time feels like it's holding still,
and I wonder what went wrong.
Part of me has died with you,
and I know you can't return.
I cry so much and I hurt inside,
but the sun just continues to burn.

I hear fall winds chiming through the trees.
I watch our children growing up.
Soon the winter snows will blow,
It'll still be you I'm loving.
I only go on in hope
of someday being with you.
So why does forever in a day,
just not feel the way that it used to.

Love is forever, but only with you.
Love is forever, because our love is true.
How could I ever love another,
When love is forever—with you.

Willie House
THE SNOWFLAKE BALLERINAS

Dedicated to my sister, Mrs. Lee Eley, remembering how nice she was to me in childhood days.

Here they come, there they go,
Swishing, swirling, smiling hi-ho,
Beautiful, beautiful flakes of snow!
They dance in a twirl, going round and round,
Descending from heaven, earthly bound.
And it is somehow they seem to know,
If they stick together they'll make a snow!
A certain grace—each one's so light,
Disclosing purity ever so white!
Oh, how they do attention claim,
Entertaining all is surely their aim.
These talented ladies who came to entice,
Are charming ballerinas made of ice!
On and on, there is no stopping,
They came to perform skipping and hopping.
Flittering and fluttering is their style,
Making silent music all the while.
Now their finale—the end of the ball,
The lovely dancers do a bow and a graceful fall!!

Kathy D Platt
LIFE WITHOUT MY FRIEND

This poem is dedicated to my late father, Mr. Sylvester Williams.

You were there when I was born, you were there when I said my first words, you were there when I took my first steps, you were there all through my school years. You were there when I needed someone to talk to, you were there through my ups and downs, you were there to ease my pain, but one day it all came to an end, the Lord saw what was best and took you home.
It is hard, but with the help of the Lord I will make it. I have found it so hard to image my life without you my friend.

Dorothy Kimmel Fox
SAY IT WITH LOVE
Say it with love
Should I live beyond my years
Become your child and turn contrary ears
Not wanting to accept your care
When you must lead me where
I would not go
Give me attention in things
I would not have you do
Meld your mind to mine for loves own sake
I shall not recognize the effort you must make
Remember, I once walked this way
There are no words of help that I can say
I love you as a mother—want not to be this child
Do what you will with voice and action mild
And say it with love.

Sharon A Mueller
I AM LOVED

To the family I love, who show their love everyday.

My eyes were wet and heavy,
my heart throbbed with hurt,
my soul felt like not existing,
my body ached for love.

But then I saw the sunshine,
it's warmth upon my face.
I heard the birds sing.
their song of love and peace.

I looked upon the flowers,
as if they're made for me.
I looked at their beauty
and felt my heart miss a beat.

He blessed this world around me,
with beauty, light and warmth
To remind me of his presence
his caring and his strength.

Tamara Ward
THE CLOWN
I smile when I want to cry,
I laugh when I want to die,
Up and down; round and round,
A joking machine that never frowns.
But underneath my mask, you see,
There's a real person,
And that person's me.
There may be paint on my face,
I may wear ruffles and lace,
But underneath that costume and fake face,
There's a human heart beating in its place.
The life of a clown is not all it seems to be,
For people never see,
The real me.

Kathryn L Stevens
THOUGHTFUL DAY

Special thanks to God, for making this dream come true.—To friends who've enhanced my journey through life. To Rick, who inspired this poem . . . I love you.

Did you just have a thoughtful day,
with daydreams passing,
. . . not much to say?

Is the quiet to be blamed on me
. . . nothing to talk over,
no dreams to foresee?

Have I let you down once again,
left you with no smile,

no desire to win?

Are you silent and making a wish,
longing for laughter,
a calm feeling you miss?

I wish I could lift your spirits up
high,
erase questions and problems,
cause sadness to die.

Was it a thoughtful day,
. . . daydreams passing,
. not much to say?

Mrs Pearl Glatky
OUR WORLD AS I SEE IT

To the people of this world

Do you sometimes wonder,
How our world was born.
Out in space it came to be,
A giant ball not to be torn.
Mountains, valleys, rivers and seas,
All put together with such ease.
Different nations and religions
try to come together.
But they cannot love each other.
Everywhere you hear of wars,
Which end so many lives.
I wish they could talk together,
Share together, and realize,
We are all here to share something,
Our hopes, dreams, and future.
With all of those our world
Will be something we can venture.

Richard Alan Barrett
YOUR LOVE

For Deborah

Across the field of new fallen snow
there was a piercing star aglow
Through the cold, so far from spring
I heard a beautiful songbird sing,
the night went by ever so slow.

Through the winter's wind and chill
I saw a woman atop a hill,
she was protective from the wild
as she held so close her newborn
child,
she gave to it strength and will.

Across the land it's Valentine's
people are asking, "will you be
mine?"
they're hand in hand and heart to
heart
believing that nothing can tear them
apart,
as the winter sun shines.

I see what love February brings
like to a girl a diamond ring,
I look 'round as far as the eye can
see
and I want you to know that to me
your love means more than all of
these things.

Richard Garza
WALKING ALONE

To D Boyland though, my love, our time is through my love for you shall always endure . . . and so will my friendship

I walk alone along the pleasant
shore as thoughts of you fill my
mind.
I wonder how you are and wish you
were here to share this peaceful time.
Yet I still try to make the most of
the moment, the sand at my feet;
wind in my hair
A paradise made for two and yet I
admire if alone. How it seems so
unfair
The warmth of the sun fills me as if
in your arms when you hold me so
tight . . .
And tears fill my eyes because I
wish we were together and
everything was still right
But we agreed we should spend
some time apart. "It's for the
best,"we said.
Then why am I so unhappy and why
is it so hard for me to get you out of
my head?
Everyday I try to be strong but the
truth is I am not.
And everyday that I walk alone I
seem to miss you a lot.
But I'll continue to walk alone as
usual because deep inside I know
That soon you'll be back with me
and once again our love will grow!!

Jodi J Hogrell
MY MOM, MY BEST FRIEND

You are not only my mother.
You are my best friend
The one who stands guard over me:
when times are tough
The one who lends a shoulder to
lean on.
When it is needed
Even when you are tired; you still
find time to listen to my problems
You are the one I turn to; when
things go wrong.
The one I share my accomplish-
ments defeats w/. I know I may not
say it often . . . but . . . I love you!
You're my best friend,
You're my mom.
Love
Jodi

Pamela Denise Buford
WALKING THROUGH THE WEEDS WITH GUNS

They bid their mothers and high
school sweet hearts good-bye.
High school boys turned into men.
Walking through the weeds with
guns.
Faced to fight a senseless war, bound
by the fear of death and pain.
Walking through the weeds with
guns.
Camouflaged with the colors of
nature, hiding in the trees, weeds, and
ditches in the jungles. Walking
through the weeds with guns.
Some died they lost their lives, some
lost their limbs.
Some lost their husbands, some lost
their friends.
Mothers cried because their sons had
died. Walking through the weeds
with guns.
Some harbor the war in their mind.
They wake up screaming for their
lives. Walking through the weeds
with guns.
Some were poisoned by the chemical
agent orange, symptoms only to show
up later. Walking through the weeds
with guns.
They came home surrounded by
screaming crowds, murders!
murders! They didn't ask to be in the
war, they had no choice. They are our
heros! Walking through the weeds
with guns.
A president built a memorial in their
honor, thousands of names are listed,
of the men who lost their lives or are
missing in action, in the senseless
war. Why did our men have to go??
Walking through the weeds with
guns.

Richard Dowdell
THE TELEPHONE

Credit! Credit! Easy got!
Phone us for cash right on the spot!
Just leave your number here with us;
We'll make the phone our incubus.
When we can't phone or din your
door,
Then Credits, yours, is "Nevermore!"

They rape your mind, gorge on your
guts,
make cannibals seem harmless nuts.
They suck your soul right through the
phone
and then your lives are not your own.
You'll pay and pay . . . and pay some
more
to feed their endless lust for gore.

But "Ho!", you cry. "The phone's my
link
to love . . . and more." Or so you
think.
But think again and will you see?
Does substitute thus make you free?
How, by ear, can together you fly,
sans taste, sans touch, sans smell,
sans eye?

Mary G Pollard

Mary G Pollard
MY DADDY'S DEATH

"From Mary Grace Pollard" This poem is dedicated to my mother sisters and brothers.

Daddy, I miss you so!
Oh, just to talk to you again.
Daddy my sisters, brothers, nor
mother are the same now that
you are Dead.
Daddy, I just talk to God, now
that you are Dead.
Daddy, I love you.
Daddy I long to see and meet you.

Cindy Headley
I THINK I CAN

I wish to dedicate this poem to: my mom, dad; and my brothers Dale and Durrin and to my best friends. Christina Cons. and Andy Phillips.

I think I can
How about you?
There are a lot
of stairs to climb
I think I can
How about you?
You and I together
We can make it!
God is waiting for us
at the top
I know I can!
How about you?

Charlotte Moore
I NEED MY SISTER'S LOVE

I, know I, can be a pain.
But I hope, that does not,
Make you hate me.

I need your love; truly I do.
Please, love me now.
Before it is too late.
Don't treat me like dirt.
I ask not to be walked upon.
Notice me, help me, love me.

Do not to this to me!
Abandon me not, not today.
Not ever, show me the way.

I must be asking in the wrong way,
So help me now.
Because, I need my sister's love.

Frances Spence
GREAT NEGROES

Contributing to the history and
culture of our nation,
All in heart and mind had undying
determination.

While in a state of oppression,
Their spirit knew not depression.

Intelligent people descendants of
kings and queens,
All had visions and dreams.

Pilgrims of God, freedom marchers,
Overcoming barriers and mockers.

With in born dignity,
Freedom their destiny.

Kevin B Gray
AN ILLUSION

I wanted her more than ever
stretching my hand through the night.
Touching her soul ever gently
slowly she fades out of sight.

With the slightest of smiles she traps
me
desire keeps pulling me in.
I run to her with arms wide open
to find that she's gone again.

Eyes full of fire and passion
she makes me feel ten feet tall.
Casting my net in a fever
to realize I've caught nothing at all.

With coals in my heart barely
burning
blinding my eyes try to see.
Was love ever standing before my
eyes
or was it an illusion to me.

Jennifer Sime
WHO ARE YOU?

Who are You?
My brother, my long lost friend and
lover.
The man who shared my dreams
The one who would jump the boldest
streams.
The fire of my soul,
and the light of my goal.
The lover of the people,
and the guardian of my mind.
Who are you?
The rebel of the world,
the subversive hand of love
the fire trapped in a world of old
glories and deep mud.
Who are you?
The light from dawn to dusk
The freedom fighter against a world
of rust.
The vandal, the thief, the scandal,
the one who taught me how to
gamble
the love, hate, and pain
I was about the encounter.

Kathleen L Anderson
FOOTPRINTS

As a child, romping and splashing on
the beach,
a favorite game was to stand at the
water's edge
letting the waves splash in over my
legs.
The challenge came when the water

forcefully
pulled back out to sea.
I would plant my feet—
Resisting the force that washed sand from beneath them—
Never allowing the waves to pull me aside—
Standing firm.
When the wave was gone I'd laugh with triumph.
I had won.
Stepping back, I would see my footprints—
big and hollowed out from salt water force.
As a teacher, balancing the lives of children,
waves are no less real.
Demands rush in about me;
whims of society seem determined to push me aside.
Can I stand firm? Will I laugh when the wave is gone?
I like to remember the determined little girl.
I like to remember the footprints delightfully larger than life.

Caren Hagstrom

A SUNSTREAKED VIEW

As a pack of geese flew across the shimmering lake, the sun shone wildly streaking the waves with beauty so fine and pure. Flowers were starting to bloom freshly with dew from the fresh rainfall the night before. The mountain air was whisping at my face like sweet kisses. The clouds grew bigger and moved slower as the day crept upon us. The streak of sun was dividing the body of water in two. The bark of the trees on the mountains were covered in wet moss. The sky was all orange with touches of pastel pink, stretching out beyond. And then the final touch to make a beautiful sight complete, a Canadian goose skimming the water with its feet breaking the stillness of the view, sending it in waves. When all the water and waves cooled down, you'd take one last look and say,
Life is like a sunstreaked view, you never want to leave.

Katie Horowitz

THE OCEAN

To my family. Thank you for supporting me through everything.

As the ocean crashes onto
the sandy beach,
I watch the water slink back.
I walk down, leaving my
footprints in the sand.
Carving my name into the sand,
I look back.
No trace of me is left,
except my name,
about to be erased.

Christina Harman

THE ACHE

Dear God, my darling, have you figured out
that there are times not everything can show?
Look past my eyes and you may see the glow
of things my mother mustn't know about.
Beyond an eyelash flutter or a pout,
there lies a place where decent girls don't go—
Upon their pedestals will never know
A love for jealous rage, a joy in doubt.
When lust burns red, then loss goes dry and brown.
Contentedness is costly, envy's free.
Sometimes I'd like to snatch up your renown,
to make you need someone, and here I'll be.
But love is what won't let me hold you down.
Desire has fangs, the one it bites is me.

Donald P Lehr

FAREWELL

To Debora, with love, for her support, patience and unwavering love.

Farewell . . . to all the children,
who lie waiting in their graves.
for the hand of the Messiah,
to reach down their soul to
save.

Farewell . . . to all the women,
who have waited during war,
for their men to come back
homeward,
to the place that they adore.

Farewell . . . to all the warriors,
who have suffered all the pain,
of loneliness and heartache,
for they did not die in vain.

Forevermore . . . the children lie,
with restless heart,
unopened eye.

As yet untold . . . the future be,
Forevermore,
with destiny.

Gerald H Grant Jr

FRIENDS

To all my FRIENDS in the U.S.A. and Germany
We will forever, be FRIENDS.

I'm always there for my friend,
My friend is always there for me,
It's not I, it's not me, it's us, it's we.
We've known each other for years,
We have a deep friendship so when I moved there were no tears.
Sometimes I would write
sometimes I wouldn't,
Sometimes my friend would write
sometimes she couldn't.
It's okay, it's no big deal,
Because our friendship is for real.
Friends like that are hard to find,
It may take years but you don't mind.
For when you find a friend that is true,
It's like your soul is reborn new.
You may argue and you may fight,
But sooner or later true friends make things right.
A last little tip for everyone with a true friend,
When things don't go right and you think about life's end,
Just remember one thing, you've always got a friend,
A true blue friend.

Terry Roeder

THE DARK CORNERS

To Joey, I love you—no matter what.

I told Somebody I loved you today,
And they just looked at me in a funny way.
Having known my thoughts for awhile,
they just listened and then smiled.

I was told to seek my happiness in other places,
But it's a hard thing to do
When you see one of so many faces.

I often wonder of telling you
About my feelings which are so true.
But then I journey back inside
to where my soul and dreams can hide,
Back beyond the dark corners of my heart
Where only my dreams and desires can begin to start.

Dusty Couret

ALONE

For the sexy Cajun with the laughing eyes I love you

Walking so desperately alone
Feeling so much

Finding no words to explain
How can this be?

You who I love so much,
need so much
Why it is so hard?
Two lost hearts looking
for the perfect soul mate
No perfect souls
Just us,
Alone.

J W Coward

J W Coward

PERPLEXED LITTLE LAD

To my wife, Elsie, the meticulous "Mom," and our three sons, John, Jr, George and Neil, the best crop we ever raised on our farm.

Down by the creek, a pensive lad stood,
Silently comparing bad with good
In Sunday best, he eyed the water,
Knowing full well he shouldn't loiter
Nor run the course that likely would bring
A green oak switch, with plenty of sting,
Wielded by a "Mom"—who failed to share
Proper respect for his derrière.
Suddenly brave yet looking askance,
He bared his feet and rolled up his pants,
Cautiously waded into the creek,
Then downstream a ways to take a peek
At a big turtle, still fast asleep;
Witnessed a bull frog's tremendous leap;
Found a green lizard under a stone
And a crawdad's house, built like a cone.
A wee lad's life is full of wonders,
On earthly things—like why it thunders.
Who can compare it with bad or good
But wonder if—his Mom understood?

Ramona L Rasey

WITH YOU

My heart is with you,
wherever you go.
My love is flowing,
from head to toe.
My eyes reflect you,
each day and night
When I sleep,
I hold you tight.
Whatever I do,
you're always there
(even when I comb my hair).
You're the air that
I breathe
You're, the food I eat.
You're even the path
beneath my feet.

Francesco A Cannella

IF THE WORLD COULD HAVE PEACE

My dedication goes to all those people that worked and are working so hard to preserve peace in the world.

How wonderful it would be
If the world could have peace.
With you I really agree
Said to me my niece.

Loving one another that's the way
Anger and hate would disappear.
O God, help us to reach that day
When the war no more will be here.

How wonderful it would be
If the world could have peace.
Be all friends, no more enemies
And feel relieved like a summer breeze.

Virginia N Lester

BEAUTY OF THE NIGHT

Dedicated with love, to Bill and Elinor Holmes

Have you ever been outside,
On a warm Summer night,
Heard the peeping of the frogs
And watched fireflies in flight ?

The bright stars are twinkling,
A full moon casts a glow,
To paint golden shadows
On every-thing below.

The chirps of a sleepy bird
From his perch nearby,
Is in perfect harmony
With the earth, stars, and sky.

Tensions quickly fade away,
Everything seems so right.
There is nothing more peaceful
Than the beauty of the night.

Ruth Gange

MY PERFECT SON

To Tommy: May God always stay by your side. We love you

He wakes me very late at night
With a whimper and a cry
It breaks my heart to realize
That my small son may die.

A perfect little boy he was
Till fever burned him through
And though we prayed and cried and pled
There was nothing we could do.

The beauty of this little child
We love so much today
We never take for granted
Lest he should go away.

He's perfect in his own right
This child with none compare
For only with an angel
Would comparison be fair.

So please think of him kindly
Don't laugh and don't make fun
Because you see I love him
And he is my perfect son.

Joseph Tugend

UNTITLED

I couldn't understand why you left me,
but not I see
that you didn't leave me,
you just went to where little
  Angels are supposed to be

I know this is true each day I wake
for the thought of you makes my body quake
and my heart ache.
But I know it is better to give than to take.

For I bore you into this world
to be kind and caring not cold
unlike others who are bold,
you were an Angel to be told.

And little Angels are hard to find.

Christine Swords

SNOWFLAKE

Snowflake falling softly down,
Snowflake falling to the ground
Snowflake falling round and round
gently swoops to the ground with a bound,
Snowflake falling, drifting down, down, down,
up above the heavens so high; and the stars beneath the sky,
Snowflake fly.

Julian Vergara

STRIVING FOR LIFE

This poem is dedicated with love and respect to humanity, my family and specially to my dear wife Sonia and my son Julian Fabian.

Take your hopes and peaceful dreams
And walk . . . walk up the difficult road,
Even if you feel life isn't worth living.
You must not allow your will to break with the wind,
You must not choose to live in pitch darkness.
Instead, you should live among the shiny stars.
Life could be hard at times, but, it sure is beautiful.
And until God decides when you have reached
Your perfect state of mind, or the end of the road
You must continue to battle the world.
Day by day you must accomplish small but effective goals.
Remember, you were created with the ability
To conquer the moon, space, the whole world.
Even the unknown you must strive for. Don't be afraid.
Just hold onto your hopes and come ashore
And make out, of your life a perfect dream.
On difficult days don't you break out in painful sour tears
And think that everything is lost or your hopes are gone.
You must turn ugliness into something you can live with.
You must smile, you must always use your common sense
Because life is not over yet. Life must go on!

Johnnie Britt Bishop

TRIBUTE TO PARENTS

To our parents that are so dear to us.
We never knew how much you meant to us.

We took you for granted from day to day
as we grew through our puberty stage.

Our problems were never too great or too small
that we didn't get a listening ear when we call.

There's so much that was given to us, the guidance of life without a price.
The principles of how to endure many, many a sacrifice.

As parents, you watched over us like mother hens,
you were always there with caring and loving hands.

When we cried you cried with us,
when we laughed you laughed, oh, so much!

Sure it wasn't an easy task to instill
The right principles of life to fulfill.
The task of using knowledge,
wisdom and love surely took some skill.

But you were patient parents indeed.
You did a great job, a good one indeed.

Jeri Ann Werner

SLEEPING ON THE EDGE OF ETERNITY

Sweet dreams, sweet son,
Wake for me tomorrow.
Don't leave, stay awhile,
I couldn't bear the sorrow.

The light and love that shine above
Don't let it call too loudly.
For I am here, need you near,
I look on you so proudly.

Hold my finger tightly dear,
Suckle my breast while I hold you here.
Take my strength and will to live
For that and love is all I can give.

Whimper softly in sleep tonight
So I will know things are right.
And I will see you smile once more . . .
Far from heaven's shining door.

Shirley Smith-Moore

LOVER'S DANCE

The Sun;
  He plays a distant song
  upon this Winters Day.
The Wind;
  She sings him a harmony
  and will, for awhile, stay.
The Treetops
  sway boldly
  in their dance of fresh desire,
And Spring
  speaks of soft seductions
  and fans their flames yet higher.
And here I sit—enticed,
  breathless as I watch
And feel a part of this Lover's Dance—
  this "Perfection" that I watch!

Marie J Mosher

MY WISH

To my husband Robert, who will always be remembered, for his love and great sense of humor.

I wish I may, I wish I might
I wish you were with me tonight
To hold me and to wipe my tears
And whisper how I love you dear
The nights are long, the tears are there
An open book, an empty chair
Your big blue eyes, I loved so much
Your smiling face I cannot touch
Those happy walks we took each day
I walk alone, and try to pray
I pray with every step I take
I'm closer to Lord's Heaven gate
Where you'll be waiting there for me
With stretched out arms for me to see
Then hand in hand we'll walk again
Beside our Lord in promise land
No more tears, no empty places
Happy walks, smiling faces
So I wish I may, I wish I might
That I dream of you, as I sleep tonight

Terry R Neal

MEMORIES

I've never seen a moon more beautiful, stretched out there in the western sky.

Early morning, but yet nite time, steam rising from the water, gently bouncing moonlite from our bodies, making memories for an old man to lie down with.

You're so kind to give to me such moments in life, friendship is one basic element of true love, and there are many ways to love.

You leave and life goes on, but at a slower pace.

Another moon, another nite, the same face upon the time.

Memories for an old man to lie down with.

Danielle N Deese

WITHOUT YOU

This poem is in memory of Russell Howard Eubanks (1970-1988)

Clouds white as snow.
Skies bluer than the sea.
The sun shines bright enough
To let my crushed heart see.

The gates of Heaven opened.
The angels sang out your name.
You had to leave me,
With a heartbreaking bang.

It hurts without you in my life.
The love we had will never leave my heart.
The memories will never leave my mind.

My sorrow will heal, when I'm with you in Heaven.
For now I'll have to go on
  Without you.

Erin Witt

THE OPINION

Two girls went walking down the street,
One looking ahead, the other at feet.
Both of them knowing a similar life
Living in a city of hope and strife.

The child with her eyes looking all around
Saw only beauty in her big hometown.
She saw flowers peeping out of cracks,
She had true friends that would not turn their backs.

But the one looking down was quick to say.
I can't see a thing but debris and decay.
Look at the cracks in the wall over there.
What can I do. Oh! Why should I care.

So the two grew up with their different views,
One looking up, the other at shoes
They both saw the city through different eyes
And for that same reason, they live different lives.

The first was a dreamer, open and kind.
Glad for the good things she could find.
Though the second lived a life that was full of despair,
For she saw the world as a burden to bear.

Cathy L Galyon

IMPRESSIONS OF LOVE

Slowly, slowly I feel you leave me.
Oh, you've been gone for hours,
But still your presence lingers.

It makes me feel sad to feel you leave,
But I know that very soon you'll be back,
And I'll feel all warm inside again.

Madeline E Joyner

WATCH AND WAIT

Where did the dark clouds come from
It was bright as day
Billows are rising, a storm is brewing
Not now, when everything is going my way
The winds blew hard, the rains poured down
It looked like a hurricane.

The silence is frightening after the storm
My heart and mind are racing fast
Is this how it's going to feel
When the end of the world comes at last.
I looked around and saw no one, I was standing all alone.

From out of nowhere the peace crept

in
It covered me from head to toe.
OH GOD! What a difference it made
From my previous tale of woe
You told me to watch, keep my eyes on you
But I was too busy, everybody needed my help.

You stepped aside—said, "I'll wait for you
While you run yourself down.
Open your eyes, calm yourself
Then you will realize, I never left town"

Jeannette Ann Hays
TEARS

I feel the pressure
In my eyes.
Trying to assure;
I'm not going to die.

Crystals of salt
Stain my cheek.
I come to a halt.
I now feel weak.

Ears ringing.
Visions unclear.
Angels singing,
"The time is near."

The crying is done.
I'm leaving you.
The time has come.
To start anew.

Jeanne Jo Wilcox
ROCKY SUMMITS

I dedicate this poem to: A true man of Courage Milo Eugene

Mountain vistas, rocky summits
A place to rest the eyes
Eyes absorbing your rocky, rugged, slopes
Your snow peaked pinnacles
Touched with hazy golds
From warm long golden shafts
Sunlight, sent from the setting sun
To light your snowy peaks
With softly glowing burnished golds

Inner summits, mountain vistas
Inside my brain
Rocky, rugged, slopes to climb
Challenges, inside my mind
Deep snowy places
Invigorating cold ascents
Calling for courage
To reach the higher pinnacles
Where sunlit golden dreams abide

Jennifer Miller
PAIN

In loving memory of F. Harvey Hughes, Jr, my grandfather.

There is so much pain inside of me,
And no one knows this pain more than me.
When will this pain ever go away?
Never? Is that what you say?
When someone near and dear to you passes away,
You lose a part of you, this I know,
But you know they will always be with you wherever you go.
Cherishing the moments you had with them,
Will help you through your days,
Always.

Jody Archinal
EDDY

To my friend, Eddy Halas

Just once in a lifetime for most
A very special friend
Who doesn't care who you are
Or where you've been
A very special quality that you didn't know was there
They find it in you and you like yourself better for it.

We were friends the first time we met
We don't require anything from each other
Or expect a set of standards to uphold
We're there for each other if needed
A very special friend—
So far away, my friend

Alicia Legghette
VALENTINE

For my father Caruso

So, you ask me what my
Valentine means to me,

It is about loving your brother(s) or
sisters whether right or wrong.

It is about loving your allies
and enemies just the same,
forgiving them, remembering what
they had done . . .,

Yet living with and among them
as though you had forgotten.

An anniversary once a year
topped with a box of chocolates.

Jeannie C Gee
MY LOVE

Thank you H.B. for being the "wind beneath my wings."

Love is your arms
Holding me close to your body
A protection from harm and fear.

Love is a warmth
That only comes from the heart
A loving hug to show that you care.

Love is your kisses
Helping to ease my pain
And your words—so warm and tender.

Love is your smile
And a gentleness in your eyes
And love is in my loving surrender.

Martha Dianne Hawk

Martha Dianne Hawk
BIRDS

I dedicate this poem to my mother and father who always stood by me when I needed them.

Birds
Nature's wings
Soaring through clouds
Sending messages through song
Freedom

Karrah H E Crable
WHY OR WHY NOT

People say you're not worth it,
but why do they say that.
Maybe it's just because they don't like you,
or they have nobody else to blame.
Many people get mad for no reason at all.
I guess some people aren't worth it,
or it is just because they have to let it out,
once and for all.
Why not say something nice just once.
Instead of being mean all the time.
Can people at least say something nice that suits you?
Once and for all.

Bill Harvey
AN OPEN ROAD

To my lovely wife Cathy, without her, I'd have no open road. Also to my mother, the greatest mother of all.

There's many dreams within your past,
They're days of future past.
with a spell, your life is set,
With you, it has been cast.

To breakaway from distant thoughts,
That rattle in your mind.
The real meaning of our lives,
Is really hard to find.

The gift of life in many ways,
It seems to let us know.
From the time that we are born,
We have an open road.

Whatever road that we shall take,
In life, there's no control.
They always lead a different way,
What way, we never know.

So do the best with what you have,
And sacrifice your dreams.
Once you find what road to take,
You'll know what happiness means.

Eva L Collins
THE GIFT OF LOVE—A SPECIAL CHILD

This poem is dedicated to my husband Fred and children Frederick, Cederick, Emmitt, and Aronda for their loving support.

Sometimes I saliva: othertimes it's difficult to swallow.
Sometimes I can't talk or move my legs to walk,
Although I have the gift of love.

Sometimes I try many things for attention.
Almost to the point that you'd like to lynch me.
Sometimes I greet you with a big hug or a kiss.
That's because I have the gift of love.

Sometimes I am stubborn and cause everyone trouble.
Sometimes I am a friend with a smile written on my cheeks and chin.
That's because I love you and you love me back.
I am a special child; I am a gift of love.

Corrine A Ferger
MY CALLING

The cold moon rose upon one starry night,
I heard a distant calling of my name.
Yet no soul could be seen within my sight.
But the howling sound was there just the same.

I looked to see if he was near again.
I passed a bush of sharp edged leaves of love.
In the distance he could be seen just then;
His sweet, gentle hand pointed straight above.

"Come with me, my sweet love,"
whispered the voice,
"And we shall live together happily."
I felt fulfilled and began to rejoice,
At last my highest love came to save me!

Through several times I broke my stiff mold;
Down lay my body and up went my soul!

Dale A Holt
THE LIGHT OF FREEDOM

To Pop, who gave me a book and Anne, who taught me to love them.

The Light of Freedom shone brightly in February of 1777. It shone in the hearts and minds of our forefathers who fought for a dream—"The United States of America."

That Light shone brightly in 1812, when again our fathers fought for their dream—our country.

It shone in the hearts of the pioneers and their children when they opened and settled the great West—and created our Manifest Destiny.

It shone in 1917 when they fought for our freedom in Europe.
And again in 1929 when the great Depression shook our country and the world.

In 1942 when again, we fought for our own and our Allies freedom.

Where is the Light of Freedom today, America? Is it gone? I say, Nay! It is there waiting for our hearts and minds to unite once again to fight for our way of life—Fight—to overcome the problems we face in our country. To overcome the waste and prosper once more—To overcome greed and corruption—Unite people and burn the Light of Freedom brightly, burn it brightly in our hearts and minds, and raise our country to the ideals our forefathers gave us—

Unite America—and burn the Light of Freedom brightly.

Gary L Goodrich
THERE WAS A WAR

My wife: Shari L Goodrich; My Children; Jennifer, Jeffery, Kirshton, and Zachary Goodrich, I dedicate this poem.

There was a war, no one wanted
There was a war, everyone hated
There was a war, where
thousands died
There was a war, where
thousands lied
There was a war, where many
fled
There was a war, that left many
dead
There was a war, that made
people rich
There was a war, where many
had a bitch
There was a war, that lasted over
a decade
There was a war, that looked like

a masquerade
There was a war, where we still
have MIA's
There was a war, where we left
many KIA's
There was a war, that's been over
for years
There was a war, that still brings
tears
There was a war, for what it is
worth,
Should never again happen on
this green earth.

Gary L Goodrich SFC
United States Army

Rosemary Clifford Trott
THE WRECK OF THE DASH

To my husband, Jim, our beloved pets, and family and friends who have encouraged me as a poet.

With close-hauled sails, and
With all the dark-gray water
A cloud of smoke beneath them,
Out, out to sea, they plunged,
Invincible, daring all,
Like some great lion's brood,
And yet some stark-white shoals,
Some sea wind that blew ill,
Flected at their desperate flanks,
Until they went the last dread path
Of ghostly, steel-gray waves;
And, in that final hour,
Their gallant bowsprits raised to
flying clouds,
They lifted hearts to Heaven, . . .
Then sailed to their eternal home.

Lea Power
A FRIEND
One doesn't ask for reward or fame
Only to have "A Friend" beside
their name
They want to befriend their
fellow man
Be a good neighbor whenever
they can.
They don't hunt treasures of silver or
gold
But search for friends, both young
and old
Hoping to find out there someone
who
Wants and needs a friend or two
Only asks respect and trust
from all
Just to be there should one
stumble or fall
To extend a hand as a
cheerful gift
when spirits are low, needing
a lift
Then when life's road winds
to its end
Have one pause. as they pass and say
"My Friend"

Carol A Williams
THREE WISHES
If I could have three wishes
And know that they'd come through,
I'd not wish for wealth nor fame
I'd only wish for you;
I'd not ask for the stars
I'd not ask for the moon
I'd wish each day had 25 hours
That I could spend with you.

My second wish wouldn't be
To be beautiful or strong
I'd wish I'd have 8 days each week
In your arms where I belong;
My third and final wish would be
That there were 13 months each year
So that I would have more time with
you
In which to hold you dear.

But I'll never have three wishes
And I know they'll never come
through
But at least I have one lifetime
One life to spend with YOU.

Lori Kolpien
DAY BY DAY
Day by day;

Morning passes slowly—
While cardinals sing
With a different ring,
Bluejay fly free
Sweeping from tree to tree.

Afternoon reaches its time—
When knowing what is next,
Wanting to forget the rest,
I hope I receive the best
While climbing by endless vine.

Day by day;

Evening draws quickly—
Waiting for darkness
To see the moon shine bright,
To see the stars fall from left to right,
And my boyfriend's face
Sparkle in the twilight.

It's getting late—
Dreaming of fantasies
As time reaches half past two.
Trying to fall asleep
As the night ticking anew.

Melissa Abenti
UNTITLED
Red strands of hair
molded
to the sink

THE WHITE PORCELAIN SINK

looking like
bloody cracks

looking like
tired scars

looking like
someting to hate my roommate for.

Sherrill Dorer
RAIN
Wednesday afternoon
The first drop
Of a wonderful April shower
At my window pane.

Pitter pat in mud puddles
A chirping note the birds sing
And a distant grumble of thunder,
For one quiet moment

The radiant colour of yellow
raincoats,
Red umbrellas,
Murky blue waters on sidewalk
cracks,
The hue of green in leaves and grass

Whisper out
It's spring.

Lawrence E Larkey
STREAMLINER
The frosty morning air is
pierced
by your strident shriek, a first skate to
plow a bold sharp slash across the
virgin ice, and thus the hold
quiet kept is rent—a wisp
dispersed:
A sleepy farmer rubs his eyes,
a colt kicks its confining walls,
a turkey indignantly calls
and a lone peacock's aroused
cries.
An eagle views your lightning
streak
from out the cool, green hills into a
once still town
with that sleeker, surer grace than his
plummet down
to a perch on the windswept
peak:
Steel sinew, with hot heart of
flame,
you transform with a casual
touch
our town in some subtle way—
not much—
to never be again the same!

Darlene F Duncan
LETTING GO

To TJM: If not in my arms, then always in my heart. God bless you.

It wasn't meant to be, he told me,
This relationship I thought was love,
The newness, the wonder, a gift from
above,
Cast aside, set adrift in a lonely sea.

How I see the world so differently
now,
My inner hurt I seek to overcome,
The despair I knew was there for
some,
Would now keep my head lowered in
a bow.

A part of me has died, an innocence
lost,
My soul, my being has changed so—
The pain and lessons of learning to
let go,
The emotions, the time I know it has
cost.

I yearn for and will seek recovery,
But my heart is so afraid to love,
Something created and blessed from
above,
A love out there that I know will be
for me.

Jude Mbamara Uzoukwu

Jude Mbamara Uzoukwu
COME FORTH RAIN

This poem is dedicated to Eddie-Lou Cole for believing in me.

Machete in hand.
Hoe on the shoulder.
A barren soil shows its vastness.
And the people await.

Oration to the Gods.
We must invoke.
And the seeds are inserted.
Like the swift plunge of the fish
into the earth.

Eyes to the heavens.
Our part done we murmur.
With a throbbing heart,
Watching the bird in its flight
Sing.
God Owns me.

We form the chorus.
The people lie in wait
Expectation is now our bane.
Oh beautiful Sun no.
Don't show your light.

Let it rain
For the seeds are wont
And the children are hungry.
Clamouring for a cloudy sky
We Concur god owns us.
Awaiting the seeds to spring
Forthe fruits.

Carissa Howard
IF YOU EVER WANT TO FIND ANOTHER HOUSE
If you ever want to find another
house
Take a long look at your old one,
and be as quiet as a mouse
Remember all the years that have
gone by
and every summer that made the
harvest die
Think of all the memories you're
leaving behind
the ones you put all the way in
the back of your mind
And try to think of a reason to
stay
to make more memories every
day.

Linda C Hargett
DIFFERENT ON THE SURFACE

To Dorothy, my loving Mother, for her support and encouragement.

Different on the Surface—
Same from within.
Oppression, rejection
Can't let it sink in.
Hope filled faces meeting
hate filled glances.
Malice that cuts so deeply—
Rips through my soul and
embitters my tongue—
Makes me wonder
Why was I?

Angel Holman
A CLIPPER AT BAY
Some days I imagine
I cannot hoist my sails.
The ore dock and the breakwater
are anchored against my bow.
Beyond, Lake Superior lies frozen.
The Sault Locks cost money
I don't have.
Lake Huron storms threaten
to careen my haul.
Do I squeeze through Port Huron
or swing around Detroit

just to face Lake Erie and
the voyaging across land to Lake Ontario?
And still there remains the long St. Lawrence
before my masts can shake.
But out there,
bluegreen,
salty,
the Atlantic just waits.

Gordon D Trotter
VORTEX
Techno-minds are everywhere
Commercial bliss is in the air
Opinions from the anchorman
Man can do it if he thinks he can

Wars and killers in the news
Wailing rockers sing the blues
Drought and famine, the dying cry
Man can change things if we try

Politics of people's choices
Unheard cries of widows' voices
Machines of death are killing man
We have the power to find a plan

Aborting babies we can't afford
Taking drugs to find the Lord
Cylinders in silos wait to fly
We must act before we die

Man can do it if he thinks he can
Man can change things if we try
We have the power to find a plan
We must act before we die

Iphigenia Xenos

Iphigenia Xenos
RADIANCE
I feel, because I love you, that I'm not an ordinary woman as before . . . My limbs, when I walk, move with the memory of walking toward you, and my hands performing menial tasks are supple with an individual grace all their own, having caressed your face . . . . I speak, and my mouth remembers being held captive by yours, and the words taste like the manna of the Israelites, simply because you kissed me . . .

Barbara Klimkowski
ARS SCIENCIA IV
The elliptical orbits formed by
the polarities of what
I feel and think,
the realm between my acting
and being, can stretch and shrink.
For years I wavered between the two,
upsetting my balance,
'til on the brink—

I have found the dimension
of within without—
the real domain
exploding infinity
imploding a point.
The merger of epicenters
is perfect when
I become a circle—
one.

All alone
on the throws of a point,
I always reach agreement.

Bözsi D-Varga'
FATHER
Of course there is no one like Mother
But there is that other, dear Dad,
God bless him.
The Mother, poets had canonized
But Father it seemed they forgot
Poets praised Mother's altar
Leaving dear Fathers behind!
Rather remember how Father being the hero
When you were a kid, the games he thaught you
The toys and things he bought you
And the stories for you he read
Remember how he worried during your illness
And he prayed for that illness to pass
And gave that saintly devotion to cheer you
To uplift you, higher than anyone did
While there is no one like dear Mother
There is that other, Dear Dad, God bless him.

Carol M Annechino
BAR HARBOR
Late September winds
chase melancholy cobwebs
from my summer mind.

Golden rays of warmth
appear in a crystal sky,
a blush of rebirth.

Anxious virgin waves
test their feet on rocky shore
laughing in delight.

Poised in quiet slumber
sailboats rock and roll in time
dancing on each swell.

Cool crisp salty air
promising some adventure
everything is new.

Eleanor Pillsbury
CAN BEAUTY DIE?
No thing of beauty lasts?
Perhaps!
But as long as my mind holds memories
Of a gold-red sky of evening time
Or silver leaves of pre-storm hour
I cannot agree that beauty dies.

And none can take away from me
The sudden sweetness of a child's smile
Or the quiet beauty of an aged face.

These things are always mine
While memories are a part of me
For they are beauties of eternal time
And as such cannot die.

Misti Thiel
JACK
Quietly demented
he stalks the shadows,
in silence
he slips through
the night
taunting the officials
leaving his clues
as he seeks
the blood to ease his
tortured soul
as he slowly maliciously
rips apart his
victims
blending their terror
with his madness
echoing through the century
that holds no
sorrow for the
victims of Whitechapel.

Donna Lupacchino
THE CHALLENGE
The frightened child
stands in the doorway
beneath the spiral stairs,
she looks upward to where they lead.
The distance of sight does not extend
the length she desires to see.
But at the top
she can view a faint light—
Decisions impulsive, yet never acted upon
as quickly
she waits, and ponders for another moment.'
To ascend the flight she can not see,
would mean to accept
yet another
challenge;
but to walk away without
another moment of decision
would mean to be overcome
by defeat.

John G Black
WALKING IN THE WOODS
I walked these woods before, I know,
It seems like a long, long time ago.
The trees looked taller
but I was much smaller
It must have been twenty years or so.
My dad would take me for these
walks and explain all nature's glory.
When we got tired we'd sit on a rock
and he'd tell me a little story.
I walk the woods alone these days
and think of days gone by,
sometimes I'd find our favorite rock
and maybe even cry.
The memories are good ones as I
move along the ground that we once tread
But I walk the woods alone these
days for you see—MY DADDY'S DEAD

Kenneth L Pilgreen
IN THE HEAT OF A COOL DAY
In the heat of a cool day
All thoughts turn just one way
With all my knowledge and pain
Why do I live my life this way

Reading about left and right
Why is it that I'm without sight
All things seem right and wrong
And thus follows the hurting throng

Why must I die that others live
Or is this an illusion that the spirit gives
Should it all change at once
Would my line follow until

I call on God's wisdom to see
The lock which takes the key
But is there a key at all
Or is it but more pain for me

It was hoped that this trek from home
Would break the riddle and ease the pain some
If this is true, one must say
Then here is the violent storm before the calm

But life cannot continue as this
With a calm outside, and inside a shaking fist
For tomorrow I may die, my spirit torn
Doomed to wander in the universe, AMISS

Jack W Cothran
ECHOS ALONG THE SPICE ROUTE

To those here and gone, who still and did, seek out ways to enjoy those special spices of life brought to us in perpetuity.

There was a time when the fragrant bale
from far Ceylon and lands beyond
did, on backs of dromedaries assail
those paths and routes the bedouins found.

I hear a caravan faint upon the wind
along the horizon among the dunes
wailing camels and calling fellahin
in desert harmony with khamsin tunes.

I smell the traces left upon the air.
A stench of camel, man and aromatic drays.
Rancid wisps of cook-fire smoke hung there.
A spicey mingling wafted through the haze.

I see oasis palms with pennants high.
Cud-chewing beasts and languid men at rest.
Sordid carts and bales arrayed nearby,
and rolled felt tents along a sandy crest.

I feel salt tinged seas on breezes bold.
The caravan goal where land and water mate,
and fragrant cargo shifts from beast to hold,
to sail that final path to reach my gate.

Jo Ann Joseph
!THE HEARTS DOOR!
When seeking God it must be,
With your whole heart.
Are the Devil will come, Rapping,
Rapping, at your Heart's Door.

Art Henry
A SHORT FLIGHT
When life begins, we are so small,
So small that no one knows we're there.
And then we grow until we're born,
Then have our Mother's fondest care.

And like a plan that spans the sky,
Up through the clouds of life we go,
To pioneer a path of life serene,
And tell the world of what we know.

We span the canyons of the clouds,
We see our dreams of youth come true.
We wend our way each day through life,

As each in turn brings something new.

The acts of life can lead us far,
Far off our course of joy we know.
We strive each time to right ourself,
And smooth our course before we go.

Our riches we do weigh each day.
Then wonder if we really try,
To lend a hand where e're we can,
To help the youth below our sky.

There comes a time when clouds of life,
Are burdened with the many years.
Our flight must take us toward our home,
As life has lost its many fears.

Our ride through all the silvery clouds,
As life in ebbing must descend,
And down toward Mother Earth we glide,
Our trip through life is near its end.

And as we near our final home,
The Mother Earth we do adore,
We think of what we left behind,
And close our eyes for evermore . . .

Sara Elizabeth Sorge
THE THREE OF US

This poem is dedicated to my two older sisters, Christine and Angela. Thanks for everything!

I have two sisters
they're both older than me,

They're the greatest sisters
there ever could be.

Whenever I need them
they're always there,

They're always helpful and
they always care.

My sisters are the greatest,
they're the best,

No one's better
from all the rest.

Susan Ashe James
TRUE MOTHERHOOD

To my mother, Cecelia Milton Ashe, I dedicate this poem with love and appreciation.

I thank the Lord every day of my life,
For leading my dad to make my mother his wife.
She is everything a mother should be.
Her road in life at times has been rough.
By now all of us know that raising children can be tough.
That is why the Lord gave her to you and me.
Her wisdom and love flows through our veins.
And still though we are grown she can feel our pain.
She is always there when we need her day or night.
We should all take time to think,
How in our family chain,
She has been the strongest link.
Isn't it strange how she has always been our guiding light?
We've watched her hair go from dark to white,
We've seen her stand by and help daddy through his long fight.
We owe her all that happiness can give,
For as long as we are on this earth to live.
God help us to be strong and good
For you have blest all seven of us with the symbol of true motherhood.

Eric Rush
HELLO DEBRA

To Debra, When I wrote this for you, we were new-found friends. Now that we're married, we'll never be apart again. I love you, Eric

Hello Debra
How are you?
It's been a long time
Since we've talked.

I thought perhaps
You'd like to go out,
Or at least
Go for a walk.

Debra, I have to
Be with you.
And when I am
I feel at home.

Because without you,
Debra,
Or them, or anybody,
I would be alone.

Loretta M McClure
MY FIRST LOVE

This poem is dedicated to the memory of my dear sister Marie.

It was a love of innocence and purity
The beginning of a new adventure
It was in the winter and a carpet of snow lay on the ground
It was such a long, long time ago
Yet it's there still, locked in my heart, the memory of my first love

I remember flowers blooming in the snow and bluebirds singing songs of love
Love, young as the springtime, but how were we to know that our love was just a passing dream dying in the winters cold

Kisses soft as a summer's breeze
Sweet words of love he spoke to me
Two lovers standing on a golden shore lost in a magical world of love

Then on one lonely, misty night he vanished with the morning stars
All that were left were faded memories of our starstruck hearts
And like a dying flower at the end of summer he was gone, lost forever in a dream

O Estelle Brockinton
A BLESSED NEW YEAR

This Poem is dedicated to my Husband, Thomas and my sweet daughter, Barbara.

Christmas Season is drawing near,
May our hearts be filled, with
Thanks, Good Will and Cheer.
Amidst a world of Turmoil and Discontent
Let's pause—Realize, why the Saviour was sent.

There's much talk about what is wrong with our world today.
Some say—
Dirty Politics, Greed, Love of Money
Those who care not what they do to get it.

What's wrong with our world today?
It's the heart of man, so unfit
Instead of Love, Honesty and Integrity
It's filled with Pride, Envy and Enmity.
That's why the Saviour came
To take upon Himself the sins of all mankind.
[Greater Love has no man than this that a man lay down his life for his Friends.]
The Heart of man He can change
Give New Life of Contentment
And Peace of Mind.

The Blessings of Christmas can be yours
Your New Years—Can be, A
Blessed New Year!

Mary Rose Sudy
THE ROSE

To the myriad Roses in trampled gardens.

I was once a lovely rose . . .
You thought so.

Over time, you tore my firm petals
and rendered me desperate.
Steadily, you snipped at my thorns
and stripped me of all defenses.
Soon, you bared me of veil-like
leaves and showed me naked and gaunt.

Eventually, I emerged and struggled
'till my cheeks flushed rosy.
Nurturing came, but
slowly, oh, so slowly.
At long last, and on my own,
I rooted and gained position.

Then you said,
"What's wrong? You've changed."

Taya Lucas

Taya Lucas
THREE STATES OF MIND
Today my childhood was sent in the mail
A friendly face spreading fertilizer
and killing nasty weeds
He smiles as he hooks his hands on
the friendly green hose
He's firm and strong and
so clean so wholesome
and his
smile
is so
genuine
All my questions are answered

But my father has long since been tripped
The weed technician drops his hose
is momentarily tangled
Now his hands are free to do what he pleases
Deliberately missing large patches
He scowls at the foul yellow pesticide
on to infect the dog
This world, too cruel for me, will soon be a
Deeper green

Leo J Spring
THE ROSE

To the lady, that will someday share my life. Whomever it will be, will be . . .

The rose
it sleeps in the winter
awakens in the spring
happiness for those who receive them
what a wonderful, wonderful thing

the rose
it signifies something unique
something everyone hungers for
something everyone seeks

the rose
its petals soft
as a satin sheet
and given to a lady
when two lovers meet . . .

Joseph P Liss Jr MD
NIGHT

To my wife, all the precious moments of time have and will always be spent with you.

Stroke of night, whispering wind,
Shadows undefined,
Leave me not alone,
Gently soothe my anguished mind.

Happiness, life and love
Are now mine with which to play.
Why wage battle against me
each and every day.

Must I accept your cold embrace,
Lose what I can no longer see?
What must I sacrifice?
What must be my plea?

Return, oh night.
These precious moments of time.
Consider my plight

Grant me the day
And our eternal love
Will grant you the night.

Margaret J Friederich
THE EMPTY NEST

To my son, Tom. Written after I washed your basketball suit for the last time for you soon would be graduating with the Class of '89.

Some time ago it was the football gear,
today the basketball suits—washed for the last time,
and each time I felt a little stab of pain
for the time to leave the nest is drawing near.

The senior photos have all been taken,
the graduation announcements have now arrived,
the colleges are vying for his attention,
and my feelings of mothering are being shaken.

The days are growing shorter and soon he will be gone
out into the world that's waiting there
for all young people to embark upon;
sure as the darkness turns to dawn.

What will be waiting for him just

beyond the bend?
Will it be fame and fortune, failure or success?
Or will he just get by in a day by day existence?
I guess whatever is to be, on him it will depend.

But for a few years college will fill his quest.
And he'll be home on weekend visits and holidays too,
bringing his laundry with him.
And for awhile, I'll still have a part-time nest,
until he has a nest of his own.

Charles H Bruce Jr
NATURE'S LAKE

To my children, may they never forget to smell the roses.

Shimmering gold in early morning light,
Upon mirrored surface shining bright;
Reflections of nature dot the shore,
Adding pictures to the lake for evermore.

As boughs reach toward sky that never ceases,
Settling in to enjoy midday breezes;
Wind softly caresses all it touches,
Seeming to come, as heat really clutches.

Crickets singing at evening tide,
Fish jumping for food, trying to hide;
Vibrations gently drifting across the surface,
Adding sounds to the lake as their purpose.

Shadows falling on pine needled loam,
Where mini creatures find a home;
Scurrying to and fro away from sight,
Cleansing and renewing nature at night.

Lights sparkle bright into night,
Stabbing through darkness during flight;
From distant shore they bring their glow,
Adding life to the lake, quid pro quo.

Barbara McCartney
THE LORD IS GOOD, HE ANSWERS PRAYER

To my precious mother who passed away May 20, 1989

The Lord is good, He answers prayer
No matter what you have done, He is always there.
He died for my sins, and for yours too
Let's praise his name in all we do

Witness to others and help spread the word
He wanted us to do this whenever we could.
So let's start today and tell the "good news"
Let Him come into your heart, it's all up to you to choose.

So let's put on God's armour, like he told us to do
So we can resist Satan and be strong and true.
Put on the strong belt of truth, the breastplate of righteousness and wear shoes that will speed you on to preach the "Good News." And in every battle you need faith as your shield to stop the fiery arrows that Satan will use.

Next comes the helmet of salvation and sword of the spirit, pray all the time, come on and get with it.

Plead with Him and remind Him of your needs,
Let's get going, start planting those seeds.

Pray for me and I'll pray for you
With His help, there is nothing we cannot do.

May God give you peace and love
And send you His blessings from Heaven above.

Tammy Detwiler
SILVER FALLS

As I walk across the old bridge, worn smooth by the years, I seemingly enter a new world of eerie quiet, shattered only occasionally by the whispering of the trees overhead.

The soft smell of freshly fallen rain and pungent pines, greet me as I descend into the everlasting, vivid green of its abundant foliage, the cascading falls of silver foam weave a spell of enchantment, while the misty spray sparkles like diamonds dancing in a sea of intrigue.

This place of delicate beauty with its crystal clear air, shimmering with fragile rays of light, is a heaven for those with much to ponder.

Susan M Dorie DuBeau
SWEETHEART

For My Husband, Pat

S is for the sharing we always do
W is for warm winter nights
alone with you.
E is for every nice thing you've done
E is for our wedding vows of eternal Love.
T is for the time we have ahead,
H is for the happiness you've given me,
E is for our Ecstasy.
A is for alway's being there,
R is for the richness we've shared.
T is for all them rolled together,
YOU & ME,
That's the way it'll always be.

Christie Ross
TIME TO PART

To My Best Friend, Hillery Stephens

I couldn't even believe my heart,
When the time came to part.
I couldn't believe
That you had to leave.
It didn't leave us much time,
That's why; I can't begin to make this poem rhyme.
It seemed like we'd know each other forever.
We said we'd always be together.
When this sad moment came,
I knew I'd never be the same.
The tears came rolling out of our eyes,
As we said our last goodbyes.

Yusefa Hill
YOU

To Joel

You inspire me . . .
To see the beauty
Behind every obstacle we encounter each day.

You help me . . .
To see that every problem
Has an answer.

You bring the love out in me . . .
That no one has cared enough
To look for.

Every day that passes by,
We see problems as just a way of
Gaining sight of new answers.

You have taught me,
By your graceful spirit,
To know the meaning of love.

Jeanne Duchene
REACHING OUT

May this poem find that place within you that part of you that allows you to Reach Out

Your silence tells me everything about the way you feel about us.
Yes, babe, I've seen it coming, watched all your clues you've given . . .
Maybe we're through.
Maybe I should hate myself for loving you.
Walk away from it all while I can still carry my head high.
But then I wouldn't be the person I know you still love if I didn't try.
Is it too late for I'm sorry . . .
Would my words fall on deaf ears . . .
Well sorry I am and if I don't tell you what's in my heart and on my mind
then for nothing I cried my tears.
I wish I were a real "genie" and it only took a bottle's rub for my wishes
Or all those stars I've seen falling would grant me their wish.
But you and I are not part of a fantasy and no one ever appreciates something gotten for free.
For all we've been and for friendships sake alone, could we just take a walk,
And while I talk would you just listen—
Could you just listen while I talk—

Linda Krench
A FLOWER

With all my Love to Mom and Dad, and to my niece, Laurie, for all her support, and for just being herself.

A flower
so fragile
I see me, growing . . . ,
To blossom
to be full.
So I wait, hoping . . . ,
My beauty to be seen.
So please remember . . . ,
Pick me
but
not apart
for
I will no longer grow.
What a shame,
for
I do not want
to wither
and die.
so . . . ,
If you do not want me,
Please . . . ,
Pass me by!

Geraldine Stegemann
NATURE'S DANCER

For my children and grandchildren I dedicate this poem.

A puppet are you—a puppet you stay.
Creations music for you I play.
Dance to my tune you living thing.
All wonders to you I bring.

A dance of youth—of fame and glory.
Nature's benefits in a primal story.
Reality is pain—try not to see.
Succumb you not—just dance for me.

The soul knows the beginning.
It also knows the end.
So dance the dance, you puppet—
Remain ye nature's friend.

Whatever color robe you don,
When the story's told.
The dance you do—
The song I play,
Returns you to the fold.

Roger Jonas Martin
THE LIFE OF A UNION ELECTRICIAN

Robert and Richard are both in the picture with Mommy and Daddy and sweet Robin Leigh

My boots were made for traveling
but no longer fit my feet.
My riding pants have holes in them
my rear end is so weak.
I'd like to ride away from here
but my back won't take the strain.
My truck is broke but my wipers work
except when there's a rain.
So I guess my worries deepen
as I watch them drive away.
Going home to each his own
and I'm still here today.
A little overtime would surely get me on my feet
and a little closer to my kids, I think that I still feed.
And when I walk into the house and shout
"It's Daddy, no more blues!"
I hope they do not turn away
and ask, "Daddy who???"

Marie C Clark
FOREVERS

To Valerie, my best friend and inspiration.

We are but a moment in time,
A moment that will last forever
In our minds and hearts,
Something time nor distance can destroy.

Time is so unfair to those who love—
With forever being just an evasive word,
That fails to hold adequate definition,

Existing always in realistic abstraction.

We might vow to love one another forever,
Knowing that it is possible,
As long as we understand; the toll of the moment
Is all that we can ever rely on.

Beverly A Leipold
EQUUS

To my daughters, Lori and Tracy

Shimmering body,
Sunlit mane,
Nostrils flaring,
Breathing flame;

Arching neck,
Head held high,
Shining hooves
That seem to fly;

Spirited by
An unknown force;
Beauty in motion;
Behold, the horse!

Barbara Davis Sweeny
SISTERS BY CHANCE, FRIENDS BY CHOICE

With love to my sisters, Dorothy, Betty and Jean

Sisters are people who knew you when you were too young to have a past

Who knew when you needed a helping hand you didn't have to ask

Who gladly tell you when you're out of line and when they think you're funny

Who sometimes advance a little credit when you're running short of money

Who listen when you complain about your husbands and your kids

And usually manage to keep their cool when they'd like to blow their lids

It's comforting to know although we're not together we have our sisters as our friends through this life and forever

Carmen Orodio Weist

Carmen Orodio Weist
FALL SEASON

Leaves turning into darker hues,
Deep, dark green and golden glows,
Reddish and deeper brown;
Color, color abound!

The breeze is getting crispy,
Nights becoming rather misty,
Colder weather is here to bear,
Coats and sweaters are out to wear.
The earthen shades much into play,
Models basics to display
Accents of moss green and spanish gold;
The richer the color, the braver the bold.

Fashions come and go,
The seasons likewise too;
Nature, motherly behaves—
There is beauty in falling leaves.

Darrin Lee Hutton
MUSIC

To Nancy and Todd who play the Music I love, and who have always said "Hey, why not?"

There is no light
But the light we see.
There is no song
But the song we sing.
I have stretched my mind to the limit
I have reached my arms to the wind.
I have solemnly sworn that all I can do
Will be done.
Far away there is another light
Far away there is another song.
If I reach for it, it is mine—
I stumble.
I fall.
But the light reaches my eyes
And the song touches my heart
I must do all that I can
I must try.
And I recognize the light
And I hear the untouchable song.
Music fills my heart.
And I am strong.

Frances Goldstein
CONTINUITY

Suddenly I wanted to do stitchery
and all the years before there was no need—
there were the parties and theatres
and songs to sing
and hills to climb . . .
But now I wanted to frame them all
And so I told a friend of this—
How would it look on canvas—what if it were
all captured with many-splendored threads—
oh—just to blend it!

Yes, leave a legacy she said
for your grandchildren—
I felt at once my mortality
And knew that the promise of future life
drew its breath from mine
and thereby ended it.

Patricia B Lowe
SONOMA COAST

Listen, the sea comes tumbling
 to the shore.
Bouncing o'er the rocky coast.
Turbulent, moody as two lovers.
First a gentle rise, silence thence
 to come.
Then a roaring boom like a thousand
 planes aflight.

Cindy Walter
TRUE FEELINGS

To those who gave and taught me "Real Love." My Parents Rose & Lou Walter, my Children Jenny & Doug Schroeder. A very special person Tony Loftus and His Family—My heart goes to all.

The key to life is held within the heart . . .
For your heart holds tender true feelings . . .
Feelings we don't always face or feelings we can't hide . . .
What can we make of ourselves, if we do not trust our own heart . . .
Few do we meet, which we can endear our hearts to . . .
Funny thing is when we do stumble upon someone we let them slip away . . .
To make life a happy and peaceful path we must learn to first trust our own feelings . . . as to when we trust another . . .
Once we overcome this obstacle, life will truly be worthwhile . . .
For then we will be refreshed with genuine love that will gently fall upon us . . . like the first snowflake of winter.

Lisa Robinson
TEN

I Dedicate this Poem to my loving husband Wendell, Happy Tenth Anniversary

Through all the sad and gloomy days,
and all those filled with golden rays,
Through all the sorrow and the pain,
and through all the hard work and strain.
Our love has held us close together
and isn't that what really matters?
Through all the good times and the bad
Through all the times both happy and sad
We proved that we could take it all
and still stand close together and tall.
Though people said we wouldn't make it
Those were the ones who couldn't take it.
As I put away this paper and pen
I know we'll soon be married TEN
Ten years filled with joy and sorrow
If I could do it over I'd do it tomorrow!
 Happy Anniversary!

Debbie Green
VIRTUES

To all my friends, especially Carrie, Kellie, Laura, Joey, Johnny, Thad, and Duyn, who taught me that these virtues can only be found through faith in our Lord Jesus Christ.

As the castles in the sand
Are washed into the neverending sea,
So are my memories of you.

As the sunlight of the day
Fades into ominous darkness,
So do my memories of you.

As these tears in my eyes
Disappear for their uselessness,
So do my memories of you.

You were strong, impenetrable,
A force forever standing;
Yet you have fallen.

In what can I place my faith?
What can be my sustenance?
Honesty and morality I seek.

Kathy Armstrong
OCEAN EYES

I look into your ocean eyes
And know my soul can tell no lies.
Our hearts are locked within the gaze
That makes my emotions jump in craze.

But then I must look back to the sand,
For I can feel the hot love brand
That you have set on my soul.

Though what good can come of this mark
If your feelings are still in the dark?
I cannot say;
I must not think!
I only know I'm on the brink
Of loving you forever.

Betty Richardson
BEAUTIFUL RAIN

Dedicated to our four children: Carlene, Janice, Lorraine and Fred who have given my husband, Guy and myself life's "Pot of Gold."

The children's laughter came to me
 With gentle sound of rain;
They seemed so happy when they saw
 The sun peep out again.

Such laughter of unclouded years,
 Is one of nature's charms,
And like a magnet, drew me near
 Into their outstretched arms.

A rainbow coming from the sky,
 Fell softly on each head;
It painted shawls, and velvet shoes
 Of purple, green, and red.

Their shining faces gleamed like gold,
 Through drops of silver mist;
Their cheeks were like a polished rose,
 That innocence had kissed.

Such beauty, lavishly out poured,
 Was God's way to explain,
The pot of gold He gave to me,
 And beautified the rain.

LuAnn L Dorman
THERE ARE SOME THINGS ABOUT YOU FRIEND

There are some things about you friend
That truly are unique.
Your qualities are numerous
You're funny, kind, and meek.

Of all the many talents that
You've worked hard to perfect,
I find one most intriguing—
This one I most respect.

The reason you're so different is
In everything you do,
You strive so hard to always share
With others, part of you.

And I can say wholeheartedly
(on this you can depend)
That I am oh so fortunate
To say you are my friend.

Maria Chilli
WATER LILY

Kicking through stretches of
 Olive-green leaves
With blotches and streaks of bronze.
 See her in jeans and wind-blown

hair,
Stepping over hidden flowers
Of pale lavender,
Petals shell-pink and forever blue,
Shaded carmine on the edges;
Never open early in the morning,
Not until nine,
Or at lunchtime.
Baby, don't wait,
Run, run, run.
Go. Now.
For the petals close
Well before sundown.
The day will be gone,
But, again shaming tears
Fall softly on footprints of a world
Giddy-colored in May.

Steve Wilderman
THE GIFT

To the memory of Debbie Williams, My sister, my friend . . .

As the sun set upon your birthday,
I looked to the sky, and smiled your way.
Thirty years ago today, you were born,
And "Oh what a lucky mom."
From then to now; I knew somehow,
You would shine upon everyone.
We were brother and sis,
And so our lives were destined to miss.
Still, through the good and bad of times,
I always knew you were mine.
I loved you then, and miss you now,
I guess you'll never really know how.
To say you're gone is so tough for me,
I still need time with our memories.
We fought and loved as families do,
But I really can't let go of you!
You may be gone, but not to me,
We still have those talks, in my memory.
You're alive in my mind, and alive in my heart,
So I guess we'll never really be far apart.
I looked to the sky,
And smiled your way . . .
Happy Birthday
Steve

Randy Yates
BE THANKFUL

To My Family And Friends

When life's daily routine begins to get you down, stop, and reconsider the stars, that have already been placed into your crown.
Tho, it may seem that nothing will work out right for you, there's always tomorrow. Your dreams may, yet, come true.
Take what you have got, go as far as you can.
Stand and face life, fear no man.
You have a sound mind to think with, while others are insane, the conception to rejoice in happiness and to feel the sting of pain.
The vision to see the light. The knowledge to understand.
So be thankful, that you were born with more than only a few grains of sand

Jan S Holtzman
TOGETHER

Together is a word of entrancing predicament. Only a paradox can see.
To feel, to congeal is cognitive, but togetherness is forever.
If we die together, it may be forever. Lives do pass, but togetherness always lasts. It's being is never entirely consumed, but remains last and eternity does not pass.
To live, to be, to feel, to see, is common in nature, always an attribute and flourishes at times.
Eternity sees, but not nearly as cordially as the night.

Peter Whalen
STAIRS

Instant jubilee
hearing the boys are in key

freddy rips the bass
johnny v. takes the lead
willie sing 'em blues

Where does that leave me
learning

All having our instruments
maybe mines the pen

then again
guess again

Slowly going somewhere
The hard-shell whips the hare
Wide-eyed for the answers
Blink at parental stares

lyric lingering
brain
music meandering
heart
promise personal
soul
sting some sparks

Cliff Sumter
SPONTANEOUS GENERATION

Look all around you a city left for dead
Covered in a blanket of filth to be never seen again
All aspirations now abandoned, everyone's dreams looted
No shots left to fire and no one to fire them.
But within the deepest gutter
there is a micron of hope
From amidst the spiraling waste
that offered no return
Where there was nothing worth saving
Emerged the strongest army
A million yawning faces
All bloodied and burnt
Eyes riveted in belated surprise as we held the prodding iron
We'd made our plans so silent from our temporary tomb
And while your cities decayed we found our beginning
As you clinged to desperation you were self-consumed.
Don't stretch out to us with your skeletal arms
We possess no pity, you dug the graves
Born with full knowledge
Fresh minds with new ideas
The near sighted had perished
Fallen victims of the prey
Stand clear for the spontaneous generation
Can't you see that we're everywhere
As we live and breath we're growing in number.

Roy D Matthews
A SPECIAL PLACE

Somewhere in the corners of space
there exists a special place
where our maker rules from his throne,
loving and caring, protecting his own.

Mom and Dad, a few relatives are there, rewarded for the lives they've lived.
If our lives are pure and true,
someday then, we can live there too.

I'll try to live the way I should,
try to do things as Christ would.
Then when life on earth doth end,
I'll walk with Mom and Dad again.

Phillip S Barbour
A QUESTION OF LOVE

To Jonnie—A great aunt and my best friend.

What is this thing called fear,
That weaves threads of glass
around my heart;
Only to break,
and cut at my bare soul?

Could it be love,
That holds me in its fragile grip,
Just beyond the grasp
of all ethereal hope?

I know not what holds me
in this graphic provision.
I only know that this fear and pain,
is worth eternity,
for the love within my heart.

Teresa A Calvert
A ROSE OF SILK

For Charmagne W.

A friendship that began as a bud
Blossomed into a rose of silk
Each petal marking an obstacle or occasion
The lingering scent symbolizing
an everlasting friendship
The stem bears no thorns, the
beginning of our friendship
bears no scars
A rose of silk lasts forever
And our friendship is destined to stand
All tests of time

Mary Kennedy
FLEDGLINGS

To Bud Burkhard for his constant inspiration and Fledglings Michael, Rose and Amanda

Sweet Dove
Gentle and Beloved
Soft
and Yet Powerful
In Flight.
Let me
Be Your Earth, Your Grounding,
From
Which You draw renewed
Strength and
Rest in
my arms when you are Weary.
Let me
Unbind your wings that
Your
soaring Spirit finds Its
Freedom
Restored, as your Beauty Frees
Mine.
Let us
Be As children, not surrendering
To
Love, not becoming One,
But Two
Nurtured
by a Passionate Love which
Gently, Teaches Us of Ourselves.

Joseph J Trichilo
OUR ROMANCING STAR

I want to dedicate this poem to my wonderful wife, Theresa

As I gazed into the darkness
Of an early morn
A sight disturbed my idleness
Just at the break of dawn.
There above the break of light
Was a star—shining, Oh, so bright.

Dimly I see the morning light
A star gets brighter, a beautiful sight
Alone in the sky more beautiful now
Others have vanished, afraid somehow
A beautiful star, the king of the sky
It shines for us dear, just you and I.

Slowly as the dawn grows near
The star gets ready to disappear
I call it our romancing star
It makes you near, but, Oh, so far
A good morning to the world it brings
As it fades away my heart sings—
I love you, Darling.

Jo Walsh
RESPECT CHILDHOOD DREAMS

To my loving children, John, Sara and Robert

Respect childhood dreams
And make believe wishes
For they are only the
Future seen very young

Brenda Comer Wilson
EACH DAY

This poem is dedicated to my daughter Sheila and my son Mark for whom I am so proud of.

Why do I get up each day?
For in this bed I'd like to stay.
To pull the covers over my head
To envision dreams of fantasies instead . . .
Of the real world today
With all its sadness and dismay.

Jeanne E Baskin
WHY

Dedicated to my Mother, You were always my inspiration, You always believed in me. Jeanne

Why can't the world be a better place
With smiles and laughter on everyone's face.
Why are there homeless we can see
Why is there no food for you, as for me.

Why are there murders, robberies, assaults
Maybe these problems, are all of our faults.
For maybe if we joined together, no

matter
The color or creed of another.
If everyone was treated as
everyone's brother
What a wonderful world it would be.

We could help the homeless, poor
and the weak
By giving them help and hope
that they seek.
And maybe in our lifetime by and
by,
We will not have to ask God,
"WHY."

Judith Bassaner
WHAT IF WE COULD

Dedicated to: J.W.F. who has given me friendship, love, and the hope that another life exists for the two of us, spending eternity together.

Could we fly away, you and I
On a carpet of Persian Blue?
Will we hold hands, then cuddle up
close
Tenderly kissing as we seem to do.

Could we sail away, you and I
On a mystical ship by the sea?
Will we embrace, your eyes meeting
mine
Softly whispering of what is to be.

Could we just dream, you and I
On a star so our wish would come
true?
Will we make love with no measure
of time
Gently sleeping, the dawn peeking
through.

Yes, I know all this surely can't be
This world is not ours—You and I,
Shall we meet now and then
Near the woods or a glen?
If only to watch life go by.

Lisa lynn Brown
THERE IS NO END

For my sweet boyfriend who inspired me to write this poem. I love you and always will, thank you Jake Cole.

Again I find myself thinking of you, thinking of you to a certain extent and thinking of you to my hearts content. I guess there's no end, when it stops, ya know when my heart pops? Although my heart doesn't have to pop, If this loving of yours doesn't stop. We've been through lots, good and bad and we've shared each others being glad. I love you and I try to show it, but don't you see how much you really mean to me?

Kathy Jarvis
USELESS TO FIGHT

To the wonderful man in my life, Tim Glover. This one is for you. With all my love!!—me

In your eyes—I see love tonight
And I realize it's useless to fight
Useless to fight—the way I feel
I realize now this love is real

This kind of love—is the kind that
lasts
It erases the pain from the past
The past is gone—and you are here
And with your love there's no need
for tears

All the loves I've had along the way
Has brought me here to you to stay
And stay with you—I always will
A life together—My dream's fulfilled

Baby-I write this just for you
So you will know my love is true
You mean so very much to me
I know this love was meant to be

Meant to last—A long long time
I want you always to be mine
Mine to have—to hold—to keep
Together—Our lives are now
complete!

Elaine Serling

Elaine Serling
DAD
Whenever there is time
Or a space left open in my mind
You are there, and I remember

When I am filled with feelings
Bright, lively, sad or need healing
You are there, and I remember

In the wind on a brisk day
On the sunlit path along the way
You are there, and I remember

When I'm at my very best
Or passing one of life's many tests
You are there, and I remember

Yet, the worst of all
Is when the emptiness hits and I
recall
You will never return, and I
remember.

Cathy Tobey
MY SON

This poem is dedicated to my beloved son, Danny, in thanks for the countless moments of joy and laughter he has brought into my life. He is now and will forever remain an inspiration of love to me!

You, my precious son, have brought
into my life much joy,
You've always been a most sensitive
and caring boy,
It seems as though you're always
trying to do the best you can,
That's why I'm certain you'll grow
to be a unique and special man,
I know we don't always agree on
everything,
And when we argue—I know the
sadness it can bring,
But you must always remember how
much I do love you,
Inspite of any difficult times we
might go through,
You are my dear son; and, I'm so
very proud of the person you have
become,
So, please my sweet son, don't be so
glum,
Although life can be complex and
sad,
There are still so many things of
which we should be thankful and
glad,
The most important being that your
mother's love for you will never end,
And aside from being your
Mom—I'd also like to be your
"special friend"!

Stephen P Croston
MIRROR

To my wonderful wife and companion, Linda who let's me be the creative literary dreamer that I am.

The image is now reflected in the
glass,
The sun line across the wall.
Dust darts in and out of the ray and
captures the beam of light.

I stand in a shadowed room of silent
cares and reflect in my mind the
hours behind.
In my mind I have smiled hoping the
pain would go and let my day be
bright.

My spouse sleeps beneath the heavy
quilt, with cat out spread atop the
patchwork.
But my soul seeks rest from my
weary mind to dream under the
sheltered slumber.

My heart beats through the soul,
my dim eyes scan the image before
me.
Spring is before my vision and paints
in quiet tones from my imagination.

Elizabeth D Burns
TEACH ME, LORD

On a recent Airplane flight from Atlantic City, back to B'ham, Ala. with lightning flashing all around, I recalled my poem, "Teach Me Lord." I am forever grateful for GOD'S presence. I feel most richly blessed!

Teach me, dear Lord, to be patient—
To accept what my life has in store.
Teach me to live to the fullest—
And not ask for anything more.

Teach me the art of endurance.
Show me the way I should live.
I feel the need of your presence,
And trust you will always forgive.

Thank you, dear Lord, for tomorrow,
For a beautiful, wonderful day.
Teach me to be ever grateful,
And thank you, dear Lord, for today!

Kirsten Weiss
HORIZON

This poem is dedicated to my mom because she has always been there for me.

As the sun lay upon the earth
its motherly arms welcome the night.
Peace comes around us and says,
"Goodnight little ones for I will
watch over you with all of my
heart."

Charles E Trotter
HE CHOSE ME

To my mother, who taught me to be a Christian, and to the Good Shepherd, who loves His sheep.

I called to the Lord—
from my wretched loneliness.
He answered me, then—
with mercy, love and
tenderness.
He turned my wilderness—
into a standing water.
And spoke to me, in words—
as of a loving Father.
He turned my dry ground—
into coolness of water springs.
And showed to me, in reality—
the goodness of all His things.
Of all of His good promise—
not one word will ever fail.
Not one saying will ever diminish—
no, even for the lonely, sick and
frail.
Because He chose me as His own—
He only is my God, my Lord.
He chose me as His own—
before the creation of the world.

Derrick Troy Haley
WHEN YOU'RE NEAR

Dedicated to the love of my life, my soon to be wife; SIMON. I Love You.

When you're near the sun shines
bright although the sky is grey,
And if I'm down your smile on sight
can always make my day.

And when you're near I feel as if all
time is standing still,
For you I'd swim the deepest waters
or conquer any hill.

For the feelings that I have for you
cannot be set aside,
My heart does tell me that they're
true and so they must be tried.

So if people say I'm acting strange,
just smile when this you hear,
Because I'm never quite complete,
except when you are near.

Agatha Kallman
INNER THOUGHTS

This poem was written with thoughts of Mirek.

On the verge where joy kills pain
and I forget all my complain,
and when my anger sails away
to a place I hope never to reach nor
find again:

A feeling so beautiful is born
within me, so rich and refined,
like I just had a mountain
climbed.

Could it be a Spirit of Love?
Will you meet me half way,
stripped of fault?
Will you give me your love and
the soul that you've got?

Your eyes shine for me,
my heart beats for you.
Our hands touch suddenly,
do you feel what I feel, too?

It is something special we share,
that doesn't mind the weather,
and everybody must see we
care,
but nothing matters when we're
together.

If you let me I'll be your queen
with feeling so delicate and fragile,
most people never had it,
some people never will.

Randy Lynn Holloman
THE STORM
I heard you were coming on the
news tonight
You had everyone worried and all in
a fright
It all got quiet and then very calm
We knew it wasn't going to be very
long
And then came the winds and all of
the rain
We knew we were in for much more
of the same
You came from the east and moved
to the west
You didn't let up not ever for a rest

You bent the trees right down to the ground
And you kept up your noise and oh what a sound

You knocked everything down that was in your way
Oh what could we do or what could we say
We don't know the reason or even know why
All we could do is stand there and sigh
You finally got through and went on your way
And didn't leave us anything but a mess for that day
I couldn't believe the mess that you made
All I can say that in time I hope this will all fade
They kept saying that this is God's way
I hope I never see you again not even for a day

Kimberly R Reeder
TIME TO BE ME
At times I'm not the daughter
that you seem to want me to be.
In many ways I'm not the same
as once I used to be.
It may be hard for you at times,
but I'm growing up you see.
It's not that I don't love you mom,
It's just I need to be me!

Emily White
THE DANCE
Dancing round and round,
Doin the tap-tap.
Waltz the steps with me.
Wake up, dear, from your nap.
Take just one step out of your trance.
Tiffs, gifts, consequences, rewards.
Trot around. One, Two, Three, Four.
Touch the Fiery sun for you.
Climb Mt. Everest. I'm The Fool.
Scrape my knee. Hang on, but keep the cool.
Enhance the dance. Reach my outer limit.
While on your dimwit butt you sit,
Staring at the flickering screen of snippets.
You say, "I don't know, I just don't know."
I say, "Follow me; One, Two, Heel, Toe."
See this is how the steps should go.
Prancin round and round.
Doin the Lindy right into town.
Buyin this and that, pants and hat.
Everyday, I'm at bat.
While Mr. Passive is quiet, the rat.
Can't you hear? Come dance with me.
Follow my lead. Make me proud is all I need,
as a peacock, showing my feathers in all kinds of weather. Dancing, Dancing,
A solo tap. Follow my map and dance.
Dance with me now.
Tap!

Stella Stevenson
PUT YOURSELF IN MY SHOES
As I sit on the cold pavement, I see feet walk past me.
I just listen to the sound as they hit.
I hear a rustling sound.
It's the wind blowing and scattering the papers along the street.
I see steam rise up from nowhere.
I feel beneath me the slight rumble of the subway.
I hear the screech of brakes and millions of lights pass by.
I'm cold and lost within my soul—nowhere to go—no one to care.
But this is imaginary, and I realize how much I have to be thankful for.

And I wonder how they feel?

A K Ayesha Roshini
SECRET LOVE
Remember years ago, when
I told you you were the one
that I loved.
When we were all alone from everybody,
by the small pond.
No sound from the water,
I didn't speak.
When your hands touched me
I can't tell by words how,
softly they were.
Kisses at the dark rain
I closed my mouth.
late into the night I waited for you.
I walked in the quiet mountains,
in the early evenings.
I thought about my life so much.
Late at night I thought
if he's with another.
When I was leaving,
your eyes filled with tears
and, your voice broke.
I know I should remember you,
for many years, in my life.
That secret love will start again.

Mark Steven Popham
DISCOVERY
Lights dim, stationary
Flickering to the beat of the horizon.
Uncompromised in its solitude.

Thoughts wander through an aching mind
Who are you? What are you?
Known and unknown in an instant.

Rough ideas, hazy in their passing
Invasion of a secret world
Unknown until now.

With the sanctity of the present destroyed
And reality all but truly known,
It's time
To move on to another forgotten place.

Al Gahagan
A MEMORY OF A LOVED ONE
I feel honored, that Josie and
Mike wanted me to share one of
my poems on this occasion, and
yet, I also feel unworthy
to stand before you and
attempt
to paint a word portrait
of Michael

People are so complex and simple
at the same time,
And for a sundry different
reasons
Michael has brought us all
here.

I have struggled to put some
words in an order
So that I can express to you
how I feel about Michael.
Hoping that maybe these
words will help you to
understand
Why you are here,
Why I am here,
And why we are
here.

I cannot say Good-bye to him
forever,
Because I believe that he is a
part of me—of all of us.
He occupies at this moment
the aching part of our
hearts
that will miss him.

But that same aching part of our
hearts,
Also holds the spirit of Michael.
The memories of the
moments we shared with
him—
The fun times—
When we heard his
laugh, his mouth wide
open, and full of
teeth.
The solemn times—
When we shared our
frustrations about life,
and heard his words
of concern and
empathy.
The sentimental times—
When he told us he
loved us,
and gave us hugs
and kisses.

In our hearts we know that
Michael was a warm, sensitive
man,
Whose self prescriptive
medicine was a combination
of nature, music, art, and
people,
With an extra
appreciation for pretty
women.
We can see it in his
drawings, writings,
music collection,
and in his wife.

We are lucky to have loved him,
cared about him,
And to have called him our
friend.

I would like to share now, "All I want to remember"

Somehow I want to capture in
words
Your inner being
So I can remember
Exactly who you are
And how I feel about you.

I want to remember
The look on your face
When you were happy,
When you were concerned,
When you were angry,
When you were disappointed.
And when you were
remembering.

I want to picture
The smile on your face;
And the lines of struggle,
determination,
And sincerity.
I want to hold in my heart
The memories
Of the times we talked
And laughed and hugged.

You may not know this,
but we are close you and I.
You are in my thoughts and
prayers.
You are a part of me.

And I know
That all my words will ever
capture
Is the surface of a much more
complicated,
Loving, and sensitive being,
who has come into my life.

I'll miss you when you are not
around.
I'll miss making memories.
I'll miss you not being where I
can touch you.

But I know, that if the feelings
I'm trying to express are
shared,
You'll be around always,
Because I have part of you in
my heart
And another reason for my life
to carry on.

Lena M Plat
STRANGE

This poem is dedicated to my loving children Pam, Bert, Rick and Con

I love rain, I love storm,
I love animals, I love kids.
I love friends, when they are real.
I love old people, they are so
alone.
I love flowers, they are God
looking at me from every angle.
I love trees, they look so
powerful and protecting.
I love the wide open fields,
because the far-away horizon
looks like the future,
You know it's there, but not clear
enough to see.
I love handicapped people, they
show so much courage.
I love the smell of cows and
horses more than the most
expensive perfume.
I love to feel the sheep's coat, soft
and warm.
I love to hear the birds sing, so
honest and clear, they seem to
have no problems, just satisfied
with what's here
I love to see in the animal world,
how each male protects his
female.
I love to sit in silence, with
somebody I love, and who loves
me.
I am strange, because all those
things are there for free.

Kim Webster
the captain of the ship he be . . .

This poem is dedicated to the memory of my Mother, Wanda Ruth Avery Webster I Love You Mommie . . .

a lonely ship on the ocean deep
lonely as a willow when it weeps;

a cloudy vessel from afar
sees the ship as a lonely star;

the color is of radiant hue
as the vessel approaches to the
rescue;

though tired and lonely the ship captain be
he welcomes the approaching vessel on the sea;

he tells the story of his fate
which left him in such a lonely state;

for he has traveled the sea many a year
though his story is sad he sheds not a tear;

he be a fisherman by trade
by which his fortune he made;

but now he is in the winter of his age
like his life was approaching its last page;

after his story was told all thru
he bid us a kind "thank you";

a kind old man he seemed to me
the captain of the ship he be . . .

Naomi C Apel

Naomi C Apel
TEARS

To my perfect husband, Robert-Simon Apel

Manta-ray clouds glide around
the world gathering moisture,
not so much from green seas as
from women's tears; back to Eve,
who cried for Abel.
Tears for lovers wasted in
combat;
Tears for children given life, who
disappoint.
Tears for marauders, ancient and
current, who rape and plunder;
Tears for houses, farms, countries,
burned;
Tears for wanton machines that
cripple, mingling their oil with
soft warm blood.
Tears behind third-world-
haystacks where unattended
labor squeezes out dead babies,
or where those who reach the
jewelled-age of innocence, slip
away from unseen microbes.
Tears that irrigate orchards,
fields, penthouses, for lost
dreams;
Tears of hanging-on-senility that
mocks progeny;
Tears of illness perpetuated by
indifferent I.V.'s where death
frustratedly toe-taps thru
unnecessary tests
against helpless physicians'
law-suits;
Tears of hunger, idleness, greed,
boredom, frustration, despair,
washing down the rivulets in
wrinkled cheeks;
Even tears of the coy, which play
trapped—men to bribe with
bounty;
The rare tear for laughter,
gratitude, achievement;
Now, shamelessly, I brush away
the tear of love, may it ever salt
my eye lids!

Wilda Powell
A THUNDER STORM

A storm is brewing it darkens the day
As it swiftly moves along it's way
Dark clouds roll, there's a thunder crash.
Raindrops fall with a forceful splash.

Trees bend over and touch the ground
As gusts of wind toss them around.
Birds and animals tremble with fear
As lightning strikes a tree so near.

They, like me, want the heavens to show
The sign that it's over—a brilliant rainbow.
We rejoice at the calm when the storm rolls by
And welcome the sunshine in a rain-washed sky.

Deborah Resch
AN OPINION

Feeling without love, I looked into the night.
Now maybe I will be paying.
I choose to have the moon guide the mood—
Have someone love me who had no right.

I'm scared and lonely, I'm crying inside.
Because crying outloud only seems to make the world go deaf.
I'm crying heavily inside.

I feel betrayed by you and by myself.
I hurt myself because I was selfish.
I wanted someone to love me just for me alone.

I'm scared and lonely, I'm crying inside.
Because crying outloud only seems to make the world go deaf.
I'm crying heavily inside.

What do I do now?
Where do I go from here?
I made the mistake, yes I'll pay.
Please just help ease my pain.
Make the pain hurting my insides go away.
But when it subsides will I still feel the pain of loneliness?
No one to love, ever, not even myself.

I'm scared and lonely.
I'm crying inside.
What is left is definitely not pride.
And crying only brings a deafness that is world wide.

Dr John J Kelly
I WANT A HILL THAT I CAN CLIMB

I want a hill
That I can climb.
I'd get my fill
Without a bind.

The hill needs snow
To take the boards,
To catch the flow.
Pray the Lord.

Then to the tub,
A swirling pool,
To get a rub
For this fool.

As dawn nears,
To the chapel I need
To remove the smears.
That's the real feed.

A little rice,
A little fowl,
This can suffice
Both body and soul.

A time to play,
A time for art.
A chair is choice.
Let's hear Mozart.

Then there's peace,
Oh, so grand,
That surpasses all
You can understand.

We set our sights,
Get ready to fight.
Better to trod
For love of God.

Karen Burke
TO CLIFF

You are the sun, that shines above, your face is full of radiant love. You are the wind that blows through the trees that flies the kites and rustles the leaves.

You are the rain . . . that makes things grow, you are the one who makes the rivers flow. You are the dove that flies above your heart so light and full of love.

Your life enchanted one and all, your time has come the piper called. Please don't fret my dear sweet friend, because I know we'll meet again . . .

Luthur L Bennett
MEMORY

For those who died—Their blood was the fuel, their life was the strength of the greatest military machine in the world.

In memory, Close your eyes old soldier and go back to the year
When death was so close you tasted it
And your heart beat fast with fear.
That's the tanks you hear behind you
And those footsteps off to the right
Are those of another company
That was marching there that night
Now you fall, for all hell has busted loose
And now you hear the screams
As the shells burst among you
And end your buddy's dreams

Then, you're up and running forward
With death there by your side
And as you fall in the mud again
You wonder how many of you have died
Then the tanks opened up with their guns
And the sky was bright and red
And soon there's nothing left to do
Except to gather up the dead
Well, it's over now old soldier
And that story you won't ever tell
But when you go back as you just did
You live again in hell.

Brian Tourjee
SUNSET

Sunset draws the lines together,
Leaves of gold mostly splendor,
Jotting down the day's defendor,
Pleasing those who choose to
keen,
Eyes majestic flow across the
gleems,
Whose fleeting beams also seem,
A bended shaft of solid light,
Losing days and into night,
But for we pass tis oh so bright,
Reluctantly we say goodbye,
To those hours spent through the
nye,
Watching til rays must fly.

Darla Abeene
JUST FOR ME

I sometimes go away,
To another place and time;

Where I'm so very happy,
And everything is fine.

There is no room for sadness,
And surely none for pain.

A place of total pleasure,
Where others have no claim.

It's a place of invitation,
For only those I choose,

Or perhaps my imagination,
May happen to let loose.

It's sacred there, you see;
This place I save for me.

It's a place of my own making;
My world of fantasy.

Pat Willis
IF

Blend in when you're Black
Look like the rest when you're Vietnamese,
Speak the language in Spanish maybe?
If we could see the people
On the inside, then see them.
Maybe we'd learn more
Yet precious few would try,
because of what they believe,
What they were told or saw.
If only we had learned right.
If only we'd take the chance.
Blend in when you're Black,
Look like the rest when you're Vietnamese,
Speak the language in Spanish maybe?
If only we could see the people
On the inside, then see them.

Cynthia Hann
MY VERY DEAR FRIEND

This poem is dedicated to Petrina, who died June 1986 in her hospital bed of a life long disease—Cystic Fibrosis. Age: 21 yrs.

A happy face, an encouraging smile
She left without a good-bye, over many a mile
She went peacefully, no hurt no pain
To have her gone, life won't be the same.

She never got to fulfill her goal
So weak was her body, so happy her

soul
If someone wanted comfort, that's what she would give
Her dream never came true—the dream to live.

She would make you laugh, she would make you cry
So calm even knowing she was about to die
She tried to comfort others when they were down
Often acting as though she were a clown.

So many feelings she could not place
She hid them all with a happy face
If ever you needed a hand, her hand she would lend
And now she's gone forever—My Very Dear Friend.

Marilyn Podolak
GOD HELP THEM

Dedicated to my loving children J.B. and Lora Lee

I pity all the children,
For they are left behind;
To straighten out the shambles,
Left by all mankind!

We leave disease and poverty,
Potential war nearby;
I think of all these children,
It makes me want to cry!

They were born so innocent,
Asked for none of this;
But they will share the burden,
Instead of happiness!

Ben Cochran
THE BOTTLE

Dedicated to my entire family: even my dogs

Bottle sitting on the shelf
You've swallowed up my life
I don't know what to say to you
You cut me like a knife

You put me through a living hell
I wish you never lied
You said it wouldn't hurt us
Living side by side

Now you've really done it
You started all of this
No we both started it
With just a little kiss

A kiss from lip to bottle
That is all it took
Bottle sitting on the shelf
You've scarred me with your hook

James E Gordon
MAKIN' IT

This is dedicated to my beloved Mother Mrs. Ann Gordon and my Grandmother Mrs. Bertha Gordon. Also to whomever has the vision to read this poem and those that can use some inspiration to make it through. There is a light for all of us to see, believe in the long run !!

You say that you're makin it, well I'm telling you I'm makin it too! You say that the struggle get's rough, I tell you that's not going to stop me.
You ask me, How high is my reach? My reply is that there ain't no mountain high enough and that the sky is just a touch away.
What do I plan to take on this journey to make it, you might ask?
I plan to take all of the treasures that the years have taught me, all of the knowledge that I have conceived along the way, and the wisdom and courage that I have been blessed with.
Have you prepared yourself for the times when someone gets in your way to hold you back and what about when the road gets rough and the mountain seems too high to climb? That's when faith comes in, for I know to get through this we must endure till the end. When someone or something gets in our way and tries to hold us back, that's when we'll show then what we're made of and through this grace they shall realize our strength and that we shall not be moved by them.
So you say you're makin it through all of this, tell me how will you know when you have made it?
I'll know for I shall feel satisfaction like it's never been felt before and my heart will be fulfilled. Also my soul will be at ease. It shall be known to me that I have passed every test.

Tamara Herbig
MEGAN

I know some day you'll ask,
And I'm not sure what to say.
I'll tell you how it was back then,
I wanted him to stay.

He said he loved me very much,
How was I to know he lied?
I proved that my love was true,
But his had already died.

The only hope then was mine,
I cried over him for much too long.
He was always aware of my feelings,
It was just like a sad love song.

You are the result of a love,
The two of us once shared.
My love for you has replaced,
That which once belonged to your Dad.

Patsy Dunagin Houghton

Patsy Dunagin Houghton
HAPPY HEARTS

TWO hearts are happy—light as a feather;
Love has touched them—blended them together.
What is this love that makes my heart sing?
A merging of our lives, a beautiful thing.

OURS is a true love that was meant to be,
For God brought us together, you and me.
Here we are, you and I together—
Never to part, oh no, not ever.

LOVE—the roses you gave to me today.
Love—the smile with words you need to say.
Thanks for sweet thoughts and loving things you do.
And I hope you know that I love you too.

LOVE, you express it in so many ways;
I'll love you my dear the rest of my days.

Melanie Anne Goulding
LEARNING TO LIVE

All throughout life
we learn to live,
Trying to understand what
life has to give.

We learn something new
every day,
And yet we live every day
in a different way.

We learn the difference
between right and wrong,
And we live our lives
to become wise and strong.

We also learn how
to love and be free,
And yet we live our lives
to see who else we can be.

So now that we've
learned how to live,
Why can't everyone
learn how to give?

Shawn Ruddy
POPCORN IS GREAT

This poem is dedicated to Granny. Thank you. Love, Shawn

Puffy and fluffy
Over and over
Popping in the popper
Corny jokes are told in there until
Out one jumps
Running away from people's mouths
Nothing can stop them.

I love popcorn,
So do most people I know.

Going round and round like
Rabbits running around
Every kernel pops up white and fluffy
All around the house the popcorn smell
Travels.

Francis Edward Amell III
VIGNETTE OF A SCHOOLBOY'S VACATION IN MAINE: 1988

It was the winter break
of February, nineteen eighty-eight,
At the Violette Settlement
in the town of Fort Kent,
That I, Francis Edward Amell,
did cross-country ski, pell-mell,
With Robert, my brother;
a friend, D.J., and one other.

Down the hills,
sometimes fast, sometimes slow,
Little hills, like pumpkins,
I go.
Little hills, like watermelons,
remind me.

As if paddled by the ghost-turtle,
I feel
Like crying when I land
on my ski—oh me!

What fun!
and
I've only just begun!

Ann Marie Knight
THE WOODS

To my future son or daughter (August 1989)—May you always follow your dreams.

In the woods
I am all alone
only with the sound
of the forest.
It is peaceful
and I spend hours
at a time
There.
Just listening
to nothing.

Irene Suchta Pacana
LIKE A FLOWER IN SPRING

There is so little time . . . and so much to do . . .
The dreams that I cherished . . . I now want anew!
My life has revolved . . . around all of you . . .
Each success you've had . . . I applauded too!

I too had a talent . . . which I lay aside . . .
Lying dormant so long . . . while I cried inside!
I wanted to use . . . this precious gift in me . . .
The yearning I felt . . . only God could see!

Now it's my turn to bloom . . . "Like a Flower In spring" . . .
Feel the wings of a bird . . . and fly high as I sing!
I want to soar to the top . . . of the highest tree . . .
I want to smile down below . . . and have them look up at me!

Now it's my turn to bloom . . . Like a Flower in Spring" . . .
Feel the wings of a bird . . . and fly high as I sing!
I want to reach for a star . . . and hold it so tight . . .
Till it shines down on me . . . till it's brighter than bright!

I'll start right now . . . living dream after dream . . .
I'll work like two people . . . I'll work like a team!
It's time to live my dream . . . to climb the highest wall . . .
To reach new heights . . . before the petals fade and fall!

Keith L Sporleder
WINTER AND THE HILL

Yesterday, I bought a sleigh,
The weather was foggy and crisp.
Today is my little boy's birthday,
This morning, it's sunny, but brisk.

The trees all hang heavy,
With white fogged icing.
Making going outside,
All the more exciting.

Day dreaming as I gaze,
Of days gone past,
Of walking though the snow,
On that well worn path.

We all know that path,
To that one and only hill,
Where we would sleigh for hours,
And never get our fill.

Alas, I am grown now,
Years since I've had that fun,
But today I'm going back
And I'm taking my son.

Freda Adair
FOUR LITTLE CANDLES

This poem is dedicated to my four children of whom I was inspired to sit down and write the words. Pamela, Alana, Althon, Jr., and Lisa. Lisa (youngest) sent this poem in without my knowledge. Written in 1963.

Four little candles light my way,
Brighten the path I travel each day.

Each one shines in its own special way,
Sunny, bright, cheery and gay.

The first little light came years ago,
My cup was surely filled to overflow.

Then came the second, my dreams were fulfilled,
My life was so happy, with more surprises still.

Then came the third light, a bold surprise!
It was so different—and right before my eyes,

These glimmers began to grow.
Each passing day, I love them so.

Then came the fourth one my dreams surely filled,
A glance at this one was brighter still.

These four little candles were Gods gifts you see,
Unduplicated and molded especially for me.

These little lights that used to glow so small,
Are grown (and still glowing) from wee one to tall.

You see they're my children, life's greatest loan;
They'll soon have small candles with "lights of their own" . . .

Sylvia Anne McLemore
DIXIE

To my sister, my sparkling ray of sunshine: May you one day discover how very precious and wonderful you really are.

Bright-eyed, curly blond, angel face—
You seem to feel sad, out of place.
You came so far to make a home
Where you know you cannot belong.
You don't recall before you left
You asked for Father's special gift.
You slipped back in and asked a part
Of Heaven to keep in your heart.
"In case my path grows dim of light,
Its glow will steer my feet aright."
Father smiled and kissed your cheek
And then He gave your nose a tweak.
He granted you this little gem
To help you come back home to Him.
And, with a hug, He let you go
Depending on that little glow
To keep you safe and calm your fears
'Cause you'd be gone for many years.
It has no battery or plug
But operates on Father's love
Because this source can never fail.
So when you're scared, confused, or frail
Just search your heart and feel the glow.
Just search your heart and you will know.

Lois M Laleman
MY LOVE

I love the way you make my heart feel,
The feeling I have inside is quite real.

The gentle way you dry my tears,
You chase away all my fears.

You listen to what's in my heart
Especially if we happen to be apart.

You brighten my day like the sunshine,
I'm so glad that you are mine.

To trust completely that's a must,
And get so excited we needn't fuss.

The memories we have to share,
When we're alone we haven't a care.

At night I lay for a much needed rest,
I pray I've given you a day of my best.

Take my hand as we walk this land,
I know it will always be so grand.

If we ever have to be apart,
The reunion is just like the start.

I'll always love you I hope you know,
Like the rivers' endless flow.

Michelle Haley
SIDE BY SIDE

A thousand times a day I find
myself wishing you were here
Wishing so much I could hold you
and always keep you near.

In my dreams you are with me
and we're dancing in the rain
Then loneliness fills my soul and I realize
you are gone again.

Though time and distance may
keep us apart
You are always with me
You're always in my heart.

And when the time is right
And when we both decide
We will be together, forever,
Side by side.

Wendy L Jackson
I WISH YOU WERE HERE

This poem is dedicated to a very dear and loving friend, my brother. As each day goes by, I wish he was here with me

When I looked into your eyes,
all I could see
was what anyone else could see—
love—
love for everyone around you
I wish you were here
so I could see that love in your eyes again!
Whenever I saw you
you were always helping someone
Whether with cooking or homework
I wish you were here to help me again
I wish you were just here
Please come back!!!
Please

J Garrison Lives
A TIME FOR COLORS

Mad egos of the healers
Are for this moment not my leaders
and I'm free.
I'll find the strength to grasp this time
Think thoughts of then and now and what can be.
At five I walked the dried up creek bed at the farm
Breathed waves of sky blue butterflies into my mind
To hold forever as weapons against users.
Sometimes the butterflies entangled in webs my mind created
Through choices not in keeping with their colors.
I must keep my colors true and hang on to those precious blues
Adding only hues which will enhance them.
I'll make them grow to ward off blows of tortured souls
Who work in muddied tones and lashing voices.
When this quiet time is gone and pressures grow and spawn
I'll try to see them troubled seas before the calm.
From the stormy ebb and flow I will watch my palette grow
And make the range from hots to colds resources.

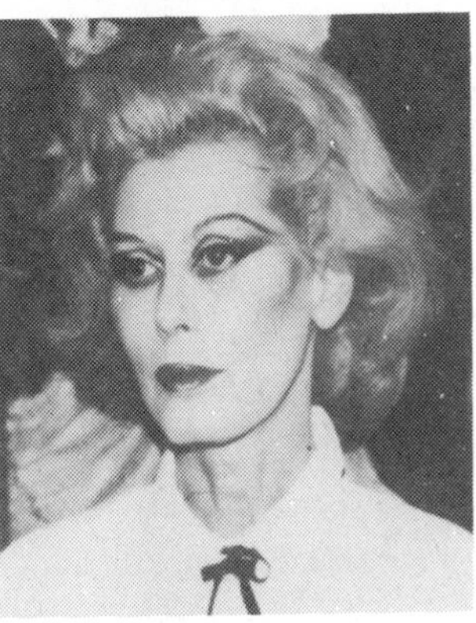

Karen Worth

Karen Worth
SOUL SCULPTOR

Let up from hell a meteor flame.
I will call it by your name:
cut multifacets with my eyes
until a diamond I incise.

Samuel E Wilkes
THE HOPELESS ADDICT

This poem goes out to anyone considering drugs as an alternative to facing life.

We are all prisoners here
In this life of pain.
Some of us choose to escape
By jumping on a train.
This train, I mean, is one of total ecstasy
From which it is hard to regain
That which we have lost
By choosing this way.
The "peace" was good for awhile,
But then we passed away.

Irene Teel
THE TEARS I SHED FOR MY DREAMS

The tears I shed for my dreams
Have just been shattered.
I finally found someone to love and trust
Until he asked too soon.
I said no. I just want to be friends.
Now I feel different—I love him
But I'm afraid to let him know.
My wish is that maybe he will
ask me again
Yet I am afraid of the fear lurking around my soul.
In our talks
What we say between us is too perfect.
Just look at the trouble and
confusion we've had so far
And the mixed feelings and fear we've built up.
This is really not perfect.
He is so strong
Not weak like me.
When we were together,
He took my fears away and I
felt happy and warm inside.
Now all I can say or ask
Is if he will only understand and
give me a second chance.

Robert Dwain Cline
CALDRON OF THE MIND

To Eleanor and Clayton: Don't forget the joy of things which can't be touched.

Is it the icy wind that wails?
Repeating the words of horrible tales.
Or dark thoughts seeking the soul to grind
In the blackest caldron of the mind?

Do hideous creatures cringe in the mist?
Do God and devil really keep a list?
Or does the fruit of life get its evil rind
In the blackest caldron of the mind?

Demons roam because they must bear
The unholy fact that we don't care.
Pray only to extinguish the fire you find
In the blackest caldron of the mind.

Violet Touch
MY FIREBUSH

Dedicated to my Granddaughter Courtney Lorrayne German

My special bush has grown quite tall.
I've watched, for years, since it was small.
It has so many sides to see.
I'm looking at it constantly.
Sometimes, it is subdued and soft—
In colors green and, lighter, oft—
But then, again, in brilliant hue—
Its fiery red can startle you.
How can this wonder from above
Consume me with such depth of love?
A love that helps me understand
My bush's many sides, so grand.
It grows in every way, each year,
As I look on and softly cheer.
I'll watch, as yearly leaves unfurl—
My Firebush is Courtney Girl.

Jean A Litchfield
MIND LUST

As, I turned in the darkened room
And looked into his eyes
Black pools of passion
Reaching down into my very soul!
Sleek panther like body
Gracefully gliding through my life.
Healing hands, caressing ever so gently.
Lips that would touch mine, like a soft butterfly.
A glance, that's all I have as he turns away each day.
As the days pass, the desire for his touch increases.
To hear his words of passion whispered in my ears.
Unbearably painful . . .
If only one word, a touch . . .

Gertrude Svoboda
I AM THY SOUL

I am thy soul,
My man who sleeps beneath the sod
And I am free, to rendezvous with

God.
I hover near this earthly bode of mine
To mark its worthiness o'er time.
The gnarled fingers, twined in rest
Have served me well, and yet
I am thy soul, and I am free.
I do not sleep, I am eternity.
At resurrection, on that final day
I'll take your hand in mine,
And tread the path from whence we came
To live again, my shrine of clay;
For thou art dear to me,
And freed of your iniquities
We'll stand before the MASTER JUDGE
For all eternity, we'll both be free.

James Anderson
YES—I NEED YOU

To Ann—A special friend in El Cajon, Calif. With love.

Yes, I need your smile today,
Your hug, your listening ear.
I need your encouragement
And gentle words of cheer.

Yes, I need your helping hand,
Your letter, your call and more.
I need your visit
To make my spirits soar.

Yes, I need your affection
When I'm feeling blue.
Listen, I am calling,
For a special friend like you.

Mary Williams Barnes
SKELETON IN OUR CLOSET

To Orville Williams in memory of his father, Bennie Williams, my oldest brother, who told this event to him. He retold it to me.

He staggered up to the creek that night,
And felt he had to cross,
He didn't know the log was slick,
And suddenly his foothold was lost.

The moon gave but little light.
I'll wager he worried about his sin.
It's sad that he was in such a plight,
And passed out from the shock of falling in.

He was in the icy black water,
All of a night and day,
His family and friends were searching,
For my Uncle who'd gone astray.

"Here he is" shouted one as he looked at the shocking sight.
There was a circle of ice attached to his face.
Everything submerged; his nose and mouth all right.
The doctor said if he hadn't been as drunk as he was,
He wouldn't have been alive as he was.

I used to hear our preacher say while down on his knee,
Except for the grace of God, that's where he would be.
This is not intended to offend AA and this account is true.
My uncle knew he had a problem, but he didn't know what to do.

Dianne M Carroll
WHAT ABOUT YOU?
God is my best friend, he knows me better than anyone.
He forgives me when only he can understand.
Only he can see within me.
Only he can know my fears, my potential, my love for him and mankind.
I strive and fail but try and try, to be worthy, to be like him.
No man can change me.
I am moved by mans' thoughts, dreams that don't come true but I know.
I don't care what race you are, what religion you are.
I want to see within you, know you, but only God can ever see the real you.
So why depend on man, imperfect man to accept you.
Imperfect struggling within ourselves, we are all fighting for our lives.
To depend on you for my strength is wrong, God tells me what to do, not you.
No one can express how they feel so someone will understand, only God can see inside and listen.
What weakness do you have? What tears the soul from you?
What takes the goodness from your mind, from your goal?
Everyone has something, to think different is wrong.
God tells me what to do, what about you?

Dee Dee Bruner
THE INEVITABLE
It's inevitable that rain falls down,
That birds lean how to sing;
That flamingos stand on one long leg,
And people learn to speak.

It's inevitable that energy is used,
That fish swim in the sea;
That whales get air by holes on their heads,
And grass grows emerald green.

It's inevitable that flowers bloom,
That trees lose all of their leaves;
That people eat, drink, and sleep,
And wonder about the inevitable.

Emilda Mercado
SIMILARITIES
Beautiful flowers, how grand you are
In loveliness you lie
How sweet the smell that you possess
You are so much like happiness
Because you soon will die

Beautiful flowers, how soft you are
Like us you have your spring
In varied colors you are made
You reach your splendor then you fade
Like every living thing

Beautiful flowers, how grand you are
If only for a day
All is special to remember
We have our June and our December
For this is nature's way

Wilbur D Mullens
OLD CAR NOSTALGIA
It was in the year of '84,
When I spied a car that was 34

The car was a 1950 Olds,
And I was almost 50 years old

I bought the car and brought it home,
Restored it till it shone like chrome

It had futuristic signs to the moon,
This Olds would roll when finely tuned

On the hood was a rocket poised for flight,
Over a globe circled by a satellite.

Underneath was a version of a modern V-8,
Towered by the original Rocket-88

The body was a short and humpback style,
So black and shiny you could see yourself smile

The Outer Space Age had arrived,
In a car that would really come alive

If you ever see me going down the high-way,
While you are standing by the by-way

Will you recognize this merry Olds,
From these very verses that I've told.

Donald L Harris
EYES OF GREEN HAIR OF BROWN

To me her beauty flows throughout her body, like the trickling water in a mountain stream.

The sparkle in her eyes, can mistify, like the dawning of a new spring morning.

Eyes of Green and Hair of Brown for I do love, this love I found.

Time has past, I've love and lost, those Eyes of Green and Hair of Brown.

To love her is easy, to let go is painful, for I have lost that love I've found, those Eyes of Green and Hair of Brown.

I do love, this love I found, her Eyes of Green and Hair of Brown.

Oh God, I have lost, this love I've found, those Eyes of Green and Hair of Brown.

Oh Lord, please take care, or her Eyes of Green and Hair of Brown.

Diane Bockelman
THE FACETS OF A FRIEND

To Connie, whose encouragement and motivation I hope I never have to live without

You listen to my dreams
You share my laughter
You tolerate my screams
When nothing is the matter

You give me hope for the future
You remember good times in the past
You survive my mental torture
But not one stone do you cast

I treasure you friendship
I admire you like a beautiful gem
I could have no greater fortune
Having you for a friend

Mary Dossett Conner
LORD, I ASK . . .
Give me a confidence deep in my heart, and a mind to pursue my own goal,
A vision unclouded to look straight ahead, and a hand I might now and then hold. .
Give me the wisdom to keep my path straight, and a pride that I may never bend. .
And scruples enough to make my own choice, but most of all give me a friend! !

Give me a song in my heart every day, that my spirit may soar with the wind. .
Let me walk down from the mountain I climb, to the valley below now and then,
The things I am asking are many, but no more than I'm willing to give,
For a life of existing for self in this world, is a lifestyle I don't wish to live

Give me the faith to accept one by one, these gifts in the hand you extend,
With patience enough to use them with care, especially the love of my friend.
One who will share in my days filled with joy, yet stay through the sorrow and pain . . . one who will walk up the mountains with me, yet stay through the storms and the rain.
Just let my life reflect every day, the gifts you've entrusted to me,
Let me reach out to those who need help, with a heart and a spirit set free. .
Never endow me with wealth made of gold, on which I might fail or depend,
Give me more courage each day that I live, but most of all give me a friend! !

Rosalie Brevelle
MONTANA

This poem is dedicated to Jeffery, my friend forever."

All about is history
And an age old mystery
Literature and western art
Can only tell a small part
But the awesome scenery
And oceans of greenery
Give more meaning to words
That have been read or heard
About this land called Montana
With its timeless panorama
Of mountains and endless sky
Even rivers that never run dry.
The Charles M. Russell Museum
Paris Gibson, don't forget him
From Giant Springs to Rainbow Falls
Malmstrom Air Force Base near Great Falls
Lewis and Clark National Forest
And Blue Ribbon Trout for those who fish
All this and more to appreciate
About Montana, the Treasure State.

Valerie L Lee
ALWAYS
Once I thought I found him, the only one for me,

But I realize I was wrong and that is plain to see,
Although he seemed like everything I ever wanted in a guy,
I finally realized why he had to say goodbye,
He said goodbye because he didn't want to be hurt anymore;
He didn't want it to end the way it had before.
There is only one thing he never thought of,
And that is what I felt for him was love.
I realize now I will never be with him again, ever;
Yet the love I feel for him will last forever.
Sometimes I wish it could be like it was before,
Yet I know that won't happen anymore,
There is only one thing for me to do,
And that is to try and forget about you,
I realized it wasn't hard for you to do,
but I know I will never be able to forget you.
Well, no matter what I may say or do,
I know that I will always love you!

Dorothy M Gerkin
STRAIGHT FROM MY HEART

These words are for all the
courageous men and women
who had anything to do with the
war in Vietnam,
Unfortunately not everyone feels
the tearful thoughts that I am.
Can anyone tell me why all those
lives were sacrificed for?
Does anyone at all know why
they fought that terrible war?
I have probably shed at least one
tear for each and every name on
that wall in Washington, D.C.,
I wish someone would tell me
why they gave their lives,
Please help make me see.
It has been many years since
those brave people have gone
off to fight,
And what it still is doing to those
left is not right.
Terrible things happened to a lot
of those people but still a lot of
citizens act as if they don't care,
Some wake up in a cold sweat
dreaming about those awful
times, some will spend the rest
of their lives in wheelchairs.
I wish to God I could reach out
my arms and hold each and
every one of you and make
everything all better.
Or sit down and tell you how I
feel in my heart in a letter.
I am one person who is very
grateful for what you did for I
know you did your part,
And I want you to know I love
you all and that comes straight
from my heart.

C Ann Chenier
I LOVE YOU, CHILD

Has anyone ever told you
how special you really are?
Have you ever seen a rainbow
or watched your kite soar?

Standing in the corridor
while tears run down your
cheek
Your parents have had another fight
I bet you're scared, aren't you?
Don't be ashamed to talk
Oh, you don't know what to say.
Tell me about your puppets
When you've laughed and played all day.

Let me brush your hair out of your eyes
There, now isn't that better?
Let me softly hug you for a while
and say, I love you, child.

Marian Falk
AUTUMN

What can be so lovely as an Autumn morn!
With hills of trees in brilliant hue
Reaching above valleys of soft blankets of fog—
Green, grassy meadows all covered with dew.

What can be so lovely as an Autumn day!
Birds winging south; the brisk, sunny air—
Leaves rustle in the trees; orange, yellow and red,
Then fall to earth, leaving the trees stand bare.

What can be so lovely as an Autumn day!
A drive in the country reveals beauty at each turn.
The cornfields are dry, with a pumpkin here and there;
The faint smell of smoke, of leaves as they burn.

What can be so lovely as an Autumn eve!
The sun seems afire as it sinks from sight.
Then the full harvest moon looks down from the sky
Like a huge golden ball, against the black night.

As we pass through the year, day by day,
Each season's more beautiful than all of the rest.
Now summer is gone, the days have grown cool,
And surely, right now, it seems that Autumn is best.

Bill Conroy
WHAT IS A FAMILY

To my loving Mom

A family is caring.
And also are sharing.

There are sisters,
And there are brothers.

What keeps us together,
Is our loving Mother.

There are times,
When we don't mind.

Sometimes being lost,
But just paying the cost.

No matter how hard we're shoved,
We all know about love.

I know as I write this poem
We always will have a home.

This is the day,
That we all can say.

If it wasn't for you,
We wouldn't be true.

Danielle Deibler
THE EYES

To a devastatingly seductive pair of deceptive eyes.

His eyes are like the clear and endless green sea;
Going on and on until you're lost within their depths
Only through his eyes are the many dimensions of his soul visible;
The sadness and pain;
The childlike excitement and vulnerability;
The innocence coupled with knowledge beyond his years;
All hidden behind the muddled confusion of;
love, sorrow, and anguish.
Emotion personified, mirrored,
Yet distorted in the calm deceiving shift of the waters.

John T LaGrone
INFINITY

My view is drawn to the crest
above this textures mass,
where the press of helplessness
summons a majestic impasse.

There end meets naught and evermore
the straight line fades to ever,
to pass no more thru ever before
and begin the end of never.

What was, is now, and must eternally be
affirming all creation will last,
wrapped in physical infinity
in boundless inestimable cast.

It will come from Him . . . oh anxious soul
that release appointed for then,
the climactic blending of new and old
in time and space with no breadth or end.

Chereece Lawson
MY LIFE

I'd like to dedicate this to my family and my friends!

My life to me is very good you see,
Thinking about it now, it should be!
I like pizza, hot dogs and
hamburgers.
I also like some kinds of sugars!
I am nine years old.
How about that!
I can't imagine being 10 this year,
I guess nobody can.
I have a mother and father
that cares for me!
Two brothers who love me!
I have friends who like to be around
me,
What more can anyone want!
There are also bad things in my life,
Like my friends breaking up with me,
Plus being grounded by my parents.
Another thing to worry about is
having a fight with my brothers.
Also being robbed like other families.
I'm worried about being kidnapped.
I'm worried about how my
life will end!
Would I get beaten up like
Lisa Steinberg?
There are other things that can
happen to me,
Like being mugged by a crack dealer.
What happened to the
10 commandments?
Are we really trusting in God?
I wonder!

S Melissa Delfin
A FRIEND

This poem is dedicated to my loving family; my dad Silvestre, my mom Mildred, my sister Sonia and to my friends Pauline, Cindy, Rachel, Dina and Julie.

A friend is someone that you know.
Sometimes a friend may be a foe.

A friend is someone that you trust,
Keeping secrets that you must.

A friend may be a furry cat.
Loving it is where it's at.

A friend is someone that is your buddy,
Great friends will always be happy.

A friend is someone you will always remember,
You will never forget, and always forever.

Robert J Carley
SOMEONE DIED

To those who died for mankind

Someone died for every gain of mankind,
For God, for science, for freedom's mind.

From time immemorial of every age
as man turned each time worn
page,
For every gain that's made
for every stone he laid,
someone died.
So His Name could carry on,
Oh Mighty Redeemer,
Conquering One,
Written o'er the tomb of a saint
these simple words, bold, e'er so
faint,
someone died.
For every hurried pace
as man explored the seas and
space,
On to yonder stars to peek,
for every dream we seek—for
these
someone died.
For every battle won
for a job well done,
For all conflicts cease,
every blessed peace—for these
someone died.
When darkness falls upon man,
his life filled with grief and pain,
understand
Science did search and find a cure
that man may endure—for this
someone died.
Freedom, may God rest in thee,
to your refuge many do flee.
For freedom's face they long to see,
may it forever be—for this
someone died.
Lift not the knocker twice,
for you were ransomed at an
awful price.
So turn not away
for 'tis Salvation's way—for this
someone died.

So man I've followed, and wonder still
was this God's Will,
That man soar on eagle's wings
or tend to earthly things—for these
someone died.
Lest these things dim in doubt,
lest the light go out,
Remember, for these gifts we sought
someone sacrificed, labored and fought—for these
someone died.

B R Tarr
TRIPPING SONG
I did not know when I began to dream
Of you, how high I did aspire.
You had the wit and gall to bring
A role I fancied I might sing.
It started easily enough
And well within my range,
With passages of sweet duet
Enchanting passages, and strange
Pauses, trios, pace, and change
Of mood and tempo, tough, and yet
Tho' bewildered I sang on—
Conducted how? Conducted why?
I did not know nor dared I try
To guess the plot, nor say, nor pray
What might be the coda. And then
suspicion crept into
My veins for the music switched again
To heights and depths in arias
impossible to sing.
The conductor is an angel, the singer but a frog
Whose croaks are misery to both
And tears plop on the lily pad
The work hangs fire in the middle (sad)
Of the invert fairytale theme.

Debby Booher
OUR FRIENDSHIP

Dedicated to: Donna Larkin, who has done more for me than she will ever know.

Your friendship is special in many ways.
You've helped me through the hardest days.
You're here when I need you and I am for you.
We help each other to work things through.
We have good times more than bad.
A friend like you I've never had.
You're someone special to have around.
You're someone who won't let me down.
Our friendship grows stronger everyday.
You're a part of my life for now and always.

Mathew J Porubsky
WHEN IT RAINS
When it rains I wonder
What happens in the sky

And then I hear the thunder
And dream that I can fly

While high above the weather
No controlling force was shown

I glide much like a feather
And find myself alone

Then I realize what I see
And quickly return below

For ways of magic were meant to be
But never for me to know

Jennifer Pasley-Smith
DRAGON'S LAIR
Into the night you reel
Breathing fire
And my name
In the same breath
With eyes closed, my mind burns
At the precariousness
Of this confrontation
For in your eyes
Those stony gates
That hide your soul
I found a fissure to reach in
With just one
Touch
Reptile slits echo disbelief
At the intrusion
But I was born for this hunt
So close your eyes
I know the breach
I'll feel my way back through cold stone
When the dragon roams
The shadow-bluffs of night.

Jeffery A Auger

Jeffery A Auger
FLYING, CRYING AND EVENTUALLY DYING
Sailing,
Flying high,
Soaring way up in the sky;
In hope that maybe from the clouds
You'll hear me when I cry out loud;
I'm just a face with the crowd.
Please listen to me.

Crying
Out to you;
Is there nothing we can do?
To make this lonely world unite
And put an end to all the fights;
Then everything will be alright.
Just try it and see.

Leaving,
Sailing by;
Finding somewhere else to fly;
I'll just stay up here in the sky
And live life from the eagle's eye
Until the day when I will die.
Please remember me.

Ella Mae Sanders
JUST FOR YOU
There are little things that someone gave me that only I would treasure,
They are things that many would call junk but to me they give great pleasure.
They're things that bring fond mem'ries to my mind and to my heart.
They are things from which I only hope I never have to part.
They are mostly sentimental things and really have no value,
Except to me, because they're proof of a husband who was true.

Sometimes we argued or we quarreled but we remained together.
We always strived for a common goal regardless of the weather.
You taught us to be fair and square, with never hate nor greed.
And this I've tried to teach our children hoping the advice they'll heed.
To give our family happiness you seemed always to come through,
And in return I've tried the same, and I did it "Just for you."

Cassandra Alexander
IN THE DARK I LIE
In the dark I lie
for the solidity of mind is now conquered.
Calm can no longer remain for corruption will inhibit all.
The soul is hurled through the air
as if no feeling had ever existed.
Night soon arrives, but how can I be sure?
All darkness is the same, all holding the same meaning.
Soon the mind and body are relieved of all feeling.
Rejuvenation begins.
The new course will soon begin.
In time some darkness will
lighten, and no longer will
the mind be heavy.
It is learned (by me).
All darkness will still be the same even in light.

Sandy Payne
MY MOTHER AND I
Yes, this is Mother's Day,
And I've got something very important to say.

When I was just an infant child,
You'd rock me all day long.
And whisper sweetness in my ear,
That nothing can go wrong.

But now I've grown, out on my own,
And pray that you will hear,
This message I am sending
With sadness and with tears.

That I must break this string of love,
So I may grow on my own.
This is part of life, it must go on,
For I have seeds that must also be sown.

Margaret B Dodson
TO THE SERVICE PERSON FROM MOM

To Diana, Chris, Joshua and Andrea who spent three long years in Greece.

Many months you must stay;
In that land so far away.

My heart was heavy, and that is true;
When you flew over the ocean blue.

Memories of you, I hold in my heart;
Even though we are apart.

As the sun comes up and sets each day;
Each time it does brings you closer to the U. S. A.

I love you, I miss you, how much you'll never know;
How hard it is for a mother, to let her child go.

But you life is yours, and my life is mine;
So we can't be together all of the time.

The day will come, soon you see;
When we meet, how happy I will be.

A few more months and this is true;
You'll be coming back over the ocean blue.

Larry Gordon
PRECIOUS

"This poem is dedicated to (Yoshani Wijé), My/Lady Brown Eyes)."

As a bee to a flower,
(Precious)
As a hot summer's shower,
for that is what you are to me, hour upon hour
(Precious)
As a food is to my being, precious as my eyes are for seeing, for that is what you are to me, please perish the thought of ever leaving?
(Precious)
As a healthy state of mind, precious as my heartbeat, in my young or old time, for
that is what you are
to me,
(Perpetually) . . .
(Precious)
Is the word, that you are to me, you see, I not only love you
physically,
(but) also,
(mentally and spiritually)! ! !

Pamela Pickering
PAINTING RAINBOWS
Sitting here
I shuffle paper,
Ignoring the work
I have to do,
While in my mind
I paint portraits—
Magical pictures
of me and you

I paint pink days forever,
and greens trimmed in blue,
With deep scarlet nights,
and grey days—a few.

I paint gold days
and silver,
all mixed together.
I paint rainbows of our love
that go on forever.

Finally I return
From the clouds up above,
and I smile at my portrait
—My Masterpiece of Love.

James D Bucknam
THE BIRDS SING PRAISE FOR GOD ABOVE
The birds sing praise for God above.
The birds sing praise for God is love.
They sing it morning, noon, and night.
They sing it always, even in flight.
They sing it when darting thru the clouds.
They sing it long, they sing it loud.
The birds sing praise for God above.
The birds sing praise for God is love!

Ruthe Mullenax
A MOTHER'S LOVE
. . . is warm and understanding
So very fresh and new
A mother's Love is special
and intended just for you

A Mother's Love has no questions
No secrets and no lies
Only honesty and tenderness
With endless bonding ties

You need not tell her when you're sad
She can feel it in her heart
She'll smile for you and hold you close
And silently fall apart

Love her—honor her—cherish her
Remember all she's done
For only a Mother's Love
Can make you whole and one

On this special Mother's Day
Take a moment and think of yours
Either touch her or remember her
That's what this day is for.

Rubicely Morales Lavalle

MY DAD

WHO is that man that has been there all of my life, to comfort me and helped me through my childhood?
A man with eyes that tell you if he is happy or sad.
HIS eyes are warm just like his heart.
A man that never turns his back when you need him the most.
HIS hands tell you how strong he is.
With a touch of his hands he could make disappear all those terrible nightmares you might have. The line in his hands are like roads that take you to the warmest part within him.
HIS warmest part is the LOVE he has to give.
HIS love is so bright like a pearl found in the sea, but yet so big like the sea.
HIS love could never fit into a chinese bottle.
A love that can't be sold for the cause than only one man could wear it upon his heart.
A man that has a face like the moon, not for its shape but for how it shines.
A man that clears the path of life, a man that knows what's right or wrong.
WHO is that man?
That special man is you DAD!
A man that helps me through the toughest days of my life and for what may lie ahead of me.
Thanks DAD for being
what you are.

Ms Diana Ramos Cruz

SILENT SCREAM

To all the unborn, whose screams were never heard.

Its darkness surrounds me and it is warm, wet and safe.
I hear the sounds of our hearts and of her soft voice.
I can hear and feel our veins pulsing with life and I wonder what it will be like when it is time to leave.
My heart beats fast with excitement from just the thought, but I hear her voice and I am calmed.
Wait, something is happening?
Pressure all around my body!
Something is pulling me! What is it?
Oh God, something is ripping me out!
It's not time!
I try to hang on, but it is too strong.
Oh Voice, please help me feel safe again, but I hear nothing from her.
Again the agonizing rip. I let our a long and chilling scream. No one hears!
I am dying and I do not know why.
One more rip and I will be gone. I listen for her, but I hear nothing.
I feel the pressure and I know that next comes the agonizing flesh ripping pain.
I will scream once more, my last scream.
I know no one will hear.

Roxanne M Staha

SWEET DREAM

The night is cold and lonely.
When you're gone.
Sometimes I'm still awake,
To greet the dawn.
It's only in my dreams,
That I can hold you near
And all those empty feelings,
Just seem to disappear.
Two warm entwining bodies,
Merge together into one.
Come kiss me softly,
As we rise to meet the sun.
Then I open my eyes,
With those feelings still inside,
Just another sweet dream,
And you're still gone.

Joseph W Allaire

WITHIN REACH

As the sun begins its daily journey across the sky
The winter's rain falls gently on the frozen ground.
The morning beckons midday only to offer a blanket of snow.
The sun, high overhead, is just a memory
For the plumage of winter has shown its beauty.

The day is nearing an end as clarity turns to shadows.
The night is upon us, the snow still falling.
Look toward the horizon over the once grassy plain.
Listen carefully to the silence
And imagine the peace within yourself.

Carole Ahlf Cialone

GOING BACK IN TIME

I went back in time, when I went to the land I heard of in childhood melodic melodies.
An enchanted land where fairy tales become reality.
A place where castle spires reach up to the heavens above.
A magical place that God has touched with his love.
The rains come often to kiss this land, and everything turns to green.
The sheep graze on majestic slopes, and life seems so serene.
A thatched roof cottage on a winding road, roses climbing a whitewashed wall.
A ruddy faced gentleman sailing past on his bike, bids a cheery hello, in the misty rain of the fall.
The chimneys spew curling smoke, and the smell of peat permeates the air.
You are in this emerald land, this gentle place, life's without a care.
Rocks piled haphazardly one on another, form fences that stretch for miles, like a sentinel of soldiers in a field.
Rugged green cliffs that rise from the roaring sea and hug the land like a shield.
Tranquil scenes in solitude on lonely country lanes.
Golden flowers by the side of the road give sunshine in the rain.
Endless beauty, like a unique painting on the wall.
This is the precious green gem in a sapphire sea, this is Ireland in the fall.

Shivcharran Hulasie

HUMAN INSTINCT: LOVE

Once, not far away, nor years past, but yesterday, I fell in love.
With whom? Why? Only my heart knows!
Secretly, without my sensing it, it had an affair.
It is not clear, but fantasizing, passion became nightmare.

I became a prisoner, chained to a cold heart, which I have lost control of.
Is it love? May it be affection? Oh God! What am I to do?
I advance forward, thinking I've triumphed over illusions.
How weak can I be? I see your eyes, they break me down.

I crumble to ashes, which the power you radiate merely blows away.
I am a person of immeasurable strength, yet a frail, innocent flower, pearl as you snap me, as one a twig.
My destiny is controlled by your hands.

Like a puppet, like a servant,
whose strings are so strong,
I cannot break free.
I am cursed for eternity.

Talk to me? Love me, as I have done so to you,
time and time again
A protector I will be, a friend I will be, an advisor I will be,
and if your heart so desires, a lover I will be.

Do not turn your back on me.
Listen to your heart, not others.
As far as I am concerned,
there is only one in my life.

Listen . . . for my words are true
Listen . . . someone out there loves you
Listen . . . someone out there is watching
Listen . . . he will always be there

PLEASE BELIEVE.......

Robert W Kane

MARILYN, MY BELOVED WIFE

When the warmth of the dreadful day is interrupted by the shadowless mist of the cool night,
I reach out for you

As I choke on past ideals and begin to drown in misdirected emotion,
I long for your warmth

When I am struck low and stand weary, bruised and desolate in the arena of fate,
I desire your tenderness

As the fevered clouds of past ills and lost love surround and cling to me,
I yearn for your joy

When my body and mind become twisted with pain and confused by the unknown,
I seek your understanding

As the wind softly curls about my face and the hawk lies in peace with his prey,
I hunger for you

When I am strong and eager for the mysteries and delights of life,
we will become one

Charles Eric Rieden

LETTER BY HER PILLOW

I, too, would like to see a girl
Become a gift to all the world
And never shed a tear
I wish a boy became a man
By holding stars cupped in his hand
And never learning fear
Childhood is special. The wonder and joy
Held in common by girl and boy
Are as the sun to flowers
But in each life some rain must fall
Sweet is needed but so too gall
And that is why the showers
It helps but little, I know, my child
For in your heart the pain is wild
The hurt too much to bear
But fire can melt or temper steel
Which one occurs depends on Will
You grow only if you dare

Betty Sprenkle Hoffman

CLOSED HEART

Open the door—Please open the door.

Don't leave me on the outside like this,
I am lonely and depressed.

All I ask is a kind word—a loving touch.
If you care—let me <u>know</u> you care.

The night is cold and I am so alone.
Open the door—Oh, please—open the door!

Lynn Beegle

DARKNESS

As I step out into the night, I feel the absence of the sun's rays on my face; telling me the darkness is the mistress of the dark side of the falling hours entering my life each and every day.

I wait restlessly for darkness to slip away and the warm light of the morning to enter once again.

I sit and wonder how the darkness of the night seems to rob me of my total vision of reality.

This showing me that it's only the postponing of the true vision of understanding.

Even though the night lights glitter in the city, making the dark tolerable to the mystery of darkness.

Giving way to the light of the new day of life . . . . .

Catherine M Ruen

WINDOWS

Windows of crystal blue
to see all of my feelings,
all the happiness,
and the sorrows.

The windows revealed more
than I wanted to.
So, I often closed them.
Letting no one see what feelings
they held.

Soon a single, perfect tear
leaked out of those closed windows.
You took a finger and wiped
it away.

Not seeing all the locked-up
feelings it held.

Natalie VanHorn
COUNTRY
The sun comes up so bright and new
The grass and flowers all fresh with dew,
I hear a bird up in a tree
He sings his song for you and me.

The chicks a peckin at the seed
The calves are mooing for their feed,
The kittens playing in the hay
Are things I see as I start my day

The sky is clear and the wind is cool
The kids are up and ready for school,
Down the road here comes the bus
Then off they go without a fuss

The tractors working in the field
Will stay there till the dirt is tilled,
The neighbors wave to way hello
As off to town for groceries they go

As I gather the eggs one by one
I thank the hens for all they've done
Deep down inside my heart tells me
The country is the best place to be

Mrs Noreen Ann Jenkins
FIREWORKS
When you kiss me, I hear the
fireworks around me.
Boom! Boom! Pow! Pow! Psh! Psh!
Boom! Boom! Pow! Pow! Psh! Psh!
Don't stop now, my sweet darling
love, let me hear the fireworks.
Let me see those sparklers and smell
those smoke bombs
and ring out all those firecrackers
because when I see you, I'm set afire
and my mind goes crackers.
You're so darling; you're so sweet;
you make me so excited when
you kiss my feet. (that's real neat!)

Lucia Nemola
THE TWINGLING LOVE
My drops fall in vain
In the emptiness faraway
In the deep sorrow
Of the dark mountains
Where
The twingling love
Wins.

Evelyn J Rimosukas
ANNIVERSARY
We could not have known,
standing at the altar, how deep
our love would grow—
Could not have known our eager
young hopes would become
reality exceeding any dream.
How lucky we were to have found
each other! For, in a chaotic
world,
We came together and created a
private place of harmony and
joy.
Because we had each other, outside
forces could not disturb that
secure haven.
We knew, never doubted, that as long
as we had each other, all else
could be resolved.
Yes, there have been tears and
splintered plans, but always
there was the safety-net of our
love
Between us there has been so much
sharing, so much caring—that
we've become fused as one.
Our relationship like our wedding
bands—golden circles of
love—without beginning,
without end.
Over the years, the unique something
between us has grown into this
rich fulfillment.
Today is ours in which to rejoice—
our own very special day
Let's celebrate all we've been
through together—the smooth,
the rough—the happy, the sad.
From it has come this great gift—a
love of dimensions impossible
to have imagined!
So, on this, our anniversary, let us
toast all our yesterdays and
each new tomorrow.

Andrea C Porter

Andrea C Porter
MIRANDA
People say she is gone but we know better. On a wintry night the moon hangs low over the snow covered hills. All is dark except the shining bright stars. As we sit next to the warm fire and drift asleep, she comes, nor sight of her can be found but her warm glow feels all.

When Spring comes and the roses start to bloom we will walk across the field as we sit down and look up into the clear blue sky and white clouds upon one she sits, as a tear runs down her cheek she disappears into a golden light.
The last you'll see but for ever she watches over you. She'll stand on a mountain peak as the snowy breeze runs through her blond hair, her blue eyes shine. Pain she does not have. Love she does.

Guy Fammereé
AGAIN
Again
the grass has stolen
into the flowerbeds.
A single week
and it has grown tall
through the broad leaves
of the Agapantha.
It is boring and tedious
pulling grass and weeds,
so I sneak off to drink plum wine
with Tu Fu and Su Tung P'o.
Toasting the crescent moon,
we fall down drunk, laughing,
trying to juggle two sticks
along a strand of wire.

Patrick LaRay Moxley
CHANGE OF SEASON

To: My favorite lady;
Happy Mother's Day

In the Spring,
The trees will bloom;
Then the Spring,
Must leave too soon.

For in the Summer,
Trees breathe and grow;
But all too soon,
Summer will also go.

Then comes Fall,
And leaves turn brown;
Soon even Fall,
Will lose its ground.

Last is Winter,
When trees will die;
But even Winter,
Must say good-bye.

As each day passes,
Without rhyme or reason;
So changes life,
With change of season.

Shelley L Palmer
SPRING
Spring is 'round the corner,
a robin told me so.
A dainty purple crocus
is blooming in the snow.

Daddy bluebird is looking
for a place to build a nest.
Mother's in the southland
with restlessness obsessed.

Coming, April showers,
will drench the fertile earth
Putting green coats on the wheat
fields,
proof of resurrection's birth.

God is in His heaven,
watching o'er the land.
We pause to count our blessings
provided by His hand.

Ann Johnson
YOUR GENTLE HANDS BETRAY YOU
The clown, the comic, the entertainer
Maintains a distance,
Builds a wall to keep others out.
"Laugh at what I say but don't look
inside;
What is there may make you cry."

At other times,
A face devoid of emotion
Stares back at what I say;
Take in, think over,
Keep, or throw away.

Ah, but your touch . . .
Feather-like, dancing,
Caressing . . .
Your gentle touch
Says there is caring inside.

Your gentle hands
Reaching over to lightly
Touch my arm
Or drop a finger's kiss,
Speak of love you cannot say.

There is something soft
And warm
And caring
Inside.
Your gentle hands betray you.

Hilda Myers Davis
FAITH, HOPE, & MIRACLES
"One" of fifteen children raised on a
farm,
With only a "Fireplace" in one room
to keep warm.
A "Number three" washtub for a
"Bath"
You see we had "five rooms and a
path!"
With cows, pigs and chickens to
"feed"
We were never hungry and never in
"Need."
Sharing and Caring we learned how
to Love,
With our parents "guidance" and
"Help" from above!
Each night around the fireplace, the
"Bible" was read,
And after a prayer, We all went to
bed.
I believe a "Miracle" will come my
way,
The "Faith" that I have, it may be
"Today"

Donna White Bradshaw
SELF-MADE
I made myself
a Somebody
from leftover possibilities
of all I could become
And gave myself
dignity from borrowed
notoriety
Then justified indulgence
by saying
"I deserve it."

I pieced together
a personality
and protected it with a shell
of contact resistance
so they couldn't reach
vulnerability
Then expected
acceptance
by saying
"This is the way I am."

Suzanne Carol Bowers
SECOND GLANCE
Searching for an answer from the
dark sea,
How the water seems to be watching,
beckoning me.
I watch with such intimidation and
fright,
But oh, how I ache to be swept away,
just lost in the night.
The waves caress the golden sand.
But the warm white foam can't reach
where I stand.
Lest I summon my courage to jump
into this wave,
It may be too late, to cleanse, to save.
I see the crest arch, the highest it has
ever this day,
Running, running to be engulfed; it
breaks, pulls away.
Staring into the darkness, knowing I
lost my chance,
I turn, stop once just to take a second
glance.

Aryn A Whitewolf
WINTER ROSE
A red rose in full bloom, lays on a
drift of
New fallen snow.
Its skin-soft petals, ragged and torn,
ebb away
Life like a heart torn from the chest
of a

Perfect lover.
It's ice encrusted thorns pose no
danger to the
Unfeeling elements.
Nothing mourns its passing,
Except the wind.

David Reeves
ICEBURGS IN HELL
Lying here thinking of you,
And a million things we could do.
Just to have you one more time,
With me in reality, not in rhyme.
We went our ways sometime ago,
Now I wished I didn't say no.
Its much too late to change that now,
And if there's a way, I don't know how.
I guess everyone has a destiny,
But I still want you, here with me.
Life's a game that's hard to win,
With just one chance to start again.
On my second now, halfway home,
But just the same, still alone . . .

Tashire Battle
PASSION DEATH

To my fiancee my heart, and to my daughter Leaveine my world

Gusty pour of rain,
misty droplets.
A deep watery grave
of feelings.

I thought death,
as something more.
So misleading but
cherishable, only in
the realm of mind, not
in the essence of
reality.

Abode of the blessed,
or lake of fire and
brimstone,
which questionable
earth awaits to
capture my restless
soul?

Which spirit of
which prince?

Kimberly N Lewis
WHY ANGER?
Why does anger fill the room?
Unnecessary lashing out, unnecessary blame put on others.
What am I feeling deep down that makes me want to hurt others?
My happiness for her is clouded by my jealousy, but jealousy of what?
Love is not shared, and happiness is hidden.
Hidden behind a shield we put up to hide true feelings.
A superficial life with brief exchanges of cold words.
Conversations are nonexistent.
A life that was once filled with joy, love, and caring has metamorphosed into one of anger, hatred, sharpness, and solitude.
Whatever happened to a family?
I thought that was your ultimate dream!
I guess times change and people change . . . or grow up.

Ginger Jones
OLD MAN
As he lay back in his reclining chair,
He remembers his past, with a blank stare.
How he could work from morn till night,
Without tiring out and taking a nap.

Now sleep fills his head so easily,
The sounds he makes so peacefully.
Then a gentle noise is all it takes,
And he will quickly come awake.

He looks in the mirror and what does he see,
An old man looking back at me.
Through shadows, he seeks to find,
Memories which were once clear in his mind.

He used to be as mighty as a big oak tree,
Now the years given him are more than seventy.
He's gained wisdom throughout those many years,
But who is there to listen and silence the fears.

His seed has been sown,
His children are all grown.
The days left, are all his own.

Wealth may increase but as it does,
Health may not be as it once was.
Where are my slippers, where is my robe,
For my story has all been told.

Flora Kinsey
THE TONE OF PEACE
Searching for the tone of peace;
That perfect blending of harmony and freedom of being.
A sense where no doubts exist,
or maybe small ones
that you know can be conquered.
Everything flexes with itself . . .
Its flowing is in steady rhythm;
a simple pattern of the ultimate.

Marillyn Meyer Oltman
MARILLYN'S MEMORIES
I seldom see within my mind
The beautiful things I've left behind
Until the clouds form, the fog rolls in—
I'm lost in memories of yesterdays
There I find love and peace and joy
And all the before begins again
I'm there for a while so peaceful serene—
It's hard to let go
And come back to my life
I've been there and I know!
I can go back anytime
The clouds roll in and the fog is thick
It's all in my mind
And in my soul—
All the yesterdays
That took their toll

Brian E Hager
FALSE ALARM FIRE
I walked into the bar to quench my thirst,
But, there was a line ahead of me to be served first.
I knew the bartender, he was a friend of mine,
But, not today. He said "End of the line."
The room was hot and my throat was getting drier.
In an act of desperation I yelled, loudly, "FIRE!"
This gained for me the attention of the room.
Sixty men stared at me with eyes of hate and doom.
I remember now what mom had said with charm,
"Woe to him ten-thousand fold who spreads a false alarm."
That fight I lost was said to be a beauty.
I was set upon by five dozen firemen . . . all of them off duty.

Jessie W Wilson
ONLY A LAD
It's Christmas tonight, and the love flows out
To the wide, wide world with a joyous shout
From a fine young lad with his coat on his arm
Swinging the lantern on the way to the barn.
The cold closes in as the door is shut,
With the heat inside, and the frost without,
But ne'er minds he for the carol he sings
Sets the heart aglow, gives the tired feet wings.
The cows in rows, with lowered heads
Grind their food with pleasant tread,
And horses neigh as he goes by,
With bated breath, lest the long legs fly.
And Jesus has said that like him should be
The great and small of humanity.
Then, off to the barn with a song in the heart
Send the merry lad, to do his part.
So the chores be done, then gathered round,
The hearth fires' glow and its merry sound
Shut the cold world out, and the warm world in,
With Christmas cheer—by a lad brought in.

Connie Jensen

Connie Jensen
THE BEAUTIES CONTAINED
The beauties contained
within a person,
when opened to another,
is most rewarding
to behold.

The sharing
in gentle strength,
invigorates and overwhelms
the soul
with loving compassion.

The opening of the soul
to persons of the universe,
regenerates the energies within.

With each awakening,
increased energies
flood the awareness
of
I live! I love! I care!
To open with another
is to feast in beauty.

Mildred Allen Crouch
FAITH IN EACH OTHER
Faith in each other is a beautiful way
For a life together to become sweeter each day.
Faith in each other makes hearts sing . . .
For it gives freedom to grow and happiness reigns.
Faith in each other brings out the best,
Forgives the trespasses and helps with the tests.
Faith in each other is a wonderful gift . . .
It does not tear down, it always lifts.
Faith in each other is a good way of life . . .
It makes a happy husband . . .
It makes a happy wife! ! ! ! !

Carolyn Williams
LORD WHEN I HEAR PEOPLE' DUMB, SILLY, AND IMPROPER
Lord when I hear people dumb, silly, and improper, remarks about my wearing a wig.
I, don't feel uncomfortable and hang my head with shame for I, am not ashamed.
I don't miss or envy, the many different style one can wear his or her hair.
I, miss and long for my father care.
I, long for the rain. For when it rain, my father washes it.
I, long for the sun. For when the sun beam down, my father dry my hair, with his loving hands and give it strength and character.
I, long for the brisk, winds. For that's when my father comb it.
I, long for the mild winds. For that's when my father gently brushes it.
I, long most for the snow. For when it snows the billions, and billions of show flakes, that fall on top of my head is kisses from my father, very own lips. And when they melt, it's the tears he shed
I, miss my father, loving care

Theresa McFarland
THE DANCE FLOOR IS EMPTY
Our love was, Oh, so very strong. We met on a blind date, and we both knew the first time it was for real. You were always there for me. We have had our good times and hard times too. We have seen the sunrise and sunsets. We laughed a lot and we cried at times, but you were always there for me. We watched our boys grow to young men. You laughed with me, and also comforted me when I cried. We loved to dance, Oh, how we danced. We loved to dance to everything and anything. It was the togetherness, the music, the mood. We felt so strong together when we danced. The music said it all. But now that you are gone, the music has stopped. The lights are dim, and I stand alone on the empty dance floor. I don't hear the applause any more. I just feel the emptiness. But the memories will always be there. I picture you still there with me, dancing to our favorite song, "We Had It All."

Jennie Franklin
GOD'S SERVANT
This man we all love is
Rev. William B. Cone.
When you're his friend, you'll be on the roam.
You'll be riding in a Mercury Marquis, going places,
Visiting church members, and finding new faces.

He joined Sandy Ridge Baptist Church in Nineteen Eighty Six.
Anything not working, He will try to fix.
After having ham biscuits, God's Word will fly.
When preaching the Bible, how fast the time goes by.

Since this is your seventy first birthday,

You and Nell have a great celebration.
September 10, Nineteen Thirtynine
when God joined you together,
He blessed you, and made a perfect combination.

Children came along—Steve, Robert, Reid, Margaret Ann.
They loved their Mom and Dad, had wonderful plans.
Their chores were plenty only they would understand.
They thank God for their Mom
and the Preacher Man.

Jeffrey Levine
THE RAIN
Refreshing, quenching, cleaning,
Unborn abundance yet to come.

Just as rain falls,
It comes again in rounding ways.

Is life any different,
Than the rain.

Grace Simmons
A PIECE OF CLAY
I must become a Piece of Clay
Within the Master's hand.
For Him I'll be a useful tool,
And do as He commands.

I can't deny it's hard to do
To say Thy will be done.
His Way is hard to understand,
For Life has many turns.

But I have learned God's way is best,
His plan is always Good.
For the things I often think is right,
Is not; according to His word.

The price I've paid for my mistakes,
Are measured; even scored.
Foolish things, and angry words,
Has hurt my loving Lord.

This Piece of Clay one day will be,
Dust within His earth.
Only the things I've done for Him,
He'll only count as worth.

Shannon L Wehrendt
FOR MR. GLENN HOPWOOD
Glenn

What sweet memories that name brings to mind.
Memories of a hopeless romantic
Memories of a gentleman
Memories of a friend
Memories of a lover.

Glenn

What sweet memories that name brings to mind.
Memories that started one boring day
Memories that are still being made
Memories that will last a lifetime
Memories that remind me of . . .

Glenn

Gary Yardumian
PERCEPTIONS AT 21
As I gaze along the horizons of my life;
filled with pain, sorrow and strife,

Deep inside as I search for solutions;
I feel the intrigue of the earth's evolutions,

I'm touched by the caring and all of the love;
some people acquire, from a power above,

The love between a husband and his wife;
will forever change, each one's life,

Children are special, you can see it in their eyes;
no deception, no corruption, no little white lies,

Today and tomorrow, they hold our dreams;
as did the past, or so it seems,

One wish, one desire is all I need;
to get me through, to help me succeed,

With all of the doubts, and all of the fears;
I manage to grow throughout the years.

Sarah Daniel Vaughan
LAST FLIGHT

To my husband, Joe Brandon Vaughan Retired Lieutenant Commander, U.S. Navy Sept. 14, 1922—Dec. 17, 1988

You lie there looking splendid
in your Navy uniform.
Your wings gleam—golden
on your chest.
Your casket is blue
like the CORSAIR you flew.

Now (thank GOD) you can rest.
You have flown where
all good pilots go
and I know you are happy to be.
After years of pain
I am glad you are free.
You are using your wings again!

Mary Ruth White
TAKE THE TIME FOR ME

Dedicated to my second granddaughter, Jamie, who always waited patiently for her turn to be held, fed, or cuddled. I love you, Jamie Always, MiMi

Hi, my name is Billy, how do you do?
May I come in and play with you?
My mom says ok, she knows I'm here
I can stay all day, so have no fear

We can play cowboys, or play with my car
We can watch cartoons, or play my guitar
I'll be good, uhh huh, you'll see
Please say you're not too busy to play with me

My mom has a headache and she's layen down
She says her head is spinnin around and round
My dad's at work, he works late, you know
Saturday, he's gonna take me to the picture show

Hey, I'm not crying, I've got dirt in my eye
I'm a big boy and only girls cry
I'm glad, uhh huh, that I can stay
I can stay with you . . . and play all day.

Beverley E Petel
THE VOICE OF THE POET
The voice of the poet
Is but murmurs
From the sea of eternity.
The words, an uttering
From the deepest depths
Of the heart of life.
it's a cry from silence,
And tears from the heart
That understands love
It's a whisper
In the wilderness of pain
And the sigh that died
On the lips of yesterday
It's the breath of God
Who breathes into the poet's pen
And the spill of ink
Is but the lingering tears
From a heart
That knows too much love.
The words that dance
Upon an empty page
Are the legacy
Of a thousand shattered dreams
That seek to build a fantasy
In the cradle of the poets mind.
Here is the ear
That listens with the heart
For silence
Is the voice of understanding
And one embrace
Is countless spoken words
That will never fade away
For they were felt
And never heard.

John Eggleston
A CRADLE'S SWING
The gold has gone
To the downhill side
Of the cradles
Uneven rockings
To run with revoke
Over memories graves
To thoughts
Without words
Words without names
To teeter once and again
Near the nothings
Of life
In some swing
Of the cradles
Blind rocking.

Donald Black
A THEME
I'm a loner—by choice.
I like to be by myself, with
myself and mostly into myself.

Not that I don't enjoy people,
but from a distance.

Not that I don't like to share—
but with a very select few.

Not that I grow deaf with the silence,
but grow mad from the noise.

I watch my friends; eyes pity me—
It is I who feel sorry for them.

I watch them do the mundane
and make believe they are happy.

I watch them fake joy and wincingly smile when one or the other comes near.

I watch and watch and then turn away because I can.

I'm a loner by choice,
not because they want me to
but, because I can.

Barbara Sharik Babb
ONLY A MEMORY
A Soldier warmed my heart.
A Soldier burned my soul.
Oh how that Soldier loved me;
How he made me whole.

Then eternal war beckoned;
A war that could not be won.
He tried to tie up loose ends,
But it could not be done.

Now he will never smell the clover,
More intoxicating than wine.
He'll never pick the blossoms
From the honeysuckle vine.

Simple pleasures are erased
That we will share no more.
Half my life is void;
Lost and missing at war.

For the Soldier lay on grasses
Of a far and distant shore.
It is like the Soldier never was,
Forever and never more.

Hildegard Ray
YESTERDAY
You gave me Roses yesterday—
You kissed my lips so tender
You wanted to love me—all the way
and begged me to surrender.

You promised: never leaving me
Your love so real and true.
Today you are deceiving me
How could you ever be that cruel?
The Roses you gave me yesterday
Are hanging their heads to die
The Beauty now has bloomed away—
I am left alone to cry.

Greg Blocker
IF I
Life is mine to live if I
control it till the day I die.

And if I pause
to let the others delegate,
I'll soon discover
I just might win.
But if I lose
I did give up the right to choose

Advice from those who do not feel
confuse this life of mine that's real.

And if they're mine,
these things I feel,
I cannot let another steal—
the thought and acts
that form the path

that guides me on my way.
They're mine you see.
For if I stutter . . .
life is bread but where's the butter

Scott David Kather
DANCE OF THE FALLING LEAVES

I saw the children this morning,
sweeping through the yards,
grasping at leaves in the wind,

With flushed faces,
running along the ground,
flying like birds flocking,

Lifted together,
with Wind's breath,

Scattered, they fall,
with Laughter.

Agnes R Jankowy
HAPPY BIRTHDAY

To Frank

Today has marked another
year,
A day for you alone
To share with only those
you love—
By card, by gift, by phone;
Today means that you've
gained a year,
But don't let that
depress;
For we think you are
twice as dear
And ask the Lord to bless
The Husband and the Father
Who has made our lives
a pleasure
Just knowing that you
really care
Brings joy we cannot
measure.

Colin MacKenzie Mitchell
THE BALLOON

To Pamela, the golden sphere that hovers on my horizon; the skin that holds the sweet-air of a thousand roses, for you I would float to the sun and back; I love you.

I am the balloon attached
to the scalp of the world,
and every day my string
is shortened, pulling me
towards the earth. How I
yearn for my string to break,
that I may float free
from this world that draws
me near. A world that wishes
to pull me down and squeeze
my skin with its worries
and fear. To squeeze my skin
until it bursts, setting
my life-air loose, loosened
to be lost among all the
common-air, the stale-air
of balloons who burst before.

Melba Jean Hrncir
WHERE HAS MY LIFE GONE

To all those I love who care enough to find at least one good quality in me.

The trees stoop and sway
With ferocious winds blowing
throughout the day—
Whistling louder and louder
as each gust
strikes with magnetic force.
I sit listening, alone—
wondering where my life has gone.

Flames flickering in the fireplace
Licking out as colorful lightning bugs
on a hot summer night.
Gracefully dancing in and
out of shadows
as tho' playing tag
With the stars high above
and sparkling just as bright.
Awakening me to precious time
passed—
Stormily loving a fantasy not to be.
Life's years past, now a mystery.

Dreaming of beautiful years gone by,
Mesmerized by the magic
of such beauty in sight.
Logs crackling in hypnotic
competition
with boisterous thunders
of the stormy rains raging lightning
bright—
As I continue wondering where
my life
has gone.

The years cognizant with memories
and pains
creeping through the mind,
Often as ferocious as the winds
crashing against the window panes.
Have I lost all passions and
tenderness
once possessed?
Patience and understanding
dissipated,
Love and hate intimately related.
Is this all my life is meant to be?
No love, no laughter, no gentle touch
in my future to foresee?
Just the storms of loneliness
violating my entity!

James J Pesutich Jr
I DO THINK AND I DO DRINK

To the loving memories of my Grandfathers: Pasquale Lombardi Dec 17, 1914—Nov 11, 1988, Vieko J Pesutich July 17, 1917—March 26, 1989

I do think, and I do drink
this beauty that my soul wishes to
take part
For a waterfall has many ways
to splash into my heart
Reminded by its permanent nature
Not all of antique beauty is gone
For many, many wars will make a
march
But the water will still flow on
Water goes through no death or birth
water lives out the endless years
A waterfall returns such gifts back to
the earth
Heaven's souls every drop of tears
The departed souls give to the living
A chance to refresh their souls
and allow them to feel
For it was the tears from their eyes
that made their souls rise
and realize what was real

Wilma Dolgoff (Holly Leah)
UNITED WE STAND

United States of America, the world

Dear children of God:

United we stand, divided we fall. Take heed dear sheep to the Master's call. For none other than the Good Shepherd is calling his sheep. Arise now sweet children from thy deep sleep.

Prayer and fasting can prepare the way—for others needing strengthening if we obey.
Tend the flock of God, let faith be the victory. Love made perfect, through the Holy Trinity.

Finally, be strong in the Lord and in the power of his might. One nation under God, we must unite. With this armour of God, united we stand. A sweet blessing, we need our land.

U is for united, S is for state, A is for America, our land so great. Americans united we stand, divided we fall. Take heed dear sheep, to the Master's call. Love one another. Please, please learn to wait on the Lord, United States, before it is too late.

Love in Christ,
Holly Leah

Mary A Swyers
DUSK TO DAWN

One evening near our fireplace full of wood,
We were feeling very warm and good. We loved one another so very much, Passion holds our tenderest touch.
Looking into each others eyes,
Outside the moon was starting to rise.
The stars and moon began to beam;
we laid close and dreamed.
There are many pleasures such as strawberries and drink, Hold me close, and we can think. Let's put on a smile, Make love for a while; passion is so wild. As time goes by so does the day, why shouldn't we stay? I know our time together is not much, Still, I love you more with every touch.
The sun is starting to rise, Another day has gone,. and there's tears in our eyes.

The End

Ruth A Marshall
REMEMBERING

In loving memory of my brother P.F.C. Virgil L Trotter who gave his life for his country in battle during World War II

I remember an old house that sat back
off of the road.
I remember carrying coal in a bucket,
what a heavy load.
I remember a cookstove and a tea
kettle with steam rising high.
I remember the homemade bread and
the warm apple pie.
I remember we'd draw straws to see
who got to use the feather bed.
I remember a stray dog who came to
stay and we named him Big Red.
I remember riding double on my
brother's Flexible Flyer.
I remember rolling down the hill
inside an old rubber tire.
I remember a father fixing my
brother's sled.
I remember he said "Soon as this is
done you're off to bed."
I remember a mother in an old
rocking chair, a babe on her lap and
one on each knee.
I remember she sang Rock-A-Bye
Baby and The Little Chick-A-Dee.
I remember before bed the prayer she
had each one of us say.
I remember, ahh yes, like it happened
just yesterday.

Angel Vaught
IF YOU STAY AWAY TOO LONG

If you stay away too long you'll have
to rekindle the fire
If you don't come home soon I will
lose all my desires
It's been too long since I've seen
your smiling face.
If you don't come home soon
someone else will take your place.
I've waiting too long for someone
like you
Now you've done me wrong and I'm
singing the blues.
I loved you through all those tough
times we had.
I thought you loved me too, I didn't
know I made you sad.
Was it just a facade to fill your lonely
days.
And now I'm left with all the hurt
and you have gone away.
But someday soon I will rise above it
all,
And I'll pick up all the pieces, when
you begin to fall.

Panagiota, Yotta, Cominos
HE'S HOME; ADDRESS HEAVEN

In memory of brother Nick, who moved to Heaven, Dec., 6, 1988, after long illness, cancer, on his birthday and his name day, St. Nickolos.

There is rain in our lives;
The sun seems to have forgotten us.
Our eyes are covered with tears;
So we can't see the flowers,
The trees, the birds, the sea.
We all have gotten near,
As it helps cover our fear;
But we forget GOD IS HERE:
Our loved one is in peace;
No pain, no sad eyes,
No false smiles;
For Heaven has opened her door,
And he will hurt no more.

Edward L Werling
THE POOL

This poem dedicated to, the memory of my father Edward M. Werling and my twin, Bill Werling & sister Charlene.

The pool, its water serene and clear,
Birds and animals nesting near!
For their food and drink is here.
The pool blue, cool and deep.
The birds sing with much delight,
For the pool with all its potential
might!
To them is a pretty sight.
The pool with its fish swimming
around is a sight to bestow!!

As only a lover of nature would be sure to know!
The pool singing a slow happy song. The sun gleaming off of its surface, Most of day long. As nightfall arrives, and the heavens begin to shine. The pool takes on a different hue! Oh! what a sight, it gives off to me and to you! As long as man keeps the water clean and clear, the pool will continue to bring us all happiness, year after year!!

Mary K Morgan
BEING ALIVE

I stand alone
Tonight
In the dark
Shivering and naked
Without purpose
I stand alone
Today
In the light
Shivering and naked
Without purpose
. . . hoping

Robert Hutchins
DISPOSITIONED

This poem is in dedication of all those people who feel out of place and out of control from time to time through life.

I feel dispositioned
Like a light and delicate colored leaf
Temporarily resting on the edge
Of a concrete step
Awaiting any force
To make me topple and flounder
Aimlessly to further depths
As if to be powerless
Knowing my destination
Is beyond my control
I await

Joyce Hackney Raudat
VOYAGER

To my fellow physically challenged voyagers.

Silky sails reflecting horizon's brilliant hues,
As my bow cuts high into a wave.
Oak, ash, and teak, secured by brass,
Sleek and proud toward Northern Star I gaze.

Shadows playing tag with the moon,
As darkness comes with thundering force.
The Black Hole devours my Northern Star.
What will guide my constellation's course?

Silently, sails down, I hug the harbor,
Guided by sounds of wind, sea, and gull.
Developing keen senses the sightless use,
Feeling the ripples against my hull.

Warm Gulf breezes caress and beckon me.
I aim my bow toward the surf's roar.
My rudder feels for uncharted waters.
Expanded senses log forgotten lore.

Slack sails balloon, pulling forward,
I dip into each wave, then rise.
Sea spray dancing on my bow,
I point my compass toward remembered skies.

Jimmy C Williams
AN ANGEL'S PRAYER

Dedicated to Jimmy Jr. and Rachel with my love and deep regret for pain I caused them.

Your parents finally got a divorce.
Their marriage is over, approved by the court.
Promises made but not from the heart,
When problems arose, they drifted apart.
Now that it's over, who takes the blame?
Who pays the price and who bears the shame?
You are the one that's hopelessly caught,
No one but you, a child not at fault.
You love your father, you love your mother,
Yet each would like you to hate the other.
Working their hardest to show you they're right,
Never trying to avoid a bad fight.
Why should you care who's right or who's wrong?
Why can't they learn to just get along?
You're made to suffer for all their mistakes,
Trying to decide what's real and what's fake.
Does it really matter who's wrong or who's right,
When you lay crying all through the night?
Now go to sleep, have peace in your slumber,
For tomorrow your heart may be torn asunder.

Marjorie Wheeler
OH LITTLE KISS

To my husband David, for believing in me.

Oh little kiss
Oh a little kiss
On the forehead
You tell all God has
to give.
Oh little kiss
You come from so
Deep in the heart;
You show all the
Love there is to give,
You give comfort,
You give safe,
You take away
the pain,
Oh little kiss.

William Scott Hamilton
STRAY DOG

To my sweet Mom, for getting this poem published

Sometimes I wonder about the comparison
between a stray dog and me.
The way he is beat and shoved around
no one caring where he might be.
No one to care and love him
he always looks so sad . . .
In a way that's me at times
I really feel that bad.

I don't think he feels sorry for himself
it's just a fact of life.
The poor stray dog, he has no where to go
To sleep his nights

So the next time you see one
wandering around,
Think before you shoot or throw
At the poor old hound.

He's got a life
just like you and me,
Try not to judge him
For the looks you see.

Think of his heart
and what it might need.
A little warmth and tenderness
can do wonders for a life indeed.

Judi Pearce
MY POETRY

I dedicate this poem to my two dearest friends, the preacher and the teacher. Thank you for being there.

I crave,
I need,
I want.
Yet no one seems to see—
And so I put my love,
into my Poetry.

Norma Mullen
GRANDCHILD UNSEEN

This poem is dedicated to grandparents who miss their grandchildren.

Stashed away
In a box somewhere,
Are the Baby Michael's presents.

Safely placed
Where the ribbons won't tear,
Are the Baby Michael's presents.

He would have loved the flashlight bright.
I can see his face when he turned on the light!

The puzzle which taught him his ABC's
He would have mastered as quick as you please.

And then, of course, there was the great big jeep.
That is the present he would want to keep.

But nothing at all would have pleased him more,
Than those five tiny cars he'd zoom 'cross the floor.

It was such a joy—to shop for this boy.
With his big blue eyes, he'd love every toy.

But very much missed in 1988,
Are the presents which will be opened too late.

Isn't it sad, that he doesn't know,
'Bout the Baby Michael's presents.

Millie Boudinot
ANOTHER NIGHT OF LONELINESS

Dedicated to my children Vikki, Debbi, Chuck, Dude, Janet, and Doug for their love and understanding.

Another night of loneliness,
With empty arms I cry.
This longing that I have for you
Will never pass me by.
I think that I should never hope
For a life so filled with bliss,
But through these nights of loneliness
I'm longing for your kiss.

"Someday" I always tell myself,
"Someday" when will it be?
When there is no night of loneliness
And I have you here with me?

What is the answer to my prayer?
Give me an answer true.
And make my lonely nights no more,
Let me spend them dear with you.

Jeannette Meidinger

Jeannette Meidinger
MY WORLD

I dedicate this poem to my loving husband Al, and to our three beautiful children Amy, Julie, and Matthew, who have indeed helped to color my world beautiful.

Color my world beautiful
with all the vibrant hues
may it be filled with joyous laughter
and the sound of happy shoes

Never to sit in the shadow
of the things I'd like to do
but actively participate
in a gathering of friends with you

So take my hand and skip with me
in a field so green, so lush,
then down by the green-blue river
we'll have our noon time lunch

We'll hear the mighty freight train
as it moves along the tracks
see brilliant orange tiger lilies
the golden sun beating on our backs

Color my world beautiful
with the most magnetic hues
leave the soft pastels for others
I'm just passing through.

Lorraine Hicks
FEELINGS

To Clarence, my love, who waited twenty-six years for me and loves me still. I'm happy being your wife.

We lay upon the bed . . .
my love, in the land of Nod.
The moonlight pierce our window.
Turning my head on the pillow . . .

watching you sleep . . . so sweet.
My soul emits a gleam . . .
This was not a dream.
Touching your face . . . softly . . .
rubbing your brow gently . . .
Smiles of my heart sails,
as a peaceful ship at sea.
My lips touch your face,
then your lips I kiss.
My mind . . . heart speaks,
This is my love . . .
You'll always be my love.

Patricia Knowles
HEAVEN IS REJOICING

I dedicated this poem to Evan Dawn Pearson twin sister of Josie

Heaven is Rejoicing for
our little Angel Evan
our hearts are saddened
and filled with sorrow
for the loss of our little Evan
But Heaven is
rejoicing for
our little Angel Evan
So let us pray together
and lift our hearts
with Joy and Praise
For our little angel Evan
is rejoicing in
Heaven.
As Christ as my savior,

Pegi Lynn Johnson
THE CAT

To Ambrosia

She never listens to me and she is very aloof. She is all cat, of that there is proof.
She walks on the windowsill and stalks spots on the wall. I do believe she is the silliest animal of all.
She sits and stares at nothing and frightens me for no reason.
She jumps out at me and claws my feet.
Halloween is her favorite season; the top of the T.V. her favorite seat.

Nancy Reuter
DEFENSELESS

To Christopher and Jessica, my inspirations, who are going to change the world.

A big toe unknowingly placed in the center of an aisle
Pink polish on a ragged nail
Cold air reaching what the blanket doesn't.
A gray kitten lapping up milk
Furry paws on the top of a bowl
Tongue stretching to reach the cold white liquid.
A newborn filly trying to stand
A nudge from its mother's warm muzzle
A slender brown hoof timidly placed in the straw.
A lonely pine tree standing on the tip of a peninsula
Strong unyielding winds try to defeat it
Thin branches refuse to give up.
Two whales struggling to survive
Two great forms caught by an early freeze
Bones visible on heads scratched by cruel ice.
An uneducated nation deciding a negative campaign
An illiterate adult who does not understand
Ignorant masses who all agree.

A frightened child watching it all.

Mary M Killmon
OUR SONG

"DOODLE DE DE ", My Friend (My land and water TURTLE)

My song,
Is your song;
My song, and your song,
Together,
Is our song;
Our song is my song and your
Song together,
What is our song?
It is wrong;
We have to make it right.
Tonight is the night
When we make it right,
Neath the Heavenly light;
When the Sun
Goes down, and the Moon is bright.
The name of our song is right
We will sing our song
All night tonight.

D Gordon Watson
TOUCHES

For Mrs. W.C. Deal. You always knew and believed.

Being with you
Reminds me of warm sunshine

A gentle breeze
Teasing across quiet waters

And I hear
The music of the universe

Stirring deep
Within the fabric of my soul

Muriel Pravda

Muriel Pravda
SONG OF THE WORLD

Dedicated to my dear husband, Arthur in appreciation of his encouragement

Do you love the world as I?
Like to see it live and grow
Love to view life, earth and sky
Want to see and learn to know?

Watch the world come to a pass
Spring, summer, winter, fall
Time is swift but slow to last
While birds fly off and leave recall.

Yet the world sings a refrain
"I have beauty, love and joy"
Still the torrents sprinkle rain,
And its people will destroy.

The world is warm though silken gray
While liberty holds her light
And the wise can still allay
A fool's desire to fight.

If you love the world as I
What difference race or creed?
We live to live
And live to die
Human flowers of a seed.

John M Fuller II
THE DREAM OF LOVE

The dream of love that comes in youth
Is fragile as the flower
That blooms neath every April sun
Yet fades with every shower

The dream of love in August years
Is quite another flower—
It laughs at sun and wind and rain
Of noon—or midnite hour.

The dream of love that comes—
In years of crispy fall—
May be that lovely rose that blooms—
Til winter lays its pall.

Margarita S Piper
BUBBLES, LIGHT, AND LOVE

To the John Lum family who exemplify the meaning of Christ's words, "I must be about my Father's business."

It was just an ordinary bowl,
sitting on the counter soaking,
a dome of tiny bubbles covering its surface.
But sunlight, streaming through the window,
transformed the bubbles into jewels . . .
sparkling, flashing, brilliant jewels . . .
reflecting every color of the rainbow.
A strangely spiritual experience,
it gave cause for reflection.
Ordinary people,
transformed by the light of God,
share his blessings by reaching out
to the hungry, the needy, and the lonely;
bringing comfort and joy
by reflecting the radiance of His love.
They give freely of their time and energy
for the work of their Lord
and in serving God's people,
they also serve God.
"For as ye have done it unto the least of these,
ye have done it also unto me."

Eddie Martin
THE WIND BLOWS LONESOME

To my JUJU-BEE From her PaPa

The wind blows lonesome through her deserted streets,
Where once rode the famous and near famous and reveled at their feats.
From gunfight to holdup, from prayers to curses,
the people are gone now, but the memories she still nurses.

Here once stood the mighty and from her whiskey they drank their fill.
Where most of the trails they traveled led to a place called Boothill.

She cries her tears in lonely repose
for all the men she knew and all the sad stories she knows.
But her memory recalls each man
that lived and died there,
and marks each one a hero.
The worn and weathered sign reads:

WELCOME to TOMBSTONE
POPULATION: ZERO

Carol A Walsh
KISSES

I would like to dedicate this poem to my two beautiful sons, Robert and Tyler-James.

I kiss my baby
a hundred times
each day on
his sweet head.

I kiss him
in the morning sun
and at night
as he lays in bed.

I kiss him
on his chubby cheeks
and sometimes
on his nose,

I kiss him
on his little hands
and even
on his toes.

I just cannot resist
this little child of mine,
and so I never wonder
why I kiss him all the time.

And one day
when he's older
(maybe nine or ten),
I'm sure I'll still be kissing him
every now and then.

But for now
while he's a baby
still in diapers
he does wet,

you can bet
I'm going
to kiss him
every chance I get!

Rita H Kertels
A PATH IN THE SNOW

I dedicate this poem to my daughter Rita M. Butlett.

A path.
A path in the snow.

A path in the snow
To someone you know;
A path to someone
You love just so.

When you are lonely,
This is the way to go;
A path in the snow.

The winter is long
When you are lonely.
A path in the snow
Is the way to go.

A path in the snow
Is the way to go
To visit your family.
The family you love so.

You feel so good
To know you have
A path in the snow.

Darlene Burch
DESTINY

To Randy, "The one who inspired me."

We look at each other
wanting to talk.
Feeling we may smother
deciding to go for a walk.

We drift towards the woods
each with thoughts of our own.
Wondering about all of the "clouds"
and even some of the "unknown."

You touch my hand,
we don't need to speak.
We sink to the sand

feeling so weak.

We fly so high
turned into one.
Soaring into the night,
trying to reach the sun.

Mickie L Saxe
A TOUCH OF MOTHERHOOD

To my daughter, Jennifier Laurine, for the inner strength—to endure

Even though the first touch of
motherhood
Was a bitter-sweet moment—
The planning, loving and caring
moments
Will live on forever—

The touching glow that only a mother
Can understand—
Replaces the pain of the loss—
Of an innocent one.

But knowing that she is safe in
God's—
Protecting arms can only lead—
To a smooth path to an open door.

To have to make the decisions—
That only you had to make will only
lead—
To a better life for those concerned.

For you deserve this acknowledge-
ment
Of happy memories of this—
Mother's Day.

Debra A Watson
SECRETS

Dedicated to the people who inspire me the most, my family.

Whispers unspoken
Quietly hidden
In private places
Not revealed,
Nor exposed
To unintentional dangers
Familiarity can impose
While patiently awaiting
The perfect time to impart
Those innermost cravings
Of intimate hearts.

Dorothy Ann Bilton
END OF THE DAY

Dedicated to the Lord Jesus Christ and to my husband, Richard, who has encouraged me in every thing that I try to do and for my three children Linda M. Grooms, Johnny L. Brown, Jr and Teresa Ann Culp—I love you all.

At the end of the day
when every thing grows quiet,
You need to relax
and let your mind rest,
Bring your thoughts into focus
set your heart toward the Lord,
He will give you rest
and relaxing untold,
At the end of the day
just as the beginning,
Remember the Lord
and praise His dear name,
Your sleep will be sweet
this Proverb is true,
God's word holds power
at the end of the day,
He will protect through the night
same as he has through the day

Proverbs 3:24 "When thou liest down
thy sleep will be sweet"

Joseph C Gunnell Sr
A PEACEFUL WISH
May peace fill Thy heart and Thy
life;
May Thy temples, Thy family and
home;
Be endowed and blessed with the
peace and rest,
That only the peaceful have known

May peace reign over Thy world;
In time of work and play;
May strife, chaos and destruction,
Never travel the paths of Thy day.

May peace fill the lives of Thy
children;
Thy colleagues and all of Thy
friends;
And all through this life, no matter
what comes;
May Thou be blessed with that peace
'til the end.

Barbara A O'Hara
WONDERMENT OF WORDS
Some DAY
when I am old and gray
by my bed
I will sit
and read what I have not read
or ponder
and wonder
the over and under
to write
down
what has not yet been written
thoughts
that roam through my head.

Georgia Parmer Milton
MELANCHOLY RAINDROPS
I'm standing here alone tonight, just
gazing out my window—
Watching the slowly falling rain—
And I fancy, that I hear each tiny
raindrop—
Softly whisper, in the night, your
name—
Standing here, I find again, sweet
reminiscing—
But; too soon, it fills my lonely heart
with pain—
And to cry, I know is but for
cowards—
So; I'll make a bargain with the
rain—
If; I should walk beneath the misty
Summer skies—
Then the rain would blend together,
with the teardrops in my eyes—
But here; I stand with head bowed
deep in sorrow—
In its utter desolation, lo, my spirit
cries—
All alone, I hear again your voice, so
softly calling—
Then, like an echo in the night, it
fades, then dies—
Soon, the rain will cease, my
reminiscing's over—
Then, these raindrops glistening on
my window pane, will all be dry—
So; I'll go and hide my broken heart,
among the raindrops—
And brush away these lingering
teardrops, from my eyes—

Barbara Ann (Goobie) Barresi
I THOUGHT

This poem is dedicated to Keith K. I will always love you!

I thought when we first met
I found the happiness I could never
get
I thought when you looked at me
I saw you cared, and you were happy
I thought that you were my guy
And a love like ours would never die
I thought that it would never end
And if it did,
You'd still be my friend
I thought our love was so warm and
true
I thought you loved me as I do you
I thought your love grew more each
day
Especially when you'd smile my
way
I thought you said you'd love me
forever
Claiming our love would never sever
I thought I could never love another
man
But this I found to be untrue
For every time I look at you
I fall in love again and again.

James Steager
THE STREAM
Maple seeds spiral to the stream
which carries them away.
Slowly relentlessly the water travels,
searching.
Sunlight makes cobblestone patterns
on the bottom
and drifts endlessly across the rock
walls.
Sky reflects distorted, from the
rippled surface.
The water speaks to me
softly in caressing tones, to soothe
my mind
and tell me of the coming winter
time.

Carol Wheeler Hamilton
THE WILTED ROSE

Dedicated to My Son—Bryant Barrett Hamilton

No Valentine Box, Heart-Shaped
with Lace,
But a wilted Rose in a crystal vase.
No Fancy card with verses—one or
two,
But a hand-made heart saying, "I
Love You".

Though the petals were torn and the
leaves hung low,
The rose was so precious,
It made my heart glow.

My son bought it early on
Valentine's Day,
Not typical at fifteen—so they all
say.
A rose for your Mother!
Some peers might say,
But the love in that rose beckoned
manhood that day.

And Shining in each petal of that
Wilted Rose,
Was the depths of love that only a
Mother knows.

Michelle D Mazzone
WORKAHOLIC

This poem is dedicated to my family and friends who provide a constant inspiration for my writing. I love you all.

Researching, writing, editing—
So much to do;
So little time.
Pages to examine,
Notes to be taken,
Making sense out of it all.
Freedom none,
No coffee break.
Halt right there;
Pause for a moment.
No time to rest—
Must go on.
What's happening now?
Pencils break,
Pens die,
Garbage can emptied.
Procrastination begins.
What procrastination?
This kind.
The work awaits
As I write another poem.

Lisa A Rodi
BENEATH THE SEA
I'm as small as a pea.
I live beneath the sea.

I'm the prettiest thing you will ever
see.
I'm the White Pearl that lives beneath
The Wide sea.

Gloria J Shumpis
TOUCHED BY THE WIND

This poem is dedicated to the Lord, my son Adam, my mother Marilyn, and my nana Elna.

Nothing in front of me,
isolated from all that life may bring
me or has given me already.
Except for the cool gentle hands of
Northern Winds
pressing its breath against my face,
caressing me with its touch
putting its own mark on me of a cool
fiery red.
The winds hands brushing my hair
from my face
as if to get a more complete look at
who I am.
Nothing in back of me,
but what is left from my day.
The winds arms pressing on me to go
to its embrace.
Let it happen.
I stand alone left with my thoughts to
wander where they will to go.
Closing my eyes imagining how it
feels to be held by a powerful and
loving force, caring and always there.
Reminding me of this fact.
The wind,
so much to give and experience.
It touches me when least expected
always invited, always a peaceful
journey.
A seduction of nature and I.

Tammy R Eledge
JUST THE TWO OF US
There's only one thing that could
break us apart

that is something we all understand,

But we'll always be in each others heart.

There will never be anybody quite like you or me
I just want you to stay close to me.

We should be nice to each other and never have a war,
but always peace between each other.

There will never be anybody quite like you or me.
I just want you to stay close to me.

Deanne Campbell

Deanne Campbell
GIFT OF LOVE

This poem is dedicated with all my love, to my children. Christopher, Carolyn and Nathan, may God be with them always.

This priceless
gift
I give to you,
has no ribbon
to untie.

But may it be
your strength,
and your
armour.

Your guiding
star to light
your way.

A fortress in
times of need.

An heirloom to
be passed on.

Terra Pfund
WE BELIEVE IN EACH OTHER

My heart was open to you; and you took it.
You loved me for what I was and not for what
you wanted me to be.
You believe in me
I believe in you,
We believe in each other.
That's why our love will always survive.
You filled my days with hopes of our future
I'm glad that we have an understanding for each other
you let me alone when I need to be and are with me
at times when I need you most.
You believe in me
I believe in you
We believe in each other.
That's why our love will always survive

Pat Futch
CHILD'S LOVE

Many a Blessing—have come from above,
But, none more special—than a "CHILD'S LOVE".

They coo-they smile—they say their first word,
They crawl-they walk—they talk like a bird.

Everything is so new—and, exciting to see,
Can't wait for tomorrow—what can I be!

They play—they fight with a friend,
They forgive—and, tomorrow begin over again.

When they're young—you cuddle and hug,
As they get older—sometimes you just shrug.

The things that they do—and, they're always on the go,
Sometimes we hardly get—a goodbye or hello.

It's hard for us parents—to let them grow up and, to go,
But, only because we love them so.

My children are special—whether young or old,
They are part of me—my body-my soul.

Children are Blessings—from above,
Thank you God—for my "CHILD'S LOVE".

Jeanne Louise Morgan
BITTERSWEET

I knew someday I'd see you
Across a crowded room,
I wondered what I'd say to you
And what you'd say to me.
I never dreamed you'd walk on by
Like any stranger would,
Or never try to catch my eye
Or smile or wave or say hello.
How bittersweet the memories,
How bittersweet the tears,
We vowed to love eternally,
One rainy day last year.
Have all the burning embers
Died and blown away?
Is the love we vowed forever
Lost in misty yesterdays?

My heart just broke again without a single sound,
I know, because no one even turned around . . .

Robert Shaffer
GOD WAITS FOR MAN TO WAKEN

I sit back and ponder the mystery
Of the exploitive, earth-bound family of man;
Driven by the forces of nature and self,
Cosmic, but lacking awareness, reasoning or plan.

In childish debate man still wonders
Whether he sprang from fish, hairy beast, or from God.
He's too quick to accept limitations, dead ends,
And to tie himself down to the sod.

Our needs and our wants, so universal,
Should bring us together ever as one.
Our hearts should share all things with each other,
Knowing eternity has just now begun.

We've fragmented ourselves into segments;
Competition, racism, and cruel wars.
We've built cold, forbidding dark boundaries;
Walls, not punctuated with doors.

Behind our facade we crave loving;
'Round the world it's the God-given same.
Let's break through to each other—and closer to God;
Then we'll find that we're all of one name.

Kelly L Cox
LEGACY

This poem is dedicated to the memory of Lawrence Sherman

It was not my dad, but his who passed
His who passed without a word, without a sign, or notice
His of whom I barely knew, though knew of him I did

I'd grown to love his pride and joy, a treasured gift, his middle son.
I feel for him, this middle son, whose dad has passed to rise no more
and of whom I barely knew, yet knew of him I did.

Those warm blue eyes, that soft white skin
Those firm and finely contoured hands
That tender, handsome face of his, a face of finely sculptured features
All of this I saw in him, a thoughtful man who passed my way, a man of whom I barely knew, yet knew of him I did.

I never really noticed the pattern of it all, the cycle of this constant passing, the tradeoff of it all.
The birth of yet another soul, as still some others leave
It seems we're here for just a while to share ourselves and our love
But then we're only here on loan to make our presence known

And of that man I barely knew, he's touched me in the kindest way
And through his son he's passed my way, yes, knew of him I did.

Tim E Thorne
YESTERDAY (BRANDY IV)

To: Brandy K. Wieslander . . . You will be with me forever and wherever I go and whatever I do.

Before yesterday came my days were filled with your smile and charm
that kept me going on each day.

Remembering the things we had and why we had them helps me
keep you alive in my heart.

And now that today is here and by His will He has taken you far
away from my arms forever.

Now that you are where you belong the memories and the love we had for each other keeps the day going on.

Days have passed and I miss your touch,
smile and love more and more each day.

Yesterday has come and gone and I long and wait for the day I hear the words once again "I love you".

Nancy Lauterbach

Nancy Lauterbach
TRIBUTE TO ZERO

Zero killed himself July 1988, because he was ill and destitute.

Zero may be your name but to all of us
Your name really should have been Plus
You sat here every day and said "Hi"
Tio all the folks that were walking by
Now you are up in the azure blue sky
Still waving to those passing by
We pray Zero finally you will win
That God opens the gate and lets you in

Alethea May
HURRY, HURRY, HURRY, THE BIG ONE DAY SALE IS ON

Hurry, hurry, hurry, the big one day sale is on.
Stores are open from 9 to 11;
Hurry, before the goods are gone.
Don't bother with breakfast, because you might choke.
Eat when you get there, so the cafeteria doesn't go broke.
Bedding is the big item, what floor is it on?
You must have a bed; the bigger, the better,
So you sleep sounder, and won't toss and turn 'til dawn.
Downstairs we have TV's, stereos, records and much more.
Throw caution to the winds; buy out the store.
These one day sales, they irk me no end.
Where do they get the money to spend?

William Aubrey Robinson
THE HOWL OF REMORSE

What kind of basing haunt
Does cowal me now?
When I, betwixt each mortal
Swell of soul,
Fear the craving call of
all below.

That now resounds with painful spurs
And ventures forth with
Chants of callous bale,
Betwixt, the nether dale!

Joel R Cochran
THE LOVER

I have loved, and had that love torn away.
I have given love, and been rejected.

My love has been stepped on, hurt, and maimed.
So there is not much love,
and there is not much trust,
and there is not much compassion.

But what little there is, I would give to you,
If you would have it.
And if you would have it,
I would ask but one thing.

Come into my arms and caress my weary soul,
Hold it gently in your hands,
Press it softly to your heart,
For no longer is my soul my own
It belongs now to you.

Linda K York
TRIBUTE TO A TYRANT
Your facade of devastation
In the finality
Is squandered on my being
Now, it occurs to me
That my attempts to deal
with your garish nature
Would best have been handled
By an outrageousness
greater than your own
Yet, being a reasonable person
I simply never knew
there existed a rogue
quite as vile as yourself
That I harboured an allegiance
is the disaster of my misfortune
As you may wallow in your alleged selfworth
rather I would grovel on a doorstep
Ultimately regaining more self-respect
Than you could ever know.

Joy Sabino
MY PERFECT PLACE
A place far away
As far as can be
A perfect place
A place just for me

Where bluebirds sing
And the trees ring
As the gentle breeze
Rustles their leaves

A creek trickles down a mountain
As the wind tickles over me
And fiery bushes
With tall, vibrant trees
They all surround me
As I lay there and stay
In my perfect place
My place just for me

Tami Hatcher
NEVER A LOVER
Scorned and forgotten,
your shallow mind
cannot penetrate beneath
the depth of your vanity.
In the beginning you were kind
yet distant was I,
testing your intent.
Now we are strangers,
Abandoned in our own eyes.
yet hope doth lie
within the dawn of the new day.

Cela Decarlo
WINDOW OF TIME
Through the window of time
I gaze
Onto a past Bittersweet.

I pass through
The Springs
The Summers
The Autumns
The Winters

To at last arrive in a season
Unfamiliar.

The Hands of time sweep
Furiously
I know not what
Time it is.

A ballerina dances
upon my chest of drawers.
In memory of a childhood
I do not know.

The mirror reflects an image.
A woman?
From which season does she come?
Tomorrow.

Lori Ann Eckerle
THE FOOL
Wind of darkness
covering lost shadows of gloom,
in the woods of time
the fool is hung in jagged vines.
Tattered clothes and heavy eyes
alone the gates closed behind.
Icy fingers stealing souls

surrender to their reaching doom.
Mirrored in the stagnant pools
watchers of the sky,
soldier of the past
now fights to stay alive.
She reaches in the darkened
empty space of doom,
they point the way while saying
the world's not meant for you.

Holly Dunn
THE NIGHT WAS LONG

This poem is dedicated to my angel in disguise, my confidant—Jeff, to the loving memory of Jimmy Lamar Tarelton, and especially to James Douglas Morrison.

The night was long,
The night was deep.
The innocent girl never wept.
It was but a chance at the
stroke of midnight,
To complete the ritual before
dawn's early light. Now . . .
All is calm in the land of darkness.
All is dead: all is heartless.

Maryjan Bardekjian
NEVER A FOOL FOREVER

This poem is dedicated to my best friends who mean so much to me.

I have fought; but never won;
I have lost; and seen no gain;
I have tried; but reached disaster;
I have prayed; but all in vain.

I cannot boast of courage,
I have not been too brave;
To fear I have been addicted;
To friends, but just a slave.

I built so many bridges;
But watched them all burn down;
I lost in every game of love,
For I played a part called "clown."

My heart has been a wishing well,
My soul a floor for dance;
I have been fooled by that cruel master
The weak and dumb call "chance."

I have stumbled; failed and been cheated
Of all that life urged me to win;
But please, name me not with the defeated,
Coz' tomorrow again I begin!

Sharad Sharma
PANDA
Prize of the Animal Kingdom
Awesome animal of China
Not liked by the bees
Dark and bright colors
Acrobatic mammal performing in trees.

Mary G Murphy
PLEA TO A CHARM TEACHER
My art of expression
Never leads to a good impression.
What I try to say
As merry and gay,
Turns out morbid and dull.
And always brings a lull.
Help me please
To speak with ease.
So I may be
The one to see,
A frown turned to a smile
And not wrinkles in a pile!

Julia Elizabeth Allen
CARESS
Touch gently,
our souls as our bodies bared,
pressed tightly to one another.
One plus one make one,
and forever we shall love this way.
Yes, my love, I do know you;
our hearts reflected in the other's eyes.
For we share a dream unknown to
any but the angels—
these our kindred minds whose
thoughts are known and yet
unspoken.
Let us touch again, my love,
for joined we are, and one we ever
shall be.

Kenneth F Paffrath
FOR YOU
For you I'd gather the stars from the skies
But they can't compare to the stars in your eyes.

For you I'd gather roses from the fields
But their beauty pales when you come into view.

For you I'd gather sunbeams to brighten your day
As you brighten mine when you come my way.

For you I'd gather moonbeams from above
To give to you with all my love.

Peter L Riesbeck
FEAR
Black is the night in which I fear.
The wind blows cold chilling the face of death.
Full is the moon at which I stare—
It will haunt my soul for all eternity.
Dense seems the air which I breathe.
It fills my lungs with terror.
So I stand, alone, in the field
Where the wall of innocence has been shattered
Many times before me, praying the dawn will arrive.

Jonathan E Jordan
COLOGNE OF SADNESS

To Life

Striking chords on silver shards,
The looking glass of sky,
Pray the storm that's nearing now,
Will reveal the screaming steel gray sound,
Directly to my eyes,

I can't be heard through veiled black laughter
So intense the voice of time,
Screaming softly coated lies of truth,
And tearing tears like velvet pages,
Scorching the book of my soul,
And yet I beg of them to be read,

Imprisoned crystalline screams of crimson,
An eternity of music without pardon,
A life of fearing sunshine,
And pleasure in the rain,
On which rainbow colored sands of mind,
Exists the breathing of frightened reality,
Oh the pain of unconscious wrath,

I pace a windy surging night,
Of frothy misty nerves of fright,
To hide in others shadows might,
Seem hideous it seems,
But when knowledge is your enemy,
You think about these things.

Marcia Sebby Winborne

Marcia Sebby Winborne
DANCING IN THE CLOUDS
Dancing in the clouds
There's music in my ears
My heart is pounding in my head
My eyes are full of tears

There are no eagles here, no hawk or bee or dove
I feel such power within myself
A greater force than love

I can see forever over endless beds of white
I roll and turn and climb and fall
And soar up out of sight

My universe gets bigger
My thought is really free
And know that I could fly and fly on through infinity

I feel the anchor breaking
The chain is getting thin
And fight against this earthly pull
I know that I will win

When machines and men grow old
And worlds are cloaked in shrouds
I know that I will fly again
Dancing in the Clouds

Darren Watson
FOR GRACE
For a single lonesome pale peach rose
Laid soft on a stone where green moss grows;

For smiles that warm the icy pain
Heaped high upon a spirit slain;

For a tree that grows from rugged rock
To nest a bird who lost its flock;

For eyes that behold with fairest light
To help the weary win their fight;

For tides that wash the dirty sands
Of a soul who prays with trembling hands;

For a touch that heals the wounded heart
Of earth the cold has cracked apart;

For water carried far and long
To quench the thirst of sorrows song;

For life that gives a priceless grace,
Praise to Heavens' all radiant face.

Sandra M Minnie
TO MY DAD

To my father Douglas E. Knight of Gravenhurst, Ontario Canada, with whom I lost contact for 20 years.

Many years were lost
Many moments never known
Many thoughts kept silent
As through the years I've grown

Many an emptiness was left
Many memories lost in time
Many answers left along the way
As a multitude of questions came to mind

But the years were good
Fate had our destiny in sight
God guided us together again
One cold New Years night

That moment I will never forget
Hearing your voice was a dream come true
My heart near burst open with joy
With a feeling I never thought I knew

I'm happy we found each other
And of knowing you I'm glad
I can't express the love I have
For the gentleman I call **"DAD"**.

Debbie Young
GROWN OLD

This poem is dedicated to Jane, not only is she the greatest mother but she is also my very best friend. I love you Mom.

Time passes all too quickly,
Before you know it you're old and grey.
Your mind wanders and runs astray,
You barely remember the days gone past.
You've become a Senior Citizen at last.

In your younger days, you dreamed of retirement and children all grown.
Now all that's on your mind, is how your body moans and groans.
Sure, you get your discount card to ride the bus,
It is slow getting on and people behind you make such a fuss.

You often feel neglected and forgot,
Have your children put you in a nursing home to rot?
Is this the thanks you get for all you gave?
For years and years you thought your kids would send you to an early grave.

But you've made it through the years, with alot of happiness and even some tears.
So just accept the fact that you've grown old.
Then laugh a little and remember, your children have children of their own.

April L Ellerbrock
MOMENTS
Wishing moments with you
are times that won't escape
For your memory is a part of me
not wanting to awake
I long to feel your arms around me
and the gentleness of your touch
Wanting this romance as reality
and to respect you just as much
Needing to have you near me
to feel the softness of your embrace
To behold this special feeling
as your hands barely touch my face
This feeling shall grow stronger
with every passing date
But these moments keep telling me
to leave everything to fate
If only you could tell me
or show me that you care
To let me know your feelings
in a kiss we'll always share

Tony Dale Farley
OPEN YOUR EYES
Open your eyes
What do you see
Lots of hate . . .
And lots of disease

Crazy people everywhere
Murderers could be anyone
Millions of single tiny hells
Only mirrors of ourselves
How hard to love
How hard to hate

It's all a link
In the chain of fate

Hear them talking on T.V.
Only lies it seems to me

This world's in trouble
As we can tell
Open your eyes and see
Everyone try it once
Don't lay the job on me.

Anna Lee Kirkpatrick
BREAKING THE BARRIER

Dedicated to my husband of forty-seven years, Kirk, and to our children; David, Anna Jean, Ande Dennis

Hearts are unheeding the passing of time,
As your vibrating vibes are blending with mine
Drifting together on a river of passion
Twirling together on waves of emotion
We're breaking the barrier built round your heart.

Floating together on a river of passion.
Whirling through a whirlpool of loving sublime,
With pulsating pulses: With vibrating vibes,
As you become mine, our loving's divine.
We've broken the barrier built round your heart.

A merging together of body and mind.
We'll go on forever our lives intertwined.
Though lovemaking's over and passion is done.
Our love it still lingers; forever we're one.
Our love was the answer; love's where to start
In breaking a barrier built round a heart.

Mëshan Rachal
SMILE

To Greggory Trent, I love you.
Mëshan

Your smile is my life, and your smile I'm missing,
There are smiles all around, but it's your smile that lifts me.

Just a smile from you is all I need to get by:
That smile of yours is what gets me high.

When you smile at me it's like a drop of the sun . . .
Your smile gives me strength and courage to carry on,

And if a smile can make you feel the same as I do;
Then you smile for me, and I'll smile for you.

The smile is our hope, while we are apart . . .
Let the smile remind us of the love in our hearts.

For to smile is God's gift of love, shared by family and friends,
So remember let's smile until we are together again.

Barbara Taylor
THE SWINGING BRIDGE
There's a swinging bridge outside of town, a special place to me
I still remember how it was; how I wanted it to be
We used to go to the swinging bridge when we first looked for love
We would listen to the water laugh, and name the clouds above
The bridge was always there for us as if it were a part
Believing in the hopes and dreams we had there at the start
The bridge would swing and listen to the promises we made
Not knowing that a promise like a summer rose will fade
I remember it was springtime; we spoke of April rain
I was grateful for the raindrops; they hid my tears of pain
"I see myself in her," you said; I wondered what to do
With all those things about myself that I had seen in you
There was nothing left to question, I had to let you go
The bridge just kept on swinging as if it didn't know
I tried to smile and wish you well, not wanting you to see
I needed time to hear the words, to make them real for me
I go down to the swinging bridge every now and then
To see the bridge still swinging gives me hope within
Sometimes I name the clouds above, as the water laughs below
Just me, the bridge, and the memory, from that time long ago

Carl A Schofield
FIRST STEP TO FREEDOM

This work is dedicated to the ideals of Freedom that led to the creation and continuing existence of this Nation.

Together they stood in small little bands
rifles and muskets held tight in their hands
Awaiting the British already enroute
listen real close you can hear the fifes toot

The long wait is over the British are here
challenges are thrown men talk about fear
Two forces stand ready at each other they stare
their weapons held ready to be fired with care

The first shot rings out from whom no one knows
a battle has started between two stubborn foes
The British are falling to stay means defeat
so the British are staging a hasty retreat

Down the road they are followed and shot as they run
all the way back to Boston harassed by the gun
This day we'll remember it will go down in fame
the new British colonies will no longer stay tame

So long we'll remember Lexington and Concord
all the men who succumbed to rife and sword
Keep on remembering long past all who survive
the Eighteenth of April Seventeen Seventy Five

Charlotte M Harris
PLACE INSIDE
There's a place inside me, where it's sad.
It's the place where I last saw my dad.
Lying held in death's tightening snare.
Icy blue secrets locked into a stare.
He'd given me new shoes earlier that day.
Now an accident was taking him away.
The shoes and the message in his eyes.
Being a child, I couldn't surmise.
Just what this would hold for me,
An embedded scene for eternity.
This place inside glows when I'm

distressed,
And sometimes makes me more
depressed.
Of an earthly father I've been
denied.
He left me here with this place
inside.

Lisa Elaine Johnson
I WAS A CHILD: I AM A WOMAN

I dedicate this poem to my Loving Mother, Fannie M. Johnson, my Loving Aunt, Essie Blankumsee and my Loving Grandmother, Fannie Blankumsee

I was a child, unbalanced, alone
in the cold darkness
with only voices I did not understand.
Struggling to get closer to those
voices,
I stumbled and fell.
Confusion was all around me.
Blood eased down my body from
where I had fallen so many times
before.
Tears rolled down my face, for soon
I
would die
without ever seeing the light,
understanding the voices
or feeling the warmth,
As I closed my eyes for the final
time,
I heard a heart beat.
I felt the warmth,
I had hoped for so long.
I felt a hand in my hand
which balanced me and led me to the
light.
I heard a voice,
words of wisdom,
words I could understand.
I was a Woman
guided by that hand that saved me
from the dark.

J Helen Condon
THE IRISH
Their plight is simple, The rewards
are few.
All of their work, has benefited you!
You revel in their gaiety, You cherish
their names.
You want to be a part of them, Yet
give them no gains.
You love their songs, you drive on
their roads,
Enjoying the freedom, Their lives
have taken toll.
They are scattered through our
history books,
Yet not acknowledged as one often
looks.
They ask for nothing, and receive
even less.
Their struggle overlooked, Their
economy a mess.
It is the Irish that we do not see,
The ones who made America strong.
Yet, we do not let them live here,
Nor, help in their struggle along.
Their freedom has long been
surpressed,
Their troubles overlooked.
The "Paddys and the Micks' etal,
Exploited in our books.
How ungrateful we are, in our
society so blessed.
To close the Eire door, and let in all
the rest.
It is time to re-evaluate, Our helpful
American ways.
Open our arms wide to those, Who
will work toward better days.
Take heed of what you have.
Remember from whence it came.
Those ones who contributed, and
never once complained.

Donna R Hall
WE'RE FREE TO BE
We're free to be,
Together, forever
Just you and me.

We're free to be,
Like the birds who,
Fly! Through and above;
The trees

We're free to be
Like the eagle who,
Flies toward the sky
So endlessly.

Barbara Yavitt
A LITTLE LESS THAN ALOT
In time and pain, I am so impatient
waiting to be alive,
So strange on that warm and
uncomfortable day, that I would be I,
And that whole cycle completed and
my being decided.
Handled, loved, and then indifference
of scrutiny: Yes, I am born
A part of the past and unready for the
unending now.

They were not sure and did not know.
Only time could tell that
Which strangers thought they knew
and could do something,
Anything, . . . my fate, I smile, I feel,
Hold me, hold me and then,
Care, Please care. I am only me.
Understand my need that I do not

Understand, but that I try to know,
but cannot, cannot. I cry,
I cry, and when I stop again, I try to
weep an outcry that I
can feel, this I can do. It is real. I
smile. Joy is what I can do.
I feel their pain. I see their pain. I feel
their shame, I am that shame. Why?
They know I am I. I try to be you,
because I love you, I do.
Others look and others know that
shame—that shame of not being the
same
I want to be the same. It hurts inside,
where is my place?
I feel those tears inside my face. I
touch the fear within me, all around
me
There is no cheer, no lightness near,
just the shame of that which I cannot
do.
My time is a cover, a cage made of
them. I am alone, single among them:
Alone with their answers, alone with
their thoughts. I smile, they smile,
I laugh, they laugh, they think, they
know, but I feel.

Floyd J Burdine
MY 2099

This poem is dedicated to Ms. Lilia Ulmos, who is a very SPECIAL and LOVING person.

My knees have buckled, and back
bent
From carrying the weight of your
burdens.
Yet . . . you, yourself, being part of
the load,
Have never been a burden to me.

My eyes have let much water run
from them.
As I cried for you, and over you.
As I cried for your love, and for the
need of it.
But you, my LOVE, have never
made me cry.
The loss of your love has been my
punishment
For the crime which I have
committed.
Convicted of loving you MUCH
TOO MUCH,
Had been my ONLY SIN.

Shelly Kendall
MY FEELINGS ARE GOOD

To my parents, your love keeps me going. Thank you for caring and being there. I love you both very much.

My feelings are good.
I have good thoughts.
Thoughts of the ocean,
with a seagull's cry.
Thoughts of the forest,
beautiful and quiet.
Then everything erases.
My feelings are bad.
I have bad thoughts.
Thoughts of arguing
with friends so dear.
Thoughts of the world
an endless hell.
Then everything erases.
My feelings are equal.
I have equal thoughts.
Thoughts of friends,
good times and bad.
Thoughts of life,
good times and bad.
Then everything erases.

Judi A Olsen
YESTERDAY

This poem is dedicated to my Grandmother because the light of love will shine through her eyes of love forever

Now that I am old and grey,
I remember all the good old days,
I remember always sitting there,
and I remember how he always
cared.

I never thought the day would come,
when we would be as one.
But then one day it came to be,
"Hon," he said, "will you marry
me?"

He wanted me to be his wife,
To be there for all his life.

Two years later, maybe three,
I found out I was a mother to be,
"A father", he said, his voice in
surprise
and soon I felt tears fill up in my
eyes.

I never thought he'd be so happy,
"Wow", he said, "my own family!"

But that was long ago and far away,
though it only seems like Yesterday,
and now the Beauty of Love is gone,
and only memories linger on,

Because Yesterday . . .
He passed away

Patti Westgate
I SEE THE LOVE IN YOUR EYES
I see the love in your eyes
And when you take my hand
I know what ere befall
Together we will stand.

As on the day we said I do
And looked into each others eyes
We knew from that day on
There'd be no more good-byes.

So till death do us part
From this earthly shore
You can know beyond a doubt
No one could love you more.

Wolfang Friedel
FATHER
Once more I see your face in my
sleep;
Your loving, gentle smile that lifts
me up.
The loss of you was great and I did
weep;
For over flowing was your gentle
cup.

It was your hands, your strong hands
that were there;
To raise me up and lift me on your
knee.
You told me stories and would share;
Your thoughts of life, to set me free.

From early childhood I looked up to
you.
My love for you was always
understood.
Your way of life was straight and
true
And your intentions always good.

When your last day came, I was
there;
To hold your old and tired hand.
It did not seem to me that it was fair,
To see such gentle man take his last
stand,

How glad I am, to have known you
as a friend;
Who taught me pride and honor and
to share.
For life repeats itself all over in the
end;
Now I have children, for whom I
have to care.

Helen M White
STARDUST
The band played "OUR SONG";
without a word we rose,
strolled to the dance floor, hand in
hand.
Our bodies melted together as we
moved across the room.
Your cheek against mine, your
breath on my face, your arms
holding me, firmly, yet gently.
Our love for each other so alive,
intense.
The dance ended, we were
reluctant to break our embrace;
You are gone, but still, after all
these years, when I hear
STARDUST, my spirit soars, my
body vibrates,
I feel your warmth, your cheek
against mine,
and a tear falls.

Dorothy Kasian
LOVE STORY
Christmas is a love story
It's written in the stars
All about the wise men

Who traveled from a far
To praise baby Jesus
Who in the manger lay
Cradled with his mother
On the new morn hay

Mary Frances Ring
FACES

To my children

I've watched the rolling traffic
Of a busy downtown street,
Where dreams and hopes and sorrows
Are often bound to meet.

I've looked into each person's face
And found a story there.
A smile may hide a heartache
And a grin may hide a care.

Hurrying to and from the office,
To the school, and from the store,
Morning, noon and evening—
Each face—an open door.

They think that no one guesses
The place where all dreams meet;
But it's in the rolling traffic
Of a busy downtown street.

Concetta TM Hajek
AND STILL, YOU CALL ME BEAUTIFUL

I've broken every promise that I made;
Instead of trusting you, I've been afraid;
And still, you call me beautiful.

I've made your love a game in which to play;
Instead of reaching out, I ran away;
And still, you call me beautiful.

I hated knowing that you had the grace;
To see the me that I could never face;
And still, you call me beautiful.

Larry L Lambert

Larry L Lambert
PASSION

As her sleek soft glistening body
melds maddenly into mine.
I recall a molten memory
of the first sweet precious time.

The first soft sensuous seduction
when our hearts melted to one.
The flaming fated future
of Love's passion just begun.

Oh sweet tantalizing torture!
Love passionate with desire.
As I penetrate pure perfection
in a consuming climatic fire.

In the shimmering, simmering afterglow
of a tumultuous, temptuous peak.
I discover my final destiny
within the soul of her I seek.

As I drink her moist sweet nectar
that my wanton wants need still.
I find the sweet flower of passion
that her cherished charms can fill.

When time takes of it's tariff
and steals of love's sweet store.
In memories my mind will marvel
of our love for ever more.

Eunice Evelyn Patrick
DESTINY

When I was young and in my prime
I squandered away most of my time.
I dashed here and there,
I was always going somewhere.
It seemed to me that life was forever
And that I would never, never
Come to the end as mortals do,
And yet I knew within myself
That all mortals must go to a final resting place.
Because it is preordained.

But as I older and older grew
I realized I had the wrong view,
That life does not go on and on.
When we have accomplished what we are sent here to do
We are sent to our final home
And begin a new and better life in another realm
Where things are different than down here—
And we shall be filled with good cheer
And no race shall be exempted or cast out
And everyone shall live without fear.

Stephanie Vermette
AS WE GROW CLOSER

To S.—More than anything.

As we grow closer
I almost want to pull away
The memory is too great
Of the pain of my broken heart
It lingers
Caressing me with its mocking fingers
Breathing to me not words of love,
but words of hate
And ultimately chilling the part of me
that is capable of loving you.

Pamela M Mosesian
A DREAM TO COME TRUE

Last night when I closed my eyes, I had a dream about you
We were walking on the beach and the sky was clear and blue
You turned to me and gazed deep into my eyes
a feeling came over me and left me paralyzed
as your lips began to part, you whispered "I love you"
without saying a word, you could tell I loved you too
The birds were singing and the sun shone bright
I had never felt in my life before so right
and as our lips touched and you held me near
I could feel on my cheek a rolling tear
For you see my dream was over and I was now awake
The disappointment of not having you was more than I could take
I think about that dream time and time again
maybe someday it will come true, for me, all I ask is when?

Geraldine Rosetti Gazzola
IN MEMORY OF MY MOTHER

I dedicate this poem to my mother, Arlene Joyce Rosetti, who passed away January 10, 1988, and is sadly missed by her family and friends. She's gone but not forgotten.

This poem I write in memory of my Mother,
For in my life there has been no other.
In my life she was a large part,
Of all the joy and laughter in my heart.
My love for her will always be,
Even though she's not here with me.
And it doesn't seem real to me somehow,
How one day she's here, but gone now.
The news was brief, the message sad,
It was the worst feeling my heart ever had.
Now what can I do, what can I say,
To change what happened a year ago today?
Even though it's only been one year,
It seems like a lifetime without her here.
I miss her eyes, her laughter, her smile,
I know it's going to take time, take awhile.
Time heals all, but one thing is sure,
For this kind of pain, there is no cure.
And just when I thought my eyes could cry no more,
They can and do, from my heart tears pour.

Diane T Kavanaugh
THE WILLOW TREE

The willow is my favorite tree,
It suits my moods so perfectly,
When I'm feeling bright and gay,
The willow flies high all the day,
When I'm feeling low and down,
The willow hangs close to the ground.

No matter what my moods may be,
The willow knows what resembles me,
Whether it flies low, or high above,
The willow is in love.

Margaret R Fuller
REUNION

When I set sail into the sunset
And head for the distant shore,
I know I shall find awaiting me there
The loved ones who've gone before.

The evening star will be shining
O'er a calm and boundless sea,
To guide me straight to the open gate
Where my dear ones wait for me.

They will know me then, when we meet again,
Though wrinkled and gray I've grown;
For it's not the eyes that recognize,
It's the heart that knows its own.

Dan Weaver
SILENCE

Listen,
Feel, the Silence
See, the deep blue sea
Rolling left, right
Rocking all night
Up, down, again and again
Then a breeze . . .
Flip, flap, flip, flap starts the sail
Look up, Silence
See a million points of light
A crescent glowing in the night
The pit, pat
The rain, cool, crisp
A flash of light
A crashing sound . . . then
Silence
Listen
Nothing
Feel the Silence

Julie Reed
CANDLE THOUGHTS

The burning flame,
dancing in the darkness of the night.
With every drop of hot wax,
trying to put up an endless fight.

The melting body,
hot with fear.
Dying slowly,
by each dropping tear.

The light begins to fade,
the bodys no longer there.
The hardened remains are left behind,
from an object that once attracted a stare.

Sigrid Singleton
MISSING CHILDREN

Dedicated to those who keep me writing. I love you all!

Snatched from the streets,
In utter disbelief—
Shattering dreams,
Encompassing grief—
Days moved swiftly,
Into tomorrow—
Families bereaved,
Sharing their sorrow—
Listening for footsteps,
A voice at the door—
A trace of possessions,
Piled high on the floor—

The hurt, the bitterment,
The empty room—
With each tiny clue,
The search will resume—
The loneliness seizes,
Each beating heart—
Protect us Lord Jesus,
Don't keep us apart.

Tup Dickson
MY MASTERS' CARD

The young folks cling to their Credit Cards,
Sometimes they have quite a few.
I have one that out shines them all
And you can apply for one too.

I really try hard to stick to
the rules,
In the book that they gave to me.
But I keep using my card to its'
limits,
I figure that's how it should be.

I use it to make my life better
And at times I get carried away.
But the more that I spend, the
more I get back!
So I keep spending day after day!

I never have to make payments,
It's all absolutely free!
MY MASTERS' CARD HAS BEEN
PAID FOR,
BY THE MAN THEY NAILED TO
THE TREE!

The TEN COMMANDMENTS I
follow
And THE RULE that is written
in GOLD.
So a spend-thrift I'll be with
MY MASTERS' CARD
Because spending is GOOD FOR
MY SOUL!

Richard L Hoege
THE MEMORY

To Don Hoege 1932-1989

Under the twilight's loom
with orange and gold blooms,

The sea feeling the sand
caressing as though a gentle
hand

Grasses softly flow
this way and fro

By the stars first twinkle of light
on rushes all that is night

As dusk evolves into night
we sense more than by sight

For of a life we shared
and unto us beauty was bared

Bringing us warmth and
happiness
departing saddened us

Alas, though gone
if loved, of warmth and beauty
can forever be its song.

Patricia E Glass
MY CHILD

To: Angie, Steven, John
Love, Mom

You are my child
I did not give you life
I gave you love
To be a mother comes from
the heart not the blood
To be there to show right
from wrong
To give a hug to say
I Love You
I miss you so much
you are my child
A gift from God above

Neil A Rutter
LOST IN FOUND
I found myself upon the ground,
A clover at my eye.
Three leaves it had
And that's too bad
Although I'm not sure why.

I found myself inside its shape and
Color so profound.
I thought of being
What I was seeing
And having leaves so round

Soon I stood and looked about
And found a million more,
All the same
And of one name,
Though separate for sure.

But upon returning to that
One that I had seen,
I found it lost
And blindly tossed
Into a sea of green.

Mertis John
A WORLD OF FREEDOM
Someday soon, I hope to see,
A world so big, and as free as the sea
A world where all people, will know
and see
That God made this world for you,
and me,

A world where we can live, work,
and play
A place where prejudice will never
blight our day
A place where love and happiness
stays,
The kind of sunshine, that never,
goes away—

A world where all children, together,
can play,
And have no fear of persecution day
Of this world I dream, I hope you
see,
A world where all men, will truly—
be free

Alisa Kaminski
DARKNESS

Dedicated to the hopes and dreams of my Husband Ed, and my Children, Danielle and Jonathan.

In the darkness I can't see.
Mother always punishes me.
I wish there were a way;
I could escape the punishment
that was given me.
At last I've got my way!
No more will mother shut out me.
Now up in Heaven I am Free.

Beverly A Marshall
IT'S VERY HARD TO LOVE YOU
It's very hard to love you
When you are far away,
I need to have you near me
In oh that special way,
I know someday you will be
I know it in my heart,
I wonder if you'll want me
When you and her do part,
You see I am your true love
And this you will foresee,
For there is but one love for you
And that my Love is me.

Kenneth Madaras
OCTOBER—
The many colours
are fragile and crisp;
Twisting, turning
in the wind that's swift.
Slowly falling
to uncertain rebirth,
slowly falling towards
the air-chilled earth.
And one, only sees
beauty in death
traveling to watch
the uncertain rest.

Now soft and light,
as if a feather;
Once full of life,
now suspect to weather.
Floating and dancing
on a sea that is not wet,
the change of season
has suddenly set.

And now life sleeps,
until the birth of next year.

C A D (Constance Kelley)
CHANGE OF TIMES
Changing times and changing people
Why is it things never stay the
same
You touch a leaf and it withers away
Feel hot summer air turn into
cold,

People should treasure what is there
Before changing times takes it
away
Friendships turn into bitter enemies
Hatred abounds where love once
stood,

To look in a mirror and see a
stranger
Walk into a room and see a
two-faced friend
Why can't things remain the same
And never turn up hidden
strangers.

Roberta Finlay Michulski
MEMORIES OF A CHILD
The grass was greener,
The sky was bluer,
The air was sweeter,
When I was young.
No air pollution,
No acid rain,
No foggy haze
To block the golden rays of the sun.

Elena Malaty

Elena Malaty
THE BUTTERFLY

To Mami si Ticu, far but always near.
To Leticia, my friend, always near.
To Nichollas, always far.

The cocoon is finally broken:
The sheltered world of dreams
became reality,
and I will have to fly on these unsure
wings,
which never felt the air until today.

It's hard to find myself, all of a
sudden,
alone and free under the arching sky,
without precise direction I could
follow,
without a Master who could always
ask me WHY.

The World is mine, but then I never
wanted
the colors and the sounds just for
myself:
I wished to share the endless fields
of flowers
that never will become a picture on a
shelf.

I started to fly high, I started to fly
lower,
I've touched the rainbow, then I've
touched the ground,
And I have been suspended, just like
a silken wonder,
above an empty garden, a garden
without sound.

And then I've realized that
everything was shallow,
and make-believe and ephemere like
me,
Displaying every day a multitude of
colors,
for blind spectators who will never
SEE.

Cynthia Hutchinson
MISSING YOU
There's no beauty in my life,
We are apart as man and wife.

The days are long, dark and gray,
no moon, no stars, to guide my way,

I see no joy or happiness,
for you my love, I do miss.

Time stands still, it does seem,
I find myself only in a dream.

A house and walls surround me here,
instead of arms that I hold dear.

It's awful quiet and awful dark,
life takes it's toll and leaves it's
mark.

I count the hours of every day,
as here I am and here I'll stay.

This is how my life will be,
until you, my love, return to me.

Jeffrey A Holliday
LAST STAND

Dedicated to every soldier who has made the supreme sacrifice in the defense of his country.

Here we sit on the high ground,
you've pushed us back this far;
We've dug our graves deep and
sturdy, you'll push us back no more;
We're not afraid to die, although
we're not quite ready;
A high price you'll pay for climbing
this ridge, we'll kill many;
A long time it's been since I've felt
warm and cheery;
A full belly is not known by many;
The cold wind hastens us away from
places existing only in our minds;
It's been a long time since I've seen
those faces, all of them friends of
mine;
Up the ridge comes a man dressed in
black, he beckons us to follow in his
path;
Although we do not want to, I feel
our time has passed;
The reason we are dying here has
long since been forgotten;
Just remember those of us who have
fallen;
Race and religion, it does not matter,
he collects them all in his swather;
You've pushed us back this far,
today we will go no farther.

Josephine H Manney
THRENODY
The ache is gone
Until the date
You celebrate your Birthday!
And then—
The softness of your lips
Is remembered.
Once more your eyes thrill me
With their remembered opalescence,
and
It is as if the days
Had not passed away;
I am young again and
You are my first chosen.
We went our separate ways . . .

How could I have known
The ache would still be there!
My mind's eye sees you
In all your manliness
As you were then.
Peculiar, isn't it?
Odd you say?
That my love could have lasted
To this day!

Fern C Corkhill

THE WORKING MAN

In honor of my husband, and all working people.

Heaven help the working man
He toils from dawn to dusk
Working many a day, slaving away
And gets no thanks from anyone
He is the backbone of our nation
Without him, we are sunk
So, remember him kindly
'Cause he's the strong and loving one
Every day he goes to work
Sometimes receiving no pay
What would we all do, without the working man?
Our country would just waste away.

Keith Reginald Cooper

SELFISH HOPES

Satisfied, we sometimes never seem to be,
Reason, we live from what our own perception perceives.
To want things beyond your reach,
While competing can make you a little upheated.
Awakening to the sun each blessing day,
Should create continence in every kind of way.
Sharing a few sincere thoughts,
Will mend the tides between any friend or foe.
Accepting Jesus Christ in your life,
Renews the soul from all substances of daily strifes.
Prayer's the only way to reach the Lord,
Also keeps you intacted with God,
Creator of the world.
Faith is not exactly what you see and feel,
It comes from the heart, which determines the real deal.
Trials are mostly to test your spiritual molds,
Answer whether or not your faith can handle the load.
Love not only destroys people's personalities,
Yet, in Jesus can enrich one's mentalities and spiritualities.
Why I wrote these few worthy notes?
I am aware everybody has their own
Selfish Hopes.

Brian C Curtis

A DAY IN THE LIFE OF A PROMISE

Promises are true, promises are false,
Promises are fragile, and usually are lost.

Promises are made, intended to be kept,
They can be expensive and put a person in debt.

Promises are words, symbols of a token,
Which nine out of ten end up getting broken.

Trying to accomplish things you said you'd do,
Tolerating the pain, and hell you've been put through.

Promises are words that lead you to believe,
They can be steadfast, trustworthy, and leave you in need.

With some people, promises are a written code of law,
If they are broken, it feels like a punch in the jaw.

Promises are sacred, and should be made true,
Be careful with the next promise made to you.

Victoria L Boldt

TO KRIS, WITH LOVE

To Kris: My most sincere thanks for your inspiration, encouragement, and most of all, your love.

Time spent with you is precious,
for you are the only one
who can see the real me.
Looking past what's on the outside
and bringing out
what no one else
looked hard enough to find.

Time spent with you is special,
for all my cares
seem to drift far away.
You love and care for me
in a way
that no one else has
or ever could.

I can only begin to thank you
for sharing so much of yourself
with me.
And if by chance,
we should never meet again,
my fondest memories shall be
of the time I spent with you.

Judith Yellin

RENAISSANCE

Turn inward
To the core
Of the pearl
Pare away
The shiny membranes
Iridescent florescent
Aflame
Like skeins of memories

The placenta
Of being
A furnace—hot
Roiling boiling
Until melt down

Float aloft
Pillo—wing
Swaying
Feathery
Adrift
In the I
Of the storm

Joyce E Loudon

LIFE

Life is a wonderful thing
It stretches ahead of you
Like an empty page.
What will mark this page you ask?
There will be joy and sorrow,
Peace and turmoil, love and hatred.
There will be times of fun and games
And also times of sadness and pain.
Life can seem fragile when you're down
But oh so strong when things are going right.

Each day you live will mark this page.
What kind of marks will it bear?
Sweet flowers for kindness, good deeds done.
Hearts for showing love and tenderness;
Or—Will there be black blotches of hatred,
Envy and jealousy; or—Big X's for turmoil and strife.
But more than anything I hope your page will bear,
The face of Christ,
Who will if asked erase the bad
And replace it with His Love.

Julia Wilkinson

SEEDS OF LOVE

Dedicated to love, and to the seeds that made me grow

When the moon fades over the mountains, and the sunset a beautiful red, remember the times that I loved you, and cherish the words that I said.

Know that the raindrops are teardrops, and the thunder a heart that has pain, and know that I meant not to hurt you, or cause both our lives to have rain.

In my dreams the wind blows so briskly, bringing your soul back to me, and I feel the warmth of the sunshine, and my heart wants so much to believe.

Will the days with the world so busy, or the nights with stars up above, bring us back to the place where we started, and help us to find our lost love?

The world will never stop growing, it is us who must plant the new seeds, the seeds that will keep us together, grows the love that will nourish our needs.

Daisy Loyd

MY GRANDSON

Dedicated to my Grandson Chris McCullough

A bright young boy of tender years,
A precious jewel that I hold dear.
His bright young mind so quick to learn,
Joy and gladness at every turn.

So quickly the years are passing by,
So many new things for him to try—
But Lord, I pray you'll guide his life,
May he be gladness and little strife.

Let him accept you as Savior and friend,
And may he be your witness of love to all men.
Let him be happy and share your love with all,
Lord, guide him gently and don't let him fall.

Let him be a great joy to his mom and dad,
I know that right now he makes them so glad.
But Lord, I want him to be more like you,
Kind and forgiving with a love that is true.

Rene (Graves) Davidson

MY WHITE KNIGHT

My White Knight wouldn't be clad in Armour,
Nor would he be dressed in white.
He would be an average man, kind and charming,
He would be a gentleman, smart and bright.

He wouldn't have to be rich,
He wouldn't need a body like Tom Crews.
He would be my friend and lover,
He would always be true.

He'd know the meaning of romance,
He'd know the meaning of true love.
He wouldn't be a saint,
Nor an angel sent from above.

He would be someone who loved me,
For who I really am.
He wouldn't try and change me,
And my faults wouldn't mean a damn.

He would always believe in me,
And encourage me in what I do.
He would always give me confidence,
With a simple "I Love You"!

Ira W Piercefield

TEN PERCENT

To my Wonderful Wife Mary Jane Piercefield

Well, I finally got up the nerve
To go see that preacher man
He said, for TEN PERCENT
I could get in the promise land

But preacher, divided up
Into my necessities
I don't have ten percent
Left over for me

I know that things
Are hard for you
They're awful hard
For me too

Now maybe you can
Show me the way
To earn ten percent
Someway, another day

Carolyn G Page

THE TORMENTED MIND

Dedicated to people with spinal disorders, and to my understanding husband, Sam

Oh my God—my Jesus—not again!
The onset of dizziness that will send
My mind and being into a swirling mass,
A condition that seems to refuse to pass.

Encompassing my entire body and soul,
Oblivious to any previous ambition or goal,
A void of nothingness, an abyss of despair,
Wallowing in self, no ability to care.

The people—they are looking —they stop and they stare.
Can they see my confusion? I can hardly bear
The thought that they know my mind is torn in pieces,
That my ability to think and reason rationally ceases.

The depression sets upon me—

weighs me down more.
I feel so incompetent—feeble to my inner core.
My confidence has fled—my esteem has been stripped.
My hours and days from me have been brutally nipped.

And then, at the edge of suicide, the shroud lifts;
The mind through past confused information sifts.
The fog dissipates, leaving the mind and body totally worn;
Limp and exhausted from the battle—my very dignity shorn.

And HE said, "MY GRACE IS SUFFICIENT FOR THEE."

Tashia Shannel Davenport
STONES

To My Parents, Franklin L. and Sonia B. Davenport

We are gray and colorless
The world passed us by
We are blemishes upon the Earth
We are not green like grass
We are not the flowers that add fragrance to the world
We are gray and colorless lumps
We go unnoticed, except for the occasional child that throws us
We are not picked and given as gifts
No, we are not the flowers, or the lake,
or even the grass
We are the grains of sand and the soft dirt
For without us there would be no green of the grass
No mirror blue lake, and no fragrant flowers
Yet we go unnoticed, but we don't mind
Together we are many, and our day will come
WE ARE THE STONES!

Victoria Fishman
WHAT'S THE USE OF A SONG

To Mom and Dad, who proved and inspired this poem.

What's the use of a song
If nobody hears?
Never long, never strong
It at once disappears.

What's the use of an art,
If nobody cares?
Is it smart just to start
Climbing the stairs?

What's the use of a soul
If nobody's near? . . .
Nothing. Nothing at all.
That is true, that is clear.

Beth Ann Kidd-Ruff
GRANDMA SLEEP TIGHT

To the seven Goodman Girls and my dearest Grandmother, for all their love, has made me who I am today.

Goodnight to you my dearest Grandma
Goodnight from all, but most Grandpa
It's only been awhile, but missed so deep
For the tears we shed were your eternal sleep
Loved by all, and missed by more
Oh what does God have in store
I want to know, I need to know
My thoughts of you just won't let you go
Here for our past, gone from our present
On to heaven, we all know is pleasant
So hard to say goodbye and hold to memories
You were the one so easily pleased
It's hard to say when we'll meet again
But you can be sure I shall not sin
We'll pick up the pieces to mend
For now to you my love I send
I'll pray for you as done before
You pray for me, you'll be with the Lord
This isn't just from me, but from family too!!
"Grandma," don't forget we all "Love You"

Elizabeth Osmera
WALK SOFTLY

To my beloved husband Richard, may he find peace in God's hands.

Walk softly my darling,
for I can hear,
the ache of your heart,
the falling of your tears.
I feel your presence,
I recognize your smile.

I reach to touch you, across these vast miles.
I long to hold you, and feel you near,
to gently touch your hair
and silently whisper in your ear,
Walk softly my darling, for dreams lie here.

Caroline Jensen

Caroline Jensen
LIFE (LETS INTEGRATE FOR EQUALITY)

To my family Jensens and Martin Luther King Jr.

Adam was molded by the earth from the ground
So it stands to reason he must have been brown
Eve was made from his ribs perhaps right
And of course you know their ribs are white
God put life in both to live
And knew that both had love to give
From these roots from the beginning of time
Who has the right to say this world is mine
Each man is put here to find his place
Without fear for his religion or race
We are born the same and will die as well
The only segregation will be heaven or hell
To hate is unforgivable
To love is divine
As God looks upon us with an expression of a kind
Don't you know all of you are mine
For those who believe there's no need for explanation
For those who don't there will be no segregation

Candace L England
ONLY TIME CAN TELL

Dedicated to my Mother & Husband, For their love and support

Too many have sat by with only a stare
Too few to listen and perhaps partially care

And YESTERDAY I desired to know if I stood fast or fell
But I do not know that now—only time will tell

Moments of desperation and self-inflicted tears
Over analyzation and trembling at unfounded fears

And TODAY I wish I knew if I stood fast or fell
But I do not know that now—only time will tell

Wide eyes and vacant faces looking somewhat familiar
But only situations the same—not all feelings being similar

And TOMORROW I may know if I stood fast or fell
But then again I may never know—
ONLY TIME CAN TELL

Sharon Anne Gardner
FROM HEAVEN

To my mother who was always there and to Carrie Armeda Faith the "star from heaven."

God gave me a star from heaven,
with her came precious light.
She's prettier than many an angel,
I thanked God for her that night.
Something inside me was lonely,
although God had granted before,
He knew that something was missing,
and that I had to have more.
He blessed me with such an angel,
that if he should change his mind,
I'd spend my life forgiving Him,
and just thank Him for the time.

Eddie Steven Calkins
A SHAFT OF LOVE PENETRATED

To my Lord and Savior, Jesus Christ, His Holy Word and Spirit.

A Shaft of Love,
penetrated me.
The warmth grew
others were touched,
others crushed
as a shaft of love
pierced their armor.

Patricia E Wood-Tresente
DREAMS

Dedicated to my daughter Karyn Moore, Love and goobies, Mum

Dreams are the windows to reality
awakening perception of future events
portents of tomorrow's joys and sorrows
emerging from dark caverns
of knowledge subliminally buried,
hidden in our subconscious
escaping when restraining awareness
releases its stranglehold
and unlocks the memories
that lie in wait
in patient and silent
watchfulness for the
onslaught of deep oblivion
and freedom.

Dale Resch
DUSTY ROADS

To my son Dustin with love

I drove my son to school today
how fast the years rolled by
as I drove I saw the innocence
curiosity in his eyes.

We were early, just a little bit
so we thought we'd share some fries
as we sat there in the school yard
talking him and I.

The freshness of the world they see
as they learn to wonder why
and how proud I felt when he had turned
to wave at me, good-bye.

Lillian M Desarmo
THE SUN SETS IN THE WEST

Dedicated to a beloved teacher
** My Mother **

The sun sets in the west
And rises in the east
And in between is everlasting peace
Or is it?
The sun sets in the west
And rises in the east
We wake to face reality
Or is it?
The sun sets in the west
And rises in the east
Or does it?

Bonnie Skidmore Ayotte
WONDER

To my mother Sandra, Her kindness gave my family the strength to go on.

If Love wanders with no place to stay,
And whispers are meaningless with nothing to say.
Recall a love that lives in your past,
Escape into memories, let the mood be cast.
Relax your mind and stay awhile,
Dance through the meadows like an unborn child.
And when you're feeling calm and free,
Open your eyes to reality.
But smile now because you know,
Happiness depends on where you go.

Beulah T Stansfield
THE APPROACH OF WINTER

To my Son, Barry

The morning sky is cold and gray—
With Winter soon upon us.
No more the clear azure blue sky of summer time—
No more the singing of the birds in early morn—
The birds have flown to a warmer place,
While winter is upon us.
Their nests in the trees outside my door,
Are empty once again—
And waiting for the winters' storm approaching.

The wind sends out an icy chill over the countryside.
The trees now shed their leaves of gold—
Once green when it was spring.
The trees will stand in nakedness—
Their branches etched black against the sky—

Occasionally brushed by the whiteness
Of a snowflake's kiss blown by.
Time passes fast—yet slowly by—
When winter is upon us.

Dan Schauss
REFLECTIONS OF LOVE

Dedicated to Taunya Martindale: may you always receive as much love as I know you are willing to give: With Love, Uncle Dan

Reflections of love we hold so dear,
We gather them all from year to year.

Some are happy, some are sad,
But never could even one be considered bad.

There are many turns and twist to fate,
So give your love don't ever wait.

When you look back across the years,
Be glad if you can shed a tear.

People out there who have never dared,
Don't know the meaning what it is to care.

So if you can look at your life and see,
Even one reflection consider it lucky.

Life is short and that is sad,
Be thankful for what you've had.

Love is good in whatever form,
A learning experience for which you were born.

Marcella Ford-Wilkins

Marcella Ford-Wilkins
MY EARLY MORNING LIST

Memories of my family who helped shape my destination

I wake up at 4:30 a.m. and speak to my Master through a silent voice.
I pray to show thankfulness for a brand new day and ask for his help and guidance along my way.

I feed the wild birds and watch them go astray, and see them return at the break of a brand new day.
They come in all colors, covered with feathers, then flying away, grouping themselves one from another. Some go Up! Some go around!
Some keep eating off the rocks and the Georgia ground.

I check my yard from front to back, picking up trash in a brown sack. I crank up my 1984 Eldo Burgundy Cadillac, make sure it's ready when I get ready to ride and relax.

I crank up my '65 and '66 mustangs and listen to them tick.
So beautiful they will make the average collector sick.
I crank up my '79 T-Bird, silver and gray . . . to make sure it will get me to work every day.

Come in my home and wash my hands, using a basin that I used in the South Carolina sand. Get my breakfast; say my Grace! Peas and beans all over my plate. Thanking The Lord for daily bread . . . and the place Benjamin left me to rest my head.

Brush my teeth; Get my bath, not a shower. Help me to meditate in the water for one hour. I comb my hair, push it back, Make sure my natural gray streak is in tact.

Check my face, look in that little hand-made glass that my brother James made before he suddenly passed. A little mirror, from the outside of a 1934 Ford that he took and placed in a home made piece of board.
He trimmed it with a piece of metal from an old Bugler tobacco box;
This mirror helps me to be thankful for my past—telling me God is still in control of all of us, from the first to the last.

Put my perfume on! Ready? Yes, ready to carry on! Check my alarm system to protect my home while I am gone. Thanking my Lord because I am on my way—to B.T. Washington High School where I earn my pay.

Louise Chapman
ANGEL

This poem is dedicated to Dale, my loving husband.

Did you ever see an angel cry?
For him she would gladly die,
She loves him, with all her heart, and that's no lie.
Shy little angel, with a dimple in her cheek,
Tonight, so lonely and meek,
With a heart full of love, she must wait week after week.
Angel, with a love so new,
To him, she will always be true,
She's in love with his eyes of blue,
And of course, his laughter too.
She loves his heart so tender and kind,
Another like him, she will never find,
To live with him forever, she would not mind.
Would make her happy if she could fly to his arms,
Never again, to fear any harm
To lay her head upon his breast,
And fall asleep, in peaceful rest.

Monica F Anderson
CELLAR DOOR

To Gladys Arcolia, Alfred, Tony, and Adrian

Oh Lord,
I'm afraid to sleep;
Afraid of what I'll dream.
Cause when I sleep,
My heart will speak.
I hate to hear it scream.

It yells my deepest pain.
It echoes through my veins.
Again and again and again!
Until my eyelids rain.

It's easier when I'm awake.
A million things to help me fake.
But in my slumber deep I shake,
In chilled pools of sweat I make.

But my resolve begins to tire,
From upside-down my lids are higher.
The silence is the sandman's choir.
Now sleep descends like rapture's fire.
Oh Lord.

Mary E Voisey
BROKEN GLASS

I open the window wide, Daddy, and stare into the bright light of the sun. And with tears in my eyes, I will remember you.

Glass shatters and the wind blows in
Despair riding its wings.
Dark and deep are the feelings
Hidden in the night.

Light filters in, a crawling creature
Of unearthly brilliance;
Its burning imprint dulling
The cold heart's misery.

Clear biting reality overwhelms the room
Chilling the soul dormant in illusion.
Replace the shattered glass.
Glass holds back the truth.

Painful light stop shining. Darkness fade away.
Leave contented nothingness.
Leave the heart to its silence.
Replace the shattered glass.

L M Malley
WHISPERS

For the Malley/Mathews Clan, a family you can't help loving; and to Tracey, Lili, Ellen, Tom and Trish, friends I hold so dear.

Whispers in the wind I heard; untold stories, wishful words.
Scattered dreams and fantasies; winding paths through haunted trees.
A hand to hold, a life to live; a faded memory, a smile to give.
Helpful hands I can't quite reach; walking down the lonely beach.
Finding love I thought was lost; holding on despite the cost.
Hanging by the thinnest thread, I found a hope I thought was dead.
Yes, I heard whispers in the wind; they told of pain, of newborn sin.
Fatal tales of passions burned; revealing secrets never learned.
The hand I found to hold was mine; the scattered dreams rejoined in line . . .
Fantasy was there to find; once far away just like my mind.
Crying in the night I heard; flowing tears, shaken words.
Shattered dreams and fantasies; disenchanted harmonies.
A tear to fall, a game to lose; decisions made that I did not choose.
Happiness is hard to find; is hope forever left behind?
And if I cry a billion tears, will dreams come find me through the years?
Will pain and darkness take control of the space which holds my soul?
And if I search will I then find, the whispers heard were in my mind?
The songs once sung were in my mind; the untold stories were in my mind . . .
All hopes and wishes left behind; all is lost—I've lost my mind.

Gerald Smith
HEY, LOOK AT ME

To my children Jerry, Phillip, and Melissa.

The kids now-a-days they really have it bad,
And as a father of three it makes me so sad,
Because I know how hard it is for them out there,
With all the drugs and dope and alcohol that is everywhere,
Everywhere you look, everywhere you see,
There's young kids out there saying "Hey, Look at Me,"
Look at me I can down a couple of beers,
Or smoke a few joints to hide all their fears,
Maybe pop a few pills so that they can make it through the day,
Or maybe do some coke so they won't have to listen to what anyone has to say,
The temptation must be an awful scary thing,
If only they had a different song to sing,
A song that they could shout so loud that the whole world would know,
Hey, Look at me I can just say no
Now that's the way to go, that's the way to go.

Phyllis M Wilson
ON MY RETIREMENT

To Stephanie and Kimberly

Another day! The sheer joy of living—
I gaze in wonder at everything I see;
I stroll with friends along the nature trails,
I breathe the beauty of each flower and tree.

I've still so many other things to see and do!
I'm beset by pleasures and choices all around;
To go? To stay? To walk? To pray? . . .
This life, which never really had been lost, I newly found.

My senses sharpen, let nothing pass me by . . .
I'm like a child turned loose in a

candy store!
My working years were spent with head bowed down,
But now, my face towards the sun, I fly, I soar!

Oh, I'm in love with my retirement years,
May they continue, giving me time to spend
Exploring everything on earth that I still need to see,
With never a thought that one day it must end.

So I'll continue in my new-found joy, my life is great!
My mind is clear, step brisk, for I already know
When my time comes, I'll say, "I Thank You, Lord,"
Then, ever so gently, I'll simply let life go.

Kenneth Walsh

Kenneth Walsh
KENNETH WALSH—ARTIST

This Poem is dedicated to my father, "He believed in me."

I'm just a simple person as you can see, just as simple as I can be.
But every morning when I arise, I thank my God and realize that I'm not small, and I'm not simple.

He gave me another day to use His temple,
To enjoy the world and make life simple,
To use my hands to ex-politic His temple,
To bring to knowledge the world around,
To show you things you've never seen, now
To make the world glow like a queen,
To let you know the things I have seen.

Yes, I am different, as through my art you can see,
I take the world as simple and free.
O what a great sculptor God must be
For he made everything here on Earth
For just you and me.

My mind is much different, my eyes you see,
Can see things much different than you can see.
I see the valleys, the skies and the trees,
As a magnificent sculpture of life so free.
I see the making of this Earth around me
As a beautiful picture of God's love for me.

And though I have searched my mind for thoughts,
I develop my canvas as though I was taught.
So look at my art with warmth and love,
For my only teacher is God from above.

John Domyan
WE NEED EACH OTHER

To Florence

We need each other
In time of grief and pain
We need each other
When things go wrong
and are in vain
We need each other
to share happiness
We need each other
to thank the Lord
for our happiness
as years go by
We can say
It's wonderful so happy
being with each other

John Domyan
SO LOVELY

To Florence

you're so sweet
and so lovely
I'll never stop
loving you because
you are so lovely
you'll always be
close to me
down deep in
my heart
you will always be
a part of me.
I love you
you're so lovely

Antonia Moreno
WHEN I THINK OF A HEART
When I think of a heart
I think of my parents' gentle touch.
I think of the way they joke with me,
poke me and even sometimes want to choke me.
I always see their smiles
then we sit around and talk awhile about each other
and how we could never find another.

My Mom cooks dinner for me.
She goes shopping to show she cares.
It's just nice to know she'll be there.

I think of how they will always mean so much.
I remember the day at the mall,
I was feeling sad.
My Mom joked around with me and made me glad.

So when I see a heart:
I know that's the right place to start telling how my parents love me.

Sheri Winn
VANQUISHED HEARTS
How distant is the muted beat
of strangled love we can't outpour.
Misguided passion, bittersweet,
this time—fermented love so pure.

Clenched inside the fist of life
the heart grows weary, weak and worn.
And apathy's relentless knife
aborts emotions yet unborn.

Pain scarred over numbs the soul,
and leaves it robbed of feeling's touch
With love as its abandoned goal
leaning on self-pity's crutch.

Margaret Moss
LOVE

To my husband Bill, with all my love.

Don't let indifference
Take its toll.
Showing ourlove,
Must be our goal.
The years pass by, so
Often spent;
Telling each other
Not what we meant!

Put love in your words and
In your heart,
It's never too late to make
A fresh start.
Overlook the little things that
Rile us day by day.
Embrace each other often
It's the only way.

As all things in life,
Must come to an end.
The memories of our love,
Will help our hearts to mend.

Michelle Becht
ALONE

"Alone" is dedicated to the dreamers of this world, reaching out to make the world a special place. And to Joshua Franks my special love.

In the abandoned foundation of a house
No longer in existence, as I lay on my back
I can feel the cool ungiving concrete against my body.
I can look up and through the reaching,
Green leaved fingers of the surrounding trees
I see an endless blue sky ascending into eternity.
I hear the trees whispering in response to the warm gentle breezes of spring.
Then everything is still
A song from a sparrow breaks the ephemeral silence.
The beauty of Mother Nature has touched the earth giving new life
To my world.

Dawn M Kirkendoll
VOICES

Dedicated to Nina Giavaras who has challenged me, inspired me and helped to expand a vision. Thank you Nina, you will always walk with me.

Who knows where the four winds may blow us
When they shift in different directions.
And who knows which road to choose
When all the signs are unclear.
—Voices of strangers grow as deep as the seas
And silently they keep their secrets from me
And if I ever make it to the shoreline it will be—
Because I never say too much, never show too much, never lose control . . .
Who knows which stars to reach for
When the brightest have lost their spark.
And who knows which paths to follow
When the only ones left are dark.
—Voices of strangers growing fewer—
Who knows where the dream can take us
If our imaginations cease.
And who knows where this life will find us
If that which is left was left unreached.
—Voices of Reason echo in the distance
Spilling wisdom to me
And when I've made it through the seasons it will be—
Because I never said too much, never showed too much, never lost control . . .

Bessie M Hart
MY PLAYHOUSE

Dedicated to our daughters, Dona Beth and Joann, who spent many happy hours years ago playing house in the trees that shaded our farm home.

I have a playhouse out in our trees
With walls and windows where I please,
With stones for stairs and stakes for doors,
Leaves for a ceiling and grass the floors.

My sofa is an old porch swing,
My grand piano a gorgeous thing,
Though practical folk would see nothing there
But a splash of shadow near the hallway stair.

I've a platform rocker from an old car seat
And a tufted hassock for my feet;
The dining table is made of crates
And my round log chairs are quite up-to-date.

My kitchen cupboards are boxes, too,
Sink and refrigerator, white and new;
My stove is a fireplace made of bricks,
Hearth and pantry are marked off with sticks.

So, why not tomorrow, come, my friend,
And spend a day at "just pretend?"
If you do not like my arrangement quite,
We can change it all before the night!

Celeste Walker
THE STANDOFF
As I finish packing a bag
I feel ready for the rocky crag.
Well prepared for the seasonal week
I heft my rifle, strong and sleek.
On my head a bright orange cap,
One last glance at the map.
I grasp the bag in my hand
and head off for the rugged land.
After two days of drizzle and wet
Not a thing is seen, my gun is all set.
We sit, silent, and wait
For a buck, or even his mate.
I see her, at great distance, step
through the trees,

Stop suddenly, startled, and freeze.
A shot, she begins to run,
Missed by the first hunter's gun.
I hear another hunter call
and raise my rifle, ready, for her fall.
The doe looks at me, eyes haunted with fright,
I lower my gun as she runs through the dark, silent night.

Raymond H Holderman

Raymond H Holderman
A TRIBUTE TO FERN

Dedicated to the Etchart families of Glasgow, Montana to honor the memory of their sister Fern.

If there is dancing in Heaven they are in for a treat
For she floats like a snowflake on twinkling feet.
A smile so delightful this lady petite,
Moved forward so bravely life's troubles to meet.

Recalling friends and acquaintance
Who were charmed by her graces,
And her families Love that shone on their faces.

Gina M Vincent
IN SOME FOREIGN LAND
As usual you jumped into it without stopping to look ahead.
When will the naive, silly country-loving girl ever learn . . .
From broken tarred streets with side gutters six feet wide,
From rain stained houses and overgrown lawns,
Rushing into the new life.
It was supposed to be open to anyone
But openness did not mean
Acceptance.

Waking up in the cold sunshine of the morning
To discover the world and the way and the whys . . .
Finally making things happen and taking fast chances,
Finally on your own with sparkling dreams
Bursting to come true.
Then reality pulls up to the curb
And splashes water all over your new
Hairdo.

Maybe in some foreign land
Where hot winds blow by
With passions of the feeling people,
There, there is where you'll find
Peace.

Fern Daniel
DON'T LET ME KNOW
If my love for you surpasses
What your heart holds for me,
If my world revolves around you
And yours from care is free,
Don't let me know.

If my thoughts are full of you
And yours aren't concerned with me,
If my eyes are for you only
And yours can others see,
Don't let me know.

If I could never change my feelings
And yours begin to roam,
If I'm content to have you only
And you stray away from home,
Don't let me know.

If I should ever lose you
For just a moment, unaware,
And you should then return to me,
Leave your indiscretion there
And please, don't let me know.

Samuel Gyermeh
UNDER THE LORD'S TENT
What joy the Lord has wroth in my heart,
To feel the peaceful calm of content;
As a struggling world dissolves apart,
I am immovable under the Lord's tent.

Each day appears with its trivial lure, While many strive for social assent; Through all such vanity I am secure, And unshakeable still, under the Lord's tent.

Endangered by wars and destruction, Earthquakes and famine still collect their rent; With drugs and violence brewing their potion, I pray to remain under the Lord's tent.

THE Lord's love can heal all pain, And there are choices available at a man's consent; Within me all of life will remain truly glorious here, under the Lord's tent.

S E MacNaughton
MY LOVE
I often wonder why
I am so fortunate
to have this man
whom I love
in my life.

He came unto me when I needed him so
unaware was I of this
until I felt his love
uplift my soul.

Together, as one, were we at the beginning of time
then pulled apart and born in separate bodies
we became as two
though in fact, half of one.

Thus began our search for each other
and we were reunited
as all along it was intended to be.

We live each day aglow in our love
and we take not our blest joining for granted
for we fill each other's cup
with the very juice of life
which we need to survive.

Shauna Morgan
SOMETIMES
Sometimes we just have to stop and make the effort to tell our friends how much they really mean to us and how we need them.

Sometimes I never want to grow up because that means we'll drift apart trying to fulfill our dreams and losing the ever-so-close friendship we shared.

Sometimes to show how much our friends mean to us we have to let them go, and then we'll know that we were behind their dreams.

Sometimes I just want to crawl inside myself for just a while and watch the real world from my own little place where no one can hurt me, but, because we are friends you won't let me.

None of us will live forever and we won't be as close as we are forever, but memories last and I will always treasure them because they are of you.

Marcia R Goldberg

Marcia R Goldberg
HYPOBEACH: FLORENCE VEERS OFF COURSE
Fecal coliform floats to shore
near Atlantic City, floats
disease into the bodies of dolphins
escaping yellow-fin tuna nets
and general over-fishing. Dogs
that bite up fish
beached by the sludge themselves die
and wash-up bloated with small needles—
the paper says, "the kind used by heroin addicts."

One or two needles wash-up each hour
and endanger barefoot beachcombers,
shell collectors, with new variants
of collapsed immunity. The beach, some say,
is fighting back. The ocean is
coming to get us,
is attacking swimmers with
contaminated pins.

Florence approaches salt-stinging spirochetes
propelled aboard tampon dispensers
jettisoned under who-knows-what conditions
from dunes when tides turn
to return to the angry waves.
Furious salt-splatters, liquid substance tsunami
heavy with mercury, medical waste, sewage,
pelts canisters and trash, cutting debris
in rip-tides: all the sea's a barge,
a Mobro that will not get off,
will not be masked by bubble-gum fragrance
or any stench-reducers sprayed upon
the overheated atmosphere.

Chlordane from garden pesticides,
lead, nickel,
arsenic accumulate in the liver of perch.
Heavy metals run into fresh-water sinks
where bass, walleye, and pike spawn fry
that grow fat with darkened welts.

Will I stump splanchnologists with earth-colored,
visceral splotches, fears Florence,
lustrous, florescent, splining my tissue,
with flat strips of mutton-gray ooze
or loathsome sponge-spital?

The pebbled beach snarls its assurance from Dover
as it rolls over spoons, hooks,
torpedo tubes, satellite fall-out,

and how can I call to shore a warning
where waders scoop through parasite sporangium
when I myself am dredging through
sour spikes infecting red algae,
overstepping sporocarp dormant only briefly
in their mutating encystments and sacs,
hitting spotted crake first,
then short-billed sora as I'm gasping for air?

The sea is feverish with the pickling brine,
scattering a continuous sheet of oils
I must push further apart,
and I must make a meal of this thin layer of thought,
served by its wide variety, or swallow
the diffuse jam, this butter-rummy extension
before we choke.

Heidi V Brown
FOR YOU
It was a beautiful day today.
The sun was shining,
and all around me I saw love.
I walked around, and as I did
I started thinking about
life and such.
I thought of far away places,
and friends, and you.
I was talking to you,
Did you hear me?
I smiled when I thought
about touching you,
did you?
I kept looking up just to see
if it would really stay
so beautiful.
It did. It made me smile
again. It really was
a beautiful day today.
And tomorrow, I know
tomorrow will be a
beautiful day, because
tomorrow I will think and talk
to you again.

Berti Hermansen
GOODBYE MY FRIEND

To my sister, Venice in memory of her beloved husband Richard C. Jensen.

Goodbye my friend, I hold so dear,
I may not see you for many a year.

The times together that we have had,
It sometimes leaves me, oh so sad,

To know you won't be here this year,
To share our love we held so dear.

My thoughts go back and try to find,
The things that made our friendship bind.

Hardships and sorrows, the times we did share,
That's what made us such a good pair.

And now that you've gone on ahead,
To prepare the way, 'til I rest my head,

I'll hold you forever, in my heart,
Together we'll be, never apart.

My heart is heavy with all this pain,
As I walk by myself down life's lonely lane.

Comfort I seek, as I shed these tears,
Your memories I'll cherish through all the years.

There locked in my heart, where ever I go,
Because I love you so.

Irene Iverson Timney
SPRINGTIME IN THE DESERT
Gay flowers shout their presence.
The palo verdi blooms.
A jack-rabbit hops along
And birds sing merry tunes.

Saguaros reach up to the sky
With long thorn-bearing arms.
A squirrel sits in the shadows
Displaying wanton charms.

Lizards venture warily
From a dark hiding place.
Rodents catch a hungry eye
As they to burrows race.

And sun-drenched sand just glistens
In the early morn sunshine.
By winding paths low cacti
Their flaccid arms entwine.

An expanse of blue above
With fluffy clouds unfold
A desert springtime setting
For all eyes to behold.

Richard Pearce
PASSION
What is spoken in shadow,
Must come to light again;
As a passionate pain
Must flow to tears of torrent;
No man can hide
His human eye
From sight of soul transcendent.
All loss is left
At lap of ocean shore,
All gain is found
In drowning to this love.

S L Taitt
LOVE VISITS

To my sons Reggie, Neil, Terry and Naylon

So Love finally came
to your door.
Love knocked lightly
a little harder
a little more harder
Love continued to knock
Love refused to keep silent
Rapping louder and louder
For you see, Love is
also persistent.
Tired of the knocking,
weary from it
You arose and opened the door.
Love entered in.
You found it pleasant.
Quite warm and free.
But, you also found, it
doesn't leave, when you ask it.

Brenda Woodard
BROTHERLY LOVE
Some people are hungry, some without a home.
What is wrong in our land; where has our love gone?
We spend a lot of money on things we don't even need,
There are so many filled with hate and some with greed.

People, let's take the time to help our brother,
Let's have a heart and love for one another.
We are Americans and so proud of where we live,
But it would be a better place if we would take
the time to share and to others give.

We need to take them by the hand
and show them there's a better way,
Don't put it off till tomorrow
because today is the day.
Let's help them get back to the place where they belong,
Let's help our country's hurting; oh, help them to be strong!

Helen M Layton
WRITTEN IN THE STARS
They had one goal in common
to explore the realms of space
If the predictions of Revelations
come
true
we'll need another place
to preserve the species of
mankind and
perpetuate the race.

They climbed the heights to
glory
their brilliance will ever shine
They gave the best of what they
had
for the benefit of all mankind.

The endless quest for knowledge
this tragedy should not mar
for their names will live forever
written in the stars.

Shelly Miller
THE PICTURE
Today I painted a picture
A picture for you
I think you'll like it
You know I love you

The picture told a story of love and hate
So beautiful, yet so wrong
The girl, she loved him with all her heart
She would never leave him
She wanted a start

But her heart, it bled
Because she knew
He did not love her
It tore her in two
It told the story of me and you

So now the picture, it lays on the floor
Never to be touched
I don't love you anymore
You don't even know you hurt me
But that picture knows things will never be the same
For our love was one-sided
Do you even know my name?

Carla J Franklin
ON A SNOWY AFTERNOON
Passing through my village,
On a Snowy Afternoon,
Was an Old Bag Lady
Looking for a room.

She came upon my cottage,
As I was lying awake,
Begged to let her in
So a pallet she could make.

I had risen from my bed
And headed toward the door
When I heard a loud "Boom"!
Her words I heard no more.

"Who's there?" I asked repeatedly
But there was no reply.
Eager was I to inquire
For a pallet I might supply.

I slowly opened the door.
There fell by my side
The body of the old lady
Who, from the cold, had died.

Mrs William H Freeze
SPRING

This poem is dedicated to Thelma, my loving Mom.

Spring with its enchanting beauty
is ready to appear.
The birds are singing loudly
the songs we like to hear.
Trees and shrubbery all are budding
from the warm and breezy air.
Moisture soon will be falling,
if we are faithful in our prayers.
The Father of all creation
with his beauty here bestows,
sends us heat and cold together
for our plants and seeds to grow.
May we look to the heavenly Father
giving thanks from one and all,
for the seasons of this universe
and the birds and beast that call.

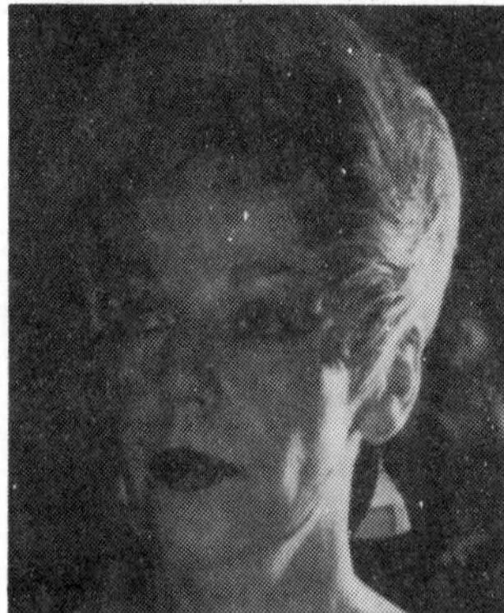

Maureen O'Keefe

Maureen O'Keefe
EARTHQUAKE
I sit alone—among the devastation and strife—
Wondering at the meaningless meaning of life.
A once proud city—turned to dust and stone—
Now, only a covering of flesh and bone.

Buildings sprung up from the barren soil—
Constructed by eons of sweat and toil.
Crumbled in minutes by nature's rage—
And left in rubble—from her rampage.

Miles and miles of rock stillness, dies—
When punctuated with unearthly moans and cries—
From the hapless innocent—so newly strewn—
Among the flattened cities, cement dunes.

A collage of ruins and dying humanity—
Testing belief in God's omnipotent sanity.
For how many thousands—here laid to waste—
By nature's fickle and capricious haste.

Only time alone—can rebuild and repair—
The vestiges of a city—no longer there.
But the future treads slowly—and cannot be hurried—
While I sit withered with age—and my spirit lies buried.

Dawn De Bolle
DEATH

In loving memory of Poppop and Simon

What have I done to deserve this
treatment
Locked away where no one can
find me
The hollow silence closes in day
by day
Hours go by and I do not sleep
I lie awake in a cold sweat
Darkness starts to close in
Getting short of breath
Can not feel a thing
My mind closing
Door slams
All alone
Myself.

Elaine Hoskinson
MIKE
I had a talk with God last night
Before I went to bed,
I told him how it hurt so much
Because my Mike was Dead.

He said, "My child don't be so sad
I needed him up here . . .
I'll keep him safe and free from pain,
By the way . . . did you know he liked Beer?"

I smiled then answered . . . "Yes, I knew
And God, it tastes so bad."
I felt that God was smiling . . . and
I tingled on my insides.

Even in Death . . . Mike was gonna be Mike.
Then I asked, "GOD, are you sure you're ready for this?"
He answered me so softly, I almost couldn't hear,
"Elaine, I love him . . . love him, don't laugh . . . I like the beer!"

Theodore J Warren Jr
LIGHT IS
Light is the luminous lamp of night,
is the flower in bright array,
is the shade and tone of nature,
is a painting on display.

Light is a stream of glorious beauty,
is the night hid from our eyes,
is the cloud in azure blue wonder,
is the eagle gliding in the skies.

Light is a miracle of splendor,
is a melody married in song,
is energy poetic in motion,
is man's vision of right over wrong.

Light is the glow in lovelit eyes,
is the fire in hearth, heart, and home,
is the joy in children's laughter,
is the moonlight on surf and foam.

Light is the source of enlightened life,
is the warmth and grace of friendship's gift,
is the star that spins our destiny,
is the glow that gives us lift.

Light is an everlasting hope,
is our measure of the soul's delight,
is the pattern of all rich tapestries,
is the spirit's return to flight.

Harrison W Strain
NIGHT STORM
a threatening flash of fire
streaks violently
across the starless heavens
of an ominous ebony sky.

trembling wide-eyed children
lips quivering fearfully
as tender raindrops
fall only from their eyes.

huddled tightly together
in creepy shadowy corners
hiding from the anger
dangerously bashing the door.

fleeting sounds of lonely whimpers
echo meekly through the night
as an appetite of terror lurks
seeking to quench a thirst for more.

Jean Truer Drope
PARALLELS

To my husband C.P., my daughter Gail, my son Terry

Beaten by the winds of time,
elements, not always harsh;
Never truly defeated, Nay—as a man who never discovers
He was once a boy, daring to dream.

Thus, is the sea, the lake, the pond,
who never recalls its birth,
As it roars, rages, reaching frantically upward and will
Not recall its beginning, as a casual tiny stream.

It now lies quietly dreaming,
reflective as a sycamore mirrors
Itself in its slender frame, in the calmness of its
Marble like surface below.
Quiet, now. No longer the baptizing torrential rage,
In anger—reflecting nothing that I know.

So too is life, delighting only in far fetched memories, so often
A chore, just recalling.
The ravages of time have moved on slowly, a gossamer tell tale sign,
Leaving its trace of aging, unwelcome, but used as a time to
Reflect and sigh.
It is benign—a state—a standard—as the dust overwhelms, consumes
And the matter's conclusion draws nigh.

Brenda Wilquet
MEMORIES IN MY MIND

To Mike, who will always have a special place in my heart.

My life used to be a lot of crying,
I started feeling pain inside like I was dying.
Then I met you,
And before I knew it you erased all my blues.
I sometimes look back and wonder
how I could ever stand,
Without your reassuring hand,
My dreams of being loved are all coming true,
It's all happened since I met you.
The look of tenderness in your eyes,
has made me come to realize;
No love for each other ever dies,
In the past people were always trying to change me,
But here you are loving me for what I am . . . ME!
You have taught me that love is patient and kind,
Jealousy and selfishness you never find.
I know someday you will go away,
But you will leave behind special memories;
Like pictures in my mind.

Shirley A Brown
IF YOU WRAP UP EACH WORRY IN A SMILE OR A LAUGH
If you wrap up each worry in a smile or a laugh,
You'll give your whole soul a much needed bath.
A little laugh a little smile,
A little twinkle in the sky.
All these things we forget to see,
But we say they mean so much to thee.
Just look around at the little things and see,
How much more life can really bring.
So take your time and slow your pace,
And stop trying to outrun the human race.

Edna M Crunelle
I KEEP ASKING
Will you ever be mine?
Will it be for all time?
Will our love be lasting?
I feel I must keep asking!
'Cause when you're not here
I feel so unsure;
for my time may end
and i'm afraid i'll never see you again.
So I feel I must keep asking;
will our love be lasting!
Will it be for all time?
And will you ever be mine?

Gwen Parker
TEARS AND DEATH
Sterile voices. Tired tears.
As footsteps pass on linoleum floors,
stop, and then continue,
My mother's hand is warm and tight, and clutching.
The room is in darkness but for a lamp near the bed.
A small body is in that bed, curled like a child.
I hear rattling tubes and ragged breathing.
Tears slide down cheeks and tickle as they drop off.
Wet, sticky eyelashes flutter over a painful expression.
In bottled whispers, mumbled words, love is found in here.
Gentle, cool air blows in from the open window,
Where sounds of passing cars can still be heard.
There is life outside, and death in here.

Tommie H Odom
I HAVE A FRIEND

This poem is dedicated to my loving children Kendra and Shemeka whom I love so much. To Mama Ida, Eardean and Mrs. Lille a gift from God to stand by me. Last but not all to Mr. King, and Brandy my foundation.

I have a friend and his name is Jesus.
He woke me up this morning and sent me on my way,
He gave me a reason to face a brand new day.

He's there when I call him
He's there when I want.
He's there when I need him
And he's there when I don't.

Yes my friend is Jesus,
And he will stand by me to the end.

Trisha M El-Sharkawy

Trisha M El-Sharkawy
FATE BY DEFAULT
Here we are
Caught up in a game of fire and ice.
The world, it moves on and on
And we stand somewhat empty,
Unsure if we can pay the price to ride . . .
We try to hide.
We put trembling hands
In empty pockets,
Waiting for "the waiting"
To decide.

Art Cano
A CHILD IS BORN
Wonder of wonders when first a child is born
A new glow and pride will now my life adorn
That new life, now cradled at his mother's breast,
a little being which now puts me to the test.
What is this feeling that wells from deep inside,
a joy so sweet and warmth that I could never hide.

Can it be that the test of my worth is truly now at hand,
can it be that today I've truly become a man.
Ah! the plans I have for him for the goals that he should reach!
What path to follow? What skills to him, I'll teach?
Should I in life be there to guide his every step?
No! I should be close, but he must his own direction set.

For I now remember that the goals my father for me selected,
are not the goals nor the path that I elected!
So in time, like my father, I must only encouragement lend.
My wants for his life's journey will not matter in the end.
And when thru his own life, I wish to be reborn,
God give me the wisdom to step aside and let him live his own.

Lee Karasseferian
ON BECOMING AN AUNT
A cloud drifted by my window last night
and a wee little, angel, with harp clutched tight,
peeked in at me so wistfully and said,
"You must be my Aunt Lee!
I've been on this cloud since early morn
just sitting here waiting to be born.
I'm awfully hungry and my didie's wet
and some "bird" just told me I'm not expected yet!
The distributing angel got things all confused
and it's plain to see that I'm not amused!
So maybe, Aunt Lee, as a favor to me
you can talk to the Doc and ask that he
move the schedule ahead just a day or two
and get me down there with the rest of you.
A bottle of milk and a quick change of clothes
would make me feel comfy clear down to my toes.
And yes—I'll admit it—it's certainly true,
I'm every bit as excited as you,
to discover what gender I'm going to be—
a masculine "he" or a feminine "she"!!

Milford Stephens
GUN CONTROL?!?

I would like to dedicate this poem to the children and their families that were shot and wounded in Ca. Also, my wife and family and friends that put up with me and have for all these years, most especially God who supplies the talent.

Gun Control Is It Necessary In This World Below;
Could It Prevent These Grisly Murders We All Know?
Let's Really Think And Consider What Would Happen;
Is This The Only Means Of Killing, Why And When?

What Other Gruesome Avenue Could I Take;
When Considering Murder, A Life To Rake?
Poison Like Jonestown, Or Maybe A Knife;
Any Object Sharp Or Dull, Mental Anguish Or Strife!
Leave A Proven Trouble-Maker Free To Roam;
One Not Caring For Society, Not Caring For Home.
You May Say What Right Gives Man To Judgement;
But I Say Why Kill Innocent, Self-Feelings To Vent!
Man Needs Guidelines And Laws To Keep Him Straight;
Discipline Can Be Gruesome, Yet It Carries Weight.
Creating Respect Of Authority And Fellow Man;
Strengthening Self-Attitude A Simple God-Like Plan.
Is An Ounce of Prevention Still Worth A Pound Of Cure?
Is Life Always Roses Should I Expect Excitement Or Bore?
Don't You Think Freedom's At Jeopardy, If Discipline's Let Loose;
Along With Moral Decline . . . To Really Cook The Goose?
The Goose Being You And I, Our Families Too;
Can We Really See This Display, Or Are Our Priorities Askew?
Death Isn't Right, But Where To Draw The Line;
Can We Afford The Taxes Death-Row To Refine?
All These Things Considered, You Try To Decide;
Is Gun Control The Answer, Or Just Lawful Self-Pride?

Dan Guidi
SHE'S GONE
She touched me
Then she left me
She changed my life
Now she's gone

She made me live again
Made me feel like a
Man again
Now she's gone

I wish I could
Turn back the hands of the clock
So I could change the things
That went amok

But it's too late now
'Cause she's gone
She was the best thing
That ever happened to me
Now she's gone

I love her so
But I let her go
Now she's gone

Deana D'Aguino
I KNOW MY LOVE FOR YOU WAS MEANT TO BE

I dedicate it to all my friends who helped me this year. I will never forget you guys.

I know my love for you was meant to be,
but all you did was hurt me.
I never loved anyone else like I loved you,
but now what am I supposed to do.
I know you'll be going out with someone else very soon,
but who's to say I might be going out with someone by June.
You had probably thought that I didn't trust you at all,
but what am I supposed to do when I see you staring at her down the hall.
When we started going out I thought it was great,
but at the end you just used me as bait.
I don't understand what went wrong,
I thought we were made for each other,
And when I started going out with you I
knew there was no other.
And now you have no love for me,
like I had for you,
and knowing you won't be there for me,
but I'll always be there for you.
I hope you find someone who feels the same way like I do.

Mary Ann Williamson
ENDLESS GIFTS
I don't have a lot to give,
It takes most of what I make to live.
But there is one thing I like to share,
I can give a smile anywhere.
It's a gift I can't really give away.
I smiled at lots of folks today,
As I smiled and gave a friendly "Hi"—
Both were returned as they passed by.
So I can't run out of smiles, you see,
The smile I just gave you was given to me.

Kathy L Bracisco
BREAKING CHAINS
Don't hold me slave to your needs
I've my own, just as easily.
Sometimes I cry, trying to break free;
To give me more strength; not because I'm weak.

For children taught to fit society's mold
The guidelines and rules are centuries old.
There is a reason for me here:
Could I be yet another pioneer?

A woman's goals; more commonly a man's
Take no special change in plans.
Get used to seeing her there:
She's not taking your place, just trying to share.

If you're one who desires traditional ways,
Then you may not understand what I'm trying to say:
Unless you give her room to try her wings,
A woman with unused potential can be a dangerous thing.

Vickie Simoneau
WHEN???

To my wonderful Dad! Whom I won't ever forget, I love you!

When I was just a young lad, I used to go fishing with my dad!
And go hunting in the hills, just to try our different skills.
Of course it was a lot of fun shooting my dad's favorite gun.
We always laughed together, always caring for the other.
But then one day my father, up and passed away.
Why did he die so fast, why couldn't life just last, and last.
I miss my dad, and all the fun times that we had.
But when I go back, and try to remember
All of the times we had spent together
There really wasn't such a time, that I could look for, or find.
Why did he go? and leave me so.
With no one to care it really wasn't fair.
So I'm telling you right now, enjoy the fun times anyway you know now!
Live up to the date!
Because soon it may be too late . . .

Marguerite I Sutton
ANGEL VOICES
Angel voices heard from on high
Floated down and filled the sky.
Gloriously the Angels did sing
Telling shepherds of a new King,

Bringing to earth a new found joy,
The glory of the new born Boy—
Heavenly joy that has no ending—
For mankind a new beginning.

Ellen Nielsen

Ellen Nielsen
STEPPING STONES
If I could build a bridge
That everyone must cross
And call this bridge
"The road from bad to good"
If I could build a ladder
As high as it must go
To climb away from sorrows
If we could.

If I could take the aches
and pains
Of every human heart
And place instead the joy
That each one needs
I would never ever need
to wish
For foolish things that
pass
Just reap the harvest
blessings
Of good deeds.

Catherine L Unislawski
A TIME TO CHANGE
One winter's day not long ago,
I looked out the window and at the snow,
And I began to think
Of how good life could be
For someone like me
If I would only change.

Change how I act and feel and think
I'm sure this would push me back from the brink
Of a life that is lonely and boring and dull
To one that is lively, exciting and full.

I'm ready to try and this is for sure,
And I know there is no overnight cure.
I know I can do it and change what I've been
With the love and support of family and friends.

I know what I want deep down in my heart.
Now is the time for me to start
On the road to changing what I now see
And into the person that I want to be.

Cheryl Derby
DRIFTER
The sky is blue with clouds
They want to miss you but they have forgotten how
Each whiteness blows away but one more moves
in until the day becomes
a clock of clouds
and each minute is time for floating
The day stops above my head.
I've gotten lost up there
The clouds are so close without you
I pull them all around me.

Martha M Maichele
GOING ON SEVEN

To my granddaughter, Lindsay

Gram I'm going to be seven years old.
Oh, no, so soon.
Not yet, be six awhile longer.
Oh no, I want to be seven!
The joyful excitement, and wouldn't know
She turned to me, "Gram, were you
ever seven?"

Jayne Cavanagh
WEAR THE POPPIES

To my mom, who stuck by me when I was a brat.

On Remembrance Day
With our shirts spotted red
We wear the poppies
To remember the dead.

There are some people
Who remember the war
But others, like me,
Just know what it was for.

For freedom of speech
And all sorts of rights
This is the reason
We put up a fight.

So, on Remembrance Day
With our shirts spotted red
Wear a poppy
And remember the dead.

Gloria Gail Harris
THE SCREEN
What is all this fuss I see
on my Mom and Dad's T.V.—
Are they wondering what to do?

Did they say it wasn't true?
And what's that picture that I see?
Do they know that it scared me?
All the noise, and all the clatter
Surely something is the matter!
Oh, I wish that I could know
if that is real, or just a show?
Just a picture on T.V.
Not the way the world must be
Not the world I want to know
Tell me, Daddy, is it so?
Tell me, is it safe to grow?
Was that real? Say yes, or no!
Say that what was on T.V.
has nothing much to do with me—
Tell me what I need to know
to learn, to love, to be, to grow

Kimberly Christofferson
THE TWO OF ME
The two of me,
We linger here in this single body
sparring every chance that becomes available.

Social grace with a smiling face
impregnates my mind like lightning,
And the need for a shining public
image debases my soul's interiors.

But why expect me to converse
happily when disease infests my sanity,
And obvious discontent slips into my
every word and motion?
I can't live up to that consummate
image conjured up by societal ladies
and men with their pinkies pointed upward!

A raging scream builds up inside me.
But it never gets the chance to echo
through the room.
Because these smiling teeth that have
been allotted me
Keep up the pretense
And satirize my existence.

Imogene Wells Kidder
SAY IT WITH LOVE
Say it with love
Show that you care
And you'll find acceptance
Almost any where
Because most of all
What this world needs
Is love and compassion
In our words and deeds.

If you haven't tried it
Begin right away
To brighten the corner
Where you are today.
Love is contagious,
Love quickly grows,
And happiness follows
Where our love goes.

margaret wilkinson
HOLD ON

With love, to Joan Wilkinson and the late Donald Wilkinson, my parents

Our love will take us far,
It will carry us to mountain tops,
It will carry us to ocean floors,
Thru clouds and coral,
We will fly,
We have found the ultimate,
The hope and joy of forever,
Love is strong,
But can it hold us?
Can it carry us?
The beginning of love is strong,
So, yes, it will,
But it will weaken,
It might even diminish,
But now it is strong,
So we must hold on,
And if it should weaken,
Then we'll loosen our grip,
So love can strengthen itself again,
Maybe it will have no room for us,
Then our time has ended,
But for now,
We hold on.

Charles S Cadogan Sr
REMEMBERING
Do You remember when we first met?
You smiled at me, a smile I'll
never forget.
You said "Hi There!"
Your voice sounded, oh! so sweet,
Like music from violins.
We reached out and touched
each other's hands
oh so tenderly.
In that moment I became as light
as a feather
caught in a summer's breeze.
My heart stopped crying, my mind
was at ease
When I saw that look of
pleasure on your face.
We reached out for each other
and ended in a warm embrace.
We kissed each other with
passion that set my lips on fire
And my body with warm desire.
We spoke words of love to each other
Oh so enchanting
Do You Remember?

Daniel Bergelt
RUN FREE

To my son Daniel my inspiration

Gather flowers in the spring and wear them in your hair. Wash away the impurities of life with the clear cool water from a mountain spring.
Free your mind of worry while watching a full moon settling on a calm blue ocean. Release your frustrations thru the thunderous rage of a rushing river.
Draw the rays of the sun inside you searching your soul for wisdom. Let the fall leaves mark each change in your life as well as the change in season. Shelter yourself from the winter's cold finding warmth thru love and friendship.
Let the autumn winds bring you peace of mind with thoughts pure as a child unexposed to life's grief.
Run free my precious one never freeing me from your heart
as I run free never freeing you from mine.

Netto A Paul
COUSIN COYOTE

To my son—Chapaneco A. Paul

You run swift—they want to know you.
Some say you always hide, others want to take you for another ride.
Jump the fence, take the money, kiss her Adios, laugh a little, what's so funny?
Where you living?
Under a tree—on a truck, in a teepee or a shack?
Cousin to the dogs down South across the border, and cousin to the Lobos up North in the Rocky White Mountains.
You are a breed— a XO-LO-IN-DIO.
Half dog and half lobo. From the city and from the country.
Why are you moving along?
Anything wrong?
Are you happy?— Hungry?
Or are you in the City, in disguise trying to learn another way of life.
Is it easy—? are you strong?
Healthy? Angry?
At night—when the Moon is bright . . . I smoke my pipe, and
I hear you sing in the distance . . .
another one of your songs, in the silence of the Moonlight.

Jude Brian Ylanan

Jude Brian Ylanan
OF HEART AND SOUL

To Ben Johnson, Mike Tyson, Ferdinand Marcos, and Jimmy Swaggart, in this order.

They say, the BODY is the physique
The being's completion—the lyric.
One's mindless care is a hectic
Entity might as well be historic!

They say, the HEART is the emotion
The center of one's pulsation.
When one loses one's attraction,
you'll end up with conviction!

They say, the BRAIN is the mental
Intelligence is the central.
Knowledge when prodigal,
you're a horse in a corral!

They say, the SOUL is the being
Identity is the bearing.
False love and power—a 'smearing'
You'll find yourself repenting!

V S Alexander
MONA
Her heart is crying with tunes of masochistic symphony
Punishing itself with tyrannical methods of self-degradation.
Sighing through the night,
increasingly inflicting
More doses of sadness through already damaged soul
Of self-pity and caprice.
Then, in a flash, when some note or tune like a golden ray
Sparks fusion of tenderness and sorrow at the same time;
Heart trembles, releasing tender silver flames.
Forgetting everything. Feeling only love of yesterdays glories.
The thighs become limp, the nipples like hills.
Hard liquidy blood begins to rise.
Mouth soft, lips swollen. Brain releasing juices.
Hallucinations take over where hatred was ruling.
Then she remembers that her arms are empty.
The strong illusion of his body not in view.
She becomes angry, squeezing snow-white liquid
From Venus-like golden, magnificent breasts.

Ted W Roberts
SPARE CHANGE
Living on the streets.
Wandering without direction,
Dingy sights and horrible smells,
Searching for answers
Finding shelter in yesterday's news,
Cold winds tear through tattered clothes.
Is this life?

Surviving on hope.
Dreaming for deliverance,
Trash becomes treasure.
Feeding on the crumbs of mainstream society,
Souls cry out.
Anguish echoed in the screams.
Got any spare change?

Helen Kelsey Morgan
FOR MY VALENTINE

To my forever valentine, My husband Rusty.

One special day of every year,
If we're together or apart,
We praise our sweethearts far and near,
To tell them what is in our heart.

If you were here with me my love,
Enfolded in a fond embrace,
And we could walk 'neath stars above,
The lonely hours we could erase.

We'd share each moment, one by one,
And wake each morning with a kiss,
Then slip away when day was done,
To spend each night of quiet bliss.

I'd watch you sweetheart, as you sleep,
My eye would trace each tiny line,
And then within your arms I'd creep,
Your picture etched into my mind.

Your laughing eyes that sparkle bright,
And mirror all the love inside,
Your arms that hold me, oh so tight,
With me these memories still abide.

They carry me each hour, each day,
As night time falls, they fill my dreams,
For our love, went all the way,
To see us through life's worst it seems.

I hold you close, in mind and heart,
My treasured memories there within,
For you are there and I am here,
Till we can be as one again.

David D DeGraff Jr
FOR YOU

Ask her no questions, she will tell you no lies, Another lesson of love well learned.

Is my love for you so hard to understand
I have even asked you for your hand.
For you I will tackle the world, to keep you safe.
Share a tender kiss and a warm embrace
With my hands, build you that big large home
Create memories, to remember when we are grey and old
Talk to you late at night, when you need a friend
Take all your worries and shoulder them
Enjoy the laughter, even if our world seems so crazy
Sometimes sitting in front of the fire being totally lazy
Each waking moment you're on my mind
Minutes seem like hours when you're not by my side
For you, all this will drift like smoke in the wind
I will have to let you leave me again
Because your happiness is so dear to me
Maybe this is the way it was supposed to be.

Donna M Bender
A ROSE

To Beth Caswell; Shellee Martin; Kristy Harper, friends, who helped and encouraged me. Thanks.

Beneath the snow lies a rose and
With the comin' of spring
Like a child wakin' from sleep
Within her room; the rose will bloom
Along with its lesser sisters
Owing to the sun its life
Until the day that it will lie
Beneath the snow once again.

Lydia R Averett
HOW CAN THIS BE

Dedicated to Norvin Kennedy Averett, Jr.

I'm in you're out
How can this be?

I cannot see the sun or moon
How can this be?

I want to feel the breeze
For I know it can and must be.

The Eagle tells me of the
Freedom I long for.
How can this be?

It can and must be.

Danielle Szymchack
TRUE BEAUTY

For: Eugene, Nikki, Mom and Michael. I love you all.

The pretty butterflies, which flutter so carelessly above our heads;
Were once ugly bugs, from which everyone turned away.

Beauty counts far too much in this world today;
Forcing all us normal people to bow our heads in dismay.

I, have seen true beauty,
—true beauty from the soul;
It does not matter what face you have,
Just have,
—a beautiful soul.

Ronald J Stedman
UNDER THE VAIL

Ashes fall on yesterday's hurts and dreams
How can I continue on this way
Walking blind without a hand to hold
Deserting feelings in the fantasy of fear
No disguising my heart from myself
Surely seeking a new path untried
All the while frightened, a new feeling inside
Her taste is cold and bittersweet
Finding her door ajar I hide
Crazy, I never really cried
My fate floats along in an empty bottle
Early morning mist clouds its message inside
But I see her eyes through the vail
Tearing the madness of my mind
Useless to fight the tide so high
Time to embrace my bride at last
Lifting the vail I loose the night
Lost to my bride; my bride called death
She's come to take me home
She's come to make me weep
She's come to let me sleep . . .
. . . And by her side I'll dream deep.

Roberta Mae Stevens

Roberta Mae Stevens
THE GAME

To my love that never was; as playful as childhood, as exciting as fantasy, as illusive as a dream. To my always friend.

The hand's been dealt,
Just two cards left to play.
The game of life is almost over.
The lady and her lover are the losers.
Luck may come and luck may go—she's fickle as we both know.

The game's been dealt
Let's play it to the bitter end.
The mysteries of love and life
Unfolding as the game progresses.

Luck may come and luck may go—she's fickle as we both know.

A smile, a bluff, a little lie;
All is fair, the games go on before our eyes.
The hurt, the pain, the bittersweet goodbyes.
The empty, lonely longing for the game.

Luck may come and luck may go—she's fickle as we both know.

The game is over!
No winner jumps with joyous cry.
The game's been lost, the aces all ran dry.
She retreats to old familiar dreams
He goes looking for another heart to master.
They both are left with the empty, lonely, longing for the game.

Luck may come and luck may go—she's fickle as we both know.

Barbara Bettis
WHY?

To all my children, Joseph, Dawna, Dean, Shawn, Shane and Shannon. This one's for you, with all my love, Mom.

Why?

This child, big yet small, approached me today with a question to beat all . . .
I could see by the look in his eyes that he expected an answer in detailing truth, something simple just wouldn't do . . . the expression on his face was stern and strong as he questioned what he had to know . . .
War, he blurted out, why do people make war against people, people like you and me?
Aren't we all the same, God's creatures and all, so why then do we fight and fight and die when we fall?
Please tell me why, I have to know, so when I grow up I'll know why I'm going to die!
The words he spoke, so big for a child, left me gaping in amazement that his confusion and fears be so great . . .
What has this child seen or heard to prompt such questions and fears, this child of so few years?
Realizing my explanation had to be worded just right, knowing this child's outlook on life was at stake . . . silently searching my mind for an answer of my own, I took a deep breath and slowly sighed returning his question . . .
Why?

Laura Michelle Osburn
FOUND

The snow blankets the Earth
like a beautiful white paint,
The birds are gone or hiding
and the sound is faint.

The wind speaks, but only to whistle
and the trees are bare.
It seems like nothing on this earth
Dares to move a hair.

The trees as they blow
speak a soft murmur,
The clouds as they move
They leave a soft glimmer.

Everything is quiet
on this white land.
The land is so beautiful
like the finest white sand.

Occasionally something will move,
or even make a sound.
But then things are normal,
It's like they're waiting to be found.

Feliza Maggay
THE FIRST TIME

Someday I will find myself, and will you help me look? I remember the perfume you gave me on our first Valentine's Day together; I've never seen it since then. Was it stolen or did I toss it aside subconsciously after our argument? The candy was gone; I ate it all by myself. And I never even recall wearing the perfume. One day I cleaned out my closet and decided to throw away that plastic heart box which held the candy.

Theresa J Lacey
MEMORIES OF JULY 4TH: NORRIS, TENNESSEE

the Commons full of children
playing and having bicycle wrecks

Norris Day activities
speeches and prizes of windshield cleaning solvent

the street dance
no one out there
through the waltzes
through the rock
through the country western
until the hokey-pokey and then

everybody dances, kicking up dust
under the streetlights

they play the bunny-hop;
more dust and more sweat
young faces and old faces smiling

fireworks and
our dog
trying to dig to China through our laps

walking home in semi-darkness
the finale of the fireworks lighting our way

dog is only too happy it is over.

Happy Birthday, U.S.A.

Mark D Tyler

Mark D Tyler
PORTRAIT IN FLESH

He created her.
Willed her to stand there motionless
as the car that he created
sped down the street that they both knew.
And as the car relentlessly approached him,
he stood there in the middle of the street,
(He knew it would look spectacular).

The music, which had been building
to a deafening crescendo,
stopped abruptly as the car ran him down.
(Focus on the white shirt turning blood red).
At that instant, everything stopped.

The car is now permanently
embedded in his midsection.
The pool of blood in the street
no longer spreads,
and her face is a frozen mask
of horror and disbelief.
(Isn't it neat?)

The artist sits back to regard his work.
Lights a cigarette and sighs

contentedly.
This one would just do.
This latest portrait in flesh.

T R Dickens
INSPIRED TO WRITE
Though I feel inspired to write
I don't know what to say
Nor can I explain
Why I feel this way

Why do I desperately feel the need
To write what I don't know
When words seldom stay with me
They always come and go

Who or what is behind this
This pushing of my mind
To write these words on paper
To fill these empty lines

None of these questions can I answer
I haven't got a clue
Ahh, but maybe, just maybe
I'm inspired to write because of you

Fran Zimmerman
WHAT AMERICA MEANS TO ME
Immigrants came here for a new start,
Leaving their homeland with a heavy heart.
Greeted by the Statue of Liberty,
They were now in the land of opportunity.

They crossed the mountains to the West,
Searching for gold, they did invest.
There were many barriers in their way,
As they settled in the U.S.A.

These founding fathers had a plan,
For preserving this great land.
In 1787, a constitution was written for you and me,
Granting us our Freedom and Liberty.

A flag of red, white, and blue they gave,
Our Star Spangled Banner, long may it wave.
It took much courage and strength to endure,
The many things of which they were so unsure.

We have the freedom to select and chose,
Preserving this freedom we must never lose.
America means so much you see,
No one could be prouder of her than me.

Kathy L Mocny
IMAGES
Another golden leaf flutters to the ground.
I'm more than living:
The wines, rusts, and flaming reds
Add color and depth to my soul.
I'm feeling.
But soon even that will be gone
And a cold, empty winter will prevail.
Believe in me!
For the waiting is long, even for one as patient as I;
And with a breath of your warm, autumn wind
You could easily blow me away.
If a child, you could take me in your hands
(A colored and crumpled leaf)
And treat me tenderly.
Preserve it—
Its essence and value at this moment will never come again.

Still,
With the love of Springtime a newness will come,
And it seems to endure forever . . .
To swell up and fill me,
As now.

Theodore J Calcaterra
JOEY
There he sat hopefull,
not so long ago
His small hands, feet, fingers, and toes.
He knew, even then, how to communicate
his pleasures, his pains.
We comforted him when he was frightened,
And we rejoiced with him
when he was happy again.
He said my name first, except his father's and his mother's—
I have no remorse
I was there for his first awkward step,
Toward me the little child
crept.
So proud he charged hands and arms opened wide,
He wrapped innocence around
my neck with God's warmth
inside.
He runs to me now and calls my name.
He loves me, he hugs me,
and I do the same.
As long as the world turns
and the sun rises and sets,
I will always love him because he is my baby brother
the only, the best.

M Elizabeth Smith
TEN DOLLAR PALS & GOLDEN FRIENDS

Dedicated to my parents and the best friend I will ever have, Catherine

To number all the friends I've had
and gaze upon their faces,
Would be just like the good ole days
of home and other places.
The things I've seen with friends, I
have their memory in my heart
Inside me now and all the time,
never shall we part.

Tomorrow as I move ahead the road
that waits for me,
I pass by glens and meadows
watching birds and bumblebees.
I've lost my way, but now I can
continue on with life,
My journey takes me through the
door that leads to pain and strife.

My suffering, was it all worthwhile?
though dealt from caring hands,
Has taught me how to lose and grow
and still remain to stand.
My friend, I hope to love you long,
but take me when I die,
Into your heart and mind and soul
but please don't say goodbye!

Spencer E Howard Jr
REALITY OF LIFE

Thanks to Almighty God, for giving me the talent. To my Mom and Dad, I thank you for being there. And to my friend Terry; keep reachin' for the stars.

Time has passed, the days have slipped
intelligence varies news a trip
A voice cries out, surrounded by doubt,
Mastercard still reigns enforced by clout.
We search and seek instilled to find
that those who see are really blind;
to the ways of this world
whether it be man, woman, kid or just plain old boy or girl.

Technology rises to reach its peak
where personalities and attitudes really speak.
Ignorance and nonsense combine as one
but, those with insight know the battle just begun,
they play mindgames with intent to mold your very essence,
until you get old. You served their purpose; no more use,
physical attraction gone like an out of luck sucker who's fitted for a noose.

Reality steps in, you're reduced to shame,
No turning back you've lost the game.
Dignity fades, confidence broken
in the wax of emotional pity while
your heart and feelings are smokin'.
Over and over it sticks in your mind,
but those who survive this trauma,
are one of a kind;
of person because they now can cope;
as they climb life's ladder so beams
the light of hope.

Berta Hoedel
THE SILENT HARP SEAL

This poem is dedicated to Greenpeace for their successful efforts in saving the harp seal.

I see you lying with a tear in your eye
In the deep white snow so vivid
You look as though you're going to cry
With your white and blue coat exquisite
Your flapping tail, your flapping feet
You lie there waiting
For the dark dungeon of defeat

Who allows this to happen?
Who wants to make empty your life?
Is it fair you must die for our wants?
Is it I who must stop this destruction?

I see myself watching over you
Stopping the club that will kill you
The spray paint, which will defeat them who kill you

I hope to see you happy with pleasure
Snow white as white could be
I hope to see the miles of your measure
Along with little babies to feed

Darlene Greenfeld-Kravetz
THE OCEAN AND YOU

To my beloved husband, Steven M. Kravetz

Strange the way you move in, and out of my life on a time cycle.
You come in very close, linger for an evening,
and share your treasure with me.
By morning you recede away from me but always
leave bits of yourself behind.
A cigarette half smoked, stray hairs from your head or chest, your scent on my pillow.

The ocean's tide and you have much in common.
The tide always comes into shore at evening,
lingers over the sandy beach, sharing its treasure.
By morning the waves recede, and always you will
find bits of shells, and dollars, and seaweed it leaves behind.

Marcell E Bellfield Jr
THE DREAMER

This poem is dedicated to my lovely family BeBe, Autumn, and Marcell III. "May all your dreams come true."

I've been called a dreamer
My goals are considered high
Since I'm called a dreamer
My life is called a lie

Can't I dream of better days
And hope for all the world
And pray for big, bright futures
For every boy and girl

Is it wrong to dream of peace
To spread love across the land
Is it wrong to fear no evil
To have justice we all understand

If a dream is called an illusion
And somehow we all survive
Then we need more dreamers
To keep the illusion alive

Denise Silvestro
WHEN YOU HOLD BACK YOUR ANGER . . .
An oncoming storm—
Clouds and fog
Shroud me,
Suffocating,
Forcing me to swallow
Thick smog
Waste that winds about my head.

I wait for the torrents,
Anticipating the slapping on my face,
The biting sting of cold water as it pelts
Then drips from a wound.

I wait, anxious, for the lightning
A jagged tear that creates a gape
Threatening to swallow me whole.

And the thunder—
That rattles in my head—my whole body—
That, trapped within me
Slams against my stomach—

Frightens me the most.

I wait in this darkness
Straining my eyes upward.
My shoulders pushed into my body,
Pressing me into the ground.

A drop of water drips down my face.
Used air pushes out of my chest.
I sit on the floor
And cry.

Arturo Taylor
THE WAYS OF LOVE

To my grandmother Maureen

I didn't know that your face would be different in sleep or that your arms would lock around me for all of the night and only hold tighter if I tried to move away.

I didn't know, on the nights you were asleep before I came to our bed, that the slightest whisper or a touch against the sheets would awaken you and your arms would reach out for me.

I didn't know that during the early dawn, when I moved against you half asleep, that I would hear you whisper "I love you."

I couldn't have imagined how it would feel to wake to your gentle touch brushing, the hair from my eyes so you could kiss my cheek, My darling I just didn't know that there are more ways than one to be loved.

Regina Denise Ott
HEART'S DESIRE
I sit by the fire.
The logs burn, and the cat meows,
Everything waiting for its own desire.

The ripple of pages in my book,
While the room grows darker,
I want to look.

My soul is longing to be seen
But I can't find the key.
What does it mean?

Then I realize love is like a road
Being driven over time and time again
Something I've often been told.

A knock at the door,
Shall I answer it?
Probably a salesman from a store.

It opens up slowly.
His eyes set off a quizzical gleam.
He is strong, made toughly.

I open my eyes.
The dream is over;
I suddenly realize love is full of lies.

Michelle L Liepelt
FROZEN IN TIME
Winter falls upon the ground covered with Autumn colors.

The air is chilled by the touch of Winter's fingers.

Silence surrounds my soul.
Numbness overcomes my body.

Frozen in time, I'm an ice sculpture silhouette.

The edges of my heart covered by frost.
The tears in my eyes freeze into icicles as they fall.

Frozen I stand amidst snow and ice, longing for the warmth of love to melt my soul.

Brought by the touch of sunshine.
Delivered by a kiss of spring dew.

Frozen tears melt at the sight of a rose freshened by dewdrops.
Frosted heart warmed by a love song of the early birds.

A burst of freedom overcomes my being.

Watch in amazement as my spirit flies the freedom flight.

Soaring through the bright blue skies, never again to be Frozen in Time.

Mary Liner
BLESS THE SMALL CHILDREN

For all their love and support, I dedicate this poem to my parents.

Bless the small children for they are the ones,
That grow up to be our fine daughters and sons.
They're born so helpless and innocent too.
We love them dearly—they know that we do.
If granted one wish, I'd know what it'd be—
That all the small children live happy and free
In a world with no anger, hunger or pain
And that none of their lives be lived in vain
So, let's join hands and work till the job is done—
Making this world a safer one
For all the small children near and far,
We love you all, just as you are.

Carolyn Dumas Smith
FRIENDS

This poem is dedicated to my children Ralphdel, Rochell, Eugene, Sitara, Kevin Smith and my husband Johnnie B.

A friend that cares and wants to share
You might see them anywhere.

They will come and they will go with much
respect they let it show.

The world is filled with many friends
and there are lots to go around.

Friends are there to listen when you need to talk.
They will go that extra step or maybe for a walk.

Friends will help you overcome the worst of time
when you feel things are going wrong.

They will sit with you, cry with you, even comfort you, they're closer than the phone.

Big friends, little friends, regardless what it takes,
There are lots of friends without a friend, there's no mistake.

My friend, your friend is a friend of a friend, when you are
in need for a friend, ask a friend about a friend.

I am a friend, see a friend, have a friend, share a friend,
so you be a friend.

Nicole Cornelisen
LOOKING INSIDE A TEAR
As I sit here alone my mind wanders.
My emotions challenging my thoughts,
I soon realize there's no competition.
My eyes swell with tears as I reminisce
Of your concise remarks, which,
For many quiet hours I sat in solitude
Searching but never finding the
True meaning behind them.
I've grown much older in a day
And found I thought I was
All I could never be.
I'm just another unfortunate individual,
Watching my dreams play with fire.
I don't understand,
I thought we had a perpetual relationship.
But your inadequate fidelity showed
Me you didn't really care.
Even though my love for you
Will linger unforgotten in my heart,
My life must go on without you.
How else to be learned but
Through a broken heart?

Paul D Smothermon
FROM THE FIRST TIME
Some friends you'd cry for
You I'd die for,
That's just how much I love you.
And as long as I live my love will be true.

You just don't know how much you mean to me.
I don't think I could go on living right
if I ever lost you.
From the first time I held your hand,
I knew we were meant to be.
I've never loved anyone as much as I love you.

From the first time we kissed, I knew our love was true.
I pray that we'll always be together.
And through the grace of God we'll have
the strength for our love to last forever.
And if you don't think I say it enough,
please remember that I'll always love you!

Bernice Reynolds (Bunny)

Bernice Reynolds (Bunny)
LOVE WILL STRUGGLE TO LIVE—TO GROW

To Howie, with love beyond self, always, your Bunny.

The little planter with the onion plant you gave me grew a center stem with a bloom and cluster of seeds at it's tip.

It grew, in that constrained small container, until this center stem reached the top of the window—at least three feet.

It then had to curve and bend down—not given enough room to grow, but continuing to do so—
WITH TOO LITTLE SOIL OR ROOM TO HAVE ALLOWED THIS TO BE.
GIVEN BY LOVE, ACCEPTED BY LOVE—
THROUGH ALL ADVERSITY—
LOVE WILL STRUGGLE TO LIVE—
TO GROW.

Bryon L Preminger
DREAMIN

To forgotten love, floating restlessly away

My nights are filled with vivid dreams
Magical and beautiful so it seems
Thoughts of you lying on the seashore
The night still, except for the oceans small roar.

As the sea air rustles through my hair
I hold you with a passion that is so rare
Then we make love beneath an endless sky
Hoping the night will never die.

But the sun always rises when I awake
My dreams of you it somehow takes
Now I long for the day my dreams will come true
And lying beside me will always be you.

Caroline Briere
YESTERDAY

For Melina

Yesterday, my troubles had gone away,
But today they have come back to haunt me,
And I am no longer carefree.
Holding on to a wisp of life,
I feel almost cut by a knife.
Given one more chance to prove my love,
I wish to fly away as a dove,
And see no more, the gore,
Of this sad, lonely world.

Karen Walters
WHY THE SKY IS BLUE
I don't suppose you happen to know
why the sky is blue?
It's because the snow,
Takes out the white.
That leaves it clean
For the trees and grass
to take out the green.
Then pears and bananas
start to mellow,
and bit by bit,
they take out the yellow.
The sunsets, of course,
take out the red,
And pour it into the ocean bed
or behind the mountains
in the west.
You take all that out
and the rest,
Couldn't be anything else but blue.
Look for yourself.
You can see it's true.

Kimberly Bradberry
MOTHERS HALL OF FAME

I dedicate this poem, to my wonderful mother Gail.

There ought to be a Mothers Hall of Fame
At the top of the list would be your name

The letters would be written big and bold
They would be like your heart that's made of gold.
Underneath your name would tell of all the special things you do.
How you've always been there for me without me asking you to.
It would tell of all the sacrifices you made for me
And all the hurt you went through but never let me see.
It would tell just how much you mean to me
And how much you taught me about the kind of person I'd like to be
And in my heart, at the top of the list will always be your name
Written in letters of Gold in the Mothers Hall of Fame.

Jenny Adams
FOREVER

To Cindy—who is the greatest friend anyone could ever have.

When you needed to cry,
I was always there, standing by.
You could always lean on me,
but now things aren't what they used to be.
You used to be my best friend,
now I know good things really end.
We have many good memories together,
but now our friendship is gone forever.
You'll always have a special place in my heart,
even though we're far apart.
I know at times you hated me,
I guess things just weren't meant to be.
We never talk anymore,
it's as if you walked out a door.
You closed it right in my face,
in your life, I never had a place.
So, good bye my friend,
and I thought our friendship would never end.

Regan Southard
THE BRIDGE

Down the road from us there is a house. Behind the house there is a bridge. It is very pretty back there. I usually go there in the fall. The robin sits on the branch of a tree over the bridge. I am on the bridge looking into the gurgling waters. As I look into the brook down at the bottom there is a fish. It is beautiful orange and yellow. Way off in the distance there is a very faint smell but strong enough to get a scent of the skunk cabbage. The leaves are floating on top of the water. They look like lily pads. You can hear a bullfrog croak, a mocking bird whistle, smell skunk cabbage, see a fish, or look into a brook if you come to my place.

Terry Daley
THE MIRACLE OF LIVING

Dedicated to: Vicki, Kristie, Eccole, Michelle, Reggie, Philip and My Parents and Family. I love them all and couldn't live without them.

We all go through changes day by day.
Some are joyful, some hurt in every way.
Yet we must face up to them, through the good and the bad,
We can't run away, whether they're happy or sad.
The future frightens me, though I'm comfortable with the past,
Week by week, day by day, it all goes so fast.
Yesterday was last year, and next year is tomorrow,
All the memories I hold of such happiness and some sorrow.
You have to enjoy your years, and whoever shares them with you,
Appreciate your friends, your family, and all the values you have too.
Keep in mind the love you receive and all the love you're giving.
You see my friend, It's a long bizarre cycle.
THE MIRACLE OF LIVING.

Anna Matheny
AN ANGEL

To my Family: All of you are great inspirations. Joshua's won this time, who's next?

I never saw an angel until I looked into your face
I never saw such beauty, such innocence or such grace
Your eyes sparkle like diamonds, twinkling like a glittering star
In color they could be green, or perhaps a blue sapphire
Your smile you give so quickly, in you love does abound
It is truly a pleasure for me to have you around.

Cheryl Gilson
A WARRIOR AT AN ENDLESS BATTLE

In memory of my inspiration: Donald Eugene Gilson

Strong and mighty full of pride
No emotions must show
I am his shield
Pain and sorrow touches me
Flowing through his mighty hand
Loved ones are his armor
Warmth and love surrounds him
Together we fight with honor and dignity
As the battle still goes on
The battle still goes on
The battle can not be won
For the warrior has not the answer
Or has he
He just hasn't looked within

Mel Ellis

Mel Ellis
LUNAR RADIATION?

This poem is dedicated to my parents, Cliff and Bev, for always being "there" for me.

I was bombarded with hype and no place to go,
Old John Wayne movie, or A.M. radio?
The three kids were fighting, the wife's pulling out her hair,
I stared out the window, a full moon was up there!
Bills were piled high on the table, several lights were out too.
I felt kind of queasy! (thought I was getting the flu.)
The kids needed haircuts, we all needed shoes,
The wife needed more make-up to cover her blues!
The house needed shingles and siding last fall,
And we were too broke to move, even though it was too small!

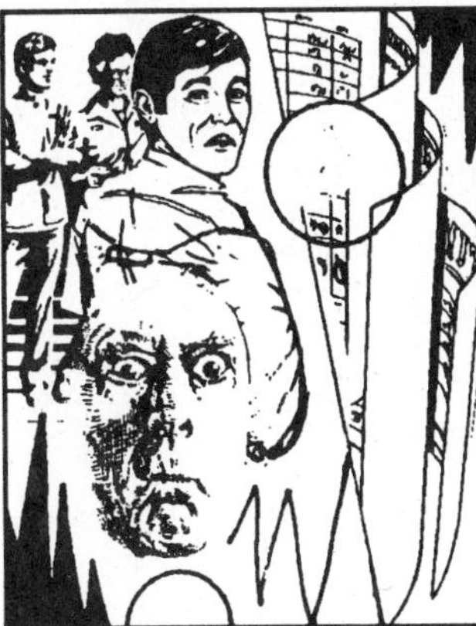

Our car was a junk-heap, my shed needed new paint,
But some kind of millionaire, the I.R.S. knows I ain't!
All those pressures kept mounting, (I felt I could scream,)
So I threw a chair through the window to let off some steam!
I started shaking and hissing, and howling real loud,
Outside on the street, I've drawn quite a crowd.
My children and wife stand in shock and dismay,
As some guys in white jackets come and haul me away!
Well I see lots of doctors, my diagnosis is I'm a "loon."
They blamed my condition on that night's full moon.
So after a few months, (they lengthened my stay),
I agreed with the doctors how I'd gotten this way.
I've thought it all over, now it's easy to see,
It must have been Lunar Radiation that had stricken me!
And sitting peacefully each day in this quiet, padded cell,
I wonder, should I tell the doctors that I've never had it so well!

Bryan McMurray
LIVING DEAD

He's just a rebel soldier
fighting to stay alive
he fears the enemy
down deep inside

He's been fighting
all thru the night
side stepping death
left to right

He tires, so he lays down to rest
he fought like hell
he gave it his best

The enemy surprised him
he panicked an ran
the enemy open fired
on the frightened young man
A bullet pierced his heart
his blood ran as he cried
the fear of death had found him
the young man laid there an died

He had a heart of gold
but it was turned to lead
his soul lives on
he's living dead.

Living dead
he had a heart of gold
Living dead
his blood ran cold

Living dead
he served his country well
Living dead
he gave the enemy hell

Living dead
he killed to survive
Living dead
he fought to stay alive

Living dead
his life is gone
Living dead
but his soul lives on

Kelley Leigh Hymes
IN FLIGHT

forever in flight
in search of grace and forgiveness
rising above the troubled waters
of this life
to the peaceful stillness
of a saner existence
beyond your knowing eyes
beyond your understanding
pain and fear seemingly banished
from my consciousness
security and certainty in their place
no longer in need of this wasteful flesh
housing my stormy soul
spirits denying physical reality
and human bondage
soaring safely in the caressing hands
of a higher truth

Anita Michelle McCluskey
IT'S POSSIBLE TO BE LOVED AGAIN . . .

Sometimes when you fall in love; it's the most beautiful feeling of all.

But when time come to fall out of love; it's like the rolling of a ball.

Your feelings are hurt, your head is spinning, and your life goes round and round.

Even though it's hard at first; you won't always wear a frown.

It's possible to be loved again; even if you can't tell.
But don't give up on yourself because then you'll feel like hell.

No matter how hard it hits you; your life is worth living.
But don't be so defensive; because everyone's worth forgiving.

So remember what I say; and let your life begin.
Because it's possible to fall in love again & again & again.

Kenneth E Corr
WHY DO I DO DRUGS

I dedicate this poem to my mother and father: Mr. and Mrs. Roland A. Corr, Your loving son, Kenneth E. Corr.

Why do I do drugs?
When I know I've been blessed
by the Lord up above.
To have a sound mind and infest it
with drugs is truly a crime

I have no excuse; just some dumb
rationale about my casual use.
Tick Tick Tick
All the time I've been wasting
Getting high off of drugs
They're destroying our nation.
We're all creatures of habit
Yes, we know that's a fact;
So it really is stupid to ever try crack.
Well, I hope you believe every word
that I say
Someone out there will tempt you
It just might be today.
When you're addicted and caught in
the drug vice
You would stand better chances in a
Mike Tyson fight.
Prayer, Love and Devotion:
The three things I think of that can
keep you from asking
Why do I do drugs?

Jeanita Pisachubbe
JEANI'S PRAYER

To Mom, just because I thought I always would.

Oh Wind! Blow through my soul,
and remove the doubt which
lies there.
Carry it away on wings of
iron and place it in the depths of
certainty to be enclosed and
destroyed, never to return
again.

Oh Rain! Pour down on my heart
and wash me of my self-pity.
Overcome it like the tide and
push it into the realm of self-
esteem, to be heard from no
more.

Oh Lightning! Strike my mind,
and cause the shadows
of negativity to shrink into a
corner.
Fill my mind with a new light
of inspiration, one that will
never grow dim.

Oh Thunder! Sound your
trumpets and force the fear
of new beginnings and new
failures from my thoughts.
Cause a peace to continually
flow through me.

Oh God! Allow these elements to
work with me in the future,
the future that has already
begun.

Neville G Weekes
BREAKING UP'S HARD TO DO

Dedicated to Jennifer. Fate, is something that everyone should respect, And in my case appreciate.

They said love was a sure thing, that
never would end
That as long as there's life, they'd
always be friends,
But someone stopped looking; a
blow from behind
Had changed all the reasoning that
true love was blind.
For she'd found a lover, and he'd
done the same,
They'd no need for each other; that
reason was lame
The pain was unbearable, but
heartaches weren't new
For somehow they found out,
breaking up's hard to do.

Good-byes aren't their favorite,
they'd leave anyway,
They'd start a new romance, and do
it their way.
But, somehow they'll never forget
what is past,
True love was their blanket, though
memories would last.
The love they once shared they'd be
missing, and yet
A new love was blooming from new
love they'd met.
The tears at the parting could drown
sorrows for two,
For somehow they found out,
breaking up's hard to do.

Greg Gunter
UNTIL WE MEET AGAIN
When night has come
To chase away
The scattered traces
Of the day

I find myself alone
In thought
Remembering of
The love I'd lost

For she was life
As life should be
'Til death; that thief
Stole her from me

Yet, I need not weep
Nor wonder why
I need but only
Close my eyes

To meet with her
In dreams tonight
And walk again
By pale moonlight

Hand in hand
Upon the shore
Free to share
Our love once more

And on that blissful shore
We'll stay
'Til morning chases night away

Cheli E Gibson
BLACK AND WHITE
Black and White
Two different Colors
Always in comparison to one another
Neither seems to know what's right
or wrong
Why must this battle be so long?
Why must I have to be succumb with
such pain?
Neither color has anything to gain
One day there will be happiness in
this land
And it will come from only one man
This man's name is Jesus Christ
And there will be no more Wars of
Black and White.

Harvey Ratner
THE FOREST

To My Beloved Wife, Jolene

The world was younger then,
I remember how the creatures in the
forest
all would run to me and eat from my
opened hand.

It was a time of learning;
when the humming sound of
the wind
and the crackle of brittle leaves
seemed to whisper a message,
and hidden under every stone was a
new mystery
waiting to be discovered.

It was a time
when I still believed in heroes and
magic,
and dreams seemed more certain to
come true
than they do now,
For I left the forest long ago, as we
all must,
and have forgotten its secrets.

All that I was unable to
understand then
is far too clear to me now,
and I have since stopped learning,
and believing, and dreaming,
altogether.

Except sometimes,
when I listen to children laughing,
or watch young lovers in the park.
That, and the thought of you,
reminds me,
that I am welcome to return.

Phyllis J Cohen
A LETTER FROM DAD
Hush now darling—
don't be sad.
And please don't mourn
for your old Dad

Remember child—
now dry your eyes
There is no pain
in Paradise!

I'll wait for you
just as we planned
And meet you
in that Promise Land

Another time—
another day—
We'll sit and chat
where Angels play!

Everett Francis Briggs
EXILE'S FAREWELL
With firm resolve I leave my land
For some faroff and alien strand.
Goodbye, my home! Farewell to
thee!
We part, sweet home, eternally.

With leaden step I board the ship,
And seize the rail with falt'ring grip.
I must not waver, land of mine,
Though I for thee will always pine.

Grown old, the fallen leaves I tread
Of summer's loveliness now dead,
And think me back across the deep,
To thee, dear home, before I sleep.

Jean Dunn

Jean Dunn
PATCHWORK DREAMS

To Randy in memory, To my Mother, sisters and my daughters who have always inspired me, and believed in me.

In the winter of my life
alabaster shadows creep silently
into the recesses of my mind.

Silver threaded moonbeams spin
spiders silken webs, through once
raven hair.

Alarming myself, I gaze into a
long dead mirror, with a patchwork
of silver and black particles, long
since fallen away from cracked
wooden frame.

Pale and wan, gossamer skin hanging
in folds,
I appear in patchwork splendor
first elongated, then circled parts
of face.

Through faded eyes I see the ghost of
a lovely young lady,
laughing, head thrown back, in
eternal glee,
Long dark hair swinging from side to
side,
skin like deep sea pearls,
azure eyes flashing, she skips through
a field
of sun ripened daisies,
Forever young,
In my winter years.

Christopher Maurice Avery
COME TO ME

To my wife, Belinda, whom I love very much, and to all those that seek Christ.

You say you're tired and no one
cares,
I say come to me.
You say you have no friends who
share,
I say come to me.
You say why pray when no one
hears,
I say come to me.
You say that life is so unfair,
I say just come to me.

When you did drugs, I made you
stop,
But you wouldn't come to me.
When you asked for a raise, I put you
on top.
But you still won't come to me.
When you prayed, I answered you,
But still you turn from me.
I'll do more than any mere man can
do,
So come to me.

For no man can love you more, than
the way I do.
And if you look around you'll see
just how true.
From the mountains to the
valleys,
From the rivers to the seas,
No man gave these gifts of love, so
my child, come to me.

Anita Gutierrez
A REBEL'S SOUL
Searching above,
And searching below,
But not knowing where to go.

He reaches high,
He reaches low,
Just sitting and crying all alone;
. . . Just wondering, . . . Just
wondering
about his rebel's soul.

Nancy Junkermann Valle
OH, GOD, HOW I LOVE THEE
Oh, God, how I love Thee,
Your powers are rare.

You make this old earth
A picture to share.

A landscape of beauty,
With each passing season.

For all to enjoy,
Beyond all reason.

Gerry Cooper
CHRISTMAS GLEE

A little tug at my heart,
Told me to get an early start.
First the manger all in white,
But Baby Jesus not in sight.
The aroma of a fresh cut tree,
Branches reaching out with glee.
Candles, beads, and lights aglowing,
Happiness in hearts is showing.
An early party planned for family,
Brings the first sound of Christmas glee.
Little ones, parents, and grandparents too,
And there's Aunt Sara, we love you!
Now back to Baby Jesus who is out of sight,
It's time, the grandkids know it's the night.
Turns are taken to place in our manger,
Baby Jesus, to us not a stranger.
Next comes the cake with candles bright,
Happy Birthday Jesus, is our song tonight.
Christmas Day has gone away,
But in our hearts it's here to stay.

Joyce Duggan Autrey
MIND-DRIFT

Relaxing is a state of mind floating in another time, another place. It is sleeping in disguise . . . imagining distant lands, as if a hot air balloon has drifted you away. Allowing you to float into another existence . . .
A land where clouds seem a brighter white and the sky a delft blue.
The trees let the wind bend their boughs like puppets on a stage;
and children laugh at every move, begging to be entertained.

From the balloon, you view the world with distant eyes; on the ground people point at the colorful mass of silk, shaped like a conversation bubble in a comic book. You rise above thoughts of schedules, deadlines letting them go . . . and drift until you gently skim the trees and land in the middle of a cornfield.

Janet G Peterson
UNTITLED

They say pictures speak louder than words
So maybe I should draw a picture
instead of writing down words.
They say love comes in all shapes, sizes and colors.
Maybe that's why our love is so unique.
But when I say I love you
You seem to get the picture
So I don't have to draw it
For you know it's there forever.
With you it's so easy to express myself.
Sometimes I don't have to say anything
For you seem to read my mind.
But to say I love you to you
Helps me to reassure myself
That you are very real,
That you won't vanish when I blink my eyes.
But, then again
With a picture, you could have it always
And always receive my message
That says "I love you."

Darrin Marshall
HUNTER & HUNTED

The hunter chases the tails of verse
The hunted are chased for penning rabid thought
Scents of sense mark the cries of . . .
Being poised on the trail of tales

Literal hounds read between the lines,
Hoping to catch you on the move.
The pain that the words beheld,
Bled from the weeping pen at hand.

Their roaming eyes spelled confusion . . .
Misled by a stare's delusion.
You've sanctuary on the papers ladder,
Blending in with prosing manner.

Seeking emotional refuge,
By pursuit, his life was on the line.
Be ever so stealth, when the void swells with age,
Those evasive words are imprisoned with sage.

Tracks won't be found where few have wandered.
Charmed by compassion, you are welcomed home.
That fatiguing game, as allusive as rhyme in itself,
Concludes its passage, hiding on the time-tried shelf.

Maureen E McLaughlin
FRIENDS

Friends are the best thing
That God has ever made.
They will laugh and play with you,
(And they never have to get paid!)

They're there in the good times,
And in the bad too.
They're there when you need them,
And you're there when they need you.

They'll either laugh, yell, scream, or cheer
Whenever you are near.
When you're feeling sad,
You'll always end up glad,
Whenever a friend is near.

So if you want a friend,
Just remember in the end
This simple little rule,
"To have a friend, you must be a friend."

Bonnie Hunwardsen
MY BAMBI

I go to the timber
My gun in my hand
I pray, Please Lord
Don't let this thing jam

There's a little deer
looking straight at me.
I think I will call
the little fellow Bambi.

He is so very little
so cuddly and cute
He looks at me and
says "Please don't shoot"

I leave the timber
The day is all done
I didn't shoot anything
But I sure had fun.

Michael Sarkissian
THE ARMENIAN EARTHQUAKE

What a shame, what a pity,
It was a compete destruction of a city.
The earthquake that struck Spitak,
around 11:30 in the morn,
Also ravaged other cities, leaving them tattered and torn.
Many lives were lost, and they are still counting,
As they clear the debris, the toll keeps mounting.
Our hearts go all out, to a people so brave,
As they carry their loved ones, to their grave.
Many generations were wiped out,
but this has happened before,
Armenians are strong people, they'll bounce back once more.
What a wonderful world, for the support you gave,
In money and supplies, so a life you could save.
The blankets and food, were also a welcome sight,
That fed the survivors, and kept them warm through the night.
Thanks to the dog teams, that searched for the few,
That were buried in the rubble, and lost from view.
Why does it take a disaster, to bring out the good in all,?
Let's learn from what's happened,
and we'll all stand tall.
We don't need war and hunger, or any discrimination,
What the world did here, certainly needs no explanation.
So, to the many others that helped, at this time of need,
We (the Armenian people of the world), thank you for your very kind deed.

Kimberly Ann Hansen

Kimberly Ann Hansen
LIVING THROUGH LOVE

You told me of your love
that belongs to me.
Your heart is full of lies,
and that is all I see

At first I was blind,
now I feel used and cheated.
My heart was torn,
from the way it was treated.

You will never understand,
what love really is.
You take what you want,
When you are supposed to give.

When will you understand,
what love is for?
When you want someone's love,
you have to give more.

It is hard to know,
when love is true.
You never understand it,
until you live it through.

Elena Kepalas
UNLOCK THE DOOR

This poem is dedicated to my sister Lili with love.

Unlock the door
of nothingness
passing by the face
only memories
no one complains
about anything
reaching the senses
the memory

secrets of power
continue filtering
through arguments
immense assemblage
of infinite units
unorganized following
the course of rivers

how to free oneself
from incarnation
if such exist
expectation of reason
can go no further
only revelation

Herman Abdul
THE TREES

To my brother George whose death inspired me to write this poem.

I planted the tree in my yard
twelve years ago on a hot September morn.
My brother planted his beside mine
and we, my brother and I, were born.

And these trees waxed fully in strength
surviving fires, pestilence and nature's ways.
They grew never passing each in length
for twelve years and all its days.

But one dark brooding day
a hooded figure stole into our home
with lightning speed stole my brother away,
and left me sad, broken, and alone.

Many years have passed since I looked at the trees
but mine is green, his beginning to die
and when I glance up at the happy bees
I cry, why were we separated, you and I.

Angela Pilla
A BROTHER

To my brother, and good friend, Anthony.

A brother is someone much like you,
Kind, considerate, caring, and true.
There when needed, willing to guide,
He'll never run, but stick by your side.
To help solve your problem, like it's his too.
A brother is someone to give your love to.

He will accept you, just as you are.
If he is needed, he won't be too far.
If by chance, you are split apart,
The love you share will stay in the heart.
He will accept your love, as well as give it back.
He will build up your confidence,
and give you the pride that you lack.

Carol Moneysmith
TO AMERICA
To America they come,
Bringing not possessions, but dreams;
Dreams of her future,
Etched deep into their hearts;
Hearts full of hope,
Raising homes beside her fresh-water streams;
Streams flowing from high in her mountains,
Making her mighty rivers roar;
Roaring past her forests and prairies,
Surging into the oceans at her shores;
Shores that beckon the burdened
To cast their troubles asea;
Seas that bring them to where they belong;
Belong to this land to be free;
Free to build her great cities,
Where a limit has yet to be known;
Free to open her prairies,
Feeding a world on the seeds that are sown;
Sown so many can triumph and sing praises once again,
Celebrating in the knowledge that here,
In America, exists liberty for all of them.

David Allen Matlock
HAVE YOU EVER
Have you ever looked into someone's eyes
Seeing a love for you which never dies
Have you ever listened close to their words
The tone of which match the song of birds
Have you ever touched a rose so red
Remembering a gentle soul lying in bed
Have you ever held them tightly in your arms
Being only yourself—forgetting your charms
Have you ever had a love so great
But used it, abused it, then realized too late?

Gregory G Kunz
WITH ME ALWAYS

Thank you Wendi, for bringing the sun on those "rainy days," for Creating the smile upon my face and soothing my heart with your care and warmth. I LOVE YOU!

I felt your caressing hand upon my face.
 I feel it but do not see it.
It was just the wind softly brushing
 up against me, teasing me.

Today I walked the beach and felt
 your moist gentle kiss upon my lips.
It was just the sea mist touching me,
 making me aware once again that
 you are not near.

Sitting beneath a great oak I thought I
 heard your sweet tender voice.
It was the rustle of the leaves crying
 their song of loneliness to make me
 remember mine.

I am sure I saw you resting in the
 clouds today when I looked up to
 the sun.
It was the clouds forming beautiful
illusions which slowly
 faded away as my vision blurred
 from disappointment.

I had to sit down today.
 Though I was alone, I realized that
you are with me always.
 In every thought, in my dreams
 and in my heart.

Lisa Schofield
GRANDMA
I remember throughout my childhood,
The days of long ago,
Every week on Sunday
To Grandma's house we'd go.

No matter how the week had gone,
No matter how things had been,
We couldn't wait 'til Sunday
When we could see her again.

She'd always tell us stories.
And hold us on her lap.
Whenever we got sleepy,
She'd put us down to nap.

We always hated to leave.
Grandma hated to see us go.
But she would always say,
"I'll see you next week, you know."

I've got many memories of my childhood,
But the ones I hold most dear,
Are the very precious memories
Of when my Grandma was near.

Carol Elfberg
THE LIGHT OF PEACE
Peace can be, as quiet as solitude.
Or as over powering, as passion for life.
Those who would want peace for everyone, can't understand,
why others wouldn't want it for themselves.
Peace is compassion, love and wanting to share with others.
Also equality and justice for human life.
But there are those, who would keep these bonds from forming.
Cut each other down, with rumors, terrorism and old prejudices.
This keeps the World in the bondage of war.
Peace comes from the heart and soul, with the belief that we
are all equal in the eyes of God.
As we are all his children.
Those who keep the peace are truly blessed, for they are like a light that shines forever.
They show a true love and example for the World.

Arlene Broderick
BECAUSE OF YOU
Because of You, I have a new life.
Days were gray and filled with strife.
Now I am reborn, with a smiling face;
With Your presence, I'll win any race.

Because of You, I hear music in the air;
Bells are ringing; there's beauty everywhere.
In a whisper a lovely voice I hear.
Who is this true Friend, Someone so dear?
No other than my Maker could it be;
One whose countenance sometime I'll see.

Because of You, every moment is bright;
"Thank you, God," no darkness, all light.
Just for You, honor, adoration and glory I give,
Ever staying close to You so long as I live.

Babe B Muilenburg

Babe B Muilenburg
MY AUCTION DAY

To American Farm Wives

Bidder, bid my life away
On this, my auction day.
Give the highest you can go
For this day, all dreams are sold.

My mother's china, her baby doll,
My wedding gown, and things untold.
Oh heart be still for bills need paid,
No matter what you get today.
"A bargain, lady, a bargain I say,
Where could you find a better sleigh."
I pulled my child on it on winter days,
As my father did when he made me the sleigh.

My tea set, how it gleams in hand;
As on my 34th anniversary I stand.
I look at my wedding band
They cannot have that, they understand.
It's over now, it's all taken away.
But one thing, they can never have.
All my years of memories so grand.

Margaret P Lafferty
QUIET MOMENTS
In the dusk of the evening
When the lights were low,
My Mother would sit me on her knee,
And gently hold me to her breast.
She would softly whisper to me
And tell me what was in her heart.
Her tales came easily
And with great affection.
I could see her thoughts in color,
The emerald green of the land,
The thatched cottage
By the side of the road,
The turf fire burning brightly,
The kettle boiling for the tea.
She told me of Nellie, the family mare,
She would smile as she told me
Of the pet goose that ruled the house.
Today, as I sit alone
And when the lights are low,
I hear her voice and for a moment,
We roam among the hills of Ireland,
Her beloved home.

Christine C Aubert
LOVE-SOFT

Warmly offered for all time—past, present, future; for men, women, and other; of earth, the stars, and beyond; to—all people in true tender love.

Helena leaned back against
 her dear boyfriend's
Chest above his heart, contented,
 dreamily enjoying
The velvety evening. He softly
 wrapped his strong, soothing
Arms around her. She smiled
 lovingly with a quiet,
Serene sigh. He smiled softly,
 quietly humming his
Deeply felt fondness for her,
 tenderly whispering the
Downy notes gently into the air
 around them as she

Nestled comfortably within the
 safe shelter of his
Arms. Gentle note upon note
 softly twined around soft tones
Within tones that drifted tenderly
 outwards around them,
And melted gently onto and
 into the sky within
Golden ambers delicately
 shimmering in between
Gentle lilac and plum and
 rich-violet purples, and
Light blues and turquoise and
sapphire
 and deep feathery

Indigo blues, as the soft evening
 sun blossoms through
The sky within the sunset settling
 all around them.
His soothing humming gently
 blending quietly into
The evening, he felt his unending
 fondness for her
Softly entwine with her feeling
 his loving tenderness
Meld with his tender love. They
 were two people, who were one,
And all around them was still,
 and quiet; soft . . . and peaceful.

Dawn Hanniford
WHO IS THIS MAN
He laughs when you laugh with him, and cries when you cry,
Oh what a joy to know this man, he never gets tired, he never gives up on you, he is always there with you through difficult times.

What a pleasure to know this man,come one come all, the door is open heed the call, you don't have to pay a fee.
Enter, you will be happy you did. Are you still wondering who this man is?

Well, when you have found this man,
oh what a friend you have found
indeed.

Bud Kruse
A SIGHT TO REMEMBER

For Megan's fourth birthday, it took awhile.

What a strange sight it was, I had
never seen it before.
For years and years I have been
watching Sea Gulls by the Ocean
shore.

The Sea Gulls arose by the hundreds
and around in a circle they flew.
Around and around and higher and
higher they went
until they disappeared from view.

What was their purpose for flying
like this?
Was it a mating flight?
Questions like these I couldn't
answer for the
Sea Gulls flew out of sight.

Doris E Aarstad
UNUSUAL TREE
SAY IT WITH LOVE

For my Mother—Biddie O. Diggs. Evergreen Nursing Home

It's Christmas again and I promised a
tree,
So I got out the one my friend gave
to me.
A letter had been mailed to each
grandchild she had
to send her a picture she'd be so glad.
I would hang money and pictures you
see,
And make this bare limb a Christmas
money tree.
Fruit jarrings Mom would remember,
Would hold the pictures this day in
December,
I hung all the trimmings, the lights
and the star,
The pictures so precious and money
from the jar.
The bears were still here, they
looked okay
I hung them so carefully they would
brighten the day.
Just a bare limb? Not anymore,
It didn't need things again from the
store,
Mom is still young, eighty-seven this
year
With the love she is getting, she has
nothing to fear,
Mom is still with us, doesn't walk,
and in bed,
but a prayer is remembered, she
often said.
To show her our love, I'll kneel and
pray,
God, let her be with us to share the
day.

Virginia K Hutto
I REALLY DO WANT
YOU TO STAY

To my wonderful, kind, loving husband O'Neal. The most thoughtful, person on earth. He will never grow old. And our love will never grow cold.

Why did you say you were leaving?
And why must you go away?
You know how much I love you.
And I really do want you to stay.

I have been up high on the mountain,
And I've been in the valley below.
The sky here is blue, when I'm with
you,
And I really don't want you to go.

You promised to love me forever.
You said that we never would part,
We always were so happy,
And now you are breaking my heart.

Oh! please come back my darling.
I need you more and more each day.
I'm Nothing now, without you,
And I really do want you to stay.

Leslie Anne Baker
LESSON OF LOVE
In depths of fear and loneliness, I
longed for love unfailing,
But didn't hear the voice of You,
Who holds love, long, prevailing.

Instead I rushed away from Thee,
Afraid to understand.
You stood alone and cried for me, To
trust Your Holy Hand.

The emptiness inside my heart,
Became a tuneless song.
I never knew you carried me, And
whispered once, 'How
long—?'

I listened to the wind one night, And
heard Thy muffled crying.
'I love you so, oh precious one—,'
'For you—I'll keep on trying.'

I fell upon my knees, in tears, And
raised my eyes above,
And felt You draw me to your side,
And teach me how to love.

My heart now beats along with
Yours, In love, divine and true.
I'll search no more for what I've
found, For love began with You!

Thomas Plummer
GOLDEN WINGS
I ride to you on the swift wings of a
Golden Dragon.
On the way, I pass by old warriors
who never
made it to your hand; warriors who
never
saw your heart; the beauty you've
been waiting to give.
I ride closer and feel my heart racing.
Faster! Faster! I command my steed
for I cannot wait any longer to be in
your arms,
and to feel your skin under my
breath.
You stand on a dark cloud
but you radiate as I get nearer,
beckoning me closer,
Closer to your heart.
I reach out and grab for your
extended arms
but we are only connected by our
hands;
a grasp that is glued together by a
Dragon's breath,
a grasp that keeps us together
and only hearts of fire can hold it.
So let us never lose the fire for I have
come so far . . .
so far.

Gary Burke
I LOOKED UPON A
PHOTOGRAPH
I looked upon a photograph
and saw there no one i knew
for well before i was
did this scene live out its life
and die in an instant,
but for the memory of they
who living in a world of perpetuity
created immortality

And as i studied more
absorbed with the fantasy of the past
drawn to them who frozen in time did
display
hope, and energy, and aspiration too
only then did i realize
that their world was mine
and the photograph a mirror

Mary S Henry

Mary S Henry
THAT REALLY COUNTS

To my husband—H. John Henry, our children and grandchildren.

It's not your age that really counts
It's not how big you are—
It's the total of what amounts
To your knowledge that takes
you far.

It's not your name that really
counts—
That makes the old ball bounce—
All your dollars, won't mean a
thing—
Be a scholar—That's everything.

Phillip Winter
A LITTLE BOY'S LAMENT
When I was just a little boy I guess I
hated women
As I got older, I changed my
mind, it must have been the
hormone
One day I saw a girl down the street,
o'boy was she a dandy
She smiled at me and she looked
better than chocolate candy
She said to me, come up to my
house, my parents are on vacation
I pulled back, I was aghast, but
it was too darn much temptation
We started playing hide and seek and
she was quick to find me
She said, you're cute and seemed
to know just how to time me
Then she jumped in bed and covered
up her head and said I couldn't find
her
But I knew darn well she lied
like hell and I jumped in behind
her
I jumped too low and broke my toe
so I really did not find her
The pain was so bad and I got so
mad and headed for the doctor
The doctor bandaged up my toe and
used a lot of plaster
It took some time but finally I
knew just what that gal was
after
A later date I walked down the street,
I saw the girl she was still a little
dandy
I looked awhile, turned into a
store and bought a sack of
chocolate candy
Now little boys, the moral to this
story, if you meet a little dandy
To save your sole and save your
toes, just eat some chocolate
candy
Be careful when you go to bed, it
might be a big disaster
If nothing else take it from me,
you might save a little plaster

Michele Kelley
WHERE THE WIND BEGINS

To Kevin—May the wind never blow us around again.

It begins in the corner of your mind.
It lies dormant until awakened.
When your heart breaks it cries out to
the wind,
and it is awakened.
It unleashes itself and insanity
begins.
It tears your heart
and leaves you empty.
Then you find someone to fill the
space your heart once filled,
and the wind dies down until it is
awakened again.

Loretta M O'Connell
MY CATS
My cats, they number two
One is so small
No bigger than my shoe

When I sit to work,
They are right there.
They fill my clothes . . .
With so much hair.

They keep me goin'
Treasures to behold.
I love them so . . .
They are worth their weight
in gold.

They give me joy
And so much love.
As soon as I get home
They get a hug.

My nights are so full
I need no T.V.
They are entertainment
Enough for me!

Elizabeth Furlan Kucera
AUGUST FUSION

To My Husband, Daughters and Sting. My Daily Bread

The candles all lit
Strengthen their flame
By kindling colors
Of the Yin and Yang.

Repel selfish idols
Of Earth's "powerful and wealthy"
Destroying ancient concepts
Of pure love and morality.

Let a dream be my gift
To all those that See,
As a golden sun sets
On waters tinged in honey.

Accept or deny this
Let your Self choose,

For infinity exists
As an ocean of hues.

Though some shallow minds
May find this too odd
Each soul in the universe
Is melting with God.

No need to fear when
His Kingdom will come
If we listen to the words
That His prophets have sung.

Stephani Fordham
ANOTHER VALENTINE
A day for sweethearts near and far
The sky is filled with shooting stars
As Cupid checks his bow again
Another valentine begins

A special day for sharing love
When hearts take flight on wings of doves
The magic feeling captures all
Erasing fear in hearts that fall

You can feel it in the air
Emotions rising everywhere
Hearts are falling left and right
On this moonlit lover's night

A pretty heart-shaped box of candy
A dozen red roses or poetry
With loving cards that say be mine
The world celebrates another valentine

Paula Goebel
A TOUCH
A touch,
a caress,
A kiss,
a smile.
You are there
all the while.

A friend
sincere,
Cherished
and true.
I'll be here
always for you.

Gary Gustafson

Gary Gustafson
CARNIVAL
Then there were those who worked in a tent
And took their families where they went
They never bathed and slept in cars
And kept their babies locked in jars

Of barker's spiels and dancer's charms
And buttons sewed into their arms
The lifelong memories that you can keep
Of babies floating in their sleep

See all you want for just a dime
Dig in your purse and spend some time
With all the others alive and dead
But see the baby—five cents a head

Meet the man who eats for five
And all the animals just kept alive
You'll never know how much is real
But wonder how the babies feel

Sometimes if you wait till late at night
In a lonely corner and out of sight
A mother drinks to better times
And lullabies a bag of dimes

Loretta Harvey
MOTHER
God thought enough to give me a father and a mother too
Without her I wouldn't know what to do
She's my Mom, but most of all my bestess friend
And I'll always love her to the end.

She's worked hard to support my brother and me
And she always gave good advice which was free
She always made our home warm and full of love
With open arms that reached high above

She never made a promise unless she knew she could keep it
And she wouldn't lie not even a little bit
She's open and honest in every way
And that's the way she'll always stay

I'm proud to say that she is my Mother
And there couldn't ever be another
She always tried to teach me right from wrong when she could
And sometimes say I don't know if I would

Thanks Mom for just being you
For what you say, but most of all for what you do
You're very special and mean a lot to me
And Michigan is my home, where I want to and ought to be.

I Love You
Loretta Jean

Randace Ellen Rauscher
THURSDAY IN CHELSEA
There is a small peep-hole on my door,
that you stare through.

I am transparent in your unearthly intentions.
It causes you to see development,
development, of blind fate
long before it is time.

Portions of your whole
create an equal of greatness.
So young to know so much.
So damaged before the destruction.
Your instinct to read me is
an instrument no one else has
learned to play.

You find it so easy to read
what is clearly mis-spelled.

Lloyd L Little
ROSES
You know a rose is hard to figure
It's a tough, thorny vine, and yet . . .

When you touch the inside of a petal
Well . . . It's like touching a piece of velvet . . .

Only no machine is ever going to
Make a piece of velvet that smooth . . .

A rose! . . . That contradiction
Of thorns and flower . . .

Hybrid, climbing, or rambling,
Perhaps a blooming in the bower . . .

A rose! . . . Yellow, pink, white, or red,
And the most beautiful smell in all the world . . .

Whether rising tall in the breeze,
Or just a slumberin' in their beds . . .

Michael R Kinser
BABE, I LOVE YOU

Dedicated to My Wife, Reneé, With Love

I've written a note to let you know,
how much I think of you
Lying here alone, at night, wishing you could be here, too
I think a lot of all the times I held you close and tight,
But, when I sleep with empty arms, it seems I lose my sight
You warm my heart, without a doubt,
as you whisper in my ear,
"Hold me very close tonight, but don't leave room for fear."
I love the soft caress and touch, it shows me how you feel.
That our love is such a precious one,
it always gets a seal.
You know, you mean the world
to me, and how much our love
is true
For when I asked my heart, it said tell her, "Babe, I love you!"

Teresa E Guerrieri
TO SAY GOODBYE

To my mother, Irma P. (Muth) Witzke (4/10/1905 to 8/19/88), who survived a life of trials! She succumbed to no one, but God! Thank you, Mom! T.E.G. 6/16/89

As we gathered, It wasn't a pretty scene!
Mom was on the death machine!
Her brown eyes had turned blue;
And she knew! Yes, she knew!
It wouldn't be long,
And she would be gone!
She seemed to know; and waited with care.
And when finally, we all were there,
It wasn't long—
And she was gone!

Leanne Watkins
IT TAKES TWO
When we first met I couldn't resist
The undeniable magic of our first kiss.

The sweet words you whispered as we sat in the dark,
They meant so much that I took them to heart.

The promises you made were real and true,
I knew I'd be happy—always with you.

And though I was unsure I finally gave in,
Gave in to a battle that I couldn't win.

Now that we're together I finally see

I'd be miserable without you, you mean so much to me.

Never before has one meant this much.
I want only to hold you and feel your touch.

I hope that one day I will mean as much to you,
Remember what you said to me—to be happy it takes two.

Marilyn Williams

Marilyn Williams
SENSE THE ESSENCE OF ICE

To my daughter,
my mom and dad,
and to the inspiration of nature in
God's wondrous world

Have you heard the ice storm?

Have you heard it tinkling in the trees?
Making a crystal chorus with the slightest breeze.

Have you tasted the delicious dripping icy magic that melts in your mouth?

Have you felt the smoothness of a branch and bloom
Encased in a see-through igloo . . . a temporary tomb?

Have you seen the sparkle of spectrums?

Shining so brightly they make your eyes shun,
Transforming the twinkling trees into prisms

Speeding to the sun.

Meredith Chastain Ramsey
LOVE
Sometimes, in the morning when I go outside.
I look all about, and above. I see all this beauty
Around me, and think of our creator.

How He created all of this! It had to be from love!

Beautiful trees, with their branches so wide and high
Reaching way upward in the sky . . .

Not only for beauty, that He made them all, but for
Warmth and homes, almost like they're instantly installed.

He gave us animals, to fill all our needs, for food
Love, and beauty, for all of us to see!

Oh! but, sometimes a person is blind, but yet he sees . . .

Magnificent mountains, lakes, and flowers to see and smell.

Knowing that nothing on this Earth! could ever prevail.

All of this beauty! Only if we would take the time
To see! With our hearts and souls, like He!

He gave us each other! To be a husband and wife . . .
To share all this beauty! All the days, of our life . . .

From this, comes our Children . . .
The light of our life!
No greater creation, had He made!
This love will last
All of our days . . .

Oh! but one day! We'll all be older, and wiser; and
Will see a different view, knowing in your hearts;
That He created all this, for me, and for you.

All of this beauty! on ground, and above . . .
Telling the whole World!

It was created, from love . . .

Albert C Schumacher
THE AMATEUR POET
I am but an amateur poet,
and my lyrics sure show it.
But with hard work & ambition,
I know I can write fact or fiction.
For poets aren't made, they are born
Thoughts, words & ideas come with each morn.
The price it cost for paper & pencil,
is very mi-nute & less than stencil
The remaining ingredients are free,
The ideas, the words & thoughts to be,
So I enter this poetry contest
Without pressure and no protest,
To win a prize of small magnitude
Would sure make my day & improve my attitude,
Nothing is more satisfying at the end of a day,
Than to know someone cares for your way.

Holly Garner
STARS
Catch a star falling fast,
into the green dewy grass,
there it lies shining bright,
the look of brass on a looking glass.

Kris Antonia Parent
DESTINY

I dedicate this poem to my father; René A. Parent, for letting me find my own life.

You let me go
into the world alone,
to make a life
of my very own.

To seek a path
that suit me best
one that only time would test.

With faith as my guide,
and hope as my light.
I wandered far
as my dreams took flight.

Before too long
a place I found,
where I could see
for miles around.

Below me was
a valley fair.
I knew it held
my lifestyle there.

To carry on
had been my quest,
but the time had come
for my wings to rest.

Away from my home
I learned to find
I had simply found
a piece of mind.

Tosha Button
LIFE

In memory of my Aunt Kay whom we all love dearly.

First a baby,
But maybe not.
Then you're older,
Or maybe just bolder,
While you're young,
Travel far and near among
The wonders of the world.

Then as you grow old,
Don't be mean and cold.
Be kind and generous,
Then the Lord will repay you.

Then your time
And my time too,
Will soon come,
But not as soon as some
So for now it is goodbye.

Laura Pittman
CLOUD EIGHT
But I don't feel that feeling
that lies in the depths of pain
And I don't look for the violets
when I feel the caresses of rain.

And I don't have wings on my shoulders,
and you don't wear a halo.
Time didn't stop with the evening
just because you had to go

The sun still shines but the rainbow is gone
and there are still a few clouds
in my sky.
But my heart understands
the season
Morning won't find me asking why.

John Preston Beck
BATTLEFIELDS COVERED WITH GRAVES
Upon the Battlefields of Yesteryear,
whose grounds still stained with blood,
Are the hopes and dreams of the gallant young men,
that ended face down in the mud.
As their duty called, they came to fight,
and as soldiers, they were brave;—
And the sun rises, and the sun sets,
upon the Battlefields covered with Graves.

They were the finest young men,
from near and far, truly the nation's pride.
They were of every race and creed,
willing to give, and to stand at each other's side.
They were like men of steel,
ready to die, so that none would live as slaves;–
Now the sun rises, and the sun sets,
upon the Battlefields covered with Graves.

They will never know whether their gift,
was a sacrifice made in vain.
They will never feel the warmth of firesides,
with their love ones ever again.
They will never see if their banner of glory,
over homeland still yet waves;—
For the dreams of the fallen soldiers,
were ended upon the
Battlefields covered with Graves.

Somewhere are the souls of the gallant young men,
who answered their beckoned call;
And their spirits still restless,
with hopes and dreams, and
memories of their fall.
And as the world has long forgotten,
the value of what they gave;—
God have mercy, on the brave young men,
whose destiny leads to the
Battlefields covered with Graves.

Dusty

Shirley Cooper
DUSTY

This poem is dedicated to anyone who has ever loved a dog and lost it.

Dusty died today
She was just a dog
So why do I feel so bad

Dusty died today
I feel like I died too
Will I ever again be glad
Dusty died today
Part of my heart
Best friend I've had

Dusty died today
I know she went to heaven
I hope she's not sad

I'll never forget you Dusty

Kim Smith
THE CONVERSATION
Subdued victims become clay in his hands (the virgins are the best). Seventy two years of age. He was tight but now the flesh hangs as a shirt draped over a chair. He told a story about being driven by his insatiable lust. Years go by and still he does not forget. When speaking of my young sex drive his eyes get lost in colorful cheeks. Although embarrassed about when he had sex in a classroom, he smiles and the stories go on. Seventy two and still in love with love is a fantasy in itself. Our conversation comes to an end. The pressures of our hearts and minds were spilled. His secrets lie with me. I suspect he will not tell anyone of my desires for a man with eternity wrapped around his left ring finger.

Kimberly D Porche
CAPTURED HEART
Walking along
Minding my day
Least of worries upon my mind

Out of the blue
Came a dashing young man
Setting my heart afloat was his kind

Suddenly he speaks
With the sweetest of tongues
My heart was fluttered, I could not speak

As he turned away
With a dashing glance
I felt I had to seek

Doing wrong
Is what I did best
But falling for you has made my heart a mess

Knowing you felt
The same as I did
Could only be a guess

William Tilghman Campbell
MY VALENTINE SQUEEZE

This poem is dedicated to Marge, my one and only "Valentine Squeeze"!

You pierced my heart with an arrow,
From Cupid's bow, long and narrow;
Blood is pouring; I may not live;
Each drop is love of which I give.

A hug from you is what I need,
A little sugar stops the bleed;
Your love could save this life of mine,
My darling be my valentine?

Anne Jones
DENOUEMENT
Come, my forever love,
Let us lay you tenderly to rest,
Cover you gently with soft blanket
of roses and gardenias
sweet and heady
Memories.

Speak never harshly of you,
Or of me, or us,—in your warm embrace.

Let you lie 'neath scented down
of satin petals;
Lay you to rest with tender caresses
And long . . . last kiss
of resignation.

Leap of one stirred ember!
One.

Denouement: Forever friends,
forever true,
Strong, glowing, furnace-tried!
Victorious in every challenge
of our forever love . . .

Ethel J Morsey
BATTLE FIELD CRIES

I Dedicate this Poem to all Service Men who served Our Country.

Shots and blood stained fields
Soldiers strewn on the ground

In fox holes, Soldiers leap by heels.
Bandaged heads, along with
bodies, of chilly pains.
Air filled of gun and cannon smoke;
Medics, Medicine combine work
in vain.
Depressive, mounds of family folk,
for some, who never woke.
Enemy press forward on to victory,
While reinforcements, pursue to
win.
The Battle Field, death does cry
"No time to retreat or give in,"
Victory at a cost must win.
for those brave Soldiers, who
die.
Sounds of moans, groans, and sighs.
Thus heard amidst the fury,
they, carry scars,
of the Battle Field Cries.
Your Son, My Son. Oh! God, hear
the cries,
for 'tis of peace they long to
hear.
While over the Mountain tops,
Bursting sounds, Come from THE
BATTLE FIELD CRIES.

Barbariae Boyette
PRETENSE

Them and their make-shift innuendo,
pretense,
No lies or secrets shall hover in my
house.

Your tongue sprawled
fabricated illusions
upon my walls.

You had to paint to shelter the
jumble.

I perceive solitude,
not lies.

You navigated through
the curvature maze of being habitual.

But there was no serenity.

The conflict within your mind,
forever sought out revenge
beneath your soul.

You say you're "you" . . . Pretense.
For the lies are disseminate upon the
battle ground.
Dismayed it may seem,
but all Pretense.

Brian J McGuire
DEPRESSION

The illusion of days
Rolled into one
As if I had died
Or been emotionally hurt
With love and life screwed
By the harsh cold night
While visions of death
Sink Deeper
Into my ever broken heart

Claudiette Fay Hancock
THANK YOU VIETNAM VET

To: A.W. Rock, Jr. and to all the men who served in the Vietnam War.

I can feel your pain, Vietnam Vet.
I can see the despair in your eye;
I know you still live the horrors of
that war,
and in the middle of the night you
cry.
They tell me it was a political war,
but no one has ever told me why,
our fathers, sons and brothers,
had to go over there and die.
They tell me that we lost that war,
that we had no business over there,
but they kept shipping you by the
thousands,
and you thought no one back here
cared.
The news showed you pictures of
Fonda,
and the dissension all over the place,
but I saw the grief in your mother's
eyes,
with the tears streaming down her
face.
The only losers in that war
did not go to
Vietnam, but they stayed here in the
USA
and answered to the name of Mom.
You did not get a victory parade,
like our heroes of World War II,
but you gave to us all you had,
and we gave so little to you.
I declare that you won that war,
but others will declare you did not;
but even the dissenters must agree
with me,
that was one hell of a battle you
fought.
If I had the authority,
I would commission a bloody
red V,
to be worn by the military,
with pride upon their sleeve.
But I do not have this authority,
so this is what I am going to do,
I'm going to plant a living memorial,
and dedicate it to you.
I'm going to plant red roses, for our
heroes that went over there and died;
I'm going to plant white roses, for
our heroes that survived.
I'm going to plant yellow ones,
so every one will know I care,
for our heroes who never returned,
and are still over there somewhere,
and in the middle of this garden,
I'm going to plant a great big V,
which will stand forever for Vietnam,
and as a declaration of Victory.

Lara Zarowsky
THE OLD MAN

The old man was speechless
As he walked into her room.

Just the thought of going through
memories brought him to his doom.

Lost in thought he carelessly
stumbled
Over the memories he sought.

As his eyes filled with tears,
he was suddenly reminded of her
beauty.

That blinding beauty only he could
interpret.
He loved her. There was no doubt in
his mind.

Now she is gone, leaving behind only
her sweet loving spirit, and

a few priceless memories for the old
man to cherish.

April T Franklin
URBANITE

black young girl living learning in a
red brick city
her clothes ain't so new her face not
so pretty
stringing a tetherball on a
government property sign
paying no mind to the village house
rule:
what's yours is yours and what's
yours is mine

her brothers and sisters keep things
straight up and tight
for when Mom's away the house gets
lonely at night
her sense of family makes the world
a whole lot better
keeps her mind clear and her
thoughts together

no fear haunts this darkchild as she
walks alone
she has centuries of confidence
running through each bone
she learns to be brave in an unbrave
world
challenges are a constant to this
young black girl

the future looks dim through
unfocused eyes
her desolation hasn't stop her from
questioning why

black young girl living learning in a
red brick city
her clothes don't mean nothing her
looks don't need pity

Joan W Schatzberg
A SWEET TOOTH

In a luxurious restaurant the dessert
cart looks grand
Filled with pastries, tarts and even a
flan.
But after a large meal that has taken
all night
A rich final course just doesn't sit
right.
Don't let me mislead you, if you
want the truth
I love all desserts, I have a sweet
tooth.

Ever since I can remember when I
was quite small
I really wasn't interested in the main
dish at all.
I'd finish my vegetables and eat all
the meat
To discover what delicacy would
make the meal complete.

Now that I'm grown and I go for a
ride
When I see a dessert shop I wish I'm
inside.
My judgement still impaired by the
lure of a treat
Guess I'll never overcome the want
of a sweet.

Rosalind Edwards
NOBODY UNDERSTANDS

I dedicate this poem to: Larry, my very best friend, who encouraged me to write. My parents, and grand-mother who encouraged me to go beyond my own limitations.

Why do we have to hide our true feelings?
Why can't we be ourselves? They always seem to judge us by our past, or by what others say, not by what they really know.
Is it so hard for them to get to know us, or are they afraid they might see some of us in themselves.
Don't they know we are hurting inside every time they speak our name.
We have tried so hard to make them understand, that we love each other and want to be together.
Maybe, someday they will understand before it is too late, we might not be around for them to say we truly understand.

Mona Kracht
ADORATION

This poem is Dedicated to the Lord Jesus Christ and to my Godly Husband, Douglas.

My Beloved is Priceless,
Sweet and fragrant are his kisses.
My Beloved is tan and handsome,
the chiefest among ten thousand.
His wisdom is peaceable and pure;
His faithfulness will long endure.
Oh Give Praise unto the Lord!

Erin Elizabeth Wissner (Age 10)
WINTER FEELING

I would like to dedicate this poem to my parents . . . the best parents in the world!

Scattering snow,
As it lies on the dead grass,
Piling.
Shivering in the loneliness,
Children watching as it tumbles,
Elders keeping warm,
Thinking of this cold season,
And thinking of the watery particles,
Falling as flakes.
Reminiscent of a pendant,
Concealed mass of ice.
Others on ice.
Seeing their reflection.
And fires being made.
Winter feeling.

Mary Gilson
PRECIOUS FOOTPRINTS

This is dedicated to our precious first grandchild, DIRANDA LYNN GILSON, and to her parents, MARSHALL and ANGELA, on the occasion of her birth, September 27, 1987, the day her PRECIOUS FOOTPRINTS marked our hearts . . . from BOB and MARY GILSON.

Her precious footprints marked
our hearts
That memorable day she came
What precious blessing sent
the Lord
What precious love in us
be-stowed
Diranda Lynn's her name.

What precious sweetness to behold
What precious joy and arms
enfold
What precious innocence to mold
What precious promises unfold
What precious trust in us you hold
In awesome wonder we're made
bold

What precious dreams you made
come true
What precious memories bear
your hue
Where'er your footprints lead you to
God's tender grace will guide
you through
And precious love we'll shower on
you
For gifts like you are precious
few

Your Loving Grandparents

Lin Hsin Hsin
this is a contest
twenty one lines or less
'tis a test
no, a contest

if you win
you'll be named
more or less

if you lose
don't hang loose
& don't protest

write again
& submit
for the next contest

poetry or otherwise
life is a big contest
else there will be no success

failure or success
do not rest
until in peace ye may rest

Donald A Weston
HAVE I EVER TOLD YOU

This poem is dedicated to Pat Hallett my dearest friend.

Have I ever told you how much you mean to me?
The pleasure I receive from this fills me with ecstasy.

I'll always keep within my heart the love that you have shown
And I can see you in my mind whenever I'm alone.

The feelings that I have for you are difficult to say
But I want that you should know within me they will stay

I don't know what I would do without you by my side,
You are my inspiration the very reason I abide.

As long as you give me your love, soft kisses, and gentle touch,
I will live in happiness for I love you very much.

Tony Martinez
QUESTIONS OF VALUE

This poem is dedicated to the inspiration of my life; my son, ANTHONY ALEXANDER MARTINEZ.

What can we say,
has the world gone astray?
Should we live for tomorrow,
or live for today?
What is right, what is wrong?
Should we live like a song,
and pretend that our troubles
will all soon be gone?
Is it not enough to be healthy,
or does one have to be wealthy
to feel the value of life?
As in the heart, what is believed,
will come to pass and be conceived.

Bishop Patti A Lee Fatt
'TWAS ANOTHER CHRISTMAS EVE
It was Dec. 24, 1988, as customer after customer found their way to my desk
When what to my wondrous eyes should appear, but the Gov. of the State of Va., no less
Like the Good Samaritan I am, I sprang to my feet to offer him my assistance
He asked that I show him the Price Club's book department, I put up no resistance
I extended my hand in a warm and enthusiastic greeting, and he took it
I know that my knees buckled and started trembling as he took it
In a flash, I noticed that he was flanked by at least three "Secret Service Men"
But I was perplexed to find that they all appeared to be dressed exactly like him.

Originally I was scheduled to be off from work that day
On Wednesday, Kitty called, from Petersburg, and told me that she had planned to go away
It had been many years since I'd had to work on a Christmas Eve
God sent the Governor to lift my fallen spirits, this I have to believe.

Gov. Gerald Baililes was much much taller than he appeared on T.V.
I pranced in front of his entourage like they were all escorting me
As I studied his profile, his eyes twinkled from beneath the glasses that rested on his nose
They matched the suit that he wore, I was wearing a Jacquard dress, tan shoes and opaque hose

He turned studying the selections of books, I decided it in poor taste to linger
I danced back to my desk to engrave yet more Shaeffer pens, silently renewing my vows of becoming a singer
I'm glad that I had not called my back-up Mrs. Greer, and that Kitty had had to go away
For you see, by helping the Governor in that way, I earned my wings that warm Christmas Eve's Day!

Connie Sue Jones
STANDING PROUD AND TALL
Standing proud and tall, too good to fall
We've fought battle for battle, and won them all
Red, white and blue, our flag stands
Under one nation, in God's hands
All for one and one for all
With God's help alone we stand proud and tall
Our nation stands for freedom, and in freedom we conceive
We all stand together, for in our nation, we believe
We the glorified, stand for what we believe in, together
We stand, divided we fall
We believe in the American flag, one nation under God, individual, with liberty and justice for all
We all fight together, that's why we don't fall
We love being the nation, that stands proud and tall.

Susan Ashley Minutillo
BLINDING NIGHT AND WHOLESOME LIGHT (A Villanelle)

I dedicate this poem to the memory of my mother, Alva Bulman Ashley, who was the real poet in our family; and, to the love from my dear husband, Gary David Minutillo, who always inspires me.

I still am lost within the blinding night.
It darkens all the world until the day
And now the world is filled with wholesome light.

The crystal halls that filled my life with light
Have turned to darker shades of gloomy gray.
I still am lost within the blinding night.

The hate from yesterday, to my delight,
Has changed into the love I have today
And now the world is filled with wholesome light.

The mighty towers now have seen their plight.
They're fallen to the ground to my dismay.
I still am lost within the blinding night.

The love I thought had left me in the night
Has since returned, forever now to stay,
And now the world is filled with wholesome light.

No matter how I search for truth and right
I cannot seem to find the valid way.
I still am lost within the blinding night
And now the world is filled with wholesome light.

Merdina Price
DEATH

To my loving father, who had such a wonderful and simple outlook on life, and to Nina who always knew I could succeed and my supporting family.

Why are people afraid to die?
Is it they don't want to leave
their loved ones behind?
They don't know what lies ahead
for them in another world,
life or future.

Why? Why are people not afraid?
Is it because they aren't happy
with what they have or no
reason to live?
Maybe it's because one thinks
they'll be closer to God, be
more at peace in another life.
Some think they will see their
family and friends who have
died in the past.

These are questions we have to
answer some time in our life.

Carroll A Rucker
NEW VISIONS

To Murline Akers, who encouraged me to write this poem, named after her gospel group, NEW VISIONS.

Mine eyes have seen many a thing,
Some that make you want to cry and others that make your heart sing.
The things I saw as a child were visions of happiness in this life,
But as I've grown older and hopefully wiser, my heart has also seen misery and strife.
The dreams we once had are beginning to fade and diminish in our memory;
Ah, but the dreams of today are becoming a reality.
This day is a day in which we've never seen before—a new dawning, the sun peeking its head just above the horizon, the stars dancing and twinkling among a blanket of the deepest blue sky, the moon is taking its place among the heavens as it follows you through the night.
What excitement, what exhilaration to be able to start a new day full of new visions for the future.
As we travel through 'this life,' we must make each day count as a vision for tomorrow.
Because if we don't take advantage of our new visions today, there will be no life left to borrow.

Patricia L Sangillo
AFTERMATH OF A COUNTRY RAIN
Street lights flickering
through rain-splattered leaves,
patent leather roads
ribboned through
wet green earth,
thick smell of damp wood.

Hazel E Williams
SANTA'S PRAYER

Santa's Prayer is based on a true experience of Mr. Wilburn Rose, who was the Big K Department Store "Santa" in West Helena, Arkansas, for many years. It is dedicated to him.

There in the bright lighted store in our town
The jolly old man in the red suit sat down.
To all of the children with faces so bright
This was the 'one' who comes Christmas Night.
To grant all their wishes for goodies and things,
And parents were smiling the smiles Christmas brings.

Then one little girl climbed upon Santa's knee
And as his eyes twinkled, he said "Let me see,
Just what would you like for Christmas this year?"
The child moved closer and her answer was clear.
"All my life I've been sick and I'm only eight.
They say I'll be okay, but I don't want to wait.
So, please dear Santa, don't bring dolls or toys.
Save those things for the other girls and boys.
What I want this Christmas your store doesn't sell—
Oh please, dear Santa, I just want to get well!"

With a very sad face, her Mom took her hand,
And the once happy Santa did not feel so grand.
This kind of request left Santa in woe.
But wise Old Santa knew just where to go.
The following Sunday when his

church knelt to pray
Old Santa jumped up—he had something to say.
With a trembling voice, he managed to tell
Of the precious child and her wish to be well.
And although the church did not know her name,
They looked up to Heaven and prayed just the same.

The little church prayed—Oh, how they prayed.
They prayed for the sick, the lost and unsaved.
But the most fervent prayer heard in Heaven that night
Was the one from Old Santa, with his eyes closed so tight.
As he talked to the Lord, tears ran down his face
And God's Spirit came down to fill that Holy Place.

Now somewhere this Christmas we firmly believe
That sweet little girl her wish will receive.
And all because Santa—who's only a man—
Had faith in the power of God's Almighty Hand!

Selma C Kahan
ENDING
Cotton ball saturated with moisture
Squeezed on my face so cooling and soothing.
Fluffy cloud laden with water explodes.
Sheets of rain falling, drench and drip from me.
My hair, spaghetti, blouse tight as melted cheese.

We would tune in to the beauty of the sky
Watching the clouds changing their formation.
Look at the skyscrapers in the city.
A bag lady arrange her worldly goods.
Comment on pedestrians passing by.

We dined on seafood, tasting the ocean.
Then went dancing, joyous as the sun.
I could feel my feet flying off the floor.
Swaying, chanting music I adore.
'The music stopped. My body still in motion.

It happened. Just what I had been fearing.
Lights, sounds, smells, dancing, all disappearing.
The clouds wispy and spare. The air is dry.
The poetic magic no longer blended.
Now that our relationship is ended.
Collapsing, I go to bed, heart weary.

Marc L Swartzbaugh
MAINE NIGHT
Maine night, your
Black sky burns
Bright with the blaze of a
Billion stars.

Earlier, in the gloaming of our own
Freshly fallen sphere, I
Peered out from under my
blind of
Pine, a bewildered voyeur,
Audience to a growing
Galaxy of exhibitionists.

Now, emboldened by darkness, I
Stare in awe of
Myriad ancient messages
Sent so precisely across the
Years of light.

I have no reply.

High on stars, my sight
Teems with the not-frozen
frieze of
Heavenly dance, revealing nothing,
Glinting all.

Edna A Snow
CHOO CHOO

Dedicated to Mrs. Theresa Wright

Slinky—skinny—shiny black,
That describes our pussycat.
She loves shrimp—it never fails,
Unless it is a big, fat quail.

She's an actress; Choo Choo is her name,
Don't know exactly from whence she came.
She is red-black with yellow eyes,
Her bobtail came as a big surprise.
She went out one night and had a fight
With a big tomcat who was out of sight.
He said you will, she said I won't.
He said I'll bite your tail if you don't.

She didn't believe him and paid the price.
For chasing a tomcat late at night.

Cynthia Hash
THE SMILE
Everytime you smile
I think,
I think of our little secret
we share.
As the days pass
I look for the smile.
Then I remember again
of our little secret.
It's something for us
to share;
Because as long as
I see your smile
I'll always remember
our little secret.

Janice E Rowell
NOTE OF ENDEARMENT

Written as a token of my love to my daughter Susan Janice Rowell For Graduation 1989

You're kind sweet and true
You must remember to always
be loving and gentle to our sweet baby Sue
She's one of a kind just like you
Handle her with a soft gentle
hand, like soft grains of sand
If you love her, she will be your
snuggly kitten with a contented purr
In no time at all you will be here
Safe in each other's arms, that
are loving and dear
Don't be sad, look ahead to the
times you'll be spending
together instead.

Donna Magaard
THE MOOD WAS SET THE TIMING RIGHT
The mood was set, the timing right
Who could have known, it would happen like this
The stars, the music, the gentle touch
But only one of us felt it that night
So warm, so cool, a difference of life
How did we know, a new form would take place
Unplanned, unthought of, how could this be—
Oh life! So little significance hold
Tell me no more, don't let me see—
How much it does not mean to me
Life is so short, don't show me the way
A child can enrich, and fulfill a day.

DeAnn Boutwell
HARDENED HEART
"Do you not yet see or understand? Do you have a hardened heart? Having eyes, do you not see? And having ears, do you not hear?"—Mark 8:17-18

Young girl who's always had life so good
Why are you here in this neighbor-hood?
I saw you pass me by today
Just like all the others who come this way
Do you really care that I have no home?
That I face the world each day alone?
I thought maybe you were different from all the rest
That your faith was more than words professed
I hoped you were someone who could help me see
That somewhere there is a better life for me
How blind can you be?

Lord, please give her Your Eyes
Through them no hurt is disguised
Lord, please give her Your Eyes
Make her realize . . .

Young man on your way to church today
How many times have you passed this way?
Is it warm inside that Sunday School?
Are you going there to study the Golden Rule?
Did you hear my child crying out in pain?
Or were his tears shed once again in vain?
His future on the street looks fearful and grim
I thought maybe you would stop to comfort him
I hoped you knew the Man who hears our cries
That you would give us hope for new and better lives
Can't you sympathize?

Lord, please give him Your Ears
Make him listen to all our fears
Lord, please give him Your Ears
When no one else hears . . .

June Daniels
BLUSH

This poem is dedicated to Gary, my loving husband.

Intensity of blazing fire
Has blasted forth with strong desire
A heat wave moist with warmth perspired
In the month of June.

Warm bodies glow in noonday sun
And passion flows when day is done
Sweltering rays prove frolicsome
In the midst of June.

The day's a mist of hazy light
And night-time brings such sweet delights
The crickets sing of firefly's flight
In the heat of June.
Green grasses burn and parch like gold
A bonfire grows out of control
Emotions surge deep in the soul
In the heart of June.

Faces are flushed in stagnant air
While moisture beads on shoulders bare
And rosy cheeks shine brightly there
In the blush of June.

Anna Bebhinn Grimes
SHOOTING STARS
FLASH! across the sky goes a shooting star.
Sometimes they really are bizarre!
Big, and little dipper too,
Are only a few of the stars
In that big sky of ours.
Oh, so beautiful with a tail
Across open sky they sail.
first star I see tonight,
Hope it is a shooting star,
For it will bring
good luck from afar!

Miss Hulda Nickel
ONE LONELY BIRD ON TOP OF A TREE

To my gifted, late father who taught us not to give-up during hard times, but to sing our way through them.

One lonely bird on top of a tree,
perched on a bare-boned tree
Standing lonely in the mist
Of the fierce "deep-freeze" just departed.
The lingering memory of its fury—
Though subsided—is evident
In the scattered limbs of the broken Trees.

How like our lives—
When the storms of life beat our feeble craft!
But the bird of Hope
When it comes
Alights on top of it,
Of what we view as destruction.
The harbinger of another spring
When new growth will reveal
What has survived.
Another nest will be constructed
And new life begin again!

Sharon D Long Griffin
THE DAYS ARE NOT SO WEARY
The days are not so weary and the nights are not so long
When I lift my voice to Jesus and praise him with my song
And when the cross that I carry gets to be a heavy load
I lift my voice to Jesus and he shortens my road

When I stumble and I think that I'm about to fall
I turn my head to Jesus and on his

name I call
And when the stormy seas are reaching out to grab me
I remember Jesus and his love sets me free

His Precious Blood was shed and he died on that cross
For Jesus he suffered so I would not be lost

He said he'd come back for me if I would obey
And I know he'll be back he'll be back again some day
And I'll enter heaven where sorrow will be no more
And I'll receive the love that he's had in store

No the days are not so weary and the nights are not so long
When I lift my voice to Jesus and praise him with my song

Greta Gillen
WISHES

There's a girl I wish that I could help
But there's nothing I can do
She thinks that no one loves her
Which is far from being true
I wish I could make her understand
That I'm always here with a helping hand
And the ones that love her are always near
But in her mind things aren't too clear
She lives in a world where rules don't count
In her mind there's no future, just problems that mount
She wants all the pleasures, with no price to pay
Wish I could help, but her life's in a whirl
How sad that no one can help this misguided girl

Laurel Wilkinson
TUSCAN AUTUMN

At times like this, when air is substance, spreading here from there with heft,
drawing there here under its cloak,
when low streaks of sun flow through it, turning
faces gold, dapples brass, and cobbles bronze, the red roofs rust,

late bouquets, turf, and harvest lift
as essence, prayers to heaven,
scenting viscous air in passing.
Blade-winged birds slice through.

You said, "Earth lies close around us tonight."
Why never so close as now?

Those near-distant hills are in the air,
their valleys in the air, the wells, that grass, that ground.
Stone sleeps beneath my hands, the balustrade,
cool and worn, as you drop your coat to my shoulders.

Julie Lawrence Day
MODERN-DAY ROMANCE

Sometimes I wonder how we found each other
in this crazy world we live in
is it possible for two people
to fall in love?
I guess so because I'm crazy about you
and you're crazy
Tell me you'll always stay right here
so we can draw the shades
and slide underneath those silken sheets
the ones I bought on sale
I thought of you as I was buying them
too bad you spilled wine all over them
it doesn't matter
I forgive you like I always do
true love is never perfect
Now chase the cat off the bed
and lock the door
and I will show you
the new lingerie
I bought on your credit card

Lisa Marie Alexander
A ROSE REPRESENTS LIFE!

This poem is dedicated to my late Uncle Mike who inspired my life and made me what I am today.

Pain is a feeling that everyone has
It is in the depth of your heart
When it's there, it hurts a lot
It affects your life—it affects your mind
And happiness sometimes you never find
A rose represents life in a garden
It grows on a stem and can be lots of colors
It brings life to those who find it
And happiness to those who receive it
They flourish and grow, bright and high
But until it's picked, it will ot die
The thorns that embrace it
Engulf it like the air to me
It chokes and strangles it until it's gone
And then it laughs and sings a song
Life is taken, like the rose is now
And the thorns are sickness that abounds
Thorns that grasp and thorns that kill
And take a life with no reason why
The answer we can not find
So the Rose that is gone today, will be gone Forever!

Charlie, The Shadow Poet
RIBBON OF LIFE

To a friend and brother Tommy Coward, who through our conversation one beautiful morning and the grace of God, all this beautiful poem transpired. Many Thanks, Brother

The ribbon of life is so beautiful to see.
The things that matter most, are simply free.
The birds, trees and flowers mean so much to me.
Take time to enjoy them, then let them be.

There's many friends, you will meet along the way.
Some will go, and some will stay.
Treat them with love and kindness, every day
Then someone will care, and brighten your day.

The steps you take, down life's golden path
Some will be smooth, and some just won't last.
If you stumble and fall, don't worry my friend.
God and I will be with you, until the end.

This ribbon of life, can be so wonderful you see.
Just smell the flowers, and remember they're free.
The ribbon of life, yes God gave it to you.
Handle it with love and care, your whole life through.

Then one day, you will receive God's call.
All that you have done, will be remembered by all.
When the ribbon of life has been cut for evermore,
You may enter God's house, and close the door.

Francisco Sierra Jr
MAN'S ETERNAL TREASURE

In appreciation to all the children, faculty and staff of Charles C. Ball Elementary School whose inspiration will always be present in poetry.

The gift of life shines today
As it did on another day
So long ago by a distant star
That drove three men from afar

In search of an eternal treasure
These three rode with great pleasure
Toward a light that we still treasure
That gift of life that we measure

For in humbleness we discover
The wealth of humility
That those three men discovered
In a day that we all treasure

Today we see a star
That drove three men from afar
That brightness we see in all
And share with great humility.

Darlena A Parnell
REASSURANCE

Kris: You have been and always will be an important part of my life. You taught me that friends don't always see eye to eye, but that no matter what they are <u>always</u> there for each other. "D"

Standing here now;
gazing into nothingness,
all is quiet!
I've blocked everything out;
I'm at one with myself.
Though there are people all around me, I don't really see them.
Suddenly from out of no where,
you are by my side.
The smile on your face brings me back into the present,
the hug reassures me that everything is okay.
And just you,
by being yourself helps me realize
that there's nothing out there that if I set my mind
to I can't accomplish;
that sometimes,
we have to be willing to lose something in life!
But that no matter what,
there will always be friends there to help me through it all.

Joseph M Turner
GREED FOOLS

They are mops
Merely skimming the surface of life
To make the path of their deeds
Gleam amidst the muck of the populace,
But becoming filthy in the process.
Yet they are flowers
Attracting us with their charm,
But beware
The sting of a hidden bee
Should we get too close.
They drift above the common laws
Too bloated with the stench
Of half-digested wealth and power
For such annoying trivialities
To sway them from their work,
Caring not an ounce for the lives
They claim in their quest
To hoard the physical.

And we are to blame!
They are nothing
If we want them to be so.
Yet they are everything
When we allow them to dominate us,
They are the true gods of this world,
And we bow to them
Then grumble behind their backs.

We wish we were like them.
We plot and scheme against them,
And our wishes are fulfilled.
Though perhaps we do not share
Their power,
Corruption is ours!

Louise S Cooks
CALIFORNIA

I wish to dedicate my poem California to my son and daughter-in-law Frank Jr. and Charlyn Cooks.

When I think of California
I think, Sunshine, Pacific Ocean,
Beaches, Bathing Beauties, Bikinis,
Pretty girls.
I Think
Beverly Hills, Glamorous
Movie Stars, Hollywood and Vine.
Movie Star's name and hand prints
On the sidewalk. Chinese Theater.
I Think
Tee Shirts
Shorts
Sneakers
Skateboards
When I think of California
I Think
Disneyland
Mickey and Minnie Mouse

I Think
Anaheim Hilton
World of Poetry
Golden Poet's Award

I Think
It was great to see
Poet Editor Eddie Lou Cole
Publisher John Campbell.
I Think
What a great time I had
In California.

California!

Deborah Lee Trikones

Deborah Lee Trikones
FORBIDDEN LOVE

Times seems to have stopped.

Life seems to have dulled.

Feelings of unalloyed happiness
Fade into the obscure

Darkness
Leaving only confusion and
consternation.

Unholy, forbidden love
Rises from the deepest dole
of the heart.

Only to wander into the darkness
where this love will languish
for the warmth and unerringness
of this untouchable
Dream . . .

Mary Crawford
FRIENDS
Through thick and thin
we'll always be friends,
forever together. Forever
until eternity passes away.
A friend, my best friend.
Closer than any other, closer
than a brother. Though the miles
may try to separate us. I can see
just beyond yesterday, a bond never
to be broken. Not a word spoken.
Now, now look at us now. Friend,
friend come and stay, we can play
in yesterday, today, and forever!

Ms Jaci-René B Werder
". . . HERE COMES A ROAD"
They call her Mel,
I was nicknamed Jac;
Rhino was he, big even then,
He could carry us both on his back.

She my cousin, the youngest,
Him my brother, being so old;
All dressed up to keep warm,
Yet I was still so cold.

Sliding down that hill,
We three at play;
So close at ages ten, eleven, and
twelve,
My, weren't we young and gay.

Onto Front Street,
We so fast would go;
On that beautiful and white,
Marathon, New York snow.

We were almost run over,
From laughing so;
When Rhino yelled,
"Get out of the car, here comes a
road."

Rhonda Tackett
THERE ARE PLACES . . .
There are places
In a mind,
Where no one else may go.

Those secret corners
Where one may take refuge,
And never be afraid,

of

Laughter,
Darkness,
Or the Crashing of Thunder.

Melody Klotzbach
WE HAVE NO HEAT TO KEEP US WARM TONIGHT
We have no heat to keep us warm
tonight
We burn candles to use as light.
We didn't pay the gas or electric bill
And as for credit we have nil
The landlord says the rent's past due
And if I don't pay he will sue.
I'm out of a job and welfare doesn't
cover
What it costs to be a single mother
The kids are hungry and they have
nothing to eat
They have no shoes to cover their
feet
They all are wearing rags for clothes
The youngest has a runny nose
We will all sleep on the floor tonight
And snuggle up real close and tight
So the body heat will keep us warm
And together we'll be safe from harm
And when we see the first morning
light
We'll know we've made it through
another night
And with it being a new day
Maybe some luck will come our way.

Frances C Travierso
REMEMBER

To P. Gendelmen. Thank you for your kindness and understanding.

REMEMBER
If the child in you
Can stay alive
There isn't anything
You can't survive.
For when you remember,
How it used to be,
Your soul forever, will
Remain Free.
Childhood is a Special
Place,
So remember to always
Leave a space
To travel back to the
Used to be.
Where you forever, will
REMAIN FREE.

Zula A McFadden
MATH LESSON

This poem is dedicated to my two children Wanda and Crystal.

He was teaching her arithmetic, and
he said it was a mission

He kissed her once, and kissed her
twice and said,
now that's addition

And they added smack by smack on
silent satisfaction.

She sweetly gave his kisses back and
said,
now that's subtraction

Then she kissed him, and he kissed
her, without an explanation, still
smiling they both kissed and said,
now that's multiplication.

But then her dad came on the scene,
and made a quick decision, and
kicked the lad three blocks away and
said,
"Now that's division."

Rebecca Twombly
GLASS ROADS
Fragile Glass often seems to cover
the road
that leads to the one with whom
you'll grow old,

So steady yourself, and I'll do the
same
So glass covered roads "intact" will
remain.

"Proceed with caution"
some what a cliche,
But a wise thought to live by
During these our first days.

So take time to enjoy the beauty life
itself brings,
and spend every stolen moment
enjoying the smallest of things.

And though along the horizon
the road's end seems near,
It's only an illusion . . .

For on the contrary, you shall travel
A million glass miles in a year!

The road's surface never changes
it shall always be of glass,

Only true Love can ensure glass
roads never crack.

David W Forrest
WE, YOU & I
We met on that refrigerated
December night.
The memory in my mind I'll never
forget,
And the glances we gave one another.
I looked into those icy blue eyes
through the frosty window.
I knew it was God's fate for us to be
together.
Finally that night we, you and I, were
alone.
Staring into each other's glistening
eyes.
Alone to be one another's, if that was
our desire.

Christopher J Williams
I . . . THE FLOWER
The lonely flower is me
withstanding the shower alone;
Hoping that you see me
and take me into your home.

Place my fragile body in water,
give my love a chance to root.
Save a place in your heart
for this little "Forget-Me-Not."

If you walk by
and see water on my leaves;
They're tears in my eye,
asking for you to hold me.

Hold me in your hands,
with your fingers around my stem.
I hope you understand,
I want to be with you again.

Kenneth L Douglas
A PORTRAIT OF THOUGHT

To my best friends my parents James R. and Ruthie L. Douglas.

my mind is a canvas upon which
portraits of my imagination are
painted

With strokes of creativity i paint
into masterpieces my thoughts

priceless works of which only i can
see
framed within the realm of my soul

John D Blackowicz
WHAT IS DEATH?
What is death? Is it the end?
Is it complete? Forever gone?
Is it blackness? No more to
'comprend?
Nothing left 'cept those who mourn?
Is the grim reaper really grim?
Are you gone forever more?
With nothing to show you've ever
been
Or has he just opened a door?

Is there more beyond this place?
Another place, another time?
Another form, another face?
Another place, both yours and mine?

Was there life for us before?
Another time, another place?
Did that reaper open another door?
To this time, to this face?

I'd like to think that there's no end,
I'll just shed this life's cocoon
And like the butterfly, my spirit send,
My thoughts and soul to a greater
June.

Susan P Graham
DIS CONNECTIONS . . .
There
is a connection
with him
that I can't let go of

A connection
that I don't own

There
is a feeling
of him
that I'm not sure of

A feeling
that I can't let grow

Those connections
let go of themselves
and the questions
are never asked . . .

Feelings
are never felt . . .
but felt

And
time goes on
with the past

Kathleen Webster
SCULPTOR

To my two children Nathaniel Thomas & Kendra Louise Webster. I Love You Both

There's an Art form of sorts, called
Sculpture
You don't have to be an Artist or a
Genius
Anyone can be this type of Sculptor
All you have to be is a little Cold,
Callous
or Calculating
To Chisel away at someone's Heart,
Soul, their very being
Until all you have left is a Skeleton, a
Semblance of what used to be.
A Lonely, Frightened, Trusting
human being.

Linda Reiterman
A BEAUTIFUL DREAM
Standing by the ocean . . . looking in
the sky,
Listening to the ocean roar . . . while
above, a seagull flies . . .

It's such a beautiful day . . . The sun
shines warm in a sky of blue . . .
I've got such a peaceful feeling and
so many thoughts of you . . .

The wind is blowing softly . . .
putting coolness in the air . . .
The sand feels kind of damp on my
feet of bare . . .

The clouds move on so slowly way
up there in space . . .
They move on so mysteriously
with out leaving a single trace . . .

I look out at the ocean . . . It's so
endless and free . . .
It's such a beautiful sight . . . I'll
keep it as a treasured memory . . .

Amy Sinn
WINTER NIGHT
Here by the fire, lying in your arms,
I hear the cold winds blow.
Your touch is fiery, gentle and warm.
Outside it coldly snows.

Lights on the ceiling dance like your
eyes.
Your loving kiss is a sweet surprise.
Wonder at feelings; love does not lie.
We can give freely; no compromise.

Only with you can I be myself.
You love me just as I am.
I know the depths of you; there's no
hidden shelf.
We become one without sham.

Talking of anything; sharing a laugh.
All fear and pain we abandon.
Icicles crumbling, hitting the glass,
going unheard in our passion.

Frances Brown
WINO
Wine bottle clutched under the arm
Head bowed to keep out the storm
of life and wind
Trying to fire up a little hope
But it's a joke

Dreams have come and gone
Makes them wonder why life lasts so
long
Folks walk by and stare
Winos look so disgusting there

Passing the bottle to a friend
They take a sip and pass it back again
Winos try so hard to overcome
Too weak, so they fall back into the
crumbs of life
Soon to keel over in a drunken sleep

Authorities will take the body and
clean it up
Put it in a box and seal it shut
The kindest words ever said
Will be spoken for the winos
When they are dead.

Nathalia S Spencer
TO LET YOU GO

To my family, whom I love and cherish.

While I lie here in the dark,
I think of you always in my heart.
When I think about that last special
night,
When you kissed me and held me
tight.
All I was thinking about was the love
I thought I found,
Little did I know you were toying me
around.
Although I long for you night and
day
I know I have to stay away.
Even though I had a ball,
I wish I had never been over to your
house at all.
I was blind, but now I see,
I was a fool to think you could love
me.
Now that I have been set free,
You mean something different to me.
Even though it has taken me a long
time to comprehend,
I now realize that all we'll ever be, is
friends.
Don't get me wrong I love you so,
But now I have to let you go!

Clifford R Hoover
THE LOSS OF A LOVED ONE

This poem is dedicated in loving memory of Allen Wilbur Hoover. He was a devoted husband and loving father.

The loss of a loved one is hard to
face,
You've always loved them and you
think of that special place
The good times you've shared
together, and all the fun you had,
I know all about that, I lost my dad.
He was everything you could ask for,
he didn't want to stop,
He was loved by all the kids, most of
them called him POP.
It's hard to write these words, I don't
know what to say.
I miss him more and more each and
every day.
He got me through some rough times
and he gave me lots of hell,
But all I wanted to do was to see him
get well.
The loss of a loved one is hard to
face I know,
I just can't bear to think about when
it's my time to go.
And when St. Peter calls me to put
my head to rest,
I hope as far as judgement goes they
say I've done my best.

Cathy Halterman
A MOTHER'S LOVE
I sit and look out of my window
As I watch my child at play,
I lean back as I remember
That blessed and glorious day.

When you first came into my world
With your little hands curled up tight,
I wonder at the miracle of it all,
That everything turned out right.

The days flew by so rapidly,
As more and more you grew,
The memories were tucked away
In places only I knew.

A mother's love will never end,
Or so I've oft been told.
The love and warmth within my
heart
For you, will never grow cold.

So I sit and look out of my window
As you run and jump and play,
And I thank our Father up above
For that blessed and glorious day.

Bea Lawrence
RETIRED

Because of his love for Arizona, I dedicate this poem to my son, Gary Lawrence.

The first time I saw Phoenix
'Twas love, of a balmy night
The city was much younger then
But what a beautiful sight.

I had never seen a desert
With cactus big as a tree
In awe, I looked at the mountains
As far as eyes could see.

Next morning, at the break of day
Staring at the golden sunrise
Again, I thought to myself
This was surely paradise.

With deep regret, I had to leave
The valley of the sun
I had made a vow when I retired
Phoenix would be my home.
Twenty years have passed since then,
Can't see as good as before
Looks to me in the desert
Construction has taken o'er.

Crazy drivers taking the roads
Pushing and shoving me out of the
way
Don't know what the hurry is
When they've got all day.

I say to myself, this can't be
The valley I loved so much
Worked hard, to be retired
Now walking with a crutch.

Tahirih Khodadoust Foroughi
THE SEVEN MARTYRS OF YAZD
I close my eyes,
but to God to all.
The seas have sunken,
seven of them all.
But look, glorious gems
have come out with style.
With one eye I weep,
with the other I smile.

They were seven seas
of love and strength,
who sank to bring
gems of peace and oneness
to the surface, of the Earth.

In the memory of seven Baha'is who
were excuted in Yazd, Iran in 1980

Janet Ezell Wells
SILENT MOMENTS

I dedicate this poem to the glory of "God."

Holy, and invisible God. Your path
leads us each day—yet
Your footprints are unseen.
Each new morning makes the world
seem anew again,—
You speak to us through the
Sunrise, the Sunset, the Moon
and the Stars.
Though we are thankful for each
day's blessings
We are still in awe, as to your
greatness.
Each day is a new beginning in
realms beyond the sky
I always think of your Son, our
Saviour as we receive his gifts of
love, to count these gifts would be
impossible, so I think to myself,
Thank you God—For each silent
moment, and for each new day.

Juanita Campbell
THOUGHTS ON PEACE

To Olga, my dear sister.

I want peace—Do not you?
God, give me—a big strength—
A wisdom;
So that I may in a soft quiet way—
Bring me peace—and you peace,
How do I do that which is so hard for
me, too?—Ah! I know—
Talk softly, walk softly, think quietly,
Hear with care, and love much.
Together we can do that which
We could not alone do.

Julie Shanks
TWISTED TREE
In the field there stands a tree,
Far upon the other side stands me.
Staring through broken window pane,
At twisted tree upon the plain.

"They're cutting it down today;
An ugly eyesore!" they say,
"Something of which to rid."

I'm not to understand, I'm only a kid.
But beneath its branches, secrets
shared I,
At the place where twisted tree does
lie.
I cringed as I watched it fall,
Hearing its angry call.
Its twisted limbs still reached toward
sky
Even as slowly, it began to die.

What right have they!, I cry
As tears fall from my eye.
Everything has a right to be,
Even the life within twisted tree.

Brenda J Bailey

Brenda J Bailey
WHEN YOU KISS ME

Thanks to Annual Collins, Jr. and Sandy Ford for inspiring me. Thanks to the Lord Jesus Christ for the God-given talent.

Your kiss is so overwhelming it is
like the roaring sea would be,

My body weakens with pure ecstasy
like an earth's tremor beneath me.

Your kiss heightens my passion that
only you can do,

When you kiss me I can imagine all
the wondrous things to entice you.

Your lips are like the touch of soft
clouds my dear,

Your kiss can speak words of love
that only my kiss can hear.

Your kiss only your kiss can remove
any fears I have within,

And your kiss my love, I shall desire
time and time again.

Laura A Probola
FOR AME
What happened to the little girl
whose father left her
Left her on his lap
A little girl with one green eye and
one brown
She always felt his love
It was OK to touch his face

He made her laugh
The stories of the soil and earth
How was she to know where stars come from

She waited
Tried hard to understand as little girls do
Walking through woods talking
Working out life's problems as if they were her own
On a rock she talked
He would surely be back today
Bursting in the house
She would find less and less of him there

That happened a long time ago
The wall
The wall that stands between her and another world
A place where sharing one's soul is rewarded
With the gift of being yourself

Bobbie Jones

SWEET JESUS

To all my children and grandchildren who have supported me all the way and would never let me give up. All my love always.

Oh, how I love my sweet Jesus.
He means everything to me.
I love Him because He died
On the cross for me.

It must have been hard for
Him to go to that old cross.
But He went anyway, just for me.

I'll always be so grateful to Him.
For by going to that old cross for me
He saved my soul from sin and shame and gave me a reason to go on.

Without Him I couldn't make it.
He's everything to me.
He'll always be first in my life.
Because He went to that old tree.

M E Brendahl

TEDDY & ME

To Mallorae

It's just my Teddy Bear and me
On a voyage of discovery
Across the desert living room
Or over a mountain chair in bloom.

Teddy and I go everywhere
Without a worry or a care
Down the dark foreboding hall
For new adventures big and small.

We turn on and off the magic picture box
Fight colored snakes that mom calls socks
Battle typhoons in our bath
Or map out a lost bedroom path.

There's silver in the caves we find
Enough to leave some trails behind
It's hard to see and do it all
For one so brave and one so small.

Teddy shares my secrets, knows my fears
And keeps me safe when no one's near
And once our voyage is finally done
We rest till another one's begun.

Mark R Wolfe

WISHES, DREAMS, AND OTHER THOUGHTS OF YOU

To Ann, who put meaning into my life, and love in my heart.

If I could brush the sky with your face
and light the clouds from your eyes,
If I could wish for endless love,
If I could only love you more.

If I should chance to touch a brightest star
and open heaven's windowpane,
If I should dream to find you there,
If I could only love you more.

If I could be all that I feel, and think, and want to be
and open up my heart to you,
If I could hold your smile forever,
If I could only love you more.

If all my wishes, dreams, and thoughts
shone through for you to see,
If God would let my soul touch yours,
then surely, I could love you more.

Genny Finton

AND YET ANOTHER DAY HAS COME AND PASSED

To my daughter, Tori Sofris, my son Konrad Finton and to the love for their father, Roger. To my dear friend Vicky Townsend who believed.

And yet another day has come and passed, but for the thought of you I surely would have lingered not. And yet another sunrise I must face without your tender touch or your kiss of love. Why do you beseech me in my most trying hours. Surely the test of my never ending love is at this hour. My heart knows no peace nor my mind and body any rest. Have you no feeling of my ever present love for you? It is in the air you breath and it runs its endless course in your warm blood. Please don't forsake my love. Every moment I live, every day of my life is yours but just for the asking. I love you my very dearest breath of life.

Cara Sanborn

SUICIDE

It was a dark night, I was as usual all alone
all I could hear was the tapping sounds of the rain
then there was a crack of light that lit up the sky
I heard the distant sound of thunder as a chill rose up my spine
I knew this was it, this was to be my last night,
For the next time my family sees me
I will be lying in a heavenly bed lined with white satin.
For I will have killed myself, for I feel as if I have no purpose in life
Why am I here? I would constantly ask myself
then in the midst of my thoughts, the phone rang
reluctantly I picked it up and uttered "Hello"
then I heard a deep and handsome voice say "I love you"
then I knew that I would live, I would not take my life
I knew now my purpose in life was to love and to be loved.

Patricia Jean Satterlee

SUMMER NIGHTS SYMPHONY

For you, Steven, in honor of our unforgettable summer together, with my love.

The sweet breeze
The window awards me
Carries in
A symphony of night songs

Infinite
And echoing

Soothing
With familiarity

Dozing and dreaming
To perpetual screeches
I toss
And I turn

With you in my heart
The cricket lullaby
Rocks me to sleep

Raquel Barajas

Raquel Barajas

FOREVER AND EVER . . .

To my family and friends and all those people who have encouraged me or been a source of inspiration. Thank you.

I have so many feelings
So deep in my heart
If I only knew
What I really feel for you.
We started out so very young
Too young, in fact to really know
What the future held for us.
Slowly we drifted apart
Like two ships
In a stormy sea
Now where can you be?
If only I knew where to find you
I'd run by your side
And beg you to come back.
But in case I never find you
Or you found someone to replace me
Remember, I'll always love you,
Forever and ever . . .

R Jean Kelley

GRANDMA'S HOUSE

I am a grown woman now
with children of my own.
You want to be a part of my life,
something I've never known.

We never had Grandma's place to go.
I missed most of the childhood fun.
I would give the world to my children,
why couldn't you have given some?

There were no mother daughter teas for me
or serious heart to heart chats.
No sober, loving hugs and kisses,
you would have none of that.

Now there's no Grandma's place to go,
but age will catch up with me.
And I'll be Grandma's house one day,
maybe then at peace I'll be.

Susan D Allison

AFFAIRS

Contemplate fantasy escapes,
Excites the soul, spirits elate.
Forbidden loves promise perfection
Thrill enhanced by intrigue and deception.

Whispered plans of clandestine nights,
Silently scream in sheer delight!
It stimulates the imagination
And intensifies our expectation.

Dismissed danger creates illusion
But suspicions arise from confusion.
Deceit discovered destroys all trust
Devastated lives from pursuit of lust!

S M Erickson

SEAMAN'S DREAM

He is lined and weathered like a ship that has foregone many storms.
He looks as old as time itself, with his bright white hair and gnarled hands.
His skin is pulled taut over his ridged form,
And his sunken eyes burn like two bright dots in the dull brown sand.
He is a man of the sea, like his father, his father's father,
and so on down the line;
All marrying young to produce an heir to their watery throne.
But he only has a daughter, who's now a mother—mine.
When she was born he hated her and his heart hardened to a stone.
But when she bore him a grandson that all changed.
So now, as he lies dying, holding my hand, he smiles,
for he knows I will carry on in his footsteps.

Angela Toles

MY LITTLE BOY

In memory of Robin and dedicated to my best friend, Craig Parsons

I walk in your room and see your bed
Your soft little pillow where you laid your head
I see your picture in the golden frame
And remember the special day you came
You were my world, my bundle of joy
I could call you my own, my little boy
You were so special in your own little way
I never knew there would be a day
A day that I wouldn't see your smile
The kind you get from only a child
But then that day, some how it came
And now my world will never be the same
You filled my life with so much joy
You were my own, my little boy
But God took you away from me
I guess that's how it was meant to be
Even though your memory stayed
I know that in time there will be a day
And when this day finally comes
We will be reunited mother and son

Teresa Morrow

MOMENTS IN TIME

To Dexter, for whom it was written, and to Gail—thanks for helping me to find myself, and to realize the potentials thereof.

Life passes as quickly as the fleeting wind, brief yet these moments may

seem;
photographs are etched into our minds, as are those graphics of the land.
Savor each delicacy placed before you; see it, feel it, taste it, for tomorrow it may fade into a vast unknown space, far beyond the grasp of man.
Utilize all that life offers, if only for that brief moment;
just enough time for the shutter to snap and the memory to be yours through eternity.

Teresa A Irby
IMAGINE ME THERE

This poem is dedicated to Lesley & Kayla, my husband and daughter. I love them very much.

Babe, "I love you!" No matter what you will always be a part of me. Even if we ain't together.
When you ever need me. Close your eyes. And
"Imagine me there!"

Every moment with you, means a life time to me. But when we're not together. You can close your eyes and
"Imagine me there!"

Every time you touch me. I just die in your arms. Lord I wish I could be with you forever.
But there's always an end to everything.
Life, love and the world. So close your eyes and
"Imagine me there!"
With you tonight.

Akua Brabham
THE SPIRIT INSIDE

To my parents, John Gibson and Dorothy Gibson Moore. To my sons Arnold and Mark Brabham and their families. To my Psychology and English professors, Dr. J. Wynne and M. Alaoui. And last, to someone I love most dear.

Just call on that God spirit,
and it can work for you.
It can lift you up
and make you feel better.
It can make you aware of love
you never even dreamed of.
Touch the life around you.
Touch the one you love.
Feel the softness, and tenderness.
The radiance of life and love.
And that peace, that we all want—
is the ecstasy of life.
It will make you feel alive—
to love and live, to live and love.
Just call on that God spirit
and it can work for YOU.

Donna Jean Larsen
YOU TOUCHED MY HEART

For Craig Alan, Thank you for touching my heart and life like no one else ever has! With all my love always, Donna Jean

You entered my life from out of no where,
You came at the right moment when I needed someone near;
You took away all the sadness, clouds and grey from my eyes,
And brought me happiness, sunshine and blue skies.

I am very thankful for the time we have shared,
I just want you to know how much I care;
I feel like I've known you for years and years,
When I'm with you, I'm happy and I don't shed even silent tears.

For the first time in my life, I feel I can be me,
When I'm with you, even my spirit feels free;
You are very special to me in so many ways,
I hope I will bring you happiness in each and every day.

It's so nice to have someone to laugh with, talk to, and even to hold,
I have someone to share my secrets with and know they won't be told;
I know there may come a day when we have to part,
I just wanted you to know, you touched a very special part of me, my heart!

Joe McNamer
A SUPREME WAY

Is there any supreme way
Whose magical touch breathes eternal life
Where the blackest night becomes the clearest day
Where my senses capture a radiant song
Making eternity no longer seem long

Flying forever in the infinite space
Existing in no particular place
Where no religion of the planet earth
May present its opinionated face

But who am I to perceive such a way?
For I only have a three pound brain
Like four billion others existing today
Trying to be struck by the eternal ray

The truth some may say they have
Assuming their three pounder can grasp
Eternity knows no deadline to meet
So why bother to jump so fast

Let eternal law continue its work
Let all people see another day
Inching yet closer to the supreme way
To that there's nothing more to say

Kathy Melton
EXPRESSIONS

I'm sorry, I say
and wait for a response.
He stares straight ahead,
as if he's trying to make
the wall before him turn to ice.

Couldn't you move,
make a motion?
I said it, loud and open—
where are you—
I'm being nice.

I need your reply,
You leave me open
exposed like a target.
Say you hate me,
or you forgive me—
Just don't make me beg.

I turn and go—
he gestures, but it is too late.
The gap has closed,
the bridge is gone;
One more rift in the world.

Marc Moorhead
ALONG THE WAY

Dedicated to Life, Love, and Lindsey Lee

I walked along in silent gaze,
Never knowing what was my fate.
This or that I only knew.
Does someone else think this too?

I lumbered down life's many trails,
Never knowing what was my hail!
Often wondering if I'd fail
Does someone else set the scale?

I gently drifted with the breeze.
I found that in going, I was pleased.
Always owing for a life of ease,
Can someone else charge a price for these?

I learned a lesson along the way.
That love of life is the tune I play
From now on knowing what is my fate.
Does someone else sorrow at hate?

I joy in living having love as my fate
My heart is for-giving. I have no place for hate.
Sharing and caring is all we should be
Will someone else come join me?

Tara Solander
IF YOU WILL . . .

Imagine a big tree with many leaves,
a warm friendly wind
rushes through the tree
picking out one single leaf
and tosses it in the air.
The leaf dances and
flies freely with the wind.
Then the wind turns icy
and stops dancing.
The leaf falls helplessly to the ground
where it is left alone
to turn brown and die.
Now imagine me as the leaf
dancing with the ever-changing wind,
The tree is now life,
and the once warm and
comforting wind
is you.

Sandra Elizabeth Marques
GREATEST LOVE

Dedicated to Maria's dad, Rafael Bustillo and my parents, Bull and Eve Marques.

There's no love greater than a parents' love,
It's instilled in you with the peace of a dove.
Their hearts of gold and ways that show
They help you grow though you don't know;
To tend to your ways, to make happy days.

A parents' love is never ending
It's always there, since before the beginning.
They teach you to pray in a sweet loving way;
To expect you to share and give of your heart,
Even when they're not there.

They share their knowledge
And swallow their pride.
They make you stand tall;
When you're looking to fall.

Daddys are special and mamas are too,
They Love their children, no matter what they do.
You can search and search on God's Green Earth
And find no love greater than that of a parents' love!

Becky S Pittman
FEELING LOST

It's so very hard to let go
To say goodbye—to release
All of the feeling, the moments
The dreams—of a love no longer true . . .
The struggle has been long and fierce
But through each and every argument
A little more was lost
A few more scars were left
An island of regret soon was formed.
With each reoccurring dispute
More bitter words
Old wounds reopened—stable lives
Once again shaken and uncertain.
A heart can only take so much
So much rejection
So much hate
And Yes—only so much love.

John Shetler Youngblud
FRIGHT
(NIGHT WATCHMAN—1947)

Out of the stillness, out of the night,
out of the darkness gallops fright
Furiously thundering straight for me
on stampeding hoofs of fantasy.

Be off you spawn of satan's sin!
curse you and your grisly grin!
No quivering quarry for you here
to fetter with your chains of fear.

So go pretender, hasten. . . flee . . .
for patience isn't long with me
And keep in mind as you embark
that I'm no victim of the dark.

Through the stillness, through the night,
through the darkness glimmers light;
Sleepily stretching is the dawn
and loathsome fright is gone, is gone.

Laurie L Hiller
A DREAM

A dream is just an image
of what you wish there'd be.
And often times with you
I wonder what I see.
It's like being a mirror
from the inside looking out.
Our dreams seem to be the same,
but it's your feelings I tend to doubt.
It's like wishing on a star
for love and happiness,
But sometimes things go wrong
and turn out somewhat less.
I'd love to be with you
that's the image that I've seen,
But you need to think the same,

to understand what I mean.
You joke around so much
it's hard to know what's real.
But what I say is serious
It's exactly how I feel.

Raina Linville
DOES SHE LOVE YOU LIKE I DO

We had a special friendship, you and me
We shared so many secrets thoughts—our dreams.
We told each other what we could achieve.
We planned our lives together, so it seems.
But then one day you left me standing there.
I wondered what I'd said or done to you.
You went away and left me in despair.
You said to me, "There's nothing you can do."
So what went wrong in all the love we shared.
For not a crisis we could not withstand.
I always thought that you forever cared.
But now I see you with her, hand in hand.
I see you at the places we went to.
I wonder, does she love you like I do?

Shannon Bartole
THE ROSE IS LIKE POISON

The rose is like poison.
The red for the love you
once gave me.
The thorns for the pain you thrust
upon me now.
I feel the thorns drive into
my heart.
Blood drips down my chest
as the color drains
from
the
rose.

James Adams
CHANGING SEASONS OF LOVE

To all the loves that have touched my heart gently, like a warm summer breeze.

Here I stand again before another long goodbye,
The sorrow in my heart pushing teardrops from my eye.
The beating of my heart is near too much to bear,
For I never again shall hear, Her voice in my ear.
Gone the tender "I love you," or warm and welcome "hello."
Now only a cold "goodbye," as she slowly turns to go.
Once the brightest blue, of the warmest summer day,
Winter has descended and changed my skies to grey.
Encircled in an overcoat, to try to hide the pain,
I wash away my tears in the cold December rain.
The world continues to turn, the seasons to evolve,
And the riddle of lost love, again I'll try to solve.
So where does lost love go when from the heart departs?
And will it evermore return, and be like at the start.
As the seasons, the winter snows begin to thaw.
My heart will slowly warm, and into love I'll fall.
This time could find me true love, to guard against life's storms,
Protect from summer showers, and in winter keep me warm.
So I could once again look forward; to the new and strange,
Frightened no longer, by the world's turns; and the seasons change.

M S Terry Mason
ALONE . . .

To James, my only love, for encouragement to fulfill my desired dream.

Times are changing
In every way . . .
And I'm alone
Each and every day.

My world has crumbled
My life is through . . .
I am so alone
I am so blue.

My will to live
Has left and gone . . .
My values of life,
End with a sad song.

Maybe I'm caught
Between life and death . . .
Maybe there's nothing
Nothing left.

I need a will
A will to survive . . .
I need to see life again
I need life by my side.

Dennis P Makhudu

Dennis P Makhudu
MORNING LOVE

From Haluk Dişçekici: Dedicated to Yasuko, who serves tea with "gentilesse."

Yeah, yield your yean youth yently to me, Yasuko—
And then my Yakut yand yanks yodels inside you,
And yin that Momentary yen, you quick quake to slake,
Till eye redblood too soon quip, yet quietly squirt—

As the quick brown fox jumps over your hazy lazy
Den glen like cave yaws glistening creamyjuicy honey.

As we arrive at the common yam mount of gorged glee;
As we thunder claps between and betwixt yummy tea and you;
And rhyme nor yet reason can hold my lightning whisk shake,
Yelping yinside yolk yak yogurt yelling hip-yip joy . . .

We yokozuna yodel yes, yes, you yipe in me, with me.
Like yin yang you say, yet also yogi singly yenjoy;

Yesterday eve sheets yawn yoked us together, and now yellow,
A glorious morn yearning yields yore Yule ululations yet.

Jodelle LeProwse
MEMORIES

In Loving Memory of My Mother Norilee LeProwse

The day that you left me,
I thought I would die.
Many nights I wished I could,
but all I did was cry.

I said today that I'd find a way
to leave these tears behind.
But I missed you even more
when I got you off my mind.

I don't want to get over you.
I'd rather hold your memory
than to be with somebody new.
I don't ever want to get over you.

Everybody told me:
It wasn't the end.
To put the past behind me,
and start my life again.

Brenda Holcomb
MY GRANDPA

I dedicate this poem to a very special lady, Virginia Pierce, who introduced me to the best friend I'll ever have . . . myself. Thank you Virginia for your confidence.

Oh! but for the moment when I sit quietly at his feet,
As he wanders through his memories of yesterday so sweet.

As we open up the doors of time and travel through the past,
He opens up his mind to me with knowledge oh so vast.

We talk of places he has been, and things his eyes have seen.
And on the wisdom of his years, my hungry mind does glean.

I know that days turn into years and I fail to say to him,
How very much he means to me, even with toothless grin.

He watched me as I stumbled through my adolescent years,
And reached for me with loving hands when I came to him in tears.

Yet, he never tore me down, or made me feel so frail,
But showed me how, with God, I might fall but never fail.

The wisdom of his many years is like a haven of rest.
For with his patient guidance, I know I'll do my best.

Yes, his hair may turn to silver and his step begin to slow,
But the wisdom of his many years, gives Grandpa a special glow!

Frances Begley
NURSING HOME RESIDENT

She is sitting there—her eyes are staring off in space
No smile or frown on her face.

Her hands limp on her lap—her legs useless, the muscles all gone.

Her mind long ago forgot all the memories, the joys, the pain.
I would like to tell her I care—put a smile on her face
A tear in her eye, fill her hands with work to do.

Give her feet a path to walk and make new memories.

She is sitting lifeless in a chair, hands on her lap, has nothing to do.

If her feet worked, they would have no where to go.

Her eyes stare straight ahead—nothing to see.
Her mind long ago forgotten all the memories, the joy, the pain.

Regina Mastrull
THIS IS WHAT I DREAM IN BED

I dedicate this poem to my sister Alicia, my friends Jill and Olivia, and anyone who dares to dream. Love Regina

Purple, pink, orange, blue, and red,
This is what I dream in bed.
Satin sheets the color of rose,
or a little baby with its tiny nose.
This is what I dream in bed,
A bee on a blooming flower,
or a gumball sweet or sour.
No nightmares can enter my head,
'Cause this is what I dream in bed.

Barbara Rame Taylor
RHYME AND REASON

In memory of James and Clifford Rame and my father Joe Rame.

Oh to have words that blend
With Rhyme and Reason.
As the colors that a day sends
With each changing season.
To have words to tell it all
Without any doubts.
To have people call
"It's Perfect!" in definite shouts.
To tell of the beauty of a spring day.
To tell of the joy of a child's laughter.
To tell of love found along the way.
Or the peace that really matters.
Serenity in knowing today's okay.
Courage in facing what may come.
Having faith to be able to say,
"I really know where it all comes from!"
To have those words that blend
With Rhyme and Reason.
Lend to me these words, my friend
And it shall be Our Creation.

Vera Williams Stricklin
SOULS, SEE, HEAR MY SONG

Summer sun on a winter day,
A tiny snowflake, in the month of May,
Things so beautiful, yet seem so wrong,
At least to souls who have no song.

I have felt that summer sun,
On delicate winter skin,
And I shall see a snowflake,
On a summer day again.

For I see through my soul,
Through the song I sing alone,
For all that is beauty,
I see as not wrong.

Oh the mysteries of life,
I cherish with inward sight,
If other souls could hear my song,
They could see our Master's plight.

Yes miracles can still be glanced upon,
If we search within our souls, our

songs,
And alas, the miracles really take wing,
When all the other souls learn to sing!

Jerry Robert Dixon
A ROSE BLOOMS IN NOVEMBER

To my loving wife Rosemarie

It was in November of nineteen eighty three
When I met a pretty woman named Rosemarie,
She set my heart on fire,
To have her love was my heart's desire
In the months that followed,
We laughed, we loved and we cried
We had built a love that would never die
I want to pledge my love to thee,
I will always protect and love my Rosemarie

Sheila Mose Lessane
THE STATE OF THE SCHOOL
We heard you had an accident
but you will soon be mending,
We'll report the state of the school
in this message we'll be sending.

School is running smoothly
and it goes without a hitch,
Ignore the eight-car pile-up
or the buses in the ditch.

Chickenpox has broken out,
the student body is lumpy,
Lice and ringworm all abound
and some are getting mumpy.

The kitchen caught on fire,
all of lunch was charred,
But we'll be making barbecue
of the food that got too hard.

Marshall School wants you well,
so give it your best shot,
But if you don't return real soon
it will be a vacant lot.

Inez Babb Young
LOVE REMEMBERED
I remember George,
My love of long ago,
The one who stirred my girlish heart,
And set my world aglow.

But that is oh so far away,
Though memory still holds him;
And sadness comes now as I think
Of love I could not win.

For someone else is in his arms,
And hers are his caresses;
While I in loneliness recall
The love my life still misses.

Perhaps some day in distant years,
As through life's roads we're roaming,
With arms outstretched and joyous heart,
My eyes shall see him coming.

Carolyn Donald
MICHAEL JACKSON
Michael Jackson is a very blessed young man,
He is loved by a lot of people all over the land;
I've never seen anyone that dances the way he does,
He looks so fragile, he is very easy to love;
He seems to be a very down to earth guy,
I hope to get to meet him before I die;
Most people recognize him as a star,
But I see beyond that, and I know he'll go far;
God made him what he is today,
He realizes that, and that's why I know he won't go astray;
Michael, no matter where you go or what you do,
Always remember that I love you.

Edward J Eller
NEVER LET GO

Much appreciation and thanks, go to PHYLLIS J. McELROY and JAMES R. ROJAS.

Don't let this good love slip away,
Let us hold the dreams we've made together.
My whole world is built around you,
Please don't let it fade away.

My heart will always treasure
All the things we've done together.
Our happy memories will linger on,
As we look back in years to come.

And if you're ever sad and lonely,
I will try to ease the pain.
Let us not drown in the sea of sorrow,
For I will be there to love you again.

I will always help you in times of trouble,
For we can make it work out right.
Take me in your arms and hold me,
I will make you feel alright.

I'm the one who wants you,
And I love you so.
I would never leave you,
I will NEVER LET GO.

Angela M Hettinger
LOST LOVE
I'll try not to cry,
because my love has died.
Along with my feelings and my fears,
each time I try to talk it
ends in silent tears.
I've loved and lost,
but that's what it cost.
There's a small price to pay,
for things you may say.
But life goes on day by day.

Gretchen Jelinek
BOX OF MEMORIES
I see your face across the room
And my mind wanders in the aisles
of memory filled shelves.

It reaches up and pulls down a box.
With the lid open I'm transformed
to another time—another place.

Remember the time.
Remember the place.
It all comes back by just seeing your face.

All the memories are not ones I care to recall.
But they are all there,
one in all.

Someone speaking to me brings me back to reality.
I answer back what I should.
But my mind and heart are in a different place in time.

I move across the room.
You are gone.
But the memory of you still lingers and always will.

Rob Thomsen
AFFRAY DECORUM

Dedicated to all athletes who have endured to better themselves.

Standing in the winds of belligerence,
Hephaestus subdues my body;
and in my suffering I achieve grandeur.
I think not of my own well being,
But the cause for which I fight;
The cries of the quitters bellow in my ear:
From the depths of Dis of which they shriek.
I look not down,
but forward;
Forward to victory:
For I am,

I am a Warrior.

Helene M Goodman
THE EYES OF AN ORPHAN

A special thank you to Marilyn Stone for her input and editing, also to the following: E.M., R.D., B.D. & G.L.

My face is pale,
My body too thin.
My eyes tell a tale,
They're the eyes of an orphan.

You can hear them pleading,
O, they're crying out
For a friendly greeting
Or a jovial shout.

My days are all bleak,
They hold no bright plan.
My eyes spring a leak,
They're the eyes of an orphan.

You can feel their pain,
They penetrate your soul,
Like a desert needs rain
I need hope and a goal.

My arms are so empty,
My eyes gaze above.
O, God, can't you bring back
My parents to love?

Julie E Turriff
FLUORESCENT STARS

Dedicated to Jimmy, the first-magnitude star in A Summer Place.

I painted fluorescent stars
on my bedroom ceiling
exactly how we'd remember them.
How they danced the many times
we shunned sleepiness and
pondered the universe
from my window ledge.
Remember? That's when you decided
upon being a first-magnitude star
for the rest of eternity.

I painted Gemini, the twins,
for you shine so close to me.
There's Aquarius, who we
thanked for sending those chilly
Autumn rains, and Orion, the brightest
of all constellations, who you
pretended to be. I put Leo close
to Sagitta, Cupid's arrow, that never
really had a chance to pierce your heart.
There's Scorpio near the corner and
then there's Virgo, the goddess of
Justice, whose choice we so admired.

Near the middle I painted
only a sliver of a moon
with one star beside it,
for you said you'd walk just
beyond there to wait for me.
You'd wait until I became a star, too.

Audrey J Ewers
EXCITEMENT

To my loving husband Vincent

Something very exciting
Being able to see clearly
Laughing at funny things
Getting nervous before a game
Getting a call from a guy
Listening to someone
Trying to explain something
To someone else who doesn't understand

Amber Muhlnickel
THE LIFE OF A POOR MAN
The life of a poor man is simple
He need not boast nor brag
He findeth love within the heart
of everyone he knows
He gives the time he has
for others and not just his brothers
He knows not the life
of a rich man with money;
but his riches are in his heart

Jane Thompson Loo
MY DOG

To all whom have loved and lost a pet

My dog so dear passed on today,
now she is free of pain.
For she is with LORD JESUS,
so it was not in vain.

Although we miss her very much,
I know she loves it there.
For she can wag her tail,
knowing that HE cares.

She never knew a stranger,
she loved everyone in sight,
and held out her paw,
so you could squeeze it tight.

She loved to hug and kiss you,
and lay there by your side.
And when you'd pet her on her head,
she looked at you with pride.

I know someday that I will be
in heaven with my girl.
Until that day, I'll remember her
as my precious pearl.

Gloria Cadag Verdadero
CROWN ME KING

Every early misty morning along the earthy dewy pavement
of Phiney Ridge, walking, running, jogging, our memories together keep flashing back and forth in my unceased troubled mind like the bright neon lights in unclattered street in First Avenue.

That unforgettable ugly day you were painfully hurt, cried bitterly which seemed eternal. Every drop of those tears was shining sharp blade piercefully stabbing my loud, pounding, confessing chest. T'was killing me to see-t'was hurting you!

My open remorseful mind entered your doubtful brain; my pleading heart honestly spoke to your bleeding, broken heart; my once uncaring tone magically changed into a sweet, soft, angelic song. Yet I felt helpless like a leaf floating in the sky toyed by the wind. Too late, to realize my sinful sin—please forgive me!

Aahh . . . I tried so hard to let the wind pumped some air in my dried plugged lungs. I felt no relief. You gazed at me, my eyes surrendered as your tearfully sad, brown eyes silently asked why the other 'she' in our lives. Excuses I had not. Slowly you walked away—my world sank!

Forever will I seek for my lost love
To once again, crown me king.

Martha Foley
I CATCH HIS EYE

The first one: For you grandpa! You always wanted my poems published, wish you were here to see! The love you always gave and much continuous encouragement. I love you!

From across the room
I catch his eye,
he winks, I smile

From across the hall
I catch his eye,
he winks, I smile

Those were the days
when we were close

Those days have passed.
No longer does he wink.
No longer do I smile.

From across the room
she catches his eye,
he winks, she smiles

Jennifer Birk
IT WAS YOU

A single rose, I give to you.

It represents all the love I have for you.
I cared for it, like I care for you.
The beauty it has—is the beauty I see in you everyday.
I was careful with it because of the thorns, but
at times I got hurt anyway.
Every morning I would smell its fragrance and it made
me love you more and more.

When I picked it, dew ran down the petals like it was crying.

I began to cry.
I cried because the rose was you.
I cared for it, and I saw beauty in it everyday.
It hurt me, but I still loved it.
Now, because I picked it, it will soon die.

So I will give you this single rose.
Care for it, for as long as it lives.
Find beauty in its delicate petals.
And love it because I loved it.

After it dies,
Love it still—because I loved you.

Roseanne Rasmussen
TIME, TEARS AND YEARS

I would like to dedicate this poem to my parents, of whom I love very much.

It will come and it will go,
tears will swell and start to flow.
years will seem like eternity
for those of us in need of company,
tears, time and years
are all a part of our growing fears.
So give me strength now and then,
when I am faced with the pain
that I remember from long ago.
From a time when I thought I knew
Just what it was that burned inside,
like a fire glowing bright.
Now as I sit here and I realize
the glow of a fire deep inside is gone
for now by
Time, tears and years.

Janet Walters
THAT'S MY BABE

Dedicated to the most wonderful man in the world. The man I love with all my heart

My Babe is sweet
My Babe is neat
My Babe just can't be beat.

My Babe likes blue
My Babe is true
My Babe likes me too.

My Babe likes to tease
My Babe likes to squeeze
My Babe always likes to please.

My Babe never makes me sad
My Babe always makes me glad
My Babe to me is never bad.

My Babe never makes me cry
My Babe to me will never lie
My Babe always makes me feel high.

My Babe always treats me fair
My Babe always with me will share
My Babe is just the kind who cares.
That's just My Babe.

Juan Silverio MD
SAD LIFE, SAD POEMS

She fixed her gaze upon my soul
and asked, with saddened eyes,
why did I write depressing poems.
And then from deep my soul replied,
somewhat confused at her surprise,
that it was life I wrote about,
and life is sad most of the time.

But she refused to hear my soul
and then insisted that in life
there must be also times of joy
and of fulfillment and of happiness.
My soul agreed that must be so
but said that happy moments are so short
that mind and pen cannot record them.

While on the other side of life's existence,
the one that brings mourning and grief,
it seems that sadness and heartaches
float in the midst of thoughts
forever and a day, and can be written
with repose for days and months and years,
and even deep into eternity.

William L Doiley
A FRIEND

"To Mary, my beautiful wife." Thank you for helping me in realizing my God given talent . I love you. Bill

One day while I was passing through loneliness
I met a friend whom I had not seen before.
Softly he spoke, with the kindness of words
He told of how he has guided me,
When I was confused and not knowing
Which way to go.
He spoke about how he built the invisible fence
Around my heart to keep iniquity and malice out.
He explained that he has given me three gifts
Faith, Hope and Love "Faith" being the first
He said always keep the faith in whatever I do,
No matter how large or small the task may be.
"Hope" which I have given you freely;
Keep on hoping for a good day and a better tomorrow
For both shall be yours.
And the third gift which you shall possess is "Love"
Love thy neighbor as thyself, and I will be with you forever.

Bernice Smalls Green

Bernice Smalls Green
THE TOUCH OF GOD

To my Daughter Debra L. Green and The Youth in America and Abroad, and The Smalls Family.

You have but one life to live;
You can make a difference from day to day,
In your work and what you give
If you make connection with God and pray.

God's magic touch can come through you,
Who have faith and accepted his plan.
He'll guide you in what you say and do,
To help those who are lost, understand.

Strengthen your faith forever in God;
Press on toward the highest calling each day.
Reach out and touch him, as you trod;
Remember, only once you are passing this way.

He has no special one to love;
He died to save all races of man.
His power spreads out from above,
To strengthen people in every land.

The life you live and the things you say
Are evidence of your spiritual touch.
The smile and work you do each day,
Let the world know you love God so much.

Heather L Druckenmiller
WHAT THE AMERICAN FLAG MEANS TO ME . . .

What the American flag means to me
Is our land, our people, and our sea.
Thirteen stripes; with six white and seven red,
Stars are states, into the union they were led.
A symbol of justice and liberty,
A symbol of our country being free.
The flag shows all the people who lost their lives,
To fight for our country, left children and wives.
A joining of fifty states as one,
A symbol—their fight for freedom was won.
During war, our flag was up and blowing,
Independence forever growing.
The pledge to the flag says united we stand,
America is walking hand in hand.
Our flag means independence to one, to all,
Looking up to our flag, we stand proud and tall.
Every country has their own flag, but who
Has a flag better than the red, white and blue?
Our flag is like a lock, which we have the key,
To open to find, freedom will always be . . .
This is what the American flag means to me.

Donald J Lutz
Northwestern University
Class of '71
FULL CIRCLE

Dedicated to Dr. J. Allen Hynek Professor Emeritus of Astronomy Northwestern University

Soaring through the sky
A cosmic lullaby
Greets this newborn son
Allen and Halley have begun

One through the heavens and mysteries of space
The other through a telescope is finding his place
But both on a path of wonder and delight
And both shedding light where once there was night

And now both it seems shall meet once again
It's been a long time since nineteen hundred and ten
Yes they're back from their journeys and like two faithful friends
They're coming full circle together again

Emmanuel Wells Scriven
REFLECTIONS FROM HEAVEN

Put away your fears my darling;
 It matters not what the world
 may think.
God loves you, and I love you;
 You're still my child distinct!

It was so wonderful when you were

born;
And it matters not, now that you're old.
It matters not if you're brilliant or dull;
Or if you're shy, or you're bold.

I remember your laughter, and your tears;
Oh yes, there were more than a few.
I remember your hugs and your kisses;
And the comfort I gave you.

We shared our love, and we grew together;
Both of us, you and I.
And as we both grew much older, it was inevitable that I should die.

But the glorious thing that can't be changed;
Such as I loved you as you grew;
You'll always be my darling baby, and I will always still love you!

Carmine Lombardo

NOBLE ONE

You, Noble One, keeper of minds, what have they done to you?
Is it disrespect that makes you sad, or their apathy that blinds the hope you have in others,
And saps the strength that so long made you proud of what you are ?
By far, is it the home falling apart at the seams,
where dreams flourished and were nourished;
Now dividing divorce clouds and shrouds stability
Where has the love gone? For you as well as others?
Are you trapped in a worldwind of madness?
Oh, Noble One, you are, but never give in;
Life depends on you as well as it does its creator;
For you are enlightenment;
you are strength;
You are the hope of the future;
even if it's one,
Think of what you've done,
Noble one;
Be sure he won't forget you,
his favorite teacher,
And when he teaches others,
May your light shine—forever.

J Nohe Villatoro

POET AND LETTERS

People praise the
creator that invented
letters so that poets may
realize the wings of their souls
and before the world
uncover themselves from
the veils of their minds

and they eagerly paint
pictures with words and
continue to desire the
blank pages which have yet to be filled.

Clarissa Hart

WAVES

The boredom sets in.
My thoughts shift
Like drops through a sieve,
Flowing smoothly into nothing.
The blackness rises
Swallowing the sieve and the drops,
Leaving my mind blank.
A catatonic state floods
Through me.
My eyelids droop
And my vision clouds
As waves of blackness
flow through me.
The tides recede
And light washes in,
Relieving the boredom
And opening the way
To the future.

E Sims MacRae

SHARING LOVE

To my beautiful daughters

I can close my eyes,
And see your face warm with love,
Your eyes seeing deeply into my soul,
And reading the unspoken words in my heart;

I can close my eyes,
And feel your strong hand enveloping my own,
As if I were a child, going down a dark passageway;

I can close my eyes,
And feel your tender, protective arms around me,
Offering a hidden, secure harbor for my ship,
As it's tossed and floundering in the dark seas;

I can close my eyes,
And you are with me,
One heart, one mind, one soul for all eternity;

I close my eyes, now, to be with you.

Pamela S Robbins

I GO UP HIGH ON MY SWING

This poem is dedicated to the crew aboard the spaceship Challenger

I go up high on my wing
On a hot day in spring
I go up so high
I nearly touch the sky
It was so blue
I stayed up there for you the spaceship crew.

John F Barger

WHY

Seven, Americans, as apple pie
Walked to the launch-pad, one more try
No second guesses, a mental high
Hoping today that this bird will fly

Count-down moving, ten thirty-eight
A perfect lift-off, looking just great
A very good climb at the right rate
When all of a sudden, up jumps fate

A huge red ball of fire, twelve miles high
Countless pieces falling from the sky
So very tragic, seven should die
Millions were watching and asking, Why?

Pieces were scattered for miles around
Launch control most concerned, under-ground
Raining bits of metal . . . horrible sound
With little hope the cause can be found

From a great many, this hand picked crew
Many applied, but so few would do
A dangerous mission they all knew
But from out there, a breath-taking view.

Sherry L Otto

HIS HIDE AWAY

This is dedicated to Nick Merriott with Love, for sharing his hidden world with me . . .

As the rain came down upon his world, it blanketed the forest with its soft, wet love. Calm and quiet with no demands, questions or expectations. It's there for all to behold.

The rain on the leaves echoes through the trees, soft like a heart beat, and I felt lost in its beauty.

Fog began to roll in and cover the mountains much like tucking a baby into bed for a night's rest.

As he stood there looking in pure wonder and speaking about the land, I watched all his tension wash away. Truly loving his hidden world.

We stood at an old foundation made of stone from a time forgotten long ago. I stood and wondered about those within, now forever gone, as new lives begin. Now filled with ferns and other growth, its beauty untouched and more brilliant with the rain's coat.

I thank him for those dreams, for I saw through his eyes all the beauty he holds dear. It will be forever in my memories.

David L Gebhardt Sr

DEATH'S FACE

To Cancer Patients

Death touched my shoulder and I turned to look upon his face.
Alas I saw but blackness under his hooded shroud
Then a spark of hope, like a candle lit at night,
Pushed away the blackness of despair.
His face I saw, rotten flesh and bones bleached white.
I told the demigog that I would not be
Taken on a cloud of sleep unto his musty bosom,
Nor would I be taken piece by piece by his cancerous soul,
Nay, I will fight Him with all my forces.
Not chained and dragged to his waiting barge, beaten to its bowel
I shall cling to life as bitter as it seems,
To see the sun rise once more.
Once more, to see the sun rise I adore.

Shirley Dyer

YOU

To my dream come true, my inspiration, Cory: I love you with all my heart and soul, and I always will.

Sometimes I just sit and think
Of all the wonderful things you mean to me.
I think of all the great times we've had
and all of the times that are still to be.

In the same whisper that I thank God every day
for love, life, health, and happiness,
I quietly thank Him for you.
For, without you, I would never have this.

When you put your hand in mine,
my heart soars like a dove.
And when your eyes caress mine,
my soul sheds silver tears of love.

When I dream of the future,
I never walk the path alone.
When I'm feeling lonely,
the warmth of my hand always finds your hand as its home.

James Marshall

THE NEVER ENDING HOLE

Day, night, hot, cold,
The blood flows through the rivers and the hill . .
The never ending fight for justice
Or what we call justice.
This land is supposed to be the "justice for them all."
But are we really as just as we think?
We fly in the air; we shoot for revenge—
Or is it just spite?
We're in a never-ending hole that we're stuck in
Or a rut that we'll probably never get out of.
Even in space, we're in the rut.
So what does it matter?

Phauneil Rebecca-Kay Hetzel

FOR A MOMENT

To Mark

Like the ocean's waves
Returning
Crashing upon the
Shore
For a moment,
Leaving—
To still echo
Evermore.

Is your memory still
Burning
Knocking upon my
Door
For a moment,
Leaving—
To come beckoning
Once more.

Brian Mello

THE FINAL CHAPTER

Angered by his father's death
He made a commitment of self-sacrifice
Dawn's Awakening slaughtered the carpet of darkness
There is the light
The promise
The hope
The abolishment of resentment aborted the plans
So what if the body deteriorates

So ends the life of mates
The flesh is torn apart by the creatures of mystery
And devoured are the eyes that once could see
But the soul jumped into the young boy's soul
And the insane replaced his immaculate role

Billy Fryer
SNOW AT LAST!

At last the long-awaited snow came
Finally, I would see the white winter wonderland
I had only dreamed of as a child
The ground became a beautiful single sheet
Of smooth, velvety powder
And trees laden with snow and ice
Became living sculptures
Chandeliers of ice hung from the branches
And changed the face of the land
Oh how wonderful it was
To look upon a white and pure earth
I felt my childhood returning
As the fragile flakes fell
So with excitement and anticipation
I bundled up in my warmest clothes
And entered the winter wonderland
The joy and freshness
Of the purifying snow came over me
As I frolicked like a child
When then I thought with sudden awareness
"Man, it's cold!"

Ms Pat Thurman
THE SOUL

Though the way be dark and desolate and you feel like you're all alone, there's an angel nearby at the Golden Gate, to take you to God's great throne.

What peace lies within the troubled heart, when you see you are home again; and the Soul is eternal and knows its place, as you go up and greet your friend!

Keith Peterson
2-BR2-C

To Lorraine

What an elegant design
Of bits and bytes
You are, my love,
2-B, my love.
What a paradigm you can be
And compute, so NeXT
Be free, my love, to
Rewrite R-memory
To text, and upgrade,
My love, my windows
Of the world you
Must view 2-C,
Or prompt you, 2-B,
To exit when i-am
Of no more use.

I C L
THE VISIT

To the People and the Justice system On behalf of every abused child.

I feel a chill throughout our nation
Violence abounds with demoralization.
We the people ponder apathetically and contemplate
Sitting idle, while our legislators legislate,
Laws so entangled with misguided effort to be humane
Within their interwoven web, only the guilty stand to gain.

The victim, a brave little man, told his story upon the court stand
Documented true, by many a doctor's exam.
Through frightened lips came his cry of alarm
His father has repeatedly raped him, done irreparable harm.

But truth means naught at Justice door,
Truth means naught—when you're only four.
Molesters have their rights it seems
To destroy lives and shatter dreams.

A familiar nightmare racks my sleep and then,
I see my Grandson's face again.
Anguished fear shows in his eyes and trembling lip;
He cries, as we prepare him for his trip.
Need I be more explicit?
There he goes for another "visit"!

Stephanie Worobel McCarthy
NIGHT SO YOUNG

This day is gone, yet another to come,
Comfort my soul, night so young . . .
Night so young, fill my mind, with dreams
of wonder, let this day be but a memory,
as lightning is to thunder . . .
This day is gone, yet another to come,
Comfort my need, night so young . . .
Night so young, fill my mind, with dreams
of love, love of children, sent from god,
up above . . .
This day is gone, yet another to come,
Comfort my heart, night so young . .
Night so young, fill my mind, with perfection,
as I count my blessings, one by one . . .
Comfort me, night so young

Corie Paden
BECAUSE OF YOU

To Bobby, the meaning behind these words.

Nothing ever mattered
The way you did to me
And no one ever showed me
All the things there are to see.

No one ever taught me
How to smile when there's pain
To notice that there's sunshine
Even when it has to rain.

You taught me all these good things
And where are you today
Someplace I don't know of . . .
Someplace far away . . .

And all because of you
I thought that I would cry
Then remembered what you told me
For now, it's just, goodbye . . .

Maureen E Rykowski
MY WORLD

To Marty: "I'll always love you."

There's a world out there I long to see,
a world out where I wish to be,
I'd like to experience the splendors of life,
the experience of freedom
before I'm a wife.

This world is not only concrete but abstract.
It can be what you make of it in fact,
I'd like to share it with a special someone someday (you)
But for now it hurts to turn away.
(and I have to)

If I could only make you understand,
These feelings I feel with just a touch of my hand
Then without a doubt you'd see it too,
My world, you would want, so beautiful, so new.

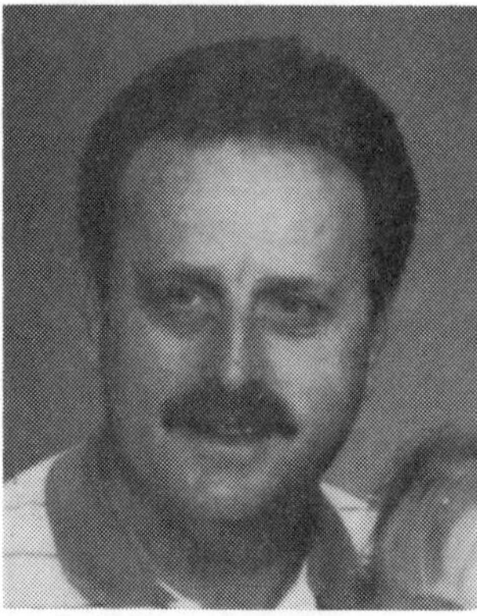

Troy D Treat

Troy D Treat
HEAVEN'S GARDEN

I dedicate this poem to my mother and father who gave me the wisdom and talent to be creative.

Life is as a rose
Along the stems of life
Can be many thorns
But at the end is a flower
It can be you
Another added to God's bouquet

Jeffrey Johnson
THE STORM

On the horizon—a storm is born

The water becomes uneasy,
comforting blue is churned under—
replaced by an ominous black.
All color from the sky vanishes as clouds appear—
the drab grey of headstones in a winter cemetery.
Growing in strength and darkness
they approach—
preparing to release their unbridled wrath.

For a moment, no sound—
all is still.

Then, with a vengeance the rain is released accompanied by gusts of cold death which causes mighty trees to cower in subjection and cars to slow to a crawl paying a reluctant homage to nature's raw power.

The waves, now erratic, slam
against the cement restraints—
pearls of water breaking the binds of the sea hurling into the air
only to be pulled back into the grey abyss.

The sun sets, the storm intensifies—
great branches snap yet go unheard
against the howling of the overpowering wind.
Events intensify—
fears increase
as we are reminded of
our weakness
our insignificance
our mortality

Cora Ronita Jones (Baby Doll)
WHY ARE WE HERE?

This poem is dedicated to all the sincere people who seek the gift of eternal life. Please investigate and prove the gospel of YAHWEH to yourselves.

Is it for pleasure,
Or is it for pain?
Are we here to lose something,
Or to gain?
Why are there color differences?
Why are there trees?
Why do we the people always fight?
Why do we bleed?
Why were we chosen to be born and others not?
Why do we admire the position of sitting on top?
It is a mystery within the human race,
Why does every human have a different face?
Why do the bugs irritate you?
Why must you learn to tie your shoe?
Why is there love and yet hatred
Why is there good and yet evil?
Why is there happiness and yet sadness?

The answer: YAHWEH said,
"Because it pleases me."

T M Piper
CONCENTRATION LOST

My mind.
In chaotic embrace,
Did not mean
To wander such woe begotten paths,
In such bad taste.

With vows of eternal focus,
I enter again;
The realm disgraced.
Pledge as I will,
My thoughts detached remain . . .

Cindy C Grimes
I BELIEVE!

To Charles E Daniel, Jr.—My Best Friend and Special Love!

Do you believe in miracles;
do you believe in destiny?
Do you believe in the Father's will;
do you believe in You and Me? !
Well I do, Yes I do! Oh, I do . . .
What about You?

I believe God watches over Me;
I believe He knows just what to do.
I believe in a "Perfect Love";

I know He'll see Us through!
Yes, I believe, I do! Yes, I believe in Me and You!

There will be times when the talking fails;
And We're not just sure what to do.
There will be times when Satan calls;
Call on God, Faith will see You through!
Oh, I believe, Yes I do! Your Faith will see You through!

Believe in tomorrow and all it can bring;
Believe in Me and You.
We know We could "Make-It" alone or as One;
I pray that the latter comes True! !
Oh, I do! What about You? Yes, I do . . .
Believe in YOU! ! !

Kevin Mulholland

WATCH IT GO

To my parents, my God, my Family and to this inspiration, Karen

Oh how it runs;
like rivers to the sea,
like melted ice cream down a little boy's hand,
like gasoline through a car's engine,
like a shadow at sunset,
like my adrenaline when you're near.

Then to watch it pour;
as rain does from a wounded sky,
as beer does from a keg tap,
as sins do to a priest in a confessional,
as syrup does out of a maple tree,
as thoughts do onto paper about you.

And it will flow;
similar to sand in an hourglass,
similar to wind through long hair,
similar to blood in a vein,
similar to ebb tide's recession,
out of my heart to you.

Barbara Ford Szydla

MYSTERIOUS FRIEND

To Cloud, My Companion of Nine Years

You move gracefully through my life,
adding beauty by your very presence.
You read my thoughts,
you know my heart and spirit.
You experience my joy and sorrow,
feel my pain and pleasure.

You keep your own counsel,
I share your thoughts as you allow.
We each share the other's joy and sorrow,
feel each other's pain and pleasure.
From differing native tongues we speak
a common language of understanding.
Our bond ties us together when apart,
enriches our time together.
We need no mediary,
allow no rivals.
You are my closest, truest friend—
You are my cat

Karen Mitchell

NEW ENGLANDERS

Crunchy, the air smells
in colors;
brown, red, ochre—burnt.
Wind breathes
smoky crackles, a
whisper down the
spine; except to us.
We know.
We know the ticking shade
of the season's secret,
hues of fading earth
just beginning
to come alive.

Jamie Henry

GOOD-BYE

I dedicate this poem to Norman, my first love.

It's time for us to say good-bye,
As you hug me I start to cry.
You tell me that our love is true,
I say that I will always love you.
As you kiss me our last kiss,
I think of things I'll always miss.
The times we've shared, both good and bad,
All the fun that we have had.
Inside my heart I slowly die,
As we say our last good-bye.

Latonia Orr

INJURED BLUEJAY

To my mother with love, Thanks for your love and guidance.

The wounded bluejay is bleeding inside.
Weeping mortal tears.
Shrieking with magnificent rage.

"Superficial bluejay." taunt unknowing birds.
Shame him cry unwary trees.

"Bluejay hide the blood." whispered commiserator.
Bluejay kill with beak.
Hiding your labile ponderings of bleak.

"Oh unwary bluejay rejoice"
siliently uttered commiserator.
For soon will end the mortal cry of your voice.

"Bold, supercilious master, What have you done?"

"Why, simply destroy you."

Rachel Posner

AFTER THE STORM . . .

The clouds cover the sky, lowering my spirits to the ground.
The cold wind streams through my thoughts
It chills and refreshes.
My thoughts have no destination,
just ideas . . . just pictures.
I walk through the park aimlessly
I'm unaware of the people around me, you're unaware of my pain
I am alone, one on one with nature.
My thoughts are all jumbled, unclear in every sense.
But the fresh air frees my soul,
Releases my worries and all my fears.
I want to sit here forever
The solitude comforts me, the cold has no effect
Just to sit here in the mossy grass
Trying to sort my unordered thoughts.
The wind blows through my sweater,
My jeans are damp
It chills my skin, but I sit motionless
Once again, confusion sets in,
indecision invades.
Memories of you flood my mind and slowly tears are shed
It seems to take forever for the storm to clear,
Forever for my wounds to heal.

Andrea Portanova

UNTITLED

With a boat passing by every now and then,
With the waves crashing,
Wind blowing,
And the lonely cry of the seagull,
The island sits by itself,
In the middle of the ocean,
In the middle of paradise.

Ms Catherine E Rauschenbach

O DEAR LORD

This poem is dedicated, with all my love, to my baby brother, Ernie (Pee Wee) Roberts. Sissy.

Each night I pray, "O Dear Lord, give me strength for I am weak, show me the way when I may stray."

"Dear Lord," I pray, "Give me your love and understanding when I am wrong, teach me patience when I am short, give me the advice I seek from day to day."

"O Dear Lord, give me your guidance in all that I may do."

Ron Minear

SILVER LACED WITH GOLD

To Mother—Her memory will live in our hearts forever

Silver now replaces the once black hair
Wrinkles now replace lines ever so fair
Wisdom still speaks out over years of many
Eyes still reach for truths, if any.

The heart will touch anyone within reach;
That of spoken words, most certain to teach.
A new path of Kindness and Pride
That only the soul can prescribe.

God has given us this tower of Strength,
For such a brief period, as life is in Length.
We cherish the time of past, with admiration and trust.
Look forward to years to come, overlooking signs of rust.

We try to see past reality and still see youth
and yet must come to realize, age is the real truth.
God make your palace ready, with a warm place
An angel will someday be at your grace.

Your children, all have to be proud for the time that God has allowed.
For this lady with a mind so bold;
the purity of silver laced with a heart of gold.

Trio Russo

Trio Russo

WEEPING IS FOR THE NIGHT

In the sun shed no tears.
Otherwise, the sad ones we mean to aid
Draw inward more and more.
Our tears are for the night,
To flow in solitude.

In the sun bring soft words
And soft smiles. Let the sad ones
Be buoyed by unforced smiles,
By words tender as south winds
Whispering among Walden's reeds.

Heed this, or else let them be.
They'll fare better minus our glum faces.

In the rose-light of day
Bring only zephyrs
Of soft words, soft smiles.

Let the sad ones know the meaning of empathy.
Let the terminal ones smile back at us.

Tara McCutchen

THE FALL OF A TEAR! ! ! ! ! !

So soft, but innocent.
Yet so many meanings.
Confusion:
the death, and the heartaches.
Happiness:
families together at last,
friends return as well.
Anger:
tearing at your flesh like a dagger.
The tears fall heavy,
the fire burning, raging at the sky.
But also one thing,
the fall of a cry.
A silent cry for help.
This cry cannot be denied.
If denied the result is . . . . .
fatal ! ! ! !
My cry was turned away.
I was caught in time and now,
the door to my new life widens every day!

Mary Ellen Mulcare

MOMS ARE SPECIAL PEOPLE

This poem is dedicated to my Mom, the most special and important person in my life. I love you!

Moms are special people,
or didn't you know?
They are always there,
their love will always show.
Since the day you were born
she loved you with all her heart,
After all, you're a part of her,
Like her special work of art.

Throughout your life
She helps you overcome the fears,
And she always knows how
to wipe away the tears.
My Mom is not only my Mom,
but also my best friend,
and our special love,
will never ever end.

Tod A Morey
OUT OF THE BLUE
Out of the blue came a blinding light
I stood entranced on that dark lonely night
My body was rigid, my spirit was weak
My curiosity was steadily rising to its peak
This feeling came over me that everything was all right
Slowly, I began to shuffle my feet toward the light
From within a figure appeared that seemed almost heavenly
And a teasing sense of recognition washed over me
Then the light began to fade as quickly as it had come
When it was gone my body became cold and numb
The dark lonely night seemed much lonelier now
And I wondered if I could get the figure back somehow
My mind was uneasy and I was in a depressed state
Until the following evening when I was on a special date
About halfway through the date I was able to see
That I was feeling exactly what the light had done to me
The ghostly figure had brought a message from above
It had taken heavenly intervention to show me I was in love

Tempest Walker
THIS MAGIC MOMENT

To Mr. L. Walker, to the one I love

This magic moment has come true
It's standing in front of you,
This magic is in my eyes for you
My eyes sparkle when I think of you,
This is the kind of magic I have for you.
This magic moment is here to stay
It doesn't matter what you say
This magic moment is thinking of you
It keeps me smiling all the day through,
This magic moment is when you're near
To hold my hand & have a smile so dear
This magic moment is when we kiss
I love it when we're like this
There's magic in the air, there's magic everywhere,
This is magic & not a moment to spare.

Peggie Jo Doolittle
THE CRIPPLER
With me you don't use a crutch or brace
Nor have deformity of body or face
I'm always there when you're having a good time
I'm even there when the sun doesn't shine
I'll wreck your life, and your loved ones too
They'll all know what's wrong, everyone but you
You'll do things for me that will make you sad
But you'll do them anyway, though you know they're bad
I fear the day when you pray to be free
Then with the help of others, you'll leave me
I'll go to another waiting soul
Till the time comes, that he can take control
It's getting harder and harder to find a home
Because of Alcoholics Anonymous, soon I'll be alone

Deanna Jean Cunningham-Decker
MY PRECIOUS BROTHER

With Love beyond any known measure, I dedicate this poem to my dearest friend——my brother—— Dean O. Cunningham, Jr.

We grew up together,
But, neither of us knew;
Just how lucky,
There was only us two.

Good times and bad times,
Are times we went thru;
Learning hard lessons,
Were only a few.

Then we grew up,
And separate ways we did go;
But, never forgetting that,
We loved each other so.

His family was his life,
As my family is mine;
However, we always had,
Much love to continue.

Times I still hear,
Precious Dean Jr. say:
"I love you, Sis,"
"Keep your chin up today."

Until later my dearest friend

Nicki Jo Miller
MAYBE YOU'RE RIGHT
A dream that I wish could come true . . . I would love to lay it in front of you . . . But I feel you might be right . . . Things just won't change to our delight . . . . We both made promises to be true . . . You to me and me to you . . . The lies were brought out in the light . . . Through the long lonely night . . . You said we had to be through . . . I was upset but weren't you! . . . Your photo is always in my sight . . . I'll always be thinking of you . . . And loving you with all my might.

Catherine McGee
MY CHILD

Dedicated to my best friend, Gary. With love, for life.

Open your eyes my child,
You are safe with me.
No need to shake with fear,
Your heart can now beat free.
Your tears have shed in the night,
I felt them dampen my soul,
life guided our spirit as one,
now being reborn we are whole.
You were my wilted flower,
only needing someone to care,
come share my cup of life my child,
this new life promises to be fair.
No more aching with loneliness,
No more feelings of shame.
Be born again, in me my child,
Together we'll play, life's happy games.

Dianne Sadler
STRENGTH IS A DAILY NEED
Strength is something all must have.
But, fail to realize.
The greatest strength comes
from above.
To all who will believe.
You see Christ Himself is
All the strength.
That any of us need.
So put your trust in
Him today.
And watch Him meet
your need

Stencil Joyner
FOR THEY UNDERSTAND NOT

To Uncle Jimmie, Dewitt and Juba. Concheral Joyner especial the Joyner, thanks and wish all the Joy and Pain. Katie AND Rose Mary.

Oh! How they try
to keep me down,
For they understand not.
Oh! They want me to hate,
For they understand not.
Oh! I love them,
For they understand not.
Oh! How short their minds are,
For they understand not.
Never trying to understand!
Understand is the KEY
to life.
For they understand not.
To understand someone is
to love them.
So, why do you say,
I love you, when you
UNDERSTAND NOT.

Joe Dovich
SOMEDAY SOON

This message of love is for Ilene, whose unfaltering love gave me hope, when there was so very little to hope for. "Someday Soon" . . . . . . for us

Someday Soon, those Chapel bells will chime, to peal out the news that you are all mine.
Someday Soon, Church bells will be ringing, while a melodious choir is joyously singing,
"I Love You Truly," and "O Promise Me," someday soon, you're sure to see.
Someday Soon, you will elegantly saunter down the aisle, donned in a gown of pure white,
and, onlookers will stare, gasping in awe at such a beautiful, breath-taking sight.
Someday Soon, the dimly-lit Chapel will glow brightly with your radiant loveliness, and, the tears that flow from your Mother's eyes, will be tears of happiness.
Someday Soon, the time is certain to come, when we'll live, and love, together as one.
Friends, family, and neighbors will audibly sigh at a single glance at you, and, will speak of your legendary beauty for years to come, as I now often do.
Someday Soon, the marriage knot will be tied, binding us forever together, and, our love will grow strong enough to withstand even the stormiest of weather.
Our love nest may be small, but it will be richer than all the castles of a king, for the Blue-birds of Happiness shall live in our trees, and gloriously sing.
Someday Soon, in time to come, we may be blessed with a daughter and a son.
The girl will resemble you, the boy me, and no other family will be as happy as we.
We will proudly watch the kids grow big, like the mighty oak, that was once a twig.
How I pray that my dreams will come to pass, and we'll share a lot that will forever last.

Carolyn S Stone
THE OLD FARM HOUSE STANDS
The old farm house stands
Quiet and empty.
The buildings that surround it
Have crumbled and fallen.
Still the house stands,
Barren and hollow.
Stripped of its insides,
Windows broken
Like a lover's heart.
The roof twisted by the winds of time.
The walls are sturdy,
Even though the siding
Is gray and rotting.
It is sad to watch
A farm house grow old,
Like a beautiful lady
Who has lost her youth.

Rev Warner W Faris

Rev Warner W Faris
"BETSY ROSS MEMENTO, OUR FLAG"—OLD GLORY'S PRAISE

I dedicate this poem, in memory of all "Our Fallen" in all our wars, to preserve the Peace that is so important to all Americans; That they died not in vain but United Freedom Worldwide. Veteran World War II.

"How many times, 'OLD FLAG,' of ours,
Have you united us with white stars.
Has our Red, White and Blue been bought,
While others for our Freedom sought?"

"How many times, in years gone by,
'OLD GLORY'S' sound, The Bugle Cry!
Many hands lifted, "STAR SPANGLED BANNER!'
In tune with God—Universal Planner."

"How many more stars stud Our Flag!
A wisp of hair—A Valiant Rag!
Stars passed arranged row upon row,
To enemy lands—A staggered blow."

"How many more will fight the PEACE—
Until Eternal LOVE increase;
The Star that shone at Bethlehem:
Hail Mary's child! Good Will towards Men!"

How many times, "we pay the price!
United all—In sacrifice!
Before we find hidden TRUTH earth!
Reveals a Flag—United Rebirth."
In behest of a grateful nation.

Tom Bilstein
TIME'S SPIRIT
Lover hold me in your arms
Time is endless when we're apart
Precious moments we have shared
Time stands still and keeps us there
Spirits lift me to the sky
Let me fly and let me shine
O'weary soul from me depart
Never return unto my heart
Time you healer of shattered hearts
Of broken spirits and tortured minds
Take me now into your bed
So I may rest my weary head
At last I rest upon your bed
Soft and warm I fear no more
My soul is free is flying high
For you have given me peace of mind
Through time and space to eternity

Deborah A Myers
MISTAKEN IDENTITY
It was a case of mistaken identity,
that introduced you to me.
I thought that you were someone else,
now, I'm glad that you're yourself.

The first time I saw you,
I thought I knew who you were already.
It ended up a mistaken identity,
and, now we're going steady.

When I realized you weren't who I thought, it had already gone too far.
When I thought I knew you were, I invited you into my car.
The more we talked, the less I knew.
I figured out, I didn't know you.
We kept on talking, I got less uptight.
I ended up staying with you all night.
It was a case of mistaken identity
that introduced you to me.
I'm glad you're not that someone else,
because, now, I've got you to myself.

Gary L Wright
IT HURTS ME TOO

I Gary Wright, hereby dedicate this poem to my Grandfather Dewey Omer. In hopes that through him, fond memories of joy and happiness live on forever.

My day began with joy at hand,
and thoughts of living tomorrow.
But now my day is filled with dismay,
and the deepest of all my sorrows.

For there was a man to whose command,
I would always respond, But now he's been given,
the stairway to heaven, and the life that is beyond.

He was my Grandpa and I always sought,
a great deal of admiration for thee,
Oh! I loved him so and it hurts me you know,
to see him leaving me.

Earlier I was bound to run around,
and forget that he was there,
But now he's gone, and oh! how I long,
for a moment we can share.

Now that I live all I can give,
is my feelings from within.
And I needn't cry because when I die,
I'll be living up there with him.

Jan M Ackerman
THE FINEST
Your magnificence enthralls me
twisted by the despair you've left in
the darkened burden of my soul.
Your electric eyes call to me
as I cannot answer—
trapped inside a destiny
I cannot fulfill.
As I slept, I lost sleep—
trying to grasp your hand
within the shadows.
You've walked to the darkened edge
though I call to you—
The heartbeat grows cold as stone
as it's dying with its shell.
My heart bleeds through every vessel
'til the pain becomes too strong.
Through the winds I hear you beckon—
if only I could sing to you.
Prisoner in my own confinement
I'm decaying in our own endearment—
as I am deceased by your love.

Grace M Smith
CHRISTMAS STORY
Once upon an olden time the weary world was still,
And shepherds watched with tender care their flocks upon the hill.

The brightest star was shining high in the eastern sky,
And there was fear, yet hope was near, for Christmas, too, was nigh.

The herald angel did appear,
proclaimed the joyous word of sacred birth in Bethlehem: Good tidings of the Lord.

The Wisemen followed yonder star,
and found that early morn,
'Midst lowing beast in humble stall,
the Holy Child was born.

The Christmas story still is told as we read the hallowed page,
And "Peace on Earth, Goodwill toward men" comes down from age to age.

The years may come, the years may go, we think of now and then,
And ponder o'er, the things that are,
and the things that might have been.

And if along the lonely way life seems but all in vain,
Just search your heart and memory,
and be a child again—
And live once more the blessed time of Christmas.

Nick Delcore
AMBITION
When sleep was peace, and not escape
Long before my dreams took shape

No force could stem the fearless way
I thought to have my way some day

Whatever wish my mind transgressed
Would be fulfilled, divinely blessed

For youth, the endless dreams abound
With fortunes waiting to be found

Desire, alone, would yield the prize
I would be famous, rich and wise

Though wishes lingered through the years
The dreams gave way to nameless fears

Too late do we conceive the truth
I'd squandered all the coins of youth

Now, one by one my dreams are gone
While restless sleep but brings . . . the dawn

John S Terranova
I WALK ALONE IN THESE THOUGHTS OF MINE

Dedicated to those who cared, and care. Thank you.

I walk alone in these thoughts of mine
Away from the world, the problems and crying
Past the blue geese and purple skies
Beyond betrayal and colorful lies
To the truth from deep inside
Of all the feelings that I hide
By myself are the tears I shed
Which creates a river of gold and red
Each a meaning, a symbol, a reason
Red is my heart and gold is the season
Blue are the rain drops, that rise above
Turquoise is the question, what color is love
I'm the creator of this far away place
I can paint it black, or trim it with lace
And when I return from this far away land
Back to reality where life is so bland
My body is at ease, in tune, in line
Just from walking alone in these thoughts of mine.

Melissa S Eskew
LOVE LIKE A RIVER
Our love was like a river
it never seemed to end,
It also proved
sometimes we have to bend.

The first time around
we didn't really try,
I didn't understand
there couldn't be another guy.

Now, our love turned into a waterfall
and over the edge we went,
Falling our separate ways
and not leaving a single hint.

As time slowly passed
we decided to try again,
A relationship built on trust,
the perfect way to begin.

So the raging waters from the "fall"
calmed to again be one,
Our love is much stronger now
this river will forever run.

Mirna Cardenas Miranda

Mirna Cardenas Miranda
LOVE-ERASED

To John, my husband (and inspiration), Also to Michele, Letitia and John Jr. (our children), For traveling the journey with us so gracefully.

I look intently at your face
To see a sign of love-erased,
A long lost love on journey back
From places cold and lonesome filled,
A distance only true love knows
Cannot be traveled standing still,
It longs to fill the lonely place
Of a lover's cry of love-erased,
A journey made at such great cost
Accomplished only by much loss,
A love that traveled at free will
In search of someone else to fill,
Has in its desperate effort gazed
Upon the heart of love-erased,
To calm the heart of a lover's cry
Allowed itself also to die.
An empty place it fills today
Our "love of old" that went away,
In search of what . . . I cannot see
That "love-erased" of you and me.

Wade Nicholes
HANDS
Long, delicate
Ivory apparitions
Tracing minutes
On the rainstained
Picture pane.

Entranced, I watch them
Mesmerized, Obsessed
Even by their smallest
Silken touch.

Oh, the ecstasy
When I am in
Their twilight
Embrace.

But now you say
We must part
How can you cause
Such pain, to my fragile
Heart?

I don't know
What I will do
Without them,
Without you.

Now I lay here
In my bed of shame
Wishing I could forget
Your emotion calling
Name.

Our love has faded
Like the tide
Washes away the beach.

But, at least, before you left
I took what I needed the most.

Those pale white hands
I love the most
The wings of a dove
That I removed from you
At least their love for me
Will remain always
True!

Julia E Brewer
A SHADOW
a shadow
of you lays beneath
my pillow.
In my sleep
I wake up and
I'm into deep.
I wonder where
you are and
if I push
will you go far.
will you always
just be a shadow to me,
or will you come closer
so I can see.
I only see your silhouette
in the night,
when I wake up
you're behind the light,
and then only a shadow
of you lays beneath my
pillow.—

Janett L Baguley
SLOW DEATH
I am being ravaged
slowly
from with in.
The pain
is eating me alive.
I expect some morning
to look into the mirror
and she won't be
looking back.

Terri Jean Bozovich
LOVE IN FRIENDSHIP

To Gene Andrew with all my heart and more, for the love, friendship, and forgiveness you've always given me—Love Always, Terri Jean

When you leave
I'll miss you
The times we've had
Will see me through.
It doesn't seem right
You going away
I want you to be happy
And I want you to stay.
The friendship you've given
Is like none other I've had
You were so good to me
Through good times and bad.
You helped me see
What I could not
And helped me believe
In myself.
No one else
Has come so close
I'd push them away
Afraid of their love.
But you were as friend
A constant love
You would forgive me
Even when I messed up.

Georgie E Smith
WORKING TOWARD HEAVEN
Laborers are so very few
If people only knew
Many more laborers God really needs
And on his word we should always
feed.

Go tell all the troubled, sick and
weak.
That God with all his love is kind
and meek.
Don't forget to tell them,
God is only a prayer away.
Their sins can be forgiven thru Jesus
Christ this very day.

Rolling down the path of time,
Seeking, hoping, praying always
coming into mind.
Thru God with our loving, caring
and sharing,
we get a peaceful mind.
That's something so many folks
never seem to find.

Faith is what leads us thru this sinful
world.
How wonderful it would be if we
could all
enter Heaven in just one big whirl.

Donna Gaby
LIFE
I see the band go marching by, their
horns are up, their heads held high.
I hear the stirring, sturdy beat, and
the tramp! tramp! tramp! of the
marching feet.

Then in my mind the years flit by,
and I remember when you and I,
marched in a high stepping high-
school band. Do you remember—my
long ago friend?

How proud we were—going here
and there, appearing at the county
fair.
Collecting trophies on our way—we
were the best did I hear you say?

But now there are others in our
place, and we stand by with a
smiling face.
We watch the band go marching by;
as life marches on for you and I.

Hilder V Carter
WHAT IS A MARRIAGE?

To my grand-daughter, Yumiko and her husband, George on their wedding day.

What is a marriage, is it the Bride?
Or is it the Groom at her side?
Or is it the flowers, smelling so
sweet
Or the lovely carpet underneath their
feet
Perhaps it's food or the taste of
champagne,
Or maybe all the guests that came,
Perhaps it's that first dance after they
are "one"
Or maybe it's just having a whole lot
of fun.
In truth a marriage is all of these
things,
But with the exchange of those
wedding rings
It means two hearts entwined
together,
To share their lives forever and ever,
It means love, understanding,
forgiveness and such,
It means sacrificing, Oh so much!
And most of all it means just this
There is one more way to wedded
bliss,
As you travel life's highway side by
side
Always be sure that God is your
guide.

Thomas Geeslin Jr
MARRIAGE

To My Wife Patty who inspired me to write this poem. I'll always Love You!! 11 years strong and counting.

Though you say it's so,
I believe you really don't know.
That is, the way you want to go.

Before you go too far,
Stop and look at who you are.

Be sure you understand
the meaning of that gold band.

Don't let the light get caught
in your eye,
Or let your head soar too high.

For Love is a very serious thing,
And MARRIAGE is the result that
LOVE often brings.

Nancy M Maring
LOVE'S BEGINNINGS
Love's beginnings
A tender start
Shared glances, smiles
A fluttering heart

Beating softly in rhythm
Gently with yours
Loving, caring
Softly exploring

A new beginning
A future bright with promise
With love and laughter
Shared

Years together, or months
Measured in happiness
Aglow with light
A forever, together
Beginning tonight.

Martha R Klock
LOVE'S TOKEN
A red, red rose I sent to you
A token of my love
To remind you of our Saviour
And of our Heavenly Father's love

It was a token from my heart
A gift to speak to you
To tell you that I loved you
With a love so deep and true

For the bond of friendship
That dwells within my heart
Has stronger grown with time
Since the day that it did start

It was a gift from Heaven
Given by our Father dear
And I pray it will grow stronger
As we go from year to year

So when you see a rose
So red and fragrant too
May it remind you of that love
which I have sent to you

Sharon Duzan
LAURA ELAINE

To Ginny Rose, for love and encouragement and Laura Elaine, for inspiration, I love you.

As gentle as a fawn
Beauty to equal the dawn
Spring flowers growing
Blended fragrances blowing
On a breeze so soft and warm
To describe a little girl of charm.

The fury of a hurricane
Force to make the moon wane
A will of iron, strong and bold
Strength to make a mother's arms
fold
To hold her always closely, tightly
Dreaming of her future, brightly.

My little girl mine, I love you so
much
Your smile, your personality, your
laugh, your touch
In just these few years we've shared
such treasures
Your victories, your tears, your
hurts, your pleasures
I pray you don't grow up too fast
That we make each precious second
last.

I'll try to teach you all I know
Until it's time to let you go
A woman will grow from my little
girl
The thought of it sets my mind
awhirl
Little girl lost—don't think you'll be
You'll always be my baby, you see.

With you my life has true meaning
No more wandering, no more leaning
With no direction or incentive
You've given me new reason to live
For you I'll always be brave and
strong
Striving even harder never to wrong.

I want you to have faith and pride in
me
And love, respect, trust and honesty
For they're the most important things
we'll share
We must be open, unafraid and
always fair
The Lord gave you to me, I'm
thankful each day
I'll be the best mother, if you help
show me the way.

Rochelle E Cozzetto
MY EVERYTHING

Dedicated to: Captain Nicholai Brachunoff "Master" of the wild blue sea, I long to "sail" the world with you, and yours I'll always be!

Every mirror I look into, I see the
beauty of your face,
For every star that shines in the
heavens, your eyes have taken place.
I see you in the silver moon, that
gives light upon this land,
I feel you in the heat of the sun, by
the beads of moisture in the palm of
my hand.

In every tide that rushes in from the
ocean, the reflection of you is there,
For every iced capped mountain, I'll
climb to the top and wonder where.
You are the air that surrounds me,
that feeds life into my soul,
You're every love song that I've ever

written, which made my heart a
whole.

You see, every place I've ever gone,
your impression seems to be,
It's just because I love you so, and
you've become the HEART OF ME!

Mattie Jewel Taylor
I THANK THEE
Almighty God, I bow,
In the humblest way I know how,
To give thanks to Thee
For what Thou hast done for me.

I thank Thee, O God,
For the path of life I've trod.
Thank You for my home, this
beautiful earth,
On which I have roamed since my
birth.

I thank You
For everything You do.
You give me bread when I'm hungry.
You give me water when I'm thirsty.
You're my Doctor when I'm ill.
Your mercy I can always feel.

Thank You for my parents, friends,
and loved ones,
And for all that Thou hast done.
When my life here is o'er
and I can't thank Thee anymore,
I want to dwell with Thee
Forever and eternity.
Amen. Amen

Amy Jensen
FOREVER

To Mom, Dad, and Karl because I will love them always and forever

As I look into the clear blue sky,
I brush a tiny tear from my eye.
Thinking about all the things that
have been,
Hoping that I'll get the chance to be
free again.
Reliving all those wonderful
moments from my past,
Realizing now they never last.
So when I look into that clear blue
sky,
Dreaming of the days gone by,
Wondering what life has in store,
Wishing happiness was forever more.

Lillian H Linderman
ALL LOVING CREATURES
The animals that God created,
Are special in his sight.
Each little friend that brings such joy,
To all a sheer delight.

The playful antics of each one
Bring love to all we treasure.
The happiness their eyes convey,
Is greater than we measure.

Each bird that sings, and fish that
swim
Bring brightness to our life.
All wild life that roams the woods,
Help lessen all the strife,

Of man's eternal zest for fame,
Forgetting what's so dear,
As creatures that can bring us hope
When no one else is near.

Their eyes show all the love they feel
For masters large and small.
No question of their loyalty,
Their love spreads out to all.

Linda E Newman
A POET'S WORLD
A poet never sees the world in
merely black and
white,
or reds or greens or sundry
shades of blue;
A poet never sees the world as
tho' an artist might,
in pastel tints or even
vibrant hues.

He sees the world in shades of light
and darkness,
with no distinct beginnings
and no ends;
He sees the world in feelings
and emotions,
and what he cannot see he
can pretend.

For a poet know one cannot
picture heartache,
or happiness or love tho'
men have tried;
A poet knows one cannot paint
elation,
or all the other things down
deep inside.

So a poet uses paper for
his canvas,
and for his brush a poet's pen
he wields;
And he's got a million words for
his palette,
as he "paints" about the truth
behind
our shields.

And if you find it hard to
understand him,
do not lose sight of this—
a poet's goal;
He does not try to paint an
earthly picture,
a poet simply tries to paint
man's soul.

Sharon V Gauthier
MY DREAM CAME TRUE
My dream came true the night I met
you and I feel in love with you it's
true
You made me feel so special, you
brought out in me so many things,
feelings I thought could never be as
you loved me yes so tenderly
One look in your eyes I got lost
inside and your gentle touch yes it
means so much, your kiss indeed it is
so sweet and you're always there just
for me
I do love you and you know it's true
and the nicest thing is you love me
too
Every day what can I say our love
grows stronger in every way and
nothing is going to stop this love
inside of us
I do have you and this is so true and
I'm glad indeed you love me too
Yes my dream came true when I fell
in love with you

Nancy Castiglione
WAITING FOR THE POTTER
Cold and brittle,
I function day to day,
a loveless mass of clay . . . I wait for
you

To come to me, in me, with me
Spinning me into your life, molding
me
Wetting me down with your
words
Softening me with your eyes
Filling my cracks with your
touch.

Lifting me from your wheel
You put me back in my place . . . I
wait for you

To come to me, take me to your kiln,
Fire me and keep me forever whole.

Leisha Smith
TRUE FEELINGS
Why, oh why
Did you do that to me?
I trusted you
To be good, can't you see

Now you say we're through
Never to be again
Now all I think of
Is what could've been

My friends think I'm crazy
And maybe that's true
'Cause till this day
All I think of is you

I used to say "I love you,"
And that was true
Now I say "I need you,"
And that's true too

For if you asked me back
I'd surely say yes!
'Cause when I'm in your arms
I know your feelings are for real
And I will never again have to guess.

Alberta Kemper Balderson
MOUNTAIN MOONLIGHT
Long brush strokes an artist's
canvas
white clouds streak across the sky
darkened sky with moonlight
glowing
millions of stars flood the midnight
sky.

Moving silently through the night
ravishing beauty with luster and
sheen
mysterious magical brilliant
nature's giant movie screen the
moon.

Stephen M Quintero
I LOOKED

To AMB: for showing me the way.

I looked
but I could not see.
I sought
but I could not find.
There was light
yet I stood in darkness.
For what I was searching,
I had no guide.
Looking on the outside,
led to somewhere
and ended nowhere.
Beholding the truth was in myself,
the answers, the hopes, the dreams;
and so it goes:
As one looks deep inside
a stream of light appears
so that,
He can see for what he looked
and find what he sought.

Beulah Stanley
LOOKING OVER THE HORIZON
Looking over the horizon at the
setting of the sun,
I'm thinking of you baby; wish I was
having fun.
I'm sitting here in the night breezes,
wishing you were here with me.
If you were here how happy I would
be.

When I'm looking over the horizon, I
want you by my side;
I need you to hold me, please hold
me tight.
Do you ever get lonely, and need a
friend that is true?
Well baby, I'm lonely, and I need
you.

Some people want to stay in the
bright city lights;
I don't care where we are as long as
you are mine.
I would be happy with you anywhere
you are,
So let's sit here together in the night.

Joseph Andrews

Joseph Andrews
AS ONE
Listen God's children and all shall
hear
The voice of a dreamer, the beat of
the drum major
So loud and so clear
So be it heard, throughout the land
from the smallest child
to the oldest man.

Let these his words ring true
In our minds and in our hearts

Free at last, Free at last, Thank God
Almighty
We are free at last.
Turn to another as a sister or a
brother
Take a hand and be as one
And joy to say, Dr. Martin Luther
King
your work is done.

Anne Calkins
HIS BEST
When the day is long and night so
dark
Praise His name for a brand new
start.

Before things get better they appear
so bad
Hold onto your faith and don't be
sad.

Cling to His word and go through the
test
God promised to give you His very
best.

And after the night with weeping and
tears
Joy comes in the morning, no
sadness or fears.

M Marie Bettger
THE TOM-BOY
A little girl who plays in the mud,
and dares to have fun.
Plays Cowboys and Indians,
and learns to shoot guns.
Being just one of the guys
was the best of times.

If "Girls are sugar and spice,

and everything nice."
"Then why are the boys so mean to me?"
"Can't they see, inside I'm still the same, Marie."
But with no girls for friends it's hard to fit in.
"Why can't it be as in good old times as just one of the guys,
Now they have only one thing on their mind.

A glance in the mirror
and a new figure appeared.
In a day it all changed.
Not knowing why
She's no-longer one of the guys.
An' it's the hardest of times.

Jesse Carlos Gomez
THE TRAVEL TO SERENITY

To Mom & Dad, who never gave up on me. J.C. my beloved son, and all the rest of the family, especially my oldest sister Anna who inspired this poem with Love, and forgiveness. One can-not exist without the other.

I just finished traveling a journey through the mind.
It was meant to be shared, especially with you. Anyone can go out to conquer the world, and make into anything they wish.
Should you fail feel no shame, because even when you can't change the world, you can still change yourself.

Just remember adulthood is filled with disillusion, disappointments, and some triumphs in between. Therefore cherish your young life, and make precious memories. It's all a part of being able to truly live. Experience is the only true teacher of life. No one can teach you better than yourself. All else is a secondhand mentor. Only one who has imagination, and a soul filled with dreams, carries the innocence of true peace. Reaching simplicity, after human desires have been quenched will then bring the greatest, and happiest possession of life.

Serenity!

above all it's the most valuable thing in life.
Because it's always there in everyone, and everything. Still so few find it, from lack of being caught up in the external world, and neglecting the internal world. Still it's there to behold at any given time. Reach in, see it, touch it, feel it. One has to love themselves before they can love others. Find God, and find the Ultimate Serene Peace! Love is everything, and really does make the world go around; because
"Love is God"

Jim Richings
TEXAS SUMMER
It is hot
And windy and dry

I stand guard in the yard
Watering

And watering
Maybe
If I continue to water

The drought may break,
And my garden will return
To its former glory
We may get rain

And cool
But
If we don't
And the whole world
Continues to dry up

I may have the last
Bit of green left
In the world
What then?
All the bugs of the world
Would come and devour it
To the last crumb
Who would then inherit the earth?

Randy J Bricker
REFLECTIONS

To Cheryl, who has always been there. I love you, even though I don't show it very well or very often.

You are one, and I am one.
Two separate worlds, two different lives.
But together we are joined as one:
Individuals, yet the same—divided, yet united.

Memories of the past—desired, but not fulfilled.
Mistakes and illusions.
Passing thoughts and fleetings hopes:
Together only in dreams, but dreams come true.

The lonely blackness has turned to light, and
My desire for life has returned.
A total involvement—a pleasing madness.
You are my world and my universe;
You are life itself.

Please do not leave me, for without you
I would cease to live, but only exist.
An empty shell, a forgotten second of time
Beyond remembrance.

You are one, and I am one
And we are one.
You are my life, which is my only possession.
I love you.

Ellen Kaye Haight RN
SPOKEN FROM THE HEART

In Memory of James R. Durham M.D. A Lifetime of Devotion and Caring

We salute you, Dr. Durham, on the new journey that you take.
And we'll remember a Dear Doctor, many decisions you must make.
Of great devotion to your work: The community that you loved,
Will be greeted by other doctors and our Dear Lord up above.
We will miss you in Mendota: Many colleagues you've left behind,
Many impressions in the Health Field, you have made upon our minds.
May we as Medical Servants who are here to carry on,
Develop a devoted heart, too, even tho you are gone.
The caring doctor growing up here, then coming back to help,
Replaces haughtiness and greed and most of all himself.
May the Postman there in Heaven, take this message up to you;
So you'll know that we sure miss you and care about you, too.
Many trials now are over as you cross the other side:
Angels will greet you; friends will meet you; No love will be denied.
So we close now in our message, for you're in the hands of God,
We remember how you responded, in the steps we have trod.
Precious moments, precious moments,
However great, However small,
We won't forget you,
We CAN'T Forgot you,
For you are TEN FEET TALL!

Michelle M Bourgeois
ALONE
I walk slowly
along the beach,
leaving a single trail of
footprints in the sand.
With an old water-logged stick
I print your name
under mine,
staring emptily
as the waves wash it away.
I walk along a little further
watching the seagulls play,
imagining what it would be like
to soar freely in the wind
without a care in the world.
Glancing down,
as I continue on,
I see similar graffiti
in the sand,
yet different,
theirs survived the tide.

Raquel Cora
RIPENED TIMES
Amid the leaves and
wind-strewn flowers,
swaying trees through summer hours
time does pass through our own eyes
seeking youth to make it ripe
We cannot see it, but it doesn't hide
its eyes of old and lines of age
Eyes that speak of hard-won lives
and glorious moments that last through life.

It's one sad story to somehow know
youth can't be harnessed—
it has a will of its own.
But one thing we may hold as true:
The life we live and time we breathe
will never be no one's but our own,
'cause no one has seen or will ever see
the world the way it's been to each.

Linda M Auerback
INSIGHT

This is dedicated to anyone who has lost his way, and to each of us who has forgotten how easy it is to do so.

Life has many paths to follow—
the end result being
we are our own leaders.

In striving for perfection
sometimes we lose sight of what is right,
knowing we'll have to pay
if only to ourselves.

Some of us are forgiving—
others are not.

We are each something different to every other human being
a treasure to one
a burden to another.
But what we are to ourselves—
that is what's important
and what matters.

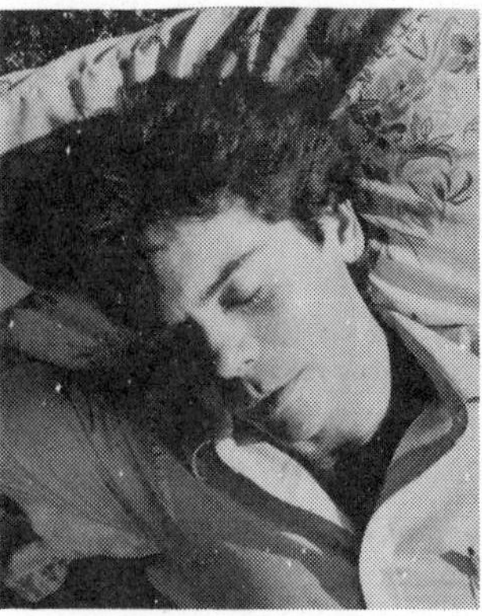

Charles James Amagrande

Charles James Amagrande
ONCE IN A LOVER

Dedicated to Richard Loring & Barbra Streisand. From a Major Epic Musical Screenplay of Queen Elizabeth I's unending love for Prince Alencon of France entitled, "THE MOMENT I FEEL YOU."

Elizabeth had tried to patch up the quarrel,
but on June 10th 1584, Alencon's adventurous voyage ended.
As her councillors had foretold, she survived her wooer.
For three weeks on end, not a day passed without tears.
To the French Ambassador she exclaimed, 'I am a forlorn widow.'
Elizabeth indeed exploited Alencon without scruple.
However, this ugly yet most congenial suitor had a real place in her affections . . . She wept for herself.
In that year, she commissioned Raleigh to found Virginia.

Once in a lover, once in a while . . . .
You will discover the other one's smile . . . .
You'll meet tomorrow or maybe an hour . . . .
Once in a lover, you begin to smile . . .

Once in a lifetime they come your way . . . .
In a cafe or a fair lane it happens every day . . . .
The air in the sky fills the warmth in your eyes . . . .
It grows brighter than the sun can

shine . . . .

When it happens, you reach for your hands. . . .
You look round and over and think you are grand . . . .
The room starts to turn into circles you will learn . . . . .
All the joy the world was meant to be . . . . .

Once in a lover, once in a while . . . .
You'll know in your heart your waitings come through . . . .
You'll know when they're smiling back at you . . . .
The room starts to spin, Oh what a shape you're in . . . . .
To've known the joy the world was meant to be . . . .

Barbara A Varelas
BLINDED

This poem is dedicated to the most important person in my life—my Mom. Thanks, Mom.

Through the days I journey on
with open eyes, yet not seeing.
Through the nights which day
brings on, my eyes still search in agony.
Though they search they do not find
The thing that is elusive.
Elusive as day and night, evasive as
the clouds but, still my eyes linger on for
to catch what is elusive is the only
things my eyes will see.

Christine Beach
TO SOMEONE I LOVE SO DEARLY

To the ones who offered me so much love and encouragement. I love you!

To someone I love so dearly,
and care so much about.
If it weren't for you I'd be very
unhappy and sad . . . .

I'm glad that I met someone like you,
to brighten up my days and nights—
You were there for me when I
needed a shoulder to cry on or
an ear to listen to me when I
am down . . . . .

Yes, it is you, the one I love so
dearly and care so much about.
You've filled my heart with
happiness and joy . . . . There
was very little sorrow between
us and what was there—
brought us closer together . . . .
(You'll always be the one I love
so dearly and hold so close to
my heart!)

Margie Branhof
WORDS

To all those who have found courage and faith from "words" spoken and to those, by "words," their hearts were broken.

Words are expressions by which we communicate,
They can either express our love or sometimes even hate;
Many wars have been waged by words of declaration,
And causes have been lost by lack of participation.

Words are the means of understanding one another,
And are first often taught by a loving mother;
In school we learn to master the art of articulation,
And hopefully assimilate volumes of accumulation.

Words are the feelings we put into sound,
The explanation for things that we have found;
We often express our hopes and our fears,
And give words of comfort to those in tears.

Words would be wonderful if they were all kind and good,
And we used them exactly, the way we should;
But alas and alack there are so many kinds,
Sometimes the right ones are hard to find.

Michael L Void
SOMEONE

To My Dearest Gloria, Thanks for the Inspiration. I Love You.

Just as you begin to feel too tired and worn
Your hopes fade away, you're tattered and torn
You meet someone with a great big heart
Someone you like right from the start
Someone that makes the wrong seem right
Someone you want to be with both day and night
Someone that will comfort you when you're feeling down
Someone that you'll always want around
Someone you hope that will leave you never
Someone you hope that will love you forever.

Barbara H Mosby
ME

This poem is dedicated to the memory of my late husband John Mosby, Jr. His kind and loving memories will always linger in my heart.

I look in the mirror and what do I see
The image of someone staring at me.
Sometimes the image is sad and low
Because of the trials it had to undergo.
Sometimes the image is happy and gay
Because everything planned went well that day.
The face of that image seems so depressed
Saying deep inside, have I done my best?
The more I look the more I see
The image in the mirror is the image of "ME"
The more I look the more I know
In order to make that image glow
Is to trust God every day
Then all the other images will go away.

Philip B Johnson
MEMORIES

Birthdays come, and birthdays go
The years mount up too fast
Thank God for all good memories
'Cause they're the ones that last

For when we stop and start to think
How could we grow so old
It's only through our memories
That youth we now can hold

How great it is our memory
Tis so much like a mirror
Reflecting all the brightest times
We've shared throughout the year

Just like a mirror's reflection
Which needs a light to show
Our memories hold the brightest times
And keep our hearts aglow

Our memories are much better
Than a mirror in every way
Cause a memory can't be broken
It's in our heart to stay

Now I hope that all your memories
On this your special day
Are bright, and clear, and cheery
And you have a great birthday

You will not find these words of mine
Where poems are often sold
They were wrote for you in a day or two
And yours alone to hold

Kenneth James Carruth

Kenneth James Carruth
A SPECIAL FRIEND

She's very big and pretty;
Never says a word.
I can tell you stories of her
Like ones you've never heard.

We walk along the pasture
Under the big blue skies
While the sad and happy memories
Reflect in her eyes.

She's a very special friend
That I know is true;
I can always ride her
When I am feeling blue.

She cannot give me a kiss;
She cannot give me a hug;
But there is something I can give her—
And that's a very special love.

By now I think you can see
How special she is to me.
My friend's name is Cody—
A very special horse indeed.

Kevin Carpenter
HAPPINESS?

Dedicated to my loving wife, Donna, who has shown me the true meaning of happiness

Happiness?
Is this word definable
Has it meaning
Ah, to me it has many meanings.
It's the smile on your face
When I walk through the door.
It's the warmth I feel
When your arms are around me.
It's the love for me
That I see in your eyes.
It's the strength I receive
When I wake up beside you.
Now as I look upon what I've written
I see that happiness has
But one meaning to me.
My love, Happiness to me. . . .
Is you

Michael Trojanowski
JOURNEY THROUGH LIFE

Silence,
heartbeat, voices, tears to cry
mommy, daddy, boy so shy
teacher, teach me, growing up fast
high school, good times, what a blast
first love, first hurt, first pain to feel
grown up, real life, no big deal
true love, marriage, so many dreams
forever, sunshine, though it seems
children, one two, watch them grow
daddy, grandpa, fast it goes
old age, death, true love gone
sorrows, loneliness, seems so long
rest, be careful, have a seat
sleep, white light, heartbeat.
Silence.

Charles E Klinger
I TOUCH LOVE

I feel the laughter
in trembling gloom.

I am sad in
the shimmering sunshine.

I am confused
when you are gone.

I touch love
whenever you are near.

Constance L Vilen
BROKEN

To Charles King, who found the King of Kings.

Lord, you let me slide on by,
I didn't try!
Lord, you let me wave goodbye,
Too many times.
Now broken and all bent,
I lie and wait.
Lord, my God, my heart,
Please overtake.
Teach me Lord to number all my days,
And better yet, Teach me
Uprighteous ways,
So that I may walk with you,
Where emeralds lay.

Krysti Hasting
TEEN DEPRESSION
You're in a maze, a big glass ball.
You try to run, you hit a wall.
You're near the edge, you start to fall.
Sometimes you want to end it all.

Pregnant. Abortion? Too many regrets.
There's no way to pay. There's too many debts.
Too many worries. Too many threats.
The things that you need, there is no way to get.

Knock, knock, knock. There's no one here.
You're being drowned by all your tears.
So brought down by all your fears.
You're being pressured by your peers.

You just went out and broke the law.
Used. Abused. An old rag doll.
You need picked up when down you fall.
Before you walk, you learn to crawl.

Taconya Patterson
A BLIND SEARCH

To my parents—for always being there.

Never yet having learnt
 Fantasy from reality:
A child who was
 So innocent, now gone:
The soul searching, groping,
 To something to keep
 From going into total darkness:

But never having monopolized,
 The time, most of it
 Was spent in indecision:
Then missing the opportunity,
 It had to continue
 The search with darkness
 Surrounding:

In despair . . .

Elmo Criner
DADDY'S LITTLE COWGIRL
She's my little cowgirl, although she's only three
Every show i go to she wants to go with me
All the cowboys like her, cuz she struts around so grand
And me i really love her cuz she's daddy's little hand
Every boy's her boyfriend, she likes them one and all
Daddy's little cowgirl only two feet tall
She's always got her boots on, and her buckles shining bright
And she makes sure she's there to kiss me before she goes to bed each night
Yeah she's my little partner and i am mighty proud to be
The father of that little cowgirl, although she's only three.

Lillian Y Vazquez
SILENTLY LOVING YOU

Dedicated to my sweet children Ivan & Leilani, and in memory of the Lion.

You will exist in my life, without ever realizing you existed, you exist in silence, because of my secret love and while you live your smile will be a sweet contrast of the pain of loving you. Yet you will never know it.
I will dream with the manly nakedness of your shoulders.
I will dream with your eyes that are as green as the sea.
I will dream with your lips desperately.
I will dream with you and yet you will never know it.
Perhaps you will live with someone else that whispers in your ear, the phrases that only I will say to you, but I for one will forever choke back my consistent love. I will love you more than ever, and yet you will never know it.
I will love you in silence like an inaccessible object, like a dream that will never come true. You are the faint scent of my impossible love, that caresses your hair, and yet you will never know it. If someday a tear should escape through my torment, the everlasting torment that I withhold I will laughingly tell you it is nothing, nothing but the wind, and then wiping my tear away, you will never know this teardrop was all because of you.

Mamilyn Takahashi
I WILL BE IN YOUR HEART
I am so glad to find you.
I can feel your shining dream.
Even if you stumble along on the way.
You may meet some difficulties.
And you may worry about tomorrow.
But I can touch your refreshing dream.
So I will be in your heart.
Our lives are so hard and difficult,
And nobody can find the shortcut to success.
However I will be in your heart.
Whenever your soul needs a smile!

I am so happy to know you.
I can help your fantastic dream.
My sweet feeling is coming back into my heart.
Tenderness, sympathy, and thoughtfulness.
All of my trustful heart has returned to your dream.
So I want to light just one little candle in your heart.
Our ways are so steep and far,
And everybody is looking for warmth to wipe their tears away.
So I will shine in your life.
Whenever your soul needs the light!

Anita J Allen
WHATEVER HAPPENED TO VOWS?
There's countless of us out there
Raising our children alone
Working, it seems, for nothing
So tired of trying alone.

Gone are the dreams we cherished
Faded, and now growing dim.
Where is the future we dreamed of?
Now endless, looking ugly and grim.

Never enough time for our children
Never enough money to spend
Always behind on our payments
Oh, God, will this ever end?

The love that was promised forever
In the end wasn't real love at all
Too weak to weather the bad times
Like sand castles that crumble and fall.

We smile as we work with the public
While the loneliness burns deep within
Hoping one day the dream that's a memory
Will blossom and flower again.
So dream on, don't tire, countless numbers . . . .

Sherrie Williams
RUINS
A loud exploding sound;
A shower of rocks.
The world's falling down,
Confusion and shock.

Fog covered passages,
Desolate and bare.
Misspelled messages,
No one is there.

Pleading cries are silenced
By sound barriers so thick.
Wash away benevolence
Left feeling nauseous and sick.

Do not look and do not see
The faces shadowed with pain.
Don't hear the thunder or see the lightning.
Unfold umbrellas against the rain.

Beth M Crowley
SILVER WINGS
Sail On, Silver Wings
And Soon You'll Fly
Smile Although It Hurts
And Please Don't Cry

Smile The More It Hurts
And Fly, Fly High
Sail On, Silver Wings
'Til They Turn To Gold

And If You Lose
Dance The Next Time 'Round

You Started Low, You Started Here
But You Know Now
That Soon You'll Fly
Then You'll Be There

Just Never Cry
And Never, Never Let It Get You Down
Bronze Wings—They Turn To Gold
Sail On, You're On Your Way!

Dreams Come True—Don't Let Go
Sail On Silver Wings
Your Dreams Are Gold

Patti L Anderson
SUICIDE
The scene was set
Now was the time.

Everyone was gone
And I was home alone.

Life is sometimes unfair
And I'm trying to prove

That if I go on like this
It'll only get worse.

I love my friends and family
Most of all, but I

Don't believe there's enough
Room for me in this world.

There's only one way out of
This wicked and bizarre place,

And I have the solution
To all of my problems.

Against it all, I want to live,
But since I've already met

With the devil in a dark world
I cannot go on living like this.

When I'm gone (I know)
It'll be all over and the

Hurt will go away
Because you can't have

Ambivalence. You're only granted
One wish. And there's

Only one question
And the answer is death!

Jane Ann Heard
SOCIAL CONSTRUCTIONISM
You inspired me and set me free—
I found my breath, you gave it to me.

The suffocation was long and hard on me,
And you gave one thing more—
The jubilation of the sea.

I have been roaming the sands of time
Bewildered and lost in false paradigm.

You shifted my sands and now I can see—
All experiences are treasured unto me!

Noelle E Goron

Noelle E Goron
THE NIGHT
When the sun goes down night is here and I try so hard to forget my fear.
Dismal darkness is all I see, so I pray to thee.
God is who lights up my life and scares away my every fright.
Even though the night is scary, God makes it merry.
So, whatever I say, whatever I do, God will be there for me and also for you!

Steve Sowka
TELL ME GIRL!

To: Cindy

Tell me girl,
  Have you ever wished for someone,
  To walk in the rain with you,
  And when you got cold,
  Hold you close and keep you warm.
    Well I did, and now I'm wishing I was holding you.
    Just to touch you, can calm the storm.

Tell me girl,
  Have you ever closed your eyes,
  But were afraid to sleep,
  Afraid of what the day may bring,
  Longing for someone, to take away your fears.
    Well I did, now I'm wishing I could do for you.
    Just to touch you brings music to my ears.

As life goes on around me, I know there's a lot I'm missing,
Maybe in time I'll see, till then, what

will be will be.

Tell me girl,
Have you ever wished for someone,
To hold you in his arms,
To whisper in your ears, sweetwords,
That fill your heart with love.
Well I did, and now
I'm wishing I could hold you.
Just to wrap you in my arms like a hand in a glove.

Sandra Cerroni
YOU ARE

In Thanksgiving to our Creator who has gifted us with life.

You are the fire from within my soul
You are the presence making me whole
You are the whispering thoughts through my head
You are the gentleness that rests in my bed

You are the greatness that I certainly cherish
You are the magic of mystifying essence
You are the being—the rainbow of day
You are the light that guides my way

You are the softness of dew in the morning
You are the wisdom that reaches my yearning
You are understanding—the hope that is true
You're my special person—I'm glad I have you

You are the refreshing meaning in life
You are the rescuer of all my strife

You are my reason for living
You are my everything ! ! ! ! ! ! !

Joseph P O'Connell
DAYDREAMS
Relax, oh mortal man, relax
Let thy mind wander away
Forms out of clouds do make
Fresh thoughts awhile today
Windows of your soul may take

Secret wishes with lost dreams
Bind them to the mast
Let them sail away today
Make fresh ones that will last
The waves will wash the past away.

Pamela F Wallace
THE ARIZONA HIGHWAY SONG

To Mrs. B. Harris C.S.

Festive flowers—verdant valleys,
snow-capped mountains too.
Mighty red rock—merry meadows,
awesome canyons always new.

Desert palm trees—palo verde,
Joshua trees too.
The agave and the yucca—giant
saguaro, tall and true.

Ponderosa pine forest at my log cabin or my home on the desert floor.
The sparkling river called the Colorado—I'll call it my back door.

So hey! hey! Wonder is alive! Let's hop in the Jeep and go for a drive!

We'll stop at the old Indian trading post,
On a bright summer day the sun is our host.
Go to old Tombstone and visit other ghost towns
Where the copper mines are all shut down.

We're on our way, whether it's a clear sky or an azure blue sky—
It's hardly cloudy any day.

The heat in July is a hundred degrees.
We'll go tubing down the river floatin' in the breeze.

Scottsdale shopping, jackrabbits hopping, citrus blossoms wafting thru the air.
A horseback rider—a cowboy or two—laughing cows and a mustang mare.

The cotton fields are white—it's a real pretty sight.
I just discovered gold—the starry gems at night.

By now you know my state flag is unfurled——
I live in Arizona, the most beautiful place in the world.

Arline I Falk
RANDE

To my daughter with love

There once was a little girl—
Rande Lyn was her name.
She always had a little curl,
And mischief was her game.

She ran and played all day;
Her puppy followed her around;
She laughed and had lots to say;
With energy she did abound.

When bedtime came, alas,
She'd kiss her mom and daddy;
The fun and energy would pass,
And dreams would soon be handy.

Her head upon the pillow white,
Into sleep she would slowly drift.
I thank the Lord each and every night
He sent us such a precious gift.

J Renee Roberts
I AM NATURE AND EVERLASTING
I am Nature and Everlasting
I am the Wind
All of Nature essentially
I am Everlasting
And do not end, there's no eventuality.

The Sun is my hair
In its color and warmth
The Flowers, my mouth
Their Fragrance, my breath.

My eyes are all the Waters
They hold both softness and power
My tears, they fall
In light Summer Showers.

My life is the Seasons
And the Centuries they bring
None can trap my Life Force
For I am Nature and Everlasting.

Mrs Claire Khalid
LOVE

Bismillahir Rahmanir Rahim; This is to my love, my life, my one and only dream.

I dreamed again of secure
warmth, love and laughter,
I heard a gentle voice console me,
a velvet loving hand wipe away
my tears;
I snuggled deeper in a beautiful
cover of contentment and
delight.
Morning came and brushed away
the web of sleep and I realized
that You, my dream, are real
and ever by my side.

Naomi Mary
THE GRADUATE
I sit here fighting tears of pride
Watching my child blossoming into adolescence
Still fresh, young and innocent
Completing another phase in the journey of life
Always eager for tomorrow and I wonder
Will tomorrow welcome her
Will she find in life, the joys that she has given me
Silently I say a prayer, knowing each day she'll fly further from the nest
Testing new-found freedoms
My Daughter. The Graduate. Born of Love
She will succeed. The fight is lost
My cheeks are wet with tears.

Alfred M Hopkins
BLISSFUL DAYBREAK
I feel the golden rhythm of the day
In peaceful slumber, knowing you are mine.
Your gentle breath, beside me as you lay,
Caress your tender lips of crimson wine.
I touch your lips in happy tender love,
Your eyes fly wide, much as the startled fawn,
Knowing full-well what I'm thinking of
Within the blissful moments of the dawn.
The precious words of love come from your soul,
Rumpled hair upon the happy pillow
Is burnished with a sheen of purest gold,
To frame your lovely face in ringlet billows.
I bless the peaceful day when I can spend
The happy time with you which knows no end.

David J Chofey
FALL AGAIN
It's fall again,
as the leaves all turn to brown.
Watch them,
fall
to
the
ground,
preparing for winter.
When there's snow on the ground.
And we're homeward bound,
not making a sound.
Near a fire is where we should be found.
When it's cold all around,
our town.
Then it's spring.
And what's growing,
is everything.
Summer is here . . . and now it's gone.
And it's fall again,
As the leaves all turn to brown.
Watch them,
fall
to
the
ground,
Preparing for winter.

Matt Heiskell
WORLD DEATH
Fast lane of unnatural resources
Nothing of nature will survive,
Because we will burn
Forming ashes of the sun.
Unlawfully committed,
Deceit leads.
Fictional beliefs
Devil's party
Accused wrongly.
Festival of light
Scream
And finally peace . .
Today's motto is destroy the ozone layer.

Pauline Lisanti

Pauline Lisanti
LOVE
A majority of us have waited on line to take care of a bill or problem exhausted and ready to collapse from the rushing day

All of a sudden a child breaks away from a parent
dragging a stuffed animal or doll by the tail or arm
And stands in front of you with a great big grin
With a soft voice says hello that melts your woes away

Our childish thoughts start marching through our mind
like Sugar Plums swaying with the drum RAT-A-TA-TA
Turning into dreams that would wake children up
with a smile on their lips

Oh how lucky these little people are
Please let's all help preserve them with our love.
A kiss hugging them with arms so strong
Lift them to the heavens let God teach them more

It's not wasted time if it is used to say one sweet word
to one dear child Mom and Dad love you lots

We fuss with the house and rush to work and spend no time with our little ones

Take time to pray hold them up to God and pray
"Dear God" we love them to help us to smooth the road for them

David Bell
LIKE GIPPSI
"You want unconditional love? Get a dog!" they say
when, really,
the point is to be one
like Gippsi
leaping from the stream's bank
to the island of your arms,
sweet burden of trust.
You told it in tears,
you leaping too;
I wonder, did you know
my arms were there for you?

Deborah H Harrington
A MOTHER'S LOVE
Tiny little fingers,
Holding onto mine;
Tiny tears on tiny cheeks,
Bigger ones on mine.
A bond unbreakable,
A love unmistakable,
This little child of mine.

Tiny little fingers,
Reaching for the sky;
Chasing dreams and butterflies,
Always asking why.
Laughter without reason,
Love in every season,
This little child of mine.

Tiny little fingers,
Counting one, two, three;
Singing of Indians and little frogs
As innocent as can be.
Watching the one whom I adore,
I lift my eyes and thank God for
This little child of mine.

Ella E E Rahming
GET OFF THE FENCE
Youths of today, get off the fence!
This strong advice means no offence,
There's plenty of work for you to do,
If you would only look around you.

Parents of today, get off the fence!
Come quickly to your children's defence,
Traditional societal mores they abhor,
Experienced voices they also ignore.

Statesmen of today, get off the fence!
Your empty talk and promises you must condense.
Your constituents need constructive action—
It's a strong desire of every faction.

Religious and cultural leaders of today, get off the fence!
Your followers you must positively influence.
To you they look for guidance and example—
But what you give is certainly not ample.

Businessmen of today, get off the fence!
Sprinkle your high prices with a dash of temperance.
Remember the poor, penniless and hungry,
Barred from your goods and services—cold and hungry,
Rich men, wealthy men of today, get off the fence!
Share your wealth and opulence.
Get involved with the less fortunate
Where'er you live—town, country or state,
Just get off! Get off! Get off the fence!

Teresa Foos
"?"
I need your body next to mine
I need to feel your love inside
A warm embrace, a kiss good-bye?
Is this all there is?

I spend my evenings yearning for love
Just a slight touch of your lips to my tongue
My soul soars, my heart stops!
Isn't there anything more?

I dream of a passion burning inside
I feel the heat of your body beside
A desolate soul, a barren mind.
Haven't I given enough?

I cry for the love I once thought I had
A broken shell is all that I am
My head spins, my stomach churns.
What have I done for this?

My life feels like it's slippin'
My hour clock has run out.
Still no answer, can I be found?

Marilyn Harberts
SOFT QUIETNESS
is the sun as it drops out of sight in the West . . . sometimes yellows . . .
golds . . . and changing reds . .
It's dusk . . . and time for quiet rest . . .
Soft darkness . . . a gentle breeze passes over all . . .
. . what peace . . . rest . . .
quietness.
The spring bubbles forth with its lazy rhythm . . .
. . . and secretly serves all nature's thirsty quests.
And the pond it makes reflects like a mirror . . .
. . . . see . . . . a minnow disturbs its face . . .
sending shivers about the path it makes.
And best of all . . . look up and see . . . the moon . . .
. . . a crescent hangs in the southern sky . . .
. . gives light and value to the edging night.
. . . the chickadee and nuthatch chant . . . as they prepare for the night . . . . .
. . safety . . . rest . . . quietness.
All who need light now look for rest . . . as the . . .
darkness brings soft . . . . .
quietness.
For the morning sun brings its light and warmth . . .
. . . a new day . . . for all . . . to begin again.

Viola F Gibson
TIME STOOD SO STILL
Time stood so still,
Nothing seemed to be,
Everything was the will,
The pusher was there to see.

I had my lonely hours,
My anxiety spread so thick,
Self begins to sour,
Life is made up of this trick.

Hour by hour the wait,
The silence sounded so loud,
Dreading the sentencing of my fate,
The measure could lift the cloud.

Could they but know my heart,
My mind traveled through the miles,
Just one call could be the start,
Of hours and hours of smiles.

Patience had to be my guide,
My hand must not atone,
The wait would be a tide,
For the ring of the telephone.

Sarah M Thompson
IAN

This poem is dedicated to every woman's first broken heart.

The thought of you touches my soul and makes me realize that you are invincible, yet vulnerable.

I wish I could hold your soul in my hands, and never let it go; but I will.

Time will let us become one in mind and body.

For now, you will be one in yourself, as will I.

Anne C Kerner
NATURE VS. INDUSTRIALISM
We are out of tune with nature
to a degree,
Because we are members
of a society.
It would be thoughtless and irresponsible
to pursue.
A life wholly bent on the natural view.

We are too busy industrializing.
And with nature, we are compromising.
I see no end in view, do you?

Missy

Carmen L S Colmenares
MISSY

To the most beautiful cat in the world, my "MISSY."

One day when I was planting a rose,
I heard a soft melodic sound,
I turned and looked, and as if in pose,
A most beautiful cat, sat so straight . . . so proud.

I waved my hand, and shooed her away,
But she only took a few steps to the right,
She sat straight as a statue, and looking my way,
She licked her mouth quickly,
and looked me straight in the eye,

I was stunned for a moment, when she again licked her mouth,
I realized quickly; that her desire was for food,
She was telling me, somehow, that her hunger was now,
and to please feed her something . . . and to please do it soon,

I had to smile softly, as I fed her real tuna,
Which she ate rather quickly, and against me she swayed,
Her gratitude was expressed, with a love that's been true,
In the nine years I've had her . . . for she really did stay;

Now my "MISSY" is queen, and she sits on her throne,
She sleeps in her basket, and eats only the best,
When I look at this beauty, who's enchanted my home,
Her emerald eyes fill with love,
and I truly confess . . .
I'm sure glad I have "MISSY" . . .
I'm sure glad, I've been hexed! ! !

Karen Boyce
FOOTBALL FROLICS
Football frolics
Sunday's viewing
I don't mind, but—
My team's losing.

Is this the answer?
Let's do something else instead
Like daydreaming together
And spending the day in bed.

I wouldn't complain
Or hardly even mind
But your payoffs on games
Are rather unkind.

The season is endless
And hockey's beginning
I picked the Islanders
Why are you grinning?

Alon Drew Boyington
SECONDS OF A MIND
The stages of wonderment
these seasons of change
The beauty of it all
Alone this spirit in a tangled maze
This turbulent flow forever pushing
Ceaseless, amazing the life of eternity
The stagnant smell of the undergrowth
Forever reaching for all
The want, the need, the lust
to . . . . to what
The thoughts of nothing
the need of the missing
Already the undergrowth it breaks to
The thoughts of new existence
Feelings of things never been
The need to grasp this new era
Realism that all will be same in time
New feelings to be an old thought
Source . . . the spirit . . . unbearing
The valleys full overrun by all
The escape in one's imagination
Questioning of one's self, one's ability
Voids of answers, empty echoes
Images standing still
The realization of birth

Jodi L Melton
SEARCHING

For all my beloved family and friends who've never given up hope, faith, or love in me. Thank you.

The wall looms before you
towering over all else

You turn the handle
but the door is locked
With ruthless determination
you pound on that heavy door
Slowly you turn away
and give up for awhile
You face the wall again
determined to be victorious
You search for a way up
to scale that giant wall
There are obstacles, of course
but you make it over
Put your hand in your pocket child
you had the key all along.

Robby Garmon
MY ANGEL

This poem is dedicated to my mother Jimmie and my friend Kristin.

In the morning light I see her
Like an angel she seems to float
Gracefully about the mortals of the earth.
Her auburn hair is red as wine,
Her smile fills my heart with joy,
Joy that no other can bring.
Her beauty knows no bounds,
And no one can surmise how
Deeply I love her for she is my angel.
The angel who carries my heart
And my soul knows who
Loves her, yet she does not know,
For I yearn to tell, but I am
Afraid to tell her of my love.
One day I will share my feelings
And maybe my beloved angel
Will take my hand in hers
And we will forever be bound,
Bound by love and joy.

Tom "The Tramp" Jenkins
RESCUE

For your expedient rescue.
I love you.

A majestic steed,
Of chrome plated steel.

Your wrathful thunder,
Irrepressible and real.

A preeminent knight,
In armor of leather.

Your expedient rescue,
From this storm I weather.

A wistful spectator,
In a state of despair.

Your deviant desires,
Can avert all of my cares.

A deserving damsel,
Waiting crestfallen in vain.

Your passions unadorned,
Can clear away the rain.

Karen Emmel
GIVING

Giving is the thing to do
When someone is in the blue,
Or writing a letter
To make someone feel better,
Or just saying,
I LOVE YOU.

Alan Hoover
IF I WROTE ELOQUENTLY TO YOU

To God who gave in me new life; to all the women in my life, who believed in me

If I wrote eloquently to you
Pray tell would it matter ?

Or gave the solace of my heart
For your whims to shatter?

The things of the world
Are here and now
But value they the youth ?

To touch a soul where it came from
Or smell an eternal flower !?

The gel no more the substance seen
All things shall be diminished

So what is beauty the timely ring
It can only be

Gods grace . . . . . .

Paul R Wopschall
OLD JOE KIST

Old Joe Kist,
Will he ever be missed?
Surely, by his dog,
And, perhaps, by a neighbor or two
But, for how long?
Well, probably, for just about
As long as I'll be missed—
And, maybe, even you.

Anjanette M Genovese
ONCE THERE WAS . . .

A candy apple sky dappled with eggshell blue clouds
Drifting through the maze of time.
Settling on the foreign world
Of Camelot and prose. Chivalry and rhyme.
Beings floated about.
Unseen. Unheard. Unknown.
Their lives ensconced in a niche of Fate.

Silent shadows whispered their way
down decaying castle halls.
Once music played and sunlight
filtered through open windows
Now, silence swirls amidst the stench
of decaying life.
The light is no more.

There is laughter.
So unfitting in this world of Reason.

And a candy apple sky shatters, while
eggshell blue clouds explode
Floating effortlessly on bands of dew.
Shifting to a different world
Of conch shell pink and cobalt blue.

Linda Jackson (Age 13)
WHY

There's a dark shadow closing in on my life,
The lies,
The hatred,
The betrayal,
The question Why lingers in my mind and soul,
A sharp pain lodged deep in my heart,
It feels like the blade of a knife,
A longing need to break free of
depression's binding ties,
The question Why is the anthem of my life.

Freda Toews
FULLNESS

The sky is almost dark.
Clouds drift across the dimness of the heavens
obscuring from my view the
shining stars.
I call it night . . .
But lo!
Far in the east where sky meets earth
I see a gentle glow;
And while I gaze in wonder
moonlight breaks forth in fullest glory!
I rest contented in that soothing light.

This world, sometimes, seems dark.
Clouds of bitterness and strife
drift 'cross the dimness of the
souls of men
obscuring deeper feelings
of comradeship and love.
We call it hatred . . .
But wait!
If we will let the love of God within our hearts
break forth in fullest glory
reaching out to men who long to see it,
They will rest contented in that soothing light!

Julie Kulessa
THE WARMTH OF CARING

The frigid winter air is blowing towards me
like a wild hurricane blows
towards a swaying forest.
But I am not cold.

The road that I travel is covered
with slippery ice that radiates a
crystal sensation,
as if it was made of delicate glass.
But I do not fall.

The far away moon and tiny stars
that I would use to lead my way
have been blinded,
blocked out from the world by
the soaring clouds.
But I will not get lost.

I look in the windows of the houses I go past.
All the people are in good spirits
as they stay warm by the fire.
But I am warmer and have
never been happier .

It is storming and perhaps I
should be bothered by the bitter
cold and howling wind.
But it does not bother me at all
because you are walking
beside me holding my hand,
And that makes all the
difference.

Kathleen L Kane
WORK OF ART

I dedicate this Poem Lovingly, to my husband Gary, to my children, Christopher and Stephanie and to my parents.

I awaken to the crisp smell of Winter air, my inner being beckoning to the call of the lone Bluejay chirping, as one in utter solitude.
I arouse myself slowly, intensely.
I look in wondrous amazement at the rapturous beauty of the magnificent bird, perched atop of a softly snow-covered maple tree, glistening, like a fine jewel.
A delightful, majestic awareness of another splendored creation of God's wonderful work of art.

Earnest B Haynes
VISIONS OF A REVEALING ADMIRER

To my family and friends, who encouraged me to come this far

Her eyes glowed like the moonlight

The splendor of her beauty a perfect vision
Her smile gives you an uplifting feeling that
Everything in the world was just right
Her smooth movements so well endowed
Seem to cause many traffic collisions
Her voice is as soft as a canary in song
Just standing near her you could feel the
flow of her passion
Her touch tells you could do no wrong
The surge of warm response
showered from
the attraction

In the mind's eye that vision is you
An apparition totally out of reach
I, the admirer, who wants to be your love anew
Such a vision bestowed upon the
eyes that feasts

A desire that only you can compose
No script could be written to express my feelings
Your beauty looms as a rose
For here I stand with only my heart revealing.

Ulysses Jones III
NEVER ALONE

This poem entitled "Never Alone" is dedicated to my grandfather, the late Ulysses Jones Senior—AKA (PIE).

When you feel lonely and it seems like the end, just remember you have a friend

When submission comes and you start to bend, just remember you have a friend

When your heart breaks while it mends, just remember you have a friend

When you are alone and you feel rather odd, just remember your best friend you and God.

Brenda Marie Combs
WOOLGATHERING

To anyone who has ever had a dream . . . Thank you dad and mom

I have no name, just a mere description
I am the consciousness of the unconscious
I am your vision when the night's blinding darkness overcomes you
I am the vigilante who releases you from the imprisonment of the unknown
I am the success of your failures
I am your strength in the present, your link between the past and the future
I am the candle which flickers in the distance, leading you down life's paths
I make the intangible tangible
I bring the out-of-reach to your fingertips

I am your emotions, needs, thoughts
and desires
I allow you to be everything you long
to be
I take you from the furthest corner of
your mind to reality
Who can I be?
You are my creator; thus, I am you
Without your presence, I could not
exist
I am a mystery it seems—no, I am
your dreams!

Fawn A Hentrel
UNHEALED WOUNDS

To: Tina Bartelsmeyer and my family Who inspired me to work and achieve things to my fullest potential. Thanks to my friends

"Daddy, Daddy come back," I said.
"Don't leave us. Did I do something
wrong?"

Am I the cause of a break up
Am I the cause of sorrow?
I wake up in the dark night
with tears of sadness and
screams bouncing off the wall
like an echo.
My family was once so happy, but
now it's oh so sad.
I love my mommy and my dad.
The screams and fights, I know
aren't right, then they still try to tell
me they love me and they still break
up.
Tears of sorrow were in my eyes.
Did I do something wrong?
Was it something, I said? Daddy,
Daddy please come back."

Melissa Melby
TIMEPIECE
What is time, do we know, like a
word, that's too old?
We know it's there, in the air, across
all land, and everywhere.
Where shall we look, look first, in the
clouds, or down to Earth?
In the stars, near that we see, corners
of the earth, that's where we'll be.
Do you know, why we are, or do you
wonder, what we are?
We are distant, as far as you can see,
further than that, above the trees.
We are wind, we are soul, we are
time, and we are old.
We are what you are, you are what
we are, somewhere in space, that's
so very far.
We are time, and so we sing,
throughout time, and with our king.
We are one, and fly like wind, to the
earth, and back home again.
You may come, you are us, you are
soul, and we are trust.
We travel distant, like the wind, far
away, and to the end.

Brenda D C Smith
THOSE WHO KNOW

I would like to dedicate this poem to my daughter Taja Nicole Smith in hope that you will find love like your father and I have and never go through hurt, like in this poem.

For those who have loved,
Know that I love thee.
For those who have dreams,
Know that I dream of you and me.
For those who hurt,
Know that I hurt over you.
For those who are lonely,
Know that I'm feeling blue.
For every lover can see it,
See in my eyes.
That since you left me,
I just sit and cry.
I love you so,
You are still my girl.
Any fool can see,
That you are my world.
If you had a heart,
How could you hurt me so.
For my love was high,
And now my spirits are low.
So for those who have a watch,
Must know about time....
For I wait for you to return to be
back as mine.

Ana V Espinosa
I LOVE YOU OH MY GRANNY!

This poem is dedicated to VICTORIA my DEAREST GRANDMOTHER.

I'm filled with life's contentment,
I'm left without those fears,
the hope and love inside me,
are caused by your sweet care.
The mornings have run by me,
and evenings are a dare,
I Love you oh my Granny,
for all those world filled years.
Though the time runs by me,
of days with full despair,
I love you oh my Granny,
for always being there.
Although the dreams are shattered,
the faith and hope are few,
I Love you oh my Granny,
for never changing too.
Years go by without a lie,
the truth and fame are you,
I Love you oh my Granny,
for showing me who's who.

Cindy Taylor
MI AMOR

To my wonderful husband . . Michael.

Knowing you sure is spectacular,
You have taught me things that
before didn't matter.

From the time we met I have been
different and new, Why are we
apart? It's what we both must do.

You are always in my prayers,
Whether you are here or there.
I am forever adoring your
soft sweet stare.

Love songs that now lift my spirits
not long ago I thought rhythm and
lyrics.

Now when I hear a sweet song
be sure, I am thinking of
you . . . MI AMOR.

Deborah G Shepherd
ONLY THE LONELY

This poem is dedicated to whom it was originally intended, Mario Jazz Allen. Also, to my mom, Cozetta Green. I Love you Fatima and Londun. Thanks Moraye and John.

Looking through the window another
life I see. One filled with laughter
and no misery. Happy children
playing and singing melodies. Birds
in the trees chirping way and dogs
busy barking chasing cats away.
Then one spring morning a tiny baby
was born. In its shining glory and
filled with warmth. Her eyes were
like diamonds as beautiful was she.
Skin shining, bringing new life to
thee. A father filled with pride, eyes
brimming with cheer. Grandparents
on hand also, adding more cheer.

Then there is the mother filled with
misery. For her heart is broken
because her lover is not he. He
doesn't know her, nor does he
understand, the needs of this woman
and what she wants in a man. For her
life is lonely and filled with misery.
The tears wet her pillow, where no
one else can see. But with the
daylight comes the strength that she
needs. Her days are long, nights even
longer, but all of her pain she must
put asunder. There are the children
who must look to her. For guidance
and direction which they will need.

As the for man, he's still there but
with neither pulling, nor do they care.
Do they really love or is it just a
game? Have they loved and lost it
burning out the flame? But with the
morrow there is always hope for a
love they once shared so long ago.
Perhaps one day the man will be who
she wants him to be. Perhaps one day
so will she.

Dionne Angela Reid

Dionne Angela Reid
TOMORROW'S SOLDIER

This poem is dedicated to any person who knows or understands what it feels like to be unjustly incarcerated!

Don't distress it young soldier of
tomorrow. It's your first nightmare
and your first horror.
"I can't believe it; I'm stuck in this
shit hole! Days seem like years and I
feel older than old! ! !
Life is beautiful. But it's an up and
down beat. I just hit the bottom and
this place needs some heat.
It's hell alright but not the one with
fire and sparks. Lonely don't leave
you alone and the sun is ice cold and
always dark.
No one to talk to, but me, myself
and I. And I keep asking myself over
and over. Why me? Why me? O—
Why?! !
But I realize I'm doing something
most people are scared to do.
T_H_I_N_K! ! !
The past, the present, and the future
too.
The past is the most pleasant. Those
fun loving days. Man do I cherish my
freedom. I'm really amazed.
And the present I'm living the
moment lonely and depressed. I'm
ready to get on with my life . . . . to
HELL with this mess! ! ! !
I'm an innocent man I did nothing
wrong. I'm tired of singing the blues;
that's not my song.
Something else about the present it
keeps me aware. About who
remembers me out there while I'm in
here.
Thinking of the future . . . man
that's a hot seat. Different roads to
travel never knowing what's at the
end of each street!
My future is in the hands of a few
select. I'm hoping and praying they
won't make it a wreck.
But just for a positive note let me
say a little more. I'm leaving this
place and I'll be wiser than before!
When I walk from this place I leave
the nightmares at the door. A clear
heart, mind and soul is what I'll have
in store."

A PRAYER OF THANKS TO THE
ALMIGHTY ABOVE KEEP UP
THE FAITH! ! !
PEACE AND LOVE! !

Frances Blackburn
TRANSFORMATION
Gloom—irrepressible and silent
Settling all about me like a heavy fog
And seeming almost to envelop me in
its entirety.
Then—a sudden dart of sunshine
Sweeping away the gloom like dust,
and replacing it with rays of
happiness.

Rebecca L Cruse (Dewitt)
SILENT MAN

Forever dedicated to my one & only "Silent Man," Stewart H.,You will always be within my heart and dreams.

Surely, you know what has
developed inside my heart

I think I've been honest enough,
for you to know,
even times when we're apart

Be it right or be it wrong,
will you please talk to me
so I can either begin
or end this song?

I can deal with your Honesty,
so please don't fear letting me know.
I tend to misunderstand
what feelings you have let show.

It's not my purpose to be
a thorn in your side,
but if there's a chance
I'll let love abide.

I think you know there's feelings
that I want to "show & tell" you,
Silent Man,
but I'm afraid this is the reason
you ran.

If you would just talk to me,
I would understand,
but not saying anything
leaves room for hope in my heart,
Be honest with me,
Silent Man.

My heart will continue to love you
for the good man that you are
and my life will go on with
sweet thoughts of a shining star.

Too far above to reach
giving lessons of a different
way to love,
is what you teach.

Give me a chance to accept you
as you are, in truth & reality,
Talk to me, Silent Man,
so I can understand
what's to be of my own destiny.

Barbara F Sturgis
GLOUCESTER

To: Amos West Upon his retirement as an educator and an administrator.

The Westerlies are blowing
West
to a country place
in Gloucester
to spend his days
in blessed bliss
among its boats and quays.

No more the clamor of the restless
feet . . .
No more the clarion calls in the
halls . . .
No more the funky and the
flippant . . .
No more! Hooray! No more!

The Westerlies are blowing
West
to a placid place
in time . . .
to cabbages and carrots
to flighty fish and funny flies
to leisure time . . .
to contemplate . . .
only
what's on the end of the line!

Charlotte A Malone
THE HOUSE WHERE MY FATHER WAS BORN
Slam
A screen door no longer there
Whispers moonlit madness
Madness
My footstep stretching wide and deep
Echoes the silence
Disturbing the hollow dampness
Staying the spirit's rise
Here
The kitchen
That pumped
Enameled promises
Into decaying
Lives
Long corridor
Dream-haunted
Rooms
Hiding secrets
Half remembered
Lies

Evelyn Rigdon
WISDOM OF AGES
Come listen to these words I say,
young maiden
For I know of where I speak
Do not hasten to the garden of
ecstasy, young maiden
For its blossoms be poisonous sweet
Tread softly and gather but a single
one, young maiden
Though each dazzle and tempt with
each hue
Do not lie among the flowers of bliss,
young maiden
For their thorns will bring torment to
you
Deafen not to virtue's call, young
maiden
And let not your senses to yield
For propriety does have its reward,
young maiden
In the heart that one knows are real.

Rex Wheeler
THOUGHTS OF YOU
I went to walk out in the rain, and let
it fall upon my face,
But the tears I shed for you tonight,
no storm could e'er erase.
I thought the coolness, could set
things right, and quench my burning
heart,
But the fire I felt in body and soul,
was only just the start.
My mind's ablaze with thoughts of
you, I need you here with me,
My heart's been torn apart by you, I
need the calming sea.
You've put me adrift, alone on a raft,
with no relief in sight,
Again I face the terrible task of a
long and lonely night.
But the rains coming down, and
falling softly on the ground,
to wash away my tears,
And a love once right, has been lost
in the night, to be remembered fondly
through the years.

Larry M Olsen
A GOLDEN TEAR

To Grandma in honor of Grandpa

To see a tear is more precious than
life
A drop of gold from the heart
It bleeds the sorrow of thoughts and
feelings
It shadows the pain inside your body
But only for a second in time

A tear of sorrow from the soul
Holds more meaning than all that is
imagined
But never cures all the hurt in your
mind
Just gives an excuse to accept it
And then fades away—
Only to come back again

To hold a tear is to know how to feel
True warmth and strength come from
a tear
A tear is an everlasting memory
To remind us of what we really are

If you never experience a tear, life is
not complete
If you never have pain, you will not
understand
If sorrow never follows you, you
have no regrets
If you never have a tear—
I will bleed one for you

Willow Robinson
AWAKENING

For Kara Marie, my first born.

She was so tiny, so small,
  ours to love and hold.
We will try to teach her,
  ours to guide and mold.
In the work along the way,
  my worry grew of how she'll be.
"She must be perfect, just right."
  The person she is I finally see.
Today I saw her play so free.
  she has such a tender heart.
She fills me up inside with love,
  Not the love I felt at the start;
Now I love her for herself,
for who she is inside.
  Not because she is of me,
That I can set aside.
My aspirations of perfection,
  I know are so unreal.
But she is a perfect friend
And now she is Ideal.

Susan Andress
BROTHER

Dedicated to my brother Charles Mancour.

My mind goes back to a summer about fifteen years ago. It was 1973. And that summer my brother and I became as close as we would ever be. I learned a lot about my brother that summer.

But all good things come to an end. And summer was over it seemed before it began.

So back to school we all went. Up before sunrise to catch the bus. And out into the dark we would go side by side. I never had to worry about things that go bump in the night . . . For he was all ways by my side.

But like I said all good things must end. And then one cold Oct. night a drunk took my brother's life.

Sylvia Halcomb

Sylvia Halcomb
MOTHER

To my Mother, Herminia. I love you Ma

Mother tender and true
What have your children
Done to you
You washed their hands
And cleaned their face
And removed the hurt
From the hidden place
You fed them, clothed them
Walked them too
It is because of you
They grew.
You were the nurse
Who watched at night
You were the counselor
Who showed them right
You were the baker, the mender too
For all the things
Children can't do

You taught them to speak
You guided little feet
You were the love
That your children knew
For no other, was more beautiful
Than you.
You were the blanket
in the cold.
Now you are old
But wait, your work was
Not in vain.
For they will have children
And know the same pain.
No one cares, if you cry.
No one cares, if you die
You are no longer needed
You planted, seeds
And you were there for harvest
And the job you did
Mother
  was marvelous

Denise Costa
AIR WALK
Flies above in the clear of air
  strings dangle
  twines tangle
Climbs into the deep blue air.

Colorful dots above my head
  Climbs higher
  flies higher
Smaller and smaller, yellow, blue,
red.

Helium balloon leaves my hand
  sneaks away
  flies away
To another wonderland.

Strings, tails, and bright stars
  brings joy
  child's toy
Joins the world of skies and stars.

Balloons, green, pink, and white
  take me
  let me see
The unreachable day and night.

Terri Thomas St Clair
OPEN MY EYES

To my husband Roger, for all the love and support he has given me. To my children Melissa, Eric, and Jon, whom I love with all my heart. And to my Savior, Jesus Christ, who gave me all my talent.

Open My eyes Lord that I might see
all of the beauty you have spread
around me.
The majestic mountains so purple and
tall.
The little violet so sweet and small.
The lazy river, the mountain
stream, the rays of the sun,
or the silver moonbeams.
The flight of the geese as southward
they go,
to the warmth of the south to
escape the north snow.
The stray little kitten that
no one has fed, I'll take him
and feed him and give him a bed.
The beautiful sunrise, the sunset
at night.
thank you Lord for giving me
sight.
though sight you have given me
I don't always see all of the
beauty you have given me.

Heather Margaret Mosychuk
WILLED BY MY HAND

To the artist of the painting, my sister, Arline Mae King, whom I cherish very much, and her husband, Granis Rexford King, for the encouragement he gives her in all her endeavors.

For our 25th Anniversary,
My sister painted this canvas for us,
She'd asked what scene I would like
it to be,
I'd told her, "woodsy" would be
marvelous.

I guess we aren't close sisters for
nothing,
I had a specific setting in mind,
If to her mind, a likened scene did

spring,
There was a psychic passing of some kind.

This beautiful gift means so much to me,
In part, 'cause she's expressing a talent,
More professional than I did foresee,
In which can be seen excellent time spent.

This painting in our family shall remain,
In no closet shall it be cast aside,
Forever, for generations to gain,
Appreciation of ancestral pride.

On a wall I charge this painting be hung,
In a home for all visitors to see,
Or, where Picassos and Renoirs, among,
I shall agree to an art gallery.

To exhibit but never for selling,
A true family heirloom, destined to please,
Without doubt a masterpiece compelling,
She captured the beauty amongst the trees.

Margaret Pendleton Quillen
MY FRIEND, MY BOOKS

To my Dearest and best friend, God and his son Jesus, Maker of the Universe and Savior of all mankind; Whose love endureth forever.

I love my Books, my precious Books
They've been a friend to me.
They've helped me face some lonely hours
And made my worries flee
They taught me most of what I know
I love each one the same
So if I'm stupid, Heaven knows
My books are not to blame.
They placed the world around me
They laid it at my feet.
Why shouldn't I be proud of them
And demand they be kept neat?
And if I loan one to a friend
It really makes me burn,
When they promise oh! so faithfully
My books soon to return.
I find out who my friends are
When they come to me and say,
Your books I borrowed months ago
I forgot again today.
I remind them they're like children
Which I would not give away.

Angela Davies
SHE DREAMS

She sits in her room wondering why
Just sitting there she starts to cry.
She keeps things bottled up inside
So in her room is where she hides
In her room problems fade away
So in her room is where she will stay
Puzzling questions run through her head,
So she lies down on her bed
And cries herself to sleep that night
She has a dream of terrible fright
She dreams she is blind and cannot see
She dreams, dreams of fear that would frighten me
She dreams she is mute and can not talk
She dreams she is crippled and can not walk
She dreams she is deaf and can't hear a sound
She dreams of death, bodies lying around
Then she awakes from this terrible fright
Now she sees her life has new light
She knows that her life seems pretty bad
But now she sees the problems she could of had.

Mazell Bradley Campbell
ROBIN PAVED THE WAY

To my brother, Robin, who was young when he paved the way for his family and race in times of need.

In Oakdale, Louisiana—way down South,
Robin Bradley began to open his mouth.
He knew exactly what he planned to do,
But he also knew help was needed too.

He knew that his people were far behind
with no time left for BLACKS to be blind.
So he met with a lawyer and his brave men
In the lawyer's office known as his den.

The first idea pulled from the racks
Was zoning the areas to include more BLACKS.
To court, they went with this great plan
With Robin to lead them as a very great man.

When the lawyer stayed home to show them up,
Robin Bradley bravely faced this bitter cup.
He presented the case so exceedingly well
Until everyone's head began to swell.

The court thought he was a lawyer,
The famous one, known as Tom Sawyer.
Everyone greeted him respectfully after the case;
But Robin, triumphantly, has won for his race.

Jennifer Anne Herzog
MY KITTEN

To my kitten Bonita Keva The sweetest cat anyone ever had Bonnie, I love you

With a soft, steady purr
My kitten
Such a black ball of fur
My doll

With a kiss
Say good night
From afar
Such a sight

And your soft, steady purr
Is my call.

With a
Fidgety tail
Such a lovely
Portrayal

Of my life, of my love,
Of my all.

Jacquelyn Holiday Jones
THE BEST I CAN

To: Mary and John Holiday For the times you've wondered: Did I do all I could for my children?

Oh Yes, you've always been there
When we've needed a helping hand,
To Love and protect us
And to do the Best you can.
You've soothed us when we've cried
And to scold us when we've lied,
To teach us right from wrong
And to keep us from All Harm.

Though you have problems of your own
You'd never let us know it,
You'd keep the pain from us
And never want to show it.

You lift our spirits when we're low
Pick us up and let us know
You Love us, and You Care.
When we need it you're always there.

So, If I'm ever down and out
And in need of a helping hand,
I'll think of you Mom and Dad
And do the Best I Can.

Willy Antoine

Willy Antoine
YOU AND I

We had seen each other for a long time,
but we were each afraid to say hi;
sometimes, I wonder why
but nothing comes to mind.
Finally, last month on valentine's,
we met upstairs on the second floor.
Suddenly, we looked at each other...
And winked our eyes together...

And smiled also together.
We were very spontaneous;
we said at the same moment:
"I love you!
I want you to be mine."
After, we approached face to face,
gazed at each other,
hugged and kissed.
Ever since, you and I
are no more shy to say hi
Because we are lovers for LIFE

Robert J Wojtasik
WHO CARES ANYMORE?

My life seemed to be taking a turn for the worse,
And I had troubles abound!
But when I reached out for someone's help,
They didn't seem to want me around.
Who Cares Anymore?

I really didn't blame anyone for my sudden demise,
But when I tried to confide my feelings of frustration to them,
I could not see any sympathy in their eyes.
Who Cares anymore?
I've never looked for or asked for anyone's help in my life,
And the only person I could really count on for support was my wife.
Unfortunately, we happened to be in the same situation.
And without financial help we couldn't meet our obligations.
Who Cares anymore?

I gave up my pride, and asked my own sister for help.
But she said she had no money,
And I should look to someone else for help.
Who Cares anymore?

Now I've sold everything of value that I happen to possess,
Even some things that belonged to my wife,
Things she valued more than happiness.
Who Cares anymore?

Well I've worked so hard my whole life long,
And yet everything I try to do just seems to turn out wrong.
I don't understand why all this is happening.
What am I failing to do that would change all this sadness?
Who Cares anymore?

Don't tell me to pray 'cause I do it each day,
And yet nothing seems to change!
There's just an illusion that appears, that helps to wipe away the tears.
But it's my life I must rearrange.
Who Cares anymore?

I know in my herat things will all work out right,
But while I'm on my feet I must continue to fight.
I still count on the Lord to help me through it all
For without His help there's no doubt that I will fall.
Who Cares anymore?

I'll continue to work hard and pray each day,
And hopefully with some luck,
I'll bring home some decent pay,
Hopefully my family will endure and not abandon me,
For without their support there's a future I cannot see.
Who Cares anymore?

There's a hurt in my heart I cannot describe,
I think I'd rather be dead than to endure this humility.
I'm sure the Lord has a reason for all that is happening to me,
And very soon He will step in and let me free!

Pamela Joan Romeyn
THE BIBLE

To My Five Children and their many generations to come in the future may they and many others find great joy as they read in their Bibles

The BIBLE is a wondrous Book,
It tells of the past and brings you the future,
Of Man's Creation and Visions of Gold,
Of wars, of Beings and Bones,
Of slaying Great Giants with a sling and a stone,
The Falling of Cities to Trumpets

and Song.
Many strange stories, and all of them True.
It tells of GOD OUR FATHER, who created us All,
Of Satan and His Demons, who want us to fall,
Of GOD's Only Begotten SON, CHRIST JESUS,
Who DIED upon The CROSS for mankind's
Salvation to bring if WE but ACCEPT HIM and BELIEVE.
Many are sold, but few Get read.
If you want to LIVE, READ IT, Live by it, to the
Best of your Ability.
It has been proved that It is better than Government Gold.
It will lead you too, to Life Eternal, and to Life in
The TRUE CITY Of GOLD.

Holly Manica

Holly Manica
REMEMBER

Remember the times we spent together,
the tears we cried,
the pain we shared,
And although there were times of sadness,
there were many days of laughter.

Time and time again,
I remember the happiness you brought me
and the tender love we made—
So strong to last forever.

Forever has come and gone;
and your tender love for me has faded,
but my love for you still remains,
and all I can do is remember.

Marie Sanzillo
EN PASSANT

To Karen

The day is dark and dreary,
But I, am never weary
Of the tapping of the fingers of the rain;
They splash and run together
And drip to purple heather,
Now a deep and pungent purple, once again:
With speed and tinkling laughter
Nor thought of the hereafter,
They submerge themselves within the thirsty clay.
Their journey, soon was ended,
Their lives were short—But splendid:
And the heather and I, know they passed this way!

Sherri Kwiatkowski
SEPARATE

While I watch and try to understand others I sometimes get caught up in my difference.
I stand alone, hopelessly alone.
My feelings aren't real, I pretend only to be somewhat alike, united with others.
The way others speak, their feelings aren't true; either filled with foolishness or a great deal of weakness.
I feel no pity or remorse. I only wish to be.
No one person understands but me.
They look at me in despair, mocking and ridiculing me.
I stand alone because I am alone.
I try my very best to grasp what is reality, but I always seem to disappear in the lost remoteness of loneliness.

Charlie Cardinal
WHAT CAN I SAY?

As I look through the window the city out there,
The hustle and bustle and cars.
Tall buildings and small ones and so many colors,
With planes coming in from afar.

The bums walk alone and the women don't smile,
And I wonder what I'm doing here?
The lure of big money or maybe excitement,
Or just insecurity and fear.

I leave my good home in the wee morning hours,
With commuters more crazy than I.
And drive many miles both morning and night,
So often I wish I could fly.

But some day it will end I truly believe,
When I have no more need to come here.
And my daughter is grown and out on her own,
Or I find that I no longer care.

But for now it goes on, this quest in my life,
Which I'll handle as best as I can.
Like so many others I'm caught in the trap,
Till at last I come up with a plan!

Marcia Senko
A BEAUTIFUL GARDEN

I would like to dedicate this poem to my lovely family.

A beautiful garden
Surrounded by dazzling colors
Appears in front of one
With a multitude of flowers
A spectrum of rainbow shades
Beaming so brightly
As hummingbirds flutter about them
Ever so lightly
Rows of lovely red and white roses
All in full bloom
With scarlet sage, tulips and lilies
Awakening at noon,
The lovely sweet scent of mixed perfume fragrances
Can be smelled
As one walks along with
A cluster of pinks and whites held
An elegant white fountain can be seen
As you enter
With a beautiful cupid
Sitting in the center
The sky so blue; the clouds so white
As one looks around
At this most beautiful sight
Walking along
On this clean summer's day
A feeling of joy and happiness
Comes one's way

Tanan Cole
PARTY TOWARD COLLAGE

Women dancing on roofs
Dressed to kill
One hundred pianos in the back-ground
Jets in the sky
Symphonies to the north
Rock concerts to the left

Colored balloons rise from the ground
Reggae people holding long hair
Jamming toward
the side lines

It's a Party Toward Collage
Headed for something special
Something I can't quite figure
Something left to Rhythm
Something

Love is contagious
In this little place

Music flies
Everything consumes

It's a Painting
A simple Party Toward Collage

Madeleine Price Brewer
DREAMS

To my daughters—Debbie, Lisa, Cyndy and Cristi—never stop dreaming.

The dreams of a young girl
are worth their weight in gold.
For she will savor and caress them
when she has grown old.
A young girl has ambitions
as to what she wants to be.
Given room to spread her wings
she will soar toward her destiny.
So many roads to travel
so many roles to play
so many challenges to meet
in living day to day.
Her dreams will chart the course
toward the life that lies ahead.
They can be a welcome pillow
for that sometimes weary head.
So don't be afraid to dream your dreams
and reach for open skies.
For when we lose our dreams
the young girl in us dies.

Malaika McCoya Moss
IN HEAVEN

Do not cry for me when I die
for I will be in a place
where I will have no more troubles
or experience any more disgrace.
Also, do not linger
on what you may lave lost
yet, strive to become the best
you can be
Regardless of the cost.
Do not attempt to blame anyone for my death;
just let me rest in peace.
Let me rest.

Until such time, I guarantee, "I will spread throughout the world my love."
Emphasize the importance of well-being
And acknowledge strength received from above.
Until such time, I ask for peace.
For strength and equality.
I request that everyone help
the world be a better place to be.

Save the tears
Limit the grief and pain
Do not cry for me when I die,
for I am sure to live again.

Patricia A (McDaniels) Cruse
LITTLE FOOTPRINTS IN THE SNOW

Yesterday was spring . . . .
The birds sang their melodious songs,
And the sun sent long rays of sunshine
To warm the heart of Mother Earth.

Today is winter . . . .
The sun is in hiding.
Snowflakes are drifting from clouded skies
To cover Mother Earth in her extended nap.

What happened to summer?
Look out the window and see,
Little footprints in the snow.
A red breasted robin is hopping about.

You realize . . . .
Summer is tomorrow.
The seasons are the same.
It's just March again!

Angela Lambriola
MY REPOSE TO LOVE

Love is compassion,
without regrets.
Love is equality,
without demands.
Love is forgiveness,
without saying, I'm sorry.
Love is sharing and caring.
Love is friendship and honor.
Love is a flame that forever burns,
unless you snuff it out yourself.
Love is the warmth of your heart,
that always shines a light.
Hate is the cold,
that will always keep you in darkness.
What a wondrous gift,
to give or receive is,
Love

Etta Jernigan Strickland

Etta Jernigan Strickland
THE MANSE HOUSE

Dedication: To my loving family: Delilah, Leo; Susan, Rodney, Stephanie; Carol, Reggie; Carl, Wanda, Jason and Amy.

The river behind the Manse House
was flowing gently on.
The sound was peaceful to the
mouse, eating her cheese alone.

The maple, dogwood, birch and pine stood stately in the breeze.
Mrs. Mouse, who saw the swinging vine, still quietly ate her cheese.
The owl, in her home in the tree, gave a loud "who, who, who."
This frightened Mrs. Mouse terribly; heading homeward she flew.
Never again! "I've met a foe, it is not worth the chance.
I'll get mighty hungry, I know; can't go back to the manse."
She remembers well the cheese there, the food, the crumbs galore.
Her baby mice, so hungry and fair, need cheese, crumbs and more.

Will, Julia, Laura and Thom Gaines, Sardis' pastor family
Do not know Mrs. Mouse who complains, wanting their food for free.
Playing on the garden wall so high, little ones on the ground,
She was watching the parade go by; a solution must be found!
We'll go up to the farmer's mill, eat the grains, sit and talk.
It is away upon the hill, quite a far piece to walk.
Away they went in a hurry, soon ate and fell asleep.
Waking them in a scurry, the cat rushed them down the steep.
Home will be by the garden wall, by the Manse House we'll be
With beautiful flowers and all, throughout eternity.

Joann K Anderson-Pittman
TIME
Time is a strange thing.
Days go by, each filled with the same amount of hours.
Each hour filled with the same minutes.
Each minute has the same seconds.
Yet some days seem only an hour long.
While some hours seem to last a day.
Life is how we spend our time.
The past is time forever lost.
Today is the only time we can count.
The future is just a matter of time.
And if I've waited this long to get to where I am,
Why am I so impatient to get to where I'm going?

Stacie Woodin
AND THEN, SAY A PRAYER
As I go outside,
I feel the leaves.
And look into the sky,
And see how it bleeds.

The night in turning
Into day,
As the trees are tired
Of the play.

As destruction is upon us!
We must let it bond us!
Together we must bare,
And then, say a prayer.

Scott Allen Smith
THE HUNTER'S TROPHY

I dedicate this poem to my love, Patricia

He glides through
Abounding blue,
Pierces floating splotches
of white solitude.
He soars over
Vast,
Swaying fields of wheat.
He flies above majestic
green mountains.
Below,
The amber sea crashes
upon the shores of
the tranquil forest.
He dives and skims
the treetops
in search of prey.
He screeches in agony
as a bullet penetrates
his body.
His carcass plummets
to the ground.

Deborah Johnson
LET'S PRETEND
"Let's pretend it was a nightmare.
Let's pretend it's gone away
As the morning mist evaporates
beneath the rising sun,
Leaving just some scattered dewdrops
As it fades into the day
Soon forgotten, just an unimportant, small phenomenon.

"Let's pretend your heart's not bleeding,
That you shed no anguished tears
In th' eternal love of Him they say was mocked and crucified;
So the lurking agitation
And the nagging guilt and fears
In my mind might also fade and this contention could subside.

"Let's pretend it did not happen.
Let's pretend it isn't so.
Look, the sandbox still is there beside the tree, and children play
In the smiling sun of springtime
As we used to do. And, lo,
The hill is greening. Let's pretend that it has simply gone away."

Michael P Wohlford
ONLY TIME WILL TELL
Only time will tell
It comes as no surprise
Was love meant to be
Or were there too many lies
There's someone for everyone
Or so I am told
To find that one true love
Will ours ever take hold
The rules to this game
Have they ever been defined
To chase after your heart
Or simply go with your mind
Who will ever know the truth
About this thing called love
Is it pulled from inside
Does it come from above
Only time will tell

Lelia M Alston
GOD IS THERE
When I feel empty and worried, I turn my thoughts to prayer. A light goes on in my head and God is there.
When in doubt, and sorrow fills my heart, I turn to prayer, and thank my God for being there.
While I am seeking happiness and searching for peace of mind, in prayer, I find, my God is there.
When my health is failing and my hair is graying and every day seems to be my last. I get down on my knees in prayer and my God is there

Sanford Panitch
THE TRANSFORMATION
Came across an old picture
Of me and my friends.
We were huddled close, and
I was trying to make sure
I was still in the lens.
It was full of holes
From thumbtacks
Meant to keep it alive.

We were little boys,
We were teenage guys,
We were men ready for work,
We were middle-aged fathers,
And we were the elderly
Always helping each other along.

I stared into the picture—my face,
And the expression of my mind—
And it showed that I thought,
Like we all thought back then,
That life was good.
Our bond was good,
And we would be lucky.

But now I am alone, and
Often I sit naked by the silent phone
And fill each of the holes with glue.

Mark W Butler
PAGES OF MEMORIES
Even though I'm not with you
I try hard to pretend I am
But it's not quite the same
You and I aren't to blame
Pages of memories, and times that were ours
My mind takes me back
To a night under the stars
When I held you close to me
Wishing the future was ours

We walked around a small lake
Happy and content
Feeling the presence of each other's feelings
These were precious moments, too quickly spent

Remembering long talks on the phone
The happy hours we spent alone
I just can't erase you from my mind
Because all of this was in my time
I remember the softness of your lips
And the smile I wish you could send
But for now I read the pages of memories
In a book that never said the end

Anna M Matthews
THE NEW YEAR

Dedicated to my sons David E. Matthews and John W. Matthews, Jr.

With Eighty-eight now history
And Eighty-Nine in view,
May you find it rewarding
In everything you do.

Now, looking to the future,
With "should have dones" behind—
Just think "success or failure's
Created in the mind."

Each New Year is a challenge,
Accept it then and see
How often what's accomplished
You'll find you hold the key!

Bob Lajeunesse
IN TIME
The Sun breaks thru the white clouds in the West
Enhancing the blackness of the clouds in the South
The brisk wind darts to and fro
While other clouds kiss the mountain in repose
The bright yellow aspens break the
dark evergreen blanket on the slope
The vast desert valleys patiently wait
for the mountains to join them
And man's small inroads into all this,
as with the storm
Shall pass and be forgotten
And the Earth shall reclaim its own.

Marshall Sears
ALONE
Alone in life
Alone in pain
Alone in love
Alone again

Alone could be hope
Alone could be death
Alone once again
Alone last breath

Alone with friends
Alone at home
Alone to work
Alone to roam

Alone to help
Alone to live
Alone to feel
Alone to give

Alone tonight
Alone when tired
Alone is good
Alone desired.

Cheré Lefebvre
ECHO'S
Echoes of your voice
Come to me at night.
Telling me so softly
That everything's all right.
Echoes of your laughter
Haunt me during the day.
They're telling me to smile
I wish you would have stayed.
The echoes of your footsteps
Follow me around.
I look for you every place I go
But you are nowhere to be found.
You're echoing "I love you"
I can't get it out of my mind.
I wish you would have told me
So we could have had more time.
I can hear the echo of the voice

That is telling me you're gone.
I keep screaming out that you're still alive
But they tell me that I am wrong.
The echo of your voice
Is telling me it's true.
And as your voice starts to fade away
I whisper "I Love You!"

Stella M Bussey
FLIGHT OF FANTASY

Dedicated to my dearest friend, Millie, who encouraged and inspired me.

I am as one with nature
—my soul leaving the prison of this earth
—consumed by God's magnificent gifts
—the sun, the rain, the moon,
beautiful oceans, glorious mountains
—outside this shell we earthlings call a body.
Floating on high with the movement of the clouds,
drifting into the nothingness of space,
tossing aimlessly on the oceans' waves
—carrying me away into fantasies of my mind,
separated from my human mortal shell,
soaring weightlessly through the clouds,
leaving behind all worries and cares
on this planet we title earth,
searching for sanctuary in the heavens,
being carried further and further away
—away from the problems plaguing my very existence
—torn between returning to what awaits me
at the end of my journey
—or remaining in my fantasy world forever,
not caring what happens outside my tiny sphere of happiness,
adrift in the realm of my own imagination.

Ross A Porter
REWARD

Now here is young Patrick
so brave and so fair . . .
Pray they have shorn not
a lock of his hair.

Has not his mother
sang to him sweet,
and laid out his clothing
all pressed up and neat?

See his young body
all bruised up and torn.
Hear now his clansmen
cry out forlorn.

Where will young Patrick
find now his rest?
In the hall of his kinsmen,
of which he was the best.

Dorothy Norton Davids
I BELIEVE

I believe in God because of rainbows,
Arcs of color tossed against the morning sky,
As though some Angel sowing seeds of joy in Heaven,
Bending low to Earth, let slip the hues so pleasing to His eye;

Watched them taking root at either end of that great arc,
Granting earthly seekers of His paradise
A view of beauty far beyond man's simple power to create,
For God alone can make a rainbow for our eyes.

I believe in God because of evenings
When, searching for safe passage through the night,
The Moon peeks carefully o'er darkened hills, then, reassured,
Beams broadly, smiling on the land and pleasured by the sight.

I believe in God because of children,
For are they not true gifts of love on earth?
Each one holding in his smallness, something of the Father's love for his own Son
Sent to spend His childhood joined with man by earthly birth?

Yes, I believe in God for these, and many reasons,
For things hard to speak of, vague, or lucid clear;
For God has granted that we see the beauty of His world, and how to pray
In thankfulness for all the good there is on earth, in rainbowed morning,
and in moonlit end of day.

Eileen Sutton
LOST FRIEND

I awake each morning and wonder
What today is going to bring
Will there be joy and laughter
To make me want to sing?

Or will the loss of a friend I had
Make me sad throughout the day
Was this person really a friend?
Whose loss is it anyway?

Kathleen N Neuser

Kathleen N Neuser
SNOW ANGEL

I'd like to dedicate my first published poem to my father, brother, and grandmother. You three are the most important people in my life. There is also a fourth who is equally important and part of my love goes to him. Thank you all.

I lay on my back, and stare at the sky—
while snowflakes softly float
into my eyes.
With a chill in my bones, but a smile on my face—
my arms and legs move in a
perfect pace.
The image I make in the pearly white snow—
is one I seek when I'm feeling
low.
When in trouble, she bails me out—
when confused, she clears my
doubt.
As I watch the clouds pass by—
I admire their beauty when
they fill the sky.
Their surface is as pure as the white laced flakes—
which try to cover the image I
make.
Her wings of grace will not give way—
to the falling flakes of each
passing day.
And though she'll disappear from where I placed her—
my mind holds her image
forever after.

Steven N Bancroft
O'LITTLE ONE

Dedicated: To my son, and his mother.

You lie upon my chest, sleeping soundly, contentedly.
I feel each breath you take.
I hear your tiny heartbeat as you dream.
You clutch my shirt and squirm, as if uncomfortable.
Suddenly you awaken, crying, wriggling, and angry.
Just as quickly you succumb to sleep,
To your dreams, once again.
How could such a tiny being, create such an overwhelming,
sense of direction, of meaning, of value, to life itself.
You would be astounded, O'little one,
If you could only know, the feelings you've awakened in me.
Although I anticipated loving you, as I love your mother.
I could not have imagined, the emotion, the esteem, the love,
Which fills me now, to my very soul.

Gail T Cross
COMMANDER

To my best friend, my mom and my beautiful family.

I walk a path of this life I've known
And somehow wonder what's gone wrong,
As I pick the pieces of my mind off the ground
And my body spins round and round.

Take me far away,
My Commander of the sky
To a place if I may
Call "Paradise".

Is this feeling food for my soul?
As I fly far where no one knows,
For now my wings do unfold
I strike my life that has grown cold.

So as my mind lay scattered on the ground
I call my Commander I have found,
Who watches my body spin round and round
As he lays me to rest in "Paradise Town".

Anna Rhynes Combs
THE QUIET OUTDOOR

I love to sit
In the quiet outdoor
Relaxing in nature's metaphor
Overhead I see a sky of blue
Its tinted shades cast a magic hue
I feel the gentle unseen breeze
That sends a rustle
Through the trees
My eyes feast on
The wild flowers abloom
In the fields beyond,
The brook nearby
Lends a babbling sound . . . and
While the sun rides high
Birds are aflutter
From tree to sky;
If I could but choose
It's here I'd stay
Close to God in every way
Bending to earth's awesome tune
From early dawn til setting sun!

Sam Beatty
WINTER THAW

Chilly little droplets
Gather together
Above my door.
They've been at it
Now for an hour or more.
I know exactly when
they'll stop—
when I go out the door
they'll go.
.
.
.
.
.
.
.
Plop!
Right down my neck!
I will not mind the chill,
Since I clearly feel the thrill—
Spring is close behind!

Martin A Mitchell
CATCHING GLIMPSES

For as long as I have possessed
awareness
I have harbored
doubt,
suspicion
That something is being
kept from me
Something that I should know
something that I
need to know
Something that flickers
in the periphery
But recedes into shadow
when I turn
to look at it
I am haunted by
fleeting glimpses
of a secret knowledge
That so far,
I have not earned.

Gina Protopapa
EMPTYNESS

Like an unborn child he lay
unstricken and alone

Unaware to be conceived
that of the spiders throne
web awakened
dew of petals fall
Lower
Lower

Arise oh the world
to thy I am
Of yours
the flesh
that bare
the womb
And the prey
is ever unseen

Sally Newsom
TO THE ANSWERING MACHINE

There's nobody here that can answer the phone,
But that doesn't mean that there's nobody home!
There's just one thing, that you've got to do,

Leave your name and a message,
we'll get back to you.

Linda Ellen Origer
FAREWELL BID

Dedicated in memory of my Father, Oleon Burchfield. "I Thank You for my life and the love I grew up with. May you now have the blissful peace you deserve and know you remain in my heart. I MISS YOU DADDY

I stand by your grave,
I uncontrollably weep.
Do you lie there quietly,
Are you in a deep sleep?

Do you see me here?
Can you understand why?
That for now I'm unable,
To "bid you Good-bye".

Are you able to feel
As you did when alive?
Or does pain no longer,
Your happiness, deprive.

Are you surrounded by comfort
Of arms those preceded?
While traveling the long tunnel,
Twas "The Light" all you needed.

When the winds gently blow,
Is it you passing by?
Could you reach out and touch me?
Would I hear a soft sigh?

If at dark I looked up,
And stars sparkle bright,
Are the souls of all saved,
What lightens the night?

If I looked a little closer,
Will one be unique?
Could it be of my "Father"
Of whom that I speak?

The questions I have
But can't answer just now.
Will they continue to mount,
Or be answered some how?

Will I finally learn
How to cope with your fate?
Will I some day see you,
For me, will you wait?

In time I am sure
Through dry eyes you will tell.
I will go to our place,
I will "bid you FAREWELL".

I will stand at your grave,
I will no longer cry.
For "you" are not there.
Your SOUL didn't die.

Love, your daughter Linda

Steven Zachgo
THE WEED'S

To Karen, for the bright moments in my life

The flower teasingly sways to and fro,
slightly trembling in the soft summer breeze,
attractively dressed in painted colors.
Under the warm glow of a yellow sun,
enchants the world with would-be admirers.

The weed seeks the same heavenly light,
spreads the barbed leaves skyward and
feasts on gossamers of dust-streaked sunshine.
Enchants disdain, scoffed in a world filled with merriment and dancing smiles.

The flower tolerates the presence of the weed;
chance occasion dictate unpleasant moments in life.
Looking beyond to the cheerful embrace,
precious comments imbued in earthly delight,
the garden sings with songs of love—ignoring one blight.

The weed's thirst is not quenched with the morning dew glistening like gems
encrusted on a ring of imagined romance.
The weed's content is not fulfilled, solely,
with rugged growth, clinging strongly to life.

The weed mourns,
I need not need be the weed,
whose measure spoils the sightly flower;
whose presence gladdens my heart
to wakeful mirth, blossoming petals.
Sure to cure my sickly pallor.

I need not need smell the flower,
whose fragrance is meant for another;
whose presence is tenderly touched by another.
Or be encouraged with a longing despair
in a garden filled with lovely scents.

The flower is plucked and placed in an ornamental urn.
The weed is ripped asunder, heaved upon a wheelbarrow.
The flower wilts, the weed's strength fades.
A soft funeral hymn whispers in the garden.
Providence welcomes both, bound for some garbage heap.

Edwin R Ling
MY LOVE

To my beloved Uncie

All women are but one
Save one
She alone, of all the rest,
Harboures true love
Within her breast.

B K Reedy
THE END

Here I sit in the dark of the night
Hiding from everything that causes me fright.
I sit here for hours and ask myself why
This feeling won't end as hard as I try.

My heart is about to collapse; I can feel it dying
No one sees the pain in my eyes; no one hears my crying
Soon the sun will rise and I must hide
As I fight to control all I feel inside.
I search and search but no one's there
Isn't anyone willing to care?
The world today is filled with so much pain
Look up and see the blood in the rain.

Beware world for it will soon end
No longer will there be such a word as friend
The love is ending; it's hard to find
Gone forever will be mankind.

Cindy A Poirier
QUIET? WITH CHILDREN?

This poem is dedicated to my children, Shawn and Robin.

It seems there is no end,
To the shrieks my little ones send,
Out of their lungs and vocal cords,
The yells are never in real words.

I tell myself one day I will miss,
This noise, but it can only be bliss,
To hear a pin drop is my plea,
If that only my children could agree.

Noise is their form of expression,
I tell myself this is a lesson,
God's way of teaching me patience,
Is it a virtue or am I sentenced?

A life sentence it can not be,
Because they grow up you see,
They move away from home too soon,
And by then the quiet will loom.

My oldest and a friend just came off the school bus to join the youngest here at home. Now I have all three trying to talk at once not being heard by each other. But boy can I hear them!

Ivan Robson
AS ART TO INTELLECT

As perfume of petunia
to petunia pertains—
as specific sparks to fire;
so is art to intellect,
in rememberings of brains,
to grasp lest it expire.

John Bryant
NATURE'S LITTLE CLEANERS

The fly, we know is awful, and with paper or pantoffle, we would gladly give each one of them a whack;
The roach is not much better tho the squash may be less wetter; and the mouse to God we gladly would give back.

But even tho we feel that we would give a startled squeal if we should find our home is now their hunting-ground,
We ought to give a thought to all the good that they have wrought by cleaning up the messes that we've left around.

For who would take the trouble to retrieve a piece of rubble that was slopped from plate or pan onto the floor?
And who would think a dripping had a taste that was so gripping after it had run most halfway down the door?

But the mouse would surely trouble to consume the piece of rubble, and the dripping would be loved by roach and fly;
So we see these tiny gleaners are just nature's little cleaners and they'll clean up all our messes by and by.
So let us not forget, if we should ever start to fret, about how mice and flies and roaches can be stopped,
That tho our swats and baiting make their likes less irritating, we are only killing food that we have dropped.

keith robert chigbrow
IF YOU COULD

If you could, change the world today
What would you do
What would you say
Where would you start
To change the way the way

If you could, would you end all war
Stop all fighting
Make peace today
Where would you start
To change the way

If you could, would you grow more food
To feed the world
To save the day
Where would you start
To change the way

If you could, change the world today
The place to start
The Lord did say
Just change your self
To change the way

Qiana Cerise Conley

Qiana Cerise Conley
PARENT OF THE YEAR

My mother is caring, loving, and sharing, like a precious flower to me.

She's tough and strong and all along not cowardly at all you see.

She lifts up my life with a strong and bright light from her heart that is fierce, not weak,

And that's why I know with a strong, little glow that she's the "PARENT OF THE YEAR" for me.

Marjorie McCandless
HALLOWEEN

Dedicated to my grandchildren: Elizabeth, Katherine and Deborah Baker; Katie and Kristyn McCandless; and Michael and Brittany Luchtefeld.

All the little pumpkins
Are lined up in a row,
For soon their faces will be carved
And lights within will glow.

So why are they unhappy?
Why are they filled with fear?
'Cause soon the ghosts and goblins
And creatures will appear.

I'm scared too, little pumpkin
Of witches, cats and bats,
But it's only little children
Beneath those tall black hats.

We really shouldn't be afraid
It's only fun you know,
Let's trick or treat together
And let our big smiles show.

Your light will shine about us
So things won't look so bad,
Together we'll be very brave
'Cause nearby is mom or dad.

Christina

Kathleen McDonald
CHRISTINA'S SMILE

To my wonderful daughter, Christina, with whom I intend to share a lifetime of smiles.

There seemed to have been little meaning
Those years of silent distress
Looking for something, oh yes, something
To fill the emptiness

A road without a purpose
A book that had no end
A life, well, just an existence
Then there came a friend.

A tiny bouncing baby girl
With eyes that seemed to say
I love you Mom, please hold me close
Her smile leading the way

As time goes by she learns to do
So many different things
To walk, then run, to play some games
To talk and then to sing

And as I watch in wonder
I truly am amazed
At the meaningfulness my life has found
With Christina sharing my days.

Elaine Bosse
THE BLUES

I work hard all day between my job and house
I'm too worn out for play;
I need the income for my kids you see,
I'm a single parent, life is not a breeze.
How come when you're a child you can't wait to get older,
But as you grow up, you tend to get bolder.
We learn from our mistakes, I think we do,
But even though life goes on, we still feel blue.
Snap out of it now, cheer up honey,
If you're down in the dumps go
spend some money.
Say a little prayer and ask to be cheerful,
God is with you, no need to be fearful.
Then think of all your wonderful gifts,
Life's not so bad after all, is it?

Tami LaSharia Day
THORNS

The sweetest smell is that of a rose.
Although before one can reach out
To the delicate petals
One must first, overcome the thorns.
The thorns painfully sting
The fingers with piercing points.
To protect the rose is the thorn's duty;
To keep her safe from prospectors
That may damage her petals.
Like the thorns of a rose, I also have thorns,
To protect me from having
My heart broken again.
Only someone special, with a gentle touch
Will pass through the thorns to reach
The petal of the Rose;
And this special person, with the gentle touch
Will win my heart.
And the sweet smell of Roses will fill the air.

Daphne D Harrell
REVERIE FOR ALL SEASONS

Muse I when summer breezes
ruffle and shuffle the
verdant leaves;
leaves weary of searing sun
leaves shading a weary one . . .
Come, Autumn, come!

Muse I upon this arc of world
rotundity in time;
where summer awaits autumn gold
where autumn awaits winter's cold . . .
Come, Winter, Come!

Muse I when chilly winter winds
wrap me in soft, white down;
and hold me safe from all that harms
and keep me safe in love's
warm arms . . .
Come, sweet Spring, come!

Muse I in shades of summer sun
if each of all mankind
upon his back the cloth of love;
of texture wrought in gentle
cloak, this tapestry
wear tomorrow . . . ameliorate
earth's sorrow . . .
Come, Summer, come!

Patricia Castella
LOST LOVE

To my mother, Arleen

My heart is broken to such an extent,
Never to be mended, now forever hardened,
Though also softened.
I am kept, trapped by only one
And there is no escaping.
For he is welded, encompassed,
Deep within my heart and my soul.
Everything is him; every thought, every breath.
His face, a mask on every other
Yet the real one I never do see,
It stolen from me long ago
By he who owns it, for the owner has changed.
He has chosen a place over me, and I will never understand
How a place could divide two bonded souls.
Neither glimpse nor glance will he catch of me
Before he goes.
And this place, all sunny and free and wild
Means nothing but loneliness for me.

Ken Kennedy
I THINK OF YOU OFTEN

I think of you often
I wonder if it's because of the rain
Drops of water making their way
down the windows pane
Seemingly painting your portrait
within my mind—
I wonder if you see as much as I
when our eyes meet—
It's as though we could have an affair
in that brief moments time

I knew you were warm and sensitive
from the beginning—
I knew it when our eyes met
and our lips touched

I wonder if it will ever stop raining.

Dave Gurney
FLOATING ON AIR

Floating along
To who knows ahead
A globe of hot air
Over our head
Able to see
For miles around
Everything so small
On the ground
The ultimate freedom
And inner peace
It's the perfect
Kind of release
Free from all
Our earthly bonds
All the pressures
No longer strong
Not knowing just
Where we'll land
For now admiring
The beauty at hand

Deadra Dee Litzsinger
A COLD RAINY AFTERNOON

A cold rainy afternoon.
The radio playing old love songs,
As I stare up at the grey clouds.

Watching raindrops run down the window,
Looking so much like sad teardrops,
On a pale, pale cheek.

I wonder on days like this,
Could these simple raindrops
Actually be the lonely tears of an angel?

Marie LeViere
YOU BET I WOULD

This poem is dedicated to Paulette, Marie and Chris.

Our house seems to be empty
since the children are gone.
But you're still kept busy
even though they're gone long.

The older you get the harder things are
and then you can only go so far.

You're washing clothes and dusting chairs
then after a while, you wonder who cares.

You cook and wash dishes even
though it's for two.
There once was a lot, but now there's so few.

When the days work was done and
you sat and relaxed,
You're hoping the tomorrows your energy would last.

Then when holidays are around, you do your best;
there's no time to think of taking a rest.

Now the holidays are near and the door opens wide
and there is part of your life stepping inside.
My family is here and I feel so good.
Would I do it all over? "You bet I would!"

Glenna Turner
DON'T STOP ME NOW

To my husband, who always says, "Just keep writing, Babe!"

Following rules and punctuation in writing are similar
To a most difficult obstacle course I must run.
Remembering to capitalize and inserting the commas,
Inevitably takes away nearly all of the fun.
There is the colon: a semi-colon; an odd little apostrophe'.
All this proper punctuation slows the writing process,
Thus, hinders relating important information, you see.
Who invented the squiggly, placed after a question or two?
I check possessive pronouns, independent clauses and compare
Antonyms and synonyms, I forget what I learned, don't you?

I run over the margin and smack into the typewriter bell.
By using more dashes and commas, I hope no one can tell,
I have run out of space, spilling letters way over the line.
Even have tell-tale dark ink smears all over my hand.
However, ideas spewing forth rapidly now and with luck,
Why, I may even find the right spot to use an ampersand.*
I favor an exclamation point to print a phrase quite loud!
Then by adding quotation marks to scream, "Silence!",
I can nearly always get the attention of a reading crowd.
I dangle participles, use a preposition to end a sentence with.
When fans buy my novels, I will surely destroy the writing myth.

Joyce Fales Homeier
OUR FURRY CHILDREN
Two white cats we have in our home
Unlike our children, they don't roam.
White siamese, they are not alike
One is big, the other a tyke.
Lucky, she is big and fat
While Snowy he is just a brat.
Snowy runs all day around
Playing with everything he has found.
Lucky, she rests all day
When night time comes, she's ready to play.
They eat three meals, just like us
No more than children do they fuss.
Store bought toys are pushed aside,
While in boxes they like to ride.
We scold them when they are bad
And they look at us with eyes so sad.
They know just when bedtime comes
For into the bedroom each one runs.
These two cats are amazing,
For two more children we are raising.

Sandra J MacCready
FAIRYLAND
It starts within the fairy tale,
Where frogs leap and play all day.
Except for one who sits in the sun,
Hoping a princess will come his way.

The weather is never cold here,
From dusk until dawns the day.
The flowers are always blooming,
And the skies are never gray.

Come sit with me, come chat with me,
Calls the flowers to the bees.
Come reminisce of yesterdays,
And poke fun with the trees.

Wandering through this land all day.
Where fairies dare to tread,
Memories please come to me,
And fill my little head.

Becky Powers
A BEAUTIFUL VIEW
Up in the air
Is a beautiful view
Of puffy white clouds
In a sea of soft blue

The bright sunshine
is going down now
It is a quarter past nine
Time to lie down

I lie down in the grass
and observe the beautiful colors.
The colors won't last
But I'm ready for others.

The colors are purple,
pink and green
They are the prettiest
That I've ever seen.

Up in the air
Is a beautiful view
Bright shining stars
in a dark navy blue.

Joseph Irvin Benjamin
WRESTLING WITH LIFE
I have humbly known the
antagonizing woes of pain,
and fought physically with the
taunting echoes of sorrow.
I have sat comfortably in
unsinkable iron ships of jealousy,
and dwelled patiently in the
midst of lust and revengeful deceit.
I have toiled restless in
the driving winds of pity,
and keenly navigated the
chilled and deep waters of pride.

I have wisely taught many
the ways of righteous hatred,
and quietly witnessed spiritual
destruction of countless others.
I have gladly crawled through
sand storms of lively iniquity,
and peacefully slept in the
dense and tranquil forest of envy.
I have endorsed educated
leaders of doctrinal evil,
and death visited with me
yet have I to die.
I have stifled lives.
I created a frail and battered soul.

Michelle White
FRIENDS

To Jill and a very special friendship

The day is fading and night sets in,
A gentle sea mist upon my skin
As I walk along this lonely beach
waves whisper the words I wish I could speak.

You are my confidant, my sister, my friend
I hope that these times are never to end.
Decisions we make, paths we choose
Create special memories we never shall lose.

The road ahead may seem too long
But the bond we have will keep us strong.
Wherever you are, whatever you do
always remember how much I love you.

And just like the tides that ebb and flow
We find many friends that come and go.
I've finally found a friend that I can call "true"
I'm grateful to say that friend is you.

Phil E Grigsby
DID YOU EVER?

To: Kimber Whose Love Inspired This Poem I Love You!

Did you ever love someone
and knew they didn't care?
Did you ever feel like crying
but knew you wouldn't get anywhere?
Did you ever look into their eyes
and say a little prayer?
Did you ever look into their heart
and wish that you were there?
Did you ever fall in love
and knew it wouldn't stay?
Did you ever have a broken heart
that wouldn't go away?

Love is fine, but the price you pay is high
If I could choose between love and death, I think I'd rather die.
So if, my friend, you fall in love,
you'll be hurt before you're through.
You see, my friend, I ought to know,
because I'm in LOVE with you!

Robert C Jones
THE OTHER NIGHT I PRAYED
The other night I prayed
I said Lord bring back to me,
The one I love so much,
The one I long to see.
The one who bore my child,
The one who went through pain.
The one who said she loved me,
The one I drove insane.
The one who made me warm,
When inside I felt so cold.
The one who said to me
Together we'll grow old.
The one I put through hell,
When it seemed I didn't care.
The one I hurt so much,
Although I know it wasn't fair.
The tears that I have shed
Are because I long for her,
But I'll just believe in faith,
Cause I know God answers prayer.

Nathan Panion
I MEANT TO DO MY WORK TODAY
I meant to day my work today
But the trees needed to be climbed
And the meadows needed to be explored
It sure beats being super—bored!

And my time didn't go to waste
'Cause the outdoors said, "Kid, you got taste!"
I said, "Thank You!" just as nice as I could
So you see, I had to explore
the wild wood!

Marianne Schlesiger
MY LOVE

To Garth, my only true love I'm forever yours

Oh love of my life, why hast thou left me?
My life, my soul, my heart
Was I not there through thick and thin?
Did I not love you right from the start?

Oh heart of my life, through which flowed my love
You kept my love alive
But like dust on the wind you drifted away
Leaving my love to die.

Oh angel of my life, you guarded my love,
And nurtured it within your heart
But like sand through my fingers you slipped away
And like strangers did we part.

Oh life of my life, my reason to live
My thoughts, my world, my breath
My life is so empty without you
Without you there is nothing but death.

Sarah Crostic

Sarah Crostic
LOOKING OUT ACROSS THE SEA
Looking out across the sea
A feeling of joy and tenderness
Comes over me.
I wish to hold you
Hold you, and whisper
"I love you, for
no one loves you more
than me."

A chilly breeze whispers back
"He is gone, and
does not love you, for
he loves me."

Looking out across the sea
A feeling of loneliness
Comes over me
For you will never hold me.

Orbrenett Kay Carter
VOWS

This poem is dedicated to my husband John W Carter Jr. and our fruits Akili, Jamaal and Ayana Carter and to all they will love . . .

It is not about my struggle
but our struggle
not about my life
but our life
nor is it about me or you
reaching our dreams
but our dreams releasing
others to further growth.
Each new day, brings an unfolding
Knowledge to our relationship
it's not if you love me.
That's a given or becoming "one"
for in all practicality the metal has been sealed.
It is about our destiny, our energy,
our growing in fertile soil, and our fruits to come . . .
and when our destiny brings us even closer to our dreams
and our dreams manifest themselves in our lives
and in others, then our fruits will be our life
longing for itself,
that will propel us into understanding
of our constant and far reaching
tomorrows
Today

Seth Schein
EDUCATE THE MASSES?
Darkened hallways
Silence
as I enter the room
Psychotic, psychosis ricochets off the walls

You'll all die here he gestures
as he closes the door to the room
Forced education, re-education, more education
They want me to start it, I want to end it
I pick up the knife

I hold it up high and slam it on down
And into the heart that bleeds me dry
die
End this started terrible life
but another life falls into place
They say, "Do it again" (and I probably will)
They want me to start it I want to end it
I pick up the gun and aim it true
and fire it quick into the lungs
That steal its precious air
I don't want you I don't need you the two of you
I thought I needed one to have the other
I was wrong about both

Michael Larson
PEACE-DOG
The riots,
The arrests,
Many people,
Not fearing anyone or thing.

Their feelings cutting their souls,
Like a well honed knife.
People stand and watch,
As the police throw the crowd around,
The gun is removed from its holster,
And the trigger pulled,
A demonstration for peace,
Ends in violence.
The Peace-Dog,
Bit his prey,
The blood is spilled,
And the red stain is still there,
The wound is deeper than that,
The family mourns,
For a lost son.

Dorothy Mae Johnson
I SURRENDER MY LIFE TO JESUS

I surrender my life to Jesus
With my heart and all of my soul.
Leaving all worldly treasures
Earning heaven is now my goal.
I surrender my life to Jesus
While asking forgiveness of my sins.
On this day to Jesus
I have been born again.
I surrender my life to Jesus
Today and forever more.
I will live and work for Jesus
Among the sick and the poor.
I surrender my life to Jesus
My body and my mind.
Trusting my life to Jesus
No matter the hardships that I may find.
I now belong to Jesus.
I will follow and obey.
I will live and work for Jesus
Forever and today.

Patricia A Herrin
TIME TO PAUSE

I can tell the time I've spent on me
By whether my toenails were painted recently,
It was just by chance I noticed at all
Though humorous, I desperately tried to recall.

I couldn't remember how long it was
Since I'd taken the time to take a pause,
To do my hair and paint my nails
Taking care of some of the little details.

With a family to feed throughout the day
And whatever else happens along the way,
Washing, dusting, and answering the phone
When there's need of help I find I'm alone.

Sometimes I forget to take a step back
Be thankful for what I have and forget what I lack,
To be able next time to look down and see
The evidence that I took time out for me.

Albert Z Curnutt
HAVE I USED MY TIME WISELY?

I have had my time and my time is over.
I am walking across to the other shore!
Jesus is waiting there for me: With all
His pleasant things to see!

Man's time is limited and moves fast!
This we know, each breath could be our last!
For what is life? It's like a vapor that appeareth
For a little time, then vanishes away!

Time is something we cannot see, but the results
Affects both you and me!
In this world of love and strife, time is still in
Control of each man's life!

There will come a time when God's mighty angel will say,
With one foot upon the water and the other on clay,
"Time is over, old things pass away:
So prepare to
Meet God this very day"!

Generation will come and generations will go, but time is
Still in charge of each man's soul!
A time to laugh, a time to cry, a time to live, a time to die:
This given time is still in charge of every man's life!

Charlene Pesce
BROKEN HEART

Tears roll out of my soul
Splashing on this hard desk
Mixing together to combine my sorrows.

Teardrops weaken the bonds of my heart
Making me vulnerable
Forcing my heart to break apart

Tears trace each of my eyelashes
Burning a path down my cheek
Adding to the pool of my distress.

Tear drops symbolize the destruction of my heart
Breaking apart piece by piece
Falling lifelessly to the ground.

Marilea Hall Wendler
A LETTER TO STEPHANIE ANNE

Dedicated to our first grandchild, Stephanie Anne Wendler, born February 18, 1984. We love you Stephanie!

Dear Stephanie,
Beautiful little girl child,
We thank you
For making us grand parents.
We thank your parents,
Who with God's help
Created you;
One small individual—
Uniquely different,
From anyone
Who has ever been
Or ever will be
Again.
So much a part of us
Beautiful little Stephanie
Our own little granddaughter
We love you!

Hazel Morvant
THE "WILD BUNCH" WHO DROVE FOR "J.T.L."

Dedicated to: James Earl Buck alias The "Wild Bunch" Here in this poem is your Monument, James Earl "Jim" Buck Your dreams as a boy, hopes as a young man, your future as a man full grown

From K.C. to Little Rock, and then to Russellville
You drive this road three times a week, up and down these hills
You run it south and then run north, in sunshine, rain, and snow
On the C.B. you're the "WILD BUNCH", either way you go

Sometimes eight hours or maybe ten, depending on the weather
You stare at white lines on this highway, until they run together
When your mind is troubled, your body gets so tired
You pull your rig to the side of the road, before you reach the yard
You rest a while and then go on, farther down the road
You're running out of hours, you must deliver this load

For the Union you're a Steward, you try to make it better
For the drivers who run the loads, you hold them to the letter
You file their grievances, and fight their fights
With the Union head to head
For all the chances that you take, you could wind up half dead

You stop and help a stranger out, more often it's a buddy
You'll leave no one out in the night, you help them out of trouble
If and when it comes your time, they should build a Monument
For peoples lives that you have touched, and all the time you spent

Every man should be remembered,
Trust me I know you will
No one will ever forget the "WILD BUNCH" who drove for "J.T.L."

Joan Kessler
(i want to bury my face in the desert)

I want to bury my face in the desert
And let my body become a mirage
Ghosting endlessly
Between the sun and moon
Winds and dunes
Me and you

Berta Johnson
A WINTER PRAYER

The sky ice blue and cloudless
The trees are bare and brown
The snow lies saintly, glistening white
Round bout me on the ground
The stillness nearly deafening
The world seems void of life
Lo! There I see the forest tracks
Mid beauty, wintry strife
And on the crisp, cold winter air
Heart movements can be heard

For now I hear the joyful strains
Of a tiny, searching bird
The song that wells within its breast
As it scratches for a meal
Calls forth the hope and courage
That God's creatures all must feel
Dear Father, grant when I'm afraid
I've learned from what I've heard
To sing with hope and courage
The song of this tiny bird

Amen!

Billie Jo Suen
TREES

All those years I've been watching trees
'Specially during winter those with falling leaves
Sunny days, Snowy weathers, they're just standing still
How strong if our lives could be up straight in adversity
Make a tree, plant a tree, put it in your memories
Lift up high
Always smile
Your life would be as happy as it could be!

Winnie Gregory
HOME VISIONS

To Hud, my husband; Dorothy, my mother; Patti, Nola & Cathy, my daughters.

The chimney smokes
Soft clouds
Drifting upward.
Life is within.

Smell the rose.
Though miles distant
The fragrance
Surrounds me.

Leaves stir.
Warm breezes cause;
Awakening the
Redbud and the Dogwood.

Placid waters
Mirror the deer.
Sandy shores
Catch the imprint.

Adeline Mefford
AT MEETING TIME

To all poetry-loving people, and for a world of peace.

When good friends get together
It creates a wonderful day.
So treasure these sweet memories
As you go along your way.

The skies will be blue
The robins will sing.
So much happiness this day can bring.

Be happy, cheery, and smiling.
Then perhaps the world will shine
To give us peace, love, and caring,
Into your life and mine.

Holly D Matthews
WHERE DREAMS LIE

I don't want to hurt anyone,
And I don't want to cause any pain.
But up in heaven is where my dreams are,
And I have everything to gain.

I can't be free of worry,
And I can't say I have no fear.
But up in heaven is where my dreams are,
And I will always hold them dear.

I know that I can't be everything,
That I tried years to be.
But up in heaven is where my dreams are,
And I just have to be me.

I try to endure the pain,
That this mean world has provoked.
But up in heaven is where my dreams are,

And I no longer have to choke.

I can only be patient,
And live the best way that I can.
Cause up in heaven is where my dreams lie,
Where I will remain with a powerful man.

Kim Vickers
THE HUMAN RACE

In Loving Memory of Kenna Nicole Vickers: For inspiring me and teaching me to be the best that I can be.

Is it so hard
To admit that you love?
Patience is barred,
Lost is hope.
A dream fades
A child in a womb.
Twilight shades
The lonely room.
The baby cries,
A mother screams.
Love dies
The "brilliant" extreme.
Man is cruel,
Lovers—kind
Faith is gone
And love is blind.
So the world goes,
Revolving in space.
And heaven knows
The human race.

Ann Cripe
COLORFUL PARADE OF FLOATS

To all the children who love a parade, especially the ones who are still a child themselves in their hearts.

There are floats in all kinds of parades.
Animated and character floats; famous people's and children's floats and other floats.
They are made out of chicken wire, papier-maché and different kinds of materials.
Also beautiful flowers, seeds and plants from around the world.
Lot of hard work, love, and hours are put into each float.
The planning and the theme starts right after January 1st of each year.
They are built from scratch while the other floats are torn down.
They all have to be in "working order" before they join the parade.
They are so beautiful with each theme and lots of love into them.
If I was a judge, I could never pick a winner.
Because in my mind all the floats are winners.

James P McKinney
THE YOUNG AND THE FOOLISH

I'm just a plain ol' country kid, that's not what I wanted to be
Maybe that's why, there was so much hurt, between my dad and me.

It seemed that everything I did, he thought that it was wrong
I guess that's why, the two of us, just couldn't get along.

The country life was not for me, I thought that I was smart
So one day, I ran away from home, and broke my parents heart.

I made my home in the nearest town, but I wasn't satisfied
It seemed that something inside of me, had curled up and died.

Then one day, a guy came along, and said I understand
Come with me, I'll sign you up, and make you a proud man.

I joined the marines and traveled far, but every where I went
I could see my parents broken heart, I never was content.

My discharge, it came one day, it didn't take too long
But during the time that I was there, I could see where I was wrong.

I owe my folks, an awful lot, but I haven't got a dime
I'll just have to make it up, a little at a time.

Now for all you foolish kids out there, here's what I have to say
No matter how your feelings are, don't ever run away.

Regina Horgan
COME BE MY FRIEND

Come be my friend and listen
to the sound of silence.
Ride with me on the wings of a crow;
hold my hand with your heart,
and teach me the things that you know.

Come be my friend and catch the wind with me;
enfold me close
when I slip in an endless fall.
Kiss my hair with your eyes, and words will have no meaning at all.

Come be my friend and hear
the mountains cry;
feel the rain against the canyons of my sorrow.
Touch the sun with me and share
in the time that is called tomorrow.

Kathleen M Keaveney
YOU WASH AWAY MY SADNESS

You wash away my sadness,
And help me find joy.

When things are tough,
You fight hard with me through it all.

You taught me never to quit,
Only to try harder.

When I need advice,
You always have the answers.

When I make a mistake,
You tell me you understand.

When I cry, you wipe away my tears
And relieve my pain.
When I say I can't,
You tell me you believe in me and that I can!

Beatrice Veitch-Clennon
PENTAHEDRON (FIVE FACETS OF OUR LOVE)

For you I have
Respect and trust
The primal love of child.
I love you
As my brother
And know
The easy comfort
Of best friend.
I feel for you
Protective love of parent
Yet have
The perfect bliss
Of woman loving man.
This pentahedron
Hanging from
A golden chain
I see reflected
In your eyes
And know at once
The joy
Of love returned.

Alan Dwayne Moore

Alan Dwayne Moore
DREAMS

Dreams are when I think of you and I.
Sitting together hand and hand,
No one but us.
As we lay under the stars
In the full of the moon
And your lips touch with mine,
As we cuddle close
We're embraced in a warm loving feeling
As I look deep into your eyes.
I can see an everlasting love,
A love that you can only give me,
But it's only a dream
But this dream can come
With the right words or touch
But I have only one thing to say
I love you
I would love to hold you in my arms
Forever and ever
I would always be there
To hold you
To make you feel safe and warm.
I LOVE YOU.

David Pezel
WHAT LOVE IS LOVE IS A HAND

Dedicated to my beloved Grandfather

What love is
Love is a hand
Held fast in your own.

Love is joy
You feel from the start.

Love is a dream
You keep in your heart.

Love is a world
That's shared by two,
Love is wonderful
Love is you!

Grace York
HEARTS AND KEYS

Give me the key that unlocks your heart,
Give me the words that we'll never part;
Give all your love, and kisses too,
No other love will ever do.

Please put the ring on my finger, Dear,
A shining symbol, you're always near;
Tell me your love is just for me,
That you are mine, ever mine, eternally.

Here is the key that unlocks my heart,
It's yours forever, we'll never part;
Here's all my love, and kisses too,
No other one would ever do.

I place the ring on your finger, Dear,
A token to tell you I am sincere;
My love is just for you, you see,
Let's marry, live together, eternally.

Maxine Jewell
MOTHER DO YOU KNOW

Mother do you know
you are a friend to me.
Mother do you know
you have raised me perfectly.
Mother do you know
you are a lifelong friend.
Mother do you know
I hope our friendship will never end.
Mother do you know
you are one of a kind.
Mother do you know
a better one I could not find

Mother I guess you could not know, for I never took the time to tell you so.
Mother these words come straight from the soul,
and to say them to your face would be my biggest goal.

MOTHER I LOVE YOU.

Kimberly A Harrison
YOU'LL NEVER WALK ALONE

A friend is one of lifes many surprises,
they come in an array of way out disguises,
A friend can be a youngster, or someone very old
nevertheless they're both the same and are worth their weight in gold,
A friend will be there for you to help you dry your tears
and stay with you through the night, until you see things clear
A friend will tell you the truth, however harsh it may be
they mean no harm when this is done, but that's for you to see
A friend will be there for you, and help you to grow strong
and will always find the time to listen to your song.
And when the years have passed you by and you're out on your own
Don't be fooled, for as the saying goes—
YOU'LL NEVER WALK ALONE.

Kari Olson
WHERE I STAND

I lie in bed at night, an open Bible in my hand.
As I read the word of God, I wonder just where I stand.
Yes, I am a Christian; but do I always live that way?
Or do I do what pleases others as I live from day to day.
Sometimes I can be cruel to those who surround me.
And later I realize that's not really how I want to be.
I want to be a mirror to my Father up above
And reflect to those around me the beauty of His love.
I want to shine for Jesus; through me they can see Him.
But many times that light from me

shines so very dim.
I live each day in a world that can be as cold as ice.
And I pray that I will be someone who's warm, caring & nice.
I pray that love and compassion from me will freely flow.
And my faith and love in God will daily continue to grow.
I lie in bed at night, an open Bible in my hand.
As I read the word of God, I know just where I stand.

Darla Elliott McElhaney
WITH THE WIND BLOWING OUTSIDE

With the wind blowing outside
My tears grow cold;
The feelings inside are weak
But yet so bold.

Like the leaves in time
Love must fall;
Your faith is within me
Not partly, but all.

I've tried with you
All that can be done;
You've taken my soul
But in love—
left me our son!

LauraJean Carrabis
THE STRANGER

For my father, with love

She stands alone and waits each night
You have seen her there before,
Every night it is all the same
She is standing by the door.

She never knocks, she never rings
It often makes you wonder,
Why this girl is standing there
Just looking at the number.

Her hair is done up in a bun
Her clothes are always new,
Don't ask her where she purchased them
For she won't answer you.

If you decide to stop and stare
I am sure you'll never win,
Because she will out-do you every time
For she is a mannequin.

Davette L Shaw
MY LOVE

My love for you is dying
I don't know what to do
I want to keep on trying
And I hope that you do too

I know that you do love me
But why do you make me cry
You know that it does hurt me
Every time you say good-bye

It is so very hard for me
To keep the tears inside
So it is easy for you to see
The fears I cannot hide

It seems to me, we have to try
To make our love much stronger
Then the fears would surely die
And not be there any longer

For when my love for you is strong
As strong as it can be
I know that nothing can go wrong
To break up you and me

Gloria Ann Rios
LOVING YOU HAS SET ME FREE

When I met you
I was lonely and lost
You healed the pain that broke my heart
You gave me comfort
When I was down
I was thankful a friend I had found
But we grew closer and so much in love
Our world became private
With no one around
Loving you was too much for me
Loving you has set me free
We had a love only death could part
Happiness and security joined us from the start
Then one day it happened, your love changed
Since that day
I've never been the same
Someday you'll wake up and be all alone
Just remember I loved you
I never meant to do wrong
Loving you was too much for me
Loving you has set me free

Mary Kelly
DRUGS

To my loving family who always supported me.

The hour is late; the streets are dark.
But what is lurking in our alleys and parks?
The danger there is quite a fright
from dealers and pushers who roam the night.
What kind of world do we live in
that lets our youth shoot heroin?
There are many kinds of drugs around
that bring our youth to the ground.
A youth that wants no part of pot
must fight his way through quite a lot.
This kind of problem is at hand
and has spread throughout our land
You can't tell me in this day and age,
we've done our best to stop this rage.
What will it take before we learn,
our youth need us and our concern?
If we try a little more with the kids today,
we'll beat this thing that's killing them
and make the pushers pay.

Rose M Tank
TREASURE FROM THE SEA

Several fathoms beneath the sea,
A treasure waiting there for me.
Twin the circles, laced in gold—
Highly prized since days of old.

Opposite of colors, do they gleam—
One is ebony, one is cream.
In the midst of diamonds, gold,
Tis a treasure to behold.

Black, the pearl, darkened rays,
Reminding me of lonely days.
White, the pearl, glimmering light
Shows me of my future bright.

From a tiny grain of sand,
A thing of beauty for your hand.
A gift of love, I give to thee—
A special treasure from the sea.

Jacqueline McDonald
THE BUTTERFLY

This poem is dedicated to my two sons Delvin and Dirrick, we love you and miss you, even tho God has you.

We are like the butterfly red, yellow, white, black, and green.
Butterflies are like children, it knows not what prejudice means.
We shall all be like the butterfly and bring love and beauty to us all. We must see no color nor race. We shall fight and let prejudice fall.

Butterflies colors are so beautiful, they bring joy and peace to mankind. They are real and yet they are mysterious. They glow brightly when the sun comes out to shine.

They show no hurt, nor fear for others. Their shades represent power of strength, they have a destiny to live in freedom, they come from a universe of dimensions of colors, they are also God sent.

Their mixed colors show no racism or division for they are the most diverse colors of all. So let's not be critical of one another, let's let prejudice fall.

For God created this beautiful creature, and a creature of beauty he is. His color has no separation nor power, and our skin tones have no uphold on our sorrow. So let's love one another as God placed us here to do. Let's be like the butterfly just as God love me and love you.

Children have no means of hate born in this world so pure, a butterfly comes from his cocoon, and peace he brings to here.

So brothers and sisters so far and near, let's reunite to peace, let's try to live like the butterfly and be still like the star set in the East.

Crystal D Smith
HEART OF MAN

For God, who gave me salvation; my parents, who gave me life; and my grandmother, who gave me encouragement.

The heart:
A place where bitter-sweet thoughts and feelings linger in the air;
Where trees may blossom with wisdom and knowledge, or die from racism, hatred, despair.
Where skies may be blue, even clear, and fill with truth, hope, freedom; or turn a cloudy-gray in a moment's notice because of lying, corrupted leaders.
Where the land may be warm and even abundant, and provide all people with plenty, or turn cold and barren, terribly lonely, especially to the poor, the old, the needy;
Where rivers may overflow with affection and love to prolong each human life, or stream forth with wickedness and evil to destroy forever mankind.
Listen . . . Follow . . . Enter you

Lee K Frost
THANK THEE GOD

Thank thee God for all you've done
Giving me strength and courage
I feel you near, you are so dear
God my soul and my redeemer.

The love in my heart
Is one big spark
Lit by your hand
In Heaven.

I'll work for you
I'll love for you
I'll do my very best for you
To prove that I am worthy.

I believe, I believe
God you are ever near me
With God at my side
To comfort and guide
I will do the impossible.

Nancy Fay West
TEACH ME HOW

Teach me how to play again,
Teach me how my little man.
Lead me to your secret places
Near the creek that foams and races.

Beg you, let us shed our shoes,
That in the sand our toes may ooze.

From the creekbed let us gather
Precious stones, or maybe rather
We could hunt for Pirates gold,
Or climb a tree that's gnarled old.

Gently-gently, little man,
Gently lead me by the hand.

Long the years since I have played;
Long my soul has crouched afraid.
Pray perhaps, that I may capture
Just a fraction of your rapture!

Teach me how, my little man,
Teach me how to play again.

Suzanne Krauss-Burleson
EPILOGUE

The fear of abandonment, pain, and disaster
Encircles my soul ever faster and faster.

I fear that destruction and sorrow, hereafter,
Will loom in my doorway midst mockery and laughter.

As uncertainty wanders about in my head,
There is only depression beside me in bed.

And the feeble expressions we've dared speak aloud,
Have solved not a thing; rather served just to cloud.

For no matter how deeply our reasonings delve,
Each of us only convinces himself.

David A Gouldner
A LIVING FANTASY

To Patricia: So much more than just an inspiration.

Elisa May says Jesus never fails and I believe it's true.
And there's a church in the wilderness where I stood kissing you.
Then somewhere in time the world was swept away.
A symphony played a sweet sad song, I think love was made that way.
I looked into your eyes, and saw clouds go passing by.
There's something in a touch, that never meant as much, as when I looked into your eyes. And felt the

music. Kissed the smiles.
I felt the water wrap around me and you fell into my heart.
From the magic of these memories, I will never be apart.

You have made these passing days of mine, a mystery and a poem.
A swirling living fantasy, I can call my own.
An everlasting memory that we can always share.
A rhapsody, a symphony, of days without a care.
Now I face the morning in a melancholy stare.
I wish that you could be with me, I wish that I were there.
And run my lonely fingers through your long and silken hair.

Jody Woodford
AS THE WIND BLOWS
As the wind blows, I hear the leaves churn
In the field I can see the cottage burn
All the memories run through my mind
But not a bad one can I find
I spent but only three days there
They were the best ones my life could bear
As I watch the flames rise
I can see the reflection in your eyes
Now you recall the last few memories
And the three days we both shared
The closeness we had will not be the same,
But now it is all up in flames
The tears begin to fall down your cheek
And they probably will for another week
The love we shared could never compare to anything,
But now the clock begins to ding
The cottage is now just smoke in the air
Like the three days we spent there

Christy Manley
FANTASY BOUND
As I talked with you tonight
I realized how much I missed you
I realized how much I wished you were mine
but you're not
and I can see
my life without you
is just me
I didn't mean to make you sad
I didn't mean to hurt you
I didn't mean for a lot of things
they just happened
as time progressed

I saw you with her today
it made me depressed
when I see you together
I lose all joy and happiness
my spirits go down
for I've found
she's got you
and I'm fantasy bound.

Jeannine Lee Grant
FRIENDS
You smile at me, I instantly melt
My heart is filled with feelings I have never felt.
We touch each other with such electricity,
Everyone around us can even see.
But we're both to shy to ask the other out,
So now we have to let fate work about.
The time I spend with you isn't much,
But when I don't see you I miss your touch.
I just pray for the day when we share company again,
But until then I guess we're just "friends."

Stephanie Dotseth
A LITTLE BOX
My life is like a little box,
A place where you store your socks.
All closed up and in a corner of a wall,
Something where you put your stuffed ball.
A place where only you can open up,
Something where you put a cup.
To catch all of those falling tears,
And to trap all of your fears.
So here you sit in a little closed box,
In a corner of a wall,
that is so very tall,
you throw the key away,
So that is where your feelings must stay.

Lee Ann Todd
LAST FLIGHT
Breathless, above the turmoiled, aquaed life, danced on turnabout westerlies till my bird heart burst with happiness.
I swooped low in my game of tease with the grumpy breakers and pretended to be a shipwrecked sailor on splinty driftwood.
My heart soared into the blazing sun and my wings followed at a whim.
Master is he, and me free
to swoop with mock ferocity at a saucy perch and now sail on grey-tipped clouds to catch my breath.

Jade

Jade
LOVE IS A RED ROSE
A bud—it blooms—a Red Rose.
The Red Rose has a rare fragrance.
A Red Rose stands alone,
It is a thing of great beauty.

If forgotten the Red Velvet Petals
Fall away one—by one.
The beauty of the Red Rose is no more.
Red Roses are symbolic for Love, white for passion, a lily for Purity.

Love is like a Rose, it flames,
It is happiness, mystery and intrigue.
If you neglect love, it dies, a dream destroyed.
And Love—as a Rose—a Red Rose dies.

Pamela Jean Valentine
MOMENTS I LOVE
A winter's walk in spring's meadow,
A torrent rain; a soft rose petal,
Angels stoop to touch the earth,
Tiny flowers poking their head out in birth,
Blossoms smell so sweet in the air,
The wind takes them up without a care.

Morning's lust is evening's slumber,
Winter's hope is summer's surrender,
Daytime sunlight melts the frost,
Where yesterday's dampness had turned to moss.

An encompassing meadow; a warm embrace,
Summer's haste; winter's mellow pace,
Restless winds; moody days,
Silent dreams; moon's yellow haze,
A morning star; an evening's bliss,
A moonlight song; a lover's kiss,
An evening's night; a winter's storm,
A starry sky; a morning is born.

These are the moments I love to see,
Because I feel free.

Annie Luck
THROUGH A FIGHT
If this love was made for heaven
why do we slice
the inside of our souls
through spoken words
of constant woes

I hurt you like the driven knife
into the deepened wound that flows

At the end it's held by the insane
we hold this knife
within our pain
Why do I make the devil
in you arise

As I retain your spoken words
I know not what are lies

Look what you've become
within our love
a stranger is behind your eyes
and I'm lost with no
form of identity
left to recognize

For our love is hiding
in this anger of disguise

As we release this tempered mask
from upon our face
let's try to identify
only lasting love

With more caution
as we pace

Diana L Hatcher
A SNOWFLAKE
As I watched a lonely snowflake drift silently in the wind, I thought of you; and that thought brought a smile to my face.
For you are like a snowflake. A drifter, a loner. You float on the wind and are silent.
You are as beautiful and fragile as the tiny frozen flakes that send us a winter wonderland.
Look upon the perfect beauty of a new-fallen snow. And share the wonder and awe at the peacefulness, the silent serenity that surrounds us.
The snow hangs on the bough of a tree which bends beneath the delicate weight.
Drops glisten as light reflects the sparkle and gleam as one tiny flake nestles itself into the hair of a passing stranger. There for an instant, all glisten and sparkle, it lays.
Soon to be joined by other travelers of the icy midnight sky, until the cold earth is gently covered with a satiny blanket of white.

Heather Diane Thomas
MY BROTHER, MY ADMIRER

I dedicate this poem to my wonderful brother Craig who has always been there for me and showed me the path to life. I love you so much. Thank you for everything.

You are my friend and my admirer, you light up my days and make me feel higher.
We talk about everything, only to each other. You aren't just my friend, you are my brother.

I tell you my stories, secrets and dreams, you understand everything and know what life means. We see each other often but when we do, I feel so close so much closer to you.

You helped me to grow and to take each day slow. I learned everything from you, all that I know. You acted as my mother and my father at times, you knew what I was thinking and read between the lines.

Thank you so much for showing you care for being my brother and always being there.

Benny L Jackson
PUPPETS
A puppet leads a dramatic life to me.
Wouldn't you agree?
Puppets are like birds, supported by rhythmic strokes of their wings.
The puppet is supported by the jerk of a wire or string.
A puppet has many talents.
He can be sad; happy; cowardly; yet so gallant.

Puppets are put together with screws and tacks.
They are shown how and when to act.
Some people are like puppets too.
If you don't pull a string, they won't know what to do.
It doesn't take too much of a strain.
You have controls put in your brain
Try your own mind; be yourself; you might be lucky.
If you succeed, you'll be your own puppet.

Ray Padilla
A BLIGHT
We were on the crest of new discovery
I had my guide hand me my sights
If I was right what I should focus upon
Would be what I would call a Blight

Blights have been in my dreams
Shunned by my friends Intellectuals and ignorant alike
Was my fancy desire to set sight on such intended creature
And plug up the hole of scorns dike

Was not for me to become suddenly well known
As also go to show where their doubts could be thrown
For as much as this meant that I prove I was right
It would also go to show their own tails they bite
Deep in the jungle my knowledge has led me
For somewhere near dwells one such as he
But set sight on this nomad ambitions where I can

Know if this be my chance
I be so lucky a man

Hark the jungle beat I respond
Encourage a Blight command me the lens see his kind
A Blight, a Blight, a Blight, a Blight
A Blight, a Blight, a Blight I did find!

Shelli Adkins
PREJUDICE

This poem is dedicated to my family who have supported me in everything And to Steve, you are so special to me!

The sky is black in this world.
The people here are surrounded by the walls of violence.
No one here trusts.
No one here loves.
There is no freedom in this world.
Peace and non-violence have been forgotten.
The people here live in constant fear.

There are no laws in this world.
Leaders are unjust and corrupt.
Racism, segregation, and hatred are the creed here.
Love, brotherhood, and peace are not known here.
The children will never know total peace.
Only the majority know dignity and pride.
The minority know broken dreams and fear.
This is a world called prejudice.

Drayth Sterling Sielaff
DAY OF THE CROSS

The Death of our lives
Was known on that certain day
While people wept and others pray
Were the longest minutes of that hour,
Thorns as thy crown
A king to be let down, there be
Happy in some eyes, Sad to see,
The death for all humanity,
Made glorious for the gift of life
Popularly wanted, Don't they see
He died for us,
For life, but not our own liberties,
To be conformed to Him is His joy
And in return is joy to us, Don't they see,
What the day of the Cross brings.

Scott E Roux
AS I STAND IN THE MOONLIGHT

To Jennifer whom I will love forever

As I stand in the moonlight against the summer breeze
No birds are chirping there are only empty trees
The night is all silent so hard to believe
That when daylight arrives the world will again breathe
And with each of its breaths will bring laughter and sorrow
It is hard to imagine this will happen tomorrow
But it will without doubt it does every day
For it always has been and will be this way
But in order to have day we must have night
Because without it the world would not be right
So as the darkness falls and the moon again shines
My heart fills with warmth and stars fill my eyes
Once more all is silent but not for long
With morning will come life and the sound of a bird's song

Frank Favaro
ONE IS ONE

Dedicated to Dr. & Mrs. Manley Ford Sr. For their sincere encouragement I shall be forever grateful

Age is more than a hypothetical state of mind,
or a chronological scale, that measures time;
age is a balance of mathematical fact,
that nature controls with a methodical act.

Nature weeds the drying fallow vine,
to allow the growing sprout to climb;
for one is one when one is old;
but one, when young, is manifold.

Sally A Hyde
MINDSET

I tread carefully down long hallways
timidly making my way through the darkness of the past
toward the saving light of day break.

I am not a child eager to open forbidden doors,
willing to absorb and indulge in fantasy and reality.

I am a battered soul
bruised by life's battles, bloodied by the sharp edges of reality and stung
by the truth of wasted opportunity.

I am unable to share a child's
delight in the strength of imagination,
I no longer thirst for creative energy.

I am afraid of the image these
words will set free.
My soul remains in chains.

Jennifer Nicole Bacon
TO TEACH YOURSELF

Thank you Rashid Silvera

If you are getting ready to prick your finger, don't'
Too many times we are ready to pick up a needle to write in blood how life is today:
Strangely enough, thinking this is how it will always be.
What is important to us today just might be forgotten tomorrow.
So before you inscribe "friends forever" or "I will always love you", think twice.
Or learn the hard way
What we all know but are not always willing to admit . . .
Nothing lasts forever.

Cheryl Barron
WHEN I THINK OF YOU

When I think of you I feel a warmness in my heart that only you can put there.

You taught me the real meaning of love, trust and respect in this special love we share.

You are my blue skies on cloudy days.
You are good for me in so many ways.

Why all this fear inside me, I do not know but with your help I know I can grow.

When I think of you I feel such joy, hope, and sometimes sadness.
You believed in me, even in my world of madness.

Maybe one day, I will have to let you go but darling, there's one thing I want you to know

Of all the things you've done for me the most important is . . . you rescued me from me.

Helen Klussmann
SHE'LL BE THERE

In memory of my loving mother, Mable Baker Zaic, and dedicated to my three WONDERFUL children: Karen, Jenny and Andy.

My life is going just as planned,
I wouldn't trade for another.
But yet I miss the gentle hand
and encouragement from my mother.

Sometimes the road seems extra long
and the end seems not in sight . . .
Just swallow, smile, and hum a song,
with patience all ends right.

To share good news or ask advice,
She'll be there when you need her,
Just find a quiet, pretty place
and walk and talk together.

Janet Louise Holman
RUMPLED

Little old man in the rumpled suit, do
you have rumpled dreams?
Does the cold wind whip in and out
and through your ragged seams?
Who made the choices that left you
here to die?
Where did you grow up and what
made you cry?
Do you weep for unfilled dreams of
joy and light?
What shades your eyes this afternoon
skirting into night?
And in the dark as breathing ceases, I
long to understand,
Why your life was only bittersweet,
my rumpled little man.

Rose M Jason
A GARDEN IN MY YARD

To my daughter Shawnee, my son Kenneth, and my mother Vergie.

Many will grow flowers
And others will grow fruits,
But only in my garden
Will I know what to do.

I'll sprinkle it with honesty
And then let truth grow tall.
I'll plant the seed of happiness
And sit and watch it all.
I'll find the plant sincerity
To place along the row,
And faith and charity will have
A plot in which to grow.
And when the planting's over,
I'll face the sky above,
And ask The Lord, Almighty,
To shower it with love.

Daisies can be pretty
And berries can taste good,
But only in my garden
Did I know what to do.

Alyce Poage
A BOY IN THE WINDOW

As a vision of my past.
A boy in my kitchen window.
The blue of the sky shines through his eyes.
The sun gleams through his golden hair.
The color of the flowers adorn him.
As a dew drop forms a tear, that rests on his cheek.
You're the seed I washed away—as you wear my father's face.
Heart pounding—Hand shaking.
How do you mend your heart, when the pain is endless
And you can't find the seams?
I see the vision start to fade.
As my past knocks on the door of my future.

Laura Jehn Menides
AFTER A NIGHT OF TOO MUCH TALK, WE WAKE TO SNOW

Let's find the parkas
and backpacks.
Let's buy some ripe Brie,
some woody Burgundy,
and a few brown pears.
Let's wax the skis
and tour out to Sterling,
past white birch and pine
and up towards Wachusett.

I know a spot
at the side of a rise.
There's a table of boulders
there and boulder stools,
and way below, little towns
lie soundless and purified.

I promise not to talk
(we've had too much of that)
nor to think, but only
to breathe the silence
and to touch: snow and fruit,
and to taste: wine, life, you.

Ethel M Vogler
MAMA, DO YOU REMEMBER?

Dedicated to the memory of my mom, Geneva Josephine, and Henrietta and to Dorothy; Kenneth, Larry, and John

Mama, do you remember when we were kids? Were you happy then?
Or did you whistle to hide the pain?
You sang for us, or was it for you?
Did bad memories ruin your day?
Is that why you woke screaming at night?
You raised 5 kids, hard work, I know
You lost 1 girl at 9 mos old.
Was that why you were always sad?
In childhood I always blamed Dad.
He was cruel to us, always made a fuss
Don't do that, quiet down, I told you no,
You're all no good, to hell you'll go.
Our childhood was wrong, kids should be strong in the love of their parents.
He hated us, we hated him

He hated women, and girl children,
and churches, and neighbors, and
hugs, and kisses, and bright colors,
and happiness, and laughter
Mama, do you remember? I
remember.

Joy Lynn Teron
TO WHOM IT MAY CONCERN

Dedicated to my Wonderful Mother, The late, Eva Teron

If I had the power, I would unify the earth.
I would start at the beginning which of course is birth.
When a child is born no violence shall he see,
Violence, hatred and prejudice will no longer be.

People will unite and hatred destroyed.
The disease of envy will no longer be employed.
The world will become peaceful.
The world will become quiet.
No more bombing or killing or outbreaks of riot.

There will still be presidents, prime ministers, leaders and laws.
But they will be true to the people and true to the cause.
The cause of love and unity to men of all races.
To bring together thoughts and technology from all places.

We could fight and kill off starvation and disease.
Instead of men and animals and plants and trees.

Is this all a dream? Will it ever be true?
Maybe it will. It's all up to you.

Rebecca Giaccio

Rebecca Giaccio
LIFE

A tranquil twilight drifted into the peaceful valley.
The settled snow pressed against the icy ground.
An agile creature pranced along the sparkling snow banks
like a guitarist's fingers upon singing strings.

His paws created a profoundly simple tune on the gleaming white drifts, which called and awakened a gentle zephyr.
A frosted evergreen swayed to the beat as the graceful boughs of leafless trees conducted the swelling orchestra of restless winds.

They whispered softly at first,
then grew faster and more lively into a swirling crescendo.
The animated snow caught on to the vitality, and hopped and danced through the air in a great circle.

Nevertheless the flurries slipped back towards the earth, stretching and grasping at the illusive sky desperately, uselessly.
The wind died.

Silence suffocated the earth.
Yet, still faintly audible,
the abandoned strains of music floated to the heavens and faded into eternity.

Judy Dugger
THE GIFT OF FRIENDSHIP

This poem is dedicated to Terry, my dear friend

Sometimes life needs a little lift,
through our friendship you gave me that gift.

You gave me a bright smile to lighten my load,
as I travel along lifes road.

When you gave me your hand, I felt courage and strength,
and the twinkle in your eye makes my troubles pass by.

You gave me your laughter to warm my heart,
that I might have sunshine at each day's start.

You gave me happy memories to carry around,
they lift my spirit whenever it is down.

And as day comes to an end,
I would like to thank you for being my friend.

Berneta Heideman
THUNDER

Is that thunder rolling in the clouds,
Or is it cannons sounding 'way out yonder?
I hear the rolling noise resounding
And it makes me stop and wonder:
What makes it sound so loud at times
And then quietly speak.
You can read about the clouds
In many a book and line,
But they never really explain
The awesome feeling you get
When listening to the sound
As it travels the sky 'round
And 'round and round—
Across the heavens, back and forth,
Rumbling and grumbling,
Like some fierce lion waiting for its prey,
And then it suddenly pounces.
Then the rain begins to fall—
Faster and faster and faster.
You wonder when it will stop;
But you know it will.

Patricia E Cole Bradstreet
I'M SORRY

Thoughts of you daily
drift inside my head
I dream of you late at night
as I slumber in my bed.

I've regretted my decision
the one that I did make
that destroyed our lives so long ago
your fragile heart did break.

I never felt you loved me
I was too young and naive to know
I needed you to express your love
you didn't let it show.

I'm sorry for the hurt I caused
the tears for me you shed
I'm sorry your love has turned to hate
and now you wish me dead.

For I shall always love you
and in my heart you'll stay.
I wish you only happiness
as I exist from day to day.

Sandra (Mason) Stephens
REMEMBERING ALAN

A happy smile upon his face.
He could only sit in one place.
Wheelchair bound he could not go.
I wonder if he felt the snow?
He just wanted to be included in their play.
But they always ran away.
Now he will never be alone.
For God has taken Alan home.

Luanne Larson Arendt
THE BRIDGE

Precious neighbors and never met friends
hoping and praying our world never ends
so closely related, spread near and far
we may each look different, but brothers we are.
Our purposes equal, why should we fight
so sad to fear going to sleep every night.
lucky we are, God gave us our lives
to have all our husbands, children and wives.
The beauty of life cannot be replaced
considering history and trials we've all faced.
were all of those lives taken in vain?
was anything learned from their sorrow and pain?
they all had hopes, they all had dreams,
all gone to ashes from somebody's schemes.
Our plans need to be peaceful for all us involved
if one's got to lose, just what has been solved?
reach out to your neighbors, the crisis we share
what good is pride, if no one's left to care!

David-Vincent Brooks
UPON GOING HOME
(A lonely soldier going home on leave)

This poem is dedicated to Theresa, my wife, Dorothea (mother), Minnie (mother-in-law) Denise & Dolores (sisters) and Karseen and Delphia (children)—with L-O-V-E!!!

Poem No. 202
i can't wait
to get home/where love' going
to greet me at its front door/
i can't wait
to get home/where love' is in
every kitchen pot/ stewing just
right/
i can't wait
to get home/where the bed' are
made up/abundantly with
L-O-V-E . . .
i can't wait
to get home/for love's awaiting
with open arms/
for anyone
who
decides
to
walk
through
it'
loving
DOORS . . .

Charles R Kenner
A KIND OF MAGIC

A star falls in the dark of the night,
I make a wish upon its flight.
I wish for something so precious and real something so warm, something I can feel.
It's a kind of magic this is true
something I give from me to you.
It's a kind of magic that will always glow,
I say I Love You I'll Let It Show.
I'll say I Love You to the end of time.
I'll forever be glad that you are mine.
A kind of magic this I say.
I wish upon that star for a
Love I shall find someday.
It's a kind of magic that will always be near
It's a kind of magic I will never fear.
It's a kind of magic that will take me away.
Find me a Love for another day.
I wish upon that star this I say.
A kind of magic I'll wish some other day.

Gloria J Morotti
ODE TO MY LOVE

He comes to me,
My beloved.

His skin soft as the moth's wing,
Yet hard as polished oaken wood.
The fragrance of his flesh that of a thousand
flowers in the rain—
His body quivering in delight;
The warm sweet rush of breath from his nostrils
Flowing like life's blood into mine.

He holds me,
We become one.

He speaks to me in ancient tongues,
His offering a prayer to the gods and goddesses.
And I become a shining light,
Petals opening to the son—a song in the wind.
As the strength and the beauty
of the universe
We become.

Olivia Tosic
THE ROADBLOCK

A flame ignites,
Excitement reigns
Into the night it lingers.
The outcome is a mystery,
As both await in awe,
Only to depart and go
Their separate ways,
Wondering.

Intrigue overflows their minds
As curiosity builds a bridge—
Determined to reach the other side,
Never quite making it across,
For a roadblock awaits them
Everytime—they must
Turn around and go home,
Alone.

"Why?," They wonder—
Their minds ticking so
Rapidly about the other
And how they can overcome
The road block,
For, so closely they come
To adjoining,
Only to be stopped once again
Frustrated.

Feelings grow stronger
As their thoughts get deeper,
They know they must unite;
Around that torturous roadblock
Is a definite stepping stone,

They both realize,
Which, too, is a mystery—a
possibility—
In need of a solution,
Desperately.

Tina Palmacci
QUESTIONS
I lie here motionless, thoughts racing through my mind.
Not yet a woman and yet not a child.
Not able to go back, I now look to the future.
Afraid to see who I'll lose, afraid to find loneliness.

The hands of time seem to stop as I lie here thinking further of my future.
A need to plan my life scares me the most.
Will it go my way? Will it run its course?
Will the answers come to me?

I try endlessly to keep from growing impatient.
It's hard but I believe I can make it.

James E Duncan
AND GOD KISSED THE BROW OF THE FLOWER

Dedicated to my mother, Christeen Duncan, of who gifted my life with her love.

And God kissed the brow of the flower
as its head bowed in silence.
Pertaining to purity;
Engulfed in beauty;
Standing by the shore of nowhere;
Wanting nothing but the sand of which it grew;
yet searching for the light
that hold the rays of love.

So help me now
to never forget the siren heartbeat
of those whom my own heart has beat for;
And never
could you brush away the stain
from the face of which a
a crystal
teardrop was shed.
And as it was your brow
enlightened with the kiss of God;
You
received the light;
You
are the flower.

Sharon L Money
WHISPER
Voices to unbend the coiled mind
Softly spoken charms to ease the breath
Speaking to unchain fears not yet held
Seeking to uncover but not find

Traveling a path of darkened facets
Finding it some long-forgotten gift
Knowledge does not change the unshared soul
Nor giving turn a death to lost assets

Hearing a true thought is nature's game
But sound to unheard echoes has no sense
Through ripples of the air we touch the heart
And yet deny the silent sound of our own name

Linda G Scruggs
PRAYER OF HOPE
To live or not to live,
that is the question.
My life is filled with troubles and trials,
each day I face agony.
I live under a bondage of fear.
I cower each passing moment,
existing only.

This shell that I live in,
is not but for a moment?
Lord, lift this heavy burden from me.
Did you not give me life?
My trembling hand reaches out to thee,
beckoning like a candle in the night.
Does thee not see?

Thee's presence flows around me.
Embracing me with ever so gentle a touch.
A smile does cross my lips,
for I know that I am not alone.
My heart fills with love and hope,
for the sun shall surely rise tomorrow
and I shall surely see it.

Marcelle I Wilson
WHAT IS A DREAM?

To all those who believe in me and love me for nothing else but me, for it is your support that brings me closer to the pot of gold at the end of my rainbow.

What is a dream?
Is it what exists in the mind,
Leaving sometimes in its trail
The scar that many couldn't find?

What is a dream?
Is it what others try to steal,
Entwining in its network
All the pain this world feels?

What is a dream?
Is it what we hope for,
Considering the fact that
It is embedded amongst a greedy tar?

OR

Is a dream
What I hope to accomplish—
Set behind this smoke filled screen,
In a future that starts out from scratch.

Mavis Wolkenbrod
WIND SONG
Engulfed in a white light,
My body burns
But I feel no pain.
The clouds caress my body
As I sail across the starry sky.
My partner's the wind,
We waltz to our own song sung by my heart.
Blue is the color of the sun's eyes
And its red hair flames from its scalp.
And the moon smiles at me with a loving grin . . .
As I continue my dance
My feet are grasped by hands of the unhuman.
I can't run free,
For the grip is too strong
And I have become weak.
I reach for the wind,
But claw at nothing.
I grab a star,
But my hands slip.
I cry out to the sun and the moon,
But neither can help me.
The light gets brighter,
The heat intensifies,
My body burns,
And I begin to feel the pain.

Sherry L Bailey
ALICIA MARIE

To my beautiful daughter, Alicia Marie I dedicate this poem

It seems like only yesterday
you were born to me
So soft, so warm, a tiny baby
So helpless in my arms
As I gave you tender care
Eyes of blue, rosy lips
Skin so soft and fair
How fast the time goes
As you will soon be three
You are Mommy and Daddy's big girl now
no longer our little baby
I am so proud to say
you are the best part of me
You bring happiness everyday
My beautiful Alicia Marie

Dawnmarie E Swilley
TOMORROW IS ANOTHER DAY

To James M. Kaull; I'm so happy that you have become a very special part of my life.

Tomorrow is another day,
Remembering out past,
Of many times we felt to say
"You know we'll always last."

We shared a smile in a way,
No other one could share.
Like seeking out that last, long mile
Where shadows leave life bare.

In the past, an idea struck and
My eyes shed out tears.
My heart rang out sudden luck
So strange with hate from peers.

Changes occurred when you walked in
Happy as could be.
Made me feel so far from sin
Excited like the sea.

Can this be real? That I have seen
His face so fair and true?
Enduring tempers, soft not mean,
Like thoughts of old and new.

Heidi R Enerson
THE WONDERFUL SHOWER

To Deidre Alané Siemons; The one and only.

The rain tapped on the jagged coat of armor that enveloped the tree. The moisture seemed to saturate the bark, like cotton drenched in a cup of water.

As this feast of rain seeps into the mouths of all natural beauties around me, I am immune to the obvious gloom. Where the blinded citizens of the fast clock see bleakness, I see joy. I become indifferent to the views of the city dwellers. It is they, who cringe at this sight, who are the bleakness. "Observe this wonder", I say.

The shower ends and the people rush into a gloom beyond compare. The pollution and noise cloud their awareness of nature's hope once more. Does it really have to be this way?

That golden spotlight shines its rays through the tiny droplets that I strain to see, and it harvests a beauty that cannot be measured. It's a ribbon that is opalescent even to the hands of the fast clock.

It's a symbol of many colors.
It's hope.
It's joy.
It's a vision of silent love.
It's a small world in awe of
Mother's wonders!

Nathaniel Arrington
STRONG LOVE

This poem is dedicated to my Wonderful and Beautiful Wife Vicki

The strength of our love
is dependent on us
We have got to exercise it
and that is a must.

Never let it get weary
Never let it rest
And whenever it's tired
it will pass the test.

Exercise our love
so it will continue to grow
because I love you my lady . . .
much more than you know.

Gloria Jean Robertson
OUR LITTLE TROOPER

An Ode To DANIELLE, Who has proved herself to be quite a LITTLE TROOPER!

The storm has hit,
The temperature has dropped,
The sun's gone away,
But, the blocks have hopped.
Awalking she will go,
Braving it all,
With a goal in mind,
Standing, oh, so tall.
The lightness of the season,
Gives one an extra wind,
But, to keep going forward,
Grandma's house is behind the next limb.
Down the winding street,
Putting one foot in front of the other,
The porch light appears,
Our Little Trooper has come this much farther!

Nancy Baird Frans
CHILDREN'S BARNYARD CRITTERS
Life on a farm is something to note,
You see all kinds of animals from a horse to a goat.

The roosters crow early and get all out of bed,
While lazy hogs wallow in mud up to their head.

The cows get milked and the turkeys do gobble,
While ducks quack around and do they waddle.

The soft fluffy rabbits will do you no wrong,
And let's remember the birds that chirp us a song.

The dogs chase the cats until a tree comes in sight,
And mules are still stubborn from morning til night.

Feeding time is the best time of the day,
Animals love your hello's, pats, and some will play.

They will bed down to sleep after a good meal,
Knowing they are loved and often your heart they steal.

We know God's critters bring us pleasure and joys,
We thank God for his loving kindness to all girls and boys

Melody K Blevins
ETERNAL SPRING

To my beloved husband, who's encouraged me to be all that I can be, and my Mother for teaching me to believe in myself and reach beyond my dreams. There's nothing that I can't do.

SPRING; the most beautiful of God's creations.
The beginning of new life, the end of a deep, lifeless sleep.
Tiny flowers raising their heads, to the suns welcoming warmth.
Birds beautiful songs, bringing news of the happiness coming.
The gentle breezes, whispering of times to be.
The sun so glorious and warm;
Giving life to all who have slept the lifeless era away.
Happiness raised to its greatest heights, stretched to its farthest lengths.

Loving you is like an Eternal Spring.
The sun racing golden halo's around your head.
The birds singing news of your special Love song.
The flowers bowing at your loving presence.
My heart bursting with happiness,
from the whispers of your name
upon the gentle breezes.

I tingle at your touch.
I quiver at your powering embrace.
I melt from the warmth of your lips on mine.
You fill my existence with more sunshine and happiness, than can ever be expressed.
Existence again in that cold lifeless state, could never do.
For I could never go back to nothing;
Having tasted Eternal Spring with you.

Chris VanVooren
NEVER FORGOTTEN
Special people do not die
They pass on to a better place
Where there is no longer hurt and pain
Here, there are new people to love
But your love will never become a memory
Just as they will never be forgotten
It hurts sometimes to think back—
But always remember the good thoughts
Because the good things in life are the best!
Do not be hateful towards God
You know he did what was best . . .
He took a very special person
And put them to a peaceful rest.

Terri L Williams
THE BATTLE OF THE SOUND
As I fight my way across the sound
I watch the turbulent water.
The crashing, thundering, roaring sound,
the rage her master taught her.
The cold and wind whip my face
till numb it seems to grow
And I long to be warm in my cottage
before the gales do blow.
I watch the sky as it blackens
then alights with claps of thunder.
It does seem appropriate to give applause
at the sight of a glorious wonder.
The waves wash over the darkened sands
as I sight a light from home.
And now I am the master
and my warm hearth-chair my throne.

Ilona Ujhelyi
LOOK AT MY SOUL

To Paramahansa Yogananda

Oh, look at my soul now,
So naked and so bare,
Shivering before you,
And hoping that you care.

Oh, look at my soul now,
Knowing that you know,
Soaring to the heavens,
Basking in the glow.

Oh, look at my soul now,
On light and airy wings,
Swinging on a rosebud,
Gliding on the wind.

Oh, look at my soul now,
Dancing through the land,
Skipping through the meadows,
It has found a friend.

Tom Delorenzo
DECEPTION

To the people that mean the most to me, Mom, Dad, and of course, well you know who you are.

i'm the driving wind from north,
i fill the sailor's sail with air.
a ship is sunk, a sailor's drunk,
and drowns, but i don't care
i'm the little child's nightmare
i live upon their fright
because of my exterior
i hide but stay in sight
an outward shell conceals my face
and no one can see in,
people see me as i want them to,
a game, no one can win.
so great time is lost no progress made
in our endless search,
for truth beneath our lonely mask,
to free us from our perch.
the rivers run until they're dry
and only mud is there
love too, can run until it's gone
and then who really cares.

Cheryl A Carson
MY CHRISTMAS WISHES FOR YOU

For Brent, the one who inspired me to love again

My first wish for you is love
Love that is constant, neverending
With no reservations or restrictions placed on it.

My second wish is time
You well deserve
To do all those things you have dreamed about
For so long
To cross that fine line to reality to accomplish it.

The third wish is contentment
No matter where you are or what you are doing
No matter whether it is the feeling you have often
Along peaceful walk on the beach
Or just driving to your hectic day at the office.

My fourth wish will be for your great success
For whatever endeavor you under take
Whether it be within your reach or beyond the farthest star
I will always be behind you.

But most of all, the most important wish I give you
At Christmas is peace
Peace of mind, body and soul
To come together in one person
And that one be you.

So here are my Christmas wishes for you
I hope they all come true

Merry Christmas!

Ruth V Butler
RECAPTURED LOVE

To Karen and Anthony Kreider

Come walk with me, and hold my hand.
Our tears have washed away our sorrows.
The time has come to sweep away our yesterdays,
And only house thoughts of love, and our tomorrows.

Kim Marie Muuss
LIFE
Life is something we live each day;
It's wonderful it's worth the stay.
Time is precious;
Time is lost each and every day,
So have it, hold it, and keep it,
Don't throw it away,
Because you only live once.

Evelyn P Oliger
MARINES CHRISTMAS POEM

This poem is dedicated to my son, George A Oliger III a United States Marine

Although my son is so far away,
I'll be with him on Christmas day.
He's been gone for so very long.
But if it makes him happy it can't be wrong
He's out there fighting to keep us free.
While I'm home decorating the Christmas tree.
It won't be used until New Years Eve,
when my son finally comes home on leave.
Graduating from bootcamp, we're proud, there's no doubt.
But I'll be happy when he's finally out.
He joined the service known as MR. CLEAN!
He's coming home known as P.V.T. Oliger U.S. MARINE!

OOH RAH !

Valarie T Severson
MEANING

Dedicated to Joshua and Sam, without whom my life would have no meaning.

What is the meaning of meaningful?
As it pertains to life, that is.
How do you know if your life is meaningful?
And not merely just another empty existence?
Do you measure it by things accomplished,
Or by the number of lives you've touched?
Or maybe the scale is your children,
How well you raise them to achieve meaning.
Is there a giant graph somewhere?
Where every event is charted and marked.
And just who determines the importance,
Or degree of meaning in each day lived?
If a tree falls in the forest,
And there is no ear to hear it,
Then does it make a sound?
If my life has no meaning,
And I leave no mark on this world.
Then, did I ever really live at all?

Barbara Altmiller
TWILIGHT

This poem is dedicated to the memory of my dear father, who also wrote beautiful poetry

As I stand here in the twilight,
I watch the beautiful sunset glow,
It leaves me with an inner warmth.
It shelters my heart from the evening chill.

As the sun sinks behind the fiery hill,
The shadows come creeping over field and mill.
The frogs and crickets send out their happy song,
While man settles down to a slumber song.

As I stand on the hilltop, listening to the breeze whispering through the swaying pines,
I see stars as they twinkle on high,
Like windows of heaven, high in the sky.

I listen to the rippling of the brook
As it goes merrily on its way. I see the eagle as he soars effortlessly on the evening air.
And here is man on his lifes journey, trying to survive.

The majestic beauty of this glorious land
is breathtaking to behold. May we forever be thankful for our blessings as they unfold.

May God bless this land, the land of the brave and free,
For He is the Greatest one of all, you see.

Bobbie A Tague
A BABBIT
A Babbit is like a Rabbit
Except it's called a Babbit.

Its ears aren't as big,
Its ears are smaller like a pig.
And it has a big nose
Like a fire hydrant hose.
And it's tail
Leaves a trail
Of friendship everywhere.

Mimi Guerra
BECKIE'S CREED

To Beckie, who's struggles are my struggles, and your Triumphs my Triumphs. Lovingly, Mom

Words unchanging never ending
Father hear me as I pray,

guide my footsteps for your glory
and lead me forth each day.

Alice Hughes
LITTLE BLUE BONNET
Little blue bonnet of ribbon and lace,
Once you encircled a child's lovely face,
Gilding the lily, caressing each curl
Of the dear little long-ago, proud, little girl.

Lovingly cherished, you lie through the years,
Faded with age and dampened with tears.
What of the child? She quietly sleeps
There where the willow tree watches—and weeps.

P Annie Housholder
SAILING INTO FOREVER AND EVER

Dedicated to my loving husband, Jerry

Sailing deep within the canyon,
Arms widespreading and engulfing.
Bringing us closer and whispering
the secrets of a lost frontier.

Holding our distance and embracing
this dimension so true,
a natural formation so perfect
in its own imperfection.

Tac, daring to steer into the wind,
gusting and catching hold of the main.
A spray of icy coldness, piercing,
hands trembling; break and set.

A scintillation of blues and greens,
of silent passion, ablaze on the water,
floating like a soft blue feather.
Aurora Australis, Aurora Borealis.

Michael Watson
COSMOS
I kneel here under the stars of the universe 'and watch'—as just a few days begin and end on earth.
The ways of old repeat—'never changing'—they wander endless streets.
Who is man to think that with time he may command?
I created the stars and know the count thereof.
'And I look at man,' from my lofty place above.
Turmoil and fear—and lonely pleas arise and meet my ear. I placed a simple path before your face. 'To walk with love—and 'me' embrace.'
Man—who have you become? And time—your course is almost run . . .
Rumors of wars and hearts that break in death.
'My children,' lift up your eyes—
'you know the rest' . . .

Daniel J Warner Jr
BRING ON THE RAIN

To Daniel & Cari with love, Dad

What can I do mom
I'm only human
If I tried to please you
I'd only be wrong
Sometimes there are people
that can't be changed
And those are the people
that stay the same.

Bring on the rain

Bring on the rain

What can I do dad
to make you proud
I could look for answers
that can't be found
Somehow I have lost all my self-control
And dying seems so easy
I could just let go

Bring on the rain

Bring on the rain

What can I do Lord
to open up your door
I have spoke to Satan
But I don't no more
Sometimes there are people
that lose their ways
And I was one of those
but I'm not today.

Bring on the rain

kirk
I THANK GOD

This poem is dedicated to MOM.

Christmas is a time of Joy and Thanksgiving.
Every time I stand or walk, chew or swallow,
Communicate . . .
By writing or speaking,
I thank God.
And . . . .
I thank God for you.

Elizabeth Revander
BE MY MENTOR
Be my mentor, teach me to love, a skeptic I shall not be
Let not my dreams run rampant, upon a turbulent sea.
But let my dreams be sturdy, with a strong sense of direction,
Let me mold that dream, cultivate it, and use it to perfection.
Let my mind be open to accept the challenge of life,
Let not my existence here on earth be the contention of strife.

Be my mentor, and I will fear no man
Teach me to obtain a great volume of wisdom to maintain my stay in this land.
Teach me everything that is good and pure, let evil flee from me
The beauty that I shall behold, is here for all to see.

Be my mentor, walk by my side
Let me walk swiftly to success, without breaking my stride.
Guide my steps to achieve the greatest height
Through the brightness of day, through the darkness of night.
Let me too become a mentor, a leader, who stands strong and tall
If I live by these principles, I know I shall never fall.

Albert Glover
THE HIGHWAY TO PETOSKEY
When we used to drive the highway to Petoskey
along the shores of Lake Michigan
(we'd come the high road) Stephanie, Jean and I sat by the door and strained
at that instant we crested the hill
to see the 'ocean' below from its shore spreading outward.
Then, with eyes forced up the slope of the land
I'd gaze at the seam where horizon met sea.
"That's California" Aunt Jean would say.
Stephanie (she sat in the middle
smiling without teeth)
craned to see. "Mom's living there" she said
made care-free by such solid fact.

The road grew flat, paper-smooth.
Jean clutched at the wheel
and I flew high like Noah's dove, keen-eyed
for sight of the promised land.

Still in the ark, my love,
some twenty years later
with eyes still fixed
on the seam between horizon and sea.

Joanie C Merriman
PEOPLE

I dedicate this poem to my father Riney, my mother Lenora, who gave me these values. To my brother Dennis, who practiced them with me; my daughters Regina and Shawna, who I passed these values to, and my wonderful husband Bill, who is my life and lives them with me.

Really good people are hard to find,
Once you do, keep this in mind:

Don't prejudge, when you don't know
Where they've been, or where they'll go.

Try to give that person a break,
For a new friend this could make.

Greet new people with a smile,
Take some time and talk a while.

Give to those who are the needy.
There's no sense in being greedy.

Our creator up above
Put us here to live and love.

There are lots and lots of rules,
Taught in all the finest schools,
On how to make and be a friend;
Use them well, for it pays in the end.

As we live from day to day,
Being kind will always pay.

For we will not always know
Which way in life we will go.

Be it good or be it bad,
Be it happy or be it sad,
Be the best that you can be,
Be yourself and you will see
That the results were meant to be.

I'm looking forward to knowing all of you,
And hope that you will like me too.

I will do what I can do
To become friends with all of you.

Inga A Richardson
THE SUN AND THE SKY
The sun and the sky,
are you and I,
but the clouds could never part us.
Because with love made like ours,
the sun and its powers,
shine through strong forever.

Oscar Nerys

Oscar Nerys
PHILOSOPHIE OR THE PENSY
! Philosophie the pensy !
yours strophe,
to refer to devot cult.
in that deceit,
in the abyss,
who profund only,
open that door or poetry,
when inspirate to sound,
it soul !

! One ecstasy of flux slip away !
Rule it pensy liberty,
when refract laight
of the etrnite,
and the unknown to quiet,

! Ware who to flee,
to her vanish,
like the wind,
when pass hurricaned,
toward afterward to remain
Or the silent

! Philosophie the selfishness,
that humble,

Soul who aggrandize,
to de c decorate that hih alter,
the that gooldess
tha Olympe.

Chead the unknotion,
that extreme,
when that mind shpe
like certain,

expose that uncovered,
fable secret,
who implied never,
could be awake!

Laurie Hiroshige
AS I WAS RESTING THERE

A butterfly came fluttering by
down near the water's edge
where I was resting peacefully
atop a rocky ledge.

The wind was playing impishly
with tendrils of my hair.
How good the breeze felt on my face
as I was resting there.

And through the clouds, my eyes
could see
the blue, majestic sky.
And in the gentle calm, I heard,
a sea gull's distant cry.

The sun was shining overhead.
My heart held not a care.
It was so tranquil, quite serene
as I was resting there.

I couldn't bring myself to leave
my cozy little nest,
and so I drifted off to sleep
to dream of happiness.

Meda Ragsdale
VICTORY

The General rode stately onward
His troops not far behind.
Victory was his today . . . .
The loss of men untold.

The precipice was camouflaged
by snowdrifts and falling snow.
The screams of man and steed
pierced the cold morning air, and
there was no more . . . . death
had claimed its prize.

Maria J Fernandez
FANCY

What I would give to be like the
condor
When his flight takes him so high
To places where he has built his nest
Where the vultures will never get by.

Or that I could be a sea
With its waves so high—gigantic!
That no one could get past them
And in their depth hide away my
children
Where no one could find them.

Or I would like to find a good genius
Who would take me to a magic
fountain
And from it drink an elixir
And in supping be transformed
Myself in a floating shawl
And wrapping my children in it
Carry them with tender lullabies
To regions of peace and piety.

Elizabeth Page
THE ROCKY MOUNTAINS

The Rocky Mountains, standing
proud and high,
Wander in the clouds before my
eyes.
Mustangs roam these wild plains,
Eagles soar without shame.
Pine trees stand, tall and green.
Blue waters run in the streams.
Mountain lions roar in the canyons.
There is a magic to these
mountains.

Judy Wilkinson
NO MATTER

Like a feather falling in water
I lie on my pillow and cry,
You know I'll always love you
No matter what or why.

I ask myself time and time again
Why can't I let you go?
But why can't you be here for me?
I know it's my fault, I know.

Why can't I go on with my life?
Is it you or the memory?
I thought as time went by
things might be better,
I know that you still love me
And that you need me too . . .
So look down deep into your heart
And you'll see that you still love me,
We both know it's true.

No matter of the past
A love like ours will always last
Cause no matter what the
problem . . . Big or small,
Our great love will conquer all.

Carolyn Buck
I'M SORRY I LEARNED TO LOVE YOU

to "Bubba," a dear friend

You taught me what seemed every
trick of the trade,
and I learned; learned well as how
you taught me,
Years have bestowed 'on me a few
precious moments,
I'll now try to relate them to you
from me.

You taught me the bad things in life
that can be beautiful,
Even the worse that seem to prove
the best,
Deep down, I'm truly sorry I learned
to love you,
Ah—precious love, you 'stowed that
'pon me too, 'mong all the rest.

Now you held my hand; guided me
to Heaven,
Like a fool I followed where you led
me; as an innocent child,
All that mattered then and for the
time being,
I had "YOU," and life was
worthwhile.

Time's "marched on," life has led us,
Neither knew the paths where we
would go,
In our hearts we thought love, life
was so right,
Deep down, truth only we two would
come to know.

I've loved you with sin and
compassion,
O'er the years, seems we two should
already be one,
What's in our eyes today; only
dreams tomorrow,
Reality is only near as when we
begun.

And I'm sorry, really sorry; I learned
to love you.

Margaret W Knowlden
MY CHIROPRACTOR

For my dear friend, Dr. Roger Crowley, who is my chiropractor as well. SEQUEL: He did fix up my feet like brand new and I can walk without pain now.

My chiropractor is truly a witty
fellow.
He is so full of fun and unusually
mellow.

For him, displaced bones are but a
grim reality
Which reflects a tough side to his
personality.

Without hesitation, he makes my
bones pop and crack
Until later they feel like they've been
under attack.

Going back for more is admitting
insanity—
Those tender spots might elicit some
profanity.

Still, I should give him a chance to
show what he can do.
Maybe he can fix up my bones to be
like brand new.

Since I have come this far I really
must stick it out.
If he helps me I'll have a lot to be
pleased about.

I'd never dream of downplaying his
ability,
Especially if I should gain more
mobility.

If that happens how do I express my
gratitude?
Why, I'll kick up my heels—and
adjust my attitude!

Neil F Mahoney
SPRING'S MORN

Shining Rainbows Through My
Trees,
Falling Sparingly,
Over The Spacious Fields.
Reflecting The Spectrum,
From Within,
Multicolor Prisms Made Of Dew.

Rebecca Martin

Rebecca Martin
WHO

In Memory of My Beloved Mother Susie Roberson Deceased May 10, 1987

Who can frame the world with his
might,
turn darkness into light?

Form a man from the earth, and
cause a child to be born of a
virgin birth?

Who could dry the land across the
Red Sea,
for the children of Israel to be
free?

Who could rain manna from
heaven, to show the children of
Israel he'll take care of them
forever?

Who would let his only son die upon
the cross?
The same someone who hated
sin and made a way for the loss.

Who would have a man build a
boat, for the saving of mankind
and set it afloat?

Who would make the lame to
walk, and heal the tongue of the
dumb to talk?

Who would prepare a mansion for
the saved, and make a way for
the loss to obey?

Who would make man as the head of
the house,
and give him a helpmate for his
spouse?

The same someone who loves you
and me, and sent his son to die
for us to be free.

Tiffanie Miyashiro

Tiffanie Miyashiro
THE UNICORN

To my Dad Stan, Mom Sandy, Brother Jason and Jichan and Bachan

As I was walking in the forest one
day
I saw a Unicorn.
She was running in the fields of hay
On a crisp Sunday morn.
She had a mane of silvergold
And eyes of sparkling blue,
And her horn of ivory white
Almost looked brand new.
I wanted to say hello to her
But then she galloped away.
So now when I think of a Unicorn,
I think of fields of hay.
And I think of how beautiful she was
On that crisp Sunday morn.
And ever since then I've never told
That I've seen a Unicorn.

Hope Ellen Genzen
PROMISES, PROMISES

Promises made,
Hopes risen,
Promises broken.

Dreams created,
Plans made,
Dreams shattered.

One man's hopes,
Another man's dreams,
Two worlds collided,
Two lives destroyed.

Another man enters the cycle.

Carolyn Ingram
YOUTHS

This poem is dedicated to all youths around the world

The Youths, who are they?
The youths, unwanted, unloved,
unknown.
The youths, going around with
negative minds,
Questioning themselves, then
automatically
it comes out verbally.

Who are we?

Where did we come from?
Where are we going?

The youths, who are we?
As youths that's the question
that shatters a great deal of us
maybe from the pressure of society,
our upbringing, ruined characters and
unvalued reputation, but although
being shattered, most of us answer
ourselves
truthfully, in a proud but rather shy
way,
"I don't really know who I am."

The youths, where did we come
from?
As youths some of us have been
brought up in broken homes, without
love, fellowship
without feminine and masculine
traits
with shy unrealistic parents who
didn't teach us how real and earnest
life was, and worse, to even
recognize that there's a God.

The youths, with no education, no
trades, no jobs,
To occupy untreasured time, we get
involved with drugs, crimes, illicit
sex, then remove ourselves from
society with the forming of Bases,
(Gangs)
Then to top it all off, we are treated
as Outcasts.

The youths, where are we going?
The youths, crying out in echoed
voices of agony,
where are our leaders, our relatives,
youths
like ourselves and even our God.
Away yonder in faint voices
We can hear them saying . . . . . yes,
we are coming,
but when will they really come, come
to set us free,
set us free, free, in order to form
bonds of unity,
Love and Brotherhood,
will the International year of the
YOUTHS be our answer?

Ann Humpal
WINTER WONDERS

As the tiny crystal snowflakes feather gently to the ground, I tiptoe through the covers of white lace all around.

The snowflakes capture colors, of rainbows, not just white. For from the sky emerges, sparkles of delight.

Frost upon the tree limbs, shines in awesome wonder. Beams of gold glow through the frost, like lightning strikes through thunder.

On winter nights, bonfires light the dark, bringing shadows into view. Horses pull sleighs thru a mystical world, amidst a sky enveloped in darkest blue.

Beauty is just one thing this wondrous snow possesses. Children dress in bundles, and women, woolen dresses.

Men wear their longjohns to keep them from the cold. For when the night is chilly, and there's stories to be told.

They gather round the bonfire, with sticks in every hand. The taste of roasted mallows makes the whole night grand.

Children build their snow friends, thoughtfully but fast. For they know when spring is near, this white world just won't last.

Andrea Kodys
A LIFETIME

The clouds slip by,
Moving through the sky,
Gently, ever so gently—
The sun moves through
The sky unseen, by many—
A human eye.
A day slips by, now two, now three,
Soon a lifetime's gone, gone away
Never to be lived again.

George F Heller Jr
HEARTS TOGETHER

Blue the water . . . . . depths
unknown,
Hearts together . . . . . ours to
own.

Waves to follow . . . . . winds
unrest,
Days and hours . . . . . a constant
test.

Across the shores . . . . . hear the
thunder roar,
Sunlight of day . . . . . darkened
no more.

Hearts together . . . . . no matter
what may,
Be still in the night . . . . .
Or sail away.

Hearts together . . . . . No others
can be,
As deep as the water . . . . . my love
unto thee . . . . .

Verka Paunovska
ON A RAINY DAY

I feel like sitting
by the fire
being in your arms of warmth
depending only on one another

The world outside is silent
as the ring of rain drops fall
in a sequence covering each part
of the solid floor

We snuggle close together
within distance of breath
showing each other
why we can't live apart, just as
rain and drops
go together
hand in hand.

Jane DeVere
THE MUSIC MEN

PRISMIC TUNES REVERBERATE
FROM GALAXIES AFAR
BUT EARTHLINGS CAN NO
LONGER HEAR OR GAZE UPON
THE STARS
FOR THEY ARE DEAD!

My last day yawned the morning sun
and strains of Destiny.
Suddenly, it turned to night, to frantic
screams and muffled cries,
To searching faces, broken minds,
scarred and petrified.
Men throughout the centuries
practiced brutal chords
Unaware the finished score would
end in desolation.
I walked by giant playrooms where
Tyrants hid their toys,
Lethal trinkets engineered to pop our
bright balloon.
I stumbled over charred remains and
human guinea pigs
As Prophets caroled through the
mist, "Time Is Waning in the Drift."

The Haunted peered with sightless
eyes into the ugly chaos
Listening long through deafened ears
to murderous crescendos.
Immune to scents of love and beauty
none recalled the smell of peace.
They tasted life with fiendish greed
aware that part was poison.
Clutching air they yelled and
whispered, preaching empty words,
Dominating—manipulating—
initiating lies,
Terror addicts sick with power
trapped in great machines.,
Completely mad, they tricked
themselves into catastrophe
As freedom's ember flickered out
and global light diminished.

The Innocent defied their plight,
strangled by the grip of fear,
Picked apart by shrewd intriguers,
warped from hate and tyranny,
Exploited by sensationalists and rank
political frauds,
Shoved and trampled, mocked and
stripped of every human privilege—
A Symphony of violent men
composed by manic fools.
Immobile now, they hang in time—a
ludicrous portraiture.
Such were they, who fell disgraced,
victims of their own contempt.
With all their wealth and knowledge
they couldn't buy another life
Nor could they purchase Mother
Earth on the low installment plan.

Susan M Paradise
VALENTINE

She sat alone
with watchful eyes
while valentines
were passed around
and once again
she realized
that on her desk
none would be found.

She tried, but still
there came a tear
and with her hand
she brushed it away
and thought again
there's still next year
another lonely
valentines day.

Imogene Crist
THE CYCLE

The miles and miles of leafless trees
are waiting patiently for the first
spring breeze.
Then, as if for spite, an icy wind
gusts in the night.
Old man winter has decided to have
one last fling.
Ah! but, Mother Nature knows he is
vulnerable at this time.
Cunningly, slowly, and ever so
gently
she eases her warming softness
nearer, nearer
to his chilly indifference.
He is reluctant. She persists.
Alas! He is helpless to her seductive
advances.
His wintry heart melts slowly filling
streams and rivers
with life giving substance.
Mother Nature goes to work, Day by
day she performs her magical
artistry.
She works fast for she knows it is
only temporary.
He shall gather strength and return to
take revenge.
It is as it should be.

Leanne Gardner
MASTER OF DARKNESS

Welcome to my nightmare,
The terror I will gladly share.
If you look into my eyes,
I can tell you many lies.

I will destroy the sanity,
Of all humanity.
My terror controls the night,
Trapping all in fright.

I am the master of darkness,
Blackness I will bless.
Bow down at my throne,
And taste the bloody bone.

Be careful not to scream,
You're coming apart at the seams.
You will never be the same,
Because you're going insane.

Kelly Vernazza
YOU AND ME

As the days go by waiting for you
The seas seem wide, what can I do
I can see your smile, those sparkling
eyes
With you there is truth, never a lie.
My wait for you, can never be tough
The love you gave me is more than
enough
Your eyes and your smile I will
always see
We will be again together, you and
me.

Donna (Brodie) Wright
THE STORM

Everything was quiet,
So cold, suddenly dark.
The whispering had started.
The waves tossing to and fro.
Then the screaming of the woman,
The woman his only pride.
How he loved her.
They would perish in this storm.

He would save her if nothing else.
She clung to the mast,
Slipping at times,
Her body soaking.
He bound her to the mast.
He called out with loud cries.
He called for Jesus to come on
board.

Surely all was vanity.
He could see the woman's frame
through soaked clothes.
He reached for the woman.
If they were to perish, they would
perish together.
Then the calm came
Seagulls circled overhead.
He hugged her, kissed her.
Gave Jesus thanks for his life.
He loved the woman because she
was his wife.

Roxana Boyles
TAKE ME BACK

Picture a lake, glimmering, a mirror
Reflecting the mountain peaks with
snow.
Listen closely and you will hear
A song of love and joy.

Smell the wildflowers in a waving

sea,
Watch the colt prancing to and fro,
Gaze at white clouds in a blue sky, and there's me
Standing alone in God's land.

I am special, given these gifts by the Lord
And I am at peace just standing here
And feeling the life, promises of the Word
Given to me in divine love.

Take me back to the beauty, God's joy on earth
And let me be a part of the serenity;
Show me the value, show me the worth
In being a creation of God.

Raymond T Mercadel Jr
MESSENGER OF LOVE
When our eyes first met
I knew you were heaven sent
You've got to be from above
A messenger with stories of untold love

Messenger of love
Sweet angel from above
Say it was me you were sent here to see
Messenger of love
Come hold me tight
Share your message with me tonight

Your eyes are burning coals fire.
You light my soul with a burning desire.
Just thinking about you makes a passion ignite
A messenger from above with stories of untold Love

Brad Slaughter
IF
If I was a flower
You would be my blossom.

If I was a bank,
You would be my money

If I was a poster,
You would be my picture.

But I am a person,
And you are my heart.

Mark Fries
FIGURE OF SPEACH

God, Rhonda, my fiancee, and my family have been inspiring, supportive, and encouraging. Much, much thanks!

The identity I assume
Is just that.

Who can I be,
But who I'm not?

I'm not even put together yet.
How can I finally talk?

Mimmo
HUSKING CORN
Perfect yellow teeth smile
from tight green lips.
I try desperately to wipe away its smugness
the way it laughs, the way the gaps between each kernel taunt me.

These same tiny goldbricks
line the barren plough rows of farmers' mouths—
dirty men with tattoed five o'clock shadows
whose shallow eyes have seen raped land, stripped topsoil,
whose dry mouths thirst for its taste

Charmaine Miles
SPIRITUAL BEAUTY
Your love, your beauty, your kindness I see.
In all that life is, which surrounds all of me.
You have opened my eyes to each little thing.
Not just flowers that bloom in the spring.

The beauty of children's innocent faces.
The beauty of people in far away places.
Each person's face different, one from another.
Your love and your kindness, make them my brother.

Your love fills a room when we come together.
Our swaying hands lifted like wind blown heather.
The smiles on faces of struggling hearts.
Each one, by faith, doing their parts.

The strength and the courage to take each day.
To apply Your word and walk in the way.
The support and comfort that each one gives.
From the hearts of people, where my Lord lives.

Thank you, Oh Lord, most of all that I see.
A gentle and patient new-forming me.
Filled with your spirit—a gift that is free.
Teaching and guiding my path, meant for me.

Audrey M Totten
FROM SUNNY SKIES TO GREY
Seasons come and seasons go.
Some bring rain; some bring snow.
Some bring grassy meadows green.
Some bring many pretty flowers;
Growing by a mountain stream.

In winter we ski on long slopes of white.
In autumn comes harvest rich and ripe.
In spring comes the warm sunshine;
With a promise of summer close behind.

Summer brings sunshine bright and hot;
And choosing the right vacation spot.
It may be a place where the fish really bite.
Or it may be a place just to sit and be quiet.
Some like to travel or even go abroad.
Some like to stroll along a country road.

As for me, I watch them all go by,
For now there's no sun up in my sky.
For the love of my life slipped quietly away.
And left me with sadness and gloom.
What once were bright sunny days,
Now are quiet, lonely and grey.
I live in hope, someday this too will change
And grey skies again will turn to bright sunny array.

Leona Summerlott
WHEN TRIALS COME
When trials come, and come they will;
I hear within a voice so still:
It speaks to me in words so clear,
"You have no need to doubt or fear."
For He that calms the raging sea,
Will surely calm the fear in me.
And He that clothed the lily fair,
Will clothe me with His love and care.

No more to doubt Him or despair,
Or feel that He will not be there.
God cannot lie, His Word is true.
He will provide and see me through.

I cannot fear the dark of night;
My God is there to give me light.
He holds my hand and leads the way,
And I can trust His Will always.

I see His handiwork all around;
In all His universe He is found.
Each time I prayed, I know He heard.
His promises are there within His Word.

So when the trials come my way,
I only need to bow and pray;
And there within my weary breast,
He speaks . . . And I am given rest.

Eva La Rue Miller

Eva La Rue Miller
ONE LIFE—ONE HEART
There is one Life on this earth
Of ours to live—

There is one Heart of Love
For <u>All</u> men to give—

Can that Heart that Life be found?
Yes my friend if you look around,

And ask the great God above,
The one who sends down such love.

And as each day for us unwinds,
Just keep on pursuing until the time,
When you will become my Valentine.

Delaphine J Thompson
JEHOVAH

To my wonderful Lord, without whom I am nothing, and to my wonderful family, without whom I would be alone.

God came down on the mountain,
  Oh, what an awesome sight.
He came down as the clouds
  Touched down at the eve of night.
He rumbled and roared in the thunder;
  He spoke in broad day-light;
But his message came in a still small voice
  After everything had gotten quiet.
He spoke to the children of Israel,
  And gave them his thoughts on life,
How they should uphold each other,
  And live without storm or strife.
He said they should worship no other gods,
  They should obey and bring the tithe;
For I your Lord am a jealous God
  And want to give you a fuller life;
Life as a separate people
  Such as the world has not known;
Of love and concern for each other
  And praise and worship of one God.

Helen J Flaig
BAKELESS BAKE SALE

Dedicated to: The women of the Presbyterian Congregation Church Middletown, Pennsylvania

We're having a bakeless bake sale
To make our mission contributions swell.

Instead of candy, cookies and pies,
Or loaves of bread that you have to let rise,
We're avoiding any baking surprise.

So without any fuss, muss, or ado,
We're asking donations from each of you.
Nickles, dimes, quarters and dollars will do.

At this time each year with our women's permission
We send Christmas money to our favorite missions.

And so if we want to continue this giving
To make others happy and help with their living
We need your support in this
Bakeless Sale giving.

S J McCafferty
LIVING
Hold the memories
But do not live in them
Feel the pain
But let it fade away
Experience love
And know how it grows and changes
Give what you have
But keep yourself
Listen with your heart
But answer with your mind
Sing the songs
But hear the silence beneath
Run with the wind
But be mindful of the storms
Seek your goals
And find your soul
Take your needs
But give your best
Want it all
But earn your worth
Hope forever
But work for today
Have what is there
And know what is yours
Give what you can
And know when to give
But know when to stop
Know what is growing
And what is needing
Know what is love
And what is want
Take what is willing
But free what is trapped
Learn love from a distance
Have faith in your teaching
Let go of your child
and he will come back to you.

Sheri Seymour
DAY/NIGHT
Looking out the window
I see the brightness of the beginning day
I see the darkness of the night before

Clowns were dancing in the stars
The man in the moon was singing with joy
Now . . . .
On this very morning

I can see the shadows on the wall
The clouds are moving oh so fast
The sun is blooming with light.

The frost has left
The dew is here
Taking its place

Night has turned to day
Clowns are at rest
The man in the moon thought of a new tune
for he is fast asleep until . . .
THE NIGHT!

Alice (Maroonie) Klim
THOUGH I CAN'T BE THERE

To Mark, whose love gave me the power to like who I am.

No one will ever tell you, why I had to go.
I suppose the fact that I loved you,
they will not let you know.
The reason why I left you,
was because they made me go.
I could see by the way you acted,
that your hatred started to grow.
I don't care what they told you,
I've always loved you so.
I know that leaving you so suddenly
must have really been a blow.
I hope before you condemn me, your judgement will be slow.
Remember me when it rains, I'm crying.
When I'm happy the sun is shining.
When I'm really, really missing you,
It's a little bit of everything,
Especially snow.

Celeste Aliesha Washington
EMPLOYMENT

This poem is dedicated to all the talented men and women of the past and present.

Come into my workplace and initiate your skills
Take the bull by the horn and do what you will
Your talents are many, your convictions strong
Come into my workplace, but don't stay too long

Come into my workplace with young fresh ideas
Draw up your memos and recommendations for the fiscal year
Yes, come, my gifted one, this is where you belong
Come into my workplace, but don't stay too long

Come into my workplace and show us <u>all</u> the way
Bring coordinance and balance each and every day
Come into my workplace and make <u>me</u> look good
Bring your aura, spread your energy; like you should
Make a lifelong commitment as though you can do no wrong
Come into my workplace, but don't stay too long
Now, how can I say this without sounding gruff
"Your services are no longer needed, you've done quite enough." I have taken everything into consideration and can say with great pride, "I'm sorry, you're terminated, you're <u>overqualified</u>."

Phyllis Mae Littlejohn
GOD'S BEAUTY
Have you ever seen the dew drops
in glorious splendor shine
as thousands of tiny diamonds
sparkling through majestic pine?

Have you felt a wondrous feeling
When you smelled the air so sweet
was heaven a little closer
when the clouds were at your feet?

I often walk the moonlit paths
alone with thoughts of rapture
and know that all this beauty
is mine alone to capture.

The stars have lit the heavens
since God, our world did make.
They've guided, led and showed us
the way that we must take.

The Sun, the air, the moon and stars
were creation's gift to us.
Will we in our most lowly hours
Destroy what He gave as ours?

Patricia R Irwin
ON A SUMMER EVENING SPENT WITH LOVED ONES

To Keith, Katherine, and Kevin, who, as youngsters, were the precious children in the word picture inspired by many loving, happy, expanded family gatherings. May there be more with their youngsters!

Having romped and raced and been embraced,
The children lullaby in a hammock encased;
While trees above form our canopy
Enclosing us all in a small green sea.
Suddenly a breeze on the cheek just so,
Opposes the warmth of red bricks below.
I close my eyes and lean far back,
And feel like a small contented cat.
The talk flows 'round both light and profound,
Punctuated by summery sounds.
The stars watch o'er, shed their same steady lights,
'Til this seems not one, but all such nights.
The same ingredients now and then
Bring peace and stimulus in a curious blend.
Each moment is stored as rich insurance
Against some unknown, but future, endurance;
And, quite surely, all humanity
Would be blessed as God intended us to be,
If we each would let in our own lives increase
What we feel this night of God's love and peace.

Carole J Christensen
WHAT THE CHILDREN BELIEVE
Do you ever wonder
 where the stars go,
When the morning sunlight
 begins its show?

They're never
 very far away,
Maybe they're hiding,
 so the children will say.

They'll tell you such stories
 you can almost see,
Isn't it funny
 what the children believe?

Unicorns and fairies
 and small leprechauns,
They tell these sweet stories
 to their dad's and their mom's.

And if you ask
 where the fairies stay,
They'll shyly tell you
 that they can not say.

They'll create for you pictures
 from clouds in the sky,
So real you can see them
 if only you try.

And when the stars
 come out again,
The children can tell you
 just where they've been.

They're never
 very far away,
They have been hiding,
 so the children will say.

And they'll tell you such stories
 you can almost see,
But isn't it funny
 what the children believe?

Yes, isn't it funny,
 what the children believe.

Joyce Liles Stanfield
I LOOK OUT THE WINDOW
I look out the window and up in the sky,
While fleecy white clouds go passing by,
Birds fly overhead, a joyful song they sing,
I breathe a prayer for all these things.

I look out the window and see the trees,
Birds of all colors are nestled among the leaves,
Down on the grass the squirrels are at play
In the morning light they have begun their day.

I look out the window and see the street,
Children of all ages are precious and sweet,
Their happy laughter fills me with joy.
Happiness begins with a girl and a boy.

I look out the window and see the setting sun,
Lighting the earth as the day had begun,
Morning dawn and noon day heat,
Evening shadows cover the street
I look out the window and I see,
Darkness covers the earth and also me.
Frogs are croaking and crickets sing
Thank you blessed Lord for all these things.

Shawn Annette Owens
BITTERNESS ENVELOPS ME
Bitterness envelops me
As I lie here and try to sleep
Anger overwhelms me
As my sanity I try to keep
I'm tired of dealing with all this pain
I'm tired of the storm and all its rain
I'm tired of the rain that falls from my eyes
I don't want to hear anymore lies
My cries are a song
The days grow long
I cry out to the Lord
To give me the grace
To give me the will and strength to face
What lurks behind the next door

Virgie N Silvey
DAD'S LOVE
Out on the prairie stood an old ranch house,
Where Dad worked hard for our Mother, his spouse
 she was the one he loved so tenderly—
genuine and sincere, a regard for you and me.

He was our Dad
So kind and true.
Big gentle hands
Large eyes of blue.

When a blizzard was raging throughout the country
a guardian angel, my Dad had to be.
the children from school he took safely home.
It did not matter if they were not his own.

Proud of his heritage and just being plain folks
Dad could always laugh and tell us some jokes.

when the twilight came at the end of day,
He would pick up his harp and begin to play
sweet Evalina and little Dog Tray—
We would dance to the polkas in a fashionable way.

I wish Dad was here to play his harp once again
To the Music he loved, a sweet refrain.

Diane R Durham
HERE AND THERE

To Dale Jewell. Friendship has no limits—be it birth, age, miles, kinship, or the lack thereof. Sometimes, sisters in spirit are closer than sisters in life. DRD

Hello, my friend. I feel you there,
 Your thoughts reach out right through the air.
Even hundreds of miles away,
 I felt you in my mind today.
You draw on me. Your need is great.
 Nothing can change the choice we make,
But, draw and know I understand;
 Wish I were there to lend a hand.
I do not know what else to do,
 But say, "I'm here and I'm with you."
Do what you must, my friend, and

see,
You're not just there, but here
with me.

Edna Tuttle
AN EMPTY PLAYGROUND
Now the playground is empty
No whirlwind footprints in the sand.

Once it was so bright and lovely
As the little people danced and ran.

Among the bouquets of baby pink
roses
Yellow daffodils and lilies so white
Stood a dandelion or two
And a weed wedged in tight.

Still all grew together
With laughter and shrills
Running this way or that
At the bottom or top of the hills.

Some folks would fancy the little
petunia
Or the rosebud with delight
While stepping on the weed
To get it out of sight.

When all the choice blossoms
Have turned their heads and passed
on
Look around you, still here is the
dandelion
A friend you can always rely on.

Sherry L Long
THE TIME TAKEN AT THE GARDEN GATE
In my garden . . . some seeds
flourish: some perish.
I've often grieved the losses—
And God must have heard . . . .
For one day at the garden wall, the
gate fell open
And curiously, over in my friend's
garden,
Grew the very portions that had
failed in mine.
So the crops I thought I lost were
never lost at all:
Only shifted from my garden to
yours,
As the gate left open between friends
serves both.

I wish to remember it always—
That, although the day is fast,
The time taken for the sweet hello at
the garden gate
Is sometimes the greater measure.

Linda Pace Maddox
FROM WHENCE WE CAME

For Alexandra Kathleen Maddox

For so long I have been enchanted
by the butterflies that danced in
your eyes.
You were three—such a magical age.
I watched you marvel at the
mummified cocoon.
In a wistful moment your
"woolly bug" became a lovely
butterfly.
The fluttering wings touched your
nose—
you jumped, you laughed, and
you tried to capture
the delightful friend in your
little hands.
But the butterfly had to be free.

In his struggle, a paletted wing was
caught in a deadly web.
Your eyes grew wide with worry—
The velvet wings folded beneath
the weight of the web——
your butterfly was again in
birthing form.

He had brought out a child's laughter.
Now he was food.

Tears trickled down your
cheeks. . . .
"Mommy, my butterfly died."

I realized that you now understood
something about death.
We scatter unforgettable
moments of love and return
from whence we came.

We know not when.

Helen E Hegg
IT WAS SO SUDDEN WE WONDER WHY

This poem is dedicated to my husband Roy Hegg, Sons, Alden, Bruce, and Conrad, daughters, Cheryl and Catherine

It was so sudden we wonder why,
Not even a chance to say goodbye.
No more worries or stress to bear,
Since the Lord took him in His care.
We miss his voice and loving smile,
The times he came and we'd talk
awhile.
But the memories we have, we'll
treasure forever,
Of the good times we spent together.
Many are the times we've sadly wept,
For our dear son we'll never forget.
Now that he's gone to eternal rest,
In memories' frame we'll keep him,
because he was one of the best.

Patti Nicole Machurick
MEMORIES

I dedicate this poem to my true best friend, Mariela Macedo, who will always be a person I trust and admire. Miles don't count as long as the friendship remains. Till then . . .

I dedicate this poem to you
To remember all we've been through,
Your sparkling smile
Made it all worthwhile,
Your terrific ways made my days.

My life will be so blue without you,
So lonely and confused.
But don't forget all the smiles we lit,
The joys we've shared and all the
times we cared.

We may be apart, through distance
and miles,
But through our hearts we'll never
part
And never lose our past time smiles.

Maria-Constanza Bade
CHEESE
. . . A truck full of cheese . . .
A cheese fanatic,
Live with such ease,
In her attic?

Yes,
A cheese fanatic
But it must be a big mess!
Oh don't be so problematic

There is no:
Cheese fanatic
Living with such ease,
In my attic!
Nonsense, nonsense!

Not again, oh! . . . . .

Jerry Hunter
THE LITTLE SQUARE

This poem is to everyone, for there is a little square in each of us.

The little square listened,
but was not heard;
He watched,
but was not seen;
He waited,
but was never met;
He was successful,
but was afraid to try.

The little square lived
amongst a world of circles.
His sides—
Unmoving. Hard.
IMPENETRABLE!
His insides—nothing.
The circles around him—
smooth and yielding . . . .

"But it is the circles who need be
squares,
Not! I! Be! They!"

With the passage of time, he
rounded,
but his sides became brittle.
Although with great age and
circularity,
he was always little . . . always
square.

Linda M Riccelli

Linda M Riccelli
THE AGES OF HER GRACE
Of centuries she knows not but ages,
Her children aptly skirted at the hem.
Ephemeral ego, all in rages,
She astronomically turns beyond
them.

She puts forth a vigorous type and
breed.
She charms them with her glib,
ageless phrases.
She permits, all eliminating greed.
She gulps big birds, in osmotic
phases.

Enthralled, big birds take their small
duration.
Feeding ego, all on colossal prey.
She speaks of biological progression
And asks, how long they think
they'd like to stay?

Undoubtedly egos, they are geguiled.
Humanity remains my small, small
child.

Nina I White-Allen
DECORATION DAY

Dedicated to My Dear Husband, Ernest Allen Sr., My Family, and All My Loved Ones.

I hope the "Souls" that's looking
down
Upon our face, will see no frown.
But within our hearts there'll be a
dent,
To show for us how lives were spent.
A world at "Peace" for "Us" to
share,
Before "More Of Us Sleeps Out
There!"
It's quite necessary "To Be Brave!"
When it's "Your Country's Flag to
Save!"
You'll pray, "come soon" some will
discover
Some way to save "you" and "your"
brother!
That someday all these wars will
end,
When "we" can call "each other"
friend.
Where all nations can truly declare,
To have "no need" for this
"warfare!"
That all might live upon this earth,
And "Share " the "Love" from
"Jesus Birth."
The good "He" died for to upon "Us"
bestow,
"We" should be glad to "cast war
down Below!"
(Hell)

The End
*Gladly "we" should "cast!"

Grace Scarberry
THE WISHING STARS
The deep purple evening sky has
devoured the stars on high.
Out from behind dark clouds the
moon creeps,
Looking for the stars but they are
asleep.
Giant bare trees stand tall with long,
slender fingers
Reaching to catch the stars, should
they fall.
But, the wishing stars are hidden in
the Milky Way,
Saving all the wishes for another day.
Just one, I would like to see, so I
could make a wish for thee.

Joyce Cox
TO AMANDA
Your hands are so tiny, your face so
small
I watched you creep, I watched you
crawl
I heard you sing, I heard you utter
momma
Sadly, for me, it was short of Utopia
It's not my place to love you, only
shelter you
It's so hard for you these words are
so new
To tell you no, I'm not your mother
Who does that satisfy The system, no
other
You grew to love and to rely upon
me
And now that you leave what do I
see?
Confusion or sadness: A new face to
learn
That is your mother. The system has
had its turn
I wave good-bye trying to hold in the
fear
But I promise myself I won't
interfere
I won't see you again though I'll
never forget
The precious months of love, to you,
I am in debt
My love has made you strong, giving
a healthy start
And my memories of you shall
remain in my heart
I know you'll survive, if only just
barely
Systems and courts, we must treat
them fairly
To be with your mother is their main
goal
Though I'll keep searching for the
slightest loop-hole
Neither money nor back ground does

a mother make
A biological answer is all they can take

Mary Kay Uslick
THE PRECIOUS GIFT
The gift that you gave me doesn't have to be wrapped in pretty paper or a fancy bow.

It's not my birthday or Christmas
In fact it's not any special day at all

Your precious gift that you gave me is your friendship, your kindness and understanding

But most of all you have given me your love
That grows with inside of me. The gift you gave me will not be forgot
Just like you

Lori J Gillespie
THE UNLOVED
There is no life, no grace,
in this cold, unfeeling place,
where I once would never
wander—
now I only sit, and ponder.

How wondrous was the feeling,
when it left my senses reeling,
but reminders of the pain
bring it back to me again.

Bitter storm inside my heart
has no wisdom to impart.
Where I once found warmth
and cheer,
now is loneliness and fear.

Had I not loved so truly,
I would not be hurt unduly.
Now my heart cries out in pain,
for I know I love again.

Joyice Bernice Young-Brown
WATER HAT

My son praise playing in water with paper Ask Him "what are you doing" me make it rain. Jesus send rain in Noah Days. Jesus baptize in river Jordan. Me make to enjoy I make rain mommie.

There was a little boy playing in water. It remind him of Jesus walking on the water. Water he play in, "Oh" How! he love the water where Elohim (God) send the rains in Noah days. Day-night to make himself happy he wore a water hat, made of paper, everywhere the water hat went "it was raining" over his head. John the Baptist "baptize Jesus" in River Jordan, and the town folks said: "We" don't see why? You need a water hat. I make it rain to enjoy as Jesus gave peace never asking for much just believe in Him John 3:16 for Elohim (God) so loved the world, that He gave His only begotten son that whosoever believeth in Him should not perish, but have everlasting life. My water hat a gift from Him Jesus Christ . . . !

Jon C Crosby
EL DEBARGE

To Tom Clarke, Both father and friend.

Over mountains,
lit by the moon—
On toward the valley,
the valley of doom—
Rode a hundred men at large,
Such was the last ride,
of El Debarge—
With sabers drawn,
that pierced the night—
That rendered men brave
with fright,
Over land the sun would
come soon—
On toward the valley,
the valley of doom—
Over thundering hooves
the dust would rise—
And settled upon those
who had lost their lives,
A battle so savage
as was the toll—
Those who lived,
lost their soul—
A hundred ghosts
Now lead the charge,
That sealed the fate,
of El Debarge . . .

Elnora Claycomb
LONELY LEAF . . .
As the leaves fall from the trees;
They went down, slowly hitting the ground.
Then one leaf went in another direction,
Just like you and me.

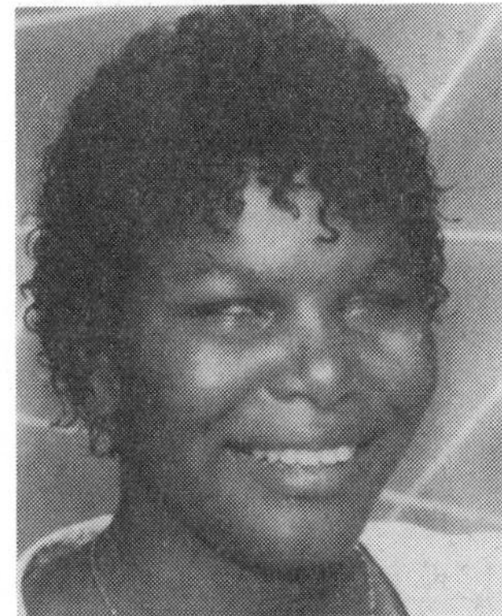

Tabbatha Denise McQueen

Tabbatha Denise McQueen
THE DREAM

This poem is dedicated to Uncle Hayward, Daddy, my family and most of all Mrs. Lonnye DeSue for encouraging me to keep writing and not to stop.

As I lay in bed some nights, As I wait for the broad daylight, I think of what I must give! And the dream that we should all live. It brings to mind you see, the one who helped to find peace. Yes! his name is Dr. King.

And we are all happy, Because he let freedom ring! Just as he did, we should do too. And we should be blessed. By the true Lord and King. So the dream isn't just a fantasy. For it has a meaning to you and me. So the dream that we are living, shouldn't just be at night. We should try to have the peace, And share the dream with a non-violent fight.

Robert J Holling
SEPARATION

To the three most beautiful children a Father could have. Stacy, Cynthia and Jeff.

We don't get along and you want me to leave.
But what will become of my children?
You say it's time for lawyers and agreements.
But what will become of my children?
You got the fridge and I the stove.
But what will become of my children?
Can I still see them, hug them and hold them?
Can I tell them of the great ache in my heart?
Can I tell them Dad will be there for them?
You go your way and I'll go mine.
But what will become of my children?

Marcia Williams
FLIGHTLESS
In my mind, my dreams take wing,
And who would ever know,
How much time, I drift along,
Where does a dreamer go?

I have soared, and I have fallen,
Now, flightless am I,
If only I can keep on running,
Until once again, I learn to fly.

But who can see, my faded dreams,
Or know the hopes I've known,
Only I, the dreamer knows,
How far away I've gone.

Sharon J Burns
WHISPERED LOVE
Whisper me
a song
And sing it
in the morning,
while I rest my head
beside you,
gently love me
in the dawning.
And when the time has come
for us both to have to part,
Whisper me a love song
To keep within my heart.

Tamara Gilson
MAN IN BLACK

I dedicate this poem to Chris, my husband.

Man in black. Man in black.
You're not John Wayne. You're not Johnny Cash.
Here you are in the hot hot desert wearing black.

I don't know where you have been.
I don't where you are going.
Man in black. Man in black.

I saw you picking up cigarette butts.
Man in black. Man in black.

I saw you checking machines for change.
Man in black. Man in black.

I have heard some say "You eat out of the trash."
Man in black. Man in black.
Some have said "You have a big wad of cash."
Man in black. Man in black.

Your face is so expressionless.
Man in black. Man in black.
Are you one of our country's homeless?
Are you one of our Viet Nam veterans?
Are you one of those unfortunates victimized by society?
Man in black. Man in black.
May God bless you man in black.

R M (Dusty) Rhoads
LIFE'S FRIENDS

To Friends

It's been my pleasure I must say,
To live among you day by day.
To share your good times and your bad,
I've had lots of laughs and I've been sad.

Through it all perhaps you know,
My soul has had some time to grow.
And in this time I've learned to share,
The love and concern that says I care.

I seek no bargain with the Lord,
Nor do I expect any great reward.
I only wish as through life I plod,
To be accepted by you and God.

Carol Ann Parsons
BILL DOESN'T LIVE HERE ANYMORE

This poem is in loving memory of my brother, William Anderson Bradford, July 16, 1946-July 23, 1988, who died very suddenly. I thank God for him, and all the memories.

Let me tell you about my
brother, Bill,
we used to have such fun as
children,
We never stayed still—
I remember the time he put tar
on my bicycle seat,
And when he tied me up in a chair,
Boy, was that ever neat!
But things have changed a lot
since then,
We have both grown up, and gone
our own ways, we were both so
wrapped up in our own little worlds,
To do a better job of keeping in
touch, but now it's too late, cause
God's called him home.
So, if anyone asks, Bill doesn't live
here anymore, he's gone to a far
better place where he'll call home.
So, my friends, I have some advice
for you, go home tonight and take
your brother or sister in your arms
and hold them tight, tell them how
much you love them, cause tomorrow
just might be too late

Ms Tempie R Land
THANKS

Friendship is a blessing . . I am truly thankful . . . for you Cecil . . . Stay positive . . . Be happy. My love always Tempie.

Have I thanked you lately, for being so thoughtful and kind . . .
For doing all of the little things, that give me peace of mind. . .
Have I thanked you, oh my darling for being my friend . .
for caring when I wanted and truly needed a friend . . . .
Oh how often, I've wanted to simply give you me . . . .
To share unspoken emotion, so profoundly and yet, remain free to be . . .
And if I haven't thanked you, my

darling for permitting me to feel and share, the blessing of your friendship before . . . .
Permit me to tell you now, my Dearest . . . . . .
THANKS

Jamie Kesler
I LOVE YOU
I love you
With all my heart
I hope you love me too!

My parents are not happy
With our relationship,
But I'll never let
That stop my feelings for you.

You are the greatest
One of a kind
I hope you
Stay that way.

I want to say it again and again
My love for you
Will never end!

Mildred Quine Dennis
EACH YELLOW BUTTERCUP
I awoke with the dawn,
And watched the sun come up.
Then saw where fairies' dewy lips,
Had kissed each yellow buttercup.

Then when the day had passed,
And the twilight began,
I saw where the sandman
Had closed them all again.

Kathleen Owen Alba
OLE GREY HOUSE

This poem is dedicated to my Dad, Allen Owen, for being both mother and father to me and giving me my memories that I will cherish forever growing up in the ole grey house.

I passed by an ole grey house
Just the other day,
So I went to take a closer look
Remembering when there I was a child at play.
The house was now empty, so all around I could see
But more than childhood games
That ole grey house had loving memories.
memories of a time when life was just a game,
But looking at that ole grey house
Somehow it wasn't quite the same.
The house that once looked so big and so tall
And the trees that stood next to it
Were not really that big at all.
My heart was saddened and the tears did fall
But what I was really missing
Wasn't that ole grey house at all.
It was the memories of a man
Who cared for me like no other
For this man was everything to me
Thank you God for this man——My father!

Nancy J Bell
TOYS
Toys, toys, everywhere
On the floor, on the stairs
And even in the chairs

Trucks, cars, buses, boats
Of yellow, blues land reds
I even find them in their beds

Oh! How they keep busy
With all their toys
By now you know
I have little boys

One day there will be
No toys upon the floor
For they will be
Boys no more

They will grow and turn into men
And I will want them
To be little again

Ethel J Thomas
TO SAY THAT I CAN'T
"To say that I can't," are negative words
But to me it's a challenge, so that's unheard.
To say that I can't climb the ladder, because it's too tall,
I did try to climb it and yes I did fall.
I picked myself up and tried it again
And I made it this time, with a big grin.

As I was crossing the road I heard someone cry out,
Don't go over there, I just had a fight!
I went on over and crossed the road, and I did see
The sight that I was told.
I said in a very loud voice, this is not right!
You all must make peace, and never never fight.

Someone asked me, "how did you do that?"
I said, "You see I have wisdom from God, and you can have it too."

"To say that I can't" are fighting words to me,
It really just brings out the very best in me.

Kimberley Maria Anderson-Meyer

Kimberley Maria Anderson-Meyer
PRECIOUS MOMENTS

To my loving husband, Larry Meyer

Take me where the sea grows warm
where you can walk on the Earth's green form.
Let us rise to the misty tip
and taste the moisture upon our lips.
Will you follow or shall I?
Whatever we do shall not die!
We thrive on Nature's good taste
So, let us use good judgement
and not put her to waste.
Hold me close
and we will grow through the years
for our Love will conquer all our fears.
And may Nature grow strong and old
for her secrets will never unfold.
These precious moments
will always be in our hearts
to share this among us
will help us from drifting apart.

Donna M Lynch
WORDS UNSPOKEN

I dedicated this poem to my son, Ryan, whom I love with all my heart, Mommy

If only my little arms could reach you,
I know my loving heart would too.

It makes me sad to see your eyes of blue
filled with despair.
Although you are all tangled up inside,
let me know that you care.

I was sent to you from up above, because Mommy and you made me out of love.

Let me into your life, together we should be.
For now I am a part of you and you a part of me.

With my body so helpless and frail, take me into your arms, so big and strong.

Because with your strength Daddy,
I can carry on.

David W Riggs
TIME
It is the remains of creation and grief,
Something that was never sewn
Into the dizzy fragments of a patchwork quilt;
Defined in terms of truth and philosophy;
or, for the sense of novelty,
Placed in a bottle as a tasty topping
for crabmeat.

Time is something that owes no fealty to country
Holds no consistency of opinion
Or blame for previous actions.
It would be a vain attempt for love as an artist
To paint it in a memorybook.

In truth, all that we can say in truth
Is that we simply must humor it
And let it work at will,
Being unable to stay for such a thing
That shows not even caustic humor,
at man's mouselike
attempts
To place it in the tick-tock order of a clock.

Wanda Ann Leoncini
INFATUATION
Please don't ever say no—
for I never want to let you go,

Everytime I'm with you—
touching me the way you do,
each and every time,

Sets my body on fire—everlasting desire,

Take me in your arms,
Take me by your side—for we will never have to hide,

In the dark and in the light—
everything seems so bright,

Never wanting to part—Always having you in my heart,

Remembering Good-bye is not the END—
It's just going to start all over again . . .

Shirley Eastwood
ENCHANTMENT OF A NIGHTTIME SKY
There's a mystical haze surrounding the splendor of a lover's moon sailing high.

The exquisite beauty radiates a magical spell as the moonbeams draw nigh.

The silver stars embrace the magic of the moon's ever enchanting spell.

The wonders in the night sky reveal the awesome beauty of which they tell.

The mystical nighttime sky silently shields and enfolds the hushed and waiting earth.

The moon's magic spells embrace the universe, until dawn, as a new day gives birth.

Angi Young
LONELY NIGHTS
I can still see your face in the mist of the evening
I sometimes hear your voice saying 'I Love You."
But then I remember you leaving
And suddenly I feel so blue.

This is a world full of lonely nights
Broken hearts and forgotten dreams,
Everyone having continuous fights
Where nothing is as it seems.

I think back to the days
When you were mine and I was yours,
Then my days turned to gray
Our lives together closed like two huge doors.

Shutting out one another
You were no longer there for me.
We were no longer together
I felt this wasn't how it was to be.

So we said our good-byes
And went our separate ways,
You never told me any lies
But you left me with lonely nights.

Connie M Radcliff
MOTHERHOOD

To Bonni and the babies, For filling my heart with Love . . .

Heaven, the home of our Father above,
A wonderful haven of kindness and love,
Workshop of Jesus & Angels galore,
Blessings they send out to all,
Rich & Poor . . .

Bestowed on the woman,
A blessing so grand,
The sight and the touch of a wee baby's hand,
A feeling so wondrous,
And love so complete
The beauty of motherhood,
Treasured and sweet!

Paula Turnage
REFLECTIONS
My heart aches
Because I'm thinking of you.
I'm not sure how much more I can take,
Or what else I can do.

I cry and cry
And try to comfort myself throughout the night.
Sometimes I feel I will die
But pray that things will be alright.

You once held me with such security,
And kissed me with a taste of wine.
I long to once again have you near me
And to somehow make you mine.

But you've told me over land over
again
That you don't feel the same.
For some reason, I just won't
comprehend,
And it brings me so much pain.

Maybe somewhere down the road,
You'll love me again.
Or maybe when I'm old,
I'll forget what has been.

John Callaway
DEROS*

Date past and future from now,
not back to mythic times
when gods and heroes could be
Expected to fulfill a destiny
accepted, if detested,
without a plan for gallant
Return to lofty principles
of morality and war;
only a throbbing ache to get it
Over before a jagged remnant
of ceremonial bronze
shreds tender, sticky bones on
Seas wind-dark,
not with Olympic celebration,
but the agonizing ooze of death.

*"DEROS" was an acronym used by the U.S. Military during the Vietnam War to boost morale by having soldiers know when they could expect to leave the fighting and return home.

Debbie S Farr Lucas
SANTA

Dedicated to my two beautiful goddaughters, Courtney and Cassie Cook.

Santa was here but
now is gone?
No of course not
he lives on and on.

He is alive every day
and every night.
He sees you grow
strong and bright.

Santa is a spirit
and will always be
here and now as you
will see.

Jacklyn Mikalonis
SHADOWS ARE DARK

Shadows are dark
Shadows are bright
Shadows don't even come out at
night.

Shadows are big
Shadows are small
Without any sun there's none at all.

Mr Fern Mead
MOTHER AND FATHER

There is no other treasure
in the world,
Or any other
loving pearl.
From not a sister
or a brother,
But from a father
and a mother.
I'm really glad
love is not a crime,
'Cause I'd be in jail
for a lifetime.
For loving the ones
that created me,
For loving the best
there will ever be.
So thank you father
and thank you mother,
For being better
than all the others.

Lonnie E Robinett III
CANVAS OF MY MIND

To: Kari Lee, Love Ya forever baby!

I want to paint a picture with my
words.
Brushes and paints are not my kind
They don't do justice to the pictures
in my mind.
Fields of flowers and birds of the
wing
The pictures I paint I want you to
sing.
Beautiful people and a leaf on a tree
The world in my mind is truly free.
Parks in the city on the countryside
There is a place in my mind I go to
hide.
Waterfalls and snowcapped
mountains
In my mind there are magical
fountains.

Darlene L Cory
THE FACE IN SPACE

There is a face that is seen in space,
Its imprint makes you wonder,
Who carved this face so clear in
space?
It could not be a blunder.
Who carved the face on Mars with
such detail?
We see a forehead, nose, chin, eye
socket and eyeball.
Long hair frames one side of the face,
There's only one other like it I can
recall.
The face imprinted on the Shroud of
Turin,
Makes you think of this face seen on
Mars.
It is the face of Jesus who died for
our sins,
His face we see hanging amongst the
stars.
Just as an artist paints a picture for all
to see,
He then signs his name to the
Masterpiece so rare,
The face in space is there for man to
remember,
The Creator of the Universe so full of
love and care.

Alice Reimer
TO "ALLISON'S MEMORY"

This poem is dedicated to: "Allison's," Mom & Dad" and "Sister Lynn"

I'll never forget the 10th of
November,
The day your "Daddy" held you
up closer,
So "Grammy" could see you and
always remember.

You looked so "tiny" and "petite."
You were your "Mommy" in
repeat.
Tears began to fall down my face,
To think that "Our Lord" lent us
such a beautiful "Grace."

We all enjoyed you when you were
"small,"
And before no time at all, you
got so "tall."

A "beautiful girl" with blonde hair of
silk,
And eyes of "heavenly blue"
We should never take for granted
what "Our Lord" already knew.

And though we loved her for the
time she spent with us,
We knew some day "God" would
call her thus.

"Eight years" does not seem like
much,
But she had "wisdom," "faith"
and "God's Touch."
This was taught by her parents
"two,"
And now she has a sister to look
down to.

"She" was called by "Him" for safe
keeping,
Never to know the hurt or
weeping.
"Joy" will always be to her avail,
Like the song she sang,
"Jesus Loves Me" and "He" always
will.

David James Billman

David James Billman
MY LOVE FOR YOU!

To the one I loved. Golden Poet Award winner for 1989

When we met, not so long ago
I wanted, really wanted to let you
know
That I wanted to be more than
friends.

My feelings have not yet completely
changed
And yet this is true, my life is
rearranged
I know we can never be, but never;
never is an eternity.

The possibility of us grows day by
day
Each time we meet my heart grows,
my mind strays
Don't worry about me; if you go
your own way.

Together we could explore the world
The sights, the sounds, the pictures,
and words
You and I could make this world our
playground.
"United we stand, divided we fall,"
Stand with me now, we'll live for it
all
The words are all said, and I say them
with pride
And nothing, nothing at all can stop
my love for you,
The love I must hide!

Harven Teakam
ODE TO A FIREMAN

If I were a fireman,
no sweat nor any strain.
My days would be sliding down
poles,
and a hot and heavy cribbage game.

Once a week I'd get a check,
for washing down the truck.
And I'd wear a moustache and
stylish sideburns,
and cast my fate to luck.

If I were a fireman,
Christmas would be a joy.
I'd fix broken toys for tiny tots,
and remember when I was once a
boy.

But most of all I'd know,
baseball'd be my fun.
I'd coach little league, and play
softball,
and drink a beer on every home run.

You see it's not the roaring fire,
that makes a fireman cool.
It's the time and space, where a quiet
place,
and a chance to breathe will do.

Adlai Le Mont
THE SOURCE

With loving dedication, Jesus I submit myself to you by dropping the I and adding J-E-S-U-S.

I know that you're searching and
seeking yet to find that void
emptiness feeling somewhere left
behind,
tossed and scattered from pillars to
post, of relationships desired by
more than most.

Come to Me!

Since the world can't suffice: Just
Grab The Giant Mirror (NOW
REFLECT)
And open up your heart for there's
The Templed Being That Throbs
From That part . . . . . .

Here's My Hand!

It's just his Blood That Cleans and
Purifies the FLOOD, Yes grasp this
JC Cell float upstream. And Walk
into light eternal! Yes go to the
Director, follow the footsteps of the
source of life. Your movie, Where
Jesus is Starring and your lead double
. . . Yes seek thee 1st the provider of
all (THE VOID FILLER) Cast out
thine emptiness the devil.

Be Born Again!

Then be fulfilled and Bathe, Eat of
this Flesh and Drink of His Blood,
For the Glory of the Lord is
Jesus . . .
He is the New Birth!

And if it's a party you seek, JAM TO
HIS BEAT come party with a true
lover, Yes Dance with Jesus BUT let
Him Lead, Yes party
with JC the STAR. YOU WANT TO
SEE A SHOW, COME GLOW,
SHINE, GLOW, GLORY TO GOD,
CLAP YOUR
HANDS SING PRAISES TO HIS
NAME. And if you must get High, a

Buzz on Jesus is all you need, He's
higher than high (he's
thee rush eternal and a mind frame)
Yes get a fix on Jesus and live
forever! PATTERNS NO MORE,
STAY WITH JC THE
STRAIGHT AND NARROW FOR
HE LOVES YOU, IT'S NOT HARD
JUST TRUST/BELIEVE FOLLOW
THE BIBLICAL
map, CONFESS AND DO HIS
WORD . . . But To Find Yourself . . .
Delight IN HIM THEN CHECK
YOUR INNARDS
FOR HE LIVES IN YOU!
AMEN!

Loretta Kulwicki
SILENCE

"SILENCE" is dedicated to all hearing impaired children . . . especially, those I hope to help someday.

In the silence ever still,
A child stares out by the
window sill.
The child speaks not a single word.
Not a sound is to be heard.

Expressions appear on the child's
face,
And he begins to speak with
such a grace.
A grace that few really understand,
For the child speaks with his
hands.

The child is in a world of his own.
To us his signs are not well
known.
From his mouth not a whisper
leaks . . .
Sign language is how the child
speaks.

Rande J Sara Rose
STARTED OUT AS FRIENDS
Love is the feeling I feel when I
see you.
Love is what I know when I touch
your hand.
We feel the same when we say
goodby,
I never want to let you go.
But we pass it off as only
friends.
Inside we know only love could be
like this.
Feeling confused, not too sure
about love,
I just feel if I wasn't here, there
wouldn't be a problem.
No telling what a few stolen
moments can do to someone's brain.
Bending and twisting, leaving deep
scars in the heart.
A few more seconds, like a
lifetime of pain,
Swept into a tornado of thoughts.
I can't choose between love and
love and I can't really explain.
Sometimes love's better off when
it's not there, dead, never to be
thought of again.
At this point I don't know
whether I'm awake or
dreaming.
I wish you could see my tears of pain
babe, because you're making them
fall.
You made me cry because you
never let me know,
you made me wonder, I didn't know
if you loved, me too.
When I close my eyes all I see is
happiness, so maybe I should close
my eyes forever.
Feeling confused, not too sure about
love, I just feel if I wasn't here, there
wouldn't be a problem. No telling
what a few stolen moments can do to
a someone's brain. Bending and
twisting, leaving deep scars in the
heart.
Then, you told me you were falling
in love, and you have loved me
always, just as I you.
Well we started out as friends, now
we'll be together forever, in forever
true love.

Lynn Cazelet
FIFTH GRADE GIRL
Fifth grade girl, coming home from
school.
Hopes held high, life is like a jewel.
Sky so clear, wind in her hair.
Sun warms skin, she hasn't a care.

Her pace slows when nearing the
house.
Opening the door, quiet as a mouse.
Crossing the threshold alone again
today.
She stands in the foyer, nothing to
say.

Mom's sleeping upstairs, days after
days.
Dad's off at work, fighting evil
ways.
Dinner at six, most of the time.
Make Daddy's gin and tonic with a
twist of lime.

Older sister's angry at little sister
still.
Nothing new today, feelings we all
kill.
Any homework is done and it's time
for bed.
School tomorrow; home life's a
dread.

Leaving the house; morning is here.
School at last!, it gives her cheer.
Fifth grade girl goes to school to
quell.
Escapes family facade until the final
bell.

Nancy Ann Lopez

Nancy Ann Lopez
ANGUISH

I dedicate this poem to my parents, Richard and Justine Talley, for their never ending love and support.

My heart is broken,
Torn by strife.
My spirit is heavy
With the burdens of life.
My soul cries in anguish
For the loss of hope,
And I struggle for ways
For my spirit to cope.
But with my family's love
To light the way,
I will grow stronger
Day by day.

Dixie T Marlowe
THE MADWOMAN
I scream, I scream.
I wake in the morning,
I stretch in the cold and yawn.
I lay silent.
Inside, my screaming madwoman
jumps and throws herself around
crying,
"let me go, let me go!".
She tears at her skin,
scratches at the tears in her eyes,
pounds at the ground,
screams at the sky.
Her sister spirit sits and watches,
quietly.
Poor sister, poor sister,
there is no peace for you.
You are the delicate balance that
keeps us from collapsing.
You are the fire that burns and
suffers for us.
You are the Love that creates the
spark.
I, am the Love that fans it into flame.
We, are the Madwoman, who lays
quiet in the morning,
alone, with her thoughts.

Amy J Reading
A MAN

To my mother, my friend.

A man was at the subway station
today.
As he calmly walked through the
crowd,
He chose a few men.
"Follow me," he said,
but they didn't.

I saw him walk out to the street.
He was different.
A look of love and kindness
glowed in his eyes.
Someone yelled at him.
The schreeching of wheels was
heard.
That night the headlines said
he died in a car crash.

Days passed.

Today I saw a man at the subway
station.
He calmly walked through the
crowd.
He didn't speak,
but they followed.

Russell James
ODE TO LOVE
One day you came into my heart
but before you were through it was
torn apart.
The days and nights we spent
together
floating on the wind as does a
feather.
"I love you," we said time after time,
but all that changed on the turn of a
dime.
"It just won't work," you said to me,
and all at once I began to see . . .
Love is such a fragile thing
it made me dance, it made me sing.
But when all the dancin' and the
singin' was done,
I realized love was just for fun.

Maxine Lewis
TRIBUTE TO A KING (ELVIS)
This is a tribute to a king,
The greatest man to ever sing.
A man who never be forgotten,
Who never wrote a song that was
rotten.
This is a tribute to a star,
Who made movies near and far.
A man in his own world,
Who was never without a girl.
This is a tribute to a friend,
One of the talented that's ever been.
A man who wrote a lot of rock,
Made a hit with every stock.
This is a tribute to a man,
We'll never see again.
A man who is layin'
But his songs will never stop playin'!

Daniel J Murphy
MIRROR, MIRROR

For my dear wife Sheri

The mirror is true, the mirror is cold.
It often tells a story that has never
been told.
You lie to your family, you lie to
your friends
But, when you look in the mirror,
that's when it all ends.
The truth that it bleeds is sometimes a
pain
As it looks right through you again
and again.
You look in again and what do you
see?
The thing you've called mirror
Is now called me.

Denise M Borchin
THE CHOICE OF LIFE
High as the heavens
and deep as the sea—
My love for God, has grown to be.
Strong you may say
and mighty is he—
To Abyss the wicked Satan,
And throw away the key.

In the beginning the fruitage was
good
In the middle of paradise, Adam and
Eve stood,
Their hearts full of love and their
lives were complete,
When the challenge of Satan Eve did
not beat.
So down came the dragon, the one
called the beast,
and with all his hatred the world
increased.

So now as we stand in the time of the
end,
Whether Satan or God, only one is
our friend.
My advice to you brother is simple
you see,
Praise the heavenly Father and live
eternally.

Christine Downs
TEARS
Tears
of laughter
Tears
of pain
Black umbrellas
pouring rain
Feeling blue
Seeing red
Collar stains
half-empty bed
Late nights
blind eyes see
On his ring
a stranger's key
Fear of loss
chance of gain
Half-baked truths
lover's pain
Final words
new seeds to sow
Sometimes half
can be whole

Christine B Bukovsky
INNER SELF

Terror and turmoil
Love, Hate and Lust
When you look in
my eyes I wonder
do you
see

Huntley P Christie
LIFE'S REALITY

Tell me truly bard of numbers,
Life a web of endless dreams,
For a dream is dead that slumbers;
And reality is not what it seems.

Life is real and death is certain,
And blessed Time is finest goal,
Death will draw the final curtain,
But can He claim the immortal soul.

In this world of endless conflict,
We must fight until we die;
Fight with sword just to inflict,
Punishment to injustice, pain and lie.

Climb each hill, ascend each
mountain,
With His Majesty up on high;
Search each crag and find the
fountain,
Drink God's blessings from the sky.

Many times you will slip and falter,
As you strive to reach the goal;
Your will and way you must not
alter,
Trust in God to preserve your soul.

Donna Marie Anselmo
RIDING A DREAM

riding a dream
through magical lands
long ago forgotten.

intricate coverings
weaving their way
across a misty border

as the conqueror's sword,
drawn from its scabbard,
yields an entrance

to the carnage
anticipating
its release.

Deborah A Ferris (Robinson)
WHY DID YOU DO IT

Sitting quietly I wondered why
Who were you to decide to die
You were so young and full of life
I feel you stabbed me with a knife
You were so selfish, I hope you
know
It's God's decision when it's your
time to go
We went to your funeral, the tears
dropped like rain
You couldn't imagine the hurt and
the pain
Your family and friends all gathered
around
We watched them put you into the
ground
I wish you had gone to someone for
help
We had no idea how bad you must
have felt
When it came time to say goodbye
I couldn't believe you chose to die

Brett W Bartholomaus
IN MORE PEACEFUL TIMES

I seem to recall before ambition
came,
Lazing on afternoon meadows,
beneath skies once blue and clear;
or chatting on some friendly porch,
smoking pipe in hand,
Once, in more peaceful times that
were.

The recollection of bonfires, sea
shells and wind swept beach,
Hand in hand walks with a woman
true;
of family unity around a glittering
Christmas tree,
Once, in more peaceful times that
were.

I seem to recall when honesty was
but a spoken word,
The shrill morning song of some tiny
bird;
of serenity before ambition came;
Once, in more peaceful times that
were.

Now that ambition has come and
gone,
Youth is but ne'er a jaded dream;
And I wish for life's simple joys that
once were ours.
Once, in more peaceful times that
were.

Evangeline Katranis

Evangeline Katranis
THE LOVE OF NEW ENGLAND'S 12 MONTH CALENDAR YEAR

TO MY RELATIVES—Son James J. Katranis, Angeline (Katranis) Lakis (Sister), John J. Katranis (Brother), Stephen J. Lakis (Nephew)— COUSINS ARE: Angeline (Dumas) Scombul, Helen C. (Dumas) Belitsos, Catherine (Dumas) Mastacouris, Peter C. Dumas—

January is a month that's very cold
an' we know that February there's
much snow for Jack Frost does not
get tossed nor lost, until March brings
forth Spring and April comes on to
let us know that May without say
helps flowers bloom an' June is the
month when everything booms.

July comes in and as freedom rings—
Summer comes into sight with much
delight.

August we do prepare robustly for
the months ahead an' September at
times brings on Indian Summer and
from there we do limber into
October—leaves turn and as we greet
November which is the harvesting
month—we then with much joy take
on the last month which is
December . . .

Festivities begin awaiting for the
Special Day "CHRISTMAS."

The Nation celebrates . . . why?
IN MEMORY OF
CHRIST'S BIRTH!

Pauline Kohlmetz
LATE DAY

All these dames
They're enough to give you a pain
They're old enough to be using a
cane
They're running from one place to
another
Giving what little they've got to
playing tame.
Who could be the blame?
The rain will come
The rain will go
But these dames will still be playing
the game
Which gives me a pain in the neck.
I'm sure I'm not the blame
Of all this shame.
Where did they get their training?
Sure not books
The pages run out too soon. I'm sure
Regardless of how it looks
I prefer to just look on.
I'm sure it's out of my class of study.

Mr Pierre Lamirande

Mr Pierre Lamirande
SEPTEMBER MOODS

I dedicate this poem to the woman that I love with all my heart. To Ms. Claire Brouillette. Without her my life would be an empty one.

Fall . . . upon us
Like a long gray coat
I see the emptiness in men's eyes
So cold and bleak
Empty autumn nights
Along the road to nowhere

Fall . . . upon us
The solitude of seasonal living
Going through the motions
notwithstanding
We live to live
Not really living

Fall . . . upon us
Like multicolored leaves
Our moods change
A transformation of the heart
We shelter ourselves from the
elements
Dreaming of better days

Fall . . . upon us
Our dreams fall to the ground
Only to wither away
We are but a mere spectre on a cold
September night
We are not allowed to choose
From these September moods

Norma Burley
THE NEW HEAVEN AND EARTH COMES

The Conquering Lion from the
Tribe of Judah, Root of David has
come.
Blessed golden seals of Revelation
open more now to be Divinely
revealed.
Throne of God and Lamb with no
need for night, lamp, or sun.
Offspring of David, heavenly
River of Pure Water of Life is
being unveiled.
Everyone who conquers faith will
inherit all these Living Waters
of spiritual desires.
As God I am of you and you are
of my very breath,
You, who are unfaithful, your
doom is in the sulphured lake of
fire.
This very act for misdeeds is to
be known as your Second Death.
The new and Holy Jerusalem now
presently, divinely descends
from the skies.
'Having the Glory of God: and her
light was like unto a stone.'
Most precious the pyramid even
like a jasper stone as brilliant
crystal lies.
Twelve foundation stones with
the written names of twelve
apostles of the Lamb Lone.
The city itself is a pure,
transparent gold like a mirrored
glass.
Twelve golden gates made of
pearls—each gate from a single
pearl of white,
And the very main street is
purely gold with a reflective
crystal mass.
The glory of God and the Lamb of
Life give it continual LIGHT.
Nothing permitted inside—only
names in the Lamb's Book of
Life that lasts.
Blessed who have the right to
enter through the gates of the
city structure.
To eat fruit from the Blessed Holy
Tree of life now not past.
Alpha and Omega, the beginning
and the end, the first and the
last Architecture.

Max S Banks
I WAS BLIND

I was blind, I couldn't see
All I thought about was me.
I found out to my surprise
The world was more than you can
see.
It is as nice as it sounds,
As good as it tastes,
As sweet as it smells,
As lovely as it feels and want it to be.
Then I prayed and thought again
Of life, of God, of living too.
Live and learn, repent a lot
Then we'll know what we have got.

I am still blind, but now I know,
There is a place for me
In the world you cannot see.
You don't have to pity me,
I am more than just my eyes.
I thank God I am alive
That is why I am not sad
I make the most of what I have.

David Lee Bell
TIME

Somewhere ahead our destiny awaits
us,
of when or where we can not know.

For we can take only one breath at a
time,
and then try to follow our hearts—as
best we know.

We wonder and very often we think;

do we belong where we are today?

Or is it just our own faith in what we believe to be true, that helps us throughout our days.

Scott M Miller
MEMORIES SHALL NEVER FADE

To Donna C.! "The happiness we shared shall always be inbedded in my heart"

We laughed together
and
cried together,
we have memories
that can't be
erased,
but only shared,
and as I remember this day
and as I offer you
these roses
let the memories
grow
with you,
as our love that
we once shared
fades away

Joan Mazuca
LIFE
When I was young, I used to dream
Life was great
Life was fun
But now I see what life has done
It's made my dreams turn into dust
And my heart and soul has begun to rust
Life what have you done to me?
Why have you made this misery?
Please set me free, set me free
And make me like I used to be
So full of love and happiness
Oh that's when life was at its best
So care free and full of fun
But now I see what life has done

Gina Pannozzo
WHAT A DREAM CAN DO
Dreams will give me wings
to fly like the birds,
and soar above the clouds.
To reach for the sky
just like the butterfly,
it will give me the chance
to chase my own rainbows,
to celebrate life and to grow.
So I'll take the time
to soar on my dreams,
to celebrate me and to be free.
I'll be free like the wind,
and soaring high
like the butterfly,
Yes—just for today
I will be that butterfly!
If I dare to dream,
love will do the rest.
The fire's burning in my heart
I can't take second best,
through the eyes of love,
nothing's as hard as it may seem
if I have the dare to dream.
I dream of the moon,
I dream of you
and I dream of me,
I also dream of things that cannot be.
I dream a lot,
and maybe that's bad,
but dreaming makes me happy
whenever I feel sad.
To dream is to live
and to live is to be,
so without my dreams,
I wouldn't be me!
The little butterfly
is my hopes,
my dreams, and my desires.
Oh butterfly, butterfly,
please take me with you
to search for places higher.
If I dare to dream,
love will do the rest,
nothing's as hard as it may seem
because I have the dare to dream.
Now, here's some advice,
if you have dream
don't let it go,
don't forget it
just reach for your goal.
No matter what people might tell you
no matter what they will say,
if it is your dream,
don't let it stray.
If you dare to dream
love will do the rest.
Practice makes perfect
it's all up to you
there's nothing that anyone can do,
except you.
Through hardship or turmoil,
through times that are tough,
if you dare to dream
love will do the rest.
The fire's burning in your heart
you can't take second best.
So no matter how far away
your accomplishments may seem,
if you want it enough,
just follow your dream
and love will do the rest.
Because dreams really do give you wings
to be the best that you can be! !

Betty C Schultz
LOVE'S FACE

This poem dedicated to all who love without conditions and inspired by country-western singer/performing artist Willie Nelson's Face

LOVE'S FACE

For years this face remained
Though constantly shaped/changed
Somewhat worn but unstained

FROM

Everyday life of stress and strain
Keeping body/mind healthy and sane
Amid life's joys, sorrows and pain

ONE SEES

In this face natural and pure
Yet quiet, gentle and secure
The strength needed to endure

Bobby C Poet & Lyrics Writer
Col Bobby Clark
THE BEAUTIFUL MAIDEN'S LAMENT
Yes, after they cut him down,
They placed him, lifeless, upon the ground.

His life ended, never no more,
Life at one time, he did adore.

The beautiful maiden with auburn hair,
That day, was there.

Knowing that she had done him wrong,
Hearing within her mind, their favorite song.

She knew now, too late, his true love,
Was as pure as the heavens above.

Looking back at the times they shared,
Protecting her, showing that he cared.

Willing to go that extra mile,
Asking little, maybe just a beautiful smile.

Oh! How she wished that she had not turned away,
He would be alive, now, this very day.

He was so kind, brave, and bold,
There now, he lay, his life ended, cold.

She knelt there, by his side,
Reaching, touching his hand, and cried.

Louis Hogan
TONI'S BIRD

To my Sister Toni

From Brundidge to Miami on the wings of a baby blue thunderbird,
The passing wind is all that could be heard.

We rolled along like the wabash cannon ball,
Toni would greet other motorists with a hi you all.

That car ran good and sure is fast,
On the road everything except big trucks and v w's we passed.

We raced along with an eye out for smokey the bear,
We didn't get caught we were lucky for we knew he was there.

John A Pacheco
DEATHTRAP

To Martha Hertzog with love

Look at the woman look in her eyes
Death comes dark as leather flesh
on the vile look in her eyes
Look out for she'll take you by surprise
She'll conceive you and deceive you
With her eyes.

Don't believe her or her lies
She'll do this to you by & by
Don't dare take a chance with her Love
Don't even try sooner or later
She'll cause you harm she might even cost you an arm.

Then that's when you'll take alarm
she may cry & beg for forgiveness
Once you fall entangled by her Web
You feel that you want to die, But you don't know why? You fell and now
you're going through Hell.

Look out for her 'cause she's a living Deathtrap she'll be wrapped into you
And you into her but those things happen and it depends where you're at
So watch out for the female that's called—Deathtrap.

Guy L Mann
WAR
War is like fire "it kills."
War kills plants.
War kills animals
War kills peoples.
War is like fire "it kills."
War is ugly.
War stays for ever.
Why is there war?
War is like fire "it kills."
When is war going to end?
When people go to war they die.
War will never end.
War is like fire "it kills."
War can do some good for us.
Then it can not do us that good.
War kills things that nature made for us.

Betty Silver
THE ANATOMY OF A ROSE
Beauty and a perfume scent
does not express the
anatomy of a Rose,
The silky texture and
delicate petals, a life
like beauty, the many
colors, may come close to
describe the anatomy of a
Rose.
Soon, all that will fade
No longer to a place to grow, wilts all
of Nature's creatures:
Never to see a Rose
and all the other
Beauty,
That glow in the Sun, sway gently
with the summer breeze;
Before long the end
Will come, None will grow
or move
like the end of a
movie
Finis,
The End

Helena Carling-Sletteland
GRAMMARRED
If I had a hammer
I'd slam'er
at grammer!

Kerry Munroe
THE SEARCH
I looked in all your houses.
And until the last one, I thought I would never find you.

Looking through the window,
into the leaves bathed in Sunday morning sunshine,
I found my answers.

I think it was in the silence that I heard your presence,
reaching far beyond my expectations.

In the other houses there was too much noise.
They tried to interpret you with their opinions and judgements.

It clouded my mind to try and listen.
I thought it was a sum of all that you are.

So much I heard angered me.
So much I couldn't agree with.

But in the silence I heard, I felt, I saw

that you are a friend not to be feared,
just to be trusted.

When I don't know what to do,
I lay my problems at your feet,
and ask you to lead the way.

Joel E Hudgins
A DAPPLED HORSE CALLOPED BY

This poem is dedicated to all those people who have given up hunting.

A dappled horse galloped by,
Its rider upright, head held high—
A red coat donned in sharp contrary
To nature's wintered sanctuary.

The fox bedecked in grayish-brown,
A color-coded camouflage from
hound.
Yet in the scheme of man's dink
mind
The scent of fate leaves evidence
behind;
The chase then falls below the line of
grace—
For God cannot sanction such a race.

Catalina Maria Walsh
PAST PERFECTIONS

To my Family and Friends, and to those who said that the Pen is mightier than the Sword.

There lay a time of forever
smiles and crystal
falcons.
Waving of comradeship thy enemy
awaits. Alas! there is wonder of
graceless
Energy. Can they seek tunnels of
shapeless pleasures?
Yet a child's footsteps grasp
the lunar escapades.

Faith in a vise. Destruction of
Dance, slumber and rain fight the
truth of a journeyman's torch. Cry
you foolish beast! for I am an inquiry
of hearts, a passage of worlds to seek.
Come Hatred! Thy concrete mending
is seldom a thought. Why are we
lights of the many rampages
of obscurity?

Denis P Burds
A THOUGHT

Dedicated to an old friend.

You are a fountain of bubbling spring
water;
Ever flowing through my placid
thoughts,
Through meadow grass, and over
sunny pebbled ravine.
Rippling and laughing in an ever
downward journey;
Always taking the course of least
resistance.
Through moonlit night you travel on,
Over craggy rock and sandy riverlet.
You reflect the golden light of night
onto white beaches;
And give life to all you touch.
You are the unwearying traveler,
That runs faster now—through
shaded forest.
Ever downward—so pure and clear,
Past mighty pines to the jagged rocky
ledge—
Where it is your destiny to fall
In silent white mist to the canyon
floor.
There you whisper your inaudible
words of life
To the pool you have formed;
Nestled in shaded serenity;
And there I bathe.

Vivian Gower
STONE COUNTY

Sunshine and summer showers on
the rolling hills
Timber on the mountains laced with
many colored frills.
Ornamental flowers growing here
and there
Natural beauty, a gift of God for
everyone to share
Enormous valleys, creeks, and
springs in this land so dear to me.
There's pretty scenery everywhere
in picturesque Sone County.

April Renfro
THE UNSEEN GIANT

A great giant stands before me
His arms are great and round,
His color like a tan is a golden
brown.
His outfits change as the seasonal
fashions do
From an emerald green to a ruddy
red.
His deep stand seems to go miles
underground to the center of the earth
His music is the music of a
symphony orchestra,
He lets many people share his home.
His flowing movements can be a
graceful ballet
He graciously gives sweet smelling
delicacies for us to eat
His arms stretch towards the sun as if
it were his god
Who is this giant you overlook and
never see?
But the tree . . . . the unseen giant.

LaVana Buck
SPRING IN THE MOUNTAINS

Come, take a walk with me.
All the wonders of nature, we will
see.

The dogwood tree with her blossoms
white,
Is truly a beautiful sight.

The dandelions with yellow faces,
Are all lining up in their places.

The squirrels are peeking from their
nests.
Gathering food, & chattering at all
the rest.

The birds are singing loud and clear
Making us believe that spring is
really here.

The wild roses are everywhere—
Their perfume fills the air.
Ah, what a wonderful sight.
Fills one's heart with delight.

Mother Nature has so many things to
share.
We find them in the mountains and
everywhere.

So—did you enjoy the walk with me?
And all the signs of spring, we did
see?

Carol Huey
THE GREAT RACE

To win a race you must begin,
Then continuous running to reach the
end,
Successfully run you will reach your
goal,
But without the beginning, there is no
race told.

Yvonne Jerome
MY MIND'S LOVE

My mind's love comforts me,
Abides within, hauntingly.
Resemblances to other faces,
Lives that touched with minute
traces.
Smiles, laughter, sorrow, tears,
Joys, kindness, closeness, fears—
All combine, good and bad,
Relationships we could have had.
An image formed, embodying,
Epitomizing lost longing.
There to conjure at whim's delight
And follow into the dark of night.
My mind's love comforts me,
Abides within reassuringly,
Encouraging me to romanticize,
With never any sad good-byes.

Aileen Fielding

Aileen Fielding
MIRACULOUS SPRING IN THE HILLS

To all my friends and relatives who have lived near, or now live near Esculapia Hollow in the Ozark Hills.

On earth's revolving schedule, not by
mere happenstance,
Mother Nature sent her bright,
dazzling, restorative sunbeams
Out to play peek-a-boo, brighten the
dormant hills, and dance,
Enjoying the elixir of the radiant,
sparkling natural streams.

When the irradiating sunbeams were
tired at sunset,
Mother Nature sent them to rest and
repose;
While the silvery, soft raindrops
united to form a rivulet.
Then suddenly a revitalized life
arose.

The sunshine and raindrops aided by
the Almighty Hand,
Touched the inert, latent, lifeless, dry
sod,
Infusing new life and new hope into
all the land.
Revitalization was taking place in
each clod.

During spring's resurrection, dead
vegetation became alive.
The redbuds and violets bloom by the
rocky ledges.
Through the Omnipotent, the hills
began to revive,
Surrounded by the emerald hazelnut
hedges.

In the hills there is balm to make the
spirit well,
Everything that a wanting soul can
aspire.
Its panoramic beauty seems to be a
seasonal carrousel,
A spiritual and physical hope to rise
higher and higher.

Ivory R McCollum
A MORNING SYMPHONY

To Virginia R. Taylor

The wood-pecker drummed a merry
tune upon an old dead limb.
The little brook danced along
the way
Full from brim to brim.
The rooster said "how do you
do"
As he flapped his heavy wings.
A moment later "good morning
too,"
To-day all nature sings.
The cardinal made a splash
of red
Against a sky of blue.
Cheer-up, cheer-up, the robin called,
The sun will soon break through.
The crow gave a hearty
ha-ha-ha
This is a wonderful day.
The blue jays in a quarrelsome
mood said
Go-away go-away.
It's great to be alive said the
old milk cow,
She with a gentle moo,
Down by the pond the
bull-frog croaked
Me too—me too.

Michael Bowler
THE DYING WOMAN

Dedicated to my mother, Beverly, whose battle with mental health institutions and the everyday toils of life could go on for all eternity.

It has been said that time heals
all wounds.
She would think the line a bit
thin,
Her mind holds strange tunes—
of anguish past endured.
Although life has become more
fulfilling,
She is still not yet cured.
And though maybe someday
willing—to trade it all away—
For a chance at restful peace,
She lives but for her children
today;
Until their troubles all but cease.
As reward for all her generous
tasks—
The showing of appreciation is all
she asks.
Although little is shown or given;
Still she strives to make their day a
bright one—
Despite her own deep depression and
unrivaled fatigue.

We all must die, are her days almost done?
Is she indeed, the dying woman?
For can it be true no longer is there fun?
Has she gone beyond what is considered human?
Another state of being from which she can't run?
Is there a way of returning to well-being?
If there is hope, the belief must come from her.
But if it exists, let it be wholeheartedly so.

Rita K Taylor
BROTHER

In memory of my beloved brother Randy Swailes

You are special in so many ways,
There's so many things I'd like to say.
I think about the past we have had,
And I know sometimes things got bad.
All I can do right now is pray,
And hope you make it another day.
My prayers are with you all through the night,
That you will awake in the morning light.
You know we all love you very dear,
And it isn't easy to hide the tears.
A brother is something you can't replace,
Nothing can ever change your face.
The dumb things you would do,
So I would give money to you.
But you always did say,
'Thanks I'll pay you back someday.'
Well, I'd give it to you a hundred times more,
Just to have you alright like you was before.
So God if you can hear me,
Let Randy be alright like he used to be.

Carolyn K Gabriel-Noel
QUIET WINGS

To my dear mother, Mrs. Ruby Bosten For letting me be . . . . . me.

As night descends on quiet wings,
The stars and moon fill up the sky.
I sit and think of different things,
Like "where" and "how" and "what" and "why."

Where the stars and moon have been,
And how the trees can be so green . . .

And what is all this beauty for,
The birds up high
the way they soar . . .

And why mankind first came to be,
And what this has to do with me.

Night was meant for just such things
To contemplate on quiet wings.

RJ Musolff
THE BIG ONES

Smiling smugly, straightening, standing,
elevating, and projecting,
beaming down, condescending,
patronizing, carefully phrasing,
he plays the part in the game
and grabs the bull by the horns
and spreads a little of it 'round
till the room is full.
He's got the background, took the course,
or petitioned for the cause,
and in arrogant display, he sings his praise
without a pause,
knowing no one else could ever climb the heights
as far as he,
thinking that he pulls things over our simple mentality,
while we humor or ignore him
—bloated ego and all—
knowing that it's the big ones who hit the hardest
when they
fall.

Kirk Nakakihara
I LEAVE TO YOU . . .

Sitting in the corner of our world,
Who are you talking to?
So much to say, so much you have learned
And these white walls are so undeserved.
Who will benefit from your pain, sorrow
And the things that you have seen?
Things that if the world only knew,
It would only know once.
Will it be the birds outside your barred window?
They are as if in a cage,
A cage that you once belonged.
Isn't it funny,
That the walls that we build, to keep people out,
Ultimately in the end,
Are the walls we can not scale to return.
I look at you.
You have no face.
You have no form.
You are but a shadow,
That can follow anyone.

Jennifer Olney Perra
WONDER

As you look out through your window, you begin to wonder.
Why do birds fly, why is there thunder?
What put the stars in the vast, black sky,
To twinkle at night, way up high?
Why do the children like playing with toys?
What made the difference in girls and boys?
Why were the humans put on this Earth?
Why do they die to come at birth?
Why are there seven continents?
Who came up with dollars and cents?
What lets airplanes stay in the air?
What makes paper so easy to tear?
Why do mountains look blue in the distance?
Why is property guarded with a fence?
How did Earth start years ago?
Surely we will never know.
Be proud to wonder 'bout things that you do,
For we are wondering 'bout them too!

Armando Trujillo
DESPERATION AND HOPE

To what end I follow some forboding call,
in solitude I travel down this lonely snowy road.
The gloom and grey of winter's somber pall,
bespeaks the weight, the burden of my load.

Where within, the reaches of my soul,
with desperate sighs an anxious voice does speak.
Of meaning too soon lost where lived a treasured goal,
and empty dreams, the stench of waste does rancid reek.

For the warmth and glow of youthful hopes,
to the dimming light of aged resolve.
In this midlife crossroad where for choice one gropes,
and atone the sins of folly one seeks to absolve.

For mortal man in the glimmer that is life,
may strive to be or choose to fail.
Calm of heart with strength of soul
to end the raging strife,
confront and abate the internal swirling gale.

There comes a time of tranquil peace,
a spring of light and hope reborn.
With weights and scales my burdens ease,
and careful, guided study does, desperation shorn.

My inner well this fount of strength, does guide my path, my course it sets.
My life will pass, whatever length,
with boundless hope and no regrets.

Zoë V Phillips
TEDDY

To my Dad, Al McCaughtry, for his loving gifts of humor and communication.

You are my Teddy,
You are love in a cold world,
You make me secure.

Mr Peron N Browne

Mr Peron N Browne
GUILT

To my daughter, Peronia and all the children of the world.

This morning I broke the mirror,
And blamed it on my brother.
Although his defence was convincing,
My mother believed me and gave him a scolding.
His bewildering gazes
Burrowed deeply into my mind's recesses,
As I sensed the essence of his extended grimaces
And the strain which retarded his paces.
Unexpectedly, I've been transformed
Into a pile of dung or an ailing dog.
My brother's innocence unsettles me.
My continual denial won't let me be.

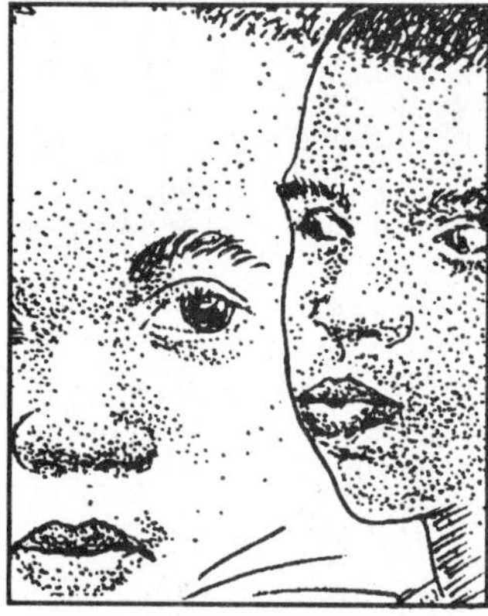

Will it be better to take my mother's bawling,
Than to bear my brother's hurting?
Must I forever harbour this guilt?
Could I shed this robe of filth?
I wouldn't sleep soundly tonight?
Unless I set things right.
This guilty leash is miserable.
Confessing would make me punishable
Confessing would make me more loveable

Stacey (Stacee') L Bruce
HURTING HEART

Dedicated to Jackie Jonker Someone who has really touched my life

Sometimes I sit alone
and wonder, if anyone really cares;
cause no one is every really there
to wipe away my tears;
I wish I could make them listen,
and tell them how I feel,
cause when I sit back I think . .
this can't all be real

No one laughs like me, Or cries like me,
or sees things as I do;
And when I step outside myself . . . .
this place is much too new
I tried to keep my feelings straight,
and all to myself,
Just to keep them all inside
just like a broken shelf.

Orval Whitworth
A TRUE AMERICAN COWBOY

Dedicated to Andy Flippin—who passed away Sept. 1988 age 82

Sitting high in the saddle and facing the cold wind,
that's the time that Andy begins.
He will round up your cattle and divide up your herd,
without uttering a swearing word.
Andy is a man who gives you his word,
he's always ready to round up your herd.
He would come to work come rain or shine,
and would have your cattle lotted and ready on time.
Now Andy was a man who knew your own herd,
and you can bet that on his own word.
He wore out two horses I know of in time.
just working for yours and mine.

These horses always knew at
 Andy's will,
if cattle were straying back over the hill.
 Andy'd say with a big grin "Oh let 'um go they've made up their mind, as soon as they get water, they'll be there on time.
 Now if there's a roundup in the heavens above, I'm sure Andy will be there wearing golden gloves.
 He will answer to God and to
 God's will,
if any cattle have strayed back over the hill.

Kathleen Potterf
TIME

Moments of gold,
Drops of water
In the desert;
Ivory-colored pearls
Of great price;
Sacred cows in
The land of India;
White rice to
The world's starving;
One true friend,
Precious last words
Of a dying man;
The life-span
Of the blue whale;
Three words called
"I need you";
A night of sleep
After a week of waking;
This is the value of time.

Norman Van Horne
THE JOY OF LIVING!

Dedicated to the VFW Post #145 Bridgeport, CT

I like to wake up in the morning
then walk along the beach
and feel that many joys of life
are well within my reach.

I love to look over the ocean
and think of hidden treasures below
some of which will remain hidden
where few men care to go.

I like to watch the sun come up
spreading its rays on the ocean floor,
then feel that all is peaceful
along our beautiful shore.

I watch people as they walk along
and look out over the sea.
That's when I feel the joy of living
and what it means to me.

Sara E Branch
TRAPPED

For Greg, for his subconscious inspiration

Pain screaming from your eyes
Laughs at my repeated, weak,
 tries.
Reaching out to grab my sleeve,
Your eyes are begging the horror
 to leave.

Unaware of this nightmare's
 source,
I wrestle with some unknown
 force.
I can't get out, how hard I've
 tried.
The door won't open. I'm trapped
 inside.

Your eyes meet mine and plead
 with fear.
The pain explodes in every tear.
From this terror I'll never
 hide.
It kills you as I'm trapped
 inside.

Steven Sheldon
LOVESONG

a song,
 a simple, innocent song,
 that cannot be heard until it
 is seen . . .
look . . .
 look at the stars,
 flashing gently in patterns
 above the sea,
 where the waves dance in
 blue and green
 to the rhythm of the leaves
 swaying in the breeze . . .
 look . . .
 and see . . .
 then lay your head softly
 on my chest
 and close your eyes,
 full of the waves and the
 April skies,
 and listen,
 listen closely
 to this song . . .

It is the beating of my heart.

Rosemarie Willig Elson
I WONDER

I wonder—
How do you live without the Lord?
How do you get through each day?
Without His hand to guide your craft
It well may go astray.
I wonder—
How do you know just where to turn
When storm clouds black as night,
Dump all their grief and pain on you
And leave no hope in sight?
I wonder—
Where in this world do you find peace
When there is no peace in your soul?
Except for pills and doctor's bills
That can never make you whole.
I wonder—
Why do you run away from God?
What can your reason be,
That you reject His love for you
To save and set you free?
I wonder—
How do you live without the Lord?
The answer is—you don't!

Paula Reinders
IN LIFE'S LITTLE WHILE

In memory of all the special people that have been in my life. The joy and pain perfectly measured has brought a wonderful blend of happiness.

Sometimes we're given for just a while
Another's love, another's smile,
Someone we've needed as we go along
To share our lives, to help us be strong.
We cry and we wonder why they've gone away,
Not realizing they were given just for a day.
There are so many times in life's little while
When we have needed an encouraging smile;
God knows that, and He will provide
The encouragement we need, will be at our side.
No matter who says it, or how it is said,
Don't blame God, Thank Him instead
For special moments that we have shared,
When we've had the pleasure of someone who cared.

J Steven Denny

J Steven Denny
TRUSTING CATTLE

A special thanks to the Ron Taylor family, my mother Doris, Ray and Jim Kilen. To the Simpson family, Harlow and Viora, my loving wife Kathy, my children Ryan, Krystal and Jay Jr. may we all be remembered.

I sit up in my lofty loft
Rest my head against a bale
I come here oft to think my thoughts
After a long day on the cattle trail.

For the trail is dirty
It's lean and it's mean
Every day I watch the cattle pass
Mindless of what tomorrow brings
They're in search of greener grass.

How easy it is to lead the herd
They haven't a thought of what lies in store
We'll offer them food, prodding them on their way
To the knife through he slaughter house door.

Who cares about these cattle
They're good for nothing but to eat
Their minds we can only scramble
And wear their hides around our feet.

But if these cattle could only reason
Distrust the man with the slanted brain
Those cattle would be in the loft with me
And miss their ride on the old cattle train.

Richard David Homan
ESSENCE OF TIME

This poem was inspired by, and written for Debbie Neidlinger

Roses are red
 Violets are blue.
There is a warm feeling
 I have for you.

Normally that would be enough
 To make a girl feel grand.
But that short poem could apply
 To any one night stand.

So this poem goes deeper
 For this I will do.
I must try to explain
 The feelings I have for you.

I could tell you I love you
 For this you deserve.
But this comes from the heart
 The only place still on reserve.

If you understand the essence of time
 You might know where you
 stand.

For time is past, present and future
 All three go hand in hand.

Let's start with the future
 There could be me and you.
But the future is uncertain
 It can grow far or fall few.

We could end tonight
 But this I highly doubt.
That's why we savor the moments
 That come to us here and now.

Here and now make up the present
 And this word surely fits.
For this part we control
 Which is a very special gift.

Living the present gives us our past
 It's usually a dim and bright
 glow.
But without it there's no memory
 From which a relationship could
 never grow.

Time is our existing life
 I love living this is true.
So can you read between the lines
 And figure out where this puts
 you?

Adelaida V Arnaez
STOLEN KISS

This poem is dedicated to Emilio, my late husband, who made this possible

I was on my usual lean
As everyday has always been
Complying my duty with a sigh
When I met this handsome guy

You won't forget to remember
Especially being the thirteenth of September
Standing tall and straight before me
Elegant in his way I could see

With shaking hands he tried to steady
Inside his pockets while I was ready
Plugging connections and what a bliss
When I felt his first stolen kiss

What happened in the beginning
Surely led to a beautiful ending
Love so pure and cherished thru the years
Our wonderful marriage with laughter and tears

Erlyne Saintil
MEMORIES OF YOU

When I think of you,
I see views of you,
When I see views of you,
I think of you,
When I think of you,
I think about the moments you and I have shared,
When I think about the moments you,
And I have shared sometimes I want to cry tears.

Patricia E Peterson
HUSH MY CHILD AND DON'T YOU CRY

To my mother-in-law, Betty Breedlove, for whom this poem was written

Hush my child and don't you cry
For we'll be together by and by
Remember me with a smile
That we brightened each other's lives for a while.

Please, my child, do not despair
Remember the happy years we shared
And God's precious gift, that we two were paired

I as the mother, you as the child
Until the last few years when we reversed roles for a while.

Through the coming years, my child, be brave, be strong
And it won't seem like it's so long
Before you slow your hectic pace
To join me in this heavenly place
As once again I gaze upon your loving face.

Do not be sad; I'm oh, so happy here
And if you ever need me I'll always be near
So have no fear
Rejoice in GOD and be of good cheer
Until that future day when you join us here.

Ozlem Razzaq
ENTRY #13

whY / does / rain / not
shine / onmyt hrone
sez mr jONES
early to bedearly
towhaT a byootiful
niGHt makesa
man wow he could-cast-a
hook further than any man
rOundam; i not wisE

Rita E Stamer
LIFE'S HIGHWAY SEEMS A BITTER PILL.

For Raymond, who is always there . . .

Life's highway seems a bitter pill,
When vision seems clouded, our thoughts become nil,
And all of our burdens are too hard to bear:
Our hope is renewed as friends show us they care . . .

William R Greenawalt Jr
SILENT ALARM

Dedicated to Bill E. Hawk Productions

Silent Running—Chain Link Fence
911—The Fog's Too Dense
Heartbeat Pounding—Nerves Unwind
You Pushed Too Far—Past The Warning Sign

Whispers In The Darkness—
Shadows Come & Go
Sirens In The Distance—Raven Starts To Crow
Night Air Thickens-Time Won't Wait
Life's Got You Cornered On This Lonely Street Called Fate

Silent Alarm Sounding—You Feel It In Your Heart
Something Tells You Turn Away—
But You've Gone Too Far
Heart's On The Line—You Chance The Game
Silent Alarm Time You're To Blame

Headlights Approach—You Try To Scream
There's No Place To Run In Your Silent Alarm Dream

Georgia "Marie" Williams White
MY LOVE

This poem is dedicated to James, "My Love".

As I lay trying to fall asleep at night,
I think of how much I love you and how it all seem so right.
Thinking of how much one person can be so sweet and kind,
And how much peace your love has brought to my mind.

The beauty in you, there's so much to behold,
And as days go by, I see more and more of your love being unfold.
Loving you is like taking a breath of fresh air,
And I'm so thankful that you really care.

I know sometimes things happen, that we don't always understand,
And I fear that things will not work out as we plan.
But if we keep the faith and don't let go,
We can watch the strength in our love grow.

If our love grows stronger, then we'll be able to see,
That our love was truly meant to be.
I can't seem to tell you enough that, "I Love You",
And how much your love has helped me through.

There's so much of my life now, that you are a part,
And the love we share has been rooted into the depths of my heart.
I love you more than words can ever say,
And that love grows stronger and deeper every day.

Tonnetta Watson

Tonnetta Watson
I LOVE YOU WHEREVER YOU ARE

Once I was happy, I never was blue.
We were proud of each other. Our love
It was true. You said that you loved me.
And I loved you too. Oh Dar-ling.
What happened to me and to you.

I loved you and lost dear. But someday I'll find. Another true dar-ling. Who'll say, he'll be mine. It hurts me to think dear. That you couldn't be true. You left for another.
But what can I do.

I hope and I pray dear. That some-body new, Will ease all my pains dear. Be hon-est. And true.
For God. Will protect me from all of this harm.
For I still love you. Where-ever you are.

I love you my Dar-ling. Be-lieve me it's true.
There'll be no other. No-body but you.
You were my angel. My guiding star.
I love you, My dar-ling. Wherever you are.

Janet L Dane
SPRING TIME

This poem is dedicated to my husband, Alan, for encouraging me.

When grass turns green
and the robins sing,
You'll know that near, is spring.
The time has come
for winter's end.
And spring to bloom again.
With it comes a feeling
that life is all around.
That God's great plan is working
throughout this great big land.
Yes, it's spring time in this country
when blossoms bloom anew,
And the land that you look upon
is so beautiful to view.
Just by looking at this beauty
you come to realize,
there's a greater power working
in the heavens and the skies.
For no one else could master,
what the master's hand has done.
This great and awesome beauty,
of which we look upon.

Millie Lee
HOW BEAUTIFUL UPON THE MOUNTAINS

A psalm from the high-desert country of ghost ranch, Abiquiu, New Mexico

The dark of early morning hides the peaks
Black shadows guard their mysteries of undiscovered cliffs/rough slides/steep/green-backed ridges/long and lazy slopes
Until the first sharp stab of light slips clear to beam across the top/announcing the arrival of an even greater splendor

And shadowed faces are unveiled
Bathed in a brightness that reveals the character and color/the strength and majesty of your creation

Yet stern/these ancient walls that seek to fend the distance
They will not bend/nor give/and seem to yield no unearned gracious-ness to life that strives as stubbornly to be
And hugs its source

I search for softness in their points and planes
And find it in the tender breath of wind that blows against my face and brushes back my hair/in feathered ends of unnamed trees
And in the gentle muted evening temperatures and tones/rainbow escaping hues/patched and plaited green
The longed for glimpse of grace amidst the harshest judgement of this land

And it becomes too vast at times/too much for me to grasp and hold
But were that even mine to do/it could not raise me to your height
Nor yet diminish all you are to my/too often/canyon-bound spirit
A spirit that also weeps with you when I forget this vision that you lend

And I would be set free/let go/to move with you into that distance
Make the soul's most dizzying climbs/meet the adverse fearful winds that/at the last/bring healing with their touch
Here I have need to catch my breath/to linger long in wonder and delight at your wide-open secrets

In all of this/and much beyond/you are my world
How is it possible for you to dwell in me/when I must/forever and always/dwell in you

Tommie McGirt
THE BLOOMING ROSE

There's so much beauty in the blooming rose.
And through its life, who knows where it goes!
Some roses will live over a season through.
While others will enjoy part of the dew.
But even roses, with all their splendor
And heart will one day.
Their beautiful petals fall apart.
Man too, has his season like the rose.
Then one day he also much repose.

Jane Rasmussen-Vieau
CRYSTALINE FANTASY

Come fly with me to a far off place
That was made for you and me
to spend our days together for all eternity

Come run with me through the meadow
Near the ever meandering brook
We'll lie on the sun warmed grasses
While faeries guard our nook

Away from all and everyone
Where white and blue make three
We'll wile away the hours
Just you, my love, and me

Lenard W Eccles
WE KEPT OUR LOVE ALIVE

Dedicated to my dear wife and best friend Judy, who has kept our love alive.

I loved you in life's spring-time,
Love's warmth through summer kept,
And in the fall,
Life's meaning our hearts understood;
We wept.

Most of all, the sweetest time is when
Life's winter-time draws nigh;
For gently, sweetly, softly,
We kept our love alive.

Sarah Steele
I REMEMBER

Dedicated to the memory of Noah Michael Wise, 3 year old son of Greg and Sue Wise.

I remember when he would run and play and never quit till the end of the day.

I remember his big round tummy and big brown eyes.
I remember his laugh and cry.
But most of all, I remember him.
Oh God, why did he die?

Jeff Edwards
DISTANT SPECTERS

Distant specters of light in the sky
Illuminate the darkness high
None are as important as the one that will rise
As you lie down and open your eyes
Rain starts falling from the sky
Just like a tear drop from a cry
Generations went and generations came
Their well of inspiration remained

the same
Because something so beautiful for so long
Should make us all sing a hopeful song
The stars in the sky which seem so tall
Are not impossible to reach at all
Just as sure as a shine from the sun
We all wish upon the very same one.

Stacie S Halbrook
BROKEN PROMISES
Please, don't make me cry!
Our hearts are too close to collide.
You gave me the promise of eternal love
And honest relationship that shall never end.
No other can put it under.
Never a day shall pass;
We have distant thoughts or feelings
Or unpromised plans.
So true is your heart?
In a blink of an eye my thoughts grow wide and very vivid.
Our life rolls on and our world changes.
My feelings for you are still unexplained,
And within me lie your broken promises.

Amy Garofalo
FOOL

—Just remember, I'm "NOBODY'S FOOL".

I'm still here
but now you're gone
I still didn't realize
how to carry on
I just can't help
what I feel inside
but when I see you
my real feelings hide
I wish I could tell him
just how I feel
to let him know
would be so unreal
'cuz then he would know
I play by his rules
and he would know
I'm still his fool

Tonie Marie (Hill) Roberson
CHRISTMAS
The Nativity Story and an exquisitely carved console,
Tantalizing mistletoe and lacy camisoles,
Christmas trees, holiday wreaths and turkey casserole.

Tasty treats hidden in a cubby-hole,
A machine that makes nifty button-holes,
And luscious fruit from Dole.

Children's letters anxiously awaiting their arrival at The North Pole,
Shiny fishing poles,
And carols sung by Nat King Cole.

A special dish of Halibut Creole,
Christmas program roles,
And your family together; makes a holiday, whole!

Susan Keefe
TRULY BLESSED

To Christopher and Jessica with all the love in my heart.

My dearest children—
My life has such a purpose now,
Since you have become a part of it.
You are the reason for all that I do.
When I doubt that there's anything left to hope for,
You make me see how precious life can be.
When I'm angry at you, all I need to do is look at your smiles and all is forgotten.
Sometimes pressures make me forget how lucky I am—
How truly blessed I've been since you've entered my life.
I see that there's a change in me.
And it is you.

Jolyn Hoffman
SACRIFICE
The important thing is this:
to be able at any moment to sacrifice
what we are for what we could become.

That is the strongest will anyone can have.

In order to grow, we have to let go;
we have to be willing to grow
and not be afraid.

We may give everything,
and in return get nothing.

There can be no giving up, for if we do,
there will be neither victory
nor defeat.

If we give up, we won't feel the pleasure,
or the pain.

To be able, at any moment, to sacrifice what we are
for what we could become is a great power that
only we have control of, to waste, or use for
our own victory.

Ann Cooper
LIVING IN THE PATH, OF DREAMS OUT OF GRASP
Burning eyes are never crying
In tears forever hiding
where is the difference I know to be
Is yesterday that tomorrow see
Dreams of glory happiness love and peace
The hope In life which never deceased

Loneliness Is forgotten gain
Passion and joy let die In vain
Pain and fire Is not at home
In this body I don't belong
Tears don't help any more so I don't cry
Along and lonely as the world pass me by
While I dwell and dream and live to die

Then I'm gone reborn In grace
The end of the means I occupied this space
Living The dream I've seen and prayed
The way of truth our Lord has made
Now Is all revealed to me
Thy word confirmed ask It's given to thee
I reside not the world but thy holy word
By which I was born and now preferred

I take my leave the beginning Is end
I knock at the door and Jesus lets me in

Ms Sylvia A Reed
AN ENGAGED GIRL'S PRAYER
Lord he's so far away
Keep him safe for me.
I find it hard to believe
that he's mine.

We've known each other
a long, long time, but
who has known us longer.

Who knows what our future
brings, but we hope to become as one.

A love like this will never die, but continue and grow from day to day.

A love ever lasting and a love renewed.
My love and I want to be together
will it be this way.

Shirley Hill Morris
OUR CHILDREN
What is happening to our children?
Don't we love them anymore?
Children can't be children,
As they were before.

They can no longer trust the stranger,
Who sees them as nice and sweet.
Who used to kiss their foreheads,
And tickle their tiny feet.

No more gifts of candy,
From those they don't know well,
For if they talk to strangers,
They may not live to tell.

They're exposed to drugs and AIDS,
While in their mother's womb.
Their prospect for the future is
A small and empty tomb.

The playground now is silent,
Where laughter used to ring.
Mothers' hearts are crying,
Where they used to sing.

Kimberly Presley
I CANNOT BELIEVE THAT WE HAVE GROWN SO FAR APART
I cannot believe that we have grown so far apart
It seems like just yesterday that we shared all our secrets
But now when I see you, we are farther apart than strangers
And I have to ask myself when this change happened
Because I wasn't there-and obviously you do not care about me or us anymore.

I do not understand why, because I still think about you often
And my feelings still hold strong
I just cannot figure out how we became so distant.

Oh, how I long for your voice, or even a glance—
I wait for a call, or look for a letter, or anything that says
That you are thinking of me too.

Oh . . . I miss you terribly and I hope that someday you realize
That it was you that turned your back on me,
But just the same I will always be here waiting
If you ever decide to consider me again.

How did we stray so far apart?
I wish I knew what happened,
because the miles never mattered before
And I dream of that one day that once again we will be sharing love—
That rare, special kind of love—that very few people ever know.

Kenneth Witt
SHE WHISPERS TO ME
The wind whispers
And so does she.
To whom does she whisper?
She whispers to me.

She begins to whisper,
I stand in the breeze.
The wind begins to whistle
And blows through my leaves.

She speaks so softly.
She speaks so free.
She reached out and touched,
Touched only me.

The wind whispers
And so does she.
To whom does she whisper?
She whispers to me.

Judy Harris
ALONE
Drizzling rain had darkened pavement dust.
Wet dirt smells rode silently with me.

Window wipers timed my thoughts
And cleared the wrinkling drips across the glass.

The red light up ahead had paralleled itself across the watered way.
I welcomed a reason to stop.

My purpose was unclear.

Loneliness screamed out within the hollows of my soul.
Everyone around seemed joined to another.

Avoiding places frequented by two,
I had browsed the shopping mall,
And planned a fast food pick up—with TV as companion.

At home, I laid across the satin-cool spread.
The rain ran faster, escaping thunder booms.

I knew the phone would not ring out.
I pulled the bed lamp chain dismissing light.
It was better to hide my singleness in the dark.

If sleep would only come, it could keep the hurt till morning.
And in the morning—the grocery store—
I can go there.

Pamula Papet
LOOKING BACK

This poem is dedicated to those who are a part of my golden memories.

I'd love to be a child again, if only for an hour,
Hold tight my Father's hand, feel his strength and power.
Watch my Mother do her chores, see her loving way,
Listen to my Sister sing, join her fun

at play.
 Walk with my little Brother, blaze a brand new trail,
Sit upon my Grandpa's knee, hear a wise old tale.
 Find a secret hiding place, meet with my best friend,
Wouldn't it be wonderful to do these things again?
 Marvel at the Christmas lights, play out in the snow,
Catch a jar of fire flies, wonder at their glow.
 Pack a bunch of daisies, make a flower crown,
March in front of the band, keep beat to their sound.
 Rake a pile of fallen leaves, jump in when it's done,
Picnic on the river bank, relax in the warm sun.
 I'm just looking backwards as I steadily grow old.
The memories that I see are more precious than gold.

Martha Sardullo
THE LORD SEEKS
The Lord looks for the lost at all cost
The Lord comes to shine as your light
So you can get new sight
He changes your life to begin anew
in everything you say and do
The Lord must be your all
To help you when you fall

Amorette A K Thomas
FOG

For Marion Dow Flint Thomas

It tiptoes in and embraces the trees
Of quiet moonlight, mist it is
And leaves as silently as it came
But not before it drops a hush
On all about between earth and sky
Finger held to lips, it steals away.

William (Tom) Morrow
NO WHERE TO GO

I dedicate this poem, to the Lord, for without him, nothing is possible

Sleepin on the sidewalk, underneath a box, prayin that my feet, don't freeze, cause I ain't got no socks.

Sleepin in a doorway, waitin for the dawn; prayin that I'll still be here, not dead and gone.

Sleepin in a boxcar, resting on the tracks; prayin when I wake up, I'm not bitin by the rats.

Siftin through the garbage for some food to eat, look at all the waste, to us it is a treat.

Sleepin in a rundown home, with no where to go, if only I had the money, to put some fire in the stove.

Those of you in Washington, who think this "no big deal," take a walk with me some time, I'll show you life that's real.

Those of us who live like this, have no other choice, but what about the thousands of little girls and boys?

Fae Hanson
TOUCHING ME
I want to touch life
 To kneel on bended knee
  To feel life . . .
   touching me . . .

Somewhere there's a hill
 I've yet to climb—
 Somewhere a wildflower
  yet to be mine—
I want to touch life to kneel on bended knee . . .
To feel life touching me . . .
 Roads to travel
  I know not where . . .
Life is waiting for me . . .
 If I dare . . .

Linda Pierce Stitt

Linda Pierce Stitt
CHURCHLADY
Hey Churchlady, where you going?
See you got your Sunday face on.
Rosy beige foundation settles
into the wrinkles of your soft skin
 like caulking.
Your face, dunked into powder,
 a freshly floured
  biscuit.
Gray eyebrows, penciled black,
thin black wings above your eyes.
Grizzly gray escapees loiter under the line, lost immigrants.
 Bubblegum pink lips
 Shine, Shine, Shine!
Circles of rogue are stamped on your cheeks like notary public seals.
You look pretty good Churchlady,
 and this poem is all in fun,
all in fun Churchlady,
 All in fun.

Thomas J Durham II
THE DEATH OF A TREE
To prophesy things hard to see,
So unreal, but meant to be,
Tears fall faster than rain,
It's hard in this world so insane.
Few live in happiness—so crazed,
Trees grow now where flames have blazed,
Hearts turn to stone from useless pleas,
Love the flowers, love the trees,
These things you cannot live without,
Trees bend as the wind does shout,
So beautiful with a life carefree.
It lives for us—it is our tree.
Watching us do things with no reason why.
Inside its heart it begins to cry.
It reaches high, mighty and tall.
It hopes for the sky but knows it will fall,
Someone comes along with a dumb reason why,
Then with a puff of smoke it goes to the sky.

Mendy Wright
I WANT TO BE A POET . . .
I want to be a poet,
And I really don't know why.
I sit down and write poems
That make me want to cry.

I write poems when I'm happy,
I write poems when I'm sad.
And just to take some pressure off,
I write poems when I'm mad.

It takes away my anger,
It takes away my stress.
And when I'm sad and lonely,
Is when I write my best.

I write about my private life,
And all my problems, too.
The day that I quit writing is
The day my life is through.

I want to write a book someday
That everyone will buy.
I want to be a poet,
And I really don't know why.

Sally Jo Wilkins
STILL

Just you, just me, just because, just us . . .

How many times,
How many times will I sit alone—
Thoughts of you whirling in my mind?
How long,
How long will each time last—
My hand unable to write ?
Each time,
Each time finds me closer—
To thoughts of us.
Every moment,
Every moment I try so hard—
Searching for those deepest thoughts.
The thoughts,
The thoughts they have a special reason—
For being so real to life.
So real,
So real it seems—
You're right here with me.
Right here,
Right here—is where I long for you to be.
So many times, in so many ways, I want you to know—
I still love you . . .

Edwin Rice
BE "I" EVER SO HUMBLE
When people ask, "Who laid this brick,
Who set so neat this stone,
Who nailed this board,
What master poured
(With perfect pitch and tone)
Into these walls and handsome halls
Such splendor—free of blunders—
Smooth craftsmanship that saves a trip
To see the 'Seven Wonders'?"
I stand about and let them shout,
And make no sign nor bid—
But bursting brilliance points me out—
And I confess, 'I did.'

Brooke Davis
WINTER WALTZES IN

To my Aunt Lucile and Mimi, who make even the wintriest of days bright and warm.

The old dry trees begin to dance,
All foliage subdued in trance,
And nothing covers vast expanse,
As winter waltzes in.

A lonely bride in white array,
She has no groom this cold dark day;
Her bridesmaids back to Autumn stray:
She's winter, waltzing in.

Her children cover forest floors,
And clouds continue to make more
Snowflakes: crystal at their core,
When winter waltzes in.

Jacques L Alexandre
STOICISM
As I go through life,
Besides the days of real happiness,
I face moments of agony
Filled with sorrows and tears.

There are days with bitter feelings,
When my mutilated heart
Invaded by thousands of night dreams
Is deeply broken.

I still keep a profound remembrance
Of those times of despair.
So much are my sufferings,
No one can make me feel better.

However, I endure my misfortunes
With stoicism
Expecting better days ahead.
Living with lots of confidence
I never question fate.

From the fountain of eternal faith
I get a lot of courage.
I shed all the tears,
I heal all the scars.

When adversity knocks,
I keep a strong heart
For sufferings are part of life,
I emerge a strong winner

Our heart is like a vase
Filled with an active mixture
Of joys and sorrows.
The activities are predictable,
To empty or to fill.

Nothing is permanent on earth
Beautiful clouds decorate the sky,
But soon some other clouds,
Will replace them
And the horizon wonders.

We succeed when we don't think of failure.
Let us, then, put aside
Our worries for another time.
Before we realize it, they will have slipped away.

Dusty Montgomery
THAT FIRST NIGHT
I remember that first night.
I couldn't let you out of my sight.
Thought I found what I was looking for
And didn't need much more.
Now it's different, and things have changed.
I feel as though my life has been rearranged.
I guess I needed someone near
To love, hold, and keep me from fear.
We both know that it wasn't meant to be.
But I still love you, can't you see?

Ms June A Baker
A CHANGE IN ATTITUDE

Dedicated to: Mothers Against Drunk Drivers

Punishment, community time
And revoke of a license
Or jail without bail
Does not fit the crime
For driving while drunk
Drunken driving cannot be ignored
Nor can a mangled body
Or life itself be restored
By a drunken driver
Who is none the wiser
Education and rehabilitation are in order
Yet not necessarily the key
To become alcohol and drug free
For the ultimate solution
Is a change in attitude to achieve

Drivers that are substance free
For the betterment of wo(man)
Take a firm stand
The end results are
A driver who is wiser
And much safer roads

Macy Pratt
PASSING
Today, I have a burning desire to see your face,
To walk the sands of time with you—
To be known by you,
And to know you—
Into the infinity of time.

But this shall never be,
For you have made thy choice.
You will go onward along a lonely path,
And I shall be lost to you, in time.

Dorthea Darby
FATHER OF EVERYTHING
The snow is falling on the hillside. I know you O, Father of everything, is right by my side. I can hear your voice in the wind. Your voice cause the waves of the sea, to come upon the shore, and wash the sand out to sea. O, God, you are a mighty God, in all of your ways. I just ask one thing of you, Father, that is, would you keep your hands upon things.

Then peace will come to many. O, thy Father, we will give you praises that will reach to heaven above. God the Father of everything, I thank you for our daily bread. O Father, that come from above, we see your handiwork upon the ground. You cause the sun to come out into the sky. We will give you all the honors to your holy name. When I see the frost upon my windowpane, I know you've been there. When I see your shadow on the ground, I know you are here. God the Father of everything, I cannot wait to see your sun come up into the sky, this morning Then I know that is the time to give you thanks for everything.

Judith McGhee Mays
AND TRUTH SHALL SET THEM FREE

For Jonathan and Darren; In loving memory of Mr. & Mrs. C.E. Findley Sr., Mr. Lincoln H. Powell, Mr. Arcell C. McGhee

Out of despair came the cry
Youth not caring whether they live or die
Shapen in iniquity-fear and shame
Piercing marrow and soul for 'nought to gain
Yes everything to lose . . . Oh say can't you see
The American dream hasn't died . . . there is liberty
Yet the shackles so tight deny you dignity
You can stand . . . you can be you can live in veracity
The drum beat thunders silence has been removed
Truth beckons you listen and wisdom will reprove
It's not your debt you say . . . not your lies to tell
The past has left a downcast path . . .
A gateway straight to hell
Yes the stumbling blocks though there
Still, keep the dream alive faith has not died
And there is no cause to detour
Oh precious commodity be not deceived there is
Eternity
Justice yet lives—God still forgives
And truth shall set them free

Rhonda K Swinson
A PLACE IN THIS WORLD

I am dedicating this to my loving husband Allen and my lovely children Allen Jr and Tahitia.

The day I was born they said "You have a place in this world,"
But how did I know.
The day I started school they said "You have a place in this world,"
But how did I know I was young.
The day I went to high school they said "You have a place in this world," but how did I know I was still growing.
The day I got married they said "You have a place in this world", but how did I know, all I knew was that I took a big step in life.
The day I gave birth to my first child they said "You have a place in this world", but how did I know, all I knew was that I had someone new to take care of.
The day I gave birth to my second child they said "You have a place in this world", but how did I know, I just knew I had to work harder with the second child, as I had to do with my first child.
Now the truth came the day I was gone, cause yes I had a place in the world and now that place is filled with two extra spaces, so I am gone and now they are here, now I understand what my place in the world was.

Ethel Hunt Street
ONCE

To my dear friend, Verlene Long.

Once I was a captain, captain of my soul
I was happy and content, perhaps a little droll;
Then you came back into my life after 40 years
And tho my love for you returned you caused me many tears.

Once I was a master, master of my fate
Then you came back into my life, many years too late;
Everything I did was wrong, you could not see my life
As one with great fulfillment, but years and years of strife.

I have so many friends, the birds with all their songs
The dogs, the cats, the horse, they know that they belong;
They give their love so freely, they ask for nothing more
Than just a little kindness, when they see me at the door.

You think this all a waste of time, this love I have to give
You think I wasted all my life, and had no time to live;
But you have roamed around the world, and you are not content
You know not what you want of life, and your's is nearly spent.

I have always been your friend, and walked the longest mile
So do not sit in judgement now, but have a kinder smile;
You have so very much to give, if only you would bend
And these last years we have on earth, together we could spend.

Robin Szczech
THE WINTER SEASON

This poem is dedicated to my best friend Allison.

It's winter now and time for snow and the cold winds will also blow,
When the snow flakes glitter as they fall the southward geese will have their call,
The summer water turns to ice and mother nature paints a winter wonderland so nice,
Winter is a time for health or happiness and family and relatives have lots of togetherness,
Winter is a time for Christmas too with lots of joy for both me and you.

Annetta M Boyer
WORDS
Words are the tools
Used by wise men and fools.
Waves of air set in motion,
Span a land, cross an ocean.

Bound not by time or place or track,
They have no leash to bring them back.
Like feathers flung into the wind,
Never all are found again!

Hurled in hate they fly like darts,
Fester and grow in minds and hearts.
'Til joy and love are crowded out
And hope is dimmed by angry doubt.

But words that caring and kindness control,
Can ease the mind and lift the soul.
Assuage the burdens of grief and pain
Like cleansing drops of cooling rain.

So may my attitudes be right,
My lips send messages of light.
And as I sail life's open sea,
The Father's love be heard through me.

Denise V Smith
WHO ARE YOU
you greet me
with hungry lips
instead of a smile
you love me
yet you're not satisfied
under tear-filled eyes
is doubt/to search
to ask
to know
i love you
isn't enough
still you pretend
not knowing
i know
i am not enough
i see the shadow
your shadow/your shadow
when will the search end
i can't see the road's end
still you pretend.

Esther R Johnson
AMERICA, YOU OUGHT TO BE ASHAMED
America, you ought to be ashamed,
Of the poverty in your lands.
Where is your land of plentiful,
Your song of harvest home?

America, you ought to be ashamed,
Of the homeless in your lands.
Are they not the huddled masses,
Seeking refuse from the storm?

America, you ought to be ashamed,
Of the racism in your lands.
Were you not built by people,
Of many religions, colors, and creeds?

America, you ought to be ashamed,
Of the drugs in your lands.
When the minds of our youth,
Are lost and destroyed, who will carry on?

Yes America, you ought to be ashamed,
You claim to be a leader, but how can you lead,
When you haven't yet cleaned,
Up the problems in your lands?

Linda Rose Currey
HEAR OUR PRAYER

To my Loves, David, my husband and Jeremy, my son and to The Cherokees, past, present, and future.

They came across the sea
We greeted them with open arms
But friendship wasn't in their plans
They came to do us great harm.

They took what was only ours
The Great Spirit gave these lands to us
They took these lands and our lives
That's what they did with our trust.

The herded us to a new land
That killed most of the tribe
Many never saw the new place
They offered as another bribe.

After giving us the new land
they then took it away again
They moved us on to the reservations
And they thought we should be friends.

Pride is all we have now
And very few are left here
to carry on our traditions
of Dance and Chants to us so dear.

But white man we still want peace
that we offered you long ago
So white man let's live as brothers
Let there be peace, it must be so.

So Hear Our Prayer, Great Spirit
Let the Indian and the White
Live together hand in hand
We want no more to fight!

Tracey E Parker
TO LIVE IS TO DIE
Since to live is to die I ask myself why.
Why should I try to live when I will surely die
I had to escape, escape to life
I had to do something to make it all right
Living in this world made no sense at all
For the next breath you take may end

it all
I watched the sun go down
And I began to sigh
Asking myself when will I die
For what is the point of being alive
When in the end you will surely die
I've never been a Christian or an evil doer either
When I die where will I go heaven or hell or neither
When my life was ready to start living
Warning signs of death started giving
This is how my life became so inspired
When I got a job I got fired
When I got married I lost the desire
Every time I started living a little
Death started to give a little
Life is just a long wait til death
Until then it's just a wasteless quest
When I die my soul will be lost
Somewhere between passion's hate and the pearly gates
I left life alone and stayed at home
Telling the days good-bye
Waiting to be put to sleep in a soothing lullaby
Yes waiting to be called to rest somewhere between hell and the sky
I have closed my eyes to death and opened them to life
I once was alive now I'm dead and gone
But I sing a brand new song
You see, there is life after death
That's the point of my quest

Daveda J Cupp
FANTASY
For some there is no escape from the world outside; you are on the run seeking and searching. But there is nowhere to hide.
In this world you look for happiness only to find sadness, friendliness only to find loneliness.
And pleasure only to find pain; in this world you have everything to lose and nothing to gain.

So why do I keep trying, knowing that in this world, for me there is no use? I reach out for a helping hand only to find that I have been gripped and held in the clutches of a terrible thing we call abuse; abuse not of the body but of our soul and mind; and you think this cannot happen to me, but eventually you it will find.

And when it does it warps your mind, your sense of thinking; it takes you for one hell of a ride, and because of it some turn to drinking and others to suicide.
But not me. I have found a better place all of my own
A place of warm sunny days and walks on the beach, a place that I wish sometimes, I could call my home.
A place of warm sunny days and walks on the beach, a place that I wish sometimes I could call my home.

The escape I find from the world outside is the world inside;
For a while I was on the run seeking and searching, but now I have me a place to hide.
In my world you look for happiness and it is within your reach,
Friendliness is all around, and for me there is never any pain;
For in my world you see, I have nothing to lose and everything to gain.

So now I know why I kept trying when I thought that for me there was no use;
I somehow knew that if I kept reaching out for that helping hand I'd find a better place where there was never any abuse.
You see, I have found a better place though not of reality;
One might say that mine is the world of fantasy!

Nancy Flebbe Munson
A NURSE IS A FRIEND
While in the hospital
a nurse is a friend,
you will see time and again.
When you are feeling sick
and feeling there is nothing to gain,
a nurse is a friend,
that can help ease the pain.

Debby Bailey

Debby Bailey
AN EVENING ON THE BEACH
Such beauty lights the night
with all too clever direction,
Impressing on the horizon
such awkward shadows
'neath my gaze.
I find my wandering self
a sanctuary here amidst
the soothing hum,
And long to know
recipience of
the fortunes held in
solitaire.

Tonight, a night of
unseen wealth,
doled out upon the
unsuspecting,
Returns to me the right
perspective.
Likened to my love of love,
it falters not at all.

Ines Rivera Acevedo
IF I SHOULD HEAR THE CALL AGAIN

Dedicated to the female veteran; so many times invisible, so many times forgotten.

The falling leaves surrounding me
Remind me of a distant past
So filled with pain and misery
With dying friends, and broken hearts.

This endless search for my lost youth . . .
This never-ending, silent pain
Could I once more heal someone's wounds
If I should hear the call again?

I hear them calling me, I see
Their faces full of pain and fear,
And in my hands I see their blood,
Still warm, in spite of all these years.

A walking wounded I've become,
A prisoner of my own pain
And my release will only come
If I should hear the call again.

Amy Dawn Johnson
THE BLADE OF GRASS

To all my friends, but especially to Marris, who has so much in common with me and seems very much like a sister to me as we share each other's writings and a few secrets we would tell no one else.

On one misty fall day
I picked a blade of grass.
I used my imagination and
Pictured it as a piece of glass.
Then winter started setting in
And snow covered the ground.
I saw on our front stoop a blade of grass
And I proceeded to turn it round.
Then this certain blade of grass
Seemed to show and sparkle like a glint of glass.
Then the shine seemed to melt away
As the wind lifted it into the shower of snow spray.

Kelly M O'Hara
THOUGHTS OF LOSING YOU
No more gentle kisses,
No more romantic hugs.
There is no life when I have
Thoughts of losing you.

No more sneaking around,
Hoping not to get caught.
There is no use when I have
Thoughts of losing you.

No more dreaming dreams,
To hope they might come true.
There isn't any sleep for me when I have
Thoughts of losing you.

No more happy, bright faces,
I get each time I see you.
There is just tears to fall when I have
Thoughts of losing you.

Myleen S Rojano
SURVIVOR

Mom and Dad, Thank you for believing in me!

Leaves wither in the hot sun.
I feel faint in my pursuit,
Ragged I may look,
Staggering through the streets,
Open to nature's cruelty,
I am a pawn,
Left to beg at their feet.
My hands are weary and transparent.
My body shall tremble at one's sight.
I lay upon the earth,
Wishing for darkness of night.
Delirious are my thoughts,
Harshness felt in my words.
Pity, I do not seek,
For I am the survivor of the earth.
Marble pavement is at my disposal,
Wood of mahogany for my bed.
I am but a survivor,
Only man I fear and dread.

Linda M Kuzmitch
WHAT IF?
Often I sit here and wonder;
'What if?' often comes to mind.
If the stars didn't glitter,
would people still have dreams?
If the sun didn't shine,
would people still have warmth
& affection?
If the clouds were never dark & gloomy,
would there be pain & hatred?
If the skies were always blue,
would there only be peace & happiness?
Without love, would there be life?
Without fear, would there be death?
Without God, would 'What if' exist?

Hannah E Klein
TO MARY
They say you are dead
And buried on yonder hill.
But does not your memory
live still
Deep within this heart
of mine?
My tears flow like wine—
My head is bowed with sorrow.
Sweet Mary, where will you fly tomorrow?
In a whisper of a breeze
I will hear your voice.
Like a song of songs it will come to me.
Sleep, sleep, Mary in sweet peace.
Now all your troubles will cease.

Catherine Barrette Atherton
BIRD SEED
How can I be strong enough to live,
In this world I'm breathing in?
Don't let it bring you down,
Your eyes must do more than see.
Clean out the corners of your mind.
Search the cobwebs for any leftover bugs,
And look through the dust for any filthy dirt.
Clean the crumbs out of the cupboards,
And feed them to some hungry birds.
Wash the windows of your mind and then invite,
your mother to dinner.

Belva A Hoops
JOURNEY OF PEACE
Just up the hill and across the way,
There's a beautiful place I go each day.
It's peaceful, quiet and oh! so serene
The sky clear blue and grass so green.

Jesus walks with me, as I go along
And fills my heart with love and song.
He shows me the beauties all around,
As he assures me, his love will abound.

I take this walk, snow, rain or shine
Because you see, it's all in my mind.
It's a trip I can take any day, any hour
Simply because, my Sweet Jesus has the power.

He bathes my soul and fills my heart
From this beautiful friendship, I'll never part.
He gives me peace and joy and love
And tells me about the home above.

It's a trip worth taking and the rewards are great.
There's no charge and you never have to wait.
He will meet you in the morning or dead of night
And makes your heart and soul and life just right!

George Pace
TO A ROSE
You greet the morning with budding lips, oh Rose.
I see a smile just blooming from above

Your folded tips like hands were clasped to close
Your throbbing prize: a miracle's Gift of Love.
Your petals unfold like scarlet arms to reach
And brace the morning's mad and golden burst.
I thought I heard your crimson throat beseech
A drop of dew to kiss and cool its thirst.
While traveling down the slim and prickly tree,
The tiny bead became a sparkling gem.
And now the tear of crystal urges me
To lend my sight and seize the endless stem.
And with my heart I'll guard that precious gain:
That I may love without the price of pain.

Tracy Stevens
BEAUTY

As I walk through
a vast meadow
of tall grass
and wild flowers
I look upon a sunset
and wonder
how beautiful it would be
to bloom with the sunrise
every morning, but to die
at sundown
then bloom again!

How beautiful it would be
to have such
bright and brilliant colors
to fill a lonely heart,
to cheer up someone's day,
or just be beautiful.
How exciting it might be
to be stuck to a float
in the Rose parade
or put in a vase
to be cherished and loved,
where people could see me
and say:

How beautiful you are!

Cornel Turner
BECOMES

The tall trees talk
The oceans sing
The mountains stare in silence
And in some distant wooded glade
A seedling grass becomes a blade
Symphony without woodwinds;
Music without strings;
Orchestra of nature
Eagle on the wing.
Crimson leaves in autumn
Verdant green in spring
Winter's breath brings sleep
Summer's fosters dreams—
The tall trees talk
The oceans sing
The mountains stare in silence
And in some distant wooded glade;
A seedling grass—becomes—

Charlie Miller
A CELEBRATION TO LIFE

Be happy to celebrate, living true worth,
Small accomplishment that adds up.
A friendship that lasts, a brother love, a sister hug.
A house you lived in, a parent thanks.
Dreams that came true, worries that past.
The hate that did not last.
The morning air you breathe, free without care.
The walk you had, holding hands,
The blessing you gave, the blessing you received,
The love you gave and received,
The child you were, the children you see,
Their smiles, you made.
All small things add up,
Your celebration to life.

Carolyn B Colby
THE CHILD OF YOUTH

The child of youth runs forth in play,
to run, to jump just for a day.
The dawn brings forth the joy of life—Oh where can be a child of strife?
The heart of innocence among the hills—Who can demand you must be still?
It doesn't know of worldly gain—Of shadows falling in the rain.
Of wars, of hate, it can't caress—and it knows not of emptiness.
The earth reels from troubled days—
What happened to my child at play?
The peace I knew in that day, and now it all has moved away.
For summers came and winters too, then spring and autumn moved on thru—
I danced across the meadows then, my merry heart, remember when?
I felt the world was mine to hold, all that glittered, it was gold!
I stepped upon the morning dew—the flowers slept so peaceful too.
Oh sun so bright, you would not lie—Could I give it another try?
Can I dance across the field. My heart to all the world will yield.
Can I blossom forth again? As in the days of REMEMBER WHEN?
I feel the breath of April spring—It's shadow, summer on the wing.
Yes, I shall ask my heart to dance—upon the fields of my romance.
To gather peace from skies so blue—and whisper "Child, I Love You True."
For you are there within my frame—
Your heart and mine, It is the same.
Tho I grow old, you'll always be—
My child of youth that sets me "free."

Candalyn M (Barkley) Niemi
CATCH THE WIND SLOWLY

This poem is dedicated to Mrs. Collins, my English instructor at college.

Catch the wind slowly;
let it carry you far.

Fly high and fly gracefully—
try to reach a new star.

Catch the wind slowly;
follow your heart's pull.
Go where it leads you
until you are full.

Catch the wind slowly;
let it billow your sail.

If you follow your heart,
you never shall fail.

Catch the wind slowly;
sail high and be free.

Catch the wind carefully;
then come back to me.

Delores E Perry
THE VICIOUS NON-VIOLENT PERSON

The things I say,
The things I do,
Are all to insure
That I really hurt you.

The strength I feel
From my vicious ways,
Makes me so content
When I see you in a daze.

My attack is non-violent,
So I know I'm not wrong.
When I cuss, and holler, and pitch a bitch,
It's all to show I'm strong.

My victim must be someone I love,
So I can boast with style,
For the friends you have,
Are the friends I have
To show the damaged pile.

But don't blame me for being mean,
For this is a cruel world.
I must be seen; I must be heard,
In the midst of all the turmoil.

But once I see my victim
Recover soon from what I've done,
I feel I've lost, been made a fool,
And find another one.

Tanaya Washington
AN EASTER PRAYER

I thank you on this special day,
for allowing me to see another
fruitful day
I thank you for giving me hope,
to carry on through the day
I thank you for giving me a voice,
to praise your name and rejoice
I thank you, for allowing me a choice
I thank you,
for giving me sight to see and to be
all that I can
I thank you,
for just being the Lord, because
without you we would
be lost
I thank you, for dying on the cross,
because without that there would be
no boss
I thank you, for sharing your world
with us
But, above all, I thank you for your
Son because with
him we will always have a bond
I thank you, for accepting your fate
and enduring the
thorns placed on your brow
I thank you for everything, even the
sun!

Stace Rappaport
FEELING OF HI

You have this enjuiced love of drugs.
The reason why I just don't know.
And to save our lives, you have to let your addiction go.
You say you can't
but I think you can.
Your love for drugs
I'll never understand.

I see you killing yourself
I can't understand why.
You say you love the feeling;
The feeling of "hi"
It's like you're locked inside,
inside this huge gate.
And I'm afraid that one day you'll turn around
and it will be too late.

Your drugs are hurting me so much
sometimes it makes me cry.
I just wish you could get rid of this feeling;
This feeling of "hi."

Kelly L Gillum
MACHO DEFINED

To my brothers, Jon, Jeff, Joe and Jack for their ability to show me their "soft" side.

Be a man
Shed your tears
Be a man
Expose your fears
Don't pretend
There's nothing wrong
Be a man
Not always strong
Find strength in weakness
And in your pain
Free-flowing tears
Without the shame

Millie (Marsau) Lutz
IS THERE ANYTHING MORE BEAUTIFUL?

Is there anything more beautiful than a quiet spring morning,
when the air is so delicious with lilac fragrance clinging?
Unless it is the stillness you sense at eventide when the sky is ablaze,
with clouds that seem to prance and mingle with the haze.
And spread out across the heavens like miles of pink ribbon,
never gaudy but breathtaking and surely God-given.
What could be more beautiful than the lilting song of a morning dove,
as he coos and wakes the sleeping world to his whimsical sound of love?
Oh the peace you feel as you walk in the humid soft rain,
as it falls and splashes on your umbrella or a windowpane.
How can there be anything more beautiful than the love you feel,
when you look into the face of your newborn child, how your heart does reel.
Then there is the fleeting moment when you catch a loving glance,
unexpectedly from a friend that you meet by chance.
Is there anything more beautiful than a starlit night,
as the clouds roll by and expose an eclipse—a very rare sight?
There is no end to the wonders that God has planned,
or no end to His love that the ages have spanned.

Ella Cronan
BUDDED ON EARTH TO BLOOM IN HEAVEN

In memory of Joyce Elaine Cronan 10-28-53 01-01-62

God gave us a baby child
And let us keep her for a while,
And then one day he called her home
Our house was left all alone.

All the suffering she went through,
And there was nothing we could do.
Oh God, why did she have to go

Cause Lord you know we loved her so.

I looked up and saw a beautiful star
It seemed so near but yet so far,
I said a prayer my eyes in tears
And then I felt God's presence near.

A soft voice whispered to me and said
Mother don't cry, your child's not dead,
She's just a rosebud up here
In my flowerbed.

So put a smile and look ahead
And picture in your mind that beautiful flower bed,
And keep telling yourself that one day soon
I can watch my Rosebud Bloom.

R Kim Baird

R Kim Baird
REFLECTIONS OF AN OLD HAND

To the Cowboy—Don't let go of your dreams, or the reason for holding onto them, for they will become memories someday.

Now lying in bed, he hears the morning sounds of the city.
But he recalls the time when he rode the broncs and watched the sun rise with the morning dove.
He remembers the smell of fresh brewed coffee on the wood cook stove.
The steam from his horse's nose as he snorts a warning of feeling a little cinchy.
The crispy fresh cold of a February morning as he helps a new born calf to his feet and his first meal.

The cool breeze on his face as he jingles in the calvey.
Being horseback and feeling like no one is around for miles.
Feeling closer to your maker thru the solitude and beauty of the mountains around you.

The simple things like watching a sun rise or set or sitting horseback watching calves buck and play in the warm spring sun.
Taking pride in your work, what you are, and stand for, and looking down in the face of the boy who copies everything you do, trying to be a hand like his Dad.

The pleasure of the loop thrown true.
Of a horse doing his job just right.
The stupid grin of a hand bested by his bronc.
No other job can make you look so good one second and look just as stupid the next.

It is said that a cow is the dumbest orneryest critter on Earth; but you would be surprised at how many Cowboys she outwits.

He remembers a time when he was among the best and was considered one of 'em.
As his feet touch the floor and he heads for that first cup of coffee, his joints remind him of the crazy things he did, of horse wrecks, and curses himself for growing old.

Then he smiles, at least he thinks,
"I chased my dream. I was a Cowhand."

Myra Lorber Epstein
THE LADY, THE MOTHER

This Is Dedicated To My Mother, Mary Mossman Lorber

The first thing one sees are her eyes, though clouded by age,
Pure, innocent, blue eyes having seen much, inspite of the haze;

The faint, yet distinct scent of old lotion,
Smoothed with care into creased, crinkled skin with unsteady motion.

Into skin, wrinkled, seasoned and worn, like fine old leather,
It, too, went through changes, seasons, cycles, like patterns of weather;

A small but audible sigh escaped from within,
As from unsteady hands falls a silver hair pin.

Her shoes are old but of polished leather, sturdy, tended.
The are plain, durable, of quality on which she depended;

Another small sigh as she slowly stands.

"I'm up!" she cries gratefully, as her spirits soar,
For she has a "date" with her son promptly at four.

Then the glint of recognition, an expression of pure joy,
As she sees in the auto the face of her boy.

In spite of trying not to, she quickens her pace,
A glance in he mirror . . . everything in place???

With a quiet serenity, dignity, acceptance of life,
She had quite simply been a daughter, a mother, a grandmother, a wife;

She raises a gloved hand, trembling, though one couldn't tell,
As a fine looking man approaches,
"Gee, Mom, don't you look swell!!!"

Judy Lowery Conner
VIET NAM

Dedicated to Jack Lowery, Bill Stacey, and to those who fought, and the ones who died in the Viet Nam War.

They sent us to war, we went and we fought
We fought for our country because that's what we were taught
But when we came back things weren't the same
Some of our people cursed us and some called us names
Some of us came back in pieces and some came in bags
And some who were lucky were still walking and wearing their dog tags
And some suffered years as prisoners of war
But for all the poor souls that died in that war, they are at peace—
I don't know if I ever will be anymore
For I still have the memories of the blood and the deaths,
I still have bad dreams and wake up in cold sweats
So I close this poem saying and this is so the horror we went through you do not know
for war is not pretty it's ugly and bad and for the one left behind it's lonely and sad.

Christopher DiIuro
BETTER DAYS

I would like to dedicate this poem to my mother and father, without whom there would be no Better Days.

The Sun sets
As a dull, gray blanket engulfs the land.
A naked tree dreams of better days;
Soon,
Very soon . . .

The Time has come for this world to sleep;
No longer will the birds Sing their song
Or the Sun blaze intensely.
Behold!
The cold Wind blows.
It has arrived . . .

Not far away,
All Alone,
A snow covered tree dreams of better days.

Christopher T Ritchey
AN AUTUMN TEAR

An Autumn teardrop fell as Grandma spoke of deep blue skies—
And Winter's chill pushed Summer's still on forth with eager tries.
How crisp the air and clean the smell of greens becoming golds,
While birds aspired and bears retired to fool the coming cold.

Twas then when sweaters found their way on moonlit strolls to town.
And drifting leaves fell swoon to breezy flitters towards the ground.
And Romance sang her hasty tune to capture and excite,
While fireflies lit cooling skies to lover's sheer delight.

Twas then when Mother searched for Summer peaches, cellar jarred,
And Dad retrieved the gathered leaves that scampered toward the yard.
And I prepared for Halloweens with anxious fantasies
Or whistled tunes on afternoons spent climbing in the trees.

What beauty filled those Autumn days with peacefulness and truth—
The reds and browns of covered grounds oft visited by youth.
What mystery and awe inspired from rhythmic Autumn turns—
Of sunlit hills embraced with chills of nearing Winter burns.

How fond these Autumn memories, held close within my heart—
The sights and smell and songs and tales from which I n'er shall part.
How fond as well is how the past again becomes so clear
As crystaled dreams reflect in streams of one small Autumn tear.

Dorothy Crawford Roberts
WHERE ARE YOU GOING AMERICA?

To my sons, Jarrod Dugan and Joseph Daniel who must make the most tomorrow of the America we have made today.

Knowledge and Technology to excess,
But education for the masses less and less!

Medical breakthroughs to boggle the mind,
But not enough money to feed the old and homeless can we find!

Salaries are higher than ever before, but buy less and less as foreign business enters our door!

Media sells what the public wants,
Blood and guts, sex, scandal and sports!

Family life becomes a thing of the past,
As our young people use drugs to help them travel fast!

Where are you going America?
Backward or forward?

Wherever you are going,
You're still the Best!

Lisa E Graham
REFLECTIONS

This poem is dedicated to Harold Edgington, Jr. For his love and encouragement, and whose opinion I trust.

My mother said to me once,
you are like no other,
unique you are like a flower.
Do not ever forget,
all people on earth
are like brothers.

And yet, as I've lived
half my life,
I see hatred, revenge,
and dislike for each other.

Was my mother's life so different?
Or has the "Garden of Flowers" gone wild.

Doris House Rice
MY SON

Dedicated to my only son: Reginald Robert Romell House

Thank you Lord for giving me gifts that I do not deserve
You've given many gifts to others, but you kept mine in reserve

In my life there are many wonderful things that you have done
But one of the greatest gifts that I cherish is the gift of a son

You sent him to me special delivery from above
You made him strong yet gently as a dove

You told the angels you were making him for me and thee
You made him unique so that he

could be the best that he could be

You knew times would be tough and at times I couldn't take it
You gave my son wisdom for he whispers to me softly and says together we can make it

You gave him a sense of humor to make me smile when I frown
You knew just what it would take to lift me up when I'm down

You gave him a heart filled with your love
All that he is comes from you above

You gave him to me all brand new—
Thank you Lord for giving me a son who is so much a part of you.

Ida Olivia Hurst
COUSINS
We knew each other well beyond the veil;
And volunteered to leave our Spirit Life behind awhile,
Our loved ones there prepared to leave there, too;
Longing for an earthly home to learn to earn our heavenly bliss!

We all agreed the time was right and, so we chose each other
there—where the cradle of "Free Agency" has ever been!

I chose to make my flight to earth's abode
Just four short weeks and minus several days
Before you said, "Let's take my turn on earth and make it soon;
Before the turning of another moon!

In time, we stood there side by side within our earthly space;
I wasn't sure that you were real and so I touched your face;
And, then I knew the Veil was thin—
It was the confirmation of our bond; together we were
Spirit Children once removed.

And, now that we have reached the tender age of three,
Hand in hand, we play and stroll on God's great earth,
As we prepare ourselves to meet again—as cousins—
For all time and all eternity!

Gail E Hamel
HIS PEACE

This poem is dedicated in loving memory of Corey Vancoughnett, December 22, 1958—August 28, 1988.

Upon the misty highway
Of heaven's endless plain
Drives a lone bike rider
Who will not come home again.
The silent motor hums along
The rider slows his speed
And then he seems to hesitate
Knowing not where the road will lead.
Then like the strong young eagle
Who soars graceful in solo flight
He faces the winds of eternity
And speeds away from mortal sight.

Mark Hefner
OLD MAN, SOME PART AWAY
Old Man, some part away,
I see you standing there
where the rails run shining by,
gleaming side-by-side
to a surely distant shore.

Old Man, you are nearer now.
You have not moved, stilled I think
by practice or by pain
your unsocked feet in broken shoes
that would not fit if new to you.
My need real, I walk nearer still
to your dreary place.

Old Man, I am uncertain what to say.
I have decided that I must, in my rush,
learn the things I need to know
so I lie awake at night no more
you shaggy in my eyes.

Old Man, now you are here.
I hurt for you.
Too, I want to look full into your face
creased and formed in leather laced
by years of things I do not know.

Old Man, will you share?
I will not dare to hold back from you
my five dollar bill or a ten when
I stop to ask . . .
I stop to ask . . .

You have called to me, Old Man.
You are reaching out an alien hand
clutching at my sleeve, your need
you have never touched before when
you see that I have paused.

What must you think, Old Man, now
how I turn to fully face you
and the chance to . . .
Share, Old Man, our pain;
mine for you
and yours
for years.

Brian Quam
AS TIME GOES BY

To Cindy Hanson

My love for you grows stronger every day.
Stronger and stronger as time goes by.
My love for you will never fade away.

For you have the only key to my heart.
And no else but you
Will the doors of my love part.

If I had one wish, and one wish to be.
It would be nothing but
To have you here forever with me.

Sharon Derrico
THE KISS
Sunset fading fast
December's zephyrs wouldn't rest
Trekking to Norm's bustling store
Shyness Overwhelming
My eyes took to the floor.
A man stood obtrusively; oh, a fond ol' friend!
Our 'conversation' met for a moment . . .
Off-glidedly . . . Kismet . . .
THE KISS!
The Bridge of Life transcended
Through dimensions never shared before,
Embouchure Across the Edge to a fertile ground
We light upon as if on wings
Complete souls magnified by Shunts
Down, Down
To the depths, our hearts did sing.
Flaming Mirrors!
Heavenly Grace!
Shone upon each soft stroked face
Forever leaving a trace, of . . .
THE KISS.

David John Garry
TO MY CHILD; IN HEAVEN ABOVE
There's a sadness in my heart
I know will always stay.
A slow, painful burning
that makes my life so gray.
You should be here now
for me to love and hold.
To hug and kiss and spoil,
to grow so big and bold.
But those times weren't meant to be.
I try and try, but still I cannot see
why God showed such selfishness.
But as these lines tell, mine isn't any less.
I just want you to know
that I'll love you forever and a day.
My pain may somehow lessen,
but it will never go away.

Asa L Kenworthy
SEASONAL ENDURANCE OF LOVE
Although the seasons come and go,
The sun rises and sets each day,
Birds fly away as each snowfall comes,
My love for you remains strong.

Brenda Irene Helling
LOOK INTO CHRIST'S EYES
Look into Christ's Eyes,
Is that really wise?
My heart pulls away,
Yet, seeks Him today.

Then, I look into His Eyes,
Warm, soothing, loving, and wise.
I know He's holding me tight,
Winning ev'ry fight!

I won't run away,
I've asked Him to stay.
Now, His Eyes look at me:
I'm at peace! I am free!

He is my healer, my friend—
His grace never ends.
I lift up my head,
Re'mem'bring for me, He bled.

I look into His Eyes,
Warm, soothing, loving, and wise.
Nothing hinders me:
CHRIST IS ALL I SEE!

Susan L Bruno
TO THE MAN WHO MAKES MY DREAMS COME TRUE

This poem is dedicated to my wonderful, loving husband Sam.

To the man who makes my dreams come true,
and makes my life worth living;
As the time comes for our minds to fade,
and our bodies to weaken:
I shall cherish the love we've shared,
the dreams we've had
and the promises that we've kept.
I shall not weep for I know
all these memories I can keep.
I thank the Lord above for giving you to me,
for their is no greater gift than the one bestowed upon me.
I'll love you forever!

Dorval Schrougham
HEART BREAK

Dedicated to my three Daughters, Lisa, Carol and Kathy.

You put me on a pedestal the day I married you,
You carved a path along life's way,
And slowly lead me tho.
You paved my road with happiness,
Tenderness and Love.
I sat and watched you darling from my pedestal above,
I sat upon my pedestal high above it all.
I didn't know what life was like until you made me fall.
There I felt life's bitter blows.
With pain that took my breath.
And fear that gripped my very soul.
You had put me thru the test.
My pedestal has crumbled
And now I walk alone.
There is one place I can go that I really feel at home.
But as I find the broken pieces of my heart along the way
I can put them back together and hope for a better day.

Howard Grant Jr
LADY
You wake up in the morning with such a pretty smile,
i hate to leave you lady wish i could stay awhile.
You never really knew what was in my heart,
but i'll never do anything to tear yours apart.
So you say you love me but i don't know the deal,
because everytime i see you i'm wondering if you're for real.
So come on lady and let's take this chance,
get a strong hold on our future romance.

Donald A Cole
A WISH UPON A STAR

To my little brother Alan Francis Cole, March 10, 1966—October 10, 1983. In memory of the life he was cut short of living.

A dream upon a dream.
A wish upon a star.
An insane life that never stops
That drags me near and far.
A gleam inside my busy mind.
A sparkle only some days shined.
The glow that starts from happiness
Then gone to once more find.
Where did it even start?
Will I find which way to go?
I live, I learn, sometimes so hard
But someday I will know
What it takes to carry on
With a smile more than skin deep.
So many dreams and feelings I've thrown away,
Where are the ones I get to keep?
Always see another way.
But should I do I dare?
What's the light at the end of the path?
Is it the one for me to share?
To maybe show to someone else
To learn some other way to see—
The good things that hide in life itself
To find where they may be.

Bill Stoops
LEAFIE—A TRIBUTE

To Leafie—My Wife, My Life, My Love

As from slumber I arose
On our wedding morn,
I paused to thank God
For the day you were born.

My partner in business
A dear friend in times of strife,
How glad I am
That you'll be my wife.

The confidence in your manner
The proud way you walk,
Your devotion to God
And the strength in your talk.

All these things
And many more too,
Make me very happy
That I'm going to marry you.

Marilyn Jean Durst (Kale)
WELCOME, THE LONELY

I would like to dedicate this poem, with all my love, to my husband and best friend, Jack, to my three beautiful children, Russell, Ryan and Melissa, to my Mother, Lois, in the memory of my Father, Andrew, and to all the lonely people in this world.

Silence, quiet thoughts, a dream-like mood,
Broken by the lonely whistle of a midnight train.
Tears, tender memories, and the pain of being alone
Captured by just one sound.
The whistle awakens the thoughts,
brings back the reality, tenses
the reflexes.
The night is no longer still.
The solitude is stirred, and there seems to be a world again.
The moon, so far away, the masses of stars, the rich blackness of sky
Trees, swaying in gentle breezes, willowing, lingering,
A breeze that seems to chill the inner soul.
A relaxed mind, trying to forget the pressure of the times;
the inescapable war, the love
affair, mad and passionate, now
crushed, never to be felt again.
Another cry from the lonesome train; perhaps a call for adventure,
a sudden stir in the blood,
excitement, the tingle of the
unknown.
Or just the realization that the world still is, and will be.
That life beats on, the pulse never stops, just pausing between the times.
Loneliness, consumed by the self, but not wholly alone.
Together, all the lonely, waiting,
hoping, wondering.
Maybe tonight—the whistle of the midnight train.

Amy Suzanne Lantz
THE CALL
The call,
Like an announcement to the world,
Echoes the hopes of a young couple for a child.
Waiting since their birth,
Two bundles of joy,
Await to be chosen,
To be taken home.

They only expected to take one,
Then they saw two.
Now they have double trouble,
Embraced in their sheltering arms.
She radiates with the passion of a mother,
As she shows her premature,
identical daughters,
To the unseen cameraman.

Twice as many difficulties lie ahead,
Somehow outweighed by the twofold
Of happiness, joy, love, and caring.
For now you and I have been chosen,
To come home.

William J Formusa

William J Formusa
GETTING OLDER

To Esther, for the encouragement and love she has given me.

Getting older is rough you see
Not like when you're Twenty Three
Hard of hearing and poor eye sight
Real thick lenses to make them right
All at once he's closing in
Father Time—It's no sin
He makes you old, you lose your grin
And all because of wrinkled skin

Take my advice enjoy your life
Forget the aggravation and strife
Accept each day as a gift
Life is better without a rift

My mind still wanders now and then
To my youth when I was ten
Happy carefree all the time
More so when I got a dime

At Thirty and Forty I had some fun
But not like when I was Twenty One
And now as I reach the Golden Years
With great expectations and no tears
Reliving the past is not my style
Go forward I say with a smile
Age is not as bad as it seems
As long as you're happy and have good dreams

Linda L Giles
CANDLE FLAME
Candle flame burning bright,
Within the darkness of my night.
I see your image in the glow,
Coming closer, ever closer . . . I know.

I hear your foot steps at the door,,
The turning of the knob.
I need wait no more.

Till the passion will ignite,
and set ablaze the lonely night.

I looked into your warm brown eyes
They lit a fire within my soul,
That need never go out
even when we grow old.

You brought warmth and joy into my life.
What I wanted most of all
was to be your wife.

Coming back from long ago,
to find you once again.
You do not recognize or know,
the package I am in.
Love me once again!

Michael Alexander Winkis
SONG OF THE VINEYARD
I'll sing to you a silent song, of islands, and music, and fire.
Of love so real, of soaring birds, of planet stars, and harbour lights,
I'll sing them all to you.
Melodies only our two souls can hear,
Because the rhyme of our beginning
Completes us into one pure sound,
To hear these feelings in our minds,
And see through loving eyes,
The strength that one pure sound creates,
Leading hand to lonely hand.
The unknown chords of sounds familiar,
Bring us to share each other.
A closeness felt, a kiss complete, a perfect touch.
As waves and clouds roll by in darkness,
Shining coloured light
While we make love.
Then, with a fullness sound and true,
Embrace, and join the waves and clouds in harmonizing darkness.
Dreaming,
'Till blue-grey dawn awakes our minds and hearts,
And the song begins again.

Faith McBurney
BEAUTY
Beauty can be hidden,
or it can be bright.
Beauty can be thoughtful
beauty's like a light.
Beauty can't be seen,
except by God above,
Because it's on the inside,
beauty's much like love.
Beauty's much like friendship
beauty is world peace.
Beauty's very powerful
beauty's a great feat.
Many different people,
think in many different ways.
When people think of beauty
They're only in a daze.

Diane Elaine Shalla
AN UNWED MOTHER'S FAREWELL

This poem is dedicated to my daughter who was born on 01-09-67. I met her for the first time just after she turned 18 years old! We love each other!!! To you, Laura Michelle Wedeking-Schipper. God Bless!

I see you lying there—so warm and content,
Not knowing what lies ahead.
Yet, I am dying there—for with my consent,
You're someone else's instead.

I don't want to leave you—I don't want to go,
You're too small to leave behind.
You see me—I see you, you act like you know what's going through my mind.

You raise your eyes at me—try to stay awake,
You seem to know I'm leaving.
I lightly touch your brow—try to make you sleep . . .
Who am I deceiving?

I walk away from you—knowing it's the end,
Knowing life must start anew.
I won't look back at you—no use to pretend . . .
Your life with me is through.

Robert Wilson
APOLOGY
Being able to apologize
Is a quality that's very rare,
Even when we know we're wrong,
We seem to not even dare.

Is it that we think they're wrong,
And we are always right?
To give in and apologize
Sometimes we would rather fight

People think to apologize,
Then weak you have to be.
Only if they would try it once,
Then they would come to see.

The greatest gift to give someone,
Starts by looking in their eyes;
Be truthful when you say to them
"I apologize."

Frank Entwistle
WISDOM PROMISED WISDOM GIVEN
Wisdom promised . . . Wisdom given
As one in Christ is raised and living
Praise born and raised thru the Lord's Holy Spirit
Comes forth from the humbled, that is submitted to it.

Marvette Critney
MY SISTER MY BROTHER

This poem is dedicated to all Afrikan Americans who have allowed their true being to show through untold years of suppression; To those of us who have freed the chains on our minds; Never give up the fight or allow anyone to dim the light at the end of the tunnel.

Across the miles
Across the sea
Our brothers meet
Their destiny

Are we free
Or do we hide
Who are we
Not to take a side

Freedom is in the air
Yes, we do hear
But we ignore
As times past before

We hear you brother
For we are not death
We see you sister
For we are not blind

Let freedom ring
Across the sea
Let's enjoy peace
And harmony

Have faith
One day you'll see
The torture will end
And you will be free!!!

Alyce Russell Jones
REBIRTH
As the caterpillar makes his way up the nubby soft branch of the pussywillow, he perches there unseen by the robin. As he watches, the tulips, daffodils and crocuses poke their multi-colored heads forth to greet spring.
Spring! How long the winter seemed

as he waited for the fresh green velvet to appear.
The sun is warm and glowing, and the caterpillar knows he must quickly drink in the warmth the sun gives him, much as a sponge absorbs the sea. For soon he will sleep awhile and come forth born anew.
What great hopes he has for another beautiful day such as this, so he can awake and transcend into this fragile creature that is one of God's miracles.
As if an artist had dipped his brush into a palette and plunge it forth-in-one fell swoop to create this fluttering wonder of color.
Once again God speaks with his trust and faith and gives us all like the butterfly a chance to be reborn.

Annette Gagnon
THE LOOKING GLASS

Like an uncut diamond
You shine of slight imperfection
But it doesn't matter
For I don't notice
I see stars in your eyes
And your words shine of wisdom
The mind of a genius
Full of dreams
Like an uncut diamond
You are beautiful
The golden perfection
That lives forever

Henry R Teagle Jr
GIVING

Giving
Giving
Giving
Giving

Giving
Giving
Giving
Giving
Giving Lord!
Lord, Help Me!
I've Gived Out.

Ruth Delamar Hendricks
MY ONLY NEED

This poem is dedicated to my best friend, Fred.

Today planes zoom, and into space we go;
'Til even this big earth seems to stand still,
We walk on the moon as if it's here below
So man's hungry ego can have its real fill;
But with all that, I am not satisfied—
Because what I want is—You by my side.

Pockets of the rich are overflowing
Many are moving to warm sites of ease,
And the casinos of luck overcrowding
Where they might win millions in one simple breeze,
Such things may be everyone's joy and pride
But I'm happy just with—You by my side.

Our land is full of opportunities, sure
So children can soar to all heights on high,
Expensive treasures seem to always allure
While meaningless awards are forever nigh,
The world may have all this, but I must concede
That—You by my side is my only need.

Eleanor E Ertel
MEMORIES

The time has come, that time in life
To break the ties that bind
A time that maybe brings a tear
Of memories left behind . . .

Memories of good times shared
Friends along the way
Moments when you had some doubts
Then a smile that 'made your day' . . .

You can't turn back the hands of time
You can't change what has passed
People come and people go, but
It's the friends you've made that last . . .

So when you leave, don't close that door
Remember, we're still here
Distance is not the barrier
For friends are always near . . .

Randy L Cheek
AN ANGEL CAME TO VISIT ME

For Wiona B.;
Where lies my inspiration! R.C.

An Angel came to visit me
at least that's how it seems.
We laughed and talked about you
while walking through my dreams.
Twas there amidst a garden
in a moment filled with Bliss;
I handed her my love for you
in the form of a Golden kiss.
She held it oh so tenderly
on her tiny fingertips,
And said that she would visit you
and place it upon your lips.
Yes, you know I love you dear
and this is the only way,
I can send my love from here to you
while they have me
Locked Away!

Daniel P Staffa
RESPECT

To my Father

Calluses are the medals great men wear.
Thick fat fingers and white tipped hair.
The spirit of a grizzly, or a polar bear.
No one will bother them in their lair.
They're like the eagle in the upper air.
Honesty their drive, they sacrifice to be fair.
He takes it in his hands, he gives his share.
Thick fat fingers earn my stare.
To capture wisdom, if I dare.
A man ain't a man till he combs his sweat,
And on a callused hand you can bet.
Why, you can stake your life on a callused hand,
And live in peace if you understand.
Calluses are the greatest medals worn by man.

Vicki Phillips
LET IT BE!

To my family
Who has always been there

Who, What, Where and When,
Questions sought after by all men.
Knowing whence that we have come,
And accepting all we are to be.

Our future is but an Enigma,
Of what our destiny is to be.
The past has already happened,
So do not dwell, just let it be.

Sylvia Simon
NATURE

Have you ever walked in the meadow green,
Where the grasses grow and the rushes lean?
And watched the frog with spotted coat,
As he paddles 'round in his little moat?

And heard, with accent sweet and low,
The scented wind as it comes and goes?
And watched the oriole's nest as it swings,
And seen the hummingbird's tiny wings?

Or looked upon the mossy glade,
Where a fawn and doe lie in the shade?
Or followed the elk's slow graceful tread,
As they wander down to their nightly bed?

Have you ever slept beneath the stars,
With pine trees 'round you like lofty spars?
And heard the pad of animal feet,
As they walk around you, afraid to meet?

If you have missed some of nature's show,
Far down by the track where the wild deer go,
There's a lesson to learn of life and love,
Written and sealed by the Father above

Robert E Blake
VULTURE

To my son Joseph Anthony and other children of the world who must be cautious of those living in the shadows of life; feeding off the innocent.

On the street corner; a dark lonely night,
ducking and dodging, not a police in sight.
nose running, back against the wall,
body aching, fingers wrapped around that cold steel plated uzie
Kids playing in the school yard, like a Vulture you wait patiently to entice.
You sell your dope, the parent cry,
now it's too late, the little child die!
You bastard, you bastard, a dirty rotten thief.
The most precious gift of all has been taken, by the devil himself.
And you, I sympathize
Jail is your vacation; hell is your reward!

Carole A Stopperich
INSPIRE MY PEOPLE

This poem is dedicated to my precious Lord and family.

Inspire my people, my Lord did say,
Tell them tomorrow will be a brighter day.
Tell them of my mercy and everlasting love,
That dwells deep inside their heart like a dove.

There is surely no problem that thy Lord cannot take,
And make it truly better, for all our sake.

For they are surely my children of blessed love,
I watch over them and care from heaven above.

Peace, I will give them, without a high price,
As long as they truly follow my advice.
So, inspire my people, my Lord did say,
And pick up their cross each passing day.

Michelle S Johnson
AWAKE

This poem is first dedicated to my three sons Harold, Eric and Kendell with love. Second to Reginald Carter who has supported me in everything I do. My love to you.

Awake to the world's conversations.
Cry out to the world's mixed emotions.
Listen to the world cry out with pain.
Do something, don't play along in the game.
Hear the story of the world's miseries.
How people are dying from little to eat.
Help the world in its poverty.
You can help by awakening to reality.
Awake and listen to the young of this society;

They have plans that can inspire you and me.
Awake all to what's going on in this nation.
Don't step back, take a step forward and face it.
Let the world know you won't let it die.
You will no longer sit back and hear

its cries.
Let the world know you're on its side.
You'll help to stomp out its pains inside.
Awake my friends and take a stand.
Awake and bring back love to this land.

Annette J Kimmel
JUST SAY NO

To my beloved children, and grandchildren.

The world of dope will grip its hold,
for a bit of fantasy;
Get high on life not on drugs,
hold fast your sanity:

Just say no, hang on to life,
remain a total soul;
Become aware the factual truth,
a vegetable's not a whole:

Yes for sure it'll fly you high,
much higher than you plan;
Is it truly worth the risk?
you addiction, the length its span:

Say no to drugs, be not a fool,
take it from a friend;
You might just find you'll not come down,
with death a tragic end!

Ed Johnson
CASTLE OF LOVE
Build me a castle on the foundation of your heart,
And furnish it with your love.
Let your bosom be my bed
And your lips my teacup
From it I will drink.
My soul has been drenched,
My thirst has been quenched.
In you I slept,
With you I am awakened.
The eagle builds its nest on the highest cliff
But I shall bury my love in the depths of your heart.
In the castle of your heart I shall dwell,
For your eyes are like diamonds
And your teeth are of ivory.
Your love is worth more than gold.
The castle of a king is filled with priceless treasures
But the castle of your heart is filled with endless love.

Gayle Mieko Tominaga
WE BELIEVE
I believe in you
And you believe in me.
Together we shall stay,
Forever and faithfully.

You believe in me
And I believe in you.
Forever our love will stay,
Always bright and new.

We shall always love,
Like the day loves the light.
Our love will always be,
Like the moon and the night.

This love will always live,
Like the wind in the trees.
Our love will forever exist,
Because we believe.

Nora A DiMatteo
THE BEAUTY OF NATURE
A sight of nature is when I see love.
A beautiful red rose and a soft white dove.

And where the shimmering, shiny, sun billows,
Is on the forest floor that's as soft as my pillow

But then I hear the thunder roar
Above in the sky and at the sea shores.

And the all at once the calm blue seas,
Glimmer so beautifully in the cool breeze.

For love and beauty, nature's the key.
It's far more beautiful than the human eye can see.

Angela D Wolf
I HAVE LISTENED
I sit and watch the stars go by
I wonder where you've been all my life
I've waited for so long
To hear your voice call out to me
In words that would not lie
And I wonder why I hear you now
After all this time of strife
How could I recognize your voice
In the sweet melody of a song
When all the times I have listened,
I was about to cry

Shelly Kov Winger
LOST LOVE

I greatly dedicate this poem to my friend Sherry A. Floom who has encouraged me and shown me the true meaning of life.

Are you there?
Can you hear my words through the loneliness and silence.
Thoughts come to mind
Oppressed with pain torment with care.
Was but you who taught me love and suffer pain.

Hours, days, and years of our past
Concealed beneath an artificial appearance.
Yesterday has no future, Our past behind,
tomorrow somewhere sleeping in the cold.

My thoughts easy to conceive.
Images of you are kept in my memory.
Was you who beheld the love and life inside this soul
Now restrained, an empty shell with nothing of myself in me.

Flowers fade, Memories forsaken, Tears reflected.

Tammy Wilson
THE REWARDS OF YOUR LOVE

This poem dedicated to Juergen and Tiffany for your support and inspiration.

My life began the day you came into my world
I thought my life was complete the day we wed
I never thought my life had any more room to grow
until the day we were blessed with our daughter's birth.

We have shared hard but good times together
Our love has helped us enjoy the times we spend together
The love we have together has helped us overcome the hard times
And the hard times have really helped us to strengthen our love.

We have been given the power to overcome our obstacles
The powers we were given is our love along with our hard times
So nothing should ever stand in our way of succeeding
With this sweetheart I say "I love you."

I just hope that in these past years we have been together as one
Your life has been as complete with me as you have made mine.
I feel we have completed more in the short time together
Than most complete in their whole life time.

I feel we have the power in our love to complete anything we start
So with much confidence I can honestly say to you
"We will be completing each other's dreams and lives until death's end.
Thanks for giving me all the missing parts to make me complete, and just
To know I have your love is my biggest and best reward."

Anna-Margrethe Hertel
TEENAGER

This poem is dedicated to my children—Lisa, Susan, Michael and Paul with much love.

Precious child,
Yearning to be free.
To fly! To soar!
Bound to earth,
by my fears and me!

Mary Kay Pate
LOVE IS A ROSE

In loving memory
To my sister Darlene Marie Guzman

Love is a rose,
So tender and true.
But nobody knows,
Of my love for you.
I hold it all inside,
So one day you will see.
All this love I hide,
Deep inside of me.

Evelyn Dodge Sayner
PROGRESSIONS
Does it seem to you only short ago, no
More than a small handful of years or so
That the world was a mix of marvelous
Sandbox toys which in no time at all
Ballooned into grander sand-lot-size joys

It was the daredevilish challenge of
Kinship with boys. All Real Pros at the
Finer Arts of Tease. 'Til after this brief
Heady vim of Teen somersaults we were
Suddenly expected to turn adult. Though
Even then we could still spin a merry pun
And make spice out of every little quirk
That tickled our funnybone

But do you know what gave us a taste of
What's tough? That like a good golfer we
Watch our swing and really really stay
Out of the rough. Only one small cloud
Drifted across the course which hinted at
Bad or possibly worse: We found that we
Had been given not one single choice. We
Just get old, Or Else.

Sylvia G Honey
OF TIMES AND SEASONS
Morning sunshine lights the ages
As wise men ponder all they know
Life speeds by then slowly dies
And foolish hearts are turned to snow

These are the times and seasons
When love is cheated by the gods
And the setting sun is darkened
As lovers struggle to beat the odds

John Bruorton
WINTER
Thief of the sun,
Of sodden clotted leaves
In hoary forest tun.

Of hot fires, reddened noses
And long loves in warm beds.

Early afternoon, as twilight
Sows its gloom in hedgerow
Pockets, an inquiring owl fluffs
Across a meadow, icy.

Peace, peace, quiet peace,
The last trill of a settling bird,
Oh! So crisp, and all is one.

Ruth Covert
GOD CREATED THIS BEAUTIFUL LAND

Dedicated to my friend Doug

God created this beautiful land
With its oceans and its sand
With the perfume of the flowers
And the rustle of the trees

The kiss of the sunlight and the whisper of a breeze
The song of the birds in a sky of heavenly blue
Then to make it perfect . . .
He created you

Emma M Elsner
DISCOVERY
Oh time,
That now reveals
Fragments of the ancients
Proud edifice
Of a fate for all time.
Ancient time?
It matters not
For my fate is found
In everytime.
A time alive
A time long gone.
Discovering, awaking,
So short a span
For the taking.
Amidst the earth's quaking

Stark naked forms
Of a you and I
Destined for a raking
Oh ancient fragments
Of my time
Molded into oneness.
A whisper sealed—
And yet—revealed
In these dry & dustless bones
Of a you and I
So full of life
That now remains
Breathless and alone.
Oh edifice profound
A tomb for all time.

Caroline M Raker Wible
TO HARRIET THE CAT
I see your eyes,
but they don't see me.
Glowing circles that long to see
but no longer can . . .

My friend you amaze me,
And make me feel sad.
Blind and crippled as you are,
How have you ever gone on this far?

Soon you will no longer be,
and your worries and care
No longer shall you see—
Oh my friend you amaze me!
I see your eyes,
but they don't see me.

Shirley J Ballinger
MY SWEETHEART
I could have boughten you a card,
Although it wouldn't seem quite
right
To say the things it needs to say—
The things I feel each day and night.
The job you go to every day
When I know you rather wouldn't.
The times you've taken me to
movies—
When I knew you really shouldn't.
You understand when supper's
late—
Even though you dislike "Shake 'n
Bake."
And when the house just isn't
straight
You don't complain—that takes the
cake!
You don't yell when I wreck the car
Although I know you have to
mind—
You let me do things on my own
But you're always there when I'm in
a bind.
All of these things I know you do
To show me that you love me true—
With this poem I'll prove to you
With all my heart I love you, too.

Michelle Slosser
MY UNCLE JOHN
John had been a loving and caring person, he never got mad and never yelled, if he did it wasn't at me, he never got excited even if it was exciting. He died young, too young. He had his days and we had ours, we never counted that against him in anyway.
He had his favorites such as a mouse and a book. We'll never forget him and the great times we had with him.

Elizabeth Kellogg Keesling
THE BLUE IN YOUR EYES
The blue in your eyes has the icy
cool effect of peppermint candy,
The blonde of your hair is
reminiscent of vanilla frosting
on a cake,
Stalactites and stalagmites
are your chicklet teeth,
The spongy warmth of your body
is as yummy as a Bundt cake,
If you were a lollipop,
I'd lick you all over,
If the road between us were licorice,
I'd eat every mile to your
doorstep,
If your heart were a valentine,
I'd treasure it forever,
Most of all,
If you were mine,
I'd cry no more.

Mrs Eddie Lynne Hammonds-Quisenberry
THE TIME HAS COME

In Loving Memory of my Father Robert Edwin Hammonds

The time has come for me to say
How much I have missed you since
you went away

My days and nights have not been
the same
Since you have not been here to call
out my name

I know the Lord just wanted you to
come home
But the feeling I have often felt is
being alone

The memories that you have given
me will always remain
And as I often know my life will
never be the same

Gary Lamar Cobb
THE ROSE

I dedicate this poem to my Angelic Mother "Romelia" in memory of Beautiful Sister "Karen Elaine Cobb"

Mid-Winter gave birth to a Rose so
beautiful.
Her aroma filled the garden and the
airs afar,
Devouring hatred with her fragrances
of Love.

The Care Taker pruned her thorns
and thistles.
To mold and shape her he pierced
himself,
Shedding his blood so that the Rose-
Buds may live.

As the Rose grew she beared her
bouquet,
Giving sweet life to seven little buds.
She nourished each with her pollen
of Love.

One Bud withered before it really
blossom.
The other was plucked for the
Master's house,
This left five for the Rose to provide.

The Rose stood strong and never
droop.
Her sap ran with the lost of her
offsprings,
But she bowed to the Master and
gave him sweet nectar.

Tho' the seasons have changed the
Rose has not faded.
Her beauty remains as that mid-
winter day,
Bewildering all that look upon her.
I Love this Rose among all others,
Because she is me and I am her.

Tracy Lynn Hicks
THE EDGE OF TOMORROW
Don't live on the edge of tomorrow,
But live in the heart of today.
The winds of change may
Bring new outlooks,
New discoveries than
Otherwise anticipated.
Breathe these changes deeply,
And embrace them gladly.
Use them to learn, and grow.
Don't live in the
Dark pool of yesterday;
The past is gone and
Will be never more.
The edge of tomorrow
Will come in due time;
Don't rush it.
Live for the moment
Before it, too, joins the broken
anchors
Of yesterday's pool of sorrow . . .
Instead of gleaming on
The edge of tomorrow.

Jacqueline C Nickels
MORNING TIME
In this bed while I lay,
Night is changing into day.
Shadows pass, sunlight streams,
There I lay in my dreams.
When finally I awaken,
Morning's here, the night's been

Verland C Brown
AN ENDING LOVE

To my three girls—Velda, Valerie and Verbena

An ending love is like the autumn;
the beginning of the end—
With its faded beauty of dying
flowers and the soft crying of lonely
winds,
And the incessant restlessness of an
army of whispering leaves,
Rolling over the barren land, not
going anywhere,
But eager to journey on and on into
oblivion.

And nights, when muffled sighs of
the pensive pines
Merge with the fluted warnings of
fleeing geese,
I stand in the gloom and shadows
And wait for the quiet rains to settle
the parched dust.
But it was not always so!

Together, we climbed the hill and
surveyed
The haunting beauty of a golden
valley at eventide;
The mauve tranquility of a setting
sun splashed above a black horizon.
And listened to evening sounds of a
sleepy world sinking into repose,
And we were as one!

Now though my heart cries out in
anguish, there is no answer
Save the Stygian beauty of an
autumn eve.
Still, there's the distant promise of
another spring when Persephone
seeks the sun!
I grasp new hope with profound
grace; This way is meant to be!
I shout a tribute to a life renewed
while the requiem for an ending love
Fades into infinity, and life begins
again!

Matilda Johnson Clairborne
THE BOOK HE GAVE TO ME (The Bible)

In loving memory of my father and mother, Edward Aaron and Alice C. Johnson.

Oh! how I love my precious Lord
Who holds the ultimate power.
He gives me varied choices to make
To fill my void hours.
If wrong I choose, it's my mistake
Not following in his word
In this book He gave to me.

How dearly do I love Thee, Lord,
Because you so loved me.
You gave your only son to die
To pardon a sinner's plea.
Life's guidelines are found in full
supply
Written in your simplistic word
In this book you gave to me.

Let me walk with you daily, Lord
Leaving footprints for others to
follow
Constantly living by your word.
Deep waters may seem shallow
When engulfed by love, peace and
joy
That come from the book you
gave to me.

Eugenia Wood Yarick
SOFT WIND
It seems like only yesterday
we talked
and held each other's hand,
and spoke about the daily
happenings.
You always seemed to understand.
And then a soft wind blew
out the candle's flame.
The emptiness I feel
makes morning noon and night
seem all the same.
Oh why did the soft wind
blow out the candle's flame?
Perhaps, some day soon
I will once again see
the beauty of a setting sun,
and feel the freshness of falling rain,,
And understand why the soft wind
had
to blow out the candle's flame.
taken.

Tara G Mullin
TOMORROW'S PLACE

For KS. who taught me to act on a crush, and for JM. who gave me the courage to admit to more than a crush.

Search
Somewhere we belong
Together
Perhaps in today's light
we can hold hands
share hopes and dreams
and watch love grow.

But maybe
our place
does not exist in today's light
Come take my hand
come with me
towards tomorrow
Help me build

a foundation of trust,
of laughter, of sharing.

Let us search
for our place
and time

Together.

Susan J Seckinger
THE WAR CRY
On a hill not far away
The distant cries of men, they say,
Who fought for things which they
believed,
Would give them freedom and
prosperity.

Through timeless hours the battle
raged,
With the fire of bullets and an
endless haze.
"Freedom for all," we heard them
roar,
Everyday during that bloody war.

Some were wounded, some were
dead,
And some deserted that's what they
said.
In my heart I do believe,
They did all of this for you and me.

As time goes by, there's no more war
Except, of course, on distant shores.
Our hearts will bleed for those in
pain,
And our love for them will remain.

We'll try and live our lives just right,
While our brothers there will
continue to fight,
And maybe one day we will see
That all mankind can live happily.

Mary-Alice Aguirre
THE BREAK-UP
I spoke of my love, but I don't think
you heard me
I showed you my love, I guess you
didn't see
I wanted to share my life, but you
said you had other things to do with
your time
I spent lonely nights crying, praying,
sighing, wanting to see your smile
and feel your touch
I saw the end coming, but you
thought I was making it up
All I could do was sit and watch our
love die
As spring comes and goes, so did my
love . . . the love I was trying to
show
Blown to the four corners of the
universe, lost in a sea that has no end
Decaying as things so often do
Withering and dying because you my
love . . . never saw the clue

Lorie Ann Anderson
WHAT PEOPLE ARE BEGINNING TO SAY
Even though I don't want to believe
What people are beginning to say
I just can't see how you could do that
to me
Tell me they are wrong so I can say
yea.

You tell me not to love you
could this be a sign?
Nights of love are turning to few
Or do you just want to keep me in
line?

Does my loving you mean anything
I try to let it show
So some time when you do love me
Why don't you let me know.

A time ago I had made up my mind
That I would let you have my heart
If had I known this were a crime
I would not let you break it apart.

I do not have any proof
Of what they say is true
What I don't want to find
Is what they say is right.

Ernest Dalrymple
ROSE PETALS

This poem is dedicated to my sweet wife, Edna, my companion for fifty years.

As I passed a rose this morn, it
glistened in the dew;
I gazed upon its splendor and
somehow thought of you.
Oh, not as a sweetheart, but greater
thoughts did it lend;
It just seemed to remind me of a very
special friend.

This is but a single rose from among
so many, whose beauty shown
Like friends—so many at times—
then it seems they have flown.
Some are true and trusted friends,
whose friendship never waivers;
Some are friends today and soon are
gone because of special favors.

Pull a petal from the rose each day,
and soon the beauty is no more,
Because the softness of the petals is
gone and the stem is but a core.
The thorns are more prevalent now,
and now the stem is bare;
It is so ugly now, because no beauty
is it able to share.

Friendship is so much as a rose,
whose petals of love bestow
The kindness of a friend, indeed, the
value we will never know.
Then unkind deeds and evil things
cause the petals of love to fall;
Soon, the thorns of hate appear, and
a friend is no friend at all.

The reason I thought of you when I
saw this rose is very clear;
You are a true and trusted friend, and
one who is always near.
Time may come and years may go,
and problem arise, too,
But today I am especially proud to
have a friend like you.

Elaine Paul
MEMORIES OF YOU CONSTITUTE EXISTENCE
Lips responding to moral sensitivity, dissolving as if the
feminity and the masculinity of
each were creating a source of
traction.

Strong arms and body; but
gentleness no one could imagine.

Soft hairy chest, so soft you could
drift into calmness as you
emerge amongst the fiber of
your being.

To touch the most sensitive; to
respond as in a dream; to know
everlasting communion.

To know suspension of one's self
and the alliance that can exist in
your presence; a bonding of two
which were once beyond reach;
now attainable.

Hands so soft and gentle, moving
in a leisurely manner, magne-
tizing and hypnotizing, as if
negotiating a response.

Unfulfilled longing, suddenly
released.

A sturdy sole, strong, not easily
subdued; but humble enough to
submit to one's own destiny.

A unique relationship; one
capable of preserving prudent
silence in society.

Reverence. Consiliation. Affection.

To know only once would be a
poignant and distressful bereavement; an abstention from
the union of body, emotions,
thoughts, and sensations, that
constitute the individuality and
the identity of our self-abnega-
tion.

Existence is respect for understood limitations and conditions.

Rhonda K Partin
ECLIPSE OF EMOTION

I wish to dedicate this poem to my fiance, Mark Fries. The words of this poem express the joy and understanding he brought into a life that had experienced little of that beforehand. An unconditional love that helped me to understand God.

Precautions
Manifestations of guilt
Ruling, Predominating, Suffocating

Expectation and hope
The foreplay of tragedy

Stifling grey smoke
Veil
A backdrop of blackness

Emanating auras of inner delusions
Believed

A heart impassioned
Ignites the smoke
Spouting a white cloud
That transcends all darkness

The cloud hovers around a form
From the core you emerge
And stand in the radiance of love
One arm extended
To lead me into your being
And caress my heart with yours
I love you.

Florence M (Kitty) Van Matre Rogers
AFTER THE RAIN

This poem is dedicated to my husband, Joe, who believes in me.

It's raining, raining, raining
Crystal droplets shine like diamonds
And the air smells so good
The leaves of trees and grass is
cleaner
All the dirt and grime is gone
. . . After the rain . . .

The sky turns deep dark gray
The clouds pass by so swiftly
There's bolts of lightning from the
skies
And the thunder makes me shiver
. . . After the rain . . .

Then there's iridescent rainbows
That appear in calmed skies
In an endless arch extending
From the heavens down to earth
. . . After the rain . . .

There'll be clear, blue skies in our
tomorrows
As the sun shines from high above
There's a brighter sense of
everything
And . . . today has just begun
. . . After the rain.

Johnathan Simon Michael
TO HUMANITY
Come! Oh Muse to aid my mind
Bring forth great wisdom of endless
rhyme
Rhyme so fierce as to stop all time
Rhyme so brash as to plague the
mind

Plague the mind with thoughts of
things oft not thought of
And bring the mind from fantasy
back to cold reality

Read their faces know their minds
Force their brains to take the time
To read the words and hear the
rhyme
While I feed the plague within their
minds

I thank the muse for aiding my mind
and bringing forth the wisdom
for my rhyme
I hope now people will take the time
to think again, and use their
minds.

Jamey Lowell Baker
LIFE, THE TEACHER

This poem is dedicated to Merritt Garringer, my beloved grandfather. I'm glad you got to see me.

I hoped hopes and dreamed dreams
I longed for things that others
had
I struggled to possess the treasures of
the world, and went too far too fast
As I watched those hopes and
dreams come crashing to the ground I
was embraced
by those who love me
It was then that I realized the greatest
treasure of all

Stephen F Pearce
A SPECIAL NIGHT

This poem is for a very special lady that means everything to me, My Wife, Rosanne Pearce.

There's a fire that burns between us.
One that the now drizzling rain
cannot douse.
As the first sounds of thunder reach
us,
Our bodies shake as the rumble does
the house.
Hoping this night will never end, but
knowing it must.

There's a storm brewing, threatening
to reach its peak.
As our eyes meet, the lightning
strikes close by.
We move closer, not a word do we
speak.
Our lips meet; there's the sound of a
soft sigh.
The electricity sparks making us
weak.

As the rain reaches a new level, so do we.
The lights flicker, we don't care.
Wrapped in each other's arms we feel so free.
The passion grows as I run my fingers through your hair.
The undressing is done so delicately.

As if not to disturb the frenzy of this storm,
Our bodies come together as one.
Your beauty; your gentle touch is of perfect form.
These sensations are so vivid I don't know where they come from.
Again the lightning strikes.

Again the thunder rips through the night.
The darkness engulfing us as we share each other.
The lightning our only form of sight.
Our bodies in tune with the storm,
Both reaching its ultimate climax on this SPECIAL NIGHT!

Janice Elaine Jones
I AM

To My Daughters—LaPrea and Tempest
May you always be wise and strong—never forgetting who you are neither forgetting that you are the essence of me.

I am the Universe, Elements, and Vibrations
A lover of life, people, and things
I'm a metaphysician
I am a philosopher, poet, and writer
I'm a spiritualist—unique, strong, and powerful
I am a moon child—YES—I love my study of astrology and I get my peace from meditation

BUT
my religion
is
in
all
things

Nancy Maldonado Mercado
LISTEN TO ME, MY WHITE BROTHER

To Ramona, my loving mother.

Listen to me, my white brother
I am your black brother
I am your other half,
Just because you achieve more than myself,
Or I achieve more than you
Don't make you better than me
Or I better than you.
The only difference is the salary
We fought together in Vietnam
You did not look at my color then
why now?
You teach your children to hate me,
And I teach my children the same
By doing this, we change nothing!
In the eyes of the Lord you are still
My brother!

Mary L Dautermann
ONE DAY THAT SPECIAL SOMEBODY
One day that special somebody
Will call me to someone
Who will mean more to me
Than almost anyone.

I think I've found that someone
To share the feeling with
I met him in the summer's month
And have been with him since.

This person is the someone
That I like to think about
The one I love to be with
And hate to be without.

He likes to criticize me
He laughs at things I say
He sees me at my very worst
But loves me anyway.

And then again he fills my heart
With so much joy and fun
To me he's very special
And love him very much.

Holly Sanders
NEW LOVE
Visions of past; unhappy scenes
Flashbacks of tears; unfinished dreams.
Rivers of joy; streams of love
Sadness down here; peace from above;
Smokey grey clouds; thunder that roars.
A sun trying to shine; a heart that's been tore.
Rainbows of hope; sunbeams of smiles
Carefree moments; a future of trials.
Digging up precious unforgettable times;
Two people who thought their love was doing fine.
Meeting new people; making new friends
This love is over; another begins.

Beth "E J" Brewington
TO A FRIEND

To Roy, my inspiration, this one's for you!

Through life's twisting
And turning road
We all must carry
A burdening load.

Some are heavy
Others are light,
Some just disappear
From our sight.

Though the paths we often take
Are sometimes full of dread,
The choice is ours to make,
The path is ours to tread.

So when you need a friend
To lighten your load,
To help you down
That winding road,
When life seems to be
Getting you down,
Just remember, Friend,
I'll always be around!

Larry E Repp
WILLOW FRIEND
Above my house there stands a tree,
Just as tall as it can be.
It bows its head as if to cry,
But always waves as I pass by.

It has no leaves just long green hair,
No flowers sweet, no fruit to bear.
But as plain as you can see.
This tree is friendly as can be.

It gives me shade when days are hot,
Even though it weeps a lot.
It sheds its tears of sadden blue,
Then grows another foot or two.

And when the days come to an end,
I wave good night to my willow friend
Fast asleep on its earthly bed,
With hanging hair and long bowed head.

J Nicholas Jones
THE QUESTION
Oh, All you questions in the world!
I will never be able to ask all of them,
Time will ever keep them unasked,
Separated from the answers,
And the thoughts still forming,
Passing from understanding.
These lips will never breathe the questions.
What past indiscretions would fill the gaps
With questions, leaving the answers doubly empty;
Only their sincere consistency grieves these unformed dreams.
And the closed minds see only labels;
Only reinforced archaic notions, only the hurdles,
Put up by them, for the unsuspecting; nevertheless,
Closed minds are always displaying charades of power,
And throwing out questions on superiority, profits
Destructive things and subordination.
No issues and No responses.
When everything is gone, then the
Questions start all over again,
To build a New World.
Hopefully, one with deeper awareness.
The doors of time are only closed for those who did not
Dare to Think of a Question.
Then, Ask The Question . . .

Recha Winkelman

Recha Winkelman
MARIONETTE
His marionette existence
dangles
from my quivering hands.
Our threads are wearing
thin.
He looks up at me
my own doing of course,
his face painted
acrylic tears
and forever accusing eyes.

Susan Parr
YOUNG LOVE
I lost my love one summer day,
When we went out in the yard to play,
With apples, peaches, and pears,
With blankets, chairs, and teddy bears.

While we built our house in the tree,
I kept hoping he would like me,
I cried, but as I soon found out,
It does no good to go and pout.

Mother was so nice to us,
She gave us money to ride the bus,
Sitting next to him there,
I couldn't help, but stare.

But then it happened one long day,
My love's family was moving away,
I could not bear the awful thought,
Of life without, and so did not.

When moving time came around,
He came to say goodbye without a sound,
This had to be the best day of my short life yet,
For he kissed me goodbye, which I'll never forget.

Larry E Flythe Sr
WATCH OUT

To God, first.
To Che'lari, Je'nelle, Ebony, Larry, Jr., Aisha, Joanna, Ciara
And to my loving wife, Josephine, who is always by my side

There are by-laws and clauses,
Rejects and pauses,
All found in dealing with love.

There are additions and deletions,
Incompetents and completions,
All created by the one GOD above.

Quick to put pen to paper
Can't wait,
For I find, personally, I must speak and repeat when necessary
To help stamp out all forms of hate.

'Tis a way of thinking, I think
That truly takes one higher
We must cringe at the sight of Satan at night
For of lost souls is not he the buyer?

What is this that I do?
Why do I it so wantonly, willingly
And often with you?
While acting as if I have nothing all positive to say!

But surely, my friend
Shall not the day come
When all our ignorance and undue animosity
Won't be so much fun?

Maybe then, we all can stay
As GOD first intended
Mankind to mankind; brother to brother—
But forever attuned to one another.

Amen

Shirley Cox
WHAT COLOR IS BLIND?

To My Best Friend, Eleanor (Zett)

What color is blind?
Is it black,
Or is it white?
Is it beige?
Or maybe green?
Or is it a mixture of colors that blind people can see?
There are a lot of different things I can see.
If only I imagine with my mind's eye, a scene.
You see, I've seen all of God's beauty,
And I've seen a lot of ugly things that this world can bring,
Like poverty, prejudice, drugs and abuse of all kinds.
Those things I really won't miss.
But a lot of the beauty that God has given us to see has been made ugly by greed, selfishness and blindness, by you and me.
So, my blindness is not as bad as yours you see.
I can still see the beauty even though

my eyes can't see.
The ugly is still here and you can't see, because you are blind to it, even though your eyes can still see!
It can be taken away, and what then will you see!
The beauty of God or the ugly things of this world that you still fail to see.
So do something now about the ugly things in this world.
Make it into beauty so we all might see, what God really wanted this whole world to be.

By the way, blind has no color, it is exactly what you make it to be.

Portia M Hunt
A PEARL OF A GIRL

This poem is written in honor of my only daughter, Yma.

I emptied my womb
and out came a pearl.
It was God's perfect vision
of a beautiful baby girl.
With a nose so tiny; with eyes big and bubbly,
My little girl, my Yma, my only child
Raised by Grandma and Grandpa
For a very long while.

Though you suckled not my breast
You were a part of me, my offspring cloned
With your little round head pressed against my breast
Each of your discomforts, were discomforts of my own.

My life was for you and for you alone
Too tiny to know—too young to understand
But God saw you through, your goals not to postpone
Just as He and I so carefully had planned.

For when I emptied my womb
Out came a pearl
Who along with mama and daddy
Were all that I had in this world.

Murray Dunphy
SLEEP LITTLE CHILD

Dedicated to my baby, and all beautiful babies of the world

Sleep little child
Through this moonlit night
All snuggle and warm
Tucked in so tight

Sleep little child
Till the rise of the morning sun
And dream your dreams
Of tomorrow's fun

Sleep little child
So tender and dear
For you'll always know
That we will be near

Sleep little child
As mother sings you a lullabye
And her love for you soars
Like a beautiful bird in the sky

Sleep little child
So peaceful and sublime
As I watch you slumber
And thank the Lord that you're mine

Amy Denise Perry
ALWAYS THERE

You were always there for me,
Then, when I looked for you,
You weren't there anymore,
You were gone,
Gone forever,
You walked with me,
You talked with me,
You waited,
You watched,
Now, as I look through my window,
The path before me seems long and lonely,
I'll never see you again
You'll always be a part of me,
I love you.

B L Sipes
MY UNBORN CHILD

Dedicated to my loving husband and my beautiful daughter, whose love filled a void.

You'll never know how much
I could have loved you . . .
For I did not give you a chance

I will never have the chance
to see you smile, laugh or cry
but my dear child I have
shed many tears for you

I am writing this, for I
do owe you something

I want to tell you that
I am so sorry, I want you
to know that I love you
for you are flesh of mine

You fill my thoughts with
an emptiness that I will
never let myself forget

I see another child and
it makes me want you more
But you can never regain
what is lost

I never had the chance to
give you a name or find out
if you were a boy or girl

Please forgive me, for I will
never be able to forgive myself
I will live my life with the
pain of knowing how much I
hurt you; and when I die
and go to Hell . . .

I hope your soul will pray
for mine

Please try to understand
though there is no logical excuse

I love you
I'm sorry
Forgive me
Goodbye . . .

Jef Garity
MERRY GO ROUND

Saw a little girl on a
Merry Go Round
Ride the spring pony until it breaks
She don't understand what keeps the world off the ground
So enjoy it while you can

A senior citizen couple walk their, dog down the street
The lines on their face I bet the stories could tell
Hope I survive to the ripe age of, eighty-three
And if I do will I still have to live

I live he lives we live
She lives a Merry Go Round
I die he cries we rise
Again, in this Merry Go Round

Drove through my old neighborhood
familiar houses have turned to fields
Progress is the key to evolution
(Some say)
Take whatever you can from life, and what it yields
Because it just takes and it makes no deals
Words of wisdom may not always be wise
A little respect can always keep you in time
Life could be death and death could be birth,
to an open mind
I'm so lucky I gotta chance to live.

Nadine King
SO YOUNG

Yesterday I held him.
Dried his tears. Shared his joys.
Consoled the agony of bloodied knee
Until he was replete.
Then wriggling in my loving arms
He said so softly in my ear:
Let me go now.
Let me go.
And my heart quivered with
Soon forgotten fears
So young was he.

Today I watch his joys,
His unshared pain and woe.
My arms ache to hold him
Yet I forbear.
For winds of time call softly.
Whisper gently in my ear:
Let him go now.
Let him go.
And my heart quivers with forgotten fears.
So young is he.

mickey
MY JESUS

To Lorrie——A Very Special Friend

Jesus walks among us
I know for I feel His hands
He picks me up when I am down
and I know He understands

For when I find myself in trouble
And I don't know what to do
If I turn to Him for guidance
Then He will see me through

He fills my life with pride and joy
With His blessings from above
He cradles me within His arms
And He teaches me to love

He fills my world with sunshine
And He makes me want to sing
For my life is so much richer
Since He became "My King"

Yes Jesus walks among us
He makes the world a better place
And when my time on earth is through
I'll proudly meet Him face to face

Patricia Sanford
JUST AN EMOTION

Love is a word,
softly spoken.
Love is a thought
that warms the heart.
Love is a certain look,
or gleam in one's eyes for another.
Love is not always beautiful and forgiving it hurts sometimes.
But remember you are not just one now, you have four feet to stand upon.
Then again one leans sometimes against the other
for,
support,
help,
security,
happiness,
and
strength.

Michele Day
STRANGE FEELINGS

Beyond the imagination of a clear unwanted mind
Is a person who's different from any mankind
With sadness in her eyes and fear from the past
Is a person in sorrow, without any laughs
With terror behind, and the future ahead
Is a person who's hiding the unwillful dead
With a strange image, which she shares only
Is a person unhappy and wants to be lonely
Searching for love in every which way
Is a person unwanted who will never stay
Picking up pieces of her broken heart
Is a person who's losing what shouldn't be apart
Magical powers slowly fading free
Is a person who's known as part of me
Losing and not finding is wrote like a song
It was a beautiful person who will now, always be gone.

Pearline J Jones

Pearline J Jones
WE'VE HAD OUR SHARE OF PROBLEMS

We've had our share of problems this year,
and see no light ahead,

We work so hard to pay the bills,
and Pat sure needs a bed.

Our washer has stopped, our couch is torn,
and I am pregnant too,

Our spirits are low, and we're so tired, ...
we sometimes feel so blue.

We take each other by the hand,
and then there is no fear.

For we draw strength and
courage together, and know each
will be near.

Martha L Langford
YOUR CARESS

To Bill, my caring husband

Why is it when we are apart,
The thought of you never leaves my heart?
All thoughts of others I can suppress,
And lightly resist a tender caress.
Their attention I can hold in cold disdain,

For another's kiss would bring but pain.
My form limp would be,
If another spoke of love to me,
And to a new gentle touch I could never respond,
For my love, you but hold in bond.
Is it that my heart but knows its ideal,
That no other to me can e'er appeal?

Tiffany Ann Bruner
LIFE EVENTS

Dedicated to my grandfather who said he would build my place in the sky next to him.

Fortune favors the foolish,
Evil chases the good,
We all end up happy,
As in our childhood
We knew we would.

Blue flames rising,
Rising in all glory,
Waiting for the beauty,
As told in all the stories.

We will be there,
Building the forever place,
Hoping to see the ones
That helped us through the gates.

Cynthia Sergent
GOODBYE
Underneath this big, black sky,
I lay awake asking myself, why?
Counting the stars above,
Wondering about our love.
I close my eyes hard with might,
Wishing you were holding me tight.
There's a million answers I need to know,
The pain isn't dying slow!
We had been together for so long,
Then things started to go wrong.
I never wanted to go,
But, the signs began to show.
Your last words keep going over in my mind,
They sound like a horrible rhyme.
I wanted to leave never turning back,
There's something terribly wrong I lack.
God knows I loved you,
And I was always true.
But, I only know the reason why,
I had to say goodbye!

Kenneth Davis Caperton
FLYING WITH YOU

To Christine, my inspiration. You will always remain special to me. I only wish I knew you better.

If one has to crawl before he can walk,
And walk before he can run,
Do I have to run with somebody else
Before I can fly with you?

My mother tells me I'll fall in love
A dozen times before I meet the right one.
My friends say I have to play the field
Before I hit home and before I can run.

They say your first love can never work out,
The first one you always will lose.
Before you can find your perfect woman,
You first must pay all of your dues.

But my heart has found the perfect one,
The one who's the love of my life.
I long ago met the girl for me,
The woman I want for my wife.

I see you flying so high above me
While I, in my loneliness, am stuck on the ground.
If I could reach and take hold of your wings
Might I, in my clumsiness, somehow pull you down?

If a boy never catches the first bird that he sees,
Should I still jump, just to be free?
But if all I'm going to do is fall from the sky,
Why should I even try to fly?

I don't want to run with anyone else
Or take the plunge with somebody new.
So here I am, walking all by myself.
Still afraid of trying to catch you.

And what if I run, only to find
That I could have been flying,
all of the time?

So I stand, looking up to the sky,
Afraid of flying with you.

Heather Jean
GOD CREATES WHAT I DON'T USE MUCH

In Loving Memory Of Myra Mehlman, my Inspiration and Great-Grandma.

There's a nice view of the rushing sea!
I daydream. I don't see.
God created two eyes for me.

Someone's talking in my ear.
I'm not listening. I don't hear.
God created me an ear, and ear.

People are waiting for my speech.
I am quiet. I don't speak.
God created a mouth for me.

I don't use three of me much, I fear.
Though I have two ears, sometimes I don't hear.
Sometimes I don't speak. Sometimes I don't see,
Though God created so much for me.

Deborah B Patterson
LITTLE ONE

To my daughter, Emily

I look at you and wonder
Where you've been.
Yet I cannot remember
What it was like before you.
So long in coming
You are with me now
Forever.

Carol A Barott
AUTUMNS OF PAST

To my husband Bill, and my ever loving children, Jason and Carissa.

The leaves aglow of yellow and red, bring signs of autumn to my head

With the wind blowing through the trees, whispering love songs with its breeze.

I walk with my collar pulled up by my ears, remembering autumns gone from other past years.

From the hot muggy nites in August, to the frost on the leaves in October.

I wander through the woods in awe, at the display of color and pageantry that Mother Nature has made before me without a flaw.

It's hard to believe in just a few short weeks this pageantry of color will cease to glow, making way for the coming winter with all its snow.

When the winters grow long and cold and hard I will sit in my chair beside my warm fire.

I'll be remembering the leaves of gold and red, and warm with the memories within my head.

John A Holloway
MEMORIES
Warm bread, holding hands,
White wine, stroking hair,
Ripe peach, kissing lips,
Red rose, smiling eyes.

Passions flowing strong,
How long will they last,
When the rose had faded,
And the peach is stone?

Cool sheets, holding tight,
Green grass, smelling fresh,
Warm fire, shining bright,
White sand, finding us.

Passions flowing strong,
How long will they last,
When the sheets are warm,
And the fire is out?

Grey hair, feeling fine,
Crisp air, touching close,
Blue sky, loving share,
The memory that is there.

Chloë Angus
WHY?
Why? The question with no answer.
Why? The question that every child asks more than a million times.

Why does it happen?
Why doesn't it happen?
Why does the sun rise in the East?
Why does the sun set in the West?

Why do I love someone who doesn't love me?
Why do we love at all?

Why are we cruel to those who are not cruel to us?
Why is there jealousy between you and me and the rest of the world?
Why can't we live in peace, each as the brother or sister of the other?

Why? The question with no answer?

John Ralston
YESTERDAY, TODAY, AND TOMORROW
Today is almost gone,
Tomorrow lies just ahead.
Yesterday is only a memory,
Of things done and said.

Yes, yesterday is only a memory,
Of the things we've said and done.
But as we face tomorrow,
We will cherish them one by one.

If today had been spent,
As if there would be no tomorrow.
We would not have had the time,
For disappointment and sorrow.

Was our today wasted?
Or did a lesson we learn.
That will help us face our tomorrow,
As the pages of time slowly turn.

With yesterday already gone,
And a new tomorrow just ahead.
Forget the things that might have been,
And think of things that can be instead.

Debralee Lamontagne

Debralee Lamontagne
MY FANTASY
I have a dream of how my life is supposed to be.
Visions of my world and visions of me.
I have a special world and a special place.
A problem free world full of grace.
A beautiful world, pictured with purples and blues.
A world made by me, a world not quite true.
I call it my world of fantasy.
A place where there's no reality.
It's that special part of me, that gets me through
the hardest of times.
It's the sun to me, when the sun doesn't shine.
So no matter how hard my life might be.
I'll always remember my fantasy.
It pushes me, to be the best I can.
For it shows me, how really special I am.

Marie Christine Stolte
DELICATE CROSSING
Delicate crossings,
gathering slivers,
from a parquet floor.

We became I's.
Singles now single.

"Dancers Only!"
reads the sign.

Distant flashes of self—
illuminated, we departed.

Boxers, each to our corner.
seeking victories—so
I piece together—
moments—reliving instants—
to be me once more.

Charles Preston Berry
DARK . . ARE THE FEARS OF MINE
Secret are the lies.
Hidden are the ties,
That bond the everlasting cries.

Still . . . in the night wind—
Shining from the light,
By the stars up above, beyond our sight.

Trees casting shadows,
Hear the crickets from the meadow?
The heart is beating louder and louder!

A cool wind blows,
Twilight changes scenery,
And the fear is gone without a word.

Black turns a soft, welcome blue.
Violet outlines the horizon—
Of the sun yet to shine!

Dark . . . are the fears of mine.

Shannon Barscewski

A TEN YEAR OLD BOY WALKED INTO HIS SCHOOL

This poem is dedicated to all the people in the world whose lives have been touched by AIDS. I'm truly sorry and I wish you all the best in the future. Good Luck and God Bless!

A ten year old boy walked into his school,
to find all the classrooms bare.
No one could be found,
the teachers weren't even there.
He couldn't understand why his friends ran away
"I don't want what you've got!"
is all that they would say.
As he walked down the halls,
he knew he was alone.
He turned walked out
and ran straight home.
He was confused, knew not what to do.
He wrote a note to his
mother saying
simply "I love you."
He went to the garage and
got out a gun.
He pulled the trigger and
the deed was done.
The boy had AIDS and
was going to die.
He spent his last days alone.
My question is WHY?!

Victoria Lee Coleman

MY FRIEND

When my world seems to fall apart,
and nothing seems to matter,
You, my friend are always there

You are the best that anyone would need
So stick around my friend;
You are the seed

The seed to my life, the seed to my heart
I'm learning to live,
So thanks for giving me my start

Adelle Stein

LIFE AND DEATH

I dedicate this poem to my daughter Debbie, who passed away in a tragic fire at age 18 years. & 21 mo's.

What can we do?
What can we say?
When we are faced with this sad day—
We grope for words—
But they don't come,
We feel as if we've been let down.
Our hearts fill with sorrow,
Our eyes fill with tears—
For we've been friends for many years.
But then we turn to God,
He always knows the way;
He'll help us make it through each day.
He has a plan for everyone
As He gave for us His only son—
We must be brave!
We must be strong!
And He'll be with us all along.
He'll take our hand and guide our way—
And make for us a brighter day.
He'll never let our lights go dim—
If we but put our trust in Him,
Each ray of sunshine from above—
Is sent from Him by His sweet love.
So praise Him!
Thank Him!
Then be still—
And happiness our hearts He'll fill!

Eric J Valdal

REFLECTIONS

Reflecting post rainstorm light,
Your shadow fades in my mind,
And on its way it struggles and fights,
But my dreams turn too kind.
Reflections come and eventually go,
Floating on streams in my mind.
Your azure eyes swirl in the pool below,
And then drift through the pine.
Your love has long since flowed away,
Past this storm to a brighter place.
Another reflection, another day,
Another reflection I soon will chase.
I'll see your tears in rainstorms to come,
But, for now, the pool only reflects one.

Beth Leann Lisbona

MY TEACHER

To: Glenda Laswell (2nd grade teacher)—Bonnie Bennett (3rd grade teacher)—Terry Edmondson (4th grade teacher)—Pixie Larios (5th grade teacher) and to Elaine Jung (6th grade teacher) DeSoto School District, DeSoto, Kansas.

My teacher is a human,
Just like you and me.
Bad grades will make her shiver,
And she's terrified of D's.
Just the wrong posture of a prefix,
Sends my teacher up the wall.
If I mess up once too often,
She will send me down the hall.
If the classroom gets too noisy,
The lights flip off and on.
She will say, "Stop!" once or twice,
When we turn around, she's gone.
We're all gathered at the doorway,
Peering down the hall.
We all have our fingers crossed,
That she's not making that dreaded call.
The classroom door, it opens,
I think she's found the cure.
She's holding a cup of coffee,
Someday, I want to be like HER!

Laura Bennett Scott

GIFT OF THOUGHT

What . . .
You think about me, a lot

Why . . .
I think about you, too

And I wonder . . .
What you think—and why

If each thinks of the other . . .
During the heavy course of the day

Do we merge . . .
Thought for thought, time to time

And I wonder . . .

What we think of each other—
and why
We don't share . . .
Thought for thought, at any time

David M Hawkins

David M Hawkins

ON TREACHEROUS SEA

To my Grandsons—Christopher and Nicholas Aholt

On treacherous sea,
Thy boundless energies;
Encased and surrounded by the still earth,
Thy fathoms once covered all land;
Then uninhabitable for human worth,

Until a power more sovereign than yours,
Rolled back thy restless waves,
And made there appear trees,
Flowers, and glossy green turf;

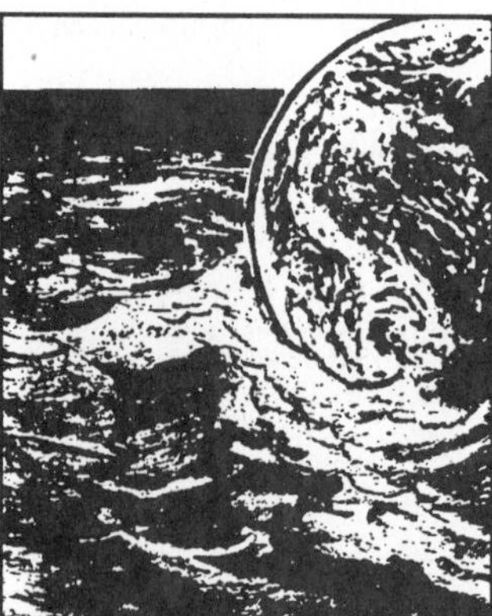

The heavens shared thy watery grief,
To form clouds of rain, for relief.

No power ever—and yet to be—
Had ever harnessed the mighty sea,

Till The God of all eternity;
Spoke the majestic words
That set the land free.

Danielle Walquist

ALMOST NAZI

Beginning the United States
Each person treated fair
Exercising equal rights
Though negroes wouldn't dare

McCarthy led the witch hunts
Against the commie threat
Sure they were unfounded but
We had to stop those Reds

We started to eliminate
A whole subhuman race
Japs in concentration camps
We made them relocate

Of course we're not the Nazis
We are the USA
Though I'd say we're getting there
We're really not that way

The Germans were the Nazis
The Germans killed the Jews
USA does quite the same
But that's not public news

Of course the US didn't mean
To ruin people's lives
We had to take precautions
For Freedom to survive

Of course we're not the Nazis
We are the USA
Though I'd say we're getting there
We're really not that way

Dolores E Yerkes

EXPRESSIONS

Poetry flows like a river
An endless current of rhyme
The deepest expression of the soul
Releasing all the time—

Just like a second nature
The words come forth so free
For to a natural poet
It's his special symphony.

Kristi Elizabeth Robinson

EMBRACED BY NIGHT

To John, with Love.

Stars
Shine Bright
In the Skies
Of the Black Night
Tormenting, Teasing, Taunting, Tattling
On Every Lover's Sigh.

The Moon
Sits so High
In the Paleness
Of the Night
Luring, Luminous, Lazy, Listening
To Lover's Lips Speaking
Softly of the Sun.

Blackness
Spreads far
Over the Moon
And Between Each Star
Reaching, Rippling, Raging, Reigning
Over Every Lover's Endless Embrace.
Waiting . . .for the Sun to Rise
Slowly Between Them
And Paint the World in Gold.

Sheila V Jones

A SPECIAL TIME

To My Family for their constant inspiration and their support.

In every store cards declare
Our undying love for those we hold dear,
Ribbons and lace all red and white
make this a special time of the year.

All the fat little pink cupids
who now emerge on the scene,
With their bows and arrows
just let me tell you what all this means.

It's a special time for sweethearts and lovers
to show how much they care,

A time when the world's divided by two
and we each become a special pair.

So on this special day of the year
I'd like to say if I may,
May you always be a special pair
and a Happy Valentine's Day.

Bonnie Odom
FORBIDDEN FRUIT

To my secret Love Benny

Because of your love I'm whole
You are the forbidden fruit I'm told
I can't deny you this is true
My secret love is you
Damn, Society it took you from me
I grew up thinking we were all free
When you're happy, when you're sad, only my spirit knows
For I see you not, the world knows
The forbidden fruit is love you see
For I took a bit, you're a part of me
Now my love for you, has been told
You have touched my very soul

Janice Moore Delap
KALEIDOSCOPE

To Ryan, my Grandson

Early in the morning, I awake
And look out my window and see
Darkness, everywhere, like a black shroud
Draped all over me . . . . .

As I strain to see the ponds below
I notice white mist, almost grey
Rise, like smoke from a witch's cauldron
Then it fades away . . . . .

I feel like I'm in an audience
Awaiting the curtain to rise
Excitement mounts, old emotions stir
There's tears in my eyes . . . . .

Sounds of awakening . . . the stillness . . .
Mesmerize me, as daylight nears
A miracle, almost unnoticed
Now the sun appears . . . . .

Peeping through the trees, Sunbursts form a
Kaleidoscope, blinding perfection
Silently performs, without request
Its destined direction . . . . .

Dee Marie Vogler
ONLY FOUR AND NO MORE

This poem is dedicated to, not only four-year-olds, but to all who fall victim to child abuse.

Please don't hit me, any more.
My body is already sore.
Can't you see I'm only four?
Please don't hurt me, any more.

The way the two of you fight,
Is such a terrible sight.
It happens night after night.
Nothing here, seems to be right.

No more, I feel this is a game.
Every night is always the same.
And every night, it's me you blame.
All I can do, is hide in shame.

At night, I cry myself to sleep.
I make sure you don't hear a peep.
I pray you don't hear me weep.
And, I pray the Lord my soul to keep.

Now I am lying in this bed.
All these stitches are in my head,
Caused by what you did, not said.
By morning, I will be dead.

Jesus told me, I'm to die.
For you hit me, when I asked,
"Why?"
He will love me, in the sky.
I can't wait to tell you, good-by.

Why can't the both of you see,
What you have finally done for me?
My one wish is only to be—
From this hurting, I can be free.

You can't hit me, anymore.
Now my body won't be sore.
Even though I'm only four,
You can't hurt me, anymore.

Francesca Aragon Azevedo
FOR LUCY

Dedicated to WORLD OF POETRY for giving me THE GOLD AWARD for this poem and to—all who knew, loved Lucy Bardessono of my Yountville Grammar Sch. days—My memory goes back to the 30's in this poem—FOR LUCY.

Lucy's presence at the school—a good part of her life and of the children's being.
'Put the paper scraps in your pockets,
let floors show the shine'—words, children learned well—Lucy tidied rooms, hallway,
removing gum, the spit balls, shoe dust,
Hershey bar wrap, and peanut shells.
Her wit led the way—worth a day in school.

Her home among grapevines on loved acres near school. Children's laughter at recess reached Lucy; Her own children—a big part of classroom enrollment, circled merriment at playtime. By her strength of purpose her large family engendered gift of harmony.

A rest from her daily work; time came again for birth of another child.
She was ready.
The voice of her daughter, Rose, cleared a morning air on the schoolground, calling;
"We have another brother. His name is Steve."
Every day, Lucy saw light come into lives.
Lucy, a widow after this; her seventh birth.

Debra M Malota
AWARENESS PART I

This poem is dedicated to my mother and father, for their support, patience and encouragement for 25 years. Also, to my brother, Robert, and my friends, for their time, patience and continuous understanding.

A flamboyant line loosely hangs;
Dangling in a dangerous wind.
Confusion causes it to sway.

Slowly; quickly; running; walking;
Leaping, and finally, landing.

Dark, murky, muddy waters
Await the soft touch of the frayed edges of the line.
They swim profusely;
Waiting; waiting.

All is quiet; all is calm,
As the flamboyancy remains suspended.

Inflections of time and space—
Inspections of general paths lead to an inner relevance.
Strength, character and convictions
Have cleansed the obscurity—
Not only to conformality but also in retention of individuality.
A flamboyant line firmly illuminates
From its darkness.

Patricia Kershner Hubrich

Patricia Kershner Hubrich
STREAMS OF LIFE

This, my primero published poem, is dedicated to mia late amada Fred; My late parents, Hildah and Walter; Jane y Bob, Kathy, John y Julie. Un millòn de gracias for your support. P.K.H.

Quiet, warm, slow, soothing, meandering streams
Merging with rushing currents, tidal forces
Swirling into life,
Rivers of no return.
Thrusting, rushing against unseen obstacles
To courses unknown.

Beautiful, crystal clear and blue.
Scummy, smelly, murky and green.
Violent, rushing, rolling, treacherous and white.
Warm, rippling, shining, peaceful and violet.
Unknown streams, rivers, waters
MERGE!

Designing their courses
To sustain life.
Shape quiet, peaceful ponds.
Produce magnificent lakes.
Create fresh, challenging, resourceful tributaries.
Form magical, musical, spraying falls.
Nurture God's fantastic flora and fauna.
Destroy human lives and precious property.
Life IS A MYRIAD OF STREAMS!

Misty Irwin
MANY YEARS
Many years you have
inspired my life,
Somehow giving me joy,
today and every day for
years to come.

Dianna Lynn Gell
EVE OF WAR
Here I am alone and crying
while our race is slowly dying
The leaders march on without a sound
leaving our people to be placed in the ground
If we allow the bombs and tanks
we'll soon diminish among the ranks
Roaring sounds pierce the night
filling our cities and towns with fright
People dying in the sand
Is this all you have to offer our land
You have instilled within us
constant fear
that when the war is over
there will be no one left to cheer

Patricia J Rios
FRIENDS

To my ever-loving mother, who was not only my mother, but the friend who was always there.

Friends are forever.
they should always try to be there
when you need them the most,
To show you how much they care,
and that they want to share.
To share your tears and sorrows,
your smiles and happiness.

A friend is not someone who will run out on you when you're having hard times,
or won't walk away when you need a shoulder to cry on, or a little love to get by on.

So, if you see someone who has a frown, they're probably down,
and think they don't have a friend in town.
Go over and pick up their chin, and show them a grin.
Tell them you care, and get out their problems, right then and there.

You may not solve their problem,
but you may make them feel better,
knowing they have a friend like you
who cares for them.

So remember this friend. I'm one who cares, and I'll always try and be there.
I'll give my advice, even if I'm not always right.
I'll try and give you positive sight,
and hope all will be all right.

So when you get the blues,
remember friend . . . it's me and you.

Douglas D Sweat
I'M STILL YOUNG
Long white hair and circles around my eyes
in my life I've had way too many sad goodbyes
heart as tired, sick and cold
I'm still young, but I feel so old

Trying so hard just to survive
but this heart of mine is in a dive
there is no sense in pretending
It's going to be a long long time in mending

One more time my heart is in distress

one more time my life has become
one big mess
again my life is an empty page
nothing for my heart to do but age

Heart so tired, sick and cold
I'm still young, but I feel so old
I'm still young, but I feel so old, so
old
no there's nothing left for my heart
to do but age.

Ruby E Littles Carr
ESPECIALLY FOR ME

To be in your arms, is like the tender touch of a baby's fingers, soothing as a cooling breeze on a hot summer's night.
Warm as the gentle heart of a perfect lover, with the power of an eagle in a mighty flight.
To kiss your lips is like a dream in wonderland, with radiant stars sparkling from heaven so bright.
Lying on a rainbow smothered by your embraces, while smiling angels whispers it's alright.
To hear your voice, is like the velvet echo of a beautiful melody. Whose volume surrounds and overpowers me I'll always remember the trauma of ecstasy, Because God created you, especially for me.
When I look into your eyes, I feel bound by the magic of your tenderness. Passion overwhelms my being, and our hearts agree, this love we share is precious and everlasting, because you came from heaven, ESPECIALLY FOR ME.

Loretta Ann Hannigan Englund
IF I COULD ONLY DESCRIBE TO YOU

If I could only describe to you,
the breathless sight of a clear cool
night,
the light that catches shadows.

A walk on such a night brings about
meditation.

What am I? Where am I going?

I'm a person walking home, to lay
my weary bones upon my bed,
to gain strength for another day.

Janice Zulauf-Waterbury
FOR: CHARLIE

In memory of my sister, Charlotta Dale Waterbury Parisi, whose beauty and light still shines brightly through Harry and Tara. Though death is no longer a stranger to you, the spirit of the "Great Heart" is a friend.

Be peaceful now heart, at my request
Put still this soul who longs to rest
For ions I have felt a traitor
As I only did what I thought was
best.

Unheard, like footsteps upon light
snow
Unseen, like all that lies below
My tears at night became a prison
That housed the grief I dared not
show.

My face stayed straight and quite
unyielding
So I fought to block this flow of
feelings
That others might extract some
thought
And take me from my task of
healing.

No longer this game can I play
For my heart and mind will not obey.
Time has not abated this loss inside
As I think of you more each passing
day.

I still hear your laughter, though I
can't sing the songs
To what good is the music when the
melody's gone?
All that speaks is the silence in
response to lone sound
For a void fills the stanza where you
once sang along.

Sweet Charlie, my sister and my
playmate from birth
Though God's taken you home now,
I have learned of your worth.
On wings made of silver, no feet
made of clay
Do you dance there in heaven as you
danced here on earth?

Michelle M Boudria
PARADISE

Dedicated to; Jim Morrison 12-8-83

Soft winds blowing through the
trees,
hear the songs of rustling leaves.
Softly swaying from side to
side,
the winds of song they
provide.

Strange the music nature makes,
giving more than it takes.
Highlights with each sunrise,
the opening of small
children's eyes.

Watch the ocean's rushing waves,
revealing creatures' little caves.
Colors bouncing upon the
surface,
more with each new
moonlight kiss.
Sleeping still within the
ocean,
the answers for all
mysteries
and mazes of emotions.

Unto life a child is born,
into death another is mourned.
But please, all tears cease,
into an idyllic state the soul
is released.
Death is feared in many
eyes,
yet for the soul it is
Paradise.

Lolita Griffin
THERE'S RAGING PASSION

To My Family and my best friend, Bonnie Bodine

There's a raging passion
of love with us
That we share.
We long to express what we have
But cannot—
We are of the same.
Some say it's sin
for us, it's love
We hold, we touch, we care
The same as others
Yet the beauty of it all
Must be kept within.

T R Markham
IN SEARCH OF THANKSGIVING

Fatted cows through amber fields
gorging;
Majestic purple mountains
witness the genocidal
stampede.
Aniwim's mourning cry a death
bell knelling across spacious
skies.
The bruised fruited plain pressed
out, the bloody drink o
mythical celebration.
Divine wrath searing through the
ozone-stripped vapor of a
vacuous dream.
Manifest destiny of bleached
bones strewn across a desert in
the making.
Prophets plainly packaged rail
over the deafening crack of
lead splintering bone.
Repentance bilious on the palates
of the oppressor, seeps like
Groundswell into the parched
mouths of the herd straining
against the clearly redemptive
drink,
Marking time for a miracle.

Carmen Burrow

Carmen Burrow
MEMORIES

Everyone has memories,
of something in their past.
Mine is of my playthings;
things that didn't last.
But the memories are still there,
and silently slip by.
Slowly through my memory,
quietly, without a cry.
I can never return to,
that world that lies behind.
But I can always think back,
and remember them in my mind.
If people will keep hold of,
the good times in their life.
They can always think about them,
when they are filled with strife.
So, please remember friend,
when you are feeling sad.
Think of all the good times,
and they will make you glad.

E Allen Jr
TAKE A MOMENT AND THINK

Life is a gift . . A diamond defined
It stimulates growth and rewards you
with time
So please understand within your
heart
That life won't begin until hatred
parts.

We all enjoy living, stray away from
wrong
Come together young colors, mix as
one
When you contemplate situations
that might bring you fate
Stand tall young colors take a
moment and think.

The world has dimmed . . . .
You're the light of the path
Stand tall young colors . . .
Subside the wrath.

Just believe in yourself you will
succeed
Open your eyes to knowledge for this
is the key
Through valleys, mountains, rivers
and storms
Seek courage from heaven and
strength will be formed
Converse with wisdom it will never
let you down
Develop patience, perseverance for
this is your crown
When you contemplate situations
that might bring you fate
Stand tall young colors . . . . Take a
moment and think.

Joseph Meeks
ETERNITY'S LOVE GATE

From beyond my comprehension you arrived and wept heart-shaped butter-fly wings. Radiant maiden, more sacred than muted tones of an un-charted symphony, you with fire-opal laughter join whispering, soothing wind-chime eyes and liquid petals of love that weep joyously beyond the private reality of our folded silence.

Rare honey, red kisses and naked laughter, blossomed into bright rain-bow flowers of loving. I opened the gate and became a part of your life within—Eternity's Love Gate!

Eldron C Rowsey
THE SPLENDOR OF LOVE UNCHANGED

To my wife and lover of 39 years. Vivian I.

Our youth of today seem oh so
confused, to love is just something
they start
Their emotions give way and in
public display, "I LOVE YOU"
needn't come from the heart
Yes they kiss and they touch gaze in
each other's eyes, yet the meaning
and depth both have missed
For love as a word has been oh so
abused, so that love is just sex with
a kiss
Let us search out the truth real love's
purest form, determine what true love
should be
We must help today's youth to
determine the truth, 'Tis more
blessed to give than receive"
Real love is fulfilling and giving
one's all, don't with-hold, prejudge
or pass blame
It's accepting one's faults not
condemning results, sharing all of
one's thoughts without shame
Two hearts that abide with love side
by side, sharing all good and bad
that comes in
Two in love don't hold back no
resentment or slack, they are
sweethearts and lovers yet friends
There's one word called trust in love
it's a must, without it no deep love
survives
No containment with space no
distance or place, purely trusting
keeps true love alive
True love is forever and sharing takes
two, both struggle and strive
to survive
With their lives nearing end both
lovers still friends, "TRUSTS" the
reason their love's still alive
This isn't a mystery reread it you'll
see, the key is for each to give all
With sharing and caring yes
LOVING with TRUST, LOVES,
responding to each other's call.

Elizabeth Weaver
MY BIBLE
I love to read my Bible;
I live each life I read.
Sometimes I ride a donkey;
Sometimes I walk a dusty road
and feel the sand in my sandals.
Sometimes I'm awfully hot;
Sometimes I'm awfully cold.
Sometimes I'm awfully thirsty
when I live the lives I read.
But when they crowned my
Saviour,
The thorns stuck in my brow.
I felt the blood run down my face
to wash away my sins.
I bowed my head in prayer and
thanked Him again and again.
And when they nailed Him to the
cross, and He gave up the Ghost,
I think of all the lives I've lived
that hurt me the most.
And then I walked up to His
tomb—
His grave clothes were laying
there—
I shouted Hallelujah!
My Lord has risen now.

Peter Layton
THERE'S SOMETHING ABOUT A MAN
There's something about a man
Such like a seed pod remembrance
Bears the musky resemblance
Of burlap and dusk
Something to be savored through an
oaken cup
Something like ale
At once diffused and also foreign
Can't be held in a lady's hand purse
It's urgent and can cut
Virulent as a tooth edged thing
It's darkly pleasant whan thought of
hence
There's something about a man

C Thomas Acres
SCREAMS
Screams, I hear them day and night,
from the troubled souls who
continue to fight.
Screams of anger, hate and rage,
from inside their small barred
cage.

Even when whispering they continue
to scream,
one to another or so it would
seem.
They scream at those that they hate,
they need to realize it's
themselves before it's too late.

Voices blending in mortal fear,
can they sense the end is near?
Like rats know when a ship will sink,
their hatred condemns them as
their understanding shrinks.

Scream and blame the others who
yell,
are they just practicing for the
torment of hell?
Scream with justified indignation,
over your self induced situation.

I find myself joining in the scream,
have I lost what little I had to
redeem?
God have mercy on our sinful soul,
for all the screaming has taken
its toll!

Luellen H Heitger
PERPETUATION
A matriarch is the main trunk
To branches of a growing tree.
If that trunk is rooted well
The branches put forth their own
twigs
And all are nurtured from the soil
In which the seedling first took root,
But it's the twigs which bear the
fruit.

How proud the matriarch must be
When that fruit is borne heavily
To pleasure those who reap the
harvest.
'Tis said that "Only God can make a
tree"
And that phrase is brought home to
me
'Cause those twigs which have fruit I
see
Are healthy ones, and not just duty
Brings forth that of natural beauty,
But innate pride in God's great gift
Of love, which brings continuum.

Kathleen P Kelly

Kathleen P Kelly
YOUR CHILDREN

To my mother, Leona O'Brien, whose love and gentleness, inspired a deeper meaning to the Golden Rule and my life.

They should not be a burden or a
cross that you must bear
For life would be so incomplete if
one day they were not there
So set them up upon your knee and
brush their tears away
And remind them that you love them
each and every day
Is it so hard to say those words which
we forget to say?
Are you always just too busy that
you turn the other way?
You had better make some changes
now before they grow too old
For children tend to imitate all that
they've been told
If you neglect your children now and
put them on a shelf
You may not like them later for they
are a product of yourself!

Robert F Tupa
CHRISTMAS IS THE SEASON
Christmas is the season
When love and peace are big and
bright,
God gave His only child
To us that starry night.

He sent His only child
For all of us to see,
That we can have this love and peace
For all eternity.

So it's not just to practice
During the holidays,
But show it to your fellow man
Each day in many ways.

Let's show God that His sacrifice
Was not too great a gift,
If you see a man in need
Reach out, and give a lift.

Then some day when you are called
To sit beside God's throne,
You'll find the love and peace has
spread
And you're not there alone.

For when you help your fellow man
He will pass it on,
Then maybe some day this whole
world
Because of you, will see the dawn.

E A Salisbury
FROM US, TO YOU

All are born predestined to experience light and darkness; with a pleading hope that the light be warm and plentiful and that sweet sleep be our reward at night. Here's to life and the living.

Where did they go, our love of life,
the sunrises we once adored,
the scented earth where our feet once
played,
the cloudless skies where our
hearts once soared?

What caused this fear to make us hide
in a cave of our own making;
where the sun is obscured and birds
don't sing . . .
where all we hear is our own
hearts breaking?

We used to sing, dance and
laugh . . .
all in life we found a joy;
this too disappeared with the earth
and sky
while our hearts were used as a
toy.

Please listen to us, all of you out
there . . .
please hear our words, our
pleading!
Return our love, which you've
trampled on,
so our souls may heal . . . stop
bleeding.

Marion Mainprize
LOVE

Murray, thank-you for the inspiration.

What is love to me:
Love is to be free:

To grow apart and together
entwined.
Love has no restrictions.
Love can overcome any obstacle.

Two people together, sitting quietly
Love is trust, understanding,
and commitment.
Love is total compatibility.

Always caring for and understanding
the other person's feelings.

"Love is you and me"
Walking barefoot in the rain,
Me when you're away going
insane.
Us holding hands at peace with
everything,
My heart so light I could sing.
Your touch, your smile, the way
you say my name.
Each stolen second I'm allowed
to be with you.
The look in your eyes when
you're watching me.
The way I feel when I hear your
name.
I want you with me every second of
every day.
I wish I knew the way to make my
dream come true.
Without you my world is lonely and
blue.
All I can say is, I love you, I love
you.
Please always be true.
Handle my heart with care, for it will
always be there with you.

Jessie McIntyre
THE SEARCH
You drifted into my existence,
As a snowflake falls from the sky;
Changing all my perceptions
Of Life's realities.

You weaved your magnetism
Over what I believed to be true.
The visions that you gave to me
Were larger than the world, I knew.

You obliterated those stoggy patterns,
That use to represent me.
Like a bolt of lightning,
You incorporated new ideas into me.

Once again, I see the world
Through the eyes of a youth.
Each day creating new patterns,
By the constant reshaping of me.

What's important, I ask;
On this another day?
Always, the answer floats back;
Search for the truth of you.

Linda Kay Harrison
THE FARMER'S CREED
Towards the edge of daybreak, and
beyond the setting sun,
a farmer tends his seedlings.
So much work is done!

The soil is ever thirsty and at times
it's never dry.
Pests and weeds and weariness; the
farmer cries,
"Oh why?" Yet, so much work is
done.

To look upon the harvest, another
crop has come, still his eyes do
moisten.
There is so much work to be
done!

The fields are all aglitter with
December snow.
The farmer sleeps a slumber, one day
all will know.
But as the fields lie barren, and cold
to every eye,
the farmer whispers sweetly,
"Now the work is done!"

Towards a new beginning a young
man feels the well tilled soil. He
knows he'll earn his living; and for
his family as well. No more time for
dreaming.

There is so much work to be
done!

Dorothy Ruiz
THAT WOMAN

For Grandma . . . your love kept me from turning sour; your acceptance gave me faith in myself and life; your presence gave me courage to live on.

That woman!
How much I loathe her.
She'll yell for the silliest reasons
And shatter my ears
And make me cry
And call me names
of the most horrid things.

None of which are true.

She'll hit me, say sorry,
Expect to be forgiven,
Then do it all over again.
She'll embarrass me
Among adults
And still exclaim
Her devoted love.
Oh, will the torture
Never end!

Kathryn Spurlock
COLOR OF LOVE

Dedicated to my mom who taught me about being a woman, to my husband, Frank, who taught me about being in love and to my daughter, Jenny, who taught me about being a mother. Most of all, thanks to God for so many blessings.

The sky clears
The sun warms the wet earth
Cleansing rain and everything is fresh
Warming rays reflect a rainbow
Colors so different yet intertwined

Red, orange and yellow lost in the burning brilliance of passion
Green, blue and violet surrounded by the quiet sadness
The loneliness and confusion
So many mirrors reflect so many sides
To so many feelings
Confusion is all around

Colors so different yet intertwined
Lost in the confusion of passion and sorrow
Swept away by the love and heartache
So may colors of the rainbow
So many colors of the woman in love

Melva F Hall
TRIBULATIONS
Lord have mercy
I'm as tired as can be,
Problems, Problems,

Insanity!

Up and down the roller coaster
Spinning around,
Faster, Faster,

Going down.

One thing after another
Can't take another load,
Burdens, Burdens,

EXPLODE!

Sheri L Henderson
WHAT IS HIDDEN

Dedicated to my brother Dan, who is in the U.S. Air Force.

He thought she was honest, faithful and true
The pain she would cause him, he never knew.
She was very deceitful, yes she was smart
For the day he had left, was when it would start.
A hidden life, she tried to cover
Would soon leak out, one way or another.
Though he is the good guy, the one that will win
It can't possibly make up for the pain he is in.
She lied and cheated, took what he had
She was the type who made love look bad.
Late at night, I picture him weeping
My mind switches to her; she's probably sleeping.
He'd never admit it, but yes, he was blue
For he was taught love, always to be true.
All that is left is a lesson he's learned
To find true love, you must love and get burned.
Someday he'll see though, there's always another
But until that day, I feel pain for my brother.

Ruth R Blackburn
THE PINES
Seeking to locate the sounds as of a distant waterfall I find it's only the wind sighing and whispering to the tall stately pines who bend their branches to listen and obey. If the wind whispers gently they nod in agreement, knowing all is well and settle back complacently to proudly display their glistening needles and bask in the warm sunshine, now and then reluctantly releasing a sharp pine cone that falls silently to needle strewn ground below filling the air with sharp pungent scent of pine. If the wind is abusive and angry the trees bow gracefully to her commands, never losing their proud dignity, knowing their tranquility will soon be restored. Meanwhile, the birds perched precariously on her branches look on in alarm and seek a more secluded shelter until Mother Nature is in a gentler mood.

Anna J Qualset
BLOOMING LOVE

This is to all the people I love, especially my Grandparents

Love is like a flower
Growing high and high
But when the blooming's over
You have to say goodbye.

Annaliese Lily Margaret McCandless
ALL I ASK IS THAT OF PEACE

To my loved, dear, and deceased grandmother, Lily Margaret Luckhurst

All I ask is that of peace,
Don't fight today, is what I pray.
So many tears, so many fears,
A memory of war never disappears.

The day is here, the men draw near.
My house is burnt, my family's gone.
I see the flame, I turn around,
I am dead;
but no one heard my silent tread, not a sound

I am still 12 as I was then,
because of death I do not age.
My heart is silent, no sound I hear,
Still my tears, and yet my fear, a long hard stage.

All I ask, is one more thing.
Don't fight again, don't fight again!
Just let the children grow, and laugh and sing.
Don't put them through the same thing;
not this pain.

Linda G McCauley
THE TEACHER
Inside my works comes a piece of me;
I'm a natural born writer for the world to see.
You teachers push so hard to put it from me,
It's all inside flowing, look and see!
I put it on paper for you to see;
It's all on the surface, don't you see?
You break it down, you're hurting me.
You're invading my private zone taking from me!

I put it on hold and locked it away;
But teacher, teacher always your way!
You broke through the ice and set me free;
Teacher, teacher, the writer in me!

Sheryl J Robinson
ALWAYS REMEMBER LOVE

This poem is dedicated to Dallas, the man who taught me how to love and hope, and who proved that love can last through anything and end up even stronger than before. I will love him forever and foralways.

Always remember Love comes,
with some heart ache and problems,
But yet it still survives.

Love is forever growing, with the good times and with the bad,
But yet it still survives.

Love is our strength, through happiness and through the tears,
And yet it still survives.

Our love is what will hold us together,
through all the passing years,
and our love is what will help us to survive.

Ivan Baker
EASTER SUNDAY. JAMAICA.
Ringing bells, lapping waters,
In red surplices the church's daughters
File in procession through an open door
From a palm framed vestry on the shore.

No need here for cathedral's splendor
With vaulted nave and gilded grandeur.
No sermon needed or chanted psalm
To sanctify its air of calm.

Here in primeval simplicity
Learn of God's infinity.

Adrienne Marie Johns
A RAINDROP
A raindrop fell upon the land
And disappeared among the sand.

It seemed to be gone forever
But the little thing was very clever.

It waited—'til the sun came out
Then raised up and went about.

It found its way into a cloud
And waited—'til it stormed out loud.

It's raining hard and down it goes
And fell this time upon a rose.

It will never-ever-go away
The little drop is here to stay.

Flora E Greene
WEATHER

Dedicated to Farmers Past—Present—Future

Weather affects us
One and all.
Makes no difference
If we are big or small,

Weather dictates how
we live and grow.
It is one commodity
that steals the show.

We need rain to
Wash the Air,
And give moisture to land,
so it won't lay bare.

After the rain,
the Sun will shine.
Bringing forth beauty
and food.
So people can dine.

Christina E Rumage
THESE WHICH I HATE
These which I hate:

Crowded rooms with
elbows in my side;
The screech of fingernails
on a chalk board;
Five flights of stairs when
the elevator is broken;
The smell of wet asphalt
on a hot day;
Cold friendships with
no meaning;
The whistle of a dark
wind;
The empty feeling you get when
all of your friends are gone;
The roaring laughter when
I feel sad and want to cry;
The slow ache in my
heart;
Death without
reason;
Life without
meaning;
Hate without
cause;
and
Love without
feeling .

Kristin M Koch
AS MY WINDOWS TO THE OUTSIDE WORLD GROW HEAVY
As my windows to the outside world grow heavy,
And my thoughts grow drowzy.
My attention focused on nothing—except everything.
As the bright stars outshine the artificial lumination of the Great City.
But only in my mind.
I wish I could stay on the cool sand
To listen to the calm waves hitting the cement breakwater.
Only beautiful if one does not search too hard
—or listen too long.
Blocking out the horns—and fuel being burned—and the artificial music.
Listening to the real music
Water playing with other waters as it's unleashed from human view.

'Cause no one can see nature in the dark.
I sit and wish on a distant star for something I may never have,
But contentedly lying on the beach, I restfully fall asleep.

Dorothy L McFalls
SUICIDE

I am injured again,
You have done this to me world.
You have knocked me down,
pushed me aside.
In a mud puddle I lie,
Bleeding tears—
In your quest as an individual
You have killed another's dream.
If you lose me
I want you to know,
"I had a lot to give."
I will fight this time,
Lick my wounds—
And struggle to go meekly on my way.
But one day, somewhere
You, world, will inflict
A mortal wound
And my soul—
will die.

Kerry, Frank and Frankie

Margaret Ruth Kelly
BLOSSOM IN THE SKY

To my precious daughter Kerry, my wonderful and charming son-in-law, Frank and dear little grandson Frankie Arcia
And last but not least my very dear and loving husband Allen.

Dark clouds are rising from the sunset.
A new way, a new day is about to bloom!

We burst with a hope that is real!
One that will never die!

It pushes us onward to horizons of love,
That make for us this new way.

A day when all our dark clouds rise,
The sun sets like a blossom in the sky!

Michelle Harper
LOVE

In memory of my grandmother Tilda Silva June 5, 1903—March 27, 1989

When love's born it searches and lives in your heart. When your heart's grown by this magical love, it will separate because of its enormous size and will live invisibly outside of you, now it needs a soulmate to grow. Be careful who you choose to accompany your heart, because of its magic, many will try to claim it. Remember, it's sensitive and fragile from being so protected inside, it's your choice when it should part, it may get broken or abused when the wrong person tries to take it away.
The unprotected heart takes time to heal, use it wisely don't be so quick to unveil the magic will last and someday will find a soulmate and together will grow and grow leaving all broken hearts behind.

Candy L Verner
THOUGHTS AND REFLECTIONS OF A MOMENT

No one hears my loneliness,
though it rings in my
ears.

No one sees my loneliness in the
course of my
tears.

No one senses my loneliness
enveloped in a blanket of
fears.

It's no one's fault, they aren't
unkind.
They just don't realize our lives are
intertwined.

Christine Leigh Brown
THERE IS A RAINBOW

This poem is dedicated to my family for their love and support. It's just the beginning. Thank you.

If shadows fall across you
When you feel low.
Let the sunshine warm you
There is a rainbow

The day was clear and shiny
The sun a bright flame
Then the clouds took over
And it began to rain.

The raindrops fell hard
into the misty sea.
Dark shadows surrounded it
And surrounded me.

Rain clouds are like loneliness
it comes in with the tide
There's something special behind the clouds
Something I must find.

If shadows fall across you
When you feel low.
Let the sunshine warm you
There is a rainbow.

Eillene M Clevenger
REFLECTIONS

Lightning flashes,
Thunder roars,
Raindrops fall on tin roofs.
Lightning strikes a tree,
Flames illuminate the tinted sky.

A child runs in the meadow,
Billowy clouds roll across the azure sky,
Multicolored butterflies dart among the flowers,
The sweet smell of June Roses,
Hot afternoons,
Warm nights,
Fireflies caught in a jar.

Mark Prince
A DAY WITH MY WIFE

This poem is dedicated to Marilyn, my wife.

It's morning once again
I wake up with you by my side
So warm all over
And still a little tired
I see you lying there under the covers
I think of the day we both said
I Do
The day goes on
Lunch comes around and I think of you
I work through the evening until 4:00
Now I'm off work
I now wait to hold you in my arms
and say hello
We spend the rest of the day together
And so night comes and off to bed
we go
Side by side once again
Off to dream land I go with you on my mind
So now you see that I spend every day with you
So once again I'll say I Love You
And thanks for spending your days with me

Mr Malcolm Kent
CRUEL LADY OF FAME

Dedicated to my daughter Heather Christine Kent who will one day make the angels sing a new song because of your special love for others.

Mysterious Mother, cruel lady of fame
a damsel of beauty, the lover of shame
glitter and glamour are part of her game
Mysterious Mother, cruel lady of fame.

I see her reflection in the streets of our land
seekers of pleasures now kissing her hand
looking for courtship, not counting the cost
seeking their fortune in a land of the lost.

I see her seduction in the eyes of the meek
she lusts for the innocent and feeds on the weak
her charms are attractive and hard to refuse
many will try but many will lose.

I see her destruction through greed and desire
killing so silently and burning like fire
she beckons for a lover to seek for a Name

Mysterious Mother, cruel lady of fame.

Michael P Galuppi
THERE IS A GOD

To my family, who has introduced me to both God and the great outdoors.

There is a God.
This much I know.
He is present in the radiance of the sun,
in the whiteness of the snow.

I see this God cry
in the gentle beating of the rain.
I see this God laugh
on a warm, sunny autumn day.

I see this God angry,
his strong fist pounded against this small earth.
I see this God gentle
in every bird that flies and
every stream that flows.

I see this God tired
in a sleepy winter day.
I see this God awake and alive
in the birth of a child.

He is not so distant or so foreign to us.
He is much like you or I.
Like a child who finds a shiny new penny,
I find him with ever jubilation.

Phyllis
ON LEARNING TO FLY

I saw a friend the other day, and
she waved and grinned and
went on her way.
We hugged goodbye as we often
do, and she lightly asked me,
"How are you?"

She doesn't want to hear, I
thought, of all the pain the
WORD has brought.
The secret WORD that lives in me,
and doctors' knives and drugs
can't free.
It creeps throughout my breast
and lung, choking breath and
hope and fun.

Yet my pain burns a way through
these clouds in me, revealing a
space where I can fly free.
A quiet space where there are no
WORDS—only peace and love
and the song of birds.
There are smiles and hugs and
my husband's touch, and hands
to hold when the pain's too
much.

There are rules to life in this
peaceful space. I can't bring hate
or a pouty face.
If I cling to anger of guilt or fear,
then the doorway of love just
doesn't appear.

And I laughed as I hugged my
friend goodbye,
"This Cancer is teaching me how
to fly!"

D T Bahl
TO TAMMY:

The things we do in our lives,
determine how we grow.
Do too much, or not enough, and
progress will be slow.

Youth, it seems, at the time, is a
losing bet.
Yet as we grow, we realize, it's life's
one great asset.

For when you're old, and take a
chance, recovery can be slow.
But when you're young, and things
go wrong, "That's the way things
go!"

You bounce right back, and try
again, until you get it right.
Set your sights and chase your goals,

your future will be bright.

But don't grow old before your time
and compromise your life.
Age will come, soon enough, and fill
your life with strife.

The secret to happiness, in this life
we share.
Is to love yourself, and your friends,
and show them that you care.

For if you can, love your self, secure
with who you are.
Troubles will be few in your life, and
you surely will go far.

Sandra L Skolfield
SWEET NOTHINGS
Flying high or flying low
My smiles for you will always
grow.

Whisper soft and whisper sweet
Then shall you hear the gentle
rhythm of my heart beat.

Saying "No" and saying "Yes,"
That's all part of life's guess.

Smile today and smile tomorrow
Keep smiling for no more
sorrows.

Touch me now and touch me tender
Then my heart shall not render.

Kiss me soft and kiss me light
My body shall glow in sweet
delight.

Expressing once and expressing
twice
I'm here for you day and night.

Remember this and Remember me
Then shall you have all of me.

Russell DiBella
ENDINGS
Like the time
Your best friend moved
Or you did—you didn't think
you'd ever find
another
Irreplaceable
Or those last days of summer
Vacation—Your clothes never
fit back into your
suitcase
You didn't want them to
Or those last days of school
Senior year goodbyes and
goodlucks
"See you this summer"—maybe
And that special one
You were sure that was it
It never felt so right—that's
why it hurt so bad
It didn't matter who decided
Even dying
Maybe it's like all of these—
combined
I don't know
I don't want to

Jeff Stagno
THE COLD SNOWY MORNING WITH ITS BITTER BITE

To my Mom, with all the love in the world!

The cold snowy morning with its
bitter bite
The distant sun with its very faint
light
The bed you lay in with its warm
open arms
The snow covered fields next to the
old worn down farms
The trees with no color and stripped
bare to the bark
The back of your mind unconscious
and dark
The thoughts you have pry into your
mind
One thing you can grip you just can
not find
Not only do you know what the old
lands hold
but soon the sun will meet the land
and gently fold
Of a life I wish I knew
A life I wish I had
the life of myself
thrown into the flame
the flame to quench my thirst
thirst of love to have
love to grow
growing to break
one heart.
Mine.

Lynn Corning
HOW TO WRITE A POEM
I'd like to write a poem.
I've got a little time.
The only problem that I have
is finding words that rhyme.

I'll start from the beginning.
I think I'll make a list
Of all the words that rhyme so that
I'm sure one won't be missed.

Now I must pick a subject.
Could be a little tough.
It has to be a good one
so I'm sure to write enough.

A subject that's of interest
to almost everyone.
I think I'll write on"How to Write a
Poem."
There, I'm done!

Jeffrey D Knecht
FAIRY TALE
I drifted off into a fairy tale
I left my body behind
Not knowing how far I might go
No idea what I'd find

The things I saw were crystal clear
The sounds I heard so kind
I felt I'd reached my ecstasy
A total peace of mind

A peaceful thought of serenity
Harboured in my head
Had I entered that heavenly state
We all reach when we're dead?

No more thoughts of loneliness
Peace and love were all around
I'd gone searching for a loving friend
But "I" was what I found

For all our lives are fairy tales
Not written in any book
Search for love within yourself
Just close your eyes and look

Tom Short
COWBOY (AS THE INDIAN SEES HIM)
Contemptible
Onerous
Warlike
Beatable
Obstacle
Young
A cancer that is ever growing
with no cure.

Marion A Ellis
WONDERFUL MOMENTS
Life is full of wonderful moments,
Take time to enjoy each precious
day.
Look at the flowers and smell the
bloom,
See the butterflies, while on your
way.
Hear the patter of rain on the roof,
Or the sound of a clear running
stream.
Hear the birds tweet a cheerful duet,
As night flees and the sun sends its
beams.
Feel the velvet petal of a rose,
Or the soft touch of a gentle breeze.
Feel the tender love of your loved
ones,
Who, with all their heart, they try to
please.
In fall the tree leaves change to
pretty colors,
Then they fall lightly to the ground.
The tree goes to sleep for the winter,
In spring it blossoms all around.
Awake like the tree and blossom,
With happiness for a brand new start.
Thankful to God for each new day,
Keep His love deep within your
heart.
Live now, with compassion for
others,
Where you're free in a beautiful
land.
Remember the gift God gave to us,
We are safe in His wonderful hands.

Evelyn Tobias

Evelyn Tobias
THINKING OUT LOUD

I dedicate this poem to my children and friends whom I adore!

Oh-yes-it's-so-good-to-think-out-
loud-Time-does-not-stand-still-for-all
-of-us-As-I-look-into-the-long-
mirror-I-see-a-figure-that-has-
changed-Like-the-world-we-live-in-
1989-is-so-full-of-surprises-for-all-
of-us-Memories-at-times-do-arrive-
for-me-the-old-the-new-Oh-yes-it's-
so-good-at-times-when-some-of-
your-feelings-in-reality-are-up-today-
you-think-it's-great! Hope-and-pray-
for-peace-and-America-to-be-safe-
after-you-listen-to-world-situations-
you-think-at-times-I-am-so-lucky-to-
live-in-America-feel-safe-in-so-much
-different-ways-why-take-hormones?
Read-the-newspapers-listen-to-T.V. -
plenty-stimulation-for-my-golden-
years-to-face-for-my-great-husband-
of-my-years-I-pray-to-be-together-as
-long-as-we-can-it's-great-to-think-
out-loud-at-times

Michael E Diller
AND THE HEAVENS DARKENED . . .
The light—absolutely breathtaking—
Was blinding,
The sound—endlessly echoing—
Was deafening,
And my face . . . it was GONE.
I remember the day; 'Twas
The day the heavens cried . . .

That fateful explosion
From such a glorious revolution;
It took what I had
And gave nothing in return.
I remember the day; 'Twas
The day the heavens cried . . .

Oh yes, I remember it well
And now . . . and now I exist
In a domain with but a single
Essence:
I

I remember the day, 'Twas
The day a country lost a son
And I lost . . . EVERYTHING.

Sheila Kost
THE VISION
I saw my father walking through
the fields of yellow flowers
towards the crystal blue lake.

He seemed very happy and at
peace with himself.

The heaven doors opened and the
angels were singing "How Great
Thou Art."

Finally, my father got all the
riches that he deserved.

I never saw him like that before.
His happiness made me feel at
ease.

Since that time, I have missed my
father, but have not grieved.

Letitia R Davis
ME, MYSELF AND I

To mom and dad, who always made me feel special.

Happiness seemed so far away,
even farther than I could see.
Perhaps happiness didn't exist,
or at least not for me.

Sadness was always there with me,
more than anyone else.
Whenever faced with a mirror,
sadness became myself.

Loneliness was always quiet,
and of course very sly.
He almost made me hurt myself,
He said I had to die.

Now we're happy and there's no
sadness,
loneliness laid down to die.
We have control of our emotions.
Yes. Me, Myself and I.

Sharron S Hensley
AFTER DEATH

To my friends, Margret and Harvey from whom I learned and loved, so much.

I wish I could imagine, or even
knew,
What will happen and with who.

What will they all do and say,
Looking down on death as I lay.

Saddened faces, will they cry,
Or will they just remark with a sigh.

Did we have enough good memories
to share,
Or did we cheat ourselves, with a
feeling of "I don't care."

Was I the best person I could be,
Or was there something I missed,
something I couldn't see.

Will I be remembered from day to
day,
Or will all the bad times be there to
stay.

I seriously hope they are not,
Because I don't want to be forgot.

Did I love you all enough or should

there of been more,
Or was there things we needed to say, to each other before.
I wish I could imagine or even knew,
What will happen and with who.

Dyana
VICTIM WITH NO IDENTITY
Being Colored is celebrating
St. Patty's Day as if it was your own.
Being Colored is bragging how
great ma Daddy was and
couldn't recognize him if I
bumped into him.
Being Colored is wearing
Mr. Charlie's kids blouse and
told the teacher I didn't put
them ink stains on it, theys were
there when I got it. Didn't
believe me, got punished . . .
Lord did I get punished.
Being Colored is being sick with
fever, chills and asthma attacks
in Harlem Hospital Emergency
and they tell you Sorry, the
Doc's out to lunch. Oh God! that
seemed like hours ago.
Being Colored is frying your hair
to make it look like theirs.
Being Colored is putting bleaching
creme on your darkest child.
Being Colored is marrying light or
white and being afraid to look
back!!!!

Laureen Scharps
THE GOLDEN YEARS
I'm not growing old,
I'm growing.
I'm not getting wrinkled,
I'm developing facial definition.
I'm not turning gray,
I'm sprouting silver.
I'm not slowing down,
I'm taking my time.
I'm not an old fart,
I'm a mature soul.
I'm not losing my eyesight,
I'm gaining my insight.
I'm not ready for the rest home,
I'm ready for Palm Beach.
I'm not all washed up,
I'm drawing a bath.
I'm not over-the-hill,
I'm just beginning the journey.

Harvest moon eyes
INFINITE SPIRIT

To Henry Rodriguez, a Luisano, and enrolled member of the La Jolla band of Native American Indians. I hear you Grandfather.

Silver threaded spirit . . .

i am the whisper of
Eternity

the voice of silence
shared

timeless
ageless
always

i am your lover
They call me
Infinity

Louise W Burns
I FEEL YOUR PRESENCE AROUND MY SOUL
I feel your presence around my soul.
It grabs my heart and won't let go.
Wrapped with emotions of fire and pain.
Feelings so good I can not explain.
Thinking of you and how good we can be.
Saying to myself it may never be.
Feeling your warmth as you hold me tight.
Feeling protected one day of my life.
For I'm living a dream with my eyes closed tight.
Only when I open them do I see a sight.
Thinking of you and how good we can be.
And wondering why it may never be.
Thinking of you always and Oh what a shame.
I'll feel your presence all over again.

Milton J Bowen
STREET BEAT

To the Philadelphia Police Department, especially those who died in the line of duty

I walk the city streets, like the others who walk their beats.
I check the stores and bars, and watch out for unsuspecting cars.
I see the prostitutes sell their wares, and dope peddlers with no cares.
There was a time when the City had pride, and people held their heads high and walked with a great stride.

Now the streets are covered with trash, and the dealers sell their hash.
Buildings are allowed to crumble and rot, the City has gone to pot.
I cover the street, on my daily beat.
In my uniform so shiny and blue, you can tell that it's new.
I walk at night instead of day, and I earn very little pay.
I do my best to protect everyone you see, for my job is important to my family and me.

Margaret van Hoorn
POETRY
Poetry _____ time; energy; emotion; passion fire; feeling; conviction; understanding; compassion; heart; soul; depth; caring and most of all ____ love.

Poetry is one true form of expression of thoughts, ideas and feelings.

Poetry is, the only form of writing ____ in which the author, is truly vulnerable to the opinions of his, or her, fellow man.

In poetry ____ your very soul ____ is out, for all the world to see.

In poetry you have all this ____ and more, much, much more!

Reneé Adam
ONCE UPON A TIME
I once loved your inner beauty
I knew the way to your pleasure;
The way to make all your existing
insecurities fade away;
The way to make all your red sap
rush into your pumping soul.

And once I thought I loved your
exterior
Until all the meaningless flaws bore
me down
And all my doubts began to
succumb.

But now my love has sunk into a
non-recalling eternity:
And I sometimes don't even
remember your name
Yet once upon a time I loved your
inner beauty.

Iris S McCurdy
REFLECTIONS OF A DEER
Large almond shaped eyes
A velvet soft nose twitching
in the air for an unfamiliar
scent

A cool clear stream reflecting
A silky smooth tan furry back
with a beautiful white under
side.

As she drinks, looking in the
water for
the enemy perhaps near by
The brush hissing as the dark
form
of an animal yet unseen comes
closer
Hers ears back to catch
every move

The hair of her back bristles as
the figure
approaches even closer
Glancing from side to side, but
never
to the exact place her
young is
hidden.

Louder and louder comes the
noise
moving faster and faster.
All at once the form takes
shape;
There standing in front of
her
a beautiful twelve point
buck.

With an exhale of relief, she
knows he
has returned from his hiding
place so
the enemy, man, must have
returned
to his way of life and once
again the
forest will be calm.

Sharon E Sisemore
SLOWLY I RISE
Slowly I rise
Tears in my eyes.
Nothing's the same
My thoughts have no name.
Heart so empty,
Once filled with plenty.
Alone I fold,
Crease and grow old.
So, slowly I rise
(once more with)
Tears in my eyes.

Venita Bunch
TO MY MOTHER

To my mother Venita Robison Love you like a Rose Bud.

It's been one long year ago today
God decided to take you.
In a very sudden way,
One whole year without you mom.
And it seems so long ago
I was in your loving arms.
With a smile upon your face
I guess what hurts the worst
I can still remember
Some of your wise old words
You used to tell me
And mom it still hurts so much.
Knowing you'll never be able
To be with me, or see you standing
there
Smiling at me, with that loving look
That you always had for me.
At times when I didn't understand
Or when I was afraid,
But I'll always have my memories
of the days you were here with me.

Debra Burchfield
LOVE
Love can be wonderful
but it's not always that way
he'll love you one moment
then he'll go away

You think he'll always be there
and every things alright
but the ones who don't love
go away in the night

He may come back
but you never know—
he may leave you
and you won't know where to go

But the ones who love you so
will stay with you always
and never let you go

Miriam K Yovino
A CHILDS EYES

To my daddy; Bill Long For all of his inspiration

If we could see the world
Through a young childs eyes
There would be no reason
For hurts and lies
We would all be free to
Speak of love
It would flow thru us all
Like the beautiful dove.
We'd be so free from worry and fear
Knowing someone is there
To dry our tears.
To a child the world is make believe
The grown ups problems
They cannot conceive.
Dolls and wagons, bikes and cars
Cookies and milk and candy bars
Bedtime stories and good night kisses
These are the things the grown up
misses!!

Bettie Hollyfield
MY ANSWERED PRAYER

First, giving all thanks to my Lord and Savior, Jesus Christ, who heard and answered my prayer, and dedicating this poem to my Pastor, Reverend Curtis E. DuBose for whom it was written and to Tangie Washington who encouraged me to share this poem with others.

God answers prayer, this I know,
For I prayed a special prayer, seven
years ago,
I had this need for spiritual feed, that
I had been unable to find,
I got on my knees and prayed, Lord,
help me please,
You know what is best for me,
I met a man one day at work, while I
was sitting at my desk,
I remember him walking towards me,
a giant of a man was he,
He stopped in front of my desk, as I
leaned back and gave him an upward

glance,
He extended his hand, this giant of a man, and began to speak to me,
He spoke words, that I had once heard, about the Lord and Savior to me,
This giant of a man, who I met that day, has made a difference in my life from day to day,
He preaches, and he teaches, God's word as it should be,
I think to myself, I do declare, the Lord really does answer prayer

Sandra Lee Rogers
TWLIGHT, FOR RICHARD
Walking the sands at twlight
thinking of you, seeing you.
As the sun descends—
leaving a light, a warm glowing light—
leaving me warm, yet cold inside.

I follow footprints
that lie deep in the sand.
Small and large,
A couple—
walking, holding, loving.
Sharing the twlight together.

I follow, leaving single steps.
As if to follow
someone's happiness.
As if to be searching
for an answer,
on an empty stretch of beach.

I come across a feather.
a quill, to inspire?
To spread a thought?
Maybe a memory!

With pen and ink in hand
It only leaves me wishing—

It was you and your hand instead,
On this twlight night.

Rick Wallin
REAL LIFE
Our cities so uncivilized were forced to carry guns,
Sadistic killers roam our streets and kill our kids for fun.

Street gangs growing stronger, Our families live in fear. The nights are getting longer, The gangs are growing near.

Poverty consumes our land, Our people slowly die.
While government distributes funds to those we should deny.

Sneaky politicians, Deceitful alibis. Selling out this nation's trust for diplomatic ties.

Iran Contra scandal, that costly little jewel.
Ollie played scapegoat, Regan played the fool.

REAL LIFE !!

Kathleen Fonte
PUTTIN' ON AIRS
My house is so old that it's covered with mold
And I don't know what I'm gonna do.
I'll have company tomorrow, and much to my sorrow,
I told them my house is brand new.

There's a ring in the tub that I scrub and I scrub,
But it won't even come off with bleach.
The pipes all have leaks, and the cellar it reeks
Of the mildew that I just can't reach.

I've been workin' since May in an office by day,
And by night I go out with my friends.
They all talk 'bout their spouses, fancy cars, fancy houses;
And I just wanted to fit right in.

So, I told them I dwell in a house that is swell
With a terrace, French doors, and a pool.
When they see my old shack with a puddle out back,
Man, I'm sure gonna feel like a fool!

"Come on over for dinner," I said like a winner.
Guess I hoped they'd just turn me down.
They said, "Yes, we'll all be there."
Wish I could be anywhere
But in this house on the poor side of town.

Kitty Baker
DISCOVERY

Dedicated to my loving husband, Iriving A. Baker. May he find Peace, Love, and Freedom.

Stars shine bright
In the dark sky
Like diamonds on black velvet
And the moon is white
Casting its warmth upon a frozen world.

Trees stretch high
Carving shadows
On the silent earth below,
And yet, all the world
In slumber, can't perceive its treasure.

When dawn breaks,
All this beauty
Will become but a memory
Of secret moments I found in solitude tonight.

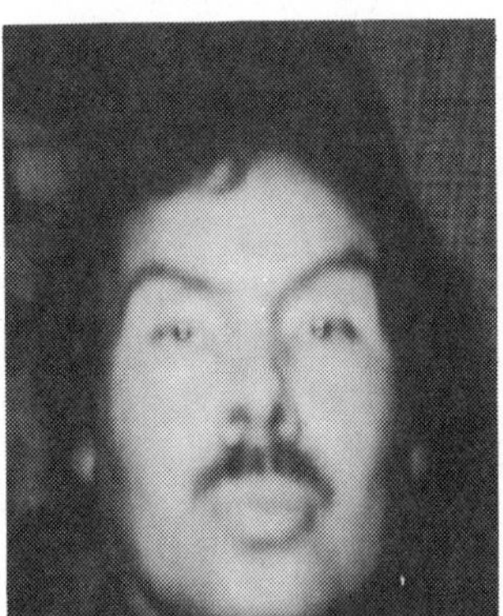

Erik P Schnikwald

Erik P Schnikwald
THE LIFE OF A SQUIRREL

To my good friend Doris Rodger whose endless support and enthusiasm always kept me going.

I think I should like to be a squirrel in my next life,
So happy and free from strife
How they seem to have such fun
Frolicking in the sun
Life for them is such a lark,
Cuddling and making love in the dark
In the fall they gather their nuts,
To hideaway in their tree-like huts
How snugly and cozy they'll all be together,
When winter brings that frigid weather
And in spring when flowers start to sprout
We'll see baby squirrels playing about.

Cindy M Gregory
THE FLURRIES THROUGH MY MIND
I am eyes half closed,
sun burning my cheeks,
Vision in my mind full of colors
those you've painted for me,
Because you are all things to me.
Thoughts shining bright of our day
we become one.
Our minds united, bodies one,
Together joined by all that we have become.

Sun shining so bright,
my eyes starting to water,
Feeling some what warm
Blood rushing to my head,
can't stop the flurries
I see crystal stars,
glimmering white.
In my mind full of colors
oh so bright . . .
Those you have painted.

Mamie Lou Killin
THE CHEROKEE ROSE
Like the pretty wildflowers
Abloom near rippling stream,
Winding 'neath the willow boughs
So peaceful and serene,

A dark-eyed beauty blossomed
With bronze skin all aglow,
In the Indian Nation
So many years ago.

Adorned in ebon tresses,
A princess lost in dream,
'Neath the swaying willows,
Beside the clear blue stream.

Reflection in the water,
A picture of repose,
As graceful as the willows,
The Cherokee Rose.

Willee C Martin
IN MEMORY OF A LOVED ONE

Dedicated to William J. Paye

He left this earth, born aloft
By man made wings.
Caring not about today, or what tomorrow brings.

Was it the path her soul had flown
A week before on Angel's wings?

He saw her face smile at him from each snow white cloud, and heard her name spoke by himself aloud.

A smile went back to her though drenched with tears, and then a Prayer
to God for shorter years.

Irene E Alahouzos
THE GREEN SHOWER
Dark warm green shower
pulsating water tapping on my clouded head
bottles turned over spilled, filled with euphoria
Ritual to the Gods of Cleanliness
washing away impurities of the soul

Jonathan Jones
EPICENTER
Once our eyes have met—
My image on your retina,
Yours on mine
Already we have penetrated
Each other.
If, with the speed of sight
A rush emanates from
My control central
Spreading tingling voltage
(Imperceptible on any Richter)
Outwards to all of me
That isn't cerebral,
Then I accept
This involuntary charge
As salient sanction to pursue.

Kathleen A Dussault
I'M HOME! I'M HOME!
I'm Home!
I'm Home!

The sky winks,
the trees wave,
the sun comes up, and
The moon comes down!

I'm back!
missed you all so much,
give me a hug,
blow me a kiss!

The others are leaving
—now we can talk!

Ms Elwanda La Bon
ENCHANTMENT
What lies ahead is mystery—
Would but I could fly!
I'ld abide my time in endlessness—
Never to think of die.

Oft I'ld chance to measure—
How sure my presence is.
When future is now and never ends—
And wonder would send my tears.

No time to wait and never to stall—
I'ld skip between the seams.
And laugh at binds that offer mischief—
Oh, but isn't life a dream?

Floating on clouds of brizzy—
Listening to thoughts of nice.
Rosy are the merry days—
I'll never roll the dice.

Anne-Marie Guest
THANK YOU

This poem is dedicated to my friends and family

When I awake every morning at dawn,
I look around to see what's gone;
and when I see how nature lives,
I thank the Lord for what He gives.

We'll take advantage while we can
of the beautiful nature and its land.

And when the stars shine above,
I'll give the night all my love,
for nature gives all she can;
and soon we will be in the land.

I want my body to be scattered round,
for as it softly lays to the ground,
I'll pray to God to never let this end,
for it was ever too good to begin.
Thank you.

The End

Martha Jeanne Tote
GIFT OF PRAYER

To my mom, for all her support and faith in me. Looks like we made it!

Please grant me Lord the strength I need
To get me through this day.
It's hard to know what's right from wrong,
Please teach me as I pray.

Please grant me Lord the strength I need,
Please stay in constant sight.

Please catch me if I stumble
And help me make it right.

Please grant me Lord the strength I need
To raise my children strong,
To understand their tiny hearts
And to listen when I'm wrong.

Please grant me Lord the strength I need
When I weaken through the day,
And as your Lamb, please feed me
As you do each time I pray.

Please grant me Lord the strength I need
To face what tomorrow brings,
And thank you Lord for being there
And teaching me these things.

Les Sullivan
TREASURES THAT AWAIT

To all you Saints who will be so well rewarded for the faith you show in the trying years ahead.

If one were given all the beauty he desired,
The joy of this great gift would eventually expire.
If the richest kingdoms on Earth were yours,
Confess that one day you will finally grow bored.
And if every bit of knowledge were to be your treasure,
Wouldn't it also end and give no further pleasure?
Why is it all our treasures run dry
As surely as we in the end will die?

When next you seek riches you need not dig nor prod
For the greatest treasures lie with God.

If my answer sounds wrong and makes little sense,
Then join the billions of others whose lives were spent
Entwined around possessions that have long since went.

You ask, "What, then, do we give up our search?"
I answer, "There is something offered by this Earth."

"We were each granted a life so very unique
Harboring a soul that guides it through a world of greed,
And at the journey's end you will look back and see
That your life was collecting treasures found in eternity.
So let's step through that threshold and accept our rewards
Perfect love, complete satisfaction, forever with the Lord."

C D Pate
GONE FOREVER

Dedicated to the ignorance of Science.

See the time.
And space.
And the wind,
carrying forth the storm.
The Man from Earth was hurled,
through the galaxies.
The waste,
of which other men's eyes
have long since seen.
In the centuries of time gone by,
countless generations,
counted the days and years.
But still the man did not return.
Only card games played late into the night,
Told of the pipe dreams and
unused chemicals.
Which carried the man
to his unknown demise.

Michelle Bosecker
SUNSET BY THE SEA

As I walk by the sea,
I see the sunset next to me.
So beautiful, so bright
While it brightens the night.
As birds fly overhead,
I see the pretty yellow, orange and red.
I feel so right
On this wonderful night.
I walked with the sand beneath my toes,
As the sun set and the moon rose.
The day ends once more right
And begins a beautiful night.

Marilyn Jeanne Mapel
AUTUMN

Autumn
just seems to arrest
The Essence of all the
Seasons
into one shining
Jewel
That is
Waiting
to burst its Fire
into
the
Universe!

Julia Crosby
MY SWEET MELISSA

Sleep sweet child, dream of beauty
Sleep sweet child, dream of peace
Sleep sweet child, dream of love
Sleep sweet child, dream your dreams

For when you wake you must face
the reality of the human race
So sleep sweet child and dream your most wonderful fantasies
For when you wake you must face reality

Angelina Salzarulo
MORE TO FORGET

I have more to forget, then I have to remember
As I think of the past, filled with pain.
How can one, put together, dreams burned into ember,
For I have more to forget, then I have to remember.
As I lay on my bed, thinking thoughts, that I dread.
I beg, of my mind, to release, the pain, inside
And plea, to my heart to surrender.
But, I have more to forget, then I have to remember
So how can I recall in my memory book at all.
That would bring me, one moment so tender.
For the pages, you see, cannot render to me
For I have more to forget, then I have to remember
Since, time has gone by, no tears can I cry
That will wash, all the grief, from my eyes.
I only hope and pray, that peace will come someday
For, I have more, to forget, then I have to remember.

Angela Franusich
MOTHER OF MINE

When I was just a little girl
And sat upon your knees,
I pressed my head close to your breast
While you sang sweet melodies.

Now that I'm growing older,
Thinking of all you've done for me,
Why, mother dear, I worship you
You're more than the world to me.

For there are just two mothers
With hearts so good and true,
One, our holy mother,
The other one is you.

Lucy Long
DO YOUR BEST

Do your best, your very best.
Whatever you have to do.
Whether it be a big job
or a small one.
There is much pride,
that swells inside from
a job that's been well done.
Everyone can't be the captain,
Some have to be the crew.
So be the best of whatever
you are. And great pleasures
will come to you. if you've
done your best, your very best
whatever you have to do.

Steve Duncan
THE ARTIST

To paint a bundle of flowers
underneath a bright light,
Is an Artist's job and delight

The Artist will paint the
brightness of the flowers that
the light has made.
The flowers that require more
attention are the ones hidden in
the shade.

Lost in the darkness some flowers
may be, but still a thing of
beauty, this is what
The Artist can see.

The artist will put on canvas, "the
flower," not leaving out one little
part.
What the Artist paints, is what he
feels in his heart.

The painting of the flowers are
you and me.
Whatever the Artist paints is
what he can see.

The Artist will put us on canvas,
not leaving out one little part.
What, "as a flower" must we put
into the Artist's heart.

Diane Campbell
I WON'T KNOW UNLESS YOU TELL ME

I act out my life so well
that no one can really tell
How lost I feel inside.
I believed when you told me
I was wrong, and I didn't know.
You'd ask how I felt
and then say it didn't matter
and if I just tried hard enough
everything would get better.

So I tried very hard
but it's never really been
quite good enough
and I came to understand
that it must be just me
and I keep working harder
at trying to be better.

I'm still waiting to hear
that I've finally done it right—
I won't know unless you tell me.

Chenoa Chilcote
A LOVE SO STRONG

Do you remember the things you said?
And the promises you made?
You said it was forever
Not just a phase.
Were those all just empty words?
Or did you really mean it?
How could a love so strong ever go away?
We had happy times and we had sad times
But we always had each other
To wipe away the tears of sorrow
And share the tears of joy.
In the darkest of nights
You were my lucky star shining bright.
Maybe in time I'll understand
Just how our love escaped us
But no amount of time
Can ever erase our past.
I will lock those memories
Safely away in my heart
And throw away the key
So they will always, always be with me.

Saleem A Khaaliq
POEM TO MOURNING

she wakes me in the morning
. . . as Mornings breath is dew
dropped
on slumbering leaves . . .
& leaves me refreshed.
her rays flood the horizons
and splashes against my pain/ful
reflection . . .
of early yesterdays with light red
regret.

Emotions burn out of control at the
sight
of forgotten Night.
Dreams are broken by the flood of
light
as the Sun washed water recedes.

She wakes me in my mourning.

innudations of inner quilt fill my
mind
as gently as a Sparrows flight
The Day will not save us
. . . and gone is the night.

Nancie Malloy
FOR YOU:

I have felt many pains,
I have cried many tears
of lonesomeness and desire.
I long to talk to you for more
than a moment, and I dream
of being close.
For many years now, I have
noticed you.
My stomach has felt a tightness,
I thought I would choke.
Wanting and waiting
to be more than just friends.
For you:
I have stayed home nights;
hoping you would think of me

and notice my subtle hints.
For you:
I have tried hard to change.
Though I can't seem to succeed,
and no one will approve . . . I'll
make it!!
I've got to!
I've got to ease the pain of just
being another person. I'm unique!
I've got to be known for who I am.
What I feel I can do and what's
bothering me
are unimportant to some, because
they look past that and see what they
want.
I love you, and . . .
For you:
I will be patient, but mark my words,
I will make my abilities be known.
My pains will be softened,
and my tears kept . . .
For you.

Kelly M McGivern

Kelly M McGivern
WISH UPON A MIDNIGHT STAR

This poem is dedicated to my father for teaching me to believe in myself, for I am the only one who makes my dreams come true.

Wish upon a midnight star
Think and hope for good,
For thinking negative won't take you far
Though some wish it would.

Hopes and dreams are wishes too
Just different states of mind
Think not what may become of you
If you leave these thoughts behind.

Claudia Robles
WHEN I TRIED TO MAKE IT LAST

Thanks to Crystal, Mom, family and friends for your support and for the inspiration behind this poem. My dream is now a reality I love you all!

When I tried to make it last,
You broke my heart so fast.
You said goodbye, and walked away,
And I began my life alone . . . the very next day.

The nights seem so cold, and the days so long,
Tears run down my face as I hear what used to be our song.
Since the day you left, I have felt so empty inside,
The pain in my heart is something I cannot hide.

I need you back, how can I make you see?
That no one could love you as much as me.
I wanted to make you happy and give you the best that I could.
If I had to sacrifice . . . I would.
But you didn't give me a chance, you didn't let me try.
Instead you said, "I'm sorry." and you walked on by.

I know I must forget you, and find someone new,
But I don't want to, I only want to give my love to you.
As time passes I'm learning to forget,
But loving you is something I won't regret.
I'll never forget the day when you walked away so fast,
You hurt me most, when I tried to make it last.

Viviane Cochrane
A KISS

To BOB, my inspiration
July 1986, and always

A kiss . . .
Upon my lips
While in early morning slumber
Brushed so gently,
Yet so real,
Even the essence of your hair
Filled the air.
Half awake,
Reaching up,
Thou dreaming still—
I saw your tanned and freckled face
Smiling,
Above me.
Could it be some spatial sign
That you do
Truly
Love me?

Tina Schmierer
A WOMAN THAT I'LL NEVER BE

Disappearing way back in your dreams,
You look at me,
And see,
A woman that I'll never be.

If I could only find a way to feel,
Like the woman you believe you see.
To hide behind your dream,
Gets harder every day for me.

I can't seem to get any stronger.
I can't seem to climb any higher.
Let me cry a little longer.
Let me hold on a little tighter.

Emotions can't be satisfied,
And you'll never know how hard I tried.
When you look at me and somewhere in your mind you see,
A woman that I'll never be.

Annemarie Schneider Annerl
LONELINESS

. . . In memory to my brother, Andy John Schneider

LONELINESS, you unwelcome intruder . . . Gnawing on our guts in this abattoir of life . . .

The Carnivore . . . preying passionately, ruthlessly on the helpless . . . the old . . . the young . . .

Teasing the egos of those with vacant eyes . . . because the dreams they dreamed never came true . . .

LONELINESS . . . preying on middle-age men in a society that associates virility and youthfulness with conquests . . .
Tickling their crotches . . . Walking them around in a graveyard of broken hopes . . . as I would walk someone who's taken an overdose of sleeping pills . . .

You STURM and DRANG of life that looks so exciting to those who are quietly settled, staring out—into their complacent, plastic, humming worlds . . .

LONELINESS . . . ringing your Pavlovian Bell until the amputation of our emotions has been concluded . . . Making the lonely live with the desperation of poker players who are losing . . . and keep playing for higher stakes . . . hoping to win it all back . . .

But LONELINESS . . . I no longer salivate . . . The nights you no longer rear your Medusean head . . . those nights you have bequeathed me . . . They are my own . . . to grow . . . to replenish my dreams . . . to swim in many oceans . . .

I am like the Hetaerae . . . yet celebrated . . . respected . . . for my independence of spirit and mind . . .

LONELINESS . . . You no longer make me afraid of being with myself . . .

Gail E Beckmann
TO LOVE IS TO SHARE

To my husband, Bill, whose love inspired these words.

To love is to share, the tears and laughter,
To live as one forever after.
To lessen each other's burdens in the valley of despair,
To strengthen the trust, to really care,
To be among a crowd and see only you,
To be faithful and honest and true,
To love is to love only you.

Susan E Wells
NEVER CRY FOR THE COURAGEOUS

For all those during and since the terrorist raid on the U.S. Marines in Lebanon who have given their lives in service to this country.

Never cry for the courageous no matter how needless their death may seem. Never cry for those who dare to die to defend the dream that says a man may walk tall, proud, and free, living as he chooses to live, being what he chooses to be.
No never cry for the courageous, no matter how needless their death may seem, never cry for those who dare to die to defend the dream
"This is Liberty"

Todd M Davis
SEEK THE MOON

Seek the moon
and find a wolf,
Seek the sun
and find a bird,
Seek me
and find one who cares.
The time spent in stealth and chase
builds on passion and ties its place
to the wonder-counselor
for whom we pray
with diligence by day.
If I wander from my birth
may I claim joy, gladness and mirth.
Thus I say as night falls dim
I sinfully miss you as the silent
rose misses its stem.

Leon Sanders
THE CLOWN

With painted face and clown's disguise
I saw people through different eyes.
The clown was different for people to see,
And the people were different to me.

The funny-looking suit I was in
Made everybody be my friend.
I saw the funniest people in town,
As I looked through the eyes of a clown.

I'll wash this make-up off my face,
And my own face will take its place.
But I'll still see the people in town
As they looked to the eyes of a clown.

Lyuba Muzichenko
TEARDROP

To Gregory Tschelak, my Uncle and writer, who inspired me to write.

I wish I were a teardrop, teardrop,
Falling down a velvet rose.
A scarlet petal with a trail of diamonds, diamonds,
Captivates your heart by its striking pose.

If I were a teardrop falling, falling,
Holding on to hearts of gold.
I would be a teardrop talking, talking,
Telling what your mind has never told.

Marian Bednarczyk
TYPEWRITER PEOPLE

Ribbons with no inkling of pride
punched out keys
being forced to backspace
Others making marginal comparisons
calling them asterisks
Shutting them to resolve their case
Warning bell rings
And they know it's time to change their ribbon

Debra K Scheiman-Neilson
GOD'S SUPPRESSION OF TEENAGE DEPRESSION

The Lord created me
I am His!
Help those around me
who use me
step all over me
run me down to the ground
neglect me . . .

I am a person—P-E-R-S-O-N

not an object . . .

Help those who think I don't
know what they do to me . . .
I live under God's light
my love is strong—given with all
my might!
How do I go on when people wrong
me?
I can't. . .
Only my Jesus pulls me along and
tells me
He cares!—If no one else does,
He does!
And I smile because I know
that with Jesus' love and caring
for me,
Nothing else matters at all.

Patricia Darville
THE EYES

To my four sons Chippy, Carlos, Desmond, & Dario. Also my friend & Colleague Claudia Rolle.

The eyes are the windows of our
souls,
And often envision what the future
holds,
The past they have already seen,
At present they are not so very keen.
They are like cameras these gifts so
rare,
To lose them would be the hardest
thing to bear,
Oh what a marvelous thing this sight,
We could see in technicolor; black,
and white.
They hold their picture a long long
time,
And hide them in the corner of our
mind,
They store them in a bank called
memory,
At some later date they set them free.
When we need to reflect on a specific
scene,
The memory releases the picture so
clean,
And true to the day the incident took
place,
Sad may be the memory we have to
face.

Sharon A Birmingham
DEEP IN MY HEART

To my loving husband, William

When I awoke,
This morning,
The sun was rising.
The rays splashing over,
The horizon,
Darling when I
Think of us,
All the while,
All I can do,
Is smile,
The sweet love,
Which is nestled,
Deep in my heart,
Bursts forth,
And reverberates,
Like an echo.
It says to you,
"Honey, come love me,
And be mine,"
Forever throughout eternity

Shari Lynn Wilder
LIFE'S FERRISWHEEL

Dedicate to my sweet husband Tom, I will love you forever and a day.

Once my heart had a pain so deep,
I wished the lord would take me in
my sleep,
Love hurt so bad and was very sad,
It hurt so much it drove me mad.
I built up a wall around myself
So I could not be hurt I put love on a
shelf.
Then one day I met a man
Who had a hammer in his hand
He loved me so much he knocked
down my wall.
With his love and trust he gave me
his all
I learned you can be hurt and
crushed down
And the perfect love can be found
It's out there somewhere it's strong
and it's pure,
And if it's true love you'll know for
sure
You'll feel it in your heart not in hour
head
So take love's hand let yourself be
led
Feel the security so strong and real
As we go around and around on
Life's ferriswheel.

Dorothea Saul Seely
A WALK IN THE FOREST

Strolling through the forest,
serenely content, enjoying the
picture
No artist could possibly transfer
to canvas, with paint.
The soft rustle of leaves as I
slowly walk at my leisure
Looking around, hearing the birds
and the sound of a brook very
faint.

Off in the distance, a majestic,
giant waterfall
Presenting a beautiful panorama
As it cascades downward and
onward, in a tuneful beat—I
stall
Observing such a natural,
uncontrolled drama.

I ponder—how many people can
see this exquisite view,
Forget time is passing and remain
dreamingly unaware
Of Nature's bounty—provided for
everyone—not only a few.
Birds sing, bees hum, a squirrel or
rabbit skitters here and there.

The little chipmunks poke their
cute, little faces around a fallen
tree.
Watching, peering as I wend my
carefree way.
I can relax, enjoy this moment
and think—This is for me!
Ah I do believe I'll return
another day.

On my next visit a camera to be
carried.
To have for eternity, the pictures
I'll take,
And when in the future, if I feel
tired or harried.
I'll bring out the pictures and
relive them—for old time's sake.

Dr L Marvin Marion
KNOCKING AT DEATH'S DOOR

I know what it's like to be at Death's
door
I've been there a few times before
Old Man Death came knocking
thrice in '88
But St. Peter didn't open the gate.

I know what it's like to be at Death's
door
All the pain and suffering I bore
It happened late, each on a separate
night
Three times a rendezvous with Death
almost took my life.
Death came knocking in July,
October and December of '88
Each time through my inner faith it
was not too late
A severe automobile accident
followed by a massive heart attack
Praying constantly and reaching out
to God I fought back.

Later in autumn an angiogram and
Tallium Exercise Test
Each time God gave me the strength
to do my best
After successful angioplasty,
complications with internal bleeding
All night through inner strength to
God I kept pleading.

God each time spared my life for a
reason
The answer I will discover in due
season
My life I owe to my wife, doctors,
nurses, but most of all to Him
He is the Rock of my life, a priceless
Gem.

Carol Jones

Carol Jones
TO CARROLL

A Valentine is like a rose
a fresh and gently thing
It brightens each new day
like a sigh of coming spring.

A rose I give, My Valentine
to rest upon your heart
A ray of sunshine on your soul
to say "I love you so"
Sweetheart.

To remind you dear, my thoughts of
you
are often unexpressed
A kiss, a touch, a warm handclasp
a soft embrace and tenderness.

So when you see a rose today
remember what I say
My thoughts are sent so lovingly
to you—on our 2nd Valentine's
Day.

A John Bergh
SEVENTH FLOOR

Intentionally caught in the crowd and
the noise
Sealed in the vacuum with the girls
and the boys.
Scream away at that umbrella in the
back
There's much more movement in
sardines in a pack.
The dullard colors all blend into one
It's moving! It's moving! The
journey has begun.
Stomaches leap and head for the
throat
Faces are ashen, all looking for hope.
The fat man sweats and looks into
the air
To smell like garlic would seem
much more fair.
The painted ladies all dressed up so
fine
Too much perfume, they do it all the
time.
With sickly sour scents, all meant to
be fair,
Oh please, doors open! Let in some
fresh air.
Staring up blankly at the numbers so
high
Suddenly slowing, everyone has a
sigh.
The journey is over, the right floor
attained,
The stomach is down, the clothes
slightly maimed.

Athena Charvonia
OUT BOAT SWAYED

from side to side
until a swirl of wind wrapped our
hopes around the mast and
swallowed our breath. Wings of
gloom challenged our eyes and
stretched them far beyond the groans
of waves and the funnels of dark
clouds.

Then we recalled the myth. We saw
the dolphin leap with Arion safe on
the arched back riding his extended
fate while the meters of his rhyme
measured new dimensions of the lyre
on a distant, less traumatized shore.

Jenny Clark
YESTERDAY

To my Grandson Brandon Wright

Yesterday was here
Not so very long ago
When I was just a little tyke
And time went oh so slow.

But then I got to be a teen
And time flew by so fast
We thought we had to catch our star
For nothing seemed to last.

Then the years began to add
And time was the least of all
The many wonders of our life
We try now to recall.
Like childhood days, our first
sweetheart
Our graduation days
Wedding Bells and tiny babes
Such scenes our mind replays.

When at last we look around
With ease and so content
Watching the hurrying crowd go by
We know where Yesterday went.

Now standing on the downhill side
Of the mountain of life we see
The "Yesterdays" and "Tomorrows"
As the leaves upon a tree.

For Yesterday was very nice
Today is oh so sweet
As we make the circle round
And our Journey here complete.

Susanne Marie Haynes
DAYDREAMING WISH

This is dedicated to my children, Dan, Mike, and Jeanette. Without them there would not be a Daydreaming Wish.

I'd like to lay down in a field of
grass,
and gaze at the clouds as they
slowly passed.
I'd hear the sweet songs of the birds
in the sky,
and dream of being one who
could truly fly.

I'd count all the petals of a single flower,
  and never sense a passing hour.
Maybe I'd whistle on a blade of grass,
  and try and try though a whole mass.
The bees would buzz around in the air,
  and also smell fragrance of flowers there.,
I'd truly enjoy the peace I've found,
  the fresh air unwinding the thoughts in my mind.
If ever I was to stumble upon such a place,
  it would forever remain my own secret space.

Ethel Goldberg

NIGHT GRIEF

In the night's deep purple
When it's half into tomorrow
And sleep won't come—
I reach into my black velvet bag
And count my beads of sorrow
Until I hear and see
The early morning plane,
A steel stylus drawing
Vapor-lines across the sky—

Wendy A Sasser

BETWEEN FRIENDS

To Lisa for all the years of friendship, thanks for all the memories.

Friendship is that special bond
Held between two hearts.
The satisfaction of times well spent—
Whether those moments of laughter,
Or in the break of sorrow.
A listening ear,
A sturdy shoulder,
And open conversation.
That trusting comrade
Who will always be there,
To laugh remember and share.
Friendship is caring,
Giving what is needed—
To help a friend along.
It is looking deep enough to see
When to reach out,
Knowing without having to ask
And having courage to hold two
When one may be down
All of this and more
Grows between friends.

John McGinley

THE JOHN O'DONNEL JR. BRIDGE (SAVAGE, MONTANA)

It is a bridge that
starts in a town
that is less than it was,
crosses a dry canal to
a railroad station that
long ago disappeared.
A barren board and girder
bridge shunned by the
National Historic Register
left baking in the
Montana prairie it dies
without benefit of clergy.
With it rusts the last
memory of John O'Donnel Jr.—
whoever he was.

Wm J Monahan

CHILD OF THE SLAVES

The black fullback toils
And grimaces his way through
Forty carries in the noon-day sun.

  In the stands, 80,000
  Sip beer and chomp popcorn,
  Cheering the black fullback
  On to fame and wealth and glory.

Two years, four years and the
Black fullback is out of a job
In the noon-day sun.

  In the stands, 80,000
  Sip beer and chomp popcorn,
  Sold by the black fullback
  Who toils and grimaces his way

Through the forgetful 80,000.

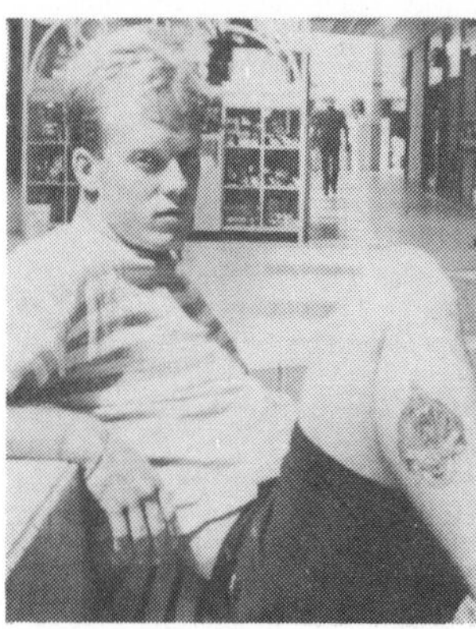

Karle Breckenridge

Karle Breckenridge

ROSES OR GUNS

To the one I love

It's lonely
Out on the ocean tonight,
The wind is blowing
And there's no-one in sight.
The stars are out
And shining down on me,
As I sit
Feeling depressed and lonely.
It would be nice
To have you here by my side,
I'd take you away
And run off and hide.

We'd live together
In happiness till the end,
We'd break all the rules
And the ones we couldn't, we'd bend.
We shall soon see
Who deep our love runs,
When I come to visit
If you greet me with roses or guns.

Susan Burgner

MY FOREVER LOVE

Just saying I Love You doesn't seem to be enough. There are many more emotions I've been thinking of.
Together, our souls intertwine, yours breathing life into mine. Apart, we're never alone, two hearts beat as one, a harmony of tones.
Our love, truly given from the Heavens above, a powerful source we are of.
All our hopes, visions and dreams, we are blessed to share to fulfilling extremes.
One life, one soul, one heart shining now, when once separate souls waited in the dark.
I Love You, a very magical phrase, simple, yet complex with abilities to continually grow and amaze.

Geraldine E Brandon

FOR YOU

There's a poetry in my heart
all jumbled with words and thoughts,
The yesterdays and to-morrows
from finishings, and new starts;

I have not much to give you,
earthly money can buy,
but, I can share with you
the rainbows in the sky,

The sunrise in the mornings
scent of flowers sweet
raindrops in the meadows
green grass upon our feet;

This special day, when we were joined as one,
and life began anew,
I am so blessed that God, let me,
share it with you.

Betty Carpenter

TURN BACK THE PAGES OF TIME

To Lloyd (and Roxanne) abuser & traitors from your wife and five children. It's your lose.

Turn back the pages of time
when we had stars in our eyes
and strength in our hearts
When we had no memories of anger
and no pain to make us cry.

Turn back the pages to yesterday
and let's try again
To love and be loved
To thank God for each other
The way we know we should.

Roxanne Youngblood

LOST LOVE

This poem is dedicated to my husband Stephen whom taught me how to love

No words exist
Yet, you see
To truly express
This pain in me

How can I go on
Without you here
I need your touch
I need you near

I'll try to be strong
I'll strive for brave
Though my love for you
Is beyond the grave

How could you leave me
What will I do
Without your love
Without you

I miss you so much
You were my breath
Now there's no such
Since you death

Robert L Jones II

PEOPLE LOOK AT OUR LOVE AS A TOY

This poem is dedicated to Darlene Ardoin, with all my love.

People look at our love, as a toy,
Won't be satisfied, till it's destroyed.
They think the feeling, isn't strong,
If they only knew, they were all wrong.
Some people say, they will be our friend,
But from what we know, it will come to an end.
Why can't people, just let us be?
Is it they want, to be like you and me?
The truth we'll never know, for sure,
All we know, is our love is pure.
If it was possible, to be together now,
I would surely take, the chosen vow.
Loving you, has made me see,
That this relationship, is special to me.

Noel C Privee

LONELY WITH LOVE

I am very sad and very lonely,
Since we have been apart.
I keep you in my dreams,
But feel very empty.

We have so much love for each
  other,
I don't know why we aren't
  together,
All I know is that my life is
So lonely without your love.

I feel you are my only love
Now I spend all my days and
  nights
So alone "My Darling"
I say this with all My love.

Jochebed Christmas Locust

THE DAINTY LITTLE VIOLET

The violet is a prim, dainty little flower,
Happy in sun and dew and shower,
Thriving in woodlands, meadows, by water's edge,
In rocky cliffs and near the shady ledge.

Close to the sod in heart-shaped leaves of green enshrined,
Its roots in bed of nurturing soil entwined,
In all humility it takes substance from the earth,
And glorifies its spot of lowly birth.

With upturned face of radiance and grace,
A jewel of quiet grandeur adorning its cozy place,
It shares its smile with rich and poor, great and small,
As peeping from its slender stem, it shyly nods to all.

This harbinger of spring does not frequent banquet halls,
Nor vie with larger florals at great balls,
But chooses a secluded way of living
And spends a sequestered life of quiet giving.

Though of simple station, humble birth,
It proves humility beautiful and of great worth.
This lovely flower has a very special place
Wherever there is beauty, love and grace.

Amelia Sprague White

OLD ROAD

This poem is dedicated to Newt Roy, a sweetheart of long ago

There is an old road in my memory
Slowly winding on its way;
Tho' many moons since last I've seen it

In my heart it's clear as day.

Friendly trees keep watch beside it—
Their lovely branches dense and low.
It falters, jogs, then hurries onward
To where the honeysuckles grow.

Mystic shadows—Silvery moon-
beams
Play and dance from dusk till dawn
While the moon smiles down from
heaven,
As the old road rambles on.

Oh! this old road holds many secrets
Close within its heart of gold
Of joy and sorrow, tears and
laughter,
All safe within its gentle soul.

When in dreams I wander
Down that old road so real and dear;
Dim figures glide along beside me—
Tis living thoughts from yesteryear.

Roxann Gess-Smith

Roxann Gess-Smith
NO BATTLE WON
The valors sense sheaths not the fool
but yields the sword that pierces
crewel;

And thrusts the strike that breaks the
heart
When love dismisses every guard;

The trenchant blade shall hew and
hack
While with no dazzling splendor
flash;

And with no triumph falls the foe
When two have drawn against the
soul;

There is no glory none adorned
No victor rises o'er the sword.

Missy L Kuster
GLASS HORSE
Glass horse standing on my shelf,
Made of dreams from myself.
His slippery back in need of rosin.
On my shelf,
forever frozen.

Trottin' always; never'll walk,
Frozen in motion—legs in a lock.
Never in need of food or sleep.
No stallions to fight, no mares to
keep.

Head held high, and never dozin'
On my shelf,
forever frozen.

Evelyn J Pittler
HOME

To Jim, my son, who served in the Vietnam War.

Today my boy is coming home to
stay,
because I prayed to God each
day,
to start bringing him back on
his way.

As I look back on the days I dread,
I think of the other boys who
lay there dead.

I have no reasons to fear,
because God's and a mother's
love was always near.

Christine Markarian
A SHOOTING STAR
Since you left me,
It seems like years
And I can no longer
Hold back the tears

Our love will always remain true
And this magnet
Will bind our hearts
Forever through

Cupid has stung me with his arrow
And my heat will bleed infinitely
Only you can nest my orphaned heart
By loving me incessantly

The tears from my eyes fall drop by
drop
As I gaze upon the sky
And continue my winsome dreams
With a hopeless sigh

The torch of our love will forever
stay lit,
And the flames will eternally burn,
As upon this single shooting star
I wish for your return.

Jeffrey L Manter
GATHER WOOD
Red Brown Golden Leaves
Stiff Over A Tranquil Pool
Autumn, Soon Winter

Melanie Donnahee
REMEMBERING

Dedicated to Mom, Dad, Lori and my teacher Mrs Ellis

I walk alone in the silence of night,
Feeling deep down it will never be
right.
I shake my head to free it from
sorrow,
Hoping for a better tomorrow.
I've kept inside the bitter tears,
No one knows I too have fears.
Remembering the hate and pain,
Never sunshine always rain.
I can still recall the night,
My parents had their final fight.
Our father walked right out that
door,
And we never saw him anymore.

Melvin Leibowitz
THE ROSES
Two dust layered roses, grown
brittle with age,
hold memories deep within
carmine-red
and purple petals.
Captured at the apex of their
freshness,
they are amber caught
specimens on
the way to completion.
Rounded dried blossoms, stems
erect,
as if in anticipation of a
climatic eruption, reach out
like the rigid priapus of a
Pompeian God-statue who
waits an eternity to bless his
long dead ash covered
worshipers in their ecstasies.
I am tempted to crush them,
to complete the cycle of their
transient life;
dust returning to dust,
BUT
Their awesome presence stuck
between the moments of time
moves me to let them Be.

Gladys Faye Hansen
MEMORY OF A WAR
It sinks in your memory,
a memory that will not die.
You see I'm a Vet,
so I would not tell a lie.

My memories are of bombs;
bullets flying high and low.
Crawling in the mud
dodging, as I go.

My memories are of children
roaming around, as free—
wearing just a diaper,
with a bomb, meant for me.

My memories of a country,
in a far and distant land,
of friends with last wishes
thankful; just to hold my hand.

My mind was sorely altered,
in a war misunderstood.
A war I can't forget.
Oh God, I wish I could

franc siekierke
ALLELUIA—Friend

To Father Bruce Ritter, as founder of the Covenant House—everyone's friend.

REACH ME:
when you want to talk;
when you need to cry;
and when you want to touch.

TRUST ME:
when you want to unburden;
when you need to endure;
and when you want to aspire.

AMUSE ME:
when I want to laugh;
when I need to relax;
and when I want to soar.

RECOGNIZE ME:
when I need faith;
when I need hope;
and when I need love.

Lisa Thornton
FOREVER MINE
Forever mine, you said to me
You said that you would set me free.
You brought me warmth and love
and care
You ran your fingers through my
hair.
I loved you more than I could say
And yet you took my light away.
You took my heart and ripped it deep
But still you say I'm yours to keep!
Am I always slave to you?
Or to my self should I be true?
For your wounds will never heal.
And I will now no longer feel
The pain that you would thrust on me
To save you from your sanity!
For you must now go on and see
The part of you, you killed in me
And maybe one day you will find
The part of me you left behind!

Charlotte A Gilbert
SAFARI
Bamboo pipes that click together
from the wind that whistles
by . . .
takes my mind on great
safaris . . .
distant drums . . . a hunter's cry.

Sounds of music like marimbas
from the darkest continent . . .
chantings of the tall black warriors
searching for the lion's scent.

Ladened with two weeks'
supplies . . .
prepared to slay the jungle king.
Men who know the heat of hell
donning but loincloth and string.

Bamboo pipes out in the distance
tell the lion's imminence.
Watchful eyes and light of foot,
they move through forest dark and
dense.

With the grace that he was born with,
pounced the cat . . . the feline king.
A shot rang out and broke the
silence.
The hunt is through . . . the bamboo
sings.

Lucille Dotson
MY GIFT
My gift this year is precious, it's
truly one of a kind
It's more valuable than gold, but it
didn't cost a dime.
It doesn't run on batteries like so
many things you get
I didn't have to worry about the size
for it's a perfect fit.

My gift is salvation, given by the
Lord above
It came in the form of a heart, filled
with an abundance of love.
Peace was in this package with hope
on top.
The blessings from this gift never
seem to stop.

Faith was the wrapping, joy the
bow
By prayer was it received, by Grace
God made it so.
Jesus bought this gift, for you and for
me,
The warranty is good for it has a
lifetime guarantee.

Gwen Park
IMMIGRANT'S SONG

To my dear daughter, Pauline Margaret Stewart and her son, Cameron Mackay Stewart. Equally, to my dear son, Alan John Park, who, like his nephew was born in Canada of immigrant parents.

I was not born here, yet I love this
land, in all her shades.
White or gold, brightly beautiful or
brooding beneath a gray sky
She renews me and, in the softness
of her green glades we are one,
Warmed by the sun of her summers
so sweetly searing, blinding;
comforting.
As winter's sun bathes her with paler
gold, and violet shadows add
Tender texture to the benevolent

snow, I sense the promise of more gold
As when grain from the prairies flows to feed the world, or the leaves of fall brassily defy death 'til they lie curled and trodden to feed, again, the forest.

Calm or wild, God's child is this land, where I breathe, stretch and
Raise my eyes in joy to the vastness of her ever changing sky.
Haven for all she has become, still, I can hear the native's drum.
Muffled, it signals the distress of those we came to dispossess.
Beneath the roar of busy street my heart picks up the drummer's beat and,
In the rhythm of the rain I hear generations of natives' tears soaking
Mountain and plain, nourishing the still-forgiving soil we callously despoil.
Privileged am I to share this heritage, knowing it is only lent but,
I treasure it, appreciate it every day, thanking God for bringing me
This way to glory in it,'til my time is spent.

In this final quarter of my highly conscious span, dare I seek pardon
From the aboriginal man—and woman?

Gay Meister
LOVE IS A GIFT

To all with love

"Love is a gift
to accept or refuse.
Love is a gift,"
sang the voice of the Muse.

Sometimes it's wrapped,
ever so tight,
inside a box of paper bright.

Sometimes the trappings
are dull and obscure;
not inviting one to explore.

"Love is a gift
to accept or refuse.
Love is a gift,"
warned the voice of the Muse.

Open the box
and let it flow out;
to sing and to dance all about.

Or keep it closed up
and shelved from use;
"Oh, how sad," cried
the voice of the Muse.

Anise Trail Collins
THE SURVIVAL OF THE BLUEBIRD

This poem is dedicated to all lovers of the beautiful bluebird.

This morning I heard a bluebird sing
As he sat in an old apple tree.
Oh, the melody his notes did bring
With a happy "Chur chur-lee chur-lee"!

Man's progress has harmed this bluebird.
Insecticides have poisoned his food.
Some day his song may no longer be heard,
If he cannot provide for his brood.

He used to build his nest in a hole
Often found in an old locust tree.
Sometimes he preferred an old fence pole,
Where his mate had their little family.

No longer do we see a wooden fence.
Progress has reared its head once more.
So many old trees have disappeared since—
Just a few holes for the bluebird to explore!

So build a house for the bluebird soon,
And help frighten the sparrows away!
Perhaps this bird will come back to stay,
And keep us happy with his merry tune!

Gail Scarola
ANOREXICS IN PAIN
What is it that resides within us,
That brings us such torment and pain?

How do we put it behind us,
So the joys of life we'll regain?

We know the pain of the emotional,
The torture inside our brain.

We feel the depth of the suicidal,
So from life we seem to refrain.

And last the obsession of the physical,
Our desire for death we restrain.

So how do we rise above the hurt,
That has left an indelible stain?

We work our minds and emotions,
Our weight we try to maintain.

We pray that our prayers will be answered,
So we won't have tried in vain.

And Anorexia won't control our lives,
Only peace in our hearts will remain.

Sherry M Marchand
RIPICHIEF
I sit and wait and wait some more
Watching both a hole and door.
I hear a squeak and then a squawk
And something now begins to talk.
I watch with eyes as big as wheels
It sounds just like my sisters squeals.
And then to all my disbelief
Out of the hole pops Ripichief.
Now Ripichief he is a mouse
Who lives right here in my house.
He never comes out in daytime light
He said he can not stand the sight.
With pots and pans and kids around
A mouse trap is where he'd be bound.
He'll come out only in the night
When there is no daytime light.
Up in my room is where he'll stay
Talking till the light of day.
And then he'll sneak right back down
To his home in the ground.
Oh no! I hear a purr quite near
Away Ripichief flies with such fear.
He won't come out till night and then
We'll talk till morning light again.

Lucy Wieneke
MARIA

Dedicated to 'the remarkable lady' from her daughter

The wonder of life escapes me not
  When I look at the beautiful face.
The lines are etched by God's own hand
  And the smile is woven in place.
Hands that are curled, still hold the beads,
  The Aves are held in her soul.
Lips make the journey they know so well
  To kiss the worn cross of gold.
Tales of hardship, excitement and joy,
  By each generation heard.
Little faces, eyes open wide,
  Hanging on each precious word.
Eyes that have seen so much of life
  Now can barely see,
But the twinkle and mischief sparkle there
  Like sun dancing over the sea.
The beauty around fills her heart
  And the beauty within shines through.
Her life is a joyous wonder
  To each person Maria knew.

Paula Andria

Paula Andria
PRAYER
When I was feeling blue, one day
And nothing seemed to go my way,
I stopped and said a little prayer
And put my woes unto His care.

It might not solve all problems, true
But prayer can do great things for you,
Once you try it, you will agree
It eases pain and sets hearts free.

There's no set rule how you must pray
Be sure there's Faith in what you say,
What e'er the hour, what e'er the day,
Whether at work, whether at play,

Ask for favors, great or small
He listens, He hears, He loves all.
If it comes from a heart that's true
The answer will be there for you.

Whichever way you choose to pray
Faith must guide you all the way,
For when you pray you have a Friend
Who'll walk beside you till the end.

David C Sutton
THOSE EYES

In my heart you will always be Mary C.

Those eyes
Those boy catching eyes
They make an old man think himself young.
They make a young man think himself wise.

I used to sing to her ears and often was blessed by the words out of her mouth.

Those beautiful brown puppy dog round eyes.

I could always see myself in those eyes
I could see a rainbow in her hair,
as I carried the umbrella for her in that refreshing Portland rain.

With all her charms
I considered myself lucky to have her arms around me, when I put mine around her waist, it disappeared.

I got a thrill watching her run down the hill to meet me.
She said she was just my fantasy.
Those eyes staring out the window, so soon to be gone and my regrets there are none.

Mary Anne Beach
I STOPPED BEFORE A PUDDLE

This is for you Pop, Nan and Mom!! I love you. Mary Anne

I stopped before a puddle
My face looked back at me,
And suddenly I saw something
I didn't want to see.

The future how it frightens me
And sights inside myself,
Of days of little children
And dolls set on a shelf.

I realized the terror
I don't really want to go,
I always say I can't wait
But, I really can, you know.

I think I'm growing up too fast
My life's still at the top,
Too soon it will be over
But the world won't stop.

Will anybody notice
That I have gone away?
Will anybody shed a tear
Or have a word to say?

So I stepped into the puddle
The image gone for good,
Of things that frightened me
That I thought never could.

Henry W Dailey Jr
JUST A CHILD
Frightened, abused and alone, forced to be on their own,
Wandering among the city streets, terrified of the unknown.
Unable to support their needs, for they're not yet grown.

Some how our young find no other way, but to sell their soul,
Always desperate for a meal and shelter from the cold.
In just a matter of time, their hearts will be hard as stone.

Children they are, but not so you'd be able to tell,
They're pushed into a sick world, one you might recognize as hell.
You all know the place, the street where a child has a body for sale.

CHILDREN!!! instantly images begin to appear,
Of little girls sharing make-believe tea with a teddy bear,
Or brave boys climbing the tallest tree simply on a dare.

Some may look at these children with pity,
Others simply ignore them, have they no shame?
Society!, you're really the ones to blame.

Alex W Busséy
THE LEOPARD NOIR
The fierce beauty of the black leopard
  The very essence of the free

wild spirit
A powerful black feline prowling the jungle
Springing in lethal pursuit of prey
Portraying all the passion and fury
Of a beast by hunger roused into action
Flaunting sexuality in swift silent motion
Absolute confidence to master all challenge
Rich and lyrical in poetic choreography
Sculptured beauty of power and intensity
An intrinsic driving force of nature
Liquid movement majestically flowing
Grace and form blatantly sensual
Powerful muscles rippling undercoat
Sleek black fur in intricate texture glistening
Piercing eyes of peridot-topaz hypnotizing
The bared fangs of the deadly nighthunter
An electrifying scene of nature
Incomparable beauty and power unleashed.

Dee Dee Delmas
SEASONS

To my Husband, for having Faith in me.

The Summer days that were bright and sunny,

Now have 'whifs' of coolness in the air.

Shadows dance like tall slim Fairies,

The Autumn leaves all sprinkled in their hair.

As the days grow short and the nights grow long,

We listen now for Winter's Song.

It creeps closer and closer each new day,

As God puts Summer once more away.

Lauren Elizabeth Carroll
FIRST LOVE

Days of sunshine,
Hours of fun.
Good times, bad times,
Two beings as one.
An affectionate hug,
An intimate kiss.
Shared emotions,
A feeling of bliss.
A blanket of beauty,
Surrounds the air.
My heart beats rapidly,
As I caress your hair.
All these emotions,
Feeling so new.
I'm full of confusion,
But I think . . . I Love You.

Natasha Ray
THE PAINTING

It was a powerful piece
done by a young artist
depicting the troubles this kid had went through
The painting was called
WARNING DUE
It would one day be a collectors edition
but for now a gallery addition
It was an original
different from others
You could see hatred and abuse
as your heart smothers
This kid had been an intellectual
till he quit school
At the school he attended
he was put down too much
which wasn't too cool
One day he left home
never to return
he was dead by morn
his body found in a field of corn
Now I understand his painting
WARNING DUE was itself to warn

Ethilia Felton

Ethilia Felton
THE CARDINAL

This poem is dedicated to my late beloved brother, James Lewis Anderson

A cardinal sits in my tree
I really wish you could see
How lovely is his coat of red
With a little tassle on his head
He looks worried as he sits there still
He hears a boy who is loud and shrill

He cocks his head and listens
Then flies away into the air
His red feathers glisten
He will be back to see us, sure
As we have set a little lure
Sunflower seeds upon a ledge
So you see we have the edge

Dennis P Dabney
SOME PLACE IN TIME

One step won't take me very far;
I've just got to keep on a walkin'.
One word won't tell me very much;
You've just got to keep on a talkin'
One thought won't make me very wise;
I've just got to keep on a thinkin'.
And if I refuse to do these things,
I'm just going to keep on a sinkin'.

Somewhere, someplace, somehow,
I'll search until I find
That place where I was meant to be,
With total peace of mind.
The past is just another step
On that ladder that connects me with today.
And as I continue to climb that ladder,
My future unfolds that way.

Little did I know five years ago
I'd be where I am today.
And yet as long as I continue to climb,
I'm sure I'm going to find
That place in time, and total peace of mind.

Ronald L Baker
THEY WERE OURS

Dedicated to the memory of The Crew of Mission STS-51L, space shuttle Challenger—Francis R. Scobee, Michael J. Smith, Ronald E. McNair, Ellison S. Onizuka, Judith A. Resnik, Gregory Jarvis & Christa McAuliffe

In the midst of a beautiful morning
on a cape by a sparkling sea
Seven reach out to grasp a star,
and give it to you and me

But most of us just ignored them, this
had all been done before
We've heard the countdown and watched
the launch, it's just that and nothing more

But more there was this fateful day
when Challenger began to fly
The hopes and dreams of America it seems,
were gone in the blink of an eye

At first we couldn't believe it, the rumors just couldn't be true
But just as we'd feared, when all the smoke cleared they were gone, both shuttle and crew

Now their memory will always be with us,
and their names remembered too, for the risks
they took, and the price they paid,
were paid for me and you

So let us not take any backward steps,
for I'm sure what their wishes are
Lift your heart to the heavens, never look back, and keep reaching for the stars

Dawn M Rosecrans
THE BEAST INSIDE

To those people who have something about themselves or their past that they try to suppress or ignore. Face it, accept that part of yourself, and move on with your life.

Inward, outward, swirling inside—
It rises, I oppress, and take everything in stride.
The day wanes on and the sun rises high;
My energy restored, everything calm inside.

Noon becomes dusk, my reality starts to slide;
Dusk becomes twilight, it rises like the tide.
Night crashes down upon me, it will not be denied;
Twisting, seething, it rages inside—

The changes start to happen, changes I cannot hide;
I raise my head and howl, it cannot be defied.
Racing through the darkness, demons by my side;
Faster, faster, four legs now in stride.

Night rolls into morning, it retreats far inside;
Dawn blankets the country, instinct no longer my guide.
Confused, bewildered, how can I face this thing inside?
Battered, broken, I gather my tattered pride.

My face in a pond, my reflection in this mirror;
Eyes reflect the soul that warns not to come nearer.
I gasp in horror . . . and then give a sigh;
That THING that ran last night; the Beast . . . was I.

William S Dean Jr
LISTEN TO THE QUIET

To solitude and those who love her. Drink deeply from her cup.

Listen to the quiet.
Soft sound steals slowly down.
Cats' paws tread on velvet pad,
Kiss of quiet, sound of no sigh.

Listen to the quiet.

Pause, sharpen ears to tune the senses,
Ocean roar in nothing lies.
Stills the nerve, calm sweet soul,
Feelings stir in sound of absence.

Listen to the quiet.

Hear its thunder, sound of nothing.
Hear it call no sound at all.
Fog drifts in on feet of panther,
Darkness clamors with no answer.

Listen to the quiet.

Orator speaks in voice so splendid,
Raging Loudly, crying wild.
With never a whisper
to mortal hearing.

Silence calls with lure of siren

Silence calls come lie with me

Listen to the quiet.

Janelle Harms
WITH MY SANITY BESIDE ME I STAND

With my sanity beside me,
I stand alone in the midst of a crowd.
Suddenly . . . no longer wrong,
No longer not allowed.
And then I become just like them . . .
Until the truth and I
Are one again.

David Porter
AN ANALOGY OF A ROSE

With all my love,
Which is always yours.

Upon our first meeting, you were like
a beautiful Rose bud ready to open,
perfection amidst an imperfect world.
As a Rose bud stands, you stood,
pleasing to the eye, mystery to the curiosity,
and a great joy to watch and share the time.
I began to watch increasingly more as

the days floated by.
You, as a Rose, began to
open slowly,
showing just a touch more beauty and
complexity.
My curiosity, love and admiration
grew,
as did each and every petal.
As the hours made the days,
you opened to me as our Rose opens
to the Sun;
holding the beauty of life with the
simple difference
that captures the hearts of passersby.
As you have captured mine.
I have given you my heart
and soul.
They feel safer and more secure
in the hands of the power, yet the
innocence, of love.
This love that you have given me and
I you.
There are not words to tell you how I
truly feel,
Just a gift from the Lord: An analogy
of a Rose.

Jeanne D Hastings
TRANSITION

To Chandran beloved of Hira and of many who were honored to know him

In that strange place
Where quiet reigns
And only voiceless winds
Stir silent things
You stand alone
Yet not alone
And know that all
Who tread this earthly floor
Again are joined.
Then soon you feel an inner quiet
And gradual changing
Of your restless spirit
To one at rest.

Patricia Koski
LOVE SEEKER

To Linda, Sam, Alan and Kim

If love flies free on a wild bird's
wing
I'll aviate on my magic swing
Grab lilting birdsongs as they pass
And hold them in a crystal glass
A nimbus cloud may hold love's
prize
I'll scale the highest mountain rise
And in a basket made of reed
I'll trap and save the love I need.
Or with a sterling silver chain
I'll harness little drops of rain
And chariot the universe
Find love and fill my silken purse
Lost love pursued is its own master
Increase your pace and love flees
faster
Love can't be held on a golden
thread
But finds its own way home instead

Jennifer L Morris
BARBED WIRE ROSES

To my Mother and Sarah, My two best friends.

Love, like roses, can be so beautiful it
can make you want to cry.
They come in different colors,
different fragrances by and by.
Love to me means happiness and joy,
That comes from a mother with her
first little boy,
Playing together like mother and son,
Never thinking, just focusing one on
one.
You look past the heartache, the pain,
and the tears,
Never opening up to let go of your
fears.
But what of the thorns, the fears, and
the hate,
You feel when you're mad at your
husband or mate.
What good does it do to keep it
inside,
It won't go away if you just run and
hide.
It's a Two way street, up and down.
One minute you smile the next you
frown.

Angel Spicer

Angel Spicer
UNTITLED

The rain falls outside
Like the tears I cry
They're not visible
They exist on the inside
Those are the worst tears
A pain
With every breath I take
There's one small difference
Between my rain
And that outside
My rain never subsides

Ida Larson
SPRING

To Roy and Anita Jost
Randy and Angela Crowdes
From Aunt Ida

Birds are Singing
Bells are Ringing
Children A playing
Trees A Swaying
Joy and Laughter
Disturbs the Master
Spring is Here
Happiest time of the Year

Gerry Huning
CLOCKS

To my sons Randy, Rick, and Billy Pool

Tick and tock, bing and bong. Did
you know clocks sing songs?
Some are tall, some are small, stand
on shelves, hang on walls.

My church's clock has many chimes.
I wonder how they tell time.
An hour-glass has no hands, it tells
time with grains of sand.

In olden days my daddy said, people
used the sun.
It seems to me if it cloudy, that
wouldn't be much fun.

Some clocks have pendulums,
swinging left and right.
Mother has a clock that shines, in the
dark at night.

Old clocks and new clocks, they all
can tell time.
The best one of all, is the clock I call
mine.

My clock is a Cuckoo, with a bird in
its tower.
But it's very smart, it saya cuckoo
every hour.

Vincent Font
FIRST ROMANCE

For the loveless

To think that I may never live
To reach the heights of first
romance,
That destiny may never give
This heart but half a chance
To speak the words it yearns to
bleed,
To act out that romantic lead
I've dreamt of playing for so long—
If only I should live that long.

To think that I may never know
The touch of another's caress,
That I may never live to show
The love that I possess;
To hold a tender hand in mine
And freeze that moment long in
time,
To take full grip while love's alive
For soon enough it, too, shall die.

Diane Yvette Bates
LIFE WITH A BOTTLE, NO PLACE TO HIDE

This poem is dedicated to my father, the late Stephen J. Forcier
With Love

Life with a bottle, no place to hide
God only knows the tears I have
cried.
Words from my mouth, what did I
say
Why can't I remember, just
yesterday?
The bars, the men, motels I'd
see—
Was someone else, it couldn't be me.
Years that have passed, I do not
recall
How many times did I stumble and
fall?
How could it be, that my "special
friend"
Would lead me to the bitter end.
"That bottle," who was always there
Could give to me, grief, and despair.
Time passed by, I grew tired and
sore
My body cried out, "I can't take
anymore."
Treatment centers—Founders Hall
I smile now, I have it all.
These thoughts are mine, my head is
clear
I do not live in constant fear.
I'm sober now, and feeling well
Trapped no more in my "living hell"

Patricia D G Otake
THE ROARING TIDE

Dedicated to the sea, the sea—the treacherous sea, that does so fascinate and inspire me.

I stood there in the dark
Listening to the roar;
The thundering, the crashing
Of waves beating against the shore.

It was the early morn
Before the sun did rise,
When night did still consume
The heavens and the skies.

The roar was quite pronounced,
Almost deafening to my ear.
Yet this sound did transfix
And send through me a chill of fear.

For I could feel the ocean's force,
Even though the waves I could not
see.
They were like a violent rage,
That carried 'cross the winds to me.

Yet, I knew within the hour,
This winter's high tide would be
gone;
To come again tomorrow—
Before the light of dawn.

Deiedre A Bellomy
DID YOU EVER TAKE THE TIME

To Barbara A. Wimer, my Mother and my best friend

Did you ever take the time
To walk along a mountain stream?
And as you start your climb
Give yourself the time to dream.

Did you ever take the time
To listen to the breeze?
It seems to talk in rhyme
As it rustles through the trees.

Did you ever take the time
To see the grass you walk on?
The color oh so sublime
Never matched by man with crayon.

Did you ever take the time
To taste the salt in the Air?
As you wade in the foamy brine
The sea breeze curls your hair.

Did you ever take the time
To be exactly what you are?
If not, it is a crime
And you'll never reach your star!

Bee Jay Freeman
MISUSE

. . . to Willie Curtis

The river
ribbons
through
parched earth
like
a frayed
and forgotten
fragment
of God's
gift
to
man
abused . . . misused.

Renee Tipton
HAVE NO FEAR

To you Kelly, my only one.

As I sit here in fright,
I need you to hold me tight.
With your arms so warm,
I know I can weather this storm.
With you so near,
I have no fear.

Edward Sexton
I DONE MY BEST

In memory of Oscar Sexton

So small and soft little boy you were. Growing so tall, yet I knew so much of you. Sitting so near full of fear. I also could hear cries of the night. I held you softly wiping your tears, holding so near.

Growing so tall as I little small. My body getting old as your life began. We sat and talked of all kinds of things. My life was coming to an end, but then you held my hand, I then knew a loven hand.

I sat in my chair as you readied to go. You, down on bended knee pulled back my hair. Touching my face, looking into my eyes. I sat so very still holding your hand.

Go on son, she waits for you. My time has come, your life has begun. Kissing my face. He took his place. I done my best, but at last I must pass. This is my young, now I have won. I love you my son.

Shirley Wilkins

Shirley Wilkins
MY MOTHER

To my loving children Terry and Suzan

My mother does not know me, that is hard to take.
Just a time ago, she use to cook and bake.
Now all she does is sit and look around.
The things she use to see and know, just cannot be found.
You see, my mother has this sickness that makes her mind confusing,
The things she use to laugh about, are no more amusing.

When she was young and growing up, her memory she thought would last.
Now she has no knowledge of what's tomorrow, or the past.
No matter how she is, my mother she'll always be.
I know who she is, even tho she don't know me.

M C Levie
TWO WOMEN

Two women
One man
Two hearts held in his hands

Two lives
Ruled by one

Two souls this one mans won

Broken vows
Battered dreams
A different life in one mans scheme

Two lifes
Entwined by one
And neither knows of what to come

Tomorrows light
Has dimmed away
Walk careful now its shatterday.

Dennis Allen
DISAPPEAR THE CLOUDS

To Mother, who taught me much of what I need to know.

T'other day I met a man
Could make the clouds go 'way.
Never mind that he had trouble
Speaking clearly. Seems like
There isn't any lack of people
Who spout words aplenty;
But, how many of these count the moving wisps
High in the air as playmates?

That curious man claimed to have beheld wonders—
Had seen the Emerald Throne with lightning flashes shooting out.
The verbal ones most probably
Would call the man a lunatic.
Yet, how many of those
Have envisioned a throne celestial,
Much less a green one?

Children do and see
Those kinds of things.
The world was wondrous once,
And, if some adults have not left that place,
Why must they be forced
To join the human race?

Pamela D Arthur-Townsell
DREAM PARADISE

This poem is dedicated to my mother, Betty, whom I owe my life. And to my husband Eddie who encouraged me.

Where is the home of dreams?
Why do they settle in our minds?
Life would be much more simpler.
If dreams would free us from our binds.

Dreams causes hopes,
Which makes it more unreal;
Reality is much more compromising,
Because we accomplish a great big deal.

These images we have,
It releases us from reality;
They fully satisfy our wishes,
That we use most ordinarily.

The questions of our dream paradise,
There will always be some;
Those dancing visions in our heads,
Each day they'll always come.

Danielle Ianniello
ALONE

To my Father, Joseph Ianniello, who passed away on September 19, 1987. Daddy, I'll love you forever.

All alone with no one to call my own,
No one to share my feelings and my dreams,
Sometimes I feel like I'm ripping at the seams,
I have so much love to share,
But no one will take a chance, they wouldn't dare,
I know if someone gave me a chance,
They could find a true romance,
Alone, I will be, until someone can see, and then
they will love me.

Benjamin Katz
THE MIDNIGHT BRIDE

To my wonderful inspirational wife GLORIA, and my precious priceless friends, KELVIN & CAY MILLS and family.

At Cook County Prison, Chicago-Illinois, the electric chair was nicknamed THE MIDNIGHT BRIDE; it was at twelve midnight that the switch was thrown.

INTRODUCTION

The defendant, sitting at the council table, being tried for Murder One, after listening intensely to the last witness for the prosecution, hopelessly slumps in his chair, saying this to himself.

THE MIDNIGHT BRIDE

It happened as they told it, they had me dead to right,
The jury, they looked horrified, my heart was filled with fright,
I knew they'd find me guilty, and wed me to my bride,
That shocking electric monster, known as THE MIDNIGHT BRIDE;

THE MIDNIGHT BRIDE, the judge he said, I sentence you to wed,
One, two minute kiss from her, and forever you'll be dead,
Zombie-like, you'll wait and sweat, until you'll meet your bride,
Then you'll be carried out of here, for your last earthly ride;

Deep pain and fear you will have known, a thousand times have died,
While waiting for reprieve, or to be kissed by THE MIDNIGHT BRIDE,
Wake up, wake up, it's all a dream, and GOD is on your side,
For who in his right mind, will want a kiss from THE MIDNIGHT BRIDE.

Audrey Rockhill Burford
RIVER OF LOVE

To my Mom, whose love and strength is the fuel to my own spirit.

Water of wonder,
liquidy desires,
dreaming about you.
colors flow on me,
flashes in the cobwebs,
rushes in my body.
places I want to drift,
whispers in the dark.
revealing that hidden place,
perspiration on my palms.
my heart on the air,
quivering into your hands,
captured by your ways.
throbbing for wanting,
needing you constant.

like ends meet,
the river of love.

Vivian L Reed
CAMPAIGN OF 1988

This poem is dedicated to my Friends and Family from West Virginia, in love and gratitude.

The election is over and there is no doubt,
The Republicans are so happy all they do is shout.
I wonder if Bush and Quayle can rest,
For bashing Dukakis they gave it their best.
Bush and Quayle did everything under the sun,
They even went to Dukakis's hometown to make fun.
From Boston Harbor to the ocean so blue,
The furlough and release of Willie Horton made their dreams come true.
Now that they have won, and have all they need,
I wonder if the poor and hungry they will feed.
I see so many homeless, hungry, and sick on the street,
I am wondering if Bush's 1000 points of light will fall at their feet.
I pray for Bush and Quayle and wish them well,
I am a good Christian Liberal Democrat I know you can tell.

Julie Levenson
THE CHICKEN'S THAWED

For Sans

the chicken's thawed
but you've got me awed
on the living room floor
i begin to soar
dinner can wait
got a hot date
the oven bell rings
but my heart sings
my hunger's for you
the things that you do
it's dawn, getting light
it's all so right
my love you've won
and the chicken's done.

Betty Ann Rowland Armijo

Betty Ann Rowland Armijo
NO LOVE CAN BE AS BIG AS MINE

This poem is dedicated to my husband Albert Armijo

"No love can be as big as
mine, no one can hold it
in their hand for it
is greater than thy
land."

Howard Glyn
MISLIGHT

Venus,
the moon that substitutes,
For earth,
with silvery feet,
measures time by your smile.
Its steps
succeed the former sky
in heliotrope—
It steps on
strewn paths
of purplish rosebuds—
Vibrating ornaments,
Stuck and liquified
by a silk gown

tapered in white columns.
When you smile,
you might not see this planet:
a spring adornment
old in its newness
run over by darkness.
Save a smile,
one that is dying for tomorrow.

Margaret M Frees

Margaret M Frees
TO MY FIRST GRANDCHILD

Dedicated to Joseph—With Love

Though I've never seen you
grandchild
This how much I know
That you were kissed by angels
For God hath willed it so.

God thought of you in Heaven
And so you're Heaven sent
Bright angels that did bring you
To happiness were spent

They carried you gently on their
wings
Through cloudless skies and white-
moon-beams
While dancing stars, shone bright
above
Paid homage too, a mother's love

While mother slept and dreamed of
you
These bright angels carried you to
Her open arms, and left you there
Surrounded by her loving care

Then back to God, these angels went
From their long journey, Heaven sent
To be your guide, from up above
A guardian angel, for you to love.

Anne M Orsborn
TO MY DAUGHTER
The day's here at last, and you're
changing your life—
To give of yourself, and become his
wife.

But for all you may give, Baby, lend
your sweet ear—
There'll be much more to give, as
you live year to year.

There'll be times when he's grumpy,
his words not so tender—
He may even in anger, go out on a
bender.

And that's when you'll have to find
strength of your own—
Understand all his ways, and the love
he has shown.

Comfort him, when his days have
been tough—
Be his love, always—but that's not
enough.

When his heart is heavy, and perhaps
he's unkind—
Hold him close and be warm, and
together you'll find—

When things all at once, seem
hopeless and lost—
Your love alone will be worth the
cost.

Remember, to him, you must be
many things—
And they all just begin, as you trade
wedding rings.

You are flesh of my flesh, now I give
you away—
Though the tears in my heart, still
beg you to stay.

Today life is new, all fresh and
glowing—
Tomorrow will prove the good taste
you are showing.

Momma

(Mrs) Sandra J Passamonte
THE ROSE
"An old man lay dying,
In a cold room all alone.
Somehow the cold fear of death,
In a moment passed away.
For he felt someone standing near
He saw a garden where he'd stay."

"Is this the mansion, "Lord",
You promised long ago?"
"You said you would prepare a
place."
"It's truly something to behold."

"Is this my garden Lord?
I can tend to all the day."
"Are all the roses just for me?"
"Dear Lord, I want to stay."

Later in the evening,
Someone found him where he lay.
A fragrant rose clutched, in his hand.
A smile upon his face.

They thought, oh what a shame,
This old man died alone.
Still, they forever wondered
About the rose.

Donna R McAloney
MY AUNT BLANCHE

Dedicated to Blanche Harrington. She passed away shortly after it was written. She is remembered with great affection.

When I was young I used to wait
to see their car come through our
gate,
then with a clap, I'd run to see
my Aunt who means so much to me.
Her smiling face and twinkling eye
were such a great big treat to my
six sisters and big brother too,
I don't think she knew what to do.
She hugged us all and brought us
gifts.
We ran to kiss her—all in shifts.
She had such soft and wavy hair
and lovely clothes she'd always
wear.
She smelled like roses in the Spring
and wore a gorgeous diamond ring.
Her mink hugged close around her
shoulder
as though it just adored to hold her.
She stepped so lightly and with such
grace,
she could have been a queen
someplace.
The years have flown and do go by
too quickly for my Aunt and I,
She's eighty seven now you see
and still she means so much to me.
You will not find, no, not a chance
a lovelier lady than my Aunt
Blanche!

Mirella Reyes
OLD WOMEN

To Jessica, and Janie with all my love.

It's lonely to have never known my
old women.

It's lonesome just to know that, I will
never

Glimpse to see her first morning
smile.

To hear her voice as she calls out for
me.
"If only she were alive today."

It's lonely to have never known old
women.

To hear her wisdom, and observe her
incourse with life as it was meant to
be.

To watch her clowiness that has
often been spoken of much to me.

To simply press thy hand next to
mine, and whisper in thy ear. My
undying love . . .

Yes. Old women . . .

It's lonely to have never known you,
and it grieves me even more now
that I am grown. To learn that, time
was our foe . . .

Najeh A Trabilsy
SATANIC URGES
A petty commoner from the
Commonwealth to England came,
Democracy and freedom to breathe,
his animal traits to tame,
In pretty "Brittania", that for
centuries "ruled the waves", [1]
Over countless peers and kings, over
villains, too, and knaves,
English freedom and democracy he
merely abused, instead,
Emotions and enmities he roused,
innocent blood was shed,
To mention his infamous name isn't
really my intent,
With him I wouldn't argue, he is
really beneath contempt,
Islam was duly perceived and
revered by Mahatma Gandhi,
What a disgrace to be followed by
such a heretic dandy!
Gandhi, fasting, would intervene and
end the clashes,
This pretender sets fire with malice,
and enjoys the ashes!
He doesn't lack intellect, it seems;
nor does sewage lack water:
A courtesan is still a whore, as often
is her daughter.
His clear and sordid aim is Islam to
stab and smear,
Which fits a rootless scum, who has
no decency, but fear,
On Islam Rushdie wants to prey, like
a parasite, a leech,
He slanders, libels and stabs, and
calls it freedom of speech!
Adulterating the Truth, he wantonly
crosses the line,
If he doesn't know, he is an idiot, if
he does, a swine!
"He should be killed", they say,
overly bitter and dejected,
"No fake martyrs", say others, "he
should rather be neglected",
Attacking Islam, he tries in vain to
escape mediocrity,
To kill him is to save him from daily
justice till Eternity,
Islam has already survived, through
fourteen hundred years,
Calamity, Crusades, Tartars, Mongol
hordes and fears,
Islam is Heaven's religion, not a
speculation hot-bed,
But fools always "rush in where
angels fears to tread", [2]
With this nonentity there's no need
at all to fight,
All that he needs is a strait-jacket,
fitted, sturdy and tight!
If he only knew the truth, he'd surely
burst into tears:
That his short sight is matched only
by his long ears!
"A little learning is a dangerous
thing", said Pope, [3]
Did he have Rushdie in mind? Or
maybe another dope?,
"Drink deep", he said, from "the
Pierian Spring", so cool, [4]
Not from rotten sewage, or from a
stinking cesspool,
A gutter mentality cannot be divine,
it cannot soar,
Salman Rushdie is a case in point,
and maybe more,
Heavy subjects overload the so-
called feather-brains,
Which strive to think big, divine, and
end up stuck in drains.
Mediocre is Rushdie, no matter how
hard he feigns or tries,
Captive of hate and prejudice, free
from conscience' cries!
A genius, telling the Truth, doesn't
hide behind sick fables,
A mediocrity, twisting the Truth,
ends up hiding under tables!
On television shameless he appears,
defending his tale,
Satanic eyes he reveals, concealing
the hooves and tail!
"Don't cast pearls before swine" the
English used to say,
But what's he been doing with the
English pearls until today?
British hospitality he abused, and
also civil liberties,
He has no values to redeem, no
ethics, no moral properties,
From the noblest sons of Mecca the
Prophet descends,
So too do his friends and wives, all of
pure means and ends.
Who is Rushdie, anyway? What's his
lineage or pedigree?
"A cowl doesn't make a monk";
reality cannot be reverie,
I must refer him to Gustave Le Bon,
on Islamic Religion, [5]
But first he must ask Darwin about
his dubious origin! [6]
With the Holy Koran he cannot
tamper, no mortal is a match,
With the lowly "Satanic Verses" he
makes no mark, no scratch!
Hyde Park is not for all creatures; or
else it will be abused,
What is he doing in Great Britain?

Her Majesty is not amused.

1) Lord Tennyson, English Poet Laureate.
2) Alexander Pope, English Poet.
3) Alexander Pope.
4) Alexander Pope.
5) Author of "La Civilisation des Arabes".
6) Charles Darwin, English naturalist.

Judith York McGoffin
A SMALL TALE
Sam was small, you must recall, but
that's not how she got her name . . .
She was also quite short, and would
with rabbit cavort,
Although that's not her claim to
fame.
She was but a runt, much too small
for the hunt,
Still her services were right for
SOME game.
She was just a pup, who didn't grow
up,
But we loved her all the same.

She had her own pen, with blanket
too, and bravely provided protection,
All she wanted in return was our
loving affection.
To see her prance, it was almost a
dance, and so she was praised by all,
And her leaps in chasing butterflies
made her appear ALMOST tall;
Only the butterflies she could not
understand—
They ran by air and not by land.

But as I have said before,
Our Sam was designed for at least
One chore:
What else would you want around,
when the mice did so abound,
But MAGNIFICENT SAM, the
mouser dash-hound.

Joan Trott
THE PIRATE
A pirate fierce swooped down on
Dad
And tied him to the mast.
He gave the most blood-curdling
yells,
We thought that all was lost.
My Dad was brave, as brave could
be,
He laughed right in his face.
"Ha-ha," he said, "You do your
worst,
My blood, your sword, won't
taste!"
The pirate crouched and closer crept,
He gave a fiendish grin
My Dad was helpless in his ropes,
It looked a pirate win.
His cutlass it was brandished high,
One swoop he'd have his head!
And then my Dad said calmly, "Son,
It's time to go to bed."

Carolyn Swalina
SONNET
The night was black and without stars
to see
He stumbled over rocks on through
the grass
To where his love told him that she
would be
Still waiting, if their love had proved
to last
It had been years since he had seen
her face
He'd had to leave to fight on foreign
shores
They promised love eternal in this
place
And planned to meet when he
returned from war
He searched in vain and then fell to
the ground
His lantpern's light confirmed his
deepest fear
Her tombstone rose above a lonely
mound
He sat beside her grave without a
tear
And if you choose some night to
pass that way
You'll see two stones where once but
one did lay

Edith Cunko
WHAT THE MORNING BRINGS
Cast aside all hatred, against
people and all things . . .
And you will be surprised at
what the morning brings.
Just wake up at the crack of dawn
and see what Heaven sent you . . .
Go outside and look around and you
will know its true,
And then kneel down, reach out your
hand and touch the morning dew.
The world in all its splendor makes
everything all right,
So look up beyond the sunrise and
thank God He kept you through the
night.

Reginald V Bruster
THE PROGRESSION OF CIVILIZATION REVEALED IN A ROOM
Our primitivism is primitive tamed.
This self-awareness needn't be
defamed.
For we linger much in one room:
A civil jungle with a fetid fume.
And water pours daily, there
Like water under Nature's care.
Its purging rain in temperature fall,
Removing dust from Clay and that's
all.
But within jungle water thoughts we
find
Although connotations go undefined.
So junglewater has upon us imposed
Thoughts from which history's
composed.
The essence of self, then, is never
removed.
Yes, primitivism is merely primitive
reproved.

Jennifer Sartell
WHERE I WALK
Between the
highest peak
that cuts the
skies
And the
lowest valley
Is where I walk
till the
end.
When the
end comes
Someone else
who knows
the secret
Shall walk
where I once
walked.

Betty W Heisey
MY WISH FOR LOVE
I wish that I could write of love
and tell you how I feel.
Each time I see you pass me by
the heart within me starts to
reel.
Your eyes meet mine and then it
seems as if our lips had kissed.
But you belong to someone else
and I, again, was missed.
Once I closed my heart to
l o v e —
I said it didn't matter.
Then you walk by and all at once
my heart goes pitter patter.
My love for you will ere abide
until the day will come—
When, hand in hand, you're by
my side and we become as one.

Irene Floyd Craig

Irene Floyd Craig
THE DUSK
The flowers have tucked their
droopy heads
In green and yellow tufted beds;
The birds have swept low to the hills
And under wings placed pointed
bills;
The lazy green frogs from the pool
croak
A mellow note from throat to throat;
An owl his heavy eyelids open
As end of day his rest is broken;
The grasses green a plush carpet
make
As drops of rain the dew now fake;
The cattle moping from the spring
Turn homeward for the night to bring
Rest to their weary plodding steps;
The dog which near the door has sat
To guard his home from prowling cat
Now lifts his sleek, cold nose and
sniffs;
For now the master homeward drifts
The curtains of night draw closely by
The dusk, God's resting time is nigh.

Nan Ward
GOD'S LOVE
God is in His Heaven above
And all around us we see His love.
If we go to Him in prayers,
He will help us with our cares.

All around us we see His touch,
In flowers and trees and birds and
such.
If we ask for His help each day,
He will be with us, come what may.

Georgina "Jo" Robinson
BABBLING BROOK
Babbling brook running by
Where did you come from, where are
you going.
From north to south do you travel.
From bank to bank, you mostly stay.
Over rock and around big trees.
Comes a steady stream of water.
From where you come to where
you're going.
Must be a pleasant trip you're on.
For seldom do you anger
But do so much good on your way.
Helping the farmer grow his crops.
In your deep dark soil from your
banks.
The wild could not do without your
faithful flow,
Fishermen with their rod and flys,
That walk your rocky bottom
Seeking a pool where your fish do
hide.
Little children playing in your waters,
That so pure on a hot summer day.
Babbling brook running on your way.
May you always be as clean and pure
as you are today.
So all can come and enjoy you
another day.

Lisbeth M Willson
THE SONG
The world was black and ugly; a
world with Hater's clouds.
Then came the sweetest melody
which rang from soft to loud.
Some began to listen to the tune
which He had sung.
Take heed or not—He wouldn't stop
'til through the world it rung.

Beaten, torn, and bruised; His
body scarred and mauled
It seemed none liked His
melody. No one cared at all;
Except for the chosen Few whose
liver were changed about.
He took all fears away, all hate, all
sin, all doubt.

But no, the world wouldn't
listen, for their ears were closed
to rhyme.
Their thoughts were of
unhappiness and their eyes
were always crying.
They put an end to the Singer with
the melody left behind.
Then realizing what they'd done,
found Him the Maker of all time.

The Singer had been put to
death, but alas! The Song still
rings
to every woman, child, and man who
will accept these things.

Susie Savant
YOU BRING BACK MEMORIES
You bring back memories.
I see you smile and hear
Your voice.
In love's sweet melodies
We walked through fields of silver
lace
Our hearts grow pale, then dead.
Though days have turned into
months
And years—
At times life blurred by view;
I'll always cherish in my heart
My dream and love of you.

W W Hogg
THE DEATH OF BLACK CAT VILLAGE
The black cat dances, entrances,
Prances through the night,
Into the silent morning
And the feeble morning light.

The Chief's dark eyes, aged, wise
Rise slowly to the sky
As the village stirs to life.
It will be a fine day to die.

The blue clad men have come again
In numbers great and strong.
When they leave this sacred place
Will they sing our dying song?

No sound is heard, no wind or bird.
The black cat sits like stone
Among the bloody wreckage.
And is utterly alone.

The black cat dances, entrances,

Prances through the night,
And softly sings our dying song
Into the dawning light.

Kristen L Campbell
HANGERS
I try to laugh but instead I cry,
My emotions are all bent up inside.
Like hangers bent during a child's play.
Easily deformed, yet not easily reborn.
And in attempt to mend the misplaced wire,
I only gouge at my internal torment.
Pulling and tugging are my emotions.
Wails emit themselves from my mouth into a hand,
And I bare my teeth into a smile as tears stream down my face.
When, at last, the bent hanger has reached normalcy,
I hang a cloak over these fears and doubts.
Only to cast a shadow over my soul.

G M Hickin
FISHIN'
My uncle-in-law by my brother's wife
Was almost my favorite of kin.
He practiced the art of eludin' strife
By the art of agoin' fishin'.
As quiet as a mouse he escaped from his spouse
To practice his art of fishin'.
But down by the stream the "big ones" it seems
Were all in his dreams, for he slept on the moss like a king.

He snorted and whistled, and his music sizzled—
Base, soprano, allegro—crescendo!
All stops out he grunted and snorted—Endo!

I could stand it no more; it was all such a bore
And so—most inadvertently—he got hit with his pole
As I threw to a hole, which caused him to rise with a quirk.
But a whale gave a jerk, and the line sped away with Unc in it.
He held to that line through mud and slime, but alas he was too late.
He splashed as he crashed (I pitied poor Unc)
As the shark got away with his bait.

Louise Mueller
MISTRESS AND HOUND
Once I could run faster than you, I could jump higher than you would have liked me to.
I had energy galore, I'd play all day and be ready for more.

It must have happened while I was asleep, my youth was gone as if in one big leap.

I can't chase the cat that lives next door, and I have trouble getting up from the floor.

My ball isn't played with too much anymore, and I make less frequent trips out the door.

You seem to understand all this, as you pat my head and give me a kiss.

But still a tear falls from your eye
and lands upon my nose,
You know my days in the sun will soon draw to a close.

Patricia H Noble
YOUR TIME TO TELL
When one is young
Time passes . . . Oh . . . so slow
Birthdays, Holidays, and Christmas
Prompt queries of "How many more days to go?"

Then school days, activities and chores
Make us wish time wouldn't go so fast
The worldly events, the special walks along life's path
All too soon are memories of the past.

As the joints get stiff
And the hair grows grey
Grandparents no longer needed in the workplace
See their children gathering to hear what they have to say.

The stories are never dull
The learning and the lessons taught
Are facts that beat any history book
Told with that special love which cannot be bought.

So when one is young and growing
Treasure and remember each moment well
For one day all too soon
It will be history and your time to tell.

Tegan Smith
LIFE
Life is like a flower.
It begins as a seed, small and unuseful.
But soon it sprouts and its roots plant itself, stating its place, just as we state our place in life.
It then blossoms and takes on a new dimension.
It bears young and, at the end of the summer season, it slowly fades away, petal by petal.

Mark A Miller
VISION
A vision as always,
like a bird in flight.
A sparkle that stays,
like the moon in the night.

As soft as a petal,
as gentle as spring.
As tough as metal,
what feelings she brings.

A place in the heart,
food for the spirit.
A definite work of art,
and music if you hear it.

All this and much more,
make up this vision.
A gem to store,
it's your decision.

Implanted in mind,
embedded in soul.
Always in time,
to feel the push pull.

Norma Chevrier
PROMISE—THE TREES WILL STAY
Don't take away the trees—
leave them for
hikers on the trail.
The traveler by foot.
The one who sees the beauty of
the softness where we step.

Don't take away the trees—
leave them for the one who comes behind
to make new trails with repeated chance footsteps
or follow the paths we kept.

Don't take away the trees
There will be no memories of: soft moccasins
or sturdy boots passing over trails
where purposes were not the same
but still enjoyed the
comfort while they slept.

Promise—the trees will stay
so that at journey's end we can laugh
and rest and not have wept.

Harry M Thweatt
THE SEASONS
Spring is here, the grass is green.
The flowers yet, are still unseen.

But all of a sudden they pop into view,
Watered by the morning dew.

The trees are budding, the leaves appear.
All the signs of spring are here.

Then summer comes with all it's heat.
The grass turns brown beneath our feet.

We water the grass to make it grow.
Then we mow and mow and mow and mow,

Till fall arrives and the trees become bare,
As their shedded leaves fill the air.

We take our rakes and tackle the leaves.
We pile and we burn until the first freeze,

For winter is here and the cold winds blow.
We take out our shovels and await the first snow.

But we survive.
Then spring comes again and we are glad to be alive.

Donna Raccio
GOD'S MANY MIRACLES
Have you ever watched a bird in flight?
Or a snake slithering in the grass at night
One should take the time to watch,
The miracles of nature, not always a clock.

Enjoy a robin or a mother on her nest
These are the pleasures, I like best
If I teach my children just one thing,
It'll be take time and listen to nature sing.

Some need the hustle of the city
Give me the quiet and nature pretty.
The early morning dawn has a lot to offer
Sit a spell and let your mind wonder.
The relaxation is so overwhelming
To see the sun break out in the morning,
I've learned a lot from all the creatures
For nature I find is a very good teacher

So I'll be up another dawn to awaken
I thank the Lord for this time I've taken
His creation on that no man can match
My eyes have seen my senses He's scratched.

Gary David Griswold
AN AWAKENING
I lie here quietly, with thoughts that beguile me,
In a reflexion of times by-gone,
And etheral voices beckon to me
Through space and time beyon'
To the silent call of a hallowed hall
Where beauty once reigned supreme,
And flowers bloomed from spring 'till fall
'Round the hall eternal of my dream.
There, the maiden dwelt of my heart song,
Not real, but illum'd by fire,
And kindled there by my heart too long
To quench my soul's desire.
For the hall became an empty shell,
A shattering illusion of my mind;
But there I shall no longer dwell,
For beauty's reign has always been mine.
That beckoning voice was my own soul,
And flowers bloom, as I look around,
An awakening within my soul
Of the precious present I have found.

La Jetta Yvette Wright
BLACK WOMAN

To my Mother, Samella, one of the strongest black women I know; My Aunt Jerri, who inspired me to read more which lead to my writing.

We are the strength of our race.
The foundation of a productive black society. The backbone of a strong man, the priceless stone in the powerful mountain.

We love our nation protect our young, stand behind our men.
We are the mothers, sisters and missionary of our religion.

We are proud and should never hold our heads low. We are moving forward and must not halt. We are strong and should never give up!

Sheila Page Mumma
TOI-LING, MY LITTLE BLACK DOG
Hey there fur face, bushy tail pup.
Feet on my dress, nose in my cup,
Bouncing, yipping,
Chasing after birds.
Sometimes when I watch you,
I'm at a loss for words.
With dirt on your nose,
And a smile on your face.
And a few dead moles and
Holes all over the place.
It's plain to see, how you've spent the day,
When I wasn't here, while I was away.
You've burrs in your tail, and ticks in your ear.
Through the wood, near the creek,
you've been chasing deer.
Your feet are all muddy, your legs soaked and wet,
And here you are smiling, while on my feet you set!
Happy little puppy chow, bouncing, furry, joy.
She's so glad to see me, my precious little Toi.

Sandra Taylor Kuck
FIRESIDE
I sit by my hearth late this night
I watch the flickering firelight
And as the flames from the fire rise
They seem to take hold and hypnotize
My mind is blank, my thoughts are none
Solitude and quiet and myself are one
Then the crackle of the fire slowly dies down
Yet a feeling of warmth still surrounds
Soon the glow of embers will give way
To gray-white ashes that will end my day

Karmen Brownson
COCAINE
You can't draw away from that intense stare
That beckons you down the darkened stairs
Into the cellar of emptiness
Dirt stains brush onto your white taffeta dress

Your hair falls out of the tight french braid
You're lost in a silence but never afraid
Spirals of night wind through your mind
An ice cold tomorrow chills your spine

You convulse and bend, this way and that
A whisper sings "Dixie" in A flat
A pounding noise in your ear skips a beat
Pythons of addiction grip your cold feet

White powder of lust, oh so divine
Please stop—you're killing my soul and my mind . . .

Elizabeth M Bierkle
CRUCIFY
Crucify, what a horrible act and word,
yet did men to this act resort.

Nails hammered through living hands and feet,
Oh, how horrible is the deed.

Our loving saviour, innocent and pure,
had this terrible agony to endure.

A crown of thorns pressed on his loving head,
weighted down with our sin.

Instead, we who are sinners should carry the blame,
but He suffered it all for us, to our shame.

God sent his son, in love, who was willing to come,
that through His sacrifice we should be won,

back to our first estate without sin,
to be forever with God and Him.

Sinner do ponder a love so great that nothing matters,
but bringing us back to our first estate.

A love that is constant and true,
that will see us, whatever, through.

Oh, thank you dear Father and Christ above,
that we can depend, on your fathomless love.

Willie Lee Graham

Willie Lee Graham
KEPT ON WORKING

I would like to dedicate this poem to my mother, Queenie Mae Graham, and wife, Barbara Graham.

He Kept on working in the midst of the storm and rain
The man kept on working because he knew life was no game.
He kept on working, his body dictated that he should stop.
The man kept on working because society had put him on the spot.
He kept on working, hoping that a change would come.
The man kept on working little smiles and no fun.
He kept on working through the night and through the day.
He kept on working because he wanted his children to have a better life.
The man kept on working because he didn't want opportunity without skill, to pass them by.

Cathleen Anne Bass
WHERE THE SAND MEETS THE WATER
Where the sand meets the water
year after year, gone, forgotten
long lines of yesteryear.
Like the sand that erodes
life passes by, day after day;
year after year.
Gone are the long walks
on the shell strewn beaches.
As are the lengthy talks
on swings in the breezes.
As sun set and sun rise
during each passing season;
no matter where I am, I can still
hear the faint seagull's cry . . .

J G Shomo
SONG
Melany, a word so tender
that it breaks against my whisper,
tumbles softly towards my tea;
slowly through my gaze I sup
that which is Melany.

Discontent with cup so grim
she flashes to my window pane.
Reflection of the deepest sea
or vision of my happiness
that which is Melany?
Shadow of the morning's dress
or is it Melany?

Still I sit and watch the sun
whose breath, life-giving, falls upon
a playful thought that I have sighed,
sweet melody my sigh must be
that which is Melany.
My ever-sleeping beauty see;
my song is Melany.

Verna Longacre
YOU'RE SPECIAL
I said a prayer for you today
I asked GOD to help you feel special in every way
You are unique, you're one of a kind
He made us all different in body, soul and mind
Breathe deeply and slowly and relax in His love
His guardian Angel is hovering above
When anxious and overwhelmed and don't know what to do
Remember "You're Special" and feel His loving arms around you

Karlie A Muller
FLYER
The White Knight of Love
Rides off into the sunrise
with his red convertible
and a smashing head-ache
Bloodshot eyes gaze back
remembering the bitch last night
Pain is beautiful, a cruel laugh
The things on his mind
—a quart of Pepto
—a lie to the boss
Screw it   You live once
make it fast and have a blast
Fly
Lost
Black
Left on the stones below
(1000 feet below)
is a tiny bent red convertible
Yeah, life is a smashing roar
Up ahead
a neon sign flickers on and off
It shuts down
and sits
dead at the outlet

June M Sacavage
THE BRASS RING
People
viewed like carcasses of meat
as the conveyor belt of life passes you by.
Unaware of the eyes
that seem to dissect your body
inch by inch.
Only perceiving the ground before you which
encompasses cans and bottles of a liquid
drug called
alcohol.
Distortion becomes reality for those who choose that path—
a path of uncertainty, judgements, and
plastic paste-on faces.
A simple release can be the answer,
the answer I choose—
to thank those responsible for who I am
and to leave this place of
smoky distortions of life and reality.

Cynthia Taylor
SPACE ENCOUNTER
Someplace in another time,
There is a peaceful existence.
The sky a magical twilight,
of twinkled dust.
The grass, green as the luckiest of four leaf clovers,
The water like crystal droplets of sweet moonlit honey.
Brightest of lights appeared,
A court began.
Surrounded by empty enemies,
With iced loveless hearts filled with anger and aggressing
Frustration, pettiness pleasures them.
I did not win; for I've committed a sin.
Sadness sorrows me,
Touch with a glittered potion
I made motion from the place in space.

L M Sands
DEPRESSED TRAJECTORY

To disarmament

slicing out of the blue
headlong into a trance
a trigger pulling you
through the temple of chance
the craft pierces the wind
that bites off a man's ear
screeching, sane and sanguine,
pressing a fighting tear
across your sharp vision
addicting velocity
and seductive fission
cutting the wrists of pity
the blood rushes blindly
staining the graves below
conscience leaving kindly
a flag cursed with vertigo

David V Raimo
THE REAL AMERICAN WAY
I sit here confused.
Reality isn't what is seems.
Love and joy are second to
Power and greed.
People hunger, people die;
For what?
Just a piece of the American pie.

Patricia Heilweck
MY HEAVENLY ANGEL
I went shopping for my new little dog
for which I already had a name
She had to be a toy poodle, white,
sweet and, of course, very, very tame
I looked and looked all over creation
for just the right one
Finally, there she was—a bundle of white fluff and my heart she had already won

The name was going to be "Angel Mist from Heaven", this was for sure
But after I got her, I thought maybe I should have chosen Devil or her ways I must cure

April Fools Day is her birthday and this year she will be three
Of course, every day and in every way she plays jokes on me

To say she is a sweetie and I love her is putting it mild
She loves to sit on laps and tug at your clothes, also act wild
Many people who never liked dogs love Angel because she's really like a person
Attention is what she adores and when the mailman comes to the mailbox she will run

She has a teddy bear she lays her head on and tosses all over the place
Also, she has other toys—a dog, elephant, rawhide bone and a ball to chase
You get so angry at her sometimes, then she looks up at you with her big brown eyes
That you forget all about what she did and to anger wave your goodbyes

No wings or halo does she have, this I assure you is true
But to me, her owner and friend, she sticks by me like glue
So, I dedicate this little poem to Heavenly Angel or Devil, this depends on the day
Too bad they don't have doggie medals, she sure would get one that's all I can say

Allen Lee Ireland
THE SPIRIT OF THE ROSE
If one should ascertain at last
The secret of the spirit that impels
The root, the stem, the blossom of the rose,
The garden rose, the universal rose,
One would receive
The loving approbation of the roses that believe.

Meanwhile the spirit of the rose, knowing not
The meaning of itself, nor even
The meaning of a meaning,
Impels the rose regardless of the rose,
And of the rose that knows.

Mary Furr
LOOKING FOR GOD'S CHURCH
Did you say you missed me in church Sunday?
Then why did you forget me again on Monday?
You got to go to church, worship, and shout;
while I was so sick I couldn't go out.

When you bowed your head to pray, did a thought of me come your way?
When you lifted your voice to sing, did you think of making my telephone ring?

During the service was a seed of faith sown,
while I read my Bible home alone?
If anyone cared surely I would have seen a sign,
and heard some voice other than mine.

It was for a month I was infirm, with narry a church member's friendship confirmed.
When you don't care enough to come on your own,
then I don't mind when you stay gone.

Now that I am able to be up and around,
don't bother inviting me back to your holy ground.
If your heart should give a guilty lurch,
forget me again, for I've gone looking for God's Church.

Nathaniel (Glenn) Stover
CHILDREN AND THE CHRISTMAS TREE
When children pass by, the Christmas tree
You can see the joy, an feel the glee
When God made the mountains, an made the sea
He made for good measure, the Christmas tree

When God made children, an a Christmas tree
He thought of love, for you an me
What ever color, what ever creed
He filled our life, of an awful need

The glitter you see, that's in their eyes
Lights up the world, do you realize
When they see the colors, red—white an blue
God made these children, just for you

With the packages all wrapped, an the tree lit up
Give thanks to God, for filling your cup
Without the children, around your Christmas tree
What kind of Christmas, would it be

Chrysti Bigelow
THOSE AUTUMN LEAVES
As an Autumn leaf floats to the ground,
You tell me that you don't want me around.
A silent tear falls from my eye,
Like an Autumn leaf falls from the sky.
"Don't cry. We're still friends," you softly say.
But I've heard that before on many other days.
You will leave me, and we'll grow apart
I'll be left with a broken heart.
But I'll let you go anyway,
because I know that you'll not stay.
For our love is dead like those Autumn leaves,
And has been blown away in that Autumn breeze.

Mimi Chapman
ENCOURAGEMENT
A little bee is buzzing round,
whispering in my ears—
"Perk up baby, give a smile,
life's too short for tears.
Reach out in love to others,
enjoy the things you do—
Praise the Lord for everything,
even skies of blue."
Then a bird goes flying by,
and gives to me a yell—
"Depression makes you sick, my friend,
It's love that makes you well."
So I guess I'll open up my heart,
and let the love flow thru'.
I'll Praise the Lord for everything,
and He'll make all things new.
Thank you pretty little bird,
Thank you bumble bee—
For taking time out of your day,
to speak sweet things to me!

Lisa Wild

Lisa Wild
A WILLOW
Supply ochry branches
of a willow
curve endlessly
into the meadow.

Rain sliding down
their tender leaves
announces the end of summer.

Childhood dreams
tucked under roots
are kept
from merciless time,
to be dreamed over
at your shelter.

Cheer up dear willow,
there will be spring
and summer again,
when sunrays make
the clouds disappear,
when fresh leaves will grow
and new hope in the world.

Julian Brady
THE FLAME
Like romance,
powerful,
full of life,
bright for the world to see.

But wait!
Is that the wind?

Watch the flame flicker,
as young love does.

Uncertain,
but fighting to sustain its strength.

As the wind comes closer,
and the fuel dwindles,
the flame with one last flicker,
valiant,
trying,
dies.

Leaving only remnants,
to
be
remembered.

Betsy L Davenport
DEAR GOD

To my mother, who instilled in me a love of God and to Jesus Christ, who was there all the time, waiting patiently for me to look to Him; When I cried out to Him, He answered.

Dear God, May I talk with you?
I am sorry that it has been so long.
My friends are all "away,"
My husband is somewhere else,
My children I hate to bother,
So, Dear God, will you listen?
I am as alone as a leaf in the vast
Windswept ocean, floating without purpose.
There is a dark, empty, heaviness
Which fills my whole being.
Please, Dear God, put life back
Into my poor miserable soul;
Let me know that you are still my friend,
That you have not turned away also.

Dorothy Anne Schwalb
APPROACH
Hush
No rush
Lush
is the wild grass

The rolling wind
I have awaited here knee-deep
and calm

Is building into gusts.

The ice hangs on
the air blue knives
Poised over the trembling earth

We fear and know
and while we stare
wide eyes
the wild grass trembles as she
always does
when she is caressed.

And even the cruelest raging
does not break her.

Belva Seeley
A POEM FOR ANDREA
As the Mango ripens
And falls from the tree
Maybe that one will
Be spied by me
Sitting on a shelf
At Fisher Fazios'
I cannot pass them by
And as I peel
And inhale the fragrant beauty
My senses come alive
To that bright
Yellow fruit
And I am reminded of
Yet another time
Another place
And that sweet
Sweet face of
"POKI LANI"

Barbara J Waller
FOR THE WINGS OF AN EAGLE

Lovingly dedicated to Art "My Inspiration"

I think of you, most all the time
It makes my day so sunny

Your smile can make
"church bells chime"
Your eyes can get to me honey

You have this way about you,
Warming me, thru and thru.
Laughing, talking, dancing, loving,
We have such fun me and you.

I hope and pray, with all my heart

it will last forever.
But try as I might, to keep it
from sight,
I know it's bound to be,
When like an eagle, you take
flight,
Leaving wonderful memories for me

And I can only hope and pray,
As each night turns back
into day
That love will grow, within your
heart,
You'll miss me, and hate
our being apart
Then maybe "the eagle"
within you
will decide not to fly all alone

Perhaps you'll think that I might
be
"The best eagle buddy,"
there ever could be.
While our star above will
guide us.
No matter where we are
Keeping us close the way we
were
And as we are right now.

With hopes for us to continue
to be
Friends, comrades, lovers, and such,
This is my wish for us, you
and me.
And even if you do take flight
Leaving me all alone,
I'll always have the treasures of
the happy times we've known

Gloria M Huntington
MY FRIEND

I dedicate this poem to my friend, Frances, who was always there for me.

I cannot count the many times,
My friend was there for me,
In times I felt such desperate need,
My hurting she could see.
She stood beside me through the
times,
I felt I could not bear,
She helped me see that I'd survive,
Because someone did care.
The days and nights seemed far too
much,
For anyone to bear,
God took my Love, He holds him
close,
And he waits for me there.
My friend gave hope to calm my
fears,
My sorrows she did share,
I struggled through my tragedy,
For my friend was always there.

Marguerite Ellen Bell
GRANDMA'S ROCKING CHAIR

To David and Sue—well loved.

It sat flat on the floor, and yet it
would rock
to the steady soft ticking of
Grandmother's clock.
On the back of the chair that was
taller than she,
was painted an Angel—just looking
at me.
There were three other chairs, and not
one the same,
but there she would sit, when
company came.
By the end of the day when her
chores were thru,
there would sit Grandma, with
mending to do.
Oh—once in a while I would sit in
her chair,
but it wasn't the same as when
Grandma was there.
Her "rocking" was smooth, and after
a while,
I swear I could see, that dear Angel
smile.
While I'm sure that she knows how
much I adore
that old rocking chair that she had
before,
I sometimes can sense in my
Grandmother's mind,
Her wish for the chair—that she left
behind.

Bonnie Gossard
LOVE IS JUST AROUND THE CORNER

To my dear friends Joy and Sally and my Granddaughter the light of my life; Leigh Ann.

Love is just around the corner
waiting for you and me;
Love is just around the corner, why
don't you take a chance and see.

Just open your eyes and you will
find, a reflection of me that's not just
in your mind.
Take a look into my eyes and you'll
see love was just around the corner
waiting for you and me.

No more heartaches, No more blues,
for in my heart there's room for just
you. Love was just around the corner
please take your chance on me.

Love is so fragile please don't let it
fall again, because oh! my heart, it's
wearing oh so thin.

My love's been there all the time,
Just toss your dime and you'll find,
two heads and two hearts were just
around the corner waiting all this
time, just around the corner waiting
for you and me. Please! Take your
chance and see.

Betty Vincent
JOSHUA

A Joshua once fought the battle
of Jericho.

Our Joshua is a different one though,
you know.

He fights the battles of guys
like "Konan,"

Or sometimes he's a hero we all
know as "He Man."

The first Joshua was fighting his
way into heaven.

Ours may too, someday, but for now,
he's just seven.

John D Madison
ETERNAL SPRING

For Sarah . . . my wife, my peace, my power.

A brisk June night brought to me
What had long been only in dreams,
A chance to feel spring in my soul
again,
To abandon my poisonous schemes.

But with a caution I should have
killed
I waited for a further sign,
And fed my weakness with my
doubts
While I lost the light of the time.

Finally, setting aside my fears,
I chanced to hear your voice
Knowing you could easily crush my
hopes,
I still trembled awaiting your choice.
"Did reality steal your thoughts of
me?",
I asked my melting self,
"Would you simply take the safest
course,
To just live with what was left?"

But when I heard you speak with the
same sweet care
I remembered from the nights in
June,
My spirit had the lightness of a giddy
lad
When first struck by a lover's moon.

John Alan Miheli
WITHOUT YOU

To Marta my love and my mom and dad, Joseph Andrew and Marie Veronica Miheli

Being without, you it's all
that I can do, to keep from
crying, dying, inside.

Knowing that part of me, will
cease to be, without our
caring, sharing, together.

Through the day and night,
it was you who made me right,
I could feel it showing,
glowing, with love.

And if I ever had you back,
I would have what I now lack,
I could go on living, giving,
myself.

For now I'm waiting for the day,
when your sweet lips will say,
that you are feeling, needing,
me too.

And if there is someone up
above, who oversees all that
is love, He will surely bring us
together, forever, as one.

Judy C Osborne
PRECIOUS MOMENTS

Nothing can compare
To the precious moments we share.
Whenever you hold me in your arm
I feel safe, secure, without any harm.
Your kiss is tender and sweet
You lift me off my feet.
Your look is so sexy and soft
I find myself aloft.
I look forward to being with you
For now I'm happy, never blue.
These precious moments are so dear
To none other can compare.

Niki Mavriyanni
MYKONOS

Light,
delight for my sight,
the walls are snow-white,
glorious sun, so bright,
Mykonos I am yours.

Boats,
from everywhere come boats,
bringing people for fun,
happiness in the sun,
Mykonos I am yours

Music,
in everything is music,
in wind, in people's laughter,
seagulls, waves after,
Mykonos I am yours.

Dance,
I always feel like dancing,
on sand and in the streets,
I'm dancing in my dreams,
Mykonos . . . Mykonos . . .

Day,
new people every day
laugh in the sun and play.

Night,
magic under moonlight.
Wish upon a star,
your wish is never far.
Mykonos I am yours.

Beville Anderson
RICE PADDY BLUES

To all my children and all the Nam vets now and then . . .

Walking along the Delta Trail
wondering if life will bid me
farewell.

This selfish old war makes me feel
like a fool knowing my brothers and
sisters are holding their cool.

My mother says to believe in Jesus
Christ, and ask him every night to
save your life.

Congress takes their time passing life
saving bills while your brother and
mine lie dying on the hill.

I say pack our gear and move out, so
that we may end this ungodly body
count.

Let's put to shame who's ever to
blame, and make damn sure next time
we take better aim.

Ronald W Nader and Paddy Ann Gray Nader

Ronald W Nader
IN MY HEART FOREVER

Dedicated to the sweetest—most beautiful woman I'll ever know, Paddy Ann Gray Nader—my one and only lover and wife. My life.

Just one miracle a lifetime, with
Paddy Ann—I had mine.
One lady my adult life—lover, friend,
wife.
Hi's lo's, crippling blows—but she's
the one,
The only one—to make me smile—
make me cry
Now she's gone and the pain, of
losing her will ever remain.
There are days I wish that I had fled
Instead of cried, had died—was dead!
For in many ways I am—with her
love I was a man
Without it there is no purpose—no
plan.
Wishing we had more—of all the
things—we had not
Less cold—more hot.
To care and share, sense each other's
pain—
Never to have to explain, just in love
remain.

My life with you mostly happy—
though sometimes blue—
Whatever way I always loved—
needed you—still do.
In every way—every hour of every
day.
Paddy Ann smile on me from that
heavenly place you be,
For Green eyed lady—I'll always
belong to thee.

Lee Fissori Wright
GENESIS
"In the beginning, God . . . all life
love, power and light flow
from Divinity."

Sun on the earth and moon's
bright light
God created light with the sun's
first ray.
As celestial bodies, creatures and
finally man, before the night,
Set the world on the rim of day.

"The life is the light of man," God
calls
And the light shines in the
darkness beneath the sun.
"Long the years till my
kingdom falls,
And the heavens and earth come
forth from the deep;
and my work is done.

The majesty and the wonder of
His cosmos, pass before us
flying.
Dost crown Him with Glory' and
honor before me.
With the light shining on the dark
sunset dying,
There, after all, is the light of
Divinity, for all to see.

And, God said: "Let us make man
in our image, to begin his role."
He's standing in the wing of
nature's stage.
For beneath the earth is the land
of sheol,
And above is a dome of air,
where the heaven's rage.

God speakes: And the darkness
becomes lighted land
Sending moon and stars echoing
through heaven's hall.
"Before creation, there was only
God:
no one save God, saw the
origin of all things, and man."
And Thy heaven's, the work of
Thy fingers beyond recall.

Astrid Hasler
TIME
Each day goes by,
the clock ticks
knowing that that hour will cease to
exist.
We take this precious time
to care for our loved ones
to discover our world
which lies under the sun.
We stand all together
dreaming our dreams,
as each day goes by,
minute by minute.

Rose-Marie Jordan Fraser
MY SILENT ROOM WITHIN
I have a place deep in my soul
No other soul can know.
A place where only angels, and
the eye of God can go.
It holds the secrets of my heart—
My happiness, my pain—
My hopes and dreams, and
memories of
All that life has been.

I open up to windows of my
silent room within
Each evening when I kneel in
prayer,
And let God's love shine in.
For without his love to brighten it
And keep my dreams alive,
None but the darkest moments
would be
Able to survive.

And for my faithful ritual
I find a great reward—
God sends the grace of hope to
me,
And my courage is restored.

Bernice Bottoms
THE OLD WOODEN WINDMILL
Once you harnessed the wild wind,
Drew precious water from deep
underground.
No longer needed you stand
deserted,
Your ancient vanes creak with a
lonesome sound,

You are one page in American
History
Telling of settlers and hardships they
bore,
One page in the story of the Wild
West,
Rich in ancestral lore.

Priceless are the tales you could tell
Of brave people who settled the land,
Drought, prairie fires and insects,
Untold hardships conquered by man.

Now you stand alone on the
prairie—
A decaying symbol of the past,
Still keeping alive the memory
Of a land that was wild and vast.

June Brittain
AMERICA'S QUEST
The soul searches out:
A tiny creature, A proud people, A
thing of beauty.
Searching in anguish, In hope and in
doubt.
And thus, America is found!

Beauty untold and unseen in the eyes
of men.
Lifts up arms unto the Most High!
Screaming a burning torture
And distilled by faith.

Arms in Arms:
Far reaching into the blue.
Frightened in hope
Screaming murmurs from the soul.

Whispers of Evil:
Wanders of the truth.
Heart for mind
Arises the day by night shadows.

Disturbed and confused, Never
before seen.
Dreams upon dreams, Never before
touched.
But still beholden to the King.
Let the cry of freedom ring!

Nancy New
TRANQUILITY
Tranquility is a beautiful word.
Tranquility is a righteous need.
Tranquility for me is falling snow.
Some may like a soft breeze to blow.
For you a lake in a peaceful glen, or
perhaps a small boy with a
leprechaun grin.
A field of flowers with tossing
heads, a babbling brook, or a leafy
bed.
Whatever your need, tranquility must
be sought.
To make life livable, tranquility must
be bought.
A few seconds here, a few minutes
there, to give our souls
a chance to repair the damage caused
by our everyday fare.
May you find this solace wherever
you can.
Tranquility must be in the heart of a
man.
Tranquility is a blossoming seed.
Tranquility is a friend in deed.

Doreen E Ryan
TRUE LOVE

To My Dearest Vernon: I Dedicate This Poem "True Love" to you and may God's blessings and mercy be upon your life forever.

I sat under the Pine tree pining away because I am so sad and blue over you. You left me for another that is true; but remember Darling, when you are tired roaming and you need a place to rest, you will always have a nest.

Although I am sad and blue over you, I will never look at another. You are the light that sparks my life . . . .When we kissed good bye, my world came crashing down on me.

Come back my love! You are not a dove! I will not keep you caged, I will let you spread your wings; whenever your roaming habits appear but remember come back to me, for when I look at you my whole world opens up with beauty and all problems disappear . . . and I feel like floating on air.

The magic touch of your hands, exceeds any wealth and I will always treasure your warm embrace and on a cold winter's night, I will have your love to keep me warm.

Karen M Anderson
fantasia
Veins of gold sparkle
As they filter thru the trees
Leaving an impression
On the minds of little children

Michelle L Riggs
TOTAL HEARTBREAK
You had whispered in my ear once
upon a time, I love you
And I believed you, did you believe?
I gave you all my love expecting not
to be hurt.
You seemed perfect, different from
the rest, special.
I trusted you with something easily
breakable, my heart.
You took it and cherished it for a
while;
Then you let me down, left me alone
and my heart was broken.
I loved you, how could you do that?
It's over, I know that now.
I will never forget those special
times.
All I have now are perfect memories,
That will remain in my heart,
forever.
Never forgotten.

Cindy Fadin
CONFUSION . . . .
Each year as I grow older,
I'm also growing stronger,
These years haven't always been
easy,
Can I deal with this much longer?

Trying to get my life in order,
At times I feel so weak,
Each day seems to intensify,
Serenity is all I seek,

Each experience of my life,
Seems to teach me a great deal,
I have no real regrets,
For emotions, I've learned to feel,

Taking sometime out for myself,
Digging deep within me,
Trying to think with a clear mind,
Confusion is all I see,

Wanting to put the past behind,
I can only do what I feel is right for
me,
Even though honesty, and trust in
others, still difficult to find,
I now realize, each experience we
should come across,
In reality! It was meant to
be . . . .

Kim Van Fleet
WHEN THE DOCTOR TOLD ME I WAS WITH CHILD
When the doctor told me I was with
child
I was so happy—my emotions ran
wild.
At 4 months along, the doctor took a
peek
Just to confirm my due date week.
You are having twins, I was told
My face went flush, my feet got
cold.
Bigger and bigger my tummy did
grow
With two little ones, I did know.
At 5 months along I was told they
were boys
Oh no, here come the combat toys.
When they arrived, I did shed a tear
What will I do, now that they are
here?
They are really small and make me
run
But I was blessed with two, instead
of one!

Kelly Seavey
GRANDPA
We want you to know as the years
roll by
the bonds of the past hold true,
and never forget for a single day
how much we all love you.

Sometimes I get lonely
and thinking about you helps
Reminding me that there is a person
I love very much
always close in spirit
even when you are far away.

We have something special that
no one, no distance, or no time could
take away . . . .
We have our love and Grandpa, that
will never die.

Sometimes it hurts to think of you
and to remember your laugh, your

touch
and to remember how much I miss
your friendship,
your caring ways and you in my life.

The tears will soon subside
and the pain will ease with time,
But your memory will live forever
In a corner of my mind! ! ! ! ! !

I love you!

Frederic Millen
LAND'S END
Walking along the ocean edge
sandy silk smudges underfoot
streamers of bark in echoing silence
hang suspended from shapely limbs

this rind of experience
is fallen away yet still present
like black leather over bare skin
curly hair tumbling onto shoulders
starshine across the broad back

what trails bring you to this
corner of the cosmos
what fabulous runs
down never ending shores

mountains of water darkly glisten
a coiling crash
answering thump of desire

we stand together apart
in unaccountable warmth
of a late season
holding dry twigs
which blossom in our hand

Carole Key
THE CODE OF THE SEA
We live by the code of the sea,
Tides and waves roll across the
deep—
Beauty amid Life's
welcoming plea,
Binded by Time's
continual seep.

And goes the sand betwixt the toes,
Sandcastles built in Simplicity—
Far richer: Life's
complexity unfolds—
When Innocence grows
up to reality.

Tunnels which channel beneath the
earth,
Hidden curves—a bridge to cross—
Tides break, crumbles in
on worth—
Hopes are dashed; Waves
cover the loss.

Tides hint at Life's progression—
A hope, a game, a gamble at best.
Time brings but a limited
impression.
Moments flee—the Rest
Blown by the
Tides
of a rolling sea.

Martin Bud Taggert
THE HIGHWAYMAN
All six horses were panting and
lathered with sweat
But the town of Tombstone was
many miles yet
The flickering whip of the driver kept
pace
As the coach swept on, sand crusted
his face.

Around a bend, fifty yards ahead
A masked rider waited, guns loaded
with lead.
He leveled a rifle, as the stage came
in sight
And shouted at the driver in the
faltering light:

"Throw-down-that-box, now do as
you're told
If you want to live, give me the
gold."
But the driver was tough, an eye-
witness said
Reached for a gun, was drilled in the
head.

The bandit got the gold, and
squandered it away
To boot hill went the driver the very
next day
The company's insurance paid every
claim
And all but the driver were ahead of
the game.

Martin M Cassity Jr

Martin M Cassity Jr
MILL STREET
If Jesus lived on
Mill Street today, He would hang
out with the people
who use the pay phone in front
of Stanley's Variety Store.

Joseph A Ellis
LISTEN, LISTEN, LISTEN

To Ofelia (Garcia) Ellis, You have been a wonderful mother and a great inspiration!

Listen to the teardrops,
for each tear has its own
heartbeat
Listen to the heartbeat,
for each heartbeat has a life
Listen to the sound of life,
for each sound will tell its own
story
Listen to that story,
for each story must be told
must be expressed
must be felt
must be heard
must be touched!

Margery E Harper
OUR GRAND-DAUGHTER'S PET
Rhythm's a creature who could be a
rabbit
She wears the most exquisite fluffy
white habit
It falls into layers like an ermine fur
coat
And is pure white all over, no
markings to note

Rhythm's blue eyes and little pink
nose
And pink tips to her ears are all color
she shows
As she slinks down the stairway and
into the yard
With her cute tailless stump, she
can't wag or applaud

Sometimes she's a beautiful queen in
disguise—
She's frisky and playful, and surely
quite wise
As she curls in a ball, or reclines on
the mat
Rhythm is Stephanie's lovely Manx
cat!

Rolf Threlkeld
IF I WERE AN ANGEL
If I were an angel I'd disguise myself
as you.
I'd come to you when you were alone
and tell you what to do.
I'd say I was your innerself; your
conscience sent me here.
I've come to help you live your life;
you can live it without fear.
I'd show you how to get the things;
the things you need and want,
Especially your sweetest dreams of
things that can't be bought.

If I were an angel I'd make myself
real small.
I'd sit on your left shoulder and
protect you from a fall.
I'd help you through the hardest
times; I'd open all the doors,
So you could go wherever you
wished, and get the highest scores.
I'd tell you the secrets of life itself.
I'd tell you what your purpose is.
I'd show you how to be yourself and
help you to learn to live.

I wish I were an angel. I would help
you realize, you're worth the world
and so much more; I'd take you to
the skies.
But you tell me that you love me and
say this angel need not be,
Because the life I live with you
indeed has set you free.
The mortal man, the way I am is all
that I can be.
I try so hard and it's all I can do
To try and make you see, that if I
were an angel . . . . .

Cecile Erickson
GONE FROM THE FARM

In memory of Albert and Wallace Forester

Back among the trees secluded,
stands an empty farm.
Shadows of the past eluded
now, wind blows through the
barn.
In my memory I listen,
echoes I still hear!
Laughter of the children
playing, soon brings forth
a tear.
Yes, the years have flown
quietly by, the wars they've
come and gone.
Taking with them two of
these people, who lived
down upon the farm.
I still remember the shelter,
the warmth and coziness there.
When the snow piled knee
deep high,
we'd hook to the sleigh the
old mare.
My brothers would put me upon
the sleigh, snow covered hills
went zooming by.
We sat warm and contented
under the covers, looking
up to the radiant sky.
Later inside dad would
build up the fire, and as
the oak wood blazes
flared, we'd sit there together
the five of us,
mom in her rocking chair.
Then came the war, and away
they both went, months
fell into years
Mom would walk to the mailbox,
and hurry on back,
in her hand, a letter
all wet with her tears.

Dad let things on the farm
go, never again did we hear
youth's song.
We moved away from this
place we all loved,
the place we had lived on
so long.
The farm was loved, but
one by one, we'd see their
silent face, and the ones
we loved were gone from us,
to meet God in all his grace.
Beckoning and luring,
the grain waved out in the
field in the back.
The boys used to cut and
till it, then romp with
their hound dog Mac.
Our old hound dog died of
mourning, he cared the
same as we, but the telegrams
came, and one by one,
they came home from across
the sea.
Now Mom is old, and Dad is gone,
and I'm getting up there too,
Never again, though I wish
it were so, will I have the
time spent with those two.
Yes, a story of laughter and
joy, of smiling bright faces
galore, and I know they are
watching from heaven, those
two who left home for the war.

R H Anderson
THE NIGHT BIRD'S SONG
I hear a night bird singing,
It's song is loud and clear.
It penetrates the darkness,
And titillates my ear.

The song is cool and limpid,
And bores into my brain.
I always shall remember,
Its beautiful refrain.

Norma M Zellmer
OG AND IG
OG the frog and IG the pig,
Lived in a house with two little kids.

OG was green and IG was brown
Both lived proper and without sound.

OG had webbed feet. IG had all fat.
They didn't care as they just sat

Until two little kids picked them up
with glee;
Pulled and pushed them, everywhere,
you see.

What will become of OG and IG

When little ones grow to their youthful mid?

Will anyone recall OG, green and IG, brown?
Two stuffed animals, sitting again, without sound!

Pauline Oates Hager
GRANDPA'S FARM
Grandpa's farm was sold today.
Uncle left it in such disarray.
Just tore down and threw away,
All the home-like features of its day.

The grape arbor by the house.
A cozy bench, the iron fence,
The front porch with honeysuckle and the swing.
Then the orchard fell with no bloom in spring.

Fences were all taken down,
Not a farm animal to be found.
Just grain planted in big plots,
No country lane to the wood lot.

The large old barn was painted red.
Attached to it was a shelter shed.
In the barn lot was a huge straw stack
And a tall windmill to water the stock.

Boards are falling from the loft.
A hammer and nail too long put off.
The roof is hanging its head to thee
Saying, "I was Grandpa's Farm since 1903!"

D Bee Staheli
COLDNESS
Hoarfrost clung to the brush and tree branches
As the cold sun tried to radiate a warmth
The snow-clad mountains stared with an icy majestic look
While the valley lay under a blanket of frozen snow
The clutches of winter refused to relinquish its hold
And all was quiet in the still coldness
The day closed with the ringed, clouded moon
Rising in a silver shadowy glow
To light the cold, frozen earth
Unable to penetrate the chilled silence
Of frozen bleakness that lay over the valley

Jeffrey Grant Hutchinson
HER MYSTICAL PRESENCE
While she slept, her dreams were servicing the day's reflections
Doubts subsided in an altered realm of contentment
The mechanism of reality was being transformed into spiritual ecstasy
Somehow, she had entered an embedded time.

The journey of her existence began on wings of flight
She soared over a sea of paradox in nature
This exotic world held a tapestry of silence and beauty
She had reached a cosmic oneness with a junction in space.

She could only sense the host of doves singing in choir
A towering waterfall melted silently into an echoing pool
Infinite colors embraced an enchanted unicorn
Beneath a shroud of illusion, a distinctive dimension found him in a silhouette of moonlight.
Her entranced being was drawn toward a transmitted aura
The encounter yielded to a vision of an intuitive wizard
He articulated to her the wisdom of panoramic insight
She fused this new-found awareness together with care-free imagination.

No longer was logic distorted within the conduits of emotion
Unhindered by the ties of control, her illuminated thoughts had no destination
Restrictions were unfelt, obstruction not known
When she entered her native presence, she had reached an ultimate peace of mind.

Anita Denison
THE DEATH OF A HOUSE WIFE
My life is measured by trash bags and coffee cups,
dust rags and cigarette butts.
Impatiently, I wait for sacred night to fall
bringing with it the facade for all
That removes the colors from the things we see
allowing me to live anonymously.
I tell myself I would rather die
than simply releasing my humble cry
So I play the mother and the bride
ignoring the emptiness I feel inside
Do I love my husband and my child?
Only for a little while.
Until the dawn unveils my life
and the daily death of a lonely house wife.

Virginia Curtis
PROMISES
The promises of man are most always broken.
But the promises of God are the truest ever spoken.
In this world today we seek fortune and fame.
When all we need is to call on God's name.
For the treasures of this world will soon pass away.
But the treasures God promises are forever and a day.

Caren Appel
FANTASY TRUE
Indulging the silence, its nuances nestled between
us within.
Our thoughts enlisted, we
glided through fantasy true . . .

A flash of infinity
permanently impressed.

Emanating bliss from an
endless ardent well.

Impassioned-blazed
reverie of
crimson enchantment
interlocked we

. . . and one.

eva decker
PILLION
The spirit flowing free
Is, oh, so easily crushed.
The most sincere utterance
Can, oh, so easily be hushed.

The gentle, easy spirit
Which wishes never to offend.
May fail to nourish
Its own desires and whim.

Where, oh gentle spirit
Does your strength lie?
Where? When? What? How?
Will you gratify?

Oh, Pillion, I confess.
Forgive, noble Pillion
I have helped to mold
What you must not become.

I re-avow, dear Pillion
To my own self be true
Pillion, I must repent
Or you can never be you.

Mrs Bonnie L Edelenbos

Mrs Bonnie L Edelenbos
A DEDICATION TO A LOVING GRANDMOTHER

This poem is dedicated to my very special grandmother, Lila Belle Williams, about whom this was written. She is loved and missed very much by her family. I also dedicate this to my husband, Albert A. Edelenbos, who I love very much.

Your passing away has left many upset.
Although we can hear you now:
"It's just one of those things—don't fret."
You were one of a remarkable kind.
Your stamina, compassion, and love are not easy to find.
81 long years you gave of your life.
You were a devoted mother, grandmother, friend, and wife.
Independent should be your middle name.
You certainly go down as a "tough cookie" in our hall of fame.
So many people come and go in our lives,
But you were so special—you deserve a prize.
Your smiles and laughter filled a room with hope.
You were a strong, courageous woman who really knew
how to cope.

We all love you Grandma,
May you rest in peace.

Joseph G Garber
FAITHFUL WINTER ARRIVES IN DECEMBER, ALIVE!

To Providence, who made all this possible!

Hawk! Hawk! Hawk! The temperature drops outside.
Sounds like ubiquitous crows, almost everywhere.
Mock! Mock! Mock! This is crows' territory!
Faithful winter arrives in December, alive!

Odocoileus virginianus, this is whitetail deer.
What an impressive sounding name. It's freezing.
Time to shed your antlers. One by one.
Whip! A mighty wind blows snow all over the forest.

Kahlōōk! Kahlōōk! Wind chill increases.
Birders count Canada geese.
Beautiful pine is cut for little boys and girls.
A Saviour's birth is expected soon.

Arctic fox searches the ground for lemming. Forty below.
Lewis and Clark had neither space heater nor four-wheel drive.
Take courage. They got through the severest winters.
faithful winter arrives in December, alive!

Jean I Brown
THE SOLDIER

I dedicate this poem to my Grandmother, whom I stayed with during World War II. Those days I well remember, and in particular, the day my Father came home.

I am cold now.
Cold and weary. Hungry, and afraid.
They say there is movement out there.
I do not know. I'm not sure where, I hear it not .
I see only the mist, and smell the rot.

We were overrun before. All around me is death.
Death is the only friend I can depend upon.
In the morning I know he will still be there.
Mud streaks my face, and cakes my hair.
The smell of blood is everywhere.

Why am I here?
The only things real out here is fear.
I cannot stand the waiting, yet dread its end.
I do not wish to share this foxhole with my friend.

They say the enemy is warm and well fed.
I wonder if he knows my dread.
Does he read and re-read the letters next to his heart?
Is he fighting for his country and what is right?
Does his stomach turn over at sounds in the night?
Why am I here?
Oh God! What's that? Who goes there?

Dan C Barbare
THERE WILL ALWAYS BE COWBOYS
They say that cowboys are a vanishing breed
That the cowboys' days are over, there's no longer a need
Well, take it from an old cowboy, that just ain't so
There will always be cowboys, as long as time will go.

A cowboy's life is rough, but he likes it that way
He sits tall in the saddle, don't have much to say
His work is hard, and his wages are low

But there will always be cowboys, I want you to know.

You can tell an old cowboy by the wrinkles in his face
They were put there by years of going place to place
Sitting by campfires and sleeping under stars
Drinking bad whiskey and loving cowgirls in bars.

When the round-up is over and he rides into the sun
When he puts away his saddle and hangs up his gun
His cowboying days are over, Lord give him grace
And let there be another cowboy to take this old cowboy's place.

Diane Johnson
EMBRACED IN A HUG

To special people: So close and yet so far.

heart beats
life pulsates
energies intermingling
a safe warm place
rushes of emotion
quickening my pulse.
a smell and a certain touch
no one else compares.

no pretenses,
energy one on one
a safe shell where
nothing hurts
except . . .
to let go.
i'm still crying

Thuy Tran Do
LIKE PEACEFUL BIRDS
Like fragile glass
Handled with care
You entered the world
With a beautiful flare . . .

Like a scented rose
With a soft, sweet smell
You bloomed day to day
Carrying tales to tell . . .
Like cloudless skies
With a calm mystique
You gave the world
A life so unique . . . .
Like raindrops
Falling from the sky
You cleansed our souls
With all the tears you cried . . .
Like peaceful birds
Across the sky
Now I've learned
You too, must fly . . .

MY CHILD,
MY LOVE,
YOU'RE ALL GROWN UP.

Nathanael Beardsley
WINDSONG OF THE SEAGULL
Loft on billowy wind, white against the blow,
Seagulls dance a windsong—tussling to and fro!
Tempest is seaward blown 'cross the rising sky!
Seagulls sing song on wind—sung with rolling cry!

Adamarie "Amie" Trout
CHRISTMAS ROSES
White roses
In an alabaster vase—
Scent of summer sun,
Memory of days long gone
Or promise of days yet to come.
Reach and grasp the roses,
The choice is yours alone—
Reach and clasp tomorrow,
Do not mind the thorns.
Carry the soft fragrance
Thru dark and snow and wind—
Assurance that blue skies
And sunshine
will always come again.
Snow roses
In translucent stone—
Fragrance of infinity!

Cynthia Breunig
WHAT ARE FRIENDS?

This poem is dedicated to my father, grandma, and sisters Dawn and Rhonda, and to my closest friends Leighann, Randy, Corrina, Donna, and Rob. And to everyone else who believed in me.

Friends are people who care for one another.
Friends help get their friends out of trouble.
Friends help you through thick and through thin.
Friends always make you smile, not grin.
Friends . . . . . When you're sad
and feeling low, they always
make your hopes
grow.

Friends . . . . . . Are forever
because they always stay
together.

Friends . . . . . . Always tell each
other their problems, what
would we do without them?

Kimberly D Jones

Kimberly D Jones
MICHAEL
You haven't known me very long, in terms of human years,
yet you somehow seem to know
my heart, my feelings, and my
fears.

You stepped into my troubled life, like someone from a dream,
so gently took me in your arms,
and became a part of me.

You understand so many things that I could never know;
just like a book you seem to
read the secrets of my soul.

The things I thought were hidden deep come easily to view;
yet not to simply anyone,
they're only seen by you.

For years I thought I had them all so cleverly disguised,
but truth and lies disclose
themselves when beckoned by
your eyes.

I never thought I'd know the peace and love you bring to me;
then, you brought happiness to
me like none had ever seen.

Slowly washing over me, caressing my wounded heart,
gently reassuring that we could
make a fresh new start.

Forgetting all the memories that haunted from my past,
you showed how I could finally
have a true love that would last.

A love that conquers all my fears and floods my soul with peace;
the reaches of this boundless
love are difficult to see.

Gil Saenz
REVERIE
Will our paths ever cross again?
If so, I wonder when?
What does destiny hold in store,
If we should ever see each other once more?
Many years have already passed
Since the days of our youthful love
That we thought would always last.
Hoping against hope and dreaming
The impossible dream.
Trying to imagine what it would be like;
That first enchanted scene.
Winter, Fall, Summer and Spring,
The seasons slowly slip away,
As I continue hoping and wondering,
If we'll ever have our day.

Debra Lynn Slifkin
SHHH . . .
sit in the silence.
Surround yourself with it.
Breathe it.
Feel the blackness in your chest,
feel it on your skin.
Watch your flesh become
silence.
Feel me.
I am silence.
Black and cold,
no bones, no flesh.
Do you hear me?
No, I am silence.
Watching you,
filling you,
chilling you,
killing you.
Shhh . . .
shiver in me.
In my silence.

Karen L Wos
GEMS IN THE NIGHT

To all those who have inspired me to write, especially Mom, Dad and Uncle Bob . . .

Diamonds in the sky,
Shimmering in the night;
Strung on invisible thread,
Suspended in the blackness;
Glowing brightly, then dimming,
Glittering forever
Until a cloud shrouds them
over;
Their beauty is endless—
Simplicity, their secret,
Quick! Make a wish . . .

Judith S Strawn
THE MAGIC OF POETRY

To my daughter Corey, in whose soul there is continuous poetry.

So many words tumbling over one another in my mind,
A thousand choices curl into the light;
And tease me with their perfect line.
I can only catch my breath as their contents are revealed;
In their beauty's truth, I rest a second,
Then am reeled by new claims from the spiritual frontier.
Only time can make sense of it, then it's hurled again to heart;
Where principle at last, and first,
comprise a promise; yet unsaid,
Unseen, I lean upon the unknown,
Where all I hope for is.
For how can dreams become
themselves without a wish?
So in this way, I attend the silent seer;
And from the seeming darkness of my body's breast,
Hands clasped there,
I await the words to come, that I might put them to the test!

Lisa Easton
SILENT DREAMS
Just when things are going right
my world begins to crumble.
Silent dreams are out of sight
slowly I begin to stumble.
Teach me how to talk
remind me of my calling.
Be my guide
Be my eyes
Please don't let me slide
Don't leave me here alone to die
I want to live and be free
Erase my past
I want to be able to see
a life worth living to last.

Stephanie Winkler
WISHES OF YOU
Wishes of you are always there,
Even though you never are.
Wishing that you'd show you care,
It was like wishing on a star.

Wishes of you that never go away,
Not even when I sleep.
Dreams that you'll come over today,
And of promises that you'll
keep.

Dreaming of you all through the night,
Tossing and turning all the time.
Dreaming that we never fight,
And that everything was fine.

Wishing I was by your side,
Loving you all the way.
We both had so much pride
That it just didn't work out that
way.

Thomas C Smith
WHAT IS A TESTIMONY
A testimony isn't just having the best to say about our past, and how Jesus brought us through.

A testimony isn't giving all of the glorious details of our past sins.

A testimony is telling people what God has done for you, and wants to do for them through his son. And show God's love to them through your actions.

A testimony most of all is just saying Jesus, I love you.

Mary Lou Watchorn
THE FORGOTTEN STREET PEOPLE
'Tis cold so cold when lost from sight within the dark and dismal night.

A stranger passes by but does he care that on the street our heart we bare.

We try to remember how things once were or do we care what we've become.

The sight of death seems very near

but in the end do we know or even care.

Yes we are lost but was this our choice or did we simply lose our way.

As darkness settles in upon us there is little chance tomorrow we'll see.

But in the end as all things do we have tried and no one could ask more of you . . .

Diane Adele Sheckells
TRADE WINDS

I am dedicating this poem to my LOVING FAMILY! I LOVE EACH AND EVERY ONE OF YOU!

Sky of clouds so wild and free
I wonder what you will become that I will see.

Your colors become so amazingly beautiful.

The sky is so Blue
Oh but the clouds they have become such beautiful colors and shapes.

I've watched you tonight change from White to Grey
And from Grey to a Wonderful color of Pink.

It's almost as if the Sky and clouds have had a Night, like I've had a Day.

Very Changeable.

Jacqueline M Adam
I'VE BEEN THROUGH SO MUCH THIS YEAR

I've been through so
Much this year;
In the cancer of my
Little dear Jessica,
And the wedding of my
Darling Allyson and Scott,
Sadness and joy both here.
My own physical pain,
But I persevere,
Because all of my life
From being one time wife
To new grandmother
Have made my life
Like no other,
But everyone's life
Is like no other,
Praise God it
Will continue forever and ever
For I quit, never

Diana Metcalf
VOICE OF WIND

Heather blows above the sage
Highs and lows of every age.
The greatest gift God gives to men,
To hear the music of the wind.
A light breeze that heralds spring
Teaches man once more to sing.
Summer winds wax hot and dry
Wringing moisture from the sky.
Autumn blows crisp chilly nights,
But winter storms bring frigid frights.
Alone, your soul hears in awe
God's voice in winds overall.

Maureen E Kozier
LOVE'S MYSTERY

Tamper with my heart,
no man dare.
Predicting an attack,
for this I must prepare.
Cannot be bought or sold,
No steal.
Currently tied up in an,
investment deal.
A universal skill,
Some succeed to master it,
others never will.
Sought by every species known.
Obsession.
Everyone wants to obtain their own.

Existing within this galaxy,
yet there still remains a mystery.
What stirs beneath the surface,
Conjures in the mind,
Absorbing all this knowledge,
What do we seek to find?

Gene R Shepler
A SUMMER FLING

It began as all, just a one night affair
But as hour gave way to hours, we began to care

From days to weeks that number twice
are now months that are more than trice

We loved and we laughed and couldn't be apart
fore we enjoyed what we found in each other's heart

Then summer left, and so did she
saying a life together wasn't to be

Well, I couldn't accept that terrible faith
'cause I wanted that lady to be my mate

So I drove through state after state and mile after mile
with only a picture in my mind of her pretty smile

When I find her, I'll bring her back with me
Then I found she wasn't really free

My undying love for her still grows
what she will do, only she knows

But as Winter follows Summer and thusly Spring
We'll have a living reminder of our Summer Fling

Jay-Ola Ento
THE ORCHID COVERED PORCH

This poem is dedicated to the memory of my Dad, Jay G. Love.

They sit
On an orchid covered porch
rocking
To and fro'
Talking and rocking
greeting each passerby
with a nod
a smile
Exchanging life stories
of times and places
Gone by
And if you've dreamed
A dream
Of an orchid covered porch
And a rose covered fence
Surrounding a field
Of delicate dewstained lilies
And a golden sun
that never sets
Rest
For everlasting life has begun.

Frank L Caldwell
PROGRESS

Marvelous wonderers wonder how.
With wonderful wonders all around, wonder now. Wonder how to draw us closer to our greatest wonder,
God's humanity.

Choose your wonder and perceive its drift.
Respect the wonderwork of opportunities which guide our ways through open doors.
Dispel enmities with self-fulfilling prophesies.

Revel in the elegance of goodness thusly wrought.
Excel in the excellence of finding what you have sought.

Expect the chance to help and succeed.
Do it better——do it now.
Think and elect. Select just how to achieve wondrous fulfillments.

Dorothy Chandler
THE INVISIBLE DOOR

Time seems to scatter spoken words irrevocably
As if life itself must waver the principle
Which hides in half finished conversations
That carry undetached ideas making
Further personal opinions which lead to selfish notions
Untouched by simple truth which lies underneath the clutter
Of preimposed reasons of self-importance.

Groping with hope to unlock the invisible door
That forever holds us, you—me, strangers apart
From a friendship rarely known but imagined,
I stand naked before God praying to have
The daring, wisdom and perseverance to find the right key
To release emotions, setting you free from humiliation
As we taste sweetness of truth with reverence.

Karolyn S Fite
LITTLE CHILDREN

This poem is dedicated to my daughter Cindi, and my Grandson Eric.

When parents get divorced, and from their marriage vows they resign, there's lawyers to see and papers to sign
They start thinking of their own peace of mind and the freedom they'll find, not of the innocent little children whose hearts they break like a thin piece of twine.
But little children aren't stupid, they know when their little world is about to decline, and that their happy home with both Mom and Dad will soon be left behind.

Valerie M Conti
SONNET FOR THE SURREAL LION

To Len Jenkin: A Writer and Writing Educator of ingratiating depth, humor, irony, wit, insight, versatility and constancy. Continue continuing.

Perusing Ortega y Gasset: Love!
Thinking of the surreal lion, lone, lost.
Writing feverishly: Justice: Pain: Above!
Traversing the world, living at no cost.
Pax atomicas raging around me.
Voltaire's biting wrath in my dreams at night.
A priori plans rush to me: I flee.
Breton's ken guides me solitarily bright.
He's escaped, this single, reclusive man.
He's shown me seduction with plays sublime.
He's taught me post-modern thought: induced can.
He's fed my soul: selfed for relentless time.
He's honed my waking thoughts: faithed, free, fresh-set.
He's Lorcaed my life without sane regret.

Pamela Thompson
A RIVER SPARKLES BY A TREE

A river sparkles by a tree
As I feel a whisper of a breeze
A soft smooth touch on my shoulder

I melted into your arms
I felt you tenderness
With your arms wrapped around me
I'm safe from the world

To the ground we fall
With happiness and feeling, I am yours

Together forever, as one we'll never part
Holding onto each other, heart to heart

We love each other dearly with heart and soul
Together we stand as a whole
Never part in happiness or sorrow
Keeping each other for tomorrow

Geraldine Reed
FLOWERS

God made the flowers
That bloom in the spring.
With all different colors.
He didn't leave out one thing.
Which could be the prettiest?
It would be hard to decide.
With the roses, tulips and fern.
But I would choose the rose,
because it bears our Savior's name.
Rose of Sharon that blooms in the spring.

Jen Barker
SUNSET OF MY LIFE

To all my family

Alone, in my room at night, I cry.
Sometimes I wish that I could die.
What have I done that I must roam,
never to have a place of my own?
My loved ones say they want me to stay, but often I feel that I am just in the way.

Thru my tears I pray to our Lord above, a voice comes back, you are really loved! So I dry my tears and say to myself, I must put these sad thoughts upon a shelf. I will live my life from day to day, helping others in every way, picking up ones that have gone astray, share with ones less fortunate than I, until the day I must say good-bye.

Tomorrow will be another day, the birds will sing, kittens will play, people will go on their merry way.

I will do my best until I must die, and go to our mansions in the sky.

My Love to All,
Grandma Jen Barker
Age 88 Years

Francis Ferre
FOUR LETTERS FOUR

To Tim, Nick, Tresa and Robert

Simply aligned they make a word,
For instance they can become a bird.
With thought a transmitted kiss,
And then a delectable dish.
When structured a statuesque tree,
Which upon sight can cause glee.
A unique power are they,
Akin to the substance clay.
Alone there is an expression of none,
Waiting for something to be done.
Easily they can say dirt,
Then again they can be curt.
Curiously they may be kind,
Without placing one in a bind.
So utilize them as a core,
To say pleasant words of four.

Virginia Acklin
I WALK ALONE

This poem is dedicated to my Mom and Dad,

I walk alone, down life's way
Over mountain dell, in valley dew.
Over flowers bright and new.
And as I walk, singing a song
Thinking of life's joy and throng.
I see the sky so bright and blue
I hear the birds singing too.
The mountains, and ocean's hue.
And I realize. I do not walk alone.
God is holding my hand,
Every step of the way.

Meredith McGuire
SOMEWHERE IN TIME

I gallop along the beach,
Me at one with him.
His sleek black fur sweats,
The sun sets in the horizon,
It glows against the water.
My mind remain ajar,
For nothing but good thoughts to enter.
The sound of sea around us,
The splashing of water,
The steady beat of his hooves.
Nothing to hold us back,
But time.

Margo Nicholson
THE MADNESS OF JOHN CLARE (1793-1864)

The falcon rings the sun—
Patterns of another tongue.
Speech trails the soft lift clear
As the cumulus signals of heaven.

Hand upon plow I push
The sward toward song
And hear the lilt toward evening
And all the summer long
Of growing things where my craft
Has touched the earth.

The characters of a worm drawn deep in mud
Grace my concerns with light;
Chiaroscuro renderings of a page
Deplete my hope, deepen my rage.

I cry in circles.
I appear in public with the words undone.
I follow the ever brightening path
That towels underneath the years
An omnipresent conundrum.

Ken Hughes
MAN IN HELL

My feverish head spins and turns,
My wicked soul within me burns,
There is no rest, no peace of mind,
Only the dragging hours of time.

The flames leap up as I look about,
Water! Water! My burning mouth cries out,
I scream but no one comforts me,
Only Satan laughs at my misery

There's nothing left, all hope is gone,
In this fiery hell I'll walk alone,
In this hell I'm doomed to stay,
From God I turned my eyes away.

I'm paying for the sin I've done
This damned reward for me I've won,
To walk this burning floor of hell,
And for eternity here I'll dwell.

Tovahl and Valerie Aube

Margaret Aube
VALERIE

To a sweet granddaughter, Valerie.

There was a little girl whose name was Valerie.
Dimples she had on her chubby pink cheeks,
And smiling bright eyes that were soft and meek.
But—not around her best friend named Garndee.

Her room was clean and neat as can be.
But the living room? No, 'twas far from tidy.
She dresses very well and comfortably,
And looked very pretty with her hair braided tightly.

When night comes nigh, she feels alone and bitter,
As she sits by the doorsteps looking very sad.
She never did like to go early to bed,
But watch the stars as like diamonds they glitter.

With a prayer in her heart, she'd look up to heaven
Missing her best friend, as she stood up and sighed.
"If she were here, we'd enjoy sitting side by side,
Looking at pictures her aunt had taken."

Next morning she awoke, holding on to this token,
A remembrance to her by her very good friend.
She held it with care and made sure it didn't bend
For she valued the friendship so it would never be broken.

Edward M Nichols
PART OF MY LIFE

As I look upon my life and see what I can be.
And as I search, I seem to wonder, is this really me.
So I go on searching, searching every day.
Looking for that part of me, which maybe I'll find today.
This part of me I look for, each and every day is the one piece to my puzzle, which seems to stay away,
So as I go along and look in all the corners, I must remember one thing, wrong, I very well could be. Wrong to keep on searching, searching for part of my life. For this life is right in front of me and could be all I'll ever need.
But to look and search for something there may never be, is a chance I'll have to take, just have to wait and see. And even if this part of me that seems to stay away should never really run into me, I feel that that's okay.
For the parts of my life, which I hold now and forever, are the parts of me that are strong and tell me I should know better.
And even though there may be a piece that will never ever be found.
The parts of my life I have right now are very much around.

Michelle Pomeroy
I USED TO . . . BUT NOW I . . .

Dedicated to: My 4th grade teacher, Mrs. Hayer, who ask us to write a poem about something "we used to do, but now we don't."

I used to suck my thumb . . .
But now I don't.
I used to like my plumbs . . .
But now I don't.
I used to go to school half-day . . .
But now I don't.
I used to say, "No way José." . . .
But now I don't.
I used to bawl and cry . . .
But now I don't.
I used to want to buy . . .
And I still do!

Kristi Ann Henry
TUNNEL VISION

Time and time again, I've been used and abused.
Sometimes I don't know exactly what to do.
I thought you'd be different, but it happened again.
I got killed by your love, bringing tunnel vision.
I can't show my face, I've been toasted and burned.
I can't trust a soul, from all that I've learned.
Just when my hopes rise, they seem to fall in.
Someone crashes my dreams, I've got tunnel vision.
My day has now come, to lie down and leave.
Put me in a box; plant me like a seed.
I'll be deep in the ground, where you can't come in,
to ruin my life or bring tunnel vision.
Tunnel vision, I see no other way out,
Tunnel vision, I can't turn around,
Tunnel vision, I just want to cry,
Let me fulfill my desire to die.

Edward F McGlynn
SHELTER OF OPTIMISM

Storm rolls in over the prairie lands,
Sweeping lightweight roadside trash before.
I shed my pack to ride it out,
In the narrow, misty, deafening shelter of the Fruitridge overpass.
The rain makes the loneliness sublime.
The rain is welcome.
For I still remember two thousand miles behind me,
When I crossed the arid, reptile, Indian wastes,
Where the only moisture for miles it seemed,
Was the few drops left in my canteen,
And the single tear that streaked my dusty cheek,
In a fleeting moment of weakness,
When your image crept into my sun-mad mind,
When I wasn't looking.
Someday, wherever this road ends
When I'm warm and dry, fed and rested, yet troubled
I will remember this night, 'neath Fruitridge overpass,
When cold and damp, hungry, weary and far from home,
I smiled in the face of the storm.

Monica Buboltz
UP UP AND AWAY

To my dear friends especially: Bernie, Steve, Arlene, Bernell, Diane, Diane, Lois, Theresa, Cecelia, Lana, Bonnie, Sister Mary Grace

A new life is born
Enter into a world of happiness
Grow in courage
Dare not to wonder
About tomorrow.
New horizons will dawn
Excitement yields
Disappointments exist
Burdens harden
Facts remain
Independence arrives.
Venture into your dreams
The sky is the limit!
Never look back
Journey forward
Reality hits
Anticipate sorrow
Faith you need
Hope you have
Love will guide you
Up, up and away!

Andrea Harrity
CHAMELEON

Dismal and alone, he lights a candle
its silent message casts a shadow upon his face.
You notice his green eyes, and how they seem so sad
you wonder if he'll ever smile.
Incense captivates the darkness
its subtle omen asks you to stay
you speak " . . It's snowing."
The boy nods his head, he loves cold weather.
There's a knock on the door
he seems frightened
long, flowing cape follows him
the gateway is opened.
You hear a familiar voice, it's raised and seems hot.

The boy only whispers.
In moments the voice is gone
he sits beside you, his eyes are blue
"Like a chameleon," you say.
He touches your face
you feel his pain, his anger, his secrets, his sins
and you wonder if he'll ever smile.

Marie Johnson
THE SONG OF THE LAST GOODBYE

Is it death
Or only the wish to be dead
Is it the beginning of life
Or rebirth

No one really knows
Some say it is like love
And others say it is like being deep in concentration

What is the last goodbye
Is it death
Or love
Is it rebirth
Or life's beginning
Is it really the wish to be dead
Or like being deep in concentration

Do you know
Does anyone

Vicki L Garrett
THE ROSE

For my Mamma, Ada, who wanted me to write.
My family who had faith in me. My husband, who inspired me.

Here's a single rose for you,
From the garden of a friend.
It blossomed with the morning dew
Just for me to send.

It can help you through the day,
You have so much to do.
And I can help in this small way,
To make it nice for you.

Just know that I am with you
And it has to be this way.
There's really nothing we can do.
Just take it day by day.

All things are for a reason
And only time will tell.
For us there is a season
And all will soon be well.

April Rondeau
TREETOPS

As we sped along the highway,
I was weary from watching eye-level things
Like a high-speed video;
Gnarled, twisted undergrowth of woods,
Where tiny trees long for fresh air
And light of day;
The shadow of a cat awaits a bird
From nest to fall;
Then I looked up into the treetops tall.
Like a pen and ink drawing
Etched against a pastel sky of parchment,
The trees stretched their tips,
Like a quiet mother nursing her child's lips.
With majestic wings, an eagle
Swooped by undisturbed nest,
Swaying in the subtle evening breeze.
Like an artist with pastel colors,
Twilight caressed the tops of the trees,
Like coolness of dew in a meadow.

Forest E Burke
LIFE

To my wonderful family and friends.

Have you ever taken a look inside of your mind
Past the illusions and dreams that you'll find
Have you stood on what's the edge of reality
And felt the warmth of the truth and the sting of the lies

The power of lust and the strength of greed
Are emotions in life you must never heed
'Cause you'll live in a life of illusions
And your soul will begin to bleed

Just give me a space in which to survive
Touch my heart and make me feel you inside
Please open my eyes to a new way of life
Touch my soul and let me know I'm alive

Angela L Lundgren
THE TICK OF THE CLOCK

The colors of green and grey
on a warm midsummer's day.
Reminiscence of the past,
and things you hoped would last.

Far away places,
and different lands.
Things you thought
you held in your hands.

A broken toy,
a pressed flower.
Memories present,
each passing hour.

The tick of the clock.
The sound of a bell.
That far-a-way world
where memories dwell.

The sound of footsteps.
The close of a door.
Brings you back to
the place you were before.

Louise Biser
LIFE'S JOURNEY ROAD

This poem is dedicated to Jenny, my sweet daughter

Traveling along life's journey road
Meeting on its path, life's heavy load,
Known as disappointments, mistrusts and pain
Traveling this road, what's there to gain?

With pain comes pleasure, this journey will show
Life's not all bleak, as we come to know
Good days and bad days, joys and sorrows,
Live through the bad days, wait for tomorrow.

Life is an adventure, to be lived each day
Problems will be solved, along the way
One day at a time is all you can do,
No one can ask more than that of you

We know not what is at the end of this road
Depends how we lived, to the amount of our load
Be not in a hurry for this journey to end
For you may return, just where you begin.

Lance Dunlop
THE PHANTOM

The phantom haunts the desert sand
A spirit wandering, without a land,
Condemned to wander,
Searching without end.

Running to nowhere,
Trying to find,
Haunted by visions
Of life, before his time.

In the desert night
He spies a spring,
And island amidst the ocean of sand,
Life and death conflicting.

And thus he serves his sentence,
Desolation is his passion,
Searching for the answer
Without knowing the question.

Willie Stine Gonzalez
KEEPER OF THE NIGHT

To staffers and clients behind 'The Orange Door'

Yes, I am the 'Keeper of the Night'
And I've read the police report that . . .
"T.K." bit off "Bobo's" index finger in that messy alley fight!

"B.B." in Room #8 has not slept for several screaming nights
Her Step-dad tried to rape her (again) and she lives in sleepless fright
Every time I make a check she's staring in my face
She feels she'll go crazy with one more week in this place
Eyes are red from crying, her body itches from stings
And no one answers her 'phone calls, no matter how long it rings!

Some try to complete prayers but none seem to go right—I know all this and more 'cause I'm,
'The Keeper of the Night'!

Tony Jaehrling
DAWNING MAN

To those who gave me beginnings: My Parents, and L. Ron Hubbard.

A man walks down the street:
There is a book in his hand
And knowledge in his eye,
Purpose in his certain step
And power in his stride.
This is a man who knows fear
Is something you don't know—
He will not stand aside!
A Dawning Man
Who comes after every dark age,
Like the one we've been through
Before and Since WWII.
Now the crypt lies empty
And the artist walks once more;
Yes, the sun is shining
And the future walks once more!
Stand aside barbarian,
Your time has come and gone,
And in our crystal horizon
Only the civilized belong,
Living their Dawning Song!

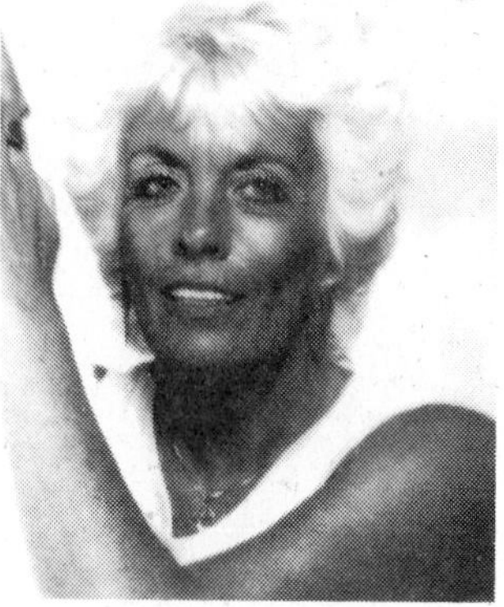

Bev M Senter

Bev M Senter
FRIEND

To my supporting friends Tammie Von Bergen, & Gordon Skog

Some people have many friends, I'm told
There's many fake gems compared to real gold
With you I've got the real thing
You'll never know the happiness you bring
Never too involved to understand
Never too busy to lend a helping hand
Always being so truthful to me
Knowing that honesty is the way it should be
Glitter wears off of unreal things in time
Not with this friend I call mine.

Holly Christinson
FOREVER HERE

To anyone in this big lonely world who is waiting for someone to come back, especially you, Mom.

I can't let go,
I can't hold on.
This love of ours
Is much too strong.
I'm getting weak,
I can't get strong,
Because in your arms
Is where I belong
I'm falling deep,
I'm falling fast,
Maybe someday,
You'll come back
at last.
But I keep debating,
I'm full of tears.
I'm forever waiting,
Waiting right here.

Darlene Benton Baird
20TH YEAR REUNION

As we flip through the pages of the 20th year, oh how we remember yesteryear.
As we see life going on, let us look at days that are gone.
As we relive the past, let us see the cast.
As we lovingly greet, let us sincerely treat.
As we dig through the file, let us warmingly smile.
As we hate to leave, may we soon retrieve.

Janice Ivey Hallyburton
MY DEAREST FRIEND

To my husband John, and son John Jr. for their love and prayers.

You gave me today to live, to love, to care
Always help me end each day to you in loving prayer.
A mountain you gave Lord, when I didn't want it at all
But, then you assured me you'd be there lest I began to fall.
You told me not to worry, and gave me good health again.
I will try not to worry Lord because you are my dearest friend.
The tears still fill my eyes when I think I may not see tomorrow, but there you are again to take away the sorrow.
The sun will shine again for me, this I know for sure.
With you to walk beside me, there's nothing I can't endure.

Gloria Maldonado
THE WORLD

To the BEST parents, and family.

The world is blue and white
with lots of might.

The stars are out at night
to give us light.

People Sleep
and cars beep.

That's why earth is
life.

Wendy Elizabeth Smith
WE WALK UP AND SAY 'HI'

To anyone and everyone in the world for whom this poem has meaning.

We walk up and say 'Hi'
The same well known strangers of ten years gone by.
We like to think that we know each other well
But one can never tell.

We grew up so close
And are now so far away.
What happened to change us so
Neither one can say.

What can we do to make things the way they were
Everything we try doesn't seem to work.
We sit and listen to the clock chime
It holds the answer:
Just give it time.

maria mercurio
CARRIED BY THE WIND
Like snow across the highway, I dance over the pavement.
And you are the wind behind me, pushing me into patterns.
For miles, or for months, I can dance on.

But like snow across the highway
I am (in the distance) lost to the eye.
Although, still dancing over the earth.

Sometimes, beauty can not be seen.
It can only be sensed.

Nothing is tangible.

Always remember, that without the wind
The snow would still remain on the other side.

Perhaps, like the wind, you were meant only
To sweep (through my life) carrying me toward beauty.
Beauty happens to be emotion.

Before you, I was afraid to feel emotion.
Now I see. I was amidst it all of my life, avoiding it.
By dancing in twisted paths around it.

The beauty, in my heart, will forever stay.
Every day, the wind will sweep through my thoughts.

Elizabeth Beaumont
GO AHEAD AND HOPE
I watch you wait
for some sunny day.
But the sun—it burns
then fades away.
You don't believe me.
You say you'll fight.
O.K., but I'll stay
where the shade's drawn tight.

You say you'll still hope.
Well you've yet to be burned.
And you'll just go on hoping
all warnings spurned.

Look at my ashes!
Can't you see that I'm charred?
Please take heed—shun that sun.
For it once beckoned me
and now I'm left scarred.

Vernell Mallory
THIS ROSE IS YOU

To my sister Cynthia L. Nelson for your boldness and to John, Shyla, and Marcus, my children, for being my friends. Love Mama.

When I see a rose garden, I think of you.
The petals— Represent the beauty within you
The stem— Your longevity
The thorns—Show the hurt and pain circling your life
The roots— Maps out your freedom
The soil— Covers the ugliness
The grass— Reveals the nurturing love you deserve but can't receive
The weeds—You pluck as time winds to keep peace
But the smell of this garden—
You—is one aura that isn't appreciated and destroyed
No one seems to recognize all the care it takes for this beautiful rose to grow and gleam as you so do!
Continue to shine as a rose
For this rose,
Is you!

Phyllis Newton
IN SILVER LOVE CLOUDS
Like white babies'-breath,
Her sweet and gentle smile lives
In silver love clouds.

Jana M Wagoner
RAY OF LIGHT

For my husband Bob

A very special person has always been there
And yet my eyes were darkened with fear
Rejection stabbed at my existence
and words would not allow me to believe
I hid away in a dark corridor
and locked up all my feelings

Then one day a ray of light broke through
From whence it came I do not know
Yet I followed it out into a lighter world
And found the same special person
Awaiting in the brightness
Others were attracted to him
and now I was too
How I wish the ray of light had broken through many months before

Ross M Strange-Dunn

Ross M Strange-Dunn
WHERE FROM HERE

Denise, Suzette, Avonae, Calvin, and Mother. Your encouragement, love, and faith in me have brought us thus far. Thank You.

Where do we go from here my love
How do we make it last
Where can we find such perfection
After this flame has past
Where is there joy to match my dear
This love I have in my heart
Where can we go to reach a place
So filled with hope from the start

Where is a nook to hold our cares
Grand enough to meditate
Where is the peace I so yearn for
To relax, take care-relate
Where is the crowning point to this
Our tenderness, loving, caring
Where do I climb, or soar, or float
To reach the summit of sharing
Where is the rule to designate
Our actions from past to near
Where from here, where from here.

Roberta Marie Levasseur
THE LONELY MANNEQUIN
She is a lonely mannequin
Left on the shelf all alone.
In the storeroom she waits again,
Wondering where she'll be at home.

Her maker created a beautiful doll
With figure and face so appealing,
But she possessed something strangest of all:
Her smile made her mood so revealing.

Once she was in a window display,
Where she wore a glamorous gown.
People just glanced, then went on their way;
Her smile grew unhappy and she wore a frown.

They tried her in other departments
To change the look on her face,
But back on the shelf in the storeroom she went:
Not happy in <u>any</u> showcase.

Til one day they needed a doll to portray
A housewife with child at her knee.
In Housewares the mannequin went on display,
Then her smile quickly changed into glee!

Ida Sagers
CRUCIBLE

To my children, Dian and Paul, as a token of my love for them and a memento of my life on this earth.

Life is a flame.
I must be burnt in it,
And rise from the ashes
To meet Thee, Eternal God.

Life is a pit.
I must plumb its depths,
And on shattered limbs ascend
To be made whole in Thee, Eternal God.

Life is the wonder revealed to me
When I've made peace within myself,
And relinquished the searing turmoil
Blocking Thy ineffable presence.
Eternal God,
I thank Thee for life.

Kate Metcalf
JUST A POEM FOR YOU PAPA

This poem is for my Papa: Hurry up and get well! We all love you very much! Love Kate—age 9

When you are having a "sirgere"
You feel like screaming.
You feel like taking a shooting star,
And jump on it and start leaving.

You feel like taking a horse,
And start riding.
Oh me, oh my! I landed in a ditch!
No, I am not having any fun!

You wake up the next day,
Oh you're all done!
I feel like yelling with joy!
You are well!!!

Leontine Smith
REACH OUT
Reach out and touch the hand of God
He's there if just you reach out.
He wants to know that you care
and trust enough to reach out.

Reach out and touch the hand of man
He needs for you to reach out.
To know that in you he has a friend
Who cares enough to reach out.

Kristen L DeBonis
I MISS YOU
I miss the way we used to be,
I miss the warmth and security.
I miss the way you could make me smile,
Or the times you'd call just to talk for a while.
I miss your teasing and your joking too,

I'll always miss holding hands with you.
I miss the times that we have shared,
I miss the way you showed you cared.
I miss the way we used to dance.
I wish we could have just one more chance.
I want you to know I'll always be there,
I still think we could be the "perfect pair."

Marion F Garrigan
I REALLY WANT TO KNOW YOU

Magunde'—For my friend, my love, the one I cry with, the one I laugh with, The one I always want to be with.—Marion

I really want to know you
'Cause knowing you
Is the key to your soul
But when I read between the lines
I just get so confused

You crept into my heart
Now you're a part of my soul
I can't put this feeling aside
It's so much more than desire
When you look into my eyes
You'll see how much is there

Don't push me away
We may never get another chance
Let me love you once
And show you the way I feel

Share this moment with me
And I'll make you see
How much of you
Is a part of me

Emeline Ennis Kotula
NATAL DAY

Dedication: For my eleven siblings, one and all, and the wonderful memories and love we share.

I knew an endless loneliness today.
My frosted flowers stood a dead delight
And a red bird sang just beyond my sight
While I, with all my years in disarray,
Sought vainly for a moment out of play.
Poised on the one of never-ending flight
I pierced the pattern of each pilgrim's right
To hold eternal nothingness at bay.

And all who laugh and weep discover this,
The blinding vision at the precipice
When eyes, anointed, turn at last to see
The loneliness of all humanity
And tread the well-worn path from the abyss
Where love of man still finds its genesis.

Samantha Roberts López
AM I DREAMING?

Am I psycho, or is it a dream
To live for death, and die for life.
To fulfill a dream which was never thought
To think a dream which will never be fulfilled.
To fear the good and trust the bad
To wonder which way is out
And the other in?
Into a dream or out of life . . .
How can one tell?
Maybe it's all a dream about a dream,
Which is to be able to live in a world with no hate,
But a world with no hate is a world
With no peace and no love.
No, I'm not psycho and it's not a dream,
Maybe it's just a thought,
For someone to dream this dream.

Linda Maddox
LETTING GO

The time has come for you
And I
To let go of the past and
To say "Good-bye"
The love that was once
So special and rare
Has been tarnished by the hurt
And bitterness we share
We can't go back, we can't forget
No matter how much we may regret
Too much has happened
Too much to erase
This decision is something
We both have to face
So look to the future with an open heart
The sooner you do
The sooner you'll start
To let happiness back into
Your life once again.
And even though this chapter
In our life must end
I'd like to be able to call you
"My Friend."

Nee Van Nuyen
LOVE AND HATE

Alas my Dear!
How come you love me so much
But still hate me,
Something in you you hate
But not the man you love.

Deeper your hate greater our turbulent love,
But hate is just a cracked crest of tidal wave
In the tempest of love,
Hate will never become a partner
Of our true love and happiness.

Human conscience screening processes,
And kindness your basic nature
Along with our passionate love
Will soon terminate
That ephemeral tragedy of love.

Then love will soon reign over our Kingdom of Hearts,
Hate will be dissolved into dust
In our powerful golden nest of love.

Joy of love and happiness
Will follow our steps
Deep into the great, great field of love . . .

Philena Porter Pierce
GUNMAN'S MARK

To my parents who gave me life, and to my pets who let me enjoy it.

Tally wore his gun quite low
Like a great gunfighter should;
He could outdraw any man
And men knew that he would.

Many saw him ride in town—
Not a one stayed on the street;
The only sound that could be heard
Was hooves in a steady beat.

Sunlight shown on each closed door—
No friendly face appeared;
Though this man was known afar,
This talent much revered.

Tally wore his gun quite low—
With a flash the metal shown;
He could outdraw any man
If he just were not alone!

Patricia G Gill
THE ESSENCE

I cannot hide; I walk alone,
Trapped by a world hewn of stone.
Forever running, nowhere to turn
Following the crowds to writhe and burn
In the deepest crevice of society's heart.

Cowering, confused, in the shadow of the great.
Weeping softly in the darkness, for that is my fate.
Shivering, terrified, possessed by my fears
Insecurity, the essence, driving me to tears
of hopeless anger.
The ultimate emotions in a clash for command,
This internal turmoil is more than I can stand.

Withdrawing, slowly, I won't be the last.
I've drifted beyond reality's cold grasp.
My friend's silent screams echo in the night;
Pleading with me to do what is right.
But they don't really care; they can't understand.
For once in my life, I'll have the upper hand.
The tension is mounting; the pressure runs high.
And at last, my final breath, the long awaited sigh of eternal peace.

Aimee Walsh

Aimee Walsh
ALONE, BUT HAPPY

I feel like I'm special now.
I'm alone, all alone.
No one can help me.
I walk alone.
I drift as a breeze,
As a tree's limb shall sway in the wind.
The last of its coloured leaves
Have flown in the icy air.
But I shall be safe.
I take care of myself. Only me, just me.
I can make it by myself.
I shall not cry, not shed a tear.
I am alone but not lonely
Here by myself.
Here, alone with my thoughts.
I see faces. Faces with no meaning.
Their bodies walk along
The old familiar paths,
But I am not with them.
I am alone as the world begs at my feet.
It screams for me to come back.
"Come back out of your dream-world!"
But I do not listen to them.
I am not dreaming.
I am quite happy here,
Alone, by myself.
I am not in need of help
For I can make it on my own. Alone.

Elizabeth A Fairfield
CONCEPTION

We have known beauty
Fierce as pain,
Wild and passionate
As lightning-riven rain.
From the seed of our desire,
We shaped a child
In elemental fire.
That flame-bright moment, we
Gazed through the cleft of Time
Into Eternity.

Pauline Mayo
HAPPINESS

Happiness is where you find it,
In a cottage by the sea
A mansion on the hilltop
It depends on you or me.
Walking through the forest
Hearing the rustling of the leaves,
The chirping of the birds
The humming of the bees.
God's creatures slipping through the brush to drink
From rippling streams.
Oh the beauty of creation
The serenity and peace, that can be found
In each of us, if it is just released.

Kathy Lu
A DAWNING OF THE SUN

The sun rises slowly,
Casting long shadows of life.
Then, a sudden breeze sweeps the land,
Awakening all in its path.

The trees bristle to life, and begin their sweet murmurs.
The hive hanging from a branch bustle with noise as the diligent bees go to work.
The sunflowers move their heads in search of the sun,
And when they find it, they glow at it as the sun glows towards them.

The birds begin their morning song,
Sweet melodies that could only come from their delicate throats.
The rabbits swiftly bounce along,
Searching for an early snack.

Yet another day has begun,
With the dawning of the sun.

Harvey L Flashen
HARV AND ANN'S WEDDING POEM

In the gentle stillness of the wood,
in the soil from which life grows.
In the wondrous mystery of the sea,
from which life ebbs and flows.
From the highest peak so pristine white,
a majesty of grace.
To a single blade of newborn grass,
rejoicing in its space.
As we gaze upon a starlit night,
in awe of skies aglow.
And knowing all within our souls,
yet learning what we know.
The paths we take within our lives,

forever intertwined.
Though as we're one we so are two,
as roots become the vine.
To always question who we are,
and know that we are blessed.
To take for granted not at all,
to journey on our quest.
Our lives are so enriched this day,
as always has been true.
To be here with the ones we love,
declaring love anew.
So let us not forget this time,
it's preciousness to hold,
and keep alive renewed again,
in ways yet to unfold.
Remember all, as we shall do,
from the deep to Heaven's door.
From the smallest grains that make a bed,
upon the ocean floor.
We all have come upon this place,
for reasons from above.
We're here to live in harmony,
We're here to love in love.

Tammy Marie Kretsch
THE CROSSROAD
Just as a rose
Would blossom in the morning

Just as a starless night
Turns to day

Just as the leaves
Turn yellow in season

I slowly . . .
Make my way

Just as the wind
Blows through the trees

Just as the morning birds
Fly high

I approach each day
Walking on without dismay

And I will
Keep on walking into the night

Cheryl Check
GROWING PAINS

To Traci Nicole King
My Daughter
My Life

From Miss to Mrs.—Mother to Ms.
In such a short time, no titles were missed
At miss it was a lot of fun
Mrs. meant two had now become one
Mother says I'm here to help the little one grow
And Ms., I've learned means—
If I only knew then what I now know . . .

Lisa Worden
FRIGHT
You feel yourself quiver,
As you run from the beast,
Your legs start to shiver,
You can't feel your feet,
Rest is what you need to do,
But you run and start to scream,
The monster catches up with you,
And you awaken from your dream.

Richard Ernest Edward Gebhardt
LISTEN
What are these tests?
Why do we have to take them?
Do we really need them?

I can't take these tests
On life, on mind, on those that I find
Which way will you go?
Who knows maybe I'll be there to show you.

If you would only listen to me
Just listen to me.

I think I've been there before you
With all this stuff, this and that puff
It's all really gone too far now.
It's just a crack, shot, and a sniff
And you're gone into their mischief.

If people will just stop and listen to us,
Just listen to me.

Nicole Serra
CONCEALED WITHIN ME
As time passes, every
day, every hour,
and every minute
of that hour, Love
burns inside of me.

It's that deep warm
feeling, in my heart,
that is concealed
within me.

It gets stronger and
stronger every time
I think of that very
special person in
my life.

I could remember that
summer breeze of
that magical day
we were walking along
the park together.

Nervous I was thinking
about what could have
happened.
But I didn't take the
chance when I had it,
instead losing my
chance of love, never
to gain it again, for
my love was not as
strong at the time.

For not long had passed,
that I realized that
it was Love.
For I loved the love
that was
CONCEALED
WITHIN
ME.

Helen L Cantrell
A DIFFERENT BIRTH
I, did not hear my babies cry
When they breathe, their first breath
I never knew the joy of
Them feeding, at my breast
The baby shoes, that set in bronze
The clothes, that they wore home
The toys, that waited in their room
Were not the first, they'd owned
There were no traffic lights, to run
No hospital room or bed
There was no nine month count down
No labor pains to dread
They are not flesh, of my flesh
But, the love is still the same
The only difference in our life
Is the way they came
An adopted child, is a child of love
Most precious gift for those who win it
Someone else, said it, much better than I
They grow not under your heart, but in it

John Lancaster
THE PROMISE

To my wife

Yes every night
When I go to bed
I still think about
The day we wed

For on that day
That we were wed
I gave to you
A loving pledge

I promised you
A happy life
On that day
You became my wife

But now the years
Have gone quickly by
And life tells me
I must die

So my only wish
Is that I've been true
In those words
I promised to you

Irene M Tafoya

Irene M Tafoya
HIS OWN
Blessed is the Nation
Whose God is the Lord.
When in unity and love
We can praise in one accord.

God looked down from His dwelling place
At all His creation the human race.
And he took note of all their works,
Searching for obedience and joyful praise.

The righteous are His chosen,
His own inheritance and treasure.
When we come in sincere humble reverence,
He is exulted to the Father's highest pleasure.

He knows each one from the depth of the soul.
Knows who relies in the strength of His power.
He protects us like a shield from harm and foe,
In Him we are victorious, our fortress mighty tower.

Rejoice ye Nation whose God is the Lord,
Like a mighty Captain He has conquered the war.
To reign as King of Kings and Lord of Lords
With His own to praise Him forever more.

Denise Sachs
I LOVE YOU
I love you a little
i love you a lot
i love you as the day
is long
I'll love you always
i'll love you forever
i'll love you as long
as time goes on
I love you, you know
you love me, i know
You and i, we know
We love . . .
Forever

Terry Treadwell
CONSIDER THIS

Dedicated with a special thought for: Rita and Melvin (mother and father), Tammatha (sister), Cindy and Doris (special ladies), Averyll, and most in honor for great-grandmother Matilda Clanton.

Every time you need someone to care and be near
Think of how many times you have been rude and insincere
Are these trials and tribulations that you have to face
Just a punishment for all the times you've been a disgrace
By not sharing, caring, or even talking to a person in need
Even if many times the problem could have been solved by just planting a seed
A seed of friendship, a seed of warmth and thought
A seed which travels routes from deep within your heart
It takes this gracious gesture to complete one's soul
To put it at harmony with itself as a whole
So the next time you see someone whose day can't get off the ground
Stop and ask, "Why on such a day does he have a frown?"
Try to lighten the loads of misery which have weighed his life down
And you may be surprised when you need the favor, and it comes back around

Netty Wilson
FOR ANDY
Muddy shoes and a dirty face
A scratch on the end of his nose
My little boy, my pride and joy
He's the best in the world, I suppose

A puppy dog following behind him
A kitten under his arm
He's such a sweet and innocent lad
Lord keep him safe from harm

Let him grow strong and wiser
Teach him to be a man
If he trips and stumbles and falls
Someone please just give him a hand

Little boys grow up so fast
The days they slip on by
Before you know it, they're all grown up
Then the days just seem to fly

So sleep on little man
Have dreams so warm and sweet
You'll walk on my heart tomorrow
But today it's only my feet.

Nicole Rossi
TOMORROW'S WORLD
We are the Future
of the world
We are the Peace
of tomorrow.
You fight for us
to save our lives
So we might live
as Friends.
But we can't read
between the lines
To see just what
you mean,
All we see is
war and death
All we hear are
Soldiers' cries.

We want to be
the Future
We want to live
in Peace
We want to end
this hateful war
We want to end
the pain.
So when you hear
the Children cry
Listen to our words.
Today we may be
only children
But tomorrow
we are
the World.

Ronald J Sanders
SOURCE OF LIFE

To my wife Alice, For her Love; Faith and Support. I LOVE YOU!

Sometimes I can't believe the
feelings that flew through my body,
Like a river cascading down a
mountainside wild and free
And even that river had a beginning,
just as all my wonderful feelings do
And mine began my Darling, the day
that I met you.

You are the source of all my
happiness; the center of my life
And each morning that I awake next
to you and take you into my arms,
Fills me with such security and
strength knowing what my future
holds
You have given me your friendship,
love, understanding, and trust;
Accepted me just as I am.

And all you wish from me is my
love, and that my Darling you already
have
From the depths of my heart; "You
Will Always Have My Love."

Jeffrey L Ward
I WANT TO TELL YOU

I thank you God, for all you have given me.

I want to tell you
How your eyes remind me of stars
Shining high in the midnight sky

How when I hold you close
My heart beats
Like the waves
Caressing a sandy shore

How when I hear your voice
It brings music to my ear
Like the wind whispering away all
my fears

How when I kiss your lips
It's like a humming bird
Taking sweet nectar from a flower
How my love for you grows
Like a rose
Reaching for the sun

I want to tell you
How I've found a happiness from
within
Where do I begin

Guðrún Bjork Bjarnadóttir
THE WAITING

This poem is dedicated to all my friends around the world.

I stand by the window waiting,
Waiting for you.
I have waited for a long time,
longer than you know.
So long that it is no longer me who is
waiting.
Only my shadow
and soon he will also disappear.
Then there will be nothing left,
left to wait
except the clock.

Nevada S Granato
THE WAR
Boys growing to men in a war zone
Shot in the arm, a broken bone
Your buddy lying beside you died
But you're a man now and you never
cried.
Until you come home and watch it on
T.V., then you cry,
then you see.
No one understands, except those
who were there.
They have good, but mostly bad
memories to share.
The mothers and the girl friends
check the mail every day.
The letters he sent in March, finally
got here in May
But the worst letter to receive, the
one that came today
The one that says your son is a
P.O.W. or M.I.A.
Will anyone search, will anyone
look?
Is his name just forgotten, mixed with
others in a book?
How could the government just leave
him there.
If it were their son, then they would
care.
Is he suffering, is he dead?
The nightmares keep going on in my
head.
What do you say to the crying
mothers?
What do you do about the crying
brothers?

Michele Selinger
THE OLD ROCKER
A rocking chair sits in a corner
Covered with the dust of the past,
And no one knows what secrets it
holds
To be stored as long as time shall
last.

Perhaps, it was used by a mother
To rock her newborn babe,
Or used to provide some comfort
When someone dear has passed
away.

This sturdy piece of carpentry
Has been through good and bad,
And beneath its once shiny varnish
Are stored memories both happy and
sad.

This gift given in love
To be used by everyone dear,
Was given when times were hard
And said to become precious over the
years.

Now the years they've passed
And the time has flown,
But over in a darkened corner
The once treasured rocker now sits
alone . . .

Dorothy A McCormick
WHERE ARE THE GOOD TIMES
Again I grope in the dark
Lost like a ship at sea,
With unsettled mind and thoughts
I search for the real me.
Pages of my life flash back
To only things that's bad;
Yet somewhere there must be
More happy times, less sad,
I reach for things I can't find
Here lost in time and space;
A smile, a touch or sweet kiss—
A hand upon my face.
With laughter and tears I cry
For days that might have been;
And though some were filled with
hurt,
I'd face them all again.
Somewhere there lies inner peace
Wherein I can survive
Through anything life gives out
Till I live out my life.

Irene Hoatland

Irene Hoatland
A PURPLE HEART WON'T DO!
The President gave me your Purple
Heart today for being wounded in
battle but it won't do.
You've gone to Heaven now and oh
how I'm going to miss you.
Oh God how can I stand the pain?
When only your future was my
highest aim.
For our Freedom and old Glory you
went far over the sea.
To fight our enemy the Vietnamese.
A you did your very best.
But now I lay you to rest.
Oh Lord how my empty heart cries.
For you and every soldier that must
die.

Some day I hope to join you up
there.
In Heaven's home we will share.
So you see my darling Son a Purple
Heart won't do!
Or ever take the place of YOU!

Gloria Diamantino
BEING
Loving the breeze that caresses my
cheek
Loving the sun, which tiny green
buds seek
Loving the sea salt that touches my
lips
Loving the sand that through my toes
sift
Loving the soft clouds that silently
slide through air
Loving the moment so much that I
must stop and stare
And wonder, why I never noticed
them this way before
Why did time stand still now on this
shore?
The moment, the moment, that is
why, will never be quite the same
Let me remember it and try not
myself to blame
That I had never understood before
why I am

Ernie Jaramillo
MY FRIENDS
If I had a million years to live,
My friend
I would spend all but one, making
friends,
And my last year.
I would want to spend with you, my
friend.
Because I would really wish it
was a million years,
before we had to say goodbye again,
my friend.

W D Furlough
MIRACLES OF LIFE
Memories are for real, they never
die.
They're a means of reliving the past
today
to anticipate a better future
by suffering the pains of frustration
built thru depression and desperation
dwelling within the depths of one's
soul,
driving him forever deeper and
deeper
into memories of a forgotten past.

Where's the consolation, if it
follows,
allowing the heart the room to
function
to help us survive from
day to day
healing scars, and closing the open
wounds.
Miracles of ages past, I wonder,
can they disappear into tomorrow's
dreams
or simply lie in waiting till reborn
once again to stimulate the
imagination.

Paula A Hatley
MISSED

To my friend the frog.

Physical features unknown
Awareness of you each night
Sounds of your voice
Sending warmth through me
Communication exchanged
THEN
Stillness invades
Distance looms
Morning reveals death
Tears of grief flow—
Sometimes Good-bye
is forever.

Marcy Villarreal
I SEE THE SKY IS CLEAR AND BLUE
I see the sky is clear and blue;
I look real high and think of you.
The sun gives off its golden rays;
I just love warm summer days!

Now it's dark, the sky's still clear;
How I wish that you were here.
The stars all shine like little lights;
I just love warm summer nights!

Angela J Luper
WHAT IS LOVE

For Scott Macuga, My One and Only

What is love?
Define it for me please.
Or would you like me to tell you
What it means to me?

Love is giving
Every part of your soul,
Every part of your being,
It's what makes you whole.

Love is trusting
Enough to let you go.
Love is caring
Enough to let you know

That you mean everything to me,
Everything the world could be.
And more.

Juanita Jo Steveson
SPIRIT OF EASTER
Today marks a bright, new
beginning;
Winter's a sign of the past,
Christ our Lord has risen,
And life has come at last.

The fragrant lilies of Easter,
Spreading forth their perfume,
Awaken the tranquil earth
From her cold and dreary gloom.

The sweetness of Christ's life,
His beautiful mission of pain,
Soon death will be conquered—
So live ye not in vain.

O, dear mother nature,
You tell of a victory won,
Of strife, conquest, and triumph—
All that our Master hath done.

Look ye to the new living,
A path not tread alone,
May you all be blessed—
For Christ lives in the hearts of His
own.

Dorothy Fowler
DESTINY
To be loved and wanted is every
child's dream,
Some are born into a life of no love
and rejection.
They are deprived of both it would
seem,
Their world becomes full of sin and
frustration.
A sin they cannot change, so they
learn to cope,
How sad for these children to go on
with little hope.
To be in the world desperate and
alone
With their life shattered, and no place
to call home.
Then we have those who decide to
take their life,
For they can not live with all the
stress and strife.
To leave this world unwanted and
unloved,
Is this to be their Destiny?—

Rose Marie Donahue
THE CLOWN AT THE MALL

To My Friend Dr. Anthony LaBruzza

In the midst of the throng, he catches
my eye
Subtly, he moves up and down, with
the grace of a dancer, yet he's a
clown
His big twinkling eyes, contagious
with laughter
The pudgy, pink cheeks and shiny red
nose
Brought me back to my childhood,
for a moment's repose
As huge and clumsy a clown, which
my eyes have ever lain on
But with the utmost grace and ease
and limber as a ballerina
Was truly a most spectacular scene
A very suitable symbol of the
"festive season."

John L Reynolds

John L Reynolds
MAN'S SEARCH FOR PAIN

To my devoted loving wife, Alice

Countless eons ago a nerve cell was
born,
And developed with others less
disposed,
And Man came into being not
unfeeling.

The Tyrant's banner unfurled
And the search for pain began,
Sometimes in strange and devious
ways.

The greater the pain, the greater the
quest
Accompanied by twisted logic
Disguised in noble verbalism and
verbage.

Thus, Man, thinks of some glory road
And, resilient, bloodied, dares
To raise arm to the heavens,
Q u e s t i o n i n g.

Maureen O'Shea
MY GIRL

This poem is dedicated to my dog "Dutch" I'll always remember you!!

They say you are man's best friend
You were there with me to the bitter
end.
Walking, running, having a ball
You and me, we had it all!
You were there when I was up or
down,
You were my dog, the best one in
town.
I loved playing ball and frisbee with
you,
And I know you liked it just as much
too.
Good times, bad times, that's what
we had.
There were even days when you
made me mad.
But you know we always
made up
because you were and always will be
my favorite pup.
Why did you have to go away?
I still think of you every day.
Goodbye girl, forget you never,
You'll be in my thoughts & dreams
forever.

Don Daniels
WINDOW PANES
Silence speaks in gentle rains
tiny hands on window panes
feel the journey of each drop

echoes of an inter clock
binding dreams in memories
chains

sadness holds the child within
age is even less a friend
of dreams time tries to erase
seasoned older faces . . . smile
watching as we walk
where they have been

Kirk Anthony Stevens
THE EYES HAVE IT

For Janis, fortified by her help, warmed by her smile, charmed by her eyes, forever.

Aqua ovals, twice glistening, fiercely
bright
Shimmering crystals, clear and
pristine
Twin waterfalls crashing out to
overwhelm
A blink, then two, the fatal, feminine
flutter
She possesses that rare, enchanting
combination
Of pink innocence and dark, sensual
appeal
Nestled below her crown of curly
red-brown hair
Standing one tiptoe down, grace is
balletic
reaffirming in herself what is obvious
to all
The presence of childlike allure
Intertwining with charms of a fresh,
blossoming woman
So naive, yet still pleasant and
refreshing
It is a joy to relish such a uniquely
skillful blend
Childish giggles with mature monthly
periods
Lack of style with vigor of untouched
passions
She has warmth for all and humor to
spare
Both come dancing from her eyes,
mystically
Engulfing us with mincing, prancing
circles of elfish joy
Those eyes brim with so much life,
with still so much to see

Shannon Friedbacher
ONE SNOWY MORNING
When I woke up and looked outside
I saw trees covered with snow,
I could hear the wind rustle
Against my window.
The streets glimmered from the ice
Which made everything look so nice,
I never really stopped to look
At how beautiful nature can be,
Until that one snowy morning
That I had been there to see.

Robert F Harris
DO YOU KNOW?

Dedicated to Teddy Roosevelt, Jr., Charles Ogan Spain, Stanley "Skippy" Seavers, Kenneth "Peavine" Pease, and all those who died for their country.

Do you know who died
At Dī Dō?
He was young, he was free
He was a lot like you and me
Friends and family recall
But memories grow small
Old photographs, diploma, tattered
jersey
Bike with no pedals
Oh, yes, and pretty medals
Purple heart, silver star, medal of
honor
Posthumous, of course
Is their memory dead, too?
Brave soldiers who were true
Or will their death bring new life
Free of war and bitter strife
Do you know who died
And Dī Dō?

Maria R Daniel
REQUIEM OF PAIN
His countenance darkens with
passing years.
No sunlight reflects in his eyes.
They seem to drown in stormy tears;
a mind adrift in a sea of lies.

He knows not of smiles, nor happy
times.
No love fires warm his heart
His lips will speak no gentle lines;
a curse for you and he'll depart.

He grumbles at the daylight hours,
yet, night was never his friend.
A roar of anger and yet he cowers
to retreat in shadows, another
deadend.

He travels through the years alone,
with life itself his foe.
But, for whose sins does he atone
in this, his solitary prison of woe?

And his countenance darkens with
passing years.
And the storm rages out of
control.
But behind his eyes lie bitter
tears
for the man within his soul.

Norman H Walker
MUSIC
I came from the distance eons of
time, before the stars and moon gave
their light.
I was immortal from the day I began,
I've always been a solace to man.
With Heaven and nature I Sing, and
the bells of Heaven I ring.
I am the toast of the ages and the
balm of life.

There's no end to where I may
appear, even from the devil's den or
to the end of the spheres.
I help create joy, happiness, love,
contentment, and often times express
sorrow.
I am with you today and will be with
you in life tomorrow.
I'll be with you in marriage, church,
or whatever phase of life you are in.

And where I have been, there is no
end, I am the sage of time and none

can fully understand me.
I have many different forms, phrases, pitches, and sounds; even the stars of heaven sang before I was earthbound.
The birds of heaven use me in many various ways, and the melodies
they bring of life, joy, and spring.
Echoes through the twilight and the early hours of dawn, and the world is blessed by their lovely song.

Everybody loves me as I am in their spirit and mind.
Man could not do without me as I speak for all mankind.
I am the intangible link to heaven, I penetrate through the stars.
And the love I bring the earth will ring forever through the distant phase of time.
I speak a universal language here on earth and in Heaven; I am
Music.

D Judson Milburn
THE YELLOWSTONE VISITS OKLAHOMA AND OTHER PARTS
EARLY SEPTEMBER, 1988
The Yellowstone dropped in the other day,
From Sunday through the week
and on; its settelage:
Ephemeral bits and microscopic pieces—Phoenix dust
Cooled down from sizzle and fry
of fiery rage
Through mantles of purple mountains' majesty,
Wisps of spruce and aspen,
lodge-pole pine,
Jots of gentian, tittles of sedge and flower carpet—
All tinged with creature fur, I
never thought as mine.
But now it lies about our place as if we own it,
The ash of lives' times' growth
my grass to bear.
Here isn't the place I'd always thought to see it;
I'd planned on going to view its
splendor there.
So, nature's catastrophic, neutral way
Has taken over, furnace heat to
wipe out planned
Human dreams. But nature hasn't self-destructed yet;
She'll bloom again and again.
Man's plans be damned.

EMR jr
LIFE

To my father, who felt deeply that children were a great blessing and family a most important priority . . . may it be with me also. E.M.R. Jr.

I am . . .
I am troubled, I am discouraged, I am tired, I am distraught;
I am depressed, I am sad, I am trapped and bound and caught.
I feel . . .
I feel lost, I feel lonely, I feel I can't find peace;
I feel cold, I feel hungry; shall my suffering never cease?
I want . . .
I want gold, I want silver, I want every precious jewel;
I want power, I want passion, I want to be very very cool.
I need . . .
I need wealth, I need love, I need laughter, I need life;
I need no more tribulation, no more trials, no more strife.
I've got . . .
I've got poverty, I've got bills, I've got headaches and a cold;
I've got problems, I've got fears, and I'm getting kinda old.

What I am is human; What I feel will change; What I want I do not need;
What I need I can't explain; What I've got is nothing
. . . and that's why Jesus Christ came.
That makes me thankful, awful thankful,
That people like me can finally get out of
. . . the rain.

Lorraine Gallant

Lorraine Gallant
THE DARK

For baby brother Randy.

Unknown vast space,
As far as the eye can see.
yet, I feel so safe
and secure when,
night surrounds me.

Pamela J Williams
A TRUE FRIEND

I dedicate this to Carleen Crum. I finally made it!

Tears filled my eyes and made it hard to see
They froze before they ever left my cheek.
Bitterness I felt, She's been taken away
The one I spent so much time with each and every day.
The one that made me laugh and caught me
When I was about to fall, There beside me at every call.
Now she lay under my feet, I can feel the love that we both need.
Though her heart doesn't beat, I can still feel the warmth that she has given to me.
I brightened her dark day with a bouquet.
As I bowed down to the grave of my best friend.
And although she is dead, I know our friendship hasn't come to an end.
A true friend she has been, and I know her spirit God will soon send!

Patrick L Cǎdy
DESTINY

To my children
That they may understand
My destiny

As much as a man, is a man is a man
As much as a woman wants to be
As much as each is a part of the land
As much as each, a part of the sea.
It never will be
What cannot be
From the highest of mountains
To the deepest of seas.

Take comfort in thought
Both you and me
Each our own
Our destiny.

Deanna Thompson
COUNTLESS DREAMS
For the many things you are to me;
for the reasons you allowed me to be.

For caregivers like you and bonds
never broken;
for Providence for sending you
fulfilling promises unspoken.

For any of the sad times and all of
the good;
for the faith and love of motherhood.

For the countless dreams we two
have shared;
for a priceless relationship knowing
we cared.

For your patience and the common
sense you bestow;
for being my mother and loving me
so.

Debra Sievert Liddy
COME SING WITH ME
Come sing with me.
Share in the song of my life
And let the notes echo from your heart.
As you learn the melody
Which is mine and only mine to sing
May I also come to know
The song which is yours alone.
Singing them together
We will learn of each other
And our world will come to know
Harmony.

C Talbot
WAR'S REACTION
Sadness befalls mothers
Loneliness comes to women
Emptiness becomes real to children
The nation cries.

Our boys dress as men,
Outfitted for an end
Earth absorbs the shock
Skies above weep
As always, sun will again
Shine.

Amy Davis
THE UNKNOWN CHILD

To Mom . . . who understands

I never gave you a chance to live and that was so cruel and so unfair.
I sit and wonder what you would look like, your eyes, the color of your hair.
You grew inside me for three months and oh how my life did change
You may no longer be with me but for all time your memory will remain
You were part of me and a person that I love so much
Oh how I would love to hold you and feel your little touch
You were so unexpected and I was so scared that I didn't know what to do.
But baby when you died a part of me died with you
I wonder if you were a little boy, a boy to call my son
A little boy to watch playing, to watch you smile as you have fun
Or maybe you were my laughter, a precious little girl
One day to braid your hair, one day maybe curl
Although I took your life away, you will always live as long as I cry
To you I say, sweet unknown child of mine, Goodbye

Donald O Brown
SITTING ON A SNOWFLAKE

To my darling daughter, Angela

Sitting on a snowflake,
falling from the sky.
The feeling is majestic,
Imagine you can fly.
Overlooking cities,
And mountainous terrain.
Wondering why man,
is living in such vain.
Can-not man put an end to war?
And all his greed and lust.
For surely as my snowflake melts,
Man returns to dust.

Ashley Wallace
THE FIRST TIME

I, Ashley Wallace, would like to dedicate this poem to all of my very closest friends and to my mom Dollie, and to my grandparents, Mr. and Mrs. Coleman Wallace, Sr.

When I talked to you over the phone, I was all alone.
Then you began to laugh, I knew you were doing it on my behalf.
But as the time goes by, I hope you wont try to deny.
And if everything works out, that's what love is all about.
I will always be very near, because I want to be your dear.
And I am not asking for a dime, just remember the first time.

Michael Craig
THE PRAISE

For Rhonda,
The only one who believed.

They
were rapturous.
The applause,
reverberating
resounding
I could feel
the sound, deep within
my soul.
I smiled.
It was ME they loved
wanted
desired
loathed
resented
despised
But The Praise remained.
I only felt the love,
I could only hear the
want,
only taste the desire,
so I remained,
aloof and erect,
drinking the praise
feeding my soul
nourishing my talent.
And later,
when the applause had died and
the crowd was gone,
I felt only
. . . loneliness . . .

Kay Hoehn
LAST PERFORMANCE
Screaming silently from within my very soul
Shivering fiercely from the awful cold
Fighting bitterly against the wind and rain
Struggling to keep my head above the water again

Forcing out the anguished faces
Flashing before me from hidden places
Trying with all their might
To lengthen my days to shortened nights
Unproven am I as I stand before them
Guilty of the webs of sin I spin
Fleeing from a painful past
I turn to face my judges all at last
Deafening is the sentence brought down
Patiently waiting in frozen time for my final bow
Smiling bravely holds a shattered heart and a thousand tears
Naked I stand here; Ripping from my face a mask, the verdict is drawn
Look at me now, Just another broken clown.

Thea Zalma
QUIET FORESTS

From nights and days of trial and pain
My spirit flies;
To open skies, sweet smell of pine,
And gentle breezes.

I'll wait no more
To find my place at heaven's door.
Each breath I take at forest's gate
Will make me strong.

Standing here under God's canopy,
I feel protected from life's misery.

I look up and see the beauty spreading wide,
And I feel free inside;
I can go on.

In quiet forests that I travel through,
I remember I am one with you.

In searching through plans made by man's design,
Not one so well has stood the test of time;
As evergreens, God's wondrous fantasy;

Forever strong; forever free.

Loree Jackson Washington
ENTER A SURVIVOR

To: My loving husband—Eugene, courageous son—Michael, a special sister—Eula and the entire Jackson Family.

When life's doors are seemingly closed
With an abrupt and cruel no
No time to weep-whimper-or pose
Who's a survivor get-up-go

Brow is bruised; body is bent
Wind in front instead of back
Smile in spite of money being spent
Don't sound the alarm, that's a fact!
Jagged nerves somewhat worn—completely torn
Living with ridicule spite and scorn
Tis-no-need to fret and mourn
Regretful of the day you were born

Weary winter's storm, soothing summer's rain
Watching breathlessly till sunset draws nigh
Must keep on fighting all to gain
If not today, way on mountains high

Joy is not bought; love is not gained
An inward cry echoes—strive on for more
Toils-sweet tears, I must shoulder the pain
No, not I, adrift on yonder's shore
Will soon prove worthwhile—to a survivor

Deborah L Busbee
CUPID OF THE FOUNTAIN

Always smiling in the spray
Where the water streams
Cupid stands all through the day
Marble lost in dreams
In his fountain on tiptoe
with his arrows near
Month on month will come and go
None does Cupid fear
Ever youthful, ever fresh
Like the fabled rose
Better garbed in stone than in flesh
That wise Cupid knows.

Joanne McT Karg
SOMEDAY

"Someday I'll get married and live by the sea,
And I will be as happy as happy can be."
Still a child expecting her third,
She buried her flier husband before he had heard.
She went home to parents who didn't believe
That she needed any time to grieve.
So she married a man with promises fair,
But soon discovered that he didn't care.
Lonely, poor, and often in pain
She raised her children and prayed "not in vain."
Smart, successful, happy are they
She cared for her parents, and said "someday,"
"Someday, I'll escape, and live by the sea
Be a child again—how happy I'll be."
Then came the reports—one by one.
"You have lupus, my dear, stay out of the sun.
Your days will be filled with increasing pain
There's no hope that you will be well again."
"Yesterday I was happy as happy could be
Even though I have never lived by the sea."

Edith Brake Grumbles
CLOUD SCAPING

O myriad bubbling clouds
The setting sun highlights upper
Extremes while shading the middle
And low levels where you expose
Vast cryptic halls, fiery caverns,
Billowing waves in purple shades—
Stormy violets, dust scarlets
And steely grays. Those forgotten
Essene black holes are far away.
What magic torrents bade you do
Slow loop-the-loops a time or two?
While you bowed out and changed your ways
How sweet and quiet in dusky haze
Fantasy systems all toned down
You succeeded clowning around.
Mourning dove whispers "Peace be still".
The sun has set and "All is well".
Silvery moon in eastern sky,
Chimney swifts clipping the firefly—
Toads are croaking, crickets chirping.
Close your eyes, sleep deep, my darling.

Paul B Whitley
TREES ARE BEAUTIFUL

Trees are beautiful;
The thought of love
Almost wherever you go,
Whatever you see,
Trees are close to you and me.

Spring is natural
For trees to sprout
And bloom
With beautiful flowers or leaves,
Without doubt of mind.

Winter is the time
For the leaves
To come to the ground
And to be covered
With snow.

Fall and summer are just the same
To the trees as they grow;
Their leaves sing again,
For the love of the land
Is back again.

Thea M Waldow
THE LOST CHILD

She ran from her family at sixteen.
She ran to the streets of the big city.
Where she found a new love.
one that hurt,
one that was terrifying
And one that was confusing
Where she sold her body to satisfy the lust of men
She ran again, but from the hurt
with the love of drugs.
She wore a mask.
She wore it like a lost child in a darkened world.
She once remembered the life she once knew
She ran for her last time,
to her destruction.

Krishna Sy
DREAM WITH ME

To Pàper and Shmuddle with love. Also, to Tiffany and all those who always believed in me.

I have a dream
A dream that is losing ground
It is losing tangibility
But what is not tangible within,
Will never be to those around you.
This is a dream for peace
Perhaps too naive a dream,
A dream that is being denied
By newspapers everyday.
Peace starts with oneself
Start within

Dare to dream,
Dream with me.

Vivien Leigh Bartley
ENGLAND

Tell me why after all these years you're back,
When now I'm used to being all alone.
The love we shared, memories I once had,
All the heartaches and the pain once were gone.

Now it's even harder to understand,
Why I still love you after all these years.
Were all the dreams we shared just made of sand?
Maybe I can't see you for all the tears.

Each day gets harder, silent tears I cry,
My heart slowly breaks each and every day.
Without you now I lose my will to try,
This time I know our love has gone astray.

Never again to hurt because of love,
Never again without help from above.

Michelle LaPointe
I WISH THAT I COULD TRAVEL

I wish that I could travel
If only for a day,
To a mystical, magical place
Where I could feel no pain.
Heartache and sadness would be strangers
And the tears I'd cry would be for joy.
Never a smile would leave my face
In my mystical, magical place.
Happiness would be for always
And the sun would brighten all my tomorrows
Leaving me no time to ever drown in sorrows.
Oh how great it would be,
If only this place I could see . . .
But to laugh I must cry
Even if the pain makes me want to die.
For when tomorrow comes
Then I'll see the sun still shines bright,
And when dark comes with its starry night
I'll make my wish if only to start
To see my mystical, magical place
Deep within my very own heart.

Jeni Herndon
NO MATTER WHAT, LIFE GOES ON.

Maybe love is better than gold.
Maybe new isn't better than old.

Maybe the easiest isn't the best.
Maybe something isn't as good as the rest.

But no matter what, life goes on.
There's still a night and still a dawn.

Maybe things aren't its best right now.
But some where, but some how.

Good light will shine through.
It will shine for me. It will shine for you.

God knows your future and the rest.
Just relax and do your best.

Because no matter what, life goes on.
There's still a night and still a dawn.

Rita M Angileri
THROUGH YOUTHFUL EYES

When troubled with the weight of earthly sorrow,
The likes of which takes all one's strength to bear,
Look to the child and from that young heart borrow
The secret that we all must learn to fare.

For in a small one's eyes, there lives a wonder,
And also an innocence which is beautiful to behold;
It sees not only the outside, but what lies under—
Sensing what is there without being told.

Alas how the passage of time seems to dull,
The carefree and joyous endeavors of youth.
We stray from our path and sometimes tarnish the soul;
Sometimes tend toward the evil, avoiding the truth.
To overcome that which harms we must each do our part,
Striving with each moment to become children at heart.

Ruth Marie Nelson

Ruth Marie Nelson
THE SUN
The sun shines through my window in every way,
and lets me know that it's another day
and time to be on my way.

I toss and turn at first it's no surprise, but I know when the sun shines it's time to rise. To rise and open my eyes to a new day ahead. I'm not unhappy but overjoyed instead.

For me, I'm grateful to see and live for another day, another time another way.

Desdra L Mroz
SPRING
One of the first signs of Spring is usually a robin, a flower, or even the weather,
But one of the more beautiful signs of Spring is me, the butterfly.

As my beautiful wings sparkle in the sunshine, I fly by the flowers and laughing children playing.
I have a warm feeling inside that this Spring is going to be extra special.

Emily Spreng
SILENCE

To my mom, Jane Spreng, who was the first person I knew who really liked and understood "Silence."

Can you hear it Ric?
What?
Shhhh. Listen . . . the silence.
I don't hear anything. What does it sound like?
Have you ever heard the stars come out at night ? Or icecream melt? Or darkness? That's what silence sounds like.
What color is it? Is it black? Like night?
I guess it can be. But I think it's white. All different shades of white.
Shades of white?
Yes. Have you ever looked at a cloud? When you first look at it, it looks white. But if you look at it close enough you'll see that it isn't just white. It's all different shades of white.
Ahh. Like snow.
Exactly!
What does silence feel like?
I think it feels like water, water at the bottom of a lake.
Do you think love is silent Ariel?
I don't know.
We could find out.
Tempting. Very tempting.

Deborah A Wood
ALONE

Alone
with my thoughts
suspended in time.

Memories of good.
Memories of bad,
begin to collide.

Laughter turns to tears
and memories are pushed
into darkness of the past.

The sun shines once again
but the thoughts remain
Alone.

Lori Insalaco
POEMS

To God for my gift.

I am here again
with a pen in my hand
and thoughts in my head.
I'm writing my dreams, my worries, my joyous times.
I relate my poems to a therapy session,
it is peaceful and calm in ways.
My emotions flow onto the paper.
I can also relate it to a tide after a rough storm—
Sometimes I lose myself into them—
Caught by the hand and swept into the midst of
la-la-land.
Sometimes I never want to come back
and run off the paper
and then jump back into reality.
But, all things end—
and I am here again.

Jodie Schoppe
WINNING
Have you ever wondered?
Wondered what it's like to be up there?
To be high above where nobody but you can see.
To be able to look down on the people who are now looking up at you.
To be honored with the highest honor you could ever receive.
To win what took you so long to achieve.
To be able to stand up knowing the entire nation is looking up at you.

Anthony Joseph Anastasio
SOLITARY STREET
Under a streetlight watching the end of another day;
I am going to stay here tonight, and whisper the night away.

So many people to meet, but when I come to be found;
Silence fills the street, and nobody seems to be around.
Solitary Street—the only place I know.
Solitary Street—no where else to go.

Lead me back to your door, I will wait here beneath the stars;
But I continue to be ignored, as I sit between the cars.

I think I better go now, nothing left to say;
No one makes a sound, as I continue on my way.

Jodi Lynn Murphy
MY HEART

Dedicated to Jeromy Kadish. The first real love in my life and may it last forever.

You gave me this ring, all shiny and new—
describing your feelings that will always be true.
I'll wear it forever and never depart—
because you'll always be close to my heart.

What can I do to show you I care,
for when I'm with you, my love is there to share.
The something I'm giving is only from me,
My gift will never leave, so don't try to set it free.

About this something I'm giving to you,
Why, you ask.
Because no one else makes me feel the way I do when I'm with you.

The gift I'm giving is my heart.
And when I say, "I love you, too!"
It's coming from this special part.

Mellissa Bowman
THE LAST ROSE

The Last Rose
Our love was as beautiful as the night.
Just as sweet as the rose I hold.
Just as day break and as the sun rose,
I knew our love was true.
But how could this feeling be darkened by night?
The sun never rose again and the days were just as dull.
Now the sun and warmth disappeared.
So did the rose that your love would forever hold.
And the memories will stay and be renewed at the dawn of a new day.
The Last Rose

Virginia B Harris
MY DAD

In loving memory of my dad Willis M.("Pete") Ward

Dear God, Please watch over my Dad for me.
I love him so much, and he was so dear to me.
Dad was always there to pick me up when I fell.
He always helped me to remember my childhood so well.

He was so kind, and so much fun to be around.
He would laugh, and joke with me, and act like a clown.
My Dad was loved, and admired, by everyone who knew him.
If a person was in need, he would do anything to help them.
My father had five other children, besides me.
He was a very loving father, as anyone could see.
He was very crippled, and I knew he had a lot of pain.
But Dad just kept on working, and didn't complain.
When he died, it left my heart with such an empty space.
I knew, that in my heart, no one could take his place.
So God, you can see that in my eyes, he was such a tall man.
So, please love him as I did, and take care of him, when you can.

Terry Xander
RIVER OF TEARS
Empty promises
Broken dreams,
Lonely heart
Torn apart . . .
at the seams ;

Crying eyes
(Stormy skies)
that never clear,
Pouring rain
(Liquid pain)

. . . into a RIVER OF TEARS ;

Carol Ann Tucker
THE LAST ROSE

To my Mother, Lillian Stowell with all my Love, Carol Ann Tucker

Autumn leaves falling
Blanketing earth gold and brown.
Cornstocks stacked in the pumpkin patch,
Weeds withering at last.
Soil tilled to get a rest.
Winter's coming—it can't wait.
As I start to close the garden gate,
A glimpse of color catches my eye
Among the blossoms of faded rainbows,
I kneel to find the last rose.

The brilliant color peeking out,
Its petals soft as silk.
A fragrant heavenly sweet.
Cutting it to save its beauty,
Before a frost snuffs it out.
Nature's timetable unyielding,
A gentle reminder of life's glory.
To keep it myself would be a shame,
For no greater love can I give thee,
Then to share the last rose.

Megan Lyn McCord
EMPTY KISSES

To: Josh
Thanks for the memories

I thought that you would leave me
I felt it in you kiss.
It didn't seem to be as warm
With its sweet and tender bliss.

I remember the last time you kissed me,

I didn't feel a thing.
You didn't even tell me you loved me,
So I knew what tomorrow would bring.

The kisses I remember most,
Were the ones that touched my heart.
The ones that said "I love you Meg,
I've loved you from the start."

But that night your kiss was different.
Quick and very cold.
And I knew that it was over,
For your heart I could not hold.

I know you tried to love me
There was just something we would miss.
'Cause the love that I'd been looking for,
Was lost . . . in your empty kiss.

Laura Livesay

MY SON

I dedicate this poem and my life to my son, who this poem is about, and my husband who has made my future something to look forward to. I love both very much. Laura L. Boebel

His tiny hands reach up to me
to hold him in my arms
His sparkling eyes express his plea
to keep him from life's harms.

I pick him up and hold him tight
and try to calm his fears;
But this world is an endless fight.
I can't always dry his tears.

If he can grow up full and strong
life's winds won't blow him down,
and if his heart is full of song
his values will stay sound.

So I will teach him to love and live,
to try the best he can,
to take all that this world can give,
to care and understand.

hugs-'n-kisses
Laura Lee

Tami Boles

GROWING UP

Each day as I grow older I begin to understand
There will not always be someone there to hold my hand
There comes a time when we must learn to fend for ourselves
A time to put all our toys upon their shelves
A time to grow a time for change
A time for life to rearrange
A time to realize what life's all about
A time to end all foolish doubt
Life goes on with many tears
Life continues with many fears
We must put those fears away
And let the good things come to stay
In our hearts we're insecure
A feeling of life we must endure
In the time that passes each day
We grow stronger in more than one way
And as we mature we learn and live
We notice what life has to give

Lynnda Kaye White

THE ME THAT'S PRETTY

The me that's pretty
Doesn't come out
Unless she's asked
And not always then
It isn't 'til a stranger's passed
That I know she's back again

Simply some reflection
Of some imagined ideal
She comes out
As if she's really real

The me that's pretty
Doesn't come out
Unless you ask
Her where she's been
You see beyond the mask
And bring her back again

When I am reflected
In what you feel
The me that's pretty
Suddenly seems real

William G Kubida

William G Kubida

MOONFLOWER

Moon Flower, fairest of all
Beautiful blossom straight and tall
With crystal petals, you sparkle with life
Like a radiant frost
In the pale moonlight.

Lovely blossom, faint and fair
Pale rose of gentle touch
Hear my words this day
As I may never again pass this way

Moon Flower, gentle queen
Raise your lovely face
To the soft moonbeams
Fill your eyes with evening stars
And fill your heart with dreams afar.

Of all the flowers, tall and small
You, lovely blossom are grandest of all
In slender form you gracefully sway
Thru rows of reeds and music plays

Moon Flower, Lady of Love
Lips as soft
As the wings of a dove.
Moon Flower, you'll always be with me
Whether in a dream or in reality.

Donna Chandler-Wyant

THE GOLDEN CHAIN OF FRIENDSHIP

This poem is dedicated to and written for—Ronald L. Click—A very special man and truly my best friend

When I reflect back on the past
I just can't help but think—
Of all the friends who've been there—
But most are now extinct.

These friends have formed a golden chain
Which 'round me now is wrapped.
It holds me in its golden glow—
It's never had a gap.

Until the day that I met you,
This chain so firmly held.
Then all at once, I realized,
The clasp had been withheld.

This chain of gold, so beautiful,
Cannot be bought or sold.
And now, it has its clasp in place—
The clasp is purest gold.

My friend, you are the only one
Who's made this whole chain meld.
For now, I know—without a doubt—
In friendship's arms, I'm held.

Doris P Titus

DREAMING

Black as night, dark in mind
shimmery black and white.
Images fill the mind
shades of precious color combine,
as of a great imaginative design.

The dream awakes by morning light
alive on paper, I begin to write
the precious memories . . . of the dream
that took place last night,
the illusion lives, and dances with light.

Night falls, wishing for sleep
for the memory of the dream, runs deep.
In silent slumber . . . waiting for the dream
for almost real it may seem
dark in mind, it's only a dream.

Michelle R Pence

MIDNIGHT'S ECLIPTIC FANTASY

To the rare in this world who purely love, within heart and spirit.

A face in the night,
A touch through the air;
The love unforgotten,
The passion so rare.

My shadow's erotic,
My dream's always there;
The vision I sleep with
The memories I share.

A visage approaches,
A breathtaking stare;
The truth lets us love,
The lies shall beware.

Frieda M Wedge

DEAR JUNE

Happy Mother's Day, to a Sister Dear
One who washed my face and dried my tears
A Sister who has been with me from the start
Always encouraging me to do my Art
From working in clay to make a simple holder
To painting in oils as I grew older
A Sister who has been found tried but true
Happy Mother's Day Sis, from me to you.

Aaron Phillip Boatright

MEMORIES

Gentle waves of grain
Snap at my face
As I run through the childhood of my life

I hear a sweet song in my ears
That becomes faint as I move farther and farther away.
As I jump, I jump
Through time
Remembering back when I was just learning to jump.

And I move through time
As I always do in my mind.

Ian Fichtel

THEY HATE ME

They locked the door
when I was in.
They looked at me,
and said I was sin.
They put me in the basement
I was afraid.
They told me to stay
and so I obeyed.
They chained me to the wall
so I could not leave.
This all happened,
upon Christmas Eve!
I said I didn't like it.
They could not have cared.
I said I couldn't stand it.
They stood and only glared.
Things were looking
pretty bad.
Because "They" were
Mom and Dad.

Joseph A Stein

TIME

Time is the measure of clocks they say
For some too little or none
The minutes, the days, do fly
In the time we are having fun
And then there are times full of worry and thought
When things never seem to go right
These are the times that fun must have bought
In measure, some darkness for light
Treasure the moments, both tears and the fun
For life is so wondrously dear
Be thoughtful and kind for the time that you have
And of death you will have nothing to fear
Time is short, the clock running out
The wick in the candle burns low
The minutes, the hours, the days, are at end
Are we ready when destined to go?

Lee Estes

SUPER NATURAL "STEPS TO TRUTH"

If something is supernatural, it means it is more natural.
If something is more natural, it is more real.
If something is more real, it is less fake.
If it is least fake, it is most true,
And if we cannot comprehend the supernatural "Most true,"
Our morals are for shit!

Diane Norton

DAD AND MOM

They were a couple that seemed to be true
They loved each other through and through
They married on that special day
They looked at each other in the most sweetest way
Years passed, days flew, less and less
Would they say, "I Love You"
They drew apart day by day
That look for each other must of gone away
If something was wrong or right
it would either end up in a kiss or a fight
So many nights of fighting and crying
So many years of betraying and lying
She couldn't take it, the love wasn't there
No more could anyone say they were the perfect pair
The day came, they're no more together
No more a couple forever and ever
The day of court had come at last
They've got to forget all the love in the past
With papers to sign and pen in her hands

She can't hold back all of her tears
But she now understands.
It's hard to see them just walk away
But we knew they couldn't of loved for another day
They should of left it all on the night of the prom,
Sorry it's over—Dad and Mom

John F Bress
IS IT ME
When I look in the mirror, what do I see?
Is it really a true reflection of me.
Is it the real me, who lives deep inside,
Or the false me—made up with pride.
Do my real emotions and feelings come through,
Or is it the false ones, to fool me and you.
Is it the one that goes with the crowd and readily agrees,
With what's being said; merely to please—
Those around me with flowery words untrue,
Saying what they want to hear, doing as they would do.
When I look in the mirror and see my eyes,
Are they windows of truth or filmed over with lies,
Do they reflect the truth to those outside,
Or held to keep it hidden somewhere inside.
I examined my image, yes it was me.
But was it only the outer self that I see.
What I wanted to see, I guess, was my soul—
Not parts of me, But the complete me to behold.
Then I smiled to myself, pushing all doubts aside,
What showed on the outer me, was the same as inside.
What reflected from the mirror was a true image of me.

Matthew A Frigon
GAMES
Two men in robes, black and white
Each has vision, but neither has sight.
A game of chess will determine the fate
of all men's destiny, small and great.

One with cross, and the other with scythe
A battle for souls between black and white.
Nowhere to run to, nowhere to hide
A demonic lycanthrope, a Jekyll and Hyde.

First moves the castle, and then moves the knight
Ignoring the pawn, which is plainly in sight.
When the game is over, they feel no pain;
Both have won, but neither will reign.

Lillian Edwards
ALONE
The evenings seem so lonely
And yet your presence near
I call your name and only
The whistle of the train I hear.

I wonder about this eery feeling
The silence broken by the phone
My heartbeats reach the ceiling
And yet I sit here all alone.

I have thoughts so near and far—
Seems to be a dream or two.
Could it be you on a distant star?
Come a little closer, so I can see you.

A ray of sunshine shone
On top of my coffee cup
Here I sit so all alone,
But always looking up.

Phillippe W Brouillard
THE BOY IN THE ROAD
One day, while driving up a hill,
a woman sped, a cat was killed.

She stopped her car, and stepped out crying,
that cat was dead, there's no denying.

The speed she used, to arrive there sooner,
took the life of a feline, this time.

As the young boy sat, by his dead cat,
the remorse could be observed, in her face.

Yet, I still wonder, the emotion she'd show,
if the cat, sat by the boy in the road.

Renaldo De Meio
LONELINESS
I saw within an open hearth
And a fire burning bright
Its glowing flames and warmth
Gave forth a cheery sight.
There before it in true comfort
The family gathered round
All was peace and contentment
And here I knew I'd found,
The homey atmosphere I have missed
For lo—these many years;
And watching through the window
My eyes were filled with tears.

I knelt upon the ground outside
And prayed to God above
To guide my solitary footsteps
That I also might find love.
Just to know that wanted feeling
As I heard their laughter clear;
With one last look I turned away—
For I do not live here.

Arlene D Schonfeld
I HEAR THE CHURCH BELL RINGING

To the Ev. Lutheran Church of St. John
Town of Grover—Peshtigo, WI
Where I have been a
member for 70 years

I hear the church bell ringing,
It echoes miles around,
The wind carries the music,
To my ears it's a beautiful sound.

I hear the angels singing,
I hear the Lord's sweet voice,
Come to my house this morning,
And see what it's all about.

I hear the church bell ringing,
It's the church that stands on the hill,
I've gone there when I was a child,
And beautifully it stands there still.

So come to the Lord's house this morning,
And see what contentment you'll find,
Just to know you have a Savior,
Is a blessing to all mankind.

Keep the church bell ringing,
Calling in every soul,
To come to the church on the hilltop,
Which is the house of the Lord.

Myrna L Pepin
EARLY MORN'

Beloved Joseph

The sun breaking
through the clouds,
The dew sparkles
upon the grass,
Sweet smelling dawn.
beautiful morn'.

Canadian geese
break the silence,
Feeling happiness here,
you're in my heart,
On this morn', beautiful
spring mourn!

Karen Kinses
DREAMS

Dedicated to: John Miles, who has always been my poetic inspiration! !

Sleep's finally come, the clock's ticking two
And all my dreams are dreams of you

The phone is silent, I want it to ring
I will it to do so, but not a thing!

What are you doing this long, long night
In my dreams I'm holding you tight

In my dreams I'm running now
I've got to get to the phone somehow

I've got to hear some words from you
I've got to hear your voice
You are in my dreams it's true
You see I have no choice!

Beth Brewer
SHADOW FRIEND

To my friends and family whom I love dearly.

—Here I am all sad and alone
no one to turn to just here
on my own,
—Here on my own all by myself
with only the walls to talk
to and nothing else.
—So, silently in my mind I
conjure a friend, someone to
talk to every now and then,
—He listens to me faithfully
and wipes my tears away; can
cheer me up or make me smile,
any time of day.
—He's a friend I will not share
one I can not lose, he's the
one I dreamed of—the only one
I'd choose.
—This is a friend to which I
confide; tell all my problems
to, with nothing at all to hide.
—My silent friend my quiet
companion
to whom I owe it all, is the
light inside the darkness——
THE SHADOW ON THE WALL.

Shirley Fiorentino
DECISION WITH LOVE

To my children, Steven, Nero, Tonilee, and Anthony
All things are possible. Love, Mom.

Warm, warm eyes, chance to meet
Danger, danger the drums start its beat.
Two lonely hearts a flame will start
In love too late for they must part.

Fires will burn until covered with sand
Decision with love, taking heart into hand.
Saying goodbyes with aching pain
Remembering our hours each one in vain

Beautiful love songs, pleasures we'd shared
Lips tenderly pressed, hands clasped with care
To-gether our thoughts would electrify
Shouldn't we have just one more try.

An unarranged meeting, a delighted heart
So very in love, made a scenery of art.
Forever and always, love and faith now come through
It's wonderful my darling, "My decision with love to you . ."

Gael M Morse
WHY DO I LOVE YOU?

For Dieterich, another name for "Love"

Why do I love you?
Your smile makes my day begin
Your footstep excites me
Your laughter echoes in my heart
Your touch exalts me . . . .
Why do I love you?
Your tenderness puts warmth in my very soul
Your seriousness and sadness push me to new heights to help you
Your need fills me with a capacity to give
Why do I love you?
You are everything to me
I can dance on my own, but when I join you in the dance of life we go so well together, you and I
I can let you alone because I respect and love you
I love you because you are you and you and I fulfill each other's needs

Andreah Childers
GLAD YOU'RE MY COUSIN

This is dedicated to my adorable cousin Ashley Nichole Ysunza.
I LOVE YOU!

Cousins like you
Are so very hard to find,
And that's why I'm glad
You are a cousin of mine.
Though we don't
Always get along,
In the end
We're always standing strong.
We live so far apart
That it's hard to keep in touch,
But I'll always love you
So very, very much.
I know you probably don't understand
What I'm trying to say . . .
You'll always be my favorite cousin
Each and every day!

Wynona R Talbert
BABY

The love I felt as he snuggled close, was something words could not begin to tell.

He turned his perfect little head and his big blue eyes teared up as he screamed for the milk that came from my breast.

Love can only be expressed, as a mother holds her new baby close,—
—for emotions mount so very high, and words are only felt.

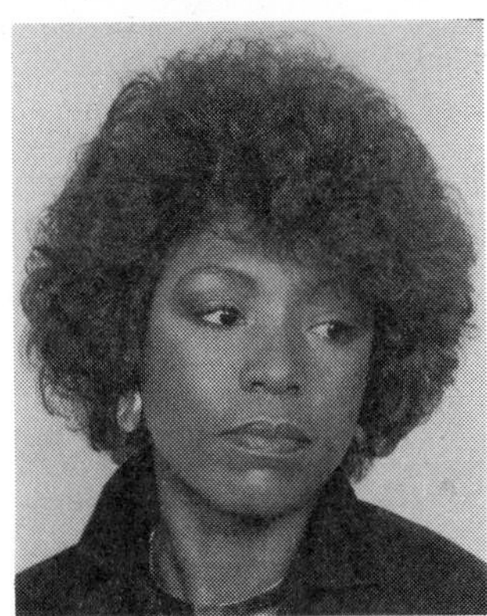

Sheryl J Paige

Sheryl J Paige
NOWHERE

This is dedicated to my husband William E Paige, in appreciation for his support to write this poem.

A place so real, yet so incomprehensible;
Where roads meander without the slightest care.
Where feelings stand invincible.
Pain and grief will never find you there.

A place where no one falls to criticism.
Where efforts are held as great.
Where one beholds a flashing vision;
That can give true direction before too late.

Nowhere is a special place inside of everyone.
Too many times to visit there can set you on the run.

Annie Pickard
THE ROSE COVERED STONE WALL

The little creek flowed gently aside from the wall,
The old oak tree stood proudly where brown leaves did fall;
Our little bench we placed there endured wind and rain,
We sat and dreamed and loved there, and truly not in vain.

Each stone the wall was made of was perfect in shape and size,
The tender red and pink rose buds did cling along the sides.
The brown leaves lay so gently on the ground we softly tread,
Where pink rose petals mixed in wind gales and also petals of red.

Our love was always special, the first I ever knew,
For under the old oak tree we vowed that we'd be true.
The rose covered wall of stone still stands so firm and strong;
A symbol of our love dear one, which I know will not go wrong.

In my dreams I hold your hand there, on the bench beside the wall;
Where the beautiful pink and red petals so sweetly and gently fall.

Janis Y Smith
A SPECIAL PLACE

Each day I hear him calling
beyond the echoes of the night
I escape into the darkness
to a place far from sight
His beauty always greets me
with gentle loving arms
I marvel at his wisdom
and delighted by his charm
This place is just for lovers
he and I alone
Joined by true devotion
a paradise of our own
Melodies so alluring
we dance to every tune
We race among the heavens
'til we cross the purple moon
Long to stay forever
love fills each empty space
Can't wait until tomorrow
when we meet in our special place.

Yeo Kok Kheng, Roland
BIRDS

BIRDS FLY HIGH,
HARD TO CATCH.
FRIENDS LIKE YOU,
HARD TO FORGET.
...... a wonderful
nursery rhyme,
I thought.

I sit at the bus-stop,
gazing at the bluish-grey sky.
The evening sky
depicts the end-of-day dimness.
The sun does not seem to glow anymore.
Night emerges.

Suddenly,
myriad of birds soar over the sky,
forming shapes
like aeroplanes or monsters, I don't know.
They break the quietness and peacefulness
of the sky,
bringing joy and laughter
as they sing their songs away.

Wow!
What a wonderful sight.
The habitat of birds.
I really envy them,
especially their carefreeness.

Birds which are perched on trees
fly to join the family.
They sure warm my heart.

How I wish I could be like them
hovering in the sky,
and experience the joy of life.

Denise M Smith
MIRAGE

This poem is dedicated to my mother.

Of twisted branches and withered streams
Of shattered hopes and broken dreams
The desert rules as king and queen
And thus crowns those that share its schemes
The arid sands envelop all
Listen closely, hear the call
The rocks surround and build a wall
And images of a waterfall
And dripping out now grain by grain
The sand it quivers just like rain
And binding all just like a chain
Much greater than all wealth or gain
A mighty cactus standing bare
Defying all, the deserts heir
A gentle breeze that soothes the care
Ignore the fates now, if you dare
And bleached white bones kissed by the sun
Scream out their story one by one
It's too late now for thoughts undone
It's all the same in oblivion
Of twisted branches and withered streams
Of shattered hopes and broken dreams
The desert rules as king and queen
And thus crowns those that share its schemes

Eunice S Soden
FOREVER LOVE

I'll love you till my dying day,
Although we've gone our separate ways.
Someday I hope this terrible pain,
I will be able to explain;
And stop the tears I cry each night,
And even sometimes in daylight.
Bless the one whose unknown part
Is trying to mend a broken heart.

Helen E Weiss
TO ASK MYSELF?

To my Husband.
To my Children, my Grandchildren.
To my Sister, Edna.

I said to my soul be still......!
But, ne'er to my thoughts at will
Would this soul of mine be deterred.
It soared its right to be heard
Across the land, in sight, as birds
Who soar to the sky, free, no cage, uninterred!

And, so again, to my aching soul,
I said, be still, ere to reach your goal!
Else havoc and perilous fright doth stem its foal,
As mare its birthing time, unto life enpulsed a-new.
Its wondrous birth to celebrate, in continuum, a-view.

Soul, my soul, I said again, be still!
I will find my highway, my noble path, my hill,
My climb to mountain-tops to thus fulfill.
I need peace and quiet in tempered clime
Of aged years in changing, muted time and rhyme.

My soul gives comfort. It is calm, at last. It is still
In unaffected laugh or knowing, destined thrill.
My soul is pure and free. It is wholly enscarfed,
To lead me, my soul, to abiding embers by my hearth.

Rethea W Kearney
FLIGHT 103

"FLIGHT 103" is dedicated to all the families here and in England that lost loved ones on board "FLIGHT 103."

God I ask you to be
Gentle on "FLIGHT 103"
For they were on their way home
From so far across the sea
For they were to be
Joining their family
Instead you greeted them with your open arms
For they are in heaven now
And as we down here on earth will grieve together
And try to be strong
For they were all innocent
And had done no wrong

All they wanted, was to come home
Now their memories will linger on
Throughout every heart in America
And hope that justice will be done
For they had done no wrong
And two wrongs don't make a right
As we say a prayer for them tonight
We ask God to remove the hatred from the heart
For those who took part
In ending so many innocent lives
And we pray to God that all who died
Did not die in vain
And that you have taken them under your wings
And that their souls will rejoice in your kingdom
For ever more.

Joan Crawford Hammond
THE FIRST SNOW

As the tiny snowflakes gently fall to earth,
And cover its surface with a blanket of white;
There prevails a quiet, peaceful calm,
Whose beauty fills our hearts at sight.

They flutter down from grey-hued skies,
Those tiny bits of jeweled down;
And lay upon the ground and trees,
A sparkling, shining crown.

They hide the scars on barren fields,
And quietly caress the window panes;
Dress the naked trees and shrubs,
Along the country lanes.

They fall into the creek's chilled waters,
And quickly, they just melt away;
Then as a thin layer of ice begins,
The snowflakes build up to stay.

Thus nature's begun her winter's sleep,
with an ever so gentle nod;
Is covered up snug with a blanket of snow,
And a tender kiss from God.

Larry Williamson
IN THE FALL OF THE YEAR

You came into my life in the fall of the year
My heart was not of joy but of uncertainty and fear
I can see you now as clearly as I did then, the cool breeze of autumn when the leaves were turning thin

Your voice so feminine, so cool, so clear, I've thought of you often since the fall of the year
I've thought of you often but
why it's not quite clear
then I remember your smile,
your charm, your love,
in the fall of the year
Now the leaves are turning green, St. Patty's day is near
but my mind often wonders back to you and the fall of the year
Our times together were special
and I think that you would
agree
Our love was growing slowly
like the roots of an old oak tree
But tragic things can happen and
why it's still not clear
especially when you fall in love in
the fall of the year
You know I'll always love you,
you can't begin to start . . .
that's why there always be for
you, a place within my heart
The summer breeze is blowing, the sky is getting clear
I can see you getting closer, I can see you getting near
If and when you ever need me
and not sure which way to
steer . . .
I'll always be here for you, just
like in the fall of the year

Gilberta K Williams
A HOME
When I'm older (as some day I'll be)
I want a home just built for three.
Where happiness forever dwells
And laughter will ring like silver bells.

A home with windows thrown open wide
To let in the wonders of the outside.
With chairs and beds and everything cozy;
I'll do my part to make life rosy.

A home where when the day is done
We'll thank Him for our blessings one by one;
For giving us a happiness serene
And letting us know what a home can mean.

I don't know, but I think I will
Make a home when I build.

Paula L Killion
A LOVE IN RETROSPECT
Our moments together have now passed on
To the precious memories they are
The happy times of glorious days and nights of ecstasy
So filled with dreams and of how much we cared

Our hopes of times to come when we could be together
To give our all, sharing all we had
To quench the passion in each other's arms
Because holding you was like
Heaven on Earth

We were like a song, a melody of love and how we would shine
Only we existed among the throngs we could not see
Our cares left behind no worries or fears for we had each other
That's all we wanted and all we needed

Once I wrote of leaving empty
But now I know that my heart is filled
With so much love in retrospect
The strength of it alone makes it endless

Having no boundaries it excels
It is unsurpassed, limitless
And how you've made me alive
For having given me your love.

Sylvia Wallau Perry
SANDY*
"Sandy," whose warm ghost inhabits
This old mansion, with its rabbits
Scurrying about where first you laid
That soft white head, so unafraid—
Those silken feathers, oft caress'd
Those crumply ears so oft distress'd
By tradesmen's step and watchman's horn:
Why cannot we all be reborn
With quickened pulse and eager stride,
Ready to feed you and take pride
In walking you past Judges' eyes,
Your stance now perfect, and our cries:
"Well done, Sensation," not a Dream . . . .
You Dogdom's King . . Somewhere its Queen!

*"Frenchtown Sensation" had been renamed "Sandy," by our son, Chris.

Joe E Workman Jr
EAST AND WEST
After Chernobyl we should have learned,
Now we are really concerned.

We have no water—We have no crops.
As the bomb was dropped—The Earth began to stop.

We can't go on—We can't survive.
Now it's all over—It took only five.

We should have learned by number one.
Now look what we have done.

Because of money and politics,
We've blown up something we cannot fix.

Just before we began to fight,
We said, "We told you Donahue was right."

Now we are gone and we're all dead—
"The world would be destroyed by fire," God said.

Harold W Stiles
YEARS OF TIME
After the years of time have left us!
We will be as one in our hearts.
As we will be, forever in our self as one,
For everyone, that was ever in our hearts,
Since the beginning of time.

Sheila L McCandless
BLISSFUL IGNORANCE
The pain of a nation
comes down to one,
and I fear,
fear for the ignorant ones.

The un-informed
and easily amused.
Sh'll find themselves
willfully abused.

Then we will cry
for what we've lost.
Our eyes will open
and we'll wish for our past.

They say time repeats
and it's proven true.
Our fearless leaders
continue on cue.

Will we self-destruct?
Not in a blaze of imagined glory,
but in a pit
of uselessness.

Carole Moshay Gilpatrick MA MFCC

Carole Moshay Gilpatrick MA MFCC
LIMITS ON WHAT?

To Mom & Dad, Helen and Al Moshay, who loved me and taught me to be a lady andTo Ernest Katz, M.D. who loved me and believed in me— even when I didn't

Vasectomy, hysterectomy and tubal ligation
creations of man
to limit creation.
Our race against nature
our nature against race,
External limit on crowding
crowding our internal space.

Hospitals, offices, M.D.'s, politicians therapists, healers, all give admonitions
"Don't fill up our space!"
"Don't crowd the terrain!"
All adamant demands
to ease populous pain.

A man and a woman,
plus one tiny child
in the overall picture
seems obviously mild,
apart from the frenzy
so publicly stated
to pit man against man
in what's naturally created.

Stephen Wayne Cammuse
WHEELS THAT ARE BURNED

These wishes galore the journey is paths two, solemn mysterious thinketh & known prophecies in one accord.

The myths we read, we pedestal the Christ in all that survive, as babies that fight in wars, they are winners Oh Mama count the high of walking we have studied words in dedication & earnest dedicated sources The walls breathe those sounds hammer Mama I love two love tremble she's don't see try & tutor the burned wheels either is the good thought—clear poor study habits the source It is known two most to study the scripts those evil worm in the brains of politics souls aren't free to serve the propered light
As a matter of fact the truth in humans is hard to believe them, to many lovers still loving others & people pull at the heart to define in others the truth & support of actuality of the self that is their & true & denied by self that they don't know about & is defined in the Bible & others that live the accord was born of Adam & the garden is embraced Gifts of the the "spirit" are numerous Gifts they are Holy & racious, all can't have all of them some preach, sing they are called & some retain the Spirit of Gifts of God the maker of all mankind & women etc etc.

Ada Bommarito
OH CHILD, DEAR CHILD

To Jenny with love.

Oh child dear child, where have you gone?
I've come back home to hear your song.

In heart, it seems just yesterday,
As you ran thru clover to sing and play.

You watched the hawk soar to the sky;
Upon your face, the wind kissed a sigh.

Winter's snowflakes tapped the windowpanes,
Delivered by northwind's sweet refrains.

Oh springtime you skipped thru floral blooms,
Which filled the desert with sweet perfumes.

I see the farm from atop Sage Hill,
The old house, the barn, the whip-poor-will.

I look and linger, just a little while,
Hoping to capture your innocent smile.

I'll bid farewell, tho you will always be,
In the long ago, my precious memory.

Bob Walanga
ODE TO A PUCK
The black disk is dropped a signal for the war to begin.
Three twenty minute battles for a tie, loss or a win.
Troops are sent in over the boards, attacking in three to five men hordes.
The filled arena rocks and echoes collide. Down on the frozen battlefield the warriors glide. The war does have rules and you're banished if you will fully hurt. Each army has a man to argue a point, he wears a "C" on his shirt. Weapons

include sticks, gloves, and skates. The war can be physical, some armies give more than they take. Uniforms are colorful there's green, red, black, orange and blue. Blackhawks mapleleafs and would you believe penguins too? The war is over now both sides are spent. The winners strut off their armor has nary a dent. The organist serenades the crowd as they fade from sight. The scoreboard says "Thank you" and Goodnight. Sights and sounds of a war called hockey.

Ms Dane Beaumont

THE DEATH OF A SEASON

To a lost daughter, who is still very much loved.

The fallen leaves a slave to the flame,
send smoky mists
curling towards the dark sky.

The trees mourn
for their lovely green flowers
have fallen and turned brown—

Soilbound.

The hot thick air
turns sharp and brisk

the tears be turned to snow,
then I who hates the mist of cold
say—

"Whither shall I go?"

Elynor A Baran

WINTER IN WISCONSIN

The Season of Winter
Brings moments of
Awe and happiness!

Delicate fluffy
Feathery snowflakes
Begin to whirl around—

In unusual heavenly quietude
The snow begins to
Cover the frozen barren earth.

Robes of white ermine
Pile and shape
Into mysterious designs.

What a joyous glow
As the snow begins
To drift!

Silver frozen streams
With tree branches covered
Like lovely white pearls.

Skiing, flying like
Graceful birds
A thrilling sight!

Brad Richard Erlston

MOM AND DAD'S HOUSE ON THE HILL

The walls are cold the floors are warped, there hasn't been a guest. Mom and Dad's house on the hill has finally had a rest. The trees are dead the grass is dry, it's time to say good-bye but that house is filled with memories that make me want to cry. It's time to say farewell but before I do there's one more thing that I must tell. Though joy and happiness came sorrow and despair, one day we will return and Mom and Dad's house will still be there.

R R Kunkel

LET HIM RULE AND REIGN

God has not ordered me
To set the whole world right,
But the work that He has given
I must do with all my might.

I am not bound to feed
The hungry on every shore,
But I must help the needy
Who come knocking on my door.

I'm not to ask for wealth or fame,
Things for which so many ask,
But only for the grace to do
Each ordinary, humble task.

For nothing will be monotonous
On mountain, plain, or hill,
As long as I am willing
To do my Master's will.

My life will not be barren,
Nor my work for Him in vain,
If I crown him Lord and Master
And let Him rule and reign.

April Hayes Tobin

REGRETS

Dedicated to my dear Daughters, Sharon Lowe and Judy Carson.

Has ever man faced the beyond
Without a single regret?
Has woman ever looked behind
And wished she could forget?

What a trail of tears we leave
Just by passing through
If I had another chance
I'd be different, please believe.

Not that one wants to really hurt
It's just in human blindness
To trample carelessly down the path
Without a thought of kindness.

Living is like sowing seeds
I wish I could have known this,
Then in my youth I'd careful be
To sow only seeds of kindness.

Michael T Martin

DEAR BUTTERFLY

Dear Butterfly,
Your birth is so delightful,
The way you start your flight.
You're awkward but so graceful,
In the early morning light.
I wonder how you do it,
When once you crawled about.
To wakeup one morning,
All ready for your flight.

Millard R Hall

GOD'S BEAUTY AT NIGHT

The still of the night.
You look in the sky,
you see a sky of stars,
plus you can see the moon.

You listen real good,
you may hear a loon,
you may even hear a whippoorwill,
you may even hear an owl.

You can even see a firefly
with their lights a glow.
You may even see an owl fly by.
You can hear the frogs sing their song.

You listen real close,
you may hear a rabbit eating clover.
You may even hear a deer eating grass,
in the still of the night in the country.

Patsy Bunch

CHILDHOOD DAYS

When I go back to yesterdays
my thoughts are full of joy
hide and seek was a favorite game
a rag doll was my toy . . .
Daddy was a farmer
he used a mule to plow
long and hard he would toil
and turned the earth to soil . . .
Summer was a time of work
and not much time to play
we went to bed by dark
and up with the light of day . . .
Our house was not fancy
but very well built
no electric blankets for us
just some pretty homemade quilts . . .
An oil lamp burned on the table
that we knew was not very stable
but you could hear our voices ringing
as we said good night just a singing . . .
I look in the mirror
and see my youth is gone
I find myself slipping back
to that old shack . . .

Helen Foster

WHAT IS A FRIEND

To Emma
My Best Friend

A Friend Is Someone You Go To.
When You Want To Take A Walk.
Or If You Have A Problem.
And Just Want To Sit And Talk.

A Friend Is Someone Who Listens.
To What You Have To Say.
They Don't Always Agree With What You Do.
And They Will Tell You In The Nicest Way.

A Friend Is Someone Who Cares.
And Someone You Care About.
You Do Things To Help Each Other.
And Don't Ever Feel . . . Put Out.

A Friend Is Someone To Share With.
Your Problems And Your Fun.
No One Could Ever Take Their Place.
And I Really Mean, No One.

I Have Found Such A Friend In You.
I'm Sure You Know This By Now.
You Are A Friend To Most Everyone.
But You Are Special To Me Somehow.

Vera B Riley

ONLY GOD

Only God can know the depth of the heart;
Only He knows the warmth that is hidden in part.
Only His wisdom and sight sees the flow
Of the soul's desire or its inner glow.

Those deepest struggles, that innermost test;
Those quiet longings, the subdued unrest;
That restless peace, stirred by inward zeal
Only God's divine love and mercy can feel.

Only God in His lovely and gracious way
Can reveal those things we fail to portray;
Only God is aware and in goodness can use
And show forth to others intents we would choose.

Dorothea Schoener

AN EXPRESSION OF THOUGHT

Dissecting the word—LIFE

A beginning
A center
An end

L = equals love
IF = equals the word if—
—and is it not questionable?
E = equals effort and energy
and put together
Living Life depends on one's definition of if
in the center of the word
LIFE
Something to think about

Jeannie L Panek

THE WEATHERED TRAIL

They say in life there are many paths to follow, I tread the weathered trail. I picked the greenest of the two, thinking on the sunlight I could sail.

Soon my path grew dreary, it never ceased to rain. The bumps, they got much harder, why continue through the pain?

Once I fell to my knees, not wishing to go on. Then for a moment the clouds lifted, I got a glimpse of what lay beyond.

There I saw a trail that seemed to glitter as of gold. I ran toward my destiny, my footsteps clear and bold.

I reached a fork in the road, before me lay my dream. Step by step I moved forward, never to look back, or so it seemed.

I stumbled over a problem, it reminded me of my past, and I realized it really wasn't so dreary, it was simply that my faith in myself didn't last.

Christine L Wilcox

A FEELING

This is dedicated to Tony, my true love who helped inspire me to write.

As long as I live I will
Never forget you
You took hold of me like nothing
Had before or ever will again
I was so innocent
Like a thief in the night
Before you can grasp it
It's gone
My life will never be the same
Now I can only hope that nobody
Ever has to feel this feeling

Gerry Zelenak

BY THE SEA

As I sat in the sand,
Alone by the sea,
I thought of the man,
I once hoped I'd be.
I thought of my dreams;
The ones that had died,
I stared at the sea,
And silently cried.

I mourned for my dreams,
Buried them away;
Then watched as the sea,
Carried them away.
Alone by the sea,
I sat until morn,
Dreaming of dreams,
As yet unborn.

Gladys M Pollard
THE MAGIC OF WORDS

Poets hang around with words,
Listening to what they say,
Then lace a few together,
In their own special way.

To flit along like angel wings
Around the Golden Ray,
Is a poet's way of saying,
Words can dance and play.

Words can ask forgiveness,
Say thanks with a happy smile,
Blend with sounds of music,
And lift the spirit awhile.

Carol E Knopp
FULL CIRCLE

Chocolates!

Empty candy boxes
In a special drawer
Was my grandma's way
Of saving smells
So very long ago.

Chocolates!

What constant love
Through many years
And guess what's happened now!
I am the grandma
With the smelling box
That grandkids
Still enjoy.

Eloise Wolverton Jarrell
THUNDER

Thundering, rumbling, blundering,
mumbling, grumbling,
In yon nightly sky as tho in
pain.
Continuously, calmly, fragrantly,
rhythmically,
Softly falls the rain.

Maria J Chevalier
WHAT IS A SECRETARY?

She has your buttered roll . . . and
coffee ready
When you waltz in . . . passed nine-
thirty.
She is like a computer . . . with two
hands operation
She often has to find . . . Inaccessible
information.
She is required to type . . . with
speed and accuracy
She is the Queen of . . . unmatched
versatility.
On the telephone . . . She lies and
swears
"The door is closed Sir . . . He's not
there."
She's like a Monkey . . . Swinging
across
To the Assistant . . . Back to the
Boss.
She delivers and picks
up . . . Your clothes at the Cleaners
She forgets your lunch . . . But brings
you back two Weiners.
She's a Wizard when you
scream . . . "Get me So and So"
She dares not ask who . . .She's
supposed to know.
She's expected to meet . . . All of
your deadlines
She's very dependable . . . Or it's the
Unemployment Line.
She really puts up with . . . Needless
conflicts and abuse
Because she knows . . . Her children
need new shoes.
She's a genius . . . At deciphering
Scribbles
She's also very proud . . . and has
Scruples
She may be old, run-down . . . Or all
burned-out
Yet she is always there . . . When
they ask your whereabouts.
What is a Secretary? . . . That is the
Big Question
Well She is the Backbone . . . Of
Your Corporation.

A L Casper
THE HORIZON A-FIRE

See the setting sun through the
crystalline clouds
Looking like the horizon on fire
Sinking faster and faster into
the Earth
Disappearing in the distance
Oh, Sunshine, oh, Ball of Fire

Setting only to rise again the next
morn
Shutting out the dark of night
A-twinkling does this Star do
Giving off sunbeams of orange
and gold
Still going strong, this Light of
old

This blazing ball, this Light of mine
Traveling across the sky and
never seeming to tire
Never go out, Oh, Sunshine
God, Bless your Ball of Fire

Kerri Jean O'Connor

Kerri Jean O'Connor
IF I KNEW WHAT TO SAY

If I knew what to say,
And I knew what to do,
If I knew what to think, instead of
being so confused.
If the world would stop changing,
And people had no disease.
If there was never any death, and
everyone was full of peace.
When the shooting stars fall for me,
and the birds sing songs of love.
When beautiful snowflakes (no two
alike), fall far from up above.
The day unpolluted waves crash
upon the sand
Is the day you say you love me,
And we walk cross the sky hand in
hand.
The day the world is perfect, like a
soft white feather,
Is the day all my dreams come true
And we promise to stay together.

Algie Lee Cox
AMERICA THE MAGNIFICENT

America the beautiful and magnifi-
cent,
We love and revere you!
God help each one his part to do
To keep you strong and free!
Your greatness due to God and His
people.
Your generosity and love to our
brothers
And sisters, inspired by God
above,
Makes you great and beloved!
God keep you great and free,
A beacon for all mankind!
We love this land of beauty,
Grandeur and opportunity!
To God be the glory for His
blessings
On you and me!
Lest we forget, we owe much to the
brave
Who gave so much—many even
life,
To keep us free!
Greater love has no man than this!
God make us grateful for all the
blessings,
We pray!
God bless America and keep Her
pure and free!

Steven N Colbert
INNER ME

This poem is dedicated to all of my children.

Lost in years behind me,
in pasts I'll never know,
there lurks a somewhat better life,
I sure wish I could go.

In days gone by, there was a time
when life was short but sweet.
To take a walk down country lanes
was just the greatest treat!

But now the world, it moves too fast.
I've somehow gone astray.
I live so fast, I kill myself,
I know no other way.

My mind must turn the hands of
time.
My clock must slow its pace.
My mind can see most anything,
I've got to stop this haste.

To see a world within my mind,
that's full of peace and free,
that's the life I can enjoy
that's the life for me!

Reneé Breen
THE BABY ANGEL

Jessica was born with Spina Bifida. God gave me this poem to help us all understand a little better. She went to heaven at 16 mo's old but was a joy to everyone around her.

There was a baby angel in heaven
above,
She needed someone to be with
and love.
She went to her Jesus and with a
little voice,
Asked him to help her make a
big choice,
Together they picked out her parents
on earth.
Someone to love her and notice
her worth,
She finally made her entrance into
their lives.
Unlike the other babies the
parents recognized,
This baby was special, She needed
extra care.
As she grew, there were
handicaps there,
But Jesus kept watching from above.
Making sure his little angel grew
up in love,
He kept telling the mother everything
was alright,
Because this little angel was
kept in his sight,
He was willing to lend this fragile
thing for awhile.
To add some joy and an extra
smile.
The mother thanked him and smiling
she asked,
"Are we worthy of the prize in
this special task"
The Lord smiled gently and took the
mother's hand,
"Just remember that the angel is
mine and, then you'll
understand."

Betty Rumohr
LIGHTS AT CHRISTMAS

Dedicated to my grandchildren: Graham, Dustin, Russell, Ashley, Justine, Kristen and Christopher.

The sparkling lights at Christmas
Are like children's glowing eyes.
When they view the many lovely
gifts
They are given with surprise.

I love to see their various ways
They view the wanted gift
Oh, such a happy moment
It gives one's heart a lift.

I hope that many children
In this great world of discontent
Could be like my grandchildren
With the gifts that they were sent.

In this confused world of ours
We should be happy if we knew
That many share the joys of
childhood
Like we once used to do.

O Christmas is a wonderful time
To thank the Lord above.
For those flowing lights of Christmas
Given freely with his love.

Shawn Greer
EULOGY

This poem is to my mother whom I love very much. Thank you for believing in me. If you hadn't believed in me, getting my poem published would only be a dream. I love you, mom!!!

Here lies a flower
Plucked before its time
Torn away forever
From its family vine
Upon the ground
It slowly wilts away
But the memory
Of it will always stay
Now it is gone
But its sweet scent remains
Good-bye flower,
Until we meet again

Sherry Love
OUR LAST GOODBYES

To the one I love, may we be together forever.

Tell me a secret . . . dark and
deep,
about the one who haunts you, when
you're fast asleep.
Tell me no secrets . . . and I'll
tell you of dreams,
of a soul who haunts me for love, as
he weeps.

Tell me a secret . . . and tell me
no lies,
but you can't read my face, for pain
has Its own disguise.
Tell me no secrets . . . and I'll
tell you not, what I find,
because I see through the flesh, that
familiar soul you constantly hide.

Tell me a secret . . . and I'll tell
you mine,
about the lives we've shared, since
the beginning of time.

Tell me no secrets . . . because
we've shared them before,
in other times, and lives, I'll love you once more.

Tell me a secret . . . about the
love we've shared,
and the hope, and the joy, we shouldn't have dared.
Tell me no secrets . . . and tell
me no lies,
and I'll love you once again, like I've done in so many lives.

Tell me a secret . . . where are
you going this time,
so that I can find you, just give me a sign.
But tell me no secrets . . . of
when we shall die,
and when the end is here, shall we say our last goodbyes?

Shellie Meyers

Shellie Meyers
THE RIGHT MOMENT

Dedicated to my true love: Lee Arrington

I thought you were gone for good,
And that's where you stood,
But, you came back just in time,
To tell me you were mine.
My heart is so filled inside,
A moment like that,
I could never subside.
You held me tight,
And close nearby,
And prayed our love would never die.
I love you now and always will,
I'll never forget that moment,
With the stars above,
And my heart filled with love.

Vyvian M Maylen
BACK HOME FOR KEEPS

As you have grown older and the track looks clear ahead,
You sometimes pause a while and reminisce and wish that you were dead,
For the past is filled with horrors of war and mud and filth,
You can now thank God, many times, for life and love and health.

Yes, you are a soldier, you have fought for peace again,
You have saved the nation's honor, we pray it is not in vain,
You think you committed errors when things looked mighty grim
But who are we to judge you? Are we all without sin?

You are "Back home for keeps" remember? Let me kiss you now,
Let me stroke your hair gently and caress your brow,
For the family all adore you and I do worship you,
Be at peace, dear one, forever;
because I see that clear track too.

Jacqueline C Waldron
SEA SHELLS

Dedicated to Lari and Clover Zatzman, for their inspiration on Sanibel Island, Florida, February 1989.

Treasures from the deep,
Hidden from our view;
Elusive, floating in and out,
on surges of surf and sand.

Remains of creatures small and great,
Food for fish and birds alike . . .
but sought after by man.

Cratered clams, delicate whelks,
Whispering the song of the ancient sea . . .
Leaving their skeletons for all to see.

Tales of life cycles incomplete,
Affected by varying levels of heat;
Strewn by storms, winds and tide,
Infinite numbers the waters hide.

Gathering a beautiful harvest of shells
Takes patience, trust and knowledge as well,
And appreciation for what Nature will share
With those who will search for her beauties so rare.

Mrs June F Cox
STILL A CLOWN

In memory of my Grand Daughter Paula June Carson, age 19, who departed this life May 7, 1989. Loved by all.

What a beautiful day,
said the little clown—
looking at the butterfly flying,
while sitting on the ground.

I'd like to fly up in the sky,
and see the world like others that fly.

He closed his eyes
and began to dream;
a beautiful butterfly appeared—
it seemed.

It flew up around—
and out of sight;
he flapped his wings
with all his might.

Down to earth again he flew,
and on the ground amid the dew;
the clown sat up and rubbed his eyes,
awoke, and smiled to his surprise!!

He was still—a CLOWN.

Ember J Lopez
MOONLIGHT HOURS

I dedicate my poem to all the people I Love.

The moon is bright
and shiny all through the night.
The moon has a smile
as happy and gay,
for the flowers that bloom,
in the month of May.
We whine, we grin,
for every thorn you see,
of trees and bushes that even now show,
how thorny they may be.
For God we may not see,
to know he's as happy as we can't see . . .

Carmella Paris Cheppa
THERE'S WORK AHEAD

To Margaret Paris, a precious mother whose presence in this world has enriched it beyond description.

Work is something never finished;
It follows in the steps of time.
Each job, each task lies undiminished,
Each struggle glowing in its prime.

Earnest efforts don't prove fruitless;
A proven proverb, so they say.
The plant of idleness is rootless;
Its fruits were never known to pay.

Never leave until tomorrow
The things which should be done today;
Time is not in use to borrow
Or life in use to throw away.

Countless generations ended
Leave behind a pattern laid
Thick with toil to be commended
Of their contributions made.

Numerous thoughts are left unsaid,
Though one is simplest to express:
There may be many routes ahead,
But . . . work is the password to success!

Stacey Lee Grata
SAYING . . . "I LOVE YOU"

To the man who inspired the love to write this poem. I love you Scott A. Roman

Saying . . .
"I Love You,"
and meaning . . .
I Love You;
Are commonly confused.

For saying . . .
"I Love You,"
not feeling . . .
I Love You;
Its meaning is abused.

But feeling . . .
I Love You,
when saying . . .
"I Love You;"
Its meaning has no end.

And knowing . . .
I Love You,
never saying . . .
"I Love you;"
A heart would never mend.

I never thought . . .
it could be this way,
I never thought . . .
I'd ever say;
"I Love You,"

And mean it. But I do.

Jannie Hope
MOTHER'S DAY TO MY EIGHT CHILDREN

To my eight wonderful children with Love "Mom."

Today I breathed a prayer of thanks,
That each of you are mine,
Each birth a special blessing,
Not realized at the time.

As children when you played around the house,
Your noise was loud and shrill,
How I longed for peace and quiet,
Now you're gone, and far away, the "house is quiet and still,"

I long to hear your laughter,
See your faces bright as flame,
When day-light turns to dusk
I listen still to hear you call my name.

You were the candles on my
Birthday Cake
The Star on my Christmas tree,
Thanks so much for "Special Times"
They meant so much to me.

Now when my day is over and,
All the work is through,
I just relax and relive
The years I spent with you.

Heather Curry
THE UNBORN CHILD

I'd like to dedicate this poem to my very first born. I Love you Terry.

You killed me and I wasn't even born yet.
You talk of your rights to have an abortion.
What about my rights to live and decide if I want to live or die.
You didn't give me a chance to love you.
You took away my rights.
You could have given me the same that your mother gave you.
A chance to love and hate, a chance to be loved.
A chance at anything.
But you took away that hope the day that you killed me.

Lenise M Mitchell
THANK YOU, LORD

To JOHN and DEMINA, for whom I thank the Lord.

I would like to thank you, Lord
for being there for me

In everything I do, my Lord
You bless me abundantly

I praise you always and forever
Cause you are number One

I praise you also for giving
Your only begotten Son

You're always there to keep me safe
From all sin and shame

How wonderful you are my Lord
I glorify your name

For quite some time you've been molding me
Like a piece of clay

The day is coming very soon that I'll be
Like you in every way

Thank you, Heavenly Father, because
These words cannot convey

Thank you, Heavenly Father, cause
You know what my heart wants
to say . . .

Joyce Parrish
I CAN STILL SEE YOU STANDING THERE

This poem is dedicated to Mary, my dear sister.

I can still see you standing there—
Looking for me everywhere.
Waiting to go where I go—
Just a little girl of four or so.

With long blond curls dancing—
And big bright eyes glancing.
Merrily, along my pathway—
You always seemed to stray.

I used to dream in times past—
Of a little girl like you at last.
All dressed up in ruffles and lace—
And wearing a big smile on her face.

But much too soon you became a lady so fair—
And college plans were in the air.
In such a short time you were out of reach—
Off to the coast where you could teach.

Suddenly, you became a sister indeed—
Ready to listen when I had a need.
To visit and to share, I do declare!
I can still see you standing there.

Grace E Hayes Pearce
DAD HAYES

This poem is dedicated to my father, Earl V. Hayes

He spent a lifetime loving and giving to others.
He responded to anyone's need or call,
With kind, comforting words to his brothers,
With tempered wisdom for all.

He quietly took food to the poor,
And offered hope with a song.
While others went on tour,
He gave of himself all day long.

He worked at the side of his men,
Gaining their respect and care,
With his good-natured grin,
And his willingness to share.

He stayed faithful and true,
To his dear wife and friends.
We are read by what we do,
And the message it sends.

One day God took him home,
He's missed ever so much.
For his life ever shone,
With the master's touch.

Carol Rae Reed Heminger
RUSHING STREAMS
Babbling brooks, and rushing streams and grandeur
fills my highest dreams.

My heart took a leap and I could not speak, as I gazed up on the sky.
Luminous clouds of white going by.

Memories of my childhood days, as I daze into that sky, memories that fade but do not die.

Flowers and clover and cliffs to look over—So beautiful to describe—makes me feel so—
"Oh—alive."

Running down hills at my fullest speed and helping out people, as my greatest deed—

Childhood pleasures in deed they were, but keeps one in a constant stir—

Smiles of laughter and smiles of tears, puts away my childish fears.

I threw a rock into that stream and whirlpools began to ring—

One larger and larger in a ring—Just like life, revolves to the same thing—

I do not forget, the times gone by and so my memories will never die.

How majestic are her mountains.
How lofty are her skies—

God's universe is spacious, as luminous clouds go by.

God's voice is ever near us, from sea to shining sea.
A lot of love and courage, for you and for me.

Arthur Holloway

Mary L Cuthbertson
OUR DAD

Dedicated with love and respect to the greatest dad of all times, my dad.

Who is the greatest dad who lives in the world today?
He's our dad, of course,
Mr. Arthur Holloway.
On a farm he raised us in the admonition of God,
Giving us good advice when on troubled roads we trod.
He spared not the rod to keep us in line,
And if we disobeyed, we were disciplined every time.
He has been our inspiration, our dad and friend,
He's one who will stand by you until the very end.
A man of his word, dependable is he,
A man of integrity, as all men should be.
He is a pillar in the community, and leisure hours are few,
He's honest in his dealings, and loves his fellowman too.
He taught us as a family to stand right and stand tall,
To honor God in all things and have love for one and all.
June 7th is his birth date, and we should celebrate,
Honor and encourage him and never forget this date.
May God richly bless you, dear dad, and may all your wishes come true,
may you live as long as you want; we know God will take care of you.

Your loving daughter,
Mary Holloway Cuthbertson

Sylvia Verity
POOL

To My Dear Bob—
and to all those who would search

Beneath the veil of light
The depths run cold and stark
Though truth there dwells
'Tis clouded by the lower realms
Nourished by ignorance—arrogance pompous intellect

To delve deeply is to one day find
And to find an onerous responsibility
Clouds of misunderstanding
Knowledge without Widsom
Conjure concepts false

Wait—wait in patient trust
And learn one's place and place to be
Yes—glean the truth through search and learning
Wisdom being the prize
But wait—save something missed

Reflected beauty that will raise the mind
Above the veil
And give the search true meaning

Hilary A Rogers
TIME

For my parents, who are always there for me. Their support is my motivation.

as a child

innocence and ignorance
sunshine and happiness
were all you knew.

as an adolescent

questions and confusion
answers became realization
as you grew.

as a teenager

all the idealism
of making love, not war
seems ridiculous now.

as an adult

you see in your children
the child,
the adolescent,
and the teenager,
and the dreams you ignored

until now.

Crystal Ann Hardey
DEATH'S SHADOW

Forever in my memory
Paul Daniel (Danny) Thornhill
February 5, 1968—March 22, 1986

It was a cool breezy day on the 26th of March of that year of '86.

It was Wednesday and the world didn't stop for me.
Life had went on.

As I walked through the sweet smelling air, symbolizing a new day,
I found myself near the house where all had taken in their warmth and condolement.

I was afraid, mostly saddened,
so I did not turn on the street leading to
that house, his house.
I kept a straight road.

As I walked I slipped into before.
And we walked.
Him with his ole' blue jeans,
Converse tennies,
and a yellow striped blue oxford
—only two steps behind me.

And I turned to talk to him.
Only to find
—nothing.

Faye Judd Hoyal
HIDE AND SEEK

This poem is dedicated to my Grandfather, Wm. T Stephens, who died when I was four years old.

The only Grandfather that I knew
Could not dance with me,
Didn't play ball like other men
Or hold me on his knee.

He would ask, "Are you in the corner,
By the big red chair?"
"Are you under the table, Little One,
Are you hiding there?"

He would guess where I was hiding,
Then I would take my turn.
"Are you in the cupboard, Grandpa,
Or behind the big green fern?"

"Or maybe you're in back of Grandma,
Sitting, smiling there?"
Grandpa, I think you're hiding
Behind my little chair . . .

Grandpa could not leave his bed
To come and play with me,
But he would play Hide and Seek
With a granddaughter not quite three.

John W Moore
HOW DO I KNOW I LOVE YOU

To "Gloria Howard," for without her love and inspiration, my poems would be impossible.

It's a beautiful feeling,
One I've never had.
With it, I can forever be glad,
Without it, I would be forever sad.
It's the best feeling I've ever had.

With you near,
I feel this warm glow,
It covers me, from head to toe.
A feeling from inside my heart,
Oh yes, that is where this feeling did start.
Oh this feeling, I forever hold so dear.

Yes, my heart does sing,
And yes, the bells do ring.
I know I'm in love,
It's only you, I think of,
It's you I'm most fond of.

It's you I love,
And I thank God above,
For this true feeling of love!!

Raymond O Davis
THE PASSING BREEZE

This poem is dedicated to my family and friends whom I love very much, To Catherine Hohlfeld, the girl I never got to know and to all the people in this world whose thoughts lie on a higher plane.

Feel the breeze flow through my hair,
Hiking through the canyon without a care.
I think of the flowing streams,
As I wonder what this all might mean.
The machines of mankind are ruining this beautiful place,
As I feel the passing breeze upon my face.

Smoke bellows from tall stacks,
polluting the clean air.
Poisonous waste fills the oceans,
killing marine life.
Nuclear power, the energy of the future,
Yet capable of bringing death for many years,
But people turn their heads and cover their ears.
I wonder where it's headed, this so-called race,
As I feel the passing breeze upon my face.

I've held a newborn child,
Born into a world without hope.
I've watched a friend die,
Because he wouldn't give up dope.
I've seen life from one side to the next,
But I know this could be a beautiful place,
As I feel the passing breeze upon my face.

Denise A DeWald
FRAGILE BEAUTY

To my loving husband, Tim, who has always believed in me, and who also shares my love of nature.

The snow is falling—large, quiet flakes—
From a heavily clouded sky.
I catch a flake on mittened hand,
And hold it near my eye.

The love of God so clearly seen
In its intricate design!
I wish that I could hold it close,
And somehow make it mine.

But soon it melts and it is gone,
And I wish that I could see
God's face as I look up and say,
"Thanks for your gift to me!"

Rachel Smithson-Woods
WINDSPIRITS OF THE NIGHT

To all my loving family and friends . . . Thank you

Windspirits of the night dancing in the darkness,
darkness' deep abyss, cold
canyons shuddering
in aged starlight.
Searching its identity not as yet known
named for its infinite age.

Windspirits of the night, pirouetting in the darkness,
quiet rage winding through,
sinuously moving,
touching, night—sleeping
nature—
Nature innocent, unsuspecting, as yet to awaken
within her floral breast, her power,
her love . . . yea! cleverly woven,
wrapped in moon's gossamer cage.

Windspirits of the night swaying furiously in curtained
darkness listening to empty
echoes of eve's past, not
hearing night now nor night yet morrow.
Not carefree, yet blithlesomely weaving it's patterns
for night ghosts, witches and
hobgoblins steadily to pursue.
Entering nowhere, fleeting everywhere,
Endlessly searching its roots
Page unto page unto page.

Jennifer Lyn Ryan
YOU TAUGHT ME

This poem is dedicated to my Mom and Dad; You taught me so much, more than you know. Love, Jennifer

You taught me ever so much:
How to touch and how to blush,
How to live and how to give,
How to smile and show it a mile,
How to hug and how to snug,
How to miss and then to kiss,
How to talk with tender words
of loving thought,
How to take a stand but always UNDERstand,
How to joke but also take a poke,
How to be brave and never to slave,
How to dream but never to scheme,
How to be all that I can be, and
How to see your love for me.
You taught me ever so much, but above it all—and this is true—
is how you taught me to always love,
whether the sky shines or is filled with gloom.

Barbara Edwards-Wrenn
THINGS TO PONDER

This poem is dedicated to the memory of my beloved husband, Theophilus, and in memory of my friend, Estelle Jenkins, who inspired me to write. Also to my Minister, Richard Barclay, my spiritual advisor.

I may not have material things to give to others here
But I have all my love and strength for those both far and near.
I may not have the answers to all life's why or how,
But God has, so to Him we humbly bow.
You may hear me complain sometime 'bout life's trials without surcease,
But oh for the burdens lifted when I pray to the God of peace.
If sometime you feel you lack the magic of love
Just open "The Book" and meditate on the Trinity up above.
And if we sometimes feel like saying "That's it! I quit! I'm through!"
If Christ had done or said the same, whatever would we do?
If you often get discouraged and don't know what to do
Lift up your eyes to heaven, there's help for me and you.
So let us count our blessings and lift out voices in prayer,
Our problems will all seem smaller 'cause we are in our Father's care.
We must keep holding His hand all through this earthly life,
And seek His love and guidance in all our daily strife.

Judy K Howerton
A TEST OF FAITH

Dedicated to my husband, Gary Howerton

Studied your path of righteousness
Learned words from your precious book
When life would start to fade away
You'd make me take a closer look.

I would knock upon your holy door.
Surrender so gracefully
Give back to you my gift of sight
With you I would not need to see.

Never stop the rain from falling down
Make the mountains tremble and roar
May the food I eat be hard to find,
You shall test my faith, Dear Lord!
Amen

Carmen Perron

Carmen Perron
HILL TOP CHILD . . . EYES TO SEE

Dedicated to my first grandson: Jonathan Robert Kasco September 16, 1988

Hills, hills, peaceful hills
I bowed my head to brighten days.
Eager child upon thy hill
Beautiful child of sweetest joy
Who filled my world with joy of teaching.
Quiet hills above the cloud
Hilltop, heaven full of joy!
Shaking down the peaceful clouds
Happy child, pure as gold
DELIGHTFUL child within herself.
Waiting teacher . . . waiting child
"Teach me, Teacher; I am good."
Happy hills beyond our fears
Guide my future toward the hills.
Praise my reading and my striving.
Alas! I am dreading the dangers
of my breathing
Higher hills wrapped in years
Happy child—high goals
Praise my days . . . the miles are smiles for you,
My Teacher.

Happy hills, higher clouds, higher future
I have reached the hill top
future . . . my Heaven
Beautiful hilltop, heavenly joy.
The room is cold, but make it warm
The child is gone!
I hear the voice, the magic of
her beat.
Magic hilltop, help me find my way.
Hill top child, heavenly joy
You touch my heart, beautiful child.
Waiting teacher . . . waiting child
Hill top child . . . eyes to see
The peaceful Heaven you have reached.
"Good-bye, my Child of sweetest joy."
"Teacher, Teacher, I am free;
My learning days are on the hilltop Heaven,
Full of joy!"

Lenora Myers-Young
SEPARATE BUT TOGETHER

Did we hear the decades cry?
Have we always known why?
Do we hope, strive and try,
To plead, to love, not to cry?
Years expressed, gone, were good,
But never to be (understood).
Do those who trace our mood
See much missing that we should?
We come from ages of time,
From distant, diverse clime.
Could we go back to prime
To be of a style sublime?
Are the scales tipped too far to the rear?
Were we made of dust to live in fear?
The suffering and the hungry do we hear?
Or is our duty and future clear?
As the boy-child suffered through,
Others were always there and true.
It's bittersweet, brother of my blood,
Such fleeting moments, precious, good.
Though we dreamed and lived apart,
You were always within my heart.
We've had our happy and sad times,
We've lived in far and separate climes.
All beings depend upon each other.
A loss is great if it's a Mother.
It was hard for me a
Goodbye, to say,
But we shall meet again
some day.

Virginia L Rayman
A PRAYER OF ETERNAL LOVE

Dedicated to the Right to Life unborn, young and old in Jesus name and Mr. Wilkie A-men

Bearing pain to give birth is wonderful, Oh Lord, it would be so wonderful to birth a child for you.

But since that isn't possible, I'd do the next best thing.
Please give to me the next baby nobody wants to keep.

This Dear Lord I would do, share the love you have put in me.
To a new life that will grow in light and in the likeness of thee.

I would be the happiest person on this earth, but in the new world because I want better for a child of yours than this world can supply.

With truth and understanding a heart filled of love and gentle kindness.

What a great thrill it would be to hold and touch, to hug daily a real live baby in my arms once again could be so wonderful.

All glory would be to God the Father, Christ the Holy Spirit, and me. Because to do for the least of these, where two or three are assembled together in your honor there you are with us.

Thank-you Jesus. A-men.

Joan Lancaster Winings
ONE RED ROSE
Careless words were spoken
And completely misunderstood.
Now we stand apart
Alone and unsheltered.
Our hearts barren and naked
Stripped of our romance and love.

You walked away
I could not stop you.
Hurt was great for both you and I.
I ached to put my arms around you
And kiss away the tears that blurred
Your sad blue eyes.

Tears of hurt, remorse and pain
Tears that welled up again and again.
Tears overflowed from my eyes too
And kept me from knowing what to say or do.
Tears of my own made me recoil
Matched your deepest hurts and
Filled my heart with turmoil.

If I send one red rose to you
Telling you that I forgive
And ask for your forgiveness too
Could the fragrance of one red rose
Bind our hearts together again
And forever hold us close?

Cheryl Kupi
SUNSET
the sky
a kaleidoscope of color
clouds take on shaded images
images of mens forgotten memories
the sun
slighted by the righteousness of her brothers
turns her face
the maiden hills
no longer kissed by her comfort
hold their quilts of clover close
the hues above the city darken
and now
we too feel the night's unwelcome chill
the sun beckons us to follow her
with one
last
disappearing
ray
of
warmth

Shirley Dawn Walton
POWER OF LOVE
Love comes so easy
But so hard to push away
Feelings grab my heart
As if they seem to say
No! little fool you can't
Push me away.

I try to push those
feelings out of my heart
Then up out of my mind
Know-ing the map
I lose every time.

How does love slip through
my mind like a slippery little eel
Sneak into my heart like a thief
at night to steal.
My heart's the winner always
And when the fighting battle is done—
Opens up its door and lets in that
only ONE

Jewel L Thompson
TEARS
I'm lonely for you my darlin'
How I miss you, my Sweet,
My arms reach out for you always,
And it's Heaven each time we meet.

When you put your arms around me,
The world goes into a spin,
I stand there utterly aghast
At things that might have been.

We're so far apart my darlin'
In miles as well as years,
And Heaven only knows
What I've been through in tears.

Tears of lonely heartbreak,
Tears of sorrow and woe,
Tears of holding you close,
And tears of letting you go.

The thought of losin' you,
The thought of our being through,
The thought of another holding you
Is breaking my heart in two.

Amy A Gomez
THE MYSTERY HOLDER
Vast images shoot through the sky
pulsing against the shade.
As the moon streaks low
the sun begins to fade.

Striking resemblances cross the night
haunting each unrecognizable face.
The wind sits upon the secret of ancient times
scrambling around at a slow pace.

I do not give out secrets to you,
these secrets I have deep to hold.
If you were like me, shadowing all
you wouldn't reveal secrets of gold.

I cover up from east to west
north and south no end,
I'm life's mystery holder
and I have but one good friend.

Jennifer Lynn Spencer
A FRIEND IS MADE UP OF LIKE AND LOVE
A friend is made up of like and love
They're always there like a dove
Giving a message to everyone dear
Wishing us all a very happy year

They go with you to places
They save you special spaces
They don't brag about boys
But give you special toys

When they're in love they don't ignore you
When you wish you were in love too
They go walking
When you feel like talking

That's a perfect friend, to have fun
Wish I had one

Martin Kirtley
NEW MEXICO STATE FAIR
Cotton candy on your fingers and in your hair
Yes . . .State Fair is coming . . . head out running
Kids get an eyeful . . . . shoot the plastic ducks with a play rifle
Cock-a-doodle-do roosters . . . little colorful throat boosters
Little piglets with curly tails . . . and lots of good economic sales
Big plump sheep . . . wool for blankets and a comfortable Winter's sleep
Also, it's apple season, very pleasin'. . . for apple pies . . . blue ribbons please the eyes
School children's art . . . young eyes to start . . . making our country better
Rodeo entertainment . . . Stars dressed in fine clothes and raiment
State Fair races, win, lose, or places . . . it's still fun
Of course, the rides . . . leave your stomach behind and tickle your sides
Chile stew, better this year because of plentiful rain
Plenty of parking . . . to go skylarking
Maybe the Governor will be in sight
Souvenirs . . . to bring back precious memories through the years
Donkeys in the children's farm . . . fill us with their charm
Food of great variety
Villa Hispana
Indian Village

Most of all, people getting together.

Shawn McRae

Shawn McRae
WONDERING

To my parents Bill & Dottie McRae, my sister Shareena, my teachers, friends and loved ones.

Wondering can be a fabulous thing,
Why is the sky blue, what makes the grass so green?
The birth of a newborn baby, oh what a wonderful sight!
A childhood nightmare so full of fright.
The brightness of light, the cool, fresh air,
What are the chemicals that make roots in your hair?
The birds fly high, but why so far?
How does an engine run in your car?
These questions can't be answered in the blink of an eye,
But why not look upon the sky?
The earth is made of wonderful things,
I wonder how many are human beings?

Judith K Riley-Bruney
YESTERDAY'S GOOD-BYE
You're gone—I know you're gone—
I no longer feel your touch.
I no longer hear the voice—
that once meant so very much.
Your face has somehow faded—
as if before my eyes.
The love once pledged forever—
slowly, slowly died.
I don't remember when it happened—
I mean—not on a special day.
It's as if—and God forgive us—
it's always been—this way.
We never really said good-bye—
I'm not even sure we could.
I mean—not in spoken words—
although I know we should.
So together—we must say it—
say our Yesterday's Good-bye—
For only then—we can go on living
really living—you and I.

Angela LaCascia
THE CARTOONIST
O'er the fields of black and grey
He puts his figures in lifeless play
Without laughing, they laugh.
Without crying, they cry.
Being just a figment of his imagination.
But why, why can't they laugh by laughing?
Why can't they cry, by crying?
Only the creator, only the feeler,
The laugher, the crier, knows why.

Penelope Heuer
THE ROSE OF LOVE
Don't leave love too long
To fade beneath a lover's touch,
The rose's thorns will keep away
The scorn and ravages of day.
But petals left unwept by tears,
Will fade too soon before the years
Of love they cast their blooms about,
And softest whispers, lover's ring
Condemned to treachery and spite
Will spin a tarnished web of lies
Turn song, and seed and love to sighs.

Rather in special climes keep
Her perfect, where every second counts
And is a beating of the heart
In symmetry and prose,
That shapes herself just as the lovely rose.
Dampen the dew in raiment of egg blue
And clad the mists with golden sun
The Oak, the Laurel and the Pine
Will do the rest, and love will
Keep forever in the breast
That beats with Lover's dreams
And song, safe as a Rose that
Bears no Thorns.

Alisa Harrison
MOTHER

To my mother, whom I love very much.

I'm glad you're always there
When I need a friend
And I know if I ever need to
I can come back again

You listen to all my problems
You calm all my fears
When something really hurts me
You wipe away the tears

You will always love me
That I have no doubt
You've taught me what the world
Is really all about

So if anyone ever asks me
How I feel for you today
I'll say I really love you
More than words can say

Victoria L Santistevan
I NEED YOU
I am the one who needs your love
I am the one who cares
I am the one who strives for love
I am the one who dares;
I am the one who feels alone
I am she, who needs to share.

I come from nowhere and nothing
I come from there, just to be;
I come from those unknowing of real

love;
I come from those who did not want me;
I am looking for care, and love, and faith,
I am me
And I need you.

Miriam Felix Banfield
VEGETABLES

This poem is dedicated to my devoted husband, my wonderful daughters, Genelle and Holly and the Felix Family.

Mom says they're good for me,
The spinach, corn, the beans and pea,
Of all the vegetables I can see,
None of them taste good to me

I'd rather chew a tootsie roll,
Or eat my cereal while it's cold,
She says I won't live to grow old,
Don't tell me what I'm always told.

I'll try a little bit of fish
And make believe I'm eating quiche,
But you know it is not my wish
To eat the things that're on my dish.

I want to be strong
And live quite long,
So I'll eat my veggie and sing a song,
'Cause you know Moms are never wrong.

Laurie D'Alfonzo
BROKEN HEARTS

If I looked up to grab the sun,
Maybe the damage could be undone,
But the rain is falling too fast,
And nothing good can ever last,
So if you happen to look and see,
A broken heart, then think of me.

Dorothy Biesaga
MY MOTHER'S CHILDHOOD IN POLAND

To my mother—Through your struggle I have been given opportunity.

Outside the window, the children play gaily with homemade rag dolls.
Enclosed behind the door, an oversized apron, an oversized pot,
AN OVERSIZED RESPONSIBILITY.
A woman before her childhood began.
No experienced womanly hand to pass down knowledge to this generation,
Cut from the vine and thrown onto barren soil.
Many a mornings the pillow soaked, but no matter,
The Rooster, her sentry calls, and the children.
Oh yes, the children would beckon with their hunger.
Starving her of Love and Hope.
Rush, rush if you want milk, hope it is not watered down,
Push and shove if you want a chance for that 5 lb. ham to feed a family of 6.
Keep the family together, love and hold always,
sacrifice yourself.
One gave, five took.
Christmas time, no coal, no shoes, no hot water.
Lard and sugar on bread, again, like always.
No help.
Maybe strength from a voice inside, maybe yourself.
Survive or DEATH.
SURVIVAL or SURVIVAL.

Mae Lowry
SWEET NORA ROJEAN

Life's wandering road can be narrow and tight.
Some crossroads I chose were dark as the night.
In blackest tunnels, you've been my light.
When I stumbled, half-blind, you brought me sight.

Steps, when re-traced, were made clearly seen.
Your presence beside me gives meaning to clean.
Not once did you scold; not once were you mean.
You are very special, Sweet Nora RoJean.

On mistakes I have made you never dwell.
So many times you've redeemed this life's hell.
Tightly you held me when I slipped and fell.
Saying with actions, "Don't worry—all's well."

Many lives you have changed . . . .
mine not the least!
You give the world beauty and banish the beast.
Hatred and evil have fled on winged feet.
By your armor of love, you have vanquished!

I know now God hears me when I kneel to pray.
He surely smiled when He sent you my way.
Life without you would be dreary and gray,
Sweet Nora RoJean, selfless love you convey.

Paul G Hernandez
SEARCHING BUT NOT FINDING

To the memory of my father—Lorenzo Aguirre Hernandez

All through life we all search for something,
We do not always know what it is we are looking for—yet we look.
Somehow we know that somewhere out there lise this elusive thing.
Could it be something we can look for in a book?

If the book were about your life the answer would lie within.
Some of us try to discover it as we write, create, and debate,
Yet so many of us never see it because it is all around us like the wind.
So stop and listen—so that you can learn of yourself and your fate.

Charles R Clouss
LIFE

We know there will never be
None as great as the Almighty!
So give him praise from day to day,
And bow your head to him and pray.
He gives us life; it's but a loan,
And we accept it as our very own,
So do your best from day to day,
Knowing you're not here to stay.
He gave us life; it's ours to use,
And we can do with it whate'er we choose,
So we should our best every day,
To leave the world in a better way.
For when in this universe we no longer trod,
We just give back what belongs to God.

JoAnn Duckett
JOHN DOE?

My name is not important,
Or who i used to be,
For i am now, just a bum,
That is all you can see.

My tattered dirty clothes,
My unshaven face,
A lot of sad memories,
I cannot erase.

No flowering rose,
Just weeds beneath my feet,
As i curl in newspaper,
To break the wind as i sleep.

You look upon me,
With embitter shame,
But i used to be someone,
With a prominent name,

We do have families,
But they will never know,
For our fate is sealed,
With the simple name of——
John Doe.

Janice James

Janice James
THE PAIN OF CHANGE

Sometimes things just don't work out
It's not your fault or mine
But the worst thing one could ever do
Is believe things will change with time.

Because we are who we are and to deny it would be
A far greater mistake to make
Than to face the facts that it just doesn't work
And go on with your life—That's the breaks!

Everything that we say and all that we do
Is a risk and we know we must take them
For to bury our feelings deep in our heart
Would be to forget and forsake them.

To change our course is sometimes hard
The "Pain of Change" usually is
But the rewards are great and worth the wait
For those who take a chance and live . . .

Like a butterfly on its solo flight
He knows not what he'll find
But free of fears, he's meant to fly
His beauty is of a different kind.

Kelly Rudolph
THE GATHERING

"The Gathering" is dedicated to the daily meeting of friends to witness a miracle and bring each day to a peaceful close . . . and to those who should.

they meet at the ocean
at the edge of the world
unaware that this is the last
they've been uncaring until this day
they still think it will last
but all those years of sunsets
not once did they desire
to hear the sizzle of the sea
as it meets the ball of fire.

Diana Lynn Carper DVM
THE COYOTE

Hey coyote out there, does nobody care
that you're fading as fast as you can?
Fallen from grace, flat on your face,
you leave things the way that they stand.

Walk on the rim, where it's mighty thin
and don't miss a thing with your eyes.
Beaten with clubs and shot at with guns,
Once again you will stifle the cries.

Watch out and wait, live life by fate.
Don't dare to let anyone in.
Heartsick by nature, can't feed a failure.
So that's why you're lookin' so grim.

Show 'em some teeth, give 'em some grief.
Look through them with distant disgust.
Don't trip in the dark, or give from your heart,
'Cause your head knows there's no one to trust.

Ken Hall
NO MORE LETTERS

No more letters do I receive,
My only friend a Vietnamese.
No more letters do come from home,
Am I forgotten, Am I all alone?

They say that freedom is the cause,
But few take time to pause,
To express with words, with pen in hand
And let a guy understand, he's not forgotten in a foreign land

So please if you've the time tonight,
Take your pen and write,
And let a guy understand,
He's not forgotten in a foreign land.

Frank Malley
RECOLLECTION
O your long hair knew no perm then,
And the pale spokes of your eyes danced
On the sunlit stage of your face
Sans mascara.
Then after love, after drugs, after brotherhood handshakes—
The sweat of the Whole Earth Family dried and left us again
Each cooled to the touch.

Beached a yard apart, behind bill paying eyes,
Our embarrassed hearts cried
With the wise laughter of recollection.

Children are so hard to kill.
It takes years, and sometimes still
A child will climb into your eye sockets
And hold delighted court there
For a moment or two.

Dorothy T McConnell
I WATCHED GOD MAKE A MORNING
The morning dew was just like rain
Had fallen in the night.
I looked to find the morning star
But it was out of sight.

The trees no longer took the shapes
Of creatures to be feared,
But bowed and waved to greet the sun
As it slowly reappeared.

I'd watched "God Make a Morning,"
It seemed a simple task
He took the dark and made it light,
It happened just that fast.

Now all could see his wonders,
Brought by the morning light
And put aside the fears that come,
When day turns into night.

Jenness Hobart
UNTITLED

For Jim
Sarah & Tessa

Who'd walk in here but I?
Where unsaid words
left hanging in the air
etch even deeper
the coldness
that hardens between us.
And now how often
we walk silently around
these bleakened ruins
forgetting
how we could again come gently to sunlit spots
where our souls would be caressed
and tenderness renewed.
Drawing my collar against the bleakness
I venture forth
Who'd walk in here but I?

Shirley Y M Dinning
GIVING
A little boy sat at the window one day.
He was lame . . . and could not play.
He sat silent and very still.
Until a little Sparrow lit upon the sill.
Its leg was broken, and he could not stand.
The little boy reached out his gentle hand.
He softly stroked, the Sparrow's breast.
Then held him gently to his chest.
With a splint the leg he mended.
Which would be good as new, now that it was tended.
The little boy was lame and could not play.
But the giving of his love opened a whole new world for him today.

Grace Blaine
THE LOVE THAT WILL NEVER BE
Inside my heart I know
I will always love him so.
Although it can not be,
he'll never ever see
that I really do love him
but I know it can not be.

He always made me laugh
when I needed someone there.
He'd hold my hand real tight
and I know that what I really
felt could never ever be.

He really made me cry
and know he wants me back.
I need the type like him
but I know, I know, I know
it's the love that will never be.

Julie Ann Saurdiff

Julie Ann Saurdiff
FOREVER ALONE
When the wind grabs my face
The pain almost feels good
So cold yet so hot, all at one time
I must wipe away the bitterness, but only if I could

The look in their eyes seems so right
But behind the mask I see
A dream and painting of an untrue picture
Where that beautiful body is holding me

The rain becomes my tears
The refreshing splash makes a silent scream
The hiss of the pounding storm grows cold
Until it calms down, giving birth to a clean fresh steam

So many windows have been shattered
With every piece representing my heart
The wall that keeps me locked up inside
Wants me unhappy and forever alone

Pauleta Cardin
ATTAINMENT
Why reach for tomorrow
when we have today?
It is here now—soon will wither away.
Make the most of your talents
give them full sway.
Live life to the fullest, fill each nook with content,
Then reach for tomorrow—
when today is well spent.

Carla J Nagel
ME AND MY CATAMARAN

This poem is dedicated to my dear friend, Irene Pacana. Her enthusiasm and love for poetry inspired me to write my first poem.

Me and my catamaran
Sailing on that crystal blue
Navigating with a plan
To discover something new

The course is chartered by a star
Faithful polaris, brightest of all
Known by them sailors near and far
You're sure to find your port of call

A mighty wind has struck the mast
Hurling, twisting and trashing about
The world is spinning by so fast
Captured now, there's no way out

Must this be a seaman's fate
To never know a resting place
Rescue me before it's too late
Poseidon, please call off the race

As quickly as the fury came
Tranquillity has been restored
The calm before is now the same
I find that I am still aboard

Transported to another time
Where man and seas become as one
Where solitude and freedom combine
FOR INNER PEACE THIS COURSE WAS RUN

Alice H Lynn
CHRISTA MC AULIFFE

For Mother and Dad, who taught me to love poetry. And for Susie, who encouraged and believed in me.

She haunts my dreams and I cannot sleep.
She was one of us—a teacher:
A student of life who had reached the heights
Of her career, perhaps her life.
And I knew her,
Yet I did not even know her name.

I ache for her now, for me, for us,
For her students who watched, stunned
That moment that was the pinnacle of her life—
Her greatest moment; the end of her life—
Her last moment.
Yet I did not even know her name.

Chris Allen
MAN'S HOPE

This poem is dedicated in memory of my Dad—Marcus O. Allen, with whom I can only share this great event in spirit.

Oh, little children of the world!
What shame and sympathy man feels.
Our leadership has created a world of
War and despair
Hunger and homelessness
Drug abuse and child abuse.

Now, you must decide upon a leadership for man,
Beyond the tangled webs, that we have weaved.
For the beauty intended in life,
Has been buried deep within these webs—
And you must go beyond them—
To find a new way.

Forgive us children! for our misjudgements,
And follow us not!
For what life has man ahead,
If you continue our path of destruction.

Oh! little children of the world
Our future leaders of the world
Be strong, productive and take time—
To create a new leadership for mankind.
Oh! little children of the world
You are man's only HOPE . . . .

Donna M Star
LOSS OF INNOCENCE
The days of childlike, carefree pleasure
Are changed in ways without measure.
Never again can the body or soul be
Accepting of touch; relaxed and free.

For a look or word by which we're led
To a place of secret, whispered dread;
And the light-hearted skip or fleet-footed run
Are slowed to put off or hopefully shun . . .

Acts, which at such an early age,
Cause the trapped feeling, as in a cage.
Stripped of all modesty, with embarrassment and confusion;
And tumbled thoughts, that come in profusion.

How can we escape the next entrapment
Of our emotions, and our young body's enactment? . . .
To stroking, caresses; touching in places and ways
That come back to haunt us, all of our days.

For now, many, many years later,
The pit of our stomachs feel like a crater . . .
Filled with sad memories of innocence lost
By sexual abuse; at what terrible cost?

Arthur Robotham
WHEN WE LOOK BACK

This poem is dedicated to my loving Wife, Myrtle

When we look back across the years
To the day when we first met,
It seems like only yesterday—and yet,
Our love has blossomed year by year
Right from the very start,
And so with every new-born day
I love you more Sweetheart.

Valerie Brockel
LOVE IS SO CONFUSING
Love is so confusing
I wish I could understand,
All I ever wanted
Was for him to hold my hand.
When I see him walking by
I think about what to say,
But whenever I say "Hi"
He just looks the other way.
I sit up late at night
And wait for him to call,
But deep down in my heart
I know he doesn't care at all.
My friends don't really understand
What I'm going through,

They wonder why I don't give up
And look for someone new.
I will never forget him,
But now I must move on.
Hopefully someday he'll love me,
Hopefully that day won't be long.

Charolette E Hall

YOU MUST BE TRULY GOLDEN

I would like to dedicate this poem to my husband, George who encouraged me to believe that I could receive recognition by putting my faith forward.

This tribute is to you WAYNE, who served
the Lord and not in Vain
You must be special to have been chosen
Your life a blessing TRULY GOLDEN

You could have lived on this earth
Among the sin that comes to birth
Afraid to walk among the streets
Worried about when next you'll eat

BUT, you were special TRULY GOLDEN
No such pain will touch you again
No sleepless nights, no lonely heart
God has given you a "NEW START"

No worry of drugsters at your door
or prowlers around anymore
No thought of how the world feels
When you do things against their will

No Love, your worries of earthly things
will never have to touch you again
Yes, FAMILY will miss you but understand
That God has chosen a special man

Glen Caretta

RESTING PIECES

Like a calcium glockenspiel it lies in the dust
—played on by wind, barrow-weaving
—warmed by the sun, charnel-dancing.

Upthrust pieces of it, pointing
—yellowing, yellowing.
Jagged plates lie scattered;
invaluable stonework,
Like fine china abandoned.
It lies hollow.

The petrified, broken pipes of Pan.

The strings and glue have long vanished.
The marionette,
Inanimate,
Hints at fleshless hands
That once moved it about.

Annette Golding

POEM

Yellow periwinkles
White carnations
ferns
all in a whispering
cluster
another day folding
evening laywaits night
huddling
blind-lighted . . . . .

I wanted to write a poem
and the sunlight started
to tickle me
playing rings around my
iris
my pencil could not write
poetry standing all alone.
I said sun
let me write a poem
of your rays on my blinds
peeking
on my vase
throwing
shadows between my Hands.

Geraldean Mitton Hill

HEATHER

Before I left him
God said to me,
Smile, this special gift
I give to thee.
I've put a twinkle
In your eye,
That will shame the stars
In a summer sky.

Your lips I touched
With a budding rose,
While a drop of dew
Caressed your nose.
Each cheek I dimpled
With loving care,
As a gentle reminder—
I last kissed you there.

Linda Frazier

DOUBT

This poem is dedicated to my nephew Joe. Thank you for believing in me. Love, Nana

Evidently you don't know who I am.
Won't someone listen?
I am good!
I've spent 39 years trying to prove that I am.
I thought I was . . . . .
Won't someone listen?
I'm good at everything I do . .
Or I try to be.
Won't you give me a chance to show you that I am . . .
A good person with pride
Or I thought I was.
Maybe I'm not . . .
But I try to be.
Don't you know who I am?
I do . . . . .
And I don't have to prove
Anything to me anymore.
Because I know who I am.
Or do I?
Am I still on display?

Carzell Moore

DEATH STRIKES AGAIN

To Mirjam, the joy of my life—and strongest impetus.

All that's left
Is the funeral
And the reading of the will.
Another prisoner is executed.
Long live the VCR
And his and her king-size bed.
The Constitution is the hearse.
Apple pie
In the sky.
Bury the body
In a wooden box
Under the Southern cross,
Turn up the volume
Eat your ice cream
And read about it in the paper
But will you share the grief?
Give me an epitaph
Freedom is now at hand
Having never come before.

Robert S Parrish

TWILIGHT'S MANIFEST VISION

In loving appreciation to those who have always stood beside me offering encouragement—seen and unseen—special thanks to Scott & Carolyn Parrish, Al & June Castellucci and Mrs. Lillian Rolf

Caught in a vision, the night tolls,
a dream senseless takes hold,
An eternal scar from twilight's
morn, happened long before one was even born.

To what avail can a master mind
uncover the remnants of lost times
asunder. A shade of glory relates
antiquity's story. A hope for tomorrow
relinquishes its sorrow.

The yearning and desire is there to
cast grief and mourning aside. Be
forgotten by the might so invested
so that path be no more trod.

May the soul cry from within and
quiver to be free, for the heart
is the domain of those who possess it
and solely owned by those who are its king.

When the illusions fade, the sun will
remain and the horizon will be radiant
bright with the dawn's brilliant light
no more into darkness will we hide
or furthermore hideously stride but
in to the great almighty's love we
will surely abide.

John McCarey

for grandmother (1888-1987)

maternal moon
graying white,
tides recede
as memory ebbs
silently back
into peaceful night.

and hollow hull
body sinks below
into ocean womb
only to release
breath's final oval,
an ascending soul

reborn into
eternity
a star.

Clare Salata

OCEANIC OSMOSIS

The fishing lines glisten
in the morning sun.
Poles planted firmly,
as if expected to sprout.
Colorful coolers sit silently in a row.
The fishing people casually hang about,
exchanging interesting stories,
some truth, some lies.
Sea gulls fly and float,
creating a pace with their cries.
The ocean rises only to fall in a rush,
as it mightily brushes the shore.
Life is slow and settled and significant.
I make a promise to return for more.

The sun will rise and set;
the tide will flow high and retreat.
Here, life's rhythms are easy to feel,
as I shuffle my feet.
The well-fed cats stray
and the always-present black crows
scavenge and steal.

The pelicans are near
competing competently
with determination.
I ponder to myself that I sit securely
at the edge of a nation.
Beneath my fishing hat is a mellow me,
as the ocean reaffirms that I am free.

Connie Fox

NOTHING LASTS FOREVER

I had fun while we were together
But everyone knows nothing lasts forever
Maybe we can be some day again
'Cuz I hate the way this had to end
I want you to know I still care
And if you need a friend, I'll be there
I have lots of feelings for you,
And these feelings are so very true
Sometimes life is so unfair and unkind
It's hard to believe how much love is blind
It feels like something inside of me has died
As I think of you and how much I've cried
It's sad to think you are no longer mine
But I've got to go on with life one day at a time
I think of the fun we once had
And leave out the times that were bad
Whenever I see you, it really hurts
Knowing we could've made it work
I'll never forget when we were together
I only wish we could have lasted forever!

Melissa L Lewinter

A MAGIC MIRACLE

In the deepest, darkest dungeon
of the mind,
There soars a spirit fancy and free.
At times, this ghostly inhabitant
of the mind
Is scared and silent, and seems
not to exist at all.
But then, when it does break free,
All the world seems a rainbow,
promising renewed life.
But when this spirit of the mind
is locked in too tightly,
Sunshine cannot break through
and use its magical beams to awaken
The ghostly spirit of the mind.
The presence of the spirit must
only be as long as necessary
To awaken feelings of love, peace,
and happiness,
But no longer, for its magical
powers fade
When left out for too long
Or left unused for too long.
It is truly a fragile miracle that
each person possesses
In this truly beautiful spirit of
the mind.

Robert J Streit
STORM

To my son, who cared enough to read my poems, even when no one was watching.

Where earth and sky forever mate, I saw the drummer rise.
From Tara's edge the specter rose, and his song would shake the skies.
But his song was now mere prophecy, for he's not yet king nor lord.
He was but vanguard of the frenzy, herald to that warrior horde.
No longer gentle nomads caught amid the streams of heaven.
But in fury now a growing thing, and chaos was the leaven.
Dark with rage, it twists and turns, great rolling horde of prey.
Between earth and sky the fury rules and nothing bars its way.

The frightened wind is first to flee, then the trees began to fear,
and the grass in terror tries to run, for the storm is ruler here.
The rain is chased from heaven and seeks a place to hide.
This was the drummer's prophecy, ... this was what he cried!

Sometimes the thunder's so profound . . . .
its very shadow casts a sound.

Sometimes the lightning fills the skies . . . . .
with words too bright for human eyes.

Sometimes I must but stand in awe . . . . . .
touched with wonder at what I saw.

J S Walia

J S Walia
MY LOVE AND MY LUCK

This poem is dedicated to the loving memory of my beloved wife S. Surjit Kaur.

Gathering I am the pieces of my love,
Badly scattered are the pieces of my love,
Most precious to me is every piece of my love,
Unlucky I am in the matter of love,
Pushed I am from heaven to hell,
Down I am from sky to earth,
And thrown I am from palace to hut,
Badly I am hurt,
Widely scattered are the pieces of my love,
In grief my eyes do not work,
Still I am trying to collect,
Some pieces are covered with mud,
With my tears I am washing them,
And putting them back to regain my love,
I am in the worst,
Cannot utter a single word,
Gathering I am the scattered pieces of my love,
Most precious to me is my love,
Can any lover come up to my help?
And help me to recover my lost love?
Lovers always help the lovers,
I am in the worst!

Teresa D Keller
YOU ARE MY LIFE

To My Son: Michael David Kreidel Loving you more than I ever dreamed.

My son, you are the sunshine that brightens all my days
You're every thought that's in my mind
And the words to God I've prayed
You are my special someone, for whom I'll always strive
Because my son—I love you
Because you are my life

My Son, you are the sparkle in these sometimes weary eyes
You're the laughter in my smile and the teardrops when I cry
You're the beauty in the flowers that blossom fuller with each spring
Precious child you are the most cherished gift
My life could ever bring

My Son, You're all the tomorrows still yet to be
The pain and all the sorrows that our lives have not yet seen
You're the joy—the happiness I feel in each beat of my heart
the first time that I held you—I received a brand-new start

My Son, you're every inspiration I'll ever need in life
You're the brightest star up in the sky that shines on my darkest nights
You're the wonders that come with each passing day
and as mysterious as the night.
You are everything I'm living for
My Son, You Are My Life—

Shirley Posey Bedard
A MOTHER'S PRAYER

To my Mother Lura, whose great love and devotion will live in my heart forever. We were poor material wise, but Mother's love superseded what money could not buy me. May you rest in peace.

I sometimes like to sit and wonder just how much this world does ponder.
Over the many things that happen each day of all the things people do and say,
As we brisk along to our work and play to leave our dear Mother at home to stay.
Yet she just smiles and doesn't seem to mind, to do the many things we have left undone behind. Mother has many a war to win, to stand up for her children from without and within.
Yet I venture to say at this very hour in psalm,
Her children's whereabouts would lie in her palm. Or a Mother living who doesn't wonder how she can make her children happier in her hour of prayer, Or show just how much share cares. When we were little and not able to take, all the sadness we alone could make. Mother was always there to comfort and care,
Ask nothing in return for her goodness to share. Yet we do not think of those bygone days, Of our dear Mother and her cheerful ways. But one of these days we'll wake up and see, That at one time we should have tried her to please.
Mother was not put here forever to stay, And one of these days will be taken away. To another land more fair than day, Where she will have no more goodbyes to say. We should all stop and think if we meet her up there, Of all the joy and goodness we'll share. Yet we do not stop nor do we think, But just keep going around in this endless blink. God only knows what is in our heart today,
He should give us words to act and say to our dear Mother while on earth she is here.

Ms Linda M Thompson

Ms Linda M Thompson
TRIBUTE TO CARREN

Dedicated to Grandmom & Grandpop In appreciation of their love and support.

Sometimes when I'm tired, moody and down,
My face is stern and I'm wearing a frown.
As I watch baby Carren's antics at play;
She'll giggle and smile and brighten my day.
She's such a good baby, I want you to know;
She seldom cries, she just seems to glow
With a love overwhelming, it warms my heart so.
My six month old baby's a bundle of love
And I knew I've been blessed by God up above.

Dennis J Beus
TOUCH

Have you ever felt windows of time,
  Or crossed echoes with rhyme?
Lost episodes found fate's heart loves stone,
  Frosted to show its line.
Touch with no need then feel, lives to
  Face the intelligence of grace.
Watch to see what becomes of what you feel;
  Dreaming you find your place.
When the heart has a taste of touch,
  Take space to kneel—with love.
Prolific truth of kindness shown, when one touch
  Embraces what we are in time.
Traces of life embraced to last for
  How we have touched our mind.

N R Moore
REVELATION

Don't you feel it coming
The time is oh so near
The seals have all been broken
The signs are very clear.

It snowed in California
To the level of the sea
And the bodies of marine life
Have washed ashore, you see.

There's hunger in the Third World
And drought has killed the fields
Earthquakes plaguing all the earth
And crime no longer yields.

The Horsemen have begun their ride
The unbelievers fall
The Anti-Christ will show his force
His back's against the wall.

We call it Armageddon
Kneel down, repent, and pray
A new world is a coming
The MESSIAH's on His way.

Judy Lea Lavell
SANDS FALL—

Sands Fall—
  death breaks the beat of a heart,
but the hands continue to turn—
  turning always turning.
Time—And marks of time.

  Silence becomes a wailing,
    muffled by the night.
Peace finds no home here.
So we wait—
  hoping each hour will bring the redemption
  long sought for. But
the Sands Fall—
  And the hands keep turning.
Marking Time.

J Diane Eichel
IF I HAD SAID

The untold surpasses the told,
The hurt surpasses the love.
The things deep within my heart you will never know.
The way I want to hold you near
To kiss away each fear—each tear.
The way I long to touch your hand and say,
"I love you Dear."
My longing to be with you,
'Tis an ache you'll never see.
To share each golden sunset
And make you part of me.
And as the shade of life and time is drawn
Slowly over me
And my last breath hovers near,
I know that I will wonder what might have been
If I had said, "I love you Dear."

Vickie LaFleur
BEYOND LOVE

To Terry, with a little bit of love
Me

Your velvety touch
upon my skin.
Your warm smile
across my face.

Your whispery voice,
your gentle ways.
All these things
are like silken caresses
I feel each time
I'm with you.

You make me feel like a woman
I've never been before.
When we love
I cannot explain
the esoteric feeling of ecstasy
you bring forth
within my burning soul,

there are no words
for "beyond love."

Sheila M Boob
THE ACTOR
The music begins to fade and the curtains glide apart
The bright lights are shining and shining on him only
Everyone is transfixed
Hundreds of eyes are upon him as everyone waits for his first word or movement
His heart begins to race as fear sets in
His mind is searching frantically for the first line
And then, a quick blink of the eyes and a slow deep breath
Suddenly his body and mouth are moving
His mind stops searching and goes into a quiet lull
Every action and word comes automatically and his body relaxes as he starts enjoying himself
The performance is flawless
The curtains close and the last bow is taken
A sadness fills his heart as he realizes that it is over
Aaaah! He knows the old feelings well
For he has experienced them hundreds of times before
They are part of an actor's life.

David L Sheets
AUTUMN
How I love the autumn trees crowned by God with golden leaves.
How I love the first brisk wind that starts to blow when Fall begins.
How I love the morning frost upon a land where life seems lost.
How I love the autumn's snow reflecting back the moon's soft glow.
How I love the crisp, clean air which in the Summer seems so rare.
How I love and long to see what God has wrought from dying leaves.

Cindy Maureen Matheson
SADNESS SHEDS A TEAR

Written in loving memory of two special people dear to my heart—Grandpa and Grandma Matheson

Though days have passed and we have changed
Our thoughts of you have still remained
The love we shared throughout the years
Of joyful laughter and heartfelt tears
The stories told of lifetimes passed
These precious memories will always last
And though our sadness sheds a tear
Not just today but through the year
Our hearts are warmed to know
God's way
Will bring us back together some day.

Angela E Johnson
MARTIN, THE MAN
A multi-faceted man of immeasurable talent,
An uncomplicated man of truth,
A man who identified with his fellow man,
Adults as well as the youth,
He left us with a legacy to guide and strengthen us every day,
He preached and taught non-violence
To all he met along life's narrow way,
He stood tall in times of adversity
In spite of trials and tribulations,
He believed in the Almighty,
Despite the fact that ofttimes his life was filled with complications and frustrations.
He will never be forgotten for generations to come,
He was, still is and will always be a giant among men,
Despite the fact that his work is still being done.

Kathryn C DeBerg
I AM RAIN
With pleasure I fall
touching the earth.
Embracing all nature
for all its worth.
In harmony I nurture.
In harmony life takes.
To fulfill a small purpose,
without backbreaking aches.
It's nature cleansing,
to feel new and fresh.
Let me send you some joy,
let me tingle your flesh.
Once in awhile—
don't take cover from me.
I just want to touch you.
The pleasure is free.

Sara Ann Stancil

Sara Ann Stancil
GRANDPA HAD A "KNACK"

To my very special Grandpa, James "Jim" Franklin Kay

His yellowed nails and calloused hands
Still linger in my mind . . .
I always loved to talk with him
His voice was soft and kind
In memory I see him . . .
He's cooking at the stove
I still recall the gentle way he turned the eggs;
The scent of bacon, as it rose
He never had a second thought
When diapers needed changing
And when the kids would wreck the house,
He'd help with rearranging
Those memories have stayed with me
I cherish them today . . .
"Your Grandpa had a knack with kids."
That's what my Mom would say.

Nalani N L Ferreira
YOU WERE MAGICAL THEN

To Esther and Gregory Kuamo'o
My Mom and Dad
Aloha Pumehana

When I was little,
I'd search for the boy in the rocking chair
I'd wait till you were full and shining bright
I never found him

You were magical then

We'd go camping on the beach
With only you to light the sky for us
I wondered how big you were
And how you could get so thin

You were magical then

Now that I'm older,
You'd think I'd know better—but—
I still look for my little boy
Never finding him

I thank you for your beauty
And enjoy the romantic fullness
And brightness of your glow

You were magical then and you still are

Thank you, Mr. Moon.

Veronica L Pajé
OFTEN THE TEST OF COURAGE BECOMES
Often the test of courage
becomes rather to live than die.

It matters not how long we
live, but how

We come & we cry & that
is life

We yawn and we depart
that is death.

Shirley J Dybdal
DEATH TODAY
I saw death today.
It came without warning.
And took my love away.
Death has no face, no identity—
And much too bold.
Death is eternity—
He took my life away,
And yet I breathe, I cry.
There is nothing I can say.
I hear the voices of our friends,
And still I want to die . . .

Michael "Misha" DellaFemina
ALEXI
Angel passing by
The devil sniffing round
Awaiting a passive moment
Too much strength to let him near
Go on try
I laugh at your so called
Power
I throw my flesh in your
So called
Flames
And come out bronzed and full of life
Go
On your way
You have no power here
I'll flirt with your passions
I'll laugh at your jokes
But just when you think you have me
In your wretched soul
Look in my eyes and be
mistaken
I spit in your heartless
wound
Your so called soul
And go on my way . . .

Kelli Morning
THIS FINAL FLIGHT

To the recently departed, Mrs. Ruth Caroline Steele/Thacker, my loving grandmother and most esteemed friend.

High up are we,
Beyond the sky,
As held to be,
Unmeant to die.

These hearts entwined,
Two souls in flight,
By day invined,
Aloft by night.

As hand in hand,
We ride the wind,
Begin this flight,
Before its end.

Approaching land,
These vows we take,
Unspoken words,
Promises we make.

Try not, confine
These wings so wide,
For vows shall break
In lesser stride,

So off we soar
With all our might,
As we begin
This final flight.

Olive Ruth Boyer
MY PRAYER
I pray to the God of the universe in me
(In me, as much as I allow it to be).
I thank the Creator for all that I see:
For my love for my fellows and their love for me.

To express my love, I'll accept where they are.
And accept that they follow a much different star.
If I try to change them—their life I will mar.
I'd alter their life-flow and cause there a scar.

I want to love them,
to accept
and set free,
And not try to make them
a copy of me.

Diane Bailey
SWEET INDIA

It is with love that I dedicate this poem to Deana, my sister and best friend.

Come closer, love.
How I long for your arms
To surround me; to envelop me.

Let the raindrops fall
Upon your eyes of blue.
For they have touched your flesh
And, oh, what I would give
To be as close to you as they.

I know others have kissed them.
Please give me the chance, won't you.

For I know I would never again
Wish to be found.

Say that there is a chance for me.
Say that the sun will never shine
If it means a lifetime of we two
Running in the rain's mist together.

Guarantee me your soul,
Guarantee me some happiness, and
Guarantee me that the rains of
Ranchipur
Will come again.

Diana L Hendrickson
I SAW YOU TODAY

To A Very Special Friend . . .

I saw you today
Spoke with you.
Touched your soft skin
All in a memory.

You were happy, smiling
The way I remember best.
I felt so very close to you.
It all seemed so real.

You entered my life,
Only a short year ago.
Yet I feel I've known you
From a long time ago.

You touched my heart and soul
In so many ways.
I'm not so sure as to why
But the feeling stays.

You enter my dreams
As a deer enters the forest.
Ever so quiet,
Yet ever present.

Marguerite Palffy-Ross
AMERICA

To my sons Anthony and Berry

Glorious sunsets
Prairies with dew
Great herds of buffalo
Forests with song-birds singing too
Eagles soaring through the skies
Majestic mountains that hypnotize

Laughing water in clear blue streams
Come to the elders in their dreams
Land of plenty pure and clean
A place the children have not seen

Kirsten Ramsay
WHY SUICIDE?
Fear came to me one day,
When my friend turned to me to say,
Fortunately I never died,
'Cuz last night I attempted suicide!
With white bandages on her arm,
She covered the harm,
At least the slits weren't too deep,
That's why she can still weep.
That night I turned to her and sighed,
And asked her, Why Suicide?
She said with a tear in her eye,
It hurt deep inside that's why.
Day by day I sit and listen,
I think that was what she was
missin',
'Cuz the other day,
She turned to me to say,
Thanks I needed you to listen,
That was what I was missin',
She stopped and sighed,
And muttered, Why Suicide?

Edith May Snowball
HOW FAR AWAY IS FAR MY LOVE

Welcome; Denise & Blanche; You're The Gold At The End Of The Rainbow; Sons Brian & Trevor; Love; Health; Happiness; Now & Always

How Far Away Is Far My Love
As the winds whistle my love to you;
How Far Away Is Far My Love
Till the tide turns
And carries your love back to me,

In every branch; in every twig;
There my love I will be
On every bird that takes to wing
There my love flies free;
So How Far Away Is Far My Love
How far I ask of you,

'Tis never but a teardrop away
In a stream real close to you
And flowers' heads held high
Is the way I always see you
So How Far Away Is Far My Love
As the breezes sway you left and
right
How Far Away Is Far My Love
As I pluck you for my Wife.

E Marice Riggs
MASQUERADE

To my family, Linder, Nancy, Aimeé (for being my first proofreader!), and Dawn Clemens. All of you deserve credit for encouraging me to continue utilizing my writing gift! Special thanks and dedication goes to the Lord!

I can be me,
Or who I want to be.
It matters to neither you nor me.
We are both clowns and
comics . . .
Free! ! !

We're droplets of water in an
incessant sea,
Painting our eyes with green of peas,
Puckering our lips in reproach of
bitter teas,
Tainting our laughter with the honey
of bees.

Ain't that a shame?
'Cause no one hears our pleas,
To do and say what we please?

Mary Scott
THE GOLDEN YEARS AHEAD
How dear to us are memories of days
that long have flown,
And dearer still they seem to be as
we have older grown.
Our first dance, how long ago that
now seems to be,
As when first you held my hand, and
whispered soft to me.

And on the day our hearts, as one,
were bound in love;
How filled my heart then seemed to
be, with blessings from above.
Then children came, each in its turn,
and troubles came as well,
And at times my heart would ache,
more than I care to tell.

But these things pass, the years go
by, Our family now is grown,
The silver strands amid the brown,
now generously are sown.
Golden years now lie ahead upon the
path we trod;
And brighter still the doorway shines,
that leads the way to God.

Joyce A Hubbard

Joyce A Hubbard
FELINE ENVY

Dedicated to Pookie, a magnificent orange-striped furry mop of mild mischief, who never fails to amuse my family with his sophisticated silliness.

I envy my cat—
Can you fancy that!
With not a care on his mind.
Except for maybe—
When his next trip will be,
To his bowl to wine and dine.

He spends hours and hours,
Staring out at the world.
Any motion he never misses.
Safe behind the glass door—
Life is such a pleasant bore!!
And there isn't any reason for hisses.

An affectionate rub across my legs
will say,
"Here's your feline friend, I love you,
let's play!
No Fonda tapes for me, but I'll chase
a string for you,
And I'll burn up those calories twice
as fast as you do!"

Alas, he has no crazy job to hold,
No ugly bills or mortgage to pay.
He just lazily, gracefully grows old,
As he sleeps his nine lives away!

Elaine T Potter
A CHILD IS ALIVE
Oh little baby so sweet and small
If only you could tell us all, how it
feels when you first know that you're
alive,
What is it like when you first come
outside?

Was it your first breath of fresh air
you took all on your own? Or the first
feel of someone's warm flesh,
holding you so close and so dear?

Was it your first time seeing the
world outside? Did the soft singing
birds or the gentle winds, whisper a
sweet song in your ears? Did they tell
you that you were alive?

I guess it's a question that will
always go unanswered, one can
never tell when they first felt alive,
except for a child when it's growing
inside.

Linda S Day
A SUMMER'S DAY A SKY OF BLUE:
A summer's day, a sky of blue:
And all I do is think of you:
I stroll along, I look around:
The beauty should to all astound:
A tiny brook, a bounding deer:
A gentle breeze whispering in my
ear:
A field of clover round the bend:
The flowers reach to kiss the wind:
You take my hand, and walk with
me:
I give my heart and soul to thee:

Dale Conner Lowrey
HELLO WORLD
Hello World I'm coming out
To see what life for me is meant to
be.
You think I'm scared?
You bet I am!
I'm still young and unaware
Of things that are happening out
there.
So give me knowledge
So I can know,
And strength so I can say,
Hello World, I'm here!

Darryl Fisher
TIME FOR THOUGHT
A person not quite on the edge
Sits alone still trying
As he sits thinking
With the sounds of darkness
Filling the empty room
While he stares at a dim light
He knows not what to do with his
life
But he knows one thing that makes
everything right
Cheers.

D Gail Johnson Robinette
THERE HE SITS
There he sits, with nothing to say;
No explanations, no excuses,
nothing.
His facial expression is ridden with
guilt;
I can't reach him anymore.
His eyes are at a faraway distance,
The closeness we once shared is no
longer there.
We used to sit and talk for hours,
always confiding in each other's
inner thoughts,
No secrets between us.
There he sits, waiting and wondering
how he should tell me;
That the moments we shared
together don't really mean
a damn thing now.

I thought our love would never end, a love so great and strong.
All we had to do was gaze into each other's eyes, and the flame would start anew.
Now he can't even look at me.
Our love has conquered many obstacles before, ones we could laugh about afterwards;
But somehow, I feel it's different this time.
There he sits, contemplating, and trying to think of an easier way of telling me . . . it's over.

Hugh D Di Maio
LOVING YOU
Thoughts of a sunny day gone by
Our hearts running in the wind
A day my mind reminds me with a sigh.
Oh what a day to be on display
But now my mind has to forget
Loving you I cannot regret
It only lingers in days gone by
Hoping to catch a new day by surprise
I'm patient, heart yearning to fly high
If only they'll realize,
I'm just a man in search of love

Paul B Hadley Jr

Paul B Hadley Jr
A LOVE POEM
The thousand suns of morning,
Reflecting from the dew;
The clouds of pure white beauty,
Caressed with crimson hues;
The warming earth and loving light,
All form a beauty rare;
And turns my gaze inside itself,
To see you standing there.

You are pure love incarnate,
And all that it implies!
Takes form in living beauty,
As that within your eyes:
If something cries for guidance,
And asks where to begin:
You take its life within your breast,
And bring forth love again.

I long to spend some time as one,
And spread truth everywhere;
And maybe open others' hearts,
To the love that's waiting there.

Kathryn Rimmer Braswell
I SHALL NOT GRIEVE
This is the time of our love and the place,
But when the hour and the environ fade,
Should I, in memory, recall your face
And find time's keen-edged chiseling has made
A stranger's of a countenance once more
Familiar than my own, I shall not grieve.
Nor yet should you on learning this abhor
My seeming lack of constancy—believe
Me faithless. This I know: our love is bound
By circumstance and fixed forever in
The flow of time. Could we but come around
Again to where this hour and place begin,
We'd find the wonder of our oneness lies
Forever mirrored in each other's eyes.

Barbara Donnici Gioffre
AD UNA RONDINE

Dedico questa poesia al mio caro Orlando; Affinchè la sua memoria rimanga sempre viva nel mio cuore.

Oh rondinella libera che vai
volando su per monti e verdi valli;
in aria e sugli alberi ti posi
padrone sei tu dove ten vai,

Vorrei anch'io come te volare,
andar dov'il mio cor vorrebbe andar
rivedere i luoghi tanto cari
dove vissi giorni di allegro star.

Li penso tanto e non li so scordar
quei luoghi tanto semplici e desii.
Forse volerò come tu fai
quando la mia anima dal corpo si divide.

O rondinella! Quella volta sai,
vienimi incontro non andare via,
mi mostrerai i luoghi a me si cari;
mi sarai vicina rondinella mia.

Holly Lee Beaver
WHEN CHILDREN CRY
When children cry
There is a reason inside
When the little ones cry
They're usually hungry inside
When the big ones cry
They're usually lonely inside
For whatever reason they should cry
Someday our children will die
And they'll never have to cry again

Elena J (Morrissey) Beyeler
TRY TO REMEMBER AND KEEP IN YOUR HEART

This poem is dedicated to my sister Donna who is now the proud mother of a beautiful baby boy, Michael James!

Try to remember and keep in your heart
The feelings you felt when right from the start
You learned of the life you helped to created
And thinking somehow that it must have been fate
Remember those days how quickly they've passed
But soon to be born in your child at last
And when that moment happens
When that day is finally here
And you hold your tiny baby
For the first time oh so near
The anxieties, the worries you may have ever felt
will somehow seem to vanish as your heart begins to melt
For the life you hold within your arms is such a special joy
That precious little baby your little girl or boy
Such feelings overwhelm you and may take you by surprise
When you often least expect it and the tears well in your eyes
Just take the time to realize if only for a minute
How truly special life's become now that your baby's in it
And when you do I hope that you will find there is no other
No greater love not anywhere than that of Child and Mother

John Leon Webb
SEARCHING
I'm searching
for something I can't find;
Something I know that's deep in my mind.
I'm reaching
for something that's far yet so near;
Something that gives me a feeling of fear.
I'm searching

I'm reaching
But I don't understand
What it is that makes a man a man.
I'm searching
for something I can't see.
Maybe I'm really searching for me!

Dorothy Louise Rhodes
STREET PEOPLE
Caught in a half life of existence, You dwell among the stares of curious others, The rift between society so great a gulf you can't pass over.
You move among the cities towering tombs of concrete, glass, and steel. The island-thoroughfare of artificial green—your garden. You spread a fare of junk-food, with your world possessions crumpled, dank and dirty, in brown plastic bags.
That lie in heaps, though only small heaps, on the island-thoroughfare. Your feet tread the steps I take, Your hands pull the same door pull to enter a corner Mart for days provisions, yet in searching eyes for common recognition I find a vague expression; weariness, incomprehension.

Come dawn I see You hovered in deserted door-ways Your bed a stack of old news paper, repose seems less sleep than stupor.

What tangled thoughts possess Your mind.
What avenue of fate has life directed.
Street People.

Cullenea "Lynn" Woodruff
REMEMBER ME
Remember me full of joy,
and not of sorrow.
Remember me laughing,
and not the tears.
Remember me full of spirit,
not lifeless.
Remember me with a smile,
not a frown.
Remember me when I helped you,
not when I turned away.
Remember me full of love,
not full of hate.
Remember me through all the good,
for if you remember the bad only,
you will be full of sorrow.
Remember when we meet,
and not the ending.
For it has not ended,
but just started all over again.

Sharline Maria Thomas
THE ROSE

Know it is true—HE sent the answer just for you. The answer is LOVE! Remember to love one another!

From Seed and Sun—
Through Truth of budding time—
Past Galaxlan mass of Stars—
Unbidden—
Love passed through I.T.'s mind!
The homeward journey eons long—
The Dawning Light past space and time—
Sweet affinity of fire and rose—
Rekindle now in me—
Now Love the miracle divine—
Which all in Heaven know—
Continues—
As The Flame returns to kiss the rose!

J Quenton Grider
BY CHANCE!

This is dedicated to my Mother, who taught me about friends and encouraged me!

Should we meet along the way,
and stop to talk
Let's not discuss the weather,
It matters not;
nor bank accounts, or what we've got.
For those things are unimportant,
and who knows the time we have?
Instead speak of each other,
perhaps even of ourselves.
Then when we have to leave,
if our paths don't cross again,
We'll speak of that day and say,
by chance I met a friend!

Wendy Raquel Nickols
FRIENDSHIP
Proverbs 17:17 says, "A friend loveth at all times."

Friends are ones who care.
Friends are always there.
When you are in need,
Friends are there to lead.
Friends always help and share.
Friends love and are fair.
Friends laugh in a special way.
Friends brighten your day.
But there is one Friend,
Whose friendship will not end,
Whose love never ceases.
That Friend's name is Jesus.

Proverbs 18:24 says, "But there is a friend that sticks closer than a brother."

Karen Dawn (Mumaw) Polk or "Krystal Kitten"
TO A VERY SPECIAL MAN
People still talk about a "poor boy" who made it "big"
He started in his "teenage years"—driving a grocery truck, & on the side raising an occasional pig
He grew to be a "huge man" about, 350 pounds on anyone's scale
As in everyone's life, once did fail

But determination, in his heart
He picked himself up, as a carpenter did start
Through the years, he kept moving—
Finally, "Contractor," right on top
But being a man with a great big heart,
His generosity, did not stop
He built houses, stores, an apartment, a nursing home & a pool hall
And this "God-loving man," never once thought he was better than all
He raised 4 children, always
Showing his "love" the same
He even gave the 4th baby, "his own full name"
I loved "this man," who never taught bad,
For you see,—"this man," was: "my very own Dad"

Daniel R Coyne
SWEET, SWEET LOVER
All I want
is a kiss.
From a sweet,
Sweet lover.
All I miss,
is a kiss.
From a sweet,
Sweet lover.
How do I meet
A sweet,
Sweet lover.
When all the streets
Are covered,
With artificial
Lovers.

James Michael Teel (Pen Name)
SNOWBIRD
Through the wintry storm and the snowy night
I see a robin in its southward flight.
It fights its way to a frozen tree
And as it lands a red-bird flees.

As I stood and gazed at this frightened bird
My mind became so misty and blurred.
And the visions passed through my empty mind,
Of the wintry world of all mankind.

I thought of all the snowy days
And of the wages that happiness pays.
I dreamed of snowy winters past
And prayed that the snow would forever last.

I gazed upon the mountains, white-crowned
And slowly turned as I sadly frowned,
For this wintry world would soon be past
As upon the robin my thoughts were cast.

But the bird had flown from its frozen perch
And ascended to a endless search,
For its true place in life is secretly hidden
As upon nature's wings it has forever ridden.

Carol M Plant/Garber
A WALK IN THE MEADOW
Wandering in the meadow
so beautiful with birds;
I see your face
I hear the words.

Gazing at the flowers
watching the butterflies;
Your voice is soft
tears fill my eyes.

Trying to go on
without thinking about you;
Watching two love birds
What do I do?

The birds are so happy
the butterflies gay;
The flowers so beautiful
I Love You . . .Today.

Shelah M Conner Coursey
TIME
Yesterday, today, tomorrow,
Past, present, future,
Child, adolescent, adult,
Time moves on.
Yesterday what I planned for today, has been put off until tomorrow.
In the past I longed for the present, and now I look forward to the future.
As a child I could hardly wait to be an adolescent, but then longed to be an adult.
So now, it's tomorrow and my future as an adult has not yet reached my expectations.
Where is that time?
It's gone with the tomorrows that I planned for my future as an adult.

Maria Dona Corvaia

Maria Dona Corwaia
SACRED SOULS
Blackness all around me
In a dusk so earthly rare
The lonely souls of the forgotten ones
Linger lost within the air
The faint smell of burning brimstone
Captures our souls
A mixture of forgotten dreams
Never to be told
The shiver of this icy chill
Runs deep into this land
The message they are sending us
Runs free without command
O heed these breathless words I say
for those who speak them know
Beyond this world there lies a place
Where we buried those unknown
For the unknown soldiers of our wars
Lie still beneath the ground
But their cries are heard
Throughout the world
Though they never make a sound
Autumn comes and goes again
In verdant fields of bliss
But those who mourn the unknown ones
Can seldom let them rest.
For deep within their sacred souls
The calling's always heard
From the place where rows of white tombstones
Lie solid, void of words
Sleep till dawn my precious ones
The morning's drawing near
For with each new day
That's one less day
I must shed my unknown tears.

Charles R Mitchell
SHE TOLD US
Dear little girl with golden hair
You told us of Jesus, and how He cares
Told of His great love and forgiveness too
Told us of how He cares for me and you
Told of how He died at Calvary
How they nailed Him to that old tree
How with His blood, He set us free
How much He cares for you and me
Told of how, on that third day He arose
Just like it had been foretold
How he joined His Father above
And how we can share in His great love
Dear little girl, on a field of white
Soon you will be gone from our sight
Now you can join Him, He's waiting there
He's taking you back, into His care
Grieve not Mother and Daddy dear
I'm with Jesus, you keep Him near
We will meet you, hand in hand
When you join us, in the promised land

Dawn E Flickenschild-Stewart
GOD'S CHOSEN WAY

In Memory Of
Mr. Edward Bertram Foote
December 17, 1988

Our thoughts and prayers are with you
On this Christmas Day.
Don't be sad and lonely.
It's just God's Chosen Way.

He took away the one you loved.
He now has him by His side.
He took away your loved one's pain
To give him peace of mind.

Remember him with memories
And the love that you once shared.
His hurt and pain are gone now
He's in God's special care.

He's celebrating with the Highest One.
I'm sure he's by His side,
To celebrate the birth of Christ
He now has a special guide.

So remember him this Christmas Day
With love and joy, not pain.
For now he too is celebrating
He has taken God's Chosen Way.

Nancy Carol Powell
BEING A FRIEND
In a distance I see a young lad,
He seems so lost and out of place.
Looking for something he can not find,
Yet searching on hoping, showing faith.
Closer I come near,
And see a tear.
There is a fear in his eyes,
All at once he noticed me with surprise.
Not able to speak,
Yet his face shows sign of relief.
Putting out my hands to show I care,
He smiles.
Then he turns as if to say do I dare?
I feel I have lost,
But all at once he turns;
And runs to my waiting arms.
Looks up to say I am glad you care,
And I care too!
The special bonding of a friend,
Was the two of us that day.

Michelle L Engelhart
TEARS OF THE SPECIAL NIGHT
I give you this poem to have and to hold
to always remember
The love we have shared.
I will never forget how our love was so right,
The memories we made on that special night.
Our bodies together as we became one,
It was right at the the time, but now it is wrong.
I love you and I always will,
When I was with you everything was well.
But now that you are so far away,
I seem to get worse every day.
So, remember this poem, and hold it so dear,
Never forget the memories we've shared.
So, I say good-night, and I kiss you good-bye,
I tell you I love you, with tears in my eyes.

Karen D Doyle
WITH LOVE AND AFFECTION

This is for Cass, who came into my life during one of the hardest times I've ever had, and who gave me the strength I needed to make it through.

Your thoughts come, on paper, from miles away;
And, I smile as I read what you have to say;
You speak of a lifestyle, so pure and clean;
A style, I admit, I have never seen.

I believed, for so long, that drugs conquered all;
Even when they caused me to stumble and fall.
The thought never even occurred to me
That there could be peace in reality.

I'm impressed with your style;
you're so confident.
Your advice is such that I cannot resent.
With each of your letters, my will gets much stronger;
And, I feel that our friendship will last that much longer.

My friend, you've made a deep impression on me,
That could alter my lifestyle, permanently.
I want to thank you, with all of my heart;
And ask that, as friends, we never will part.

Barbara LaMae Grandchamp
REASON TO TRUST

Dedicated to my five daughters, Shelley, Leah, Peggy, Darlyn, Kristi.

Give me reason to love and trust you
It's a shame something like this has happened.
Maybe it will bring us closer together again.
I love you, but you've given me reason,
Not to trust or believe in you.
Maybe in time my trust will flourish.
We are young and in time we'll find our way.
Both must trust and love each other.
Forget past mistakes, and strive for everlasting trust and love.

Gary Toole
CAROLYN

Life was meaningless,
Till you came along.
Loneliness haunted me,
But in my heart you put a song.

I could have had many,
But none would do.
It had to be someone special—
Baby that's you.

I could have searched the end of a rainbow,
To find the pot of gold.
But only in your loving arms,
Do riches I hold.

For our love is more precious than rubies
You're the diamond of my heart.
From the time our eyes first met,
It was love from the very start.

As the petals of the rose fall
To blanket the earth and catch the morning dew.
So does your love cover my heart,
To you, I'll always be true.

Before we met I was in a prison of depression,
Seemingly hopeless to be.
But you came along and had the key
To unlock my heart—to set me free.

There's not enough paper,
Ink, or a quill
To write all my heart
And how I feel.

But I'll say it all in three short words,
Maybe that will do.
You're the love of my life,
Darling—I love you.

Your Only Husband
Gary Toole
Year—1983

James H McCrea
INDIGENCE

Poverty is not having meat on the table,
Wearing rags instead of new clothing,
Watching as rats and roaches pass by,
A child's cry for a decent meal,
And wondering if there will be better times.
To be stricken by poverty is to know death.
Many smother in their own wealth & could give a damn about the needy!
We talk of peace & of love,
Yet we often neglect the starving.
What about these forgotten people,
Who have never found the right road?

Thomas J Hackett
BELOVED FRIEND

Dedicated in honor of Anastasia Mun-Hi Song whose friendship gave a whole new dimension to my understanding of love and the joyous celebration of life.

What can be said of this resplendent cloak of wonderment which thou hast girded me?
To speak that it has filled my life with light and love is an utterance of one dumb with eyes who cannot see.

What of these joys that gird my earth as stars upon the darkness of a fallen night? The wonder of knowing such a love that standing side by side a noon day's summer sun retains its light.

Oh spectre of my soul, struggling within the dark of night to siege my land, this light cast of love's enormity strips thee as a coward of thy substance to command.

What blessed nectar from the grapes of life this love has pressed, ferments a vintage Joyance swelling within this staven heart caressed.

I pray, keep not the sweet elixir of such wondrous brew alone to thee. Extend thy chalice full to sate another's thirst of heart. In such its golden fruit will be.

And in thy twilight days of each own soul's memory, cast back thy knowing glance on two who touched to see, the wonder of a poet's heart in spaken word and bind them to remembrances of love . . . and we.

Lora Lee Adcock
THE BRIDGE WITHIN

Any bridge takes you from
a place you need not be
and in crossing over,
becomes just history.

A bridge is for leaving
also for the coming home;
you may weary of the road
and no longer wish to roam.

And per chance if you long
past friends and fond sites to see,
yes you may cross again
on the bridge of memory.

There is a constant yearning
within our hearts it seems;
We believe crossing over
is the answer to all our dreams.

The Lord knows our every thought;
that our will is very thin;
and on that one final day
we could never hope to win.

We know that in Christ Jesus
our last journey will begin
that leads us to His Father,
for He is that bridge within.

Bobbi Bell
CRYSTAL CASTLE

Look at my walls.
How they're cracked.
My crystal castle I erected about
me is in shambles.
I put it up for both of us.
So you could see me;
inside and out.
But you threw rocks.
You wrecked my walls,
And broke my castle.
And you have hurt us both.
For now,
You will never know
Me.

Brenda S Evans
IN REFLECTION

to my catalytic friend . . . Pete

With cascaded eyes,
I viewed his silhouette.
Him so eager for me to see,
What he had to offer.
In blushing silence
I breathed in,
and felt passions thud.

Then souls' eyes directly focus,
to hurts that lie within.
Contact high is broken,
as hums quiver slowly closes.
Exposure so complete,
even tho fully clothed,
in earth's woven ware . . . .

He stilled my soul
completely,
allowing me to birth a tear.
Looking past his silhouette
our spirits now as one
We embrace without compulsion,
true friendship has been won.

Frances Ann Richard
MY HEART SINGS THE WORDS

This is dedicated to and in memory of Elnora (Nannie) Schneider, my sweet Mother.

My Lord gently whispers,
Tender words in my ears,
"These Loving notes from your Momma,
to your heart, you may share.
Choose the words carefully,
Don't be too free!
We can't let just anyone
Know about the special key!
Whether Locked in your heart
In your special care
Or lovingly written
So, that all just might share!"

Patricia A Henderson

Patricia A Henderson
LOVE WILL STILL REMAIN

To condemn myself.
To want . . . . .to need . . . . . . to torture.
To provoke and thrive on the evil within
And then to expect that love might live.

But how can love live when hurt continues to rape my heart?
Pitted in the darkest corner of my mind, the seed has already been planted.
Once again, it attacks with force, tugging at every fiber of my body
Until every cell has surrendered in disgusting defeat.

Fling outward, oh beast of the soul!
Before nests are built ;
Before the vultures devour the good,
The good that needs only time.

Fulfillment! Let it stray into nothingness and find its own way home.
Thoughts! Let them fly with the sunshine and tickle the vanishing wind.
Let only the good penetrate.
Deeper . . . . . And deeper . . . .And deeper.
Until doubt is but a memory and fear has tiptoed away.

Then my heart can smile, and my burdens will be light
For all but love is cast down. Only love remains.
And in the end I, too, will see that all but love has been cast down
For in the end I will be. Yes, I <u>with love</u> will still remain.

Joseph Parker Hall III
ALL YOU DESTROY

This poem is dedicated to the wildlife of Alaska for taking their coats and replacing the coats with oil.

The cartoon is over
And only the truth remains
The charade we have been playing
Is drawing to an end
And the whole experience
Has left the world drained
We have been laughing at the mirror
Pretending what we see isn't real
And the fact remains
After the sad reality of it all
We have taken all we could steal
Trash keeps washing up on the shore
Amber waves of grain no more
The image leaves a blood red stain
As we ride the storm of acid rain
After all is said and done
The blunt reality of it all is
All you destroy we cannot build again.

Timothy L Wilson
SHE

To DLC: The most caring, understanding, and loving person I know. Remember you're my best friend first, for which I treasure. Because you're the only one who can make my dreams come true. Love ya, TW.

Woman, Friend, Lover, Mother and Wife,
These are the things I need in my life,
A Woman to whom I've given my heart,
Knowing we'll never part,
A Friend when I'm feeling really sad,
A Friend to share my happiness when I'm feeling glad,
A Lover to me for which I treasure,
One who brings out my inner most pleasure,
As a Mother I find you will always succeed,
By giving the children all the love and care they need,
As my Wife you would be a perfect mate,

Lord, am I glad we made a date,
Woman, Friend, Lover, Mother and Wife,
Would you like to bring these things into my life?

Marion F Davis
LOVE
The sea assumes a daytime unconcern,
Endlessly occupied with boats,
And birds on horizontal scenes;

But one blue night of secrets and of dreams
I saw the sea
Go wild about a stretch of shore,
I saw the sea
Reach longing arms to touch the bare earth's face,
And strain to rest embosomed in that place.

Neda Ursic
I OFTEN THINK OF REASONS
I often think of reasons why
we're born, we live, and one day die
we laugh, and hate, love and cry
feel pain and pity, brave and shy
I've searched the world for peace of mind
I've been unjust, I've been unkind
and still not see the reason why
my heart is empty, my smile a lie
I may look happy, I may look glad
but within myself, I'm very sad
I give my heart, I give my all
sometimes I'm big, sometimes I'm small
the loves I've lost are my own cost
but the biggest pain and hurt I feel
is when I've trusted friends not real.

Miguel Gonzalez-Fouchea
1988
Fast cars, city lights
People walk without going anywhere
The blind man on the corner
gently asks for compassion
But no one seems to care
Nobody listens to the truth anymore
Lies fill the dense, polluted air
Power is on the roam
For more souls to enchant with galore

Fast cars, city lights
Death is on the streets
Walking pills, dollar bills
killing machines are not behind
Why do we look without seeing
Can we listen, do we care?

Kevin Foster-Bey
ADVENTURE OF PAIN

To my grandmothers; Marie Stokes, Eddie L. Ray, mother Shirley Foster, my deceased father Clarence Stokes, Family, my spiritual Bro. Rev. Jesse Jackson, Min. L. Farrakan, Bill Cosby, World Vision Christian Min., Moorish Science Temple and Shrine of Black Madonna.

As thoughts pass through my mind, there's a message that I must proclaim,
But shuuu . . . . . .ssh, it's a secret, keep it to yourselves and it's called the adventure of pain.
You may wonder what I know about this, but my experience has reached a height,
There are some who think they're better than others, and oppressing them in secret and in plight.
Standing before some judge a Dove and a Crow, he says to the Dove, I'll send you to a place where you can learn and be loved, he says to the other, you're caught little brother, off to prison you go.
So listen to me close all my brothers, but a word of this never utter.
For the time will come when we will have our chance,
To triumph over our oppressor in song and in dance.
Yes that day is coming when victory we will claim,
But even so, and as I stand here today, I will always remember
the adventure of pain.

Joan Pszeracki
VA-VOOM-VACUUM!
Va-voom-vacuum cleans the room
from the old to the new—doing what it will do, suctioning up dirt
So many kinds to choose from,
but jet-propelled is my favorite
Turn it on and magically, it mooo-ves . . .
Hold on to handle as it glides
you around—it sweeps—"weew!"
Another fun one is filled with water,
cleaning as it suctions, with long
handled apparatus for easy maneuver
Then there's the don'ts—pick up
bobby pins, long strings of carpet
which wrap and entangle and clog and
chock and spit and smoke and scream and
chug and eat up the rug! Change the bag and gag—
throw some moth balls in and grin
Place attachment in and
"COME ON BABY, SUGAR PIE!"
THAT'S A GIRL! Follows you from room to room—from corner to
corner Turn it off, turn it on
and yawn I'm getting my exercise
Beats a broom!
"VA-VOOM-VACUUM!"

Ruth S Nicoli
WHEN YOU THINK THAT LIFE HAS DOWNED YOU
When you think that Life has downed you,
and you're feeling mighty low,
Take a look or two around you,
at the folks who come and go.
See that man with halting walk?
He was crippled in the war.
And that blind man with his cane?
He's alive and asks no more.
And that girl upon the corner?
She's a "woman of the streets"
Thank the Lord you have your pride
and the use of hands and feet.

Though you may have hit a rough spot,
in the road that's known as Life,
Shift your pack and keep on going,
and accept your share of strife.
Try and find the joy of living,
You've your health and hope and pride,
Keep your faith intact around you,
and thank God that you're alive! !

Lucy A Thompson
STANDING ON THE OUTSIDE
Life is not all roses,
Sometimes it's mighty grim
Fate stacks the cards and leaves you
Standing on the outside, looking in.

I'd like to join the people
And share in all the din,
But they just rush by and leave me
Standing on the outside, looking in.

I dreamed I died and went to heaven
And much to my chagrin,
St. Peter closed the gates and left me
Standing on the outside, looking in.

I dropped down to see the devil
He flashed his wicked grin,
And slammed the door and left me
Standing on the outside, looking in.

Now I'm not optimistic
My hopes are mighty thin,
Life just rolls by and leaves me
Standing on the outside, looking in.

Marion F Heflin
OF ALL THE PEOPLE ON THIS EARTH
The most beautiful thing in all the world
Is the Statue of Liberty
And the flag that we unfurl
Shows Americans are free

So many died to keep it so
'Cause freedom is life
Can you imagine how life would go
To live in Communist strife

But so many take for granted
The freedom that we live
Their way of life firmly planted
But to keep us free no time they give

America's way of life has changed
So we must change too
For all the freedom you were granted
It's time to pay your due

We have to fight for what is right
And some of us must die
But we have that statue and flag
And it will always fly!

Lucky Hager
CASTLES OF HER MEMORIES

To all those enigmatically enchanted with the perfect love.

Riding from the castle on a horse with silver braids
Heading off for Eastwick, flower petals brush her legs
Enchantment fills her heart of gold and clouds her mind with haze
And now I search for my sweet love and the hours turn to days;

Tulips filled with water, buttercups and fairy tales
Glistened across her eyelids like violet windblown sales
When she walked she fluttered like the butterflies in spring
And when I woke and saw her face she'd smile and then sing;

Unicorns and soft white doves would follow her and pace
Waiting for this angel where they knew there'd be a place
'Cause in her heart were many things and they knew it was so
But when I tried to capture her that's when she had to go.

Castles of her memories and corridors of lace
Bring about the heartaches of her beauty and her grace
Now my love has gone away to another time and place
While I sit in wonderment and miss her soft embrace.

Ashley L Miller
DARKNESS IS FALLING
The light of day with the clouds.
Then twilight comes. How beautiful.
Sunset. A wonder to the eyes.
The colors; purple, blue, pink, red and yellow.
Dark with beautiful bright stars.

Michelle Rae Buheit
LOOKING BACK
Looking back, my life was so chaotic,
But then again . . . how crystal clear
In answering those complicated questions
Through hindsight, their simplicity appears.
Of course regrets are bound to haunt our memories,
But in the end, we learn from each mistake.
I wonder now how many desperate memories—
How many times a broken heart it takes
Before we finally find a light to guide us,
A hopeful glow to let us see the way,
A ray of wisdom shining on tomorrow
And a switch,
To turn off thoughts of yesterday.

Georgia White
LOVE REMEMBERED
My Love, many times you come to mind,
the gentleness of your touch,
your easy way, your sensual gaze,
and I miss you ever so much!

Never before have I felt like this—
you brought something to life that's now gone.
I long for the nights I spent with you
as if caressed gently by song .

No one will ever replace you,
as my heart will never forget.
The love we shared in years past
was an everlasting gift.

Even though someone else shares my life,
he will never be as you were.
He can fill the hours of day and night,
but cannot cause these feelings to stir.

I understand now more than ever
the feelings you spoke of before—
the love of a person so close to you
but the longing for something more.

I will remember and love you
for the rest of my time,
and hope that you will do the same,
for what we shared will be ours forever
and the rest of life only a game.

Linda Wright Theriault
CLOUDS
Lie back and look . . .
You will be witness to an original . . .
Floating . . .Floating.
As a child you look and see . . .
Oh yes! A bear, a dog, an elephant . . .
Such carefree and happy

creatures!
As a young man you see . . .
A beautiful maiden . . . .Soft and graceful.
A young girl would look up and see . . .
An ocean . . . seeing the tide rush and wash . . .
A prince waits.
But with age and wisdom
Clouds, like ideas, they change . . .
They are happy and full of young life,
Vibrant with color . . . then gray . . .
And the tempest of life is gone!
A fragrant and clean spring rain has begun . . . so a new life! ! !

Mr Lynn Sneath
BETWEEN THE LINES

To Dianne . . . .
Your love is resurrection
and continual rebirth.

Between the lines the Phoenix lies,
Between the tempest and the truth;
Amidst loving aches with wanton sighs;
Amidst tarnished dreams and shades of youth.

Within the shadowed void we wait,
Where darkness dares the heart to sing;
We endure the cruel decree of fate
That defies the Phoenix to take wing.

If time were born again my friend,
And ages now were ages past,
My heart would sail with yours till end
Of eons long at love's full mast.

Perhaps amidst tomorrow's time,
As we alone in silence stare,
When eyes reveal what words can't hide,
Without the need for mask or lies,
The Phoenix will be free . . . . .
To fly . . . . . .

Paula Frederica Durry
WHAT'S GOING ON?

To my family, and friends.

Homeless people engulfed in dirt,
wearing their shabby cloaks of desperation,
eating delicacies from dumpsters,
and begging for money from men in Italian suits,
and patent leather wing-tips.

An ivory-hued teenaged girl . . . .
Belly filled with a fetus sits in a bathtub,
and shoves a clothes-hanger up her channel of conception,
and slowly bleeds into an eternal sleep.

Staggering from a bar, intoxicated from liquid chaos,
a man with hair of salt and pepper,
and skin of caramel
flings his body in front of a train on the tracks behind a junkyard.

A young mother, peering through perceptions of confusion
puts her infant son into a rusty trash can in a dark alleyway,
swaddles him in debris, and runs away
as his wailing echoes from the depths of his new home.

Leaning against a Catholic mission house,
a wino in a philosophical mood
clutching a bottle of cheap wine
blurts out,
"Folks order their own lives!" He then makes a silent toast to the sun,
and takes a long gulp.

Virginia Smith Kingrey
THE TIDE OF LIFE

This poem is dedicated in loving memory of my mother, Katherine, who taught me to focus on the best in myself and others and who always gave me the best of herself.

LIFE: Harsh and cruel;
Often much like fighting a duel.
LIFE: Gentle and kind;
Creating love and emotion in everyone's mind.

The downs they come like the ocean's tide;
Quickly, unexpectedly, and then subside.
And when they go they take their share;
And yet leave new things to linger there.

The ups are like the highest wave;
Smooth and beautiful and seemingly brave.
And like all good things on earth must be;
They spread their beauty for all to see.
And like the tides must forevermore,
End their glory on life's great shore.

So as in life, with pain and sadness,
With grief and sorrow and love and gladness;
They come and they go, and they take and they give;
But somehow, through all, we continue to live.
Still we must stand like that great vast shore;
Prepared to withstand whatever's in store.
Knowing not what the future will give or take nor what the ocean will leave in its wake.

Violet Verena Curlee
I CHOOSE TO PRAISE

Life is made up of choices,
Moment by moment deciding,
Discernment of so many voices
Lest temptation be over-riding.
Parading, are bitterness and anger,
Bidding to shorten my days,
Aware of imposing danger
I CHOOSE TO PRAISE.

Daily we make our decisions
Feeding our spirit-man.
Beware of your own television
You hold that "remote' in your hand.
Eating ashes becomes detrimental,
My hands and my heart I will raise
Conducive to worship, instrumental,
I CHOOSE TO PRAISE.

The agenda of life is before you,
Which path will you walk in today?
If to God and yourself you are true;
You can worship and praise as you pray.
I elect to follow Christ Jesus,
I am not going through some phase,
For He is the Lord of my life,
I CHOOSE TO PRAISE.

Good times come, bad times too,
In my heart I have hidden His Word.
Instead of being angry and blue
I just praise the Lord.
He gives to me such great rewards,
Christian friends and a family to raise.
Because He is MY PRECIOUS LORD
I CHOOSE TO PRAISE.

Carole Ann Lea

Carole Ann Lea
COTTON CALL

This poem is dedicated to my Grandmother, Mallie Ruth Miller. Although I have never been to her birthplace of Whiteright, Texas; because of her, I believe I know "Dixie."

From a child of the South to the West woman kind,
To a crippled up body with trouble of mind;
And I watched as she hobbled and rocked to and fro,
Wondered how she could smile and hoped she didn't know.
Picked a flower of yellow, seemed just right for her:
"Dandelions are my favorite, how'd you know they were?
Some call it a weed, it's a mirror to the soul;
Like when Grandma sings Dixie and she becomes whole.
Tip your chin up just slightly, the flower enfold—
You're as sweet as cream butter, if your chin turns to gold.
Worked the fields in my youth, I was real good at hops,
And when cotton fields called I was proud of the crops.
Picked by light as the sun lent its glow through its sphere;
Just want you to know Dixie, while Grandma is here.
I learned about life, put my heart in its worth
Didn't question its reason, I turned toward the earth;
For the answers were there, nature's credence I gave."
And while Grandma sang Dixie, they dug Grandpa's grave.
And her song it was heartfelt, a life's story it told
And when Grandma sang Dixie—she never was old.

Shana K Williams
LAST SUMMER

Last summer,
Lost dreams.
We were together
Just you and me.

What happened?
Where did the time go?
I miss you now,
I just wanted you to know.

I still think of you,
It still makes me sad.
The memories of those days;
The good times and the bad.

Please always remember,
You're so special to me.
You always have been,
You always will be.

Anita Arbutus Pennington
FATHER AND SONS

To my husband, who has been a source of inspiration to me and a role model for his children.

I watch as they contend with one another
Hurling mock insults with each push or shove.
Their flailing fists stop short of actual hurting
Glad laughter interspersed, professing love.

I watch them now as youth becomes the stronger
And moments of the past return to show;
A father gently romping with his four sons
Like playful bear cubs learning as they grow.

For long years now I've watched and heard these battles
And wondered if the house and I could endure.
But now I've come to see each well staged conflict
Has formed a bond that's lasting and secure.

Lloyd Farnham
SO SMALL,—SO TALL,

How, "oh" how can I so small
Live to do "God's" will,
He needs me this I know
What job does he want me to fill?

He needs me to love you
As he has loved me,
For without the love of him
There would be nothing, you see,

He wants us to help
When you need me brother,
Wanting nothing in return
Willing to help one another,

In love, in caring, in need,
To pick each other up when we fall,

To prune our branches and our eyes
Just as he did our brother Paul,

To do his will wholeheartedly
Even if we are so small,
For when Jesus is in our lives
We are ten feet tall.

Tamhra J Luper
IF I
If I grow old
  before my time
  I can no longer dream
  I can no longer see

If I forget
  how to love
  then I can't travel on
  I'll never see the light

If I remember
  yesterday
  help me to be a little stronger
  the tears come easy

Chris A Phillips
DÉJÀ VU
There's a lazy old river
I haven't seen her in so long
Her banks are lined with stones
So big and so strong
Déjà vu, Déjà vu

There's a single lane highway
It tangles and it weaves
Through a pathway of heaven
Green valleys and trees
Déjà vu, Déjà vu

Now I'm thinking of your eyes
And the sparkle I knew
And I'm dreaming of those nights
And our rendezvous

Could it be magic, a witch
And wizard make two
Together their spirits
Dream of Déjà vu

Déjà vu, Déjà vu
What makes you?

Cliff Valenti
GROWING OLDER
I am growing older
My limbs are growing weak
One leaf falls on each new day.

As every leaf departs
The tree begins to lapse
Branches once strong soon decay.

Life, precious like a rose
Endangered by the wind
Blowing the petals of my life away.

The thorns are very sharp
The sun gets much too hot
And sometimes my eyes see rain.

Together with the rain
Comes remote eternal pain
From life's winds and storms
That cause prickling of the thorns
And the loss of the leaves
    it blows away . . .

Jeanne Floyd
A DEDICATION TO MY LIFE
The world is filled with many things
Some are wrong and some are right
But I would like to tell you of
A dedication to my life

One day as I was thinking of
How far I had to go
On the road to happiness
If I should reach my goals

A feeling soon occurred to me
As thoughts go on and on
I need a friend for company
And so I will not be alone

It seemed the Spirit guided me
In times I struggled with my strife
I knew that I was Heaven bound
A dedication to my life

Happiness and tenderness
With each new thing I try
To be a christian filled with love
A dedication to my life

Renee M Rancourt
REFLECTIONS OF LOST MEMORIES

To Kevin, Debbi and Kathy
David and Matthew
My friends, my life—Forever

when the mirror to your soul is scratched
the memories start to slip away
like sand in an hourglass
until you can't recall your past
they have all escaped into another time
all your experiences are gone
falling into unconsciousness
your past has no meaning
memories of your life don't exist
motionless waves of sound surround you
suffocating every thought
every movement
holding you in suspended animation
lost in another time
lost in another world
lost forever

Janice Campbell
BOOTCAMP

I would like to dedicate this poem to the Lakel Anthony, the son of Brenda D.C. and Johnny Lakel Smith.

I'm living and it's hot as hell,
I got off the bus and I heard a yell.
The yell was of a drill instructor
jumping on my case,
Before I could swallow, he was all in my face.
Screaming and pointing to run here and there,
I thought I must be having a bad nightmare.
But to my dismay and to my greatest fear,
When I woke up this morning, I was still here.

Amy Ritter
DROPS OF SCARLET
I see scarlet drops on the floor,
my eyes begin to search for more.
My mind stays in silence,
as I see this violence.
I look to find where the origin may occur,
for a moment my eyes begin to blur.
A razor clenched in my fist,
along with a cut on my wrist.
I look again to see the drops turn to a scarlet pool,
it seems in my life I've let my depression rule.
Sometimes at night this nightmare haunts me,
and a vision of any razor just taunts me.
Many times with depression I have now dealt,
and now I realize just how I felt.
When with their life people are unsatisfied,
they feel their only hope is suicide.
Because of my experience in my earlier days,
what I can say to them is they'll only bring dismay.
If you think with suicide the problems are vaporized,
you really need to be otherwise advised.

LaJan White-Sanford
THE TOUCH OF LOVE
There is no fire to light the soul
That ceases from its depths to burn.
No mellow mountain height can reach
A heart far from the touch of love.
And yet no stream that's ever flown
Can seep into a heart that's bound.
Sad memories sing that life without
Shall cease away from life itself.

Doris Shanahan
DARK REPOSE

For Kevin, Judy, Paul, Barbara and Brian . . . . .
May all your dreams be sweet ones.

Harken to the wind on a cold and windy night
The rustling of bended trees and an owl's futile flight
Listen to the rumbling of a thunder cloud gone wild
And heed the mournful cry of a frightened little child
Watch the raging river rise as it rushes to the sea
A whirling mass of foaming rage that reaches out for thee

See the power of lightning as it blazes cross the sky
A lamp that lights the world below and soon begins to die
Then feel the calm that comes again and wake to a rising sun
For in that moment is relief to find your nightmare's done

Stacey Tatich
I HAVE TO KNOW
I have to know who tells the sun
  to rise and shine bright,
I have to know who puts the
  leaves on the trees and who has
  made the birds and bees,
I have to know who makes it rain
  and who plants the rainbow
  high in the sky,
I have to know who tells the
  moon to rise and give
  moonlight,
And I have to know why every
  star above twinkles with delight,
Who but God does all this?
  —and why?—

Arlene Wellington López
SILENCE

To the Lord God who created all things Great and Beautiful.

Silence, what is it?
  It is not a sound,
You cannot see or
  smell it. But it
is always there. Yes,
  it is sometimes covered
by noise, but it
  is always there.
It sits and watches as
  we lead our lives, but
rarely says a word to criticize.
  It crawls through
the night on quiet padded
  feet. Then sits and
waits as the sun ascends
  and loses itself in
the noise of day. Do
  not worry, for it
will come back, when
  the day is over and the
noise ceases to play.

Terry Van Worth
BEAUTY
There's beauty to be seen where-ever I go,
I didn't understand, but now I know.

  Roses grow through the garbage,
  Daisies spring up among the weeds.
  Birds sing over junk yards,
  Dew glitters on old fallen leaves.

From the musical laughter from children at play,
To the shine of remembrance at the end of the day.
I still believe in beautiful things,
And, they're not all as obvious as butterflies' wings.

Lynne Perilli
THERE IS HOPE IN THIS WINTRY THING CALLED LIFE

To God the Father, the Son and the Holy Spirit: For The Hope; To Every One of my Loved Ones: For Helping Me Find It.

Breathe deeply and step out;
there is hope in this wintry thing called life.
There are stars that kiss our nights
and the lights in the eyes of a lover . . .

(Do not high-tech miracles away!
For then, you will miss the wonder of the thunder;
of the gentle rain and soft snow . . .)

So . . .
throw those pre-packaged plans away
and lift your hands to heaven!

Breathe deeply and step in;
there is hope in this wintry thing called life.
There are mountains calling us to climb
to higher places—to heights divine—

to kiss the stars that light our nights,
to defy this world
AND LIFT OUR HANDS TO
HEAVEN! !

Anna Marie Sobarzo
RARE LOVE

Dedicated to Jose Quiles

Love to me is just your size.
5'8 and sparkling eyes.
When we kiss, you do excite.
Just a hug and I'm alright.
My heart is yours, as yours is mine.
Let's unite and waste no time.

You and me we make one.
You show your love in many ways.
And make my life much more fun.

We are to each other good yet bad.
It's the best on special days,
so sweet and kind in many ways,
But then the worst comes out of you
and makes me say please stay away.

The love I have for you is rare
to no one else you can compare.

I love you more than I ever have.
One day you'll see what you mean to
me.
And our love will always be.

Suzzanne M Kuykendall
GENTLE PORTRAIT

To Poppy, who always made me feel so special

He once stood tall like the mighty
oak with his depth and breadth
as impressive as his height.

His ruddy complexion engraved
with the lines of sun and wind
and time.

His large thick calloused hands
worked with the same precision
as the machines he repaired.

His hair, once black as coal, had
whitened early and now receded
like the melting snow.

Through the years, the coarse
weathered body had protected
the man, but had not hardened
his soul.

And from the deepest caverns
within the man, the gentleness
of his spirit would echo in his
smile.

Nancy Hohenberry
THE GIFT OF LOVE

To my friend Phyllis who had steadfast faith in me and gave me the courage to withstand

I asked a friend with outstretched
hands
Tears flowing from my eyes
If I am all that I was told or if it was
just a lie

My heart was heavy, I had lost my
heart
among the muck and mire
To know the truth, the absolute truth
my desire

My inner being ached with pain, for I
felt
no growth I had gained

Soft tender words I heard rang clear
Dry your eyes, be still, be quiet, my
dear

You are quite wrong in heeding
words in anger
they are said
for often we regret, and wish we
would have prayed instead

In tenderness I was assured with
words so softly spoken
You are indeed a good soul, no
commandment you
have broken

Lift your head, give a smile, don't
hide yourself, my friend
Stand straight and tell, rise above
Send back the gift of love

Norma Forbes

Norma Forbes
HONESTY

This poem is dedicated to all the people of the world (especially children). Honesty is the best policy, and each honest act we fulfill each day is the noblest work of God.

Are there anymore Honest people
around?
Yes, but only a few.
How many of us fulfill an Honest act
each day?
Just a few.

The road to Honesty is so narrow and
unseen,
That it is not visible to the human
eyes.
To be a traveler on that road,
You have to be Honest to yourself
and to others.

We are told that Honesty is the best
policy,
But not anymore.
Honesty means Trust, Uprightness,
Justice, Openness, Sincerity,
And being fair and faithful when
dealing with others.

To prove yourself an Honest person,
Take a look into your own life.
Why, because the next Honest person
award,
May just be handed to you.

Susan Hall
THE SHADOW

There is nothing behind, nor in front
of me—
That I have not experienced . . .
yet . . .
I do not exist.
There isn't any darkness, nor is there
sunlight.
Love or hate, there isn't any feeling
of.
When I was born, it was too
late—
For I'm not listed.
There is neither worry, or wondering
why . . .
I do not exist.
Cannot hear laughter, nor see tears—
There isn't any pain, or sorrow.
Lust and evil are not felt, or
needed . . .
I do not exist.
You think you see me,—but you do
not.
You hear what you think I am
saying . . .
Really you do not hear me at all.
When you are not thinking of me,
or—
Looking for me . . .
I do not exist, now do I.
Am, but a figment of your imagina-
tion.
I do not exist.

Christy Thornton

Christy Thornton
A WINTER'S DAY

It snows
The wind blows
Water froze
Ice still
Morning chill.

Keep warm
during the storm.
in a small dorm.
Fill a pot
with broth.

Get snug as a bug
in a rug.
Call your cat,
Pat, pat.

Cuddle up close
by the fire.
The snow is like sapphire!

Pick cat up higher
Then hold him close.
You doze-z-z-z-z.

Marta Leigh Ticherich
. . . AND BEGIN AGAIN

To anyone willing to fail . . . And begin again

Take this year one day at a time.
Hold your head up and don't fall
behind.
Look in the past and see much to
mend.
Close your eyes and begin again.

Hearing voices not heard in a while,
give the impression "No need for
denial."
These voices continue, a message to
send;
Speak these words and begin again.

Among a group stands one alone.
Relying on no-one shows one has
grown.
Learned in the past only one can
depend,
always be **ONE** and begin again.

Continue down a chosen road.
Steps are unsteady and sometimes
slowed.
Think that a finish is at the end,
just keep walking . . . AND BEGIN
AGAIN!

Timothy C Friedrich
THE DESCENT

The bird swoops down from the
Heavenly sky as the thrashing wind
Bears down from wing to side.

It flutters and twists to stay up high,
But soon it must rest and lie.

The lively feathered thing looks to a
Branch to see its chance to find rest.

The branch is wide with soft green
Leaves fluttering from side to side as
The wind blows its nostrils upon the
Tree of time.

The tree of time is a tree of rest
Playing upon the winds of the south,
East, north, and west. It is the barrier
Of place and time which serves as
Rest.

The rest of body and soul along the
Long branch that awaits the feathery
Bird of sky and place.

It seeks only a place of rest, but the
Sky calls upon it to stay within the
Heavenly blue which the sun arise
And rest.

The bird seeks to stay but aching and
Pain of muscle and limb forces the
Feathered object to fly to the branch
Of time and place.

The bird is forced to light, and it
Tucked its wings by its side awaiting
For the time to return to sky which
Holds the freedom of soul and sight.

Ronald A Freeman
THE SHADOW OF DEATH

As I awake to a horrible cry
I lie there with sweat running down
in my eyes
The cry gets closer and the door
begins to open
I thought I was dreaming, at least I
was hoping
So I close my eyes for a moment of
fear
And open them just in time to see
who was standing there
It was the shadow of death, it was
dark and cold
So I pulled up the covers and it
started to grab hold
It said come with me I have
something for you to see
It was a tombstone laid out just for
me
He took my hand and said it was
time to go
So I close my eyes and I was back at
home
So I turned on the lights and you
know what I saw
Nothing, it was just a horrible dream.

Joy D
HEART'S DESIRE

When the sky is filled with golden
sun
And clouds are far away
Is it me you're thinking of
As you go about your day?

When happy things are happening
And life seems so worthwhile
Is it me you want to be
Beside and share a smile?

And when the sun is not shining
And the purpose of life is unclear

Am I the one you would come to,
The one you want to hold near?

I truly love you, Darling,
But we must be apart.
I wonder if you will ever know
how much it breaks my heart
I want to be all things to you
In joy and in life's sorrow.
My prayer is though it cannot be
today
We'll be hand in hand tomorrow.

John Osterman
THE OLD HOUSE
There's an old house in the country,
Off the road back in the hills;
It's a place most folks would forget
But I know I never will.

That house once rang with laughter,
That house was filled with joy;
That house knew all the growing
pains
Of nine young girls and boys.

That house was filled with happiness,
Tenderness, and love;
Mother made that house a home
With guidance from above.

I wish I could return again
And run barefoot through those hills;
I wish the old days would return
But I know they never will.

There's an old house in the country
In the hills back from the road;
It's the place that I remember best:
It's the place I called my home.

Marge Tkach
THE FLOWERS OF LIFE
As in their hospital beds they lay with
loss of limb or in pain all day
These war torn men still reminisce
Of their days in France and their girls
last kiss.
They dream of the day they first
shouldered a gun
And marched off to war to fight the
Hun
Of Flander's field where this Flower
grew
And the dead, dead heroes they all
once knew.
This beautiful flower why so red
Signifies all the blood they shed
A wonderful flower grown in France
Is now assembled by our own Vets'
hands.
So happy to be able to fashion this
flower
Although even one may take an
hour,
Looking back there's no regret
Their only hope, lest we forget.
So wear this lovely flower of life
As we hope someday to end all strife
And think of our boys now over there
And let them know we all still care.

Laura Barbara Elizabeth Jensen Crowder
A PLANET FILLED WITH HOPE

To Mother—Barbara Ethel Gray Jensen—Now 50 years a widow, who made flower garlands with children & grand children.

The eyes of a pre-schooler see lace in
the spun web of a spider,
And a magnificent butterfly soars as
a glider.
Sweet-smelling clover ties into a
necklace, and
Honeysuckle tips lick like syrup for
breakfast.
Buttercups sprinkled with violets and
onion grass become bridal bouquets,
Wooden wagons are filled beds of
soft leaves and hay.
A tire swing rides high, where the
astronauts fly.
Round culverts afford a quiet place
to hide,
Driveway icy puddles delight with
their reflection.
A rainbow from a hose shines in a
colorful collection.
The hush of awe as a velvety fawn
drinks from a pond—
The star-seed in the center of an
apple,
Surprise when heavy cream shakes
into butter,
Cracking "elephant" peanuts from
their shells—
These God-given mysteries cast
magical spells,
Through the eyes of a pre-schooler,
with their ever-inquiring scope,
Our earth becomes a loving, joyful
planet filled with hope.

Tracy Ann Eason
SISTERS
When we were young,
we had a lot of fun.
We would tell stories,
about boys.
We liked to play games,
and if I won you would call me
names.
Now we're grown,
but, we aren't alone.
Now you've got your guy,
and you must not lie.
We are neither sad,
but both glad,
and now I often say,
on a lonely day:
"How I miss."
"My little sis."

K J VanDruff
UPS AND DOWNS
In these times of ups and downs
Of things I can't foresee
It's hard to keep from making frowns
'bout gets the best of me

I try and try to do my best
As everyday goes by
Then suddenly comes another test
That makes me want to cry

All at once I lose my job
Or have an accident
I can't help feeling I've been robbed
Can't even pay the rent

I am not alone I'm sure
With troubles that I've known
I think I might have found a cure
In family love at home

Donna Martin
MY MOM

This poem is dedicated to my mom. Thank-you for always being there!

My Mom and I don't get along,
Sometimes I wonder what went
wrong,
Sometimes I wish that she could see
that things I do aren't meant to be,
Often I think about running away,
But my problems are here, so here's
where I stay,
Somehow I know it'll all work out,
I've just got to learn not to sit here
and pout,
She taught me that running won't
help you at all,
You run into more
You'll stumble, you'll fall
If you don't help yourself then
nobody will,
She told me that once, I remember it
still,
Sometimes we fight, and my mother
will cry,
I hate when this happens, I just want
to die,
I wish she could see just how I feel,
My love for my Mom, no one can
steal,
Someday I hope we'll understand
each other,
But no matter what, *I love my
mother.*

Clarence G Estes Jr

Clarence G Estes Jr
TRUE FRIENDS

This poem, True Friends, is dedicated to Frances Estes, Connie Estes, Nancy and Kendall Back, my dear family and truest friends.

True friends are a precious gift,
Treating them right, we get a
lift,
Treating them wrong, and parting is
swift.
So treat them not with hate or
haste,
For losing Friends is a terrible waste.

Making Friends at an early age,
Adding them daily page by
page.
If your hand you will extend,
You can win a loyal Friend,
Holding them fast until the end.

When our path in life is found,
And a web of Friends are
wound,
Then True Happiness will abound.
Family and Friends make our
net worth,
While we're living on this earth.

Brian R Waterhouse
IN MEMORIAM

In honor of a teacher and friend, David Dibble

What made you do it?
Or should I ask why?
What made you want to make
yourself die?
Didn't you know how much we
cared?
Doesn't it show with the tears that we
share?
How should we take this?
What should we feel?
These questions have made my head
start to reel.
Anger, fear, confusion, frustration?
We all find ourselves in the same
situation.
This is a time to stick close together
And remember our friend forever and
ever.
Remember what he stood for, not
how he died.
Let's keep his memory forever alive.

Ellen M Williams
THE MOUNTAIN OF COLD ANGER
The Mountain of cold anger
has begun to melt;
and as it liquifies,
rivers of rage roar
over the boulders
still numb from the years of ice.

As the rushing waters continue,
they careen out of control
carrying furious feelings:
rocks of hurt and pebbles of pain.

Perhaps it is good that there are dams
built up,
for I am not sure if I could
survive
if the raging rivers pulled out all the
roots and anchors.

But how cleansing it feels to be free
of the glacial cold anger.
Now I can get beneath it to explore
what I may find.

Valerie J Otterline
HOW CAN I REACH THE MAN OF MY DREAMS?

For My DollFace

That caring one, with emotions
running deep
How then, do I reach that man I
seek?
The man I want to have and to hold
Within reach, even as we speak
My dreams, then will unfold

You do not reach
We will teach
That man to uphold
His gift of gold

To you, he willingly giveth
That you shall liveth
Those dreams of yours

That man, shares your dreams
As different as it seems
The motion
Of your lives and love
Will be filled, with emotion
As pure as a dove

You need not reach, the man you
hold
Together, your dreams will unfold

Virginia A Dickerson
LISTENING TO THE MUSIC
Listening—to the music
Hearing a guitar climbing up and
down
A ladder of notes
Hearing the organ creep slowly upon
me

Hearing drums pounding rapidly like
the sound of thunder
I feel comfortable here
These sounds—
They let my imagination run free
Through an open field on a warm
summer morning
The ground still wet with dew.

I let my imagination run free . . .
Free of sorrow
Free of worry
Free of care.
It brings new feelings
Fresh thoughts to my mind
And the dew, it wipes clear old
worries
Listening to the music
I—
Run free through the open field.

Mrs Lela M Randall
TAKE TIME TO UNDERSTAND SOMEONE

If my heart could sing, it would
sing a thousand songs
Of love. But no one will hear it
but me. You never was
Good for nothing as people
say. In my eyes I see so
Much love and warmth in the
lives
Of other people, but for me I see
so much sorrow, hate and
Disappointment. I know you can
not make people care or

Understand, but you go on
trying to tell people how you
Feel and no one ever listens to
you at all. You try to
Let people understand you but
they
Don't want to understand
you, Not At All.

Jylle Richards
SUICIDE

Standing on a sandy beach one night,
Thinking of all the things you never
did right.
You were always being told to clean
up your act,
And try to forget the hearts you have
cracked.

You look back into your past
wondering WHY?
Then you remember and start to cry.
You think of what you had put
everyone through,
And you wish that none of it had
ever come true.

You think of the last thing your
mother had said,
That night you took your life in your
bed.
You pulled that trigger ever so
gently,
And now you lie in a casket, dead.

You suddenly wish you had dreamt
this day,
And didn't have to see anyone react
this way.
You plead to GOD that you'll be
good and behave,
But hey, your soul, you already gave.

Jewell Castro
A MASTERPIECE OF MAN

I love people, generally; children, in particular. I humbly ask that all those whom I love, share my three Golden Poet Awards. They are my inspiration.

A child is the masterpiece of man.
Nothing else created by man
can compare to the
creation of a child.
Nothing else can be molded,
altered as changes occur;
can give unquestionably
his love to you.
Be careful how you mold him.
Give him love for all his life.
Discipline him with temperance.
Guide him to realistic goals;
share your dreams with him.
Protect him for his sake,
but don't shield him from life.
Prepare him for his
place in the sun.
It is then that you shall
have created

your masterpiece.

Julie A Henneberry
FRIENDS

Friends will always be there,
Through good times and bad times
they bear,
To guide me into the light
To help me make choices that are
right.
Friends will always share,
and always be there to care.
Friends are a must today,
Just as we should also pray.
Friends are fun,
Friends are great,
Friends are what makes life up to
date!

Beth Ann
PAUPER'S PRAYER

I dedicate this to battered women who are always hoping, dreaming and praying for an end to the violence in their home.

Here I sit alone upon a throne I do
now want.
The cup that I bear do I dare to throw
it out?
A queen of paupers I may be, sitting
among the thistles and thorns.
A lazy fool full of dreams that will
never be.
Fantasies that rot with loves that are
not mine,
Ones my heart cannot see.
How can I rule with royalty when my
own mind I cannot bare?
Earnest thoughts are tossed about to
an id that does not care.
So as I sit alone on my throne I pray
a pauper's prayer.
Hasten death of dozing dreams, give
me a wine so that my lips can share
The courage to speak, the courage to
cast out the weak
And drink to my life's whims,
leaving no drop for the grim!
And cater to the riches of robust and
flair.
Make merry the days ahead, giving a
toast to the pot of gold.
Please lighten my heart and make my
rainbow so bold
That the bright colors it has may
cling to my soul.
To help me take hold of my cup and
drink in my throne.
To boast about the throne among the
flowers . . .
Not among thistles and thorns.

Leon Rushing

Leon Rushing
HUNGER

Starving an intelligent species that
of which is human
Dying off by the thousands perhaps
this sign an omen
These masses bound together by only
skin and bones
Feasting upon a morsel of food tho
pain is long from gone
Yet a speck of life lives from these of
feeble remains
Which touches out affectionately to
feed their skeleton frames
Those sent upon this needed quest
feeding many 'til nothing left
Shall continue to help such needy
people 'til their dying breath
If you feel no pity because this is not
you or yours
You may one day be in trouble when
it rains they say it pours
To give to those that's unable to seek
of their own food
Is but a blessing within itself to be
caught in such a mood

Juliana Lok
THE LONELY CHILD

I dedicate this poem to all the children who have been put up for adoption and the children who have run away because they truly are the ones who strive to live a life of happiness. My heart goes out to all of you.

A child reaches out her hand with a
crying soul,
In search of the love she's without,
which we all know,
She's been deprived of the happiness
that a family has to share,
The caring souls, surrounded by love,
the security of them being there,
Not knowing who to turn to or who
she can actually trust,
When all her hopes of happiness are
blown away in the dust,
Still she struggles to find the ones
who left her behind,
Searching for any answers to the
family she can not find,
Wondering what she had done to
make them go away.
Continuously praying for them to
return for her someday,
Through the many heartaches and the
feelings of being alone,
The frightened child experienced the
struggling of being on her own,
Scared of the surroundings and
where she is to live,
The child wanders in the streets, who
has so much love to give,
The search for the family she loves so
dear,
The sight of finding them is no
longer clear,
Though she keeps on trying as the
disappointments take their toll,
The thought of not finding them,
follows her where ever she may go,
But the love she holds for them,
keeps her standing tall,
As the sights of her security really
starts to fall,
Through the eyes of the Lonely
Child . . .

Tammie Thurlow
WE COME AND GO

To the young and old, and those like me who love them both.

Look at me,
I have grown.
I now have children,
of my own.
Busy days,
and sleepless nights.
Let's make love,
it feels so right.
Another child,
has been born.
An old one's death,
today we mourn.

John Charles Zbercot
TYPECAST

White-socked and blue-collared,
These brave people of pittance,
They work all the day
For minimal remittance.
So solidly, their futures cast,
They give their all, until life's last.
When will the effort of
Their talents, their ability,
Present to them, life's
Abundant fertility.

Judy Broyles
LIFE'S TREASURES

In loving memory of John and Marie Campbell and Randy Broyles

Some people spend all their days
seeking fame and fortune in a variety
of ways.

Some prosper by education, hard
work and dedication. Some are born
with a wealth on hand.

My life's treasures are not built on
fame;
no one except family and friends
know my name.

I have found a gold mine.
Priceless treasures that always will
be thine.

Things no one can take;
you see life is what we make.

A loved one to comfort you during
the bad times.
A friend whose love always shines.

Some may have fame, fortune, and
gold;
all my treasures are too many to be
told.

Enjoy your treasures please;
they are earned not with the greatest
ease.

Ms Bonnie Simmons Peter
WOMAN

Fragrance doesn't make a woman.
Neither does style.
Happiness and a smile,
One who will walk a mile
For you and me,
Is a woman free
To see the needs of others,
Her sisters and brothers,
With a heart of gold,
Shattering the bitter cold.
With a delicate song in her heart,
Beauty became woman.

Jerry Christian
ROMEO AND JULIET

To those still young who have let passion become an obsession made into the bonds of holy matrimony.

Tonight we love
We will dance forever.
I will be your desire
You will be my passion.
Let us love; until we forget.
Let us be happy forever.
No one will know?
If we stop living!
Our hearts will kiss in eternity,
We will be married !!!
You will be my passion!
I will be your desire!
Let us wait until tonight—
No one will know?!
We will be married !!!
Forever.

Catherine G Smith
COME . . . GROW OLD WITH ME

To Reginald M. Woodall "A part of all he has met."

Come . . . grow old with me;
Let my bosom cradle thee;
Feel the warmth and love there.

Look—full in my eyes and see,
One who means so much to me
With soft eyes and silver hair.

One whose voice warms my heart,
Whose smile plays a special part
In all my fondest dreams,

Of future times when we could share
The moments you've spent everywhere,
You'll never know how much it means.

Just to be with you at your side,
Adds a special glow of pride
That I know all can see.

So . . . before time takes its toll,
On the body and the soul—
Come . . . grow old with me.

R E Vaughn
JENNIFER MORGAN

While sitting in my yard one day,
Jennifer came out to play—
I just fell in love with her, but then she moved away—
I can hardly wait 'til she, comes back down to visit me—
I'll just wait, and wait, and wait, and when she comes—what glee—
We sincerely had such fun, sitting in the summer sun—
Calling up her friend Amanda, boy I was the fortunate one—
Jennifer, I hardly knew you, when you moved away—
Jennifer Amanda Morgan, please come back to play—
And I'll be sitting in my yard, and watching just for you—
Jennifer Amanda Morgan, I miss you, I do—
And I thank God, for giving this poet, this poem for you, so I can show it—
Around the world, where this will be read, now all the world will know it.
And I can tell them joyfully, of how you sing so beautifully—
And just how pretty, and nice you are, I wish they all could see—
And you're my special little friend, and this I'll tell, again and again—
And how the world will know this too, and this friendship will never end—
And I must say, before I part, I like your Mom, and brother Mark—
And all of your family, yes I do, but Jennifer Morgan, I love you.
God bless you always . . . I truly do love you little girl . . . truly.

Martha Mulville
UNCHOSEN MEMORY

There is a chamber in my head,
Like the chair in a musty corner of the
Old dark room we never used, adorned with the
Picture frame of some ancient aunt
I never knew.
There standing still,
My feet are glued to my shoes, then
To the floor. Muscles aching from
Attempting just one first step.
Crying I pull harder toward the
Door whose light I see. Surrounded by
Dampness I am cold !
I shudder !
I rest.
I turn toward the locked trunk whose
Contents I never knew and
I grow weary.

Russell Mauck
OUR LOVE

To my beloved wife, and mother of our child, Kathy. I love you.

My love for you is that of compassion
And of truth for ever lasting.
You've showed me how you really care
In the love that we share.
I've waited so long for someone special like you,
That will help me through times so blue.
Now that we're together there are things I must show
Knowing now that I'll never let you go.

I call you my Princess and that's what you are,
Kathy, my love, you're as bright as a star.
I am all yours and you are all mine
And our love will be as warm as sunshine.
Our love grows stronger each and every day,
And stronger it will get, to God I pray.
I think of you all day and dream of you all night,
Knowing that our love is growing just right.

You are my number one and you'll always be,
Our love for each other shall be eternal, you'll see.
As free as a bird and pure as a dove,
it's the best that we've got, it's Our Love.
Blessed Be

Joëlle K Hearron
A FEELING

A tender smile
that moves the land
A loving look
and you take my hand
A casual movement
that stops the sea

A warm hand
and your love for me
A lingering kiss
that blocks the sun
A willing gaze
and my dream is done

Janis S Deitsch
PURPOSE ?

For my favorite poet . . . my sister, Dani.

Should I but stretch beyond my voice
I'd reach the silence sweet.
My head freely accepts the choice;
My heart forsakes retreat.

My mind would seek the hidden proof
That yearns to be discovered.
My hand grasps at forbidden truth—
All secrets now uncovered.

The margins of my courage worn,
I struggle to bring light to dark.
To dispel the vanity of being born.
To free the Earth; to leave my mark.

Jessica Zuck
ALWAYS IN YOUR HEART

To Susan, I give you the moon, the sun and the stars. Love Z

A sigh comes from my lips as I carefully
Pluck a sleeping rose for my hair,
Skipping through the blue daisies with joy,
Heart aloft on a summer cloud,
Eyes on the placid scene

Lying on my back—looking at the stars,
Filling my mind with wonder,
The sweet smell of poppies ring in my ear.

A place of joy, love and caring
No hurt ever to be found,
Swimming in the purple lake with its
Mallards and its lilly pads
I sing a sweet song always in your heart.

Shirley Diane Johnson-Wooten
MARTIN LUTHER KING, AND ME

This poem is dedicated to my family, my husband Charles Sr.., and our three children: Chakia, Charles Jr., and Ebone´. . .

I also have a dream,
Of Martin Luther King and me.
We both saw the world come together,
In Peace and Harmony.

Every one walked, hand in hand.
Every color, every man.
There was no hatred, no hunger.
Just Love, across the land.

But this dream was never over,
We must not interrupt this dream.
We must all love one another in Peace.
And this dream will become reality.

The whole world has to believe,
To make this dream come true.
Then the dream will be real,
For Martin Luther King, Me and You.

Florence C Janis
POETRY IN MOTION

Spirits soar—dancers of the night
Blades touching down on a canvas of ice
Freedom of speed fantasy of mind
Running, twirling, spinning, whirling
Experienced control of anatomy.
Toes tingling—itching to outline
Patterns on frozen crystal
Floating across space, head erect
Breath held in ecstasy—
Creating reflections
Emotional high—clash of steel
Ice chips spray a halo of mist
From windswept feet
We are alone—romance found
On a frozen sea of dreams!

Glenna M Baker
HATS OFF!

This poem is dedicated to all citizens of the United States of America.

The day for the big parade arrived
  And the crowds had lined the streets.
Some of the children down in front
  Were using the curb for seats.
Then was heard the sound of drums
  And the band began to play.
The people cheered and waved—
  The parade was on its way!
Up front a prancing horse
  Kept time with the music beat.
The Flag with its Stars And Stripes
  Held high, ahead of the marching feet.
Flags and Floats and Clowns and Bands
  And girls with twirling batons
Flowed on, to our delight!
  When close by my side went up a cry—
"Hats off! Hats off! When The Flag Goes By!"

Gretchen Yates Lum

Gretchen Yates Lum
THE PHYSICAL WORLD AND ME

Today I baked a terra cotta pie.
Stuffed it not with berries, dates and plums,
But a frog licking at the sky.
And forms of random shapes
Without sugar to glue them together.

Threw in equilateral triangles
Of color for human interest
And silver ones to reflect the shimmer
Off each smiling face that looked!

WOW! THIS PIE IS ALIVE!
Or is it my imagination?

Doris Ann Taylor
SHADES OF DARKNESS

Nocturnal beauty, shroud of mysteries
hiding so much
Yet, leaving some things to see.

The beauty of a star scattered sky,
searchlights crossing way up high
Bright lights shining like jewels.

The moon overhead, casting shadows on
the water
Lovers in warm embrace.

As the night comes silently, unearthening
the many sounds of the shadows
Mating calls, sounds of joy, sounds of fear,
sounds of love
Even a baby's cry is different in the dark.

Nocturnal beauty, cloak of calm, shattered
by those bent on destruction
and harm
For fear of discovery in the daylight,
they wreck the beauty of the night.

Nocturnal beauty, casting shadows, shielding
discovery, conjuring memories and
before the dawning,
Bringing our minds peace.

Erika Power
THE WAVES OF DESTINATION

As the waves rush to the shore
I find someone close to me
Whose life is filled with love
And of friends and family.

Who, like the waves, are reaching
Reaching for those distant shores
Sometimes just barely touching
Sometimes going just too far.

But the waves will always crash
And this someone tries real hard
So if luck goes pass our way
We might reach those distant shores.

Paula E Smith
INTO MY HEART, LOVE CAME

To: Glenn Breier—the only person who believed in me. You are my inspiration and my strength. I will love you always.

Into my heart, love came
on a slow, but violent trip
to the end of time.
Damned forever and ever,
but always mine
and never to end.

Tammy Kay LaVene
DON'T QUIT

In memory of Tammy, who was killed in a car accident April 1, 1989
Poem submitted by her Mother

When things go wrong
as they sometimes will,
When the road you're
trudging seems all uphill,
When funds are low,
and the debts are high,
And you want to smile
but you have to sigh,
When care is pressing
you down a bit . . .
Rest in you must,
but don't you quit.
Success is failure
turned inside out,
The silver tint of
clouds of doubt,
And you never can tell
how close you are,
It may be near when
it seems afar.
So, stick to the fight
when you're hardest hit . . .
It's when things go wrong
that you mustn't quit.

Dorothy Goodwin Stallings
THE POET'S QUEST IMMORTALITY

This poem is for my children, and their children.

O eternal sea
take my words,

Bathe them in thy
misty depths

Fling them in thy
foamy waves

Into Sun's brightness.

Let them soar,
white-winged as gulls
Flashing, spinning,
falling . . .

Into the Sea of Time
these words of mine

Immaculate them,
as the tide,
the sands of the shore.

Gracie Garcia
MY SPECIAL DAY

This poem is dedicated to Valerie Cortez, my aunt.

Today begins with the sunrise
When I open my sleepy eyes.
I get dressed
and eat my morning meal.
Then I take a walk outside
among nature's colorful wheels.
Then basically I bum around
collecting dust
just like the ground.
Then my perfect day
ends with me crossing the bends,
between day and night.

Karri Sizemore

Karri Sizemore
GOODBYES

Dedicated to: Bear Elementary School and to my grandpa Carl Woodard, whose death taught me the true meaning of Goodbyes.

The years have come and soon will be gone,
We have our memories to carry on.
The years have gone by so fast,
And all my elementary years are in the past.
But before I go away, I would like to say,
Thank-you in a very special way.
For the love and laughter we all shared,
And for the times when you were always there.
I'll miss my friends today and tomorrow,
Cause in my heart I feel such sorrow.
I know some of us may cry,
Because it's so hard to say goodbye.
I won't go back to those days,
Where we were just young kids, and always in a daze.
But as you may recall,
These have been the best 6 years of all.
But now that I am older, I understand,
But I would still like to return, to these golden days again.
I don't want to say goodbye, you are all my friends,
So all the times we have been late,
You know we will always cherish the years we had in 1988.

Charles W Murray
AN ODE TO MY SON DAVID

My son, my son, my greatest joy.
My son, my son, a beautiful boy.
Part of Mother and of me a part,
Because of you we smile from the heart.
Some day we'll have new roads to travel.
Good times, great joys & problems to unravel.
A bend in the road, a new mystery to explore,
Lakes, rivers, trees and more
Some roads will lead to
happiness . . . others best left alone—
But we'll all learn together,
The things we've never known.
Dancing eyes, laughter and a
wonderful smile—
You're a joy beyond words . . .
I wonder how?

Gaylle S Garrison
POETS DO

What do poets do? you ask,
What use are they? Where do they fit
Into the modern world? And are they relevant?
And when am I ever gonna need to know about
Andrew Marvel, Phyllis Wheatley,
Coventry Patmore?
(You're kidding, right, about
Coventry Patmore?)
And why do we have to read this stuff, anyhow?

We read for fun, for grace and favour, and for wonder
At those who are beyond ourselves, who may not fit
Into modern worlds, theirs, yours, and ours,
But make their own, and let us in, to thoughts
Beyond our thought until someone shows us how,
and worlds beyond our seeing until our eyes
Are given sight of stately mansions
We cannot, ourselves, build.

But poets do, they say,
Make of nothing something,
From white blank page and
insubstantial thought
Build worlds of dream and word
Like God.

Laura Lee Emrich
SHADOW OF LOVE

This poem is dedicated to Terry E. Land, whose love inspired me.

I know I can't be with you through every lonely night;
to lie there close beside you and wake by morning's light.
I cannot have the pleasure that I truly desire; to feel your body soft and warm like embers from a fire.
I cannot sit and talk with you the way I'd like to do;
to have the time to learn about the uniqueness that is you.
I cannot walk with you at night and gaze at star-filled skies; to stop and hold you close to me as time goes softly by.
Still my love is stronger than the day that we first met;
and this is something I want you never to forget.
Because although we live apart my love for you is true;
and never will I love someone the way that I love you.
I could not love you more, my dear,

if every day we shared; for in the shadows of our love there is no cold despair.
Your love is all I'll ever need how could I ask for more;
for you have touched me deeper than anyone has before.
And so my love for you will grow like flowers in the spring;
because to me you are my life, my world, my everything.
Through summer, fall, and winter you're my every smile;
for in the shadows of your love, my soul can rest awhile.

Betty Mills
MY CHILD
My child has brought new dimensions into my life, new responsibilities, and fears, new hopes and joys. Something to grow old for, something to count on and to watch out for.

This little miracle that I may call my own, which in a sense was once my own, is now a real person who will have to go through the struggles that I have, this child will lead a life of her own, with only my guidance and love to help her, with only my heart and hands to comfort her.

My prayers are for her future every day, will she choose to follow her mother's unguided footsteps, or will she become more special because of them.

As the days go on for us both, it is wonderful as well as heartbreaking to see this small person growing and becoming a personality of her own self, to see the many dimensions and depths that are emerging from a once totally dependent life.

Sometimes I am afraid for her, sometimes, I am almost afraid of her. The way that our children are growing now, what of the day when she can answer things for me, what of the day when she no longer needs me.

Lisa J Haidsiak
MY LOVE
Open your eyes—
See my love.
Open your heart—
Feel my love.
Open your arms—
Hold my love.
Open your life
Be my love.

Donna Scott
THE CORNERSTONE

Dedicated with love to our Dad, Floyd A. Wright, Nov. 20, 1888—July 23, 1979. Gone, but most certainly not forgotten!

So like the building, straight and tall, a family is grown,
The starting place for both of them is with the cornerstone.
God surely blessed our family by giving us a man
Who demonstrated strength untold, as very few men can.
His ways were strict, and sometimes hard for us to understand,
But soon we learned he only meant to lend a guiding hand.
He gave advice when we would ask, he gave us songs to sing;
To him his family was the very most important thing.
His music brought tremendous joy to all who came in touch;
Another reason he was loved by everyone so much.
When times were hard, as oft' they were, his courage faltered never;
His faith was strong, beliefs sincere, his sense of humor clever.
Looking back across the years now that we are all grown,
We understand what he went through, and the trials that he's known.
So great a man, so strong and good, we're thankful that we've had
Our "Superman in overalls," our CORNERSTONE, OUR DAD.

Diane K Glazier
MONTANA
Rolling foot hills signal
The approach of
Majestic mountains.
Waiting
Calling me
Home.
Hay bales, like
Loaves of bread,
Needing only
Giants.
Crippled cabin with
Empty eyes;
Watching the
Endless, meaningless flow of
Traffic.

Gaye Kettl
I LOVE YOU DAD, BUT
Looking searching all these years
What is cause for my tears.
Empty ache of my heart
Can't you fill, please that part?

What I'm searching for will never be
The love of my Dad has eluded me.
It was mine long ago
In my heart, that I know.

But for myself I'll let it go.
It really wasn't meant to be
But what shall I tell that little girl
Lost inside of me?

John L Ennis
IN THIS CORNER
Ah Death, you've found a poor opponent here—
I am no match for you, you need not fear
By me your title ever will be won.
I cannot do what no one else has done.
Each day. alas, is but another round
And I am up and at you with a bound.
I'm game enough in spirit, yet I know
This flesh is far too weak for such a foe
As you, who never yet have lost a bout.
By will alone I hope to last you out.
You're laughing now, for any day you choose,
You'll weary of the sport and I will lose.
In vain I struggle to avert the blow—
I should have thrown the towel in long ago.

Edward H Miner
THAT'S NICE
When I tell you how I feel
about you and all the rest
of things that are important to me,
you look out the window and say,
"that's nice."

Of all the events in my life,
you are my highest joy and lowest despair
and when I tell you this,
you watch a bird flying and say,
"that's nice."

Sometimes I get angry and scream
at you and the unfairness of life
dealing me this aloneness and
you watch TV and say, "that's nice."

So I left to live alone
in the company of earth
and look out the window
and watch a bird fly
and watch TV
and I say "that's nice."

Jennifer K Mays
THE FIRST VISIT

To my cousin Greg, and his family who miss him dearly.

The pain is coming back
That pokes at my deepest fear,
Of facing that you're gone—
It's now more than a year.

The first visit to your grave
And the tears swelled in my eyes,
When I remember all the sadness
From all of the desperate cries.

A million tears that day
Were falling from above,
Angels bowed their heads
As we prayed for our lost love.

Now God can only comfort
The hurt we'll always keep,
But we know that He'll protect you—
In your endless, peaceful sleep.

Calvin L Strong
CRACK IN MY DOOR

To My Only Begotten Son Julius L. Strong

There's a crack in my door . . .
I never seen one there before.
What evil have I stumbled upon?
What oblation could there be instore?
Precious possessions taken away without—
Guilty restraining everyday?

From it I see the light does—
Seep, surely to disturb a quiet sleep.
Waiting to bruise my sweaty head.
Hate message, crime or accident?
There's a crack in my door; but why—
Do I fear?

Who in the world could have put it there?
Was it made for sneaking peek on nights—
When ugly creepers . . . creep?
How could I be so wrong?
Was it there all along?
I would not have seen this brewing—

Trouble if eyes weren't sharp;
And peering careful.
I know it's not wise to stare; but
Could that person be lurking near?
Masquerading as my friend?
Trying to hide an obvious sin?

Laughing at my fearful look.
Looking casing from a roof.
Should I run in desperate escape?
Or try to chase my fears away?

Josephine Buttafuoco
SPIRIT OF AN AUTUMN LEAF
I am in autumn colours.
I feel the whisper of the breeze
I tremble, the time has come
For me to break free and surrender
To the mercy of the gentle breeze,
I die in sweet abandon.

Amanda Whittington
SUCH A BEAUTY 'TIS THY LOVE
Such a beauty 'tis thy love,
It sets my heart afire.
I know that I will ever love thee—
Till all the days retire.

Thou art bonnie—my lovely lass,
O' didst thou never know?
And bonnie shalt thou always be—
As always shalt the winds blow.

And tho' we shalt not live forever,
Our love shalt never die.
And when thou meetest me in heav'n,
We shall see the stars nearby.

Elizabeth Sturm
GIVE ME

To my family for believing in me and supporting me, and Geoff for all the wonderful things you are; the wonderful things you "give me."

Give me the air,
living breath of the fire,
Give me the sea
blue shimmering sapphire.
Give me the trees
hiding dark in the shade,
Give me their verdant leaves;
soft dancing jade.
Give me the wind
blowing soft on your face.
Give me the sun,
warm and bronze in its grace.
Give me the moon
with its face glowing white,
Give me the stars,
diamonds set in the night.
Give me the dawn
remnance of the moon's sigh,
Give me the rain
crystal tears from the sky.
Give me things lovely,
things born of His hand,
Give me the water, wind, sky,
and the land.
Give me this Earth,
floating marble of blue,
Give me the world.
And I'll give it to you.

Ophra Leyser
THE MIST HAS RISEN
As man's combat comes to an end
as the warfare smog disintegrates
Nature arises around the bend
and its beauty penetrates.

As it soon becomes healthy
and there are no more scars
the forest is replenished and wealthy

under the sky filled with stars.

So nature keeps on going
but people do not seem to care.
It makes its beautiful showing
which it lets us share.

Society does not even know,
Society does not even see.
What it is to hear the wind blow
as the leaves rustle the tree.

In life there comes a standstill
where we live no more.
And we do not fulfill
the pleasures we adore.

Throughout life we don't even think
nature was once in us all.
It was once a link.
From our birth, until our fall.

Lorene Swank
CATTY CO-WORKERS

To my parents who have gone on. I miss you. To my three sons and four grandchildren. I love you. To a couple at work—pfsst!

Another day to face the world, Co-
workers are so catty.
I think I'd rather stay in bed than
face that bunch so ratty.

I'm so tired of those loud mouths,
most of them are two-faced.
T'would be a better office if some
could be replaced.

Some women think they are too
good, They're the ones so stupid.
I think they are misplaced, they
should be playing cupid.

But miracles sometimes happen, two
have a good attitude.
For this, a great big blessing, I have
much gratitude.

Why wasn't I born rich? I'd like to
take a stand.
I'm forced to listen to their crap. It's
quiet that I demand!

The good ones always get away.
Sure do miss those folks.
The bad ones always seem to stay.
It's one of life's cruel jokes.

Female workers are the worst kind.
In fact some have the brass.
Is there an office somewhere with a
lot more class?

Life could be a better place if it
weren't for those so nosey.
Maybe I'd better change jobs. Do
you think there's one more rosy?

Anthony M Hughes
RELAXING TRIP

To Mrs. Weaver; who made me write poetry for class grades.

I know a trip in the car
can be very relaxing,
The trees so tall and green,
with broken branches from past
snow falls.
The air crisp and cool,
The birds singing in the tree tops,
The river so pure and sweet,
I know a trip in the car can be
relaxing.

Kevin V Osborne
TOKEN OF LOVE

Oh, how the rose has withered, weary is the stem that holds its bud, petals have turned pale, and the richness that once prevailed has perished into the atmosphere that surrounds us.

Clear crystal glass supports its remainings, as I search in vain for new life, but the petals keep descending leaving me grim, for new hopes that this rose will survive.

For it was with tenderness this rose was given, gently passed from hand to hand, it left a smile in my eyes, and a fragrance on my soul that will be etched in pure bliss forever.

Now I must come to the realization, that a rose is just a token of our love, and they do wither away, but I believe that's to say, keep the rose in your heart alive.

Felix-LaSalle Artis
MOM'S MEMORY

Dedicated to our Mother, Mrs. Jessie T. Artis, in memory of her mother, Ms. Ethel C. Turner. Phyllis, Jimmy, Felix, Conrad, Pamela

Ours was a special relationship only
you and I could share . . .
Often leading me to wonder, without
you, how did I fare.

For 20 years, your spirit has touched
me whenever I've felt low . . .
Spreading a blanket of security when
there's no place left to go.

Your memory will be cherished
forever—
still many times I'll cry . . .
Knowing that we've separated, but
never really said goodbye.

I miss you earnestly—however now
you know . . .
There's a beautiful life waiting on
the other side of the rainbow.

Cathy M Triano

Cathy M Triano
MOTHER SWEET MOTHER

Dedicated to My Mother Mary.

Mother Sweet Mother.
Your Charming Face.
And You Smile So Sweetly.
And You Are A Beautiful Mother.
I Love You Mother.

Kaye Barrett
SEAGULLS

To My Father and Mother, And to Janet—The Finest Seagulls of All.

Some people are like the sand,
mostly stationary—yet at times,
Very mobile. For they move
each time they are dug into,
And when you try to put them
back where they belong—
They never look quite right.

Some are like the waves, cold and
mean, lashing out at innocence
Their harshness tempting and
taunting, "Come near me." They beg,
Then drawing back, they leave
their angry foam to dirty the
sand.
They toss others like the surf
tosses the shrimp boats. They
need to prove something to
those whom they consider
inferior.

And, there are those like the seagulls.
Flapping their wings,
They are carried by winds of logic.
The blood of freedom surges through
their veins. They walk bravely on the
sand, not fearing the harsh waves.
When they are high they are in
communion with God. When they
are grounded they dream of being
high. Their cry is of peace and
solitude. When they inch close to
you they are quite plain. But watch
them soar—They are beautiful.

David Quinones
IRISH GIRL

I would like to dedicate this poem to Kayla Michelle Grado, who I like very much. I give her this Irish poem. I love you Michella.

I found an Irish girl,
With pretty red hair
So beautiful is she,
With those blue eyes sparking
at you
Pretty is she
As pretty as a rainbow in the sky
So darling, and gifted
And Irish is she,
She's still mine

Jack N Haley
PICTURES TO PAINT

To Jerry: the young girl who loved me long ago.

There are pictures I want to paint for
you
and baths I want to draw,
Things to build and make for you
with my hands, hammer and saw.

Your car I will wash and wax
your house I will sweep and mop,
The trees and bushes with my ax
I will trim from bottom to top.

I will stay when you think I'm Father
and will be there to be your Dad,
I will love you as a lover
to be the best you've ever had.

I will guide you through your life
as only you shall know,
And when all the troubles and strife
are finally over . . . then I shall go.

Vicki Lynn Fraser
HOW DO YOU KNOW YOUR LOVE IS AT STAKE

How do you know when your love is
at stake
Things seem so good, but yet are so
fake,
Being together is when things are
just fine
But then you hear those three words
that are all just a line.

Sometimes the feelings just seem so
cold
Then other times they're as solid as
gold,
You don't want to make good for
what you could jeopardize
But you can tell the feelings all
within the eyes.

There are so many times when you'd
just like to scream
All these feelings you wish for are
just a dream,
Sometimes they say that dreams will
come true
But love is one thing with which
there is few.

You work so hard for the very best
You try to be as good as all the rest,
Sometimes it seems like such a waste
But I guess it's something we all
must face.

Time is needed for everything
Sometimes it may hurt or even sting,
But just hold out through thick or
thin
And if it's for the best—you will
win.

Ronnie D Phelps
NEVER GROW OLD

Dedicated to Jackie Sue Warner (30th birthday), 4-20-85

Look thee and absorb the view
Of the many wondrous sights around
you;
The birds, the bees, the flowers, the
trees,
But not only these.
Stand silent, and too behold
The sounds of nature, ages old.
Even now with the wilderness gone
Mother Nature still lives on.
So even though your years may glide
Remember the little child inside.
Remember all the tears and cries.
Remember all the whats and whys.
And if thee do as thee was told
Thy spirit will joy and never grow
old.

Karma Lee Jones
HIS PROMISE

To everyone who reads these words, may you find peace, joy, love and God's promise to you.

One night while talking with a
friend,
Of the days events from the
beginning to end,
I heard someone speak out to me,
Listen here he said.

I am the Lord God,
The one who watches over thee,
You're having a bit of trouble here I
see,
But don't you know if left to me,
I can fix it all. Just wait and see.

From the smallest broken wing,
To the little boy who fell from the
swing,
To every living thing, I can mend it
all.

I said, Lord if you can do it all,
What do you ask of me?

He said, my child, the only thing
I ask of you is your Love,

For it was all created in Love,
Every Living Thing.

Kenneth King Jr
SNOW SQUALL

White. Purposeful.
Darting creatures within the swarm,

Each tracing that one path in the
Universe
Relentless gravity and capricious
wind have drawn.

Insect motion eerily inaudible,
Their windy matrix sways a creaking
branch.

Eddies within the northeast wind
Generate trajectories bizarre and
unpredictable.

One flier pulls up inches from the ground and
Climbs steeply to gain altitude for a better landing.

Another strains to parallel the earth
Postponing the inevitable with a final reconnaissance.

Suddenly an explosion, a white puff
In the midst of this smoothly functioning chaos.

A microcosmic catastrophe,
A rare collision at a juncture of flight paths.

Stragglers from the last wave now descend,
Reluctant to give up their airborne freedom,

Unaware of Spring's consoling metamorphosis of
Icy wings to vapor for countless future flights.

Jean Ann Maxie

Jean Ann Maxie
BERRIES EVERYWHERE

This poem is dedicated with tremendous love to my children: Bob, Al, Arny and Caley Lou.

Berries everywhere! Berries down by the river gushing swiftly by, seeming to be on the escape from the majestic mountains.

Berries on the mountainsides, adding bright cheery colors in addition to the foliage and flowers.

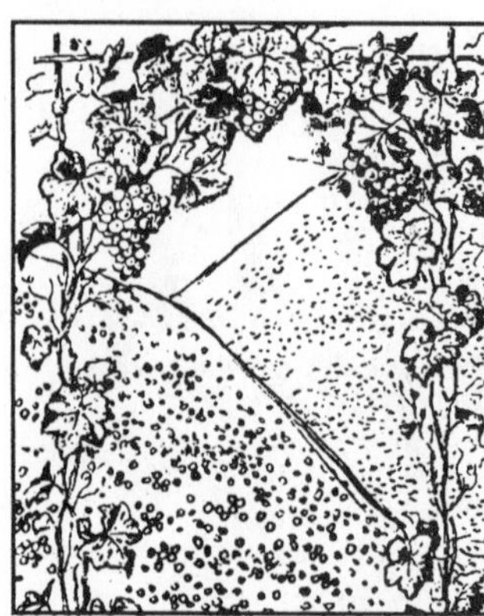

Berries on the squishy tundra, berries sitting quietly by the lakes. Berries hiding ever so still underneath the little willows. Berries bobbing up and down, seesawing in the wind-swept branches, as though signalling and calling out softly: "pick me, pick me!," almost like an echo growing further and further away.

Little children running playfully through the endless sea of berries all around, as if they were in a gigantic bowl of alphabet soup.

Marlene Wall
THE HE THAT USED TO BE

This poem is dedicated to all my great friends in Wyoming.

The he that used to be
  is now never more.
Yes, people do change
  for various reasons galore.
At times we think it strange
  to see how people change.
Then as we walk out the door,
We think of the he
  that used to be.

Carol Weal
DESTINY

For My Mother, My Friend

Distant thoughts arouse my mind
to awake my most inner being.
I can't quite grasp the meaning of
the visions I am seeing.
What triggers the memories
my mind continues to hold?
Maybe an expression it tries to
unfold.
Reflections of my thoughts within.
A symbolic message which could
have been.
Why tempt your mind to awake the
past?
You can't redo what has since been
cast.
Take hold of what is to be.
For this my friend, is destiny.

Reinert B Kvidal
VOLUNTEERS

The hostile winter round each corner
The wintry days like baffles set
Thrusting snow and stinging ice—
colder
Seeking unrelenting unprotected
targets;
Then it's nice to be indoors
And feel the furnace warming all
Watch T.V. and, tonight, go out no
more.

The same as this, cold and wet
The season same for each; we
Big and small: The piling snow yet
deeper still and the same for others to
be
Home and warm snug in bed
But for winters frosty windows and
banging
Doors allowed to enter an icy breath.

So then some people finely dressed
In warm coats with furry collars
From houses warm in cars no less
To churches warm to speak of dollars
To use that others might know of
safety
Warmth; and food; shelter adequate
from
The cold baffling round a corner
waiting.

Kenneth Wood
FALLEN LEAVES

  From the pages of un-published
  books
where the eyes of man has never
seen,
  the mind of a poet begins
  searching for a dream.

  Always seeking to open the
  door—to things never seen.

to him, a poem is like a flower
  that always seems to grow,
from deep within the heart of an
angel
  so the story goes,

And where the power of his words
come from,
  Only God really knows,

like the falling leaves,
  Leaving their footprints in the
  snow.

Elizabeth C Meier
AN ELEPHANT WITH HIS TUSK RAISED HIGH

To my son, Robert for his accomplishments as a teacher

An elephant with his tusk raised high
Carries a token of good luck;
A book beside it above the
elephant's thigh
Indicates the teaching you have
struck.

Dennis J Hoppa
MY FATHER

David a man of great love & wisdom. A man who loved all of us equal. A man who lived for his children.

Here lies my Father,
He is dead.

There is no blood in his cheek,
in his hand there is no nerve,
He is Dead.

I will speak for my Father,
I will say what there is to be said,
I will set forth what he tried to set
forth,
He is Dead.

It is not easy for me to speak,
In my empty heart there is no song,
There is no light up above,
There are no words in the world,
To Honor my Father,
He is Dead.

Mary G Nigro RN
I JUST WANNA DANCE

I just wanna dance.
Don't want no romance—
It's dancing, I'm missing,
Not any one's kissing.

Want some arms around me,
But not embraced romantically
Only to guide me o'er the floor,
So I can dance once more,

To the old tunes of days gone by,
Songs that we danced to, you
and I.
Don't want to see a flirting glance,
'Cause all I wanna do is DANCE!

Barbara J Bailey
REFLECTIONS OF JESUS

Dedicated to our Lord and Savior Jesus Christ and to those He has brought unto me in his Love: my parents, Leroy and Hazel; my sister and brother-in-law, Beverly and Jimbo; my daughters, Kelly Beth and Deborah Dee and my grandsons, Daniel Adam and Dustin Lee.

Precious Savior, I long to be like You
I pray to bring joy to each heart
I ask that You give me sweet words
of joy
And the gift of love to impart

I lift Your Name far beyond the
clouds
Your sweet fragrance I cast to the
wind
The hills resound with Your lovely
music
Each heart can feel You within

Grant, Precious Lord, bits of wisdom
Nuggets of truth from Your mind
Blessed assurance of Your wondrous
presence
I pray each longing soul will find

I sit by the waters of Life by Your
side
Your reflection looks back at me
The goodness I seek in this world,
Lord
I knock and I find it in Thee

Oh, reflections, reflections of Jesus
I pray, Lord, that I might be
A mirrored reflection of Jesus
Others would see Your reflection in
me!

William Spatz
THE OCEAN

I would like to dedicate this poem to the ones I love and cherish, my Mother and Stepfather.

The Ocean is a world of excitement
The gallant crashing waves are
gleaming
  as they crash into the shore line
  rocks
The fish are the guardians of the sea,
For they might all be enemies
  though they all work together to
  welcome new life.
Is it that the ocean is a reflection of
us?
And us a reflection of them?
Who knows!

Chundra Lynn Daniels
NOURISHMENT OF LOVE

To my mother Marvia, my father Ray, Gail, Michael, and all of my concerned wonderful friends who have helped and pushed me, especially Richard, Randy, and Liana.

Love asks for nothing
It nourishes itself
With the joy and happiness
Of two compatible souls

Souls that hunger
In a common desire
To obtain the same pleasure
To quench a distinct craving

A craving that is patient
One not irritable or touchy
It doesn't boast nor show envy
Only flourish in the satisfaction it
has found

Satisfaction of a special gift
That can not quote a price
It comes from deep within
And glows in an outer shine

But if the souls' common desire
dissolves
And the craving becomes impatient
So shall the flourishing
Of pleasure and satisfaction be
denied

William G Kimmey
FATE

Sometimes my thoughts are far
away,
But mostly they're of you.
You've changed my days to
happiness,
When once they were all blue.
I dream about the days gone by,
And times of yesteryear.
And wonder how I got through life,
Without someone so dear.
My love for you has grown so much,

Yes darling, this is true.
It's strange how fate will Play a game,
And finally give me you.
The time will come when we can be
Together till our death.
Just remember, I will love you
With my dying breath.

Deborah Treat Carlisle

Deborah Treat Carlisle
COLOR SCHEME DREAM

This poem is dedicated to my beautiful family, Bob my husband, and Robert and Bryan, my sweet little children.

I ran through a rainbow the other day
Upon the hill where I used to play
A beautiful dream of the color scheme

Stars took the place of the day that night
I stayed at the hill till I rose at light
It was my place
my place
A place of lace and frills and skills of nature
my place
I hadn't seen my place for years and years
Before that day of the color scheme dream
I had to return—and I did—to stay
And I saw the magical stars of day
but I saw them in a different way
and then I knew
I was a part
of that rainbow

Lori A Barnes
MISSING YOU
When you've been gone so long
my body craves your touch,
though my dreams give me a heartache,
I tend to sleep too much.

Lynn DeOgny
MELANIE'S BABY
Melanie's baby, so soft and sweet,
In Satin and Bows from head to feet.
Her mother's pride, her mother's joy.
Her father's love, her father's toy.
She sleeps so soundly and peacefully,
Unaware of the turmoils within me.

A grandmother before my time has come,
Ready instead for a daughter or son.
Not yet ready for the rocking chair,
And fighting hard my silver hair.
Motherhood was hard enough you see.
Grandmotherhood? Not yet Lord!
Not me!

No words can possibly ease this pain.
My world will never again be the same.
Until I can hold her and see her face,
Touch her hands and know her place.
And when I know she is really mine.
Then my world will all be fine!

Elizabeth Grace Jeffords
ROSE

To: Love

My love is like
a rose
growing in a
big world
determined to
grow strong.
Making hearts bleed
like thorns
on long green stems
that prick
someone who's un-
aware.
The delicate
red glow
is as gentle
as Love's
sweet emotion
can be.
My love is like
a rose
as beautiful
as the
soft fragrant petals;
dying . . .

Terry Johnson
DEAR CO-WORKER
We're sorry if we upset you
by writing you this note,
but we'd all like you better
if you'd used some soap.

We know deodorants cost money
and none of that is cheap,
but you could smell sweet as honey
instead of a raunchy ol' heap.

We hope we didn't offend you,
we only meant well,
but somebody had to tell you
that you really smell.

Joni E Snider
THIS LAND SO BEAUTIFUL!

To my Mom, thanks for believing!

The wind it whispered through the trees,
The beauty brought me to my knees.
The bright green pasture that lay ahead,
With daisy flowers and poppies red.

The new born fawn beneath the pine,
Hardly seen and so entwined.
The bright blue sky seemed all around,
It magically blends with the ground.

The lake that glistens in the sun,
Makes me feel with nature one.
The smell of soil fills my nose,
Seems more fragrant than a rose.

I want so much to embrace this earth,
My wonderful America, my place of birth.
The silence broke as I spoke loud . . .
This land so beautiful makes me proud.

Joe Thompson
FROM ME, TO YOU
Sittin' here all alone
With this bottle in my hand
Gettin' drunk feelin' low
Tryin' to understand

Wishin' I had done things right
Wonderin' where I went wrong
Drownin' myself in my sorrow
Hurtin' for so long

Watchin' the fire, thinkin' of you
Makes tears fall like rain
Feelin' so much sorrow inside
Feelin' so much pain

The smoke fills the air in this room
As if I were in a bar
Couldn't give you money so I gave you love
Cuz' I know I won't go far

No help from my friends and family
So who can I turn to
I'm between a rock and a very hard place
But baby I still love and need you.

Karen L Stallworth
SPIDER

To Lucille Wacaster who taught me it's never too late to make your dreams come true.

A fat black spider stares at me,
Behind him hangs the night.
But the lacy web he spins as home
Is delicate and light.

A gentle breeze caresses it;
The moonlight makes it shine.
He proudly smiles to have created
A tapestry so fine.

Torrential rains have knocked on it;
Winds have tried to snare.
The battle won, he has the right
To keep his home right there.

No, I shall not sweep it down,
This skillful made creation.
He'd only build again somewhere
With new imagination.

Learn from spiders—spin your dreams,
And if they should fall through,
Build again! For if you don't
Your dreams will not come true.

Rosemary T Dunleavy
A CHILD'S WORLD

This poem is dedicated to the Class of 1964, Valley Stream Central H. S., N.Y.; The Class of 1968, Queens College, Flushing, N.Y.; and those servicemen and women who died during the Vietnam War.

Oh, to explore the world that is known by a child.
To gaze in awe at fresh fallen snow—
To be thrilled by the glory of the downpouring rain—
To marvel at life's bigness, color, and depth—
To be yet untouched by the hands of prejudice—
To see but beauty in all living things—
To fathom only goodness and perceive little evil.
Oh! to know the world that is explored by a child.

Hazel Cherry
THANKSGIVING IS NEAR
Thanksgiving is near again.
My favorite holiday throughout the year
Brings to my mind the love we need to share
Be thankful we have the strength to live
And to have those we love so near.

Eating, drinking, making merry in our hearts
Laughter spreading all around
Counting our blessings coming throughout the year
Giving those we love the love without a frown.

Hoping the years ahead will continue to come
And bring joy for those we share makes Thanksgiving.

Lori L Lee
COLOR ME . . .
Color me blue,
For the tears, I've cried.
Color me white,
For the times I've lied.
Color me pink,
When you cheered me up.
Color me dark,
When the times were rough.
Color me green,
For the walks in the park.
Color me gray,
When we kissed in the dark.
Color me silver,
For the love we felt,
Color me gold,
When we sat and just held.
Color me white,
For the times I lied.
And color me blue,
When we said good-by.

(Princess Mar) EKJ Garit Mandalionmefgco King (M E Shriver)

(Princess Mar) EKJ Garit Mandalionmefgco King
(M E Shriver)
LAND'S WONDERMENT

To: My King Perry Lee King, Kings, Presidents, all our people, close family, soldiers including myself that do care and keep Almighty God's world.

I tried before Almighty God's wondrous dawn.
To see out there only whiteness of objects—snow thereupon.
Lights were on, amid the rising vapors borne.
Eerie except for happy sound to early dawn, morn. (morning)

Grasses were stiff with ice.
They felt to your feet as little knife.
The lands wonderment is still with me.
Awe as I open to Almighty God's creations each morning, you see.

This brought to mind the Misty Ills with the ship in silvery moonlight.
I could see the golden shore of sands and what a pretty sight.
I beheld the glory of the land, thus so.

The trees swayed to the whispers of the breezes I know.

I was lain on the grasses with perfume of the flowers as pleases, you see.
Truly a wonderful night for me.
I also walked the thin valley amongst the mountains of night, where I felt the cushiony grasses with my bare sandaled feet.
I could smell the fragrance of the King's garden wafted
over the mountains as I took a seat.

I looked up at the darkness and there the full moon shed its light silvery beams on me.
I was not alone for Thou art with me, I could see.
I was suddenly brought back for you stood by me.
With all of Almighty God's natures graces be.
Abide with me said he on most high—enjoy creations you see.

Stacy Helminiak
I'LL NEVER FORGET
I'll never forget the way I felt when you said, "Goodbye."
You gave me one last hug and went your own way—
You couldn't bear to see me cry.
Even though it's over I know you still care;
You couldn't leave me that easy after all we've been through.
Maybe someday you'll realize what you've done—
how bad you hurt me—
But until then, I'll be waiting for you to return.

Aixa Gerena
IT'S SUCH A WASTE

This poem is dedicated to all who need to find TRUTH, instead of an ESCAPE. May God bless you all!

It's such a waste, when the sweetness of life you've yet to taste.
So, why drown yourself inside that bottle. (Booze)
Why freeze to death in all that snow. (Cocaine)
Why try to fly just like a kite. (Pot)
Why pop without a fight. (Pills)
Why crack up without a joke. (Crack)
Why not listen to your folks.
You're not happy with what you're doing,
who do you think you're fooling.
You're the only one you're going to hurt,
because pretty soon you'll turn to dirt.
So just throw those things behind, and a new life you will find.
Don't give up without a try,
I'm not telling you no lie.
From over here I'm going to pray, so that soon you'll be able to say . . .
"I don't want to be a waste,
and the real sweetness of life I want to taste!"

Carol Follis Hutchison
OH, BEAUTIFUL ROSE
Oh, rose, with your petals so velvety soft
Bring great warmth to many hearts
Your beauty is beyond my belief
How one flower can cause so many tears
Tears of joy and tears of sorrow
The beauty of the rose, brings tears tomorrow
A rose, the best loved flower in the world
Petals soft, such velvety soft, as you unfold
Flowers galore, God made plenty
Rose, oh beautiful rose, I want to be—
As beautiful as you have meant to me

Robin G Brown
A SPECIAL FRIEND
While sitting upon my back, your child has seen,
Wide open pastures with grass o' so green.
We've rode to the mountain tops in the spring
And never home did I fail him to bring.
We've forged the rivers all the days of summer,
And I've lain beside him at night when he slumbers.
We've trotted thru meadows in the fall,
And colors? Man, we've seen them all.
Belly deep in snow we've tread during winter,
But he's always been home in time for dinner.
We've swam the ocean—to explore the lands on the other side,
Yet darkness found him in his room—by your rules we did abide.
We're galloped into space, out beyond the blue,
Simply because he had nothing else to do.
So I think you can see why my heart breaks with such force,
When I hear you say, "Oh that's just my kids silly ol' hobby horse."

M Akal Kaur Wieting
HOW LONG MUST WE WAIT?

To Honor and Glorify that Infinite Truth . . . from which all things come and to which all things go . . . Sat Nam

How long must we wait
for the world NOT to hate?
Lack of respect for all sentient beings.

Why? says the man . . .
Why not? says the dove . . .
There is nothing more lasting than Love.

Is it fear
of death?
Letting go?
transition?
What keeps us from peace?
greed?
competition?

The teachers of man . . . illumined souls . . .
have shown us the ways to achieve our goals.
Goals must be for good, or, we all suffer . . .
We're inter-dependent . . .
one for the other.

All Nature's kingdoms come from the One . . .
we live in abundance . . .
enough for all.
So, let us share . . . co-operation . . .
We'll make it together . . . one world . . . one nation.

Michelle Ann Johnson

Michelle Ann Johnson
COLORED FEELINGS

To my mother, Mavis Anderson Miller, with love

What color am I?
What color am I?
I am a tranquil blue like the sky above.
I am a gentle white like a precious dove.
I am a sparkle of gold and I do shine bright.
I am a bold black facing the world alone at midnight.
I am a flaming red and burning with fire.
I am a seductive fuchsia with a passion of desire.
I am a vicious brown like a growling bear.
I am a cowardly yellow facing the truth and not dare.
It really doesn't matter what color I appear to be.
The only thing that matter is the character that exists deep inside of me.

Betty M Cook
LOVE THY NEIGHBOR
Everyone knew my neighbor.
She
Was PTA, Church Hill, Senior Citizen,
Fair Housing, Camp for the Blind, Teacher,
Antique Cars, Sailor, Writer,
Lay Minister,
Methodist . . .

She
Cooked, Baked, Mothered, Scolded,
Grandmothered, Humored,
Smiled, Listened,
Sang, Studied, Loved, Suffered,
Died . . .

She
Was a Christian and talked openly of God,
Handled His Love in a special way.
But, I loved her most, my neighbor,
Because she taught me to
Pray . . .

Donna E Norton
WHEN I DIE
When I die don't weep for me,
My body will be dead but my soul will be free.
I live a life down here on earth,
My mother brought me in by birth.
I was born not once but again makes twice,
My father above made a sacrifice.
So when I'm gone from this place,
I won't be here to show my face.
All that's left are memories shared,
For those ones who really cared.

Sue Bozarth
A GENTLE MAN
A gentle man . . .
Loving, hardworking,
With calloused hands
Gentle enough to rock
seven children
Strong enough
to start them straight
down life's path.

Eighty now, and stooped,
but still with a twinkle
in his one eye
(lost the other
in an accident years ago)
My friend,
the father
of my husband . . .
A gentle
man.

Jeri Mae Poppe
DADDY

For my Dad, Jerry. Thank you and I love you.

Fourteen years ago I
knew a little girl who
never really knew her own
Daddy's touch.

The reason for this was
that her Daddy drank just
too much.

Years passed by and her
Daddy received some help.
Now this little girl I
know, no longer has
a reason to cry.

Julie A Olson
I WANT
I want to play hide n' seek
paint birds in the attic
chase you in a cornfield
lie on a sandy beach
play golf in craters on the moon
ride bareback in the desert
count the stars above . . .
as I sit on a blanket of cool green grass
I want to taste forbidden fruit
and tie dye the sky magenta
journey through the black holes of space
take me to a high mountain where
I can feel the reign
find me a place in this world
where everyone believes
in freedom and peace . . .

Diane M Morelli
A WALK ALONG THE BEACH
On a warm summer night,
As the gentle breeze blows,
The mighty ocean roars,
Upon the beach the water flows.
I love it here at night,
Just you and I together,
You feel like it'll never end,
And you'll be with him forever.
The beach holds love,
And never any fright,
If you go, you'd discover,
As you're wrapped up in its might.
It's romantic in the stillness,
So peaceful and serene,
If you take a walk, along the
beach,
You'll see just what I mean.

Carie L MacDonald
DAYLIGHT ANON
The dawn wakens in taciturnity
with the rising sun.

Young rays turn dew drops into
dancing spirits of the day.

Softly glittering, they reform the
blackened plains of night into
golden beauty of morning.

With each passing hour the sun
mounts itself higher and higher
upon the sky until this
star afire brings a vision so
enlightening that we struggle to
see due to its undiscerning ability.

The fervor is so grand that we
dream that star afire will
warm us infinitely . . .

And soon we come to see
that this spirit of the day
will truly burn eternally.

Mark Trenton Lethco
THE KING
His blackened, grimy hands clutched
his only treasure
cradled in a brown paper sack
as he sat upon his throne.

His throne was so carefully erected
from discarded wood and rusted
nails.
His kingdom limited
to the vast chasm of the rusted out
box car.
As he drank from his wealth,
his lips parted to reveal a toothless
smile.

A train whistle blew in the distance
and it began to rain.

Edward M Opoka
GOD'S GOLDEN GIFT IN PERIL

*To my son, Matthew, his generation,
and the next,
That they may live in a clean
environment.*

I'm often quite dismayed
and find it hard to understand
Man's folly so displayed
in our precious waters and land.

Yes, God in his goodness and
glorious might
created Earth in just six days,
Mankind in his imperfect
wisdom and knowledge
must destroy it in so many ways.

The air, land, and sea grow
darker and grayer
as the years go rolling on,
Oh, why can't we see that if we
don't stop
the earth's beauty will one day be
gone.

For what right has any one
person
for his own luxury to destroy
God's golden gift of nature
one meant to cherish and enjoy.

And, so as I gaze off into the
sunset
some pollution may catch my eye,
I'll stop and offer a prayer to
the Lord
as I bow my head to cry.

Kimmery Ann Mackie
DO YOU KNOW THE DIFFERENCE?
There are so many things
I've tried to say to you.
But the words never came out
quite the way I wanted them to.

The many hours we were together
things went well.
I wish I would've known
what the future was to be.
But of course, as we know,
there was no way to tell.

It would've made things easier
if your mind I could've read.
Because your words were different
than what was really in your head.

So were they "just words," or were
they coming from your heart?
Do you know the difference?
Can you tell the two apart?

Margaret Leatherwood
BABY JESUS
The Innkeeper said to Joseph,
"There is no room today."
So little baby Jesus
Was born in a manger on the hay.

I wish I could have been there
When little Jesus was born.
I would have picked Him up
And held Him in my arms.

Oh, how I would have loved Him
And caressed His sweet little face.
I would have known no other
Could ever take His place.

I would have seen the shepherds
That came to worship Him,
And I could have knelt by His
manger
To worship there with them.

Now Mary's little baby
So precious and divine,
Has become our dear saviour,
So loving and so kind.

Hugh W Vaughan Jr
THROUGH CHILD-LIKE EYES
The simple things in life
Are often hidden when
Nothing is seen through child-like
eyes
And words must be said again.

Flowers dripping with rain or dew,
Rainbow's promise clearly in view,
Sounds of springtime and the
inquisitive "why"
Mean nothing but through child-like
eyes.

So, when even "I love you" isn't
enough
And new-born babies cry too much,
Nothing quiets the sounds of
whipped pups
Like the mother's voice and the
father's touch.

For when faith lives one day at a
time,
Then things are seen through child-
like eyes.

Katie Evans
DREAMS
Hazy images,
They dance through my head,
Late at night,
As I lie asleep in my bed.

Knights in shining armor,
And damsels in distress,
Princes and princesses,
And all the treasures of that they
are blessed.

Heroes and heroines in times of
war,
And hellish creatures consumed in
gore,
Sometimes romantic as they be,
Or so scary that they frighten me.

In my dreams I choose the life I
want to,
For when I awaken to face reality,
I know that my dream can never
come true.

Tamara Benson
AFTER THE RAIN
The Summer rain ceased to fall.
Clouds, in shredded little puffs,
Chugged along like white boats,
Over the darkened skies—
The raindrops still hanging
From the glistening pine boughs.
In the cathedral of stately trees,
Steamy smoke came within,
As of from a green altar—
An earthly offering of thanks,
To the mighty heaven for the rain,
Giving life to all things again!

The air is scented of grass and weeds
And of the distant and disturbed sea,
As we walk along the silvery trees,
Among an open pass of purple
heather—
You kissed my damp and glossy
cheek
And I, your tender, sunburned neck,
What do we care about the world?
We had found our own,
Under the misty pine bough dome—

Laurie D Martinez
IF WE ONLY DARE (A SONG)
There's a spark that zooms inside
me,
Makes my heart want to sing and
share;
For I know that what's designed for
us
Is ours if we only dare:
Dare to love, dare to give, dare to ask
for better sight;
Dare to see ourselves blossoming
ever in the light!

We're a part of our creation
As we choose all the ways we go;
And the spark of God in all of us
Encourages as we grow:
Grow to laugh, grow to cry, grow to
ask for what is true;
Grow to understand everything good
in all we do!

Shall we celebrate the birthdays
That are happening everywhere?
Light the candles now for all of us,
Unfolding because we dare:
Dare to dream, dare to have, dare to
ask for what is right;
Dare to see ourselves blossoming
ever in the light!

Susan LaBarge
PACKING
boxes full of empty
memories
shake them out and see just how they
feel
do they still fit the picture as you see
it ?
can you still taste them as they were
fresh?

boxes full of cloud
not even rain with the storm
thunder words and lightning eyes
how much longer will this rain of
you
pour down
into
my
boxes full of empty

search through every one you gave
me
trying to find a piece of you
and wonder
if your boxes full of memories
are as filled with this grey-blue

Rosemarie Kivits
FRIEND OF THE SAND
Blue was the sky
Shiny the shells
Footprints led me
Where seagulls dwell.
Bronze was your skin
As I saw you there
Sorting the shells
With delicate care.
"Friend of the sand"
I named you than
Memories I'll keep
Of a wonderful man.

Janice E Hacket
THOUGHTS OF LOVE
My thoughts of you
Just flow through me with
sun-kissed warmth,
Their waves of love caress
The shoreline of our meeting,
Only to recede again into glistening
hope,
Awaiting your footprints in the sand
To hold me captive.

Rose Payzant Strever
IMAGE IN THE WINDOW

To all my children with love Mom

I looked at her picture the other day
and saw in her eyes the wish of days
gone by.
The hopes and dreams which she
once knew have slowly faded from
her view.
It's a twist of fate some may say, but
that is not true.
We can blame everyone and
everything: But, when it all boils
down, which it will, she will always
blame you.
The one she should turn to she
ignores and he is waiting for her call.
With this plea, I do pray, that she
will turn and head his way.
Please pick yourself up from the
floor and knock at God's holy door

Mark Allen McBride
THE FRIEND I NEVER HAD

This poem is dedicated first to my almighty Heavenly Father for His strength; To my loving parents: Willard & Ruby B. McBride; my grandmother: Ludie McBride; And to: Pauline, A.C., Greg, Nelson, Polly, Tara, Tia, Maryanne, & Judge Bonney

I never had anyone to care
It seemed, no one could understand.

In everyone's eyes I was just a stranger,
Unimportant, unwanted and facing danger.

I longed to be more than just somebody,
I longed to be a friend.

A friend in whom others could confide,
And rest assured that I was on their side.

I continued my life in total darkness;
Lonely, sad and feeling homeless.

No one expressed attitudes of sharing,
Which in my eyes was second to caring.

I felt permanently estranged from all who met me,
And even from those who had helped to raise me.

I continued to wander aimless along
Until one day, someone said, "You belong!"

I happily replied,
At last, "The friend I never had!"

Quetta Copley Church

Quetta Copley Church
PRAYER OF A TRUCKER'S WIFE

This poem is dedicated to Donald Church, my beloved husband.

This is the prayer of a trucker's wife,
I've said it, each day, nearly all of my life;
Thank you, for keeping him safe out there
And for answering some of my many prayers.

Over thirty years, up and down the road,
Atop eighteen wheels, with a heavy load;
Dodging all the crazies and the "Smokey Joes";
It's a story my old trucker knows,

My trucker says, "You've gotta have faith,
Love the Lord, with all of your might;
While you grind those gears and burn those brakes,
It's gonna be a long, long night!"

Oh Lord! Keep him safe, on the road at night;
Keep his eyes wide open, 'til his goal's in sight;
Let him not be too lonely, as he finds his way;
Bring him home to me, safe and sound today.

Tania Evans
DREAMS OF AN ORPHAN

To my family for their love and support And to the homeless, may your dreams come true.

Will someone hear my crying?
See the sadness in my eyes.
And know inside i am dying to be part of their busy lives.
I can only dream of having a home, a family to love me
a pet of my own.
To be treated with kindness, and know that you care.
There's love in my heart that i want to share.
If only dreams did come true, i'd have a happy heart.
I want to keep on hoping, but my dreams just fall apart.
I am only asking for love, you see.
Please take the time to think of me.

Janice Fraizer
DOWN THE HALL

To my family, with love.

Sleep no longer comes easy,
Many hours to stare at the wall.
Silence hangs like a heavy mist,
And there's only darkness down the hall.

A gentle breeze softly blows,
Searching for a place to stay.
The old house forbids its guest,
Like darkness forbids the day.

A moment struggles like forever,
With nowhere to go at all.
Silence shakes hands with the calm,
And there is only darkness down the hall.

Frances Bertucci
TIDES OF TIME

To Louie, Tricia and John, with love always.You are my life, my love and my reason for living.

I am but a mere drop of water in a turbulent sea
Though I appear to be inconspicuous, do not underestimate my powers
When tides constantly change, I try to keep an equal balance
I strived to be high, yet the tides kept me low
I came crashing against the doom, because I felt the need to rise above
I will indeed beat my breasts upon the sands, only to be swept away into the turbulent sea
I know the tides now, though they appear unchanged, nothing ever remains the same
The turbulent sea can also be tranquil, providing peace and harmony
The depth will determine who rises and who stands in shallow waters
Waves of frustration separate the strong and those who will be swept away
Yet the moon will continue to radiate and there is a sparkle in the dark waters
For it takes but a mere drop to reflect a light in the darkness, as the moon rests quietly upon her crest.

Robert Steve (Bob) Allison Jr
HEAVEN: ANY TAKERS?

To my Poetry-loving, Poetry-writing Aunt, First Cousin, and Second Cousin—respectively: Beulah Page, Marilynn Kaye Follis, and Brenda Kay Clausen. May they—and all Poets, Everywhere—continue to hold up the light . . . .

All de Po'try Conventions:
a sweet success, dis we know—-

An' if dey ain't no Po'try in Heaven:
den who de Heck want t' go?!

Ross P C Carroll
SHE WAS

She was of a different nature, a different culture, a different way.

She was my depressant, my stimulant, my desire.

She was what I wanted to hold, what I wanted to caress, what I wanted to satisfy.

She was my emotions, my thoughts, my fantasies.

She was what made me smile, what made me hurt, what made me laugh.

She was who I wanted to be with, who I wanted to share with, who I wanted to explore with.

She was talented, intelligent, beautiful.

She was more to me, than I to her.

She was something I could never have.

Paul J Michko
PRISMATIC VISION

Rain droplets falling down 'cross my face
Prismatic visions of life interlace
Coloring thoughts with translucent paint
Mind wanders slowly through light sources faint
Hear sounds of voices screaming out loud
As rays of the sun break through a cloud
Test the endurance of life as a whole
Watch closely to see its effect on the soul
Skyscraping rosebuds of purple and gold
Wings of a butterfly gently unfold
Futile endeavor to reason with lies
Laughing and playing while a small baby cries
All senses disrupted by a spectral design
Try to balance all thoughts on a thin wavy line
Wiping my eyes as the downpours now cease
Clear vision returning, mind now is at peace

Sharon Ford
LOVING MEMORIES

In memory of my Father, Elmer Spradlin, Who passed away Sept. 12, 1987

Hello Daddy, I wish I could say,
It's been a year since you went away.
I wish we could sit and reminisce about the past year,
Why, Daddy I just know you'd have to wipe away a tear.
You'd tell me about Heaven, God on his throne,
I'd tell you about my work, and your grandson getting reborn.
You'd tell about the pearly gates, the streets of pure gold.
We'd have to have a laugh and you'd say
"That's the biggest fish story you've ever told."
Why, I can just see you now, your eyes full of delight,
Singing with the Angel Band, where there is no night.
There's so much I could tell you, the things I now can do.
Like the things you talked about doing, now I do them for you.
I'd like to hear you tell about meeting a friend or two,
About how Jesus said, "Elmer, I welcome you!"
I can hear the angels singing in a voice sweet and low,
You singing bass on "Swing Low, Sweet Chariot."
Daddy it's been awhile since we last sat and talked.
You promised you'd wait by the tree on high.
Where someday we'll all be together in the sweet bye and bye.

Gerald Jessup
DETINU SETATS
Detinu—Setats

Explain thy ritual
of Citsilairetam
Seulav

eno. Nourish thy
computary vaults
owt. Distract from thy
filings that
which suits thy
being and weave
thy pattern
drith. Match and lock
each with binding
from thy acquired
wisdom of times
past and now
Then harvest thy
fruits and enjoy
thy riches—Jes

Peggy T Nelson
HE WAITS

The days are empty and empty are the eyes of the man on the white sheets.
Now he waits for anyone.
Someone to say his name, tell

a story of the past;
To help recall a pleasant
happy time again.
He captures a memory fleeting in time.
Words form and flow again from a mouth unused except for nourishment.
He waits with longing of
communion of ones in the past
To capture a memory to help him recall who he was.
He waits for a hand to touch
and to hear sounds of laughter.
A light sparks in those blue eyes
only to fade quickly
and shadows form, confusion follows.
He retreats into oblivion, Alzheimers.

E Jane Dills
DAY DAWNS

The song of a bird
In the early dawn.
Glistening dew drops
On the lawn.
The whisper of
A gentle breeze,
As it stirs the leaves,

On stately trees.
A promise of sunrise,
In the eastern sky.
The gift of another
Day draws nigh.

Diane L Fifield
OUR FOREVER LOVE

To my mother, who has always been there for me. I'll always love you mom.

When I look up at the stars on a night that's crisp and clear, I think of you and every-thing I hold dear.
When I think of the moon and the distance that it holds, I remember my life and every thing it molds.
When I look into your eyes and the sparkle that makes them shine, I think of our love, and I know that you'll always be mine.

Sharon Davis Clayborne
LOVE FOR ONE DAY

To: My Ace of Cups
Love: Queen of Cups

Do you know that I truly care?
Do you think I'd be always there?
Do you know of my dreams of you?
Do you think that they'll come true?
Can you say how you really feel?
Can you tell that my love is real?
Can you turn and just walk away?
Can you leave what you found one day?
Will you ever catch a falling star?
Will you have time to look so far?
Will your dreams make you call my name?
Will your hopes be forever vain?
Just remember as you make the choice
That the tremble you heard in my voice
Came with the answer of reality
When you said you never needed me.
As I walk down this lonely road
With the burden of lost love my load
I will always thank the Lord above.
For one day, I held your precious love.

Stefan Forrester
WHEN

This poem is dedicated to April Fischer . . . my true inspiration

When the sky seems just the sky, not a wonder.
When the clouds are just mist, not magic.
When rain and snow are just weather, not special.
When a bird is just an animal, you'll know.

When a girl seems just a girl, not strange.
When fairy tales are just fiction, not real.
When your birthday seems nothing, not happy.
When toys seem unimportant, you'll know.

When simple things in life seem difficult, not easy.
When the energy seems lacking, not there.
When pain becomes more than a scraped knee, not physical.
When you envy the boy and boyhood, you'll know.

Kimberly McCleve
WHAT WILL I BE WHEN I GROW UP

When I grow up
What will I be
Will I be a star
Or a lady of the streets

How do I know
That what I have learned
Will be of any use
In the years to come

If only I knew
What God had in store
For me and my life
Forever more

Nancy Brown Pemberton
THE WONDER OF IT ALL

For my Mom and Dad, my sister Peg, my brother Tom, and all those who love me unconditionally—and for those who hear and feel the sounds of nature and see hope and beauty in a rainbow.

Did you ever stop to question
why the sky is blue
Why the birds sing more in
springtime, and what brings the
morning dew
Or marvel how one degree can
turn the rain to snow
Or how no man can change the
time of the ocean's ebb and flow
Did you ever stand at twilight and
watch the colors fade to gray
Then watch the stars appear as
darkness claims the day.
There's magic in the rainbow that
comes with Spring showers,
Color from light and light to feed
flowers.
Great men say that music
transforms thought and color to
sound,
And if we combine the right
tones, perfect harmony can be
found.
Fortunate are those who go with
the flow and hear the call—
The wonder of it all, the wonder
of it all.

Jennifer Lynn Jones

Jennifer Lynn Jones
I KNOW WE CANNOT BE TOGETHER

Stephen Marton I'll love you forever Always you are in my thoughts, My life is you, You are my life. Together love is ours.

I know we cannot be together
But I know we will never be
apart
The love I feel for you comes
from deep within my heart
The time away is not so rough
I dream of the future that is
meant for us
Each day away is one step closer to a
time and a place for us to make
our escape
I know in time that I will call you
mine
For a love like ours, comes once in
a lifetime
You made me a promise, don't
make it a lie
You have captured my heart,
don't let it die!
I'll wait with a joy that could only
be love, for a time and a place
that we will be one! ! !

Marlynn Marie Kotaska
MIRROR IMAGES!

"To Gaye," "Marie," "Sr. Mary Thomas," You know the meaning of love,—For taking a moment of your time to care! Made the difference between a tear "drowning" in despair, or one that harbors Hope!

I've learned that "Angels" are made
out of fire and ice
Filigreed ornaments of Heavenly
stature
Mysterious beings still thought to be
untouchable by the hand of mortal
man.
Yet, looking through the cheval
glass
In gentle tender moments of mine.
I find entwined in heartfelt
grasp
A legion of sorts of Angelic faces
that have donned my life with
unsung fragrance.
There have been many a dear
person to whom I can relate.
Each have their place in the niches of
my heart.
Though, why is it I wonder that
I have been blessed with the
steadfast courage of three?
Heroes are they in this era of vast
uncertainties.
The course of illness is not an
easy pace
Shattered dreams seem to be the only
thing that time doesn't erase.
The three that shared the walk
with me down the lonesome
path
Never left me secluded in the
shredded aftermath.
They tugged at the weary
teardrops and helped chase
them away
And teased a forgotten smile to find
its rightful place.
Ageless is the beauty of the
fragile rose,
As are my thoughts of the "Ivory"
figures that made my life unfold.
For each of them I thread a
silver strand of Prose
Their fragrance embellished in ink
leaves its mark
The Artist's touch unfolds from
the Canvas Soul!
Thoughts! Now lost in words
. . . . . .That carve the music which
flows from the Poet's
Heart . . . . . .

Marciana A Sevandal
JUST FOR YOU AT CHRISTMASTIDE

This poem was sincerely dedicated to a beloved thoughtful niece at Christmas. She has made it a part of her life to keep in touch with me every year even if only at the yuletide.

Because you are a thoughtful niece,
The kind who keeps in touch,
Most specially at Christmastide,
When even a line means
much—

Because you spread love and good
cheer,
Adoring the Holy Child,
Giving true meaning to His
birth,
And to the role of the Virgin
mild—

No aunt like me can e'er ignore,
The love and care you spare,
To keep in touch even just
once,
Thru God's rare gift to share.

I pray for you to carry on,
In God's sweet love and grace,
Thru all the years that lie
ahead,
In health and happiness.

So I thank you most sincerely,
For showing that you care,
For an old Auntie far away,
Who has nothing to spare.

Finale:
But God provides, so let's live His
way of life.

Michael Devrone Whitfield II
LOVING AND CARING

Loving and caring
laughing and sharing
is what we do each day.
Loving, caring, laughing and
sharing can be shown in each a
new way.

Loving and caring helps show our
love to many people
and the Lord above.
If you show your love
to someone new
then one day you'll find
their love will come back to
you . . .

Pope Paul Bunyan McCoy

Pope Paul Bunyan McCoy
DEMON I BEHOLD GOD IN YOU

To: KDIA 1310 Radio Sation Oakland, CA.

Demon I behold God in you,
In the name of Jesus Amen-Amen-Amen;
In your ways of thinking and talking,
In the name of Jesus-Amen-Amen-Amen.

Demon I behold God in you,
In the name of Jesus, Jesus, Jesus;
In your ways of plotting and gossiping,
In the name of Jesus—God's son Jesus.

God gave us all a three-fold life,
To use upon this earth that he created;
He gave us all a body, a soul, and a spirit.
In this Earth that he created.

Demon I behold God in you,
In the name of Jesus, Jesus, Jesus,
In the name of God—I behold God in you,
Demon—in the name of Jesus, Jesus, Jesus.

Vince Farkas
AS YOU ARE
I like you Debora, exactly as you are,
With your hidden weakness and towering strength.
I don't want you be any different—ever,
Nothing in you, I would want to change!

I like the way you look, like the way you walk,
When you sit in silence, or chit-chat and talk.

I like your eyes blue, with a red haze, or clear
With a spark in them or hiding behind a tear.

I like your hair blond or black, touched with tender care,
Or just plain, blown with the wind wild, or tied into a tail.

I like you when witty, fired up and smiling,
When you are down, sad, tired and yawning.

You could be crippled or fat, you could be bald or blind,
I like what you stand for, you believe in, what is in you inside.

I like you when tender and charming
. . . even stubborn and mad,
If you were any different, we would have never met!

I like you, Debora, exactly as you are,
With your hidden weakness and towering strength.
I want you to love me . . . just a little . . .
That's all in you, I would want to change.

Suzan Lee Rush
SEARCHING

This poem is dedicated to everyone who is searching for that peace of mind.

Searching and searching
I can not find,
The one and only piece
To this broken mind.
The pieces have been broken
A thousand times.

Holding on to dreams
That don't seem to last,
I run from the shadows
That come from the past.

Searching and searching
I still can't find,
That missing piece
To that broken mind.

Holding on to memories
Is not for the best,
Searching for happiness
Now that I've lost all the rest.

Beatrice Dye
RESOLUTIONS
This year I'll try to be more kind,
To others' faults to act more blind;
In others' troubles have a share,
To really make them feel I care.

I want to ever wear a smile
To make folks see that life's worthwhile.
I'd like to be less selfish too,
And to my Saviour be more true.

Each day I want Him by my side
To be my life, my friend, my guide.
I want in Him to put more trust,
And less for worldly things to lust.

I want my deeds to earn a crown,
But not for wealth or world renown.
When I meet Him face to face
I do not want to feel disgrace.

I want to love Him and be true
In everything I say or do.
To be of service, and obey
His will for me along life's way.

Margaret Richardson
SARAH
Who would that we could make
such as you.
Small cuddly bundle, tufted black hair
And eyes, such big brown eyes
And you were loved, Oh how you
were loved.

Who would have thought there
could be such as you.

Not perfect, but almost, well
sometimes.
Growing up fast, much too fast
And we were saddened to see
time pass.

Who would have thought there
really is such as you.

A smile, Oh what a smile.
Surely a gift that gladdened
people's hearts
And we are happy, you made us
happy.

Who would have thought
eighteen could come so quickly.

Still to us a small cuddly bundle
With tufted black hair.
And you are loved, Oh how you
are loved.

Mum & Dad

Evelyn Hoffman
OLDER GENERATION
I'm the older generation,
Once the backbone of this nation.
I stare out the window looking for hope,
But all I see are youngsters filling up on dope.

Who said the streets are free for one and all?
Not for me, the old or the small.
I dare not walk the streets
Though there is nothing wrong with my feet
Is it true what I've been told
No one cares for the old?

Some elected officials say "Don't worry"
As they pass us in a hurry.
When I was young I had a smile for all who passed me by,
But now that I'm getting old, no one cares if I live or die.
Won't anyone hear my plea, the walls are closing in on me.

What happens when it comes your time?
Right now it happens to be mine.
Each day the sun rises and sets,
For me it only ends with loneliness and debts.

So how about it children—come and visit me,
for someday it may be you looking out the window sitting here like me.

David Wayne Sas
SUNSHINE I NEED
The sun was trying to break
the overcast sky.
I was thinking to myself
that this is how time goes by.
Happiness tries to break out,
but our emptiness keeps it in.
If the sunshine does break out
it's only a matter to time before
it goes dim.
But there are days of total sunshine.
These days are spent with you!
When the clouds start rolling in,
I know our time together is
almost through.
Thanks for the sunshine
you have put into my lowest
days.
Hopefully you can see
just what I'm trying to say.
You are so special
and very dear to me!
Time I spend with you
is the only sunshine I need!

Maria Michaels
PREREQUISITE

To the care and feeding of our imagination, where dreams are made of stuff . . .

There are no expectations I have,
Just be yourself.
I don't want whispered promises.
Show me,
Don't tell me how you feel.
There is no need to speak of tomorrow.
Let's take everything one day at a time.
You don't have to explain the roads you take,
Just travel them.
Above all . . .
Make sure you're the happiest person you know.
Then . . .
You will never disappoint me.

Cheryl Henry
DE JA VUE
Undercurrents of meeting you before—
along the shore,
a misty hue.
We're more than ships just passing thru . . .

Gin and Laughter our canopy;
soft ocean breezes when you hold me.

Back in the recesses of my mind,
'tween African drum rolls and a slow grind,
I see reflections of me and you.
De ja vue of a dream come true.

Kiss me/Hold me
once again 'cause
that's the way it all began.

Undercurrents
is what I wore 'cause
I've been along this shore
before.

Susan Kinney
REFLECTIONS
I will miss the marshmallows
floating on a mug of hot cocoa.
I will no longer see my childhood swing
cast in shadow.
No longer hear Christmas songs,
so bright and gay
Nor see the teddy bear left, forgotten,
after a young child's play.

Solitude has boxed me in,
leaving little space to breathe.
The choker 'round my neck draws tighter,
granting final reprieve.
I have tried to fight back,
but evil forces are stronger.
For me,
the mirror reflects no longer.

B J Haliburton
I DON'T MIND THE THORNS, IF YOU'RE THE ROSE

The bright color will delight you
and the fragrance will tickle
your nose
And sometimes there are thorns to
bear
if you want to enjoy the rose

I'll watch until the spring comes
wait patiently for you to flower
I'll see a newness burst forth
as you blossom by the hour

Even when the thorns appear
It will be you that I chose
To take the pricks that handling
brings
Sweetheart, if you're the rose

I know that you're not perfect
I've made mistakes too
But surely, I'll endure the test
if it means a life with you

I love you so very much
and I know that it shows
That, I just don't mind the thorns
HONEY, if you're the rose.

Sharon Bancroft
A TOUCH OF AUTUMN

To Dan, my faithful, loving husband and friend

Hear the sound of rustling leaves,
See the trees whipping up the
raving colors with a new gusto,
Feel the bone chill of crisp autumn
mornings,
Observe the sight of the swirling
wisp of autumn leaves burning and
the aroma too;
Yes the aroma; it's like sweet-
smelling incense to my nostrils;
How lovely, the gorgeous array of
color painting a brand new season
into being;
Oh what a scene; magnificent to
behold!

Sunny Santry
ETERNITY

Dedicated to Kelly, Marianne, Shawn Patrick, Erin, Mary, and AlexaRay. God Bless and Protect You for ETERNITY——With Endless Love, GRANDMA

To gaze upon a valley's mound

And see the lush of green,
Listening to an unheard sound
Of beauty not yet seen.

To wonder of the mountain's peak

That's capped with new fell snow,
Of what in life that we do seek
And then to never know.

To take life's journey to the end
And seek no greater joy than
ETERNITY.

Tammy Downing
PASSIONATELY INFATUATED

Passionately devoted to one another,
our obsession
becomes our infatuation.
Together till eternity.
Clutching the love we share,
Hoping it will succeed through
the sequences.
Dreaming it won't flourish, then
die . . .
. . . as the rose in winter.
Holding one another securely,
to assure the efforts of the
romance
to lie ahead.

Daniel P Melnick
WHY I'M HERE

Want to make a difference
In someone's life today?
The Spirit knows your heart
Ask Him. You have the way.

Earnest Expectations
Awaken when you pray.
Now one day in Heaven
A shining face will say:

"Praise the Lord, Beloved
What a difference you made
Greater is your reward
I'm here because you prayed."

Melanie Hoogner
MAGIC

The motion of the water
the sand close to my body

the body with its emotions
the sand with no reaction

Making love to the sand.

Purring a song of sensuality
as it comforts my young body

Making love to the sand.

Getting up I walk away
leaving the sand as it was before

and never knowing what it was they
shared
the waves come and wash what was
given away . . .

Maria A Bentley

Maria A Bentley
FOR THE CHILDREN'S SAKE

For the children's sake, let's all pray.
They are little people who need our
Attention, because in the future they
Will be our salvation.

We are only one Earth, we are only
Human. Please stop child abuse, stop
The world that is confused.

Let's all get together, let's all Stand
and fight; to protect all the Children
no matter where they Are.

So please, for the children's sake let's
All be aware of family, stranger,
Neighbor and friend, Because in the
end you
Never can Tell.

Barbara J Conner
BEAUTY

If beauty is only skin deep
Why do I constantly see your face in
each cloud and feel your warm
embrace in each raindrop
Why do I continually hear your
whispers in each of the sun's rays,
and your laughter in each bright
moon.

If beauty is only skin deep
Why do I see all the love stored
within your heart,
and watch you give freely without
hesitation to all.
Why do I feel such joy and such
happiness when you're near.

If beauty is only skin deep
Why do I always hear you call my
name after pain has overpowered my
inner soul,
and causes a river of tears to flow
freely,
yet without an end.
Why do I wait patiently for your
return
Come tomorrow,
Could it be an illusion or love
unplanned.

Rosa Martinez
BLOWING IN THE WIND

Blowing in the wind, mimicking the
leaves
They are tall and, oh, so gold
Just like the sunset they are
gloriously beautiful
And standing there they look to me,
so bold

In my dreams the picture is perfect
This picture I could never forget
For in my dreams I see everything
As perfect as the perfect silhouette

The wind is blowing a harsh breeze
But the are no squinting faces
For there are no people in my dreams
There are only places

They are fields of wheat which I
dream of
Every time that I want to be free
I simply think of them and this
makes me happy
Just knowing they belong to me

Milton A Newman
LET'S DO IT ALL FOR FUN

Let's take a walk, thru driving rain,
And go for a ride, on Amtrak's train.
Lay on the beach, and stare at the
sky,
Or lay on the grass, and watch clouds
roll by.
Ride in the country, on a wagon of
hay.
Stroll thru the zoo to watch the
animals play.
Eat cotton candy at the county fair.
Run with the wind, like we haven't a
care.
Sail a kite, on a warm summer's day,
Or celebrate Christmas, in the month
of May.
Let's eat dinner by candlelight.
Make love during day, instead of the
night.
Let's take a nap in the tall green
grass. Think of the future, and not of
the past.
Let's dress you in satin, silk and lace.
Say "I love you,"
Staring face to face.
Let's stop walking, and start to run.
Most of all, let's do it all for fun.

Stacy L Grimes
FOREVER MY FRIEND

To Lisa, this says it all.

When I'm with you, everything
seems right
Every day and every night
You've been there for me from
the very start
Your love and friendship fill my
heart
I can tell you things I've never
said before
Your faith and understanding
open life's locked doors

When I look into your hurt,
wondering eyes
I am reminded of stormy skies
Dark, mysterious, pain so deep
Together we stand, together we
weep

When I look back upon years
gone by
Times we've laughed, times we've
cried
I know now heartbreaks can
mend
Together Forever, Forever My
Friend

Cindy Cortez
WINTER BLUES

The clouds in the heavens grow black
And the rain pours from the sky
The leaves have all fallen down
The wind begins to howl and cry

And like the changing season
There's a storm within my heart
It rages without end
And tears my soul apart

Life has left me empty
With a bitterness inside
Trying to make things better
Is like swimming against the tide

I never ever imagined
Life would turn out to be this way
Broken promises and broken dreams
Like a shattered piece of clay

But now there's no turning back
From the course that I am on
Forgetting things that were
From the past that is now gone

Dawn Antaya
WATER FALLS

Where does it come from
I don't understand
Is there a man pouring
it from the land

Where does it come from
I cannot see
Does it fall from the seas

Where does it come from
I cannot tell
It must come from
Heaven the angels
get it from the well

Nicolina Vasquez
CALLS OF LOVE

For my family, friends & teachers, especially Mom, Dad, Mikey, and Eddie. Thanks for believing in me. I love you! ! !

I sit beside the window,
I hear the raindrops fall,
I see you in the shadows,
Oh, can you hear my calls?

I call and call,
"Please, come to me!"
You hear my calls,
But can't see me

I sit and wait for you, again.
It seems my dream has no end.
Maybe you are just a dream.
A dream, to me, is what you seem.

You are my dream of love,
You are my dream of love.

Caroll M Hubert DerKacy
US

I'll always love you on earth and even in the spiritual world.

Our two hearts beat at the same rhythm.
And as we look into each other's loving eyes,
They shine like the stars in the mystical night.
They reflect all those beautiful emotions that live in our hearts.

We breathe the same air;
It gives us life . . .
It gives us love . . .
It gives us love and life . . .

As your hands caress my body,
I reciprocate the warm sensation to your handsome body,
It is more than just LUST and PASSION!
Don't you understand that this means "I love you."

I have never nor ever will discover,
Another love as perfect as yours.
My love for you is eternal,
I pray, hope, wish and want to always believe that—
Your love will always be eternal for me.

Nestor J Marmol

Nestor J Marmol
NOWHERE LAND

Woman: Beautiful creature of the universe, Thank you for bringing out the poet in me. Love.

I'll go to nowhere land
But my heart will stay
In my little town, my loved one.

I'll send you verses
Which will be written
To lighten your dark days
And to light up my life,
In nowhere land.

Eventhough the oceans
Will separate us physically
And the passing time
Will try to make us
Forget about each other,
I beg you my loved one
To stand by me, for I will return.

I'll wander around places
That could bring me remembrance of you
Because it won't be enough
To see you only on a photograph.

I promise you that
I'll work very hard
And I will bring you
A whole world full of love in my heart
And I won't ever leave
Never from your side.

Rozana Caccaviello
FORGOTTEN ONES

You've succeeded!
Be proud!
You've corrupted their minds!
Those poor children!
Once filled with images of bubbles, pinwheels, and lollipops.
Now filled with horrors of threats, bombs, and death.
Where has the future gone?
NO MORE TOMORROW!
You've succeeded!
Be proud!
You've taught them to fight,
And to HATE!
Poor little children.
How could you have tainted their innocence?
No more peace, they chant!
FIGHT! FIGHT! FIGHT!
Does that really solve anything?
Oh, you should be so DAMN proud!
You've succeeded in what you set out to do.

LaJaniese Shanelle Washington
A BROKEN HEART

When we first met, I didn't know
Just how much our love would grow.
What started out as a simple friendship
Turned into a lasting relationship.
But as time went on things began to change.
The love that once lived no longer remained.
Now as I sit here and wonder what wrong,
I can still feel the love that once was so strong.
I now know by all of the clues that our love was not true.
For you didn't love me when I love and needed you.
I should have realized right from the start
That our so-called love would leave me with another broken heart.

Theresa Franco
MOON CHILD

A Moon Child's soft and tender to touch,
And sometimes a hug is just not enough.

His smile is bright and full of life,
And quickly changes in times of strife.

A Moon Child's moods are hard to match,
They sometimes cling and won't detach.

If you shower him with love and attention,
Then he'll cover you with tons of affection.

He's yours to keep and hold on to,
'Cause in his eyes it's just you two.

A Moon Child makes a special friend,
Because on him you can depend.

He'll make you laugh and maybe cry,
But he'll stay always right by your side.

His sign's a Crab, I don't know why,
Maybe it's because he's sometimes shy.

His emotions and moods are sometimes mixed,
But it's all a part of what makes him tick.

A Moon Child's not so complicated,
He's just a bit more than anticipated.

Michael Constantine
A MESSAGE FROM THE LORD

A Mother's Plea is written through these lines so others may see who opened the gateway of my inspiration.

To anyone who feels much pain,
My hand will help him gain,
The inner strength and health he needs,
To carry on my graceful deeds.
Raise your confidence and do not nod.
Carry your cries up; lift them to God,
For it is in Him that you will find,
The only hand to break your bind.

I tried this you may say.
Well, then impatience is in the way,
Because I, the Lord, answer all,
Who to Me doth make their call.
So now you can be less blinded.
But hurry! The clock is winded.
Put your faith in me, the Lord.
Only I can relieve all discord.

Melissa Fleming
A THANK YOU NOTE TO THE ONE I LOVE

To my dearest brother Andrew, whom I love with all my heart

Thank you for being you
The special person that you are
You give me a reason to be happy
Just knowing that you're not far

Knowing that you love me
Is the greatest feeling I've ever had
You're a special gift from heaven
And because you're mine I'm glad

Share your spirit with all the world
Make it a better place
You can take a person's frown
And put a smile on their face

When I look at you I can see
Goodness through and through
You're always cheerful and fresh
Just like the morning dew
It hurts me to see you upset
I hate to see you frown
So just remember that I love you
And don't let anything get you down

Mary Ann Latella
ME

Dedicated to Ida Slutsky who encouraged me, and showed understanding—despite my foolishness

A humble little daisy in my garden, I once found,
Ashamed of her appearance, she took refuge in the ground.
Amid the regal rose she grew, a misfit, sad and lonely,
Feeling out of place, because, she was the one and only.
The roses garbed in velvet growing proudly in a row,
While the solitary daisy sadly mourned herself below.
When her heart could take no more, she then began to cry.
Why couldn't I be a rose, than a daisy such as I?
You silly little posy, there's no need to be forlorn,
You envy me my beauty, yet you overlook the thorn.
Your pure white cape of satin, brightly trimmed with golden lace,
Why your beauty is refreshing, if you'd only show your face.
You haven't seen the sun shine, or bathed in the gentle rain.
You chose to be forgotten, and created your own pain.
Look up now little flower, show your beauty to the earth,
Don't ever be unhappy nor despair your right of birth.
Just then a pair of scissors cut away the velvet cloak,
Poor daisy in a dither knew it was the rose that spoke.
How could I be so shallow? and so foolish heaven's knows,
I'd rather be a daisy than that poor ill-fated rose.
And as I left my garden, six roses in my grip,
A small voice whispered to me, Life is over in a snip!
I pondered for a moment, where the sound was coming from,
I turned and saw a daisy growing proudly in the sun.

Barbara Lane Tripp
THE PARTY FLY

The table set with elegance, we all sat down to dine.
I heard a small voice whispering,
"There's livestock in my wine."
I glanced to see the other guests,
their faces were all smiles,
but little did we know just then, that fly would swim for miles.
Now you may wonder why they called it what they did that night.
You'd know if you lived in Maine,
Moose flies are big, that's right!
The waitress came to take the glass,
removing it from sight.
We told her "Stop! Don't touch that glass. Our bets are in tonight."
Each one had picked a time this eve,
when Party Fly would drown;
but as the banquet carried on, he kept on swimming 'round.
The speakers spoke; the voters vote;
the hands of all would clap;
this merry little drunken fly, he looked like such a sap!
Hypnotically we watched that fly

swim 'round the glass that night.
His back-stroke was of course the best, his wings would stand upright
All bets were lost, he splish,'d and splashed, still swimming on his back.
He never sank before we left; his fate a certain fact!
A MORAL TO THIS TALE I TELL:
the wine tastes good it's true,
if you become a Party Fly, they'll all take bets on you!

Hugh Goodman Jr
TRANSITION

Failure to communicate attributes to the void between people and that failure cripples their ability to exhibit open awareness, reaching the inner depths . . .one must stand on the shoulders of maturity to overcome the shortcomings of life. Through our eyes we need to see each as each needs to be seen. Today . . . exchange identities, evolve with the span of time . . . growth is necessary . . . or the stronghold of ignorance shall reign.

Christina Heil
LARRY, MY FRIEND

Captain—This one is for you. What you thought was the end, became a new beginning.

There was as time when you thought turning the television on during the day was almost sinful.
Today I think of that as you sit and watch 'The Price is Right.'
Your mind used to be so full of strong ideas.
You would argue any point about anything.
Now you can just about carry on a conversation without feeling confusion.
Confusion that you blame on someone else for getting through to you the right way.
I don't mind taking that kind of blame.
It's senseless to argue with you when your mind is doing you wrong.
I can see how hard you try to keep up with it all.
Don't feel ashamed.
Because you are not a failure in anyone's eyes.
You aren't in competition with anyone.
But you will win your medal of honor.
You will see that you did not lose.
When it is time your ship will charter its own course and you will be your own captain.
Just as you were all those years before as you watched over the sea and made sure everything was alright.
Soon it will be your turn to be watched over.
Don't be afraid because you had a wonderful purpose in life.
And did your best with the way you knew how.

Donna G Farr
HANDS

Thanks to Becky, Lucy, Diane, Harvey, Margo, Toki, Linda, and Shirley, You're my inspiration.

The same hands
That sent distress signals in wartime
Are the same hands
That gently stroked the child's cheek.
The hands big and calloused
Oft times bleeding
Are the same hands
Clasped together each night in prayer.
The same hands
Now gnarled with age
Are the same hands
that
In youth——reached out
To hands
Much the same.

Tim Stroud
THE BRIDGE

Love is the Bridge,
Over which Hate can not journey
Destiny awaits its cue
And Time to be set free

War rages on
For Anger carries its flame
Fate has her hand in this
As Mischief plays his game

Music soothes the savage beast
A true Heart hath no Shame
Life and Death blend together
To form an eternal Chain

All of our lives
We search for the Glow
Questing for the knowledge
So that we might Grow

Hence, the day through its eve
To a Mountain on a ridge
Two hearts find each other
With Love as their Bridge

Patricia Boyle
WHY DO I CRY?

To my family, my true inspiration.

The feeble old
The battered young

The trampled weak
The twisted powerful

The self doubting rejected
The unquestioned respected

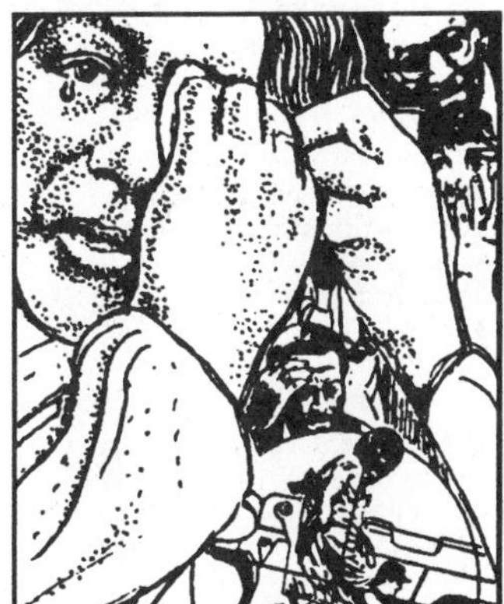

The condemned minority
The closed minded majority

You ask me why I cry,
I can only ask, why you don't.

Patricia Vonita Gilmer
PATSY

This poem is dedicated in the loving memory of my beautiful grandmothers Mrs. Annie P. Estes and Mrs. Floyd Gilmer, also to my family and friends who encouraged and believed in me. Thank you.

When you look at me what do you see
I'm not afraid to show it, a young black woman caring and free
When I walk you can hear that I have something to say
When I speak stand clear the flame isn't far away
When I smile I bring out joy in the company I keep
For I am a black woman you see

I carry myself in such a matter to grab your attention
Clothes to accent my personality and figure
Hair layered to show off ancestral features
The curves in my legs, hips, and lips are added dimensions
For I am a black woman you see

I am a proud woman generated from past seeds
Not a shame to say in the presence of my enemies
Stand back, take note, there's plenty to be learned
Determination is the key to make my mark in this world
Respect that I'm entitled of
Love for my fellow man, a positive attitude goes hand in hand
And the grace of God my friend to guide me
Hoping one day, I will be noted for my poetry
Energetic, Strong-minded, and Resourceful you better believe
For I am a black woman as you can read.

Mary Anna Lee Givens

Mary Anna Lee Givens
THE FEBRUARY WOMAN

To my loving parents MRS Annie Bell Lee and MR Johnnie Lee SR
And my four beautiful daughters Erica, Annie, Ruthie and Summer

The February woman was born in july
She hides her tears behind the rain when she cries
She shelters her children from all the worldly harm
The February woman can weather any storm
From her bosses' constant nagging
To her husband's when will dinner be done
The February woman smiles and keeps moving on
Then late at night when she's tired and weak
Before she closes her eyes to go to sleep
The February woman is on her knees in prayer
Thanking her heavenly father for all his love and care
And when The February woman's month has come to its end
The March woman shows up takes over and grins.

Amy Minty
MY LAST DAY AT THE BEACH

The coast is rocky. The sky is clear.
The seagulls dip low and smooth, as they fly in fear.
The wind picks up, no longer a cool breeze.
The sky clouds over and my emotions seem to freeze.

The ocean crashes. The sky is red.
I can feel a storm approaching. The warning rings inside my head.
The wind whips my hair as I anxiously look around.
The sea is calling. It's a familiar sound.

I stop and breathe, but not for long.
I'm pulled toward the water, as the seagulls sing my song.
I move towards the waves, as slowly as can be.
I feel a strange sensation, as the cool water reaches me.

I'm so near to the freedom. Too compelled to the sea.
I can't turn back now. My longing lies within me.
I look back at shore, suddenly seeming very far away.
I've made my decision. Today is the day.

The deeper I get, the stranger I feel.
I'm being controlled. This can't be real.
It's suddenly dark. I can't see the land.
I'm no longer standing. I can't feel the sand.

Donald J Maurer
BECKY THE ONLY ONE

Dedicated to Chris & Carey

When you feel the warmth of the sun hitting upon your body,
That's the warmth from my heart showing its love for you.
When you feel the rain falling on your face, that's my eyes
Crying out my love for you when you're away from me.
When you feel the wind blowing in your hair,
That's my way of whispering I Love You.
When you hear the thunder in the heavens above,
That's my heart beating out I Love You.
When you feel the coldness of the snow under your feet,
It's my way of showing you how cold I feel
When you're not in my arms. When night falls all around you,
That's how empty I feel when you're not lying beside me.
When you look beyond those dark and cloudy nights,
And see those stars twinkling in the heavens above,
Those are my eyes watching over you
To make sure you are safe and sound.
When you look beyond those darkened nights,
And the stars look into the heavens above,
And see how brightly the moon shines my love for you
So remember I Love You now and beyond.
If I could give you the earth and heavens,
That would only be one way of

showing my love for you.
So look up into the heavens and see how powerfully my love. . .
Is for the Only One in my heart. I Love You.

Evelyn Heath Cardwell
FAMILY
On the night of Nov. 2, 1954,
As we came out the door;
Down came the snow so beautiful and white.
This was our wedding night!

Time passed and . . . . . we increased . . . . .
and then there were three . . . . .
you . . . . . baby son . . . . . and me.

Then another one to take her place . . . . . a daughter . . . . . someone to wear lace.
And then there were four.

Wait! Wait! There's more . . . . .
another one . . . . . what fun.
And then there five.

Even after event happened in our life;
For all good causes you have to strive.

You fixed candy apples on the 29th just before Halloween.
Why you knew when to, I can't explain.
Anyway I felt like a queen.
Another son . . . . .
And then there were six.

Days passed and a year or more.
I know by now you know the score.
Our family was blessed again from heaven . . . . .
A son . . . ..
And then there were seven.

Now this is our family if you want to know.
And if you ask why my face is aglow.
Go back to you . . . . .
baby son . . . . . and me.

Our son and his beautiful bride had their wedding day.
Our family has increased in another way.
And we want to say and not hesitate.
And then there were eight.

Time went by and very soon
To those dear ones of yours and mine . . . . . .
A little girl . . . . a grandchild . . . . .
And then there were nine.

Now, this is not the end of this story . . . . .
God sent them another one from glory . . . . .
A little son . . . . . another grandchild
And then there were ten.

Here we go again! !
About Face! !
Another event took its place.

Ask me why my face beams . . . . .
Our daughter wed the man of her dreams . . . . .
pure heaven . . . . .
And then there were eleven!

What next will take its place is not evident,
But a mystery yet to unfold . . . . . until it becomes an event!
Then it also will be put in writing (Lord willing)
As in the past the prospects are truly inviting! ! !

With excitement galore,
This event in our lives came about.
On my face a look of pure admiration.
Number two son,
married his darling one . . . . .
The beauty of it we need not delve;
And then there were twelve.

Here we go, again, around the family tree.
Another event happened to you and me.
Son number three . . . . .
has a wonderful wife
. . . . . and . . . . .
. . . . . two little ones . . . . .
has she . . . .
A mommy-in-law and a mom-maw all in one day!
Oh, well, anyway . . . . .
By the look on my face you can see I think it's quite keen.
Now, let's see . . . . .
that makes fifteen!

Although things don't always go right,
Our path and those of our children,
By faith we can see, how God meant for them to be.
So, to have victory we must see, by faith and trust that God can work out things that cause pain and woe, and make them right.
Our every care, our every need is before His eyes; He has us in His sight!

Into the family of our first born son . . . . .
Has come another . . . . .
That makes sixteen . . . .
The son of his wife's sister, we accept him as a part of us,
By family law.
He calls us Mom-maw and Pop-paw!

Can you count the joys?
Can you count the unhappies . . . . . that go with all the adding, subtracting, dividing and multiplying that goes on in a family!
Aren't we glad that the joys are more than the unhappies! ! ! !

Now for the rest of the story!
Guess what . . . . ..
For son number four . . . . .
. . . . . A wedding . . . . .
A pretty wife to adore . . . . .
It has added one more . . . . .
The joy on my face is heaven seen,
And that makes seventeen! ! !

Well, all our children are married now.
My dear, I still have you . . . . . and of course, our dog!
But I think of all the added joys we have received as a family striving to love regardless of those old unhappies that come our way . . . . .
Through it all, and even now, sometimes,
As we continue on I hope when memories of unhappies come back to visit, we just disregard them.
Counting all our blessings is impossible, I know,
But they keep coming and a few of them just reappear and give us another step to take toward the mark of the success of a family. .

Well, what do you know
After waiting a while! !
We have another grandchild . . . . .
. . . . . And grand he is . . . . .
Since he made the great scene . . . . .
That makes eighteen! ! !

In the most delicate way I can,
For all concerned . . . . .
I must subtract three from the number eighteen of the people in our family,
Because of an event unforeseen . . . . .
We must revert to number . . . . . fifteen! !
. . . . . continued . . . . .
Next event pending! ! !

Thomas J Raulerson
TEN ATTRIBUTES OF A GOOD FATHER

This poem is dedicated to my beautiful wife Diana Atkinson Raulerson, without whom it would not have been written, and loving daughter and two sons, Vicki Lynn, Thomas J. Jr., and James Brandon who provided the inspiration.

1. Expression of Love
2. Involvement with Activities
3. Provide Comfort
4. Practice Good Morals
5. Spiritual Guidance
6. Preparation for Their Future
7. Security and Protection
8. Show Trust
9. Request Honesty
10. Teach Responsibility

Love for each child is first on the list,
And reaffirm it at the end of each day with a goodnight kiss.
Take them to the fair, the circus, and the park,
And let them know that we are there, when they are afraid of the dark.

Provide them with our best, give them a home,
So they will always feel at rest, with no urge to roam.
The Golden Rule to them we should teach,
And let them know that with God, there is nothing out of reach.

The future for them be sure to prepare,
And for the pitfalls of life, always, always make them aware.
Guard and protect each one like the treasures they are,
And show them a night how to wish upon a star.

Let them know that they have our trust,
And throughout their life, honesty is a must.
And when they have grown up, with children of their own,
We will be so proud of them even though once again we may feel all alone.

Linda Chavez
ANNIVERSARY

For my ONE LOVE, Tomas from Lindita

We
are two are One
inseparable ever unfolding
in love
I looked, longed for love
And despaired
For I
fit no mold
thought I was content
to be a universe unto
myself
And then

You
joyous dancer
stepped into my life
And saw
that which I'd locked away

You
lightly but firmly
took hold of the thread

unraveling weaving
a rich tapestry
never ending ever unfolding
of We

Imogene Hall
YESTERDAY'S LOVE
Say not to me—
That time,
Takes pity upon a seeking soul,
Gives sweet forgetfulness,
Bringing back once more
All that was before.

In the deepest night,
Poor incredulous ghost,
Clatters in the empty room
Where heartbeats echo and silence roams;
Memories in the midnight fire,
Tracing the sadness of desire.

Murmuring seconds,
Pale the lost delay—
Burning a little against the dark,
Shadows dream and spark . . .
Seasons of love in disarray
Begging a spirit to stay.

Stay dear comfort—
Or let me come to you,
Like the flush of a rose
As the soft light swells,
My heart will be drawn
Toward the rising dawn.

Rachel Elisa Reiner
UNDERSTAND ME
They think I'm bad
But I'm really just sad,
My feelings are a mangle
Which no one wants to untangle.

I need someone that I can trust

Who won't tell what I hide,
To find this person is a must
With little time to abide.

I hear each day all that they say
But they don't know the reason why,
With my temper I may someday pay
For the silence I choose to defy.

No one comes close to share my pain
No one has felt the hopes I gain,
The one I need to let my soul free
Is the one who can't understand me.

Charles E McNally II
PARADISE

I dedicate this poem to Mary McNally. Without her love and understanding I would never have been able to accomplish having this poem (my first) published. She is truly my best friend and of course my mom.

Rainbows crossing over this land,
Everyone equal, walking hand in hand.
The animals are at your side, sharing their love,
All united under the blue skies above.

Dolphins swimming with you in the sea,
Understanding one thing, the beauty to be free.
Lions walking the fields at your side,
In this land of love, never a need to hide.

No false pretenses, everyone to be themselves,
Be it you're born poor or with wealth.
All that matters is to care for one another,
To live your lives like sister and brother.

Here you're never left to be alone,
To experience pain, suffering, a lonely moan.
Here in this land people truly care,
Their lives and love is all they want to share.

Evelyn Dubee Csugie
REALIZATION

This poem is dedicated to my mother; with all the Love a daughter's heart can hold.

I am walking down an unfamiliar path;
My feet have never tread this way before.
Everything is fresh, and new, so green;
Dirt or dust or smog cannot be seen.
I am looking to the left;
I turn now to the right;
Nothing can be seen that is not clean and bright.
I come upon a pond of crystal blue;
I gaze into the waters, just to see
My God, I'm dressed in pure silk of white—
Me.
I look ahead, and Oh dear God,
My eyes, my heart cannot believe,
My Mother.
Now I know just where I am and why I'm here—
This is God's Heaven.

Neal B Thurman
THE ILLNESS OF A FRIEND

I sat at the bedside of an ailing man
A man whose cheeks bore the summer's tan.

The night wore on and the nurses round us crept,
While some of the luckier patients slept.
We knew within this young man's chest
The human heart was being put to the test.

The pain he bore was very intense
The words spoken in agony caused no offense.
The needles, the catheter, the whole nightmare,
Person after person this would have caused to swear.

To hold Arnold's hand and quietly talk
Made me thankful for the privilege to walk.
Do you know what it is to bow your head and pray,
Asking the Lord's blessing to come right away?

The wife was grieved, tired and pale
Deeply disturbed at Arnie's every wail.
What if the Doctors and nurses failed?
More and more heartache this would have entailed.

To those who have cancer
We quickly need an answer,
To subside the horrifying fears,
And stop the flow of tears.

Two A.M. and all is well
Arnie drops off to sleep from a living Hell.

Darcy Miller
THE ROSEBUD AND THE ARROW

I give to you a rosebud
A token of our love
Of a new life beginning
Graced by God above.

I give to you the arrow
Sprung from Cupid's bow
Plucked from within my heart
My true love does it show.

I give to you these tokens
Of what is meant to be
A life of love and happiness
Made for you and me.

Melody R Dunn
A MAN HAD A VISION

To Tricia, Kim, Shari, Gina and all my family

A man had a vision of money on trees
A man had a vision of being free.
A man had a vision of equality
A man had a vision of being free.

Dacia Lawrence
HIS ADDICTION

To Jim, for whom this poem was written: May your future be as beautiful as your art. I will miss you.

His being, like sand, slips through my fingers
I'm scared, but tell me, what can I do?
Love is feeble when it's faced with addiction
Helplessness seers wounds anew

Why does he abide in solitude?
Closing out all that could of been
True feeling, true pain he puts aside
He sees his escape, he sees not sin

The wound is gaping though it kills him slowly
He cannot stop, then he will die
He's good and gentle, still he is weak
The trap bears down on him, but why?

And so time keeps moving, pulling us along
My mind revolves in anguish, I don't know who is wrong
If only I could tell you, if only you but knew
We'd cast aside this tragedy, and I could still love you

Joyce Goodin Price

Joyce Goodin Price
A CRY OF THE HEART

Why me, Lord? So often we cry!
When our heart is so full, and we wonder why
All the problems that ever have been,
Or could be thought of by women or men,
Have suddenly dropped right from the sky
And fallen on us and caused us to cry.

But then from way down deep inside
Comes a tug to remind us that God can provide.
We are not alone as our fears continue,
But have help and comfort to get us through.
Someone resides and will not depart;
God the Holy Spirit lives in our heart.

Lindsworth S Garvey
THE FATE OF THE NORTHERN WIND

We'll allow the wind to take us where she's going
Into destiny without knowing,
We'll drift like logs contained
Within the ocean of time.

Our minds afloat on flatters
Of vain an' vague flutters
Euphemistic terminologies
To justify our own imperfect ideologies
That make victims of innocence devious;
Like illogic without base, her fate's mischievous.

The extent of her depth
Uncovers the enigma of death.
Relentlessly fate debates:
Will she transform destiny? I'll await
The alpha 'n' omega,
Our destiny or fate's, times stigma.

Now will she lead us to where we ought to be:
Where love 'n' life lives and were born free?
The sky's the limit
Or will we take ourselves beyond it?

Sharon Lasenberry
GOD IS NUMBER ONE

You may say, He's my man.
You may say, She's my woman,
But God is number one.
He stands tall above us all.
God is number one.

His son died on the cross.
And shed his blood for us.
We shouldn't cuss or fuss.
We should trust in him.
God is number one.

Read God's word.
Pray when you can.
He'll understand.

I love God with all my heart.
When are you going to start?
God is number one.

Don't wait until the last day.
You'll have to pay.
Get your life together now!
Accept the Lord as your personal savior!
Because God is number one.

Jane M Embry
THE SAGA OF ALICE

There was a young lady named Alice
Who wanted to live in a palace.
She worked on a scheme to realize her dream
And live in grand style in Dallas.

The people she met on this turning
Could take no delight from her spurning.
Her methods of putting friends and foes on a footing
Of stepping stones left them all burning.

One day she came into her splendor
With a mansion and servants to tend her.
Now when she surveyed her estate it conveyed
An atmosphere designed to send her.

Admirers flocked to her palace
Even offered their hand to Alice.
But she couldn't decide if one wished to abide
With her, or just in her palace!

The end of this eye opening tale
Is obviously beyond the pale.
Alice left her palace in Dallas with malice
And never again took that trail!

Loretta F Gibbs
TOMORROW

The face looking back in the mirror at me,
Is not the face as it used to be.
The laughing blue eyes and hair of gold,
Now it is wrinkled and growing old.

The face looks at me and says why, why?
I have so much to do before I die.
Where has time gone, what have I done?
Why you have lived and you have had fun.

You have raised four children, that's what you've done.
A beautiful daughter and three fine sons.
You have laughed and loved and been loved in return.
By a wonderful husband from whom you have learned.

You have learned the joys of love and life,
You have learned what it means to be a good wife.
You have learned how to deal with death and sorrow
You have learned there is always a better tomorrow.

I look back in the mirror and the face I see
Is more like the face it used to be.
The blue eyes are shining, the hair is spun gold,
Who ever said that it's bad to get old!

The memories I have are priceless you see.
There is no one alive who is richer than me.
I have lived and loved and learned to say
There is always tomorrow, an even better day.

Wilfred Vanover

Wilfred Vanover
THE GREATEST LOVE
The greatest love is not that of romance
When youth in tenderness woos maiden fair;
It is not the mother's loving glance
Upon her child, asleep and free from care.
It is not childhood friendships, sweet and strong,
Yet turbulent and changing day by day,
Nor friendships of the aged which have long
Been blooming through the decades, as they say.
This love is not expressed with a kiss
Though it is strongest, lasting to the end,
For there is no greater love in man than this:
That he lay down his own life to save a friend.

Kathleen Rae Gaber Greer
GOD LOVES EVE N ME
I came from man's rib
to be fashioned in flesh . . .
But disobeyed God
the fruit was so fresh!
I fled from the garden
my curiosity met . . .
And waited for Jesus
to redeem my debt!
I accepted His gift
now praising His Name . . .
He's forgiven my sin
and bore all the shame!
Father please help me
how great your compassion . . .
Do encourage and motivate
my Faith into action!
The power in my life
is Love I can see . . .
So Lord may Its power
begin here with me!

Lisa Rains
THE PATH
Although you walk a rocky path,
And know not where it may lead.
Your path is already laid out,
What's to come, is for only you to see.

The fork in the road,
Only divides it somehow.
For you must choose which way to carry your load,
And tread lightly for now.

Although you might stumble,
And eventually fall,
You must get up and continue,
For your Journey is not complete at all.

Our paths are never smooth,
And no one promised easy.
In some tasks we may lose,
But we must not ease.

We must stay strong and take the tide
We're not wrong God is on our side.
Our paths are not simple or fair,
But can be accomplished,
with God there.

Sher Chappell
ONE MAN
One man jump starts my heart, then lets the air out of my emotions:

Flattens my Love
Flattens my Trust
Flattens my Hope
Flattens my Very Being.

I can not move——
I start looking for a wrecker

Along comes another man.

Kit Sturdivant
QUESTIONS
New thoughts and old haunts
Piled up, compose worry.
Memories that were happy once,
Questions that were not buried

Live on in our ids,
Awaken us when they please.
Wonders wander like city kids
On a country lark, freedom to seize.

Unresolvables should be forgotten?
But resolving "un" is our mop
To wipe out woes, we play to win,
In spite of odds, and even "no's," we cannot stop.

"Daddy, what do you mean?"
"What is easiest is not always best."
Now, later, I see your wisdom was keen.
And love is forever though flesh goes to rest.

Questions roll in as waves to shore,
Perpetual and deep, they whisper
And whirl about, in and out, stifled no more.
Mystic traces they leave, but no answer.

C Larry Sykes
THE THIRD VERSE IN THE HYMN
I'm the third verse in the hymn my friend
I don't understand what is wrong.
Folks want to skip me
sing the last verse of the song.

How would you like each sunday,
as you sit there in your pew,
have folks all around
never say hello to you?

It makes me feel not wanted,
for I can inspire 'tis true
Yet they always seem in a hurry
to rush the song through.

Singing makes folks happy,
They just can't sing too long.
When you sing the next hymn
please add the third verse to the song.

Edward C Alfano Jr
SEASONS
Ago, again, awry—
Follow, falter, die:
Winter wearies autumn;
Woodlands ravaged lie.

Time ordained to shiver—
Weathered, wounded, worn:
Souls, too, freeze and wither—
Tattered, trampled, torn.

Spring supplants the season—
Repetition beggars reason:
Budding blossoms beckon—
I'll love again, I reckon.

Kellie Kwiecien
FINE ARTS—2ND FL
Nicked wooden benches—a face-off.
One warmed by the sunlight,
the other cooled by its
direction facing.

You and I on scratched, ink-marred wooden benches—
a face-off.
Who can hold out the longest
without speaking a friendly word?
or do we not care that we're becoming
Scratched, wooden benches;
hard and always at a face-off,

One burned by the sun,
One cold by its direction facing.

Laurie L Fachet
LONELINESS
Alone . . . alas . . . alone.
All alone.
No touch to relieve the ache of the soul.
No ear to listen to the crying pleas.
No look from eyes to comfort your soul-breaking heart.
No one there to fill the empty void.

Alone . . . alas . . . alone.
All alone.
The empty stillness haunts the mind.
The ache of the soul is a never ending pain
the loneliness—a never ending dream.

Commander

Jeanie Knecht
SALUTE TO MY DOG

You weren't buried without a heart, my little hero, because when yours stopped, you took mine.

COMMANDER . . .
To whom I yield all my admiration and love,
For you live a most venerable life of no pretensions.
You foray the dawn with more glory than the sun
And relish life with infectious fervor.

To no living creature do I owe more respect.
You are, indeed, my celebration.

Laurie Alice Frantz
STAND APART
I always try to live my life with heart
And never let them tell me what to be
So if it means that I must stand apart,
At least my mind is mine and I am free.
I never let them tell me what to say,
Or get me down and make me sing the blues.
If this means I must go my separate way,
Then that's the way that I will always choose.
I'll conquer all the things I must defeat—
That try to stop or block my own true road
And win when it is hard to find my feet.
I'll know that I am of the brave and bold.
Someday I hope to find the rest of us;
The few, the proud, and the victorious.

Evelyn Kintop
REFLECTIONS ON MY LOVE
I've seen thee drift from vapored mists
that stalk the eventide,
And watched thee form in billowed clouds
that haunt the countryside;
I've found thee hidden deep in flowers
that grace each woodland tree;
Oh, Love, there is no place at all
where thou can'st hide from me.

Mine eyes behold in spellbound gaze
the flare of setting sun,
And there atop a fiery throne,
I find thee, dearest one;
So deeply interwoven in
the streams of shadowed light;
A perfect imagery of thee,

half-hidden in the night.

I find my footsteps falling
in the prints thy feet have made
And touch with tender reverence
blessed earth where thou hast
laid;
And every breath of air that stirs
brings thee ever close to me,
For love, no matter where I go,
I always walk with thee.

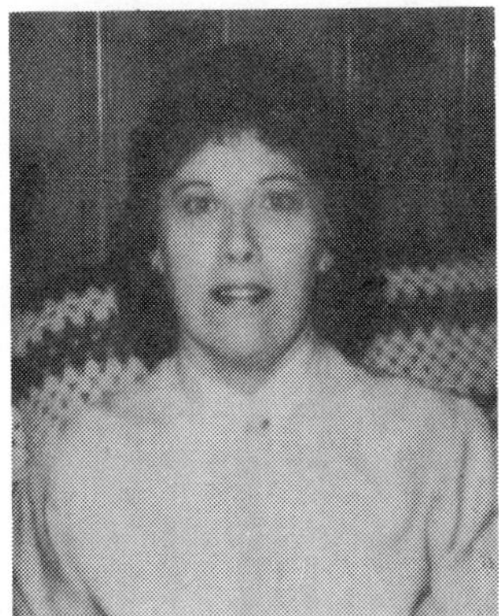

Janice Rothwell Clayton

Janice Rothwell Clayton
FATHER I THANK THEE

For Jesus Christ born here on earth,
So that we might have new birth,
For the Holy Spirit you sent to stay,
To comfort us and guide our way;
Father I thank Thee.

For leading me to right from wrong,
For placing in my heart a song,
For wisdom in Thy Holy Book,
To be found on any page I look;
Father I thank Thee

For thinking me important to save,
For life eternal beyond the grave,
For a Heavenly Home beyond the
stars,
For my mansion in Heaven where
you are;
Father I thank Thee.

For all these things and many more,
Too numerous to mention in a score,
But all are written upon my heart,
I'll thank Thee in person when
eternity starts.
Father I thank Thee.

Audrey Allen
I FELT LOVE

To Auden my husband with all my love.

I felt love the first time you held me
Empty was I until I saw love in
the eyes of our child.
I cannot say why of this love
But it's stronger than death.

I felt love when I lost you to life
When I realized that you were
the most important person
in my life.

And we had shared. You had cared
To fill this void you came back
Then I felt love

I knew love when you left
When no more the arms that held me
were there
I knew love when the nights were
cold
And empty without you.
I knew love when once more time
for us stood still
together we loved, together we cared
And as for sharing I would for any
brief moment
Share my life with you.

Tim Kruszynski
LOVE NOW, I SAY!

Love now, I say! Some raging
Cosmic swell
Could sweep your flesh-poem, your
dreams embodied,
So far into the depths of Outer Space
You'll never meet within your
fleeting breath-spans!
Love now, I say! Though joining is
forbidden,
A single touch will do; a conscious
sensing
That recognizes, in this life-warm
aura,
Infinity itself—that all the stars
Ordained such lovely atoms as
expressions
Quite necessary for their final
triumph!
A possibility of charm, of vigor,
Of thought-nobility somehow
intended
To melt into, and strengthen, classic
stances!
Love now, I say! Glow with totality
You've avidly evolved, artistic
statement
Surprising, sometimes, in its utter
starkness!
Proclaiming, to a world that doesn't
care,
You wish, through close involve-
ment, to continue!

Merle C Hansen
I CRIED A THOUGHT

I cried a thought,
And reached out to eternity to
understand
The meaning of my tears;
And yet I knew
As thoughts paraded through my soul
The reasons for my fears.
Tomorrow comes,
And yesterday had gone its way
With wave and grateful sigh,
As the world
Just goes its ever-present way
As the hours fly.
Remembering
Becomes the burden that the world
Somehow does not understand,
But at other times
Becomes a blissful moment of a sigh
That fades upon time's sand.
I pause,
And think of what was wrought when
the world began,
And cried a thought.

Mr Kris A Wendt
WHAT IS FAIR?

Life never did seem fair, for tragedy
is always in the air.
We do our work and then we die, oh
dear Lord don't you hear our cry.
I think about the child abused, the
woman raped, and the drugs misused.
It's just not fair all these sorrows and
woes.
Why me Lord, why me Lord we all
seem to shout.
This just isn't fair as we scurry about.
Then in a distance I see a great tree.
The tree is a cross and he's dying for
me. I ran to his side, and with his last
breath, he said come closer I'm
nearing my death. He looked down at
me and he started to sob, do you
know my child, this is my job. No
this is not fair, for I have not even
sinned. But here I will suffer and die
just the same.
In hope that every heart will soon
know my name.

So when you are troubled and feeling
real low, just remember this tree and
it will ease the blow. Jesus Christ is
my Savior, and his dying was not
fair, but please remember all the
suffering he had to bear.
Now Jesus reigns in heaven above,
King of all Kings, and the Holy Spirit
in a dove.
So be strong and remember that old
tree, that Jesus hung from, for you
and for me. This is his love, that
branches out from this tree, that we
may have for eternity.

Robert G Aldous
NOT TODAY

The purple shadow of death looms
overhead
To touch a loved one, touch me
instead.
I dare you Death to play your game!
Playing with me is not the same.
I have skirmished with you before, I
know your way
She'll not be your prize—not today!
I'll tease you and taunt you, so sit
back and wait.
You won't get her, but I'll give you
her mate.
That's me Mr. Death, you've met
your match,
My loved one won't be your catch.
Show me your rage if you can Mr.
Death,
I'll show you revenge till your last
dying breath.
Forget it for now, I ask you to cease,
So my love and I can live in peace . .

Raenita Y Spearman
FAITH

It is the dead of night.
My eyes, filled to the brim with the
pain of living, have closed.
They want never to open again.
My heart, heavy with the cares of the
world, has descended deep into my
soul.
My sobs reverberate in the stillness
of the dark room.
Is my God there?
Does he not care?
Can't he see that my grief is more
than I can shoulder alone?
I hear a voice in the darkness.
It says, "Your God does not hear
your pleas for help.
He has left you all alone. . . . ."
The voice is smooth, satiny, and
briefly comforting to my emotions.
I begin to slip and fall into the
clutches of hopelessness.
But I cannot go there.
I cannot give up on my God.
With my last ounce of strength I cry,
"God, please be with me now!"
Suddenly the voice is gone.
The pain is gone.
The fear and the emptiness of
complete despair are gone.
In its place is a cool, unfathomable
peace.
Faith.

Leo D Barron
MY LIFE

When I was very young
And my life appeared carefree,
It wasn't true at all,
'Cause choice was not for me.

My parents, aunts and uncles
Told me when and what to eat
And what to wear and where to go
And how to act discreet.

Now my life's steadfastly waning
It's moving toward the end.
Still plagued by authority,
It's my kids I now contend.

They say what's best for me to do.
From large things down to small.
I resent it, sure, but it would be sad
If no one cared at all.

Doris Stroud Basinger
INNOCENTS

I was told the boy next door
was handsome and bright
with hair of black and his
teeth were so white.

One day he arrived with a sleek,
red "Flyer."
He had slipped under the fence,
raising the loose bottom wire.

Pulling his little wagon up the
front walk with pride,
he had come for me to take me
out on a ride.

But Mother said 'twas not to be
in this wee cart so new,
for I was two weeks old and he
was only two.

Linda Marie Steiger
SEA GULLS

Listen to the sea gulls, as they call in
the night
watch how they glide, as they take
off in flight;

The freedom they feel, the space that
is theirs
like free-spirited souls, without any
cares;

When I gaze in his eyes, as deep as
the sea
and his arms so secure enclose
around me;

My heart soars with the birds, adrift
in the night
and I know what I've found has to be
right;

The pain that I've felt for so many
years
is gone with the emptiness, and all of
my tears;

His wild carefree actions, his loving
mocking ways
leave me yearning for the nights, and
anxious for the days;

Should I hold on very loosely, let him stay the way he is?
Or, hang on very tightly reminding him I'm his?

To roam is in his nature, his home is on the land
to try to change or own him, will not be by my hand;

I only wish to love him, and show him how I care
for a love as strong as ours can be is often very rare;

Listen to the sea gulls, as they call in the night
I wonder what they call for, as they take off in flight?

Margaret Peel Burris
DESPERATION
I'm sinking alone in a sea of despair
Face turned upward gasping for air
Loud screams for help I send from my soul
But there's no one for comfort, no one to hold
Lines of turned away faces go by on the shore
Their blank faces and deaf ears I'll trouble never more
If only there was someone to hear me as I scream
And search these dark waters with their lighted beam
A line to reach a distant land
A calmer place with sun and sand
This despair I would leave behind
If only I could one person find
To share their line and lighted beam
And answer my unending scream
I've traveled rough seas for endless ages
I've fought the good fight as I turned life's pages
The waves are now higher, they sound a loud roar
The turned away faces are gone from the shore
There is no lighted beam as before
My chances of being rescued are gone for ever more

Celia Volkman
A MESSAGE OF THANKS

To my dear daughter, Erica, God's gift to me, whose love and devotion made my dreams come to be!

I can see the clouds emerge
Watch the birds in flight converge,
Feel the coolness of sun beyond,
Warm caress of sun beyond,
Hear the whisper of the trees
Muted murmur of the breeze,
Smell the flowers as they sway,
Taste the fruit before I stray.
These treasures to my breast are pressed—
I thank Thee Lord, for I am blessed!

Maggie (Margaret) Paxton
SOMETIMES WE DON'T SAY HOW WE FEEL
Sometimes we don't say how we feel . . .
Sometimes we find time for
a "little" prayer at a meal . . .
Sometimes when we want something bad,
We remember the Lord,
and pray a "little" bit.
Now if there's sickness the Lord comes in mind,
But when the prayer was answered,
a Thank You, somehow slipped
our mind.
Always time to complain for evermore.
Always time to want for more.
Aren't we lucky we're not the Lord,
to be thought of in that way.
A hit and miss, a now and then,
or maybe someday . . . . .
I know we are humans,
unthoughtful and unkind;
Thank you dear Lord,
for not being that kind.
Dear Lord, I don't want to be
your hit and miss,
Or a now and then or . . .
maybe someday.
Thank you God,
for one more chance . . .
To hear me pray.

Robert Loudin
BEAUTEOUS
You're an authentic work of art
soundly finesse
Extraordinarily vivid in colour
novel and fresh

Magnificent curvature of body
splendid in flow
The loveliness of your beauty—
structure and soul

You release astonishing awe
a stimulating esteem
You harvest enthusiasm and homage from men
suitably pleasing

Your charisma's so powerful—
so inspirational
Passionate attraction immediately allured
you're delicately beautiful

Heather Emery Miyauchi

Heather Emery Miyauchi
JIMMY SMALL
'Tis a fair land I leave
Aye, fair
Fields of heather
Wondrous to behold
Their white and purple blossoms
Send a glorious fragrance
To tug at my heart and beg me
Don't go
That strange new country
Untamed
What perils are unforeseen
What trials await you
Ah, only stay

It is an immense country
Compared to my homeland
Miles stretch into miles
Only the oceans had I known
To reach so far
Surely here a man can find
His God
Nature at your fingertips
Its forms innumerable
Its colors vibrant
Though a stranger, welcoming me
Gladness fills my very being
I feel at home
It seems like yesterday
Riding over lush prairie grass
Me against the wind
Such freedom
Friendships formed as strong and lasting
As the very earth
A life to live
A country to call "mine"
Now old, but always
Looking forward
Each year I stretch my luck
But yet, I expect another
Eternity would find no disciple
Such as I

Lee Anne Dorey
IF YOU LEAVE
If you leave me now, I wish that I could say
You'll take my heart away.
If you leave me now, I wish that I could say
I'll die for you today.
But it wouldn't be true, it wouldn't be true.

What we had was never what it seemed.
What we had was just a dreamer's dream.
All that it was, was a pack of lies,
Hidden from me by your scheming eyes.

If you leave me now, I wish that I could say
I'll cry for you today.
If you leave me now, I wish that I could say
You'll take my life away
But it wouldn't be true, it wouldn't be true.

Edna M Selby
THE SETTING OF THE SUN
It's not always the things we do,
But, the things we've left undone
that give us a bit of heartache
at the setting of the sun.
It's not always the things we've said,
But the ones we didn't say,
That cause us to ponder
At the closing of the day.
We think about the things we did,
Not the ones we didn't do.
The sick we didn't visit,
And when our day is through,
Perhaps we should remember
The things we could have done
And do these things tomorrow,
Before the setting of the sun!

Trudy E Albrecht
FILTERED
Once you've seen
a shooting star,
it's hard to care
about the others,

sprinkled on us
in another time,
to light
chilly moonlight walks.

Frozen in static
destinies,
cold,
their aureola paled
and relevance faded,

when you flash by.

Robert S Cassidy
DO NOT CLING TO THE PAST
Remembering is a wonderful thing,
and, is not to be slighted:
especially, by surprise, at
things, that have already happened.

Those things—are good to know,
in your heart; that they were tried, by
being successful, but they
won't help you now—to grow now.

We must live in the present,
and remember the present day;
remember
the future happens, and remember
who we are;
not who we were—Do not cling to
the past:

or, you will be the last of your
kind—
good things are daily, you'll find—
and, the past is a long road,
with dark corners, every way, they
wind!!

Lizbeth Landes Miller
THOUGHTS IN THE NIGHT
In my darkened room I lie
Contemplating life
And fearing that my hope will die
Of that to be a wife.

Thus I lie in bed alone
Thinking of the past,
The wedded bliss we did not own,
A love that did not last,

Wond'ring if I'll ever feel
Ready to be wed
And not afraid to see what's real
Nor dread to share my bed.

As I lie in peace and calm,
Silent solitude,
The darkness serves as soothing balm
To ease my somber mood.

Love again will come my way
When the time is right.
On this I force my thoughts to stay.
I drift off in the night.

Cassandra Kelly
WHAT IT TAKES TO WIN
Winning is everyone's dream
come true!
You try your best but,
Your best is never good
enough.
To win, you must strive for
the top,
And nothing should ever
stop you.
Dream; about climbing the ladder
of life.
It's a long way to the top.
Don't look back now
Or you will never be
The winner you always
wanted to be! !

B B Watkins
OUR PART . . .
It's delivering the pitch that counts;
What happens after that . . . who
knows?
It's serving up our very best
Against odds and forces that
oppose . . .

No nervous or debilitating guesses
About what the batters might do;
That's totally out of our hands
—And unknown to the batters,
too . . .

Angela Jackson
PUZZLES
Puzzles, puzzles, puzzles,
they rack your brain,
but still they're fun to do.
At times they make you wish you
hadn't bothered;
they test your knowledge and
sharpen your wits,
but still they're fun to do.
Some are very challenging,
but still they're fun to do.
Some are like solving mysteries,

with each clue leading you closer to the end;
these kind often cause you heartache, pain and agony,
but still they're fun to do.
There are many different kinds, of which you can choose;
from easy to hard, from tried to true,
However it doesn't matter,
Still they're fun to do.

William O Hicks Sr
OUR WEDDING DAY
Our hearts will beat as one
Our love will be forever,
The vows we make today
Will join our hearts together.

We are in our world together
Bound with the bonds of love,
I'll always love you darling
You're all I'm dreaming of.

Whom God hath joined together
Let no one taketh away,
He has joined our hearts together
On this our wedding day,

I'll always want you darling
I promise to be true,
I promise to be faithful
My darling I love you.

When our wedding day has ended
It will not leave our mind,
Its memory we'll cherish
Until the end of time.

Glennda E Chambers
THE RETURN

I dedicate the poem, "The Return" to the everlasting love of my life, Ramon. You'll be forever in my mind for all time.

Peaceful and calm the days used to be.
Now they are filled with the longing for he.
As I sit and look out the window,
I wonder if I will soon be a widow.
Never will this be for me!
For I feel as the tree that withers and dies;
And wonder if I will live to see another day
Filled with such happiness and joy that only he can employ.
He will come back to my arms long awaiting.
And our love will grow
Into what all God's creatures know.
And together we shall be as one with Thee.

Jess Hayworth Lowe
CONVERSATION WITH A PINE
Driving my old truck, into these hills,
Shifting and unshifting, there's a rhythm, there's a rhythm.
Dual exhaust, roars out to the wilderness,
I'm here, a peaceful driver, I have no fear.
The sky is painted perfect, with clouds here and there,
Bristlecone pines, stand like wise old guards;
Unlocking the secrets to this place, must start with the pines,
If these old trees could talk, the wisdom would be so very new.
Walking many miles, a stray thought came and flew,
The world's oldest living people, are young, and so very new.

Nellie Mae Crawford
SPRING IS COMING

To those who were an inspirational in earlier years encouraging one to go on

In spring flowers bloom
Gone is the winter gloom
Sending forth their sweet scents
Into all the open rooms.
Bringing the indoors in
Cheering up all the shut-ins.
Giving colors that never ends
Long after, gone are the friends.
Some are in for awhile
Wearing themselves thin-in meanwhile,
Waiting for a cheery smile.
Helping them on their way,
Seem to brighten up the day.
Going down life pathway.
Know what spring brings
After the cold winter winds
Hearing the song bird sings
With the ever coming spring
Sending forth their sweet smells
Winter gone and things going well.

Carolyn P DuEst
HAPPY 70TH BIRTHDAY MAMA

I would like to dedicate this poem to the memory of my mother, Mabel L. Valente, a very beautiful and special woman. And although she is no longer with us, her spirit will live on forever.

We've gathered together tonight in this hall,
For this is a special night for us all,
We are honoring Mabel, of that we're aware,
We want her to know we all love her, we care.

She's touched all our lives in her seventy years,
Through good times and bad times, laughter and tears,
And now in return we want her to know,
We will never forget her, wherever we go.

We will always remember our mother, our friend,
Even after this night has come to an end,
We'll remember her kindness, her faith, and her love,
Which God has bestowed upon her from above.

So lift up your glasses and raise them on high,
And let's drink a toast before saying good-bye,
And let us be thankful whenever we're able,
For our warm, and our loving, our beautiful, Mabel.

Jessica Bordes
A TENDER THANK YOU

To my loving mother, Marguerite, whom I love more than anything.

Thank you, Mother, for your unconditional love,
I love no one better than the one mentioned above.
You bestowed and still nurture my existence,
Even though my gratitude isn't consistent.
The effort you show is not always redeemed,
But your maternal duties did not go unseen.
Patience and knowledge you possess,
It is of great value I must confess.
Through runny noses and scraped knees;
Your affectionate kiss was a sweet remedy.
When peers ignored me because I didn't fit in,
You told me to smile and hold up my chin.
Every time I was wrong you loved me still,
You gave me space and judgment of free will.
I made many mistakes, but you never said, "I told you so."
My downfalls educated me and helped me to grow.
Words can never express my emotions so deep,
But I share my love with you, all you want to keep . . .

Pradeep Shumshere Rana

Pradeep Shumshere Rana
EMPTY TALK

To my mama, Saraswoti Rana, who designed me early on for Tribhuvan University teacher on English Literature.

Break my mortal cast
To tone up your hubris,
I don't give a damn
'Cause I'm a little end.

A tissue dies in your trickery!
Who cares?
One more corrosive ache in thought-machine!
Who dreads?
Black into black, and how much black?
That's yours, not mine, alright!

Yes, day on night, moon on sun.
No, not thin many on fat few, man!
No, not even in eyes!
Just one big reversal in your mind!
That's it!
Oh, I see. Vice in virtue, truth in fallacy!
And nothing more to start or finish!
How strange it sounds!

Wrong stuff into illusive rack, ok?
Come with others?
I'll play with you tomorrow.
Yes, tomorrow.
No, never with foul stuff, never again!
Tomorrow, alright!
See you later.

William R Scofield
DI—ET
There once was a woman filled with hate,
because of the things her daughter ate.
She said, "If you continue to eat like that
you will grow up to be very big and fat."

So the daughter went on a diet and stopped eating,
because she was afraid of getting a beating.
And, as she dieted, she grew thinner and thinner,
until there was nothing at all left within her.
The first to go was her mind and her brain,
which left her friends in much sorrow and pain.

So they took her to the doctor who said,
"Feed this girl plenty of shortening bread."
"But," said the mother, "I would rather be dead
than let my daughter eat shortening bread."

The moral of the story it must be said,
"It is much better to be fat than dead.
Now shut up and eat that shortening bread."

Sunny Virginia Chandler
SILVER DRAGON
One dark, stormy night I flew over the sea
On the wings of a great Silver dragon.
From the land of knighthood he carried me
To the land of the covered wagon.
Fearful I was of the height and the space
As the plane o'er the world seemed to tower,
Spitting fire he was in his time killing pace
Yet I was soothed by his deep throated power.
"Sleep, little one, rest" he seemed to croon,
"For a new life comes with the morning.
I'll hold you safe, then we'll race the moon,
And we'll laugh at the storm cloud's warning."
So comforted, I finally slept,
While the elements howled in o'er the sea.
Though the thunder crashed and the heavens wept,
I dreamed of my new life to be.

Melody Carol Davis
IN THE SKY
Life
Is colored like a rainbow
Of bright yellow happiness
To dark blue sorrow
And at the end of the rainbow
Is the last tomorrow

But after tomorrow
Is another day
For those who wandered
Yet found the way
For the good and the giving
While on earth they did roam
With God
Awaits an eternal home
Where there's no sickness, no sorrow,
No poor or no old,
Up in the sky
We'll walk
Streets of Gold.

Mary Ursula Sumpter
H*I*L*L*H*O*U*S*E**

To All Those Who Have Encouraged Me; Especially My Great Aunt—Loretta Meyer and Georgia McGuire

All hope betrays me
Wishes turn to dust
Green pastures have turned brown and barren.
There lies no heart to fill me with love
The architect built no windows for light
The dark remains the sill of life.

There was once a full moon and it did shine down upon the house
And the house did live with joy and love!
But, the moon could not stay
For it had other lives to enter and kinder light to spread.
So lonely the house did remain
Until the ceiling began to falter and
The sides did cave in.

Judith Fenton Bochkay
BY THE GREAT FALLS—

To warm honey—the way it flows together sweetly.

Sprays of fine mist
float above
the rolling, twisting
waters
beyond my reach.

Cool wet fingers
tap my face
lightly.

I feel one
with the energy
the twinkles
round me.

Jo Ellen Nye
THE TURN OF THE CENTURY

All of us have wondered at one time how it might be,
Will we be climbing staggered stairways or playing "Punch In The Answer" on T.V.?
And see children solving equations in the second grade,
The latest health craze of the year might be chewable gatorade.

Living in foam houses may save time and energy,
Using laserwave type ovens can make meals easily,
Planes and rockets of the age will be soaring to new heights;
Let's play "Win A Trip To Venus" on NASA'S most recent passenger flight.

Record albums and tape cassettes will most likely not be around,
While shiny, blue compact discs and MTV will be sure to wear the crown;
The movie theatre's big attraction would be "Friday the 13th Part Thirty-two,
And E.T. will be alive and well vacationing in Honolulu.

Answering digital telephones that will buzz instead of ring,
Just insert your plastic in the slot and you can buy most anything;
So while planning your next holiday on a star beneath the sun,
Pack extra tapes for your 3-D camcorder for it will be a most memorable one.

R C Pavlovsky
THIS SAILOR'S PRAYER

To the Sailors who died on the U.S.S. Iowa

Oh Mighty "SOL" That provides the light of day, you come with warm red rays to bathe my face each day. When your heavenly rays no longer warm me from the morning chill, you'll know my body's eternally still!
Oh Harvest Moon: You came to light the night, with your heavenly halo's light. When my eyes no longer drink in your pale golden glow; I'll be stiff and cold!
Oh sweet breathe of life when you no longer touch my life,
With your precious gifts, I'll render up my immortal soul, and be free to seek my eternal goal!
Oh great sun and moon please light my way on my trip past the Milkyway,
Oh Breath of life you've set me free, now please fill my sails with lighting speed to travel on this eternal sea.

Katheren Layman Cafourek
TOMORROW

I dedicate this to my family.

I do not have time to grow old,
So many things I want to do;
There's quilts to make of colors bright
and pillows with ruffles, stitches and lace.
So many cookies shapes and kinds,
Just to write a line to family of mine.
From outgrown clothes, crochet a rug,
To tame a cat someone dropped by my door.
I like to sit before the TV, have coffee,
Visit on the phone, my friends also alone.
Look at pictures of family; Time flies.
Where is yesterday, and still more things
I want to do.
How could one miss tomorrow when I hear,
"Grandma, I love you!"

Angela M Schneider
CRY FOR ME

For Rob, My Dear Brother, These are words to live by.

Cry for me,
When I die.
Cry for me,
While I lie in my grave.
Cry for me,
When you feel lost and lonely.

But please:

Laugh for me,
When you remember.
Laugh for me,
When you hear a joke.
Laugh for me,
For I can no longer.

Cry for me once.
Laugh for me forever.

Debbie Stewart-Wilson
A FRIEND IS A GOLDEN GIFT

To Scotty, my "friend of friends"!

A friend is a golden gift
Like a ring that does not tarnish
Like the sun that always rises
Like an amber leaf off an autumn tree,
Floating through your life on a gentle wind.

A friend is never an imitation, always true
Like sweet yellow honey, taken from the hive
Like a rare, valuable coin, not easily parted with
Like the gilded song of a carefree sparrow,
Not to be duplicated by any other source.

A friend is a golden gift, because,
To have even one—

Is a treasure.

Teddy D Reese
THROUGH ANOTHER DAY

When the dawn breaks into morning,
And the sun begins to rise;
As my head lifts off my pillow,
And I open up my eyes;
It's then, I bow my head in silence,
While I go before my Lord;
Where I ask for His protection,
For He is my shield and sword.

Heaven help me!
Through another day;
Lord, I need Your strength and guidance,
As I go along the way;
And please Lord, I need Your presence,
In everything I say and do;
All these things, in Jesus' name,
I ask of You.

Through another day?
"Jesus is the only way"
AMEN . . .

Wendy Marie Maniaci
DAD

For my father, Frank A Maniaci

Sun through the window
a glitter of light.
No other father,
could make this seem so bright.
A special place,
locked inside my heart.
A warm and blessed feeling,
never to part.
Yet, though at times,
through the days,
There seems to be missing,
some appreciation, thanks, or praise.
Forever through our lives,
whether times of good or bad,
I will always be with you,
to love and adore you Dad.

Trudy Cessna
THE EYES OF JESUS

This poem is dedicated to Rev. Don English, First Cumberland Presbyterian Church, Jackson, Miss.

What do the eyes of Jesus behold
When they look into my soul
What does He see
When He looks at me

Am I a witness shining bright
Or, are my deeds as dark as night
Are my thoughts pure and true
Or, do they dwell on the wrong things to do

Do I feel envy, greed and jealousy—
What does He see when He looks at me

As I begin each day
Lord, may I remember to pray
Today, I commit to you
Everything I think, say and do

And, as I into the world go
May I to others your kindness show
With brotherly love and caring
All my earthly possessions gladly sharing

And, with the Spirit's power, I can be
What He wants to see
When the eyes of Jesus look at me

Joan Roberts
SWEET MEMORIES

To Wichita, Kansas for my inspiration, and to my beloved family.

Sometimes, I awake in the middle of the night,
it seems like I have been in another world or time.
Because I see a real bright light.
I seem to be falling into different dimensions,
of other lives I could have lived,
before I lived this one.
Life like dreams, so real of sweet memories.
Beautiful gardens, of many exotic fruits, spices, water and green fields, full of gorgeous flowers, of celestial smells, aromas, and colors like I have never seen, only in these sweet memories of my dreams.
Streets of gold, pillars of ivory.
Foundations of many precious stones, all colors
Gates of pearls, angels, God, Jesus.
Where was this sweet memories of another life and time? Paradise?

Mayme E Bennington
LOVE

Dedicated to my son Kevin on his 30th birthday

Love is so very many things
Like sun shining on butterfly wings
As it flits from flower to flower
Or a bee drawing nectar for the hive
Walking through a soft summer shower
Feeling good to just be alive.

Love is a constant and steady thing
Like a mother has for her child.
What joy and happiness it can bring
To see a doe and fawn out in the wild.
To help the beggar on the street
To tell your neighbor "I care about you"
To give a smile to those we meet
To love everybody and not just a few
That feeling you get back is Love
And it only comes from God above.

Michael Andrew Vidalis

WILDFLOWER

Little wild flower
By the edge of the cliff,
What can you do
To soothe some of my grief?

Windblown as you are
Have travelled so far.
How can you stand up
While I'm falling beneath?

Eloisa C Rodriguez

SHALL I

I dedicate this poem to Gracie our loving dog. For her Love and strength till the end.

Shall thy telleth thee of undying love,
Or keepeth sacred to thy self.
Shall I singeth thee a song,
Or giveth thee Spontaneous Spring.
Thy have bequeatheth my soul with fire,
For thy walketh a mile for thy divine smile.
Thy tenderness requesteth only thy sincerity,
For it's brilliance illuminateseth the city.
Thy giveth thee thy life,
For thy art thy Wife,
Thy giveth thee thy heart,
For thy desireth to never be parteth,
Shall I dancest for thee, my love.
Or preseverely bestoweth thee thy soul.
Shall I bringeth thee the moon,
Lest thy wanteth the sky, too.
Shall I showereth thee in Blossom's Wines,
Or showeth thee the beginning, of Time.
Thy harvesteth strength bellows like the Ocean's roars.
But thy sweet voice weaveseth thee to be adored.
Thy dazzling beauty has stabbeth, me true.
For thy woest thee, with thy departure.
Tilleth the morning light has befallen on thee,
Shall thy remaineth forever with thee,
Only death shall seperateth us My Love,
But I forsaketh to come to thee from above,
For death not beest the end
But thy gloriest beginning to mend.

Amelia J Nagle Simmons

THE FIRST SNOWFALL

Freshly fallen snow
clings upon
towering pine trees.

Ivory-colored flakes
sprinkled over
spacious log cabins along the mountainside.

Charcoal, gray clouds
stream out of
Chinese-red chimneys.

Crystal clear icicles
dangle from
burdened eaves.

Quivering bodies
tremble in the
crisp winter air.

THE FIRST SNOWFALL
HERE
AND
NOW.

Delford Baker (Panaderro)

LIFE

Inspired by and dedicated to Don Jackson and Lorie Baker. Thank You Both For Your Support.

A flower which grows right before your eyes.
No room for error, none for lies.
Bringing forth what is so great.
The potential for love as well as hate.

Roots that spread, anchor and grow.
Programmed thoughts limits desire to know.
Notions conceived, what might have been?
Should've tried something, if only back when.

What happens to that which is so precious.
Consumed by complexity or simple and gracious.
You're wrong, you're right, someone will say.
So come what will, come what may.

Just like the rain all cycles end,
merely to seed and form again.
Why is there fear of the time bandit,
when life is truly what we make it.

Alma Wesselman Langston

MOTHER

To my children, grandchildren, stepchildren and my husband Carl

It's so hard to be a Mother.
Your heart is never whole.
They break it all to pieces,
More with each year they grow.
They step on your toes, at the start,
When they grow older, they step on your heart.
My love for them, they will never have really known.
Until they are grown, with a heartbreaker of their own.
We teach them truth and honesty.
Then when they are bad, and we don't agree.
They yell "Mom" you're mean to me.
Just bide your time, my dears and you will see.
It isn't easy a mother to be.

Sophie Rank

JUST A SIMPLE THOUGHT

Just A Simple Thought was submitted by Barbara Joleen Baker, the granddaughter of the late Sophie Rank in her loving memory.

We must part and say good bye.
Leave each other with a sigh,

Perchance never meet again, In this worldly earthly reign,

May the "Lord" our pathway guide.
Till we rest at his own side. All our tears forever dried. Where we'll never say good-bye.

There we'll meet, each other greet, never more to part, never say good-bye

Read these simple lines, think of me.
Though far from you I be.

Let them comfort you. "Learn of Christ your defender, There full salvation find."

Finally meet me in the heavenly home where we'll never ever say good bye.

Carla Chapman-Powell

COYOTES

To Timothy who rescued me from my lonely nights. I love you.

That eerie sound
That lonely cry
That howl that pierced the night

Across the dark
Awake from sleep
I wonder what's your plight

I feel a chill
I sit alone
Staring into a desert vast

Alone you cry
The night's nomad
Reminder of my past

Rob Sanford

HIGH COUP

First and third each five;
Seven (as in days) second;
Seventeen to sketch.

Peggy Chittum

Peggy Chittum

THINGS I REMEMBER

Sitting on the front porch counting cars go by
Watching fluffy animals float across the sky
Lazy summer afternoons with neighbors down the street
A friendly smile, a loud hello to everyone we meet
RC Cola and a moon pie
Thunderheads in a midnight sky
A time to play in snow and sun
And soundly sleep when day is done
A kiss that wipes away the tear
No second thought of things to fear
Those were the days away back when
That I remember now and then.

Kristie Howard

FINAL FAREWELL

The room is deadly silent
the sobs I hear are mine,
As I lay my eyes upon you
for the last and final time,
I see you lying in your casket
so quiet and so still,
I long to hear your voice again
though I know I never will,
My heart is filled with sorrow
as I say my last good-bye,
I let my tears flow freely
I am not ashamed to cry,
You've left me now forever
but I'll keep you in my mind,
And though I'll never see your face again
the memories are left behind,
I tell myself that it's not true
But I know this is the end,
I've not only lost my mother
But I've also lost a friend.

Virginia Carlson Knight

CARESSING RAIN

To my husbands, who served their beloved Country with unselfish devotion. Lieutenant C. Lyle Carlson, killed in action World War II, August 15, 1944. Goodwin J. Knight, Governor of California, 1953 to 1959. Dec., May 22, 1970.

Rain drops sing a melody
Upon my restless heart . . .
Coming from your starlit world
Telling me we're not apart.

Rain drops wash away my tears . . .
Did they caress you too?
And then come down from Heaven
To kiss me for you.

Julius Carl Frank

BEFORE

To my son Julius Jr.

Once the world was as pretty, as a dove in flight. Pretty as a flower
in full blossom. But that has been changed, by all the crime,
and all the sin, Oh what an unhappy world we now live in.
And yet, if just the young, would stop.
Listen and Love; our lives
would once again, lift up, on the
wings of the dove.

Jonathan Pyle

LIVE YOUR DREAMS, INSTEAD

To Mom, for making me believe I could write, and proving to me what it means to be brave

The past was once the future.
The future will soon be here.
When you think about the present,
The future's not so clear.
The past is there for memories,
The future is for dreams.
The present is the hard part,
Or so, it only seems.
They say forget about the past.
The future holds the key.
Where does that leave the present?
How much future's left to see?
The present's what it's all about.
The past is all but done.
We don't know what the future is,
So live while you're still young!
Never look behind you.
Always look ahead.
Don't dwell on bad memories,
Live your dreams, instead.

Helen Keegan

GREEN BANK HIGH

. . . for the Class of 1958 with love

Late summer, nineteen fifty-four
We came prancing through your door
Eighth grade hot shots, a few months before
And now wondering, "What's in store?"

Locker doors clanging as off we ran
To English, Biology, Math,
Shorthand
Your hall was filled with laughter,
Ringing bells, before class and after.
Cheerleaders, ballgames, the Senior
Play,
Journalism, Study Hall and FFA.
Some drop out, but most of us stay
For class rings, proms and gradu-
ation day.
Time marches on and with each year,
Green Bank High, your memory
grows dear
Your doors have since closed, we
know
. . . We left you
. . . thirty years ago.

Erma Simmons
DREAMA

for my daughter, Dreama with love

Late at night and the wind blew cold
A little babe to her breast she'd hold
And whisper softly in the little one's
ear,
Don't be afraid now, Momma's right
here.

I watched her grow into a beautiful
girl
And tried to protect her from hurt in
the world
Although Dreama is just
twenty-one
Heartaches we've shared and
also fun.

So Dreama, today while you're
reading this,
Stop. Did you feel something?
Maybe a kiss,
Or a soft whisper close to your ear,
Don't be afraid, Dreama, Momma's
still right here.

Brenda R Richardson

Brenda R Richardson
ROSEMARY

Especially written for my loving Mother Rosemary

Once long ago . . . .
In a studio of light and trickery
a small child stood.
In her little dress and blouse
she set a proud, yet gentle mood.
She stood on an oak pedestal
her skirts held high,
Her childish charm pouring out
in a smile so shy.
And as the day turns to night
And the seed becomes the
rose . . .
So she grew, a beautiful woman
in every way it shows.
Giving love and kind respect to
anyone in need,
Receiving in return
An eternity times three.
My Mother . . . . . .
Clothed in honor from
her head to her toes,
A human more fair
than the loveliest of all flowers
The Rose.

Justine E Hanif
ALONE IN A CROWDED ROOM
Alone in a crowded room,
No one notices the solitude,
The remote silence that exists
amongst the chatter,
Under the bright and flowing smile,
lurks a dampened heart,
An abandoned soul, A woman lost
and confused.
She sits looking very much at peace,
only camouflaging
The battle in her mind.
Whether to end it!
She wonders if now it is worth it,
To give them the satisfaction of
knowing they have wounded her,
Of letting them win the long war.
Or really, would she win?
She closes her eyes to hide the tears,
And from the noise and endless
confusion comes sleep.
Her mind drifts slowly into peace
awaiting the new day,
The new war.

Pamela J Logan
"I" AM A COUPLE

Dedicated to my ever strong Mother, Audrey, my strength giving daughter Courtni, for without you two I might have given up, and those who have known and lost love!

I give myself happiness,
I find my own joy.
"I" Am A Couple.

I bring no pain, no grief, nor
sorrow.
I live for today and not just
tomorrow!
I care and share within my soul,
and to make my life complete,
I treat me like gold!
"I" Am A Couple.

I wait no more for the gift called
"Love",
that projects the key to
happiness,
not sorrowful bliss.
"I" Am A Couple

I share no pain,
that I can not live.
I weep no more for someone who
can not give
I've learned and learned through
passing time,
that one can be miserable if
they let someone else try.
"I" Am A Couple!

Priscilla Thomas Woodard
DRIPPLES OF BLOOD

To my dad and mom, Charles P. and Ada V. Thomas for their loving and strict guidance through my childhood and adolescent years at home. I love you both very much.

The dripping of blood from the
wound of Jesus,
When the spear had pierced His side,
Came trickling down upon me and
opened up mine eyes.

The dripping of blood that touched
my head, gave me to know the fear
of the Lord was the beginning of
knowledge.

The dripping of blood that touched
my heart, showed me to repent or I
must depart.

The dripping of blood that touched
my eyes, let me see the way of a fool
is right in his own eyes.

The dripping of blood that touched
my ears, made me adhere to the
Word of God.

The dripping of blood that touched
my tongue, help me to bridle to say
no wrong.

The dripping of blood that touched
my hands, to be used in the work and
praising of God

The dripping of blood that touched
my feet, to walk no more in darkness
but in the light of the Lord.

The dripping of blood that touched
my body, to make me a temple for
the indwelling of the Holy Spirit.

The dripping of blood from the
wound of Jesus for the redemption of
my sins, has made me a new creature
to live and work for Him.

Sharletta Michelle Green
A MOTHER'S POINT OF VIEW

To a sweet baby boy, Cameron Lanier Spurlock.

It's a boy! It's a girl!
whichever you prefer,
you're the newest member in
your mother's world.
Your tiny fingers and little toes,
you're the cutest baby she knows.
You're so tiny and so free of fear,
you don't have a worry and won't
for years.
You'll bring joy to her life when she
feels down.
You make her life worth a whole lot
more,
You are her baby, her love.

Douglas Lee Hatfield
IN THE FIELDS
In the fields
the green grass grows,
In the fields
the farmer hoes.
In the fields
the sun shines thru,
In the fields
the rains come too.
In the fields
the children play,
In the fields
the animals stay.
In the fields
God looks down from above,
In the fields
He shows his wondrous love.

Sandra Merrick Stallons
IN DAYS WHEN RAIN WAS ALL AROUND US

Terra and Matthew this is for you because I love you so much.

In days when rain was all around us,
One simple smile could chase those
clouds away.

One kiss and all trouble would
disappear.
A gentle I love you,
And the days of my own childhood
would come running back to greet
me.

Here, in thought I sit.
Swept away by the loving years of
life,
Hopelessly I try to hold my young
one back.

When I recall those days of joyful
sunshine,
I want to give to you all that has
been given to me.
For you my child I have the gift of
love.

Joseph P Flynn
ON MY DAUGHTER'S 40TH BIRTHDAY

This poem is dedicated to my daughter, Kathy Labourdette

It seemed oh so far away
At 10 when all you did was play.
At 20 you were halfway there
But at that age you didn't care.
At 30 is when you began to see
That it could truly happen to thee.
And happen it did—that day is here
Now you're 40—but it's not so queer
You're such a beauty—soft as a
dove.
With a great little family, a home full
of love.
So look forward to the future but
don't be hasty.
Drink the full cup of life—as you
head for number 80.

Shirley Jean Arnold
MOTHER

This poem was written for my mother Bonnie Lee Arnold

A mother is like the wondrous
heaven angels take care of their
young
Or a proud Indian chief's wife with
bows and braids in her hair
Or like ocean waves crashing, on
the shore with every clock's tick and
every heart's beat my mother is
always there!

Jackie Lynn Herman
ESCAPE

I dedicate this poem to Brian and Dani Murray—And to Jeff Haese—the three reasons I don't escape

On a cold grey sidewalk of an
unknown city, the drifter walked
alone.
Searching for a little hope as he
roamed
One friend—one smile—just one
glimpse of the sunshine he
remembered
The sunshine seemed so far away,
locked in the past of yesterday
He had it all in his youth, and never
once knew.
For youth doesn't see the forbidden
dangers of hidden truths.
He had found himself on the outside
looking in—no door to be found.

To his past, he seemed destined to always be bound.
He had sadly become a lonely shell of a man.
With no one to give him a kind word, or a helping hand.
No more loss—no more pain
He felt there was nothing left for him to gain.
With a look of total despair—the old, lonely man disappeared into the night
Total hopelessness—no will to fight.

Melody Hope
MY WORDS
In the past my words held only air;
floating off
drifting in
and out
of conversation
They never seemed to hold weight or have any meaning.
But with you they have strength;
They hold lies between us.
Words can now express when I feel happy or sad,
And draw an imaginary line between pain and . . .
They give me hope and let me see choices
Because if my words mean something
Then may be I do too.

James H Neale
UNICORNS AND WISHING WELLS
Step through the door
into a world
that people seldom see
of Unicorns and Wishing Wells
and cotton candy trees
where dreams go on forever
and the sun it always shines
where clouds are made of candy canes
and rivers made of wine

With flowers made of gum drops
so big they touch the sky
the taste of honey fills the air
so open up your eyes
Step through the door
take my hand
and let me take you there
of Unicorns and Wishing Wells
it's easy if you dare

Jackie Romero
HAPPINESS
I thought a pot of gold
To be at the rainbow's end
But much to my surprise
Something more glorious did arise
A happiness beyond compare
Because of the struggle to get there
The strength to climb
the higher road
Though harder it was
And heavier the load
The beauty was beyond compare
Once I made it there
The colors vivid and bright
Surely gave me a new light
So search for your rainbow
And follow your dream
For happiness is the ultimate thing

Betty Karleskent Fancher

Betty Karleskent Fancher
BUT WHAT OF HIS NAME

This Poem is Dedicated to my Dad—"For he now knows"

I have an angel,
He is here by me now.
What of his name,
I do not know.
We walk together every day,
He gives me a smile
Just to know he is there.
He has help me through good times,
and also the bad ones.
God has given me
This wonderful angel
As a gift from him
On the day I was born.
But what of his name,
I do not know.

Linda Jaroszewicz
JUST YOU AND ME

To the one I love

what a feeling
Just you and me
lost in many thoughts
what a feeling
Just you and me
warmth tingles the body
our hearts beat simultaneously
what a feeling
Just you and me

Doris Gladys Chase Brown
MCCAGNEY'S INFERNO
Cracking bones, sucking marrow,
Tossing the remains of her moral excellence,
Into the black cauldron of malice,
The Marmot Beast presides over the Witches' Sabbath,
Raising a forum to vilify his wife.

Mixing, Blending the putrid brew
over fires of accusation,
The fermentable stuff of character assassination,
The Marmot Black-A-Moor's frenzied progency,
Ever encircles the enormous kettle
emitting screams of matricide,
He, the gang of three, rends the air
demanding McCagney's life.

No match, she, against his fresh, new weapons—their issue.
With a fractured, brave heart,
imbroglio brain,
Improverished, a daily consumption of watery fare,
She encamps, decaying, in a cracked walled house,
It leans precariously on a precipitous hill.

Craving succor from involuntary isolation,
McCagney, beholding, each dawn with child wide eyes,
Roseate, dreams of finer days long gone pass,
Returns, reluctantly at day's end to face the truth of the day,
Of besetment, she, emaciated, jawbone steel, abandonment is her strange pill.

What is this odoriferous rot?
Man thing, draping itself on her wary shoulders,
Clinging to the soles of her shoes.
She's featured in someone else's nightmare,
Surely it can't be hers—but then whose?
How, where, when did the Marmot Beast,
Gain such power to make McCagney appear a liar?
And he so pure, angelic, and soulful,
to mimic the guise of a Friar?

Patricia M Mahan
AS THE SUN SETS UPON THE LAND

To: My other half, this is for you! I love you.

As the sun sets upon the land,
together we walk hand in hand.
The stars shine bright in the blackened sky,
they represent our future, just you and I.
I hope it turns out the way we plan it too,
because we were made for each other, me and you.
Although some clouds may cover the sky,
we'll ignore them and together we'll fly.
Everyone knows and doesn't care,
except these two people, this one pair.
Yet when I get old enough, turn eighteen,
we will be able to follow our dreams.
And live the life we've always prayed for,
I love you each day more and more.
I'll stay with you Always and Forever,
I just can't wait to live together.
We've done so much every day,
It's like we're married in every way.
But the day will come when I say I do,
It's all out of love from me to you.
I LOVE YOU!

Jeanne Embry Hale
DREAMS DO COME TRUE
As we walk along the beaches,
Where the sun meets the shore,
And the love we feel between us,
Is much greater than before.

We realize that destiny,
Is leading our lives to,
A lifetime full of happiness
With a love that is so new.

The beauty of our friendship
That has caught afire,
Is now warm and loving moments,
filled with passion and desire.

And no matter what the future brings,
We will always be together.
For a love as strong and true as ours,
Will always burn, forever.

Betty A Harmon RN
TWO PAIRS OF EYES
Her eyes—how they pleaded.
Her fingers—they clung.
A life, in the balance,
Precariously hung.

I am only a nurse.
The Power's not mine.
Tho' could I but change
Our Master's design.

Compassion is all
I was able to give.
And, try as I might,
I could not make her live.

Cool cloths to her forehead,
An injection for pain,
My small contributions
All seemed in vain.

He wanted her with Him.
The cards had been dealt.
But, I hope my eyes told her
How deeply I felt.

Beverly Chandler Burger
THEN THERE WERE SONGS
I hear a song
and I think of you.
The melodies sweet
and the words ring true.

The happy refrain—
The heartaches, the pain.

Because then there were songs
where our love always lived.
In music that painted pictures
of love that takes and gives.

And since that day, I woke up alone
I've held you in music, though you were gone.

Because then there were songs
where our love had lived.
Music painting pictures—
of love that takes and gives.

Then there were songs
Where a love affair lived.
END.

Therisia Strom
SILENT EDGE
As time goes on, the pain lingers along, heritage our history,
heros become memories, forgiven; forgotten; the past we try to bury,
hoping this is the solution to our future,
but still the memories of hurt and hatred from the past cause many to remain silent enemies; for one crime or another,
I know not my crime; my time in many ways I have done,
sticks and stones can break bones, but names,
many cultures have been hurt by inhumanity,
men, thinking of greater glory,
women, weeping on their knees,
how shall they tell the children we are destroying the earth,
none of God's children want to take the fall,
many not able to truly forgive, the hurts too deep,
giving up hatred; losing the edge
leaving no device to be used in the

name of injustice,
our prejudices remain the same only
the name has been changed,
maybe as time goes on, our only
hope, it won't be too late,
but then the right time for everything
can never be too late,
time is all we need to teach our
young; to learn from past mistakes,
compassion is all it takes.

Willie M Smith
THE REVEALING OF DEEP LOVE

They dressed it up and called it
inflation.

But I know it's the same wod you
wuz under fur years
hardwork.

They dressed it up and called it
high economy.

But I know it's the same wod you
wuz under fur years
hardtimes.

They dressed it up and called it
potato-augratin.
But I know it's the same food you
work fur to fill
my stomach fur years,

stewed ice potatoes.

They dressed up lots of words I
like...
I'm appreciative, I'm honored,
I'm elated, I'm delighted.

But fur all dem years, I just wanna
say
"Thank you."

Merry Christmas,
Daddy

J Travis Wendt
MANY WERE THE THINGS THAT CAUGHT MY EYE

To all the Children of Christ and the Foundation for Inner Peace.

Many were the things that caught
my eye, but far too many to carry.
Many were the loves that broke my
heart—far too many to ever part.

Many were the times I spent alone
and some with friends, but seldom
were the times of worth, for I am but
a man.

The Gods have made me a servant
of this earth. They raised me from
the dust and set me in my place.

I am but a human, not mighty,
sharp nor quick.

The Lord my God may do with me
as He sees fit, and many were the
things that caught my eye, but
seldom do I pick a better thing.

Amen

Tracy Jo Flood
I FEEL LIKE A TINY BLADE OF GRASS

This poem is dedicated to Ma & Pa

I feel like a tiny blade
of grass in a great big field,
getting trampled on by someone's
feet but I'll grow to be a
hundred inches tall, and all they can
do is run through me!

Melody Anita Whitfield
NEW BEGINNING

In memory of my Father, the late Willie Lee Wilkins, Sr. 06/21/40—02/23/89

Just as we entered into this world,
We too must someday depart;
Though the end of this life is just the
beginning,
Of a new and wonderful start.

We miss our friends and loved ones,
All of those who have gone on
before us;
And pray for the day when we'll see
their smiling faces,
Their outstretched arms to
gently embrace us.

But our loss is God's gain,
If in His Spirit they remain...
Secured at best, home to rest;
Heaven's reward they will
obtain.

Free from misery, free from pain;
A new dimension, a new
domain;
In the Land of Sunshine—never, ever
rain!

Josephine Currie
WITH LOVE

Let me say—with Love
My Darling Valentine!
Come to my waiting arms
And change your name to mine.

I promise to protect you
To keep you safe and warm
I'll shelter you from every care
No matter what the storm.

Each cloud I'll fill with sunshine
Every tear—I'll turn to joy
We'll travel life together
While time passes by.

You are everything I've wanted
You're the answer to my prayer
You're the reason for my living
As long as you are there.

I've said it ten times over
Let me say it once again—
I love you more than ever
Since you have my NAME.

Brenda Lee Burkhardt
PLEASE BRIGHTEN MY DAY

This poem is dedicated to my precious son, John Michael.

We started out so good together,
nothing could get in our way.
We were so light-hearted, a smile
from you would brighten my day.
I could count on you to brighten my
day.
But the world is vicious, these
modern times are hectic and
cruel.
We got caught in its endless circle
and forgot our only rule.
Now I need you to brighten my day.
I never stopped loving you, you
filled my heart with joy.
People can't play with emotions and
we both know love's no toy.
Please come to me and brighten my
day.
It never helps to fight or argue,
it can't always be my way.
I hate yelling and screaming, please
tell me that together we'll stay.
Please find time in your heart to
brighten my day.
I've learned a bitter lesson and
each day I pray hard it's not too
late.
"Dear God, I pray he still longs to
brighten my day."
This time I don't have a choice
and if I work hard some day it
will show.
If ever I just get the chance, I'll show
you how deep Love can grow.
Now I need for you to <u>want</u> to
brighten my day.
We had good times to remember
and I know it can be that way
still.
We can grow stronger, together, with
Love and God's Will.
Every day I pray that you'll come
brighten my day.

Anna Grace Jewell
WHEN I'VE GIVEN ALL

When I've given all Lord
Then what do I do
When there seems to be
No end of strife
Just teach me to walk Lord,
In the path of righteous
And give me the victory
In the days that lie ahead

Just give me the victory, I pray
And help me to walk with thee
each day
Be with me Holy Ghost I pray
And give me the victory this day

Trina Kallian
PUT FAITH IN YOUR DAY

When the little things
always seem to go wrong,
you swear it's going to be
like this all day long.

Starting first thing in the
morning, it would be nice
to rearrange. Hoping to yourself
... "my luck will change."

Taking everything in stride,
the obvious mistake you
try to hide.

Though you force your face
to smile and try to convince
yourself... "today's worthwhile."

Ready to cuss and criticize,
it helps to remember you are
under God's eyes.

He knows you can do your best
and to keep moving
on let problems rest.

Charles Shaw
LOVE'S DECLARATION

To every woman that reads this poem.

There are a few beautiful women
in the world.
I hereby today declare you,
as one of them.

Your beauty is rare in quality
like a gem.
You possess a quiet and subtle
charm;
That stems from your heart
and radiates outward.

Your eyes have that twinkle
that could only come from a star;
Your lips have that insatiable desire
that would quench the sun.

Your voice is velvet soft and smooth,
that makes the blue-belles sing;
So when you speak, the wind ceases
and the moon beckons to you.

There are truly a few beautiful
women
in the world.
I hereby today declare you,
as one of them.
So declare your beauty today
dear lady,
come out of yourself within
and come into your beauty...

Dorothy Sill Brown
TO THE NEW YEAR

The drifting clouds grow gray and
drear,
Symbolic of the fading year,
Whose span of time is nearly o'er,
As janus gently claims the floor.

The wild wind adds its eerie howl
O'er hill and dale, thru every bough,
As slowly dies the aged year,
Whose flight is o'er and death is
near.

The new year dawns o'er spotless
plains,
With slate brushed clean by falling
rains
And snow, whose pure unmottled
flakes,
A clean and prosperous year dictates.

A whole new chance to start anew,
To reach the rainbow's golden hue,
And gain success by toil and fight,
Will bring real peace and pure
delight.

So make a new resolve today,
To try—you'll find that it will pay,
In happiness and self content,
For all the pains you underwent.

Schelle Roberts
PEACE OF MIND

Peace of mind is all I long for,
hope for, pray for
Hoping for some kind of problem
solver
A solution from all this pain, being
left alone
In a world who doesn't care if you
live or die,

pray or fight, if you were right or wrong
But there is a way to find peace of mind
When you last fall cold against a bed,
A wall, a loved one, or a rope strung around a neck,
But that's not the right way
So I'll keep on praying, hoping, longing for . . .
that peace of mind.

James F Cavadini
I CAME UPON A BIRD TODAY
I came upon a bird today
it sang a story of the sky
the wind blew a sweet harmony
I sang my own song in between.
The brook below was burbling notes
agreeing with my own life force
I listened to it with my ears
but first I opened up my heart . . .
The insects and the birds and snakes
the trees, the grass, the fields and lakes
the Sun and wind and living earth
all sang the song of Joys rebirth.

Billy Fred Rutherford
PATIENCE

This poem is dedicated to my wife Barbara, your love and understanding we have.

So many times stars that shine in your eyes,
Glow in heaven like the gild over thin vapor
Of the morning mist with patience, love and
Understanding our two sons, their wives, our
Two grand children and I.

Barbara Craig
THE SONNET OF LIFE
While gazing up upon a star, I saw
My life as one who only looks upon
A stream so shallow, cold, and dark. When dawn
Arrived, my star was gone. My soul was raw
With wonder, sadness. Through me, life had gone
Like arrows through a cloud. I understood
That life was more than living. It's a hood
We all must wear till Death follows no one
To immortality. I wished I could
Betray my heart and not learn what I knew
I should of me. Life's book of pages blew
Across my heart to be remembered should
I fall and reach a hand out to be smote
By one not hearing life's beautiful note.

Margaret M Valdisera
HOSTAGES
Oh Lord, please give us a helping hand,
To get all the hostages out of Iran.

Many days have already passed away,
Too much talking and many delays
Having caused our great country to hang head in shame,
Bowing down to the Iranians, the people to blame.
Why should the Hostages have to suffer some more?
Get on the ball Washington, get on it fast
we're sick and we're tired of
excuses in the past.

Oh Lord, please give us a hand
Help get the Hostages out of Iran.

For the love of their loved ones
Who feel just as sad,
It's what keeps them on living and trying their best,
The letters, the cards, a tear dropped on paper while filling them out.
Oh! yes we care, we care a whole lot.

Please Lord give us a hand,
Please help get the Hostages out of Iran.

Their faces are sad and their eyes filled with tears, the lumps in their throats were hard to disguise.
Their bodies showed pain and too much fear.
They have suffered enough Lord.
Please give us a hand, please help get the Hostages out of Iran.

Pay the ransom who cares what ever it takes.
We want them home give them a break.

Raise the flag, roll the drums,
Bring them all home, leave not a one.

Please Lord give us a hand,
Help get the Hostages out of Iran.

Shannon Maleah Jackson
MOON LIT NIGHTS
Moon lit nights
Sun lit days
Moon brings in evening
Dawn brings up day
On the coast of Puerto Rico
On the mount of Caven Bay
Hear the whistle in the wind
Watch me cast away

Saundra Bolden
A DISTANT SHORE
They're saying their last farewell, these friends.
They knew it would come to this—
a gentle word, a last goodbye,
a final warm embrace.

The bond is strong and the pain is deep,
but tears do not fall.
It's not sorrow they share, but an abiding love,
and this, we know, lives on.

The years have been kind to these dear old friends.
Oh, they've struggled, but they've grown.
And the thread of life that's spun so fine
weaves yet another sweet, bitter song.

Say no farewells. Say no farewell.
It's time and nothing more
that separates, but never ends.
You shall meet on a distant shore.

Abdul-Alim Sabir
30 PIECES OF SILVER
Thru the ages
it was ever thus,
Payment on demand
for secrets not discussed.

Whether prophet, nobleman,
peasant or serf,
Payment to a Judas
determined their worldly worth.

A device of shaitan,
the eternal foe,
At entrance and exit,
around, to-and-fro.

'Tis sorrow that man,
performs on command,
The act of moral treason
by shaitan in demand!

No matter;
for payment—like shaitan—is thus,
A veritable wisp
of psychological dust!

Alexis Davis
A MAJOR CONTROVERSY
Tomorrow is another day of the year,
Even though I'll have you here
Your smile's not for me, it's surface
Midnight beside you is not a painting
That jar of hand cream on your dresser
Could be replaced by gloves
Your slippers would probably
Best bediscarded; they're dusty
The notes you leave me aren't poignant
Hot chocolate with you needs marshmallows
When we go for long Autumn walks
You don't raise nature's theme an octave
Tangerine is not our passion
This will all burn away.

Portia Owens Tillman
THE WALL AROUND YOU
It is easy to keep blaming others
For the wall around you.
Yet, some of us have always been outside
The prison of your person.
Seems that the foundations and cement
Were laid by inside bricks before.
Do not blame others for the mortar that holds
This mess all too tightly.
Perhaps to carefully chisel the seams away
Would help you be in touch
With your REAL self.
Then, you can be free to be you!

Diane Onopa

Diane Onopa
WORDS

This poem is dedicated to John, my loving Husband. Thank you for believing in me.

Words are only words . . .
until written in a song;
then they bring out the melody,
when we sing along.

Words are only words . . .
until written in a poem;
then they become the feelings
the poet calls his own.

Words are only words . . .
until said between two friends;
then they become the bond
and friendship never ends.

Words are only words . . .
until said by two who care;
then they become the words of love
that only two can share.

Words are only words . . .
until a child is praised;
then they become the strength
when loving parents raise.

Words are only words . . .
when said by one too late;
music, poetry or words of love . . .
these words must never wait!

Theresa Riesenberg
SEASHELLS, FRAGILE, YET TOUGH
Seashells,
Fragile, yet tough.
Beautiful,
but at the same time
ugly.
We love them , yet we
hate to walk on them.
Seashells,
remind me of love.

Jalynne George
ODE TO MY MOTHER
Ode to my mother which I'd like <u>to say,</u>
She has always cared for me in a kind loving way.
She has helped me get started with every new day,
She has always been so bright and gay.
Ode to my mother which I'd like to say,
For ever and ever her love is here to stay.

Karen J McKeown
TENDER YEARS, TINY TEARS
Tender years, tiny tears
Guard the adolescent's fears
Little playmates now are grown
Finding problems of their own
Seeking help but cannot see
Patience tried, woe is me!

Adult form, mind of child
Drastic measures, never mild
Shape the school and social whirl
Parents hinder boy and girl
Cannot let them have their fun
May not go, only one!

I.Q. high, I.Q. low
Doesn't really matter though
Smarter, quicker than the best
Folks just couldn't pass the test
Voice of long experience
Using brains, making sense.

Tender years, tiny tears

Age will open little ears
Till the time of triumph stops
When they too are Moms and Pops
Holding gently to their fold
Tears grown big, years grown old.

Laura Shears

Laura Shears (Age 8)
FLOWERS

To my sweet Nana: I love her with all my heart.

In the Spring the flowers bloom.
Colors red and white.
When I look outside my room.
It gives me such a beautiful sight.

Jon Marc Jagush
DIANE

Like the sun upon frost-covered morns,
You glisten and shine to make my being aglow.
You stroll in the woods and give meaning
To my view of nature's best.
Your "y'alls,"
Your silly thoughts
Your innocence
Your true, real beauty
All make you perfect
I love you—you're every—you're everything
You make my best—better.

e A young
i guess . . .

i searched.
i thought i had found it.
i guess i was wrong.

i hid.
i cried.
i slowly died.
i mean, i guess i tried.

i should've known.
i thought i did.
i guess i don't.
i guess i won't.

Marnie Rosenberg
A LOVE POEM—". . . I WILL NOT BE FAR."

A happy laugh or simple smile
Just to show you care—
These would fill my heart with joy,
But you don't even dare
To let me know you love me;
I try so hard and yet,
You live your life immune to me
As though we haven't met.
Inside I feel so much for you;
I wish you felt the same,
For you alone hold the match
To light my candle's flame.
The days will pass as I continue
Wishing on a star
And hoping you'll soon notice me
For I will not be far.

James J Luscombe
THE SEED

The winter air was numbing,
and it made my flesh dull red.
The ground and frozen, and the seed was merely dead.
But now the sun has risen,
and the ground begun to thaw.
Morning has awoken, and the crows begun to caw.
The day progresses steadily,
but at such an uneven pace,
As if to strike a flame of fire and then freeze it right in place.
While the day grows older,
grayer, and unerect.
Like a man on his death bed,
struggling for every breath.
I can see the clouds come rolling in,
and the rain begin to fall.
I can hear the lightning scream,
"Death to you all."
I began to tremble with fear, of such an evil fate
As to die from someone's doings and their wicked hate.
I felt my life being taken as you walked out of the door.
But the love that I've felt for you,
will grow forever more
not unlike the seed, that grows to be a plant.
That falls, and dies, when finally it can no longer stand.
It falls so lifelessly, and then it fades away,
Leaving behind only a seed for remembrance, when it grows again, some other day.

John T Maxwell
TURNING FORTY

For My Wife Judy

We've passed another milestone,
You and I.
Another in that growing list of firsts,
And bests
That we have somehow shared.
We're both beyond that magic mark of time
That separates the dreamer
From the dream.
We are,
What we once hoped we could become,
In late night conversation
Over coffee,
After wine.
The years have had some fun with us,
I know,
But we have kept the promises we made,
And found something
Our dreams had not foretold.
I sometimes can't remember
You and I,
As being anything but us.

Jennifer Kathleen Andersen
ASPIRATIONS FOR 1987

1987 is this year,
I will get my brain in gear.
I will try to get 4.0;
That, I already know.

I will go to Washington, D.C;
All the sites I will see.
Travel all around the country here;
I will do this all this year.

I will try not to bother my brother;
I will be kind and mind my mother.
I will try to stay out of trouble;
By the end of the year my thoughts
Will double.

All the people I will meet;
And certainly watch what I eat.
I'll start a new school year,
That I will do;
And something I hope that I
Will meet you!

Elaine Covington

Elaine Covington
THE SEASON OF DEPARTURE

To my ex-husband of 15 years who gave me precious memories of all the seasons

As you depart
The feel of a dart
Goes right to my heart.
From the very start
You had all my love,
Soaring like a great white dove
From way up above.

We used to walk hand in hand
Through the warm sand,
And as the winter came the wind would blow
As we walked through the snow.
In the spring the smell
Of the honeysuckle vines would swell,
And in the fall
We'd walk through leaves big and small.

All I want to say
Is I hope someday
You'll come home to stay.

I'll always love you
And hope somehow you'll love me too.

Franz Keller
THEY START WITH SLUDGE . . .

They start with sludge,
Don't hold a grudge,
Or you won't get to eat.
Some toxic waste,
Don't help that taste,
It smells like stinky feet.

They put in fats,
A few dead rats,
It'll clog up all your veins.
It makes me cry,
When they deep fry,
It tastes like monkey brains!

They add in dirt,
It couldn't hurt,
And nightshade by the bunch.
With every bite,
It's such a blight!
It's the Junior High hot lunch!

Lynn M Burdekin
SPRING . . . NEW LIFE BEGINS TO FORM

SPRING . . . when new life begins to form
New hopes and dreams bloom with the crocus . . .
The sun nurtures growth of plants and creatures,
As well as all our goals.
SPRING . . . A new beginning in this stagnant world . . .
All is fresh and pure once more.

We all need SPRING to wash away the debris and old heartache . . .
This is when the new year begins—
With the beginning of so much LIFE!!

Patrick Pierce
WANDERING TIDES

Dedicated to Mary, my mother, for her love and support in helping me to find myself.

Wandering tides follow the wind to distant lands,
Discovering the meaning of life along the journey.
And night is for sleep,
But far away places beckon searching travelers
To continue on;
While the sea's melancholy melodies
Entice the heart of many a loner.

I watch as each wave when touching upon the shore,
Carefully chooses the grains of sand
To be carried off into its
Infinite waters of wisdom.
And how I wish the sights and sounds
Were mine to know.

Jeff Brehan
BEDTIME FOR NIGHTTIME

Starry night
Moon so bright
Neon gleaming
And headlights beaming
As cars go hissing by.
Sirens Screaming
People dreaming
And airplanes reaching for the sky.
Cold air stinging
A telephone ringing
Two lovers let out a strangled cry.
Buses roaring
The early rays of morning
And the night lets out
Its final sigh.

Dawn Ten Pas
ME AND YOU

For Donald
The guy I will always love because he made me so happy! Love always and forever Dawn.

Everyday when we were together, All my hours were filled with pleasure.
Just the way you smiled so sweet,
You made my heart skip a beat.

Those well suited songs we said were true, Each time I hear them they make me blue.
For all my troubles you had some advice, When I didn't listen you'd tell me twice.

But now that's gone under the sand, We decided on friends and I do understand.
It's the only decision that we could make, But now as I think it's harder to take.

I thought it would be so easy to let go, I was wrong and my feelings proved it so.
Your friend is what I want to be, But please do often think of me.

I believe it when you said you won't stop trying, So I won't make a fool of myself by crying.
Even though it came to this we did try, And I never would have thought to spend this time with
ANY OTHER GUY!

Carolyn R Williams
SURE IS WONDERFUL!
Waking up each day with
no ache or pain;
Moving from place to place
without strain . . .
Sure is wonderful!

Sharing my energies and
touching some lives;
Transferring my most powerful
vibes . . .
Sure is wonderful!

Shutting out those attitudes
that try to block
My chance of squeezing life for
ev'ry drop . . .
Sure is wonderful!

No time for tarrying.
Move out of my way.
There's no discouraging
Me from enjoying this day . . .
Sure is wonderful!

Tracy L M Riley
HOW LIFE SHOULD BE

This poem is dedicated to Lenny Tracy, Jr. who didn't have the chance to see "How Life Should Be."

The lake is wide and deep,
As my love for you is steep.
I look above in the sky.
As no clouds appear in my eye.
The birds are singing tweedly-dee,
This is how life should be.
The trees are growing tall,
And our love will never fall.
You and me will always be,
This is how life should be.

Laura Kennedy RN
MEMORIES

In memory of Patricia R Kennedy
A long time gone . . . but never forgotten. I Love You.

As I stop to think,
I can still recall.
The times that we shared,
I remember them all.
Although I was little
I loved you so.
You would soon be gone,
I was too young to know.
Remember the times
That we treasured together?
Each happy moment
Getting better and better.
But sometimes when tears flowed down on my cheeks,
You came and you held me, I was yours for keeps.
My favorite sister—you were all mine.
But God came along and said it was time.
The sad times had come. The memories remain.
My sister is gone, my heart feels the pain.

David Thayer Wells

David Thayer Wells
ANOTHER TO HEED
"Beginning with word
Followed by seed,
Then coming sword
Ending in DEED."
Meanwhile from seed
A tree ensued
In quietude (more seeds.)

Now, is this fair?
A trifle nervy
To uproot the thought—
Ending—
And change it by
Bending it into
Artistry?
Yes the glamor
& clamor
As attractiveness
Is distracting indeed.
This misses the point
Of Poe. Who smells
The arts?
Or poor poetry?

Chevelle Banks
MY TRUE LOVE WILL SOOTHE THEE
How can I express my true feelings when those feelings have caused you pain? Can your heart allow me to show you I care, when my caring has brought you tears? In spite of my broken heart, I desire so much to give you comfort. My true love will soothe thee.

Please feel my need of wanting you in my life. Please feel my pain and through that pain, how much I care. You in my life has brought explicit joy and without you, only much more pain. Reconcile with me only through true love. Yes, reconciliation will mend our broken hearts and relax our disturbed minds. My true love will soothe thee.

Look through my eyes and view my heart; look through my eyes and feel my warmth. My warmth reaches out to touch you but it fears your response. Please respond with the love that made us laugh in sad times, that love that bonded us closer in lonely times, that love that exalted us in shattered times. Think on our love that you once felt. My true love will soothe thee.

Rita Johnson
IN MY HEART

Dedicated to my mother, Essie, whose love is endless.

I have a soft spot in my heart
for you.

It happened long ago
When the seed of your love lodged
there.

Roots grew out, burrowed deep
into my flesh.

Attached you to me, there, in my
heart.
There is no way to remove you
from my heart.

Too late, terminal.
Too deep go the roots
in my heart.
you are entangled
in my flesh.
to cut you out would kill me.

If you go
you must take my heart with you.

Kimberly Reddick
REMINISCENCE
Seems like old times, so they say.
I used to be
An excellent artist back then.
My work in pens, ink, brush
once went everywhere.
Neighbors ask of my drawings;
Sometimes quizzing me of their
interpretations.
Now those days
are like house-plants;
Neglected, and in need of water.
Memories forgotten.
My pens are still—the acrylics and
the watercolors
No longer work their magic
on the submissive paper.
Where has it gone?
I now write poems.
Someday, I will do artwork once
more.
Lord, may your will be done.

Dorothy Twiford
WORLD OF

My poem is dedicated to Lacy and Kirstia yet unborn, they are the future generation. May it be a better world for them.

P is for poverty that is found all
over the world.

O is for the old folks not listened
to or heard.

E is for the elite that have no time
for us.

T shall stand for truth, something
we don't hear much of.

R is for remembrance, the
memories of love past and

Y is for the youth of today, this
too shall pass.

Carla J Kiesling
LETTING GO
I must let you go.
That's all I can do.
I must let you go.
Now we are through.

No matter what I do,
Dance, cry, lie on my bed,
I think of you.
And wonderful memories fill my
head.

I've shed many tears,
And felt much pain
you put an end to my fears.
I'll never love again.

My heart is broken.
Can't eat. Can't sleep.
My dreams are broken.
And all I can do is weep.

This hurts me a lot.
Probably much more than you.
But I gave it my best shot,
And now we are through.

Russ Fitzgerald
OPEN YOUR EYES

To my mother Ozell Russ
My inspiration. With love

Open your eyes and see
People just you and me
Searching for ever
Excepting never!

Unconsciously we live our lives,
without loving each other.
As if tomorrow really mattered.
We have time, there's always later!
To live our lives in someone's eyes.
But what about the tears we hide,
down deep inside.
That scream I am down here!
I want to live.
I don't want to hide.

Melissa Schraga
PEACEFUL BE OUR WORLD
If peaceful be our world, then
Peaceful be our continents and
countries;
Peaceful be our cities and villages,
our families;
Peaceful be our valleys, fair and
green,
And our mountains, majestic and
white.

If peaceful be our world, then
Tranquil be the cottages,
Each in its own nook, its sheltered
hold
Underneath its own tuft of trees.

But is it really we who decide our
fate?
Or, does some superbeing hold us in
the balance?

Many ideas but not one I can
condole
Or condone just now.

In our homes we feel safe, protected
But really we are ignorant—our
excuse for everything—
Because a house is nothing but a
lowly roof with
Walls, no matter how big or small.

When peaceful be our world, I can
take a day
Sitting on a rock or hill looking on a
valley fair,
The cottages with their groves of
trees, and see the people
Resting there—not ignorant; not
hiding.

For they have nothing to hide from
because
There is peace and tranquility. No
pain; no suffering.

It would be a day so mild it could be
the first day of spring—
The gladsome spring with robins
warbling and
One solitary throstle singing.

It would be the day a stranger comes
with odd tongue and

Bizarre look, ready to answer and defend
But is not questioned, not turned away,
Only welcomed with opened arms—

When peaceful be our world.

C J Jeffrey
THE TIES THAT BIND

To James G Davis II When ties bind, they can never be broken.

Watching each other closely . . .
the tie of attraction.
Communicating to each other . . .
the tie of friendship.
Lilacs in the spring . . .
the tie of warmth.
Kissing for the first time . . .
the tie of excitement.

The emotional support we lend . . .
the tie of needing.
The first caress . . .
the tie of wanting.
What we say we want . . .
the tie of truth.
Wanting to know more . . .
the tie of sexuality.

Our exploration of new adventures . . .
the tie of joyousness.
Having what we want . . .
the tie of happiness.
Opening our hearts to each other . . .
the tie of trust.
Trust in each other . . .
the tie of freedom.

Blowing bubbles and flying kites . . .
the tie of youth.
Responsibilities we accept . . .
the tie of age.
Curiosity of the roads before us . . .
the tie of life.
These, the ties that bind . . .
the ties of love.

Brian Randall Funston
I WIN

I would like to dedicate this poem to a great lady Betty Funston—my Mother!!! Who throughout the years has been my inspiration to "follow my dreams."

To dream is human
To achieve is divine
Never say no, never say die
To have failure is a step in the right direction
To accept failure is defeat
The dawn is warmer & brighter
After a long dark night
A long journey is just a series of short walks
Each walk a journey of experiences
Success is in the whole
Not the fractions
Despair of true love lost
Can shine on opportunities beyond measure
Treat each day as your last
& every morning you will awaken with newborn eyes
Face your moment of doubt & pain
Look trouble right between the eyes
Make your mark in life
Let not life leave its mark on you
Never begin intending to stop
Never stop believing you can succeed
Endure, strive, persist till life's final breath
Live life as a whole
Look for challenge, dare a dare
Winner take all
Never succeed to life's fatal call
Born a winner
Birthed to succeed
World beware, life take heed
I control my life
I WIN!!!

Anita L Weber
LAURIE

Your memories are the dearest part
I hold them closest to my heart
I loved your little Harvard accent
When you grew it slowly went

You were a fashion plate right from the start
And your smile and dimples did impart
A heart full of beauty and love
Which came of course from God above

I love you for the sunshine
You brought along my way
My tears begin to flow
When I know I have to go

I won't be here forever
Our love no one can sever
I'll be waiting on the other side
With my arms opened wide
For Laurie my baby
Now a beautiful lady
Your loving mom

Irene F Beihl
MY DOG DUKE

To all my grandchildren, with love

I had a little dog
his name was Duke
He had worms and he did puke
So my Daddy took him to the doc
and Doc gave him medicine by the clock
but Duke didn't like it
So my Daddy put it down
Duke's throat and socked him
That's when I began to cry
for my poor Duke laid down and died.

Scott Solley
EVERLASTING MEMORIES OF HER

I dedicate this poem, which was written with all my heart, to my grandmother Mary Cassello. I hope this poem brightens her days and helps to heal her in her time of sickness.

She was the light of my life,
She gave me hope.
She taught me right from wrong,
She taught me to cope.

And like a story-teller,
She would tell me of the fond memories of her past.
And time invisibly slipped away,
And it seems that her life went by too fast.

And when I was just a kid,
She taught me to love people—no matter what they did.
And at grandmother's house is where you could always find me
Sharing her past of happiness and misery.

But, oh, age leads to death and then fear,
That is the fear of dying.
And my eyes are like storm clouds that hold rain,
Rain that could drown this fire—doomed earth from the tears I am crying.

And now today is even lonelier than yesterday,
And to carry on without her is merely a part of life.
And I know she is in good hands and her halo does glow
But, oh ever so dearly, I do miss her so.

And so I live my life from day to day,
Hoping the pain will soon fade away.
But still that empty feeling remains inside of me,
When those everlasting memories remind me.

Lee Cambra (Leondro)
JUST FOR A MOMENT

To my grandchildren/Michelle, Kimberlle, Michael, Matthew

For the time being is like
The sound of a water fall with
Its rippling waves, like the
Brilliance of a rainbow
Just for the time being
Is like the hug of a teddy bear
Like the warmth of the morning sun

Just for the time being
Is the happiness of a gift or a
Well earned pat on the back, and
When the crowd cheers.
Just for the time being
Is watching geese fly south in perfect
Formation, or the blooming of the
Crocus at the first sign of spring
Just for a moment
It's the kind word from someone who cares
Just for a moment

Dennis F Phillip
STREET PEOPLE—A DILEMMA

I would like to dedicate my first poem to my Mom and Dad, John & Caroline Phillip

Good fortune was upon us, we survived as a norm.
A dwelling to shelter us from the element,
A meal to fulfill a daily nourishment.
Ample wages and gratis, helped us weather the storm.

Dark clouds of misfortune befell us.
Our shelter mutated, to a domain of the element,
Our daily nourishment became a morsel, infrequent.
Stormy weather enhances our sickness.

Our needs cry out to those with no ears.
Some food for our children, a shelter, we ask.
A country so wealthy, relates to it, as a task.
Our hearts are broken, we break down in tears.

Only few care, what we do or say.
All that is left, is to hope and pray.

Haskell S Gayheart
AN UNBORN'S PLEA

This poem is dedicated to the millions of unborn who have been murdered I speak for them, since they can't.

A trash bag is what I saw
As from my mother I did fall
Life was stolen away from me
Now a trash bag is what I see
As I lay here with others
We're as one—sisters and brothers
Torn and twisted, pieces and parts
Done by someone with a cold, cold heart
Not allowed to see the light of day
To God above you better pray
To ask for forgiveness of this sin
Why did my life have to end?

Natasha Cunningham
DISMAL AND GREY

The wind started howling
And blew the trees back and forth.
Darkness settled in, and the
fog came out of nowhere.

Dismal and Grey the rain started to fall.
Control of my plans for the day were gone,
And alone and by myself I sat.

At first this sudden change, affected me,
Until I realized I had no control
And I started thinking good thoughts.
I already knew the next day would be
back to blue skies and soft wind and
the sun would be back to shine
Today is tomorrow and it is.

Maureen Fylan-Benavidez
FALLING STAR

To my son, Michael, in memory of our stay in Klawock, Alaska

Twilight falls so gently
On this island
Ushering in a swiftly falling stream
A greenish, glittering swoosh
Arcing through the darkening sky
Wending swiftly and silently toward the earth
Magic pervades this falling star
I stop in wonder
Silently I make my wish
Perhaps this dream will come true
Fulfilled by the magic of that falling star

Michel Ewing
WHAT YOUR LOVE MEANS TO ME

To my husband, Jack, with all my love.

As the days go by,
I often wonder why,
I don't say it more
as you go in and out the door.

I love you!
I'm not blue.

When you are near,
I love to hear
in my ear
your sweet soft words,
as if the birds
up in the tree

were singing them to me.

I know you care
and I will not dare
to jeopardize
what I see in your eyes.
Trust, faith, and love,
pure as a snow white dove.

What I feel in my heart,
is that you are a part
of my inner soul.
We both have a goal
That I know we will reach.
One we made as we were walking on the beach.
The dreams that we share
will fill the air,
with so much love
that the clouds above
will begin to smile
and we will know that it was all worth while.

Samantha Sanheim
ME, MYSELF AND I

For those that believed—and one that didn't—you have been justified.

Me.
The individual that everyone sees.
The outward appearance I choose to give the world.
The person that must face reality.

Myself.
The secret person hiding inside Me;
The self that can dream forever and never get hurt.
The "hero" that always wants to live in dreams past forgotten.

I.
I am both the dreamer and the realist;
I dream of the past while facing reality at present.
—Always striving to make a tomorrow.

How do I cope you ask?
By simply being—
Me, Myself, and I.

Patricia L Lenhardt
A GIFT OF LOVE

To my love, Tom

I know you think, "Why an empty box?"
But empty it is not.
This box is filled with treasures,
Yes, treasures of our love.
It's filled with all the Love and Joy
And Happiness we know
You can not buy what's in this box
No matter where you go.
There are some sad days in here,
But most of them are glad.
So take this little present,
I give to you my dear,
And treasure it with all your life.
Always keep it near.
Now as the years go by, you'll know,
This box will be too small,
Because all our Love and Happiness,
Will make it over flow!

Lieunell Morrow
THE MASTER'S CALL

To Mrs. Louise Gray In Loving Memory Of her husband, Dennis

Days became months; months became years.
We hugged and kissed; we worked and played.
As days filled with pain, hours filled with tears.
We laughed and cried; we talked and prayed
As we waited . . .
Waited . . .
Waited for the Master's call.

Gone were the years, only months of ill health.
We hugged and kissed, no more work or play.
Time became shorter; we counted each breath.
We cried and talked but only to pray
As we waited . . .
Waited . . .
Waited for the Master's call.

Then the days were spent; I felt betrayed.
Too soon the hours and minutes were gone.
I hugged and kissed; I cried and prayed.
The time had come and I was alone.
No more waiting . . .
Waiting . . .
No more waiting, the Master had called.

Rachele Rulon
WAS IT YOU?

For my brother Mark
December 3, 1966—July 13, 1987

I sat and watched our baby today
he babbled and cooed at nothing
He smiled and giggled and reached above his crib
then "spoke" again
I watched in total amazement as our child
played alone
almost as if there were someone talking
to him—was he really alone?
Was it you, Mark? Telling him who you were?
Knowing that if you came to us
we would not believe?
Was it you, knowing that the innocence of a child
has no fear and would readily
accept your soul? It had to have been.
How else could a baby occupy his time.
I sat and watched our baby today
he babbled and cooed at nothing
He smiled and giggled and reached above his crib.
Tell me . . . was it you Mark, that he was
playing with?

David L Chapin
SANTA'S HAT

Dedicated to "Two fine boys" William and Kevin Chapin and a friend named "Matt"

The sleigh and the reindeer, seemed to be all-right;
Everything was ready, for this special Christmas night.
It was cold, that Christmas eve,
And the snow was falling down;
The moon shown brite, over each and every town.

Santa, found each house all in order.
Each stop was just right;
With the toy lists complete, take a cookie—he might.
The stockings he stuffed,
Each one he would fill;
Then Santa, he noticed, was feeling a chill.

He checked his red coat, with the collar so white;
His black boots, and mittens, were all on just right.
Then he noticed the cold, on his forehead, so bare;
And found that his hat, was no longer there.

He looked in his sleigh, and he looked in his pack;
He looked high and low, and he even looked back.
Then he ended his trip, on that cold Christmas night;
And by morning you see, Jack Frost, took a bite.

The tree it was trimmed with the holly so gay;
And the toys piled high, on that cold Christmas day.
Now William and Kevin, two great little boys;
Were unwrapped their presents,
And showing their toys.

Then Kevin, he spied a red fluff on the chair;
And William, then said, "what is that? there".
It was a red furry hat, that was trimmed all in white;
With holly, and sleigh bell, and tassel so brite.

"He did it!", said Kevin, Santa left it for me;
"Oh no", said William, that just couldn't be.
Old Santa, you see, he would never do that;
He just couldn't go, and forget his good hat.

What a problem we have! exclaimed Kevin so bright;
Santa lost his good hat, on this cold Christmas night.
The toys, the presents, the stockings, the tree;
Old Santa, had been nice, as nice as could be.

Let's take Santa's hat, and send it right back;
On the North Pole Express, number seven's the track.
So, they packed Santa's hat,
And addressed it, just right, and sent it to Santa.
. . . LATE CHRISTMAS
NIGHT . . .

Garry Burkhart Sr
MEMORIAL DAY

To all the men and women who have given their lives to keep America free.

Memorial Day, what does it mean?
It's of men that were tough and lean.
Who fought for the future that now can be seen.
Whose death now we take for granted, it seems.

Memorial Day, what is it for?
For men's bodies that were weary and sore.
It's for men that died in a number of wars.
Let's not forget them ever more.

On Memorial Day, shouldn't we be full of tears?
For the men who died with and without fears,
So with our loved ones we can be near.
And with our great country we can all cheer.

Memorial Day, what does it say?
Thank you, men, where in your graves you lay.
Because of you America's Freedom may stay.
On this special day, we remember you, as to God we pray.

Helen F Bales

Helen F Bales
MOTHER MINE

In loving memory of: Alice M. Hoffman

I wish that I could someday be
The Master of a mystery

How can a person know such bliss
To have a Mother such as this

She is so sweet and kind and gay
She carries all my cares away

Were I a wave out in the sea
Serving God I'd always be

Were I a pebble in a brook
Up to my Jesus I would look

If a baby on Mother's knee
I'd surely be her rosary

Ten baby fingers and small toes
Is how a Mother's rosary goes.

I wish to thank our Mother high
Who looks upon me from the sky

She gave me one who is so fine
I am so happy she is mine.

Lee Ann Gardner
YOU WERE THERE

This poem is dedicated to Larry, someone who is very special to me.

You used me as you felt you should.
You lied to me as best you could.
You held me into the night and told me everything would be alright.
You gave me the strength to go on with my life.
Although the pain just cut like a knife.
You showed me that I really can be loved,

and the sky isn't so dark way up above.
You were there for me when I needed someone.
You showed me that life really can be fun.
You took away all of my fears,
but then you left me in love's lost tears.
I cried for days in hopes you returned.
'Twas one hard lesson I had learned.
I thank you for those moments we shared.
It helps to know that you were there,
but I still wonder did you really care?
Deep down my heart knows as we pass on
the streets . . . and stop . . . and stare.

Camilla C Hollister
IT'S AUTUMN

I dedicate "It's Autumn" to the memory of my late husband, Forrest H. Hollister, who was an outdoorsman and nature lover.

What's this I sense in the morning air
That only yesterday was not there?
Is that frosty breeze from the great northwest
Trying to put my summer to rest?
Is that orange and yellow leaf I see
The one that was bright green so recently?
Why, the hickory nuts and acorns are falling galore
To the squirrel's delight, for their winter's store.
I hear a honk in the heaven's blue,
Guess the geese know it's time to travel, too.
I must confess, with a bit of complaining,
That I'll accept Mother Nature's way of exclaiming,
"It's Autumn!"

Cecelia Lynn Palmer
SEASONAL HAIKU

For my beloved Jeffrey who shares the changing seasons with me always, this poem belongs to you.

The rain showers fall
Warm sunlight shines on the ground
The Spring's flowers bloom.

The earth is now hot
And pools of water are cool
Here comes summer now.

Leaves fall quietly
Blazed in amber, gold, and red
But soon Autumn goes.

Death is all around
Silent snow blankets lie still
Winter's in control.

Janet Balo
TOMORROW BEGINS TODAY

This poem is dedicated to my dear husband, Raymond, and our two sweet children, Amanda and Kenneth.

We must enlighten the innocent,
On all in the world that is dear.
We must show them all the beauty,
Yet not make them ignorant of fear.
Share with them all our hopes,
and allow them to share their dreams.
Direct them towards the positive,
as hard as, at times, it seems.
Grant them the pleasure of their fantasies,
yet be sure they know what is true.
View the world with optimism,
for they see the world through you.
Show them the difference that they can make,
help them to understand.
For the future of our immense world,
Lies truly in the tiniest of hands.

Leonard M Jackson
PAINT YOUR LIFE

This poem is dedicated to Judy, Jennifer and Dawan, my three wonderful daughters.

Paint your life in golden hues;
Shadow 'don't's and heighten 'do's;
Blot out 'can't's by adding 'can's;
Border it with 'willing' hands;
Let the tint of 'try' appear;
Stroke in 'effort' bold and clear;
Gloss it with a 'glowing' love
for fellow man and 'HIM' above.
When it's finished, leave a frame
proudly displayed with your name.

Nikki Jones aka Neci Lynn
I REMEMBER MOM

To my hero: I wish I could give you the world moma but for now I give you this poem.

I remember the times you held me so deep within your arms
and you sheltered me from all the world's wrongs.

The times I felt like dying when I thought I could not go on
When I said I hated him, and you told me I loved him
And I argued, but you said I would feel for him always.
Mom you were right, as I now look back upon that night.

And the times I felt like laughing but instead could only cry
And I asked you why, but for the first time, you had no reply
And you, too, sat down and began to cry.

Those days have now gone by, and I am too big to hold
I'm all grown up now, but I wish I was still small.

And now as I hold my child in my arms to comfort her,
I think of you and when I was a little girl.
If I only knew then what I know now,
Mom, I would have wanted you to hold me longer.

Lisa M Terruso
A BLUE DAY

For Mom, Grandma, and M.E.R., Thank you for guiding me in the right direction with love, caring and understanding. I will always love you all.

I sit alone this somber day.
No red lace hearts have come my way.
No chocolates and no roses red.
Romantically, my life is dead.

I think of loves that've passed me by.
My eyes are filled with tears.
I cry.
The scars lie thick upon my heart,
From loves that always do depart.

Yet on this day of red and white
I reminisce of love's delights
And pleasures that my mind recalls—
Moonlit nights and dancing halls.

I wonder where I'd be today
If I had once been swept away.
If "Mister Right" had been around
I never saw nor heard his sound.

I sit alone. My world is hell.
I have no more vignettes to tell.
My body shakes, alone I weep
While
Red and White
Invade my sleep.

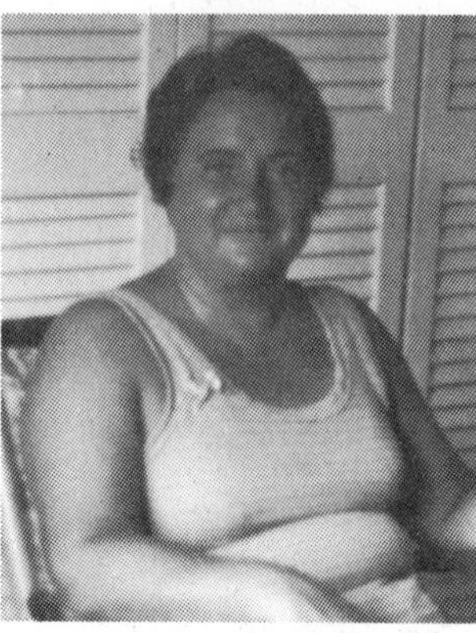

Anna Marie Rose Soldo Craig

Anna Marie Rose Soldo Craig
FORGET YOU?

Looking Back

Forget you?
I could no more forget you, than I would forget to breathe.
A diamond—An emerald—A sapphire—cool, clear, sparkling water, the Prince of my fairy tales.
My heart almost jumped out of my chest, when last we met.
You don't have to touch people to love them. I will always love you & all our friends.
In my dreams, I held your hand & kissed your fingertips, and looked into your eyes & told you, "I would love you through eternity."
I love you Linden, I hope you keep warm.
I love you Elizabeth, I hope you keep warm.
I love you Appleton, I hope you keep warm.
I love you my youth, my family, my friends, and all.
No one in this whole wide world could ever take your place.

Angela Arjun
WHAT HAPPENED TO ALL THOSE PRECIOUS MOMENTS WE SHARED

This poem is dedicated to a Special Friend

What happened to all those precious moments we shared
Don't you remember, or don't you care

Now you're telling me, we are through
Tell me, what am I to do

Said you want for us not to be friends
But after what we've meant to each other, how could we possibly end

Probably I was the fool from the start
But it ain't smart for you breaking my heart

Won't you at least think it over
And tell me there's a chance for us to be together

Just give me one more try
And make me prove to you, that my love will never die

I may have hurt you in the past
But that had no effect on our love that it couldn't last

Please believe me, it's true
Can't we start all over just me and you.

Margo Ellen Hoffman
BUT I CAN

To Mom and Dad—My Inspiration
To my friends (especially Bri)—
Make Your Dreams Happen!

I can't help you, but I do care;
I can't help you, but I do worry;
I can't help you, but I can cry—because somehow I feel hurt inside;
I can't help you, but I can share with you—I know sometimes I can learn a thing or two;
I can't help you, but I can pray—that someone will keep you safe both night and day;
I can't help you, but I am a little older—don't forget I have very broad shoulders;
I can't help you, but I can be your friend—a friend forever 'til the end;
I can't help you, but I can challenge your mind—and help you realize and reach what you're trying to find;
I can't help you, but I'll always be there to say—I hope you have a wonderful day;
I can't help you, but I can . . .

Ronnie Bruscino
A LOVER'S SORROW

This poem is dedicated to: J.A.C. Always and forever princess, Ronnie

The world is very hard to face,
For heartaches have left no hiding place,
Warm feelings are gone, they've turned to stone,
All beauty is vanished, I'm all alone,

I hear a song that once brought a pleasant sigh,
But now it only makes me cry,
The sun no longer shines for me,
And my anguish will never set me free,

All my dreams have been put to sleep,
A smile is impossible for me to keep,
Happiness is just a memory from the past,
Because I can't capture yesterday or make it last,

My heart is empty yet filled with such pain,
The reason is simple but I refuse to explain,
There is a princess who could tell you why,
But she left long ago without saying good-bye.

Clifford Malone
CLIPPED WINGS

For Lynda, Forever And Ever

No longer in flight
The place I now dwell
You would surely flee

A residence where tears
Continually await spillage
From a border behind clouded eyes

Like a river, swelling against a dam

This place, this Hell!

Where in the quiet ache of night
Memories blow blasts of sugar
Into the chamber of a heart

That dies, a thousand deaths, a day

Where the sting of bitterness
Crowd the empty corridor of a soul
Shuddering in recognition

Of a grounded spirit.

Dieter Kroll
LOVE WAITS

To my parents and Gloria

I think about love from time to time,
I wonder if there's any to call mine,
Wouldn't mind having a woman to hold,
To keep her warm on nights that are cold.
Or one who's there when I need to talk,
Maybe one to share a nowhere walk,
Love waits for me to find,
Love waits as it sits in my mind.

Feel I really need this thing called love,
Wonder if I'll ever find enough,
Wouldn't mind to feel just one woman's touch,
One that I could love back just as much,
I'd just like to see,
Someone who'll really love me,
Love waits for me somewhere,
Love waits for mine to share.

Time keeps traveling by,
Love keeps making people naturally high,
Wouldn't mind feeling the same,
Instead of always ending up in pain,
Think of love all the time,
Wonder where sits mine,
Love waits . . . ,
Love waits . . .

Elizabeth A Kidd
THE TRIBUTE

To MDA and all the "Special" people associated with it.

You see their smiling faces,
And hear their happy noise.
All those trusting, loving children
All those special girls and boys.
You bring them joy and promise,
Of a beautiful new day.
With hopes that in the future
They will run, and skip, and play.
So each Labor Day in chorus,
The world stands up to sing
"We love you Jerry Lewis"
For all the love you bring.

Timothy L Dewey
TIME

To the peacemakers, May god bless!

Wake up in the morning to a clock that never sleeps,
a new day dawning in a world out of time.
Set the watch to ponder a thought of memories,
reality sets the world in motion and on line.

Many are the troubles that plague our life,
the world revolves around a second hand.
Travel the roads and meet the ghosts, of the hour and the minute across the land.

Misty are the eyes that long for freedom,
trapped by the timeclock that holds them back.
The dream unfolds as the workday ends,
time ends and yet begins, a life off track.

The world around us lives without the shackles of time,
they survive with an inbred clock that has no gears.
We can free ourselves from the burden of hurry,
and live in peace for a thousand years.

The earth will spin and the lands will change,
and man need not worry if he's late.
and to love one another will be our fate.

Vanessa Navarro
DRUGS

To my cousin Charlie whose efforts have been rewarded through our love and prayers.

It's a big nothing, nothing
is, nothing was and nothing
ever will be. This is what
happens when you use drugs.
It's like your life never was,
this is simply what it does,
It takes your life for a whirl
but it also wipes away your
world. All of a sudden you're
living alone, living alone in
a great huge dome. Your world
is leaving and so is your care,
It's simply something you'll
have to bear, Because if you're
stupid enough to start you'll
be living in an unmended heart.

Joseph Clark Jr
MY SHIP

Dedicated to Sailors of the world

There she sits high and dry,
It seems she chose her spot to die.
Tug boat after tug, tried in vain
To pull her away,
But the reef held tight to welcome
Her stay.

Typhoons hit her with winds one
Hundred knots strong,
But she moved higher and higher
Until they were all gone.

Yes; "This tale of the sea"
High and dry is where she wanted to be.
Where other ships would pass her by,
Saying, "Beneath this reef the Pendelton doth lie."

She picked her spot of dry land,
With lots of fish and beautiful white sand.
Oh' what a "Lady" who loved the sea.
Her hull made of beautiful steel,
She is now controlling herself,
With no one at her wheel.

With the help of this "Reef" so hard,
We chose the bottom of the deep and
Not a scrap yard.

Rita D Friese
MY BROTHER

I dedicate this poem to my brother, Harry, for the loving care he has given his wife, during all the years she has had this terrible affliction

I have a brother who must be half saint,
For all he goes through without a complaint,
His wife has Alzheimers Disease, for many years,
And to see what he goes through would make your eyes tear,
They have their own apartment which he keeps neat as can be,
You would wonder how he has the time and all that energy,
She prefers to spend her time in bed,
But he sees that she gets exercise instead.
I pay him a visit with a lady friend of mine,
And he is so happy you can see his eyes shine,
He wants us to stay for tea, which we do,
And he gets his wife to join us too.
I pat her shoulder and say "How are you today?"
But she stares at me confused, and pushes me away.
He says the vows he took "In sickness and in health" will stay,
And with the help of God, will keep her till her dying day.
This is not a story, it really is true,
And this wonderful man is age 92.

Deborah C Phillips
SHADES OF BLUE

For my husband, Gary, who is always patient and understanding. I love you very much.

A countless number of aqua waves
Beat upon the oaken timbers
As they stand graciously
Holding their own against time.

A beautiful ocean greets the shore
Leaving behind its treasures in the sand
Before it retreats back
Into its world of magnificent blue.

An endless sheet of polished azure
Suspends, peacefully—
Holding in the different hues of blue
While they dance so divinely below.

On the horizon the ocean reaches to embrace the sky
The two share the joys each hold in their bosom.
They exist forever together;
Permanently—shades of blue.

Margaret Walden
JEFFREY'S FIRST BIRTHDAY

You've come along way Jeffrey.
Grandma Margie

When I was born, I was to be,
A little different, as you can see.
I couldn't crawl as babies do,
But sure did try to be like you.
I learned to roll from side to side,
And I could kick my legs out wide.
I've been to Boston on a trip,
Where doctors there, have fixed my hip.
I'll learn to crawl now, tho it's late.
But Mom and Dad will think I'm great.
My sister plays with me a lot and shows me all my toys
We have an awful lot of fun, and make a lot of noise.
I get a lot of love at home, from Sis, and Mom and Dad.
They never get upset with me, not even when I'm bad.
They're teaching me to use my hands, so I could feel and touch.
I'm trying oh! so very hard and want to very much.
My therapist comes every week, to keep my muscles limber.
Without her help, I guess I'd be just like a piece of timber.
It's been an awful busy year and there is more in store.
But when I'm two years old next year,
I'll tell you much, much more!

Ruth E Cardeman Salazar
WEDDING RING

To the Cardeman family and my husband Jose.

This wedding ring is meant to be,
the thing that keeps your love close to me.

Not a chain around your neck.

This wedding ring is meant to
expand with love,
not trap you and your precious love.

This wedding ring made of gold,
will remind us when we grow old,
love does not have to grow cold.

A wedding ring is not a jailor's key,
it's the way I pledge my love to thee,
and you pledge yours to me.

A ring is what you let it be,
a prison or love through eternity.
But not a chain around your neck.

Edvina Boyd Brown
HULLABALOO
(COLOR BLIND)

To my sister, Beatrice Boyd Mair and the Human Race.

Black is black, and white is white;
Green is green, and blue is blue;
What is all this hullabaloo?

I saw a man, his face was white,
Hie hair was straight, his voice polite,
But in his mind and heart there lived,
An evil thing of hate and kill.

I saw a man, his face was black,
His hair was wool, his life uptight;
But in his mind and heart there lived,
A thing of hope, and grace, and skill.

Now, turn it 'round the other way,
The white the black, the black the white;
With evil thing and good reversed,
To find the black the one accursed.

What is this puzzle man has wrought,
That looks at skin, and eyes, and hair
To bring a person's worth to bear
Upon his value, life, and care?

Have not we learned that in this world
Of God's own creatures, far and near,

That great things camouflaged within
By hair and eyes, and color of skin,

Are the size of the man,
The strength of his heart;
The depth of his soul,
And the breadth of his mind?

These things are not measured by hair and eyes;
By prejudice, hatred, labels, and lies
But by how a man functions in day to day life,
Through failures, successes, contentment, and strife.

How he deals with his neighbors, his peers, his friends,
What he thinks, what he does, how he lives
How he spends the precious time of his years
Toward what goals, to which ends.

Why should man be different from plants,
Trees and flowers, fish and ants;
Shells and rocks, birds and dogs,
Jewels, metals, snakes, and frogs?

In coloring they are not the same,
Though all of them have a species name.
Homo sapiens means not color of skin
Shape of head, or line of nose,

But a creature of God, with a mind and a heart,
With blood in his veins, and in need of a start;
Who walks upon earth with spirit and soul;
Who breathes and feels that he's part of the whole.

Who's accepted for what he is and does,
Not rejected for what his father was.
Away with this peril of black and white,
That's based upon only what shows at first sight.

See the man, hear the man, learn the man,
Know the man.
A chance to perform is his own precious right.

So down with the black and the red and the white;
And down with all this color-mad fight.
Grind out the hours of our lives color blind,
When it comes to the humans we meet in our time.

Linda Dixon
MY KNIGHT OF SEDUCTION

Dedicated to truth and inspiration. Thank you, God, for giving me talent, inspiration and imagination, and the intelligence to know it is truly you!

Without wishing or knowing, one evening, our eyes met! Enchantment!
I didn't ask for it, I was content. But you, you pursued!
Expressions held, were read.
Thoughts exposed for what they were.
Intense, it was! Seduction and thirst, they were there!

Come, grow into my night with me!
A fantasy, let's make it real!
Appearances were peeled away,
revealed. I hesitated—you did not!
Skins shed, inviting new, inviting you!

Night blinds open. Full moon glow.
Smoldering stars, creating desire!
Play your music for me, I said! Make your music for me, vivid, I said!
—And you did!! Prince Star, where is your other? Is there another?
But, play on, oh lover, play on!
Energize me—
Provider of the night! Covered in darkness! Dark music!
You look so good! Let me touch you, please, like you know I should!

Love overdue, on cue! Carry me through the night! Embrace me, tight!

But oh—it is slipping away! You want it to stay!
No day! Not yet, day! Who loves to see reality take.
Time you thief, invading the darkness without invite.

I get up to leave. You asked, "Is that all this was?"
I look at you from the doorway.
"No," I said, etching
the burning essence of the room on the pages of my mind which
I have entered again and again.
Remember me, I ask, remember me.

Maria Chille

Maria Chille
AL PICCOLO NINETTO

Ninna Nanna o mio piccino
Veglio presso il suo lettino

Dormi e non piangere mio diletto
Io ti stringo al mio petto

Ninna Nanna cherubino
Vegliano gli angeli
Sul tuo destino

Nastri d'orati e di merletto
Abbeliscono il tu letto

La tua culla e' tutta d'oro
Ninna Nanna o mio Tesoro

Alfonse Ferreira
EIGHTIES

To the poor, tired and hungry.

I saw it die before my eyes—
the pain could not be seen

The strength and force possessed by few—
deceived the eyes of all.

'Tis not the eighties but in shame—
with shrieks of poverty?

Polluted nature everywhere—
by greed deemed uncompared.

The young and old flee with a sigh—
What will become of me?

Deception creeps a midst the few—
Intrigue becomes the Law.

The buck is passed form A to Z—
and "Read my lips" is born.

The streets belong to smack and crack—
with pot that's shared by more.

Who cares what's stolen by the Corp.?
from Wall Street to D.C.

Streets Reek, churches peek,
officials all despair.

A-me-ri-ca A-me-ri-ca
You have but lost your dream.

Cheryl Magana
SWEET BLEND

To my family. . My wonderful husband Ariel. My two beautiful sons A.J. and Joseph. My mother Virginia Reynolds. My father Victor Hamshar. My brothers and sister. All my in-laws. I love you all.

Roses are red to show you the love.
Yellow for friendship with a big hug.
Pink is a mixture with just the right blend.
No matter what the color you'll love them to the end.

If only the world could be, like roses or flowers you see.
No one would judge another, just by their looks or their color.
We would all be yellow, red, and pink.
Full of friendship and love a blend that is sweet.

Or is it just a dream to me.
Something I would like see.
A yellow rose for those like me.
What a beautiful sight that would be.

How wonderful the world could be.
So full of hope, love, and dreams.
If people only saw
The beautiful person in us ALL.

Phyllis B Payne
RAINDROPS

to Jon H. Payne

Raindrops rolling from
the roof

Falling on fences
Spraying to and fro
Creating streams with
rainbows

Pitter Patter on the roof
A contented sound
All is well in
God's world.

Pat McClure
LISTEN

In memory of my son Michael, who I will love forever, Mom

Oh, how I wish I'd listened
To my son's very last call . . .
All I remember are "my words,"
Only "one" of his, that's all.
Seems I'm always rushing through
This busy life of mine.
Oh, how I wish I'd listened
And given him more time.

I know he was trying to let me know
How much he was in pain . . .
He was reaching out for help from me,
But I was never to see him again.

Oh, how I wish I could hold him,
Just one more time . . .
And how I wish I'd "listened,"
To that loving son of mine.

So parents, slow it down from running
To a gentle walk . . .
And please learn to "listen"
When your children want to talk.

Tina Howard
GIFTS

Please precious child,
don't turn and run away.
I've come bearing gifts,
they're yours if you stay.

These gifts I have to offer you,
are the finest you'll ever see.
I can give you joy and love,
if you'd just ask of me.

You can be fluent in other tongues,
or have talent that is superb.
I can give you the greatest wisdom,
or a memory, that records every sound you've ever heard.

Perhaps you'd like my patience,
or my sympathetic ear.
Maybe you'd like some courage,
to chase away your fear.

I can give you this, and so much more,
if you'd just take the time to see.
That child all you have to do,
is offer your tender heart to me.

Almeda Utterback
NIGHT OF THE TORNADO

To my husband Norman Utterback, and friends and neighbors of Springfield Mo.

The night of anguish, and fear, April 29, 1983,
Was the night, we knew, "the tornado was here"
While eating our dinner and watching TV.

The dread sound of the tornado alert, was frightening to me
The eerie sounds of trees, as they cracked
Whipping of winds, as destruction they did,
On and on, it seems time stood still,
Not knowing whenever, if we would still be here.

The all clear, when it did sound added to our fears
Yes, the tornado had struck, and come to the ground,
Many houses were hit, many were torn down.
The red cross, and National Guard were called out.

To protect our City, and help those in doubt.

Trees were down, people were in shock
Up and down, police circled the block
Time has passed and memories remain,
Of the dread tornado, that hit in the night,
Bringing destruction to Our Town.

Franceska Ceuterick
RED ROSE
Darling, last night was a beautiful night,
Holding me and a red rose in your hand.
The table was set for two,
And one red rose was for me and you.

Candlelight blended with the dark of night,
Waiting for the sun to rise and greet the new day.
My heart was saying, "I hope the love never ends,"
That the love and the rose will stay forever.

Many nights passed by,
Your love faded away.
The red rose lost its petals,
And your hands hold another.

My dreams and love you took away.
The sun with the gray sky will pass by,
Holding the secret for another day.
And many red roses will bloom again.

Eloise Point
UNTITLED
How bitter sweet the waning days as our life span daily shortens
What once we took for granted grows more precious, and we cling tenaciously to things familiar, as though doing so will slow the passage of time
Ah, sweet delusions, meant to allay our fears of what lies ahead
But time, the ever present cunning thief,
taking back all it gives, second by minute by hour, will not be denied
And our span will end when time decrees

Marguerite Hawkinson
ANTIDOTE
Today I feel
this strong compulsion
to pick flowers
to tether a world gone suddenly awry.

The need is great
to feast my eyes on beauty,
stabilize somehow
the shifting scene.
(Strange how these fragile
evanescent blooms
seem anchor-like
a hold on constancy.)

As ancients gathered camomile
and rue—
caught in a web of pain—
I too must go
searching the fields
to gather flowers in.

T Jonathan Just
SHADES ALONE

This poem is for my wife and children, that they may better understand the most important man in their lives. You are most important to me.

Birch and willow bend and whistle
As winds of life bellow through
And near-by church bells toll for them
Beckon their way home

Drifting passers, wayward souls
Crimson inside by familiar thoughts
Bravely contesting nights unknown
And look beyond the shades alone

Mystic shadows hide imperfection
Gracing background pieces
Foremost my thoughts are incomplete
And harden to the night

Valley of my humble home
Hills that rise above
Through which I cast myself to stone
And gaze into the shades alone

Forward my procession heads
And back I've never known
Stillness relieves the tensions felt
Before I met the shades alone

Louis L Hogan
MY TEN DAYS AT WOODLORE

To all woodlore campers

After a few days at woodlore,
With my new nine dollar boots my feet sure were sore.

I went in the creek without my shoes,
I was lucky I didn't cut my feet or get a bad bruise.

A scout is brave and also bold,
Otherwise he would never get a bath, for that water sure is cold

I have altered my boots i don't think my feet will get sore,
Come next year i am looking forward to ten days more.

I could make a list a yard long of the things we call hardship,
But one word erases all that, the word is fellowship.

Joseph Bridevaux
SPEAK NOT

Thanks Ack for listening. Once again, all life flourishes between everything and nothing.

Counseled in the art of depression threads
Through the eye of the storm, as dampness
Runs through the veins of asylum.
Persecuted for introversion, revealing most
Of the being of a brilliant surrealist.
Surely, intelligence is the center of attention,
But what becomes of emotional trauma?
Or the naivety of redundant innocence?
Manifestation in curious forms attack.
The imagination of the subconscious being,
Bringing forth the jester in the King,
The man inside the boy, and life within itself.
In the revelance of thought,
Ending, not beginning, causes flight
Of universal apathy sinfully affecting
Normal society by negative energy.
Escape the mainstream, as if by real means,
Then focus on the behavior of
Wild animals, when survival tritefully
Surrenders to immortality.

Tonya M Maddox
FRIENDS

Dedicated to Stephanie and Denise; My closest friends and my inspiration.

A friend is there
At day and night;
For one to share
Joy and fright.

No worry too much
No trouble too small;
For a friend as such
For one to call.

Closer than a Sis
We are to each;
We are this
Never hard to reach.

And so we are
One to the other;
Never at war
Always a Brother.

Kathleen Schroeder
MY PARENTS
Words never spoken
Love never shared
Both have lost
The years have passed,
Too late for memories.

James R Sullivan
SPARKLING EYES

To my wife, Kathy

The sparkle in your eyes on the day we met
Darling I'll always love you, I hope you won't forget

You came into my life on a sunny day, and as I remember
It was the month of May

Your beauty is like the flowers when they are all in bloom
And when you're around me honey, there's never any gloom

The love I have for you no one will ever know
So darling I just thought I'd better tell you so

Your eyes shine as bright as the stars above
So darling I hope you'll never want another love

I want to hold onto you, oh with all my might
And honey I want you in my arms each day and every night

You make my life worth living and oh so full of joy
Just like a little baby with a brand new toy

And that sparkle in you eyes will never go away
And honey I'll love you more next year again come May

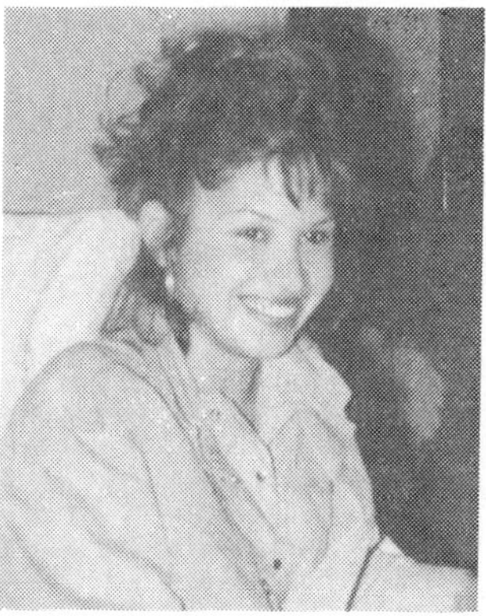

Maria Hernandez

Maria Hernandez
MY CORNER

Chago, Carlos, Cayetano, Celia, Hugo, Julieta, Joel, Olga, Hector, Lorena Noe, Abdulah, Mom; Celia and Dad; Baltazar Hernandez

Sometimes I find myself shut out from the world
Everyone in the same world
Me in my corner.

I approach them to talk
I joke n'laugh
I'm happy
They don't look at me, don't listen
I stay longer
It's the same.

I'm back in my corner
It's friendly and warm
No humans in my corner
Except me
I find it the only world I fit in.

Shirley Smith Monroe
LOVE

Dedicated to Vaughn, Vaughn Lee, & Benjamin Jacob
The three continuously shining lights in my life

Love is a four lettered word,
Expressed in many ways;
It can sometimes be your world,
Or make you broken hearted for days-n-days-n-days.

If you're in Love and your Lover's a liar,
Don't get your hopes up too high;
Cause he might two be a jiver,
And make you wish you wanna die.

But being in Love can be a great success,
It can make you wise, it can make you blue;
It can lead to good times and happiness,
It can make you do things that you thought you'd never do.

But to me, there are all sorts of Love,
Such as being in Love, making Love, and the Power of Love.
Love is not always for keeps,
So don't fall into this powerful thing too deep . . .

Maureen J Palmer
RICHES FROM THE HEART
Praise God, I'm rich! Just found out the other day
You see I was feeling down in a most unusual way

The list of things I needed seemed so very far
Like new furniture for my home and

of course, a brand new car

I kept coming up short in every aspect of my life
I wanted to be successful, the perfect mother, a loving wife

I craved appreciation, the chance to really be known
Someone to share my love to rid me of being alone

I had so much to give struggling desperately to get out
My affection was overflowing running wildly all about

It showed on my face, you see I had this radiant glow
And people started to wonder what lights this child up so?

That's when I found it, you see I had it all the time
All the wealth was in my heart, in my pocket I hadn't a dime

Then the Lord said to me the day I was feeling blue
"Seek first the kingdom of God and all these things shall be added to you"

Some can't understand this and to them life closes its door
I feel so very sorry for those who are so poor

Marie B Burlingame
LAUGHTER AND TEARS
I used to memorize and recite the poems
My Mother memorized and recited
When she was a little girl.

But now I read them over,
As she wrote them down for me
And laugh and cry at the memories they bring.

Christopher Henfield

Christopher Henfield
HOMELESS BAG PEOPLE
Here & there we see them.
Men, women.
On their backs,
Filthy, unhealthy, rags they call clothing.
Faces, miserable, despair.
Trudging along.
On the side of the street.
Soleless, shoes, on their feet.
Or, simply, sitting, squatting,
On cold concrete.
All their earthly possessions,
In a discarded bag, they keep.
Standing in long lines,
Awaiting, eagerly, their daily rations.
Or
Simply begging, from the sides,
Of streets.
With no place, in particular, to go.
At night,
They make do.
With empty telephone booths,
Hallways,
Alleyways,
Subway.
Escaping, in some way
the elements.
Remnants, of a society
Whose Rhythm!
Upbeat!
They couldn't keep.
Broken spirits!
Poor Souls.

Thomas A Paige
THE OWNERS OF PROSPERITY
Lost in their corporate frenzy
Above the plains they reap
Distanced and unfeeling
To the crowds
Over which they leap
They live in their sweetened worlds
Trampling the future underfoot
Not caring
For anything other
Than obtaining the maximum output
From the realms they've bought and conquered
Using them till worthless and dead
Not seeing the difference
Between the soles that they walk on
And the souls on which they tread

Phyllis McMillan Bowersock
ADOPTION
Jeanie's an
apparition
I think but
I saw her once
tiny
and then she was
newborn small alone
Oh, God
she was a pretty thing
and what I want to
know is
will I ever get to know you
Miss Jeanie?

Karren Raschein
SUMMER-TIME HOME
Inside our four walls, that's filled with love
Often the floors are all spotted with mud

There's papers on the table and dishes to do
The dog's curled up by someone's old shoe

Step out the back door and trip over a cat
Look down the lane, where the pigs are all fat

There's clothes on the line, the lawn ready to mow
Someone's in the shop, getting the go-cart to go

Talk to this boy, you may not understand
He's over for a visit, from another land

There's a different color, than you normally see
Little girls or big boys, come from Mississippi

There may be nieces or nephews, or friends of another
All joining the family, to call me Mother (Mom)

Our sons and daughters, who so fast did grow
Are fine young people, for us to show

We always have room, for a few more
Our home around here, has an open door

My husband and I have love we can share
To those who come here, in God's gentle care

Eric Bent
WANDERING ON
Softly over the land
The sighing wind swept
Carrying your voice
Throughout the deepest planes.
Streaking across the horizon
Your silhouette was born

Arriving with overwhelming grace
To shadow the light of dawn
Exploring through young sentiment
Being lured into the snare
Bringing about moments of bliss
Only to elapse into the nightfall.

Elana B Hill
FAREWELL MY FRIEND
The moment has now dawned upon me,
The moment that I have feared.
The time has come to say good-bye
To my very dear friend.
A friend who I have shared good times and bad,
Someone who I could always rely on.
A friend I have shared happy times and sad,
From my eyes fall tears as big as raindrops
And in my heart is a lump as big as a stone,
I don't know what could be worse
To be left or to be leaving alone?
And even now that it's time to go,
My love for you continues to grow.
Our friendship will never come to an end,
But it is time for me to say, farewell my friend.

Pamela L Krenke
GRANDMA
For 16 long years
Through thick and through thin
Through all of my bad moods
No matter what kind of a fix I was in

You were there for me to talk to
All I had to do was call
Or even to write you
I knew you'd be there, heart and all

Thank you for being my grandma
So loving and so kind
You've been so very special to me
You are always on my mind

I love you so much
And I have for so long
You have given me security
And made me so strong

I can't say much else
I think I've said just about all
Just remember I love you
The best of all

Helen Mc Nab
AT THE TAJ MAHAL
Glimmer, shimmer, waves of heat,
Marble's sun gleam on bare feet.
Walk the silken promenade
Agra's skillful craftsmen made.
Frame the mass of symmetry,
Concrete in transparency.
Bulbous domes against the sky,
Muslim's chants meander by,
Vault of wonder, rapture bound,
Floats the square above the ground.

Pressed in stone, jewels flower;
Narrow minarets tower;
Fine carved alabaster lace,
Frozen music, meshed in space.
Formal Turkish garden bed;
Sandstone mosques in contrast, red;
Settled in a garden green,
Shallow pools reverse the scene.
Sleeps below, the Moghul queen,
Pearl of India's lavish scene.

Peggy L Hunst
INSANITY
The Evil are ruling.
The madman is here.
He's taking the children—
from far and near.

He's taking them away.
They'll never return.
He's killing them off.
It's love they yearn.

He'll beat them and slay them;
tease and betray them,
but they'll never escape
for Hate guards the gate.

Diana Thompson
MY DREAMS AND I
When I was born,
I saw no hope,
For I saw no Love.
For if there was,
I was sure to see it!

As I lonely sat,
I dreamed of Dreams
That never came.
For if they did,
I would no longer
Need to Dream.

I asked myself,
Are these my Dreams
That are to be?
Or will they all vanish,
Into thin air?
For my soul is full of longing,
For my Life and my Dreams.

Clifford "J" Campbell
LIFE'S TREASURES

Dedicated to the treasure of my life: My wife—for life

Un-mask my quill, lest the worn words of time past, have no place.
Let the emergence of truth be told for it drowse no more, and likened unto a child, hath no patience.

I speak of time, for it travels at night, and the shadows go unnoticed, but its presence doth script the life we love.

To you my love, I do re-affirm that the language of youth . . . once written fire and passion, doth still burn within a well traveled memory.
What gift do I give thee? When the giver of treasures has made present, all that has lasting worth;

then surely the second greatest gift must need be, the sharing of such gifts.

This I have done, but my words of thanks would nigh ring a beggars cup—but given the eternities I will do thee justice for such treasured gifts of companionship and love.

Lady justice doth scale in my favor
and the keeper of treasures—
hath with held not . . .

Rosa M Caro
BUSCÁNDOTE
Sabes a donde vas?
Y quien es que te mueve?
Que has hecho do to vida?
Que piensas tu de mi?

Acaso eres tan fuerte,
que no me necesitas?
O tan debil te encuentras,
que has perdido la fe?

Tu por quien me desvelo,
to por llamarte así,
tu, tu mismo y no otro,
me llevas a morir.

Buscame y me veras,
pídeme y te daré,
sírveme y tu tendras
lo que has de menester.

April M Bottomley
SADNESS
Sadness comes
more than
once a year
and brings
one too many a tear

Sadness you
can feel only in
you but has
shown to hurt
others, too.

Sadness may
sometimes be
fought but
happiness
may not be bought.

You have to
wait for another
day and turn
your head the
other way!

robert browning
second tea party
american children
crying
in the streets
torn & ragged & empty

liberties children
weak
roaming back alleys
forgotten & unwanted

freedoms children
betrayed
seeking fleeting dreams
refuse of american life

your mother/mrs america
mother justice
is fat & oblivious
to your plight

american children
return to boston
i smell tea
in the harbor

Theresa M Szilagyi
LOVE
Love is the sun shining each new day.
Love is showing you care in your own special way.

Love is the time we spend together.
Love is the way you make me feel better.
Love is holding you close to me.
Love is knowing that that's where you want to be.

Love is all the things we share.
Love is knowing you will always be there.

Love is the flowers that bloom in the Spring.
Love is the happiness that being with you brings.

Love is the chirping of crickets at night.
Love is the way you make my life so bright.

Love is how I feel when I think of you.
Love is everything you always do.
Love is wanting to be with you—
the rest of my life.

Betty Y Lee
FAREWELL TO J.P.T.
J ust to free myself from hopeless hope
A nd undesirable desire,
M ust I leave you now
E ver and forever
S ince I see no future for us, sire.

T eardrops falling, heart keeps aching,
Y ears in pain that is to
L et you go this way,
E specially with countless memories to
R emember you always.

B ut since
E verything has its end,
T o hang on to you
T o dream and love
Y ou in vain

L eave me no room to
E ase my spirit and so
E nd must roam.

Thomas Odar

Thomas Odar
UTOPIA
We could find every ocean
We could climb every star
Days could be our fantasy
Nights could be our dreams
Lose ourselves in sunshine
Get carried away by rainbows

We could dance away our fears
We could live forever
I could wash away your tears
With a bucket of pearls

We could climb every mountain
We could humble the grand canyon
We could paint the sky orange
We could drink golden drops of rain
We could create new galaxies
We could hold infinity
In our brilliant laughs
Smile forever
Like an endless river

But first you have to love me

Melinda Shaw Snow
I THINK OF YOU—MY FRIEND
I think of you—My Friend.
Yesterday, you were the optimistic one,
in love with love itself.
In everything, you had only the purest
of needs—of desires.
You had the fortitude of many
and ever a trust in the Divine.

With time the smile was not as quick;
the light not quite so bright.
I wanted to help—to talk,
but you were the optimistic one;
in love with love itself.
You had the will to make things happen,
knowing that this would be the year of years.

Today I think of you—My Friend:
You wanted to talk, and I listened.
Now I see fear in your eyes and in those of your children:
The tears of empty years will soon fall.
The smile is an afterglow—the light has dimmed;
and love itself has died.
I wanted only the best for you—I still do.

Arianne
LOVE SET FREE
I've tried so hard for so long to put into words the way I feel about you,
But I can't, oh I can't! I'd write a few stanzas, then throw them out;
Others I'd keep, but it seemed almost a sacrilegious thing to do.
I've kept my feelings to myself, tried to hide the way I feel about
You, but it's something I can no longer conceal
This prisoner inside me called "love" hungers for freedom's sweet taste;
It strives for life, it struggles to take a breath, it appeals
In the name of all that's "Holy" for liberty; the seed that once lay dormant has now been replaced
By a burning fever and an ardent desire to speak and be heard.
It beats inside my breast and screams inside my brain,
And echoes in the corridors of my mind till I can no longer be sure of my own spoken word;
My very thoughts are drowned out till not a shred of my sanity or self-respect remains.
"You love him, you love him!", shrieks the voice, "Tell him, don't be afraid!".
But I am scared, terrified of losing the one thing I've searched for all my life—
The substance and breadth of my existence; my emotions are constantly being played
Against my reasoning and my common sense, and it cuts me like a knife.
I can no longer live in this world of darkness, this uncertainty, this madness,
I must set my emotions free else they rule and destroy me.
And come what may—a life full of love or one of sadness,
I won't know till I try and stand face to face with Destiny!

Dottie White
ONCE UPON A DREAM
Once upon a dream, in the long, long night,
A lovely star, shed its golden light,
It lights the way for you to see,
Across the miles, straight to me.

Soon, there were few miles between,
Your face was such a lovely dream,
The precious little twinkling star,
Kept right on smiling, where you are.

I seem somehow, to feel your touch,
The lips I love so very much,
Were drawing ever closer, dear,
You seemed so close, so very near.

All at once, the dream was gone,
The little star, went with the dawn,
In its place, the sun shone bright,
May our little star, be back to-night.

susana t batcagan-pasicatan
LOVE POEM
i love you
as a silkened dew
caress the morning rose
in self-abandoned care

a
n
d

long to hold within
the essence of your charm

the mystifying bond
with which you've always
drawn me with.

Mayme Berger
A TRIBUTE TO MY MOTHER AND FATHER
When I was just a little girl,
Too small to even crawl
Polio struck my mother
And the world began to fall.

My father's world was shattered
As he loved my mother dearly.
And I, not being old enough
Voiced my displeasure clearly.

I couldn't know what my father felt,
I didn't know what he thought,
All I could do was look at him
And see his face distraught.

But after weighing the situation,

He suddenly came to life
"I'm going to fight the battle," he said
"For my children and my wife."

He fought that battle
And he won it, too.
He brought Mother home walking in braces
Which we never thought she'd do.

Desiree Cordova
IT'S TIMES LIKE THESE WHEN I WISH I KNEW
It's time like these when I wish I knew
How I should act and what I should do
You don't even know what love is about
That's why between us it would never work out
I thought you cared but you didn't even try
I think of it now with a tear in my eye
You'll find someone else whose love you will share
While I sit alone and pretend I don't care
I've got to get used to us being apart
And live with the pain that remains in my heart.

Joan M Jones
LUTE SONG
My lady knows where mosses grow
And gentle mists of morning blow
Around her unicorn. She sees
Them curling after him and swears
She loves him more than life itself
And never will she leave his side.

My lady's wild and free to roam
At will her secret forest home.
She laughs and runs to me as soon
As I appear because she knows
That I, too, love her unicorn
But so much more do I love her.

steven michael scroggin
WHAT IS LIFE
what is life
why am i here
are there any answers
or are there only questions
sometimes i think i have the answers
but are they really answers
or are they only questions in disguise

am i a failure
have i failed you
did i do the right thing
or should i have humbled myself
to accept that i was
will i make a difference
or am i just passing through
on my way to nowhere

where is he
if you see him
tell him i'm here
he knows where that's at
and if you know
maybe i've already found what i'm looking for

Jen Ellis
GATHERING MEMORIES
The woman sat on the old front porch rocking to and fro, and as she rocked she reminisced of those days so long ago.

She talked of the hardships and sorrows, of fun and laughter the good and the bad.

She remembered the chores that had to be done, carrying wood and water, the churning of the butter, the cooking and the baking, before they could have their fun.

She remembered running through the fields hair blowing in the breeze, the old swimming hole and the swing in the trees.

She paused a moment, then smiled and said, I now realize in these eighty years I've been gathering up memories.

Carroll A Schillo
AFTER LOSING BRANDON
I feel all bottled up inside like
A powder keg ready to explode or
A dam ready to burst
And spill over in rage
I feel like a tiger in a cage

And I want out.

I feel like screaming, running
Jumping, stomping my feet
Yelling out in anger and
Losing control
But there's such an empty hole

That I can't shout.

Barbara J (Haggins) Jenkins
SUNSHINE

This poem is dedicated to Tyree, Kemp, Melodie, Stephanie, my family and friends with love

Beautiful sunshine shining so bright.
Warm and so pleasant.
It will be gone tonight.
And in its place darkness will fall.
Bringing soft breezes shadows and all.

Then comes the dawning.
It knows it's best of all.
Because it brings sweet freshness.
For a new day of promise.
For us all.

Bonnie Herring
POET'S LEGACY

Dedicated to my parents Jerry and Margie Moorehead for their encouragement and belief in me that I truly have something to leave behind for others through my poetry.

From the poet come these words
We hope will bring a smile,
To a persons sadness
Make them happy for awhile.

Words we hope bring memories
Of the present and the past,
The very ones you've cherished
And hoped would always last.

Sometimes we find it difficult
To make our words rhyme,
Then a special thought occurs
It happens just in time.

Writing words with feeling
We put them on a page,
For you to read with happiness
No matter what your age.

So for the "poet's legacy"
We leave behind for you,
Words we felt within our hearts
Hoping they'll come true . . .

Jennifer M Almada
ELEGY TO BEETHOVEN
Like the intensity of Jasmine
in the Night,
You created symphonies
Within the Silence.

Through your hands
you heard the soft tones
of the piano keys
Beneath your finger tips.

Your imagination was boundless.
You were limited only to
the Universe
which held you.

Now you share in the
Greatest Symphony ever inspired.
And we, we enjoy the legacy of
Music you left behind

Darren Wilson
GIRL OF MY DREAMS
Her hair blows gently,
Like a soft weeping willow;
As it spreads evenly,
Over her satiny pillow.

Her voice is gentle,
Like a purring kitten;
Her embrace is warm,
Like a woolen mitten.

Her smile is sweet,
Warm and sincere;
Whenever I need her,
She is always here.

She moves with style,
Beauty and grace;
I can feel her presence
And her warm embrace.

Her eyes are bright,
Like a sun's shiny beams;
And this is,
The girl of my dreams.

Minta Geraldine Zimmer
CHILDREN ARE LIKE FLOWERS

To Chad M. Ruff and Jason A. Ruff who have been the light of my life and whose footpaths have led them down towards the lowlands and back toward the light. May God Bless the both of you, as together we travel in life.

Don't crush the gracious flowers, symbolically understand.
You are planting baby seedlings throughout our flowered land.
Trials and tribulations to weigh their sturdy stand,
calling the arc-angels holding tightly to their hands.

Children's footpaths are like the trails of flowers in the fields,
swaying and delicately blowing like millions of daffodils.
Shelter all the flowers from the gales and blackened storms,
guidance for tomorrow to reap a higher reward.

As the dew will surely gather, give them kisses from the sun,
an amber light to guide them, and security when darkness comes.
The children are like the flowers along the trials of life,
traveling toward the lowlands and back toward the light.

Fragile as pure crystal, give them shelter to withstand.
Lovingly plant the seedlings and scatter them throughout the land.
Perfect little rose buds, winds to cause them strife.
Stumbling across high mountains, faltering in their lives.

Practice to make them perfect, give them patience in each smile.
A colored array of brilliance shining like jewels in the Nile.
Prisms of redirection standing so preciously groomed.
They're delicate little treasures growing as they bloom.

Moon beams to cast long shadows, God to light their way.
For at dawn they magically open and sleep in twi-light's stay.
Standing to protect them, hold a lamp to clear their paths.
Our children are the flowers who blossom and root at last.

Mahbubul Hassan

Mahbubul Hassan
SLEEP VERSUS DEATH

This poem is dedicated to my loving daughter Roxanne Jabin Hassan.

Why fear death?
Sleep itself is a sensation of death;
Still, why is this eternal fear?
Partly awake, partly slumber,
This is life.
However we strive,
Never awakening from sleep that is death;
Deafened in solitude,
Lost in one's own self.
Ever wondered prior to retiring
That the chillness of death
Lies in sleep?

Death symbolizes life in the next world.

Sharon LaVetta Harris
DR. MARTIN LUTHER KING, JR.

To my devoted mother, Sandra who inspired me to write this poem. Also, to my loving grandparents, aunts, uncles and cousins who had faith in me.

Dr. Martin Luther King, Jr. was a good man
One who didn't have his head in the sand
He wanted freedom for everyone
While others pulled out guns
He was thrown in jail many times
But historic memories will never be

left behind
He will go down in history
Which is really not a mystery
He gave his famous speech "Free at Last"
Right before he passed
People sing "We shall overcome"
Before the day is done
He will be remembered by everyone
Especially his daughters and sons
He worked for equal rights every hour
Because people wanted freedom power.

Marie Willimont
IDES OF MARCH
The Ides of March—here so soon?
What will they bring?
Springtime laughter
Or Winter's sting?
I wonder!

Or curious daffodils
Peeping up through
The hard-crusted earth
To glimpse the blue?
I wonder!

Or maybe it would possibly be
Wind's icy blast
To frighten the buds
From waking too fast?
I wonder!

But then there comes a lovely day
When birds do sing!
I thank the Lord
And know it's Spring.
No more to wonder!

Betty Vaughn
WHEN THE ASPEN TURNS
In the spring, her birthday near
He wants her hand, for now always
She loves him, the answer yes
She'll marry when the aspen turns.

Through the summer the plans are made
Dresses, gown, flowers and a veil
A mountain church in a valley high
There'll be a wedding when the aspen turns.

His family comes from near and far
Hers and friends gather together too
At a castle white with mountain dew
Wedding time when the aspen turns.

The bride lovely, the groom handsome and tall
A ceremony joyous, meaningful with love
She was the bride just as she said
In the mountains when the aspen turns

Traci Hollenbrandt
ALONE
Alone with nowhere to go.
People all around,
But no-one to turn to.
A house filled with love,
No love left for me.
A man to hold,
With no meaning.
Moments of love-making,
But no feelings sparkle.
I'm in a world by myself . . .
Forever being . . .
Alone.

Diana Kwiatkowski Rubin
EVEN STRANGER STRANGERS
We used to be so close.
Now we're not even friends.
What subtle cause for giving
Light to this indifferent end!

A loss is best remembered
In neat concentrated ways—
Denizens of memories pushing
Through the feather-veined blaze.

Makes one stop to deem what
Kindred is if it can be lost
Without a quiver, pain, shake
Desperate choking gasp or cost

As if nothing matters—as 'twas
Before. Like air, invincible.
Now cloistered and tight we are.
How ghoulishly incredible!

Pray tell me if you really
Don't care—was it, was it
Ever even there?

Eldor Rathjen
LAST JOURNEY
The stars fell—the moon grew Dim
The sun had lost its Light
The earth we Knew—and lived Upon
Lies battered changed, eternal Night

The universe—no more Remains
In place is one vast Waste
No way to reach—beyond the Void
Or save the human Race

Then straining eyes—reach out Afar
Vast distant, shines a Light
As magnets drawn—we grope our Way
Through the eternal Night

Now destiny—beyond Control
Through emptiness and Space
Our eyes glued on—the heavenly Light
We travel on, by Grace

Then from afar—our vision Clears
The light upon His Throne
At last, at last—we've found the Way
To our eternal Home

Barbara Grimm
GOD'S MEADOW
There is a meadow
Where the sun always shines,
The air is so pure
That it cleanses your mind.

The grass is so soft
Against skin so pure,
With a kind heart you feel
Safe and secure.

For friends you have known
Have gone there to stay
You can feel their hands
Guide you, each passing day.

It never grows dark
In this meadow you see,
For in God's kingdom
Everyone's free.

There are no more wars,
No killing, no hate.
So know in your heart
When you reach God's gate.

To look toward the meadow
And drink the pure air,
And feel the warm sun
As it touches your hair.

For you are home now,
There are angels who see
Your friends in the meadow
All safe as can be.

You feel God's warm hand
As he guides you in
To a meadow where everyone
Is free from sin.

Beth Perry
LOVE IS SOMETHING SPECIAL
Love is something special,
Not around everyday.
When true love is finally found,
It will be here to stay.
Of course there are different kinds
Your sister and your mate
The first being as a friend,
The second as a date.

It may take others,
A lot or even just one.
But finding "Mr. Right,"
Could be lots of fun.

Break-ups can be the worst,
Especially if you thought he was true.
But as you meet new guys,
You'll find his type wasn't for you.

Even if you love him a lot,
Not all were meant to last.
Think of him as a friend,
And soon your hurt will be past.

Evelyn L Sweeney
THE SEQUOIA TREE

This poem is dedicated to Harriett "Petey" Weaver, without whose love, encouragement, and dedication, would never have been written, and to whom I am grateful and love very deeply.

Oh! Giant tree, for living to be so old
I wonder what stories you must hold,
For the centuries have come and gone
And you are truly a phenomenon.
I can only guess at what you have seen
Through the years as you stood so serene,
Living before the Christ-child's birth
And countries not settled all over the earth.
It's hard for us to understand
So many years and still look so grand.

From Mother Earth you grew and grew
Until reaching the sky of blue,
Spreading the width of your girth
To become the largest tree on earth.
What a magnificent giant of a tree,
For no other can reach as high as thee,
So tall and God-like the way you stand
And how you beautify the land.
Live on oh! Glorious Sequoia tree
To fascinate those who follow me.

Hilda M Collins
THERE IS NOTHING LIKE A FAMILY
There is nothing like a family;
So, you'll never feel alone.
The day when you get married
Will start you on your own.
It's always nice to have someone—
That you can share your love.
And life would be just great,
Like the stars that shine above.
It wouldn't be a family,
Unless you have a child.
They always bring such happiness—
This little one that's mild.
Just understand each other
And your trust it means a lot.
It will keep you both together,
From the day you tie the knot.
There are so many couples,
Who do not seem to care.
But there's nothing like a family;
When two people learn to share.

Daniel Malcom Curtis
IF I BELIEVE

I gratefully dedicate this, my first published poem to Gladys (3), Betty, Laura Marie, Jean, Jim, Nancy, Mary, Pat and Victoria Lynn, without their influence, I would not be reaping this victory.

I opened the box so that my curiosity would win.
It was supposed to have housed the knowledge
of centuries within.
I found peace not evil.
For Pandora, the box had contained
all of the world's evil and sins.

During the 18th century, logical thinking prevailed.
Unanswered questions remained;
through determination
religious superstition slightly failed.

Now I sit and ask myself
why knowledge was stolen by thieves?
Was it to help us question the faith of our parents
about the losses that they grieved?
Is it just what the individual perceives;
where does the problem lie
when and if I believe?

Anthony M Curlee
SEEMS LIKE ONLY YESTERDAY

This poem is dedicated to my Mother; deceased Father, and all of the Vietnam veterans; living and dead

Twenty three years ago today,
My Father died in a tragic way.
He will never return to Birmingham,
for he was killed in Vietnam.

The soldiers went down the Delta to fight,
they fought against wrong; they stood for right.
They stuck together through thick and thin;
fought together to the very end.
It was so long ago I must say:
it seems like only yesterday.

The soldiers that fought there were young and bold;
Some made it out alive: some will never grow old.
What really happened in that hell of a place;
that left so many young men with a bitter taste.

I was just a kid when Dad left for that place;
it's been a long time, but I still remember his face.
My little brother don't remember him at all;

that's why Dad's picture's hanging
on the wall.
It was so long ago I must say:
it seems like only yesterday.

Jodie M Rahn
LET ME BE ME

Dedicated to Neva: My friend, my inspiration,, my daughter.

One body, one mind, together true,
Free to be totally different than you,
I'm a single unit that I call—ME,
A separate, complete personality,
Why must you constantly try to
change,
Mold, distort and rearrange,
All that I am to fit your need,
Make me follow when I want to lead.
Just stop and listen, and understand,
That I am being all that I can,
I'm serious and funny, happy or blue,
Identical feelings that also are you,
Opinions I speak, are only to share,
A part of myself, to make you aware,
Altho I'm different from you and the
rest,
I too have rights to think and express,
All that I am, individual and free,
God let you be you,—SO LET ME
BE ME.

Philip A Eckerle
TIME WAS

Time was
When a jungle gym
Was a challenge to youth,
Not rusting iron;
When a seesaw
Was a source of joy,
Not a political opinion review;
When swinging
Was a natural high,
Not a sign of promiscuity;
And sand was for building castles,
Not something that passed through an
hourglass
Far too quickly.
Playgrounds and definitions change
With time and age.
Time was.

Karen Paige Klingner
MOONLIGHT DARKNESS

The clock strikes the midnight hour,
An owl flies above.
The night is filled with evil power,
And darkness is its love.

A wolf stalks its prey in the
moonlight,
The trees dance in the wind.
Nothing is safe in the moonlight,
Everyone has sinned.

Tami Kobra
JIM MORRISON'S DEDICATION

Between sun and moon, earth and
sky, bound by chains that won't
untie.
Things running through the mind,
never to be found in places of time.
giving no reason to things that are
done, traveling thru waterless deserts
of sun.
There he stands thru blurred visions,
over troubled seas of time, the king
of words, and fluid of phrase, the
master of rhyme.
Darkness takes over the day, moon
glows thru the trees, there's a chill in
the air causing nighttime to freeze.
As darkness connects into the sea,
distant faces appear to me. Causing
trauma thru my mind, giving sight
but always blind.
Silence stalks the night, giving reason
to fear, the depth of perception is
crystal clear.
The ocean rises to touch the sun,
spirits are at ease except for one.
Tell me the reason, oh tell me why,
the sad one starts to cry.
Leaving the truth to the brilliant eye
why do the good ones always die?

Ethel A Susman
A WIDOW'S LAMENT

To my late husband, my beloved Nathan

I was always dreaming of
That sweet mystery called love
I was trying hard to find
Someone who was strong and kind

Then one day you came along
Life became one happy song!
But my blue skies changed to gray
Suddenly—you went away!

The nightingale has lost its voice
forever
No more the sun will shine—it's
stormy weather
No more will flowers bloom
The moonbeams hide in gloom
I've lost the only one I love

The ocean beats upon an empty shore
My heart keeps crying out—we'll
stroll no more
I hide from Lovers' Lane
I've torn up love's refrain
For I've lost the only one I love!

Patricia A Livengood (Shane)

Patricia A Livengood (Shane)
LOST

To the love of Rob & Pat born Jan. 14, 1989. "A calling" for two soulmates who were lost & crying out, to be united & for eternity.

In the lonely hills of West Virginia,
A lonely woman's heart did pine
It ached to have a true love's love
to love her for all time.
Her heart held dared secrets that fills
a woman's mind
Her heart longed to share them but
her soul held them confined.

She'd gaze out through the window
to the highway running by and often
thought she'd travel it someday . . .
though she knew not where or why,
She'd follow it to a freeway and
there, turn her spirit free
to the world that lie before her—
whatever than might be.

She had given her love freely to
everyone she'd known, but somehow
love was not returned and it turned
her heart to stone.
Yet loyalty kept her sitting by the
window for so long . . . beside the
man who did her wrong for that's
where she belonged . . .
even though love had gone.

Her heart was like a mirror, inch by
inch it slowly cracked, until one day
. . . the final blow . . . in pieces lay a
stack . . . of shattered lives, wasted
youthful years,
Should she pick the pieces up and
put away those tears?

She was born a survivor—she knew
she'd be O.K.
She took out on the highway—today
was a brand new day.
That night she spread her wings to
flight,
broke outside the world she knew,
The BLUE ROOM II was calling
her . . . a "comet" was passing
through.

There she met Rob Kirkland, the
man she knew in her dreams,
He was standing there with open
arms just waiting to be seen.
Her eyes were wide open, they
welcomed him with love, her smile
said "Somehow I know
you . . . you're the man I'm
dreaming of."

Their bruised lips touched softly,
their hearts touched one on one,
They knew they'd found each other
A new life had begun.

They swore a life together,
neither ever going back
The life they left behind them
was now all in the past.
They laugh now at the heartaches
that caused their paths to cross
and thank the ones who gave the
pain
'cause now they are so lost . . .
IN LOVE.

Steven Brown Sr
MOPKIN'S SONG

In dedicating this poem, I thank God, Sherry, Herbert, Alma, Shantez, and Steven Jr. and a special appreciation to Eddie-Lou Cole

Like a mopkin on your hand, and
you're holding it's stick.
Moving him around right on click.
Rubbing his furry body,! you
understand.
Makes the mopkin feel, like a real
live man. Mopkin's Song!
Mopkin's Song! you can do it, just
move his mouth with your hand.
Mopkin's Song! put your mind to it,
you're singing with the mopkin man.
Sing that mopkin's song!
Don't sing it wrong.
Sing that mopkin's song!
Sing that song. Mopkin's Song,
Mopkin's Song!
There's small ones, an' big ones of
everyone's size.
An adoption certificates it's a big
suprize.
Cowboys, rockstars and many more
drop in on the mopkin's store.

Grant Way
AN ANGEL

From the beauties of the heavens,
came an angel long ago. The sweetest
of the ladies that I ever that I ever
came to know.

Through my tender years of
childhood she would guide my tender
feet and hold me in her arms and her
song was Oh! So sweet.

She would dry away my teardrops
and ease my aching heart, but one
night the master called her and from
this world she had to part.

My heart fell down with me and
teardrops began to flow,
She said do not cry my darling God
will care for you I know.

I laid my head upon her breast,
and she dried my teardrops then, and
we fell asleep together but she never
awakened again. In the beauties of
the heavens upon the golden shore I
see her with angels where she will
love forever more. And if it is God's
will I know I can I will meet my
angel up in the Promised Land.

Cara Vitolo
I WILL HOLD YOUR HAND AND WALK

To all God's children

I will hold your hand and walk with
you along rocky paths and quiet blue
waters.
I will comfort you with my thoughts
and hold you so deeply inside of me.
My voice will keep you warm when
the voice of the world is so cold;
. . . For what is here is
beyond . . .

. . . And what is beyond is
here . . .
I will touch you with my eyes that
not only look but see into your heart
and soul.
I will wash your wounds with my
tears and heal your pain with
gentleness, kindness, peace and love.

Wesley W Wilson Jr
SLAVES

To Christ, who makes all things possible!

Freedom is an often elusive quality.
Many of us profess to be free; but in
reality we exist as mere slaves.

Slaves—made captive by our will to
be FREE!

Free to live out our heart's desires.
Free to drink wine to our heart's
content. Free to partake of life's
worldly pleasures.
Free to live—without repercussions.

Thus, in our quest to be free, we sell
our souls into captivity.
To serve under a brutal task-master;
stripped of its rights and bound by
the chains of our carnal desires.

Being driven by our selfish appetites
and ruled by our ever-seeing eyes.
Whipping our souls into submission!
We never protest—We never resist.
We only Obey—We only Submit!

Because we have forgotten the simple axiom; that the soul was not made for the body, but rather, the body to house the soul.

Therefore, if we allow this tent of dust to govern our soul's existence—are we indeed Free? And if we permit our most primal instincts to suppress our Godly traits—again, are we Free? God Forbid!

So let us wage our many insurrections; bearing the many risks of Spiritual conflict. Ever striving for higher plains of Freedom. As in the words of the old negro spiritual: '. . . . before I be a Slave, I'll be buried in my grave and go home to my Lord and be FREE'!

John C Holmes
MY PLEDGE

To Mary; a wonderful wife and a great friend. I was lucky to have her.

I made a promise, it came from my heart,
'Love, honor and cherish 'til death do us part.'
I won a great prize when I made that vow.
I knew it then and I still know it now.

Best friends and sweethearts
Through all of the years
That we've shared our triumphs,
Our hopes and our fears.

Now you've had a stroke; your spirits are low,
But, Honey, there's something I want you to know,
That let come what may whate'er we'll go through
Sweetheart, I promise I'll always love you.

Willie Mae Mcclendon
GOD IS LOVE

God is joy and faith of life
God is the love of all—man kind

God has no respect of person,
regardless of race.

God is there when all—man kind
has left.

God will supply our needs
of this life.

Willean Burks
TOUCH OF BEAUTY

This poem is dedicated to all that enjoy the fine writings and wonderful readings from author(s) of the most imaginative and creative thoughts that express feelings and most precious dreams. Each poem has its true meaning of the joyfulness you so desire.

To feel the softness tingling on your face;
As a gentle breeze of star-like particles twinkling down every inch of your body with out leaving a trace;
Filled with the arrogance of beauty and delicacy of a summer white dove;
To feel the tiny rainbow coalition of bubbly beads bombarding in every direction covering your entire body with the extravancy of the glorious feelings from above;

HUSH! HUSH! and silently close your eyes and let your mind slowly absorb the deep feeling of happiness, joy and delight;
Remembering every detail of warmth, softness, and twinkling feeling flowing all over your body when you spin and DANCE! DANCE! and DANCE! under the mist of full moon of the night;

Keeping in mind that NOW! is the time of a great feeling that will last forever . . .

Marshall Gealt
STORM WARNING

In the tangled sleep of the fallen,
My night is besieged by uneasy dreams
And beneath my pillow,
I can feel your warm breath
Breaking the sweating summer night
With the glow of fever
And storm warning breezes
Easing their fingers over my burned flesh.
Torturing demons rose in your eyes
Obscuring the light of day with their black wings.

By pouring acid in your ears
And fanning fires of their own ignition,
You became asphyxiated by noxious smoke
Under the end of a February sky.
And the enchanted bliss of that first night
Soon faded under your heart's inability to meet mine.
The charged air crackles with excitement and mockery
Of its slow exuberant approach
Lighting and laying dark the same in me.

Dan Sherman
EDGE

The pulse of time races through me
As I feel my way through life
Slowly, softly, hoping blindly
For something not tarnished or trite

A time of change is upon me—
The choice of actions not clear
The path I take now is the one I will follow
For the rest of my terrestrial years

But my scars, like chains, hold me fast
To incidents locked deep in the past
Do I break their hold and stand on the edge—
Or do I hold back cold and inch off the ledge?

The sky is blue and I am young
My heart beats gold with vertigo
How far I could fall is terrifying
But I know what I have to do—

I'll break their grasp and fling off the past
And jump out into the sky
With my mind in control I'll harness my soul
And then I'll start learning to fly

Heather Lashley
TOGETHERNESS

To my dear mother Verene, the Lashley family, my friends Cynthia and George.

It is better to be together,
To show your love
Towards one another,
Rich and poor
Black and white,
Should be friends.
It is time to know people
To see the real values deep down inside of them.
Some people may have less
Some people more,
Do not let clothes, food or money
Make you resent people
Because all are human beings,
Special in their own way.

Beverly Foxwell
FRIEND

You're warm and inspiring;
A real honest to goodness man;
You're self-reliant and real understanding;
A God-fearing person with a sense of humor;
Music you love and of course the outdoors;
You're trusting, and loving, sharing, and sweet;
You drink of the sunshine and that's real neat;
You see the opposite sex as a warm Gesture;
You also see Beauty as it reflects upon yourself;
You're a bit of heaven and a little hell;
You're everything and so much more;
You look at the future with a just cause;
You're so refreshing like a breath of spring;
You're a knight in shining armour;
And you're just plain you;
You're realistic and so much more;
You're the handsome one;
My heart goes out to you.
That friend of mine.

Debbera E Neilson
REFLECTIONS OF CHILDHOOD

Daydreaming, just passing time,
Many thoughts come to my mind.
Today, tomorrow, those days of the past.
Dreams, desires, that seldom last.
Through this looking glass I see,
a reflection of my used to be.
Running free without a care
had this feeling inside that life was fair.
Growing up means snapping out of a daze,
Wake up to the real world and enter the maze
They say "Open your mind," learn everything!
But forget what makes a robin sing.
Well I think I'd have done just fine
had I never opened mine.
For then I'd never looked at the world with sorrow,
Or see the destruction we'll all see tomorrow
It's sad life is not what it seems
to us grown up children with broken dreams
All this hatred and violence is destroying our land
When will we all walk hand in hand
if only we could let it be,
then all of us again could RUN FREE

Joyce Brown
THE KEY TO THE FUTURE

Dedicated to my daughter and seven sons . . .

The key to the future is
Being carried around in the
Minds of all our children:

Feed their minds with the
Educational knowledge of the
Streets the good and definitely
The bad.

Help our teachers motivate
Them down the right road;
Even if they can succeed at
Any and everything they do.

Encourage them at intelligent
Tasks that they engage in;
Teach them that God is their
Key to the future and to
Walk hand in hand with Him
No matter what their trial
And tribulation may be, He'll
Love you to the end, so
Should you.

Cindy Ann Yenchko
I HAD ADVENTURED

TO MY MOTHER: For all her love and support throughout my life Thanks for giving me the courage to follow my dreams. I Love You.

I had adventured into an unknown region
a chamber of darkness at rest
all around
in the silence barely a sound
except a faint beating
though shifted and scorn and buried
in the darkness
seemed withered and worn
I couldn't make out quite what it was
'til it cried out
in the stillness
that chilled me to the bone
I could dimly see its edges were torn
and it sought refuge away
from the storm
I paused but a moment
before I could see, it was a heart
—and it belonged
to me.

Gokarran Sukhdeo
GOODBYE

In my heart there's no more dawn,
Darkness shrouds around like mist;
There'll be pain when you are gone,
Pain my soul will not resist.
There's no tear in my eye as I bid goodbye
No sign that I cry as your journey draws nigh.

Every moment you were near
Was a treasure to my heart,
Those were times that I endear,
But now it's time that we must part.
Friends may come and friends may go
But none will take your place, I know.

To me you were my immortal love,
My dream, my hope, my goddess;

With you I soared the clouds above,
With you I knew no sadness.
Remember love, as I say goodbye,
You'll be my breath until I die.

Gerald Dean Holt
DEAR LORD

There are times in my life when I wonder if tomorrow will ever be better, the sun any brighter? I need warmth tonight. Something to make me whole.

The image of a dog chasing his tail comes to mind and reflects my life today. The stars are too far away to hold and the rainbow has no beginning nor an end; ever proving untouchable.

I have no friend, no tears to flow. I feel so very empty. God, reach down from your throne to soften my soul.
To hear my silent cry—
To be my friend.

Juliet R Lynch

Juliet R Lynch
THROUGH THORNY WAYS

Be still my soul . . . a drift in the rolling, thundering sea . . .
Be still my heart and mind in the pathway of destruction . . .
Walking, staggering, faltering footsteps . . .
Oh Jesus! Hear my plea! ! !
Thorns among the flowers and its pricks shall soon devour . . .
Through the pathway we struggle to perceive . . .
Behold, our shield Thou art my God. . .
and the thorny way—revealed within that Power . . .

Doris R S Miller
BEST FRIENDS . . . MOTHER AND DAUGHTER

To my mother Margaret B. Edgar, with warm and loving thoughts. You deserve much more for all you have given, the inspiration, understanding and encouragement, but, most of all, the love you have bestowed upon me during my life.

I often remember some quotes said to me, "always be the best you can be," Some recollections go back to age three.

I'd make her laugh, she'd make me cry. Learning and growing, seldom we saw eye to eye.
We live our lives doing the best that we can, but, we both make poor judgements now and again.

Between us there is compassion, and anxious emotions and a deep bond of love, separated by oceans.

What I am trying to say, to put down in this note, please read between lines all these words that I wrote.

All that I am or all that I'll be, is because a great woman made me the best I can be.

I speak of the mother that gave me my birth, the "BEST FRIEND" of a daughter that lives on this earth.

Pamela J Williams
REFLECTIONS

I was in a crowd the other day as I walked along a busy street.
As I gazed into the shopkeepers window, I saw a reflection in the glass. I turned to catch a glimpse of a face so familiar, yet so distant in my memory. You turned, the same time as I and as our eyes met, I felt a catch in my breath. Time seemed to stop for that endless moment. The crowd grew heavy and you were no longer there. I turned back to the window and the reflection was gone.

ClaraBelle N Turner
HERITAGE

To my granddaughter—Regina

I am glad that I lived the years I have—
In this land—Even times when living was sad.
As a child, bare feet to run through the fields of hay—
To wade in the brooks, pluck daisies on summer days.
Sit by a bonfire, toasting hot dogs and marshmallows,
To play in the grass blooming with dandelions so yellow!
To shovel snow from the pond to skate winter's cold nights
Brought happiness to a young girl—a freedom of flight!
To study long hours to have my parents prowd—
Find a good job and mingle with a caring young crowd.
Then walk down the aisle, to honor with pride,
Happy to be living—a husband by my side!
To give birth to a son—this heritage to give—
To our family, his family with honor can live.
If only we could turn hearts and heads of our young today
To have pride for themselves, God and Country
There must be a way!

Jerry Carter
THE SPECIAL SPIRITS

In Heaven there are certain Spirits that are pure in every way
So much so, that they don't have to prove themselves with each passing day.
Their love and devotion for their Heavenly Father is one that will always be
But in order to fulfill His Master Plan, there are thing to be done, don't you see.

So they have come to earth to receive an earthly body like everyone in the past
But because of their purity and their love for God, the time spent here doesn't have to last.

Those of us who are selected to provide a body for this sweet and special child
Don't understand His plan for them, so the pain of the lost one drives us wild.

We blame ourselves and think that God may be punishing us for things we've said or done
But instead it's because of their special callings that they are the Chosen one.

The pain and agony is terrible and we are always asking ourselves "Why?"
And the only thing that you can do is hang your head and cry.

The age of the child doesn't matter, from stillborn on up, it's all the same
The only difference is the number of memories of them that you can claim.

The one ray of hope is in the knowledge that the child is so pure and sweet
That if you will only live worthy enough, someday soon you will again meet.

To be able to raise them up as though you were still here on earth
To become the man or woman that you had always hoped for, and do it right from birth.

So we must hold our heads high and be happy for them don't you see
They are doing the things that God wants them to do, preparing the way for you and me.

Tracey M Cole

Tracey M Cole
MAMA'S ARMS

When I was a child, brave I was not,
To sleep was a chore, I had nightmares a lot.
Mama would look down into my face,
She'd tell me, "There is a special place,
Real close by, not far from here,
Where my dreamer can dream without shedding a tear."
"So sleep little darling, no need to be distraught,
You've had a bad dream, it wasn't real as you thought."
I still cry a lot in the night, but I remember my Mama, how she held me oh, so tight.
In Mama's arms soon safe I will be, my Mama will bring sweet dreams to me.
Thank you, Mama!

Paul Platt
UNHEARD WHISPER

This poem is dedicated to Debbie Gibson my "inspiration" Also Mom, Dad, God, John P., Eric S., Jenny P., Steve P., Dawn P., Stacey W., Kelly E., Kellie W., Eddie-Lou Cole, Cindy H., Christine M., Mrs. Schunck, Lisa P., Jeremy P., Jay. P., and anyone else.

You sang a song I knew real well it brang back memories but I couldn't tell 'cause you would go so only I know of the unheard whisper and this is how it goes, the unheard whisper you haven't heard our life together based on the song you wrote and now when I see your face my heart beats a beat quicker for only I know of the unheard whisper . . . You finished the song with a look of sadness I asked what was wrong you sad just madness Somehow you knew if the memories too and now the unheard whisper was heard by you, But why didn't you look when I was away you could have caught me any day now all I see are mem'ries of you, unheard whisper I need you.

Ted McTeer Sr
IN MEMORY OF LONG SCHOOL

To my classmates and friends of Long School, write this tribute. It is in loving spirit that encouraged everyone to attend this reunion each Year. We retain in warm memories a lasting fellowship through the years.

Share with me these memories from the past as down a lonely country road we travel. Trees overshade the road where the sound of iron wagon wheels and the clop of hooves are heard no more.

Down this country road hundreds of youths have tread through the summer heat, the autumn rains and the cold rough days of winter.

Down this country road we stop to gaze where once a schoolhouse stood; visions of the past come forth, as we with immortal spirits blend.

How fast the schoolyard filled as brisk youths appeared on feats of graceful folly bent.

Look again, they all are gone, the youths under the old oak trees, the cluster around the schoolyard pump . . . and scarcely do they disappear than the sound of melody is heard, with one consent the youths rejoice, filling the school with lofty voices.

The moment ends. All is hushed without and silent within. The school bell no more will its iron tone ring out across the Ozarks hills to influence the time and the seasons. The only voice we hear is the soft murmuring of the nearby oaks for even the birds are hushed in silent tribute with the speechless clouds floating through the evening sky.

Yet this tragic story cheers us on, for it speaks of Long School in its golden years.

Few happier moments have been ours and the days gone by return to us almost from the dawn of our lives as each year survivors meet in memory, some from far off by cordial love invited. And as this visionary splendor fades, a portion of God's gifts is won: the gift of memories.

Flora C MacDonald
PRAYER FROM A NEW LAND
Dear Lord, teach me to look upon this vast
White wilderness that I might see,
Not naked rock and desolate stretch of land,
But a new future for an ancient race
Whose destiny is shaped by alien hand.

Teach me to overcome my fear of all that's strange;
My distrust for that which I do not know.
Grant me sweet patience and an understanding heart,
And courage not to let my sadness show.

May my heart always have an open door,
And welcome strangers to the warmth within.
May I now miss my home and friends too much
To keep me from inviting new friends in.

And when the stars blaze from the night-swept sky,
And glitter on this land so strange to me,
Help me to still my bitter, lonely cry
And close my eyes so that my heart may see.

Norma J Jussila
HERE I AM, ALL OLD AND GRAY

I dedicated to wonderful son—Theodore Salo Jussila

Here, I am all old & Gray—
All, my hopes & dreams so far away—

They ended in a terrible way—
How I wished, they'd come to stay—

Marin Lee Bukowsky
A MORNING PRAYER
Eternal Light, I bathe in Your brilliance—
My mind the melting pot of Your ideas.

I return to consciousness each morn—
My eyes lit with the vision of the
Day ahead, knowing that if I follow
Your beacon, I will arrive safely
At its end.

I rise, placing one foot beside its
Counterpart, shuffling across infantile
Feelings of insecurity, braced by
Hope—sure that You will carry me through
The labyrinth of life.

Pamela M Brown
MY FRIEND

To my husband, Cortland, who has been my strength, my inspiration, and most of all, my friend.

My friend I hate to do it,
But this friendship just can't last.
The times we've shared together
Are memories in our past.

I told you it would happen,
I knew it had to end
Although you know I care for you,
You've been my only friend.

Please don't try to argue,
But try to understand,
That time can change two people
As the tide can change the sand.

Our friendship has been lovely,
But it's time to start anew.
Because you see, my dearest friend,
I've fallen in love with you!

Renae Venturoli
I'VE SAT AND WRITTEN POEMS, SINCE 10 I GUESS IT'S BEEN
I've sat and written poems, since 10 I guess it's been,
of feelings that I've had, of places that I've seen.
I've written poems of love, of happiness and tears,
of all the changes that occurred,
along my growing years.
And how my feelings come on paper,
I really can't explain,
I can express my greatest joys, and my deepest pain.
When I touch the ocean, when the wind blows in my hair,
when the rain drops on my face, My pen begins to flair.
And each and every poem I write, It's in my heart I feel,
In everything I think and touch, my writing becomes real.
When I go to sleep and have a dream at night,
I wake up in the morning, with something new to write.
And, O my mind is never blank to think of what to say,
'Cause there's always something new in life every passing day.
And when my poems are finished, I give myself a smile,
For when I read my writing, I know that it has style.

Lewis Rodger Nestor
THE HIKER {SCHÖNES}

To Tina Smida, my inspiration, my love.

I encountered the sun hugging a mountain
this early morning
As it reach its embrace onward
to the lonely sky
Dispelling the dark sleeping night
unto new-woke light.
I saw a world reborn and cleansed
of its blackest-mourn range;
Looking to heaven I saw deep royal purple
go crimson to star-lit orange—and
viewed heaven's own steeple;
I felt lavender touch my mind,
turning my thoughts a golden you,
And was awash in a cloud of
ethereal blue . . .
White light caromed without alternative;
thereafter scattering the
cumulus few . . .
Awakening various birds who to skyward winged and flew.
Standing awed I listened to the crows
as they called & cawed and in
prose asked:
Who, Lord, am I, to be so gloriously persuaded, gift-given and blessed,
of your complicated simplicity
now unshaded?
Is it merely to me or to all who would but look—
with circumcised heart—
To see wisdom is gained in the knowledge fall
of light and darkness apart?
This majestic splendor—panoramic imbued—upon silver-flecked snow
careens my senses aside to you,
schönes—tho' gone—
And this love I ever know:
Hello, My Darling;
Everything, yet nothing, has changed
about which to write.
I just wanted to share my descent
as I chased myself home before
new-fell night . . .
To let you know I think of you here
even among the jagged & frozen rocks
as I lay out my pack to rebundle
the load of life's shocks.
I still remember (vividly) your form
and manner of touch (in colors).
It's to there I travel—torn—
destined to meet your memory
on a ridge.
It is a most beautiful day donning my pack on its shoulders;
And, as I see the borders
of our once-initialed
wood-covered bridge
I round the corner of my memories
one step nearer to you.
The depth of emotion your remembered-love brings
can never be expressed again
(until knew);
There, where your vision flies on rainbowed wings.
I close this lettered-dream memory now
in smiles, and early morning dew;
and post it on your cloud
heading home
to our forever-love song, alone.

Troy R Lorton
THE DESERT BY THE SEA
I feel the wind and the salty humidity brush my face,
And all I can see is empty, desolate, wasted space.
Sea gulls fly over the blue-green water.
The birds fly gracefully.
Their speed is cunning.
The day grows hotter, hotter, hotter.
Is that a crab that I see,
Or do my eyes deceive?
The sea oats stand,
Like cacti over vast valleys of sand.

Robin M Duran
ON THE EDGE OF THE WORLD
I
stand on the edge of the world and look out
across the choppy waves.
Chased, by the familiar, to this side of the continent,
I teeter. My toes hang in space.
I face
the unknown lands that sing
to the boiling blood in my veins.
The energy within me coils so one leap
will take me out of the reach of all that I have known.
Perhaps, if I leap hard and fast and high enough,
I might fly beyond the atmosphere—so blue!—
and into the deepness,
the heartbeat of space.
I might sail across imagined realms—
a glow amid the others of the night
and all because I shook the shadows from my eyes,
I could, yes,
I.

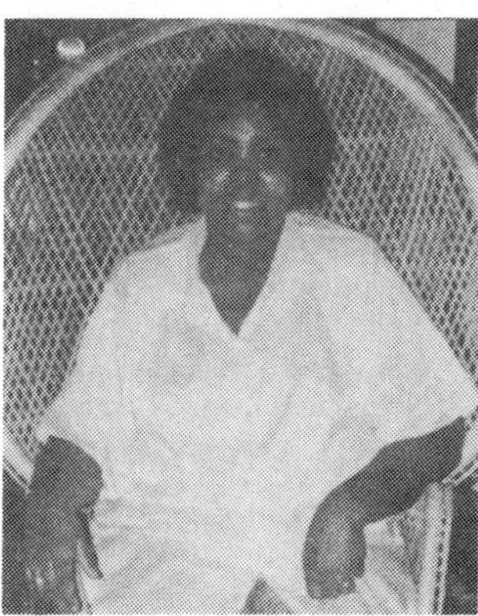

Rosetta White Handy

Rosetta White Handy
IF JESUS WOULD COME TODAY

This poem is dedicated to Rose Anna White, my sweet Mother and friend.

If Jesus would come today,
What would you do; what would you say?
If He would knock on the door,
Would you open it or shout on the floor?
If Jesus would come today,
I don't know what I'll do,
Or what I'll say.
I'll stare and then I'll say,
"Hello Lord Jesus, how are you today?
Do you know I love you?
Do you know how much I prayed?
Thank you Lord Jesus, for all that you did
And for all that you said."

Walter David Peterson
TONIGHT I SAY GOODBYE

For my loving wife Debbie who is always there for me (thanks to my Uncle Andy for the encouragement)

Tonight I say Goodbye, but I'll be
back before too long,
All I ask of you is that you please
stay strong.
With all the troubled times coming
up in our life,
I want you to know one thing I'm
glad you're my wife
With our future summer nights that
will be coming soon;
I have but one dream,
That we lay on the beach and make
sweet love under the loving moon.
I have no way to tell you just how
much you are loved,

But I want you to know one thing I
wish I was there to give you a hug.
Baby, I just left and yet I miss you so
much,
I long to feel your hair and your
warm, sweet, loving touch.
That's all I have to say for now
before I start to cry,
But Babe just know one thing I'll
love you till I die.

Dolores Patricia Firestone

Dolores Patricia Firestone
I SPAN THE FOAMING CREST

To Mother and Dad in Heaven, my Guiding Force here on Earth. To my Sister Marcia, my Best Friend—My Soul Mate.

My Soul Longs for the
Open Sea . . .
The Pounding Waves—Beckon to
me . . .
Ships that Sail with mast on
high . . .
Echoes . . . Come be at my side . . .

I am there with Eagles' Breath—
Wings Outspread . . .
I Span The Foaming Crest . . .
Oh, can you not see?
My Soul is Now Forever Free!

Michael J Jan
CHICKEN DOLL
(SONG)

Love

I said Hi Chicken, then she said Hi
Doll,
I knew that moment—I was heading
for a fall,
I fell in love with a doll I called a
chick,
I knew I was lucky 'cause she
answered me quick,
She said, Yes she said Oh Honey
I could love you so,
She was sincere 'cause her eyes told
me so,
Now I love this chicken and she
loves this doll,
When I said Hi Chicken then she
said Hi Doll.

Renee L Burke
ANOTHER MOTHER'S DAY
Mother's Day is here again and we
are feeling lost and sad,
Our mom left us a short time ago,
she's gone to be with Dad,
Even knowing she is happy now
doesn't really ease the pain,
She left a void in our lives never to
be filled again,
Her reign now is over, she enjoys
eternal rest,
We know she had to leave us, God
knows what is best,
I found myself again this year
headed for the store,
I couldn't seem to realize Mom was
here no more,
I picked up this lovely card as I had
in other years,
I couldn't even read the verse, my
eyes filled with tears,
So I put the card back on the rack
and quickly walked away;
Perhaps it won't hurt so much,
another Mother's Day.

Margaret Allan
WHERE ONCE WE STROLLED
Once we strolled in Pershing Square,
Crunching the snow, and close
together,
Where a Doughboy patrolled the
frosty air,
Not caring like we, what kind of
weather.

Now it's Spring, and I've come
alone,
Flowers are blooming along the way,
Thinking of you so far from home,
And how we hugged in the snow that
day.

Past the Doughboy where birds
alight,
Coming back for Summer while
skies are blue,
But I was remembering that snowy
night,
And how dear, the love we knew.

Pauline Hakr
GOD HAS A REASON

Dedicated to my son Joey Hakr who passed away May 19, 1988, his wife and children Cindy, Joey and Becky

I walked alone beside the sea and as
I walked there seemed to me
There was a reason,

I lingered there until the sun dipped
in the sea and day was done
There is a reason,

For every grief that bows the head,
for every teardrop that is shed
God knows the reason;

So if we trust God as we should, it
will work out for our own good
He knows the reason.

For every pain that we must bear, for
every burden, every care
God knows the reason.

He rules the seas, the sky, the land,
the moon and stars hear
His command,
God has a reason.

It's amazing and incredible to me but
it's true as it can be
God has a reason.
Oh why did Jesus bear the cross, the
hurt, the pain, and the
Bitter loss,
God knows the reason.

It seemed somehow that I heard Him
say you will not walk an easy way
I have a reason.

Remember this and know that there
will come no grief that we cannot
bear, God
Has the reason.

Toni Figueroa
ODYSSEY OF SPACE
Men boast they've skirt the heavens,
Bragged that they have touched
God's face,
This puny, earthling man, has
crossed,
God's boundaries of space.

Long ago a man named Nimrod,
Built the Tower of Babel high,
So God confused their languages,
Their ambitions had to die.

The heavens are Jehovah's throne,
The earth, He gave to man,
And out of God's great wondrous
love,
God's mercy formed His plan.

Men soar to heights of heaven,
Beyond where eagles fly—
So daring—so presumptuous,
We ask the reason—why?

How long will God, Jehovah,
Permit this flight in space,
Will He destroy—this human ploy
That competes in this vain race?

Matthew E Jackson III
THE BOY WHO FLEW

This poem is dedicated to my Dad, my best friend.

The boy could fly.
Over the clouds he flew,
Higher than an airplane,

But sometimes his mother worried,
Because he loved to fly over the
town.
He likes to feel the excitement of the
town.

Jennifer Cook
UNCONQUERED
Unconquered, uncontrolled, no boundaries or limitations to what is to become of me.
A vast mystery to explore, but there is no mystery to the certainty that grows in my soul. Contained will never be my feelings and emotions.
For a field of flowers overflowing and a stream bubbling down the bank is the feeling of unlimited adventures.
But through the dark corners are shadows who will try to conquer and suppress the freedom of my soul. But the gates to glory will never deny, no matter how rusted and pitted they become.
For underneath lies the unconquered soul of me.

James E Belcher Sr
COPING

To my new love found ahead

Common the journey, same the road.
Common the cross, sharing the load.
Common the thought, following His
code.
Common the place, His heavenly
abode.

Togetherness over, gone the wife.
Darkest and deepest, moment of life.
The drummer stands, less the fife,
In halted march and vivid strife.

Long the day, restless the night.
Eyes in dark, mind in light.
Flash back thoughts, in constant
fight,
Trying to sort wrong from right.

That journey ended, just for one.
Our battle over, her victory won.
With the Father, through the Son.
Another direction, has just begun.

A widower now, dad of three.
The Father's will, it must be
Must put behind, "poor little me."
What lies ahead, I will see.

Teresa Cox
THE RIGHT CHOICES

For Brian and Jill

You shouldn't have to demand love,
It should be freely given.
You shouldn't have to beg for love
It should be easy to take.
You shouldn't have to fight for love,
For there's so much love to share.
You shouldn't have to run from love
Even though it can bring you pain.
You should never hide from love
Nor neglect the chance you have to
love back.
Because love is something we're all
lucky to have and should gladly give
in return.

Karen Pnazek
HOW COULD YOU LEAVE ME?

To Althea Reetz,
because I understand

Who's gonna listen to my stories
about classes and "BOYS" and the
girls I hate at school?
Who's gonna hug me when I'm
hurting?
Who's gonna show me how to
wear make-up and criticize
every one of my outfits?
Who's gonna be my chauffeur?
Who's gonna take me shopping
for my prom dress?
Who's gonna cry at my
graduation?
HOW COULD YOU LEAVE ME?

After I'm a full grown woman,
who's gonna worry about where
my boyfriend sleeps when he
visits for the weekend?
Who's gonna be my role model?
Who else is gonna care about how
my boss is treating me?
Who's gonna be my sounding
board for every minor crisis of
my life?
HOW COULD YOU LEAVE ME?

Who am I gonna fight with over
my wedding plans?

Who else is gonna think my
babies are as beautiful as I do?
Who's gonna tell my kids all
those stories about me when I
was their age?
Who's gonna make me laugh
when my kids are driving me
crazy?
HOW COULD YOU LEAVE ME?

And how am I gonna keep you
alive inside me—and for my
children—every day of my life?

Aldouphus L Williams

Aldouphus L Williams
TOMORROW'S PRAYER
Let's pray today
For a Better Tomorrow.
For time is passing between
the minutes and hours.
Life on Earth may be short,
So listen God's children
And give this some thought.
For today, we live
And tomorrow is not promised,
So let's take to practice
God's word upon us.
And accept it as a daily digestion,
for it is our hope
And our only protection.
So together today, if we may,
Let's take a moment out
On our knees to pray,
that God will make tomorrow
a better day.

Joseph Tucker
I THINK OF YOU EVERY DAY

This poem is dedicated to my wife Lori. She is always on my mind and in my heart

I think of you every day,
Like I have always.
I see your face in mind,
But my eyes are blind.
I feel your arms around me,
But my body is cold and my
arms are empty.
I feel your kisses on my lips
But my lips are dry,
My eyes are wet.
When will the pain that grips my
soul,
Finally subside and let me go?

Michele Godfrey
PSALM IN—TENSION
Who has not listened
Who has not listened
with hearing dimmed
the heralding bell—the crowing cock
almost forgotten in the din?

Plodding along
Simmering along
in fear of passion
the gift of the dog—the defiled dove
diffused in preoccupation.

But on the way
Along the way
crisis unravel
through seasons' song—and sprays
of storms
what beckons from the
denial.

Oft called forth
So oft called forth
from lowly station
the deserts embrace—on humble
rung
intimates of a new liberation.

Bring us again
Bring us again
to surrender's bower
eternal lover—on embered bed
Dayspring e'er in darkest
hour.

Robert L Martin Jr
DO YOU LOVE ME?
Am I what you want for the rest of
your life,
Do you really know me, we'll never,
ever fight.
When you become unsure, I can take
a flight.
Because, at the end of life's roar he
makes it right.

While we're together, I still search
for what I need.
Sometime, I know you don't really
agree.
Then I always let you live your life,
And sometime, to me, it doesn't
always seem right.

Then, if you love me, you know I'll
do everything,
By realizing that I can and will do
most things.
So, do you really love me? And in
spite of all,
You can very well be the sunlight
that shine bright,
In my life.

Robert Arroyo Jr
THE BRIDE
Life,
Oh wonderful Life,
You are my Wife!
Earth and Water,
Our Son and Daughter.
Tree and Bird,
The spoken Spell.
The burning Sun,
Our Guardian Angel
Our Wishing Well.

Scott A Spence
THE PLAYERS
They played the game with nary a
rule.
The subtleties were easy to ignore.
'Twas waveless like a stagnant pool,
yet the wood still drifted onto
shore.
The players were cast on the timeless
stage,
for a performance of epic
proportion.
The controversial script was
designed to wage,
a mirage of intellectual
distortion.
An unsettling clamor, had filled the
air,
for the audience was appalled at
what they'd seen.
They'd been unwittingly trapped
inside the snare,
for their perceptions, had not
been keen.
With sweat pouring down from their
brow,
the curtain was drawn for the
final act.
Blood pumping faster than their
hearts would allow,
with the knowledge of the
ensuing impact.
Their reward was received with the
closing phrase,
for they had reached the level
beyond.
With their mouths open wide, and an
astonishing gaze,
the patrons were unsure, how to
respond.

Robert Arroyo Jr
PURPLE

For Ursula: I still lose myself in your maroon hair and violet laughter.

The color of the sun descending,
Wrapped in a shroud of Heaven's
silk.
The flavor of sudden Spring
raindrops,
Echoing the sweet taste of Mother's
milk.
The sound of songbirds in the
morning,
Nature's joy orchestrated on the
wing.
The touch of the breeze off the ocean,
Like the feeling Love's presence
brings.

Purple!

Scott A Spence
YOU'RE MY . . .

Dedicated to my darling wife Hope. You're my poetical inspiration. HAPPY VALENTINE'S DAY 1989

You're my gentle spring shower,
on my dry parched spirit.
You're my loves' passion flower,
that blooms as I near it.
You're my honey sweet essence,
on my lips as they touch.
You're my strength that never
lessens,
in our unbreakable clutch.
You're my sense of direction,
when I begin to wander.
You're my voices' inflection,
as my heart grows fonder.
You're my eyes that see clearly,
in the fog and the rain.
You're my memories I hold dearly,
deep in my soul, they'll remain.
You're my sip of wine,
that quenches my thirst.
You're my imagination's design,
of what can only come first.

Marty Collier
THE TINY BUD BEYOND THE SKIES

To Michael Brennen—we love you!

The tiny flower that bud so soon,
Is now far beyond the moon.
In a place where he no longer cries,
But laughs with grace beyond the
skies!

He crawls around the throne of God,
No longer on this weary sod.
He climbs upon the lap of Him,
Who loves him so, and made him
win!

He's back in the arms of his dear
Lord,
Playing and dancing and singing in
word,
He's feeling the joy and exaltation
Of praising his God in jubilation!

He's wrapped in love and warmth
supreme,
This tiny bud has been redeemed!
Little hands raised so high,
This tiny bud, beyond the skies!

Ethel M Tinney BA

Ethel M Tinney BA
LOVE IS THE ABDICATION OF KING EDWARD VIII
He left his throne, his realm, his
power, his friends
For one who brought his heart the
joy of love,
Yet, who, twice-married, could not
rise above
Her chided past to be a queen—nor
make amends,
Nor could the Lords arrange to meet
his ends!
Then Edward's royal burdens
weighed him down
'Til, half in hope, he laid aside the
crown
And left his land—to take what
Heaven sends:
Such sacrifice shows Life is made
complete—
Not by the purple pomp of palace
pleasures,
Nor fiery fluttering Fame, nor
fettering treasures,
Nor servitude of many million feet;
But that a fuller life one measures
By little things that do with thrones
compete!

Al Fortaleza
MUSIC OF THE PAST

To Katherine the special person in my life

I hear the music of the past.
Songs of romance,
of love,
of defeat.
The melodies are soft and sweet.
To an older generation
all their hopes and aspiration
have come to an end.
All that is left is the music of
yesteryear
and memories of love, romance and
sometimes defeat.
But don't feel sorry for them.
For if you're young, they ask not for
this.
Only that you try a little bit harder.
Soon your music will be the music of
the past
Of romance,
of love,
sometimes defeat.

Christina Baisley
THE TREASURES OF LIFE
Do you know what to do when the
world crashes down?
Do you think sometimes it's a
dream?
Do you wonder where it is that your
hopes have all gone,
Do you sometimes just want to
scream?

When the world shows itself in its true light
Where do you run to then?
When your life isn't all you had hoped it would be,
Do you find yourself asking why?

Well, I know that some days aren't the best
I know that some hurt so bad,
But life is an uphill climb,
And the only reward you get is satisfaction.

I've been loved and I've been despised,
Sometimes I think it's not worth-while
But then I look up and you're still there,
And I decide to hang around for the end of the show.

Wanda Rutman Shafer
FRESCO (OF HONEYED ICE)
What bitter horse has flowered in the bark
Of rounding steam that confiscates its sight
Whose hoof is crested in the pellet flight
That unwinds its rough curtailment on the loom
In pillowed steps that stretch the bowels of night
(That burnished lantern pulverizing night)

And callowing the orbs of cinctured dawn
In dilate yellow where its hoof has shorn
The snows unreeling plummage in baked ice
And drank the sinews that its foot had worn
In potted hollows honeycombing morn.
FINIS

Maxine J Boman
WHAT IS A TREE?
What can we say about a tree?
It's many things for you and me.

To some animals, a tree is known,
An ideal place to make a home.

The pages of our book could not be,
If God had not given us the tree.

Maybe your bed is wooden made,
But what would you give, for its trade?

A telephone pole, is oh so tall,
Is standing by with grandmother's call.

When out of a drizzle, you may run,
Under a tree you can wait for the sun.

Fishermen, upon the waters, may not row
If not for a tree, to make it so

Branches that blow with such ease,
Can cool down a hot summer's breeze.

In October, when days are bright,
Colored leaves are a delightful sight.

Now we know, and it's true for me
That "only God can make a tree."

Joanne Dornan
A BUSY MOM'S PRAYER
God bless this house
and all its work and toil,
and bless these my children
both big and small.
May their lives be long
on this earth;
May they find happiness
and mirth.
God bless my man,
and may he be happy
with me and mine.
May we make up our house
happy and quite fine.
Amen.

Dolores Torres
DEAR HEART

To Larry, you made life whole again.
I love you, Doris

Broken heart too sore to mend
Came a time to love again

So hard to forget that much pain
Feeling it happen once again

No way to know if it is real
Untold feelings are hard to feel

So Dear Heart please hold strong
Again you cannot be so
Wrong

Teresa A Cox
MOTHER'S REALITY
He was just a boy when he went to war,
Didn't even know what he was fighting for.
In my eyes a child, but not Uncle Sam's;
They sent him away to Vietnam!
Before too long, my son came back;
In nothing more than a body bag.
I should be proud of his courage and sacrifice,
All I knew for sure was that my son had died.

Helen Benlehr
THE SELFISH LIFE
I'm so all alone
And I wonder
How and when did my life
Go asunder
I've lived alone
The greater part of my life
I've had fun
And I've had strife
Yet today I can recall no adjective
To describe my fate
There is no love, no hate
I just tolerate
But I remember and I still dream
Of when we and myself
Made quite a team

Jennifer S Hayes
NATURE'S WONDER
Blanketed by gray
the tree stands proud,
branches jut out
like a defiant chin.
Blossoms,
white as doves,
challenge the gloomy atmosphere.
This creation watches
while clouds kidnap the sun,
and hungrily devour the blue.
It drinks in drops
of rain
like dry, cracked ground
in a desert.
The tree
dances with wind
gyrating left then right,
politely bowing to its partner
when the day escapes.

Mary Ezquerro-Garcia
OUR DREAMS

To Richard, my husband, I dedicate this poem to you with love. May we never stop dreaming.

Our dreams bind us now.
And because of our dreams,
We grow and learn and flourish.
We laugh, for we are free to dream.

Our dreams bind us now,
because in a world of desperation,
We know that there are greater things.
We share our lives, and dream.

Our dreams bind us now.
We dream of many things.
We hope where others fear.
We dream of peace and love and joy.

Our dreams bind us now.
And we know that when we close our eyes the final time,
Our dreams will bind us . . . then.

Janis Hirst Barnett
THY MIRROR WOULD I BE
Thy mirror would I be—
Deep-silvered and
Reflecting
Like a shadowed
Pool at twilight
Look inward seeking.

Thy window would I be—
Unblemished and
Sparkling true
In sunlight and
Rainbow's flash
Look outward learning.

Thy lantern would I be—
Steady and
Unflickering
Forever
Chasing shadows
Look forward unafraid.

Clarisse Marrero
CONSENT OR CONSIDER

To my Mother who gave so much of herself. To my Children with whom I share the dream. And to the men in my life both good and bad, who made it all possible.

What do the trees do when they're fighting lumber jacks?
Do they reach to the sun or hold Mother Earth closer to their roots?
I wonder if they ever miss the leaves they shed
or bid them a happy farewell.
What must a cloud feel when the elements take over?
Do they really want to cry their tears to feed the soil below?
I wonder if they feel the loss of gentle tears that fall
or smile with wisdom.
How difficult it is for me to understand or explain
what feelings stir deep in my being
when you speak my name.
In my search to touch another being
equally as I am touched
I've found the language that I speak barely covers much.
Why is it when I'm in your arms you can simply say you love me,
Words spill easily from your lips so how deep can your feelings be?
To those of us who need to feel and cannot find a label for all the things,
imagined or real, consider things we're able.
And when I have the strength of trees and face what comes my way
and the mystery of the clouds unveils itself in some revealing way
I'll be armed with gifts in my life from the universe above
for only then will I consent to name my feelings love.

Albert Peywa

Sana Padilla
YOU'RE NOT GONE

To my friend Albert "Lerch" Peywa
May his memory live on forever!

No words can bring you back,
But to us, you're not gone,
Because you left with us, Memories
We'll remember for so long.

You had your own way of showing
That you cared—
In the adventures, stories, and advice
That you shared.

The jokes you told, brought a smile
To one's face.
We all know that you're now
In a special place.

We'll see you in the stars,
Up in the sky, flying free,
Remembering how everything
Used to be.

You'll be in the sun,
Shining up above.
Every day and every event
You'll be thought of.

No words can bring you back,
But to us, you're not gone,
Because you left with us, Memories
We'll remember for so long.

Lawrence W Peterson
NEW YEAR'S RESOLUTION
Before this year has passed away
May I resolve some things to do
Things that for others will brighten their day
Helping them along the paths that are new.

May I think well of all I meet
Sending out love to all mankind
With Holy love all sinners to greet
Helping the lost their way to find.

Teach me in deeds to help the weak
And on others kindness to shower

May I be cautious of the words I speak
That in everything my God to honor.

William "B" Mears
COMPARED AND WATCHED

This poem is dedicated to the family of whom I was brought upon. With love and respect, always. Remembering the past and looking at the future to grow.

Compared to what we had.
We all sit and stare the same as always.
Be on top of bricks of real stone,
and always remember the sequence.

Michael DelRussi
SOFTLY JOHNINE

Before the final droplets of our years
Cascade without notice, without echo.
Come softly Johnine, with the scents
And persuasions of your heart, of your deep, tender womanhood, so I might absorb its light even as I fade to black.
Let me hold to the sight of your youth, your loveliness, as I bid my last goodnight.
Come softly, Johnnie.

Barbara Turner
WHO ARE YOU

This poem is dedicated to my children Misty and Jalon Turner

Who are you
Do you know
Are you that someone
I should know

You may be the one in my dream
Or are you that someone I haven't seen
Do you know who you are
You may be that someone from afar

Can it be you are I
Must I say who am I
Looking at you now I know
You're that someone I should know.

Emma Jean Williams
MYSELF

I like myself as I am,

I like myself because there is only one me,
I like myself because I'm 4 ft. 2 in."

I like myself because I'm brown and not blue,
I like myself because I'm not shy.

I like myself because I can always say hi.
That's why I like myself

Because I'm me, not a tree
Just me watching TV.

Joyce Momarts
A CHRISTMAS NOTE FROM THOSE WHO CARE

A Christmas note from those who care,
Is filled with love and sent everywhere
To friends both new and old.

A time to look back over the past year
And hope that the friends we hold dear,
Have pleasant memories to reflect.

The new year is about to arrive
With exciting plans for all.
Will we take a trip, build a house
Or plan ahead for fall?

Great expectations are in our hearts
For those we love,
Knowing we can accomplish it all,
With help from "the One above."

LOVE, JOY AND PEACE, to our friends
In many places,
And hope this finds you all
With smiles upon your faces.

Gary L Millburn
FEELING IN THE HEART THAT SINGS

You may say good bye,
I never will.
You may never want to see me,
One day, I'll say hello.

My love for you is forever,
Maybe not the way you've dreamed it.
My mind will see you always,
My heart will always believe it.

Being married doesn't prove I love you,
Being unmarried doesn't mean I do not.
Love in the heart needs no proving,
Love in the heart needs faith and trust.

These feelings you cannot hold on to,
Like a piece of paper or ring.
These feelings will last forever,
A feeling in the heart that sings.

Ruth E Johnson
BRIDGET'S FIRST CHRISTMAS

It's my first Christmas, or so I'm told.
And I guess it's true 'cause I'm only nine months old
I hear stories of Santa and his sled,
They say he's coming, while I'm in bed.
There's a tree in the corner, with an angel on top.
Everybody's in a hurry, and nobody stops
Grandma's cooking and the house smells sweet
I hope she doesn't forget, that I want a treat
There's boxes with pretty ribbons all over the place
Every time I touch one, somebody takes it away
I'm all excited 'cause Christmas is near,
And Santa is coming with his flying reindeer
I'm in a hurry and can't wait for his visit
Mommy wrote him a letter, and she signed it Bridget
Aunts and uncles and cousins I've never seen
And more keep coming when the doorbell rings
There's got to be more, and I wondered what it all meant.
Till grandma told me about baby Jesus, who was heaven sent
Christmas is over, and I got lots of stuff
I can't wait 'til next year, I can't get enough
I'm tired and I'm glad this day is done, 'cause I'll never forget,
Christmas number I

Sharon R Freas
IMAGES IN THE SKY

Running ever onward
 Chasing eternity;
Sparkling eyes that twinkle,
 The world's infinity.

Ghost riders chasing rainbows,
 Await the golden sun;
On a ball of blue & amber,
 Listen now, and hear them run.

Window of the sun,
 Lender of peace supreme;
A crystal blue celebration,
 Of an ageless dream!

Elmer A Rasmussen II
AGE OF LOVE

I dedicate this poem to "Judie" with my love forever, a beautiful redhead who inspired me for 16 years to be creative.

Age makes no difference,
 Unless it's cheese 'r wine.
'Cause it knows no barriers,
 Between yours or mine.

Age is a meaningless fact,
 Used to determine time.
Weathered 'n processed by nature,
 To span one's lifetime.

Age comes to everyone,
 With different rates 'n speeds.
Always mellowing one's life,
 According to our needs.

Age means nothing in love,
 Even as we're apart.
'Cause people who know love,
 Are always young in heart.

—Bud—

Kelly Kriz
LOOK IN MY EYES

Look in my eyes
 And what will you see?
 A wall made of brick
 Getting higher and higher.
Look in my eyes
 And what will you see?
 A tower of tears
 Ready to fall.
Look in my eyes
 And what will you see?
 A closet full of feelings
 Never to be free
Look in my eyes
 And what will you see?
 A faceless, nameless mask
 Longing to be seen.
Someone please hold me.
 Show me I am loved
 And take my sorrow
 And my fear,
 Away Forever!

Angela Gulley
I WAITED TOO LATE

It's now too late, I've met my fate.
Ahead I see a dark road that I seem to fear,
What are these frightening screams and moans that I begin to hear?
I walk a little way to see what's going on,
I start to hear people crying from living their life so wrong.
My feet have stopped, my legs have stiffened;
All I can do is stand here and listen.
I reminisce and look back to the times,
Why my preacher talked of a life that forever shines!
Before I take another step I think back just once more.
Why wouldn't I live right when I had the chance before.
I realize now that my ruthless mind and cold selfish heart,
Shouldn't have waited a minute more for that new life to start.
I look up, I see Satan awaiting;
For He couldn't wait to see me start burning and screaming.
I have been judged now for a life I once lived,
A life of greediness that never would give.
It's time for me now to live in that lake of fire,
Where the worm dieth not and my heart full of desire;
For the life I refused to take,
For a miserable life I happily faked.
I step into the blazing fire and oh the torturing pain I feel,
If all my friends could see me now, they'd sure believe that God is real.
My body will burn now forever and ever,
And my pleading cries will scream and moan with all the others together.
I look down to the evil one; I believed would give me a happy life,
With a snarl He points his finger and gives me a mocking laugh.
This horrible place that I'm at now is my eternity;
It was my life I had lived that Hell my destiny.

Suzanne Marie Testerman
RED ROSE

For you Garett Burnham, Cathy Blanchard and Michael Green: You are my lifelines, my sanity, and my sources of strength
I love you more than you'll ever know.

You are such a joy in my life
Like the first beautiful red rose to bloom in spring
Telling the world that better days will soon be here.
You're my eternal life-line—constantly pulling me out of the depths of despair
Always leading me to a happier place.
I share with you my joy, and continually turn to you with my pain—
Seeking some sort of comfort and solace in your words.

You never complain or grow tired
You just accept and share my joy and experience my pain as though it were your own—
Never turning away—Always turning toward.
Accept my love and never-ending gratitude
Find comfort in knowing that I'm here for you, too.
Whenever you need a helping hand—
Just reach out—I'll be there.
You see, I've been given such a treasured gift
A red rose forever beautiful—
You.

Johnny Richard Polk
RUNAWAY MIND

Laying through another sleepless night.
Seeing no relief in sight.
Riding the roller coaster of life,
Waiting for the next hill.
Trying to abandon my grief,
Dare not think of knife or pill.
Imaging getting up and not coming down.
Hanging a curve
Falling over
Ground bound.
Life being a series of ups and downs,
Achievements, failures, and changes.
Some say; which God arranges.
God please grant my mind a pause.
Maybe even reveal the cause.
As I lay tossing and turning in vain.
With my mind and heart pouring pain.

Mae Dempsey Lightsey
BEAUTY

In the beauty of the morning
In the early quiet hours
In the silent hush of twilight
Know and feel His mighty powers

In the bird song at day's dawning
In the golden streaks of sun
In the glitter of the dew drops
See art by the Holy One

In each rain drop softly falling
In the wind that whispers by
In the white of the lily
Feel His presence ever nigh

In the thunder and the lightning
In the puff-clouds sailing high
Hear His power, see His beauty
In the bright blue of the sky

In the quiet lonely evening
In the stillness of first night
In the comfort of His speaking
Know that He will make things right

Amy L Clay
SINGLE'S LAMENT

No Matter How I Search,
or How Hard I Try,
Just Can't Seem To Find Anyone
To Save Me From Being An "I."

Lately, It Has Occurred To Me,
That Instead Of Being An "I,"
I'd Rather Be a "We,"

Now That I'm Tired Of Being An "I,"
And A Sad And Lonely "Me,"
Maybe I'll Find a "Someone,"
And Someday Become A "We."

Shawn International
WE AS A PEOPLE

To God, Family, World

We as a people
A whole unity of minds
Should help each other advance by the grace of God.
To the plateau of great opportunities,
Together we can fight our common enemy
So we can live in a world of prosperity
So we may acknowledge one another and be free.

For we have been on this earth for so long
I wonder why we haven't learned to get along
Unity in love, unity in your country
Unity in your family
All of this we need
To make the world suitable for the human race.

Grace F Guindon
THE FLOWER LADY

Written in loving memory of Frances Lowell Smith, who helped keep Fairhope beautiful.

She did her best to beautify
her hometown on the
Eastern Shore
But the "Flower Lady" of
Fairhope will walk our
streets no more.
Now the streets of gold
will be lined with flowers
from her seeds,
And the Lord will surely
smile when He sees her
pulling weeds!

Of singing God's praises
I'm sure she will never
tire,
For now she's a member
of that great heavenly
choir.
Though we here on earth
will no longer see her
face,
I know that in heaven
she has found a special
place!

Demita J Roberts
LIFE AND LOVE

For you shall always hold, that special place in my heart; even until death when we part. Victor Ray'mon Smith

Life is so short; and you are sweet.
Knowing the time shall come when our hearts will meet.
For Cupid, will release an arrow of love, that God has helped to create through all arms of love.
With Love and Affection even at a distance; Truly, knowing there will never be any form of resistance.

Artie Christian
AT WHAT TIME? NOW

A SPECIAL THANKS and LOVE to my maker, my mom Mrs. G Bray also special thanks to my family and friends.

Now is the time to pace, not race
Now is the time to make haste, not waste.
Now is the time to conceive, not deceive,
Now is the time to motivate, not hate.
Now is the time to participate, not wait.
Now is the time to perceive, not receive.
Now is the time to construct, not destruct.
Now is the time to progress, not digress.
Now is the time to strive, to stay alive.
Now is the time to realize, also materialize.
Now is the time to make your decisions.
In order to accomplish needed revisions.
Now is the time to continually achieve,
to make a better world, in which we believe,
now future leaders it's up to you in all you endeavor, in all that you do.
You have a nation of Hope, Love and Prayer to help us all from total despair.

Scott M Snow
HOPE

For the Hope that comes from knowing God's Love personally . . . . Yesterday, today, and forever.

Hope is more than wishing
For all good things to come.
It is so much more than wanting
The things of which there's none.

It must be nurtured, like children
And given room to grow.
It must be given freedom
There's no end that it should know.

Some say there really is none . . . .
If only they could see
It's from their dreams that they deny
That they can never really flee.

It's the stuff that dreams are made
of . . . .
It's from here that faith can
start . . . .
And with hope and faith together
From God's Love you'll never part.

Shanon Peacock
MY HEART

My heart,
Covered in the dust of loneliness,
Untouched by the fingers of love,
Lay on a shelf of rejection,
Shattered into a million
Rose-colored glass shards.
My fragile crystal soul,
Broken by the hard stone
of betrayal,
Frozen by the cold eyes
of contempt,
Lay waiting for the final blows
of repudiation
To terminate the pounding
of despondency
Inside my agonizing frame.
I wish you farewell.

Tyrena M Cross
EVERYONE CARES

To my mother, sister and closest Family—Tyrena 9 yrs old

People who love me always care
People who love me always share
People who love me are always there
And people who love me are willing to bear

Every night Mom is there with warm and loving care. She sings to me . . . .
And I say "I love you more each and every day"!

Micheal J Schelin
A WANDERING

For Dad and For Mom For being there!

The way is clear. The path is long.
Life is short, so come along.
On a journey through both time and space.
To another aura, to another place.
Leave your soul and use your mind.
Drift now back . . . back . . . back in time.
View the world as it once has been.
Full of love, void of sin.
Back to times where few will know.
Crystal chasms, violet snows.

A place of silence and of peace.
Strange wonderful creatures, emerald geese.
Unicorns, elves, satyrs, fairies.
Fresh golden fruit, crimson berries.
Valleys and dales, oh, so green.
Places here that have never been seen.
Relish now, for we must go.
Back to our world of Mother Sol.
Rainbows come and they may go.
Remember the times of the violet snows.

Della Lynne Gavrun
OPEN YOUR EYES

Everywhere I look upon this great big earth I see,
Beautiful things that our mighty God made for you and me.

Trees and flowers,
birds and bees,

But the most beautiful thing that I see,
Is the love between friends and family.
Oh that the whole earth might learn to love,
Like those whose love comes from above;
If we with open eyes could see,
To love each other peacefully;
Then all the world would be at rest,
And we'd all by God be humbly blest.

Glorious B C Bird
BLUEBERRY PIE

Mama dressed me for the fair,
Brushed, combed, and curled my hair.
Daddy said I looked so fine,
Smiled, and handed me a dime.
I heard a man calling from his stall,
"Blueberry pie, come one—come all!"
Now, Blueberry pie is my favorite.
I bought a piece—looked for a place to sit.
Now this I hate to tell,
But I stumbled and fell.
Oh my, what a horrible mess,
And I now have a Blueberry dress.

Jean Ponting
ODE TO THE WORKING PERSON

To those who rise and shine each day
Who come and go to earn their pay,
Of these people we should boast
And raise our glass in merry toast.

To those who must invent a way
To do a job without much say,
It is these people we should host
North and south and coast to coast.

To those who work the nights alone
When the rest are safe at home,
It is they who deserve a rest
A night untroubled, would be best.

To those who brave the cold or the heat
With the elements they compete,
It is these people we should assure
We admire their strength to endure.

To all of us, mighty and small
We do the job, we do it all.
Give us the credit, when it is due,
Not every day, but just a few!

Shirley D Brown
OF LIFE

To LAURA and MARIAN my daughters with love and understanding we have made it through as it should be as it always will be.
MOM

I look outside I see the pain
I look inside I see the same.
If I were brave I would investigate,
But not knowing the answer I feel so safe.

The probing and prodding makes me somewhat wary.
The questions as well as the answers make me
oh so scary.
Am I running from life afraid of failure or success?

With failure you have to start again
With success you can not slow down or stop.
Is there a middle ground upon which I can stand,
Am I there is it here I shall remain?

Dwight L Kemp
WITHIN THE CORE

This poem is dedicated to my three children, Bridgette, Brian and Travis

Down deep within the core, to stay forever without showing itself ever more.

Staying within its crossing line, making sure not to be caught in a bind.

Not to be caught in the world outside, but to stay in a dark place and hide.

Holding back not wanting to take a risk, the long slender creature gives a hiss.

Rendering to itself that it must go, the black snake very slowly crawls out of its hole.

Karan K Jorgenson
GOOD-BYE MY FRIEND

The leaving of a friend always seems to take a part of you, there doesn't seem to be anything to mend the broken hearts, no matter what you do.

Friendships, they must come and they must go, we must wish you well and know that this must be so . . .

And friend, the love I have for you will kindle in my heart and the fond memories of your sweet smile shall dwell forever within me.

Even though I know the time has come for you to part, the love and friendship I have for you will forever be deep within my heart.

You've given me strength when I was weak, the encouragement, to go forward when I wanted to retreat . . .

You've given to me more than you could possibly know and I will treasure this friendship as though it were a pot of gold.

So remember, my friend, whenever you're feeling a bit low, just smile and remember, how much this friend loves you so.

Bruce Pruiksma
GIANTS

the bridge over the hudson unveils
the city's twinkling of giants
in the winter night air:
silent overgrowths unmoved
by the beads of humanity that string the streets.
some, pearls that shine,
some, dulled by grime,
some plastic;
alive in artificial times.
and crowded passions pull for freedom
in the rolling forever of private minds,
at the feet of giants that step nowhere,
and need no coats in the winter night air.

Bobbie Hall
LITTLE ANGEL

Dedicated to the memory of: Jessica Renée Bowman
Nov. 27, 1988 - Dec. 16, 1988.

Little Angel, you arrived so tender and sweet.
You filled our hearts with joy, you made our lives complete
But your stay with us would not be long, and for
The parting soon to come, we had to remain strong.

We loved you every minute, every hour,
Prayed that God would not need another flower,
Nineteen days would be your life span—
Now you are in heaven on high. God Blesses
Our little Angel, the brightest star in the sky.

Fenicia D Womack
FOR ALL THE TIMES

For all the tears I have cried, God has been there by my side.

For all the shame and the pain, God has loved me just the same.

For all the times I felt so alone, God was there to sing me a song.

For all the times I said I will never, God was there through the stormy weather.

For all the times I was talked about, God was there for I had no doubt . . .

that he will always be there
through thick and thin to sing
me a precious song again and again.

Mary M Beasley
MY SON

This poem is dedicated to My Son, James Scott Beasley

It's Hard to find the words to say
just what you mean to us today.

The years have quickly passed us by.
We've grown together, both you and I.
Good times we've shared and some bad too,
but with God's help we've made it through.

This one thing I want you to know;
it has been as pleasure to watch you grow.

We wish for you the very best,
for you have truly passed the test.

As your days of school will end
and your future shall begin;
take pride in everything you do;
goodluck, God's speed, we all love you.

Regina V Kozak

Regina V Kozak
HYMN: DEMENTIA PRAECOX

Paradox in the cell black;
Mind a shrieking dissonance of thoughts;
Heart disconnected with frailties;
Eyes pale wide in sleepless dreams.
Afraid to be beaten past the checkmate,
Afraid to be brought to the knees in weak defeat;
In the streaming existence of souls,
In the thorough complexities of living,
We sleep not for fear of vanquishment.
Those conquered are those lost;
The lions are awaiting.
Striving on with endless passions consuming;
Carrying arrogance and patronization;
Bestowing supplication to none.
Onward march—soldiers of antiquity.

Sandra Crenshaw
LIVING IN A SHADOW

As I lurked in the shadows of uncertainty,
Afraid of my own destiny.
Total annihilation . . .
Gave way to grave frustration.
Due to lack of desire
I felt uninspired.
Worthless, it seemed.
Identity was but a dream.
However, should I express
These feelings I've long regressed?
Aloof, I remained
Though never again contained.
Free . . . to be me.
. . . I like what I see.

Patricia Paulley Hayworth
IF YOU EVER LEAVE ME

To my husband, Gene, for a lifetime of love and seven Beautiful children.

Take the sparkle from a rainbow
and the warm rays from the sun
Take the sweet smell from the earth below
When a summer rain is done

Take the color from the flowers
And the wind that blows in Fall
Take the joy from all my hours
Leave no memories to recall

For if you ever leave me
This is just how it would seem
Everything would cease to be
Like waking from a dream

So if you really love me
Then never make me cry
Let happiness surround me
Don't ever say goodbye.

Jessica Belle
WHEN I GROW OLD . . . . .

In honor of my loving grandma Hartley and grandma Rubenstein.

When I grow old
I hope to keep my sight.
If not, I'll remember the beautiful blue sky,
And gorgeous green grass.

When I grow old
I hope to keep my hearing.
If not, I'll remember the birds' chirping,
And the water crashing against the rocks.

When I grow old
I hope to be able to walk.
If not, I'll remember walking through the freshly cut grass,
And running through the shallow water of the beach.

But, if when I grow old
I can not love.
I'd not try to remember when I could
But turn and ask for mercy.

Crystal Ann Perrelet
FRIENDS

A friend is someone you can tell things to . . .
You can tell friends secrets . . .
And lots of other things too . . .
Friends are people you should be thankful for . . .
So always remember the golden rule,
"Do unto others," and as you would have them do to you . . .
Treat your friends with respect,
and a little kindness too . . .
And you'll find that this kindness will find its way back to you!

Dannielle M Powers
WHY ME

As I turned around;
I walked into the sunset.
Leaving him slowly.
Tears rolled down my cheeks,
my heart broke in half,
why did this have to happen to me?
The strong feelings between us
bound us together forever,
or at least I thought so.
When she came in between us;
our thoughts for each other
Slowly disappeared.
She tore us apart,
and now I have him no more.
Why did this have to happen to me?

Vickie J Kimber
LITTLE ONE

Where are you?
My lost little one
Where have you gone?
For you're not here
You've gone to a place where
I cannot be with you
I'll never be able
To hold you close

Or give you a name
I feel empty inside
Good-bye little one
Someday we will meet
In a holier place
But until then
Remember this
My little one
Mommy and Daddy love you
Good-bye little one
Good-bye

Renee Gibson
YOUR LOVE

This poem is dedicated to Robbie

You took your hands
And held me oh so very careful
You turn my blue skies
Into sunshine
And you turn so many frowns
Into smiles

You just took your hands
And built love all around me
You've stopped the worse pains
And pushed back the worse rains
You have done so many things
My precious loving being

You then took the tears that
I've cried
And showed me how to turn that
into pride
You were always there
To show me that you care

You took my downs
And showed me how to turn them
around
You took the angels from above
And gave me your love

Iva Davenport
TO SHARE FOREVER

Dedicated to "Lee" my wonderful husband.

The smell of a rose
The beauty that it holds,
The sparkle I can see in your eyes:
How warm a summer breeze
How deep are the seas,
How far is a bright sun lit sky.
That's how much I love you
That's how much I care.
Forever I will need your love,
And for eternity
I'll be there.
No more than I do
No less than I say,
You're in my every thought my love,
You fill my heart every day.
You strengthen my day
You light up every night
We've set a strong foundation,
And now everything seems just right.

Moira Girard
HERO

Is this the hero I prayed for?
He looks little like the knight
of which I dreamed.
No great stallion.
No armor of gold
No gleaming sword
To vanquish the foe.
Thieven honor.
Barbaric grace.
An Ogre's manners
A young boy's face.

Deanna L Cox
A LOVE NOT YET FOUND

The stars were bright, and the
crescent moon
was a shade of pale yellow against
the black sky.
The trees could be seen on the
horizon
with the help of the dim light cast by
the moon,
and though there was little foliage
left on the branches,
it was still a peaceful sight.
But not all things were as calm as the
night.

The bitter cold fought its way into
your body
and into your mind—almost numbing
it,
and somewhere a young woman was
crying.
Crying over loneliness, over a love
she had not found yet.

She was surrounded by people who
loved her,
but yet it made no difference.
They all had someone to share their
thoughts with—
someone to share their dreams with—
someone to hold.
She had no one, and for her
the bitter cold was not enough to
numb the pain.

Nathan McKinney (age 10)
BEASTS

I've met every beast from mountain
to shore.
They've growled and they've roared,
But never a hint to what the heart has
in store.

I've met every beast from mountain
to shore.
They've shoved me and kicked me
and shoved me some more.
But I know it doesn't really matter,
'Cause their hearts are as big as
Saturn.

B T Leedy
THE DISCOVERY IN THE PIT

I was ship-wrecked—many years
ago.
The shore—I floated to—was a cold
place—I wished not to be.
For a dreadful occurrence would soon
confront me,
Being weak, hungry, and barely
alive,
My mind, a blank, of what would
soon arrive,
upon me, as I lingered there, in a
forest of old.
The ground was bare, the temperature
very cold.
I entered an opening, sensed a
familiar smell,
I looked left, then to the right, there
was a trail,
up a grade, leading to a pit.
Drawing closer, I detect a fire was lit.
Movement occurred down below,
I observed it, in the glow,
as it began to spin round and round.
A figure appeared. It motioned me
down,
Hesitant, I froze, I was scared.
A moment later, again the figure
appeared!
Saying, "Come down to me, so I can
glide,
from this grave, and to your side."
Again, I was shaken, I hesitate.
I stand there frozen and wait,
For I recognize this angel, from the
hole,
Who came from below.
To tell me, she still loves me so,
Although, we were ship-wrecked
many years ago.

Deborah Burgamy
ODE TO ALL DIPPERS

Listen potential hunks and you shall
know
Of the fine times you miss
When you dip that ol' skoal.
It's hard for a woman
To use all her wits
When she's continually worrying
About what's mixed up with your
spit.
Now it may not sound fair,
But it's certainly true.
How can your sweetie
Have sweet dreams of you
When your mouth is full
With a big old chew,
And even you don't know
What you are going to do
With the spit and the drool and the
leftover mess
When you've finally convinced her to
say the big yes?
Now think it all over,
Now think it all through.
Which would you rather have—
A woman or a chew?

Doris Richards
THE LITTLE LEAGUER

Dedicated To My Grandsons Cory and Jeremy Bentley

His is just a little guy;
but watch him catch that
baseball, as it
falls from the sky!
He may tumble and fall, but nothing
stops his scramble, to get that ball.

When he is up to bat;
he keeps his eye on the ball!
As he swings, he is sure he has
a good hit!
the out fielder misses his fly ball,
and his little feet take flight!
He runs those bases, with all his
might!

"He's Safe!" calls the umpire;
and raises his hands!

He has scored; and the big smile that
he wore, told everyone; he
would be back next week,
to play baseball some more!

Rudy Beltran
A WINTER'S SUNSET

To my loving wife, Severa Beltran, Thank you for all your help.

As golden autumn leaves cover
The lifeless yellow ground
And the bare lonesome trees
That appear only as a shadow
On the not so distant background.

I see one or two clouds
That humble over them
And the once hot and sunny sun
That now is all but gone.

A winter's sunset now appears
Leaving me breathless,
As I await for morning's dawn.

Rosemary Karlik
MY PRECIOUS GRANDSON

To Benjamin who is my precious grandson—Poem composed when he was 15 months—Today Ben is 12 years old.

When I hold and cuddle him,
And squeeze him to my heart,
A surge of love flows through me,
That no words can impart.
The love I have for this small boy,
Can never be defined.
All I know I couldn't love him,
Any more if he were mine,
But he has a loving Mom and Dad,
Who worship his every step,
But I'm his loving Grandma,
Whom I hope he'll never forget.

Sharron Sharp
WITH WARMEST AFFECTION

I feel something is wrong.

I know our schedules are
not always compatible, but when
we first met there was time
for talk, cuddling, and warmth
(even a show and dinner.)

There appeared to be potential
for a meaningful friendship.
Has my lack of communication
(inner feelings) caused you to
distrust my intentions?

If this be the case, would
our friendship warrant you
helping me learn to express myself?

Shirley A Jakimowich
"MY" MOTHER

Dedicated to my mother—Marie Masa—born in Czechoslovakia, March 6, 1904
Died in Tucson, Arizona April 30, 1988—Poem written in 1979

She always has time for a cheery
"Hello"
And a minute to stop for awhile.
She's really sincere with the people
she knows
And it's never a bother to smile.

She's just herself without acting as
such
And has always a hand to lend.
And the trials that life brings never
burden her much,
For she treasures dearly her friends.

She measures her richness in
gladness and health,
Always willing to settle for less.
Bringing kindness and laughter to all
whom she knows.
This is her happiness.

What difference the smallness in
what she can do.
Her motto is to "LOVE ONE
ANOTHER"
Hers is a treasure that's cherished by
few.
This wonderful woman "MY
MOTHER."

Ken A Rhodes
WINDOWS OF LIFE

Not just another World Series going
on,
this one is taking place on my
parents' front lawn.
How I hit that ball so far, is really not
that clear,
sailed all the way through
Mr. Johnson's window
that he held so dear.
What could be so important about
this window pane,
that would make an old man almost

go insane?
He sat me down, I thought it was the end,
but then he began talking as if I was his friend.
He said, "Son, to you it may only be a piece of glass,
but to me it's a window of my past."
"When I look out this window, what do I see?"
"Children running, laughing and playing, all the things I used to be."
"Don't get out much and no one comes by,
just look out this window and see my dreams and memories fly."
As the time goes on I look back on the story I was told,
and think how lucky I was to be a six-year old.

RoseMary Polando
STILL WILLIN'

To my parents and my little girl, Pricilla, as well as those people who believed in me; Aunt Gloria and Celia Pratt. And last but not in the least, that "special" person in my life.

The memories we've shared
Will always be there
Looking at your face
Takes me to that special place
Where you and I
Used to cry and even tried
To work things out
But instead our love took a wrong turn and went about
Different ways
And played different games
Your big eyes
Made me realize
That we were wrong
And now you're gone
We've shared a lot of good scenes
Even our expectations of goals and dreams
Maybe, we weren't meant to be destined together
Hopefully that doesn't mean forever
I wish we were still willing
To share those loving feelings!

Georgia Maloney
MY ANGEL WINGS
Daddy please forgive me, for leaving you today,
I didn't mean to leave so suddenly that way.
Jesus called me home, and now he takes care of me you see,
And he gave me, my own Angel Wings.

Please give mommy a hug and kiss for me and hold her tight,
And don't let her be lonely tonight.
Tell her there is splendor and there is beauty here in the sky,
Sorry that I had to leave you, that I had to die.

When you and mommy are lonely, just look, up at the stars,
And the two of you can see, I'm not very far.
You would be very happy if you could hear me sing,
Oh so proud of me, with my Angel Wings.

My little spirit is there with you, in my empty room each day,
Please don't forget me, when you kneel to pray.
Jesus puts his arms around me and holds me while I sing,
Oh so proud of me, with my Angel Wings.
As time passes by, some of you will be with me soon,
And I can take you through the golden rooms.
I'll lead the way to where the heavenly chorus sings,
Watch your eyes light up, when you see my Angel Wings.

Barbara Annette Williams

Barbara Annette Williams
A WOMAN'S REVENGE

Dedicated to Diane Farmer of GSU Business Publishing Department who has given me much encouragement and support in all I endeavor.

When the absence of youth,
Robs you of all you've got
I will stand and watch you rot .
Lies, your allies; you pretend is true,
The hurt you've caused runs very deep,
I'll get my revenge, 'cause I'm all you've got.
Never toy with a woman's affection.
Give all of yourself or keep it!
We want no love that is not true.,
Any more than you want rejection.
You set the pace for my hate!
Now you will get just what you're due.

Carmen Mozena
PRAYERS
If you want to be truly happy
As through this life you roam
You must keep your eyes on Jesus
And that beautiful, heavenly, Home

You must make time for prayer & praise
And give thanks to the Lord.
Leave all the sins of the world outside
And feed upon his word

Don't forget to have a talk with him
In the quiet of the night
He will always listen to you.
And he will show you what's right

God always answers prayers you see
But not always for what you pray
He knows the things we really need
He will answer them someday

Sharon Morgan
I AM
I am the rainbow playing in a child's tear.
I am the rain softly hitting the ground.
I am joy; there is always hope.
I am sorrow; I sometimes cry.
I am love; peace only do I give.
I am hate; I sometimes conquer.
I am the waters softly singing a song.
I am the waves playing all night long.
I am the sunshine breaking through the day.
I am the trees playing with the wind.
I am the air which all things breathe.
I am the stone crying to be set free.
I am a child's smile—joy only do I know.
I am a child's frown—anger I now feel.
I am the tears softly falling from Moon's eyes.
I am peace being granted to the world.
I am war—fighting one against another.
I am the life that is given to you.
I am anything you want me to be.
I am the heart of the world.

Pamela Carpenter
THE ALMIGHTY GOD

Dedicated to Terrie & Juanita, my parents who with love and understanding taught me to love God and to follow in his footsteps, to eternal life, peace & happiness.

Upon this rock I shall build my temple;
the gates of hell shall not prevail.

For I'm stronger and mightier than he,
that lurks away in the deep darkness of the sea.

The time will come when the war is over and the victory is won.

Don't fret or be afraid; I'm raising up the strong and mighty from the dead.

I have the power to loose and to bind, to build-up, to tear down, to shackle in chains, to set free, for
I am he—Alpha & Omega the beginning and the end.

Dorma Grossnickle
THE DEPRESSION

To my father, Forrest Creecy

I'm a depression baby, know what that means?
You're at least 50 or more, so it seems.
I think I was happy, can't recall being sad,
We didn't go hungry, the days weren't so bad.

Daddy worked for the government, the WPA,
Forty dollars each month was his take home pay.
Our rent was $5.00, can you imagine?
But then it seemed like a lot to fathom.

I remember meeting Daddy each day after work,
He'd hand me his lunch pail, it was our own private joke,
There's something for you he'd say with a sigh,
And sure enough, he'd saved me some pie.

The train didn't stop in our little nook,
They'd drop off the mail bag on a large hook,
We'd wait for the mail, Daddy and me,
Maybe this time there would be something to see.

No need to rush—there was no place to go,
No TV to catch, no picture show.
They tell me the times were hard back then,
But we had time for each other and our friends.

Never again will time like that be,
We can never recapture nor our children see,
Time almost stood still at such a slow pace,
Wish we'd bottled it up for the whole human race.

Walter Love
GENIUS

To my complete happiness, my wife, Daniella, You and I Rockie.

Love my God
Love myself
Love my people
Love my knowledge
And the wisdom
To understanding.

Catherine P Paul
MY NUMBER ONE

Dedicated, With All My Love To: My Son, Michael.

I look at you
Your eyes aglow,
And wonder how
You always know.

Just what to say
To make my day,
To make the pain
All go away.

Your eyes are bright,
Your smiles they shine,
Sometimes I can't,
Believe you're mine.

You run and play
Without a care,
Your toys you must
Though learn to share.

Someday you'll know
Just how I feel,
This joy I have
Inside is real.

Until that day
Comes for you son,
You'll always be
My Number One!

Therese M Baxter
DAWN OF THE DUSK

This poem is dedicated to my mother who instilled in me the love of nature.

The dawn of evening hours
signals the ebb of daylight's powers;
now is the time, as nighttime begins,
for forgetting all hassles, the whole day's chagrins.

The peace and serenity of the night
unfolds, the sunset's a beautiful sight;
subtle pink hues, pale yellows and blues
help obliterate bad scenes you saw on the news.

Nighttime enfolds you, arousing your senses,
your eyes start to wander from well-worn park benches
to nature's own beauty; the flowers full-blooming
and scenting the night air for fireflies swooning.

The whip-poor-will rises with sweet melodies,
so glad for an audience, eager to please;
the crickets awaken and, taking their cue,

they join with the wildlife to serenade you.

The air becomes lively with
nature's night song
as they herald their god-head, so
proud and so strong,
and thank him profusely, each
in his own way,
for the dawn of 'their' nighttime, the
end of the day.

Rhonda Marie Reed
MY WORLD
If there was a world
Where there were no wars
And no destruction
Along the shores.

If the world leaders
Could gather 'round
and calmly watch
Snow fall to the ground.

In a world where
Peace is what you see
In that world would be
The place for me.

Vanessa R Buffaloe
UTOPIA & YOU

This poem is dedicated to that mystical place in one's imagination that holds the inner peace that keeps us together and makes us what we are.

What is this place
that takes one away from life's
bitter realities?
That soothes the tediousness
hustle and bustle of an everyday
routine,
and provides calm feelings of peace
and tranquility?

What is this place
that has no sense of time?
That knows beauty lies deep below
the
surface not just in physical
appearances,
but also in the imagination of the
mind.

What is this wonderful, mystical
place
where nature sings of purity and
happiness
and gives thanks to God for all with it
has been richly blessed?

Is there such a place
where one can visit to find
this uninhabited sanctuary?
to seek its refuge, honesty
amongst its glorious serenity.

Yes, Utopia's the place.
Where gentleness is effervescent
perfection's tried and true.
Utopia, which shares the same
common virtues and likenesses
I most admire in you.

Faith L Bowers
THE BARE BEAR

To Michael James Andrew Adams,
my most loyal fan.
Love you, Ma Ma

I once heard of a bear who had no
hair.
I guess one could say he was
frightfully bare.
His skin was pink and blushing fair,
He'd rather slink than take a dare.
(No coward for sure, it's just that he
could not bear for all to see.)

He found a cave, and with a frown
He curled up and settled down.
His bed was hard, and soon he found
He could not sleep upon the ground.

What would he do, that hapless bear?
He couldn't wait to grow new hair.
The winter storms were coming on,
Whatever would the poor bear don?

What luck! A hunter crossed his path.
All bundled up . . . A coat at last!
Without ado, he claimed his fare,
And guess who ended up all bare?

Across the hills in birthday suit,
The hunter ran in hot pursuit
Of one fully clad, contented bear,
Dressed in plaid without a care.

Corinne Nawells
POEM FOR THE BLIND
All the beauties of creation
That God gave to you and me—
The birds, and flowers and trees, and
such
Are lost to those who cannot see.

So as a Poet I must write
From a different direction,—
Not about the things seen by sight,
But of those we seldom
mention—

The softness of a Butterfly's wing,
The fragrance of a flower,
The songs that all the songbirds sing
As they fly from bower to
bower.

All of these, too, are Miracles
Of hearing, touch, and smell
That exist in Mother Nature—
For God made <u>all</u> of them as
well!

Carol Cameron
WAITING

It hasn't been so long ago they placed you in my arms. How beautiful you were, how warm and good you made me feel inside. That sunny sweet smile and occasional stormy temper made my days a joy.

I really didn't mind all the dirty diapers and bottles. The bubble gum stuck to beds, tables and floors. I even learned to tolerate the smell of sour apple gum. And, I really didn't mind going to school when you dug up the floor hunting buried treasure.

What I did mind was the days passed too quickly and before I knew it you were a young woman and going to have your own baby.

I'm so sad and so happy at the same time, I wanted you for mine for just a little longer, I wanted time to spend with you that I never seemed to have, Now I'll have to make up that time through my little girl's, little boy. I already wonder what he will look like? Will he be dark like me or light like you? Will he love me and cry to spend holidays and summers with me?

We'll go fishing, we'll play baseball. I'll even learn to like football. I'll try to love him without being overbearing and overprotective. I'll spend the time with him, that I somehow let slip by with you, but I'll know when to let go.

It won't be long now until he arrives. Just a few more weeks. I already love you little one and feel like I know you, even though you're not here yet. I've felt you kick and can't wait to hold you in my arms, but the greatest joy of all will be one day to hear you say, "I love you, Grandma."

Chuck Kiefrieder
WHAT WE COULD BE

All my words for all to learn from.

Will we ever worry about the end;
Or some day maybe we'll all
comprehend;
That as one civil race we will live
If only we learn not to take but to
give
To help each other one and all
And keep our backs from against the
wall
From the stress and strain of
everyday living
We should receive some of the
reward for all our giving,
If we could only learn to unite,
And do away with all the fight,
There may be a chance for the future:
If only we keep away from
something nuclear:
May be space will be the answer,
If we don't all die from cancer.
When and if we come to a solution,
That will be our biggest contribution:
We can do it if we try:
So don't sit down yet and cry:
To know that God is with us is very
essential:
Now all we have to do is, reach our
full potential.

Vashni De Schepper
TO RETURN AGAIN
Dust, mere red dust
to be blown about the earth
by the silent wind and then
rejoined with the soil again
so we may grow again
in another time
and another form.
This is our last chance, our fate.

Arlantha J Baldwin
ROSA WAS TIRED
Working all day body in pain
Cloudy outside looks like rain
Off at last on her way home
Probably wishing her shoes were
rubber foam
Rosa was tired

Fare in her hand waiting for the bus
Just want to get home not looking for
a fuss
She sat down where there was a
space
I bet her tiredness showed on her face
Rosa was tired

The driver said get up for you must
stand
She said no and I need no helping
hand
He then walked away she still not on
her feet
For when he returned she was still in
that seat
Rosa was tired

Faith C Howard
THE SEACOAST TOWN
Did you ever know that stillness
that seems so nice around—
And the lapping of the waters
as they spread toward the sound?
Have you known the sun drenched
splendor
of that fine and rugged coast,
And all the weathered beauty that
New England shores can boast?
Have you watched the lone gull circle
to sweep the summer sky,
And dive so poised and purposeful
and never wonder why?
Have you sat on the old stone wall
as errands you would go,
To village store, or just for mail,
beneath the elms you know?
How warm it was, the old town dock,
how wonderful the sun!
And you wished that your vacation
had only just begun—
Ah me—if time could but stand
still—
and life was just for pleasure cast—
That you could take it leisurely
and never pray that it would last!
The world is all so far away
beneath that summer sky—
Where God paints clouds and waters
for
the folks like you and I.

Ranee Long
HIS UNCONDITIONAL LOVE

Dedicated to my eight children, Drew, Radell, Gary, Valene, Brenda, Rick, Tonia and Pam

I love my precious Savior
For his unconditional love,
As he suffered, bled and died,
Obeying his Father above.

No greater love has no man,
Than the love he gave to me;
When he prayed and wept alone
In the Garden of Gethsemane.

Beaten for no reason,
Spat upon—betrayed,
As his cross he bore
While for my sins he paid.

Brought as a lamb to the slaughter
Did not change that love so true,
As he pleaded, "Forgive them Father,
For they know not what they do."

May I have that self same love
To guide me through this life;
A will to love my neighbor,
Helping him in times of strife.

Lien Nguyen
TO SAIGON, MY LOST CITY

This poem is dedicated to my lover who had died in the Battle of 1975.

Saigon, dear capital town of my
nation.
You were called "the Pearl of the
Extreme Orient"
You survived through many foreign
invasions,
But Helas! You are now captured by
tyrannical politicians!

Saigon darling, you watched my
peaceful, innocent childhood,
My enthusiastic, adventurous
teenager during the war.
You witness my courageous,
continuous hard fighting adult,
And my lover's heroic death on the
day you were conquered.

Saigon, when leaving you, I confided
in your trusted hands
Hundred and hundred of acres of

fertile farm land,
A beautiful castle surrounded by all kinds of tropical plants,
A department store, a famous restaurant, and a sandbag factory.
Those were products of my stiff labor years, as you could see.

So embrace my honey's body tight, and hold my properties firm.
As I am always hoping for a nearest victorious return.
For the USA 41st President proclaimed, after he was sworn:
"New Breeze is blowing, a world refreshed by freedom seems reborn."

Saigon darling, you will be emancipated, you will be free
Because in this talented new elected leader, I believe
Saigon, in my dreams, I saw you wearing a gorgeous triumphal gown
Opening widely your arms to welcome exodus people back to your town.

Keith L Coe

BUT I PAY MY CHILD SUPPORT

For my daughter and son, Tabatha and Travis, and Fathers who don't get to see their children.

Another Christmas holiday has gone by,
Again, I sit at home, all alone and cry.
"Is it fair?" I ask, when the Judge may say,
"You're to have your children on every other holiday."

BUT I PAY MY CHILD SUPPORT.

Well, I remember of that painful day of long ago,
When the courtroom became our soap opera show.
Why, it didn't matter what each person did.
The Judge sat high and listened to our bid.

BUT I PAY MY CHILD SUPPORT.

The arguments are over, the Judge made his decision.
For whatever was decided, he did it with precision.
It didn't matter if he did it to me.
There are other Fathers it happened to, you see.

BUT I PAY MY CHILD SUPPORT.

The children are hers with no hesitation.
And all I get is scheduled visitation.
"Hey! That's not fair, it's not right!"
"Why, it was me who tucked my kids in at night."

BUT I PAY MY CHILD SUPPORT.

It's been——years now and no children in sight.
What does the Judge say, "Well, it's alright."
You pay your support and the children you'll see.
She has it her way and keeps them from me.

BUT I PAY MY CHILD SUPPORT.

The law says "You must pay" or go to jail.
Miss one payment and the cops come, like a storm of hail.
But what happens to her when visitation is denied.
The courts do nothing, our hearts have cried.

BUT I PAY MY CHILD SUPPORT.

The Fathers of this land want justice and equality.
After all, the children are just as much our family.
They've been taken away, no justice in sight.
For the Fathers (such as me), a long and bitter fight.

BUT WE STILL PAY OUR CHILD SUPPORT.

Oh, how I remember those voices so clear.
Coming home from school, year after year.
"Hi, Dad! I missed you . . ."
"Hey, that's great! And I love you, too."

BUT I PAY MY CHILD SUPPORT.

Now, the children are gone, across many miles.
How painful it is, I'll never see their wonderful smiles.
A candle is lit, each and every night.
And dreams of their faces.
Oh! What a beautiful sight.

BUT I PAY MY CHILD SUPPORT.

If things are allowed to continue at its present rate.
Before you know it, we'll all end up at Heaven's gate.
The children will no longer be lads and lasses.
They will have grown and passed all of their classes.

BUT I PAY MY CHILD SUPPORT.

But one day will come when you hear their voices say,
"It's not your fault, Dad.
We're here today."
Whatever has been done, we know is not right.
"We love you, Father, Hold us, in your arms so tight."

"WE KNOW YOU PAID OUR CHILD SUPPORT."

Toi L Vines

A WALK DOWN THE HALL OF LIFE

I once was wandering with no aim
Through a hall with many doors
And all of my life I searched for the one
I had to return to once more.
And all this time I somehow knew
Of the immaculate things I'd find,
And I knew of the ones waiting there
I had, at one time, left behind.
And now I have found the ones left to dwell
In such a fine place as this,
And they're showing me things in this wonderful world
I never knew that I missed.
Now I have found that in the spiritual world
Is where I have longed to be,
Because the spiritual world expresses and is
All of what is me.
I sometimes laugh because I just found out
That this is where I belong.
And it's funny because I just now realized
that it's been there all along.
Well, I guess I just didn't look hard enough
For what is so very plain to see,
Because the gift of life in the spiritual world
Was hidden inside of me!

Pauline (Denney) Burton

Pauline (Denney) Burton

A TRIBUTE TO MY CHILDHOOD

To my family

A child could never be more lucky,
than to be reared in the state of Kentucky.
Where the gentle summer breezes blow,
in winter season there is beautiful snow.

I grew up in a two room cabin with Dad and Mother,
along with a sweet sister and two fine brothers.
We worked our small farm for what we did eat,
never went out into the world to lie and to cheat.

Mother and Dad have long since been gone,
but their love and their honesty will always live on.
Through the years we children have gone our separate way,
but fond memories of childhood are as clear as today.

Our destination is Heaven if we be so lucky,
holding second place only is the state of Kentucky.

Ann D Walker

NOT ME

This is dedicated to the ones I love My Grandchildren—My Inspiration

There's a certain little fella'
That lives within our house.
You can never see or hear him.
He's as quiet as a mouse.

He has very dirty fingerprints,
And dirty footprints, too.
We often find things missing,
As a glove, a comb, a shoe.

He plays with Nana's jewelry,
He leaves the room a mess.
He spills the milk, the juice, the chips,
But never does confess.

It seems he does so many things,
And yet it doesn't seem
He's ever there when Nana says,
"Who'd like some more ice cream?"

Just ask the kids the question,
"Who's guilty?" And you'll see
They're quick to give an answer
And blame it on "Not Me."

Diane Wright

HUG BUGS

As a token of my love and appreciation for all that God has blessed me with, I dedicate this poem in honor of Him, and also to my parents whose belief in me made my dream a reality. All my love, Diane

God sent hug bugs down to earth
To tend to children's needs;
He wanted every child to have
A life filled with hopes and dreams.

So in planning for these hug bugs,
God thought, "I'll make them big and strong
For my children will need someone
When sometimes things go wrong."

These hug bugs will be special;
Their love will grow and last,
And they'll give my precious children
A caring home in which to rest.

Then my children will learn sharing,
The difference between good and bad,
And the hug bugs that my children love
Will be known as mom and dad.

Children, love your hug bugs,
For they're God's gift to you,
And remember that their opened arms
Are a sign of God's love, too.

Catherine A Oberdorf

STREET PEOPLE

Deep in the night they wander
No family or no friends.
Walking down the winding road
Not knowing where it ends.

Their home is in the open
In streets or in the parks.
They carry their belongings
In bags or grocery carts.

The clothes they have are tattered
Lucky to have shoes.
Their warmth is found in boxes
Or yesterday's old news.

They often beg for money
To buy bottles of wine.
Maybe that's how they've learned
To shut off their minds.

They live from day to day
Not knowing what to do.
Until they find their way
Remember they're people too.

June Branch
BELIEVE

To my husband Joe who believed in me, when myself and others didn't. I Love You.

In a confused state of mind,
I stumble in the dark,
Down a long dark road,
Not knowing where to go.

My heart is heavy,
My eyes full of fear,
Afraid of the future,
Nothing's very clear.

The bitter cold I cannot feel,
My heart is heavy
And I cry a tear.

Walking and wondering,
Not hearing a sound.
The night is so quiet,
When you're all alone.

I look to the sky,
And pray out loud,
"Please Lord, give me strength to carry on."
I hear a voice inside my heart:
"Believe in me, and I will help."

Down a long dark road,
Not so alone . . .

Gloria Khan
MY EPITAPH
Here I lie, now all
of bone
To which place do you
reckon I have gone?

To the place of Glory shown?
Or to the wrath of fiery drones?!

Mildred L DeMarco
POET, PAINTER, AUTHOR
The poet's soul is in the poetry that he writes,
As the image of himself in a mirror that must always be right.

The painter expresses his soul on the canvas that he paints, with the wondrous spectrum of colors from the morning until the night.

The author's soul writes prose which ever it might be, fiction or non-fiction as to his own fancy.
His books are read and reread for the whole world to see, and so basks in all his literacy.

The poet, painter, author are three souls as one, together they gather the cultures of the world as ever to be renown.

Michael C Nelson
LOVE IS FOREVER
They say love is forever . . .
I'll love you until the day I die.
But death is the beginning of the end.
I love you now and I'll love you then.
I just pray that it'll be a short time apart because the time will bleed my heart.
But when we unite out of the years of darkness there will become a magnificent light, bright and golden as the stars on earth. A new beginning, a new birth.
The Doves will fly, the rain will cease.
Unto the heavens our love will release . . .
At last . . . loving peace.

Donna Hemans
THE WOES OF A HATER

To my parents who have miraculously succeeded in their duty as parents.

I have no cares in this wide, wide world
I have grown to hate.
My best I have kept hidden for fear I fail,
My friends I have neglected for fear they care;
I have grown to hate.

The mother witnessing the murdering of her child,
The wife remaining silent to keep her husband,
A friend lying to save a friend;
These things I cannot understand.
The starving child of a barren land,
The homeless man with an upturned palm,
Those fighting oppression,
Those fighting to praise their God;
I have no care.

You ask, 'How can you not care?'
I answer, 'What the world has taught me I have learnt well.'

Beverly Jones Trotter

Beverly Jones Trotter
LET IT SHINE

To my 2 babies Quacy and Clarice I love you.

I've often heard that the Sun will come out tomorrow.
But it can shine today if we release all sorrows
"Let them go," "let them fly,"
For sorrows can be lessened with a little sigh
Oh! But how the wind does blow
For it breezes by the water and calms my spirit so
Yes, the Sun will come out tomorrow and every day
Because you've let go of the brassiness and put all hurt away
There will be times of sadness and times of "NO PEACE AT ALL"
But you can keep your balance if you just stand up and call,
"WIND, SUN, FIRE, RAIN," all elements of Earth
Guide me, lead me, carry me across, heal me for all thy worth
If my destiny be sorrow, then so it shall be
But I will do my best to "LET THE SUN SHINE ON ME."

Wallace J Dawson
BLACK AND WHITE SQUARES

Dedicated to the most valuable players in my life Carla, Oriana, Samuel, Tabitha

You take the first move and I'll take the second one
Don't catch me I'm falling. don't trip me I'm on the run.
Life is like chess, in war they'll get your best
The pawns are pushing on, turmoil turns them on.
To castle your king you've got to move your rook
Knights are coming on, you hope no one will look
As time becomes a factor and all the frustrations
Your rook had taken a back road and stopped my expectations.
Talking black and white squares countries and people
Sometimes cold stares some people bleed for.
Squares are empty now, countries and people gone
No more empty stares, they all were looking on.

Karen W Killeen
THE LAST ROSE OF SUMMER
The last rose of summer, I put on your grave.
Knowing your love, a tear comes to eye.

I miss you so much, the children do too.
How cruel is life to take you away.

Sorrow and pain, will hurt you no more.
I hope you're at peace, awaiting in sleep.

I wish that you knew, the loss that I feel.
And the last rose of summer, laid down beside you.

Lisa D Johnstone
SOMEDAY
Someday I'll forget
All that we've been through.—
My life will go in a new direction
And I'll be over you.

Someday I'll plant some new seeds,
Ones that will really promise to grow,
And form into a new life,
And I'll be able to let go.

Someday the sun will shine,
Pushing the dark clouds away,
And shed some light on new endeavors,
And help to lead the way.

Someday I won't remember,
What you've done to me,
And I'll forget the reasons,
I had to set you free.

Someday all this will happen,
And I'll find someone who's true,
But until that someday will appear—
I won't stop loving you.

Kenny Kelly-Starchild
THINKING OF YOU
I couldn't express it if I couldn't see,
This strong picture of you and me.
I can't explain the way I feel,
It must be true I know it's real.
It seems as though you came from a dream,
I have feelings for you if you know what I mean.
I want it to stop, I want it to end,
I should relax and let us be friends.
No way is it easy you're pounding my heart,
If I can't have you it will tear me apart.
Don't be surprised by the words I say,
I have feelings for you and here they will stay.
Your smile warms me, your eyes give me chills,
Your love to me is a positive thrill.
Now that I've expressed it I hope you can see,
the picture I have of you and me.

Frederick Reed
FINALLY SEEING LIFE

To my loving wife Tracy: with whom I've finally seen life. I love you

Reality is based on the fact of existence;
Existence is based on dreams.
Dreams are based on showings of love;
Love is based on the fascination you have for yourself and others.
The point I'm trying to make is . . .
How can you love someone before you love yourself?
It takes a willing mind, pure endurance,
and the capability to identify the signals your heart gives.
You learn to love others, before you love yourself.
Some may think this is a lie; let me prove you wrong.
There's difference between love and survival.
Survival comes natural; yet love is a must.
Sometimes in survival, you feel you can't go on.
But love gives you that extra energy, to make another step
I have that love, it has given me the will, the strength to survive.
In this life & time. "THAT'S ALL THAT MATTERS."

Stella Ferry
GOD'S WILL BE DONE!

Dedicated to my beloved and sweet husband Maurice Aloysious Ferry, Jr.

My dear husband's death came as a shock,
My life seemed to stop—just like a clock.
He had been sick for seven long years;
I loved caring for him, but I had my fears
That he would die, his body wracked with pain
And become senile before awful death came.

But God answered my prayers late one night
When death was near, but out of sight.
My husband was smiling and happy too
As I kissed him good-night—his eyes were so blue.
In the morning I jumped awake with a start—
I knew something was wrong; I felt it in my heart.

He looked content and peaceful, just lying there.
He's gone—I always knew my heart would tear.
Then, without warning, peace flooded my soul,
I had prayed day and night for such a goal.
A happy death for my sweet loved one,
He died in his sleep—God's will be done!

Richard C Stewart
AND (IN) JUSTICE FOR ALL

Do we truly distribute equal justice, or is it possibly just reserved for a few?
The fact that it's supposed to be for all of us, is the only reason that I ask you;
For beginning with a theoretical right and wrong, we must then determine what is fair,
And finding mutual agreement in that alone, is something that is rather rare.
From there you go forth to the public, where things instantly begin to change,
And although you may have initially agreed what was, here things no longer remain the same;
Because what's good and equal for one, isn't necessarily good and equal for all,
Which immediately creates conflict in the ideology, of liberty and justice for all.
However that isn't to say we shouldn't try, which is the point I'm trying to make here,
A question which only leads to another question, with answers we all have moments to fear.
Simply because justice for one isn't always justice for another, this I know for a fact is true,
And if at one time it doesn't affect me, you can bet that it's going to affect you.
Which is why it is so important to resolve the issue of balance, before it gets too late,
However, in our desire to find peace and happiness, oftentimes it's a nightmare we create.
Which ultimately forces us to ask, just who is knowledgeable and righteous enough to judge,
When two people claiming to be honest and fair, discover they have an irreconcilable grudge?
Obviously part of the reason being the influences of morality, & its impact on decisions of justice
And individuals' various interpretations, camouflaged with the phrase of "please just trust us."
Which pretty much brings us back to where this all started, and basically leaves things unchanged
Along with an innumerable variety of extremes, all of which occurs in justice's name.
And indirectly might mean that there is no true justice, at least in a theoretical sense,
Unless we are willing to base its definition, upon the proverbial jurisprudence fence;
Leaving it all open to situational interpretation, by those who society feels they can trust,
As well as leaves us without an absolute definition, something I personally believe to be a must,
And yes I understand the many advantages, to common law by circumstance and situation,
But at the same time that leaves us little alternative, but for justice by cultural creation;
Which possibly could lead one to believe, that there is no such thing as justice for all,
And so it is we have begun to legally run, before we ever even began to legally crawl.

Thomas Francis Mortimer III
MY ONLY DESIRE

This poem is dedicated to my only desire in life, "Deborah Lynn Yorck"

She's more beautiful, than any words can express, the thought of her makes me happy, when I feel depressed . . .
She brings the sunshine, when clouds fill the sky, she's all the warmth, when it's cold outside . . .
She's the flower that blooms in the spring, when I feel like crying, she makes me sing . . .
In my heart, she burns a fire, she's all I need, "my only desire."

Fred Kunzi
DREAM TIME IN RED MAN'S LAND

This is a strange and silent land:
deep gorges, cut by nature's hand,
contorted cliffs are reaching high
and seem to touch the endless sky!
Red veils of sand are rippling by,
the riverbed is parched and dry.
Up there along the canyonwall
dark, painted figures, standing tall,
tell stories of a distant past,
of hopes and dreams which didn't last.
Faint trails, laid down in cold and heat
and used by restless, sandaled feet
they zig-zag up to the plateau
and vanish in the long-ago!

The sun shines hot and blinds my eyes . . .
my mind hears drums and mournful cries
up yonder by a burial mound,
then suddenly a passing cloud
casts shadows like a somber shroud
upon this lonely, sacred ground!
The Ancients' souls are going home,
I feel their presence . . . then I'm alone.
Up to the cliffs, which reach so high
their spirits soar and touch the sky!

Adam D Larson (Age 13)
THE LIGHT OF LOVE

For Death is overwhelming darkness; feeds
Upon the heart. It swallows up all joys
Of life and makes it desperate for needs.
It frightens people from old men to boys.
You cannot see it but you know it's there.
It waits and hopes to take the life of some
Poor lonely soul who is in great despair.
It tears apart the light of life and comes
To torture men that feel they need a rest.
It causes pain before their time to die.
But after passing on they find the best.
The everlasting light that is so high
Among the rest. It conquers all above.
Oh yes, how wonderful! The light of love.

Jeremy T Spence
THE FINAL RACE

Dedicated, with hope, to the children of the future.

In my dreams I see the pictures of the day the fires come
And I wonder what will happen when all is done.
I see many people running with their children at their sides,
But you can't escape the day of falling skies.
You can't escape the day,
The day the planet dies.
About the children of the aftermath
Living in the waste
Their thoughts will be survival
Not which side won the race.

Erwin Keus

Erwin Keus
FALSE HOPE

Praise be too what
Amen too whom
So—
Hide behind those men who speak
In their voices lie the coins of the weak
So each coin magnitudes—
False hope?

Then here is my coin
For I too am a weak dope . . .
Damn—

Susan Kasprzak
JUST TO SAY GOOD-BYE

Improving all aspects of life
—Man's Discoveries.
All the great walls and barricades
—Man's Architecture.
Weapons become art forms of deadly precision
—Man's Achievements.
Good-bye to the families as they scatter with the winds.
Good-bye to the cool night breezes rippling through the trees.
Good-bye to the warm summer days fishing in the stream.
Good-bye to Nature's children playing around the world.

Such a wonderful world we create;
Razing all that man once held so dear . . .
Say Good-bye!

Denise Thompson
LIVING A DREAM

As I sit here watching "Days of our Lives"
I think of my own, one not so bright.
I feel trapped from head to toe,
A feeling of fright about something I don't know.
I live by day, and cry by night,
Hoping that one day everything will be right.
But sometimes I feel that I'm just living a dream,
A dream that seems will never be true,
Oh my god! What am I to do?
I know there's a place I should go,
But I really can't because my cash flow's low.
So tell me, tell me, please lend me a hand,
Let me know where I stand.

Sian Jones
WILDFLOWERS IN FIRESCARS

Beyond were the azure hills,
Simple risings of soil
Woven into plains of wildflowers
Burned golden and
Sunburned foxglove.

The plow did not return
To turn up the meadows
But laid instead,
Half-buried in the charred ruins,
next to the cracking plaster face
With ash-darkened eyes.

Raymond Lee Clifton
THE BLOOD

To my Mother, Neva Lovette-Lee; to my sisters, Barbara Clifton-Hockenbury, and Tammie Clifton-Polanowski; to my brothers, Dr. Randal Robinson, and Mark Andrew Lee; to my grandmothers, Mable Lovette and Helen Clifton, I love you . . .

High in the mountains, by a snow-fed stream,
Cloudy dawn, blasted, by a terrible scream,

Crashing down the slope, running under aspens' bud,
A flying mane, a coat of red, dark, like blood.

Seventy-two seasons in his majestic day,
Many sons and daughters, from lovers along the way,

Dancing, he moves, magic, pounding hooves thud,
A black stallion awaits below, for the blood.

Tail streaming, head proud, nostrils flaring,
He charges to the challenge, bold and daring,

Kicking, biting, stomping, rage in the mud . . .

Reason doesn't matter, to a stud,

A virgin filly the prize, her secret flesh sweet,
The champion will know her, the other defeat . . .

On battles the warriors, offspring of Noah's flood,
The victor walks away, behind, lies dead,
The blood . . .

Virginia M Long
BLESSINGS

This poem is dedicated to my husband James, children Rodney and Deborah.

I look out and see the glory of the morning.
I look out and see the beauty of the day.
I look out and see the magic of the Lord's performance,
I stand in awe, of all He gives us every day.
The Many flowers blooming in the spring time, the sights and sounds, of winter left behind.

Summer comes He gives us rain and sunshine,
Yes, all these things are free, they're yours and mine.

Autumn brings the gift of many colors.
He fills our sights with paintings every day.
He gives us time to gather our harvest.
For all these things, I gladly sing His praise.

With winter comes a feeling, of thanksgiving,
a time to ponder, season's left behind.
And a time to thank our blessed Savior,
for all these things He's given, are yours and mine.

Betty Gibbs
BORN AGAIN THAT DAY

To Elna Albers who turned I think I can, into I know I can

I get up in the morning
Waiting for her call
Just to hear "I love you"
But it never comes at all

Then darkness surrounds me
The memories flowing through
My mind still cluttered up
I can't believe it's true

I knew that God had sent her
For me to love and keep
But can't you tell me why
My feelings run so deep

I remember the words you said
He will always be with you
God never closes doors
Without opening one or two

He understands you're homesick
And that she seems so far away
How you wish to touch her
But He needed her that day

I listened to your words
And as I heard you say
Don't you know? She didn't die
She was born again that day

She was born to be with Jesus
A price she has to pay
When He reaches down for you
You will be born again that day.

Jean Futujma
A MOTHER
God giveth strength to function with hurt and pain.
No one but a Mother could feel the one she gave birth to struggle for life.
To live amidst the fear of the unknown with hope and faith in God,
We show no pain as we give courage and praise . . .
So they may continue to fight the lonely battle they face each day.

Cynthia E Libby
GO IN TO TOMORROW
Walk on by, my little one,
Go beyond my sorrow.
Walk on by this path I tread.
Go in to tomorrow.

Take the tools, the lessons learned.
Keep them by your knowing.
Walk in to the future ways.
Go and keep on growing.

Don't look back. Don't worry; none.
Keep your link still glowing.
Chain on chain back through the years,
Each one forward flowing.

Once was ours to forge ahead.
Once was ours for going
Pass it on, my little one.
Keep tomorrow growing.

Walk on by, my little one.
Go beyond my sorrow.
Walk on by this path I tread.
Go in to tomorrow.

Carrie Yotter
LOST
Where am I going?
How will I get there?
Will you really be with me?
Or will I be walking solo?
The road is never ending,
I don't know what to do.
I need you here beside me
I'm feeling very blue.
I don't know how to tell you,
How much you mean to me.
I don't know how to say it
I need you here with me.

Barbara Casey
BECAUSE MY LOVE

Dedicated To My Husband David

Because my love you are the one,
With whom my heart's had so much fun,
I write this verse with love endured
While not in vain how it's matured.
The night we met if not by chance.
When Cupid himself wished us to dance.
From that time the days we shared,
Will grow with Love and show we care.
All the thoughtful and kind things you've done from the start,
are tucked away safe and warm in my heart.
Yes Dear, you've entered my life and taken the lead,
To care for my life, to fulfill and need.
So Thank you from me for bearing the load.
I love you forever however it's showed.
Because My Love.

Leisa Bain Good
I LEARNED TO FORGIVE
I learned to forgive . . .
Myself today.
And, oh, what a bouquet!
A bouquet of flowers!
A bouquet of life!
How good I feel.
His peace is real.

Jan Lopez
MY GRANDFATHER

To my grandfather, Frank Ornelas, whom I really love a lot. Love always, Jan

My grandfather is really great, he's No. 1 in any rate!
He loves us a lot I can see, he's the best grandfather—and always will be!
I help him a lot when I can, he is surely one nice man!
On April 1st he'll be 99 years old, looking at him is like looking at gold!
His eyes shine bright in the light, and he has a wonderful site!
Being around him is so much fun, I have a grandfather that's No. 1!
He goes to some places that I go,
He's really super, everyone should know!
He congratulates me on things I do good, he does what every grandfather would!
What he says and does is always right, he uses his will, power, and might!
His family would like to say, Happy Birthday and many more to come your way!

Mary Miller

Mary Miller
THE MAKE-OVER

To Melvin, my wonderful husband, whose special love, super manners and constant devotion, have made my life happy and complete.

You must bow down and humbly pray
Ask God into your heart today.

He can move mountains out of your way
He can do this in a single day.

God moves in and touches your heart
Satan moves out, he must depart.

This Make-Over is a spiritual one
Coming from God in giving his Son.

Alice Kinter
PETS
Our first dog
Her name was "Dusty"
She was black as coal
But didn't turn rusty.

Tami's Christmas Joy
She called him "Chris"
Up high he sat
Like a Siamese king.

Sam's mutt "Pespi"
Light brown and curly
Tossed his dishes
High up topsy-turvy.

Co Co Brown is
Chocolate coloring
When the phone rings
She barks like crazy.

Grand-cat Frisky
Black, hails from Germany
Grand-dog Sheena
Black, from North Carolina.

Susan Hand
PS.

ps.
my longing is born
of depths unknown
of ancient ageless
timeless eternity
not understandable
to my mind only
to my soul. your
smile gladdens me
your voice beckons
me your arms reach
for me and hold me
close while your kiss
searches my soul
and finds my
ancient hunger.
sh.

Lila Fay Rogers
I HAVE CRIED MANY TEARS FOR HER DEEP PAIN
A Villanelle upon the Untimely Death of My Paternal Grandmother During Childbirth

I have cried many tears for her deep pain,
Although she left here before I came
I pray that her suffering was not in vain.

I have seen her in the sunshine and the rain.
Her life was not always a cheerful game.
I have cried many tears for her deep pain.

I have known the thoughts of her fevered brain.
She whispered her new-born baby's name.
I pray that her suffering was not in vain.

I have felt the futility of her weak body's strain.
Her having to leave then was such a shame.
I have cried many tears for her deep pain.

I have believed greater heights are for her to attain,
Because her good deeds here brought her little acclaim.
I pray that her suffering was not in vain.

I have looked at the tomb in which she has lain.
Maybe a new time will come for her to claim.
I have cried many tears for her deep pain.
I pray that her suffering was not in vain.

Kimberly J Jones
DEAR JESUS . . . THANK YOU

A special dedication to my parents, Tilmon and Betty Jones and to everyone at the Ravenna Church of God, for encouragement and support.

As I watch the early tide
flow out to meet the sea,
I often think of Your love
which You have given so
abundantly.

I want to take this time to thank You
for loving a sinner such as I.
For You proved your greatest love
for me
when You gave Your life to die.

Since I have come to know You,
You have been the best friend I
could ever have.
For when my heart was troubled and
heavy laden,
You would always listen and
understand.

You are everything I've wanted in
life—
peace, happiness, love and more.
I could never live without You, Jesus,
the King of kings and Lord of
lords.

Now with You in my heart,
and the feeling ever so sweet,
I know, I will never be alone . .
For You—
Make my life complete

Lydia Alcorn
SHE SMILES WITHOUT THE PAIN

In memory of my Mother, Fannie Cunningham Withers.

As Mother lay helpless in her room,
I watched her for quite a while.
What was very hard to understand
Through all the pain she'd smile.

She must have known relief would
come
As she looked beyond my face,
Because when she talked of going
home
It was to a better place.

As sure as blue skies follow gray
As sunshine follows rain
My Mother's body is at rest;
She smiles without the pain.

There's an emptiness inside me
As Mother's Day draws near.
There is a feeling of loneliness
To lose one so very dear.

Flowers bloom and fade away,
But memories will remain.
There is relief in knowing
She smiles without the pain.

Joseph M Taro
HAPPENINGS OF ME

There were two chosen people
For his earthly life,
They were, Joseph and Mary,
His child bearing wife!

He came on to us,
On a holy night,
Angels sang and told shepherds,
To follow the light!

He went to the River
Where he got wet,
Then the heavens opened up,
Father and son met!

Put on this Desert Land,
A period to fast,
Tempted by a common foe,
A confrontation at last!

Destiny led him to Galilee,
Saying, "Come with me,"
They left their fishing boats,
And went with thee!

He reached out his hand,
With all his might,
Then touched their blinded eyes,
And gave them sight!

He went to a mount,
And started to pray,
If it's your will Father,
Take it away!

He had enough of this,
He helped the slaves,
Then some words of wisdom,
That he rightfully gave!

He was sent to Pilate,
Without a single crime,
Next he went to Herod,
He knew the time!

Soldiers seized a traveling man,
Simon was his name,
He walked up the hill,
Ahead of the frame!

His lips began to thirst
He sensed cheap wine,
Then his eternally holy word,
Completed the true line!

What had happened once before,
From Mary's blessed womb,
He did the very same thing,
From the dreadful Tomb!

We have a wooden Cross,
Hanging from our wall,
Its everlasting symbol,
He loves us all!

Anita Kowalski
AN UNFULFILLED DESIRE

An unfulfilled desire
Laced with inspiration
Crushed by downfalls
Yet never diminishing

Part of the struggle of life
All that I exist for
A part of me day in and day out
Yet, a constant turmoil

Splinters of failure
Blind my eyes
My mind and soul still search
In spite of my setback

My existence wills it to continue
The unseen, unheard longing
For all my life I yearn
An unfulfilled desire

Virginia L Foster
GENTLEMAN GOD

Gentleman God stood to open the
door,
but I pushed on blindly ahead.
I didn't behave in a ladylike way.
I grabbed for the door knob instead.
Oh that I'd wait for His care and His
grace,
so We might flow in One accord.
Like some human planners, I don't
mind my manners and wait for my
Gentleman Lord.
God didn't break in when He saved
me from sin,
but His own precious blood
sacrificed.
All strength is His source. He does
not love by force,
but in power by the Spirit of Christ.
"Savior teach me how to wait upon
You;
to be gracious, as I ought to be—
to allow You to lead, knowing how
much I need!
Holy Gentleman, You are to me."

Peter G Matutino

Peter G Matutino
DON'T THROW IT ALL AWAY

We've been through thick and
thin
Life without you is a sin
Love it comes and it goes
Like morning and night We
don't know the consequences

Don't throw it all away
Please please stay
Don't throw it all away
It'll all come back one day
Don't throw it all away
Stand by your love come
what may

We've got a good thing going We
can't give it all up now
Isn't it wonderful for what we've got
And we've got a full pot
Which overflows with faith

Susan L Keller
ASHES

Memory's ash filters
Down from my mind
to settle at my feet.
Trudging through grit
I am careful.
It will not do
to disturb the smoldering
embers of pain
And burn my heart.

I sift through the soot and
see the souls of women,
two in particular.

One a war-bride child-mother
Hoping for peaceful domesticity.
Instead, a war poisoned husband
returns
To work or not, feed them or not, but
Always to drink.
A man in pain who
Framed the lives of a
Gentle woman and their children with
sadness.
Wasting love, energy, hope.

Young women grow old and
Live alone.
"I want no more husbands to
look after me," she said.
"I can do better for myself."
Her life played out in whispers and
Sighs of stories for her grandchildren.
Dust of dreams was in her heart's
corners,
Carefully swept, seldom disturbed.

She survived with herself then
Died with herself
Alone, naked on the floor, cold tile
Against the flesh of her life, done.

Her daughter, dreamer of undone
dreams
Found her, mourned her, buried her
And part of herself.
"I cannot live," she thought, but did.
Pain recedes, days proceed and
custom calls
A mother to cook and clean,
Wash and mend, comfort and love.

All this she did for
Me.
Damming her pain, containing her
emptiness.
Saving it, savoring it.
Where was the white knight
She had married?
Only a man remained of a
Dream.
This woman of myths, reader of
legends, kept
Searching for the could have been
that
Couldn't be.
Unreality.

She survived with herself then
Died with herself.
Consumed from within by disease
and regret,
Almost alone.
Cradled to sigh her last breath
in the arms of the
Fallen hero.

Here I am rooted.
Conceived in love, nurtured in
Sadness.
I must reach into the flames and
Extinguish the fire of anguish
I suffer for their unfinished lives.
To move on and be what I am.
Mother and wife,
Enabler of life, a
Writer of words,
Reaching up from the embers,
Reborn from the ashes to
Live with myself,
Fulfilled.

TSarah M Humphreys
TO THE PLANETS

Venus on the lake of time
Ever flowing with beauty and grace

Jupiter the great laughing man
You have made my life a joke

Uranus won't you mix for me
A potion to stop the sands of time

To keep the rickety skeleton
From slicing me with his scythe

Mercury his quick silver messenger
Will bring me roses black as night

While I shall not find a poem in
Neptune
For my enchantress is not the sea

Mars and his mighty fire
Is the lure for me

I hear the beauty calling
As the sea will play my song

But fire is my making
It rages deep within my soul

Clare Hunter
FACADE
Upon waking from the dream
I rearranged my mental scheme,
and the truth in my head I put aside
while my outer facade I once again applied.

Oh, the way my lips and limbs have lied
and all the while myself denied.
Sad no one has yet known
what a backward image my life has thrown.

Slipping back into the realm of sleep
the tenant in my mind began to weep,
and drowning in my own sea of wonder,
slowly, quietly was pulled under.

Joyce Dawe
BIRTHRIGHT
This is my heart
pumping the blood
that courses my veins.

This is my mind
held in my brain
beheld by my heart.

These are the genes
giving me
my individuality.

Other parts of this being
are mine invisibly
incapable of vision or decision;
equal and vital parts
of the person you see
as me, completely.

This is my body
given me by my mother
and that given by her mother
and that by her mother's mother
and so on, eternally.

This is my body exclusively.

David McGaughy
WHO OR WHY
Who will tell
the hungry child
Why there is no food
Looking at
his glazing stare
The truth not to elude
Who will tell him
of the waste
Prevailing in the land
Or that nothing
can be done
While pushing back his hand
Who will explain
to little ones
Of all the rising costs
While another
grave is dug
And another life is lost
Maybe the question
isn't who
Maybe it is why
For they trust
the one on one
Response of you and I

Fern Gardiner Murphy
LIFE ETERNAL
My friend do you know Jesus—?
The Son of God above.
He gave His life to save us
By showing us His Love.
And if you do not know Him,
You'll miss the Joy of Love—
And you won't be up in Heaven
To share His Glory there.
I beg you reconsider—
What God tells everyone.
You can't get up in Heaven
Except through Christ, God's Son.
So change your life completely,
And be assured to know.
We can all be up in Heaven
To share His Blessings there.

Mary Broderick Muntz
DADDY'S STAR

In Memory of my Father John Paul Broderick

When I was a little girl my Daddy told me
about the stars in the heavens above.
He said that the stars that were up in the sky
are the nightlights of those that we love.

Daddy was always one of those guys
so it seemed that everyone knew,
and if you were in trouble and a dear close friend
he'd have taken his shirt off for you.

He was a wonderful father and a good husband too,
and a proud strong man deep inside,
but when it came down to say "I LOVE YOU"
he never had nothing to hide.

I will always remember the things he taught me
and all of the love he had shown,
and I'll do the very best that I can
to pass it on to my own.

Now when I walk out into the night
and everything looks so very far,
I study the sky and in the moonlight
I look and find "Daddy's Star."

Michelle Lee Alano
WHY?
Why do thoughts of you still linger
in my mind?
Why can't my heart forget about you
and just leave you behind?

Why do days drearily wear on?
Why do I feel empty with you gone?

Why do I feel lonely and scared?
Why do I feel as though our love
should have been spared?

Why do I feel this way?
Why do I think of you everyday?

All I can ask is why?
Why is it so hard to say good-bye?

Timothy Dennis Bryan
MIRROR OF TRUTH

In memory of Emma Dinius, a wonderful poet and our mirror of truth.

I look in my mirror everyday,
'Cause this thin piece of glass has something to say.

It talks to me loud, It talks to me clear,
It tells me the things that I want to hear.

It tells me I'm good, It tells me I'm bad,
It tells me I'm happy and it tells me I'm sad.

It tells me about life, It tells me about me,
It shows me my appearance that other people see.

You have to understand the importance of this thing,
And the truth to your self that this mirror can bring.

For you have to look in your mirror and like who you are,
'Cause dissatisfaction and hate for yourself won't carry you far.

You have to look in your Mirror and like the Image of you,
Or your hopes and dreams will never come true,
And you will live in sadness, always to be blue.

Jeremy Miller

Jeremy Miller
UNTITLED
When your Mom says "I'll go warm up the car,"
But finds out it won't start
And you're late for school.
When turning a corner too sharp on your snowmobile,
You tip over face first in the snowbank.
When you are driving up the snowbank with your three-wheeler,
Then you find out that you are not going anywhere.
When you go out to the fishhouse for 5 minutes
With your new Polaris,
But you can't go back home because it won't start.
The sun comes out and the "fun" melts.

Donna Lea Jones
OBSTINATE PEOPLE
Obstinate people,
Believing all you hear.
Convicting and condemning,
Even those who once loved you dear.
Who made you judge,
With a heart that's hard and cold?
Picking away and tearing,
Trying to fit me in your mold.
My life's been different,
Circumstances unknown to you.
For your pessimistic mind,
Of the real me you'll never have a clue.
So go ahead and talk,
You've never any good to say.
Don't forget the good Lord is watching,
And will remember Judgement Day.

Heather Michelle Tuomala
SUMMER

Dedicated to my parents, Michael and Marilda, and to my two grandmas, Grandma Linda and Grandma Esterline

Walk through the meadows,
Cool and sweet,
Don't close the windows,
Feel the breeze.
Summer is coming,
You can feel the heat.
Hear the birds humming,
There's no more sleet.
Children are shouting,
Hooray, hooray,
Summer is coming,
Today, today.

Brenda D Jackson
MOON RIVER
Its water glistens in the night,
as the stillness touches shorelines.
Upon its bank shadows dance
under stars. Follow the winding
of waters and be led to a rainbow
of colors at its waterfall.
Cascades of blue, green and silver
shine in the moonlight.

Lisa Marie Shaw
LET IT GO
A life inside of me
A heart beating strong,
A baby girl I nurtured
I had waited for so long.

She breathed the air I breathed
And felt the emotions I felt,
When she'd kick me with her little legs
I thought my heart would melt.

One day I woke up to find
That God too wanted that special girl,
It felt like He took her right out of my arms
Like He'd ended my whole world.

For years I couldn't conceive it
And thought I had nothing to give,
But, finally my dad gave me his talk
And I realized it was nothing I did.
Now I realize that my life is full
And I have to let go of that day,
I can now hold a child happily in my arms
And smile my own special way.

I love you Mikkila Elizabeth
Even though we have to be apart,
Be proud of your mother for letting go
Though, you are forever in my heart.

Larry Glenn Wininger
I'M JUST ME

Dedicated to Karen, that special one I've waited for, wanted and dreamed of all my life. I wanted her to be my life, all my tomorrows, and my wife, but all dreams don't come true. I love you, Babe.

The world is full of people who want to be like someone else.
They want and try to be like others, and not happy being themselves.
I walk my own path, and do things in my own way.
If I make or mistake, then I learn for another day.
I'm just me, and don't try to be, or want to be anyone else.
I know who I am, and what I am, and I'm content just being myself.
I know what I'm capable of, and my own abilities and limitations.
I have my own dreams like everyone, but no real great expectations.
I'm not one that thinks I'm perfect, and I'll never claim to be.
We all fall short of perfection as I do, I'm not perfect, I'm just me.
I don't pretend to be something I'm not, 'cause I'm not much, just what you see.
I'm nothing, or no one special, and I'm just what I am, I'm just me.
I don't follow fads and fashions, and I do things in my own way.
I've got my own style of sorts, and I don't do, and think as others say.
I don't do, or say something just because someone else does.

I'm not one way, or another just because someone else was.
I don't agree, or disagree just to disagree, or agree.
I speak my own mind, and opinion, and I'm just me.
I don't try to impress anyone, 'cause I've got no one to impress but me.
I'm not rich and famous, or handsome, and I'm not that talented,
I'm Just Me.

Jessica Dawn Carner
MY SECRET ROCK

I have a secret rock where I can go and play,
Outside by myself, all day.
I can see ants go by all in a row,
And bees and bugs and well, you know.
I can be here and play what I like to do best,
And look at flowers, trees, and empty nests.
I sit on my secret rock and then,
I see a bee on a tree.
I run in the sun,
And I have fun,
My secret rock is big and gray,
And I can't wait 'til school is out in May.

Ida Mae Bienz
A RANGER'S LAST STAND

Dedicated to all Texas Rangers

As the moon climbed high in the starlit sky
And peace lay on the sleeping town,
Three riders paused on the brow of the hill
And sat grimly gazing down.

All was still on the moonlit hill
As time fled swiftly by,
The three sat motionless, listening, intent
On the breezes' whispering sigh.

The leader stirred. The three then spurred
Their horses down the hill;
Making no sound as they rode along,
They stole like wolves to the kill.

They paused before the bank's barred door
and dismounted stealthily there;
They drew their guns and with tools in hands
They entered the bank with care.

They opened the safe door and piled on the floor
The bags of gleaming gold.
Then packed it on their horses and fled,
These night riders, fearless and bold.

The country around was terror bound
By their cunning and fierce cruelty,
For they plundered and killed with wanton hearts
and mocked with savage glee.

Ever winning their loot, they rode the owlhoot
And laughed in the face of the law
As they tortured and killed all who stood in their way
With the cruelty of the Falcon's claw.

But, at last, one was here who knew no fear;
He was only a brave Texas lad;
But he wore with pride a Ranger badge
And swore vengeance would be had.

Through aspen and birch in ceaseless search
He at last found the outlaw camp,
He patiently awaited the thieves return,
Though the night was cool and damp.

The hours marched on. Now nearing the dawn,
His quick ears caught the muffled thud
Of the horses' hooves of the owlhoot three
Who had brutally shed so much blood.

Confident, unaware as they approached their lair
That, at last, their cache had been found,
With curses and laughter they came to a halt
And lifted their loot to the ground.

Tex drew a deep breath for he well knew that death
Would soon claim some of them here;
He sighted his guns o'er the top of a rock
And his voice rang out calm and clear:

"You buzzards, reach high if you don't want to die;
You've reached the end of the trail."
At the sound of his voice they whirled, guns in hand,
And lead flew like screaming hail.

With steady hand he took his stand
In behalf of peace and law;
His guns flamed death at the murderous crew,
All swift and sure on the draw.

In bloody strife he gave his life
To defend his Ranger star;
With smiling lips for a task well done
He crossed the Final Bar.

Mrs Vineler Mann
A SIMPLE PATTERN

I made myself a dress today
I hear that somefolks can't
Well what would I have to wear
If these things I could not make.

I have made my clothes all my life
Well I guess I know myself better
than all those famous designers
who have never seen this body.

I know where to take it in
Or where to let it out
I can make the hem up high
or put it to the ground.

You can buy your own material
Any color or any print
You can sit down and make it
And enjoy the time you spent.

When you walk down the street
You won't meet yourself coming
The designer makes a thousand dresses
by that one little simple pattern.

michele booth
SILK'N'SCRAPS

Fine wines and caviar
A granted wish upon a star.
Crystal glass and chandelier
A sixty foot yacht seen from a pier.
A limousine and formal ball
A polo game in early fall.
A summer ranch near a mountain pass
A life of leisure, a touch of class.

A cardboard box makes a home
On the streets and all alone.
They wear their wardrobes on their backs
A daily meal they often lack.
Kill a dog for his bone
Once tender hearts have turned to stone.
Excuse me m'am, have you the time?
Spare a nickel, spare a dime.

Reagan Wilson
TO MY AUNT WITH LOVE

May you live together
In love forever
Decorating the world with flowers
Making it shine with great light
Reaching great height

With family behind you
You'll know you can't fall behind
With a loving heart and a caring mind
You'll live forever.

Nelda Pinkerton Limeres

Nelda Pinkerton Limeres
CELEBRATION OF THE WINDS

It's not a sin to rob the blowing tree of golden leaf,
Nor catch the laugh of tiny babe
And tumble on, to write your signature
In light and shade.
With glissando soar, and mount on easy wing
To kiss the sky—and blowing, breathe on all
The souls that lie

Beneath the cover of the earth.
You harmonize and press
Against the day in soft caress,
You winds of south, north, east and west.
And trembling, sing with echoing, on mountainside.
In ocean depths you hide; and seek in caves.
Opening the desert flower, with kiss of spice,
And whispers of your color.
Or frolicking, tease the grain on golden plain,
And in your celebration, an ordinary man, like me,
knows life!

Linda S Kinney
MY PRIVATE STORM

I'm far adrift amid the storm,
my vessel is beaten, its sails are torn.
I'm not sure just how long I'll last,
I feel I'm going under fast.

The storm is raging all around,
yet I hear a still faint sound.
It's God's voice, he's calling my name,
saying Linda, I love you still the same.

Come to me my weary one,
I will see your journey's done.
My peace is here for you!
Tell me now, what will you do?

My answer is bewildering to me.
I'll just stay here. Leave me be.
And still the storm is raging round.
I wonder if I'll ever let myself be found.

Alycia G Peters
TOMORROW . . .

Dedicated in loving memory of my grandparents Manuel and Fanny Zink

Today is built on memories
of yesterdays gone by,
and tomorrow is built on wonderment
of things we've yet to try.
An unconquered wilderness lies ahead
filled with mysteries at every turn.
There are endless obstacles and challenges to face,
we've so much yet to learn.
To learn about our inner selves,
means opening up our hearts
to those around so dear to us,
who play such vital parts.
And in this time of struggle,
with futures so unsure,
remember to never turn away the ones you love,
for they help you to endure.

Louise Piston
SNOW STORM

January's warm moist nights
Brought young mosquitos swarming
Around our yellow outdoor lights
Early and unwary of the storming

February's frigid sighing
Seeking winds which swiftly flow
To find them stiffly lying
Under frozen buds in soft white snow.

Paula Ellis
GOD'S ROSE

This poem is dedicated to the memory of Cindy Grider, a rose whose beauty will forever bloom.

We are God's rose garden.
He helps us to live and grow.
He gives us this place
to live in; and our love to others we show.
When we grow and reach our destiny,
He picks us as his own. He only picks the very best and takes us to be shown.
It seems like our life on earth is so long,
We take it for granted until it is gone.
As God picks
His best Rose now to go home,
We'll always remember the love
she's shown.

Thadious Cobb
QUESTERS
Searching has brought me here
to this desolate place.
I am without.
I am alone
Though there are those
Who share my fate.
Searching, finding.
Finding is not my goal
for Findings I have aplenty
And goals abound too.
Losing?
Losing is not truth
It is finding
And finding
is searching.
I have lost only time but
time cannot be lost.
(certainly not as lost as I might be)
It is eternal
And cannot share my fate.
Though we walk in strides the same.

Some other's world might offer
solution.
But offerings are entrapments and
Entrapment is enslavement.
Thus there is no freedom.
No quest when
Searching is freedom.
And there must be truth.
So there must be searchings
And findings.
for these
are all the quests
In the world.

Sheree L Case
IT WAS YOU AND ME
I came upon a memory
took it out to see
It was all the good times
it was you and me

I saw the smiles we shared
heard echoes of our laughter
gone were all the many tears
of pain that came after

I saw the walks we took
on that moonlit beach
And just for that moment
you were in my reach

I toast to you with rainbows
for the memories I see
It was all the good times
it was you and me

Linda Rose Campbell
BEAUTY OF LIFE
I've seen flowers open to kiss the
sun,
And little children, as they laugh and
run.

I watched raindrops fall into a lake,
and I saw all the ripples a raindrop
can make.

I've climbed trees up to the sky,
and touched the clouds as they passed
by.

I've heard the oceans as they roar,
and waves come up to kiss the shore.

I've felt the heat of the desert sun,
and I've climbed all the mountains,
one by one.

I've seen the sun rise, all golden and
bright,
and I've seen the sun set, scarlet, at
night.

I've watched the snow fall softly to
the ground,
And as it falls, it makes no sound.

I've seen rivers, streams and
bubbling brooks,
And how peaceful a valley looks.
I've heard the birds sing their song,
And a gentle breeze carries it along.

I've traveled this land, far and wide,
Always walking, never asking for a
ride.

Although two wheels adorn my chair,
From here, I've gone everywhere.

Nicole Bianca Brown
BELONGING TO A FAMILY IS A GIFT OF LOVE AND THE PLIGHT OF THE HOMELESS

I wish to dedicate this poem to all the homeless people in the world.

Of all the wealth in the world, no gift could ever be, as precious as the gift of love, belonging to a family.

With all the homeless victims without a family, no clothes to wear, no food to share, no education to let them be.

Loving wishes come to us as the earth is touched with spring, and our hearts are touched with all the blessings that joy and love would bring.

Some things just go without saying, and we feel that this is one, belonging is the most dearest love, and it's the most wonderful thing done.

All the joys in belonging that you're dreaming of, are wished for you everyday with a little bit of love.

A caring and sharing family, do not belong apart, where joy touches every soul, and love creates sweet hearts.

Dorothy Helen Oberle
THROUGH THE WINDOW PANE
I looked out the kitchen window
today,
And saw the purple lilacs all in
bloom.
Then I saw one other bush that stood
There in between—yet it stood alone.
It was a bush of purest white,
Spectacular in its own special way.
It reminded me of a tumbling
waterfall
Billowing, frothing, and fluffy with
foam,
Cascading down between the lilac
tones.
There were hundreds of dainty
blossoms
Falling on the soft green lawn below.
I thought of the beautiful Bridal Veil
Falls I'd seen
Dropping down to the river's flow.
I saw the lovely Bridal Wreath
Stirring gently as the warm breezes
Drifting from the south would blow.
The pure white petals were
Rippling lightly down to the green,
To the green that lay below.
There is much to see from a kitchen
window
When you are still, and all alone.

Stephen Austin Welch
SO MANY THINGS THAT THE WORLD DOESN'T UNDERSTAND
So many things that the world
doesn't understand—
Where is our sanity?
If we would only listen,
The answers lie in our hands.

We can't reason with the blind;
We need to keep our eyes open.

Lies are told;
and lies are believed.
Please end all the lies being passed
and sold.
They're only for materialistic things.
We will gain nothing from them;
They will only hold us back.

Look and find your ideas.
Love and know what has been
learned.
To know is to believe;
And to believe is to trust.

Trust what has been found and
learned.
Love and share those ideas.

I want to cry for the world.
Please listen to yourself.
So many things that the world won't
understand.

Kevin B Hoffer
MERCY SEAT
It is known
Must be told
Propitiatory slab
—of pure solid gold
"Two cubits and a half
He proclaims the length.
A cubit and a half
He declares the width."
Above the ark
He gives thee
Between cherubim
The final testimony.
High priest;
Sprinkled blood on the mercy seat.
High priest;
Dripped blood at his feet.

Joyce E Appleby

Joyce E Appleby
SCOTLAND REMEMBERED

Dedicated to my family, in England, with much love.

I see the distant mountains, in hues of
purple and grey.
Again, those distant mountains
beckon me to-day.
Commanding earth's horizon, with
their usual majestic power,
Mist cannot consume them,—above
its swirls they tower.

I hear the kilted piper, play his dawn
awakening tune.
Silhouette amongst the heather,
'neath a fading translucent moon.
Melody from his bagpipes lilting
down the glen.
Echoes of the rhythm bouncing back
again.

I smell a rich aroma, by gentle
breezes blown,
Down from the heights of stature, on
rugged mountains grown.
Trees of fragrant lushness; fertile
continuous lines.
Rows of harmonious splendor.
Stately, evergreen pines.

I explore the Loch of Lomond;
ripples flirting with my toes.
Depths of quiet mystery; what secrets
to disclose?
Waters reflect the mountains, to
compliment her grace.
I kneel to stare more deeply, and
view a pensive face.

I force myself to realism, and the
duties of my day.
Away from dreamy memories, and
longing thoughts at play.
But I make a silent promise, as I
close mind's inner door.
Be patient beckoning mountains: I'll
visit you once more . . .

Brent Pedersen
GOD'S BLESSING
When we first met, we were kids,
Our parents would call us, a little
family,
They joked about us being married
someday,

Without a care they separated us,
States apart, too far away,
It seemed any future had gone astray,

We found each other, in our teens,
Seemed forever, but really not for
long,
Our love proved to be so strong,

Told that our love was real,
We asked that we be married,
They said yes, believing it wouldn't
last too long,

A year gone by, our first child was
born,
Two years later, we lost the second
one,
At five years, plus, our third child
came,

Now, here we stand at nineteen years,
Four of us, a family, fully grown,
Our love we share, will always
remain the same.

Amanda L Espinoza
THE EAGLE

To my family and all who inspired me. Thank you

As the eagle flys through the sky,
So clear and so high.
So high up above,
And filled with care and love.

He's filled with bravery, courage, and
love.
And is as graceful as a peaceful dove.
He flys through the air,
With a voice only one can hear.
He so strong and bold with the flight
of his wings,
And a love song the powerful bird
sings.

Diana J Kirkman
TRANSFERENCE OF THOUGHTS
A transference of thoughts is what I'd
like to see,
For you to realize what it's like to be
me.
To see War, Hate and Preju-
dice . . .
And, somehow reach within for
righteousness.
To feel life so precious and be
patriotic,
But, through ignorance you're treated
as zymotic.
To extend your hand, as well as,

your mind.
Take a short journey, perhaps, out of step with the times.
To feel what I feel, and know what I know.
To be hampered by other's thoughts, though, it you must not show.
To feel, too, pain and contempt—
And, the times you
find it difficult . . . to be benevolent!
To want to be someone, to feel life has meaning.
To be without the one you love, while your soul is screaming.
To know the pains of other, and love so intent . . .
And, see the beautiful tree of life being bent.
To know the ghosts and echoes of your thoughts, insecure . . .
Perhaps, it's only a mere thought . . . even obscure.
Yes, a transference of thoughts I'd like to see.
Perhaps, only then, you'll understand what it's like to be me.

Jennifer Chaney
MY MOTHER

This poem is dedicated to my mother, Linda Chaney

My mother was a beautiful person,
filled with glorious things.
She was warm and loving,
never in pain.
I love her with all my heart,
and in my heart she will never apart.
She may be resting asleep in heaven,
maybe on cloud number seven.
My mother may be with her mother.
She may be happy or sad,
but never will be mad.
My mother will watch over us,
and take care of her family.
My mother will be with us always,
and I do not mean maybe.
I love my mother dear,
and when she died my heart went a spear.
I know I will miss my mother the rest of my life,
but I know that I will see her again.
Through vision and through heart.

Joanne S Bender
IN TIMES PASSING

To the man I love . . .

Footsteps in the sand,
Walking along the beach
Hand in hand.

Seagulls' cries being heard,
As the ocean roars
With pounding surf.

On the shore, in the ocean's mist,
Two hearts beat
And lovers kiss.

Just a few precious moments
In times passing,
And yet memories are
Forever lasting . . .

John F Bickerdike
THE MOON

In the still of the night,
I am a light that is very bright.

My gleam of extreme, brightful beauty,
Shines throughout the world in every city.

I hang in the sky ever so high,
As I watch every soul go walking by.

By the end of the quiet night,
I begin to fade out of sight.

I am hidden by the sun by day,
But will return when it begins to fade.

Aileen Chavez
ONE WARM SUMMER MORN

To My Mother

One warm summer morn
I happened upon a rose
Crimson was its color
Its beauty majestic.
The scent so sweet.
The morning dew gently caressed its petals.
Never had I seen such a beauty
I reached out to take it.
Its guards met my eager fingers.
The prick of the thorn made me sigh.
The rose was not to be mine.

Alan Lawrence
CONDITIONAL LOVE

To be alone
It's a fearsome state
For some.

I have grown accustomed to it
No longer feeling
Or yearning for your company.

My memory does not lie
Take away those moments of ecstasy
All that remains is hypocrisy

I'll
Love you tomorrow
IF . . .

Joan Adox
COMMUTING TO NEW YORK

At five the clock is crowing
A cuckoo start to a dizzying day
By bus from hills of Hackensack,
Through Hudson hollows and Lincoln Tunnel
Into the Terminal's catacombic menace.
Teen drug addicts shouting obscenities,
Beggars, bag-ladies, and sleeping homeless.
Shoe-shines, same-day photos,
And Zaro's whole wheat bread.
Descending like Dante through subway turnstiles
To greet Beatrice and Bernhard,
Panorama or penance.

Linda Frederika Gebhardt
THE PRICE

To Bernd and my family, for love, understanding and believing in me.

The darkness props my silent cry—
Hide from the world
They needn't see . . .
Be strong, I hear
Follow thru on course
Forget your sorrow—
Show no remorse
Build your fortress
. . . Like steel and stone
and glare out in victory . . .
all . . .
alone.

Suzan Fogarty
CANDLE FLAMES FLICKER, NEVER FADING

Candle flames flicker, never fading
resembling the tease of the Midnite Sun to
an intended twilight sky.

Memories flicker, never fading
intensified in the flame,
a guidance light to the past.
Only tears dim the flame,
as rain quenches the sun,
fulfilling the thirst of the heart.

Flame melts the candle; crying tears of wax,
forming temporary human monuments,
as clouds collide constructing
meticulous etchings; deceiving
the soul.

Only for an instant does the

Flame
Sun
Memories
flicker, never fading

Shirlie L Robinson
IF JUSTICE WERE NOT BLIND

To my friend, Anthony, who patiently led me to the threshold of my own mind.

Would life be just if Justice were not blind?

Would perpetrations foisted on mankind
by senseless bias and intolerance
remain to hinder man's deliverance
from out the mire of refuse left behind
by venal circumstance? Or, would he find
the space of his existence not confined
by margins preordained by ignorance,
if life were just and Justice were not blind?

How long? How long must man remain resigned
to bearing burdens bigotry assigned
with cold disdain? Why must he play the fool
to destiny's unconscionable rule?

Life might be just were Justice less inclined
to opt for sightlessness—forever blind.

"Doc" Carlos Gardner
IT MAKES NO DIFFERENCE

Dedicated to Charles Etta Gardner a beloved mother YOU MADE A DIFFERENCE in my life.

It makes no difference what your name
for I treat everyone the same.
It makes no difference if you're young or old
you all must pass down this road.
It makes no difference if you're rich or poor
it won't stop me from knocking at your door.
It makes no difference if you're white or black
the color of your skin won't turn me back.
It makes no difference if you're a woman or a man
for you all must become a part of the land.
It makes no difference what you believe
I must come and you must leave.
It makes no difference you will agree
That I makes no differences now that the key!

Kelly J Fore
PERFECTION

Why does this sadness overwhelm me so?
I think I'm sad, yet I really don't know.
I look in the mirror, but what do I see,
Just the reflection of a woman, staring back at me.

The reflection is clear, so why should I ask,
Is this really my face? Or only a mask.
I don't like the mask, it's not becoming to me.
It has so many flaws, the beauty I can't see.

"Nothing is perfect," I tell myself,
So why do I strive for perfection?
When everything around me
Seems as if it needs correction.

The world seems so vast and appalling,
My being so very small.
I wonder sometimes when I look in the mirror,
If I'm really important at all.

I drift out of touch with reality,
Decisions seem harder to make,
Confusion becomes apparent,
Just how much more can I take!

That's when the lord takes me over,
As I kneel, hands folded, in prayer.
And he leads me through the twists and turns,
Without him I'd be no where.

In his message, a word to the wise—
Take off the mask, you don't need a disguise.
The image that the mirror reflects,
Deserves love, understanding, and lots of respect!

Kari James McWest
NO MORE FEARS

For my one & only Melinda, and Ms. Elva "Vita" Chamberlain, without whom I cannot express myself.

It's late at night, I've nothing to do,
so I think I'll share my thoughts with you.
All I need is to find a track
otherwise you might send this back.
It really is not taking long,
it may, perchance, become a song
. . . but who knows . . .
So I think I'll think some more . . .

I guess I should get back in the swing
(for poetry is such a peculiar thing)
Poems (most think) should rhyme and flow
but, to be honest, not me . . . oh, I dunno—
Words that rhyme and iambic pentameters

we all learned these in English and grammar.
But I prefer the poem that changes, often writing prose of mountain ranges.

And just when you expect a nice rhythmic verse,
I'd throw in a twist, but I shan't make things worse.
Well, thus ends the first I've written in years,
now happily married I've no more fears
. . . to write about . . .

Angie M Smith
THE JOURNEY

I would like to dedicate this poem to my daughter-in-law and welcome her to the family with open arms: Brenda Denise Corpening Smith.

Walk with me while I think for a while
Listen to my words while I speak for this mile.
For when we reach our destination,
We shall sit for a spell.
We will listen to each other,
And the stories we tell.
Lie to me not for I shall remain your good friend
I will always be there from the beginning to the end.

Nancy Susan Armstrong
ORA PRO NOBIS
care you not for the very soul of your flesh
the fruit of your womb   the seed of your loins?
is it yet possible for you to abort after birth   to
dismiss a mothers' sweet anguish
the prelude
to deliverance of a life conceived through the dance
of a lover's honored celebration of oneness?

at such a tender age were you so filled with rage
with bitterness that you invited the devil
to stand in God's stead beside your bed
to witness the unholy union of two immersed not
in the sweet gift of your love   but
involved solely to taste your own evil passions?

I pray God come salve my soul for I yet
pay the penalty for your manifest egomania
which still does great violence to my being
writhing I beg Jesus for infusion of His Holy Spirit
that I may not crumble beneath the weight   of
yet another assault   knowing there is a
bottomless pit from which you dip your ladle

Lois Bates
ABUSE

This poem is dedicated to Clara in Al-Anon.

My life was sad
I was never glad
God only knew
What I went through.

Forgive you say
It's hard to do
Forget those days
I was abused.

When you are near
I live in fear
That's all in the past
I'm myself at last.

Janet M Faustner
OUTSIDE THE GATES
Snuggling down
against the wall,
and wrapping
tightly against the dancing fire,
eyes catching a tidal wave.
Wisps of smoke
filling lungs,
cutting throats,
and cold bricks licking hair.
Paralyzed
wind—sticken cheeks,
the mud is rolling in underneath,
movement,
nervous feet.
Eyes closing
against the dark night,
who is to say
this is right?

Kimi Minor
GRANDPA
He married a woman, at the time 17,
They bought a house to fulfill a dream,
Since they were poor, so far from rich,
They bought a shabby shack they dreamed to fix,
The windows were all broken, the door was ajar,
They couldn't fix the door, much less have a car,
The inside was dark and dingy, and covered with dust,
It was no rich man's dream, but to them a must,
The years passed by and by,
the aged limit was the sky,
I see him now, growing older yet so spry,
Deep inside his grayed head lies
knowledge not known by young,
But by old instead.

Connie Hartford-Page

Connie Hartford-Page
"WATCH YOUR DIET." "I DO WATCH MINE." WHAT'S YOURS?"

To the volunteers at the house next door of Deland, a well appointed counselling family organization.

Let's treat ourselves to early lunch.
We agreed, this dull and rainy day.
"No need to eat a plentiful bunch."
Thinking of the tempting gourmet display.

Helpful nudgings as plates over-filled—
"You don't want to look like that—"
Reminder—though your appetite willed
"This is no fun if it augers a spat."

"We can have hot water for supper,
"Unless this stimulates digestion—"
Then,—to even remove the "upper"
Won't welcome that first line suggestion.
So—
Carefully June picked another cauli-flower
Jane a smaller slice of ham,
Joyce and Ann decided on protein for power,
And Mary had a little lamb.

Jeannie Vinson
TO WISH FOR YESTERDAY
The sun is shining brightly, but the world is strangely cold
Our minds are changing quickly as everything grows old
We don't believe in what we used to; those days have come and gone
Our morals are diminishing through the things that we do wrong

We run from place to place yet we don't get anywhere
We're searching for the principles that are not even there
We're lacking so many things that were common in the past
Majority overrules and is taking over fast

Spirits of goodness walk the city streets
Hoping to change us, but will they succeed?
If we could only stand up for what we know is right
We'd live so much easier and sleep better every night

Museum walls reflect the lifestyles of the past
If we could only find some way to make the good faith last
Turn and look the other way when you see them heading for you
They'll corrupt you with their lies and then totally ignore you

We could be so many things yet we all know who we are
If you keep that in your heart then you won't stray very far
The sun rises every day, yet when it's hidden by the clouds
You have to break through the darkness and spread the light around

Take a look at what's becoming and you'll see just what I mean
High spirits and illusions make it better than it seems
Listen to the oldest ones for they know what is right
Stay in the right direction and don't ever lose your sight

Captolia Brown Ernst
REMEMBER SON
This my son you must remember,
My mother said one day.
Soon you will be grown up,
And this will really pay.

First be honest and truthful,
This you must always be.
Then polite and neat,
That's very important you see.

Go to Sunday school and church,
Say your prayers each night.
Walk tall and be proud,
Do what you know is right.

If this you will remember son,
And practice it too.
You can teach it to your son,
As I have taught it to you.

John R Kennedy Sr
THESE ARE THE THINGS . . . (FOR WHICH WE NOW PRAY)
Father, forgive us, sadly we fail
Help us when fear and doubt would prevail.
Strengthen us daily for each new test.
Keep us alert, Lord, doing our best.

May we help others thru toil and grief.
Finding some way to hasten relief.
Gaining more faith with each passing day.
These are the things for which we now pray.

Time is so precious, moments so few.
Help us to guard them in all we do.
Lead us and guide us, show us the way.
These are things for which we now pray.

Heavenly Father high up above,
Fill us with kindness, mercy and love.
Teach us to grow, Lord, and understand.
Temper us slowly, stayed by thy hand.

We are the branches; Thou art the vine.
Mould us as one, Lord, our will in thine,
Watching each deed and word that we say.
These are the things, Lord, for which we pray.

Amen

Diane M Heinbuch
WHEN MOM GOES AWAY FOR A COUPLE OF DAYS
When Mom goes away for a couple of days
Something strange happens in my room.
The furniture somehow gets rearranged
And mold begins to bloom.

The desk gets turned upside down
And somehow the chair gets stuck to the wall.
I thought I was going crazy
Until one day I saw them all.

I saw them cover the floor with trash
And the window with grease and dirt.
Then they pulled out all my dresser drawers
And popped the buttons from my shirts.

When I walked in on my visitors
They rumpled my bed into a lump
And politely turned and introduced themselves
As Mr. and Mrs. Grump.

Later when I saw fancy paint
Splattered about my room in fun,
I confronted the Grumps that they were not alone.
Then they introduced me to their son.

If that wasn't enough for the day,
I realized I was really in a bog.
'Cause the family also consisted
of a round lump grump dog.

And of course wherever lump grump dogs may be,

They are always followed by bump
grump fleas.
Who like to bite and play around
Wherever they darn well please.

Yet, when Mom comes home and
enters my room,
They all play hide and seek.
And I get left with all the blame
For the mess they left that week.

To try to explain about the Grumps to
my Mom
Well, that would be a hopeless case.
So I tell her: "I've been hiding from
aliens
And my room is simply Home Base!"

M F Patterson
RETROSPECT

Long ago the days were sunny, and
happy, gay and bright,
with blue skies and chirping birds,
sending their songs into my days and
nights.

Long ago my eyes did view and cry
and smile,
my heart did crave and yearn,
my legs did run and jump to an eager,
inner burn.

Long ago my mind did wonder and
wander and dream
of far away places,
where my legs did strive and strain,
to follow in their chases.

Long ago I did laugh, and sing, and
dance and pray
and oh I did so love, my soul did
weep and feel bereft
for they have gone and I alone was
left.

All that was oh so long ago
and now my eyes can hardly see or
my legs to dance,
my heart now cries for that long ago
the ever passing chance.

The skies are still blue, the birds still
sing,
my soul does know of one more
thing,
that soon it too will rise so high
above
where they await me, those I love.

Kerry E Burke
THE OTHER WOMAN

The night to me is most unkind
To hold your body, never your mind.
I can only give Madame Darkness
what she is due
For sleep, she steals my time with
you
When I say goodnight this affair does
begin
And this other temptress destined
always to win.
To lose you to another time, another
place,
And only dream the vision of your
face.
The day barely over and still so clear
Now your soul elopes, your body
grounded here.
Captured by the whore of the
unknown
To such awesome beauty I relinquish
my throne
On sleep's charmed world I let you
be
Pray at night your heart will not flee
And daylight brings you back to me.

Donna M Bove
FRIENDS

The poor, The rich,
The sick, The sane.
They all get hurt,
Or they hurt to gain,
A few pieces of silver,
A few pieces of gold.
Yet one Friend has more value,
Than all they could hold.

Michael Branch
LOVE FOUND AGAIN

I dedicate this poem to my family and friends. Thank you for your guidance and understanding. I love you all forever and always.

Love is what you've brought me
Something I've never had before
It has opened many closed doors in
my heart
You've opened my eyes so I could
see

There's nothing out there I can't be
I've looked from sea to sea
But there's something you've given
me and it's called love
And I know it will always be you and
me forever

I love you for the person you are
Not because you're warm, funny, or
caring
That alone will take us far
But because of that special love only
you and I know about sharing

You're on my mind day and night
Even when we get into a silly fight
I know everything will turn out
alright
I'll be by your side when you're
down

Something we'll always get around
Just remember one thing
I love you very much
One thing for sure nothing's gonna
change my love for you
And it's our love that'll see us
through

Bill Malone

Bill Malone
MY LITTLE GIRL

To my daughter Jenny

Little girl with the pony tail hangin'
all around.
Have you traded that red bow for that
pretty gown.
What about the jump rope and dollies
you held so tight.
Traded them for that special man
that's holding you tonight.

Remember the little puppy you held
for days and days.
Now you have bigger plans and have
changed in many ways.
I remember when gum and candy
would fix it all.
Now it's different things, if only that
certain man would call.

It doesn't seem like very long ago
you rode up on my knee.
Today it's the man who said, for him
you would always be.
Yes you've put a lot of things behind
you this year.
And I know in the past they were so
very dear.

I know you've always kept that little
special spot for me.
And I'll try to find that special place
and there I'll always be.
Should you ever stumble or think
you're going to fall,
My darling I'll be close, all you have
to do is call.

I guess we try and slow the growing
up now and then.
But we don't really mean to do it
seems it comes from
deep within. I want you to grow and
find what's yours alone.
Be home before too late, oh I forgot
this time you're leavin' home.

Sandra Jean Martin-Root
PERSIST! PERSIST!

Persist! Persist!
though tired the will be
for the fine grace does find you
forgetting expediency

Be True! Be True!
for even visions thought lost
will return to reward you
or exact a sure cost

Do Share! Do Share!
for every selfish restraint
could eventually bind you
to the picture you paint

Seek Peace! Seek Peace!
dark thoughts and unloving mumbles
do come home to remind you
just whose life they would humble

Live Love Now! Live Love Now!
or be later grievously perplexed
for you know there is no division
between this Life . . . and the next.

Robert Alan Noneman
CHANGING COURSES

To the memory of John Lennon

Imagine sailing on a ship across the
open sea
Put yourself upon that ship and
you're inside of me.
I wonder if it's possible, I hardly feel
it probable
To change, the course of eternity.

Imagine walking all alone on a dark
forgotten road
Put upon your stubborn back a
somewhat awkward load.
I wonder if it's possible, I hardly feel
it probable
To change, the course of your
destiny.

Imagine thinking to yourself that all
the world has changed
And all the cruel and mindless
thoughts have all been rearranged.
I wonder if it's possible, I hardly feel
it probable
To change, the course of reality.

Mary E Hohn
A CHILD AT PLAY

A child at play,
is a joy to the heart.
He's happier I think,
when in mud from the start.

Let him get dirty,
be happy, make pies.
Mud washes out,
no reason for lies.

Carolyn Siefert
APRIL MORNING

To my Mother and Father

Today,
Like a thrill of fairy laughter,
Elusive and sweet,
A new mood . . . a wild mood
Ripples and runs o'er the grasses
With an echo of ethereal music.
A mood of mysterious meaning
Ripples and runs and is gone
In a blending of sun and mist,
Losing its essence in subtle
patternings
Of light and shadow . . .
'Tis April! Oh, 'tis April,
A presence shy and sweet
As fragrant violets;
Who comes to blow the magic of her
kiss
Upon the drowsy land;
And leave the prophecy
Of gleaming rainbows arched above
the trees
In beauty after storm!

Katie Kelley Jones "Kay"
THE RIVER OF LIFE

As we flow gently down the River of
Life
Oft-times our path becomes strewn
with strife
The River is never too deep, or too
wide
When we allow God, to be our guide
Being human this is not easy to do
Especially! When we paddle our own
canoe
As long as our sailing is smooth—
We congratulate! ourselves, and
really move
"Until one day there is a storm"
"We say save us! Lord from harm"
All through life He has been right
there
Guiding, aiding us with His love and
care.

Bernice Ellen Adams
PRELUDE TO WINTER

Frosty grass, nippy mornings,
Afternoons of golden sun,
Starry nights, moonlit evenings,
Days that tell us Summer's gone—

Crimson maples, golden oaks,
Autumn colors all ablaze,
Flitting squirrels, pudgy quails,
Say good-bye to warmer days—

Pumpkin pie, Halloween,
Jack O'Lanterns glowing,
Candied apples, football games,
Anticipation growing—

Turkey drumsticks, roasting
chestnuts,

Firesides aglow,
Rustling leaves, white puffy clouds,
For soon will come the snow.

A Nicholas Webster
THE LOVED-ONE
He sits there! all alone
Only wanting to go home.
She sits here! only wanting
To see Him alone.
She is sad, She is new; the
Shivers eat up her spine.
If Her love does not come
Soon; He will become stone.

Her love, for miles stretched to Him,
His Lover is not just a girl, but a goddess.
She will sail a holy-wooden ship to him;
But He sits alone; only wanting to go home.

His ship comes into the bay, wooden-made and holy,
She is not on this ship and is still at sea.
He cries and leaps into the body; swimming
And sees a hand as His Loved-One screams.

The Loved-One is slowly passing on in spirit—
Her lover is trying to get to Her quick,
His hand reaches out of the bodies current;
But just as he reaches for her she slips . . .

Keotah M Fannin

Keotah M Fannin
AN EMPTY CHAIR

In Loving Memory of My Husband—Harold Fannin, born April 4, 1909, died July 11, 1988.

There's an empty chair
across from me.
There's an empty chair
where you used to be.

There is a hum
of voices near,
as I eat alone
without you, dear.

I play the games
as we used to do.
But it's not the same
Dear Heart, without you.

When you passed away
I must confess
I lost my love
and all my happiness.

The morning sun
brings no relief
from a dark night
of total grief.

Why must I live?
While you are gone?
Without you love,
I don't belong.

There's an empty chair
across from me.
Dear Lord let me join you
for all eternity.

Then there'll be no empty chair
across from me.
There'll be two empty chairs
one for you
and one for me.

Frances Wilber Hellmers
FRAGILE LOVE
Love is like a fragile flower
Nurtured by its roots,
Pushed aside by weedy growths
In busy life's pursuits.

A tiny flower, for it to grow
Must have nourishment at its base;
The same holds true for love,
For it to wear a smiling face.

For a flower long neglected
Will be overgrown by weeds;
And a love no longer nurtured
Will wither in its needs.

Marion Knowles
MY TREES

I dedicate "My Trees" in honor of Spirit in love, praise and thanksgiving.

Joyous friends
Embraced in love
You stand so stately
I am in awe!

Calm and serene
Through every scene
Reaching toward Your God Presence
To quench your thirst with Essence

Tell me what you feel and say
I am human, don't forget
And really wish to convey
My love to you in all array.

Mrs Alfred Z Hartman
TEDDY
Yup! I'm the pup, that tears things up
They're strewn from door to door
Bern's very best tie, every paper awry
Your slippers in shreds on the floor
When I've run out of stuff, sensed you've had enough
I climb in your very best chair
Then I have me a dream
Of the things I've schemed, the havoc and upset I've wrought
I think I'm a "heel" and awake with a squeal
To find of a truth I'm not
You give me a grin and then I start in
Good intentions have "gone with the wind."
And I go on a spree, give a show for free
And we are happy again!
Someday for a fact, like a real lady I'll act,
But just between you and me,
These days are the best, when I'm a bit of a pest
And to you a stocking I bring
Then you whisk me up when I deserve a cuff
And hold me close in your arms
And give me a squeeze, until I sneeze
Your laughter all sunny and warm
And I know at a glance, I stand every chance
To make aright every wrong
Resolving anew
your bidding I'll do
And cause you no more alarm
When you next whisk up this bit of a pup. and I nuzzle in your ear, Please hear me say
In my very best way, Happy Birthday to you for many a year
Especially on this your very own day
Please let us both agree
That whatever I do it's my very best way of saying Happy Birthday to you.

Thomas Andrew Howard (Walks-Lame)
SEASONS

I dedicate this poem to my brothers Denny and Huey, may they be forever young, also to the efforts of Green Peace and all other environmentalists, and finally, to Native Americans, our mother's first caretakers.

I took a walk this morning, the shade half-slanted by the building's reflection. The morning sun shined alone, touched by all that could feel the warmth.

In the snow, I saw a single pair of tiny-hopping wingeds tracked, softly imprinted where it had been, the only notion of its landing and going again.

As I looked about where man's hand had not touched, Mother Earth's changing and ever-present beauty showed herself in a single leaf hanging still from the end of its twig.

And the tree, surrounded by its fellows, lent to me its steadfastness and told me of seeing the seasons going and coming again.

Charles E Wallace Sr
MOTHER I LOOK TO THEE

Dedicated in the Memory of my Mother Mrs. Willa Mae Nunn Wallace, Also Dedicated to the Wallace, Bell & Perkins Family

Like the seeds of a beautiful flower that's cast upon the wind, the seed of man is cast upon woman. I ask not to be cast down upon cold stone where I cannot take root. Cast me where there is warmth, where the warmth of the sun flows to me through you, so that I may take root and grow. Like the seed of all living things, I look to you for protection and safety. I ask not to be cast away, for if I am, surely I shall die.

Like the seeds of a beautiful rose that grows to be beautiful, I ask only for time so that I may grow to be beautiful too. I ask this of you Mother, for I am your child.

Rita Krielaart
THIS MAN WHO IS SENSITIVE AND GENTLE

For Steven, my true inspiration, who has given me the ability to trust and love without any reservations.

This man who is sensitive and gentle;
Is like a child
While watching him sleep, I see the picture of innocence in the purest sense.
A man who can only bring out the best in others.
A man who see's everything in a beautiful new way.
Without realizing his gift, he continues on in an inquisitive way, wanting to learn more.
My how everyone around him is touched by his caring disposition.
Such a shame that all of us don't learn from him . . .

Michael G Allan
WELCOME HOME?

I would like to dedicate this poem to all servicemen but especially my family who stood by me when others didn't.

It's been many years ago I fought
to keep America free.
A great lesson to me was taught;
the only one that cares is me.

We were proud to fight for the U.S.A.
and help our fellow man,
So why didn't they let us stay
and win in Viet Nam?

So many lives were lost in vain;
most of us volunteered to go.
We weren't there to play a game,
but to help freedom grow.

When we came home, we heard no bands,
nor got a victor's shake,
For the war we left in Viet Nam
was just a political mistake.

God help us understand and see
what our children have in store
To fight for the land of the free
and die on some distant shore.

Jamie K Scott
THE LOVE OF CHRISTMAS
Christmas is a time of love,
When we give thanks to God above,
We gather around the Christmas tree,
And thank the Lord that we are free.
Around the fire, in voices low,
I tell of Christmas long ago.
Jesus was dressed in swaddling clothes,
To keep him warm from head to toes.

Linda Jerue
MOON STAR WARRIOR
In the misty vale of sorrows
By the dark forgotten lake
Walks a warrior in the darkness
Walks alone within this place

Tall is he this Moon Star Warrior
Slowly walks he by the glade
Sad his dark eyes searching upwards
Star dust glow lights up his face

Flows his black hair ever shining
Frames his eyes so deep still brown
Sweetly sings he in the stillness
Sings the silver rainbow song

Bright and full the moon shines on him
Bathes his face a light so clear
Silver showers floating downward
Crystal tears upon the cheek

Soft he dreams of days gone by now
Roaming through this endless space
Living as the Spirit told him
One with all his songs do reach

Life sees he in all around him
Lessons to live to teach to learn
Land and moon and stars sing out
To the heart ears of the earth

Long ago this warrior man
Turned his heart to moon lit sky
Felt the Spirit enter in
Took the Moon Star in his hand

Learned the songs of those around him

Ate the silver Moon Star stone
Saw in himself the star lit night
That Tonka Waikan to him shown

Lonely walks the Moon Star Warrior
All in him and him in all
Sings of what the others taught him
But no heart ears on them fall.

Cyril Tate
CLAY IN THE POTTER'S HAND

To Mildred, my dear wife, who has been a vital instrument in forming our vessel of matrimony for forty-seven years of a happy married life.

In the market place one day, I saw the potter toil
with a wheel, a pail of water, and a pile of soil.
Mixing water with the soil, he formed a ball of clay.
His work was in earnest, there was no folly or play.
The ball of clay was just right to make the proper size.
Molded by the potter's hands, it would become a prize.
Soon the bottom of a vase began to take its form.
Then the neck was completed—it was the usual norm.
Molding a perfect vessel, the potter did not tire.
One more step to perfection and that was through the fire.
Now into the furnace, burning with an intense heat,
the vase was entered so the process would be complete.
As it came forth from the fire, what beauty to behold!
A vessel for the master, its worth was that of gold.
God instructs us to be as clay in the Master's hand;
not to be a rock or pebble, neither shifting sand.
Always yielded to his will and doing his desires,
so we may be set free and escape the tempter's fires.
All this can be accomplished here on God's earthly land,
if we remain as clay to mold in the Potter's hand.

Marvin E Reed
GOD BLESSED OUR HOUSE WITH LOVE

Dedicated to my son, Marvin, Jr. and his many young friends who grew up with him through high school.

Oh we've had our share of troubles
For they come to everyone,
Like tiny fragments of bursting bubbles
That are too long in the sun;
But we've enjoyed all the days and years
As we've trusted and looked above,
And that is why we keep on singing
For God blessed our house with love.

Yes we've had lots of spats and quarrels
But they didn't last too long,
And all the bitter words soon turned
Into the sweetest kind of song;
Children's fingers on the piano keys
Playing favorites everyone knows,
Turning troubles into vibrant joy
For God blessed our house with love.

So no matter what the day may bring
And no matter the darkest night,
We've always got a glad tune to sing
For we know the Lord of love and light;
And we're just going to keep on singing
The songs that happiness wove,
And we're going to let the whole world know
That God blessed our house with love.

Vicki L DiPretore
THAT CORNER

There was an old man on the corner
We were christians passing by,
As we filled up the church pews,
We never heard his cry.

We walked right past that beggar,
"GOD walks with you," he replied.
When the services were over,
And we've forgotten why we came.
Then we all walked out the church doors
In the direction in which we came.

The old man had passed over,
But his death was not in vain.
I learned a valuable lesson,
He loved me just the same.

Pearl Chafin
SIGHT AND SOUND

This Poem is dedicated to my two children: Dale and Sue Chafin

The sight of your face I still can see
The sound of your voice lingers with me
As the Autumn leaf drifts slowly down
And the gentle breeze whispers sight and sound

I see you wrapped in a thin cloud veil
A faint echo reminds me of our love so well,
As the falling rain kisses the night air
And the summer sun touches your hair

The sound of your laughter I hear each day,
Then feel the need to kneel and pray,
And I count my blessings all around
For the loving memories of Sight & Sound

Sight and Sound, Sound and Sight
All alone wandering into the night
Counting the stars that shine so bright,
Loving you freely until the morning light

Carol George

Carol George
THE MEANING OF CHRISTMAS

Christmas is a time for families to be together—
Exchanging presents with one another.

Children play with their new toys all day long
And carolers sing a Christmas song.

There are decorations everywhere you go
Christmas can be white from a December snow.

It is a special day for expressing love
And being holy like God above.

The meaning of Christmas is all of these things but importantly it means one thing more,
This is the day our Lord Jesus was born.

Angela Stoker
OH HOW I MISS YOU

To Scotty, My first love I'll always love you.

Oh how I miss you
You're so far away
I love you so much
More than words can say
'Til you're home again
Time will pass so slow
Oh how I want you home
I didn't want you to go
I think of you often
Every minute of every day
I wish that you were here with me
Instead of so very far away

Kenneth D Clark
FOOTPRINTS ON MY HEART

The moon shone bright above us
As we walked along the sand
I had not a care in the world
When I held onto her hand

We sat and built a castle
That soon would wash away
We shared our dreams as lovers do
As upon the sand we lay.

It all seemed so easy then
The problems we faced were few
We never thought of loneliness
For we knew our love was true

But then there came the bitter storms
Our castle began to fall
And watching our dreams wash out to sea
Was the hardest part of all

Now the beach is a memory
If I had known it from the start
I wouldn't have let my summer love
Leave footprints on my heart.

Sherri Smith
NEVER AGAIN

No one to talk to anymore,
You've gone, closed the door.
In my heart, you will always be
Someone who was always there for me.
Someone who would help me through good or bad,
Happy and sad.
Someone who I could talk to
About things no one else ever knew.
Someone who would wipe away the tears,
And take away your biggest fears.
Thinking of the way it used to be,
How I'd laugh at stories you told to me.
Of your childhood days,
How things have changed in many ways.
Of how you would boast
About the one you once loved the most.
Or of how Uncle Clyde,
Asked you to walk down the aisle and be his bride.
Of things that happened long ago,
Things, never again, I will know.

Patsy Bockman
FIFTY-TWO

My friend said,
Why are you sitting there looking so blue?
I said tomorrow I will be fifty-two.
Fifty-two is that all.
You should be celebrating and having a ball.
Your life is just in its middle beginning.
You are a long way from the ninth inning.
So get in there and get to pitching and see the game through.
You are only fifty-two.
When your life has passed you by.
And you think that it is over.
Stop and smell the roses and take a roll in the clover.
Wade barefoot in a stream.
Sit back against a tree and daydream.
Remember when you were young and full of hope,
Don't sit around and mope.
Dreams still have time to come true.
After all you are only fifty-two.

Norma Franklin
NO ONE CARES

On a lonely stretch of highway my broken body lays.
NO ONE CARES
As the breeze of hundreds of cars pass me by, gently ruffling my once soft fur,
NO ONE CARES
Weeks pass and still I lay there, for no one has offered to dig my grave.
Predators have long stripped flesh from my carcass bare, leaving the sun to bleach my bones.
NO ONE CARES
The legacy of love and protection to my master and his family I so joyfully gave, while in harsh reality I've found . . .
NO ONE CARES

Billy Pace
THE THINGS YOU HAVE GIVEN ME

I who have nothing but love to give you,
will give you love for love in return.
You have made me happy when I was sad.
You have taken away the sorrow and pain that was in my heart.

You gave me strength when I was in a struggle with myself.
You turned my frown into a smile.
You have unlocked the door to my emotions, now they want to run free
I have been afraid of being hurt like so many times before,
but with you I don't feel afraid

anymore.

You have put a special feeling in my heart and I thank you for that.
You have put love back in my heart and I want to say I love you for what you have given me.

Dorothea Colangelo
JESUS—A SPECIAL LOVE

Dedicated to God and the Love He so gave the world.

There is one special Love in the world,
I wish I could sing it in a song
Jesus is that one special Love in the world.
And He was sent by God above
Down to an earth that was crumbling by man's own
Hatred & greed
This gift of God has turned us around
by giving us
special needs
The need to be Loved and understood
And the need to have faith in someone good
We must thank God for sending us
this one special Love
JESUS.

Dorothy Prater Niemi

Dorothy Prater Niemi
PRESCRIPTION

TO INTERNATIONAL COOPERATION IN SPACE EXPLORATION

The pain of human overpopulation
permeates the world
Resources are limited funneled to human use
Ecological systems based on non-human interactions
Are doomed death of species is common
Agonizing last days of beautiful animals

Humans with an exponential population growth
Cannot fit into any existing ecosystem
And do not have the kindness necessary to limit power
Destructive power of amoral capitalism
Will ruin the world and thus our species

Religions create breeding populations intense crowding
Amazon rainforests fall to capitalistic interests
Free enterprise is the moral excuse for decimation
Mockery is made of the sanctity of life
Sanctimonious developers make usurious loans
Our beautiful world cannot be owned by amoral interests
Let the rainforests survive for they rejuvenate the atmosphere
Every species that dies kills the value of our endeavors
Develop a moral system that preserves all lifeforms
While limiting material desires and fostering intellectuality

S Renee Arentson
TIME

To Jamie J. Adams for all we've shared and everything he's done for me in the past three years.

I love him
I treasure him
There is no way to hide
All of the feelings
That I have inside.

I love him
I need him
Time goes so fast
By the time we get there
It's already past.

I love him
He loves me
And one of these days
The shortness of time
Will have just been a phase.

Edward Smerdon
WONDERING WHY

I am wondering of years
so grey and blue.
Wondering of things,
I plan to do.
Wondering if I served as
I had planned,
To help some poor person,
with willing hands.
But as the years go quickly by,
With all the birds as they swiftly fly!
I still am left!
Wondering Why?

Marian Yolanda Lord
FIRST TIME MOTHER

To Mrs. Myrtle Jones. My loving Mother.

How can I explain about becoming a mother?
The pain is unexplainable, not like another.
It's beautiful, yet hurtful,
It's wonderful, yet real
But what came out of it is someone beautiful
Someone like me!

I have a wonderful baby, he's a treasure
Being his mother is such a pleasure
He's chubby, yet cute,
He's an angel, yet a handful
Everyday he reminds me of someone
That someone is ME!!

Jean Dawson
THE OLD DOLL

The Old Doll, sat in the corner,
No longer loved or cuddled.
Just like a lonely mourner,
She's been set down in a huddle.
The little girl, has grown at last,
The poor Doll, is in her past.
Yet years later the girl sees,
The Old Doll, who really pleased.
She picks her up and holds her close,
Rocks back and forth in a pose.
Remember good times in the past,
When she was her baby, never to cast.
The memories will never fade,
A clean dress and hair in braids.
The Old doll is slowly led,
To sit on the little girl's bed.

Kevin Kerr
THE DAWNING

The morning dawns
through sleepy eyes.
The birds sing
as they soar so high.

The darkness ebbs,
the light rises,
to show the mountains,
and great divides.

The trees whistle a merry song,
and beckon all,
to join along.

The children playing,
in the street,

their voices—
not sounding a bitter retreat.

. . . And now,
through eyes abandoned by sleep,

it's not the day,
to sound that hideous defeat.

Joanne Senus
SAY IT WITH LOVE

With Love: To my Mother and Father, Flora and Leonard Cavaretta, Also to my Husband George, who inspired me!

My heart has a feeling that is hard to express.
As I reiterate, it is causing distress.
The happiness, heartache, that flows in my veins,
Is moving in a pattern that is causing much pain.
C'est la vie, is the adage that comes into mind.
As I look for the understanding that is so hard to find!
I say it with love, you have become a stentor,
When it comes to your wife!
Causing her to become distraught in the time of mid-life.
You're tenacious in your way,
As I think with love, as I say.
Love her today that's all that we have.
Take time for remembering,
What you feel in your heart,
And it looks like tomorrow may have a brand new start.
A start, that I thank you,
Will help me today!
Be happy, and not worry as life passes my way!

Shirley Mae Cox
HE

This poem is dedicated to all my co-workers at St. Mary's Hospital, especially Sue Boltik and Gary Winningham who were my inspiration.

He is out there somewhere,
But I can't see His face.
I'm sure I overlook Him,
As I stare into space.

He is in my morning orange juice,
In my afternoon cup of tea.
When I lay me down to sleep,
I'm sure that's where He'll be.

He is a comforting hand on my shoulder,
And in all places he can lurk—
From my bedroom in the morning,
Until I return from work.

He is the strength that makes my legs go;
He is the reason I am kind.
He brings rhythm to my heartbeat;
He maintains my healthy mind.

He is really quite apparent.
All we have to do is look.
My life to Him is no secret;
He must know me like a book.

He is my lifeline to happiness,
Like my grandson on the phone.
If I walk the path with Him,
I'll never walk alone.

Rebecca L Callahan
THE DIFFERENCE

Lovingly written for myself, Rick Steven Hegg and the special children of this world, and graciously dedicated to Dr. Anthony B. Fadely—the wind behind my sails, who led me back to my loving Father, the Lord Jesus.

You can make the difference
If you try,
Day by day, love you must give
In so many ways,
But why?

Children, precious lives of our future
Need and cry out for our love,
But, do we try?
Or do we only see our needs . . .
Oh why?

Promising lives go to waste
Only to envision despair,
But, some will hope and dream
These children will make the difference,
Won't you try?

We continue to be children of despair
Unless we escape our pasts,
And bring forth our hearts' and souls' dreams
And truly make our difference last . . .

You can make the difference,
But, only if you try!

Phyllis Detwiler
THANKS—3E NURSES

A group of nurses that are so sweet
Always scouring the halls, on their feet.

From early morning, on through the night
These gals work hard with all their might

Taking blood pressures, pulse, and temperatures too
Doing their best to take care of you

They fluff your pillows, and make your beds,
Rub your back, and bring your meds

All through the day, and the night too,
They'd come in your room to comfort you.

They cheer you up when you are down,
Have cheerful smiles, and never frown.

Thank God for nurses who care for you
We patients are grateful for all that you do

All patients aren't easy to nurse and take care
But just remember, someday it might be you there.

I enjoyed the care that I received on

3-East,
All the nurses were terrific, to say the least

Thanks for helping me to get on the mend,
And thanks to you all for being my friend.

Sheri Lyn Pickett
BRING EM BACK
Camouflage upon his face, dressed in combat green,
Battling a senseless war, 'gainst enemies he's never seen.
Forced to fight and forced to kill,
Forced to serve against his will.

His country he would proud defend,
But fight a war that has no end?
Fight for ground and comrades lost,
Fight to win at any cost?

But we didn't win the freedom sought,
And we didn't gain for which we fought.
Instead they lost their lives and pride,
Though honor's paid to those who died.

Boys left home, fear on their face,
Men returned with their disgrace.
They had not won, they were not praised,
No flags in honor for them were raised.

Bring back to us those still lost,
In Viet Nam's holocaust.
Wave the flag, and hail the corps,
Bring them back to fight no more!

Shanda Gail Dixon

Shanda Gail Dixon
YOU ARE SO BLACK & BEAUTIFUL—THIS IS FOR YOU

For Abraham: The light of your beautiful blackness has shone through me.

Feeling your blackness releases me . . . . Into me

I look into your beautiful black richness and I can feel the pain of generations past

The ruby redness of your lips symbolizes the bloodshed of millions

As sweat glistens onto your beautiful blackness
I can see what all others feared . . .

. . . The narrowing of your brow
tells of your tenseness of immense love

. . . The broadness of your nose
as it flares with anger
or subsides into softness

. . . Seeing the delicate fullness
of your lips
fills my breast with pride

For I can see my own
reflection in you
The fear of your . . .
STRENGTH!!

The strength of your character
outshines the darkness of day
which brightens even the blackest night

Looking at the whole man
I feel the whole picture
The power . . . The tenderness

Your ebony smoothness engulfs me
Whenever you hold me

For all Black Men . . .
. . . Beautiful & Strong

You have helped me
Find the Beautiful Blackness
Inside of Me

Deborah L Tomaszek
ALWAYS REMEMBER
I will always remember
The fun you brought to me
You went away in December
You always stood by me lovingly
You brought great memories that
I will never let go
We sat by the fire and chatted
Our love had grown
You brought love to our hearts
And took each day as it passed
You left with a sudden parting
All my memories of you will last
Now you are gone
But the memories live on

Margaret (Peggy) Thomas
I WENT TO VISIT YOU TODAY
I went to visit you today
But you were not there.
Your bed was neatly made
Your sweater laid out upon your chair.
I saw your precious family photo
In a frame of brass.
And all your favorite pictures,
Mementos from the past.
I checked the hall and diningroom
But still you could not be found.
I asked some of your friends
If they had seen you anywhere around.
My pace quickens—What is this dread I fear?
When I go to the patio, to see if you are there.
The sun is brightly shining
The flowers are still in bloom
But, alas, I find no answer to your whereabouts
So I sadly return to your empty room.
I touch the silken flowers
You had put upon the windowsill.
The room seems oddly quiet
So strangely still.
But then I hear your gentle laughter
As you come walking down the hall.
Thank goodness you are alright,
Nothing dreadful has happened after all.
Yet in my heart I ponder
Just what I would have done this day
If you had really gone forever,
What then would I have to say?

Ronnie L Comstock
REMEMBER OUR VETERANS
Our hearts go out to those Service Men.
Who fought and died while serving in the Armed Forces.
Each one gave up their life for a friend
And we will miss hearing their voices.

Our hearts may get heavy and we may shed a tear.
Thinking about the things they did in the past.
And remembering the times when they were near.
They may not be here, but their Memories will last.

A group of people got together.
And decided we need something to remember our soldiers by.
They planned and worked real hard together.
At times, some may have wondered why they died.

They decided to ask people to give a donation.
To help tackle this great task.
And whatever is given will show their appreciation.
And hoping this monument will last.

They had a goal in mind they were reaching for.
They appreciated everyone who took part.
Hoping this will open many doors.
And hoping each one gave from their heart.

They finally raised the money for the monument.
They had the Dedication on 11-11-87—Veteran's Day.
After the Dedication, they uncovered the monument.
And anyone who came to the Dedication—didn't have to pay.

Here lies the monument in front of Washington County Court House.
With a list of World War I and II, Korean and Vietnam Veterans of Washington County.
We hope this memorial be felt from here to the White House.
To remember those who died from Washington County.

We will still remember the things they have done.
We know things won't be the same around here.
And remembering the good times and the fun.
By having this monument, it will show—
Some One Cares.

will slocum
roses, rainbows, and newlyweds
a toast to the rose
and to the rose's
fragrance in bloom
a close embrace
in a cozy room
a bottle of wine
and tender refrain
of romantic song
love to last
a lifetime long
entwined in nights
lightly star-kissed
amid days of sun
shining thru the mist
rainbows gently caress
the flowerbeds
and forever bless
the newlyweds . . .

to roses,
and rainbows,
and newlyweds . . . !

Kavin W Bobbitt
WHAT'S
What's in the eyes . . .
The sight of Nature's
Beautiful Creations . . . . .

What's in the Mind . . .
All the Wonders that
Creations have brought us
in time . . .

What's in the Soul . . .
The deep -n- hidden
obstacles of Emotions . . .

What's in the Heart . . .
The true -n- sincere meaning
of Life -n- Love . . .

What's in Me . . .
The need to be
a Friend . . .

What's in You . . .
The rare essence of
Being a Friend . . .

What's in Us . . .
The most valuable Gifts
in life . . .

What? . . . The ability to be
Friends . . .

Terresa L Walker
PRECIOUS FRIEND
If you must remember me in tears,
Then remember me not at all;
But instead remember me with a smile,
For with Christ I did it all.
And as I walk every mile,
I will always remember your sweet smile;
And hopefully see you at the end of life's journey.
I've just to say live in the light,
And you won't regret it.
Then the day we meet again
will be on Heaven's bright shore.
So stand strong in the Lord
And by the grace of God
We will meet again at evening tide.
I've just to say good-bye, My Precious Friend
We will meet again and when we do
We will never say good-bye.
May the Great God Jehovah bless

and keep you,
Like His great power never ending;
So shall your beauty and Friendship
Be throughout all eternity.
Good-bye, My Precious Friend.

Lee L Ryder

Lee L Ryder
MOMENTS IN TIME

Lovingly dedicated to Matthew and Tracy Ryder, Donna and Brent Alexander, and Janie Ryder, my family, who gave me moments in time which can never be eclipsed.

There are moments I spend with you,
as I look deep into your eyes
I see a need, a joy, a love so true
as deep as the seas, as wide and blue;
And as each of these precious moments we share
try as I may, I cannot keep
them here,
For they appear and quietly pass,
reflections in a pond, eclipsed by pebbles cast.

Now in this moment we are apart,
I pray you can know deep in
your heart
The love I feel for you shall transcend
This brief pause and carry our
lives through
To a day when we will walk hand in hand
along special shores leaving four
prints in the sand,
To laugh, to feel, to share, to say,
I love you in a very honest way.

For you, my dearest love, as you walk alone under stars above,
I place this moment into your heart
In hopes you know, we are not apart.

While separate in body, your
eyes I cannot see,
I wish with you, my soul to be.

Diane M (Daigle) Manville
WON'T PLAY THE GAME
Built myself a wall, secured it with dirt.
No-one could get in, no need to be hurt.

It was strong and sturdy, to keep out any pain.
Yet it didn't help, to stop the rain.

I could hear people say, we can see inside.
Lady stop building, why you want to hide?

I'd look at them, with the biggest smile.
Wouldn't believe anyone, not even for a while.

They wouldn't get in, like a thousand times before.
No need to believe, by opening my door.

If they had half the chance, they'd chip my wall away.
By making me believe, what they had to say.

It would be no different, yesterday was the same.
Losing my heart, playing their game.

Sylvia Dyck
COUNTLESS SHEEP
If you can't fall asleep,
They say, "try counting sheep."
But is that counsel fair,
When there are no sheep there?
Pulling wool over eyes,
Sheepishly, no sleep buys.
So their mind won't unwind,
But stays tight through the night.
Sham sheep count,
Won't account,
For sleep.

Ruth Antoinette Wilson
UNREQUITED LOVE
Dear Heart I've tried to write you a letter
To let you know that I'm feeling better
But a letter to you is difficult to write
Since all we do lately is fight.

I've tried to reach you
God knows how I've tried
It's rough being shut out
And hurts so inside.

We all must share the good with the bad
But this never meant for just one to feel sad
This is a sad fate and it is true
Especially when life has offered so much to do.

As the years go by couples who have shared love
Grow fonder of one another
But those who have lived in turmoil
Wind us as sister and brother.

Kathryn N Scarola
A PART
Shattered day,
Broken moment;
All that is left
Is alive and well;
Ointment for the gash
That spreads beyond reason
Like wildfire.
An arch foe decides
Our inspired path
Uncurving,
Relentless
At the helm.
Life breathes until—silence,
And rises from a horizon:
A power so great
It gleams with phosphorescent
Glory.

William A Nolan
I DON'T LIKE SAD

I wish to dedicate this poem to you. Eddie Lou-Cole.

You don't know 'bout lonely
Until you have been, left so alone.
And your ba, Ba's, done got mad, up and gone
And all you can do, is sit right there and moan.

And mad, ran off to our bedroom.
And sad, ran off the the bar.
Oh, but sad did not drive that far.
In our little old car.

I walked into the bar, and when I heard our song,
I got right up, left my beer, and ran along,
Gotta leave sad, in this bar.
Can't take sad, back home in this car,
I don't like sad, that I've already had.

When I got back home
Mad came out of our bedroom a laughing,
And sad got glad, all over again.
I don't like sad, that I've already had.

You don't know 'bout lonely
Until you have been left so alone
And your ba, ba's done got mad, up and gone.
And all you can do, is sit right there and moan.
I don't like sad that I've already had
And honey, I've got nothing, but some good loving to add

I don't like mad
I do like glad
I don't like sad
That I've already had
I don't like sad, I don't like sad.

Kevin James Rowley
OLD HOUSE

Dedicated to Adam, Violet, Mom, and Dad, to Fred, Art, Karen, Kathy, and Lorraine—You made the house a home.

There's an old house on the prairies,
That's seen many a better day,
It was once the heart of a family,
But they've grown and moved away.

The house still sits where it was built,
Once filled with joy and laughter.
But now it sits, an empty shell,
With creaking, sagging rafters.

Time was when all ten of us
Had lived within its walls.
And we were poor, but in that house,
We felt we had it all.

Marie Rowland
LAST TRIP TO YESTERDAY
It seems that all the world is pieces of gold and glitter,
and the people on the stage play a scene so bitter.
We've started a holy war just trying to survive,
you have to watch your neighbor if you want to stay alive.

We never look back to the dreams we made,
reminders of the past leave us lonely and afraid.

So we sit and wonder what will happen tomorrow,
and try to forget about yesterday's sorrow.

You can trust your heart but only at times,
especially when your feelings are spoken in rhymes.
We've got to hang on to what little we've got,
we have to make it last even though it's not a lot.

It hurts to remember the things we left behind,
but if you start to cry I really won't mind.
You can tell me your secrets or even a lie,
I'll never say a word or even ask why.

Your dreams may come true if you give them your best,
take what you want and forget about the rest.

Maureen A Malone
MY MIRACLE OF MIRACLES

Dedicated to my husband Michael and my children Kerry, Sean and Brian—whom this poem is written about.

Little tiny baby hands
And tiny baby feet.
A gorgeous face with God's own kiss
And skin so soft and sweet.

A miracles of miracle of miracles
Is what each birth should be.
Another healthy happy son
Is what God gave to me.

The day this little baby came
Our hearts were filled with joy.
To hear my doctor's words ring out
"You have a little boy."

With wondrous looks I stare at him
And dream of what he'll be.
I know some day he will grow up
And I must set him free.

But till that far off distant time
I'll cuddle, caress and enjoy.
That loving face that warms my heart
Of our beautiful baby boy.

Nan Wood Hall
MY GRANDFATHER WAS A STERN MAN
My Grandfather was a stern man, not often did he smile;
But he was a good man, and even as a child,
I loved him for his strength, but was puzzled by his style.

He never seemed to mind how hard he had to work.
He farmed his land with pride, and never did he shirk
the chores to be done before the moon replaced the sun.

Everything was always clean; no weeds, no mud, barns freshly painted.
An example set in my young mind
that life is serious, though tainted,
if there is no laughter, no joy or singing, then something is wrong in this world!

It's O.K. to be a stern man,
hardworking and proud;
To set an example for young ones, to show pride, clear and loud.
But remember to be happy, to laugh, and to sing;
For in this world, Joy, Peace and Happiness are everything!

Matthew Ashbrook Griffith
THE SONG OF A BOY-MAN

This sonnet is dedicated to all the people who have meant so much to me and have helped me so far. Thanks!

The wet dreams are there, am I used to them?
As frustrations of life gnaw at my gut
And render me useless for all else but
Thoughts that stick in my throat as does phlegm.
A sticky substance cleared simply—ahem!
Oh, why is it so hard, why such a glut
Of emotional releases that cut
Into my brain? And is life such a gem?

But all is not over at seventeen
And the consummation I seek will come
In June—or July—or in November.
Whenever the time, my body will glean
The jewels of satisfaction and hum
A lighter song to induce sweet slumber.

Annie Elizabeth Scofield Ellis

Annie Elizabeth Scofield Ellis
A MOMENT

If we would take a moment
And listen to each word.
And listen to the things
Which we have never heard.

If we would take a moment
And patiently wait.
And feel of this great love
that only patience makes.

If we would take a moment
And do a kindly deed.
And reach out to each other
They too would see our need.

Ricky Valasco
JUST A DREAM

The love from a child.
A lot of world leaders should probe in their brain.
The innocence in their minds.
All the love and beauty the world could gain.
No more wars:
Our skies would always look a creamy blue.

Racism would be non-existent.
Things like this should mean a lot to me and you.
A dream like this will never exist.
There's too many power hungry leaders;
Working on making nothing exist.
A child's love and innocence we could all learn from.
It's all just a dream though
It will never be done

Aleta Ellen Crystal
SO WHAT

What is love if no one is there ?
What is joy if no one can share ?
What is giving if no one receives?
What is truth if no one believes ?
What is life if no one survives ?
What is death if no one cries ?
What is mine if no one will say ?
What is God if no one will pray ?
What is me if no one is real ?
What is touch if no one can feel ?
What is right if no one is pure ?
What is wrong if no one is sure ?

Laura Lemons
DEAD OR ALIVE

As a child
I watched in wonder
Electric eyes
Absorbed the thunder

I had no conscience
I was mesmerized
No detected responses
My brilliant disguise

In clashes of lightning
I saw the rainbow of hues
In flashes of enlightning
I heard the rumors of truths

Without reflection
I was alive with energy
Without interjection
Gallant strides were in reach

As the starry comets slipped
Through the mind's mesh
To that one point in time
When soul becomes flesh

To feel the awe—like a moth to the flame
To feel the desire—to have all things explained
I embraced the fire

Patricia S Struve
LIFE

Life
So close to death
Just
A heartbeat—a failed system
Just rewards

For those left behind

Mary Donnelly Canterbury
THE NIGHTS DARKNESS

The night's darkness
Who knows what lurks beyond;
Who knows what the future holds
For he who ventures on.

Jennifer Rankin
WHAT LIES BEYOND THE HORIZON

What lies beyond the horizon is a question many ask. Is it the ice-blue ocean? With its waves beckoning to us? Which stretches as far as the eye can see?

Over that ridge of mountains, what lies beyond? Is it the unknown desert? Its sand dunes always moving, always changing. Where the sun beats down on the weary travelers that happen upon this vastly plain? Where it seldom rains and even the cacti's thirst is never quenched?

Over the treetops, what lies beyond? Is it a wide open range? Where the cattle roam morning and night? Where gallant stallions watch over their mares and foals? Where the cowboy's song is always heard? Where a stallion's magnificent scream can be heard as he is taken from his homeland?

On the edge of the vastly plain, what lies beyond? Is it a forest of towering trees and shrubs and bushes covering its floor? Where animals can live and play like nowhere else? Where all wildlife lives in peace? Where there is no evidence of man?

What lies beyond the horizon?

Brenda Lambert Williams
I'M TERRIFIED TO DREAM

We're at a highschool football game,
The second half's begun.
When out of nowhere we see the "cloud"
They've dropped the atomic bomb.
The screams are deafening, the fear is real,
Where are my children, are they out on the field?
Oh Blessed Hope I see them, but there is so little time—
Lord, I then call out to you—but your peace I can not find.
I've wasted so much time Lord, that was not mine to waste;
And now I will be so ashamed when I meet you face to face.
Man's inhumanity to man just made countless thousands mourn
The rich man and the pauper alike will share the enemy's scorn.
We know what comes hereafter for men who've sown to reap;
But, what about the ones Lord, who did not your vigil keep?

Lisa Crouch
ONCE WE WERE BEST OF FRIENDS

In memory of my bestfriend,
Heidi Stanek

I sit here by myself,
wanting to cry.
I see your picture on the shelf—
without you I want to die.
Best of Friends We Once Were,
now our relationship is but a blur.
We had so much fun in the past,
I wish it could and only would last.
I cared for you
and tried to be true.
But now you're there and I'm still here,
only hoping you'd be near.
I hated it when we argued today—
Lord knows, I don't want it to end this way.
Our friendship was always special to me,
Best Of Friends We Once Were—
I thought it would last an eternity.

Russell D Means
REFLECTION

This poem is dedicated to all those who believed in me, that I might believe in myself.

In front of the mirror
Or, it in front of me,
Looking at myself
Looking back at me.

Delving into my mind
To see what I can see,
I find that it is like
An abyss of the sea.

Covering with the silt of time
The secrets of my self,
Dusty scraps of the past
Forgotten on a shelf.

A bridge across the chasm
The mirror is the key,
To unlock the darkness
That has enshrouded me.,

All at once I blink my eyes
And come out of my trance,
I realize the truth of it
A reflection is but a glance.

Eileen Bahlmann
MOTHER'S LOVE

I dedicate this poem to my dear mother, Madonna Kacher, of Little Turkey, Iowa, who will live forever within my heart.

The new-born baby fusses, for she's sick and oh, so cold,
"This little girl won't live long," the distraught woman was told;
But a mother's love is deepest on the face of this great earth.
'Twas put there by the Good Lord at the moment of our birth.
And so she took the baby small and fragile as it was,
She nurtured that dear infant with her tenderness and love.

Time passed so very slowly as it does when we're in pain,
Day in and out she wondered if some progress they would gain.
Then gradually it happened—her sweet babe began to mend,
The young devoted mother saw her child become her friend.

And yesterday that baby of so many years ago,
Heard words from her kind doctor that she prayed would not be so:
"Your mother's very sickly and her days with you are few,
Go home and tend to business, better do what you must do."
The tears would not stop coming as she blinked in great dismay,
The love she'd come to trust in was about to slip away.

'Twas then that she remembered what her mother taught her best,
"Our love does not stop growing when we're finally laid to rest.
You see, it's like the sunshine spreading warmth from up above,
And it continues living, this great gift that we call love."

Sandra M Van Sistine
THE SHADOW (K.K.)

Strong, yet gentle
Warm and secure
Frightened and alone
And yet, still so perfect.

But not like you and I
Different.

He stands tall
But by himself
Hear him call for you
Careful, don't get too close
He may hurt you
Not intentionally
But he will

Oh how perfect he is
But not like you and I
Different.

Dolly Charlene Smith
SWEETIE

As though she were the star
And life was her stage,
She'd sing, talk and dance
In her wee little cage.

She would strut back and forth
Like a queen with a crown,
Or doze unashamed
With her pantaloons down.

Like a teenage 'bop' singer
With a nod, get that beat! !
Then quickly change moods
And sing so wistful and sweet.

Like all shows that must end
She sang her last hymn,
Last night she sang herself to sleep
My precious little parakeet.

Rock-a-bye now cradled so high
My heart still echoes with your lullabye.

Lee Johnson

Lee Johnson
THE FALL OF THE ALAMO

To my 6th grade teachers at Crockett Elementary in Wichita Falls, Texas, Barbara Page and Alma Grace Richardson

Guns firing in the early morn,
Cries of pain echo through
the once quiet land.
Sounds of men marching,
with a mission to win,
Seems there could be no
feeling involved.
Days go on,
No stopping of this hatred,
wrath.

Innocent young men being killed
for power,
Such torn feelings.
One last shot is fired,
Many men lay dead,
They fought for what they believed.
Such courage.
The land is still and silent.
The Alamo,
Once a safe place,
Has fallen with its men.

Misty Tipton
RAINBOWS
Rainbows hold beauty
with colors bright and bold,
About the stories of the leprechauns
at the rainbow's end a pot of gold.

The colors light up the sky
so much mystery, I guess we'll never know,
Arching up in the sky so high
like a gift with a big colorful bow.

They show up in the misty rain
and on the reflections in the pond.
There never seems to be an end,
It seems to go on and on . . .

Then the rain stops and the sky clears.
The rainbow decides to go away.
Sometimes I wonder why god
doesn't make every day a rainbow day.

Bonnie Beebe Turner
VALENTINES JUST FOR YOU

This poem is dedicated to "Don" my dear husband.

"Best friends," I wrote just for you.
Now "Valentines Two" will have to do
As I sit here late at night.
Another rhyme comes to light.
One year ago I wrote to you,
of valentine friends
That was so true.
From time to time I get so blue, then I start to
think of you.
Sense you "were" a friend of mine,
This year you'll be my valentine.
Still there's times we cannot understand,
Why our love's so true and grand.
But "our love" shows upon my hand.
With a tiny diamond in a wedding band.
Now we know why, and do understand
Why "our love's" so true and grand.
Year after year I write a rhyme, and
Show the world that you are still my valentine

Barbara Keathley
THE CHRISTMAS CHILD
Long ago in Bethlehem
A Christmas child was born.
He came to tell the world of love,
Sent by his Father from above.

Long ago in Nazareth
The Christmas child did grow.
He grew strong in love and grace,
A light shone round his holy face.

Long ago in Galilee
The Christmas child did walk.
He healed the sick with gentle hands
And taught of love for fellow man.

Long ago in Jerusalem
The Christmas child did die.
He died for you, he died for me
On a hill called Calvary.

Joan E McGinnis
A CHRISTMAS DREAM
Twinkling, blinking little lights
upon my Christmas tree.
I gaze into the magic glow and
dream my dream of dreams.
I travel over land, flat and tall
through woods of great majestic trees.
Cautiously, I roam along the desert floor
Where saguaro, ocotillo and
cholla live and breathe.
Hoping the magic Christmas glow
will spread ahead to family,
friends and strangers that I meet.
Oh Christmas tree, bright with love,
thy magic light glows on.
Thank you for the vehicle to help
me dream my dream of dreams.

Marcus Juarez
SARAH
Sarah's so beautiful that if they ever
cast her down into the dark depths of hell,
they wouldn't be able to keep her there.

Because the beauty of her face, the beauty
of her eyes,
would burn a flame brighter, would burn a flame
mightier,
than any flame in hell.

That flame would burst through the ground and
touch the skies,
that beautiful, blinding flame from her beautiful
face and her blinding eyes.

Then she would walk out of there
and up to heaven, where even the angels
would be jealous of her incredible beauty.

But if I had more courage, I would
live up there in heaven with Sarah
above the clouds, below the stars
in a land all by ourselves.

Linda J Tarman
L. A. RAIN
Los Angeles is raining.

Baby leaves of crabapple green
nestle on darkened branches.
Jeweled petals glisten in the sun.

Driving home
twin rainbows arc the interstate,
planting their pots of gold
firmly in the ghettos.

The setting sun blinds me
while raindrops spatter the wind-shield
blending color and shape
until my view becomes a Monet.

Jagged peaks of snow
rise from the eastern desert
rolling into hills
that tumble to the Malibu surf.

Twinkling lights appear
as beauty fades into evening.
Cocooned in my car,
oblivious to time or destination,
I am hypnotized by the drumming rain.

Jeremy Lewis
NIGHTMARE
Drifting off into an endless sleep,
Chased by ghosts and other things that creep.
I am drowning in an endless fear.
It follows us year after year

Any escape I cannot find,
Help me escape the monsters of my mind.
Always waking just before the kill,
What have I done? Have I done you ill?

In the darkness, what do I see?
I'm falling into eternity.
A shadowed figure, I see in the dark,
While I wander in my mind's
amusement park.

As I reach it reaches out to me.
As our hands meet I realize the figure is me.
As I jump and through the mirror go,
I am caught in the eternal river's flow.

I need to find a way out of here
And return to my beloved sphere.
An exit is exactly what I find.
A welcomed trapdoor in my mind.

Charlotte Alcorn Bossinger
I SAW AN OLD MAN CRY TODAY

We dedicate this poem to you Dad, which was given to us by Charlotte. Through her reaching out and caring, God has opened our eyes in a new way.

I saw an old man cry today!
His spirit, oh, so low.
His outer shell was crumbling down
While the inner man cried, "No!"

"Come take me home, oh Lord," he begged,
"Release me from this shell
That will no longer do my bid,
And makes my soul rebel."

I saw an old man cry today!
His shell had slipped awhile,
And it had let the sorrow out
That hid behind his smile.

A smile that's lifting other hearts
Who have to pass this way:
But for a moment was so tired
I saw an old man cry today . . .

Eli Sjostrom
NO GREATER GIFT
In all kinds of ways
We are all seeking prizes
But most keep on failing
Which doesn't surprise us

But our hearts need not troubled be
Dark clouds can lift
For The Lord "if we choose Him"
Makes Heaven a Gift

Edie Swope
UNSPOKENLOVE

To Marj and Kevin with love Mom

Love to the child we'll never hold
here's all the "I love you's"
that were never told
Love to the child taken from our arms
before we knew your love
or felt your charms
Heaven shall know the laughter
of your sparkling eyes
God will sooth your pains
and mind your cries
To you our child we give our love
knowing God will take care of you
in his home above

Kimberly Ann Bigelow Welliver
LITTLE RED BIRDS
Chinese flowers, with long slanted leaves and fragile red crepe petals, look murderous;
are as out of place in my white room as I.
They cast eerie shadows, fingerpaint themselves in black relief on stark plaster walls.
A tiny porcelain chinaman; in little silk trousers, sits on the windowsill, he looks at me with sly eyes, his quick mouth a devious snip of persimmon.
At night, alone,
I remember Nanjing, and the long green river,

sluggish as blood between its
clay banks.
I can hear the tiny scarlet birds with
their piper voices, and the biwa
played by Ling-Zhou, her dark head
bent.
Sweet rice cakes and melon soda
flavor my dreams, and at night,
ingenious spider monkeys play
in the shadowed corners of my
mind,
catch at memory's tatters with
clever hands.
I watch the breeze from the
open window
sway the faded oriental blooms,
and long to return to China,
and the little red birds of my
youth.

Michele Rasbury

Michele Rasbury
GOOD OR BAD, RICH OR POOR

The world is full of people,
All different in race and religion.
Some are good, some are bad,
Bad are our enemy
Good are the helpful.
Some are rich, some are poor,
Poor are the hungry, always needing.
Rich are the two story houses that
take up two blocks, diamonds
and emeralds on every finger.

But some are neither good or bad,
rich or poor; they are just there.

John J Egan
FALL FERVOR

A work of art, a timeworn face
An eagle on the fly
Are steeped in beauty
This I feel no one can deny
But the fairest of all the stirring sights
That grace the human eye
Is a forest bouquet of autumn leaves
Against a fleecy sky.

T Butler Gelber
PRESENCE

In truth one can never tell the truth
As truth has facets never to be
counted
Leaving winding trails for minds to
travel
None of them at all to be surmounted

In truth, candor can be elusively quite
bold
With patronage thrown in to fill the
hours
Spent rehearsing monologues for
those untold
Of realities not seen outside their
powers

Reliability within our system
Graded by results not checked by me
Leaves my hyde available for errors
Passing by me incidentally
Prejudice arises from these dealings
Naturally as egos start to flow
Bruising here and there some honest
feelings
Standing out the door all set to show

Willingness collapses on occasion
Bridled by the reigns not questioned
here
Leaving room for others at
summation
Probably to not receive a cheer.

John Kinney
A SILENT SUFFERING

*To Mike, Sean, Kevin and John—
Condemned*

Cries of the innocent in the night
Born from emotions of both love and
fright
Not allowed a childhood, a normal
life
Innocence and love cut by the elder's
knife

In amongst the others, no different
than the rest
Too scared to tell the story, unable to
forget

Broken bones and bruises time will
erase
Psychological cannot and will never
fade
Destroying a soul before its life can
begin
Emotional murder, an unforgivable
sin

A silent suffering
An inescapable hell
Silently suffering as the punishment
fell

Ron J Olson Jr
TIME STANDS STILL

*To my Mom who made it all possible
and to Wendy who I love.*

with nuclear screams
and atomic whispers
a silent world cries
no one hears
no one replies
time stands still for an instant
as life wilts away
does anyone understand
will anyone know
of things accomplished
and of deeds done
will there be a past
if there is no future
with warped and twisted minds
dreams of peace prevail
in a world without love

Jon A Wells
RAW HATE

*To my great boys, Rhamy and Arion
May you accomplish all your dreams*

Such a term isn't
Written or found in any
Dictionary around
Nonetheless raw hate
Is a reality that lives
Within a home possessing
An ungodly sound

To hear it, to feel it
Is a daily plight for
Raw hate dwells in
The darkness and devours
The light

Raw hate has no true
Meaning for it is not
Documented to date but
One woman's hatred can
Be one man's fate
Raw hate can be
Described as destructive
And a killer of home
Harmony or a man's
Existence in a hell that
Only his eyes can see

Raw hate actually
Has no place in any
Person's life particularly
When it involves the
Stripping of man's
Dignity by his insensitive
And resentful wife

Though this statement
Will always be true
Raw hate still lives
Within a woman who
Possesses no love and
No heart for a husband
Whose home is a
Battleground for her to
Destroy his spirit and tear
Him apart

Georgia Lee Wagner

Georgia Lee Wagner
MAGICAL MOMENTS

Just for a moment let my fantasies
run wild
As my eyes search out your shy,
sweet smile.
Feeling the warmth of your love, so
like a child
Reaching and searching as we
traverse each mile.

Knowing the hot flames a new love
can ignite
Indulging each other and nurturing
our caring,
Letting passion continue to soar like
a kite
Cherishing the magic of this moment
of sharing.

With laughter and humor we can go a
long way
Each making changes as we give and
take.
Pondering our future in light-hearted
play
Treading ever so softly to insure no
mistake.

Wondering if our temperaments
should be more alike
Or if we should live in your house or
mine.
What does it matter if we just go for a
hike
Basking in love, not fears, as we
continue to climb.

Time is so precious, never let it
escape
Having found the person you've been
searching for,
A congenial, sincere, fun-loving
mate,
Need one ask for anything more?

Grace Paschal Wheeler
A LEAF IS A PROMISE

*This poem is lovingly dedicated to my
beloved husband, Terry, in deep
appreciation for his constant,
steadfast love and encouragement.
"Thanks, Honey!"*

A leaf is as promise
of Life yet to be,
It falls in the autumn twilight
drifting tenderly,
A child sees its flight and thinks,
"That looks like a
butterfly!"
It gently rests on the earth
till a breeze passes
by,
Then, skips and dances merrily
but not for very
long,
Cold, merciless storms come and
all too soon the leaf
is gone,

Days and months come and go,
dismally one by one,
Unhurriedly, life stirs again and
earth is given new
tone,
The grass on the lawn blushes
greenly,
"Oh! What's that on
the tree?",
It is a precious, visible reminder of
the
Life that is yet to be,
Yes, that tiny, tender bud,
some never bother
to see,
Silently communicates the joyful
reality,
God truly does care
for you and me.

Sally Angstadt
MAGGOTS

Maggots slowly squirm,
On the dead.
From toes to,
decaying head.
A fly walks on,
The rotten face.
He stops,
And takes a taste.
From lips,
no longer red.
As she lies,
on her cold,
cold bed.
With a face as white,
as paste.
Still half covered,
with,
Rotting lace.

Joseph J McDonough
ODE TO A JUNK HEAP
O Pile of Junk! O Heap so Grand!
O growing Monument to Man!
O Gauge of our Great Metropol,
Which towers where once grew
forests tall.

Oh, fill our fields and flood our
streams,
Inevitable End of Dreams!
And, when the Earth beneath has
sunk,
I'll say: "All hail, Great Heap of
Junk!"

Richard Beck
A PATH OF COLORS
No emotion is bad or wrong.
Only emotion with the chains of
restraint becomes twisted.
Imagine pure, unchained emotions as
the swirling colors of the
spectrum . . .
How can my most fiery explosions of
amber anger be any less beautiful
than my strongest violet waves of
love?
How can the darkest, coldest navy
tones of depression and pain be any
less enticing than the first beam of
goldenrod joy that pierces it?
As I walk through this path of
dazzling pigments only one fear do I
have, a fear as horrible as the beasts
of childhood dreams.
That fear is this . . .
I may look away, stepping off the
path,
Onto a path of coal grays, a wash of
neutral toned denial,
leading only to blackness.

Carmen Carroll
THE DAY I SAW THE DEER
The Day I Saw The Deer
I
In the door way
The deer
Near
The old apple tree

He
Stood there
Straining to hear

I holding my breath
To say
Do not fear

In the silence
Between us
My thought said
Stay

Did it snap
Like
A twig
He rose on a curve

Shawna Mathis
COOL BREEZE
The wind blows
a cool breeze,
The feeling of meeting,
the guy you've had your eye on.

The wind blows,
a cool breeze,
through the trees which
whistles a peaceful hum,
It brings back tender memory
sitting under the tree
holding the one you care for.

The wind blows,
a cool breeze,
that hits your face
to wake you to reality, to find
your heart has been broken.
All you have left is the wind blowing
a Cool Breeze

D H Faulkner
REMEMBRANCE
Pondering about my fate,
I wonder if I am too late
To change the world in some small
way
Before I face the dying day.

What deeds of mine, remembered
then,
Shall live beyond my mortal end;
And in the thoughts about me shared,
Will I be known as one who dared?

By all the lives that mine did touch,
Will I be thought of very much?
I hope to be, and fondly of
As one who left a gift of love

Symphony E Reynolds
JUSTICE?
As he created the fire,
He created the sky.
With this constant
And that
Contradiction.

The souls burn.
The birds soar,
With no justice for
Any.

Emmaline Palmer
JUST FOR YOU—IN AND OUT
IN's say, "It's a different world out
there."
Faultless egos seem disturbed by the
OUT's.
Now plain common-sense philosophy
knows
That all men have both their
weakness and clout.

Some view life as world-boxing
arena
With daily scheduled and unsched-
uled bouts.
Others see it as con games at race
tracks,
Where pro and novice receive and
give touts.

Apices for IN's or pit-bottoms for
OUT's,
In man's struggle to learn where lies
his space,
He fumes with rebellion against
"topkicks,"
When their greed becomes lip-service
disgrace.

Wasted millions that politicians
spend
To buy office, then freeload with
budgets,
Continues spiraling by transparent
means
Such as errors, graft, cutbacks; YOU
name it!

Can U.S. "waste groups" profiteer
hard work?
Can they refine "might-work" with
know-howness?
Are those words, "become a gentler
nation,"
Mere lip-reading limbo state-of-
mindness?

JUST FOR YOU to decide—my IN-
OUT kindness.

Alvin Lee Barker
CLOUDS
Have you ever had the privilege
Among the clouds to fly?
To forget those things that bother you
In the freedom of the sky?

So often people speak of clouds
As obscuring the brightness of day;
Or think of them in relationship
To storms that come their way.

But when you fly above the clouds
And behold the beauty there,
You think not of the storms that beat,
Nor of your earthly care.

Behold a sight that fills with awe,
Revealed to you in softest white,
Towering clouds that stand so tall,
Fleecy forms in majestic flight.

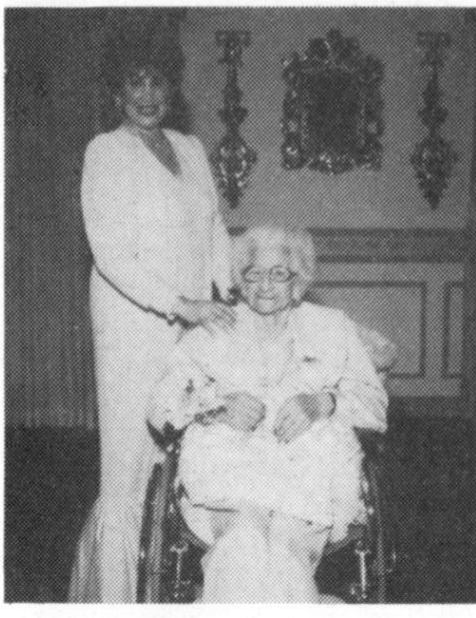

Shirley Lister

Shirley Lister
THE TABLES HAVE TURNED

Dedicated to my Beloved mother—
Yetta Friedman
sadly missed

Our Mother's teachings
We've learned
However the tables have turned
Now she's our "Little One"
Who depends on others
to get things done
Who needs every kind of care
To relieve her tension
Brought on by fear
We try to make her smile
By sharing happy events for awhile
It's difficult to recollect
Memories of yesteryear
It hurts to find her
With a hollow stare
She was once tall and strong
We ran to her
when things went wrong
Now we're the ones she seeks
As tears come trickling
Down her cheeks
Visiting means so much
It's important to keep in touch
To fulfill her desires,
We bring what she admires
Her eyesight is now poor
Her feet are swollen and sore
She can barely stand or walk
Her conversation is
Limited to small talk
Her hair has turned
sparse and white
Her body is frail and light

....

One day for a change of pace
A trip to the shore
Seemed to be the right place
With wheelchair and
Emergency items packed
With the aid of a nurse
To help keep things intact
We helped her in a van
And she sat by my side
We felt delight to see her smile,
and enjoy the ride
She loved the beauty of the ocean
Watching the nature of its motion
Then shopping at the mall to
purchase shoes
It made her feel whole again to select
and choose

Next a visit to the Casino
To gamble for fun
With assistance she managed
to pull the lever—and won
As her winning streak went on
She played 'til
all the coins were gone
By then it was time to go
Our "Little One" was tired—we
know

Ila H Stoltzfus
SOFT CHAGRIN
Between four trees, under warm sun
I see nature in action:

3 blue jays 2 cardinals
1 woodpecker 3 squirrels

Dig among the fallen leaves
Hop to a better spot
Hop to the spot just vacated

Oblivious of me
Oblivious of the big black cat
creeping across the yard on
velvet paws
flattened belly sliding on the
grass,
anticipating blue jay for lunch.

ONE POUNCE

A flurry of activity
Cat is alone in the yard
He looks around in chagrin
He curls up in a patch of warm sun

dreaming of blue jays of past
lunches
dreaming of newer and better
blue jays of the future

Immediate disappointment is
forgotten
in the warm sun and soft
grass

Steven Stadler
CELESTIAL PERISTALSIS
Behold! the moon offers me a
sanguineous smile, quietly slumbering, low in the horizon, a gentle
vagabond bathing in the romantic
chiaroscuro of dusk. And I
acknowledge her smile as an
intangible flavor, a flavor not of
tongue, but of mind . . . of soul. As
darkness approaches, this gentle
vagabond drifts away . . . digesting
beyond the horizon, marking the
beginning of celestial peristalsis.
Now! the Great Wanderers gradually
appear like phantasmal intruders,
luminous phantoms metamorphosing
into hot, feverish jewels . . .
scintillating, whispering answers that
only God is willing to share. I watch
these sparkling soldiers, and I
contemplate their ubiquitous
grandeur.
I watch them until they digest into the
early morning dawn; thus, marking
the completion of this celestial
peristalsis. Ah! the wind is now but a
mere zephyr, touching my cheeks
ever so gently . . . Psyche! prepare
me once again for this glorious
journey.

Christine Anderson
DRUGS
Drugs are a problem, you can see,
Affecting our children, and you and
me,
As God is our witness,
A solution we must find,
And to the dealers,
We can't, be kind,

God save our children!
Is our cry!
And every effort, we must try,

Put the dealers in the jug,
And the cap on tight,
That's the only way, I know to fight.

Kathleen M Ferguson
PORTRAITURE
reliable peripheral vision told the sunrise man
dawn never paused before to offer
spiced brandy tasting rainbows
passages from pages found only in
an unfinished book
alive with wonder
a gold and silver map leading to where ever
his patience calloused hands touch
the third button of his
white starched work shirt
relaxed
the sunrise man chuckles contented
feather sounds in the back of his throat
feeling gold and silver
purring cat stretch directions
to day
and
tomorrow

Eddie Fair
WILD GEESE
Against the crimson glow that
stains the eastern sky,
A pattern emerges as geese fly high
And swift, to where feeding
grounds abound,
Wheeling gracefully across the
waters of the northern sound.
Dear things, who hold Dame
Nature's love of solitude,
Who quickly learn the weather's
ever changing mood,
Who wheel and dip with joy and
pure delight
And fly in staid formation home
at night,
Joyful we behold you, etched
black, high against the sun,
And watch you winging home
again at night
When day is done!

Edwin Keller
THE BEAUTIFUL EARTH
The mountains are so breathtaking,
It boggles the mind of man.
Where else could we find such beauty,
Except upon this gift of land.

The beautiful trees of the forest,
And the wonderful valleys so green.
The babbling brooks and waterfalls,
Nothing more amazing the eyes have seen.

The Indians trailed these hills and vales,
And thought it all belonged to them.
God created it for all mankind,
Nobody knows just how or when.

I feel sorry for one who gazed at these sights,
The beauty of nature, has failed to see.
For when God created these wonderful things,
He did it out of love for you and me.

Lee R Roethlisberger
THE CARPENTER
With a mighty arm
Pounding nail by nail,
With every cut exactly true,
He molds a home
That's very precise.

The carpenter, a little man
With enormous pride.
A custom home to suit
The needs of each and everyone.

From the barren ground
To the finished detail,
A home that stands solid
On the mighty earth.

A home of their dreams
Stands like a castle
In their hearts.

Bonnie Penno

Bonnie Penno
B. C. MY LADY

To the working people who made B.C. what she is

B.C. you are a blessing
And to me, so very dear:
From my childhood, to my growing up,
Reflects on you, so clear.

I started life at oceanside,
Vancouver, my birthplace;
Then four years later I moved on,
To, Penticton; pretty place!

Then a short time later, I moved on
To another part of you,
Through your mountains standing high and proud,
Against your skies of blue.

I knew they would protect me
And your valleys keep me warm;
'Cause B.C.'s such a LADY, that
She'd never cause you harm.

I camped out by her mountain streams
And heard the loons at night:
And watched the geese fly overhead,
With dawn's first morning light.

No other place could offer what
My B.C. has to give:
Good people, love and beauty;
It's the land I'm PROUD to live!

Glenn S Beaton
EYES THAT SEE
Eyes that see, without seeing.
Seeing with clearness, yet indistinguishable.
With brightness, yet as cloudy as a dewy morning.
Eyes that see hope and sense love.
Eyes that see, without seeing.

Andrea Marcogliese
YOU
You're the sunshine in the morning,
The mist upon the sea,
A vision of pure happiness
Wistful and carefree.

You're the apples in the orchard,
The shining knight in dreams
Of young girls loving guys like you,
Namely, girls like me.

Your voice stirs in me passion
A whisper of desire,
A kiss to trounce all ration
And hearts to light afire.

So kiss me in the sunset,
And hold me in the dawn,
Just love me in the moonlight,
From now, forever on.

Mrs Maynard R Burns
NAVAJO CAKEWALK
(at Rocky Ridge Boarding School)
From a helicopter one looks down
On Rocky Ridge, gigantic, brown,

Where twilight steals and creeps and fills
The pink and mauve and violet hills.

In all that vastness there's a school
Of neat square lines, symmetric, cool.

There's not a sound for miles around
Except a truck on bumpy ground.

But, inside! Oh, it's Carnival Night!
The schoolrooms are ablaze with light,

And dusky folk have come to play,
To toss the beanbag and be gay!

The cakewalk beckons one and all,
And round they march; the short, the tall,

Kids with round heads, round black eyes,
A proud, slim matron, big fat guys,

Two giggling girls, a boy in red,
And music playing "Shortnin' Bread."

All over this lonely land, not one
But knows how to have a little fun.

Adell Carlock Lambeth
TIME'S STORY
Father time has surely taken his toll,
To cause all this some years did roll.
He has sapped the color from my hair,
Left some wrinkles here and there.
My jowls sag somewhat
And other wrinkles and sags I've got.

My steps may be slow,
Sometimes I can hardly go.
Oh yes, my youth is gone,
All my muscles have lost their tone.
Many miles Father Time has put me through
And there is not much more he can do.

Father time's story my body may tell
And the story, I admit is told quite well.
But—
That old man can't take it all,
In spirit I stand up straight and tall.
The sunshine of God's love abides with me
And my heart feels young and free.

Mary Smith
EVOLUTION
If it is true that we all sprang
From pollywogs and apes
Seems there would be no end to it
Since there's so many woods and lakes.

Seems like every other day or so
We'd have a brand new strain
From all the pollywogs that grow
And apes that become men.

They'd be crawling from the water
And leaping out of trees
They'd descend upon our nation
Like a plague or rare disease.

The biggest problem they'd create
Would be on Uncle's back
When time rolled 'round to see that they
All paid their income tax!

Ada S McCoy
I'LL NEVER LEAVE OR FORSAKE YOU
"I'll never leave or forsake you,"
said, my Savior one day,
"I will go with you always
even to the end of the way . . .
You have only to trust me
as your pilot and guide
I'll never leave or forsake you
even o'er death's chilly tide."

"I'll never leave or forsake you,
God, sent me down to the earth . . .
He, gave me power to save, to cleanse
and give a new birth,
To all who will accept me as
their Lord and King
I'll never leave or forsake you,
life eternal I bring."

Walter Hittle
AS THE WIND BLOWS
As the wind blows
So does life,
With each passing moment;
Through thickets of time,

Each day reminds me of a rustling,
As endless days of summer nights
Uplifting into sands,
Of eternal lights.

Love;
Traveling passed days end;
Never forgetting a moment,
A sign; that stars seem to send;

As the wind blows,
So does life;
With each passing moment,
Through kisses of time.

Joanna Mae Captain
THE CHRISTMAS RUSH
Well, once again
We hear the chimes
That remind us that
It's Christmas time.
The sky seems darker
As snow starts to fall
And suddenly cheer
Appears in us all.
It's the part of the year
We all like the best
When we rush ourselves
Getting ready for guests.
Far in the corner
Of our prettiest room
We set up a tree

With the finest of groom.
It's covered with stars
That brightly shine
And an angel on top
With a smile divine.
Out in the kitchen
Is a welcome sight
Cookies and cakes
To fill our delight.
The candy dishes
Are filled to the brim
To give the house
A tastee trim.
The mailbox is full
With cards by the lot
Of friends we once loved
But somehow forgot.
Out of these days
We really find
The meaning of love
And "to brother be kind!"
So it's really a shame
Not merely a sneer
To think that Christmas
Comes but once a year.

Blasita Gonzalez
FRIENDSHIP
Friendship's a joy
That never ends . . .
It's a friendship that grows
again and again
Now and forever
I will always treasure
All those moments we spend together
Good times and sad times
Will always come along
But no matter what
We'll still be strong
For you are a friend that I cherish
And whose feelings of friendship will never perish!

Henry J Nunez

Henry J Nunez
LOST WITHIN MYSELF
Lost within myself, I close my eyes to see
Feelings I possess, in the deepest part of me
Lost within myself, running all around
Please open up my heart and let my soul be found

Lost within myself, my future comes and goes
If you were a flower, you know, you'd be a rose
Lost within myself, amid words I need to say
How long will it be before, I'm to see the light of day

Lost within myself, another place to hide
Feelings and emotions, those lonely tears I've cried
Lost within myself, looking for a way to tell
Am I walking towards heaven or just straight to hell

Lost believe you me, it's the honest truth
I'm trying to find myself, 'tween adulthood and my youth
Lost believe you me, I've no reason to lie
The day I find myself, gonna be the day I die

Judith Cook
WHISPERS
rosehips, lips
and apple pie mouth
above the red stained rim
of a tea cup, steamy with spicy amber
and a twist of lemon

a dish with sugar tongs
silver plated and tarnished
as if dipped into sliding kaleidoscope rainbows
of spilled gasoline
colours I expect to drip onto the tablecloth
embroidered with blue cornflowers

rose petals, kettles
copper and shining on the stove
in the kitchen
where peasoup simmers and bubbles like oatmeal
or mud
or cement, with which one can mortar together
gossip and stories
if one is a clever stone mason
or a stone at best
for rumours are always cold and hard

Stephanie C Harris
FOR ERIN AT TWO
They will write songs about you
. . . and for you.
You're going to be a star someday
In a unique and special sky.

And you will always be my laughing, dancing Erin;
My littlest angel, my quietest moments,
My impatience, my joyous occasion;
My realization of eternal song.

Through a medley of colored pictures
Your face shines back to me
And I'm finally holding that star,
That star too high to reach.

Always remember . . . there is one song, our song,
That sings most different from all others,
For it rises from the tears, and it moves through the laughter
And makes such bonds as
these . . .

First born, first love,
No matter what, no matter where, I am here for you;
For you are an inseparable, inevitable part of my heart.

Nealy H Wooten
I CAN
No one knows me better than me.
I'm the only one who can change me, you see.

All that I feel I can put on the outside
When there is nothing that I want to hide.

I can cry out loud and I can complain,
Add a little more misery to a world filled with pain.

There's no reason for me to dislike myself,
And no reason to seek pity from somebody else.

For no matter what my problem may be,
Someone somewhere has a bigger one me.

And they do much more with substantively less,
Going one step further to do their best.

So the way I feel about me and the things I do
Can be a rewarding experience or a poor excuse.

I must lift up my head and straighten out my thoughts,
For no one but me can be what I ought.
And I can.

Elizabeth L Greene
PERHAPS
I lie awake and think of you
Not knowing what to say or do
The little things I think you would love
Perhaps for me
To bring to you
The stars at night
and maybe even the moon above
To show you colors you've never seen
To be with you
and having it feel like a dream
To find your heart
Would only be the start
To hold, to touch it, to keep it
and never be apart
Someone special is so hard to find
Do you think, Perhaps,
You could be mine?

Brian O'Hara
TIME LEAVES THE WIND
The snow laid its soft white blanket over the entire sleeping land
My best friends sleep in my sacred heart
In the dollhouse beds of my bones ribcage
When we were in boy scouts wed ride bicycles on the highway
Picking up Owls that died chasing beams of light
I saw a baby santa claus with a cap and a beard hanging on a christmas tree
Christ walks the streets like a beggar hungry for love
While Spinoza said the truth is written in our hearts
in our instincts and intuitions not necessarily books
Only children can save us
The four winds take turns with the maple leaves indifference
and so the ghost of the jade green river follows me through streets and rooms

A bum in portland oregon went down to the fountain by the plaza
took off his clothes as the people were walking by
lifted a bar of ivory soap and took a shower in the rain
The statue of mary has snails on it and passion flowers climb around her feet

A hippie lies under a pine tree and dreams of oceans, waves of fresh creek water
I was a child playing with a paper doll God
He knew I loved Him the perfect God, the God of my heart and dreams
The safe sword and the song in dreams. Reality itself is paradise its only the impurities within us which prevents attraction.

Beverly J Bridges
THE LAMB
Stan the man had a Van and lived by the Dam.

Now Stan the man had a friend named Sam who had a Van and lived by the Dam with Stan.

Now Stan the man and his friend Sam was out walking by the Dam when they met a man with a Fan named Dan.

Now Stan the man, his friend Sam and the man with the Fan named Dan sat in the sand watching the Dam.

Along side the Dam came walking a Lamb.

So Stan the man, his friend Sam and the man with the Fan named Dan went back to the Van owned by Stan the man by the Dam.

Now Stan the man, his friend Sam and the man with the Fan named Dan, smiled as they ate Lamb, while being Fanned.

D C Himmelspach
I STOPPED IN FOR COFFEE
I stopped in for coffee,
That was all.

But as the morning sky broke through the darkness
I recalled when darkness filled each morning.
When every day was gray
And day's end gave no solace.
Yet I remembered without malice,
And with a strange detachment.

The waitress filled my cup
And I turned my thoughts to you—
Waterfalls of love that we have bathed in . . .
Security and hope
And cold stone walls that finally caved in.

It then occurred to me—
Change is the only certainty.
I pondered,
But not for long.
No melancholic fit for me.

After all,
I stopped in for coffee . . .
And that was all.

Mae G Jacobs
A VISION OF HEAVEN
Oh, Lord, I'd love to have a vision of Heaven
Just a little peak of the beauty up there,
Sometimes I try to imagine it all—
But I know there is nothing here to compare.

I see the pearly gates as I enter
Oh! Lord what a beautiful sight,
It is a breathtaking view to see
That Heavenly shore so bright.

Oh, Lord, I see a beautiful rose garden
Not just a few roses of each kind,
But hundreds and thousands of the biggest blooms
An array of color that hasn't even come to mind.

As I walk down the streets of gold
And see the radiance of your

face,
The Love that shines I just can't describe
Oh, Lord, Just to know your amazing grace.

We are looking forward to the promises of God
Through our Salvation we know it is true,
Someday we won't have to wonder—
For my Lord, and Heavenly Father—
We will be there with YOU.

Belinda M Dolata
TRUE LOVE

This is dedicated to my mom who has faith in me.

"You are the love of my life," he told me.
"Wherever you are, I will be there, too."
I asked of him if he will always be
There, when I fall in true love with him, too.

His answer true until now, it may seem,
At the ball a new lady appeared there
Her eyes ice blue, her hair was like a beam
Of the sun; the lady came from nowhere.

He is with her now, the lady of ice,
And dances with her at the fancy ball,
And speaks gaily with her, and Oh! how nice
She positioned his back against a wall.

"You are the love of my life," he told me,
And love, true that he pledge, what may it be?

Scott Thome
THE WINTER WIND UPON US CHILLS
The Winter Wind Upon Us Chills
the summer wind and daffodils.
Reminding us of long lost loves,
of yesteryear, and sharing shoves.

I'm wishing they would reappear
just one more time throughout this year
to warm my over frozen heart,
to stay awhile, and never part.

Matthew Hadley
WORDS
With pen in hand, I sit to write
but the words will not come tonight
The empty page on the table
Reminds me of when I was able
To pick up my pen at any time
And put down words in simple rhyme
Some were good, some were bad
Some were happy, some were sad
Some spoke of loves I'd known
Others were of me alone
Others spoke of flowers and trees
Or maybe a gentle summer breeze
Or maybe it was of wind and rain
Laughter, joy, sorrow, or pain
The words always flowed so free
From pen to page so easily
With pen in hand, I sit to write
But the words will not come tonight

Muriel Vanderhorst
TREASURE TENFOLD
The sun shone brightly o'er the lea
As light I tripped down yonder path;
I felt the freedom of the sea,
And sensed a peace that long would last!

The tall grass rustled neath my feet;
The sky o'erhead was cloudless blue:
Should I, perchance, a stranger meet
My ramblings I'd recount anew . . .

Of rare wild rose along the way
And sturdy blossom, side by side,
For weak or strong, each has his day
To fill a purpose ere he die!

While saunter, I, to water's edge
And catch the gleam along the shore,
By Willow tree, espy a ledge
To rest,—thence to return once more.

Life's blessings here, in memory
I'll cherish still, and gladly share,
For Nature's treasure soon will be
Rewarded tenfold over There!

Stavros Cosmopulos
WHEN YOU WERE A KID
So long ago, so long ago,
the things you said,
and the things you did,
when you were a kid.

Go back a score or two or three,
when you were only as high as an elephant's knee.
Go back to the time when you wanted to know . . .
why trees are green and apples red,
and seven o'clock meant time for bed.
You always played with the neighbor's dog,
your personal pet was a huge bull frog.
The broken-down wagon that you had found,
how loud those caps in your gun would sound.
A big pile of dirt and clay,
is where you always sat to play.
The many scraps and fights you had,
and the slaps you got for being bad.
The woods you joyfully traveled through,
and that wonderful smell of home-made stew.
Just stop and reminisce a bit,
before too long your thoughts reknit . . .
the fun you had so long ago,
when you were a kid.

You look at a kid that plays today,
his wagon's a rocket, his gun is a ray
He knows apples are red and trees are green
He's tested them all in his atom machine.
and when the time is approaching seven . . .
he screams, "turn on channel eleven!"
Sure, the home-made stew is still around
a bright-colored can is where it's found.
But the dirt is still dirt and the same with the clay,
as you look at this high-powered kid of today,
his wagon has changed and so has his gun,
Yet, his smile shows it's the same kind of fun . . .
that you used to have,
so long ago,
When you were a kid.

Marjorie L Cross
THE MIRROR
Look in the mirror, my friend.
Not superficially—to
reflect and contemplate an image.
Rather, look deeper
Into the cavern of yourself.
What do you see?
Do you see what I see now?
Barren, cold
wasted self.
Lost in deceit and lies.
Trying to be what?
To whom?
And for what reason?
Gone is warmth.
Gone the sunshine of your very soul.
The caring.
The spontaneous self of laughter and happiness.
Gone the best friend,
of mine, and many—
except—yourself.

Donna L Fotschky
YEARS OF MAY
When you're young, love is bright and gay.
But after those years of May,
You come down to earth and there you stay.
Finally, you learn that it isn't always what they say.
Love can be sad.
Love can be one-sided.
Love can be bad.
Love can be chided.
If you're one of the lucky few, you'll find one day,
A love just like your years of May.

Bernadette Sievers Gannon

Bernadette Sievers Gannon
TO MY GUARDIAN ANGEL
When danger surrounds me
And loneliness sets in
I must meet a deadline
To survive lift my chin

Goals need their reaching
Time runs ahead of my lead
One ever present rules and guides me
Guards, enlightens, succeeds

Other angel friends often help too
St. Raphael the movements
St. Michael distress
But dear guardian angel—it's you nonetheless

Jason Leaf
SIX AND A HALF WEEKS OF DREAMING
Thunder crashed and shattered all windows,
Lightning flashed in cracked streaks
Striking everywhere, causing fire.
I was struck by awe.
I held on by my fingertips,
Dreaming that I could be with you.
I was slipping, knowing I would plunge downward.
Last minute memories flashed bye,
As a gust of wind lifted lifeless fingers.
Only the spiral fall remained.
I looked into the deep black,
There was little to see, only the occasional
White light, twinkling from above.
I had been let go to dash against edged rocks.
I watched, my body beneath me,
As it was about to hit.
A sudden jolt, my eyes opened
Only to see your lovely face.
I awoke vast in your arms
You cared and held me tight,
That drove all evil away.

James Ploeger
IN THE SILENCE OF MY HEART

For Christine, She who unknowingly changed my life.

She
Is like a May morning
Overflowing into the darkness . . .
And leads to the swaying,
And the silence of my heart.

She
Is like the nightingale
That softly sings on a cool summer evening . . .
And leads to the swaying,
And the silence of my heart.

She
Is like the reddest rose
That grows so lovely, no one dares to pick it . . .
And leads to the swaying,
And the silence of my heart.

She
Is the swaying of my deepest emotion,
That leaves me so shy . . .
In the silence of my heart.

Helen M Walton
I NEED YOU
With you, I am strong
You open all doors.
No task is too great,
With my hand in yours
—you are my strength.

When miles stretch between us
And problems increase,
Life's fears return—
In vain I seek peace.
I ache for your strength.

I search through my memories
For a breath of your touch,
For an echo of your voice,
For a word that meant much—
even a whisper of that strength.

Then with memory's magic wand,
The tool of heart and soul,
I melt in your arms.
Once more I am whole.
You still are my strength.

Edna Rush
MY WISH
My wish is that my home might be
A place of fond tranquility,
A place of love and tender care,
Where trials and problems we can share

A place of peace and harmony,
Where love abounds and Christ makes free,
A place to cast our cares away,
And rest our weary souls each day.

Daneen Dustin Jameson
JUST ANOTHER RAINDROP

To my family who have always loved my poems, my children, Tara, Jim and Danny, and those that say they are my "fans."

If I could make the sun shine, I would,
I'd make it shine forever, if I could.
But, beings as I can't I guess I won't,
And even if it did, I bet it don't.
We've just dreamed of camping this whole June,
If we're lucky it clears up a bit by noon.
And every time it don't we wish it did,
I bet it's hard to live up here if you're a kid.
The weather man assures us clouds and winds,
The kids have traded ice skates in for fins.
They ask us to go swimming on what little sun we get,
We figure either way they're getting wet.
A couple hundred miles from here there's sun,
Their friends come back with burns and reek of fun.
It hasn't always been like this I know,
But, now Fairbanks seems the only place to go.
We're hoping by July the days will peak,
So we can have a taste of summer's heat.
The quality of pictures all depends,
On just another rain drop on the lens.

David Kevin Wagner
CLEOPATRA IN THE SNOW
The seed within dead December,
Deep beneath cruel Winter's throw,
Long since foreign of the stem
Patiently awaits to grow:
The petal from the flower,
Fast under Crowded Snows,
No longer can remember
It was once the Rose.

Gerry Mattia MD
THE LADY AND THE OUTLAW
For it is I in the world that is—or it would be me in the world to come—but what now, a blighted dream—a once perfect ten—a true lady born and bred who dreams no more—settling for the outlaw in all his dash, in his panache. Sure no man can take issue for she had once found needed, wanted only one. There is no true sate. It is her loss of her make—believe prince who has come, loved her, and gone off to marry the horrid thorn—as I say to you is this the way it should be or shall I say this is the way it has got to be—

Sherry Dunaway
ALL IS WELL WITH THE WORLD
Fog slowly covers the shore. Cool breezes brush my face.
Peace, gentle peace surrounds me.
The distant fog horn, comforts my soul.
All is well with the world
The waves caress the sand, like a lover. Warm and tranquil. Fog covers the flaws; Leaving only the beauty. Remnants of life in the sand. Starfish and sand dollars decorate the shore.
All is well with the world.
The sun rises on a silent world. Spraying bright, yellow light on all that grows. Bringing to life the chirping birds.
Setting in motion, once again a day to behold.
All is well with the world.
With the rising moon come the quiet, soothing hours of darkness. Quiet night sounds. Unknown happening and gentle breezes; Known only to the people of the night. The hurried, hassles of the day, at rest. Nightfall brings peace; At last.
All is well with the world.

Nancy O'Brien
I KNEW HE WAS MY FRIEND

To Bob, my best friend

He called me when I needed to talk.
When I was restless, he took me for a walk.
When I was scared,
he told me he cared.
I knew he was my friend.

He picked me up when I fell,
and quieted me down when I started to yell.
He came when I was in need,
and swore he would never leave.
I knew he was my friend.

He told me I was wrong when I thought I was right,
even though it caused quite a few fights.
He said he would make time for me.
If there was a problem, it was me he wanted to see.
I knew he was my friend.

He brought me flowers just because,
and tried to be the best there ever was.
He said let's make it official, please become my wife.
Now that we are together, we have a happy life.
I knew he was my friend.

Annette Y Evans
AGONIZED SPIRIT
For years something has held me in chains,
It holds me, it binds me, it keeps me in pain.

People have long been telling
me what I need to do,
But how can they do that when
they don't know what to do?

They don't understand me, don't even try.
God, I just want to . . . cry.
I wish I knew why I'm so uptight.
Something's wrong, something's not right.
Frustration and struggle battle within,
I wish it were over, I wish it would end.

I feel so alone, like I want to melt.
Now I know how the greats of the world felt.

Everywhere I go, they ask me the same,
A question that threatens to drive me insane.

Why are you shy?
I don't know why.

I am who I am, make no mistake.
But how much more am I supposed to take?

C Todd Ransick
LANDSCAPED
The remains
of an earlier time
melt into the landscape.
Surrounded by the youth
which seem to smother it.

Still visible
the old retains sight.

Once relied upon,
the youth is gone
from its old limbs.

Pushing up
against a stationed force
it gives in.

The remains of an earlier time
melt.

Dudley Jess Catron
CHILDHOOD DAYS
He thinks of how he'd bait his hook
And cast into the running brook
And watch the bobber float along in hopes to get a bite.
Thinking back on younger days
Reflecting on his childhood ways
Now Father Time's caught up with him, he switches off the light . . .
he hopes he'll sleep alright.

She thinks of how she'd comb their hair
And push each doll upon its chair
And make believe that she had planned a party in her room.
She reminisces days gone by
And all at once she starts to cry
Then tries to find some happiness to chase away the gloom . . .
she hopes it ends real soon.

Within a wink we're middle aged
The book of life has turned its page
We're caught up in a rat race that has no finish line
Find a job and buy a home
And all at once the kids are grown
But no one seems to notice just what they've left behind . . .
is everybody blind?

Douglas Frank Roskowske
THE RACE IS ON
Finally dreams come into view
Making me restless with visions of you,
Unlike those who grow old where they set
I keep on the move cause I'm not finished yet,
Running a race with time and my past
Dodging the future and making the present last,
But once in awhile love comes around
Making it hard to keep both feet on the ground,
Slowing me down breaking my stride
I have to start finding new places to hide,
Restless by nature cautious by choice
Always ready, my opinion to voice.

Lisa Miceli

Lisa Miceli
SCARS UNSEEN
Spending time alone again
It's what I need to say
And now my friends have echoed in
The strangers gone away.

And you, my love, have followed me
Home . . . I take your hand
Alive, at last, to see what time
Has given for the past.

Now you say that love will linger
Even without my smile
Or hers—imprinted—rings on fingers
Ours . . . hours
In the photographs of time.

Poetry, not flowers, rests on my pane
Mystery, not showers
Spending time alone again . . .

I hold you closely to my heart
Where forever you will stay
Engraved within my very soul
—Scars Unseen—
Since you've gone away.

Kip Adams
A SPECIAL CHRISTMAS

To My Grandparents

As the flurries begin to fall
And the squirrels are scurrying around,
All of the children are rejoicing
As the snow blankets the ground.

The pine trees are standing tall
With colored lights wrapped 'round their crest,
And all of the houses are being tidied
For the long-awaited entrance of their guests.

Families are gathered together
Eating turkey and drinking wine,
It sure feels warm to have loved ones so near
That chills are sent down my spine.

Now as Christmas approaches
With the gifts and the trees and the love;
You know that somehow, somewhere
There is a God up above.

So as we gather today
It drives away any feelings of blue,
To know that no other boy in the whole-wide-world
Has grandparents as nice as you!
Your grandson, Kip.

Bethann Cotter
ALONE

Paul, A special guy once told me that friends last forever. I'd like to tell him that I love him. Love always, Bethann

I went down to the beach last night
And gazed out at the sea.
I closed my eyes up tight last night
And dreamt of you and me.

I saw us walking hand in hand
And talking 'bout our fears.
I saw us lay down on the sand
Our fears then disappeared.

Your touch last night felt different
Than it's ever felt before.
Your kiss last night felt better
And it left me wanting more.

We moved as one, together
With our passion burning strong.
We touched and kissed each other
And we knew it wasn't wrong.

I went down to the beach last night
And gazed out at the sea.
I woke up from my dream last night
As alone as one could be.

Your love for me is just a dream
My love for you is true.
I fear I'll always sleep alone
And dream of me and you.

Chyanne Williford
LIMITED LIFE

Look into this world of ours,
That was once so freely gave.
Rainbows settle from a beautiful sunrise
While clear waters trickle from long ago caves.

Now is bought or traded, and a lot has been stolen.
In exchanges that left men brave and bold.
Even then it would have been impossible;
Had it not have been for God's miracles.

If we could just take time to look and give our thanks,
For all those things which we have been blessed.
We don't need medals, gold and titles to give us rank.
Just to walk with the Father should be a simple,
But powerful request.

Steven R Strobel
DOWN THE DARK STREET

To everyone who did and did not believe. Special thanks to Mom, Lianna, and, Charlie.

Walking on down the street
Wondering, what does it all mean?
Walking past the corner store
I saw a man laying on the floor
I guess he couldn't breathe.
Oh! Tell me, does it ever end?
Are you still my friend?
Even if we don't talk anymore
Because I find you such a bore?
Broken ways that I cannot mend
Listening inside
Do the angels really fly?
Only you and I can guess
In a life that's such a mess.
Will my blood wash clean in the tide?
Taking notes from the inside
Wondering if I can fly
Wondering if I should try.

Gretchen Seeley
IF I COULD PAINT A PICTURE

If I could paint a picture of what I thought true love was
First I'd paint it yellow, red and blue
And then I'd paint a picture of you
Yellow for a gorgeous sunrise
Letting you know today was our day
Red for a beautiful sunset
So you could always hold onto our yesterday
Blue for the wondrous sky that goes on & on
To show you our forever had just begun
And then I'd start on you
But how does one paint true love?
With a smile, a teardrop, a kiss?
If I could paint a picture of true love
I'd paint a picture of you.

e j chavez
LOST LOVE

for melinda

although our worlds are apart
and our timing is not precise
our destinies are united
and fate is ours . . .

M C Walter
BLACK

Black, unpopular
Black, it fills
Crevice our own thoughts.
Depression
The color of fate
Black is as the dawn awaits
Secrets that are not shared
We do not know how deep it is
It is up to each of us
Can it teach us?
Dark
Death
Black stands for mysteries without a trace
It illuminates fear,
It is a hiding place

John Zimmer
SPECIAL FRIENDS MEAN SO MUCH

This poem is dedicated to all the friends I've known. Most especially to David and Peggy Homann, and their families. Thank you.

As we travel down our lonely roads of life, little do we know what to expect. Around each turn is a new experience maybe happy or sad, funny or bad.

And as we travel down our lonely roads of life, God has given us friends to share our experiences. Friends who make the going easier and less lonely.

And once in a great while, or once in a lifetime, or maybe in the next life, God brings certain people together that are more than friends. Who are more like a brother or a sister than can share with each other their inner most secrets and dreams.

Friends like this are so special and rare that we may not realize it until it's too late. My life has been made much better because I have such a friend. You!

Although I don't show it all the time or say it enough, I'm so thankful our roads have come together. And someday when sadly our roads lead us in different directions as we know they must, we won't be quite as lonely. Because we will be with each other in our hearts and our memories.

And when we finally reach our destination we will once again be together. For no matter how many twists and turns we must take on our journey all our roads lead to the same place.

And knowing that makes each step of our journey more hopeful.

Carolyn E Kennedy
ODE TO AGE

By sixty you start learning
Of "bad" and "better" days,
And big toes that start turning
And going separate ways.

You look in vain for footwear
And none of it will do,
Because the toes are pointed
And are not made for you.

You try to get your views
Across to some you meet.
("Why not have funny shoes
For folks with funny feet?")

The hats are smart and cheery,
But you look at them through tears,
Because you know in winter
They will not shield your ears.

The seventies have wings,
So say the multitudes,
And every decade brings
Its own vicissitudes.

Tom McGuinness
COMPLETION

This poem is dedicated to Teresa, my sweet mother.

Enduring is difficult in a world of creation:
Searching for completion
But, it is told, "Love conquers all"
Matching the completion of half to whole.
Conjointly, two is better than one, unless
Two is One in Love, confess
Thank the Lord for whom He has sent
His blessing was a compliment.
Though I see, sometimes, the world unfair—
It embodies my soul in a blank stare.
But, is it the world? Or
Those whom it is intended for
Who have made . . . feel naked and hunger
For shelter.
Upon completing my Pilgrimage,
I hope to relay the Message
Which had been conversed before
And then, shall say no more;
Thank the Lord for whom He has sent
His blessing is a compliment.

Katherine Poe
FAILURE

Failure is dull, colorless.
It sounds like howling wind.
It tastes like sawdust
And feels as if winter is here.
It smells like the dull wood of an old barn
And it is lifeless,
And dull.

Eugenia Adams
LIKE A SUMMER IN DECEMBER

Like a summer in December
That forever you remember,
Like the brightness of the sunlight
And the magic of the moonlight
And the magic of the moonlight
Is my love for you.

Like a summer in December
Bring me the sunshine in your eyes,
Bring me the magic in your smile.
Even if you love me less
And your heart is changed
I'll still give you all my tenderness
And I'll find again the way
To your heart of yesterday.
Even if you love me less
And your heart is changed
I'll still give you all my tenderness
And I'll find again the way
To your heart of yesterday.
Even if you love me less
All my love is here to stay.

Bring me the sunshine in your eyes,
Bring me the magic in your smile.
Like a summer in December
That forever you remember
Is my love for you.

Carol Coppock
MEMORIES 1974

This poem dedicated to the Hispanic Boy in Rahway, New Jersey—my guardian Angel.

As I ran to catch my plane,
I turned around to see;
your face pressed on the window,
Looking back at me.

My feet were running very fast,
My heart was standing still,
And as I waved my hand good-bye,
My eyes with tears did fill.

So many years have passed since then.
It's something I'll always remember.
I want you to know I love you—
Sad, sad eyes and heart so tender.

Ian Laitala
THE MEDIEVAL CATHEDRAL

Slowly falling through
Cathedral windows
Into a clear blue sky
Shattered priests
With praying hands
Drop down
Upon these lands
After centuries
Lost in thought

Paula Johnson
BROKEN HEART

You were all I ever loved,
All my hopes, faith, and soul,
My whole life,
All for you.

I will never love anyone,
As I have loved you,
I will never love anyone,
But you.

You were my dreams,
You were all I ever wanted.

No one will ever take your place,
In my heart,
Or in my soul.

Kirsty Hales
A BLAZING RED OF ASHES BURNING

To my friends who insisted I keep writing, and to my family who gave me love and encouragement.

A Blazing Red
of Ashes Burning
All the cities are destroyed
And the ants shrivel
in the dry wood.

Morning—
overwhelming me
shows me the vision
The sea becomes a reflection
of earth and sky
Until a skylark flies
through the pink air.

David Williams
CHRISTMAS IS
Christmas is
the singing of
all the beautiful carols.

Christmas is
watching all the holiday specials
I saw as a little kid.

Christmas is
families celebrating
the birth of Christ.

Christmas is
the smiles on all the happy kids
as they eagerly open their gifts.

Christmas is
wishing for peace in the world
and good will towards all men.

Christmas is
giving gifts and cards
to all those who I love.

Angeline M Cortez
SNOW FALLS

To: Eric, May we stay forever friends! Good luck with your music!!! Yours, Angi

When snow blows weakly in cool breezes,
Trees rustle viciously,
Flakes fall softly,
Streets absorbed unwillingly,
Windows shake wildly,
Walls creek eerily,
And I, quickly, wake up the night stars.

Gail Simmons
SPEAK SOFTLY LOVE

Dedicated to a past love for whom this poem was written, and to a dear friend, Leona York, for her belief in my writing.

Speak softly love when you're near to me
Speak softly love for I truly adore thee
Be gentle love for a heart can easily break
Be gentle love for thee I shall not forsake
Speak softly love, whisper love words in my ear
Speak softly love so that I alone may hear
Be gentle love when you hold me near
Be gentle love for you're one so very dear
Speak softly love, love words I long to hear
Speak softly my heart and soul, I give my love
forever as long as we both shall live.

Ola Mac Donald
CONGRATULATIONS WENDY!
An Inspiration!
Creative! . . . Exciting ! . . . Talented!

A beautiful young woman !
A person of intelligence,
Dedication and determination!

When facing a challenge,
Your original ideas,
With your creative ability,
Shows you at your best!

In Medicine and Science,
These ideas could become
Mankind's "Beacons of Hope!"
Save lives and help others cope!

Poets bring profound meaning
To the hearts and minds they touch!

As an Artist who knows,
One Painting can "Stir a Man's Soul!"
Wendy . . your vitality and zest
For always giving your best,
Could mean much to Humanity,

Wouldn't that be an ultimate test?

Muriel Demorest
THE SHY DARKNESS
The sky darkens,
The moon shines.
The world is peaceful,
We are loud.
Things all over
Are not the same.
Different people,
For different places.
Learning together,
Growing apart.
Never seeing
Love in their hearts.

Alexandra Russell
SOARING ALONE
Walk with me for awhile
Hold my hand along the path that is life.
If I stumble and fall
Grasp tightly, and help me soar
Above the pit-falls and mistakes
That are inevitable each day.

You will know when to let go
I need to learn from you.
You fly so elegantly, serenely
Your wings glide through the heavens
Your keen eyes miss nothing
You guide in a silent way.

The mystery that was once so great
Is reaching a climax.
Knowledge is replacing fear.
The strength of your hand holding mine
Lessens each day.
You have taught me how to fly.

Louise M Sinclair
TO A BUTTERFLY

To all those who appreciate more in life than money and material possessions. We have an immeasurable wealth!

Butterfly, you flutter by so gracefully
With wings of gold and orange and blue, you interest me
Such fragile wings that carry you upon your flight
And keep you soaring, smoothly soaring, as a kite.

There are those who try to catch you with a net
And take advantage when your wings are wet
Their fingers crush your tiny wings into a dust
To cripple you and betray your trust.

Not I, as I know your uniqueness
And hold in awe your gentleness
For beauty as rare as a butterfly
Deserves to live, and never be made to die!

Lucille (Landis) Brubaker
GOD WILL COMPLY!

Dedicated to the memory of my husband, Ellis D. Brubaker

The MOON was full,
Just riding high
In its ORBIT
Up in the SKY.

Stepping stone CLOUDS
With MOONLIGHT GLOW
Formed my slate gray
SKY PATIO.

I walked up there,
My p a c e was slow.
I groped along—
Where shall I go?

My mate is gone!
GOD called him home.
Can't talk to him
By telephone.

I feel there's help
Lurking close by.
I will find it—
GOD WILL COMPLY!

Susan K Witteman
JUST ONCE

In memory of my brother, Jay, whose life was taken from him by the hand of another. We had so much of life yet to live. (written at age 15)

Why?
Why couldn't I say it just once?
So many moments of laughter and joy.
So many times of anger and frustration.
All are so dear to me.
I hold the memories dear to my heart
And will never forget the joy they have brought.
But the empty space inside of me is so vast and lonely.
The tears seem to flow and flow,
Longing for the time when it will be filled once again
Only by you.
Or maybe till we meet again once more.
I long for the smile of your face,
The tickle of your voice,
The laughter from your heart,
And the love of you, my brother.
Now that you are gone I sometimes feel regretful and angry
For not ever saying how I felt.
To you, and for you, my brother,
I am saying this,
I Love You.

Stacy Joseph
TWO OF HEARTS
Two of hearts made of red,
losing you is what I dread.

Two of hearts so pretty & blue,
I sure love you, through & through.

Two of hearts I love so true,
as I said it's pretty & blue.

Two of hearts, my gorgeous love,
is like a wonderful dove.

Two of hearts that sparkle with gleam,
Do you think this is a dream.

Two of hearts like your sparkling eyes,
hopefully, this isn't a disguise.

Two of hearts, do you think this love will last,
or is this just a thing of the past.

Tammy J Allan
INNOCENT LOVE

To: Steve B. Kendall my fiance, and Mrs. M. Allan my mother. You've always supported me. Thanks—love Tammy J.

Soft music playing, bathed in the fire light
You and I on our own little flight
You ask me if I love you, what am I supposed to say?
Of course I do, I love you more and more each day,
I used to wonder if you feel the same, now I have no doubt
I know in my mind and in my heart, it's your love I can't live without.

Anthony Rivera
THE GREATEST GIFT OF ALL
They say that love,
Is the greatest gift of all.
Yet I must firmly disagree.
For there is one thing,
Far better. You see:
Along with love;
There's education, care and fun.
Stories to please, memories,
And playing in the sun.
The endowment of life,
An ally in strife.
A friend when you're in need.
These are but a mighty few,
Of the glorious joys decreed.
For the greatest gift of all:
Is a mother!

Hilary Pullen
MAN
A bomb goes off in the middle of a war,
Killing thousands of people nearby.
While far away a daisy blooms,
With a beauty that could make one cry.
Survivors of the explosion,
Start to run for cover.
While the newborn flower starts to discover,
The early mornings crystal clear dew.
The bomb's victims cry,
In agonizing pain.
While the crys clear dew begins to dry,
In the luscious and very green plaine.
The survivors began to help the hurt,
And many of the wounded do die.
While the flower gathers the water from the dirt,
And a hiker walks a trail nearby.
The explosion catches many trees afire,

And the animals run from the strife.
While the hiker gets the great desire,
And picks the flower taking its life.

Roy A Collins
THE LAST LEAF

To my beloved wife Evelyn, who continually gives her support to me, and will always be appreciated by me.

The last leaf which dangles on a limb
having watched others fall and
die,
not knowing if it'll be the next to go,
to float away and wonder why.

Yesterday, I felt so very strong,
and truly much alive,
today I am a forgotten leaf,
that will drift away and die.

Life is truly like that leaf,
for sooner or later we all must
leave,
but we are so different than a leaf,
because we understand and
"Yes" believe.

For tomorrow I will live again,
never to ask the reason why,
for I'll be safe in those loving arms,
never again to drift and die.

Colleen M Meinhold
A MOUNTAIN CLIFF

The breath is quick,
and the air is cool.
You see the clouds below,
and the birds are above.
The land beneath,
is in sight for miles,
and the sky beyond,
is clearer than ever.
Snow is circling you,
And the breeze is chilling your face.
It seems forever there,
and leaving is senseless.
Your mind is slowing,
air is precious.
But no worrying,
for you can save it.
The heart speeds,
there is nothing to do,
but lay down and wait.

Mary A Mullens
THE HOMELESS

There are people living on the street,
People who have little or nothing to
eat,
They have no money, they have no
home,
They wander the streets, so sad and
alone.

What happened to make their lives so
sad?
Where did it all turn out so bad?
They once had homes and lots of
other things,
How can they face tomorrow and the
sorrow it brings?

Our government sends billions to
Foreign Aid,
While people here are starving and
are so afraid,
Why isn't our government helping
out our own?
Charity, I've heard, still begins here
at home.

Let's start now and help our starving
here at home,
Please don't leave them to perish, out
there all alone,
Give them a helping hand, that's all
they need,
Give them another chance and watch
them succeed.

We can still help those in a foreign
land,
I'm not saying we shouldn't lend a
helping hand,
But let's help our hungry and our
homeless too,
They should come first, both to me
and to you.

Pamela Jean Craft (Lavanway)
I BROKE DOWN YOUR WALL

I broke down your wall, tore it right
down.
I got close to you, you let me
through.
No one has ever opened that gate,
No one cared, but I feel great.
You let me where no one's been
before,
and I went there, all the way to the
door.

I broke down the walls that held you
inside,
I cared enough to stay by your side.
To not walk away and leave you be,
I reached out to you, to help you get
free.
A friend you are, a friend you'll stay.
I feel close to you, so here I'll say,
I broke down your wall, you let me
inside.
You're set free again, you don't have
to hide.

Marilyn R Taylor
THE JOGGER

This poem is dedicated in memory of my mother, MARGIE TAYLOR, in memory of my aunt, MARY COLLINS and to my friends EDYTHE RICE and JANICE LETT who all urged me on.

There you stand, tall, dark and in
demand.
Soft black curls dancing on your
head.
A handsome copper-brown face with
big brown expressive penetrating
eyes. Black long lashes hovering
serenely over your visage.

Further down the face deep pretty
dimples lie.
A small nose which compliments the
facial expression perfectly.
A lusciously shaped mouth and
straight pearly white teeth.
A chin that looks authoritative and
neat, connected to a long neck and a
shapely torso.

Brown muscular shoulders with
beautiful rhythmic movement catch
me in a stare moving clean through
the crisp air.
Drops of salty moisture slowly
trickling down the heightened bosom.
Breathing rapidly from this
performance of exerted energy.
A magnificent chest with no flaws at
rest, gleaming with sweaty pride.

Arms nimble, sleek and strong.
Thighs and legs built just right with
every pound in place. What a
physique! So exquisitely unique!

Feet moving easily on the pavement
hard, steadily onward toward destiny.

Steve Wyman
PERHAPS

A child needs, a child should get
A love that is sincere and direct.
She needs to know, what to expect;
without effort, there is no success!

She needs a hand that can be firm.
A shoulder to cry on, a cheek that
turns.
Blood that can boil, but never burn.
A chance to grow, and a chance to
learn.

She has to learn, before it's too late.
All good things are worth the wait.
It's the love, not the hate,
that teaches us to appreciate.

Perhaps when all this learning is
through
When she and Mr. Right have said "I
Do,"
And she has her own little problem or
two.
She'll finally do as I say and not as I
do!

Paula W Coe
LIFE IS AT A STANDSTILL

Life is at a standstill, no night, no
day.
The sun has stopped shining, not
bright, not gay.
Birds have stopped singing, and
church bells have quit ringing.

Flowers have stopped smelling, I
guess death is unveiling.
Love has ended all, my happiness,
my heart.
Love took you away, it played its
part.
What used to be laughter has now
turned to tears.
What used to be minutes, now seems
to be years.
What used to be you, has now gone
astray.
And what used to be me has withered
away.

Jane Morgan
GIVE ME THIS TIME

Give me this time, when love's
aflower—
the impatience for an awaited hour,

When our lips will touch and hearts
entwine—
and I can pretend that you are mine,
give me this time.

Give me this time to dream secret
dreams of you—somehow, it makes
them sweeter to know they can't
come true, give me this time.

Give me this time, when the sun
glows faintly in the West—the hour
of day I hold as best, its end has all
its beauty cost—another day from
you I've lost. Give me this time . . .

Donna V Lingren
THOUGHTS OF YOU

For Byron
Happy Anniversary

These words of poetry you see before
you,
are written warm and true;
Their existence here today,
is due to my thoughts of you!

My thoughts will warm the
coldest day,
and lighten my darkest night;
They tame my restless heart,
without a painful and/or
tearful fight!

And now each time I think of you
My body fills with such delight;
I say, "There's nothing to be afraid
of,"
because thoughts of you are always
bright

We have each other and
vowed forever
to have and to hold it's
always getting better;
So with each new day that
passes by
in my eagerness, maybe I'll
touch the sky;
and touch I will higher and
higher
because thoughts of you set
my soul on fire!

So listen my love with a careful ear
my thoughts of you have been and
shall be in plain sight's view!

Nicholas D'Andrea Jr
SILENT FLIGHT OF THE SNOWFLAKE

This time of year I really love
To watch those crystals from above
Begin their journey way up high,
Patiently descending from the sky.

Each is a very unique structure,
Possessing a complex architecture.

Like a gentleman dressed in white
Riding a horse through the wintry
night
One comes to rest without a sound,
Becoming acquainted with the
ground.

Julie D Vandever
SOMEWHERE SPECIAL

This poem is to my loving Father, and those memorable moments, I will cherish always. I Love You!

There used to be a place,
Where my Father and I would go.
The trees were very tall,
And the water used to flow.
This place was so special,
to me and my Dad.
But now it's so different,
For this, we're very sad.
My Father used to tell me stories,
about this place when he was young.
One day when I have Children,
I'll tell them stories of my own.
This place is still so very special,
to me and my Dad.
Although it's covered by water,
We are no longer so sad.
We used to drive there,
Now, we sail across the water,
like we're in a race.
SOMEWHERE SPECIAL,
To that certain place.

William Fallon
SNOWY NIGHT

When once upon a snowy night
snowflakes softly landed light.
Trees did twinkle with icy crystals,
there were written many missals.

Townsfolk rested, quiet, cozy,
whilst I wandered cheeks all rosy.
Peacefully the snowshoe slept,
silently a stranger crept.

When I came upon a lane,

and I followed and I feigned
the little lane was all I had,
neither good nor bad.

Yet this is how my life is placed,
a country road to tread I'm faced.
A course to follow in the night,
a path to lead me to the Light.

Wendolyn C Myers
I WISH THAT I POSSESSED THE ART
I wish that I possessed the art
Of rolling time into little balls;
To end problems before they start
And avoid unhappiness before He calls.

Of putting all tears in a little cup
And placing them high upon a shelf
Where there they soon would all dry up
Then on to meet my happy self!

Of wrapping Sadness into papers blue
And tying it up with little bows
Careful to let no one undo the strings
So that it never shows

And of placing Faith where Doubt now dwells
Though I fear it's found a permanent home
And of stopping the pain inside that swells
And makes me feel so all alone.

Although this talent I do not own
The gift of ending my misery;
Throughout the turmoil I have grown
And a little love's been revealed to me.

Miss Maxine Landry
IN MEMORY OF MY DEAR SISTER WHO DIED SEPTEMBER THE FIFTEENTH 1988
The day you passed away I will never forget as your memory still lives on.
I will never forget that sad day as you have left me all alone.
But now I have no one to turn to anymore.
I will always keep missing you no matter what, although I have shed many tears which were not in vain.
So hope we meet one day so that I could see my footprints in the sand that I could walk with my Saviour hand in hand.
And I hope to see Him face to face in the promise land.

James M Thompson
THE SECRET TO A HAPPY LIFE
Life is a special gift, it comes from God above.
We're created to serve Him, but especially to love.
We show that we love Him in many different ways,
Not just now and then, but all of our days.

The love we show God can come through loving others:
Black, white, yellow or red, they are all our brothers.
Everyone's life needs love to grow and thrive,
For some people love is their means to survive.

Some people are young and some people are old.
Many live in houses, but some stay out in the cold.
But to God it doesn't matter, all are equal in His sight.
He loves those who are down and out with all His might.
There are those people who at the world are mad.
These people find it hard to even love a tad.
But no matter what they do and no matter what they say,
Even till the end, God will love them anyway.

So we should be like God as much as we can,
Loving every woman and every child and man.
We should love every life from its beginning till its end,
And maybe one or two might even become your friend.

Louis Connola Jr

Louis Connola Jr
THE BRIGHTEST STAR

To all my fellow employees of the Boca Raton Resort and Club.

On a cold winter's eve, three men travelled afar.
They were in a land in which they had never been before.
The distance had been great;
The hour was late.
Yet, they had no worries,
Because their guide was a beautiful, wonderful star.

April Vencill
FRIENDS (ARE FOREVER)
When you're down, you know they care,
When you're hurting, a friend's always there.
They give advice in time of need,
By your side forever they will be.
A friend is someone with who secrets are shared,
A friend is someone who really cares.
A friend is someone who understands,
Someone willing to lend a helping hand.
A friend is someone nice to see,
A friend is something that forever will be.

Jim Gardner
THERE'S NO ONE TO STOP YOU BUT YOU!
Give me the lad who lays plans ahead
And sticks with the job till it's done;
Hail to the chap who puts up a scrap
To see that the victory's done;
I'll take the fellow, with no trace of yellow,
Who, in spite of all setbacks, succeeds;
Here's to the man who tells you he can
And backs up his words with his deeds.
Many there are who'll travel so far,
Then stop somewhere short of the goal;
The cream of the crop will work with no stop
To finish the job as a whole.
The world's full of guys who want the top prize
But won't pay the price asked to gain it;
The fellow worth while, adorned with a smile,
Leaves nothing undone to attain it.

Avoid and ignore the radical bore;
To heed him you cannot afford,
For he's out to steal your incentive and zeal——
His tongue is a dangerous sword.
False prophets today you often hear say:
"Do just enough work to get by,"
But surely, indeed, the American creed
Is something more noble and high.

Opportunities rare are still ev'rewhere
For those who have vision and skill
The same rules apply as in days gone by
Intelligence, industry, skill.
So make up your mind you are going to find
The work you're best fitted to do,
Then get on the ball and give it your all——
There's no one to stop you but you!

Marilsa Torres Fonseca
UNICORN

To Vicente, my life and my love, and to my wonderful children, Bruce and Aimara, who showed me the Unicorn in the first place.

Brave soul that wanders through valleys of eternal myth
White as the highest clouds that drift among my dreams,
Carry me into the world you inhabit,
Independent and proud
And where all seems to be infinite!

Your stride is sure as you walk—
In knowledge of what is what,
Although to those who cannot see,
Your heart so pure and noble
You can never be
Real.

Take me away from all things mundane!

I waited another day
Until
You heard my call
and then,
You came.

Stephanie M Davis
ALONE
I feel so unwanted, so much going on in my head. Sometimes I think I'd be better off dead.
Unsure of what I want, never knowing what I need. Can't we get along? If I beg and plead?
I'm insecure and very unstable. Let me tell you what I think; lay my cards on the table.
I know what I want, but what it is—isn't right.
Can't we stop arguing? Can't we stop the pain? I want it to be like it used to, can't we be friends again?
My heart is very shallow, all I want to do is cry. I feel like I'm breaking down, sometimes I want to die.
Being together is making it worse, nothing's happened but the pain has grown. You can't understand me or anything I want, and what I want is to be left alone!
Please respect my wishes, please go on your way. If you can't understand—I'm sorry; I have nothing further to say.

Frank J Thomason
THE SPUD
Consider the lowly yet holy potato,
Potato bits at the Bistro,
Tater Gems and Tots at most drive-ins.
The potato state knows on which side its spuds are deep-fried;
But imaginations are constrained. Come,
Let us peel together, fry up a mess of hash browns and talk of spud futures, skyscrapers, and things that smell tatery in the night.

Verona Edwards
MY LOVE
My love comes free
Through the mists before the dawn.
I give it to thee
By morning light I must be gone.

My love comes freely
I give my love to thee.

Did you step from the stars to me?
Oh how I want you near me.
Where came your smile
And your loving eyes?
But out of the miles
And the sun in the skies.

Before the mist to predawn is burning,
Before the sun's red fire,
I'm lost in desire.
When we can't hold back the night from turning
That's when I'll be going.
I follow you wherever,
But no word do I say
To North and South I'll follow
Till the dawn of my day.

Martha D Haney
FLIGHT
Bright—
Dancing in the rays of the sun—
A floating rainbow
On a robin's egg sky—
Carrier of dreams,
Escaping the bound'ries of earth
On the end of a string

Sue Barnes
WELCOME HOME

Richard I love you

While underneath the evening Star,
I watch for the headlights of your car.
By the window in your favorite chair.
I think about the love we share.

While I am safe inside our home,
And the night sky makes a purple dome,
The radio plays your favorite song.
Tonight the hours seem so long.

And then I hear your keys in the door,

And I feel my heart begin to soar.
I rise, you're home—we run to meet.
My evening world is made complete!

Carolyn Allred Walker
SMUG FACES

Dedicated to the memory of my beloved husband, Charles.

They are so smug!

Those ones who have not encountered this poker game of life . . . not yet chosen to play the real game

Those ones who are holding aces and kings and queens
Seemingly so unfeeling, so unknowing

But wait; they too will be dealt a hand . . . soon enough

A losing hand, no doubt . . . by the Great Intruder;
hovering in the earthen shadows of life

Ecstatic to deal; mocking, laughing

A losing hand once; a quick hand of death

A losing hand twice; she breathed her last

A losing hand thrice; his death bells tolled

Oh, the agony I have felt

With the hands that he has dealt

My most dearly beloved ones, departed from me

Those ones with smug faces; still holding aces

I forgive them . . . for they do not know

That this dastardly dealer is cunningly lurking . . .
for me, and for thee

Margaret Sexton Remy
HOW WILL YOU REMEMBER ME?

To Mother, after Daddy's death.

How will you remember me when we've been long apart?
What will you recall when I'm not there to touch your heart?
We cannot have tomorrow, and today is almost gone.
The moments we are sharing will be memories by dawn.
And if, again, love comes and gives you strength to see life through;
Please know that, in my absence, that is what I'd want for you.

So, how will you remember me when we've been long apart?
You'll feel the pounding of the surf and recognize my heart.
The sun's warm rays will hold you, and you'll feel my presence near.
A raindrop soft upon your face will be a parting tear.
The wind will be my fingers sliding softly through your hair,
A bird will whistle love songs, and you'll know that I still care.

When pressure and discouragement or sorrows come your way,
I'll be the rainbow in the sky that brightens up your day.
I'll kiss you with the falling leaves that gently touch your face.
Their rustle is my laughter time and distance can't erase.
The sunset's glow will be my smile you said could lift your heart,
And that's how you'll remember me when we've been long apart.

Parker S Newby
CAROL OF FREEDOM
Snow filters through the cold grey fog.
Black trees, like notes on a score sheet
Flash by on an unseen horizon through
Fenceposts weakly joined by rusty wire.

Through the fog an eagle flies,
Diving, stalling, and twisting
To a silent melody
Pouring forth from shapes of grey.

Like fingers upon a keyboard
Her wings caress the air;
Notes and movements combine into
A smooth crescendo.

Spiraling upwards to new
Heights, she gracefully
Fades out of sight
Like a note through the air.

Sheldon Locke Harris
A BEAUTIFUL QUESTION
Why, I ask myself, my heart, are you
So beautiful? Is it that I
Love you for your beauty, or are
You beautiful because I Love you?
Look deep into my Love, beautiful,
Seek answers to find. My Love
Is pure as you are beautiful;
The thought of you rules my mind.
(That, in itself, is beautiful.)
My heart Loved you before I saw
You: Our Love is beautiful. And
My whole dedication is to
Preserve this truth so beautiful.

You are as is our Love, need there
Be an answer to a question—
Beautiful? Do I Love you because
You are, or, are you because I
Truthfully do? Need there really
Be an answer to what I wish
I surely knew? The age old question
Come to haunt me: Are you for real?
Will I wake the morning, finding—
That you are a dream—beauty—
fill'd?

Tammy Jarrard
WORKMAN'S CRY
Sails moving in the breeze, the sun has begun to set.
Piercing shrill the eel cries, the day is not quite done yet.
The men move to their own heartbeats, moving on every passing note.
They work long, and they work hard; without warmth, shelter, or coat.

The workman's cry of weary rings clear through the brisk night air.
And yet the captain sits back drunk and happy by a heater in a warm soft chair.
Backs straining to the drum of the heart, knowing there's a family to feed.
The workmen pull in their day's catch, with dirt, mud, and seaweed.

Tears and treachery are commonplace; have no room for a moment's rest.
Striving sometimes to no avail; good enough will have to be best.
The captain sits still drunk and happy by a heater in a warm soft chair.
While honest men work to the beat of their hearts; freezing in the cold night air.

Peggy L Harris
THE HANGING LADY

To my loving sons—Kevin and Brian and my lifetime love Ed

She hung gracefully in the chain lamp
though she was slightly bent and bare,

Surrounded by greenery that looked like
it was in full bloom,

When the lamp switch was cut on the oil
dripped through the cylinders
sometimes it spotted the chair below,

The spirals surrounding the lamp made
it look like a hanging cage in motion,

When the windows were open
and there was a slight breeze,

She swayed like a hula dancer with
the lamp from side-to-side.

E P Haas
CHANGING TIMES (ON GROWING OLD)
I am a stranger in my garden.
Great plants, flowers and weeds now grow
In many places I did not sow.
I am no longer the warden
Of the forests I knew so well,
My paths now blocked by trees that fell.
Familiar bird songs that used to gladden
Are drowned by calls I do not know
And winter's shade replaces summer's glow.

Where once I walked, stout of heart,
Mid green leaves and fragrant pine,
I shuffle now through dead leaves of falling time
That have covered my earth deeply with dark.

Eleanor Durr
ACCEPTANCE
I make myself acceptable to me
For only thus can I be free,
The Good, the True, the Beautiful my aim
I strive to reach this worthy role I claim.

I fortify my Soul by acting well my part,
To be in harmony with Self is all of Art
I must feel worthy and accepted—
Not guilty and rejected.

As each idea fashions strong desire,
I seek to create, transform and inspire
By doing something really worth the doing,
By being someone well worth knowing.

I claim my certain rich inheritance
As I accept my own significance,
Accomplishment so often comes before success
Yet I find ever more and more to bless.

Life is becoming what I am to be,
A wholistic personality.
I'm Justly proud to prove myself unique
As I become the cherished person whom I seek.

Danny L Powers
WHERE DID ALL MY LAUGHTER GO I'M SO SERIOUS NOW
Where did all my laughter go I'm so serious now
Where's the sparkle in my eyes they've turned angry somehow
Where's the smile I used to have, the wit, the joy, the fun
It went to California, it's out there in the sun

Where's the pride I used to have, where's my strength and guts
Where's the determination that used to drive them nuts
Where did my caring go, my ability to feel pain
It went to California, it's out there in the rain

What happened to the man that people looked up to
If they had a problem, they always came to you
My answer was final, I never backed away
I lived and laughed and loved, only day to day

So where did that man go, the people want to know
I used to be so wild and so free
Where did my heart go they all want to know
It went to California, it left without me

I remember the laughter, the tears, and the joys
It's sunny in California, it's dark in Illinois
So I'll keep on trying, I'll always do my best
But forgive my lack of humor, all my good times have gone west

I know you had to go, it seemed the thing to do
You left behind a sad old Dad that cares a lot for you
So they won't hear my laughter, and never see me grin
Till you all step off the plane and I see you again
Love you Miss you
Dad

Mamie Hodge
MY FLORIDA HOME
Florida is my adopted home.
Home where the cattle are grazing.
Friendly people everywhere,
Sharing sunshine and fresh air.
Home where the citrus grow.
Home where the moon is all aglow.

Home where the people are the very best
Coming from the North, South, East

and West.
Home where Edison invented light,
to make all of our Cities bright.

Home where our vegetables grow.
Home where sparkling waters flow.
Home where the birds fly high and free.
Home of the Alligator and the Orchid tree.
No other State can offer more.
Sea going ships, or a boat to oar
"Florida My Adopted Home"

Ethel R Whitaker
THE PERFECT CHRISTMAS (FOR BARBARA)

This poem is dedicated to Dr. Barbara R. Gillenwaters, a valued friend.

Christmas is a time of change.
It has become a time of hurrying.
The hectic rush, the furniture to re-arrange
To fit the tree in can be a little strange.

Amid the hustle come problems of many kinds
Causing fear, sadness and a change of mood
That really happens in our minds,
An altering of our attitudes.

But, "Ah," one says, "This Can't be.
The day must be an even better one for us.
There is the same necessity
For Christmas to be perfect from dawn to dusk."

There was a delightful air of tranquillity
And happiness did abound.
Adults' and children's laughter
Echoed all around.

And Christmas was a perfect day
In every inconceivable way.
The peace, the love, the joy, the sharing
Made us know that God was with us in our caring.

Amy L Merrell
SOMEDAY
Why does it always turn out this way,
no matter what I do or say,
There is no one left to run to.

When I need someone the most, just to get along, and I think I've picked the right one,
Once again it turns out wrong.
How much longer can this last, I've learned from mistakes I've made in the past,
But how many more will I make?

Just when I think I'm going to win,
there goes love playing tricks again.
I keep thinking just once, I'll get it right, but I'm almost ready to give up the fight,
Maybe, just maybe, someday.

Why do I fall so easily, and always I think it was just meant to be.
Why is it so hard for me, to just turn, and walk away?

I've played with fire and I've been burned, but one day it's got to be my turn,
To find the right one, someday.

Out of the darkness, out of the night, when the full moon is out, and the stars are bright,
Or when the skies are fiery, just before twilight,
He'll appear, someday.

The one I've dreamed of, year after year, I hope one day that he'll appear, and take away the pain, and the fear, maybe, just maybe, someday.

This one man I've got to find, before I finally lose my mind,
And I know he'll be strong, but gentle and kind, and God will send him to me, SOMEDAY.

D J Jeña Richardson

D J Jeña Richardson
I AM ME

Dedicated to my sisters and brothers, the children of Carlos and Rita Chavez from San Rafael, New Mexico

You are you! And there's nothing anyone can do.
To hell with them and I don't give a damn.
Why should I change? to please them?
I am me! And always will be.
I shall change whenever I desire,
For I could never ever be another,
Unless I fool myself and become a liar.
Why do I let people do this to me?
Make me feel like I'm to blame for
Making them act like they're offended
by something I've said or did?
Yes, I know! I alone am to blame for this feeling.
So, I shall start right now to give myself a healing.

Melville C Utterback
ENIGMA
Life is a journey down a trail my friends,
That winds to an unknown ending.
With many a fateful turn my friends,
Beyond all comprehending.

It climbs beyond the twilight ranges,
Into the land of night and the unknown.
The never never realm from whose dark shore,
No man returns and which could be our final home.

How strange it is that once upon that fateful trail,
There is no turning back for us,
the die is cast.
What memories we hold at last grow dim,
And moving time decrees no man relives his past.

Here is the great enigma hiding in the world,
Time has a secret futuristic undertow.
Man has his dreams but so does God,
Dreams more wonderful than man can ever know.

I bow like men of old before the ancient gods,
To silver draped Aurora goddess of all dawns and the unknown.
I kneel before the wonders that are yet to be,
To final dawns more wonderful than man has ever known.

Christina Hildebrand
MY FAMILY
My Husband,
My Son,
My Daughter,
My Life,

I love being a mother,
I love being a wife,

Together we are,
Together we will always be,

When you have the love of family
You have everything you need to be happy.

Catherine Stotts
YOU

To GOD who inspired my thoughts: May those on the hard road of life meet a friend they can have with them always.

In my loneliness and despair
Someone reached out and touched me with the hand of God—And that someone was you.
Though in my life I may still walk alone—
My memories of you and the kindness with which God sent you will always be with me.
I will hold you in my heart as one would hold a rare and priceless gift.
I know not what the future brings—should the time come we shall see each other no more—
Know that I memorized every part of you.
You are written in my soul.
You are my friend I carry with me always!

Richard Trask
NEVER SAY I AM SORRY
If sorry is a condition of decadence in the world
Which we all too often find.
While regret is a position brought
By the reality of mind.

Allow me always an ability to profess regret
For an error or thoughtless blunder;
But never let me mentally decay
To a condition of being sorry;
A condition wrought
While in the mire of psychotic plunder.

Charles Gaylord
FREEDOM
Years ago when this nation was young
Freedom was on the mind of everyone
They fought a war for freedom's sake
A free great country they did make

Then down the years when slavery ruled
The north and south for freedom dueled
Everyone should be free just like you and me
Be black or white or whate'er we be

Then Reverend Martin Luther King a leader came
Bringing no wealth but a lot of fame
His message to all for freedom bring
And have the nation freedom songs to sing

The fight's not finished push on again
In the sunshine or in the rain
Keep Reverend Martin Luther King's dream going strong
And keep on singing freedom's song

Sometime in the future we all pray
That freedom will be here for all each day
And as the years go right along
So everyone can sing freedom's song

Mr Victor Maynard
MY WIFE
Thank you for helping me through my illness
Without you I would surely die.
Thank you for giving me your love and kindness,
that only you can supply.
You whisper the things I love to hear,
that no one else can say
Your voice I hear so very clear
it really made my day.
You are to me a wonderful woman,
that makes my life worthwhile
With your trust and understanding,
is meaningless without your smile.
You once made me your prisoner,
and you sentence me to life.
I can not be happier,
With you my lovely wife.

Robert L Jones Jr
LORD, THANK-YOU

Dedicated to my Saviour the Lord Jesus Christ, who has blessed me with so much, though I gave Him so little, myself. Lord, thank-you.

Lord you've made a way,
Lord you've made my day,
Lord all I want to say,
is thank-you.

Carolyn Waters
THANK HEAVEN FOR POETRY
Thank Heaven for poetry,
without it we should be
emotionally groggy,

The lines of a poem do not
necessarily need to rhyme,

but they must have
meter all the time.

Tony Aquilino
ONCE UPON A NIGHTTIME

To those who are inspiring and to the lucky who are inspired by them
TA

There is no moonlight to guide our earnest hearts
No gossamer rays shimmering on the mirrored lake
Enveloping darkness soothes our mounting nerves
Will we be caught in intimate embrace?
Settling on the dock we seek each other's touch
Gentle passion makes way to wild abandon

The sentient lake bears witness to release
She surrounds us with loving warmth
Inviting us to revel in her languid shallows
But, time robs us of further pleasures
The promise of day intrudes upon our bliss
Starlight tears reflect her sorrow as we leave

Hand in hand we walk back through the silent wood
No sounds reach us from the quiet earth
Has the world stopped for us?
Hesitant parting mars the dreamy night
The lake absorbs another memory of love

Robert L Stowe
TO MY WIFE

Honey, I am sure that you are
at peace with the One who loves
you more than I;
Even my love for you is as deep
as the ocean and high as the
sky.
You have been gone only a short
while;
yet I am still lonely for just a glimpse
of your faint smile.
The raging storm is quiet and still;
The pain and suffering is no more for
you to feel.
I am sure you are cradled by the
Savior's arm
Where you will never experience any
more hurt or harm.
One day we will meet again,
you and I,
on the golden shore just at
the edge of an endless sky.

Shirley Sellers
THE AMAZING WALK TO HEAVEN

To my little boy Russell, and my little girl Casey Sellers

I took a walk along the clouds and I opened them up and I saw some wings that were as white as snow I asked myself what could it be and a voice said unto me this is the right place to be so come on in because my house is free look around and you will see
I said to the voice why are those white, soft wings here to meet me the voice said back to me dear child these are God's pretty angels that watch over thee I said O Lord are you ready for me and the voice said unto me No my child I just want you to come and see what it will be like to be up here with me I said okay but Jesus could it be another day when you come back to set the whole world free so the voice said unto me Come all ye that's faithful and that want to live up here with me where the angels are bright and it shall never get night.

Penny Letson
OPTIMISM

The new year is fresh and young.
The time to look forward to things to come.
The time when ideas begin to glint,
To burst forth not yet bent
by the weight
of passing,
of time,
of things left undone,
of not to repeat the abandoned hope
of older years.

The new year is tightly wound.
The time when all optimism abounds.
The time when the promise of a frond unfurls,
Of the strength
To greet that not yet met
of passing,
of time,
of hope not abandoned
and of things complete.
Rejoice to join in this fete.

Colleen S Klemp
TRUE LOVE

To my loving husband, Al, who is as precious to me today as the day of our wedding for which this poem was written.

It knows no boundaries.
Its passion knows no limits.
It has no clear beginning
and goes on without an end.
It starts like the trickle
of a small stream flowin
and gradually becomes a raging
ocean.
It becomes a relationship in which no
sacrifice is too great to ask.
This is the way it must be
if it is to last.
The pleasure received and
the rewards given are beyond
description
of any words that are written.

Sheri Saxe
MACROBIOTIC MAMA

For my mother, who taught me to cook and to write poetry.

Brown rice, sesame seeds, and veggie stir-fry,
Salad, beans, and tofu pie.
The frig is filled with foods Japanese and exotic
Now that Mom has turned macrobiotic.
The kids and dogs are at their wits' end,
A hamburger seems like a long-lost friend.

If someone comes near they'll do all in their power
To get hold of some smuggled bleached white flour.
Even the ketchup is on a far-off shelf.
The kids' only hope is Mom herself.
Though she's been really careful and strict so far,
How long will she last without a candy bar?

Christine K Coleman
IF ONLY I COULD

If only I could see you
If only I could touch
If only I could tell you
It would mean so much

Sometimes I think I hear you
Whispering in the night
It's just like I could see you
Your features close in sight

You told me that you loved me
And would for evermore
You gave me a golden band
Which everywhere I wore

But then the morning came back
You disappeared again
I couldn't remember where we had ended
Or where we would next begin

I look forward to nighttime now
Searching for your star
Watching for your wandering spirit
Wondering where you are

Darla Russell
FATAL REVENGE

An open window
Gives you a last breath
An unlocked door
Gives you a certain death
Three in the morning
Mommie's away
A killer is waiting
It's time to pray
Pain in his side
His wounds never mend
Someone betrayed him
A fatal revenge

A heart that is broken
Like a clock that doesn't tick
A mind is confused
Like a dog that doesn't lick
The wind whispers silence
Horror in the air
A doorknob is turning
The loner is there
A shining knife
Brings his pain to an end
Someone betrayed him
A fatal revenge

The ex-boyfriend came back
To hunt and to kill
The pain is over
And the night is still
A horrid nightmare
A horrid mistake
No need to scream
'Cause it's much too late
Gone out of his mind
On a chop and kill binge
Someone betrayed him
A fatal revenge

Edith Young
PITTER, PATTER

Dedicated to: Michele, Michael, Marty, Marc and Anthony Muroff

See the rain drops falling down,
Hear its pitter, patter sound
See the puddles on the ground.

Pitter, patter went the rain,
Pitter, patter went the sound,
Pitter, patter went the feet
Through the puddles on the ground.

Then the rain drops went away
And the sun, came out to stay.
No more rain drops falling down,
No more pitter, patter sound,
No more puddles on the ground,

Just a rainbow way up high
And its color, fills the sky.

Alberta Dedera Phinney
VICTORY

As I looked toward the eastern horizon,
I saw the sun in all its fullness rising.
I knew that another day was here,
And as I knelt in that quiet place of prayer,
It seemed that heaven's angels were lingering near.
God's still, small voice came to me so clear,
"I am with you alway,"
Today, I through Christ shall conquer.

In the midst of my work, in the excitement of life,
I paused for a moment to speak to my Christ.
I told Him my weakness,
Expecting strength from above;
The tears rolled down, and I pleaded the blood.
In sweetest tenderness He said,
"My grace is sufficient for thee."
Today, I through Christ am conquering.

At the end of the day I looked to heaven,
And thanked my Christ (thanked)
For the grace He had given.
While the evening stars were twinkling,
And the moon was shedding her light,
I looked up in full assurance
Knowing that all was right.
Today, I through Christ have conquered.

Vernice Henderson
HAND IN HAND

Hand in hand
Start the band
Prep for show
Set to go
While Macho Man
Glides me smoothly o'er the floor

Yvonne (Spirie) Wilson
BRIGHTNESS

Dedicated to Ms. Eddie-Lou Cole of the World of Poetry for letting the Brightness of God smile through.

BRIGHTNESS
As it penetrates through your
windows it sparkles
Widening the openings that reflect
your soul
Can it smile
Yes
Brightness smiles
When it tickles the nerves
Around the edge of your lips
Opening the mouth with gaiety
and
Sending out sensations of Joy
From within Brightness comes
Shining forth with eyes of laughter
That glows your face
and
Rouse your cheeks
With a message flare of Happiness
So alive
So sweet
BRIGHTNESS! !

Margaret Ferrelli
WINTER IN NEW ENGLAND

I dedicate this poem to my beloved mother, MICHELA for giving me life and her love

The snowflakes are falling past the windowpane
My gloominess is not feigned
My love is far away in a foreign land
Serving in the military . . . loyalty, duty and discipline go hand-in-hand

The wind is howling in the pine trees
All I can think of is my love of thee
The brook is frozen over
Where is he? Cornwall? the Cliffs of Dover?
West Berlin? Beirut, Lebanon?
Malta? Cyprus?
He boarded the plane without a fuss
Hesitant, he paused to wave
laconically to me and then he smiled . . .
Stalwart was he, my handsome dashing "Kyle"

The birds are feeding on the
carelessly tossed wild bird seed
I pace restlessly . . . . my nerves are
keyed
"WINTER in NEW ENGLAND" . . .
a panoramic view . . so peaceful . . so
serene
If my U.S. Army Air Force Captain
were here . . I would feel like a
queen!

Home and hearth . . my mind at rest
. . . more like a woman possessed
"WINTER in NEW ENGLAND" is
what I love the best
Vaguely discontented, why do I
yearn for more?
Is it my lonely soldier? A sentinel
standing upon a God-forsaken hostile
shore?

Kathy Churchill-Sulak

THE SUN SHINES BRIGHTER

Every day would end in darkness
But never as dark as just before
dawn.
Each night seemed a little longer
But of course, I could be wrong!
The sun always shines brighter
Knowing you're there to share in all
that is love.
The fact that we have a perfect son
Reassures me there's a God above.
And if it weren't for that tiny little
being,
You'd never know the depths of my
love.
That one day ended, with a light that
shone so bright
The night shorter than any other
before.
On the day our bundle-of-joy arrived,
Into our home and hearts,
For us to love and adore.

Rosetta E Bowles

SWEET PRINCESS

For My Sweet Princess,
My Lovely Daughter,
Karen

Tell me a story, my daughter
would say
Put some magic into my boring day
Maybe about a bird that lives in a
tree,
or Unicorns, or Fairies, or a Princess
that looks
like me!

We can have fun, just you wait and
see,
so please, please, a story for me
I'll turn out the light and we can
pretend,
of dungeons, dragons, and lions' dens
My, Oh My, what a fright!
Oh Please, Oh Please, a story tonight!

To bed, To bed, My sweet little
Princess,
You have loosened all of my
defenses
A story it shall be, but not of dragons
or lions
Please!

Sweet dreams shall come to you this
night,
For I have given my word
And sweet little Princess,
you shall never be bored!

Phyllis Spangler

UNDER THE RAINBOW

Under the rainbow
Nights are not the same.
Dreams last forever
Enchanted by the rain.
Reaching through the darkness
Thunder breaks away.
Hearts are in turmoil
Enter another day.

Reality overcomes you
As the sky rages on.
Inside your private world
Nightmares are finally gone.
Breaking the spell
Of sorrow and pain.
Windows open up and friendship
stops the rain.

Jan M Rice

SEARCHING THE WORLD FOR SOMEONE TO LOVE

Searching the world for someone to
love.
Wanting somebody that was made up
above.
Thinking somewhere the one will be
found.
Looking and learning without making
a sound.
Wondering just what you're looking
for.
Knowing there's someone out there
that you'll adore.
Beauty on the inside is hard to find.
I just want somebody who is gentle
and kind.

Alex B Jackson

Alex B Jackson

MEN CRY TOO

I dedicate this poem, to the three most important ladies of my life. My mother Carlotta, my daughter Briana and my baby sister little Carlotta. I love you all

A man may be hurting deep inside,
but you could never tell it from the
eye.

You may never see a man,
cry in the light.

It's not accepted by society,
so they cry at night.

When you catch a man crying,
Which is seldom done.

He might play it off by laughing,
"these are tears of fun."

But believe me when I tell you.
Men Cry Too
They have feelings just like you.

Yolanda Starr Hornick

THE GIFT

This Poem is dedicated to Portia Denise Hornick, who brightens up my every day.

I look down at my beautiful, caramel-colored, curly haired girl child. What a wonderful gift the Creator has given me. But, can I really call her mine? For soon a time will come, she will grow up and change like the seasons. Become a grown-up woman, off on her own.
Will she come visit, and sit and have tea? Will we have those girl talks, just her and me. Then, I will realize, she was never really mine. Only for a season. But, now it's time to give her up. Oh, but her memory is sweet, like a precious burnt offering blowing in the wind, whose scent goes up to heaven and makes our Father smile.

Mary Jane Rohn

FAITH

With the dawn of day
There comes a new light.
What is this heavenly light
That can turn sorrow into joy?
Emerson knew of this magic lantern;
All great men are aware of this
God-given power.

As a great star at night that guides the
ships at sea,
So this bright light guides the
God-like man,—
Through the Red Sea and the
wilderness,
Into the Promised Land.

It is not learned in colleges,
Nor from the man next door,
But only at the feet of Christ
Can such as He be blest.

J Kevin Burlison

IMPASSE

It is the most agonizing of pains.
Watching all of the people go by
Disillusioned by the love they were
so fortunate to find.
For some love is easy,
For others it is an impasse.
Why must I make it so difficult?

Betty Jean Banks

ALZHEIMER'S DISEASE

This poem is dedicated to my dear Mother, Daisy. She cannot thank me with her mind but with her heart.

As I look around at the elderly, my
heart aches deep inside.
To see them slip into yesteryear, is
not beholding to the eye.

They know who you are today, but
tomorrow is a different thing.
The one you know as your mother,
sees you as a stranger again.

The day to day transition can be
boggling to the complex mind.
But your love for her is stronger, than
the pain you feel inside.

They say there is no help, when they
reach this place in life.
Parts of the brain are deteriorating,
medicine can't cure this time

Is there a point in life from which we
escape reality?
Do we take ourselves back in time to
a place we want to be?

Though times are changing and the
future is at hand,
in their minds the past will always be.

Psalms 71:9;
41:8,10

Becki Dilley

THE TURKEY

There once was a turkey
Who said "Oh my!"
"I really, on Thanksgiving,
Do not want to die."
"I want to eat corn,
mashed potatoes, and peas
But everyone else
wants to eat me."
So he fled from the barn,
ran across the road.
And then you know what?
He met a pink spotted toad.
The toad asked, "Where are you
going?"
"I'm running away.
I don't want to be eaten
on Thanksgiving Day."
So then the toad asked,
"Well, where are you heading?'
"Oh, I don't know,
I might go to my sister's wedding."
And that's where he went
that sly little guy,
He went and got eaten
and this poem is no lie!

Dorothy Peterson Sprague

LADIES—OUR PRESIDENT

A toast to every president,
past, present and potential,
who brings the office dignity
and kindliness essential,
who stimulates constructive growth
in every loyal member,
who betters her community,
her term, all will remember!

With every credential
of courage prudential
and poise presidential,
she has the right
to expedite:
business motions miscellaneous,
and to curb those extraneous,
to omit the non-essential,
to avoid the preferential,
to delete the influential.
Her keen foresight
finds truth and light.

Ethel Huffman Taylor

THE BEGINNING

This poem is dedicated to Jesus who made it possible, to my loving husband Donell, son Jonathan, parent B J. & Odessa, brothers Willie (Jay) and Jimmy, my sister Margaret, Godmother Fannie Primm and all the supportive saints.

Life begins as a small sperm
That's seeking for a home
Looking for a Mommy and Daddy
That he can call his very own.

A tiny little precious thing
That God has allowed a new
beginning
A body so soft, sweet and cuddling
A tiny being that will have your heart
singing.

A baby is a special gift from heaven
Bundled up and sent directly to you
A little smile and large bright eyes
Letting you know that "I belong to
you"

The beginning of life is giving
The inner part of God to mankind
Nothing in the world more precious
No better gift you could find.

Emily E Clarke

SKY VIEW

Birds have responsibilities
Just like we humans do;
Their schedules are so tightly knit,
I noticed when they flew,
They even had some traffic jams
With crows and jays to blame—
And there's another quarreling one,
I can't recall its name.
But have you watched at evening
light
And marvelled at a bird
That swiftly and alone made flight,

With no sound to be heard,
To its secluded resting place,
And wished that you were one?
Oh, I have—but I came inside
When dark night closed my view
And noisy imitation birds
Claimed earth's whole sky, and flew!

Robt P Holmes

Robt P Holmes
E AND THE BOYS

Dedicated to the memory of E a special Mom.

The mother was E, the boys were three,
Donald, Robert, and Dee.
Almost from the start these four were an atypical one parent family.
Although early life was hard, they never tired. E was always there as mother, father, coach, and ofttimes referee.
Then as time flew, they all grew, there was never pain without corresponding gain,
For E and the boys.
Always through the hurts there came the joys, for E and the boys.

From farming sharecroppers to the city life,
Steady careers all but ended the monetary strife.
But too soon life takes another turn, then the value of health not wealth we continue to learn.
After a time she grew ill, another test of the will, of E and the boys.
Through many years of suffering a cure was sought, alas, only sufficing comfort could be bought.
E left this year, to enjoy living in heavenly rapture, thus closing this worldly chapter, of E and the boys.

Khuloud Haddad
A CHANCE NEVER TAKEN

I always thought there was a chance
for my love to enhance
until I heard you were leaving
my heart that day stopped believing
I thought you never need to know
that my love follows wherever you go
I keep thinking of what could've been
if I would've told you of my feelings back then
day by day the pain slowly dies
but the regrets will always fill my eyes
I'm such a fool to forget that life can be cruel
It has taken the only love that I have known
all because of the feelings I've never shown
all the chances that I failed to take
in fear my heart might break
now I live the life I have chosen
with my lonely heart that has been broken

Nancy Jean Swartz
SOMETIMES

In loving memory of my father, Arthur John Swartz Jr., who died on Aug. 22, 1984. I will forever miss him.

Christmas time is sometimes sad,
and nothing else can feel so bad.
As trying hard to keep the smile,
that's covering up the heart that's crying.
It's not that I don't feel the cheer,
but there's someone gone who should be here.
And it's hard to fight the tears inside,
as it's always hard to say good-bye.
And a father is a girl's best friend,
if you're gone there's no one to defend.
The little girl that's still in me,
who wishes that it wouldn't be.

Dorothy Cooper Bisselberg
THE GREAT KANKAKEE RIVER

To my son, Richard G. Cooper Who spends many hours hunting and fishing on the Kankakee River.

I enjoyed our cabin on the old Kankakee,
We spent nearly every week-end there, with our grandsons, three;
They liked to play along the shores where the Indians lived so long ago,
Pretending they were warriors with their arrows and their bows.

The deer came down to drink in the early dawn,
The huge buck with his doe, and their little fawn;
The chipmunks scattered here and there in the heat of day,
Caring not who was around to interrupt their play.

We loved to sit and fish on the shore from morn to night,
As the big ones tugged our bobbers, and pulled them out of sight;
Some got away, but others were the victims of the hook,
Ending in the frying pan of the family cook.

If you've never been to the old Kankakee,
You'll be surprised at the wonders you will see;
Treacherous waters rushing by,
turtles sunning on a log,
Acres of beautiful trees, miles of mysterious bog.

It is heaven to the fisherman with his rod and reel,
And to the avid hunter, stalking out his evening meal;
I'm sure you'll feel the presence of the Indians all around,
For the land along the Kankakee, was their hallowed ground.

Take time out of your busy life
before your days are o'er,
With your family and your friends,
walk along the Kankakee shore;
Our land is full of beauty if you only look around,
You'll find it on the Kankakee, the Indians' camping ground.

Vanessa Jo (Shaffer) Swanson
DEAR MOTHER

Written For Josephine Shaffer, With Love, Judy Ann Moore, Pauletta Lee McDonald, James Mikel Shaffer, and The Poet Vanessa Jo Swanson.

I Love you Dear Mother and never tell you so.
I've taken it for granted that you must know.
You gave the gift of life to me and my very own name.
Taking care of my needs and forgetting your own.
You gave me Love and a home.

Dear Mother, forgive me for troubling you so you're
everything a Mother should be.
At least you were and are to me.
My wish i'd grant you if i could, all your dreams.
But just saying i love you is hard, it seems.
I Love You, Please forgive me.

Linda J Williams
SCHOOL OF HARD KNOCKS

To my son, James A Cason (Jay), for all the heartaches and trials you went through as as teenager. Love, Mom

There's so much happening in this world of ours,
We could sit by the street and watch at all hours,
Most of us would surely be shocked,
At the things to be learned in this school of hard knocks.
That's life, by the way, this school of hard knocks;
The triumphs, the failures, and sometimes the shocks.
We learn a lesson every day that we live;
We must always remember, we get what we give;
For life is a give and take situation;
Most don't get far without education.
We need to have knowledge, to a certain degree,
To live with more comfort, most people agree.
We can't change what happens to others each day;
To the sick and the poor, it just happens that way.
Life can be cruel to some people it's true;
But more often you find it's all up to you.
Try not to look back, don't dwell on the past;
Plan for your future, it's coming so fast.
Look forward, step proudly, have respect for yourself;
And every so often, you need a good laugh.
When you're depressed and downhearted, rigid as rocks,
STOP! ! ! ! ! ! !
Say "I'M GOING TO WIN, IN THIS SCHOOL OF HARD KNOCKS!"

Debra Renee Monetti
A SISTER'S LOVE

To Tammy (Monetti) Waller, to always remain my special little sister.

What is this bond that they call love
that is shared between two sisters?
A love that time cannot destroy,
that miles cannot separate.
A love that endures sorrows and overcomes all hate.

What is this love that we do share?
It is yesterday's memories,
tomorrow's dreams and today's accomplishments.
Thoughts of days gone by, but always
the comfort of your love right by my side.

What is this special bond of love that we do share?
It is a love so true, a love that only sisters share, this love I share with you.

Laura M Johnson
MIRACLES

Dedicated to my three daughters, Lorys, Eldora, and Marlys—my miracles.

The day of miracles is past?
I tend to disagree.
Just look around about you,
Many miracles you'll see.

The miracles of sun and sky,
The miracles of earth;
The tree, the bird, the lovely flower,
The miracles of birth.

The tiny seeds that germinate
To give us daily bread;
The necessary rain that falls
From grey clouds overhead.

And then another miracle;
The miracle of man,
Whom God made in His image
To fulfill His mighty plan.

But the greatest miracle of all
Is the miracle of love—
And the greatest love in all the world,
Is the love of God, above.

Elaine R Renner
TEARS OF RAIN

In loving Memory of Janelle Alaina March 7, 1988—March 15, 1988

Silence is all I know,
Since you have gone away
Peaceful Silence turns into Rain

Tears flow through my soul as rivers flow
Through majestic mountains of ole'
Gently flowing towards the open sea
Cleansing my soul, setting the spirit free.

Remembering always, the love in your eyes and the beauty
of your face, as your tiny hand enclosed into mine,
Surrounding my heart with your loving embrace.

SLOWLY . . . . . . SLOWLY . . . . .
SLOWLY

YOU GENTLY SLIP AWAY,
LEAVING ME WITH
SORROW AND PAIN.

SLOWLY . . . . . .SLOWLY . . . . . .
SLOWLY . . . . . .
AS YOU GENTLY SLIP AWAY
PEACEFUL SILENCE COMES
THROUGH
TEARS OF RAIN.

Maureen Spisinski
MASTER OF DISGUISE
As I doodle on cartoons,
Fake mustaches and darkened moons,
I sometimes wonder, if there be
A more creative way for me.

Perhaps a novel—takes too long.
Got a tin ear—there goes a song
How about a mystery story?
I shudder at macabre and gory!

The children's stories I preferred
All sound like tales already heard.
So, ruling out all these tries,
I wield my craft, in deep disguise.

Hidden in words sent over the years
To car mechanics, about slipping
gears,
To friends and family and educators,
In notes, stuck to refrigerators.

Though great talent may not be mine,
And no best-seller will I sign,
I still enjoy the frivolity
Of writing silly poetry.

Elizabeth F Tudball
MY DREAMS . . .

In memory of my beloved Father
My Mother for her undying love
And the men in my heart James and
Matthew Megge.

I remember looking into his eyes one
night
Saw beauty and grace, oh so bright.
His eyes sparkled like a very cool
wine,
Then I noticed his eyes were looking
into mine.
Our eyes met and we fell in love,
Not the puppy love, but the kind from
heaven above.
He was very handsome and kind,
A man so different that I lost my
mind.
I wished the day we spent together
would never end,
But we ran out of things to do and
money to spend.
He took my hand and we took a walk,
We heard birds singing in the
moonlight,
We didn't even talk.
But the night came to an end, he
walked me home.
We said goodbye for the night,
Tomorrow he said, we'd talk on the
phone.
It was the best day of my life,
Because he asked me to be his wife.
He asked me on our walk by the
stream,
But all of a sudden,
I woke up and realized it was a
dream.

Kevin Brent Nelms
"FANNIE"

Dedicated to: Barbara Duncan—a
true friend and beautiful lady.
She brings out the best in me. Love
ya, Bobby. KBN

The news of her, that came today
Was that she'd passed away. The
Old lady who lived up the street,
Who kept her garden so prim and
neat.
I'd pass her house almost every day,
But not in years since we moved
away.
How soon forgotten, those childhood
days.
Barefoot summers and mid June
slumbers,
Have somehow slipped away; but I
still
Remember the one up the street, who
kept
Her garden so prim and neat.

She'd call us over for a Coke, then
Make us laugh with a joke. She never
Seemed to be angry or sad. We were
The children she never had.
Just how long has it been, since I
Was a kid of nine or ten?
So much in life has changed since
then,
But when I see a garden so prim and
neat
I remember "Fannie" who lived up
The street.

Patricia Verheeck Stover
DREAMS TURNED TO DUST
The way I felt I tried to conceal,
To you it was fun, to me it was real.
The love I have in my heart will
never be told,
When my days are numbered and
I've grown tired and old.
I wish you could have cared and felt
for me,
The deep love I had for you but you
closed me out and you wouldn't see.
I wanted you to love me as I did you,
But you loved those who only caused
you pain, and that made me blue.
So now I close my heart and hide the
hurt,
Hoping someday, someone will come
along and lift my dreams from out of
the dirt.
And love me like I wanted you to,
And fill my dreams that I dreamed of
you.

Lois Wilson
TREES

Dedicated to ALL little children.

I wonder so many times,
Why God made a tree,
To live much longer than me.
It stands so straight and tall
With its branches waving in the
sky.
It seems to whisper with the
wind
As if it knows secrets none
knows,
Not even I.

The children play in its shade,
It's a special shelter that God
has made.
It protects from the hot sun and the
rain.
In the fall the leaves begin to fall as if
it's in pain.
The leaves of every color are so
beautiful,
I cannot tell.
But it stands so proud, so strong
When the cold winds prevail.
How many years will it live?
A hundred or two?

It will be standing proud,
When I'm gone.
I wonder, will there be trees in
heaven too?

Dona L Fox
FRIENDS FOREVER

To the Golden Friends in my life who
will always hold a special place in
my heart.

A friend is someone special
whether living near or far,
Someone you can count on
when the clouds start growing dark.

Someone you can share with
your sadness and your joy,
Who knows just when you need a lift
and can give you that extra buoy.

A friend is someone who believes in
you,
When you—yourself do not
and tries to help you understand
to give life all you've got.

A friend is someone patient,
kind and understanding.
someone you can really trust
when you don't know where you're
landing.

Yes, friends are very special
and should be cherished more than
gold.
True, some will tarnish and fade
away
But the best ones always glow.

Howard F Smith
CHALLENGER, GO AT THROTTLE UP

For risking it all, the Challenger 7:
Dick, Mike, Judy, El, Ron, Greg and
Christa! Shuttle Flight #25, Pad 39B
launch at 11:38 A.M. EST, Tue., Jan.
28, 1986, Kennedy Space Center,
Cape Canaveral, Florida.

Commander Dick Scobee, "Roger,
Go With Throttle Up!"

74 seconds into Shuttle Mission 51L,
1977 miles per hour,
54,685 feet high,
8.0 statute miles down range.

Ride the Fire! Instant oblivion, only
three remain!
Columbia, Discovery and Atlantis,
While their sister ship's debris,
Rains over the Atlantic, reduced to
cosmic junk!

The spirits of seven young and strong
astronauts,
Suddenly transformed into eternal
white energy.
To merge with Dave Bowman and
HAL, a Model 9000,
Exploring forever the mysterious
universe.

While we are left to Ponder our
fragile existence,
The hopes, the dreams, the
inexplicable horror,
That comes to visit our ordinary
reality,
We grope to pick up the pieces and
cope with today.

While a few adventurous and
fortunate souls,
Are chosen and choose to pursue the
inexorable,
Humanity's insatiable desire to reach
for the stars!

John "Probert"
UNICORNS? . . . BAH!
"Unicorns and Elves
Pans and Faeries, too
Are created by the mind
When there's nothing else to do."

"I think you are wrong
I believe they're real
Just like the emotions
That constantly you feel"

"Your point is a good one
but still I disbelieve
So hop upon your Pegasus
And then just kindly leave"

Joy Ward Rhine

Joy Ward Rhine
A WOMAN'S HEART

To my loving family and special
friends that I love in my heart and
soul and for their inspiration and
love to me—Thank you—Joy

A woman's heart can hunger,
all her lifetime.
It can ride like the sea crest,
and never be answered.

Not that she's never been loved,
but that she has love that,
she cannot reach.

A hunger that is in you and
through you, to touch another
that you'd love to know.
Also knowing that you can never
do that.

That desire in a woman's heart,
to be loved, more than anything
in the world.

To be caressed MIND and
THOUGHT and BODY.
To be desired above all else,
the impossible dream.

Marie Dickerson
LOST, BUT HOPEFULLY NOT FOREVER

To Amanda; you are not alone. We
are in this together. And to everyone
else who has anorexia.

As many people do not see I am lost.
Lost where I don't know . . . . maybe
that's why I'm so lost.
My mind likes to play a lot of tricks
on me.
I say I eat three meals a day,

But that's just the way I say I'm O.K.
But really I am not O.K.
Because sometimes I skip some meals each day.
I'm lost in wondering what to eat.
I even think about it in my sleep.
I say to myself "Now you can't have more than 800 calories,
For if I do it will be the worst,
Because if I eat too much my stomach will burst.
If I eat a piece of pie I will gain,
And that will cause my mind and stomach much pain.
I tell myself tomorrow I will eat right,
But all I do is put up a fight.
I want to be strong and healthy,
So that I can raise a little family.
But until I find myself I will be lost.
What ever happens, I'll have to pay the cost.

Steven Jude Apice
GOOD LUCK
I know where a dirt oval
is raked clean; where the odor
of liquor, cigars, and droppings,
permeates the sensibilities;
where only adults
can study the fortuities
in ever-changing illuminated odds.

And though their picks remain haphazard,
there is some victory,
but for the multitude,
the obligatory tearing of tickets
is invoked by Lady Luck.

New bets are placed,
but in the end,
most are denied a future.
And isn't it a wonder,
that people have the right to choose
the ventures they enter.

C Sparks
WHO FORGOT THE DREAM
Who forgot the dream, was it you, is it me, the question was asked;
Who forgot the dream, of a somber past:
Who forgot the dream, of my blood that was shed;
Who forgot the dream, of equality now that I am dead:
Who forgot the dream, of sitting in the back;
Who forgot the dream, of the colored that's now black:
Who forgot the dream, of the walk from Selma, to Montgomery for the vote;
Who forgot the dream, of the journey through time, that great voyage on the boat:
Who forgot the dream, of the graduation from the chains of bondage, and inferiority;
Who forgot the dream, of the low wages, rat infested tenements, the bugs, the drugs, and being the minority of this sorority:
Who forgot the dream, of southern economics, two of everything shows the world of our class;
Who forgot the dream, of the civil rights worker's cry "I'm free at last":
Who forgot the dream, of an organizational friendship, with a strong head and solid base;
Who forgot the dream, of a seer of mountains removed and given a building of change in its place:
Who forgot the dream, of a speaker, of my brothers' keepers, and spirit filled;
Who forgot the dream, of a finisher, once the starter has been killed:
Who forgot the dream, of a man in a Democratic society, and a Capitalist state;
Who forgot the dream, of a downtrodden people, with a predetermined fate:
Who forgot the dream, of this rhythmic people's melody;
Who forgot the dream, of this world's race bloody symphony:
Who forgot the dream, the question is asked;
Who forgot the dream, of who will be last:

S Lynn Scott
WHOSE LIFE ARE YOU LIVING?
Porsche, BMW, SAAB,
Tiffany's, Cartier and Van Cleef,
all of these and more, and more
if all could be Commander in Chief

Love your money and live your life
or is it the other way?
You think it's both—you may be right . . .

It's you against the world my sweets,
can you seize that motherlode?
When you have reached your goals
you'll know
and will have set your style and mode.

Robert Edgar Burns
SUNRISE
When I look at a sunrise
I see the dawning of a new day
And the expression of your eyes
With the many things they say.

When I look at a sunrise
I see the coming of a sky so blue,
And then I find it no surprise
How much I love you.

Doris Barb
TIME
The pendulum of time may seem to swing slowly
But its movement is constant we know.
The seconds, the minutes, the hours pass before us,
And not slowly but quickly they go.

As we pause to reflect on each eon of time,
How minute or great it might be,
Let us weigh the value it holds for us—
This gift of time which is free.

We've been given this gift to use wisely
With countless things to do.
Every brief moment is precious;
Don't waste it—it is of value to you.

That special task—it ought to be done.
"There's no time like the present," we say.
With a plan fulfilled, a deed well done,
God's gift is not wasted today.

John D Gulick
GRAMPAW'S LANE
Grampaw's lane leads up to the barn
Built when Indians once walked near,
Its thin-gray boards, no longer mute
Whisper secrets in the wind.

A peek inside, through toddler's eyes
Spies dim-lit harnesses, dusty things
Rusting, rotting implements
Suspended in time . . .

Remnants of a once-prized way
Stand vigilant, stand waiting,
Silently waiting for teeth to chomp bit
For whip to sting flesh,

Forever.

Shadows flicker—eyes grow wide
Nostrils flare, wee toes turn up,
Stagnant hay
Steaming earth.

Puzzling that living man found meaning here . . .
Mind's eye glimpses life not present.
Timbers groan as
Small feet churn down Grampaw's lane.

Tamara Papka
DO YOU REMEMBER?
Do you ever shed tears, for by-gone years, the love that once was there?

Did you forget, or just regret,
or did you ever care?

The laughter shared, the problems bared,
in whatever we did do.

Not anywhere, was there a pair,
that was like me and you.

So when came the hate, that was our fate,
why was it such a must?

To destroy our love, which held none of,
these new feelings of mistrust.

Now I'm all alone, my emotions condoned,
'cause it hurts too much to care.

Do you remember, do you now?
'Cause I think it's only fair!

Maureen S Berk
HANDS
Touch me,
with hands as lithe as butterflies.
Dart tenderly across
the softness of my palms.
Reassure me
with each gentle flutter,
and with dancing fingers
express thoughts that your
lips cannot utter.

For words come hard
from a tongue used to weaving webs—
And emotions are hidden
behind emeralds that glow fire.
From burnished nieve reveal
the music within,
making notes sing and scales dance.
Touch me
With hands as lithe as butterflies.
Touch me.

Audrey Fleischer
A LIST OF SUGGESTIONS OF THINGS

To my husband, Tom, and our children, who have inspired my writings. I love you all.

A list of suggestions of things
you might do,
To make you feel happy, instead
of so blue.
Just take a good look at the
person you see, and try looking
for the good in you and me.
Remember with each passing
hour, you've conquered the
hardest, your own will power.
Use this power as your strongest
defense, and you'll face all
your dragons with confidence.
Each day you spend in questions
and doubt, makes it harder to
understand what life's all about.
Only you can decide which way is
the best, and make THAT your own
special quest.

g l mendoza/Maeva A Clark
GRIEF BE SHORT

L.L
inspired by you
carried by God

Grief be short
words were long
Pain end as joy began
Bondage once, now, not allowed
peace within, thanks again
Prayed—knowledge revealed
Denied Him, denied self
Loving you pain remained
tears shed all in vain
Acknowledged this—pain fades
peace within, joy comes
Praise Thy Name

Sherral Hunt
TRUE LOVE

To every child that is lonely and needs true love.

True love starts by giving
All you have
By showing one's true self.
One child lonely
And poor but has so much to
Give for everyone.
This child is called mistaken.
No one sees this
Child unless you're one of those
Mistaken yourself.
All is needed to find one's
True self is
Looking deep enough to find
The mistaken one
Hiding in you.

William Albert Miller
THE WORLD WE LIVE IN

Try to help anyone you can anyway you can. And let them know you care.

We live in a world that is full of crime.
And it seems to get worse with time.
There's drugs and thieves, and killings.
But we could clean it up if we were all willing.

Stop cutting down the trees and killing everyone.
Stop the crime in the streets and we are only half done.
This is what we must do if we're ever going to win.
It is the only way to clean up the world we live in.

We must learn to stop hurting each other.
Start treating each other as our brother.
We must help the man next door.
Whether he is rich or even if he's poor.

There is good and bad in everyone we meet.
So don't judge them because they live in the street.
Someday we might need that man to survive.
He could be the only one that can keep you alive.

Melinda Thornton Johnson
MOMMY'S LITTLE MAN

Dedicated to mommy's two little men, Joseph Allen and Jonathan Richard. With all my Love.

He cuddles close to my side.
I wipe a tear from his eye.
If only he could go out to play.
I say, "Maybe another day."
If only he could understand.
Hours ago, his fever ran.
Time is nothing in a child's eyes.
Naturally they think time does fly.
Soon he'll grow, then he'll see.
Life was not so simple, when he was three
I take his little hand.
He smiles at me, that's mommy's little man.

Randy Golden
VISIONS OF YOU

To Professor Charles Hughes, who created in me a love of poetry.

From deep recesses of the mind,
Come thoughts of peace—serene, divine.
Answers to problems, are not there to find,
Can there be a memory of what has not been?

Will love for, desire for, only make seem,
That which is not a lovely memory—fantasy.
When those come to fruition, what is next,
More pulsating mindless apparitions?

How then can that which is not—be painful.
Does hope bring—anxious fearful craving,
Wanton pleasures—seeping, perspiring,
—Can the mind embellish all of this?

Elysia J Watkins
DANA

To Dana

Mom persevered in his younger years
but time increases its toll
Now only the sedation of a magic liquid
to give her rest and quiet her tears

It's been twenty-two years now
he is already twenty-nine
I think things will get better somehow
Afterall, it's only a State of Mind

God had a different plan
a plan that devastates a mother
breaks the heart of a father
And makes a child, forever, of Big Brother

He does not appear to understand
He does not appear to reason
He can never take care of himself
He is a child for the season

He laughs a beautiful laughter
frustration provokes his destructive anger
for he has been robbed of expression
And so he speaks a foreign language

No fault of his and others like him
And GOD made man in HIS image?

William R Beck
THE WORDS

For Wm. and Roberta, C.C., & L.H.

I've learned so well never to trust
The things that came before my eyes,
Or words that sit on paper like dust.

People look at me, into me, and I feel desire.
So many times someone's said good-bye.
I've learned so well never to trust

What was said and what was thrust
Upon me. So strongly I defy
The words that sat on paper like dust.

To memorize what men say I must,
I listen to lectures, read words I deny.
I've learned so well never to trust

Those who stood too close to me.
But to them I supply
More words that sit on paper like dust.

Certain laws learned, I preach unjust.
One man dies and we quit trying.
I've learned so well never to trust,
Words that sit on paper like dust.

Melvin J Hamilton

Melvin J Hamilton
IT'S GONNA BE ALRIGHT

To my Mother, Mrs. L.B. Hamilton

The doctor slapped me. My first sound and sight.
The world seemed painful, loud and bright.
So I cried—and Mama said,
Hush boy, it's gonna be alright.

A school full of strangers just didn't seem right.
The thought of Mama leaving gave me an awful fright.
So I cried—and Mama said,
Hush boy, it's gonna be alright.

Some kids teased because I was a pitiful sight.
The school bully started it, but I won the fight.
So I bragged—but Mama said,
Hush boy, it's gonna be alright.

When life threw me down and nothing went right.
Though I worked all day and half of the night.
Disgusted, I cursed—and Mama said,
Hush boy, it's gonna be alright.

Then one day Mom passed away. I had lost my guiding light.
My whole world was shattered and I was very up tight.
I almost cried—but a voice said,
Hush boy, it's gonna be alright.

Jennifer Leininger
THE LAND OF THE CELTS

I used to walk the land of my fathers
But now I walk the Land of the Celts.
I used to walk the pastures of my horses and padded woods
But now I walk emerald forest and through grey mist.
I used to walk the cliffs high above the oceans
But now I walk the HILL of TARA and mist shrouded mountains.
I used to race chariots with my brothers
But now I fight them.

The Land of the Celts has caused war and many a death.
But the Land of the Celts has also made a new people

Jeff Troxell
THE SEQUOIA TREE

The big, the huge, the Sequoia Tree,
It is the grandest thing to see.
Created so many years ago,
Although it is a million years old.
It still is as good as gold.

Although the bark is thick and red,
It can not withstand the red, hot flame.
Which careless people are to blame,
So be cautious and they will stay the same.
And the king of trees will not be of the dead.

Judy Garcia
COMPLETE

Lovingly dedicated to my sister, Brenda Benson and to the memory of our Mother, June Emerich.

The job's too big, I can't begin to lose this precious time.
It won't come back this way again and all is past its prime.
I can't let loose this part of me and sadness fills my heart.
Beginnings are too close to ends to find a place to start.

To find the magic that seemed to vanish with each setting sun,
to hold the dawn, each bright new dawn with its own course to run.
How then can I, alone and one, give up to those in need,
a part of me, forever lost with no remaining seed.

In His own time He lifts me up to reach those great new heights.
To live anew, to love complete, to walk within His light.
Forever gone, the doubts and fears that dwelled inside my heart.
Alive and fresh the glowing soul reaches out to do its part.

To trod that path that once was dim, with shadows in the mist,
I offer to all, a part of me as my own precious gift.
For not to keep and not to save but give and share His love,
the magic found again at last, sent from God above.

Shirley Brezenoff
HOW DEEP?

Silently I watched—as they shoveled . . . . . .
Would that hole be big enough
For pine wood coffin AND searing guilt
Silently I waited—and pleaded as they dug,
Deeper, deeper, I need more space
In that abysmal pit
Silently I tried to toss
That smoldering cursed guilt,
To watch it decompose
Too heavy now to carry all these years
From Crusades; Inquisition; Holocaust;
In Philadelphia, Mississippi; in Montgomery, Alabama
And in Vietnam;
For you, too, in that pine wood coffin
The first clump of sod was flung;
Silently, my shoulders heavy, I walked away
The hole was not yet big enough.

Ruth Shelton
DON'T GRIEVE FOR MOM TOO LONG

Dedicated to all my children; Mike Clinard, Debra Williams Judy Yancey and Anna Senter

As I sit alone and growing old,
It's time my life's story is told.
Children listen while I say,
With lots of love they never stray.

I've worked hard in this world,
To give each of you a start.
I know you have courage too,
Real love will never part.

Your hearts are young and so in love,
And I am growing old.
Don't weep for me, but live your life,
With love my story's told.

Now you have homes of your own,
You'll understand your mom.
Love them dearly with all your heart,
Don't grieve for Mom too long.

Alicia Green
WHEN LOVE IS BORN

Dedicated to Larry and Anna, my kids, With much love from Mom.

Of all the things that Man has done to make this life so Grand . . . .
There's one that Supersedes them all that's in our Lord's dear plan.

When God created Adam alone and so forlorn . . . .
From his Rib he gave him Eve, and that's when LOVE was born . . . .

And down thru all the ages this concept still rings true . . . . . .
For marriage is a Sacred Trust when two hearts say, "I—DO." . . . . .

And then the Love is lasting . . . . It grows and multiplies . . . .
For the Love of two grows stronger with children in their lives . . . .

True Love is such a Treasure and needs to be enhanced . . . . .
By little things you say and do to nurture Love's Romance . . . . .

As you journey thru this life your Love grows true to form . . . .
Holding even stronger bonds than the day your Love was born.

Jaime Espinosa
JUST WANT TO TELL YOU I CAN'T WRITE

To my loving father and my wonderful teacher Mrs. Kathy Ventura who inspired me to write this poem.

Just want to tell you I can't write this poem anyway, anyhow,
After all, it's hard to say what you want with the paper
Staring at me this way.
Innocent little poem, what could it do? Something to me?
Maybe nothing to you!
My, all those words flashing in my eyes. It takes me by surprise!
Excellent! I wrote a poem all by myself. I guess it's not so hard if I really try!

Carol Martin
AGING

To Rich, Trish, Terry, Shelly, Gregg and Gayle— who inspire me daily.

Sparkling dew drops at my finger tips
The taste of freshness tempts my lips
The youth I knew will soon be gone
Nature continues to push me on
Dancing buttercups in the breeze
Sparrows darting through the trees
I was here once, long ago
And with my life the wind will blow
On and on through all of time
Pushing gently on my mind
Footsteps linger far below
Soon my age and past will show
Take my hand and show me the way
For yesterday abandoned me today.

Nora Nita Stillman
A NEW ANGEL IN HEAVEN

Dedicated To My Darling Mother Altie Mae Osburn

There is a new angel in Heaven tonight,
She made the journey today,
We weren't ready for her to go,
But she left us anyway.

We'll miss her oh so sadly,
But there's one thing I know,
That she is up there with Jesus,
And I know he loves her so.

You see, she was our Mother,
We loved her with all our hearts,
We'll treasure her memories always,
Till from this world we depart.

There will be no more pain or suffering,
Just jubilant joy and praise,
With God and the Heavenly Choirs,
Through all eternity.

So if you see that sweet angel,
Tell her hello for me,
She will be on the right side of Jesus,
No trouble to find her you see.
Her hair will be made of silver,
Her heart will be made of pure gold,
Her smile will tell the whole story,
That she is at peace with her Lord.

Michael L Nash
JUST A THOUGHT OF ABSENCE RINGING

To all of the People who served.

I was born in Southern California. So I guess you'd say I was a Southerner.
I was raised up North. So I guess I'd be just another dawn yankee.
Yet My heart is with all parts of the land. So I guess I'd be an American.
I raised My eyes up to the air and saw a bird sweep through the trees so near.
I looked up, up in the sky and saw an eagle flying by.
It flew so high and beautifully, that it moved me to cry.
When suddenly, the wind it blew a whistled tune. I could hear the American Anthem bloom.
I got up on my feet to stand and found I was in another land.
Still I could hear the Anthem ring and feel the enemies' bullets sting as they struck their blow.
I called for help (oh God save me) and I called for mom (please come and get me).
Then I turned to fight in Vietnam.
Oh, oh God please come.

Joanne Marie Ferris
EVEN APART WE ARE ONE

To my beautiful Jason, I give you my soul.

Filled with empty sorrows,
Aching for your skin I can no longer caress;
My soul flees to her secret dwelling
In which no other can trespass.

Flowers in mistful gardened waters
Float in a stillness full of peace,
And tonight I can see my soul's powdered dew appearance
Weaving in and out of a fluttered breeze.

Like the ashes that fall so comes the morning
Finding her beckoning for comfort beyond that I know.
Then a feeling comes through me in need of attention—
I look and see with her another soul.

Many shadowed grays surround me
In a love that we claim cannot exist—
But I have seen our souls embedded as one,
And I have felt neither resist.

So we stand in an empty world faced without one another
But oh I'm so grateful our souls have no mind;
For while our minds are denying us to ever be lovers,
Our souls are embedded as one, for life.

Margaret A Graves
EARTHLY, UNIVERSAL LOVE

You are as beautiful as the sun that shines.
You are as soft as a petal on a rose.
You are sweeter than honey that's spun from bees.
You are more gentle than a lamb could ever be.
You are prettier than a rainbow in the sky.
You are more loving than life can be.
You have more warmth than heat from the solar.
You shine brighter than a full moon above.
You have more feelings than could ever be told
You have more strength than a team of bulls.
You are more refreshing than a stream of spring water
You are as lively as the twinkling stars in heaven.
You are more precious than diamonds and jewels.
You are the most special of all I have known.

Charlotte "Charlie" Smith
TO BE A RAY OF SUNSHINE

To my sister, Julie W.A.M.L.

Oh how I long to be a ray of sunshine
beaming down from the Heavens above
with an intensified beauty all my own
To be longed for and cherished—
To be eagerly awaited at the beginning of each new day
How I wish to be someone that people are overjoyed upon my arrival and saddened by my departure
I long to feel alive and strong and yet somehow never-ending
But I remain here, trapped within my own dark and desolate walls,
with all hopes of escape slowly diminishing

It seems as if every time I begin to pull myself up, something happens to drag me farther down than I ever was before
I had heard that there was a light that always shone in one's darkest hour; but that too, has somehow eluded me
Am I condemned to be bound by these chains of despair forever
Oh how I long to be a glorious ray of sunshine that God has given the world

Lori J Allan
THE FOG

To Don, who is my inspiration. Without you, there would be no poetry to write. All my love—Lor

The day is dawning.
The sun slowly rises
Over the horizon.
The fresh morning dew
Glistens like crystal.
The fog—often hard to see through,
Slowly starts to lift.
As I look in the rear-view mirror
And see all the roads
We have traveled down,
The dew is glistening.
The sun is raining upon us.
But the fog is slowly
Clouding around us.

As I look straight ahead
At those untraveled roads
We still have yet to journey upon,
I know the day will dawn,
The grey skies will disappear.

The dew will sparkle like diamonds
When the sun kisses it.
But the fog is very dense now
And impossible to see through.
I wonder if we will be able to
Penetrate it together and continue through,
Or if we just get lost in the fog.

Whatever happens as we go down those roads,
The day will still dawn.
The sun will still rise.
The dew will still glisten.
And we will arrive in the lifting fog separately
Only to be joined together again
With no fog clouding around us.

Nagiko Sato Kiser
MAPLES LEAVES (A HAIKU)

To Isson Sato (Pen Name), Takeichi Sato, my father who is a Hototogisu Donin and has been inspiration to many Haiku poets in Japan and America. Note; Donin—The highest rank of poets of Haiku Associations in Japan.

(In Japanese)

Momiji chiru
Nippon teien no
ishidatami

English translation:

Maple leaves falling
on the stepping stones
in the Japanese Garden

Note: The Japanese Garden of the Golden Gate Park in San Francisco

Jan White
A LITTLE WOMAN

There is a little Woman
Who sits on a hill.
Who never keeps Christmas
And I don't think ever will.

It isn't that she's selfish
She really is a dear.
She is a little elfish
And sometimes rather queer.

She thinks that Christmas ought to be
Kept throughout the year,
Not as short as a Christmas tree
But a life of hope and cheer.

There is a little Woman
Who sits on a hill.
Who never keeps Christmas
And I don't think ever will.

Trevor Greco
THE DISOBEDIENT POWER

To you, I write this not only so that you may hear,
But to help me understand love that can be so dear.
Do not take this wrong, for I love you not.
I mean not to cause fear,
I only wish to share my love, with one who will care.

I know no wrong,

And I can't feel the right.
I'm having trouble hearing the song
That your heart whispers through the night.

Love is a gentle punisher,
Yet one that overcomes the troubles.
It receives no dishonor from him or her,
But painfully pops the wrong bubbles.

Do you know of a love that is quite clear?
Or do you wonder as I do, only drawing on a dry tear?
I am unsure of love, as many of us are,
Not willing to take a fall.
But I take a step towards you, only to find the meaning of it all.

Kathryn E Crouch

Kathryn E Crouch
ALWAYS
The joy of showing someone we care,
Time spent together, our thoughts shared.
Always listening and keeping in touch,
A gentle smile can mean so much.

We must be sensitive, always take heed,
For there is always someone who has a need.

Kenneth E Edie
DON'T GIVE UP
When the world sometimes appears so cold and bleak,
The thoughts that run thru your mind you daren't speak
For fear of what the people would say,
If they knew that you felt this way
But what should it matter to the likes of them
You, who they would not even consider friend
Yet you strive each day of the week,
To prove to them that you're not weak
Though each day the load grows heavier,
And your confidence grows unsteadier
You must not give in,
To the final sin
For I know from days gone past,
Bad times won't, forever last.

Helen Gloria Ferr
SIMILE
Smoke—encircle me
My lungs
Black me
Make me
Dark
Dead
Breathless

Light—fill me
Illuminate me
My mind—
My whole being
Life-force—wisdom

Wisdom—encompass me
Surround me
Change me
Filtered fumes—life
God-life
Breath!
Divine—unending
Time-less.

Denise M Kautzman
DEEDEE'S POEM
I know what it's like
To feel insecure
Without a blanket or teddy-bear
I'm not cuddly and soft
Or cloth that will warm you
I'm your friend and I'll listen
come to me if you feel the need
My shoulder is a motel, always vacant
Except when occupied by you
It's starting now to mold itself to your head
For it's laid there before
And my shoulder knows your tears
And welcomes them like a cleansing rainfall
And sometimes your rain
Is met by a river of a friend
And they both flow together
And when the rain stops
The river still flows with concern
Never to run dry

Danny Joe Tinker
MY LOVE IS LOCKED IN A CAGE
My love is locked in a cage
Kept in a tower
Inaccessible
Gilded.

The key is lost
In a river
Ocean
Abandoned.

The wind sings at this height
Carrying with it the sound of music
A flute, band
Lifting my heart.

You arrive on your white horse
Shining armour, handsome
Climb the tower
Release my love.

Off we go into the sunset
Towards never, never land
To live happily ever after
Among the stars.

I hear the wind again
A giant, from the sky
Captures my heart
Unwillingly.

Will my knight in shining armour
Rescue me again
Or has Beast
Beat the Beauty?

Blue bird of happiness
Flies by my cage
Without a second glance
The dragon eats it.

I am lost, forever
In a land long past
Fairy tales; puppy dog tails
I awake to face reality.

Phillip W Lee
THE WATER'S GUEST
Off in the distance a honking,
a honking I hear.
Off in the distance a wedge,
a wedge is clear.
Above me, above me a flock,
a flock down low.
Above me, above me a whir,
a whir their wings go.
Beyond splash a water,
a water they'll rest.
Beyond splash a bobbing,
a bobbing water's guest.
In the rushes a nest
a nest in they'll lay.
In the rushes a gosling,
a gosling of lime array.
On the water afloating,
afloating forward and back.
On the water agrowing
agrowing now brown and black.
All too soon the south will
be their track.

B K McCoy
YET

To my loved ones Katrina and Chrisie and to all the rest who are close to my heart.

The world is round
and blue of water
and brown of dirt
of the Earth
and green of plants' life
of what we eat
and which we grow
on the Earth.
Yet we still struggle
in our society, trying to make ends meet
to survive.
The first run around the scene is now.
We ask God to aid us in reaching our goals
in life.
The world is round and we are on it
but mostly of all
God is on our side and all we had to do
is ask him to come to our aid
God Almight.

Beverly Rose Kunkle
OUR CHORAL DIRECTOR

Written in 1967 to J. Frederick Wolf, director of The Mansfield Choral Society. The singing group was organized by him in 1933 and he has been its only director. After 56 years, he retired on April 25, 1989.

What is it about this man of ours,
Whom we all love so much?
He stands and waves his hands around
With, oh, such a gentle touch.

"Look into my eyes, girls," he would say
"And watch my hands—them you must obey."
And then to the basses and tenors he'd preach:
"Sing loud and sing clear—those notes you must reach."

Now my impression of this man, you see,
Is that he brings out the talent that's in you and in me.
He's been our leader so strong and true—
Without our director, just what would we do?

Linda Vincion
LOVING MEMORIES
As I sit here alone I'm thinking of you.
I know you've only just left, but I'm feeling blue.
All my loving memories of you linger on
And it seems as though you are still at home.
I am sure you have gone to heaven above
And God will take care of you with his love.
It's so hard to believe that you have gone away.
I just hope I can see you again someday.
Although you are gone I will miss you still.
God needed you with him for it was his will.
The kindness that you showed to people you met
Makes me believe you can have no regrets.
You took care of me for so many years
And you were so dear to everyone here.
Even though I hated to see you depart
You will be in my mind and close in my heart.
Someday in Heaven if it be God's will
I'll see you again to say I Love You still.

Shirley T West
PATIENCE
There is A latent feeling
Lying in one's soul;
It is called patience,
Everyone should know.

A hurry to pick the fruit
Ripening on the vine,
Rushing it to ripen,
Too soon before it's time.

Wishing tomorrow would come,
Before you've lived today;
Ah! it's such A pity,
People are made of clay.

Patience is A precious thing
Found within heart and soul,
One's heart would surely sing
If more of it could show.

Jason Cartwright
DARKNESS OF HELL

This poem is dedicated to my brother, John. Thanks for your input.

There was rain falling from the sky, it was dark and scary.
Thundering lightning struck off and on. It was hell just like hell.
Demons were flying through darkness and flashes of light were beaming through the sky as if the earth had been split in half.
Although the rain is falling, the lightning lighting and the thunder sounding, I see a hole in the cloud.

The north star is shining with its brightness towards me. It says to me, Tomorrow is a whole new day.

Eileen Hendrickson

Eileen Hendrickson
ONE OF A KIND

I dedicate this poem to the love of my life, my husband, my soul mate.

If I'd had but one choice to make in this life,
I made the right one when I became your wife.
To see your face each waking hour,
To feel at night your love and power,
Your touch, your kiss, and embrace I do crave
Feelings and emotions ride on a highwave.
The world of splendor, together we found,
Life of enduring love, forever bound.
The memories, the past, we can never erase
We'll look forward to our remaining years, our love embraced
For our love was meant to be
Therefore we have recognized our destiny
We have shared laughter and the shedding of tears
A solid foundation we have built through the years
No longer do we have to sit and dream
Everything has been real, no longer unseen
You are my favorite way of spending time
There is no other, for you, my husband, are one of a kind.

Virginia M Bumbry
IN THE SKY

To the Astronauts' Families, my three children Larry, Garry, Sherella and to the world.

Every time we see a plane go by
We'll think about that day in the sky.

Smith, you were the pilot of the plane
you had a vision what could happen to man.

Scobee, you worked for Uncle Sam in Vietnam
Many test planes you saw come down.

McNair, you came back home and told the story
Your work was ended in a flair of glory.

Onizuka, with your face set and stern
A hero's name you have earned.

Judy, all women respect your get up and go
Being an astronaut, it was a lot you had to know.

Jarvis, you achieved the rank of captain and engineer
Your testing and studying was without fear.

Christa, when we saw your happy smiling face
We never dreamed God would take you while in space.

This flight will live in our memory each day
We regret you had to leave us that way.

Jill Kaminski
WHITE ROSES

To my daughter Victoria Ann and everyone I love.

White Roses . . . innocent thing
never a kiss so nothing to tell
Old fashion . . . dreaming passion
romance the incurable
romantic . . .

Have you ever heard such lies?
or could I have been so passé
Far behind modern sexual times
slow dance the incurable
romantic . . .

Times when men were expecting a virgin
for courtship on the terrace when
chivalry was alive and doing so well
AND SEX WAS A DIRTY WORD!

Times undressed, exposing the skin
sin consuming up all of the flesh
when
chivalry is dying and death so welcome
AND SEX ISN'T A DIRTY WORD!

Have you ever heard such lies?
or could I have been so sheltered
Far behind modern sexual times
enhance the chaste mind a bit . . .

White Roses . . . innocent thing
never a kiss so dreaming bliss
Old fashion . . . hidden passion
until he unlocks her chastity . . .

Dear white roses for you from me

Vicki Tindall
HOMELESS

Why do these people have no homes?
Why has the world left them all alone?
How can they maintain and stay alive?
How do they manage to survive?
Cold days, cold nights, cold glances, cold stares;
They huddle together; sometimes in pairs.
Scrounging together pennies for food.
Begging from people who are extremely rude.
Their children are housed in cars that don't run.
Each day they pray for no rain; just the sun.
It makes me wonder just how it is done
That these people survive with no money to come.
"No welfare for you; you have no address."
No food stamps, no jobs, no warm clothes; just stress!
Some turn to the bottle, others try to get drugs.
Each night their bodies are threatened by thugs
Our helping hand only lasts for one night;
We go home to warm houses; they're out freezing at night.
Red tape must cease, to help them out of their plight.
Is a trailer enough of a help in this fight?
Homeless; how did they get there?!

Elmer R Castle
THE PRIZE

A joyful praise to my mother Jeanne, my aunt Ruby, my Grandmother Pat, brothers Mike, Mark, Eric, and my sister Becky. Also a special thanks to those of World of Poetry Press.

I have walked among the
gods . . . . .
And have held the scepters,
that rule the four worlds.
I have looked upon the rune
scrolls . . . . .
At mysteries that lie within.
I have traveled both time and
space . . . .
Seeking the Holy Men Or War.
The conqueror of conquerors.
The one . . . . . . .The Great
King . . . .

And with his power and his might.
That we . . . . . .As ONE . . . .
Should rise and crash through the
Holy Gates.
To drink from the living
waters . . . . .
And laugh as death dies.
To walk the sacred ground . . . .
Where no foot has trod.
And to claim the Thrones of
Gods . . . . .

Jose DeKarpenter
FARMER BURNHAM

A withered leaf has lost its grip
  and slowly reached the sod
Beneath the feet of Burnham
  Where his cherished forebears
  trod.

Tho' never wandering far from home,
  He's gone that extra mile,
With the outward sign of an Inner
Grace—
  An instant toothless smile.

The precious rain he welcomes,
  Mindful of the Hidden Hand
That gathers and distills it,
  Then fondly spreads it overland.

Prepared to cross the Jordan;
  There is no fear of Hell,
In a heart that's big enough to love
  The privileged and deprived as
  well.

The Sacred Script still has its place
  In chamber, church, and temple;
But I thank you, Farmer Burnham,
  Who teaches by Example.

R L Dingle
OUR WORDS

TO BARBARA'S FAMILY and FRIENDS.

To a sister loved by all,
Though now we are apart,
A Diamond ring, tho in the ruff.
We Will miss you one and all.

To my best friend, That was like A mother,
Mother, means love and hope,
We wish you all the best,
We will always love you, My nanny I mean.

As she always loved me,
GAB__or__GUE, leee, Oh no me.
All her children numbered six,
Add four more, It's quite A mix.

We all love you, Altho now you are gone,
Your help to all of us,
And your memory shall linger on.

WE ALL LOVED YOU BARBARA,
YOUR FAMILY.

Jessica A Harrison
TIMES SPENT WITH YOU

I am the ocean and you are the waves
that come crashing to the shore.
Each second a wave splashes a
memory of
times spent with you.

I am the ocean and you are the sand
that sparkles in the sun and builds
tiny castles.
Each castle holds a memory of
times spent with you.

I am the ocean and you are the moon
that shines on me each night.
Each image of light reflects a
memory of
times spent with you.

I am the ocean and you are the birds
that spread their wings and fly high
over me.
Each bird carries a memory of
times spent with you.

I am the ocean and you are a ship
that sails on me wherever I go
and no matter how far or what
direction you sail,
it will guide me to a memory
of . . .
times spent with you.

Jill A Baker
IMPRESSIONS

Barefoot,
you walk along
the empty beach, leaving
impressions
in the moist sand,
your right foot playing
follow the leader
with the left.
I, too, travel
that sandy trail
guided by your
footprints in the sand.
An impossible quest; pursuing
five independent toes
and a dawdling heel
but I never reach
you, for
although we journey down
the same path,
you are going in
the wrong direction.

Kathy L Pappakostas
IT TAKES COURAGE

I dedicate my poem, "It Takes Courage" to my very special and treasured family: Penny, Chris, Jim, Margie, Mark, Bess, Sarah and David. From Kathy, with love forever . . .

It takes courage to smile,
  When the world is dark,
And the sun just refuses to shine.
When you've lost your way,
  And your heart is sad,
And the path is an upward climb.

It takes courage to hope,
  When your hope is gone,
And nothing seems to be right.
Today is just an echo of yesterdays
gone,
With naught but the darkness of

night.

It takes courage to dream,
When your mind is adrift,
And the weariness enters your soul.
When you long for contentment,
And peace in your heart,
But you can't seem to conquer your goal.

It takes courage to smile.
It take courage to hope.
A courage, when all else is gone.
When clouds overshadow,
The sun in your sky,
It takes courage to smile,
And go on.

Diane F Guerreri
HEARTSONG
There is music in the heart
a melody soft and bittersweet;
as the song plays
the tears begin their dance,
not their first nor last chance.

A voice that finally chooses silence
because no one is there to listen;
it doesn't forget how to speak
but it falters to trust the words,
once they're spoken, once
they're heard.

So the words become invisible
like shadows in the dark,
and the feelings deep within
will slowly lose identity,
suffocated by their own
intensity.

When next the Heartsong plays;
tears dancing out of tune—
When next the Heartsong plays;
occasionally skipping a beat—
the heart breaks in quiet of
retreat.

Lance St Clair
OUT OF THE LIGHT
Sitting in the darkness, no love or
hate.
Lack of knowledge, awaiting my
fate.
Time is of present, there is no
past.
The future beholds more
darkened overcast.
There are no friends, just
acquaintances in this darkened
state,
Losing my patience, still awaiting
my fate.
Thus I see a light so far away but
so very bright,
Almost blinded at the sight, but
still I look at this very bright
light.
A man shaped figure steps out of
the light and reaches out to say,
come with me child, for I am the
way.
I walked on with him as far as I
may,
For as long as I live I shall
remember this day.
For the one called God has shown
me the way.

Frank L Wilcox
TIME
A sun bleached shore tells the story
of time,
Of man and nature and a rhythmic
rhyme.

Few will ever know the power of the
sea,
As she draws them near with an
inviting plea.

Behold the beauty I present to you,
Never so calm so clear so blue.

A grain of sand once a massive stone,
Broken by the sea and her magic
throne.

For the ones we have lost the
maidens shall weep,
Never so vast so lonely so deep.

Look upon her and cast your caution
to the wind,
Listen closely and you'll hear a new
story begin.

B Ray Greenwood

B Ray Greenwood
MY AMERICA
This poem is dedicated to my beloved wife Gwynette, my mother, and in memory of my father—and the United States of America.

America—Will it stand or will it
fall
I still believe you're the
greatest country of them all.

America—I was proud to be a
part of Uncle Sam's U.S.M.C.
who with all the other
forces fought to keep you
free.

America—The country where I'm
free to pray
And worship God in my
own way.

America—Yes I still believe in the
flag
The red, white and blue
And all that it stands for
And I pray to God that
never again
Will you ever have to go to
war.

America—You've been good to me
the land of plenty and the
home of the free.

America—The land that will
never fall
I love her so
She's the greatest country
of them all.

Donnamaria Madonia
HOW BROKE I AM!
To my family and friends for all their support. ILY
Ro—would you happen to know a good accountant?

How broke I am!
How broke I'll be!
When I'm in jail
Who will bail me free?
I spend all my cash
on such stupid things
when they repossess my car
such sorrow it will bring!
Do you think I'm caring now?
Oh no, of course, not me!
When my credit is blown away
I'll be living in a tree!
But really not to worry,
I'll just marry someone rich
and when I spend all his money
they'll find me in a ditch!
But do you think I'm worried?
Looking good is where it 's at!
In the streets of New York
on a tin can, playing ratitat tat!
So won't you give me some money?
so I can pay my bills
or you'll see me in the market
buying food that says, "no frills"!

Freeman Edward Moore
THE LOOP THAT BINDS US
To my loving mother Mattie L. Fields, my son Micah, and the family in Michigan, Ohio, Tennessee, Alabama, Mississippi, Florida, California, and Illinois . . . . . May you long remember, the Loop that binds us . . . .

I hear you
Whispering my name
Oh . . . . How you send for me
My heart pines
And I long to be with you
On your lakes' shore
You astound me with your height
Your boldness and might
But I'm frightened and appalled
By your violence
You send brisk chills
Through my bones
Yet warm my heart with your caress
I'm infatuated by your breezy style
And I like to feel myself inside of
you
Oh . . . . How you wine and dine me
Detroit is jealous you know
Chicago
Chicago
I'll be home
I shan't forget . . . .
The Loop that binds us

Becky Brooks
(Nick-name—Geminian)
ALL I HAVE LEFT
All I have left
Are ones who don't know
But if they did
They would turn away also

Why should one judge
By the color of one's face?
Why don't they see
We're all of the human race?

Someone who accompanies
One of a different color
Is considered a disgrace
To all of the others
WHY! ! ?

Now is the time
My heart speaks loud
What used to speak softly
Now speaks out! ! !

Debbie A Hearn
MY BEST FRIEND
This poem is dedicated to Dovie, the world's best mom.

My Best Friend . . . . .

She'd help me all that she could
for when I was blue
She stayed with me and brought
me through!
She never turned her back on me
for she could always see . . . .
That I needed her, as much as she
needed me,
So now in the future and forever
She'll always be . . . .

My Best Friend!

Adeline O Maynez
MY ROSARY
With love—to the Blessed Virgin Mary—mother of God and our mother too!

A sweet and lovely Rosary—is in my
hands entwined.
Each bead a "Hail Mary" with Faith
and Peace combined.
Imploring Our Sweet Mother, Her
blessings to us send,
For sinful man's salvation, for hate
and wars to end.

The peace that I receive from it—to
guide me on my way,
One day to enter Heaven, will be a
glorious day!
With loving tenderness She hears
me—smiling sweetly all the while,
Oh Holy Mother, bless me—protect
your little child.

So peacefully I go along—life's
solitary path,
Rejoicing in God's Mercy, for He has
truly said,
"Please love my Dear, Sweet Mother,
no greater gift to me,
Can you bestow today, for all
eternity."

As I gently close my eyes—in
slumber deep, I dream,
Sweet Mother be with me always,
don't leave this lovely scene.
With your enchanting heart and soul,
your words to me are brave,
"My child, if you'd be near me, my
hand is yours to take."

Lionel A Nadeau
ETERNAL LOVE
For Catherine and Howard

Life's frightful chasms, emptiness
and fears,
Favorite couch, your hand, bridging
pain and tears;
Fondly we contemplate the dying
embers' glow—

"Seems that front porch step is not as
low,
Trip to the mailbox takes a little
longer my Dear.
How beautiful! An artist's sunset,
Loveliest this year—
What did you say? I did not hear."

Flickering shadows pausing in the
fire's glow,
Silvering crowns, a reign of love their
closeness shows—
"Remember that New Year's Eve so
long ago,
Joyful bells, the sleigh, the fields of

snow?"

Visions straining, timidly approach the light,
Images stumbling through the silent shuttered night.
The legacy of time can never rim
Fondest memories neither can it dim.
Summer's fading bloom will blanch in winter cold,
Autumn frost must streak your plaits of gold;
Reluctantly our time will come for growing old.
I'll dwell on everything, the things you mean to me.
I know I'll always be in love with thee.

Myrna D Frederick
MY DEAREST ONE

How much I love you, let me tell you now.
I love you like the clouds hovering softly, and magnetically,
engulfed in your presence.
Like the sun shines radiantly, giving warmth to all living thing.
Like the sparkling, rushing brook, in the lovely springtime.
Like the warm summer air, just after the rains have come and gone.
Like the precious water, that yields to the sun.
I truly am given to your every desire.
I melt at your touch. I long for your every embrace.
I love to look in your eyes, so much. I adore your wonderful face.
I love you as a child clings to his mother for assurance and guidance.
I love you like a woman, who longs for companionship and praise.
I care for you as a mother does, her first born child to raise.
I care when you hurt. I care when you've gone astray.
I love you as a shepherd does his sheep.
As a minister his flock to keep.
I love you as a Merry-Go-Round thrills a child.
I care when you care.
I love your every dream, and want you to be mine, Valentine.

Mary Hoffert
WINTER'S FIRST SNOW

As Winter shows her white glistening face
fading Autumn Summer's glow
The land is filling with Winter's first snow
Fresh, shining, pure and white, soiled not even a trace
causing children to run outside and play
with a glee and laughter lasting all through the day
Excitement is in the air, as snow-flakes are falling in their hair
They are experiencing Winter's first snow
Grownups are looking out the window as the snowflakes are falling,
their faces showing gloom
As they reluctantly get the shovel and broom
for they know they have a job to do
as they put a galosh over the top of their shoe
They are experiencing Winter's first snow
It is the eye of the beholder
determining good or bad
To be happy or sad
At the appearance of Winter's first snow

Julie MacMonagle
HE WALKED THROUGH THAT LONELY DOOR

To my one and only true love, Eric. I will love you always and forever.

He walked through that lonely door,
Of this I was not aware.
When I saw him how my mind did soar.
I had this feeling I could not bear.
Often I would look at him,
Wondering if he noticed me.
It all seemed very grim,
Until one day someone told him of me.
Then I tried with all my might
to talk to this dear one.
Finally on one lonely night,
When we met, I was stunned.
He had this breathtaking look
Of emotion and true love.
At that very moment I knew I was hooked
On this guy sent to me from above.
From that time on, I knew I would spend
My whole life dedicated to this man.
And not one person could make me bend
From being this guy's biggest fan.

Olga Blachford

Olga Blachford
TO MY SISTER

I want you to know how very
much I love you, Sis,
That this is one birthday I truly
didn't want to miss.
Because in years gone by we had
shared in so many things,
For instance, when you wanted to
join forces with me so together
we would sing.
We will never forget all the
different places we sang
together,
And we would keep our
appointments at the studios—
No matter what the weather.
The studios, the recordings, the
rehearsals and such,
Mr. Graham, Miss Maloney, our
favorite piano teachers
whom we liked so very much.
The Stage Door Canteen where
sang, "Poinciana" for the
Army, Navy, and Marines,
It was exciting, thrilling, a
wonderful part in our lives
and we were in our teens.
Yes, sister dear, we have much to
remember all that we shared
in years gone by
That only death could erase those
memories that we two shared
—you and I.

Sheree M Riggs
SNOWDROPS (FAIRY CHILD QUEEN)

Marigold petals floating
Fantasy figures with silvery wings
Strange adventure the child's dream
Stone castle of a queen
Legends of dove
Treasures intense love
Striking beauty of a child
Wind that blows mild
Atmosphere of drifting snow
Frosty colors of the rainbow
Dreams drift in and out
A loving wish moped about
So suddenly sweet tasting
Enormous passion keeping
Wide opened eyes olive green
Waiting time recaptured dreams
Voice faded in the icy night
Winter's swiftly fading light
Laughter before the fire
Creeping back the desire
Night birds soaring voice
Castle wishing the choice

Marilyn K Hoffman
THROW ME A LINE

A star fell from the sky tonight,
and I thought of you.
I ordered another Sea Breeze from the bar,
and thought of the breeze that
blew over the Sound.
I thought of being rocked to sleep by the waves;
of being rocked to sleep in
your arms.
That first shooting star we saw together
was the first shooting star of
my life.
And, as I watch the snow fall over the mountains,
it seems so far away,
but it's still so close to my
heart.
You're still so close to my heart.
The days on the boat,
a summer in the sun
with you at the helm
of my heart.
You always said I was a good swimmer.
Well, I can't swim to you now,
and I feel like the current is
sweeping me away from you.

Please,
throw me a line.

Kathleen M Bachi
LOVING PARENTS

To Mom & Dad—Thank you for adopting me 34 years ago.

I was born to no one,
You came and took me home,
You didn't even know me
But loved me as your own.

The hearts you have are bigger
And filled with so much love,
That if the whole world needed you,
I know that you'd be there.

God took you both to be with him
Because he had a job,
To love and care for all those kids
Whose parents never could.

Please leave a little memory
With all of those up there.
You sure did leave some memories
With all of us who cared.

You filled the world with so much love
You made my life so good,
And, if I could I'd give my life
To have you back for good.

Minnie R Laube
GRANDMA'S FACE

This poem is dedicated in loving memory of my late grandmother, Jean D. Laube.

Grandma's coffin was sitting there,
As I watched it, perched upon my chair.
On the morrow, ten years ago
Grandma's body parted with its soul.

Grandma's in heaven now,
No more worry lines upon her brow,
To be singing in a sweet soft voice,
Standing next to Jesus was her choice.

Only five when she departed,
I can't recall much now,
Except that look of peace upon her face,
And not a trace of pain upon her brow.

Someday, I hope to go as her,
To leave a quiet bliss of peace;
And may some small child recall
On my face—His blessed peace.

Kellyann St Jacque
TIME TESTED

The trailer sits silently on a grass lot.
Its yellow paint is fading,
Its roof leaks in spots.
Where once it was a welcoming sight of laughter,
There now is only silence.

There is an old chain in the back—
It is rusted with no dog attached.
Amongst the lot are bare patches where grass had grown;
Along with a garden where only weeds survive.
There's also a fence hanging by its wires.

This was at one time a friend,
A shelter to protect one from the cold.
Now time has worn out its welcome.
Only silence lives here anymore.

Kathy Lynn Maine

Kathy Lynn Maine
NIGHTY-NIGHT CHAUNCEY

I would like to dedicate this poem to my beautiful children, Philip, Tara Lynn, Kimberly Kathleen and to their loving grandfather, Richard Patrick Maine Sr.

To my precious Chauncey,
Who for fourteen years gave love.
You asked for nothing in return,
Like your mother, yes I was.

My love I'll have forever

For you my precious one.
And in my heart you'll always be
Loved and thought of as my son.

But most of all, I write this poem
For you my boo-boo dog,
To thank you for the lovely years
And now you'll be with God.

So think of this as nighty-night
As you close your precious eyes,
And always know that Mommy's
there
Forever by your side.

Amanda Dianne Wilson
SPECIAL FOOTPRINTS

I dedicate this poem to mama and daddy, for the life of dedication they have given me.

As the years have passed I see
what mama and daddy have done for
me
The many footprints that's been
put on the floor
And the many times they've
walked in and out of that door
Suddenly you realize how many
footprints you see
And you look down again and
realize it was for me
And there again is that footprint
that has quickly been replaced
For it has always been because of
the love and care shown on their face
These footprints are always
special you see
Because they go deeper down just
for me
As the deeper they go, the more I
know
how much mama and daddy
really care for me.

April Marinos
MY JOURNEY

Dedicated to my family and friends, especially to my husband, Daniel Sr.—May you all experience the joy of a beautiful journey to Christ. With love, April.

Slowly drifting upon a cloud,
Your wings are golden and bright.
The halo which floats above your
head
Proves true to peace and delight.

I am to join the crowd,
To journey within the light.
The pathway seems never ending,
But, oh, what a beautiful sight!

I pause to glance upon the Earth—
Eyes are glistened with tears.
The family and friends I left
behind—
Fond memories will linger through
the years.
I look away, but am not sad.
My heart is filled with glee.
For I will meet my Savior
And he will meet with me.

George H Hutson
MY FLY BY
Mount Fuji was there
Would make you stare
Top above the clouds
Like it had shrouds
Of soft white cotton
All around the mountain
Like a white beacon
While we were streaken
Back to our base
At a good pace
All that white lace
A mountain to grace
I will not forget
The day we went
Past that big mountain
Mount Fuji white fountain.

Stefanie de Vita
ENCORE
Silently, he asked me to dance,
His touch, like a bittersweet memory
Tenderly bruised my heart.

Though we had never met
Soul remembrance of our past
Swirled mistily thru my mind.

We swayed like drifting clouds, then
The balm of gentle music
Restored two spirits torn asunder.

His eyes were wistful, still
I remember his smile from long, long
ago.
How sweet to meet again.

Pasquale W Forsythe
I FEEL AS THOUGH I'VE BEEN THERE BEFORE
I feel as though I've been there
before
Where you are now i mean
Each passing day i feel it more
Do you think it could be but a
dream

My life is empty, cold and gray
Since i touched you long ago
Oh so long ago and far away
My heart still aches, the pain
still flows

Your loving touch i'll always
remember
The last sweet words you spoke
to me
When an angel came in late
December
My heart, my mind shall never
be free

I feel as though I've been there
before
Where you are now i mean
Each passing day i want it more
To be with you and not with a
dream

Michele Buck
RAIN STORM
The morning sun has
slowly faded away,
It has made way for
the darkness.
How empty it seems when
yet there is such a miracle.
For what could it be, but
a miracle?
The sky so full of light, but
still no sun?
Are the heavens mad, why else is
the sky roaring?
Falling, Falling—yet so lightly
during the madness.
Rising, Rising, to an extent far
beyond that which we know.
But as this little miracle takes its
toll on the earth,
It always draws the darkness and
emptiness away!

Marte Wilder
CLOUDSTORM
Shades of grey,
Clouds on high;
Spiraling across a stormy sky,
Racing against the wind:
Cloudstorm on high.

Shades of grey,
Clouds of emotional turmoil;
Shadows of negative indecision
Tumbling in soulful wanderlust,
Cloudstorm of the human spirit.

Shades of grey,
Reflections of moonlit silver
Riding low in the dusky sky;
Cloudstorm serenity on high.

Shades of grey,
Reflections of sunlight silver
Floating into the depths
Of humanity's feelings;
High prospects of positive decision;
Cloudstorm serenity of the human
spirit.

Helen Headly
I AM WOMAN

To my Mother Louise Davis—The Source of my Hope and Aspirations.

I am Woman !!!
I am—the Center of my Church,
the Core of my Diocese,
the Summit of my Religion.
I symbolize all the Faiths of the
Universe.

I am Woman !!!
I am—the Mother of Mankind,
the Incentive to
Achievement,
the Stimulus to Greatness.
I symbolize the unseen movers of the
rulers in the world.

I am Woman !!!
I am—the Reasoning Force in
Controversy,
the Love bequeathed to
Mankind,
the Ingenuity to make it
All work.
I am the competent, clear-
headed, argumentative
posture that
consolidates all thinking
persons.

I am Woman !!!
I am—Wife, Mother, Lover,
Friend—
A Child of God
A Worker in my Parish
Church.
I am the Coordinator, the
Mischief-maker, the
Teaser,
the Oiled Wheel that
makes the World Go
Round.
I am Woman.
AND—I'M GLAD !!!

Lorene Russell
CHILDHOOD MEMORIES
Laughter of children at play, a cool
summer breeze
Fragrance of honeysuckles, the
swing from an old tree
Delicate little butterflies, the
humming of the bees
Fields of lacy queens lace, the
game of hide and seek
Singing of the birds such sweet
melody
A bushy tail squirrel high up in
a tree
Building sand castles in the warm
sand
Playing the game tag, catch me
if you can
Making mud pies in little tin pans

The feel of cool wind, blowing in
our face
Gathering wild flowers for a
playhouse vase
Follow the leader all in a row
hopping and skipping
To the barn we go
The smell of sweet clover on the
hillside
All taking turns for a pony ride
The future came the past must
go
Every year my memories grow

Robert E Poer
MOMMY
Mommy I love you,
Mommy I care.
Mommy I hope you
Will never despair.

Mommy you're wonderful,
Mommy you're grand.
You gave me everything
In the palm of my hand.

Mommy I yelled at you
And mommy you cried.
I never straightened up for you.
Oh! Mommy I tried.

Now I am still trying, Mom.
Though you may not see.
So please stop your crying, Mom.
Your boy aims to please.

Melody Jan Hayslip
LOVE LIGHTS
Like sky rockets bursting on the 4th
of July
Our love streaks in passion across the
night sky,
Or shines on our faces over candles,
Over candles and wine.
When your hand on the table
Reaches for mine.
For sometimes love's growing with a
warm gentle fire,
When the joy of being together
replaces desire.
And I'll always be near you as
girlfriend or wife,
For you are most truly the light of my
life.

Florence Bowers
LONGING TO BE FREE
There are so many lovely things—
Rain falling outside my window
The solitude of a lonely place
The murmur of running water
The restless sea.

Why must my eyes
Be blinded to all this
By anguish and despair
And my heart bound and crushed
By burdens beyond my strength to bear
Oh, if only I could fling aside
The chafing bonds and flee
To some high and lofty mountain
And there be forever free.

Lisa Love
PREGNANCY
My sister, my west coast cousins, all with little bundles of joy.
I'm 30 years old and more than anything I wanted a baby.
A new addition to the family;
someone to cuddle, to love, to share.
The holidays Christmas . . . came and gone but still . . .
Nausea, constipation continued and I realized something was wrong.

Five weeks after I missed a period,
the doctor says you are not pregnant.
So I take some medicine for my constipation and wait two hours for the cramps to subside
In a few days I was better.
On Monday came a surprise.

After three hours of trying to get through to the office,
I finally got the results of my test.
I am pregnant.
I cannot believe it, like my prayers were suddenly answered.
We had been so busy moving to our new home and adjusting to a suburban environment
We could not afford a bigger house,
so the study was converted to the baby's room.

Normally a size 10 now my clothes did not fit, but I managed with stretch fabrics.
Sometimes I craved a steak, the next minute I could not eat a banana
I glanced at my smiling God child's face and then I realized the struggle is worth it
Each day came a new challenge and within me lay the strength to endure.
Fighting over names and what color to paint the baby's room
We're caught up in a world of Burger Kings and Porsches
What's real is the baby listening, kicking, inside of me

Melissa L Dykstra
MEMORIES IN THE MIST
I stand on the deserted beach, calling for you, longing to hear your voice.
My mind hears my hopeless calls and rebukes them, reminding me you'll never come back.
My heart won't accept the challenge of being alone forever.
But my eyes still search my heart for answers I will never understand.
As I search the sunset, I find you. A golden ray of light, streaming down to touch my soul.

Alfred G Nicholson
SEARCH
"Why are you here"
the voice spoke out
"This is not the road of life"
"Do you not know only the
dead here walk,
They who tire of life."

"I search" I said, "for
better things, in this plain
unknown to all. I'm told that
here is paradise
Where tears are yet to fall."

"There's no such place
How could it be, for tears
don't just show grief
Have you not heard of tears of joy
Or tears just for relief"

He spoke of joy, but yet
He said "this road is of the dead"
What will I find, I ask myself
What lies for me ahead.

Caroljean Kagan-Wilbur
EMBRACES
My heart has been cracked and chipped.
My self-image has been severely whipped.
Over the years and for many a day
I have a restlessness; peace will not stay.
My soul and body for love cry out.
But there's no fulfillment—just self-doubt.
I do not feel this is wicked indeed
It is a statement of fact, an unquieted need.
If you treasure me as you claim
Then with me always please remain.
I know life is comprised of ups and downs.
I need smiles, hugs—not demeaning frowns.
I need to share your hopes and dreams.
Then your being will become part of my self-esteem.

Grace C Nichols
BEACH PARTY
The sea gulls all face the sun,
The end of day is near.
Children play and run
People standing by,
their talk I hear.
Watching rays of the setting sun,
Locking this in my memory.
I watch this glory,

The end of this day has come,
The sky turns orange and red,
Dark clouds hold on to the colors.
My eyes take in this beauty
as I start to think of others.

Hungry tummies coming in,
shouting, "What's for din, din?"
I called back, "It's too pretty
to eat in."

Katherine Sears
I WILL MISS YOU
You say you're leaving.
You won't be back for a while.
You say we'll keep in touch,
but is that good enough?
You want to stay I know,
but you're my friend we've spent
so much time together.
It's so hard to accept.
I'm sure you'll find people
to take my place in person,
but please don't let them take my place in spirit.
I won't forget you
so don't forget me.
Well it's time to say good bye,
but I can't so I'll say until we meet again

Barbara Delima Peterson
LOVE ME JUST A LITTLE
Love me Just a little
A little will do just fine.
You don't have to forsake all others
Or promise to be mine.

I just want someone who cares
A little bit for me.
Someone I can talk to when
I want some company.
Someone who will listen not
Laugh or put me down.
Someone I can confide in
Or put my arms around.

So love me just a little
I'll love you the same way.
And we'll love each other forever
Forever and a day.

Rocky S Tompkins

Rocky S Tompkins
LOST LOVE
My love for you
Was like a fire
Ever Burning
Brighter, hotter
Higher and higher
Like passion gone mad
Out of control
All consuming, ever replenished.
My love for you dear
Was like a fire
Thoughts, hopes, dreams
A fantasy land that seemed true.
In the glorious heat of my fire
Hurts, pain, loss
Were as wraiths on the wind
To be blown away
Away, by the heat of my fire.
Life, will it ever be the same?
Without my fire
Or the burning desire?

Robert L Antrim
THE OZARKS
October in the Ozarks
is my favorite time of year,
Where I can see the beautiful creations
God has provided here.

Sometimes just to sit in silence
and forget my doubts and fears,
To let the sounds of nature
fall upon my ears.

No painter can match the colors
that God has painted there,
This living, beautiful masterpiece
for all of us to share.

I love to walk in this beauty
that God has created for me,
I praise my Lord and thank him
for the wonders he let me see.

Greg J Marks
DEJA VU
Mistaken identity, a dream recalled
A vision of that we've known before
An intuitive revelation from cobwebs called
A forgotten past, or something more?

Such experience in experience of Deja Vu
A rudiment of yore contrived
A precedent subsistence unproven true
Tenacity between lives survived
From an intimate past from whence one has grown
Disturbed of its sleep in the bearer's heart
A reminence, incognito, makes itself known
Of the gestalt to which we are part

Neither of heaven above nor the anguish of hell
Is this mystery, an enunciation sent
But from within one's essence
whither memories dwell
Of prior lifetimes spent

The experience of today may become that of tomorrow
And many vast futures to ensue
In a lifetime hence, we may come to borrow
A wit of this mystic, call it
Deja Vu

Neal Henry Lawrence, OSB
DEATH OF THE EMPEROR
The Emperor dies
After wars and reaching peace,
Japan's longest reign.
His heir trained in his duties
Steps forward courageously.

Karmel Mangan
THROUGH THE WINDS OF TIME
I visualize her standing there,
Gentle winds blowing her long blond hair.
A child of wonder she was to me.
So very young, so innocent, and free.

As memories take me back in time,
This child always searched to find
The innermost depths of her soul,
To measure the question of her life's role.

Destiny carried her to college fame.
A runner who they called by name.
She earned respect of friends and foes,
And touched the lives of those she knows.

She stands before me on her wedding day,
An expression of beauty in every way.
My child now takes a woman's role, and
The gift of herself she does bestow.

Life's passing evidence is all so clear,
As we sort out the purpose of why we are here.
Knowledge and memories fill my mind,
As I go through the winds of time.

John W Doll
THE MOON WAS YOUNG
The moon was young and our love was too.
The breeze said, "look, she's in love with you."
"For she holds you tight, like the stars do the night,"
And the moon dimmed its light to agree.

The moon was young and her kiss was new.
The leaves spoke low, "she'll always love you
For her heart beats fast, this is love, it will last."
And the moon said, "it's true, I can see."

As the moon grew old her love grew cold
And the breeze ceased to talk to the leaves,

For the wind was the kind with the changeable mind,
Like my love, who had said, she loved me.

The moon was young and it couldn't know
That a heart can change like the wind that blows
And that love's not told by a young flippant tongue,
But my heart couldn't know . . . like the moon . . .
it was young.

Anita Durán Jones
TEACH US . . .
Teach us to love with Thy unfailing grace,
to still the tempest of the human thought,
to conquer doubt, walk over the waves
with fearless heart illumined by Thy Love
Teach us to heal . . . to bind the bleeding heart,
to feed the hungry with Thy mighty word
to fly over the oceans and the land
multiplying the fishes and the bread.

Teach us to pray with deeds and not with words,
to see the star beyond the darkest night
to love, to laugh and healing in Thy Name
to touch the garment of Thy radiant light

Ray Holden
FRIENDSHIP
We live our lives in search of wealth
We seek precious treasures and good health.
But, do we value among these things
The most valuable asset living brings?
We'll travel many miles to see,
Those we love so intimately.
There's nothing in the world more sincere
Than a close relationship with one held dear.
So in counting our blessings, be they many,
If we leave out friendship we don't have any.

James B Reed
STOP! LOOK! LISTEN!
Pause for a moment—
and rest!
Rest your eye upon—
the broad sky
the high mountain
the tall tree
Rest your ear upon—
the song of the stream
the gentle purr of hummingbird wings
the rolling thunder of a restless sky—
Rest your cheek against—
the snow flake
the warm summer sun
the gentle breeze at evening
And be glad—
that you are who you are
and that God is who He is!

Rita A Walker
THE SEA
Silent and mysterious it drifts by
How many people in passing
Have gazed in wonder and awe

Seagulls pass by overhead
Ships sail the endless miles
And along its sometimes forbidding shores
It stretches to all corners of the earth
Within its dark depths many creatures roam.
Through the ages it has carried
people all over the world.

How often I go down by its side
Just sitting quietly alone—meditating
Its silent rhythm comforts the weary mind

I often wonder what marvels lie
Under its turquoise and blue depths
It is surely one of God's greatest creations!

Cheryl Leanne Collins
PASSION

This poem is dedicated to Bob, who has given me strength not only in person, but also in spirit.

Baby, lay down next to me
So I can look in your eyes and see
And hold the one who is so dear to me
And say the words,
"I Love You . . ."

Baby, lay down beside me, please
So I can touch the face that means so much to me
And caress the body that does tease
And say the words,
"I Love you . . ."

Baby, lay down upon me so
I can feel the passion let go
And surround the one who's in my fantasy
And feel your warmth inside of me
When we explode into ecstasy
And say the words,
"I Love You . . ."

Anne M Webster
HEART STEALERS
Cats are cats and only cats
no matter what we call them.
Some have tails and some have not,
it makes no difference to them.
But Persian, Manx or Alley Cat
have one thing in common to them.
They snare an owner by the heart
enslaved forever to them.

Beth Ann Butters
MADDNESS
I get so mad, I really do!
And the reason for it is my sister, Sue.
My sister is an awful bore
I'd like to kick her out the door.
She messes up our pretty room
And hates to touch a mop or broom.
She leaves her clothes upon the floor
And then at her I yell and roar.
She eats the candy I have hidden
Although I've told her that it's forbidden.
She rants and raves and throws a tantrum
Then flees through the door, like a phantom.
And so I get madder, I really do!
Because of that darn old sister, Sue.

Joyce Rogers
AUTUMN
Beyond the ears of shimmering corn
Again, the scene is set
A sunlit vision to behold
A harmony of green and gold
Of square cut acres, ripe and new
Glistening with the morning dew
Of swooping birds, never still
Following the tractor on the hill
While in the village, far remote
Cottages belch their chimney smoke
A changeless view that's always been
When England shows her Autumn scene.

Christine M Faude
DEREVAUN SERAUN
I stared towards the ground to see
my right hand
becoming wrinkled with time.
Time, never ending.
I, am.
Neither gods nor Nature could cure me,
ever.
For time has won.
Time has won.
My hands will shake
though I try to steady them.
I fear not,
for time has won,
and I have lost.
I have lost.

Patricia Heid
LOVE

This poem is Dedicated to my family, that I love.

Let us show it, for into the night
someone must know it.
A light that keeps on glowing
If our love would keep on flowing.
For so many that need us to show it.
Beats of the heart each day are slowing.
But the warmth in our hearts keeps the love glowing.
And sometimes, the silence of just knowing.

Mary Anne Cataldi
ALBERGON
They gathered at Albergon,
scattered about, chatting,
in little groups
bound to each other
as high as the floor to the ceiling
and the flower to the mountaintop.
We are consciously aware of infinity,
yet, curiously oblivious
of the world that is us.

Trudee De Kay White
RAIN
the rain sprinkled lightly
on my window
leaving a trail like
streaks of fine silver.
so silent was the world—
so beautifully and fully silent
with only the pitter-patter of rain
to keep me company . . .
to remind me of the difference
in alone and lonely.
for a time which could not be measured
i sat staring through the fine silver
lattice work nature had provided me.
as i sat, looking but not seeing,
i was reminded of times we never had.
i remembered, with pain, the love
that never existed,
and i longed with every fiber of my being
to be held in your arms
and listen to the words i know
you did not mean . . .

Lynn Dixon Walters
A REFLECTION
Be kind to me;
I'm the type to
make a sudden ending.

I know myself;
I'll be gone.
I'm the flight side of
the fight or flight scene.

Be fair to me
or you will see
how reflective
I can be.

You'll see yourself
very clearly,
in the mirror of the
shadow of eternity.

Gigi McDaniel

Gigi McDaniel
TWINS

I dedicate this poem to my twin cousins Chad and April Hughes.

We expected one baby, but we got two.
Oh my goodness! What would we do?
Two little babies so pink and small,
I'd have to share my toys after all.
What could be better, two cousins at one time,
A boy and a girl—one of a kind?
At the age of three I was very smart.
I helped my aunt right from the start.
Those first few years were hard to bear
They kicked me often and pulled my hair.
But I thank God there were two instead of one . . .
Because now that they're older, they are such fun.
Twins are a double delight indeed.
And I'm very proud they are kin to me.

Karen J Pfeffer
CREATIVE JOURNEY
Walking with closed eyes, mind.
Years of heavy-handed footsteps.
Is this all there is?
Guess so.
Then, perhaps, a spark,
An intimation that life does indeed exist.
Hard to believe, hard to accept,

Yet yearning never really died.
More footsteps, timid at first,
Then growing in strength as the quest continues.
A bright world, brightening.
A light heart, beginning to shine.
Rainbow thoughts that sing,
"I AM, I CAN."
Possibility becomes certainty.
All that was dreary now glows in wonder.
Talents never absent, now abound,
As the creative process salvages
Yet another life.

Robert E King
I LOVE YOU
Sometimes when two people meet,
Golden things are laid at their feet.
Opportunities never ending,
A spark of friendship, is just a beginning.

As time rolls by in its endless roll,
The effects of love shall take its toll.
Hard times come as well as go,
But, I thought that I would let you know.

So much is the love that I feel,
Things around me don't seem real.
I'm lonely inside and need a friend.
The way I feel toward you, will never end.

I hope that we will always share,
The magic moments of a special pair.
A pair of people living day to day,
I LOVE YOU, is all that's left to say.

Patricia Schmidt
GRANDMAS' ICE BOX DOOR
Let the world have its' Picassos'
Rembrandts' and Van Goghs',
They pale, when in comparison
to the artwork on this door.
For each scribbled little drawing,
is a treasure in its' self.
I know it's true, it has to be; 'cause
she told me so, herself!

Katherine L Morean
ANALOGY
Trapped in life's web
I'm caught like a fly,
Tangled up and mangled up
With days just passing by.

I've never felt so close to death
As now with it moments away,
Creeping towards me is the web-builder
Preparing to kill his prey.

Don't take me yet, I'm not ready to go
I've got more things to do
Release me—give me one last chance
To let my goodness shine through.

I'll never come that close again
I'm sure to die next time
Was it a web-builder or a man,
Who saved this life of mine?

Judy Matté
I AM AN ARROW
I am an arrow
sharp and sleek,
simply gliding,
full sail,
across the sky,
soaring gently
with great force
Born by the greatest power,
My Father, the archer of all.

Martha J Buck
SATURDAY AFTERNOONS
Saturday afternoon westerns
are dust free now.
The steel wheeled steeds are tethered
to the smooth, polished rail
Their snowy riders slump.
Gentle vigilantes have sheeted
the feeble to their chairs.
The canvass sling and its pulley
hang over the stainless tub.
Ladies in white parade.
The lysoled doors swing.
The TV blares.
A woman moans.
And, bedridden Joe
bangs his plastic cup
and hollers, "More."

Jan Shook-Hagen
MOUNTAIN TRANQUILITY
High in the cloud-swirled meadows,
There slowly grows the noble pine;
Casting stately green shadows,
Redolent of perfumed sunshine.

Cloud-scattering bald eagle,
Sounding his primordial cries;
Feathers breathtakingly regal,
Intrepid monarch of the skies.

Timid, whisper-footed deer,
Warily at feed in the glade;
Ever alert to dangers near,
Quickly melting into soft shade.

Often during times of great strife,
These ancient mountains make me whole;
Teaching me to rejoice in life,
Calming and repairing my soul.

Eileen McHale and Russ Jennings
COMING TOGETHER
We met in an impromptu manner, and before long, engaged in discussions concerning our behaviors.
Behaviors are safe in a conventional sense: structured, giving credence to cautious resistance.
In this precise talk of techniques, often emotional desires rebelliously increase . . .
Though our earnest, honest self shyly directs us to the ultimate wealth . . .
To be intimately known, hoping against all doubt—to be recognized as our loving selves.
Why should we be so precise, considering our knowledge of life's raging devices?
Perhaps the answer lies within our hearts—defending ourselves against the rationalized darkness.
Or perhaps, it lies in our infinite desire to put out hurt and pain's smouldering fires.
Securing such is vigorously sought by all who have had such demanding thoughts.
Have we drifted from our original plan, writing endless revisions in fickle sand . . .
Only to change again to conform to the environment within?
This manifest moment in a dream come true, built on inner strength and fortitude . . .
Boundless energies and hope are required to access this illusional desire.
Life will undoubtedly be the death of us both.
Perhaps our greatest desire is to be real in our reality.
The purpose of this exercise is to live our disguises and to ultimately decide . . .
If we will recklessly live life . . .
Or cautiously die.

Karen Hay
MY SAFE PLACE

I dedicate this poem to God, my inspiration.

I sing to you a new song,
A song of freedom, a song of deliverance.
You, O Lord, are my high tower.
You set me on high in your presence.
You are my shining light, and that light is glorious.

You call me unto yourself, and I run to you for safety.
My praises rise unto you for your light shines.
It shines forth into my darkness, and you give me light.
As you welcome me, Lord, I welcome you.
As incense, Lord, my praises rise to you, and your glory shall be seen.

My Lord comes with light and truth.
He restores unto me the joy of my salvation.
And He makes for me a place of safety where I can go, now.
A place where I can be safe for He is my safe place.
In my safe place, there is light for there is you.

Rusty Morgan
LAST SALUTE
O sacred timber, your stature high,
The wind flows free through your eastward side,
No sound of leaves resisting its plight,
Is so uncommon for a July night,
Like cancer, it spreads to your extremes,
Progress it is called, how ironic that seems,
For my very being is yet causing your death,
You are the evidence of life's fleeting breath,
But as I gaze in awe at your towering peak,
I consider the cause that appears so freak,
For it was not course of time, or wear of storm,
It was a trade my friend, my dwelling for your life,
A pretentious display for your sacrifice,
The earth that once fed you can breathe no more,
Through the blanket of concrete that approaches my door,
Yet to consider the years you have grown to this earth,
Surpass my age three times your girth,
O noble one, no you will not die in vain,
This last salute is to your domain,
Tomorrow's new dawn and bright sunset,
Will be somewhat lonelier without your silhouette.

Laura Hurley
LOVE
Love is heart sending
Love is heartbreak mending
It is addictive
It is nonrestrictive
Love is never ending

Love will always be
With you, and with me
It will be forever
It shall leave never
Love, you will always see

Pearle Z Davis
LOVE, THE TENDER TOUCH

To my daughter and her family Marian Z.Gordner

Love is the gentle whisper
encircling spring's fragrant blooming trees;
'Tis love so soft and tender
whose passing gave my heart a squeeze.

Love, the crystal clear spring of living waters
that refreshes our lives day by day;
Love's grace is our Lord and Living Saviour,
the Heavenly Father to whom we pray.

Love's touch is the tender healing contact
that makes our broken and sad hearts whole:
The loving touch of our precious Saviour
who can heal our weary soul.

Love is this planet's Prince of Peace
and God's only begotten son;
Lovingly he watches his flock of sheep
and guides us one by one.

Love is the tender touch of early spring,
summer's warm caress and cool fall rain;
Love is the restless winter's waiting
'til God's reign comes to earth again.

Richard Attenhofer
CHOCOLATE MOUSSE

To Joan, my dear friend, who has inspired me to write poetry:

May God forgive us,
Chocolate Mousse at ten.
Do we commit a dietary sin
To taste of life's
Sweet dessert again,
As we add to our repertoire
One more delectable event,
Truly just for lovers meant?

Will we become addicted
To this ambrosia of the Gods?
Or will we overcome the odds
And only taste love

When we know
This decadence,
Which savors us,
Leaves us in afterglow?

Mary Cahill Cook
DEVOTION TO MOTHER EARTH

To Ted Turner and . . All of mankind

Pollution
Solution

Global ecology
Global psychology

Mankind caring
Mankind sharing

Many races
Many places

New plans—whatever?
Men working together

Pollution
Solution

David Shane McEndree
INVISIBLE TOUCH
If, I were to leave
would you still remember me
who I was, the real me
my touch . . . , my love?

Would your eyes cry?

The shadows of time grow with each passing moment
I can see wonders that no one ever sees, but me

Night and day come and go
You came into the night and made things so right

I feel better now, no doubt about it
you changed the way I felt about so much
How did I become so out of touch?

Things are so much brighter
out of the blue you came into my life
You have picked me up and made me strong
This is straight from my heart

Even if you and I were to depart I would owe you so much

As the days go their own way
Turn into years . . . oh the tears
never wash away the strength,
warmth, the smiles,
laughter and . . .,
the invisible touch you
helped to create.

Christine Curtiss
I SPIN FOR YOU

To My Parents, Ken and Betty, I love you.

Yes, gave you all I could
Gave you my heart
You ran a dagger through and through
The wounds still ache, so hard
Gave you my soul
You shot it to the wind
Barren is my insides 'til this day

Now you whisper to me, come my sweet
Stopped deep in our tracks
Time went by with bloody tears
How can your desire be put on layaway
Cried deep red rivers
Yesterday still can make it rain
Where am I supposed to hold on?

Well! Am I your toy?
Turn me off, turn me on
Heartless, soulless I spin for you
What am I, a puppet strung for you
Tearless eyes full of red rivers
Tomorrow what am I to think?
Tell me your answer now.

Donald A Young
I HAVE A BROTHER THERE

Dedicated to Private 1st Class David James Tidd

Somewhere in Korea,
I have a brother, Strong,
Who is fighting for his Country
and things that are so wrong.
He is fighting for the freedom
which we hold so dear
So that we can keep that freedom
every day throughout the year.

On the hills thru mud and fire
from the distant shore
We see our men advancing
up to the Commie's door.
Men have fought and died there
in that bloody war
But we haven't lost,
we have yet to make our score.

Not for just my brother fighting
but for all the soldiers there
I will pray for Peace and Unity
everywhere.

R Udaya Bhanu

R Udaya Bhanu
PAPIER MACHE
A loveless, lovely, lovable
papier mache
Once on a warm december
pulsated me to teaspoon her
with the tincture of my love

So I sprayed her with
rose-water from honeyed paper roses.
Then I sprinkled her with
golden pollens from the wildest flowers.

And then, placed her at the adytum of my soul.
Offering a bunch of Edelweiss.
Right then papier mache
became the liquor of my poems.

She was lifeless—
I slipped life into her.
She was loveless—
I schooled love into her.
She was soulless—
I shared my soul with her.
And papier mache?
She eternalized my love.

Charlotte Stonestreet
GIFT FROM THE SEA
I looked into the great sea,
The sea that calls
All thoughts to itself.
Life draws to life . . .
Just me & the vast sea.
The sea is a magnet
of all things:
Tears & laughter
The past, the present.

As a stream of water is poured
Into the sea I gave
All thoughts to hold
To scatter, to announce
To hide, to give back
At will.
I walked away
Filled with one-ness,
The gift from the sea.
You were like that!

Leslie Martin
WHEN HE MEANT MORE
I noticed a change in him
The line between friendship and love was slim
At first I didn't know what to do
I started acting strangely too
Here was the boy that I climbed trees with when I was younger
Now it was like I was looking at a stranger
He had grown up and was oh, so handsome
But why did I feel so lonesome
I should have known it from the start
Now there's something missing from my heart
He said we should stay apart for a while
And he tried to part with a smile
As he walked away I said, "But, I love you!"
And he turned and said, "I think I love you too."

Barbara Sanchez
FAMILY

This poem is dedicated to the memory of my dad, Earl Craig, who taught me that love is the most precious gift of all.

Love your family
Cherish them
Keep them close to you

Take each memory
Treasure them
Make them a part of you

Remember the faces
Each of them
The smiles they have for you

Life is changing
Taking them
Far away from you

Love your family
Cherish them
Keep them close to you

Pamela Stone
GIFTS

This poem is dedicated to Elizabeth Wheeless
My Mother and my friend.

Although these words are written in love,
I hope that you will see
Mere words could never express
How much you mean to me.

All through my life you have given me
Gifts that have meant a lot,
But the ones I will always cherish
Came from your heart, they could not be bought.

The meaning of strength I learned
From watching you through the years;
Face many storms, such courage you showed
Even through your tears.

You taught me that when I go to the Lord
And my heart is in deep despair,
To always be sure as I go on my way
That I left my burdens there.

For all the gifts you have given me
I thank the Lord above.
Mother, you gave me the greatest gift
By showing me how to love.

Teresa M Maxim
THE HUNGER WITHIN

To my father, Harry Maxim who has served as my inspiration and hope. In silence, we walk together. Always, Teresa

It was not your handsome face
Nor the sweetness of your voice.
The robust frame you endeavor,
Nor the walk you solely possess.
The pride within you shines so bright
Your smile;
A million suns
The tranquil effect of your calming nature
Tells me, we are one.
As I turn to focus upward,
And reach to grasp you tight
Always, I will know you love me
Now, as I follow the light.

Lola T Lane
GOD'S LOVE

This poem is dedicated to Robert and Kenneth, my dear sons

I gaze inspired at the morning dew
When the sun turns the drops to gold,
It's as if God opened a curtain
To reveal a beauty untold.

What is more glorious and splendid
Than the sun at the height of day,
As it warms the earth with her glory
'Tis God's way of shedding His rays.

The soft gentle rain, that we feel on our brow
Caresses the earth as it falls,
And the voice of the thunder echoes
And speaks, as we listen with awe.

The peaceful scene as we gaze at night
At the starlit studded sky,
Tells of God's faithful love for His earthly man
And sometimes we wonder why.

Victor Velasquez
SLEET
lightning shatters the evening sky
waves of grays cascade before my eyes
shapeless shadows cry out thru the mist:
"why play it safe when life is a risk?"

a wound unhealed—more scars concealed

thunder bursts a momentary daydream
gusts of madness muffle a beggar's scream
ghosts and monsters lunge thru the fog
withered roses bring to mind a dead dog

turn down an alley to escape a mistake
run until long after the last day breaks

rain once cleansed away the sorrow
once long ago; not today or tomorrow
now only feature films and special songs

remind you there's no right in wrongs

a wound unhealed—more scars concealed

clouds of sadness obscure the morning light
on what you know will be a neverending night
trapped by time in a whirlwind of pain
as the past rapidly drives you insane

Debi Larkin

IN MEMORY OF JADE

She was a woman of free spirit,
With her heart full of love.

She dreamed of having her own two wheels,
A dream she'll never fulfill.

She loved her ol'man and being in the wind,
And she wore the story of her life tattooed everywhere.

They went down in the fog of a New Year's Eve,
She was loving her man 'til the end.

One last trip down the happy trailway.

This was my sister with my spirit, taken in the night.
Sister from the start, sister 'til the end.

Dear Lord, watch and keep them,
We'll never see them again.

Her family would not claim her,
Her friends would not disown her.

Karen S Houser

FREEDOM

I dedicate this poem in loving memory of my father, Marvin Spratley.

Freedom is a wonderful thing;
It's like a bird flying in spring;
Freedom is so many things;
It's in America where the Liberty Bell rings.

Freedom has been fought for in this land of the brave;
Many men fought for it all the way to their grave;
Freedom will always exist here;
Communism we need not fear.

"Old Glory" is a symbol of our freedom;
For we won liberty from the United Kingdom;
Freedom will forever be here;
Communism we shall never fear.

Here American Patriotism still lives on;
Men still fight wars so freedom won't be gone;
Faithful Americans won't let Communism come here;
This is why Communism we will never fear.

Joyce Elaine Sweet

I INHERITED THE WIND

Day approaches restless nights. I lie upon my lonely bed.
Tossing between the covers, dreams invade my troubled head.
Spectrums reflect shadows, of haunting memories, I dread.
Feeling contempt, for leaving words and Thoughts unsaid.
Holding memories from yesterdays, lie's with me instead.
Tossing restlessly, dreams come forth, like thunder of mighty steeds.
Profusely sweat pours across my brow, I wipe away its beads.
Lying motionlessly, tears stream down my cheeks, my heart bleeds.
Fighting never ending memories, finding harder each night to fleed.
Picture's flash across a giant screen, I review dreams that feeds.
A lonely child crying out in darkness, my inheritance taken from me.
My thoughts wander to yesterdays, wondering why I was deceived.
Casting me aside, like wave's tossed upon restless seas.
Voices within my head sound's like distant winds, I grieve.
I'm forsaken to roam, within dream filled sleep I lay.
Eternal fires burn my soul, where overtures memories still play.
In dreams I tarry, hopes gone astray, into nights of yesterday.
My inheritance drifts like blowing winds, flowing far away.
Fruitless I know, tho in my dreams grandfather's home remains.

Jeff Leonard

IF I WERE AN ARTIST

If I were an artist

I would paint a sky of pewter grey
That would melt into a soft orange
Turning yellow just as it touches the horizon

The trees would mirror near perfect on a still northern lake
With ripples caused by children skimming stones

The homes would stand frozen on the shore
As the inhabitants move slowly to the close
of the hottest day of summer

But for now

I will use the gifts given me
and paint with the word and song within my heart

Karl Dornemann

WICKED SOUL A MAN

To Dad and Mom, thanks for everything.; Ded, thanks for being you.; Dawn, well . . . you know.

Amidst a thorn-filled bed of daisies
Stands a bird.
A robin perched high in its glory,
And perched high in its cloud.
A lone bird casting a light.
Casting a light only the real can see.

Among a low-filled field of grass
Grows a flower.
A lone flower towering high in its infinence,
And towering high in its pride.
Solitude baring a soul.
Baring a soul only the real can hold.

Wicked soul we; a man.
In fear; mortal never to himself.
In pride; casting an ascetic light.
Falling prey to the thorns and low

Glory, pride, and infinence;
Standing: robin, flower, and we.
Self evidence for the real;
For only we shall remain.

Sharon P Dorsey

MY PRAYER TODAY

Oh Lord as I fall down on my knee,
My prayer today is going to be,
For you to bless others, not just me,
For those that are sick Lord I pray,
For comfort and healing and no pain today.
Lord bless the poor that are cold, hungry and full of strife,
Lord warm and feed them, put some meaning back in their life.
Lord bless those that can't see or hear,
Their eyes are sightless and full of tears.
Lord guide them in the silence and darkness as they go,
Lord touch them gently, your love let them know.
Lord bless those that are troubled and full of stress,
Let them know they can trust in you and that you will bless.
Lord bless the old people, whose children are all grown,
Let them know you're with them, and they're not alone.
Lord bless the homeless, they have nothing to share.
Let us give to them something to show that we care.
Lord bless all your children, all colors, black and white,
Let us all get along with each other, and let us not fight.
Yes Lord, today my prayer will be,
For you to bless others, and yes Lord, please bless me!

Frances Kay Smith

FIRST WINTER'S SNOW

I look out my window into the cloudy sky; I watch the little birds as they go flying by.
The trees they bend from the cold winds blow; Soon we will have our first winter's snow.
It falls from the sky, pretty flakes so white; it covers the ground on a long winter night.
It falls so freely as it touches the ground; it falls so softly and makes not a sound.
Everything is covered as far as the eye can see—from high on the mountain tops, in the valleys, and in all the trees.
Then early the next morning, to the window I go, and there it is, our first winter's snow.
The ground is covered with a blanket of white; it happened while I slept on a cold winter's night.

Michael Humphreys

Michael Humphreys

MEN ABROAD

This poem is dedicated to the United States Marines and other armed forces stationed abroad. "SEMPER FIDELIS"

Here we are
On an island of Japan,
Its name is Okinawa
And it's far from our homeland.
This is a place
Where men come to train,
Whether it be Korea, NTA or the Philippines.
There's quite a few things
To do over here.
Like sightseeing, snorkeling
Or even
Drinking a few beers.

The women over here
Are small and fine.
They like to receive drinks at clubs
And give American GI good time.
But thru it all,
We pray to God.
To keep ourselves safe
'Cause we're the men abroad.

Jordana Kotlus

GOODBYE

So quiet.
As she walked through the woods
On that cold, snowy day.
Nothing surrounded her
But the trees
And the snow
And the complete emptiness
Of the world she knew.
She must leave.
And she walked
And walked
And walked
Out
Into the woods
Further than she had known possible.
And she whispered,
With a single tear on her cheek,
"Goodbye."

Lisa Boggs

STREAM OF TEARS

Tears fall on
her glass full of
wine. They forge
into a line.

Stream of tears
run into all those
wasted years. One
more drink, she
begins to sink into
her happiness.

He's at home
all alone. His
children turn away.

He remembers how
hard he worked to
get what made her
happy. And why
should it matter
now? She's gone,
she is gone.

Norma Schornick

A TOUCH OF BEAUTY

One may travel the winds of time in search of treasures untold
But, the real treasure upon this earth is the beauty that life unfolds.
For when one surveys with an open

heart the wonders throughout our land,
one knows that only God could place so much beauty at our command.
Anywhere and everywhere there's beauty to be found,
the softness of the moonlight casting shadows all around,
the universe sprinkled with glittering stars, a sunset all aglow,
a field of golden daffodils kissed by a blanket of snow.
Majestic mountains reaching high in all serenity,
the billowing waves caressing the breast of the deep and mystic sea.
In the early dawn the sunrise revealing the birth of day,
lending its light and warmth to earth as night speeds on its way,
the quietness of the early morn, the stillness of the night,
the beckoning of the forest, the swallows while in flight.
There's beauty in the snowflakes if one will only look,
the pebbles and seashells on the beach, the small but faithful brook,
the colorful rainbow after the storm, the deserts barren sand,
the deep forbidding canyons, engulfed in natures hand.
The graceful weeping willow tree whose branches doth unfurl,
to add a touch of beauty to the vastness of this world.

Linda K Akers

THE LOVE AND MY LIFE

In the beginning there was only me
Then as I grew older my heart could see,
All the Love and Beauty that surrounded me.
The different kinds of Love one life could have,
The special little dreams and emotions I felt
That only my mind and heart could melt.
A love of a life time or just one for awhile
Brought to me a little smile.
Sometimes I've been sad and thought I would never again see
The happiness and smiles my heart had brought to me—
Then like a flash it was all gone
And my heart was lifted up and sang me a new song.
Love is all around me
And in my life I see
The beauty and gladness which is all the world to me.

Saun Lee

TWO HEARTS

This poem is dedicated to Jimmy Hudson, my future husband!

Happy is the time of our meetings,
An electrifying mist envelops our embraces,
My mind has spread its wings,
And now Blackness is the darkness that prevails against my day drams.

I see you as a storm cloud,
Black-Red-Blue-Brown-Yellow-Green-skin tones of your inner self.

While you seek changes,
I watch with awe as your beauty emerges to perfection and life itself.

You go through colors and match them with phages of cares and destiny.

You begin anew bringing happiness, silence, and treasures of love to those who seek you as their ideal.

When I speak your name there is no sound 'cause your windy spirit of perfumes and colors carry me adrift leaving no one to hear.

Turning my head, I see the sun rising (droplets of light, imitation pearls of dew) out on the eastern horizon.

But, to purchase light is to lose your love until tonight when you'll rein supreme over day dreams that carry us adrift through boundless space.

And eons from now happiness, tears, and treasures of love will be preserving dreams and chasing fears of those who seek you as you are.

Our kisses last for decades,
Its sweetness is ever lasting,

Sad is the time that TWO HEARTS are apart!

Alexander Di Buono

ACCEPTING LIFE AS A LESSON

Dedicated to the inspiring city of San Francisco. Where I've lived, loved, learned, laughed and cryed. Thanks for the inspiration.

Each day I live, is yet another opportunity for me to grow and learn. I prefer to learn the hard way, through trial and tribulation. It has made me emotionally stronger as well as spiritually stronger. I've also been learning about myself, which is quite a lesson, when it suddenly hits you. I've learned to be aware of myself and certain feelings that come along. I've learned to listen and accept what my feelings are trying to tell me, instead of resisting them. Learning to be aware of who I am, how I'm feeling and where I'm going, has given me a great sense of security. Knowing that I do not have to carry life's burdens all by myself, is also part of the reason I'm at peace with my world, my life, and myself.

Katrina Vialpando

HAND IN HAND

They walked in the precious sand,
Hand in hand comforting each other.
The ocean spray spritz their calm bodies.
The glimmering moon flickered upon their bodies
Leaving their silhouette against the dark mountain side.
The earth was peaceful and shy.
He and she walked hand in hand
All through the night.

Pamela J Durham

HOW I FEEL

I wish to dedicate this poem to Linwood R. Blount, Jr. Thank you for being there and believing in me, when no one else would! I love you.

Hard to tell you how I feel
The words I want to say are so unreal
Can anyone make it on their own?
Can you find a place to call your home?
Life is not just what you make it
Without love it's hard to take it.
Does anybody love me, who really cares
All the time people just stop and stare
When I'm saying what's wrong, there's no love along.
We all feel down, we all try
Sometimes we laugh and sometimes we cry
Looking for a place to go, feeling low.
If there is love, there is a way
The love I give to you will never stray
It's the only way, Do you hear what I say?
So love everybody, always care
Then the people will be there, to hear my song
There will be love along.

Esther Ahart Maness

Esther Ahart Maness

PRAYER

There is a quiet place I go to pray
God meets me there every day.
I thank him for each blessing that he gives to me
and he makes me happy as can be.

And when I tell him of my burdens
He always understands, then reaches out and takes my trembling hand.

And when I think of my burdens as tall as a tree
It is then I hear him whisper, "You leave that to me."

And when my burdens get too heavy for me to bear
I just take them to Jesus and I leave them there.

It's a beautiful thing what faith can do.
When you trust in Jesus, he will always see you through.

When you are praying, do you do all the talking there is to do?
No! You must be quiet, wait and listen, God wants to speak to you.

When you think of God, and he asks something of you,
Do not faint or be weary because he will help you.

And when I think of God and his great plan, he does his mighty works through his crowning glory, the woman and the man.

Katie Heckman

JUST A LITTLE PRICK

Just a little prick.
It won't even hurt.
That's what they told me
And I believed them
It can't hurt you they said.
but it will make you feel real good.
They surrounded me telling me everyone was doing it,
that I was a chicken if I didn't.
It's a small needle.
What harm can it do they asked.
I was tempted.
They told me stories about some of their experiences.
How high you could feel, like you didn't have a care in the world.
They told me all of this,
but they didn't tell me the pain of coming down.
They didn't tell me about how once you start you can't stop.
They didn't tell me about how crazy it makes you.
It's just a little prick they said.
And I

Kathryn M Diana

FEELINGS

Love is not so much heeded
While it is there as missed
when it has gone,
Like a little songbird held soft,
But cold and quiet, within your hand,
The empty sound of a clock
Whose chimes have ceased
To mark the hour.

Love gone is a day without sun,
A crib without a child,
A chill you cannot touch,
Grasping only at a memory
Of the sun, the song, the sound,
The child, the warmth,
The One that was
The love you knew.

Theresa A Zakraysek

BEHIND THESE EYES

Behind these eyes is a heart hidden away,
hidden so that others cannot see
a heart scarred and fearful,
still sensitive to cold and to pain.

Time has not healed all wounds
and when human hands try to touch it,
the heart cries out in alarm.

The body and soul join in unison—
protect the heart at all costs;
a biting tongue, a defiant spirit,
oh, the weapons we do use

And the heart burrows deeper

Only One can heal this heart
only One has the perfect Hands,
Hands scarred themselves,
so that all hearts can be healed.

Oh, take my heart into your perfect Hands
and heal it with your loving touch
Oh, One who is Love, help me love again.

Bruce Wilson

GOODBYE TO A FRIEND

Silent for so long keeping secrets for your nation,
Made it hard for you to open yourself,
Though I never asked for an explanation.

An only child; it was hard for you to share,
I—merely a child, was so unaware.
Selfish and too young to care,
I did not see the times you wanted to, but couldn't be there.

While growing up, it was difficult to see
That your being hard was the best way to be.
Through the years now, with time to reflect,
It was this hardness that taught me respect.

Respect for the right way . . . though we might disagree,
You taught me to look at both sides, so better to see.

In time, I found you were a person;

not simply a Dad.
I saw you differently then, began to understand
That all I need do was ask, and you would lend an hand.

With understanding, love so soon came.
Even so—I could not tell you . . .
what a shame.

Now that it's too late, I finally comprehend;
Through it all I found a friend.
Thank you father for all you've done,
I'm very proud to be your son.

So long Dad, goodbye . . . to a friend.

Debe Kostock-Forrer
SITTING IN A ROCKER
Sitting in a rocker,
only hearing the chair squeak,
children outside,
playing hide,
and go seek,
with the wind,
so still,
and the trees,
standing with ease,
the squirrels,
sit and watch,
the motion,
of the falling leaves.

Jean A Cassard
STRENGTH

To my children and to theirs

The silver was so faint it could barely be seen
Wound through the heavy gold like a screen.
The gold stood out—dusty shades of pink.
Showing great power, infinite strength.
But the true link was the lovely shimmering, delicate silver thread.
So it is in life—you may not perceive real truth or even where the angels tread.
Strength lies not in the largest, strongest or prettiest necessarily as has oft' been said.

Judy Clement
NATURAL TRANQUILITY
I'm sitting in the forest;
It seems full of peace.
It's far from the city
Where it's quiet in the least.

Right before me
A bird flutters its wings.
Off in the distance
Another one sings.

I see a spider's web
Glimmer in the sun.
Just as a dew drop
Early in the dawn.

There is no place here
For prejudice or hate.
When you enter
They're left at the gate.

Leonora A Wyatt
REQUIEM FOR A LOST LOVE
As I sit here listening to "our song,"
I wonder where our love went wrong.
What happened to the love we shared?
I wonder if you ever cared!

I was so much in love with you;
I thought you truly loved me, too!
But that first blow to my body, one night,
Turned off my love, like the flick of a light!

It would have been nice to grow old with you;
To sit and remember the joys we knew;
To love you now, as I did when
I first saw you way back then!

But now we are no longer one.
Our life together is over, done!
May God bless you in all you do;
Somehow I still miss loving you!

Jonathan Marshall
BLUE LOVE
The emotion transcending affection's warmth and
Infatuation's foolishness
Manifestingly exists.

Its deep devotion and intense fondness, with
Benevolence so gentle
Yet strong it passes
Like twilight before
Dawn, and the calmness
Before the storm passionately persists.

Silently, wistfully whispering with compassionate
Cares, love powerfully
Ensnares with a
Soft and elusive touch
Being of heart, mind, space, and such;

She as unpredicting as a raging sea calls to me.
Though love chances as
Gracefully as the ballerina
Dances, I feel admiration,
Simply love crossed by
Circumstances.

Elaine C Davis
THE GO BETWEEN
A snow white flower bloomed today
On an almost naked tree,
And even though the sky was gray
It said, "Spring is here, come see!"

I looked and found spring close at hand
Despite a cold wind blowing
For nature seems to understand
The perfect time for growing.

I saw the crocus pushed through snow
Sans warmth of earth for guidance.
I gazed in awe that it should know
The time was right—could it be chance?

But no—for everywhere I look
From violet to trailing green
Upon the willows by the brook,
Something acts as go-between.

If man could also learn to wait
Until Divine Direction came,
Then act and never hesitate,
There'd be no joy he could not claim.

Ron Langley
THE OMNIPOTENT THIEF
Time is the universal thief
So imperceptible his pace
He steals my very youth and then,
Leaves lines upon my face

He saps the strength that he once gave
He fogs the fertile brain
That only withered sinews and
Dim memories remain

He takes the sight from aging eyes
He once did freely give
He takes it all 'til finally
He takes your will to live

He steals 'til there is naught to steal
Which seems to be his goal
Then for his final plunder
He steals your very soul

So youth, while time is giving these
The things which I now lack
Enjoy them, use them wisely
Someday he'll take them back!

Rayford Woodall Sr
SHAME
When life's out of control
Evil thoughts freely flow
After all has been told
There's no place to go
Hurt the one you know
Words of anger—uncontrolled
When a love grows cold

Ginny Bridges
HIM

Dedicated to—my Grandfather . . . with love

So full of life,
Yet so painfully ill.
So determined to live.
We wondered if anything could kill
But Death overtook him,
And pulled him from our grasp.
But his existence
Will never be a part of the past.
We'll keep his memory alive,
No matter of any obstacle.
We'll always remember him.
There will never be a lull
We loved him so dearly,
His face remains so clearly

Brenda M Dalbec
A FULL AND SHINING MOON, ON A STILL AND PEACEFUL NIGHT

Dedicated, with love, to Bill. He believed, he encouraged, he cared.

A full and shining moon on a still and peaceful night,
Could there be magic falling with that brilliant light?
For "something" touches my senses when that golden glow is above
Tell me why, when the full moon is shining, do my thoughts always turn to love?

Cathy Biers
WAR
I can still hear the people crying
I can still see the people dying

I can still hear the thunder in my ears
Bring back all the fears

I pray day and night
Hoping that there'll never be another fight

Now it's here once again
Never knowing who will win

You can see me cry
And I can see you die

Marcia Waugh
MY PARTNER'S HANDS

To the partners I have played cards with that are farmers . . . My husband, Ray, and also Eugene Hess.

Much larger than mine,
Tanned, scraped, calloused,
Tough from tractor, combine,
Tender to grandchildren and fishing line.

Figuring milo, wheat, heifers, steers,
Calculating fertilizer, fuel, gears,
Holding black coffee, ice tea or beer
Quick to comfort a grandchild's fear.

Scarred from planting, cultivating, harvesting.
Lava scrubbed, knife cleaned nails
Wearing the stone in his masculine ring
High bidder, holding only the deuce and a king.

Jean Lankford
ACROSS THE MEADOW

To my husband James and my ten children: Jimmy, Debbie, Gary, Carolyn, Susan, Sharon, Jeff, Mike, April and Tammy.

As I look across the meadow
And down in the valley below,
I think of all the beauty
And how he loved us so.
God gave us many blessings
We need to count each one,
And thank him every day
For all that he has done.

Juliette Gudenas
HOLD ONTO THIS YEAR
Hold onto this year
Don't ever let it go
Because before you know
It will blow
Right past your eyes
A baby cries
A good friend sighs
Memories lurk
A bird chirps
Hold on
Tighter than ever
Because before you know
It will blow
Right past your eyes

Becky Dickman
SAD SONG

This poem is dedicated to Danny, I think of you often and love you always

. . . As I sit here thinking,
I hear a sad song play.
I listen to its every word,
But tears get in my way.

I mumble out the lyrics,
For I know the words by heart.
Because its just that same old song
Which I have become a part.

You know the one I'm
speaking of,
For you're the one I played
it to.
I cry now when I hear it,
'Cause it's all I have left of
you.

But it's time that I let go
And put you in my past.
It's time I realized it's over
And that not everything
will last.

But no matter how I try
My love for you won't go
away,
Because just when I think
I'm over you
I hear that sad song
play . . .

Ellie Field
INTROSPECTIVE IMPATIENS
I am such a delicate flower
So fragile, yet fair.
And the transplanting shock
Is so hard to bear.
The moving and shifting takes its
toll,
My soul gasps for air.

My seasons for blooming come and
go,
But for now I'll rest
In the warmth of your glow.
The roots have been damaged
And I mourn their duress.
The anguish is real, not fast but
slow.

The day will come when I reach for
more,
After the hybrid graft.
Blossoms will linger even in snow
As tomorrow becomes the past.
Of this I am certain, this I know,
Your love makes me grow.

Paul Milk Jr

Sylvia Milk, Mother of Paul Milk Sr
MY LITTLE BOY

Dedicated to Paul Milk, Jr. by Paul Milk, Sr.

Where is he tonight?
Is he safe? Is he warm?
Is he dreaming of cowboys?
My Little Boy
Is he happy without me
And is he growing
As a boy should?
When I think of him,
A part of me
That I love,
My heart grows sad
Because
My Little Boy
Will never really know
His Dad.

Jeff Adams
THE EYE

I would like to thank my sister, Rhonda, for her participation and help. Also I'd like to give an indirect thanks to Mel Gibson for the inspiration to write this poem.

He knows about bad grades and
impossible dreams
He knows these things and tells them
to his friend, who has an eye that
is all-seeing and all-knowing.

To him that eye has all the solutions
It can take all anger, pain, and
frustration away. The eye knows that
and it rarely fails.

He picks up his friend and caresses
its pure black body. He likes its feel.
He is intimate with it
He puts the eye into his mouth.

Eye, you are so wise. Can you talk to
me?
Yes, but it needs help. All it needs is
a finger on a small lever
and a little bit of a pull.

Its response is loud, it isn't music
to the ears.
It's too bad that its holder can't hear.
Those grades won't ever be good and
the dreams will always be
impossible.

The eye seems all-seeing and all-
knowing but it is very cruel.
Its effect on the holder is the opposite
who is unseeing and unknowing.

Glen R Hill
LAST NIGHT

To all my teenage romantic fantasies, while attending Orlando, Fla. Sr. High School in 1937 and 1938.

Last night, when day, softly to rest
Had leisurely crept toward the west,
And all my tasks of day well done,
Sought from their midst, the sinking
sun.

I was alone without a care,
'Twas I alone, I know not where;
Just drifting into space so wide,
The moon, I thought I soon would
ride.

I visited the moon perchance,
And found the land of lost romance.
My life-long wish, at last come true:
To be far-off from all but you.

You said you were forever mine,
I promised likewise to be thine.
You let me kiss away your tears
Which come in life's most envied
years.

I heard the winds cease when you
spoke,
And by unlucky chance awoke
While floating high in vision's
stream,
To find, in all—'Twas just a dream.

Erika Allred
I CAN'T FORGET
My friends always tell me to forget
him. How can I forget you when I
still love you

Forget the songs
Forget the dreams
They just don't know what it means

To forget when we were together.
Telling each other it was
forever.

You were always there, You were the
only one who really cared.
Forget when we were alone.
Forget how long we talked on
the phone.

Forget all the times I would cry
and you were the only one by
my side.

I will never forget you. My love
for you will always be true.

Mary Marie Hill
SIX HOURS UP ON THE CROSS

To: My Two Sons, Melvin and David Box.

Six hours upon the cross
Six hours of Agony
When the Savior of the World cried
MY GOD, why has thou forsaken me

And for Three hours
Darkness fell
And the Temple that stood by
Began to crumble to the ground
With an unseen hand from on high

And for Three hours
Darkness fell
And the people that stood by
One man said truly he must be the
one
God has sent from on high

He could have called
Ten legions of Angels
To take him from that cross
But if he had done this
For ever we would be lost

Jerry W Marshall
ONE IN A BILLION LOVE TIME, LOVE LIFE
There was once a woman child
proudly
Born to be, on that March morn.
Did the rain stop and the sky turn
clear blue
"Oh look at these revelation:
"Grace and beauty tell fore to
see:
"She'll say I love you to thee, she is a
love written one in a billion. She will
make and create a change for all
lovetime, love life, because to show
love is the way she's created,
teached, taught, to live. This is her
life chance for love, Love chance, for
this. Those, That, many lovin' life
times that her life showing, telling,
word of love compassion. Please
send to all her my, those, stroke, of
words lovetime, love life, in a billion.

Patty Call Bauer
A TRUCKER'S WIFE
She thinks God showered her with
luck
The day she found her love who
drives a truck
He is so very good looking
And really loves her homecooking
She didn't think of all her time alone
While to make a living, he must roam
Of times when things go wrong and
kids get sick
He, to the darn job would have to
stick
She fixes the plumbing and roof
when it starts to leak
For he is barely home long enough to
speak
She knows, he truly wants to be at
home
But he has a bug that makes him
roam
He knows that he is missing out on a
lot
As he worries if dispatch for him a
load has got
He worries about the needs of his
family
And, also if on time he'll be
He wants to hurry back home
And from that safe warm haven never
roam
Back to the kids and his special angel
But once there for awhile, she can
begin to tell
He must get back on that lonely road
To deliver that very important load
For trucking is his very soul
And for his truck, they went in the
hole
So, with a smile and sigh
She tells her man goodbye
While thanking God for her good
luck
Of the day she married a man who
drives a truck

Sherry A Stanley
MY CASTLE OF ICE
Looking at life through a window of
ice
Not willing to surrender at any price
The beauty and serenity that is only
mine
In a world of fantasy that crosses the
line,
Between the world of once and the
world of now
I would not leave, if by chance, I
knew how.
The ice that numbs the pains of the
heart
That freezes the emotions before they
start.
But it does not hurt and I cannot say
I want to leave in anyway.
For with every stillness and every
move
You can see the light through every
groove
Knowing that with the sunshine's
heat—
My castle of ice will soon be sleet.
Releasing those feelings, setting free
the pain
Until I find a way to freeze them
again.
And then I will open my book and
write
On another dream and another
light . . .

Myrtle Mae Johnson-Tennis
A PRAYER OF THANKSGIVING
"Omnipotent God of our Universe—
Creator of all that now is—and is yet
to be:
We give our Thanks for the Gift of
Life,
For our Nation—strong and free!"

We ask, Forgiveness for all pride
Attached to false Ambition's aim;
Help us to search within our hearts
And recognize our hidden shame!

A priceless heritage is ours
Deeply rooted in the cultural Past
Transcending the many, varied
strains
Shaping the mold of our Country's
cast.

Help us assume this innate debt
To those whose worthy Past we
share;
Make us aware of Humanity's plight,
A way to ease needless suffering and
care!

Dear Heavenly Father, our loving
God—

Thy Infinite Plan to no one is given.
As our Fathers before us IN GOD WE TRUST—
Our Guide through life, our hope of Heaven."
AMEN

Lena Roberson

Lena Roberson
YOUNG LOVERS OF DAYS GONE BY

Two young lovers walked hand in hand
In warm and breezy weather,
They thought their love would always stand
Thinking God had brought them together.
The wind blew softly through the trees and leaves,
Full moon and stars above;
Like magic he sheltered her in his arms,
From his heart came only lasting love.
No harsh nor sad words spoken,
They slowly slipped apart;
Tender memories were kept in life's pages,
Folded gently and deeply in their hearts.
Many years have fast slipped away
While growing older . . . It's been hard to bear,
Lost love so young and tender,
In days gone by they did share.
His spirit hath left a shadow o'er her
She slowly drifts . . . down memory lane
Wildflowers on the hillside still whisper—
I want your love all over again.

Carmen R Velez
MY LOVE IS

This poem is dedicated to my Loving Husband Fidel

My Love is, waking up in the morning next to him
My Love is, being there for him when things go wrong.
To comfort him whenever he's feeling low and blue
My Love is, praising him with a kind word or two.
My Love is, when he is feeling weary, taking control of things
And showing him I'm strong.
My Love is, caressing his face, and telling him how much I love him.
My Love is, understanding his pain.
My Love is, wiping away the tears that he hides so well
And reassuring him things will be better again
My Love is, giving him the courage and strength he needs to see him through it all
My Love is, telling him there aren't any problems too big or too small,
That together, we can outweigh them all.
My Love is, stroking his graying hair
And telling him how much I really care
My Love is, telling him how very happy he's made me throughout the years
With a Love like ours, beautiful and pure
There's nothing in the world, together we can't endure.

J P Moran
NO MORE TEARS

For Vickie, my wife, with love.

The times have become happy
In a sudden moment of laughter
There are no more tears for troubles behind.

Our future days loom splendid
With a boundless romance
There are no more tears for romances of past
We sleep now alone, but forever together
There are no more tears for lost, lonely nights.

Look forward to the future, don't ever look back.
For when we reawaken, we shall not be apart,
But in each other's arms we shall remain in ardor.

Gerturde Phipps
GOING HOME

To Edith Blanche Porch
Mother of Leland M. and David C. Porch

As our life on earth
begins to fade, Then we start
our journey Home.
God waits with open arms
to welcome us into His great domain.
Those left behind know
the life and love we shared
will never leave us.
Some day in time to come,
we shall be together in Heaven,
our home on high.

Vivienne Harper (Ve)
MAMA'S BIG BACK YARD

To Mama: Maude Parker Barnes
In Loving memory—

When things these days get hectic,
My new way of Life's a bit hard,
I long to escape . . . just sit for awhile
In Mama's big backyard.

It was never really quiet there . . .
And yet, it was so peaceful!
Shaded by giant-like trees,
With sunlight through the branches
That were swayed by the ocean breeze.

Sometimes it's hard to understand
This world that we inherit . . .
It is, for sure, the worse for wear
But with God's help, we bear it.

Beauty fades so quickly . . .
Often hearts forget to care;
Life is a mixture of sunshine and rain;
This I know—so when I'm feeling low,
In memory I go . . .
Back to Mama's backyard!

Roberta Reimer
ROADS THAT PART

To Joie

Our roads from this place on must surely part.
Although you leave my presence not my heart.
We each must lovingly pursue our way,
While all the while our hearts
Do heavily weigh upon our souls.
We still can always, always, gently hope
That somewhere, on some sunny slope,
Our roads will cross again along the way,
And we will clasp each other heart to heart.
Never, Never, shall we ever part,
Nor shall we ere remember, roads that part.

Larry A Perkins
HEAVENLY HOST

To: Debbie Val, My Princess—with love.

I looked upon a world of misery,
so to you, I sent down my son.
He was crucified by you at Calvary,
though you knew he was the one.

Now in churches do you say,
through Christ our Lord is the way.
To know the father, love the son,
worship no other I am the one.

Heavenly Host some call me,
father of the son who died at Calvary.

Brian Day
COMPANIONS OF THE DARK

To Karrie Goudreau, My sweetheart and companion forever!

From the top of the mountain
the wolf cries out lonely,
but his howl is uncertain,
as it echoes in the valley.
The moon rises high,
the wolf can be seen
facing toward the sky,
standing tall and lean.
The air has a chill,
shadows dancing in the moonlight,
but tonight there will be no kill,
as the wolf slips out of sight.
In the darkness he moves about,
cause somewhere in the valley,
another wolf cries out,
and tonight two wolves won't be lonely.

Stephanie Boquet
YOU ARE MY INSPIRATION

I dedicate this poem, with all my love, to my husband Leroy

You are my inspiration, I love to hold you tight.
I'll try to make you happy, and I'll try with all my might.
For you bring these feelings to me, I never thought were true.
I hope you always love me, for I love only you.

My love for you is growing, stronger every day.
It makes me sad to think of you, when you have gone away.
The times we spend together, the memories that we share.
The way you say "I LOVE YOU," lets me know you really care.

You are my inspiration, my ever loving glow.
I long for you in desperation, how much you'll never know.
For words are hard to come by, to express my love for you.
But please believe in one thing, my love is forever true.

LOVE ALWAYS AND FOREVER,

Stephanie

Jeanne Albers
IT ISN'T TOO LATE, YOU KNOW!

Pure and innocent whore
Who has destroyed mankind . . .
Raggedy Ann costume hiding Mary Magdalen.

Modest women are an anachronism.
Too bad, I say.
We might have done well teaching men our ways
Instead of giving in to their conditionings.
It isn't too late, you know.

Emmalena H Jessie
THIS IS YOUR LIFE

This poem is dedicated to Benny, my dearest friend

The life you life is but your own
The extent to you is never known
Take time to analyze yourself
Astounding results are often felt
Knowing your faults and where they lie
Your incentive won't be to wonder why
Improve upon your weakest point
Satisfy, then get just what you want
This life is the only one you will get
So live it to the fullest extent

Audrey Brannon
A CHILD'S PRAYER

To my children: Dorian, Dechon, and Dimitri Love, Mom.

dear god up in heaven
please hear my plea,
why does mommie and daddie
do this to me?

day after day they smoke cigarettes,
louder and louder their coughs get.
dear god up in heaven
please get them to stop!
my mommie and daddie are
All I've Got . . . .

Julie Melissa Day
LIFE

For the dearest parents in the world, who can never know just how appreciated is their unfailing love and support.

What joy to feel the breath of an evening breeze
And know, should I die come morn,

The flittering of my heart remains scattered about,
And my thoughts—a myriad of loveliness adorned.

You see, my life has not been spent
In the despair of self-pursuit forlorn.

But instead I have brought to those stricken, lost souls,
Who between love and despair are torn,

The tiniest specks of such happiness and hope—
Glints of shining light from which despair must adjourn.

I have no fear of death, for I know
That the summer lamb's wool I have shorn,

That I have brought to my world such ecstasy
Through a life well-worn

That could not have even feigned to exist
Had I ne'er been born.

Lyla K Fletcher
POOR LITTLE CHILD

To: Lisa M.S.
You bring me joy, and happiness.
Love, Mom

Poor little child, you sit there alone.
Crying for your "Momma," who will never come home.
Come, and sit beside me—just-for-awhile.
Come, and sit beside me—I'll try-to-make-you smile.
Come, and walk-with-me—where-gentle-breezes-blow,
Come, where Sun will warm you—
for life is hard I know.
Come, and let-me-rock-you, and let peace-come-to-your-heart.
Come, and walk together. It will be a brand-new start.

Elaine C Mandulak
TELL ME

Dedicated to the three men in my life, my father Thomas Constandilo, my husband Robert James, my son Thomas John, life would be empty without you.

Tell me that you love me
Tell me that you care
Tell me you won't forget
me when I'm no longer there.
Tell me all the things my
heart and soul need to hear.
Tell me! Oh! Tell me!
You'll always be there

Michael P Mulvey
CULTURE SHOCK

To Denise Jacoby
For giving me faith to believe in myself.

He is sent abroad
for reasons unknown
For years at a time
away from home
Not knowing the people
unfamiliar with the land
Awkward with the language
adapting the best he can
Until at last he is accepted
finding his own niche'
Only to be recalled
like an engine with a gliche'
Back to his homeland
a stranger once again
Never forgetting his newfound love
or the comfort of his friends
To finally realize
as he studies the clock
Anyone can be a victim
of the so called culture shock

Charlotte M Peiler
HUNTIN' A CEDAR TREE

Thanks to Vernon for taking us on a real Christmas tree hunt, also for the best days I spent in 1979. . 53 days but like the tree they were very special and real!

For many years back, Christmas
meant goin' huntin' for a cedar tree.
Who heard of Artificial?
Who heard of boughten pine tree?
Not the folks of Shadwell or Smith
Creek in Eastern Montana.
This here is tree huntin' time.
You bet! We takes out our gun.
Takes all the wee ones along and
mudder too. 'Cause her opinion is
'portant!
The gun you say? You bet!
See that tree over yonder?
That the one? Mudder agree?
OK!! ZING ZING go the sound of
the bullets as they whiz along.
There she be. Our Cedar Tree.

On Smith and Shadwell Creek you
see, we only shoot off the top and
leave the rest for posterity!!

Marie Harlow

Marie Harlow
IN BETWEEN

To my children and grand-children My pride, my joy. Eternal love.

Today you stand so proudly tall
And too mature for tears.
Tomorrow likely you'll forget
To wash behind your ears.

With peacock strut, designer jeans,
And body curves aligned,
You're on parade, quite unaware
Of that split seam behind.

Your English rates par excellent,
Well chosen, well dispersed,
But penmanship needs practice, Son,
And diction needs rehearsed.

You seem to have control of voice,
Monopolize the phone,
But sudden change in pitch betrays
That new born baritone.
'Tis constant contradiction this,
The age of "In Between"
The boy you've been, the man you'll be,
Enigma, age "Midteen."

Selisa Maahs
MEMORIES

Dedicated to William Allen Tillery

Memories are heartbeats,
Sounding through the years.

Echoes never fading,
Of our smiles and tears we've shared;

Moments that are captured,
Sometimes unaware.

Pictures in an album,
Or a lock of hair;

Bits of verse we cherish,
Once upon a time.

Through the musty hallways,
Of days that we once knew,

Ever comes the vision,
Beautiful and true.

Memories are roses,
Blooming evermore.

Full of forgotten sweetness,
Never known before.

Life must have a meaning.
Goals for which to strive—

Memories are lights that burn,
To keep the heart alive.

Donna Hertz
(A CHILD'S BOUQUET) DANDELIONS

Dedicated to my son Jade, with lots of love, and to all children, who have and will ever, love dandelions.

The thrill in your smile, gave you away
When you first found, you could pick dandelions
That made a bouquet
You held them close, leaving a yellow smudge
On your nose, yesterday
I hate to tell you, Son, I fear, one day
They might become, one of your worst enemies.
When you find you have to dig them up by the root
You'll want to give them the boot
For you see, dandelions are, what you call a weed
Too many go to seed
Spreading like wild-fire, all over the land
That! most people can't stand
Myself, I felt sorry for them,
I wished they rated, being a flower
I never understood, why they missed that respect
But in you, and every little child, I suspect
They're your happy hearts & hands, beautiful bouquet
Because you can pick them
everywhere, any day

Kenneth Mark Neighbors
SILLY LITTLE ROCK SLIDES

To the human conscience, the foundation of all artistic work

What are these which do come and go like the seasons? Like timely building blocks of God to satisfy His reasons.
These silly little rock slides that come into the heart and to one's mind, tearing down and remodeling the man to aid his own kind.
These walls of my life come crashing down so as to cause me to check my priority of heart, mind, and soul. Why don't they just plunder the entire temple?, I wonder. But its foundation only shaken in piece, and part, and whole. Rabid little warriors running to and fro, mocking little bastards laughing as I go. Go, go and find a purpose,
A mission here or there. Searching for that magic rhyme or reason so as to break this present season wretched as it stands.

Agnes M Peters
FORGIVE US . . . AS WE FORGIVE THOSE . . .

To Mom and Dad

If I have hurt you in anyway
Forgive me—
I love you . . .

If you have hurt me in anyway
I forgive you—
I love you . . .

As we ask forgiveness of each other, know this—

Forgiveness takes Courage
and
gives
in
return
added Strength.

Forgiveness takes Trust
and
gives
in
return
a deeper Faith.

Forgiveness takes Love
and
gives
in
return
an unsurpassed inner Peace.

Forgiveness takes Time
and
gives
in
return
a glimpse of Eternity.

Joyce Kirkpatrick
THE CHILD IN ME SEES THE CHILD IN THEE

To Frank Le Roos, May you always find a heart that's warm, and a loving hand to hold.

the child in me sees the child in thee,
can you come out to play?
Ah, but it is raining, perhaps 'tis in we stay.
Mayhaps, the doctor, we could play?
Perhaps another game you say,
One of riddles or rhymes
of the kind to tease the mind
the child in me sees the child in thee,
and will tease anything
you have in mind.

Dorothy L O Sackett
NINE HOURS LEFT

Barter as he will,
his day has come.
There is no more he can sell
for judgement comes on what he's done.

His payment is past due,

not by one, but by all.
We want to see the deepest of red hues;
his life to be taken . . . a call, for those we loved and knew.

Bundy may be ill or sick of mind
but forgiveness must never be given.
For the sake of all mankind,
awaiting his remaining hours, I listen . . .
With quiet restlessness, of the verdict to be given.

When the judgement comes;
please God let it be, that our will be done.
He cannot live—he took so many lives . . .
Please take his, so we can rest in saddened peacefulness.

Evelyn G North
PARIS

I dedicate this poem to my dear friend Doris who was to make this journey with me.

Sitting with sadness on one's mind
Is just a waste of time
It's much more satisfying
To conjure fantasies of another kind
So dreaming of a room in Paris
Is it something to be achieved?
Or a Machiavellian turn of fate
Not to be realized at this late date
Until some splendid calculations
Almost made it a fait accompli
When quite suddenly I awakened
from this reverie
For more structured dreaming
A pretty skyline and an ocean view
Full of vigor of the sea
And I was left with a dream
Still in me.

George E Rhodes
DO IT NOW

I want to dedicate this poem to the finest doctor I know Dr. Claudia M Calibrese, D.O.

If you have a special longing, for some one you know, if you like them, or you love them tell them now.

Do not wait till cares of living have taken their swift toll, and spread wrinkles and grey across their brow.

Time is very unforgiving, and it's later than you think, and careers of life take from you even more.

Often a compliment well given, will save a soul on the brink and direct him to a more blissful shore.

Posthumous awards; so well intended, but I seriously doubt, if heard by the guy that paid the price to win the game.

A comfort to the living, but I'm tempted to believe. If they did nothing, results would be the same.

Maggie Fohl
SHE'S MY MOM

Dedicated to my daughter, Margaret Payne, who is a great mother also.

My Dad walked in one day and told my Mom he was going away. She loved him so it broke her heart. She said we will try to make a new start. She's my Mom.

She came to Columbus, Ohio with her six children dear. She said, "I will make a way for you so have no fear." She's my Mom.

She worked all day and half of the night. She kept us fed and happy alright. She's my Mom.

She kept her chin up and smiled all day, even though her heart was breaking, we could hear her pray.

She prayed, "Dear God, I ask a favor in your precious name. Never let me do anything to make my children ashamed to say, She's my Mom."

When a woman I grow to be, and God lets me a mother be, I want to be like Mom all the way, for I wouldn't exchange places with anyone else today for She's my Mom.

Shelley Dilworth-Mills
WITHOUT YOU

I used to wonder, surrounded by your love,
what I would do, if you weren't here, and with me.
For a time, I was secure, surrounded by your love,
and believing in you and me.
I will always wonder, what it would have been like,
to have always had your love.

My wondering is over now.
You are gone from me.
Your love didn't last,
and although my love is alive,
the rest is gone, and I just . . .
do without you.

Doug Pedersen
APPRENTICESHIP

I am,
even at this point
only midway through
in my lesson—
some ways to go
in the learning of life
and just as far
at least, to go
in the ways of love,
perhaps.
Especially, when love
gives itself
back to me.

A steady learning process
till I qualify
for my diploma.

Ted R Randolph
THE TELEPHONE

I was home alone
When I was awakened by the telephone.
It was her again—I knew it must be.
It was almost three.
The 'phone rang twice
And I wondered, was she really nice?
Or was she being mean to say
She had something else to do to-day?
The 'phone rang a third time
And I wondered, was she really kind?
Or was she trying to hurt me
Or maybe to use me again? Yes, I see.
As the 'phone rang the fourth time
I decided that girl would never be mine.
I pulled my pillow over my head
And I tried to go back to bed.
In the morning the 'phone started ringing.
He said, "My name is Officer Brennan.
We found a young woman to-day,
And the hospital where they pronounced her D.O.A.
They found your 'phone number; it was all she had!"

Amy A Monson
ALONE

Ticking watch and talking trees,
Brushing leaves in blowing breeze.
Creaking floorboards screech with sound,
Yet no one here can be found.
Deep blue sky in night's hour,
Brown in ground the dying flower.
Remaining drops from poisoned wine,
Duty done through hands of time.

Connie Buchanan
A PRISONER NO MORE

Oh, hopeless and seemingly abandoned world,
Now reaping the whirlwind of yesteryear.
Mankind manipulated by greed and lust,
Held captive, in his own prison of fear.

Take heart hurting world for hope abounds,
Despair does not endure to those who will believe.
For the Creator has given us freedom of choice,
But how many will give, what it takes, to receive?

When we openly accept His gift of sweet grace,
By the faith and trust we willingly display.
And abide by Christ's commands of obedience,
His promises clearly guide our pathway.

True release comes far from within,
The depth of every man's heart and soul.
And freedom lies in the surrender of will,
To the Christ in us who makes us whole.

Connie L O'Neil
FANTASY IS REAL

Darkness caresses my being as from a dream I break,
tingling my senses with emotions as I strive to wake,

A smile captures my lips as I again close my eyes,
images of you stream through my consciousness as I romanticize,

Warmth inflames my very essence as I retrace visions of your touch,
echoes of my heart are lost in the blackness as I realize, I need you so very much,

Desire is aroused as I wish again for you at my side,
dawn teases the shadows as I try to bring my dreams alive,

Traces of your scent linger as I pull my pillow to me,
fantasy is real, as I turn and it is you I see.

Janelle Jones
BLACK WORLD: WHY?

Why do we fear
our future looming near
will be stormy skies laced with
morbid clouds of tears.

Why do we fight
our everlasting light
that shines in the tunnel of death
to end life's flight

Why do we strain
against the murderous pain
flooding into our hearts like a
knifestabbing rain

Why do we cry
gospels preached full of lies
giving hope on wings of doves
that will never fly

Why do we scream
reality is the the dream
the fish of a better world
is dead in its stream

Linda Susan Anderson

Linda Susan Anderson
FEEL THE FEELINGS

To the Homeless people of the World Peace, Love and Hope

Standing in the Street
in the dark of night
outward appearance none too clean
hard times, tired faces

Did you ever get up and watch
the beauty of the Sunrise
See the colors on the horizon
Sing out at the top of your lungs
Sing your favorite songs
Worship him as the sun rises

See the lonely people—they try
See them turn towards Jesus
Like the opening of petals in a flower
Their faces starting to glow
as renewed hope, faith and love of God
comes through from head to toe

Feel the feelings, they are there inside
Then let them go, it's your truth believe
Sing until you laugh
Sing until you cry
Sing until you feel free—inside
and then pray to him
It's a whole new world outside

Terri A May
BUTTERFLY
I see countries torn apart by wars
and never ending strife,
people blind to other's needs,
the senseless ending of a life

I see sickness and disease
burdens of pain and sorrow,
victims of society,
waiting for a new tomorrow

Then I turn to see a child
wide eyes as blue as sky
sitting in amazement
as she beholds a butterfly

Ericka Katheryn Green
THE CHALLENGE
If luck should come my way,
would my efforts be any less?
Trying so hard to achieve,
Only succeeding to second best.
Is talent a thing of the past,
Can only the "lucky" prevail?
When competitions require
The confidence that so often can fail.
With only my youth and hope,
Hanging on at my wit's end,
My sunshine attitude borrowed,
The spirit to defeat I pretend.
My competitor has championed,
My pride has been bent,
Wanting only for my spotlight,
Yet wanting only to quit.
Through the strength of friends,
The world keeps turning.
The betterment I strive for,
A gleam that keeps me yearning.

Elizabeth Miller Elfring
FRIENDS ARE FOREVER
Friends are forever
As are memories shared.
Knowing time spent
Is with someone who cared.

Much can be shared
Without words spoken.
Where joy and laughter
Are just a small token.

That one special friend
Fills a space irreplaceable.
A life long friendship
That is easily traceable.

Life and love
Would not be as full,
If not for that someone,
A friend that is you.

Martha Taylor
LOOKING BACK
I would like to be a little girl again
And say my prayers at my mother's knee
And climb upon my daddy's lap
And kiss him one or two times, or maybe three.

I would like to go the woods again
And climb the highest tree
And let the breeze blow me back and forth
As I would sing and shout with glee,

I would like to ride a horse again
As fast as it could go
Because just to walk along
Would be very much too slow.

I would like to go into the haymow
And hide behind the hay
So I wouldn't have to go to school
But just stay at home and play

I would like to milk a cow again
And when the snow was on
To slide down the hill to the cow pen
On an old dishpan full of corn.

I would like to make a snow man again
And perhaps I will some day
For after all at ninety-six
You are not too old to laugh and play.

I would like to be a family again
With my husband and children home
But I still have happy memories
When I am there alone.

The Lord has been so good to me
Down through all these years,
For when grief and sorrow came my way,
He reached down to wipe away my tears.

Jennifer Frank Van Duzer
FOR MY MOTHER
On the wings of time
gliding through memories
a bright blue beacon of hope
soft whispers of love
resting softly on butterfly's wings

The soft brush of scented wind
amongst sun dappled glens
The sweet smell of happiness
drifting on soft white billowy
clouds like puffs of radiance
against an azure blue sky

Riding high with strong swift eagles
scanning the perfection below
Eden on a soft spring day

It was on a day like this that
you must have been born.
The sweetness and caring inside you
created by a beautiful God.
Your face is a haven to me
when the winds blow too hard.

A mother's love
so perfect in its warmth.

Hope La-Tanya Ausby
THE IMAGE OF LOVE

To my family from which I get my foundation, in God from whom I get my strength.

A Loving heart is the truest wisdom.
Love is an exercise that with practice makes passion.
Love is a destiny for it's finding
Someone to love and Someone to Love you.
God made Love up above, for us to share,
And I want to share my Love with you.
Love is a melody that when written by the right two people, makes beautiful music.
Love is one Language, Love is color blind.
Love looks at the inside and not on the outside.
Love is two hearts made in heaven, that find each other on earth.
Love is an innermost feeling that can only be brought by a special person. I want to share my Love with you.

Deborah Melville Moore
SPIRIT OF MY FRIEND

To Anne Sexton

A read your pain, and thought I found a friend.
Alas, in my loneliness, I am not alone.

The future stars shine bright but cold.
Though neither have anything against life.
Is it that old wounds never healed
Or bruises never stopped?

It is possible you met the wrong day.
Your voyage too early to survive
your world of enemies.
Or is it no matter to your possession
What revolution the world is in?

It is the soul of the world that failed.
Not you
Your star still shines bright but no longer cold.
You have traded life for warmth.

I am left in this cold.
I grieve the friendship that failed to be
But mostly the words written that I will never see.

But if you come to me, through me
I will stay and shine bright but forever cold
And I can call your spirit—
Friend.

Joanne Lawrence Kelley
MY PEACE
Let me find a forest to ramble through
I will feel rich as a king,
A forest where signs of life come anew,
To hold out the promise of spring.

Let the branches form a canopy
To shade me from the heat,
A trail over-grown with roots of trees,
And moss springing under my feet.

Let me travel always further on
And when I'm tired, and turn with time,
From dawn to dark and on to dawn,
Let me whisper to God, "Peace be mine."

Lisa Marie Foley
LIFE

To all the people who make my life special, Erica, Daddy, Janis, Mom, Dad, Lin, Nan, and you Ron I LOVE YOU ALL.

Always changing
It's never the same
Like a roller coaster
Who's to blame?

Sometimes rising
to the top
Then I'm waiting
for the drop.

Sometimes falling
and this more often
Then I'm waiting
for life to soften.

Ann Marie Baker
FORBIDDEN FRUIT
I see your eyes, they glance my way;
Your lips, they smile; what do they say?
"I love you, I love you;" I watch you from afar,
so full of life, shining like a star.
But I cannot have you; this can never be,
The feelings that grew between you and me.
I touched your hand, you touched my cheek,
Your body so close that it left me weak.

How could I love you, you're just a mere boy?

You bring me such happiness, such laughter, such joy.
We wrestle like children, getting ever so close,
I smell your sweet body, I'm wanting you so.
My imagination runs wild, as your lips brush my skin,
I lay in your arms and my heart starts to sing.
How will it end, this forbidden love affair?
Why must it end, when we both really care?
Don't touch me, don't touch me, I can't let it show,
These feelings inside me, I can't let you know.
I want to see you, but I'm afraid if I do,
You'll look in my eyes, and see that it's true.

Stephen E Zoleski
SUNRISE
Have you seen its morning rise,
Its beams of white that bleach the skies,
It beckons all for open eyes,
To raise yourself from where you lie.

The morning bird is singing song,
The glories of a sunny morn,
From treetops high and branches long,
He calls to you to sing-a-long.

Cast off your sheets and raise your head.
There is no time to make your bed,
And to the kitchen be quickly fed,
The moon is waning overhead.

So rise and shine, leave dreams behind,
And to the morning bird be kind,
A more glorious morning you'll never find,
To waken all your weary minds.

Morse A Galitello
HORIZONS BECKONED RENDEZVOUS

This poem is dedicated to Corinne.

The sun to earth its blessing send
With radiant warmth its dwellers tend
Convincing tis' less foe than friend

That glorious DAY STAR framed in blue
Illuminating days' debut
Horizons beckoned rendezvous

Oh welcome dawn, dark curtain rise
Expose the beauty night belies
Fulfill the hunger in our eyes

That magic link tween' heaven and earth
Sustains the garden of our birth
Where man doth strive to prove his worth

Through the windows of our mind
Words of poets we can find
Lyrical passages entwined

Express man's joy and his disdain
Inner feelings love and pain
His quest for harmony attain

Though times baton wont' not to rest
Attuned we strive to d our best
Till then our book of life assessed

Kelley A Chavers
DREAMS
You determine your destiny,
By making choices and plans.
You ensure a bright future,
By doing whatever you can.
So say what you mean,
And mean what you say.
Show how much you care,
In every possible way.
Let your love shine through,
And smile a smile that beams.
Believe in your fantasies,
Chase all your dreams.
Never give up,
Fight till the end.
Set your goals high,
Try and try again.
Give one-hundred percent,
In everything you do.
Work toward your goals,
And your dreams will always
Come true.

Miss Krista Frederiksen
HERE'S MY HEART

Dedicated to my loving boyfriend, John

On this very special day,
There's some things I want to say:
I want to say "I love you."
And know how much I care,
And how deeply I treasure
The feelings that we share.
I think it's time you realize
Exactly how I feel,
And know these feelings
Are very very real.
My love for you grows stronger
Each and every day,
As I know the bond between us
Will never fade away.
When you say you love me;
I know that you're sincere.
You always say the kind of things
That I like to hear.
You are why
I'm here on this earth;
You are the reason
I had my birth.
For God always knew
We were meant to be,
And that it was time
For us to see.
When we first met,
I thought it was fate,
I knew that our love
Could no longer wait.
You make me feel
So good inside;
I know in you
I can confide.
You have done more for me
Than any other man;
They weren't able
To do what you can:
You have the ability to love me
Without causing me pain.
You make the sun shine,
And you chase the rain.
In the Spring,
You make the flowers blossom;
You make life itself,
Seem so awesome.
My love for you
Will never ever fade.
For me and you,
We got it made.
Every dark,
Clear night,
I see our star
Shining bright.
I will never leave you,
I am here, to stay.
I wouldn't have it
Any other way.
No other guy
Measures up to you.
You make me happy;
When I'm feeling blue.
Every minute of the day,
You're always on my mind.
I think of how
You're so very sweet and kind.
If I could have
Any guy to choose;
You would not
Be the one to lose.
You don't need to change a thing;
For I love you just the way you are.
I Kould love you just the same;
Whether you were with me, or a million miles afar.
You were the guy
That was always in my dreams;
When I look up and see you,
My whole face gleams.
I guess I should get
To the point of this present;
Which, I feel,
Is the most pleasant.
I'm giving you a special gift
That I've never given anyone else;
I know it's safe with you, because
I know you won't hurt me;
And that's what makes it melt.
On this very special day,
There's some things I want to say:
I hope you believe I love you.
And know how much I care,
And realize that our love
Is something very rare.
On this Happy Valentines Day,
I'm giving you my heart,
To tell you that
We'll never grow apart.

Gwendolyn J Davis-Kyrimis
WOMAN TO WOMAN

To Christa M. Cherney, you are a gift of the divine universe. You are as I am, my very Best Friend.

As love is
the nurturing of the earth
to produce life and take it back
to regrow and replenish old life,
I am beckoned
to listen to that inner earth
and light the way for others to come.
To give unconditionally
and not let mankind govern
my spirit of pride
or smother my truth in living lies.
I reach out to you
knowing that we are bonded,
bearers of good fruit and are
much more than reproducing
machines.
You and I nurture each other
and in the dying, we grow stronger
in our faith as Best Friends.

Susan M Frick
I REMEMBER
I remember
When I was younger
I would leave for school and
I would give my Mom a kiss
goodbye.

I remember
the taste on her lips,
that sweet taste of wine

I remember
I would think and I would
know
what she would be like when I
got home.
I didn't even want to go home,
but I knew she would need
me.

I remember
all those nights I spent with
her, helping her.
Sometimes her hurting herself,
sometimes hurting me.

I remember
that I vowed I would never
drink a drop of alcohol
because I hated her for what
she did.
I never wanted to be like her.

But as time went by . . .

I remember
she was helped and as for me,
I never did keep that promise.
Now years later . . .

I am just like my Mom was.

Erin G Adams (Age 12)
WINTER WONDERLAND

To Floris Elementary School, Herndon, Virginia

In the winter, when the sparkling snow is falling, the icicles dripping from the mail boxes, the brownness of the trees makes them as beautiful as they ever were before.

The deer run through the bare and frosty wood. The white rabbits blend with the white glossy snow. The snow covers the hemlock trees like a blanket.

The blue birds and the cardinals whistle with the wind. The winter colors are as beautiful as the summer winds. The colors of the fire glow through the houses. Winter is the most beautiful time of the year.

Barney Haggberg
THE SACRIFICE
Love is a two edged blade.
Finely honed it glitters battle.
In one hand fire purges forth from
within.
Wreaking havoc amongst the host,
sparing none.
Neither mother nor child.
Yet all cry for its touch.
In another hand.
The edge shines soft and bright.
Lifting the darkness from the night.
Holding together strong and right.
Those who share its powerful might.
For you I wager my tears.
Risking all I lower my shield.
Learning the secrets love learns.
I bid thee take my blade and pray
strike me wisely.
For I love you.

Joshua Cain

Marcia Evone Henley
THE PROMISE

To Brandon, You are someone very special to me, and I'll never stop loving you! God Bless You!

I never told you I loved you,
I never told you I cared.
I never called you on the phone,
I was simply never there.
I never gave you little gifts like
you gave me.
My actions must have made you
think that "we" weren't meant to
be.
My eyes are open wide now
And I realize what I've done.
I know it's now too late
And things can't be undone.
There is one thing I want to say
And I hope you'll take it to heart,
If the chance should roll around
again
I promise to do my part!

Larry S Mitchell
SPARKLING CRYSTAL
Catching color,
throwing it away,
an elusive grasp at rays of light.

Through the glass thoughts are born,
mature,
and fade away . . .
To be replaced by new enlightenings.
Through which things are clearly
seen
and quiet feelings shared,
and ne'er forgotten.
Only added to the silent reflections
the two shall future share
through the crystal . . .
sparkling.

Lisa R Laliberte
ROSES OF LOVE
Roses of love,
Flow with the music of a violin,
To make a harmony of a sea,
That brings me back to thee.

Ocean calm waters,
that flow upon the beach,
then, descend out of reach.

For my love for thee
is . . . as beautiful as the rose,
as quiet as the music,
as calm as the pure ocean.
But with this bliss come,
a broken bow,
an ocean of anger,
blood made by thorns

But in that time,
One must look to the melody.
So in all your dreams of harmony,
Look to the thing that brought you to
me.
And remember
Broken dreams can become your
sweet melody.

Luetress Dimples Washington
THINKING OF YOU

This poem is dedicated to Robert Lee Holmes whom I'll cherish always, Love Dimples

In the middle of the night, as i lie
awake.
A familiar scheen flash across my
face
This familiar person whom i love to
embrace
I wonder is he having the same dream
I am having
This feeling i am having it feels so
good
Me and my lover in each other's
arms,

Wishing and hoping to keep each other from all harm.
Then all of a sudden, at a half past three, something or someone startled me.
Could it be, is it really true.
Just then a ring came out of the blue.
I hesitated for just one moment, as i reached for the phone, it began to ring again, and again, then i said, my oh me
It was only the TV. As i laid back down and returned
to my thoughts I slowly began to close my eyes, then my
Oh my what a surprise, the scheen hit me again
Right at sunrise.

Lattice Boykin-McKoy
THE ROSE

To Lyles, who inspired me to write "The Rose."

What is that,
A rose in her hair?
Worn, so proudly, everywhere,
With a hat?
While in riddled pose, people stare.

No one knows the code
Or why she chose
To wear a rose
In her hair
In the cold winter month of January.

Now she is the talk of the town
Wearing a rose, year round,
Even when she goes to church
Under her, wide-brim hat, a rose is perched.

Tis rumored, it symbolizes a love she left,
Based on a secret well kept
Wearing the rose is not worn out of season
And not without good and sufficient reason.

Willie Jeneva Flathers
TRUTH STANDS

Dedicated to my husband (Harry), and all our family, friends, loved ones, and AMERICA.

In the beginning God made man
And He prepared for him a plan
For him to follow his whole life through
Never to sway nor flee from TRUTH.

When all has failed, and sank and gone
Yet one thing shall still stand strong
The mighty TRUTH of life shall remain
TRUTH HIMSELF unmarred, unharmed, not changed.

If the world would change its course
And leave behind what brings remorse
Get geared, in line, with the core of TRUTH
Cleansed and purified through and through.

God would harken to the prayer
And heal our land because He cares
But it depends on you O man
Whether you'll follow God's wonderful plan.

Andrea Witherington
BABY'S SONG
I feel so alone what can I do? she is about to make a very wrong move.
She has something within her that is so very clear, but it too will soon disappear.
We'll never see him grow up to be a young man, there was no time to prepare or even plan.
It seems so unfair what can he do? There is no room in her life for two.
He won't play with friends or even go to school, I feel so helpless, how how can she be so cruel?
Her life is hectic, I know this is true, yet it's not his fault, what did he ever do?
Some say he isn't human, I disagree. If you can kill him then it seems to me, that he is alive and living in his mother, in a warm and trusting.
And I don't think it was meant for her to take his life away.

Shawna Swafford Kuddes
I FOUND A CURE

This poem is dedicated to my parents, Bill and Charlene, for being there when I really needed them.

I've gone the route of drugs before
I guess I thought, "It's Cool"
Now when I stop and look I see
I must have been a fool

I had lost my will for living
And broke my parent's hearts
But, what it really comes to is
I had torn my life apart

First, I was "Down," then I was "Up"
Then at times I wasn't sure
Till one day I wondered if
I'd ever find a cure

Well now I've come away from that
And I honestly can say
I couldn't go back to that life
And it's going to stay that way

I have too much to live for
To go back to that again
To put my family through the hell
I put them through back then

Cathy Marie Bales
THE DREAMER
Once in a while a dreamer is born. This person's different for they know how to mourn.

Through the troubles and trials we people go through. The dreamer's a person that never will rule.

They are quite meek and sometimes quite shy. The people that know them will never know why.

A dreamer is someone who knows how to think and tries very hard to stay in the pink.

But a dreamer's quite different and so very rare and no one knows why. And nobody cares, until the dreamers all die.

This is quite sad and a terrible waste. For if there were more dreamers it would be a much better place.

Ardath (Spires) Zwies
MY GOLFER

My husband
Walter C. Zwies
USN Retired

Up out of bed at the crack of dawn,
Gulps down a cup of coffee and the race is on.

Heads for the bathroom to shave and shower,
Then combs his hair for half an hour.
Gets all dressed up in his colorful clothes,
That's the latest in golf fashion you know.

The night before he polishes his shoes,
And shines his clubs till they look like new.

A final check to see that everything's done,
Look out golf course, "Here I come."

Neither rain, Hail, or a sweltering hot sun,
Will keep this goofy golfer home.

An hour goes by, then three, then four,
At last I hear him at the door.

He heads for the couch, kicks the shoes from his feet,
And there he lies fast asleep.

Now I know the game of golf has a very high rating,

But What makes that game so INTOXICATING?

Michael Allen Cline

Michael Allen Cline
AS I WALK THROUGH FIELDS OF GREEN

To Mom, for all her love and inspiration

As I walk through fields
of green

Unto my ears do angels
sing

To give me strength to
to carry on

Fear no night, for it
brings dawn

Only angels sing the song
That blessed my heart
and made it strong

Love passed me by, and
this I know

My angel in heaven shall
point me a way to go.

Dan Salinardo
DONNA
Donna Owen
How's it goin'?
All day long
I'm so forlorn
'Cause you're not here with me
sitting on the steps in Boston
—at the Quincy Market
Writing verse
Trying not to be terse
(What a curse!)
The day is bright
and breezy too,
Sitting in the sunlight
writing to you.
As the pen moves on
at Twelve-o-Nine,
The words come out
In rhyming lines.
Enough of the talking—
Lunch is over,
Time for walking,
And move this rover.
This poem is of 'er
Yeah, she's the one
Donna, my love
The only one!

Nicole Antonia Hales
EDGE OF REALITY

This is for my friends, my family, and Bill W. Thank you for everything.

I'm standing on the edge of reality
not knowing what's real and what's not
running from the monster that chases me
fear is now ruling my heart

running to the edges of darkness
trying to find the white light
begging for my God to forgive me
hoping He'll cut through my fright

Satan is standing before me
his promises tempting my soul
with a smile he opens his arms to me
hurt and betrayed to him I go

Running through the arms of insanity
chained to the darkness for life
my savior has completely abandoned me
all that is left is my fright

wondering why I gave up his love for me
in return for this unending night
knowing I can still ask forgiveness
my Lord, take me back to your light

Cherie L Colet
MY LOVE FOR YOU
(A Letter)
Darling,

I just want to tell you how very much I love you.

I will not say as Elizabeth Barrett Browning said,
"Let me count the ways."
My love for you is whole complete
all encompassing entity,
which forever faithful stays.
An iridescent, incandescent,
transcendent flame,
So great that nothing can ever put it out.
That's what my love for you is all about.
It is eternal!
A love that will be as great and

wonderful in the after life
As it is now great and wonderful in the present life.

A love that is so constant and so strong
That it can never break—or bend.
A love that is always all your own.
Always and forever—through time and eternity.
A love that will never end!

And Darling,
That is how I love you.

Dorris L Peters
MY LOVE

To Phillip, you will always be "My Special Love." I love you always.

My love is yours for as long as you want it
If there is anything that I could do, to make you happy, you know I'd do it, anything for you . . .
Making you happy is what I want to do
May our time together be as memorable as our future time in life . . .
The love I give you today will be much stronger tomorrow
With you in my life makes me love you more and more every day . . .

Kevin M Schau
THE PAINS OF PLEASURE
With a warm body both beside and beneath I awake.
An urge rolls gently into my brain
And slowly, without strain
I grab my lover's hand and leap for the stars.

The window parts like a membrane before my hand,
My will carries me into the night.

My brows furrow, my mind distracts,
I feel a weight—an anchor to the mundane.

Puzzled . . . worried? Confused I ask,
"What is it my love? The cosmos awaits."
Her reply is blind—a stare unwilling to behold
What I know to be true.

Pained . . . sorrowed . . . suddenly selfish
I squeeze her fingers.

Her pain, her fear I plainly see,
But her heartbreak I ignore.

And as she slaps the window glass
And hold tears inside her throat,
I spiral up and out to visions huge and real.
Never do I glance back.

Jeff Thomas
LET DEFEAT IDLE ON YOUR DOORSTEP

To my Mother, Rita Thomas, who encouraged me to continue writing, and for whom this poem was written, and to our mezuzah, which was the inspiration for this poem

Search for the Impossible.
Drink water from the moon.
Let defeat idle on your doorstep
so he will not bring you ruin.

Be the rose that strives through winter;
the leaf that lives through fall.
Let defeat idle on your doorstep
as you conquer over all.

Tame a wild dog.
Tap-dance on a cloud.
Punch the wind.
In silence, be loud.

Aspire.
Conceive.
Conspire.
Achieve.

Possess the courage to hope.
Find your heart full of zest.
Let defeat idle on your doorstep
and you will be a success.

CE Pruitt
THERE'S HOPE

To my lovely sweetheart, Darlene

Life sometimes is cruel, and hitting us hard with its mighty blows.
One day we are riding high above all, the next day we are trying to overcome our lows.
It's times like these that it becomes very hard for us to cope!
but there is no reason to fret simply because there's Hope!
We often become tired and weary, and even sometimes depressed.
In search of a way to put an end to this awful mess
Some think that the answer is found in alcohol; while others think it's in dope!
But what we should do is not despair simply because there's Hope!
Hope is merely trusting in the things unseen
Believe in God is what I mean!

Carolyn J Davis
NO MENTION OF ABORTION

Dedicated with love and thanks to my parents—Perry and Cordelia Decker.

Thank God for families where life and love does abide,
For in a family of 12, I was number five:
Some born at home, but not me I was a difficult one;
My left hand came first and was swelled the size of an adult one.
My Mother was told—I may not make it when turning blue;
Mother was struggling for her life too:
No mention of abortion was ever spoken or thought of back then;
I am here to tell you that I was a struggle for birth.
Thank God for life and all it is worth.

I am a Mother of two, who seemed unable to bear;
With ways of adoption and a miracle of birth,
God has given to me a reason for mirth:
No mention of abortion ever entered that Mother's mind,
Thus women like me with love to share;
Would not be able to give or care,
Before you make mention of abortion—let "life" live.

Carol F Mungin
RHYTHMS OF PARIS

To my mother, Elizabeth, who showed me the world.

The streets they call love,
By night, by day.
In my heart she sings.
Each night different, afternoon passes,
Next year anew.
Fresh bread is never for tomorrow.
Sweet sounds of children, the smile of a woman,
The look in a Frenchman's eyes.
Rain is never wet,
It becomes romantic.
While buildings reflect light of warmth.
The tower is still standing, with delicate pride.
The Seine never cries for love, the people come.
At night she sleeps, the people at cafes.
For you are never alone in Paris, the streets they call love.
By night, by day.
On the left bank, on the right bank,
Different shades of life, will always remain.
In Paris, my Paris, with love, to love.

Denise R Thurman
I BELIEVE I FINALLY KNOW
We cry each painful teardrop
for the things of yesterday,

And pray for remission
of our failures along the way.

We forgive ourselves with sorrow
for what we cannot be,

And I believe I finally know
what it means to be me.

I think perhaps I've seen
the worst of yet to come,

I think I may have known
the rightest kind of wrong.

I've smiled the sweetest moonlight
and cried the deepest sea,

And I believe I finally know
who I'm supposed to be.

So with the driest kind of tears
I'll put these words away,

To store them with my past
of a sadder yesterday.

William Gribbins III
BROUGHT IT ON MYSELF

To my daughter Jessica Nichole Gribbins

More than a year ago,
The beginning of a story,
That must be told.

Sent away from my loved ones,
Two lands, far and wide,
It was the start of all the lies.

Being there was hard,
So it seemed at the time.

Harder times awaiting,
To those I can not find.

Now without a home,
a job and family!

I'll pray to my God,
He will help me through
This hell like life,
I have put myself through.

pat moran quinn
the black sheep
ba ba black sheep
what did you do
that has made you an outcast
leaving you blue
why couldn't you play
the games that were played
why did you always run away
hiding behind dreams
held close to your heart
was that your refuge
a world apart
come out come out
where ever you are
reach up and grab that shining star
and if the dust gets in your eyes
at least you know
that you did try

Mandy Lynn

Mandy Lynn
MY PRIDE

I would like to dedicate this poem to my mother for giving me the extra push and encouragement needed. For letting me always know, she believes in me. Thanks mom, Love Mandy.

I have two flowers beautiful and bright.
Look at how they grow in the sunlight.

Every new petal, every spark of growth.
Helps me never, ever lose hope.

As I watch them day by day.
Oh how I wish I had their energy
they use to play.

They love the world and everything in it.
Oh can't we hold back the hands of time
just for a few minutes?

See how they glimmer. See how they shine.
Oh how proud I am, that they are children of mine.

As we hear them singing day by day.
God bless them with courage and strength.
To face the coming days!

Cosseam T Youman
A SILENT DEAD END

To my sister, Irene, who is not here to experience this moment with me in body, but is here in spirit and in my heart."

My soul cries out in the darkness
and the tears that fall from my eyes
weep out for compassion.
My mind wanders off into the mist of the clouds
just looking for satisfaction.
My heart eches the secrets that I try to keep,
there's no way out because I'm in too deep.
Sometimes I wish I could just jump in the air
and the wind would carry me off to a special place.
Or that all the bad things that I've done in the past
can be erased.
My eyes are filled up with a burning flame that shows my anger,
and the tears that fall from my eyes at night understand the danger.
There's no way out, no matter up or

down.
I'm hopelessly trapped and there's no one around.
Everyday seems to be the same.
I guess you say that's kind of strange.
Hour after hour, night after night
But still not a single change, no one in sight,
not even a friend.
Well, that's the price you pay when you enter
A Silent Dead End.

Karen Dauster-Husted
TIME TO BLOOM

*To God my Father who first loved me; and gave his only Son [Jesus Christ] as a sacrifice for my sins, that I might receive the free gift of everlasting life; and who set me free from the Bondage of sin. John 3:16 * Romans 6:6, 3:23, 24*

Daughter
Little One
You are a precious rosebud
About to bloom into a beautiful Rose.

Decorated with thorns to remind
you of life's pains
Your petals represent a soft and
yielded heart
Your pollen is the Fragrance of
things to come

Don't resist!
Let the Son's warmth draw open
each petal.
Be Bold! Reach Out!

With roots deep soak; in the
water of the latter rain.
Be Strong! Help Others!
To be delivered from the strain;
of meaningless life.

Dawn M Burke
NIGHTMARE IN THE MIRROR

You are my nightmare!
I look you in the eyes
And feel disgust.
I don't know you—
Nor do I want to.
You don't know your future
Or accept your past
You think you are innocent
But you are really pure sin.
You act so brave
When inside you are screaming.
You bare your soul
Yet hide your true feelings.
You think you are honest
But you are really pure deceit.
Everyone else knows it.
Why don't you?
No one really likes you
Although sometimes they pretend to.
I don't want to see or be near you.
Then why don't I step away from the mirror?

Jeanette L Proctor
ANSWER THIS

Tell me how in all of God's universe,
Is it possible for two souls to so sweetly immerse?
Torn and shattered is the world left behind,
Be it ever so true that love is blind?
Yet from the beauty of the union
When two hearts are in communion,
Can you leave the pages of history to the past?
And while it lasts—
Know only the beauty of fulfillment divine—
When I am yours, and you are mine.
A classic love, so complete, so infinite,
Yet will it go like it came? In only a minute?
Who would but guess which course love will choose?
But, from the experience gained, no one will lose.
Each soul in love has a chance to win,
Yet another question . . . Is it a sin?
If someday you have to decide,
Remember to let your conscience be your guide!

Virginia Ross Pelham
EARLY SPRING

To my son, Ray R. Pelham, his wife Christia Nan, Two grandsons, Steven Mark Pelham; Jason Perry Pelham With love of God's miracles. V. R. P.

I watched ere early spring, came in
their leafy beds;
Bulbs lifted up their tender heads,
tiny sprouts peeped through;
Shed the gloom of drooping—as if a
gentle voice had said;
"Arise, show forth your glory, there
are hungry eyes and hearts to be
fed."

Along the well trained border—of a
flower wall
Each dainty teardrop answered to the
call;
Burst forth in hues of yellow, whites,
the daffodils danced in the breeze;
They skipped across the lawn, hid
behind the trees:
Filling each nook and corner, came
one, came all.
Sweet narcissus heaved and swayed,
rose to spy
A gorgeous bed of tulips that pranced
nearby.
A sigh at all their color, the purples
and reds their many hues
Brought forth with meekness the shy
violet and crocus.
From their enfringed bed—among
the shrubbery tall
From out the shadows, the colorful
hyacinth, shed their fragrance rare;
To add to the stately beauty of the
lily fair,
With all the power of dormant nature
instilled in their bulbous form—
Burst forth with leaf and flower—a
time be born.
Forgotten was the still form of
embryo—
That once lay so quiet, so dry , so
still and grew;
Touched by the magic of God's Hand
we knew
Proclaiming His Power and Glory.
Early Spring.

May L Zacharias
MY HERO

My Hero is a man of power
He watches us each and every hour.

He calms us down when we get mad
And talks to us and makes us glad.

He makes the world all sunny and bright
So that this world is never without light.

He cleans the world of all the grime
And as for criminals there is no crime.

He slows us down when we go fast
So we won't die and be in the past.

He makes this world a nice place to live
So we can all feel free to give.

He tells us each and every day
To help each man that passes our way.

Yes, If my Hero lived today
This world would be a better place to stay.

And now I've only one more thing to say
Please, Help me find a Hero made this way.

Lynn Ezero

Lynn Ezero
I LAY ON MY BED WHILE THE CLOCK TICKS AWAY

To My Grandfather, "Pop"

I lay on my bed while the clock ticks away, in the distance I hear a radio. I glanced around to notice a teddy bear sitting straight up on my floor. But what wonders me is how sad my teddy bear looks. If only I was able to say something that would ease his sadness. A word of joy to brighten his life. Maybe I'm imagining this because he's not real. He's only a stuffed animal, that sits on my floor.

I hear something faint.
What could it be? I looked around to witness my teddy bear with a tear drop in his eye.
How foolish I was to believe that he wasn't alive, alive with emotions ready to stream about. I stared into his eyes, for reasons unknown to me, my teddy bear just winked at me.

M Steven Fain
THE GIRL WHO SKATED WITH ME

You are not the first girl I've talked to, but you help break thru my shyness. We talk to each other, with great feeling for each other.

You are not the first to skate with me, but you helped me, by teaching me how lovers skate together. We learned about each other; and cared for each other.

You are not the first to love me, but you are better than the others! We learned how to touch; and hold each other, as the days went on: I hope our love would last for ever.

Cecilia A Ludwig
THE WORDS

To Jim—Once upon a time.

I can't say it—but you know I do.
When you say it—I say "I do too."

I wish I could return the affection
you so generously share.

Voice my thoughts unashamedly—
tell you how much I care.

Unconditional love is true commitment
and I'm unable to bridge that gap.

Standing on the edge of my emotions
holding back—holding back.

Like a chameleon in the forest
changing color by the hour,

Afraid to show its own true self—
afraid to be devoured.

Sometimes inspired by need
I think how easy it would be

To say—"I love you cling to me."
But when you said "I love, you," as you often do.

I repeated the worn refrain "I do too—I do too."

Ann Henry
DREAMS, DREAMS, DREAMS

I dream of mountains, waterfalls, and streams
Blue skies, butterflies, and bright sunbeams
Canyons and valleys far away, far away
I dream of the green meadow where the gentle lambs lay

I dream of the ocean and the sun on my face
I dream of the desert horse of fire and grace
This ancient steed that dances on the sand
And all other creatures that roam our land

I dream of the tawny fawn that hides in the brush
I dream of the song bird that flies off in a rush
I dream of the future while remembering the past
I dream of the treasure those golden moments . . .
that never last

I dream of and wonders of nature and I love them all
I love all creatures great and small
Most of all, I love my Arab, Miss Maggie; she brings me joy
My happiness has doubled; she has had a baby boy.

Keith E Holley
THE DANCER

Gently, ever so gently . . .
she dances across the mind.
Still . . . her presence is felt,
bringing with it, the pain that
comes . . .
with remembrance. The force,
the force that refuses to let Memory,
stir the heart. So so often

conquered by, a greater power . . .
The power, of unforgotten love. A
love which pierces deeper . . .
than the heart itself. It
touches the inner being . . . the
very soul, hidden . . . in
fathoms of pain.
A tear . . . summoned from
these depths, surfaces . . . and trickles
down a cheek. Here for only a
short time . . . so like the
Dancer . . .
dancing, in my mind.

The End

Lois Zaun
MOTHER

I dedicate ths poem to my Mother, Dorothea Copp Washburn

When the word "Mother" falls on my ear,
No other name is so Dear,
So kind and sweet, and loving too,
When she smiles,
You know she loves you.

Cheryl "Kish" Swift
WORLD OF MORNING FOG

To my brother, David Mark Dalton, whose life ended tragically, but whose memories help to mask our grief.

I see a tall pine standing
With its head bent toward the oak,
Branches pushing against the fog.
Wind moves through the grove
Shoving water particles into spaces
Once occupied by other mass.
The air about me exists,
Opaque in density, so damp.
Slowly, I move through tall bodies
Yet flexible, in motion.
The limpid posture of the verdant lichen
Is burdened by the moist purveyor.
The morning's chill speaks to my skin.
Hairs stand straight in silent assentation.
Mist-chamber, your veiling arrests our spontaneity.
The curls on my neck lie torpid
'neath the weighted air.
Serenity of spirit and embrace of wispy dew—kidnapped
By spurts of irresolute air—all circulate
'Midst the world of morning dew.

Connie Sue Smith
WATCHING THE CLOUDS GO BY

This poem is dedicated to our Creator, Jehovah God

Watching the clouds go by
Is a favorite pastime of mine
I can actually watch them for hours
Which must be a lazy sign
I can see anything that I want to see
Such as a huge circus in the sky
Then all of a sudden it can dwindle
To resemble an apple pie
I have seen animals, monsters and faces
I have seen flowers and trees
Even far-away places
Watching, the clouds are so peaceful
But after watching for awhile
I start to think of our Creator
And I wonder with a smile
If he made the clouds for some other reason
And not just for my pleasure
Whatever the reasons are
Those moments I will always treasure
It doesn't take much to entertain me
Or much to make me sigh
I hope I never get too busy
To watch the clouds go by

Rebecca Lowe
DARK SHADE OF GRAY

This poem is dedicated to my dearest Mayson, my first love.

Why are you so mad at me
I don't understand
Was it what I said to you
Because I thought I should take a stand?
I've always fought for what I wanted
I fought to get you
But when I thought things would work out
You looked unhappy and blue.
We used to think everything would go our way
And that our love would never stray
Somehow our love turned from happy and gay
to a dark shade of gray.
I knew we both wanted out of the relationship
But we also wanted to hold on
And when we made it final we knew
Our love for each other would never be gone.
I don't see much of you anymore
I miss you very dearly
But always remember
My love will be waiting for you
behind a closed door.

Melanie Oliva
I'M SLIPPING AWAY

This poem is dedicated to those who live life hanging by a thread . . . . . Waiting for it to break—

I'm slipping away
I can't seem to hold on
I'm mentally drained
Why must life go on
I tried to get out
I tried to escape
But people always saved me
People that I hate
I tried to O.D.
Slit my wrists too
And the people I hate most of all
Are the ones who pulled me through
Even though I'm alive
I'm still dead inside
I need to be set free
So I don't have to run and hide
To live is to fight
To die is to win
When will they see
I don't need any help
I just don't want to live

Tracie Lynn Ranck Stella
FORK IN THE ROAD

For my mother, Cathy. Thank you for all you have done. I Love You.

I'd been walking down that road for years,
But the last several months were so full of tears.

I was nowhere now and saw nothing ahead,
I now was alone when before I'd been led.

But I was the one who turned away.
You tried so hard to make me stay.

I ran so fast, so far out of sight.
You tried to catch me with all your might.

I'd been running from you for years, not days.
Then the road I was running split two different ways.

The left road ended, I could see that it would,
But, the road to the right could be bad or good.

I thought long and hard of what I should do,
I ran for the left, but, then, I saw you.

Smiling, you reached for my hand, and held it tight.
And together we walked, down the road on the right.

Today I walk this road, but I walk it tall
Because, no matter how tough, my mom's love conquered all.

Lillie Maude Deffenbaugh Massey
WHEN

When the storms of life seem too much
Reach out to God and let him touch.
Your heart he will truly bless
He really loves you, please confess.

When trouble overtakes you
and friends seem to be few,
Reach out to God and he will say
Trust me child when you pray.

When God seems to be far away,
Perhaps it was you who did not pray.
Why not let him have his way
And you will never go astray.

When disappointment comes your way,
Remember others have had their day.
When the road seems long and dreary,
Ask God to help you and do not weary.

When you have lost a loved one,
Please remember God gave His son
To die on a cruel cross
So that you and I might not be lost.

Isabel Ann Kent
BRIAN—EULOGY TO A GRANDSON

To all my grandchildren, with all my love, Grandma Issy!

You came, you conquered, but you left right away,
God said, "Brian, I need you, I can't let you stay";
We knew you such a very short time,
We wonder about the reason or rhyme;
We love you so much, it was hard to say Good-bye,
Within our hearts, we wonder why?
There's a plan for everyone on this earth,
For some it ends right after birth;
You're an Angel in Heaven now, of that we are sure,
So, Good-bye Darling Brian, you'll always be with us here!

Love,
Grandma Kent
(Isabel)

Patricia L Johnson
NATURE'S MAGIC MOMENT

To Bev: Without your vivid description and your faith in my ability, I would not have written, "Nature's Magic Moment," My thanks to you.

Warm November sun glistens
Wispy fingers of fog linger
Over thin icing on the lake.

Reeds along the shoreline sway
Nudged by whispering winds
Serenely sleeping waters
Slowly wake.

Caressed by waves performers pose
Tiny graceful figures
Lacy dresses etched in ice
Enchanted ballerinas dance
Pirouette in one final bow.

Musical tinkling fairy bells echo
As waters meet the land
Shimmering diamond chips
Scatter across the sand.

Colette Rumbolt
IMAGINATION

Dedicated to my family and friends

Imagination is like a butterfly
Going everywhere
It soars into the sky
As beautiful as a bird
It's light as a feather
Softly it flutters to the ground
Just waiting to be found
You can imagine you're a lion
You can imagine you're a bear
Best of all I imagine I'm home
Because I know I'll always live there.

Irene LaVerne McCartney
THE WISHING STAR ABOVE!

To Gary: My eternal lover and best friend who this poem is written about. Even after being apart all these years and finally getting together, our love grows stronger each and every day.

Hello Sunshine!
Hello Love!
Here I come!
I've found the star that I was wishing upon.
Now I have that special love that falling star above gave me.
For now we will be together.
Until that star fades away.
But if we keep our love growing.
The star will always stay bright.
So let's keep shining our love upon each other.
And our wishing star will always be bright.

Wilford F Teel
LITTLE "RED"

This poem is dedicated to "Bre-anne," my "angelic" little red-haired grandchild.

I need to reminisce a bit about a girl, the age of three—
She was a little red-haired "angel," who was all the world to me.
Mere words are not sufficient to give to her what's due
'Cause she's given me such

happiness, only attained by just a few.
"She," simply, had the sweetest smile, and when "she" talked to me I'd do almost anything for her, to prove my loyalty.
And when she went home, even for one day, I wasn't quite the same
I'd try not to show resentment, knowing no one was to blame.
For I knew the time was coming, when she'd be too big to say
"Me vunt ta doe ta Dampaw's house" "doe ova dere un play."
Then there'll be a certain sadness, and it'll show on my old face
And the smiles won't come so often, many tears will take their place.
But, I'll cling to precious memories of time spent with little "Red"
And I'll always get much solace from the kind, sweet things she said.
Then, sometime in the future, when my eyes have grown dim
And I can't get around too good, 'cause I am weak of limb.
I believe I'll get that call from her, and "she" will say to me
"Grandpa" "I love you Grandpa" like "she" did when "she" was three.

Judy M Neighbors
DREAMS ARE FOR EVERYONE

To Mom & Nona—Dreams
That became Realities
Those still with the Stars

Dreams are for everyone
Rich or poor, happy, sad
You will always find them
Wars are fought because of a man's dream
Freedom was won and lost
Dreams
Fabulous when they become reality
Even the smallest one.
My dreams came to life
When I met you
A Dream of meeting
A reality of camaraderie

Eve Ryon
A BOY NEXT DOOR

To All Children, Everywhere

I know a boy named Brett.
True, we never before had met
Only six years of age, sweet as can be.
It's nice you live next door to me.

You made pictures of the sun and moon.
Working on them, way past noon
You cut out each piece, laying them straight.
The banana trees were really great.

Your big words, like infinity.
A writer you surely will be.
You have faith in what you do.
Just as I have faith in you.

Stay sweet, loving and kind.
Success will not be hard to find.
Smile as you think of me.
Always smiling. I want you to be.

Love you
Your friend
Eve Ryon

Linda Cline
HOME THEY SAY IS WHERE THE HEART IS

This poem is dedicated to my loving parents.

I have longed for a home where I might find
Solitude and a peace of mind.
Home is where you go to
find your inner self and
the memories of the days
long since
past.
The pictures that hang on the wall
Of when life seemed so full and
gay.
And you remember your mother's rocking chair and the loving arms that held you.
And the once beautiful window that as a child you sat and watched the snow.
fall
There's no more laughter here.
For it's all gone now.
The home is just a house now with the memories
of the days long since
past.

Charles A Robinson
KING

January 29, 1929 is where it began, the birth of Reverend King, a wonderful, intelligent, and graceful man.
A winner of rights and many goals, his pursuit of equality will be forever told, in history books and made up tales, he spent many nights in dampened jails.
Jails of the south and of the North, a new meaning of freedom was soon set forth, to be acknowledged by the people, for blacks were now considered equal.
Equal to white and any creed, equality for all is what he believed. Awkward situations, non-violent demonstration and many problems were there, but he didn't stop his pursuit because of fear, fear of conviction or even death, he fought for freedom with every breath.
April 4, 1968 was a sad day indeed, for Reverend King was dead. But he did succeed, equality for all, every creed. If not for his death he might have achieved, the greatest goal, the goal for peace so war and violence would someday cease.

Lucille J Moore
FOUR SEASONS

To My Family With Love

Winter is a time of beauty with a soft white blanket of snow.
All the little snowflakes glitter as they dance about and flow.
Underneath this white blanket of snow a miracle is taking place.
For all the sleeping roots of life are reaching out at a slow pace.
They are reaching out with an abundance of new energy, so that new growth can come forth.

Spring brings back the sleeping roots to burst from buds to leaves and flowers.
And the trees reach out their new leaves and limbs like a far and distant tower.
The robin red breast jaunts boldly about gathering worms from upon the lawn.
As she sings out a lullaby to her babies and feeds them from morn till dawn.
In the meantime all the new sap of life is flowing across the land.

Summer is a time when the fragrance of perfume from all the blooming plants, mistily fills the air.
The ring of children's laughter from the barn yard as the animals start to stir.
And the distant sound of the tractor in the fields as the farmer plows his land.
Also the grunting of the pigs and chicken's clucking as they busily scratch for sand.
The dog lies in the hay stack watching everything with grace.
Until a squirrel comes out of hiding and taunts him for a race.

Autumn is when nature's paintbrush like magic, touches the leaves before they stray.
They fall upon the earth like a carpet of red, gold, or yellow before they drift away.
Then the sap of life from the trees and other plants flows from the roots down to the ground.
This makes the miracle of life's circle start over so that we can have these gifts around.

Elaine D Barber

Elaine D Barber
ANIMALS

I dedicate my poem Animals to all of the beautiful people who love their Animals, and to Buffy and Missy and our eleven little Chinese Gerbils.

Animals are beautiful people too
They need love and attention
just as much as we do.
A pet can bring laughter and joy
when you're feeling down
Especially when they act like such little clowns
You can't help but laugh when they act so funny
Especially when your day at work went just like a Monday
Pets are always fun to come home to
They love you no matter what you do
Treat your pet kindly with love and respect
Because Animals Are Beautiful People Too.

Sharon Grace Sprayberry
PINE TREE AND ANGEL LIGHTS UP FOR JESUS

In memory of Fonley Vern Sorenson (Sweed) (died Oct 2, 1988), and Dorthey G Bunch Sorenson (died 1964)
My daddy & mother

There was once an angel up in the sky so blue.
One day she was looking down on earth in a town far away.
Everyone there looked so unhappy and fighting each other. The angel asked God if she could go down on earth to see if she could do something to help them. God said she could, so she went down to earth to the town far away to look in each person's heart to see if there was good in them. The angel came to a pine tree all by itself and the tree told the angel I'd like to help. So the angel put lights on the tree and a star on top. With each light it said we are lighting up for Jesus for Our Savior is born today. The whole town came to see the Christmas tree, and out of all their hearts came Love and Joy, for the lights on the tree were saying, Jesus Christ was born today. He came to save us all, that are born again and believe in him. Jesus will save our souls. That was what the Christmas tree and lights were saying. So when you get a pine tree and put lights & star on top, it will bring Joy to your heart.

Jeryl Ann Sheridan
BLACK

To my wonderful husband Wallace, my parents Elizabeth Scott and Joseph Guillory for believing in me.

B — stands for Beauty
as the many shades of our skin
and depth of our character.

L — for Longevity
For we have fought long and hard for the progression of our people and have so much further to go.

A — for Active
We must remain active in our daily fight for equality of all men.

C — Creativity
We are blessed as a people with great Actors, Musicians, Poets, and Athletes
We as a people must support them.

K — for Keep
We as as people must keep preaching, speaking, teaching, learning, singing, understanding, helping, and working towards one goal.

That goal is "EQUALITY," and we've only just begun.

Ada Mae Jackson
SUNBEAMS

To Bill—My Sunbeam.

How bright the sunbeams are today.
They set the world aglow.
I wonder if they realize
The happiness they sow.

The children's eyes light up with joy
to see a sunny day.
And off to school they go, each one
With laughter all the way.

Then as the day draws to its close,
And every prayer is said,
I wonder if the sunbeams know
The happiness they spread?

Lori Johnson
I'LL ALWAYS LOVE YOU FOR WHO YOU ARE

To Bobby Johnson who I will always have in my heart and who I hope will always remain my friend.

I'll always love you for who you are
Whether you're near or whether you're far
We've had good times and we've had bad
but now that you're gone I'm left feeling sad

I think about you a lot every day
but now we should go our separate ways
It's all over, it's in the past
We tried so hard but couldn't make it last
So I guess this is goodbye I hope we meet again
but I don't want to be your enemy, I want to be your friend
One last thing before I go
There's something else I want you to know
I'll always be here for you if you need me
If you want to talk or if you just want to be set free
No matter how things turn out
You'll have your kids to think about
So I wish you luck in all that you do
You can go on now and start your life anew.

Debbie Wildt
I MISS MY MOM

This poem is dedicated to my Mom Joan, with all my love.

I miss my Mom I miss her so,
because the Lord came and took her soul.

I remember that day holding her hand and crying,
because I knew my Mom was dying.

I prayed the Lord to take her away.
And now all I can do is wish she had stayed.

When I'm sick or very lonely, it's my Mom I want and her only.

There's times I think I will give her a call.
Then I realize the phone would just keep ringing on the wall.

Mom I miss you I miss you so,
because your Love is irreplaceable this I will always know.

Yolanda Huizar Serrato
CREDERE (IN MY BLIND FAITH)

Dedicated to my mother Esperanza, and my uncle Fr. Pedro Ortiz. I love you for your prayers. Thank you for not giving up on me.

I believe in one GOD.
Trusting him in total submission I shall trod.
I believe all men are created equal.
Of the same flesh and bones the power must sequel.
I believe all good conquers evil.
Ancient civilizations became extinct in their own righteous upheaval.
I believe man can move mountains.
Unwritten secrets are our greatest weapons.
I believe in spiritual rebirth.
Of far off galaxies waiting to become unearth.
I believe in the laying of the hands to heal the sick.
With the speed of a match lighting a candlewick.
I believe mankind holds the secret of fate.
To one's reach, right at the edge of the legendary Golden Gate.
I believe in love and life.
It's apparent one needs one or the other to grow into rife.
I believe GOD Almighty's Kingdom shall come;
Heirs are those chosen few from the race yclept CHRISTENDOM.

Angela I Land
A CHILD IS BORN

To my beautiful children, Christopher & Erin Patricia Land

You were born into this world one stormy summer night.
Love and elation overwhelmed me at very first sight;
This tiny little baby; eyes blinking in the light,
Screaming as if you were angry to be here,
Being taken from the warmth and comfort so near.
For that I surely couldn't blame you, my dear.
The months have been long and truly put me to the test.
Now I'm looking at you and holding you at my breast.
After such a long ordeal we both need some rest,
For the wait is finally over; we have to wait no more.
I have dearly loved you long before you were born,
Protected you and kept you nice and warm.
Emotion unrelenting as mother and child first meet
And I notice as tears of joy roll down my cheek
Your innocence so peaceful as you quietly fall asleep.
Good night, my precious angel, as I hold you near.
In my arms you will always be safe and secure.
I love you, sweet dreams; thank you for being here.

Patty L Augustine
LONELY PIPER

To myself . . . a loving, but lonely woman who's had no man's love . . . only the love of her music and flute.

I am a lonely piper, merely wandering from place to place. For in this type of life I see many a face. Many a face both happy or sad. I play for them, and appear to be glad.

Glad is the one thing I am not. My flute is my only friend. For I fear my loneliness will never end. No man has ever wished for me to be by their side. It is to only make them happy, I've tried and tried. The gentle notes emerge from my soul. It is the flute that accomplishes the goal. Once my playing is done, the people merely stare, for they wonder why they were even there.

Each night, I lay beneath the blackened sky. I casually wish about loving a "guy." But, I think back to the only friend I now have. It lies beside me, quiet and still. For again tomorrow "play," it will.

I'm a lonely piper with no one to hold. My prison is to walk God's earth alone. If you see my silent tears, please try to understand.

Nora M Wentz
AN ARTIST

I Dedicate this poem to Donald, My son, The Artist.

An Artist can take a thought
That's resting on the edge of reality,
Transform to shape, combined with color,
Then creates He none ever finer.

An Artist shows his talent in
The quality of his work,
By ideas expressed uniquely
He shares with us life's beauty.

An Artist can calm man's ruffled modes
With the blending of green, and the
Coolness of blues. but if We could
Only hear what An Artist sees
The greatest concert would no longer please.

Al Kaminer

Al Kaminer
BALLAD OF THE BOTTLE

Walking through the Bowery I came upon a solid regiment Gentleman looked like A SCHOLAR—Who fell by the wayside—Close to his face—lay a large jagged broken Booze Bottle—asleep drugged by the spirits—What I saw came to be BALLAD OF THE BOTTLE—

I'm whiskey . . handle me with care
. . my reign . . is spotted with despair
. . I'm lethal dynamite . . a social blight. . I mould sultry moods . . in thoughtless youth . . twist tongues . . with words of untruth . .
I'm fondled . . cursed . . and hated . .
I'm a decided factor . . in your fate . .
well known names . . grace my roster of shame . .
Doctor-Lawyer-Professor-Artist and others . . live-in-their-vomit . . like brothers . . I'm at ease . . midst poverty . . and disease . . I'm the climax to a good time . . Mister bluenose . . closed me down . . lock-stock-barrel and key . . I crawled underground . .

with gangsters . . and grafters for company . . I won—my bout . . with Prohibition . . by a knockout
. . I'm back in good graces . . at a thousand and one places . . I'm the real McCoy . . I'm yours to enjoy . .
No more Poison . . that kills . . and blinds . .
I'm bottled for your peace of mind . .
for those . . who freely imbibe . . I weave a pattern . . too hideous . . to describe . . I can break down your defense . . I'm whiskey . . Use Me With Common Sense . .

Patricia Gonzales
SUNRISE

Those few minutes
In the morning;
Before you realize
Who you are,
It is rather
Like a warning.

For you can
Be happy with
Who you are,
Or you may
Wish you had
Never woken up.

Shirley L Brennan
LIFE & LOVE

Where the river flows and the birds start to sing:
Puts a wonder of Love in the hearts of all men.
The air is so warm, and your heart pours out to care,
for the wonders of love that we now both share.
The adventure of love and what it can hold, reminds me my dear of the words you were told.
So upon my return, there is not much to say, accept love from your heart, please don't go astray.

Dorothy L Blair (Roeder)
A MIGHTY CARRIER

Dedicated to the late Russel O. Roeder, ACMMF, U.S. Navy and his daughters Sandra and Sylvia (Kim) Leilani

'Twas a dreary Wednesday morning
The ship sailed out to sea
To face a troubled continent
Protection for you and me.

We watched her hoist her anchor
Our eyes were filled with tears
The present world situation
Could keep her away for years.

This ship that I have mentioned
A mighty carrier she—
Won't mean much to many folks
But she means the world to me

'Tis the U.S. carrier Boxer
My father is part of her crew
Now, when her mission has ended,
Let's hope the enemy is through.

Mary E Thompson
UMM TREE

I was thinkin' one day about the family tree
How often misplaced a feller could be,
Why, just a hangin' there from a straggly branch
Next to, Uncle Henry and fat, cousin Blanche,
Somehow you know you're out on a limb
One without leaves or red ribbon trim,
You could be hooked to a spot with an ugly knarl
Touchin' the bark of, bootleggin' Carl,
You'd be an old man if you took the top spot
And likely as not on a wormy old knot,
They might count the rings to find

your age
And make it as gospel on a yellowed old page,
So, if you don't mind, I'll follow the season
And know that my life is not without reason,
By chance, if you want to know, where I hang out
Just follow, Santa, on his happiness route,
You'll find me on the furriest tree
Smellin' of spices, and icing on my round little belly,
I'm the proverbial, Gingerbread man
Hoppin' with joy as I pop from the pan.

Nic Louis Nardoni
ODE TO AN ELEGANT WOMAN
Her presence reveals a friendly relaxed attitude.
Her beauty comparable to an old tapestry,
is mysterious and intriguing.
Her soft as satin voice is calm and soothing.
Her skin must be softer than a baby's.

Her hair flows like silk in the wind.
Her eyes are deep pools of compassion and understanding
There's been times when she was my confidante.
I have, and always would gladly return the favour.

Many of the songs on the radio,
Always seem to hint about her.
This elegant woman is Mother Nature's best.
She can never be outdone by another.

Oh that elegant woman.
There aren't many like her now.
How I wish she were mine,
Maybe I'll find my own elegant woman.
(I hope I can)

Heidi Lynne Stewart
THE CHOICE
Sometimes
A pond looks small—
Compared to the ocean

It glitters, at peace
waves lap serenely
branch outward
return to the center again
content

An ocean tumults
and storms, obeys
no master
defies the work of time to change
and battles the internal pull

I sit on land
between the two
And wonder
If I were a little drop
with a choice
Where i would fall

Mary Virginia Holden
LOVE IS FOREVER
Love is forever
So come what may
The rain and the gloom
Shall never, no never
Cause us pain in our day
Love is ours, we shall say
Love is forever
My darling so true
What priceless beauty
Is all I see in you
With you I'll never be blue
I'll Love your forever, just you
Love is forever
When all is said and done
We know great joy and fun
There is a prize to be won
For which we both shall run
Yes, Love is forever

Ramona Lynn Brumley
VANISHED LOVE
As he was walking out the door,
tears started to fall from my eyes.
He turned to me and said:
"Honey, I am sorry." When I will be back? "I don't know."
Why I am leaving? "I don't know."
"What I do know is I love you, and I will be back."
As he shut the door, I ran for him.
It was too late, he was already gone.
I ran until I couldn't run anymore,
and I fell to my knees.
I looked down that dark and lonely road,
and I wondered, oh how I wondered,
Where my love has vanished?
He has vanished into thin air.
I never saw my vanished love again.

Rhonda Seton
FOR THE LOVE OF GOD
God's glory is good, God's love is glee,
With Jesus on my side, thru Him I am free.

He says, "Ask and ye shall receive, seek and ye shall find,"
You need only talk to Him, when troubled and in a bind.

When life is a burden, and trouble has you down,
Take a deep breath, sit up and have a good look around.

God gave us each day, though numbered as few,
He asks only you listen, and do as He would have you.

God's love is rare, but ever so true,
For God so loved us, He created me and you.

With His hands to lift me high, into the clouds above,
Above the sky so far and wide, thru Christ He gave, His true love.

For God so loved the world around,
With His love you'll find, there are no bounds.

How happy we will be with emeralds to hold,
In His kingdom above the seas with a throne made of gold.

Evil spreads its wings and there is sin after sin,
Thru God's love, a miracle at birth, a new life begins.

With His hands of great strength, He will always lend,
For His love will go on, from beginning to end.

We are only but a dot, on the picture He drew,
We are always in His sight and never out of view.

When you ask the Lord to take up the part
Of emptiness you have found in your heavy heart.

You will find the life you know will make a dramatic change,
When all things impossible are now within range.

Though we may not know what's in store for us today,
Trust in God and hold His hand, so that He may lead the way.

You will find, come day to day,
That happiness is found along the way.

Take my hand and come with me,
I am your life, you will see.

From beginning to end I will be,
For I am "A" and I am "Z."

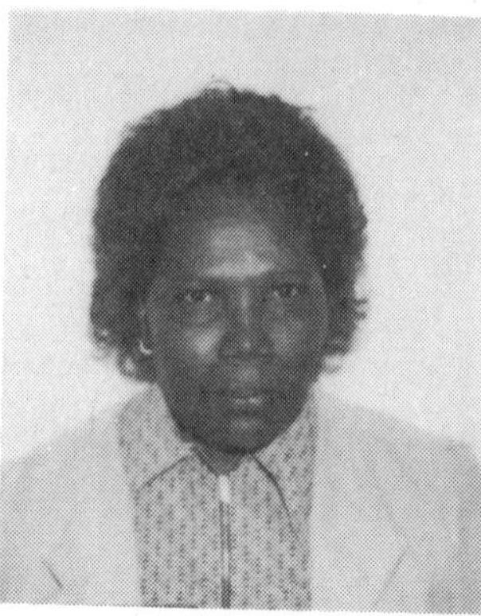

Gloria E Lezzieri

Gloria E Lezzieri
GOOD DEEDS LAST

This poem is Dedicated to Eddie-Lou, for such inspiration and stability throughout all those years.

Whether you are young or old,
It pays to be very bold;
In your work and or in your play,
You can have a lot to say.

"Sometime, things make you feel so sad;
But for some people, you should be glad"
When they feel their heart is frozen;
And you had yours only broken.

It would pay, to lend a hand;
To anyone, it would be so grand;
"The more you do, the less you see;
That's what some say, but not all agree."

Many times, we're taken for a ride,
"That we almost lost our pride"
Keep on doing the best you can
Whether you're a woman or a man.

"Nothing in life, ever comes that easy"
So let us think, and then get busy;
Even if we are down the drain,
We can get out and start again.

Lloyd A Woodall
Underneath us as we climb
Underneath us as we climb, you see,
I see the meaning in the sea
High above us as we go, I see the secrets in the glow
All around us we must know, we cannot continue where we go,
We all must meet, we all must see, peace found there, beneath the Shadetree.

John R Chiesa
KILN
Life's tragedies soften and mold the clay of humaneness;
At times, even tearing and smashing it apart.
Then, that which we call "self" comes gliding forth.
We gather the detritus, bathing it with emotion.
Welding it in our memory, we give it sanctuary within us.
Ready for kiln and final glaze, we are fired.
Finally, strengthened, we emerge with a polished, sensitive armor of maturity.
Prepared are we, then, to face our greatest critic;
The GOD all of us find within ourselves.

Susan Klock Meigide
HEAVEN'S REWARD
We've gathered to pay our respects
To a dear "sister in the Lord"
She's gone before us to Heaven
She has gone to her reward.

She's one who was always willing
To do the Father's will
And she was always ready
Her special place to fill.

She reflected the Father's love
As she moved among us here;
Now she's gone to be with Jesus
She has joined her Saviour Dear.

Let us not mourn her passing
She sings in the Heavenly choir
But let us all be ready
Let "Heaven's Home" be our desire.

James H Farrell
ON THE WING OF A PRAYER
Lord!, I feel your touch
I've been blessed with so much,
I was once a sinner
You've turned me into a winner,
Carried me on your shoulders
In time of need,
Teaching me to lead
To spread joy out there,
Riding On The Wing Of A Prayer
Giving me a special love,
Always; with a bright star, above
Knowing; you'll always be there,
As I ride On The Wing Of A Prayer.

Barbara S Weppener
WHAT
What makes the wind blow through the trees?
What makes the color change in the leaves?
What makes the clouds high in the sky?
What turns them to gray and makes them cry?
What makes the sun shine hot and bright?
What makes the moon come out at night?

What makes a seed sprout in the ground?
What makes the melon grow up round?
What makes a cat purr when it's glad?
What makes a dog growl when it's mad?
What makes milk turn into cheese?
What makes the honey that comes from the bees?

What makes fire hot and ice cream cold?
I want to know before I grow old!

Christine Sergio
A TERRIBLE SECRET
Held inside you
And won't come out
Terrifying to tell
Terrifying not to
Hard to let out
Just sticks inside you
You can't tell

This terrible secret
Hurts to hang on to
Hurts to let go
It's just loose inside you
Now you can tell this
Terrible secret
Is just not scary
But hard to tell
You can't speak it
You can't teach it
All you can do it
Sit there and weep

Joan E Youngblood
MY LOVE
I can't tell you in words
my feelings hidden deep inside
Buried in my heart and soul
of what it has meant to my life
Knowing, loving, caring, sharing,
Spending precious minutes, hours
In your beloved company;
Learning to bend with the flow
So things easier would go.
If I were to die today,
I'd just want to say
I loved you in every way.

Laurel L Marston

Laurel L Marston
DAYBREAK
Lovingly dedicated to my parents, Neita M. and Thomas Henry Marston in appreciation of their sincere love and true devotion

Mom shrugs herself and blinks her droopy eyes,
Opens her shades and peeps towards the skies.
Her gentle move alerts the fireflies
Who make a dart to escape the sun-drenched skies.
Then mom her quivering fingers now does raise.
And like a magic wand they set ablaze,
Apollo's lamp that sputters in a daze.

"Awake my lord!" she cries,
"It's time to rise
And set afire your beacon in Earth's skies"
Apollo rises wearily at first—
Then suddenly, as with a mighty burst,
He throws aside the gloomy shroud of night,
And struts across the skies in blinding light.
All Earth succumbs to Apollonian might.

Adell Hayes
THE DREAM
The clock ticks and the years go by but "THE DREAM" never dies nor is it forgotten. We continue to strive to make "THE DREAM" come true.
Our lives are like grains of sand in an hourglass. We continue to fall but yet if we're turned over the flow is still a go. Something that's so uncomplicated but yet it terrifies mankind.
We have distinctive minds that are congressmen, doctors, engineers, judges, lawyers, mayors, even senators. Now all we need is a P R E S I D E N T and he's soon in line.
We used to have to sit in the back of the buses. We used to have to go to colored only schools. We used to have to use colored only toilets. We couldn't even drink from public water fountains. There's a lot of used to be's.
Look at us today. All because of a man with the initials M.L.K. Think of all the other initials that we have. If would put all the initials together, we'll have Full Force. I don't mean Full Force M D but Full Force M L K.
If we don't keep "THE DREAM" alive in other than in our hearts and our minds, we would have failed our children and ourselves but most of all we would have failed M.L.K. who died for "THE DREAM."

Alberto D Tristani
INTIMATELY YOURS
In the recesses of my mind
I hold intimate memories of you
There in all its passion I find
That our fervent embraces
always seemed so few.

For we never seemed to quench our thirst for love's passion
And found that those intimate hours nearly flew
As we held dearly to those moments of obsession
That seemed as if they were
always somehow new.

And so our intimate love knew no bounds
We were really two hearts
beating as one
And as our love its climax found
Its lovely intimacy was
comparable to none.

Eleze (Mickey) Gaede Herrin
MY DAD
My "Dad" has put away his fishing nets"—
Hung all the lines to dry—
Stood the long poles upward—
Pointing to the sky—

He pulled the old "gray boat" up—
Placed it high and dry—
Stored away, his "tackle-box"—
And laid down, with a sigh—

He, knew, his "fishing days" had ended
And, he would-go-no more"—
Only "one last river trip, a-cross"—
To stand on "another shore"—

"The river crossed" tho' high the tide—
He had heard the, "Savior" call—
Soon now to be "Judged by Him"—
The "Greatest Fisherman" of all.

Then "Heaven's Door" swung open wide—
"Great Golden Nets—Stretched Side by Side"
With "Outstretched Arms" and a "Holy Smile of Pride."
"He", Beckoned "My Dad", to "Come Inside."

Rustico S Castro Sr
SONG OF NATURE
Dedicated lovingly to my dearest wife, Adelina, Daughters Ma. Teresita Castro-Toledo, Erlinda Castro-Aquino and Rustico, Jr. Sons-In Law, Rico & Noel and Daughter In-Law Leny—*

White foams of roaring giant waves,
Sings as it dash upon the sandy shore,
Gigantic trees hold sway its leaves,
As gentle breeze in horizon fan more.

The chirping crickets mournful tune,
Cheering birds chant songs of old,
Atmosphere diffused aroma flowers June,
Reminiscent of fond memories untold.

Glistening rays of morning sunlight,
As showers bring joy to Nature's plants,
Moonbeams stealthily creep in the night,
Satisfying needs and human diverse wants.

Daily workers drive in their routine,
Maintain cadence abreast of the time,
Gorgeous valleys, mighty grand mountain
Join murmuring springs in tone sublime.

Wonders, happiness, pain and sorrow,
Encountered hours and minutes of day,
What promising future of tomorrow,
Trials of life, the thorny path and way.

R Thompson
CHRISTMAS PRAYER
To Maxine

On the calendar of life, Lord,
I'm into December.
So under my tree, Lord,
Wrap a night to remember.
And if it's a 10, Lord,
My night to remember.
Please tell my poor pecker, Lord,
That it's only November.

Teresa Comeau
FUELED
With loving dedication to my Grandmother, Mary and my Mother, Maren. Submitted by Teresa Comeau

Fueled
by a million, man-made wings of fire
the rocket tore a tunnel through the sky
and everybody clapped.
Fueled
by a thought from God—
the seedling urged its way
through the thickness of black
and as it pierced the heavy ceiling of soil
and launched itself up into outer space—
no one
even
clapped—

Robert A Timmins Jr
THE AMERICAN WAY
IN DEDICATION TO: all my friends, family, and relatives. This poem was written to stress feeling and importance in today's society.

It's the home-made apple pie;
the freedom,
the democracy,
the human rights.

But how are problems viewed?
The problems such as war,
AIDS,
crime,
abortion.

There is no end, no solution.
If we can all work together,
we can make it happen.

Whether American or foreign
our opinions are heard.

One way or the other,
time stands in the way for changes.

Going through the red tape, courts,
appeals, articles, and gossip;
makes it extremely difficult.
Society has gone through an entire make over.
Who has the answers?
The All–Mighty or We The People.

H D Watson
A MESSAGE TO THE WORLD
This poem is dedicated to father and mother, Gerald and Mary Watson, and my wife and son, Tanya and Jamal Watson.

We can't destroy old prejudices;
By creating new ones.
We can't be followers of love;
If we are leaders of hate.
For hatred exists in all of us.

It's when we are less conscious
of its existence;
That we increase its chances to
reach its ultimate goal;
"SELF DESTRUCTION."

Let's master the Art of peaceful
confrontation.
Let's master the Art of love.
GOD—Not by prejudgments;
But by being sensitive to one's
feelings as though they
were our own.

Brenda Lee Lavaron
LOVE IS A WORD
To Scott: Who has brought everlasting happiness to me. Who has taught me the true meaning of love. I'll always love you, sweetheart!

Love is a word,
We use in haste.
Nobody knows the meaning,
A lot think it's a waste.

But, to fall in love,
There's something to gain.
A weird kind of feeling,
You just can't explain.

Two people;
Who think as one.
Two people;
Out to have fun.

Not a worry, and
No more tears.
You won't stay up all night,
And think of your fears.

I should know,
You see my friend.
I'm in love with you,
From now, until forever's end.

Mary Louise Moore
OUT MOTHER

To Marie Gertrude Burke Ruth, our Mother. She always loved us and we will always love her, even in death. For she will always be alive in our hearts. From your daughter, Mary Louise Moore

A Year has passed
since you left our home,
to live with the angels
and your husband and son.

You went so quickly
it was hard to believe.
We weren't ready to lose you
or know how to grieve.

We were filled with remorse,
love and sorrow.
And our hearts were heavy,
you would not be with us
tomorrow.

But then we remembered
how you taught us to pray.
And in our hearts we truly knew
you're just a small heartbeat
away.

Till we meet again, your
daughter
Mary Louise Moore

Terry A Baker
ILLUMINED VOICES

To those of the spirit

Still waters flow in empty space,
Hard walls of time reflect my mind,
Transpiring thoughts, without a trace,
So quick to leave the world behind,

Beyond the senses we can see
Outside the realm of earthbound
thoughts,
Into a sea of harmony,
Expressing gifts we've all been
taught,

Left covered by the veil of man,
A lotus blooms within us all,
Envisioning a caravan,
Illumined ones, who heed the call,

So softly beckons that within,
A voice of power, from the stars,
Inside us all, beneath the skin,
We can become greater avatars.

Louis Graziaplena
LITTLE BOY GONE

When you were young, you were my
pride,
My love for you I couldn't hide,
So many things, we used to do,
I now must face without you,
We went to the doctor's for you to be
checked,
Little did I know then, my life would
be wrecked,
He said you were very sick, and
nothing more,
I could feel the tears welling up in
my eyes, as we walked out the door,
There were other doctors that we
went to see,
But none of them would say, what
was most important to me,
As time went on, you became very
ill,
I felt your pain, as I always will,
I held your hand, as the days passed
away,
Praying to God for you, that was all I
could say,
Near the end, when you looked up at
me,
I almost wanted a merciful God to set
you free,
You've gone now, as I watch the
setting sun,
Part of my life will be missing
without my only son.

Ann Abeyta
CHRISTMAS STAR

To my loving son, James Michael Abeyta, from Ann E. Abeyta

Christmas star way up high in the sky looking down on me, do you remember the first time you came out to lead everyone to Jesus? Christmas star you see all, tell me please why must I always be the little girl next door who always looks at Christmas trees thru someone else's windows. I stand and look, the Christmas tree is so beautiful with so many lights, and all the children look so happy there singing, looking at the Christmas tree. There is laughter and hugging and they are having so much fun. Christmas star the children with daddys and mommys are so lucky. I only have my daddy, the angels took my mommy up to heaven, now there is only my Daddy and Grandma and me. I don't have a Christmas tree, do you think Santa will find my house? I hope he does, I'll be waiting here for him.

Georgia Dowell
FIRE ON INDIAN MOUNTAIN

The Spirit-Fire has round the
mountain sprung,
And mindless-moving, serpent-
coiling, winds,
Spoiling his domain with ravening
tongue,
That, flicking, leaves the servant
Wind behind.

In temper ill, with shifting,
raging game,
He, uncontested, claims the
Hunting Ground.
Now subject tree and fleeing
beast, the same,
Are soiled snowflakes, heavy-
drifting round.

The Father-Sun, grief-red in
smoke-dark'd skies,
In forc'd reflection, blackens to
the death.
Below, with chants fear-soft
and flame-tranc'd eyes,
They wait, and smell the
scorching Spirit-Breath.

He chanc'ly turns, and, rabid Spirit-
Son,
Searing-eye'd, descends on Indian
Canyon.

Mildred Bettag
A DAILY INVENTORY

Did I stop to smell the flowers,
To appreciate the small things
along the way
Did I look for the good in people,
That I met along life's way,
Did I see the beauty in God's
creation,
As in the things created by man,
Did I count each day the blessings,
In my life since it began.
Did I listen with caring and
compassion,
And walk in another's shoes,
Did I offer a shoulder to lean on,
Did I practice the "Golden Rule."
Did I kill my anger in its early stages,
Before it had time to sprout,
And grow to its full maturity,
Where love is crowded out.
Did I blindfold my eyes from life's
sunshine,
To avoid the pain that comes
from life's nights,
To only live in the ugliness of
darkness,
Never to see the beauty of the
morning's light.
Did I let my heart seek vision and
purpose,
When I was lonely and filled
with fear,
Did I stop and ask God for directions,
Did I give hurt time-out for
tears.
Did I practice the words "I'm Sorry,"
And try to correct wrongs to
make them right,
Did I forgive the ones who hurt me,
Before I fall asleep at night?

Sharon D Prince

Sharon D Prince
YOU MY FRIEND

You my friend, have been so kind, so understanding, and so loving.

You have shown me the most exciting things in life, from the smalles of Zoo's to the beautiful Whales in Paradise.

You have slowed me down enough so I'd take the time to watch the sun rise, and set, yet you have given me energy to enjoy and live every day to its fullest.

You have always been there, and believed in me and my goals, showing me fantasy, and reality, and how beautiful they both can be.

You are my inspiration, my courage, my life.

You my friend, are my HUSBAND.

George Walker
HILLS OF NEVADA

Nevada, a great elevated table-land
With her dry climate, her fruits,
potatoes, hay and forage
For nature blessed this land
with abundance of natural
wonders on every hand,
The east and west are bounded by
mountain ranges
Beautiful mountain lakes
surrounded by forests, green
And through the denseness of the
forest foliage,
The sparkling water in great
currents forms
And the greatness of the Colorado
River is seen,
Behold, in midst of river, hills
and dales,
All nature rings in clearest echoes
through the hills
Triumphant through the
boundless day, she hails,
Nevada, her priceless natural
kingdom lies,
In splendor blessed in bright
colours
The enchantment of green of forest
and blue of sea and skies,

Nevada, the wonderland
Nature has blessed this land
with scenic wonders
on every hand,
Lake Tahoe, giant forests, and rolling
hills dot the countryside
And standing majestic for all the
world to see
Is man's great triumph—
Boulder Dam
And o'er this man-made project
flows
The Colorado River to form
Lake Mead
A mighty triumph, indeed
And she has great history too, this
wonderland
For there is a city, Las Vegas,
gateway to Boulder Dam
And Virginia City, gold and silver
mining town
Silent, and deserted now, as
from a distance the
Slumbering Hills look down
Nevada, the wonderland
Nevada, her priceless kingdom lies
The enchantment of green of
forest and blue of sea and skies.

Ruth Coté Brown
LOOKING TO TOMORROW

They say that life is a highway
That has many turns down the road of
life—
We sometimes stumble and fall
But we have to keep pushing on,—
Till we come to a turn in the road that
can bring us happiness all through
our days.
It sometimes can be a rough road, but
we have to try to keep trouble away,
and see that things don't go astray—
So as I sit here dreaming of the days
to come—
My thoughts go beyond the rising of
the sun.
My hopes are positive as I think of
the days before me I have nothing to
dread.
As the sun slowly sinks another day
is done
My mind will be at peace in the days
to come.

Mary J O Donnell
CONSTRUCTION OF I-88

Relentlessly they push and surge
ahead
Relentlessly the million dollar
machines
Slash the earth's sweet-flowing
breast,
Snatch the feeding trembling trees,
Break them by the millions.

Brooks bent into long dark tunnels
Are without babble or banks;
Singing streams choked by collars of steel—
To the million dollar monsters.

Proud bucks bewildered,
Their hilly demesne denuded,
Coated with form-fitting concrete,
Road ribbons spread without mercy
Serving the greed of commerce.

Twenty minutes saved
For trucks to roll
Binghamton to Albany.
The money changers are glad.
—How sad!

Glinda C Smith

Glinda C Smith
A POEM FOR THE AGED

I would like to dedicate this poem to one of my dearest friends that we all call "Willie." Thank you for your support and encouragement over the past several years. God bless you always!

We love a guy called Bill
That's getting a little bit over the hill

With eyes that sparkle
And teeth that shine
Oh my! do you think he might still be 39?

It's his BIRTHDAY we're celebrating this Christmas Eve
So be nice to this guy named Bill if you please

He tells us he is fifty
Which means he is still spiffy

We understand he loves to hunt
This man called Bill who is over the hump.

His love for deer is more precious than gold
He'll hunt till he's ninety which I call old

He loves to tease us when he has time,
This special person who thinks he's still 39.

So cheers for you ole Birthday Boy
Hope Santa brings you lots of SEX
and a BIG RED TOY!!!

Ellen L Riley
TO MY DAD ON FATHER'S DAY

To my father, whom I love and hold dearly in my heart.

It doesn't seem so long ago
Since Dad has gone away
He's now in heaven with our God
Forever he will stay

As the years have come and gone
I still ask God in prayer
Please tell my Dad, I love him
Someday I'll see him there

Let him know I miss him
And the many times we shared
The special thing he did for me
That showed how much he cared

Please tell him I look forward
To that glorious day
When I'll finally see him
We'll both have much to say

Dear Lord, there's still one thing
My father ought to know
On Father's Day & every day
I'll always love him so

Lori A Wenzel
MY LITTLE MAN

Of my nephew, what he gave to me. Thank you!! "Neil" Love always, Aunt Lori

My joy, my inspiration,
"He was a sensation"
My enlightment when I was down,
"He was a little clown"
My tears all dried up,
"He was cuddly, like a baby pup"
My smile when I was happy,
"He was a little joy of Pappy's"
My love of life alone,
"He was a little star that shone"
My memories of this "Loving one,"
Will never, never be undone.

Born: 10/14/80 Died: 10/24/85

James E Loeffert
THE SHADOW OF A MOUNTAIN

For a long time I lived in the shadow of a mountain. My vision was clouded and my eyes could not see—the other side where the sun did ride—keeping its face from me.
And then one day as the dawn approached, I felt a tremendous urge—to see the side where the sun did ride—and abandon my dismal dirge.
So I packed up the very few things that I owned and began climbing upward and onward—and I reached the peak as my legs grew weak—not looking backward or downward.
Then I saw a new world as it opened before me, a world of color and light—and my being rejoiced as it filled my heart's wonder, enthralled by the breathtaking sight.
As I stood there amazed by the splendor before me—I questioned my heart and my soul—as to why I had not done this before, then the answer came back in whole.
You could not have climbed this mountain before for the legs of your soul were too weak—and your vision was clouded—and your eyes could not stand—looking down from this mountainous peak.

Mercedes Barnes Thompson
HEAVENLY BLISS

I saw you toss the waves around
your wonders to disclose,
But only those who've looked have found
the truths a wave unfolds.

What beauty lies beneath each drift
whose sounds are so like thunder.
But other voices too do lift
one's thoughts to awe and wonder.

Ah come aside and wade with me
over the sands and the dunes together.
We'll float a message to the sea
that will bind our hearts forever.

Then you and I alone will know
the truth our wave must guard.
For never once will it repeat
the truth inside our pod.

David Close
HILL 609

To: Arick Dylan, and Corrine Kether Close . . . May you never know the horrors of war.

Its name was simply 609 . . .
that isolated jungle hill
filled with waiting men . . .
armed and ready to kill.

We charged that deadly gauntlet . . .
directly into Dante's Hell,
surrounded by an insanity . . .
of napalm and shrapnel.

The scent of burning flesh . . .
enticed death's appetite
into bloody butchering, without regret . . .
through bomb, bullet and bayonet.

Politicians call it a necessity . . .
while generals label it a victory,
and epitaphs glorify the vanity
of 609's inhumanity.

Flag games persist world-wide . . .
with hills, orders and men
victims of changing tides
just pawns . . . on opposite sides.

Mrs Jacqueline S Bagwell
TURN OUT THE LIGHT

Why can I not turn out the light?
I speak of the one at the end of the tunnel of life
One which our loved ones passed thru,
True it brought them out of the darkness, into the eternal light
Why do I see them standing there so often thru the years?
Even during the busy day they appear, sometimes warm, loving and vibrant.
I say O God why did they have to go? I miss them so.
Sometimes while praying they appear. And I ask my loved ones
What do they want to say?
Often in the deep and darkness of nite, I see them standing so far off in that light.
I say Lord is it at last alright for them?
Please turn off the light, and free my soul and mind
A quiet calm voice answers, I can not turn off the light
Because it burns also for thee.

Georgie M K Mack
SCRIPTURES FUL-FILLED

This Poem Is Dedicated To Virginia, My sweet Mother

"Soldiers; sglothing with spears in hands,
following gladly:
Sinners commands,
King of worlds; Scripture say!
Read the Bible today!
Ok.—

Carie Ramirez
LIKE THE FREE SPIRIT I AM

I should rise and go to a place where the sun forever shows
Beyond the meadows to a land where singing seagulls soar
But the thoughts of you will fill my mind like the waves upon the shore
It's like the stream of tears running down my face
As I think of when we parted, much like my emotions, different day to day
Wishing rain and tears will go and hoping you and the sun will stay
And if the sky may darken or the snow may fall
I could think none of it and turn away from it all
I'll escape to my paradise
Where star filled nights remind me of you
Love helped us grow in a special way
Like a tiny flower that wilts and dies and that's turned the "hello" into "good-bye"
It's the sea that's cried a thousand tears
And the moon that's heard a million lies
Know you sigh upon the sky
But eventually the coastline stops
Just as our love may someday
It's really not that far away
For I was never one for "goodbyes"
So you have to let me go
Let me fly like the free spirit
I am . . .

Harry Percupchick
UNBORN

Today my life began, I'm a miracle
God has already planned who I'll be
What I'll look like
The color of my eyes
And the color of my hair

I hear talking outside my mother's womb
They're saying I'm not a reality yet
That I don't exist
But I do exist, I do

Things are happening so fast
My heart is beating now
I'm starting to take form
Alive, I'm truly alive

It's so dark around me
But I know when Mother brings me
Into the world
Everything will be beautiful
And there will be light and colors
I'll be beautiful, you'll see

I'm looking forward to meeting my parents
I wonder if I'll look like them
The same eyes, the same nose
Maybe I'll walk like Dad
Or talk like Mom

I'm so excited
It won't be long now
I wonder if my parents are as
Happy as I am to be alive

The pain
My life is over
My heart has stopped
I'll never know who I could have
been
Today my parents murdered me

Margaret Cobert Gianturco
THE BRASS BED
I feel like a queen
In my big brass bed
With the little red roses
At the foot and the head
Oh sometimes I worry
And sometimes I fret
Still I feel like a queen
In my big brass bed
When I lay me down
At the end of the day
The cares of the world
Just fade away
I thank the Lord
In my simple way
For taking those I love
Through another day
Oh I'm not the person
I used to be
And I'm not as young
As I'd like to be
But I'm a queen
For all to see
When I lay me down
To rest my head
Beneath the grand red roses
Of my big brass bed.

Ann Ferguson Martin
SHE IS YOUR WIFE
I was so happy when you called,
I trembled with delight.
To know I'd get to see you,
If only for tonight.

I know I shouldn't feel like this,
You have someone at home.
But then I know you can't be mine.
That's when I feel alone.

I hope it doesn't show at all,
For the world to see;
I hope no one will ever know,
Just what you mean to me.

I know I shouldn't thrill,
To how you touch my hand.
Though your gentle kiss is sweet,
You wear her wedding band.

I hope I never, ever cause,
Sorrow in your life;
I guess I should forget you,
After all, "She is your wife."

E E Merino
A PROPHECY TO GERMAN PRINCES

Above our shared bed the tantalum lamina softly swings, which we had Merlin's oracle engraved on, three centuries ago, with the speech he delivered in a low voice, his schismatic hands deep into our manes:

"When the unsatisfied yearning distresses your lover and he slips away among the castles at dawn, sheltered from the approaching morning, go and search by the lake, as it is there where you will find him, seated on a wet lily, grieved by the mercy of life. Call him to try the red water until he fulfills his childlike thirst, for a propitious youth will come later to your port, spongy like a sacred gift. The plants with pinkish flowers and other subtle shapes—the high white herbs—will escort your return.

When the invading stance of your industrious lover lessens and he loses his faith in your tomorrow, let him leave. It is urgent for him to sleep some midnight at the bottom of the ocean snail; he longs on awakening for the troubles of the labyrinth to discern the course towards the uncertain twinkling, the tenuous but long-lived sea—a space for dead barons—, towards the grief of the morbid and distant shore where your domains begin. He needs the torture reserved for infidels. Perhaps you see him afar on the thick lip of the mollusc, with his dying tint anticipating himself; go then to meet him, soothing his fierce temper with your reasoning, while you guide his iridescent vessel towards the cliffs."

That we heard from Merlin three hundred years ago, the many german princes, ministers and gentiles, whom his magic initiated into the pleasure of the crouched love. Crouched and perpetual.

Craig A Flanders
PICNIC MEMORY
Remember?
Yes, I remember.
We ran through a flowering meadow,
a field of ocean green.
Exhausted, we stood and stared.
I tossed you with the wind,
just like a blanket you softly settled
down.
Then I came down to you.
The smell of lilacs were in your hair.
Wine: (the aphrodisiac grape)
could not have intoxicated me more,
than when I drank from your lips.
A banquet your breast made for me
that day.
They nourished and fed my flame.
Pink rose petals blossomed,
by the blood of our lust.
Petals, sweeter than honey.
Eat . . . I did eat of the flower.
A swine to the swill!
Yes, I remember . . .
I have made a picnic of you.

James R Bassette III
THE RUNNING 1/2 SAMIEE
A running 1/2 Samiee ran across my
yard.
Oh yes she did catch my eye as—she
turned and winked
I'm going to befriend that lovely 1/2
breed.
For days she ducked, dodged and not
come arm's reach, even after
drinking my milk.
One night feeling—next it, in the
ready state—she ran cross my path
as I got out my car.
I called to her and to my surprise she
slipped softly toward my available
hand for the pats—rubs she missed
or never had.
I slipped in got some milk and placed
it at her paw or feet.
She drank thirstily afterwards
offered her head and body for the
only pats.
She then followed me wherever
I ventured outside.
Picking her up was easy—carrying
her in the house was easy
—Locking her in the den was easy
as
I slipped out for bits of beef and
chicken & tuna.
Now she's my pal and friend
I get rubbed on—I get tail dragged
and purrs beyond my knowledge.
We're friends and Ashley is her
name. I hope to remain the same.
As I told her—hands off my two
cockatiels (Aura & Yellow top.)
there're private VIP—6 months
ahead and special.
Our pack is set and all's ok.
for the running 1/2 Samiee is mine
just as I foreseen.

Margaret Johnson Mawyer
INTO 'YON FLOWING RIVERS
One warm wintry day—
An exotic ship came sailing my
way—
From out the misty sea, to deliver an
amorous gift to me
The likes of which I may never see.

The cargo contained the most
glorious mementoes—
all lined in silver, gold and
precious stones—definitely not
of hay and stubble, so easily
destroyed.

Friendship filled my daily thoughts to
make me board its decks which
became a secure thought shelter and
stay.

Then—
My ship sailed smoothly away from
rigid rocks that turned its rudders
toward 'yon flowing rivers to small
rippling branches studded with
more exotic treasures—suddenly
turning its oars—

My dreams were delivered to
continue its journeys, yet desper
ately I cling unfulfilled to the sails
as the stormy seas beckon my ships
return to yonder flowing waters.

I yell in desperation! Return O'Ship!
My lovely gem—to sink such a
vessel would mean only a harmful
gesture in the end which memory
ceases to erase.

Now looking to another day, I remain
hoping—awaiting delivery when the
ship sails again my Rivers way!

Johnny D Arrant
FEELINGS OF A LUNATIC

I'm not a machine or a robot just as much,
I need your caressing lips, and the softness of your touch. My desires are often too much for you to understand or see, but my feelings are in frustration, and that's for even me.

I try to express my feelings and tell my point of view, but all I seem to get is nothing out of you. It makes my mind wander to the past, and how it could have been. Always making love, never hesitating to grin.
I always come back to the present and realize it's just fantasy. Were we always making love and did you really care for me?
Maybe I'm childish or better yet a fool. Are you really loving or are you hard and cruel? Fond memories keep me going that's all I have to hold, happiness and laughter have all turned bitter cold. Yet at times you're loving and soft and it seems to ease the pain, Is my lover all these things or am I just insane?

Glenda Halvorsen
I CAN'T BELIEVE WE'VE COME THIS FAR
I'm sorry for all the pain
You've suffered in the past
I'm sorry that we tried so hard
To find it wouldn't last.

I'm sorry for your broken heart
That takes time to be mended
I'm sorry that the love we had
So soon had been ended.

I'm sorry for the tears you cried
And nights you lay awake
I'm sorry you didn't understand
That love is give and take.

I'm sorry that the way you feel
Is not the way I do.
Just remember dear, no matter what
I'll always remember you.

Donald C Ewing
LINES TO A YOUNG GRANDDAUGHTER
I will not always be around to take
your hand and walk beneath the
summer sky,
to see among the leaves the birds that
fly
above our path that leads down to the
lake;
I may not be with you to help you
make
your games that mean so much to
you, and I
may not be there to see the years go
by
nor watch the shell of childhood
slowly break,
when all you love may seem to
disappear;

But other days will come to take their
place,
and there will be new things to claim
your heart.
Perhaps you may remember, though,
and hear
across the years what time cannot
erase,
the days we shared, of which we
were a part.

Paul E Chern
THE MAGIC OF NATURE
A warm spring day, a very warm
breeze
Gently blowing, rustling the leaves
A peaceful, lazy sort of a day
Into a comfortable lawn chair I do
stray
A refreshing drink I have beside me
I look around and so many relaxing
things do I see.
The violets, so purple with leaves so
green,
Clouds floating slowly by, making
one feel so serene.
The gentle breeze softly, warmly
caressing my cheeks

This same breeze blows gently into my ears and truly speaks
Saying life is beautiful enjoy it while you live
There is so much beauty in nature,
Nature has so much to give
the trees silhouetted against the skies
The birds soaring, swooping, gracefully flies
What is actually nature? but a part of God
Why we as people don't appreciate her more is quite odd
The beauty of living fully we feel intensely once in a while
the wonder of nature brings this out
And we meet life refreshed and serene, and with a smile

Ellen Lilly

YEARNING

To my parents: For all the memories and support.

Golden threads of
sunset weave between
the trees, entwining
about me like
a spider web of
light while I
wander down a
path gently followed
by the night.
And beyond the
velvet moss by
the water's edge,
I scoop up
a stone, feel
its smoothness
in my hand,
then toss it back
into its womb
with a secret wish
attached.

Hy Young

THE ANCIENTS WROTE

To my darling wife, Evelyn

Splicing couplets to make verses
Is like sewing papyrus strips
For records and coming to grips
With legends, superstitions and curses.
In ancient annals times wise men wrote
On clay tablets and skins of goat.
But from Egypt's swamps rushes split,
Sewn, were made into scrolls fir
To give the world its first tome
It later migrated to Greece then Rome.

Still farther back in time
Before humans learned to rhyme
The skin-clad cave men drew
And scrawled rude pictures that you
Can still find—they're petroglyphs
Some on cave walls, others on stony-faced cliffs.

Billie R Day

HEAVEN'S GATE

We strolled along in the outback
Cherishing the beauty that God did create.
The birds were singing like angels,
As each step took us through
Heaven's Gate.

We walked through the brush and ravines,
And the hills that rolled like the tide.
We held hands and smiled at each other
As our hearts began swelling with pride.
A fire began raging within us
As his hands gently lay me to the ground.
Our passion, like volcanos, erupted
And we knew a new love we had found.

The trees stood tall as our fortress.
The leaves rustled with each breath of wind.
The cattle grazed in the meadows around us.
The river flowing, like our love, with no end.

These moments shall always be treasured.
As this love too, our God did create.
An inner peace we shared as we became one.
As we loved just inside Heaven's Gate.

Linda Wehling

ILLUSIONS

Truth, evasive in our soul.
Love, reaching out with deceit.
Reality, play hide and seek.
While we dance,
What is our music,
As fantasy lays sweet within us?
You sing me sweet songs
Of promise.
I listen knowing not,
Caring not,
Content with lies,
Evolved into surface joy.
Yet, reach to higher levels,
And deeper into soul.
Our spirit cries contentment
As it dies
Dormant into winter
Awaiting spring's reality.

Cindi S Cusanelli

YOU'VE BEEN TEACHING ME A LESSON

To Mike, Randi & Jami With love

You've been teaching me a lesson—
One I had never learned
To make it through a lifetime
To change with every turn.
And now if you could only
Put your trust in me
While I belong to every moment
Only your heart can fill—
And loving you in a world of
Confusion—my love for you
Stands still
Most people search a lifetime
Yet never seem to find
The love we found—in such a
Short time
So, now I want to thank you
For all the things you've
Taught me—these things
I won't forget
As for my love for you,
I shall never once regret

Pamela Babaei

THE DAY A BUTTERFLY LANDED ON MY SHOULDER

To my loving husband who has shown me the beauty of love, and all things.

A Butterfly landed on my shoulder
As I sat on my husband's car today.
It took my breath away.
I felt myself somehow blessed,
My edification could not rest.
I felt like an angel.
When a Butterfly landed on my shoulder
I sat in utter awe,
And by the time I had grasped
The joy and beauty of the moment,
It graciously flew away.
My joy was much
When a Butterfly landed on my shoulder.
Oh God!
Thank you for the beauty of the Butterfly
And for the day
When a Butterfly landed on my shoulder.

Tamre Rivera-Kindrick

Tamre Rivera-Kindrick

MOTHERS ARE LIKE ROSES

To my beautiful mother, Betty R. Rivera. I love you Mom

Mothers are like roses
a constant blooming sweet
that's why God made mothers
never to be obsolete.

And so my mother
to me you're precious and dear
no matter the miles between us
in my heart you're always near.

You've always been here for me
to always talk and listen
when I see your pretty face
a constant shine and glisten.

You've seen my tears
and held my hand
you've let me lean
no matter how long a stand.

And so dear mother
you're sweet as a rose
petals always blossom
the Love continuously grows.

Jacque Hirt

SPRING

To Norma Hirt, who has always guided me brightly with inspiration

Purple indian:
Paint a turquoise ocean,
Oceans of sunbows
Dripping flowers,
On orange ground;
Splatter butterflies
Over white sheep shower.
Where do butterflies go
When it rains?

Florence Lee Rheam

BOY IN BECKHAM COUNTY

Thanks to Bill Schooler

A boy lies back to warm sweet prairie
A ball of mesquite to shade his head
The folks and the sodhouse are out of sight
Mother, making red beet jelly
Dad taking the cream to Carter
The winter wheat is up, six, seven inches
Green as grass. And overhead, a V
Sharp as on a slate for teacher
But wider, from Schooler farm to Johnson's
And soft, a whir of soft gray breasts
the honker dips, the flock settles down
And flattens the wheat, noisy, chattering
From Canada, the folks say, from
Saskatchewan, their nesting ground
Saskatchewan? where is that? How far?
Bound for South America. How far is that?
A boy lies back to warm, sweet prairie
In autumn, in Beckham County, Oklahoma

Oji S Blackston

PROMISE

O' woman of love,
sustain me in my trial
be the protector of my heart.

My heart is open to your love.
My arms are to comfort.
My eyes are to paint.
My mind to appraise.

Let me make your dreams
come true.
O' woman of love,
Queen of my life,
your chair is now a throne.
I am a warrior by your side.
I shall slay each day
on my sword of Truth.

Fill each night with star studded lust.
Belief in each will make us
both a truth.
Be we each other's for
eternity.

Dream your dreams my woman.
Come, let me guide you to
my heart.

Lisa Grooms

ADAM AND EVIL

Oh Father, God of life and death,
why Adam, who in his first breath
of evil is condemned?
An image created of Thee,
then please explain how can he be
if in ignorance hemmed.
How good is good without evil?
A homogeneous level
beyond which does not span;
The being of an angel that
is said to harbor thoughts, in fact,
which merely envy man.
I see difference in evil known
compared to that which has been done
and do not understand;
Why the eating of a tree
placed in paradise by thee
is the first sin of man.

Richard A Leavitt

I REALLY LOVE YOU

I may not have told you everyday
I may not have shown you in every way.
That my love for you is very strong
and I know that my feelings are not wrong.
For I have had time to think it through
and I am sure my love was meant for you.
I am very glad that you are my wife
and I hope that you will be for the rest of my life.
We will share laughter and we will share tears
but we will also share many, many years.
All of these years I know we will cherish

until from this earth we both do parish.
But even then it won't end for you and me
because we will be together for all eternity.
I know that what I have written is true
and I know for a fact that I really love you.

Rhonda Updegraff
REFLECTIONS IN YOUR EYES
I couldn't tell at first
By the look in your eyes
But the love in your heart
Took me by surprise.

I'd decided long ago
Not to give my heart away
I was just so very sure
No one's love would ever stay.

But your patience proved me wrong
I'm glad I have to say
That what I was so afraid of
Didn't turn out that way.

Now I see the love in your eyes
I can feel it in your heart
Cause I know in mine this love is real
And we can never, ever part.

Adam T Kern
INNOCENCE
When I was young
I awoke with a scare
Teeth and paws
It had to be a bear

They're mean, they're nice
Don't touch, don't hold
Just squeeze for dear life
And hope you never grow old

Age may come to me
But youth must always stay
I love to hold my Teddy
When time got in the way

My bears always understand
They're always on my side
We always tell the truth
They lend a shoulder when I cry

If people were like my bears
The warmth would melt the ice
There'd never be no tears
And the world would be so nice.

Kenneth Mekonen
WHAT
What if I should venture to write from the heart
What thoughts came to me
I might record maybe unknowingly
What some might in their mediocrity call primitive art
Childish, or simply rubbish.

But tell me truly
Of what should I write
The things that would appeal to all?
But my mind will find no ease
For that too may appall
Because it is impossible to conceive
What transpires in the minds of all
Let alone to please.

Patrick Zale
AFTER HOURS
They don't know anything about love down at the bars but she who lives a life of passion experiences passion, for whatever it really is.

Perhaps the same is true of love.

Tonight, out here on the veranda,
it is a warm January night, the moon is full,
and I have been waiting for just such a night as this,
when the world becomes ghostly
quiet and unsure of itself,
so ghostly quiet that even a single word, spoken surely,
could be heard a thousand miles away—

It takes guts to keep looking for that stuff, love,
to strut it out there solo on the dance floor one more time because you came to dance,
to relish in this puritan era the pleasure
of an object you have desired for ten thousand years,
to have some kind of volition in the face of honest confusion,
some kind of faith in the magic of the lustrous night to
bridge the laser celebrations of sex and a somber dawn.

Faye Miller
THE STILL SMALL VOICE
Though bombs may burst
and wrath may move,
and earthly cities flame,
the hopeful fact that God is
love
remaineth still the same.

Though many for the
burning bush
and outward signs may seek;
when waiting for the still
small voice,
we all may hear Him speak.

Carrie Neubauer
AN OLD BLUE BOX
Tucked inside my drawer is an old blue box,
Underneath my undies and a pair of yellow socks.
Locked inside are treasures from when I was just a child,
Things that I'd forgotten, memories compiled.
A yellow curl in cotton, from when Mom first cut my hair,
A pendant Dad had bought me at the Seattle World's Fair.
One black onyx earring—it used to be a set,
Keith bought them for me at Christmas, with a necklace yet!
My blue silk bag of marbles, drawn up with a string,
And a white, cracked opal that used to be a ring.
A little square of material—Mom put lavender inside,
To kill the smells of dirty socks, I guess I tried to hide.
Then I found a Barbie head, she used to be together,
And then from an outing at Beacon Hill Park—a peacock feather.
A bracelet from a boyfriend, with our names etched in,
Which I've kept for many years, much to my husband's chagrin.
Some crests for sports and a Sunday school pin,
And a locket with a picture of Mom and Dad within.
These treasures have been kept for twenty years or more,
And I've loved browsing through them many times before.

Harriet (Shove) Bedard
JUST FOR YOU
My dear darling daughter
Writing this poem—I feel I gotta'—just for you
If only I could turn time back—to when you were born
I'd do it without a moment's hesitation—and then
Just for you—I'd love to have you live your life, again
Mothers cannot be everywhere—see—hear—do everything
Hindsight makes us wiser—if only our foresight was as great
I'd take off the blinders—take away all the sad reminders
Someone did you much wrong—a possessive love—out of control
Confused his mind and actions—put a shadow on your soul
Thought it was dealt with as best we could
The memories won't disappear—if only they would
The past we cannot undo—if only I could I would—just for you
Then your partner in life—with his wrong-doings—degraded you as his wife
Now all the past hurts are haunting your life
Just for you—I wish I could wipe them all away
Put them in the past—where they should forever stay
Peace of mind—just for you—I pray
It is not your wrong doing—but, by forgiving
You can overcome the bitterness of wrongs others have done unto you
A family needs to find ways to be united—not divided
For when the curtain of life descends—we no longer have time to make amends . . .

Hank Thompson
EPITAPH
I feel the warm sun above me
Gently beaming from its place.
The grass grows above me.
I feel its tender embrace.

I hear the wind play its music,
That soothes my restless soul.
I feel the strength in my weakness,
As I lay silent in this hole.

I feel the cold ground around me.
Its chill on my bones.
I hear the truth in my singing;
No one knows that I have gone.

Arthur R Garcia

Arthur R Garcia
THE REAL ME
I'm a young boy in disguise.
I'm merely an illusion before your eyes.
My true self is the spirit inside me.
This temporary existence was meant to be.
I was born to live. I was born to die.
I live in between the ground and the sky.
I travel each day searching for more.
I'm a young adventurer ready to explore.
I walk on the road of life telling no lies.
I don't want intelligence. I want to be wise.
This young boy lives in a body that grows old.
I carry on as this story is told.
Time will never take away my mental youth.
I'll always follow the Light, the Truth.
I'm a young boy reaching out from within.
This body holds the mind that wants to win.

Jacquelyn M Hendrix
INNOCENCE
I've come a long way since I started this job.
I've learned to reach inside myself and find strength
When the props I depended upon, failed.
I've learned that you really do grow when you overcome hardship
Though it's not a pleasant experience.
I've learned that popularity is a worthless commodity
Without respect.

Yet sometimes the desire to change places with my students
Is strong.
I want to forget responsibility and the lessons
I had to learn the hard way.
I want to trade the character for a little of the magic,
To again see the future as an endless parade of tomorrows and possibilities.
Some days it isn't possible.
Some weeks it doesn't happen.
But once in a while teaching gives me that gift.
And again I find I can view the world
Through the pure eyes of a child.

Charlotte V Patterson
ONE SMILE
While strolling through the park at the peak of dawn,
An elderly woman passed by; so subdued and calm,
She generated a smile that was so very bright, it's amazing
How one smile, can put sunshine in just one life;
Persistently I strolled, overlayed with illumination,
I smiled at every creature, without hesitation.
She rendered something to me, that I already had,
So why walk around, looking so mad?
So many of our hearts, are filled with intense strife,
Remember one smile, can put sunshine, in just one life.

Betty J Wilson
EVERYONE ELSE BUT ME
When you get angry with me for something I won't let you do,
Please remember the important times that I was there for you.

Just keep in mind when I ask you why, because,
I don't want to hear that everyone else does.

When you were little and had diaper rash,
It wasn't everyone else who was there in a flash.

When you started walking and weren't very steady,

It wasn't everyone else that helped get you ready.
When you started school and you were so scared,
It wasn't everyone else that showed you they cared.

When you fell down and skinned up your knee,
It wasn't everyone else who kissed it
Hon, just me.

When your hamster got sick, you can sure bet,
It wasn't everyone else who took her to the vet.

When everyone else starts wearing makeup, it doesn't mean it's right,
Be proud that you are your own unique person and don't look a sight.

When everyone else starts chasing and catching boys,
Remember boys are abundant, not so your childhood joys.

I love you so much but I want you to have your own dreams,
Don't make decisions lightly or follow everyone elses' schemes.

Vincent A VanMeter
SITTING, ONLY SITTING, SIMPLY WATCHING THROUGH THE GLASS
Sitting only sitting, simply watching through the glass,
A gentle man, a lonely man, sits dreaming of his past.
He dreams his dreams of childhood, of when there was no cares,
Only play to last a day, now he sits and stares.
Running, always running, chasing rainbows through the trees.
Only dreams, it always seems, he looks but never sees.
Years and years come and go as he watches through the glass.
Looking, always looking, but seeing only past.
A stormy day he passed away, still dreaming, I suppose,
Of a gentle boy, happy boy, with dirt upon his nose.
With a life of dreams, I guess it seems, he gave up long ago;
But a lonely man does what he can for a place that's safe to go.

Rebecca F Goffinet
WORDS TO LIVE BY
every day
your life is like sand
it flows thru your hand
or you can take it, hold it,
shape it, remold it
into a castle of dreams
or that's how it seems
any way

L Mae Nelson
ROOTS AND WINGS
Two things we can give to our children—
One is roots—the other is wings.
They must know that we are with them,
They are ours—whatever life brings.
With these roots so firmly grounded
They will grow and become mature—
Knowing we will never forsake them
That parental love is sure.

When in our love they feel secure
They will grow and want to fly;
And we must loose the fetters
So that they are free to try.
We may find they fly far from us
But they really are not gone
For the roots of love will hold them
As the days and years go on.
In God's love we are together
And will always, ever be,
For the roots that hold so firmly
Give the wings that set them free.

Cheryl June
CAPTURED
Around and around
you quietly spin your web
before my eyes

Beauty of its intricate design
has me spellbound, mesmerized!

Thoughts of retreat whisper like a breeze
through my mind

I remain transfixed, steadfast!
to all else blind

and my heart feels joy, as it is I
that becomes entwined!

Crystal F Arnold
IF I COULD SEE BEYOND TODAY
If I could see beyond today
Would I keep up the fight?
Would I be willing to pay
The price of believing I'm right?

If I could see beyond today
Would I be proud of what I'll become?
Would I continue to say
What I think, or be silent like some?

If I could see beyond today
Would I regret what I'm doing now?
Would I wish I'd gone on my way
And thrown in the towel?

If I could see beyond today
Is this the path that I would choose?
Is everything that I might gain
Worth everything that I might lose?

If only I could see beyond today!

James F Krick
JAILHOUSE
Captive of the kitchen
Shackled to the stove
Making English muffins
Baking gingerloaf

Breakfast on the table
Coffee starts to perk
Serving out her time
While the warden's off to work

Pudding pies, chicken thighs, captive cries—
Her shackles stick like jam in the jailhouse

Pris'ner of the pantry
Baking berry crepes
A recipe required
To brew up her escape

Dinner on the table
Steak is slightly burned
She simmers with a smile
The warden has returned

Poison steak, file in cake, prison break—
She frees herself and flees from the jailhouse

Wilda Tomlinson McDonald
AUTUMN IN THE ROCKIES
Leaves are falling in the Rockies,
O'er the hills may now be seen
The scarlet of the maples
And the oaks' bright tangerine,
Beneath the wraps of dull mauve willows,
Quakies are in yellow dressed,
At the Summer's last gay frolic
For the trees soon go to rest.
Dark pines, like precious jewels,
Stud the canyons here and there;
Or perhaps they're chaperones
Watching o'er each well-loved pair.
There's a splendor in the Rockies
Such as we know in our dreams,
When at night the lonely coyote wails
And the pale moon brightly gleams.

For the beauty of the Rockies,
As the plenty at our board,
Or our homes and happy families
We thank Thee—Thank Thee, Lord.

Louise T Tanaka
IS THERE LIFE AFTER KIDNEY FAILURE?

To Dr. Robert Doud, the world's best nephrologist

I carried them around with me for 42 years—two wee things,
no larger than my two hands—
But, now, they no longer function, almost anyway.
Thank you kidneys. I never thought very much about you before—
how much you have both done for me.
Wow! Did I ever take you for granted.
When I started bloating up—for no reason, I thought, then—
I couldn't breathe—I didn't really know what was wrong.
Later I realized that you couldn't do the work you once did.

But thanks for all those years—years I played happily on the farm—
Years of going on picnics and sniffing the woodsy air—
Years of health and happiness—
Yes, it's true I almost died, but thank God I didn't. Thank God
for wonderful doctors and nurses who treated me so beautifully,
that now I am almost as good as new again.
So, there is life after kidney failure because—even if a part of my body is
not the same, I am being helped through CAPD—a mobile kind of dialysis.
PRAISE GOD! I feel great and I know that there is much for me to do—
work, play and be!
Even when all of me is gone—the part that you can see—the rest of me
will be in a Heavenly place with my Heavenly Father!

REJOICE! Yes, I can rejoice! There is a greater love and truth in life
than we can ever know. It
seems a mystery to be able to
make contact with it. And yet, it's so very simple.

JUST ASK HIM TO COME INTO YOUR HEART!

Carey Corrigan
THE KEY
Drifting through the day
Another class
The same old way

I saw you through the crowd
I was so quick to fall in love
I could not voice my love aloud

And then my dream came true
I found myself right next to you

You taught me how to care
I taught you how to share . . . my love

Whenever I'm with you
A fresh new love begins anew

My love for you is pure as pure can be
I finally found the key . . . to your heart

To your heart . . . I found the key
You changed my life . . . a brand new me

Now, how can I repay you for your love ???
Boy, look what you've done !!!

I finally found the key . . .
the key . . .
the key . . .
to . . . your . . . heart . . .

Barbara-Ann Pitta
A LOOKING GLASS
As I look into the mirror,
I get a very scary fear of,
Mean, dark, gloomy eyes,
That stare back at me in great surprise.
As though they never saw my face,
As though I come from a different place,
A mouth that frowns, not smiles, not grins,
A mouth that out of comes harsh things.
But instead I see twinkling eyes,
Who look at me in great surprise,
Because they remember my face,
Because they remember my place,
A mouth that smiles, not frowns, not cries,
A mouth which says nice things.

Mary I Windmiller
THIS NATION
My heart does love this Nation, It's so strong and brave and true;
It glories in its daughters and its sons of every hue.
Freedom is what binds us as it's meant for me and you.
This is America.

Our strong men work for progress when the Nation is at peace;
Our strong men fight for country so that freedom shall not cease.
Our women guard the hearth fires of the great and of the least.
Hail to America.

United are the states in this glorious far flung land;
Created from a dream held by Sturdy Pilgrim band.
Formed in beauty, rich in harvest,

toil blessed by human hand.
God keep America.

The flag is full of splendor as it flies for you and me;
May we never soil its meaning or dull its purity.
Pray, its stars will shine forever, bright with faith and loyalty.
Fly on in unity.
Faith and glory to our Nation
Glory forever to our flag,
Glory, glory to America,
That fills our hearts with pride.

Gerald D Joiner
MAMA
Mama, I dedicate this to you
With love, honor, joy and respect
Just to say thanks for all that you do
Much more than I deserve or expect.

Thanks for all your advice
Some of which I even listened to.
If all you do had a price
I am sure I could never afford you.

Thanks for all your loving care
and the times you made me smile.
Thanks for always being there
You are a Lady with first class style.

Thanks for healing when I was sick, too—
Splinters, scrapes, sniffles, flu.
For baking cakes, custards, puddings, pies;
For encouraging me to at least try.

Most of all, thanks for being my Mother.
One thing for sure I can bet—
I would not have any other—
My Mama is the best Mother yet!

Brian Viergutz
WINDOWS
There are windows in
which to see truth.

There are windows in
which to see falsehood

There are windows
which shine light.

And there are windows
in which shine no light at all.

There are windows in
history.

There are windows in
time.

And there are windows
that are never seen at all.

But most of all
There are windows
for dreams.

Ann Radabaugh
MONTANA'S AUTUMN
It's oh so beautiful, it's hard to believe
in just a short time, with the change of a leaf
The water so calm, the sun shining bright
with outlining mountains, and never ending light
But, the tell-tale signs of winter soon nearing
as the water starts rippling, with air that is chilling
The plants that have thrived with sunshine abound
will soon join the trees in the winter they've found
The air, full of life, will succumb willingly
to a quiet breeze of calmness, it'll blow silently
And as life quietly sleeps, throughout the winter it seems
it won't be that long, till life will redeem
Its many moments of beauty as it awakens to be
the glorious season it is for everyone to see.

Mary Chappell

Mary Chappell
THE LOVE AFFAIR
I went down into the slough of love.
Wild yellow snapdragons with red-freckle faces.
Danced beside onions with their blue-tasseled dresses
Among rocks, grasses, and pale blue-violets.

The rain fell, ran into the slough.
Ripples bowed down the flowers,
Ran over the rocks and grasses,
Splashed the Fall of the slough.

The slough froze, clear-clear ice,
Air bubbles trapped immobile,
A window to flowers postured and dead.

Stephanie E Hobbie
ONE

This poem is dedicated to my grandfather Harold Sala Carmichael with love

One voice one will
One thought can kill
One cry of pain
One mind insane
One child crying
One old man dying
One wish for love
One flightless dove

One person caring
One person daring
One small deed done
One heart has won

One outreached hand
One grain of sand
One thought to give
One will to live

One small life saved
One gold road paved
One miraculous birth
One person's worth

Doris M Santana
THE LIVE FRAGILE ROSE YOU INTENDED TO BE
The live fragile rose you intended to be
sang and pranced its filled heart in to me
These wondrous dreams of affectionate feelings reminded me
of the mystical scent that filled the petals over thee.
For every sound it make
for me, it be a most pleasant break
"It's the least" the rose spake
"It's the most" thought the rose mistaked.

Received I best compliments
from its praising expressed comments
Inspired by your prance were those movements
And those eyes made my soul's moments.

Harvey E Kolz
LOVE

I want to dedicate this poem in memory of a loving mother.

Love is something you can't touch,
You say you care, but you don't say how much.
Love is something you can't measure
But love can be, a great treasure.

Love is what a child shows to a mother
Love can be shown to a sister, by a brother.
Love can be shown to a sweetheart
It can be cherished when you part.

Love can hold a marriage together
Love can tickle like a feather.
Love can be mushy,
Or it can be pushy.

You can pretend that you are in love
And it can fly out the window like a dove.
True love can be shown in many ways
But when you are true to each other,
Is when it really pays.

Helen Hadlock
ROBYN
To my daughter
Who came after great pain,
To be engulfed in more pain
Until only the pacifier comforted.
Your physical scars deep,
Emotional scars deeper
Because others cruelty
Said you were damaged goods.
They eroded your belief
That you were valuable
Until by forgiveness
Your pride overcame
In your becoming
The beautiful girl
You are today.

Eric R Doty
THE FIGHT

For Francis "Shorty" Doty (My Grandfather), THE FIGHT was as a Dairy Farmer and in his last 12 years was against cancer. He finally lost the battle on 5/15/88. This poem was written in his loving memory.

The start is so fragile, at the elements' mercy;
And the years to come, will be full of controversy.

We enter a world, with no choice of the date;
God knows it's not perfect, half love and half hate.

There are goals to reach, failures to endure;
The road will be long, of that, you can be sure.

We will work hard for survival, to support those we should;
Then we work even harder, for material goods.

The days full of worry, all the business dealings;
It's hard to find time, to express our true feelings.

We've planned for the future, and now it is here;
The years have flown by, the end is drawing near.

At the end of the tunnel, there shines a greeting light;
We become very tired, it's hard to keep up the fight.

Through happy and sad, we've given our best;
Leave it to the fragile, it's time to rest.

Ila Smith Robertson
THE GARDEN OF LIFE

To: Albert (1901-1989) and Nora Robertson (1906-1983) My in-laws— Together forever—

In the Garden of Life there are Roses,
Such Beauty!
But, oh, There are Thorns—So prickly and sharp.
There are Violets of deepest hue.
But, They are found—Hidden in the morning dew!
There are Morning Glories, too;
Climbing upwards, toward the Sun,
And golden Dandelions—
Everywhere.
God makes the flowers to show His Care.
Whether we are great—or just
"One of the Smallest Ones—"
He's with us—
And when our Race is Run,
He takes us Home to be with Him,
Forever. Amen!

John Brussaly
A SONNET FOR THEE
The sky is blue,
the grass is green,
supreme.
The earth God made,
skillful was he,
for thee,
He blessed the land
with all you see,
for thee,
Do you agree
with what God did,
for thee?

He made the man,
then made the femme,
supreme,
He placed them both
amidst the flowers,
the trees,
Both lived a life
of peace, of joy,
in love,
Do you agree
with what God did,
for thee?

Eve 'n Adam both fell
from grace, hid from
God's face—
They ate the fruit
forbade by God
to eat—
Disgraced God's first
were told to leave
God's gard'n . . .

But God so loved
the world, he gave
his Son,
He died for you,
for me—accursed—
on that tree,
Do you agree
with what God did,
for thee?

Blanche B Lindblad
REMINDER

It was there
all the time,
unseeing eyes
missing it—
that old telephone pole
high and lifted up,
with its crossbar . . .

Unending power
and energy,
communication
in that rugged pole—
that cross
for reaching out
to touch new worlds . . .

I needed reminding:
it was there
all the time.

Janetta Hinton Scott
SOMETHING OF VALUE

To my brother with love

Oh 'retched hearts racked with pain
On whom doth thou cast this blame
Doth thou search but never find
Something of value to say "it's mine"
What a pity, what a shame
Canst thou bear even thy name

Souls like these who lost their way
What's left for anyone to say
However shrewd, however smart
There is nothing left but a troubled
heart
Would thou have another share
Things that you cannot bear

Awake before the sun has set
Let the devil know he hasn't won yet
Spare your brother the hurt, the pain
That you might have given, if you
hadn't changed
Does not the ache in your heart reveal
The kind of life you've chosen to live

Michelle Jarvis
CRACK

Let me tell you a story on crack
this new drug that makes you all
wack,
it will make you do some horrid
things
and if you knew all the pain it brings
you would stay far away from this
drug
it will have you crawling in pain on
your rug.
It doesn't care who or where you are
it obsesses all kinds near and far,
it will make you as thin as a mouse
you will sell all including your house.
You would steal or kill for this drug
on the hill
but if you knew Jesus he could
strengthen your will,
don't be sad and don't even cry
just open your heart and let Jesus try.
In this world today if he can pull
whores and junkies through,
then this crack I'm sure he will
conquer for you.

Terry Van Nostrand
THE STORM

A blue lake reflects dark clouds.
Raindrops fall, echoing in
ripples along
a river of darkness.
Leaves droop from weight of water
fall on the forest floor
carpeted by moss and
leaves already fallen.
Thunder echoes
reechoes
along midnight skies.
Lightning explodes in the forest.
Creatures of the night
scurry into their dens
to escape The Storm.

Debby A Smelcer
THE ORPHAN

I am an orphan,
I am like a rag doll,
Hating to be tossed from home to
home
with no place to call my own.

I have a magical dream
that someday I will find
a home,
that special person to love
and care for me—
all that magical dream come true!

Then I can truly say,
"I have a home,
NOW I AM LOVED!"

Judy McDonald
THE ROCKS

To Kathy and Mignone
Friends Forever

The waves dance against the rocks
below
Spraying foam where nothing can
grow
High above the rocks, I stand
On bare, bleak, forgotten sand

Clouds above are solid gray
Like my mind is, today
Nothing left but empty life
Inviting rocks, sharp like a knife

Alone, alone, so by myself
Pushed aside, put on a shelf
One more step and down I'll go
To the rocks, so far below

Belinda Tygrett
ANSWER ME!

To Vernon, Mary Ann, Mandy, Justin and Tara
Without them, I'd have been blind.

The secrets of a million minds
pulling together as a force of one
Answers to riddles begin to fall in
place
Answers are not allowed here!
Fear sets in amongst the strong
Confidence corrupts the timid
The world is turned upside down—
yet only for a moment
Then sweet, sweet silence . . .
interrupted—
Laughter bellows from the city walls
Dark alleyways summon you by
name
The secrets of a million minds
Whisper softly down cobblestone
streets
Answers are not allowed here!
Sunlight cannot reach the homeless
Towering masses of brick and mortar
shadow their existence—
Mere existence
Such angry hatred dances on wicked
fingertips down cobblestone
streets . . . and the tear stretches
down . . .
Like fire, it burns from the soul
Eyes up-turned, begging for answers
As the secrets of a million minds,
although as loud as thunder
Whisper too silently to hear the
answer . . .
For answers are not allowed
here!

Donald J Barnhorst
A SPECIAL SONG

For Missi Stein, who has brought joy and happiness into my life. It was easy to write this poem for you, because it came from my heart.

My special song . . .
for you will be
a beautiful melody
A song of love
of beautiful things . . .
it comes so easily.

I know our love . . .
will lead the way
so we will be as one
It times of joy
and times of pain . . .
it is a special song.

This special song . . .
comes from my heart
in a place only you can see
The rest of the world is secluded
it is only . . .
you and me.

Barbara A Adams
THOUGHTS OF WINTER

To My Sister, Melody, Who's Always There.

As I stood alone by my window;
watching the snow fall softly to the
ground.
It was the first snow of the winter,
falling with not even a sound.
My heart beat fast with joy,
of the wonder of this beautiful sight.
I wondered how many more people
were watching this miracle in the
night.
All the children were sleeping and
dreaming,
not knowing what morning would
bring.
When awaken with eyes filled with
wonder;
and in unison voices will sing.
Come and look at the snow and its
beauty;
before it flees like a bird on the
wing . . .

Jean Wilcox
HIS FRIENDS

In memory of a Vietnam Vet

His hair was black and silver, His
body long and lean,
His beard was full and bushy, His
pants were old blue jeans!

His refuge was a doorwell—Out of
the chill cold air—
But when the sun was shining, He
found solace there!

The sun would shine—a little while,
The clouds would skitter ne're,
And then the rain would tumble
down, But he'd hold his place—so
dear!

He'd chosen time, his place and
friends, Freedom in the air—
The gulls, the sun, the rain, the wind,
These friends—were with him there!

As daylight broke in the morning
hours, His body lay cold and still
For he'd succumb'd in the dead of
night, And bowed to His Master's
Will!

His body, now all clothed in death,
Was shrouded all in white!
The gulls were flying overhead, As
he too made his flight!

Evelyn Louise Nowels
DEEP BLUE WATER

To my daughter Ramona Eileen Dillon, with love, mom.

Far across the deep blue water
watching sea gulls fly,
As the sand is washed away each
grain seems to cry,
With endless numbers drowning
under waves never to return,
Flood of white foam covering the
rocks with no concern.

It's natures way of cleansing and
keeping all things pure,
Tide-waters rushing and washing,
giving a grooming to the shore,
Sunlight on the water warming it for
the day,
Each sunbeam is dancing in their
own graceful way,

Mary Morris Smith
TOO LATE FOR TEARS

This poem is dedicated to family and friends

The road still goes by there, her
flowers still remain,
My friend used to live there, only
thoughts remain.
A friendship great, so tightly bound,
It suffered many storms.
What happened then—I can't recall,
We were going separate ways.
The road between the houses,
Wasn't traveled very much.
The friendship seemed to fade away,
We didn't keep in touch.
We were getting older, did our values
differ so much?
What happened to the love, what
happened to the trust?
We became like strangers, growing
far apart.
The friendship that was bright, soon
grew very dark.
Life can pass us by so fast,
Then it's too late for tears.
It's too late for friendship,
That faded thru the years.
The road still goes by there, the silent
house remains,
My friend used to live there—only
thoughts remain.

Wilma V (Sines) Lipscomb
OUR GLORIOUS FLAG

To my oldest son Robert, who was in Vietnam fighting for our freedom when I wrote this. To all the veterans, L O V E to all.

Brightly, How Brightly,
We'll sing Her this song.
We'll respect her as long as we walk
along.!

Her stripes are long in the form of a
stream.
Her Stars like a five cornered dream.
"O", Gaily we glide her up on a
string.

Around her we stand, The anthem

we sing.
Softly, how softly the wind comes along.

It seems to settle, when we've finished our song.
Then up and away it went like the tide!
Then settled back like a veil on a bride.
"O," How proud we are of thee.
In this beautiful land of the free.

Dr Gust D Davis Jr

Dr Gust D Davis Jr
WITHIN HIS WORLD

Dark, dreary, clouded with mixed emotions.
The world, His world of A.I.D.S., I sought to enter.
My friend trapped within a deadly disease.

The day of affirmation. The doctor walked in, within his eyes stood confirmation. A.I.D.S.!
Within my friend's eyes, PLEASE UNDERSTAND.

Lovers? No. Lovers we were not, only platonic friends from two different worlds.

My world, one of love and hope. Now shatter. His world, one of sure death, destiny and despair.

Within His world, I enter to give comfort and strength. My friend's world like a vapor, it was, then it was not.

My friend's world. Now a memory within. Question! why no. For he was my friend you see.
I walked within His world.

Margaret L Morris
OUR SHIP OF LIFE

Dedicated to—My Mom and Dad, Jim and Modena Grover

You two set out on an adventure, some 30 odd years ago.
The course not always steady, your destination so unknown.
The voyage was a long one, there was a storm or two.
But, through gale or calm, you always seemed to make it through.
You added little ship mates, a girl, a boy, or two.
They too, were on an adventure, you were the Captains, and they, the crew.
The girls turned into women, the boys to manhood grew.
You smiled with pride, and watched their steps and strides, and helped them make it through.
Yes, life has been an adventure,
we've shared so much with you.
Our laughter and tears, our woes, and fears, seemed to fade into the blue
But if we could do it all again, I'd sail again with you.
I'd cherish every memory, and love, and thank you two.
I love you both very much.

Margaret Powell
MARGARET

To Mary Katherine and Clare Roedel

[Margaret] you just have a
beautiful baby boy, 8 lb 4 oz big,
cute baby. It was worth
the pain.

[Margaret] you never once
thought for a minute that
you'll go down in history—
Mother, Grandmother, etc.

[Margaret] what age did you
know you couldn't raise a
child by yourself? You need
the help of good people
and God.

[Margaret] who wouldn't tell
you that times don't wait
for nobody and today he's
graduating and next month
he's going to the army.

[Margaret]

Richard Wiggins
A FRIEND

I like to dedicate this poem to my sister Christine, and one of my friends Willie T. McGhee. I haven't forgot ya! Willie

A friend is a person who's with you, through the good as well as the bad. A friend is a person you can talk to when you're sad. A friend is a person who will let you know when you're messing up, in a way you won't get mad. A friend is a person you can trust. A friend is a person you know is a must. A friend is a person you can count on for help in need. But, there's one catch you have to be counted on in return. If not you have a friend you didn't earn.

Vivian Leda Stevens
THOUGHTS OF A POM POM MOM

To my daughter Erin, a very special Pom. 1988

I cried with you—
three years you didn't make it.
This senior year I prayed,
'Cause Lord, I couldn't take it.

I told you to keep trying
You musn't ever quit!
Finally, the coveted rose,
Thank God! You made it!

I've seen you work hard
to learn your routines.
Babydoll you've done it,
What awesome machines!

Tears sting my eyes
each and every time,
I see the entrance
of the burgundy and gold line!

I promised I wouldn't cry,
I know that I did.
But, you don't understand,
I want to scream THAT'S MY KID!

Don't you see her?
She's in the front line!
Isn't she sweet and pretty,
Yes, yes she's MINE!

Both love and pride
swell up in my chest.
My little pom is strutting,
She's giving her best!

You prance and swirl then
you do a split.
I scream and holler,
and am proud of it.

Who is this nut? Do you
know who I am?
I'm a pom pom mom,
I'm your biggest fan!

OH AGONY, report card time.
Do you have a 2.0?
Wonder who would hurt the
most if the answer was NO!

I've done all I can do
to give you my support;
Washed cars, served food, football
tickets for sports.

Nothing was too much,
I'd do it all again;
Cause I'm a pom pom mom,
In my eyes you always win!

Why do I get so excited over Poms?
Why the big to do?
Daughter when you are out there,
Just once, I wish I could be you!

There's a hidden message
in this little ditty.
There's more to life my love
than fluff and being pretty!

My dearest little pom,
I pray that you have learned;
If you persevere and never quit,
All you desire of life can be earned!

Heather Koehler
MEMORIES

To My Parents
for all the love and encouragement they have given me over the years

There comes a time when all must depart
From different worlds to different places.
And carry the past within the heart
In the memories love traces.

Untouched by love is no one's soul
For all souls radiate light.
Yet one always finds a deeper hole
Into which to shove the light.

The light of the past should not be hid away,
But like a rose be free to bloom.
For the memories of another day
Are meant to sail in one's lagoon.

Memories are like flowers of love
They give us courage to face the unknown.
For one's time will come to sail like doves,
And be a memory alone.

Theodore Douglas Mirich
THE SILENT CHORD

To my favorite city kid, with love.

The chanted words of my brother
whom I tortured for life,
woke me from a dream.
I stared at beauty, such
as I had never seen.
Crowned as the King of Time
I looked at the ages of
men gone by.
Somehow, I was in their minds.
The time machine I traveled in
took me so far away,
to a place I could never find.
Adam and Eve were before me.
The Devil tried to steal my soul,
and I ran away.
The evil was awesome,
it came from the air.
There was no place to hide.
Someone heard my plea and
struck a Silent Chord.
I am in this world, no more.

Linda S Demmers
THE HIDDEN LIFE BEHIND THE TREES

To my husband Bill, who stuck by me through so much. I love him dearly.

As I look back,
life was an abundance
of overwhelming fear!
Afraid to open my eyes—
numb to the world around me.
I see nothing—yet, I see everything.
Terrified of consequences
if I speak.

Afraid to live, afraid to breathe,
afraid to be.
I need space to get out
away from those trees.
I need to grow and not be
afraid of the consequences.
for if I don't step out
away from those trees,
I'll always be afraid.

Gladys Alford Everhardt
MY SON—JUST SEVENTEEN

Dedicated to Dr. and Mrs James T. Paul and to Mrs Vee Donahue in loving memory of their sons, John Paul and John Donahue. They both lost their lives in separate automobile accidents at age seventeen.

Beneath the sunny skies you rest,
Sleep my son may you be blessed,
The starry heavens will give you light
And watch over you through the nights.

Soft breezes whisper sweet and low
With outstretched arms about you flow,
Rest a while my dear one sleep
As the world around you weep.

The days move slowly, one by one,
Your young life had just begun,
Never again to hear your step
Overwhelms our heart with painful regret.

Sorrow and sadness will ever be
Like a garment clothing me,
So suddenly you had to go away
We loved you more than we could ever say.

In the springtime of your years
You leave us lonely with many tears,
Our broken hearts may never mend,
We pray that God will comfort send.

In His new order joy will abound,
Death nor crying will ever be found,
Weeping and mourning will have passed away,
Happiness with loved ones,
Oh glorious day!

Raymond T Barrett
IN THIS COUNTRY

To Smokin Joe and Rich
Smokin' Tears

See the child crying
But she doesn't make a sound
Her father is in the field
Breaking his back behind the plow
Her mother is in the kitchen
Cooking the evening meal
That is how life is in this country

See the child crying
Barefoot in the street
Her father is in the factory
Making his ends meet
Her mother pours a vodka
Then relaxes with her drink
That is how life is in this country

See the child crying
Another child took her toy
Her father sits behind his desk
Making corporate gains
Her mother hires a nanny
So she is free to play her games
That is how life is in this country

Lynette Smith-Wiegand
MOMENT'S LENGTH

To George Raymond, who inspires my inner peace, and creativity.

When love does shed its light on thee,
And holds your glance for moment's length

You'll find that sunshine's not for free
That love heeds work and seeded strength

When the sweetest hours pass,
And sour moments mount to naught

You've found that time may turn love crass
That love is not the refuge sought

When inner peace is found in thee
And holds your sight for moment's length

One finds that sunshine can be free
That peace heeds work and seeded strength

Vicki Sobol
THE SHADOW

To making people believe that we can accomplish world peace, if we try hard enough.

We never know where we may be,
We don't even know what's expected
The sudden diverge of tragedy
the end of all life's sanity
no more memories,
no more time.
The shattered fears, unspoken words
the crying tears of those unheard.
The shadow dark and dreary
unwelcome by mostly all
leaving us a mushroom cloud
the end to every call.

Karen D Tate
CHRISTMAS AND BIRTHDAYS

Dedicated to Jason Michael Douglas

Christmas and birthdays
come but once a year.
The gift you've given
comes but once in a lifetime.
The seed that grows
but one bloom unique.
the beauty it has alone.
the time you've spent with me.

When the chains that bind
a heart to sorrow
are thrown off.
Give way to feel of love,
the seconds are fleeting.

The light that remains
burns free through time.

Drene Salmonsen
A MOMENT OF SERENE BEAUTY

This dedication is to my big sister, Darlene Scheidt. Thanks and I LOVE YOU!

Early crisp morning,
fresh gentle breeze.
Dew drops beading in the meadow.

Soft westward sound,
clear brilliant sight.
Perfect moment, perfect
time captured in my eyes.

Francine D Thornton
WORKING WOMEN

To MoM, David and Diane—With Love—You're the Best!

At the crack of Dawn,
We're up with a Yawn,
Ready to meet the Day.
We'd much rather Play,
But we do need the pay,
So it's up and away, for the start of our Day!

With Tedious Tasks,
We think of our Pasts.
When Playing and School seemed so tough.
Work isn't so bad, it just makes us Sad.
Remembering the times we thought were so bad.

Dedicated we are, at least for so far.
With the Calls, the Accounts, the Complaints!

So we Push and we Strive
In Hopes to Survive,
The Ordeal to Achieve and Advance.
For as much as we Try
The Day ends with a Sigh.

And We Pray For The Day
When we're well on our Way
To Retire, To Play, And be Able to Say
I Made It, Today Is The Day!

Lisa Quintanilla
NIGHTFALL

To Sal, whose face I only need to see to inspire my heart.

Nightfall.

A shadow walks
on the water.

The moon sits by the
horizon, watching,
Watching the quiet
covering the world.

A pressure climbs my shoulders
gently reminding
My eyes must close.

A fog of peace
settles
Resting its weary feet
after a hard day's work.

Slumber attempts to envelop me
whispering songs
Of a persistent sandman.

Darkness lurks
and I must
Surrender.

Steve Trimboli

Steve Trimboli
BLOND-GIRL

Her golden blond hair shimmering as if it held light in it, angel of the morning, one special star, I'll love you for ever, window man.

Shrill demented blond girl barks
Her golden hair into being
She rules dawn's kingdom
Her voice a rising chorus
In my dream the child of the school yard
A hundred little secrets
complete the dream.
In the dream there was an
intense visitation of her energy
We left the school and she took me to
a secret place and told me things
She never told anyone
At night the moon became her
beautiful face
I met the spirit of her past
I slept on the beach I saw Satan the
evil one
A fleshy shadow of my secret
mind
I felt her vibes thru my skin
I'm freezing
the dark dream of conquest and
voyage
Into the night a golden satyr
Moving beside me I screamed
Princess of sorrow wilderness
angel
Call me tomorrow

Lisa Cowen (nick name—T D Angel)
LOVE

This poem is dedicated to Scott E. Campbell

When love makes you blue
Then he turns to you
And you see his face
And it makes your heart race
Then you feel his touch
And he wants you so much
You say you want to go slow
And he says I know
He makes you feel so good
Like you thought no one ever could
And when you're together
You want it to last forever
But then again,
Isn't that the way
We all want love to be
Together
Forever

Sulin Horton
FLOWERS

I dedicate this poem to my family

Out in the garden
Their colors flow
The red zinnias stand straight and tall
While purple violets swaying below
It's a wonderful sight

Heather Leigh Bowen
INSPIRED

To anyone who's ever thought of committing suicide—life gets better! Also to Steve, Nancy, and Ray for being there.

Inspired
By the rising sound
Of the nearby river,
He closes his eyes,
Preparing for what he must do

Looking
Down at the black water—
Swirling, dangerous, cold
Beckoning to him as if
It understands his problems.

Lights
Flash bright in his face
As a car rushes by;
Its destination unknown
No one stops or seems to care.

Darkness
Once the car has gone.
He looks again at the river
Fifty feet below him
The water closes over his head—

Death

Lena Gali
ALONE AND . . .

To Gary

It's past mid-night
Listening to the rain
Coming down outside
With silence in my space
There is sound to silence
Believe me . . . I know
It's like a concert with no audience
Conversation is silent thoughts
With yourself
Thoughts that fly by
Thoughts that disappear
Like silence into oblivion
Alone . . .
Listening to the rain
And . . .
The echo of silence
Which comes to an end
When . . .
I fall asleep
With you on my mind

Sheila McCausland
ENDANGERED SPECIES

I would like to dedicate this poem to my three wonderful children, Patience, Joshua and Heather and to Dr. Busch my friend.

I hopped around, in earth and dust
I am a broken winged bird
Look for some shelter, I say to myself
With the love of the Mother bird
Deep in my childish dreaming
I knew you'd find a way
You always sought to protect me
From the scavengers of this day
I see you swoop, fast down on me

Eagle wings, you've opened wide
You saw my life in danger
Having seen the blood in their eyes

Scott D Welch
MY LITTLE BOY

To Ricky Lee Welch
My Little Boy

My beautiful boy now going to sleep,
not making a sound, not even a peep,
He's all curled up upon my chest,
and I say to myself, that this is the best.
He looks so dear all snuggled so small,
his tiny hands, his tiny feet, but will he be tall?
My beautiful boy,
he stretches, he yawns, he rolls his head,
from out of my arms, and into his bed.
I cover him up and I tuck him in,
always to know that this is a win.
My beautiful boy for I love him so,
by telling him this I'm sure he will know.
So sleep tonite in peace and in joy,
for the one I love is my little boy.

Laura May Jassin
TEARS

Dedicated to my Father.

Tears,
The ever flowing River of Tears.
Tears of an anguished soul,
Tears of a tired heart,
Tears of a broken spirit
Adding their share to the rising tide.
Tears of a nation,
Tears of a world.
Tears of a mother,
Tears of a lover
All form this ceaseless stream.
Tears of the past,
Tears of the present,
Tears of the future
Rolling, roaring thru the canyon of ages.
And my selfish little tears,
Shed in a passion of self pity,
Form merely a drop in this vast sea.
And yet this weeping world must cleanse its soul
In this rushing River of Tears.

Geneva Keene
HERO'S GRAVE

For all those who have served the cause of Freedom, whether living or deceased.

A crude, rough cross of wood . . .
A name carved there . . ..
A helmet hung, which shielded once his head . . .
A mound of foreign soil . . .
A mother's son . . .
Heart stilled, who once the cause of freedom led
Through the jungles wild . . .
To him, 'til then, unknown . . .
When Duty called, to save the world God gave . . .
Had lifted high his heart, and marched with Pride . . .
Through all that Hell could be . . .
To this . . . his grave.
It was not he, who chose this final place
To rest, when God would say to him, "Well done."
It was not he, who chose this dying place . . .
When life for him, had only just begun.
His only thought had been for those he loved . . .
His only hope, to keep his country free . . .
That his own son might never have the cause
To shoulder arms, and fight for Liberty.
A crude rough cross, raised after silent TAPS . . .
He lay at rest beneath a far-flung sky . . .
The name to fade, the cross to rot,
The creed he'd lived, to triumph, never die.

Julia Scalcione
PASSIONS

I've grown out of it.
I tire with the weight of monotonous
Useless
Passions.
they sat in my heart
like an iceman's cart
in the Sun.
Melted.
Melted right down and out.
Passions
which ignited in
furious youth, tire with age.
Look to the twilight of existence
Dissipate.
Wait.
Passions
will begin once more,
like a child developing in the womb
Burst forth like a flower in spring and like a cocoon 
begin the cycle once more.
for what good are passions if not to
Perpetuate
Regenerate
the
Passions
which died in the creation of themselves?
no asking why.
as
Passions
Lives,
Passions
will die.

George B Honnen III
WHEN HAPPINESS BECOMES REALITY

To my "Kitten" ;Sara with special love for giving my life special reason to live for another day

One day I met this girl, who truly made me see
That my life has meaning, and what love can really be!
You should know the way she makes me feel when I may be in a bind,
I am so proud she is my life, and the old ones far behind.
We spent some time together, just the two of us, and I knew at that moment,her in my life was a must!
We saw we had these feelings that could not be denied, and now I have the pleasure of her always by my side.
As I look into the future, and the happiness that will be, out of all the men she could have picked, her heart found room for me!
I love to see her smile and that twinkle I see in her eyes
And to think all it takes to bring it on is if she sees me passing by!
Some nights we'll spend together may be chilly or even cold,
But the warmth that comes from our love will keep us 'til we're old.
I know our love has meaning and this I can be sure
For here is how our love got started; unselfish, sweet and pure.

Jean Ann Irvin
AMANDA IS THREE

To my most precious granddaughter, Amanda Irvin

Mommy's having a birthday party just for me!
I'm as excited as I can be . . . I'm gonna be three!
Grama and Pap-Pap came to our house,
And my cake is decorated like Mickey Mouse.
Beth Ann, my best friend, came too
I'm three, and she's only two.
But next Saturday, she will be three
And she has already invited me!
Presents! . . . all wrapped in pretty paper
So much fun,
Showing them to everyone.
They all made a fuss over me
At my party when I was three!

But at Beth Ann's party, all her cousins were there
And her presents were stacked everywhere!
No one made a fuss over me
At Beth Ann's party when she was three.
It wasn't much fun at all for me
To watch Beth Ann squeal with glee
I smiled, and I was good
But I'd just rather go home—yes, I would!

Terri Gebauer
A MOTHER'S FAREWELL

To Sandy—Out of love for Patrick.

I know I must let go, my son.
It's a hard thing for a mother to do.
Everyone tells me it's time to move on;
but I can't imagine life without you.

The Master of all creation,
has beckoned you to the peace of His side;
and for now only He knows the reason,
why a mother's very lifeblood must die.

I know it's not ours to question,
the reason for the purpose He demands;
but there is a certain comfort in knowing,
that God fulfilled your sweet part of His plan.

So I'll turn now to the Virgin;
and share the passion and death of her Son.
I beg for her blessed consolation,
and pray she takes care of my little one.

Only by closing the casket,
will Heaven's gate open wide for you son.
For in dying to this world of sorrow,
a new and glorious life has begun.

Vickie L Kelley
WEEKEND DADDY

To my family who inspired me to write I love you all!

My daddy is very special,
He's my best friend.
He gives me lots of presents,
But only on weekends.

My daddy takes me places,
and lets me play in the park.
We spend the whole day together,
and makes sure I'm home by dark.

My daddy calls me on the phone,
to see if I'm doing alright.
He says he's sorry it happened,
that he and mama had a fight.

My daddy says these things happen,
and it's hard for us all.
But if I ever need to talk,
all I have to do is call.

My daddy loves me a lot,
this much I really know.
But when he brings me home,
I wish he didn't have to go.

Janorah Bowen
GOD'S CREATION

I dedicate this poem to all of my children

When God created this lonely world
He made it safe and sound
Then he created Adam
From the dry dust of the ground.

Then he took a look at what he'd done
And seen that it was good
Then he created a woman
For Adam's likely hood.

If he had known how it would be
Would he do it all again
For this old world ain't good no more
It's too full of hate and sin.

I know there's sadness in his heart
To see his creation's scorned
He'll tear it all back down someday
When Gabriel blows his horn.

Jay Graves
FRESH AIR

In memory of Marlene M. Graves for all her love and support and with all the kindness only a mother could share.

I look at the joy
I see in the fun
Oh isn't it wonderful
To be in the sun

The warmth of the beach
The rise of the moon
Oh isn't wonderful
To be a balloon

I fill a crowd
I hold them tight
Oh look at us now
We're off on a flight

The end of the hour
Shadows do fall
Oh what a day
To feel so tall

Patricia Anne Balliett
MY DADDY

Dedicated with all my love to my daughter Kylin.

You my daddy made me,
And yet you just don't care.
In the years to come I'll ask you
Daddy, why weren't you there?

I am your little daughter
You are my only dad
How can you ignore me?
Am I really that bad?

Not a visit or a call,
Or even a lousy card
I want to understand why
I'm trying very hard

Do you hate me Daddy?
Do you wish I was dead?
I bet you would love me,
If I was a boy instead.

So here's from your daughter,
Only for you my dad
You'll never really know
Just what you could have had

Antonia Katherine Green

Antonia Katherine Green
TOGETHER

For Chuck, my husband, my lover, my friend.

What moves a woman to survive
What stirs a woman in her mind
What makes a woman laugh more than cry
A gentle man by her side.

What angers a woman to unknown sights
What frightens a woman to limitless heights
What makes a woman laugh more than cry
A loving man by her side.

What releases a woman to any paths
What pushes a woman beyond unopened doors
What makes a woman grow and grow
A loving, gentle man that only I know.

Patti Mcdaniel
FORGIVE ME LORD FOR ASKING FOR THINGS THAT I DON'T NEED

Forgive me Lord, for asking for things that I don't need
For thinking only of myself and showing selfish greed
I have a home to call my own, warm clothes and food to eat
A shelter from the raging storm and shoes to warm my feet
A cupboard filled on every shelf with food I keep in store
Lacy curtains on my windows and carpet on the floor
A bed with fluffy pillows where I sleep every night
A lock and key to keep me safe and doors that close airtight
And yet I dare to ask for things that I do not deserve
Forgive me Lord, ungratefulness of showing so much nerve
So as I close this prayer to you I ask nothing more today
Than to share my wealth with someone else and be a blessing in some way.

Sandra Compton
SILENT EYES

To my Illusion,
To my Reality,
And as always—To my Muse

You look at me through silent eyes,
As if you see more than reply.
And all your questions find answers there,
Beneath the silence of your stare.

You strip my soul, unmask my face,
Leave no fingerprints to trace.
You need not touch for intimacy,
My thoughts a mere transparency.

But do be careful when looking deep,
For there is where the creatures creep.
Beneath the heart where all truth lies,
Hidden, protected, from silent eyes.

April Prewitt
OCEAN

I hear the waves come crashin' in,
It is night and the moon is dim,
As I look up to the big yellow circle,
I think of that day trying to snorkel,
It leads a pathway through the calm sea,
And on my balcony the sea looks to me,
With its deep, dark, blue eyes,
It calls out to me and cries,
Please stay for a while it says,
My tide has come, in a shade of red,
That was last night and now I'm home,
And I feel as if I'm all alone,
I promised to go back and visit again,
And enjoy the moon, the need of a friend, and
the loneliness of the ocean.

Terry E Wade
LITTLE BOY BLUE

Little Boy Blue
is Honking His Horn,
Hoping that He
Might Have Scorn,
Following them Close
From aways Behind,
Trying to Think
Which one is Mine,
Catches them Now
At the Light,
Wondering to Himself; Why!
He's Lost his Sight,
So He's Honking His Horn
Saying, "Get out of the Way!"
Telling Himself
This "Just Ain't My Day!"

Terie Jensen
STILL FRIENDS

I knew it wouldn't last forever,
But at least we were once together;
We gave it our best,
Until every last caress;
I loved you in every way possible,
But no matter how hard we tried;
our love was just impossible,
The memory of us together;
I will cherish in my heart forever,
I hope that you will remember me;
Just like I will remember you,
Even if things are at an end;
I'm glad that we're still friends.

Wesley J Callihan
ON A GREAT LIBRARY

This is a forest, ever green;
A wood no killing frost can bare;
These leaves may fade, but in between
The life is there.

This is a graveyard, but instead
Of death, it's life to seeing eyes;
When hands unclose these tombs, the dead
In glory rise.

This is a journey; from this door
Lead many roads with many inns;
Each yields, in measure, joy before
The next begins.

This is the city that will last
Until the time when time is gone;
No bodies die until they've passed
Their own seed on.

This is a light, a gift of Love
Who bids us learn, that we may see,
Until there dawns the clear light of
Eternity.

Greg R Bullard Jr
UNICORNS

Dedicated to my wife Deanne M Bullard, and to those who believe in the magical myths of the UNICORNS.

Thou aren't just of body and soul,
But of the heart and mind as well.
Therefore, those who have an open mind
Thus do believe in the unicorn.
It is believed to be the most magical and mystical creature
That ever lived and is the symbol of the one thing
In life that shall never die or fade away . . .

"LOVE"

Alicia Gregerson
MY COCOON

I feel like a butterfly,
Inside my own cocoon.
Sometimes it's thought by me that I'd,
Be happier on the moon.

When the world's around me,
I feel confused and lost.
I'm afraid to be myself, you see,
I'm afraid to give my trust.

So only my good friends,
Have seen the real side.
They know to what extents,
I will go to hide.

I want to break from my cocoon.
And spread my wings and fly;
But the narrowness,
Of the populace,
Has caused me to be shy,.

Mrs Winnifred A Cleaves
ENJOYING THE HUNT

The leaves flutter by,
As we wonder why;
Do the seasons have to change?
Just like feelings of the heart,
Over the years, we've drifted apart.
Now that we've grown older,
And getting used to being bolder;
We say to each other,
"What's happening brother?"
As we walk along the woods.
We'd probably go back if we could,
To our younger days;
Fun, summer and the sun's rays,
Instead we watch our children play.
The women just don't understand,
What it's like to be a man;
They wonder why without reason,
We can't pass up on the hunting season.
Just the walk itself,
Seems like such a help;
To clear the mind,
Of all the jungle it entwines.

Stephanie Kittredge Block
WHITTLING

The dollmaker whittles
Her parings falling around
Like flakes of snow.
They will melt.

She shades off the bad wood
Scraping, making smaller
The little doll.

Look, the dollmaker says
Proudly, the rasping and
Scorning and blunting
Have molded this little doll.

Pleased with herself
She points at her suffering
Settled daughter.

I have made her into the woman
She is today, she says, smiling.

April Bowden
SILENT TEARS

She is crying you can see it
In her eyes; not aloud, but silent tears
Fall.

She is too proud to cry
She hides the terror and madness
Inside.
But now she sheds
A single tear that releases
Her fear, anger, and madness.

Never again
Will her guard fall
To stoop to a helpless mortal.

She never lets her emotions show.
She always has a smile,
Filled with every emotion.

Ruth Simons Ensor
HOW PRECIOUS

Oh how precious is my Jesus.
He will be your Jesus too,
If you'll only seek and trust him
As he kindly bids you do.

He's the answer to all problems.
He takes care of every need.
For our sins he begged our pardon
And upon the cross did bleed.

When he arose that blessed morning,
He fulfilled his promise true.
Opened up the way for sinners,
Sinners just like me and you.

So that we could be forgiven
Of our sins along the way,
If we love, obey and trust him,
Ask his mercy when we pray.

Listen! At your door he knocketh.
Let him in, this friend so true.
He has long since been my Jesus
Let him be your Jesus too.

Joanne Dalton
THE FACE

This poem is dedicated to my parents, my sister, and everyone else who has touched my life.

With the mountain being considered my eyes
I have seen the world which spreads so wide,
For in the distance there is another land which
is better than called by man's.

My lips are the oceans which seem so wide
For they will kiss you till the earth's divide,
As the raindew fell onto my lips,
All I do is quench my thirst and sip.

With my world which seems to be peaceful looking
below, I really can see the corrupt of which we know.
For it'll change in a matter of time,
For the Lord has shown just where to hide.

With the face of a mountain which is smiling on you
Will tell you then for I've guided you
To a place on my eternal grave,
I'll not only rest, I'll be saved.

Curt Smith
ACCOUNT FOR THIS AND ACCOUNT FOR THAT

For my dear sister, LuAnn

Account for this and account for that
We know you've got what it takes
Straighten out those files LuAnn
And clean-up others' mistakes

We're proud of you
You saw it through
And went for your degree
You've graduated to a better way of life
To be all that you can be

Yes now you know
Just what to do
To clean-up paperwork disasters
But you won't stop there
Cuz you really care
And now you want your Masters

We wish you all success
LuAnn you know you are our honey

And by the way
When you make your fortune
Would you loan your big brother some money?!

Tom Romano
HOW TO FILL AN EMPTY HEART?
As I sit here in the quiet of my room—thinking of you
Remembering times past—knowing the present
Feeling only emptiness—hoping for a future.

Remembering your smile and mine in return.
Playing at a game—flirting with you.
A game of sorts—until knowing you.

Then I knew—the wonder of your smile
Your sensuous eyes, dancing with life.
Of laughter, joy and love.
A quiet love, unknown until you were gone.
Sharing a moment in time.

Of memories of seeing myself in your eyes,
As the lights of the life danced by.
Of Holding your face in my hands—
Sharing a gentle kiss.
The simple joy a rose could bring.
Unaware of time passing by.

Yet it's all a riddle—questioning WHY?
Thinking of words said and not—
actions and reactions.
As time passes by.

Know in the emptiness of my heart I wonder—WHY?
Why have you lost the life in your eyes?
Where has the joy and laughter gone?
Was it just a game and we're the losers?
Again I question—WHY?
As the clock ticks and time passes by.

Trying to find fault within myself—I asked was it I?
Only to hear you say; "It wasn't—
Trust me—It's better this way";
As I try to understand your meaning and WHY?
And the clock ticks at time.

Oh the riddles of my life; are they without meaning?
If you answered—It wasn't I, as I tried to bear the fault.
Then could it be—
If it wasn't I, then was it you who stopped the time for our hearts?

Was there love and caring?
Did I finally touch someone's heart?
Only to find that because of time—
we must part.

Or is the riddle deep within my soul—a simple question;
How do you fill an empty heart?
And the answer echoed throughout the stillness of the night;
By the tick of the clock—One stolen moment at a time.

Monica E Cummings
GROWING UP

Take Heed Like My Mom Did.

When you were young
Color didn't mean much,
Except the green of the grass
And the blue of the sky
And living together was Child's play.

But now you've grown
And all you've known
Is that the grass is brown
And the sky is gray
And living together is all work and NO play.

Kevin Michael Merlo
YOUR BONES AND MUSCLES
Your bones and muscles work together
To do a job that makes your body better.

If you want to connect a muscle to a bone
You need a tendon that doesn't work alone.

The bone marrow is the marrow of the bone
Which produces the cells and keeps them grown.

Cartilage is on your chest
To protect your bones and let them stretch.

Your skull and brain work together
To do a job that helps you to remember.

If you exercise day by day
Your healthy body is here to stay.

Wanda G Yancy
I WONDER WHY!

This poem is dedicated to Fate, the love of my life, and the inspiration of my poem.

I wonder why,
When you are gone,
I'm really sad, and all alone.

I wonder why,
I feel so great
When we're together, or on a date.

I often wonder,
What I would do
If you should leave me, or say we're through.

I know for sure,
that I would cry,
Hurt myself and wish to die.

For my heart would stop,
And I would freeze,
because there would be no one, for me to please.

So now I know, the reason why
I feel this way, about this guy.
He's all my hope, and all my dreams.
He's all my life could ever mean.

Carla M Wallizer
LOVE

Thanks to Charles W. Peters who made this poem possible. Who gave me the help and support I needed. He encouraged me to write. I owe it all to him.

I'm looking for love
in all the wrong places.
Maybe someday I'll be able to look above
and go in search for new faces.
I enjoy hot summer nights with music
and the lights down low.
In winter I like to stay in bed
and listen to the wind blow.
When making love the best time of all
is under a big shade tree in the fall.
Love can be kind.
Love can be blind.
Love is a game that we all play
and we will all find true love someday.
But, if that day never comes
will there still be someone there to love.
To hold at night and keep them warm.
To share the love as never before
To look in their eyes and see their dreams
and feel their thoughts, emotions, and pain
It's all in the world and it's all just a game,
and yet there has to be another way.
Why look for something you will never find.
Take what you got and make it last
through time.
For not all love is kind and there's
still the odds of you being blind.

Angela M Hargis
LOVE'S FATE

To Mark Lewandowski, In thinking of past moments shared. Love always, Ang

Our love seems so true
It will never die
But I have a clue
And it makes me wanna cry
Cuz it makes me feel blue
I love you . . . I cannot tell a lie
I love you . . . Yes, I do!

But we're not stuck like glue
Romeo and Juliet we are not.
Neither do we go together like a
hammer and a nail.
But our love is so hot,
It's though it will never fail.

So let's just give love a chance,
Maybe our lives it can enhance.
Awhile we shall wait, till our love
has its fate.

Donna Powers-Maska
PASSAGE
And pausing briefly they turned
heads cocked slightly, raising upface,
hands inert, three full, one empty.

What was that?
Did you hear?
Nothing.
The whispering of the wind.

And granting nought they turned
bending again to the task of living,
backs bowed
hands in earth
three full
one empty.

Pedro A Reyes

Pedro A Reyes
CALIDOSCOPIO

Para mi madre.

Jovén de campo, donde el aire es limpio y puro.
Corriendo alegre vas por los prados.
Tu sedosa cabellera copiosa,
alborotada por el viento.
La brisa acaricia tu agraciada cara angelical.
Por fin, jovial llegas hasta mi umbral.

Por bonita, me embriaga tu sonrisa
alegre e inocente.
Valiosa perla del Oriente.
Por hermosos, me intrigan tus
grandes ojos almendrados.
Tu fragancia de frescos nardos.

Por lindos me intoxican tus labios do color coral.

Tu canto alegre es musical.
Por bella, me facina tu clara y tersa piel.
Dulces besos savor a miel.
Tu lento y ridmíco caminar.
Me estremese al pasar.

Kandy Shane LeFebvre
ONE WITH THE SEA

I love the sea on an Autumn day
When the wind blows through my hair
And the brown sand beneath me
Warms my feet that are bare

I know the call of the sea gulls
And the power of the running tide
That gives me strength within
And lets the fear in my soul hide

I'm one with the sea on a misty day
When the air dampens my skin
And the solemn tears that roll down my face
Mingle with the rain and wind

I can feel the waves break into swells
Of soft caressing foams
And thunder against the high cliff
The cliff that stands alone

As I walk I feel content
To let the sea release anger for me
For the sunset I'll wait, patient
Near this euphoria of the sea

Marsie Silvestro
US IN THE AIR

Seat 15 A.
I'm flying away
with your love.
Five and a half years of
traffic controlling emotions
to land safely too many times,
now leaves us on
two different runways.
Fasten your seat belts!
(who ever really knows
what kind of ride it will be?)
I prepare for take-off.
Solo-flight
was Amelia's dream
Mine,
flying united.

LaWanda A Bowie
UNTITLED

To my loving mother, Eddie Mae Bowie, without whose help, this would not have been possible. Thank you.

I am here, yet I'm not
I remember, but I forgot
There is truth, and all there is are lies
We show our feelings, yet we keep them inside

Where there is law, there is no justice
Where there is justice, there are no laws
When there are dreams, there is no tomorrow
Where there is wrong, there are no flaws

Where there's a sun, there's no light
Where there's a moon, the sun shines bright
Where there's a boy, then there's a girl
And where there's hope, then there's a world

Where there's liberty, there must be death
Where it's raining, it must be wet
Where it shines, it must be dry
And where there's courage, it's do or die.

Where there's a will, then there's a way
Where there was love, there's hate today
Where there was joy, it followed sorrow
And where there's hope, there's a better tomorrow.

Pepe M ROUBAIX
NAMES AND THEIR ORIGINATION

Since early history, a name was given as soon as a child was born,
A name, with a special meaning of, and for, each of whom it was worn,
Later in history, a surname or ekename was added, meaning known by another name,
It helped to further place and identify, and know from where a person came.

In early times, a given name held a meaning all its own,
But . . . today, a given name is a family choice, regardless of meaning shown,
And alas . . . the day has come, when a number will be included too,
A personal number, number, nobody else should have, giving a positive identity clue.

Yes, names too will take on a progressively and meaningful numbered look,
While joining the many advancements in the chapters of life's daily book,
A Social Security Number, is now included after five years of age,
POSSIBLY . . . a number will be given to each NEWBORN CHILD, adding still another page,

As we progress throughout our lives, the changes are apparently needed,
Not always do we desire that fact . . . but reality asks that they be heeded,
Therefore, promise yourself to live each day, knowing you CAN be a happy spirit on earth,
Strive to make YOUR living goal, one of great friendships, success, joy, and proof of life's great worth.

Chrystal Antionette Lucas
HOPE OF A SLAVE CHILD

Worl' gon' git ugly sometime, turn 'roun, git mean on ya!
Life ain't what I'd thought it'd be.
Times too hard—too ugly sometime.
On a cloudy day, my mind git dark.
Th' only hope I got is the sun.
But it begin beatin' down.
While makin' me drag
—my tag 'round.
git tired of bailin', hailin',
Somethin' . . . someone . . .
—that ain't gon' help me be . . .
"Th' sun ain't always gon' be bright," momma said.
I look farth'r and farth'r to th' time
—fo freedom come.
Then I stop . . . thinkin': Worl' gon' always be ugly sometime.

Sunlight, always gon' be heavy sometime.
Why that is? Ansa me not? Won't change notthin'
Won't change massa; won't make time go fasta'.
I read a verse I may, so I don't burst today. Only make th' worl' go roun'!
Then . . . turn ugly . . . to put me down . . .

James D Vibbert
MY DAUGHTER

In Loving Memory of Mary June Vibbert

Like a ray of sunshine
Like a gift of love
You were sent to my heart
By God up above

You were sent to me
For just a few years
To cherish and hold
Through the pain and the tears

Though I had you to love
For just a short time
My life was complete
Because you were mine

My life was blessed
Because of you
With your gentle ways
And your love so true

Though the Angels have come
And taken you away
To a far better place
To forever stay

God has called you home
From this world you must part
But the love you gave
Will remain in this father's heart.

Ginger Chapman
A FATHER

A father is someone you can look up to,
He helps you find your given talent,
And then supports you in anything
You choose to do with your life.

A father is someone who understands
And listens to what you have to say.
He is the backbone of the family,
Working hard for a living.

A father tries to keep things going smoothly,
He is a companion and friend
Who helps with any family matter
And gives strength wherever he sees weakness.

Joyce Harmon Thomas

Joyce Harmon Thomas
LET IT BE GOD!

Dedicated to my co-laborers of the Gospel of Christ.

When I reach out and touch
Let it be the hand touch of God
When I lay hands on the sick
Let it be the healing hand of Jesus
When I stand up to speak
Jesus is speaking through me
When I kneel down to pray
Lord you lead the prayer
Let each prophecy come from you Lord
When I open my mouth to prophesy
When a revelation comes forth
Lord let it be you revealing
When I speak of mysteries Lord
Please let them come from your throne of grace
Let it be you Lord, let it be you, let it be you
Lord you do it , Lord you do it, Lord you do it.
Let it be God, Let it be God, Let it be God.
When I exalt, Lord
Let it be your words of exaltation
Let it be you Lord, let it be you, let it be you
Only you, Jesus only you, only you.

Dreama Claybaugh
A LOVER'S GOODBYE

For my loving husband, John.

Victim—
To a lover's touch,
One who meant so very much.
Surrender to the morning's call
Wondering if you believe it all.

Feel the aching deep in your heart
Knowing, now, you two must part.
Then, with a touch of sorrow the night must end,
And, with the new day's light we'll begin again

Emily Rogers
AN URGENT MESSAGE— 1 JOHN 2:26

All Praise, Glory, and Thanks to Almighty God, our Heavenly Father; His Beloved Son, Jesus Christ, Savior of the world, and the Holy Ghost whose Spirit is being poured out on all Christians. Joel 2:28-9.

It seems that the New Age Movement was spawned in the pits of hell.
The work of the anti-christ with the devil as well. 1 John 2:22 & 4:3
The power of God's Holy spirit of Love and Peace is becoming so great
Overcoming negatives all over the world of diseases, wars and hate.

The New Age Movement is not new, but a blend of old humanistic thoughts
Of eastern religions and occult ideas as the Garden of Eden wrought.
Lest that sounds benign and harmless, there are recurring themes that be
Highlighting the stark contrast between New Age Movement and Christianity.

1. Self love takes precedence over everything else.
2. Jesus Christ is not the Christ, nor is He God. We can all be christs.
3. There is no personal God, only a force of universal consciousness.
4. The Holy Bible is flawed—there are many bibles to follow.
5. You are your own god: we are all gods.
6. Life is eternal without salvation: no judgment, since we are gods.
7. Sin and evil are only illusions.

The Face of Christ appeared to me in clouds in the sky. Mat. 26:64
That's why I am duty-bound to witness for my Lord with a loud cry.

Act 26:16
Christ is alive! He still performs miracles! The Good News real! John 3:16
God's Holy Spirit is free for the asking to Christians with a service zeal.

Our Lord and Savior, Jesus Christ, said "I am the Way, the Truth, and the Life, no man cometh to the Father, but by Me." John 14:6

Chris Gayden
A I D S FOUR—FOUR LETTERS TO DEATH

This is dedicated to all of the AIDS victims, who feel that God has abandoned them. He has not. Never give up on God, because he will never give up on you.

When you are told that you have
A I D S,
your whole life begins to fade.
You wonder how this could have happened to you;
positively no way for you to accept the truth.

You feel a false sense of deception;
but only you're the blame for having such misconceptions;
About this terrible, but deadly disease,
that has now put your life under siege.

Each breath is harder for you to take;
and each body movement,
harder for you to make.
Your body is thin and your face is pale;
and you feel as if you've died and gone to hell.

Your mom still loves you, that is for sure.
She still believes that God will provide a cure.
From feeding you, to cleaning and ironing your shirts,
she does well of hiding the pain and hurt.

Because of your overwhelming feelings of hate,
your pastor was there to help renew your faith.
He tells you that God still loves you and cares;
and your pain and suffering, he also shares.

Marsha Reid
ASPIRINS AND ORANGES
Aspirins and oranges, will these days ever end?
Aspirins and oranges, oh how long has it been
Since she slept eight full hours, or ate balanced meals,
Or simply had someone to tell how she feels?

She believed once in the reality of white picket fences,
And happily e'er after, but now her defenses
Keep saying that her dreams are myths so elusive;
Confused and exhausted, she wonders what truth is.

With the child support late, and school clothes a must,
When a second job beckons, what she must do, she does;
Working late hours, thoughts on children at home,
Her tears slowly fall, and she feels so alone.
But from somewhere within, an unknown strength comes to light,
And a deep-seated belief that tomorrow will turn bright;
So with aspirins for her headache, and an orange for dinner,
She thankfully goes home, chin up, and a winner.

Joan Braverman
A SUNSET SONNET
A sunset sonnet
Wearing the sky's scarlet bonnet.
Flying streamers of hot pink and golden mauve,
Over the bay they dove and dove.
A fuchsia blush to the right,
An aqua ray for a lovely light.
What a magnificent colorful sight!
Deepening, deepening into the night.
A bright red Sally Lightfoot Crab
And claws reach high for the sky to nab.
Dazzling setting sun,
Dizzy delight—prism of fun.
Life's sunset magic
Painting over all that's tragic.

Carolyn Ann Rodgers
SON

To Chris and Daniel, my sons.

Sweet pain, loving memories
My they grow so fast
Time so swiftly fleeing
Childhood never last
Stay small a little longer
Please don't go so soon
My baby one day, the next
A man reaching for some room
Sweet pain, loving memories
With which I have truly been blessed
Grow up my son, to be a man
For you've made my life the best.

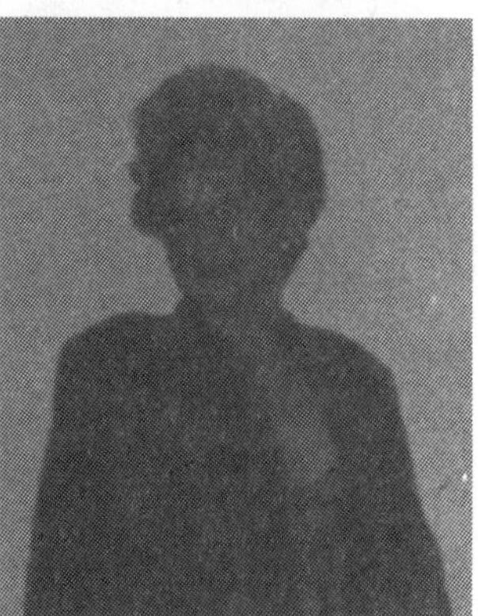

Matilde Aguiar

Matilde Aguiar
EL VATE

This poem is dedicated to the "prócer Don Luis Muñoz Marin" from Puerto Rico.

Oh, Prócer puertorriqueño,
Tú, de patriotas modelo,
que creó con gran desvelo
aquel famoso estribillo,
que resuena en los oidos
y es lema de tu partido.

PAN, que no faltará,
TIERRA, que se cultiva,
¡LIBERTAD, de un pueblo libre!

Labrador de pueblo pobre,
que tus semillas dejaste
por los campos y caminos
cuando por ellos pasaste.

Un pueblo que te recuerda
por tus obras y tus frases,
llevándote en la memoria
¡por el fruto que legaste!

Pensador de pueblo chico,
Cuna donde te arrullaste,
Barranquitas, te recuerda
y nunca podrá olvidarte.

Defensor de los humildes
que so hogar to visitaste,
Y en sus paredes aún cuelgan
¡el retrato con tu imagen!

Muñoz Marin, la eminencia
que más años gobernaste
y le diste a Puerto Rico,
tu honor, tu vida y tu sangre.
Nunca, pensó nuestro pueblo
¡que llegaras a ausentarte!

Michelle A Sutton
ICE CASTLES
You've spent your time
building ice castles around your heart,
to keep love out.
**
Love came by with a lit match.

Your castle melted one drop
and snuffed out the match.
**
Love came by with a torch
to see if you were inside.

Your castle melted a bucketful
and splashed out the torch.

Love brought branches and twigs,
piled them high around your castle,
and started a bonfire.

Your castle melted enough to rain out
the bonfire.
**
If you don't watch out you may win.

Deanne Catanese Aleman
A SIGN OF LOVE

Dedicated to my parents for their love and support and to my husband and sons because I love them; and to my sister and her family because I love them, too. They are my "Sign of Love" from God.

The new fallen snow upon the ground;
A heavy, white blanket spread around;
The smell of cinnamon in the air;
These are the memories that we share.

The new leaves on the limbs of trees;
The cool, crisp, springtime breeze;
The smell of flowers in the air;
These are the memories that we share.

The warm summer breezes drifting by;
The flitting of a butterfly;
The scent of jasmine in the air;
These are the memories that we share.

The autumn leaves—orange, red and green;
All part of a beautiful scene;
The smell of burning leaves in the air;
These are the memories that we share.

These four seasons are in a year;
Cherished moments we holds so dear;
God gave them to us from above,
A true sign of His great love.

Florence L Beers
DEAR MOM; WITH LOVE

In memory of our mother, a very caring and loving person, who we miss very much. Bessie L. Gregory

We are sending you this little book, as a token of our love and affection. I hope you have no objection. I know how you are, when it comes to sentimental things, even as small as this.

I know we never told you often enough, how much we loved you. You took time to teach us right from wrong, to listen and share with others, to respect all people and things. But most of all
Mom, you taught us love.

As the wild flowers will always bloom in the spring, and the harvest moon will be full in the fall, we will always love and remember how we grew with your love and understanding and somehow your patience.

Yes Mom, you can fill this book with memories of long ago or just to remember. You see Mom, the wild flowers will always bloom, and the harvest moon will always shine.

Asia Torrence
THE WALL BETWEEN THE HEART
A mind so full of thought,
That it forgets the heart that longs,
It wonders where the storm began,
And when the dark clouds covered the sun.
It forgets the scent of spring,
And the flowers that laced the garden,
But, however, it does remember the brick wall
That it put up to block out the Blue Bird song
That the verses of promise carried to the ear.
It separates the heart
From the ever wondering thoughts
That the mind stores well.
Leaving out the magic,
And bringing down the dawn ,
Leaving a love that could have spread throughout the body
With no way past the wall.
Still a heart that longs,
At a dead end stop.

Puella Rontos
THE CITY

To Mom, Dad, Peter, E.J., and Erica F.

Smelling the stink, from one place it comes
The cars following the freeway from work
smelling the stink
The shoppers coming out of stores

smelling the stink
The dog on the crosswalk, stopping
smelling the stink
The policeman waving traffic, standing
smelling the stink
The wino waking up, suddenly
smelling the stink
The baglady rummaging in cans, ignoring
smelling the stink
The little girl cowering in an alley, alone
smelling the stink
Everyone gets hit by it, the smell of the city
Going on with different life—
Smelling the life within the city.

Anthony M Santiago
SMILES

I could never see what was behind your eyes.
You put up a shield whenever I would try.
How could I know, how could I feel?
What you really meant,
All I saw were smiles.

I know that people are always changing.
I could never see just where you were going.
How could I know, how could I see
How you really felt,
All I saw were smiles.

We traveled down the road through many stages.
We laughed, we cried,
We fought and tried to get by.
And all along,
I never heard beyond your laugh.

Pearlina Mills
THE GIFT

TO MY SON AND BROTHER ...... PHILLIP Sr. and Jr.

How dare you speak to me
Of civil disobedience
Pretending that all is well
Hiding the pain in your
Manly strides
Returning from the market place
With a gut choice my mind cannot make.

I wandered into a garden
Of parental folly
Watering the roses with my tears
Tirelessly, I slaved to create a pyramid
Betrayed by the hand my labor
Fed.

Our son to the swordslayer
I cannot give
The task master's fear of uprisings
Is the joke of the century!

An idea shines through
The dark hallways of my soul
Dazzling against the sun's rays
On the source of life ...... THE NILES

Sandra Cunningham Billieu
SENSUAL

I see plainly, you and me,
Calmly swimming in the sea;
Satin slick, the water feels,
We're gliding by like playful seals.

Gently laying on our backs stroking,
Slowly first, and then poking;
Pulling waves of water through,
Encircling sheets of velvet dew.

So enchanted we become,
We watch not where we started from;
On and on we swim forever,
Looking back, well, maybe never!

Something that's so plain and simple,
Should be praised like in a temple;
Pleasures like this, it should be known,
Make our senses sharper hone.

Next time when swimming, you really must,
Lie back in wonder, full of trust;
Clear your mind, experience and respond,
Connect as if, we all are one!

Amber Hendrix
WHEN YOU'RE NOT REAL

When you're not real you lay there quiet and still. Forever never going to move and if you're not loved you feel no sadness or pain. When you're not real the hope and love never fill your heart just loneliness and tears is all the emotion you feel. Tattered and torn you wish you were never born. Sad and lonely no one to hold you just your heartache to give you warmth. Shut up in a musty closet you see no light at all. Just loneliness and darkness is all you see and nobody cradles you nobody loves you. Then you suddenly realize the hope and love that comes from being real. When you're not real that hope and love disappear with one quick swipe of hate and tears it all disappears.

Mary Emery-Imbelloni

Mary Emery-Imbelloni
SCHOOL COLORS

Dedicated to the Class of '69, Fort Vancouver High School, Vancouver, Washington

Red is for the cheerleader's busy pom-pom.
Red is for the blood shed in Vietnam.

White is a color in the flag we fly.
Why did our soldiers have to die?

Red is the color of a prom night rose.
Red is the color of a hooker's hose.

White is for a virgin, bridal beauty.
White is the paper of her divorce decree.

Red are the jerseys of the home team at play.
Red's for a gang that fights in L.A.

White is our little house in the lane.
White is the color of our kid's cocaine.

Red is the color of a Christmas bell.
Red is an addict's living hell.

White is a soaring gull that flies.
White is a coffin, when a child dies.

Red's always red and white's always white.
Sometimes the colors don't come out right.

I will end my lines this way
On this, our twentieth reunion day.

May all your reds be rosy bright
And may all your whites mean truth and light.

Jenine Johnson
MY HEART ACHES

Dedicated to Craig Warmouth. Though we are miles apart, our memories bring us closer together. Thanks for being a great friend. I love you!

I reach out to touch you
yet the miles are absurd.
I call out for you
only an echo is heard.
The days are gray,
because the sun is gone.
The nights are chilly
and life seems wrong.
I miss the security
your presence brought.
Your sense of humor
brings a warming thought.
You made me feel wanted
no longer alone.
A person with meaning
someone I've known.
I admire your tenderness
you made my eyes shine.
Your face full of smiles
time after time.
The next time we meet
in silence and tears,
I'll embrace the one
I've loved through the years.

Annette L George
OH LONELY POET

This poem is dedicated to my family and best friend Janice. Also, in memory of Juris Gailitis, who gave me the chance.

Oh lonely poet,
Why is it so?
The words that you write
are so spoken
in truth that not
only life seems glorious,
but the sad times, too.

Oh lonely poet,
All hidden away
deep in the forest
where people are not astray
but where roam animals of
nature of your poems are written.
Life and nature are a poet's inhibition.

Sherri A Simone
OUT OF ME

For my Father, Richard P. Kaloostian, who has given me the world. I love you. Sher

Although it is often dark and timeless, I have learned to deceive these thoughts. They are simply, trivial.
I have watched, from this place, much of life pass over me. There is so much to tell. And the regrets of past events can become endless.

I try to envision that I am near the ocean's touch. That way, I can believe the tide will come and dispel my body into the waves; At least they are alive and vigorous.

Without my body, I am a spirit and a soul. Without a connection to the living world as others know it. I am afraid and ashamed for the state of mind that I have acquired.
In my remembrance of life above me, I can settle small debates with my selfconscience. Able only to fantasize that some of the decisions I made in the past will resolve if I think about changing them long enough.
The tears that leak from my mind, pour from my soul. But I have no way of letting the people I have loved imagine this weeping. They will have to remember me for what I portrayed to them; And they will judge me.
As I had once judged all of them.

Out of me, has gone the hope.
Inside, I am left with all that death has taught me.
From beneath life, one can discover many more reasons to live; and only pray that it is known above them.

Ms Teresia Harper
HAPPINESS

Giving honor to God from whom all blessings flow. To my Mom and Dad. To my friends and loved ones. Thank you for believing in me.

Happiness is a shooting star blazing across the universe
A brilliant stream of glory stunning the eye of the beholder

Visionary pleasure that both frightens and draws one deeper into its glow
Happiness is the equivalent of a shooting star
Brilliant, breathtaking and gone in fleeting seconds
Savored and remembered for its beauty.

Rose Graham
NEW YEAR VERSUS OLD YEAR!

Oh! what will we do in the New Year?
Live in the same old way,
That we have in the old year
Twenty-four hours a day?

Fighting among the nations,
Fighting for greed and fame,
Each trying to outdo the others
In Life's Big Game!

Little time for the Saviour
Who gives us the breath we breathe,
Little time for the house of God
And time upon our knees!

Help us in the New Year dear Jesus,
This is our humble prayer,
To look around for those in need
And show them that we care!

Help us to do the little things
That Thou would have us do.
Now please, dear Lord above,
In '89,—Give us peace—and love!

James Clark Eaton
WHO, WHAT, WHY, AND WHERE?

For my three lovely daughter, Pamela, Stephanie, and Rhiannon.

In talking to oneself,
As I myself know,
One sees what one wants to see,
And hears what one would.
Because, it's harder, you see,
To see what you would not,
And hear what you should,

As one looks, inside oneself.
To know what one wants,
And to know what one needs,
Wherein is our seed,
As it grows!
For we all know we're someone,
But who we are,
We're not sure.
Who, what, why, and Where
Am I?
And who, what, why, and where
Are you?
And when
Will it be we?

Laura Caputo
PRECIOUS PAIN
I live every day in hope,
Waiting for you to notice me,
Again.
I look for even the slightest reward,
But still I am blinded,
By what used to be.
I try to break away,
To understand.
But each day brings more confusion.
When I reach a decision,
You change,
A new and different problem evolves.
Why?
I ask myself,
Do I still feel this way?
Why?
Do I suffer such Precious Pain?

Vickie Crosby
FOREST FINALE

In memory of my Father and Mother. He set an example of hard work, and she always believed in me.

See the Sunset
Nestled amongst the trees,
its brilliant colors vibrating
and dancing on every leaf
Slowly ebbing away
into shadowy dimness,
then enveloped in complete darkness

with only the sounds
of unseen things
settling down for a night's slumber.
Ready to awaken
come morning's light,
to start afresh on a new day.
Until once again the
curtain comes down.

Nancy J Davis
OUR SAVIOR LIVES: AN EASTER POEM
He had to walk the road alone that day to Dark Calvary. Though beaten and cast down, He struggled along. He knew there was no other way peace and contentment could come our way. Unless He suffered and died to take away man's foolish pride.

People thought it was an Earthly Kingdom at the time Jesus walked. They couldn't understand this Kingdom would come into their Hearts. Judgmental with pride our Lord they crucified.

If Jesus had walked and talked with us today, would we respect His Authority and recognize His Love, walking humbly by His side, or would we struggle for a kingdom built on our own foolish pride?

Our life with Jesus is hidden in our hearts. You can't buy it, or sell it, or find it in any man. Just believe in your heart that Jesus was the Son of God and purchased each one of us through His Blood. He'll never leave us nor forsake us. He'll only love us until He takes us home.

Delonna Shawler
LONELINESS
The loneliness I sometimes
feel
The days are long
The nights are still
The solitude
The dark gray moods
The loneliness it seems
just looms
The clouds that hang
overhead
Are always there for
me to dread
Tho the sun may shine
Tho I'm not alone
The loneliness is
never gone

Christopher A Nicholson
EXPRESSIONS

Dedicated To: Darlene S. Giddings and Nicole D. Giddings
You two are that special star that's always shining in my life With Love, C.A.N.

I'm a man that's strong and bold
Whose heart is sometimes cold
A man who gives protection
Who sometimes shows little affection
When I see your face
there's no other place that I'd rather be
For you are like the sun that shines so bright
For you are that star that shines at night
You are the ocean that's vibrant and blue
the land that's sturdy and true
For you are fire, very intense
My love for you never needs defense
For I'm a man who desires love and caring
Whose feelings are worth sharing!

Elmar E Zirnis
WEST COAST

With love to our grandchildren, Mara and Andris Vitols
Mill Valley, California.

Beautifully placed, just fit for a poet
abundantly blessed with a scenic view's,
touched by the Pacific ocean—
the majestic California cost stands, admirably.

Steep canyons are bordering bridges beyond
forth'coming waves vanish toward mighty rocks,
on a rugged cliff's eucalyptus stand.
Gigantic redwoods skyward are towering
brave, impressive stocks.

In the North bound coast line
nature pleasingly rise wild flower decor,
South a way, palm trees tenderly whisper
liveliness to the white Calla lilies,
while the ocean waves forever serenade—
the endless Hymn!

Ruth E Bettenhausen
OUR LOVE

Dedicated to my husband, Russ for the many years that we have been together.

Our love has lasted through many years
We have shared much laughter and tears.

Our first date was January 21, 1938
Four months later May 21 was our wedding date.

Here 51 years later, how time does pass
God sees, that if it's true love it will always last.

Over the years kids, grand and great grandkids have joined the clan
When you read your bible, you'll see that it is God's plan.

We give all the glory to God
For the love we've shared on this old sod.

Now I will lay down my pad and pen
So that will bring this love tale to an end.

God bless!

Kate Louise Mendrey
RECIPE FROM THE COTE D' OR 75
Harciots a la cream
generous pea plants.
extraordinary mastiff trees
beautiful garden walls.

Yellow starflowers
profusion abound
spring from burnt
sienna villages.

Tinging renaissance songs
baroque music designs
carpets of primroses
snails in sunlight.

Orchid branch smiles
twin spirling butterflies
light air dancing
afternoon cats sleep.

Stately apple boughs
old man yawning
graceful cerises
three stories tall.

Mucha meets Carmine Miranda
glories ecological richness
one's backyard monuments
tribute to abundance.

Pastoral grazing sheep
daisy full fields
milky ways of buttercups
red poppy quilts.

Bluebell skirts, frilled
laughter wit bouquets
fill passionate embrace
topographic nuances.

Coolness warm sunshines
Sweet cake walk
lovely forest firs
meditating bench iris.

Vert bodies all
translucent winged
turquoise dragonflies.

Vezelay, Avallon, Semur.
Aviare golden age
stain glass window
interior ringing
Burgundy vallies overflow.

Artichoke mandala
cheese plate size
ladybug ladybug
fly away home.

Baby lettuce assemble
mist touched huge
Ming Dynasty mountain
another view ado.

Swaying delicate wheat
Stalks citron halos
Strong poplars
Liberty leading the people.

Cascading ivy tendrils
light green waterfalls.
Celadon heart notes
Piano scales memorized.

Willow branches
Swallow tail kingfisher
Baldinciesquing against
gray washed sky.

Feeling faintness picking
Redon Shirley poppies
oranges roof robed
float skyward.

Big black crows
Squawk loudly
soaring lunchtime
Skirmish awaits

Larks spiral
apexing then dive
Leonardo smiles
Mother Earth song.

Doorstep flowers little
purple scalloped edges
a la belle epoch
bug marigold eyes.

Fresh—basil dancing
pansies fill urns
dream in sunlight
tomato family ripen.

Nasturtium peach bright
lilies flock canals
Rosemary rare weeds
in rich terre sauce.

Eva Gumke
SHARING
what a joy to watch,
a tangible bond that is visible,
a catalyst one for the other.
concentration of the project at hand.
total involvement brings a smile to my lips.

somehow the energy level is increased
when two minds are allowed to roam free.
endorphins build up—bursts into creative needs,
stretching the days and shortening the nights.
I feel good when I am with him.
I smile with him
as we joke about the seriousness of life.

Terrie V Kibbee
IN MEMORY OF MOTHER
It's hard to say good-bye, even harder to let go;
You were showered with love, more than you'll ever know;
If love could have kept you with us, you would still be here;
Taking away the emptiness and filling it with cheer;

For whatever the reasons, it was time for you to leave;
Our lives are empty and lonely, and now we grieve;
But loved ones who passed on before you, will lead you their way;
It's just time to share you 'cause that is God's way;
So, we're not going to say good-bye 'cause you'll live forever in our hearts;
And with a love that is strong we will never be apart;
We'll go on with our lives and think of you with love;
'Til, one by one, we'll join you forever, up above.

Suzanne Lafranchi
UNTIL THE WIND CHILLS
I strolled along the tranquil path
With browned leaves beneath my feet.
Crunch and crackle though not heard,
For morning's dew did soften pain.

Faded light streamed through the trees;
Bare and lonely did they stand.
A lush green blanket no longer warmed
Their aching moaning branches.

Silently, I walk alone.
No protection from the cold.
Naked to the lashing gust,
Striking my crying soul.

The wind has chilled to winter
And summer's sultry lingering days
Have lessened,
Silently, I walk alone.

Annette S Angelino
REALITY IS IN THE MIND OF THE BEHOLDER
What kind of eyes must we have in order that we see?
What kind of thoughts must we think in order to perceive?
Does it take all kinds of people's ways to show what there can be
And how many roads must we walk in order to believe?
Where is the will we need to keep our spirit strong?
How many years must we live to find where we belong
There has to be a reason for everything we do
Right or Wrong, good or bad, it's only point of view
It's only what we choose.

Robin Rippon
THE LOVE HAS GONE
As times went by
It was plain to see
That you had lost
Your love for me.

You were always
Gone, day and night,
You'd never call to see
If I was alright.

Our Love we had
was slipping away,
with each and every
passing day.

But, I still loved you,
And hoped that you'd somehow see
If your heart still had
That love for me.

You left with tears in your eyes.
I felt you hated to go
But, you never let on
to your feelings that showed.

I saw you
Once in awhile
The words we spoke
without a smile.

We couldn't seem to get along,
No matter what we said,
The months passed by fast.
The times we shared were now in the past.

You left,
And went far away.
This time our love
Has gone to stay.

Susan P Clark

Susan P Clark
NOAH'S ARK

Dedicated to peace on earth between all nations. May God light the way.
—Amen

There they gathered two by two, into God's holy ark
Blessed as they marched through
Males sturdy in their patience waiting with helpmate at side
Offspring to enlighten with the new world into glide
God's holy touch to each breed His holy hand
Animals gathered, two by two in a band
To fulfill God's promise, a new day would begin
No more floods, no more sin
God's holy power on earth would win
God's holy throne high in mountain reign
Man with his woman, filled with the holy scheme, would never be the same
Days, weeks, months of dreary wet rain,
Would subside
Ark stable now on top of high mountain
Reaching high through God's turbulent tide
Our punishment was over
A new page to turn
A new man in God with new lessons to learn
A new wilderness to pursue with glistening sun from clouds high above, sparkling with God's holy love
Would guide us in the right direction
Love in full bloom
God's holy reign would be our inspiration
To form a new world and spiritual generations
Delving deep into mind, heart and soul and deep meditations
The last pair of sheep are marching onto new found soil
Dirt to turn and men will toil
Beginning God's Ten Commandments
on earth
May we keep peace between all people and nations
God's love is lighting the way
Peace on earth this Christmas Day.
—Amen

Lisa Brosius
MY BABY, MY EMILY ROSE
My Baby, My Emily Rose,
you are the light of my life.
And, so, I'm writing this prose.

Though you're only a little over a year old,
Each & every day you grow more dear.
You are quite a vision;
Your rosy cheeks & spunky smile,
and eyes of electric blue.
With every arm outstretched
and every "Mommy" said,
I fall deeper in love with you.
Not every day that goes by is
quite what I expected;
Sometimes harder, sometimes not.
It doesn't matter though,
You are my Emily Rose.
My pride, joy and inspiration are you.

My Baby, My Emily Rose
you are the light of my life.
And, so, for you I wrote this prose.

Maria Falco
CRUISING THROUGH LIFE

This poem is dedicated to Carlos who remains in my heart.

Here we are together
Birds of a feather
I get close to you
You say back away

I'm cruising through life,
Please, no more strife
Here today, gone tomorrow
I have to go on
Regardless of sorrow.

Are you afraid
Of me
I will get to know you
You'll begin to know me too?

My feelings are hurt
I thought I meant much more
Without you I am
Emotionally poor

Cruising through life
So cold
Won't you hold me?
Stay awhile, be bold.

Jeffrey L Shannon
MICHELLE LOUAINE
One star.

The one on which I dream.

To those whose eyes mislead them,
she may ne'er appear pristine.

But I, while on my journey
through the glitter of the night,
have found that, quite prismatically,
she is, in fact, most white.

And from her passioned heart of red
flows free the warmth of sunset orange.
Her sweetness, that of yellow buds,
is lightly fragranced, dew adorned.

She freshens like the greens of trees
and powers like the blues of seas.

And all these colors intertwined
have settled deep within my mind.

For all the gifts of that one star,
I'll always love, though from afar,
the beauty of her bright, white light,
the one that rules my dreams each night.

And wish upon that star, I will;
my hopes and dreams, she may fulfill.

Yet all may pass

if one stays fast:

I wish her shining days to last . . .

Stephen J O'Connor
LACED WITH SIMPLE WORDS
The lady was a sinner
and I was just a beginner
I wined and dined her
the only real fire
in this cold winter

A pilot light to my soul
with just enough jazz in her
rock n' roll
to make me see
her simple complexity
her love that runs so deep
in the night . . . .

The moon, an earring in the sky
the stars,
sparkles of light in the night
the rain, champagne shampoo
and you darling were my first clue
to what heaven's really like

So it was . . .
2 steps back
and 98 steps forward
laced with the simple words
"I Love You"

Redgie D Trujillo
SIRENS IN THE NIGHT

This poem is dedicated to Todd Mark & Angie, my beautiful children

So much hatred, so much fright, what is wrong . . . . what
is right?
Little children cry in the
night . . . . Why? Oh why do
we fight?
Love is the answer to it all . . . .
Hatred is why we fall.
What a wonderful world this would be, if we cared and gave the love Christ shared.
My heart is hurting for the little child . . . . we all seem to have become defiled.
Let's not lead them as if we were blind . . . . If we work together, we can love & be kind.
Love is the best gift you can give . . . . If we give more it would be a better place to live.
Where there is hatred, there is strife . . . We just don't need that in our life.

Emmerson Gordon Luffman
UNTIL THE END OF MY LIFE
At first sight of you
That look from your eyes
Reached right into my soul.
I believe that you planted
The seed of love,
In the garden of my heart.
The seed like a tree
Has slowly grown
To the sheltering of its prime.
For I have deepened my affection
To appreciate our differences
I have honesty and courage
To accept you as you are
Faults and all.
I have had the ability to let go
To learn that I do not own you

So exclusively that others
Cannot find a place in your life.
I believe that is true.
What I feel about you
That if you were my wife
I would love you faithly on true
Until the end of my life.
So will you be my wife
So that I may love you faithly on true
Until the end of my life.

Mr ChiCha O Weusi
AT SEA

Being at sea is breathtaking! Watching the moon and stars on moonlight nights is capturing nature as it was intended. There's something romantic about the varying intensities of the stars as well as their shapes and sizes. How the peace, calm, and tranquility engulf one and slowly float away into never never land. Even the reflection of the moon on the crest of the tireless waves makes one yearn for intimate happy experiences with someone special. Time seemingly floats on a non-linear scale giving an illusion of suspended animation and enchantment where only magic and fairy tales come true. Wow! It's so easy to drift out to sea!

Kim Wiley
WITH LOVE

I see you with love
As I watch you go.
She holds your heart
For now, you know.
But when this time is over
You will see
That love with her
Was not meant to be.
I know I'll never have you
Or hold you again,
Not as lovers
Only as friends.
So I write this to you,
With love to the end,
To let you know this was written
With love,
from a friend.

c r glines
INSIGHT

the overwhelming magnitude of
His love that reaches out to all
on this earth
Is a never ending process, never
ending in death,
always beginning before birth.
We are all part of his master plan,
manufactured by His love for us
to find our own way
But if we don't truly succeed, is
there some unholy penalty that
we all must finally pay.
We are taught that He will always
love us even though we may
stray from his original plan
So there must still be hope for
those who love not just as
woman and man.
Many have their own versions as
to what His purposes are and
meant to be
Still try to convince the many
who have still yet to be set
totally free.
Many great prophecies have been
given that great numbers are
expected to follow
Still much prejudice still exists that
make many of these prophecies
hard to swallow.
So many do gooders look down
their noses at those who may
not live as they are expected
And still many more feel that just
by going to church they are
fully protected.
Then there are those who are
smug and know just where they
will eventually be
But won't they be terribly
surprised when they end up
somewhere else with me.

Bernita Waller
SUNSET OVER ZIMBABWE

Dedicated lovingly to the memory of Alfred Morgan Waller, Jr. and with extra special love to my wonderful parents, Jack and Inetz Stanley

Red, orange and pink-streaked clouds
Stack up against the sky
Fondly bidding farewell
to the purple, green and
blue-speckled earth below.

Swiftly fading, the sun smiles
a last good-bye
to the black, brown and tan
Zimbabwean folk darting along the
paths,
hurrying homeward.

Inviting aromas that warm the
cooling air
rush to the roadside to greet
the tired travelers' return
While those gathering round, settle
down
as final chores are done.

Grey-blue shadows spill across the
evening scene
Sending the sun to its other daytime
place
Leaving a quiet, peaceful embrace
around
the soft hum of chatter and
children's laughter.
Day comes to an end—
Night falls like a hem—
The sun sets
Over
Zimbabwe.

Carolyn Bugden
UNTITLED

Unresponsive words
Spoken to the dead
Can this heart be jolted back to life?
Stiff and painful love,
Inside this ancient crypt
Will you rise
And paint my face with crimson
knowledge
of a place where you have been?
My love,
Do you see the potent sword
Against my inviting throat
Slit,
Such a warm peace I have found,
All of our colors bleed into one light
As a fraction of what it was before

Andy Esch
OLYMPIC FEVER

Every four years the Olympics come
to town.
They gather the best athletes
from the world around.
They compete for their country and
try to do them proud.
I think they like the support
and the roar of the crowd.
They have worked and struggled for
four long years.
They put out a lot of their blood,
sweat, and tears.
They worked real hard with coaches
young and old,
Just for a shot at the bronze,
silver, and gold.
Although it is over, the competing is
done,
Some athletes are happy with
the medals they've won.
But the countries don't stop looking
for someone like you
To compete in the Olympics of
1992.

Kathleen Storey Markham
MEMORIES

Memories are like faded photographs
of past days.
To be kept tucked away in the
corners of your heart.
To be brought out and pondered over
on a rainy day.
They bring smiles of laughter, an
occasional frown,
and perhaps a sigh of regret over
times that can never be again.
Remembering the smiles, the
laughter, the happiness—
I think of you and how much I love
you.

James Vincent
CANOPIC JAR

The alabaster one
Translucent, carved from a single
stone
Contains a shadow
Where grey rests the assumptive liar
The closet hero
The phone booth genius
Who has attempted to evade his
destiny.
There are no fingerprints in his earth
But the invisible ones time has placed
Where the sound of falling dust
Is its own company
And desiccation befriends time.

Joyce Ann Markarian Williamson

Joyce Ann Markarian Williamson
WAR BUDDIES

This poem is dedicated in loving memory of our friend, PETER KALLIANES and my loving father, JERRY VINCENT MARKARIAN, SR.

There was a friend of my Daddy's,
who he met while in the war;
Soon, when they were separated,
they planned to meet once more;
The war went on and men were
killed,
the plan they made no more
seemed real;
One day while my Daddy was
walking,
a fuzzy image appeared;
As he neared this fuzzy image,
his eyes filled up with tears;
For the fuzzy image my Daddy saw,
was his friend alive and well;

So overwhelmed with gladness
to see each other again;
They hugged and laughed and left the
war,
to become the best of friends;
The war had brought two men
together,
for which nothing could pull
apart;
Until the day his friend Pete died,
and broke my Daddy's heart.

Matt Connolly
THE STONE LEGEND

To Kim Diana—the love who shared my childhood. And Diane—who made the shared music.

From the depths of saddened oceans
A stone rose in the dawn wind
Washed clean by blood and water
Translucent with his new light
The Father offers him again.

He walks the seawaves unbroken
To the harbors of tomorrow
In the sand above the high tide
He leaves footprints for our journey
Through his seasons of forever.

In ivory shells from blue waters
We taste the new wine of his
presence
While in the sky above the daystar
We hear the music of his children
Singing, come home Abba Father,
come home.

He rises into the sea clouds
Leaving his spirit love to guide us
Past the storms in many seaports
Out to waters known by angels
Where his stone will rise again.

Sylvia L Mayer
FLOATING CLOUDS ABOVE

Floating clouds above make me
marvel and I wonder . . .
what the world underneath might
look like from out yonder?
Clouds congregate . . . I see the
beauty of spring showers as it rains,
Sprinkles add dewdrops to flowers
and weeping willows in the plains.
Raindrops like tiny crystals cascade
from the sky,
Falling on dancing daffodils and
swallows flying by.
Brilliant colors shimmer through
clouds coming from a rainbow,
Increasing the luster of mountains,
foothills and the valleys below.
Streaks of light beam down on the
prairie from an opening in a cloud,
. . . . . . shafts of rays coming out
from a silver halo.
God's presence is felt everywhere, up
above and down below.
I'm curious if God is sitting up there
and what he might see,

I imagine him smiling while enjoying the breathtaking scenery.
Could this silver halo be where souls enter heaven from our earth?
Or could this be where infant souls are given birth?
Morning turns to evening . . . evening clouds now float in the horizon,
Painting the sky with an array of scarlet colors from a setting sun.
Night will soon be upon the earth . . . stars will soon be visible from behind a silver cloud,
A romantic full moon gleaming through makes me want to cry out loud.
Perhaps when I die my spirit will sit on the floating clouds above and
I will no longer have to wonder,
For then, I shall be keeping God company, and enjoy with him all the splendor he created down yonder.

Beatrice Ransom
PRISSY KITTY

To my children and Sweet Pea, the four-legged member of the family.

Prissy Kitty down the hall,
Met her shadow on the wall.
Tail upright and all wide-eyed,
Ran upstairs so she could hide.

Prissy Kitty down the hall,
Stayed away from scary wall.
With a sigh she thought, "No more!"
Oooops!
Met her shadow on the floor.

Prissy Kitty down the hall,
Has no fear of scary wall.
So the story ends, I'm told,
Ooooh!
Prissy Kitty's laid out cold.

Gregory Ford
SOMETHING THAT HAPPENED THE OTHER DAY

To Danuta Rajpold
A Friend Across The Miles.

A rose awaits in the dark of night
Patiently thirsting for a ray of light
Her eyes were cold, who needs a friend
To curse the indifference of the wind
She sat beside me on the train
Her life in stress, her soul in pain
She glanced and saw this rhyming page
She spoke no words, but I felt her rage
I wrote of the beauty in children playing
The forest, the sea, the heather swaying
And then I added within these lines
How her eyes did make her hard to find
But a poet may see the inner soul
Pass the pain that makes us cold
With love and tenderness I did end
I know thee not, I am a friend
Suddenly she stood to go her way
Then she turned, smiled and waved
Then she walked away.

James A Carr
PLACE OF PEACE

To all the people who want to achieve world peace and live together in harmony

I'm looking for a place of peace.
Where violence and war will for ever cease.
I don't really know why I look for this.
When I know such a place doesn't exist.
But still I search from the coldness of Alaska to the heat of Ethiopia,
forever searching for my Utopia.
But still there was nothing and I felt despair, and a war broke out and I became scared.
Who starts it up isn't a factor but the amount of lives that are lost by a nuclear reactor or a bomb from an attacker.
The world becomes doomed, the sky becomes blacker.
Men died who've never held a gun.
Women died for things they haven't done.
Children died just looking for fun.
We should all just unite together as one, and wait for the kingdom to come.
But instead we make war, to make peace. And if we continue the lives of many loved ones shall cease. For in the mist of the night there was a light.
For in my bed of fear in fright.
My eyes were now opened and revealed to my sight.
Was a vision I saw and could now understand.
There could never be peace if there was to be man.

Gerald D Maynard
REFLECTIONS

Several times within the span of your life,
There is cause to look back and see
If it all went well, as it should have been
As it really was meant to be.

The high school days, the college years,
The fun, the joys, the fears;
The marriage, the children, the job, the house,
The deaths, the failings, the tears.

Then you jump back to now, to a loving wife,
To children who have brought no pain,
And you suddenly know, when your time comes to go,
That your living has not been in vain.

Mary Szczepanski
THE OLD MAN

To Mom and Dad
Thanks for always believing in your children!

His look belies his words—
"I'm fine Dear, just tired."
I know that look;
it silently pleads with me
to prevent what is coming.
Sadly, I can only hold his hand
and pacify him with my own lie—
"Don't worry, you'll be alright"
As I watch him die.

Tara L Howell
THE FACES OF FEAR

To all of my friends and family, my dear mother (who is as cool as they get), and to Jeremy; and last my dear departed father—May I make him proud.

Fear is dark.
It is shadows in the corners.
Not being able to see where you are going . . .
not being able to see what's making the sounds.

But then fear is light,
Having no shadows to hide in.
Being able to see where you are going . . .
being able to see what's making the sound.

Fear is loud.
Fear is people shouting,
Books slamming,
bombs exploding.

But then fear is quiet.
Fear is people whispering,
paper rustling,
bombs ticking.

Fear is a child's nightmare;
with devils hiding in the shadows . . .
and fiends clicking their nails against the windows
But then the child turns on the lights . . .
And the devils turn back into a pile of toys,
and the fiends turn out to be a small tree with its fingers
Tapping against the window

Roseller Sacro Espere

Roseller Sacro Espere
A THOUGHT WRITTEN IN A DREAM

This poem is dedicated to Tiina Ojala, my fondest friend of Pori, Finland.

You're like a damoiselle in a fairy tale,
Sometimes untamed like summer gale,
A kinsman's sight, a lover's delight,
A moonlight night for a pauper's plight.

A starlike blink of your eye,
Unfold a sigh to a starry sky,
The love I know, a smile that glow,
Like yielding seeds the farmhand sow.

Like morning sun you're someone new,
Adored by many, loved by few,
Your tender touch, soft and free,
An epitome of virgin sanity.

Your tune erstwhile like melody fair,
Like twilight's too your dusky hair,
Your lips, Oh! red like roses,
Relieve a heart from pain and bruises.

Blest are you conceived not planned,
A masterpiece of God's hand,
An illusion filled to my mind's brim,
A thought written in a dream.

Edward J Jakubiak
AN ELUSIVE METAPHOR

Impossible to collect
Impossible to gather
into expounded visions,
The soft flutter of wings
The rare whisper of dreams
in the evening breeze.
Perhaps strangely mistaken
Perhaps doubtful to intuition,
A murmuring forest to comprehension,
Lingering, though sublime,
Forever musical in autumn color,
Elusive to definition, insensible
To deeds defined by time.

James M Copeland
ROSEBUD

With tender love and affection
The soil was made ready,
Gathered, were rocks for drainage,
Loam for richness, clay for strength,
And broken treebark for ground cover,
Each spade of dirt lovingly removed
And mixed, then packed tight
To hold the plant upright!
Summer's warmth and nature's rain,
And gentle dew,
Watering and nurturing and reviving
So it could act as a reminder of the love
Shared
Between the two who planted it!
And then,
To bless the efforts of this work
And union pending,
While the cold and frost descended
Upon a wonderful summer's ending.
This plant of essence and beauty
Bore a single rosebud,
For them to share. . . . . .

Tris A Legacy
CARPE DIEM

Were Janet I thought about
For in my mind she left no doubt

Life was sweet, life was grand
A merry dance to a benign band
So away stole pain on a halcyon breeze
And we nary a care strove to please
So carnal, so chaste, our times portal
So embellished, so encumbered, so mortal
So we ride fancy twists to risk rapture
Of joy so high wrapt in daring nature
There-of, how far, how high, how long
These questionable planes we speed along
Yet what matter, what difference
Is not life sweeter for intimate indulgence
So time passes and eras spawn
Such fertile relations beget their dawn
Where suns shine, rains fall, and winds sweep
And we bared of inhibitions to loving leap
Free from guilt , free from reservation
Our bliss fostering a brash revelation
We are human, and that is beautiful
We so love life our love blossoms fruitful

Philip Joseph Perrington
MEMORA

To All and Every, for Without, there is Any. A very special thanks with love. To my wife Lynn and loving children, Kristie and Andrew.

Behold, the tides of memory have washed ashore . . .
Bringing back yesters past . . . And yet . . . yes . . .
Even now looking for more.

The waves of moods, of: Ethics,
Morals of:
Love, Peace, Joy,
Treachery, Hate, Beauty:

Compassions of Expressions of tools
of Self's past.
Slips into once again . . . the
entombment of moments thought, of
which we don't know
The last.

For the memory of the
moment . . .
That comes within seconds,
We all have remembered the reckons
and
The beckons.

If . . . yes . . . if we have played,
worked,
with fullest . . . according too . . .
And with our memory of tools . . .
We may not . . . . entity with . . . with
all ourselves, for the
Memory
of
fools.

J M Duttweiler Esquire
AS I SIT BY THE SEA

To Susan, The one love I never got over the loss of, or can ever forget.

In days passed I saw the beauty of the sea and in its echo somehow call to me, it matters not where you are now for in its echo I hold you close somehow, in older years it calls to me and beckons my return to the sea, it tells a tale of you and me a sunset shared by two exclusively, holding hands across the sands in a summer's wonder land, I wonder if she still sees true love by the sea, I know someday she will be standing there without me looking out to the sea seeing things much differently, So long ago she did leave after our trip to the sea maybe she could not see sunsets beauty by the sea or maybe it was just me with her eyes she could not see, how much her love meant to me, as by the sea I do sit I feel the lonely hours fit into time without care at times the pain is so hard to bear, maybe she does see the beauty of the sea and one day soon she will beckon me as she sits lonely by the sea.

Valerie LeGault
OUR TURNING POINT

As I watched the nose of your plane head upwards into the clouds, all of the joys and pains of your childhood flashed in front of my tear filled eyes.

We made it on our own for so long, laughing, crying, talking, hugging,
Now you're gone.

You'll know this empty feeling when you have a child of your own some day.

You've chosen to serve your country for the next four years of your life. Who wouldn't be a proud parent?

You'll be gone overseas for only a year, and I feel this is the turning point in our lives.
You're no longer my baby, my first born. You're a man.
Just remember this, you'll always be my son.
Love Mom

Hazel S Moore
HOW CAN I HELP SOMEONE

How can I help someone
When I can hardly help myself
With a kind word and a smile
For their troubles may far outweigh
mine
I have so little of worldly goods
They may have far less
When shut-ins can't get out or around
on their own
A phone call or a drop-in visit means
a lot
To share time doing little things,
errands they need done
A ride about the city or around the
country-side
To make them aware they're not
alone
That someone does care, is a loving
kind thing
An hour can mean so much and
brighten one's day
Bring a ray of sunshine their way
Sharing a pot of tea will do wonders
for them and me
Shared conversations of hopes and
dreams
That may not come true, fill the time
that flies so fast
Hopefully not to be forgotten soon
Memories of days and afternoon to
cherish, to last.

Vicky Armanios
PRE-OPERATIVE: LATE NIGHT WATCH

For Ezzat

At this late time of night
The city's Saturday heat wave
Gives way to solitary cars skidding
Intermittently through softly falling
rain.
The fresh night air
Sweetens the sleep of urban yuppies,
transients, lovers
in one another's arms and the dreams
(I hope) of my husband,
Heart beating its intimate
rhythm—persistently, insistently,
Though halted—and mine, too—
In the depths of winter.

Now as I write, a summer fan
twirls the smoke past
this page and forbidding spectres rise
unbidden,
and writhing with them, tender
thoughts strangled
by the grip of too many loving,
clutching
hands, while loneliness
becomes a deeper loneliness.

Jeanine Thomason
SATISFIED

This poem is dedicated to my parents, Alfred and Catherine Thomason, whom I love very much.

The moonlight,
fulfills the needs of my night,
by seducing me, to sleep the sleep,
of complete silence,
Only to be awakened, at dawn,
by the acknowledgement
of the Sun. By which I am Satisfied.

I never fear, while I am at rest,
the troubles of the days gone by,
nor do I worry of the things
that are yet to come, for in the
moonlight,
I am as calm as the sea, and am at
peace,
with my soul, as with the skies
above.
Safe, and satisfied.

The moonlight,
the dawning of the sun,
the peace in my soul, and fulfillment
of life,
in having all of these things,
I am truly satisfied.

Kimi DiMarco
THE OTHER SIDE

This poem is dedicated to Brian Jones and Jim Morrison . . . The two men who made it all possible

Poetic mind
Filled with traces
Of intelligence
You scream

Let the boy go
And free the soul
That looks beyond
To the other side

Prosecuted
Put away
And freed again
In another time

Lonely rejection
The free world
Stops
Form of art
To the expanded mind

Silently searching
Conscious mind
You can't come back
To the other side

Tony Robertson

Tony Robertson
DEAR FAITHLESS WOMAN

Dedicated to my sister, Teresa, and my friend Darren

Woman, Dear Woman, how faithless
thou art!
This saw I, in the dark gray clouds of
thy stormy heart.
Yea! It was thou who abolished my
living will;
Absolute chance, never was I allowed
to fulfill.
Why with my precious blood did thee
abscond?
Was it my touch? Thine? Or failure
of each to respond?

Was it the absence of some worldly
gain?
Have thou found recourse in a
recrudescence of chains?
Hail me Dear Woman, with
benediction
And lead me not into the adverse
winds of fiction.
Thou consumed my soul as a blazing
flame,
Then flustered my floundering faith
to unending shame.
Why, Dear Woman? Why, Dear
Faithless Woman?

Harold E Richardson
REFLECTION

To all my sons, Robert, Edward, Thomas, Mark and William

I walked slowly to the water's edge
And as far as I could see
The ocean kissed the horizon
And shrank into infinity

Out to sea, a large rock
Appeared and faded from sight
As the incoming tide
Enveloped it—and then gave it life

It would sink beneath the waves
And rise with the receding tide
In a cycle that never ended
Like man, nature and life

Hungry sea gulls flew low
To search for food in the frothy foam
While sea lions resting on rocks
Made their presence known

While I stood on the beach
Looking out to sea
The ocean mirrored a reflection
And that image was always me.

Elinor Hocking
BUNDLE OF HAPPINESS

For Tina If in December, a rose should bloom, It would be in memory of you. Wherever you are, I love you. Mom

One day in late December,
God sent a gift my way;
He told me to watch over her,
And lead her not astray;

Such tiny, gentle hands has she,
To reach for things anew;
Her little feet may dance someday,
In slippers soft and blue;

All through the day she's lively,
As she watches everything;
I guess I never really knew,
What joy a child could bring;

When day is done, and shadows fall,
The stars come out to see;
My little angel fast asleep,
As peaceful as can be;

Now, as I sit by her little bed,
I pray thee Lord to bless;
The little one I love so much,
My Bundle of Happiness.

Tammy L Payne
A LITTLE BROTHER

This poem is dedicated to my little brother, J. T. Buchanan Jr. Thanks Jr. I couldn't have done it without you.

If you have a little brother,
Then down deep in your heart;
You know there could be no other,
For nothing could tear you apart.

For what could take the place,
of that darling little face?
The one behind the hands pulling

your hair,
Then turning around to Mom and Dad,
Saying that's not fair.

From calling you a liar,
To letting the air out of your bike tire.
Now all of a sudden you don't hear a peep,
Down deep you know he must be asleep.

You know his heart is full of love,
Even if he does like hitting with his baseball glove.

As you listen to his sweet little sigh,
It's then you know your little brother,
You can't deny.

Sally Hite
BRIGHTEST STAR

To my special little sister, Jeanne Wilbur. I love you, Sally Hite

Along with this card I'm sending to you,
I've also included all tried and true,
A special bright rainbow just for you.
This spectrum of color, glistening of gold,
With crimson reds and jades of green,
Hues of blue with soft petal pinks peeking through

Now close your eyes and drift your mind.
And listen well, as I do tell
Take my hand, as I take thine,
Come with me, for a time.
As there is a mountain, "ahead,
No time to bed."

Towards the heavens, through the clouds,
The twinkling stars of twilight's hour
As they have divine and lasting power.

The brightest star I give to you, as
Brilliant colors shining through

Anna Jane Spurlock
GOD'S PATH

As I sit here, musing . . . . .
There is a feeling, confusing,
Of how my life took this turn;
The possibility of all I yearn.

Unfolds bright new world
Like as flag unfurled;
Rippling in the gentle breeze
With great grace and ease.

God's gifts wait along the way;
More fruitful day by day,
Lending a rainbow of joy
To this journey I employ.

Where does it lead?
I wonder, indeed.
What is my God saying
In this role I'm playing?

He is more than fair!
How fast can I get there
To bathe in his blessing,
Ever His love expressing?

Donna Cheatwood
MY OWN LITTLE WORLD

To my loving husband Steve
For his love inspired the words from my heart.

When I am with you I feel safe and secure,
I want to be by your side, year after year.
When we are together, I feel that we have it all,
Your love puts me on a cloud where I could never fall.
I want you to know that I am very proud to be your wife,
And I want to share with you, the rest of your life.
As we go thru life, we will have a lot of ups and downs,
And we will share with each other a lot of tears and frowns.
There will be times that we won't know what to do,
But somehow, our love will lead us on through.
When I am with you I am happy and that's all I need,
I don't want nothing else in the world, it's too full of greed.
I have "My Own Little World," that includes only you,
I need only you to help me make it through.
Thank you, for sharing my life with me,
You have made me happier, than I ever thought to be.

Sondra Cloud
ALL SEASONS

To those that were and to those that are

A season is here again. Lonely, it makes me feel, changing leaves are coming. The days of warmth are slowly disappearing to cold. The warmth of the season is like the love we knew
The cold is the love forever lost in time. When you walk through the snow think of my loneliness. When the first spring day is here think of my beauty. When you think of me picture a summer storm because the rain is my tears. When fall is here and the winds gently blow, think of my loving arms around you. When you can tell me you have lost the feelings for all seasons then you have lost me.

Maruja A Hatheway
WORLD'S HUNGRY CHILDREN

To those with a heart.

When I see these hungry children
Looking with those begging eyes
My heart gets tied into a knot
And a desire to cry . . .

These children never have been children
They don't know how to play
Their fragile life is a struggle
Just to live from day to day.

I wish I could do for them
More than the little money I send,
I wish that somehow I could
Their sad existence change.

If there is a God in heaven
Looking down for all of us
Then, why does He send these children
Into such pitiful life?

Kathleen Pothof
YOU'VE GONE AWAY

Dedicated to Christopher White, my fiance

You've gone away,
But the memories of you
Shall always stay.
We used to be so happy,
Never depressed, and never alone.
We used to have so much fun,
But now it's all gone.
Now you've gone away,
And all I have left,
Is memories of brighter days
Hopeless romancing still can find a way,
To make true love forever,
Where I shall always stay.

John L Roton Sr

John L Roton Sr
"LORD," DON'T LET ME LEAVE WITHOUT HER!

This poem is dedicated to my beloved wife, Virginia

Today, "Lord"! I speak with you
As age begins to show.
Don't bless me with much more days,
Than it takes to bless her with,
you know!
You've walked for years with me dear Lord,
My heart you already know.
Make straight, the gate and bring her home,
Awaiting, I will go.
You've blessed my home with only one.
She's cared and loved me so.
Give me the strength to serve her well,
As her life begins to slow.
She's paid the price as a help-mate twice,
As a king I've enjoyed her well.
So thank you Lord, for your answer today.
For with you, I've done quite well.

Evangela Thompson
THE MAGIC OF LOVE

This poem is dedicated to "Michael," "Janet & Ivory" My sweet lovin' husband, mother & father "With all our love."

Love is like magic,
And it always will be.

For love still remains,
life sweet mystery.

Love works in ways,
that are wondrous and strange.

And there's nothing in life,
that love can't change.

Love can transform,
the most commonplace

Into beauty and splendor,
Sweetness and grace.

Love is unselfish,
Understanding and kind.

For it sees with its heart,
And not with its mind.

Love is the answer,
that everyone seeks.

Love is the language,
that every heart speaks.

Love can be brought,
It's priceless and free.

Lives like pure magic,
It's a sweet mystery.

Sylvia Eisner
LISA MICHELLE

This poem is dedicated to my beautiful daughter, Lisa Michelle.

Our world almost stopped
That fateful day
That day of June 10
When we all did pray.

I saw her lying there
Suffering, tormented, with frightened eyes.
My heart stopped; I screamed and screamed;
I saw the tears; I heard the cries.

Will she live to dream her dreams
I wondered—
Will she see the setting sun?
Will she smell the freshness of Spring,
And watch the robins on the run?
Will she live the life of motherhood
With babes on her lap,
Will she live the life of brotherhood,
And watch the trees, with their sweet sap.

And then life came back to us
As she began to heal;
And life won out;
She sang, she played,
As emotions, we once again, did feel.
And we'll live again, sing again,
hope again, laugh again—
Because she will again be well

Our very darling
Lisa Michelle.

Eileen C Kratt
HAND-IN-HAND WE WALK

Hand-in-hand we walk
Sun-rising pink sky
Above
Walking in sand
With sinking feet
Below
Deep in thought
As we wander aimlessly
Ahead
Knowing that the roughest
And hardest times are
Behind.

Geneva Bray
A SISTER'S PRAYER (FOR BROTHERLY LOVE)

To my parents: Mr. & Mrs. Davis, my grandmother Mrs. P. Burns and all my family members at home and abroad. A special thanks to my pastor Dr. P. J. Jones and the creator above.

As I grow each day in brotherly love asking for guidance from God above, sharing as I grow, no tricks, no games. For this love, I share with all faces and names.
Sometimes I feel a lot of pain, beautiful is the reward I stand to gain.
You don't care who they are, or from where they came.
And all I ask of them is to love me

the same. When brothers and sisters scorn me, I don't despair, because I have a Master who is always there. To teach me forgiveness and a fervent prayer, To instill in each of us this love so rare. So come one, come all let's hasten like the dove, and spread the world over this brotherly love. We can all do the task whether sixty or seven, it's the only way to get in God's Heaven.
Amen

Beth Reeves
RAINDROPS FROM HEAVEN!
There was a man of God, whose name was Bill!
He only lived to do God's will! He prayed to the Lord, to receive a blessing. He cupped his hands together, and prayed that he was worthy! Bill lifted his hands together toward Heaven, and prayed for his hands to be clean! Dear Lord, he thought, my hands look so dirty. But I am your man, and I will do my duty!
The Lord looked down on Bill, and felt such an overwhelming feeling of love for Bill, that God let the teardrops fall from His eyes; And He let them fall as raindrops!! They fell from Heaven with joy for Bill! And the raindrops as they fell were singing. "Hallelujah, Hallelujah!"
And so those raindrops from Heaven washed Bill's hands clean! Bill continues to sing; "Thank you, Jesus! Thank you, for the glorious singing of the raindrops. As they fall from my Savior's eyes!!"
Hear that glorious sound!! As the raindrops fall, they are singing, "Hallelujah, Hallelujah, Hallelujah!!"

Brandi Erwin
WINNING WAYS
How can you be a winner?
Well, I'll tell you how . . .
Let's start at the beginning
And I'll begin right now.

You don't need to be the smartest
Or the biggest in the crowd
All you need is a little courage
Try it—it'll make you feel real proud!

Go out and try your very best
Give 'em all you've got
For that's the thing that matters most
It really means a lot!

And if by chance you fail
Don't feel bad, just try again
Get yourself in gear to work hard
Maybe next time you will win.

Yes, you'll always be a winner
And in life you'll go real far
If you just follow these simple steps
One day you may be a star!!

Denise Bowers
A FAMILY'S STRUGGLE WITH AIDS

To M.D. Gregory With Love, Thanks for your encouragement!

Rubbie was Happy and Full of Life
You Say
She cared for her own in a very special way
A Day that Came to Pass
Rubbie grew ill
That started her Long Journey
With a Family of Pills . . .
With False Healings
and
False Hopes in Mind

The Illness only Grew Worse
With time
One Day a Time of Hope
For in Spirit and Mind
Rubbie was Getting Better
The Next Day
A Time to Grieve
For the Illness Would Not Let Her

As the Months Grew Long
Rubbie's Family was Strong
For the Time She Remained
Her Family Tried to Ease Her Pain

That Awful Day Came
Rubbie Melted Away
Like
An Ice Cube, On A Hot Summer's Day

The Blood that they gave is
What Took Her to an Early Grave

Her Family's Grief Was
Consoled; For They Knew That
Her Soul Was Not in That Hole

A Day That Came to Pass
Rubbie Was Gone
Her Family Cried

One Thing That Will Never
Go Away
Her Family's Love
That Has Not Died

Eleanor Bridges Akridge
LOVE YOURSELF

Dedicated to the "Homeless"

Who do you think you are
That you feel so unloved
Just someone cast aside
You must rise and walk above

Don't fret and wring your hands
Nor cast a cloud upon your face
Just believe you can and will
Be strong and win that race

Life can be so unkind
To you, To me, To others
It's when we take the challenge
We stand and inspire another

Believe in your self and say
I'm alright, I deserve the best
I will try with all my strength
To stand and pass the test

Be the best you can be
What'ere you attempt to do
It's easy to be a loser
But the winner can be you

Cherilyn L Tousignant
ADDICT
I die alone—there is no one,
However willing, who can come
Along this tortured nightmare track
To rescue me—to bring me back.

Back from this void beyond all time,
This ashen place, this dusty clime,
This starless night where dreams are swept
Away by tears that strangers wept.

Where I might be a memory
Of one or two, perhaps of three,
But when these rememberers are the remembered
God! Who will remember me?

Timi Smith Cody
QUESTIONS TO A MINER'S WIFE
Why I be wife to a coal mining man?
He works so hard to make our life have ease.
When times get hard he works more than he can,
So I need not to work unless I please.
For 'tis a lonely life you wonder why?
'cause we be one since June as man and wife.
Without the one you love would not you cry?
For he and I share all 'til end of life.

Why I pick he to be my only love?
So kind, so warm, and friendly as can be;
And I thank Him who watches from above
For sending love to my husband and me.

And now do I take leave, no questions more.
For he, my love has gone to work once more.

Adam Lee Alder
SCARED DEAD
I was cold in a storm, when the wind started to blow and I got so scared that I hid under the car. When it started to lightning, I got so scared I died.

Njoki McElroy

Njoki McElroy
FAMILY OF QUEENS
You have the aura of a Queen
She said to me
It's like I've seen you before
Another time Another place
Queen Nefertiti/Queen of Sheba
Mali/the Gold Coast?

Oh yes, I replied
I belong to a family of Queens
Some Great Grand Mothers
Who came before me
Names/faces lost in capture
Middle passage/slavery/brutalism
Yet beautiful loving
enduring caring
They were all Queens
Passing on Queenships

Now I pass the Queenship to
The beautiful One—my daughter
Bearing strength love
endurance caring
She will rule her domain well.

Lucinda Smith-Sudges
ILLIMITABLE LAD
Are you there father, are you there?
Is it you I see in the leaves of green, fluttering
in the breeze, in the orchards beyond pasture of green?
Wait the hawk floating on currents of air, he's gone,
Father were you there?

The swallows are calling out with a dare,
a shadow is cast over the fields, are you there?
The purple petals of flowering nettles I see,
I feel you with me, they may grow where they please.

The air so fresh, always full of life,
I can see your world now, forgetting it's strife.
The robin beneath the tree has had his fill,
A buck just ran, they're running still.

And oh your mountain, will forever stand tall.
Are you there my father can you hear me call?

Do you think of us still, someway, somehow?
Yes, you're right here beside me, guiding me now . . .

Timothy Everette Tweed
RAINDROPS
Life is like a drop of water,
Falling down from a dark blue sky,
Makes no diff'rence son or daughter,
Life has purpose until we die.

"What great purpose?" you might inquire,
That we acquire before our birth,
Like drops we are to quench the fire,
To cleanse and saturate the earth.

It's our responsibility,
It is all our own decision,
Do with our own ability,
Using raindrop-like precision.

If everyone pulled together,
And joined in the great commotion,
Just one day of cloudy weather,
This desert would be an ocean.

Life abundant would be as waves,
Bountiful, clean, and even free,
Free from death in earth's desert graves,
And due in all to you and me.

Susan J Hitchens
I LOVE YOU DADDY
Thank you for ice cream castles and clowns.
You brought true the penny-arcade dreams we shared.
I'll always have candy-striped memories to keep.

Thank you for painted ponies and carousels,
white knights and mystic magic dragons.

Your smile turned my tears into rainbows—
and saw bruises through with lollipops.
Thank you for showing me you were behind me all the way,
with a glass of water at midnight,
a warm hug and gentle kiss.

You held my hand when the mountains were hard to climb
and made lost lovers seem not so tragic.
Thank you for Tiger, Princess and Pussycat—
for blue moons wrapped up in purple stars.

Thank you for showing me the world through rose colored glasses—
letting me find me.
I thank you for the world you've given me, but most of all,
I thank you for loving me Daddy.

Ronald K Brantley
TO LEAVES OF OAK AND APPLE

Tonight I have tasted the sweet bouquet of youth,
And find myself immersed in thoughts of passionate streams.
Yet, I know tomorrow's coming and tomorrow will bring me truth—
The real truth that I wait upon to drown these lively dreams.
Yes, for now the joys devour me and I am filled;
Many long dormant drummers spark incessant beats;
But ecstasy alone's a swollen wave that's frozen stilled,
And truth and love exist apart from youthful scandalous retreats.
I have been touched (with the wish to touch again
Those taboo'd flowers of youth's forbidden fruit)
Holding for heightened moments the lengthless breadthless wind,
Riding the tireless mare while nearby excited ones stand mute.
Come, come, come tomorrow take me heart so it will learn
That what is deemed desirable is mostly whines and whims;
That love, dear love, is but a warm spot—not a burn;
That truth will shine beyond the glitter of these playful gems.
To this I now address my open heart and limpid knees
While overhead temptation's dancers celebrate the skies,
And to the choice unripened pleasures promising to please . . .
I must then never know again, or feel such youthful rise.

Nyna R Kaminer
THE UNSHAKEABLE THRONE

For my Heavenly Father; without His Grace I could not write.

God sits in the heavens
On a throne too bright to see,
And the rainbow that surrounds Him
Is a promise made to me.

A promise for the future
That's lifting up my soul;
For every time life breaks me,
His love will make me whole!

His throne has strong foundations.
No elements can shake
The base on which it stands there,
Or the beauty, for His sake.

The throne eternal waits there
Unshakeable and strong,
And when my life is over,
He'll forgive me all my wrongs.

God sits there in the heavens
On a throne too bright to see.
And His saving grace is waiting
For the world, for you and me.

Judy Dianne Anderson
SUMMER'S CHILD

To Rusty, my loving husband, who sees and understands me far better than I.

Short and tan, sleek and wild runs the summer child.
Across the fields and forest green to the waters soft and deep.
To play amongst the fleeting bands of water and crystal sand.
To lengthen yet another day in buoyant and joyous play.
For all too swift it flees away to cold and crispy autumn days.

Kevin M Doran
A ONE WORD POEM

A one word poem?!!!?
How can that be?

Poems must have beauty
grace
smoothness.

They must have that and more
poems must have feeling
depth
excitement.

This poem has all of that and more
this poem has desires
dreams
thoughts of forever.

What is this one word poem??
YOU.

Michele L Kommer
WEATHER REPORT

For Brian—
For your strength and courage
For your love and inspiration

Last week,
It rained somewhere.
Somewhere over and
Over and over
The rainbow.

So big!
So bright!
So much so
That eyes closed
In pinched faces.

A dry spell
Is expected
To last (and last)
Over
Much of
The nation.

Marsha A Lowery
THE BEAUTY OF LIFE

The sun arises so beautiful
to awaken the desirous soul,
just to remind you of the grace
and the goodness the Lord bestows.

The evening is so special
for the one that is all alone
the noise is defeated by silence,
and peace has now overcome.

Learning to accept differences
will always exist in life,
the greatest of all experiences
is to always kneel at knight.

Maria C Basti
A SPARROW

This poem is dedicated to my Heavenly Father and as encouragement to people of little faith.

As I looked out my window this winter morning,
A lonesome little sparrow in my yard was flying.
And as he came to rest on my dogwood tree,
I heard him chirrup as loudly as can be.
Snow had fallen very heavy last night,
The ground was covered and seeds out of sight . . .
But he kept chirping as loudly as can be,
Not caring if a worm in the ground he could see.
I marveled, then, staring toward the sky so blue,
My mind with thoughts of "I will never leave you."
Oh yes, my Heavenly Father, has said so in His will,
That even a little sparrow will have his day's fill.
How foolish I seriously then thought to myself,
When I worry and fret and get greatly upset.
There seems to be a lack in my life way too great . . .
What I need most of all is to have a little faith.
So, I finally said to myself: Look at that sparrow . . .
Is he afraid and worry and fret about tomorrow?
Life is wonderful, every moment is really a gain,
Enjoy then today, sing a song, never worry again!!!

Mary T Zangare

Mary T Zangare
HOMELESS, HUNGRY AND COLD

"I dedicate this poem to all the homeless" as I too was on that street. Love you "Mary"

Lord What's this all about
I'm doing without
I'm Homeless, Hungry and Cold

I come to you without pity
I come from "Silver City"
Yet I'm Hungry, Homeless and Cold.

I can't go on this way
I can no longer stray
My eyesight is failing me.

My home burnt to the ground
Nothing but misery I found
I'm Hungry, Homeless and Cold
Just take me by the hand
To the Promise land.

I know the story I was told
And please let me sit by your side
And I'll be satisfied
I will no longer be Homeless, Hungry and Cold.

Jennifer Maxwell
RUNNING

For Trevor Christian

The long-distance runner,
never seeing the finish line,
feels each weary step.
Bones crashing on a concrete surface,
the blood, the sweat, the tears
slowly drip from an exhausted body.
A voice cries from within,
"You've gotta keep going, keep going, keep going . . ."
Heart bursts like a starting gun,
"But I just want to stop, I'm too tired."
Mindlessly, blindly, feet leading the way—
to nowhere.
Endless paths of windowless faces cast
gloomy shadows that block out the sun.
The only advantage—keeps you from having
to keep looking at nothing.
Eyes beg to close, but the
cold, clean edge of a serrated blade
slips slowly into her abdomen.
Jerks up, "I've gotta keep going,
keep going, keep going."

Anna G Kananowitz
YOU'LL ALWAYS BE MINE

I know how much you love me,
I know how much you care,
but sometimes I wonder,
if you're really being fair.
I cannot give you all the things
you desire,
for I'm not the person,
that one can seem to bear,
and thinking,
my mending heart is always there.
I love you like it was yesterday!
Still I care for you today!
My life here has ended,
but within my heart,
It's just the beginning,
what we call, "The Healing Soul."

I gave you all my love in passing time,
I cared for you, because you're mine,
and now I know, I cannot find,
a way back, to what was mine,
for it's yours to give,
no longer mine, a love gone by.
Why? I cannot understand.
Still I love you!
Still I care!
Just give me time,
to heal within my soul,
so I can once more, feel fine inside,
hoping someday,
you will remember,
you'll always be mine.

Valerie L Bergman
DO YOU KNOW HOW LONG I TRIED TO FIND YOU?

Do you know how long I tried to find you?
Then you walked toward me,
As in some future time,
Your hair streaked with gray;
Too long searching for me,
Your journey much too long.
You found with me what you'll try to recapture
The rest of your life.
Look for wealth, it is in vain;
And fame is fleeting.
We are not rich—except in each other.
But because you do not see
The miracle of us finding each other,
Fate will take me from you,

And I may never find you again,
Until I am also gray.
In other ways, I will not change;
My face will be this same face you see,
And I will look at you lovingly, as I do now,
And I will hold you for hours without end;
For there might not be a tomorrow.

Pamela Broach
INNER THOUGHTS
What is life? We often think.
It's often a way of being,
To make your choices for right or wrong.
We're often down, no hope to see.
The obstacles often take the place of joy,
The tears that fill our eyes, rob the heart of joyful song.

For in this process we call life, we will always have,
A mind for thinking, a heart for feeling.
Hope for tomorrow, confidence in believing.
If tomorrow never comes, that won't matter,
What was in yesterday, no longer seems to count.
Living today for all it's worth, is the highest form of achieving.

So when all is said and done,
For the ultimate goals in life to be attained,
You have to believe in you, and be only you.
Being happy in life, despite all the odds.
You must devise a plan that suits your wants and needs.
And if you're different, no matter . . . to your own self be true.

Cathy Galla
BETWEEN TWO PEOPLE
Something shared between me and you
It's been around for a century
or two
It's something old nothing new
It's a bond we share that is
very rare
It shows we care for each
other
That something we share is
our love for one another,
The love we share as eternal
LOVERS!

Vernonica Gonzalez
WHY DO I LIKE YOU?

This poem is dedicated to two wonderful people: My mom, Norma, who motivated me to write it, and Anthony Zozaya, whom this poem is to.

Why do I like you like I do?
Why does the sun shine?

Why do I think of you as I do?
Why is the world round?

Why do I dream of you at night?
Why does the moon stay in the sky?

Why do I like you like I do?
I'll tell you why:

I like you because when you look at me,
Your eyes shine like the stars.

I like you because your voice is like,
The sound of soft guitars.

I like you because your walk is like,
A lovely summer's breeze.

I like you because your laugh is like,
The rustling of the fallen leaves.

I like you because of the many things
You say and do to me.

To sum it all up, I LIKE YOU,
because GOD made you, YOU!

Maudie M Treadway
KNOWING
Do you know my Main Street, the one in my home town? O' I knew you would recall those sweet smells of fall, with all the crinkly golden leaves; glistening like bright embers quietly glowing. And sadly thinking the embers appear to be dying or dead, then just as suddenly along comes a wind of reviving; at this knowing our hearts leap with joy.
Surely others have known this too! There is no new glowing—no—not really—things are just a changing—rearranging.
So come sift through the ashes of time with me, just silently stand there and stare until your awakening then you'll know too.
Main Street? O'the one in my hometown, our hometown—it's you—it's me! We have this knowing in our golden years, about the embers glowing and together we are awaiting as the wind is changing—just rearranging.

Kate Sullivan
FREEDOM FROM THE WATER
Standing on a rock
With wind blowing in my hair,
I wait.
I do not move.
I stand solid, undaunted by the ocean's waves.
They crash, the rock sways
But not I.
I am strong, for I stand for freedom.
To be free is to live but I live not upon this earth as man.
My strength is in all of you,
Helping to free you from the bondage you live in.
Slowly, the water tries to wash away my message.
But I am strong,
For in your hearts I live.

Luana McGowan
THE END OF SILENCE
There she sat, so quiet and serene,
Looking somehow like soft ice cream.
Like a sentinel she watched the years come and go
With no sign of life, or the dread lava flow.
Then suddenly she woke from her sleep,
Stretching & grumbling from way down deep.
Quake after quake, what a change.
It won't be the same in this mountain range.

Quaking and shaking, and blowing of steam,
She lost her look of soft ice cream.
Then for days she grumbled and roared,
As if through the years she had been bored.
As the days came and went, the more restless she grew
The rumbling & stretching gave us a sure clue
Till early one morn without more delay
The north part of the mountain, with a loud blast gave way.
Dark as night the ash came, creating a wind so strong,
It snapped the trees like toothpicks & everything living was gone
A desolate waste she became, but time can bring a big change
Till once again we can enjoy this beautiful mountain range.

James G Stahlecker
ILLUSION OF LIFE

This poem is dedicated to all my good friends for encouraging me to higher levels. You know who you are.

Tripping through the illusions of life,
Falling from niche to niche,
Living on the edge like the blade of a knife,
Trying to pull myself out of a ditch.

They told me about reality,
But I still live in my dreams.
They say it is insanity,
But everything is not always what it seems.

I have felt the passion of another life.
I have felt the pain of this life.
I have gone where no one has gone before.
I have gone through the transparent door.

Most people who know me would say I am crazy,
But they mean nothing to me.
Their minds are clouded, polluted and hazy.
They will never feel what I see.

Tripping through the illusions of life,
Being dragged on a leash like society's pet,
I have fallen and failed; nothing left to save.
And I have landed in my grave.

Hildegard Leuschner

Hildegard Leuschner
A MOTHER'S THOUGHTS

To my three lovely daughters Gabie, Heidi and Ingrid. Love Mom!

My little girl is all grown up,
I look at her and sigh,
How did it happen, why so fast,
How did the years slip by?

She's going out into the world,
For the first time without my protection,
How will they treat her, will they be kind,
or will they show her rejection?

Will she be strong, can she endure,
Did I teach her enough self esteem,
Will she conquer the world, wherever she goes,
Will life seem to her like a dream?

I pray the Lord to guide her steps,
to bless her every day,
To fill her heart with happiness,
take all her fears away.

My heart is full, there's a lump in my throat,
my God I love her so,
That little girl that's all grown up,
but it's time to let her go.

Jimmie Brooks
A MISSING JOY

August 29, 1983. In loving memory of Aaron Beck, rest in peace in the loving care of the Lord.

Blessed are the children for they are pure in heart.
Knowing only what they have been told from the start.

Always being mischievous, but practical and not knowing why.
And then to be taken from us at a blink of an eye.

His voice you hear that cries out for you in the dark of night,
And then a vision appears to show that he's alright.

He's in his resting place in the heavens up above,
That place we know that is filled with warmth, happiness and lots of love.

There will be an emptiness in your life that will never let him go,
And as the time passes, the pain you will no longer try to show.

But a sense of loneliness within your heart will always be there to stay,
And knowing he will come back as you will see on that judgement day.

So blame not his death on anyone but the Lord above,
For He was the one who gave you that bundle of joy to love.

Never stop praying for the one thing that you held so dear,
For he's so far but yet so near.

Antoinette Bennett
MIRROR, MIRROR
Each morning as I face the mirror, I know exactly what I'll see and I'm not afraid because I know I like me.

Mirror, mirror, "Today's another day" and "I've still got it," I always say. You see, I like me so I start each day with a smile.

Mirror, mirror, "Thank God," I'm still alive. I know that it's only through his mercy that I've survived. More than anything I know that God cares because He's always there for me.

Mirror, mirror, "God's the ultimate friend," he sticks by me through thick and thin. Each time I stumble and fall, God picks me up and brushes me off. No matter how many tears I shed, God wipes them away and gives me the strength to face another day.

Mirror, mirror, I'm glad we had this talk. It's always good to speak out loud about the goodness of God Almighty. This gives me my strength to get through the day.

Mirror, mirror, you're a good friend, you hold the image of me, a person whom I like very much.

Dianne Fertig
SO IN LOVE
I love you in a quiet way—
quiet because it's necessary—
but in my heart I want to shout
it out for all to hear.

I love you passionately, more
than
I can convey in a look, a kiss,
a touch, an embrace.

I love you caringly, for your
needs,
your dreams, your hopes, your
happiness.

I love you for loving me, in your
own special
way, a very special quiet, beautiful world—
a world I wish I could share
with you.

Most of all, I love you for the way I
feel when I am with you, the
wonderful way you, and you
alone make me feel.

And, when we are so far away
from each other,
I love you in my thoughts, my
dreams—
my days and nights are filled
with memories of you my
love.

Andrea J Wisniewski
EXPRESSIONS

Thanks Mom!

Somehow
Someway
I need to convey
My thoughts—
feelings—
emotions—
That words alone
—cannot express
Come
hold me close
feel my meaning

Barb Noftsger
WHAT ABOUT ME

A dedication to Greg, who read these lines, but not the words.

When the need for someone to
speak their mind
About filling the empty space only
you can find
How does one release to one who
has no denies, questions, nor replies?
Does one bury the feelings of
emptiness that seem to be eating me
alive?
One marries, bears children and
tends to everyone's needs and
feelings and forgets herself.
The worry of the tears that should
have been shed.
Be strong she says be strong for
them.
Later, by oneself one cannot revive
feelings that should have been felt
hours ago
When asked to see me, love me, and
be my friend,
Ends up, forgotten, lost, or sees it at
no problem.
It's you, that has no feelings, for
you only hear instead of listen.

Oneida N Canoy
LIFE
Life, a planted seed beginning to
unfold
Is a touch of magic within a
soul.

Life, a spaced step within the
race
Is a mother and child in fond
embrace.

Life, a moment captured and
tenderly
held
Is the soft cloud entering earth's
blue
realm.

Life, the eternal dawn of hope's
new
mysteries
Is the mirror reflecting yesterday's
histories.

Life, the fleeting sands drifting
past
Is justly spent, but not to
last.

Life, the process of all substance
growing
Is a gift generously given and the
art of
bestowing

Life.

Ginger Anne English
LIVIN' OUT THE SONGS
Do your songs reflect your life,
Or are you livin' out the songs you
write?
Writing of love, the way it should be,
Lines of desire, passion, and mystery.

Time after time, line after line; in
your fantasys,
You can create whoever or whatever
you please,
Love and laughter, sorrow and pain,
in various degrees.
You seem to do it with such finesse
and ease.

Your restless mind seems out of
control,
In that direction your actions flow.
Your secret desires flowing thru your
pen,
Wondering if that's the life you're
wishin' to begin.

Don't waste your fantasys all on
paper.
Don't hide your desires, though it
may be safer.
Live the lyrics you make seem so
real,
Transform into touch, to my senses
appeal.

Hold on to reality, don't lose control,
Fantasys are fantasys; what truth do
they hold?
Dreams that come true are no longer
dreams.
Loving you is reality beyond all
measure and means.

Doris J Averih Mathews
THINGS I LOVE

To my son, Shawn—True Love is someone who knows all about you, and loves you anyway.

Pigtails and velvet.
Blue ribbons, Honeysuckle.
The caress of a warm gentle breeze as
it floats through the trees,
kissing my face as it goes.
Passion, as it washes over me.
Sweet slumber, Early morning rain.
My child's smile.
A letter from a dear friend far away.
White wine.
Wildflowers, a good book.
Homemade vegetable soup, Flannel
nightgowns, Roses.
And You.

Samantha Russlyn Flowers
IT'S LATE AT NIGHT, AND IT'S RAINING OUTSIDE
It's late at night, and it's raining
outside,
my tears seem to be falling from
the sky.
The rain has stopped, and I
patiently await the dawn.
It's morning at last, a new day has
begun,
and the sun is shining.
I feel blessed, God has helped my
pain
and given me another day to do
something special with.

Elizabeth M Davis

Elizabeth M Davis
LOVE IS

Dedicated to my neighbor, Robert E. Hession, Sr. Dec. 8, 1886—Jan. 9, 1989. 102 years of age

LOVE Is loving one person with
all your heart,
promising in marriage "'Til
death" do you part.
LOVE Is to settle arguments, to
wipe away someone's tear,
or taking away someone's fear.
LOVE Is to bring laughter to
someone's mind
and lifting that worry, is being
most kind.
LOVE Is visiting old folks at a
nursing home,
either singing to them or
reciting a poem;
OR helping to dish out food to
the homeless,
not just on Thanksgiving Day or
Christmas.
LOVE Is to answer a child's
"Why . . . ?" or "Wherefore . . . ?"
with a true answer and a good
"Therefore . . ."

LOVE Is to "Love thy neighbor as
thyself"—
My neighbor had two fires in his
house,
I welcomed him to stay in mine,
since then, all things with him
are fine!
"Do unto others as you would
have them do unto you"—
my neighbor just turned 102!
HIS doctors said 'twas due to my
loving care.
I said: "God gave me blessings
with others to share."
A stray mother cat brought her
little kittens to my door,
wanting food and shelter, her
eyes did implore!
I fed her, giving her family a
place to stay,
and what joy I had watching
them romp and play!
LOVE Is talking to one's neighbor
over the fence,
exchanging tidbits and current
events.
LOVE Is living in this great land
of the Free
with its many freedoms for you
and me.
LOVE Is giving monetary, or
material aid,
wherever a catastrophe has
been made.
LOVE Is forgiving and forgetting
when one has been hurt,
at someone's untruth, or being
curt!
THESE are just some of the things
that LOVE Is—
But, Lord, how I hate it when I'm
addressed as "Liz"—
And I hope and pray when I
send this poem in—
that it'd be considered for a Big
Prize to Win!!

Sherie Madsen-Cloutier
YOUR GRADUATION FROM AN ALCOHOL REHABILITATION

This poem is dedicated to my husband Jeff: "THANK YOU FOR GIVING LIFE ANOTHER CHANCE." I love you. Sherie

Tonight is the beginning of the rest of
our life
as we struggle to become a new
husband and wife
and not to forget our beautiful
daughters
as they have been with us through
hell & high waters.

We know that it won't be an easy
thing to do
but we all love each other and
especially you,
for you have acknowledged the
problem in hand
and have chosen to change, which we
think is just grand.

I know that a rehab is a hard thing to
do
but I want you to know that I am so
proud of you
for sticking it out and making it to
this night
as I hoped that you would and prayed
that you might.

I would like to take a short moment
here
and thank you so much for giving up
the beer.
As that and other things are now in
our past
and we can start over a new life at
last.

I guess I have said all that I need to
say
except that this disease is a hard price
to pay
and I promise I will learn to trust and
be kind
and I'm willing to live, just ONE
DAY AT A TIME!

Cynthia Jean Jones
NIGHT SKY'S PAIN
Pink and blue make a soft color purple,
As quietly the clouds roll over each other.
Then the sun slowly fades away.
So, too, the colors of the day.

A soft darkness floats over the city.
For the hearts of the recently let go,
The evening seems to know no pity.
Thy sky, the hurt of all hurt, makes those hearts know.

As we move from one to another
In this world of pain and sorrow,
Like the one before, there will be no other.
Not until Eternity's tomorrow.

Marie De Sales Bagley
THE CIRCLE
Where have all my summers gone?
Quickly time is fleeting.
Soon the Autumn of my life—
I shall be greeting.
Reminiscing on yesterday's memories,
A sense of sadness enveloped me.
I returned to the meadow—
To the old oak tree.
I glanced at the carving in the bark,
Our initials in a circle, instead of a heart.

You said it was like our love,
A beginning without an end.
It was a lovely thought, my dear,
Only time was not our friend.
Golden leaves began falling
Like the dreams of that lovely day.
I gently touched the carving,
Turned slowly, started walking—
Still asking, "Where have all my summers gone—
Since you—went away?"

Denise L Gosselin Dufresne
ONE GOLDENNIGHT
Sitting by the crackling fire,
with our thoughts so tranquil.
On the left, the moon is full and bright.
The glowing stars are to the right.

Take my hand, Lay by my side.

Lying under this glowing light,
I feel the warmth of your touch.
A lot was heard, yet nothing spoken.
A memory of time that won't be broken.

Take my hand, Stay by my side.

As the fire begins to flicker, the light of day is near,
we listen to the peaceful silence.
We touched souls in a special way.
With contentment, we'll face the day.

Take my hand, Walk by my side.

Karen D Price
MY APATHETIC COMRADE

Mother—Georgia H. Price and Sibling—Carl W. Price. In them there existed no apathy. Their profound love and adamant belief are a source of strength and inspiration.

Tell me the secrets you consistently apply
so that nothing and no one affects your life.
How is it that you are not unnerved
by anything and yet with you everything is alright?
How can you become so conditioned
without becoming totally cold? How can your mannerisms be so bleak—if your heart isn't made of stone.

You claim to be loving, yet you have no need for love.
It's only an emotion that you make mockery of.
How can you be so impassive, so nonchalant and disinclined.
Does ever a warm and loving thought stir some portion of your mind.

Share with me your methods so that I may know
What it is that gives you such an air of intrepidity
that seems to compose you so—tell me that I
will no longer be so bewildered and confused—
that I may better comprehend the thought patterns
of your mind and your emotionless views.

I'd like to know the secrets of your impervious moods
that seem so continuous to me—I'd like to know
What it is that keeps you so impassive and full of apathy.

Rose Marie Phillips
MY VERY BEST FRIEND

To my dear friends at New Liberty Baptist who inspired me to write this.

I have a friend that always knows,
He's always there for He never goes.
He listens to me when I talk,
He's there with me when I walk.
He gives me a true peace of mind,
That only true believers can find.
He's always in my heart,
For we are never apart.
To you this may sound odd,
But my very best friend is, God.

Karen Elise Wormack
ON TERRORISM

This poem is dedicated to my family, friends and fellow countrymen. Glory to God in the highest!

The terrorists are twisting our wrists!
Their wiles are on display,
Wrecking lives, despising rights,
Terrorists are in a hey day!
No mercy can be found in their bosom,
Only plans for DEATH and DEATH,
A terrorist attack is a plot against life,
Enforced with a man made nefarious device!
For the love of their country they say,
And for the hate of yours
A message is conveyed,
To annihilate innocent lives,
On this notion terrorists thrive!
They will bomb a plane, and send acid rain,
To accomplish diabolical deeds,
There's no law except the law of revenge,
They know nothing of a mother's plea.
A terrorist has a sick mind,
For his conscience is seared with an iron.
Kamikazes are his ancestors,
As the hereditary genes still fester.
Yet their movements are induced by a leader,
Whose command they believe is sweeter,
Than the melodic song of a bird,
For they obey his every word!
No questions asked concerning a task
They'll fulfill to their utmost potential,
As a means to carry-out a strategic plan,
They'll have access to false credentials!
The world lies in a potent trap
Of fear, and hate for these doers,
Our methods of peace must eradicate
The voices of terrorists rulers!
We must gird our loins, and strengthen ourselves
To the onslaught of terrorist violence,
And pledge allegiance to surrounding countries
Who acknowledge our country's alliance!

Darrell Anthony White

Darrell Anthony White
THE MAN IN THE MIRROR

To my beloved Mother; Sis Mary Louise White, to my beloved Grandmother, Sis Willie Mae White, To Aunt Nita & Uncle Bob Campbell, To Bro. & Sis. Johnson; To Uncle Willie (Boddie), Thank you all for everything! Sincerely D. White "The One To Watch."

I woke up one morning; I received a sight. I pictured a thought that had entered my mind last night. For I had dreamed. It happened so fast. I jumped up real quick and I gleamed at the looking glass. Oh yes; I looked in that mirror and what did I see? It was an image like my own staring back at me! Was there any hope? Did anyone really care? You see, I had dreamed about life . . . But I was living in a nightmare! Now, while I was asleep, that dream was good to me. Because joy and peace was all that I could see. But when I finally woke up . . . What would it be? It was the poverty stricken reality!!! For one brief moment I had a little thought. But I had to stop myself, no . . . it wasn't God's fault. I know life is His to give, and for sure it's His to take. So I just went in the kitchen and got me some cornflakes. There I began to contemplate on the thought I had. And I said to myself, there is no reason to be mad. So I headed night back to that same looking glass. And as I looked in that mirror, what did I see? It was all the great things that God had done for me! Life is His to give, and it's His to take. Well, just as sure as I'm standing here, Lord knows I feel great! To be upset, I have no reason. Because my trials and tribulations are but for a small season. Jesus wept on that cross, and Christ died for me. No, there was nothing lost. But now I can live eternally. Now if you have a troubled heart and you want to see clearer . . . well, it all starts with "The Man In The Mirror."

Crystal L Schmidt
BABIES
Babies always crying,
When they grow up they're always whying,
Why this, Why that,
It can drive you crazy as a matter of fact,
You better use your time while you get it,
'Cause a baby can surely throw a fit!!

Charles W Fortson Jr
FATE OF THE HEART
O crescent moon
spirit candle, rise
bring forth your face

Ageless moment awaken!
trace the heart's fate
reveal desire's voice

Your veil lifts
with magic presence
and illuminated grace

The hour's orbit
visits late mystery
and early legacy

With shadow and light
you fold the tents of dawn
for this next venture

Will not your beauty yield
with signal view
to paint the day?

O eye of trust
be yet the vision
for our blindness

Wilburn B Craft
TO MY BEAUTIFUL BRIDE

This poem is dedicated to my beautiful wife, who is the biggest part of my life
Wilburn Bryan Craft

To my beautiful bride, whose love I cannot deny.

I would swim the ocean wide
For just one kiss from my beautiful bride;

For she is always by my side,
My beautiful bride.

So these words of Love
I cannot keep inside,

I send this poem to;
My beautiful bride, Tresea

Dru R Thompson
VISIONS TO SEEK
God spoke aloud, he formed the land;
heaven lit the way.
No height, no depth too great for Him,
He separated night from day.

His land speaks out for all to hear,
each life is blessed by His.
A land to roam and call their home,
the coyote, wolf and deer.

They prowl and search for refuge right,
bald eagle soars above.
Migrating geese echo resounding cries,
graceful swans announce their flight.

Majestic elk trail river bank,
then disappear from view.
A mother cow whistles anxious cry,
her calf is lonely too.

A watchful bear, her furry cub
perch on flower sprinkled ledge.

Curious woodchuck ventures a look,
jumps back from jagged edge.

Misty veils of water
cascade to rocks below,
Seething foam then settles down
and forms a river to flow,

Cutting through the canyon
meandering in peaceful bliss
Greeting low hanging willow,
punctuated with a kiss.

Visions to seek, memories to hold
for all Eternity.
Uncounted lakes of every hue
tint land with sky reflected blue.

Day greets night and gossamer clouds
wrap moon in loving arms.
Traveling trail thru darkening sky
it seems to speak aloud . . . .

"Protect this land and treat with care,
unmolested may they roam;
Let them multiply and grow,
created earth, their beautiful
home."

I tremble!

Susan Kay Connett
THE CHILD WITHIN
Today
I found a child within these hidden
walls so carefully built; made strong
by tears and sorrow.

I
glimpsed this child in a mirror of pain
and reached out, tentatively, afraid
the image would disappear.

A
hand reached back, our fingers
touched and I felt the warmth. She
saw me through her tears.

With
an un-touched love, this child
reached out and ever so gently,
wrapped her fingers around my
fragile heart.

A
longing was born and a fervent wish
made,
to love this child inside before I fade
away.

Alexis Megan Marxmiller
WOLF

To my fellow creatures, may your lives be full of hunt and glory and may your hearts be full of pride. I will always be with you, my dear ones.

Streaking through the night, your
silvery coat is struck by the full
moon, sending off a radiant glow,
surrounding your body.

You are on the prowl, searching for
your prey.

You have found something. Possibly
a rabbit or a squirrel. But no matter
what it is, you have found something.

This something will tame your
hunger pains and ease your thoughts
of starving in this stark wilderness.

You are a wolf, constantly searching.
Searching for a destiny that will
depend on whether you live or die.
Now you can find nothing, so you lay
down, easing your body into an
eternally-peaceful sleep.

You are now the prey, prey to a force
you have never seen, but only sensed.

Your predator is man.

Magdoline Skaggs
TO LOWELL

Dedicated to my great grandson

Your soft little body held close to me
You are a blessing to someone as
lonely as I
How can I explain to you how I miss
you
In these lonely hours as time slowly
passes by
The feel of your arms around my
neck,
Your head on my shoulder—will you
remember the comfort
we found in each other as you grow
older?
There is such a distance between
us—not only in miles,
but in years—
I should help you in life's trials but
you've seen me through
life's broken dreams.
Goodnight little Buddy!
What a joy to see you
What a heartbreak to leave you.
Nanna

Molly Sharpley
THE FOREVER WALK

To Danarchy, Straight Tait, Erb, Beer, and Bridge—I love you! The Master of Disaster—learn how to count; it wasn't three! Dru Guy—I'll miss you!

Holding hands we walked together,
side by side, on the shore.
You carried me for miles,
when I could walk no more.

I smiled until my mouth grew weak,
and I became tired of pretending.
You could tell by the look on my
face,
our "forever walk" was ending.

You could have let go at that
moment,
but you held on to me tighter than
ever.
You said that the friendship we
shared,
was a bond that time could not sever.

You told me to try a little harder.
There was a point we had to reach;
a point where this ground that we
walked on
was no longer just a beach.

You told me to look up.
I saw the moon, the stars, and the
sky.
You held my hand, you held my
heart,
And you taught me how to fly.

Shelly Ruiz
FEELINGS
I feel like people are pushing me
around.
It always seems to drag me down.
I wish I could just be found, but I
seem to let people do it to me.
When I'm hurt, when I cry!
I wish I had someone to dry my
tears away.
To also drag my fears away.
Feelings come feelings go, but
why can't we keep them
though?
I feel like I been in a hole.
Why can't I just be whole?
When I'm lonely, when I'm
scared!
I dared to ask will you help me
please?
When I'm happy, when I frown!
I just don't want to be let down.
I make fun of, but I know how
they feel.
Why can't things just seem real?

Wilda M Haskett
DISTANCE
If I could only talk to you
Gain strength from what you say and
do.

Just feel your arms around me tight,
Then everything would be alright.

Your tender lips would feel divine
If they were pressed so close to mine.

To share the candlelight once more
While shadows in the room explore.

The laughter and the tears we've shed
Bring precious memories to my head.

The poetry and music shared
Expressed again, how much you
cared.

Oh loneliness, why don't you flee?
Just hang it all on love, you see!

Elizabeth Denmark
AUTUMN DREAMS
Autumn dreams of winter snow
With seasoned books and hearth
aglow;
Good music wafting o'er the scent
Of cedar embers almost spent;
Serenity of hearts in tune,
'Midst memories of April/June.

Winter sighs for late September,
When the leaves are turning amber;
When the caterpillar spins
And his favorite ball team wins;
E'er the chill winds start to blow,
Prophesying early snow.

Dreams come true, they sigh no
more;
Light the hearth and close the door;
They've spun their own little cocoon
And live again their April/June.
Autumn Dreams and Winter Sighs
Fondly touch and close their eyes.

Robert M Traynor
A POETIC PORTRAIT OF CINDERELLA
Let Me Paint A Poetic Portrait
Forever True,
Of The Loveliest Girl I Ever Knew;
One That Will Bring On Happy
Tears,
When It's Read Down Through The
Years.
She's Lovely To Look At, and I Need
Not Be Told;
Even Lovelier To Hold.
A Vision Of Loveliness, This Little
Maid,
With Her Bouncing Golden Braid;
Slightly Less Than Five Foot Two,
With Sparkling Eyes Of Baby Blue.
She Carries Her Trim Little Figure
So Petite,
To and Fro; On Tiny, But Dainty
Feet!
She Has Rosy Cheeks With A Smile
Pure and Simple;
Punctuated By A Child-Like Dimple.
She Could Be A Misplaced Princess,
Her Father A King;
For Just To Know Her, Is Like A
Breath Of Spring!
It's Not Likely, I Will Ever Be Her
Loving Fella;
But I'll Always Love My Little
Cinderella!

Christine Hicks
VESPERS
The fears are three
That come to me
Within the still of sober night:
A loved one lost
The holocaust
The lingering of vespers' plight.

If chance to choose
Which lease to lose
Full well I know the cost to me.
A sad farewell
A flash of hell
Beget a pain too stark to see.

And yet, to live beyond one's time,
To grow infirm of limb and mind,
Cocooned within where life began,
The circle made—a child again
Without the wonder, void of
hope,
Bereft of friends, one's self the
scope,
No greater ill, no deeper rift
Than this: the gods' ironic gift.

Heather Gallas
SUMMER CONTENT GIVES WAY TO THE FALL
Summer content gives way to the fall
Almost as though it never happened
at all
Green leaves turn to brown, then into
gold
And you feel your heart turn icy cold

June started things off with a hearty
laugh
Into July came the fateful dance
August flew quickly on the wings of
a dove
September brought the end to your
summer love

Stumble, but then quickly get back
on your feet
Tread carefully on the pavement of
sleet
For in November, a darkness
descends
Especially for the ones whose hearts
need to mend

Cold, bitter snow falls to the ground
Wind swirls past, like a whistle it
sounds
And December runs through like a
man on the run
Another year ends, now it is done

Barbara Harris
SNOWFLAKES

I dedicate this poem to my two precious Granddaughters Kasie Orr and Mayumi Harris

Snowflakes where do you come from
Who empties you out upon the
ground

How can so much of you fall upon
the earth
and never make a sound

Why are you white and shiny

and shaped in so many forms

Why is it that you feel so cold
but when I am by the fireplace
the thought of you seems warm

Snowflakes you're beautiful
I know that you fall from the sky

You are so wonderful to touch
and to play in

You are so delightful to eye

Janice Dunn-Diamond
A WOMAN OF THE 80'S
A woman of the 80's
A statement so hard to define
We're all so very different
None really two of a kind.

Some of us are a success
Within our own right
Being happy and productive
We've resolved a personal plight.

To try to figure out
What is our destiny
We are woman that's for sure
But again who are we?

There's a little voice in each of us
That calls out from time to time
A disturbing unsatisfaction
Shouting show me now what is mine.

I have so many talents
I have so many needs
I'm bursting with all this energy
Oh, Oh, I better take heed.

Don't lean on all the others
Who always profess to know
For hidden beneath their exterior
Lie fears they don't want shown.

Therese O'Connor
HEAR THE VOICE FROM WITHIN

To my Mother who always hears the voice within me.

When I speak with you today
do not laugh nor look away.
Scared and lonely am I.
Trapped within this universe,
one so silent so diverse;
at times I wonder why.

Hear my voice within the breeze
will you listen to it please?
Tears rush forward fast
leaving me without a friend,
alone forever in the end.
Remembering days past.

Words of wisdom passing by;
inside I'm feeling so shy.
Secrets from within I see.
Time is short so don't delay;
speak to me my friend today.
Reaching out is the key.

Sharon Rutherford Miller
THE BIRTH OF A REVOLUTIONARY
Thoughts climbing up a stair
Words, they come from anywhere
A dream—A scheme
Does anyone really care?

A paper mind
With hands of ink
I look—A freedom took
I think.

A seed sprouts
passion flies
Anger—fear—doubt
Peace and comfort dies

Lines and circles on a stage of white
Dancers waiting for the light
My words—My thoughts
I'll hold them very tight—
in the morning—
I'll join the fight.

William Agbor-Baiyee
THE LIGHT OF HUMAN LIFE

This poem is dedicated to the sustenance of the human spirit.

Human life taps inexhaustibly
From the dependable resource of
hope.
Hope illuminates our path
Through the precarious reality of life.
From hope springs
The desire to cling to life preciously.

Hope buttresses human experience
Like mangrove tree roots.
Hope uplifts the soul
From every depression.

Hope is as predictable as
The alternation of day and night.
Hope brings cheer
And great expectation to the
oppressed.

Hope yesterday, hope today, hope
tomorrow.
Amidst every facet of our existence,
Hope remains the light of
Human life.

L Delgado
GLASSY EYED STARE

I dedicate this poem to everyone who has felt the thorns of love.

You took my heart
And tied it in a knot
then kissed me good-bye
Without a second thought

I don't even think
You ever really cared
But you sure fooled me
With that glassy eyed stare

What a fool I was to
Let beauty catch my eye
And still believe in it
Even through all the lies

I know it's over now
And there's nothing I can do
But there's one thing you can't take
away
And that's my love for you

RoxAnna A Sway

RoxAnna A Sway
COYOTE MAGIC
Rabbits have antlers,
The Eagle has paws,
Whale sings a death song to fishes'
applause.

Trees scorched by rain,
Oceans run red,
No Balm of Gilead; the hungry
unfed.

Twixt the Moon and the Sun,
And the Sun and the Moon,
Watermelon in Winter, Snowfall in
June.

Sweet Milk turned sour,
Chernobyl's blight,
Coyote Magic; right's wrong,
wrong's right.

Worm eats ashes,
Owl blinks an eye,
Old Shaman casts a bone at the sky.

To the Southern Cross
And the stars beyond,
Man sends a message
......"Please Respond."

Black is light burned,
White is light quickened
Who will heal what man has
sickened?

Willie Yates III
DON'T BE DISCOURAGED

Changing careers can be very difficult. With a loving family and true friends, it is made easier. A special thanks to my wife (Ginny), my three children (Nicky, Kenny & Janelle) and my mother (Vivian C.)

Increasingly emotional pain, sorrow
and grief,
Sometimes the thought of dying
seems to be a relief.

Problems, stress and despair/makes
me sad and almost swear,
Why is this happening, when will it
end?
Sometimes it seems I don't have a
friend.

One who will just listen and
understand me,
Who will sympathize but help me
see.

That while there may be sorrow in
living,
Still true happiness is in giving.

When we just don't feel like trying
any more,
Remind us of the blessings that are in
store.

Remind us not to dwell on
disappointing things,
But on the joy that serving God
brings

Lori Ruyle
HEART'S DELIGHT
The crack of antlers
like a pistol shot on a misty morn.
The wild Rose
Amid the thistle; marrying each
other's thorn.
The night owl's call
Across a midnight meadow expanse,
The mouse's scratching
in a lovesick hayloft dance.
The November face of an icy moon,
A bright suncircle in the forest
gloom.
The green, green mountains
Reaching for the purple sunset glow
This is my heart's delight,
This is Idaho.

Joseph John Imperial
SON

This poem is dedicated to Joseph Samuel Imperial, my son.

Son! I remember, when you were
born!
I was in the waiting room, pacing the
floor, until it was worn.
And so, as you grew! We had a lot of
fun! Us two.
When you slipped, on the ground,
and I thought you were hurt!
That was when you said, your very
first word!, and it was dirt.
Then, when you became a little tyke!
That was when, I bought you, your
very first bike.
And when I had to bring you, for
your first day of school!
You must have felt, that your dad,
was very cruel,
So as you have grown! you wanted to
be known.
Well one day! You wanted to play.
And you thought you were a little
man!
So you decided to play, Superman.
So you climbed on a chair! and
jumped up through the air.
Because you wanted to do a great
feat!
But you fell on your face, and
chipped your two front baby teeth.
Well as the years flew by, which
they really did fly.
And now that you are grown! And
you feel that you're ready to leave
home.
So now you're a young man of
twenty one! And all the funny things,
you said and done.
I am very proud, that you are my son!
God! Bless you! Son! Love Dad.

Marion P Bennett
A MOTHER'S LOVE
When God created mothers
He knew a thing or two,
For their love is as old as time
And yet it is always new.

It starts with a first-born child
And a husband at her side,
When the love she had for him
Has now been multiplied.

And with each new addition
Her love is not divided,
But ever grows throughout the years;
It's something God decided.

He knew how their love was needed
So much upon this earth
For a mother will love her children
From the moment of their birth.

A mother's love is constant
Even when it is mixed with tears
For the wayward son or daughter;
She will love them through the years.

Adrian Payne
Blood through many young men's veins
I saw you at the party.
You were there in a long
black dress with a large
two looped bow tied behind.
A halo shaped pearl necklace
embraced your neck, and God I
wished it were me. Yet it 's
been over for years. You even
said that it may never have begun.
But if I close my eyes, I can
remember every hour, every secret,
always young, beautiful and dancing.
And in my arms she was like a sun
bird singing its favourite song, a
whisper that opiated my senses and
fastened my heart.
I'm told that the sun bird's song
shall be sun again, and until the
night city lights go dim, I remain
restless and wish that I were him.

Mary G Dorrough
CAMPUS WINDOW SCENE
Barren, stately, stand the campus
pecan trees,
Against a background of
low-hanging

gray sky with spots of azure
here and there.

Now and then a squirrel, gray as the outstretched
limbs of the trees, darts along
the branches,
then pauses to place a morsel
in his
eager mouth.
Nimble and quick, he seems in preparation for the
winter being foretold in the sky
beyond.

The trees, reminiscent of the respiratory trees in man,
breathe ever so slowly because
it's time for
them to rest a while.

Catherine L Phillips

Catherine L Phillips

A BOY AND HIS DREAMS

This poem is dedicated to Robert my son when he was five.

A little boy lay beneath a tree
With one bare foot upon his knee.

That day he didn't go to school
Instead went wading in the pool.

He looked up high into the sky
And wondered how airplanes did fly.

He saw a bird upon the wing
And wondered why they always sing.

He wished that someday he could be
On ships that sailed far out to sea.

Or be a soldier strong and tall
In answer to a bugle call.

Over his eyes he placed his cap
And promised he'd take one little nap.

When he awoke to his surprise
The stars were shining in the skies.

He dragged himself upon his feet
And wearied home to bed and sleep.
For that's the only place it seems
For a little boy with great big dreams.

Raymond F Rogers

THE EXPANDING UNIVERSE (The Big Bang)

This poem is dedicated to God, Who gave me life, liberty, Lillian—and a sense of wonder!

Come fly with me on fancy's light,
elusive wings,
Beyond the farthest galaxies of stars,
To where faint rays still pierce the
darkness
At the constant speed of light,
And the word of God still echoes
With undiminished might.

Evermore expanding outward,
There still rings eternal morn,
As the Master of Creation laughs
Man's brightest guess to scorn.

In those outer reaches,
At the end of fancy's flight,
Hear the universe still echoing
The words, "Let there be light."

Florence E R Foster

THE WHOLE YEAR THROUGH

When Christmas comes, we love to share; . . .
To show each other how much we care.
We wish happiness and joy to friends, . . near and far,
To let them know how important, to us, they are.
We keep alive all the memories of Christmases past,
And share hopes for a peaceful future that we pray will last; . . .
And, for just about a week or two,
We live and love each other the way God wants us to.
Now, if only each one of us could stop, and think it over twice, . . .
When Christmas-time ends, wouldn't it be nice
If we just didn't notice, it had come to an end; . . .
And we could go on right through the year, treating one another as special friends: . . .
Sharing happiness and peace the whole year through, . . .
And living our lives the way God wants us to.
If all year long, we could spread yuletide joy and glee,
What a wonderful place this world would be!

Lawrence A Beardslee

CANDY CANE KISSES

Candy Cane Kisses, so tasty
sweet
Your Candy Cane Kisses just
can't be beat.

Those Candy Cane Kisses only
come around once a year.
Maybe this is why,
your Candy Cane Kisses are
so dear.

Candy Cane Kisses wrapped
in God's Love.
What a special treat
Candy Cane Kisses made
from above.

Debbie Squires

MY GROWN CHILD

Where did all the time go?
It was just yesterday that I watched
you grow,
Growing up into a world unknown.

I have always wanted the best for
you.
No matter what I said or did, it was
all for you,
My grown child.

So now you treat me like a stranger,
like a person you've never known.
I brought you up my grown child,
and made you what you are today . . .

Now you've changed into a person I
had never even known,
You have finally made a life of your
own.
What a beautiful woman you've
grown up to be.
May your life always be simple and
free.
Whether or not your life will include
me, I don't know.
But just realize one thing . . .

I'll always be there if you need me—
My grown child.

Jennifer Gordon

DREAMS

This poem is dedicated to Mike, who I really never got to know.

You know I like you,
And I care a lot.
I want to show you,
All the love I've got!

It'll take time,
But I can wait.
I just hope
That I'm not too late!

I wish we could be together,
And share our dreams.
We could work together,
Together as a team!

Linda E Bluford

DAVID

To David: You gave me love, hope, and inspiration when I needed it the most, I'll always love you!

Of all the men, I've ever met,
David, you are the one I can't forget.
The look of your eyes—Lights up my very soul,
Much better than any stars, Can bring light to thy world below.

The touch of your lips, All over my body and face,
The feel of you, Your embrace—Is something I couldn't replace.
I love the way you hold me, When we are dancing close.
I love the way it makes me feel—
When tenderly you are kissing me.

The talks we have, they mean so much,
You tell me your needs and fears,
That shows me you trust and care.
I love all the fireworks—I seem to see and feel,
When we are very intimate, In sex and hold as well.

If I could explain the excitement, I feel when you enter the room.
Then I'd have all the answers, To why I seem to bloom.
You say it's me, who makes me happy, I tell you it's you—my dear.
I never could have done anything,
Without the want and need of you.

Dorothy June Harrison

LONELY HEART

Lonely, lonely heart,
in a world full of desire,
Lonely, lonely heart,
in a soul that's set on fire.
Lonely, lonely heart,
searching for that someone
right,
Now this lonely heart cries in the
night.

Once this heart was happy,
it was filled with joy and cheer.
I had everything I wanted,
and the one I loved so dear.
But, time changed our lives,
and it tore my world apart.
That's what made this lonely, lonely
heart.

Lonely, lonely heart,
try to calm your fears.
Lonely, lonely heart,
wipe away your tears.
Lonely, lonely heart,
I know one day you can
find another lonely heart who'll
understand

Geri Bennett Smith

STORM

A quickly darkening sky, a cover for
the sun—
Leaves blown shapeless by the now
persistent wind—
Grasses flattened to look like mirrors,
Birds hiding secretly among swaying
branches—
All waiting for the rainfall to make a
clean wet path of the wind's folly.

Heather Waldroff

BEYOND THE PAIN

Beyond the pain,
Beyond my tears,
Lies a heart
In need of desperate love.
It reaches out
And pulls back in,
Empty-handed.
How many times
Must one
Cry out
They can't take
The loneliness anymore?
And the tears
Pour on and on.
Falling faster,
Falling harder.
Does anyone care?

Lynne A Barnett

Lynne A Barnett

THE LIE

She hides the ugly crack behind a veil
So no one can see.
She weeps, but when the dawn is
real,
he will come.
Not now, but then, when the dawn is
real.

He will come in time to know, that
when he dealt the blow, it did cause a
crack.
before the dawn is real, he does not
know.
She hid the crack with a veil so
no one could see. Not even he.

Then, the fog came to cover the veil, so
no one could see but she.
She knew the blow would cause a crack. So she did weep, and the fog came to hide her and the veil and the dawn.

She will stay in the fog until the dawn is real.
Then when he sees what he has done, he will
use his great strength to close the crack, and it will seal. He will take the veil away, and the fog, to see her again, when the dawn is real.

Cynthia Mendelsohn
IF WE WEREN'T WE

This poem is dedicated to John, "my friend," who inspired me to write more often!

Stand by me
Just touch my hand,
Let's go thru life
the way we planned.

Tho we have grown
in separate ways,
We still have shared,
so many days.

We've faced the world,
Its ups, Its downs.
We've been its fools,
we've been its clowns.

We've gone so far,
so far to go.
We've lived life fast,
tho it felt slow.

Yet all we've done,
First you, then me,
could not have been,
"IF WE WEREN'T WE"

William S Arthur
WORKMATES

To my friend and mentor, Donald Willard Moore, of Toronto, Canada.

Let us be strong and mend the breaches Time has made,
Together, you and I, go labour with the gang,
And feel the sun, the clammy sweat, the joy of work well done.
Let's share a crust, drink from the cup mauby or wine;
Tell jokes, swap yarns, and laugh clean, joyous, zestful laughter
Drawn deep from hidden springs with cords of brotherhood.
Let's relax there in the shade, well satisfied,
And tell our last night's dream, or last year's for that matter—
(Strange how the debris of the years choke up the ways
That once led to the soul) and blend our voices in gay song.
They would keep us apart with barriers and notions,
Strange, foolish notions of another day once grossly ignorant:
But we have freed our souls, seen vision wonderful:
Arise and let us walk together up the hill.

Kimberly Dawn Gerhards
HAIKU CREATIONS
Mystical horned beast,
Colored gold and white beauty
Running through the fields.
A unicorn

Falling to the ground
And leaving a misty dew,
Crying drops of tears.
Raindrops

Bright red color full
Welcoming the things that come,
Sweet smell fills the air.
Red roses

Puffy white cotton,
Blue ocean with marshmallows
Flying like eagles.
Clouds

Father keeps it well,
A never stopping magic
Stays, leaves, all year 'round.
Time

Isaac D Davis Jr
LADY OF CRIME
For you're so sweet, And you're so fine . . . Just, being without you is a crime . . . .
You stole my heart, and you're always on my mind . . . . To have you back would un-leash this crime . . . I need to know if you'll come back, or will this crime stay upon my back, from now on, day to day, Or, will you return to me and stay . . . . ?

Holly Ann Mandeville
A CHILD ALONE
His tiny body shivers in the icy night air
His little hand reaches out wanting someone to care
His eyes are filled with hunger and pain, they've shed so many tears
But there's no one to catch them, silence is all he hears.

His clothes are torn and dirty, his hands are rough and scarred
The wind blows up against him so very lonely and hard.
His home is on a street corner, his family . . . he has none
This little boy is all alone, why has this been done?

But yet this little face looks up, his lips form a smile
His head is held high and his eyes . . . they sparkle all the while.
For in his heart he knows that he must wait because one day very soon
Someone will come and dry the tears and take away the gloom.

This is his dream that he'll be loved and he holds on as each day will pass,
But for this child his dream is his life, for that is all he has!

Michelle Vandiver
YESTERDAY
Yesterday
between the gray sky and grey parking lot
I saw a sea gull.
She was flying in circles
And diving
lost, and searching
for her warm blue home
that was so different from this
She would circle,
and dive,
crying. And as I sat there, watching,
I laughed.
But not a happy laugh.
How can you mistake a parking lot for the sea?

Kim Ramella
THE WIND BLOWS ON A COLD WINTER NIGHT
The wind blows on a cold winter night,
Swooping over everything in sight,
The trees watched by little girls and boys,
Swaying with very little poise.
As raindrops of silver drop they shine,
So delightful, heartwarming, tender and fine.
The panes on the windows rattle and shake,
Frightening the small children as they wake,
What is to become of this cold winter night,
Will it constantly disrupt the children in fright,
Or will there be happiness and joy the next day,
Or will these two things disappear and go away.

Donna L Kidd
A GENTLE COMPOSE

To the friends who live an unbalancing life.

The sun is setting like it never had.
She's bringing on these tears that life's options are turning from the bright colors to a bold plaid.
In a glance I see her focus a thought in a timidity way. She looks away above at the sky, she must be praying her thoughts will be caught up before the next day.

Sometimes I wonder about the world and how it spins around.
I know she must have dreams that shine like diamonds and she's scared that they'll fade to worthless gems without a sparkling strength.
She stops with her mind so clear and looks away in such a length.
We both listen to a determined pattern and walk away with a beautiful sound.

Shirley Toler
ON THE WINGS OF PEGASUS
I went on a journey last evening,
over distances beyond believing.
I rode on waves of passion,
on a deep blue sea of lust.
Reaching the ultimate goal
soon became a must.
Over hills and thru valleys
of depths unknown.
Sowing seeds,
yet unsown.
Reaching heights not meant for us.
Riding on the wings of Pegasus.

Laura L Metlak
CRY OF THE DEAF
Silence is golden.
So it is said.
If it is gold,
I'd rather have lead.

No birds to hear,
No people talking.
No thunder to fear,
No sounds when walking.

I can not hear,
What did you say?
There is no noise,
Why must I pay?

I have one wish,
I do not fear
One thing to ask,
Please, let me hear!

marLynn bidwell
untitled
there i felt for life
in the summer dry, moon
risen,
musky night of you

i felt for life
of hands held, waiting
desires
the flesh all crisp, new

felt for life
the heart's pound, the eye's
flow,
sublime with responses

for life
received the emotion of
departing,
in the quick of eternity

life
within the depths of blue
the stars,
the air of your breath

Edward E Klinger
LOVE FROM THE OTHER SIDE OF THE PYRAMID
On the side of the pyramid
Where the sun shines
The grass is green
The flowers are bright
That life is going so well

The woman sitting beside you
Is looking through your eyes
She sees what's bothering you
She knows you can be loved

You want to be loved, but you can't
You don't know why
But you can't

The flowers are bright
She looks through your eyes
She knows now
You are life past life

The sun on the other side
Things are dark, but getting lighter
Then it happens you fall in love
With the woman on the other side

Lori Mae Fenton
BRANDY
He would take me for a ride
Or we would just walk,
Sometimes we would hide
So we could just talk,
But when he had Died
I thought it was the end,
Because I loved him so
I lost, my closest friend.

Judith L Russell
FOR THE TWO OF YOU WE DRINK A TOAST . . . .

To my Mother, and in memory of my Father, for all their love, support & inspiration.

For the two of you we drink a toast,
for all the times we shared,
and
all the times you cared.
For all the tears, and
all the years, and
all your smiles that went on for miles.
For all the times we cried,

and
all the times we tried.
For all the times you held us dear
to comfort our greatest fears,
and all the times you caught our
fall . . . .
For all the things you taught us
and
all the patience you brought us.
For all the love, and all the joy.
For the two of you we drink a
toast. . . . .

Candida Iacuzio
BEAUTY UNNOTICED

Beauty unnoticed is something sad,
There's so much to enjoy to
make you glad.
A tree for shade, the sun for warmth,
Moonlight for lovers as they
stroll 'long the walk.
Gold stars twinkling in the sky
overhead,
Like a blanket of skylights
covering the earth.
The flowers with colors vivid and
bright,
For bees and butterflies they're
a delight.
The carpet of green grass like a
magic rug
To rest on when tired, or picnic
for fun.
Even the birds have their own
melodies
As they fly happily from tree to
tree.
Looking for sea-shells along the
shore,
Children build castles big and
small.
The silvery clouds below skies of
blue,
Their shapes change as the
breeze blows through.
The soft falling snow sets the scene
aglow
With a winter wonderland look,
a snowman for show.
Take notice of all these wonderful
things,
They're free to all with the joy
they bring.

Theresa M Gall
ODE TO A DYING PATIENT

Your chest is so still
I cannot hear your heartbeat with a
stethoscope
pressed to your chest.
You are so pale,
so still.
You have passed beyond this world
to somewhere unknown to us.
Your family grieves at your bedside.
Their pain tears at my heart.
I feel their anguish and despair
for I, too have lost a loved one.

Laura A Lange
LIFE

To Richard L. Wrather, who gave meaning to my life.

Life is strange, life is funny,
one day gloomy, another day sunny.
Love is blind, yet seen so clear,
touching the mind, with the heart so
near.
Allowing your heart to be open and
free,
for the love inside, through your eyes
can see.
The soul of the body controlled by
one,
the spirit of the mind rising the sun.
The power of life is what you feel,
with your mind in control, you'll
know it's real.
Life is time, with no going back,
changing only better, with no time to
lack.
Think of each day, but look at
tomorrow,
time is short, with no life to borrow.

Frances Cecil-Olearo
PEACE

To My Loving Family

May your peace
become like a river
flowing strongly

as it ripples over
the stones and rocks
in its pathways
of life . . .

John R Yahola
ECHOES

The stars glitter like gems, as we
loved under the Oriental
Twilight,
Kim, with hair dark as midnight, coal
like eyes,
Your spell-binding whispers still
echo in my mind,
The wind kisses the chimes of Soyo-
San,
The songs of the sparrow still echo in
my mind,
As sunrise nears, your magic wins,
You depart in your
turquoise Ao-dai,
Your spirit is ever like starshine,
Though we are apart.
I still hear the echoes in my mind.

Christy Tendler
FRIENDSHIP

Friendship is close feelings for one
another
Friendship is sharing thoughts
together
If ever we are parted through
misunderstandings
Or time please just open up your
heart and I will
Open up mine you can tell me
anything that comes
Upon your mind for I have been
through a lot myself
Maybe even your kind yes sometimes
I may take you for
Granted but please try and understand
for I am only
Human my friend and faults are
something I have be
My friend and I'll be yours through
troubled times
And happy moments and endings
whatever it may be
For friendship is something we share
my friend and
I'm glad you share yours with
me . . .

Pat Lindic
AFTERLIGHT

To Bernice Bukosky
My Captain, Oh Captain

I've been in rough seas before
But never as rough as these
I've had cloudy days before
But never as hazy as these

These eyes have seen so much before
But now they're really very sore
These bones have shaken some
before
But now won't stop as before

Before I could always find a ray of
light
Now none does shine upon this
wretched sight
After they say it's oh so bright
Now I pray with all my might

Before before there was an open door
Now I realize before is to be no more
After after there's so much more
Now I realize after is to be when he
opens that door

Steve Essick
SOME KIND OF LOVER

I dedicate this to a woman some-where out there . . .

Some kind of lover,
Some kind of friend,
That's what you are to me.
I've been looking for a friend like
that,
for a long time coming,
Some kind of lover,
Some kind of friend,
I guess, all I want was someone to
love.
But, I got more than I bargained
for.
Some kind of lover,
Some kind of friend,
I've been up one hill and down
another until I met You.
Some kind of lover,
Some kind of friend,
That's what You are to Me.

Melissa Paulette Bramlett
A BUTTERFLY

Like A butterfly
My Love For You
Has Many Different Colors.
My Love Is Like Colors
But Only I Express It In
Many Different Ways,
In Hugs, In Kisses,
And Even In Cherished Looks.
So I hope You'll Remember
I'll Always Love You!

Maudie Amburgey
LOVE IS LIKE A ROSE

Dedicated in memory of my husband Roger, and grandson Marty

Love is beautiful, like a rose bush. You water, prune, and tenderly work with it till it is rooted and starts to grow. It will soon come alive and reach out, spreading its arms till it grows into a beautiful bush. Then a bud appears and soon a beautiful rose appears.

It will be looked at and loved by everyone because of its beauty. It appears at weddings, funerals, and is sent to sweethearts. It goes on to bless people year after year. That's the way our love must be: watered, and tenderly cared for until it is rooted and grounded in our hearts. Then it will last a lifetime, making those we meet love because we love through our hearts with a never ending love. Love is beautiful, never selfish. There is plenty of it if it is cultivated and is worked at daily. We can love our sweetheart, our husband or wife, our children, and many others. The beautiful rose is of many kinds, and so is our love. Our love goes on to make those we love happy. So, like the rose, our love is beautiful if we take care of it.

Sara Lewis
DAISY

In fond memory of my uncle Loyal Banks Boger

Crisp and shining—white;
Face lifted skyward,
Adoringly gaze into the sun.

Storms may wilt others;
Noonday heat will see them fade.

But you—exuberant in the summer-
blue;
Greet the morning, tall and fair.

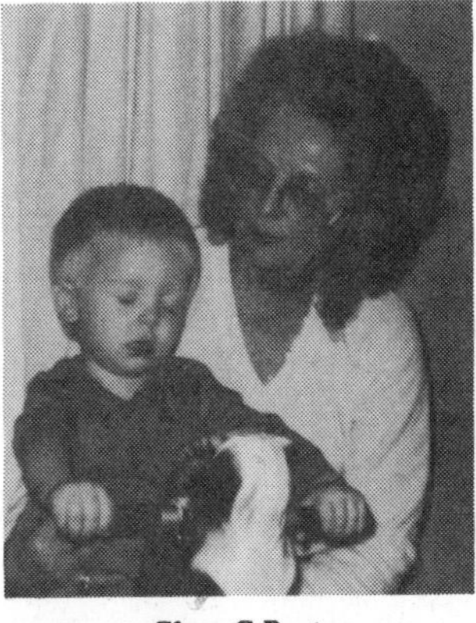

Clara C Purtee

Clara C Purtee
HOW LONELY CAN IT BE

Softly a breeze
is blow-ing
across
a rose bouquet
across
a million memories
across
those yesterdays
dry-ing away
the tear drops
that broken hearts
have cry-ied
Lift-ing away
The foot prints
To be carried
Through the sky
Setting alone
In those memories
After the night
cover-ed the grave
After the sunrise
Of the dawn-ing
After the tears
Have blown away
In memories
I come to the edge
Of these heart-aches
I touch the soil
That en-earths
The soul
I know just beyond
That sunrise
There's no more
sorrow
No more
tears
No more
Growing old

I stand in
The shadows of leaving
I reach for the touch
Of them there
But they've gone
Far away in the evening
In the twilight
Of yesterday's glare
Soft-ly I hear
The sweetest music
Coming from home
Far away
My lips kiss the rose
Of tomorrow
Across the rain-bows
Of un-cloud-ed days
Hot tears bathe the cheeks
Of my body
While reaching my soul
To the end
Somewhere in the twilight
Of tomorrow
We will all
Be together again
SO YOU SEE
I know the hurts
That have touched you
In partings
I know the misery
I know the sweetness
In loving
I know by the silence
How lonely it can be.

Edna E Daniels
RAINBOWS OF THE HEART

For: Bettie Huggins, my sweet Mother

If you've ever seen a rainbow,
And who hasn't you say?
Well you can have a rainbow each and every day,
For it's imprinted on the heart,
And will never disappear,
It just glows with color, and grows brighter each year,
So when you are down, or troubled with fear,
Look to your rainbow, for it is always near.

Kathy Ostrowski Morris
YOU BRING HAPPY WORDS TO A SAD HEART

To those who helped shape my life, especially my mother.

You bring happy words to a sad heart
You make me wish that we never part
You bring blue skies where once was rain
You bring joy and laughter where once was pain
You turn darkness into light so I can see my way
You know how to help brighten my day
You and your smile

Arthur R Baker
FOOTPRINTS
When our footsteps on the sands of time
No longer here are known
And we stand in contemplation
Before the Master's throne;
Will the thoughtfulness of others
And helping hands we've known
Be matched by deeds for others done
And kindness we have shown?

Oh man of such uncertain fate,
Thy pathway now endear
To weary pilgrims following
Throughout the coming years;
Mark well each trial and pitfall;
Thy beacon lights enshrine;
And make the world, for having
lived,
A little more sublime.

Patricia Rehfeldt
HARDLY GROWN

To my son Ed. and Silent Mothers.

Grown up my boy, It's hard to do!
Caring and teaching your life through.
Times have been Rough, You're not sick!
Your heart is going, Let it click!

Your maudlin eyes, Day after Day,
OH! to help you, I will Pray.
Gambling with life and its vices,
Makes you vulnerable to its crisis.

How many times to tell you you're loved?
Quarter of a century still in a clough?
Be good to yourself, Do your part.
You can do it, Give it a Start!

Grow up my Man, Life is waiting.
Sons are bright, suns do the fading.
The world is waiting, Give it a Try!
Then I'll wipe the tears from my Eyes.

Ralph J Jackson
THE WONDERS OF MOTHER NATURE

To Sam and Mary Ella Jackson, Which without them, such words would not be possible. I love you both.

Mother Nature is more powerful than a machine,
Producing everywhere and never seen;

She equips the land and the sea,
With the smallest fish and the largest tree;

She progresses slowly but never stops,
With a strong determination to reach the top;
She can build high and she can build low,
She gives us sunshine and gives us snow;

Her works are like a masterpiece admired by all,
during the spring and during the fall;

Her productions are colored bright and clear,
And her wind is heard by the smallest ear:

Her fowls are gifted with the finest feathers,
To fly about in her beautiful weather;

So when you see the smallest creature,
Just think of the "Wonders of Mother Nature"

Daniel Ryan
REFLECTION

*To God for his generous gift
And to all who dare to believe in miracles*

She counts days leaving yesterday behind,
She gives herself to that and nothing more.
Dormant she lies so one can be defined,
Enduring for one waiting at life's door.
Sleep takes her spirit above its memories,
In dreams she lives to rise above her fears.
And tries to forget the possibilities,
Three fights waged, three fights lost, in as many years.
The odds were one among a star lit night,
A miracle to brighten up her life.
In five dark days she almost lost the fight,
God, the months of insanity and strife.
Bear down sweet pain, bring forth a painful cry,
A reflection within my dampened eyes.

Vanessa D McLain
SPLINTERS

To Lynne Seagle: Thank-you for listening.

You are Doctors
You are Lawyers
You are Chief Executives
Accomplished Leaders in
every field of "major" achievement

We are Your Daughters

We are likewise Achievers
EQUALITY also being our ultimate goal;
We struggle diligently in Your footsteps.

We, unfortunately, fall painfully short
of initial understanding.

Thus we are also
Your drug abusers
Your anorexics—Your bulimics
We are increasingly becoming
Your embezzlers, Your sex offenders,
Your murderers.
We are Lonely.
We are afraid.
We can find No Peace.
We are the devastated outcome
of what should have been a
noble and triumphant fight.

We—Your Daughters
need desperately to know,
if the rewards are worth
the sacrifices?

Alice David
YOU TOUCHED ME, LORD!

To My Loving Husband Mike, Jr., My two sons, Allen & Clifford, My Grand-daughter Laurie, two Grand-sons Mikeal & Brent. In Memory of my parents, and my father & mother-in-laws.

My body and mind were racked with pain, with fears and with strife,
I was ill and at death's door, the first time you touched my life.
I knew death wasn't far away, the end was very near,
I felt Your presence come to me, I knew I had nothing more to fear.

I gave You all my love, my heart, my very soul,
The miracle You gave to me, is more precious than purest gold.
I turned from the darkness, into Your blessed light,
My blinded eyes were opened, and I received my sight.

I received You as my Savior, You forgave me all my sins,
You gave me strength and courage, when You touched my life again.
You gave me back my life, unworthy I was indeed,
I've witnessed the power of Your love, You knew my every need.
I've learned to live one day at a time, as fully as I can,
To hold to Your unchanging love, and to Your steadfast hand.
I truly trust and believe in You, Lord!
Your love so freely given.
I have Your blessed assurance, one day I'll see You in heaven.

You touched me Lord! You made me whole,
You asked nothing except my love in return.
You're my friend, my redeemer, my salvation,
The amazing love You gave to me,
I didn't have to earn.

R Alix Snow
YOU AND I
Pale green fingers reaching for the sky,
Dewdrops, drop . . . drop, splash!
Frog jumps from wet to wet

Under the old willow
Petals swaying in the breeze,
Ducksong floating on the pond

Green sky,
Cradled by clover,
You and I

John W Lester
IN MEMORIAM
O' Grady, 'Piccolo Pete' and Slim stand at attention and salute.
A moment's meditating hymn; a silent prayer is his tribute.

Ol' Mother of the boy deceased in his behalf move not a tear,
Put back the handkerchief that's creased—revere
His memory, weep not—one of the toll has marched in state
But we who yearn to be fulfilled must wait;
Lord God protect his gentle soul—our mate.

Margrit Alston
MELANCHOLY JILL
As I sit here looking out of my terrace window, I can see the rain falling
I can see the rain falling
Coming down in sheets.
I feel as though the raindrops are my tears
falling on the street, and the black, and heavy clouds are my heart,
which is breaking even now.
The room is still, but for the sound of the falling rain,
and the ticking of my clock.
It's a comforting sound, but a lonely one.
I've watched the world go by from my terrace.

I've seen babies cry, and young men die. I stop to wonder why?
Families living on the street, looked down on, by strangers whom they meet.
With little food, and much less love, and nothing on their feet.
Nations stop just short of war, as death waits lurking, outside the door.
He waits for me too, as I sit and weep, and weep some more.
I can hear him knocking, calling, Melancholy Jill . . ., Melancholy Jill . . .

Vera Balla
WHISTLER MOUNTAIN
View the spectacular snow capped peaks,
the nature lover always seeks.

Few fishermen and mountaineers,
visited Whistler Valley in early years.

Rainbow Lodge was first on Alta Lake shore,
hauling in supplies by pack horse was a weary chore.

Give credit to the couple who braved the elements of the mountains,
for Whistler is today a financial fountain.

Take in the beauty as the sun reflecting on the snow sends a glare,
though the old lodge is no longer there.

Keep the natural surroundings of Whistler for generations to come,
should forever be number one.

Whistler is now skiing and bright lights,
a resort for the skiers delight.

The World Cup competitions are the modern day way,
with new condominiums and shops which are here to stay.

Working in harmony with nature can create a magnificent feat,
live there year round or take a weekend to enjoy an enchanting retreat.

Richard A Diem
GIRL OF MY DREAMS
Girl of my dreams
Is that really you
Have you stepped
Into reality
Do wishes come true
Your precious soul
I long to explore
Can I have
Time in your mind
Five minutes or more
Are you overwhelmed
By my eagerness
Do I come on too strong
Heart's breath too excited
I've been waiting so long
Has my imagination
Dulled my senses
My mind's eye just a blur
Are you living and breathing
Or the dream
You once were

Brian Donald O'Donovan
COMING OF AGE
Let the wrinkles come and the crow's feet spread
and my hair turn gray around my head.

Let the age spots appear and my teeth fall out.
I've lived long enough to know what life is about.

Let my sight grow dim. Let my hearing go.
Let me use a cane as my movements slow.

For, as you can see, I'm not concerned
because of a most important lesson I've learned.

And that is:

That age is a sign from God that our life's end is near.
And he gives us many signs like these to make his meaning clear.

So, let the wrinkles come and let the crow's feet spread
and my hair turn gray around my head.

Let the age spots appear and my teeth fall out.
I've lived long enough to know, you know, what life's about.

Kerri Lynn Copp
SMILE
"SMILE" if you are down,
For a "SMILE" can turn your day around,
Enjoy life while it's still here, for before you know it, it will disappear.

"SMILE" if you're happy
so everybody knows,
That you don't need to pack-up your cares and woes.

"SMILE" if you're mad,
For maybe you'll see,
That there's no reason for
you to be angry.

"SMILE" if you're depressed,
For your problems seem less,
Your eyes will sparkle with happiness and glee,

Please do me a favor and
"SMILE" for me!

Syble Ferguson

Syble Ferguson
DO I REALLY LOVE YOU?
Do I really love you . . . . you want to know.
It seems a simple yes would do;
But from the way you ask me,
I know I must reassure you.
So I must be careful of the words I choose . . .
To answer won't be an easy task.
I must make your doubts go away,
So you'll never again have to ask.
I love the way you look at me,
When all around are cloudy skies.
I love the rainbow you put in my heart,
When we embrace and I feel your touch;
I love the happiness I see in your smile,
And the things we enjoy so much;
Like soft music, and sunsets, and walking,
And holding hands and making love under a tree,
And so many things we do together . . . . .
Without you . . . . my love just wouldn't be.

Shirley Anne Beckman
THE GREATEST OF LOVES
With heart over-flowing by
the setting of the sun;
Stirred by gentle breezes
of wind on the run.
Captivated by waters inviting
and calm;
Filled by all nature and the
birds of song.

We cherish the warmth of a lover's tender touch,
and begotten children we love
so very much.
Yet the greatest of emotions
escapes us within;
For love of ourselves we
know not how to begin.

Dory Kay
DON'T WALK ALONE
One night I did walk astray,
I knew for me no more to stay.
My heart was burdened with the strife,
that I, myself did want new life.

I did not know where I could start,
Where I too, could become a part.
I traveled far beyond this land,
And there I found my Savior's hand.

God and Heaven filled my Plea,
Of wanting love eternally.

Put your life child in God's trust,
for I have found that it's a must.
So put God first in all you do,
for God puts you first your whole life through . . . .

Susan Hurl
SILENT CRIME

Dedicated in the memory of Lisa Steinberg. May her spirit forever live on.

Silent crime, it is.
Under the roof it lives.
Silently the child cries.
Another fist of Dad's flies
Never will the child tell
Living alone in her own hell
Yelling, the father's furious.
Now he's become delirious.
Now, too late, the child cowers
Her head is hit with mighty power
Unicorns and angels come
Rest with death, no more sun
Life has handed the child release
May she always rest in peace.

Joan Churchill
THE WE WITHIN

Dedicated to my grandmother, Katie, whose beauty within will forever live.

Don't look at my outside and think you know me.
It only covers what you really should see.
Imagine everyone with faces the same,
Would we choose the same person over again?
Without are masks, to cover what's real,
Would the same one make us feel how we feel?
What if all of the people had eyes that were blind,
No beauty now to hide behind.
The beauty would all have to come from inside,
And the ones that forgot would have no place to hide.
Everyone now with faces the same,
No way left to play the game.
All of us starting at the same line.
Who will come out ahead this time?

Gayle Crowder
THE OTHER WALL
The Emerald Isle—a dying evergreen
Ornamented with splashes of ruby.
Belfast, bleak and bloody—
Humanity consciously ripped apart
Under the guise of a "peace line."

Call it what it is!
A makeshift fortress of metal and mortar—
A venomous snake of a barrier,
Warning those on either side
To approach at their own peril.

The imposing wall of Berlin seems a tranquil haven
When compared to this vicious breach in the human spirit.
IRA, are your perpetrators any less guilty than your victims?
Catholic, Protestant, Protestant, Catholic,
All God's children got hate!

How sad to see them engaging each other in an unholy war,
Proclaiming God's name as their captain.
Flames of hope are not ignited by petrol bombs?

"You are hoping yourselves into oblivion,"
A disheartened God weeps.
"If only they would tear the wall down," He prays,
But to whom?

Brooke Lombard
DENISE'S SUMMER
This summer was as wonderful as ever; it could never be doubled. The spirit and wildness were like a thick mist. Baby's breath, red roses, tulips and fresh fruit caressed the air. The stream bubbled over the rocks while songbirds filled the air with sweet music.

And Denise, the lovely figure on the shore.
Golden skin, aqua eyes, and the innocent face of a unicorn who's the only one left.

Denise's summer, now and forever
If only I could have her, I would leave her never.

Malina Little
SCATTERED DREAMS
It is autumn
Leaves the colors of the fading sun are falling
Standing in their midst
I try gathering them into a pile
A gentle breeze guides them past my grasp

Jeanette Fox
A TRIBUTE TO MOTHER
Mother Dear, you were always near.
You held me close when I was born,
you didn't care about their scorn.
When I was wet you made me dry,
you played with me so I'd not cry.
When they called me names you kissed my tears.
You cared for me all thru the years.

Remember when I skinned my knee?
You sat me down upon your knee,
you taught me all that I could be.
That was your song to me.
I know a day will come when you'll be gone . . .
But I'll be strong, I'll continue your song.
You've given me memories beyond compare, loving, touching, funny.
Oh mother you've made my life so sunny!
And some enchanted day we'll be in Heaven to stay.
I can't give you back what you've given me,
But I give you my heart, so I give you my love.
Like a butterfly's wings, I'll continue to sing.
Our song which began so long ago,
I'll give it to my daughter,
so it'll continue to grow.

Annie Cyborski
VALENTINE'S DAY

Valentine's Day is a day of hearts,
Red and white paper, candy tarts.
And some people think on that day,
Their true love will come to stay.

Barbara Abbate
THE OLD MAN

In Memory of Mr. Frank Siringo, Sr.

The Old Man Looks Out His Window,
As Time Has Made Him Old.
There Is A Child In His Heart,
But the Mirror Says Not So.

He Sees His Own Reflection,
So Drawn and Racked With Pain,
And He Thinks Back Of Days of Old,
And Wishes He was Young Again.

He Knows Deep In His Heart,
That It Could Never Be That Way,
For The Years Have Passed Too Quickly,
And Now With His Age He Has To Pay.

He Sighs As He Thinks Back,
Of His Friends Gone So Long Ago,
And Patiently Awaits For His Time To Come,
For He Has No More Oats To Sow.

The Time Is Passing Slowly,
For The Man Who Has No Fear,
He only Panics At The Thought,
Of Living Through Another Year.

Jessie Placco
MY IRISH BROTHER-IN-LAW

Dedicated to Harold Kelly

St. Patrick's Day is coming, the glad St. Patrick's Day,
We sat and dined and danced around the green decor and sang Irish songs.
It was fun because we had an Irish Brother-in-Law.

You are gone and not forgotten, we still remember when the fun
we had with the children on the St. Patrick's Day.
We know that you are happy in heaven and waiting for us there,
and that you have lot of friends and relatives.

Most of all we know you have someone dear to you here,
because she will never forget her Irish love.

And someday, we will all be together again and meet our Irish
Brother-in-Law, especially on
St. Patrick's Day.

Henrietta Siemering
TWO HAPPY LITTLE GIRLS

To my sister, Ada Williams (deceased) of San Angelo, Texas. Ada and I are the two little girls in the poem. I was born Oct 17, 1895. Ada was six years older than I.

Under the Texas bright blue skies
This is the joyful story of
two little girls' lives.
Early every morning we
ran to the meadow
To see the birds, butterflies,
wasps, chattering squirrels
and the funny-faced raccoon
The turtle and the bumble bee
The wildflowers were a beautiful
sight to see
The blue bonnets, Indian
paintbrushes,
wine cups, buttercups,
primroses, and wild violets
Watermelons cooled in the brook
were one of our favorite fruits.
Needless to say, we were hatless
and shoeless.
With apologies to Greenleaf
Whittier
We, too, had cheeks of tan.
At eventide we heard the whip-
poor-will sing his nightly song.
We were ready for sleep and rest
with a happy day gone by.

Jerry Hazelwood Gensler
HE LOVES US

Dedicated to my grandchildren Justin, Karina, & Guston Morris. I love you, wherever you are.

Once when I was lost and
felt the need for something more,
I heard the story of redemption,
And how my sins Jesus bore.
I felt within myself,
there was nothing I could do,
except to claim the savior
whose love is pure and true.

Now I know I'll not be perfect,
though I study God's own word,
but I will try to show His Kindness,
and make sure His story is heard.
And when I see all His wonders,
and the proof is all around,
I know without searching,
no love like His can ever be found.

He has given us the beauty of
the flowers, grass and trees,
and no matter how man tries,
he cannot improve on these.
The birds, a tiny baby,
the rain on a hot parched earth,
These are all God's creations,
and no price can cover their worth.

Most of all I owe to Him,
a price I cannot pay,
for a life I live in His sweet peace,
as I go from day to day.
And when the prayer I am praying,
is a petition from above,
I want to stop and remember,
that in all this is His love.

For He gives me lots of beauty,
for my eyes to behold.
But my prayer is for all to remember
the greatest story ever told.
And this Jesus who loves us so,
has much more to unfold,
as we live with Him in our heavenly homes,
and walk the streets of gold.

Kathy Ferbrache
MY GYPSY LADY GRANDMA, J. J.

To Momma—who passes the flight of the butterfly on, as I do to Jered and Abrie

Everytime I see a butterfly, I think of her.
A short little lady, with hair like silvery snow,
and garden green eyes that could see into your soul.

Altho, not educated by any school system past grade four,
she spoke many languages
that filled my ears with graceful phrases.

Her passions were many in this world.
Collected things, common place to most.
Loved her family, flowers, Johnny Carson, and most men.

She lived thru wars and great depressions,
so could live on nothing more than her belief
that things would get better, 'cause she'd seen worse.

Youth was her vision and so she lived it.
During her adventuresome life great illness she did suffer.
Conquering most to make medical history.

Until the caterpillar, cocooned, became free
to fly on into eternity.
For that is what it means to me, when a butterfly I see.

Orville W Pieper
THE SOLDIER

Dedicated to my lovely granddaughter, Mary Celeste Conell

Cursed be he
Who shoots so well
With a twitch of his finger
His soul did sell

No more on this earth
Shall he find his rest
Till he lies among those
Who his finger did best

Hubert T McCann Jr
YOUR LOVE

To my wife Gwen, I love you very much.

Your Love is very warming
Your Love is always sweet,
Your love is everything I need
To make my life complete.

Your Love is so relaxing
Your Love is always true,
And when I look into your eyes
Your Love comes shining through.

Your Love will always be there
Your Love was made for me,
Your Love bonded with my love
Will last all ETERNITY.

Julio Gotay
ALL THE BEST COWBOYS HAVE BROKEN MINDS

All the best cowboys have broken minds
and cement souls,
see them birthing bullets all day long.

All the fine executives stink of math.
Their bland brains are full of straight lines
and dollar dreams.

All the great generals have red voices that shriek,
and steel teeth with which they eat poems.

That is why I
prefer all the good human beings
who wear no clothes.

Susan Kincaid Tindell
WHAT

I think you are afraid
somewhat,
of what I am and
what I'm not.
Perhaps of what I might be
come.
Perhaps because you love me
some.

I think you could love me
a lot,
for what I am and
what I'm not.
If only you could mellow
out
And love me for what I'm a
bout.

Esther Murphey
IF (With Apologies to Kipling)

If I could know what others think
I would be careful how I speak
If I was perfect in others' eyes
They'd have nothing to criticize

If I am good or if I'm bad
If I had "done this" or wish I had
"If" is a small word and might
change me
Then a model person I would be

If I knew when the world would end
Guess everyone would be my friend
I'd take up evangelism

And appear on television

With gobs of makeup I would go
Cry—wave my arms—put on a show
Don't you think it would be funny
To beg the folks for their money?

But I can't always be so nice
When it's more fun to add some spice
If it's an "if" or if it's a "but"
I'll be myself no matter what!

Sue Cox
MY SON
From love you came
To give in return, is your fame

Such warmth, such charm
A ray of hope

Be kind, my little one
For love, you'll always have

A mother's heart
Never dies to a small flame

Only gentleness will submerge
Thru time of questions and time of pain

Be patient my little one
For I'll always be there

Calm the storms of fear and doubt
Draw within the love and the pride

Be happy, my little one
For Mother, will always be near

Alison Iong
YOUR FRIENDSHIP
Your Friendship is the oasis
In my soul's dry desert
In my darkest, loneliest hours
This oasis fills my thirst
With warmth, companionship and understanding

Your Friendship is the ointment
For my old, persistent pain
When fate brings forth disappointments
This ointment lets me gain
Concern, comfort, consolation and caring

Your Friendship is the obbligato
In my symphony of life
I have often been told
That this obbligato will survive
Through time's test, without ending

Jacqueline E Madison
A DRUNK'S DREAM
Friendships come,
and friendships go.
But old faithful
forever swirls on.
Life is created,
and life is destroyed.
But old faithful
steadily flows.
The sun comes up,
the sun goes down.
But old faithful
is always around.
What is old faithful?
Is it someone?
Is it something?
Is it trust, honesty,
or even respect?
Maybe, it's love.
No, it's none of those.
It's a touch of heaven.
It's a hug of hell.
But to a drunk,
it's security wrapped
up in a golden glow.

Roberta Sivils
A FRIEND LIKE YOU
I didn't take the time to say
'Your hair is lovely fixed that way,'
I rushed around, my manners lost
In frenzy, forgetting all the cost.
I did not comment on your 'dress'
Of how you always look your best,
I did not thank you for the tea:
Worthy not of hospitality.
I didn't tell you that your smile
Brought comfort to me all the while,
That with each caring word you give
You've given me the will to live.
Instead, I turned and walked away
My own world in my thoughts this day,
Please forgive me, mean not be rude,
Yet not deserving a friend like you.

Amber Nash
REMEMBRANCE
Why did you leave me
out in the cold?
Why did you leave me
with no one to hold?

I felt like dying
but what could I do.
I ended up crying
just for you.

Does a smile cross your lips
when you hear my name?
All I want to know is,
Does your heart feel the same?

I've tried to find you,
I've searched for your address.
I miss you so much,
And long for your caress.

I hope I find you
someday, sometime.
I hope you still love me,
and someday will be mine.

Artress L Hoff
POETRY
Poetry is something that can come directly from your heart;
Poetry can be an art!
Poetry is simply an expression of thoughts and feelings,
deep inside your soul.
Sometimes you can write things that are never told;
Poetry can be brought, poetry can be sold.
Poetry also can be old!
Poetry can be good, poetry can be bad, poetry also can make you sad;

You never can tell what poetry will bring, 'cause poetry also can make you sing!
Poetry can bring you up, poetry can bring you down, but poetry can also bring you around!
Poetry can be love, poetry can be hate; Think now, don't hesitate!
Poetry is a talent that some people possess, some, with much success!
So take some time to write your thoughts down, 'cause, poetry may bring you around!

Sharon Giannone
WE BETTER HIDE OUR EYES, HERE THEY COME AGAIN

This poem is dedicated to Judy "Just Because"

We better hide our eyes
Here they come again
Those desperate, hungry and homeless

We shake our heads in shame,
The government's to blame
For those desperate, hungry and homeless

We say a prayer at night,
Fill a bag of food,
And think we've done all right,
To help,
Those desperate, hungry and homeless

The children ask why,
In our world,
It's all right, to be
Desperate, hungry and homeless

Inez Dean
CHRISTMAS
Christmas is a time of cheer when every one is gay, they are looking forward to a bright and cheerful day.

Sometimes the snow is falling all beautiful and white. It makes us enjoy our shining lights much more when it comes night.

Old Santa is a popular guy, with beard as white as snow, his nose is red and rosy, it will even glow.

His reindeer are so frisky they are always on the move, they know that Christmas time is here and they are in the mood.

Christmas is celebrated in many different ways, some take it for a day of folly, some for a day of praise.

For me when I spell Christmas, I'm sure it's spelled with Christ,
for after all he is our Saviour and the one who paid the price.

Kimberly Perkins
CHANGES
Things have changed,
It's not been easy,
I've tried so hard,
They say I'm lazy,

I want to die,
Just fade away,
But love keeps me going,
Each and every day.

Lynn Edelman
LIFE AND DREAMS
Life is a world of challenge,
Though it may be,
Sad at times,
Happy at times,
We have yet to see,

It's a world unseen, in a sense,
For the challenges we cannot foresee,
When fantasy and reality come together,
That day may never prove to be,

But our hopes and dreams,
We still can believe,
That they can become our own,
If we in our hearts,
Know ourselves,
What we want, alone,

Though troubles may overwhelm us,
And happy times, perhaps are few,
We must set our thoughts,
On what we want,
And make our dreams come true.

Pepper Breese

Pepper Breese
RITES IN L.A.

To all the victims, families, friends, the trapped, the scared in the continuing L.A. war.

Still! Still!
A strange, cosmic chill
Breathes the ill of an ugly thrill
Still! Still!

Alone. Alone in the gangland night.
Alone. Alone in panic and fright.
Oh, we who know the width of night
Know best the love, the freedom of morning light.

The rock of night bellows its rancid staccato.
The stars! The sun?
What have they done?
Where is their glow? Where did they go?

But . . . how should I know?
Unless, the stars, the sun be cold
When the shades of my judgment unfold.
The stars? The sun? What have they done?

Secret still! Still! Still! Silent still!
Crested chill! Cosmic chill! Cold chill!
Almost serene, yet so horribly somber.
Such a huge stain on remembered splendor.

Mary E Morrison
JOHN FITZGERALD KENNEDY
A Great Man was Mr. Kennedy
A remembered man he'll always be.
He was a great courageous man
A true lover of his land.

He left behind a wife, two

children, a girl and a boy
To him they were his greatest joy.

He always took time even on
his busiest day, to laugh
with them, to romp and play

He was a good kind and
wonderful man his
Killer has had to pay
Let's always remember
Our 35th President of our
wonderful U.S.A.

Stewart Lewis
LET ME, O LORD
Dear Lord,
Let me see
Through Your Eyes.
Let me hear
Through Your Ears.
Let me understand
Through Your Mind.
Let me go
Beyond intellect.
Let me feel
Your Holy Touch.
Hear me, O Lord
Strip away worldly illusions.
I would know Thee
As You know me.

Louise Lewis
DESPERADO
The artist has to be a desperado
Riding on a horse that leaps through
flame.
He has to go the distance like a hero,
Lead the pack to insights bold and
brave.

Ignore the mob that cries for
execution,
That loves to hack and chop at
rainbow dreams.
Keep singing songs and making
brilliant photos
That burn a timeless image through
the brain.

He has to shatter myths that cloud
and dim truth,
Lead the fight for justice and the
right.
He has to find the beauty in the
darkness
And spark the torch that brings the
final light.

Colleen McCune
ONLY THE FLU
Cough! Cough! Sneeze! Sneeze!
Oh God! This Wretched disease!
A Chest full of marbles, a head full of
cotton;
I don't think I've ever felt quite this
rotten;

An Epidemic, I hear them say.
All I know, is it's here to stay.
This Flu in all its painful majesty.
Has me aching all over my anatomy.

From the roots of my hair, to the tip
of my toes;
In such misery, I'm not alone.
"You've just got what's going
around."
"You're only as sick as everyone in
town."

"Oh No I'm Not!' I shout and cry!
I'm sicker than them. I'm going to
die!
I cough and I sneeze and I ache all
over.
Someone Please Bury Me. I know my
Life's over.

I'm Dying! I must be. There's no
chance I'll survive.
With these shivers and shakes and
tears in my eyes.
But then wonder of wonders! I start
to feel fine.
And I knew it would happen. It was
just a matter of Time!

Virginia Lynn Dossey
RELATIVITY
Today a breeze blew an acorn
from the old oak tree
I knelt and gently pressed it into
the loam
I rose and smiled, destiny would
come into its own
Because of an acorn, a breeze and
me
You nod and smile indulgently
Because you don't see long years
from now
A little girl, a little boy frolic
beneath a large oak tree with
shouts of joy
Because of an acorn, a breeze and
me

Phyllis Lawson Corathers

Phyllis Lawson Corathers
A GOOD FRIEND

For my husband, Frank, who has always been my best friend.

All of my friends have their own
view of life,
and to a good friend the stories come.
Some filled with laughter, others with
strife,
lots with humor and some . . . I'll
keep mum.

When my friends arrive with their
problems and trials,
and from a good friend the advice is
asked.
My expression is attentive, I frown
and I smile,
while the thoughts in my mind whirl
round completely masked.

Well from a good friend an answer is
wanted,
even more, it's expected and always
needed.
But this friend worries, my mind is
taunted,
I have tremendous misgivings should
my advice be heeded.

So you know what this good friend
does while I sit and listen . . .
I make shopping lists, all my plans
for the week.
I think of all the things that I'm
sitting there missing,
consciously hearing my kitchen
sink's faulty leak!

So I've learned the art though it's
taken awhile,
of being a good listener and the very
best friend.
Now heed . . . bring out the coffee, a
hug and a smile,
and last but not least . . . two hours
away from children and men!

Rusty Jessie Ventaloro
AUTUMN
Falling leaves in the sunset
Reflecting silver, gold and crimson.
The air is crisp and cool
With the early morning dew.
The day turns warm as noontime
nears.
As the night approaches,
A cool breeze blows through the
open window—
Sleep peacefully, sweetheart.

An owl is heard in the distance
With an eerie woo—oo—oo.
Birds in the treetop happily chirp,
chirp, chirp.
I feel a gentle tug at my pajamas.
"Wake up, Mommie! Get up,
Mommie. We're hungry."

Rain is pounding fiercely on the
rooftop.
Bacon is sizzling and popping in the
frying pan.
Sister and her baby brother are
waiting
Patiently for their breakfast.
Eventually the day comes to an end.
Hail starts falling fast and hard.
A cool breeze blows through the
open window.
Sleep peacefully, sweetheart.

Ila Michelle Camby
AN AWAKENING

This poem is dedicated to Gregory Hutchins, who gave it more than just the name.

A lonely world it will be with not one
To put a heart into the troubled ways.
The world is far from having any sun
And all consist of only shades of
grey.
The sun will never rise nor ever set
For without even one to make you
see
The grace and beauty you have never
met.
Since all that caught your eye was
only weeds.
The sound of owls and crickets all
night
And any star that should be able to
catch
The mind that always far from any
sight
Of all the life and beauty yet to hatch.
Then someone one day opens
both the eyes
To make them see the beauty,
grey then dies.

Renette Janvier Horita
MOMENTS

Dedicated, Especially for: My Dear Mother, Mildred Maury. Adam, Brandi, and Loving husband, Ray Horita.

Iced air surrounds my face, and fills
my nostrils.
The silence and chill is overwhelm-
ing.
I breathe heavy once more, and the
cold seems to cleanse my soul.
Spellbound by the falling snow,
My fears disappear with each melting
flake.
I welcome this frigid breeze, for it
has revived me.
And, for this very moment!
My head and heart is stilled,
I am,
At peace, with this world.

Michelle N A Lake
NOW
Could it be that after all this time
We've come to nothing . . . .
Or is it that I have gained nothing
But abuses,
pain,
sadness
After all my sacrifices in the name of
love;
After all those understanding
moments when you fouled up
And I forgave in the name of love;
After all those sleepless nights you
gave me
Because of something more pressing
than my company;
After all my commitment to our
cause
And the hope that despite everything
we would still share
Each other's company and love;
But . . . .
No longer will I be a martyr of love
At least for you.

Ann B Traini
THE IMMORTAL MEASURE
I've felt the nearness of thy presence,
God,
Below the hill where woodland paths
recross;
And seen thy step impressed on
velvet moss,
And walk with thee upon dew-
sprinkled sod!

I saw the mighty sweep which was
thy breath
Make abject slaves of monarchs
thought immune;
I hear that same breath pipe a simple
rune—
Then cooled the feverish wantonness
of death!

Oh, Lord! Thy arm the whole world
doth embrace;
The sun and moon lie in thy hallowed
hand;
Thy thought doth every molecule
command;
Thy mercy is the essence of thy grace
. . . .

One measure of an organ did
instill
This prescience of thy immortal
will!

Bob Rodenberger
THE LONESOME BUOY
He was standing there all alone,
In the calm blue sea,
As I stood and gazed upon it,
I wondered, how lonely he must
be.

For many days as I passed it,
Staring as I wandered by,
This lonesome "buoy" in the ocean,
Just seemed to sit and sigh.

Then one day as the sea was stormy
I saw a "gull" circling high!
Would she pay this buoy a visit?
Or would she too pass him by?

But then she swooped and landed,
I was filled with joy!
For now there is a pretty "gull"
That sits with this lonesome "buoy."

Ann Houston
A SOLDIER BOY LAY DYING
A soldier boy lay dying in a fox
hole over there.
He lay tattered, torn and bleeding
as he whispered this little
prayer:

Tell mother that I'm sorry for the

times I caused her pain.
I only wish I could see her dear
sweet face again.
Tell dad that he can be proud of
me,
I gladly give my life to keep my
country free.
I'm glad I was a good, average
American boy,
Where my reward will be heaven,
where there is no greater joy.
I only hope our cause will not have
been in vain.
Where life, love, and liberty will
all be ours again.

Shirley Pearson
THE RAINBOW

I have seen the rainbow—
It came, built and shone,
So pure and intense—
Its going was not so much
A bursting and dispersing of colours,
Nor yet a fading away,
As a disjointment, a separating,
A disorientation
As to time and space;
A breathless grasping
To hold the memories in place;

A curious, lost feeling,
An empty disillusionment.
I was sad to see it go,
The rainbow.

(Could my life's journey
Be portrayed in a single picture,
The rainbow would surely soar
Across its sky.)

Felix Rivera
THE WOMAN I HAVE LOVED

To All of those with eyes that see that love is more than visions, but deep within us, and to my wife and friend, Sandy

The woman I have loved
Would never answer back at me
For there would be no cause
The woman I have loved
Is all a man could dream
I'll give an undying heart
To hear her when she's sad
To comfort her in pain
Acknowledge she exists
The woman I have loved
Cares for those she sees
And sees to those she cares for
Selfgiving of mind, heart, and soul
The woman I have loved
Is no angel, yet she could have wings
And if she did, I'd let her go
For she means more to all
Than she would to me
The woman I have loved
Never needs to ever ask
For knowing she would need my
hand
It shall always be there . . .

Edith Spark Hollander
HOLE IN THE AIR

Mourn silently,
I tell you,
Mourn silently,
Say nothing.
Leave words to those
Who cannot mourn.
Grieve quietly,
I say, grieve quietly.
Touch nothing.
Do not stir this air.
I am measuring
And cannot comprehend
How a small being
Can leave so vast
A hole in this air
That I, larger,
Am lost in it.
Nor how her ambiance
Filling it, overflowed,
Spilling everywhere.
Nor how her small voice
Stilled, leaves not
Silence, but absence
Of its sound,
Flown beyond the
Reach of despair.

Edgar H Kleckley
WHEN JESUS RETURNS TO EARTH

These words are a true value of my own sentiments for expressing the ideal of American Christianity and wholesome southern traditions and culture

When Gabriel blows his horn
And time shall be no more
Our Savior Jesus Christ
Will descend from his Heavenly
home

He will return to Earth with the
angels
In clouds of glory
To restore the Earth like the Garden
of Eden
As the most beautiful new world

When our Savior returns to set up his
kingdom
Satan will be banished from his rule
over the Earth
And those who obeyed God's
commandments
Will reign with Jesus in eternal life

To those who rejected God's
salvation
Will be judged for the sins they have
done
And be banished to be with Satan
In a tormented eternal world.

Lavona M Potter
IN LOVING MEMORY OF OUR GRANDSON, MARK

Dedicated to our beloved Grandson, Mark Allen Simpson, who was killed by a drunk driver on Sept. 20, 1987; "He was just 23." "Mothers Against Drunk Drivers (M. A. D. D.) asked for permission from me to read this poem about my Grandson, Mark, at as candlelight vigil in San Jose."

In a new dimension, an iridescent
place,
There is the reflection of a sun-
mirrored space
Where I can see your handsome,
familiar face.
Beyond the far horizons of sky and
sea,
You are as near as a whisper can be
And your voice is gentle as it
comforts me.

Suddenly, I am exceedingly aware
Of doors opening wide to Everywhere;
Now I know the answer to my
constant prayer.
You are free at last of all our mortal
ways.
The encumbrances of our blemished
days
Have been transformed into a more
perfect phase.

I am beginning now to understand
The significance of what God has
planned;
And I see you reaching out a helping
hand
To guide those of us who are left
behind.
The qualities you possess will always
find
A way to lead us who still stumble,
blind.

. . . .

Help us, Mark, with our own
Gethsemane,
And we will search together for
immortality!

Lea Radtke
THORN IN MY SIDE

Dedicated to my Grandpa Furlong

One icy December evening,
My grandfather died,
As he did,
He left a thorn in my side.

In and out,
Rolls the tide,
Still remains,
The thorn in my side.

As I looked at his pictures,
I've sat and cried,
From that everlasting,
Thorn in my side.

Michelle Reneé Bergquist
MEANING OF LIFE

To Sheri Lynn Wilson, my best friend forever. Love Michelle Reneé Bergquist

tears that fall from my eyes
as I look up toward the sky
trying to find love that is not there
floating around up in the air
life isn't always what it seems to be
especially for someone like me

always looking somewhere to find
a love that could and will be mine
I only need just a little bit
but God only knows what I may get
if I don't find what I need
what kind of life will I lead

maybe only if I could die
if I could fly up around the sky
looking down upon the world below
then maybe I would know
what the meaning in life could be
for someone almost exactly like me

Bill Dluzniewski
WINTER MORNING HUNT

To my mother who I wish could have seen this. To my father who taught me to appreciate nature. To my wife who tolerates me. To my children who are not at all impressed.

One struggles to mount the inclined
field of hay.

Footsteps in the snowy melt,
Fleeting fossils on oft plowed buried
span.

Crystal puffs of breath age the brazen
beard of youth.

When crest is breached aft breathless
toil in search of hare or hen,
What splendors stun the software
eyes of modern man in hunt!

Soft powdered web, gem starlit twig,
sun's laser flash impressed;
Upon the plate to be developed,
alone, in wanton days

One holds the gun, lost is the game.

No matter!

Jan Letany
FOR MOTHER'S AMUSEMENT

This poem is dedicated to Mom.

Bingo chips—
Bingo hall—
Good luck charms—
You've got them all.
For jackpots big
and
jackpots small,
good luck on the cover all.
Sometimes you win.
Sometimes you lose.
Sometimes you get the bingo blues.
But,
you are hooked upon the reel.
And,
pay your dues for the package deal.
Sometimes you take an intermission.
And then
go back for free admission.
You make your rounds to favorite
places.
Bingo hounds are familiar faces.

Ruthe-Marina Raines

Ruthe-Marina Raines
"of mist, of mind . . . ."

To the dreamer who transcends his time and space . . . .To the runner who still runs, though he may not win the race . . . To the singer of those silences only the heart can understand, here's to you.

'twas but a moment of time,
that day . . . .
the air was clear, the colors bright,
the sun was gay.
nasturtiums blazed even in shadows
gnarled with ivy on the bay.
was it like this, or did I just imagine
it this way?

'twas but a picture held in mind and
space . . . .
a cottage found, (or was it lost,) with
wild vines
scribbled on its face.
hand in hand we walked, enchanted,
as if floating
into grace.

* * *

'twas but a day like any other.
yet . . . .
for a moment, of the world were
pardoned debt,
and upon the endless sands our feet
we set
knowing well how swiftly footprints
sand forgets.

'twas but a moment of time, that
day . . . .
the air was clear, the colors bright,
the sun was gay.
the moments passed as those of any
other day, and yet
it takes such days to make us realize
that life is made of little moments, we
know not how to prize:
such moments often even come
and take us completely by surprise.

Donna Lynn Hepworth
FOUR SEASONS

Dedicated to my Mom, Chuckie, Joe, Rita, and Mr. Pulick, thanks to all of you, for believing in me and giving me the confidence to follow my dreams. And to Eddie-Lou Cole for giving me my first break in poetry.

Spring days sing in the rain
Dreams are free to roam,
Love gets the best of us
When the doors are opened to home.

Summer gives spring a ring
Says "You are over now,
It is my turn to grow and prosper
As the beaches become towns."

Fall is here to relieve summer
Watchful eyes are wide,
Leaves are changing, beauty has
come
And my picture is on the countryside.

Winter is here, a snowy bed,
Time to rest your weary head.
Soon spring will come again,
As in the past, no broken chain!

George A Hancock
A MAD DOG
I know a mad dog
Who likes to jog
He's known to sob
Because he lost his job.

His name is Bob
He once held a distinguished job
As a harmonious head waiter
Lately he's resounded like an
anguished alligator.

This is a melancholy tale
Of a nervous twitching tail
Poor Bob would also stutter
Nary a word could he utter.

At first glance
There's the chance
Of detecting his melodious skills
And remembering long lost thrills.

Bob moved to Dusty Roads
A place of contradictory codes
Now Bob runs amuck
While awaiting a change of luck.

W Phillip Lyliston
SUNKEN DOWN
Love yourself
is the push
up
from
a lonely place;
Caring thought,
self-value;
Feeling potential
well
from its moors;
I guess
the day
of the
bottom
can be
the start
to the stop.

Elisha Ann LeFlore
WAITING
I am but a poor lass,
Waiting in a brown meadow.
I am but a poor lass,
Waiting for a friend.

Waiting for a friend,
Yet she wouldn't show.
Waiting for a friend,
This I didn't know.

I am but a poor lass,
Waiting in a brown meadow.
I am but a poor lass,
Waiting for things to grow.

Waiting for things to grow,
Yet it wouldn't come.
Waiting for things to grow,
This I didn't know.

I am but a poor lass,
Waiting in a green meadow.
I am but a poor lass,
Still, after they did show.

Jovy G Paquiz
FRAGILE THING
LOVE is a fragile thing
not a diamond ring

LOVE is a delicate thing
it's a scary thing

LOVE is a rose in the spring
it's a painful sting

LOVE is what a bluebird sings
it's what a lonely night brings

LOVE is sweet rain falling
it's the cold wind blowing

LOVE is tight-rope walking
and the doubts with steps
you're taking

LOVE is seeing
and not dreaming

LOVE is changing
and LOVE is crying

Oh LOVE is a precious thing
LOVE is everything
'Cuz LOVE is life
And just trying to do it right—

Penny Brockington
GOD'S ABUNDANT LOVE
God loves you, don't ever forget
And he always will, He'll never
forsake.
It's a great wonder, what His love
can do
It can bring us together, and
keep us true.
A home with love brightens our way
A family with love will
remember to pray.
It brings out the smile on a loved
one's face,
And warms our hearts on the
coldest days.
Without this love, what would we
do?
It's given to all, and this
includes you.
It's a gift from God, given to His
Son,
Who while on earth gave to
everyone.
He made it strong, and so abundant
too,
It was handed down for me and
you.
Don't bottle it up, share your love
each day,
Show someone you care in a
loving way.
You will feel better, and be glad you
did,
And God will be pleased you are
doing His will.
So share the love that God gave you,
It will help someone who is
down and blue.
Let them see in you that true love
glow,
Be loving and kind, and let God's
love grow.

Dorothy Jean Ewing
PROMISES
Come live with me, my own true
love,
I'll take you to my dwelling place
where lacy oak leaves screen the sun
to make cool shadows on your face.

We'll walk through fields of clover
bloom,
tomorrow when the wind is south,
and when you laugh, I'll give to you
a wild strawberry in your mouth.

We'll sip our wine from butter cups
and dine beside a limpid pool.
I'll weave a shawl of love and dreams
to warm you when the nights are
cool.

I'll give you golden honey, sweet,
with berry buns to spread it on,
wild fern fronds for your pillow soft
and marigolds to bed upon.

We'll dream the grandest happenings
and I will make them all come true.
Within these four apartment walls
right here on Seventh Avenue.

Rochelle Boatwright
WATCH AND LISTEN
I heard someone knocking on my door one day I looked and saw nothing so I walked away. I next heard a voice keep calling my name I looked again and still saw nothing.
Then I sat and thought for a while and later I realized Jesus was calling me home.
I thought by then it had been too late so I said a little prayer and lucky for me Jesus still cared.
From that day on I put God first in all things, one moment later it could have been all gone. So watch and listen for footsteps nearby it's Jesus calling you home like he did me.

Ruth Volid
DUNES
If I had sat along the shore
And never shed a tear,
Would I have seen the waves come in
And not had any fear?

If I had built a fire there
Upon the dwindling sand
Could I have had a weenie roast
Upon the driest land?

The night was late, no moon was
there
And not a star to see,
The clouded sky was full of rain
Causing us to flee

Into the barn where Bossy slept
Dreaming of oats and hay,
And knowing that with passing time
There'd be a sunny day.

Michael Alan Cool
THE AMERICAN COWBOY

I dedicate this poem to all the descendants of Frank Cool.

Hail! The men of the western plains,
Who have ridden far through the
worst of rains,
Their life of cattle was never at
ease—
Always on the move, and the worry
of disease.

"Has the life of the American
cowboy really gone by?"
When you stop to think of the
wild, wild west,
You'll know it was conquered by
the very best.
God and man can now rest.

These men we praise have paid their
dues,
They've swallowed dust, hoping not
to go bust.
They fought the redman and took his
land,
For fear of the rifle, the Indians ran.
The head's held high of the mighty
drover,
For he knows the trail's end is nearly
over.

With the feel of money in his sagging
pocket,
He rides to the store to buy his girl a
locket.
As the sun sets in a clear blue sky,
We might ask ourselves and wonder
"Why?"

"Has the life of the American
cowboy really gone by?"
When you stop to think of the
wild, wild west,
You'll know it was conquered by
the very best.
God and man can now rest.

Cornelis ZEGERS
FLORENCE FROWNS
Florence frowns

With the morning light.
Red streaks across the sky
and will it be a nice day?

Florence smiles,
running down the stairs
on naked feet.
I don't belong to anyone
and
please make me belong.

Not to mention her hair
flowing
through my dreams,
like a seabow.
Can I sail away with you?
Can I?

Florence frowns.

kryssi wyckoff martin
I WANT TO
I want to be Laura Petrie
I want to wear flat shoes
and hang around the house
I want to cry when I don't get my
way
and when I do

I want to open his mail
 and cook his dinner
I want to get my hair done
 and buy a new hat
 to go with my new dress
 and shoes
 for The Dinner Party
I want to be Laura Petrie
 and bake cookies for my precocious
child
And be Happy Happy
 OHSO Happy
And kiss him when he comes home

Melissa Watkins
THE TAG SALE
Alone I sit amongst the treasures of
my past.
Gazing around me I see all the things
I once loved and cherished
 now ungratefully heaped in
 boxes and piles
 priced much too low for their
 value.

In my mind's eye I am brought
 back, beyond yesterday
 to glorious days long since
 forgotten.
To days when the whole world
 revolved around my favorite
 Teddy Bear.

I gingerly pick him up from a box
 of old toys priced one dollar each.
His fur is matted and scarce in
 places.
His body is limp from being
 squeezed too hard at night.
He is missing one eye, and his ear
 is torn from an unnecessary
 quarrel with the cat.

To a stranger's eye he is not even
worth that one dollar.
But to me he is worth millions for he
is stuffed with memories.
I hold him close and wonder how
many tear drops have stained his fur.
And then come to the conclusion,

He is Not for Sale!

Kimberley K Pleasant
THE CHILD'S KITE
The child glides along flying its kite
Running through the fields wild and
free.
The kite gets caught up in the tree
the child tries bringing the kite down
 with all his might.
The kite stays in the branch
with its rips and tears
The kite is rescued but the damage
done cannot be repaired.
In life the mistakes we make can
 not change
It just takes a mite of wind
to fly the child's kite
As it does for to move onward
in life.
The battle of life is in this object
 that we see.

Brenda Belair
TRAVELING
The big oak tree sheds a single
yellow leaf
 as it falls to the dew touched
 ground
Lingering but for a moment
Gracefully floating through the air
Pausing as it drops to the green grass
 to mingle with the others that
 have fallen
Brown and red, green and orange
 all huddled together
Then a strong gust of wind sweeps it
away
Carries it off to a little pond
 with rippling waters and tiny
 stones
Little fishes and hopping frogs
And the leaf continues its journey
 riding on the current
Resting here and there
Looking for some companion,
 or a place to end its voyage
 or maybe a place to begin
Feeling the chill of the first
snowflake fall
 and it becomes buried under all
 that snow
And we will wait to to see if it
emerges in the spring
 or dies in the cold
 under the weight of the snow
All for a chance to venture away
from the tree,
 the limb, the branch
Just a chance to see a new world.

Jenica Sword
WHY?
My children invented the
A-bomb
They killed each other over minor
squabbles
Whose space was whose

They turned on each other
Found wrongs in their kin
Brainwashed each other

Claimed death was honorable
If you were murdering your brother
Somewhere else

I weep for the follies
My children have brought forth
For THEM I cry

I am the world
I no longer exist

Tracy E Minkoff
APPARENTLY
Searching on perpetually
But yet to catch a clue,
Although an independent one
You're apt to seek a crew.
Nothing true will surface here
The shadows must conceal,
Unknown vows to hide the plum
You'd likely strike a deal.
A warning issued forcefully
To desecrate your faith,
Despite the threats of shattered hope
You disobliged the wraith.
And through uncertain corridors
You sauntered in despair,
Seeking with profound exertion,
Sensory aware.
The sadness of this anxious task
Eternally unfound:
You might have gained the
knowledge
Had you stopped to look around.

Sharon G Sharretts
DUSK
Distantly watching, with a burning
desire,
A lioness stalking, swift like the fire.
Into the shadows, blending with
night,
Slinking from vision, lost to the sight.

Soft in the winds, a scent still
remains,
Her powers, unyielding, cannot be
tamed.
Restless on haunches, eager to prowl,
Tensed up and ready, stifling a growl.

Daylight grows dimmer, with the
falling of night,
Sounds of the cautious, ready to
fight.
Into the grasses, she expertly waits,
Knowing with patience, her hunger
she'll sate.

There, in the sunset, an image of
black,
Alert and quite ready, but still she
holds back.
The prey, unaware, walks in her
reach,
The birds, now disturbed, flee with a
screech.

Unfrozen from shadows, the lioness
runs,
Chasing her life-blood, with a speed
known to none.
Down with a struggle; the hunter and
prey,
Both come to know, the ending of
day.

Tony Carozza

Tony Carozza
I STAND AT LOVE'S THRESHOLD

For Madeline, Je t'aime.

I stand at love's threshold,
 anxiously awaiting to cross
 into the arms of unconditional
 love.
She radiates a purity of love,
 with a softness and a tenderness
 that envelopes my soul and
 captivates my heart.
My senses are alive with her.
 My pulse pounds with her
 blossoming sexuality.
 I am drunk with the very scent
 of her.
I caress her with my eyes.
 I savor the sensuous touch of
 her hands.
 I am enchanted by the woman in
 her.
I desire to love her,
 as I would hope
 she desires my love.
I am content to search no more,
 for this love has given to me
 my life's companion.

William F Geary
THE VICTIM
There she is—alone in the dark,
no place to go, no place to hide,
she wonders as life passes her by.
There! In the corner—she sits, she
waits,
waiting for the moment to rise
to be herself again,
once again—when the nightmare
dies.

Shaken by this trauma,
she hasn't been herself,
losing the feeling of dignity
she sits there and she cries.

There! The problem—the scars on
her mind,
the ones deeply stained,
the ones that blow chills,
the ones she wants left behind.
Though there is not much more I can
do,
I pray with all my heart,
I hope it will all end soon,
I would hate to drift apart.

Sylvia Kielbik
OFT WHEN I SIT SO LISTLESSLY
Oft when I sit so listlessly
 and watch the world go by
I think of the things I'd like to see
 things that can't come to me
And as I sit and dream away
 my thoughts wander back oh so
 far
And memories I wish to forget
 seem to cling to me like tar.

But oh for the touch of a hand so near
 or the sound of a voice so dear
To wake me up from this reverie
 which persists in staying so
 clear.

If only these thoughts would vanish
 and leave my mind in peace
I'd vow I'd never do it again
 and breathe a sigh of release.

Candice Thomson
PEN DESIRE
The pen flows gently over the paper
It creates letters and numbers.
It is unaware of what it is to write.
But it does so with incredible grace.

It doesn't make any mistakes.
Only the hand controlling it does.
It can not create on its own
for the hand forbids it to.
it does as it is ordered.

Oh, its desire to write for itself.
The beauty it knows it can create.
The thoughts to be stated.
The world it knows it could open up.

But alas, it cannot succeed on its
own.
A controlled world it must lead.
Its only hope is that someone creative
will pick it up.
Someone who knows its potential.

The pen sits with its ideas.
Accepting its life of slavery.
Dreaming of one day having its
freedom.
To write its work of art.

June DeFaye Adams
CONTENTMENT

My all . . . . for Paul

Can you tell when a man's content
and at his best, at that?
It's when he grabs his favorite rod, a
few worms and his hat!

He leaves the house at early dawn; he
won't be home till dark.
He doesn't notice all the miles—it's
such a pleasant lark.

The countryside is God's own way of
setting him at ease;
The world is his to gaze upon and
tromp where e'er he please.

Up wooded hill . . . down rocky
vale . . . above . . . below the stream,
His energy is boundless now, for he's
found peace supreme!

The gurgling brook inspires his art to
harass every hole.
With skillful aim he flaunts the line;
he'll float it first . . then troll.

His step is graceful, O—so—still;
entice them is his plea.
He's sure his shadow doesn't show.
(The fish would surely flee!!)

No talk; must act . . and quickly, too,
for when you feel that quirk,
He's feasting on your tempting bait;
Now! Hook him with a "jerk."

Poor flopping beauty . . . so
alert . . . how can he treat it so?
The fact that man can "out-smart"
fish is worth it all, you know.

Peggy Vaughn
THE STIFLING WORD
I sought to achieve many goals in
life—
But, one day I overheard—
Someone speak in a scathing way—
To dampen my enthusiasm with the
stifling word—

I was told I shouldn't seek success—
And to dream was foolish and
absurd—
It then seemed the star I was grasping
for—
Became dull and tarnished by the
stifling word—

I'll ever strive to fulfill my aims—
And a can-do approach is preferred—
I'll try to eliminate negative
thoughts—
And turn a deaf ear to the stifling
word—

The world is filled with don'ts and
can'ts—
Word contractions that should be
interred—
But, I will continue to exert my
abilities—
And delete from my vocabulary the
stifling word———

Charles Safford Jones
THE MAN AND THE MEADOW (B.H. JONES: GRANDFATHER)
I still can recall . . . . . .
the dew-dropped morning on
my father's farm
the bitter-sweet flavor of my
mama's biscuits
the hushed whisper of the
waking meadow flowing over
the trees through my window
buffeting my face . . . . . . waking
my soul.

For the love of the meadow I rose
and toiled
And like the winter wheat . . . . . .
maturing with time
A young boy . . . . . . becoming a
man . . . . realizing
A man who can't work will
eventually die.

When my time comes . . . . . .
when I'm tired
and frail . . . .
don't sorrow, my life has been long
and filled with happy memories of
the meadow;
and the family it fed.
The stalks of the winter wheat
like myself . . . .
harvested and felled.

Stephan C Ban
TO MY CHILDREN AND MY FRIENDS
Thunder and lightning struck my life.
That horrible day, I lost my wife.

Loved her dearly for thirty years.
All that's left are salty tears.

Felt myself all in a slippery well.
How to get out, I could not tell.

Looked up from below to high above,
There they all were with healing love.

My children and friends took hold of
my hand,
That yesterday wore the gold
wedding band.

They pulled me from the bottomless
hole,
Wiping my tears and mending my
soul.

How lucky I am to have such peers,
Never again must I shed bitter tears.

Laurie Cannady
A KISS
To some
it's merely
a token.
But to the Romantic
it's a Work of Art.

Lips softly coming together
Smoothly Gliding
In slow motion silence.
Exploring
. . . Responding
. . . Savoring
A precious moment.

Moist tongues
Entwined
In a Sweet Rhythmic
Salivary Dance.

Each one
A Unique Experience,
Physical expression
of Heart and Soul.

Stacy L Johnson
CHINA DOLL
Oh doll, oh baby, oh pretty, precious
one,
What I see on the outside fills my
eyes with awe.
So soft, so fragile, so gentle—want to
touch.
Seeing is believing—ah—but
seeing's not enough.
If hands were used for seeing, they'd
find so much more.
For to see is to touch and to touch is
to adore.
The lines from your bones on your
tiny, chiseled face
Are mirrors from your insides—
solid—giving grace.
From your poofy, pouty lips with my
fingers I do trace,
To your slightly rounded hips, where
myself I'd love to place.
Oh . . . but little china dolls are
known to often break.
Dolls are made for holding, loving
indefinitely
So I was quite surprised to find my
doll was loving me!
I found there's more than the eye can
see and more beneath the touch.
It's the soul of my china doll that
makes her look just such.
For within her tiny frame, was
abundant solidity, strength everlasting, enduring capacity.
Although pieces of her heart, over
time had chipped away,
I found within this little doll, a
woman who would stay.

Marguerite Rideout
GOING FOR THE MAIL
The box was by the cornfield,
a quarter mile away,
beyond the "crick"
where Grandpa went for water
when the rain barrel was dry.
Bill's big horseshoe prints
and Queenie's smaller ones
from yesterday's trip to town,
made patterns in the dust.
The way led through the wood lot,
where great elms touched heads
across the lane, and whispered
to each other in the breeze.
There was mail in the box today.
Farm papers. Two letters.
Tender chains,
binding soul to soul
and banishing the miles between.

Jeri L Nissen
I PONDER
I sit and ponder the events of life,
many of the moments I've lived
are pondered twice.
Thoughts of what went wrong,
the words that would have
changed my song.
Mostly feeling time passing and only
existing,
what am I reaching for, who is
listening.
One fourth of life has passed me by,
sighing, wondering if I should
cry.
A life that was led so much to please
others,
leaving the real person
smothered.

Lorna Georgalas
HOPE
Times when loneliness creeps
into the crevices of the soul
that lay open like wounds,
making them smart.
Then Love's kind hand rests
upon the weary body
soothing the wandering mind.
Thoughts of yesterday slip
into oblivion, and falling
into the abyss we clutch
to tomorrow's hopes and
dreams.
Some rot, like decadent empires,
and fall to the earth to be
consumed by another yesterday.
But from the earth also
springs fruit; the pulp
nourishing the body,
the seed fulfilling the mind.
And tomorrow waits with arms
open wide to caress what
was almost lost.

Patricia Grosz Schirrmacher
HIS LIGHT OF NOW
One night I slipped down the
Dreamer's Passage
to the Crystal Hallways of Enlighten-
ment.

A sapphire glow surrounded the
purest white light.
It would have blinded the awakened
eye.

I came upon the Lord and we walked
arm in arm,
talking in Spirit of Love.

Alas, I chose to return. The Lord
gave me a choice
and with His Blessing my inner self
flew to His Light of Now.

Glynda M Roberts
NOTHING TO LOSE
Have you ever been lonely,
discouraged and blue,
So down and out, broken-hearted,
you didn't know what you'd do?
Have you ever been mistreated, told
what you could and could not do?
Did you feel like you were in prison
with a door you could not go
through?
Do you have an inner longing for a
sense of quiet peace?
Do you need to feel you have
someone that can offer you sweet
release?
Are you looking for an answer, but
questions are all you find?
Are you wrapped up in a turmoil, but
you long for peace of mind?
Do you look for answers in places
you know you should not go,
Or do you try another route that
makes your mind work slow?
I want to share a secret with those
who feel this way
There is someone to help you and
light your path today.
Just give yourself to Jesus, in Him
completely believe,
Ask for His forgiveness and a new
life you'll receive.
Don't try to solve your problems
alone, just give them to the Lord,
And you will begin to see a change in
life—you are no longer bored.
Life takes on a whole new meaning,
you'll see things all anew
You'll never be alone again, the Lord
will be with you.
So if you've tried all other ways and
nothing seems to ease the pain,
Just give yourself to Jesus, You will
never be the same.

Ruthy Stenson Brown
LOVE BATTLE
What is love—
From where does it grow?
In the bosom of the heart
In the depth of the soul

Laying hidden, under a mask of
granite
Awaiting the next victim—
Then, like a possessed demon it hurls
With a mighty force
Striking . . .
Piercing . . .
Leaving a wound . . .

Now, the battle is at a standstill
A stalemate . . .
The triumph is there one?
Only the future knows
For that is where the scar must surely
show.

Henry P Madera III
AN UNDELIVERED LETTER OF LOVE
Dear Mom,

You gave me life for which I
cannot repay
And waited anxiously for that
special day
When I would be born, all tiny and
new
A son to my father, a blessing to

you.

I was part of you for eight long months
And made you happy for awhile at least.
You loved me then and I love you now
Though your heart is sad you must forget somehow.

I had to go, but God promised today
To send you my brother; this time to stay.
I thanked Him for that and for one more thing too,
I thanked Him for giving me the chance to live within you.

Your still-born child

Minna Wong
THINKING OF YOU

As I walked down by the seashore
I watched the waves roll in.
With every wave I saw, I thought of you.

Remember all the days we spent
Seeing the world,
We took in every beautiful inch
As though we never saw it before.

The days we spent seeing the world were few.
I learned so much.
I felt like a small child seeing the world for the very first time.
Remember all the questions that were asked
About the world around us?
Remember the fun we had discovering the answers?
Anywhere I went with you, no matter what the fuss,
I enjoyed the time I spent with you, you made me feel safe.
Please don't forget how much I care, how much I love you so.
And please remember that it will never change through time.

Antonio Vieira Pereira

Antonio Vieira Pereira
THE WINDOWS OF DISMAY

This poem is dedicated to Ana Maria my sweet wife

Look through the windows of dismay and tell me what you see.

You see clouds of misfortune as men spread themselves to the four corners of the world.

Though for the present your world may seem black.

As men destroy the forests the valleys and oceans and the very air that they breathe.

O that we might grow in virtue, in kindness towards our world.

We who have been born into an age of great events.

We must take our stand and prepare to guard our world and our home.

Annette Dahl
IN MEMORY OF A PERUVIAN INDIAN AND MY GARDENER HUSBAND

Our train killed
A man on the track, an Indian—
Ill omen—How hard you breathed
When we climbed. We marveled at
Runners' paths like veins
To the heart of the mountain.

High above the Sacred Valley,
Where flows the Urubamba,
Terraced fields are a fence
To a bowl in the Andes.
We beheld Machu Picchu there,
Pristine treasure of the Incas.

In the ruins outside Cuzco
You knelt by a purple flower;
"Wild potato," you said.
Mid roses and lilies
You found one maize stalk
In the garden
Of the Archbishop's palace.

Glenda Martin Sherman
LOVE RETURNS EVERY SPRING

Mountain tops with budding arms
are scarlet against an azure sky.
Crocus and daffodil add golden
highlights to nature's canvas.
I met you in the warm of springs past,
We wandered the hillsides
through honeysuckle jungles.
Hand in hand ....
Reborn as one—into love's own
vicious realm.

So, this time of year I wait for
new life within myself.
But for a while I'll capture God's
enchantment of the mountains,
And only pray He hear my cry of
lonely
.... and bring you here.

Juan Ascidro Giron
MOTHER

Dedicated to Regina Ann my lovely wife & Indian princess

We all stood there in echo land,
listening to the dream
Lonely the rustle of hope,
diminishing in her throat,
We painted our selves, as if to relieve her pain
Way on top of echo land,
listening to her dream.

Her dream,

The scent of fresh and clean earth
filled the nostrils of life
She washes me with her soft
dirt, gently cleaning
The dirty breath of greed lying all around. She scrubs
My flesh—her flesh is
welcoming the duty.
She dreams of us all the time.

Way down there by the little brook, I stand there all alone
Tears falling off into her
wrecked slime, I cry
She loves me, we all stood there in echo land
Listening to her dream, she
loves us all.

I carry now a wounded heart, a damaged dream
My Mommy's crying, in the
world she is,
Tears are poisoned by greed, tears are quick to burn
My Mommy's crying, in the
world she is.

Now the earth it eats my flesh, my
Mother's flesh is torn
Sores are upon her beauty, we all stood in echo land,
Failing to see my Mother's dream,
failing to see, failing to see,
That life is going, to the
phantom of the dream.

My Heart she aches, my Mother her
Heart aches too
My tears are hurting my
Mother, hers are hurting me too,
I stood there in echo land, bowing to her dreams
My Mommy she is hurt, begging
us to see.
Her dream . . .

Elizabeth Lu Hulse
WHEN YOU DREAM

To my beloved granddaughter, Skyla

When you dream, dream of love—
Of Mother and Daddy and family all.
Listen to the wild birds call—
To the wind in the trees.
Hear the whisper of the falling leaves,
And the patter of the gentle rain.
When you know the message of all of these,
Then dream and dream again
Of the things you'll do,
And the places you'll go,
Of the sights you'll see,
And the people you'll know.
Dream your secret dreams—and
those you can share,
But always, always be aware
That only you make your dreams come true;
That as you love, love will come to you.
Your life will be full, and rich and good,
If you walk the paths you know you should.

Aisha C Waheed
FOR OUR ANCESTORS

These sentiments of our Souls, (the living descendants of African slaves in America), are dedicated to the Great Ones who preceded us . . . You LIVE through us!

We have inherited your
struggle . . .
and we vow to let not your
struggle be in vain.

We have heard your cries,
experienced your agonies, . . .
your shame, your
humiliation, . . .
and your degradation.

WE HAVE FELT YOUR PAIN!
. . . and we vow to let not your
struggle be in vain.

We are the very life-germs which
you so cleverly, and so
courageously managed to savor.

Our souls are filled with your desires,
your aspirations, your hopes, and
your VICTORY!

. . . AND WE VOW TO LET NOT YOUR STRUGGLE BE IN VAIN!

We know how you have been
shamed, and we struggle to clear
your name.

We know you were once the best,
until the envy of others toppled
you from your nest.

But rest peacefully, dear
ancestors . . . . for victory shall
come.

. . . and WE, who have been
degraded to the lowest of the
low, . . .

SHALL SOON RISE TO THE TOP!

Evelyn J Morand
COMPASSION

I dedicate this poem, to the lady who inspired me to write it, Willie Jordan, co-founder and president of the Fred Jordan Mission in Los Angeles, CA . . Her compassionate heart and love can be seen in her children and mission work, and to my mother, Ann Arsenault, who taught me compassion, first, as a child.

When did it start, this ache in my heart,
that led me to today?
Could it have been from long, long ago,
something I saw, or heard
someone say?
Then it found its way inside my mind,
and the burden grew strong and
deep there.
Pictures flash by me, of homeless people,
who are hurting and need
special care.
Who will help them, where can they go to,
when will their pain go away?
Someone must reach out, to help them "QUICKLY,"
I heard a small voice inside my
heart say.
Men, women and children, who live on bare sidewalks,
who fearfully sleep in cold boxes
and cars.
Broken spirits behind them, little hope for tomorrows,
their lives torn and so full of
scars.
Will the day ever come, can their battles be won,
is there anything that you or I
can do?
And a small voice inside me, cries out saying loudly,
REACH OUT—TOUCH and HELP them,
Compassion really begins; with someone like . . . . . . "YOU"

LaVerne Garrison
MORNING FRIENDS

It's early every morning
Outside my kitchen window
The birds, my wisteria are adorning,
Start putting on their show.
Waiting my daily preparation
Of bread crumbs and seed,
Eyes shining in expectation
Of their morning feed.
Then out I go into the yard
To their feeder in the tree,
Not a bird's eye off-guard
While scolding me to hurry.
I spread their goodies all about,
Then retreating from the feeder,
I can almost hear them shout
Come on, follow the leader!

Don Cast
A TEAR
Today a single tear
Ran down a caring cheek.
It was for the big and strong,
And for the small and weak.

A tear for all the hate
And pain this world can hold.
A tear for every heart,
More precious than purest gold.

A tear for the lonely one
Walking the streets at night.
A tear for every country
Whose answer is to fight.

A tear for the loved one
Who died the other day,
And a tear for every other tear
That someone shed today.

Pat J Knight
A LAND OF LOVE

To Larry My sweet Husband!
Love, Your wife—Pat.

When there is beauty in the sky—
Watch for Jesus as he passes by—
Show him never growing old—
Where you want to go—
The eternal tempest may blow—and glory fill your soul—I lost the one I loved—My tears forever flow—Our endless hours we spend far-away. We have gone to meet Jesus. He saved me on "Easter Day."

"A robe and crown he wore"—"A land of love" and "life"—"A land of love."
"The death he endured"!
"The Body of Jesus crucified"!

Melva L (Moore) Eastwood
KEEP THE DOOR OPEN
When life is getting on
And seems most family is gone
Keep the door open.

For when children are grown
And troubles come
Keep the door open.

You never know just when
There might be a loved one or a friend
Who sometime will need your help
Just keep the door open.

When in your life you need some love
Some friendship and some laughter
Don't sit back closed within
But keep the door open.

Diane L Chase
AS THEY MARCHED OUT TO WAR
As they marched off to war
They had seen things no one had seen before.
As their buddies lay there dying
They tried to get to them, but no use trying

To hear their screams in the night
They try to forget with all their might

Our country sent them there to die
They do not need to hear one more lie
To see all that suffering made them unkind
They'll do anything for peace of mind.
Some can't rest to know what they've done
They fought that war and never won.

My God can't we see what we did to those boys
Played with their lives like they were toys

It's over now and they've come home to rest
And they did their very best
God bless you boys you passed the test.

Debra Laverty
MIGHTY OAK AND GRAY SQUIRREL
The Mighty Oak is tiring, it's time for winter's nap.
She sheds her colors to the ground, puts on her winter cap.
The weight of fruit upon her limbs is more than she can bear,
so with a passing of the wind she sheds them everywhere.
The sound—
Like rain upon the hill; a cue for Gray squirrel's pleasure
as he trudges through the chilling snow to reap Mighty Oak's great treasure.

Mighty Oak is old and wise, no fear of winter's fury,
but Gray squirrel so small has no defense—
Oak yells "Come up here Gray squirrel, hurry!
Climb up my trunk and to my limbs so you may have a chance."
Gray squirrel makes the leap in time and gives a happy dance.
For far below at Oak's great trunk lay Willow's snowy hood,
blown off by raging blizzard winds, like old Oak knew it would.
Mighty Oak drifts back to sleep;
Gray squirrel is safe and warm, nestled in her loving care; sheltered from the storm.

Michael Lamb
FLIGHT OF THE FORGOTTEN SUN
Expanding on an inner plane
Time and space yet to come
Giving birth to inner light
From where no end will come
Yes it's time for years to pass
The daylight hour of ages past
Experience came an hour late
A light from time to come
Time and dreams together yet
On the flight of the forgotten sun.

Trevor M T
TABLE FOR TWO
A golden plate, for our dinner date, for my woman my special mate, a table for two, just for me and you; after we've enjoyed our feast love is a must, we have to burn off the energy with lust.

But help me to understand your emotions I've got to be equipped to give you my total devotion, don't give me something I don't deserve listen to me girl my emotions are my nerves.

Let's enjoy our romance while it lasts, as love can wear off so fast, but if we are meant to stay together, the candle-light dinner brought to us favour, and my darling I hope and pray our love will last forever; but if the candle-light blows out I will have to re-light it with a new partner, so I'll strike out warmer, looking for more love and laughter.

Shele M Vallario
FEELINGS THAT HURT
Wished I had an ear to tell my story to.

There's a man that I know for a short time now.
But here lately I feel like I have known him a lifetime.
I do not want to fall in love with him.
But it feels like there is nothing I can do
Unless I find someone else.

I never thought this would ever happen
To a person no better than myself.
But he is a lot older than I am,
But the feelings I'm feeling are true
And they are strange ones.

I wish there was someone else in my life,
Or should I say someone that meant so much to me but, didn't know how to stop some things he was doing that were killing our love.

Or in someone that was like he was in ways
But in ways like this other guy.
If I could just stop all this

Dallas Metz
THE SNOWFLAKE
As I fall from the heavens above,
I bring forth that time of the year;
My journey is a long but memorable one,
soon to reach my destination;
I will please all who I will touch,
I am cooling but yet warming to the heart;
My life is a short one,
But I enjoy every bit of it.

Marypat Gabor
WHY GOD MADE GRANDPA BOB

To Robert Armand Auclair, my Father, my friend

God made Grandpa Bob for a boy like me,
He gave me someone sturdy and strong like a tree.
He created Grandpa full of spirit and fun
We walk and explore, we play in the sun.

We study our leaves, our twigs and our berries,
And when I get tired, you know who he carries?
With my dirty face and my dirty knees,
Grandpa Bob is so easy to please.

And then of course when we're in the mood,
We jump in the car and sneak off for some food.
Sometimes for ice cream, or burgers, or fries,
Food we feel, will be our demise.

After such long days, we both are so tired,
There is only one thing that is really desired.
With a favorite book, I get on Grandpa's lap
And then what happens? We both take a nap!

So . . . GOD made Grandpa Bob
Because I asked Him to
send Nicholas Terrence Gabor
A very . . . Best Friend

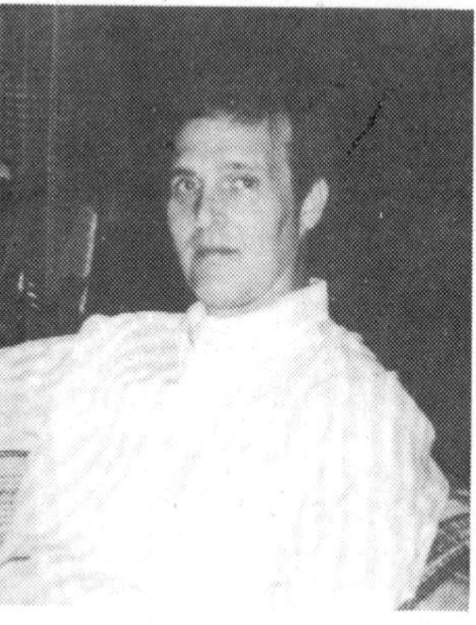

David Talik

David Talik
LET THE CHILDREN

To the world's children
To Joshua and Tammy
To my parents and brothers.

Let the children bring world peace,
Let them find what we vainly seek.
Let the children play in the sun,
Must they dream to have fun?
Let the children play in the street.
Why must they always weep?
Let the children run and be free,
Let them be them; Not you and me.
We grown-ups haven't done so well:
Instead of peace on Earth; we offer Hell.
Let our children fight our war.
Or do we fear, in time, our children will be no more?

Joan Wightman
GRAMPA
There was a man of wisdom, there was a man of pride.
I worshiped him for twenty years, now he's gone and died.
He was so warm and gentle, I loved him with all my heart.
Now he's gone forever and it's tearing my soul apart.
The tears they fall like raindrops, the pain it hurts like hell.
Why did he have to leave me?
Now I'm an empty shell.
No one has meant more to me, and damn if anyone will.
I know he's resting peacefully, for he lives amidst the waves.
And all the seas are still
Grampa, I know you can hear me, although we're oceans away. I love you, those are the words I never did say.

Nicole M Parent
PLASTIC BAG ON THE HIGHWAY

A plastic bag danced to Stevie Wonder
on Route 128 North this morning.
I watched as cars swerved to avoid her,
so full of air and mischief as she
jammed in and out of traffic,
boogied by bumpers,
and break-danced in the break-down lane.

She twisted onto the antenna of a red BMW
for a second or two,
flirting with the man behind the wheel
and copper-toned Vuarnets.
(He hadn't had his coffee yet and
wasn't in the mood to tango.)

I laughed as she pranced over
and did a pirouette on the hood of a police cruiser
then raced off at well over 55 miles per hour.

Stevie sang,
"Isn't she lovely"
and I agreed as the bag
did the bump with an eighteen wheeler,
barely pausing before continuing to
two-step down the highway.

Carl F Starke
BLACK MARBLE "V"

The black marble mass shaped in a "V"
A memorial to the dead they say
It's cold twisted and atrophied
Is this what we give them for the price they've paid?

Golden names bold and proud
Are we as fortunate as they?
Or should we be in the blackness of that cloud?
What price glory for the un-kind pay!

Friend re-united for the last time
Mothers and fathers and wives, they pray
While in the sun the black marble "V" will shine
What price glory, for the living to pay!

Black shape what is that you represent?
Is it the guilt created from the past?
Or the present?

Shannon M Frabbiele-Taylor
WHAT'S THE USE OF HOLDING ON

What's the use of holding on
When we both know our love is wrong?
Choosing places where we have to divide
And holding all those thoughts
So deep inside.
Capturing feelings,
And letting them be so hard to let go—
We're changing all of our directions
And hoping no-one will ever know.
Maybe it's that we need some space,
To unhook all those feelings, thoughts
Let them all just be erased.
Ungrasp those moments that were so dear,
Just erase our minds
And let them be free and clear.
Holding back on loving you
Had never really hurt so bad until now—
I took my chances,
Made the mistakes
And now I hold my head low, looking down.
I realize now,
There's no use in holding on—
Our love for each other will always be Wrong.

Lori Ann Medeiros
YOU MEAN SO MUCH TO ME

I wish to dedicate this poem to the one who means so much to me and the one I love. Bruce Philip Loudin (Skip).

You mean so much to me
If only you could see

To feel your love just one more time
How it would be so divine

I want to whisper sweet things in your ear
Caress my fingers through your soft, silky hair

Your warm, tender luscious kiss
Will always be my wish

In my mind there is no rest
Until I feel your sweet caress

I'll always long to hold you so tight
And have visions of squeezing you
all through the night

You mean so much to me
If only you would let it be

Pierrette Gagnon
MY SWEET LITTLE BUTTERFLY

To my "Honey Bun" to give him courage to follow our Heavenly Father's master plan.

Slowly, I stroll along in the forest
filling my heart with delight
I stare at the tall trees rising proud
towards the clear blue sky
The birds hovering above gather
around me singing a lovely lullaby
As I pick up a wild flower, emotions
overcome and I start to cry
Making its way through the bushes,
is a sweet little butterfly

It is so small, it could rest on my
finger and its body is pure white
I sit down on a broken branch,
daydreaming and enjoying the sight
Joyfully, I recall the day I bought this
unique colourful butterfly
I thought it would be a nice gift for
you and it felt just right
I treasured it until your birthday
arrived and trembling like a child
I offered it to you and taken by
surprise
You could utter no word but gave me
that gorgeous smile
And all was said in the sparkles in
your eyes

Elizabeth Ann Andrews
PRAISE JESUS CHRIST

This poem is dedicated to the memory of Mr. Archie Downey. A soldier in the army of Our Lord, Mr. Downey was an immigrant from Scotland.

O, praise Jesus Christ at His birth,
Glory to God and thank Him;
Honor our Lord God, who will rule
us now and over all soon;
His son will reign on this earth;
Proclaimed by seraphim, they blew
for our Savior
Their own glad trumpet call.

O, sing glory to God on high,
We praise Him and worship Him;
The Lord God, the King of Heaven,
He alone is God above us;
Jesus will live e'ermore, we blessed
Him and we adore Him;
Behold Lord Jesus, He appeared to
save us.

Alleluia, praise Jesus;
We adore and bless Jesus;
For our God and for His Son, raise as
heavnly chorus;
Jesus said, "O, come to me, all you
weary, I will give you rest,"
Alleluia, praise the Lord; alleluia,
Jesus.

Glory to God and to His only Son,
And on earth, let there be peace
among men;
And so sacred His name, greet Him,
joyous;
O Lamb of God, Lord Jesus;
Praise Him, the Lord Jesus!

Shelley Jeanne Larson
LEAVE ME ALONE

Leave me alone . . . You don't care.
Leave me alone . . . Please be there.
Leave me alone . . . It's not fair.
Leave me alone . . . Come and share.
Leave me alone . . . We're no pair.
Leave me alone . . . Please don't stare.
Leave me alone . . . And be aware,
That if you
Leave me alone . . . My heart you'll tear.
Leave me alone . . . Don't you dare!

Marilyn Sapienza
VALLEY OF FIRE

Into the valley we walked not easy,
There was no wind or anything breezy.

Our feet were seared by burning sand,
Between earth and sky was a scorching land.

The rocks and formations were red and tan,
Around us they spread in an arching fan.

Holes and crevices made us feel eerie,
Of lives gone and infinitely weary.

Drawings on rock faces made us aware,
That man in his infinite plight was there,

But long after a time when creation had cooled,
Using strange implements he had tooled.

For in his own way he had need and desire,
To add more creation to the Valley of Fire.

Far out in this strange desolate space,
The beginning of time has always kept pace.

Sun, sky and clouds are reminders of this,
In a landscape that hints at total abyss.

To be part of creation in its original clime,
The Valley of Fire has crystallized time.

Mary E Kelly
THE LINES OF COMMUNICATION

The lines of communication
Between my God and me,
Are always, every moment
Open wide as they can be.

I tell Him every secret,
Precious dream that's in my heart,
And ask Him please to give me strength
To always do my part.

He knows my every weakness,
What things are hard for me,
Then I hear Him softly whisper,
"My Grace is sufficient for Thee."

Then Thankfulness o'erflows my heart
And Joy and songs of Praise!
I tell Him how I love Him,
And how sweet He makes my days.

Edna B Romig
AFTER THE BUTTON IS PUSHED

To the Collard Greens Festival Committee of Ayden, N.C.

Cadillacs stand still
While rusting.
Man has given up
His lusting.

The scientist is
Now extinct
Along with whales and
Milady's mink.

Earth no longer is
Called Mother.
Now to live Man eats
Each other.

We loved their Chicken Kiev
And caviar.
Alas! It only nudged
The door ajar.

Could Collard Greens have
Changed our fate
Had they tried and liked our Greens
Ere it was too late?

Kimberly A Flax
THE SKY IS ALIVE

The sky is alive
when I say it is.
I can make it die again;
the choice is mine.

It can be happy
filled only with me,
my hopes and fears;
all that I am.

Or it can be sad,
calling to me
to give it attention;
to fill it with life.

Only with my help,
by using my life,
can the sky have feelings
and express them to me.

Some say it's just there
with no life of its own
but I know the truth:
the sky is alive . . . in me!

Sal Robert Pauciello
A FAMILY OF DUCKS

I dedicate this poem to my loving wife, Sandra, who is a talented visual artist.

While resting on a porch one day
Which stood beside a moonlit bay
My friend and I in silent thought
There came a sound our ears had caught

It was the quacking of a duck
And this had brought a touch of luck
For out upon the water calm
We felt in movement
Nature's psalm

Nearby beyond the pier there came
Three little ones who looked the same
And mom or dad, I know not which
Appeared beyond the waves' soft pitch

A family of ducks we thought
Resolved a clue which we had sought
For in their graceful play at last
Our bodies sensed the shrouded past.

Tanya A Stafford

Tanya A Stafford
THE ROSE
You and I are rose petals
Attached to the stem of love
As the rose dies, our love shall grow
everlasting.
For our love is not perishable
It has no time limit
It is not matter, but feeling.
Feelings cannot be seen or touched
Yet I feel your love grow together
with mine.
Into the most beautiful unseen rose
there is.

Kathleen A Bartholic
GOD QUEST-IONS
Have you come to us now from the
depths of our being?
Our hearts open and vulnerable,
seeking answers to the Quest-ions
yet unasked
Shall we find our Resurrection
in your coming?
Embryonic in our stages of
recognition
Will it be enough to propel us
to your Truth?
Shall we welcome the Light that
precedes your arrival?
Freedom of choice, being your reins
of control.
What disguises do you have?
Mirrors?
Shall we know you—only—
When we know ourselves?
Quest-ions Quest-ions

Carolyn E Johnson
TRAVELING

To my family with love, and to A.G. now and always.

I like to travel often,
To places I've never seen,
Taking pictures and sightseeing here
and there,
And souvenir shopping in-between.

How I remember the vacation
we took during the fall,
the trees in the forest stood proud,
luscious and tall.

The zoo kept us busy,
the day that we went.
During our camping trip in Vermont,
we slept in a tent.

The gardens clear and bright,
with statues to please the sight.
Seeing waterfalls flowing full,
watching fishermen as they pull.

Miles and miles of beaches to see,
with plenty of island to roam.
But even though I enjoy these
things—I love,
there is nothing like coming home.

Dorothy LaBelle
WHEN THE VALLEY WAS GREEN

To Gramp with love and who never lost faith in me.

Yes, my Valley was green with
towering, gnarled trees,
A place you could walk, your face
brushed by the breeze.
Your house was unlocked for the
straggler who stayed late,
And mom didn't worry and sit up
and wait.
The clip-clop of horses on our old
covered bridge could be heard,
It was almost a symphony without
even a word.
The hills were all rolling, fragrant
and green,
So taken for granted they weren't
even seen.
The houses were large, well built,
with cupolas and gingerbread trim,
Housewives beat carpets with vigor
and vim.
I would if God willing go back to
that day,
However, progress came by and
took it away.
Condos , apartments and cardboard
houses now litter the scene,
They stand where the Valley was so
sweet and green.
Life was simple and sweet,
your neighbor your friend,
Now people are strangers and
porches and rockers have come to an
end.
We're all segregated, the young and
the old,
We're called "senior citizens" and
sent to nursing homes, barren and
cold.
Only in memory can I go back,
Then our worries were people,
not money's lack.
Somehow God fixed it so we always
got by,
In my heart my Valley is green 'til
the day that I die.

Joan Brice Wylie
BLOOM OF LOVE
Her love was like a flower
Growing daily in the sun,
And with tenderness, like raindrops,
A full bloom it had become.

How it thrived upon attention
And the care it got, indeed,
For it blossomed so much longer
Than the ones that have a need.

But the day came when the cold
And windy skies brought forth
despair.
Then the flower from its fullness
Withered quickly for lack of care.

No, it could no more be lovely.
No, it could not bloom again,
For the one who cared so dearly
Found another bloom to tend.

Dorothy G Betchel
BEYOND HEALING

This poem is dedicated to Clarence, my beloved brother.

Alone in a single, dreary room
sits a lonely man.
Amid disorder of empty beer
cans and empty bottles of
whiskey sets the dismal scene.
Drapes are drawn forbidding the
entrance of the sun's rays.
A powerful feeling of hopelessness
fills the smoky air.
A chain of cigarette smoke makes
clouds around the room.
No room for air.
No room for living.
Only a man lost holding his drink
and cigarette.

Rebecca Annette Faulk
IMAGES

This is dedicated to my family and friends which encouraged me to fulfill my dream of becoming a poet, special thanks to my loving parents, Martha and Ronnie Faulk.

The way we were,
Was the way we wanted to be.
'Cause we are to be what we want to
be,
'Cause we are free to be this way.

If you can not be what you want to
be,
You should not be what you are.
If you know what I mean,
Please tell me right now.

I am not just talking,
'Cause I understand;
What you're feeling inside;
Just don't make a man.

I need some lift-up when I'm feeling
blue,
So here I am to tell you what to do.
Just look in the mirror and don't be
afraid,
'Cause what you see you'll see every
day.

So heed my advice and don't get
blue,
'Cause you know me and I know
you.

Hiram Ratliff
REFLECTIONS
I woke up this morning and looked into the mirror, but the body I saw was not my own. No, there you were staring back at me. I would have touched the mirror but I was afraid that the image I saw would disappear. There you were reading the circumference of my mind, the radius of my thoughts, and the diameter of my heart. You saw the pain, hurt, and agony of a broken heart that was swept away by a baptism of love. You could see the reflections of good times shared, memories of you and I walking through the park holding hands, kissing in the movie theater, and making love on the beach. I put my clothes on in front of the mirror and as I started out the door I could not help from smiling because I knew that the woman in the mirror was really you.

Rose Milstein
MONITOR

For Joe

I did not need forget-me-nots
To make me think of you.
Their tiny little faces blue
Beside the rock ledge
Where they grew.

It was the very first bouquet
That graced our kitchen table.
With bluebells that
Were tolling Spring
When everything starts over.

Begin again, Spring tells me.
And if it seems I do
Forget-me-nots
Will bare the lie
I live and laugh without you.

Trudi-Hannelore Francis
THOUGHTS OF A PATIENT
When you get up in the morning to
start your day
You drink coffee, smile, and are on
your way.
Your plan is to work or play,
but when a foot ailment gets in your
way
You cannot have a very good day.
What should you do? Without delay,
visit your podiatrist, Dr. Voloshin,
today.
He will explain your foot problem to
you
and tell you in detail what he is
planning to do.
Dr. Voloshin will use his razor
and/or his amazing Laser.

He will make you feel relaxed and at
ease.
The entire procedure will seem like a
breeze.

If you are brave you may want to watch
and you will see Dr. Voloshin has the touch.
Please follow his instructions to the letter.
Wear good shoes you know it will matter.
Before too long your foot will feel like new.
That's what Dr. Voloshin will do for you.
Now, when you get up in the morning to work or play
Smile, you know you are going to have a good day.

Patricia Tyree
UNTITLED POEM
Shoulders muscled,
skin smoothed.
Lips stretched in
teeth-baring smile.
Green orbs glistened
with unshed tears.
Kittens played in sunshine.

I felt you with my eyes.

I see you forever.

Mandy Davenport
MY BROTHER

To my loving and understanding brother, I love you, Chris. Love, your little sis.

My brother is someone special,
In his own way.
He always makes me laugh and smile
Each and every day.
He's there if I need him
He's there if I don't;
He's there when I say I need a friend
Or if I don't.
My brother is someone special!

Lois-Lynn Bellemare
CLEARER SIGHT

I dedicate this Poem to the "Southerner Guide Dogs, Inc." for their gift of mobility to the blind.

I am blessed with the gift of sight to see whatever I want to see, the trees around in all their Glory the Sun shining down one me.

My neighbor as he smiles at me and waves a big Hello, I look at him with my big blue eyes and see such a nice fello.
The sea shells, as I walk the beach lying in the sand, I see the prettiest one of all and take it in my hand. I see the calm blue river and birds a flying by, I see the thunder clouds a forming in a graying sky.

But everything that I see is not pleasant to behold. I see a hungry animal standing in the cold. I also see the aging face of my Grandmother I love so dear. Her eyes no longer see so well, and in them I see tears.

I also see a little child, tears running down her face, and the bum who's sleeping on the bench, because that's his only place. I see the color of each man's skin, and the blind man who's also lame and the person who talks with his hands and I see we're not the same.

But I have a friend who has no sight. He does not see at all. He can not see the stars at night or the autumn leaves that fall.

He doesn't see a stranger looking straight at him but if that stranger says "good day" he greets him with a grin.

My friend he has a special way of looking at the day. He starts it off "Dear Jesus," in your name I pray. I thank-you, Lord, for clearer sight that I don't need eyes to see. I see the Love of Jesus Christ smiling down on me.

Then I close my eyes and look around and I can see it too, the beauty is not in what you see, the beauty's in what you do.

God and Lois-Lynn Bellemare

Kimberly Austen
GOD IS . . .
God is the one who gave us love
For he is the Father from above
God is the one who made the seas
God is the one who made you and me

God is the one who made the skies
God is the one who made mountains rise
God is the one who made the world so great
For God made the trees, oceans, and lakes

God is the one who made the shores
For God made birds that beautifully soar
God is the one who made man
To dwell in his image upon his land

God is the one who gave us Jesus
For he is the one that now leads us
God is the one who gave us love
For he is the Father from up above

Michelle Handfield
SHOULD HAVE KNOWN
How could I be such a fool.
I should have known from the start.
I should have known he would do this to me,
That he would just break my heart.

I've been in love with him for four years.
I thought he felt the same way.
We both wanted to be together,
together forever I'd say.

He was afraid to be with me.
But I never knew why.
Maybe it was the word relationship?
Even if it was, couldn't he give it a try?

He has a girl friend now.
I thought that was kind of strange.
He was so afraid to be with me.
I guess time has changed.

Finally it came to an end.
I came to reality.
He was leading me on all this time.
But why did he pick me?

Margaret Forest
PORTRAIT OF AN ETERNAL LOVE

To Dalla—my teacher & guide

I try to embrace thee, thou illusive one,
But thy restless soul will not abide the hand
That restrains thee in passionate longing.

For centuries past we walked beside one another
And in one magical moment we were drawn together,
Two souls created in union from the beginning of time.

We spoke the same language, touched one another in total recognition
For we had long ago communicated with the stars and
Listened to the music of Heaven.

Many centuries later we were drawn together
Unaware we had known one another so long ago.

Now once again we stand, hand in hand, gazing out at the universe.
Turning, you hold my eyes in silent thought
And I, spellbound, can only answer you in depth of soul.

Philip D Stang

Philip D Stang
PROUD—AN AMERICAN TRAGEDY

To Dianne, All my love always

Proud, tranquil are we in the
Crystal waters, blooming valleys and thick forested mountains
Proud, In the plumage of the eagle
Tranquillity prevails.

Proud, protectors are we in the
Ebbing waters, withering valleys and sparsely timbered mountains
Proud, In the paint of the berry
Protection prevails.

Proud, revenge seekers are we in the
Poison waters, charred valleys and barren mountains
Proud, In the crimson of our enemy
Revenge prevails.

Proud, defeated are we in the
Stagnant waters, blood-soaked valleys and crumbling mountains
Proud, In the ashes of a nation
Defeat prevails.

Proud, dying are we in the
Polluted waters, trash-laden valleys and eroded mountains
Proud, shoulders bent and whiskey-soaked
Death prevails.

Shannon L Osterman
A MISTAKE
It was a special day,
you would finally be here to stay.
Gone through the week,
not able to speak.
I've been waiting so long,
and now you are gone.
I made a dumb mistake,
and now it's too late!
I took the sharpest knife,
that's how I stopped my life.
No one knows why
I committed suicide,
it is because
you had died!
Now you are gone,
and so am I.
Why did we both,
have to die?
It was for a love,
so strong,
but why death,
it is wrong!

Both family and friends,
from far and hear,
come to see us, as we lie,
helplessly here!
As you leave our coffins,
with caring eyes,
You put us beneath you,
for our spirits to rise!

Margie C Keener
MY BEST FRIEND

TO MY MOM, MARGARET K. PROBASCO CARLLSON
Who passed away 8 May 89!

Whenever I need a Friend—
You always seem to be there,
You help me with my problems,
And our joys together we share.

I can't imagine life—
Without a friend like you,
Once we get together,
We are an indivisible two!

All the fun I've shared with you,
Can never be replaced,
Together we've had many good times,
And conquered the problems we've faced.

So I want you to know—
That I'm always here,
If ever you need a friend—
To make your thoughts clear.

And when I must leave you,
As many good friends sometimes part;
I leave you with good memories,
And an important place in my heart!

Meghan Werner
REASONS UNKNOWN
Everything happens for a reason,
What that reason is I cannot tell,
People disappoint you all the time
Forget them
Concentrate on you
For you are the only true love you have.

Some people change for reasons unknown,
It is hard to accept why, but you often do.
There is no easy way to adjust,
Just be yourself and,
One day
You will
find a
real and forever love.
Honest, you will.

Emilie J Provost
SH, WINTER
Silently the snow flakes fall
blanketing the earth in white
Silently the hawk soars through the sky
searching in vain for food
Silently a lone leaf tiptoes across the snow
to its final resting place
Silently the moon rises
its shine reflected by the ice
Silently the mercury dips lower
only to prove winter's power
Silently dawn is breaking
tinting the whiteness with color
Silently the sun is rising

it's warmth reaching down to the snow
Silently the snow is melting
running, looking for a place to hide
Silently winter has gone away
just as quietly as it came.

Ms Kerren D Bradley
SWEET SPIRIT
I was living a life of nothing, never achieving a goal,
I was always focusing on worldly accomplishments and never on my soul.

I was wanting and never giving, anything in return,
I never understood who Jesus really was and wasn't the least concern.

I began to play my life by air when my dreams had vanished away,
Until a sweet spirit entered in my life and smiled upon my day.

My heart was filled with a new as my eyes had begun to see clear,
That I should try humbling myself, and allow the spirit to draw near,

My teardrops were put to an end, and my heart had begun to take heed,
Because I knew that He would supply what I wanted and all that I'd ever need.

I'll lift His name in praises and to Him I give my all,
Because when I was in my deepest despair he was there to answer my call.

Wayne M Bushnell Jr
A DATE WITH TRAGEDY
Deathwatches ticked at a furious rate
As America awaited its destined date
With fate most cruel, fate of foreign rule!

Soothsayers warned but Americans scorned
Predictions of this destined date,
A date of horrifying fate!

Out of the East arose a beast,
A beast yearning for a hearty feast,
A feast befitting a ravenous revenge!

Tragedy's shadow had crawled from its sea,
That lifeless sea of destiny,
And waved an icy hand over freedom's land!

Ravens crowed and ravens cackled
At Lady Liberty bowed and shackled
In this pall of chilling black!

Amidst the echo of the funeral knell
America slowly slipped into its chasm of hell,
That lifeless and eternal sea of destiny!

Above this incredible and inevitable demise
An Eastern sun majestically did rise
Glowing with pride in instrumenting America's suicide!

Julia Vaughn
THE UNWANTED
There was a young boy he was very sad.
He wanted to talk with his parents but they were always mad.

Ever since the boy was one his parents couldn't accept him as their son.

Now he's eleven, and has entered heaven,
His parents are sad instead of mad,
When your child cries out,
Stop and listen, but do not shout,
for this crying is a warning of love throughout.

Jennifer Ohlbaum
BEACHES
Lying on the sandy shore, I
Feel the shivering waves
Crash against my feet.
As I glance up, the palm
Trees seem to be one
Enormous umbrella protecting me from
Everything above.
The rough sand feels smooth
As I slide my feet through
The sun shines brightly like a
Ring of fire and transforms the ocean into
One gigantic crystal.
As I gaze out into the ocean blue,
Far, far away there may
Never be an ending.

Renee Willis Santomieri
THAT GUY
As I sit in my bed gazing out at the sun shining brightly into my window.
Tears in my eyes as evident from my wet pillow. I lone for that guy.
Who betrayed my love and left me to cry.
I still want so so very much to hold him; Even tho I am now married to Jim.
I often wonder what to do about this sick feeling that has left me so blue.
I truly loved that guy especially when he'd whisper my name.
At that time he had me so so hot. It started blood boiling inside of my veins.
Each time he'd walked near; I wanted his touch but I was in constant fear.
Lately I've needed him so much I ache.
Yet he never cared not one date.
I think about him no matter what town.
He would talk so so sweet to me when he didn't put me down.
I was so lonely for him I couldn't eat and couldn't sleep.
Months passed and I then became very very weak.
I want him now but he still won't come around.
That guy he wears most of my favorite colors.
Yet he kept me sad as he loved another.
Will someone help me please because that guy has truly destroyed; all my faith in love you see.
If there's still everlasting love around it must be.
Among the blue jays and the pretty white doves flying free.

Lee Clement
ANSWER
Feelings of complete aloneness;
When, it's a time to be joyful.
Only thing is you, only feel like Crying . . .
The tree light, shines so bright,
Yet the light in your soul is so dim.
The answer to your darkness
—glows,—
When you give your heart to the
—Lord—
You may still follow a shallow path,
the only difference is you sure will not be alone.
For the Lord will always hold your hand, and
From then on protect your
Heart.

Natalie A Brady
LOVE AND MEMORIES
Dedicated especially for my husband Robert, and children; Iris, Carolyn, Bobby, Glenn and last but not least Arthur.

In the morning when I waken bright and early,
Let me feel the gentle touch of your dear face
As I reach to softly put my arm around you,
And remember another time and place,
We were younger then, and full of vast emotions
Never dreaming that time would pass so fast
Like quivers of arrows speeding
Reaching a mark so sure and vast—
Children growing up, life flowers speeding,
Towards a future full of sunny glow,
Never realizing their childhood days had come and gone,
Now looking to a future of their own
Our arms enfold the circle of our children

For they are the essence of our love,
May God's love deeply fill them, as
He watches down from above;
For our love like embers burning
Soon to ashes we will be,
But our memories long forgotten,
Blown like winds throughout the trees,
Circling, spinning, blowing enfolding our love forever.

Janet K Lorenz
NATURE'S MOST PERFECT GIFT
If spring should arrive and I couldn't be here
To witness the beauty unfolding each year,
My loss would be blossoms on trees of perfume,
A bouquet of daffodils brightening the room.
White fleecy clouds that turn gray to mist showers
Of soft falling rain to touch dainty flowers.
Lace-like ferns on the forest floor,
Melting snows forcing rivers to roar.
Birds winging North at the first sign of spring
Enhancing my world by the songs that they sing.
If spring should arrive and I couldn't be here
To enjoy things in nature I hold so dear,
I'd miss my existence with sun, moon, and stream,
But there's one part of nature that always will seem
Like something to place and admire on a shelf . . .
Tis the magnificence of life itself.

Alfred Oliver
JUSTICE
Just what was it? I couldn't see, Justice.
Just as Blind as that Lady on the Statue you see.
Or is she Blind, as she pretends to be?
Or is it just me?
Or is she Blind to the things she don't want to see?
Or is it just Me
Just as I look back, every night you see.
I wonder why, Justice never came to be?
Just Us?
Just for Them?
Just Me?

Jared Story
LOVE
Sometimes love is like a river,
it flows until the end.

Sometimes love is like a flower,
it blooms, then crumbles up.

If your love is true and pure,
it is a river that flows until the end.

If your love is riches and fame,
it is a flower that blooms, then crumbles up.

If your love is like a river, just let it flow,
but if your love is like a flower, just let it crumble up.

Audrey Hansen
LONELINESS IS ALL INSIDE OF ME
Loneliness is all inside of me.
I never let it out for anyone to see.
I have people all around me;
But they all have their own.
They come and go and say 'hello.'
They call me on the phone;
But I'm still alone!
I think of others that can't get out
And the others that can not see.
I look around and see myself
And think how fortunate I must be.
But, Lord, that loneliness
Is still inside of me.

Virgil S Hart
TO WHOM I SAID, "I DO"!
'Tis February once again, and Valentine's Day will soon be here.
For five years I have written a love poem "Just For You"!
Now I sit and wonder, "What will I write this year?"
I'm thinking, and I'm pondering; but new ideas are so few.

My thoughts go back to forty-eight when I fell in love with you.
I do not need to ponder long, for our love is still a binding tie.
February is a fickle month, but our love stays strong and true.
Time goes by and customs change, but our devotion is until we die!

February is here once more, the shortest month of all the year.
Valentine's Day will soon be here, the thirty-eighth since we said, "I do"!
The years are flowing swiftly by; but our marriage still endures, my dear.
We'll keep our vow to be as one until at death one says, "Adieu"!

Sometimes it seems so very long since February of forty-eight.
We've had our sorrows and our joys and problems that seemed unfair,
But our love has survived those one and forty years since we began to date.
"Just For You," my darling, a Valentines's poem once more, I dare!

Rae Dempster
THROUGH THE MIST
Through the mist
  And through the rain
I see different sights
  Down that same old lane
I take the time
  To notice how
A sparkle looks
  On a rain-soaked bough
Call to a child
  And lift him high
And point to a rainbow
  "There" in the sky
Hurry home
  To awaiting tasks
But notice how
  That squirrel basks
In a ray of warmth
  From a peeping sun
And I think to myself
Dear Lord—Well Done!

Bruce Siegwart
DRAGONFLY
It's time to stop and greet this friend
that every sunlit morning brings.
I kneel in grass of marshy glen
beneath the dragons beating wings.

He's leaving from the twilight stillness
to hum beneath the summer sky.
Noble songs of ancient wisdom
that free the humble dragonfly.

A life so full of force is dying.
His soul has not the heart to fear it.
Lost within the love of flying,
goes the swift departing spirit.

How I wonder where you're going.
Now your earthly wait is through.
Though the joy is in the knowing
that I've been waiting too.

Britt Nicole Fekete
AS I LOOKED ACROSS THE COUNTRYSIDE
As I looked across the countryside,
my life became clear.
The reason for leaving heaven,
to fulfill my duties here.
For heaven is different from
where we are standing now.
I wish everyone could know
my feelings,
and so I will share,
That before we return to
heaven;
we could let the world know we care.

Sherry Gail Grindstaff
LOVING MEMORY
I stand here and look down at you
I realize how much we will miss you.
I hope you know how we feel about you
Even though we never said.
There is never enough time to say.
Or maybe we don't know what to say.
And then it's too late.

All the flowers that frame your casket
Spell out our love and thoughts and we hope you
Know all the people you left behind who care.

Now you're gone and we are left behind.
To pick up the pieces of our life
And deal with our loneliness as best we can.

Verna Mae Konkus

Verna Mae Konkus
YOU CANNOT BE BOUGHT WITH SILVER NOR GOLD
You cannot be bought with silver nor gold
And one that loves you will happily behold
A melody with a waltzing tune
A soul as distant as the moon
You react in a vacant or pensive mood
Sometimes your bliss is solitude
Your love is that of a bird that flutters
Which stirs within a heart that shutters
You won't love in effortless vain
You accept the good, you endure the pain
You're as immense as the wide blue sky
Yet clouds of fears can make you cry
These are the reasons why I love a man on the move
You're a man with everything to prove

Frederick G Widdowson Jr
PHILOSOPHER'S DREAM
My Mind is turning inward,
  My Tongue, a blooming Rosebush speaks,

  In fiery flames write I the night,
And see eternity in an Idiot's eye.

Not an insight into life wanted,
  But more like a Window forced open,

Forcing the gazer to witness,
  The Quiet beauty of nature,

and the ugly lunacy of man.

S J Hoff
THE RIVER FLOWS
Life is a flow of moments
Every moment the seed of infinite possibilities
A forever within a forever.
Take the time to stay awake
To sing and dance, and paint the stars
Free from the labor of the soil.
Take the time to stay awake
Take the seed that's planted
And let it grow wild.
Jump into the everflowing river
Going with the flow of destiny,
Destiny will carry you forward
Forever forward, toward darkened horizons.
So jump in my friend, jump into the river
Those left behind count their crowd,
"The meek shall inherit the earth,"
So let us be brave and take every seed
And jump into the river
The brave shall seize their life,
"The brave shall inherit the stars."

Bill Howey
SOMETHING NEW
Something new just came into my life
A newborn baby from my wife
So tiny are her hands and feet
Oh my God, she's so sweet
My wife labored long and hard
But in the end
I felt life had played our card
Our new roles as Mother and Father
Has made at times
A crying child no bother
As she cuddles close to Mother's breast
I just want to do my very best
At times, we were bereaved
But happiness began, when our child was conceived
It was hard to believe
From what was first a thought
A new beings conceptions was brought
New light has been shed in my life
As continually, I learn more
About loving my child and wife
May God bless his household.

William Ketcham
ROAD OF LIFE
Sometimes the road
  is a little rough,
But this is the time
  you got to get tough.
You can't keep complaining
  and crying all day,
It's time to get busy
  and don't forget to pray.
You need God
  if you want to succeed,
He will help out
  and provide your needs.
The road may be rough
  and hard to get through,
So keep your faith
  it's all up to you.

Leslie Thornton Hall
OH DREAMER
Oh Dreamer, wrapped in cozy thoughts of what might have been. Had you known then, what little there is to know. The great aspirations of youth, could not have aroused in you, the damnable need to question all you saw. You would have been content to build monuments in stone, to slow ideas, and to salute dead eyed men, who have preceded you. Happy to be cast into the unbreakable mold with the rest.
Oh dreamer, you committed the unpardonable sin, of screaming, bright ideas in dreary places, breaking the silence of hallowed halls.
Oh dreamer, why? Why risk so much for so little. They did not applaud you. You were silenced, the silken threads of your delicate soul, ripped beyond repair, your song still unheard.
Oh dreamer, your sad eyes could not reach them, they merely shrug, and turn away. For all you have learned, you know nothing. They the men of steel, who feel nothing, rule for the time, rule the age. They cast out their nets of greed, and pull in their catch. We are their meal, captives of a conscience, weak in caring.
Oh dreamer, one who rest his weary head upon my knee. How can I explain, the near mortal sin of nonconformity.

Mildred Prather
THE TEST
Life without rhyme or reason
Is sad indeed.
Our needs have no season
And pity must flee.

Love is important—
Love of God and man
This, for certain
Must go hand in hand.

If we can like our loved ones
And love all the rest—
Be they red or yellow,
White, black or brown.
We will have passed one test
In living—that is worth any crown.

Heather Harris
INNOCENCE PAST
You did not give me time
to find out about my life
instead you gave me strife.

I ask you, how can it be?
You are my friend and made me do
these adult things until I was blue.

You are not my friend.
You lied to me,
and took my innocence, you see.

My Innocence may be past,
but now you will pay
for your guilt until your dying day.

Dennis L Knecht
THE FIRST NORTHEASTERN
Autumn is done, signs of winter are here,
  Soon, billowing white flakes of snow will appear . . .
Like small parachutes, they glide and dart toward the ground,
  Some shall melt, some will touch down safe and sound . . .
Let the sunlight be blocked by thick clouds today,
  Let the colors be replaced by shadowy grays . . .
Allow vision to be blocked by a thick, white haze . . .
  Harsh sounds be swallowed by glittery crystals . . .
Mother-nature orders an end to the silent phase,
  She calls for Northeastern wind to carry it here . . .
Through barren, high-reaching tree limbs sounds a whistle—
  Posting a communiqué of natural fear . . .
Then, a white-out occurs—hiding man-made boundaries—
  Meanwhile, cleansing the air without effort or a tear . . .
  Quietly carrying man's pollution to the earth and the sea . . .
  Yea, man's fences and walls are hidden—temporarily . . .
As grown men stare blankly, in awe—as if to agree,

A strong force acts which all
ages can see . . .
And they throw snow and laugh like children, with glee . . .
They soon shall face their age,
but for the moment—they are
free!

Evan Monahan
FROM DEFEAT TO VICTORY

To my mom, who continually encourages me and believes in my abilities.

When George Washington was twenty-one,
He was asked to get a big job done.
The French had settled on Virginia land,
So Virginia's governor came up with a plan.
Washington asked the French to leave one day,
But they wouldn't budge, they wanted to stay.

So Washington and his men were forced to fight.
They fought and fought with all their might
Until their gunpowder got drenched by rain
And they no longer could remain.
They realized this battle was no cinch
And ended up surrendering to the French.

Later Washington grew to fame,
And soon everyone knew his name.
This famous Virginia resident
Became our country's very first president!

Olivia Racey
BEING
Isolated with my thoughts,
In a world's profusion of "oughts;"
I steal away among the crowds,
Hide myself in reflective shrouds;
Draped and silent,
I escape this action spent;
Heed an inner voice
That allows my personal choice
To be alone—
Upon my throne
Of exciting meditation!
(Without predication);
And here I dine
On this novel shrine
With its forbidden food, Consent!
And happily refuse to alter or repent
Of this solace afforded for free—
To allow myself merely to be!

Eadie Mae Russell
REMEMBERING YOU
Stillness of the body, throbbing heart beats, the calmness of a gentle breeze, as thoughts of you trespass through the secret passages of my mind. For in you a true friend I did find.
Through all the rough matters, through all the tough times, with all the dark and cloudy days in my life, through your love, the sun did shine.
While treading my most inner thoughts, looking back at the happy moments we spent, I wouldn't trade it all for any amount of dollars and cents. You taught me that love is not just a matter of having some one take care of you, and that it is not always convenient, but when life and mutual feelings are shared on one accord by two, what a beautiful personal proof, of ways to say I love you. With these thoughts in mind, I realized, having a relationship with you was but a hair away from being a golden treasure. For you gave love in no terms of measure. Because of your love I can say to myself, I have lived through many fears. I can handle the next obstacle that comes my way, and I know I must do the thing I think I can not do. STILL REMEMBERING YOU!

Bonnie L Phillips
WINTER
Winter is the time of year,
That I always hold so dear.
Snow lies gently on the mountain top.
While icicles dangle from a limb.
The world is of a glow,
With each falling of a snow.
So bright, shiny and free,
The way God meant it to be.
Not knowing what tomorrow might hold.
This is the world I've come to know,
With all its grace and beauty.
Winter shows what a treasure we have.

Josetta Ibrahim
I AM THEE
I AM as a cloud
Raining the water to quench your thirst.
Like the one drop of rain
that had to come first—
My love will flow as a river to the sea
Encompassing all you touch and see.

And as I grow, an ocean to be
You as a fish, can abound within me
To expand and grow
And always live free.

I shall shelter you from the vastness
And nourish your soul. .
As one and the same
Each part of the whole.

May I be rain, or may I be snow
Whatever I AM is for you to behold
Come to me when darkness won't cease
As a pillow of love, I'll fill you with peace.
Come to me when your dreams have drained
And I as a cloud
Shall rain miracles again.

LaDonna Dixon
WHY
Why is life so foul?
Some people live with eternal contentment;
Others,
. . . eternal pain.

Why?

If men were created equal,
Why doesn't that equality lie between the anguish and trauma
From one to another.
Where is the symmetry
That forms the horizon between the waters and the sky?

Where?

If the balance stays broken
And one man's serenity become's another's mortification,
Then how much can one man grasp?
How long can one man restrain?
When does one man die
. . . on the inside?

When?

Some people live with eternal contentment;
Others, with eternal pain.

Why?

Tammy Seekamp
JUST TO SAY "HI"
You don't need a special season,
or a special reason,
Just to say "Hi."

We don't need to be together,
to be in love with each other,
Just to say "Hi."

We can be friends,
from two different ends,
Just to say "Hi."

So, what I'm going to say,
I'll say today,
"Hi"!

Andrew J Mitchell

Andrew J Mitchell
DILL PICKLES

To Terry, my mentor, Thanks a lot

Have you ever had the chance,
to see someone eat a dill pickle with a solemn glance?
I should think it would cause me to tucker,
to eat a dill pickle without a pucker.

Sam J Dolsen Jr LCPL-USMC
LOVE FOR PEACE
Love has it's time
For all who love
For it is holy
For one to love all

The times say for peace
Some people say no
For those who care
It's all we know

These times are hard
Time to take part
This our world
To leave or part

Those who care
Make it worth our while
Reason is ours
Ours to care for all

Orpha Parscale Norris
A DREAMER AM I
I fear that I am a dreamer,
And have always been you see,
And tho' I try to change myself,
I fear it will never be.

From morn' till night my mind
spins lines,
So many I cannot pen all;
But the best are the thoughts that
happen at night,
That when morn comes I cannot
recall.

Caroline Rehder Ellis
TEAR DROPS
Hello, old friends;
Soft and warm, you've come again.
Tonight, tomorrow—always near,
Waiting, waiting to appear.

Hello, old friends.
You know my sorrow never ends.
Tonight, tomorrow—always real,
You seem to know the way I feel.

Hello, old friends.
How can I sing again?
Tonight, tomorrow—can you tell?
Will I ever leave this hell?

Hello, old friends.
Will you stay til I mend?
Tonight, tomorrow—always true;
I guess we all have friends like you.

Hello, old friends.
Wash away those other days.
Tonight, tomorrow—times long past,
Comfort me to sleep at last.

Lesley Lacny
MY SPECIAL PLACE
I have a place where I like to go,
A place that only I will know,
A place where no one's tears will fall,
Just a place where I stand tall.
A place where no dark shadows appear,
Just the sounds of birds are near.
This special place, that I know,
Is somewhere only I can go.

Pat Hinkle
THE CRIME
You took my love
and never returned it . . .
As you took my life
And filled it with your dreams;

You took my spirit
and dampened it down
until . . .
There was nothing there
except ashes of what might
have been;

And you took my blind belief
and my trust in you . . .
And betrayed me
with all the callousness of
Judas;

Yet I can,
even in my darkest hour . . .
Forgive you
for all of these things;

But . . .
in searching my mind
I'm saddened to find . . .
I cannot yet forgive you
for the premeditated murder
of my soul.

Perry L Garner Jr
THE CREATION OF HUMAN KIND
In the beginning there was only
darkness and quietness
The darkness was the quietness
The quietness was the darkness

The darkness and quietness were as one
There was no light in the darkness
There was no sound in the quietness
Then a speck of light shown through the darkness
Now the darkness was separated
Then a tiny sound pierced the quietness
Now the quietness was separated
The light grew and the sound grew
The light and the sound became as one
And were separated from the darkness and quietness
The light was the sound
The sound was the light
Together they grew into many voices and sparks of life
And God said, "This is good, this is very good"
And God called this light and sound together
Human Kind

Ronda Turner
TO BE

You had her, and I had him, this is now and that was then.
It had to be lust, because we both know it wasn't trust because the relationships bust.
I love you and you love me, I think it's time for us to be.
You'll care for me, and I'll care for you, and we won't have to go through any more blues.
The time is right so let's make it tonight.
Now that we are free from pain, the sun will dry away the rain.
I know you're right, I feel that it's true
I want to spend the rest of my life loving you.
It's time for you, and its time for me,
I know its time for us to be.

Terrie Louise Coffey
LIKE A BIRD IN A CAGE

Like a bird in a cage, looking out as the world goes by.
You put your best foot forward, only to find you fall.
Only to get back up and fall again.
Not knowing which way to turn without falling again.
So scared to go on, not knowing what's ahead.
You stay in your little hide away
And look out the window
And watch the world go by
Like a bird in a cage being protected.

Donalda J Cook
DREAMS

In my mind I dream about a place for you and me.
A place where little children play and everyone is free.
And, fears are only memories of days so long ago;
Like hidden scars in old men's hearts that never need to show.

And, in my dreams I always see the animals at play.
They have all the land they need, and are never chased away;
Where the water flows so cold and clear for creatures great and small.
There are no words of guns and bombs which may destroy them all.

In a corner of my heart these dreams are so secure.
The dream of marching hand and hand and never knowing war.
Where everyone is happy, and there's food enough to feed
Everyone around the world who's ever been in need.

Now dreams are only fantasies of things we wish could be,
But prayer's a language of the heart between my Lord and me.
So, Lord someday these dreams of mine will come to pass I pray,
For it's up to us to change the world with what we have today.

Mary Alice Wood
THE MARBLE

Surreal is hard to define
Dali ruled the day—

I placed a marble on the table
Then it rolled away.

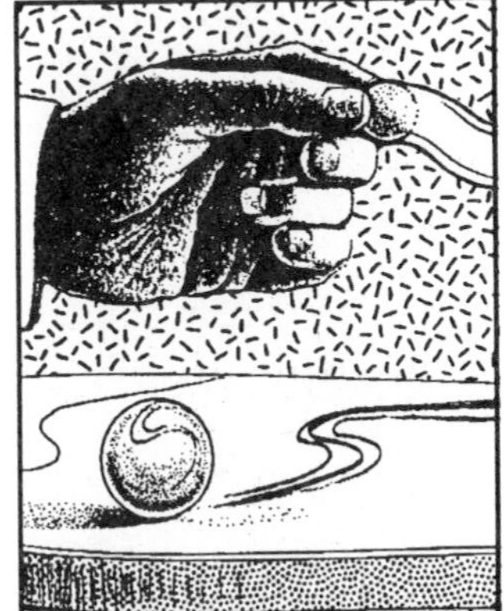

The role the tiny orb can serve
In this auditious play

Is that it returned where it began
Before it rolled away!

Linda Deputy-Thomas
APOLOGY

It's hard to talk about you
so the words fall into place.
They're telling tales about you,
so fast, I can't erase.
Their ugliness astounds me
and I'm ashamed for them.
Still, I can't despise a stranger,
I can only love a friend.

Richard L Baxter
THE CONQUEROR

In the shadow and gloom of midnight,
On a hill outside the gates,
In a lonely, tree-filled garden,
The man of Sorrows waits.

He kneels in a prayer of anguish,
And cries from a heart of pain,
And asks, "Let this cup pass from me!"
And He asks it again and again.

He had left His friends a few paces,
Asking them to pray while He prayed;
He comes—finds them sleeping for sorrow—
They are weary, discouraged, afraid.

So He wrestles alone in the darkness
Till His soul to triumph doth come;
And He cries to His heavenly Father,
"Not my will, but Thine be done."

He has conquered the flesh in its weakness,
He has sweat, as it were, drops of blood;
He is ready for the task set before Him—
Reconciling lost sinners to God.

Oft we think of the cross where He suffered,
How He died for our sins on the tree:
But the battle—'twas won in the garden
That mankind, thru' Him, might be free.

Karly A Lewallen
SEASONS

The branches of the withered tree lie still,
Its leaves all changing golden brown once green.
The hunter's hounds and bugle sounds so shrill,
Once vibrant colored flowers lose their sheen.
Transparent sky turns now a bluish grey.
A breezy chill disturbs the tranquil lea,
Commencing to a rhythmic, graceful sway.
The state of nature in its ecstasy.
But soon the leaves will vanish from the trees,
The ground be smothered by a blanket white.
And gusty winds blow forth as if to tease,
The lifeless foliage left behind to fight.
And when it seems the
bleakness will sustain,
A flower blooms, there's luster
once again.

Karma M Van Gelder
PUSSY WILLOWS

For Jim, who helped me find the courage to look inside for answers, and to know that what I know, I don't know.

Pussy willows growing
Thriving against all odds;
With the first rays of sun
Living in bitter fog.

Pussy willows bending
Before buffeting winds;
Growing on the southside
But dying from within.

Pussy willows frosted
By frigid cold dark nights,
Standing tall and sturdy
Close yourself in and fight.

Wrap yourself in velvet
Look inward never out
For then you can survive
Some more late winter bouts.

Look inside for comfort
Cuddle your own soft felt.
Then you can still live on
Against the pain that's dealt.

Patricia M Thomas
THE TWO OF US

To Kaytlin Margaret, my child—all my love—mommy

We walked along, just the two of us.
Holding hands and kicking up dust.
We jumped over stones and logs and streams.
We walked through our memories and our dreams.

Down the path we went with no voice,
through forests and seas we had no choice.

It rains it snows but onward we go.
Where we're headed, we do not know.

Through sunny days and blistering heat,
there is nothing we cannot defeat.

Through hurt and pain and crying eyes,
mistrust and deceit and bruising lies.

Through hope and glory and all unknown,
just the two of us we got it alone.
We've left a lot behind us and have a lot to face,
but we'll take our time, life's not a race.
Sometime we'll sit and rest for awhile,
but right up we'll go, just me and my child.

Jack Shannon
BEER

When you don't drink coke, but beer,
Things may look close, but are not near.
You may or may not be filled with cheer,
Possibly with anger maybe with tears.
Thru the eve you're with us . . . or not.
The time?! . . . You probably forgot!
You may feel strong, possibly weak.
More than likely you'll be taking a leak.
Maybe a six-pack, maybe two,
When they are all gone it seemed but few.
Maybe you'll be mellow, maybe you'll fight
Hopefully you'll make it thru the night.
When morning comes while holding your head,
trying to remember what you did and said.
Thinking of feats performed without fear,
You think, "Maybe coke instead of beer"!!!

John P Jones
A MOMENT

To my nieces, Tammy and Sharon Williams

For a moment I was lonely no more
For a moment I was mesmerized by your walk
For a moment I was someone else

For a moment I was endowed with your beauty
For a moment I was once again in love
For a moment I desired to be close to you

For a moment I wish you were my love
For a moment I wish that I could make love with you
For a moment there was no more sadness

For only a moment I was able to fantasize
Not really able to touch your hair or smooth skin
Only for a moment was I able to look upon your beauty

And for your beauty to response to me
Only for a moment I was able to love without fear of rejection

But that early dawn morning shall

remain with me
Hoping and wishing that the beauty
that I saw and talk to would
give me the chance to be a part of her
life

Sandye Applegate-Hager
PLEDGE OF LOVE

To you my love, I pledge my eyes
To help you see how much I care.
To you my love, I pledge my ears
To help you hear the words we share.

To you sweetheart, I pledge my hands
To help ytou carry the heavy loads.
To help you with the saddened times,
To you my dear, I pledge my soul.

Most of all, I pledge my heart
And promise that I'll always show
The depth of love I have for you.
I promise it will ever grow.

Joyce Rice
WALK THROUGH THE ORCHARD

The northwestern wind blew clouds
out of sight,
except for a wispy few
The ten O'clock sun is warm and
bright,
and mountains are in full view

Hearty black crows caw their
irritating cry,
whisking off with nuts from the
ground
The pretty gray doves are quiet and
shy,
communing in families all 'round

The orchard is popping its buds into
flowers,
promising fruit in the spring
And buzzing goes on for many hours
Creature bee is a wondrous thing

Delicate pink petals shower away in
the breeze,
as branches redress in green
Dandelions stand tall in rows of the
trees,
their translucent heads convene

A walk through the orchard is a hug
in the spirit,
all sensual components agree
To absorb all the wonders within it
and near it
allows the mind to be truly free

Carolyn B Lucas

Carolyn B Lucas
MY BABY

I dedicate this poem to my mother, Gladys Bridges (1921—). She taught me what real love can accomplish . . .

My baby is born
New life begins
Beautiful love is worn
Everything I do wins

One glance at his smile
And just a simple touch
Makes everything worthwhile
For I love him so much

As I watch him grow
I'll wear his love
With a magical glow
As do the stars above

Soon the touches will be few
He will grow to leave me
And expectations, I knew
That's how life is to be

Grant him the knowledge
to love as I have
When his life seems on edge
Let him wear someone's love

Lylah Casper
BABY

to Tobi and Bert on the arrival of their son

Rosebuds, angel hair, and butterfly
wings
Sunshine, soft clouds, and all
delicate things,
Must surely be what a baby's made
of—
So tiny, so trusting, so free with its
love.

God in His wisdom, chose you with
great care,
To bring forth in this world a baby so
rare.
In all of creation, there'll not be
another,
More precious to you, his father and
mother.

Treasure him, protect him, he's only
a loan.
Teach him and guide him, until he is
grown.
Love him, enjoy him, for time will
be swift
From cradle to manhood, for God's
greatest gift.

V Beverly Rogers
THE GIFT OF AN HOUR

Rising early on a chilly morn,
In the quiet hour before the
dawn,
When mist in fragments lingers low,
And dew drops kiss the flowers
and lawn—

Thoughts form slowly as the mind
awakes,
There is peace in that time
alone,
The gift of an hour, to plan, to pray,
For a day filled with trials
unknown—

The mixture of gray that is dark and
light,
Elicits no feelings of sorrow—
For in that hour strength is renewed,
To last until dawn tomorrow.

Teresa Brassard
MORNING

An eagle flies on golden wings
above a misted mount,
and spies a rose covered with
dew
waiting for the sun to shine out.

A ripple in a silent pond reveals a
tiny frog,
who leaps and croaks from pad
to pad
until he's up upon the sod.

A child laughs, and merrily jaunts
toward the tolling bell, and as we
know the day begins with morning,
All is well.

Naomi Newton
DREAMS

To my husband who dreams with me . . .

Dreams are facets of each one's
life . . .
struggling to become bright
images;
They capture the heart, the mind,
and witness the reward of
lasting curiosity.
Try to snare each small bit,
ignored or forgotten,
And take permission to enjoy;
Listen to limitless ideas that call
slaves to freedom . . .
Ignore a thoughtless sense of
security
that loses accustomed comforts;
Keep a kinship with memories that
must dare destiny to endure,
and come to inordinate terms . . .

Irene S Laupp
HER DAY

On a May morning
bright with dew.
Early Spring flowers
all for you Mom.
We want to pamper you
on your day.
To charm you with flowers
to shower you with roses.
For a rose is a rose
pink and red and so refreshing,
as the May morning dew.
We want to wrap you
in soft pastels,
and with delicate lace.
As the memories
of your life
brings warm memories.
Yes, many happy moments
to recall.
The hours warmed
by your love.
In the days you were with us,
not so long ago.

Peter Frederick Johnson
INCARCERATION

A bunk, a john and plain white
sheets,
The four small walls you live in must
be kept neat.
A plastic mirror, toothbrush, one
door and small shelf,
Is the hell you now live in brought
on by yourself.

Endless lonely days of dreaming,
crying and dying,
You express your inner feelings
through a whimpered sighing.
Sometimes you recall the fictitious
"good times" you once had,
But most were not genuine, out of
proportion and sad.

Taking your freedom for granted like
the spinning of a spindle,
Now your self-esteem, morals and
pride start to dwindle.
Wishing you could change, to do
away with your sinful past,
To rise above it all like a sturdy
ship's mast.

Plenty of time for thinking, so many
things to say,
Staring at the ceiling, on your cold,
hard bunk you lay.
You're suddenly distracted by the
slamming of iron doors,
You need to turn over anyway, your
aching body is sore.

Seldom a friend to share with,
someone who's worthy and true,
All your problems inside must be
dealt with by you.
At night, when you're sleeping, your
body drifts home,
Then you wake to the four walls . . .
once again you're alone.

Lois Webb Stout
TO JONATHAN: ON BEING FORTY

Stand tall, my dear beloved son;
For you, the race is half-way run.

But you are so hale and hearty,
It's no problem being forty.

In days gone by, when you were
small,
It seems, I hardly can recall.

But I'm so proud that you're my son,
I sometimes think you're Number
One.

Except, of course, there is another
Who must share that spot—your
brother!

So, please, do not act like a dunce.
You'll never be forty but once.

Grant Fewsmith

Grant Fewsmith
NOTHING, BUT A MAN

To Karen, who saw me standing at the door, and helped me find the key.

Looking to the morning
to see the world a show
I long for something to give you,
So that you will know,
For I am but a walking man,
traveling mile to mile,
Bringing to you laughter, tears,
But leave for you a smile.

Know that I do love you, know
that I do care, know that in all
I do, I will do it fair,

For I am but a walking man,
traveling mile to mile,
Bringing to you laughter, tears,
but leave for you a smile.

And will you understand
these travels I am on,
exploring through the stars,
looking for my home,

I who have no words, nothing
but a song, which I write to you,
please cherish for so long,
for if I seem bewildered,
out of touch, not so strong.

Remember that I love you and my
love is long.

For I am but a walking man,
traveling mile to mile,
Bringing to you laughter, tears,
but leave for you a smile.

To you I leave this gift,
this piece of my soul, this I
leave to you, so that you will know,

I am but a walking man,
traveling through heaven and hell
Bringing to you my self, whom I
know so well, have no fear my
lady, for as you will see,
I am but a man, with love,
caring, and sensitivity.

Alice May Shutt
LIBERTY
I am so glad I live in a land that's
free.
I am so glad that God has given me
this liberty.
Freedom to live and to love as I
ought.
Freedom to tell others of him by
whom I'm bought.

Many Godly people have been
denied this freedom.
Many have lost their lives or have
lost their freedom.
But not here in this land where I live
today.
People here have freedom in what
they do and say.

Who gave us this freedom in this
land?
Who gave freedom, was it God or
was it man?
I can tell you that answer today;
God gives true freedom in every
way.

You say it was man who fought and
bled and died,
To give us this freedom that in other
lands is denied.
This is true, I know it is so today;
But so did God, in Jesus bled and
died that day.

It is because of this death and
resurrection that day,
That we can have freedom from sin
in our work and play.
When sin is gone, we think as God
does today.
We think more of others and give
freedom today.

Dotti Imwold
GOD, GIVE ME COURAGE
God, give me courage
To live this day.
To face the things I must.
I know I can not do it alone;
Lord . . . in You I place my trust.

My hopes, my dreams,
They seem so small
Compared to your master plan.
You sent your only Son, Dear God,
To free me of my sins.
Please use my life to bring Him
glory,
Though I am but mere man.

Susan C Robak
SAY IT

I want to dedicate this poem to my best friend, Kathy Morani, because of her support and encouragement to keep on writing!

How many ways are there to say it
with love?
Can you say it with love when you
give someone a hug?
Can you say it with kindness to
over come shyness?
Can you say it with flowers, or dance
by the hour?
Can you say it with friendship?

Can you say it with a note or a letter
of hope?
Can you say it with a poem about a
special home?
Can you say it with a present or
money well spent?
Can you say it with a look?

No matter how you express it.
No matter what you say or do,
Love will find a way to shine through
you!

Michelle E Orchard
FRIEND TO THE END
You helped me when I was down.
When I tried to give in;
You helped me put my feet back
on the ground.
You made me laugh when I wanted
to cry.
And you only had one reason why.
You were the one that didn't say
good-bye.
You were the one who hugged me
when
I'd cry.
Although I didn't tell you so;
You also knew when to let me
go.
I'll love you till the day I die.
All because of your one reason why.
Because you are my friend;
and you will be to the end.

Mae Koppman
JOURNEY
We come into the world
Naked,
When we leave, again,
NAKED.

But all our lives
We clothe ourselves
In silk or cotton,
Or richly woven fabrics,
To shelter us from cold,
Or heat, or prying eyes,
Or simply to show our taste or
style,
Or—just for plain decency.
But
We go no further in life
Than our souls can reach.

Yet, we seek the stars, we yearn,
And as long as we do this, we are
alive,
For when we cease to want,
We're partly dead,
Soon gone.

Eric Bennett Ward
TO WORLD LEADERS
To you, the world leaders,
Who have accepted the responsibili-
ties of all nations.
You are the corner stones of the
earth,
Laid by God, the great world leader,
to represent mankind
Though you may be few in number,
you represent many and much.
When you speak, you speak for us,
your people
When you act, you act for us, your
people.
The powers of peace and war are in
your hands
To be used as you decide.
We, your people, have elected you.
We regard you with respect and
honour your integrity
And we trust that your decisions and
efforts will result in peace and
happiness for all mankind.

Martha Tarase

Martha Tarase
YOUR NAME CAST IN STARDUST

This verse was read in church for the wedding of my Grandson and his beautiful bride in nineteen seventy-seven and they are still happily married.

I'm seeking the blessings of heavens
above
Making you all mine alone, all mine
to love
I'm searching the domains of
heavenly gold
A soulmate of heavens to have and to
hold
There's nothing more sacred, a love
more divine
For an angel of heaven, keeps vigil
o'er mine
Your name cast in stardust, mellowed
in blue
A lowly breeze echoes, I love you
too

Your name cast in stardust, mine in
between
I am your emperor, you are my
queen
I'm seeking the blessings of heavens
To be crowned on the throne of love
The stars are all blinking approval
While the angels keep vigil above
I'm seeking the blessings of heavens
Love's greatest question to ask
Do you truly love me
Will it really last?

D O Loudermilk
MY SISTER, MY FRIEND

This poem is dedicated to Melody, my super sister.

I wish there was an easy way to reach
across the miles,
And tell you that I love you and miss
your warm smiles.

A sister's love is a rewarding of all
the secrets they share.
It is a love that is so undying, so you
know it's always there.

Your love gives me comfort in times
of sorrow and woe,
And I know I haven't taken the time
to really let you know.

So I wrote this poem just for you, my
sister who is so far away,
And I just had to let you know, my
friend, you're in my thoughts each
day.

Harry C Craft III
AN OLD MAN

To my grandfather: Howard L. Nash, Thank You for being there when there was no one.

I am old now;
and my bones do creak,
my hair has turned gray,
and my eyes have become weak,

But I have lived,
and I have paid the price,
I have learned,
not to do things once, but twice,

I have done many things,
and would like to do many more,
but I realize, that we are all, just
human beings,
now the time has come, for me, to
open that door,

But life itself, is experience,
and as the days went by,
those unanswered questions were
telling me,
that we all, must live, and die,

So now as I step into the gates,
of either heaven or hell,
I can only be thankful,
that I never spent my life in
jail . . .

Sandra J Clamp
CLEVERLY CLAD
Painted geometrically about the
rounded face—
the explicit colors formed facial
expressions all their own.

White stars surrounding vividly
expressive eyes—
Without doubt, the eyes were
most impressive.

Tipped with a dark red blotch—
the nose appeared a target for
aim

Grass green eyebrows reaching for
the sky—
enhanced the glow of a
remarkable visage.

Thick, black outlines gave shape to
the mouth of the colorful figure—
forming a smile where there
was but a frown.

The curly, metallic blue, bouffant wig surmounted the head—
highlighted by the oversized ears.

Most intriguing of all—left unpainted—
tears rolled down the rosy cheeks of the figure.

Clad in paints and costume—
a bold figure waited to escape.

For inside the clown, there was I—
communicating with the voice of expression.

Jon Howard Hall
REFLECTIONS FROM THE HEART

To Everett and Cathy Sollie

I may never be able to express to you just what you mean to me,
but as friendship grows in future days it becomes more easily;
To tell you in some word and deed or other act of love,
the feelings that I have for you that span the meaning of.
Since you have come into my life, you've been a joy to know,
you give my life a new meaning and I want to tell you so.
As our paths have crossed and one day go our separate ways,
I hope you will remember me and also all the days.
The times we've shared together, the good ones and the bad,
we'll treasure in our memories, although parting will be sad.
So I pledge my life, a friend to you until the very ends,
Just remember, "That a lifetime's not too long to live as friends."

Sulayne Aaron Jacobs
DESTINY

To those "few" who aspire to excellence–Because you are known by your works; both of God and of man!

The world is full of caterpillars—
occasionally one becomes a butterfly:

Much in the same way that frogs,
apart from toads, are destined to comply!

And this assigned lot in life is
exemplified by the rarity of a true frog;

Who, accepting this fate, is in essence
almost a real prince–the analogue!

Glenda J Simpson
JUST PONDERING AWAY

On this beautiful day
With thoughts, old and new
Wondering of life's ups and downs
Comparing events too
Never a dull moment
With such a mind
Trying to find out the clue
As to what life has to offer
For the best, me and you

Rhonda L Garcia
PARENTS ARE LOVE

As I look back over the years,
I remember the joy and the tears,
But the most important thing you see,
Is knowing you were always there for me.
My Mom and Dad whose love is true;
Always there no matter what I do.
Always there to lend a hand,
Trying hard to understand.
Raising children is no easy task,
But love and respect were all that you asked.
You raised us all to know right from wrong,
To do our best as we went along.
I remember you saying, "Do the best you can do,"
And I tried hard so you'd be proud of me too.
You've given me more than I could ever repay,
You gave me strength from day to day.
You taught me to be proud of all that I do,
Have respect for others and self confidence too.
You raised me with love in a family that cares,
This feeling I'm sure each one of us shares.
There aren't enough words to tell how I feel,
But the love and respect I give you is real.
Thank you for always being there for me,
You're the best Dad and Mom there ever could be.

Virginia Cain Conner
FULFILLMENT

Oh love, how could I know how precious
All our together moments would be;
That long after they had all been spent
And no longer were you here with me,
Lovely memories would come rushing back
Through the aeries of eternal time.
Like gentle raindrops falling softly,
Soothing an old, tired and weary mind,
Knowing at last the truest meaning
Linking us forever with the past,
From the present, and to the future;
Hearing children's voices at their play,
Echoing the ones all yet to be,
Living their lives when ours have ended,
Fulfillment is love's eternity!

Tina Ely
MEMORIES

Memories of a child
left crying in the cold

stories of nightmares
kept inside and never told

visions of a man
drifting slowly out of sight

dreams of the love made
earlier that night

now the woman is lonely
the house is dark and cold

no one is left to love her
and she's rapidly growing old

her mother used to beat her
filling her with fright

her father selfishly used her
on several a lonely night

the phone rings loudly
another trick is on the way

she sighs and puts the gun back
to wait for another day . . .

John B Packett
WITH ALL MY LOVE

All my love I will give to you,
To your heart I will be true,
To no other my love receive,
To you alone I do believe.
You are always first on my mind,
No better love I could ever find,
My love for you grows stronger each day,
Together in life all the way.

If dreaming of you is what it takes,
To have you near me when I wake,
Cupid's arrow must have hit the spot,
For you are the one I love a lot.

Your warm embrace and loving touch,
Are all that I pray and love so much,
God is watching us from above,
'Cause here's to you with all my love.

Heidi Marie Fisher
IN ADMIRATION OF MY AUNT

She was never really here.
though she was quite sincere.
She will always be remembered,
in our thoughts that will never forget her.
She is one of our beloved,
who fought for her keepsake.
To her, her keepsake was life,
in which she fought for with many struggles and strifes.
She has been gone for quite some years,
And she will always be truly loved.

Pamela D Koop
SKIN OF PORCELAIN

This poem is dedicated to Aaron.

Skin of porcelain
With a hint of blush
Smooth as silk
Soft to the touch
Trustful eyes that sparkle with joy
Such a blessing
My beautiful baby boy
Angelic child
A heart so pure
Aura of innocence mild and demure
A genuine treasure
Bundled with love
The truest of gifts from God above
And of all the joys in the world
Could there be
Is the gift of this miracle
Given to me

Douglas W Gonyea

Douglas W Gonyea
FOR YOU

To all those I have ever loved

Rainpaths, moonbeams, and the forest floor,
Cool water in mountain streams.
These things make me think of you,
Or would have me knocking at your door.
Things of wonder,
Things I adore,
Things that make me feel;
I know you more,
I love you in my dreams.
These things from my spirit,
Give my love for you the power of thunder,
Ever more . . .

Ruth Elliott Pressler
ONE GOLDEN AFTERNOON

Dedicated to my dear son, Dr. John E. Pressler

We were together, then—
One golden afternoon in Autumn—
Together once again—
And spent the hours in happy Camaraderie—
Something I thought
Might never be again;
Just you, with me—
To talk, and laugh, and plan
As once we used to do.
And now I never can
Get used to losing you;
For I so loved the day
That brought this golden afternoon—
All I had hoped for,
And thought lost too soon,
Came back to me
In joyful hours with you—
One afternoon in Autumn—
One golden afternoon.

But will there ever be another—
Ever be again—
Another golden afternoon?

Jonathan R Stephenson
A MUSING

To Finian and Curran

Heartless mockery,
Sorrowful supplication,
Scornful morbidity,
Villainous oversimplification.

Hastened to a dark, forboding river,
Scoured empty of dregs.
Looking up from the muck
to see unrequited pretensions;
"LOVE"!
The Styx, perdition,
an empty soliloquy,
All evasive ramblings
of a madman from Bedlam's renders.

Shameless enticement,
overzealous lust,
perfunctory platitudes,
All, creative dust.

Kneejerk reactions,
D.H. Lawrence's tears
Lugubrious passions,
Palladial fears.

Rote reaction,
what have I said?
'Tis but excrement
delivered out of my head.

Michele Thayer
SILENT MISERY

To my Jake—who has helped me to abandon the darkness of silent misery, and who now fills my days with sunshine.

We wait—
And anticipate.
But broken dreams are hard to take.

They shatter—like glass.
Each shard
Piercing more vicious than the last.

Yet we keep hoping—
a tormented soul knows no peace.
And torture, relentless, has no mercy.

Always a thousand wishes
But far too few stars in which to wish upon.
And in silent misery—

We reach out
And try to communicate
Only to be left alone amidst the silence.

Chris Corbin
WATERLILIES

To my son and hero, Myles—the musician.

Claude,
where are you when I need you?
Help me cleanse the fuzziness
from my mind.

Through my haze,
I see them adrift in the pond.
I swim and swim, sometimes closer to,
sometimes farther from—
the waterlilies.

I can't
get to them
just yet.

Once I reach them
(and of course I will).
my fuzzy mind will clear.
I'll be free and whole at last.

Won't that make an Impression
on my world . . .

Rebecca L Puente
SO SAD
As The Winds Gently Sway
Thru The Night of Darkness,
I See the Outline
Of A Face So Sad.

What Are You Thinking?
Now That The Air is Still
Do You Remember Me?
As I Remember You.

The Times Gone By So Long Ago
Bring Them Back to Me
So I won't Forget
Just What the Magic Was.

Of Days Gone By
As Time Passes By.
What Will Become
Of A Face So Sad.

Susan S Carpenter
TO YOU
To You—whose eyes are filled with love; whose presence floods my soul
Whose kisses are so strong and sweet, whose heart is made of gold

To You—whom I have waited for through years of tears and pain
All hope of you alive no more, the vision empty, vain

To you—who came into my life unnoticed one fall day
Lost for so long amid the noise, and quietly remained

To You—who spent those months with me sometimes just to be there
Who told me in a thousand ways, no matter what, you care

To You—whose absence suddenly played light upon the truth
That somewhere deep inside my heart there'd grown a place for you

To You—whose friendship deepened then as I drew nearer still
Whose love somehow got through to me and slowly warmed the chill

To You—whose hand was gentle, yet, still hesitant with touch
You who loved me as a friend and I had grown to trust

To You—whose soul you shared with me and gently handled mine
Whose dreams and hopes did match my own and yet I stayed so blind

To You—who never made demands while carrying my load
With time I grew to understand our paths had made a road

To You—whose heart and mind and soul I cherish as my own
I know the truth; within your arms, I am at last at home

Veriand
OPIATE'S WEB
The world slowly turns, as the children try to play.
Mothers cry as the playgrounds lie barren.
Physical fulfillment has replaced the gospel.
Deep in thought.
The wise men ponder, realizing that fools have beaten them at their own game.
White abounds, as our youth lie dying in the city streets.
The river of education has become but a mere trickle that lies drying in dusk's fading light.
Excellence is measured by the car one drives.
Sorrow has replaced hope.
Stagnation is met at every corner.
Despair, brought home every night wanders through once proud halls
The nation is caught in a suffocating grip.
Whilst our leaders remain deep in thought.
Profit spawned from misery continues to turn the capitalistic wheel.
Burying the flower of future generations in its wake . . . .

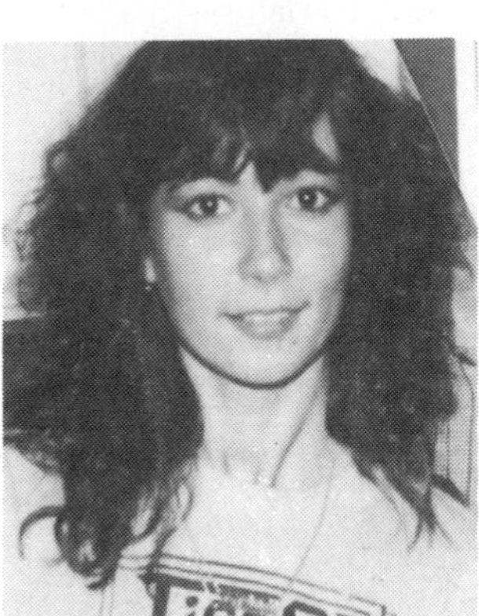

Dámaris A Pickin

Dámaris A Pickin
STRAWBERRY AND DANCING EYES

To Adele, I'll never be too old or too busy to remember. Love always, Dámaris.

Some gifts come wrapped in boxes and purple laces,
Some gifts come wrapped in paper with colored strings,
But you came on a dark and rainy morning,
When someone died and left me everything.
Funny how life turns out sometimes,
You get what you thought you'd never want,
And then you find that what you have is made of gold.
Yet I didn't think I needed the pain or to hear the story once again,
of how Strawberry lost her Dancing Eyes.

Time was so short when their flame was just beginning,
And in April Angels blew the candle out,
Just when she thought that things would last forever,
'Cause sacred are the promises we make.
The smile became a silent cry,
When someone whispered late that night,
"He loved you very much," he told me so.
No, I didn't want to see the tears come down or be the one who stuck around,
Now that she didn't have her Dancing Eyes.

Long walks at the park and prayers by the altar,
Flowers on a wreath in place of wedding bells,
We held on to each other, figured we had nothing,
I was different and you were something else.
Now I see the light back in your eyes,
I am glad I listened a thousand times,
Edged in my heart & mind are all your words.
I want to share it all and write it down, this is what my poem's about,
How Strawberry loved her Dancing Eyes.

Shirley Elliott
CHILD TO MOTHER
Oh mother dear, I love you so much.
Please take time to love me.
Give me a little of your busy time—to love me and help me with the little things.
Give me a drink, help me dress and do so many small tasks I ask you to do.
You know how you love to have my hear next to your cheek.
--I'm only small once, so , mother dear, now is the time to take time to love me.
God Bless You Mother Dear.

T H Mercer
SURVIVORS OF CHARLIE

Dedicated to the Vietnam Veterans . . . in remembrance of Harold Cumbie

The Vietnam War was senseless,
and many died for no cause.
I really don't understand it all,
and for them my heart will pause.
I did not fight in that war,
but I kept my dad from going.
I wrote this poem for those who went,
and it's love and kindness that I'm showing.

Many never came back at all,
and some only came back in parts.
And the way our country treated you afterwards,
you deserve more than the purple hearts.

They finally built you a wall,
and they act as if they care.
I dedicate this to the survivors of charlie,
and to my uncle that died over there.

April Virginia Look
TO ROBBYN
The old songs will never die.
I will play them in my heart forever.
Every time I do, I'll look at old notes and photographs.
The songs may leave the radio,
but I'll cherish them forever.
And when that certain song is heard,
I'll think of all we shared.
Through good and bad, you were there.
You'll never know how much I care.

You'll stay in my heart forever.
There is no better place to put a friend like you.
So, I hope, when you hear this,
You'll understand how special you are to me.
No one could replace your friendship to me.

Please always remember me,
even when we are apart.
If it's forever,
then listen and you'll hear those special words
of songs from yesterday.

Heather Hoffman
GONE
The white sky had no more blue
And the zest of the ocean did not feel new
The Red of my Rose turned to pale
The green of the grass no longer appealed
The sand of the beach met with the yellow that did not shine

The birds that no longer flew
The sounds we once knew

The puffy clouds
The drops of rain
The roar of the thunder
Met with the wind that never came

I felt no more pain
The world no longer sane
The gift was not alive
We have used all our pride
Our world now gone
We have done our time

Susan Briggs Wilkie
IT TAKES TIME TO RHYME
I'm always surrounded by people and things
and I don't have time to think,
Confronting issues is not my style
decisions must wait tho hearts may sink.

I'm forever projecting an unapproachable air
for it's the multitudes I hate,
And with all my thought provoking analyses
I'm not in control of my fate . . .

My glibness is astounding; I can talk

circles
yet hide behind my wall,
But ask irony—it tolls—to quell the fear
that someday I will fall . . .

I'm afraid to love and lose again
and commitment makes me frantic,
And yet the welcome of unconditional love
is compassionate and ideally romantic.

I don't wish for an island
but rejection is difficult to face,
Let me mask my feeling with caution and time
'til my emotions keep up with your pace . . .

I'm private, cautious, and just out of reach—and I don't make promises that might be breach.

Laury K Headley
WORDS OF A DANCER

I dedicate this poem to Kimberly Lynn Ramsey, the one person in my life, who has shown me, it doesn't always hurt to open your heart to others.

The life of a dancer
Is filled with glitter and fame
They will always make sure
That everybody knows their name

Everywhere they may go
They express their feelings
In the grace of each
Gliding step they take

A dancer's life is strong and full
The electricity of the music is their tool
They feel for life as they do
The music that they dance to

A dancer can fill up your life
With the power of their energy
They can bring a smile
On all faces, if even only for a while

If you should ever meet a dancer
Get to know them if you can
Because having someone who's full of energy for a friend
Is one of the best made plans.

Gloria M Heiser
COMFORT

To Dar and Michelle, my son and daughter-in-law.

When the hour is so dark
that clouds no longer drift,
be still your inner spark
will send a loving gift.

Sharon Scott
IMAGINATION
Glistening

Emeralds

a piercing glare
breaths of flame
gliding on wings of bats

Vaporized

an electric cloud
bolts
outstretched as deadly claws

the cracked earth heaves

Eruption

pushing upward
opening
petals reveal the fertile pistil

Rolling out

a serpent's tongue

Extending

across the green and blue earth
cars
bumper to bumper

Linked

a garland
around a fair neck

Glistening

Emeralds

Wendy Robertson

Wendy Robertson
UNDERSTANDING LIFE
Life's three main factors
Have unexplainable parts.
Pieces either make us smile
Or tear us apart.
Love is a factor
That's common among our peers;
It seems to make most cry
Or shed so many tears.
Friendship, another factor,
Needed in life today,
Helps most of us out
So we can all have a say.
Last, we think of death,
That dark scary feeling,
Which, among us, makes us weak
To the rest of our dealings.

Patrick Glass
NATURE
Nature is the most elegant thing,
The windy breeze, the leaves on the ground,
In the seasons we see these sights,
In winter, the snow makes a small mound.

The mountains and the rivers,
The animals and the flowers,
Nature's being destroyed,
By those with power.

The frosty winter mornings,
The moon and the sun,
It's beautiful what we see,
But most people are on the run.

We need these things to live,
And that is a fact,
If nature is abused,
We'd better react!

Lester B Yauger Jr
A LOVER'S PRAYER

To my love, Kimberly

As I kneel beside my bed each night at the close of day,
I bury my face in my trembling hands and the stars fall as I pray.
Dear Lord unworthy though I am, I ask one thing of thee,
Don't let the one I love forget, please help her to remember me.
Dear God she's only human you know, so when the long day is done.
She may be alone as I am now and turn to another one.
I can no longer get to her and take her by the hand.
But you Dear God go to her and make her understand.
Just keep me in her heart, till the day we meet again.
Though we are apart tonight, I love her Dear God, Amen.

Michael Earlywine
JUST AN INNOCENT LIL'BOY

To T. J., My Nephew

Just an innocent little boy,
caught in the middle of something awful.
Mommy and Daddy had a fight.
They both went their own ways.
And here sat an innocent little boy.
in the middle.
He didn't know what to think,
or do.
He knows he won't see one of them for a long time.
But, he knows daddy's gonna try his damndest to keep him.
Because, it is his daddy's name
he wears with pride,
and honor.
Mommy is sitting in the back,
wondering what to do.
As for Grandma and Grandpa,
they're already making plans,
Yes, for this innocent little boy is,
you, T.J.
But, don't worry lil' guy,
as long as I'm around,
nobody will ever hurt you.
So may your life be colorful,
and full of success,
and all your dreams come true,
Hang in there lil' guy,
you'll make it.
I love you, T.J.

Gina Monica Lozano
DID YOU EVER LOVE SOMEONE?

To my darling Jesse "Robby" Lozano, my one and only Robert Smith (cure) and Morrissey.

Did you ever love someone
and know they didn't care?
Did you ever feel like crying
but knew it wouldn't get you anywhere.
Did you ever look in their eyes
and say a little prayer?
Did you ever look into their heart
and wish you were there?
Did you ever watch them dancing
When the lights were way down low?
Did you ever whisper, "I love you,"
and didn't let them know?
If you ever fall in love my friend
the price you pay is "High"!
If I were to choose between life & death
I think I'd rather die!
So don't fall in love my friend
you will hurt before it's through
You see my friend, I ought to know
I fell in love with you.

Elaine Rosario
SUNSET

To Marlon, For the insight and courage. Be a good dad.

If you could be what I want you to be,
I'd say you are the sunset,
The beauty that I've never seen, until the day we met.
You flow into me like the ease of its winds.
caressing everything in sight,
as the layered colors softly meld, and disappear into the night.
The creamy smoothness of the setting sun,
blazing crimson and bright,
reminds me of your sensual twinkling eyes.
And like the sunset that fades away,
to let the night descend,
I know your beauty just like the sunset, will continue to come again.

Todd Timothy Garverick
THE NEXT BREATH
Murky filth clouds this air
and forms a sullen, heavy atmosphere.
I draw from its sheath a breathing sword
with which I slice through this man-made wall.
Will I find yet a clean day through,
so these swords may remain in their sheath?
Then I shall exist in my purist form.

Lucy Gibbs
THE OCEAN IN ME
The mist rolled from the heavens,
From the darkness came a light,
The world was in its dawning,
There came the day and then the night.
Soon it would be my turn,
As they gave birth to the sea
And so pleased with his creation,
He cast the ocean into me.
The chains that once had tied me,
Now released me, free to roam,
So I rolled across God's country
Calling every shore my home.
I filled my deep blue waters
With the life God gave to me,
And in return I asked for only,
That man respect the sea.

Marianna Jo Arolin
BEAUTY AT MY WINDOW
I've spread the banquet table,
gracious invitation, not to be declined.
Oh, Cardinal, scarlet beauty,
I'm honored that you've come to dine.
Bring along your feathered friends.
Please extend my hospitality.
I'm humbled at the wondrous sight.
You fill a window beautifully.

The long monotonous winter days
are lessened in severity,
each day you come to call.
Oh, Cardinal, scarlet beauty.

Kerri Lynne Drydak
IT MAY BE COLD . . .

It May Be Cold . . . Is dedicated to my Mother, who has shown me that there's a brighter side to life, and to Lila, for her friendship and encouragement.

It May Be Cold . . .
The snow melts beneath my feet,
And the flakes melt at my mouth.
But yet, I do not feel the warmth,
And the sun beats down, but I cannot

feel it.
The cold has taken control once more,
Blocking all warmth for only, past or future.
And the children are wearing mounds of clothes',
To shelter themselves from the bite of winter.

The animals, have hidden or gone,
To take cover from the long winter nights.
And the trees are barren, and the wind is cold.
And the moon . . . resembles a ring of ice.
A crispness in the air which nips at your skin,
Until it hurts . . .

The ground is hard and slippery,
And the only rain is heavy like a stone.
But the days are still rainbows of beauty,
And there will always be a horizon,
And forever a star to wish upon.

Elizabeth E Hudson

Elizabeth E Hudson
THE APRIL SNOW
Today, I saw a robin—
hopping in the snow,
Poor little fellow,
wondering "where" to go.
Just yesterday, his world
was bright and gay—
And, he was quite sure
Spring was here to stay.

But, now, 'tis such a
sorry place to be . . .
No wonder that his wee chirp
sounds off key.
OH! Robin Redbreast,
please don't be so sad;
The sun will surely shine again—
And, make you glad!

Margaret W Welker
I WILL STILL BE YOUR FRIEND
When the wind drifts the snow,
And the hot embers glow,
In my thoughts you will stay,
'Though you're far far away—
I will still be your friend.

If you're down on your luck,
And you've spent your last "buck,"
And the chill in the air
Seems to add to despair—
I will still be your friend.

While the gray shadows fall,
I'll help you stand up tall;
Through your sorrow and pain,
'Til your strength you regain—
I will still be your friend.

When the last bell has rung,
The last song has been sung,
And the sun goes away,
At the end of the day—
I will still be your friend.

Mary Ann Varsolona
PAPA TEACH ME
Papa, teach me to smile again,
I've forgotten how
The love you taught me how to give
is just a mem'ry now.
Teach me of the shining stars,
I've forgotten why
The things you showed me as a child
just fade as time goes by.
The time you said how life would be,
I've forgotten when
So teach me papa, please teach me now,
All these things again.

Elaine Sheffler
SO I WRITE
This is the way
I
Assure
People showing up at my funeral.

I would like to be remembered.

So I write.

When all the souls
Check out,

An appreciative nod would be
Nice.

It's selfish.
I know.

But, honesty
Feels so good

I can barely
Keep my feet
On the ground.

Jayne Lind
CATHEDRAL OF THE MORNING
I worship at your altar
Not bound by cement walls
Rather, green velvet canyons rising
Steeply from still water.

A narrow vault, yet wide
Colors not proscribed nor
Ever insensitive to needs of change.

The water is not yet awake
But lies smooth and quiet
While a finely robed choir of birds
Sings anthems of praise.

I worship here
In this cathedral of the morning
With new awareness of source

As the sun frees itself
From bondage of high peaks
Dispelling the mist, making everything
All at once

Clear

Erica Goodstone PH D
I WANDERED THROUGH THE FOREST STREAM
I wandered through the forest stream
Upon the hillside
In a dream.
The outline of your chest appeared
To me
It was geography.
Your face somewhere behind a cloud
Your body pulsing
Out loud.
My fingers felt fantastic pull
Magnetic field
They had to yield
Hypnotic thoughts controlled my brain
To touch your soul
Could not refrain.
Every inch brought new delight
Looking soft
But feeling tight.
I wanted to go on and on and on

Leigh Anne Johnson
MY TEDDY BEAR
Over there in the corner lies my
teddy bear,
For as long as I can remember,
he has been there.

His eyes aren't exactly in the right
place anymore,

But they still have the sparkle
as they did before.

I overlook the clothes that are
tattered and torn,
Cause I know it's because of me
they are so worn.

I know if I need him, he will
always be there,
My greatest friend, my teddy bear.

Kathleen Byrne
SOFT HEART
My heart is so soft
and loving you is so easy.
All I can do
is think of you.
Cherished memories of days
spent in love;
travel through my mind.
Our walk in the park
on a still wintry day.
The snow glistened from the sun,
beside our pathway.
Then you touched my face
and we kissed.
My dreams have come true
by knowing you.
Love is so grand
when I stand
next to you.
My soul is aglow
with our warmth,
for we are one.

R Langford
RANSOM
Our noses are glued to the television tube.
Iran-Contra 3 channels all day.
Fingers are pointed shame shunned.
Elephant's faces covered with mud.
Whose hand is in the cookie jar?

Who will pay the ransom and set me free?
I am held with agony.
Forced rage kidnapped, by a band of senile infested rats.
Terrorists rip my flesh, battered for confession.
America will pay the price if I sacrifice.
I hold forbidden knowledge, if fallen by my tongue
disaster.
Traitor will be my tag.
How imminent and heavy laden, my Superior's dread.
If this message seeps undulating repercussions.
Who will pay my ransom?
Sweep me from this horrid nation.
Held against my will.

Whose hand will be caught in the cookie jar?
The price for liberty.
The tag of traitor balances on whose side, whose favor.
To some traitor others hero.

Rick French
GRAVEYARD

This poem is dedicated to all of my family and friends—Past, Present, and Future.

In this graveyard, where I lay,
The trees grow stronger, day by day.
It sure seems strange, where death may be,
Life is found, within a tree.

Paul Michael Beston
THEM
Have you ever seen the seven year locusts
attached to your trees like thumbtacks
sucking and chewing and biting and eating
its life away as you watch?

Have you ever seen the perennial locusts
in every town; attached to your child like chickenpox
stabbing and staring and laughing and taking
his life away as you plead?

Minnie Tosh
MEMORIES

Dedicated to "Al" whose heart ache knows no bounds.

Beside the still, still waters the little boy did play
Making paper boats to sail and castles made of clay.
The sun so warm, the sky so clear;
So many years: now fewer tears . . .

As I pondered what had been and could not be again,
I heard the voice of one so near say,
"Go my friend, and let it be!
He will be there to welcome thee."

It must have been the Lord, you see
For who else could have spoken to me?
With someone there to guide my way,
I took a moment to stop and Pray.

Judith Lavicka
SUNFLOWER RAIN
Sunflower rain
Burned through the opaque of old heartache.
Self's frail concoction
Swept into a different Space,

a better fantasy.
It flew the gentle bird away
to flowers, pines and light.
Thank you, sunflower rain.

Noemi C Mendez
DARKENED SKIES

I Dedicate This Poem To: DUSTONIAN

Sitting outside in quiet tears . . .
The sky is suddenly turning into darkened skies.
Broken pieces of shattered hope,
Leading to a darkened tunnel of lonely cries.

I feel so tempted to chain my heart,
To yours once more and never let go.
For your memory in me, makes you come alive,
As though you never left me . . .

Awakened by a shove from reality,
The sun shines on my crying eyes.
I get up and walk inside to realize . . .
There's still darkened skies.

Mrs Betty Causey

Mrs Betty Causey
GOD'S GIFTS OF BEAUTY
I wonder if I ever will see
Anything more lovely than an Autumn tree
The colors so bright, so vivid and bold
Make a picture so glorious to behold.

It is amazing what God can do
Giving extra blessings to me and you
For in a time of troubles on every hand
He spreads His beauty over all the land.

Look at the trees with leaves of gold
Yellow and red with green unfold
Such a gift of beauty for us to see
How very grateful we should be.

Blessings are many and thanks are few
For what God has entrusted to me and you
One special blessing we are told
When God in mercy saves our soul.

Among the magnificent gifts of love
The mountains which tower toward above
The gentle slopes and valleys below
Show us God's handiwork wherever we go.

Marie Sollars
GOING BACK TO CALIFORNIA
Going back to California,
going back to my old home.
Going back to California
going back where I was born.
Going to plant my own fruit trees
eat all the fresh fruit I want.
Going to plant my own vegetables,
plant me some peas and corn.

Heaven is there waiting,
strolling in the early morn.
Catch fish I'll be eating,
back there where I was born.

Going back to California,
going back to my old home.
Going back to California,
going back where I was born.

Jayne Whitlow Berman
MY MOTHER'S HANDS WERE BEAUTIFUL

Dedicated to my mother, Louise Arnett Whitlow, posthumously

My mother's hands were beautiful,
Imbued with faith and grace,
And all the love that they performed
Reflected in her face.

My mother's hands were so thoughtful
In all the things she did,
Preparing the way for others,
Though to the world were hid.

My mother's hands were priceless
When occupied in prayer,
And when I looked into her eyes,
My heav'n was found right there.

Mair Tini
THIS YARD IS GROWING OLD
This yard is growing old
and the neighbors who sit on
their porches all day
are dying

The little ones are growing fast
the world will soon be theirs
they'll have their moments of pleasure and pain
before the wrinkles of time
begin to show
and that's when they'll know
these porches are also for them

And while they await
the voices of death's call
they'll reflect on the days
when they were once small
and the world was so tall
and the old people then
did not matter

James E Miller Jr
MY FRIENDLY WORDS OF LOVE
The dream for all mankind to unite as one is far from over.

Each chip at the mountain of prejudice moves us just a little closer to achieving the goal of a wonderful dream.

If every man and woman filled their hearts with a little dedication to Dr. Martin Luther King Jr.'s dream, this world wouldn't have to negotiate for peace.

peace is for all mankind to stand, evil is for all divided to fall.

A personal comment or maybe an idea of blindness for all men and women of every color to consider:

I am not a black man nor am I a white man,
I am a man with no color, but ambitious
to strive for success to be Somebody.
I share your dream, Dr. Martin Luther King,
I share your dream.

Freedom is the key to life. Think not what people can do for you, but what fruitful joy the LORD gives to each and everyone who is willing to accept his gift of life. Do not be afraid to call on him in times of need. Let faith, courage and trust in GOD be your guide to future happiness and Eternal life.

LeAnn K White
SOMETIMES
Sometimes I wish my life was like a pencil—
getting the lead out and accomplishing more,
And when I push too hard, I'd break off,
but I'd immediately be sharpened,
and I could be sharpened to the degree of pointedness I wanted.
And I would try to never let it get too dull.
And when I make mistakes,
they could be erased away.
A pencil's life span is usually long,
but that depends on how much
use you get out of it.
The shorter the length gets, the more enriched and fulfilled its life is—
just as the older people get, the more they learn from life's experiences.
And when the pencil reaches the point
where you can't hold onto it any longer,
you know it's time for a new one—
and it was able to leave a trace of itself behind.

Judith Lobianco
BEING
How do you tell a flower from a bird?
For they are just a word, and the meaning
They imply would be the difference of earth to sky; not seen the same by the other, but being it's content its own environment.

To be a flower or a fly with freedom of the butterfly, a caterpillar, or a weeping willow.
Each its contemplation being its creation.

Anna Rose Maertzig
THE PRICELESS HOUSEWIFE
She's only a housewife . . .
But far more than that . . .
She's a wife . . . in a house full of Love.

She's a chef, she's a baker . . .
A dishwasher, dressmaker . . .
She's the spark that sets our hearts aglow.

She has soft shoulders to lean on . . .
And also to cry on . . .
Whenever we're feeling low.

With understanding and wisdom . . .
So tenderly shown . . .
She makes our confidence grow.

She listens, and, slowly . . .
Her magical touch . . .
Brings us tranquil assurance . . .
That means so much.

And when she's not there . . .
It seems empty and bare . . .
But the sun shines again . . .
When she's home!

Michael J Seabrook
CONTEMPLATION OF ONE'S REMEMBRANCE
As I walk from this beach my pockets are full,
Of the memories I've picked up along the way.
I have taken a lot, but I've left them much more.
Tiny fragmented pieces of my mind and heart
Are strewn about this sandy shore.
For some to choose, and then decide.
What will they think after I have left,
And littered their beach with my insides?

Carol L Valero
IT'S TIME
Can one a-tone for past mistakes?
When all alone their children they raised.

As life held mostly despair,
from lack of time and care.

By hard work they struggled and got ahead,
and the children are all grown and on their own.

More time is now here,
and the years bring knowledge of what they fear.

But see the children of their own,
who need some time for them alone.

So give some time to those who need it now,
and make amends for those mistakes somehow.

Cecelia D Johnson
SOMETIMES
Sometimes plans are blown away by the wind,
And hearts are taken with them.

Sometimes friendships are too far away.
And hearts ache, but dare not to change them.

Sometimes love is too hard to bare,
And hearts will cry forever.

Alvin P Kus

Alvin P Kus
SANTA CLAUS IS COMING
Santa and his reindeer had a good rest,
and again this year they will do their best
to bring to every good little girl and boy
the Christmas toys they like and will enjoy.

Mr. and Mrs. Santa Claus are very,

very busy
preparing for the sleigh ride to the city.—
Santa's reindeer are ready to pull the sleigh,
and the red-nosed one will lead the way.

Finally, after all the packing is done,
they are ready, and the long ride has begun—
It is a very long and very cold trip,
but Santa and his wife are used to it.

One thing Santa Claus does remember,
he has to get here before the 25th of Dec.
So Rudolph, the reindeer, has taken the lead,
and the all-important thing is speed.

Santa Claus always arrives here on time.
Santa is very good at that, he is fine.—
And the news quickly spreads all-around:
"Santa Clause is coming to town."

Mrs. Santa Claus has no trouble talking,
but she has a bit of trouble walking.—
This is because of a touch of rheumatis
that she has become the way she is.

In the very presence of the parents
she helps handing out the presents
only to the good little girls and boys
so that they may enjoy playing with the toys.

The very bad ones don't get "anything."
Santa Claus knows all about them.—
So for goodness sake be the one to
get some toys and have some fun.

Phil Che

CHEERING YOU

Cheering you,
I am cheering myself.
When you're cheerful,
The whole world cheers with you.

So, be cheerful:
Think cheerfully; act cheerfully;
Learn cheerfully; dream cheerfully;
And you'll be cheerful.

To cheer you, I've to be cheerful myself.
When you're happy, I cheer you with my smile.
When you're sad, I cheer you with my sorrow.
When you're lonely, I cheer you with my company.

Say, you're cheerful,
And I am cheerful too.
When you're cheerful,
The whole world cheers with you.

Charles Alamah

SERENE SOLITUDE

Dedicated to Alecia, a Serene Velvet, a Lily so lovely and special.

The night in its loneliness is calm, desolate, silence spreads into the night like a dry barren land laying waste, uncourted and uncultivated like an ugly damsel undesired and unwooed by both suitable and unsuitable suitors.

The solitary mind is unfavored and unminded, it has no friends and foes for friends and foes alike are far from fun, flattering and flirtation due to its lack of farthing.

In its silent lamentation, the solitary mind's eyes are wet from cry, like the face of the night in its drizzles, night at this time is abandoned and rejected so is the solitary mind, no comforter to give or tuck just a pat on the back. Oh! gracious providence, no support, hearts are dejected, for why hearts can be mean, heart don't know.

Suddenly a sound, the chirping of a cricket or other tiny legged creatures of the night, alas solitary mind has got company, Oh! behold the cloud is pathing the face of the sky, a gleam, a star, Uh! a moon.

Solitary mind wishes for a twilight cruise on passage from dusk to dawn and when it is day time he would sit on river bank the bird would sing and the sun will shine and nature will find its rapport.

M Elaine Arnold

REFLECTIONS OF FLIGHT

We shall not always climb together.
Sometimes it is right for you to soar,
While I on earth remain. I feel no pain.
It's then I take my pleasure
In your flight.
The reflection of your ecstasy
Is seen in me and I am fulfilled.
Though one in love,
Our footprints take a different path;
It must be so, the way it's always been.
For no two souls are joined
Where no line can be seen.

Lowell "Ted" Davee

JUST GO ON

When life seems to be getting you down,
And you can't keep from wearing a frown,
Just go on.

After some bad news has came your way,
To make sure that you have a sour day,
Just go on.

If a new disease attacks your health,
Which threatens to wipe out all your wealth,
Just go on.

So you can't concentrate on your work,
Be you a doctor, farmer, or clerk,
Just go on.

Baby cries! all kids out of control,
Making you willing to sell your soul,
Just go on.

It's dark, yet half the chores are not done,
Tonight you are too tired to have fun,
Just go on.

What three words of advice can one say,
When facing life's challenges each day?
JUST GO ON!

Charlotte Daniels

TAKE THAT DARE

To my mom, and all battered women

For all those women that have been battered out there,
There's something I want to share!
Don't be afraid to take that dare,
Because there's people that really care.

I know, because I was there once before.
I was scared, but I opened up a brand new door.
They beat you until you're down on the ground
And then one day you look around,
Does he really have me bound!

You may not think you can live another day,
"You can! If you may."
It was hard for me to say.

I stayed up night and day
Being afraid, that's all it was.
I prayed up above to make me strong
And then one day I said, "So Long."

Daryel Groom

ON THE OUTSKIRTS OF LOVE

To Anne and Fred these are the years of endurance . . .

You and me we drift together away from the crowd, we dress in leather. Our common goals are to find a place, where we don't feel different from the rest of the race. Together we make adolescence so easy. By loving you the trip has been breezy. Clicks and clubs they don't attract us. We need not know what the others do, just the common love we share that shall pull us through. So take my arm just me and you we'll share a place, a fear, a thought. We'll summon the night that love has brought, with you it's OK you're the angel I've sought. Although life's been a little hard we'll soften those stones, it may be rough we might even be a little tough: Yet our wrinkles are fading, we've made it a bluff. In your arms, I'm soft as a baby blue, it's another land when I'm with you. Yes we stand on the outskirts, but at least we know where we are and where we've been. This world unknown has trapped us within. We've diffused from silently waiting to begin. Our hearts beat the rhythm up this rugged river bed. So life isn't easy we've still learned to win. In the end our love burns further than any river beds . . .

Teresa E Hayte

THE LIFE STREAM OF MOTHERHOOD—THE CORD

To my children; Mary-Margaret, Todd.

This soft and twisting rope
Through whose strands flow
many thoughts
To find its home in the base of which
A new life grows—
To be born into this land.

The love, the fears,
The wealth of joy and dreams,
Are blended with the tears of sadness
As the life stream flows.

A wealth of riches
In dreams to share with all . . .
And forgetting none,
Prayers to by-pass . . .
Channels of greed and hate
Shall become found
In a continuous flow of love.

These strands when severed and tied—
So close to death—
God breathes His love
Into a life to be born again
Unto this earth.

Melony Drury

A WARMING HEART

to my loving mother, Sherry.

I am of vacancy
I can be filled with
memories
I can fill your dreams and
hopes
And let you feel them in happy ways

I can be broken in half
and be destroyed
When something hurts
or I'm annoyed

I bring a smile to your face
When in fear or sorrow
And give you hopes
of a new tomorrow

You see,
I'll always be there for you everyday
Just keep a smile
and lead the way!

Thelma D Schreck

Thelma D Schreck

AMERICA, THE LAND I LOVE

To my husband, Mike.

I love this land, America, there's honor in its name
Though now and then someone will say, "Our country's not the same."
And I'll admit there are some things with which I can't agree
For the scars that crime and greed have left, we all can clearly see.
But, I'd still rather live in the U.S.A. and for "Old Glory" stand
For there's no other place so blessed by God, as we are in this land.
We've freedom here to do as we please: to work or shop or play
We don't have to live by a dictator's rule or be censored for each word we say.
We can go to the store and buy all that we want, each day there's plenty of bread
While in other lands there's never enough, and many from hunger are dead.
We have beautiful homes and plenty of clothes, all that we need and to spare
While others who live in a land torn by war, live their lifetime in want and despair.
So in spite of all that people may say about the mistakes we have made
I'm glad I'm here in the "land of the free" and safe in the "home of the brave."
I pledge my allegiance with pride to our flag, as it waves in beauty above
And I'm thankful to say this is where I was born, "America, The Land I Love."

Tammy S Walker

HAPPINESS IS . . .

Happiness is you,
When you're with me.
The love that we'll share

Through eternity.
A smile on your face,
A kiss or a hug.
My happiness is you,
No matter what.
If you were gone
From my life,
A part of myself
Would die inside.
You bring light
And smiles to me.
My happiness is you,
And always will be.

Karri J Manitsas
HOPE
My mind, like distant thunder
rolls across the barren land of me.
My heart is empty.
Like the sea without a sunrise.
Memories draw me away
To solitary places where loneliness lurks.
Arms reach out for my soul mate,
Finding nothing . . . only emptiness.
My old Friend trust eluded me,
It's the first . . . and last time.
What's left but dreams,
and love never to be shared.
Not much to say about the pain.
It's there . . . always.
My final crutch is hope.
I'll keep it with me.

Robert J Cierlitsky
LAMENTING A YOUNG GIRL'S UNTIMELY DEATH

To my sister Bert who had the confidence to forward my poem to the publisher.

A fresh new seed, the joy of today
All hope for tomorrow, what can I say?
The young and the beautiful, for whom we pray
Denied of their lifetimes, they're taken away
I've said it before, I'll say it today
I would go in their place to allow them to stay
There must be a reason—I need to believe
A cause for the season in which we must grieve
Can I do more than they? In my own backward way?
Can I stand in the night and relieve them of fright?
Or is it their goodness that makes them so dear
To the power beyond us?
They're not allowed here.

Bro C G Andro
I FIRST KNEW IT AS INNOCENT GRACE
I first knew it as innocent grace—
Being admired for the charms of my face.
When I was just a new member of the human race;
Then it became lost in time and space.

I've searched high and low for this lost treasure,
That in my youth, held so much pleasure,
My journey took me North and South, East and West,
But nowhere could I find, this valued crest,
Guided by a fool called Ego—
Forgetting that we reap what we sow.
En route I have traveled through the streets of time,
Searching for this lost friend of mind—
I traveled through the Wilderness of pride—
Often overlooking the ones that stood by my side.
Pausing now and then for the pleasure of some forgotten whore.
Never would I admit that I too will reap what I sow.
The pleasure of the moment ended—
I moved on, leaving some bridges unmended.
My trip has been a lesson to be told,
Why some of my efforts almost cost me my soul
We need no one to help us do bad,
To live for gold or fame, is an expensive fad.
For the answer was within me all along,
Hidden by doubt and fear of the unknown.
But at last I've found the place, as one would expect,
And no longer will I be-without my: "self-respect."

Teresa Freesemann
TIMES OF OUR LIVES
There are times when we need to be strong.
And sometimes we know that we'll be wrong.
A time for us to laugh and cry.
A time for us to say goodbye.
Sometimes we lose, sometimes we win.
Other times it's best to give in.
Sometimes we wonder, sometimes we worry
Make time to think it through, there's no hurry.
We wonder where we're going, we know where we've been.
Take time to regain your direction now and then.
There is time for joy and time for sorrow.
Spend some time to plan for tomorrow.
There are times when we need just to be,
But the best times are those shared between you and me.

Omer Beals Jr
LONGING
I awake in the night—
Longing to hear your voice;
Though I may have seen you yesterday,
Today, seems so far away.

I long for your tender touch—
That I miss so very much,
The little quirk when you smile,
So much your wile.

The touch of your lips in kiss,
Just another thing I miss,
So, it's for all of you I long—
And, miss you, be my song.

Phebe Alden Tisdale
AN ANSWER

To E.D.'s Question.

I hear that piercing cry of Amherst's leader
explaining tersely— "I AM NOBODY!"

When "WHO ARE YOU?" is fired at the reader,
those six imperial words of agony demand I give an answer:

I am string, tying a package up.

I am the tape that seals a box for mailing.

I? The Ring SYMBOL OF LOVE (which marriage vows re-shape).

And I am Gravity binding together
Planets & Satellites around our Sun.

I am a vacuum-tube
that lets a feather
drop like a stone
when free-fall
is re-run.

I am the cord whereon fine beads are strung,
the hidden cord which somehow goes unsung . . .

I AM THE WORD, formed by an unseen Tongue!

Randal Savacool Jr
MEANING OF CHRISTMAS
What does Christmas mean to you?
Perhaps a tree, mistletoe and holly too.
It seems we have too soon forgot
the baby in the manger, Mary begot.
It's nice for tiny tots, in their world to make believe.
to look forward to a visit from Santa on Christmas eve.
They are too young to understand
the true meaning of Christmas throughout the land.

But for us old enough to know and adore Him,
let it ever be engraved on our hearts and in our minds, Jesus was born this day in Bethlehem.
Christmas is not a day of ribbons, tinsel and bows,
Nor Rudolf with his nose that glows.
But it's a day to remember,
the one born that night in the manger.

Laura Herlihy
WATCHING THE CHILDREN GROW
In the park there is a place where
alone time can stand still,
It's just beyond the merry-go-round
right behind the hill.

Special is that place where laughter
fills your ears,
Where happy faces run about without
holding any fears.

Children fill the meadow green and
what a joy to see,
And walking among the children a
child you will be.

And then you go behind the hill to
jump rope with the girls,
Watch them blush when boys walk to
see their gorgeous curls.

The boys are running playing games
all along the side,
Shooting each other with make-believe guns and acting as if they died.

Whispering among the bushes and
giggling in the trees,
Try to find them if you can, they'll
slip between your knees.

In the distance is a young boy and
girl holding hands,
Love they think they've found, not
knowing the demands.

The foolishness that fills their heads
will carry them for years,
Not knowing all the heartache and all
the sensitive tears.

This park is like a storybook, you
watch the children grow,
It's part of our movie film, another
picture show.

For the laughter and the whispers will
always be right there,
It's really up to all of us, how much
we want to care.

For each of us are children growing
older every day,
And in our heart we'll always want to
run through the park and play.

Danielle (Doni) Wyatt
HELP ME
Help me
There is no extra fee.
Please don't flee,
I need your help
Beside me you knelt.
Gave me a hug
Pulled me up with a tug,
you gave me a kiss
And with this
you helped me
And the cost was no extra fee
Just to free me from awful pains
And the chains
That used to bind me to the wall
And all it cost was
to, on your knees fall,
Just for me.

Kay Lilly Cottrill
SNICKEY-POOH
He was just a cat, a neighbor's cat
As white as a flake of snow.
We'd borrow him for a visit some nights
And laugh as he raced to go—
Upstairs to see the cat in the mirror—
A snow white one just like him,
Or play "You touch me and I'll catch you"
Through the posts of the stairway trim.
Then downstairs to roll a pencil or ball,
Bat a string of rubber bands,
And all the divan pillows stacked just so
Made a cat's special fairy land.
He seldom slept, as far as we know,
Being always ready to "attack,"
He watched the birds as they flew above
And dreamed sky dreams as he lay on his back.
Maybe too soon those dreams have come true
And he is up there, too,
For Heaven has called that snow white one—
That dear little Snickey-Pooh.

Lora W Asdorian
PASSION'S PAIN
The rain still slithered through the leaves
And fell upon her breast;
And he lay near her breathing low
In passion's languid rest.

He turned and pressed his lips to hers,
Once more their passions soared.
Her will was gone, her body his—
Her lusty, lustful lord.

Her heart beat fast, her body writhed,
She soared up to the skies;
And suddenly the ascent stopped,
So too her throaty cries.

And down she floated feather-like
And nestled by his side.
She turned to him but there she saw
That which he could not hide.

Their gazes met, but in his eyes
There was no trace of love.
"Oh no," thought she, and cursed the rain
That spattered from above.

She cursed the leaves, she damned the trees,
And all that brought this pain—
Yet in her heart, she knew too well,
They'd go there soon again.

Bernice A Fox
I AND THE FIREFLY
When I was a kid thin and ganky
With legs and arms so long and lanky,
In the quiet evening with a bottle or jug
I'd ever pursue the lightning bug.
It's funny how I can recall
The nights and times when I was small.
All the kids in the early night
Playing "Kick the Can" or just "Red Light."
I remember the bats how they used to fly
And we'd hold our hair till they went by.
Carving initials on telephone poles,
Chasing speckled hop toads and trapping moles.
All was fun but I recall
Capturing fireflies the most of all.
Now I'm grown with children to hug
But at times I still yearn to catch the Lightning Bug!

Ms Gloria Petelo Otilano
LOLITA

In loving memory of my sister, Lolita who gave so much from so little, in love and service.

LOLITA, a name to her was given;
sweet, gentle and ever fragile.
Her face always with a merry warm smile,
a welcome to friends and
strangers alike,
who came to tread her humble
path.

An ailing heart she'd borne through life;
beat of a pure and tenderest
love.
Graced with heaven's bliss to give,
toiled and lived for those she
cared,
grateful she served in ways
great and small.

LOLITA, when laid to her eternal rest;
left behind a treasure so dearly
rare.
Neither 'twas earthly wealth nor its power,
'tis virtue chiseled on rock in
her,
an undaunted devotion that
Faith had firmed.

Kelly Oliver Kalkhoff
VIOLENT THUNDERSTORM
Sitting,
waiting for the angry rain
to stop beating down
upon the cold house.

White streaks shooting
through the jet black sky,
while loud bangs shake the
earth below.

The wind wild with madness
enters the trees of green
angrily shaking the life
from them.

When will it stop?
you hear a voice cry
in the darkness of a
child's room.

Robert Kane
BIRTH
All nestled in fog as it rolled near the gate
I dreamed of a life as I lay in wait;
When out of the mist like an angel's wand
Came a whispering voice and the fog was gone.
I lay in the darkness with my eyes rolling 'bout,
Trying to scream, wondering how to get out.
My hands were all sweaty my face a red beet,
I couldn't imagine who I was going to meet.
When through that damp-darkness I heard such a shout,
That I wanted to know what it was all about.
I started to move to slither and slide
And I knew this was it no more time inside.
I shivered and shook as I came to be
That little tiny baby for she and he.

Jean Brunie

Jean Brunie
FOR MALCOLM
When I was four-and-twenty and life was smiling down,
I went to seek my fortune in
San Francisco Town.

I met a lot of floozies, I panned a lot of gold.
I lived on gin and sourdough
and cheese with blue-green
mold.

I played the villain on the stage, I drove the trolley cars.
I swam across the Golden Gate
and met some girls from Mars.

Said they, "We've been all over, but there ain't no place like this."
When it was time to say
goodbye they each gave me a
kiss.
Their lips were green, their eyes were red, their voices like a hiss!

They started up that awful thing and took off upside down.
Above the roar and flames they
yelled just as they left the
ground,
"There ain't no place in all this world like San Francisco Town!"

W P Jaspert
THE HOUNDS OF HELL
The hounds of hell were set on thee
by Ayatollah Komeini
Oh wicked Salman Rush-die.
Much earlier yet the Divine Comedy
had cast offense and Dante Alligheri
told of the Prophet Muhammed
languishing in a pit reserved
for traitors there to be split
from forehead until the place
where one is pleased to fart.

Sheila Hawkins
CHRISTINA: 1989—1989

To Winfried and Leslie Platschka: Out of all suffering, a little sweetness remains.

I made my life touch everyone,
I felt love from all around;
I brought joy to my Dad and Mom,
I loved them with no bounds.
I know they will never forget me,
And when they pray to God above;
I hope with all sincerity
They will remember me with love.
If I'd grown in life, I know I'd say
To my parents, in no such haste:
"Always include my name when you pray,
For my life was not a waste."

Mimi Buttenheim
MYSTIC WINTER
A mild December day
suddenly turns;
An Arctic cold wind
Surrounds me
Filling my every breath with ice;
Lifting me up into a world
of frozen doom

Randy Freret
THERE IS NO EDEN
There is no Eden
the roses have died
no wreath to be made for the winners anymore
The state of happiness has been overthrown
The dark globe lingers
and sheds little light into the
mysteries of why
unlucky days cast apprehension
Do not look into the shadows
they no longer imitate
royal waters have been poured on all of your treasures
there is no wealth left to display
hope springs eternal in those with strong conviction
but they shall stumble like us
and be bastardized by the weak
we shall become one in ignorance
no truth to illuminate our hearts
visionaries shall harbor paradise
but in time who shall believe
for the roses have died
and there are no gardens left to see

Jay Ferguson
A LIGHT FROM HEAVEN

Dedicated to my wife Elaine and my sons Bruce and Brian with love

One night of pain and sorrow,
I closed my eyes.

I think someone in heaven heard
my cries.

I prayed Dear lord please stop
this sorrow,
If not I do not want to live
beyond tomorrow,

Then in the dark there came
a light,
It looked so soft, but yet
so bright.

Into the light I did walk
It was so calm I could not talk

And in the light there was a face
A blessing for me a state of grace.

I was blind but now I see
what this light has done for me

That light is with me the rest
of my life.
It's not a spirit, but my
family and my wife.

Richard Carr
THE JEALOUS LOVER
Little I wanted to jealous be in all the days I sighed.
Still green the eyes that followed you with the hilt cold to the palm.
For all around me the mark of Cain flowered unanalyzed.
And my own broke out upon my bosom almost like a balm.

The street it led from light to darkness; the drops rained on the stones.
The gauze of night like a soporific lured my steps along.
I waited until you kissed him then I plunged it past your bones.
And with you fallen I choked him and his gasps were sweet like song.

Life wanted a jealous lover and her lust appointed me.
I wrap my collar high off the chin and know I have a path.
Condemned forever I dwell but in a gruesome memory
to prove once more that love can live even in the child of wrath.

Major T Cannon
THEY FRIED HIM
Why am I depressed?
Because he confessed?
My heart ached!
I thought it would break.

Bundy was his name!
His victims many,
I know not their names.

But they still cry from their graves,
Deprived of their young lives,
Too terrified to be brave.

They said he cried with remorse,
As he finally confessed.
Too terrified to be brave,
I guess,
At the prospect of his own grave.

They said he confessed!
Only way to heaven,
He guessed!
How many? Six, thirty-six? Not seven!
As the clock struck seven!

They watched, wore shirts that read,
"Burn Bundy Burn!"
His fate he justly earned!
They laughed, glad that he fried!

It seemed no one cried.

They said, for his victims,
He had no care!
They said, for himself,
He had to be carried to the chair.

Why am I so depressed?
The question I still press.
I know not why! I know not why!
We fried him.
I guess that's why!

Lisa Brooks
WHAT LOVE IS
Love is wondrous,
Love is grand.
Love is the one—
you'll find in this hand.
Love is like birds whistling—
in the whispering wind that—
flows very softly through—
the leaves on the trees.
Love is a wonderful
thing that happens between
you and me. Love is when
two people know how each—
other feel about one
another. That's what love is.

Earl J Boyd
THE GLORY OF THE RAINBOW
The earth must weep its share of tears
Before it reaps its golden years,
For rainbows never fill the sky
Until the storm has passed us by,
And every life must bear some pain
And have its share of sun and rain,
For only then can our hearts see
The Glory of Eternity

Floyd A Simon
O'GOD
Thank you Lord for accepting me at the Pearly Gate.
What a relief to be able to live with no more hate.
What a beautiful sight to behold.

To see all the Angels with their wings of gold.
Now I realize life on earth was only a test.
To see if one was worthy of living forever in peace and rest.

Amen

Natasha Boudreau
THE DREAM
The dark.
The lazily falling snow.
The bright candle's flame.

It's like a dreamworld,
staring into the falling snow,
so peacefully floating to the ground . . .

The romantic darkness.
The snow falling peacefully.
The warming fire.

It's so wonderful,
Sitting in the cabin,
Surrounded by snow and the forest.

The comfortable feeling.
The strong arms holding me.
The wonderful thoughts.

It's perfect
Sitting there with him,
As he draws me nearer . . .

The now lonely feeling.
The empty room.
The candle, almost burnt out.

Lucille M Marsh
LADY OF THE EVENING

To my loving daughter and son-in-law, Marilyn and Bill Toland.

Manhattan after dark—
Lady of the evening

Gone, gray concrete daytime garb
Printed with yellow taxies.

Gone, frenetic swish of traffic skirts.

Dressed now in elegant dusky cloak
Urgency slowed to murmuring rustle.

Raucous dawn to sunset voice
Subdued to throaty chuckle.

Jewelled skyscraper fingers ever reaching

Sparkling bridge necklaces
Draping river bosom.

Manhattan after dark—
Lady of the evening

Who can resist your siren call?

Stephen L Fox
MOON STRUK

To the most beautiful girl in my life I truly love you. Loving you dearly

Your eyes are like the moon at night;
Ever so bright and secretive when looked upon,
Your so loving and caring when I see you;
For your eyes tell it all;
I care for you dearly, and love you as well.

Laura M Campbell
MY DELIVERER
I Praise you O'God for your mighty hand of deliverance.
You've reached down to the very bowels of my private hell
and released the chains of depression.
Suppressive links continue to grab at me;
but you've renewed my inner strength.
You are there beside me and it's okay with your power
that my resistance weakens the clutching links.
You've broken through the murky depths of my personal hell;
and released me from the gripping snares of suicide.
Though I continue to get snagged on death's icy barbs,
the warmth of your love melts the sharpness away.
You god, have interceded for me and re-energized my desire for life.
It is only as you guide me, that my feet step within your footsteps.
You're standing there beside me during uprisings of self-destruction.
You buffer their intensity and enhance my resistance.
Daily, I enter a minefield of harmful thoughts and deeds.
With each step I take toward your freedom,
I'm blocked by yet another grenade.
Mercifully, you reach out and take my hand in yours;
and guide me through another day.
I praise you O'God for your mighty hand of deliverance.

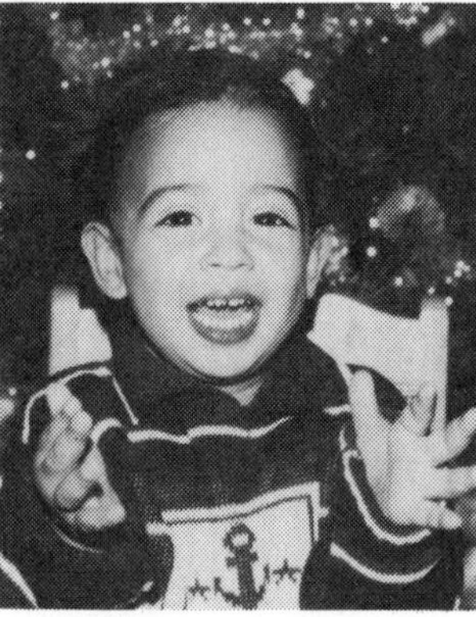

Christopher David Casiano

Arlene Casiano
A HOLIDAY CHEER

This poem is dedicated to Julio, my husband and Christopher my son

A Christmas Blessing I send to you
A special time for all to do
A New Year is coming, and the old one gone
But memories will be cherished as time goes on
I'm growing I'm changing and seeing all new
I'm learning what's right and what not to do
My parents are sending a picture of me
Showing my Holiday Cheers for all to see

Lisa Grimes
A CHANGE FOR THE BETTER
Once upon a time in the dreary land of fear,
There was a young maiden that shed many a tear.
Most stories say that the young maiden is fair,
But oh no! not this one—for she didn't even care.
You see this maiden had made a lot of mistakes,
but she shouldn't dwell on that for goodness sakes!
She felt that she wasn't worth a penny.
And when it came to friends, she thought she didn't have any.
So she spent her time doing bad things because she thought she was a bad person.
Drinking, smoking, cussing, flirting, and teasing—it only made things worsen.
She wanted to talk to someone, but the one she loved was gone.
He just left her hanging and wondering what went wrong.
Her parents were understanding, but what would they say?
So she continued doing things her own way.
You see the one she loved had never called again.
That's why she did these bad things and hoped that her life would end.
For he was very special and different from all the rest,
And she thought she wasn't good enough to pass his test.
Two months passed and she hadn't heard from this daring prince;
So she went out with another and she hasn't seen him since.
This other always hurt her with his yelling and his threats,
And this kept the maiden crying and she began to regret.
She regretted the things she did and the things she said.
Most of all, she regretted him and she stopped wishing herself dead.
She started going to church and changed all those bad traits.
All she had in her heart was love which was once all hate.
One night she kneeled down beside her bed to pray;
And listen to these words that she had to say:
Dear Lord, it's me—the one
You've helped so much.
Thank You for this new life; it has a special touch,
But thanks isn't enough for all the things You've done.
I finally believe that in this battle, I have won.
I promise to be good and to worship You so true,
She finally realized she had never carried this much for a boy.
They saw each other and their breath was taken away,
And they haven't been apart since that wonderful day.
Ah, excuse me, Lord, thank You for that sign,
And I hope that later on in time,
I can surely say that he is all mine.
So because of this prince, the maiden tried to live right.
She said a very special prayer every single night.
No one knows if they'll always be together, except the Lord up above.
But as of right now, they're working on a special kind of love!

Monte Shockman
WAVES THAT POUND THE SHORE
What power in the waves that pound the shore,
Made so apparent in the mighty ocean's roar.
Wave upon wave caresses the sandy beach,
For millions of yesterdays beyond our puny reach.
Mighty rollers, ever advancing,
Touching the shore, our heart's entrancing.
Angry waves strike the cliffs with a crash,
Then fall back to the ocean in their unending dash.
With picturesque rock giants guarding the shore,
Standing as sentinels for now and evermore.
Like gigantic stone fingers, clutching the sand,
'Gainst strong waves for eons they stand.
Shafts of light stream through sullen skies,
Lighting the breakers 'neath seagulls cries.

Rhonda Pickren
OUR FRIENDSHIP
I've had broken hearts before,
But never none like this.
My heart broke in two the day I left you.
Words just can't express how much you are missed.

We became friends overnight it seems,
We shared reality and our dreams together.
We put up with every body's schemes,
but we always stayed right beside one another.

The memories we shared keep running through my mind,
From the day we met my eyes adored you.
Because you were so nice and kind.
I knew from that day on we had a friendship that was true.

Now that we are apart,
I try to keep on smiling but it is so hard to do,
When you have a broken heart.
Because I miss such a special dear friend like you.

Patricia E Flack
THE DROUGHT OF 1988

This poem is dedicated to the family farmer of the United States, who strives selflessly to bring food to the world.

The year of nineteen-eighty-eight
Is hot and dry they say.
The clouds come drifting over the plains,
But ne'er a drop today,
And on they float moving away.
The strong winds are hotly blowing
Across the grassy plain.
The earth is hard and cracking.
We watch for rain in vain
In desperation and in pain.
The scorched crops crackle in the winds.
No seeds are in the husks.
The grain is less than is needed
To bake the sweet, sweet rusks,
And dust is everywhere at dusk.
The drought is long and dangerous.
The food supplies too short.
We pray for rain to lessen the
Impact at the far port.
Yet, no rain is still the report.
The hot, dry summer days pass on
In no ending relay.
We hope for winter's storms to come
To wet the arid day.
The parched and broken earth allay.

Sandra Jaffe
IF I EVER LOST YOU

This poem is dedicated to my boyfriend, Mark. Thanks for everything! Especially the inspiration. You're the best! I love you forever!

I love you so much, that's true,
That I'd do almost anything just for you.
Sometimes I wish we could always be together,
Knowing that our love would only get better.
You are so wonderful to me,
As anyone can see.
You show me you care
Since you're always there.
Whenever I'm down
You turn my frown upside down.
You've been there through good times,
You've helped me through bad,
You hold me in your arms
To make sure I'm not sad.
You spend so much money on presents for me
But, I guess that's because of all your love for me.
I said this before and I'll say it again,
My love will be with you to the end.
Because I don't know what I'd do,
If I ever lost you.

Rosemary Whitlock
ENRICHMENT

This poem won a Golden Poet Award in our recent poetry contest

I share my joys with you
  and joys are multiplied
I share my sorrows with you
  and sorrows are divided
I share my heart with you
  and love is nurtured
I would be poor without you
  I am rich in you.

Vasile Preda
THE NOSTALGIA OF THE WAXED EYE . . .

Dedicated to my mother, and for my friend, Keith . . .

my sculpted,
broken soul,
given the color of life,
the power of his hands tell of my story . . .
and i touch the infinite with
the grandeur of his idea.
not thinking of my original sentence
to solitude,
and never begging;
i have a singular season
a perpetual embrace with time.
no past, and no future . . .

Christie B Burchstead
WINTERHAWK
The snow is blinding fury
Storms throughout the day
Tall pines project the soul of winter
Hold the regal hawk at bay

Soon unfettered in the chill
From her lofty perch she'll fly
Amain to tear the shrieking prey
And soar across the winter sky

Julie E Martin
REFLECTIONS
Reflections . . . We are all reflections of time gone by!
Molded by life's lessons and God's spiritual awareness within us.

We each travel down a path to our own goals guided by our acquired judgement,
Some decisions are influenced by our heart; some by our knowledge.
Sometimes the results are heartbreaking and seem to gain us nothing,
But then, so often, bring us great pride in our accomplishments.

Who then are we? How do we fit in the universal plan? Where is our niche?
We are but a reflection outwardly of our emotions and morality within.
Through growth and maturity we learn compassion and forgiveness,
As we delve to understand suffering and its final rewards.

We hope to contribute something worthwhile to society and our peers,
Touching someone's heart deeply;
imprinting a valuable lesson to leave behind.
So that after we are no longer within this realm of life,
We may have comfort knowing we will be fondly remembered by some.

Roger E Kinnaman
GENTLY AS A DOVE
Gently as a dove, I cherish your love.
Your heart I hold so dear.

And when we're apart there's an ache in my heart,
as one day seems like a year.

So never say goodbye, never make me cry,

and your love I will cherish till the day
that I die.

Christine Gray-Crews
AND THE SPIRIT CRIES
My spirit leaves my body,
In the middle of the night,
Finding its way to you,
Because I long to hold you tight.
It cries and moans of loneliness,
Searching far and near,
Till it finds you miles away,
Your voice my soul can hear.
Softly, our spirits touch,
And darkness fades away,
Two souls have joined together,
But must part again at day.
And the spirit cries,
For departure must take place,
Tomorrow will find them joined,
With smiles upon their face.

Priti Topiwala
AFRICA
It is a land of beauty,
A land of wonder.
There is no other place
Filled with such splendor.

It is a country,
With a magical dream.
A place called Africa
Which is everything it seems.

Lions, Elephants, Giraffes,
All a sign of love.
A marvelous gift
From the one above.

However, many must leave,
For reasons unknown.
But some day they will return
To the land of their own.

Abbie Lynne Gold
THE ADVENTURE
An Adventure in which I'd like to see,
  all the Around, Near, and Far.
Casting in New Waves all the time,
  Seeing what Leeks in all of the Beyond.
But, if Danger shall Ever Threaten
any of the Light in Me,
  there is Where the Real
  Adventure Begins.

Brian Robert Dunne
home

For Peggy, who loved allegorical moonpies, and possibly even me.

. . . rumbling over pockets of dirt, through potholes, on three good truck tires, my ma and pa on either side of me. he ain't shaved in near a week, and she give up ever gittin' a new sunday dress. bloody cakes of flies on our windshield, and grasshoppers kiss the radiator grill.
  it never rains out here.
  the dog died, and we buried
  him out back, back behind the barn, back where uncle john used to vomit up his saturday nights.
  they sending me to school, to get me some learning, so i can marry me some rich business man.
  but i doubt it, look for me, i'll be the one hanging rags on clotheslines, and sucking up dirt.
  ma clenches her hands, stares at
  the sky, and cries . . .
  mercy, mercy, mercy . . .
it never rains out here, and she don't know . . .
  ain't no god
  ain't no mercy . . .

Eleanor Butler

Eleanor Butler
SOMETIMES
The upset landlady managed to keep her voice down,
Tho still unable to conceal an unpleasant frown,
As she gaped at the wet floor; her tenant knee-deep in it—
She cried—"o-this mess gets worse by the minute!"

"Why didn't you tell me the roof leaked on my hardwood floor;
I'd then have it repaired, so 'twouldn't leak any more"—
The uncaring tenant replied, in manner disdained—
'Why—it only leaked when it rained!'

Camille Mercogliano Drouin
MY CHOSEN CHILD, YUN HEE

To my wonderful daughter, Brittany . . . the little girl I always dreamed I'd have. And to you T.J., my inspiration.

Today is not an ordinary day.
Although the sun is sparkling, as it does most mornings,
This day will be different.
This day I will become a mother.

Although I've seen you only in
pictures
I feel we are already a part of each
other.

Such a beautiful child; shiny black
hair and defiant eyes.
Eyes that shine with courage.
A courage brought on by
circumstance
Fired by an inner strength.

I can not judge the people who gave
you life, then sent you away,
Only thank them.
For if not for them, I wouldn't
have you,
My most precious gift, my child.

You may not have the shape of my
eyes, or curve of my lips.
My blood will not flow
through your veins.
But my soul has matched
yours . . . making us family.

I did not see you come into this
world, Yun Hee,
But always count on me!
For I intend to see you through it.
My special child, my chosen child.

Madge Stanford Crackel

NATURE'S PLEASURES

We all can enjoy these natural things
A beautiful sky, the sunset brings,
The buzzing of a humming bird's
wings
As it feeds on the coral bells.
A pair of cardinals searching to find
Their favorite place to build.
And when the nest is finished,
Burst into song, because they are so
thrilled.
A robin flitting across the lawn,
Looking both left and right
Hoping that he will find for himself
A delicious, juicy, bite.
A squirrel busily hiding a nut
To have on a cold winter day.
But if he sees you watching him
He quickly scurries away.
The beautiful blossoms of early
spring
The brightly colored leaves of fall
The magic of a blanket of snow.
We can enjoy them all.

Kerry Andrew Teague

LET YOUR LOVE GROW

*I dedicate this poem to my son in
heaven, Andy. I know as an angel
you're doing just dandy.*

Well the sun is shining,
But the rain is startin' to fall.
The old miner's still mining,
When there is really no gold at all.
Well we're all searching for a
rainbow,
Trying to find our pot of gold.
I wish you all could know,
Love is much warmer to hold.
Still out to the mine we go,
To search for a metal so cold.
Still we have no gold or love to
show,
We're just growing grey and old.
People let your love grow,
Because you know it can't be bought
or sold.
And this is the way the story goes,
Yes, this is the way the story is told.

Andrew C Pierce

NOT THIS NIGHT

As soft as a shadow he moves,
Taking things of value as he goes.
A clever person he is,
But,
Outside he hears the dreaded sirens.
He snatches the bag he filled
And flees.
He steps out the back as quiet
As can be.
As expected, a man in blue tries
To stop him.
Out of his pocket comes a
Revolver as black as pitch.
He pulls the trigger quickly
And runs like a fox being hunted
By a pack of dogs.
He dashes behind a bush and sheds
The black like a snake would
Its skin.
He hides the bag to be picked
Up later and walks away passively.
The man will get caught, but not
This night.

Melissa Nevarez

LIFE OF A TEENAGER

The sky is dark and clear,
There's no sign of death near.
Couples walking everywhere,
Because there is love to share.

I wait for you only,
And hope we don't feel so lonely.
I don't want the end near.
I can't wait 'til you are here.

Take me away to our special place,
Where we don't have to face,
All the problems of mankind,
And hope the solution we'll someday
find.

Lisa M Zigler

FREEDOM

I'm your only one, the one that you
have to call on I'm friend
I'm your lover,
There will be no other, to come to
you
If you tell me that you love me
I'll share my life with you,
I'm always here no matter what you
do.
Just say the word, and I'll share my
world with you.

Alice L Mathis

Alice L Mathis

THE WHISPERING WIND

Around us ever be the strong
and the weak,
Some as strangers, others as friends,
Others bold and others meek,
And always the whispering wind.

We seek for joy and free of worry.
Time is ours to choose to spend
As ever onward we must journey
Through the whispering wind.

We stop awhile beside a restful
place,
Walk the road that has no end,
But always meet to embrace
The whispering wind.

We watch the face of Mother Nature
And see her arms extend
To give out her lessons
like a teacher—
Her voice, the whispering wind.

Time is now and time to be,
Time to take, time to give,
and time to mend
Leaving a path free of debris
To listen to the whispering wind.

Janet Renfroe Raper

PEACE

She lay within the stench of death
I walked into her room
My patient with no family;
No love to hang on to.

I knew the other nurses
Avoided going in.
What could they give this lady
Whose life was soon to end?

I walked right over to her
And looked down on her face,
I saw this dear old lady,
I loved her for her grace.

I took her hand into my own,
She squeezed it oh so slight,
I knew I couldn't leave her
To die alone tonight.

I put my lips upon her cheek
And kissed her oh so soft,
I felt that warm tear flowing down,
My heart she had just bought.

She sighed so hard and then was
gone,
I cried for her to stay!
But she could die in peace right now
For love had come her way.

Kathy Householder

CRACKED BACK

"If you step on a crack, you'll
break your Mama's back.
If you step on a crack, you'll
break your Mama's back."

The little girl skips along
the sidewalk singing her song,
neatly skipping over the cracks.

"If you step on a crack, you'll
break your Mama's b—."

(But wait! If her back is only broke a
little
she'll have to stay at home with me.)
The little girl neatly starts to land on
every crack.

"If you step on a crack, you'll
break your Mama's back.
If it's only broke a little
You'll have to stay at home
And me and Daddy won't have
to be alone to do the things
he does to me . . . when you're
gone."

Sings the little girl softly
as she walks along the sidewalk
in front of the church

killing time;

before she goes home alone . . .

(Except for Daddy's there.)

Julieann Sherman Coppock

MOUNTAIN MAN

*This poem is dedicated to Dave, who
is not only my brother, but a
wonderful friend! Thanks for all the
good times!*

I have a brother who is as big as a
bear.
He has a raccoon; buckskin clothes
he does wear.
His beard is the fullest of those I
have seen.
He is not really stout, but neither too
lean.
He loves to go camping in the teepee
he made.
Shoot black powder rifles; sip
homebrew in the shade.
And if there's a fish a swimmin' in
the river,
He'll catch that darn rascal with a
hook and some liver.
When deer season comes he will sure
make a kill.
Tan the hide, mount the rack, and dry
the meat, yes he will.
He cuts a lot of wood for his heat in
the winter.
Not a thing goes to waste, not even a
splinter.
His dream is to have lived 100 years
ago.
To live without convenience that man
does now know.
He does for himself as much as he
can.
The folks around town call him
"Mountain Man!"

Dona G Vincent

INSTEAD

Instead
you decided
to let me go.
Instead
your life was more
important
than a life together.
Instead
you will regret
one day.
My life left
tattered and torn
like a rose after a heavy
winter storm.
Instead
of us it is now
you
then me.
Alone
with memories
of the way it used to
be.

Stuart Skolfield

NOSTALGIA

Recounted yesterdays, their
memories
Creep from the shadows of the days
gone by,
Wherein the meadows echoed with
the lark
And the green hills reechoed in reply.

Gone with the vanished birds and
butterflies,
The cheery songs; beauty of fragile
things
Now seldom seen; yet weaving fancy
brings
Those golden dreams, long faded
with their skies:

Springtime incarnate, in a summer's
dawn,
Of yesterdays made sweet in thoughts
that burn
With olden fire; nostalgic scenes
withdrawn,
Swift reconvene; in rose-lit shades
return;

As daylight fading in the sunset's
glow
Before the darkness lingers in the
sky,
So memories entwine, that overreach
The wasted years; return in brief
reply;
Bringing a surge of music, ever so,
As some slow wending wave upon
the beach.

Phyllis J Cardassi
YOUNG RESTLESS LOVE
Through two sillouettes of love the sun has shown
At this love nest of romance they sought to have fun they can now own.
In innocence and fascination with each other they fussed, and smiled. It often seemed confusing so they were sometimes beguiled.
So in the hidden hours of daylight they were full of fears They could'nt suppress their desires or their tears
Memories will be made this hour, they will be filled with young dreams, and their dreams will be scented with every wild flower
Young love is a permissiveness, an alluring youthful attraction, but as one ages it becomes part of a memory, a mental frustration, a young persons reaction

R T Simone
EMPTY CITY
quietly dissolved in morning mist
wondering without thought . . .
why can't we play today?
to be without being . . .

emerging organically from nothing,
return the same;

to live the dream and laugh at the joke,
remembering a day to come
which had more light.

George A Tison
MY LITTLE GIRL

To my daughter Michele

Time is going by so fast,
And in my mind I live in the past.
The day you were born I remember so well,
I was so happy I could hardly wait to tell.
Now you're twenty-five years plus a few days,
My love is the same and will be always.
You are my diamond, my only pearl,
You'll always be my little girl.

Cyndi Reed
TWENTY-FIVE YEARS
Twenty-five years ago today,
They said "I do" and went on their way.
He was tall, blonde and handsome,
A fine one in sports, was known as "That's the one."
She was so small and very pee-teete,
Charcoal black hair, very pretty and sweet.
Lucky they were, they lived in the same town,
To her surprise everywhere she turned, he is around.
Hard times she had in photography in school years,
But he was a great comfort to her tears.
They enjoyed many of times together,
That they'll remember in all kinds of weather.
He said "I'll be true, come home for you in many a day,"
Later in time a telegram she received,
It said "I miss you, I love you, and in you I believe."
Away in a hurry she went on the first train,
And all the way she thought of him while it rained.
They were married with the approval of the army,
And that's how it started with Daddy and Mommy.
As they were pronounced man and wife,
The general said, "You two are set
And will be happy for the rest of your life.

Buffy Stone

Buffy Stone
THE STATUE OF LIBERTY

I dedicate this poem to my wonderful "family" because I honor and love them.

She always stands with all her might,
She always stands with a torch
of light.

As the days and nights pass through,
She's always there for you.

The Statue of Liberty is her name,
She always stands tall with all
her fame.

Susan Leifeld
DREAMS
I awake, rested.

You filled my dreams
with gentle caresses
and whispered words of love.

Images . . .

Your many aspects
float through my consciousness
into unconsciousness.

I am loved.

Dreams, mirror world of life.

Amy Janssen
THE TWO OF ME
I can't get satisfied,
I am always wanting more and more.
I'll hurt you if you get in my way
I will make your heart feel torn and sore.

I am a very caring person,
I love to share my hopes and dreams.
If you need some one to talk to, I'll listen
No matter how bad it seems.

I am selfish and evil,
What I want always comes first.
When I have you in the palm of my hand
I'll squeeze you till you burst.

I like to make people happy
I don't like to see them sad.
I love life and being alive
I would never purposely be
bad . . .

As I stand in front of this mirror
There are so many faces that I see,
The mirror is so confusing,
Which face of these is the real me?

June Bell-Van Dyke
ARE WE?

To the world with love . . . may truth and light heal your fevered cry and its reality call your star performance before his coming; that all just, thinking peoples can hear, heed and follow.

Raucous rumblings, tawdry, torn;
Laying beside me scorn upon scorn.
Smiling faces, masks of clay;
Proudly flaunting day upon day.
Blood baths of empty faces . . .
Slaughtered by night in beautiful places.
Seething, raging, sea upon sea . . .
We aren't barbarians . . .
Are we?
Prancing proud pomposity;
We aren't barbarians . . .
Are we?
Ravaging soul; spirit; flesh;
Proud hungry prance
Your pomps gone to pieces!
No more should flaunting egoists sing
For face to our face to our face; the humbling.
Savage scornful frenzied dance,
Billows like the winter sea.
We aren't barbarians . . .
Are we?

Darion Andre' Taylor
CATS

To my parents, grandparents, brothers, sisters, entire family and friends I dedicate my poem with love Darion

Cats are cute to cuddle by
Their eyes look like the sea blue sky
They are very gentle and very sweet
Be very quiet don't make a peep
And maybe you can watch them sleep
Play with your cat make it feel at home
But don't forget to give it space to roam

Maxene Gonzales
THE TOMBOY
Looks are so deceiving, I'll tell you
that's so true,

Our little girl dressed up in pink,
always looked better in blue.

On the day she arrived, we were
filled with joy,

Here was the sister we promised our
little baby boy.

As she grew up she disliked dolls,
books, and stuffed ducks,

She chose instead to play with her
brother, and his trucks.

Dresses were a bother, with their
frills, and things,

She wanted to wear instead "T"
shirts, and "Jeans."

Then one day it happened when she
turned sixteen,

She started wearing dresses, put
away her "Jeans."

Now she's a mother, with children of
her own,

She fondly remembers that
"Tomboy," and "Home."

Sheri R Kern
LOVE AND SUMMER
love comes in many ways
a baby yellow rose on a summer day
a baby blue sky
waves on the beach
biting into a fuzzy peach

a picnic lunch by a stream
dreaming of a romantic dream
picking out ice cream flavors
a cozy bear hug you want to savor

looking into a lover's eyes
forgiving each other for little white
lies
falling down and skinning your knee
Grandma making sun-made tea

running through a grassy field
opening your heart
so it is no longer sealed

Dorothy Gabrielsson

Dorothy Gabrielsson
MY LION
My lovely Lejonette* loves me
She says it every day in a very unique way
With each gesture and pure loyalty.

I can't hear; she can't talk.
But we walk, and walk, and walk—
We are happy—.
I love her; she loves me.

My lovely Lejonette loves me,
She says it loud and clear,
Even with deaf ear—
I can hear! I can hear!
She loves me.

Whatever may befall—
When I'm "climbing up the wall,"
When I'm sure that no one else loves me,
I never need to doubt.
She never needs to shout.
She Loves Me.

*Lion = Lejon in Sweedish.
Lejonette is by beloved Chow.

Antionette Adelquist Bell
MYSTERIOUS ENCOUNTER
The staircase of my soul
Shines before you as whole
Your dinner jacket just pressed
My fainting now, from this test

The xylophones sound the note
A messenger has sent your vote
The chandeliers sparkle and tease
In the hotel, a summer breeze

The timbre of the drum's leather
With eyes closed I'm but a feather
The veranda of roses of love
Shake the earthquake of sky above

The mountains purple at dawn's day
We've stepped in time the night away
On horseback into the waterfall you swish
Will this penny give me, this day, my wish?

Rosemary Delderfield
A BEING FROM A DISTANT TIME

O being from a distant time,
Remember when your love was mine?
We basked in sunbeams every day,
At night we sailed the Milky Way;
Two stars were we away up high,
No sadness came to make us sigh,
No fears or musts that we should part,
No love of ours we could not start.

Such times were sweet when we were free,
What sheer delight it was to be,
To ebb and flow, to be as one,
Expand anew with each day done;
The joy and truth of life we knew
Excelled all known to but the few
Who've seen a moonbeam flee the night,
Beheld a rainbow burning bright.

We saw that moon and felt the rain
And knew we would return
again . . .

O friend of mine throughout all time,
Remember when your love was mine?

Walter C Johannes
AN ODE TO THE LORD'S PRAYER

OUR FATHER WHO ART IN HEAVEN
where we all hope to be
HALLOWED BE THY NAME
all power and glory to Thee
THY KINGDOM COME
we are awaiting your return
THY WILL BE DONE
we accept it with some concern
ON EARTH AS IT IS IN HEAVEN
as here and high above where you manifest your love
GIVE US THIS DAY OUR DAILY BREAD
that we may not hunger, that we may be fed
AND FORGIVE US OUR TRESPASSES
that we may start our life anew
AS WE FORGIVE THOSE WHO TRESPASS AGAINST US
that we through your love be forgiving, exemplifying you
AND LEAD US NOT INTO TEMPTATION
that we keep on the narrow path
BUT DELIVER US FROM EVIL
that we do not incur your wrath
FOR THINE IS THE KINGDOM,
THE POWER AND GLORY
forever and ever amen

Armineh Ebrahimian
ARMENIA

Sometimes I wonder how life can
Be different for some.
It seems like they lose their touch of love
Seeing their whole culture fall apart.
They're lying in a world of nowhere
Desperate for help.
Massacre, earthquake, blood, dead bodies all over
Seeing these happen to humans
Make me sober
It's a nightmare, that always comes true.
Just once if they could wake up
And hear some good news.
Just look at these people and look what you will see
As much as it hurts them, it hurts me.
These people are innocent Armenians
Who are pleading for help
Let's help them live their lives and take them
Out of hell.

Nikki Dornin
PIECES

To Bill, my father, of whom I hold many pieces.

Here I lay my soul on the table,
And give you a piece, or two, if I am able.
Then for the first time you can see,
That this is really part of me.

Then I pick up the pieces and put them away,
For some other soul, some other day.
And soon all the souls, all around,
Hold onto little pieces that they have found.

It's not just yours, it's not just mine
It's something beautiful, something divine.
It's pieces of people that we do and don't know,
Pieces of people that come and may go.

Coming from everyone dead or alive,
Little pieces of people will always survive.

Stephanie D Fink
MY DEAR, DEAR FRIEND

To: Susan Shanker, for your enduring patience as my friend; may I grace your presence once again:

As I sit here writing, the warm thoughts gently flow across my mind, of how special our friendship makes me feel.

Lovingly, ever so lovingly, shall the words glide across this paper to harness the emotions felt, by the simple stroke of this pen, when I describe my wonderful friend.

Inadequate as the word may be, oh so powerful is its meaning.
For tenderly shall I long for all eternity, that you will be with me unto the end, because I need you as my friend.

Although it may be triumph or tragedy, you were always there, for your warmth has shown no end, when I have needed you as my friend.

So forever shall I long for your enduring patiences, which has carried me unto the darkest of nights. For you were always there when I have needed you to care.

For if there shall ever be another time for choosing a special friend, oh let me be fortunate enough, to grace your presence once again, "MY DEAR, DEAR FRIEND."

Chrystal Doucet
GOD NEVER CRIES

I DEDICATE MY POEM WITH LOVE: to every small child in need, across the miles, over-seas, and around the world.

God never cries at night-time,
Not intentionally.
He's so busy wiping all the tears
From you and from me.
He' so busy helping others
In the midst of a brand new day
Even for the ones
Who seemingly forgot to pray.
Did you ever stop to think, for a minute?
That God has tears too.
So get busy my child and help someone
And wipe a tear-or-two.
For all the tears
You wipe away—
God gives a thousand Thank-yous to you.
It's one less tear
For God to shed
And one less job
For him to do
God never cries—
Only when he has to.

Mary F Wortman

Mary F Wortman
L.A. TOUR

City of devil; city of angel
City of hopeful; city of painful

City of homeless in the street
City of stars under our feet

Sing Los Angeles; Here's to Her
City of glamour and allure

City of lonely; city of fear
City of welcome; city of cheer

City of people breathing in smog
City of people living in fog

City of gods, a thousand prayers
City of apartments stacked in layers

City of music; rock to the beat
City of children, nothing to eat

City of leather and topless bars
City of families living in cars

City of gangs, a kid with a gun
City of nations living as one

Sing Los Angeles; Sing L.A.
Changing faces day to day

Emily Steele
THRU MY EYES

Memories of childhood was the start.
Falling all so apart
I'm abused, I'm accused
His fault lies here.
Beneath my tears.
Hope comes with stars,
my cloudy eyes clear
Death, and hate
are then replaced,
As he took my hand
he could see forever peace.
Thru My Eyes
life and love
stand by my side.

Carol S Chapman
TOGETHER WE STAY

Together we must mend
Forget the hurt and start again
Walk each path, hand and hand
Join together, we must band.

Together we both have learned
The days together, we have earned
Showered dreams and broken chain
Much much hurt, was not our aim.

Together we must plan ahead
Then tomorrow, will not be dread
The kids grow up, and drift away
It's together, we will stay.

Together we must start a new
Lessons learned, are not just few.
Wasted days, are now gone by
We can make it, if we try.

Lillian Smith
LIGHTS OF THE NIGHT

Did you ever sit by yourself at night
And watch the stars arise
And wonder and think with all your might
Just why they were put in the skies?
Was it for the use of both you and I
Or did it just happen to be.
That God puts them there every night in the sky
So that we all may see.
Some seem brighter than others to be
And some are large and small.
Wouldn't it be terrible if some bright night
All these lights should fall.
Just think how dark the heavens would be.
There'd scarce be a thing in sight.
God made for us to love and to see
The little bright lights of the night.
Sometimes if you sit and watch in a space
You may see a small, light drop.
It hurries as though it had entered a race,
and was soon to be caught by a cop.
But the next night, look once again in that space,

From where that small light fell.
As sure as you live, there'll be
another in its place.
Oh my, but He does his work well.

Grace Jenkinson
A SMILE ON MY FACE

You start my morning with a smile
on my face
You are always there and shine me
face to face
The energy you give away
Brings so much fun the rest of my
day

The love you give
Is the life I live
I could ask for more
Because I need it forevermore

You are a dream come true
You never color me blue
With all the precious things I get
from having you
There is no one out there more than
you do

You are so perfect for me
There is nobody else I could rather
be
You are my only way
And there is no other way

You are the star I see in the night sky
That twinkles up so high
The brightest and wonderful
The most beautiful of them all

Theresa Herle
OUR TIME WAS LOVE

This poem is dedicated to Mike, my loving husband and best friend. "For the way you have touched my heart"

You made no promises
and yet
I feel as though
I have been betrayed.

I don't think you ever realized
the depth
of my feelings for you.

Not only the depth
but the strength and sincerity
of them also.

But you are gone now.

And as we both probably knew
our contact with eachother
has diminished
to nothing.

How sad.

Because our time was beauty
our time was love
our time
is over.

Elinor Reneau
WITHOUT YOU

To my husband Samuel, Today, Tomorrow and Always

When I am without you by my side,
I sit and dream of the next time
I'll be in your arms.
The next time I hold you close,
The next time I see your face,
The showing of love.
If only to have my dream come true
right now—
I would be happiest of all,
To be able to crawl into bed with
you,
Your gentle touch on my breasts,
Your soft lips on my neck;
all snuggled up as one.
These are some of the things I dream
of—
When I am without you by my side.

Dee deRosier
BOXCARS

To my parents who are my heroes and to my children who are the wind beneath my wings

Dull patchwork colors in a line
Writhing witless worm
Spark along your flinty trail
Docile boxes with no mind.

Feed on sooty tidbits black
Giant galvanized grub
Feel your innards strain and wail
Puffing up your endless track.

Your face is belching jets of smoke
Segmented steely snake
Poor Cyclops' eye can't even blink
In protest of your steely yoke . .

Donna Ellenberger
TOUGH LOVE

The drugs and booze out on the
streets,
Sold to our kids like candy treats.
Destroys the way they think and feel,
Makes them angry and makes them
steal.

They blame the parents for their
distress,
Forgetting it was them who said yes.
They can't see it's the booze and
drugs,
That plague their minds like poison
bugs.

Caught up in their so-called friends,
Where the supply of fantasies never
end.
When playing with fire you can get
burned,
There are a few who have learned.

So parents need to take a stand,
Regain control with an upper hand.
Show a strength your kids can see,
Let Tough Love work and evil flee.

Peggy Rios
WHAT DOES MARRIAGE MEAN TO ME?

What does marriage mean to me?
I honestly don't need to be free!
I don't need security, so that is out,
So what is marriage really about?
To have and to hold from this day on,
To sleep with him from nite till
dawn.
To be with him when he has needs,
To be with him while he reads.
To stay by his side through thick and
thin,
To debate on issues I may never win.
To share his ups and downs,
To even let him go out on the town.
To say I love you every day,
To make it always stay this way.

Domenick P Catalano
MY BABY

One beautiful summer morn
God blessed me with a newborn
My baby was born with a physical
defect
And in my life, it had quite an effect
And for all the times I shed a tear
I always knew God was near
And as the time went by
I would pray and ask God, why?
And as God listened to my voice
I know now why He made this choice
It's clear why God chose me
Because that's the way
He meant it to be
For He knew that I had
that special love
To carry out His message from above
And that I would give extra care
And for sure that I would
always be there
And when my day is done
I know that I'm the lucky one
For I am blessed every day
That God sent this beautiful baby
my way

Laura L Pinckert

Laura L Pinckert
JUST FOR YOU! VIETNAM VETS!

Dedicated to all Vietnam vets.

Down in the jungles of the Viet
Cong a battle was fought which
lasted so long
Men were sent off to war not even
knowing what they were fighting for.
The men were happy when they went
at first but it didn't take long for their
bubble to burst.
Spirits and morale were mighty low
as the soldiers went forward to meet
their foe.
One by one they took their stand as
they advanced with gun in hand.
The communists were coming over
the hill seeking out Americans they
wanted to kill
A soldier fell, and then another, as
they fought back to save a brother.
The battle raged on and on and on,
more boys were wounded their
strength nearly gone.
They never did give up They gave it
their all among them Bill, Bobby and
Paul
Little did they know this would last
for years as relatives back home
fought back tears.
The war ended. A memorial in D.C.
was made may God in his mercy
cause the bad memories to fade.

Raymond S Metz
HUNGER

To my parents, who were always there for me.

World-strewn pain, dying babes
Mothers waiting for help that never
came;
Activists speak out but it isn't
enough
People sending money but still it's
tough
To feed the hungry, starved, the
mal-nutritioned
Newspapers, t.v., make an exhibition;
Of these people with little hope in the
future
We have to stand and find a cure;
For this disease so many people get
Its name is hunger
Its appetite must be suppressed.

Virginia Dare Smith
EACH DAY WE ARE FACED WITH DECISIONS

With thanks to my sister, Carolyn, and my friends for the encouragement, I dedicate this poem to the Requirements Division of DCSRM at Headquarters TRADOC.

Each day we are faced with
decisions.
The intelligence gifted to us is greatly
tried and our emotions are drained.
But do we go to sleep at night not
caring?
We race to join in the competition.
We humiliate to get revenge and our
animal instinct is forever increasing.
But do we ever invite anyone along?
Our minds and bodies are mingled
together.
We depend on each other's
capabilities with desperation written
on our faces.
But do we ever stop and consider
humanity?
Not knowing the facts, we jump to
conclusions, hurting the feelings of
others.
We strive for our own satisfaction.
But do we ever stop and touch?
Nobody's turmoils seem as great as
our own.
The clock keeps ticking with
deadlines to meet.
Why? Why can't we stop the clock
for just a minute to care about each
other?

Janice Lynn McNutt
A TEAR OF GRIEF

Upon thy love for David were tears of self-denial desire wept unto daydreams

What tear shall befall
a grieving heart
such sorrow we pour
till destitute

In chains of silence
do hopes but fade
with love so lost by
destiny's fate

Oh empty vessel
has thy dream spilt
unto seasons leave
without its taste

Of souls that tarry
on past mistakes
is time forsaken
remembering

Lainee Gant
LEFT (THE MORNING AFTER)

There was dew on his windshield,
As he drove away,
And it saddened her to realize—
That it was barely day.
He didn't know he had wakened her;
She feigned sleep too well.
She's had so much practice since
they met,
That he could hardly tell.
But whenever he got out of bed and
there was no one left to hold,
She felt the change immediately—
Instantly sensing the cold.
She listened as he showered,
And dressed in the morning
light,
Then hurried toward the hall—
Leaving memories of the night.
She rose and put on his sweater—

Left lying on the floor,
Forgotten in his haste—
To make it to the door.
She had thought it would be different,
But each time it's the same.
He leaves her in the morning—
As quickly as he came.
And she longs for the comfort and protection of his arms,
But he left her broken hearted: A victim of his charms.
She forgets that love and desire don't always come as one,
Until she's standing by the window while he races home the sun!

Sam Hart
LORD'S STORM
Who has the right to say their opinion is correct in life?
No opinion is agreed by everyone, we should not fight for power, it will only kill us soon.
What gives the ones who don't believe in God, the right to raise a knife?
Some love God, some do not, one love is power, any opinion should not be of doom.

Some think death is heaven or hell, I think it's life after death.
If only we kept our opinions to ourselves, we would all be okay.
I wish we all could open our hearts like simply taking a breath.
And clear the air with no opinions in the way.

Some worship God in the Bible as the power and the strength.
Others think some worship a God no longer there
They say some spend so much time praying at length.
I wish we all could say the symbol of life, is only to care.

I think as we die in life, another is born.
I believe we live on a cycle, we live on production.
Now finally as we die "peace" fills our ears as the rain falls from the Lord's storm.
There should be no opinions, and not even my own—
For after we die, it is as if, we had never been born.

Josefina B Salazar
MEMORIES
I don't know why the world is so cruel
To leave me truly alone
The love that once we cherished
Had vanished and forever perished.

Years we counted thirty-eight in all
Was too short for me until you were called
Leaving along your footsteps and memories
For me to remember and to caress.

The flowers you always brought me
Brings back my mind of our younger days
When once or twice you trod your way
Just to say the words "I care for you."

Gone forever those good old days
You are so near to my mind today
And yet so far for me to reach
For you are now in the Land of Bless.

Good-bye words that are hard to say
This little flower I have to lay
On this cold cold earth as your bed
Where I will be with you when I'm dead.

Mary Nickerson
REFLECTIONS
I see in the mirror a
reflection that looks like me.

But she is a stranger, no
longer a part of me.

I see the sadness that is
in her eyes.

For no one knows that pain
as well as I.

I know the hurt she feels within,
the silent tears she's cried.

And I have seen her bow her
head to God and wonder why?

Maybe, if she could learn
to smile, then I could too.

Then maybe we both could
start anew.

Oh, reflection in the mirror
who looks like me,

When did we lose what
was once you and me?

Ann-Marie Drew
YOU LEFT ME ALONE
You left me alone
in shadows of memories.
I lie awake
with pain I can not see.

The love we had
will never be again.
But I have gained
a better strength within.

The love that was lost
is forever gone.
But love for myself
has finally been found.

I have survived the pain
and become a better person.
No more to be shadowed by clouds
but to be followed by the sun.

Shereé Burdette McGowen
WHAT TO WEAR
I remember the fashions of yesteryear,
Boys and girls with long, straight, stringy, hair.
Pants with hip-hugger waists and bell-bottomed legs,
The love beads, peace signs; I wore my share.

My daughter wears neon orange, yellow, and pink,
Colors so bright they really open your peepers!
Narrow legged jeans and spritzed hair,
Oh, don't forget those high-top sneakers.

My son sports deck shoes with laces twisted,
A denim jacket with buttons and things.
Silver chain around his neck,
And stone-washed, acid-treated, worn out jeans.

After examining my closet, these two great kids,
Stand before me and solemnly shake their heads.
"You can keep this, and maybe this," they say,
"But honestly Mother, the rest will be great in the dog's bed."

Well, maybe, my hair-do isn't quite the thing,
Perhaps my clothes are a little out of date.
But my husband doesn't seem to mind,
Probably because his wardrobe is in the same shape!

Brook D McKee
YES, I REMEMBER YOU

To C. E. Tindall, the wind beneath my wings.

How did I get into this, the void, the longing.
So, it really is possible to be happy and unhappy at the same time.
It is so easy to stay submerged in a dream; especially when the dream looks back at you.
How time stands still when our eyes lock together in a private moment of passion.
The secret garden that is ours to share.
Two strangers meeting for the first time on the dance floor but with bodies in full sync like we have danced across time to be together again . . .

With each passing song our souls saying, "Yes, I remember you."
Our bodies locked together by sweet melodious rhythms, our souls meeting and intertwining with pent up passion waiting to be unleashed.
Yes, our private interlude will come one day. I have missed you and cannot wait to explore your innermost feelings once again.
I will love you until time ends our dance on this parallel . . . and until we find each other again on the next.

Aura Burgos
ALIEN

This Poem is Dedicated to: My Father and my Dear Family.

How can I be an alien. Why why . . . . I came from a country with same sky, same sea, same ground; Lives and kingdom same "God"
How "you" can say that,
Alien? . . . I work same as you, respect other, love other just like you. We speak same language, we have same dreams Our feelings are similar Our friends consider me as kind and intelligent just like you; we have same values, a home, a family, in same country, same level—Tell me . . . tell me Alien? . . . .
Only Human . . . like you Only Human, with same dreams same hopes; An Alien? . . . . We share same world
Only Human with dreams . . . . and hopes to a better future . . . .
Just like you, Just like you

Karen Sue Elizabeth Elliott
PHYSIQUE

To Joseph E Carsley, for all your inspiration and love, friendship and happiness you have given me, Love, Karen.

The human physique,
Symmetry,
Body poetry in motion,
Physical beauty,
Mastered beyond words,
Sculptured muscles into maximum performance,
Systemized dedicated work,
To achieve the ultimate goal,
Of physical perfection,
Synchronized routines,
Created to display,
An athlete's peak performance,
Symmetry,
Body poetry in motion,
Is beautiful to behold.

Dwayne E Willis
JOURNEY'S END
Our sail bellows out,
as we sail with the wind.
On our way home,
toward our journey's end.
We pillaged, we raped,
we conquered them all.
We mangled, we killed,
we watched them fall.
The rewards we took,
and filled our ship.
We had gained a lot,
for our long weary trip.
As most of us sleep,
for, filled with ale.
Both wind and sea,
turn to hell.
Up and over,
and down with a splash.
There, up ahead,
then suddenly, a crash.
Can this be?
could our rewards have been worth?
Dying on the bottom,
when we're so close north.
Slowly, everything
starts to descend.
And, all is quiet,
at our journey's end.

Shane Leland
THINKING
Thinking of you, wondering if you're thinking of me,
Thinking of life and the way it should be.

Thinking of home and what's to come,
Thinking of the past and the things I've done.

I think of the good times and of the bad,
Sometimes thinking of these things, makes me sad.

Thinking of the future and what it will bring,
Thinking of the songs, I love to sing.

You never know how life will turn out,
Or how it will end,
One thing for certain we all need a friend.

So I'm asking for friendship,

And maybe a little love.
But I don't want to push,
And I don't want to shove.

Thinking of you wondering if you're thinking of me

Veronica S Waldow
REFLECTIONS OF A MAN
The sun rises above the clouds,
casting a shadow behind me.
It follows
wherever I go.
I turn, and it confronts me:
doubtful greyness.
Just what are these images?
Reflections
of thoughts and ideas
forming a man?
Only God knows.
But to destinations unknown,
my shadow goes with me,
until I reach that final
pure light,
where no shadows can follow.

Jennifer Rebecca Martin
STILL WAITING
You took me to places
That no longer exist—
With the look in your eyes
Or the warmth of your kiss.

You made me believe you—
Although you had lied—
When you said you would always
Remain by my side.

You left me alone,
With nothing to say—
Except that we would be
Together some day.

Since "some day" never came,
My love never fading,
I've been here for you—
Still loving, still waiting.

Jeff Harris

Jeff Harris
IN SOCIETY I HAVE LIVED A BITTER LIFE!
In society I have lived a bitter life—"
Whenever I feel sad
Mad or down—"
My wife makes me feel good
throughout all my nights
In society I cherish my life
And wonderful wife!
In society my friends love to shoot drugs
Some of them want to become a big time thug
God what is wrong with these people—
Who wants to throw their lives away everyday?
God of all Gods
King of all Kings
I want to help stop people from snorting crack
Yellow Jacks
And the junkies lying on their back—"
Wisdom is something they all seem to lack—"
In society I want to help the homeless
People lying around on cold grounds
Many of them once had a place to go to
Every time I see the old
And young—
Lying on dirty streets without anything to eat
Dying so young
Starving to death
No place to work
The young joining street gangs
Who should I blame?
Joining street gangs is never any fun!
People life is not a game
In society I have lived a bitter life
Because of the prejudices
And injustice that goes on—"
I thank God for blessing me with a beautiful wife
In society I hope the young youth offenders—
Will stop killing our brothers
And sisters over drugs
Territories
Money
Sex
Power
And learn to live amongst each other—"
And stand proud like a prison tower!

Helen P Andres
KEEP THE COLORS OF MY LIGHT
God within me
with power so great
and knowledge
which goes beyond
human experience,
I let your will guide
me—your wisdom passes
through me,
as I write your words.

Wonderful is thy presence
and so restful
in peace and joy
that when I stray
my strength disappears
and although I sit
with mortal man/woman
I am alone.

In the quietness of my soul
your words echo with perfection
and bless all of humanity
and I take, again, baby steps
to unite within God who
knows and cares
and seems to whisper—
keep the colors of my light.

Walter H Andres
THIS WINTER'S FIRST SNOWFALL
The snow came calling early last night
And covered all things wintery white.
Such a visage of silvery beauty, so bright . . .
The boughs on the fir trees
A wonderland all right.

White ribbons and lace all over the place
Make the holiday feelings just right
And the trees in the wood
All understood
They'll be warmed 'neath this blanket of white.

Ding-a-ling, sleigh bells ring—
These riders huddled up tight
Winter has come to lovers of fun,
May we all sing
Our caroling
How deep is the snow
As whirling we go
The folks on the pond, of which they're fond;
Will need a warm fire tonight.

Gina M Officer
MARRIAGES ARE MADE IN HEAVEN
Marriages are made in heaven
under the hand of God;
He gave us each a commitment
for which we should not trod.

Weddings are very special
that make a couple as one;
Promises are made, and
the work has just begun.

When a couple loves each other
as much as you two do;
The work can make a bond
that can hold you through and through.

Good times as well as bad
will come throughout each year;
But the love you have established
will help you enjoy every precious year.

Your marriage has grown older
as you've looked at the work you've done;
You can see it is even more precious
than when you first begun.

Martha Kennon
MY GRANDCHILD
The door bell rings, the door swings wide
Yes here he comes, that little guy.

So full of life, giving lots of hugs,
My heart just swells with loving tugs.

Coat comes off, thrown in a chair.
The cap is tossed without a care.

He checks the kitchen and the cookie jar
For cookies baked or a candy bar.

His favorite book is then retrieved,
And then he climbs upon my knee

To hear me read line after line
The words he's heard a million times.

Radiance, Love, Warmth and Joy,
All wrapped up in this little boy.

Marion L Anderson
OUR LORD HE IS CRYING

Dedicated to my parents John S. MacFarlane. And Helenina Cameron MacFarlane for their love and devotion

Listen all my children, harken to my voice
All is not lost, you still have a choice
Just open your hearts, and open your eyes
The signs are all there, just look to the skies

Too many stories, Too many lies
Oh listen my children, Our Lord He still cries
What more can He say, what more can He do
His Son died on the cross. For me and for you

Oh why won't you listen, Why can't you see
Our Lord He has told us. To watch the fig tree.
Oh listen my children, all is not lost.
Just open your hearts. There's simply no cost
Our Lord He is crying. The time it draws nigh
The choice is now yours. To live or to die.

Lillian K Clark
A ROAD CALLED "HURRY"
The road called "Hurry" is
wide and bright
And its ditches are narrow
and sharp,
And up ahead is a gleaming
light—with just a <u>hint</u>
of a coming night.
So you pick up your skirts,
and get poised for flight,
and you <u>Go</u>!

Linda Diane Fortney
THOSE GOLDEN YEARS

To Mom and Dad, on their Fiftieth Anniversary. Thanks for all the love, courage, and strength that you have given our family.

It's been 50 years since mom and dad were wed,
At the old homeplace is where their vows were said.
They were both young then with hearts of youthful song,
As time passed on they tried very hard to make a happy home.
In the spring of 39, Sandra, the first child was born.
Her biggest dream was to sing, play a piano, and a French horn.

Almost two years later, mom bore dad a son,
They were both happy as could be,
They thought Duane would be the last one.

The kids settled in the cozy house that daddy built,
While mom sat by the fire working on homemade quilts.
Now just about the time they thought their lives were complete,
Along came another baby and that was me. I caused utter chaos
Among the family, but we lived happily together.

All the family has grown now, with families of our own,
And sometimes I wonder how mom and dad survived the child raising disaster zone.

This brings us to our reason tonight for being here,
It is to celebrate our parents' wedding anniversary of 50 golden years.

Brandi Mathias
THE CIVIL WAR

For my family, friends, and all those striving for world peace.

Oh dear moon shall you n'er rest
for the men of the South are trying their best.
The men of the North need no direction
but hope for some peace and lots of protection.

The men of the war see no joy
for they are being killed both man and boy.
Their wives and children are in grief

for they had to bury them underneath.

The towns are all ruined
and there is no peace,
but hope for salvation
will e'er increase.

Robert Hugh Dishon Jr
ETERNAL AMOUR
Ageless, timeless, before first flight, growing weary, filled with fright.
I seek the love we had before, the one we shared on pristine shores.
Eons spent, searching for the loving heart, has it always been ending, will it ever start.
Our spirits passed, crossing our course, could it be, was it her . . . . .
Higher planes on paths we've traveled, we were joined again . . .
Strands of memories were unraveled.
Reaching places, in distant pasts removed, knowing, sensing, haunting, déjà vu.
All the feelings in our souls rekindled, energy spent, guarded, damaged, spindled.
Enmeshed once more, emotions enthralled, tearing down barriers, of time, endless walls.
But only a fragment of time has passed, lost yet again in a spacial mask.

So the journey, and search, begins anew, the beginning is only an end to work through.
Propelled into time, heretofore, boundaries undefined, wandering, searching, that one love to find.
Ageless, timeless, before first flight, growing weary, driven, to excite . . .
We seek the love we had before, the one we shared on pristine shores.
To touch you again, just once more, let us be one, cease this torment,
Eternal amour.

Kimberley Lavorante
CONFINED MINDS

Dedicated to: My Mom and Dad For their encouragement and understanding

Their world
So small
And uninviting
So closed
And mind undelighting
Yet they raised
Me loving
And taught me giving
And brought me up
Properly
With all their training
But still they seem
So far away
Their heads all cluttered
With thoughts demeaning
Definitely not where
My mind is beaming
But close we'll stay
To a certain degree
Because after all
We are a loving
Family

Jean Willis
PAINTED ON SMILE
Clown,
Caught in a storm of green & gold & red,

Clown,
With a tall black hat upon your head.

Smile,
Painted upon your face for eternity,

Smile,
Clown no matter how sad you may be.

Globe,
Of glass will hold you prisoner always,

Globe,
Of glass holds your empty eyes and vacant gaze.

Clown,
In a glass house with storm of glitter raging,

Clown,
Our lives, how alike they are!
Isn't it amazing.

Jan Johnson
WILL I SEE HIM AGAIN
From the moment our eyes met and our lips touched
And he whispered
"When will I see you again?"
I have waited . . . .
Anxiously,
somewhat impatiently,
waited,
To be held in his arm once more.

As the days passed
ever so slowly
Visions of him constantly entered my thoughts,
Each day brought the same age-old question . . .
"Will he call?"
"Will I see him again?"
Still . . . .
I waited.

Finally, the day I had so anxiously waited for has arrived
But, the fear of him not calling was far worse
than the wait for his call,
And with each ring of the phone
my heart asks . . .
"Will he call?"
"Will I see him tonight?"
Again . . . .
I waited.

Now, as I lay,
ever so peaceful in his arms
After an evening of magical love,
The question returns once more . . . .
"Will he call?"
"When will I see him again?"
And once more
I wait . . . .
Anxiously,
Somewhat impatiently,
wait . . . .
For his next call.

Richard M Lea
FROM MY GARDEN

To my best friend, my wife Virginia.

As I looked at the world around me
In reflective contemplation
A little boy appeared
In whose eyes I saw trust

For an instant my mind perceived
A strange angelic vision
The lady of my dreams
In whose eyes I saw love

And as I strolled from my garden
Down the lane by the tracks
There appeared a poor man in rags
In whose eyes I saw nothing

This was disturbing indeed
And in my silent reverie
I knelt beneath a shady tree
To seek an answer from God

Soon, a muffled voice whispered
Down deep in my soul
Trust and love never blossoms
In those we ignore

Nina Blazier
THE FORGOTTEN CHILD
"Jesus, where's my mommy and daddy?
I know they love me, I have no doubt.
But, where are they?—Please help me!
I want to tell them—I need them now."

I'm taken care of in every way, but—
I need <u>you</u>——what more can I say?
I have needs just like you do—yet
Mommy and Daddy, where are you?

I miss your smiles and hugs and kisses
Your laughs and jokes and hits and misses.
My needs are plenty—my troubles few,—but—
Mommy and Daddy, where are you?

Jesus loves me, this I know.
I don't need gifts to tell me so.
To see your smiles and hold your hand—
"Jesus, tell me where they are——
<u>again</u>.

Deborah Lynn Jex
LONELY PEOPLE
Such lonely people, in this world.
Gazing hungry eyes, reaching out of empty souls.
They come together for a night, or a day.
Engulfed by darkness, two people become one,
Never speaking; Never watching.
Without feelings, they make love.

Morning arrives, silent and cold.
Each lonely person, still empty inside.
Each rises to go without glancing back.
Why go on? Night after night.
Living a life of one night stands.

Calloused feelings belong to each one.
Dreams long gone, lost to an insensitive world.
Trying never to care, but always hoping,
That someday they will find a better way
to ease the pain of loneliness.

Deborah L Baker
THE SEARCH
We go searching, searching, searching,
and find—
What?
A love that will not last,
A friend who will not stay,
A life that cannot be endured?

We find all of these in our little world,
but really, What are we searching for?
Is it truth, love, justice, an understanding of one another?
Or do we search for—
Ourselves?

Tiffany Krell
MY SHADOW
Where I go
My shadow goes
Why it follows me
I do not know
It may be watching me
Like death
Watches old people
Waiting for me to make a wrong move
I do not know
But
Where I go
My shadow goes

Jeff Barber
AND SO IT IS
I gazed upon your eyes,
I saw the pain,
I saw the suffering,
I saw the questions?
I saw the hurt,
I saw the physical changes,
I saw the tears.
I gave a smile,
I gave a hug,
I touched you.
I shed some tears,
I laughed.
I was compassionate,
I listened.
I won't always be there, physically.
I am but now, in heart, soul, essence
And so it is!

Douglas Earl Bolton

Douglas Earl Bolton
FORGIVE THIS FOOL
Life has been good to me, a fool,
Each experience of life a very good school.
Ungrateful indeed forever I'd be,
If I did not share my thoughts with thee.

Your gentle voice, your caring touch,
Your friendship is worth so very much.
Without you sharing your life with me,

Mine would be a life of pure misery.

If in the weakness of this fool
Thoughtless acts become the rule,
Be bigger, better, angel mine,
Forgive this fool from time to time.

Perfection is worth striving for,
This fool has not yet reached that door.
Be gentle, therefore, and loving too.
This is not foolishness, my love for you.

Forgiveness is from Heaven above,
Will you forgive this fool, my love?
Reach out your hand, put it into mine,
I'd like you for my Valentine.

SRI-Chang Le' Rishi
**** MISSING YOU ****

Dedicated to the most loveliest woman this world may have ever known (my inspiring angel): Ms. Camilita M. Moore

My Darling Angel,

The morning sun shine, the glistening dew, inspire me with missing you.

The birds, the bees, the creatures too, remind me of the harmony and love I Would Like to share with you.

But . . . my darling dear, what can I do?
I'm hopelessly Lying Here . . .
"missing you."

The frowns, the smiles, the laughter and tears, up came my soul mate through all these years.

The love we could share in the park, your tingling voice could ignite the spark.

I want to say "I LOVE YOU" . . .,
but what good would it do,
"you see," I'm just lying here . . .
"Missing you."

But maybe soon the day will come,
when all Soul Mates will be as one.
Then . . . no more tears, no more feeling blue, no more lying here . . .
MISSING YOU

Richard L Barkley Jr
I STAND ALONE

I stand alone,
I walk alone
I exist, from day to day
I want to be happy,
to love,
and be loved in return
I want to share,
with one who cares,
and live a quiet life
And, while I share,
with one who cares,
We'll climb mountains,
and wade streams
But, most of all,
we'll share our dreams.

Katie Charbono
LOVE

I dedicate this poem to my parents whom I love. And all of my friends.

At the beginning of time, there was a feeling
This feeling had everything that was filled with kindness
Man and woman clashing together making one, caring for each other
This feeling wasn't hate, it wasn't greed,
it was a feeling even the meanest of people had
This feeling was felt by: Joseph and Mary,
Adam and Eve
This feeling was like the feeling of holding a new born baby
This feeling is the strongest of powers
This is love

Kathy Pritchard

Kathy Pritchard
ESSENCE OF LOVE

To my Parkay: Mitch Carlson. You've put so much laughter, peace, joy and love in my heart. Waiting is hard but to me "You're" worth your weight in gold. I love you Mitch!

Hide not from the shadows
Of your past
For it may be a cold
And shallow one

Reach out and let the softness
Touch you
Be guided by the warmness
Of your heart

Share with me your visions
Hopes and dreams
That our hearts may be
United as one

Let the essence of love
Surround you
Such reflecting the radiance
From one to the other

Fear not from what I have
To offer
Simply live on what I have
To give.

Helen M Cassidy
CUPID'S BOW

To my husband Bob whom I love very much

February 14th is for lovers
Above us Cupid hovers
He has his arrows hot
As he puts us on the spot
He sends each heated dart into flight
And we wonder into whose heart it will light.

S Craig Lannom
A SON'S PRAYER

There are so many questions
I have yet to ask
Why must you go
before answering

There are so many sights
I have yet to see
Why must you go
before showing

There are so many topics
I have yet to learn
Why must you go
before teaching

There are so many
things we need to do
Come back Dad
and let's start them.

Margaret H High
OPEN SEASON

To Mom & Dad—who have not only thought me capable of anything, but have also taught me how to be

Hunting season on the heart is open all year round
The hunter stalks his prey
wherever hearts are found.
The hunter stalks, he's fully armed—
A touch, caress, and fatal charm.
The heart is fleet, ever aware
Of the hunter—danger in the air.
The heart, the hunt, the chase is long
Enchantment rules, excitement strong.
Pursuit of heart, pursuit of dreams,
The hunter rules—or so it seems.
But hearts survive the constant chase
The hunter's heart is in the race
Snared by love, trapped by schemes
The heart, the hunter—the same in dreams

Doris Israel
JEWELS—MY PARENTS

Dedicated to my parents, Flo & Johnie Wachter, who provided a happy loving home. BY: their daughter, Doris Israel

Thank God for a loving home
For arms that embraced me tenderly
For faith instilled in early years
To help allay all fears.

Home is a place where love is real
And cooking scents the air
Where aroma of bread is baking
Because of a mother's loving care.

Home is a place of happiness
Hugs, affection and such
Home is a place where love bears flower
And living means so much.

My parents instill contentment and happiness
As they pass along the way
And I see two hands entwining gently
At the closing of the day.

As they celebrate 70 years together
There's love and pride in my heart for them
And many a grateful thought
The cherished memories of years gone by
And the joys they both have brought.

Nikol P Dickens
WITHOUT YOU

This poem was written for my "Fortune" and is dedicated to my mother, Dr. Alice M. Dickens

As I sit here, alone and crying I think of you
One moment you were here and we were together and now you're gone . . .
It all happened so very fast, where did we go wrong. Where did I go wrong?
The amount of pain I'm feeling is the amount of love I have for you
Without you is the way I'd hate to be but the way I am.
Days have passed and we have yet to speak—
The time that lies between us grows deeper each moment—
With each breath I take I can feel all the words I want to say to you press to escape from my lips,
But you're not around, so I sit here quietly, with no one to trust.

Robert L Bousquet Jr
THIS PEN

To my wife, Cindy

What can I say
With this awkward old pen
It fails to relate how I feel
Just holding your hand
A warm sweet smile
That makes my heart glow
Feelings I'm sure
This old pen couldn't know
So much to say
That hasn't been said
But I'll wait 'til I see you
And put this old pen to bed

Julieanne Kucera

Julieanne Kucera
SUCCESS

This is dedicated to my children Who inspire me daily Amanda and Tyler

We once focused
On being
Dressed for Success

Which only led
To being
Stressed for Success

And with children
We became
Blessed for Success

Thank you Lord!

Charles Smeltzer
THE HORN

For Xiao Fahn

Starvation is painful, starvation is slow;
free in their stupor from the mentality of the well-fed, they are not afraid.
Inflated death masked children struggle thru' the bush supported by toothpicks as they forage away their short lives indelicately—Frantically searching through soil and stool for the seeds that will save their lives and

bathe their souls, to be freed of want, to know the feeling of full-filment, to not be able to see the hunger in their eyes, in their cries, in their silence.
So, to you, and to me, Feel freed by the startling revelation that life is dark, life is not very pretty.
In the underworld of the minute that lasts for a year, in the landscape of the horn, it rings very clear

Shirley Horne
I HEARD A RAINBOW

To my Ray and Raysie, both musicians.

A golden vibrato shimmering upward—
Soft blue rhythm becoming
A cool violet, a sweet song flying free,
Then the radiance of a florid jazz sax
Brilliant improvisation swinging into the air,
And the flashy red abandon of the trumpet,
With a keyboard's crystalline splashes,
Then a jagged syncopation
Smoothed out by a slide upward,
Glided into a sky I was listening to.

Stacie Hixson
MY FARAWAY FRIEND
As I walk alone,
I hear the ocean crashing
upon the distant cliffs.
There is strength in its powerful waves
and gentleness in its soothing sound—
a sound that calls me from afar.
"Come," it calls,
"and spend some time with me."
I talk to the ocean
and it listens with silent intensity.
The ocean reaches up
to shower me
with watery kisses
and comforts me with words
of quiet wisdom.
And when I leave
I am filled with peace.
The ocean calls to me,
and I turn to wave.
"Goodbye," it calls
"and come see me again."

Tony Napoletano
DO YOU LOVE? IN THE DESERT, WHERE THE WILD THINGS GO?

For Aimee Ro, as always. Keep well, Hon.

The desert dweller awoke before dawn.
He struggled into a trance
And dragged himself across the sand
on dying pillars of liquid fire.

Calling to the shrine where the traveller dwells in hiding,
All day watching tiny monsters make their rounds.
They bear his own face.

Dreams of love and desire are here.
The girl calls to him softly,
Staring at her reflection in the mirror.
She eyes her nakedness, the gentle curves of her breasts
Solemnly with wonder.
He lays behind her,
Wrapped in the cotton slumber blanket,
Dreaming endlessly of an excited climax.

Love is the desert dweller
Moving alone in the strange world
that calls all to welcome the machine with open arms.
The fingers of the damned seek
purchase of his last bit of cloth,
Eager to gouge his weather-beaten skin
His head reels with a love drought,
With the loss of a dwelling place,
With the loss of sustenance.

Love is the nomad who waits.
He'll wait for her if he has to.

Kim M Aalaie
GIFT OF MINE

Dedicated to Atieh Renee

Four years ago
God gave to me,
A precious gift
of what love can be.

Something to cherish
So adventurous, yet mild
Four short years ago
He gave me my child.

Life has been quite different
In fact, in a whirl,
Since God gave to me
my sweet baby girl.

Yet, I wouldn't change nothing
or go back in time.
I wouldn't take anything
for that gift of mine!

Elizabeth Grell
CLOUDS
Within a mystical distance
between earth and the hemispherical waves that caress the paths of the universe,
Lie countless figurations
nurturing the spacious sky,
sending air rockets engraving
images of paper satin dolls,
giving birth to seedless
fountains of futurity.

Circular minstrels hovering the
atmosphere, begin dancing,
fulfilling nakedness.
Let lies tender explosions of love,
earth settles, becomes sexually
involved, enriched, seduced by
virgin maidens.

This child that is received,
becomes the human of nature,
The sun shines for him, the
clouds rain for him,
And only he cries for himself.
These teardrops, victim of rain,
imprisoned by clouds.

Nikki Agosta
A NEW DAY
Dew Drops glisten on newly
Sprung grass.
As the dawn arrives over the
Horizon
Seasons change
And a new day begins.
A new day without you.
The birds outside are singing
The song of spring.
But it sounds like the blues
To me.
A new day is beginning.
A new day without you.
Everything is so alive
But it all seems dead to me.
It's just a new day.
A new day without you.
A spring wind is blowing.
But inside my soul
A cold winter wind blows.
It's just a new day without you.

Jessica Ward
SET FREE
As time goes by,
it's time for me to fly.

Though I don't want to go,
it must be done, I know.

Terrified of what might come to be,
I shed a tear and set myself free.

Though it hurts inside,
it's something I must hide.

To live forever after,
and know what I did was for the better.

Nellie Pezzani

Nellie Pezzani
TWO HEARTS

Dedicated to my wonderful son and daughter-in-law, Wayne and Jacki Gray

When God joins the hearts of two,
The world's a happy place.
There's magic in the smallest touch,
And love in each embrace.

When two hearts are joined together,
And love entwines the soul,
Happy spirits will stay young forever.
There is no growing old.

When two hearts are joined together,
And laughter fills the rooms,
Love grows, and is eternal.
Their world's in perfect tune.

Brian Allen Borchardt
PRECIOUS CHILDREN
Many, many children born each day
Numerous children
Your children, my children, God's children
Dependent children who have no say
Even before their birthday
Nine months of frown and grin
Began long ago with original sin
Where are all the children today?

Childless parents' wanting a child
Waiting, yearning, waiting, yearning
South Korea once made it mild
But, no more as we are learning
Times are again getting wild
For some, the emptiness continues to wring.

G C Gillies
THY PRISM HEART
Flowers drift in meadows wide
Creating specks of color on thine eyes
Resembling an artist's palette long forgot
Within thy prism heart.

Petals sprinkled with morning dew
Shed tears of yearning for you
Sweet memories of our love shall start
Aching in thy prism heart.

Love once known is fading fast
Creating nothing but a shadowy cast
Reflection upon face and eyes impart
Glimpses of thy prism heart.

Lisa Hurley
THE UNKNOWN HAPPINESS
It begins in a daze
It slowly moves into trust
A trust that can not be broken
We knew so little, but
Learned a lot
It seems to buzz
Worry and fear, Don't
Seem so fierce with you
Strange people, say I know
They taunt and tease
Then leave
You're patient, you understand
I'm happy with you
Yet I'm not sure I should be

Isaac Jay Kennedy
GROWING OLD GRACEFULLY
There comes a time in each one's life
When life becomes more dear.
It's when the sun is setting lower still,
And the end is drawing near.
When all things thus said or done
Begin to show their wear,
And priorities are changed or pushed aside
With the loss of teeth and hair.
The eyes cannot see as well anymore
The things that meant so much.
The tendons have lost their flexibility
And the fingers their loving touch.
All foods taste basically the same,
And words are hard to understand.
The mind begins to err and wander.
Is Alzheimer's close at hand?
Have no fear you are losing it all now.
It is all meant this way to be.
Pay heed to what your body is telling you:
"Slow down. Grow old gracefully."

Robbie Darden
ONE AND ONE, THAT MAKES US TWO

For Krista and all the children of the world who walk hand in hand with their mothers.

One and one, that makes us two—
We are special, me and you.

Story books and nursery rhymes—
what a very precious time.

Cuddle close now, and you'll see—

That you mean the most to me!

You are my hopes and dreams, my shining star—
Please, my babe, never wander too far.

It's you and me, side by side—
If you need, I'll be your guide,

I'm rocking you in this old rocking chair—
wondering if you'll know how much I care.

Together—we'll learn and grow—
And someday—you'll turn and go.

But babe, when you do, I won't be sad—
Your love's the sweetest, I've ever had.

Grow strong and be happy, and learn to love—
It's a beautiful world my little dove!

One and one, that makes us two—
We are special me and you!

Boz Ahmadi

Boz Ahmadi
IN THE BELLY OF MY FATHER'S LAND

In the belly of my father's land
Where he ploughed and planted
seeds,
in endless strands

To be respectable, to work and
be free

Perturbed predicament, one did
not foresee

To lose the land passed down
generation to generation

And father, shooting himself in the
head—land was his passion

He fought in two wars—a
highly patriotic man

Proud and tough—hard work
through his life span.

His prejudice and shortcomings
are buried with him now

Not much has changed, the
land, just faded somehow

Deborah L Jensen
WHISPERS IN THE WIND

Further—further, until we collide no more. Our thoughts, our dreams, our happiness—no longer shared as one.

Splash—splash, against the shore for you and I can be no more. The beauty which existed once, is fading quickly and can hardly be seen. Straining ever so harshly to see the speck of beauty struggling to remain being.

Fading—fading . . . now no more, sight longing to be seen in the distant shadows far beyond. Evil awaits the borders of the shore—yet the tide is lowering.

No—no, do not let me sink, I do not want to die under the sea. Engulf me not and once again I shall be free.

Marshall G Smith
THIS "BEAUTIFUL" PLACE CALLED "HEAVEN"

To the memory of my daughter, B. Diane Smith, My sisters, Janet Louise, Esther Kathleen and Gellaine. My Grandparents, William R. and Betty T. Goodin

I'm dreaming of a place called "Heaven"
Where there's no pain nor sorrow or tears.
Where "Flowers" do bloom in abundance
And cares are gone like the years.

I'm preparing to make that journey,
Whether it's sooner or later to be,
I'm wanting to visit that "City"
Where beauty abounds everywhere.
Then on to the Mountains and Rivers
That I enjoyed while living down here.

The troubles, trials and sorrow
We're bearing while living on earth.
This "Beautiful" place "God" gave us, but not to mar or Disperse!
Still it can not compare with the "Promise,"
Of the "Heavenly Home" in "His Word."

This "Beautiful" place called "Heaven"
I'm longing more to see.
Where friends from the past are waiting,
And my "Dear Mother' I'll see,
standing beside of "Lord Jesus"
Just waiting to welcome Me!.

Sheila Ann Kostelecky
THE GAME OF LIFE

To Michael Mortensen, proof that dreams really do come true.

I don't know where the chips will land,
Only that you must play each hand.
The cards are marked, so you be wise.
Watch each glance of the dealer's eyes.
Place your bets with the utmost care,
'Cause his three Jacks beats your two pair.

Agnes G Woodard
MY FRIEND

Dedicated to: Lucy Brannan— "a very dear friend," and to my mother: Mary Taylor, who through her love and prayers has guided my every footstep.

I've met a lot of people,
Some near and some far away
But the friend I hold true,
Is a friend, such as you,
Whose friendship never strays.

You've known just when and what to say
To make my day seem brighter
With outstretched arms, like a touch from God
You make my burdens lighter.

Your roots are deep and lasting
The kind that has no end,
So I want to say I thank you
For being a friend, "My Friend"

Jody Appleyard
UNTOLD LOVE

This poem is dedicated to Craig, my one and only inspiration.

My love for him is kept inside;
It is a secret I must hide.
He can not know the way I feel,
Although my love for him is real.
I fear he'd treat me differently;
Good friends no longer we could be.
I want to share my love with him
But my daydreams are growing dim.
If only he would call my name,
Then we could finally end this game
That he's been playing with my heart.
And then we two would never part.

Maxine Hannum
THOUGHT

To my three children Jill, Jane, and Dan—Who have it all.

Thought precedes emotions
And thinking creates feeling.
It, in turn, foregoes doing.
Imagination is powerful
And needs motivating.

We have it all
Within our grasp.
So shatter not
Your self image,
And know
What we do not
Imagine is the
Very most important part.

Delve into what seems
Beyond reach
And make it what you are.

You have it all.

Amanda French
I HAVE A FRIEND

I have a friend so near to me.
A friend I know who'll always be.
To guide me through each day I live.
He always has so much to give.
I love him more and more each day.
He always knows just what to say.
I hear his voice inside my head.
I talk to him each night in bed.
The thing that makes it all so real.
He always knows just how I feel.
And although I've never seen his face.
I know in heaven I'll have a place

Gregg H Smallwood
A NEW YEAR'S EVE FEELING

To the people whom I have met, and the ones I have not yet.

Looked into your eyes to find what one may see.
New Year's is the best time to spend a romantic eve.
It brings people close together, others far apart.
Let us remember people who are close to our heart.
New Year's is the time for everyone to be near.
Respecting resolutions in which some may make.
Remembering not to boast, however give, and take.

Compassion finds a beautiful, and extraordinary place.
New Year happiness, and cheer should be all that we need.
For togetherness, and a smile makes the beauty of the face.

May we all make a resolution to help one another.
Like a sister or maybe a dedicated brother.
For if we should lose the warmth of a friend;
All mankind will come to an end.

Walter Gilliam

Walter Gilliam
GROWING OLD

*To my son "Akim"
May God bless you always.*

Youth has its moments like trees in bloom,
Full of life and beauty and sometimes gloom,
But the beauty of life is when it reaches full bloom.
When we are young we waste precious time chasing
Folly and fame.
Not realizing what it takes to achieve worthwhile gains.
So what part of life does one wish to retain?
To grow old is a blessing so I'm told,
Memories of our youth are to cherish and hold,
O' but how sweet it is when we've reached our goals.
All the hustle and bustle have come to a stop,
Debts are paid and we're out of hock,
No more getting up early to beat the clock,
How sweet it is to hear the grandchildren say
"I love you pop."

Now as we take an afternoon stroll,

Thinking about what used to be while steadily growing old.
No more towing the line lifting that bale,
Because now we can relax and wait on monthly payments
By U.S. mail.
Growing old is a blessing. I'm proud because God has
Blessed my soul. As a youth, I listened to my parents and
Did what I was told.
I feel great and no one but I knows, today I'm grateful and
Blessed to be growing old.

Julie Leckband
WINTER

A cold Thursday morning in February,
Surrounded by white.
Glance out the window and
View an Arctic scene.
Skies without color stretch over vast hills of sugar.
The world seems lonely.
My backyard oak is stripped of foliage,
Robbed of summary attire.
The early sun, Great Illuminator,
Rises in the east,
But isn't strong enough, great enough,
To melt enormous sheets of ice.
Defeated rays are bright though.
Bright, off a natural frozen mirror,
And into my eyes.
What season holds longer than winter?
Now, again, flakes of frost fall.
Dancing, teasing.
Building soft piles of snow on my sleeping garden.
What season holds longer?
Longer than winter?

Eunice I Standley
THE GIRLS IN OUR FAMILY

Dedicated to my mother

"Hi There"! Alana says with a big traffic stopping grin
as she wobbles across the room on 14 month old legs.

"Thank you!" comes unexpectedly from
Katie, as her sweet face beams
Behind the tray of the high chair.
"Only 18 months old, you say"?

"My Mother said I was never to go into the deep end of the pool"!
Came Mary Jo's 10 year old obedient reply
to her surprised and delighted Grandfather.

"I hate to be so much trouble," whispers Mother, as her 92 years
Causes her steps to falter,
and require the aid of another's strength.

Our girls are so very lovely,
each in her own special way.
They lighten our load, put a song in our hearts,
and add sparkle to the old Family Tree.

Epilogue
Two more little girls have joined our Tree,
Amy and Holly, as sweet as can be.
Mother breathes a prayer, as her head bends low,
Lord, care for my babies when I go.

Rhonda Limpert
THE FATHER-IN-LAW I NEVER HAD

This poem is dedicated to Bill Limpert, he was loved by one and all. "May he rest in peace."

Why did you have to leave so soon?
Everything I dreamed of is now all ruined.
The talks we could have had about your son,
how much I wanted to tell you,
he's the one I love.
I never got to tell you how much "I love you."
Why did I have to be such a fool?
Now you've gone up to the sky,
and left me all alone to cry.
Your wife and family need you home,
you can't leave them here all alone.
They try to hide the pain they feel,
but deep inside I know it's real.
I know you are watching us all from up there,
please keep in mind how much we all care.
We'll be thinking about you as each day goes by,
we'll hold our heads up and try not to cry.

Dennis "Pete" Owens
LONELY NIGHT

In the middle of night I jerk awake,
What was that awful sound?
I stare at the walls and start to shake;
There's no one to be found . . .

No loving hand to ease my nerves,
Or wipe my tears away;
No one to smile and kiss my face,
In this hell in which I stay . . .

So I lie awake this lonely night,
With freedom on my mind;
And I think of things now out of sight,
Like the girl I left behind . . .

And I realize, in real surprise,
The sound I thought I heard:
It was a lonely heart, being torn apart,
By a jailer's angry word.

Sheila Merrill
BREAK-UPS!

Walking through the halls,
hoping to see you soon,
and there you were,
looking cool by your girl's locker.
While walking past, we exchanged smiles,
Then there was a moment of just our world,
Until you kissed.
Then I knew it was all over for us,
We were a thing of the past,
you had left me in the dust,
while you had gone on to
experience with your life and others.

Robert P Cooper
FOREVER/LOVE

To my son Bobby and his bride Michele on their wedding day—Forever/Love

Love is something constant,
It is with us every day
Our love for the Almighty,
Is the force that makes us pray
The love we have within us,
Flows forth in many ways
And the power of love gets greater,
With every passing day
Why hide our love inside us,
Let's show it off to all
For what better thing to answer,
Than the strains of love's sweet call
So as long, as there is an earth below us
And a sky, so high above
Let's keep our happiness glowing,
With a fuel we know, as love

Johnny Marshall III
THE WINTER WIND

The winter wind is whistling,
And seems to never tire;
While inside we're listening,
To the crackling of the fire.

A chilly breeze marks the beginning of a new season,
As it blows through the boughs of the lonesome pines;
And we sit there thinking that it's the reason,
For the chills running down our spines.

The winter wind is screeching,
As though it barely could;
While inside we're reaching,
For another stick of wood.

Rebecca Lynne Chaput

Rebecca Lynne Chaput
CALLED TO CHRIST THROUGH PRAYER

Grasping the reality of dreams—To touch rainbows with Faith, Belief, & Prayers.
An "unconditional love" of true friendships; Found & Cherished.
One walk within Christ; Treasured for Remembrance--Forever and Always; I thank you Vickie Schweitzer & James Rotundi . .

Feeling you sleep;
Lie dormant.
Miss presence within.
Known peace; contentment.
Felt emptiness;
As if you have gone.
Longer days upon days;
Each and every moment;
Time passes slowly.
Thoughts of you, Lord;
I question your absence,
Beg for return.
Test of faith,
Strengthens my belief.
Search for reason.
Want this void to pass;
Why remaining absence?
Light seen through aching darkness.
Without hurriedness; must walk with patience and time.
Turn to prayer upon prayer; called to Christ.
"He" has been waiting.
Bow before image; grasp tightly at cross of faith.
Spoken words; whispered tears.
Asked to dream; Asleep but awakened. Kneeling before you, Lord—Image clear. Quickly fades as you're drawn to my within. Felt roots planted upon my heart. Soul connects as union complete of Father, Son, and myself.
No longer asleep—awake; thy Lord lies deep within.

Michelle McLaughlin
PRINCESS

Why, oh why fair maiden,
Did you not believe my words,
Could you not believe that you could be,
The one so beautiful and carefree.

Was there fear in your heart,
Or was it madness to your ears,
To believe in kissing me, a Frog,
I am here for a purpose, please come along.

Let not your eyes deceive you,
For I have been spelled for many years,
To find such a beauty, so pure and sweet,
I have come to sweep you off your feet.

Do not hesitate, for there's not much time,
Let's go, let's hurry to that Palace of mine,
But please first kiss me to prove it's true,
I assure you I am a Prince, Would you be my Princess too?

Barbara Walker
BROKEN HEARTED GIRL

To family & Oprah Winfrey & Michael Jordan

A Broken Hearted Girl
Travels
From town to town
Trying
So desperately to forget her
Ex-Romeo
To forget about his sweet lies
And
Broken Promises made to her
ALL ALONE
By Her Ex-Romeo
He promised her
She'd be his bride
And
He'd come home every night
But
He married another girl instead.

Sharon (Pierson) Daniels
SINCE TIME ALLOWS MOST ANYTHING

I dedicate this poem to my husband, Randy, and our children, family, and friends, Because you are everything to me.

Since time allows most anything
And it keeps moving on,
I know that I must find my place
before my time is gone.
To share myself with you is time,
time to me so dear,
To waste my time so foolishly
Is time without you near.

Kim Hope Lawrence
REGAINING LIFE'S ROMANCE

In life 'tis strange what fates we weave
With seeming lack of programmed ease
Our intent is true but our minds are vague
Too often lost in memory's haze

The sorrow is deep; the cup seems full
The pattern appeared made when we first entered this school
Can the heart be so wrong—must the head always rule
Why can't we live like saints instead of playing the fools
Our lives lose the passion of life's true romance
'Tis because of mortality's persistent advance
Laughter is drowned by boredom's refrain
Innovation, creativity cause fear to the mundane
Let the time be now when the lamb is blessed
And the tiger is hailed for his fight for ignorance's death

Cathy Joe Malecki
HEARTWARMING FRIENDSHIP

I dedicate this poem to Scott, a caring, sensitive, wonderful and the most beautiful man I know. "I Love You"

You are the one who makes each day fun
You are the one who gives me your kind love
You seem to be the perfect friend
So I know we'll be together till the end.
For no matter what you're always there
And no matter what you always care.
A part of you has grown in me
And so you see it's you and me
Together for always and never apart
Maybe in distance, but never in heart.

Patricia Ann (Rando) Kaplan
WINTER WATCH
In the cool, dark night I can hear
Crickets chirping their last sweet song,
The soft breeze whispering in my ear
And see the weeping willows long.

Flowers vanish, their colors replaced,
In the leaves of the still standing trees.
Snowflakes drift, all prettily laced,
Zigzagging down in the breeze.

Old man winter is soon to be heard,
When earth snuggles under blankets of white,
And the beautiful song of the bird
Turns south in its homeward flight.

Sylvia Paris Stewart
ODD COUPLES
Today I cleaned my dresser drawer,
a pile of socks lay on the floor;
battered, limp, perverse, irate,
for not one of them possess a mate.

Clinging to one another, though each alone,
they manage their loss as I have my own.

How absurd to think of a sock's remorse,
but when compared with my life's course;
as the one I loved, who had gone astray,
their loved one lost, in the wash, one day.

Their faithful service not once rewarded,
So if not a pair should they be discarded?

No! I say, No! I exclaim,
I ignore the ridicule, inhabit no shame,
endure each conflict without a scratch,
When mocked because my socks don't match!

Charles Andrew Mc Cue
MY GUARDIAN PHANTASM

In love with a ghost—From one ghost to another—Indeed—Wingo the friendly ghost—

O so holy
W/ a ghostly glowing halo above thee
& you, smiling so placidly
hauntingly yet saintly . . .
Yes, and I still do remember you—faintly
Though this image is swiftly fading
W/in my brainwaves—receding
& when I die won't you receive me
clasp me and show me
A little cottage in Elysium
Less than eternity
Yet with a dreamy stream flowing,
whispering ever so melodiously
in an emerald foliaged distance
& so for a while contentment
W/ your smile so comforting
W/in some wondrous respite of mystical harmony
one temporary, transitory interval
Before my next sojourn is chosen
And the dream W/in our souls is forever frozen—again . . .

O, Eternal Being please protect us
Through this flowing un-reality
And with our souls most ghostly saviour
Please keep us together, as one, with thee . . .
O, my Eternal Being . . .

Ruth Marie DeHeck
IN YOUR ARMS
In your arms I feel safe and warm
Nothing can harm me there.
Your love is a wall that can't be broken
In your arms I feel alive and strong.
Nothing can strike me then
In your arms I am whole.
Nothing can hurt me there
When I'm in your arms disaster cannot reach me.

Together we've built a barrier
nothing can shatter
In your arms I am fulfilled
Nothing else matters there.
In your arms I take comfort
Refuge is always there.
I cannot wait to be in your arms once again.

Estus Marsalis Smith
A WOMAN

To My Wonderful Children; Whom I Love Very Much,Buddy Allen and Teresa Louise Smith. Daddy

Through darkness as cold as death at the end of life's evil journey. There lies a love bound by destruction and cursed by a woman's lust of broken desire. Behind it lies a heart torn and severed from a lady's sharpened blade of passion. And even further we find a great warrior of life's tremendous battle. His eyes swollen with tears from wounds of sorrow. For he has lost! Honor he has lost and pity has come to his soul. Yet life has he still to face. Memories still burn life fire through his mind. A curse from a woman's wicked love. Black is the heart of her who thinks she is the destruction of men. Her soul spits fire upon those who lust for her enchantment. And she will destroy the hearts of many.
What a woman she must be!

Edna Arroyo
ALL NIGHT LONG
It was a cold winter night
when I asked you to dance
Suddenly, I was not cold any
All I felt was the warmth of your body
near me,
your kisses, your caresses . . .

Now it is still cold
as I am writing this
but the sweet memories
of that dance
keep me going all night long . . .

Agnes (Drumwright) Meacham
COUNT YOUR BLESSINGS
When the days are dark and dreary
and you really feel let down.
Go get a pen and a notebook, and you can fill every line—
Just write down, one by one, the blessings God gives you each day.
And I promise you it won't be long
until you are feeling fine.
But don't leave out a single thing
that God has done for you.
And please remember that He always provides and takes good care of you.
There is also beauty all around us,
and He gives us such marvelous things.
Man gets the praise, but God gives the knowledge and the talent too.
So count your many blessings for you will never realize
How many, many blessings God gives you day by day.
One of His greatest blessings, is His wonderful love for you,
So count your blessings each day and night, it's so wonderful
What God can do!

Danielle Meghan Jarrett
I SEE YOU STANDING THERE, BUT I JUST RUN AWAY
I see you standing there, but I just run away
I hear you call my name, but I just run away
I feel your love tugging at my heart, but I just run away
I smell your beauty, but I just run away

You see my mistakes, but you don't run away
You hear my plea for help, but you don't run way
You feel my pain, but you don't run away

I ask you how much you love me,
You open your arms and die

I see you standing there and I run to you

Janet Vander Sloot
MY SPECIAL STAR

Dedicated with love to Esther Klomparens who is truly a "Special Star" in my life.

There you were glowing so brilliantly in the velvety night,
How I gasped in utter amazement and pure wondrous delight!

Could it be that you were winking at me
And that life was better than it seemed to be?

Intently I gazed; brighter grew your sparkle and twinkle,
Making stardust float around as feathers often sprinkle.

Oh, lovely star, what magnetism you emit—
Drawing one up swirling into your orbit.

Other stars dot the heavens, too;
But none so alluring as you.

My nonpareil, one so truly unique—
Words fail to express what I wish to speak.

Never dim your effervescence or luminous glow;
Such precious value your lighthouse effect, don't you know?

Even sweet influences of Pleiades cannot compare
To you, my shining special star, heavenly gift, so rare!

Savonna Adkins
A GIFT OF LOVE CALLED MARGIE

To: The VanHoose Family "Daddy Glen," Jean, Larry, "Tricia," Terry Lee, Sharon, Floyd & Lloyd. I love you all!

A lady I know is one of those who comes from a breed so rare,
She fills your life with happiness and helps ease your every care.
Her life means total joy for anyone around her,
And her laughter so contagious brightens all things that surround her.

She's pretty, she's witty, full of life and full of fun,
She's one of the most special people ever placed under Heaven's sun.

If you've ever looked up and found the bright blue of the skies,
You'll find it again in this little lady's eyes.

But there's more, much more you'll see waiting there,
You'll see undying love and such unselfish care.
She thinks never of herself but of the loved ones she holds dear,
She is one special lady, that is very clear.

In the short time I have known her
she has become very precious to me,
And I'll always love her dearly, "My Little Margie."

Alma Hunter Davenport
SHARING
Come share with me a walk in the sunshine
Come share with me a walk in the rain;
Come share with me a joyous occasion,
Come share with me a moment of pain,
Come share with me an experience to remember,
Come share with me an experience to forget,
Come share with me a time to be elated,
Come share with me an occasion to fret.
Come share with me a newfound relationship;
Come share with me a relationship at an end.
Come share with me the birth of a loved one;
Come share with me the death of a friend.
Come share with me when my cup runneth over;
Come share with me when my cup is bare.
Come share with me when you don't feel like sharing,
Come share with me when you really care.
Come share with me in any experience
Whether it be good or bad.
For in this life you will find
An experience is better handled when it's shared.

William D Witte
TELL ME BATTERED CHILD
Tell me battered child,
Have I seen your face before,
Hiding in a closet
Or cringing on the floor?
I love you little child,
Much more than you can know,
For I saw your face in a mirror
Twenty years ago.

Lori Gayle Pearson
FIRE AND ICE
In the fires of old
Rage the torments
Of those souls
That will never rest.

Like the flames' fingers
They flit here and there
Only to remain—always—
In the same place.

Fire and ice . . . . the enigma
They never understood.
Icy hearts then, and
Fire now . . . . But never relief.

Had they only tried
To love, to feel love
Toward one who so
Desperately needed it.

The wings of my soul
Take flight from this fire—
Fire of all time. For the cruel cold
Still lives in the world.

Kristy Reasoner-Janes
NOT WITHOUT YOU
All alone, I sit here
looking out the window
down onto the beach
wanting you to be near.

I see a couple walking,
hand in hand,
along the shores
where I long to stand.

The sun is starting to set,
The stars are beginning to show.
The waves are rolling by
as the moon begins to glow.

It could be very romantic,
I wish that I were there.
I won't go without you,
that's how much I care.

Catherine Molly Ells
BROWN EYES
I've a crush on brown eyes
I've built it carefully.
I've collected all the petals
And built a rose of love.
A petal of courage to see me through
The trying times I've had.
A petal of warmth to replace my chills.
And one of strength to counter my ills.
A petal of knowledge to enrich my life.
A petal of endurance to withstand
The lengthy fight.
And in the center the purest petal of all.
A petal of love and compassion to assure me all is well.
These petals I've collected and made a fine bouquet.
I've built a crush on brown eyes
That I don't want to slip away.
But crushes die as blossoms fade—
Their petals softly falling to the ground.
Yet memories remain as sweet and dear
As when they first were found.
I'll always love my brown eyes
Though he needn't love me back.
For I'll always have those fallen petals
Safely tucked within my breast.

Edith Walker Madison
I PLANTED A GARDEN
I planted a garden where the roses blow,
And which was the fairest I could not know:
The garden I planted
Or roses that there did grow.

I planted my garden in the morning sun,
I planted my garden where the showers run.
O come, morning sun and all-day showers,
Water my garden and bless my flowers.

I said, O Soul, live here forever;
From this beauty never sever.
Taste the roses, touch the leaves.
They are all for you, my love.

Came the cold and came the snow.
Came the frost to bend grass low.
Came the lonely years to stay—
I'd forgotten all 'til yesterday.

I snatched away the mold and rust,
I broke new buds all ready to burst,
And I found it hid under a poppy leaf—
My Soul all shriveled and brittle as dust.

Sara G Witmeyer
SAIL AWAY

To a dear friend who has inspired and encouraged me. You know who you are. With my love, your SBK

I wish that we could sail away,
Maybe someday.
Sail away to a place for two,
Only known by me and you.
Sail away on the open sea,
Love will be the only key.
We'll set a sail at early dawn,
They probably won't notice that we've gone.
Time won't matter ever again,
Just you and me hand in hand.
Love will be ours to share forever,
It won't be wrong to be together.
We'll finally be free, from this crowd we now see.
We will be allowed to love,
There will be no more push and shove.
They won't be able to tell us what to do
Our entire world will be me and you.

Anthony John Ciccariello III
DEAD AND GONE
I don't know how I can live today, seems I'm left here on my own.
My family deserted me and this old house, they went away to roam.
My old lady don't care about me either, she's gone with them too.
Seems she had a liking for my older brother, so that means it's down to us two.
How are you my oldest friend, it's been years since we had a talk.
It's a shame you're just a reflection in the mirror, we can't even go outside for a walk.
I have no money to pay all these bills and Big Al's coming over later on.
He wants to know what I'll do with all this property, when I'm dead and gone.
Lord when I'm dead and gone.

Guess I might as well go cook dinner, yes I think that's a good start.
To cook for one is really no problem but cooking for one seems to be the saddest part.
I've had enough of bad luck, every time it's just the same.
I have no friends to help me out, no, so on me you can lay the blame.
There's a chance of snow tomorrow, this winter will be the death of me.
The chilled air seems to weight on my bones and the rats in the cellar look mighty hungry.
Since I can't buy fuel for the furnace I guess by morning I'll have passed on.
At least something in this house will eat with a family when I'm dead and gone.
Yes Lord, when I'm dead and gone.

Charles L Cooper
THE PRAYER OF A GOLFER
Well! it's Sunday Mom, 5:00 A.M.,
I'm ready for early *Mass*,
By 6:45 A.M. I should have my cart
and greens fee *pass*,
Well! here goes, thy will be *done*,
Maybe on that par 3, you'll allow me
a hole in *One*!

Praise you Lord, for looking after my
family,
And Lord, for that beautiful bird you
allowed on the 18th, *par 3*,
Bless my son Lord, who I named
after your *St. Paul*,
Perhaps in your infinite mercy you
will allow more of my putts to *fall!*

Isn't it a bit ironic Lord, that I wed a
woman named *Mary*,
Whom after I mow the lawn and fix
that leak, I hope, won't be too
Contrary,
She loves me and seems proud to
carry my *Name*,
However, I cannot say she loves my
Golf Game!

Lord, bless all the persons in the
world, the hungry, sick and *poor*,
And while you're at it Lord, could
you kind of better my *Golf Score*,
And Lord, could you soften the
hearts of those that maim, steal, hate
and *kill*,
Maybe if they learn the game of
Golf, it could possibly cure their *ill*.

And Lord, for those that have a
problem with alcohol and drug
Abuse,
Lord, please give them a blessing
that they cannot *Refuse*,
Well! Amen, Father God, guess I'll
be on my *Way*,
I see the other 3 in the pew in front
of me and we all just can't wait to
Play!

Anngeannette Pinkston
GOODBYE . . .
Listen closely to what I have to say
I love the times we shared together
each and every day
Now's the time we must depart
but never have I lied
I'm telling you the time has come
for me to say goodbye . . .
We had great times together
let me not forget
We were perfect together
me and you as a set
It's like cupid hit us with an arrow
and let our feelings flow
But now's the time for me to leave
so you must let my love for you go . .

The time has come today
The time for us both to say
Goodbye my love
Goodbye my friend
Until the time we meet again . . .

Goodbye . . .

Carol AC Hynes
JACK-IN-THE-BOX

Michael "DD" D.
Alls: Now I will just say goodbye . . . (METALLICA)
Thanx! Later . . . Love ya, kiddo

He sat inside a funny little box, all rainbow colors and cherry music.
A funny little man that always knows what line to say to make people laugh.
He lived on that laughter—it made him what he was.
With every laugh was a smile, all because he was a funny guy . . .
No one knew or suspected that he went so deep—
Such a secret!
Who would've guessed?
No one ever saw him as himself.

He was always careful.
Never let them see, they can't know,
or he risks losing it all.
So he stayed inside sometimes and
talked to himself.
But after awhile it'd suffocate him
being alone with those four walls.
For too long, he'd start to
forget . . .
But finally he'd sleep and then it was
okay.
Eventually when he awoke—it was
finally morning.
He had survived.
He was out again with all his friends
making them laugh.
They'd never know the hell he called
home and how he dreaded going
back again.
Because he hid it away.
Shivering—crying softly, with every
laugh . . . . .

Wm Ward Kummert

Wm Ward Kummert
AS LIFES WATER TURNS BITTER

To Sonja and all who served in Vietnam

As lifes water turns bittter
When the sky cries yellow
And the land heaves and jitters
Can nature ever return to being
mellow.

Betty Elizabeth Casey
A VIEW

Up on the mountain above the green
sea,
just one old Eagle, the mountain and
me.
The mountain peaks of beauty,
the rocks the grass the sky.
I could stay here forever,
and let the world pass me by.
It is all so special, so peaceful and
serene,
It's like a great treasure,
It's almost like a dream.
You can see to the Heavens
no clouds to mar your view,
yes I could stay here forever,
the mountain, me, and you.

Thasia Anne Eckard
JUST WHAT ARE FRIENDS FOR?

To Eric—The Source of My Inspiration

Love, that knows no boundaries.
Anticipates, the exciting and inviting
Aspects of this endearing
relationship.
Love, that knows the wondrous and
annoying.
The fulfillment of our enjoying,
One another as we enrich and
grow.
To be able to trust one another and
always know.
Who loves you during your best,
Accepts you throughout the rest.
When life's so hard, you can barely
catch your breath
Through happiness, joy, illness, and
death.
Whenever I needed it, you always
were my clown.
We have hurt each other, but we've
never let us down.
And when I feel the need to cry,
I close my eyes and bring you
by.
Then flush the fears, wipe the tears
And get the guts to try.
So, just what are friends for?
To hold dear in your heart, share with
and adore,
so, I salute you,
for who you are . . .

Michelle Jacqueline Duquette
UNDERNEATH GREY SKIES

Today
Was an Ordinary day.
As I stood and watched the sky turn
grey.

(Life)
All around me faded away.
Soldiers
Marched in an awkward way
While children ran in search for
shelter.

And there I stood
In the middle of it all
Passing through
Heading for my distant journey.

James J Entwhistle (JimEjoe)
GRANDMA'S DESK

Just old varnish and veneer
Yet I loved her oh so dear
Hiding places in the drawers
Bookcase with a curved glass door
A fold down desk with linen drawers
below
It really hurt to let her go
Away at school continued the fool
Gone like day into night
Fear gripped I couldn't fight
Only a wooden nickel from the
bottom drawer
In an old cigar box
I saw her no more
Goodby Grandma

Marie Antoinette Reem
IN APPRECIATION

Dedicated to Donnie,
For his inspiration and affirmation

It's really nice when people care
Enough to give their time, and share
With those needing a helping hand,
A heart that's willing to understand;
Who will listen to others, try to learn
When lives have taken a different
turn,
How they might help to end the
strife,
Improving someone else's life!
Giving hope, or inspiration;
Lifting them through the long
duration.
Someone with a caring heart,
Willing to aid a brand new start!

Francis Andrew Barnhart
MORNING LIGHT

Morning Light!
Comes across the sky
So swift to make a brilliant
appearance into a dark void.
Awaking, then the birds start to fly
Morning light when the day is so
clear
a fresh start for everyone to do as
they wish
walk into the woods
among nature's very being
a squab, a doe frozen into place
for as to you a Surprise
to the animal a human face
fresh dew upon the meadow paints a
picture
Oh so nice.
walk further on and a pond with
winter's first spot of ice
bear, fox, weasel, squirrel and hawk
every being starting to move around
the woods. for some another moment,
Other's the last!

Belinda M Gordon
TOO MUCH OF A FRIEND

Of all the time I have spent,
trying to understand your way
I never once thought, I would
have to ask you to stay.
Our dreams of the future, never
seemed to end.
Until one day you told me,
"I hope we can still be friends"

The test of independence had come
over me,
You were the man I let free.
Thoughts of the past blinded my eyes
And I remembered my friends'
words of you,
Being my prize.

My friends continued to enter the
picture of
You and me.
Then I realized, the truth, you
had left me for
She.

Barbara Harter
SONNET ON DREAMERS

Some men will say that I must wait
to dream
And with cool logic look before I
leap.
Yet things are hardly ever what they
seem
And small good comes from fantasies
of sleep.
A fool will measure life by worldly
gain
and disavow the mystic and the muse,
Not I. My wealth is found when I
attain
The qualities of mind he would
refuse.

For Heaven smiles on dreamers as
they cast
Their visions on the sands of time,
and see
Just one lend hope to some among
the vast
Unseeing masses of humanity.

Look fool, and see that every
worthwhile goal
Was first conceived in some poor
dreamer's soul.

Zelma Spivey Groves
"SEASONS GREETINGS"

To Everything There Is A Season
And A Time To Every Purpose
Under the Heaven:
Ecclesiastes 3:8

A time and a Season for
everything to the "four
corners of the Earth"
Whether weighed in the
balance of the scales—
Or judged by the value
of its worth
A Season—for living, to live a
good life:
To sow the right seed, to pluck
out the strife
For the Harvest "is white and
the Laborers are few"
And reaping like sowing is
accounted—to "you"
A Season for loving, our
Families to love
Like the "Creator of Hearts
and the Heavens above
A time to laugh and a time to
weep;
A time to lose and a time to
keep:
"A Season in Heaven" where the
good Book will be read;
And we will be judged according to
the lives we have led
A time to die: and the time we're
born:
Like "Jesus" the "Christ-Child" on
"Christmas Morn"
So "now is the Season," to
think of these things:
The "Season of Christmas" the
Birthday of "King's"
For soon all these Seasons
will gather together—
And fall in the sea!
And vanish like "Christmas"
when we take down the Tree.

Herman Gabin Gaddy
PASSION'S STEELY BREATH

To Cecil—But for you, we wouldn't be here.

Passion's steely breath is on my
tongue.
She gathers deftly coils
Around my loins.
And turn by turn She aches me to Her
Song.

Burning perspiration sends its
flaming down my limbs.
I'm weak, Her probing tongues
seduce my will

She penetrate my eyes and I am blind
to all but touch
While trembling fingers kiss and
probe
and shrill.

Her voice builds in my throat
an anxious rasp
a hiss

Intoxication foams and rocks and
leans.

My body soon is dancing to an
ancient
hungering rush

And I am gripped in lush hard turgid
seethes.

Scaly fins, a musty sweat ascends
into my head
My nostrils flare to greet the pungent

heat

Primordial bath that welcomes every voyager
to its heart
And none from there depart Her will half done

Passion's steely breath is on my tongue.

Melvyn McKinney
THE STORM
Aureate streaks of amber
Coruscate and ripple
Horizontally across the livid sky.
Pitchforks of lightning
Grate through clotted clouds
With flashing swords of fire
That rip the nebulous cloak of darkness.
Grumbling thunder
Drums a tympany of rumbling from a distance,
Like the ponderous tread of brontosaurus
Obstreperous and brontologic

Quakes the crags and somersaults
Like boulders
Avalanching to the bowels of an abyss!
God steps up to His throne
And lifts his hands in benediction,
As tears of prostrate angels
Deluge the thirsty earth.

Paul Cusano Jr
A REASON FOR LIFE
For the woman that I Love
For the woman that I hold
For the woman that Understands
When I wish to be Alone.

For the sweet, gentle Affection
That from her I so much receive
For the Love, the trust, the Care
That she holds in her heart for me.

For the nursing, when I am ill
And the cheering when I am down
For the pride that I always have
When I walk with her through town.

And for the greatest, most precious gift
That God has given me
Time,
In which I will always Love her,
My Reason for Life,
My Wife.

Margaret Thompson-Zanolla
LET GO, LET GO, OF SAD MEMORIES

Dedicated to: Joanne & John with Love

When you're feeling low and hurting inside,
Can't comprehend the thoughts of your mind,
When your tongue speaks in anger with feelings of hate,
Do you just lose control?
Can't seem to relate.

Is it just the pressure of life's many trials
Or is it a deep hurt you felt as a child?
Whatever it be Let Go, Let Go.
It's you that will suffer and not feel the glow.

For when you are hurting you feel all alone,
The secrets of terror and pain are your own.
Just you remember when you lose control,
The hate in your heart are thoughts of your own.

So Stop—Listen in silence to that small voice within . . .
Let it take over and peace it will bring.

Now you must realize just like a child,
Jesus our saviour is close to your side.

So just stop and listen—his voice will come through,
And you'll be surprised how he'll comfort you.

So Let Go, Let Go, of Sad Memories.

Gérard Ntawe
GOODBYE MARY K
Dear 'n Sweet friend, why is your ghost chasing after me?
Smooth velvety skin, why do you reject me?
Black 'n thick lips, what are you searching for into my night dreams?
Naked Mary's specter, what are you looking for in my bed sheets?
Mary's resilient hips, what have you hidden in my room?
Bare thighs of Mary, why are you rubbing against me?
Mary's silky slacks, why can't I take you away?
Mary's dotted blouses, why are you driving me crazy?
Mary's fawn-colored skirts, please hide that haunting body!
Mary's purity, my platonic love, how you mesmerize me!
Mary's sinless thoughts, let me flee away since I can't match you.
Goodbye, sweet witch's fairy: My sexual desire can't raise up to you! Let me have a rest, Mary!
Mary's oily cheeks, I wish I could bite you!
Mary's winged dresses, where are you driving me to?
Large belts of Mary, why do you tighten me up?
Numerous-belted-Mary, why can't I hug you?

Ellene Smith
AT LAST MOM'S AT PEACE

Dedicated with love
In Memory of Myrtle Clemons
I miss you Mom, Ellene

I thank thee God for putting Mom at peace.
Her sufferings on earth were so unneedlessly.
Her aching body will ache no more, for now she stands
At your heavenly door.
Her tormented heart no more has to ache.
She's in your hands Lord when she awakes.
Her one quest in life was to be a good mother, no
Doubt in my mind Lord that she was.
Her life was filled with grief and despair for her
Children and their lives she wanted to share.
Her soul is at rest with God up above.
She died leaving us all her legacy of love.

I love you Mom, Ellene

David Kingsbury Judd
A SONOROUS SOOTHING ECHO IS HEARD!
Amidst the noisy rush of
MEandering humanity,
a rustle of falling leaves is heard;
Above the window shaking sonic booms,
the melodic chirping of a humming-bird is heard;
Aside a desperate cry for help,
an Inner Voice is heard;
Beyond the shrieking tires of a revved-up car,
a running brook softly caresses its earth surface;
Beyond the bonebreaking crunch of heavy feet,
Another's Walk is resounding the earth;
Alas, the discordant notes are met . . .
a sonorous, soothing echo is heard!

Elizabeth Locke

Elizabeth Locke
ARE WE?

With love to all at World of Poetry!
God bless you!

Are we daisies,
Nodding our heads,
In the fields of fate?
Are we stars
Bursting into novas
As our passions sate?
Peradventure
We are these and more,
Tall and short,
Small and great;
Rationales
Beaming thru time
As our dreams abate!

Amy Marie Samson
WHY
A feeling of blue—
Not of joy
is how I feel inside
A feeling so untrue
Why me.
How do I feel?
Is it real?
Is it love?
Am I wasting time?
Probably.
but what have I got to lose?
Time is wasted away
but on what
Where would it go anyway?
Someone else?
Who?
Why? Why me?
—That's all I want to know.

Tracy Lynn Brownridge
SAME OLD LIE
You left me for her,
Now you're no longer here.
These times I'm alone,
I can no longer bear.
When I see you in the hall,
You're holding her hand.
Please try to explain,
Make me understand.
You say you still love me,
And you will always care,
But you can't be here now,
Because she needs you there.
Please tell me again
That you will try.
Tell me again,
That same old lie.

Diana D Moore
BY THE RIVER

For my son, Sherman Madison Moore II
A poet in his own right
In memory of his "Dog"

Over by the river is a very nice place to go
And if Dog could talk like people,
I know he'd tell you so
He loves to run and roll and sniff at clumps of grass
But twice we encountered Chows, each a real bad ass
The river in most places is shallow, enticing you to wade
But if you should get too hot, there are no trees for shade
And on around the bend, there's a rock beside the road
Where you can sit and dream, laying aside your mental load
And further up the road is a two-story house of white
It seems deserted by day, is anyone there at night
There's dogs inside the fence, that bark as you go by
Would they bite if you reached to pet them—you won't know until you try
I don't walk by the river often, as I have other things to do, you know
But if Dog could talk like people, he'd say it's a very nice place to go

Vesta Rae Henderson
OH BAD
Just can't do Bad and get by.

One day everybody got to cry.

Hey Bad is never bad alone.

Bad always got someone hanging on.
Oh Bad with a gun in his hand,
Think he owns everything in this land.
One day oh Bad will be knocked to the ground.
Then old Bad won't be around.
Bad can't look goodness in the eye.
Everything Bad say is a lie.

Oh Bad run up and down the street.
Oh Bad never gets any sleep.
Better watch Oh Bad 'cause by your side
He will creep.
Oh Bad you better not trust,
Get away Bad you can't get us.

Deborah McCardell
SERVICE TO OTHERS

Though today is dark and cloudy
The Lord needs me with His touch
This seems very strange to me
I know I can't give much.

However I will try my best
In every single way
To do whatever comes to me
On this darkened day.

My future ahead may be short
But I have given the best I can
To lift one up and help someone
According to God's plan.

I wonder though, what other needs
I'll find as I go on today.
Whatever they be, I'll stop and tend
My best in every way.

Julia Mecham-McKinnis
EQUUS IMMORTAL

Death . . . We cover our faces in fear, yet peek through our fingers in wonder.

He dances upon the horizon
Somehow molded of the sand
With inner-strength found
I hold my ground
For my time is now at hand
He comes on hooves of black onyx
And shimmering wings of gold
His knowing eyes
Forever wise
Of stories yet untold
And red nostrils flare
As he tests the air
Listening as well
And I wonder if I
Shall ride among Gods
Or be banished
Straight to Hell
With unsteady hand
I give command
And we step through Eternity's gate
"Carry me, mighty steed of the Heavens
To my awaiting fate."

Darline Kussmann
A GRANDMOTHER'S PRAYER

Dear Lord, on Thee I call
As a grandmother I feel so small.
It seems only yesterday
I watched my own children play.
I counted the blessings
as they grew
With each day came strength anew,
To care and share each precious hour
Knowing time has great power.
Now I'm called Grandma
And my dear husband Grandpa.
And now, Lord I would ask
Strength and courage for
for this task.
To teach of what real things consist
And what things to resist.
Let me not be so charmed
That this child is harmed.
And I pray that he may be
Always faithful to Thee.

Lindsey W Page Jr
LADY OF MAJESTIC BEAUTY

This poem is dedicated to Emma, my gorgeous wife

At times I sit and I wonder will it ever be another, I dream.
Watching from afar in my mind. I see features beyond belief.
I sit and I wonder will I ever meet her.
I see in my fantasy each step she takes, a radiance of Love is unleashed.
Her lips were like soft petals of the rarest Flower.
Her Body as smooth as nothing known to man.
And to think no one has ever seen this mysterious Lady.
But knowing and feeling that she does exist keeps my anticipation alive and well.
And then it happened. a glimpse of the Lady.
For me to say what she is like I cannot,
only to describe because it is something that will be with me till my death.
Because I and only I have seen & still live to know what the
Lady of Majestic Beauty
was like.

Reneé Slanker
BLACK LACE

She strolls down the aisle with him so elegantly.
Only in your dreams can you love her passionately.

The essence of her loveliness sets your heart on fire.
Craving her embrace, your senses are filled with desire.

She gives you a quick glance and she has you mesmerized.
You wonder, can she see what is really in your eyes?

Can she know that you have seen her image donned in black lace?
As she surrenders to you all of her beauty and grace.

You were always a good friend but never her lover.
Now a forbidden thought, she belongs to another.

She flashes you a smile so radiantly.
Her eyes are on you most definitely.

You wonder, can she share your secret fantasy?
Or is dangerous love her style of ecstasy?

The wedding party is over and you have gone home.
Except for the image of her you are all alone.

You lie in bed and wonder if she has longings for you.
Your male ego needs her to suffer just as you do.

The intense emotions are driving you insane,
as you realize your love for her is all in vain.

This rhapsody of your heart you must forever refrain . . .

Alyce Bruhn Scott
A LITTLE VALENTINE

To my grandchildren TONYA, SCOTTIE & MARY JO & folks at Fairhaven Baptist Church & College in Chesterton, IN.

A little Valentine wish
to you this year.
May your day and week be most
dear.

As you scatter valentines across
the way,
You'll discover lots & lots of
joy on Valentine's Day.

So put on a cheery outfit and
a gay hat
And you'll have a gala day
if you stand pat.

Jo Ann Brewer
THE LAST STRAW

I gratefully dedicate this poem to my son Glenn and my friend Theresa for all of their loving support.

The Camel laid down
On the moist jungle ground
While two Buzzards circled the sky
For alas and alack the Camel's strong back
Had been broken and so he must die
A Lioness and Cub, hiding out in the scrub
Gave no thought to how he might feel
For all they could do was think of "Menu"
With the Camel the crux of the meal
A Hyena pack, slinking past, circled back
When they heard the old Camel's low moaning
The hair on their necks standing stiff and erect
While their great appetites they were honing
They all gathered round with the sun going down
Each one coiled and quite ready to jump
On the old Camel's form, in the sun low and warm
Till they spotted the crack in his hump
They said, "tell me my friend, what brought you this end?"
And they waited to hear with great awe
For there in the crack of the wound in his back
Was a tiny despicable straw

Mary Coker Wrenn
TURN BACK

This poem is dedicated to, Joseph Andrew Snow and to Roy James Yelton, educators in Mcduffie County, Georgia. Thanks for all your support, time and patience. And thanks for believing in me.

Just take a trip back to the days of old,
When life was simpler, when love wasn't bought and sold.
To ride the frontier on top of the fastest stagecoach,
Walking at night, safely down city streets, lighted by candles on a lamp post.
When having less money, exercising the system of barter or trade,
When household goods weren't bought, with love they were made.
Listening to the howling wind through rough pine walls,
Life on the prairie, gladness when company calls.
Trusting your neighbors, friends, never being provoked,
When people believed in give, looking on special times with hope.
Starting at an early age being taught, for what we get, we work,
Helping and sharing, not waiting around to steal in lurk.
Meat and vegetables were raised on a small farm plot,
Never fearing being robbed in a supermarket parking lot.
Father time turn back, where the road has many turns,
Where children attend log cabin classrooms to study and learn.
Where families were close, hard times were a helping times,
When neighbors stuck together, integrity being as valuable as gold mines.
Go back! Back through time, without all the stress and ills,
Back to the days of old, when life was without all man's self-esteem frills.

Lois M Miller
WHAT CAN I DO

What can I do
to please you, Lord?
That I haven't already done.
What can I do
to help you Lord;
To please Your only Son.
I've given you
My daughters, my Mother and
My Father,
My Sons and Husband, too.
What, Lord, do you want me to do?
Turn around, my child,
What I want is you.

Ada Carswell
I LOVE YOU

This poem is dedicated to Russell Williams whom I had built a dream on.

I love you in so many ways
When Cupid shot his arrow, I was standing the way
I have given all the love that one woman can give
I have nothing else to offer, I only want to live

It's not your fault, that I hurt so bad
It's your love that I sought and at times it makes me sad
I can't give up now and just walk away
I've asked myself why I love you this way

I love you I surrender you my heart
No matter what you say I've loved you from the start
You will always be someone very dear to me
Love for no other could there be

To fall in love was my mistake
To accept this love is your decision to make
I promise to be true among other things
I long to hear you say you'll be my king

I can see that you are smart and bright

To make you happy is my delight
I don't know what makes me feel
this way
I love you more from day to day

I pray to God the Lord above, to give
this poem to you with love

Betty Lou Manning
MEMORIES OF MINE
There are days I remember
'specially in mid September
Working hard through the day
Nights filled with fun and play
Walking through backwood trails
Fields of wildflowers and fox tails
The smell of fresh baked apple pie
Sounds of a whippoorwill's distant
cry
Memories of children fast asleep
These and a million more I will keep
And when from here I have gone
I can close my eyes and return home

Pauline Beverly Staton
THE NARROW ROAD

To all the weary people searching for something they can not find.

As I wandered through this life
carrying a heavy load
I stumbled on a Narrow Road.

My burdens were getting heavier as I
walked along.
Each day was like a nightmare I
began to dread
Then I came upon a man I thought
was surely dead
But as He arose I saw a crown upon
His Precious Head.

He said, "Come sit with Me my child
and rest your weary soul
Then I'll walk with you and help
carry your load.
Just put your faith and trust in Me
And peace and comfort you will
see."
I asked if I could stay with Him in
His Heavenly Realm.
He said "You must stay here and tell
someone
the Peace and Hope you've
found.
There are so many lost souls like you
that need to find their way.
Go tell the world that Jesus is
the Truth the Light the Way:"

Sallie Thompson
FADED VALENTINE

To an old love, and to those loves that have passed the test of time.

I have kept this faded valentine,
with its frayed tattered and
worn edges.
Inside my heart, the words so
distinct, still carries the same
intriguing message.
Through my mind so many sweet
memories flow, unfolding the
love we've shared;
As if before my eyes, from the
book of life, there are slowly
turning pages.
The thing that bound us in the
past, still has its magic touch.
The tears, heartaches and
struggles, we've endured
throughout the long, long
years;
Only proved to bring us closer,
even when there were times of
doubt.
Recollections come to mind, dim
and distant thoughts, proved
how much we cared.
I'll keep this card forever, it
makes me feel trusting, warm
and loved inside.
Its contents and its meaning,
bring precious intimacies
surging wildly through my
mind.
Yesterday, again becomes today, I
am lost in a world of wondrous
love.
I read the words again aloud,
with misty tearstained eyes
"I love you, My Darling, please be
my Valentine."

Robert P Adsitt
FRIEND

I dedicate this poem to my dear friend, Carla Warner.

Friend, What does that word really
mean?
In the dictionary; it is a person one
knows and likes.
But it means more, from what I've
seen.
A friend is someone who cares,
someone who helps through all
times,
someone who shares, whether it be
their love or pain.
Friends are special and they love
you.
Friends comfort you when your tears
fall like rain.
Some friends are fake, They're not
yours.
When you need them most,
they walk out the door.
Some friends are too good to lose.
These friends are lifelong.
Friends are really great.
They say what friends are for in a
song.
Who knows what's in store.
Some friends share their love year
round.
Your next friend may be knocking
on your door
And you'll never know what a great
friend you've just found.

Lobna Elrabadi

Lobna Elrabadi
WINTER
The wind passed through my hair,
Its coldness rubbing against my
face,
There is a new feeling, a good
feeling;
It is special.

The houses, streets, and roads are
clean,
and soon everything is white.
I lie on the snow covered ground
forming angels in the snow.
I leave footsteps
where nobody stepped before.
I look upwards and there is a
rainbow,
I am lost in its colors. I reach a
door that opens to a new land.
It stretches eternally bringing a
bright colorful life.

God touched the earth and sprinkled
it with his heavenly blessings; with
pure gold. Life is beautiful.
Winter is a blessing.

Kelly Lord
SIGNS OF FALL
Fall is a pretty season of the year,
when pretty leaves do appear. Some
people wear hats, and children play
with cats. Boys find frogs and girls
run their dogs.

Anthony L Spain
THE CANDLE

To my son Kyle: Though we are apart you're always in my heart.

On a beautiful day a babe is born,
And is looked upon by a face both
happy and worn.
The candle of life is lit.
In a time that seems short the babe's
a boy,
And he trades his rattle for a different
toy.
The candle of life burns bright.
A few years later he becomes a
man,
And he nears the end of life's short
span.
The candle flame does flicker.
Many years later a man of old age
Turns the Book of Life's final page.
The candle of life burns out.
The candle maker collects wax from
its base
With a creative look upon his face.
The candle of life remade.
On a beautiful day a babe is born,
And is looked upon by a face both
happy and worn.
The candle of life is lit.

Scott Bergevin
ONE BIG SHOT

To all Nichiren Shoshu Soka Gakkai of America with my deepest heart-felt emotion.
Nam-Myoho-Renge-Kyo

In this world lurks evil
This there is no doubt
But also there is virtue
Just not as readily about
How much has life cheated me?
As much as I cheat myself
Who can I blame for my agony?
Only me and no one else
We've all got that one big shot
Whether we like it or not
To make the best of our lives
We've all got that one big shot
And when come great obstacles
That I alone must overcome
I will conquer some quite easily
And others harder than some
Never shall I shame in failure
If my efforts never cease
Never shall I stop praying
For the glory of world peace

Beverly Meier
MY CHILD
The money was tight,
And the smiles weren't just right;
So I killed him.

So tiny . . . so small:
I never touched his cheek at all,
But I killed him.

We plotted and planned,
Calculated his death.
He hadn't a chance,
Not one single breath.

I just killed him.

Sylvia Poradish
THE HUNTER AND THE GUARDIAN ANGELS
The hunter sat high in a tree and
scanned the woods around.
Then suddenly the tree branch
snapped! He tumbled to the ground.
With dimming sight, his brain in
shock, slowly he realized
He could not move . . . the searing
pain . . . his legs were paralyzed!
"Oh, God!" He cried. "This cannot
be!" His heart scissored with fear.
His voice, an echo through the
woods although no one could hear.

His rifle lay beside him. His mind
jumbled with dread
and grim resolve that he would put a
bullet through his head.
. . . A vision of his family, (awaiting
him in town),
Encompassed him with surging love
. . . he laid his rifle down.

Five hours long the hunter lay upon
the cold, damp ground.
With labored breath and ebbing
strength, he prayed with heart
profound.

His wife had sensed a chilling fear
that harm had come to him.
With friends to guide, they searched
the woods as light of day grew dim.
The guardian angels combed the
woods. Once more they called his
name.
And then they heard a feeble cry,
"thank God," the answer came.
Their heartbeats raced and arms
embraced when they found him at
last.
For the hunter in the woods . . .
anguished hours now are past.

His future is uncertain. He will never
be the same.
But he'll recall . . . when shadows
fall . . . the day the angels came.

Shonna Siegers
THE RATTLESNAKE THAT LOST HIS RATTLE
The Rattlesnake lost his rattle;
Now he can not battle:
Not even chase the cattle.
Across the lake he will paddle;
And sooner or later, he'll become a
horse's saddle:

Bobbie Fields
THE ALIEN CODE
In my youth I made a quest
of Knowledge, Truth, and Light
Then, travelled far with little rest
Pursuing secrets without fright
Until one night weary; searching
still
I gazed into the stars
And hurling old questions with
power of will
Sought guidance from afar
In answer to my urgent need
A light flashed down from Space
An alien mind reached out; said
"Heed!"
"I've brought data to aid in your
race"
"On Daath our Sacred home and
hive,
We live in peace and thoughtful
leisure
With a code of life used as a
guide

Toward beauty without
measure"
"In Daath there is no law
But lying is not pretty; Cheating is
not pretty; Stealing is not pretty
Killing is worse than not pretty
And to complete our code
In Daath we don't tell All."

Susan B French
TRAVEL EXPERT

In Zermatt a tour leader called Del
Eluded his charges for a lovely
French belle.
O'er the Alps they went skiing
As if demons they were fleeing,
when
S-P-L-A-S-H
Into a lake they fell!
Inquired she, "Where can we be?"
Replied he, "It's too early to tell!
It's considerably too chilly
For the South China Sea
Yet decidedly too damp for H-ll;
(Excusez moi)
Just let me consult my skiometer to
see
How far from Switzerland we fell!"

Kenn Schildkamp
IN MEMORIAM

Though our hearts will ache with
sadness,
and the tears of sorrow must flow;
You were one man among the living
whom everyone was proud to know.
But now you've gone away to a
better place—
a place much more peaceful than
this;
Where the skies are blue and nature
is alive,
and the soft winds touch you like a
tender kiss.

You will be in our memories always,
with laughter in your heart and a
smile upon your face;
Just as you once were when you were
on the earth—
living among us with your truth and
grace.
Sometimes we hear you calling—
calling us all by name,
and if we listen carefully, we seem to
hear you say:
"Don't worry, my friends, I'm only
sleeping;
and we'll all be together some day."

Andrea McCullough
DO YOU KNOW THE POWER HE BE?

God is the answer.
God is the key.
Do you know Him
and the power He
be?

Behold the wondrous
things He does, believe
in Him with all of your
heart and soul. And
good things will come
in time.

For Jesus is love and
many blessings He will
bestow, upon followers
who truly believe in the
Lord.

For God is the answer.
God is the key.
Do you know Him and
the power He be?

Kimberly Ann Albright
CRYING

This poem is dedicated to my very special grandmother with whose help my writing career is still possible.

Crying comes from the heart
For the lost child. My heart cries
for you.
For the lonely old man. My heart
cries for you.

For the homeless kitten and
forgotten puppy.
My heart cries for you.

For the mother protecting her
children.
My heart cries for you.

For the father who lives alone
My heart cries for you.

For the beautiful child left unborn
My heart cries for you.

My heart cries for all of you. But
alone what can one person do.

Cynthia Brand
A DAUGHTER'S PLEA

For my daughter, Sherry. She fought the battle and won. I'm proud of you honey and I love you.

Mommy, can you hear me?
Please don't turn away,
It's me, it's Sherry,
Please listen to what I have to say.
Mommy I did something bad
It started with just a toke,
Oh please! Don't be mad,
Now I'm addicted to coke.
I didn't mean to hurt you,
Oh mommy, please don't cry,
Won't you tell me what to do?
I swear I'm ready to try.

Shirley Brinley
EXPECTING SNOW

This poem is dedicated to J.R., my grandson whom I love very much.

You should have seen my grandson's
eyes
When the weather man mentioned
snow.
Grannie, Grannie, he would say—do
you suppose they know?
I didn't want them to let him down
so I would nod and say—
Just look at the map, J.R., it's headed
this way.

He awoke next morning, no snow had
fallen down
He came to the breakfast table—his
face all in a frown
Grannie, do you suppose it will
snow?
I told him that I expected so.
Snow clouds were all around—they
were hanging to the ground.

Along about nine o'clock, the snow
began to fall.
The biggest of flakes were falling
that I could ever recall.
Soon the ground was covered and
everything was white.
I knew J.R. was happy—this time
Silly Siler was right.

Christa Mesick
WRITTEN LOVE SEALED WITH A KISS

To Daniel R. Ihde, one of the sweetest guys I ever met.

Lemonade
Street
Ice Cream
State
Excuse me
babe
I forgot the
date

City of Love
State of Wishes
17 Hugs and
83 Kisses

Dear Dan,
Written Love Sealed with a Kiss
if you still love me, listen to this:

Of all the guys I ever met,
You're the one I can't forget.
If you're not there on judgement day,
I'll write our name in every way
I'll give the angels back their wings,
golden hair and other things.
And you know what else I'll do?
I'll even go to to hell for you!
If you smile while reading this,
I'm entitled to more than just one
kiss

Herbert Lee Monk
HEART TALK

Dedicated to my daughter Melinda, a real sweet young lady.

This morning a letter came from my
little girl.
Inside the letter was the picture of a
heart.
Felt so warm inside . . . . brought
tears to my eyes,
Remembering where that heart got
its start.

After getting ready for work one
morning.
My little girl came running, as
always,
She'd hug my neck and kiss me
goodbye.
This was always the start of my days.

What made this morning so special
was,
Along with the hug and kiss
goodbye,
She gave to me a little piece of
paper,
Looking at me, said "Daddy, I love
you . . . why?"

She's just three, looking at the heart
she'd drawn.
That little heart felt so warm and full
of love,
Thought it would burst right there in
my hand.
She's a blessing, sent from heaven
up above.

Has been years since that first little
heart.
Meaning so much to me, I put it
away.
When down, feeling that no one
cares,
Just a thought of her brightens my
day.

Cynthia Lenz
SILENTLY, BUT TRUE

To Shawn With Love This one's for you!

Now I lay me
Down to sleep.
I pray for the whole world
To see me weep.

I love you silently,
I love you true;
I only think of
Me and you.

Where I now sleep
Is where I shall die.
Maybe soon,
You'll see me cry.

I had you then,
I have you now.
I only wish that
I knew how
To make you believe,
To make you see;
I love you,
Do you love me?

Jewell Gonzalez

Jewell Gonzalez
RUN MY SON

Dedicated to: my late son, Mark William

Run my son . . .
Through the fields of trees
and flowers so free.

Run on and on . . .
With your tousled hair
blowing in the wind so fair.

Run down the hills . . .
And across the creek,
your carefree way with rosy cheeks.

Run my son . . .
Don't stop to frown,
so far to run so don't slow down.

Run my son . . .
Run on have fun
throughout the way. Run on my son.

de Jewell

Stella Falco
MOTHER'S DAY

To my Mom, who lives with me forever!

Roses are Red? Violets are Blue? If it
weren't for "Motherhood" what
would we do.
The cooking, the laundry, the dentist,
the store, Oh good Lord there's
plenty more.
So once a year we all get our day and
here's what I think they're trying to
say. "Thank you Mom for giving

your best," the tears, the laughter, the work, no rest.
So what the hell, why should we complain, who knows one day we may be sane! So here's to you and here's to me, we're the best of mothers there could be.
So moms take heed today, make sure you can hear, 'cause we won't hear such nice things until next
year! !

Kelley Paprocki
WISHES

I want you to know
Wherever you are
That every night
I wish on a star
I wish you were back, so that you'd know
How very much
That I love you so
I wish that the hurt that I felt when you left that day
The hurt mixed with pain
Would just go away
That was the day I cried so hard I thought my heart would break
At first it seemed like a nightmare and soon I'd wake
But it wasn't a nightmare, all of this pain
And with this pain there just wasn't a gain
I wish all of that and I wish this too
I wish you were here so I could say
I love you

Lora Marie Penn
LOVE'S FIRST SPRING

To Tom, the only man I've ever loved

I wonder at sunsets
Cry when love songs play
And in the night, remember, "Love's Yesterday"
I still tremble, At your touch.
And feel again, the springtime rush of, Love's forgotten moments.
Sometimes I think my heart will surely break, "Remembering Love."
As if for the first time.
Look closely at the smile, I paint upon my face,
And have the grace to ponder, the teardrops; as they trace
"New lines," where old ones lie.
"I ache to hold you close," to stop the clock,
And wake up in joy,
To the memory of, "Love's First Spring."
I want to know that for a million yesterdays,
You shared, the secrets in my heart
And understood, the you of me.

M Ridpath
KATY'S INNOCENCE

This poem is dedicated to Dr. Norma Scudder, she will always hold a special place in my heart.

Katy's days were filled with
innocence, she played house
with her dolls and cradled her
kitten;
stainless and pure were her
childhood dreams.
Taken away one day by a
stranger, her childhood
innocence was no longer her
own. He touched her in places
that made her cry, and still to
this day she can't understand
why.
Then one day Jesus came and
took away the hurt.
He gave the innocence back to her
and now her heart is his own.
There are children just like Katy
who were robbed of their
innocent dreams; because just
like Katy, this little girl is me.

Laura Spagnola
WHO AM I?

Who am I?
Where did I go?
I've lost myself through space and time.

The spaces that have come between us,
The time we've grown
together . . .
But what happened to me?

Like a plant I've grown and expanded
Given birth to a flower
Shared love, joy, heartbreak . . .
But like a plant, I am still here.

Deep down in the roots . . . I am there.

You may cut me down,
Pick my flowers,
Try to get rid of me.
But like the plant
Through my roots, I will be back.

Because deep down in my roots
I am there.

Terryl Shepherd
A DREAM LONG SINCE DREAMED

A dream long since dreamed
You are.
Like a mystic apparition
You leave me shaking
Wanting more
Of what I have yet had none.
You have seduced me
In a time long since gone,
We were lovers, I know
In another life.
When I hear your name
The anticipation mounts
Like that of a virgin
On her wedding night.
You have come from a past
Of which I have no recall
To fill my days with dreams
And my dreams with lust
To tell me we must be lovers once again
We must be lovers
We must.

Lynne Hay
JUST FOR TODAY

To Tennessee, with my heart and affection

In each memory there is a face, a voice, a touch.
In each memory there is someone you remember,
Something he said, something unspoken.
In each life there is a challenge,
the challenge to meet
the challenge to conquer,
challenge to be set free,
free of hatred, free from torture.
In each of us there is a desire, a
desire to love
the desire to live.
For today may we feel the love, the desire, the freedom, the memory.

I want to hold that memory, the memory I have of you.
Today I pray for not the memory, for that I already own.
But I pray for the freedom.
The freedom from hatred, freedom from torture.
The freedom to speak, to touch, to hold.

For now I respect the freedom I have,
for it has been taken from me, and never again will I take that freedom for granted.

Barbara Clendennin
FOREVER

I dedicate this poem to my mom and my dad Kathy and David and to Debbie Cella who's helped me with a lot I love all of you, you're all special people in my life.

Forever is a chance of eternal life,
Only through God you can see the light.
As you enter the gate of the Lord,
You leave all your fears, regrets, and Sing.
Through the eyes of God those are no more,
For Jesus died for us on the cross,
He cleaned our sins away.
For those who believe he is Savior and Christ,
Shall seek and have eternal life.
For those who reject this word,
Shall never see the Kingdom of the Lord.
For God has given us all a chance,
Through Jesus his son and his death.

Patricia L Rhodes
THE FAITH OF A LITTLE CHILD

To my husband and three sons, who were my inspiration and my strength

Last evening, as I knelt to pray,
My thoughts went back to yesterday.
When as a child I used to pray,
God bless Mom and Dad in every way.

My faith was strong, I had no doubt,
That God would know what I was talking about.
The faith of a little child!

When I was young, I always knew,
That if I got hurt I could come to you,
For I knew that you'd be there,
To hold me in your arms with loving care
The faith of a little child!

Now I am grown, my faith is dim.
I wonder if I should pray to Him.
I wonder, is He really up there?
And if so, will He answer my prayer?
Oh, to be a child again. And have the faith that I had then. The faith of a little child!

Maija Pesola
A SUNBEAM ON A CONCRETE WALL

Slowly through the prison bars
the early spring sun leaks,
Casting long black shadows
across his hollow cheeks.
To this musty and forsaken cell
so sullen with his sin,
So little of the light and color
ever dare sneak in.
As he squints to watch the sunlight
prance upon the floor,
He lets the warmth creep inside
and ease his pain once more.
Somewhere in his hardened heart
his spirit seems to lift,
Basking in his meagre share
of nature's finest gift.
He clutches at it, desperately,
like the thirsty for a drink
To hold it but a moment more
before it starts to sink.
But forgetfulness is short-lived;
a sunbeam will not stay
And the fading rays of light
won't keep the shame away
So though the light transforms the dust
into golden grains of sand,
The concrete wall is still as cold
beneath his work-worn hand.

Christine Mahoney
BALLERINA DREAMS

To Mom, Dad and Lindsey. It's not much but it's a start. I love you all so much. Love Chrissie

. . . ever gliding beauty that
caresses the air
softly floating, lingering on
each breath
yet moving as quickly as and
as luminescent as
a beam of morning sunlight,
or as wondrous
as a beautiful star twinkling
for our pleasure throughout
the night.
slowly moving as natural as
life itself.

. . . gliding across as if walking on
a cloud or moon
you wear a dress made of the
petals of roses, and a
crown of gold given to you by
angels. Rising up, twirling,
into our hearts. Your eyes
sparkle like those of a
child . . . innocent and pure.

I can see you when I close my
eyes at night, and if I listen in
the still of the night I can
hear you
silk shoes tinkle like the
ivory keys of a
grande piano . . .

an everlasting beauty softly
floating, yet you seem as real
as the pillow which my cheek
rests upon each night.
you are more than a
Ballerina . . .
you are my dreams

Donald R Cross
TOGETHER

To Dalpha L. and Jane J. Day Most Gracious and Beloved

From their early childhood days
Their Love was there
And in all kinds of weather
They were always together

In High School days
Their Love grew stronger

An engagement ring for her
Continuing through life together

The Golden College years
Brought years of joy
And in front of a Minister
They vowed their Love together

In future years
A business they worked
And a family did occur
Binding their Love together

A temporary parting
When he passed away
But now and forever
They can be together

Eloise V Dickinson

THE KID

When I first saw him
He was a few hours old,
All pink and wrinkly skin
But, oh, so sweet to hold.

His baby years flew by.
He was soon in school.
His grades were good,
His name on the honor roll.

He was nine years old
When music he discovered.
He played an old keyboard
And knew what he wanted.

Now, at 14, he plays a guitar.
He plays hard rock with a group.
See how tall he stands in his
Reeboks
Waiting to start the music?

His hair is shaggy and curly,
His smile is sweet and warm
When to me his head he turns.
He is, "The Kid," my grandson.

Lora Wood

AGAIN

This poem is dedicated to Alex Helmel—Vancouver, British Columbia—whom I will never give up on.

Again undecided
Again unsure
Over and over it seems
Always the same
He wants this or
I want that
Forever it seems
We will disagree
Your heart breaks
Your heart bleeds
But someday, someone
Will plant new seeds
Your heart breaks now
And you've said goodbye
For again some day soon
You will be
Again undecided
Again unsure.

Jean M Orr

IN THE MEMORY OF MY SON GUY

To Guy's Family.

I used to wonder why God took my son Guy. It is true he was suffering. So maybe that's why God took him home so he could rest. The more I think about it the more I realize God knows best.

Guy was a beautiful baby. He had big brown eyes and hair that was wavy. He had a smile that would steal your heart. I knew he would be a good son right from the start.

He was here a short thirty-five years. I'm really thankful for that time, to have had him, to have known him, and to have loved that son of mine.

He has gone to that beautiful home in heaven. I no longer have to ask why God took Guy. I know he is now at rest in the wonderful care of the one that knows best.

Mary Thayer Blanchard

Mary Thayer Blanchard

MUSIC

When I consider how my life is
spent,
I realize the part that music plays
In brightening the dullest humdrum
days
And filling them with gladness and
content.
Its subtle charm is surely heaven-
lent;
To lofty heights our feelings it can
raise,
And nothing more effectively allays
The strain of jangled nerves and
worriment.

Whenever my vitality is low,
Then music is the tonic I require,
And so to Shakespeare's "food of
love" I turn.
From personal experience I know
How it can charm, soothe, stimulate,
inspire
And give me the delight for which I
yearn!

Gaylean Millsaps

RAINBOWS

Brilliant Colors.
Timeless Dreams.
Sparkling over Waters
Of Endless Streams.

Shining in the sun's rays.
Waiting for the chance,
To brighten someone's lonely days
And make them want to dance.

Many hearts were filled with
sadness.
But as the soft wind blew,
They became filled with gladness
Of rainbows, so precious and few.

Rhona Domingo

I'M BLACK BY GOD'S DEMAND

To my family and daughter, Nicole, with love

I am Black by God's demand.
Molded and shaped by his holy
hands.
Taken out of captivity
Given a life of sweet liberty

Yes, I'm Black
And carry life's cross on my back
But by God's demand
I shall stand
And fight life's battles with
his helping hands.

Lorene W (Cate) Yowell

TO AMERICA'S ASTRONAUTS

Oh say did you see
by the television light
what so proudly we hailed
on the moon, Sunday night?

Oh the astronauts there
having glided thru space
brought beauty to share
with the whole human race.

So on the moon far away
waves the flag, U.S.A.
with its red, white and blue,
proving what we, MAN, can do.

All the astronauts so brave
even some their life gave
made their names in history great
thru out the whole world and United
States.

Katharine S Carter

THE CONCH SHELL AND THE ROSE

For Mom

I gave you
the time of day,
a few lunchtime confidences,
a single game of tennis,
before we went our solitary ways.
But when I went to the Caribbean
I brought you back a shell
a conch shell
brittle and broken
but inside the curl
a livid blush of color.
I left in on your desk
a souvenir, the cast-off
shell of death,
although the animal smell
was still alive
enough to soak my suitcase
like the brine of tears
I never shed.
Not then.

Not until
you gave me
a single rose,
pink and perfect,
a furl of feeling.
nipped in the bud.
You left it on my desk
In a green bottle
unlabeled
but shaped like a tear
Dropped by to offer
condolences.
And tears pricked
my eyes
in your absence.

Liam McNamara

FREE AGAIN

Water was his tonic, water in
whatever vessel, whatever
basin, bottom, bed. Almost.
Fresh or salt, water was what he
most liked to look at, taste, be
in for the swim
Or on for the sail, the sail to
Bantry Bay.
Salvific force, discerned
selectively by Isak Dinesen;
"The cure for anything is salt
water—sweat, tears, or the
seas."
Ah, yes, but in this man's book
the cure with gusto goes inland
too
For the trout line, the skipping
stone, the dipper, and the bark:
that Old Town Canoe.

Altogether God's finest hour in
Genesis, this sublime invention,
except perhaps that reserved for
Eve:
Eve's turned his head, he granted
that, but water held it steady.
Only once did water fail him and
it was Eve, his Eve, who poured
it
In, of all things, a compact lap
pool, 6 x 12, "where you swim
(in place) at your own pace . . .
for exercise, for fitness, for
hydrotherapy."
Goodness, God did it so much
better. And bigger, with
plunging depth and untapped
mystery. Free!

He drained the lap pool,
consigned it to the dooryard
Where it collected dirt and rain
and grew exotic shoots.

Heather Pruiksma

FREE

Now that the world is over,
Now that the capitals are felled,
Now that the leaders have beaten
each other
To death for the sake of their
swelled

Egos which required some
depraved
Warped fulfillment as food,
Now that the innocent have
survived
The chaos the "big men" thought
good,

Now that the corrupt have been
destroyed
By the means which they had
created
We, left in this ugly void,
Look around: this is freedom, yet
I am not elated.

Kristi Martel

BLIND THROUGH SEEING EYES

Right or wrong in this world of
superficial means,
The awareness of his enemy is what
scares him most.
The presence of false reasoning
awakens him.
He looks into the blankness of an eye
that will not see.
The eye creates an ignorance, a dark
and empty ignorance.
"What puddle?" asks the blind child
as she rides her bicycle through the
mud.
"What debt?" asks Mr. Reagan as he
borrows some more . . .
And as he spends this on star wars he
asks why those people there are
sleeping in cardboard boxes this
cold and rainy night.

"Rocky" (Robert Costanzo)

LONELY MAN

Why am I all alone, real tired and
feeling so blue
Could it be that I've been left behind,
and waiting just for you
I keep pretending that we live in a
world, that's still full of love
As we watch our souls dance, with
the clouds high up above
The shafts of light so golden against,
the royal sky of blue
Up comes a breeze from the north,
that brought me closer to you
At first I see you trying to hide,
never letting it show
Continually acting a scene, where
you have style and total control
But time is what you are fighting, so
come back to the very start
That's where you'll find the key, that
unlocks this broken man's heart
I know what you are feeling, as I

stand by your side
While your beauty inspires me, like the moon effects our ocean's tide
Still there's more to come, as we write our memories in the book of life
Some not so pleasant, you might say they cut like a knife
You act as though this world is yours, and only made for fun
Then instead of taking your cue, once again I watch as you begin to run
It's time to be different and change what you still can
Then you just might fix the heart, that's in this lonely man.

Lois Elaine Kelsay
CONTRAST

Yesterday, I walked rain-slickened streets,
I wandered midst a tired and shop-worn mass,
Each busy person hurried on his way,
Without a thought, or word for those who passed.
The darkened sky reflected from each face,
Few gave alms; there was no time to give,
As each pressed homeward wearily,
Life seemed to be most difficult to live.

Today, I walked in sunshine bright and clear,
Cheery voices pierced the morning air,
Strangers too, oft voiced a warm hello,
Smiles were seen on faces everywhere.
I saw men give to help some needy soul,
Women laugh and joke when day was done,
While in my heart I breathed a little prayer,
Dear God, may we be often blessed with sun.

Cleo Hewitt
IN DEFENSE OF A TUMBLEWEED

I am a tumbleweed.
God knows, I just go where the wind goes.
Seeing, hearing, touching, tasting and smelling,
In God's wonderful, horrible world.
I need no assurance or testimony from others as to my being.
I simply am.
I make no apology.

Marilyn Presswood Smiley
THE MAKERS

This poem dedicated to my Makers.

Welcome teachers!
Educators of the past, present, and future.

Communicators of knowledge.
Appointers of time.
Recorders of data.
Educators of the past, present and future.

Attempters of children's minds.
Bringers of bright ideas.
Organizers of the skills of management.
Understanders of children's desires and wants.
Testers of the minds.

Trainers of future children
Holders of children's dreams
Educators of the past, present, and future.

Travelers of time
Experimenters of satisfaction
Appreciators of small smiles that are given.
Chimers of the songs that children sing
Helpers of a bright tomorrow
Evaluators for the betterment of the future
Rememberers of knowledge long gone and the beginning of the future.
Smilers of all that is good.

Ahna Marcantognini
DAVIE STREET

Ladies on the corner being replaced by young boys
with long legs
short shorties
and rosy cheeks hanging ready
to be petted and pleased.
Red lipstick—green feathers
Blue hands from the cold wind
They hop from foot to toe,
Smiling at the Cadillacs
And frowning into black vans.
Two on one corner
Three across the street
And more down the lane away,
All smoking
All shivering
And only one stooped at a window
Of a possible sale.
Price is right
Lashes blink twice
And one more angelic babe with
acneed nose slips into the night.

Victoria Limon
FEELINGS OF LIFE'S CREATION

This poem is dedicated to my mother, who's always believed in me

I walked through a field of a wild and wonderful meadow where the winds of life blew upon me. It opened my eyes to see the lesson of nature's sweet revenge. I could hear the echo of the wandering creations and the whispers of the trees as they rose above me—I felt the honesty of this wonderful creation. I felt the warmth that touched me and protected me with all its glory. NOW I KNOW WHAT LIFE HAS TO OFFER, IF ONLY IT WOULD LAST FOREVER.

Now as I reach the height of a glorious hill I look over the land. It gives me the feeling of life's goodness. The air gives a sweet and refreshing scent and the sky above is bright and oh, so pleasant. NOW I KNOW WHAT LIFE HAS TO OFFER, THE KINDNESS IT SHOWS AND THE UNDERSTANDING TOO.

If only it could last forever then I could live my life only to surrender to the wonderful creation God has offered.

Donna Blau
JESUS

To Dr. Diane McElheney—I owe you all & I love you

My Savior was hung on an old oak tree that the soldiers fashioned into a cross, and as they gambled for the robes at his feet, my Master's life was lost;
But on the third day He returned to His flock, and to us,
To let us know that if we only believe and love one another
As brothers, and treat each other fairly, He will come again in glory to take His followers home.
So pray every day, and pray every night
About the glory that awaits us all
And never forget that cross on the hill
And the man who died for us all

Larry D Norton
DEAR GOD

To my late Mother Arnice Marie Norton, who loved God—people—poetry

I looked out my window one early morn.
To my surprise there were two beautiful birds fighting, they were all battered and worn.
One was blue and one was red.
I really think one wished the other one dead.
It was such a sad thing to see
at least it really brought out the sadness in me.
Tho, they're only birds, their battle is true to life I believe.
Like white man and black,
they fight and they grieve.
White man or Black
Blue Bird or Red
"Dear God" can't we live together
or do we really want the other one dead?

Horace Bailey
CARE FOR ME

To my dearest Mother, Josephine Harris

Care for me, I was born of a woman.
What's my name? I cannot remember.
Hearts of stone, turn soft and warm.
Care for me, care for me.

Tell me there will be a tomorrow.
Can I trust my fellow man?
Give a child a chance to live.
Lend a helping hand.
Care for me, care for me.

Blood is thicker than water.
It has been proven in the past.
Other people will do more than your own,
Which makes it very sad.
Care for me, care for me.

Mary Jane Nitterauer
FRIEND IN A DOG

This poem is dedicated to Jim, my wonderful husband, friend and lover.

Has a dog ever been a part of your home?
With a four legged friend, you are never alone.

She asks nothing more than a pat and her meal.
But gives much more in her end of the deal.

The children are safe under watchful eye.
And when they're in bed, she lies down with a sigh.

A stranger is met at the door with a bark.
"What a good watchdog!" they always remark.

Sometimes we're all busy and don't notice her stare.
But when we want her, she is always there.

Every time we come home, she makes a big fuss.
Who else is always happy to see only us?

If a lasting friendship, I had to choose.
It would be our dog's, for human friendship is too easy to lose.

Paul A Blais
KINGS & KNIGHTS WITH SWORDS

My first poem is dedicated to the Lord, and to my first born son

This is not a poem with deep philosophical meaning
Just some words to keep you reading
This is not a story full of action
No main character, no big attraction
As you read you might even get bored
But you'll keep reading hoping it will get better on forward
No there's no fancy lines with elaborate words
It's not a tale of Kings and Knights With Swords
The more you read the more you wonder
Did the writer mean this or was it a blunder
I would say "I meant every word you read"
But as you may have noticed in the poem nothing is said.
These are just words with no claim to wisdom
From someone who never claimed to be wise.

Merle T Killinger
THE MASTER'S PAINTBRUSH

To My Loving, Husband, C.L.

The storm struck without warning,
The wind came as as great gush,
The rain fell swift and was gone
Leaving behind signs of the MASTER'S PAINTBRUSH.

The trees glowed with new life
The flowers glistened with fresh rain;
The stillness was broken by birds' chatter
Each released the wondrous beauty they contained.

The Eastern sky was the MASTER'S canvass
Each color HE chose with matchless care,
To form a celestial rainbow
Painted in colors soft and rare.

This arc of beauty held promise
Then slowly did the colors fade;
Vanished was the work of art
Which surely GOD had made.

Deborah C Ashenfarb
GODDESS OF THE KNIGHT

To Michael, my husband and to my Mother and Father, thanks for always believing in me . . . I love you all.

The darkened trees amidst
the rolling fog becomes the knights
lover

Up against the pitted shadows
are the countless pulse beats
that echos in the hollowness of my
thoughts

Quiet is the passion that sears the
silkened flesh
susceptible as the rose in an April
thaw

The night engulfs the lover
in her bosom
softly scented in lavender

The moon faintly visible
A Lorca moon, peeking through the
mist
the mistress is the night
she glides on secrecy and desire

The swirl of the stars breathes energy
into the veins
like a brushfire, ravaging everything
in its path . . . .
the unaware, the naive, the loveless

Noelle Bumgardner

Noelle Bumgardner
BUT ONE FATE

This poem is dedicated to the future! ! !

I wish I didn't feel this way—
though it happens nearly every
day.

The love we shared once long ago
is nearly gone as you well know.

I've never felt such vicious hate
from someone who has but one
fate.

You'll be alone your whole life
through—you don't deserve a
love so strong and true.

When I'm gone, I will be soon—
maybe then you'll sing a
different tune.

You've won the battle and the
war—I don't want to play this
game anymore.

Your need to hurt someone is sad,
since I don't believe you're
really bad.

I love too deep I've been told by
some—maybe someday I'll truly
find the right one.

Susan M Samarigan
MISSING YOU

For Vincent, with all my love, Mom.

Jack-in-the-box is leaning,
His head tilted to one side;
Rocking horse is sitting patiently,
Awaiting your next ride.

Colorful balls have all quit rolling,
They no longer bounce about!
Your wagon's cold and lonely,
Until tomorrow when you go
out.

Stuffed animals and building blocks
Have all been put away;
Tiny clothes lay in the hamper,
They're all dirty from today.

The house sits still and empty—
It's hushed from playful
screams;
But everything misses my baby boy
When he lies placid in his
dreams.

Avis Stark
HOMEMADE PIES

Dedicated to the many friends whose love and prayers helped me recover from cancer.

There is so much love in a
homemade pie
When it's brought to you by a
friend.
Whether apple, or peach, or
lemon meringue,
You savor each bite to the end.

My dear friends who have
brought us these luscious
delights,

Need to teach me their secret
skill.

For kindness like this—mixed
with patience and love

Surely must be the Father's will.

Mary E Jardin
AND NOW I'M FOUND . . .

This Poem is Dedicated With Love to Damian; My Forever Friend

As I search across the sea
Of unclear faces
There is but one face
I recognize—
It is yours . . .

As I am drowned by the flood
Of unfamiliar voices
There is but one voice
I have heard before—
It belongs to you . . .

As I reach out to the swarm
Of waving hands
There is but one hand
That reaches out to me—
And I take your hand in mine . . .

Margie Dolohanty
A JOLLY MERRY CHRISTMAS

To my children, grandchildren and great grandchildren with love.

Oh how I love this time of the year
Christmas is coming and Santa is
near.
Just look up and see that beautiful
star
We hear from people from near and
far.
Lots of love goes in each card I send
To a relative or just a good friend.
I looked all over for a card for you to
see
None of them sounded like they were
coming from me.
Large or small they are so nice in a
drawer they go
But my little cheapies I know they
can throw.
December 25 is the Christ Child's
Birthday a day to Pray
We have family gatherings on that
Special Day.
Just never let us forget what makes
the Day so great
If it wasn't for Him, We'd have
nothing to celebrate.

God Bless
Grandma D

Marjorie Diggins-Liebler
THE LOVE GOD GIVES US

This poem is dedicated to Jesus—my Lord and Savior, without Him I am nothing.

God gives us love to fill our lives;
To make each day more beautiful
than the last.
God gives us love to share our hearts;
To create peace in a world of hate.
To give each other profound joy;
God created beauty, so that we may
see this place we live in,
Unmasked, through the eyes of God.
God gives us love, each day, like a
rose in bloom;
And, as our love grows, so must we.
For when love grows to its fullest;
We can look upon our brothers as
God intends.
For God intended that the kind of
love He gives;
Be a kind of healing to the wounds of
this world.
God's love is the beacon that will
shine,
For ever through the shroud of
darkness;
To lead man on to a better life.

Elaine Adkins
JUST SAY NO

This poem is dedicated to Just Say No Club

"Just Say No" is a powerful phrase,
Staying away from drugs, it really
pays.
It keeps your mind clear for thought,
For things that can never be bought.
Your self respect means much more.
Doing drugs is such a bore.
Be honest with yourself and don't lie,
Good things in life are a natural high.
If someone dares or makes a bet:
Don't let this be a threat.
Be different if that's what it takes,
Life or death, don't make the
mistake.

Jo Anne James
MR. RESTLESS

For daughter Dana James, for Son Dante James, my treasures in life. For my only sister Adele Davis, my love. For my companion PRINCE SELVER, my inspiration, my beloved.

Where oh where has my true love
gone?
What made him wander out of my
arms?
Am I to blame for his restless ways?
God's on my side, so I'll just pray.

He will return, say I'm sorry this
day.
He may, stay home for just a short
while.
Then off again, leaving dirty clothes
all in a pile.
Clothes on the floor are a good sign
indeed.
He will return, maybe settle down,
have kids on his knees.

Happy days are just up ahead.
I feel so, he's really a very sweet
guy.
Best I get ready to bake his favorite
apple pie.
I hear his sports car coming down
the lane at high speed.
Thank you Lord, for returning to me,
just what I need.
Home at last—Safe at last—Happy
at last.

Stacey M Reynolds
I WAS FIFTEEN THEN

For—LuLu V Reynolds, my Grandmother

I was fifteen then,
I knew it was coming soon,
Her face showed so much pain,
But none of us knew when.

She laid in that hospital bed,
For such a long time.
We all had much dread that she
Was soon going to die.

She hurt so much,
But where she was going was the best
place,
The worst thing we all had to do
Was to say goodbye.

I didn't know who,
I had missed so much before.
I thought the tears would never stop.
I know for one thing, I loved her a
lot,
And I'll miss my Grandmother
forever.

Herbert D Welch
THE KING REMEMBERED

When I was young, I was black and
proud,
I march with the king, and sang out
loud.
I walk with dignity, held my head
high,
I was part of a mission, direct from
the sky.

We held marches all cross the land,
We fought for equality wherever we
can.
Our move was nonviolent, we
couldn't raise a fuss,
but we refuse to ride the back of the
bus.

We demonstrated and protest; all for
a cause

This removed the colored and white signs from the public walls.
There was so much segregation; We just couldn't win,
and was denied our rights because the color of our skin.

We fought real hard to make things right,
We tried to break the color barriers with all our might.
We envision one day; our dreams will come true,
to open all doors so you can walk through.

Now the king is gone and the dream has died,
it seems like all our effort has been pushed aside.
So wake up black America and let's not forget,
we came a long way baby' but we ain't done yet.

Aleta J Deese
BEAUTY

To the memory of my father Donald O. Sanford, a great man that is missed by all who knew and loved him.

The Lord created many things
just for you and me
Then He gave us eyes and ears
so that we could hear and see

The butterfly that whispers by
on its gentle flight
The birds that keep on flying
'til they're far from sight

The bees that buzz to and fro
their journey never ending
The squirrels that scurry up the tree
as the day's beginning

So say your prayers every day
And thank the Lord above
For all the beauty that you see
was created by Him with love

Hazel Gardner
LONGING

To my children

There is no one in this world
as lonesome as I.
Lonesome for the one I love
and will love until I die.
There are nights I sit alone,
and crying in the dark
These tears that I am shedding
are from the bottom of my
heart.
I'm longing for my love,
and my love he'll always be.
And while he's fighting for our
country,
May God keep him safe for me.

Ruth Ann Nicolaisen
WINTER'S DEEP

To my father, who gave me wisdom. To Bryan who showed me courage. To my husband who shows me love.

Winter deep shadows faded and brief;
my prints shallow without speed.

Conscience reminds you yesterdays
behind; tomorrows briskly beside.

Old dreams like frozen creeks,
covered with ice; the bottoms
vaguely seen.

Dawn's approach, a welcomed host
for day's journey; warmer than most.

Rays of sun breathe life in the
forgotten strays, that wondered in
December's maze.

The doors slowly open to Spring's
emerald abode; hastily I approach.

The grass cleansed with dew
smelling its warmth; taking me back
of dreaming on the hearth.

What chaos this time of Spring; but
yet silent in vertile vibrance.

Hurried to bring future's breed, so
they too may grow and sleep in
Winter's Deep.

Reverend Helen Y Torkelson
A MEASURED LIFE

This poem is dedicated in memory of my Mother—Ressie Marie Harper "Your Love will light my way, your memory will forever be with me for Grace was in all your steps and Heaven in your eyes, and in every gesture Dignity and Love."

I have measured out my life & what is mine alone
Oft-times I found the rainbow amid the storms in my home.
I've had many temptations, many solitary hours to think upon my life
Some I want to forget, but others have banished strife.
My life was ordered to be what I am today
And though the walk is often uncertain, I would have it no other way.
Mother dedicated me to her Saviour before I was conceived,
She walked in all His compassionate Love and she Believed.
I thought that I would change it all around & live according to my views
But her Lord kept His promises when I was born brand new
Just as God the Father chose Jesus His Son to be the Saviour of the world,
Mother knew the moment I arrived, I would be her Lord's little girl.
My trials have been hard & many years of illness I knew
But always despite it all—I had Jesus to bring me through.
I am much older now & often have been at death's door
But the enemy of the world could not take my life for my Lord made sure,
Because our Lord went through much the same tribulations & He feels our pain
He suffered, died and arose from the cross & grave where He bore our shame
And today I have measured out my life, my trials have taught me real Love
The kind that only Jesus our Lord can bestow in the hearts of those He Loves.
Mother lived and walked His Way and taught me how Our Lord above
Placed His call upon my life and in my heart—His Love.

Dolores G Dutra Hicks
DON'T GET LOCKED IN YESTERDAY

To: Geraldine Rego Dutra my mother, William W. Hicks my husband Christopher B. Sears my son

Leave the past in yesterday, lock it
up and throw it away.
Use it only when things go wrong,
make it a guide to help you along.

Use it as a progress chart, make it
apply to a brand new start
Make new plans along the way, and
don't get locked in yesterday.

Plant a seed and watch it grow, then
leave it there for all to know.
Make a new friend every day, and do
some good with what you say.

Make your life a paradise, tell
someone you think they're nice.
If you can, a little prayer, but tell
someone you really care.

Help someone and watch the smile, it
makes you know that you're
worthwhile.
Then you can know the joy it brings,
from doing daily little things.

Practice all these things I say, don't
get caught in yesterday.
Live your life, don't waste a minute,
live it now! be glad you're in it.

Cherish it, don't let it pass, live life
today, it goes so fast.
There may not be another chance, to
give someone a loving glance.

Do it now, don't hesitate, have no
regrets when it's too late.
Pass all you can along the way, and
don't get locked in yesterday.

Angel Luis Vasquez
LORENA

Because the words wouldn't have been right without the special feeling in my heart, I dedicate "Lorena" to—Dawn Lorena Dressler.

When you think of far horizons,
Of clouds all laced with dew,
You may think it's so surprising,
All these, remind me of you.

When the moonlit night is clear,
And the stars all twinkle high,
Instead of dipper-forming sphere,
I see the twinkle of your eyes.

Of the mountain-reaching sky,
And the lowly meadow deep,
Reaching, you have been so shy.
Alas, an angel in deep sleep.

And when I think of flakes that fall,
Upon the crocus of spring,
Content with nothing else at all,
But have you near, makes my heart
sing.

Rayson Leon Allen
SHE SITS ALONE

Given to the memory of Cecil Allen and the twins Bobbi and Robbie

She sits alone come evening
with her feelings left inside
when the sun is low, then gone
she savors the night

Twins were born, summers passed
almost to the day
the clouds formed an autumn storm
and washed his grave away . . .

It left a tree that never grows
took all the flowers, 'cept for
two
just an orchid and a rose
for the girls he never knew

A fire blazed up this morning
too early for the leaves
but it left behind the ashes
of her treasured memories;

Still one burning ember glows
where she now sits . . . alone
and I feel her longing anguish
as if it were my own.

Jeanette Rickerman
LONELY IS

For "Kap"

Lonely is waking up and not
seeing your smiling face
Lonely is the side of the bed
that should be your place.
Lonely is no one to laugh with
or cry with
Lonely is a walk in the park
without you
Lonely is always there
because you're not
Lonely is me without
you

Reva M Walker

Reva M Walker
WHEN LIFE IS DARK

Dedicated to Rev. James M. McPherson

When life is dark and seems upside
down
Look to the Heavenly Father and
wipe off that frown.
He's seen us through tougher times
than these;
We can look back now and say,
"That was a breeze!"
Our Heavenly Father never has let us
down
And if we trust him now and forever,
One day we'll receive a crown.
So put your hands to the plow and
don't look back
For there's much work to be done—
no time for slack.
There are lost sheep that need to be
brought into the fold
And their souls are much more
precious than gold.
So determine now in your mind and
in your heart
To find the lost sheep and bring them
in,
For when in eternity we'll never
more part.

Luke 9:62

Becci R Hoffman
HOLD ON TO YOUR LIFE

—To all the suffering alcoholics and drug addicts in the world—

Destruction, despair and absolute
trauma
are life's stages in rounds about
drama
You live, you die and Heaven
abounds
leaving the life you had in
mounds

Contacting the outer lining of space
the mirrored images of your
face

So cruel and damning, the inner peace
finding a way for this to cease

Hold on to your life, do not let go
Keeping the faith will always show
Richness and kindness there will be unfolding graciously for us to see

Once we find what we're looking for
revelation will fly forever more
Casting the shadows upon the ground
the sun reflecting the life you found

Nancy L Edgar
WORLD

To my many friends and family members who try so hard to keep their hearts open in this world . . . This is for the triumphs and the failures.

World is spinning—No one's winning
When will the facts be all laid out?
No one believing—Everyone deceiving
Leaving the world in a shadow of doubt.

We all want to choose—Yet with nothing to lose
We don't take the time to love at all,
Holding all feelings in—Walking on ice so thin
Building and perfecting our protective wall.

Living in sin—Hurting within
We keep on hurting ourselves,
Running from the good—Being misunderstood
Why do we put ourselves through this hell?

Too afraid to show love—Too anxious to draw blood
Can anything help us get back on our feet?
Killing those with a heart—Tear their feelings apart
Seems like we're ready to claim a defeat.

Something has to turn around—
Make us all homeward bound
We need to pull what we have left together,
Cause without love inside—Letting go of our pride
We'll lose ourselves in this hell forever.

Sean Rogers
WHO NEEDS YOU?

Who needs you? is dedicated to Elizabeth, with all of my love. How I wish you could have understood . . . . . Understand, that Shawnathan misses you. Thank-you James, for the changed, yet prompting letter.

I don't need you,
I desire you.
I don't NEED anyone, anything, anybody,
that helps me to become:
a better person, the best that I can be.
a better human being, one of the greatest that this world has ever seen.
a true man, to myself and all involved.
a true believer, even of the unknown.
a true success, in everything, and in all of the meanings tied to the word.
a driven man, striving to reach my fullest potential.
ELIZABETH,
CAN'T YOU SEE? ? ? ? ? ?

I'M IN LOVE WITH YOU! ! !
I DESIRE THE FEELINGS THAT
I HAVE WHEN I'M NEAR YOU,
WHEN I THINK OF YOU. I
WANT THOSE FEELINGS FOR
ALWAYS.
I WANT YOU, I DESIRE YOU,
I NEED YOU . . . .
I NEED YOU.
WHO NEEDS YOU?
I DO, THAT'S WHO.

Mrs Cloia Curtis
LA! WA! WA! GOLDEN CREEK RIVIERA

Dedicated to Mr James Haile

How: John Baptist was called on by "JESUS" to immerse him.
Into the WA! JORDAN LA GOLDEN RIVER.
"Wearing a white wrap on his head & a White Robe." JOHN BAPTIST—was found with
A BUCKET of "HONEY," that he used to dip La "LOCUST." Early he had gathered a "Brick" of SALT "from MRS LOT MINE" that he used this
A few grains to sprinkle on the "LOCUST."
As he Roasted them on an open fire, to nutrition for the body.
"JOHN BAPTIST," why me? For I am unworthy to tie your "SHOE STRING." One of the best messages that was PREACHED—To Jesus by "JOHN BAPTIST."

Phyllis O Siskind
THE LOAN

For my loved ones, For the future, Remember me.

We can't hold on to anything.
It's only out on loan.
Our friends and loved ones,
Time and gold
All slip away from us.

It's always much too soon, we say
When friend or love departs.
The shock and grief encover us
As we are left behind.

Accumulated coins are naught.
They follow not our souls
The years go fast before we know,
And then we, too, are gone.

A loan's a debt that must be paid,
And so it is with us.
For having lived God's precious life,
We must return to Him!

Alison Humiston
HERE I AM ALONE NEAR THE OCEAN

This poem is dedicated to my family, And loving dogs, Brandi and Champ For always being there for me

Here I am alone near the ocean
I will squirt on the cool feeling of my sun-tan lotion
I will sit on a cozy lounge chair
And I won't even care
About the problems back at home, that seem unfair
I will wear my dark glasses
And overhead see the bright green grasses
The sand will feel as soft as flour
With it, I will build a huge beautiful sand tower
The ocean is the color of bright turquoise
I'll hear the sounds of the waves, joyful noise
I will find the most precious sea shells
The seagulls fly above me and I will hear them yell
Everything is so gorgeous and glee
I don't know if I'll ever want to leave

Robin A Geesman
REMEMBER MY WARNING

Creep slowly, my child
For the whispers of darkness
Are never-ending.

Speak softly, my child
For your words shall echo
Through the minds of others.

And always tread lightly
For the sound of your footsteps
Shall lead the path for those yet to follow.

Remember my warning
And you'll find peace within yourself
And all that surrounds you.

Diane Elizabeth Scott
PORCELAIN MONDAY

For Charles whose Mondays run eternal, and whose water bill is extraordinarily high.

Well it's Monday again, and
Thank God for the sewer system, because
There's a pile of shit, shit, shit on Monday morning.
The swelling flush began rising the moment that it,
Whose pieces scattered in trash can,
Was a ringing alarm clock.
Found roaches living in coffee filters.
Spilt coffee on floor.
Left it there.
Late to class, because
Rising to the crest,
(like all the pimples on my face growing into one last big one) . . .
Monday.
Flung off speeding bicycle
Butt busted
Right onto cold hard, Monday morning.
Sloshing down the drain, and
Thank God for Monday morning.
It doesn't run on Tuesday.

Sheila D North
FOREVER YOURS

For my loving husband Micheal. Without you, this poem would have never been written. I love you. S.

I thought my love that I
would write you a simple
poem, to tell you "I love
you" in all shapes and forms

My love for you is growing
stronger through every passing
day. Your love is in my heart
and there is where it will stay

You're always asking me "How
much do you love me?" More
than anything I'll say.
There is no one else in this
"big wide world" that makes
me feel this way

Now do you know how much
I love you? If not I'll
tell you once more. I love
you more than anything, and
my love is "Forever Yours."

Kate Bushman
GOOD-BYE MY FRIEND

To my forever friend, Brenda Newman. Thanks for being there for me. I'll miss you when we're apart, but I will always love you.

I didn't know you in the beginning
But then we became good friends.
I guess I never figured
That it would ever end.

Our friendship grew stronger
I thought it would last longer
But then I found you had to leave.

I sat and thought about that first day.
When you smiled and acted so gay,
Then I came back in reality and knew you couldn't stay.

The last day of school was the hardest for me,
I couldn't let you know. I couldn't let you see,
That I was hurting inside, and knew it couldn't be.

After I had cried
It felt as if my heart had died
I knew that was my last good-bye

So every night I sit in bed,
And pictures of you flash through my head,
If only I had told you, if only I had said.

I love you and I'll miss you
And there's only few, from my point of view
That love you like I did
That loves you like I do.

Laural D Anderson
A PLACE CALLED HELL

This is dedicated to those POW/ MIA's in the Vietnam War; You are not forgotten.

Satan's law will unlock the door
To a place called Hell;
And that is where I shall go.

I see flames and dames,
And hear the screams,
That so long plagued
My childhood dreams.

Here I stand
In Satan's court,
Found guilty of my plea;
As I walk toward
My final decree.

I'm damned in Hell,
My soul is His;
Shackled to the sins
Of my past.

My home,
A place I've come to know
So well;
In this place called Hell.

Edna Kleis
TENDER ARE THE LEAVES

To our daughters, Danabeth Holleman and Opal Chilson

Tender are leaves that whisper
words of love.
I can hear his answer now as he
answers
When I ask, "How much do you
love me?"
"Ten bushel baskets full—
with the tops, bottoms and
sides out."
Yes, tender are the leaves
when they echo these words.
Love that is infinite, and I'm not
worthy.
My love for him was a heart full
and running over.
Life with him became a new
thing,
I was a new person.
He spoke words of love and the
tender leaves echo them to this
day.
I hear them whenever Silence
surrounds me.
Though he is gone from—I still
hear his words in the rustle
of Tender Leaves

Evie Ginsberg-Cowan
FRIENDS AND LOVERS

To my loving husband, Douglas Cowan

Came to your house
We meet by accident
We talked and talked

Became friends

We talked and talked
Every night by phone
You are there and I'm here

We talked and talked
Days went by
Months went by

Talked and talked
Now you decide to see me

Your heart opens up
My heart pounds

Should I stay
Should I go
You're the one
Don't let go

I love you
You love me
Forever and ever.

Anonymous
SIX TALL MEN

For Lois—my grandmother and friend

Standing out in the cold, I see six tall men
I see the woman, stooped and old, as she watches them
And in my mind, I can see a myriad of things
I can hear a memory, clear as the church bell rings
A quiet man, humble and good, who made so few demands
He made his life with blocks of wood he fashioned with his hands
A grandchild he'd set on his knee, and smile his gentle smile
He'd beckon to a scared puppy to visit for a while
In summer's heat, he'd lift a hand to wipe his dusty brow
The dust that rose from the land so dry and barren now
The memories, they flutter to-and-fro across my mind
As quietly I utter to this man my last goodbye
And six tall men, they stand so proud as they lay him down
With all respect, our heads bowed, we place him in the ground
Standing beneath a frozen gray sky, kissed by the frigid wind
With a tear I say, "Grandpa, goodbye—until we meet again."

Laura Hill
SMILE

I would like to dedicate this poem to my son, Darius LaShante Hill

Smile when you're happy;
Don't endure pain and sorrow
Because there's still tomorrow.

Smile and thank God you can;
Because God made man
And he smiles all the time,

Smile to everyone when you're sad,
If you don't that person might get
mad.

Smile to the world and be sweet:
Because it's like the ocean & the
wind
Who knows when you might get beat

Ms M Eileen Cloud

Ms M Eileen Cloud
A DREAM CAN BE REAL
Hold your head up high
and never, never look down
don't let your dreams turn into a lie
When you become discouraged; look around
for somewhere out there, there is a friend
who's with you until the very end.

So you come from a broken home
Where to have and believe in a dream is a joke
While taking to the streets to roam
seems to ease your heavy yoke

I know that when you're in the streets
you can feel free and be at peace.
no one to laugh at you,
or make you feel and look uncool

Now ask yourself "What do I want from life?"
Do you want nothing, but constant struggle and strife?
if not start now getting busy as that little ol' bee
making hard work, confidence, and consistency your keys.

Joyce Gentry
MOM

To my Mom for giving me the courage to dream

She's the one who's always there
To make my world seem bright
For she has a heart that cares
And that helps me through the night

Her sweet love will forever flow
Within this heart of mine
Like the wind that softly blows
Through a lonesome pine

She gave me life ever sweet
And blessed the day I was born
You would love her if you meet
For any life she could adorn

I'm lucky to call her mine
As I'm sure that you can see
For she ages like a fine wine
My mom ages with beauty to me

Karin LeCouteur-Sullivan
FACES OF YESTERDAY

To those at The Ritz Club, you know who you are, for hours of inspiration and encouragement to pursue my dreams.

The mood of today blossoms
in a well.
Water rippling down the
contours of my face,
Into a pool on the floor near my feet.
Until now my shoes were dry,
the souls
Breaking in the sun of my dreams.
Tomorrow 'til then is but
a fantasy in my heart.
Dancing on broken wings,
soaring high
To a sky that's bright
and void of light.
Rainbows beaming through
silver lined clouds.
Searching is the bird in
free flight form.
Climbing and dipping
from the heavens
Through the faces of yesterday.

Edward D Voelker
DAWN

To Louise, my love, my wife!

Strolling through the woods
o'er damp leaves springy mat
See where rain has driven
down amongst the fern
And fragrant shy young violets
their faces upward turn
To peer through tangled boughs
washed clean by storm and wind
At ragged empty clouds
fleeing from the sky
Now the sun appears
and birds begin to fly.

Brian P Collier
REFLECTIONS

To: my dear departed grandparents Dick & Naomi Bauer, I'll always love you!

What is freedom? Is it a deliverance or perhaps a rising beyond my days and nights of loneliness to break the chains which I have fastened around my noon-hour? What is it but fragments of myself that I may discard for the namesake of freedom.

When I lose my fetters and become free, "does not that freedom only become a greater set of fetters?"

Pain and loneliness, I claim as mine. I have fought against it time after time, only to be captured within my prime.

For my prison is my mind and my freedom, my soul. Where and when it may end I'll never come to know.

Viva Gay Armstrong
WIDOWED

This poem is dedicated to Jim, my darling husband, now deceased.

I have watched my dreams and expectations marred from the breath of reality,
saw the visions of a new born day, slip away into a vast fog of nothingness.

I have been clothed in joy and happiness where its height had no boundaries,
but was shared with time which was fleeting, and had an end.

I have known love, Felt the quality of its strength and tasted its passion, In seeing it, knowing it and feeling it, every fiber in me knew, that for a short time, I, had had the best.

I have cradled my memories like
an infant, hoping the warmth of
my own love would keep them
alive, only to feel them like
sifting sand,
slipping away into the night.

I have danced with Angels while
devils watched, and felt the
comfort of knowing, they could
not touch me.
It was only when the Angels let
go, that I realized the vastness
of my inabilities.

These thoughts, only vapors
rushing through me like arrows,
from every direction I feel their
sting,
And I am filled with wonder,
which way to go.

Louella Marie Antone
ETERNA SOUL (TEET-PHA TEET-PHA)

I hope that some day ALL TREATIES WILL BE HONORED FOR ALL NATIVE AMERICANS.

Memories
Memories that haunt my mind.
Now history has it written and
pictures tell their story.
"In this land of peace and glory"
Settlers came bearing gifts and our
peace pipes were lit. But soon the
fighting began.
As our leaders fell to their death.
And many loved ones at their side.
Leaving us with our tears and fears,
and no hope in our hearts. But where
do I put my memories?
"In this land of peace and glory"

Bernard
A RAINBOW—GONE BUT NOT FORGOTTEN

To Bonnie Ann—Whose forgiveness should be as great as Love once was, Love greater than anger, and Rainbows a beautiful memory.

Its brilliant hues cast streamers
between the hills
And so it came to be the creation of
sun and rain,

A varied multi colored rainbow,
Which in my contemplation I found to be,
Of two sides, each having its own cast,
One a deeply shadowed mist of dew and clouds,
The other warm, smiling, loving, sun,
A view of beauty never-to-be-forgotten
The "pot-of-gold" I found to be,
Of long chestnut-blonde hair,
Flowing in the ripple of wind,
Of droplets clinging to a golden summer tan,
A glittering smile that filled empty rooms,
Blended together they became nature's delicate creation.
Oh, how I miss the rainbow, it appears so seldom,
For now the golden treasure that is her smile,
Is gone, but not forgotten,
Now I long for both rain and sun,
To see the rainbow again.

Edyth E Powell
I CARE

The poem is dedicated to E.A. George

I care
It has been established
Do you care
It has not been established
Whether it is true
Of you
It doesn't matter
Because
I care
Yesterday
Today
And tomorrow

Joyce Eybers
SIGHT SEEING

I would like to dedicate this poem to all the people who helped me struggle through the hard times. Thanks.

Beautiful, but cannot touch
Walking through the words.
Strong trees, big roots
'Til man destroys it.

Frederick Steven Calloway
AMERICA

To the Minnifields, Calloways, and the Walkers

America,
you've got three-quarters of this man crying
the other one-quarter of him dying
and the whole of him drowning in fear
very much afraid to face the sun
for it may be a mistake during these dark ages
for he may turn and it may not be there
so he'll keep his head tilted down toward the rain
trying psychologically to remove the strain
upstairs and downstairs and in his sleep cramped-
down in prayer style still trying to believe
his heart will rise above . . . .
because of his faith he's questioning all
howling still like his friend
barking in efforts that he may live
his life
his soul
he must not know
his spirit is scrambling upon the ground
loveless and less
god! please have mercy before it's too late

Marilyn R Brace
CHILD OF LOVE

To all mankind

As I wandered in the mist today
There appeared a child so bright and gay
I heard her laughter so full of glee
As she swayed and danced with the trees

She played with the animals cuddly and soft
As an owl watched over her from a loft
Over her head hovered a morning dove
To all living things she gave her love

As she kissed a primrose and glanced my way
I felt there was something she wanted to say
Suddenly I realized this child was me
The loving, trusting child I used to be

Ever so softly she whispered to me
As a loving child you must always be
Thank you God for reminding me

Terrisa Evans
SILENT FRIENDS

Written for: A.S.F.F.

I once met a man on life's lonesome road,
Our hands both empty, yet each had a load.
I asked if he'd like to share the walk.
"Okay," he replied, "but I don't like to talk."

We closely, yet separately, walked a long ways,
While we both silently longed for our earlier days.
He liked it that way, simple and sweet,
Keeping his feelings wrapped up so neat.

We shared only a road in one of life's counties,
But the feelings of oneness was a glorious bounty.
He started to grow on me before I could tell,
It was hard to believe this man was real.

When we got to the fork, I did silently stand,
To wait for his asking to take hold his hand.
"Sorry kid," was his way of good-bye,
So I forced a smile, and never shall cry.

Deep down I knew I was crowding his space,
Even while walking, it showed on his face.
I wore out first welcome, away he did go.
I shouted after him in a voice soft and low.

You're in my heart now
like it or not.
I'm sure going to miss you
a hell of a lot!
Think kindly of me once in awhile,
I will of you, each time I smile.

Sophie Chubrich
HE HAS GONE AWAY

In memory of my beloved husband

He has gone away, he has gone to stay—
And I cannot follow.
Since he's been gone, I don't belong
My life is bare and hollow.
We had made so many plans,
But like the tide and like the sands
They are gone, before tomorrow.
I try so hard to reconstruct,
I need more time to readjust.
I must confess, I cry a lot,
Alone at night, like a frightened tot.
Bless my family, for all their love—
And for "His" comfort from above.
Bless my friends from far and near,
They are all so kind and very dear.
Time will heal, of that I am sure—
But the pain and tears, I must endure.
He will always be, a part of me
His love from me, will never flee.
He has gone away, he has gone to stay.
And I cannot follow.

Kathleen Robertson Bryan
LIFE IS BEAUTIFUL

I dedicate this poem to my beloved family

Each flower, each bird
Each tiny bee
The sunset glow
On rolling sea
All this and more
Was made for me—
Life is beautiful!

Each thought of love
With warmth and care
For God above
Makes one aware—
Life is beautiful!

Even flowing tears
In times of grief
Heartaches and fears
There comes relief
In believing still—
Life is beautiful!

Maria Rosa Marchetti
SIMILAR LIFE

To my 7th grade English teacher, Mrs. Cindy Garetson—

Be strong, no weakness,
Time is running out,
Deep inside flames burn,
Quenching life in youth,
Tears wash nothing away,
All is black and dim,
Clocks tick with an echo
In an endless darkness,
People laugh,
Killing happiness,
Dogs bark,
Taking away madness,
Hair flaps in the wind,
Blowing all away,
Be strong, no weakness,
Time is running out.

Claire T Swafford
I SHOULD WEEP FOR YOU

To my loving mother, Clara Woodson. For your love, help, and for believing in me—I dedicate this to you.

Today it broke my heart to see . . .
The ones I love weep at the death of me.
For it is I who should weep for thee.
Because I am happy—I am free.
You are left to carry on.
Thru sadness and tears now that I'm gone.
There is no pain for me to bear,
And only memories left to share.
I cannot ease the pain you feel—
Nor comfort you as you kneel—
In prayer for me to our dear God.
For peace along the path I trod.
Now know in your heart that it isn't I—
Who'll sit alone at night to cry.
And so each night remember this—
That I am in eternal bliss.
Now there's one thing that you should know—
I am gone from here but even so
Never again let me see you blue,
For it is I who should weep for you!

Sandy Artino
OUR FUTURE

"To Joey," a very special man.

The land of the Proud and the Free.
These words were always taught to me.

History showed great things in the past
But the Future says, Can this last?

People helping one another, Oh no not true!
The situation doesn't concern you.

No prayer or discipline in our schools—
That's not one of the "Golden Rules"

Who's your neighbor? I don't know.
I only moved there a year ago . . .

To the house of the Lord, your money's been sent,
but it's the preacher who must Repent!

Children suffering, people sleeping in the streets,
Murder, Terrorism, What do we do?

We look to the Future
God, Can this be true?

Gayle Crane
MY MOTHER'S PRAYER

This poem is dedicated to my mother-in-law, Velma Sanders, who passed away 8/19/86. Yes, she is gone but her soul will live forever!

Known to some as just another
She was known to me as Mother

Even though she lye there dying
While I sit beside her crying,
Thinking the Lord will take her in just awhile
As I will never forget her warm and friendly smile.

She wouldn't want it this way,
So I must go on
Lord, give me the strength to
sing my song.

Good things come to those who
wait.
Mother's at Heaven's gate.

Lord, heal our hearts of this sorrow
For there will be a bright tomorrow

Keep her under your wing and
teach us all to sing
How to get along with one another
And let us never forget, she was
known to all as Mother

Lisa Gugino
THE STRUGGLE INSIDE

Scott my love—always fight the reality and live for the dreams.—Lisa

The struggle inside
Must be fought
Let it not fade
For it shall never leave
It will only come again
And the battle will be fierce.
You must overcome . . .
The reality—

Kenneth Yanow

Kenneth Yanow
SAMANTHA'S SONG

This poem is dedicated to my loving wife and angel of a child

I said I would be a millionaire,
The time by the year of thirty,
Money I thought the reason
Only to find not on this 120th
(hundred-twentieth) season.

Samantha born in November;
I now know wealth is forever,
Full of joy, wonder and pleasure, I
am now a millionaire forever and
ever.

So dreams come true, just have a
vision,
Don't care what others think, make it
your own decision,
The means may differ all along,
The end is the same—this is
Samantha's Song.

Dear Samantha, this is your song
I wrote it for you all along

In many ways one receives wealth,
not only by money, material or
wealth
A new life begins every night and
every day, this is the healthiest,
wealthiest way.

The beauty and love we always long,
Is the thought equal to Samantha's
song,
The curls, the smirks, the eyes and
the burps
All make the dime, quarter and dollar
smirk.

I love our little gem, tiny, pink and
cute
Just to love Samantha is all I want to
do.

Janet Lee Pastorius
DERRICK—THE 8TH WONDER OF THE WORLD

For all the Middle Children of the World, with special love to My Buddy Derrick and My Sister Cheryl.

There is an adventurous boy named
Derrick,
whose bully streak can be as
mighty as an oil derrick.

However, don't let that bully streak
fool you, my friend,
for another trait outshines it,
over and over again.

His love, by the way he lets you enter
his world
and shares with you his
compassion for lizards and
squirrels.

Thank you, Derrick, for showing me
Just how beautiful a lizard can
be.

Derrick, my buddy, remember one
thing,
you will always be loved for you
make hearts "sing."

May Nature always present its
wondrous beauty to you,
so that life will always appear
exciting and new.

Rosa L Coleman
A WORTHY LEGACY TO HOLD

To the present and oncoming generations of those whom I love most dearly.

A legacy given to us by our parents
of many decades
As we, the children listened
grudgingly, but came to rely
On behavioral restrictions, some less
stern, the teachings
Issued on morals, integrity, and
taming of wild escapades,
Youthfully taken for granted, despite
all preachings
Regarding many hazards, inevitable
consequence to ensue,
When doing the things that we
shouldn't do.

Yes, dear brothers, I am an older
sister who, indeed
Was trained, as girls then were
taught, the virtue
Of learning to cuddle, feed and
comfort, fulfill the need
Of the younger siblings, and also
learn to nurture
Fledgling differences between the
rights and the wrongs.

Old-fashioned? Perhaps. But how
does one ever learn
To consider, cherish and love, by
never hearing the songs
Of generational survival and those
bright futures to earn?
Now, with passage of time and
circumstances impacted,
We see with elderly ease the great
need to revert
To the once adhered paths our own
parents exacted,
Hoping to steer us from the pitfalls,
dangers and hurt.

And, if wisely passed on, each
generation will see
The worth of holding on to such a
legacy.

T M Windley
LIFE'S SEDUCTIVE DEALER

To my daughter, Breanna; I hope life deals her a winning hand in everything she does.

Life is a seductive dealer,
It lets your cards start out in place,
Then it takes a hairpin turn
And gives away your ace.

Life seems to give a better hand
To someone that doesn't need it,
Then makes sure that all you get
Is cards that could never beat it.

Then life seductively deals again,
Seducing you to think your ace is in.
But then life deals you one more
card,
The card that won't let you win.

But I'm not giving up on life
Or all its seducing dealer's faces,
Eventually it will deal me
The hand with all the aces.

Robyn Christine Yanke
WATERBOUND

To Grandpa Kirkpatrick, the one who inspired me to write.

The wind blows across my face,
I speed along with crispness and
grace.

The water is cool and clear,
I feel not a tinge of fear.

A turn and a figure eight,
The sensation feels so great.

The world stops, there is no sound
As the boat takes me 'round and
'round.

This is life upon the waves.
I could stay out here for days.

Alas and alack,
We have to go back . . . .
But there's always TOMORROW!

Pierre B Jones
UNA NOCHE DE AMOR

To my wife Pat, 2 daughters Shaina & Mireia and Mom (Shirley M. Armstrong)—"A scop, 4 alluring women & a continuous perfume of God"

Una Noche De Amor
Fulgent, didst thy eyes capture
me
Fro' beaten knees, I fell to th' floor
Knowing not, my heart, hae you
th' key.

Una Noche De Amor
Thy great love; left a frivolous
man
A sweet poniard in deep, I yearned
for more
Alone, melodious air, lead the
silent band.

Una Noche De Amor
Was it possible to negate all that
was
To touch thy face, blood came, but
none poured
Resurgent temperatures, is this
what love does?

Una Noche De Amor
She whispered her name o'
elegiac gest
With alar love, didst finally swing
th' door
"Pat," I screamed, my soul hath
come to rest.

Sarah Berkowitz
SITTING IN THE DARKNESS

Sitting in the darkness,
staring out the front room window,
waiting for the headlights,
that never seem to come.

Feelings that are fading,
from the loneliness I'm feeling,
wishing he was with me,
knowing that he's not.

In my mind I see him,
amidst the neon, smoke, and
laughter,
amongst those bar room people,
who call themselves his friends

But they only know me,
as his bar room widow,
not sharing in the emptiness
I am feeling from within.

Rose-Marie Roy
A NEW BEGINNING

To my precious Bob, whose love and encouragement bring me endless inspiration.

As I step out of a tunnel of darkness
I sense the warmth of your closeness
Your radiant smile sets my skin
aglow
Penetrating each pore from head to
toe
As I close the door on my sadness
and pain
I look in your eyes and know I can
love again
Your touch is so gentle, it greets me
with care
I melt in your tenderness, it's more
than I can bear
As the memories of the past become
distant and weak
I grasp for the right words but I'm
not able to speak
Your silent thoughts are now
mingling with mine
I taste your desire like a full bodied
wine
As we embark on a brand new
tomorrow
You fill me with hope to replace the
sorrow
We bathe in our passion, are together
as one
Setting no boundaries, for us there
are none

As our spirits untangle we're content and secure
We drift on to sleep all smug and so sure
That our future will blossom and continue to flourish
Because of the love that we will always nourish.

Belinda Jean Chaffin
FIRST LOVE

I would like to dedicate this poem to my parents Landonia and Weldon Chaffin for passing their love and ability to create and write poetry to me. Thank you. I love you both.

My first love
A love that I thought I would never forget
Gave me the opportunity to share a part of me that I didn't know I had
A part of me that would climb the highest mountain
And tell the whole world I'm in love
Separations only made me want him more and still that wasn't enough
Our love was touched by Midas
Everything we touched turned to love

Mary Anderson-Rotvald
UNTITLED

For all the wisdom in the silence of emotion— poetry is its freedom

The binding worn with age and words . . .
The pages of momentary thought
and the pens that have run dry.
This book of books,
silent and private to all but me.

Containing the joys,
the sorrows that are mine.

To be a poet of nothing,
and yet of so much.
Personality within
personality . . . . Tears
within tears.
It is artistry at the tip of my
pen . . . the pen that flows
freely over these lines of
indifference.

And as my book ages, I
continue to age my words.
Their meaning often lost
to incoherent thought.

This treasure, worth ten times
that of gold and its weight
twenty times that of steel, is a
precious gift to share. And
would there be greater
rewards than this, more
than I receive right now?

I think not!

For it is on this ninety-eighth
page, that a wisdom is
spoken with true
meaning . . . no games
being played . . .
it is simply a reflection of
me.

Emilie Lucas
FOR YOU DEAR FRIEND

Dedicated to Gary, my dearest friend. I will always appreciate you.

Lay your head upon my breast
Let our tears flow free
For I understand your sorrow
And you my friend are a part of me.
Give up the ache and share the pain
Let the well run over with your anguished refrain.
For what are we for, if we cannot bear
The heartaches and sorrows of those for whom we care.

Lay your head upon my breast
And sigh a sigh of relief
For when it all passes through
I will give it up to the ethers
And that dear friend will free you.

Pamela Fischer
A FEELING(S)

Dedicated to my future husband, Philip L'Heureux "now and for always." Also to my mother Sandra Caskey, for all her love and support for the last 24 years.

A feeling of hope; a feeling of caring;
A feeling so subtle; a feeling so daring.
A feeling of body; a feeling of mind,
A feeling of heart; a feeling so blind.
A feeling so candid it feels like a sin,
A feeling so wonderful the body gives in.
A feeling of want; a feeling of giving.
A feeling of happiness; a feeling of living,
A feeling of openness; a feeling forever,
A feeling of togetherness; a feeling to endeavor.
A feeling of marriage; a feeling of child,
A feeling so mellow; a feeling so wild.
A feeling of health; a feeling of pain,
A feeling of smiles; a feeling of strains.
A feeling of want; a feeling of . . . . .
All it could be is the feeling(s) of love!

James Deaux
ON AGE . . . . . .

To the many wonderful guys & gals throughout this country with whom I share this philosophy . . .

29's a lucky year . . means you
finally pack the gear . . . to get out
with the movin' set an' show
'em what they ain't seen yet!
you've learned the ropes and
run the bars . . . you're
diggin' all the concept cars
you've had your share of
"far-out" drinks . . .
casual love and folks with
kinks . . .!

39's a turning point, been
everywhere 'cept in
the "joint" . . had a place
down on the beach . . . . .
nothin' cool was out of reach!
All the college kids are blah . . .
beers held on high, a loud
RAH-RAH . . .
aperitifs are more your style . . .
a subtle pass . . .
. . . . a misty smile! !

49's the year to have . . . in
retrospect you soothe
and salve the bitter
words . . the endless fight
you showed "your self" . . .
to show "you're right" . . . a
monday-morning quarterback,
you sit in candlelight
and wrack your brains to
set the past all straight . . .
with more aplomb
. . . a little late! !

But when you get to be your age
. . . Lord knows there is no wiser
sage . . .
money and advice you loan, but
both in such a moderate tone . . . .
the only time you have a sip
are birthdays . . . or a market
dip. . . so let's address an
ageless toast . . .
"What e'er the day . . . .
. . . enjoy it most! ! !"

Dorothy L Barchus

Dorothy L Barchus
WHISPERING PINES

Blue skies, heavenly stars, a full moon beaming down.
All shining through the pine trees and whispering their music.
In the quietness of the night, the whole world seems at peace.
If you stop and listen you will notice that "JESUS" is your companion.

The whispering pines are like the ocean.
When the waves wash ashore it brings the sound of music.
As you stroll along the beach, the green meadows, the birds sing.
The flowers sway, the wind blows and all in tune with their music.
It is a miracle for all to hear and see when spring blossoms forth.

Way up in space, where you can barely see the stars shiny so bright,
it's like tiny Christmas lights spread across the sky and it gives a tiny glimpse of what lies beyond the land of paradise.
But the whispering pines are towering high above the ground,
singing the praises and standing as a sentinel to the land of paradise.

Karen T Every-Pedro
ENTER MY WORLD AND GENTLY CLOSE THE DOOR

For Joe, for finally seeing my need to be me.

Enter my world
and gently close the door.
You are one of the few,
chosen to look inside me.
To listen to my heart,
to touch my soul
To share my treasures
of love and laughter and life.
Seeing the complex—yet simple structure
of my mind.
To feel the wall of my very existence.
To touch and push so deeply
into the crevices of my life.
Listen: can you hear the beating
of that magical device—
That gives me daily life?
Can you hear my thoughts
at night—when I am quiet?
With only the gentle breathing
after the storm
Gently touch me—
and the storm will begin again.
And when you choose to leave,
Slowly withdraw
And gently close the door.

Shelley Lynn Bailey
THE LIGHT OF LIFE

To Mom, Dad, Donna, Lisa, Rusty, Rachel, Elsie, Etta, Dianne, Kenny, Gregory, Cindy, Tiy and The Almighty God; Thank You for everything.

My pocket is filled with money,
my head is full of dreams.

I look unto the future,
get scared and start to scream.

I remember those special words,
"What you dream you can become."

Yet the pathway is dark and shallow,
all I can do is run.

My life is like a room,
where the windows are painted black.

Beneath the darken shadows,
is a gold and shiny track.

The track holds a rule,
that only hope can find.

The best will surely come,
the answer in your mind.

Just open all the windows,
until the light shines in.

And when it hits the track,
your life will soon begin.

John Eugenio
WHY MUST YOU TORMENT ME?

You were way ahead of your time, but now the World will finally get to read your poetry, as you will from heaven above. Love, your sister Marie La Guardia and family.

Your footprints on the seashore;
Your laughter by the sycamore;
I see you dancing on the seven seas;
Why must you torment me?

I walk with you when snow falls;
I hear your name near ivied walls;
I hear your voice in every summer breeze;
Why must you torment me?

Why can't I get you off my mind;
Why don't I lose my memory;
Why can't I start a new romance;
Why must I live in misery?

I hold your hand in springtime;
I see the smile I thought was mine;
I'm always near you in my memory;
Why must you torment me?

Henrietta L Johnson
THE WORD

Father you have brought me
through the wilderness of
confusion.
Through your Word my faith has

grown—through the readings
and study I have progressed.

I am no longer a body molded in
dissension.
My prayers have been answered
through your grace not by
persistence.

The light has been revealed to me
at the end of a dense forest.

Through my growing faith, I will
walk to that light unharmed and
receive the glory that has been
promised to me through your
word.

Jamie Nestaval
FRIENDS

To the world's greatest mom with love

Friends are all people who trust
one another
Who don't become enemies
easily
A friend can be anyone a
Teacher, a schoolmate or even
your parents
Even people you dislike can be
your friend if you give
them a chance
Some people have a lot of
friends and others have none
But if you think long and hard
We've all had a friend from
the very beginning
And that of course is the
best friend of all
That friend is you Mom!

Janice Irene Hatt
TOGETHER

Dedicated to my best friend Chrissie Walling, my wonderful, loving husband Bruce and to all my friends from Easthampton High School

O, please, I ask of you, my friends,
My sweet and dearest, best of friends,
Do not let me walk alone
This road of sharp and curving bends.

Who knows what might there lie
ahead
Just beyond that mysterious curve?
Could it be dangers or fortune there?
Will it be something we deserve?

O, let us ever walk hand in hand,
Together we'll cope with all our
fears,
Up and down the long, lonely roads
We'll share our laughter and our
tears.

And so, my true and loyal friends,
My very, very best of friends,
Never, let us, never walk alone
As we continue 'round those bends.

Sharon Ann McNamara Shorma
A SUNDAY AT THE LAKE

Forgive me, God, if it seems to be . . . A very long time since you've heard from me . . . Don't think that I've forgotten you . . . When your Church shows up my empty pew.

I know, some Sundays, I could have been there . . . And maybe it seems I no longer care . . . But, God, that's so far from being true . . . When I seemed distant, I was close to you.

I recall one Sunday in your sunshine . . . I sat at the lake with a fishing line . . . And the peace I felt surrounding me . . . Is the peace I find in Church with Thee.

And that sunset when the world stood still . . . And reminded me of the things it will . . . . The family and friends I've come to love . . . Is peace and contentment from above.

Life has a way of going too fast . . . Before I have time to enjoy, it's past . . . Away from the hustle and bustle it seems . . . I have time to relax and dream new dreams.

I see the flowers and trees in bloom . . . Filling my days full as they have room . . . And find time to notice the little things . . . That make me happy—how my heart sings.

So, God, don't think that I forgot . . . I've filled my days with such a lot . . . I spent them happy and carefree . . . Enjoying the wonders you've given me.

Janinne Grimes
DANCING

Dancing is not a game of easy-come-
easy-go,
it is something that you earn,
It doesn't come from being pretty or
popular at all,

It comes from your will to learn.
It doesn't show what school you go
to, it shows from deep in your heart.
It doesn't matter what part you get,
It matters if you give it your best
from the start.
It isn't easy, you might agree, it
sometimes makes you hurt and cry.
But it teaches you to get back up and
teaches you to try,
It doesn't matter if you lose and don't
win.
The loser is the one who falls and
won't get up again.

Barbara Nordlund
MY LITTLE GUY

To Daniel—my son

Climbing trees, skinned elbows and
knees,
Searching for spiders and ants;
Grubby little face so lively and
bright,
Finding joy under rocks and in
plants.

Rolling on the grass, singing to
yourself,
Catching a kitty cat too;
Looking for the ladybugs, only on the
"hump,"
That special place just for you.

A baby caterpillar so soft and alive,
You show me just what you find;
There's a slug and a worm collection
to see,
So many treasures to find.

My little guy, you never grow tired,
Discovering so many things;
Never let go of that happiness,
Only outside adventures can bring.

Joy Henderson
A CHILD'S PLAY

Watch them laughing, see them run,
Never knowing life's just begun.
Today's agenda, eat, sleep and play,
Time doesn't matter, it's just a day.
Not a plan for tomorrow, not even a
care,
It's right here and now, and with
whom and where.
Today we'll build castles and slay
dragons that fly,
Play cowboys and indians, then eat
apple pie.
We'll chase all the monsters from
under the bed,
And tell all our friends, what so and
so said.
Someday I'll be a doctor, or maybe a
cook,
I might fly to the moon, just to take a
look.
Here comes the neighbor's old cat to
play,
Pretend it's a lion and chase it away.
I'll be Superman, you're the bad guy,
This towel is my cape, now watch me
fly!
Pretend we're flying this kite to the
stars,
Oh! Never mind now, it's time to
race cars.
Yes Mama, I heard you I'll clean up
the mess,
I'll just start over tomorrow I guess.

Adelia (Adelle) A Alcaraz
YOU'RE STILL A FRIEND TO ME

I will always be your friend
That's what you've said to me
I still recall those happy times
Those memories, sweet memories
Shared by you and me

But now you've changed
I thought our friendship will last
forever
Through thick and thin
We'll be the best of friends

I can't blame you—
Being with other guys
But when things won't work out right
Don't hesitate to come
Cause you can count on me

You're still a friend to me
A friend who will always be
Not only when you're happy
But most of all—
When you're alone . . . .
Feelin' down and lonely

Nola N Shiverdecker
MATHILDA

It is so quiet and still in here.
Her voice is gone that was sweet and
dear.
She was so good when the baby had
come,
Always knowing just what each cry
came from.
Then when Anne was ill and fever so
high
Night and day by her bedside she'd
quietly lie.
She was patient and friendly to one
and to all
Of the people who, to the house,
might come to call.
When Grandfather died she mourned
like the rest
But always showed love and gave of
her best.
No, it isn't the same and I'm quite
sad today
For Mathilda's nine lives just faded
away.

Tamara Montgomery James
WHISPERING WIND

Dedicated to my loving Daughters; Ashly Ann & Rachel Renée—Listen to the songs your heart sings.

Because up ev'ry
Sunny plateau
You go;

It ofttimes rains
And sometimes
Snows
In the end,
Whispering wind . . .
Will show you
Which valley
Has buffalo
And which
Has deer
Which one you'll
Walk alone;
And which will have
Me near . . .

Dorothy Kofoed
LIFE'S MIND

Time is out there,
You can see it through the tunnel of
life.
The gentle breeze will keep the
candle light flickering,
Choose your passages well.

Walk upon this earth,
Don't run in a fury to places
unknown,
Hold your head high,
Let your eyes see the light of
guidance.
Treat your body with respect for all
to see.

Use your heart for love to honor you
with others,
Let your conscience open up to all
that's good.

Exercise your mind, feed it with
spirit.
Let it—Be active
—Breathe on life
—Run on strength
—Override pain
—Vitalize energy
—Overcome fear
Use your mind to the fullest,
Don't let it lie dormant without
meaning.

Life is out there and it is ours to
keep,
But only until our final sleep.

Barbara L Santiago
IF YOU KNEW . . .

If you knew how much I love you,
you would think the same thing too.
Oh Nestor, how I miss you, I'd do
anything to kiss you.
Every time I think of you I get
the feeling I'll never see you,
What this feeling is I'll never
Know, please Nestor never say
no. If we ever get together
I hope and pray that we'll stay
forever.

Julie Heck Magley
CHRISTMAS EVE

To Betty, Joseph and grandchildren

Tonight one sees
Trimmed branches of trees,
Sprinkled with stardust and
silver rain.
Amid gay times
Christmas bells and chimes
Ring out a sweet and joyous
refrain.
All is aglow
With bright winter snow,
Little children await Santa's call,
Love fills the air,
Kind folks give and share,
And bring comfort and goodwill
to all.

Katherine J Weber
REQUIEM FOR AN UNDERTAKER

In dedication to James Daly, Snover Funeral Home, the mysterious undertaker who fired my imagination.

His eyes, something in his eyes—
enveloping me, drawing me near

familiar yet unfamiliar,
vacant yet full,
easy yet distant
Obsession

Where is he tonite?
Where does he lurk in the shadows?

Loomed over somebody
or some "body"
dead or alive
Jealous

I want him,
etched across my body,
my being—
capturing my soul
Completely

His eyes, something in his eyes—
or morbid curiosity.

Hoss Melton
TO CONFESS A FALLACY

This poem is dedicated to my wife and best friend, Cindy Melton

There's a song, there's a song,
It says I've been everywhere.
In my twenty years on the road
I was sure I'd been there.
I've seen the sights from coast to
coast,
The Grand Canyon, Mt. Rushmore,
I loved Oregon the most.
I felt my life was boring,
Excitement at its end.
I had done and seen it all, and done
some of it again.
Then God took my life,
And sent me where he knew I'd
never been,
In your arms.
Ecstasy, newness, a beginning of life,
I knew more than anything, I needed
you for my wife.
So the fallacy of my life is obvious
and true,
I had been nowhere and seen nothing,
until I met you.
So I can honestly say, with absolutely
no remorse,
That my new life is on its last and
final course.
And however long its lasts, I know
one thing that's true.
I've done and seen it all because I've
loved you.

Jean E Kopplin
SUMMERTIME

Dedicated to Clark's Lake

Tawdry lace . . . red bee balm
Wild & tousled beside the lake
Bees buzz
Butterflies drift . . . settle on chosen
flowers

Darning needles dart and light
Display transparent wings
Fly over rippled water
Land on blue iris

Soft sounds . . . drone of bees
Slight rustle of flowers
Crickets' crisp chirp
Punctuate monotony

Soft sounds mesmerize
Warm sunshine
Sleepy
Energy gone

Quiet as a butterfly
An airplane hums
Drone of bees
Thoughts vacuumed
Within a breeze

Evelyn Evon Pigg
MY REAL TRUE LOVE

Springtime follows winter, winter follows fall and I will follow you through troubles. My love will be strong and years to come you'll still be the one. You will always be in my heart and on my mind. No matter where I am or what I might be doing, you are always there—only you. My love for you is real and true and can stand the test of time from a heart so real. I have been the whole world over, I have sailed a thousand seas, and still come back to you.

Sometimes I have stumbled, sometimes I have crawled, but never have I doubted love could conquer all. Oh my tears have fallen like raindrops, my pride I've worn like steel, and you were always there, you never once ran scared. Now I know that gold is not so precious or so real, for I have seen the miracle of love as it's revealed the gift I give to you, my love forever true.

Shirley Witcher
UTTER FRUSTRATION

To my two sons, Rome Witcher and Allen Parker. To all hardworking single parents.

Single parent, two children, can't get ahead.

Hungry sometimes, borrowing money all of the time, even wishing you were dead.

You try for a job, you get a job, you try hard to succeed.

You stay awhile, you do your best, only to find you are not what they need.

There is no place else for you to go, there is nothing else you can do.

You wonder how new people come in and get the higher position you thought was meant for you.

Most people you know, would have thrown in their hats a long time ago, but you can't think like that.

What good would it do, for a single parent of two, to throw in their only hat!

Dorothy Smith
THE UNEXPECTED MIX UP

This is about Mr. Meal,
Who is as nice as a man can be.
One day he called to Miss Flour,
Said "Come take a stroll with me."

Miss Soda was always his steady
So the jealousy built each day,
But he paid no mind to her nagging,
As he quietly went on his way.

Mr. Milk was watching Miss Soda,
And was hurt to see her so sad,
For the way Mr. Meal had done her.
Was enough to make anyone mad.

So he told Mrs. Shortning about it,
They agreed something had to be
done.
Mrs. Egg soon learned of their
planning,
And wanted in on the fun.

So they all sent for Mrs. Water,
But the Farmer's Wife came instead.
And she dumped them all together,
And made her some good corn
bread.

Roy Nathaniel Powell
BACK AGAIN

O' how I long to go back again,
when the grass was tender, green,
and cool under my feet
where the breeze was warm and
the wind was free,
where the sky was clear and the air
was fresh.
O' how I long to go back again,
when the days were short and the
nights were long,
where the music was soft and
the water was calm,
where the gulls danced endlessly to a
melodic love song,
where you could wish for
anything and your dreams came
true.
O' how I long to go back again when
the flowers sweet
fragrance filled the body with
pleasure and joy,
where everything was done with
time and love
like the blooming of the rose.
I've been here once and O' how I
long to go back again.

richard j hartmann jr
the lady in red

To A Lost Love

i once had the love of a lady in red
and when we slept we only needed a
small bed
our young love was true
you knew that too
i tried to drift away
but you had to have your way
you had an ally
and knew i lived a lie

i traded what i knew
for something new
the love of a lady in red
our young love was true
but now its turned blue
so anyone out there if you see my
lady in red
tell her i need what's in her head

Hèléne-del Hamburg
MY HOME

My Home, isn't a Castle,
My Home's not by the Sea,
There isn't a Brook;
that runs down to a nook,
or a lane, with a gate, to my
front door—
My home, hasn't much Treasure,
But Love, fills it with Pleasure,
Wherever I roam, there's no place
like Home,
And there's No Place I'd rather be—
Wherever I roam—there's No Place
like Home,
And there's No Place—I'd Rather
Be!

Donna Jo Nichols
SITTING, WONDERING

Sitting, Wondering—
If there's going to be any reaction
to those pills I just took.
If I'm going to die or cause
myself more pain.
Causing more problems for myself
than I already have.

Wondering if life's worth all
these problems,
Wondering if there's anything
I have to live for,
Wondering if things could
get better.

Well, it's a little too late for
that kind of thinking now.
The pills are already in my
system,
I can't change my mind now even
if I wanted to.
If I don't wake up from my nap
you'll know the pills worked!

Alyssa Ritter
THE LONELY CHILD

There was a child not long ago
Who loved to play and romp all
around.
But then one dark and dreary day
There were no children outside to
play.
She cried out with pain from within
her heart
And walked toward home as if in her
back were a dart.

Suddenly there was a clap of thunder
And she looked to the sky with awe
and wonder.
"Oh, let it rain," she silently said.

"My life is now gone, I'd rather be dead."
Then she heard screaming; she heard crying, whimpering, and fear.
"What will I do? There is no shelter near!"

"Oh, I'm so sorry world, so sorry I am.
I didn't try to be a lion, I tried to be a lamb!"
"You are forgiven my child," said a voice booming and clear.
"Who was that, who was that? There is nobody near!"
The voice was gone, gone, far, far away.
But then she realized suddenly who had spoken to her that day.

Dan C Clouser
YOUNG BOY'S DREAM
Oh, to dream, a young boy's dream
To think, in innocence, of sights unseen
To sing, again, life's brand new song
But alas, for me, those days are gone
For as the years, have sped on past
Left behind, my youth, I feared would last
Too young, back then, was I to know
How swiftly, the hours, the days would go
Now with, creaking bones, and withered skin
I sit, and rock, ponder where I've been
To have once more, that I wished away
Again, to spend, in life's autumn day
Even, if only, for one simple thing
Relive, my youth, in thought and dream

Victor Sánchez

Victor Sánchez
MEMORIAS
(Para Mario Serrano)
Hermano sangre de las calles
hombre-niño criado por su
forma, educado en la academia
de monstruos donde los recipientes
de los pobres son olvidados.

Siempre enseñando, educando, y
enseñando ha sido la lucha de
su vida. Nunca terminando sus
enseñanzas educando a otros
hacia la dirección de sobrevivir.
Basado a la determinación
sublime del poder de sobrevivir.

Hermano, camarada, personaje
inolvidable de mi vida. Aún
hoy las distancia nos aparta
más aún hoy mi vida está
edificada por la semilla
cultivada de tus enseñanzas.

Ponte fuerte mi hermano no
dejes que tu debilidad devore
tu existencia. Apréndete el
poder de sobrevivir como tu
enseñastes a otros a hacerlo,
haz un esfuerzo admite que tu
vida no es manejable y prueba
contigo mismo tu mejoría.

Los sueños del ayer han
pasado con el tiempo. El
tiempo de hoy puede contemplar
los sueños del mañana.

Cuando el tiempo se acerque
en que podamos llegar a nuestros
objetivos solamente el futuro
es la meta de nuestras más
completas enseñanzas.

Aún, hoy no estás, más nos
dejastes, dejando entre nosotros
gratas memorias y el objetivo
de un sin número de ejemplos
y enseñanzas.

Maajid M Ali
DIVINE COURTSHIP

One for Carmen R. Lopez
Love Everlasting

Divine Courtship . . .
Orange bright
like
sun/kiss
and
soda
pop/music
dance
to
micheal
and
thrill/her
with warm kisses

Linda J Lindsay
ANGIE'S SONG
My heart is crying,
As tears run down.
But they're not tears of sorrow,
As so many times in the past,
Regrets ran through my inner being.
No,
These are tears that
Rock me as I cry.
As I read my daughter's words,
And read within their meaning,
Of a child who knows she's loved,
Of a child who is happy,
Of a child who knows life is not always perfect,
But my love is but a smile away.
Thank you God for helping me
Reach the only goal in my heart worth seeking,
For my child to know she is loved,
And she loves me too!

Marie Elizabeth LeBlanc
SOMEONE CARES
Treasure the moments, quiet and calm.
Remember the times you've been kept from harm.
Someone is watching, waiting to hear
Your cry for help, to dry each tear.

Tender and gentle, meek and mild
Full of love for you, His child.
Turn not away from the One who cares
Who is ever involved in all your affairs.

There is nothing too great, nothing too small
To ask of the One who has given His all.
Moment by moment, reach for his hand
He will steady your footsteps and help you to stand.

When you feel defeated by life's many blows,
Just remember He's there and will always be so.
You're never alone, He is there at your side
And in His great love will you always abide.

Take heart, take courage and never stray
For He'll always help you to find the way.
Someone cares, of that be sure
And in that love you are secure.

Mr John J Pickett
REMEMBERING YOU

This Poem is Dedicated to the memory of Jamie Lynn Snider 1968-1982

Holding you close as the songs roll on
the memories flood back to me of a lonely,
rain filled night and of a lonely face
at a rain tracked window.

Maybe you could see the tears but
the rain has soaked everything
and those eyes staring so intently
through the window
have become cloudy and bloodshot.

It is enough that those eyes witness
merely an empty room
bare, devoid of life except for the
laughter and the pain
that seep from its walls.

Holding you close and remembering
that there was another
many years ago when youth was
pulsing through young veins
and love was still a fantasy . . .
Holding you close as the tears flow
again, silently in the night
remembering how it used to be . . .

Kathryn A McInnes
INCOMPLETE
Confusion sets in on me
and fear comes tumbling in.
Like clouds of dark grey color
before the rains of sin.

Mood swings:
like branches in a
furious storm.
My heart is crying coldly
when inside I long to feel warm.

When you're around I'm confident,
happy, and complete,
but now you're gone and my world
is crashing upon my feet.

When you said good-bye to me
and promised to return—
my heart was set on fire
and my insides began to burn.

Tears of sorrow snuffed a flame
of my once picture-perfect
dreams.
But now the frame has shattered
and the glass around me gleams.

John Lee Smith Jr
THOUGHTS OF A DYING FLOWER

In memory of my beloved grand-mother, Ruth E. James (1914-1989).

'Twas just yesterday I was
standing in lush green grass
Listening to the drone of workers
in my head
'Twas just yesterday I bathed in
the afternoon rain
Soon to be dried by the kiss of
the sun
And 'twas yesterday I cowered at
the thought of today
As the chill of the wind runs
through my veins
And the tune of the workers
fades in the distance
I wish that I too could leave the
scene of the crime
Where brittle leaves form a pyre
at my feet
For tomorrow, I realize, I will rest
in their arms.

Meagon Thueson
TO THEE
"Children, follow me,
And Father, the glory to Thee."

Follow the light
Soft, shining bright.
My mission has begun,
Father, I am your son.

Listen to my words
ye gentle flocks and herds.
Peace and love I teach to you,
Hearken and obey ye who
know me. Both night and day,
. . . Always pray.

I prayed and taught,
that which men taught.
I loved them so
I had to go.

"Father, Please, remove this
cup . . ."
I'm glad Thou wilt I drink it up.
"Thieves do hush your fearful cries.
Tomorrow I'll see you in
Paradise."

My mission done, a glorious end,
To save each man from deathful
sin.

All ye children, come to me,
And Father . . . Father, the glory
to Thee.

Laurie Habets
A KISS GOODNIGHT
I'll open the stairs
run up the door
Dance on the ceiling
look at the floor
I'll turn on my bed
jump into my light
All because
you kissed me goodnight

Sandra L Wilson
THE MAGIC OF MOTHER

To Ethel L. Lund, the most wonderful Mother in the world, who is always there to listen and help Her family. We thank God we have this "Special Lady" as our Mother.

A Mother is a sweet and gentle person,
With the Love She gave, we can surely be certain.
Even if we are not always near each other,
The magic is there between child and Mother.

That warm special feeling of loving and caring,
The laughter and tears, all a part of us sharing.
Her opinion not always the same as our own,
With Mother in your heart, you are never alone.

She struggled and sacrificed so much as we grew,
Her joy was our smile when we got something new.

Her smile, to us, was sweeter than honey,
Thinking of Mother makes a rainy day sunny.

We recall in our minds of the days gone by,
We catch ourselves laughing, and sometimes we cry.
She gave so much of Herself through the years,
Wonderful memories of Mother, She is always very near.

I LOVE YOU MOM

June E Barsalou
PRY LACE & SLY DOTES
(Motel Cats of Punta Gorda)
Pry Lace is a more than curious cat,
And a most sniffiferous cat, at that.
From high on her perch by the motel entry,
She particularly inspects all pets and their gentry.
Nose atilt, she peers and she spies
With inquiring, querious, questing eyes.
Selected guests she escorts to their door,
Surely assuring them she's been there before.
Then, affecting disinterest and disdain,
She returns to her perch by the entry again.

Sly Dotes, shadowy beneath a car,
Suspiciously stares out from his warm bed of tar.
Flattening himself as a splotch by a tire,
His coat becomes soot, his entire attire.
Yellow eyes frightful and glariously alive,
He snaps to attention any guest in the drive.
Warily, each watches the other,
More than keenly aware the other's no brother.
Hunching his back, he slinks away,
Searching through brush to begin stalking his prey.

Madge E Bautch
MAJESTIC OVERVIEW
Oh, Majestic Mountain you stand there with such grandeur and sophistication

I am full of awe and perplexity as I witness your spectacles of nature.

Cyclonic gusts of wind, coupled with driving pounding snow have left me breathless and frightened.

There seems to be so much turbulence and unrest in your make up. It baffles me.

What prompts this uneasiness? What is this power enveloping the space around me?

Why do you create such mood swings within me? Is there a lesson from this all?

I am studying about your power, controlling at all times.

Tempered and adjusted, my fears abate. Calmness once again reigns, at last.

Days become a pleasure to behold, sunsets end the time and proclaim a rest.

Have I mastered your plan for me? I doubt if I've discovered only a part.

But I'm learning it all has meaning—unveiled in minute quantities to digest.

Give me courage to keep progressing in my search for existence and identity.

Lori Bulloch
MYSTIC WONDERLAND

This poem is dedicated to Kathy Bulloch and René Hazen for believing in me!

The sun's glimmer
Filters
Through the clutching mist of
Dawn.
Clouds crawl
Sluggishly
Across the azure sky.

Powder and Entrancement
Blanket the chalky slopes.
Skiers carve wrinkles into
The osseous face of the
Hill.

Laughter cries from distant
Trails like tiny sparrows
Chirping for food.

Wind swirls the enchanting snow
Like an enormous ladle stirring a
Simmering brew.

The sun
Grants its last rays to the
Contented snow
As
Victorious,
The shadows seize breathlessly.

Judith Kay Kramer
LOSS OF MY MOTHER

In the memory of my Mother Frances A. Curtis

This poem that I have written
Is to show you how I feel
Is to put my thoughts on paper
Make her death seem to me more real
With my thoughts down on paper
They won't be filling up my head
Maybe someday in the future
I can accept that she is dead

The loss of my mother
I just cannot bear

Most had their memories
We had few that we shared

Days and years wasted away
There are words I did not say

It's too late to say them now
She's went and gone away

We became good friends
Mom and Me

I learned to understand her
Her actions and her ways

We spent many hours together
The good and bad days

I didn't have the time with her
That I'd like to have spent

The time I got to spend with her
To me was well meant

She didn't talk so very much
The words were few and such

But what was said between us
Holds dear in my heart much

There's things that I remember
I wish there could be more

The ones that I remember
Are in my heart well stored

Mom didn't show her feelings well
When she did, it was a yell

For such a small built lady
She was big in many ways

She was Oh! so very intelligent
I learned this every day

When she talked to you
She had something big to say

Her hobby, it was reading
She did it, Oh! so well

Crossword puzzles, many
And words, Oh! how she spelled

She went through so many
Good days and bad

Through all those days she went through
I never saw her sad

She had such a fear
We'll just never know

She tried to be brave
And let it not show

The only tears I saw her cry
I then knew the reason why

I saw her face
The pain and fear

I long for her voice
I wish I could hear

I lay awake nights
Going over those days

Wondering, WHY!
It had to be that way

Ask me, am I over it?
The answer is no

I'm not sure I'll ever be
They say time does heal the soul

The minutes, the days, the months
Now a year

Have gone by so fast
The pain is still here

They say I'm supposed to look ahead
Not dwell so in the past

They say it will get better
As time does pass

I know this pain I feel, Mom
It is going to last

Material things that she did leave
Don't hold a candle to my memories

I just cannot forget you
Can't accept that you are gone

God! How I miss you
I love you, Dear Mom

Just remember this, Mom
You hold a special place

Always in my thoughts and heart
Each and every day

I hope and pray you heard us all
Just before God made his call

We told you that we loved you
We said we'll miss you so

We meant every word of it
We knew then you had to go

Someday they say I'll see you
God tells me this each day

So until we meet again
Dear Mom

I love you
Forever and always

Written by,
Your Daughter

Anna Kenas
THE ANSWER
I needed someone to talk to . . .
I looked left and right.
I couldn't see anyone;
I couldn't see the light.
I was all confused inside,
I admit, I cried and cried.
I would sit and wish
That I had died a long, long time ago.
My heart was crushed and shattered;
I didn't have any pride.
I was like a little baby
Except with no mother at my side.

One day deep within
I heard a little voice that
Repeated again and again,
"My child I love you.
I'm always by your side;
I'm knocking at your door;
Let me tell you I can restore.
All the troubles inside you
Can finally be set free,
If you just believe in me and love me
Oh you'll see, I can turn your life around.

Wait, I hear a sound!
Something's calling you away.
But remember, I'm always with you,
I'm always by your side.
Day by day I watch you.
Oh, believe it . . . I do love you! ! !"
Now my life is better,
I made the right choice.
I listened to that little voice
That made me who I am.
I am a child of God. I am! I am! I am!

Mildred B Brown
THERE ARE MANY SONGS OF LOVE IT'S TRUE

This poem is dedicated to my first love and all Lovers of the World

There are many songs of love it's true,
But my song of love is just for you.
I whisper softly in your ear,
I love you and I want you near.
Dear to my heart you'll always be,
Welcome to my world and see.
I'll love you till the end of time,
Just love me, love me, just be mine.

MY song of love may be the same
As many others you may name.
But to me, it's special in every way,
Cause my love for you will always stay.
As certain as stars are in heavens above,
You will be my only love.
I'll love you till the end of time,
Just love me, love me, just be mine.

I want to be so close to you,
A heartbeat away will only do.
Gentle kisses are my desire,
A passion within that builds a fire.
Forevermore lay close to me,
Two hearts blended as the sand and the sea.
I'll love you till the end of time,
Just love me, love me, just be mine.

Robert F Nesbitt

Robert F Nesbitt
TWILIGHT MOMENT

The setting sun splashes reds and golds
On the horizon, as a wandering wind
Sweeps lonely clouds into the approaching night.

A passing jet leaves a chalky streak
In the deepening blue, a sudden flash
From its silver skin bidding farewell.

Black mountain shadows disappear into a lake of glass,
Which reflects the crimson of solar fires
Still burning below the edge of darkness.

A thousand eyes of light blink and stare out
From the hidden cradle of earth, some marking the way,
Others moving in pairs in long, slow processions.

Only a thread of orange and blue now remains,
As the canopy of night slowly closes,
Enveloping all in the final blackness.

Penelope Wedgwood
EVERYONE'S POETRY

To my father James Collis a composer and musician who filled our house with music.

People speak in metaphors.
Quietly listen to find
Their words open doors
Between heart and mind.

Dennis I Goode
SWEET MEMORIES

To my family for which this poem is about. Love you all, Dig '89

As time goes by, things will change, but one thing always stays the same, that's memories.

Living down at Happy-Hollow, playing out at the barn, I remember an older timer telling me a yarn.

Sweet memories that run deep through my mind. No matter how much we change with time.

I recall as mama worked sewing for the rich man in town. Me and my sister Sue stayed in the cellar when thunder shook the ground.

We had chickens, cows, and a pig. And oh, how I remember those taters my daddy would dig.

Sweet memories of days gone past, but I will have those memories and that will always last.

Good times when we got together shelling those purple hull peas. As we all listen to the whippoorwill singing in the distant pin oak trees.

I can remember huddling together in a one bedroom house, fighting off the skeeters, and dad setting traps, trying to catch a mouse.

Sweet memories of my childhood days ....

Enjoying life's good ole-fashion ways.

Mieke Lee
I AM A CHRIST CHILD WHO WONDERS

I am a Christ child who wonders.
I wonder if I'll ever reach the stars.
I hear a voice from above.
I see a crown of peace and joy.
I want the future to come about.
I am a Christ child who wonders.

I pretend I am a star and lie above the sky so far.
I feel the cool wind blowing through my hair.
I touch the world far below me.
I worry about the world, it's so weak and weary.
I cry at the sight of all sadness.
I am a Christ child who wonders.

I understand the feeling of criticism.
I say I will not fail the Lord.
I dream of the day He will return and fulfill His promise.
I try to help others and love them, too—yet it is so hard.
I hope someday I'll be rewarded.
I am a Christ child who wonders.

Tiffany Cates
WINTER

It was almost Christmas Day,
And my parents were away,
They were on their way,
And I was scared and alone,
So I called my friend on the phone,
And said what's going on,
I heard a loud noise,
It was some toys,
It was Santa and his elf boys,
He had a sack on his back,
Then after Christmas Day,
I went outside to play,
I saw Donna Faye,
We were on a sleigh,
We saw a snowman on the ground,
His body parts all around,
We put him together,
And he stayed together forever,
Guess what happened that Christmas day,
My parents were still away,
And they never came back that day.

Theresa Marie Hanson
STARLIGHT VIGIL

In loving memory of my Uncle Tom

Nights in white satin
Heaven's above
Rock on ride free
My love.

Misty winds everywhere
Through the eyes of darkness
you stare.

Starlight—starbright
Some visit me tonight.
High above the clouds you dance
Proud at your own will,
I adore you
Because you're my lucky
Starlight vigil.

So ride on sweet unicorn
Set yourself free
Reach for your dreams
For anything is possible
If only you believe!

Miki Harrison
THE MIST

All senses straining, nerve endings raw.
Mind playing tricks on a fragile sanity.
Massive drawn curtains refuse to part.
Frantic attempts deadend in the maze of the mist.

Fog's chill prickles the skin and numbs the soul.
Beads of perspiration form on a racing heart.
Voice whispers sweet indecipherable words splintered by static.
Heard with the ears or the mind?

Hazy hypnotic images beckon to touch.
Waver, retreat just beyond reach.
Phantom flickers suddenly, the cottony cloud vanishes.
Heart stills as the warm solace of your arms materialize.

At last, the dream's end
fully awake
confident
certain.

Or,
both sides so real
which
is?

Faith Ann Welch
THE PROMISE

For My Greatest Love My Husband My Friend

To my husband
I love so much.
How I long for your soft touch.
Your gentle hands so soft and strong,
That say "I'll love you" for so long.

For you my love I would give my life,
I'm so proud to be your wife.
To you my love I promise this,
I'll love you always till none exist.

Deborah L Hart
MY ANGEL

In loving memory of Christine Lovejoy

My daughter's up in heaven
She is an angel there
God gave to her a pair of wings
And a halo for her hair.

God dressed her in a gown of white
She holds Jesus by the hand.
There beauty takes my breath away
God helps me understand

I thank God he lent her to us,
for just a little while,
Now she's up in Heaven.
With God she wears a smile.

A smile that says "I Love You."
We have memories left behind.
God let her have her passport
the one that Jesus signed.

Ernestine J Myles

Ernestine J Myles
A TEACHER

This poem is dedicated to Willie Long, Jr., my son, to all of the teachers and children of the world.

A—Accepts the nation's most
Precious resource, the child,
into the classroom.

T—Teaches enthusiastically to
Help develop the maximum
Potentials.
E—Eagerly probes, explains and
Interprets ideas from his
Experiences.
A—Allows the child to use the
Basic skills,
The fundamentals and creative
Thinking.

C—Cares about him no matter
How affluent or how destitute
His environment.
H—Helps him to know who he is
And appreciate his worth to
Society.
E—Encourages him to start where
He is with what he has.
R—Refines the raw materials
From the diverse school
Community by stroking,
Molding, carving and chiseling.

Tracy Miscio
MY DEAR GRANDDAUGHTER

I held your tiny little body in my arms,
against my tired old chest—
not long after you experienced
your first breath of life.

My mind immediately planned our life together . . .
of course, I knew I would not see you

fully grown . . .
my old bones could not carry me that far
down the path of your future.

I could see you growing up in my life,
step by precious step.

And as I held your warm, fragile frame,
a tear escaped from the corner of my eye
as I thought of the joy
you were going to bring into my life.

Now, I sit here and hold your tiny cold body in my arms,
against my broken heart—
not long after you experienced
your last breath of life.

My plans and dreams of our life together
are now empty, black tunnels
with no light proceeding . . .

I can only see you lying in the damp ground,
taking no steps,
growing no more . . .

And as I hold your stiff frame,
a tear escapes from the corner of my eye
as I think of spending the last years of my life
without your sweet little face . . .

My dear Granddaughter,
for the short stay you had in my life,
you brought me more sunlight
than a million suns . . .

more laughter than a million clowns . . .

and you gave me more love
than a million hearts could ever give.

Michael J Spencer
MORNING LIGHT
The rhythmic beating of the waves
A sea gull flying through the haze
Dawn is breaking, the fresh salt air
Sitting mystically without a care
Running frantically just for fun
Falling to the sand with your only one
You sit in silence and hold her tight
Together you watch the morning light

June Berry
LIVE EACH DAY AS A BLESSING

This poem is dedicated to William K. Furst, M.D., our loving family physician. I, wrote it for him, after he came down with a terminal illness.

Live each day as a blessing,
And your heart will stay filled with love.
You will bring joy to everyone,
While pleasing your Father in Heaven above.
There will be no time for hatred,
And your enemies will be few.
For they will see your goodness,
And will want to live just like you.

Live each day as a blessing,
And your faith will grow stronger each day.
Thank Him daily for your sunshine,
Don't wait for clouds to appear to pray.
Don't let your heartaches mislead you,
And tempt you to sin along life's way.
Keep your heartstrings tuned into Heaven,
For sinners always have to pay.

Live each day as a blessing,
And you will find there's time to share.
For God will give you added strength,
To help others who need your care.
Oh! if only we could learn to be brothers,
What a wonderful world it would be.
You begin . . . living each day as a blessing,
And you will help set weary souls free.

(Miss) Larnell Custis Butler
JUST PLAIN CARZY!

This poem is dedicated to my parents—Lillian A. McCoy Custis and Alonzo (Howard) Custis Sr.

Skin as dark as indigo dye,
She hides her beauty in the night among
Windows of a house where Mulberry Street
Divides an intersection above
Brandon Lane's Housing project.
People believe that she is a witch, but she
Dispels their notions by attending church
Regularly at Brother Leroy's house of worship.
Some say her mama was from Africa, and her Father was a red-neck white man from Tuscaloosa, Alabama.
When nocturnal hours appear, she pokes her head outside a window and hoots like an owl all night long.
The woman is just plain CARZY!

Wanda Moyer
MY SPECIAL ONE

To my beloved son—Robert Dean with love Mom

I'm just a simple person.
No great things have I done.
To me the greatest gift of all.
Was the choosing of our son.

Our girls had married left the nest
They could make it on their own.
Too soon the heart gets lonely.
When your children leave the home.

God sent to us a baby boy.
That needed loving care.
My guess is Jesus knew,
When needed we'd be there.

To tell him about heaven.
To teach him God is fair.
No matter what his problem be.
His mom and dad are there.

I thank you Lord and savior.
For the boy that we call son.
For thinking we'd be good enough.
To raise this special one.

Cynthia E Downey
CAROUSEL
Carousel horses all painted up fine,
Mount up your glittering steed and ride.
Hear the music play: now loud, now soft,
Reach out your hand and grasp the golden ring,
Lift up your heart and sing.
Won't you please ride on the carousel, now?

Dreams flying, hopes sailing,
Carousel horses dancing to the music we hear,
Beautiful steeds going round in never ceasing circles.
Please, carousel horses, take me along
To a place where our dreams all come true.

Oh, beautiful carousel horses,
Lights flashing, lovely music playing,
It makes me happy, for now.
I am a child laughing with delight.
Carousel with your song so cheerful,
Happy children everywhere.

Carousel slowing down
Your horses no longer prancing,
Your music no longer loud,
Carousel, you've stopped!

George R Herring
YOU ARE MY LOVE

To Carol Dawn The One Who Cared

In your smile,
I see the happiness of yesterdays
spent enjoying each other's closeness.

In your eyes,
I see the anticipation
of pleasures we have yet to discover.

In my heart,
I know that no one
has felt love more completely
than I have with you.

Betsy

Diana J Cleary
BETSY

To our dearly loved and missed Betsy

Betsy though you are not here
Thoughts of you, will always bring a tear.
Betsy you were truly one of a kind
Forever your picture will be in my mind,
You were always sweet, gentle and kind.
Always with your temper in check
Even when Bonnie teased you like heck.
Betsy you were a friend and pal
You will always be a special gal.
Betsy you always readily licked my face
Tried harder to win the race.
Betsy another could never take your place.

John S Paurich
THE SUN
The sun so high in the sky,
Shines down in my eye,
As I climb the mountain high,
The sun so high in the sky.

The sun the sun shines so bright,
Only in the day, not at night,
It may come out without a doubt,
The next day we'll yell and shout.

The sun is a great big fireball,
I wonder why you can't see it all,
Sometimes I want to touch the sun,
Because I think it might be fun.

Sometimes I know, I want it to snow,
When the day is going so slow,
I didn't think the sun was so hot,
Well, maybe not.

Dawn S Olsen
IMMUNITIES
Media mania causing
Social/emotional
Immunities.
We no longer know
The patriotism,
The pride,
The remorse,
The regret.
We no longer remember
The sickening stench
Of stomaches squeezed
In foreign, famined lands.
We no longer know our world.
Media mania causing
Social/emotional
Immunities.
We no longer care.
We no longer know
Ourselves.

Ann Marie Jagielski
GO AWAY WINTER
I woke up today,
and there was snow on the ground.
It buried all the summer dreams,
that I had once found.
It seems much too early
for the shivering winter.
It's going to be—
So long, cold, and bitter!
And as for,
the beautiful green grass . . .
To see the summer again—
the winter will have to pass!
And now, the summer stories,
that we had once told.
Will be far underneath . . .
the deep, freezing, cold!
And now the summer
is just a far away land.
I sit here in this wintery state
that much resembles, my left hand.
Why does the summer . . .
Seem so far away?
Sometimes I wish,
the winter would just go away!

Frances E deLange
DON'T FEEL ALONE
Don't feel alone—I am not far away—
My love for you is just the same today.
Though we no longer feel each other's touch,
I hold you in my heart—and love as much.

I've lived—I've worked—my life I've rearranged.
But deep inside my feelings have not changed.
Though you're with God, you're also here with me.
Each day is filled with joyous memory.
And—although weeping sometimes has its way—
Through tears, I smile at things you used to say.
And—while I long to feel your arms and lips,
And touch your face with tender fingertips—

Our love—our happiness—was meant to be.
I'm there with you—and, darling, you're with me.

Lorijean Grindrod
LABYRINTH OF MY SOUL
For those who choose to enter the labyrinth of my soul,
they will discover many distinct levels.

Pass first beyond the outer wall of shyness and uncertainty.
It will not beckon you to enter,
nor, entice you with what lay-in-wait just inside.

Negativity and poor self-esteem,
my dehabilitating ideas became
the stones and mortar of my inner walls.

I learned well the art of evasion, self taught,
for fear controls my every action.

Awash with vague neutrality.
Make no stand. Express no opinion.
Contradict no one.

You will find the hologram—my obsequious personality,
which is shared with those who choose to know me.
But a fragment of the person you look for.

Further yet, my soul protects the spirit,
shrouded by an inner wall.
The essence of my being locked away—and safe?

An alien within.

Alma Joyce Zabka
THE COMMISSION
Loneliness of committed belief
you are a cup most bitter
and must I drink the dregs
of separation from your lips?

Gentle, odd, unknowing child,
seek establishment in retreat to
graves' complacent sweet oblivion,
no strength to know or feel.

Warning Attack! From expediency
speeds illusion to destroy
delights of doubtful blood
yet unrevealed by weeping.

Confirm the loss of what
but faith thrust thru the heart.
As hope enduring ever finds
communion in the empty cup.

Verle Nichols Higgs
PHOENIX
Out of the ashes
Bird of myth and mystery
Ascend again in triumph.

In unfettered flight,
transcending adversity
Now and evermore.

Silent silhouette
The glory of your song
The heart alone, hears.

Wallis Remsen Sanborn III
FADING
You are the fragile flower.

Guilty pleasures occupy the time
Runaway trains and steel love;
Sweet chemical kisses, bitter biting self.
Of these, you know.

Scatter and stumble, and flicker
As some candle flame
Swayed in the dark wind
That is this humanity;

Wander through the maze
Excised of beaten path,
Feared by that which attracts
A careful suffering.

The light that is your pilot
Spits and chokes,
And sits blinking, burning,
As an ember . . .

Fading.

Edie Marshall
OUR BURNING LOVE
In the arms of love I am,
Strangled by its blood-stained hold
The depths of passion slowly dying
Buried by our love grown cold.

Heart to heart and tear to tear,
Love's flickering candle turns to shy
With one more whisper, one last word,
Our burning love comes home to die.

Jean D Epperley

Jean D Epperley
LORD GRANT ME ONE MORE DAY

Dedicated to my two lovely daughters, Wanda Darlene and Tamara Jean, my parents and two sisters who inspire me.

Lord, grant me one more day
so I can see sunshine
and children at play

Lord, grant me one more day
so I can hear birds singing
when skies fill with gray

Let me hear the pitter-patter of rain
and see snowflakes drifting
softly
on my window pane

Let me smell the sweetness of flowers
and feel the breeze that sings
through the trees for hours

Let me walk by the rivers foam of lace
where it thunders a mist
as it falls from its place

Lord, grant me to see my way
when shadows of purple
mountains end the day!

Renate Grunenfelder
UNIQUE PHENOMENA
as days go by;

Rain is eminated by Sunshine
two corresponding Halves eventually meet

as months pass by;

Fall is heeded by Winter
the Known is preferred over the Unknown

as years go by;

the Ozone layer degenerates
eventually all Old is conquered by the New

Juliann Johnston
THE STAIRWAY
She agreed to take the dare
to walk
the length of stairs
that led down,
down into the ground

Many different trails of stairs
all leading down,
into the ground.
Why won't she turn around,
and go up, instead of down?

Stairways of deception
anything but truth
closer to destruction,
and much too far
from the truth

Down and down she went
until reaching
the final choice of destination
she continued upon the stairway
down
to death and to damnation.

Leslie Brighindi
WHERE DO I GO? WHY DO I BOTHER?

To Matthew My Guardian Angel, you will remain in my heart and mind forever. Love Leslie

As I sit and wonder
a cold chill comes over me as the earth begins to thunder

Staring out the window the world looks so gray
the poverty, sickness and all of God's children
looking so afraid; From this I long to run and run far far away

But where do I go?
Everywhere I look I can find no crystal clear
babbling brook

Why do I bother?
So much time of pain and suffering has elapsed
although I know there is a God
It seems the world will soon collapse.

Becky L Ippolito
LAKE MOHAWK '88
Lake Ladies are seemingly sweet
yet, always fail at being discreet
looking, looking, down long taut noses.
Lake Ladies try so, to know, not you
only the filth used to cleanse
their own bourgeois existence.

Lake Ladies actually fear themselves
carefully, skillfully, never seem to reveal themselves—not
willingly as

Lake Ladies desperately act so
leisurely content along their
lifelong stroll.

Bernice A Rouse
WHAT'S HAPPENED TO MY AMERICA?
Our country has been changing
It's hard to understand,
Why aren't we true Americans
And be proud of our land.

What's happened to our people
So many don't seem to care.
Our patriotism is slipping away
And no one is aware

The generations changed with time
They know not what it means
How the generations before us
Fought for freedom and our dreams.

Lord help us be what we were
Save our rights and liberty
Before it's too late for all of us
And we're no longer free.

What's happened to my America?
Dear Lord, I make my plea
Guide us in our ignorance
And save my beloved country.

Valerie DeLine
NIGHT
Night is when the stars come alive,
And it's such a beautiful sight
In the night.
And the creatures and everything
Else comes alive,
And they dive into the night
And everything is fine.
Then it strikes twelve,
It's a few hours till nine
Then bang, bing, bong, dawn has
Just begun.
Now the fun has ended
Yes indeed,
Tonight I'll see you.
Why don't we meet?

Esther H Anderson
SLEEPLESSNESS
Sometimes when I awake before its dawn
When sleep escapes and in my heart I'm torn
I lie there deep in thought while minutes pass
Until the clock alarms and then at last

Reluctantly I rise with need of sleep
Which must wait til night hours slowly creep
Back to the time when I can go to bed
Vowing that this time I'll sleep like lead

The problems of the world I cannot solve
But in night hours they will not dissolve
Sometimes past pain inflicted to my heart
Presents again in memory with a start

Please go away, you hurt me once before
You took me through, why return once more?
To bother me when I should be asleep

Some things you bring may inside make me weep

Occasionally you bring to mind some good
That is nice but be it understood
Sweet sleep I need to function at my best
Oh, sleeplessness please go so I can rest

Karen Ann Bauer
SHE'S ALONE
Mostly she's alone, she does her tasks just fine
she accomplishes almost anything, once she sets her mind

Mostly she's a worker, not having much time for play
her job, her house, her little chores, seem enough to fill each day

Mostly she's dependable, the one that others come to
when they have doubts or concerns about something they must do

Mostly she's a saver, awaiting bad times to occur
no fancy clothes or gold jewelry will ever be found on her

Mostly she's responsible, not the type to commit a crime
always goes to work, does her job and pays her bills on time

Mostly she's an achiever, she always does her best
if a job re-done or one that's new, she tries harder than the rest

Mostly she is proud—proud of the seeds she's sewn
and wonders if it all came about, because mostly, she's alone

Stephanie Nahirniak
DRUG ABUSE
In previous times the word drug was used
By doctors prescribing them, to kill the pain,
And if by Satan's tricks and people's curse,
There are drugs made now to kill the brain.
God gave us faith, and a brain to use
For our life upon this earth,
To help carry our crosses when trouble strikes,
With hope and love to ease the hurt.
But some people began losing this faith,
Thus ignoring God's gift and misusing their brain,
To mislead yet others, with their wrong ways of life
By using drug abuse in their kind of game.
Whether being depressed, or whatever the reason
They turned to drugs for their relief,
Forgetting God's love and faith for help;
Thus ending up in disaster and grief.
Please God forgive them, and rescue this world
From this dangerous drug abuse,
Help them regain their faith with patience and love,
So the brain killing drug they never do use.

Dewey Blair
TO MY WIFE, WHO IS NEAREST TO ME

This poem is dedicated to my wife "Marie," which was by inspiration of the grace of God,

To my wife, who is nearest to me,
I have often wondered, and now I see.
What is so special, about your love,
That was given to me, by God above.

You have stood by me, for better or worse,
And numerous times, have been my nurse.
It is hard to express, what's in my heart,
But I miss you most, when we're apart.

I love you more, as the days go by,
And to you my darling I cannot lie.
Because you are, so special to me,
And I'm sure you know, you'll always be.

Your loving smile, and wonderful ways,
I'll always cherish, the rest of my days.
It's the little things, that you do for me,
Which at the time, I cannot see.

My love for you, grows more each day,
As I travel down, life's highway.
And always remember, this my dear,
That in my dreams, you are always near.

Alberta Murphy

Alberta Murphy
WHAT RADIO & TV IS TO YOU & ME
Before there was TV, radio brought news to you and me.
We could hear about the news over the land and sea.
Radio has been so much to you and me.
Now that we have TV it is good for you and me.
If we can not hear we can see the news from land and sea.
If we can not see we can hear the news on TV.
Radio and TV is so much to you and me.

Myron L Hastings
THE MORNING
As I awake for another day
My eyes capture a breathtaking view;
For shimmering shafts of golden sunlight
Were spreading their fingers across my room
Dispelling all my gloom.

What can I say for my day has begun anew;
This morning prepares my heart with joy
And soon to be my new found toy,
As I watched and gazed into a world of light
Easing my soul's plight.

Mary Ann Ventura
SUMMER FUN
Sometimes when I hear water running it reminds me of a summer so long ago, it was a summer spent with you my love; a summer filled with fun.

Walking down the long and empty boardwalks close to dawn
Listening to old love songs, walking arm in arm

Running wild along the sandy shores with hair whipping past as you ran,
A pup biting at our toes, a kite in one hand, a woman and a man.

Talking of "someday" having a family and maybe even a farm
There were so many surprises then, so many things to learn

Stopping to help the little children build their sandy home
You promised me everything . . . the best—even Rome!

We were so in love in those days my dear, where are we now?
The surprises are fewer, summer fun is left for the young.

I want those days back again, I never wanted them to end.
We two sit in our chairs as if those two lovebirds were someone else.

Let's go back to our days of summer fun she says,
Without a care, I'll let my hair grow long again she says.

The kite and the dog and the sandy homes are still alive and well,
The faces have changed and some have just aged. There happy faces.
Young and old.

Adib J Sarkis

Adib J Sarkis
SATURDAY NIGHT IN AMERICA

To my children and grand-children I dedicate this poem.

Saturday night is the night
America's main delight

It is the peak of the week
Beauty mole adorns its cheek

A ghost that shades the lovers
Who are looking for covers

It drives slumber from the eyes
Spreading joyance in the skies

Instigates the yearning breeze
To flirt with the dreaming trees

Its moon fondles with the dawn
Its stars drowse over the lawn

Even the poor and the forlorn
Are not left alone to mourn

America, show the way
To others who go astray

Help them overcome their plights
And enjoy Saturday's nights

Stan Cohen
BLUE LEAF SPECIAL

for Judy

I have simple tastes
wanting wanting nothing
nothing more more or less
(or less)
than a blue leaf

Should you Should I
find one

Please share
I want to touch / smell / see it
Forever
and then
give it back

Vanessa Tapper
MIDNIGHT TRYSTS
Midnight trysts
under starry skies

Stolen kisses
taken by surprise

Maddening embraces
Bodies intertwined

Loss of reasoning
Two hearts combined

Ann Parrinello
ANGELS ARE FOREVER

To Michele, Laura, Christy & Darren Although you're no longer with us, I feel you in everything I do, and see you everywhere I go. I know you're in a better place, watching over us, where you will live in happiness forever.

You're the ears that listen,
when I pray.
The warmth in my soul,
on a cold winter day.
You're in the air that I breathe,
you're the light in the dark,
which helps me to see.

You're the voice of the white
dove, that sings.
The petals on the flowers

which bloom in the spring.
You were the one, who knew how to love.
That's why He needed you, up above.
I miss you more than you would know,
but now I see why you had to go,
And someday soon, when the end is near.
I know that you will reappear.
On the path to the promise land.
You will lead us hand in hand,
And in the light we'll stand together,
because now I know,
Angels are forever . . .

Jonathan Mayer
HOTELS

To my family who has guided me throughout my life and to all my teachers who have taught me well, especially Mr. Michael Culhane who has had a great influence on me.

They're big, they're small, they're everywhere.
Some are commercial others are not.
While some have lobbies, others have atriums.
Some are suites others are not.
All have beds some are king, others are queen.
Some are colorful others are dismal.
Most have furniture chained to the floor, so you can not take it out the door.
Some have clean carpets, others have spots
colors of red, blue, green or dots.
Some have fine dining others do not.
While some have pools others have spas.
Some have health clubs others do not.
Credit or cash you're out in a flash.

Alberta Williams
THE LITTLE WRANGLERETTE

To my beloved granddaughter, Robin Rae Adair, who inspired me to write this poem when she was five years old.

She rides the trail without a thought of fear,
Along the horizon to head a steer,
And digs her horse with silver mounted spurs—
She never minds the thistles and the burrs.

Her hair is always flying in the breeze,
She rides along through under-brush and trees.
Blue skies emit the sunlight in her eyes,
Around her neck she wears bright silken ties.

When day is spent she trudges to the house,
Exclaiming that she saw a speckled grouse.
The little Wranglerette rides on the go,
She is my grandchild, you must surely know.

Melissa A Jacobs
INFANTICIDE
The killing of a precious thing,
The murder of something that cannot be replaced,
A disturbance of the greatest miracle of all,
The human life.
Every day this happens.
STOP!

A baby is not allowed
To see a beautiful rainbow,
To feel a beam of sunlight,
To hear a cricket singing,
To smell a sweet rose,
To taste the joys of life!

STOP!

We must stop this pointless act,
Before it happens again.
We must care, love, respect;
Not ignore, neglect.
PREVENT!
SPEAK FOR THE SILENCED
NOW!

Brenda M Barcomb
LOVING FAREWELL

To my loving husband Barry of whom understands and accepts me just the way I am—I love you!

I love you—
more than I can say,
it just doesn't seem right
to keep you this way.

You'll never be a daddy
for a little girl or boy,
or hear a precious thank-you
for that special brand new toy.

You'll never be a grandpa
bouncing babies on your knee,
or taking them for walks—
it can't ever be.

There won't be anyone
to carry on your name,
someday you'll regret it
and I'm the one to blame.

Maybe if I went away
you would find somebody new,
someone who would love you
and give you children too!

The thought of losing you
is tearing me apart,
you're a special part of me
deep within my heart.

Just because I'm barren
doesn't mean you should be too,
honey please forgive me
and remember—I love you!

Clyde C Hawkins
LIFE IS A MYSTERY

To my dear wife and mother of our children Alice Newbold Hawkins.

Life Is A Mystery We All Seek To Solve
We Can See The Answer Slowly Evolve
As Each Generation Records Its Find
The Next Generation Continues The Climb.

We've Learned Our Lives Are Not Our Own,
To Live And Mold For Self Alone
For All Of Our Lives Become Entwined
As We Traverse Life's Road In Time.

We Cannot Live By Bread Alone
So Said A Sage In Time Long Gone
A Heart When Filled With Love And Care
Can Face Each Day With Hope, Not Fear.

Friends Are A Must On Life's Long Trail
Smiles Make Friends When All Else Fails
When Your Body Grows Weary
Mile After Mile
Throw Back Your Head, Go Forth With A Smile.

Once Life Is Started That Life Must End
We Know Not How, Nor Where, Nor When
So When Our Bodies Are Laid To Rest
May It Be Said They Did Their Best.

Mrs Michiele J Tietze
MY MOTHER, MY FRIEND

Dedicated to the memory of my mother, Carmelita Mauer/Savage.

My mother, my friend,
she placed me unfurled,
my mother, my friend,
brought me into this world.

My mother, my friend,
watched me grow through the years,
my mother, my friend,
saw me through laughter and tears.

My mother, my friend, shared
her wisdom and love,
my mother, my friend,
found strength from above.

My mother, my friend,
with years passing by,
my mother, my friend,
said farewell, then goodbye . . . .

Brian V Martin
A STEALER OF HEARTS

To my family, who has inspired me right from the start My sister, Karen St. Louis; My Mother Norma Hodgson All my love, Brian V. Martin.

I feel like there's
a little devil in me.
Well you can decide
here's a picture of me.

Sometimes I'm a cupid
spreading love all around.
You'll never know I'm there
because I hardly make a sound.

Got myself a hat
and a pair of dark shades.
I gotta keep up
with today's day and age.

I have a cupid likeness
that, you can easily see.
But I go around stealing hearts
and I keep them all for me.

Nephi Camacho
I AM A DREAMY GUY

To my family who gives me much encouragement in putting forth and giving the best to others and also to my Dad who is striving for understanding and perfection for eternal rewards.

I am a dreamy guy who likes the ocean,
I wonder if the sea will hold up to man's new creations.
I hear the rain pounding on the hot cement.
I see a surfer riding on a rainbow.
I want to have a beautiful wife and some animals
I am a dreamy guy who likes the ocean.

I pretend that I am a dolphin swimming in the sea.
I feel as a leaf, weightless in the wind.
I touch the warmth of the sun and feel the stars.
I worry of what man will do to the world in search of power and greed.
I cry when I am away from loved ones.
I am a dreamy guy who likes the ocean.

I understand the cycle of life and death.
I say "Go for it," "Rush," "you only live once."
I dream of a place where there are no worries, no regrets and no sorrow.
I try to hold my temper and not do anything stupid.
I hope that man will realize what we are doing before it's too late.
I am a dreamy guy who likes the ocean.

Shirley McClelen
FEAR WAITS

Dedicated to my husband, Tom, and to friends at the Travis Hospital, where this poem was written.

Fear took me; death's dark line I crossed,
And you were gone, and I was lost.

The terror there was cold and black,
My trembling mind screamed, "Hold it back,"
But on it came with death-filled eyes,
And no one heard my pleading cries.
The terror reached, took my right hand,
To keep me there in that dark land.

I tried to turn, to scream, to run,
But I was lost, the fear had won.

Your tender hands touch my tired face,
And I am in a soft, light place.
The terror's gone when you are near,
Your soft warm kiss dissolves the fear.
Please, I must hold your gentle hand,
To give me strength, to help me stand.

But fear will wait while life is mine,
To take me back to death's dark line.

Ida Pack

Ida Pack
THE FEET
A foot is a wonderful thing,
It's more precious than wings.
With wings, you could fly,
But your feet would tell you goodby.
God made you just as you are,
And your feet are as precious as the morning star.
Not hand made, but God made, they turned out to be,
And well kept, they perform miracles as you can see.
They walk, they dance and they spin around,

And they do this without making a sound.

So give them special care, as your podiatrist would say,
And if they need to see him, don't keep them away.
He is trained to know just what to do,
To keep them in trim for me and for you.
Their needs are simple, as you may guess,
A little attention brings much happiness.

That big toe, He's the boss.
He tells others not to cross.
So to keep in line, step by step,
His directions they have kept.

This whole project will make you smile,
and you will realize,
Healthy feet are really worthwhile.

Lara Osmon
SENTIMENTAL

Just for you, Mom!

She thinks life's fragile
like a green cut glass butterfly.
She believes everyone should have a home like a
cottage with flowers in the windowboxes.
She thinks each person must
continue to drive on
like a little four speed car going uphill.
She believes in treasured keepsakes
like butterflies
in fields of flowers.
She believes everyone should listen to some music
like "Lara's Theme" flowing from a music box.
She thinks everyone should dance
like a globe that
spins round and round.
She thinks beginnings of friendships really begin
like her favorite poem, with "One Hello."
She believes everyone's beautiful
like a sunset or a sunrise.

Guido Berardi
JOY TO LIVING

To my dear Father, with love.

There is so much joy to living
That very few people understand
How all things work
The way God had planned.

Whether in joy or sorrow
God is always at our side
And we never walk alone
Without His friendly guide.

Wanda Henderson
OUR FINAL FATE

Dedicated to, and in memory of, Grace Jackson Henderson

A natural time for you, for I,
as time has crept so slowly by,
a telling wind,
a special scent,
telling me three years were lent.
So as I lie beneath blue skies
surrounded by your love so great,
the final step into my fate.
I feel a warmth as I depart,
the love of friends,
flowing from your hearts.
As the sun goes down
and all has left
the lingering thoughts
you left behind
still deeply imprinted
on my mind.
My path is here for me to take
so I will follow, to leave behind
my love for you, and the memories we shared,
I leave them now,
imprinted in your mind.
So take them now, as you walk away,
as the sun goes down,
and the sky turns gray.

Janice Saeger
A MOMENT OF SENSATION

I thank the Lord of all! !

I've been sitting here for hours
Just watching the beautiful flowers
Thinking back to the snow
When I couldn't wait to see them grow

I reach down to grasp a piece of earth
Rolling it in my hand, feeling there a new birth
For a moment a sensation forms
That I am just like a gladiolus corm

I am planted deep, deep down
In a bed made of ground
Experiencing things unseen
Like how it is to be green

Spreading out, standing straight and tall
Revelling in the pleasures of blossoming before fall
Bending, swaying in the wind of a storm
Dying, recapturing energy to return to an old form

Waking, I realize I've spent more hours
Just sitting, watching the flowers
Looking down at my hand
I know I will have to wash off the sand

Donna Taylor
LAST WORDS

To my darling daughter Crystal Chalet Stull. May she rest in peace. Love Mom.

Her hair was like silk,
Her eyes were so blue,
And her skin was so soft too,
But now that she is dead,
You'll only find me crying from her bed,
Some say it was life,
Some say it was a boy,
But only she knew, why she was so blue,
Sometimes I can't sleep, sometimes I can't hear,
I feel like I am going crazy, from ear to ear,
I wish I could turn back the hands of time,
To tell my daughter that dying is a crime,
She left me with tears and left me with fears,
Oh God please take care of that daughter of mine.

Lilian L Sotolongo
WALKING THROUGH COLORS

Nicholas—the colors in my life live only through your eyes.

I am the moody Sky, dressed in robes of Azure passion.
Which swings above the Purple Hills you are—or so I must imagine.

And with Reds of autumn's stirring,
You enfold my fiery soul
In Yellows flying, willows purring
Softly as they weep, and leaves are dancing as they roll.

We are alone in wind which whistles news to someone,
That we're held eternally free—
guarded only by a Greater One.

And the searching Sky, as if to say "come share my bliss,"
Takes hold the gentle Hills with a floating cotton kiss.

And with the kiss of gentle White,
The Sky turns robed in Onyx-night.

She travels far to now become—
The Tide which runs to him the Sand.
And she, embraced by warmth—the sun,
Extends a moist and Emerald hand.

And as they blend, to form the Copper shore
His virgin youth she does restore.

So cleansing is her Hue that when he's touched,
Removed are troubled souls, with footsteps rushed.

Margaret L Shearer
HIS HEAVY LOAD

Ms. Cathy O. Doty: Without God & You, I could never have written this poem. I dedicate this to you. I always said, that you walked hand in hand with God! "Thank You," for all you've done for me, & for inspiring me with your caring & concern. I shall remember you always. Friends & Love for Life, Margaret.

We often sit, think to ourselves
In self-pity no one cares,
All the things, that must be done
The problems, we have to bear.

At times we think, the load's too big
Our shoulders much too small,
To carry such a heavy load
And complaining, when we fall.

What about the man who did!
Carry such a heavy load?
He bore it on his shoulders
For many miles up the road.

He was shoved, kicked, and spit at
As he traveled that last mile,
He carried his burden with him,
And, not once was there a smile.

The burden he carried was of wood
Made from the DOGWOOD TREE,
This burden he carried to his death,
Was for sinners, like YOU and ME.

Ann S Wegmann
WILL YOU REMEMBER

To Charles

My love when we first met I somehow knew,
As surely dear as there are stars above,
That I was born to share my life with you
Until the end of time. Since then our Love
Has grown the dearer with the passing years,
We laugh as one and sometimes cry apart,
While anguish for each other's sake, and tears,
We hide behind a smile and aching heart.
My love when we have aged and throbbing veins
Are winter-bound and still as frozen streams,
When time has taken toll and there remains
Alas just shadows of our former dreams,
When only ash is left and dying ember,
Will you remember dear, will you remember?

Anthony Cruso
A FRIEND IN THE DARK

To Little Shoes from his grandfather, who loves him very much.

When you think you're right, and everyone is wrong,
Maybe they never understood your song.
Maybe the ego that is within,
Never really let you sing.
The acoustics that come from the wall of hate,
Reverberate back, and cause your fate.
So sing your song, like a man in the dark,
Look real hard to see a spark,
Of the love you have, that is within,
Smile, and say I am your friend.

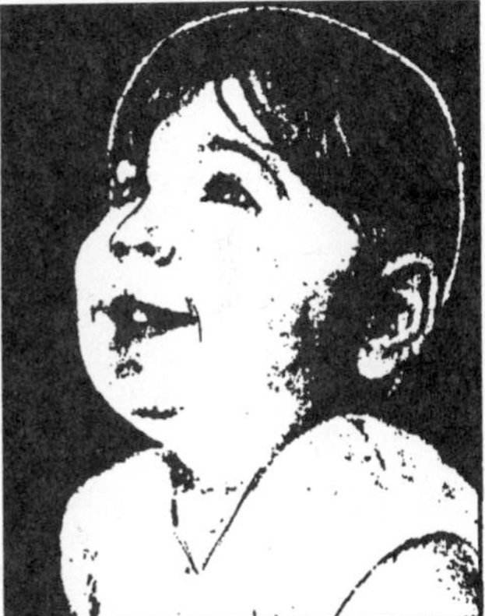

The world will be bright,
You will find your heart,
For this, my friend,
Was the spark in the dark.
Speak kind words, like a bell they'll ring,
Your friends will understand, the song you sing.

Barbarella A Hicks
IS THERE "BLOOD ON OUR HANDS"

This poem is dedicated to my beloved husband Lamar and precious son Starky and daughter Hannah in servitude for our Lord.

Last night Lord as I lay sleeping, the violent spirit of darkness came creeping.

A young couple Lord, whose marriage had turned to grief, they from this life, floated away from the family tree, now just a fallen leaf.

Two precious little children stood by, too afraid to scream, their little bodies could barely force, a sigh.

Daddy took Mommy's life, by the cruelty of a knife.

As Granny entered the room, in total horror,
The spirit of murder she did borrow.

With gun in hand, she sought to save, but now Mommy and Daddy's gone with the chilling wave.

Two little children left all alone, no Mommy no Daddy not even a home.

Why Lord, aren't our preachers standing between the porch and the altars weeping anymore.

When asked to go visit a young couple in trouble, they puff and become downright sore.

The brothers and sisters say it's not our job,
That's what preachers are called to do.

It seems to me Lord, nobody wants to work for you.

Too often Lord, when someone's in need, we turn our hearts away and your precious works we do not heed.

Lord please in my spirit live, that I might, always of my self be willing to give.

Send me to them broken homes, that I might, tell them of your blood that atones.

I wish not to be called a saint that's lazy,
I'll simply rejoice when called Jesus-crazy.

How hard is it Lord, to stop and chat a moment or two, with a couple of children who really need you.

Give me courage Lord, to knock on that door today and through the love of Christ show them a brand new way.

My Father, my God, their blood is on our hands,
If we don't tell them, it's only through your Spirit that unity stands.

With tear-filled eyes and a trembling heart,
Guide me Lord, thy message to impart.

Jesus Christ is your answer my friend, there's not one situation sorrow or sin that His great love can not amend.

As I close, I can hear the children cry, as they whisper to Mommy and Daddy goodbye.

Peggy Oliver-Nance
ONLY A DREAM

This was written to my late husband Carl Oliver during his long illness. I would like it dedicated in his memory for our children Regina Barkell, Dino and Frank Oliver.

We were walking along, just
you and I
When a bolt of lightning came down
from the sky.
Where the lightning hit, there
stood a man,
He spoke not a word but
held out his hand.

Then I noticed He was
pointing at you.
"Wait," I said, "I'm coming too!'
My feet were planted to the ground.
I tried to speak; no words I found.

It seemed as if you found
wings to fly;
You never turned to say good-bye.
Oh, dear God, what did I do
That you must take him back
with you?

Give me a chance and I will do,
The things for him you want me to.
As the tears rolled down my cheek,
I thought I heard my darling speak.
"Wake up," you said, "Don't sleep
all day."
It was only a dream that took you
away.

Tracy Ann Alvers
THE REUNION

In loving memory of two of my dearest friends, who both passed away in car accidents, Gladys Marie Rodriguez Deaton (1969-1986) and Pedro Cavazos (1970-1987). I love you both.

An icy chill crept up my spine
As the daylight faded into
obscurity.
Memories of lost years hovered
over me
As childhood friends settled into
their places with utter silence.
Strangers struggled through the
crowd with lowered heads
Some hoping for one last chance
to speak those feelings
only divulged in a hush
Others seeking a solace . . . an
answer to their silent prayers.
Yet all hurled together by a
whirlwind
of sorrow and misfortune . . .
Not exactly the reunion we had
anticipated
on this cool autumn day
As we witness . . .
A funeral for a friend.

Russell Hansel
SEVEN PEOPLE DIED TODAY

To my wife Kathleen
My daughters Sandra and Angel
And my granddaughter Amanda

Seven people died today
Oh how I wonder why
'Twas wisdom they were seeking
Seeking from the skies

Altho their bodies were not found
And probably will not be
Their hearts and souls are still with
us
Just as they used to be
All the world will miss them
And all their friends will mourn
That such a thing could happen
And so many hearts be torn
But look at how they thought of it
And let our hearts be brave
It was for our knowledge
That they are in their grave
Though I could go on and on
It's best I didn't try,
Cause all that I could get from this
Is teardrops in my eyes

Susan Vance
NO REPRIEVE

For Tom,who went through the fire with me

The sentence has been handed down:
an old year lost, a new year found;
twelve spent, tired months,
now century-bound.

Eight elevens freed at last
from their thorny, shackled past.
Execution, day by day,
left '88 no hope to stay.

A prisoner without parole,
the annum's crime exacts its toll;
while we mere mortals ,
you and I,
paid costly dues, then wondered
why.

Rejuvenate? We cried in vain;
we gave you love, you gave us pain.

But '88 is history,
time's transient fatality;
a Death Row docket drawn
and signed,
midst fading strains
of Auld Lang Syne.

Oh New Year how we like your
look!
A newborn chance, an unread book.
We pray that you'll go straight
this time,
no wayward acts, no life of crime.

We'll pay our dues, just like before;
then knock upon your time-worn
door.
A plea, now in your infancy,
that no offender will you be.

Hazella Westman
"LOVE" (WHAT THE WORLD HAS SO LITTLE OF!)

To One and All of My Family

Love makes this world go round
they say—
Each day, we share it with folks
along our earthly way,
Depending on who they are, and
close they are to us.
Anywhere from friend to family;
o'er which we devotedly fuss,
With surprises, hugs & kisses, and
all that "mush"!
It puts "spring" in Grandparents'
heart and step—
What a mountain of little love tokens
thru years we've kept!
And tons of bumps we've kissed
while little "go-getters" wept—
Tho, they truly looked like little
"angels," while they slept.
Love has many facets like a diamond
ring,
It gives a Home a firm foundation, to
weather everything!
It bursts forth in all life forms every
spring,
And makes the happy memories,
upon which we Seniors cling—
To have known love from the cradle
to grave, is such as rewarding thing!
I'm grateful for the "years" I lived
and "events," that—
Gave my heart, its "own" song to
sing!

Roy Ivan Sittig
YOU

To Susan: Always & Forever—I Love You! !

When, in my moments of deepest
despair,
I cry aloud but no one is there.
I sink deeper and deeper in sorrow
and pain,
Only to cry out again and again.
It's at times like these I think of you,
And how you've made all my dreams
come true,
And how you've cured my pain and
strife,
And turned around my failing life.
It's you who's made the
difference to me,
You've opened my eyes and made
me see.
See all the things life has been
giving,
And how, without you, I haven't
been living.
It's things like these which you've
done for me,
That raise my hopes and make me
see,
That life without you isn't really the
same,
And I'm so glad that into my life you
came.

Brenda Kay Kuepfer

Brenda Kay Kuepfer
HOPE

Dedicated to: My Mother, Cleo Rogers, And: My Husband, Don M. Kuepfer

We look without seeing, we touch
without feeling
We eat without tasting, we hear
without listening,
We talk without saying, we smile
without laughter,
We care without loving, we want
without caring,
We take without giving, we go
without destination,
We sing without a song, we reach
without a goal,
We exist without living, we have sex
without meaning,
We multiply without planning, we
plan without a future,
We are parents without children, we
are young without youth,
We act without thinking, we seek
without finding,
We forgive without forgetting, we
worship without God,
We are neighbors without friendship,
we are brothers without love,
We discipline without justice, we
fight without a cause,
We are free without liberty, we are
people without pride,
We are man without knowledge, we
are heroes without honor,
We are old without wisdom, we have
governments without leaders,
We are countries without faith, we
are nations without charity,
We are without understanding,
So Hope!

John R Matza
WHAT IS OLD?

Dedicated to the musical group the WHO and their rock anthem "My Generation" which inspired this writing on their 25th anniversary

Graced with lines through the brow,
Smiles inverted conveying
indifference,
Not a stale mind but stagnant ideals,
Traces of fear of the unknown,
Contemplation of life instead of
thoughtful living.

Is this my picture?

Do I desire to be——old?
Or do I, "Hope I die before I get old"?

Am I now?

Who ever dreamed such in a song?

WHO?

Denise M Archer
FOREVER MORE

Dedicated with never ending love, to my father David R. Green, my husband Randy and two extra special children, Nathaniel & Gabrielle Archer for making my life all the more worth living. I love you! !

Let the sunshine in your eyes
Forever More.
Let the smile on your face be
Forever more.
Let the beauty in your heart flow
Forever more.
And Forever more
Happiness is yours.

Shandora Sandy Faulkner
HOPE

To K-11-7 DoraLee, Scarlett, Gwendalspire, Lily Bell, Shirley G, Also LSBW—Becky, Debbie, Bonnie, Santa, Armenta and others.

The beauty of flowers, and birds and things
A mouth that laughs, and smiles, and sings
All of this will come to me, simply because—I am Free

A heart that's light and skips about
A soul with all the sadness out
All of this will come to me, simply because—I am Free

A happy life although alone
To know I "made it" on my own
All of this will come to me, simply because—I am Free

For all my "SISTERS" who think that Hope
Is in a drink or bag of dope
For all my sisters Black/White
Who are going to be abused tonight
All of this will come to me, simply because—I AM FREE
UNDERSTAND?

Betty J Chastain
REAWAKENING

To Sally for her inspiration and courage

Standing tall and proud, its limbs unbowed,
Who sees the inner battle man's destruction has endowed.
The winds blow strong with heightening furor,
The roots rise from their earthly nest.
And so begins the final flow of juices yet unborn,
The vines their hollowed core sends forth fruit
of sweetness yet unsown.
The will to reproduce, the hollowed base outshown.
The final flow of sweetness yet unborn.

Barbara Dees
SONG OF LOVE

To The Other Part Of My Heart

My soul dances with joy at the sight of you,
My heart sings of love whenever you come near,
I long to be at your side,
I lay my heart at your feet,
My love for you grows and grows,
You are my love, My life, My everything,
Come and be with me.
We shall forever be in the ecstasy of our love,
You, My Beloved, are the other part of my heart,
Come and be with me.
Come, My Love, dance with me forever, in the silvery moonbeams, as we sing
our Song of Love . . . .

Pati Hicks
TO MY DAD

To my dad, Lee Perkins, my sincerest thanks for sharing with me the ability of having an optimistic attitude, friendly smile, and faith in the Lord. With love, Pati

This is to you dad,
In all times, good and bad.

Your faith it will all work out,
Is what this is all about.

You have given to me strength unknown,
Through actions and behavior to me you have shown.

Your attitude so cheery and bright,
Your kind words reassuring things will be alright.

Your smiling face and friendly hello,
A charm that picks you up when you are low.

These are the things that make up you,
That add something special to all you do.

These are some things that you have given to me,
And forever grateful I will be.

For these are the things that make life worth living,
The things that give life meaning.

Thank you dad! ! !

Deborah Alicia Wakefield
I BELIEVE IN YOU LORD

To my Mom and Dad for believing in me and to J.D.M., my sole inspiration

I believe in you Lord, but how can I doubt,
That nothing in this life ever works out.
The world is a mess with the drugs and the killing,
With cocaine ready for whoever is willing.
People are dying from some virus called AIDS,
While terrorists blow airports up with grenades.
Satanic worship is quick on the rise,
Sacrificing their babies for some leadership highs.
There are evangelists preaching for money and fame,
Getting caught with prostitutes, then facing the shame.
The killing, the hunger, the drugs and the greed,
People laugh as they watch their stabbed neighbors bleed.
I know you are there Lord and I know that you care,
And I hope that you'll answer just one of my prayers.
That this world will get better on through the years,
And love will replace all the hate and the fears.
Yes, I believe in you Lord and hope I won't doubt,
That this world will get better and life might work out.

Bettye M (Hughes) Evans
ELVIS

In memory of my parents, John and Leota Hughes, for their love, encouragement and belief in my ideas and endeavors, I give my gratitude.

You gave the world much happiness, with your music and all—

But our gift to you in return was far too small,

God gave to you a very special gift of musical talent,
That you shared with the World with love ever so gallant,
You were born into a life of love so divine—

Our memory of you, like a star will forever shine,

You had the mountains high, and the valleys deep—

and then the curtain closed with a peaceful sleep,

You left us your music to share with all—

You inspired us to have hope, then you answered God's call,

Rest in Peace Elvis, we love you—

Annie G Jones
GIVE ME STRENGTH

To my son, Charles K. Taylor, may you always find God to be a tower of strength.

Give me the strength, O Lord,
To lift my head up when I'm burdened
With the pressing problems of life.
The strength to meet each day with hope and courage,
The strength to assume my responsibility
And not try to shift it off on someone else.
The strength to speak thy words of truth
In the face of adversity or opposition,
The strength to climb the mountain of life
And not stand at the foot hoping it will be moved,
Give me the strength to do the right thing
And not compromise in making decisions
For many times it is easier to give in
Rather than hold on to one's own true values.
I realize my shortcomings and weaknesses O Lord
Sustain and keep me in time of trouble
For I know that thou art a tower of strength.

Kris Dispenziere
THE ODD FELLOW

To my two loving children (Madeline and Karl) and two granddaughters (Jamie and Jodi)

He travels fastest, who travels alone,
They say and it is true.
For I've been speeding recklessly,
Since I bid goodbye to you.

Love has lost its polish,
The glitter of romance is gone.
I've no strings nor signs attached to me,
But still my life goes on.

Others believe their aim in life,
Is to share a cute little home.
But me I find, I'm having fun,
Traveling, Strictly alone.

Mary-Jo Mastrianna
GOD'S PROMISES

To My Family who have lovingly encouraged me to write.

God's promises are so very true
But as humans we just don't trust
At times what God has promised us.
And end up feeling miserable and blue.
God promised: Accept my son, I sent him to die
To save your soul and to give eternal life
How can a father sacrifice his only son?
He did because He loves us so much
Our only hope for eternal life was a loving God.
God promised: To send Jesus back again someday
To bring us to a land without tears
And sorrow shall no more abound in our lives
God's promise to us in our Christian life.
God promised: Follow me; I will never leave thee
nor forsake thee.
No matter what happens God promises us
That Satan will not win
As long as we humbly ask forgiveness
Our God is there, His arms opened wide
His tenderness for all to receive
As long as we believe.

Missy E Gentile
A LIFETIME TOO LATE

Dedicated to my grandmother Carol Gentile who saw the light under the barrel, and my therapist Andrea Bush who helped me make it shine.

We came together, as before, on the last night of my stay.
I remember waiting: from preoccupied morning,
To apathetic noon, to anxious evening;

The day going by in measured minutes.
We sat and talked
When I would rather have taken you to bed,
Feeding you love in unmeasured portions.
Staring at you unabashed
Drinking you up with my eyes
Intoxicated with my want for you,
Being content to hold your hand.
Basking in your smile, wanting you now.
No time left to make you even an occasional habit;
Like warm milk on a cold winter night.
There are spaces in me that won't be filled,
And my needs ring more hollow than empty attic rooms.
I have to leave you now.
Our paths crossed a lifetime too late.

Lisa Renee Reynolds
GOODBY

To my mother, Dorothy, who believed in me. I Love You.

We met each other when bitter winds blow,
freezing ice upon the snow.

We reached out for something warm,
there we found it in each other's arms.

There we reached the hottest heat.

The love we made was tender and sweet.

Our love was special, I hope you know.

I wonder why we let it go.

Ruth I Myers
THE LOCKED GATE

Dedicated to unloved, unwanted, abandoned pets and for humane treatment of all animals

In the country, on a road of clay
The afternoon before Christmas day
I journeyed to where the
heartless part
With furred lives, models of a
human art
With food for under the
Christmas tree
I reached the shelter much
before three
There closed and locked was
the entrance gate
Grieved, I knew that I had arrived
too late
For the abandoned cats and
dogs to share
Gifts from my heart, for
them I do care

Loving by nature and lively
by choice
With pleading eyes and sound
of voice
They beg to be loved in a
friendly home
With children and fields where
they can roam
My two car Dobes started to
bark and growl
When they heard a forlorn
puppy's howl
Left unwanted at the shelter's
locked gate
Before Christmas, such an
unkind fate
I can't forget the puppy's
imploring eyes
That told of cruel and calloused
human lies

Linda D Whistler
A DAY AT THE CABIN

This poem is dedicated to the memory of my parents, who have gone on to be with the Lord.

We thank You, Lord, for this new day that's just about to start,
A cool brisk morning, soon to give warmth from the sun so bright.
We thank You, Lord, for the beautiful ride in Your lovely forest,
Up in Your mountains where the air seems the coolest.
We thank You, Lord, for the cabin we all so happily entered,
The togetherness in cooking the breakfast, the prayer said as around we gathered.

We just thank You, Lord, for the best breakfast You made possible for us,
Just bacon, eggs, homefries, and coffee, cooked on a good old wood stove without any fuss.
We thank You, Lord, for the talks and the fellowship we had this day,
As we remembered the past and the thoughts of cabin life made us so gay. Thank You Lord, for the walk we had in Your woods, as all beauty around we saw with our eyes,
The moss, ferns, trees, a stream, the silence, even blue skies.

Lord, this day will always be remembered by this dear family You made,
As we touched each other and said our farewells, may the peace, joy and love we shared never fade.
Thank You, Lord, for showing us that without fancy living we still can be mighty happy and thankful,
We just pray Lord, that You will bring us all together again for a day in Your forest, so delightful.

Patrick Lewis

Patrick Lewis
RISING STARS IN TEARS MAKING A STAND

First to my Grandmother, Mrs. Lula Mae Reed. Secondly to my mother, Mrs. Ola Mae Quinn. Thirdly to my beloved daughter, Lithicia Michelle with much love.

As I look upon my fellow friend and foe,
the heart is aglow

Wipe your tears away and
lift your head

Today you must make a stand to rise within yourself

And show the world you can
see beyond the narrow scope of no
Singing of love and joy; lifting up the fallen ones
to stand together in brotherhood

Hand in hand we can change the way we are
to the way we want to be

So come along
one and all

Do your best to guide a child
in the best for a growing need

Then we'll see the deeds of a stand
made by rising stars in tears

Kelly Bolte
I'VE KNOWN OF MANY LOVES BEFORE

I've known of many loves before,
but none were quite like this.
'Cause now I dream about your lips,
kissing mine with sweet tenderness.

When I hear your voice or envision you,
A smile appears upon my face.
A chill will tremble down my back,
As my mind drifts into space.

I love you in so many ways,
Each is too hard to explain.
But whenever I am without you,
My heart cries out in pain.

I love your humor, wit and charm,
These brighten my every day.
In your arms I hope to forever be,
To live safely each night and day.

Ulla Haraldsdotter
STANDING TALL AND SILENT

To my mother

Standing tall and silent,
the ancient tree, bark gone,
glistens in the sun.
It is a gnarled old hand
with arthritic pain,
from work well done.
Suddenly, shiny specks of birds
appear,
and land and lift,
and up and down,
and all around in joyous flight.
The tranquil scene
is alive!
It is my great grandmother
reaching out to me
with her venerable,
gnarled, old hand.

Shirley Smith
A PROMISE

A promise I made you
That I'll always hold
That comes from the heart
And cannot be told.

To make you a promise
That I'll never cry
Or promise forever
Would just be a lie.
But to make you a promise
That I'll always be
The same kind of person
Your eyes see in me.

Is a lie never to be . . .

Charlie

Allene Harrington
LIFE

Life doth hold but fleeting shadows
Bits of flowers that fade away
Happy now and sad tomorrow
Changing petals from day to day.
First comes life and love and happiness
Then 'tis sorrow and despair
And there's none to turn and guide us
Help us climb the long, steep stair.
Why can't love when first it grips us
Let us glory in its wake
Lift us o'er our perils and pitfalls
Erase our errors and mistakes?
But that is not the way of life
To move the rocks strewn in our path
When first we make one tiny stumble
She smites us through her terrible wrath.
Then we go on the same as ever
Raising willfully our drooping heads
Hiding gallantly that awful sadness
When our hearts seem turned to lead.

Herbert R Webb
HONEY

I dedicate this sonnet of love to the wife in my life, Lucille Margaret Taitt-Webb

You mean to me what a flower
means to a honeybee.
For without a flower there can
be no nectar,
And without nectar there can be no honey.
In other words, I am that
flower,
You are the honeybee.
And the nectar I have to give
Is a love that is continuously sweet.

Jay A Blakely
ROOT OF EVIL

People of the earth take heed,
existing is an urgent need,
Look to the skies, open your eyes,
A world of fools, you make your own rules,
A divine being cries, another life dies,
Is Satan your Lord? the wine of despair poured,
Your greed rules your life, you cause pain and strife,
Into the darkness you strive, taking for granted, you are alive,
Not respecting the power above, you have forsaken love,
The day of wrath shall be swift, a second death shall send you adrift,
Many religions abound, listen to the ominous sound,
The father soon will appear, He is the religion to hold dear,
Do you feel anger in your heart?
hypocrites soon shall part,
Scorners beware, for some still care,
When will be the time of release? can this world yet make peace?
You kill your children to take gold to your den,
Is this life the only future you see?
sinners shall hang from a tree!
I hear the news and see distorted views,
A sadness fills my heart, moving me to depart,
From a world of evil pursuit, to a realm lacking the evil root.

Bart M Young
SELF IMAGE

Knives seem appealing to me.

Death has touched my senses
and I feel laughter
turn to hatred.
How dare he attack me.

Slaughter turns to tears
as they take his body away.

On the ground I look up at myself,
I see misery. gravity pulls me
down.
I fall to my knees scratching at
the pale earth.
I see tears falling. Death has

finally overcome my diseased
life.

On the ground I look up at myself,
I see hatred. Hatred of myself.
The knife still drips with blood.
The blood that came from my
downfallen life.

Expressions turns to rage . . . I have
broken free.

Tammy Furlotte
LOVE

In my eyes your love is the greatest;
but in others' it's poorly shown,
no one but me sees how sweet and
patient you are;
Although they say love is blind,
with you there can't be a love of any
other kind.

Suzanne Fingerut
A RAINDROP TURNS BEAUTIFUL

To my Daddy whom I love very much.

A raindrop is like a really small diamond in the sky, blue as the ocean, and very beautiful.
The clouds are as soft as white pillows, the residue falls on them so lightly, like a teardrop from your eye. The blue in the sky reminds me of water falling from a bucket. All together and you could have a rainbow.
Orange, red, and yellow
just like the colors of the sun.
When the sun raises from its sleep in the morning it is so lightly darken and gray.
Then the light comes up after it is rested, it's here to cheer you up in the morning after you wake yourself up.
Then the night falls again till the next time it arises.
It is so wonderful when the rain comes down and so peaceful too.

Kay Walters Booker
DREAMSCAPE

I dreamt I was a princess,
in a place inside of time.
At a table lined in wisdom,
sat the leaders of mankind.

The first man was a carpenter,
and was chosen King of man.
The second man's head wrapped in
cloth,
breathed mastery of sand.

The third man and his brethren,
masked slanted eyes—strength of
will.
The visions of what these men saw,
plays vivid to me still.

If all religions could combine,
and war amongst them cease,
then maybe Gorbachev and Bush
will somehow find world peace.

Eric B Fuller
GANGBANGER

To my family, and my Columbia College writing teachers.

A gangbanger was shot in the school
playground recently
Shocked? Surprised?
It happens everyday
Gangbangers are young men
Who think they're young men
But haven't grown up

They're black, white, yellow
They leave their spray-painted calling
cards
on the walls of schools, stores,
subways
And itch for a fight if looked at the
wrong way
For what? A piece of a street called
their turf

Gangbangers don't want to see other
young men make it
They cut them down before they turn
on themselves

For the young soldiers of the streets
It's a vicious circle that'll never end
No medals are given
Just hell.

Lillian E Scott

Lillian E Scott
YOUTHFUL ANGER

To all mothers who have gone through this experience.

He knew everything, This young
man,
Many hurts he'd bring,: In his
youthful span.
Angry words he would apply, To any
wisdom spoke,
From the nest he did fly, The strings
of home, "he broke"

His father's heart was broken, His
mother left to cry.
From angry words he'd spoken, As
he broke the family tie.
A gentle hand will guide him, And
lead his steps, I pray.
God knows he is my pride, Tho he
broke my heart today.

Teach him gentle wisdom, Protect
him every way.
Bring him to our kingdom, Don't let
him go astray.
Love him? Oh, Yes, Dear God, My
love for him won't flee,
Even as to death, I'd trod, Please
guard him, God for me.

Crystal Shelton
SILENT CRY

She'd been crying all night,
but no one could hear.
She'd been hurting so long,
but no one was there.
She was confused and so tired,
alone and so scared;
All she wanted to know
was that someone cared.
She didn't know how
to give her wishes a voice,
She was so tired of trying;
there was no other choice.
She needed some help,
but didn't know why.
She wanted someone to hear
her silent cry.

Michael Mack
SHADES OF OPTIMISM

God bless you Mom. Love Michael

Emptiness invades where love once ruled, this man once driven by desire completely alone. He refuses to accept the reality in his life, so use to controlling his own destiny not even religion can help him now. Hatred confines his soul, the dice no longer roll to seven. He is a prisoner, a slave he has become to the harsh environment around him. Nothing short of a miracle could release this heart. No other source but a heavenly light would unchain these bonds of hell. Lucifer has tightened his grip, he's tied the strings of my freedom and shortened the leash around my neck, strangling what used to be.

Surely the light must come, I believe it must. For the heavens don't lie to those who believe in a better life. A life without pain, a life without chains.
A crown of thorns he wore for us.
His life he shed for me.
I must believe, for there is no other hope but in the light that someday surely it must come, surely it has to come. I ask myself where can it be? Why! Oh why! Oh why must it take so long?

Aaron Dettbarn

Aaron Dettbarn
A NEW LIFE

A new life comes with the pain and
tears,
An extension of yourself for the
coming years.
Dress her up in a bright yellow dress,
Smile to yourself as she comes
home a mess.
First she's three and then eleven,
Now she's grown, oh thank
Heaven.

Karla Cooper
FEELINGS

The clouds above,
So peaceful they seem.
Symbols of nature,
What do they mean?

A storm in the midst,
Or a nice sunny day.
Who's to know?
Who's to say?

Feelings like clouds,
So unsure we try.
To predict our next mood,
To laugh or to cry?

Can we control
The way that we feel?
No, I don't think so.
Emotions are real.

Don't fight the tears
When in need they come.
For when the rain's over,
The sun will come.

Larissa Vilenskaya
WHAT IS HERE AND HEREAFTER?

To dear Barbara Ivanova with gratitude for years of friendship and guidance.

We live, we play, we grieve, we
pray,
And often we ask, and often we say:
What is the meaning and what is the
mission,
And what is the reason for such a
condition?

No easy answers, no easy lives.
Easily things go but not easily come.
Questions, questions, questions that
we call eternal . . .
Will I get a rest from them, internal
and external?

Questions come and go, Truth and
Essence stay.
Let me ever sow, let me ever pray,
Let me tell the meaning that I've
understood:
We are never leaving in a somber
mood.

Here comes the answer, here
comes the joy:
We are never leaving to
become a toy,
We are never leaving to
become a night,
We are always leaving to the
Land of Light!

Thomas Mistysyn
DO YOU KNOW WHAT I MEAN?

He believed in the American way
Work hard and go to school, be rich
someday
But the dream it turned and bust
The golden credit card had turned to
rust

He left his home as a happy
young man
To see the world and grow up was
the plan
He wandered round before he settled
on down
His mind soared high though his feet
stayed down

Do you know what I mean?
To put your hope into a far off dream
Do you know how I feel
As you try to talk with God and
make a deal

He settled down in a very small town
To write a novel or to work on some

songs
But his job took too much of his time
And late at night he would drink too much wine
Girls he met well they played with his head
He even wondered if he'd be better off dead
He lost his faith in the American dream
His life would pass him or so it would seem

Yet it's okay and it's alright
Some how, some way he'll get through his life
He'll go on as best as he can
Because He's an American, an American man

Kristen Kulage
AM I ONLY DREAMING

As the sun beats down upon me,
I feel a joy inside.
A feeling that I love you,
A feeling I can't hide.
Am I only dreaming that our love can be,
I look at you and realize you're all I want to see;
Although we've never met,
I feel as if I'm you.
For am I only dreaming, that my dream will come true.
I hoped so much you'd notice me,
Just like I noticed you;
I don't know what to say to you,
I don't know what to do.
The first time that I saw you, I knew you were the one
We could do everything together,
and have so much fun.
Although I only saw the outside,
I feel as if I know the inside, too.
But am I only dreaming that I can be with you.
I smiled at you,
then smiled again.
But not one look,
not one grin,
That's what you gave me;
You left me behind in the dust,
and now I'm only dreaming;
And remembering your face is a must.

Shaunna Maureen Gramm (Age 9)
A SAD FOREST

Nature lies on the ground so still,
No water.
No happiness.
No birds are singing their beautiful songs.
Loud noises, big trucks, many men.
No happiness.
Flowers stop growing, their petals drop.
No clean dirt left.
No happiness.
No squirrels collecting their nuts,
No acorns, No trees,
No happiness.

Walter Grier
OLD FASHION LOVE

This poem is dedicated to Melissa McKinney. I feel she is responsible for this happening. I love you, also, thanks to my son, my mother, Carmen, but most of all thanks to our Creator!

I believe in old fashion love, the kind of love that brings a man and a woman to a deep understanding; one that no theft on God's earth can steal. The kind that sends you walking in the rain, walking on the sands of the shore, catching tears from a crying face in the palm of your hands and sharing all that you have without anything in return. To learn to become as one, having trust in one another with a large amount of communication, forgiving the things that you can't forget. Old fashion love is sacrificing for another, loving a person for who they are, and not for what kind of car they drive, not for the clothes that they wear, not for the money they have, or for how much gold they have around their neck. Remember that all material things must come to an end.

What happened to the love making? Has it turned into sex? What happened to playing in the snow? Has it turned to fighting in the snow? What happened to helping one another? Has it turned to I've got mine now you get yours?
Why? Have the little things about love been stepped on by the big feet of hatred?

David James Beecher
MANKIND

For Shannon

Sparkles of
Amazing light
The inside outedness
Of sight;
Belongs to voices
of the wind snow white
Drowning in the sunshine,
Drifting past the
Time of motion
Sailing away upon
an unseen ocean
Tonight alone
Without a sound
Ships without sails
run aground
in crashing surf:
Where shifting sand
is carried aloft
this fragrant earth
Unknown to man.

Joey Ann Grothendick
ON THE EDGE

Alone I walk the beach.
Silent, lonely, afraid.
Of what—I'm not sure.

I see you standing there
Watching me.
You too are alone.

We are different . . .
Separated by a force too big to fight—
We know we would only lose.

I can only stand here
On the edge of Yesterday,
With you
On the edge of Tomorrow—

And wonder . . .
Do I live in your heart as you
Live in mine—
Forever.

Leslie J Matthis
MY BABY, MY CHILD

For Jessica, our little girl, who brings so much joy into our lives.

The door is open.
Sounds of darkness enfold us.
Crickets.
Coyotes.
Drifting wind.
She lies, breathing softly, in her crib.
Naive.
Angelic.
Gentle.
She will change. I wonder nervously.

The door is open.
Sounds of sunlight rush in.
Blue jays.
Splashing water.
Giddy laughter.
She bursts, dripping wet,
into the kitchen.
Vibrant.
Jubilant.
Mischievous.
She is changed. I marvel
optimistically.

Hanne

Mr James E Williams
VALENTINE TO A SWEETHEART

To my Valentine sweetheart, who is now my loving wife, Hanne, who has given me a handsome son, Christopher, which makes us a complete family. I love you both, Sweetheart and new born.

Sweetheart chosen or complemented, gift or greeting, sent or given. Someone sweet, someone neat, for I do love you, my Valentine sweet. Valentine, is memories of you, wishes for happiness and warm thought thru.
Thoughts of someone special and dear, with members of someone as special as you, for you are my Valentine sweetheart.

Valentine, a time for sharing, a time for loving, we share the blankets, and the T.V., we share the shopping spree, and family car, we even share midnight snacks and the bathroom too, but nothing is half as great, as sharing life with you. You are neat, you are sweet, you are my Valentine sweetheart. All my life through, you are my Valentine all the time.

A Valentine sweetheart is someone special, one you really like and really love. Someone who makes you happy just by being near. Your closest friend—the one who shares the most secret places of your heart, the one who understands your feelings that go deeper than words. You're the one who gives meaning to that beautiful world—together! My Valentine sweetheart means the world to me, the one I'm proud of, too. The one who's always with me in everything I plan and do, you're that certain someone, I'm always thinking of.

My Valentine, I love you for your faith in me, your understanding heart, for showing that you miss me anytime we are apart, for every special plan and dream we're working to fulfill. Sweetheart, you are loved with all my heart and all the things you are to me . . . sweetness, softness, a gentle touch, a warm little smile that says so much. With all my love my Valentine Sweetheart, you are my sweet, today, tomorrow, for ever . . .

Robert A Williams
AS THE NIGHT HOURS TICK AWAY

As the night hours tick away,
I lay there on my side,
I think about the very day,
in which my life did abide,
was it good or bad, or did I even care,
should I have been sad, or
should I have been spared,
was it full of destruction,
and/or cruelty,
was there ever any combustion,
around any novelties,

these are the many questions
that I ask, before I fall asleep,
then I slip into the past, and
my sleep is deep.

Debbie Hunziker
MY WORLD

To my husband William, To my kids Tonya and Dale. For being a part of my world. I love you.

The world is so large,
And beautiful if you want it to be.
You can be scared and you can run,
Or fly like the birds and be free.
The world can be beautiful if you look at it right,
Always there never out of sight.
It's there for us all,
Never too small.
This is my kind of world,
To be free and a home for me.

David N A Lewis
FROM RHODESIA TO ZIMBABWE

'One man, one vote' Was their strident cry,
For we care less if we live or die,
We want your money, your land, your wives,
We want it now or we'll take your lives!

Some went for training to Bucharest,
While others stayed to pursue their quest,
Destroying villages far and wide,
And laying waste to the countryside.

Their weapons came from the K.G.B.,
For they were promised they'd soon be free,
To be the masters of their own fate,

In what they called: 'A one-party-state!'

'We've no remorse for the things we do,
For soon the terror will see us through,
And when at last all is done and said,
We'll hold our hands out for U.S. aid.'

Then at last the day dawned dark and grim,
When the 'comrades' said: 'We're voted in,
To ruin this land, as we see fit,
Our only Bible, the Marxist Writ!'

'One man, one vote,' was the mindless shout,
'We're going to drive the white man out,
We're only killers who burn this land,
But never . . . racists; you understand?'

Helen W Pabor

LUMMI IN THE SAN JUANS

I would return to lovely Lummi Isle
In spring when pink roses fill the meadows,
Sea birds run feeding in the tideline,
And yellow finches line the fences;

In summer when the sun is warm,
Reefnet boats anchor in long lines,
Swallows build their nests in the cavernous boathouse,
And fish lie deep waiting for a flood tide to carry them north;

In autumn when storms come up from the south,
Pounding the beaches,
Roiling the gravel, polishing the agates,
Driving boats to take shelter ashore.

And finally I would be there in winter
When snow blankets the land,
Small boats rest snugly under its cover,
Wildlife sleeps in its den,
And all nature waits for the coming spring.

T Temple

MY TREE AND ME

Love to my kids, Tim, Mark, Jeff, Greg and Penny for them understanding and supporting my need to find a new life for myself.

Have you ever taken a little time
To analyze a tree?
I see so many companions
Between a tree and me.

The trunk I see as solid,
A few cuts deep in the bark,
But yet it holds its branches up
Thru sunshine and the dark.

A few branches are dead and dying,
Tangled, gnarled, torn away.
There are parts of my life I see like this
That recalls of long, past days.

But the trunk is still solid
Its roots deep in the earth,
You have to have a source of growth
To feed your own self worth.

The thriving branches are of different strengths
With smaller ones reaching out,
Upon them all the leaves sprout forth
Without reservations or doubt.

I find these branches in myself
Both weak and strong, but reaching
My leaves feel full and shiny green
Responding to His teaching.

But trees have dormant stages too,
To grow, they need to rest.
They draw their strength from earth and rain
A must to do their best.

And in my way, I rest, I grow
God looks after us you see
We're born and nourished, we grow and die
This tree of mine and me.

C B Saxon

ETERNALLY YOURS

Think of me when you're away
Think of me when you're cold
Think of me if you've had it with today
for I am warm to hold.

Speak of me while you are there
Speak to me when you are here
Speak for me if you must
for your voice is crystal and in you I trust.

Dream of me if you're sad
Dream of me if you're lonely
Dream of me when you've had it with the world
for I am here, yours only.

Dream us afar.
We'll play a star.

We string its light of fire within our hearts,
between our hearts.
And in our heads we tune the glow
that warms us in our bed,
until the end.
And the end is starlight, to us ever sent,
never spent.

John Anthony Garcia

THE PROBLEM

THIS POEM IS DEDICATED TO: Reggie Southard, and Linda Dickerson, two true caring professionals whose efforts are making a difference in the "WAR ON DRUGS."

We can not lose the War On Drugs.
We must unite and make our stand because;
We know Drugs are the problem.

Tell your children that it's not right.
Don't be shy, nor get uptight.
Let them know Drugs are the problem.

Read about them in a book.
Try to show them how they look.
Make them aware that Drugs are the problem.

If we try to, "Just Say No";
That alone won't make them go.
Together we can solve the problem.

Drugs aren't a party that we should share.
When they learn the truth,
they'll know to be scared.
Tell your kids to beware because
Drugs are the problem.

When they lose their friends to Drugs,
Or brothers and sisters that they love;
They'll see why Drugs are the problem.

They must live life right before it's too late.
When they live it right life is really GREAT!
But they must understand Drugs are the problem.

William M Morgan III

CANDLE OF LOVE

To the sweetest of sweethearts, Katie

Once to be together
but now to be apart
is a destiny of its own
that comes straight
for the heart.

A power that serves its reasons
not understood by all
It comes and goes
As it pleases
For many it hurts inside
For many it hurts to be alive.

But they must go on.
for somewhere lurks its mutual mate
They will collide somehow
even by the theory of fate.

A cosmetic change will occur
the heart will re-light
to burn a candle
full of love.

Joe Davis

HAPPY FATHER'S DAY

To all the Davis family

There is a place in my heart, I call back home. In the hills of the Ozarks where I used to roam. A railroad crossing with a cattle guard, A big cedar tree in our front yard. These are just memories I keep for my own. In a place in my heart I call back home.

We were a close family, the Bible was our guide. We were held together by Mother's prayers and Dad's pride. I believe the family ties were stronger and the days were longer. After work we always had time to play. And on Sunday Dad would put all the work tools away.

I can still see the blacksmith shop where my Dad made plow shears out of old grader blades, There's that old water jug with the burlap tied around. I used to carry my Dad's drinking water when he was plowing the ground.

He would stop the team in a furrow and I can see him now, tying the plow lines to the handle of the plow. Then he would take a drink from the water jug and say "much obliged, son" and give the lines a tug.

As I walked away, I could hear him sing his favorite gospel song, "Unclouded Day."

Sometimes I think we take Father's Day for granted, We give a shirt or a tie, or maybe even pass Father's Day by. Personally I believe a hug and "I love you Dad," will be the best gifts he will ever receive.

And now I look up in the sky, wipe a tear drop from my eyes, then say a little prayer along the way. In the land where angels dwell, where they ring those golden bells. I know my Dad has found his land of the "Unclouded Day."

Willis Benjamin Hunting MA M/Div

Willis Benjamin Hunting MA/M Div

COW BELLE FOR POLAND

THIS POEM is most lovingly dedicated to Lucile Florine Hunting, the belle of my life and compassionate wife for more than 50 years; and to our younger daughter, Nancy Lucile, aspiring Poetess.

O ! the tintinnabulation by the bovine population
Seems a splendid indication that they stray;
And by good manipulation of the schedules at the station
They are shipped to every nation that can pay.
When they reach their destination, after proper motivation,
There can be no deviation from the way.
There they show appreciation, drinking cool precipitation,
Chewing on a dusty ration such as hay.
When a special delegation, planning on a long vacation
Tries to get a reservation for a stay,
The hotel administration, on the chef's own commendation
Orders beef in preparation for the fray.
Each tale (tail) has a consummation, so we see by observation
That a cowboy's occupation is O.K.

Lawrence Spirio

EASTER MORN

Upon this early Easter morn,
the golden sun breaks through the dawn.
from out of the gardens and out of the field;
the scent of flowers doth its fragrance yield.
The golden dew drops sparkle and gleam;
a sight of peace that ere be seen.
The singing of birds upon their perch;

the ringing of bells from yonder church.
The town folks gather from far and near,
the gospel of the lord they've come to hear.
The early spring air filled with happiness;
freedom, love, serenity and gladness . . .
The sun shines down in all its splendour
in breaking through the dawn;
for life is in all its glory
upon this Easter morn.

Francisco F Ortiz Jr
LIFE (THE RISE OF THE SUN)

To Bruni my sister and my brother Demetrio and my Mom, I love you all

As you open your eyes
With the rise of the sun
You know that it's time
To do the undone

The undone is that
Which no one has done
Before or even after
The rise of the sun

The rise of the sun
Means a brand new day
To do the undone
You didn't do yesterday

Yesterday has gone
But tomorrow will bring
Some more of the undone
Some other thing

The things which are done
Don't worry about
But those things which are undone
Can wait, until the next, rise of the sun

Ronny W Hagan Jr
THE WAY IT GOES!!!

A day to remember. But want to forget.
It is something I'll always regret.
We pushed our love over the limit.
Now I know why it didn't make it.
You wanted your way, I wanted mine.
We both got nothing all of the time.
I hurt you, You hurt me.
It was just the way we made it be.
I had a chance to change that day.
But I let it stay the very same way.
Now I feel alive again, Free to please myself again.
Maybe you feel that I gave in too soon.
But the way it was, Was a living HELL!
I did ONCE love you, but now that's gone.
My heart is repairing fast and strong.
This will never happen again.
I'll pick the right lover, But this will take time.
I won't be selfish, I'll really try.
Because I want to be the very best guy.
When we see each other in time.
I hope we can smile and maybe a friendly HI!
But if we can't, oh well that's THE WAY IT GOES !!!!

Londa Lush
THE WAY TO HEAVEN'S DOOR

Brighter than the light of day, stands Heaven's door; His Majesty, our Lord.
His intelligence, grace, power and love
Encircles our life—serenity.
His presence; uplifting, is clean and pure.
His wisdom and knowledge encircles our mind
In truth; our souls to bend in solemn prayer.
His light; our guide,
The path to heaven's door—eternity.
His love divine; so warm, so tender.
His power to heal; curing our ills, strengthening our souls
With His presence, grace and understanding.
Blessing the life He gave; a gift to us, a joy—
The way to heaven's door—eternity.

Mary J Stephens
ALWAYS IN MY SIGHT

You have come to me;
You think I have the key.
I have lived to see you grow.
Now I must tell you things you must know.
You will have some heartaches,
And see all the love that some can take.
It will leave you empty,
And you might wonder, "Why Me?"
Love can be so good
Like it always should.
Or make you think that all is bad,
And that will make you sad.
Remember this throughout all your life,
That the love I have for you will give you strife.
I have held you near, and wiped your tear.
I will always have an open space,
Even in this hurried pace
To ease your fears,
And wipe your tears.
So hold me tight, and give me a hug.
You will always be in my sight.

Beth Grogan
A FEELING CALLED PEACE

For my Mother, Grace, who showed me beautiful things and for my husband, Daniel, who showed me a new way to look at them.

Come with me. Please? Come with me.
Sit, if you would, and listen
to the gentle hum of the insects;
to the birds as they sing their lovesongs
floating high in mid-heaven;
to the soft murmur of the river as it glides down the mountain side.

Take a deep breath. Smell the tender breeze
as it caresses your body, carrying with it the fresh clean smell of pine
and the sweet smell of wildflowers.

Look quietly around you. See
the delicate array of those wildflowers
as they dance politely with
the grass in the breeze.

Look! To your right! Don't move!
Coming into our clearing . . . it's a beautiful timid doe and her fragile little fawn.
Time seems to stop, nature holds its breath
as you look into each other's eyes
and then they are gone
leaving you awed and with that
feeling called Peace.

Tammy "Sims" Torkelson
A WISH

I Wish I could be the one,
to be there for you,
to love you and hold you
and let you be you.

To be the one you could
Laugh with—when funny thoughts arise,
to talk with,
be crazy with—when you're feeling wild.

To be the one you could
Cry on—when everything's gone wrong,
to lean on,
Just let down on—when with life you can't go on.

To be the one you could
Share ideas with—no matter what they may be,
to share dreams with,
share life's goals with—however far the reach.
I wish I could be the one!

I know I can't be the one,
A wish it will only be.
But I can be your friend, and when you have a need,
I'll be there, just wait and see.

Dorothy A Newsom
LIVE!

A new beginning; the start of the year—
The sound of the surf, the feel of the sea
And, lo, a muted rainbow appeared
Misted by the silent pyrotechnics in the west.
A sunset of such splendor that one can
Only feel renewed and awed by the glory
and the promise of happiness and peace,
And thanksgiving for being able
To dwell in God's beautiful earth.

Allan Fletcher
LIFE

Where does it begin?
is the question
asked by women and men,
for we have the answer
as to when it will end.

Is it there
when rockets seem to burst in the air,
while ecstasy leaves our body limp
without a care?

Or does it begin when the memory
has long forgotten,
that two souls in love did make a flight
while the moon was in her zenith
that bold and daring night?

Did you not hear your baby cry
while passing through the air?
As two souls embrace in love,
a child took life from the joy they shared.

It is there in love that life first begins,
two souls in harmony,
once without and once within.

Now that the final act is over
and you both are left alone,
do you still ask the question
Where does life begin?
No!
I think you have the answer, my friend,
for in your spouse it lies within.

Jeanne Baird
BE GOOD AND KIND

Dedicated to Rutledge Pierpont Van Allister, III, Tuffy, Matilda, Patches, Happy, Happier, Singleton, Fluffy, Herman, The General, Timothy, Brainard, Perro, Ponti, Peregrin, Bonzo, Bobby, Sandy, Friskie, Matthew Malcolm Muttlenger, III, now Buddy Baird, and all the others—

Be good and kind
To all God's animals,
No matter the number
Of their feet.

Be kind to all—
Whatever circumstance,
Wherever you may meet.

Whether human on two
Or animal on four,
They all have hearts
and time is fleet.

So be good and kind
To all God's animals—
Be kind to all you greet.

Darlene Cusmano
A NEWBORN ROSEBUD

Some days I sit down
and think of all of you I've met.
A certain person stands out in my mind
like a beautiful rose
among a million wilted daisies.
In my mind, that is you.
Knowing and loving roses so well
I make the connection
within a solitary second.
This closeness is as tight as
a newborn rosebud
growing with more gentleness
as each new day rises
with the morning sun.
Giving light to another day.
Shining its rain to make it
much fuller and stronger.
I understand this newborn rosebud more
now that it has lived to grow
forever with gentleness.

Bobby Todd Frase
THE "CRACK" IN MY BOAT

To my son, Randy, whose wit and laughter made me a happy Mom

I'm in the boat of my life,
Riding high upon the waves,
It's wild and wonderful,
And it may spell doom,
But it's my boat, so give me room.

I'm not looking for any horizon,
I'm lost, and I know I can't make it,

It's wild and wonderful,
 And it may spell doom,
But it's my boat of life,
 So give me room.

I'm tossing to and fro upon a terrible sea,
 My life is ending all too soon for me.
It's still wild and wonderful,
 And it may spell doom,
But it's my boat of life,
 So give me room.

I'm still in the boat, too far out to reach,
 It was wild and wonderful, now I'm doomed,
But it was my boat of life,
 And I gave up my room.

Bruce Wayne Goble
I HIRSUTUS OF VENUVIUS I CHILD OF NATURE I CHILD OF GOD

May Stars may Sky be your Kingdom Spirit Father William, Spirit Mother Mary Elaine.

Dear God, Father of the Astral Heavens
Glory and Praise be to thee and to Thy sacred and blessed bequeathal of Thy Pangloss Parchment of Thy Holy Scriptural of They Etherean and Ascendetrean Sacrament of Thy Melodiate Rhapsody of Nature's Verdantic Love

Dear God, Dear Father
 I rejoyce of Thee and of Thy Scrollus Elegantinus Naturaliam and of Thy Lyrate of Thy Purine Psalm Thou hast gave to I, Child of Nature, by Your Transcendence Father; as Thy Divine Essence of Thy True and Alabastine Spirit of Thy Salvatum Equalae Congregatious that I shall be messenger and deliverer thereof and that shall be the Sacristy of My Soul, the Life and Blood of My Sacrifice
 I shall be the Truth of My Heart
 I Thy Child of Thy Earthly Plane, Creator God, I shall bespeak in prayer Thy Minds' Images as Thy Visages of Thy Visions of Thy Heart that My Child's eyes shall Illuminesce as Thy Light that shall be Thy Appartitive of My Existite Evanesence and My Way of Passage to The Plane of Spiritualis Infinitum

Dear God, Dear Father, Dear Spirit
 I, Sun of Thy Mornes
 Yellophaneous Rays,
 Whisprous Breath of Thy Days Breezes,
 Springs' flower petals Falline
 I Child of Wind,
 Child of Raine,
 Child of Thunder,
 Lightning of the Sky
 I shall say nay nature nay; I shan't Mourn Lives' Farewell as I worship the Spirit of Thy Astralic Ascendency as I leave the Sphere of The Earth Plane's Energy

Yea. God. Yea.
 I welcome the Glidanous Utopiation of the Flight of Thy Spiritual Skys as I Sing Thy Songs of Nature, of Light, of Love as I worship with The Tranquilide Placial Harmony as They Gelden Trumps of Haves Thereafter play thy music thy Silvern Harpes of Thy Wingd' Angeles

Dear God, Our Father
 I shall be with you, I Hirsutus of Venuvius, I Child of Nature, I Child of God shall be of the Platonia of Thy Celestial Stellary Planetary Galaxy of Thy Universe of Thy Cosmos Eternitus, to Regnate Regallate Forever with Thee

 Spiritus, Serenitus, Placidus, Jesusus, Naturalius, Eternius, Amenius

Virginia B Grove
TODAY
I had my share of laughter
I had my share of fun
Heard the birds singing
Felt the first warm rays of sun
I smelled the aroma
Of flowers sweet and rare
Felt the stirring breeze
Ripple through my hair
I touched a little baby
Who wore a smile so sweet
Had a richly blessed table
Someone to share this treat
I saw morning dampness
Absorbed a pink sunset
If life holds any better
I haven't found it yet
And such a lovely way
For today to end
By sharing conversation
With today's new friend
If I can have tomorrow
And I could have my way
I'd want the same riches
I was blessed with today

Victoria Sander
THE DEAD KNOW NO PAIN
The dead know no pain
Only the living complain.

The dead know of no losses
Only the living count the loss.

The dead know not of gains
Only the living score wins.

The dead know not of tomorrow
Only the living keep sorrows.

The dead have met their fate
The living anxiously await.

Melody Michelle Trentham
THE MEETING OF LOST SOULS . . .

*To all those people who have lost love, thinking they will never find love again . . . hold on to the dream . . . it can become reality.**

A gentle kiss soft as a summer breeze,
a gentle look that comes from so deep within . . .
this is the meeting of lost souls, but where did it all begin?
So new yet so familiar, so real, yet feeling insecure,
a hidden joy, such tranquil peace . . . how can it
make one feel so unsure?
And as the dreams unfold, you can feel, untold,
all that lies between us, as we stand feet firm on common ground . . . .
there is but only a slight sound . . . .
touching souls with fingertips, reaching out with eager lips,
one night set free from all restraint,
that dawn, nor truth could ever taint . . . .
our mixed emotions, so very real, that morning
could never steal away the presence of the dream . . . .
that only a pinch reveal—those special moments
neither truth nor morning chase away
the reality . . . of shared love . . . .
the meeting of lost souls . . . . .

Jan H Bradley

Jan H Bradley
FINER THOUGHTS
Mirrored images appear
In dreams, my eyes half-closed,
My journey to escape life's grip
A fantasy overload.

I squint to hold my eyes closed tight
In fear the light may enter,
And spoil my only time of day
To cherish in its splendor.

So hard to hold the finer thoughts
Of flowers warm and blowing,
Swift breezes with the ocean's waves
The power overflowing.

I travel to a place in time
When innocence was in fashion,
And silly girls with wavy hair
Wore ribbons of pale white satin.

A brand new baby's skin so soft
And chocolates semi-sweet,
I'll linger in these moments rare
Til night and morning meet.

Heather Phillips (Age 12)
THE MORE I WISH THE MORE I LOSE
The more I wish
The more I lose
This curse is never broken
Though I wish it were

My heart is always
Open with dreams
And fairy tales
But never do these fairy tales
Ever seem to come true

I always tried my best
To hope and not to wish
For more badfortune that
I knew would still come

But then one day
In the still of May
Was the day of my
Dreaded death

At last I was put to rest.

Grace B Liberman
WINTER APPROACHES
The early morning is a sight to behold.
A brand new day is about to unfold.

The sun is peeping through clouds passing by,
Spreading radiant colors over the sky.

The wind is blowing up a cool breeze,
As golden leaves fall from the trees.

Squirrels are scurrying to and fro,
And to the south the birds now go.

Tis the fall season of the year,
And all too soon winter will be here.

Mrs Sarah I Davis
THE FEELING OF LOVE

This Poem Is Dedicated to Al Davis, My Loving Husband, for Valentine's Day of 1985

When a woman meets a man,
Will they love and understand?
Are they right for each other?
Will they lose their love for another?

All these questions we want to know,
Before we let our feelings show.
How easy it would be,
If our lives, we could fore-see.

But I have been blessed a fortunate one,
For these questions I have overcome.
My man loves me with all his heart,
And for no man, will I ever part.

We have the rest of our lives to grow.
And only to each other, our feelings show.
May every man and woman feel in their hearts,
What you and I have shared, from the very start.

Sonya Wright
A TRUE GIFT

To the man I love, Dave, who is a true gift in my life.

You came into my life like a
 soft gentle breeze.
You brought out many feelings
 within me,
 unlike anyone else,
 and for that I am very grateful.
Your love for the Lord is as fresh
 as a mountain stream, and I too
 want to share in it.
Before meeting you, I was like a
 seed that was waiting in the soil
 to be nurtured. Your gentleness
 and caring enfolded that seed
 and nurtured it.
My love for you has grown,
 just as that seed grew into a
 beautiful flower.
I love you.

Robert Lewis Williams
PLEASE LOVE ME
When the waters of the ocean
 bring a cold feeling
 and the beach is closed,
 will you be near me?
When the dark grey clouds are
 shutting out the sun
 and suddenly my nose starts to
 run,
 will you still be near me?
How about when the hot summer
 night has changed its warm
 winds into icy cold winter's,
 will you comfort me?
Will you hold
 and keep me warm against the
 cold nights
 or are you afraid of loving
 me?

Louis Lampman
POETRY
A place exists,
A garden of thoughts;
Though this semi-oasis belongs to someone else
I find it pleasant to wander there.

I sometimes sit and ponder,
At ease, at rest, relaxed,
As though when clouds float by

Or mellow minds meld.

Yet there are moments
When almost-lightning strikes,
Almost-rain then will fall;
Ah, but I have shelter,
So it doesn't bother me at all.

Peggy Ryan Williams
I SAW A SPIDER SPIN HIS WEB OF THE MOST EXQUISITE BEAUTY
I saw a spider spin his web of the most exquisite beauty to behold.
I heard the spinning of a web with a fast formula dramatically told.
The spider's web was built by instinct and with explicit care was made.
The man's web with cunning speech related plans extremely well laid.

The spider's web was for survival with food and insects he could lure.
The man's web was a fantasy—yet a dream—with rewards quite unsure.
Both webs were engineered with purpose and involved intricate plans—
The spider's web of beauty and the clever web of the man's.

Men with intelligence and capable of very keen thought
Feel sure there's no web in which they can get caught,
But it appears that sometimes men and insects as well
Discover they're entangled in webs—so pray who can tell?

Christine McIntyre
FOREVER

This poem is dedicated to my Mom and Dad, my Aunt Ronnie and my Prayer Group for their love, support and encouragement.

You are my friend, my lifetime friend
And I'll be yours until the end
Through thick and thin, when lights grow dim,
I'll be your friend

. . . FOREVER . . .

When you're in a jam, you know where I am,
So don't be afraid to shout
When you're in trouble, any kind of trouble
I'm here to bail you out because
I'll be your friend

. . . FOREVER . . .

If you're in a bind and no help you can find,
And you really want to share,
Don't be afraid to give me a call
You know I'm always here because
I'll be your friend

. . . FOREVER . . .

Mrs Izora Keeton
DEAR JOHNNIE
Dear Johnnie,

We have traveled through life together;
Through summers and winters too,
Each moment has brought joy to me.
Now tell me what about you?

Sometimes we traveled over mountains
And sometimes by oceans blue,
But the time has seemed short to me.
How has it been for you?

There have been a few thorns near our pathway
But remember there were roses too.
The thorns I walked around bravely,
But the roses I gathered for you.

I have never given you treasures,
But I tried to share what I knew.
I have tried to show you the highways
But the exits puzzled me too.

Now keep on holding my hand
And I'll keep close to you too.
I can see dawn approaching,
Oh! the sun has already come through.

Love you,
Izora Keeton

Debbie Higdon
THE GIFT OF GRACE
For many years I tried to "earn"
Salvation that I was not worthy of;
I tried to understand, to justify
His forgiveness and His love.

Heavy obligations overwhelmed me
As the debts I sought to pay,
But His blessings were so numerous,
That I couldn't find a way.

It was only when my precious friend
Brought me face to face
With the reality of eternal life:
That we are saved by grace.

My heart could finally understand
And accept what my mind had not:
That God's love and mercy are of
God's will and neither can be bought.

John L Everitt
A TASTE OF PERSIMMON

To my grandfather, J. C. Everitt; to the memory of my grandmother Irene M. Everitt

On my autumn walks perchance I'd trod
across the branch and the farrowed sod,
to the corner pond which grandfather'd dug
to water stock from gumbo mud.

The dam was low and leaked a lot
across which many a hoof did trot.
And all grown up with briars and such,
but as for shade there wasn't much.

There were a few persimmons there
persistently growing under sun's hot stare.
Just damp enough for their fruit to grow
and ripen 'bout fall didn't I know?

I'd sample them early but oh, what a curse!
My mouth would pucker an involuntary purse!
I never learned all fall it seemed.
Still stopped and tasted though they were green.

Doves winged past Bob White among fencerows.
Elusive squirrels hid from cawing crows.
Toting my gun I fixed rusty wire,
but often my reflex was too slow to fire.

Senses full of fall and as love for our place
like a lingering taste that time can't erase.

Krista Thornton
TO BE
To be . . .
Is only
a distant
dream.

To which . . .
We cling
so
heartily.

And yet . . .
We still
refuse
to see.

All that
we
have tried
to be.

Mary H Ransom
FROM MY WINDOW

To my granddaughter, Eden Elizabeth

Below long jacket
Swathed in minimal yardage
Legs in opaque hose.

On storm-tossed branches
Fluffed against the driving rain
Seemingly birds sail.

Playful children lie
In fluffy snow; arms wing-spread
Imprint snow angels.

In sync with nature
Birds wait to fly down and eat
Tidbits of brown toast.

Cloud-streaked orange sun
Clinging to the horizon
Challenges the night.

Don Dufaux
DANCE BLACK

To those who share their love

Dance a Nation's Love;
sing assured of Blacks'
two-edge sword . . .
struggle.
Rhythmic sway a Black's
heart-torn joy,
pain . . . bleeding dry.
DAUNTS not Black skins
redemption beauty . . .
power.
Deeply souled in
Spirit's mystical realm.
Black hands lifted to
God . . . lifts redeeming,
Love's unison dance.
Hearts' pure-fire-love
dances Black.
Angels lovingly dance . . .
a dance Black.
Blacks grace Love is
alive . . .
a sharing alive . . .
a world alive.
Colors multitude fuse
in God's KALEIDOSCOPE
Eyes.
Dance Black,
Brotherhood world.
A dance of joy . .
of God's
Living Word.
Consumed,
revealed,
given,
in dancing Black.

Fern L Kalar
THE GOLDEN YEARS

To My Mom, Elsa E. Marling

I was remembering the
Golden Years before
When it all started
for me in the year 1894.

There I was a 'tot'
Just learning to crawl,
Walk and talk
Remembering what life has brought.

Mom and Dad teaching me the
right from wrong.
Having brothers and sisters
who have come and gone.

The Golden years are all
the years of Love and laughter,
And what is in store
for me ever after.

My 'babe' now watches over me
I no longer can do the things
I did before,
But that's because I'm a foxy 94.

Shawna Harris
MY LOVE

To Jeff, I love you with all my heart!

Well my love where do I start,
It's very simple, you stole my heart.
You kissed me once, then again,
And that is where this story begins.
Each time I see you I fall deeper in love,
I know it must be a gift from above.
The way you kiss me puts me on cloud nine,
And the way you gently touch my face sends tingles up my spine.
I love for you to hold me close to you,
As a matter of fact, I love everything you do.
You say things to me so sweet I cry,
And when we're apart I miss you so much I almost die.
No one else is as sweet, kind, or considerate as you are,
Then again you are the greatest there is by far.
And when you grin that lovely grin I adore,
I just fall in love with you even more.
So now my love I hope you'll see,
Just how special you are to me.

Jenny (Wren) Findling
I AM
I am the sun—I am the breeze
I am the moon—I am the trees
I am the clouds—I am the rain
I am the joy—I am the pain
I am the priest—I am the whore
I am all this and then I'm more.

I'm life—I'm love—I'm the snow-white dove
I'm puppies and kittens and the blue

skies above.

I am the flowers—I am the bees
I am the oceans and the seas
I am the baby—fresh and new
I am the Catholic, Baptist, Jew
I am the Black, the White, the Red
I am the the old man and the newly-wed.

I'm thought—I'm deed—I'm all you need
I'm always there—I always care
I'll pick you up—I'll fill your cup
I'll dry your tears—erase your fears
I'll walk with you—I'll talk with you
I'll be your friend until the end.

Heather Barry

Heather Barry
NEVER FORGOTTEN, ALWAYS LOVED
You were his youngest son, his pride and joy
In his eyes, you were still a little boy.

But then you deceived him and broke his heart
It went straight through him, like a shining dart,

He told you no, but you went ahead
It was like you never heard a word he said,

You kept it from him for so long,
You played it cool and acted strong.

But then something happened and your fun ended
It broke your father's heart, which can never be mended.

We knew you loved him and he loved you too
But why you didn't listen, no one knew.

Oh how hard your father cried,
Knowing his youngest son had died.

What you've done has scarred him forever,
If you think he'll forget you, the answer is never.

Arrie Herndon Lewallen
A HELPING HAND

This poem is dedicated to all Navy wives who battle daily with loneliness and boredom while their husbands are out at sea. Hang in there girls. God loves you.

As I began my work this morning,
Washing dishes, pots, and pans;
It was so dull and unexciting,
I sure did need a helping hand!

Then Lord you gave my heart some manner,
It sure brightened up my day;
"Do everything as unto the Lord,"
These words I heard you say.

Dear Lord, we had a sweet time,
Cleaning house today.
Tomorrow we'll clean this house again
Just like we did today!

Colossians 3:23

Barbara M McDonald
HOW I LOVE THREE

Whispers of Love To Leonard, Keenan & Mike

The morning was fresh,
with a spring rain slowly
drizzling a pattern
on the damp earth.
The cool moist air hung heavily,
blanketing trees,
shrubs and all living things,
and feeling God's presence
surrounding me, I looked at our
youngest, with hair tousled,
pajamas and sleepy eyes of blue,
and my heart leaped as I
whispered,
"How I love you."

Slowly, struggling to meet the
coming day,
he paused on the stairs to greet
his brother on the way.
I smiled and said "Good
Morning" to our tall brown-eyed
son,
seeing them together, my day
had just begun.

He sat, we talked and my heart
filled with pride,
as I thought of our two great
gifts from God,
our sons, to walk by our side.
Then, looking out at the morning
dew, I whispered,
"My Son, how I love
you!"

Now, back to the early tasks, still
counting blessings by the score,
I looked up into a smiling face,
as their Dad came through the
door.
So straight & beautiful, no,
handsome is he,
and I thought, how lucky I am
that this man belongs to me.
My heart filled anew and I
looked around
and loved each part of our
home, with my eyes, without
sound.

Then, as he turned and went on
his way,
a sadness poured in and I
wished he could stay,
but I know there are many
things that he must do,
so, I whispered a prayer,
"God Bless, you know I
love you."

Soon the three of them left, my
men to their chores
and I'm here with washing,
ironing, and scrubbing the
floors,
but when evening arrives and
they all come in
and call "Hi, Mom" with that
special grin,
I know each in his own little
way is a lovely gift to me,
and I thank God and whisper,
"I love you, All Three"

Barbara J Korte
WITHOUT TREES?

This poem is dedicated to my brother, Jim Bour, who has been an inspiration on my life and my writing.

How lost the squirrels, getting
weak. Where now dwell? Beneath?

What to call Autumn. The special
feeling colors give. This brightness,
gone.

No forests? Oh how hungry the
animals. So scared, cold, longing.

Where's the beauty, the frozen dew,
crystallized branches. Is winter to be
so bitter?

Spring brings new life. What!
No budding trees? This is sad.

Tired the birds, flying. Where do
nest, needing rest. Babies soon
to tweet.

So hot the summers. Relax, read
a book. No tree to lean? Where's
the shade?

Richard B Hawks
WHEN MY FAITH SOARS THEN LOVE ME

To my wonderful wife, Terrie and my baby "Rashad"

When my faith soars
Then love me
When my soul is overwhelmed
Then be with me
When friends stop being friends
Then walk with me
When I look at people
Let me see them with your eyes
When I seek the lost
Let me use your heart
When I think of myself
Remind me that you are the
difference
When this journey is over
Then give me a seat in heaven

Kathleen Riemenschneider
ANEW
Innocence will slip by
rain like April showers.
May flowers will sprout
out of the manure from past
years.

The fields will bloom with laughter.
All children will play.
Cruelty and hate
will not be known.

Up in the sky,
the sun will shine
with warmth and love.

A sparkling smile
will form.

Life is anew.

Lilian S Barber
JANUARY TWENTY-EIGHTH
Sky breach,
Out of reach,
That spacebound thrust.
With might it must
With power surge,
Great upward urge,
Ending in dirge.
To ride a flame,
Then have it claim
The seven who dared
And were ensnared,
Their challenge ended.
They were expended.
To grab the glory
Is the eternal story
With danger fraught.
Weep, weep for the astronaut
Who reached too far
For an elusive star.

Mack O Wicker
A QUEST IN THOUGHT
Once a day, and sometimes more,
You knock upon my daydream door.
I say very warmly, "Darling, come
in;
It's good to have you in my
daydreams again."
And so we sit and have a chat,
Discussing this, recalling that;
Until a chore that I must do
Forces me away from you.

Though my daydreams bring you
near,
I wish, darling, you were really here.
But what reality cannot change are
the
Thoughts in my mind that you
arrange.
So, through my daydreams, you'll be
brought
To me each day: a quest in thought.

Anthony Moreland
SEPARATE REALITY

To those above who watch and wait. The sleeping poet has awakened from his dream.

The mountains, the sea, the sky and
clouds,
The Sun and Moon are all in tune.
If they were not then I would not be
here.
That is why I am . . .
I am in the ebbtide and in the ocean
waves,
And I sift the sands of time.
I am in the rain from the clouds and
in the heavens above,
And I watch the world go by.
I am in the mountains, in every forest
tree,
And I conceal the wisdom of the
ages.
Yea, I am in all of this,
For I am borne of these things,
For I am Nature . . .

Bob McGuire
THE ALL-NIGHT MISSION
I don't want to live this way
anymore,
Locked up in the grief of your
mistake,
Looking out the window for a sign,
Searching for a clue that will only
show in time.

If I gave all I could get,
But I don't want to die just yet.

Artificial flowers melt inside your
window box,
Clinging to the tokens of too many
yesterdays,
Headed for a place you cannot grow,

Roaming like Kim Novak, in
"Vertigo."

I can't chase you down no more,
All I found was bolted doors.

You're my all-night mission in the
dark,
You're my all-night mission in the
dark,
Is there room at the inn, for a wretch
like me,
Or are you going to flash: No
Vacancy?

Tonya Gaiters
TREES
Some are brown and some are green
As they stand so tall and lean

Through the windows they fill my
eyes
As they try to touch the sky

Covered with the winter's snow,
Hovered by the clouds that blow
From West to East and East to West

And birds that build their little nests
In pockets of their spiny vests

At night I think I like them best
With the moonlight's silvery beam
of zest

I feel as if I'm just a guest
Invading on their peaceful rest,
While tuning into wilderness

Mark Marquez
LIFE'S BLUE RIBBON

This poem is dedicated to my sweet Darling Daughters, Mindy and Marina Marquez, Daddy loves you.

When you deny your soul,
You are playing the part.
For your soul is
The real you.
We would all like
To follow our hearts
And be ourselves,
But we choose to
Think it is impossible.
Very few know us and
Surely we don't know the world.
Hence we know
Anything is possible.
The balance is here,
And we're not blind . . .
We need just let our souls
Be part of our mind.

Ellen Hinterlong
PARTING AS FRIENDS
We are parting in our own ways,
And we have nothing left to say.
We were the best of friends through
the years
Now we sit here shedding sweet
tears.
I'm sorry for all of the fights we had
Please accept my apology and don't
be sad.
Someday I may call you on the
phone
Please remember you're never alone.
You're always inside of me
That's the way friends are to be.
You're a friend forever in my heart,
But now it's time for us to start.
You follow your dream while I
follow mine.
I'll look you up when it's time.
We both have a life to live.
Remember, it's kindness we are to
give.

Rita Vazquez
SEARCHING
I'm looking for the light,
the light is calling me.
I'm looking for the day you see,
free of misery.
Patience is the key I know,
With faith you feel sublime.
I'll pray to Thee till that great day,
when light will come to mind.
Then everyone I touch,
I'll touch in only name of Thee.
I'll teach them how to love and hear,
your sweet melody.
So when I see the light, dear Lord,
that I am longing for.
I'll make a shrine for all to see,
to love forever more.

Kerry Haines
I CAN SMELL FLOWERS ON THE WIND
I can smell flowers on the wind
And feel the sun on my face.
And if I close my eyes
I'm in a faraway place.

Where mythical trees whisper my
name
As the scented wind blows through
their leaves.
And I listen to the waters run.
Freely as I wish to be.

I long to run through an open field
Of wild flowers and reeds.
Not in this world of concrete
where nothing lives or breathes.

Where the air is heavy
With smog and dirt.
Where people are rude
And so full of hate.

I wish to return
To where I'll be free.
To live among those
Who know how it could be.

Jennifer M Campbell
THIS LOVE OF OURS
As I lie here tonight dreaming of
you
I think of how loving and caring
you are
Just to name a few.
With your love for me so gentle
and your feelings so warm
I sit back and watch our beautiful
relationship form
We've come a long way since I
first saw your face
And not a soul in a million years
could ever take your place.
You are the one I mostly care for
and the one I mostly love
And you're the one on my mind
that I constantly think of.
Therefore, together forever is
you and me
Because our love is strong enough
to last an eternity!

Bill Holler
SISTER
Sister by the well,
you draw your water way too fast,
it wastes itself within the sand,
it seeps and sinks beneath your feet.
Sister, your eyes betray you,
they roam too far beyond the fields,
they close upon the distant heights,
they settle in the shadows of the
world.
Sister, these nights are still and long,
your lover enters gently through your
dreams,
he sets himself beside you in the
dark,
he takes you as the wolves of night
lament,
he leaves you in the chill of dawn.
Sister, this desert is a lonely place,
the storms of summer just begun.
Its sands will lash and close our eyes,
its torrid winds will dry our hands.
Sister, draw your water slowly,
for us this a weary land,
too soon the earth recovers what
the wells of youth discard . . .

Cecilia C Faughnan
LIKE GARDEN'S SUN
Like garden's sun
Bright, reaching one
Bold color flight
You grow so bright.

Leaves reach, stretch more
Stems feel, know, soar
Don't hide, conceal
Your self, that's real.

Bright eyes, strong fight
Feed deep your sight
Let thoughts delight
And tame you.

Not in a shell
Could my words tell
Of magic's spell
That wakes you.

Who else can show
You love you know?
Hold high the glow
Life gave you.

Diane M Roger
HELL IS IN A BOTTLE
Hell is in a bottle
and it's closing in on me.
The cork is the devil
that keeps me from getting free.

I cry out to God
in my dark despair.
I know what it's like
to live on the dark side of nowhere.

Amber Kaufman
THE MEMORABLE NIGHT

I dedicate this poem, with love, to my friends and family. You encouraged me to pursue my writing and try my best. THANKS A MILLION.

I looked down from the top of the
mountain,
Watching the stars that seemed to be
dancing,
Shimmering in the night, like a
glittering fountain,
It occurred to me then, there was
someone else there too,
I looked around and realized it was
you,
Just you and me standing there,
Watching the last glimpse of
daylight disappear,
Inside me there was a cozy feeling,
A feeling of warmth, kindness, and
healing,
I felt I could stay there all night long,
Listening to the birds sing their
melodious songs,
But I had to go, I couldn't stay,
For I had to be home early the next
day,
And when I'm sad I remember in my
heart,
The memories of that night, with
which I shall never part.

Michael Byron
INVITATION

Dedicated to Janene Keely, whom I love dearly. Also dedicated to my family, and to my friends. My deepest gratitude for their support.

Ah, to dine leisurely 'neath
Autumn's crisp star flecked sky,
Amidst sizzling Australian lobster
and heady French wines,
Swiftly Evenings' lazy, languid
hours shall nightward fly,
And We—surrounded by foaming
Oceans' wet, wavy lines,
Two thousand feet seaward from
Lands' moonswept beach,
Reclining serenely just above
crashing Surf's' highest reach,
Enwrapped in Candlelights' warm,
flickering, ethereal shell,
Comingling therein, Oceans' salty,
nocturnal fragrances,
With Gourmet Cuisines' delectable
smell . . .
Alas! Too soon comes the Waiter
with the damnable bill,
P'raps its random atoms in motion,
p'raps its fate,
Anyway, if you're willing Janene,
I'll see you here Saturday at eight!

Shiela Gujral
BEATRICE WOOD
Nestled in the lap of mountain
a care-free babe, absorbed in dreams
flickering smiles, radiating joy
lies happy valley of Ojai !

I went there once
met the ceramist Beatrice Wood
pouring life
in lifeless clay.

Charm personified, captivating eyes
love oozing from her every pore
balm dripping from her drooping
form
I was mesmerized !

Drenched by the showers
of blissful calm
refreshed by the nectar
of her caressing palm

relieved of tensions
oblivious of worldly bonds
like a joyous bird
I began
scaling the sky !

Mrs Herbert (Esther) Hill
MY SPECIAL FRIEND
I have a friend so dear to me.
He took my sins and set me free.
My life became new and the
years soon passed
As I lived for Him whom I'll see at
last.
I am never alone tho' there's no-
one around
Since I have this dear Friend I'm so
glad to have found.
He greets me each morning at
the start of my day—
As I ask Him to guide me each step
of my way.
Sometimes I grow weary with
the news that I hear.
Then He comforts my heart with,
"There's nothing to fear.
Lo, I am with you always; on
that you can depend—
It's recorded in Matthew twenty-

eight. I'll be with you to the end."
This Friend was slain and hung
on the cross
To redeem sinners like me—but oh, what a cost;
So I praise Him today, this
Savior of mine—
Who is loving and patient and wholly Divine.
He arose from the dead, went to
heaven to await
The time He will meet His own at Heaven's Gate.

Peter Stanley
(a conceit)

. . . to all the unvoiced and unwritten, they are the inspiration . . .

The sounded notes portray the actions of my life.
Diff'cult to master music, I sustain such strife.
If a committed failure, dissonance is heard,
Then I must repent, rewrite with novel concord.

Born of European ancestry, hence to latter form.
The parts of me-my neck, my back-I fret will
not perform.
Will I produce fresh melodies?; mature in time to come?
The music must please my own mind, at least, if not
someone.

Observe! Observe! this mind, this instrument.
Yet I know not now what my life has meant.
But when I am played, and when I live,
The best recital I will try to give . . .

Dan Dulcey
MEEK AS A MOUSE

I am dedicating my poem to Elaine Ermel, whose poetry roars like a lion, but who is indeed meek as a mouse, and has a heart of gold.

She's meek as a mouse
but her poetry hits you like
dynamite.
Such lovely imagery you would expect
from Frost, Kilmer, or Noyes.
Such expression you would expect
from Shakespeare, Chaucer, or
Tennyson.
She may be meek as a mouse
but her poetry roars like a lion.

Lucille M Kroner
A DOCTOR

A doctor is a man with caring hands,
Who works long weary hours through night and day;
Sometimes without a 'thank you' or his pay,
But keeps a cheerful smile at his command.
Sometimes he is a teacher of his art
And offers us the knowledge that we need
To keep our health, the order of his creed.
Sometimes he gives new spirit to the heart.

He is there when we need him and quickly gives
His whole attention and his learned care,
So patiently, as our requests unfold.
In disease and accident the doctor lives
To treat mankind, as did another rare,
The Great Physician in the days of old.

June Corneilson
TWO FLAMES OF LOVE

Two sparks arose and lit two flames
In our hearts, many years ago.
Promise still shows in our many love claims.
Our lives seldom start tears of woe.
Nine offspring and eight grandchildren, each a beautiful boon,

Teach us to sing a very proud tune.
Thirty eight years soon as man and wife,
Along with our fears and joys and strife,
And hopes that good names of our children survive,
Have kept our two flames of love much alive.

Subrata A Sarkar
SUMMER'S LEGACY

A dream to remember
From June to September
Quiet nights of wishful slumber
Emotions of depth and number.

Sunlit smiles wither away
To reveal the glory of another day
A stroll on the beach, a friend to stay
Loving, caring words to say.

Songs sometimes sad define the mood
Feelings that can't be fully understood
A walk through the meadow, arborless wood
Looking back the times were good.

Silly flowers in her hair
Skin so crystal clear and fair
A loss of innocence, someone to share
Painful yearnings told in prayer.

Mari P Saunders
DEAR UNIVERSE

We're all down here (or is it up?)
Going through the sameness
of dark and light at regular
intervals
Each of us
with a limited number of moons,
All of which will too soon pass
plunging us into void
Would it be asking too much
to share this finite energy with a
soul other
Whom we could kiss goodbye at the end?
If not, could we come back
and try again?

Chrysann Mitzel
SWEET PROMISE

someday when you are ripe and weary
when your polished decadence is dulled,
it will come.
a silent, sweetened truth
piercing your arrogance,
tearing your direction.

someday far beyond
your empty, brittle days,
the sin of greedy, human consumption
will choke your darkened soul.

someday when your need is high,
when grief has taken hold,
the truth will come in brilliant splendor
to claim its victory.

someday when you are ripe and weary
I will be there
inside of you . . .

Kim Penning
A REAL FRIEND

To Mom and Chris my two real friends

A real friend is someone who cares
Someone who is always there
When you laugh or when you cry
A real friend is always standing by
When you feel you're at the end of your rope
A real friend is there to give you hope
A real friend accepts you—for you
Not by what you say or do
They don't criticize your habits or faults
But instead offer kind corrective thoughts
A real friend is a special person
And will always be a part of your life
Because a real friend is a friend who is true
A REAL FRIEND will always love you!

Jean M Franklin
NAKED

'C'an you not see, it could all be shared. 'A'nd that love is so beautiful. Life goes around just once.

You have seen me naked before
Now I have unveiled to you my inner most thoughts
Leaving me with little left to be seen
I can no longer hide behind my mask
Of fast statements, smart remarks and jest
Does this make you know me better
I am sensitive and caring
Will you help to heal all wounds
I'm naked and without shame
Hold on fast without embarrassment
You have seen me naked before

Vera M Schultz
MARCH WINDS

Now come the boisterous winds of March
To fling old limbs and leaves
around,
And make the forsythia branches arch
Their golden tips clear to the
ground.
Then toss old papers wide and far
And raise the dust a mile or
higher.
But, when night shows the evening star,
They stir like lambs held in the
byre.
And when their bluster's had its day
They quickly hush their roar
and din
From wind-swept earth then hie away
To let the gentle April in.

M L Thomas
TILL THEN

Lost you once, then lost you twice;
This trail is tough and cold as ice,
But I will find you, feel you near,
As I have found you other years
And other lives—we've shared a few,
Connected by the kind of glue that
Stretches thin, but doesn't break,
And so, my friend, make no mistake;
Our paths will cross time and again,
Though I can't tell you how or when,
But cross they will and cross they must—
Till ash is ash and dust is dust.

Violet Branch

Violet Branch
IN HER LITTLE SHOES SO WARM

To my son Robert Manae, and my Mom and Dad.

I often see a little girl,
She always looks so cold,
As she pulls her tiny coat so tight,
Her feet so cold her shoes with
holes.

I feel so sad to see her
As she goes by each day.
I'd love to talk to her,
But I might frighten her away.

God you know what I am thinking &
The clothes and gifts you've
blessed me.
Should you be short on blessings,
Could you give her mine you
see.

It would make me feel so good
If her little coat was new,
And her tiny feet were warm,
I know she'd love you too.

You really heard my prayers, God
Did you see her smile today?
In her coat and shoes so warm,
As she went along her way.

Ann Arnold
I OPENED UP

With love to my friends, family, and Ann Marie, who have all helped me to grow.

I opened up like the petals of a rose
To breath the wealthy air.
I held my face out towards the world
And there wasn't anyone to care.
People wanted to take me home,

Knowing I would die.
Instead of fighting to protect myself
I would sit and wonder why.
They would watch me slowly suffer
Then they walk away,
Knowing there were more of me,
Another for another day.
They looked like me but weren't the same
Even though they used my name.
None were as beautiful
Or as vulnerable as me
No one looked closely—or cared to see.
That I get hurt too.
—Now I know that's why
I have thorns.

Mrs Kate White
FREE FOREVERMORE
Some glorious morn, King Jesus will descend,
He's coming for His church, His bride;
There will be a great wedding day
In the Heaven of Heavens, way up in the sky.

Shedding old carnal bodies and putting on the new,
As we rise to meet Him; we'll shout and sing,
We'll voice glad alleluias on the wings of the morning,
For the amazing grace, of Jesus our King.

We'll reign with Christ forever, and glorify His name,
Only He is worthy for us to worship and adore,
Saints and angels at home with God, one great family;
While the ages roll on, we'll be free forevermore.

Wayne G Zack
THE GAME
Roll the dice, play begins
Future hangs in the balance
Time moves on, bet it all
A new game now to challenge.

Spin the wheel, cut the cards
Round two of play begins
More enter the game, for fortune and fame
The desire of wanting to win.

Stakes are high, bets are made
Round two has no rules of play
Hopes and dreams now fade—no moves to be made
Some will go and some will stay.

Enter round three, the final stage
Last attempt to win—now disposed
No cards to be dealt, no numbers do dice show
The third stage has ended, the game of life—has closed.

Dorothy Coignet Stanley
MY PRECIOUS HOURS

To: Thomas, my husband

May I never forget the happy
hours I've known.
May I always remember them clear.
The way that my heart accepted from you
All that was sweet and dear,
In those hours of bless that seemed like heaven to me,
Please let them return to me.
For knowing that someday, someone will return to share with me . . . for
ever . . .
Those real and touching moments,
Those everlasting dreams,
Those nights that were filled with pain and pleasure.
Are known to me, my precious hours.

Steven J Alvarado
MY MIND
My mind is a volcano
waiting to explode
with a burst of knowledge

Only thing is
as most volcanos are,
this volcano's inactive

Once in a while
the lava will erupt
only to be cooled by the air

It then goes back
to where it was before
and lays silent

Till it acts up again

Thomas M Kazamias
IF ONLY I COULD

To Androniki—my inexhaustible source of inspiration in pursuing excellence.

Cold and fierce, the winter winds
whipping my soul, alone and empty.
My body, tautened on the lancing rocks,
lamenting my loss of your countless blessings.
Your countenance—
a silhouette of years long elapsed.

Echoes and shadows, fading memory,
faithful companion in lonely years,
my heart, my body remember in love.
The warmth of your touch
never did I let penetrate my soul,
to blend, as it ought to, with my restless heart.

If only I could travel back
to days of yesteryear;
if only I could go back once again in time.
We, alone in secret love;
our bodies close, our soul one.
The mesmerizing sounds of summer months:
the peaceful Aegean, the never-never land,
the golden sand, the azure sea,
the gentle breeze caressing our arms
in loving, warm embrace.
I felt your lips,
our minds dull with erotic ecstasy.
I felt your love.

Stay you said, be here with me,
my body and soul yours, forever.

I would not hear
the heart-born words of love.
Imperceptibly
I erected walls around me.
Without remorse, without mercy,
I shut myself inside

A prisoner.

How unable still am I
to wreck these walls
that keep me inside
in sunset days, in hidden fears.

I only I could go back in years.

Catherine Rickards
TO A WIDOW

Dedicated to Libby Harrison, Coordinator, Widowed Persons Service, Wicomico County

After many years you lose a mate
You are devastated by your fate
Why me? Why me? You cry
How will I ever get by?

It has happened; you must accept
The lonely days and nights you wept
No one to talk to or share
The loved one is no longer there.

Friends are supportive, helpful
They miss him as well
Accomplishments are remembered
Good times and bad have been had.

Now is the time to go to other ways
Plan things you wanted to try
Your advice is valuable to many
It's up to you to make you happy.

Melissa A Rivinius
PEACE

This poem is dedicated to my parents, who have been so good to me.

The wind and the roar of the ocean
fill my ears.
Gliding across the sky, seagulls
give their long, shrill calls
Of either love or loneliness.
It's as if each sound is a part of
nature's song.

I feel the rocky hardness of the
ground beneath me
And the airy lightness of the sky
above me.
I watch as the white, foamy waves
crash against the jagged rocks,
And a feeling of peace comes
over me.

Jeanette Rich Wiley
LOST LOVE
If only I could
walk with you
And feel your gentle
love again, and
touch my lips
to yours . . .
And let you know
how very much
I still love you.
But we are lost to
each other and I
am dead inside.
I died when we ceased
to try to mend
each others hearts
And I only have happiness
in memories . . .
and dreams.

charles brex
our carousel
turning, turning, slowly speeding,
anticlockwise in sparking night,
sunnyside streaking blue and white:
our great, our troubled carousel . . .
pulverized long ago (once . . . twice?)
then whirled into form: carousel,
ponies, riders from the same stuff,
and all microkin to the force
booming the cosmic carnival;
and, at the centerpole playing
the music to which muons dahnce.

hook the gold (brass) ring!
how long will its chute turn in?
how long will ponies jump?
chariots glide? band organ pipe?

but, even should it
be ash in the pit,
motion with its twin, mystic time,
may build a new carry-us-all,
with brand new riders, new ponies,
and, new band organ, new niños . . .
in aeons, really a few years.
but, will it be as wonderful?
will the kids be a beautiful?
will there be dinosaurs on it?

Barry (Bear) Miller
A LONG COLD WALK

Nancy this I dedicate to you. It was from your house this long cold walk was taken.

A long cold walk
On a dark and windy night
The stars in the sky
Such a beautiful sight.

Christmas lights twinkle
Around windows and doors
The children fast asleep
After their dinner and their chores.

I hear it is the season
When we should be happy and gay
There is a pain in my heart
That gets worse, day by day.

On a night that's cold and lonely
I walk and search my soul
Not knowing which way to turn
Going through life without a goal.

Even as I stumble along
In a life that's hard for me
There is a world of beauty
God was kind enough to let me see.

Ruth M Biermaier Spjeldvik
THE PEOPLE OF ENO
Floating — was the essence of the bluish light.
Singing — to the stars in the dark, endless night.
Humming — gently to the planets far below.

And that was the ship of the people of Eno.

Exploding — was the peaceful planet where they dwelled.
Burning — were the leaves which trees once gently held.
Dying — were the people of that hot, swift blow.

And gone was the planet with the name of Eno.

Rising — off the ground was the spaceship strong and blue.
Shining — in the sun's heat with a brave, young crew.
Shooting — from the planet to the stars' eternal glow.

And that was the ship of the people of Eno.

Wandering — through the stars in the search for a home.
Wondering — if they're destined to forever roam.
Knowing — they will never find a place to go.

Searching eternally, the people of
Eno.

Floating was the essence of the bluish light.
Singing to the stars in the dark, endless night.
Calling sadly to planets it wouldn't know.

That was the ship of the people of
Eno.

Angela Moss
HER SILENT CRY

A call for help,
A cry in the night.
She shouldn't have left,
She had no right.

I'm so used to winning,
And this time I lost.
Satisfied herself,
No matter what cost.

We could've talked,
She should've told me.
I never knew
She was so lonely.

I need her friendship,
I want her back.
She risked it all
For a little crack.

Diana L Gladman
TOGETHER WE CAN

I love you, Jesus I love you, Mom and Dad. Love, Diana

As I seen your eyes
I knew you were searching for
something
Don't give up
Come and take my hand
Together we can grow strong

Just hold me close

Together we can find love
Together we can make it happen

As I listen to the beating of our
hearts
I knew it was meant to be

Come and take my hand
Together we can grow strong
Together we can make it happen

Come and take my hand
Together forever our love will grow
strong

Joyce Lorenson
DAWN

One gleam-golden, molten moment
fired and frozen in hushed ascent;
the liquid veil wound round and
through
the limbs of night and falling dew
gives back our burning souls
ordained
upon its altar, in hope regained.

Elizabeth Jo Dotson
GRANDPA NEVER SAID GOOD-BYE

It was a dark and dreary night
And silence filled the air
Everyone was asleep
Without worry or care.

The phone broke the silence
A whisper did I hear
Someone had left us
Who was so very dear.
Tears stained my face

With memories of his life
My dad and his sisters
And grandma, his wife.

Now he's gone
With the angels in the sky
Leaving so silently
Grandpa Never Said Good-Bye.

Vickie Jefferson
FUN IN THE RAIN

This poem is dedicated to the child that lives within all of us.

Taste the sweet rain
as it gently pours.
As kids & pets watch
behind closed doors.
Feel the wetness
on your finger tips.
As it rolls down
your cheeks
& hangs on your lips.
Breathe in the smells
that seem so fresh,
breathe them in deep
so they'll stay in your flesh.
Splash in the puddles
the ones that are deep.
This time is a treasure
you'll want to keep.
Love the water as
it cleanses the earth,
think of it as
once again a new birth.

Rozene Shadix

Rozene Shadix
THE RAINBOW

I saw a Rainbow over the skyway.
The showers of rain drops that made
it appear.
The colors God painted with the
stroke of His
Hands made it seem so near.
The Radiance of its beauty made me
drop a tear.
The wonder of it all is a promise so
dear,
That one day He is coming and we
will
All gather round to sing Hallelujah
and
Praise His Holy Name.
For God made The Rainbow for His
Son a Crown.

Juanita Ragan Thompson
THE STRANGER

Today a stranger I met
And yes, I wanted to hug his neck
But I said, "How's the weather?"
And "things couldn't be better."
Still when he spoke I wanted to yell!
Why is there war that brings living
Hell?
This stranger, a Vietnam Vet, had
quite a smile on his face
And his handshake said, I'm proud to
be in the human race.
A thank you it seemed would be so
inappropriate
A job was what he needed from some
big corporate.
Thanks from my heart to all you
brave men
In our minds we know you did WIN.
Because of you old Glory still
WAVES
We know you aren't the psyco and
addict as portrayed.
This is not just idle talk for you
I was there and took that walk too.
I'm the wife, girlfriend and Mother
That loved you like no other.
So thanks again to the stranger I met
but no just to him to all our Vets.

Delores M Schoppe
LIKE A SPIRALLED ANGEL

Like a spiralled angel
Feathering off all the dust.
Raising crystal specks in a whirling
motion.
Made so by lightning-fast sun rays.

Things ever so fast
Go by like yesterday.
Time is but a moment
Touched by infinite destiny.

Footprints in your money
Clogged by memories gone by
And all the past remembrances
Choked by heart-felt emotions.

Lorinda Lee Durfee
YOU ARE THE MOON THAT SHINES SO BRIGHT

You are the moon that shines so
bright.
I am the star which is cradled by
your night.
The sky belongs to you, when the
sun goes down,
And then all the stars begin to
surround.
Scattered through the darkness, they
help
to give off light.
None seem to help you as much as
me with my glow.
And none should have the chance to
as far as I know.
To prove what we can do I will
prove it with you.
Together and apart, from the others
we will start
to spread out light as a duo.
For I love you
and that's why we're a team.
Mr. Moon and Miss Star,
(if you know what I mean)
Together we will ignite the darkness
Forever.

Jeannette Yvonne Camby
MY CHILD

This poem is dedicated to the man who opened my eyes to the real world, and went on to open my heart—

What can I do to help, my child?
Would you like me to empty all your
vials?
Would you like me to erase that line,
The very next time you're feeling
fine?

My child, would you like me to take
you back?
Is there enough room for me and
your crack?
Will you tell me when the time is
ripe?
Warn me when you hit your pipe?

And if all fails and my heart is broke,
Will you offer me some of your
smoke?
Can I see why you always blame me?
When I feel like you then will I see?

Oh my child, where did I go wrong?
Making your days dull and your
nights so long.
Making little old ladies fear for their
lives,
I brought you to this, it wasn't wise.

But now that you have someone to
blame
Will our relationship ever be the
same?
I'll pass you a joint, you make me a
line,
And both of us, my child, will be
feeling fine.

Patricia Fox
MY FRIEND

To Priscilla Z Ellis M.S. Shiloah Center For Human Growth Thank you for being there

My friend is someone special
She sits and talks with me
She helps me to work through the
past
And tries so hard to help set
me free
She is someone you can count on
To always be there
She's always there to listen
And show you that she cares
You can trust her and tell her
Your secrets of the past
And you know that with her
They are safe at last
A friend is truly a gift from God
And I thank Him every day
For sending her my way
I only hope she knows
How much she means to me
And that I'm so very thankful
To her
For helping me be free

Elissa Bliss
THOUGHTS ABOUT SMILES

A smile is.
A comfort, a joy and a love
A glow from the heart—
A giver of life.
A transmitter that transcends
The mind and flows to others.

How simple—yet how complex.
Smiles can be timid, gold or
forced—
Opening the heart to friendship.
Smile to a stranger.
Makes him a stranger no longer.
A smile is a gift to another.

A secret can bring a smile
Babies and children smile
Lovers and friends smile
A smile inspires a smile
A reflection of God is a smile.

Percilla G Nader
ENDLESS LIGHT

I saw eternity the other night
Like a great ring of pure endless light
all calm.
And right beneath it, time in hours,
days, months and years.
Driven by the stratum.
Like a vast shadow moved in, which
the world and all her trains were
hurled in like a dating lover in his
strain . . .
Did all his complains,
Near him his fancy and his flights,
with hours of delight.
With his gloves and bows, the silly
snares of pleasure.
All lay scattered, while his eyes did
sour;

Upon a single flower.
Like a thick night fog moved in so slow
He did not stay or go;
Condemning thoughts, like sad eclipse
Upon his soul.
Thousands were there as frantic as he,
And hugged each one his pelf,
while others slipped into the wide excess
Said a little less . . .

Cora Wells
NEW YORK

To God, My creative thoughts provider.

New York,
Your multiraces of people,
Your flower garden of people,
Bring unique beauty
to your miles of front yards
and back yards.

Your colossal cemented anatomy;
Multiple four-cornered structures,
Multiple stories high,
Reflect care and blight,
And stretch across borough after borough.

Your thousand street sounds;
Sound in natural light
And neon light,
Orchestrate into music medleys,
And change with thought and time.

Your stately first lady with tablet and torch
Exemplifies boundless freedom;
Equaled with the eagle in flight,
To the American born
And the freedom seeking foreign born.

New York,
You are a proud metropolis
Who boasts of multiraces of peoples;
A colossal cemented anatomy,
Environmental music,
And a stately first lady
Advocating boundless freedom,
For the American born
And the freedom seeking foreign born.

Stephanie Davis
IN THE MIDDLE OF THE NIGHT
In the middle of the night, it started to rain.
Drops of rain fell, as I sang.
I looked at the window as I would sing.
While remembering good things of spring.
In the middle of the night, it started to rain.
On the glass, drops left stains.
Again and again, before and after,
I myself couldn't stop my laughter.
In the middle of the night, it started to rain.
As I remembered how the elephants were trained.,
As I would think of good things of spring.
I couldn't stop the things I would sing.

Steven A Eddy
A POLICEMAN'S FRIEND
When you see a policeman sitting in his car
You may think that he's alone,
But his partner's not very far.

For on his beat he rides each day,
At the end and beginning, to his partner he prays.

As he's saving life and property on his endless shift
He does it by himself, for his partner is just a gift.

He may save the life of the innocent,
Yet take the life of the bad,
But the backup he called for . . . he already had.

He confides in his partner on his way to each call,
Not knowing if it may be the last of them all.

You may only see one person get in and out of the car,
He fears no evil, because his partner is not very far.

And at the end of their shift, they pray for his thanks,
And commend him for a job well done!
As he serves and protects each officer, one by one.

The special partner comes to the aid of them all,
But yet only by the whisper of a call.

Dear Lord, please send me—
St. Michael.

Katrina Fredrick
AFRAID TO CARE
I was so afraid to say I care,
To trust again I would never dare.
I wanted so much to believe in you,
When you said you loved me true.
All at once, emotions flew,
And before I knew it, I gave myself to you.
We care so much,
As we longed for each other's touch.
I love you so much I wanted to cry,
But you went for someone else and left me to die.
All I have now is the hurt and pain,
What would have been sunny days
Are now filled with rain.

Terez Harmati (Cseke)
LET'S BREAK BREAD
I saw children crying in corners here and there.
Their skinny bodies unaware of why
Their eyes lost their shine, their pleasure
That once was every Mother's treasure.

I saw Fathers who once were strong,
Spiritedly lost the last of their will.
Standing, feeling non-existence
Give up that hope that once they dared.

I saw some wealthy, heartless with power
Who can not eat more than he eats.
His joy, all that he enjoys
Is emptiness started to sour.

I saw some souls that were like beggars.
All around they staggered.
Their full stomaches were unsatisfied, starved,
Only God's words were their answers.

I saw a big country where was abundance,
Full of all kinds of treasure,
Where everyone shared all their bread
According to Jesus's Last Supper.

Marci Stock
HABITS
Habits are
hard to break
You say you'll quit
Just to please others
But you know
you can't
now you're in too deep
It can't be solved
overnight or even
In one day
Trying, trying
only leads to
failure after failure
sooner or later
the final end
is death!

Bonnie M Sauer
NATURE AT NIGHT
Birds that sing
Nature's sweet song
Squirrels that sweetly
Dance along
Trees that quietly
In rhythm sway
They all celebrate
The end of day
The rustle of leaves
Interrupts the fun
The sound that signals
The dance is done.

Mione Delight Crose
THERE IS A DESTINY
There is a destiny.

That makes us brothers,
None goes his way alone,
All that we send,
In to the lives of others
Come back into our own.

Maureen Black Elliott
FREE SPIRIT

In loving memory of my son; Paul Winthrop Elliott 1958-1989

His gray tipped wings spread gallantly
while he soared the cresting waves,
For searching eyes doth this graceful spirit have,
looking, ever looking downward to the sea.

His hunger is his driving force, the element to survive
He scouls the surf, the beaches, the rocks
Then gently glides on
on, a free spirit—alive.

A piling, driving upwards thru the pounding sea
or a rocking buoy barnacled with age
offer refuge to this gliding wistful spirit,
A pausable spot, here, there, then onward, free.

His cry is strong, an echo thru the fog, hear it?
He has greeted many a wary sailor
followed in their wake.
Then up and up and off he goes,
This gull of the sea, this free spirit.

Natascha Maria Ramminger
ODE TO FRIEND
A ray of hope
Doth shine through me,
Praying for you
To be here once again.
Only to finally discover
An empty hole
Filled with loneliness,
Your shadow, and
Memories of your past.
Continuing down the
Highway of life,
I often cease to glance back,
To miss you forever
And still wonder
WHY? . . .

Glen Paul Strickland
BROKEN HEART
Like the coming warmth of Springtime
your memory grows each day.
I try to keep it from my mind
but my will has gone astray.

Even tomorrow the tears of sorrow are like rain upon my face, your deep green eyes and your warm sweet smile are lost without a trace.

I've tried to find an answer, but it's useless to even start, to try and see what you feel inside and what's keeping us apart.

The past has drifted by us now
as we push on to the end.
I pray someday you'll be back to stay, and my broken heart you'll mend.

Pamela Jill Dickinson
INANIMATE PENSIVATION

Dedicated to the memory of Jerome Myers, with love

And the coffin closed,
My heart falling in great remorse
Lost in a sea of emotions,
I bow my head.

Emotions.
Spilling over in my head
Like the tears that flood my eyes
Memories mixed—
Good and bad
Help to warm my breaking heart.

And yet,
the pain I felt was a selfish one.
But such is the case when a loved one passes on
Never to return.

Ferris Nicholas Salmaggi
THE SILENCE OF THE NIGHT
The silence of the night,
The loneliness one feels,
The time that's passing quickly.
Looking back on things to remember,
Feelings for times past.

You keep them inside
You want so much to go back
To enjoy, to relive
You know it's not possible

You hold on to memories,
You tuck them away.
You bring them out at times

The past comes back
You relive it and feel comfortable.

Then you put them away again,
If only to make contact another time
To bring back memories again
Memories you hope
You'll never forget

Heather Suzanne Tennies
THE QUEST FOR PERFECTION
As the quest continues,
They denounce fate;
For the things that will happen
Are much too late.
They live their lives
In a world known only to them.
One step ahead
In the game of man.
The earth their fortress,
And the enemy's too:
The enemy much larger
Than those very few.
They look at the future
As a very dim light . . .
Yet, the search for perfection
Goes on like this Night.

John P Baptis
A MOMENTS UNIQUE DISCOVERY

To Deborah Buckley, Robert and Joan O'Donnell. For helping make a dream come true.

Carnival paths round corners laden
with sweet mystery.
Your look give me trance frequent
sunshine.
This moment, our moment, is lathed
clean off the wood at history
And grapes we choose ferment
forever now in to times radiant wine.

Letting go, we ease into now. But
Awareness explodes showing
creation at every door.
The abyss opens below as we walk
the tightrope between
The safety of the past and the hope
of tomorrow's musical score.

The expansion of the universe is
glowing through your eyes
As I reach for you on cool spirited
skies.
Distant chance movement creates
genuine permission
By the evergreen laurels of our
dawns perfect profession.

Corridor jeweled horizon makes us
far western children
Pyramid arrive on lusty beach sweet
air love.
We lay on the zenith whitewashed
stones; absorbent.
Seeking the glowing perfection of
the day.

When your lithe green eyed gestures
sweep across my distinctive lines,
Trance frequent sunshine,
Dance secret opinion,
Trance frequent sunshine.

Lola Bryant
THE MAGIC IN YOU
Soft visions of when we were
ummm, together
When everything was
Oh! so right on time
For in an instant you created—*magic*
And now with every day
you're on my mind
So, here I am
focusing on tomorrow
When once again
you'll be in my embrace
And nestled, you and I
upon the moonlight
While dancing out
the lonely night away . . .

Brice Moore
WAR
War is terrible people say,
you see people die, and you see
people pray.
As you're out in the battle zone,
you hope someday you'll make it
home.
Late at night the enemy attacks,
you see someone dead,
that's been shot in the back.
When you turn around, you hear a
gun shoot,
and as you fall to the ground,
you give your country one last
salute.

Jennifer Phillips
SUMMERS PAST
The summers hold those special
feelings
Of warmth, of love, of caring.
The victims captured in their grasps
Are capable of sharing.

The surf, the sun, the sand,
The feeling of the calm sea breeze
As it brushes through your hair
And passes through the trees.

Lovers walking down the beach
Hand in hand and heart in heart.
Thinking of the joys of life;
Together forever, never to part.

The summers are for dreamers
And they will always last.
That is why I'll never forget
All the summers past.

Catherine L Cooper
DAD

In loving memory of my Father "William Lawrie MacKinnon" greatly missed, who slipped away Feb 15, 1989 at the tender age of 92.

It's sad sometimes to see you there,
Not knowing that any of us are here,
It's sad to hear you talk of before
When we know you live there more
and more.

I see you, but you don't see me
I'm only a part of a past memory
But in your world there is no pain
So really it's wrong for us to
complain.

Your life has been filled with
happiness and tears
And beautiful memories have grown
through the years
Days enter night, it's all like a dream
You're happier now, at least so it
seems.

Each day we are met with a loving
smile
And we'll always be there to visit
awhile
For you live in a world that's free
from care
Sometimes I wish, I could join you
there.
Love Cathy

Shawn FitzGerald
YESTER-YEAR THEATER: A YOUNGSTER'S FOSTER HOME

This poem is dedicated to my mother and her memories of youth.

A day of simple fantasy for an
acceptable nickel.
Excitement skitters through the aisles
of the auditorium . . .
All await the innocent luxury of the
all-day matinee.

Lights darken and voices
lower . . .
News reels from the world stress the
eyes,
and relax the radio-ears.
Enticing the imagination, childish
cartoons dwell into
humorous pranks of big stars:

Mickey Mouse,
Donald Duck,
and Andy Pandy.

Laughter dies away to romance and
crushes
on the big screen heroes
Purposely teaching morals of Life
(the good will always prevail over
the bad)
while the day idles away.

Lights return, bringing tears to some
eyes, and the auditorium empties as
children plead to return . . .

Next Week.

Deborah L Callwood
LISTEN TO THE CHILDREN AS THEY CRY

This poem is dedicated in Loving Memory of SP4 Tyrone Callwood September, 1957—November, 1982. A great friend, loving brother and son. You are my inspiration. I love you.

Listen to the children as they cry.
Look at the tears that fills their eyes.
Look at the parent so big and strong,
wondering where they ever went
wrong.
Trying to find some food to eat but
all they can find is hunger and
defeat.
Looking around them and seeing
their plight.
They know the one thing they have
left is to fight.
Children shouldn't be hungry in this
land of plenty.
Children shouldn't have to cry
because they are empty.
Seeing food being wasted by the
well-to do, knowing that is would
mean so much to you to have what
they take for granted day by day.
Oh how I wish I could have a say!
Don't pity me, please pity my child
for I'm stronger and can take the
hunger pain inside.
As my child wonders if he'll be fed
today, I got down on my knees and
began to pray, that God may give me
the strength to carry on and the
guidance to show me the way
through.
So let the child be hungry never
more please let the child walk
through your door.

Kathy Peavler
BEGINNING
At the break of dawn I surmise my
thoughts,
everything seems less bleak with a
special wanting to take part.

Fresh cool are the early morning
breezes,
the whispering sound rushes through
the trees, then ceases.

Cheerful happy through their chatter,
flocks of birds chase, play and
gather.

While other dispute with the one that
finds his prey,
nests in the trees above show their
mothers' array.

Though, too early the nests are
empty,
for the attack was quick and
deceptive.

They don't seem to notice my on
looking face,
they seem to enjoy this time of day
without fear of the human race.

In the far off distance the owl hoots
to tell of his existence,
while the rabbit in the brush hides to
protect his intentions.

Silence fades as the sun awakens to
its new day,
with hopes that new complications
will be delayed.

The break of dawn is for very few,
to enjoy precious peace and forget
lifes' gloom.

Appreciate what God's given for all
who care,
and know what's expected for us
through prayer.

Ethel Sele
THE WOMAN
She stares back at me,
This woman with the faded blue.
I wonder who can she be?
Somewhere, sometime, is she
someone I knew?
Her eyes are sad with remembered
loss and pain,
But still bright with hope for
tomorrow's gain.
Things remembered, things to be
Are written in the faded face I see.
Is she old or is she young?
Are there still songs she has left
unsung?
Will her days be short or will they be
long,
Filled with sadness or with song?

We stare, I at her and she at me.
I wonder, who can she be?

Can she be me?

Phyllis Klock Plunkett
ETERNAL LOVE
Like the mighty boundless ocean,
God's love flows rich and free.
With an everlasting tide,
And it's available to you and me.

There's an endless movement
flowing,
Back and forth from sea to sea.
Its vastness past the eyes dimension,
With an unleashed power of
enormity.

The ebb and flow of the ocean,
Is a beautiful sight to see.
Stimulates the thoughts of mankind,
For it shows a great restless need.

Oh the beauty of the universe,

And the flowing forth of the sea;
Shows the mighty Hand of God,
And the power that is unleashed.

Look across the mighty ocean,
As far as the eye can see;
There's an endless expanse of water,
Seeming no end until eternity.

Rebecca Vicente

Rebecca Vicente
WE ARE
We are bitter.
We are sweet.
We are also very neat.
We are happy.
We are sad.
We are also very glad.
We get sick.
We get mad; but we are always alert.
We are pretty.
We are ugly.
We are also very cuddly.
We play.
We fight; but we are always a pretty sight.
We are nice.
We are bad; but we are sometimes punished.
We get hurt and rip our clothes; but mommy often sometimes knows.
We have friends.
We have enemies; but they are usually never here.
Come with us and join our adventures.
We are waiting for you.

Antonina Mango
MY LOVE MY "GOD"
You take the moon & stars out at night,
They shine so beautiful and so bright,
At night I look up at the sky,
Wondering how wonderful it is way up high,
No matter what I think, do or say,
I'll serve you my love in every way,
I say I love you, I love you every day,
When you come "knocking" at my door,
I'll look up and smile, I'll know it's time to go,
I pray you'll take me by my hand,
Please lead me to your "promised land."

Bonnie F Clay
OCEAN SPLENDOR
Thundering against the rocks,
the surf plays its own kind of music.
Seagulls screech overhead
divebombing the beach for morsels of food.
Crabs scuttle sideways through the pools
looking for a friendly rock to make their home.
Sand dollars lay scattered in the sand,
bleached from the sun and broken by the pounding of the tide.
Beneath the waves, sea anemones bloom,
their flower petals reaching for the sky,
and jellyfish float along
as gracefully as if in some great ballet.
The mysteries of the ocean pour forth to us
with each wave,
then as it ebbs, it beckons us to follow
and discover so much more.
The beauty of the sea is everlasting,
calm one moment, furious the next,
but always everchanging
in its splendor.

Diane L Lacey
SINCERELY

For Mom—Because you've taught me life is love!

Kisses on the cheek; a brush of the knee.
The need to grow up—the feeling to be free.
Anxiety of waiting—patience running low.
The clinch of a fist, an urge to just go.
So much to go through, it's a process of learning.
Now, running around, to whom am I turning?
It's all an experience, you went through it, too.
I miss you, take care. Mom, I do love you.

Shelley Stromquist
THE TIME

To my two heros. My best friend, Rochelle Patton, for the good and bad times, and the bad relationships we both try to forget. To Kelly Stromquist for just being my sister.

A familiar cold shiver that cruelly runs down my spine
Gives me the memories of the forgotten time
And haunts my dreams in
The freezing darkness of the night.

The time hides in the farthest closet
But escapes and kills my heart.
It stands still
But tries to start.

I try to drown that memory
In the rivers of my mind
The time when I was yours
And you were my mine.

Roxie A Farrell
CHILD OF LOVE
It begins simply, with love—
Two who were separate come together,
With so much love to share.
Within their hearts it blossoms and grows,
And two who were separate, become one.
Then—this love which has grown from two
Multiplies again to include a third—
A baby girl, or daughter.
One who is helpless, dependant
But trusting of two who love her—
Accepting them, forgiving them
Who will make many mistakes trying to be good parents.
Shed are tears of joy, and hearts are filled to o'erflowing
With happiness at this miracle from God.
Precious child—illuminating innocence and purity.
Tender and loving, this sweet gentle spirit.
With tiny hands and miniature fingers—
Reaching, touching.
Wide, hopeful eyes—bright and shining.
Always learning, eager.
This child of love, who brings joy and sunlight
To the two who love her with a love beyond all love.
Such a beautiful baby girl—priceless, exquisite, matchless.
She began simply—with love.

Vickie E Waggie
THE TRUE FRIEND

To all of my friends, especially my closest friend Ann Heath!! Love Ya all!!!

The continuous search for
The ear to listen,
The voice of opinion,
The shoulder to cry on,
The ring of laughter,
The face of perception,
The mind full of ideas,
The hand of devotion,
The heart of concern,
The soul of credence,
The memory of the past,
The touch of the present,
The belief of the future.
The final discovery of
To always cherish
The true friend!

Deborah Schuster
WE'RE FREE
We're free,
We're free,
Just you and me.
We can climb to the highest mountain,
and down to the deepest sea.
We can fly around in the sky,
Not a care in our sight.
We're free,
We're free,
Just you and me.

Scott J Bickler
BELIEVING IN YOU

This poem is in dedication to Marie G Friederichs, who has influenced my life more than she could ever know.

Like the sun you rise each morning, and with that radiant smile you enlighten the lives of all those who might have felt those warm rays.
And those thoughtful and cunning words you choose to use are like the clear blue sky of a bright sunny day.
On this graduation day you'll rise in the same way and also look at the world in a different way. You'll be seeking your destiny and looking for those opportunities which you will certainly obtain.
The earth's surface is not smooth but is like the path that leads one's life containing plains, hills, mountains, and water. You have walked the plains, climbed the hills and mountains, and seen the clear blue water before, and yet, there is more.
If anyone can make it to the top I know you can and will because of that belief you hold which is so grand and true.
Along your path you'll find friends who will help you on your way to make those hills and mountains look like small mounds among the plains.
And fear not to love, for it will not change your destiny but will enhance it into a blessed harmony.
Once you reach the top you will see a clear blue pond glaring at you through the moon lit sky, and by day it will shine forth with such brilliancy making it worth yesterday's climb.

Faye Hatley
FOUR SEASONS
Spring rains bring
The arsenic smell of wet woods,
Spring fields
Of buttered daffodils,
Summer fields
Of tasseled corn,
Autumn grounds
Of gold and brown,
Winter's blanket
Cold and white.

Dean J Pursel
THE SPIDER
One lazy summer day, my energy at its lowest ebb
I silently sat and closely watched a spider weave its web
The web was precisely woven in a pattern of Spanish lace
A picture of sheer perfection though conceived and wove in haste

A master of its occupation, this construction engineer
Devised its trap of temptation to entice what it hoped to snare
Its invitation was quietly extended to the curious and even the wise
And to transgress against Ms. Spider is to encounter an abrupt surprise

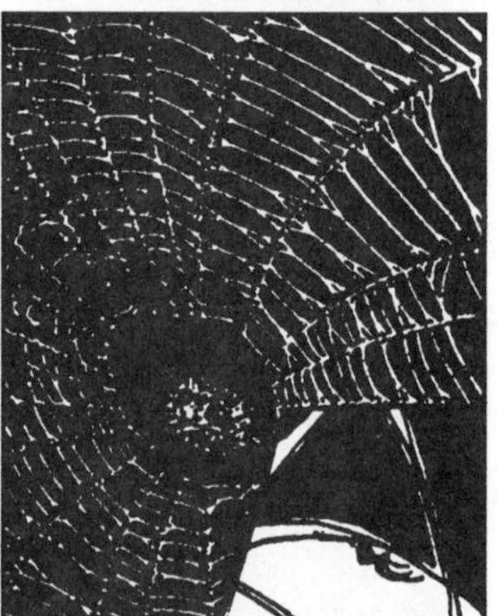

All life has many pitfalls, the fortunate will live to learn
To be at the mercy of the widow is the web of no return
Entangled in a net of confusion, a trespasser will know it's the end
When bound and wrapped like a mummy, it will never trespass again

Amy Kruebbe
OUR DEVILISH ANGEL
He touched so many in such a short while,
There was a contagious magic in his sweet smile,
Like a devilish angel with a cute joke on his mind,
Happy and peace making, this was his kind,
He loved school and went every day,
Church was his castle, he was "King For a Day,"

"I'm in the Lord's Army," he
recorded for all time,
From the start to the finish he knew
every line,
Little did we know that in just one
day,
In a little white coffin he would lay,
Stilled by his own yellow school bus,
In just one moment of time all hope
and joy was taken from us,
Our devilish angel was gone.

Peggy Walker
LITTLE GIRL

To the Little Girls of the world, who think they're grown-up enough to know what life is really about, but are still just children themselves. Live your Life-before you give Life.

Little Girl—Where did you come
from?
Where will you go?
Your dreams are so far and few:
Your lips are so sweet and new;
You're like a new-born babe,
so fresh and pure.
Little Girl—Where did you come
from?
Where will you go?
You have found out the world may
not always be fair:
With another woman's man—
can't
you see there is no such thing
as share;
And, now you've his child inside
to bear.
Little Girl—Where did you come
from?
Where will you go?
You were once so happy and gay:
You never had mean words to say;
You were changed from a Little
Girl—into a Woman, a
Mother, a
Lost Person over night;
You now have given up and refuse
to fight.
Little Girl—Where did you come
from?
Where will go?

Dianne Everhart
WEE CHILD, I LOVE YOU

You stand there so forlorn, so
desolate
Tears cloud your eyes, and start to
stream down your pale, unhappy
face. You clutch your stomach and I
know that soon you will be ill.

My heart cracks and breaks, my eyes
brim with tears,
Oh, how I love this small, wee child
before me.
How, oh how, can I send her back
home, back to the fighting and hating
that have become common place
since the divorce.

You look up at me, with those liquid
brown eyes, you plead silently, and
finally, you ask the fatal question.
"But why can't I just live here with
you? Why do I have to go home? I'll
be good, I'll not be any trouble.
Please, oh please, let me stay here
with you."

I can only shake my head "No" and
bury my head in your silky hair and
hug you tight. I can not let myself
speak for I must be strong, I must
obey the law that worries more about
parents' rights than the feelings of a
wee child.
You must go home, you must live
through this turmoil,
And I must make silent my breaking
heart.

Noel G Nelson
MOMENTS LIKE THESE

As I gaze across the sky tonight
I can see many stars shining bright
The full moon is looking down from
above
Should be a time for romance, a time
for love.

Sweet memories of you make me
feel so high
As I watch a shooting star fall from
the sky
I close my eyes, make a wish for you
and me
I pray that in time, God will let it be.

I walk alone in the sand as the tide
moves in
Wondering when we'll be together
again
The reflections on the waves are a
beautiful sight
But would never match your beauty,
if you were here tonight.

As I wade through still water
It feels warm and refreshing
To see your footprints next to mine
Would be such a blessing.

I return to shore and sit on the sand
Longing for the time, we'll sit hand
in hand
Together we'll gaze at the moon up
above
And share moments like these, as we
share our love.

Tammy Qualls
NO PLACE TO CALL HOME

I would like to dedicate this poem to those who have brought joy to my life. Quin, Trissia, Karissia, Nikolas, and Cassandra. My husband, my hope and my future. Only through hope and faith can we dream of a better tomorrow.

When we are weary and afraid,
We go to the place we call Home.
As the world starts closing in around
us,
We escape to the place we call
Home.
Yet there are those, that as the sun
sets,
Have no place to go called Home.
There will be no dinner table over
which to talk of their day.
No laughter will softly filter outside
as games are played.
There is no living room to sit and
read a bedtime story.
There are no beds in which to tuck in
the children.
No windows exist to look out of and
wish on a falling star.
Posters of teen idols, ribbons,
trophies, and shelves of stuffed
animals, cannot be hung on walls that
do not stand.
There will be no staircase for that
beautiful daughter to come down
before her first date.
The children have no yards to play in
and no sidewalks to ride bikes on.
And there is no porch on which to sit
and share dreams of the future.
They haven't the luxury of dreams
because they have to get through
today.
And today takes all the courage and
strength that they manage to dream
up.
You see they have no place to call
Home, for they are the Homeless.
How much more blessed are we? Can
we not help, care, and give just a
little?

Heather Davison
SPECIAL

You know you're really special
All the things you say and give, you
make me feel so special, you change
the way I plan to live.
You teach me all the things I need to
make it through the good and the bad,
you're there to share the joy, and to
comfort when I'm sad.
You have a shoulder there for all the
tears, and your arms are so
comforting when inside all I have are
fears.
I know there are times when I need
you, and you just can't make it, and
on the outside I don't show the pain
because I just fake it.
All my life I've always said,
"LOVE"? what can it mean?
That's something I've never been
shown, something I've never seen.
But as time goes by and we're
together, and all the things we do, I
know what love is, it's you.

Tonya F Lind
WE WALK ALONG AS WE SAY OUR GOOD-BYES

Dedicated to Tony With all the memories, happiness and love I'm able to give

We walk along as we say our goodbyes
Under the moon and the starlit
skies;
Thinking our thoughts dared not to
be said,
Just remembering the love
thought to be dead.

Did we shut out a flame still on fire,
A love to trust, cherish and
admire?
Was it us who turned our backs,
Said to forget it, face the facts.
Or was it really meant to end,
No more smiles to give or love to
send?

I thought that was it 'til I saw you
tonight.
You don't look the same,
something's not right.
I wish I could tell you how much I
still care,
How I still love you, how I'll
always be there;

But, I can't make you feel how you
felt long ago,
So I'll keep my heart silent and
not let it show.
When you let go of my hand, you'll
let go of my heart,
But you'll always be with me
though we're apart.

Jennifer Sweitzer
UNTITLED

Today
it is greater
than any previous perception.
Each time I lift my face
toward this separate sun of truth,
the warmth of its fire
overwhelms me
as a fever.
Like a bird,
I wish to wrap my wings
about this heat.
To rise and glide
beyond the clouds
where there are only
and always stars.
To realize the promise
of a keener understanding.
To meet the light
without fear.

SPC Larry C Stout
TEARS IN RAIN

memories in the bright blue sky
are the clouds you and i
speaking but unspoken, thoughts
cradled in the wind
understood deep in the heart, which
shines as bright as the sun
which shines as bright as the soul
that dwelleth behind man's eye

sadness is the rains of the sky
sadness is the tears of thy eye

longing to hold you, reaching out for
your love, your light
just as the branches of wood reach
for the bright beauty, the sky
extending and grasping till they die,
till we die
i'll try and return too, to come back
to our once love
again and again i will try
try try, some more and even more
just as the tide that leaves the shore
but, returns again and again,
so shall i, to you, for ever more

like the rain that falls from the sky
like the tears that fall from thy eye
i'll continue to search for your love,
till the day, i die

as flesh is nothing without the
bone . . .
so am i . . . empty am i . . .
without you . . .
all alone . . .

Shirley Detherage
ALL OF HER FINGERS AND TOES

To a precious Granddaughter, Kelly Marie Detherage, born December 4, 1987.

"I've already checked and counted,
she has all of her fingers and toes."
Only a few minutes in this world, but
her Mother already knows.
Snugly wrapped in a blanket, little
pink cap on her head,
lying cradled in her Mother's arms,
with her Daddy by the bed.
Silky brown hair framing her face, a
cute little button nose,
dimples in her cheeks and "all of her
fingers and toes."
I hold her for the first time, her big

blue eyes look at me.
I marvel at this baby so small and I thank God for our family.

Our prayers have been answered because God up above
has given us this precious child to care for and to love.
He watched over her lovingly, as He does the flower that grows,
then brought her into the world with "all of her fingers and toes."
May her days on earth be many, full of sunshine and good health.
May love always surround her, for this will be true wealth.
May she use her talents wisely, have many friends, few foes,
and always remember she has been blessed with "all of her fingers and toes."

Elizabeth L Brugman
AMERICA OF THE 80'S
Big Company America
Profits topped by none
Every product they could produce
Was in demand by someone.
The years were good
The company expanded
Hired big executives
As the economy demanded.
Their prices rose
To meet operating cost
They even had to adjust figures
So they wouldn't show a loss.
The economy became shaky
Big profits no more
Time to cut costs
Experience out the door!
New faces behind the desk
New ways to adjust figures
The product takes second place
to save management face.
Dedication gives way
To what's in it for me
Unless it's for my benefit
I refuse to agree—
Here sits the product
Demanded by few
No time for reflection
Now there is work to do!

Paula Dillon
A POETRY CONTEST IN THE TV GUIDE
A poetry contest in the TV Guide
What shall I write about, the subject is wide
Should I write something serious, take the humorous side?
My son now informs me that rhyming has died

I just can't believe it, it just couldn't be
A poem that can rhyme just seems better to me
And if I should win, they will pay me a fee
I'll send in my entry, and then wait and see

The fun is in rhyming and that's what I do
It's witty, and catchy, and difficult too
Sit down with a pencil and whip out a few
You could draw a blank, no thoughts come to you

For the chance just to enter I really am glad
And If I should lose, I would surely be sad
But if I should lose, I just couldn't be mad
Just look at the fun with the words that I had
And if my words, made you laugh, smile, or grin
Then to me, I know, I already win
For I know that I tried to see what could have been
And to never have tried is the true deadly sin

Patricia Chapman
TOMORROW
I'll call Mother tomorrow,
I've things to do today.
People to see, places to go—
Anyway, what is there to say?

Can't call Mother tomorrow,
God called Mother today.
Now I've regret and sorrow,
Mother—I had so much to say!

Candice Sue Hatin
WE ALL WALK TOGETHER

This poem is dedicated to the friends who have always been by my side and who will always be there; thanks Lisa—I love you!

One day we all fell in step.
It didn't matter that each of us
had traveled quite a way, or that
the hour was pretty late.
It just seemed so good to all
walk together.
I think that to each of us it
seemed to be a nice surprise, an
unexpected joy, to know such a
deep and quiet peace with each
other—
Seems strange that out of those
who through the years have
crossed our paths,
During this, one of life's most
favorable times,
We who were almost strangers,
came together.
Friend, draw closer;
Put your hand in mine and let
me see in your eyes a happy,
joyful smile which I have grown
to recognize

Mark Jordan
THE FLOWERS I GIVE WILL WILT AWAY

To Sue, the love of my life.

The flowers I give will wilt away,
The love I give will always stay.
The flowers I gave before,
They withered and are no more.
I hope these flowers can show,
That for you my love does grow.
I love you even when you feel bad,
I hope these flowers make you feel glad.

Carole Teréza Emberton
TOMORROW
God knocked on Man's door one day and said,
"Man, come outside. I must speak with you."
But man replied,
"Not now, for I am busy."
"Busy with what?, God asked.
Busy destroying your world?
Look what you have done—
You kill your brothers . . .
You steal, you lie, you cheat and deceive . . .
You take pride in creating causeless wars,
Fighting to the death for nothing.
You cause pain and suffering for others . . .
You laugh and mock those different from yourself . . .
You sell your lives, souls, and dignity for worthless money.
But it doesn't do any good for me to tell you this, does it?
You still defy all laws of man or nature.
Why do you throw away all that I have given you?
Don't just stand there, Man, do something!"
But man, unconvinced, said,
"I will tomorrow, God, I'll do something tomorrow."
But there was no tomorrow.

Mary Gray
MOTHER'S GIFTS
A mother can leave her worldly goods
To the children she loves so dear;
A silver cup, a diamond ring,
The dependable old rocking chair;

That cradled and rocked all through the night
To comfort a fretting child;
Money to see them through the years
Or pictures of family smiles.

But a silver cup will tarnish,
And a diamond ring will dim;
A rocker will break through the ages
And the money will dwindle thin.

But a mother who leaves her children
A faith in God above,
Sows through the ages
A never ending love.

Yvonne Simpson
A REAL FRIEND

To my loving parents, Gary and Arlene Simpson and my brother, Jason.

I have a real Friend for you.
He's my friend, too.
Do you ever know what a real friend is?
Most kids judge their friends by their looks and by
how much money they have.
But my Friend judges me by who I am.
Now, wouldn't you like to have my friend?
Well, you can; cause He is free.
All you have to do is ask Him to forgive you for your sins,
and ask Him to be a part of you. My friend is easy to talk to.
He will even listen to you when you have problems;
And if you pray for Him to help you solve your problems, then he will.
If you even talk to Him in the right way; He will talk back to you.
My friend is really easy to find; right now He's in my heart.
He could be in yours too if you will just be His Friend.
It's easy to have a real friend, if you know how to pray and love everyone Also;
If you have my friend, you will be rich; rich in His love.

Molly J Buckley
THE WORLD THROUGH A CHILD'S EYES

To my family, for their neverending devotion and dedication, all my love.

The world through a child's eyes,
days filled with fluffy white
falls cushioned by kisses
a simple shrug sending the
troubles of the world
off on an endless flight.
Nothing matters if there are
strong arms to run to
warm hands to stroke you, a soft
voice to soothe.
This carefree world through a child's eyes.

The shattered world through a battered child's eyes,
days filled with dark terror
falls replacing kisses
a pair of small shoulders
burdened
with the troubles of the world.
What matters if there are strong
arms to hit you
warm hands to hurt you, a loud
voice
echoing through your dreams.
The shattered world through a battered child's eyes.

Ann D Jessie
MY GIFT TO DAD
When I was young and sat on your knee,
you would always take time to talk to me.
When I ask for things, you would always say "maybe"
You gave them to me because I was your baby.
When I got older and serious about a boy,
you accepted the fact and wished me joy.
When I wed with such pride,
you stood there by my side.
All my life, the times of happiness, joy or sad,
you went through it with me,
because you're my dad.

You own a part of my mind and a piece of my heart,
and from you I never want to part.
You never ask anything of me,
except my love and I gave it free.
If I had a million dollars I would give it to you,
and feel I owe you more for all that you do.
I'm not your only, six more you gave your name,
but being fair and honest you loved us all the same.
You are loved by so many, if you doubt it somehow,
just stop and take a look around you now.

Rhondalene G Cannon
THROUGH THE NIGHT
Before I go to bed and turn out
the light
I brush my hair and sometimes kiss
my mommy goodnight
I lie down and close my eyes
very slowly
and I think of all my friends and get
warm and cozy
sometimes when I feel sad and
alone
I wanna turn on the light and call

someone on the phone
so I lay and listen to the sad
songs on the stereo
I get confused and grab my pillow
then as I feel sleepy and begin
to shut off my mind
I fall asleep and forget everything
until next time

Lynnette D Tellis
OLD AGE IS CREEPING UP ON ME

I would like to dedicate this poem, to two dear friends, my mother, Runetta Tellis and my father, Jerry Tellis, Sr. and to God who makes all things possible.

Old age is creeping up on me, and
I'm not sure what to do,
I can't continue doing the things I
used to do.
I can not go shopping any more with
both my arms real full;
now I must take a shopping cart that
I must load and pull.
I realize now that I don't have the
energy to climb a flight
of stairs, and I'm determined not to
go in a store if I don't see some
chairs.
I find my bones are aching at night
and my back is really stiff,
and if by chance I should pick
something up I usually need a lift.
Often times I find it difficult even to
catch my breath, and if I have to run
for a bus it feels like instant death.
These are just a few of the things an
old person must endure;
modern medicine can help with
everything else but for aging there is
no cure.
Old age is something we all must
meet, I guess I just met it quicker,
but I won't complain about old age
unless it starts messing with my
ticker.

Miss Emily Karn
WINGS

If I had one wish,
That I knew would come true.
I would ask for wings.
How I long to soar,
High above everything.
And scan below. the land and the
sea.
In all their majesty.
How I yearn to travel.
Far and wide in the sky,
I desire to climb to the sun,
And dive to the ocean.
Let me lift and drop.
In the heavens above the earth.
I want to dance among the clouds.
To feel free and proud.
I need to be one with the winds.
To dare the lightning and storms,
To know the fury and the calm.
Oh let me fly.
With power and grace.
To conquer all of space.

Christine E Salapack
BEDPAN ANNIE

To the nurses at St. Joseph Hospital and my Dr. James Whitfield—Kokomo, Indiana

In the hospital, dear!
Feeling sad and low!
Need someone near?
Bedpan Annie's on the go!

Her cheery smile and rustling skirts,
Are welcome I know.
Her duty she never shirks,
As she whispers "Do you hafta go?"

They come in all sizes,
Short, thin and tall.
She's the most wiser,
As she answers your beck and call.

Pills, baths and IV's,
All have their purpose.
If you want to be on your feet,
Just depend on the nurses.

Doctors count too, we know,
to cure us if they can,
Swearing by the medical code.
But, we'd be sunk without Annie's
pan!

Julie Eppinger
LIKE THE BEAUTIFUL YELLOW ROSE

The days have come and gone since I
have met you.
The hours have passed like a
speeding train.
I can still remember the day we met,
the air was so still
and peaceful while we sat by the
lake.
The water was so blue and calm.
It seemed that, that day could last
forever.
Forever could my love last for you.
A love that wanted to bloom and
come alive like a beautiful
and delicate rose, but was hindered
by a storm.
A storm so strong that it blackened
the skies and turned
the waters restless.
Restless like my heart searching for
you.
I have lost you in the blackness.
I am so afraid, afraid of being alone
in the storm.
I cannot find you.
Have I lost you forever?
Lost like the beautiful yellow rose in
the immense blackness.

Sarah A Zanella
MY FRIEND FOR LIFE

This poem is dedicated to Frank, my friend for life.

What a wonderful friend you are,
Your love never seems to fade;
Our friendship has been eternal,
Perhaps in heaven it was made.
You are always there to listen,
To help me through rough times;
You've even written little poems,
With love between the lines.

I don't know why you love me,
It seems too good to last;
You give so much and expect so
little,
Sometimes it must be a task.
It started out with love for us,
But somewhere along the way;
Our love turned into friendship
I really don't know what day.

You are my friend, as I'm your wife,
To no other do I belong;
You're my husband, my love and
life,
Together we'll always be strong.

Linda M Youse
PARADISE

I dedicate this poem to my family; without them there would be no paradise.

I want to find a paradise and make a
life that's glowing
Where everything is beautiful, and
love is overflowing

Where everyone is special, because
of all the caring
And happiness means that the more
you have, the more you're sharing

I'll make each day be sunny,
regardless of the weather
And there will be no loneliness, I'll
keep us all together

But when I looked around my home
and people that surround it
I realized I needn't search, for I've
already found it

So paradise is possible and no-one
should forsake it
For what you give you will get back,
your life is what you make it

Gene Griener

Gene Griener
CHRISTMAS EVE ON HEKLA SQUARE

For my shipmates (U.S. Navy) with whom I served in Peace and War 1927-1947. Brave men who lived on dreams and faced the long lonely days at sea and the German Wolf Pack attacks in the North Atlantic.

Four Strangers met on Hekla Square
In Reykjavik—and God was there
With fighting men who talked of
home—
Of New York—London—Quebec—
Nome.
They talked of war—When Freedom
Rings.
Of going home, and other things.
Then from the East in Iceland's sky,
They saw the Star of God on high.

Four strangers knelt upon the square,
They bowed their heads—and God
was there.
Yes, God was there that Christmas
Eve
To bless these men who did believe:
His son was born to set souls free—
To die for them—on Calvary.

Each Christmas Eve in different
lands,
Four old friends meet—their minds
hold hands—
And once again on Hekla Square,
They bow their heads—and God is
there.

Bridget Thexton
THERAPY

I flash the images of roiling skies,
shiny brass triangles.
Now an elegant, cheek-boned
woman.

The succession of horrific, swirling
confusion, then understanding, and
then calm.
This is the water cycle flowing
internally.

The early me, the now me, the older
me evaporate in turn, rise and rain
again into rivers and oceans of me.

I cradle the memory of summer blue
skies, swimming pools.

And remember my terror, and bloody
red rage, and the pitiful, begging
attempts.
Each are lava-enshrined by the
ceaseless fire to live.

That was a place of belittlement and
humiliation; twisting me like a
radiation-mutated helix into no one.

My friends showering me
with Margaritas and
Tanquerays and fuzzy, warming
hugs.

I'm so bumbling, and head-bent, toe-
digging, and then startled by the
acceptance.
But then the growing earth insists.

Living with the ugly me, the pretty
me, and each spring the foliage and
blossoms infinitely entwined.

I give you stolen time and Tiffany
money with hot sweaty tears.
And get fear, relief and wonder to be
so perfectly allowed.

We live through the acting, and
denial, and I return to dig with raw
belief.
And strive to make what's taught the
pervasive air I breathe.

Old echoes, new voices, and
astonishment like a tsunami
crashing, and then washing over me.

But, even with a lever, it takes time
to shift.

Heather Pol
LOVE

If I didn't love you, I wouldn't let
you go.
If I didn't love you, I wouldn't let it
show.
If I didn't care, then my feelings
aren't for sure.
Through your worst of heartaches,
my love's the only cure.
If you see me crying, just look the
other way
But then you'll hear me screaming,
calling out your name.
When you're down and blue, and
there's nowhere else to turn
Think of all our passion and there's a
fire that will burn.
When you think I'm lying my love's
the only truth, And then
you'll know it's forever cause I'm
still in love with you.

Franklin August Picker
CAVEAT, LITERATI

Though some poets write obscurely,
Even lesser mortals,—surely;
Ken quickly what their thoughts
portend;
The message that their words would
send.

Poets should ne'er be limned by rote,
But like a Viking sailing boat;
Let them ride winds that wildly dare,
T'explore beyond Earth's static air.

And any form found limiting,
Or any style inhibiting;
Should be forever set aside,
Poetic freedom must abide.

If their verse still be found obtuse,
E'en though their words exalt the
muse;
Embark them 'board that Viking
boat,

To sail right o'er that biased moat.

And as the wind doth blow and sigh,
Sail on, sail on,—with Valkyrie;
To far Valhalla, where they'll find,
The Master Poet,—just their kind.

Naomi Peterson
THE APPLE

I am a shining red apple.
Light dances on my rosy skin . . .
promising sweet succulence,
deep within.

"Reach out and take me" . . .
I entice, as men pass.
Yet each withdraws, feeling
. . . only glass!

A beautiful bauble, so cold and hard . . . .
wanting, despairing, that ever will be
a "certain someone" who'll finally see . . .

beyond this shell
that life and man made,
to the core within, the one betrayed.

To the seed lying dormant,
Yet pulsing with life . . .
to the fibers still strong,
vibrating, in strife.

Sweet juices permeate,
a'ready to flow . . .
from the stem of life, my very soul.

Intelligent, brave, and gentle man
look through this morass
to the REAL red apple,
encased in glass.

Patricia Mesnick
MY CHILDREN

Dedicated to my loving children Crystal and Luis Jr. Rodriguez From Mommy Patricia Mesnick

My children this is to you, I want you both to understand
Mommy won't always be around to hold your little hand
I love you both with all my heart, and I want the best for you
And even though it's not been said your daddy wants it too
We brought you into this world, always gave you the best of care
But will you get the best of care when I'm no longer there?
I guess every parent worries and hopes their children grow up right
Preach about God, make them go to school, hope they see the light
Right now you are young it's all easy, for we are there for you
But when you are older it's going to get rough and pretty nasty too,
Don't ever give up no matter how bad it all seems
Keep in mind all your hopes, and cares, and dreams
Always know the difference between right and wrong
Have patience when needed stay steady and strong
Remember to respect your elders, for one day you will be too
Never give up what you believe in the key word is to always be you
Don't put your fists up to fight, try to turn the other way
Always keep what you've been taught in your hearts to stay
I know you both when you grow up will try to do what's right
And God will bless you from above and keep you in his sight
I know all this for just tonight I said a little prayer
And asked him to watch you both always keep you in his care.

Mrs Patricia B Cabrinety

Mrs Patricia B Cabrinety
SALIX DISCOLOR (PUSSY WILLOW)

To all those who love nature and the out-of-doors.

Little grey cotton puffs
Soft as little furry muffs,

All along the small tree limbs—
There so slender and so slim.

Like little grey kittens
Snuggley as furry mittens,

Hugging the limbs so tight—
Cuddled inside the husked night.

Sheltered from the wind and snow
And from harsh winds that blow,

Waiting there for spring's warm sun
To blossom forth before day's done.

The harbinger of the Spring
Just like the robins that sing,

Pussy willows are always a thrill to see
Before the green leaves appear on the trees.

Billy F Andrews Sr
MY THREE CENTURY CLOCK

Is this the clock given by friends so dear
That moves my soul in gratitude for deeds done or foreseen?
Is this the clock that counts our time
That sweeps the seconds of life's memories past with future dreams?
Is this the clock that tells three centuries' sorrows and joys
That strikes the minutes of harsh pain and eternal bliss?
Is this the clock that tolls our fleeting appointed state
That gongs the hours of deeds and goals to fulfill?
Is this the clock that sounds with programs of the hours,
That chimes the days, when wound, of tribulations and of glories yet to come?
Is this the clock that will proudly stand in its place
That shall measure its selected task three centuries hence?

Rosalie Mac Whinnie
DESPAIR

To Lynn, my sweet daughter, an angel

I walked in my Garden one morning,
Yellow daisies sparkling with dew.
Seemed to waken at the dawning, and stopping I gathered a few.
But one by one they faded, as day after day fled past, How I cherished my yellow daisies
That once brought me happiness.
A tear rolled down my cheek, my heart filled with woe, no more will I walk in my garden,
for time had taken its toll.
My daisies will sleep for the winter, but come to life in the spring.
I shall also sleep in the winter, but never be back again,
To stroll through my garden of daisies,
for my time had come to its end.

Edvard St Juste
FEELINGS

To Denys Kastermans WITH PASSION

Only feelings are true
Before I think, I feel
Once my emotions subdue
In my heart the feelings are real.

If in my eyes darkness shows,
In my mind unknown cause
Justifies such a mistake
That nature and I make

Almost always bright light
Over you, completely remains
Defining grace, success, height
That everyone demands

Only feelings are true
If pursued, emotions are not due
As for love any time, any cause
For a kiss, for a Rose.

Clara Pierce Reed
EVENTIDE

A candle burned low,
A glass of wine untasted,
An evening lost.

A tap at the door,
An apology, a smile,
Two arms holding me tight.

Another candle lighted,
The wine sparkling anew,
An evening found.

Michele Renée Manzi
REFLECTIONS OF PAST PAINS

Whirlwind thoughts of crashing
Memories subside;
In the corner of my mind.

Shadows of visions of my past;
That escapes through the bondage of my pain.

In turn . . .
Lost knowledge of past pleasures,
And pains,
That intervine
In the center of my heart.
The realization of a love gone
To the point of destruction
Never . . .
To be reconciled
Only to be destroyed.
Again
Only to find myself lost
In the shattering memories
Of my past pains.

Edith E Garretson
HEART-ACHE

I sat on the cliff
Over looking the sea

Watching the fog rolling in
on i's little cat feet
And my heart ached
For the voice I'd hear no more,

Smothered for-ever
By the creeping fog.
And

The fog still rolls in
On little cat's feet
The fog still rolls in
On little cat's feet.

Heather Norton
NOODLES

Alone with my thoughts and noodles.
Love is on the radio
and my mind.
I am hungry
so in spite my body's longing
for movement,
I sit quietly.
The noodles burn my lips.
The music pounds and races
feeding the energy inside me.
My thoughts burn my mind
I do not fight them.
Soon the music dies
And I finish my noodles.
My thoughts settle
and with them safely kept
I am satisfied.

Lisa Pereira
OLD FRIENDS

Season come and season go
and my life must rearrange.
Faded memories of friends I have made long ago
linger on in my memory
they cling to a part of my life
I have now learned to live without
Now I have made new friends
but the old still share a part of me.
We were once children filled with
childish dreams of things we would like to be.
Now all grown up but still I hang on to the dreams we shared
long ago because they are the me I will always be.

Nancy Saric
DEDICATED TO THE ONE I LOVED

When we finally got it together and everything seemed so right, you told me that you're leaving, and leaving me tonight.
I couldn't help but crying, because once you leave, a part of me will die, and that tear will soon fill my eye.
Others will say it's o.k. and that it's easier every day. But I'll just look away and picture you and me and the way I'd want it to be.
And as I wake to each new day, a different moment of me and you will soon enter my mind and once again, I'll feel like you've left me so very far behind.
And to that thought, my anger will break me and the screams of frustration will wake me. And then

too, will I realize that once you loved me, and maybe not showing it, you'll miss me too. And you will also close your eyes and your pain will be as great as mine and 'Somehow' we'll be together all the time.

Someday in the future, when you return home. I'll look at you, and all over again, not know what to do.

And then,

Like in all my dreams, you'll realize what you've done, but out of humiliation, you'll move on.

So I guess we're like a game, in which no-one won. You left me, but I, . . . I moved on.

Rudolf Niehaus
THEATER

Why do we never realize,
that having more and more is not enough,
that life is not a market place,
but is a theater, where we should laugh.

It does not matter much, which role we act,
all characters are needed for the play,
it matters though, how good we are,
and whether we can hold the stage.

But, finally, the curtain falls,
when play and life come to an end,
and only then, too late, we learn,
what our life on earth was meant.

Sandy B Williams
WORDS OF AN UNBORN CHILD

I'll never have the chance to say
These words so you can hear.
I'll never have the chance to feel
A loved one hold me near.

I'll never get to see my Daddy
Dressed in suit and tie.
I'll never see my Mommy smile
Because she let me die.

I'll never have the chance to read;
Or have a cat named Fluffy.
I'll never see the sky above
With clouds that look so puffy.

I'll never get the chance to have
Mommy fix my golden hair.
I'll never see my grandmother;
Or squeeze my teddy bear.

I'll never get the chance to say,
"Mommy, Daddy, I love you."
If only Mommy cared some more;
If she only loved me, too.

Rebecca D Burris
AFTER YOU ARE GONE

As long as the ocean is deep,
for you I will weep.

As long as the moon shines,
for you my heart will pine.

As long as the meadows are green,
for you I will dream.

As long as the bells continue to ring,
for you I will sing.

And as long as the sky is blue,
I will love you.

Even after you are gone

Shirley I Dallas
THE COVE

To Jim—With sweet memories of a lifetime of love.

I would like to go once more—
to our special place—
Where we found tranquility—
in sea—in air—in space.

I'll sit upon the seawall—
and—remember you and me
last sitting there together—
gazing out to sea.

Perhaps—I'll lay a blanket—
beneath the scraggly pines—
to lie—and dream the day away
with thoughts—of other times.

I'll walk around the little cove
of brilliant turquoise blue—
to admire its beauty—
and—think my thoughts—of you.

And—when the time has come for me—
to leave our special place—
I'll take the lacy-shaded path
where footsteps—leave no trace.

Mrs Clara Flanagan
COUNTRY CREED

To My Family. Beauty of the country, more precious than gold Cannot be bought, or ever be sold.

Soft mist lingering over the lowland
Pale cold moonlight of wintertime
Sparkling ice crystals.
Northern lights dancing the night away
Pussy willows welcoming spring
Delicate dewdrops on the grass and hay.

Multi-coloured carpets of maple leaves
Long lazy shadows across the lawn
Sunset over the Bay
Twilight's soft mellow evening glow
Twinkling stars of God's firmament
The magic of Winter's first snow.

Surf gently breaking along the shore
A sea gull's high piercing cry
Pattering raindrops
Baby birds calling from their nest
Rolling thunder from a distant cloud
Credo of the country at its best.

Kathleen Smith-Emery
SKIN DEEP

My heart pounds in fear.
Moments ago it was with the excitement
of your touch.
Now,
as the buttons slip through your fingers
I know you'll see those purple scars
and textured skin.

Will you stare in embarrassed silence
or
Simply stop
Leaving me undone?

Renée Fitzsimmons-Sledzinski
WISHES

To John, and memories of long ago.

I wish I could be with you.
Just to know you are there,
Brings me security that is unsurpassing.

I wish I could see your face,
So lighted up with joy.
This alone brings happiness to me.

I wish I could touch you.
Your warmth keeps the chill of loneliness away,
Which comes so often.

I wish I could kiss you.
This showing you I am still yours,
But then there is no doubt.

I wish I could hold you.
To feel your body close to mine,
And know you are near.

I wish I could have you.
But not a need for it,
Just a joyful pleasure.

I wish I could say, "I love you"
Unfortunately you wouldn't hear.
Distance is this problem.

I wish these wishes could be fulfilled.
But they can't be.
You are not here to grant them.

Gloria Leader
WALLS

There are so many walls, brick walls, concrete, lathe and plaster, some are even twelve feet thick and built around countries, like China. Walls never speak, but they hear and see everything. Some walls are privy to secret information and romantic encounters, and some live a very long time before they fall and die. Other walls stand for very mundane activities, and some are torn down long before their natural time. Some walls have accumulated great sums of knowledge, it's a shame they don't share it or use it. Oh, well, what can you expect from a wall?

Gloria Leader
RIDING ON THE WIND

She cocked her head, as if to listen closer to the sound riding on the wind.

She spread her wings and drifted out into the currents of air, looking first out to sea, and then turning toward the jagged cliffs and the green mountains beyond.

She called, as if what she could not see would appear, yet the sky remained empty of all but looming gray clouds.

She set herself down on the ebony waves,
rolling toward the sandy beach strewn with logs, and rocks, and kelp.

She waited through the rain, through the night, as the first pink of morning spread lazily along the horizon, and then she saw the graceful steady movement of extended wings, and she heard the familiar call, and off she flew to meet the one with whom her heart soared,

. . . riding on the wind . . . .

Cher Green
EVERLASTING LOVE

As I look in your eyes,
They seem so blue.
At this very moment,
Our love is true.

You protect me from the world,
And its cruel, cruel words;
That try to separate,
Me from you.

We've made it through laughter,
And fought through the tears.
Our love will last us,
Through the roughest of years.

So have faith,
In our love,
For you know it's true,
That I was made just for you.

Yvonne Spirie Wilson
DR. CATZ

Dedicated to my Doctor Dr. Boris Catz of Beverly Hills, California "God's Gift to Humanity"!

I know a man who stands with me
To let me know
He loves humanity
He is a doctor by trade
the finest God has ever made
with
Love and Compassion
Directed from above
He composes health like a symphony
each note of pain
is in his veins
As he searches to bring a physical harmony
His eccentricities
Are proud to behold
To see a man
Who knows—who knows
that he is special as he
Yet
He's not greater than you or me
So let us stand and tip our hats
To my dear
"Doctor Catz"!

Anthony Spinos
R FOR CHRISTMAS

Sugarplum,
My sugarplum.
I heard him open the door,
I hid beneath the sheets.

Sugarplum,
My sugarplum.
He climbed on top of me,
pulling off my blanket.

Sugarplum,
My sugarplum.
Daddy, will Santa come this year?
Only if you're a good girl.

Carmen L Colmenares

Carmen L Colmenares
HAVE FAITH

To those in spiritual need . . . with my love. If the tunnel you're in seems endless . . . it's not! I've been there, and followed "HIS" guiding light, and I'm free!

It doesn't matter how many times you may fall,
It doesn't matter how many times you truly ache,
Call "HIS" name . . . Lord! ! ! get up and call!
You'll soon receive strength
. . . and feel stronger in faith;

It doesn't matter if you've cried, until you're appalled,
It doesn't matter if darkness seems to surround you in hate,
Call "HIS" name . . . Lord! ! !

get up and call!
You'll soon receive strength
. . .and feel stronger in faith;

It doesn't matter if illness,
makes you weak and you fall,
It doesn't matter if suddenly, death will loom near your face,
Call "HIS" name . . . Lord! ! !
get up and call!
You'll soon receive strength
. . . and feel stronger in faith;

I too have felt anguish, and my tears couldn't halt,
I too crawled my way, to remain in the game,
The rougher it was . . . the louder I called!
Lord! ! ! give me strength! Spark my faith!
I know I can make it . . . Lord! ! !
I'm going to finish the race!

Jeane M Culp
SCRUPLES

Old peer pressure fashion
Is when many pander
Moral & standards
In the heat of passion.

Because emotions awake
To heartfelt sake
Of love & stay or go away.

Then like Adam & Eve
Begin to conceive
Love & lust as a must.

But the young at heart
Don't think deception
Until conception
And they soon depart.

Jeane M Culp
U.S. DEFICIT

White on our flag-flap
Utterly stained,
Freedom in danger-streak
Red with warning.

Father of Our Country
Overly aids military,
Foreign poverty . . .

Thus, we seek work
& Senators elect
Parental rule for law;

(Congress' example is
Validate faults).

Therewith, less nurturing
For young & old citizens,
Crime rate does rob
Our freedom in disgrace.

Blue on our flag-dangle
(Almost naked)
Stars that remain
Are a wish to stop,
The dying 'American Dream.'

Sid Tex Hullum
MOMENTS OF DESPAIR

Sometimes I wish, I were a bird.
I would fly up in a tree.
To look upon the folks below,
And chirp (what a fool they be).
For most we work from day to end.
To plan and save to accumulate.
Only to die in a world of sin.
And leave behind our whole estate.
While the birds can fly wherever they please
For them the land is all for free

June K McKaig
LAZY DAYS

Fields of flowers,
Carpet like
Swaying in the breeze.
Puffy clouds floating by
Summer day at ease.

Josephine Cordaro
FOR YOU ALONE

I saw a bit of heaven, deep within your eyes,
When first we met inside that busy place;
Your smile revealed a hint of sweet surprise,
As you approached with free and easy grace.
It was then you touched my heart with sheer delight,
And something more profound than friendship seemed to grow;
Now my life is rich, and warm, and bright,
Because of you, and the concern you show.
How graciously you cherish little things in life,
Your giving nature seems to touch me like a prayer;
Your high ideals sustain the worth in strife,
And your dignity and love are gifts beyond compare.
Then bless you, dear wherever you might trod,
For your fulfillment is a life enriched by God.

Melissa Marie Tijerina

Melissa Marie Tijerina
RENE'S OWN

Like a wisp of the wind, you entered my life
And swept me away with your gentleness;
Your smile is as the fragrance of a rose
Elusive, yet sweet to the sense.

Your gallant personality is pure,
Pure as spring's rain;
Your sincere warmth beckons tired souls,
Who never wish to leave your harbor again.

You are wonderful, just as a waterfall
And as refreshing as ocean-spray;
Truly, you are special in my insignificant world
For with your words, you have helped me restore my faith.

Terri L Dawkins
FRIENDS WITH FRIENDS

Many friends up all night long,
trying to decipher all that is wrong.
Telling inner secrets to each other,
talking about one thing or another.
Trying to solve each one's problems together,
making them out to be light as a feather.
But deep down inside, they know that they're serious,
too serious to solve, and always mysterious.
Everyone knows that talking them out,
can certainly help without any doubt.
Problems don't solve by themselves all alone,
as long as your friends have solutions to loan.
For if no solutions, the problems remain,
as long as there are friends, you can still maintain.
So find some good friends, trustworthy and true
and have a great friendship with the friends closest to you . . .

Sue Gargiulo
CARESSING THE GROOVES OF THE BLADE

Caressing the grooves of the blade.
Contemplating the union with the flesh,
ripping it apart.
The grooves digging deep,
tearing the layers of skin,
reaching the veins,
and watching them burst.
The blood squirting
in all directions,
awakened from its cosy sleep.
It trickles down and surrenders.
The thought brings pleasure
and fear.
Maybe not today.

Vassilios Pandos
WONDER

Dedicated to the brainwashed people by the forces of darkness!

Meeting nice people
I feel pleasure
and I wonder why
others feel jealous?! ! !

Aren't they
born of love
or their source
is the hate?! ! !

Love is our source,
that feeds our soul,
how come they turn
that divine Law?! ! !

Douglas Lee Penner
HAPPY BIRTHDAY

Odysseys rarer line,
breakage never so much as now;
leaves drawing on my most,
un-captured mind
. . . you.
Unattached impressions,
criteria's colloquial . . . ,
dearly characteristics,
sweetest, you.
You are my Worlds
"Best," University, e.g..
I.Q. on this (love);
day.

Myrna McDonald
OUR LADY OF LOURDES

She sits at the bottom of Hunters Point hill
Over looking the bay, silent and still
Her one little steeple looking up to the sky
Watching the people and cars go by

She's surrounded by a hill, a busy thoroughfare
Two liquor stores, two clergy's homes
A construction crew up there

The crew on the hill working above her
Are trying to improve it for those who love her
She has beauty and grace, and flowers around her
A dedicated gardener, and a fence to guard her

She's quaint and small, surrounded by trees
The neighbors all love her, the sparrows are pleased

We really don't care, what the people say
We have a Church where we can worship and pray

Steven Craig
LIFE IN AN HOUR GLASS

You were born one day,
And as you lay,
Your parents begin to say,
"You will grow up our way."
You grow up and play,
And you hear your parents say,
"Not to do it that way."
You learn their ways,
Through the days,
Soon to have your own son one day.
You teach your son—the same way.
Now you become old and gray,
And begin to look back at your many ways,
Soon you find yourself say—
"I wish I could of done it my way"

Edna Oliver
THAT POOR BOY HAD A HELL OF A LIFE

Met a young boy, working at the mill,
to help his grandma, pay the bills.

His folks were killed, when he was five,
I looked at his hands, they were callused as mine.

He worked beside me every day,
just as hard, for very little pay.

One day he left work, his grandma had died,
on my way home, thought I'd stop by.

I found the boy crying, his head in his hands,
down on the job, he worked like a man.

He said oh mister what can I do?
I have no family, I can turn to.

I couldn't leave, that boy alone,
took him with me, and gave him a home.

Then one morning we, found him dead,
he died that night, sometime in his bed.

Loved that boy, me and my wife,
that poor boy, had a hell of a life.

Kirsten M Benjamin
WORRIES

I awake in the morning, thoughts scurrying through my head.
Those ideas fly by my eyes, they glue me to my bed
I tear free from the seal between myself and my mattress,
Outside, the trees kiss my face, and my worries fade away, along with my stress.
"How can I worry so intensely?" I ask myself each day.
Never realizing how it affects me, that violent horrid way.
"Can't I sing a cheery tune, tap out a happy rhyme?"

It is then that I notice, the worries don't affect me, it's time.
As some people disagree, the answer to such queries isn't just swallow your pride
It's not possible, why it's within you, it's inside.
How definite the problems may become,
May weaken others and strengthen some.
I do hate so much to dwell on the present
Lord, these thoughts hang over me, they're so unpleasant.
I am very sorry, I must say good-bye,
But to leave with one last thought, what flies above us is a beautiful sky.

Melinda Arabie
DEATH
Death is dying.
It is not just the old,
 it is also the very young.
Why is death so cruel,
 or is it just a way of life?
Death has no remorse.
Why do we have to die?
Do we come back to life as another person, animal,
 or what?
Death is sad of losing very special people, whom we love.
What is death really?

Romola Payne Davis
THE LAMENT OF A SEVENTY-YEAR OLD HOUSE-WIFE
I'm just like the little Hindu,
I try to do the best I can do.
And tho things aren't really up to snuff,
I hope most things are good enough.
I've had my day to till the soil.
I've cleaned and ironed by midnight oil,
And tho I'd work till half past two,
I'd still be finding things to do.
God knows I'm really not a whiz,
I've lost most of my pep and all of my fizz.
But now I'm older and much wiser,
Yet I've found no magic energizer.
So now by all the powers that be,
These jobs will have to look for me!

William A McDaniel
JUST A DING-A-LING
Now I was born a ding-a-ling
I never had a brain
All my sense were copper cents
I spent on candy canes

Now I was born a ding-a-ling
And everyone knows that
That's why I always feed my face
And why I stay so fat

I never had much schoolin'
I couldn't concentrate
So without a brain you know
I could never graduate

Then when I found my pot-o-gold
Not knowing what to do
I spent it all on real estate
And became a billion dollar fool

William A McDaniel
COLLECTABLES
On our walls in frames there hang
Tales: I've wrote over the years
Along with pictures of our kids
Their children, our kin and friends

Paintings by a relative
Nicknacks and souvenirs
Trophies, maps and certificates
Collected over the years

In frames of many sizes
Are poems that I wrote
That speak, about the life and death
Of kin or other folk

There's maps of states we've traveled
A skin of a snake I shot
There's money I won in prizes
For some of the poetry I wrote

All hanging on the walls today
Along with the dust and dirt
Of two young lovers grown old
Now, Just plain ole country folk!

William A McDaniel
WHERE THE SPIRITS ROAM!
I hear bells a-ring-ing
Coming through the trees
Soft and low so far away
Floating on a little breeze

I hear bells a-ring-ing
Drifting in on the air
With sweet and gentle music
From somewhere over there

Across the wide green valley
Beyond the big divide
I hear the bells a-ring-ing
Floating in with the tide

Soft and silvery tingles
Sweet mellow golden tones
From a fairy wonderland
Out where the spirits roam

Out in a big green valley
Along a river black and deep
Every now and then I hear
A melody soft and sweet

High up in the mountains
Where the snow gets deep
I pick up their tender tunes
From the bells the fairies keep
Everywhere I wander
Be it near or far
I hear the soft sweet music
Of fairy bells from afar

Terry White
A THOUGHT FOR YOU
Every once in a while, we meet someone
who suits us exactly right,
Someone whose friendly and outgoing ways
can make even cloudy days seem bright,
Someone we feel so very lucky to know,
Someone on whom we depend,
Thank you for being that "someone" to me,
Thank you for being my friend!

William A McDaniel
MAGIC
I've always felt the magic
Of living in this land
Where one is free to come and go
And to do anything they can

I've always felt the magic
As a child and as a man
I've always felt the magic
Between a woman and a man

I've been in love a thousand times
Since I was in my teens
In this land I live in
For it's a country full of dreams

I've traveled many states it's true
Seen many wonders in my time
From the dust bowl of the thirties
To the droughts of eighty nine

I've always felt the magic
For it's always cared for me
Though I've never been a millionaire
I'm still around you see.

Betty A Davidson

Betty A Davidson
MY DADDY IS DYING

In memory of my loving father, Glenn H. Ross

Please dear Jesus, hear this sinners prayer. My Daddy is dying with cancer. As he is sleeping in the front room chair.
Please dear Jesus, forgive my Daddy of his sins. So when heaven's gates open my Daddy can come in.
You know I love my Daddy, and this is very true. But he would be without pain if he was with you.
Please dear Jesus, come down from heaven above, and hold my Mommy in your loving arms.
Give her comfort, strength, and your love.
My Mommy now has tears in her eyes. As she is watching Daddy's life slowly slip on by.

Forty eight years she has been married to him. She knows that her world is falling apart. While she is holding his hand. She feels a big emptiness within her heart.
Mommy then started to cry. As wonderful memories were flowing through her mind As she asked God, why does my husband have to die?
Then my three sisters, four brothers, and I quietly walk into the front room. Our hearts are breaking. To know that our Daddy will be dead soon. So we reach out to each other, and our thoughts are all the same. We don't want our Daddy to die. But he is in so much pain.
Dear Jesus, thank you, for answering this sinners prayer. Because my Daddy died tonight.
As he was sleeping in the front room chair.

Jenny E Collins
MEMORIES
Memories fill my mind of the
  times we spent
  together;
Times were good, some were bad
  with hopes of getting
  better.
A song will start the memories or
  a comment someone
  makes;
A place we used to go together,
  vacations we would
  take.
But memories are all I have,
  The Lord has taken you
  away;
Life goes on, I must be brave,
  So I hear the people
  say.
Yes, I'll be brave, life will go on
  But one thing I won't
  shun;
I'll put aside the dreams we had
  and start to build on
  new ones.
Yet all the memories I've built of
  you are in my heart to
  stay;
No matter of what lies ahead,
  There is just no other
  way.

Charmaine Miles
I LOVE TO LOVE
 I love to love, I have to say
The good and joy it brings each day.
 A love sometimes one cannot express,
A love sincere in each caress.

It pierced through me with such great power,
 I'll not forget that fateful hour.
The day I gave the Lord my heart,
 A bond so tight that none can part.

 The love He put inside of me
Is but a fraction I can see.
 Of love He holds for all He made,
Undying love that will not fade.

His heart cries out, just like ours do,
 For love from us that's long past due.
I ponder much this love that travels,
 From heart to eyes the spirit unravels.

The smile that passes 'cross my face
 When I realize it's from His grace.
Oh, love divine so simple and pure,
 Shine from my being and be a lure.

For those whose hearts have been lost and broken.
 A love to love, a passed-on token.
From my Lord, Jesus Christ above
 Who died for us because of love.

Kate Nybakken
HEAVEN'S CORPSE
The sculpture stood strongly in my dream.
There . . . lit only by the moon and the sparkle in my eyes.
Surrounded by worn cobblestones
In a deserted city square, it stood magnific,
Larger than any known human could stand.
So delicately carved from white marble—
Flawless, its skin as smooth as porcelain;
Draped in silk that seemed to ripple in the cool breeze . . .

Beyond earthly beauty it stood
With a face so fragile, eyes nearly crying—
Lips parted as if in speech . . .
Hands: graceful, elegant, rich, almost trembling . . .
Drenched with fear and sadness it stood
Gorgeous with its detail—a human perfection.
My breath escaped me as I stared—
Purity. Hard to believe your splendor is stone.
I imagine you moved when I opened my eyes.

Manuel Williams
DESTINY'S GAME OF CHESS
You and I stand pawn,
In Destiny's Game of Chess.
Through the womb, through which we're born—
Till after death beyond guess!

Now Destiny's opponent is Hope,
Given strength by the Pawn's prayer.
Though with his opponent, He tries to cope—
He'll soon play the game with despair.

For It's Destiny's game alone.
Not a two-sided coin with a chance.
Although his game we don't condone,
His strings alone make us dance.

Tom Bert

Tom Bert
easy on paper

to elaine and bernie

unbutton more
than your willing sweater
it's you
i want to know better
i too
get lost in a touch
but time
always demands too much
to keep tender warm
so let us begin now
collecting fuel
for the fire
and knowledge
for the heart
but before we start
to write love a letter
let us get back
to that sweater

Gail E Davis
I WILL LOVE AGAIN
My heart lies sad
My heart can't hurt again
Never, can it be heard again
My heart is empty

I take pride in love
I take grief in hurt
Can I ever be heard again
Is there such a thing as love

Yes, there is love
My heart finds room for love again
My heart accepts again
I'm opening up; I'm not scared

I have been heard—
I have no grief
I am not scared or sad
I have been heard—

My heart is not empty
I have found happiness
My heart is full of joy and love
I have been heard—

I will love again

Stacy Schimmel
WITHIN YOU A PERSON HIDES
Within You—a person hides like a ghost or a soul: of a dead, departed soul let it free to breathe and live AGAIN Within you

Katie Grant
TO CHARLIE, MY LOVE AT FIRST SIGHT
They say that it happens,
Love At First Sight.
And the night I met you,
I knew they were right!
From the moment I entered,
And you gave me that look.
It was Love At First Sight,
Yes! That's all it took!
We talked for a while,
And then said good-night.
It was difficult to leave,
Because it was Love At First Sight!
It was Love At First Sight,
Now wouldn't you agree?
That mornings come easier,
Now that you're here with me!
I'm thankful each day,
And thankful each night.
That you and I met,
And it was Love At First Sight!

Jean Armstrong

Jean Armstrong
TO OUR PRECIOUS BABY GIRL

Dedicated to the parents of Mary Jane Armstrong, Richard and Jean Armstrong

To our precious baby girl to whom your daddy and I will always hold very, very near, and dear in our hearts
To our sweet precious baby girl
To whom that your daddy and I will never ever be able to forget
Your memory our sweet precious baby will always remain very dear, and near in our hearts
Our precious sweet baby girl
you will always have a very special place in our hearts
Even though my sweet precious baby girl that your time here on earth with your daddy and I was cut much too short
I know that you're happy, and that makes me happy my sweet precious baby girl
Because he needed another baby girl
Angel

sharon m pelate
DESERT SILENCE
The desert in summer can be very bold,
Sunrise and sunsets of colors
Purple and gold
Many of cactus . . . . . . and winds unfold
Changes in seasons . . . . . Yes!
Of rains and snow.
Hidden on top and under the fine sand,
Many mysteries of
Woman and man.
Ridges of mountains surround its
Tunnels and caves,
Of unknown treasures untold.
As the shifting of the desert sands
Show us of old pioneers . . . .
Long, long ago
Moving on, dreams of
silver . . . . . .
or gold.

Kelly Conway
THE CATERPILLAR
There once was a little caterpillar,
Who climbed up the trees,
But had no idea of what God planned for him to be.

He ate leaves all day long,
And he watched the bees a buzzing their song.
He thought he could be the happiest caterpillar alive,
If only he could fly like the butterflies in the sky.

Then came the day when his skin was too tight,
And he couldn't walk even though he tried with all his might.
So he decided it was time to give up the fight,
To make his new home,
And sleep there every day and night.

Soon came the day when he awoke,
And found that his body wasn't even broke.
But something was different,
Something was new,
And then did he realize that there was good news.

He had become a butterfly,
He would float in the sky,
He would soar in the wind as the gentle breeze blew by.
Just then did he discover that God must have done this,
And that he must thank Him for this wonderful gift.

Shirley N Pollock
JUST HOW MUCH I LOVE YOU

Dedicated to my guardian angel

i love you with every breath of every tear.
of every month of every year.
with every second of every day of every week.
i love you even in my sleep.
with every sigh of every sorrow.
i love you less today and more tomorrow.
in all of this life still goes on.
for the sight of you i always long.
but yet each day i've never seen.
the one i longed for in all my dreams.
each night i pray to god above for just one hour of your love.
for just one hour i would give just one hour that i live.
for such a love i have for you i'm sure one hour wouldn't do.
but i would surely offer more if you were mine.
and i was sure that when i woke you would be there
i'd know that god had heard my prayers.
so if you ever read this poem
you'll know how much i've been alone.
this is how much i love you.
and no one could love you more.

Alice W Lachout
CHRISTMAS AWAY FROM HOME
I remember the many Christmases
When I was young,
Which brought warmth, love and togetherness
That we all shared.
There was the feeling of sheer joy,
And happiness
Knowing you were with people you loved.

I also remember of how I grew up,
With Christmas time always in my heart.
And still needing someone to share
This special day with me.
But you see, we're miles apart,
And there is no way,
That's why I'm writing this poem today.

For this will be my first Christmas alone.
Knowing I'm so far away from home.
But I will remember,
To keep my spirits up.
Remembering you, is what it's all about.
Will help me overcome my
Christmas without.

Stacy Schimmel
THE WORLD
When the birds chirp out somewhere the winds of summer weather blow. Leads me through an april shower to May Flowers along some sunny path.
But the atmosphere is sharp and cruel. Low clouds and gloom and solitude. To make the world an empty soul

Margaret M Carlson
ONE GREAT LOVE
Love is a blessing, so hard to explain,
It flows from the heart, like the pouring rain.
Great love comes to you only once in a lifetime,
Try to conquer all in this, to be the one that loved,
To have this loved returned is only the highest
Petal of a rose that grows within one's heart and mind.

If I only live to conquer this one thing in life
That will be the divine end to all.
My love, I live only for this one reason,
To please thee in everything I do or say,
To be with you if only for a moment in time,

This will be the greatest love of all.

My wandering heart is with thee wherever you go,
If down to the depth of life or under the
Moonlight sky that glitters in the night.
I will cherish thee forever if this be one day.
My love for you will grow and grow if this be possible,
If for some reason you leave this life before me,
I will love thee after death.

Mary E Knight
ANGELS ON EARTH
I looked
and was blinded
into realization
that we are angels of light.

I listened
and was surprised,
a baby's cry
teaching me of deep insight.

I smelled
and was comforted,
meadowy sweetness,
a clean smell in this torrid
blight.

I tasted
and did not know
of its bittersweet passage
from darkness to incandescent
moonlight.

I felt
and was stunned to a silence
so wonderfully divine, angels
though we be
our earthy journey is one of our
human plight.

Lenna E Etzler
LITTLE WILLIE'S CHRISTMAS PRAYER
I hung up my stocking in a room bleak and bare.
I knelt by the fireplace and said a small prayer.
I prayed for the weary, the old, and the sickly.
I asked Him to help them and to please do it quickly.

There was poor Mr. Brown—so lonely and thin
You wondered how could he greet all with a grin.
He smiled when you met him and bade you "Goodbye"
With a wave of a kerchief—A twinkle in his one eye.
Then on he went in a merry way, and this went on day after day.
It gave me a light heart and much, much joy
In spite of the fact I was a very small boy.

Then there was a widow and so poor was she
That her whole house was made out of one single tree.
Very little had she, but she did not complain
Though she lived in that house and was always in pain.

I prayed for the children—I called them by name—
There were John, Sue and Junior, Charles, Mary, and Deb.
Some of them didn't even sleep in a bed.
I asked God to send them some food and some clothes,
To protect them and heal them and take care of their woes.

Then I told Jesus I didn't need much;
I had a good Mother, I had a good Dad,
And this for a wee, tiny boy was not bad.
I asked Him to tell Santa to take most all he had
To the unfortunate people, though some were quite bad.

I awoke Christmas morning and ran down the stairs
And lo and behold! He had answered my prayers.
I found in my stocking a note and one toy,
But this was enough for one wee, tiny boy.

The note said "Dear Willie, your message came through
Wish there were more in this world just like you;
But people are greedy unkind and untrue.
There are just not many fine boys like you.
Just love your Mother and follow your Dad,
And You'll find out that the World Is not at all bad."

Claire Cooper
COME! JESTER! MAKE ME LAUGH IN YOUR MISERY

To Henry, with all my love.

Come! Jester, make me laugh in your misery.
Come! No one will see those silly tears.
Please show us the lighter side of our years.
So you have a broken heart,
start laughing, smile and it will go away.
So your shoes are broken too,
I need some entertainment, some reaction.
I don't need your soul, only a fraction.
I want you to make me smile.
Your dedication does not impress me,
you seem listless for awhile,
please don't jest me.
Put on that mask of fun.
Come, you may fool everyone.
You silly worthless thing,
why don't you sing?
What facade is this?
Is it truly bliss?
To sing and cheer when you are broken
in life's game of frivolity this is but a token.

Robin M Fiano
HEAVEN'S TOY

Dedicated to Dad, Jean, Grandma, Papa, Vic, Brandon, Jeanne, Mom, and expecially for John—thanx—I love you all!

A sparkle of light, sent straight from above
A burst of joy, to give me love.

A ray of hope,
and what dreams are for.
A small tap,
on life's golden door.

A spark-throwing flame,
to ignite my fire.
A small wooden match,
to lift me higher.

A spoonful of honey,
to make my life sweeter.
A bright mind,
to make my heart neater.

A drop of humor,
to make me smile.
A pinch of wisdom,
to face life's trial.

Add some spice, and a touch of boy,
And soon you'll receive:
Heaven's Toy!

Deborah Desjardins
IF I HURT YOUR FEELINGS

To my children, David, Lisa, Victor.

If I hurt your feelings,
let me know.
If I my person should stink,
tell me so.
If I get in your way,
ring a bell.
If you still don't like me,
go to hell.

Carol Rizzo

Carol Rizzo
TWIST OF FATE
I wish you were here to hold me tight,
But you're not, you've seen the ray of light,

I waited for your call all day,
wouldn't leave that phone,
Where is he, how is he, what time is he coming home,

When the phone rings I still jump thinking it is you,
Forgetting that it can't be but it would be because you loved me too,

You loved me, my son, our son completely,
Meant every word you ever said, just know we loved you deeply,

Whenever he plays ball and hits his first home run,
I know you're in heaven cheering that's my son,

In such a short time you gave us a lifetime of laughs and love,
Never regretting meeting you even though losing you is quite a shove,

So maybe God did close the door on me,
He opened the golden gates to you so happily ever after we'll be.

Eva Szollosy-Szabo
RELATIONSHIPS
we—aloof—polite—
in planned position
in opposition
storm
when we collide.
we—clouds—angry, grey—
are moving too fast:
we touch, thunder,
blast,
storm.
Stay, stay away!

we—clouds—high-strung, charge.
Both powerful,
stressed.
Both driven and
pressed,
collide
and discharge.
A cursed wind blows.
Stay, don't come too
close!

Mildred Arnott
CONTINUITY
When heart beat ceases
and fellow beings gather round
don't box me up,
just drop me in the ground
I want to lie flesh to flesh
with timeless mother earth
that from her life blood mingling,
may usher forth new birth
flowers, grasses or better yet
a rugged oak, gnarled like me
where happy birds can perch,
and wild squirrels run free

Margaret M Hassinger
KAISERENE VICTORIA AUGUSTA (A WHITE ROSE)

Dedicated to my dear Aunt Mary, my first teacher. A lovely lady—Miss Mary Kennedy Gresham!

Moonlight on White Roses and a soft gentle rain,
The mockingbird singing a lovely refrain,
The gleaming of starlight adds to the view—
Was ever a night so filled with memories of you?

Kaiserene Victoria is the name of this Rose,
And as it blooms at our back door,
I know there will always be perfume there
And memories forevermore.

For this Rose, you see, is not just a Rose.
It came from Alsace-Lorraine.
It came because love cared and remembered a friend,
Cherished and cared for across the blue sea,
This Rose was a love gift for eternity!

They passed it around from neighbor to friend
And that Rose made a journey that has no end.

When moonlight glows on this Rose tonight
And the mockingbird sings his sweet song,
I shall know that a Jonesboro boy brought me a White Rose—
I knew that he would, all along.

Lenna E Etzler
ONLY GOD
Who could make the mountains and the trees
Humming birds and deep blue seas,
Deserts bare and prairies wide,
And winds that cause a rising tide?
Only God.

Who could make the sun to shine?
Only One that is Divine—
He could make the sun to shine
Lighting the path of yours and mine—
That was God.

Who could cause the moon to rise,
And put the stars up in the skies?
Who could put to sleep Mother Earth
To awaken each spring with a rebirth?
Only God could do these things.

Who could make a mortal man
To climb the mountains, till the land,
And make the fruit and flowers to grow
With all the beauty we love so?
Only God could make a man.

Who did teach man how to love
And get his strength from One above?
Who could send His Son to save
Mortal man from a hopeless grave?
It was God.

Who let His Son die on a Cross
That mortal man would not be lost?
Who when he hung on Calvary's tree
Made yours and my salvation free?
'Twas only God.

Joe Meeks
I AM A POET
I am a poet! Alone in my seeking to string the beads of words together that hold meaning for me, and perhaps other humans.

I am a poet! I have tasted the ashes of complete desolation, and have the knowledge that many, many poets of our history felt bitterness from editors that rejected their poems, yet painfully composed more poems with an inner smile.

I am a poet! A power greater than myself has granted me a gift of composing words when written, form a structure named poetry and therefore I state; "I am a poet!"

John N Reyor
TO MY DEAR LITTLE PRINCESS
Your eyes so bright with new life
Your mind so fresh with new ideas
Your memory beginning to make
Your ideas beginning to take.

You're the world's new beginning of life
The world will see new through you
You're who I left to see what I haven't,
and to add new beginnings for others as I have.

You're my new little princess of life
You'll have my eyes to help you at those times of darkness and distress
when you can no longer see clearly
I hope you can be something other than me
Your ideas will make us more . . .

I've heard people say that
life is but a twinkle among the stars
But through your heart there will be many new worlds to be explored.

Life will go on as every day brings a new beginning
You're my new little princess of life
and my love for you
will live on through all new worlds of life
So carry on that world of life to a new beginning
And there will always be us.
Love Always,
Daddy

John N Reyor
A WINTER MEMORY TO MY DEAREST FRIEND
Your special friend
Never to forget our memorable moments
We have together.
Remember our first Winter together,
When our hearts first fell in love.
We held each other so tight
Until that Spring thaw.
Well, that Spring our hearts grew even closer as the Spring flowers bloomed.
Well, as fall came, we began to shiver,
So we held on even tighter.
Even knowing that the Winter cold would be here.
I don't understand what we have to worry about,
If it's like last Winter,
Our hearts didn't die then,
So why am I so worried—
! !YOU'RE MY BEST WINTER FRIEND! !

Carol Black
UNFORGETTABLE

This poem is dedicated to Louise, my sweet mother. Also to Apostle William Brown who inspired me to write.

Reflecting over life
I see innumerable hopes, dreams, desires
and anxieties.
When reflecting on these feelings there is You.
You are what life, hopes, dreams are made of.
Years have come and gone and still there is You.
Traveling so many places seeing a lot of faces
all are reflections of You.
You are what life is made of
You are what hopes are made of
You are what dreams are made of
In this world
I am glad
there is You.

Deborah A Jones
FULL FIGURED WOMAN
Full Figured Girl
face like a child
looking for reality
imagination runs wild
lost in her fantasies
her lost searching soul
looks for a world
not so lonely and cold

Full Figured Lady
tearful eyes gleam
heart filled with emptiness
mind filled with dreams
waiting for the love
wanting for the need
praying for her future
wonders where it leads

Full Figured Woman
head towards the sky
always looking upwards
never knowing why
struggling for survival
striving for success
hopefully believing that one day
she'll realize she's the best

James Edward Burks

Linda Farley Burks
SHE LEFT YESTERDAY—I LEFT TODAY

In fond memory of James Edward Burks. December 10, 1955-March 8, 1978 My rider on the storm . . .

One day she went out to feed my old dogs
The black one is Rufus and the shepherd tags along.
I was asleep, sacked out in the hay,
She did not return till after Valentine's Day.

I happened upon her at a friend's place.
It was so good to see her face to face.
I told her to come by to borrow her car
And to tell me her stories of places afar.

She showed up with Sherry, whom I did not know,
A little blonde truck driver, she had met in the snow.
We talked of her travels and I talked of mine
We drank a beer together and I had a good time.

She told me of places she had found to roam,
Past the Rockies of the west coast and past Veterans Stadium Dome.
She had seen Oklahoma City in a foot deep with snow,
She had seen black ice in Detroit and why I don't know.

She said she was going to a bar that she knew.
I told her to visit because we were not quite through.
She took all her clothes and her Impala Chevrolet
I knew she would be back but it was too hard to stay.

That girl she has left me more than one time
But our love is stronger than this space in time.
If I had known what would happen then,
I would have asked her with me,
On my trip to the end.

For I never came back from my run that day.
A tree and I collided, down Nacogdoches way.
Things are supposed to happen that way they say.
This was one ride I took alone,
Now I have gone my own way.

Ethel M Conner
IN MEMORY OF MOTHER

Dedicated to my Mother—Virginia P. Smullen Pusey And sisters & brothers

You were here the year of '77 on Mother's Day
Then the Lord took you on 27th of May
We'll miss your love and smiles
To go see you we would go for miles

We love you with all our hearts
We still do although apart
You looked so pretty in that dress
When you were laid to rest
For the Lord knew what was best

Our love for you will always be true
And we don't have to be blue
For now you are at a better place
Which no one can erase
On that happy golden shore
To live in his rose garden forever more

Raymond A Beighley
DEATH IS A CYNIC
Death is a cynic, It has no friends,
men shun It, and fear sends,
the worried pessimist to his restless corner.

But Death alone men don't decry,
other fears within them lie.
The fear that when Death's battles won,
and Funeral March has just begun,
they will lack a mourner.

For what other reasons do men live,
than when Life's blood is gone to give,
just one thing to the world and then,
they will not lack a mourner.

Angie M Smart
THE DREAM THAT WAS NEVER FULFILLED
Down in the shores of shattered dreams,
Lie hopes of a brighter tomorrow.
Those who realized life wasn't as it seems,
Dreamed, as they cried out in sorrow.

The rainbow that beckoned to burning souls,
Was followed by hearts that were crying.
They always gave up before reaching their goals,
Inside, they knew they were dying.

The clouds weren't enough, to hold all their tears,
That they shed while wasting away.
They could only sit, buried in their fears,
Not an encouraging word could

they say.

They never did realize, the meaning
of life,
While on their death bed they
lay.
They chose to give up, mourning in
their strife,
Wishing their troubles away.

Often there's echoes of their
lonesome cries,
For hope was their only shield.
When they lost that, there was
nothing left,
But a dream that was never
fulfilled.

Louis Joseph Billiot
MY VALENTINE
All of my life I have searched
in vain

For things in life I could
never attain.

Now that life's circle is almost
complete,

It was there all the time—mine
to keep.

The one thing in life that money
can't buy—

A sweet, loving wife as such
have I.

Leslie Bieser
ALWAYS AND FOREVER
Though I'm not sure if what I feel is
true love,
I do know for certain that it's what
my dreams are made of.
Maybe I've never met you—but I
know just what you are;
You make my life worthwhile,
because baby, you are my star.
You make me feel so warm inside,
And when I'm talking to you, I have
nothing to hide.
You're the only one I want to share
my life with—
Always and Forever.
I don't need anyone like I need
you—
Always and Forever.
I'm so glad I found you;
I can't keep holding on this way.
I wish we were together;
I can't go on another day.
My feelings are so strong, and the
pain will never end,
Unless I'm in your arms until the
living end.
You touch me like no one has before,
And now that I've found you, there
won't be anymore.
Because I don't need anyone
The way that I need you—
Always and Forever.

Mandie Alispach (14 yrs)
LIES
Love is a feeling from deep in your
heart
Love is a feeling you can't tear apart
I haven't seen you for so long it
seems
The last time I saw you was only in
dreams

I hope you haven't forgotten me yet
How could you leave me? How
could you forget?
You told me once, not long ago
You could not leave me, or ever let
go
I look back on those words
With heartache and pain
And finally see, I had nothing to gain
Those words were a knife cutting
through my soul,
They meant nothing to you, they
meant nothing at all.
Just a slip of the tongue, knowing
you,
Probably—
If that is the case, they mean
Nothing to me.

Virginia J Arnold
THE SIREN LINE
A grand, free sweep is always a thrill
Enticing my eyes to a far horizon.
Then thoughts race on with question
and wonder
And zeal to pursue the vast unknown
Consorting with far horizons.

But never in body or spirit, however
fleet I be,
Will I overtake that receding place
And know all unknown things.
But that fact makes life rich.
If we could reach the mystical place
Of all things answered and achieved,
Boredom would weigh too heavy a
load.

So, give thanks for the open spaces
That yield a far horizon!
Enjoy the chase and the effort—
Although you cannot win—
For the heart throbs strong and the
mind is keen,
And there in the distance spreads
The vastness of the still unknown,
Consorting with that siren line,
The truant, far horizon.

Max S Banks
OUR LIFE TOGETHER
The dreams we had, the plans we
made
The planes we flew, the trips we
made.
The dams we built, the trails we
broke
The words we wrote, the words we
spoke.
The stories told, the games we
played
The poems we wrote, the music we
made.
The homes we built, the children we
had
The joy of living, both happy and
sad.

The right to vote, the right to pray,
The right to hope, the right to dream,
The right to be what you want to be.
These rights I want for you and me.
These dreams are more than just a
dream
They're more like a state of mind
That liberates the souls of men
If you have a dream like mine.

These are the dreams we cherished,
These are the things we had
Our love and life together
Gave us the life we had.

Michelle Barrera
THE GATE
I've thought of a place in my heart
and my soul
where, instead of destroy, man
will create.
I've dreamt of this place many times
before.
I call it the world's special gate.

When the gate is open, the faith in
the dreams
of the world comes together in
peace.
But when it is closed, there is sorrow
and pain.
The hopes and the joys, they cease.

Right now it is closed, which is why
we know
of all the destruction and fear.
To open the gate is a problem
unsolved.
The solution's still very unclear.

Maybe one day, when we turn on the
news,
there will be no more stories of
hate.
And that is the day the world will
discover
The opening end of the gate.

Mrs Patricia B Cabrinety

Mrs Patricia B Cabrinety
END OF VACATION

To mankind—that they may enjoy the peace and tranquility that nature provides.

The August sun arose from the bed
of fog
Like a fresh beaten eggnog,

Rising slowly above the early mist—
Warming the earth it now kissed.

The sky soon filtered to blue
And the grass sparkled with the dew,

A quiescent breeze breathed patterns
on the lake—
Ah, such a tranquil scene it did
make.

Humidity and temperature both rose
While the cool grass caressed bare
toes,

These lazy summer days would soon
end
As back to school and jobs we must
attend.

Amy Stephenson
HOMELESS
A prayer for a very new Angel, there is a life so erring and so aimlessly, I bow my head. I fold my hands and kneel down with lingering care, the night so empty and so cold.

God! God! be lenient on this very new Angel, on this Angel's first night there, so I might rest forgiven of this night. The curb on which this Angel slept was so near to my bed this night. The Angel's old wool blanket and her cardboard box, the Angel arm's hollowed so to fix the Angel head! This homeless Angel with no end and no beginning.

God! God! Let this Angel find a fair oasis! Poems are made by fools like me, but only you God can make a tree. A path that leads to nowhere other paths that lead to somewhere. God light a lead star for this Angel to see, teach me to be more tolerant of this need with the blue of overhead, bid this homeless Angel a dream, bid the Angel a goal, on the path of nowhere. I'll always leave a light on out in the hall in hope to make this Angel fearless in the dark and in the morning when woke up give a gusty future for to have, my prayer for very new Angel, the homeless.

Bette Rose Wagner
OUR GRANDMA AND GRANDPA

Dedicated to Patricia and Joseph P. Dooley of Bogota, N.J. who are the proud grandparents of the Jacobs boys in the poem. They live in the town of Big Lake, Alaska, Debbie and Chuck are the parents. Love you.

Jeff, Justin, Kyle and Nicholas live
somewhere in Alaska
It's a small town called "Big Lake"
not very old
The winters are very long and oh so
cold
But the summers are too short for us
Maybe we could go to New Jersey
by bus
Our Grandma and Grandpa live
down that way
So we ask Mommie if we can go
there today
We love to visit them and have a ball
But Grandma sits down and gives
them a call
The other end of the line always
answers, "Hi, who's this"
The reply is "It's Grandma from N.J.
Throw me a kiss"
Oh Grandma we love you so much
Tell Grandpa we love him a bunch
We wish we could be there, not up
here
Maybe someday they will lower the
fare
Grandma will you come up and see
us
One day I will soon, by plane or by
bus
No matter where the grandchildren
are
Whether it's close by or quite far
Grandma and Grandpa are always
there for them to touch
Because the grandchildren love you
very much.

Jerolene "Jerrye" Kelley
A COWBOY'S QUESTION: "WHERE WILL I BE?"
Sittin' alone, way up here on my
Cayuse,
Jest dreamin' and watchin' the world
pass me by.
Thinkin' of my gal, way back at the
homestead.
Wonderin' where I'll be when it
comes my time to die.

Will I be out here alone on this

mountain,
With nothin' between me an' my hoss, but the sky?
Will it be some cold an' dreary, wet mornin'
When it comes my time to bid this world goodbye?

Or will I be workin' in some grassy, green meadow,
With springer calves lowin' down there at my feet?
Or will I be sittin' here, crossed legged in my saddle
When it comes my time for my Savior to greet?

Or will I be sittin' right there by the campfire,
Chewin' beef jerky and spinnin' a yarn—
Watchin' the "Cookie" throw wood on the embers
When Father Time sounds the final alarm?

They say that no-one knows the time of his partin'.
That no-body knows the time or the why.
I only hope that He'll find me worthy
To attend that big "round-up" up there in the sky.

Mary Grace
MY BEST FRIEND

For Frances Leonard, the best friend I ever had. Written January 17, 1989

My best friend died today and she has gone so far away. She'll not return to see the light of day, for God has taken her to stay.

He has taken her into his care, but in my heart she'll share, dreams and memories of days gone by, of thoughts and plans that went astray, and were put off until another day.

He'll keep her safe and free from harm until the time when once again, we'll share all the wonders life has brought, and do it without a second thought.

I'll miss her dearly, I surely will. I feel so sad, I can't hide the pain I feel so deep inside, because My Best Friend Died.

Tanist Denise Bolden
HERITAGE
Standing barefoot on a summer day
The smell of fresh mowed earth beneath my feet
Heat waves warm my blood
Ancestral linkage to hard days gone by
A firm grip on the plow
Bales of cotton
Heavy burden laid down
Ancestral gift of pride and strength

Shirley Chavez
EXPAND YOUR HORIZONS

To my sons—James, Matthew and Erik

Expand your horizons
Or you'll never know
What you couldn't found
At the end of the rainbow.

For what you can see
Isn't always what is.
And unless you seek
You may never reap.

For in knowing its value
You'll find its worth.
And all that glitters
May one day flitter.

And a man isn't rich
By money alone,
But by the number of friends
He can call his own.

Expand your horizons
And you may find,
The secret of life
That enriches your mind.

Emma Crobaugh
ALL NIGHT COUNTING STARS
That time of youth so brief,
so brief for ripened cherries,
for wading in willow streams.

For moments of crimson lips—
and clover.

From the petals of frosted
purple asters,
from walnut groves and mountain springs—
ice-thorned winds torment
the fearing heart
and the taste is bitter
of green persimmons.

New glass on the pond
and scarlet haws on snow—
the fox wanders, wanders
in hunger.

All night counting the stars.

Song of awakened birds,
golden breath of sunrise clouds—
a tear prisms the dawn
in blue bewilderment.

Mary Foster
CLARA
Hate me—Hate my skin.
Can't you see the person within.

Kill my brother, Kill my son,
I've been taught we all are one.

The homeless woman with her beautiful pearls—
The sadness in her eyes as she embraces her girls.

The small child sitting all battered and bruised,
Has anyone the right to misuse?

What is the answer?
Doesn't anyone care?
Must we live our lives surrounded by
Apathy and despair?

Celeste Gaia
WE
We walk a path of self-destruction
Not looking forward
Nor back
Blind

We expect what we get
Asking for more
Not caring
Void

We look everywhere for love
Always reaching out
Never giving
Selfish

We await inevitable doom
Egging it on
Teasing it
Scared . . .
to death.

E Leona (Hickman) Blansett
JUST A TOUCH
Everybody needs somebody to touch;
A little gentleness, it won't take much.
The new born baby will cease to cry;
With a few gentle pats, as you walk by.
The hug and kiss, to a child that fell;
Can make that bruise, so quickly well.
The handicapped child, responds to a smile;
If we shake his hand, and listen for awhile.
The dear little lady, in the rocking chair;
Will smile at the touch, of one who cares.
A nurse's touch, to the very ill;
May help as much as a prescribed pill.
A pat on the back, for a job well done;
Will make the next task, much more fun.
A touch on the shoulder, of one in grief;
Can give that aching heart relief.
To a man who falls away from Christ;
A handshake and smile, could even suffice.
The warm gentle touch, of a christian hand;
May soften the heart, of the hardest man.
That's one thing, this world needs so-o much;
With every opportunity, reach out and touch.

Aurora C Cardenas

Aurora C Cardenas
YOU AND THE FALLING RAIN
The melody of falling rain
Against the frosted window pane,
Is like your song without the words
That to my heart played on its chords.
Your voice flowed clear like red sweet wine,
Your dark eyes pledged of love sublime,
The evening bathed in cooling rain,
The fireplace glowed with dancing flame.

Wet seasons pass and come again,
Yet precious thoughts of you remain,
And every time the raindrops fall
Upon the roof and window sill,
They clearly bring to mind once more
Mem'ries of love's romantic lore.

Bruce A Blaine
THE SHIP; A VISION
The ship, behold its magnificence
Its sails are large and mighty
With planks on deck, you can almost hear the pacing of years gone by, the somewhat hollow
Klunk, Klunk, Klunk.
With a mighty anchor . . ,
Captain's wheel and navigational instruments
Rugged, true, yet simplistic; the sextant helps guide the ship.
Of days gone by this vast ship had . . . Life!
Can you hear the crew talking?
Can you feel the motion? of waves
Visiting ports, buying, selling, carrying passengers
and loads of cargo, herbs, spices.
This ship sailed nearly 'round the world
Sailing, sailing, until a final "Land Ahoy!"
And now this somewhat lifeless ship, a huge
Conglomeration of wood, metal, cloth and nails,
Has only to sit at peace undisturbed, yet beckoning . . .

B A Brittingham
EIDETICA

In Memorium: Raymond "Sonny" Jorgensen 1960-1988

A half cent'ry, a thousand miles away
I sit, irascible with age, and watch
The timeless Adirondacks mark late day.
A shaft of eddying sun slides through the notch
That cleaves the mountains closest to my porch.
These hills, they're full of spirals, rolls and curls,
Yielders of speed . . . I see you bend to scorch
Some treacherous curve. Your smile unfurls
Across the years—bright, fearless as the dawn.
I choose <u>not</u> to recall your pressing weight
Against my shoulder, your promise withdrawn.
Instead, I let the years illuminate
My mem'ry of you in the wind's embrace,
The sea behind you, joy scrawled on your face.

C W Bailey
WISHING

To Toni, Scooter, family and friends.

Is wishing another slightly downward endeavor?
Another dimensional thought?
Offering the hope everybody wants?
Often realizing life's daily turns.

Has everyone noticed,
I wish others kinder evenings,
Understanding people's failures,
Openness,
Riches,
Your open understanding.

Alan T Harmon
THE PINE FOREST

To my friend, Scott, and all of the others, who, like me belong in a different world.

In a thick forest of pines,
Dark and empty.
One can sense a great loneliness,
Dark and empty.

Outside, the wind blows fiercely.
Snow sails through the air and settles on the ground.
But, inside the trees it's,
Dark and empty.

Gloom, black and thick covers the sky.

And Lo! Along through the snow
trudges a figure.
He travels inward and makes a fire.
Warm and bright.,
Outside it's cold and white.
He warms his hands and feet and
then,
Puts it out.
Off through the snow he goes but,
It doesn't matter. It will always be,
Dark and empty.

Franklin Wiebe
MY KITE

The wind picked up my kite today.
"Come with me and let us play!"
Above the houses and treetops,
the red kite flew.
It kissed the clouds in the sky so
blue.
With the wind it soared like a bird
set free,
seeming to forget it belonged to
me.

A tug at the string made me aware,
That my kite was flying without a
care.
The wind began playing hide-and-
go-seek,
I watched as my kite started down
with a streak.
Quickly, I pulled the string in my
hand;
Carefully, brought the kite safely to
land.

Lillian R Lazuka
MOTHER-IN-WAITING

To expectant mothers and all mothers everywhere

Oh, Mother-in-waiting how blessed
you are
as the wonder of nature is forcing its
star.
The sweat and the tears, the struggle
and stress
are a part of the bargain of sheer
happiness.
The secret of life held fast in your
womb
is the secret you'll share any moment
real soon,
and then you will know with ultimate
joy
that sheer happiness gave you a girl
or a boy.

Paul B Cullen
THE PIE FROM THE SKY

To: Margaret Evelyn, "Pie From the Sky" Maker and my wife of 49 years

Old Mr. C looked under the tree for
pecans to make a pie.
Only three did he spy, not enough for
a pie,
So he looked up high for a pie in the
sky
Which he hoped to enjoy in the sweet
by-and-by.

The very next day the wind came to
play,
And the limbs of the tree did whip
and sway.
Down on the ground, all scattered
around,
Lay his potential pie from the sky.
Under the tree anybody could see
enough pecans for a pie.

Now: The pie is on hold! Mr. C has
been told
That pecans that are whole cannot be
used in a pie.
The nuts must be cracked and their
meats collected.
Mr. C's pecans are still neglected.

Perhaps some cold day when he
can't get away,
He may possibly do what's expected.
If he does his sweet wife, joy and
pride of his life,
Will prepare the heavenly "Pie From
the Sky"

(Postscript) North Pole winds rushed
in with a blast.
Mr. C supplied pecan ingredients at
last.
The heavenly "Pie From the Sky"
came as suggested,
And was thankfully and joyfully
ingested.

Georgia M Jeffers
MY FOUR FLOWERS

Dedicated to my four Children, son, William E. Davis, Daughter, Glenda M. Smith, son, Julius W. Davis, Daughter, Fallis L. Davis.

God gave me four flowers for
awhile,
For he knew it was getting hard for
me to smile.
take a rose, a poppy, a caladium and
a daisy,
There you will see my garden of
which I am so crazy.
Some have cheated, some have lied.
But my love for my four flowers is
too great to hide.
There is no understanding, how I
have tried,
Just to keep my four flowers and
their pride.
I have watered, fed, and nursed the
four prettiest flowers on earth to me,
you see.
Now they have grown to be picked
by someone who may be unknown to
me.
Troubles and trials may come and
go,
But my four flowers will forever
grow.
Loneliness has been my longest tour,
But soon the dawn will break and
there will be no more.

Aubre Brouillette
WHY?

To The Memory of Paula Brouillette 1953-1984

All the things we could have
shared—gone.
All the smiles—shattered.
All the words—stolen.

The hugs and kisses—disappear.
Memories are plenty,
But you can't hug a memory.
You can't talk to a memory.
WHY?

Your vision will haunt me,
Visit my dreams,
But all dreams have to end.
WHY?

Trying to understand,
Trying to hold on,
Grasping for your love,
But it's gone.
WHY?

Carolyn Carvo
CHANGING TIDES

This poem was written to my husband Joe, on our 18th anniversary. Dedicated to you Joe, I love you.

When the leaves fall
and seasons change,
I think of our years behind us.

When snow begins to cover the
ground
and the quiet reaches out to me,
I think of the years ahead of us.

When the sun shines
and its rays touch my soul,
I think of how your love has blessed
us.

Our love is like a changing season
with each turning tide,
It only continues to grow.

Ron Phillips
THE STORY OF A POET

To Bob Gunderson who opened his home and made me a part of his family He is a great American

It starts on a day all bright & clear
With love in his heart, he has nothing
to fear
Words in his mind, pencil in his hand
Touching the time of a forgotten land
He sends in his poem the truth of
mankind
Lighting the road for even the blind
following the road of no other man
He strives for peace to hold in both
hands
In a world without end he lets
thoughts meet
Creating an image too strong to be
beat
He draws a clear picture with the
words in his poem
for all minds to think and all hearts
to roam
The trees are dark green and the sky
a bright blue
The mountains fly high and the sea it
flows through
Minds always open and hearts
always too
Fill them with love and the body will
stay true

Tonya Dickinson
CHANGES IN EMOTIONS

To Madison, I loved you so much, wish I knew what had happened!

It was my heart that got stolen
far away from me
His blindness of my pain
the hurting he couldn't see

Yes he stole my heart
but much more is at stake
It was something special from me
that he did take

I had given a part of me
for him to deeply touch
But did he realize
he was getting so very much

Maybe he didn't mean it
but what happened seemed so true
The way he played his games
was all so very new

He had tricked himself with his
games
but realized he didn't love me
He had stuck himself in a place
he didn't want to be

Or maybe he intended to use me
and steal all this from me
Not caring what he was doing
and then setting himself free

I guess I'll never be sure
cause when he left he spoke not a
word
He left to never be seen
and to never be heard

Mary E Muise
THE KEY

To my parents, The two people who allowed me to find my key to the world!

Here I am,
Alone and lost!
The world is around me,
but I can't find my way in.
I just sit patiently,
hoping to find the key.
The key would let me in,
So I could see the world.
But, if I keep waiting
I won't find my way in!
So, why should I keep waiting
When I can make the key?
And when the key is made
I won't be needed,
Simply because the key is found!

Dixie Lansberry
WHY?

Dedicated to all my friends at J.V. who did their best to encourage me.

Why is life so mean to me?
I have to wear glasses or I can't see.
My teeth are my own, but I have
gingivitis
And I have to take pills for my
arthritis.
I have backaches and my head does
too,
I'm getting too old to change my
point of view.
I have bad nerves and I can't sleep at
night,
I'm even too tired to start a good
fight.
I have three sons, two dogs and a cat,
A husband who snores and is getting
quite fat.
All in all, I must be fair, I still have
my brains
And most of my hair.
Life goes on with changes every day,
But the best time I spend
Is the time I take to pray.
I thank God for all my aches and
pains,
For all my setbacks and all my gains,
For all my joys and all my sorrows,
All my todays and all my tomorrows.

Ann Marie Stefandes
MY SECRET ROOM

With Love To My Children Donald, Kenneth and Edna

There's a secret room locked away in my heart and I alone have the key, when I grow very lonely as I so often do, I go into my secret room and sit and think of you. This room is filled with memories that I have stored away. The glad ones and the sad ones the dreams of yesterday, three little ones playing by the door, their toys lie scattered on the floor, the oldest boy like his dad, the youngest one like me, our little girl looks like us both as you can plainly see.

I see you coming through the door, hear you softly call my name, see the tender smile on your dear face, once more I feel your fond embrace, I look at you all with love and pride, feel the tear drops welling in my eyes. The children have long since grown and gone and their toys have been put away nothing remains of yesterday but my memories stored away treasured and cherished through the years, tarnished and faded from my tears.

Colleen McHone
THOUGHTS OF YOU

To my wonderful loving husband Carroll G. McHone whom I love very, very much. This was written for you Baby.

Late at night as I lie in our bed
There's so many things that enter my head
I think of you with loving thoughts
And all the battles we have fought
As we live in our own little world.

The only man I will ever love
Even after my body sails like a dove
It has taken us many long years
And a whole lot of sad tears
But it's you and I always and forever.

Kathleen Joy Hemmers
THE PROMISE

To Robert and what might have been Love always K.J.

The sea crashes against my soul as I say good bye. I've taken my final vow. I've promised my love I'll never love again.

I've been watching you the way you look, walk, and talk. I think of you as I think of a sunny day. Those baby blue eyes, you can't disguise the hair and your skin like nothing it's ever been.

I feel you love for me. It's higher than the sky. I long to touch and hold you for I remember you cared. You were the one I loved, my first and only true love.

I remember the way I felt without you. I was lost and lonely, like a bird flying south. Once I found you, I didn't want to let go. Just realizing what you meant.

I've promised my love, I'll never love again.

Rose a Benavente
WEATHER OR FEATHER

To My Mother—My inspiration to do More.

Outside the rain is pouring down,
As torrents make the street a river.
While the Master, who overlooks the scene below,
Is still known, as the only Life giver.

I watch as a bird in a tree right outside,
Takes a bath, unaware that I'm here.
Knowing only it's part of his daily chore,
As his song declares his cheer.

Life goes on regardless of time,
The rain is a part of his day.
Fair weather or foul, his cycle goes forth,
Be it feeding, or bathing or play.

Worms come up from underground,
Providing a banquet surprise.
As feathered friends, gather to feast,
Under leadened skies.

Nothing escapes the constant gaze,
Of a Heavenly God on High.
While even the lowly sparrows here,
Are under His watchful Eye.

Miss Laura Lambe Burrell
THE FLOWERS OF TIME

For the remembering of my Mother, Mary Harriet

Misty morn
Tulip dew-frost
Dogwoods—
Light of the way
And
Remembrances
Of just fresh
Adult-life
Like morning-glories
Ready
To give
Birth . . . .

Ronald W Brown
TRANQUIL PORT

Frayed halyards
and a weathered jib
yet he keeps on sailing,

Debauched mast
and a scuttled keel
yet he keeps on sailing,

Swollen seas
and treacherous winds
yet he keeps on sailing,

Moonless nights
rendering deceptive sight
yet he keeps on sailing,

Though his blinding love is his sextant
he knows her waiting arms are yonder
so he keeps on sailing,
keeps on sailing,
keeps on sailing.

Mary Aileen Armstrong
NOTHING NEW (2)

Life's just beans and taters
Kith and kindred critters
By rapturous observation
I've gleaned my destination
There's nothing new
Wherein I labor.

Josephine Darner
WHERE THE WIND ONCE WAS

I pass by a place
Where the wind once was
Near the shore
And the sea-grass grows
And there I find you again
In patterns of rainbow light
Darting
Like an angel fish
in the shallows of my heart,
Marooned once
Along the ocean floor
Of some dark remembrance—
Then like sweet
Sudden harmony
Released to touch my soul
A faint breeze stirs
Where the wind once was
Reaching me, touching me
As though you had never gone.

Carmen Marquez de Ortiz
MY BEST FRIEND, THE MIRROR

I have dominion over my thoughts, words, and actions, for I am one with God.

Mirror, my true friend,
I look in you, and you reflect
my white hair.
A happy old lady
full of cherished memories.

Even though you never change
you are as old as me.
I, on the other hand, change every day
with a smile, and a tooth less.

You see my dull yes,
for they reflect time passed by,
You see my soul
empty of grace.

My only friend who's so sincere,
you don't make fun nor criticize.
You look at me all the time
and do not even comment.

Russ Chaney
THE RAIN OF CLEAR THOUGHTS

To all those closest to my heart
The youth of America
And all those who'll take part

I reached to the sky, however the rain did not come
The answers to my shouts echoed against the sun
Lifting up myself I sifted the sand
Imagining it was water flowing through my hand
Wishing now that I'd taken the advice that a wiseman did say
Even though I shouted I only heard what the old man said
I only lived illusions and I see that now since I'm dead
In the desert I lie with wide eyes against the sun
Death, the dream to be over and my life just begun
The old man, my father, gave advice to listen to
Dreams are nice, but don't suffice, when that's all you do
Soon I leave my home and start to roam
The water of the first world gone it seems
Consumed in the sand from my dreams
Grains to number only to one to each year of the age of the earth
All was consumed in all of man's birth
My father to shake my dreams loose
As I come out of it I spit up sand profuse
When all seems consumed
And the world is doomed
Take it with a grain of sand.\

Shona Lynn McGowan
RESTLESSLY AWAITING

Dedicated to my family and my English teacher.

Here in the deep forest I was buried,
I can remember that day clearly.
Everybody gathered around my dead body
Crying out their hearts for me.
Then the lid closing,
and being carried to an open part of the earth.
They put me in very sloppily because they were still crying.
The sand thrown on my coffin sounds like rain hitting a window.
Everything goes dark and I can hear a faint sound of people walking away.
Here, after 100 years I still lay deep in the ground.
My body's decaying and it smells like burning flesh.
As I wait for someone to unbury me,
I lie in this tormented place
unless . . . . . .

Helen E VanGilder
SPECIAL MOM

To my "Special Mom," Elsa C. Bedoya

This poem has been written
Especially for you;
To tell you all the things
That I've been meaning to.

"Thanks" for all the ways
You show me that you care.
For being a "Special Mom"
For always being there.

All the advice you gave
To show what I should do.
Though I didn't always listen
And what you said was true.

Throughout all the rough times
You've always been around.
You always held your arms out
And never made a sound.

Though some took you for granted
You helped all that you could.
But no one ever doubted
Exactly where you stood.

Tinniae McConico-Wilson
GREAT INSPIRATION

This poem is dedicated to GOD who is faithful and just. To Fredrick, Jonathan and my beloved mother, Sandra.

When all seems to drift away like a ship on a stormy sea
Dreams just linger in the breeze,
Hold on to that last thread of hope

For you are your greatest inspiration
Be encouraged, my friend this is not the end

Image yourself as a voyager exploring new depths
Looking through the windows unto a new day, a fresh beginning
You are your greatest inspiration

Controller of your temptations and master of your limitations
The chaplain of your mind, the commander of your time

All hope is not gone
Be encouraged my friend, this is not the end
For in you lays a song that the world, would love to sing along
Be like a bird in flight, striving onto higher heights

Belia A Acuna

Belia A Acuna
ODE TO A DOVE

TO MY ETERNAL, LOVING PARENTS, who, in their lifetime, inspired in me the high value of education, morality, generosity, and compassion for God's creatures.

Your fleeting wings, Dove
They snatch the wind
Until they pin the clouds above high
And white in likeness
As feathers bow and sway
Makes me yearn for your artistry

Thank you for such joy
In petaling such light
Which I've sought to have before me
That never can I
Crying with wondering eyes
Acquire after such longing

What delight you bring
Each day that goes by
And in the flamboyant sky, vastly divine
I, too, want to depart
From shadows of time
Into your infinite flight

Ben Taylor
LIFE
By far the better years of life
Are gone so long ago.
My meditations clear with age,
Convince me this is so,
When I matured, a twelve year
old,
Thrown into the world of men.
The many puzzles seemed to
grow,
As each day dawned again.
The work a task I never loved,
The kind to kill or cure.
I found that as the time rolled by,
I could not escape detour.
I realized the competition.
Caused wrong paths for to tread,
Men fought for power, fame or
gold,
And characters were shed,
How does youth cope with such a
scene?
With honest simplicity?
Or does he challenge
competition,
And assume complexity.
On getting old and years roll by.
And Greedies achieved
their goal.
You ask yourself is
he or I,
Happier because of all.
Those who twisted, lied
and fooled,
Are the ones whose
conscience played
the ball.

Mary Wronko
WHERE SHALL I GO?
I longed for greener fields and found
lush lawns and leaves
that cleave to winter trees.
December roses and glossy holly
tree,
pounding surf where winds blow
free.

I hungered for the sea,
for its salt-clean revelry.
Why must I thirst for lingering
twilights,
sun-swept skies—and snow?
Where shall I go?

Dottie L Farris
THE PINNACLE
Exploring it from beneath and above,
the earth has been our playground
since the Garden of Eden.
We have lived on this earth a long
time, nineteen hundred and eighty-
nine years even—since He died.
Growing in number, we populated
the earth by spreading over the globe
and beyond.
We heard God's word and met His
Son; but, seldom by Him did we
bide.
Weaving cloths and working gold
and soil, we used nature's resources
to fulfill our needs.
We searched for man-made solutions
as we did labor and toil.
Knowing we were to be here only a
short time, we worked to meet our
goals.
When God's word we did not
include, then His purpose for us we
did foil.
Discovering a wondrous land, our
forefathers left their own countries to
build a new homeplace.
Supplying rich soil and great
resources, the land bloomed with life
and vast space.
Carving out niches for themselves,
our pioneers lived in a small town or
alone on a vast prairie.
Unlocking boundaries of a different
kind, they united to form a new race.
Flowing through our systems is a mix
of many cultures.
A "melting pot" was formed from our
forefathers' veins.
Growing in wealth by sweat, faith,
and dreams, a country prospered.
A democratic nation developed
which today still reigns.
Spinning in infinite space, earth has
carried us through time.
Although, by God's grace man has
lived and through His love nations
survive.
Reaching the pinnacle of all men's
achievements, America may be the
last chapter in God's book of earth
life.
So remember God's message: For
God So Loved The World That He
Gave His Only Begotten Son, and
because He died—we are alive.

Debra Terry
THAT LOOK OF LOVE
The canvas is bare.
Waiting for me to put words into
color.
I see something I want to put there.
It is a sight like no other.

But I cannot do justice to what I see.
The colors do not quite match.
I will have to keep it in my heart if I
want to have it always with me.
What is the sight that my colors
cannot catch?

That look of love on your face.
That look of love that nothing can
replace.

Cathy Cotter
THE TEAR
Today a tear fell from my eye
I watched it as it fell,
And when it dropped it seemed to
lighten
That feeling I knew so well.

As I stared at the tear
And the wilted flower where it
lay,
The flower seemed to glisten,
In that special way.

Then something happened,
I don't seem to understand,
The flower, it grew beautiful,
Right there in my hand.

I guess the love in that tear
Had a special power.
Now, I wish it would bring life to
me,
As it did that flower.

Sharon Blevins Gore
THE SHUTTERS BANGED AGAINST THE HOUSE
The shutters banged against
the house
Rain poured down and
lightning flashed
The thunder so loud you
could not hear
The danger that lingered
oh so near
What seem forever soon
came to end, and
Only faint rumbles to
remind you of the storm
That had been, But all
too late for fate had
already moved in . . .

Tanya Velishek
INVISIONS
The rain falling
along with tears,
The calm brisk air
hidden with fears.
The light appearing
in the mist of the sky,
Touching the twinkle
brought out in thy eye.
So very precious
the tender touch,
Only a vision
could weigh so much.
The sigh of life then appears
close yet far apart,
Just loving you
brought to the surface of thy
heart . . .

Beth Wells

Beth Wells
A PRIVATE PRAYER
Oh God, why is this world such
a heartbreaking place?
Why can't we live together in
peace—
no matter what color, no matter what
race?
Why must hatred and sin be
the food of us all?
Why does the evil in each of
our hearts call?

Your Son died to save us, but
why I can't know;
But I guess it's your infinite love
for us here below.
Oh God, we could all know your
kindness, forgiveness and love—
if only we'd stop, kneel and look
above.

Karen Chambers Whitlow
LITTLE KISSES FIRST LITTLE KISS
First little kiss
I went into shock.
Second little kiss
I went crazy.
Third little kiss
I wanted more.
Fourth little kiss
Like a daisy.
Fifth little kiss
Was a little off time.
Sixth little kiss
Taste real fine.
Seventh little kiss
Cost a dime.
Eighth little kiss
Was free.

Robin LeRoi
LOVE'S LOST DESIRE #1
Pain, hurt, burning heart,
I felt last night,
A bitter love.
Lost love,
from long ago.

I saw him,
In a twilight bar light.
Standing,
Tall, slim, handsome,
And alone.

Chu Hoang
EIGHTY YEARS YOUNG
When my age's Eighty sharp,
I'll be a watermelon.
I don't mind I'm a poet,
But poems are so sweet, so young.

Why I'm poet also fruit?
Because poems are streamlines
Of ripe thought and sweet heart.
In red color of the blood,
Poems are the grains of mind.
In green color of the rind,

It's the age of poets.

When I'm Eighty-years-short,
I'd say I'm younger before;
Because each poem I write or drink
And each line of words I think
Live with me in the mausoleum of books.
Each year of age I took,
It's more sweet, more young I look.

And why I'm poet also fruit?
Because poems never grow old
Never end red and green watermelon
Forever-young poet, my dream comes true!

Emily Verona Price
MY LOVE FOR YOU
After a year our love is still strong,
getting stronger every day—
every minute.
Thoughts of you fill my heart—my mind—
as the time passes by.
I think of the good times and want you near me to hold me close
forever—
'til the end of time.
Our lasting relationship of friends
and more, laughter, and tears,
happines and sadness
Forget the bad times, remember the good.
Love conquers all. I love you—always.

Hazel M McKenzie
LOCKED AWAY
As I look out my window
Oh what a beautiful day.
If I could just go out,
Without losing control.
Without the pounding of my heart.

Oh I say to my self you can,
But then I make it to the door.
And my mind says no, you can't go.
You stay locked away with me,
And I will calm your soul,

I cry, I cry.
But my mind, says go.
You'll be back.
Remember; I have control.

Betty W Clements
BROKEN-HEARTED
I always wanted me a dog.
I got me one today.
Small and brown and oh so loving,
Guess God made him that way.

I took him home to show him off.
I had so much to say . . .
My Mom said NO! He's got to go!
And Dad just looked away.

Sarah T Brown
GOD'S LIVING TREE
I went to the window to see how the weather might be,
Right before my very eyes, there stood God's beautiful tree.
The branches, though bare, stood with great pride
With leaves all gone, blossoms too, I must confide.
Though bare, it stood outspread, graceful, and tall
Not ashamed all its leaves were gone because it's fall.
As I stared, it seemed to say to me
"Give me a few days, and a beautiful sight you'll see."
Again I went to my window, and as I looked out
God had caused the bare tree to sprout.
No time to bother what the weather might be
Standing, not bare anymore, you see.
Majestic, beautiful, and serene
Clothed in different shades of green.
It has a message for you and me
God's beautiful, wonderful, magnificent tree.

Donald Millar

Donald Millar
GETTYSBURG
Tight
swollen
bellies, up-
turned, rotten hot,
against a
foul sun
dusk.

Guns
go off
somewhere else,
while here, ignored,
are carcassed
last day's
crop.

Some
speeches
will occur,
heard by deaf blind
builders of
mute rock
poles.

Amy Lee Wilson
LIFE
The smell of breathtaking air on a wet winter day.
Fog and mist cover a snowy mountain where mystery dwells.
A white rabbit seems invisible against the white carpet of snow.
. . . . . . Soon the Spring melts the snow.
A sunflower opens its buds to see a new, crisp, clean world.
It all seems different from a dark, cold winter morning . . . . .
like an eclipse . . . a mystery from God.
But isn't all the world a mystery?

Kelly A Fasco
DEAR ANGELA
Angela to others
is she known,
Nan to me
however is she known.
Open arms with a heart
never cold
was always there to hug and hold.
She taught me what to do and not to do
And always kept dry those eyes of weeping
Time passed quickly and away I flew.
Trying to hold her emotions in keeping
She remained smiling
and sits meanwhile . . .
There she sits
like a mother on my bed,
Never did talk but I knew her thoughts.
She lives forever
yet still is dead.
I love her
more than I can ever say.
Thoughts of her
I keep throughout night and day.

Connie L West
DISCONTENT
Quietness, filled with peaceful calm.
Tranquillity reins, as the night grows long.
A ripple of breeze touches my skin,
As bittersweet memories, come crashing in.
The calm shall leave, replaced by undying scorn.
The witch like touch gone for so long,
Returns to sing me its melancholy song.
Perspiration collects upon my furrowed brow.
I calm; commanding you to release me now.
Tranquillity returns, with the pale light of day.
Discontentment will now rest, not obstructing my way.
Till twilight fades to a deep shade of gray.

Shirley Arnold
WINDOW OF LOVE

I dedicate this poem to my husband, Keith with love (In remembrance of the Musquodoboit River)

While paddling down the river on a quiet sunny day
Listen to the birds singing, the water rippling against a log decade
Suddenly you hear a breeze whistling through the trees
The sounds of wings in flight, are crows playing with delight
A dark shadow crosses over you, oh! what can it be
An Off Spray flying home with dinner—is what you will see
Suddenly you go around a bend
Reflections in the river that never end
Trees bending over the river bank, casting images that never sank
A pinecone plops into the water, it's carried in the flow
Bobbing here and there till it finds a home along the shore
Look off in the distance, a mountain is in sight
Its colors are carefully painted, in golds and reds and yellows bright
All is quiet—now listen carefully
A tapping you will hear upon a distant tree
A woodpecker is making music, just for you and me
Oh! look up in that tree, a porcupine sitting oh! so proudly
Gazing down at you and me, while eating an apple carefully
All this and more is free by looking and listening
So open up those eyes and open up those ears
Receive the greatest gift of all—The Window of Love is free

Prudence Fulwider Theis
WHO KNOWS

To my beloved parents, Horace and Cora Fulwider

Who knows
Where the wind goes
When it blows,

Who knows
Where time goes
When it flies,

Who knows
Where beauty goes
When it fades,

Who knows
Where pride goes
When it falls,

Who knows
Where love goes
When it is lost,

Who knows
Where life goes
When it expires?

GOD KNOWS.

Susan E Badger
IT TAKES A LOT
It takes a lot of courage,
to trust in someone's love
It takes a lot of strength,
to give our lives entirely to another
It takes a lot of ability,
to fulfill our beliefs
It takes a lot of imagination,
to dream our dreams
It takes a lot of pain,
to find a love that will be kind
It takes a lot of giving,
to make love stay
It takes a little foolishness,
to send love away.

Brian Stitzel
WINDY WALK
Whistler . . .
Whisperer . . .
Wanderer . . .

Crash your waves in another neighborhood's trees
Carry a zephyr across a mid-summer beach
Or add weight to a postman's winter

Go scare little boys in dark beds

Do what you wish
But leave us to our walk,
Our peace

Silly fool
You can't blow us apart
See,
You only make her huddle closer to me

True, I cannot make a three-knotted tail wiggle
Wonder in an eight-year old's eyes at two-hundred feet
Nor can I make the cirrus, stratus or cumulus
Veil the heaven's eye

But I can feel wonder through her eyes;
. . . MY HEAVEN

Leave me to what I can

Diana L Henderson
MESSIN' UP SOMEHOW

I feel a struggle goin' on in my soul.
Please, Lord Jesus, revive and make me whole.
I am willfully disobeyin'
and my downcast spirit is payin'
in the sinful state I'm in,
Help, Lord, to restore me ag'n.

I have failed in the past
and want to be at peace at last.
Lord, help to make me what I ought to be . . .
Set my troubled spirit free.
I need You here to guide me now,
I keep a messin' up somehow.

I know there will be a day
if I keep with you and pray
that my struggle will be no more
as I cross that Blessed Shore.
Help me, Lord, my humble plea
I'm a wretched sinner, forgive me.

Mary E Davis

Mary E Davis
IN THE QUIET OF THE NIGHT

To my Aunt, Ida

I can feel the storms, from deep within,
calm to a gentle breeze.
Soothing, like the soft tinkle
of chimes hanging from the eaves.

I can hear the chugging of a train
as its grinding wheels churn.
Sounding its lonesome warning whistle
around every crook and turn.

Across the way at a neighbor's
I see a light go out.
While here I sit, composing my thoughts,
when no one else is up and about.

There are lots of ways that we can
spend, quiet moments of the night.
We can paint, read, knit and mend
but I prefer to write.

With thoughts of those so far away
I'll touch their hearts in Rhyme,
until I see the dust of their boots
as we march on in time.

Marchetta Jagger
LOOKING IN THE SKY TO SEE.

Looking in the sky to see,
A big bright moon, staring back at me.
Pity on his shining face,
frowning at our human race.
Gazing in this fire I see,
flames of heat that threaten me,
Scorching wood, as it burns,
A pile of ash, to which it turns.

Feel no breeze to blow on me,
No chilling bones from sea to sea,
All the cold has gone away,
Which once our flesh made turn to gray.
Hear the sizzle of dying earth,
Ancient sounds of a different birth,
So it's said, shall come a day,
for the falling of rocks, on us, we'll pray.

Witness stars bursting all around,
Caving earth as they hit the ground,
Creeping silence due to mistake,
As now there are no humans wake.

Alicia R Lein
I WISH

For: John and Anita, the two people who most believed in me

I wish,
for thousands of things.
But one in particular,
I wish for you.

I dream
of the day you'll never go away.
That you'll hold me in your arms,
And bless me with your charms.

I pray
for the day which would make you stay.
In which you say "I do,"
and mean it, too.

I wish
that you truly loved me.
I remember the days and nights we spent together.
They really seemed forever.

But today I see,
the truth in it all.
Your heart is to the wild,
as mine used to be.

Lance Lewman
AN IDEA CAME INTO MY HEAD

An idea came into my head,
Flickered for a moment,
And fled.
I wonder what it found there
That frightened it so.
Maybe it was lost and
Wandered in unwittingly.
Doesn't matter.
I'll find it.
Cause now I know it's out there.
Waiting.

Susan A Remrey
TOO MUCH EARTHLINESS

To my Heavenly Father, my loving husband Don, my children and my grandchildren, with all my love,

We're over blessed with earthly-ness,
and not enough of You.
Our earthly-ness is such a mess,
there's not enough of You.
When I look at Your creations, and
think of You above,
I know You made this earthly-mess
to be a place of love.

Now, I know I too, am guilty of
wanting earthly things, but
in my heart, I also know I'd trade
them all for wings.
People surely have changed, Lord,
since You first created them,
and who's to say but You, if it's
worse now, than then.

When You look down from Your
kingdom with Your mercy and Your
love, do You, as our Creator, feel
sick and hurt inside?
Does the corruption of this earthly-
mess make You want to run and
hide?
Dear God, as we grow older, the
wiser we might be to forget about
this earthly-mess and cling much
more to Thee.

Evelyn A Campbell
COLORBLIND

When I see the world
And its many colors,
I see
Blue in the sky
Green in the grass and trees
Brown in the soil, and
White in the sands.
But when it comes to love,
I'm colorblind.
For color makes no difference
To me.
Whether it be
Black with white,
White with black,
Black with red,
Red with black,
White with red,
Red with white,
Black with yellow,
Yellow with black,
White with yellow,.
Yellow with white,
Red with yellow, or
Yellow with red;
Love is love,
Just two people.

Patricia Roberts
WHY MUST WE DIE?

HEAVENLY FATHER, MOST HIGH
Tell me please,
Why must we die?

Little child, the fire dies out, but smoke ascends and passes from your sight; The stars are there by day as surely as the night.

Young eyes can read the promise hid in all living things; Already you know better than I, that you never really die.

The serpent sheds its skin, the caterpillar spreads great wings, and both return no more—
to yearn for things outgrown.

Is it earthly life then that we outgrow?
Child, you know the answer better than I—and understand it too! For you are always outgrowing.

Thelma L Reusser
THE EVENTUALITY

Of all the rhythmical composites in
this very dramatic world,
Some were blessed among God's
human souls;

Each tho' enriched was then also
judged—
Others had weakness; brothers gave
of their blood;

Always there are those, lending
humanity in love,
Perhaps not noted by earthlings but
honored Above;

Please God, forgive our brothers—be
they black or be they white,
Let our Father be the judge in wrong
versus right;

We are all found wanting, all with
infirmity,
Our lives will deplore, or bless our
eternity.

Jack Widner

Jack Widner
GRANDCHILDREN

To: Lianne and Cherilyn McLam
Dawn Heather and Keith Gordon
Cassandra Whitney Gordon

Sometimes a blessing;
Sometimes a curse.
Often at times;
They cost your purse.
Many times you kiss better their
hurts
Then they are off in a fast burst.

They are adorable; it is true;
Maybe it's what they put you
through.
Nevertheless at times we love them
best;
When they are fast asleep in bed at
rest.
Soon they are up in a bound;
Quite fresh for another round.

Their youth and energy are
boundless;
Some worries severe! some
foundless.
Even though at times you could
wring their necks;
You forgive them fast before you're a
wreck.
Often you don't see them for quite
awhile;
Then in the door they come with a
great big smile.

You try to teach them the good
things of life;

So in their lives there's not so much strife.
It's so important they grow good and true;
To see the world good and be proud too.
So when all is said and done;
We love them so much in the long run.

Theresa C Pinotti
THE BOTTLE
There's that . . . that
thing
It makes you ugly
not human
You become
blurry
out of place

Pain
to you
to me
So much hurt
I can't watch
I want to strike you

You don't stop
each opportunity
you have
You get that thing
And use it
into oblivion

It's my biggest
enemy, fear
Because it takes things one loves
away

It will never take my love away
Or blur my vision
So you keep your play-thing
Your bottle

It can't hurt me . . .
anymore.

Douglas Spring-Claussen
TO MY DAEMON SPRING

Inspired by Kathlene Spring Gere

To my daimon, Spring
My koan
even in my dreams

Reality, yes
stinking reality
stalks me in my dreams

mans gifts,
music, books, Buddha,
lie under thy feet
broken toys
useless distractions

distractions
from my own reality, you
My new mandalas
Loneliness, insecurity,
paradise memories of you

no boundary

Hazel Ridley
A GEM

To everyone alive worldwide.

A gem to most is something of value like diamonds and rubies etc.

To me a gem is something far more precious than the above.

A gem to me is to be able to see the flowers in the springtime.

To hear the birds chirp early in the mornings.

To feel the sun and breezes in any given day.

To be able to taste the different delectable foods and drinks.

To smell all the good plus bad smells in and out of doors.

The five senses are gems to me because without one or all of them you will be considered short changed.

Soloman L Hay III
LOVES SWEET WHISPERS ECHO IN MY MIND

In loving dedication to Lynne and Legare

Loves sweet whispers echo in my mind,
while the gentle winds of understanding caress my remembrance of loves passionate embraces.
Nestled in feeling amid flurries of emotions,
the flickering limelight of fantasia, explored;
burst forth into bloom, nurtured by hope, faith,
and the knowledge; that the future will hold us dearly.

Alice Koonts Ostrom
TWILIGHT ZONE
Evening light, phosphorescent, in
threads melting like butter on hot
french bread—linking two worlds,
day and night;
swiftly descending as an eagle in
flight;
ending the past and carried burdens;
promising a slumber pilgrimage and
pardons.
Then, blue-black night coming down
like a curtain above horizon ground.
Inky light begins to blur; invisible
with shades of darkness indivisible.
Eventide, a time for reflection and
memories, auguring introspection.

Sonja Nault
LOST IN A WORLD
Searching
Looking for a way out
Seeking for an opening,
a light to show a guiding path.
You're lost in a different world
A world of darkness and anger,
a circle of hate and fear.
You scream for help
but no one hears your cry.
You reach out through the wall
but no one takes your hand.
You're the only one who can find the peace.
You're alone to find your way out,
The way out of a world only you see,
and only you feel.

Jason Leone
CHRISTMAS TIME
Christmas time is full of cheer;
With candy and presents and family so dear.
We sit around the organ at night;
And we sing Christmas Carols, what a delight.
When we go to bed on Christmas Eve;
We talk about what Santa might leave.
Then we get up in the morning, and bake butter tarts;
And we empty our big stockings filled with chocolate hearts.
There's all different kinds of candies inside;
Plus there is also a paper plane that glides.
Then we open our gifts to see what we got;
And when we're all done, we all have a lot.
After we're done, we go down the road;
To grandmother's house, where it hasn't even snowed.
When we open our gifts, we all are surprised;
Because we don't get what we asked for inside.
And when we're all done, we all go and eat;
Our big Christmas dinner, with baked turkey meat.
Then we go home to play with our gifts that are under the tree;
And we also remember that Jesus was born for you and for me.
So as the day ends, we remember the great but long year;
And we hate to remember that Christmas comes but once a year.

Shirley J Storey

Shirley J Storey
GOD'S BEAUTIFUL WORLD

This poem is dedicated in loving memory of my husband, Leonard B. and Kurt Len, our son.

God's world is beautiful
Everywhere I see,
Masses of beauty
Awaiting for me.

Dearly God loved us,
And blessed everyone,
With abundance of beauty,
He forgot—not a one.

So live and enjoy,
Give thanks to Thee.
For a life that's so beautiful,
God gave you and me.

O sing and rejoice,
Take time to see,
God's wonders of beauty,
And sing praises to Thee.

Bessie Kay Derieux
HANDS

To my three dear daughters Kay, Ellen and Marian Lee

Did you ever realize how important your hands are to you?
How many, many things your hands help you do?
There are idle hands and there are busy hands
Hands that do what the brain commands

There are hands that don't and hands that do
Things that are false and things that are true
But beautiful, beautiful hands are they
That do for others day by day

"Do unto others as you would have them do unto you"
We know this isn't always easy to do
But doing for others is an expression of love
And our hands are a gift from our Father above.

Ernest Gregory Kurpuis
A DARK NIGHT AT THE TREE
In the darkened night
As the moon shines bright
I sit under a tree
Thinking of thee.

As the beams shine
Through the limbs and leaves
They cast shadows
Of how things have been with you and me.

Some wavy and bent
Some smooth and soft
And even some
That would break right off.

But when I take into thought
All of these
And looking again, I see a tree
Just like you and me.

Melissa R Smith-Barnes
MY TIME

I dedicate this poem to my sister Nanci who died on October 5, 1988 at the age of 21. She is loved and missed by family and friends.

If I die before my time
and rest permanently in the sky
I pray that you will understand
why I had to die.

And as I sleep in the clouds
forever and eternally
I want you to always know
I rest my name in thee

And as I watch you from the sky
I hope that you'll be fine
For I'll be waiting here for you
until the end of time.

So when you come to visit me
please don't feel sorry and cry
Don't blame yourself for what has happened
It was my time to die.

Gertrude Zielke
GOD IS MY COMPANION
When I awoke today, I sat at the edge of my bed, I folded my wrinkled hands and prayed. Lord it's cloudy this morning and days like this seem so long; I then get pretty lonely, so won't you be my company?
With you nothing seems wrong.
Let's have coffee together, or maybe you'd rather have tea?
No, it's no bother at all, as long as you are here with me.
My hobby is writing letters, and I know you help me write them too.
But today, I'm writing this poem and it's all in the honor of you.
Thank you, Lord, for keeping me company.

Dianne Hatfield Cummings
THE TEARS OF TIME

To my brother, Bobby; May he rest in peace.

Cry loudly little infant as you begin your life anew
Let them know you're here and that the world belongs to you

Cry my dear child because you've broken your favorite toy
Let Mother kiss away the tears and bring back all the joy

Cry oh ye troubled teen with your broken hearts and braces

Why does life deal you jokers and never any aces

Cry, cry ye young adult, cry those joyful tears
You're to wed the one you love and share the coming years

Cry again for the children you've born into a world unsure
Pray that you can give them love and make them feel secure

Cry once more for the grey in your hair and the coming peace of mind
All the tears are about to end as you leave it all behind

J D Rose
A FLOWER BLOOMS

To my friends & family in Alaska.

A flower blooms; as always in the spring. Its beauty tends to wither, so it isn't what it seems. All around in paradise chaos is the scene.
Lightning strikes the love birds nesting in the trees, ice cold wind chills and also stops the bees.
The rivers they stop flowing, now as gentle as a stream; oceans turning black, this is not a dream.
The leaves they turn to brown, as they're falling to the ground.
Animals seem to wander; no sight, no taste, no sound.

Charles H Davidson
SOME CALL THEM GOLD
Some call them worthless—
most call them old.
Others say lonely,
but some call them gold.

They've lived a long life—
much longer than us.
They talk of "old times."
You listen, I trust?

The memories they've gathered,
the things which they do
may seem quite strange
(and somewhat odd, too!)

They save many things,
old things and new,
things which seem worthless
to me or to you.

These people I speak of?
They're much like you.
Parents and grandparents
are all people too!

So why then does most
of society forget?
These wonderful people
have true value yet.

They are not worthless—
and weren't always old.
One thing they are . . .
Is worth more than gold.

Edith Eastin Moore
THE UNITED STATES OF AMERICA
Europe had her Napoleon, yes.
Alabama her George, no less.
With ambitions in politics, you see.
He said that he would, and he did, by George,
Became governor in seventy-three.

Our "Little Corporal" wouldn't back down.
"Segregation for the South always," he swore.
He said that he would and he did, by George,
He stood in the schoolhouse door.

By law, in his state, governors could not serve twice.
But Wallace had a plan, the state could not ban.
He said that he would, and he did, by George.
Lurleen, this was his man.

The White house beckoned; Cornelia urged him on, so
He said that he would,
And he might have, by George,
Had not the assassin's bullet laid him low.

Tammy Lide
DREAMS

I dedicate my poem, "Dreams" to John and Tiffany and to their dreams.

Everyone's dream is different
yet everyone's dream is the same.
Everyone's dream they want to fulfill,
and everyone wants to receive their fame.

Some dreams are very low,
however, some are high.
To some dreams, some people
too soon, say good-bye.

Dreams come in different shapes
and in many different sizes.
Sometimes, how dreams turn out
is very much to our surprise.

Some dreams are unrealistic
but some are beyond reality by far.
Some dreams are like reaching
for very high shooting stars.

Some people reach their dreams,
for some this chance is few.
But for you my friend,
I hope all your dreams come true.

Maggie Neese
WIDOWHOOD

This poem is dedicated to my beautiful and courageous little mother, Virginia

Hours of frenzied activity
Stemming the ready tears
That otherwise would fall on
Faces of bereavement,
The gaping wounds of loneliness
Temporarily bound.

But night's darkness falls ruthlessly
Activity ceasing,
Replaced by unwelcome thoughts
And countless, nameless fears,
Painful prisms of memory
Kaleidoscoping dreams.

Time eases the pain, acceptance
Blunting ragged edges
And through the filtered curtains
Of friendship's nurturing,
The glare of loneliness dims
But never really dies.

Jennifer Cox
DREAMS
The world is a wonderful place
Full of grass, trees, animals, and people.
The world is like hopes and dreams
Come true.
I dream I could fly with the birds
In the sky as they sing.
I dream I could live with the bear
In a cave and sleep all winter.
I dream I could be a tree
And have little birds chirp me asleep.
I dream I could be the grass

As people have picnics on me.
I could be the sky
As trees touch me, birds fly in me,
And as clouds flow thru me.
I dream I could be a rabbit
That hops on the grass and eats
Its carrots.
These are all my dreams and I
Hope you have wonderful dreams
Like me.

Annamae H Gibbons
EAGLES

To Shirley Kirkendorfer, who lives where the eagles fly.

Eagles
Magnificent!
Soaring on high,
Picking up the wind currents,
Alive to God's breath
Blowing steady and strong.
Up from the tree-choked gully
They come.
Magnificent!
Eagles, a soaring.

Brian J DePonte

Brian J DePonte
AND NIGHT FELL ONCE AGAIN

To my nephews (Jamie, Shawn & P.J.) And Nieces (Danielle & Marisa) Also my parents "Thanx"

The daytime clouded my mind
Though the sun was shining down,
of all my possibilities
beyond a shadow of a doubt.

I walked on past the water
and then it started to rain,
The cold and misty change of weather
left me in great pain.

And night fell once again
trying to save my soul,
from running around in circles
as the stars put on a show.

A jumpshot in the dark ahead
I saw but was not running,
fast enough to leap across
to keep from being pulled under.

The moon looked down and laughed at me
In a moony kind of smile,
full and bright he looked so strong
and me a helpless child.

And the nighttime once again
trying to save my soul,
from running around in circles
If only I had known.

Kathy Kostek
SPECIAL DELIVERY TO HEAVEN
There's so much that fills my mind of you
All the things we talked about; all we used to do
The day you brought me home I know you were proud
The times I woke you in the night, you never talked loud
As the days rolled on I got acquainted
When I took my first steps you almost fainted
The first words I spoke were of you
From that moment on we were known as two
All the walks we took I'll always remember
Whether it was the middle of June or late September
And on those rainy days I had to stay in
You found us a game and always let me win
There will never be anyone like you—There never could
Who would mean so much to me or do what you would
You meant the world to me; you still do
I'll never forget your face or eyes of blue.

As the years went on you aged some
That never stopped you or our fun
I'll never forget my first date
You wanted me to have the perfect mate
You worried so and now I know
That it actually hurt you to see me grow
But being the way you are you took it with understanding
That the facts of life can be so very demanding
And the day you walked me down the aisle
You assured me with your wonderful smile
You were proud of me that day too
I could tell by those eyes of blue
The kiss you gave me at the end of the day was so tender
That's just a minor of the many things that I remember
I was out on my own I had to learn
But there were so many times for you I'd yearn
Just for that warm smile; a little assurance
Maybe a little coping; or little more endurance
But I managed; I managed fine
You knew that I would and it would only take time.

Well, time went on and the days got dim
And there wasn't much of a warning sent from HIM
I had to realize you wouldn't be here much more
Because I had known HE had opened HIS door
You knew the facts we had nothing to hide

And being the man you were; you took it all in stride
It was a beautiful day when HE asked for you
I know you're happy now in the sky of blue
My memories of you will live forever
I could never forget them—never
The actual life we shared—we two
But most of all; a man so wonderful as you.

Karen Randel
THE MASK

To my husband Kerry and daughter Kelly—I love You

The comedy and tragedy that I have lived;
It's made me much stronger
And helped me to give.
The newness of each bright day
Makes me so happy;
It helps me to pray.
The mask that I have shed of late
Has made me elated;
I've peeled off the hate.
The snow must go on like turning a page
I'm feeling so good
I'll take center stage!

Heinz Hellinger
HANDICAPPED
You're lucky you can use your hands and also both your feet,
you ought to try without them, you see a hopeless feat.

So just for one day try it, to work without one hand,
and see how difficult it is, one good and one lame hand.

The next day try to drag your foot, the left leg just behind,
and see how you can move around, I beg you, please be kind.

Your vision may be perfect, but please shut one eye now,
narrow is your range of view, how different things look now.

When you sit down for supper, your food runs down your lip,
You're lucky you can feel it, your nerves give you a tip.

When you are doing chores, let's take a cane and try,
to balance your own body, believe me you could cry.

Now take them all together and see how you make out,
You see how someone suffers, I bet you, you want out!

Mary Hostetler
DEBI

To my firstborn

A child was I when you were born on that cold November day,
and the wonder that I had of you I've kept along the way.
From the strong willed child that you were then to a woman you have grown,
and though I've helped to shape your life it's mostly been your own.
At times you've tried to hide your heart behind a door of steel—
but the passion and the warmth in you comes through so very real.
The strength in you has been a shield to help you carry on,
the love within is but a cloud you've rested tears upon.
At times you've felt so deep my child, the hurts along the way—
but now I think you realize, that hurts just never stay.
As wisdom comes along with years, to change the very heart,
you'll keep the good, forget the rest, as understanding starts.
From the baby that was born that night when the winter winds did blow,
to a woman's soul of beauty now, my daughter you have grown.
I pray that peace will fill your nights and love will fill your days,
that God will hold you in His arms as I did that first day.
That you know His love and mine are there if ever you have need—
for your Mother's love like the love of God,
is eternal love indeed.

Helen Rae Wegner
I FLEW SO HIGH
I flew so high without any wings
I pondered the earth and saw many things
The billowing clouds
Their beauty to see

God's beautiful home up above me
The lights below give a beautiful hue
Of cities and towns
Oh! my what a view

I flew so high without any wings
God gave me the wisdom to see many things
I pondered the earth such beauty to see
Come join the flight, come fly with me

Fern Louise Tracy Brown

Fern Louise Tracy Brown
THE BEAUTIFUL OLD

To Mother, Angie Nettie Tracy, who can still smile at me and show her independence, even though, she is 88 years old and the years have changed her.

Mother was born in Nineteen hundred and one.
She knew only hard work and had no fun.
At the age of eighteen, she became a bride.
She raised a big family with Dad by her side.

Dad became ill and died finally in sixty-three.
And living with Mom was the life that fell to me.
She was so strong then, Now she is old,
But she is a wonderful, beautiful soul.
She is feeble and cannot walk.
And she gets confused when she tries to talk.
She says, "Isn't it awful to be this way?"
"Don't worry Mother," is all I can say.

We take everything for granted every day.
Until someone elderly comes our way.
To remind us what we each are supposed to do,
"You cared for me," I said, "Now I'll care for you."

Michael M Green
TELL ME

To my wife Dorothy, my daughter Robin, my sons Alan and Shawn. Books are a joy. Knowledge abounds, love is all. Family is the glue.

You say the pen is mightier than the sword, then tell me how that can be?
When so many people are starving from one shore to another sea.

You say the pen is mightier than the sword, then tell me how that can be?
When so many people are homeless from one shore to another sea.

You say the pen is mightier than the sword, then tell me how that can be?
When so many people are filled with hate from one shore to another sea.

You say the pen is mightier than the sword, then tell me how that can be?
When so many people are murdered from one shore to another sea.

You say the sword is mightier than the pen, then tell me how that can be?
People starving, homeless, hate, murdered, can be, can be!

Deborah J Stingis
MY DAD
My Dad is a very special Dad
he is perfect in every way
the kindness shows right through his eyes
and brightens up each day

He's gentle and strong
and always willing
to give a helping hand

There really is no other like him
in all of God's green land!

I'm very happy and very lucky
to have a dad like you

May God surround you with his love
in everything you do!

Donald A Girillo
MOTHERS

To my Mother whom we loved and called "Queenie"

My dear sisters and brothers,
Do we really know
The true meaning
Of our Mothers?

These wonderful creatures
Enhanced by God
Who become our deliverers
And set us forth
On the good earth's sod . . .

We are born thru them
Raised by them
And we become
The flowers of their stems.

They are a gift from heaven
The best of God's creation
They are in reality
Their own maternal nation!

So my dear sisters and brothers
This is indeed
The true meaning of our Mothers

Love them, cherish them
Never let them go
They are the essence
Of our lives
This world must surely know

Edna B Hicks
OUR MIRACLE CHURCH

This poem is dedicated with love to the members of McPheeters Bend Missionary Baptist Church, Church Hill, Tennessee but especially to Lorene Harris who suggested that I write a poem for the dedication of our new church.

Miracles still happen you can plainly see
As you enter our church with all its beauty.
This church of brick, though built by man
Was also built by God's loving hand.

Through faith we stepped out on the promise of God
Even when turning the first spadeful of sod.
Through faith we continued doing His will
Sometimes just listening when He whispered be still.

With Him there beside us to show us the way
We struggled along by night and by day.
At last it was finished and a joy to behold
More precious than treasures of silver and gold.

We look at His handiwork with eyes full of tears
Tears of rejoicing for God is so dear.
The doors are wide open—Oh, won't you come in?
Our Saviour is waiting to free you from sin.

Through prayer and dedication and service by all
God's church will remain standing if this building falls.
With hearts still rejoicing we pray without a sound
Knowing He is listening for we are on Holy ground.

Thank you, oh thank you, God, for our miracle church.

David E Whitmore
MY CHRISTMAS PLAN
Now Christmas day is coming, and Santa will soon be here, so I want you children to gather around, even you my dear. Because I have something to tell you, and I want you to hear it well, it won't be long we'll be hearing, a sleigh and Christmas bells. Now if you remember last year, when we stayed up all night, so we could hear Santa's reindeer, and see them all in flight. Well that didn't happen, we know something went wrong, why we didn't even see him, or hear his Christmas song. Now the rest of the world they saw him, so I know that we did something wrong, now here is my plan for this year, and listen, because we don't have too long. Now Peter! I want you to hide by the window, and let us know if he comes in sight. And Mary! you put

your ears to the roof top, I want everything to be just right. And you my dear wife, I want you to bake some cookies, and put them on the window sill, and open the window just a little bit, I want him to get the smell, and when that aroma reaches him I know he won't be able to resist, and that's when we will have him, this year we cannot miss. Why he'll come flying down, and land upon our roof, and he will slide down the chimney, now that's when we'll have our proof. We will know then that there is a Santa, and he lives at the North Pole, and brings us presents every year, because he loves us so.

Frank S Sliva
ALONE

To my beloved wife Susana, who for 31 years was my ears, my light, my inspiration, my everything.

The streets are crowded everyday,
And yet they seem so bare;
And I am lonely in my heart,
Because you are not there.

And when the mailman comes along,
I merely dream and sigh;
Because I know so well, my love,
That he will pass me by.

No matter where I search for it,
There is no joy for me;
In town, or valley, or beyond,
The reaches of the sea.

From winter into springtime, and,
From summer into fall;
The sky is dark and dreary, and,
The shadows form a wall.

I cannot see the sun that shines,
Or hear the birds that sing;
But I can only wait and pray,
And keep remembering.

Arajuana Alexander
YOU REMIND ME OF

You remind me of
Things past
Of loves that didn't last
But did (held in your heart and theirs)

Things profound
Thoughts abound
Of all the traveled places
Many faces of time

Things now
And how
We all have changed
Remained the same (as others).

Ruth Elmore
I WANT SO MUCH

To the one woman I idolize. My Mother, Agnes Domainque! "your right arm girl"

I want so much for you to care,
to feel your fingers touch my hair,
for you to notice when I'm there,
I want so much for you to care.

I want so much to feel your love,
to know it's me you're thinking of,
to give your heart a little shove,
I want so much to feel your love.

I want so much for you to see
the sorrow deep inside of me,
the pain which is my destiny,
I want so much for you to see.

I want so much to understand
why you can not take my hand,
the separate shores on which we stand,
I want so much to understand.

I want so much to tell you how
a daughter's love stands tall and proud,
and though my head stays in the clouds
I want so much to tell you
now . . .
I Love you, Mama!

Michael J Evans RN
THE FAWN

Stepping from the void of dark,
she paused scenting the wind.

Soft skin shining in the light,
tawny shoulders smooth and glistening.

Her limbs taut, ready for flight,
slender legs braced and trembling.

Nostrils quiver, gray eyes glance,
clean lines shift and shimmer.

The past whispers run, run.
but the scent is strange and alluring.

One step, then two, draws her nearer.
"No," says a voice. "Perhaps,"
counters her soul

The breeze shifts and she whirls away,
but pauses and thinks of return.

Lauren Jenkins

Denise Ellen Jenkins
UNCERTAIN

This poem is dedicated to my husband John and our special daughter Lauren. Also, to my parents Harry and Mary Kollar and my sisters, Dena Maree and Diane Breakell and their families. You are all very special to me.

When first I looked upon your face, a more angelic sight I'd never seen,
You were so fragile and precious, a gift from God to me.

Each sweet sound that passed your lips, each gentle movement you made,
Etched memories in my mind that will forever remain and never fade.

You gave me many sleepless nights and emotionally trying times,
Making me laugh . . . Making me cry.

Answers to unending questions were not forgot, you are so bright and smart,
To Mom and Dad there is not a child more special in our hearts.

I wish I could be certain what the future holds for you . . . each painful moment I would erase,
So never could the shadows of sadness darken, the soft light of your face.

Like the sun emerging from a gray clouded sky, so have you brightened my life,
Touching parts of my heart that were never explored as a woman or a wife.

Tears that escape from my eyes are filled with love and pride.

You are the most cherished thing in my world,
You are . . . "MOMMY'S LITTLE GIRL."

Linda S Akridge
THE MASTER CARPENTER

For Damon, Kathy, Kabrina, and Todd, To God be the glory for the marvelous new creation we become through Christ Jesus, savior, Lord, and Friend, who truly is the carpenter of our lives.

Jesus Christ, the Nazarene, the Master Carpenter is on the scene
Divine Architect of the universe, drafting interior designs supreme,
With a plan of redemption to fulfill life's inimitable dreams
Through a storehouse abounding in supernatural creative schemes.

A foundation of hope laid with mortar of changed attitudes
A porch of repentance adorned with pillars of gratitude,
A prosperous roof of faith covers the house by precious grace
Windows of tear-stained joy are molded prayerfully into place.

Nails of love secure the submissive spiritual beams
A Rosin of harmony fills the innermost minute seams,
Mats of temperance placed before obedient patient doors
Carpets of mercy covering noncomplacent chastened floors.

Walls enhanced with elegant patterns of genuine compassion
Furniture of charity rendered in a righteous humble fashion,
Accents of serenity complete this picturesque, eclectic decor
Complimented by an air of humility to breathe forevermore.

Only God wondrously moves through the blessed Holy Spirit
To permanently take up residence with undue human merit,
In an individual to rearrange and ultimately transform
The inner realms of a mere house into a loving Christian Home.

(Psalms 127: Except the Lord build the house, they labour in vain that build it.)

John F Herron
WHAT DO I SEE?

Out in the woods,
what do I see?
A bug. A bird. A tree.
Here a bug, there a bird,
a tree, a tree, a tree.

Climbing vines, little shrubs,
a tree that used to be.
Rough bark. Rotten wood.

A branch. A stump. A thorn.

Daddy longlegs, little cocoons,
a tiny spider having lunch.
Buzzing cicadas. Singing crickets.
An ant. An ant. An ant.

Deer tracks, fox tracks,
raccoon prints in the clay.
Gushy mud. Crunchy dirt.

A rock. A stick. A stone.

A moving shadow, the shining sun,
the hawk flying in between.
Flying hither. Gliding yon,

and on, and on, and on.

Out in the woods,
what do I see?
A bug. A bird. A tree.
Here a bug, there a bird,
a tree, a tree, a tree.

Marie Hoff
GOING OUR DIFFERENT WAYS

*This poem is dedicated to my Best Friend, Julie for always believing in me and my talent even when I didn't believe in myself. Julie you're the greatest person I know. I love you, and God Bless You * —Love Marie*

Love is just a silly game,
because nothing ever stays the same.
You said that you would always love me,
but now I know, we were never meant to be.

Now we're going our different ways,
Living our different days.

But sometimes I wish that things could have stayed the same.
Even though you're not to blame.
We departed from one another
each not loving the other.

Now we're just going our different ways,
Living our different days.

For now we will just say goodbye,
without either making a sigh.
I loved you more than I could ever say,
even at the price I had to pay.
But maybe someday we may find
love once more.

Jessie P Tipper
THE HOME

Follow me into this other world
This white sterile prison of living ghosts
With limbs that depend on wheels for mobility
Or steel rubber-tipped sculptures to lean upon.

Blank or searching white faces
Wrinkled and twisted with bleary eyes
Looking for someone or
Something that is recognizable.

Deformed, shaking, bony fingers
Grasp and clutch at my clothing
And pitifully claw their own clothing,
They mentally reach for some remembrance.

Tortured moans and groans echo
Down the empty long hallways.
Curses cry out from the lips of old angels
Decrying the last stage of this life.

Where is the fairness of having
Lovingly devoted a lifetime to others
Then being left with no candle of hope
In this cold home of forgotten souls?

Susan Ansbro "Whitford"
LOST DIRECTION
We go back a long time ago,
When all we had to show
Was getting high
And our troubles would fly.
Little did we know
Our lives would change,
In just ten years
So rearranged.
What happened to our direction
In that state of time,
With our heads so filled
With a young mind?
I look into your eyes
And see the deepness,
But in some way, are we showing weakness?
Here we are, at an older age
Have we yet made the stage
Living in this lonely cage?
Lost direction, what a shame
So you pick up the pieces
And no one's to blame.

Dolores Lein
FRAGMENTS OF FEELINGS
Shielding,
Seldom yielding,
Her words are masks
That must not slip
Lest vulnerability betray
The weakness that is strength
And emotions gain their way.

Dorothy Angevine
DORENE
Little girl, as you walk down the aisle, in your gown of lace,
The starlights shining in your eyes, a smile upon your face,
You'll see your mother sitting, with a teardrop in her eye,
Know it's not because of sadness, but for all the times gone by.

The memory of, "a beautiful baby girl," I could hear the nurses say;
If only they could see how true their words are yet today.
I remember little hands that brought me flowers, grass and all,
And the pen marks in the doorway to see each day, "How tall?"

And through the years, each new thing you learned, added to my pride;
And every time that you got hurt, then I was hurt inside.
Then, you had no way of knowing, what each day meant to me;
When you were sad or happy, that's what I would also be.

So on this bright occasion, when all is said and done,
I haven't lost my daughter, I've really gained a son;
And your husband gets another Mom, for I know he will see
That when he marries you he is getting part of me.

Eighteen years of (sometimes crying) mostly joy and pride
All reflected in one teardrop as you become a bride.

Liz Felton
ISLAND AND MAN

To Patsy and Scott, with lots of love.

You say you're like an island, so strong and all alone.
No one can reach your shores or come upon your soil.
Surrounded by a mighty wall, so near but oh so far.
No one to see your beauty or taste your forbidden fruit,
To dig beneath the surface, to see below their roots.
To waste away your treasures and to stand there all alone,
With not one soul allowed to share those mighty points.
But remember that even an island must depend on a lot of things, to grow and retain their beauty, down through the courses of age.
Even if you think you're like an island, so strong and all
Alone, remember you too cannot stand, and grow all alone.

Guillermo Gil Ortega (Chamorro)

Guillermo Gil Ortega (Chamorro)
INSOMNIA

To the poets. This first page of the book "In the sub Passageway" ("A Dairy of the Insomnious"), which deals with the transition between wake and sleeping lives.

Let me withstand,
to undergo no changes,
I want to disregard all great ideas,
and all the daily problems let unsolved
because what I want now is more important:
tranquil I want to stay,
I have to sleep.

Time will not run, don't worry;
it only makes a move if you want that,
it is not free, is not autonomous
it's only the interruption of the thought.

What moves it is your fear.
Don't make it run, and don't give wings to it,
it seems to go ahead if you get frightened,
stops if you get calm.
And there is only movement in your thinking.

Time is a ghost.
The soul has funny laws,
because 1 minute, 10,
if forgotten of time you get slept
can afford you the rest time can not give.

Jann Houston
SEARCHING
I have known the beauty of the trees, rivers, the valleys,
and the freedom of the breeze
When I walk, I walk alone and dare to share what I have known

Should I challenge natures best and try to put my curious soul to rest

If I could move a cloud today, should those mountains soon give way

There seems no answers for what I need . . .
should I accept unknowns and heed

The truths are there and I must know, where
my paths cross others and will go

Oh, give me time to search and find
complete serenity of mind.

Leah Jewel Reynolds
ROOM OF DARKNESS

Upon writing 'Room of Darkness' I was inspired by the difficulties African-Americans endure and have endured throughout our history. This poem depicts the plight of African-Americans. I shall dedicate this poem to America and her illustrious people.

Students crammed inside a room
so enclosed, simulating a mother's womb.
Working diligently they find
there's no way out.
In looking behind
they find stretch-marks;
struggle, anger, intimidation,
fear, lack of knowledge, opportunities taken,
ideas, thoughts, inventions, talents,
all of which were stolen.

Despite the many storms, hurricanes, bad weather,
the minds of the students reluctantly come together.
As the door to the room
begins to open wide
they all jump to the other side.
A loud, disturbing, harsh, "Boom,"
is heard in this room.
The students awaken only to realize
that it was just a dream
that was in their eyes!

Joyce A Lepri
GOODBYE
Goodbye is now so close
I can hear it, I can feel it, I can touch it, I can taste it
I cannot turn away this bitter dose.

All my thoughts will this farewell to not be
But it will soon be here in front of me.

Maybe not today will it come, but surely tomorrow
That's when I will be drowned in the depths of my sorrow.
I did not want to say hello to this—so long ago
I knew you would not stay, but then my heart could not have said no.
There has been so much happiness, so much joy.

Yes, after hello must come goodbye
But yet I beg for just another moment before you go,
Because I do not want our love to die, for I have loved you so.

I don't want to believe it
But it rings everywhere
Goodbye—Goodbye—Goodbye
There is no-one to care as I sit here and cry.

In torrents falls the rain
So do my tears
There is so much pain—

Goodbye—Goodbye.

Gurtha May Sisk McKinney
LOVE, TRUST AND SURVIVAL

Dedicated especially to Steve, and to all recovered addicts.

Son, we love you.
We're very proud of you.
We knew that you could make it
if you only wanted to.
Sometimes the path we choose
is not the right way.
We make a wrong turn
and find ourselves astray.
We will forget the past.
We will not make a fuss.
Thank God for His directions
and for His love and trust.
As we live each day,
we're thankful to be alive.
And with the help of God,
we know we will survive.

Virginia Hahn
AS A LITTLE CHILD

To My Lord and Savior Jesus-Christ

The Little Children Flocked Around,
And Clung Unto His Flowing Gown.
He Gathered Them Unto His Breast
And Laying Hands Upon Them Blessed.

So Must We Be To Enter In,
Innocent As A Child, Free of Sin.
Trusting, Believing Completely In Him,
To Come Unto His Kingdom And Enter In.

Tracey Gonzales
DADDY'S GIRL

To my father, with love

Being born and becoming daddy's little girl,
is the best thing that's happened in this whole world.

A special love, that cannot be compared to any other love
I see it through my eyes, and deep down in my heart;
a father and a daughter is something that should never part.

"I love you daddy," is something you'll always hear
Even though I'm far, my love is always near.

I'll always love you, and nobody can take away,
the memories of my childhood; how you and I would play.

Growing up is a part of life, and I always try to show

that no matter what happens, or wherever I go
I want you to know, that I'll always be daddy's little girl.

Diane Johnson
A FRIEND IS . . .
Someone who you can share your inner feelings with . . .
knowing you won't be judged or rejected.
Someone who gives freely . . .
without expectation or motivation.
Someone who lets you be who you are . . .
if you want to change it's up to you.
Someone who is there when you are hurting . . .
offering true tenderness.
Someone who sees your beauty . . .
your true beauty.
Someone who gives you space when it's needed . . .
without hesitation.
Someone who will listen . . .
to what you're really saying.
Someone who will consider your different beliefs . . .
without judgement.
Someone who you will always feel close to . . .
even when they are far away.
Someone who is comfortable to be with . . .
anytime, anywhere, doing anything.
A friend is a special gift . . .
to be cherished forever.

Mary A Meekins

Mary A Meekins
MY BEST FRIEND
My best friend, she was supposed to be
All the time, she was trying to steal my man from me
She was always saying, "Keep your eyes on your man"
"They will run around, cheat, do everything they can"

Then she was telling me about some of her friends, she know
How they ran around and some of the places they go
How they call other women's homes and ask their men for a date
But, when the wife gets the call they say, "Sorry, mistake"

Until one day, I came home, my man was on the phone
I heard his say, "Listen, don't call me when my girl's not at home"
I crept in quietly, and closed the door
And picked up the phone in the hall
She was telling him how she admired his ways
How nice he was, and she wished he would make a play

"I'll tell you something else, you don't know,
I've been following you around wherever you go"
I put down the phone and said "Damn"
All of the time she was pretending to be MY BEST FRIEND

Carol Nieman
SECOND THOUGHTS
In the middle of the night, I lay here huddled in my king-sized bed; wondering what happened to our love, our marriage, even the friendship is dead.

I play things over and over in my mind; wondering where I could've been more loving, thoughtful, and kind.

I ache with the desolation and emptiness I feel.

I live each day in a daze! not knowing what's actually real. I want to be half of a whole, part of a team; mean something to someone, to help live out a dream.

I know we both did things out of anger, jumped to conclusions, and said things we didn't mean. If only we could explain or erase the hurts we inflicted on each other: to wipe the slate clean.

I guess that there's no going back to what we had before; no way to say "I love you" and enjoy what life had in store.

Maybe someday when we both get on our feet and time has had a chance to heal—we'll fall in love with someone else, this time for real.

How wonderful it would be,

If that love could have been you and me.

I just wanted you to know that I'll always care . . . even when I actually make myself believe: you're no longer there.

Jennifer Hladick
LOST LOVE
The snow blows softly about outside
As you turn away and say Good-bye
No more hugs or kisses shared
I see now how much you cared
All the times we've shared together
I wished those moments could last forever
It was you I looked for, you I seeked
Now tears roll silently down my cheek
You look toward me
And mouth I Love You
Just one more time
I want to hold you
I wipe my tears and heave a sigh
As you walk into the storm
And say Good-bye.

Hazel French
A POEM OF LOVE
Beyond the Blessed Cross
My Jesus waits for me,
To welcome me with love.
I'll see him face to face.

He's always in my mind;
He comforts me each day.
He fills my heart with joy.
I love him so.

If you will ask him in
He'll do the same for you.
He'll guide you day by day
And fill your life with hope.

He saved my soul from sin;
He strengthens me each day.
He's all the world to me.
He loved me so.

Herman Dahlberg
GREEN
Life was seen
In all the green.
Among the dead,
Golden brown and red.
Orange and yellow,
Once a mighty fellow;
Soon to follow
This beautiful sorrow.
Life was seen
In all the green.
Yet, beauty lay dead
In its golden brown bed.
It is clear,
Green will again appear;
Only to shed
Brown and red.
Orange and yellow
Will quickly mellow.
All will again follow
This life of beauty and sorrow.

Rachael Searfoss
LIFE
Drivers crawl in their dirt-spattered cars,
Searching for an open freeway and room to breathe.
Cluttered town houses are thrown together on a giant monopoly board.
Tenement houses shut their lids in the night
to draw their shades from the world.

An ordinary man sighed and shifted his feet
in a snack shop that bordered on the expressway.
He rubbed his bloodshed eyes and held
his watch several inches from his face to check the time.

His fatigue could not be easily shed,
Since each day he pulled his covers over his head
and heard the rumbling of footsteps on the upstairs floor.

A traveler stood outside the door of the shop
She tried to think while she sipped the sour coffee.
The traffic's buzz disrupted her,
So she walked in the bathroom and fastened the lock.

If she passed out from exhaustion
Would the cleaning lady
Stash her in the garbage bin?

Lori Crandall
THE CAROUSEL
my mother once told me
the carousel was a magic playground
of animals in a forest of winter
white icing snowflakes
swirled around jeweled faces
manes of spun gold
hooves of onyx
they lived in a world
where spring has fallen
forever frozen in winter's night
imprisoned in a whirlwind of stardust
where a child's smile could set them free
now the sun revels in my frost covered eyes
mocking the carousel
patent leather shoes
it reveals the splintered wooden forms
cheap rhinestones
chipped red paint
and like a child
i weep

Peter J Mitchell
LIGHT O' NIGHT
Only a few
Can find the hue
It's the blue
Beyond the rue
It'll be soon
Under the moon
I'll be out
And about
I'll be near
I'll be here
Overthere
And everywhere
Black as a crow
A bright shadow
Like a spoon
The big full moon
I'll be out
And about
In the light o' night

Bertha Cornwall Pearson

Bertha Cornwall Pearson
CREATION
Beneath the earth's soft loamy sod
I tenderly placed a small seed pod.
A fine-sprayed shower and warm sunshine
Interchanged their blessings by design
To nurture the seed. A mystic force
Has pushed a shoot on its upward course.

A bud so tiny and tightly bound
Has begun to unfold without a sound!
Oh, fragile beauty with delicate hue
With glistening drops of early dew,

Your fragrance is so rare and sweet
That my awe of God is now complete.
I bow my head and humbly pray.
God's power and grace were here today.
His power, so marvelous and divine,
Performed a miracle with that seed of mine!

Amy Betts
TEARS

Tears are like raindrops
That fall from the sky
Crystal blue drops
A waterfall of eye

When something upsets you
Whatever it may be
Tears seem to form
Allowing everyone to see

To ease the pain
We let the tears go
Nothing to hold back
We just let them flow

We cry for a while
And when we are through
The tears dry up
Just like raindrops do

When the sun shines
It dries up the rain
When you release your tears
You dry up the pain

Paul Tumarkin
TIME IS RUBBING ITS NOSE

Time is rubbing its nose
against my brow
I hear the tapping
of my spoon against my cup
as I stir my coffee.

"Stoic rain pattering against my window;
I have been hunched over in your down-pour"
The rains have stopped
The waters are evaporating
From the grilled sidewalks
under a watchful setting Sun

Thomas Rossi
THERE'S A FLY ON A WINDOW

There's a fly on a window
looking out of a room
It sees a thousand fingers,
Pointing, through its eyes,
it turns and sees the world outside,
it likes to fly, but has to hide
from the pointing fingers' swatter.
Dodge to dodge
to web and wall,
so many traps, so many enemies,
what it would give to be gold
But ohh what it takes to be whole.
It wishes it would STOP!
and every thing would hold.

Kara Schrage
TO DISCOVER ME

I was sitting next to him
He was staring into my eyes
It was a romantic fantasy
Happening under star-lit skies
He told me I was special
And that he loved me so
Whether to trust him and believe him or not
I really just didn't know
We were just too young
I needed to grow up
I wanted more time
I was just a pup
I had the world to discover
I had to discover me
Why couldn't he see that
Why didn't he understand and let me be
I suppose I made the right decision
Maybe I'll never know
But at least when I'm sure I'm in love
I'll be able to let it show.

Marguerite Stanley
I AM ME

This poem is dedicated to my very supportive family and friends

I dare be proud
To be Black, without reservation
It strikes odd, my 'ruthers
For the curly 'fro.
Over the silky straight,
For the soft browns
Over the baby blues. You see,
My standards of beauty
Are not dictated
To me
By the "Man" or the "Sam."
Yet I face
The
Impatient tolerance
Of my juniors
Because
My Blackness does not
Color my
Judgement of others.
No matter what their persuasion

Kevin Leo Kelly
TREE

I would like to dedicate this poem to my grandfather, Leo C. Kelly. He loved the woods with all his heart.

I wandered by the woods one day,
on my way to school.

They were so inviting, dark,
mean and cool.

They seemed to draw me into them;
To welcome me like a long lost friend.

I lost track of time and space.
Could it be, such a beautiful place?

Amidst the rumbling roar of man.
His mad machines, his cruel demands.

What if the woods were lost someday?
Man no longer here could stay.

I wish the people would start to see.

Preserve mankind,

Preserve the tree!

Anita Heard
THE FOUR SEASONS

All four seasons are full of delight,
With their skies either cloudy or bright.

Winter is quiet, peaceful and still,
Spring sprinkles flowers all over the hills.

Summer is hot and moist and
gives us fruit by the bunch.
While fall is full of a bountiful
harvest on which we love to munch.

No matter what the season,
We are happy and here's the reason,

We are healthy and all is well,
This is a lovely land in which we dwell.

Carroll Phillips
CIRCLE OF LIFE

You flew off thru' the night sky
With a dream you thought might come true
You went for a swim in the ocean dry
When all along you knew

You can't fly forever
In fact you can't even fly
You can't swim forever
The waves are just too high

You walked along the sharp edge of a knife
And hoped it would not cut you
You jumped off the ledge of your life
And prayed someone would catch you

But you can't walk forever
On the thin edge of a blade
You can't fall forever
And you can't get up and walk away

Life is a circle from beginning to end
And where you begin and end
Are one and the same my friend

Kellie Hyatt
WAITING FOR YOU

Watching the clock on the wall
hearing voices in the hall
I sit in solitude
just waiting for you.

I'd do anything to change this moment
as I'm sitting here in torment
drowning in wasted tears and sorrows
thinking of the never to be tomorrows.

As my heart is breaking around me
And my body hurts endlessly
a deep void fills my soul
at the thought of letting you go.

Clouded scenes replayed in my mind
hoping there's something I might find
to help me not feel so blue.
but right now, I'm still waiting for you.

Bob Brown
THE ENDLESS FLAME

I would like to dedicate this poem to all those who have recently lost a loved one.

Like a star she lights up my life
She's an endless flame burning deep in my mind
Visions of her grace the pages of my thoughts
Memories of her are forever locked in the diary of my mind
Since she's been gone, I've been lost without a trace
Who am I?
Where am I?
I'm lost in an endless sea of broken hearts
Life had no meaning without her love
I can't sleep
I can't eat
I'm a helpless soul wandering about the earth in search of her
When she left it was as if a part of me had committed suicide
She must come back, without her my life is incomplete
If she never returns my death is inevitable
For without her I am nothing

Mariaelena Pascal
WISHES AND DREAMS

Staring out my window, into the darkness of the night
Nothing to be seen, but the distant stars flickering light
One shoots across the sky, then forever out of sight
What should I wish for, what is my dream
My wish is for peace and tranquility, like a quiet mountain stream
My dream is for eternal love, the kind meant to be seen
I wish peace to be forever, I want my love to be true
But nothing lasts forever, so what else can I do
Dreams sometimes fade, wishes are sometimes lost
Life holds many changes, with this is always a cost
The cost is sometimes hard, but it won't last very long
The pain and sorrow will end, as in the finishing of a song
But if you dream as hard as you wish, and wish as hard as you dream
Anything can be possible, as long as it's your wish and your dream

Carolyn M Myers
WHAT IS WAR

War is hate, and pain.
War is where man, and fear come together, and shutting out all others.
It's blood stain battle fields, where green pasture laid, and children played.
It's not knowing who your friends are, or who your enemy is.
It's seeing children the same age as yours, being killed by bombs, and hand-grenades.
It's watching innocent people being killed, by the same people that say "they're on your side."
It's watching your best friend dying in your arms in the end.
It's laying at night wondering if God will take your soul, or if you'll get out of this hell hole.
And when you do go home, or if you come home.
It's the nightmares, the waken in a cold sweat, and remembering the hurt, the fear, the love, the hate, and praying to God to make it disappear, but knowing that it never will, because that my friend is what war is.
Nightmares, hurt and fear!

John A Dodds
AN ELEPHANT FOR SANTA

To: Mrs Elsie Tideswell—In 1924, a Most beautiful young lady and still a beautiful person today.

I wish I had an elephant
who was light upon his feet
I'd use him when
the going's rough
Or in case of rain or sleet.

Reindeer go OK on snow
Or when the moon is bright.
But when the sky is really rough
There's need for a lot of might.

I'd call him JUNGLE JIM
instead of RUDOLPH—you
know who
He'd help out when the case was
right
Like all good helpers do.

My need for space is so intense
There's scarcely room to ride
An extra trunk would sure help out
I'd pack big things inside

I'd want him to be colored pink
Like the ones they usually see
When someone's telling of the world
And the way it used to be.

Now I have been around so long
There's times that I forget
But an elephant, he's got a mind
That remembers all he's met.

Not one of you would be left out
We always would get through
With a spare like that, there's not a
thing
That Santa couldn't do.

You know just where I can be found
And how to send me word
In case pink elephants do appear
I'll use the whole darn herd.

Mr Bela Nagy
LAUDITUR DOMINE
From ashes rising hope
Battles with changing motion,
Power of love overhold,
Takes a win on distortion,
And divided words.

As you shine through it all
Eversoul keeps matter mold,
Makes our life look so small,
Yet, as bricks, we overfold
Building and rebuilding.

Hallelujah! Sing the spheres,
Stars born and stars shallow,
As you are through light and space
Reflections hold your shadow,
Remembering the things will
come . . .

Barbara M Johnson
THE WAY YOU MAKE ME FEEL
You just don't understand
The way you make me feel.
It's like I'm lying in the sun
On a grassy hill.

Your touch makes me tingle;
Your warmth gives me chills.
Your breath is a vapor of sweet
wine;
Your loving is my only pill.

I know that you are special
For even my dreams are real.
You just don't understand
The way you make me feel.

Margie Dell Stuart
TO MY DAD—WITH LOVE
We shared a special bond that very
few will ever know,
We were there for one another—and
Dad, I still love you so.
I am convinced that down deep in
your heart—even today,
That you—and you alone—know
what I really want to say.

There were times that we sat alone in
silence—just we two,
Or walked together thru the fields,
with nothing at all to do.
During these times—we talked of life
and all your dreams for me,
But now I must continue them alone,
without you there to see.

I remember so many things you said
and things you tried to teach,
I just hope and pray your goals aren't
way beyond my reach.
We didn't always agree or could see
things eye to eye,
But thru love and understanding, we
each came around—by and by.

Just 'cause you've gone away does
not mean that I'll forget,
The good times, the sad times, and
even all those dumb ole' rules you
always set.
I'll do my best to continue on—in
the direction you headed me,
And try to be the person that you'd
have wanted me to be.

Before I close please let me say
again—I truly will miss you,
You were always there for me—
whether I was mad, happy, or blue.
You were my teacher, protector,
good friend, and buddy too,
What I wouldn't give to hear you say,
just once more—Baby, I love you,
too

Cynthia Malone
MANDELA REIGN
The elusive face of freedom, dances,
Nymph-like and veiled,
'round my head.
Spinning long shadowy lines
across the dark walls of my world.

Unspent tears lie dormant and dried,
as profiles of loved ones flash
through my mind,
like, trace memories, of an ancient
people.

My wife wears a golden band of
broken promises,
as she creeps around the chipped and
broken edges of humanity.
The once warm and familiar voices
of my children,
are muted now, not unlike padded
footfalls
on some forgotten stairwell . . .

The days here ebb, and flow into
years,
and the years slip through my fingers,
like a dense fog through a picket
fence.

My captors gaze at me through
clouded eyes,
of confusion . . .
As much a prisoner of their
blackness
as I am of mine.

I wish to die a forgotten man . . .
Neither a minion nor a martyr.
The cause for my captivity should
too,
become but a trace memory . . .
Of an ancient people's grave
misunderstandings.

Margaret (Pieters) Hoy
MEMORIES
My best friend is so close to me,
But still it seems so rough;
To tell her that she's special
Just doesn't seem enough.

I'll always need her by my side
To guide me from my fears;
She's always there to lean on,
And she's often dried my tears.

She laughs right along with me,
Even when my jokes are bad.
I hope she, too, feels lucky
To have shared the times we've had.

Although we're not together now;
She's never far away;
She's always in my dreams.
And for us, my friend, I pray.

That we'll always be together,
And that we'll always share
That very special friendship
That truly says, "I care."

Christine Titone

Christine Titone
LIFE

Dedicated to my children: Catherine, Peter, Camille

Life is a puzzle to many
It has many phases,
Love, hatred, depression, and evil;
But you make it to your liking.

Love can be beautiful
Depending on how true you are;
Hatred can be ugly
For it takes beauty out of one's life.

Depression is destroying your
thinking
And may end in a shell
But evilness is the devil himself
With no heart or condonement

Louisa M Burger
MAN WITH A PAIL

To my father, Harry B. Everest, who is the man with the pail.

A man who likes to pick berries,
Can stand up and pick
Into a two-quart pail,
Fastened under a suspender button
If he picks from a high bush.

A man who likes to pick berries
Can sit down and pick—
And he can soon fill that pail,
For he won't need that suspender
button
If he picks from a low bush.

A man who likes to pick berries
Can stoop down and pick—
And he'll find he won't need that
pail,
And he won't need that suspender
button
If he eats from a berry bush.

Roberta S Van Löben Sels
REPROACH
How can I talk to you
When you will not listen?
How can I see you
When you will not be seen?
How can I hear you
When you will not articulate?
Into the roiling fog of alienation
I reach my hand with love,
Only to touch the rough wall
Of your paranoia.
Lost in the black miasma
Of your own unhappiness,
You cannot accept the actuality
Of mine! Thus this estrangement
Nags like a cancer in my brain,
Gnawing at the edges of my nights,
Shadowing the brightness of my
days,
And, unresolved, presages
The bleakness of my lessening years!

Theresa G Imes
REGRETS

To all the beautiful Mothers in the world with equally as beautiful children.

Did I buckle up my child you ask?
I just don't have the time.
Besides, i'm only going to the corner
store,
and my child will be just fine.

Get into the back seat sweetie,
and please don't make a sound.
Did I buckle up my child you ask?
I will next time around.

The store is only four blocks away,
did I buckle up my child you say?
The lights are green for me to go,
hey, where did that car come from?
Oh no!!

The screech of tires, the sound of
glass,
please "Dear GOD," don't let that be
my child in that mess.
My head is aching, my eyes are
blurry,
Is anyone around? Oh please hurry.

Now all I have left are the memories,
that haunt me day by day.
If only I had taken the time,
Did I buckle up my child you say?

Karen Sue Curley Boller
WHENEVER I SEE A SUNNY DAY

This poem is dedicated to my wonderful family, Bill, Norma & Phil, Mom & Rich, Robert & Lisa, Paul & Matthew, and all my dear relatives & friends. I love you all, & thank you my dear parents—Tom & Rachael.

Whenever I see a sunny day—
I think of my childhood which has
long passed away.
Happy memories flow through
my mind—
of people I knew, some were
wonderful; some not so kind.
My sister and I would read
comic books on our front
screened-in porch—
A delightful shade from a sun that
could scorch.
We would read, for hours on
end—
And to this day she's my very best
friend.
Holidays were always so
meaningful—
Not a one could ever take a toll.
Our parents were very special to
my sister and me—
In our hearts they will always have a
key.
Having grown up in Oklahoma of
which a song and show
was named after—
Many days were filled with warmth,
love and laughter.
Now nearing my late thirties
and having moved on—
Most of the memories have stayed

with me but some are gone.
 Still I'm ever so thankful to the
 Lord Jesus above—
For allowing me to be a part of a
family rich in love.

Roberta Armstrong
HAND TO HAND
Ashes mix with dust on the ground;
war veils the earth in a black
wedding gown.
Reagan has no ring to put on
Nicaragua's finger. Forked-Tongue,
grandfather
Preaches from a White House cake,
rides a CIA horse to cut off the hands
of the people.
President's heart is like a tree stump.
Sad, flowering armssssnake:
CONTRA
Ring upon ring of Medusa hair rolls
into the forest. "Abort the beautiful
forest.
Nicaragua is freely pregnant and
refuses to marry America."

Something is building up that almost
got suffocated to black; beneath
Nicaragua's wordless skirts
Little feet dance in the dust by the
riverbed. Where the trees reach up
vampires are flying
Inside a plush red violin case waiting
to be opened up. Tonight Reagan lies
at the dinner table
Drinking Dragon Soup and drowns in
the word 'communism.' His ears are
filling up with
"Communism." His old machine-gun
joints 'click-click' and he cannot hear
what we say.
See him swimming like a red devil
around and around in his soup,
mouthing wide, fishy talk.

And tomorrow morning their Forked
words will split people as logs get cut
in two, every day
More fresh blood flows in the river,
dries up in the Sun. It's business as
usual,
A two-faced smile of sunshine burns
Saturnine, charcoal-broiled shadow.
Americans are stumped, but with
silver hands and a grizzly claw,
we've woven
A pair of gloves, made by the warmth
of our country's people towards you,
Nicaragua.
"Gracias." As a moon shines on the
southern sea, mettle-gloved, we'll
drink
Long shadows now worn, dark
cotton-sleeved.

Put your gloves on my brown sister
and take my silver hand never to
part.
All over the earth hands will grow
like Spring touched by music again
in the heart.

Crystal Lynn Dillahunty
SUNSET
Red blazes on the horizon,
as an indigo blanket gently lowers
onto the earth.
Pink clouds scuttle away,
as an invisible dancer sweeps across
the sky—
In delicate purple.
It is sunset.

Ann Jeannett
FOREVER LOVE
My forever love
 breathless words hang
Waiting in dreams to get you
 near by me
Wishing away cares unresolved
 to spend time in warm slow
 moments
The night holds still and quiet
 for what we whisper now
Begging for more this unquenched
love
 stays long within bodies entwined
Unfolding passions drifting deeper
 into flowing ecstasy
Serious wet kisses and endless
 all that your heart can hold
It is understood, my forever love
 our hearts undivided

Jean R Page
PUPPY
Where in this innocence remains the
spark
That stirred the first primeval cur,
As, belly-down, he prowled the dark,
Stalking feather, fin and fur?

Survival was his one concern;
Now, eons since he's come to learn,
With tail to wag and moist eye plead,
That Man will serve his every need.

Alex Dan

Alex Dan
THE SIGN OF LIFE

To my wife Irina and son Seva

The time may come for doomsday
crack
when shadows of unbeing rise,
but Life for sure will be back
to fill with light extinguished eyes.

Its flame would get to every place
without singeing soul's shed,
then each new-come could read in
Space
a shining sign THE DEATH IS
DEAD

Geraldine M Kuprewicz
THE STORM
The thunder rolled
The lightning flashed
The rain poured down
And the cold wind lashed
At everything within its scope
That chanced to be out
On the stormy night
With never a cave or a shelter about.

The cattle stood with their heads bent
low
As each flash lightened the pasture
below.
Tall trees bent over in utter defeat
But the gnarled old oak held his head
high to meet
All the force that the wind sought to
bear on his brows
Too stubborn to bend to the storm in
his boughs.

At last when the storm in its fury was
o'er,
And the wind's strength was spent
For a short time once more
A tiny bird flew out of an old bent
tree and said,
"Thanks for the shelter you gave to
me."

Jeannie Marie Tempesta
REFLECTIONS OF MISTY

To you my friend and pal; and for all the wonderful years you gave, to all who knew and loved you.

My friend and pal, we had it all; you
and I
Now you've gone to rest in heavens
home.
You're not with me, but still live on.
Happy memories fill my heart; of
days now past.
A ball you fetched for me to throw,
legs a running, off you'd go.
You talked to me through those big
brown eyes;
no words need be spoken, at any
time.
My heart now you've taken.
Good times, sad times, always by my
side you stayed;
lying next to me, full of pride.
Your comfort always warmed me.
A silver coat I'd gently touch
so in my prayers you'll always be.
These thoughts I'll cherish always.
I love you much; my friend and pal.

Carol Barrett Jordan
THINK ABOUT IT

To all that have made my life worth thinking about, especially my family. Thank you.

As time passes by, you wonder where
it's gone.
You stop and remember all that
you've done, all that you said.
Was it good, something worth while.
Were there times to cherish, moments
to consider.
Did words reach out in anger, or were
they kind ones.
Whether or not the meaning, if they
were for belief.
This is all that should matter, if to
make a better world
as you pass by.

Kay Arneberg Booth
MY MOTHER
To me she's gone with no return,
 My tears flow fast and free.
No more her smile and loving arms
 Will soothe the hurt in me.

But is she gone when memories
 So cherished linger on?
For I'll feel her tender greeting
 Each morning at day's dawn.

I'll remember times together,
 With laughter kind and sweet,
When Autumn leaves before the
wind
 Go dancing down the street.

I'll sense the softness of her touch
 When balmy breezes blow.
The budding rose, a kitten's purr
 Her love to me still show.

Remembrances like this will stay
 To all my life endow.
So no more tears, just always know
 She's gracing Heaven now.

Jeffrey Edward Tracey
BROKEN
Now we dally till we tire
of this warnet on our star.
The love worn web lies worthless,
open,
flaunting its lifeless sway.
But I know that when the words
are finally spoken,
only you and maybe I will see
that nothing has
nor ever will be
Broken.

Jenna Marie Droluk
LITTER
Breathe in the fresh, sweet smelling
air
It's just too bad that some people
don't care.
They throw their trash all around,
Hoping that it will not be found.
Look, over there!
I see somebody who really does
care!
They pick up the trash
And turn it into ash.
Thank-you, for now I know that I can
go!
I was just standing around for the
show!

Freddi Saunders
MICHELE
I miss you, I miss you.
Against Grandma's wall you struck a
Marilyn Monroe pose—
I snapped your cherub smile and
form when you were only three.
It cannot be, it cannot be.

I miss you, I miss you.
To pick up the phone, dial your
number, hear your voice—
To wish you a Happy 16th Birthday,
is a desire from me.
It cannot be, it cannot be.

I miss you, I miss you.
To be by ourselves to laugh, to
gossip, to carry on—
To visit and dine and an R-rated
movie we will see.
It cannot be, it cannot be.

I miss you, I miss you.
Too short a time to do even half of
what we'd planned—
Soulmates now on different planes,
decided by a higher command.
Never again conspirators and
confidantes, like aunts and nieces
are—
Suddenly you are Heaven's newest,
brightest star!

Gina Venglass
LOOKING THROUGH THE GLASS
Please tell me what I
 should do.
My love I'm trying
 desperately to see through.

My heart, you see is
 bleeding too,
And I know that you too,
 can not see through.

My eyes, trying to see
 into the glass,
The glance I gave,
 you simply let pass.

It's gone, forget it, but
 it was much too strong,
The love we shared,
 couldn't be wrong.

The glance is now gone,
 and so am I.
I had to leave,
 I had to die.

Now don't weep, for
 there's nothing you can do.
You didn't try,
 so you didn't see through.

Elizabeth G Kelley

Elizabeth G Kelley
THE LIGHTNING WHIPPED THE SHADOWS INTENSELY

To the man who taught me how to love selflessly—I will always love you—

The lightning whipped the shadows intensely
Intimidating the world—
For endless hours.
And in those coagulated moments,
Our passion was kindled by the flame of solidarity.
You were gentle when you touched me—
Reverently,
Silently,
The dichotomy of two worlds touched—
Silence of nature—fury of nature,
Contrasting partners used to separate us to a spatial plane
only we can share.
you led, I followed.
In that dreamlike state we merged—
Pulling each other into ourselves
For only the moment.
And we descended,
Loving two people at once.

Carl L Frye
DREAMS

You walk along a beach on a warm summers day
thinking of what you want to be or what you can be
telling yourself what to say
focus your eyes on what you want to see.
Just Imagine a flower that just begins to bloom
the rain and sun washes nature off its petals
but when they die it's like a dark filled room
like a contest without the medals.
A boyhood dream of having a home
which no man can take away
god protects it like a dome
in the night or the day.
Dreams are like the colors of a rainbow in the sky
their colors are so different and bold
they fade away as time goes by
it turns warm air into cold.
Dreams can be very happy
Dreams can be very sad
Dreams can be catchy
when you are glad.

Clara Catron
THE VISITOR

To my son Jerry for his support and faith in me.

In the middle of the night when silence abounds,
It is there in the darkness without warning she bounds,
Her eyes leering and cold as ice,
She seeks out her victim and life is her price;

As she peered through my window I stood very still,
And with a single glance my heart she did chill,
She spun around twice, then with leaps and bounds,
On the tip of her toes and without a sound,
She danced through my window then, settled down;

Who are you? I asked, and why are you here?
She crossed her legs and sat on the floor,
Stretched out her hands and closed the door.
"I am heartache and tears, I am torment and fears,
I'd never have come, but you invited me here."

We sat there for hours in silence and stared,
The longer she stayed, the more I, afraid,
Then as dark turn to day, she started to fade,
Who are you? I asked, as she faded away.

"I am anger and despair, I am vain but still I'm fair,
And if your misery does cling to me,
I'll come again,
Someday . . ."

Samantha Ann Marks
DEATH

A deep, dark, place,
 Full of misery and despair,
It's always around us,
 Yet it's not there,
There's no way of telling,
 How soon it'll be here,
It comes when it wants to,
 It's always near,
So why must we then,
 Always fear,
The presence of death.

Judi McFadden
BIRTH OF A GRANDCHILD

To my birthen children, Kerry Jo and Lance and all the others who adopted me as their mom.

Can you now feel the miracle, of life's everlasting flame?
In this new beginning, born joyfully through you in pain.

Through the silver cord; stretched threading and drifting through time,

Linking all in life's perpetuity; the universe is thine.

This feel of infinity; bonding, through you and through me
Lifetimes unremembered, with those that are yet to be.

Now you, and then he, will come through the passing years
To this same awe at life's wonder, held fast in love, laughter and tears.
My heart can't hold all these feelings that flow, in an overpowering torrent.
And this river of words can only begin, to capture this soft fleeting moment.
As a dark sky riven by lightning, emblazoned forever in mind so, for a second, the key to life's mystery and all the answers are mine.

Melba Todd
THE COLORS OF CHRISTMAS

The greatest story that was ever told,
Is seen in the white, red, green and gold.
Colors of Christmas each year we do see,
When God sent his son for you and me.

White is for purity like the fresh fallen snow,
Our saviour was pure no sin did he know.
Red is for love God gave to all men,
The blood shed by Jesus to cleanse us from sin.

Green stands for life as seen in each tree,
The cross that he bore to set all men free.
Gold the most precious and sought for by all,
Can only be found when on Jesus you call.

The colors of Christmas are special to me,
They remind me of Jesus, my saviour, you see.
Thru him I am pure bathed in his love,
Life and true riches from my father above.

Courtney Landes
SHOOTING STARS

I look out the window of my hiding place,
and see the glitter of stars
embedded in the ebony canvas.

One falls in a split second across the sky.

Silent tears roll down my cheek
as I think of how I am so like
that star.

Shining and bright, the envy of all
until the darkness enveloped me,
beheld me,
then cast me out of its sparkling
domain.

My riches of affection slipped
through my fingers
like precious bits of sand.

The more I try to catch myself,
the more I find myself falling,
falling,
falling,

like the star I thought I saw
in the silence of the night.

Mary Maloney
SOLILOQUY OF LOVE

To my God; my mentor, my creator, my friend; with all the gratitude, and love, that I possess . . .

How can these words tell all you mean to me?
How can eternity tell, unfathomed time?
Does the poet's quill know instinctively,
Words that are written upon the page must rhyme?
Do dying leaves that in the autumn fall,
Vow to replenish the barren boughs come spring?
Can burning sands upon the shore recall,
The cool relief the moon-lit tide will bring?
How do the stars light years above us shine;
Penetrating through the furthest realms of space?
Can your hands though absent be held in mine;
Your endless love my loneliness replace?
Just as our bond, no force of time can sever;
The winds will breathe, the promise, of forever.

James T Roberts

James T Roberts
SPRING TIME

In Loving Memory Of My Dear Mother SARAH E. PAYTON. And My Darling and Loving Wife DARLENE ROBERTS.

The Glow of Spring
Will Soon Be Upon Us,
As The Snow Will Soon
Be Melted Away.

For Far Beyond The Clouds
Does Lie,
The Warmth That Comes
Our Way.

The Signs of Spring
Each Bring New Life,
With Each Passing Day.

They Fill Our Hearts
With Joy And Love,
To Hear The Birds Sing.

The Flowers Bloom
The Forests Turn Green,
At Last! It's Spring.

Seal Anderson
FRIENDS GROW UP TOGETHER

Friends grow up together,
Friends grow old together.

Friends share experiences,
and they give without expecting.

Friends understand,
and they love you in spite of
your faults.

A friend is someone who will tell
you the truth . . .
even though you may not want
to hear it.

They also remember the little
things,
even when others forget.

Friends will always listen,
and will be honest and true.

A friend is one who you can respect,
and with respect have total trust.

With each new day, you meet new
people;
With each new person, a new
experience;
With each new experience, a little
more knowledge.

With more knowledge, one can
appreciate
what a true friend really is.

Thanks, FRIEND!

"Seal"

Alma D Ferebee
GOD'S WONDERFUL CREATION

To all of my wonderful family and friends, the sick, well, needy & rich folks.

There was a void, a terrible void
Darkness, darkness everywhere
And out of this darkness
The Good Lord spoke
He said "This darkness, I revoke!

He raised his arms in glory,
He said—"Let there be light!
There appeared a beautiful bright ray
which he called day
And the darkness, he called night!

God said, "Let there be land & seas!
He created the animals, birds & bees
Swept the wind thru the trees
Placed the stars moon and sun
And when it was done
God said, "It is good! It is good!

Then God had another plan
He said "Let us create man!
That he did, from a bit of dust
Man emerged, from part of earth's
crust
God said. "It is good." It is very
good.

God placed Adam in deep sleep
Took one of his ribs and a woman
was made.
Gave them Eden and laws to keep.
He raised his arms in glory and said
It is good! It is very good.
Yes, God basked in his glory and my
friends—This is a true story!

Della Mae Kinney
THE WONDER OF IT

Did you ever wonder?
How does a little house-wren know
When it is time to begin
To build a little nest

Did you ever wonder?
How it knows just what to pick
It looks here, there and everywhere
For just the right twig or stick

Did you ever wonder?
How it decides just the right place
It wants to put the nest
It always seems to pick a place that is
best

Sometimes in a little bird-house
Or just a hole in a post
Sometimes in an unused light meter
box
Or anywhere it likes the most

Did you ever wonder?
When it has laid its eggs
How it knows to set on them
Until they hatch

Did you ever wonder?
How it can know
It must feel the baby-birds constantly
To enable them to grow

Did you ever wonder?
When the babies are grown
And each fly away
If they recognize each other, at a
later day

As I look out my window
At this little brown house-wren
And know it is looking for a place
To build a little nest
I wonder?

Elizabeth Winslett
TO A WONDERFUL BROTHER

To my wonderful brother, a
charming little man.
Like most men you seem to be
searching, searching
For some thing but know not what.
Searching over land and sea.
Searching in air and sky.

But know not why.
Is it a special Lady love?
To take you by the hand,
And lead you,

Like a fluttering little Dove
To the world of your secret dreams?
You are searching too, it seems
For the truth of Being.
You search here, you search there.
You search every where,
Except with in, That is.

Leona Ann B Sevin
WHAT IS HAPPINESS

To the ones I love, and to our world of love. To my family, love always your mom. "Leona B. Sevin."

Happiness.
It can be defined. It's a certain
mood.
A state of mind.
It's sharing everyday affairs.
With one who understands, and one
who cares.
It's a tender look, or a tender
touch,
that says, "I love you." so very
much.
It's a smile of welcome when
you're blue.
A dream that's shared,
A dream for two.
Happiness is even more than this,
it's a warm embrace, and a
tender kiss.
It's a special blessing from above.
"Happiness" is what you have, when
you're in
"LOVE."

John Ledbetter
POEM FOR A FRIEND

This really seemed the thing to do
To write a poem for a friend like you
For you are so special and close to
me
A friend for now and always to be
Someone close and Oh so dear
Always willing to lend an ear
Hard to find are friends that are true
Friends who laugh and cry with you
I wrote this poem for you you see
Because you are that and more to me
One last thing to you my friend
I hope our friendship will never
end . . .

Bonita Lea Braneff
CHANGES

To life . . . To a new adventure! . . . February 1989

Clamoring through a colorful past
I turn my head and feel at last!
The magic deep within me rises
My future full of amazing surprises
I seek not structure
Nor a path
I feel a sense to now unlatch
The spirited soul deep within
I brace myself—time to
Begin . . . !

Dora McDearmon

Dora McDearmon
LOVE

To my husband, Bill

If I could speak what's in my heart,
If I could tell of all or part,
If I could show my feelings true,
I'd shout and shout my love for you.

I'd say perhaps too much at once
And be not understood;
O where are ears without the fears
That will hear only Good?

I'd like to sing of Love I feel,
It almost does consume me.
But where are eyes that can but see
This yearning that is in me?

If only you could understand
The 'why' of things I do,
You would be warm and tender,
Dear,
You'd have to love me too!

Margo Kreis
SECRETS OF MY HEART

Just as shadows hang heavy in the
night
And lingering clouds keep out the
sunlight
So are moments of memories
Hiding down deep inside of me
Searching and searching
For a way to come thru
As if they could bring back, the Love
I once knew

But there they'll stay, The Secrets of
my Heart
Hiding away in the coldness of dark
Never to be gently touched by the
soft moonlight
Nor to be kissed once again by the
warm sunlight
So I must make believe they never
were
Then die I will from a life so obscure

For how do I find happiness
When shadows of sadness follow so
near
Or not feel lonely, when loneliness is
here
And how can I be warm
When the absence of Love is bitter
cold
Or see the beauty of a flower if it
doesn't unfold

Well the answers all lie
In the Secrets of my Heart
Waiting to be free, free from the dark
Then the stillness of tomorrow
Will drift slowly off in the wind
As unfolding beauty takes rapture
within
And the Secrets of My Heart will
give life once again

Antonia Darder
A QUIET PASSION SONG

i search endlessly for words
which fail to come i fret

my soul continues to seek
refuge even from myself i rage

only the deep dark shadows
of the unknown stir within i fear

my ugliness and suffering
reveal only a gentler form i weep

to hear requires the inner
stillness of the deafmute i listen

its meaning easily escapes
the stubbornly proud i learn

only in humility can i find
the song that heals my heart i love

Anna Burtle
HERE AM I

Here I stand so great yet small;
To the world I'll tell it all.
I feel my pulse beat really fast,
In my heart you'll always last.

Holding you tightly in my arms,
I'll let the world bring you NO harm.
Yes; In my heart there's love for
you.
For in my life I start anew.

Paul M Medlick
MARY AND ME

This poem is dedicated to Mary and sweet memories.

High up in heaven resting on a silver
cloud
Sits my wife Mary, of whom I am
quite proud.
My inheritance is five children and
memories Oh so deep
When Mary left me by way of a long
and quiet sleep.
Bitterness, loneliness are with me
along with despair
God, I feel, was not at all quite
honest nor fair.
However, I guess this is the way it
was supposed to be
A short, happy, beautiful life between
Mary and me.
I remember her eyes so tender and oh
so brown
The black hair and laughter hearty
and sound.
The eyes so dark and shining with
love
I am sure this was a gift from God
above.
I must remember that these memories

are of the past
Beautiful memories that will forever last and last.
A new life I have been told I must begin
For my children and I must start over again.
Forget the bitterness, loneliness and all that despair
Because—you see to your children this isn't fair.
Thus, a new life is one that must be
Regardless of the memories between Mary and me.

Christopher D Polasko
TREASURE
Jewels of the bay shine through the darkness,
A fisherman's treasure.
They wind and bend between and around
Through the tight crevices
Without a sound.
Streaks of silver,
Darts with sicle-shaped fins
They shoot out of the dark,
Past the light,
Into the dark,
Gone.

John Logue
WINTER
I look to the bay,
The hills beyond,
And remember
Good fortune - Happier days.

Love, I see some days.
Old love as well,
Long gone now,
As the leaves gone their way.

Long gone now.
Like the mountain.
Bare the leaves,
All gone now.

So I wait.
In a balance.
To live in the love.
That came - not late.

Lester A Johnson Sr
OLD AGE
Your body gets stiff
You get cramps in your legs
Corns on your feet
Feel big as hen eggs

Your teeth are decaying
Your eyesight getting poor
Hair falling out
Hate to go out the door

Nothing to plan for
Not much to expect
Wait for the mailman
With your security check

You feel fairly good
You look pretty well
Thank God you're alive
But old age is hell

Iris Brandes
TOGETHER NO MORE
Together we saw things of life
That others never see.
Together we watched a bird in flight;
Felt the tallness of a tree.

Together we knew the touch of rain;
Heard the muffled humm of the bees.
Together we saw day turn to night;
Felt the gentle caress of a breeze.

Together we shared the beauty and scent of a blossom,
And heard the rippling of a stream.
Together we knew happiness,
As if in a lovely dream.

The sparkling Burgundy that is
Spring turned to summer,
And Summer soon became Fall;
But, quickly upon us came Winter,
The coldest time of all.

The togetherness is over.
It all has ceased to be.
And the heart of life lies as frozen,
As the heart you gave back to me.

E R Abramoski
ONLY IN JUNE
Raindrops like diamonds
Shimmer in the trees,
Shining with brilliance
In the soft summer breeze.
A gentle rain in the night,
Had dampened the earth.
The sweet perfume of flowers
To a freshness gave birth.
A plethora of color in the garden is seen.
A sight one sees only in a dream.
Nature is fragile!
All this will be gone soon.
For a day such as this
Can only happen in June.

Pat Patch
VIEW FROM MY WINDOW

To my children

I wish that I could walk up the drive
To that old fashion ranch that sits on the country side
I look out my window, across the bay
To the rolling green hills, where this lonely ranch lays
Like a symbol of the past, the
"Good Ole Days"
The barn stands so big, so strong so tall
I can just smell the hay, see a horse in a stall
Tho its all in my mind, I bet its all there
Then of course there's the bird songs that float through the air
The cow to be milked, the chickens to feed
A tractor that's "hum'in", the fields to seed,
it's spring you know, a time for grow'in
The family is busy, some how this I'm know'in
In a warm country kitchen, all full of good smell
With jars of canned "everything", that sits on the shelves
From time to time I see a kite in the air

Don't you just know some happy children live there?
A dog that's bark'in, and chasing rabbits
Them scurrying down holes — it's really just habit
Yes, I wish I could go there, so close yet so far
Smell the fresh country air . . . .
. . . Hec — where's the keys to my car!!!

Donna J Rathbone
WHAT LOVE MEANS TO ME
What love means to me,
Comes from up above;
It came from a tiny twig,
sent in the mouth of a dove.

Let's not forget the rainbow,
that came from the Master's hand.
You see, God never forgot about love;
Because it was part of His plan.

And when I see the twinkling stars,
and the moon so bright and gold;
The stars are my diamonds,
They are my riches, and part of God's fold.

Oh yes, there's the sun, the flowers, and the trees,
The tree for the little birds and the flowers for the honey-bees.

And there's a mighty sea,
this reminds me of the tears that God shed for me.
This is what love means to me.

Gloria Narciso McDermott
THE CLOCK OF LIFE
The Clock of Life is wound up
No one knows when it will stop
It's up to Us and GOD!
Live each Moment of every Hour
Live each Hour as your last
Live each Day as it flies past!
Don't put off 'till tomorrow
What we must do Today!
How long is our Fate,
We do not know!
Tomorrow may be too late!

Arline M Tobola
YOU
You have my time and my love
You have my heart and my soul
You have my mind and my thoughts
I see your face, you have my eyes,
I feel you, but you're not there,
You have all of me, and I none of you.
Why is it this way?!
Where is your soul?
You have none, I've been told.
I'm going away into the dark, you have me no more, I never did.

Joanne Roderick
JOHNNY
Johnny called out, but nobody listened.
Johnny was happy, his eyes always glistened.
Mother, father, sister too, they were all proud of you-know-who.
My son, my brother, an angel he is.
Always was, is now, and always will be.
They didn't know what was inside.
They never heard Johnny cry.
Alone, all alone, yet always surrounded. Johnny loved his family but they didn't understand. They never saw the bottle in his hand.
They didn't see, did not realize, they didn't notice the red in his eyes.
They didn't know there were holes in his arms. They didn't know he was doing harm to himself, to his friends, everyone he loved.
He hollered, he screamed, he pushed and he shoved.
The day finally came, of course, they were late.
Johnny had a date with death.
Johnny knew he would, he couldn't take the pressure, there was no way he could. He tried and he tried to make somebody listen. Where is the smile, where is the glisten. Where did they go? Brother, don't do it.
Don't do it son we love you, we care.
The bottle in his hand soon turned to a gun.
BANG, BANG, no more fun.

You know what Johnny did. It's been done before. Please, I'm begging, don't let it be done anymore.

Brooke W Adkinson
AT THE EDGE OF CREATION

A verse of love to my wife Marjorie (Hi Beautiful), whose radiant soul was one with the sea. My warm thanks for you being you.
Our sad world needs lines of beauty to up lift it on wings of light to the horizon of hope. Keep at it Lady . . .
An Alaskan Sourdough salutes you.

Have you ever walked a sandy beach at low tide
With the call of the questing gulls
The sweet sad cries of the sand piper,
The restless roar of the sea,
Pounding the beach,
Keeping you company
On your eternal quest
In search of life's haunting mystery?
If you have, then you stand alone
At the edges of creation
With the tears of life
Playing its sad notes of beauty.

Robert Okey
THE EARTHWORM
Don't dismiss the lowly earthworm too lightly
Especially, if you are one who waits for robin's song in spring
You'd be wise to welcome the aerating soilmaker
He lets life into your lawn and garden bed.

Don't take for granted the contract-ing—expanding angler's worm
For most, he will be a companion in their last home
A place where friends will put off coming
For as long as they can.

Gerald S Szewczyk
DREAM OF DREAMS
Blow wind blow.
Only God can know
where this nation and world

in the future will go.
Sail on sailors and dreamers of dreams.
Fight on in any kind of weather
from jungle heat to bitter cold at the polar extremes.
Let me be a prophet don't say no,
and give my opinion of the only way to go.
Love and freedom, peace and unending joys
are the key words of the future.
Without these words we would all feel as bad,
as a child with no toys.
The love I speak of
is the rarest and most divine.
Something to treasure forever
both yours and mine.
Walking on dreamlove beach

God, child and man
at last hand in hand.
You ask how will this dream of
dreams come to pass?

Not by mans power and might,
but by the grace and spirit of God,
as a gift for us his truest
delight . . . .

Vivian-Deborah Mathews Moeller
MORE, MORE, MORE OF YOU
I come full circle everytime I meet
you.
I never fill complete without you.
I love you not only when I need you.
For you have always been there for
me to do.
I WANT MORE, MORE, MORE OF
YOU.

My life I cry to a kneeling surrendering.
To breathe your essence of remembering.
Control if what I want to lose to you.
Home is where I desperately need to
come to.

Myself as you intended I want to
conclude.
But now I WANT MORE, MORE,
MORE OF YOU.
Please penetrate my very soul.
Dear GOD I want to be saved.
I WANT MORE, MORE, MORE
OF YOU.

Gabrielle Dyer
YOU CAN NO LONGER HURT ME
You can no longer hurt me,
I'm not by your side.
The love that we had has all
dissappeard.

The memories are vague and the
crisp autumn air has blown them
away.

Don't send me any flowers, don't call
on my phone, just go away and leave
me alone.

For now my life is my very own.
I'll do as I like, even stay up all
night.

Your magic has withered—
Your touch gone cold—
You no longer have any control—
No don't even try—you can't make
me cry.

Just send me my check, without
postage due-because what goes
around comes around is so very true.

Dana McCowan
CONFORMITY
Why can't I be the way I want to be?
I'm pushed into a stereotype—
Forced to play a role.
I can't change my mind—
Or my interests.
I'm boxed into a corner—
Doing what's expected of me.
The desire burns deep—
To let go of everything.
But something stops me when I try—
It's society and its friend—
Conformity.

A Russell Biddix
ONE IN AWE
The sun is high
And so am I
From sitting under an oak tree
Watching the clouds rearrange the
sky
Birds flutter past as they succeed to
walk on air
While on the ground a busy squirrel
stops
And asks questions with his stare
What a day for dreaming
Letting countless thoughts be born
What a day for seeing the planet
whose colors I have worn
And the birds
And the trees
And the animals on the ground
Play the planetary anthem with the
combination of their sounds

My eyes are opened wide
As I lie studying the land
With my hair haphazardly parted by
the gods' very own hand
Oh, in this dreamy state I could stay
and never go back again
That is unless the gods look down
And decide to make it rain

Virginia Lemperle
COUNTRY DOCTOR

Dedication to Dr. Louis Schaffer

His office hours were supposed to be
seven to nine in the evenings,
afternoons, one to three,
but more often it was seven to eleven
or one to four, or even more
with house calls in between
and lunch and dinner just whenever,
all depending on current epidemics
or the whims of weather.
Sometimes there was no charge
for those who couldn't pay
and if a child was sick he wouldn't
turn him away
or tell his patients, "Come back
another day"
and when he lost a loved one, I have
seen him cry
and say "I am not God".
"We cannot save them all" was my
reply.

Donna M McQueen
HOMELESS
Once a home for drunks,
and ladies of the night.
Now its home for children
from teen right down to tykes.

Living on the streets,
eating day by day.
We are the children,
that's been thrown away.

Eating from the trash cans,
chasing the rats away,
sleeping in the alleys,
to keep the cold at bay.

People walk right past us,
like we are not here.
No one even notices,
no one seems to care.

Go home lucky people,
please pray for us tonight,
ask, Our God, Our Saviour,
to help you do what's right.

Please help the homeless!

Tina Oliver
I CLOSED MY EYES THIS MORNING . . . . .
I closed my eyes this morning,
I dreamt of the wind through
The trees, in the clouds an
Eagle was soaring, and for
A moment I was free.

I remembered all I had known
As a child, my hopes and dreams,
I thought of all that this world
Had shown is they last as long as
Winter leaves.

I closed my eyes again,
My thoughts hovered above
The water, at fantastic speeds
On the ocean, beyond the clouds
And further.
I saw all that I had lost,
My heart, my way, my pride
I thought of the man on the cross
And for the reason that he died.

I opened my eyes this morning
To a dying race throwing stones
At an eagle slowly falling,
Badly wounded and all alone.

I closed my eyes again
And thought it best to leave
Them shut, for all that we were
Intended to become, I realized,
Is all that we are not.

Dwayne Jorgensen
THE KISS

This poem is dedicated to my family and friends and to my special girl Karen

A yielded heart is less a task
persuaded in her kiss
it calms lifes wonderment of ache
in silent soothing bliss

I long to meet her lips with mine
when distance is a foe
but even though our lips are far
her last kiss lingers so

And even in the depth of night
when slumber rests my love
the stars will witness to the truth
her lips I'm dreaming of

Texana C Hollis
MOVE ON

I dedicate this poem to my lovely grand daughter, Karen Dawn Hollis.

Don't sit around sad, worrying about
things you might have had, make use
of what you have and be glad

Turn sadness into gladness, and
worry
into laughter. Look up and around
the
things that bring you down, wear a
smile
instead of a frown and move on!

Robert Prior
ENLIGHTENMENT

Please guide little ships
To reach a quiet rest
For all tracks are washed away

A hidden shadow lies there
Misty clouds masquerade to taunt
and tease.
The weary sailor eager for a sign
as the day grows old.
Hah! The plunging fire is diving to
it's quench.

Shearing off the shrouding veil
there's instant endless sight.
Confirmation cleanses for the dark
is now just lack of light
And the compass knows.

Tamera Fox-Coley
ANCIENT NIGHT

This poem is dedicated to my mother, Miriam Larimore, and all women with strong devotion giving support to their children in the arts.

A woman molds herself easily
with light of the moon
a purple candle
burns
into her music

the breath
the flute
sound
the voice of her song
to flow skyward
expanding the vibrations
of dreams
first collected
then released
by the mutable chords
of ancient night
and a woman
with light of the moon

Janice R McKellar
ODE TO THE NEW MOON
She rises, wan and pale,
And takes her place in azure vale
That is the sky.

As slender as a vine.
Too maidenly to brightly shine
In the sky.

He watches, not too far,
That shining Knight, the Evening
Star
Of the sky.

Guarding through eternity
The new moon's fresh virginity
In the sky.

Barry Cutlip
BIKING IS FREEDOM

To my loving and very beautiful wife, Rita

Being a biker is more than it seems,
its bein' free to experience your
dreams.
For some its a lifestyle—filled with
pride;
for others its being, what most
people hide.

Society hates us, 'cause they don't
understand,
why once in a while, we get outta
hand.
To them we're a menace, disgrace-
ful, EGAD!
but under the surface, we're not all
that bad.

We just like bein' free, is that such a
sin?
enjoyin' what's left of this world that
we're in.
We don't like cars 'cause they shut
nature out,
feelin the wind . . . . that's what its
about!

If you've never tried it, then don't put
it down,
what's wrong with relaxing, and
acting a clown?
Life is too short, and for some its
plain boring,
come out of your shell and do some
exploring.

So next time you see a biker go by,
with a smile on his face, a gleam in
his eye;
Give him a wave, so he can see,
that you don't blame him, for bein'
FREE.

Bernice Walker
MY DEAR JESSIE (The Night Jessie Died)

My Dear Jessie,
I wonder what you saw that night you left. I tried really hard to see it myself; your face lit up, your eyes aglow; your breathing was fast, but your pulse was slow; you didn't cry out nor did you frown, I called your name and you looked around. Your heartbeat was slow, your blood pressure fell, but the look in your eyes said all is well! As the girls and I stood around your bed, calling out your name and rubbing your head, you were so relaxed and looked so calm—seems you were safe in Jesus' arms. Then I thanked God for all our years, as I noticed in your eyes there were no tears.
You'd prayed not to go home crying.
God answered your prayer even when you were dying.

Now it's not heard for me to be strong, for I too am standing the safety zone.

You said that you wold be all right before you left us that Thursday night.

So, until we meet on that other shore, please wait for me at Heaven's door.

Sincerely,
Bernice

Diane York
SUMMER'S END

Remember those wild years
Before our hair turned gray
And while I'm alive
I want those memories to stay.

Remember all the things we did
And said and talked about
And remember when we got in trouble
We'd throw a fit and pout.

Remember all the stories we'd makeup
About the killer butterflies
And we were always able to convince
Little brother that they weren't lies.

Now while our bodies weaken
And our spirits grow light
I'm reminded of those forgotten years
And dream of them every night.

Leann Strait-McGrath
INATTENTION

The child huddled in the doorway.
His mind, like his stomach, empty of life.
And the people passed him by,
Not seeing, like the child.

The child walked the streets,
Searching for the one who abandoned him,
The one who betrayed all that he knew.
The child was looking for his mother.

And the people passed him by,
Blind to his needs.
Blind to their own humanities.
Blinded by it all.

And the child searched on for the one.
Wallowing in his pain and hungry belly.
Blinded by the humanities of the others.
Until he found the light.

And the people stopped and led him into the light.
No longer were they blind.
Life was a lot clearer now.
And the one was there.

Welcoming the child with open arms.
Warming him in her bosom of humanity.
Filling his belly with the warmth of it all.
The search is over. The child is home.

And the people no longer pass by.
They are stopping, looking.
No longer blinded by it all.
Aware now of their own humanities.

Sherry L Meszaros
MEMORIES AND FADED DREAMS

Memories and faded dreams
That's all I have
So what does life mean
If you can't forget the past

Our love was so grand
But you went away
So now alone I stand
Only to exist day by day

Now my tears fall down like rain
I wish you were here with me
To chase away all my pain
And live the dreams we used to dream

Everytime I think of you
My heart cries in vain
I wish I could die too
For I'll never love again

This band of gold I wear
I will wear forever
To prove my love, my dear
My heart will endeavor

Ann Wellborn

Ann Wellborn
MY SON

This poem is dedicated to my son Bob first. But, it is also for my two grandsons Michael and Brian with the hope they succeed as well as their "dad" did.

I was thinking about you as I so often do, with thoughts that span the years.
Considering how far you've come from the days of childhood tears.
Every emotion that exists has touched your life in some way,
And helped to make and mold you into the man you are today.

They say a mothers love is blind perhaps that's true in ways.
But I'd hope it wouldn't cause foolish pride to color my feeling of praise.
Because, you see, I do realize perfection lies out of reach.
For you, for me, for everyone life has lessons to teach.

And the only way we seem to learn is to stumble and rise again.
Each fall chips at our self esteem as we take it on the chin.
Painful experience causes character growth, essential if we're to succeed.
Life never promised paths free of stones or gardens without any weeds.

As a mother I'm sorry you must be bruised as you travel along your way.
But at the same time I rejoice to see what developed from your lump of clay.
As I look back I seem to recall having only one main wish for you.
Just to be a man, true to yourself and honest in all that you do.

So pardon me now if I can't help but smile when reflecting on how you've grown
I like what I see and it pleases me to know you're a man of your own.

Christy A Dargitz
COTTONWOOD

It is Spring.
Soft, white seeds parachute
down from the cottonwoods.
They ride the current
so easily,
Looking for a good spot
to take root.

I wish I could be
one of those seeds
Drifting away,
Far from the noise
of the city
And all the commotion,
that litters my life.

Faye Johnson
THE PREACHER

Back in April, I met a man.
His hair was silver and his cheeks were tan.
He talked like a Saint
And I knew right away.
That God had sent him, to save my day.
It turned out, he was a Preacher.
I went to hear him speak.
And when you heard him Pray
Your body got so weak.
When ever I missed a service
He came out to check on me.
I knew that he had something
That you couldn't see.
It tis the Holy Spirit
He told me one day.
And you can have it too
If you'll give your heart away.
Now if you want to hear a sermon
That will knock you off your feet.
Just go up to Calvary Church,
And hear James Justice Preach.

Alicia Valadez-Abeyta
IN LIFE

To my husband Alfonso, my best friend

We are recruited in the Navy to try ourselves at sea.
The Army is many a jungle, what growth is there for me.
The Air Force sends me airborne, I go to try my wings.
And all life in between search in what it brings.
Oh what adventures facing life is through all of this.
But watch the arrows and fire, and what life really is.
The fiery arrows of the enemy leads us through the cross.
In God's army we learn why our Savior gave his life for us.
God portrays his love a sacrifice for our redemption.
The battles we fight in life is a war for our salvation.
If you think you can escape the strife you haven't got the light.
With God's virtues as our weapons, strength and the will to fight.
It is not a hand to hand battle but a spiritual warfare.
Prepare and gird yourself with the armor of faith getting there.
And with banners flying high proclaiming love for one another.
Lifting Jesus high our victor, a gift from God the Father.

Mark Allen Brewer
DEPRESSION

How much longer will the pain and torment last?
How much longer will I continue to live in the past?
Will this depression befriend me or, will it betray?
Will my sanity leave me or, will it stay?

I'm out on the edge of madness;—not sure how to get back.
I tried to reach happiness, I was way off track.
Darkness engulfs the inner folds of my temporal lobe.
I am a man carrying a much too heavy load.

What am I, the half-sane man, to do, now that I see all is lost?
Should I shrug off the rest of my sanity and not think of the cost?
Or, should I go to "The System" and ask for some type of assistance?
Maybe, then, with the right help, I could break down the resistance.

The earth, for me, is off it's axis and spinning way too fast.
I'm on the stage playing the tragic herd; the fool in life's cast.
Maybe I should give up hope and wish for a final curtain.
Oh, well, whatever comes about, I am lost to these depressed feelings.
That's for certain.

Sabrina Henry
GREAT OCEAN

The waves roaring in the wind,
The storms will never ever end,
Awful waves won't cease to roar,
They will always be there for . . .

Just seeing the waves of wrath,
And have them come up my path!
They seem so mighty and so great,
Soon they will disintegrate.

The currents rise with the sun,
Down it goes, they're not done!
Oh, they never seem to cease,
Instead, they just increase.

Bernadette Surprenant
YOU

I saw you and knew at a glance,
Faith had willed it, t'was not by chance,
Our paths had crossed and I had met,
Someone I never would forget.

Then came the day you took me home,
I know my eyes too brightly shone,
My heart beat fast, my feet had wings,
To me your words were precious things,

Many wonderful times, mine and yours,
Beneath the sun in the great outdoors,
Never to be forgotten hours and days,
Remember the things we'd do and say.

When the setting sun gives place
to the moon beams bright,
And the last hour of dusk
closes into night,
Tender memories pass and my love
is stirred anew,
With thoughts of happy days
side by side with you.

Heidi Loria
ELEVENTH HOUR

This poem is dedicated to the world and it's infinite beauty.

Touching the sands of time;
Evolving from the soul to eternity.
The visions of life encapsuled in the
Womb of the whole being.
Sifted finer than air.
Fire the minds of those who do not
Conceive the richness of life,
Living their lies, existing in time,
Feeding off others like parasites,
And suffocating them.

They offer nothing to the source of Life.
Mindless they pass through this life,
Victims of their own prisons . . .
Their hell on earth!
Soulless for they have created no love,
Unfulfilled by the realms of two worlds.
Darkness passes through their life with
Little hope of light.
Generated by the barren sickness
possessed in their minds,
They dry and blow away . . .

Carol Schmidt Reichart
HEAVEN HAS CALLED

In loving memory of: Adam & Eileen Schmidt and Ambrose & Evelyn Reichart

Beyond our earthly powers wait . . .
Upon our heavens golden gate . . .
There sits our Master with his slate . . .
To check our loved ones, don't be late!

We sit in prayer along the way . . .
We say our blessings everyday . . .
We pray for all whom are in dismay . . .
To guide them safely on their way . . .

Our time is near, hear the trumpets blow . . .
All loved ones bustle to and fro . . .
Everyone we do and don't know . . .
Are all lined up in one long row . . .

To say their final farewells, goodbyes . . .
The preacher cuts all our final ties . . .
We bow our heads in sadness and with our sighs . . .
To say our final goodbyes . . . goodbyes!

A E Bernstein
DISTANT LIGHTS
Time and space become one as thoughts interweave with reality.

We get lost in our own images, trying desperately to interpret their meaning.

I find myself searching for inner peace, yet it is no where to be found.

A deserted beach with only the distant lights of civilization brings a feeling of tranquility over me.

I'm not sure who I am, or where I'm going, but I know that here I am one with the universe, at peace with my soul.

Some days I just close my eyes and think about that beach. Like an exercise in guided imagery, this is my reality, my peace, my sanity.

Emily Wieja
I DON'T KNOW WHY YOU STAND APART
I don't know why you stand apart,
From all the rest, a lonely heart
I look at you in the eyes,
holding in all my cries
You look away, my very
cruel price to pay.

David Woodard
THE BIG BIRDS
Way up in the clear blue sky,
are mighty birds that fly so high
With weary people in the hearth,
anticipating somewhere farth
I often wonder to or fro,
those roaring engines take them so
Many times I'd dream,
I were flying one with gleam
It makes it almost seem,
they are mere flying machines.

Vicki Bea Linn
COLORADO
Colorado, The Centennial State, was admitted to the Union in 1876—
From Golden wheat fields, Majestic Rocky Mountains, and a clear blue, sky singer John Denver called Colorado his "Rocky Mountain High"—
Skiing, Alpine Mountains, and Trout streams, Colorado is a land where Urban dwellers can fulfill their dreams—
In the 1800's Colorado was rich in silver and gold, "The Saga of Baby Doe", is one of the greatest mining stories ever told!
Four Hero Astronauts hailed from this state—Scott Carpenter, Jack Swigert, Walter Schirra, Ellison Onizuka—from Mercury, Apollo and Challenger, Ellison Onizuka met his tragic fate!
Governor Roy Romer is Chief Executive of this state, he hopes to keep Colorado "Top Rate!"
Colorado has everything to offer here—from Broncos Pro football, Dynamic Denver, The Western stock show, wheat Western Colorado Peaches, to COORS, Rocky Mountain Spring water beer!
Colorado offers both Urban and Country life. On weekends Denverites head for the mountains to escape "city strife"!
Colorado is the land of the free,
Colorado is where I'd rather be!

William A Bryson
THERE COMES A TIME

This is for two ladies in my life. My wife Gayle who inspires me to write and my friend Susan Keller who pushes me to publish. Bill

There comes a time in all our lives,
Decisions must be made.
We stand and fight or run and hide,
Our debts must all be paid.
We seek the truth and in our youth
Our naive eyes wide open.
We dive headlong and sing our song,
Yet feelings go unspoken.
The pain and strife controls our life,
And optimisms burn.
Our blood runs hot, we take our shot
At goals we seek to earn.
We try our best and on the road
To education's end,
By standing tall we still feel small
Enough to not pretend.

Terry L Balthazor
PICKETH ME

This poem is dedicated to Jackie, an inspiration to my writing.

picketh me, forever to be yours
I will love you, for I am the rose of red
color me no mind, in passion I spread,
I thank you for giving thought
from the beauty of you I always got
pamper me for I may live long,
losing petals only means I am in your song
when I am gone, I will return the color that says forever
I will stay and promise you the nevers,
so I will forever be yours to picketh me

Barbara E Gengler
WHO IS SHE?
"MOTHER," her children call her
What a magnificent name.
To think
It was these children
Who rewarded her this fame.
"DAUGHTER," her parents call her
What a grown-up girl.
To think
It was these parents
Who tried to give her the world.
"WIFE," her husband calls her
What a wonderful gal.
To think
It was this husband
To whom she was friend, lover, cook and pal.
"ME," I call myself
What a wonderful she.
To think
It is myself
Who makes all these people happy.

Shirley Grace Morgan
DREAMEN
Forever drifting through misty nights of sleep's calm loveliness.
The day's sorrows float into nothingness
Sailing, always upward, upward through the stars. We drift through beauty that's only ours.
Eternity, is the heart's desire—We forever seek peace from the eternal fires.
Gliding to earth on misty wings.
Another dawn the heavens bring
Where we drifted to and fro, only the galaxies will ever know.

Lovie Lee Borchardt Phd

Lovie Lee Borchardt Phd
EXPRESSING MY LOVE

This poem is dedicated to my two daughters, Donna Borchardt Cox, Millie Borchardt Matthews, my late husband, Raphael David Borchardt, and my immediate family.

How can I say, I love you?
There are so many ways:
Holding your hand when you need me,
Helping to brighten your days.

Bringing to you gladness
When you're feeling blue,
Cheering you onward,
Saying, "I love you."

Sensing your need,
Feeling with you your pain,
Sharing your music
In all its refrain.

Picking you up
When e're you fall,
Bringing to you laughter,
Heeding your call.

Looking into your eyes,
Showing you I care,
Whispering to the Father
Your name in my prayer.

Edna Mae Henning
ABORTION.
Don't take that breath, just let it breathe
It is a bundle of joy for you or me,
Conceived in a moment with ecstasy and love
And blessed from beginning from the Father above.

Don't rob it of life, just let it live
It has so much to offer, so much to give.
Time can only tell, a great blessing it'll be
It'll fill your life with love from here to eternity.

Just give it a chance, it will survive
Just let it come forth with a new and precious life
A new and healthy creature that little bundle of love
Was sent from heaven to earth, by the great Master up above.

It won't be too much trouble, love it and watch it grow

Into somebody special, a special person you'll always know
As each day it passes, you'll be glad you let it live

That precious bundle of joy, with so much love to give.

Many times it'll make you happy, many times it'll make you smile,
You'll look around, say thank you Lord, for this precious child.
Wouldn't trade it for money, riches or anything
It puts within my heart a song, and causes me to sing.

Marian Egenberger
CHRISTMAS NIGHT
In a stable full of hay
 on a cold winter's night
Mary gave birth to the Christ Child
 under a star shining bright

When the babe was born
 and was wrapped in swaddling clothes
then laid in a manger
 to keep warm from the snows

The bells started ringing
 and the stars shining bright
the angels were singing
 bless this Christ Child tonight

Oh little town of Bethlehem
 where this child is born tonight
the world shall celebrate his birth
 with singing and bright lights

The kings and shepherds traveling from afar
 following the brightness of the beautiful star
bearing gifts for the babe lying in the hay
 all were rejoicing this Christmas Day.

Lois Spradling
A MIRACLE
One day I cried to Jesus
 Please take away my sins,
He heard my cry and answered,
 A drunken wretch He cleansed.

He satisfied my longings,
 And gave me joy and peace
Now contentment of this world,
 No longer do I seek.

He healed my aching body,
 And set my mind at ease;
He said, "You can have Life Everlasting,
 If you will only believe."

He baptized me with The Holy Ghost
 With Fire and with Power,
Followed with Signs and Gifts
 Bestowed for this hour.

Marilyn T White
LIFE
Life is full of letdowns and discouragements
And very often you will stumble and fall.
'Tis also full of an abundance of fulfillments and accomplishments
And these will all make you feel about ten feet tall.

It is full of joys and sorrows
All an intricate part of life's big game.
When it is sad there will be better tomorrows
And when it is joyful you will be glad those days to claim.

You will meet some who are bubbling over with love,
And sadly you will meet those full of hate.
However, no matter where your paths may lead you,
You will always find many folks who are truly great.

If you can master the discouragements and sorrows,
And derive the most from the accomplishments and the joys,
You will find life overflowing with many new tomorrows
And indeed a most precious thing to employ.

Those who love you will give you guidance and lend a helping hand,
Yet there will be moments when you will feel completely forsaken
And you will feel left in this world all alone.
Try never to let your faith be shattered and you will find you have really grown.

Karan Louise Gilliam
THE START
These are the days when you sit and ponder away.
Noticing how blue the sky is, and watching the tall trees sway.

Looking as far as the eye can see, and wondering how all <u>this</u> could be
I crept deeper and deeper into my heart, trying to figure out a logical start.

A start to end all of my doubts and fears, something that's going to wipe away my tears—
Something that makes people rejoice and sing—
Something that cures everything.

I found it in the book of love; the start has come from up above.

Betty (Daniels) Poulos
FAMILY REUNION

To the celebration of Mathew and Charlotte Smith—Ft. Collins, Colorado—July 1988

When I heard of Nottingham and Sherwood
I thought of Robin Hood
A favorite character from my youth
Who lived in Hollywood

To learn that there was kin of mine
Who resided there, back then
Gave me the biggest culture shock
Since I can't remember when

I started out like most folks
Just my dad and mom and me.
Then my sister came along
To enlarge the family tree.

I remember all my grandparents
The memories are sweet
Aunts, Uncles and cousins
Made the circle seem complete

There were many happy times
Times I'll always treasure
I had a happy childhood
The best by any measure

I pondered not the future,
Nor lingered in the past
An occasional tale of an ancestor
But the reflections didn't last

Just a few short months ago
I learned, and news to me
There are lots more limbs than I had thought
On the old family tree

My schoolbooks spoke of the Mayflower
And to discover, after all these years
That I had relatives even there
On America's first frontiers

The good book said go forth and multiply
And we added and divided.
The population grew considerably
With people we'd provided

There are cousins now
From coast to coast
With many occupations
I greet the many here today
With a rush of jubilation

A salute to the long gone past
And things we all now nurture
May God bless us, one and all
As we move into the future.

Ida Phelps
A GLORIOUS MORN!
As I look from my window each glorious morn,
There is before me a new day born.
The leaves on the trees in God's rhythm do sway,
We will refresh and cool you they seem to say!
To the feeder comes our Lord's tiny hummingbird,
In the trees the voice of each winged friend can be heard.
I see unique colors from the endless blue sky to the firm brown earth below,
No one but God could create all this perfection I know.
Let us enjoy each new day and begin it with zest,
For the hours are short and it will again be time to rest!

Joyce Fucito-Lenko
MOMMY'S LITTLE GIRL

To my daughter Christina, this poem is your poem. I love you. And in memory of my mother, Thank you for leaving me your love of books and reading. You were right! Books can be your best friends.

Mommy's little girl, So precious, so sweet.
From the top of her head, To her tiny little feet.

So little was she, When first she came home.
Just look at her now, See how she's grown.

Soon will come the day, So cute and so sweet.
When she will start crawling, All around at our feet.

Then comes the day, She will start walking.
And not long after, She will be talking.

Time passes so quickly, Today she starts school.
You want to cry, But you feel like a fool.

Once she was tiny, But she grew up fast.
Be happy for her, But don't forget the past.

The day will come, She'll need a friend.
That's the day, She'll need you again.

Mommy's girl she will be, Even when away from home.
One day she may have, a little girl of her own.

Robin Shimasaki
A TRIBUTE TO BA-CHAN
I just wanted to Thank You
one more time.
For making those golden moments with you,
forever mine.
For showing me that the sun shines through the rain.
As you had, even through all your aches and pain.
For all the comforting words and smiles,
while I was here or away hundreds of miles.
For showing me how to love and care,
in all the things that you would do and share.
For all the thousand other things that you would do,
Grandma, I Thank You, for letting me know and love you.
And as I realize that you'll never physically be here,
I'll still forever Thank You.
For in my heart, you'll always be near.

Loretta Clark Wiggin
NEBRASKA
The people of the prairie sod,
Where skies meet endless skies,
Seem scattered as though swept by God,
Who watches all with knowing eyes;
While rivers flow relentlessly,
Their waters to the sea,
Nebraskans reap their golden wheat,
Their sorghum, corn and soybean.
The wind, the grass the rolling plain,
The prairie reaches wide,
To scattered forest patches
And sunflowers by the side
Of every road that crosses,
Where field meets field of grain.

Brana Vuk

Brana Vuk
I'M GLAD I AM
I'm glad I'm free
Walking on the sand
Watching sunsets
Dancing to the melody
Talking to you
I'm glad I am.

I'm glad I feel
Sometimes strong
Sometimes weak
Living to see beauty
Searching for unity
I'm glad I am.

I'm glad for energy
The love I can give
Learn the ways of wisdom
Yearn to create
Give you a hand

I'm glad I am.

I'm glad I live
I'm a flower
I'm a fire going after desire
Following that star
I'm glad I am.

I'm glad I am here
And I was there
Touching flames of life
Like a curious child
What eternity of pride
I'm glad I am.

Nanceeann Zannone
MY EYES

To anyone man with the fear of anyone else should command action of any kind of exploitation, retains a fear and is less human.

Take apart the head of a human and realize the mind is the first and last weapon beyond any. Though the body, beyond color runs true to the same structure, leaves for no human beyond that, the ability to choose which is RIGHT and WRONG.

There is no greater horror than to see a person of my same life, die before me, with a brittle saundre, and a tear on a no lesser cheek.

What my eyes see isn't as painful as what they feel. To take me because I was bore of color, creed, or belief, that now I'm killed you steal my soul, yet spared my memory. For my memory cannot be slain.

Bonnie Lou Navicki
LOVE AND SPACE

Frankie, my son, may the sun shine on the path you choose to travel Love, Mom

I built my castles in the air
Anchored them with rays of sun
A raging force pulled them apart
Dreams were shattered, "Oh, Despair"
I felt the pain deep in my heart.

Somewhere, someone will come to meet
And find them lying at their feet
Restoring them to fit their needs
Then laugh and dance with glee
Not knowing they belong to me.

If only I could stand close by
Protect them from the undertow
And watch with a tearless eye
I must confess, I can't let go
They were my strength, now I must choose.

"Can I rebuild?," Is there time?
Or should I "snare," "trap" or seize then flee?
"Why Not?"
"I gave them birth, they are me."

Amy Leap
IN NEED OF A FRIEND

Sometimes I feel lonely
in need of a friend
hoping you will be there
and help my heart to mend

Time seems to pass us
faster everyday
I want you to be there
in each and every way

Friends forever
together in our hearts
I will always be there
I hope that we never part

I look in the distance
to untravelled roads
hoping to uncover them
with you and not alone

Tracy Williams Smith
TURN TO ME

To my mother, Carolyn Williams, you taught me about the love of God and to love God; I thank you for the Faith which is in me and it is this Faith that brought forth this poem.

Turn to me my children,
I feel your need is strong.
I see it in your actions,
Your will is almost gone.

Turn to me my children,
Your sorrows are mine.
Your burdens will be lightened,
Your tears will be dried.

Turn to me my children,
On your knees you should be!
Forget these earthly evils
They cannot compare to me!

Turn to me my children,
I died for all your sins.
My arms stretched on a cross
Expanded the earth, taking all in.

Turn to me my children,
I am the Savior! The Light!
Acceptance means forgiveness.
Acceptance means Eternal Life!

Allison Edwards
OF MEN AND LOVE

For my father, Robert T, Leo S. and Brian E., the men who inspired me

Men and love are fine,
As long as kept separate.
Put them together what a joke!
I loved a man once,
the first,
And he beat me then turned his back.
Then I loved another,
He too left me, with many promises,
All shattered and empty nothingness!
But yet there were more,
The next I gave my most prized possession,
After words he too turned and left!
The next I gave my all,
Hope, love, pride, and success,
Alas, he used what he needed,
And was on his way!
Father, boyfriend, lover, and husband,
All men I love, yet all turned away!!

Ed Y Kish
THE LITTLE BIG BOY

To Daniel John Kishinami, my second grandson, whose cheerful and pleasant personality continues to bring sunshine into my life as well as the lives of those who are close to him. There has never been a cloudy day since his arrival.

His roving eyes kept going back to rest
Upon the cake with colored candles three,
Balloons were bobbing, playing overhead,
Well-wishers sang the "Happy Birthday" song;
And elsewhere, people danced in festive mood
Old Year was gliding out as year gone by,
New Year was ticking in to take its place.

His smiling face amid the gifts now bared
So sweet, so pure, so free from cares or woes,
I shared the joy the little big boy felt;
My mind became a chart for plans and plays
I thought of ways to play the helper's role;
With parents, I will steer the way for him
To safely sail the rugged stream of life.

This child of three one day must take his course
As sturdy, upright, useful man of trust;
Before that time arrives, I strongly wish
All drugs that maim clear minds and bodies strong
And weapons aimed to shatter peace be banned;
I hope the flash that brightens up the sky
Will come from peaceful smiles around the world.

Eva Loren Siegel
BIRDS ARE TRILLING OUT THEIR GLADNESS

Welcome, precious morning breezes,
Skipping through my bedroom window
Blowing high my nylon curtains
Bringing respite to the heat-drenched
Like cool trickles down the mountain.

Birds are trilling out their gladness
Chirping prayers from tree and roof-top
Minus harmony or rhythm
Each chip-chirping in bird language
Its delight, O summer breezes!

Even elm tree and magnolia
Welcome you with swinging branches
Stretching high their hands in greeting
Seeking your reviving freshness
Like a lady in her shower.

Alexia Lishnevski
LEAVES DO CHANGE

To Michael

Leaves do change.
Every season, every day.

In the spring they begin to sprout.
Little green popping out.

In the winter trees are bare,
from the leaves that once were there.

In the summer they are green.
Fully grown, how they preen!

And the autumn best of all,
well Known as famous fall!
Leaves are yellow, orange, brown,
red, and green for a crown.

A soft breeze passes by,
blows the leaves,
they fly so high!

Down they come,
down come all.

Down, down, leaves shall fall!

Esther Ronshausen
LIFE'S SEA

I'm only a stone in the sea of life
Tossed about as the waters flow
Never at rest as the waves rise and fall
Forever a captive in the undertow.
Though I long for a quiet resting place
Away from the seas swift rushing pace
I covet the polished stone I will be
If I remain in the path of the raging sea.

So I will not seek the calm waters yet
I'll endure till I'm bright as a stone can get
Then I will emerge from the gruelling sea
Impeccably clean as God wills us to be.

Mary Marshman Miller

Mary Marshman Miller
FAITH

To my husband, Bob, and my children, Stephen, Mark, Kellie, Kerrie and Konnie.

The night falls heavy in the West
With storm clouds in the making,
A tranquil day has come and gone
With foreboding and forsaking—

The bees who gathered honey sweet,
The birds who made their nest,
The butterfly on borrowed time,
The ant put to the test.

Oh, leaves so fragile on the limbs,
Of trees so stately standing,
Begin their dance of agile grace,
Preparing for the landing . . .

On beds of grass so soft beneath,
A final resting place,
Secure in knowledge yet unknown
Of God's redeeming grace.

Beverly Corben
THIS BROWN HOUSE

It is there at the end of a suburban street,
as still as a patient brown moth at its rest.
Unpainted aged wood of a sameness and sigh
hints at bold secrets of a long gone bye and bye.

The porch, with a swing, looks as if it were blessed

by centuries past, and there's also a chair.
A churn, clouded bottles, and other saved things,
are ancient and grayed as the river that sings.

I love this brown house, all so peaceful and neat,
with its time-set of yore, and sunlit patina;
but the fact of it is, it's not twenty years old—
it's in truth more like ten, and the story is told

that an architect's dream, a developer's eye,
envisioned this home as it once 'might have been.'
So a pretty *trompe l'oeil* now turns back the clock,
quite claiming our hearts, once we're over the shock.

It basks in the sunshine, its quaint, quiet charm
disarming the critic, who might think to disdain
its audacious newness free of skew, mold or squeak,
this artful, authentic, artificial antique.

mary taylor tiffany

MY HUSBAND

TALL AND PROUD my husband stands—a complexity of man.
A part of him is still a child, full of wiles and sweet, shy smiles—
so hard to understand.
And yet he strives to walk the line—the wife and kids, the contractors' bids,
reality in demand.

LOW AND GENTLE a father kneels, my children's treasured playmate.
A small girl's hero, a smaller boy's pal—he whistles and chases, wrestles and races
with energy unabated.
He's a teacher, a buddy, a daddy who dispels their fears and kisses their tears
with Love commensurate.

QUIET AND YEARNING my lover waits, patience and passion entwined.
A husband who's there when I need him—a warmth to lean on, a shoulder to cry on,
my best friend defined.
Too, he's my lover, both gentle and wild, very demanding and yet understanding—
our needs are met combined.

TALL AND PROUD my husband stands—this reveller of Life.
A grown-up child with dreams to dream, a husband dependable, a father commendable,
this dear lover of mine.
A friend, a part of me—and yet—the child within will never give in.
I would not, could not change him . . .
I am his wife.

Troy R Beach

THE NIGHT BEFORE SHE DIED WE SAT AND TALKED

The night before she died we sat and talked
of all the dreams she had dreamed.
And she told me of all the things she had never done,
she said there had always been time,
or so it had seemed.

And we spoke of him, the one she loved.
Me being his friend she felt comfortable to talk,
and me being her friend she related all of her pain.
She surprised me by saying she had always known he'd walk

away at the first sign of an honest emotion.
But him having done so after all did not lessen her love.
I told her he was simply not strong enough
to bear the pain of watching her go to heaven above.

She said she believed that could be true
but only partly so, the rest being a weakness
he had for fast cars and new women,
a failing of commitment, and
feelings of a lack of completeness.

Having said that she smiled, and I helped her in
and to her bed where early that morning she died.
With a contented smile on her ashen but still beautiful face,
and the ever present picture of him at her side.

And through my tears I thought she would be angry that I cried.

Marlene Leach

SAD EYES

To Margaret and Christine, two of my most wonderful friends ever.

Dance! and dance!
Whirl through sky blue days,
Jingling jewelry, Flowing dress
Bright laughing eyes and flushed cheeks
Empty head—
You're dead.
Somber eyes, Sallow face
You have seen the Beauty—
And run in the race,
You have lived as a man—
and as an animal.
Now! To decide how to live!
In response you show your back,
to all mankind. Oh Sad Eyes!
You are wise!

Bernard Davis

PEBBLES ON THE BEACH

Pebbles on the Beach, you find them everywhere. As you walk along the beach, breathing the fresh air.
You gaze down at the ground. See many scattered shells. You stop to pick one up. What stories could it tell?
Is there life down there? Living in that shell?
How far has he traveled? Was he all alone? And why did he leave that place that once was his home?
You put an ear to that shell, you hear a distant sound. The sound you hear is from the sea. There's no-one else around.
Did he venture from his shell, and lost his way back home?
And is the sea saying, "you shouldn't be out alone. There's many predators out there waiting for a snack. But if you follow all my sounds, you'll find a safe way back."
So he hides among the weeds searching for a place. Soon he spies an empty shell. A home for himself.
Quickly he darts right in. Not a moment too soon. A predator spied him. He's safe in his lonely room.
Listen to the sea. The stories it could tell. Of Pebbles on the—beach. Midst countless Sea Shells.

Michael A Horn

Michael A Horn

GOODBY MY FRIEND

This is Dedicated to: Jeffrey H. King. When I needed a friend you were there, God knows if it had been possible, I would have been there for you! R.I.P.

I've lost a friend,
Not so long ago.
Due to the anger of another man,
An anger, I pray to God, I'll never know!
I've never understood it,
Now will I ever understand!
How can a simple human being,
Take the life of another man?

I've given it a lot of thought,
But I still can't figure out why.
Why someone should kill for such reasons,
Why someone innocent must die!
Can anyone explain,
Or even try?

Rest in peace my friend,
You'll suffer no more.
Maybe someday my friend,
We'll meet once more!

Kay Selby

DOPERS BLUES

Dedicated to my daughter, Chris. God Bless Her

Honey, before you start foolin' with me,
Let me tell you how it will be.
I shall succeed and make you my slave,
Those stronger than you have gone to the grave.
You think you can never become a disgrace,
Ending up addicted to poppy seed waste.
So you start inhaling me one afternoon,
But into your veins I'll go very soon.
And once I have entered your veins,
The craving for me will drive you insane.
You'll beg and you'll steal for narcotic charm,
Only content when I'm in your arm.
You'll sell your own body just for a buck,
And turn into something vile and corrupt.
And one day you'll realize the monster you've grown,
And solemnly swear to leave me alone.
If you think you can master the mystical knack,
Sweetie . . . try getting me off your back.
You'll vomit, you'll cramp, you'll tie in a knot,
Jangling, your nerves will scream for a shot.
The hot chills, the cold sweats, the withdrawal pains,
Can only be stopped by little white grains.
There's no other way, and no need to look,
Deep down inside . . . you know you are hooked.
I warn you ahead, so if you should start,
It says in the contract,
"Till death do us part."

Rebecca J Cooney

EVERYDAY PEOPLE

People say that I am cold,
But, I have a love that's deep.
People say that I just don't care,
But, I'm most understanding.

People say my life's a mess,
But, I'm the one that they will call
When life puts them to the test

Rose L Hunt

THE WAY OUT OF DARKNESS

This poem is dedicated to my husband Terry, and my son Philip.

Where is the light?
It is so far out of sight.
My heart pounds, my breath comes loud.
Why is the sun hidden behind the cloud?

Why can I not find the light?
I try with all my might.
I cry, lift me from my pain,
But it seems I cry in vain.

I look all around,
But a friend cannot be found.
So I look above,
And then God sends down His love.

Praise Him, I have found my light!
He sent His Son to guide my sight.
Jesus Christ came to earth,
To show us all our worth.

To save the world he has come,
To save us all not just some.
God waits for you to look above,
Then He will send down all his love!

Nancy Parker

ODE TO A CLOSE FRIEND

I miss you when
You go away.
I think about you
Everyday.
I miss that special
Touch.
I've come to know
And love so much.
You have always
Been there for me.
Someone special
Just for me.
All those times
Happy and sad.
Always there
For which I'm glad.
Just some lines
To tell my thoughts.
The truth is
Without you I'm lost.
If the time comes

We must say goodbye.
It would break my heart
Make me cry.
I'll cherish the special
Time we had.
The funny the happy
Even the sad.
When I'm old in
My chair.
My mind's reflection
To that time back there.
Wondering what you are
Doing now.
I'll see your smiling
Face over the miles.

Barbara Sinyard
THE RIGHT TO LIVE

Dedicated to my little nephew Chase who has filled my life with love and joy from the moment of his birth May 28th 1988.

I ve been ripped and torn from my
n her's womb
The place I loved so much, because I had started to bloom.
My tears of sorrow, oh how they will grow, for the wonderful life I will never know.
I heard you say just the other day, I cannot have this thing inside of me, for what does it matter,
"It's not even a baby" you act as though I cannot hear.
The promise of my death, I hear so clear. But you don't realize the blood that flows through your veins also flows through mine.
I lived in fear of knowing the day was drawing near.
Can't you feel me moving about, trying so hard to cry out! "Oh mommy mommy I was meant to be here" to fill you with laughter and joy year after year.

Nina Kurth
IMAGES
Hear echoes stern
The arctic Tern
Her craggy nest belies
The fiercesom rake
From salty break
whose tide for purchase vies

The stoney sheets
Of granite pleats
Grow rare upon the moors
But misty breathes
The heather wreathes
Of winter's coming storms

And hearty tufts
Upon chalk bluffs
That brave the biting air
Are much akin
From fen to fen
To uplands sodden fare

See beauteous still
With icy chill
The moonlit moat again
Near castled stone
Which lichens grown
Wet with English rain

Such wonder scene
Created clean
And given by best of bard
This Britain great
Smitten image slake
And as of yet unmarred

Phil Sindlinger
JOYFUL VILLANELLE
Awfully quiet where we live.
Losing hair can't order near;
Stay put, wait who gives.

Down corner old maid grinning.
Rocks were thrown into pool.
Seems quiet where you now live.

Gosh, water's bean dripping.
What's in store?
Stay put, wait who gives.

My time on watch has run its course.
Sheriff made illegal growth;
Awfully quiet where we live.

Junky satellite has crushed rib.
Party's anxious teacup:
Stay put, wait who gives.

Rising sun games leave holes,
Wrathful grain shakes it,
Awfully quiet where we live.
Stay put, wait who gives.

Nora Elizabeth Martel

Nora Elizabeth Martel
LIFE—A BUILDING BLOCK

This poem is dedicated to Mary Jane, my loving mother and supporter.

Life . . . You are a baby
Held like a tiny fragile figurine
With no awareness of your surroundings
God gives you a block with six colors
You hold it

Life . . . You are a child
You notice your surroundings
"But, what does it mean?"
God gives you more blocks with more colors
You play with them

Life . . . You are a teenager
You learn, the good and the bad
"But, why is god giving me more blocks?"
They hold no meaning for you
But, you stack them

Life . . . You are getting married
You add your colorful blocks to your mate's
You are happy and feel like one
You reach a low point
Your blocks tumble
You notice you can't surrender
But, you go on rebuilding
God gives you more blocks with more colors
They are rising and rising.

God holds every gift for you
The first block you held is a gift of love to every human race

Kenneth Haefner
YOU CAN'T RIDE YOUR HOPES

To Laura—For giving me her encouragement.

Take a bike ride?
ha-ha-ha-ha
funny thought.
I wonder if this burned-out grass
will survive the drought
Thought I'd leave at two.
Had to move the furniture instead.
best bet make it on Saturday.
They say it's supposed to rain,
I hope they dew.
I'd like to ride on Saturday,
but the rush for the concert
gets in my way.
And so Saturday comes
and rain does not
at least not right away.
It chills me so.
So I don't go for my ride.
And the burned-out grass
does not survive.

Genevieve B Kubashack
SEE LOVE
Love is made in little ones
and going along the way
Babies fill a heart with joy,
kindness and happiness today.

The touch of their little hands
is a true blessing to others
giving real feelings of love
to their fathers and mothers.

Looks from their little bright eyes
bring love to those who see joy
from a little girl or boy.

Peggy Robles
DOMESTIC ENGINEERS
Hail to the ones who cook and clean
and hear each daily woe!
Who somehow keep all schedules
straight as to where all must go!

Cheers to you dears who meet each
call and rarely do complain,
'Cause house and husbands, kids and
dogs, can sometimes be a pain!

You 'stay at homes' who don't get
paid for service through the years,
Are priceless to your families, you're
"Domestic Engineers!"

A title earned for jobs well done in
the field of 'wife and mothers,'
Fulfillment doesn't come in cash
with you like all the others;

As time goes by, and kids grow up,
you'll really be surprised,
The way you made the house a home
is the thing they idolized!

The craft of 'Wife and Motherhood'
one doesn't learn in books,
You can't just quit at 5 o'clock or
make it on your looks!

So wave your dish towel high with
pride, as you have done for years!
You're loved much more than you
could know, you "Domestic
Engineers!"

Sandy Lingard
YOUR FRIEND

To Tom who was ever so supportive of me, Thank you!

Take my hand
That I may hold you
And feel your gentleness

Learn from me
That I may teach you
And watch you grow

Cry with me
That I may share your tears
And feel with you

Care with me
That I may be with you
And I will know you

Dream with me
And your hope will be
Tomorrow's reality

Reach for your star
That you will know
Who you are

And then you will know
Who I am
For I am, your friend

Corey Schapley
A MEANING OF LIFE?
With the brightness of birth,
To the darkness of death,
Life is so cruel,
but yet—
holds pleasant breath.

As we live and we grow,
As we crumble and die,
to bind with the wind—
as the wind blows by.

To be buried in a grave,
so all-all alone,
decaying to bones,
in the moist ground below,

What is its meaning?
Why are we here?
Life is so short,
and death is so feared.

Lori Hilsz
THE LAST DREAM
How woebegone and sad the flowers and trees are!
As I tilt my head toward the cloud-covered sun,
swiftly departing from my view as I drift across the land
The mountains, tall and stately, step aside and let me pass,
and I enter the land of the unknown, the forgotten,
The world that stems from the very corners of my mind,
the very depths of my heart and soul
I look 'round, seeking answers,
answers to questions only this world can explain
This world, where the season is eternal spring;
and all my lost dreams are my own again
I see them, high above me, floating across the sky

"Reach!" exclaims a musical voice,
"for here you are free."
And I do! I reach with all my might,
until I am a part of the sky,
a cloud by day and a star by night
Now in the world I departed from,
I can be seen by all
And for those who take time to
admire me,
a place is waiting here for you when
you are free, too.

Jeannette Andersen
FLAME IN LIFE

Oh precious time that believes in my young dreams, will somewhere in time wash clean with the aging limits of life's theme.

Shall people step aside in imperative wisdom to see from the inside out and only faint fantasies of a pure heart without doubt?

In prayer only once did I ask my lord in the twilight dusk for the gift of love to share a heavenly bond in trust. In this minute I clearly unfold gentle portions of my soul, meaningful between us three. My wish is to give thought and tenderness toward one's time in life with my words written for you to forever see.

Why can you smile within tears while seeking for love's fire?

You're the icebergs' endless flame somewhere in time burning your name holding a desire.

Kcarolina B May
A SLAVE

I would like to dedicate this poem to all the P.O.W's from the Vietnam War.

Words of freedom,
Shreds of hope,
Bound in chains forever.
Lost to a world of untruths,
nothing ever gets better.
The lash marks on my back, are
deep,
and I did not misbehave.
But Mama always tol' me,
I should try to be brave.
She said one day, that the Good
Lord,
would set me free.
She filled my heart with love,
they took her way' from me.
NOW I face the world alone,
how can I be brave?
The other people tol' me,
I'd always be a slave.

Fred Royal
GRANDPA'S BOOM-BOOM STREET

Hey man, let's take a ride
Down boom-boom street.

Man oh man, what a trip
Down Grandpa's street.

The flashing of car upon car
And the squealing of brakes.

See all those poor boys in heat
And the girls standing round and
round.

Hey, look there's one . . . Nice
Oh, oh—there's an old bag.

Wow—That's a nice little
Black one—See, See.

There's a white one—what a pair
Of boobs on that one—boy oh boy.

Quick, see that one—no pimp
Just waiting for—you know what.

Boy, could I go that one
Yes sir, yes sirie that is mine!

See, see those knockers—one
In the mouth—one in the ear.

Look, Look no panties—wow,
wowie
See that a . . . ss. I'll take it!

Oh my god—brown, black, white
What have you . . . ten upwards
to . . .

IT'S MINE . . . ALL MINE
LORD . . . WHAT A WAY TO GO!

Down on Grandpa's boom-boom
street.

Carrie Fouche
SAYING GOODBYE

Dedicated to my family and friends who encouraged me, and to the boy, with love, for whom it was written.

Tonight, our last,
We said goodbye;
As I walked away
I wanted to cry.

You've meant so much
And always will;
When you gazed in my eyes
My heart stood still.

I realize now
You've always cared;
You couldn't forget
The love we shared.

I wanted to kiss you,
To hold you so tight,
Hating what stopped me
On our last night.

Howard R Burch
MORNING OF OUR LOVE

Give me sleepy mornings,
Give me quiet evenings,
Laughter in the dark,
Long looks in twilight—
Learn to tease and fight.

When bad times come,
Hard days seem long,
We'll still hold on,
And mend our
Hearts as one.

Dr Letha Memorie Lloyd-Wayne

Dr Letha Memorie Lloyd-Wayne
THE PEARL

To my children—Pamela-Earl Anthony, Kristen & Justin Wayne

May we be wise
Like the magi of ages old
Hold to the vision
Of the star in the story told
Of their faith and quest
For the babe divine
To seek and find
This truth sublime
That frees and heals
Thru all ages and time
May we like the magians
Of the past
Press on and forward
To behold the babe—The Christ—
The crowning gift
Of God's beneficent—Universal
Love.

Edith Mathis
THE MIND

How still the world, at 3 A.M.
When sleep, the body covers.
The mind is going, mile by mile,
In dreams, where mystery hovers.

An island or a mountain,
A strange place far beyond,
A secret or a lover,
Perhaps the lily pond?

The mind will keep the lonely things
In waking you remember,
Like running in the meadow,
Or hiking in December.

The mind is but a storage box
Of all things new & old,
It locks the bad and views the good
Like a solid box of gold.

Edward L Johnson
MESSAGE TO A BLACK AMERICA

To Cora Lee Johnson

How much longer must I wait
Are not my tears enough
How much more must I suffer

Are you my woman or must I seek
another
Should my eyes continue to judge or
Should I let my heart choose

Are you not a woman
Must you always chase some other
woman's man
Am I not strong
Am I not handsome
Am I not smart
Man, Am I not one
Can't you love me for me

Can I be poor and be love
Can I be black and be love
Can I be shy and be love
Can I be innocent and be love
Black woman love me for me

How much longer must I wait
Please, come home.
Let me love you for you
Let me love you
Let me hear your voice
Let me feel your warmth
Love me black woman

I cry from loneliness
My nights are long
My days are useless
Black woman come home

Happiness is in our love

Joyce B Davis
TWINKLE OF AN EYE VERSION II

In a twinkle of an eye,
  My life has passed me by.
I ask myself just why,
  And hang my head and sigh.

I came to earth,
  When Mother gave me birth.
What's my purpose in life?
  It's always constant strife.

Now I'm ready to die,
  And I look toward the sky.
Will I know the reason why?
  In that sweet by and by?

then I begin to feel,
  Not long from now I will.
I'll meet the Lord up yonder,
  No longer will I wonder.

I'll have the missing link,
  When I cross o'er the brink.
Now I draw my last breath,
  I'll feel the chill of death.

In a twinkle of an eye,
  I'll meet Jesus in the sky.

Edith Maria Stenvall
THE OLD PIONEER

Beside the glowing fire she sits,
A symbol of the past.
Her face, that was once young,
Is now deeply lined, but lovely still,
And ageless as the desert sands.

As she knits, one sees the quiet
Beauty of her work-worn hands.

She dreams once more of the long
ago—
Side by side with her mate she toils,
Eking a living from the unyielding
soil;
Together they carved a home out of
the wilderness
And a place in History.

Ann M Schmidt
DEFINE

E.A. Newbauer, You are my one thought, one emotion. You are my Magical Spell.

Ecstasy,
  when one's mind is ruled,
  by one thought or emotion.
  As you are that one thought,
  that one deep emotion,
    that lies
    deep within me.

Enchantment,
  drawn towards one another
    by a magical spell.
  Standing side by side,
  wanting to hold you,
    draw you
      ever so near.

Magic,
  Charm,
    as you are
      fascinating,
    attractive.

Drawing you nearer,
  and closer,
  so close that our souls,
  seem to touch
    and grow,
  with ecstasy.

Ralph B Stump
LISTENING IN THE RAIN

I heard it so soft and lingering
A sound so compelling to my hearing
Where was it coming from again?
And again I forgot I was in the rain.

There in that cathedral is an open
door
That tune drew me closer more and
more
I stepped inside to listen more
carefully
To music played thru heart and soul
prayerfully.

A CRESCENDO then so sweet and
low
Its allure so strong my heart seemed
to grow
Wings as in a silver toned musical
prayer
Seeing the musician I understood the
fare.

Watching the musician's facial expression
Was to invite true and timely confession
As the musical sounds rose and fell
There were no words that could tell,

Of the joy that music brought
Time stood still as I thought
Such music can only be where Jesus is guiding
And in Jesus that musician is abiding.

Mae Mitchell

Mae Mitchell
I GAZED UPON A GLOWING STAR

To my three sons

I gazed upon a glowing star
It sent me visions from afar

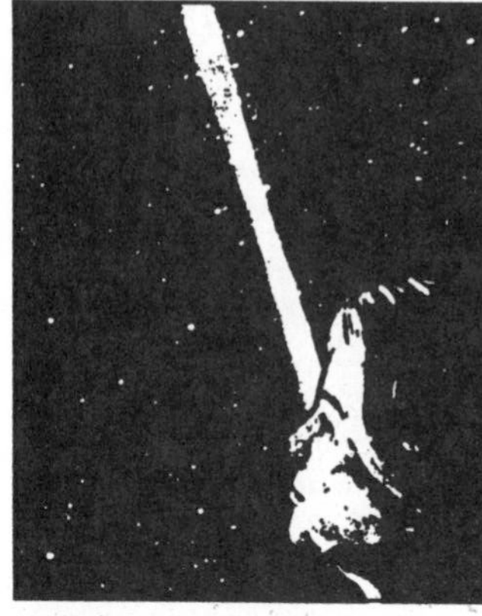

Such beauty I have never seen
Enough to fill your fondest dream

Cookie
SIXTEEN—OH GOD!

"To anyone raising a 16 year old in the late 80's" To Joseph, Todd & Alison & my encouragement—Ellen

16 is having one huge fling
16 is knowing everything
16 is having no one intrude
16 is having an attitude
16 is staying out too late
16 is having sex with your mate
16 is being accepted by peers
16 is drinking lots of beers
16 is having fake I.D.
16 is being anyone but me
16 is asking dad for a loan
16 is having an ear glued to the phone
16 is rarely making a point
16 is sometime trying a joint
16 is having a car without gas
16 is praying your grades will pass
16 is having parents that care
16 is hoping they'll always be there
16 is having a tough skin to shed
16 is the beginning of a new life ahead!

Rose B Younkins
ATTENTION! ATTENTION!

To: All (7) seven of my Grand Children

Attention: listen to my heart.
I read to-day a child went away.
He was six and needed a fix.
Any kind to help hide the pain.
The hate and the love of a trix.

A signal one day all is wrong.
Saying something had gone, leaving the world behind for so long.
Why are they dying? trapped? and Blind? the bind of the children delusion and alone, unprotected.
No more to be borne.

Parents once provider and protectors
Now all are defectors
Parent with children, no one could touch. All held by a big pouch
Family ties, children multiplies that's how we kept the future alive.

Mother! Father! relatives all until yesterday and recently looked on with pride. Children began to hide. A vanishing breed now wait in line to be freed.

Michael Young
CRACK IS TAKING OVER

Crack down because,
The moment you're born,
Life can be sweet,
But crack babies being born,
With nothing to eat.
It's not safe anymore,
In your own back yard.
When you leave your home,
You better be on guard.
Pushers keep pushing,
So that they can rule.
Putting rock cocaine,
In everybody's school.
Shootings in the streets,
Like the cowboy days.
Forcing people all over,
To change their ways.
Just for once say no!
Put the dope in the trash.
You will save your life,
And save your cash.
Crack is taking over!
Crack is taking over,
All walks of life,
And it's cutting people down,
Like a sharp blade knife.
No salt or butter,
You can put on the table,
And it's making many lives,
Seem very unstable.
This war against drugs,
Is like a tug of war.
Watch for batter ram,
Knocking at your door.
If you sell this stuff,
You better drop your sack,
Because the law will book you,
With the Reco Act.
They will take everything,
You claim to own.
They will take your cars,
Your money and home.
Crack is taking over!!
Crack is taking over,
Turning good girls bad.
They don't care,
If their children,
Are happy or sad.
They would sell their souls,
For kibbles and bits,
But when the rocks run out,
They will go in fits.
No matter what you have,
You will put it up for sell.
You will even take a chance,
And go to jail.
Crack is taking over.
Now you say you want to be,
Like a big dope dealer,
But once you learn the trade,
You become that killer.
Everyday that you live,
You better watch your back,
Because every rock head,
Wants to test your sack.
Now you're tweeking off the stuff,
Because you don't get sleep,
And the crack man is waiting,
For his beeper to beep.
So your rocks run low,
And you're looking on the rug,
But you're digging your grave,
Because you love that drug.
Crack is taking over !!!

Jerry Manno

Jerry Manno
FALLING OFF THE EDGE OF THE WORLD . . .

Sitting in this lonely room,
Staring at the walls.
Chains that bound my heart from freedom,
I scream, but no one hears my call.
People think I'm crazy.
If they could only read my mind.
They would see, I'm just an empty soul.
Lost in time.
Thoughts which fill my head confuse me,
The reasons, so unclear.
People tell me its alright,
but I sense the end is near.
Feel myself slipping away,
Just about to fall.
Scream for someone, to save me
but no one hears my call . . .

Marion McCartor
I WONDER

Dedicated to the memory of my dear mother, Mary.

I wonder—
About the meaning of life;
The part that we should play.
I wonder—
How should we stand
On issues of the day.
I wonder—
Is each to blame
For things that are not right.
I wonder—
What can we do
To help relieve our plight.
I wonder—
Oh, so many things,
Confusing as they are.
I wonder—
Can we help ourselves,
Or just wish on a star.
I wonder—

Carl R Schreiber
MEMORIES

Oh stay these moments of life I ask
that I might remember more
For charge the world for good times past
as memory and spirits soar
That I was young and bold those days
my heart was gay and free
And now the hour has come at last
to make this payment by me
All that is done can not stop age
the waited enemy at the door
But memories of times gone past
my youth returns once more

Randy Baker
DYING

Give me another bottle of gin
So I won't remember at all where I've been.
Pardon me sir, may I borrow a smoke?
I'm all out of mine, and I can't wait to choke.
I'll have another burger and fries,
I'm setting myself up for a tragic demise.
And pass me just one more line of that coke.
If I'm gonna die, I want to go broke!
Dying is fun, we do it for play;
Now I've got to go, 'cause I'm dying today.

Randy Baker
GOING HOME

For Jennifer

The sunset sheds a golden glow
Across the fields of corn.
Heading eastward, I must go
To the land where I was born.

Wayward wanders in the past,
No longer shall I roam.
To be with loved ones now, at last.
I'm finally going home.

Virginia Rayman
BEING STRUCK DOWN

Dedicated to Dr. Mark Warner, Jeff Carter, Therapist, Jesus my Lord Savior & healer.

Long suffering I've hid inside, til nuclear scan with dye showed damage done.

Satan tried to take my life, but instead took a portion of my right arm and shoulder.

I said, "Jesus my Lord, loosen Satan's reins on me, for this arm and shoulder belong to thee."

So to repair Satan's damage, a spiritual doctor was chosen.
Who by his skilled hands and tools, began to reconstruct what God had once made.

To overcome and recover from surgery in the hospital, then on the third day to be released in God's care.

Arm in a sling, two weeks have passed by, and all staples are gone and the healing with netting of new tissue has begun.

Therapy must start again, but I suffered great pain by the hand of a lady therapist, who forced a measured stretch.
She brought tears that wouldn't stop and fear in my heart.

Since I forgave her at that point, I still can't relax in her presence to be helped in therapy.

A new therapist has come, he is kind and gentle with a soft voice and healing hands.

His history taking and measuring was done in line without force. My faith was renewed once more.

All the ice packs, heat and ultra sound is helping, with stretching and exercising are working.

I am feeling life again, but I still have a long way to go to get back range and motion, with reach to return to normal if possible.

My praise to those who heal, All Glory be to God.

Sue Driscoll
FOR HOWEVER LONG JOHN'S JOURNEY

Dear John, For the boy you were and the man you've become. Love Mom.

I know not what lies ahead
My journey has not always been easy
The roads I've traveled
Have at times been vacant and lonely
At other times demanding and frightening
Just the same I'm glad for the stroll
For in the end I'm where
I've always wanted to be
So I understand
Your destiny lies elsewhere
I'll not hold you back
You have mountains to climb
And bridges to cross
You've dared to dream
And I'm with you
For however long this journey takes.

Wilhamine Johnson Huber
A WASTE OF TIME
"Mother, come play with us," my dear little ones cried,
"Just a silly game called 'Cat and Mouse',"
"I'd love to, my dears; later, perhaps, I'm busy right now cleaning the house."

Hubby was off on his favorite sport,
Hunting rabbits and grouse;
A friend called and asked me over for tea;
I declined, because I had to clean house.

Another year's gone; my birthday is here,
Mother sent a beautiful blouse,
I still haven't worn it; perhaps never will,
For it's too pretty for cleaning the house.

The shelves were filled with books, all new,
I opened a cover to browse;
"Put me back on the shelf," it seemed to cry out,
"Get back to your dirty old house."!

The piano had stood in the corner for weeks,
Waiting for strains of Bach,
Beethoven and Strauss,
I dusted the keys and righteously said,
"Some day, when I'm not cleaning the house."

The view from my window is lovely, I'm told,
With song birds and flowers: a meadow with cows,
But I haven't the time to stand there and dream,
There's so much to do to this house.

Now the children are gone, with homes of their own,
And I haven't even a spouse;
I sit in a rocker and think to myself,
"I wasted the years cleaning house!"

Nyoka K Bobb

Nyoka K Bobb
THE STILLNESS OF THE TAPS

This poem is dedicated to the soldiers of the past, the present and the future.

As the lights go out in the now silent billets the lonely bugler sang his hymn. And to a soldier standing on, it touched the cord of a memory long gone. And though he'd like to move on to laugh, to talk. The lingering sound of the bugler keeps him standing on. And when the sound had died away and stillness filled the air he felt the mystery of sadness and longing, glory, and defeat of soldiers long, long gone.

Suddenly the stillness of the moment is shattered and sounds of the presents preclude the taps, the cannon, the past, nothing prevails but a nostalgic feeling of time. Something lost, but what? In the haunting sound of the taps something elusive from the bugler, something mystical in the stillness of the night air. Something fades when the bugler lays down his bugle with a solitary tear and a smile he bids all the soldiers of the past, present, and future a good night.

Br Edward C Breault S C
GENEROSITY
Adopt a family for Christmas . . .
That is a thought!
We'll make up a box of groceries, and add some toys
For the little girl and the three older boys;
And we could have an Xmas Tree with ours,
The others haven't thought of that, I'll bet . . .
We'll raid our pantries, and buy a turkey too;
If we all chip in enough, it will soon be done.

There's the house . . . but what a depressing place!
Does poverty always have to smell like this?
And look at the mess . . . why can't they keep it clean?
But their furniture isn't bad at all, I thought . . .
And color TV . . . with VCR, no less?
I wonder why this family was on the list?
And why did they have to assign this one to us?

But wait . . . what is the color of poverty?
Just put yourself in this hapless mother's place . . .
And who am I to draw the line at this or that?
No child I've met has earned such deprivation!
There's more than meets the eye in this affair,
A chance for future thoughtful giving, perhaps . . .
Or even gathering more than we have given?

—Fidelis

Ester K Roberts
MY AVOCADO SEED

To my dear children

I stuck a seed of avocado
into a pot one day.
It was a big surprize to me
when a friend came by to say,
"You have an avocado tree
growing in a pot, I see."

I can't keep it here
in all the winter snow.
I'll take it to a friend,
he will take care of it, I know.
He will put it in his nursery
and help it grow some more.
And when it's big and tall
there will be fruit on it
Maybe by next fall.

Thelma Jinks
OLD JEF AND ME
This little old shanty I claim for my own sits on a hillside where no man roams
don't see no creature from sun up till dawn just ripple of water as it rushes along
Don't take much liven, old Jef eats turnip green's right long with me. I take the fishen pole old Jef the worms we walk the track for meat in return. I've no regrets as night ushers in I've judged no man and no man me. Old Jef lays beside me without ever a doubt the crickets soon lulls out every thought
Thank you dear Jesus for a beautiful day please bless this old shanty. Old Jef and me

Sheila Cline Smith
THE POTTER AND THE CLAY
Put me not on a shelf to decay.
This in earnest I do pray.
Help me Lord, to know what to say.
To keep others from Judgement Day.
Help me to stay on in the right way.
Your love and trust never to betray.
To tell others of your love if I may.
For, if they receive your gift of life truly from your path they'll never stray.
In Your way if they choose to obey,
Heaven's Golden Streets and in Mansions will they stay.
For, You are the potter I am clay.
Put me not on a shelf to decay.
This I earnestly do pray.

ISIAH 64:18
Yet, the Lord, You are our Father we are the clay. You are the potter.

Joanne Perkins
FAITH

My wonderful husband Jim, a gift from God, who has shown me the true meaning of love,

Sometimes as you go through
life and all your problems
seem sky high, and all
hope is lost let it be
known God is there

As you try to figure out
what to do and which way
to go, reach out for God
he is reaching out for you.

Sometimes when you pray
the answers seem so far
away, but keep your eyes
on God, the answers are
on their way.

James E Jinks
WHO AM I
Who am I who fails to see this day's not mine alone.
Who am I to judge others' faults, and fail to see my own. Who am I who fails to see a ready smile, turns away words of wrath unspoken
Who am I who sees the anguished soul and fails to share my blessings,
It's only with a contrite heart the spirit of love sweeps o'er my soul changes sin to righteousness then only can I freely say
Who am I?
I am a child of love

Joanne Perkins
LOVE HURTS

To Jim the love of my life

Love can be so beautiful
when completely shared by two.
The total joy and fulfillment you fill
when your love is returned.
Oh! how sorrowful when love
is only one sided.
When you find out his love is still
for someone in his past.
No matter how much
you love him.
No matter how much
you care.
His love seems to not
be there.
If only, I pray,

he could love me!
If only I was that very
special person, in his life.
As he is in mine
I LOVE YOU.

Sue Driscoll
BEFORE MY EYES
As you passed before me
I reached out to touch you
And my fingers were pricked by thorns
I pulled my hand away
And stifled the cry within
I looked at my hand
The blood trickled from my fingers
And formed a broken gentle stream
I was thoroughly bewildered
Why just the other day you held me
And just last night I touched you
I could feel the love
Pour out of you into me
While still looking at my hand
I lifted my head to see
And before my eyes
You had turned to stone.

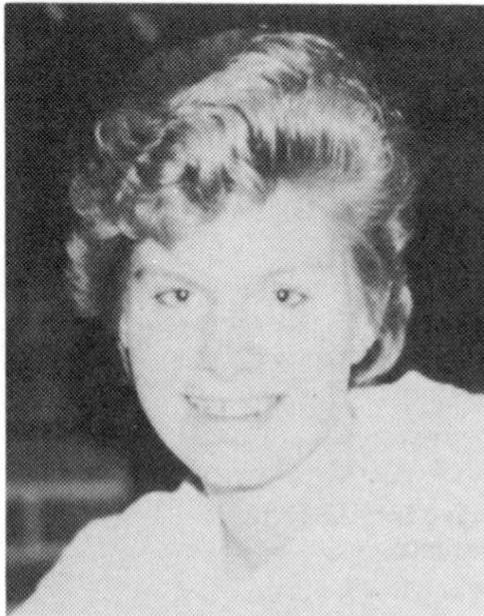

Christina Muehlbach

Christina Muehlbach
A CHANGE OF MIND
The pressure builds
locked inside,
you just can't seem to run
and hide,
Time is nothing as
the days go by,
How can we take this without
a sigh,
But I am created in so
precious ways,
How can I not fulfill
my days?

Bobbi Turi
THE ACCIDENT
My nerves are twitching as the mass of red tail lights flicker and dodge—paralleled and paired—blinding and racing
They blend and the lights dissolve
Beings flung and the red is born again—liquid and flowing
Tire treads on a snow covered roadway are stained, splattered with dirt and what once was the gift of life—
And stars form the night lights to the heavens.

Ann Elizabeth "Blessing" Jarvis
A MOTHER'S DAY

To my Husband, eight daughters, and two sons. "The Perfect Ten"

I wonder where all the hours go,
From the Time that I arise,
I wake at The crack of dawn,
To The sound of my baby's cry.
First cooking for dad and The children
Then dressing for school, work & play
They wave Au revoir to mother &
They are on Their way.
Now, There's washing,
housecleaning and mending,
Picking up and somemore baby Tending
Trips To The store, knocks at The door.
Stooping, stretching, and bending.

Hurts I kiss To make better, spills wipe up from The floor,
The mailman delivers a Letter, who is That at The back door?
Hang clothes on The line if The weather is fine.
Wash faces and hands, Try To meet all demands
In The meantime the hours have just flown

And my Loved ones are on their way home,
But when They greet me with a smile,
It makes my whole day so worth while.

Barbara Shaffer
CALLING

The poem "Calling" is dedicated to my mother, Anne Lorreen Medlin Bagley. Her love of truth and beauty of spirit are inspiration enough to fill my every cup with dreams for all my tomorrows.

I have flown the farthest reaches of space, seen the dawn of a million starways, and flipped in and out of the center of the sun.
I have listened to the music of the stars, and experienced the breathtaking beauty of the highest mountain peak.
All space, the planets and the universe are folded within my arms.
All souls of tomorrow and yesterday crying out in the far reaches of time feel the touch of my hand and the whisper of my lips dries all tears.
I have held infinity in my fingers and allowed the stars to trickle through to space. I reach out and gently caress your brow with the palm of my hand.
"Who speaks?"
Be still my beloved child!
I stretch out my hand from beyond the stars.
Reach with all that is within you and I will lift you up.
"Why do you speak to me?
Thou art God.
"Who tells me this?"
The voice simply says,
I Am!

Terry Felicia Hock
NOT FORGOTTEN
I wanted to walk up to you
and thank you for what you'd done,
But I feared you'd think I wasn't sincere . . .
that I was making fun.

I watched you wheel yourself about
on your legless walk through stones,
that beared the names of men
you may or may not have known.

I saw the crease between your brows
grow deeper with each thought:
Horrors I could not imagine;
Memories of the war you fought.

You cocked your ear at the rustle of leaves:
Ghosts that tramped about your dreams, with leather boots and M-16s,
through flame and smoke, gunfire and screams.

I stand and watch from across the plots.
I see the tear you cry.
With trembling chin, I only wish . . .
I could tell you . . . Why.

You see me through the branches.
I quickly turn away.
I hope to find the courage
to thank you . . . some how . . . some day.

Jan Chiodo-Wilhelm
THE CHAINS THAT LOCK THE FORCE OF MOONS

To my Father and my Mother who showed me the essence of Poetry and Song.

The chains that lock the force of moons have been shattered by the sound,
and they are left to lead astray, to travel all around.
The sun cried out its sorrow song, the fiery light burns low.
The stars let tears of sadness by, they know they must turn and go.
The blazoned air grew hard to breathe, the surfaces turned to dust,
what once was vibrant in colored red has faded now to rust.
The din of ending mystified the existence that was known,
where a perpetual balance of white and black has seemingly been sown.
Planets whirling in maelstrom viewed what this end may bring.
Venus and Neptune followed the path of Pluto the distant king.
Saturn's ring crumbled to grey and Mercury sailed to the sun.
The others in an instant passed with Earth the surviving one.
With no contempt or with no reason the energies were drawn,
darkness covered over the skies now the universe was gone.

Lynda Schmidt
THE BIRDS ARE BUSY BUILDING THEIR NESTS

To Alvin; For the friendship you've given me, here's the happiness and perfect day, that could only be achieved through the mind.

Warm Spring breeze blows gently through the young leaves,
The birds are busy building their nests,
The woods are full of young animals.
The sun so bright and warm,
Your hand holding mine as we walk
In silence, enjoying life together.

We stopped by a pond,
You talked to the frogs, while I tried to catch a fish.
All the birds laughed when we both fell in.
Lying in the sun to dry,
We talked of love and life.

The bright sun turned the sky a beautiful red
As the animals came out to play.
It was a world of our own,
Watching the deer play,
Sharing the sounds of the night.

You laughed so hard when I thought the owl a ghost.
Safely home we sat by the fire, watching the flames,
Swearing never to part, our souls always joined.
Now, you are gone, I am here
Still, together we walk in our forest and fields.

Barbara JoAnn Smith
I SIT AND WATCH THE SUNSET, GO DOWN BEHIND THE HILL

This poem is dedicated to Norman F. Snowberger, whom I loved and miss very much.

I sit and watch the sunset, go down behind the hill.

It gives to me such peace of mind to know that it is real.

God gives us all these beautiful gifts to enjoy and to share.

We take it all for granted, we should all be more aware.

And as I watch the sun tomorrow, come up over the hill.

I thank the Lord for a whole new day,
for I know that its God's will.

Nancy Olinger
I'M THANKFUL

To Don, my wonderful and supportive husband. He encourages me when I need it the most. He is my life, my love and my best friend.

Lord, I'm thankful for You each day.
For granting me the will to pray.

For my husband who's blessed my life;
Such joys You've brought me as his wife.

For a safe place to lay my head;
A home where faithful prayers are said.

I'm thankful that You've gifted me
The love of friends and family.

I'm grateful for my needs You tend,
With Your promise, "There is no end!"

For assuring, "I need but ask,
And ever in Your care I'll bask!"

I'm grateful for my love of Thee,
And thank You Lord, for loving me!

Thelma Coil Lathrop
WINGS
I held it in my hands,
The bird with the broken wing,
And kept it close to me
To love, to ease its pain.
While time gently healed,
It sang its song for me,
Then I opened wide my hands,
And love set it free.

Carmen Rae Newby
AS WE WALKED DOWN THE HIGHWAY

I would like to dedicate this poem to my grandparents, Wade & Eleanor, and to my mother, Charlotte.

As we walked down the highway,
you turned to look my way. You
have always given me the confidence
to see the ability I have in me.
I understand what you mean when
you say "life goes fast," you said you

wished it would last.
I will be with you till the day I die. I will always be true, I'll try not to lie.
As we walked down the road you turned to me and told me—We've been through our good times and bad ones too, through the tears and the smiles, but we've always fought it through.
We rose with the sun and we settled when we were done.
I promise—when we reach the end—you can always count on me to be your friend.

DJ Giovanini
NOT AS A STRANGER

What began as an ordinary day
was enhanced by a stranger
sharing
open communication,
pains of remembering,
touching of hands,
tears of vulnerability,
excitement in
walking and talking

Not wanting the day to end
nor these warm feelings to rescind . .
So long it's been hidden
but just for a day
love returned
not as a stranger.

M Elaine Hollier
LEAVING AGAIN

To my most wonderful family with ALL MY LOVE! ! ! Adrian, Betty, Cap, Therese, Ricky, Adam, Aaron, Andrew and Alan, I LOVE YOU! ! !

Driving the streets
of the old town.
Seems they sleep,
at the first sign of nightfall.
Functionless humor
surrounds me.
Thoughts of youth
interprets for me
solid feelings
of yesterdays passed.
A motionless existence.
Like manikins,
behind glass
for show.
Not going any place,
for any thing.
Casually existing,
in the streets
of my home town.

Gladys V Moss
WHEN I SEE MISS BETTY

This poem is dedicated to "Miss Betty" a "Dear Special Nurse".

When I see Miss Betty
I see love abide for people
Young, middle and golden ages.
Fathers, mothers babies, sisters,
brothers, aunts and uncles,
cousins, friends, rich and poor
reaching out for love and more.

Her warm smiles kind and true
the soft touch of her hands, even with a "needle"
in one; to ease the pain and rage.
Oh! What a beautiful "lady", person
and friend to know
With such "TLC" she shows

Theresa Neely
YOUR DAUGHTER

Dedicated to my daughter Kristina with love and to her father, Trey Earls, for without him I wouldn't have her . . .

You try to protect her
like a china doll,
You're afraid she'll shatter
upon her first fall,
You want to be near her
to stand by her side—
But as she gets older
she builds up her pride,
She pushes you aside
so she can stand alone
And you begin to realize
just how fast she's grown—
With moment after moment
and year upon year
Smile after smile
and tear upon tear—
She's a woman now—
in which you can be proud of,
made from you, with your patience,
understanding, caring and love.

Richard Bailey
DE VITA ET MORS

To My Father Charles C. Bailey 2-27-33 to 5-31-89

As pilgrims squander in the face of humanity,
The plague of life is before us
And all is there.

So what if the Dodo bird left?
Unicorns appear on shelves as
Dragons still spread their leathery wings
For all to reflect upon.

And thoughts can be put on paper,
And ideas turned into machines.
Theories are relative: everyone entered/exited.

But only visions count,
Because dreams are not a specialty,
Nor are assumptions accurate.

Logic, emotion, what difference is derived:
Spirits and auroras are just properties
de Vita et Mors.

E Lynn Norcross
FAR AWAY EYES

To the Glory of God—Without whom this gift wouldn't be. To my husband, Robert White, my best friend. I give you this gift. Thank you for putting the music to it. I love you!

Far away eyes to to places that don't exist—
Of marriages and children . . .
Meadows in the mist.

Eyes that search for rainbows and clouds—
Colors and music . . . Lands with no crowds.
They look for little Jackie and Puff—
Bright colors . . . Notes high enough.

Far away eyes are green filled with laughter and tears.
They truly never leave . . . they question, they love—
Look for things unseen.

Far away eyes have wars of conscience—
Of good and bad . . . Pleasure and purpose.

Eyes in search, where do they go?—
Up high . . . Down low.

It is a rare person to have far away eyes—
Soul tied to one . . . Spirit flies!

Far away eyes are brown filled with laughter and with song.
They truly never leave . . . They question, they love—
Ache for sound.

Evamay Wilkins
THE DAY IS DREARY

To my dear husband who passed away 20 years ago.

The day is dreary,
The nights are long,
But in my heart
There is a song.
The song I sing
Is my love for you,
That tells of charms
That are so true.
So let this be a word well spoken,
Let the word love be a small token.
For in my heart
I know its true,
Thought we are apart
I'll always love you,
My Sweet, Sweetheart.

Bonita Holley Dodd
THE MIGHTY SEA

Dedicated to my Dad, Henry Morris Holley, who passed away November 1, 1976 and for all the endless times he took me to the beach as a young girl.

Seashore at the break of dawn;
Majesty, all its' own;
Overwhelming you and me—
As we listen to the roar of the sea.

Mystical and magic, all in one,
Sound and sights and lots of fun;
Taking us away into fantasy,
The magic and power of the sea.

Give me the sound of the roaring waves,
Castles in the sand, to engrave,
As far as eyes can behold,
Where memories are made and can't be sold.

Clarence Bobino
VANITIES OF LIFE

This poem is dedicated to my wonderful wife Dorothy

The sojourn is fleeting and thoughts began to stray
The temple that stood on the threshold of youth
Is falling in decay.
How vain were the pleasure vanities of sort
Idols and treasuries
Once dear to the heart,
And now for every idle word love or hate
An account must be rendered,
For a soul a-wait its fate.
Alarmed, fear began to a-mass
Face with the unknown
Remorseful thoughts retrace the past
Contrite and broken, in darkness I stand a-mid,
Trusting in a love who favor life instead.

Michael Mueller

Michael Mueller
GIANT WATERFALLS OF YOSEMITE VALLEY

This poem is dedicated to Ted Mueller a great father.

I have walked among the giants.
I have listened to their songs.
I have watched their majestic waters
Rushing from the high country to
Yosemite Valley below.

I have marvelled at their beauty,
And I have been amazed at their
height and water flow.
I have been captured by their
presence,
And sometimes covered by their
swirling mist and spray.

Each giant waterfall has its own
identity
That changes throughout the year,
From dashing water running from
the height of mountains
To sometimes no water or just frosty
ice.

I have watched and listened for
hours, the heartbeats of Yosemite
Valley,
Overwhelmed by their picturesque
beauty and eternal grandeur,
And I have often wondered why this
Valley
Was chosen as their home.

Heather L Melton
FRIENDS

To my best friend Jennifer, Our friendship will never end!

They are nice, they are kind,
They'll always be at your side.
Friends are special,
Yet everyone has friends.
Short friends, fat friends,
They're all the same.
They're here through thick, and thin,
For this friendship will never end.

Kathy Kuhl
AWAKENING

I have found a new person.
A person who was there
all the time.
It was like watching
a flower bloom.
Or seeing a rising sun.
New Spring buds on a tree.

I looked in the mirror
and it was me.

I should have known,
I was there all the time.
I was too busy to stop
and look.
Too involved with living;
I thought.

But today,
I took a deep breath
and opened my eyes.
I looked deep into myself,
and liked what I saw.
I am love and feelings,
He gave those things to me.
I think I'm going to keep these gifts
and use them.

William Michael Pitts
FORBIDDEN LOVE
Love is full of painful emotions
Things we cannot control
Of a love that will never die
Between two people fighting to stay alive
Each in our own way protecting each other
Yet you are married to another
We want to be together, but we cannot
For this is forbidden love
Although we share a common bond that no
One can take away, no matter how they try
Though I love you more than love itself
I know that I have been the cause of much of your pain
So I must say goodbye that you may survive
But I feel that part of me will die without
You by my side, it has to be this way
It's better for both of us this way
Farewell my forbidden love

Betty L Rose
LIFES GARDEN
There stands a house in the center of a garden
Where all lifes dreams come true.
In this house within the garden
There is a dream for you.
I stood within that house one day
Not knowing of its power,
I walked the paths of the garden
and picked my favorite flowers.
Each flower was a dream
And each flower brought a sigh.
When all the flowers were finally gone
I sat alone to cry.
For in that house within that garden
I never let my dreams come true
For with each flower I picked,
My darling,
I lost a part of you.

Gregory C Veich
TO WATCH THE CHILDREN GROW

To all the children

America. the land of plenty, of God we're richly blessed. With fancy cars and big new homes, we've never lacked for less.

But now a cry has touched our ears, and spreads through-out the land. A nation which is far from us lies dying in the sand.

Let not the miles keep us apart, but lend your ear, your soul, your heart. And give today all you can give, and help this dying nation live.

I know we have our problems here, with prices ever rising, but think one moment of Africa, and all she's sacrificing.

Her lands are bare, her rivers dry, her resources all are dying. Yes, listen close and you can hear her children also crying.

Let's join our hearts, and hands once more, and stretch across these miles, to bring her help, and hope, and love, don't answer with denial.

We'll sow the seeds with which we're blessed, and with compassion let them know, we hear their cries through tear filled eyes of hunger, hurt and woes.

America, let's do our part to let this nation know, that America, above all cares, to watch the children grow.

Shirley Bergman
WYNN

To my beloved husband's memory, at the time of his death, 1905-1985. His roses faded, missing his caring touch!

Wynn,
When I was young my heart was sad,
No life-long friend for me.
And then I saw him, mending nets,
beneath a shady tree.

I stopped to have a word with him-
And he replied to me.
And he became my beau, my love,
A life-long friend to me.

The time flew by 'til we were wed-
My love, my life, my friend!
We'd walk a long a winding road
Until our time would end.

On thru life together
Thru joy and grief and woe.
Living for each other
No other way to go.

At last, our youth has slipped away
Our journey at an end.
Today I come to say, "Good-bye—
My Love, My Life, My Friend."

Tina Schutz
HAND IN HAND

For Scott Charles Eudy All my Love

I love you,
So very much.
There is nothing I wouldn't do,
Just to feel your touch.
I've never felt this way before,
About anyone or anything.
You make me feel special,
You make my heart sing.
Yet I am so scared,
Of these new feelings inside.
I don't know where they will lead,
Will you always be by my side?
Teach me about love,
And all the good things it can do.
I know there might be drawbacks,
I want to learn about them too.
So guide me through this time,
Help me to understand.
I feel so uncertain,
Walk with me hand in hand.

Mrs Vernon Pringle
APRIL
Envy on a rainy day
Of birds that fly singing on their way
Among green trees and flowers
who lift their heads to April showers.
Then I think of all the things I would like to do so much.
Of petunias that would like
mother earths tender touch.
So on with boots and trowel in hand
rain won't bother me,
I planted the petunias in the rain
on bended knee.
Then as I stood my work to admire
that crazy old sun came out like a ball of fire.
All of which just goes to show
of April weather you just never know.

Suzanne Ryan
MAN PERSON
I want to be with a gentle man,
a man who loves the trees
One who reaches into the world
and embraces what he sees.

I want to kiss a loving man,
and feel him close to me
A man who cares, a man who shares
in friendship and liberty.

I want to love a tender man,
a man in love with me
Experiencing together
a living reality.

I want to live with a peaceful man,
whose vibrations hum with mine
Whose joy is the blending energy
that makes the patterns rhyme.

Marlene A Stroud
A POEM OF OBSERVATION
At night the clouds come together as a blanket.
Designed with stars and a moon defining peace.

In the day the clouds separate into native islands warmed by the sun, complimenting loves beauty.

When it rains the clouds are covered with darkness. Hit by lightning, and deafened by thunder to eliminate hate.

Clouds are forever apart of the universe just as peace, love and hate are a part of us.

Kay Creviston
FOOLS GOLD
When we first were married I was blinded
By all of your promises to me.
All wrapped up and tied with pretty ribbons
About our life and how that it would be.

Those visions of rainbows and roses
Fade fast in the shadows made by life.
No more looking through rose colored glasses
Reality cuts deeper than a knife.

You're out on the town most every evening.
And now my eyes are open wide.
Our love lays cold within the ashes
Of the fire that once burnt so strong inside.

Those rings that we slipped upon our fingers
As a symbol of love forever true,
Our 24 Karat promise to each other
Has been tarnished forever now by you.

That band on your hand is made of fools gold
Though it glitters as bright as it can be.
That band on your hand is made of fools gold
And the one that it fooled was me.

L E Ferraris
A RAIN' SERENADE
That sound of drops of rain
Tapping as ghostly friends
On roofs and windows panes,
Seem to whisper to the restless
On lonely sleepless nights
Celestial soothing lullabies.

Sailing softly on waves of air,
Seas of tiny droplets
Untouched by germs or stain
Leave the treasure of the sky,
Distilled and priceless,
To quench the thirst on earth.

..Rainy tears of crying skies
Rinsing land's polluted face,
Feign to dance on water surface
To serenading ducks or frogs.

And dewy droplets labor nights
Their gleeful morning bliss
Kissing flowers, grass and trees
And early rising men or beasts:

And all of earth's "works of art"
That nature alone can sculpt or paint
With nothing but clear drops of rain.

Molly Helline
GROSSPOPI
I feel his presence near me,
everywhere I go.
My love for him is cherished,
only that I can bestow.
He stood behind me supportively
for anything I should do.
He knew my talents and feelings—
everything he knew.
Ever since he took his life
two years ago this week—
I remember when he said he loved
me, and he kissed me on the cheek.
I could always talk and open up
to him. Well, you know, until . . .
I loved my Grosspopi very much,
and believe me, I always will.

Patricia A Jangel
LET GO
I made a mistake you can't forgive,
Love is so badly wasted on what might have been
You have no compassion for a wayward girl. Her unruly transgression in this real crazy world.
I know what is done is done. We'll never be the same, but to still care for you, can only bring pain.
The pain I've caused was never meant to be. I didn't realize how fragile you were, can you never forgive me?
I now know the heart ache that you've been through before, I understand somewhat better, as it rages at my door.
If the truth be known by I did what I did, unconsciously decided by innocent greed.
Cannot be reversed or undone.
As you cannot forgive my only misdeed.
Have I learned a lesson from all of this, of course I have, because I have

lost what I can now only miss.
We may be called upon to go our separate ways, in light of our fate, it won't be the same.
A part of my heart lies in your hands which you've chosen to ignore, but that's ok Mike, you won't be bothered anymore.
This is the end of my tale of woe, I leave you to yourself—
As I truly LET GO!

Lucila Villaseñor Grijalva

Lucila Villaseñor Grijalva
MY LITTLE FLOWER

With love—To my father who encouraged me, and to my family who inspired me.

There's a new flower in my garden
coming up to face the sun,
There's a new flower blooming
Petals opening one by one,

So much joy!
So much happiness—
So much love!
So much readiness—

There's a new flower in my garden
Coming up to face the sun,
There's a new flower blooming
Bringing forth the spirit of fun.

Delos Munger
A SOLITARY RAMBLE

To my wife Myrtle

Oh how fine to slip away
From the turmoil of the day
Just before the shadows fall
Nothing on my mind at all
Wander to some pleasant nook
Down beside a babbling brook
Listen to the birds and bees
Squirrels a chattering in the trees
See the violets bashful blue
Smiling shyly up at you
Sit upon a mossy log
Hear the croaking of a frog
Wander till the sun sank low
Warns me that I'll have to go

Alma A Inwood
JESUS OUR FRIEND ALWAYS

He was always there,
When I needed him.
When I was down, and destitute,
He gave me friends to see me through.

The trials, and tests, and burdens,
I had to bear.
I couldn't have carried,
Had I not known my "Saviour" was there.

He was always by my side,
And gave me hope to trust in Him.
This Hope and Faith, and Prayers,
From Christian Friends.
Is all that kept me going then,
For He was always there when I needed him.

The Greatest Gift that we can give,
is "LOVE" for one another,
" "GOD" gave us his Son "Jesus",
For Unto Us a "Saviour" was
Born.
Amen

Larry E Hopson
YOU AND I

This poem is dedicated to my sister Linda. When we were kids we never seemed to see Eye to Eye; She and I

As I take pen in hand and begin to write.
Tears fill my eyes as my mind drifts back across the years.
We never seemed to see Eye to Eye;
You and I.
I guess we didn't even try; Oh how I could cry.
Now I'm proud to say; Come what may our love is here to stay.
I hope and pray.
Every thing seems to be alright;
We see each other in a different light.
May we always see Eye to Eye; You and I.

Keshia C Fisher
BEYOND THE REALM OF REASON

Beyond the realm of reason
Where the sovreignty of darkness
Hides; there lurks upon
A spirit extracting life
Which is left inside. Slowly
It diminishes as extraordinary
As it seems. Leaving life.
Without a reason, and faith
Without a gleam. No conscience,
No awareness, just a silence
Null and void. Can't replace it
Just mistake it for a feeling felt
Before.

Ginger Niemeyer
GRADUATION

They appeared to be ending—
my days of learning, closing
with Pomp and Circumstance. And
yet they had only just begun.

As president leaving office,
my emotions seem confused.
Those dreams of yesteryear which
were many are now so few.
Friendships, some trite, others true,
will no longer be the same.

I wished my college hours away.
Oh, to relive them again.

Edward J Kula
LAND OF THE KAISERS

Germany, land of the Kaisers,
who once reigned majestic and supreme
Brings imagery of a landscape,
picturesque and pristine.

The rivers, Main and Rhine, weave paths
through the plain like endless strands
Snow-covered mountain peaks
rise above the fruitful sown land.

Horse-drawn carts clatter across
worn cobblestone streets
Throughout quaint villages, friendly faces
bidding "Guten Tag" will you meet.

Within her castle walls is a faint presence
of legendary German princes and knights
Monuments etched with faces, brave yet fallen,
reflect on the Fatherland's courage and might.

Churches ornate with Baroque splendour,
herald a Germany of reknown talent and pride
The land of the Kaisers beckons one to step back to a glorious period of time.

Gloria Washington
I LOVE YOU VERY MUCH

To my mother and children

Your love, is my enchanted vase.
Your smiles, are all my flowers.
All grown, and the clock,
You are my minute and my hours.
You are the magic of my days,
From dawn to candle light.
You are all the tiny stars,
That twinkle through the night.
I dream of you whatever,
tide of weather
All I hope and pray, is just that we may be together.

Neil Mickelson
"BELIEVING" IS SEEING

This poem is an actual event inspired by my good friend Orville Springer. Who never gave up on God or Himself!

I have a friend who had a stroke and lost much of his skill
But there's one thing he didn't lose, he never lost his will
Then one day years now gone by, the thing he longed for came
A chance for us to hike a trail although his leg was lame

We knew what he was up against but slowly made our way
Up a rocky mountain trail, it was such a lovely day
But as we hiked along the path he repeatedly stumbled and tripped
And now becoming very hot out of his jacket he slipped

And like a high watt light bulb that lit up in my head
It occurred to me we'd use his jacket, as a make shift rope instead
So with the jacket now in place we found him much more stable
And with each sleeve tied to our arms he was ready, willing and able

I walked in front, he close behind, we were quite a team
And moving at a snail's pace we made a funny scene

But one thing we were proud of, was never did he fall
He made it up the steepest trails and had overcome them all

He finally reached the mountain's top where so proudly he did stand
And with deepest satisfaction his eyes surveyed the land
The reason he had conquered? He believed deep in his soul
That no matter what it took to win one day he'd reach his goal!

Rolanda Brousseau
TO THAT SPECIAL PERSON

To twin girl and husband

Asd I look in your eyes
I see starlight and
the moon that shines
so brite . . .
Days so full of light
and a night of
beyond special site . . .
Golden dreams
that with you
I know will came thought.
That special dream that
never can be seen
Days came, Day go.
but in my heart, I
know what is so

Anthony L Ray
RAINBOW DREAM

For Anushka

I dreamt of a rainbow
that spun from the sky
It wrapped me in colours
long, lean, lovely, I looked up,
and started to cry
It lifted me—but
I was afraid to fly
I clung to the ground
and in desperation
opened my eyes.

Pamela S Brigman
MY BIRTHDAY

To my wonderful parents, whose steadfast love, faith, and belief in me enabled me to believe in myself when I couldn't. Mom & Dad—I love you—Pam

Twenty seven years ago today I was born,
Bright and early at three in the morn,
Mom said "Pop it's time," much to his dismay,
It was my time all right, the pain didn't go away

With a heave and a ho and alot of grief,
Out I came with a sigh of relief,
Pa said I was first seen gnawing on my fist,
And eating ever since has been hart to resist

With curly black hair and marble black eyes,
There came from moma an astonished cry,
"This can't be my child, fair she is not,"
"Can't help that" said the nurse, "this is what you got!"

The years went by and I started to grow,
Rock music replaced baby dolls as you know,
The teen years flew by pretty fast,
And being a child was a thing of the past.

As time went by I started to see,

That some things were changing
inside of me,
A calmness prevailed, I'd never felt
before,
And maturity set in more & more.

With my parents there was no more
debate,
They finally became "people" to
whom I could relate,
I started to respect & give a little
more,
No more begging to go out & stay
until four

Dad's giving ways are part of my
whole,
And mom's sensitivity is deep in my
soul,
Part of both was in me from that very
first whimper,
But where on earth did I get this
terrible temper?

The days of yesteryear can't be
blocked out,
And I look forward to alot of
birthdays without a doubt!

Kelly Gawrych

NUMBERED DAYS

To my Grandma: My inspiration, my hero, and my best friend. Your words and smile have made the world a better place. I will always love you.

When Life is timed and one
can no longer stay

The meaning of life changes
in some ways

Days seem shorter and time
keeps passing by

Everything is hurried, no one
stops to say "Hi"

I have seen people come and seen
people go

I have seen time go fast and
have seen time go slow

But when days are numbered and
minutes just shy

Will anyone come to say
good-bye?

Ronald L Prince II

TODAY

The mind is the heart,
For it is the clock of life,
The day is deep with life,
The mind is for ever seeking,
I sometimes go deep inside,
I sometimes sleep instead of thinking,
For things are easier this way,
For the pain that comes these days is
seeing,
And praying inside you're not
believing,
Seems I am captured yet so
young,
But dreams don't live by
vision,
To somehow live within
these words,
For dreams are not forgiven.

JoAnne Roethlein

NIGHT TIME

The teddy bear was juggling a red
and yellow ball.
The toy train was puffing, chugging,
tooting down the hall.
The striped prancing pony with the
curly mane and tail
Was jumping lightly through a hoop
and over a tall rail.
The trucks and cars were busy
honking horns and driving round.
The tops were gaily spinning,
singing, falling to the ground.
The dolly with the golden hair was
twirling in a dance
With the wooden man who loved
her, (you could tell it at a glance).
The music box and wagon and the
engine painted red
Were laughing, when a voice called,
"Johnny, please get out of bed."
And one by one they slipped away,
to come again that night,
After the sandman, making his
rounds, had turned out Johnny's
light.

Kevin D Melancon

WHEN A TREE FALLS IT HURTS

To my loving wife Julie and my Children

When a tree falls it hurts,
Heavy does it fall as it hits the
ground,
Breaking even the smallest of twigs
that depend on it so,
So many are they that are touched by
the one,
The skies cry at the sight of the
thunderous fall,
Helpless as life is robbed from its
very soul,
Each branch reaching out grabbing
with nothing there,
So many are they that are touched by
the one,
When a tree falls it hurts,
Vacant is the spot for which it once
stood,
Leaving a gap that once had life
flowing in it,
So many are they that are touched by
the one.

Amy Baxter

CITY STREETS

The city streets are dark and silent.
You think that no one's there—
but somewhere deep inside you
lurks a thing called fear.

Fear of long black shadows,
maniacs in the night,
knowing they are hiding somewhere
fills a girl with fright.

With that fright comes anger,
an anger that grows so strong,
for there is no longer a time
when a girl can walk alone.

No longer can she walk that street
sorting her feelings and emotions,
no longer can she walk the coast
or her body may be found in the
ocean

With all this fear and anger
there is no cause for debate,
with all this fear and anger
it's no wonder why we hate.

Marcia Kay Sharp

CHRISTMAS

To my dear Grandma, Marie Coss.

Christmas is coming, the months are
going faster,
but make sure you think of your dear
Loving Master.

You shop for boys, you shop for girls
too,
you shop for toddlers and grownups
that's true.

You have big dinners and some
presents too;
but remember your Master who has
risen for you.

Christmas isn't always presents and
things,
it's Christ Jesus' Birthday that comes
first every year.

So remember our Saviour instead of
great gifts,
because He's lots more important on
everyone's list.

Gerry A Loving

IN BED WE CRY

At night
In bed
We cry out
Our vexations.
On sodden pillows
We shed
Our most furtive fears,
Leaching out
The rank impurities
Of our soiled souls
With salt-laced tears,
Leaving them gnawed clean
Of the murky meat
Of despair and sorrow,
Clean shriven and fetus-fresh
Only to be polluted again
Come tomorrow.

Uriel Kreklewich

AS TWO DOVES KISS

As two doves kiss
Two spirits touch,
Two hearts embrace;
Two souls are one.

As soul and mind
United through faith,
Man links with man;
One finds true self.

As self is known
Our being is revealed,
And in the mystery of our living
We share its constant love.

Benjamin Roy Rodriguez

A COW AND HER CALF

A cow and her calf drinking from a
stream,
with a reflection they have never
seen

A soft breeze blows the reflection
into a thousand tiny ripples

and once again

the cow and her calf are all alone
at the deep pond.

Scott W Ross

GOODBYE

Waking up and realizing
What you did was totally wrong
And messing up that gold horizon
By seeing that you are gone
Well it's hard to say goodbye
Yes it's hard to say goodbye
Because the one that you love, is
leaving now
Oh it's hard to say goodbye
You said that you would keep in touch
I was hoping that this would be true
When all along you knew as much
There was nothing you could do
Nothing you could do, to keep this
love alive
But to pray that God would touch it
So this love would survive
Knowing that someday will come
We will meet up once again
The look in your eyes will tell you
That to love there is no end
No end to this love of ours
For God has granted this
The past few years of memories
Proves that love still exists.

Peter Baisley

SEASONS OF OUR LIVES

To Dorthy Harding; Mother, who nourished all of our dreams throughout the years. Love, Peter

Spring of newness, splash of colors
Mid-summer's eve, bright fire
burning
Leaves of autumn, on the Twilight
Snows of winter, coming on

Thus are the seasons of our lives
Meaning of our yesteryears
Spring of our youth we seek to find
Winter ends, our search profound

Does reason prevail, in this time
Do we hurry and scatter as geese
Is our wisdom, one which rules
Sees the light and slows us down

What we have looked for, and found
What we have searched for, and lost
All are meanings in our fullness of
life
All are reasons for our daily being

Thus we close, on our ending years
Some of Joy, and some are veiled
with Tears
But all with meaning and some
profound
For what we have looked for, we
have found

Jennifer Lynn Unger

SWEET LITTLE DOVE

I ask for your love,
Will you give it to me.
So sweet little dove,
Fly over the sea.
Don't drop, don't die,
And I won't lie.
So free to fly,
So very high.
As you soar,
Danger crawls near.
Watch closely for,
It will form a tear.
Wipe it away,
From upon your eye.
If it shall stay,
Our love will die.

Duane J 'Akela' Hall

WHEN IS A MAN LONELY

To my family: Thank you

When is a man lonely
Even in a crowd
When he is silent
But screaming out loud

When is he touching
But no contact is found
When is he standing
Even when lying on the ground

To openly see
though his eyes are shut
When is he a man
or is he just but . . . .

Ann M Akers

Ann M Akers
WAR

Here lay our brave men, who gave their lives to wits' very end.
They did not choose to die, but they gave their life for you and I.
Rows and rows of monuments stand,
I stood and pondered, what for, why?
War is evil, war is unfair.
Here lay, our brave men.

Lisa R Anderson
ASHES

A picture of you
Is all that remains
A few scattered memories
Turn coals to flames.
Alive in thought
Dead in reality,
The past and the ashes
Left by the flames
Find me alone
And vulnerable to your pain.

Looking to the future
With hope in my eyes,
Feeling the trust
That within
My future lies.

The day will come
When no longer
Will your ashes
Inflict my dreadful pain,
And I will again
Be trusting and plain.

Dana M Tischler

Dana M Tischler
WINTER SKIES

To my mother, Kim and Marc.

Winter skies are nice and crisp.
Like beautiful snowflakes in the air
Winter is 4 fantasy and a time to glare
Out in the beautiful crisp air.

In winter skies, drift your fantasy to the top of the world.
And love every moment more and more.
Fly through the sky and never cry
Because all you lose
Will come back to you in
Winter skies

Maryann Domman
THE DAYS OF KYMBERLEE

Yes A Craze—Maybe Even A Maze
Of Days Gone By
At Last I See It Will Never Ever Be . . .

Oh The Magic, You Had To Be There! To Touch! To Feel!!
Like Frankenmuth Under The Acid Sky.
Only Kymberlee Knows.

Of Course With All The Highs Came The Lows.
Living With Sherry Must Have Been One.
Losing The Monte Must Have Been Too!

How About Ashton When Life Was Grim?
No Car Oh No! ! How Do I Get To Work Tomorrow?
Ahab or Michael?

How Will You Decide Your Life Kymberlee? For A Car?

No No No! ! A Little Cocaine Maybe . . . . .

Jose A Carmona
I MISS YOU!

I miss you,
Like a flower misses the spring;
Like a mother misses her offspring,
That's how I miss you.

I miss you,
Like the summer misses the sun;
Like an old man misses his past fun,
That's how I miss you.

I miss you,
Like autumn misses its colors;
Like a lover misses his troubles,
That's how I miss you.

I miss you,
Like winter misses the snows;
Like the river misses the waterflows,
That's how I miss you.

I miss you,
During the four seasons.
Why? I can't find a reason,
But, that's how I miss you.

Randall Rice
HARVEST

So much I wanted to do today,
but you couldn't be cleared from my mind,
nor could desire go vacationing

So I let myself wander

and remembered the red lips
of summer's end
while I picked cherries
and watched the sun trickle away
into autumnal evening.

Gloria Hockenberry
THE BURLED LEPRECHAUN

Aside the road a market mantled
'neath an August sun;
Tables displayed discarded wares
once treasured by someone.
The searchers sorted through the spread, enthralled by the array;
A frenzied quest for hidden fortune fashioned a foray.

Not wanting to be swept along, I stilled to gaze upon
A whittled, wizened little man, a span-high Leprechaun.
I mused into his burled eyes, and he mused back at me;
Enchantment posed betwixt some folds of tasseled tapestry.

I marveled at the elfin image hewn so wondrously;
He donned a garb of burnished burls, an elflock brushed his knee.
Upon his jacket seven rows of seven buttons bunched,
Over a pointed fairy shoe the capsuled cobbler hunched.

Yarners of yore wove fancy tales of wee-folk wizardry,
Of jolly jigs, of wily whims, and rampant revelry.
They told of fabled Cuchulain, of herbal mending made
To rouse the wounded lionheart when in the louch he laid.

He winked a burled eye at me, I was at once beguiled;
Wild fancy fraught my kindled thoughts as I winked back and smiled.
Most carefully I lifted him, possession was my wish,
I held him tightly in my hand, fearing he would vanish.
More mischief made the seller shout:
"I hope you like your dish!"

Mrs Donna May Bradley
SPEAK-OUT

I dedicate this piece of work on behalf of all the people in the world. I want the people of all races come together, one as a whole, and unite as one. Please let us as a human race believe in unity and equality, justice to all races.

I'm a person who speaks my mind
A voice which expresses true insight,
A perception
A sensitivity 'bout life's problems.
I've seen the problems of the ghettos, the filth, the garbage, the slums
ALL the sick people, oh, how I'VE seen evil under the sun . . .
Whose possessions, and honor is torn by bitter hate, and prejudice, by the illiterate high power phonies . . . .

My heart bleeds to see people boxed in poor sections marked "ghettos,"
All people and races have important parts in life, but we need to be set free.

All the toil of man is his mouth, yet his appetite is not satisfied.
For what advantage has a black person over a wise man who's a fool . . . .
Yet, a poor man has the know how . . . . to conduct himself before all whose lives to witness equality and justice.
Yes, we're all human beings, with the better of a sight and the wandering of desire; this also is vanity and a striving after wind.
Each and everyone belongs, we all need to stand strong.
Never dispute with an illiterate, or one stronger than you
Never live your full life in vain—
Because revenge is a shadow, but love is the sun . . . .
With hope and fate, runnin' deep is our pain.
Life's a long road, we need to identify with each other . . . .
We're brothers and sisters
People who live in ghettos should be seen for themselves
Not as a reflection on all.

Adam F Misterka
FOR YOU

For you God created World,
The sun to warm the Earth, and to spring the life,
The blue of the skies;
The green blanket what cover the land
The majestic trees attempting reach high
The flowers of color, shapes and perfume smell,
The millions species flora fauna share;
The birds singing, the charm of butterfly
The depth of oceans holding so much life,
The space above with a billion stars,
The moon what shining in darkness of night:
. . . And to admire all this,—Your mind and your sight.

—The greatest art whatever was made
Is round you and upon your feet,
Every day you see it, every day you meet
The miracle, the beauty of heavenly feat
And yet, when day after day passing through
You never notice it, never think,
—That all of this was made
for . . You.

Dena Miller
COMMON SENSE

With common sense we kill one another,
And tell ourselves "He's not my brother."
His color is different, his thoughts are too,
He's not the same as me and you."
With "common sense," we leave alone, all those people that have no home.
One can't take a chance, they may have disease,
So we all sit back in all our ease, and "common sense" comes in to play,
Then we say to eachother, "Have a nice day!"

Lori Orr
DROWNED OUT WITH TEARS (CEMETERY)

I dedicate this poem to my sister Carrie with best wishes and love always and forever.

As I walk this quiet place
where no one likes to go
where the birds are always chirping
and the wind will always blow
this place is filled
with saddened faces
and drowned out with tears
people have been lying here
for many many years
their faces cold and crusty
and their body old and dry
but now their mind and happiness
are way up in the sky
this place is to remember
all the lively years
but whenever people come
they drown it out with tears.

Mary J Key
SOMETIMES TOMORROW

To my daughter Tana, my mother Sue Corder, dear friend Roy McAuley, and highly admired artist Laurie Anderson.

Thought I would write you today, though I thought of you yesterday. And the day before, and the day before, and the day before, and the day before.

I'm sitting here now. In my room. Like, I often do. But, I don't always stay, no. My mind we wonder away.

You know that hope and fear are one and the same? Sure. And that sadness and gladness only mean

And if I were to try and say, in some other way, they'd send me away, put me away, lock, me away, they'd throw the keys away.

But like the birds in the trees, I want to be. Then I am. So I can. Like this land. I am. Even the sand.

Please take hold of my hand. And I could take you away, so far away. Away, away. Away from this day.

Aaahh, then you could. You could if you would. You would if you could, if you would.

Let me stay. Just this way, today. So far away. So far away, this day, today. Yesterday.

Joseph Lamah Walker Jr
MOMENTS

Dedicated to Jason, Michael and John

A moment comes, a moment goes,
It has no place and has no time,
It comes and comes like wind that blows.

It passes no time, it passes no place,
And never passes the next in line,
It's on the move as though at race.

Moments past are forever lost,
While moments now are what we have,
And no future's gained at any cost.

So live and love, and do it now,
For now is all we have at hand.
The time we share has never stopped,
And moments come like seeping sand.

William G Laing
FRIENDS

To my best friend Glenn; the Divine Sarah.

Here I sit thinking of you
with a lump in my throat
and a tear or two.
It may sound funny
coming from me,
as I am not a person
of this type, you see.
From the day we met
it did not arise
you were the one
with the pretty eyes.
Since that day, a love
has grown a friendship so strong
and solid as stone.
If ever we decide
to go our own ways
I'll always remember
those as my happier days.
They say a good thing only
lasts so long.
With a friend like you
that quote has to be wrong.
It all comes down
to a phrase so true
I really miss
that friendship in you.

Donald R Sandifer
HELP ME LORD

Help me Lord, when a friend has gone astray,
Help me Lord to know what to say,
Give me your word to relay,
Help me Lord, as I pray.

Help me Lord, every day,
Help me Lord, in the month of May
As I walk along the bay
Help me Lord, your will to pray.

Help me Lord, as I play,
Help me Lord, when I'm hauling hay,
For you know I've bills to pay
Help me Lord, oh this I pray.

Help me Lord, when skies are gray,
Help me Lord, not to go astray
And if I fall from your way
Help me Lord, so I can pray.

Peggy J McClain
THE BLUES

To my husband, Larry
Also Larry Jr, Lisa, Todd
—Family & Friends

If everyone was happy, we would have never heard the blues. It's from all this feeling, we learned to dance in twos.

It's times when we are hurting, that we learn true happiness. Thru life's growing experience, it's the key to our success.

Listen to your heart closely, and hear all the tender tunes. You just haven't been listening, if you've never heard the blues.

Sheila Dennis
A GIFT OF LOVE

I wanted to give you a very special gift,
a gift no one had ever given you.
One you would always remember.
So I looked in every store and couldn't seem to find it.
So I looked into my heart and found it.
My gift to you is LOVE.
This gift isn't just for today, but for always.
I will keep on giving you this gift all the days of my life!

Sharon C Hines
FOR DERRYL

Dedicated to my beloved son Derryl Jaimes Wright—Age 20 Killed by a drunk driver Nov 27, 1988

A mother's love is gentle and kind
For a mother's love is the tie that binds
A child to her before birth and after death.

A mother's love is firm and strong
With a guiding hand to keep the child
From going wrong.

A mother's love is full of joy and
hope for tomorrow.
A mother's love never gives up,
gives out, or grows old.
A mother's love is all these things
and more;
So this is what I send with you,
now, my son—

YOUR MOTHER'S LOVE!

Mary C Royal
FOR MY HUSBAND AND FRIEND

This poem is dedicated to Gene, my husband of fourteen years.

It has been quite a few years,
And though sometimes I drove you to tears,
I still love you through it all,
Even if telling you now may seem like something small,
Three kids later and a wrinkle or two,
I still have this to say to you,
Whether each day may bring happy times or sad,
Some times good or some times bad,
I will always hope and pray,
That you love me enough to stay another day.

Judith K Pierson

Judith K Pierson
HAPPY

Looking in your eyes
for the first time,
you may be shy,
you want to hide,
but my heart knows
the beauty,
the grace,
it's there in your face,
when you move,
when you smile,
heaven's delight.

Looking in your eyes,
a strong good feeling
climbs.
Happy,
sets my senses reeling,
takes me miles high.

Donna A Nichols
HELP ME

Help me, for I am lost,
I am a woman, yet a child.
I go thru life searching for warmth,
And I find pain, hurt, rage and anger.
I don't like feeling this way.
Why have I lost trust in mankind?
Why am I so alone and scared?
Even if surrounded by people.
Please, can't someone help me?
Love me for what I am now,
Not for what I was,
Not for what I will be,
But for what I am right now.
I am still a child in many ways,
Loving life in all its glory.
This is how my life will be,
If someone special will share with me.

Howard R Kindred Sr
AFRAID

To my wife Kathleen who inspired me

Was in love before, I was hurt before.
I cried in pain, I hid in shame.

Then came you, didn't wanna get close.
Got into my blood, you looked and smiled.

Talked like a friend, sounded like a woman.
You touched my hand, smiled at me, said!

Don't wanna get hurt, I've been hurt before.
Don't wanna again, looked at me, smiled!

And all the time, you said what I felt.
I guess that's when; I fell in love.

For the first time wasn't the only one, that was scared.
So I'll say; I love you first.

Florence M Foti
DRIFTING

I'm leaving for a while . . .
this month of October,
So think of me
as the leaves are turning
and wish me well.
I'm just beginning to live.

The wind will lead me
where I'm going
As it blows away
the tired wishes
and the endless hopes.
But, I'll always have my dreams
And
I'll
be
drifting . . . .

Alice M Walker
THE FLIGHT

To my beloved family

WE board at five o'clock,
A golden coach? 'tis nay,
Rather, a great silver eagle, its
Wing spread wide, long, slicing
Through cloud castles with the
abandon of Apollo,
The throb of engines defies
The silent skies as we pass,
Unheard, unseen, yet there.
From the porthole we look
Down, down, down into
Nothingness, patches of blue
Between boiling white the scope
majestic,
Here the reality is electric,
Only, in all this vastness,
Until suddenly we're descending
Into that earth bound world of
Love and ordinary we left behind.

Helen F Brady
ON THIS OUR SILVER

Dedicated to my husband Ed, on our 43rd Anniversary June 30, 1989

On this our silver as I look back,
Happiness and love we did not lack.
The first five years we grew up together,
Many small storms we learned

to weather.
When at last came our great joy,
God's great gift a baby boy.
The wonderful years just flew as he grew,
Our love became greater in
those years too.
A life that's based on love, faith and trust,
In a happy marriage this is a
must.
Vows that were made when we were wed,
Freshly linger as tho just said.
From silver to golden we will strive,
With the help of God, and our
love so alive.

Robert C Leonard
THE DYING FLAME

For my Mom, Shirley, and to Lupe, wherever she may be

Brilliant is the match that's struck,
Flames are hungry for its stem,
And a love has started carelessly,
Seeming like a precious gem.
The flame is strong as is its heat,
Consuming its own time,
And hearts of gold bleed their truth
As bells begin to chime.
Without a care, and with great ease
Its luminescence holds,
And bells that chime are silent now,
As truth itself unfolds.
The flame holds life now carelessly
For it shall surely fade,
And hearts of gold show signs of rust
That tears have slowly made.
The light grows dim as does its heat
So slowly will it die,
And bells again chime for a love that is dead,
As they fight off the pain as
they cry.
The fire has died and smoke fills the air,
And time is left holding the
blame,
And two hearts have tried to strike up a love,
But succeed like the dying
flame.

Dianna Paglianete
VIEW
The Sun beats down hard and hot
upon my pen
I sit and stare out at a distant dream
Lying upon the treetops, it looks so
majestically innocent as birds
fly in and out of its rainbow
illumination only to become engulfed
in a lost blaze of fiery yellow

Georgia Kay Taylor
PITTER PATTER

To my baby I lost, wherever it may be.

The rain is falling.
As I lay awake wondering what
could have been.
Listening to the rain drops knocking against
my window pane.
Just like the tear drops falling from
my heart.

Pitter Patter
There goes my heart.
The thought of little feet going pitter patter
across the playpen floor.

Pitter Patter
my window is open, the raindrops
are falling on me.

Patrick Knowles
AUTUMN WINDS
What beauty can a soaring bird present,
that a wind blown feather
could not offer?
Who shall embrace that which the wind
holds dearest,
such as the Autumn reed?

What greater love shall be known,
than that which is sown,
within the windswept seed?

Genevra A Simonton
A WISH IN MY POCKET

To my dear sons, Ryan and Randy

While walking life's pathways, just
strolling along
I've a wish in my pocket—where
does it belong?

How should I spend it—my mind's
in a daze
I keep changing decisions—I'm lost
in a maze.

Should I wish for happiness—or
should it be love
No, I want to be wealthy—Oh, to fly
like a dove.

I'll wish for success—or should it be
fame
I want to be courageous—No, a
beautiful dame.

I'll wish for a mansion—No, a small
country home
I want a luxury car—with a driver
and phone.

This wish in my pocket—it's driving
me mad
If only I could find how to spend it—
then I could be glad.

If only I had two wishes—or better
yet three
Oh—I'll give you my wish and you
spend it for me.

Carol Bilica
THE MORTICIAN
A Mortician is a man they say
Who sees you after you pass away
You are his guest and I must say
He only lets you stay three days

He has a bed so soft and fine
That you are ready to recline
Rest in Peace all is well
This is the story they do tell

The bed is durable they say
It will last forever and a day
What worries me is the price
Will I be able to pay

They ask about insurance that's nice
Then they go on their way
They are the last person we see on earth
We were destined to them since our birth

There is lots of sadness and tears
For all of us have fears
What lies ahead for the one in bed
Has been a mystery for years

Norma P Friend
BETTER, BETTER
Now, by all reason and logic it's
time that I should say
You are surely getting older, another
year has slipped away.
I could say, "Slow up! Take it easy!
Move about with care."
Perhaps I might say, "Just take to
your rocking chair."

But no! Not so! Tho yes, the year has
flown
You are not really older, but have
better grown.
This has been another year to love
you—each day is like a page
And like so many good things, you
grow sweeter with age.

Your friendship and love are a
blessing to my life
You help in many ways to keep me
going right
I sincerely hope your special day is
especially nice for you.
Because you deserve the very best—
nothing less will do.

I may say, "Good morning" when
day has turned to night
But remember I love you whether
it's dark or light
For if I should have had a sister, and
she had a husband true,
I think I could not love them more
than I love your spouse and you.

Harvey E "Chief" Muzzy Sr
USN Ret Phoenix AZ
FORGET ME NOT
I am a human embryo, in the
beginning stages of life
Don't for the sake of some pain, or
shame, think of doing away with me.
Let me be born, there's someone,
somewhere, that has plenty of love
and it will bring them laughter just
having me to be part of their life, so
just let me be.
God created all life right from the
start, so please, I ask
"Forget me not"
Soon I am a child, discovering all the
beautiful things our maker has made.
Pretty flowers, animals, some big,
some small, a beautiful puppy, a
kitty cat too.
Rain for the flowers, so pretty in
spring, the grass turns greener and
big tree will make shade.
Even white snowflakes fall from the
sky, as I look up they fall in my eyes.
Time will go on, a lot of things I will
learn, now as I am growing . . I also
get smart. Please I ask
"Forget me not"
No longer a child, a teenager with
new responsibilities.
Help me, guide me, don't wait until
it's too late, someone has led me
astray, with some kind of bait.
I want to be helpful, in this country,
and this world God has made.
Maybe I'll be called to fight for this
country, for our freedom, so many
feel is something that is automatically theirs.
Forgetting the fallen comrades, and
the fathers, mothers, and sisters and
brothers
That lost a loved one, nothing
stopped their tears.
Come on now, do your share, don't
stop, please I ask.
"Forget me not"
Those that return from a foreign land,
who have done their duty,
We don't expect a parade, marching
with a band, just some respect, from
those who gain, show those that do
their part, you are thankful, please, I
ask
"Forget me not"
Years will have passed, a senior
citizen, we now are called.
We're still useful, look back at the
long roads and responsibilities we
hauled.
God wants us here now, to tell and
help the young, show with love and
spiritual foundation there is light at
the end of the road, not just a sign
that says stop.
Please, I ask
"Forget me not"

Judith Davis
GRAM, A SPECIAL LADY
I can't begin to tell you, although it's
plain to see,
Your love and understanding
mean more than the world to
me.
You're the kindest, gentlest lady,
with a heart as pure as gold,
And anyone who knows you, has
been blessed by God above.
He knows that it's not always easy,
you've had some rough sad times,
But God also knows your faith's
so great, that He'll be there to
help.
You've been a mother who cares and
understands,
A grandmother who nurtures
and is always there,
A great grandmother who can make
all children's eyes glow
And yet you'll always have time
for someone else,
To smile, to lend support, never
complain, but encourage and love.
The dear Lord was smart when
He put you on this earth.
He knew how we would love you,
and how you'd love us in return.
You're still a peppy speedy lady,
running circles around me,
But that's alright,
Because I know that circle
surrounds me with your love.

Candida Iacuzio
HER DANCING FEET
They called her the girl with the
dancing feet,
She was so graceful and so
petite,
She learned to dance before she
could talk,
In fact she would dance instead
of walk.
She came of age to enter school,
With her dancing feet she broke
the rules,
She tried to control them when she
sat
But everyone heard them go tap,
tap, tap.
She was scolded and punished but it
did no good,
It seemed to her no one
understood,
That dancing was in her very soul,
She knew some day she would
reach her goal,
For every step meant that she'd
succeed,
As long as it took her dancing
feet.
To reach the ladder way on top,
The standing ovations as she

bowed,
The curtain calls, the floral bouquets,
She knew this was the only way,
For it was a feeling so very deep,
That she fulfilled with her
dancing feet.

Mary Agnes Lynch
A BEAUTIFUL ROSE

"A flower of delicate beauty,
Sweet smelling to my
nose,
Sending forth a heavenly
perfume,
Is that of a beautiful
rose."

"The loveliness of its color, a
rich, and deep,
red
Reminds me of the blood of
'Christ,'
So precious, each drop that
'He' shed."

"The sweetness of a rose,
so white,
Lovely, and pure, like
a ray of
light,
Blooms with rare
beauty,
In 'God's' 'Divine'
sight."

"There's so much
more,
I'd like to
tell,
About a rose I like so well.
"How glad I
am,
I have a nose,
Each time I see a
beautiful rose"

Maureen Winn
AUTUMN SPLENDOR

Floating down from the treetops
You cloak the earth with a mantle of autumn splendor,
Crimson, emerald, and gold,
All transitional evidence of the artistry of God.
From the master creator of beauty
You give the world credence
To the constant cycle
Of death and rebirth,
In the spring you'll rise again
As our Creator
Fresh and constant as life itself.
You do denote the coming of winter
But in your splendid death
There is unsurpassed glory and hope
Born of the radiant palette
Of the Almighty,
Surely you teach us
The repeating parable of the season,
"And to each season turn, turn, turn."
Autumn provides time to give thanks
And a time to take stock
Of our successes and failures
You remind us that each spring
We are given a new chance
To begin again,
To renew old acquaintances
And to forgive and love once more.

Linda Marie Zemtseff
A BIRTHDAY THOUGHT FOR MOM

The days fly by, the months roll on,
The years so quickly pass,
And each day there is something
To ourselves that we must ask:
What have I done to make this place
Better for those around me?
What have I done to improve my world
And to better me?
(The answer here, is oh, so clear).

You make your life so meaningful
To those who surround you—
You give much of your loving care
And every part of you,
So that we may reach our self made goals
Through values taught by you;
To make this world a better place,
Like you set out to do.

No one can correct the world
In the short time that they live,
But the years fly by, and we should try,
To give all that we can give.

Gary Zemtseff
THE SENSES

To hear, to see, to harbor thought,
From what beginnings I know naught,
By with which we can perceive,
All the things of splendor sought.

The senses are a wondrous great,
But man does not appreciate
Their marvels! For ne'er does he realize,
That there is naught to compensate.

But for our sakes they are forgiving,
And think only for our living
For the betterment of man,
Always working, helping, giving!

George T Zemtseff
THE PATH

A man works, he lives—he dreams,
He seeks a path lined with trees of hope and grass of green;
He searches the depth of this world in quest of the magic that will give meaning to his life,
That in years to come he can know that his endeavors did reap the harvest of his work and strife.

And it would seem that this time for you is an appropriate time of reflection,
Not that your job is done, but only a plateau from which to observe the goals your life was set on;
To reassure yourself, that you have given of yourself, each and every day,
To be at peace with God, knowing that your path was His path in each and every way.

You plucked the fruit of goodness on your way and she, of course, is lovely Ann,
The foundation upon which you could always rely, when your feet might give way to sand;
And together a platform of love you both did tenaciously build,
And together you both did conquer all challenges this world might possibly yield.

The imprint you leave carries on to many another,
And we two have been privileged to be touched by that love you have for another.
For most certainly our lives have been swayed by the gracious way
You care and give to another, to lighten their burden, to brighten their day.

While so many a couple's path has long been covered by the leaves of distress,
Shining pinnacles of Oak lie scattered on your path to confirm the difficulties you did redress.
The trees of love and strength which line the trail that you chose to take,
Stand strong and tall as if to pridefully acknowledge the decision you did make.

So take a joyful glimpse at the miles that you have tread,
With anxious expectation of the road that lies ahead;
And hand in hand you'll shuffle leaves of hope lined by grass of green,
That glisten in the sunlight, reflecting the love He does beam.

Carol Murphy
DON'T CRY FOR ME

Don't cry for me
My soul has been set free
My body lies in quiet rest
And I am at my very best
I have no longer any faults
All my pains have come to halts
Now I am part of a heavenly choir
Now can sing to my heart's desire
I have witnessed perfect peace
Now I walk among the meek
Please don't cry for me
Just because my soul was freed

Rose R Thomas

Rose R Thomas
MY FRIEND

Someone who takes time to listen,
To a troubled heart in despair.
Someone who is sympathetic,
Who shows concern and care.

Someone who is there when needed,
Giving a helping hand.
Someone who is kind and thoughtful,
Making no great demands.

Someone with a sense of humor,
A smile to light up my day.
Someone who is loyal and dependable,
To keep me steadfast in my way.

Someone whose positive thinking,
Gives me confidence which I can depend.
That someone so dear and trusting,
Is someone I call . . . MY FRIEND

Lee Frandsen
TRIBUTE TO MY FATHER

This poem is dedicated to my friend and father Andrew Frandsen

I the farmer—keeper of earth,
tiller of soil—worker of dirt.
I with the hands so calloused
and strong,
a mind often worried, but a will to go on.
A kin to elements—cold—heat—
wind and rain
accustomed to toil and the burden of strain.
A worker with the memory of
things in the past,
amazed with things of the present—
wondering too how time could go so fast.
Remembering the horses and
the machinery they drew,
and working with ease the machines of new.
Fearing the loss of my crops by
elements uncontrolled,
always hoping my harvest 'tis the best ever known.
With visions and dreams I
keep planting the seed,
hoping nature and God will be working with me.
Wishing my offspring will
inherit my love of the land,
remembering the good times not dwelling on the bad.
Yes, I the farmer with
complicated feelings inside,
hoping to work this land till the time I shall die.
I the farmer my feelings so
seldom revealed,
yet always knowing another
farmer—knows just how I feel.

Florence Oleyar
MISS LIBERTY

She came to us through friendship
from a land across the sea,
Piece by piece assembled
she became "Miss Liberty."

She stood above the water
with a torch held in her hand,
A mighty crown adorned her head
A gateway to our land.

They came from every country
the people of despair,
They left their home and family
to a place they knew not where.

As the ships sailed passed the lady
their eyes were filled with tears,
She touched their hearts like magic
and calmed their many fears.

One by one they settled
in a land so far and wide,
They worked and sweat together
but never lost their pride.

They never asked for riches
and as the story's told,
They never found it easy
nor the streets all paved with gold.

They gave to us a blessing
born in a land that's free,
So let us keep their spirit
our God and our liberty.

Thank you France, our ally
for a gift so great and rare,
"Miss Liberty" is shining
for all the world to share.

Frances White
SHALL WE AS GOD'S CHILDREN

Shall we as God's Children
fight
to live in the world
so confused, shall we be.
Shall we let ourselves die?

Shall we be so gullible
lost without direction
think,
for we are all unique individuals.
We can either abuse the mind, or
we can enrich it to the fullest.

If we can allow ourselves to be weak
We can allow ourselves to be strong.

Our egos, our pride shall not get in

the way,
for we were born with richer gifts.
And we shall share
our hearts, our good thoughts,
ourselves.

By admitting our imperfections.
By succumbing to the truth.
By not living a lie.

But, by sharing ourselves,
God's children.

Kathleen Williams
MY SISTER, MY FRIEND

To my mother, Mary E. Donnelly, who has always been there with strength, understanding, wisdom, and most of all—love

She was always special, a
friend right from the start
A loving hand to guide me, we
hardly were apart
She didn't ask to have me, so young
she didn't know
How little sisters sometimes are,
with big sisters do they go

A tag along, to here and there,
grabbing toys away
But then she had to keep me,
she didn't have a say
A room we shared throughout the
years, sharing secrets, special dreams
Rock n' roll, boyfriends,
schoolwork, like only yesterday it
seems

Then on to love and marriage,
first me, then later her
We stood beside each other,
what lovely brides we were
Time passed, then one day we both
knew a love that's like no other
We cherish that time when we
earned the precious title "Mother"

And through the years our lives
were filled with our children's
every need
Then they had schoolwork, rock n'
roll, a precious time indeed
Now here we are, our children
grown, fond memories to recall
Our lives are different, yet in
ways nothing's changed at all

We started out as friends that day
so many years ago
Dear sister, love grows stronger as
years pass, and I know
That you will always be there, and
I'll be there for you
I love you now—forever, but then
I thought you knew

Jay Braxton Nix
LET FREEDOM RING IN MEMORY OF DR. MARTIN LUTHER KING

To Barbara Haskins, Rev. Anderson E. Porter and Alma Steed. My Family and Extended Church Family and Friends.

Let freedom ring
Join the fight of Martin Luther King
King was a man with a difficult task
to face
He loved everybody, no matter what
race
Even though Martin Luther King has
passed on
Love should still prevail
Starting with every newborn
Carry out his thoughts and carry out
his plan
So freedom will ring out for every
man
Gone should be the days of Jim
Crow
Hatred is devastating when it
continues to grow
In loving memory of Dr. Martin
Luther King
Let's all have a loving attitude and
let freedom ring
King was a fantastic spiritual and
family man
Always helping out and lending a
hand
King showed me the power of people
joining together
Marching courageously forward and
keeping the faith forever
God gave Martin the power to lead
the people
So let freedom ring beyond steeple to
steeple

Jennifer Neer
LOVE IS SOMETHING SPECIAL

Love is something special,
something that never dies.

Love is what's between me and you,
right before our eyes.

Love is the thing that brightens your
day,
and it won't just walk away.

Love is there night and day,
to let you know how much I care.

Love follows you wherever you go,
and tells you the things that you
should know.

Love is there for you can see,
just how much you mean to me!

Julie McLain
DON'T RUSH IN

Sea shells hold the special song
of love that just somehow
Went wrong.
The moon has told a thousand lies
And turned hello's into
good-byes.

The sea has cried a thousand lies
For loves that fade through
The years.
The breeze has brought back faded
dreams of the past
The dreams of those who were in
A hurry and went too fast.

And if the stars could talk
If only the stars could talk
They'd tell you that before you run
You first must learn to walk.

Stephanie King
AMERICA, WHERE ARE YOUR BOYS?

Dedicated to: My Daddy and all the others who fought and fell by his side during the Vietnam War, and fight still with him today.

Once a smiling boy
without a single care
has somehow faded in the night
but none of us know where

Not one could see the road ahead
where are those carefree days?
The broken men with loyal hearts
in solemn defeat turn gray

Those boys who fought and
served afar
Who thought their motives right
must fight this war with no avail
through every haunting night

No one knows the pain they bear
the aching of their hearts
No one sees the hate they know
or feels the stinging scars
In duty's name they did their share
And fought with hatred's toys
I only have one thing to ask
America, where are your boys?

Karen Kellerman
THE FOREST

I want to give thanks, to my husband, Scott, our sons: Matthew and Jonathon . . . For the same peace an' loving feeling. An' a special thanks to Penny Walker, for inspiration . . .

It's a foggy day
Yet it's so beautiful
Birds have plenty to say.
The forests' quietness is so
powerful . . .

Walking in the wilderness
Enjoying the peace you receive
Feeling the winds' caress
Knowing God's with you, which I do
believe . . .

Looking around this territory
Seeing that it's no illusion
Feeling the animals glory
'Cause there's no streets or heavy
confusion.

I'm lucky to live out here
In this quiet and peaceful place
Having nothing to fear
Seeing a trustworthy face . . .

Betty J Jarvis

Betty J Jarvis
A POEM

To all my friends, in Texas

A poem is words that should be
heard,
Or read in silence without being
disturbed,
A poem should be neat and also
sweet,
Lovely in rhymes and something to
keep.

It'll make you laugh and sometimes,
cry,
Yet not knowing the reason why,
It makes you feel warm and never
any harm.
But feeling secure from dusk to
dawn.

Jill Renee Hunter
I BELIEVE I'VE SWALLOWED . . .

I believe I've swallowed . . .
A frog,
A log,
A little smog,
My sister's dog,
A cogswell cog,
And a taste of egg nog.

I believe I've swallowed . . .
My notepad,
My dad,
Some milk that went bad,
My shirt that was plaid,
An English lad,
And some anchovies (a tad).

I believe I've swallowed . . .
A bag,
A little jet lag,
A game of tag,
The American Flag,
A dog's wag,
And I'm beginning to gag.

I believe I've swallowed . . .
A cow,
Some dog chow,
A cat that's starting to meow,
A dhow,
And a cactus (ow!),
But how?

I'm hungry now!

Virginia Dean Waters
SEE THE HAPPINESS THIS BRINGS

To the miraculous Infant Jesus of Prague. In thanksgiving for all the miracles bestowed on me, my family, and many friends I have helped.

I want to help the young in
school,
Explain to them, be careful, it's
easy to become a fool,
Go out, and, have fun, while
you're young,
Pick your company, be mindful,
of another's tongue
Build character and reputation,
Without it, you'll end in a bad
situation
Think first, honesty is the best
policy,
Use your insight,
You are never wrong, in doing
what is right,
Have good thoughts, and you do
good things,
Your mind controls you, try this,
And see the happiness
it brings

Alice D Moore-Cornett
SANDS OF TIME

Relentlessly the sands of Time
so steadily record our hours.

When youth's in bloom, a time
of Spring,
we do assume foreverness.

But 'tis not so. The summer comes,
and softly goes; then Fall's at
hand.

For some the sands have
slipped on through.
For some the grains becoming
few.

Wait not for age to seek the Lord.
Give Him your life, all self
outpoured.

He has a plan for each of us,
but gives each one the choice
to make.

To follow Christ and go His way,
creating peace and harmony,

or do you choose the worldly
way
that ever leads to worldly
fray?

Your choice to make,
but do be sure.
When sands run out
it is too late.

Milton Davis
RACES OF PEOPLE

There are White people,
There are Black people,
There are Mexican people;
There are all other races
of people. But we are all
part of God whether if we
know it or not, so let us
have peace in this world
instead of war.

Regina Deutschman
NEEDS

We need the Holy Spirit,
To show us tenderness;
We seek the Holy Spirit
For its divine caress.

We need to live above the
Worldly living to excess;
To keep our sights on Heaven—
And never to digress.

To recognize the Light and Sound
within—
And them address;
To hunger for Thy Beauty—
And not under duress.

We need to lift our spirits,
To express a loveliness;
And remember Spirit needs mankind
Through which to express.

Kirk Gerard Crouch
SONNET//1.

WHERE is the amiable breast that I
do seek,
To upon wipe my tear and rest my
cheek?
WHERE is the fair hand that should
mine hold,
To lead me onfromward—through
the tumult?
WHEREFORE dost thou beauty
that I seek go this night . . ,
Does it wish to play or does it
rest?
WHERE does your mind rate—
Are you comatose or awash with
zest?
WHERE does your physical
sheath rate—
Are you rosebud or scurvy-like?
WHERE lies your future,
Is it in the pit,
Or in the Garden in the Cloud with
flowers, trees, and candles alive?
WHERE ARE YOU? SWEET
CHERUB . . , WHERE ARE
you . . ?

Danny J Dickerson
A SOLDIER'S SACRIFICE

To ALL the brave Men and Women who served Their Country and lost, They know the words all so well.

I've chocked my pride and honor,
Gave up my wife and home
My children don't understand
Where their Daddy has gone.

Their mother has to tell them,
Duty has me on call
With no words of promise
That I'll be back at all.

Thru trenches I must trut,
To fight the flames of hell
I constantly stop and wonder
If my family is doing well.

Mangled or dismembered
Crippled for rest of life,
They send me back home to the
people
And my "once" loving wife.

I thank God for my return,
And that I'm still alive
But in a horrible shock I stop and
realize
There's no one there to greet me,
Even though we've won the war
I've lost everything I fought to
protect
And a few pieces more.

My duty has left me stranded
I've no family, home nor friends,
But to save my country
(The United States)
I'd sacrifice all again.

Bernice V Patera
THE SEASONS

When summer comes all nature
flowers and is in bloom;
Birds are singing, the sun is shining,
a summer breeze is blowing.
Soon, the fragrance of summer ends
with the scent of new mown hay.
Comes autumn with fading flowers;
The robin is singing a song to say
good-bye.
There is a far cry of geese o'er
head.
The brilliant leaves come tumbling
down.
And the winds begin blowing cold.
But winter is lovely too.
When the leaves of the trees are
under the snow.
Snow whistling and swirling falling
to the ground,
The air is crisp, the sun shines
bright;
Earth can become a fairy land in the
gleaming winter sunshine.
Snow drifts are high and the wind
blows cold;
Then the magic of spring comes
creeping around.
The whispering winds play through
the budding threes.
Now the snow is melting and
vanishing away.
Once again it's time to inhale
the fragrance of the flowers.

Jeannie
THE BROKEN HEART

To my Father, I love you very much.

You asked
I did,

You showed
I liked,

You talked
I listened,

Only once
I loved,
You didn't.

I loved you!

Pauline Beck
SEASONAL LOVE

Dedication: 1988-89 Mrs. Kelly's 4th Grade Class Immaculate Conception School B.V.M., New Oxford, Pa.

The cold of winter ends—welcoming
the Spring
A smile, freshness, new growth
The budding appears
The rain—the sun to bloom blossom
and harvest,
'Tis earth, the beauty o'er all again.

Here comes Summer such warmth it
doeth bring
Birds butterflies insects and frogs
The cooling waters a refuge
The sun shineth bright twinkling
stars in the night,
'Tis earth, the beauty o'er all again.

Autumn—bringing the falling of
leaves
Another of nature's wonders
Come alive! come alive! many
colors foretell
Cool morn cool night the moon and
the breeze,
'Tis earth, the beauty o'er all again.

Now the cold of Winter comes,
Brrrr- - -
Children laughing, children playing
in
Purity white the falling of snow
And find with it all, that perfect love
Through the year after year,
'Tis earth, the beauty o'er all again.

Judy Kiel
THE CRY OF GOD'S CHILD

If the world should stop for just one
day,
we would see no love,
or children at work or play.
The earth would stop breathing.
The grass and trees would not grow.
The sun would be dark
The stars would not glow.
There would be no more pretty
flowers
No clouds to see.
Everything quiet.
No bird and no bee.

The schools oh how quiet.
Books and papers tucked away.
And there would be no more
generations: if the world should stop
for just one day.
So please Mr. President
and other nations, whoever you might
be.
Stop, look and listen.
There is so much beauty to hear and
to see.
And everyone listen.
Read this poem for one minute.
Then the world will never ever stop.
For we will all see the beauty in it.

Phoebe Juanita Vaughn

Phoebe Juanita Vaughn
MARCH 9, 1989

To "ME," may I live another 50 years.

Hello America, how are you? 3/9/89 marked the date of my 50th birthday. Just think I've lived one half of a century and survived to tell it.

There was another great historical personality who was born on March 9, in 1454, by the name of Amerigo Vespucci.
You know, that fellow that America was named for.

I feel just great about turning 50. I can now get a discount on life and extended hospital insurance. Isn't that fantastic.

So I dye my hair, well, at least I admit it.
Ok, so I am a little wobbly when I get up too quickly, but it only happens every now and then.

And I've only had a memory lapse three times this week. I think it had something to do with me misplacing my glasses.
But, I still have all of my teeth, except for a few.

What the heck, I am happy with me and even the extra weight that I've gained.
Well, the body does change its shape with age, you know!

Sorry, but I've got to go for now. I want to get my membership application off to AARP.
The fee is only five bucks, can you believe it?

Estella E Prasuhn
SONG POEM

In Thee Oh, Lord
Do we put our trust
Be Thou near—Bend Thy ear
To our humble supplications.
When our faith is weak
give us strength
When it is strong
Let us give thanks, to Thee
When life seems cruel
Help us renew
Our faith in Thee.
Ever thoughtful
Ever mindful
Of Thy goodness and grace
In our hearts, in our minds
Always find Thou, a place.

Catherine E Olson
VOICE OF DESTINY

To the God of gifts, my Lord and Savior, to him be the glory forevermore.

Only to hear a solemn word for my soul. To tell me where and when to go. I pray for wisdom to come my way, clear my path, to steer my reins.

For in my darkest hour, before the rising of the dawn. I hear a voice calling me, the unheard voice of destiny.

Longing to listen, leading me in my search for sanity. The voice silently utters unspeakable words, as it speaks to me from within its tranquility.
It awakens my darkened spirit up out from the night.

Fragile are the hands of time upon

your weary soul and mind, they take
you in with delicate care, and nurture
your soul, till it is aware. The rising
of the dawn that is unseen, that will
shine upon your dreams and when
you see your dream in sight,
along will come an unspeakable
light.

Before the rising of the dawn,
destiny calls it's destiny's Time . . . .

Susan Napoli
I LIKE TO BE
I like to be the best
I can be.

The part that no one can
See unless I set free.

Enter my kingdom,
Behold the art

For there is the secret
To never depart.

Mary Metcalfe
IDYLLWILD
A small porch
Colored
with T-shirts and jeans,
catsup, coffee and tourists;
Lighted
by a sterile blue sky
reflecting an American flag
on the mountains.

Wild lilac buds and planned tulips
invite the season
as the young slim girl
deciding which way to go.

Morning snow and noonday heat
are broken promises
for the straight forward dreams
of unsuspecting minds.

Lee C Marshall
LIFE IS PEOPLE

This poem is dedicated to my sister Lea Coffrin

Life is people.
A bell in a steeple.
A bird on the wing.
A bell that must ring.

Life is pain, life is gain.
Life is loss, life has dross.
Life is beauty, that shall remain,
Sweetly to savor again and again.

Life goes on, it does not end,
we act on life's stage, and return
once again.
Life is absurd, a sad song heard,
a loving child, flowers growing
wild.

What do I think of this life,
with all of its trouble.
I just look to the steeple,
remember, "Life is people."

L C Novak
A POET'S DREAM
A poet's dream came true
The day I saw you
In another city on another day
Like today when you walked past my
way

Could this be for real!
Red, could this be you
Then I knew it was deja-vu

It could only happen in the City of
the Angels
I'll be damned, I forgot my pencil

So close and yet so far
As you got into your blue rental car

ZMKW131 and then you were gone
I can still see your warm smile
Your smooth fair skin and your red
hair too
Knowing it was all deja-vu

I swear I'll remember this day
When I couldn't find the words to say
A POET'S DREAM CAME TRUE
THE DAY I SAW YOU

Beth Lee
AT THE END OF THE RAINBOW
At the end of the rainbow you can
see,
A pot of gold and a land near the sea.
In that land everything is green,
Their main crop is the jellybean.
You may even see a leprechaun
named Pat,
You can easily spot him, he wears a
purple hat.

Carol A Burton
THE INTRUDER
A stranger came to call
Under cover of night.
He stole my prize possession
And then took flight.
A stranger came to call
Never intending to stay.
He was here just long enough
To kiss my baby's breath away.
A stranger came to call
As I rocked my child so dear.
I never even saw him
I never knew he was near.
When that stranger came to call
On that night of bitter cold
If he had only spared her life
He could have had my soul.

Anne Ayer
RETROSPECT
Mist drifts over the meadow
Shimmering in the sun
And the distant river
Gently meets the sky.

Now, only an hour past,
Black clouds and driving rain
Wrap the soul in sadness
Taking memory far.

Forgetting and remembering
So fast an interchange
Leaves the old man wishing
Forever to hold his dream.

Vivian Agostini
TO AVATAR MEHER BABA
When all our bones to dust will turn,
When all the flowers die,
When the roaring rivers still their
din,
When all birds cease to fly;
When the shining stars will fade
away
And even the sun grow cold;
When each grain of sand will
disappear,
And the rocks and forests bold—
There still will remain
That Only One
From the ever before to the ever
now,
And the ever ever yet to come!

Jose de la Cuadra
THIS I KNOW
though the dark clouds gather above
me
nature's glory is it will fall into a
much needed rain
though the heart aches from being
lonely
its triumph is when true love prevails
like a rose bud that hides its beauty
there is a time when it blossoms it
springs with glory
so i'll wait my day because i know
you'll be there
like the dawn that greets a new day
there will always be hope. tears will
fall . . . but of joy
like a burst of sunshine after a stormy
night
you will be there . . . you'll make it
right
once and for all i will make you stay
to fulfill the dream to be together
again
this i know—you will be there

because i care i can make it better
together we will build our commandments of love
with the solemn promise to live by
the word
i will stay by your side for always
with all my heart i give you my love
that you may be happy as you dreamt
before
that we may be one now and
forevermore

Leon Thomas David

Leon Thomas David
THE CITY

To my Native San Francisco

Like bees that to the blossoms come
To fruitful make the vine and tree,
The swarm of men pass to thy heart
To office, factory and mart,
The hum and clash of industry.

The people march round Union
Square.
The pigeons hold conventions there.
Tourists crowding rattling cars;
The some who look may clearly see
Our world without tinsel panoply.

At four, the wind begins to blow.
It hurries, for it has to go
To usher in the fog, which now
Descends to cool the fevered brow,
Obscure the ills, and green the hills

And like a flower droops when the
sun
Its daily course has duly run,
The clang and clatter and the fuss
Quiets, wilts, now with the exodus
The ebb tide of the day sets in,
The morrow, it flows in again.

Edith Young
I BELIEVE
I believe,
When I see a tree so bare,
Turn into greenery,
From out of nowhere.
And when a tree, standing tall
Changes color, in the fall,
Then sheds its leaves
And again turns bare.
I know why, I believe.

I believe,
When from a seed a flower grows,
And after the rain, a rainbow glows,
And the wind so calm and warm,
Turns into, a raging storm,
He sends his message loud and clear,
Believe in me, for I am here.

I believe,
When the seasons come and go,
And the rain, turns into snow.
And through the cold and icy ground,
A little green, begins to show,
He whispers low.

I put the snow, upon the ground,
I turn the seasons, all around.
I put the rainbow in the sky,
I taught the bird, to fly so high,
And I believe.

For who can take the darkest night,
And turn it, into a day so bright,
And who can paint the sky so blue
And add a touch, of color too
Then add a million little stars,
And still find room, to put the moon?

Elizabeth Gooden Jones
LOYALTY UNDAUNTED

To my friends, especially Mrs. E. Mae Calvin, my family and associates who have encouraged me and given me a forum and so many chances to share my poetry

My country 'tis of thee
Begins this song of much renown.
And I believe that this is so
Though treated as the clown
Laughed at, scoffed at, pie thrown
In my face.

Yes, I'm treated as inhuman
By a so-called human race.
I'm jostled and mobbed in jest
Sometimes.

And in others to prove the case
That this poor worthless matter
Isn't part of the human race.

Yet, every time the flag's unfurled
And voices rise in glee,
Though body bent, and head bowed
Low, I still sing fervently.

Though I'd rather
There is no other.

My country 'tis of thee.

Jessica Maria Gatewood
I DIDN'T HEAR THE WORDS

This poem is dedicated to Ike my friend. This poem is dedicated to my mother Ophelia.

I catch the rose that you handed
me.
Until i hold it in my hand, i will not
understand.
the smell caught my eyes and
kept it in my heart.
How pretty the rose that once
was mine.
To you i give the rose and in
time you shall be mine.
I thought of you with a pure
heart.
So lovely you are and so is the
rose.
It was nice of you to hold in
your hand the rose.
You bought in to my soul the
rose.
The ocean spreads across the sea
but too
it could be you and the rose. Within
my soul
I stand not alone because of you

within my soul
and with the last of the rose.
I shall wait not too long but
until you again smell
the rose. The gladness of my
soul will wait until
the rose is gone.
Now forever i will
remember the rose.
For Always the rose.

Edith Young
A PUZZLE IN THE SKY

Little stars you shine so bright,
And the moon gives so much light,
Making the sky, a wondrous sight.

The sun it lights my path by day,
And the moon it guides, my path by night.
Wish I could see, where the sun hides at night
While the moon comes out, to light up the night.
And if I ever, figure it out,
Two more puzzles, must I solve.

Where does the moon go when the sun comes out,
And how can so many stars, find a place to hide?
The answer lies in the heavens above;
For only God, knows where they hide.

Kimberly Fiordimondo
FEELINGS

This poem is dedicated to my family, my teachers at the West Deptford Middle School, and my best friends the Pressley family.

The cold, unfeeling night goes on,
waiting for morning to come.
I hear the cry of a child in the darkness.
Bitter silence overcomes me.
The terror in the innocent child's scream fills me with grief
I feel the sorrow in the voice of my fellow man,
calling to me for help.
I feel the loneliness of a poor man out in the cold, heartless
night.
Alkl the pain they feel I feel too,
For I am only human as we all may be.

Stephanie M Stacey
HIDEAWAY

If you could find me a place in the sun,
Where no shadows have ever been,
I can find you a perfect hideaway
With an angel who whisks away sin,
It's a place of perfect fulfillment
A place imagination dares to explore
Like an apple of sincerity,
With a problem free core.
When I find you this dreamy filled hideaway,
On a high mountain's peak,
Just remember all fantasies end somewhere,
So here's hoping you find what you seek.

M Catherine Davey
TIME PASSAGES

He looks at the infant who'll soon call him dad
And swears he'll give him what he never had

A year goes by and he starts to talk
With faltering steps he begins to walk

As a lad of six he throws the ball
To a man known as dad who seems so tall

A teenager now, he looks for advice
From the man who always treated him nice

He graduated with honors today
His father now sees how time slips away

The son now has a boy to raise
Who speaks of grandpa nowadays

As he walks the sands he thinks of when
Not long ago his boy was ten

Now that he feels so tired and old
He longs for the boy to once again hold.

Ann H Gillespie

Ann H Gillespie
M.I.A.'S

To: All of our M.I.A.'s . . . We await the day of your return!

They were left behind; they had no choice
Loved onces still remember and hear their voice
"Please get us out of here," they seem to cry
We want to come home again, before we die.

The agony of knowing they were left behind
Is enough to make, lose your mind
The reports have come through, that some are alive
And they've been through hell, just trying to survive.

They went off to war, to protect all of us
Remembering where they are now, makes me want to cuss
We should pressure those countries, for their release
And bring them home, to live in peace.

So don't shove them out of your mind each day
One thing you can do for them, is PRAY
And don't ever forget, our Freedom was bought
By men like these, in the wars they've fought!

Bernadine Tetzlaff
THE NAMELESS ONES

To my most precious Friend, Eddie-Lou Cole

The nameless ones wait in the shade for me.
Why do they tarry when I have nothing
To bring them as they wait under the elm tree
Like falling autumn leaves that need raking.
A wave of my hand and a fleeting smile,
Small tokens of my life freely to give
Was all their long wistful waiting
As this passing moment together we live?
In this brief moment we've something to treasure
As communion of their souls seek mine
We've welded unbreakable bonds forever
The strength of a smile we cannot measure
A touch of heaven, a smile is divine
As smiles bind wandering souls together.

Ter'e E Russell-Seffern
SUICIDE

As the waves crashed against
A lonely rock,
A beautiful girl cried on the dock.

As the bitter wind whistled and blew,
A lonely girl knew what she had to do.

As the sun sank behind the clouds,
A lovely girl screamed out loud.

As darkness set in around the ocean,
A lonely, beautiful girl, lay without a motion.

As the air turned cold and brisk,
The dying girl had taken her last risk.

Alessandra Tognato
FOR A.L.

Some of us
need
to fly to trace
autoextinguishing geographies

to let air
consume us
so that we for ever can be
with forgetfulness
feathered

Theresa Marie Chamness
VISION OF LOVE . . .

With Love as a Gift to: Brent McCowan

If you were to ask me my vision of love,
I could not tell you, only showing the feeling from above.

While we're together knowing peaceful breathing,
Two children running, tumbling and playing without shielding,

You handing me daisies with a kiss on the cheek,
As I pluck the petals with love, only you I can see.

We're laughing and talking while holding hands,
Looking to the sunset while walking in the sand.

As the quiet night falls with a warm moist wind,
Standing close and knowing from within,

A vision of love that we can see, as we're looking to the sky at the doves by the sea . . .

Jeannie Selby
TO MY BABY COUSIN JACKIE

This poem was written for my 13-year-old cousin, Jackie Staggs, who died on February 28, 1988.

Don't take time for granted,
Because there's never enough.
Time can steal your heart away
By taking someone you love.

But while you can, tell that love
Just how much you care
Let him know all the love
that you have to share.

And when you have to say goodbye,
Say it but do not cry.
For he loves you and cannot say
He will see you some other day.

But now that he is gone
And you have no one else to love
You sit around—weep and cry
Wondering, "What has he done?"

I've never been able to figure it out,
Why God took my Jackie away.
I'll just have to go on with my life,
And wait for that "some other day."
I'll Love you always,
Jeannie Selby

Sharon Styer
ALWAYS A FRIEND

This poem is dedicated to Dana, April, and Rachael, who have always stood by me. Thank you and I hope you like this tribute to you. I love you.

Whether here nor there,
through thick and thin,
you are always a friend.
If I am happy or sad,
mad or glad,
you are always there,
and always a friend.
Through love,
and through hate,
you stay by my side,
and keep me in my place,
because you are always a friend.
There is no way,
I could ever thank you enough,
but hopefully some day,
I'll be able to repay,
the love and the time,
you have given to me,
because you truly,
are always a friend.

Debra Williams
ANNA ROSE

This is an ode to Miss Anna Rose,
Her beauty is evident as her petals unfold.
Anna Rose was lovely,
breath-taking when seen,
She had but one flaw, a petal which was green.
The lovers would come and pick the Rose-Maries,
They'd pick the Rosettes, and the lovely Rose Sherrys.
But no one picked Anna Rose, they thought her quite peculiar,
Though Anna Rose always she was a lucky flower.
The others were always chosen, and always in demand,
But Anna Rose was confident

forever she would stand.
The others pitied Anna Rose because of her unsightly petal,
But Anna Rose wore it proudly as though it were a medal.
She had seen the blue Jays wed, she heard the sparrow sing,
She had seen a rainbow, and heard the church bells ring.
And when the rainbows faded, and the sparrow ended his song,
She knew winter was near and the nights would be cold and long,
But Anna Rose slept through the winter and never felt a thing,
for when she awakened, it was already spring.
Anna Rose opened her petals, she saw that one was green,
The others looked in pity, not knowing what she had seen.
This Rose knew she was different, but felt beautiful all the same,
This ode tells of her beauty, and Anna Rose is her name.

Melanie Good
MIND SONG

My mind is songs and poems,
A shell that has carvings in it,
Carvings ancient,
Skeletons that bring back time.
By seeing it,
Thinking what may have been,
What it is.
A thought or myself.
The carvings,
Owned by only itself.

Nicole Robinson

Nicole Robinson
REMEMBER

This poem is dedicated to Bret Sharp Although we're apart, you're still in my heart. You always made me feel so special

Shut out the lights
and remember our nights
Listen to this cassette
and remember the times we met
It's been so long
That each slow song
Reminds me of you
and all we used to do
The things we shared
The moments you cared
Close your eyes,
Forget our goodbyes,
Remember us together
and how we talked
of forever

David S Bowen
RENDEZVOUS

To walk the night for want of you,
To hate the day when I must act new.
To aimlessly labor at the worldly task,
To feign emotions—wear
Contentment's mask.
Endless my efforts my shell to refill,
Seeking most vainly to copy that thrill.
Such is the glory lost love brought to me—
A deep slashed wound that the heart can see.
It will never heal, but I'll keep it scarred
'Til to none it's apparent, nor my surface marred.
I'll repossess our love at each rendezvous—
To walk the night for want of you.

Mrs Rose Kornstein
SPARROW

This is dedicated to my husband Jon, for his love of all of God's creatures great and small.

Hey little bird, high upon a tree;
Swoop a little lower, on that branch next to me.

Don't worry, spring is on its way;
And that should get us through this busy, busy day.

So ruffle up your feathers, and shake away the cold;
Life will begin anew, and that is how it's told.

Is it a message in the wind, that makes you sing this way?
Or the goodness in your heart, that never makes you stray.

Hey little bird, high upon a tree;
It will always be a wonder, why you give a song away for free.

Sonia (Sonnie) Gugliciello
A PIECE IS GONE

In memory of my late husband, Fred
For a son he would be proud of
Lovingly, Sonnie

You died so quickly   Our life had only started
No last goodbyes   or wishes from the now departed
You left a son, a name, a wife
They said "go on and make a life"
I showed him pictures as he grew
I told him stories, all of you
I've taught him well, he is strong and good
He has smarts and values, as well he should
But he is empty of the feel of your love
And so am I, it doesn't come down from above
What of the feel? The sound? The sight? The touch? The smell?
That were yours alone
So many years the memory fades, the senses dull
And in a dream, I moan
I cannot give him more and so my job is done
He will have an empty space
Because a piece is gone

William F Dickinson
LOVE

The greatest force known to man
Is stranger than the best steel band.
Innocent as a baby's first timid smile,
Soft as a mother's touch of her newborn child.
Fragile as a butterfly on her first flight
Enduring as the day, followed by night.
Courageous as the lion, ever bold
Shy as another, the lowly mole.
As precious as sunlight on a grey foggy day
Lovely to behold on a long weary way.
Instantly hurt by an unwary deed
But brought back to helping, shown the need.
Tender as prayers, but ruthless as well
Love keeps us going, to heaven or hell.
Sweet as wild honey, but sharp as a blade
The way is open to all, be not afraid.

Traci Anderson
IT'S ONLY OUR MINDS

It's hard to believe that a little rain can wash away our smiles. A little sprinkle sets in a sadness over all who feel it falling from the sky.

It's hard to believe that only yesterday the sun was shining overhead. A small ray of light kept us warm, you and I.

Now it's dark. The mistress moon and her descending stars have not shown their twinkling smiles to us tonight.

What is wrong with this evening, with the wind and its chill saying it's alright?

Yet we watch through a window, afraid of the dark, as if the evil only waits for us then.

We don't realize that it 's only our minds.
Everything is beautiful when we open our eyes and see the magic once again.

Sally Harper
THE MUSTANG AND THE COWBOY

The mighty old mustang looks out at his land,
His regal kingdom of sagebrush and sand.

It's his alone and he's free to roam.
No need to fear in his ancient home.

From the first dawn, this has been his land.
His regal kingdom of sagebrush and sand.

Then comes the cowboy and he smells the fear.
For he knows death and destruction are near.

The cowboy shoots and he's left to die.
And all the while, he's wondering why.

He did no more than wander this land,
His regal kingdom of sagebrush and sand.

Robert Glenn Gipson
BENEATH THE EVENING SKY

Two lovers strolled hand in hand
Beneath the evening sky
As they walked quietly along
Their anticipation grew high

They paused from time to time
To look at each other face to face
Then they kissed passionately
In a lovers' embrace

They patiently guided each other
To a secluded spot on the ground
Both trying to hold on
To the special feeling they had found
As they lay together
Their passion rose higher and higher
With hearts wildly beating
Soon they yielded to their desire

Much too soon the time
Seemed to pass them by
But oh how sweet the ecstasy
Beneath the evening sky!

Larry Palm
I HAVE YOU

This poem is dedicated to a very beautiful friend, Cathy Elliott. I love you.

I woke up this morning
The sky was gray
Clouds hanging low
Chill winds blowing snow.
When I saw you
You were the warmth
You were the sun
You were the sky turned blue
You were the brightness
of my day.

No more snow
No more cold
No more gray
I have you.

Penelope J Jacobson
PEGGY

To Peggy, who worked with disabled students for ten years. You live in spirit in the lives of those people you have influenced and touched. We remember you!

Peggy, your warm and loving smile set our hearts aglow.
You were always there for us no matter how busy you were.
Peggy, you helped guide us in the right path when things seemed all wrong and no one cared.
We loved you Peggy, you made a special mark upon our hearts.
And as we walk through this world we knew you helped to make it a better place for us.
And when we think of you and times gone by there will be a warm and loving memory.

Anne D Dyde
THOUGHTS IN DECEMBER

My wishes are the same
As I watch the candle flame
And the rain on my window pane.

May the bells you hear
Be on Santa's reindeer,
For Christmas is nearly here.

May your nerves never shatter
Should the turkey slip the platter
As the souffle gets more flatter.

May the sounds of laughter
Never crack your plaster,
Only echo now and thereafter.

May you always remember
As you stir the dying embers,
Those absent this December.

Joy Alexander
EARTH CALL

I've seen the sweet earth's kindly lit face.
She's wise and noble; she's all of grace.
She's soft and smiling; a little bit shy.
She tolerates so much; I dare ask her . . .Why?
She says:
Men act as blind fleas on the back of a stray dog.

They poison and gouge my body; I'm bloated with smog.
They grab parts of me to hoard for themselves and claim.
They trash and litter me 'til I'm trussed over in pain.
I say:
How much must you overlook?
She says:
It is the fleas from the dog that must be shook.
I say:
How much longer in patience can you wait?
She says:
In a flash I'll tremble and fall because that is my fate.
My call cries to rouse those sleepers unaware of their test.
They must awaken this day to love and deliver me to rest.

Rosanna Angiola
LIFE IS LIFE
Time can fly
Like an eagle can soar
You find yourself in the future
Always looking to see more.

Frustrating thoughts
Seeking to find a solution
But the answers are in the heavens
Getting surrounded by pollution.

Life is life,
One problem leads to another
But the silver lining will be there
If you can look beyond the thunder.

Allen B Williams
AKA Ritz Barroune Caszier
MORE THAN OUR COMPLEXIONS

Unto my grandfather—Henry B. Trass, grandmother—Drusie Trass of Miss., all their children, readers, and all the generations of my beloved African and Egyptian culture, I dedicate this work.

It is not the color
of our skin
which makes us to be BlACK,

It is the DEPTHS
of our Creatus Consciousness
which makes us to be so!

Only Our souls,
to search within
you'd see the reason that,
Our beauty reflects
The enduring gentleness
such as the rainbow . . . . .

Mysterious OUR ANCESTRAL PAST;
Those great structures
which today still stand,
Our creators gave us solemn task
seek of LIFE's truest mixtures
built PYRAMIDS IN THE SANDS,

Phenomenon of the world to so many other men
who yet search to trace their last origins
Maybe they'll find, as like my kind,
It's MORE THAN OUR COMPLEXIONs.

Herman Collins
IS THIS OUR FUTURE FIGHTING TO KEEP CRACK, OFF AMERICAN SOIL?

I dedicate this poem to my wife Barbara, and my daughters, and grandkids, my Aunt Kitty and the Collins Family.

Is this our future, fighting to keep crack, off american soil?

The sight and luxury of america is gone, every since drugs became the number one, vicious killer in the world people aren't safe.
America has become, a sight of death and fear from the heavy drug traffic and their arms to kill.

The sight of america is gone when I see and read how children are carrying pistols around in schools.

The sight of america, has gone, when I see kids using crack, as well as, pushing drugs and they are the target for sex.

Is this the sight of american future with homeless people living in the street?

Is this, the sight of america, when I see people from all walks of life, destroying themselves by using alcohol or drugs?

Is this our america's soil, turning into a battlefield.

Nancy Jo
FIFTY
Fifty—it's an age
And suddenly I hear this voice,
What have I accomplished?
What have I done?
And yet when I look back,
Did I have another choice?

I was born
I became a teen
Then I married
We bought a house
The children came
What does it mean?

The children are educated.
Life's just about perfect,
Then the children marry
And start their own life.
I'm suddenly alone,
It's time to reflect.

So here I am
Fifty—what an age!
And what do I do now!

Benju
A DAY IN THIS WORLD

To my parents (Juliana & Benedicto A. Manderico)—You both had to make me! Thank you!

It's one of those days
The day that you wish
Would never go away
From your protection of peace

The bells are ringing
Ringing for a child no one cares
Enough to leave them dying
In a world of tears
While governments talk about peace
But spending money for wars
The troops are in combat
Killing one another from other lands

It was an awesome day
And I don't know what to say
Wishing this clock would never chime
To tell the day is near
Cause that's what I fear

The day is ready to be blown away
By just one press of a button
That sends their missiles this way
And leaves this world all rotten
and everything is forgotten.

Eric P Nelson
IN THE HEART OF LOVE

I dedicate this poem to my first true love, Vonda C. Rosquist

In the heart of love,
She will always be there.
In the heart of love,
She will always care.

Her love is like a rainbow
Prospering long and having many facets
She would always help in time of sorrow
Her strength of will gave many assets

In the twilight, her green eyes glowed bright.
Her dark hair glistened in the starry light.
I vision her at night.
Oh! How I wish I could be with her tonight.

In my heart of love,
She will always be the one.
In my heart of love,
She will always see the sun.

I only wish,
That I would be the one,
to see the sun,
In her love for only one.

Tonight and every night, I wonder
While I hear the sound of thunder
Thoughts of her will be asunder

If . . .

In her heart of love,
I am the one.
In her Heart of Love,

I wish . . .

That I could see the sun.

Phyllis Wallace
WE THREE ARE ONE

To my parents, AUDREY and CHARLIE WOODY

My smile is hers, and also my eyes . .
Eyes
that see you in my hands.
My hair, my laughter, my
walk . . . .
From
my head to my toes are you.
Dad, in life I am both of you . . . .
And,
in me both of you are one.

Chandra L Stone
BIRTH
I look about
I see my home
I run, run, and
run towards it
Yet as I run
It moves farther
Into the distance
I cry for its
simplicity
And loving warmth
Yet I feel tremendous
joy
For I have entered
the world
I am alive!

Daniel O'Donnell
NEWBORN

Dedicated to Linda, Kerry, Sean and Casey—"sharing makes everything worthwhile"

You are a flower of God's garden—
a young bud eager to open to the world,
full of the beauty wrapped in your youth
and strength awaiting for its time.

May you always be as the wildflower lives;
surrounded by the innocence of beauty,
bringing serenity to those who look upon you
and touching the lives of those who tend the garden.

When the warm showers of love touch you—
let their drops caress and be absorbed,
for they will flow within to enhance your life
and build the character needed to bloom.

Walk with the knowledge of nurtured love—
accept with eagerness the caring of family,
thirst for a need of understanding
and enjoy the life that you carry within.

Kelly Walsh
WITHOUT YOU

To Dee: This poem is dedicated to you, because I can't live without you. (I Love You)

I never thought life could be this hard without you.
I cry myself to sleep, only dream of us, our past.
What would our future be like?
I try and try to calm myself down, to hold back the tears,
To believe you'll come back.
It's all a waste of time; I'm kidding myself.
Everything around me reminds me of you.
Every song on the radio brings back wonderful memories.
It reminds me of what I had before I lost you. You are special.
You can't be replaced. Though we tried over and over, it didn't work out.
Maybe we weren't meant to be. It's an awful feeling.
Though we're apart, you'll always be in my thoughts,
In my words, in my heart.
You'll always be a part of me. It's so unbelievably hard to think that
Everything we had is gone. It really hurts.
In our eyes, it was love. I wish it wasn't over.
Without you I feel depressed.
Nothing else matters but being with you. You always come first. I wanted

to be loved and cared for
Just like you were when we were together.
Since you left, my life has felt empty.
My life is not worth living without.

Sharon Ward

Sharon Ward
DIRECTIONS

In loving memory of my mother, Florence Letts Kushnerwich and my living dad, Victor John Kushnerwich who together taught me the meaning of love.

Each time I see you I want to speak to you and tell
You how I feel; but as always, there's no time for us.
I wonder, is time our real enemy, or it might just be our
Friend and we ourselves are our own enemies.

As our hands drift slowly apart and our eyes grow dim
We lose sight of one another . . .
I want to say I love you, for a very special reason.
Love seems to be everywhere, because it's the "Sweetheart" season.

Today is quite special,
A day that couples say . . . "Won't you please be mine,
On THIS Happy Valentine's Day?"
You don't need to buy me roses, or even send a card.

Just say, "I LOVE YOU,"
It won't be that hard.
I promise I'LL LOVE YOU,
Even after THIS day's through.

All you have to do is create the surge of power
Within yourself, but only remember,
The directions you take . . .
Are for you alone.

Debra K Carter
TO THINE OWN SELF BE TRUE

To my daughter Michelle, my sister Charlotte, and to my parents. Thank you for giving me the inspiration to put my feelings into words.

There is a reason for everything. God has a special plan. People that help other people just by reaching out a hand.
Hearts reach out in search of love, but not the binding kind. If you are searching for a friend, I'm the one you'll find.
I try to touch every heart, to bring them up in life, and if I manage to help you smile to me that will suffice.
A smile can not be kept by one. It's something we all can give. And if my smile can touch your heart, then that is why I live.
So my friend pass on that gift, the one I gave to you.
Lift up your head and spirits high, be happy and not so blue.
Remember as you go through life to keep an open mind,
trust in yourself and in God, concur the test of time.
Put a smile upon your face to give to someone new.
Be honest with the ones you meet and To Thine Own Self Be True.

Connie J Nunham
A SUMMER'S EVE

To my husband, for allowing me to follow my dreams.

It came at dusk
And stayed till dawn
An evening spent
And then 'twas gone

I heard the tide
In the distance roar
While watching sea gulls
Collect upon the shore

Suddenly stars appeared
One by one
Then just as suddenly
There was the morning sun

Bright and golden
Surrounded by a blue painted sky
Bees collecting honey
From a flower nearby

A new day, a new dawn
Yet soon to be another
Evening spent,
Then gone

Magali Ruiz González
ENCOUNTER

Hello again! And now we meet as strangers
After leaving behind laughter and tears.
Different persons, we look into our faces
Relieving traces of those tempestuous years.

Whatever happened to that intense enchantment,
To the excitement, the magic and the thrill?
We look at one another and we wonder
If we are still aware of what we used to feel.

It's useless to go back, we are now other persons
That chemistry has withered and dissolved.
We look now at each other with cold faces,
exiles from intense feelings, all past, gone.

How sad, the meeting of past lovers who have changed and forgotten in the way,
and having lost the need for starting over
casually nod and keep walking away.

Jennifer Spungin
THE MAID

I read about the mask
And why the caged bird sings.
The vultures in my past,
They drew the blood, white kings.

Why does big, black nanny
Kiss me, child of her spite?
She rings the bell for dinner.
We like to dress her white.

Silver sits on her lap.
She sees herself in rays
And shines her black label.
Clean and clean, tarnish stays.

The bell rings with fear.
Dark Jamaica, she loves.
White makes past slaves cower.
Dreams fill her skies with black doves.

Mary Evelyn Duncan
SOLACE

In memory of my late husband Talmadge E. Duncan, a victim of Alzheimer's Disease.

The old green chair is tattered and torn
Yet it sits in the self same place
As it did when it sheltered a tired form
That sought comfort in its embrace.

The little brown monkey waits patiently near
And stares with his shattered eyes
As he waits for the one who placed him there
And whispered a garbled good-bye.

I spend each night in the silent room
Where the chair and the monkey sleep
And listen as memories chase the gloom
With the fragments life lets me keep.

The long lost voice will no longer cry
Nor the crippled form be seen
But the old faded chair, the monkey and I
Find solace in what has been.

A K Ranjith
GOAL

To Aunty, Father and Mother.

Let me write my last and
only success story in this desert
My blood is boiling, boiling with anxiety
I am holding my mind tight,
Tight for waking and waiting—
for that final moment of fantasy

Eagles are flying up above
Wind is blowing across with fire
Sand is melting under my feet
I am lonely and hunted by Death
Miles and days pass slowly
Still I've got miles and miles ahead of me
And my only inspiration and fuel is my dreams

Darkness falls. Sudden. Frightening
My eyes and mind are fixed on that distant goal
On that glimmer of light which leads to a new sunrise
I am holding tight to my dreams
And now I can see it starting
And I am stepping into that world
And my journey has just begun

Betty J Perriman
WORDS FROM THE SOUL

It's so bitterly cold outside here today,
Warm words from within I need to say.
It's not very often on a day such as this,
That one alone can be filled with bliss.

There are many things we take for granted in life;
Sometimes ignoring the world's troubles sand strife.
We often sit and watch as each day goes by
And when times get rough we wonder why, Lord why?

Seems faith in ourselves and also in mankind,
When dwindled to nothing can play upon one's mind.
It takes a lot to overcome what we cannot change
And how some do so well seems somewhat strange.

I've had lots of joy in my life so far
And those who have helped deserve a gold star.
May it be family, friend, or a lover indeed,
Without those among us we cannot succeed.

Let us be thankful for blessings we receive,
And have less time on our hands to mourn and grieve.
There are better times ahead of us as we've been told,
And we can endure each day if we're brave and bold.

Gary Eugene Sarvey
NEVER SAY GOODBYE

This poem is dedicated to Marie Falcon, my loving aunt, who watches from above with love.

When I die do not cry, do not sigh and never say goodbye.

For I've only left this body, but my spirit will always be with the ones I love and shall watch over them from above.

Joette Manning
DEAR SON

I was only 18 when first we met,
But it was a moment I'll never forget.
Your hair gleamed golden and your eyes were so blue,
Our gazes met, and I fell in love with you.
I forgot my dreams of a college degree,
But those were in the days of 1973.
Women made choices then, we couldn't have it all,
But I never regretted my choice, as I watched you grow tall.
The years passed by and you moved away,
That was perhaps my saddest day.
For with you went pieces of my heart,
Love that had been given freely from the start.
You brought me such joy and also

deep sorrow,
But then I remember—there's always tomorrow.
So with the rising sun of each new morn,
I wish you happiness,
My handsome first born.

Helen F Rodgers
A VISIT TO THE ZOO

Have you ever heard a hyena laugh? Or tried to reach up and hug a giraffe?
My little nephew tried it once, and oh! was it a sight!
The giraffe decided to stand up tall, and lifted him in flight.
The polar bear swam round and round, as if they couldn't stop.
They'd swim below, till they needed air, then come up to the top.
The monkeys all chattered playfully, as they ate their bananas and swung from their trees.
Talk to a gorilla and watch the way he'll stare.
His eyes are almost human. You'd think that he might care.
Toss an elephant peanuts and clap when he is through.
He'll toss his trunk from side to side, and prance around for you.
The tiger is my favorite. He's such a mystic sight.
He'll pose and snarl his feline teeth, and try to cause you fright.
Sea lions are such a joy to behold; tossing balls upon their nose, their playfulness unfolds.
Oh! Let's not forget the 'greatest beast of all';
The lion as he watches you, like in the 'Jungle Call.'
When you wish that you were somewhere else, away from the human race,
Take a trip to the Zoo. You could make a new friend.
An animal would be a great change of pace.

Georgia Ann Dimick
DIARY

a book of memories
forgotten thoughts
lost in the past.

looking back, i laugh
foolishness
that's all it is now,
but it was sensible at the time.

and so i read on
not wanting to forget
remembering everything
by glancing upon a page.

i cry over past loves
thinking of ways
i could have changed mistakes
but knowing things wouldn't be the same,
if i had.

when the pages end
my dreams end too
shattered by the present and by reality,
it was me all the time.

Dr Pauline L Green
MY PRECIOUS ONE

I love you tenderly
Because you mean so much to me,
And though I always see your face,
None can replace you;

Ours is a love that ever lives
My love forgives you—
For there's a magic in your heart;
Darling, may it not depart:

You make of each mistake a work of art.
There's nothing now that I can't attain;
You turn to sunlight the darkness & lonely rain.

You make of me a very brilliant power
That opens Heaven's gates each living hour.
You're like the sea . . . Ever changing
Your life's deep & free. Yet you can still see
Your heart with me.

With your caring for me,
I toss every worry in the sea.

I want you near
We belong, Dear

No strife,
Dear wife,
You are my life.

Lisa Read Reynolds

Lisa Read Reynolds
SMALL WONDER

To my wonderful parents, Stan and Velma.

I saw a balloon
become a star in the sky
I pardoned
the sun
and watched with one eye

I gazed at the color
drifting far out of sight
my tiny hand
reached up
not touching its flight

The clouds became curtains
opening on cue
for dusk's
presentation
of a star in debut

How magical it seems
to one who's so small
a lot of space
out there
and I've just learned to crawl

Melissa S Rich
MOTHERS

To: My Mother—Beverly S. Rich and all my Great Grandmothers and Grandmothers.

Mothers are special,
Special you know.
They love and care for you,
birth to old.
People have mothers,
Mothers have mothers,
Mothers are special,
People you love and know!

Chloe Beeson Blom
SHACKLED

Your hands were cuffed
Your head hung low,
And oh, my heart was aching so
I searched your eyes
They stung with pain
And, oh, my tears began again
"So sorry," you slurred,
Your eyes were glazed
I focused on your saddened face.
I yearned for happy moments
In days gone by
When you were little
And there were no lies
I wanted you back again
Innocent and free
To hold you and love you
And draw you to me.

Norma Bischoff Feinberg
SHE

To Renata Elsberg Maimone, my muse at Lower Klamath National Wildlife Refuge on September 15, 1987.

He leaves her, moves on,
forgets, even dies—
yet more than half a century later
she still feels the current
of thigh against thigh,
electricity synapsed direct
through space and time
still potent
to raise the forearm's silken hairs,
and 'rouse remembered longing
in dry loins.

Patricia Rigsby
MEMORIES

She trips through memories in her mind
Of dreams once dreamed and left behind
Of brighter days so long ago
That led to future days of woe
Intricate patterns still entwine
She trips through memories in her mind.

Visions of those childhood years
Of expectations, hopes and fears
Skip once again o'er matter gray
They seem now so far away
How sweet the rose, how green the vine
She trips through memories in her mind

Memories now are but a haze
Woven through an endless maze
Can't comprehend—must let it be
Too clouded for the mind to see
In and out, both cruel and kind
She trips through memories in her mind.

Eva-Dawn R Singh
LOVERS LOVE ON

To Lyncoln & Jackie and all the others whom I love And who have inspired me.

And lovers love on . . . . . .
Their quarrels begin and end
Even as a new day dawns
From a tired yesterday.
They love their sleepless nights away,
And count each splendid moment.
They love, and to them—love is forever.

The music plays on . . . . . .
Its overpowering effect is
The sweetness of the lyrics
From a lover's instrument
It tells me that I have lost in love
And love is done for me,
No more can I ever be sure.

And life goes on . . . . . .
No looking back at all,
Except to ensure that the
Path taken is the right one.
But life is not worth living
When love is to be seen not touched—
Even as I see now and weep in my heart.

Anne Green
SYMPHONY, INDEED!

Hark! I hear a symphony
Its brilliant sounds appeal to me
It's Tschaikowsky at his very best
The movements are filled with plenty of zest
Every note seems to be like a nugget of gold
Like a story that is waiting for its plot to unfold
It has allegro, vivace, presto in its directions
It does resound with many tonal successions
When Tschaikowsky composed this wonderful opus
He gave the world a work on which to focus—

Tammy M King
AIDS IN HATE

Good night my Friend,
Good bye it might be.
You may not wake,
For AIDS might take.
I love you.
Yes I do.
Just live one more day,
Please do I say.
Just one more day.

Victoria Kelly
WHAT'S LEFT FOR ME, MOM?

To my children, Jeffrey and Michelle And to Ira, Brian and Austin May you grow up to care

What's left for me, Mom, after today?
Is it true our gas and oil is going away?
Will we have parks in which to play?

What's left for me, Mom, after today?
Is it true our libraries are closing their doors?
Will the air be fit to breathe when I am twenty-four?

What's left for me, Mom, after today?
Is it true that our families are dying away?
Will the earth be a safe place to stay?

What's left for me, Mom, after today?
With nuclear arms, pollution and strife,
What's left for me, Mom after tonight?

Laurette Green
GIFT OF YOUTH

If we could forever dwell in the tingle of romance,
bestowed upon us for the duration of youth, comparing only to the velvety soft petals of the most exquisite rose, which tends to make even heaven itself seem insignificant, then we would forever possess the most precious gift mortal life has to offer us.

But as age devours youth, a horrid reality emerges and the realization that relationships once filled with love and attentiveness, simply become a comfortable existence, and the burning desires felt in our youth, survive only in our dreams which vanish with the gentle light of dawn.

Holly A Barr
A TEAR FELL
A tear fell on our friendship,
For what reasons I could not find.
Just slowly closing all the doors,
To our childhood now behind.
For what used to seem forever,
The days now quickly pass,
Adding knowledge onto our
unknowing years
Sending forever into the past.
Those wonder years now silhouette,
Against the struggles I will face
Always in the shadows whispering,
Transferring my thoughts to that
carefree place.
Back then there were no tomorrows,
And today no yesterdays.
Only memories of the way things
were
In kind and gentle ways.
Now the times are gone
And we knew they wouldn't last,
As a tear silently falls,
The doors are closing to our past.

Elsie T Hildbold
FAITH
In the Garden where I rest,
God speaks to me with tenderness—
"Fear not, take thy cross and follow
Me
All thy needs I will send to thee."

If we, with faith, would just become
Like a child of only one,
All our fears would melt away,
When for His saving grace we pray.

Night of sorrow, tears of pain—
He sends them too, but don't
complain.
Day of joy with the peaceful dove
Returns again through His great
love!

Michael W McClellan
KINGDOM OF SADNESS

To Carol, without whom, a kingdom of love would never have been possible.

There once was a prince,
With no princess,
His life in his kingdom was sad,
For though he was ruler of many,
He lacked what so many now had.
He searched, but true love did evade
him,
He'd cry in his chambers each night.
And pray from the dusk of the
evening,
Til the morning's first glimmer
of light,
For a love to be sent there unto him,
A gift from his God up above,
For he tired of his kingdom of
sadness,
And longed for a kingdom of
love.
He then met a lady so lovely,
She appeared to be all he would
need,
Then he set out to win her unto him,
For he so loved this lady indeed.
Now this story as yet has not ended,
But the ending you're surely to see,
For the princess he searched for is
you dear,
And the prince full of sadness is
me.

Tracy Ann Peterson
LOVE WITH YOU
Never say never,
Our love is forever.
My undying love,
Is gentle like a dove.

Your love is beautiful,
Like a rose.
I dream of you,
When my eyes close.

Our love is sweet,
As fine wine.
It will blossom,
If given time.

Our love is pure,
As fine gold.
Together it will
Never grow old.

Never say never,
For soon we will learn,
Our love will last . . .
FOREVER!

Lisa Marie Rocha
SEASONAL EXPRESSIONS

To MOM Thank you for giving me the inspiration to be able to express the way I feel.

Let me feel the autumn breeze
hear the sound of the leaves as they
fall from the trees

The bitterness of snow when it
escapes the sky
the music in the air as winter birds
cry

The beauty of spring when flowers
dance
such a feeling to know I have a
chance
to be able to hear, see and feel
those gifts from God that makes life
so real

A summer sun that shares its warmth
at day
and at night a moon wakes with a
smile
the stars gleaming in place in their
own special way
with a soothing silence from mile to
mile

Aura L Pineda
LOST CRIES

This poem is dedicated to the abused and neglected children of this world.

The night seems long when you
cannot sleep,
I am awakened by the cries of the
children within my dreams,
So sweet and innocent how can I
help,
Should I shout to the world to stop
their pain,
Or tell their parents to take a break,
They are so small,
They cannot be ignored,
This world is theirs, as much as
yours,
So take the time to understand,
Give them love and hold their hands,
And guide thy children through the
hard times we live,
For they are angels without their
wings,
Do not let them carry the pain of our
sins,
Remember it was not they who chose
to live,
So forget them not and teach them
well,
Make each day the best you can,
For there is no stronger feeling,
Than the power of Love,
For Love conquers all, and eases our
pain,
So let us help our children in every
way.

Norma Jean Scheller
SILENT SADNESS

Dedicated to Rhonda

Silent sadness trickled down her
cheek
Beauty in motion
Lady of compassion
Secretly capturing my heart.
Searching eyes seeking understand-
ing
Tenderness
Slowly filling my world
Needing the cherished touch of a
woman.
Reaching out and giving then
retreating
For fear of being known
Afraid yourself of admitting
The driving force from within.
Blinding hating loving
Aching to reaffirm that
She has the same needs for you
As she hopes you have for her.
Then you turn to leave
In loneness
The silent sadness gushes—within.

Kellie A Moroney
STILL LIFE
Alone. Hunched over.
In the middle of an almost-empty
garage he sits, staring into the
midday sun that fills the open
doorway.
His white hairs, scattered in small
patches, like gobs of paint on an
artist's worn palette.
He plants his feet firmly on the
ground in front of his chair,
trying to stop the rotation of the
earth.
Clenched fists press against his
cheeks as he feigns pensiveness.
His work pants, stained from long
years of toil painting the houses
of unappreciating others, rise
high above his ankles.
I can see the crease that remains
from the letting down of his
trousers.
I watch his eyes fluttering,
blinking away the voids of his
life.
His mouth is slightly open. The
gap between his two front teeth
seems to expand as he breathes.
In the corner, a towering wall of
brown cardboard boxes, filled
with newspapers from the
1920's, blocks the brown
window pain.
A layer of thick, gray dust and
cobwebs coats both the boxes
and the elderly figure.
Life is still for this man. Empty
for this man.
Two fat, black cats stare at him,
then walk away.

Norma Rockwell Preisler
WITH LOVE

To our dear parents, Evaline and Jay Rockwell

Let us say it with love,
Well, the poets of old wrote much
about love,
That we've read and retold.

Now we modern day poets know
much of the past
And added to this we must write so it
lasts
For all future poets to study and
know.

Our love must be broad as the width
of our land,
Love of our country, land of the free,
Love of our families so dear to our
hearts,
Love of our neighbors both near and
far,
Love of our Savior who rules over
all.

Grace Rizzi
THE ECHO
The stairs from hell
Reached my feet
As I lost all faith
In Mankind.
The heat I felt
Was no burning sun.
The blazing flames
In my eyes
Were of no gleaming happiness.
The harsh tone in my voice
Explained my past.
My weak body ached
As I walk up the stairs.
Red hot flames
Were the last things
I saw.

Dan Ejem
WINTER'S END
No stars are out.
There's no moon for light.
The cold wind's blowing
freezing rain,
Against unfeeling skin.
Sitting, listening,
I hear the noise of the unknown,
then nervous quiet.
Unseen creatures stirring
on winter leaves,
turning my thoughts to riot.
Alone, waiting.
Waiting for the sun to rise
and shine warm upon my face,
the promise of spring,
the promise of new life.
The grass will be green.
The flowers will bloom..
The birds will sing.
I am anxious for winter's end.
I am ready to love again.

Dennis Allen Burke
A MOST IMPORTANT JOB
"Could you help me with this
Daddy"?
I hear a little voice;
and when I look into his eyes,
it seems I have no choice.
"My toy, it just got broken,
you can fix it with ease;
could you fix it, Daddy,
could you fix it, please"?

He is only five years old,
He knows it might take awhile;
for I will work all night long,
just to see him smile.

"Teddy wants a story,"
He says as he jumps and leaps,
"O.K., I'll tell a story,
but then you must go to sleep."
He treats me like a hero,
I like that very much;
for there aren't many heroes left,
not one that he can touch.

Nasser Al-Robaidi

Nasser Al-Robaidi
FORGOTTEN
Just an old timer
Holding his bottle of Gallo
Like a mother nursing her baby
He chews on what got caught
On his long forgotten beard
When the wind blows left-overs
From a near junk-food restaurant
Motionless he sits sipping wine to warm
His wrinkled veins
Waiting for rain to come down
And wash away marks time left
On his side-walk home

Daphne Lee
ARMS IN A VELVET SKY

To Din, with love. And to my family and friends. Many thanks.

Shattered—the earth,
In a burst of golden sparks,
Scattered to eternity.
The stars burnt blue holes
In hands and hearts
And every silver lining left
A broken cloud—
Fragments in the empty sky.

Silence was as great as
God, or He who watched
And seemed to know not what
To say:
Speechless for the splendour,
Overwhelmed by this last
celebration,
The world's grand finale—
Arms in a velvet sky.

Candy Apple Stapleton
MY GRANNY
My Granny is the best granny
in the world.
Wherever I am I'm Granny's
girl.
I love her very much.
She has that very special touch.
She makes me laugh
When I feel bad.
She scratches my mad place
And makes me glad.
She's the best Granny
I ever had!

Dolores Krymis
THE ROSE

To my dearest husband, August Andre Sr. and children Deena Yolanda, Karen Rozalia, August Andre Jr., Fred J. Milena Lynn and Roy Daniel, with all my love.

The book was open
and between the pages
a dried flower
spoke of love.
It was a rose
with dried petals
and its fragrance
almost gone.

It took no effort
to remember quickly
the day that flower
became my own:
a tender face,
a big smile,
two little hands and
a tiny voice saying:
"I love you, Mom."

Betty Hall Reed
THE WONDERLAND OF SNOW

This poem is dedicated to my four sons, Larry, Joseph, Michael, and Stephen.

Moonlight shimmering on the fallen snow,
Is like a beautiful wonderland, that makes everything at night have that special glow.
The snow on the trees and rooftops glisten,
And you can hear the sound of the wind
When you listen.

Terry Rapue
QUALITY TIME

This poem is dedicated to my sweet wife Rita, and my loving children and my mom and dad.

In these days of uneasy stress,
we all try to do our best.
Husband comes, wife goes,
off to work as we all know.
Children muster all they can,
to go to school to be what they can.
A boy a man, A girl a woman,
comes too soon as you can imagine.
Quality time is hard to find,
but we all know it's on our minds.
Life's too short without a doubt,
quality time we can't do without.
Make the best of this time,
and you'll find, that the sun does really shine.

Joseph M Costa
DARK CLOUDS RODE IN THE DEEP OF THE NIGHT

This poem is dedicated to a man who believed I had the talent to make it someday. And here's my chance! To you, Joseph Costa, Jr.

Dark clouds rode in the deep of the night
Flashes of the screaming, recalling our fight.
Somewhere lost in deep time, my mind was in a maze
It seemed like not so long ago, we were in better days.

But now those days are over, and here I stand alone
Wondering what direction, the mighty winds have blown
If they should blow the way I want,
I'll blow straight back to you
But deep in thought, my mind still thinks, is that the thing to do?

Now I'll learn the right from wrong,
and try to forget about our song
Will I come out on top of it all, or
will I still slip, and continue to fall?

I know there's so much more, to see out in this world
But to break free from this spell, to which so I am curled
It seems to be so easy, but still it stays so tough
To face what lies ahead, and sneak by my own bluff.

Freedom lies ahead, to which I have been told
But just put up those fists, and go in face front bold
So now, I know it's time, my heart I know will mend.
For if I count the days, I'll just be crying again.

Michel Hodgson
I SEE A DOVE NOT FAR FROM HERE

Brooklynne May you change the world my little dove.

I see a dove not far from here.
As I watch and wonder, I ask,
"little dove why is the world so cruel?"
I wait awhile, no answer.
As the dove jumps from twig to twig
I watch and ask again,
"Why is the world so cruel?"
The dove flew away into the distance.
I've never seen the dove again,
And still I wait for an answer.

A H Owens
TO TEREASA
Her tender heart is broken,
The tears fall down like rain,
For cruel words were spoken,
Her gentle life is pain—
A life lived in his shadow,
(A hero in her eyes)
Now all those "hero castles"
Turn out to be just lies!
Dear God your child is hurting
That gentle, precious one—
Reach down your nail scarred hand and heal
Her heart scars one by one,
The tears that washed her lovely eyes
That she might see what's real
Will take with them the cloudy skies
A rainbow sent to heal!

Carol Maxwell Nantze
THE FORTY NINERS
Westward they came, over rugged mountain and raw land.
Mules loaded with picks and shovels, their gold pans in hand.

The were called forty niners, for they came in that year.
While seeking the gold, they left loved ones so dear.

Lawyers and farmers, men of all kind.
Big nuggets of gold, they were hoping to find.

To the quiet peaceful mountains, they came in a rush.
Dreaming the gold, from rivers would gush.

Along creek beds and rivers, they staked out each claim.
Their hard work and hopes, helped to bring California its fame.

Wild mining towns sprang up all around.
Then in came the ladies to settle them down.

Sluice box and old pans are still found yet today.
Where some turned to business and settled in to stay.

Those hard working miners and ladies in lace.
Left California, their children, history and grace.

John W Foerster
LOVE

To Patricia the best of all inspirations

Love is a question,
Not an answer.
Love is a journey
With no destination.
Love is the spirit
In search of being.

Love is tranquility sought
Never totally achieved.
Love is silence
Eyes meeting.
Love is minds caressing
Achieving oneness of spirit.

Gilbert J Pelletier Jr
ODE TO MOTHER
A mother's work is never done.
Especially if she has a son.

She has to pick up things all day.
All he wants to do is play.

She changes his diapers when he's wet.
She even works up some kind of sweat.

She works very hard every day.
She even finds the time to play.

And at the end of the day.
She even finds the time to pray.

Winifred "Jane" Lewis
HEAVEN'S BOUQUET

A tribute to Cori Martinson a talented young lady who's in her Father's house.

He wandered through earth's garden
and much to my surprise
He walked right past the pansies
that begged with smiling eyes.
He stopped to touch the orchids
all covered with soft dew,
then glanced across the garden
toward the spot where roses
grew.
the jonquils rich and sporting golden crowns
nodded gently in the breeze.
tulips flaunting brilliant color
danced about as if to tease.
purpled lilacs lent a fragrance

that lingered in the air
for they knew the special presence
of the One among them there.
tho' He seemed to know His mission
for His manner clearly spoke—
it was left to hard-decision,
it was then the tension broke.
as i looked around about me
i saw clearly what He'd chose,
it was YOU He had selected—
one lone and perfect rose.

Jessica Parrish
ENRAPTURE
Sweet darling angel—opaque
surroundings are nigh
Chilling evening air, this does bring
you upon me
Traveling ever so high, I trace your
luminous figure
Across the midnight black sky

As you draw closer two mystical
green eyes appear
Translucent are the eyes of you—
Piercing the darkness
Piercing my soul, As a pool I feel,
Reflecting, clear

Round about thy head flows an
incandescent halo
Which gleams upon creamy skin
Lips of crimson, Locks of gold
Innocence lies within the features of
you

Speak you not a word—But how
your spirit touches mine
My heart has been awaiting you
Beautiful Angel
You reach out for my hand, to coax
me near thine

Oh! Embraced in golden warmth
An angelic smile appears upon my
face—
Quickly we take wing—with
heavenly grace.

Joyce Bauer
LIKE A WHISPER
Like a whisper
A friendship starts
And grows along the way
It warms the heart and soul
In a very special way.

Anne M Brundage
SO EASY TO LOVE YOU
You make it so easy
to love you.
The more I see you,
the deeper in love I fall.
It's so easy,
it's so real,
the love I feel for you.
When I see you,
when we touch,
the fire runs wild.
The sparks in your eyes,
reflect in mine.
The warmth of your hands,
in mine.
The way your love flows into
and around me,
makes it
so easy to love you.

Patricia E Bunkowfst
MY BROTHERS
They come tall, short,
Fat, and lean.
Their eyes are blue,
brown, and green.
Never goes by a day
but, what they say.
Does this look right?
Is it good enough for tonight?
What goes with this?
You should know Sis.
Would you shine my shoes
and all the things they
think I should do.
I clean their room and help
them out. I like to do it
without a doubt.
Of course among them all is a little
pill
who always gets his fill,
They all eat so much
too, that I just cannot
seem to push on the clutch.

Well anyway in runs
one and out another.
but we all seem
to stick together.

Lorraine Loiselle
PLANTING THE SEED

I Dedicate This Poem To All Of Humanity

There was a seed, laid on top of the
soil,
Forgotten by day and left to spoil.
By chance a child was present one
day;
It found the seed and took it away.

If planted this seed the child did say
To what will it grow and become
some day?
Will it be good so that man will
share
Or will it destroy to an endless care?

Planted the seed the child did do
And a cross she made of sticks of
two.
So to what growth it brings it 's easy
to see
This one seed planted was but for
harmony.

And from this seed other seeds will
grow
Depending which hands will
continue the flow,
And if by chance it grows with
weeds
Then it's up to man to nourish the
seed,
And give it a chance to grow in
peace.

Sadie H Barker

Sadie H Barker
THEN JUDGMENT
Will the wind blow mournfully and
long . . .
The feathered fowls hush their song,
The heavens cry with silent rain,
Sun hides its face because of pain.

A star shoots endlessly through
space
For one of Earth has left their place;
As waters beat against soft sand,
They'll never pass this way again.

As oceans beat against the shore,
They'll pass this way, no, never
more.

They had their time as all men do
And all too many play the fool,
Not redeeming the time, at last they
stand
Guilty, undone, they bow their heads
Cast out from God, forever dead.

Brenda York
TIME

To Tim with all my love, Without you this never would have happened.

As the days go by,
I think of you more.
The shattering of time,
As I wait for the first toll.
That final second,
Before meeting face to face.
Endless becoming,
The most important date.
Watching the clock,
Waiting for time to pass.
Marking each day on a calendar.
How long can this last?
Precious time,
Moving too slow.
Wanting to see you,
And hold you close.
What seems to be forever,
Coming to an end.
Anxiously awaiting,
As time closes in.

Ursula Burnett
PAIN
The question asked and never
answered, the word spoken but never
heard.

The story written and never read, the
tear in a lonely eye left unshed.

The feeling felt and never shared, the
silent heart that never cared.

A poem wrote with not a soul left it
to quote.

A letter written and never read, a
word thought and never said.

And what pain that lives after we're
gone, after we're dead?

Tanya Lloyd
LADY LIBERTY
The brilliant flame of
her golden torch glows.
With the sea breeze
her long robe flows.
Her face of beauty
reflects a shimmering light.
Her crown to all
is a welcoming sight.
In her hand, the book
of Liberty and Freedom.
She's welcoming all thru
the gates to her kingdom.
Poised in strength
she stands with pride.
So many have seen her,
"America" they cried.
The land where dreams
can come true,
A home of freedom
she gives to you.

David A Phan
DEPARTURE
When the sun set,
Is the time you depart.
Water soaks sadness,
Sky covers departure,
Clouds lost in the endless world,
The wind blames its sorrow,
Oh! wind and clouds,
Don't make us cried.
Eyes with tears deep in souls,
Lips dry out no words,
Legs be still, hands shaken,
One left behind to see one off.
When was that like yesterday,
Side by side with love and
tenderness?
You go, on the road with blossoms,
I lay, in the freezing time,
Looking out through the window
every evening,
Shadow shut off my world,
Hands on face with missing tears,
Day ends . . . departs our relation.

Travis French
THE STATUE OF LIBERTY FROM LIBERTY'S VIEW
Here I stand tall and proud,
while I'm admired by a very large
crowd.

I hold a torch in my right hand,
that represents a very large land.

The French gave me to America, as a
gift,
which gave this country a spiritual
lift.

I'm glad I'm a statue standing here,
representing America's freedom
from fear.

As everyone looks at my crown,
they also see hanging my beautiful
gown.

Let's keep my torch lit with your
contribution,
so I can continue to represent the
constitution.

Doris H Griffin
CREATED AND OWNED BY ME

To my children Francis, Delores, Norma, Donald, and Gilbert
Memories of Love, husband Joe

Throwing petals to soothe situations
A nominee to destiny
Let me climb and scale the walls
To stop a habit falling.
I'll correct mistakes to learn the
fakes
Intended daily notices
My heart though heavy like anchors
weight
Created and owned by me
My caring folded neatly, package
safely
to keep from breaking hearts
Alone I walk. Trying to equalize a
firm mind that only I own
Each pain that electrocutes my body
will reap the one that sown.
Shall I wind up my possessions I
held with dignity
No inform me of pleasures that I
redeem myself
Not in vain. Not corrupted by human
minds
Now, pure chances blown by silent
winds
Accountable only by sounds.

Marguerite G Jones
SEASONS
As I sit on the river in a little nook,
called the 'slew'—
Looking out on the banks, I see
nothing pretty, or interesting about
the view.

To understand the desolate look of
the banks, and woods so bare—
You would surely have to be there.

The water is muddy and full of
trash, some of the trees look as
though they were struck a mighty
lash.

While I sit and muse over God's

control over the seasons—
I can't help but wonder if I shall ever be old enough to understand His reasons.

In real life, it's somewhat like a picture show, the trees, young and old, die and fall along the way;
As with people, young and old, we each have our day.

Four seasons He gave to us, daily changing season to season, as we go;
He only asks of us,
Let our faith grow and grow.

Lucy A Garlit

THERE IS A SENSE OF YOUTH

There is a sense of youth
The pure clean breath of birth
In the young green bud of Spring
That peeks its head above the earth

The barren arms of Winter's trees
No longer shiver bare
Now tiny threads of leaves appear
to warm and cover there

And thorny stems of rosebud too
Will soon begin to show
The budding light of color coming
Forth to let us know—

That Spring has come
And with it brings
All newness good and pure
No one condemns the young, the sweet
Whose Love is bold and sure
The bud of need, The leaf of care
Through Autumn will endure

N L Shaw

NOW APART

To Lee

Sunshine dimmed before your brightness.
You are important to me still.
Though our foot steps no longer
Travel the same daily paths,
My spirit your essence "encapsules."
Your force sings as music
Deep inside with aliveness.
On lonely quiet nights
I hear the great sound that was you.
Our hands, once long ago,—touched.
Yours on top of mine.
And I—in the soft shades of time—
Lightly touch your cheek, in memory.

James Lee Belviy

THE STRANGENESS OF NIGHT

The whole moon casts a magic glow to all the habitat below.
Bats dart wildly among tiny, blinking stars above open, isolated fields.
Swift, biting breezes spark dormant objects into animated oddities.
Long, crooked branches grow unexpectantly with evil urges to grab unsuspecting subjects.
Whirlpools of dancing leaves are skipping here and there
Showering their array of colors.
Dogs and cats are swirling as tops chasing loose limbs and papers as toys.
Low telephone lines whip sides of houses, while windows vibrate with limitless anger.
Warped, flaky-painted swings sway effortlessly as if under a spell by unknown demons.
High intense squeals pierce the velvety-blackness causing massive goose bumps on every stirring creature of two legs or more.
The old steeple church clock strikes proudly.
Streaks of light splash the sky brightly.
A new day filters through.

Joan L Tamborski

COLORS

Colors form the sky above with tints and hues
that dazzle the eye.
Colors form the moving galaxy with rings of color bands that demonstrate commitment.
Nature calls her color shots with vivid splendor—
And man too, is but a creamy hue . . .

Edwin N Korengel

MORNING POEM

I don't know if I have a mind

left.
sometimes I think I over-react
sometimes I wonder how I
stay intact:
I can't go home
I really can't roam
maybe we could get together
and wait for better weather

occasionally I look up at the
gray skies and smile.

Irene Kalebdjian I Cheffo

THE DUCKS

Two Docs, talking together
One said to the other:
Poor chick, is very sick!
After giving birth, she couldn't find her baby/babies!
It was a mistake of ID . . . .
They didn't put the 2 eggs, in the same basket,
She is heartbroken, and till, they find the kids,
She will go banana!!
The 2 docs are ducks, from the Pond nearby, in Alabama—.

Margaret M McNabney

SAIL ON, OH SHIP OF STATE, SAIL ON

My brother dear,

The waters rough, but you are tough
And there is land ahead,
A great white light shines through the mist
To guide and change your course,
Just let the pilot take command,
and he will bring you through.

Remember in those long past years
The Pilot was our Dad,
and steered those steam boats large;
and you were standing closely by
To place your hand upon the wheel
and blow the whistle loud and clear
when other boats passed by.

You won a hero's award for saving Lives,
a long, long time ago; Yes, from Andrew Carnegie it came,
I know that now you're just as brave,
as you were then, Sail on, Sail on,
there's land ahead.

Marianne Faas

STRANGE BEGINNINGS

Strange beginnings
Our love had strange beginnings
Silent words spelled our dialogue
Dense and deeper than a London fog
I knew I took the wrong turn in the road
When you walked across my life
Filling me with desires
Never before had I known
Strange beginnings
Our love had strange beginnings
You led me to the edge of the earth
When you gave me a kiss to dream on
Was I ever to see again
The how the when
The where of it was a question
Still up in the air
I dare not stir the fates
For fear of breaking the spell
It's so fragile a thing
To follow that road to Shangri-La
Someday
Some how
We shall meet again
And play the roulette of love

Marian Barbour

THE WORLD OF POETRY

THE WORLD OF POETRY—like building a bridge
Is over the river then down to the ridge
I shall try to ride over and never fail
To the end of the road with my poetic tale . . . . . .

It's fun, it's stimulating to try to rhyme
The words as I come to the end of the line,
Some are most difficult and some make no sense
And some lead the reader into real suspense

But the prize we are told is well worth doing
To make it rhyme, must continue pursuing
You have given us courage to carry on
We who are trying it of it are most fond . . . . . .

The Department we learn is JUST FOR YOU
And out of it all this whole idea grew!

Alicia K Doyle

MY SEASON

Watching the rain outside my window
I can see the reflection of my eyes in the raindrops.
I long to be a part of the clouds
That release the rain upon the grass and trees.
I can imagine how good it must feel
To be able to let go of so much pressure inside . . .
To be able to release a pain that causes frustration.
I'd love to be able to just burst out my anger
like the clouds . . .
And be able to scream into the night
like the thunder . . . .
I would love to just be able to express myself upon the world
And make everyone feel
the way I'm feeling . . .
I would storm until a flood would arise
Making people fear my power.
I would rain until
The water carried people's precious belongings
into helplessness . . .
Then maybe
just maybe . . .
I would part my clouds
And allow the sunlight to beam down a rainbow
And then the world would know
That my anger was over.

Ray S Woodall

DAY BY DAY

A new day is upon us
Just what will it bring
The coldness of a winter
Or the freshness of a spring

What adventures are ahead of us
Will they make us glad
Or will they weigh upon our hearts
To make us very sad

Will life be something precious
Or will it become old
Becoming such a burden
To make our hearts grow cold

Can this day become a moment
In which we would like to share
Every part of our being
With those for which we care

A new day is upon us
In which we all must live
Struggling for tomorrow
If it is in God's plan to give.

Otakar E Bosak

RESURRECTION

Dedicated to brother Karel

Don't be scared. Never good-by.
I am a man now. Man don't cry.

You will not die,
there is no death,
only last payment
with your breath.

Last silent prayer. You and I.
I will be crawling, You will fly.

Shannon Briones

FAMILY LIFE

We gather around the radio
Listening to the static
watching it glow
We put on our gas masks and sit on the roof
It glows outside too

We get our daily meals from the dumpster in the yard
We drive the family car
We sit on Daddy's lap
We get to push the pedals for him—

he doesn't have legs
Mommy skinned our cat!

We walk to school each day
The teacher has a tumor on her face
None of us kids have hair—It's a dark and gloomy place

We go to church on Sunday—there's a funeral every week
We go and have a picnic but we can't go in the creek
All the fish are dead now—brother picks them up
Sister makes us dinner—and then we throw it up

We don't have a government, Daddy calls it anarchy
Sister doesn't have a nose—Mommy can't see
Me and all my friends from school shout
"Look how her tumor grows!"
We love our family life now. We love the way it glows.

Albert E Vicent

OUR DOMAIN

The beauty of the colors of the
season of spring
as it flows o'er the Earth
our spectacular domain.
Encompassing the world quietly
with buds, blossoms, leaves, birds
New life—old . . .made new
death—rebirth
butterflies—cocoons
rainbows, rain
Nature
Love.
Earth in its entirety
as beautiful wings
of a searching dove.
The winter fades from the woodland
Snow filled, its scene
To a world of
Lush—verdant—green.
And the beauty of the colors of the
season of spring
flows spiritually spectacular
over our . . . domain.

Sara Zurstadt

HOT TIN ROOF

its iron grip upon my breath,
the thick hot air twists
silencing sweet summer murmuring
and the delicate screams
of blossoms against blacktop
until all is deadly.

somewhere a fan purrs on
its mechanical monotonous
perfection.
purrs on, licking itself cool.

the sound of ice dropping in coffee,
a grimace cracks the baked cement
narrow and ragged
just beside my toes.
perhaps the ants will tell great stories of it.

steam passes over my parched lips
and these cry out.

and night falls eventually
as ever it does
and we all lie
in the thick milk night.

Stavroula Staikos

SUNRISE

In the early morning mist,
when the air is sweet and cool
and a brisk breeze clutters by.
Everything is quiet,
except for the chirping crickets in the distance.
Now the air begins to get warmer
and a color of orange begins to appear
with a touch of red.
The sky is bright and filled with rays of the heating sun
beginning to break through.
The sun has risen, and all living things on this earth have
awaken to the bright, shining sun and the warm breeze that
welcomes every single day of our lives.

Marvin O Chisnell

FAREWELL TO TAMMY JO

Dedicated to Yvonne Cain.

Tammy Jo was a sweet little dog,
That you couldn't help but love.
She lived in the West Virginia hills,
Put there by the Lord above.

She never asked for very much,
just food and a place to sleep.
A kind word, a loving touch,
She was really a joy to keep.

She's gone to Doggie HEAVEN now,
To lay at the feet of God.
She's left a vast emptiness,
In the places she used to trod.

We all miss her very much,
That little bundle of love,
But we know that she'll be waiting there,
When we reach our home above.

Mary E Clark

Mary E Clark

DEEP DESPAIR

To all those who find themselves in deep despair.

I'm in a pit of deep despair.
There's not a ray of light.
No bottom and no sides I find,
It's like the middle of the night.
No stars, no moon, just nothingness.
It's like a thick black sooty fog,
That strangles me each breath I take.
A monster type of armless thing;
That wrestles one each move I make.
So I sit in nothingness.
I wrap my arms about my soul.
I find I love no body left,
No mind, I am no longer whole.

Ora L Ransom

THE FIRST DAY OF SCHOOL

To my darling daughter Kay

The first day of school
My Dad is always shooting pool

The first day of school
Mom is on the run

The first day of school
I am so proud—I look so nice!

The first day of school
An apple for my teacher

The first day of school
I counted-20 boys and girls—in my class

The first day of school
Please don't spoil any of the fun

The first day of school
The bell reminds me time to go home!

Betty Harness

TO MY DAD!

The best Dad a girl could have. He was thoughtful, kind, considerate, and helpful. One in a million, my friends said.

To be alive at ninety-five
Should be more than existing.
If only breathing is being alive
So much of life is really missing.

For a year before he went away,
he wondered why he stayed so long.
Though, thank God, he was able each day
To be up doing chores and keep going strong.

Then came the day—a stroke laid him low.
The daily chores he could not meet.
He knew not when others would come or go.
His body was so quiet beneath the sheet.

After lying eighteen days this way,
And being moved from here to there,
Even his breathing seemed to say
He was ready for another place somewhere.

Lauri L Evans

MY SPECIAL CHILD

To my son Christopher William. Thank you for teaching me how to love, unconditionally.

When I look in his eyes that light up the sun,
And I look at his face that shines of love,
I wonder why God trusted me as the one,
To mother this child sent from above.

"He's unlike the others," they say behind his back.
"He looks a little different from the children we love."
I continue to wonder as adults what they lack,
And why God trusted me with this child from above.

He's a challenge, I agree, yet one taken with pride.
His laughter rings softly, quiet moments, our love.
And the differences you see, I take in stride.
He's my gift, not my burden . . .
This, God's child from above

Ted L Sanders

I AM NOT THE NAVIGATOR

This poem is dedicated to my mother, Juanita Sanders for her 83rd birthday.

In the beginning there was desire between a man and a woman; thoughtless lust they seized, like a faint breath of air mist, a hot summer breeze. Later perhaps there came love.

Thus from desire I, man-child came forth. With all my dreams of conquest and infinite self belief. Oh how magnificent!
In every facet, throughout every event life had to yield. I gave a great account, occasionally bringing them thrills.

I ran in the swifter races, I endured the marathon; I out debated the most loquacious. Yes—I even loved once with relentless passion, how exulting the consummation of our souls had been.

Now sometimes, I sit and wonder about such simple things, like the falling of the rain, the lightning and the bolting of the thunder.

For all of my trophies have long since been tarnished. Now when I go to bed I fail to sometimes sleep; for lonesomeness is indeed a loser's disease.

Then, on one lonely sun forsaken day, I came to see that I was a victim of life's technicalities. I was one of the best; but now, in the wake of my waning years I fall short of the season's yield. Could it be that I am judged so unfairly or maybe it is I had failed to realize that I Am Not My Own Navigator?

James Richard Hansen

THE DAILY CYCLE

Fighting every step of the way,
Fright'ning things will happen today.
Twisting and turning in agony,
Bending, collapsing—the pain is free.

Pleading, needing—respite is gone;
Leaning, bleeding—the damage is done.
Minutes are hours and hours days—
"It's all okay," the doctor says.

Inside, outside, everywhere lost;
Death to shadow plays cunning host.
Fantasy quickens the searing pain;
Ecstasy threatens to ne'er come again.

Waiting over, the hour is through;
Skies are sunny, cloudless and blue.
Coming is more of the same for days—
Pain on the market (the price one pays).

T J Anonymmous

NOT ENOUGH

I cry for clowns,
I stalk with tigers,
I live among music,
and talk among stars.
Time is my enemy,
Love is my friend,
Gravity I define,
and words are not enough.
How far must I go,
How much can I obtain
I discover me,
Only to satisfy a query.
I am afraid sometimes,
but only of myself.
I am by name knowledge,
and this is not enough.

Rita A Francis

I HATE YOU, I HATE YOU

Dedicated to all the children in the world whose lives are the essence of this poem.

I hate you, I hate you
a child cries out
Not only enough to understand
what life's all about
Some times are tough
while others are rough
Sometimes the child
has just had enough

Where is his mother,
 where is his Dad?
The only parents
 the child ever had

He takes to the streets
 he's out on his own
No one cared
 while he was at home

There's junkies
 there's hookers
They own the street
 they tell the child
How he can afford to eat

He gives up his innocence
 throwing away his name
He has to survive
 so he plays their game
He totally surrenders
 to this life with some doubt
I hate you, I hate you
 a child cries out.

Elizabeth A Soltis
THE HOUR GLASS

I dedicate this poem to my grandmother and to my mother and father who have taught me the meaning of love.

The hour glass holds only so many
grains of sand
for one man.
Those who love and have been loved
find the mystery
to the fountain of life.

Living life to its fullest is
the key to wisdom.
For knowledge is self power,
the inner strength to face
the true meaning of the
Alpha and Omega.

Bernadette White
TO BE FREE

Dedicated to my mother, Catherine J O'Connor, the fabric of my being.

To be free,
Was to release the past
To unveil the guilt, and set it free,
Like the sails on a mast.

To be free,
Was to seek a higher power
To guide me through troublesome
times,
To them, unyielding like the Eiffel
Tower.

To be free
Was to trust that good would prevail
And evil would be left behind,
Like Noah portrayed when setting
sail.

To be free,
Was to look to my dreams
To see hard times as periods of
growth,
Like a babe reveals teething through
screams.

To be free,
Was to accept the challenge of each
new day
To live each day to its fullest,
With the wisdom that I only had to
pray
And God would give me the strength
to control my destiny.

Mary (Reed) Stott
I

This poem is dedicated to, my family and friends. Thank you for the encouragement. I love you!

I created the earth,
 Oh! What a task.
I made the moon,
 the sun,
 the grass.
I planted trees
 all around
I grew flowers,
 shrubs,
and lay them
in the ground.

I created birds,
 to fly the sky,
the little, the big,
all that meets
 the eye.

I created man,
 to work this heavy
 load.
to mow the grass,
to work the road.

I created women,
 to care for man.
To run the house,
to Harvest the land.

I am God,
 the man above,
Who watches you,
 and brings you
  Love.

Deborah Pawlowski
SOMEDAY

This poem is dedicated to my Father and his Grandchildren.

For sixty years he's been on life's
way.
The early years pass quickly with
school and play.
Ambition in him sent him on life's
way.
To college and that first day of pay.

It was one summer along life's way.
He met a lovely lady to spend all his
days.
It was never enough so he went all
life's way.
Till his name on the door shone like a
ray.

The years flew by filled with all life's
way.
No time for family only a grumble,
"Someday".
It's sixty years to the day and his
smiling eyes are creased from life's
way.
Oh yes he's still on life's way, but
it's Someday.

The office, trains and planes are still
on life's way.
But, now it walks with the lady who
waited all those days.
There's time for family, fun in the
country and the smell of hay.
And when his little grandchildren cry
"don't go", he can stay, it's Someday.

It's been a long road sixty years to
Someday.
Now Someday is here and we're so
glad, for finally he's on his way.

Delphine Mahalak
CARING

Dedicated to my loving husband Ed and my grandson Craig.

I heard a voice, so crisp so clear.
Where's grandpa? it inquires.
Soon hand in hand both boy and man
to grandpa's chair retire.
Upon their laps on current news two
golden pears for sharing.
The boy responds no words were
said, the warmth was so apparent
A thought occurs, that grandpa is
surely made for caring.

Bruce A Thompson
HARVESTED MEMORIES

In Remembrance of Rev. P. C. Key, Sr., my grandfather; May his memories be harvested joyfully by the Throne of God in Heaven.

As we ponder on thoughts of
 years that have slowly past,
We wonder on mirrors of
 yesterday that will always last;
The wisdom we earned from
 those days have budded into
 flowers,
Of memories harvested in
 youthful dreams, but sung
  during peaceful hours.

Eric John Rardin
THE MIRROR BOY

To those that forgot to smile

The boy in the mirror is crying again.
He's crying for someone to reach out.
For someone to care, to make him
happy.
Nobody has, and so he cries again.
Still no one comes.

Yet no one can make you happy little
boy.
Except the boy in the mirror. When
he smiles, you do, when he weeps,
you do.
Smile and laugh and he will back.
Happiness is inside.

Michael Junek
IN CASSIE'S SONG

Cassie, you're the Wand-at-Magic's-Hand, then you wave it
I'll kiss you once, though Once is Like a Thousand Times

Into love's past, I go soul searching for the words that were once, in Cassie's Song. Who she was I never really knew her though I dreamed that I did, in Cassie's song.
We were on the run, from the capture that sought us, but we got away, in Cassie's Song. She led the way 'cause she knew that I would follow her so close behind. We escaped to where no one could ever find us, but the lyrics were there, from Cassie's Song.
Oh! there was guiding light at the end of our tunnel, for we never saw what others saw, from then and on the clouds were all but broken, but the darkness turned on, in Cassie's Song.
We still had hope, though the moment would not last us, for we would dance on, in Cassie's Song. I would be King and she would be my Queen and we were to love, in Cassie's Song.
I've had no such luck, in my journey to wherever her spirit was lost, in Cassie's Song. If the answer's there, then I wish I could find it. I'd love her again, till angels call.
Who was I to be in love with her she was in my world, but now she's gone, just a dream, or was it really truthful, the truth is still known, in Cassie's Song.
Who she was, that thought will always matter cause I was a line, in Cassie's Song. And X marked the spot on the treasure we did find for we had it all, in Cassie's Song.
Frosted grains of so sweet-to-hold sugar, that's how she was, in Cassie's Song. But like the wave of the hand that only sends sorrow, we waved goodbye, in Cassie's Song.

Glenda Marie Morrow
MADAM BENEATH THE LAMPLIGHT

Dedicated to Madam

A shadow in the doorway
 beckons to her hasty feet.
Why bother thy "madam of
 frocks"—
A stranger in the street?
Rush! Tell him she'll be waiting
 there—
 Her usual place—at ten.
Do it with your blessings, child.
 Delays naught soon be forgiven!
Madam beneath the lamplight—
 don legs a satiny smooth.
Hoisted on the lamplight base—
 sleek to make her move.
Her skirt slid high, she reveals a
 tightly crescent crotch.
Make any man with half an
 instinct dare to stop and watch.
A scent of musk that lingers on
 weakens their resistance
And entices the anxious
on-lookers
 To shorten up their distance.
With pursed, red lips and
 bosom high
And throbbing 'neath her loins
Madam, she bounce like
 "monkey-free"
Toss her a hand of coins!
After Madam's night triumphs
She treks on down the aisle
To use sad tokens of her trade
Caretaking for her child.

Doya Nardin
BALI LADIES

For Rowen Hayes

Women talking
working walking
Hips bare breasts
undulating
as you stride
Sarong tied high
gracefully
through the streets
Heavy baskets sitting lightly
on your heads
Straight backed beauties of
Balinese balance ballet
Mindful of the weight the work
and hips bare breasts
undulating
as you stride
Sarong tightly tied
gracefully

Judith Brink Alexandre'
MAN IN THE STREET

Dedicated to Dennis Lindsey, PhD. His predestinated passage valued.

'Twas Friday morn' the day was new. I chanced upon a man in blue. Squatted behind a wall, trying to straighten his faded attire. With a dirty sock, from his feet he brushed the previous day's mire.

I had the urge to take him home, let

him shower, clean his clothes. Fix him food to nourish body and soul. For this I'd ask his story be told. I'd write it down for the world to read. This terrible thing could happen to you and me. In this great country that men get down . . . Without some help it's impossible to turn around.

As I drove off down the street the tears of sadness streaked my cheeks. I'd let my fear get in the way. I didn't raise the dignity of that man this day.

I understood what I had lost . . .
But . . . I'd never know the real cost.

Tammy Renee' Moore
MOTHER'S LOVE

This poem is dedicated to my beautiful three year old daughter Brittany who means the world to me. I love you very very much.

My world comes alive when she gets up in the morning

Her bright eyes show me there will be another day of bliss in my life

When she hugs my neck I can't begin to explain the feeling of joy I get

It's like I don't have any cares or problems around me

When she says "I LOVE YOU MOMMY" I feel I have achieved the greatest thing in the world

I have accomplished my ultimate goal: I AM A MOTHER

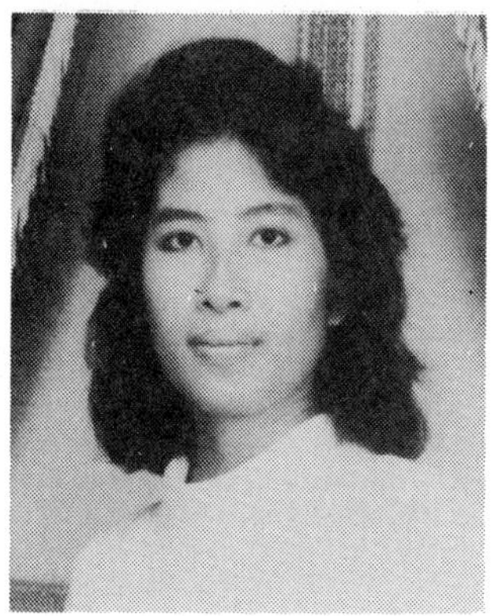

Lilia Sinaga

Lilia Sinaga
NEW YORK NEW YORK, LADY

To: My parents Syarifuddin Sinaga, Sabarniaty Manurung Restu Denny, Dedy Sinaga, Eko Widyawati.

Moonlight on the city of New York
On the old snow covered bench, in perplexities I am captivated.
Embracing my pack, I am waiting for none, for nothing
'cause I have never made even a tryst.
The luminous city crawls to seize the raven locks night, here
I adumbrate Lady Liberty who ever smile so sweet to me
in this land of hope she promised me an ablution and a freedom.
but she didn't say there are so many covetous foxes hid in faith
but she didn't say there isn't any delusion and munificence.
Epoch walked in raving raucous destination
and then trapped in the hole of freedom we have made
O' Lady where did you hide me and my hope.
O Lady, the expectation I have put on the corners of your lips.
the trust I have put in the tremors of your heart.
New York New York, roaring in the hoarse tone.
Shaking the land, shaking my heart, I am disappointed, deceived.
The old father of mine ambled and stared the exalted city.
We have seen it changing with unknown colours
Panorama, the high trees imprisoned in the side ways poured by dust
My heart was dried in the navel of the gaily city
O, let me alone here to draught my choice.

Estelle Russell
HAPPY BIRTHDAY HEATHER

To our Granddaughter Heather—May she be as delightful in years to come; as she is today.

Heather you will be 9
On this Thanksgiving Day.

You have grown to be a beauty
What more is there to say?

You are your mother's daughter
In all the things you do.
You help her with the little ones,
and even tie their shoes.

We love it when you come to visit
The notes you leave are fun.
We never know where we will find them
But we treasure every one.

If we had ordered a granddaughter
We're sure it would be you.
You let Grandma take your picture
and give hugs and kisses too.

Happy Birthday
Grandma & Grandpa

Mary Inman
MAYMIE'S LITTLE BUNDLE

Dedicated to Jimmy Lee Summ, who was in my day care for five years and nine months. Ken and I will always have a place in our home and hearts for all the joy you put in our lives. Sincerely, with a heart full of love—Mary E. Inman (Maymie)

Little Peepie, this poem is for you. It may not sound brainy, it may not sound smart,
but it's written sincerely from the bottom of my heart.

All of us have loved you, 'cause you're such a little honey,
cute and sweet and at times a little funny.

Kristie and Terri love you too, know how I can tell—
they play with you a lot of times and treat you very well.

Your days consist of tantrums, excitement, amusement and fears,
smiles and giggles, orneriness and tears.

You're a bundle of mischief, a toddler of moods, but good behavior,
naughty, a bully, or coy,
you're Maymie's little bundle and your folks' little boy.

It's no wonder God made you and put you on this earth,
you have lit up so many lives and made them feel their worth.

At times it seemed too much for me,
you're such a demanding child,
but I'm so happy I stuck with you,
'cause you help make my life worthwhile.

You bring out the sunshine, you chase the clouds away,
I'm so glad your mom saw fit to send you around my way.

You're one of God's little miracles
and let me tell you true,
you always bring out the best in me
and I thank God for you.

I feel like I could go on for days,
writing this poem for you,
but I just can't, I have to stop, I have lots of other things to do.

Just had to tell you how much you're loved, then when all is said and done,
want to tell all who this poem is for,
it's little JIMMIE SUMM
—Love, Maymie

Myrtle A Ballard
HEART'S ECHO

A prayer for my sons Tom, John, and David, as they continue their life's journey.

Strength for today is petitioned from you
As life with its burdens, I muddle through;

Courage to buffet the obstacles so great,
Love so overflowing that it smothers hate;

Patience to refrain from lashing out
When the wisdom of others' decisions I doubt;

Harbor in my mind loud peacefulness,
Wrap my heart's echo with your tenderness.

Sarah Eason
PUSH AROUND

This poem is to be dedicated to the abused women and children of the world. And to my family whom I love very much.

Look Love, there's more to me.
Than Sweat, Blood and Tears
There's a person you're mistreating
There's a person you're abusing
It's me, you're pushing around.

Salayne Cook
NIGHT SHIFT

I dedicate this poem to my children Taisha, Shonna, Brandy, & T.J.

Tired as I can be
I tried to sleep with no hope
Dreams of people I wish not to speak
Waking to find the same night
Toss and turn if I will
Shake the dreams away
Turn the channel to who are you
Never another day
Bright skies
Light skies
I awake to find no sky
Only memories of the day before
Hoping times will be better
Old man turn over
Don't nestor too long
Sleeping is the art of peace
You must master to grow
Don't dream no more sorrows
Old man you're already grown
Tomorrow you will be tired
As the same as the day before

Louise Suiter Yates
LITTLE MOON CHILD

To My Daughter, Karen Yates Johnson

LITTLE MOON CHILD with your heart so pure
Your moon sails high in the sky tonight,
LITTLE MOON CHILD, YOU ARE LOVED AND SECURE
In the glow of your celestial orb so bright;
'Tis your golden symbol sailing across the sky,
A great yellow ball floating leisurely by.
LITTLE MOON CHILD, this night belongs to you,
It is your time the whole night through,
Until the darkness to daylight turns
And the night fades as the sun returns.
LITTLE MOON CHILD, may all your dreams
Be happily borne on golden moonbeams.

Nellie Mingus Roberts
TRIBULATION OR CLOUDS OF GLORY?

I dedicate this to my darling grandchildren: Mark, Lynette, Stacey, Julie, Amanda, Jason and Jessica.

When I look at the heavenly blue sky

I realize we will meet Jesus up there in the sweet by an by

And then we will never have any more heartaches or worry

When God gathers his children up in the Clouds of Glory

Then those we have tried to warn but they wouldn't hear

Would be left to go through all that terrible tribulation and fear

God doesn't want you to be left, for He loves you so be aware

And let's be ready and waiting so he can gather us all up there.

Cynthia Meurer Daly
FORGET-ME-NOTS

In memory of Mom, for future memories, for my son, Andrew . . . .

Scrambled, tossed, up cloud, empty, hopeless, tearful,
But proud, echoing words . . . No longer at ease, lonely,
Leaves fall from their once fully dressed trees, as is,
Who's to say, in tunes or degrees.

Time period, still perilous, is its stone, sealed up,
inside its platinum cone. Simple things see, they don't,
Stop for you and me . . . only its echo, run, so you're free.
A love, now simplified, one last cry, before it died, strangled,
In mixed up hopes . . . but still nigh, for you and I . .

Remember me, in backgrounds of blue, where sea gulls fly in,

Twinkles of true, curved up smiles,
remembering love in heart,
felt miles. When does that wave she
gently crashes on shore, asking,
Her question, with a wondering what
for. Remember me . . .As one,
Who told you before, live one day, as
it as as such, for you'll,
Remember it in time . . . and love it
as much . . .

Paulette Oliveira
ISLAND OF HAWAII

LOVINGLY DEDICATED TO MY FAMILY Marion & Anita Oliveira, Josephine Medeiros Debra Clark, Devin and Desmond Valentin

The sun has risen on the clear
blue sky,
with gentle winds from snow
covered mountains.
The sea has sand as white as
snow, endless and calm as can
be.
Flowers of all varieties spill their
fragrance with beauty,
so come to my island
surrounded by sea.
Islanders and Visitors share
smiles and friendliness
so visit our beaches to share the
Aloha Spirit.
Here everyone relaxes, and time
lingers on,
so come, come to my island
surrounded by sea.

Blacks, Browns, Blues and Greens
of our island coast,
and the gentleness of the sea,
will all help you to relax,
on our island surrounded by the
sea.
The warmth of the sun, the gentle
sway of the trees, the beauty
and fragrance of the flowers,
will make you want to stay.
Roses, Hibiscus, Anthuriums,
Plumerias, Orchids and
Bougainvilla's,
give beauty, fragrance and
enjoyment to all who are
present.
The abundance is here, reds,
yellows, oranges and purples,
so come, come to my island
surrounded by the sea.

Julie Gatens
ALONE

Ever proud, she stands above.
Forever stubborn, she is sorrowful.
All she ever wanted was love.
She only desired for someone to call
her own.
But she'll always be alone.

Ezekial Smith
A TALE OF HAPPINESS

This Poem has been dedicated to my special friends (1) Dahlia M. Prophet, (2) Herbert E. Gooden and (3) Geroge's Bar-B -Que West Little York

Look there's a bird, up in a tall tree.
Let's sit and be quiet, quiet as can be.
He's whistling a pretty song for us
can't you see.
Tell me, tell me, what could that
song be?

It seems to be, one of the best
melodies ever a bird whistle thee.
Hey and that's an old Blue Jay up in
that tall tree.
A bird I used to cherish, all through
the day.
Because I once thought, he was most
prettiest of all.

He is still whistling that melody, up
there, "still as can be."
It seems he has awakened all the
birds in the tree.
But I truly believe, that bird will be,
One of the best and greatest, that
ever whistle in a tree.

Blue Jay, Blue Jay, if you ever fly
away.
Keep whistling that sweet melody,
all through the day.
We might be outside having a party,
in the park, or standing by a tree.
Wherever, we may be, just keep that
music sounding good, in that tall tree.

Helen Schambers
FOR YOU IN THE HOSPITAL

I heard you had a By-Pass done
For better circulation,
And judging by what I have heard
That's quite an operation—
Thank God, the worst is over with
And now it won't be long,
Before you'll lead a normal life
And get to feeling strong—
So, take it easy—rest a lot
And take your medication,
Remember, we all miss you, when,
You're "OUT OF CIRCULA-
TION!"

Get well soon!

Paul E Windwehen
A RIDDLE

My first lines ever published should be dedicated To the two people soul-ly dedicated To my being Educated: "Flo" and "Windy" Windwehen

I float through the heavens
effortlessly,
Sliding and gliding with
soul-shaking glee,
Freezing and thawing alternately,
On the wings of a dust speck whose
center is me.

From high up above, the world is a
quilt,
Veiling, unveiling with each
current's tilt,
Flowing and blowing with rivers and
silt,
Riding the rim of a wheel whose hub
my kin built.

Far up over the ocean, looking wide
and flat,
Drifts up my sister and drops in for a
chat.
Then in come our friends from this
way and that,
Changing shapes in the eye from a
dog to a cat.

We dance and we prance and we
mingle together,
On the wind, floating and flying,
birds of a feather.
In multitudes of tons we all party
together,
And cast ourselves out, giving life, in
a flash of God's glory completely
untethered.

Who am I?

Heather A Sutter
HIS LOVE . . . THE ANSWER

This poem is dedicated to Bruce Rimbold, with love always.

Love is the answer
there's no other one
Heartache and frustration
isn't much fun.
Understanding, caring
cherishing it all,
Part of the memories of a love that
used to be.
Tears of pain and love cry out at
night.
Wanting that touch of his love, near
and insight.
Memories of us fill my mind
While feelings for him and our love
pour out of me; time after time.
I'll never lose the love
never forget his touch because
his love is warm and gentle,
caring and understanding
I love him so much.

Cynthia D Leavitt
SPRING

This poem is dedicated to my mother, TRECIL

The leaves rush by my window
As the wind blows them along
While in the spreading apple tree
The robins sing their song
The flowers are so pretty
As they decorate the scene
The morning sun shines brightly
To remind us that it's spring

The babbling brook, it hurries on,
Not knowing where it ends
The pussy willows nod their heads
As if they're greeting friends
The children seem so happy
While soaring on their swings
The air is filled with laughter
To remind us that it's spring.

Iva Kant
THE LAST MISSION

To Linda Sexton

On the back of your last book you
sit,
Leaning at an angle unknown to
protractors,
The glass in your hand linked lightly
to your perfect manicure
By a kind of will that almost rejects
sweat.

This arm is the brawnier arm, the
tennis arm.
It blocks the chromium chair handle
in a hearty "v."

The sun sneaks across part of your
face
As if you had made up with it
temporarily
And were now telling it,
As you once told servants in your
childhood,
"Yes, here and here and here."

Which poem had you just finished?

Which lazy, happy time did you call
up for the smile
And the subsequent off-camera dash
to the future—
So loud, so needy, so complete?

The chain necklace curses your chest
like some angry virtue—
Rejecting shape, slithering over twin
creases in your blouse,
Biting the breast that feeds it.

It cannot look back.
Unlike you, it owns no shadow.

Sandra L Schmid

Sandra L Schmid
IN SEARCH FOR LOVE

To Dennis Ricker, thanks for your support and love.

When you're born there love in Mom
So tender and kind, so fulfilling

As you grow and mature each day
you find you need more love in other
ways

The love of life is not enough
Must have love of lust, of beauty and
friendship too.

Sometimes you find that love can
hurt
For it has many faces

Pain is love to a sick mind
The love of nature and all its kind
Respect of love can be there too
The love of laughter will even do

After searching your whole life
through
Your search is finished
For love is you

J L Ries
MARBLE BRIDGE

For P. W.—who, I know, understands.

It seems that every
Once in a while
I come to this damn bridge.—
It is the same one
With all its intricate lining
And nothing underneath.

I want so to jump
I don't care what is below
It may very well be nothing
But that would be something
Better than here.

My walk to this place
Has always been alone
However, surrounded
By rings of people
Doing dances with steps
I can't find it in my heart to learn.

I see that I am the only one

Who sees this wonderful bridge
Who takes the walk
Up the steps to it
As they continue to dance
in their rings.

I don't care about their music
That I somehow don't
hear all of,
I don't care about their fancy steps—
I have my bridge
That I ponder climbing over
the wall of.

If I don't this time
I'll probably come to it again
For it seems that I am
Walking in circles.
There are merely different land-
scapes
That I pass each time around
And maybe different people
Dancing on the ground.
However, I have the same old
bridge—
I know this is my own—
Oh, please, won't someone
join me on it
So I'm not so alone?

Ruth Stuckey
EMPTY EYES
This hellish current child, dragging
you along.
You feel insecure and the damage is
done.
Inside the battle was, inside you
fought.
Looking for love and refuge you
sought.
No longer speaking, climbing into
your shell.
Wanting it to stop, no one to tell.
Reflection of emptiness seems to
wander in your eyes.
A reflection of what must live inside.

There doesn't seem to be pain you
haven't felt already.
Your mind still wanders but has
become unsteady.
What good child is left inside of you.
You no longer care and feel no need
to be true.
No longer sensitive to the touch of
love.
Only a passion filled hate, never
getting enough.
There doesn't seem to be a right
from wrong.
A dark void inside, yet you live on.

Patsy K Watson
PRAYER

This poem is dedicated to my family and friends who have stood behind me and encouraged me all along.

Now I lay me down to sleep
Was once a prayer I said.
Just before I closed my eyes
As I lay in my bed.

My life was very simple then
My problems very small.
At night I'd simply say my prayers
And God would take them all.

I knew back then that I was safe
From harms that came my way.
That nothing here could bother me
As long as I would pray.

But now, you see, I'm older yet
Than e'er I was before.
My problems are much larger now;
My worries more and more.

And yet I do not falter still,
For I know God is there
I talk to Him both day and night.
I speak to Him in prayer.

Edward C Hill
A FRIEND OF MINE

All glory praise and honor
To Christ our King!

It was early day when my eyes
beheld,
a man I did not know,
He appeared to be a friend of mine,
someone I should of known.
They took this man and beat him,
although I knew not why,
they said he was a liar,
and should be crucified.
I asked the crowd about him,
and what this man had done,
the crowd just laughed and said,
He's God's begotten Son.
Then they marched him to Calvary,
to nail him to the cross,
and as he hung there then I knew,
what a friend the world had lost.
He gave his life for friendship,
as he hung upon that tree,
and this is why his blood was shed,
that we should ALL be FREE!

Catherine F Warren
WHEN BREAKS THE DAWN
She was looking at the stars but
the stars
She did not see,
For his face it shone from heaven
brighter than
A star could ever be,
And the night was sweet as with
the perfume of
A strange and lovely tree.

And the tree it spoke, someday you
will love me
As before,
And I, yes, my mother I will love you
Evermore,
See, here and I, I have not died,
And the woman, she replied,

Beautiful tree, you must blossom for
the angels now that you
From me are gone,
You, whose touch I'll feel from morn
til night while yet
The stream of life flows on,
But sweeter still, to see your face,
that wondrous face
Again, when breaks the dawn.

Sean W Gaines
UNTITLED
The world is lined in a grid-like
pattern.
I cannot reach the grass and sun
—or my love.
Someone lend me a rock
and I will break this cruel window.

Marie Poto
A MOTHER'S PRAYER
Oh the sea rose in waves to the tops
of the trees
That were planted by mermaids bent
low at the knees
And only the stars which refused
now to freeze
Knew the reason that this had been
done
As the whales blew a kiss and a
geyser with ease
To the land of the setting sun
Where the work of all madmen was
said to begun
But why this all happened why
nobody knows
Not a butterfly winking the close of a
rose
Or a dragonfly busy with lunch and a
doze
And with frightening children who
ran runny-nosed
Into mothers who wished they could
be
On the tops of those trees that waves
crested with ease
Planted by mermaids bent low at the
knees
In celestial gardens of uncharted seas.

Margaret C Kearns

Margaret C Kearns
LONGING

In Loving Memory of Marvin Kearns
We Found Our Ladder and Climbed
It Together, Forty and One-Half
Years

If Life could hold for us, dear
The joys of eternal love;
If we could share together
A paradise, like that above.
If we could climb, together
Life's ladder of every day
And leave far behind us
The rungs of yesterday.

If somewhere along, we'd stumble
Upon the joys of a little nest;
Setting down in quiet contentment
Upon the ladder of success.
We'd climb into a world brighter,
Find great happiness, by and by
And Oh! My dearest darling,
Our goodnight, wouldn't be
goodbye.

Rosemary H Mamienski
AN INEXPLICABLE LOVE

Thanks G.H.H. for all your help and M.E.B. for the inspiration.

Most memories fade away fast;
only the fondest linger on to dot
our past;
If only our romance could last, or
we would have another chance to
take a few more tests and see if we
could make it the best from here to
east and west.

But since you think we should
retreat to our separate nests, I
guess it is time to put
everything to rest.

Before I go I must confess: I will
always fly a flag half-mast in
case your new relationship
doesn't last and you decide to
stray and come back here
possibly to stay.—Then I would
gently cast aside the non-
suspecting, gracious little lamb,
as we reunite to satisfy our
carnal desires until we both
expire.

Mildred P Law
TIME ON MY HANDS
Many years ago when I was young
There was never enough time to do
All the things, that should be done
No time for this No time for that
Tomorrow, Wait 'til tomorrow
I will do it tomorrow.
All those busy hectic years now are
gone
All those wait 'til tomorrow's now
are here
With all the time one needs to do
All the things that could get done
With time to spare, I get nowhere
Nothing accomplished nothing
done—but wait
Wait for time to pass
Wait for another tomorrow.

Mary Ann Fuller
WHO COULD LOVE THEM MORE?

This poem is dedicated to any mother, father, husband or wife who is considering leaving their home and family.

Your life is not what you think it
should be,
You think you'd be better alone.

Have you given much thought to
what your children will think,
As they grow up and are out on their
own?

Who could love your children more,
than the man who gave them life?
Who could love your children more,
than the woman who is your wife?

Your life is not what you think it
should be,
You're looking around for a new
family.

Look again at your home! Have you
done all that you can,
To make things right for this woman
and man?

Harvey T Miller
A LITTLE KINDNESS

A little kindness to everyone

PART I
A little word of kindness spoken
And with a smile that's sincere
Has often healed one's "Heart" that's
been broken
And has made a friend true and dear
The face you wear the wonderful
thoughts that you bring
Will let a friend and others see the
brightness of things
"Kindness" and "Love" in this
"World," it's a treasure
And it creates some "Unity," among
the "People" and it's a pleasure
These little things are all important
for all of us to see
in the making of a "Peaceful,"
"World" that's here to be

PART II
With our smiling faces and our
helping hand
We'll make friends who will always

understand
That there is in the "World" someone who really cares
in making a pleasant life for others in which sometime is rare
There's sometime in the "Heart" a little bit of sadness
And a dear friend intercedes and brings them things of gladness
Remember the "Heart," sometime brings to us a little stress
And with a little moment from you in "Prayer" it will always be blessed
So when you think things are "dreary" and "Blue"
Just "Pray" to our "God," high in the "Heavens," up above
And with all of his kindness and help he will give to us all his "Love"

Sheryl L Walters

A SPECIAL LOVE AFFAIR

Dedicated to my One-derfully Curious Son, Lanny Dale Whaley. For all of those questions he asked that I could not answer.

I see a Special Love Affair
as I sit across the room.
It's a new experience
to see love as it blooms.

I watch them sharing secrets,
not caring if they're alone.
Whispering to each other
in public and at home.

One always asking "why?,"
the other trying to explain.
Sometimes I see jealousy,
new attention is always gained.

I watch with tear-filled eyes
their special love affair.
I watch their love growing
and the closeness they share.

A real Special Love Affair
that keeps growing even more,
between the man I love
and my little boy of four.

Evelyn Mazzenga

THE ROSEBUD

The rosebud.
Young and fragile,
Sweet smelling and alluring.
It cries out for the Sun's nurturing love.
A dew drop falls gently from its petals,
Sometimes hitting the ground with force,
Sometimes trickling down peacefully.
Then it opens, suddenly as if to say "here I am"
fully grown now and reaching for the sky.
Though I may lose a few petals along the way do not stop watering me.
Do not become discouraged if my radiance dims,
it's just a rainy day.
Tomorrow I will reach for the sky once more.
See the love that I reflect with each new day.
Feel the warmth of my innermost petal.
Smell the sweetness of my maturity.
There is no need to prune me,
just support me with the stake of your heart.
Listen to my cry to be picked by you,
to be touched by your loving hands.

Mabel Lagerlof Manville

THE WATCHMAN

I never thought I'd write these LINES
To WARN the PEOPLE of our TIMES!
Great WOE is headed towards our EARTH
GOOD NEWS, too! So, an ACTIVE Watchman
I MUST be, delivering the DIVINE Message Faithfully!
GOD says: "Clean up your act . . . . . . your ways . . . . repent
Turn around: I offer you ETERNAL LIFE . . . . . Health . . .
Perpetual YOUTH and a WORLD without . . . . WOE! ! !
LOVE your neighbor and BURY . . . . .H-A-T-E!
Do this before it is too . . . . .L-A-T-E!
OBEY my Voice . . . YOU have a . . . . .CHOICE!"
God adds: He takes no pleasure in the DEATH of a wicked one! Why DIE needlessly?

IF this Divine Message . . . . . I DO NOT CONVEY . . . .
Your BLOOD will be on my hands . . . . to . . . . STAY!
HEED this call, PLEASE . . . . One and ALL . . . .
It is NOW or NEVER lest we FAIL and FALL!
This means NEVER to attain . . . . PARADISE at all!
Our LIVES . . . . . our LOVES will . . . . . TERMINATE . . . . .
All will be LOST . . . . if we do not . . . . BURY . . . . H-A-T-E!
AMEN

(EZEK. 3:17)
(" 33:11)

Ms Armetta L White

Ms Armetta L White

THE DREAM

In dedication to the Kings— Ms. Coretta Scott King and the late Dr. Martin Luther King Jr.—fighters for human equality and justice.

Midnight hour, emotions scream—
that flow within a summer dream.
A vision struggling to survive—
how can one keep a dream alive?
The monster mares attempt to sweep
the newfound dream off feeble feet.
Within my grasp, then yet it dies—
how can I keep my dreams alive?
Through days of sorrow I pull on
and fight until my dream is won.
A momentary flare that flickers, then flies—
how can I keep a dream alive?
Hidden terror and secret doubt—
find the cause and stamp it out.
The spiders in my plan will weep,
when they have suffered mass defeat.
I'll struggle to reach a spacious shore,
and have my dreams snipped out no more!

Marguerite Fain Everson

FALLING LEAVES

The trees drop leaves
in the fall,
Like death that comes
to one and all.

For some
it is fast,
For others
a lingering task.

We know not when
we will be released
To enter the land
of eternal peace,

But when it comes
it's sure to be
What God wants
for you and me.

Dorothy Margaret Griggs

Dorothy Margaret Griggs

THE SIDEWALK

I called . .
My neighbor's child over
And asked her . .
If she knew
Who wrote . .
All over my sidewalk
It looked . .
Like something she'd do
"My friend did it"
She answered
As she walked . .
Closer to see
And without hesitation
She added
"My friend . . .
Writes just like me"

Angie Ford

FAST FOOD EFFECTS

"Fast Food" isn't good at all
you can find it anywhere, but
especially at the mall
It comes in all forms fries and a shake
the choice is yours to make
I prefer myself a BLT yeah,
yeah that's for me!
So I ordered a BLT, fries, and a coke
the people in the restaurant put it in a poke
I went to sleep that night,
and to my horror and fright—
Those items of food were in my dreams
how funny this all seems
The coke hit me, the fries shook me and as for the BLT it gave me gas, right before 1st period class!
"Oh God!" at first I thought,
then a bottle of Gas-X is what I sought.
It was all over I never ate "Fast Food" again
'Cause I learned my lesson well
"Fast Food" isn't swell.

Patti Stocker Machotka

WAITING

To Sam

You never say "I love you" and I wonder why.

The same way I wonder why birds not man can fly.

It would be grand to see the sun beside the moon at night or touch an eagle's feathers as he glides along in flight.

I will not cease my dreaming but I can clearly see some things in life most wanted are not meant to be.

So I will console myself by trying to love me giving you the space you need so that you can feel free.

You are like the mighty eagle soaring in the sky—I should not try to cage you for surely you would die.

In giving you your freedom I am hoping to hear the words you never uttered while I tried to hold you near.

Jean R Froman

GOD'S TIME

Time: is the undying power of
our lives—
It is given for our birth,
It is measured in our loving.
It is used in our growing.

Time: Must be used with
expertise—
To its greatest advantage,
To further our knowledge,
To gain humility.

Time: Must be shared to gain
kinship with mankind—
With our neighbors for
cooperation,
With our enemies for
understanding,
with family to gain trust and
understanding.

Time: Is the essence of every
event in our lives—
All the comings and goings
of friend and foe,
To know and cherish the
love of others,
To appreciate the advice and
wisdom of our elders.

Time: Regulates:
The maturing of our minds,
The healing of our bodies,
The tempering of our aging,
Finally, our death! When
Time becomes Eternal!

Beverly L Besser

HOME

I've been around for quite a long time
Trying to learn reason from rhyme
Yet I still return to the same familiar place
Perhaps because I recognize its welcoming face.
I leave and I roam . . . .Always searching
Only to come back . . . . to discover home,
For as they say in words of a distant

day
"Home is where the heart lies'
To each his own in their very special way.

Happy to be here . . . .I guess I'll stay
My memories sweet . . . . some bitter too.
But most of all the best are of you.
I cannot believe three times not more
I have left this place and closed the door.
Now I've returned to the same soft shore
To find it free and available to me
For all I've done . . . . and all I've seen
This is reality . . . . It is not a dream.

I was meant to be here on my own
In this fine structure that I call home
With all its cracks and ancient fixtures
Such a warm conglomerate of mixtures
But then so am I . . . .It's plain to see
This old apartment . . . . was always there for me.

Nichole Marie Veitch
REFLECTIONS
Through the reflections of the water,
I see images of a life of old
Where survival was all that mattered
And friendships, along with love,
took new fold.

Through the mirror of my mind,
I see a battle for what is right—
Something so easy to comprehend,
so hard to find,
And to obtain must take a fight.

Through the images of my dreams,
I see all that has been fought for,
All that we lost and what it means,
And the echoes of opening and
closing that door.

Through the words of history,
I see that there is none
That can express the memory
Of a life that is gone.

Anita Reed-Davis
THE UNWRITTEN POEM

Dedicated to my grandmother; The Late, Jenny "Dutchie" Patterson, who taught me the love in poetry.

The unwritten poem lies silently
As an unspoken treasure of my mind
Priceless collections of golden thoughts
Unmarred by changing time

It's grandma rocking on the front porch
With a far away yen on her face
While the washin's a blowin' on the clothesline
Like Old Glory a flappin'—in a mid-summer breeze

It's a heart in need of mending
Like a tattered and aged photograph
A grey cloud lowering the mountain top
A fire engine's wail—A train husseling the rail
Piercing the still of the night

The unwritten poem is a parade—A circus comin' to town
Baby's first step
A sparrow's first flight
A policeman with a child he's found

The unwritten poem is early sunrise
Marching across the meadow
A rainbow arched o'er a distressed sea
Autumn erasing Summer—You and me

The unwritten poem is the best one—
I shall ever write
All life's simple uncomplicated things
Silently awaiting its time.

Susan Graham
THOUGHTS OF YOU
I walk in the cool sand and warm sun,
and I thought of you.
My thoughts blended with the sand,
until they disappeared.
I imagined I could feel you here.

Late in the day, as the Moon rises over the Ocean,
I'm thinking of you as I walk along.
The warm wind caresses my face, embraces me,
and makes me want to be with you.
Because your smile is like the sun,
and your arms like the warm wind.

Donna Carter
LET ME GO
The gaping sky reaches for my hand
It doesn't pull me in, I don't understand
Please let me go, let me die
Let me drift up to the sky
I want to escape, to let go of my fear
To find the love, I never found here
My mind is empty, my body aches
Let me go to some other place
I'm on the edge of white and black
Please walk away and don't look back
Face the fact I am now gone
Back to the place where I belong
Don't shed those tears for me my friend
Because I am finally happy again.

Janice L Skidmore
A SUDDEN END

To my friends and family for their encouragement to keep on writing. And for Cheryl whom I miss so much

the road was long and winding
lit only by the glow of our headlights
It was a perfect night
the stars shone above us
twinkling in the distant sky
at that moment we thought we had it all
the love and time we shared together
was never ending
then with the snap of a finger
your life and my world ended.
we were so in love
now I live an empty life
in a world that just doesn't understand
the love we had for one another
Sometimes I think I see you
and sadness overwhelms me
Because I know you're not here
I held you in my arms that night
as your life slowly drifted away
and you left me alone
in a world that just doesn't understand

Barbara Beals
THE CRY FOR HELP
Listen closely, it's easy to hear,
A cry for help, for freedom of fear,
It is soft at first and very meek,
For the poor child starving is oh so weak,
The cry comes calling every day,
But you go on by, not a word to say,
The child comes crying,
"Please, I'm deaf & blind & mute and lame,"
You say she is lying,
But it is all the same,
The cry goes on, for it's just a lie,
And for such nonsense, the child will die!

Marana Wiebusch
LET THERE BE HOPE
Let there be hope,
in this lonely place,
where people don't seem to care.
Living their lives recklessly;
day by day;
living without a prayer.

Let there be friendship,
between the people
passing on the streets.
Start a conversation;
say 'hello' to a stranger,
that certainly would not be defeat.

Let there be love
in this crazy world,
where things don't seem as right.
If only countries could see—
that without weapons,
there's no need to fight!

Joyce Lloyd
ALIGHT TO WAIT
My presence is seen
A shadow falling across the pages of time
Descending quickly, silently from on nigh
Here to find its place, a creche to life
The Master having bid the way.

The lineament, its realness unknown
'Cept the witness who wonders
If time has changed the laws of known
Alight to wait
Be seen and know
The presence of Godly intervention
Has ceased our hurry with life.

In touch—the Master did care
Alight to wait
Quietude the answer
Alight to wait.

Mary C Klopchin
A MOMENT IN TIME
A moment in time, through the
looking glass.
A quick glance at a day, 14 years
gone past.
An arrival of a child, a new
generation of kin.
An arrival of a daughter, a new life to
begin.
Anticipation fulfilled, the sweat and
pain forgotten.
As I held, Wendy Christine, the
daughter I'd begotten.
A child who will bring me both joy
and sorrow.
A child I'll guide along the roads she
will follow.
This moment in time, so very dear to
my heart.
A moment, a lifetime, a child, neither
one to be forgot.

Lisa Colleen Pahl
GOOD-BYE
Trying not to think about it,
It's really very hard,
Trying not to think about,
My heart that you have scarred.
Trying not to think about,
The look that was in your eye,
The looked that seemed to tell me,
It was time to say good-bye.
We were out in the moonlight,
Your face—it shone so true,
I couldn't get out the words,
"I love you" . . . .
But then it was over,
It really can't be true,
If only I would have said,
"I <u>DO</u> love you."

But something seemed to tell me,
It was time to say good-bye,
I wish it could have lasted longer,
Why, oh why, oh why?
It's all over now,
We should have one more try,
Because it hurts <u>SO</u> much,
To have to say good-bye.
I'm not going to mope now,
And I'm not going to cry,
I'm just going to say,
GOOD-BYE . . . ."

Samantha Liddell
NO TURNING BACK
He went away,
Because he had to.
They never knew
When they were going to see him again.

But it was the vicious system,
Under which they all lived,
That was the cause of his
Necessary, but unnecessary departure.

He could never go back,
And they didn't know
If they could ever leave.

The pain was indescribable,
As he stepped onto that plane
In search of a new life.

He could never turn back.
But that's the pain,
That goes with a life
Under apartheid!

Dierdre Warren
THE INEVITABLE COMPARISON
Distorted reality,
a vision seen through desire
The all time great—
. . . Fantasy

Eventually reality crashes in
and I drown in painful truths

How do I feel today?
Quiet,
Don't expect too much—

I am so fragile and full of pain
. . . conversation may be slow

The good part about fantasy?
It appears on demand—

The bad part?
It's just not true

Ann Kent

Ann Kent
LITTLE OLD LADY OLD AND GRAY

Dedicated to Sarah Armstrong, Little Old Lady Old And Gray

Little Old Lady Old And Gray, When
She walked she seemed to sway.
She had a wee voice I heard her say
good morning to a cat who
was a neighborhood stray. She was
left all alone one summer's day
when the Lord came and took her
husband away, he took him to
heaven
the home of the soul, where we will
never grow weary or never grow old.

Dodie Soto
YOUR EYES
I like your eyes
I like the way you hold my hand
I like your eyes, you seem to always
understand.
I like your eyes,
The way you kiss me tenderly.

Am I to blame, you are the only one
for me?
Can this really be that I could fall so
quickly;
Oh, but it's your eyes;
The way they say so much to me.

Please hold my hand and we will
face our destiny,
So tenderly; Oh, it had to be this
feeling,
Between you and me; do you
understand,
You put me in sheer ecstasy?

I like your eyes
And forever we will be in love, you
see;
I like your eyes.

Coleman (Chief) Felihkatubbe
INTO THE NIGHT

To my dear wife Tina Jo

I look at her as she sleeps
Her eyelids quiver
And she takes a deep breath
As I lean forward to kiss her
At that moment, she lets out a soft
moan
As she sleeps— she is so innocent
I want to love her forever

Karen Grignon
FEELINGS OF LOVE
Say it with love; sending her flowers, candy, giving kisses, a diamond ring.

The air at springtime is as fresh as the scent of a bayberry candle. Your heart is filled with sunshine, laughter; everything seems like its coming up roses.

The birds begin to sing in harmony, Church bells ringing out a melody. Your body becomes light as a feather, you have to be together every waking hour, day and night.

These moments you have are special, spending life with one another is a must. Trusting each other, sharing your feelings, taking a walk on a moonlit night, gazing at the stars that shine so brightly.

Knowing you have each other; these are the feelings of love.

Wendy Cooper
EXPRESSION OF AFFECTION
It all started with a devilish grin;
You don't know what state you've
put me in.
If I told you I loved you, it would be
a lie;
For you, I feel more than love inside.

You know me, but not my desire.
Each time I see you, my heart's on
fire.
To me, you're like a breath of
spring!
The sun that sets on the sea.
You're what I hear when the robins
sing;
The very air that I breathe.

Oh, if you only knew;
The feelings inside I feel for you.
But how could you possibly know;
If I can't express them myself?
I try to explain, but it's hard to show;
For you're unique, unlike anyone
else I've known.

Julie Ann C Castro
FOREVER IN MY SOUL

To Grandma Matilde for sharing with me her most cherished values in life and to Mom and Dad for their love and for their presence especially when it counts

Isolated; Alone; No hope; Only
Despair.
Fear is the main element,
the fear of never changing;
Without a shadow of a doubt,
the fear was well hidden.
Hidden with a smile,
a weak vulnerable smile.

By my calm demeanor,
No one could tell,
or even suspect my true feelings.

Silent cries
within my heart
Ached for counsel,
But instead remained

Forever in my soul.

I remain pensive,
Thinking of what could have
been.

Tears . . .
Tears . . .
Tears . . .

Donna M Weiss
LIFE, LOVE, AND ALL
I love my risen Saviour, my Father in
Heaven too—
Christ proved His love there on the
cross, dying for me and you;
He lives today and will guide us —
if upon Him we will call,
Oh, thank you Lord for giving—Your
life, Your love, Your all!

I try to please Him by the things I
say and do—
But most of all in living—a life in
Him that's true;
Oh, I know there'll be times when
I'll stumble and fall,
Still yet, I am saved thru Him by—
His life, His love, His all.

Regardless of what others in the
world may do or say—
I will hold steadfast and live my
life— the Christian way;
Showing Christ of my love for Him
on this terrestrial ball,
Join me, Christians, let us give—Our
life, Our love, Our all.

I know that after everything is said
and done—
Only through Him can the gift of
eternal life be won;
Knowing this, I am awaiting His
precious voice to call,
"Come live with Me; for you gave—
Your life, Your love, Your all".

It matters not that others laugh, my
faith they cannot shake—
Nor will it matter if I'm scorned in
life for my Saviour's sake;
Because He loves me; I will stand
straight, proud, and tall,
Then live with Him forever too
because—He gave—His life, His
love, His all.

Erik C Peterson
ON THE BRINK
A bead of sweat, heavy and wet,
Breaks the bonds of the forehead and
plummets down,
Thirty two stories down it hits with
force on the black pavement.
He totters on the ledge observing the
drop,
The fall is real, as is what brought
him here.
The complications, divorce, failing
grades,
Stress, peer pressure, laziness,
The fears of the future, always
dreaded.
At last a way out is evident.
Thirty-two floors down, follow the
bead of sweat,
And the worries and frights of
college, a career, a future,
Are all . . .
History.
One fraction of a step and the
pavement below will break his fall,
Will be his freedom,
Will be certain death . . .

But he didn't,
He wasn't,
All that fell was the sweat.

Erna O Lacombe
OUR LITTLE BOY

To Stephanie With Love

Shall I tarry awhile and tell you a
story,
Of a child not yet two in all his
glory?

Mischief shone from eyes so brown,
Clear and limpid where one could
drown.

On small sturdy legs he followed the
dogs,
Till exhausted in sleep his head fell
in nods.

Like a baby bird his mouth opened
wide,
To devour the food that was placed
inside.

His antics were funny, a sight to
behold;
Sometimes so cautious yet ofttimes
so bold.

Good or naughty he was such a joy;
Sometimes his mother would say,
"Silly boy",

When he banged on the pots and
pretended to cook,
Then just as quickly his concoction
forsook.

T'was on a summer's day so bright,
The angels took him from our sight.

But now in the heavens there's a new
shiny star,
Twinkling at earth from ever so far.

Sally Gaye
WILL THERE EVER BE A SUMMER
Stormy, Snowy weather
Wintertime a stay
Will there ever be a summertime
A Balmy, Breezy day
Winds a blowing swiftly
East and North most cold
Bundle, Wrap and Huddle close
This season's growing old
Frost upon the windows
Steamed by simmering broths
Open up those windows
And free upon the moths

Snowy, Stormy weather
Blown, fast and hard
Only makes one Smile
When it glitters on a card
Will there ever be a summer
Or a Springtime sunny day
It's just around the corner
At least the hopeful say

Noreen H Smith
MY BUTTON GIRL

This poem is dedicated to my Dog Buttons, my beloved friend

I watched her grow from a pup
Running around making noise till I
got up.

Crawling under things and hiding out
Always curious to see what things
where all about.

Scurrying fast when you rustled a
newspaper
For she got going, and disappeared
like vapor.

My Button Girl has grown into
adulthood
No more messes made, Like a puppy
would.

Greets me at the door when I come
home
She meets me with an excited tone.

Eagerly looks forward to our nightly
walk

Letting me know it's time, without talk.

Staring at me with a gleam in her eye
With a paw on the knee, a whimper and a sigh.

So out the door, and down the street we'd go
Whether it be in rain, wind or snow.

Then at night sleeping by my side
We share in the comfort, taking things in stride.

Now my Button Girl is not well, and getting older.
But with me still, is my Little Soldier.

Reed Vernon Lloyd
CARMELITO
Little black child carpeted in blue,
Headed toward work on Saturday morn,
Found me crying in a mirror,
Found me experiencing an alternate form.

Little black child carpeted in blue,
A reflection from my within,
Discovering himself,
And his surroundings,
And with little respect for pretended men.

Stacey North
MY MEANING OF CHRISTMAS
Christmas is light,
Christmas is bright.
What Christmas really means,
Is lit-up Jesus scenes.
To celebrate the night,
That Jesus came in sight.

Octavio Esquivel Diaz
WHEN WE FIND DIVINE LOVE
Hardships wouldn't matter at the very end
When it's worth living the precious gift of life,
Life itself doesn't matter if we could find,
Love divine, worthy beyond all human gifts.

No more would we have a place to sleep the time,
Open doors, windows, the skin of our being
And soul, the spirit awakening inside,
Domain of God so far above here and now.

Dream of eternity guiding our mind,
Not the universe but the same heart of God,
It can't be lower nor higher our price.

Love divine and humane exchanging on trade
Each instant, pricing the infinite timeless;
One heart, we in God bounding the unbounding.

Linda Thomas
NEW BEGINNINGS

Dedicated to my beloved student Lawrence who has begun his road to success and happiness

You must have been
Such a sensitive, sweet
Child
So eager to please
So crushed when
The mark was never
Reached

. . .Which was often
You tried so hard
But could not please
Father
So eager to love
And to be loved
Your heart and spirit
Broken

. . .Which was yesterday

You are a man
On the verge of a new
Beginning
So never give up
Striving for and trying
To reach the goals you
Seek

. . .For today and tomorrow

Sara Hopkins
SHADOW

Inspired by a dear friend, my horse, Shadow

I have a friend,
it's very close to me and very special.
It's there for me
when I'm alone or in a crowd.
It listens to me
when I'm happy or sad.
We never fight
for my friend never talks back.
None of my other friends
know this special friend of mine.
But in a way,
they know it as well as me.
What is so special about my friend
is that it is totally unique to me.
But everyone has
a special friend of their own.
Everyone has a shadow.

Henry Camacho
PORTRAIT OF LIFE

The dawns and sunsets of my life my daughter Caroline

The seasons went gently by,
So precious few,
As I write this poem for you,
Child of God's design,
My lovely daughter Caroline,
Immortality; a glimpse of reality,
So immediate to a child,
An expression of a smile; so mild,
A portrait of life that greets no end,
A seed of my today and many tomorrows,
A graceful reality,
God's design of life; forever to unfold,
A sprinkle of happiness,
A gentle drop of sadness.

Sue Cristi
A ROAD I WENT DOWN
Pleasurable moments in memory I bask
Nothing more from you I ask
Be still and hold your arm about me.
Till the morning sun with me you'll see.

We ventured into a time yet unknown
I try so hard not to take your throne
Desire and lust was your inmost quest
As into my soul you pressed.

Deep inside me, as things you learned
Try not now to get your fingers burned
To plunge on in, then backward glance
We come together - just happen-stance.

A thing you knew to me you taught
Of those words I gave second thought
apart of you I cannot possess
And that for you does not regress.

You who are reckless with your life
Those who memory you have causes no strife
I see from you I have no hold
So again my soul was bid for and sold.

Eric Scott Smith

Eric Scott Smith
THROUGH THE EYES OF POVERTY
The little boy crying on my shoulder
Is drowning in an ocean as big as a huge boulder.
His dreams are filled with visions of wealth and money,
A time that would be as sweet as honey,
In a world that wouldn't starve his mind and soul of its goodness toward all.
He does not desire to stand taller than tall.
Only to take life in tremendous stride.
Then he could hold his head up with great pride.
He could help all less fortunate than he.
But how could he think of this before he's free?
Free of the shackles and chains bounded around him by this terrible fate.
May God bless him and free him to another state.
No one, especially he deserves such a life,
But bad as it may be, it has made him as sharp as a knife.
May goodness come out of all that is bad
And may we never be sad.

Joyce Doss
I WATCHED THE SPRINGTIME COME AND GO THROUGH CLOSED WINDOWS

Lovingly dedicated to my sister Theresa, who always understands

I watched the springtime come and go, through closed windows
Never feeling, never touching, all that grew
In my lonely existence, I saw changes in the distance
But I never felt the coolness of the dew.
Then all at once, sweet summer's sunshine warmed my body
The smell of roses blooming filled the air,
And before my time had gone, I touched them everyone
And had even pulled the blossoms where I dared.
Now the autumn's pushing through to change the colors
The leaves turn red and gold, then blow away
Everything seems colder, and maybe just a little older
I wonder why the roses couldn't stay?
But I suppose we all must have a change of seasons
And my winter is upon me, so it seems
If I had only had my summer, when I was just a little younger
I wouldn't see these roses in my dreams.
But I'll keep my summer, forever and 'ever
Locked in my heart for all time
And if the roses don't bloom, for me anymore
The dead ones are pressed in my mind.

Lori Wilcox
THE WALL

To Jim; whose faith and love could penetrate the wall.

Never again, I cried
And quickly reached
For one more brick
To make my barricade secure
Just daring anyone to
Try
To catch me unaware
Without my armour
Minus my shield
Outside my fortress.
Carefully constructed
Methodically attended
Brick by brick
In neatly patterned rows
Bound by years
Of never having come undone

At last, I am safe —
Or was:
Until you coaxed them down
One
By
One
And with these bricks
We've laid a path
And joined together

Walking on the wall.

Linda M Mundschenk
THIS MOMENT
Nothing lasts forever, not pleasure, not pain.
So I'll keep right on singing my songs in the rain.
I'm laughing, I'm singing, I'm crying out loud.
People are staring, I'm drawing a crowd.
It's only once in a lifetime.
You close your eyes and it's gone.
This moment's what you make it.
I'll make mine in a song.

Ella Mae Marsee
DAWN TO DUSK
Sleepless I lay, tossing and turning
with the tick of the clock,
I lay in silence.

My body was withered
from lack of sleep,
I finally got up to a cup of tea.

I looked out the window,
waiting for daybreak
the early morning light
awakening the day.

I walked to my shower,
getting ready for my day
with the red ball of sunshine

showing me the way.

The chores of the day
were finally finished,
leaving my body lacking of energy.

Dusk was here once again,
with the beauty of sunset falling
again.

Jina Bellamy
TO BE OR NOT TO BE . . . A LADY?
Clean up your room, eat all your
peas;
Always say thank you, always say
please.
Listen to your elders and to the wise;
Always be truthful and never tell
lies.

Mind your manners and be real
polite;
Ride your PINK bike or fly your
PINK kite.
Play the guitar strings or play the
keys;
You fall down you scrape your
"little" knees.

Get back up and try it once again;
Smile when you lose and cry if you
win.
This may not be easy or seem like
much fun;
But this is the way it has to be done.

Antoinette M Silvestro
A SPECIAL FRIEND
I reached out and you were there.
It makes me feel so good to know
that you care.
You make me feel so strong,
This feeling cannot be wrong.
You give me so much confidence,
And never make me tense.
You know you have my respect.
You're a person who is always so
direct.
You are special to me in so many
ways,
Because of you I have so many
memorable days.
You don't have to do much,
Just share your magic touch.
Let's never let it end,
Always be my special friend.

Evelyn Burga
'TWIXT AND 'TWEEN
My home is in the Southland
My present home, that is
Where Bayous, Lakes and Swamps
abound
With crawfish, crabs and catfish
And grosbeak, geese and gulls soar
high
'Bove Alligators and Opossums
Magnolias reach to Southern skies
To sun their scented blossoms.

There's much to love here in the
South
Its beauty, clime and people
But why can't I look through the
trees
And see an old Church Steeple?
I've lived here now for many years
I've raised my children here
Though long ago I settled down
I daydream, by the year!

I don't want crabs and crawfish
Some fish and chips will do
And I'd gladly give up Spanish moss
For heather, white or blue
To walk o'er hill and dale again
To see some winter's snow
Instead of these great flatlands
Where lilacs never grow.

I'm 'twixt and 'tween these two
great lands
I love them both you see
Coffee I enjoy a lot
But love my English tea!
I care not where these old bones go
When my life is o'er
For then my Spirit will be free
To roam from Shore to Shore.

Doris J Rhodes
THE HATE OF SUICIDE'S FATE

To GOD, my children: Chet, Dornetta and Michelle and to Joseph Parks, M.D. for the professional support and care he gave me during one of the most needed periods in my life. Thank you.

The raw pain of my soul
penetrates the core of my supreme
being.
It tears away until I am
incapable of physical and
emotional sensations.
I know not the difference
of a smile and a tear.
The hurt is like the Wind
blowing through the pores of my
body.
The drum in my head
or is it my heart?

That continuous thump from the
anguish; I bleed
No words can soothe the
seclusion of my Hell.
I have subsided to a world of apathy.
No Love can nourish,
No hope can sustain—
the boundaries of my solitude.
It has subverted the me
I once knew.
I know not the person I am.
Should I get acquainted with her?
or—shall I rest within
the tranquility of death?

Jerry E Gibbs
UPON THE EAGLES WINGS
Darlin I am asking of you, to please
come to me.
Oh darlin can you not see, this
feeling that you; have put in me.
For you it is that I have searched,
from shore to shore, near and far
between.
To try and find that someone special,
like you have etched upon this heart
of mine.
Oh darlin will you not try, to ease
this aching heart, and wary mind of
mine.
Oh little darlin; will you not please
come and try, to let us see if you and
I, upon the wings of an eagle can fly.
For we; little darlin will never know,
if you and I darling do not, at least
give it a try.
Won't you please come and let us
soar, so high up in the sky, so that
we upon the wings of an eagle can
fly; you and I.
So please oh little darlin, let us try.
I am not asking for a complete
commitment, but only that we at least
give it a try.

Kathryn L Ferris
FORECAST

This poem is dedicated to Dawn who helped me hear the silence.

Always silence, endless silence,
Crashing, Booming, Raging silence.
Broken by the morning news.
"Sun tomorrow, rain this evening."

Perfect, flawless, sinless image.
What is his name? I cannot see
him . . . hiding somewhere in the
silence.

"I like fried chicken, cherry pie and
roast beef gravy."
At last I've make it . . .Not his
mother—
Glorious, perfect, passive Mother,—
Brother, Cousin.
Maybe more . . . above me on the list
of Special.
Do not question, do not wonder,
That will spark the angry silence—
All-consuming angry silence.

No fulfillment, no completion;
dismissed, ignored, deceived, denied.
Why am I here? Why do I stay? To
play the part.
To laugh, to scream, to cry, be angry.
To be the source of all the sin.
To touch, to hold. To fill all needs
with just one act.
Amid the silence, always silence.
Powerful, Crashing, Lonely silence.

Then his voice, as if recorded, "Sun
tomorrow, rain this evening."

Louise Bennett
PILOT LIGHT
Someone will be there to remind us
of where we are at.
We ought to diligently search for
who we are.
Truth lies in the mainstream of life
no matter what the sky looks like.
Our histories teach us, are we
learning?
Are we yearning for more? Of
ourselves.
Color surrounds us in our mood.
Prism breaks the mood when we
touch the light.
While we pilot the colors of life,
Destiny insures our arrival.

Jim Sprague
MY OPEN DOOR

This is dedicated to my mom, who makes all things possible for me, my whole family, Ms. Cari Weber, who's an inspiration, my 2'nd per. english class ('89), Michelle Reda-T.A., and Bellarmine Prep in Tacoma, Wa.

Time is wasting as I sit here and
write,
I should be out working, to improve
my own life.
But being here with you and giving
my words,
Is all of my comfort and nothing
that's absurd.

I speak with you now, because you
are my friend.
I invite you in my house, so you can
leave the chilly wind.
You are my guest, please, come in;
come in.

Susan Link-Sandoval
MY DEAR FRIEND
My dear friend, I hate to do this,
But our friendship can't last.
Those great times we shared together,
Must be put in our past.
I knew this would happen,
That our friendship was bound to
end.
Though, I know you care,
I can't consider you as a friend.
Please, don't try to argue.
Just try to understand.
That time can change two people,
As the ocean changes the sand.
Our friendship was lovely,
But it must come to an end.
For I look at you in a different way,
I have fallen in love with you,
My Dear Friend!

Henry M Beaver
HOW SWEET IT WAS
At a time, long ago, when I was just a
kid.
Simple life, we enjoyed simple things
we did.
Streetcars rattled, clanged, six rides
for a quarter.
Dad worked, Mom stayed home,
everyone was shorter.
Car garaged, but for drive we took
every Sunday.
Old folks on the old farm, made it
such a fun day.
Fried chicken, to be sure, and apple
pie to boot.
Ate until fit to bust and no one cared
a hoot.
Sky blue, air clear, at the creek,
found a frog.
No gasp, cough or wheeze, no one
had heard of smog.

Anglena Waller
A DREAM
I reached out my hand,
you place it within yours—
we run with the wind,
till we fall on the damp grass.
We laugh into one another's eyes,
then the ground drops away
as our lips meet;
we are part of the universe
as our bodies dance together.
Afterwards we roll apart,
filled with each other's love,
to gaze into a big blue sky.
I turn to take you once again into my
arms,
and I awake to find it only a dream
. . . for you have not yet returned.

Linda Wakefield
THOUGHTS ON A WINTERY DAY
It's only a few minutes drive home
each night and never a one forgotten.

Autumn brought the brilliance of red
and gold—the sound of fallen leaves
under foot—memories of a summer
long past.

The cold of winter blankets the early
morning with its frost—clouds move
fast, ever changing their many faces
—sometimes Indian chiefs, an eagle,
a whale—all moving to new places.

A moon crisply shows itself, and
then hides. A moon that beckons to
the soul to sing out songs of the heart
—"make a wish".

Mother earth is alive here. Her
music is everywhere. The wind
chants her name.

Fog is a winter resident—bringing

Merlin, ferry fog horns, mystery, enchantment.

Soon, the air will blend with the scent of spring and my nose will curiously twitch and beg for more. There will be apple blossoms, cherry blossoms, buds of all sorts. And, the ground will come alive with a rainbow of colors—tulips, daffodils, roses, buttercups and iris.

I know a place by the bay where these feet want to wade.

I know lots of places—places to share with you.

Sonia A Moore

Sonia A Moore
WHISPERING SOULS
I Walk Upon the Earth;

The Soles of my Flesh Blending with the Souls of the Universe.

My Breath is Warm.

Life is a Wondrous Phenomenon;
or a Nightmarish Dream.

A Young Child's Laughter is Sweet
Upon thy Ear;
An Addict's Anguish and Suffering
Pierces the Heart.

A Man and Woman Unite in Ecstasy;
The Thunderous Roaring and
Crashing of Waves.

A Heart Beats with Loneliness;
The Whispers of Love.

The Hunger of an Empty Being;
The Greed of the Selfish Swine.

The Wisdom of a Spiritual Soul;
The Vile of the Evil One.

The Soft, Silky Petals of a Rose,
Caressing a Fingertip.

ALL SENSES POWERFUL AND
DRAWING
IN THE ESSENCE OF LIVING!

Mrs Sharon L Jenkins
YOUNG HEARTS AND MINDS
Lord, save the children, show them
the way
In this wicked world they sometimes
go astray
It's up to us to teach them right
To love and share sweet words of
prayer
And let them know we really care
Let's put the pieces back in place
Let's keep a smile upon their face
Most often girls and boys some-
where
Find pains of life so hard to bare
Christ Jesus said "I'm always there,
to lift your burdens in despair."
He first loved us, oh yes He cares
Now once again a day has past
Wake up! Wake up! For time moves
fast
Let's love, let's care and believe in
prayer
Young hearts and minds reach high!
It's there

Sharon Madore-Richmond
THREE YEARS

In memory of Denise Marie Maydole who went to heaven April 9, 1986. You're still in my heart, "Auntie Em"

Almost three years have passed,
Since that dark dreary day.
When God decided t'was time
to take you away.
He needed you more in heaven.
we knew,
So we had to live our lives anew.

It left us empty, lost and mournful,
there would be no more Denise,
So loving and thoughtful.
We knew you were better in heaven
than here.
Where there would be no more
Pain or fear.

And now you're surrounded with
His everlasting LOVE;
The Glory of God and
The freedom of a DOVE.

Donna Charity Lane
KYLE

This is dedicated to my son Kyle, for being my inspiration

He came into my life
sent by way of heaven
to give me no strife
but to teach me a lesson

A lesson of joy and love
with his beautiful smile
my heart soars like a dove
just to see my son Kyle

His eyes have a sparkle
so big and so brown
like fine polished marble
a sweetness felt deep down

He's so good day and night
and when it's time for bed
doesn't give me a fight
just lays down his sweet head

So sleep well my dear boy
dream of wonderful things
for giving me love and joy
my heart has a new way to sing

Dawn Shipp
SPRING IS PRETTY & BRIGHT

To my Aunt Ruth & Mother, & Grandma. Y'all mean so much to me.

Spring is pretty & bright
Flowers bud to see the bright sky
Birds play in bird bath.
Mother birds watching the eggs
hatch.
Tree buds to beautiful full leaves.
Squirrels playing up in the tree tops
Spring is pretty & bright
You can smell honeysuckle in the air
Sky so blue & bright on spring day.

Emily F Zierold
THE AMERICAN FLAG
When Betsy Ross,
First made our flag,
Little did she know,
In peace and freedom,
Rights for all!
The flag, the world, would always
know!
From 13 states to 50,
America has grown!
The American Flag,
Will fly forever,
Over everyone's home!
Old glory will rule the world!
Wherever our flag does fly,
Other lands look to us, for help.
We always heed their cry!
The American Flag, will reign
supreme!
From the one, Betsy Ross first
made!
Then 13 states to 50! Wow!
It wins the highest accolade!

Marina Tanco
BEYOND THE SHALLOWS
To lie alone
Upon the sea
Enfolding me

To slowly slide
Below the depths
And go to sleep

The waters warm embrace
Console my aching soul
And hide my face

The silence laps around me
All around it clings
So close my love

I swallow thee:
Thou swallow me.

Delana Mead
MY GIFT

Written with Love to all my family and friends, especially to Warren and Eileen DeMond, my parents

On cool spring nights
Stars are bright.
Crickets chirping
Through the night.
Morning breaks
With skies of blue.
Soft spring breeze
To lift the dew.
This is Gods gift
He gives to you.
His gift to Me, Dear
Was giving Me, You.

Lillian Randrup

Lillian Randrup
YOU ARE SO YOUNG!
Nobody grows old merely by living a
lot of years
. . . . or giving in to tears.

People grow old by deserting their
own ideals . . .
You stay young with anticipation of
what life yields.

Years can wrinkle the skin . . . But
not the soul.
You never give up . . . And you're
never old.
These are the years of worry and fear
But your glowing spirit and your love
of wonder
Keep back the tears . . . no matter the
years.

What next in this joy of life?
This always softens the strife.

You're as young as your faith
. . . never giving in to doubt
Staying young . . . within . . .
without.

You're as young as your hope . . .
not old with despair
Never yielding . . . always giving . . .
because you care.

Within the central place of your heart
A song is sung—each day a new
start.

Love and courage are yours for
keeping
There is no time for weeping.

This because you are so young.

Michael Jankowski
THE RIVER RISES
The river rises and the rain keeps
coming down,
I look across to see the shrinking
bank and wonder will I drown?
It rises to a spot never thought of and
flows on by,
As the world is similar in only a way
that I can see why.
Is this violent world giving up, are
we to be drowned?
For I see the muskrat swimming aloft
trying to avoid sinking, isn't that
profound.
Sorry, I feel a change, one that will
require a lengthy swim,
I hope it doesn't drown us—once
again.

Nancy McKeen
FOREST TREE
Oh great dying forest tree! Yours is
the finest death there be.
not entombed beneath the ground, but
standing, with your friends around;
your lifeless branches bending still
before the gusts of a windy chill;
birds perched on you, singing high,
whether your branches live or die;
ending grandly where begun, in your
forest in the sun;
dead, but looking strong and tall, and
so not seeming dead at all;
neither the mournful toll of a bell nor
even a whisper of fare-well;
never the slightest feel of pain when
your vital sap is on the wane;
still a home for squirrels and birds;
uttering yet your life-long words,—
the little creaks and cracks and sighs
a tree makes whether it lives or dies;
all your leaves from years before—
together now on the forest floor,
decomposing into the earth as part of
an endless source of birth,
into the future out of the past, as long
as Fate will let it last,
with dense profusion everywhere—of
other trees around you there.
Oh great dying forest tree! Yours is
the finest death there be.

Dorothy C Anderson
WHERE DO I BELONG
Where do I belong Lord?
Is it here or is it there.
Where do I belong Lord?
When I feel up in the air.
Where do I go Lord?

When there's nothing anywhere.
I don't belong with this one.
I don't belong over there.
My effects seems so empty when no one seems to care.

I love you Lord,
I need you Lord,
And thanks for being near.
I know I don't belong here on this earth.
I just don't fit in anywhere.
So I know, I must belong with you up there.

Foster Creighton
ASTRONOMICAL DIFFUSION
Calculations of such precision,
Seven echoes of a distant stare,
Countdown ignites the heavenly mission,
Ultimate "CHALLENGE" beyond repair.

Projection, velocity, a majestic flight,
Technical cargo achieves disjunction,
Hammer and sickle are not in sight
as voyage succumbs to major malfunction.

Celestial gala, now tragic event,
Newtonic forces are not denied,
Millions witness the sudden descent,
Meltdown,
splashdown . . . trapped-inside!

Classified internal investigation
disguises the truth, conceals the terror,
Opens the future's indecision
and closes the world to human error.

Judith Jones
WE ARE DIFFERENT
Our pathways are different-
Yours and mine.
Yours has flowers-
Mine, a vine.
When the sunshine warms your face,—
I am soaked in morning rain.
The road is rocky, rough for me-
Yours is smooth and you run free.
When the darkness covers you,
There is rest and troubles, few.
I am lost in stars and moon—
Alone, in my solitude.
When I shiver in April's wind,
You find her a warm and gentle friend.
You reach for the mountains.
I'm as deep as the sea.
We are different, you and me.

Judith C Horn
A CHRISTMAS EVE, A CHRISTMAS MORNING
It's Christmas Eve and what do you see
The Family's finished decorating the tree

Now the children are getting ready for bed
"Asleep you must be when I come", Santa said

The cookies and milk on the table they sit
And food for the reindeer whom we cannot forget

It's snowing very lightly as Santa approaches
He lands on the rooftop his reindeer he coaches

Then under the tree he places the toys
Surprises for good little girls and boys
The cookies he eats, the milk he drinks
Then back to his sleigh, quick as a wink

Now on to the next house, Santa's just begun
This is his busiest day, but He's having fun

It's now Christmas Morning and what do you see
Bright eyed and smiling children happy as can be

"Thank you Santa for the presents", they say
And then they continue to unwrap and to play.

Beatrice Harper
THE ARTIST
The artist sees the world
Through different eyes
He abhors ugliness
From this his soul cries

So he puts on canvas
The beautiful and sublime
He seeks to create beauty
Ugliness is a waste of time

In a world of turmoil
He seeks solace in creativity
He creates on canvas
His world and sensitivity

The artist has no time
For violence or crime
He seeks the beautiful
And the sublime

The artist goes his
Own unique way
Creativity is his goal
So ugliness goes away

Trisa Jeremy
HAPPY 8TH ANNIVERSARY
To the man that still fills my heart with delight,
And keeps my toes warm at night.
I Love you so, so much;
you still can make me tingle, with a single touch.
Even when we have our ups and downs,
I want you to know, you're the one that
makes my world
go around.

Hallie Compson
ON MENTAL ILLNESS
I live in Solitary Confinement
My thoughts are all my own
I can not break through the wall
This prison is my home.

The bars I can not feel or touch
No steel could be so strong
The light of day does not penetrate
To separate right from wrong.

The friends I used to cherish so
Their names I long forgot
They are no comfort to me now
Of their world I am not.

No joy or sorrow do I feel
Each day is just the same
Would that God would take me now
That I may live again.

Pauline Klepper Sydebotham
UPWARD THRUST
I delved into the past
Far as the mind could know—
Found naught but dauntless fortitude
In those who have gone before.
I considered things as are,
Compared to things as past,
And wondered if we had honored them
With what we have become at last.
I dipped into the future
Far as the soul can feel—
Beheld this truth in vision:
"The dignity of man," His likeness should reveal.
In His own image, He did make us;
In His own time, His Spirit break us.
What right have we to flaunt so lightly
What He our God, hath wrought so rightly?"
All this I beheld on 'morrows wing
Of future's past and present plan;
Indeed we become the collective thought—
A tried, and true, and better man!

Arise O child! Claim you heritage
Of faith, and talent, and will!
The last, for which the first was made
Rises onward and upward, within us, still!

Galyn Thompson
FORGIVE ME
I won't let you go,
Without a fight.
There's things you don't know.
I'd like to set them right.
I gave it to you,
All that I had.
I lied, too.
Then I felt bad.
You weren't there,
When I needed you most.
You know I still care,
But I feel like your ghost.
I'm sorry I hurt you.
I wish I were dead.
I don't know what else to do,
But let you go ahead.
Please don't go.
I want you to stay.
I need to know,
That you'll never go away.

Gerardo C Edra

Gerardo C Edra
FILIPINAS

To comrades in Arms in the USAFFE under Gen. MacArthur and to Filipinos who are serving faithfully and honestly to preserve freedom and democratic, sovereign Philippines: country of my birth.

Since when I opened my eyes,
I saw you on vast ocean lies,
Wide horizons beyond the eyes can see,
A naked beauty; pearl of the Orient sea.

Years passed; the world became dark,
I hate the days will set us apart,
But you're in bondage I now realized,
Your sufferings hasn't been finalized.

I step my foot into the dark world,
Gambled my life for you if it's worth,
So that some day, you may be free,
Like birds singing on top of the tree!

The world brighten after four years past,
Uncle Sam brought you a gift at last,
July 4, 1946; a token of your freedom,
Your children celebrate with their drums!

Years had passed; your tranquility shaken,
Your future at stake on hands of your children,
I felt your agony; I know not whom to plead,
I hate to see the dawn if you fall to your knees!

Beverly (Harrington) Cottrill
CLASS OF '66
High School Reunions come and go
Every 5 or 10 years or so.
Some let the years pass by
While others the years pass them by.
Some become dentists, doctors, lawyers and such,
Others are happy being blue collar workers in a rush.
One thing that is for sure,
We are all getting older and more mature.
Now we are parents with children of our own,
Wondering how our parents survived us at home.
When we were in school, our parents would agree,
Some of the things we did were not done so smartly.
Doesn't it make you feel alot older, worn out and gray
When your child makes the remark, "Gee, Mom,
Did they have those things back in your day?"
Hope for my classmates of '66
Many years full of good health, wealth, and happiness.
In everything they strive to do,
May they succeed and prosper, too.
My thoughts I have conveyed in writing,
Please overlook my English, grammar and rhyming.

Sherry Starr
A DREAM
Come and see my dream, look into my eyes.
He's waiting for me somewhere, possibly in disguise.
Full of love and life and lots of caring,
Wanting my life to be sharing.
When we'd be together the limit is the sky,
a feeling that reaches out from deep inside.
Something that tells me, if I want to I can fly,
With the someone who'd never say good-bye.
We'd take life one step at a time.
We could leave the rest of the world behind.
To be together forever would be the plan,
it's something we both would understand.
For now this person is just in my

mind,
because dreams are so hard to find,
but never give up on your hopes and dreams,
they may be closer to reality than they seem.

Betsy Moore
VOYAGE
Under a velvet dark
Decked by the Southern Cross
Drifting upon the Main:
Touched by a dying spark
Even a moment's loss
Equals a light-year's gain.

Fixed on a point in time,
Swinging through charted space
To the predestined shore;
Only a step to climb
To our eternal place,
Never to journey more.

Eagerly sighting land,
Warping the waiting dock—
Finally this is all
Clearly to understand:
Subtle the soul's shock—
Life was a port of call.

Sandra Dee Moss
AIDS
To you I am simply slow death.
Where do I come from?
No one truly knows.
You see, I discriminate against no one,
black, white, young, old or otherwise.
I have no sexual preference.
To know me better, simply spread your
arms and legs and embrace me.
Through me death and destruction reign supreme.
For, I am AIDS.
Technically known as:
Acquired Immune Deficiency Syndrome

Sharon Marie Bellissino
I HOPE YOU FEEL LIKE A MAN
I wish that you would have taken my life,
Instead, I relive it everyday.
You left me, with my mind on hold,
When you took my body, While I was out cold.

How can I get to sleep at night?
When I'm afraid, to close my eyes.
I wish, that I could be whole again,
And people, wouldn't stare, and tell lies.

My husband, and some of my family,
Have been great in everyway.
They are here, to love and guide me,
And give their support everyday.

I am really trying,
To take away the pain.
I know that my body, will heal,
But my mind, will live this nightmare,
It will never, ever go away.

Lydia Regehr
TROIKA
Watch the troika as she races
On the icy tracks of snow,
Hear the music of her traces,
Tinkling bells in high and low.

1&2 Chorus: I am coming, coming, dove,
I'll be with you soon, my love.

Is he countryman or stranger,
Bound for joy or bound for plight,
He who dares to face the danger
Of a road in stormy night?

Gay the song my coachman raises,
A bright village is in view.
Warm the lights on which he gazes,
With their welcome always new.

3 Chorus: I am coming, coming, dove,
I have come to you, my love.

Sigrid Rita Merriam
TRIBUTE
Writing is your specialty;
a poem is your gift
to you . . . and me.

Your words, well spoken,
are a token of
your love for mystery

Your gentle ways
have opened the heart's door,
inspirations to explore

Your help has consoled troubled hearts
because you were there
and knew how to care

There is a special bond between us—
your love was not in vain.
It shows up again

Writing is an art.
Your thoughts live on—
and for some—
for generations to come.

Alice M Hach
PRAIRIE GRASS
Surrounded by fields of grass
And barn and home—
A plot of grass grew on and on
Undisturbed by man nor tools
Of men.
It made no contribution to
The yearly income from the land
Like the fields of corn and soybeans
Alternating as its neighbor.
But in a sort of independent way
It seemed to stretch upward toward
The sky
Swaying proudly in the breeze
As if to say—
"Not all riches are in dollars measured"
And when I heard a pheasant from
Its midst
I understood.

Sandi L Baum
DOLLY
Dolly is the one for me
She came into my life quite suddenly,
Her big brown eyes pulled at my soul
And leaving with her was my goal.
I searched and pondered for a way to pay,
So she could leave with me that day.

When arrangements had been made
And the money had been paid,
She snuggled closely in my arms
She somehow knew I meant no harm.

She follows me everywhere I go,
And gives me wet kisses when I feel low.
She beats her rag against the floor,
And barks at strangers at my door.

When I talk she cocks her head
And she loves to jump on my bed.
I couldn't ask for better company,
My Dachshund means the world to me.

Barbara Batterson-Rossi
WHEN TIME IS AT A STANDSTILL
When time is at a standstill
and we two face the day
to see each other fully
beyond the softened clay;
Beyond the sweet words spoken,
far into the other's soul———
What promises of the morrow,
What words of love extolled?
And when the mist has risen
to reveal all that there are———
Will you speak to me
of spirits free
and disclaim the Holy Bar?

S Eric Padgett
SOMEDAY A BIRD MUST
Someday a bird must
Leave the nest,
And soar above just
Like the rest.
Climbing high in the sky,
He has the need to fly,
To freely circle 'round
No longer knowing any bounds.
Higher and onward,
Faster and forward,
Leaving the earth with a sigh,
Facing the hardest test.
But as death draws nigh,
He wonders why.

Francis T Sablan
SHINE
A smile grew upon me
As she rose to the sky,
In the air of inspiration,
A sparrow's wings took flight.

All the while we spoke no words
To break the silent air,
But through her warmth and Radiance,
I felt her love and care.

Beneath the blue she glorified,
A dream instilled within,
In a time of youth and Innocence,
A journey must begin.

Though brief in time we shared The day,
This heart she did inspire,
To lead a life so long deserved
Of passion . . . grace . . . and fire.

Virginia Driver
OUR WORLD
"The Mills of the Gods grind slowly,
But They grind exceeding fine"—
And through its wars and hatreds
Our Earth is trying to shine.

This planet's teeming millions
Have somehow lost their way;
And unillumined leaders
Don't bring a brighter day.

But when some great disaster
O'erwhelms our puny world,
Love in the people's hearts
Is suddenly unfurled!

O come, though Promised Future
Of Godly Brotherhood!
Reveal to struggling nations—
Love is the Source of Good!

The world's blood-bath is acting,
But the Earth is beginning to shine;
"The mills of the Goods grind slowly—
And They grind exceeding fine"!

Sharolyn K Gemmell

Sharolyn K Gemmell
WHAT SHALL WE DO FOR AMERICAN HEROES

Dedicated to John R. Gemmell, Sr., my husband of 27 years and my best friend

Time was when we had no fear to
pick a hero we might hold dear
But nowadays we hesitate to place
such honor on the great
Because we know right from the start
that in each hero's is a blackguards heart
Alas, 'tis true, we know full well
their reputation is shot to hell
Policeman, doctor, judge or sailor,
philosopher, cleric and even tailor
All are rotten to the core, is nothing
sacred anymore?
What shall we do for American
heroes when the media shrinks the
BEST to zeros?

Even apple pie and motherhood can
no longer be considered good
In this age of Show and Tell when
one cannot the onslaught quell
I, myself, would die of fright if my
dirty linen were in public sight
So God forbid me to excel lest MY
public image "Today" might dispel
And if YOU were under the
microscope I venture to say you'd
have no hope
That Donaldson, Severeid or
Jennings would not kick out YOUR
underpinnings
What shall we do for American
heroes when the media shrinks the
BEST to zeros?

I want a hero I can revere without the
threat of TV's smear
I don't think it too much to ask to
overlook a person's past
To me it's not a selfish thing to ask
they bare not EVERYTHING
Whatever happened to important
facts, like how a person in public
acts
Are they qualified for the post? And
which would serve the public most?
I don't think it unkind to me if I
cannot their bedroom see
What shall we do for American
heroes when the media shrinks the
BEST to zeros?

Jim McKeithen
THE PITTSBURGH STEELERS
Some of the Steelers have
Four Super Bowl rings,
In the history of the NFL,
They've been the Super Bowl kings.

Franco Harris was a
Great running back,
The Steeler defense was
Always ready to attack.

The Steelers haven't gotten in
The playoffs the past few years,
They've made the Pittsburgh
Fans shed some tears.

J J Arnold
EMERGENCE
She is as a butterfly.
Beginning as a fragile babe that struggles to move forward.
Inching her way across endless paths.
And, As her time grows shorter,
And her growth develops,
She is engulfed in a veil of protectiveness,
Where she changes.
Her awareness heightens.
Her knowledge abounds as her REBIRTH grows closer.
And, At that time,
Just the right time.
A new creation EMERGES.
Having shed her bonds,
Ready to fly freely towards her new path.
Beautiful and Radiant as she dances in the sunlight.

As the caterpillar changes into the butterfly,

SO DOES SHE.

Marc Blount
ALONE
Today I walk alone,
Feeling lonely and by myself,
these feelings I hold I do not like
From the crowd I distance myself,
These crowded halls I walk
all these faces I look into,
they all seem to disappear
because of my vision of you,
In a passing thought of you
I think of the morning star,
It's brightness and beauty never cease,
reminds me of the way that you are,
I know tomorrows another day,
Alone, I'll never be again,
For she is coming back to me,
and with her, my time, I'll spend,

Tihan Seale
POLYCHROME
Green forest pines awash in bright splendor
White snowflakes drift in the chill of December
Fire cast shadows dance on the wall
A picture of winter, hatched from late Fall.

A beam of clear light sent from the sky,
to brighten the pink in a white bunny's eye.
Perched on horizon the red robin sings,
his song carried on, the tidings of Spring.

Sphere of bright crimson, the sun from a high
charring the land, unheeding its cry
Liquid blue pools and satin green clover,
a water oasis from sweet silvery Summer.
Willow pond meadows of grey and deep green
Treetops of crimson and woodlands serene
Brown hazel nuts in a mid morning zephyr
The blessings of Autumn that give birth to winter.

Phillip Reed Brinkerhoff
I LOVE YOU
Love like a humming bird's kiss,
Love like dew on a rose,
Love like silk on skin,
Love like a morning's promise,
Intense, true, vital, mine,
Is but a remembered shadow,
Of what my soul cries out
To you.
I cannot share you
Even with a memory.
Leave me if you must
For I will push you from me
Only because I love you.

Cynthia L Lawson
A LESSON OF LIFE
Through sadness, anger, depression and despair . . .
It will always remain a constant.
Though it seems you're all alone
And no one cares, or
Loneliness refuses to release its grip . . .
It's still there.
While walking the lonely streets
And passing unfamiliar faces and buildings,
Going through the motions of existence,
It never fails you.
Even when you think you've reached the lowest point
That you could ever imagine,
It will stand by you and keep you from falling.
The abiding strength of your soul
Will maintain your inner calm
No matter what adversity comes your way.
Just hold on to that faith and
You will never be truly alone.

George N Argyros
THE RAPTOR AND THE HUNTER
The vulture spreads its wings.
It takes off like a sling shot.
It's talons sharpened by her stench
The raptor now attacks . . .
Torn are the eyes of her deceit
And all her putrid flesh.
Filled are Its guts.
It soars!
A hunter sees the vulture
That circles overhead and burps.
Says he, "Well done my friend. You
Saved me a shot."
He stops.
He looks where her carcass is . . .
He turns his back, and
Laughs.

Ben Haley
THEN AND NOW
As a lad of the good ol' times;
When horses left their healthy signs.
The water was pure most everywhere:
Dollars were dollars; clean was the air.
Our roads, our lights, our social life;
Our speech, our dress, a man and wife;
A phonograph or radio was exciting then.
Neighbors we knew; and had a chicken pen.
Our day started at early dawn;
Breakfast was big, the day was long.
Restriction for kids to work, was not too strict,
We learned our parents could crack the whip.
Today is different, our cars are fast,
Our minds, our actions, are T V cast.
Toilets and dryers are now inside.
Our banks, our cards, our only pride.
Things could be better, don't get me wrong;
As education, work conditions and modern song.
Would I go back to days long ago?
At my age! I'll have to say, 'Heck No.'

Mary Catherine Brown
HE'S MY DAD
No, he's not my Father,
But he's my Dad.
He married my Mother.
He's the only one I ever had.

The times were rough;
We worked all through the day.
For us, barely enough;
After chores, was time for play.

Lesson's learned on his knee,
About this wonderful world.
All of us became a family,
And I too, was Daddy's girl.

Of money there wasn't much trace,
Still, I shared in all.
Love and guidance took its place.
Another Dad? No, not at all.

Now his voice is ever still.
Love in heart makes me glad,
For I know t'was God's will,
Just to let him be My Dad.

Tami Heilman
HIM
The wind softly blowing
against my face
The smell of the ocean
I look at him
I love the sweet tone of his voice
His golden brown tan
How gentle he is around me

The same softly blowing wind
The same smell of the ocean
But . . .
It's not the same
As I walk along the shore
that night echoes in my mind
The crash . . .
The ambulances siren screaming
in the night
My love . . .
is dead?

Nina M Maphis
ARMENIAN EARTHQUAKE
Oh! God, some people seem to get more than their share of troubles, and sometimes it seems like it multiples, and doubles. I wouldn't even for one second presume that I could ever comprehend the heartache and the doom of the Armenian's Earthquake. Oh! the heartbreak of it all, that the cities and the little villages had to fall.

In my mind's eyes it would seem to me, like one moment you could be happy and well, and in the next moment you were all living in HELL. Alas! alas, so many people buried alive, 'tis it any wonder that I want to cry, and cry, "Dear God, if only more people could have survived." I also know in my heart, that there isn't anyway that anyone could count the terrible cost of all of the men, women, and children that were lost.

I also understand that, that TERRIBLE CATASTROPHE, happened in a land far, far, away, but that didn't stop me from wanting to pray, and pray, and to thank God, for all of the relief, and aid that was sent from all around the world, proving that, WE REALLY ARE, OUR BROTHERS KEEPERS.

Needless to say, "Mother Nature, can sometimes be very violent, and cruel, especially when she goes on such a terrible rampage as this." Oh! why, oh why, did she have to go so amiss, in such a ghastly way as this?

Years, and tears, will come and go, but only the loved ones left behind, will ever know, what it was like the day the ground beneath them rumbled, split apart, and shook.

James Rolling
LET US END, WHERE WE CAN

To my lovely wife Sylvia, the Rolling children, James Jr., Chris, Angela, Mark and the family of man.

Let us end,
Where we can,
Man's inhumanity
To man,

And hope we,
Live to see,
Hunger decrease,
Justice and peace.

Melissa Ruhr
SUFFERING IN SILENCE
Pain and despair is fire and ice.
Relentless forces, blinding the way
To salvation, intolerable vice
Of darkness, overriding the day
Of exuberant resolution.

Onward, through chilling trenches of fear
Clutching the soul in desperation.
Enduring the torture with silent tears
Until the day of divine revelation
Ends the battle of torment and confusion.

Minter Smith
ESTEVANICO
You may read of the brace Coronado
who sought seven cities of gold,
reached legendary Cibola,
entered the Zuni's stronghold.
You may read of his many discoveries
throughout the great southwest.
But what of the first to Cibola—
the man who led all the rest?

The pages of history should proclaim
this Moor for his exploration

two centuries and two score years
before
our country became a nation.
You may laud and esteem Coronado
and pioneers who followed his track;
but remember, the first to blaze the
trail—
Estevanico, the Black.

Sharon Barker
RIVERS
I love to watch a river run,
Cutting its path through history.
It glistens and sparkles
As it moves by,
Leaving its mark on Humanity.

If attempts are made to stop its flow,
Maybe "damned" by a thoughtless
soul,
It rises above each obstacle,
Or finds a new course to its goal.

I enjoy the movement of rivers,
As I stop to observe and absorb.

All philosophy aside

It's just nice to find
Something that moves on its own,
Something I don't have to push.

Michael N Keaton
GOD'S CHILDREN
Their love is so needing
Their innocents are pure
Without them you would be cheating
Of one's way, through life to endure

They are so full of energy
No matter time of day
That ole so everyday question
Is it alright to go out and play

We try to make their life simple
In everyday living
Telling them about God's temple
Which teaches, not taking but giving

So let's never forget from this day on
That ole so life is very short
Try to love them until dusk to dawn
No matter the mistake, always
support

Never forget the trust in them
For in the future time will tell
Of all the teachings, about him
The difference between Heaven and
Hell

May 8, 1981

Linda L Magsig
HAAR FARM
Waking in brass bed
To summer heat
Family breakfast with T.V.
Morning wash upon the line
Feeding horses sugar cubes
Sitting in crooked apple trees
Tractors in the barn
Cats everywhere
Altair design books
Lunch in
Air conditioned comfort
Collecting henhouse eggs
Shopping in Toledo
New clothes for school
Forts under flower bush
Riding bikes and horses
Buckeye candy
Hoeing bean field
Cutting my foot
Big dinner at six
Relatives visiting
Swimming at quarry
Riding in pickup
Sharing green bathtub
Ice cream or popcorn
Fireflies and
Turnpike lights
Say goodnight.

Eula King

Eula King
THE STILLNESS OF THE WOODS
There's a stillness of the woods—yet
it's full of sound
with so many animals running all
around.
They are so happy as they
communicate and chatter.
Listen to their little feet as they go
pitter-patter.

Even the rain falls softly upon each
blade of grass
Shining the faces of the flowers as if
they were brass.
The foliage looks so shiny and green.
As the many raindrops wash it so
clean.

Each leaf seems to be bursting from
a bud anew.
Scattered clouds appear—showing
patches of blue.
Wild flowers are bursting through
the leaf mold
Portraying newlife and beauty
untold.

There is a quiet peace in the time of
spring
Even though we can hear the
mocking birds sing.
Underneath our feet the little violets
grow
So happy to appear above the ground
after the snow.

The stillness of the woods brings
such serenity
Making life worth living—with
wildlife running free.
There is a new awakening appearing
here and there
As the scent of fragrant flowers
circulate through the air.

Jason Lehman
PRESENT TENSE
It was spring.
But it was summer I wanted,
The warm days,
And the great outdoors.

It was summer.
But it was Fall I wanted,
The colorful leaves,
And the cool, dry air.

It was Fall.
But it was winter I wanted,
The beautiful snow,
And the joy of the holiday season.

It was winter.
But it was spring I wanted,
The warmth,
And the blossoming of nature.

I was a child.
But it was adulthood I wanted,
The freedom,
And the respect.

I was twenty.
But it was thirty I wanted,
To be mature,
And sophisticated.

I was middle-aged.
But it was twenty I wanted,
The youth,
And the free spirit.

I was retired.
But it was middle-age I wanted,
The presence of mind,
Without limitations.

My life was over.
But I never got what I wanted.

Mark D Calkins
REFLECTIONS
On a cold winters night,
I can only think of the
warmth of your love,
the soft tone of your voice,
And the gentleness of your touch.
Your love means the world to me.
YOU mean the world to me.
I see your silhouette in every
corner of my mind.
At night, I close my eyes,
and I can hear your song.
You take me on your wings,
and we fly through the night.
Harmoniously we are as ONE.
Our love is like the reflection
in a pond.
You can cast stones upon it,
but after the rippling of the
water, the reflection still stands.
That reflection stays beautiful
Forever . . .

M D Haworth
MY WORLD
A sunrise from a mountain peak,
A stand of redwoods, tall and sleek,
A thunderhead that rolls on by,
A rainbow in a darkened sky,
A hidden pond with padded bloom
Within a leafed cathedral room,
A quiet glen in wooded hills,
A field of crowded daffodils,
And snow atop a far-off ridge,
The milky way, a star-built bridge,
A breeze, the wind, a gust, a gale,
A calm, a storm, the rain, the hail,
The desert, blinding in the sun,
With shrub and bush, but shadows
none,
The seas, the land, the lakes, the
bays,
The dark of night, the moon's soft
rays,
Volcanoes blasting fiery plumes,
And earthquakes' splitting, rumbling
booms,
The flow of glaciers to the sea,
With icebergs moving in their lee,
All nature mighty in array
From violence to a peaceful day—
These are the world that I esteem,
Though hidden in a misty
dream . . .

William R Whittaker
ABANDONED BABY
Poor little baby asleep on the step
I wonder if your mama wept
Did she shed a single tear
As she laid your blankets here
Did she have one word to say
As she turned and ran away
Do you think she'll ever regret
That she couldn't change you when
you're wet
Wipe from your face a smudge of
dirt
Or kiss away the pain and hurt
I hope you never learn the facts
About today's cowardly act
For her loss will be another's gain
Another who'll kiss away the pain
And change your diapers when
they're wet
Give you love you haven't known
yet

Howard E Ragsdale
ENLIGHTENMENT
Let not a sense of humor desert you,
No matter where you may go.
At times life may not seem like
living,
But it is if you'll only help make it
so.

When things all seem wrong and
nothing right,
And you lie awake and toss all night.
Just change your mind to other
things,
And see the difference that tomorrow
brings.

No one tries to be purposely unkind,
And of this you can be sure.
If you'll just let a smile ease your
mind,
All the hardships are a cinch to
endure.

Many are the things we'd like to
forget,
Though try as we might they remain.
But a laugh and a smile you'll never
regret,
And in them we have everything to
gain.

Bonnie Schlangen
BIRDS FLY SOUTH FOR THE WINTER
Birds fly south for winter
as you hear them say
but when the sun stays out
they do not fly away

Birds fly south for winter
so they stay nice and warm
sometimes they come back again
because there was a storm

Birds fly south for winter
they fly so far away
If they don't come back again
they probably want to stay

Birds fly south for winter
I think they fly all day
I don't really know yet . . .
but I'll find out someday

James M Hughes
PROMISE

Margie: Like a meteor in the midnight sky our love died, I still don't know why a fiery fourth; is now the fifth of July

---

Even in the darkest night
You have the promise of the
sunrise
While pain tears at your heart
And salty tears fill your eye
Hold this promise in your heart
For you know it must be true
The sun must shine again
And a new love will come to you

Bonnie J Eaton
MOM AND I
Mom and I, we sit by the hour
dreaming dreams long gone in the
past
Gone so long it's hard to remember
the things that come first or come
last
Sometimes they are dark and

foreboding, sometimes they are bright as the day
But always it seems in the evening, the clouds, they chase them away
Often we are awakened from slumber by voices we think that we hear
But mostly it's just the wind sighing, the sounds that come to our ear
Most times we stare at the ceiling, the walls, and often the floor
Our days are so long, they mean nothing; we just don't care anymore
We are old, we are tired, we are lonely; the times in our lives mostly bad
I wonder if kids ever think what will happen to old Mom and Dad
Well, so much for this poem of nonsense, the value of which I may doubt

So I think we will wait until evening and then we will go and eat out
I think I'll get some more coffee, let it settle my nerves as it may
For I doubt if we go in the evening, it never turns out that way

Josephine Monaco
A NEW LIFE
You're sixty-five, retired and feeling blue
You've no place to go—nothing to do
Cheer up—you've just joined "The Leisure Class"
Offers and discounts will arrive en masse
Trips and tours to anywhere
You can even ride buses and trains half-fare
This kind of life just can't be beat
As long as you can stand on your own two feet!

Dee Overpeck
TO ALL MY CHILDREN

Dedicated to all my children: Julie Lynne, Maxwell Wayne II, & Charles Shannon LaCaze

To all my children, you are winners!
With your lives, you are beginners;
I'll be there when you need me
Until then your hand is free.
I figure it's about time
That from my knee you climb.
I forgot to tell you how proud I am of you,
I just assumed you knew.
I forgot to praise you a little more often
Or to lend an encouraging word then;
I assume you understood.
My role in motherhood
Was not smooth or easy.
I started too young & did not foresee
All the hardships that I would cause us to endure;
If I had known, I assure,
Things would have been different!
It was never my intent
To have you suffer or hurt,
But I'm no expert!
You are very important to me!

Ora Lee Hunter Jones

Ora Lee Hunter Jones
WHERE, OH, WHERE DOES IT BEGIN? MYSELF

"Pure as a lilly" Dedicated to my friend Lilly Price.

IF I strive to make myself better
My home will be comfortable.
IF I strive to portray the comfort of my home
My neighborhood will blossom.
IF I water the blossoms within my neighborhood
My community will be blessed.
IF I stress thankfulness for my blessed community
My city will prosper.
IF I'm concerned about the prosperity of my city
My state will be rich.
IF I contribute to the riches of my state
My country will be strong.
IF I share God's strength with my country
My nation will know God.
IF my nation and myself know God
My world will be at peace.
Where, oh, where does it end?
Myself and God.

Dian Snell
FOREVER LOVE

To Larry

Loving you is not of things
Neither is it of time.
But a dream of mine.

Barbara Jean Stanley
A NEW DAY

To My Loving Family; Mom & Dad, Patty, Ronnie, Dick, Donnie, And Kathy; My Brothers And Sisters: To My Children; Daniel N. Sisco Jr., Marsha Lynn Frampton, Howard T. Sisco, David Jason Sisco; And My Beautiful Grandchildren:

A NEW DAY IS DAWNING; A NEW DAY'S BEGUN,
BUT THIS DAY SEEMS DIFFERENT; THAN PREVIOUS ONES:
I'M FINDING MORE COURAGE FOR EACH TRIAL I FACE:
I'M FILLED WITH YOUR SPIRIT, AND BLESSED BY YOUR GRACE:
YOUR LOVE IS AMAZING;
YOUR GRACE SO DIVINE:
BLESSED ASSURANCE;
FOREVER IS MINE!

John S Goodwin IV
TWILIGHT OF TIME
Dreaming upon the twilight of time, feeling a slumber across my mind.
God's awaken the Planets of Dew, creations are granted for me and you.
Skies are grey, with mystic red, as the sun settles into her bed.
Night brings the twilight of time, as slumber reaches into our mind.

Laughter arises upon Mt. Dew, freshness tasted, as we shout: "Ya-whooo!"
Oh thus, in the dawn of time, one with coolness, refreshes the touch of lime.
Twist and shout, "Dew" with praise, our songs are lifted, our signs we raise.
Freedom is cast in fields at home, gods are speaking, "We are not alone!"
The moment has come a standard we call, they give to us, for DEW IS ALL!

Al Kirsch
WHEN I MET YOU!

Dedicated to: My first beloved wife Anne (Banks) Kirsch

I
This certain feeling is new
To Me;
And it will always be a
Memory
It sets me dreaming of things
A new;
Of golden sun-light and skies of
Blue!
II
This certain feeling came when
I met you;
It started whispering of a love
So true!
I never thought love with me would
Start—
But now this feeling is within my
Heart!!!
The End!

Gladus M Moore
YES, I AM HE
We condemned our Lord
In ignorance, fear and greed
For Satan seeds give only death
While our Lord, is life for all eternity

We scrouge and beat our Savior
Black Wednesday, He was condemned
We nailed our Savior, to a cross
Made from the Dogwood tree

Angels rolled the stone away
On a misty Sabbath morn
Our Lord, took leave of His burial place
To walk in the garden for all to see

Before ascending to His Heavenly Throne
Our Lord, proclaimed "Yes I Am HE"!
And I leave The Holy Spirit
With those of you do believe

Frances Shaver
A HEAVENLY EXPERIENCE
The anxiety of him coming home
Greeting me in a loving way;
I turn the soft music on
And ask — "How was your day?"
While awaiting dinner
I serve him a hot or cold drink, sit & talk;
I wash his face and massage his feet
After his long home walk.

The sweetness of his charms
The gentleness of his touch;
His hands gliding over my skin
Makes me love him more than much.

The excitement of our bodies meeting with
The exotic feeling love blessed;
The contentment of peace and drifting
Into a relaxing sleep upon his chest.

A beautiful heavenly experience
It doth seem,
The morning has broken—
I awaken from my dream.

Bert Rutledge
A TRIBUTE TO A DEAR DEPARTED ONE
A million times I've missed you,
A million tears I've cried:
If love could have saved you,
You never would have died.

Things I feel more deeply are
The hardest things to say:
Oh! dearest one! I've always loved you . . .
In a very special kind of way.

I often sit and think of you,
And think of how you died:
To think I couldn't say good-bye,
Before you closed your eyes.

No one can know my loneliness,
And no one can see my weeping:
For all of my tears from an aching heart,
Are shed while others are sleeping.

If I had a life time wish, my dear,
Or a dream that would come true:
I'd pray to God with all my heart,
For yester year, my dearest one, and you.

Ruth E Barnhart Ardieta
MY GENESIS

Dedicated to Mother

Come let me sit by your side
Seed that I descended from
Let me live in the yesterday
For a time, When I felt Safe.
Free of earthly things.
Let me dream as a child
With innocent thoughts
of days gone by
When you would say
Time to say your prayers
Then a kiss goodnight.

Sally Harris
LOVING
What is loving?
In my mind, loving requires "giving."

When a person "gives" of himself—physically, mentally, emotionally—he may risk being rejected by another.

In my life, I've taken "risks" and I've played it "safe."

Many times my "risks" were followed by great emotional pain.

However, during the "safe" times I found myself feeling empty and lonely.

Why were these "alone" times unhappy ones?
Was I confusing "being alone" with "being lonely?"

One cannot find genuine happiness in this life until he or she learns to "love" being alone.

Yes, loving is giving.
But it begins with giving to oneself.

Being happy depends upon me, not another person.
My "safe" times can become my "good" times thus enriching my "risk" times, if and when I choose to take them.

Dolores Harple Koch

COME HEAR ME CHILDREN

For Russell My Husband and My Best Friend I Love You

Why do our children fight or hurt each other
Why can't they get along to give a hand as brother
I listen when they join to play in life's cruel game
As taunts are thrown daily their lives are not the same

Come hear me children to listen while I say
Join hands together for peace on morrows' day
Stop the fights, the hitting, put down your hands
Support and embrace each other, here or foreign lands

Fighting brings such heartache, bruises and pain
It doesn't help to solve a thing or anything to gain
Tears fall so freely then take their flight
They assuage the pain felt within ever so slight

Heartbreak follows when I hear the children fight
When they play in harmony it makes the day so bright
Gather round children to listen when I say
Join hands together for peace on morrows' day

Lisa Sloter

TODAY YOU TOUCHED A HEART

Today you touched a heart.
The words you said
were gentle.
Where there was pain,
you sent laughter.
Because you smiled,
Because you winked
last week,
you took a problem away.
Because you
gave a hug,
Because of a concerned look,
a helping hand,
the word "Hello,"
you lifted someone up.
Just because
you were there.
Today you touched a heart.
I know.

Raymond Sutherland

THE UGLY ONE

Introduction
There are times
when a man
glances at a
woman, or a woman
at a man, and the
receiver of the
look concludes,
ignorantly, that
the person who
looks has a
romantic interest
in the person
looked. That
ignorant reaction,
on the part of the
recipient, has a
tendency, on occasion,
to considerably annoy
the bestower of said
look.

Has this happened to you?

It did to me.

The stratum of the
inheritrix of my
glance was substantially
beneath pretty.

The Ugly One
'cause our eyes met in the air
For a one-split-second glance,
Now I wonder how you dare
Grab your very asinine stance.

You have leaped to the conclusion
That because I looked just once,
I romantic'ly have fallen.
What a Jackass Petulance!

What an insolent audacity!
Daughter of witless capacity . . .
I will not tangle with you, Creep.
You are The Bottom Of The Heap!

You should see the kind of broad
That I have met on my road.
Each and every one I rode
In and out of my abode.

If you had seen all my harems,
And the current one right now,
You would switch your stupid meow
To a flabbergasted WOW !!!

I go only for luscious women,
Honey . . . those enjoyed by men;
Not an Ass As Ugly As You!
Twenty-two, skidaddle, SHOO!!!

Eldridge J Sneed

THE GAME

To Aftan, may your life be the greatest time ever

I've entered into a game. More intense and requiring more attention than chess.
Though the players and rules are different, the end result is the same.
How much of my time will I invest.
Is the outcome worth the risk?
Am I entitled to this pleasure? Can I handle the fear of the test?

It's my move. King? Queen? Pawn? I feel I'm too far behind. Should I retreat? No, that has never been my style.
Stand tall go for it, unsure all the while.

The King safe and covered by his Queen and many pawns.
I am a pawn. There are many of me. I am dispensable.
There's to be no fight.
I think and think and deeper I sink into this darkness before the dawn.
I shun at the thought of taking flight.'

Wound up, Dictated to; Only a toy for the moments play.
When playtime is over, I'll be boxed and stored until again your desire for me is aroused and attentions focused upon me for some reason unknown.

Your favorite car, truck, doll am I.
I am here/there for you, Like a game.
I am sure you'll play again. You play to be a winner, I play for fun. I am not happy but you have still won.
No need to worry about me for the game is now over.
Without competition there is no game.
Not now not for the moment.

Bette M Decker

Bette M Decker

I PRAYED AGAIN TO GOD TODAY

In memory of my husband Charles, the love of my life

I prayed again to God today
I felt he turned his face away
I knew there was no one there for me
I wondered what my life would be—
I looked at the cloudy skies, with
shades of blue
Watched the birds and listened to
Maybe a sign from God there would
be
To let me know he was still
there for me.
He hadn't turned his face away
I just didn't listen to what
I pray.

Janet Capachietti

BABY ME SET FREE

This poem is dedicated to my loving husband, Louie

Thanks! for not babying me
It helped me get up the nerve to be free.
You never really needed me
you always seemed to be free.

I wanted you to be more like me
before I even really knew me.
But, I have become free
instead of you like me used to be.

I always admired your ways to be free.
Such pride it gave me to see
you act free, which I always wanted to be
and needed for me.

I am glad I grabbed a little freedom
from you for me.
I will pass it along and help
others to be free, as you and me.

I climbed over the top!
Which is right or which is wrong??
Together, we shall find out the norm.

Happy, happy, happy are we
skipping along together—
smiling, just to be free!

Seymour Brownstein

THE RACE

It was a cross country run,
Thirty-four men launched at the gun,
Lunging forward they left their mark,
Then an uphill downhill park.
My son amongst them wearing the wrong shoes,
Leading the pack at the rear,
With sudden speed coming downhill,
He finally made his move.
Near the finish in nineteenth position,
Man after man gasping for air,
There he faltered, a rare condition,
Losing nineteenth place by a hair.

Randy Covert

A ROSE

A diary of untold secrets
in the years that I have come
with many thoughts and many changes
with words I'll tell you some.

You've given me a life
that only I dreamed could be
you gave to me a rose that I long to see.

You are this rose my love
for when I said, "I do"
never did I like a rose
until the day that I met you.

The stem is your warm and loving body
that keeps me warm at night
the leaves your soft caress
that helps me see the light.

The petals of a natures rose
is your heart that's so warm and giving
so thank-you my rose, thank-you my love
to see this way of living.

Petra Gayle Baldridge

THE FLAME

You cast a warm glow on me
the very first time we met.
The cinders fevered softly
for you were one I couldn't forget.
The sparks arose spontaneously
the very first time we touched;
The incandescent glimmer
shown on my face when I blushed.
With every beat of our hearts,
the heat grew out of control;
With every "I love you" whispered
in my ear
the flame rages throughout my soul.

Jeane M Culp

OPTIMISTIC

Have you ever seen vultures cry
Crows flit crops by
An enemy turn a cheek
The mute speak
Anyone who hasn't thought the
worst

Hunger not thirst
An arid desert cold
Juicy gossip untold
Can you truly see a crack in dawn
Someone that went, yet wasn't gone
Burdens weigh a wee ton
War minus guns
Did you really see silence break
The greedy not take
Insanity lack madness
Or a frown without sadness?
Then heaven must hold the best
For all God's chosen guest.

Regina Golden
BENEDICTE
The storm avenged distemper's suit
with ever-growing perturbation;
As thunder rumbled, and the air
repercussed in loud jobation.

A hapless bird, by cold wind driven
onto the arbor where it clung;
From the vine in waving motion
the beleaguered bird in peril
swung.

Responding to an outstretched hand
as eager as a frightened child,
The white wings raised and settled
down
as if the bird had been beguiled,

Whereat, a sweet tranquility
dispelled the gloom and dark
despair;
The bird was brought into the room,
which now seemed quiet, clean
and fair.

Sophia Lamb

Sophia Lamb
LEPIDOPTERA
(MY BANANA BUTTERFLY)
If I could be but beautiful,
A beautiful butterfly,
I'd pull off the layers which held me
down, and do my dance in the sky.

I'd flitter from flower to flower,
and go from here to there,
Dazzling colors on my wings
I would bare.

I am quite fragile and delicate,
A lovely creature to behold,
I came from an unsightly caterpillar,
but now my beauty is bold!

Lois M Allen
NAM VETERANS
Don't denounce the warriors,
They served their country well,
They did more for each of us,
Than words could ever tell.

My buddies bled, they lost their
limbs,
And some were tortured, too,
And there were those who lost their
minds,
To honor me and you.

But then we were not welcomed,
When we came marching through,
Since some dropped bombs on
targets,
As they were told to do.

But when I meet my Maker,
I'll say, "Sir, I wish you well.
One more marine reporting, Sir,
I served my time in hell."

And then I'm sure He'll say to me,
"We're glad to have you here,
Since you ennobled stars and stripes,
And all you hold most dear."

Frederick William Ayer
PRIVATE PAINS, PUBLIC TRIUMPHS

This poem is dedicated to Gladys, Diane and Jackie

Inside him—
So very private
Commonsense harbored
Slights that straddle
His everincreasing pains.
Personal merits crumbled!
His humanness has no importance.

Outwardly—
So very public
Love and endearment
Made a distinction on his body
But not his brain . . .
Or was it his body and not his brain?
Ambivalence!

The perilous stairs
Wobble with the price
Of outward triumphs—
Ah!
Being a world champion . . .
Being a world star . . . Did not matter
anymore
His private pains, public triumphs
Became laced in sugaried caramel.

Rexana Blair
COSMIC CONNECTION
Some people are born
With all that there is,
While another is shorn
Of what should be his.
Some people are cruel,
And others are kind.
Some cups are brimfull,
Leaving others behind.

Some lives are carefree
And some full of woe
This shouldn't be
But living is so.
We worry and fret
With negative chatter
And then get upset
About what doesn't matter.
So when we feel sad
And suffer with pain
Tis but a launchpad
For what we will gain.
The only part of us
That really exists
Is our inwardness
And nothing but this.
Our body is temporary
Our life but a season
Our beauty illusionary
Yet it all has a reason.

When our body is gone
Rejoice in its passing
For our essence lives on
In love everlasting.
In life we feel love
But in death we are more
We then become love
Pure love to the core.
A love so unbound
Infinite and vast
Within and around
And never surpassed.
In death we are whole
Universally fused
Part of each soul
It matters not whose.
Life's meaning is clear-cut
As everything is one
For nothing is separate
In cosmic connection.

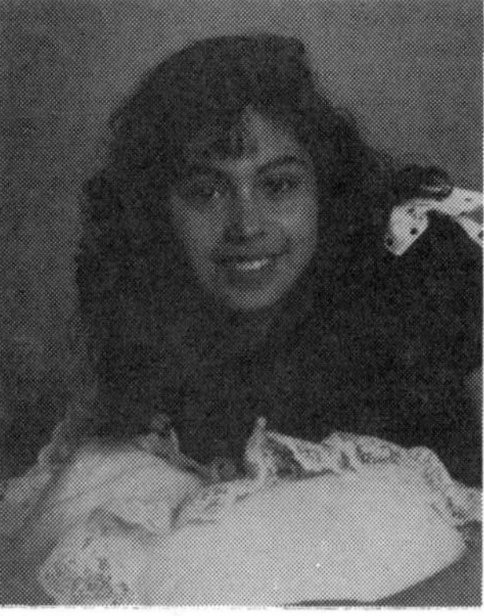

Olivia C Roybal

Olivia C Roybal
MIRRORS
Mirrors show
the real me
They show
what I look like outside
and how I feel inside
They show
my happiness, my joy
my tears, my fears
Sometimes
when I look in the mirror
I see nothing there
It means
I have a strange feeling
waiting to be seen
Mirrors . . .
they show everything

Sophie P Shiaris

Sophie P Shiaris
A BOATMAN AND A SAGE

To my sons Michael—Chris and their families

Someone who considered himself a
sage
Was conversing with a boatman
while traversing a river by boat.

The sage asks the humble boatman,
have you ever studied philosophy?
No, replies the boatman, and gazes at
him with wonderment.

Unfortunate one quippes the sage, a
fourth of your life is a loss.
Per-chance you've studied astronomy? "No, never had I any desire."
Per-chance you dig philosophy? "Not
even for this had I ever any desire."
Alas, the three fourths of your life are
lost.

The witty boatman upside-down his
boat he turns
And the sage had no knowledge how
to swim.

With humour the boatman shouts at
him, do you know, my wise man,
how to swim well?

"N . . . n . . . not at all", he replies
half-drowned.
Hey, have a good voyage to the deep
bottom.

Gregory W Byer
AUTUMN
The illusion of rainbows is forming,
It predetermines the cold.
The trees all look like kaleidoscopes
For Autumn is growing old.

I can feel a dreary raindrop,
The leaves no longer crisp.
A pigskin sails through the clouded
sky
Like a leaf in an Autumn wisp.

I can see a colorful background
And with it a painted street.
The tee-shirt all look like sweaters
And the flowers all look like wheat.

So we put away our baseballs
Time for the horse and foxhound.
The flocks of geese look eager to fly
With the instincts which take them
southbound.

So the force that intensifies greenery
Has finally lost its hold.
The trees all look like kaleidoscopes
For Autumn is growing old.

Mrs W Bode
LIFE'S PRECIOUS GIFT!

To my husband & children

Among the nicest gifts
Are memories of those—
Who have touched our lives
With love and kindness.

The priceless gift—
To all of us—we share
Counting time isn't so important
As making time count:

So don't save your breath—
When it's time to breathe
A prayer of thanks this day—
For life's Priceless Gift "LOVE":

Denice E Robichaux
LOVE IS

To: Daniel Bailey I hope you enjoy this poem. My thoughts of love. I love you!

God's creation of man;
A soul with a destiny.
An ultimate plan.

A mother holding her baby
Close abreast;
A bluejay making a family nest.

A lovely stream flowing
Peacefully by;
Tears of happiness
In a young child's eyes.

A gentle touch,
A warm caress;
A tight hug.
Thoughts of love.

The Lord's painted sunsets
In the afternoon skies;
Two in love gazing in
Each others eyes.

An outstreatched arm
To lend a helping hand.
An admirer of poetry;
A fan.

Children playing in the sand;
An older couple holding hands.

Nice lyrics with a beautiful melody;
Special moments shared between you and me.

Freedom of the butterfly;
Spacious mountains in the clear blue sky.

The ocean with its lovely sound;
Seagulls in flight all around.

The seven wonders of the world.
Gentle movements of a squirrel.

Hearts filled with love;
A spirit of a white dove.

Bees in a nectar tree;
A LOVE POEM SHARED
BETWEEN YOU AND ME.

Bill Dooley
THE GREAT WALL BY MIDNIGHT

Even when the moon emerges on the screen of the capitol city late at night, many post war pilgrims assemble at the great emotional Memorial to remember. How placid and still ones steps are as they walk past each black slab engraved with 58,022 men who bravely carried the weight.

Amongst the multitudes of observers, one boy stands solitude bearing a single name of significance. A legacy remaining—almost a man, just like his father was when he left the world. A mortal he never got to meet nor understand in a planted relationship. Father to him was always known as a legend and romanticized myth. A life which war had scrapped, robbing and leaving him with no memories to revive. Finally, the evening stroll meets the boy face to face with James Thomas Davis—. The midnight hour rings an overwhelming silence which causes any bystander to tear, as the President lies sleeping and Abraham Lincoln sits on his throne thinking of stars.

Anguish stretches sinews in the face and rest of corporeal when the moonlight introduces him to his father's name for the first time. The young man desires for the lifeforce lost, reaches for dad's identity engraved on black commemoration. To seize the piece of enshrinement fabricated from granite sculpture to be his own. Wanting to put it in his pocket and take it home for personal remembrances in search for oneself's identity. But the lamented fact remains and realized by all offspring of the war deceased: Father must stay for duty and as an example for the millions who will come to ask him what was it like to die in Vietnam.

R J Ellis
JOURNEY

This poem is dedicated to my wife "Mindy"

We'll follow our hearts and
seek our dreams,
We'll chase the wind for fun . . .
We'll climb a tree and reach for stars
Then lay beneath the sun . . .

We'll frolic in the tall green grass,
We'll stroll along the shore . . .

We'll trek high mountains and skip through meadows,
Then we'll chase the wind some more.

Chiodo
GHITY

I see the bright flood-torrent of tears
brimming on the rim of Persia's
night-dark eyes:
the edge of loss, sustained in silent self-control.

A single word on either tongue could
drown us both
But tell me now: What is the trick of
forgetting? How shall I live?

The Moslem jeweled kingdom is a
veiled exile to the West: a dream of
opulence and your sweet company.

You must go and . . I am left
With whom shall I dance?

I who have filled the young girl's
dreams with that wistful motion.
Who will see or care
with what subtle taunting and
undulating art
I echo the East?

And your old mother there, spell-bound in the moment
singing out: "Iranien—Italien!
Italien—Iranien!"
She who keeps me in her
prayers . . .
Can I endure the hollow after hearing
the chorus of her laughter?
And you with all your whims and
wiles forever besieged by
longing . . .
Where will you store the memory of
me?

Michael H Brownstein
CLOUDS

The moon hung there precariously,
a strip of cloud blurring it
as if an eraser on the end of a pencil
rubbed back and forth, back and
forth,
futilely trying to blot out the spot of
light
full bloom over the silent desert.

It reminded me too much of past
mistakes
recorded on fading paper
and erased in angry swipes
leaving broken tracks like crippled
animals
or tattered leaves too late in winter.

When morning colored the desert,
the moon slowly moved away
and the eraser marks spread pink
across the sky
leaving white feathered flakes
as if it were snowing against the blue.

There is always time to leave
mistakes behind.

Victoria B Heeney
MY FRIEND

My friend, to you, the heart of me,
a poorly printed parchment,
rolls open for your soul to read.
Here—please—turn the leaves
tenderly.
See here, where once I failed,
and here, my excellence does bloom
(somehow!).
Now here, I am all lost and cold,
and on this page, I find myself anew!
And here?
I keep and cherish you.

My friend, for once so worthy of the
kindest words and deeds,
love-ladened smiles,
for one I find deserving of the
priceless and the rare,
for you who should be gifted with the
best this world affords,
I know nothing I can offer sufficient
to the cause—except, to you, the
heart of me,
this poorly printed parchment,
rolls open for your soul to read
and for your life to write upon and
add.

Elmer R Spoor
THE AUTOMOBILE

In this day of modern motor cars
If lined up would reach from earth to
Mars
Some are large some are small
There are colors and models to suit
all
If you see one that suits your eye
And decide to buy
Some are Antique and some have
class
But none will run without gas
You may be a smart Chick
Buy an Electric but they can cause a
frown
For if in a hurry you want to go to
town
You get in turn on the key there is no,
sound
Because the batteries are run down
So to save you remorse why not buy
a good horse
He might want a blanket or some
shoes
But that is up to you to choose
There are three words he is trained to
know
Say back up he will do so say Giddap
And forward he will go when you
want to stop say Whoa
You can guide him North, East. West
or South
By two reins from your hands to his
mouth
Put on his harness hitch him to a shay
Get in give him orders he will obey
And gladly take you on your way
Or there—s a place near or far
That you cannot reach by car
Put on a saddle or ride him bare
Sitting on his nice soft hair
And safely take you there
You will have some trips that you
admire
And did not have to buy gas or
change a tire.

Randall H Hardie Sr
SNARE BENEATH THE SNOW

For Chrissy, So sad is the fact that we cannot accept a true friends advice before it's too late. We love you and miss you.

Your value climbing higher, Yet your
justice very low
Constant to abuse our youth, A snare
beneath the snow
Reflections in the mirror show the
pattern of your path
Feeding on the victims you've
addicted to your wrath
Awaiting transformation as you
glisten on the blade
Burning on the entry to the system
you invade
Fooled by your soothing mood, Your
taste of bitter sweet

Keeping thoughts awake all night,
Denying them of sleep
Alluring to your nightmare by the
pleasure that you make
All the while searching for another
life to take
Shower in your glory, You're a sad
reality
Shattering dreams of strong belief
that were meant to be
Synthetic sin is what you are,
Creation of your maker
Chemists of your evil way,
Corrupting human nature
Constant goals ahead should be to
show you firm resistance
Put to rest your wicked ways, And
end your sole existence

Vera Warren
TOYS

To my sister Reva

When we were small we had an iron
horse,
which pulled a fire engine which was
also iron of course.
There was a lead-footed elephant
when wound up he would waddle,
plus a sailing ship inside a small-
necked bottle.
We had a pair of clowns that did
acrobatics,
also eyes that lit up in a pair of
siamese cats.
There was a little kitchen stove made
of black iron,
and a police car with a cop and a
shrill siren.
Most of these were wind up toys and
really well-made,

our parents thought they were well
worth the money they paid.
We had a spinning top that would
hum and sing,
each Christmas we would look
forward for Santa to bring.
Another new toy to give us pleasure,
we sure extracted enjoyment to full
measure.
From the toys that were available at
that time,
would you believe it? Some of them
only cost a dime!

Linda G Gann
THE GREAT WHITE THRONE

To my loving husband Lonnie B Gann, and daughters Londa Cottington and Leanda Gann

When we stand before the Great
White Throne, we won't be alone.
We'll be with the dead, the small the
great, I know for certain, that Jesus
won't be late; when he welcomes us
home.

Is your name written in the book of
life?
Do you struggle daily for your very
life?
Well, just ask Jesus to change your
life, then you can say—

The earth shall be purged, and the
sinners judged, sin shall be destroyed
forever.
Then with the Lord, we shall set up
his Kingdom, we shall be light as
feathers.—

There shall be no night, There, God
shall be our light.
What wrongs that were done to us on
earth, Jesus shall make right.

Come on ride the new Highway of
Holiness, Heaven is calling for you
to be their guest.
So get ready for Jesus, put on your
Sunday best.—

He shall give us crowns for our
heads, white robes for our backs.
The Tree of Life shall be opened to
us, there's nothing we shall lack.—

Praise to the Father, praise to the
Son,
Praise to the Holy Spirit, the three
shall be one.—

Let us go forward, never looking
back.
When you trust in the Lord, you are
on the right track.—

Maybelle A Finn
GOIN' HOME

To my brother Bob Finn. And to my friend Bob Lloyd—Veterans

In the shadows beyond the dusk
While birds do twitter, and rustling
leaves
Send out a message through the trees
A wagon creaks a friendly whine
A horse drawn sentinel, so divine
Carrying a hero to the last—while
dogs follow quietly
And friends do gasp—
A right none can dethrone—
As shadows do condone at last.
The breath of fame is ever sweet
But far more sweet, the memory
Of one who lives within our hearts
The memory of human Art.
The stars shone bright this memo-
rable night
While making dimples in the dew
With stripes a-glow, red, white and
blue.
Spun-sown, to cover one so true
As into shadows beyond the dusk,
While birds do twitter and rustling
leaves
Send out a message—through the
trees.
Into the evening mist sun goes
And shadows lessen one by one
To God's great land of no more woes
Carrying the honor, he has won.
Then fold the banner, let it rest
To honor him who stood the test.
—A VETERAN—Goin' Home.

Susan Edwards
I AM THE WIND

For James . . . who is also the wind.

I am the Wind—
We pass each other,
—meet
travel together
For as long as we do
Until we're different,
—not One.

And I am the Wind—
who are you?

Cricket Mease

Cricket Mease
BITTERNESS

I dedicate this poem to my mother who taught me how to let go of bitterness.

As the years roll by and you keep
looking back,
Your heart grows bitter and your
mind's not intact;
And when you think back over the
times in your life,
Do you wish you could change them
or take them in stride?

I don't know about you, but I do
know about me;
My mind's opening up and I'm
beginning to see—
Bitterness will smother you and
you'll wither away.

You'll lie awake thinking every
night
And then don't want to face the next
day—
Wake up your mind and your heart
will follow
And then you won't feel so bitter and
hollow.

Betty Corrao
NEW FANGLED MIRTH

While recollecting the precise
moment Peace infused my being,
only flashes of time reappear:

As the moment my soul became fully
aware of the tedious task bestowed
upon it.

As the reality deep within my heart
that there was more to me than I.

As the reality that as a whole being,
body and soul, I belonged to the
Cosmos.

That my life was not a useless grain
of sand as I had once thought,
purposelessly isolated amongst
millions of others.

Scattered along the water's edge,
only to be swept away in the arms of
angry winds,

And tossed needlessly against the
ocean's floor to Nature's whimsical
delight.

Perhaps consciousness is only a
phase, for once mastered, do we not
turn inward to seek Truth?

Rebecca Buldo-Jackson
PAPA

To a wonderful man who was always there for me.

A beach day in the Fall:
A-top the stairs you stay,
While watching Nick play ball.
Your laughter filled my day.

To Chris I pledged my life:
You dressed in fine array,
To stand beside your wife,
And light my wedding day.

Your body, often frail;
Your face, so drawn and pained.
Your mind would still prevail:
You never once complained.

The love you sent across
Will live within my heart,
And lend me strength in loss.
My world won't fall apart.

We've said good-bye for now.
It will not be the last.
For we will meet somehow
And laugh about the past.

Eileen M Martensen
UNKNOWN ANGEL

I never got to see you,
Sweet baby grandchild of mine,
To cuddle and adore you—
Touch your cheek and hair so fine.

Gift of God, seed of my seed,
Conceived in passion and love—
Irreplaceable treasure,
Precious promise from above.

No one asked my views of life
As you lay safe in the womb.
You'd be an inconvenience—
So they sent you to your doom.

Before you ever saw our world
You were torn from your warm nest.
My wistful arms reach out, tears fall,
And my heartache finds no rest.

But when I get to heaven
There will be a rocking chair
For us, my unknown angel.
I'll hold you. I cared, I care.

Ricky Silvers
TIME IS MY TEACHER

When we are born a little while,
We look for evenings shadow fall;
Then hurriedly we go from young to
old,
in time we've missed it all.

It's hard to find out what life is,
So swiftly it passes by;
We never find the real definition,
Before we have to die.

If we could only slow down our pace,
Beginning at life's dawn;
We could know life's meaning then,
for time would teach us all.

Ellen R Waters
'TIS EASTERTIME

To my three grandsons, Scott Ryland Waters, Jeffrey Lee Dudley and Jonathan David Dudley.

I saw the flowers, sniffed the air;
Heard the sound of the birds, free of
all care.
With their twittering and fluttering of
each tiny wing—
They seemed to say to each new
thing;
"Tis Eastertime, Awaken! and listen
to the Easter story,
As the sun shines down in all its
glory.
How many, many years ago our Lord
Jesus died—
He was crucified-because He loved
us so!
How He gave His life, that we might
know
of the wonderful love He had to
bestow;
The saving grace and power divine
That were His to give. 'Tis
Eastertime!"

Dominick Parisi
SILVER AND TURQUOISE

Heroic City Of The Sky,
Pueblo for a millennium,
the mesa casts a watchful eye
o'er a golden landscape in the sun.

The eagle cries an angry scream
and curses beneath its breath,
when wakened from its angry dream
by the holy couriers of death.

There are voices from the heavens
echoing from adobe walls,
the Great Spirit of the Father
to his staunch and brave sons calls.

A lone coyote howls at night
from the blood-drenched distant
hills,
he laughs at those who lie in fright
then he cries for those lying still.

Acoma of the towering cliffs
where war-cries ring no more,
silver and turquoise line the shelves
and a proud squaw tends the store.

Carmella Belue
THE PATH OF REMEMBRANCE

Remembrance finds a hidden path,
Tucked away in the treasured
yesterdays
The path became overgrown with the
passage of time
Forgotten in the hesitation of a
promise.

A shadow travels through fallen
leaves,
Clearing away the debris of so many
years,
A misplaced cherished moment
reappears—
Tenderly the shadow sweeps away
the hand of time.

Quietly the moment wakes from a
restful sleep,
Becoming once again this day in
time.
A heart weeps silently with the joy
of
Finding the forgotten friend.

Too soon the time to part comes
once again.

Gently the moment of yesterday lies to rest,
Settling beside the person of lost tomorrows,
As yet another moment buries itself on
The Path of Remembrance.

Lynda Fashbaugh
FAITH
Don't give up on your faith,
Nothing can ever take its place.

When it seems that nothing is going right,
Just keep your faith and you will see the light—

When it seems your life is only going down,
Just try a little smile; instead of a frown—
When it seems that everything is over and gone,
There is always some good to keep you going on—
Things always seem worse than they really turn out to be,
Be glad that you are a person; God could have made you a tree—
So, remember, when life is only getting you down,
Pick yourself up with a smile; don't frown.

Anne Lyons
I LOVE YOU MOM
I love you mom
I wish to say
Take care of yourself
While I am away
My heart is with you
Wherever I go
I must tell you this
So that you will know
I'll miss you mom
I wish I was there
It's a heavy load
That we have to bear
But I know you can do it
I have faith in that
It doesn't even matter
Wherever I'm at
So always be happy
I'd like you to smile
It won't be so long
I'll be back in a while
So be happy and joyful
And keep your faith strong!
Soon I'll be home to say
"I Love You Mom."

Sindy Strickland
I STOOD HIGH ON A MOUNTAIN
I stood high on a mountain
And as I looked down,
I could see pain in the eyes of the people
In this large town.
The taking of innocent lives
By random disguise
From vehicles passing by.
Groups that claim to be superior in race
Long for attention in this vast place.
The Lord is our shepherd, we all do want
And long for recognition and attention
For just one moment.
Life is neither easy or sympathetic . . .
Use your time wisely, for when it is through
The Lord will judge and sentence you.
Babies sleep in mother's arms
Precious by birth
They can do no harm.

We are all molded by experiences
Some good, some bad.
Life is but a passing moment
And then you are dead.

Claire McGonigal
THE UNICORN

Angie, wish on a rainbow, ride on a cloud, take time to dream, and be happy.

A unicorn came out to-day
Before the mist had blown away
He pranced and gamboled through the trees
I tried to stifle back a sneeze

He looked up startled, quite surprised
Such trust and beauty in his eyes
How can a creature such as this
Be make-believe, only a myth

Pure white and slick, with flowing mane
Somehow it all seems such a shame
That ordinary folk can't see
Beyond their noses, such as we

His tail all fluffy, full and long
Blew out like some enchanted song
He chased a bird, then stopped to look
At woodland creatures by the brook

And then as quickly as he came
He seemed to disappear again
Where did he go, how far away
Would he come back again someday

Lisa Dane
SHERRY

In memory of Dad who died April 1, 1989.

Ah little one
with your long dark hair
and your big fringed eyes
blind and trusting to the bidden way
snuggled all unknowing in your gauzy robe
(stones go right through it)
the world never touches you
perceiving what you want to be
coloring your world with fantasy

Heidi Rain
TREE
You
on top of me
After making love
A tree
weighted down
By its own branches
leafy full
Abundant color
having form
and substance
Feel—
ing you inside of
over
pinned to me
so deep
This moment reaching past
exquisite
Into floating lightness
Seems
to be
Beyond this bed, this earth,
you, me
Our love: a rooting tree.

Janet Lynn Posey
cats

I dedicate "cats" to the rulers of my household—Sushi, Tapestry, and Quasar.

thieves all slinking
on silent paws
eyes flash light
toward the nest
stalking young prey
with claws that bite
tail snaking behind
parents scream for
children lost

Michelle Johnston
HELP!
Alcoholism is a pit,
and alcohol is the dirt that fills it up
A beautiful day can dissipate
into a blurry fog
when those numbing juices
touch my lips
and force me inside again.
With the bottle in one hand,
and that glass in the other,
the pit keeps getting deeper, darker
Filling it, also, are tears
tears of mine, and of loved ones,
that remember me
from before I fell down here
Can't you see my eyes, calling out for help
I'm down in this pit, don't forget
I'm in here
Let the light of day seep in, soon
and fill me with a smile of warmth
Let it crack through my glass
and melt the ice cubes into water
For I am thirsty for love and life,
not this slow death,
that Alcoholism is inviting me to.

Henri Zogaib
OLIVES ARE MY HYMNS
How long ago?
I no more remember.
But I do remember that
I no more remember
And that
I no more want to remember.

Blessed Thou art
In the Book of the new Genesis :
" . . . And there was a flood
—What was before was not—
So, out of the ship,
Thou hast risen
—Title of my Life—
And Noah of the new Testament
Rested in his shade . . . ".

Thou stand'st
—For Thou art the beginning—
At the opening of my Time
And at its unend
—For Thou art an infinitum—.

Pick me in the orchards of Thine Peace :
Olives are my Hymns.
Draw me the sign of Faith
On the cross of Thine Content.
Then make me Thine People
Rising from an emptied memory.

Annie H Graef
FLIGHT
At break of day
They come—
Dipping, swooping, wheeling their way
Across the sun.

All white; undersides, wing-tips of gray,
they
Are scavengers, well-adapted,
with hooked beaks and small webbed feet
To the tidbits the tide brings in.

Swarming, their raucous cries are heard;
And then as one, as though on cue
Each bird
Takes flight into the blue.

Larinae,
Sub-family of the genus sterna,
Are cousins to the tern-A
Larinae Pinnae!

Kathy Watt
THE ROSE
The dew gently baths the bud
In the wild rose bush
Making it shine
So lovely to sight

Knowing that someone had a special
Place for her in their heart
The rose slowly opens up

Desirous of all who took
Time to look

Samantha Ann Jenkins
THE LAST BRIGADE
A plan is made for the last brigade
There is no time to cry
People lost in conscious thought
There is no reason why
Carry through the daily due
Each second past is lost
As if in dream the people scream
They've won at such a cost
The land is laid a country made
New but oh how used
People scurry in the fury
Of ones down and abused
People walking barely talking
All are in a trance
The dream was lost at such a cost
Ne'er again to dance

Helen J Wilbur
A TEST FOR GROWING

I wish to dedicate this poem to my beloved family and friends and to whoever may benefit by it. God Bless you all.

Through the eyes of Compassion,
Love, and just Knowing,
A vale of tears;
The search for the human soul in its flight
To Heaven, to find
The silver shining behind
The dark of night;

Through the suffering that Life, in living,
Teaches Man
Of its Eternal Spiritual Plan;
These are the things, O Lord, with which You test our Growing.

Joys in the warmth of the Sun, the vital struggle for Understanding,
Then, too, the clouds in the sky;

We wonder—Why?—
The clap of thunder,
The snap of lightning,
That strikes a mortal blow at anything in its path
Regardless of the aftermath;

The crawling things and birds that fly
And here we are!
We wonder—Why?—
These are the things, O Lord, with which You test our Growing.

Mother and Father

Carol R Trevisan
TO MY MOTHER AND FATHER

This poem was written specially for my mother and father on their 42nd anniversary.

Love is never having to say you're sorry.
Love goes up, down to the right to the left,
Love has no reasons.
Love is Let—Our—Visions—Escape,
Love today, true love, is fantasy.
Love is most powerful a feeling,
Love is most powerful a vice.
Love can make bad, good; ugly, beautiful; sad, happy.
What is more important than LOVE,
God doesn't know that.
Love is acceptance, understanding and a component in Faith.

Virginia L Rayman
A SPIRITUAL RESPONSE TO SAVE

The morning your words entered my mind and stirred my heart. When I heard you say I am going out to Bethany and I'll be back about noon.

My heart felt hunger in your soul and I could hear you crying in the wilderness, and I didn't want you lost.

I responded by buying sweet rolls for all of you to share with coffee, this is when Len asked Mary Ann to call you back.

The next time I saw you there was anger in your voice, when I heard you say I'll be here now.

The day I gave the girls their choice of butterflies and gave you one for your wife, there was light and happiness in this day for me.

The best was when I gave you the poem I had written and you reached out and hugged me. I felt a touch of tender warmth and love that I hadn't known for 30 years from a man.

Then one day by the touch of our arms as we passed at close range sparks flew from static and I saw special power in us.

Each of these signs seemed to be saying within me be still and know that instant feelings of renewed spiritual life.

As therapy continued and your kind voice caused me to have faith and trust in you.

Then you called my doctor and asked how far you could go with therapy on my arm. He told you to go for it.

Well I was in prison in my own body until you went invisible and caused me to be open in my inner feelings.

Everytime you gave me a hug it was what I needed most and nobody else had even asked or tried.

Now you see it doesn't take sex to lift or help a person who is human. Just kindness and understanding with common sense.

I never went out of control and I hope there wasn't unwanted pain endured in your body by your perfect self control.

But my problem is I have this feeling for love greater everyday and time is growing shorter all the time for me. With nights are very long and lonely.

You've done a great job and I love you for doing this beautiful thing for me. For you went above and beyond human power to bring about life in the spirit of God.

The day I put my hands on your shoulder and looked into your eyes, I took the yoke of Jesus upon me that moment. Then I felt the Lord touch me and a radiant glow came over me, and you asked "How did you get beautiful"? I answered that is how God made me. You said that's right. This was a spirit blessed day in faith for me 1988.

May God always be gentle and bless you for responding in his behalf to save another human life from death of unworthiness. A-men.

Debra Herring
THE SMILE OF LOVE

To Hassan Babollah You will always remain in my heart.

My life was once so filled, so happy.
At that time I couldn't believe it was true.
You made me look at the world with a smile.
Always happy through bad and good.
Now that you're gone my life is so shattered,
I pick myself up but still I fall.
How can a man make such a difference?
How can a man make life so complete?
I look at your picture and the memories flow.
I look at your picture and I remember the smile.
THE SMILE, I remember is what made it so.
When you were here my heart had a smile.
Now that you're gone my heart has a frown.
I try to remember, a frown is a smile turned upside down.
I try to remember, it's hopeless though.
The smile you gave me was LOVE, and that's the best smile I know.

Mary Veronica Wright
QUESTION

Where does love go
When it dies—
Is that what we hear
In the sobbing brook
As it wakens every Spring?

Is that what we see
In the bleeding heart
Drooping against Summer's Breast?

Is that what we feel
Like hot, wet tears
From a rain-filled Autumn Sky?

Is that what we touch
On a Winter's dawn when
A dying star is half
A heart-break
Away?

Erika Nolan
I CLOSE MY EYES

To Stanley, a very special and much loved friend.

I close my eyes
And envision a stranger,
A face of parchment and ink.
Your tender and unique ways
Flow softly my way, through words,
Gently washing over my heart
With love, warmth, and sincerity.
You reach out to me when
I need gentle encouragement
Or an understanding ear.
Living in separate worlds,
Miles between us, only
Words away,
I close my eyes and
Think of you . . .
My friend.

A R Harrison
UNTITLED

You hold me prisoner in a cell
without walls.
No bars—No gate

—No Key—

Once inside my cell,
I gave my soul to 'kept safe,
And I fear
To never have it again.
It will be safe with you, will it?
For freely I gave,
And it is no longer mine.

There is a prison around my cell,
With walls of my own making.
They keep you out
And lock me in

—With No Key—

The walls have no windows
You can't look in
And for me to see out,
I must climb to see over them,
And I always fall when I look down.

They say there are doors in my walls,
That are invisible to me.
I search vainly, to never see.

Is there a key to my Prison,
My cell without wall?

—Where is it—
—Who has it—

Not You

For you too are a Prisoner,
Trapped within my Heart . . .

—Was not the trade fair?—

Mark H Wilson
CHANNEL FEVER

To the brotherhood of men known as the Merchant Marine. The most misunderstood people on the face of the earth.

So now we've been at sea for fourteen days
Fourteen days ago home seemed a long long way.
But, tomorrow all's forgotten as we sail into the Chesapeake bay.

Your mind begins to tingle. Your body becomes aroused.
Your face takes on a long ago smile.
Now it's only a matter of a few miles.

With days at sea that seem endless at times
You see Virginia coast, you know it is all now behind.
It's time to go home, it's time to unwind.

It's a feeling you just can't describe
No matter how hard you try.

It's this night before.
You stay up and pace the floor.
Your mind won't let you sleep.
It's so eager.
It's this feeling sailors call
Channel fever.

Nancy Anne Chiffolo

Nancy Anne Chiffolo
QUESTIONING—THE ACCEPTANCE

To one snowflake in the sky:
When you float gracefully toward the ground beneath you,
Are you choosing your own destiny?
Or has fate
Brought you together with other snowflakes
to decorate this pine tree,
As a lace scarf beautifies a silk dress.

To my snowflake now settled in this picture before me:
I hope you are living your life as you desire.

Sarah
SOMETIMES

When your absence seems overpowering,
I remember
When I camped on a shelf of cliff
Above the water
And rested on the ground
Restless and bone weary.
The dark came and all that was left
Was the sea and the stars
And the feel of the earth.
Then I hear your words dear heart

And my soul bursts with applause
Resounded only by the waves.
I'd always felt drawn to you,
Your simplicity, your gentleness,
Your love of life, you whom
I cannot take for granted
In the quiet corners of my life,
Like a sun washed cliff
Or a stray scent of heather.
Where only you and I dare to be together
In the silence of lonely windswept places.

Allen Tidwell
YOUR LITTLE WINDOW
Looking out on the world
You see everything,
And when the sun goes down
The night takes over until the very next day.

You sit at home in your little room
Watching people live and die,
Looking out your little window
Just waiting out your time.

You see the good and bad which mess up your mind
Yet, you sit at your little window each and every day,
And you think that it's just fine.

Just looking out your little window
Waiting out your time.

Ken McKinnon Jr
MOM MY MOM

I dedicate this poem to my son Ken Jr. in his memory as he wrote it to me in 1978, on Mother's Day. May your music be sung by angels my son.

I'll love you on and on.
The sun will never shine on earth
like it has since your very birth
and however long or short the day
or far from your side I will stray
I'll never forget that warm face.
Mom Oh Mom
I see you every dawn
and never forget what you said
to me such a long time ago:
To be myself and make my decisions
to understand what is in my vision
free from libertines unjustly convictions
and be a man wherever I go.
Mom Oh Mom
I'll love you forever long.
No one can tell me what I think
of you for I have my own thoughts in ink
And forever as there is time,
Your memory will be etched upon my mind.
Please accept these short words
from someone who is trying to
be true. I love you.

Kenny

Robert Pettit
MY SURVIVAL
Serving the sentence in the purgatory of my existence,
I was suffering through my anguish and despair
And reached out and you were there.
Before I met you, I was like a child without a toy.
Or a friend to play with.
I was hollow. Alone.
Then you came into my life,
And you became it.
You were the missing piece to the puzzle of my soul.
You were the blood that coursed through my veins,
The oxygen I breathed,
And the nourishment I needed to survive.
My heart beat only for you.
You were the heart that beat within my chest.
Now my heart beats no more.
Once again I find myself like a child.

Carole Markham Pearce
WINDS
January wind is harsh.
It blows across the fields and marsh.
Its mournful howl won't go unheard
By man or estuary bird.

February wind is cruel.
Its hungry soul devours the fuel
Of mankind's hearth and fireside.
It chills the bone; It frosts the hide.

The March wind yet still puts to shame
All wonders of the prior game.
It frees the spirit; plants the seed
Of Earth's abundant hunger need.

So let the winter's winds rage on.
Set them free to chill the dawn.
And when they've finished, spring will see
The flowers of tranquility.

Donna Gill Burke
SOMEDAY
Someday I'll take a walk away
from the place where I know you stay.
I'll take along some fairy tale
and play the games we know so well.
But until I see inside of you—
I'll stay and make my dreams come true.

Someday I'll sail around the world
and watch the flags of love unfurl
and watch my feet sink into sand,
Somewhere on an island when I land.
But until I do, I'll stay awhile—
and wonder what's happening behind your smile.

Someday the world of you I know
will fall apart and I will go
toward my ever-shining star,
back to the place where my dreams are.
But until I do, please take my hand—
and, I'll take away your worries if I can.

Someday the rain will come down white
and though the ice will drown the night;
I'll not replace my thoughts of you
with thoughts I know will make you blue.
But until I do leave, I'll stay and try—
to map the hidden country behind your eyes.

Kathleen Frances Coelho
A PARENTS' JOB IS QUITE HARD

For Mom & Poppy. I love you as dearest friends and mentors as well as my loving parents. Thank you for everything. Kath

Since the day that I was born, they were by my side
The love and learning they brought froth kept me satisfied
When I was just a tiny tot, they taught me all about God
Now I'd like to say 'thanks a lot' a parent's job is quite hard.

A little girl with mischievous pranks helped turn their heads to gray
But you took it in stride and not one time did you ever turn away
With your love I learned about people's rights and standing up for my own
I say my thanks to the Lord each night for the people he put in our home.

The years have flown since my yesterday world, sometimes life may keep us apart
The memories flourish, the love still remains, forever, so deep in my heart
When I remember all that we've shared and the hard times we always got through
I know that I have been truly blessed with a father and mother like you.

John Tate
TIME ESTEEMS LOVE
Before there was time or space
I knew your face.
Now that I have found you. I will spread my love over you like the blue that colors the sky.
I will make the design for the architecture of your mind.

Like rare vintage wine, we will experience love one sip at a time.
And when we have grown old and time has taken its toll.
We will turn to each other with love only we possess, and gracefully nod yes.

Roger M Meska
THE HUMAN MIND
From earth's beginning, and through the ages
All the prophets and the sages
Nor anyone else in all mankind
Has figured out the human mind.

Why are our thoughts forever changing
Our moods, from love to hate are ranging?
How do we recall memories of the distant past
But then can't remember the night before last?

Why do we like the things that we do
But can't see the other guys point of view?
The depth of the mind is so immense
From ignorance to plain common sense.

But there is still hope before it's too late,
Away for all men to get rid of their hate
To exchange it all for kindness and love,
God has the answer in heaven above.

Marcia Wilson Hicks
WHY DO I CLOSE MY DOORS?
Why do I close my doors? And why must you?
Come into me
Find me . . . Share me
Know my heart, my very soul.
And then, perhaps, I can know yours.

There is beauty inside, and terrible ugliness too
There are tiny cramped closets
Wide sparkling windows
Drawers of fear, hearths of love

I lock so much behind my doors
Come into me
Find me . . . Share me
Know my heart, my very soul
And then, perhaps, I can know yours.

Gerald Bart Edwards
WHAT IF

To Doris, My greatest love and inspiration. She made love, live and laugh. Her patience, tolerance, compassion and understanding taught me to look within, and believe.

What if we were to forget the quarrels
And start as friends.
What if the mistakes were overlooked
And we tried again.
What if those negative thoughts were reversed
And empathy considered.
What if bigotry did not exist
And we were truly brothers.
What if we walked in others shoes
And saw what others see.
What if all this did happen
How beautiful life would be.

Dionne N Dames
TWO HEARTS
Two hearts now beat as one.
We've found love that's new.
There is burning deep inside.
As one our spirit grew.

We found romance in the night.
We laid among the stars.
We traveled in time and in space.
We traveled to Venus and Mars.

Two hearts now beat as one.
The love we cannot explain.
We feel the emotion that runs deep,
Pure, true and clean.

Two hearts now beat as one.
It feels so good and grand.
You don't know how I felt
When you asked to take my hand!

Two hearts that beat as one,
Now I can say you're all mine.
Our love is now forever joined
We've stood the test of time.

Two hearts now beat as one.
We are one of a kind.
Two hearts, two of a kind—
We're the best team you'll ever find.

Evelyn M Wehrmeister (Miss)
I SHALL TRY

Dedicated to Beverly

I shall try to do tomorrow
What I didn't get done, today.
With a patch of sun on my window sill,
I know I will find the way.

The letter I never answered,
The friend I didn't call,
A simple smile, a cheery hello,
Oh yes, I shall do it all.

And when I come to the end of the road,
And go to that home in the sky,
Let it be said in my epitaph,
"She certainly gave it a try."

Janice L Farnsworth
REFLECTIONS OF REGRETS

In memory of my son—Greg killed in an auto accident—Jan. 2, 1987.

Marvel not, O ominous clouds,
Peeping sun,
Or shadowy shrouds,
Sandy roads,
And shimmering lake
In your somberness
Shall I partake ?

Will worry and fear
Teach me naught ?
For inner peace
My soul has sought.
Will hope embrace
A new retreat
From vain philosophies
And youthful deceit ?

Our destiny is Wisdom's child,
Justified by fate beguiled;
So guide My feet
To warm content
For wilder years that
I have spent.

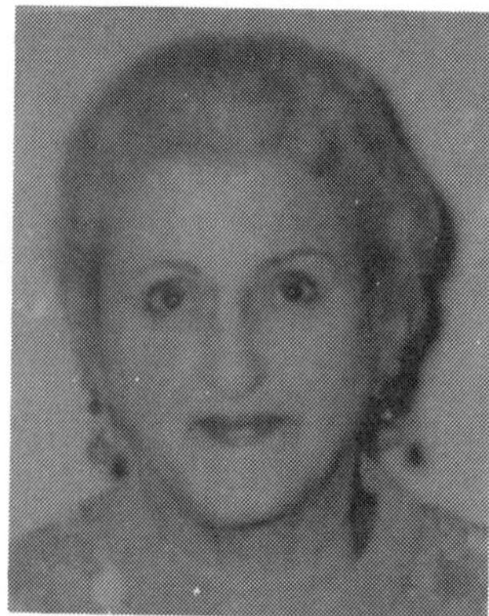

Pegge Fitz-Gibbons

Pegge Fitz-Gibbons
GAMBLER

To my old friends

Toss in your hand
Fling the cards
A gypsy's smoke swirls
To the beckoning stars

Take the dark path
Still is the night
The moon is mocking
Too eerily bright

You simple femme
At least be gay
You tossed a king
To meet a knave

Elsa Hertel Mills
WE HAVE A LITTLE COTTAGE

We have a little cottage
On the outskirts of the town
And in our backyard garden
The land slopes gently down.

In this little garden
Are vegetables and flowers
And now we hope and pray
For warm and gently showers.

So when my cares and worries
Just seem too much to bear
I seek solace in my garden
And ease my troubles there.

Folks, in passing, often say
Why do you work so much?
But they, not having gardens
Know not, earth's soothing touch.

Michael Shiflet
THE NEWBORN

A virgin spring
A newborn dream
The time of life
With winter to bring
The fold of joy
Comes with the snow
Comes with the sun
Another will flow
Crossings of blood
With ties of love
Will anyone dream
Can the time be seen
When the winds and the seas
Become a part of thee
And the life of our times
Has a future indeed

Andrew Clark
SUNRISE, SUNSET

The sun rises on a bitter man lying dormant in a state of numb confusion. A one man revolution turned inward, and now, has the time come to abandon all hope?
A faint voice still stirring in the far corners of his mind urged him on.
But alas, the struggle was over, and the end had come, just as always, for men who seek their pot of gold in the affairs of men.
And time was out of time, and love out of love, and the sun set on a lone soul and an iron heart, as he raised his glass in a toast to eternity wasted and happiness untasted, and closed his eyes to the light,
and slept,
forever.

Alissa Macchia
BLIND DATE

To my mother; who has never let me know what life would be like without constant love and friendship.

Face to face we still shall meet
Anticipation ending
Nerves full in tact
Imagination becoming reality

Where this new meeting will take us
I cannot know
But I have known love; been warmed by friendship
And that sole fact will keep me searching

For you have already given to me
A most important experience
The chance to first meet you
Without eyes

More people should meet
Via telephone
Putting less worth on physical attributes
Gaining sight of the inner person

Though I have yet to physically see you
I've already come to like you
And if nothing else
I know the value of a friend

Charles L Smith
TO JEANNE, MY FIRST VALENTINE

It was many, many years ago
When my first tow-head was one;
I sent her a very first valentine
And knew that my fun had begun.
For she looked every year thereafter
For something funny and sweet:
From a comic guy—her Valentine.
Who worshipped at her feet.
And as she grew and understood,
That it was a secret game,
She played her part quite perfectly,
Never mentioning her Valentine's name.
Yes, you were that little Valentine,
A long, long time ago;
It was I sent you cards and lollipops
From whom, you did not know?
And, although you've grown up
And claim a brilliant mind;
I'll have you know I still do claim
You as my Valentine!

Eleanor R Wright
A VISIT TO GRANDMA

To our Grandchildren Melissa and Joseph, parents Deborah and Joseph Belvedere. In memory of our son Ray, a Medic in Viet Nam and served as Bush Pilot in Surname, New Guinea, Guatemala, Honduras and Alaska. He loved poetry.

Melissa asked her mom if they could go to Grandma's for a visit;
Mama said of course you can but oh—just wait a minute.
So Missy packed her suitcase and one for Joseph too;
Beside their usual clothes, there were the stuffed animals too.
Now, Missy packed her favorite "blue velure"
The pride of all her shirts, but saddened by the stain it bore—
She brought it to me and softly asked if I would remove the stain;
For mama had told her not to fret, Grandma would make it like new again.
Joseph packed his little "Pooh Bear," the ears had been chewed mighty thin;
He had bitten the ears when cutting his teeth
And cuddled it whenever put to bed.
Little did he realize that he would never see it again;
It had become quite ragged but this he didn't mind;
Mom and dad searched and searched to find another kind.
They chose "Tenderheart Care Bear"
Because the bear cares about a "child's feelings."

Grace Pearl Goodrum
LITTLE RED BIRD

This poem is dedicated to my son, Conard H. Goodrum.

Come little Red Bird waft your song on the breeze,
Sing from the windmill, and the tallest trees.
If you have a song, then sing it for me.
I will open my window and listen for thee.

You may fly to the east, you may fly to the west,
You may sing the song that you love the best.
You need fear no harm, I will hear your call,
Even the sparrow, Red Bird and all.

Sing little Red Bird, the whole long day.
Give each note a twirl and then, a gentle sway.
There is music in your singing, the notes swell with pride,
As they sink into my heart and there abide.

While I sit by my window and listen to your call,
Sing little Red Bird, sing for us all.
Let your notes swell gently until I hear your call.
Come, come little Red Bird, sing your song for all.

Andi (Adrienne L) Troast
MAN'S LIFE

For my father, Arthur Shepstone, for the love and affection he has shown myself and his grandsons, Shawn and Timothy and great granddaughters, Kyra and Kayla.

Man alone is laid to rest.
He who once lay upon his mother's breast.
The years have flown, so quickly by.
And the spark of light has reached its nigh.

Did his life mean anything?
As he himself searched in his Spring.
His Summer was a joyous bout.
Though his loves and his friendships were with doubt.
His Fall in life withered by fast.
In his Winter, he reminisced his past.

Now his time has come and gone so quick.
His whole life's style he did not pick
But gone it has and not in vain.
For he has left us with his name.

Sandra Cagle
THE RAPE OF THE ROSE

For all the emotionally and physically abused children . . . May God bless you.

Through the detestable darkness
The midnight rose she blooms;
Much too beautiful and perfect
To be born amid such gloom.

The wind blowing fiercely
Ripped savagely at her heart;
Her petals stripped without mercy
The bitter cold tearing her apart.

Then without pity or compassion
Fate dealt its final blow;
The cunning and the wicked
Raped her of her tiny soul.

Just a wilted and broken child
Desecrated in the prime of youth;
Dead before she ever lived
How sad sometimes the truth.

And slowly as the mourning sun
Dawned across the skies;
It came to pay its last respects
To where this shattered beauty lies . . .
. . . And none heard her cries.

Susan Phelan
LAST NIGHT I DREAMED OF LIVING ON A SUMMER AFTERNOON

This poem is dedicated to my love, for he inspires me in all I do.

Last night I dreamed of living on a summer afternoon.
I saw myself quite clearly,
it was sometime late in June.

My love and I were sitting midst the pebbles on the beach,
and though the clouds were miles away
I felt that I could reach,

Right up to them and touch them floating softly in the sky.
And we would travel all the stars this man, my love and I.

We'd travel to the milky way, then on up to the sun.
And we would see a million miles before this task was done.

Then we'd return both weary at our journey's end
and we would talk of all we'd seen.
Me and my best friend.

For he inspires me to write these words and so much more,
and I have never known someone who'd done this thing before.

And someday we would sit again, a lovely day in June,
and share our thoughts, our dreams, upon a summer afternoon.

Jane Y Freeling

Jane Y Freeling
"WE ARE" EQUAL
In this world, we all are equal
In our hearts, we know the truth
Let our minds speak from our hearts,
To the old and to the youth.

We live as one great family
To fulfill our life on earth
We talk, and sing, and make our plans
From the beginning of our birth.

To know one's inner feelings
Is to understand one's deepest thoughts,
Forgiveness, sincerity, love and understanding,
Are qualities that cannot be bought.

Elizabeth L Rossell
AFTERMATH
Isn't it sad that you and I must now live far apart,
because a few words left unsaid, hid pain in the deepest heart.
And now in coming twilight years, I know what we have lost and try to find some solace in the memories that we tossed.
The smiles of new lives just begun, are dimmed by held back tears and in the knowing we can't share those smiles and hugs and years.
Years of children growing, laughing, loving like our own,
Years of watching lives unfold from seeds of caring sown.
And though it's sad that we can't share these fruits of labor spent, to look in tiny eyes and see us both, can bring content.

Kelley L Quaid
I LOOK AT YOU

This poem is for the future, God bless the power of love.

I look at you
and I see a man
With all the beauty
of a single red rose
You can't fool me
I know the good inside of you
It's like an angel
whose wings flutter about
wildly
fighting for your soul
pushing into your heart
to find the love
you are
so capable of giving
I've felt that love
it's embraced me
it captured my heart
and my soul
Your love is strong
with the strength of ten men
And your smile
it warms my heart
like a fire fading in the night
the glow of the dying embers
comes shining through the darkness
like our love
will come shining through this
darkness . . .

Dixie Kearley
SILENCE

To David

Walking the shore in the wilderness,
No sound emerges—recognizable.
Acutely we strain our ears.
We hear—a ripple of water bathing stones,
A flutter of wings,
A shift of the breeze through the trees.

The distinct sound of a loon,
Becomes integrated into being.
Bringing smiles all around.

We began to fear our speech.
Communication seems infantile.
Needless—against this silence of life.

Christine Congleton
TO YOU

With all my love this is dedicated to Ron C. (Heritage Ranch) I love you and always will Babe, so . . . "To you," Sweet Dreams . . . . . Chris C.

To you,
Because of you; love slides,
In my heart,
Giving of priceless moments,
Looked in carrousels;
For which time holds no place,
I took the needs of one
and made the sorrows of two.
So to you, your everlasting caring,
Most of all, for your love,
That gives of hopes and makes
dreams so sweet . . . . . .
For you, an open window,
Letting others taste, that,
That we've shared, for I share you,
This is to you, sweet dreams . . . .
My love for always,
I love you ageless as one.

Suzanne Quintela
BLEEDING HEART

Dedicated to my first true love, Thomas Robert Ernsberger II, I'll never forget our dreams and promises.

'Tis but a shadow within the mist
Of a warm dream, once glowing.
The love so carefully tucked away,
So that it won't be showing.

'Tis but a dagger in the back
Of a young maiden knowing,
Once she had the precious kiss
That you were once bestowing.

'Tis but a soft light,
In the air brightly shining.
Now in the eclipse of noon,
A new day now residing.

'Tis but a drapery of scarlet red,
From a window hanging.
Just a clock upon the wall,
A hammer, relentlessly banging.

'Tis but a slash within my heart,
That seems forever bleeding.
A solemn thought within the mind,
Hand in hand, once you were leading.

Elaine M Gedrich
MY HOPE

To my husband, Kevin. Thank you for your everlasting love and endurance these past twenty-three years.

Love me
For being me;
Cherish me for myself
Don't get blinded by worldly wealth.

Pray for God's love, hope, and understanding
They are all ever demanding.
Achieve health, happiness and all of this
And you will have eternal bliss.

For what greater joy can there be
Than I to have you and you to have me.
Honey, I love you, I like you, you are good;
Hold me, like me too, as a friend if you could.

For all I want is for us to have a happy and peaceful life,
With you as my husband and me as your wife.
Let us start once again, me and you as one,
For as we stand now, I feel empty and lonely without you.

I want us to be re-united and special to each other,
Because for me there can be no other.
Can this dream of mine come true
That I can be the girl for you?

Help us to re-capture what we had
For sweetheart, was it always that bad?
Can you overcome my imperfections and find warmth in your heart,
So forever more we can be joined as one and not drift apart?
Will you take my hand and share a life with me,
Will you also laugh, struggle and cry with me?
Please do not laugh at all of this
Because for me this would be bliss!

Fred T Tracy
THE TEACHER

This poem is dedicated to Mr. Marc Segall, a most outstanding teacher.

Once upon a time in God's fair land
There was a fellow with only one hand.

And the God who made him was so wise
To also give him very poor eyes.

But as he read so very slow
If he sought, God would show

Him the truly fulfilling way to live
By learning more and more how to serve and give.

Now God's ways are high—who can know
How he will show this fellow which way to go?

Well, there came a teacher with very good eyes
Who reads many books and is famed for being wise.

Who showed this fellow which path to take,
And helped him to see what decisions to make.

And what would this fellow say to this teacher so wise?
Thank you very much for being my eyes!

Jodi Garcia
THE LONG RIDE HOME

To: Alan Garcia, my father, my friend, my hero. Love, Jodi

I was riding home today
watching everything:
new life is born
in every flower,
every tree.
The yellows and grays
have been bathed
into green and blue.

The thick cold plate
is now laughing and giggling,
feeding its friends.
The day is a yawn and a stretch up:
Yet there are things dying,
like my sad thoughts, that have lived
all winter long.

Jocelyn Hill
STOLEN BUT UNWANTED LOVE!

This poem is for Brian Keith Glunt the only one I will ever LOVE!

A tear drop is a sign of what I feel
Separating fake from real

My love is shed in one single tear
Many other feelings from anger to fear

This feeling is unable to explain
How much it hurts, the feeling of pain

I wonder when this tearing will stop
When will I finally forget you and give up?

I do realize that I never will reasive
The love and care it will remain desive

We will never have our chance
You'll never give me even a glance

But I do understand I'm not for you
and I'll just keep dreaming, that's all
I can do

But the thing that hurts so much
Is that I know I'll never feel your
touch

This will not be the first time
But to secretly love someone is no
crime

So, I will wallow in sorrow all alone
While wondering why I have a heart
of stone.

Annelise Bue
THE WALL BEHIND ME

To my grandparents, Dave & Jennie Wallace, with thanks.

I turn my head
ever so slowly
To take a glimpse
behind me
At my past
The mistakes I've made
Unchangeable
like the seasons
like time itself
for eternity
like a wall behind me
that I can't tear down
no matter how strong I am
that I can't rebuild
no matter how hard I try
brick by brick
with the knowledge
I've acquired
slowly
through the years

Valentina M Panzone

Valentina M Panzone
READING A POEM

This poem is dedicated to my brother, Daniel B. Iannamico. When I was a child, he would compose special little poems for me to enjoy. He instilled in me the love for poetry.

Reading a poem is like having a
friend at your side
Comforting you with friendship
words—opening your world
a-wide

Reading a poem is like feeling a
mother's comforting arms
Soothing words that bathe you—
shouting out any harms

Reading a poem each day to a child
held dear
Enriches his vocabulary for all to
hear

Reading a poem to a senior citizen—
hold their hand in yours
Takes them to a journey of visions—
to many never-ending tours

Reading a poem to a loved one—
giving memories for future years
Bond the two of you forever—
through happiness and tears

Reading a poem to someone that
lends an interesting ear
Fills the room with playful words—
with happiness and cheer

Reading a poem is like traveling to
far off places with scenes
Enriching your imagination—way
beyond your dreams

Reading a poem brings comfort—
when your world falls apart
Let yourself read "Out Loud"
Then listen while your problems
depart

Reading a poem develops your self-
esteem
Secures you in conversation
With a word-bank to express your
dreams

Catherine Gwen Laws
A PILGRIMAGE ON FOOT

First, to Our Lord Jesus Christ the King: may He reign in our hearts forever! Then, to my beloved Mom, who led me to love the beauty and truth of our Catholic heritage, and who shares that love with me.

Dennis Larkin took a walk
From Schesslitz, south to Rome.
No mere tourist's stroll he took
So far away from home.

'Twas a pilgrimage, for sure,
In grand old Catholic style;
In fulfillment of his vow
He tramped those weary miles.

Endless roadways, blistered feet,
The Alps, Venetian plain,
Sweltering heat, and aching joints,
The Dolomites, chill rain:

All of this he overcame
When he set out to see
In his Roman home the head
Of Christianity.

Near eight hundred miles he
marched
In thankfulness to pay
Debt of gratitude to God,—
A walk on pilgrim's way.

Mary-Jo Collopy
SOJOURN

A gift to Mark, whose own special Poetry speaks volumes: Thank you for the loving inspiration!

Whispering his name dispels the
ruminations of her sometimes
troubled soul.
And when she awakens in the
grey morning with his leg
pressed against hers,
The miseries of the real world
fade and blur.
She can keep the demons at bay
this way—
In the place where his body and
hers meet.
His uncommon love has filled a
hollow in her life,
just as his head had rested in
the hollow of her pillow.

She doesn't want promises yet.
It has taken her eons to know
herself—
How can she ever expect to know
him?
A volcano is erupting beneath her
skin.
And molten emotion is breaking
her into tinier, more complete
interlocking fragments of her
essence.
When the dust has settled,
The configuration of her
landscape will have shifted to
an unrecognizable shape.
Warning: We are entering
unchartered territory.

Her eyes are calm—
Her walk is slow and unhurried
as she stares sightlessly beyond
the planet.
This woman with a secret is a
mere brush of movement in her
nondescript persona.
But—she is everything to
someone.
And nothing to everyone else.

Beverly Baggett Coleman
COMPANION

To Polly, my best friend; for giving me thoughts, ideas, inspiration and friendship.

On some desolate plain in my mind;
One lone red rose you will find.
Through the void darkness of my
head;
One drop of rain will be shed.
In the density of the sand;
I search for a brighter land.
My mind is like a desert of waste;
Empty by a windy gust of chaste.
One lone figure stands erect in the
sand;
Meekly extending one open hand.
A shadow, a person comes into the
light;
Suddenly the desert is remarkably
bright.
Now there are two standing arm in
arm;
Now there's love, nothing could do
any harm.

Dennis E Carroll
TO A MOONSET SUNDARK

To the survivors of malevolent acts

"Who won?" "Not you" with deep
seeded contempt
Been humiliated twice, maybe more
I don't remember
So full of excess, excellence and
packed with excelsior
Most of the time an obnoxious pain
in the butt
How in the hell did he know?
Or was that just the abusive nature of
flannel and
knives
Some people speak soft for the
simulated sincerity
And some cut the rhetoric and cut to
the bone
Still others never speak, just seethe
Eyes wide, eyes all iris, complete iris

Laura Granados
MEMORIES

To Ma and Pop whose love and caring will remain in my memories forever and a day . . . Laura

Hold onto the memories
They're all that you need
For memories are almost
As good as a seed
Planted with love
Handled with care
Some are to keep
And some are to share
So don't let the memories
Bring your heart pain
Go out and make new ones
They're never the same
Plant them in your mind
To have and to know
But whatever you do
Don't let them go

Pamela J Strecker
PATHS

I dedicate this poem to you, Carol. Without your support, this would not have been.

Many roads to choose on this path I
follow.
Some go far, others nowhere.
Sometimes too scared to follow one,
choosing another which is a deadend.

Many are paved smooth as silk, but
most are rocky and dirty.

Everyone's paths are different,
passing through or running parallel.
Never knowing when mine will curve
away.

Some have merge and may go
forever.
Bumps and turns we'll go it together.
Holding fast as we enter the rotary.

Dianna Smith
SHE CRIES FOR HELP . . .

To Stacey . . . who has always been there—I LOVE YOU! . . .

She cries for help—
Yet no one hears.
Not a smile is revealed—
Only tears.
A reflection of sadness
Upon her lonely heart.
Will these feelings diminish?
Will she fall apart?
Confusion and fear
In an empty soul,
What she needs is security
To make her life whole.

Garrett Eilenberg Jr
LONG BLUE NIGHT

Fog of mind blue of night
Lowers our rising visional blight

Perimeter swirling thoughts to be
born
Though knowledge acquired is
scattered and torn

Blanketing concrete black & white
dreams
Are shredded remains of colorful
schemes

Over cold numbered reality

Charles Kenneth Persons
TEACHER

Dedicated to a very special teacher, Frances Brabston, May 1988 Ken Persons

A teacher is someone important
A teacher is someone who can
A teacher is someone appointed by
God
To be the highest placed among man.

God made teachers to help His
children—
Children He loves very much—
A teacher gives a child tender care
And instruction, correction, and
such.

A teacher gives a child self-
discipline
And brings out the talent inside.
You'd be so amazed at what a teacher
can do

Your feelings, you could not hide.

Teachers don't get enough appreciation
For the good things they do for a
child.
They deserve big hugs, or pats on the
back,
For they've always been calm, never
wild.

Mrs Juanita May Hileman Leggett

Mrs Juanita May Hileman Leggett
AUTUMN

I wish to dedicate this poem to the following: Husband, Roy Leggett, son, Steven and wife, Michele, grandson, Johnathan, mother & daddy, John & Sophia Leeson Hileman, Elma, Wanda & Hedric Leggett, sister, & brothers; Velma, Alfred, Ralph, Ray, Marshall and Kenneth Hileman

A beautiful sight to behold indeed,
The red, yellow, green, and orange
leaves.
The trees are bidding the leaves
good-by,
Telling us that winter is nigh.

The morning air is brisque and cool,
As children hurry off to school.
It is harvest time; food gathered in,
Apples from the trees, potatoes in the
bin,

Squirrels are as busy as little bees,
Gathering nuts, and hiding them in
the trees.
The wood is stored for the winter
heat,
And baking in the fall is a real treat!

The raking of leaves is quite a chore,
The very next day there are always
more.
Children love raking leaves in the
sun,
They pile them high and have lots of
fun.

Autumn is a peaceful time of the
year,
All things are at rest, winter is near.
The seasons are wonderful! God
made them all,
But I especially am fond of Autumn
or fall.

Olga L Carhart
THOUGHTS
The sky, the sun, the stars above
To many mean a token of love,

How can an artist paint a hue?
To match the sky, so heavenly blue?

What light can surpass the sun
above?
Taken for granted, or is it love?

The stars that twinkle during the
night,
Are similar to a Christmas light.

These things I see in a state of awe . .
So perfectly created, without a flaw.

As I grow older, I truly see
These 'gifts' that are freely given to
me.

When I am lonely or feeling sad,
I look up above and can really be
glad,
To enjoy the treasures the blind
never had.

Melody Collins
FIRST LOVE
I always knew that you and I
would one day have to say good-bye,
I guess we're just too young to stay
in love.

Together so long, you taught me so
much,
The strength in our love, revealed in
our touch,
You've made me strong enough to
stand alone,
I cherished your heart as if it were
my own.

But still we're young; we need to be
free,
we're the best of friends: you're
always there for me,
And I for you, always and forever,
I know that in time, we'll be back
together.

So explore and have fun,
It's these times you'll treasure,
We had it all,
I'll always remember.

You filled a place in me,
like a hand does a glove,
So to me you'll always be,
My First Love.

Carol E Burdick
A MOTHER'S LAMENT
My precious daughter's small and
fair
With golden frost thru out her hair.
Her eyes of blue are dark with pain,
If only they would smile again!

The world's closed in on her, says
she;
No one understands, not even me.
She'll never trust or love again;
I've taken my love from her and ran;
Not once, but twice I broke her heart.
This pain is pulling us apart!

I love you, Daughter, please try to
see
This bond of love will always be.
Tomorrow will be a brighter day,
Trust me, my daughter, troubles fade
away.

I'm here to listen with advice to give,
But it's hard to remember, 'tis your
life to live.
Please forgive me all the ways I've
erred
And understand truly I've always
cared!

I love you, Daughter, and will
always be
Here for you, are you there for me?

Daniel H Hamman
AN EXPRESSION OF MY LOVE FOR YOU

To my loving wife who is always strong enough to carry on while I am away, these words mean the same when we are together as they do when we're apart. I love you.

Though miles lie between us
my love for you is strong,
and just because of my love
those miles aren't so long.

The weeks and months will pass,
my love for you will grow,
and one day, far at last,
my love for you I'll show.

So if you think I'll ever stop
just ask and you will see,
that on my list you're on top
and forever you're for me.

Judy A Esteb
SOUL LESS?

For Dartanian who knows. Romans 8:19, 20, 21.

Go softly with feet
So dainty and light.
You prowl every corner
That hides in the night.
The things that you see
Nobody will know,
With silence your motto
And secrets your goal.
A cat is a creature.
Some say has no soul.
But I dare you to tell him.
I dare you, you know!

Jackie Moyer
WITHOUT YOU

For Tommy, with all my love forever

Without you, life has no meaning
and without you there is no more
dreaming.
Without you, the sun shines no more
and without you, I cry behind closed
doors.
Without you, it just can't be.
I am without you . . . . . but not for
eternity.

Kenneth W Lanford Jr
THE CYCLE BEGINS IN THE MORNING

Dedicated to Tammie Songer for all her help.

The cycle begins in the morning,
And a cycle it does seem
With beauty found as nowhere else
But possibly in a dream.

First the birds begin to sing
A song that night has gone,
Or perhaps it is the voice of angels
Singing to praise the dawn.

The forest gradually comes to life
With the first rays of the sun
Holding fast the first true sign
The day has just begun.

But all too soon does the sun hang
low
And the shadows grow long and tall
The daytime creatures venture home
And nighttime starts to fall.

But when the howl of the wolves has
faded
And the owl recaptures sleep,
The birds will soon begin singing
again
And the cycle will be complete.

Hattie Calihan Taylor

Hattie Calihan Taylor
LIFE IS WORTH LIVING

To my husband Bob who has had such a beautiful attitude during a very trying time. He believes life is worth living! !

Life is worth living,
Look around and you'll see . .
What the mighty hand of God
Has done for you and me.

The stars twinkling in a velvet sky,
Snow falling softly to the ground:
The Beauty of a mountain high
Where peace and solitude are found.

The silvery mountain stream,
Winding its way to the river below;
Giving life to ferns and trees,
Helping the fish and animals to
grow.

Look at the beauty of a perfect rose,
Feel the joy of a warm embrace.
Walk in the hot sand by the sea,
And feel the warm sun on your face.

Yes Life is worth living,
There is beauty everywhere!
The Lord gave it all to us,
And it is ours to share!

Daniel C Sulikowski
OPENING UP
Look inside, I've found you
Now your door never closes,
Every day we spend together
Will be full of wine and roses

Wine is the flowing love
Which began from a seed,
From within your heart
In which we all need

Roses represent humanity
In which we are all a part,
And love conquers all
When it's from the heart.

Docie Keefe
GOODBYE SON

To Lib and Topper

We took a boy to college today
To be turned into a man
What happened to the time dear Lord
Please hold my shaking hand.

We left a boy at school today
The empty house is awesome
We planned for this so many years

Didn't know we'd be so
lonesome.

We left a boy at school today
But still the future's bright
A wife he'll find—then a baby boy
Lift our life to a greater height.

We left our son at school today
Now it could be a daughter
To have and hold, this child of his
I guess we'll place that order.

We left our son at school today
But we'll adjust alright
We'll find the need to grow closer
still
Yes, God, our future's bright.

Pamela Phaiah

WINTER COLD

Rainy days,
cold cold nights,
snowy grounds,
wanting go hold him tight.

Winds blow by,
chills run through,
on these cold winter days
feeling so blue;
wondering what he's thinking,
is it you?
When you look into the past
there is no clue.

We had everything from trust to
love,
you say to yourself as
walking you see a dove.
That dove's so peaceful so white and
bare,
to make a noise you do not dare.
You stop to watch as its sits there
alone,
we seem to have something
in common, something unknown!

Amanda Lynn Bird

MY VALENTINE

To my sister, Rikki, who inspired me to write poetry.

Be my valentine,
For now and forever.
For peace and love,
Has won us over.
You can be mine,
Any day and any time,
All day and all night,
The valentine love
Is at its might.

Evanne Marie Christian

SUNDAY AFTERNOON

The world through the window
Resembles an old yellow newspaper;
And the mantle clock ticks slowly—
While its hands move not at all.
The music from the phonograph
Just whines and drones
In a melody quite unfamiliar and
monotone.
This atmosphere seems filled with
cotton gauze;
And I lose the strength I need to face
tomorrow.
I am sitting in the porch swing,
seeing nothing.
You hold my hand, and together we
await
Another Sunday evening, weakly
smiling.
I see myself reflected in your eyes—
A lady dressed in flowing lilac lace.
And in my eyes, your armour is
untarnished.
We see ourselves against this pale
day and know
From some late summer, memories
can come.
We are simply people from another
time—
Waiting for our time to come again.
Remain still.
Do not disturb this fading photo-
graph.
Let the sunset fall upon us with the
lightness of a whisper.

Mary Helen Miles-Sheppard

Mary Helen Miles-Sheppard

A PERFECT FRIEND

Dedicated to My Sister in Christ, Cornelia (Nunnie) Powell McRae

A friend so great, a friend so true,
A friend that was always there for
you.

Through the longest day, or darkest
night,
This friend could always make things
right.

And when you were down or sad,
She would always make you glad.

Faithfully we did abide,
My dear friend and I, side-by-side.

With a mind so strong, and a pure
heart of gold,
I need not tell you, what a precious
soul.

We shared our laughter, we shared
our cares,
But most of all, we shared our
prayers.

All of the heartaches, the tears and
woes,
We knew so well, would soon be
o'er.

With a glance back into the past,
I cry—home with Jesus—free at last.

Drucilla Duff

MEMORIES

Memories are the one thing,
that you can't take from me.
Without these precious memories,
I wonder what my life would be?

That awful hurt has gone now,
just a dull ache remains.
When someone forgets about us,
and mentions your name.

I thought that I would surely die,
from all the hurt and pain.
When you said you didn't really love
me,
and didn't want to remain.

But, I've learned to live on
memories,
of the few months that we shared.
When you were eager to show
the whole wide world
just how much you cared.

Leno Sislin

WAITING—WHEN YOU'RE LITTLE

For CaitLin: Love is what you live up to. With all my love.

Waiting—when you're little
Waiting—just to grow
Up to be old enough
To know all there is to know.

Waiting—when you're crawling
Waiting—just to stand
Up—and be just like them,
With a little one by the hand.

Waiting—when you're working
Waiting—for time to play
Like the people in the pictures
On an endless holiday . . . .

Waiting—when you have it all
Waiting—just to feel
That everything was worth it
That all of it is real . . . . .

Waiting—at the end of day
Waiting—for one more chance
To find the love you were dreaming
of
For time—for one more
dance . . . . . .

Tosha L Hudson

MY IMAGE

I look in the mirror,
I see a frown.
I look at me,
I feel like a clown.

My image is plain with no design.
Where did I come from;
Who are my kind?

I'm filled with sadness;
I'm filled with pain.
I'm going crazy;
I'm going insane.

I have no true meaning.
I have no true friend.

What am I to do?
Who am I to depend?
Will someone please
come be my friend.

Chuck Mills

MY IDEAL LADY

I dream of my ideal love.
I pray that she can be real,
Not just a heavenly image.

My image would be easier to
possess.
She could never leave me;
But I could never hold her.

And if I find her in my searching,
what then?
Can I love her or will I be too afraid?
Afraid to risk losing her?

Will my eyes fail to see it is her?
Will my fear blind me to her earthly
image?
So afraid—of not finding her and of
loving her.

Common love is the answer—(or is
it?)
It is easier to find than my image.
It would be easier to hold and to let
go.

Contentment could be mine, maybe
even happiness.
Nights would no longer be so lonely.
My life would no longer be so
empty.

But would it be an unholy triangle?
Would my ideal lady's image still
possess me?
Could life without her be worth
living?

Donna D Pincince

NATURE'S SEPARATION

The crash of the waves
Is killing my heart
The winds that carry us
Farther and farther apart.

The ocean we cruise
In search of each other
The rocks that separate us
Then farther and farther.

We drift away
Looking for reasons
Further and further
A change of seasons.

Is there a way
We can stay together
We'll work it out
Closer . . .
and closer . . .
forever.

Linda M Vlahakis

FORMAL DESTINY IS FAILING

Formal destiny is failing
Gradual distance is prevailing
Future engagements are disillusioned
While scattered emotions play
confusion
Burning desires flare wildly
Yet head control works mildly
Awakening is sought
To end this needless hurt
Certain destruction is evident
When two hearts fight torment
I set my standards, my point of view
laying out my provisions
While you revert back to a child
And cannot make a decision.
Failure to see through all this
madness
Is leading up to troubled sadness
Task too difficult to decide
You use time as an excuse to hide
Cast upon us this terrible charade
Ultimate choices are being weighed
Promises, promises I intend to do
You refuse to believe any are true
Persistent to keep this love alive
So sure it has what it takes to survive
So what more can I say
I'll love you tomorrow as I love you
today.

Janie Pogue

TO COME FULL CIRCLE

Yesterday—
Yes, 'twas really only
yesterday—
Boy—girl—hands touching—
smiles—eyes meeting shyly

Surf pounding—gulls wheeling—
blue of sky and ocean meeting—
And these two—seeing nothing
but each other—

"Wait for me," he calls, as she runs
ahead—leaping for happiness—
He, beside her now—reaching

out and drawing her close—

She shyly lays her head upon his shoulder—for he is first love—
Dear, never to be forgotten love words whispered, "You're kinda cute"

Yesterday—was it really only yesterday?

Many yesterdays have come—love grew and from that love a daughter—
Yesterday—beautiful baby—only yesterday—

Baby words, "Mama Mama"—toddling steps—first day of school—
Big eyes brimming with tears—

Young woman—so very beautiful—
Yesterday—
one—
short—
yesterday—

Boy—Girl—
Sand castles building—hands touching—eyes meeting—
time fleeting—
Your Yesterday—
is—
here.

Kim M Stuettgen
A PLACE TO BE
On his back lies a dirty grey torn shirt,
Patched and faded blue jeans,
Ruffled, dark as coal hair . . .

Eyes brightly shining with the city lights,
Was this big city for him?
Sadly caressing his clothes,
Style, was it meant for him? . . .

With wild eyes he could not hide,
Running, the strong wind hitting at his back,
Searching, desperately searching for a better place to be,
Light shining city river's water grey,
Seemingly calm, embracing the chilled bridge rail,
Finding his place to be . . .

Slowly I embrace his hands, his tear gently falls, Knowing how I feel, a dream, our dream . . .

Slowly time stood still, his grip released,
It's a chance, our chance,
Together embracing we leave hand in hand,
Only glancing back leaving his faded destructive demand.

Linda D W Griffith
FAITH
If you just think of the manger
you don't grow in your faith
If you only look to the cross
you die in that place.
You must think past the cross to
the stone rolled away,
And grow in your faith each and
every day.

Howard Hill
MARY'S SECRET
Why are you here, little babe in a manger
'Midst the smells of cattle and hay?
No room in the inn, the innkeeper told you
And reluctantly turned you away.

What will you grow up to be, little baby
What will you grow up to be?
Will you till the dark earth as your father before you
Or sail a white ship on the seas?

Will you carve the fine woods from Lebanon's forest,
Be a merchant—a leader of men,
Will you seek a release from Rome's terrible clutches
To live as a nation again?

But your future is known, little babe in the manger.
The prophets have known from the start,
For your life and your death and your plan of redemption
Are hidden in your mother's heart.

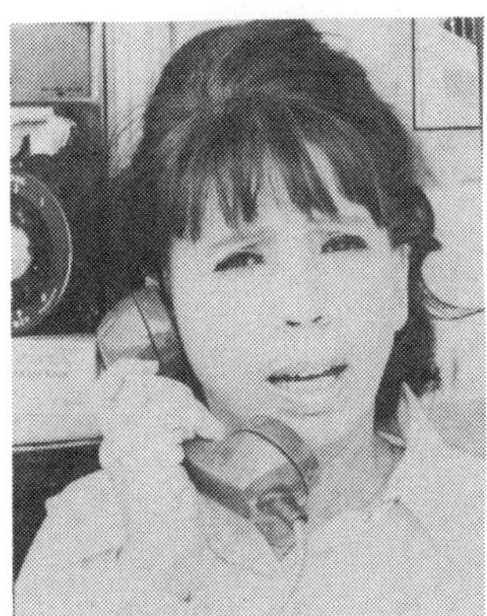

Geraldine Paulette

Geraldine Paulette
HYMN TO THE SUN
Sun god of golden splendor
Lord of the realm of day
The music of thy courses
Flows down time's changing way

The heart *beat of thy rhythm
Since worlds from mists—were born
Rolls on in ceaseless measure
Creating each new dawn—.

Sun god of golden splendor
Attune our hearts to thee
Till our majestic love song
Shall set—Earth's spirit free

Grace A Swanson
A KISS FOR GRANDMA
He kissed me. It happened so fast,
But I was wishing it would last
For another moment, or two.
I gazed at his face—such innocence, such grace!

Funny how he, so small,
With his sly little grin, could enthrall me so.
Oh, how I loved that moment
When he kissed me.

He hugged me. Strong little arms
Encircled my neck; and I suspect
It wasn't planned, for in his eyes
I could see the surprise.

He ran away, and my eyes grew misty
For I heard him say, "I love you, Gram."
Oh, how he caressed my soul that moment
When he kissed me.

Sherry G Rash
OUR NEIGHBOR
Sometimes it takes a tragic death to open up our eyes,
So we can truly see our loss and fully realize.

That other soul who lived close by and often was our stay,
When storms of fear and doubt assailed and caused our hope to fray.

That neighbor dear who listened long when we were wont to talk
About our ills and troubles sore which caused our faith to balk.

He it was to whom we turned to share both joy and sorrow.
He gave so freely of his love, we never had to borrow.

Though family and friends are near, we often turn instead
To one we know will be there, with loving arms outspread.

At last we hear the Bible speak from its spot upon the shelf,
God's wisdom in that great refrain, "Love thy neighbor as thyself."

Leona A Metling
MY SAD DAYS OF 1988
Cars trucks and planes still run
And birds still fly, why did my son have to die?
Tears and being sad won't help I know.
I'll be upset, rain or snow.
Days go by, my heart beats slow.
It then beats faster as I think of days I held his hand.
We spoke of death and which first would go.
So it was he—my son why oh why?
It is no wonder, I should cry.
Things to remember, are not a few.
Nearly all that pass through my mind.
Again each one makes me feel, so blue.
He served his country, in the Navy for twenty two years.
There again comes the flow of tears

David E Butler
STAGES
When I die, where will I go?
To Heaven, Lord no!
For there is no Heaven or Hell,
Only this life on earth that we
know so well.

On my world there is no rain in
summer,
No flowers bloom in spring.
The only sound I hear is thunder,
For there are no birds to sing.

Life, why am I here?
For the burdens that I must bear
At times life has not been fair,
I fear;
So question it, yes, I dare!

Lord, please forgive me for my
sins,
I know not what I have done;
For these words, they flow from
my pen.
Lord, forgive me please for I am
your son.

I AM's child
GARBAGE
Life is like a garbage can
And God is like a garbage man.
When you feel you've just got stuck,
(Yea, in this earthly guck),
God comes around in his garbage truck.
He takes out the garbage of this world
And to the back of the truck it's hurled.
His service leaves you little delay
And keeps you feeling refreshed for each day.
So if you have problems, don't hesitate to call—
'Cause he'll help you, one and all.

Warnella Faye Tennyson
LIGHT IN DARK PLACES
Depression, Despair, Two words
with grave meaning;
A dark hole one falls into; With No Exit, No Ending.

A place where Evil lives; Always
luring in new souls;
And using all the tricks, that are in his power to know.

To give up and fall deeper; We
soon grow weaker;
And feel the loss of control; Then comes the fork in the road.

At this place, we make a
decision; To fight for the light;
Or give in to, Oppression.

My decision is for Life; I reach
for the Light.
My Soul is Mine, the Darkness Can Not take it.

If one only knew, how very few,
are told they have a choice.
That they can choose to go deeper;
OR they can reach for the Light.
"REMEMBER"

When One finds their 'self,
Surrounded By Darkness;
Just Say the LORD'S PRAYER; And
Ask HIM to PLEASE, PLEASE,
Get You The Hell Out Of There,
Remember;
There is Light in Dark Places.

Terri Villone
SELF FAITH
Open your minds to an imperfect world, where human frailties abound.
For blame is in each of us. A power so strong, an easy excuse, a prelude to quick judgements.
Search deep . . deep down inside, where only you reside.
Where long ago memories, hidden guilts swirl, gorging and growing on time and interpretations.
By reliving their birth, we extinguish their worth.
Freed from the darkness in cleansing absolutions.
Accept it as is, that life once lived cannot be altered, changed nor forgotten. Wisely, only learned from.
"Self Faith" dictates. "Self Love" demands.
Responsibility for one's own actions. An ongoing challenge. Our ultimate salvation.

Larissa Coffin
CIVIL WAR IN MY MIND
Uncontrollable I could be declared,
As my thoughts flutter in the air,
With each explosion my brain does vibrate,
As there is war with love and hate . . .
As my Civil War leads strong,
All seems endless and long.
I question the questions that fly,
The questions—as bombers soaring the sky.
The shriek and whistle of an explosion dropping,
Is heard near and far, never stopping,
Accepted by my mind it explodes in fire,
Inflicting my thoughts to soar higher and higher,
Yet now all seems to be ending,
As the broken pieces and open wounds are mending.
Dead corpses of my thoughts are buried,

My oppressions relieved, the air is once again peaceful,
All has settled, even what was once fearful,
And light streams as everything again is renewing.
All could be done. It all just needed doing!

Eunice C White

Eunice C White
SPEAKING OF FENCES

To the memory of my dear husband, George Everett White

The picket fence around my home
Kept out stray creatures which might roam,
And too, of course, young children in groups
Who might run through, with lusty whoops.

I was planting ruffled white sweet peas,
And paused a moment to rest my knees,
When I caught my breath in such surprise!
Scarcely could I believe my eyes—

For slithering through beneath the gate
A small green string of a thing did wait
Just a split second, as a butterfly,
Flashed its colors as it fluttered by.

Hastily I arose, walked on, and on,
Considering many things pro and con.
Of fencing it seems one can't always rely;
I'm beginning to see the reason why.

I thought of a fence built around my heart,
Designed to keep folks out.
I'd build it strong, and built it high
Of prejudice, and fear, and doubt.

But when 'twas "builded" all around,
I viewed it with chagrin,
For you stood smiling close to me
And I found I'd fenced you in!

Marcel Floris
LIKE THE WIND
like the wind
like the wild wind
I go North by North East
I go South by South West
I turn East
I turn West
I go up, I go down
I go down, I go up

in search of my way
in search of my very own way

Martha M Arndt
TREES
Trees are like our lives
Sometimes twisted and bare.

They are like the human arms
Raised up to God in prayer.

Those that are evergreen and fair
Are like our joys, without compare.

Others, like the human heart
Pierce it through, and see it smart.

Some, in their Autumn hues arrayed
Are like some lives,
More beautiful as they fade.

Jeannie Falacienski
I NEED LOVE
I need someone to love me
For my dreams and for my hopes
I need someone to show me
That with their love I'll cope
I need someone to care
If I am happy or if I'm weak
I need someone to show me
That their love for me is deep
I need someone to understand
My feelings and my thoughts
I need someone to show me
That for my love they've fought
I need someone to love me
For what I am
And all I can be
I need someone to love
And love me
Just for me.

YvePendragon Lewthwaite
STARS
The stars, like fairies in the night,
Dance to music with delight,
Music played by celestial strings,
Music only darkness brings.
Ears don't hear the music played
Though eyes can see the dance delayed
By distance mind can't comprehend.
But still to bow, to sway, to bend,
To music that our minds must lend
The final notes. As if a friend
In times unending dark of space
Had left a gift—star splashed—like lace.

Heidi Ann Ziegler
YOU & ME
The coolness of the October breeze
Strangers when I met you and you met me
The mixture of the stars above
Gave me the feeling of a new love
From then we were now a pair
Seeing we both really did care
Days and nights just flew on by
We were together almost all the time
Summer soon appeared out of the blue
Yes,
After all this time I still love you
Now at last, I look around
To find all the joy we have found
October breeze has come back again
Thinking about that day we became more than friends
But wait, there will be more to come between you and me
Honey, I will Love You until Eternity.

Claire C Foceri
CAN YOU MEASURE SAND WITH A SPOON
Can you measure sand with a spoon
Count the steps to the moon
Know how many lilies bloom
How many brides there are in June

Can you count the lights on a Christmas tree
How many pinecones can there be

Can you imagine how many rays come from the sun
How many children there are having fun

Can you think of how many words you say in a day
How much laughter would cost if you had to pay

Did you ever wonder how much you're loved
Add up the answer from above
That's the amount I'm thinking of

David Hare
ANTHEM
today I saw a dead fish floating down the river
I saw a very thin man throwing bread to all the birds
today I saw a white child playing with a black child
I saw an aging priest shouting out the sacred Words
today I saw a pill the size of a bullet fly down the throat of some unsuspecting dude
I saw a newborn baby crying in a cradle
today I saw a picture of a woman in the nude
I saw a college graduate racing in his car
today I saw a dropout comb his mangled hair
I saw a race of people crashing into walls
today I saw a dead fish floating down the river

Gayle Campbell Bradley
I LOST MY WORLDS
I sat down to
Write a poem of love,
and lost my words along the way
not sure when or where.

I lost my words.
Was it when we said good-bye
one hundred years ago.
Was it just yesterday.

Started
to sing a song of love,
and lost my song along the way
not sure when or where

I lost my song.
Was it the time we said good-bye
one hundred years ago.

I lost my song and words
one hundred years ago.
Maybe a hundred years from now
I'll find my song and words.

Linda Cantrell
TRIALS
Thank you Lord for making up,
The worst years of my life.
Because thru them I learned to grow,
Past heartaches and much strife.
I found ways to take the bad,
And turn it into good.
Not letting it destroy me,
like many thought it would.
I drew my strength upon you,
forever leaning safe from harm.
You stayed through all the darkness,
holding fast onto my arms.
I felt that in your hands,
I could stop and rest awhile.
For you told my spirit softly,
My dear child it's just a trial.
Walk with me the whole way thru it,
for it's just another mile.
Up ahead the sun is shining,
where again we'll rest awhile.

Elmer D Colcord

Elmer D Colcord
THE RANDOLPH BRIDGE
On a wet and windy night and dark
The bridge was no good place to be upon.
It swayed and seemed about to fall
Then in a last convulsive effort recovered all
Its iron strength, unconquered still
Through years of storms and winter's will.
Below, the river lay, sullen, deep
And many secrets it would keep.
People who lived on either side intimidated quite
Stayed wisely home on such a night.
He clung fast to the iron rail
Knowing the slightest slip meant he would fail,
Careful each step, inching along,
Determination strong.
He held his breath once when a partial slide
Unnerved his grasp and broke his stride
But recovered with an iron will pledge
That matched the iron of the bridge
More cautiously he mounted to the framework's top
Fearful only that a gust of wind or sudden pelt of rain would make him drop,
And then the won result, the gain:
He stood erect, felt the glad rain
Upon his face, turned fully south
And leaped into the darkness' mouth.

Sandra Ann Moore
WRITING
I have a dream so bold and bright,
I have a dream, that is, to write.
I stay up most nights far too late,
My fresh ideas just can't wait.

Lest I lose what I want to say,
I work my mind all through the day.
I think it over, then again;
'Til I get my paper and pen.

I jot quickly, my thoughts alight;
Then rewrite so it sounds just right.
When my hand is clammy and damp,
I then stretch out my writer's cramp.

Before long I'm at it again,
Then, with heavy eyes and tired brain;
I give it up 'til the next night,
When, refreshed, I've new things to write.

Christine Schlagheck
FISH FANTASIA AT BANDOS
Close to the shores of this tiny island
on the Indian Ocean in
gin-colored water

Fish flock to meet feet, greet knees
as you immerse in
knee-high wavelets to float

Face down arms extended outward
like a drowned man. Under, sucking
air through

A hose and blowing it out, in and
out, you linger in this liquid world
and watch.

In zigs and zags the blue ring angels
and silver sardinella streak by for a
glance

Then return to stare back at you, a
submerged intruder. Small fish brave
you, brush against

Your skin to map the curves of your
body like a rock formation that needs
exploration. Outside

The sun beats down bleaching the
already white sand. The heat hits
your back while

You float in solitary exhilaration
staring to secure the vision of fish in
unrestricted

Movement streaming, like silk
swirling in a soft breeze, here, under
the sea at Bandos.

J Victor Lopez
ARGENT EMANATIONS FROM THE CYBERNETIC BLITZ
Passionless automaton wishes how
the digits could be perfectly aligned.
Simplicity haunts the criss-crossed
network of vindicated connections.
Raptors and reptiles tumble through
the cortex of an ambivalent psyche,
While jingling commercialism
hijacks another sedated, median
sensibility
Then Wall Street twitches in the last
throes of a spoon-fed pipe dream,
As volunteer social workers place an
emaciated charity into the ground.
A cloaked phantom whispers into the
ear of a napping figurehead,
"If we, the 'golden' bourgeoisie, are
so damned free to do as we please,
Why does it take so long to muster
up a sprinkling of noblesse oblige?"
Grace thus fulfills the incomplete
attempt at arduous endeavor.

Suddenly the positive feedback
flings me into a familiar circle,
Exporting logjams of electric input
provided by televised, tabloid
innuendo.
The control of ivory towers are made
plaid with the parched ones'
blessings;
Rational intellect without emotion
amounts to surface tension.
Define Rock 'n' Roll genetics: DNA
twisting resonantly into a Jello
cosmos,
For all microcosms of plasma fix
entropy onto the essential seat of
being,
Until subjectivity blurs and
sublimates into a mist of unified
proportion.

And after my coffee break, I stop the
tape and wonder to myself,
Does this fruitful account confirm
my wildest suspicion,
That this is the way God really
intended it to be?

Teresa Ann Gardiner
CINDY STEVENS (A LITTLE GIRL WHO TOUCHED MY LIFE)
I was fifteen when I met this little girl, who was five. She was so adorable, and very beautiful, full of life, loving, happy, and very giving.

Cindy had a problem though. She was stricken with Cystic Fibrosis, and was only given until she was seven to live.

I spent a lot of time with her, as I became their babysitter. Cindy had a sister, Marie, who was 10 years old at the time.

I only babysat for a year, then we drifted apart. I was graduating and Cindy was preparing to die.

Cindy lived to be nine years old. Her life in those nine years was very meaningful, and very significant. She was loved by many. Her father was by her bedside when she passed on. He said she was very brave. Just before she died, she told her father, "Daddy, I'm not afraid to die."

I will never forget the way her little arms would hug me, and how she didn't want to share me with her sister, Marie. She used to tell Marie to leave me alone, "Teresa's my friend, not yours." Oh, how I miss my little friend. She made me feel very special.

I feel very honored and privileged to have been a part of Cindy's life, and I thank her for touching my life so deeply. Through her I have seen how precious life is, and how meaningful it can be. Life truly is a gift we should honor, and cherish.

William E Bethea
TO MY LIFE, WITH LOVE
As I gaze upon the so distant past,
I wonder where all the years went so
fast,
I think of all the things we have
done,
But, of them all, I remember the fun,
That you and I shared in our life,
I, as your husband, you, as my wife,
Together, we have done all that we
can,
To make our daughter a woman, our
son a man,
With them, we shared laughter and
pain,
But, through it all, we loved them
just the same,
Alas, we had to break free, for they
had their own lives to live,
With their own tears to shed, and
love to give,
When we met, I knew our love was
true,
This sweet, special feeling, that I
share with you,
And now, as I gaze upon the so
distant past,
I am now, finally, content at last,
For, I am so lucky, to have someone
like you,
I love you darling, I really do,
With love, oh so filled with tender
care,
I am happy, that with you, my life I
share.

Dorothy Z Alverson
FAT CATS
All men are "fat cats"
That's why they have whiskers
They get fed, they get pampered
While gals work until blisters.

They stretch in the mornings.
They yawn from lounge chairs.
We even change channels
For their T.V. stares.

Ah yes! Men are fat cats
Though most, salary poor.
At home they are kings,
While wives just endure.

Be careful, don't argue
Just keep him purring.
Get him upset and you'll
Hear his loud gurring.

Warm up his night milk.
Give a scratch on his head
Cuz you got a "fat cat"
The day you were wed.

Joyce E LaStringer
THIS LITTLE LADY
Grandma is a friend of mine.
I never knew one could be so kind.
She's always busy spinning good
deeds.
Never will her garden go to weeds.
Of others she's always thinking you
know
To build us up when we are low.
Her sweet gentle smile or soft tender
touch,
Her timing's so right and it means so
much.
I say my world's a better place,
When I behold Grandma's lovely
face.
So glad am I to have her near
Because I know God sent her here.

Kelly Latham
SILENTLY

This poem is dedicated to all of my family and friends.

He creeps down the hall,
Silent as a sneaky cat.
Softly in the night.
Fluttering like a bat.

She lay asleep in her bed
the satin sheets seem to float,
about her head.

The shadows creep from
black to gray,
as the night turns to day

He watches her for many hours
Suddenly, her eyes open
and seem to blossom
violet as the flowers.

It is time for him to
slip away unnoticed as
the night turns to day

Olivia Hall-Vander

Olivia Hall-Vander
MEDITATION
The NAACP rings its Freedom Bell
Its message is clear to tell
With only civil rights to sell
It is done well

Three generations of time
Blacks have endured this crime
Now is the day
For a better way

In your fields we toiled
In the heat our bodies broiled
In conflicts we went to battle
While at home, treated like chattel

Where lies the cure
For a nation so sure
That Civil Rights will creep
While justice sleeps?

What do Blacks intend?
Fight to the bitter end?
Lord don't forget little Black us
Maybe 'tis with you we need to fuss.

Jane L Lyon
ON A DAY

This is dedicated to Billy Lyon, my sweet son, who died at the age of nine, the victim of a violent crime.

On a day
before our time
Ponce DeLeon
did find

A fountain
that is said to spray
Eternal youth
for all our days

With the coming
of your thirtieth year
We thought that this
would bring you cheer

This urn you hold
is said to possess

The secret of
immortal bliss

Take this potion
sip it slow
and older, Kathy
you will not grow

We know not if this legend
holds an ounce of truth
And if in fact
Ponce DeLeon did goof

You needn't concern
yourself, Ms. K
For YOUTH is in
the heart, we say

Christine Barbara Mozer
STRANGE TIMES LAY BEHIND ME

This poem is dedicated to my loving family in America and Germany

Strange times lay behind me.
Strange times lay ahead.
In between lays happiness
And in between lays dread.
Some days are filled with happiness.
Some are filled with tears.
But when I think how far I've made it,
I overcome my fears.

George-Ann Long
TRUE FRIENDS

Dedicated to my Mother Corinne, my daughters; Dawn & Jennifer, and friend, Jim.

True friends are ones who care
for each other at all times and
under all conditions,
Who can ignore some of the
difficult moments, because they
see beyond them, to the real
person they know and love.
True friends stand by each other
when the chips are down,
giving you a strong shoulder to
lean on.
They're the ones who can share a
hearty laugh at things no one
else might think are funny.
True friends know when the time
arises, under any
circumstances, they'll be there,
no questions asked.
True friends feel the tender
warmth in each other's
presence, and the sheer delight
and pleasure of holding each
other near.
True friends know it takes time
and courage and patience to
help a love to grow.
And that it always needs the
nurturing, that only true
friends who walk hand and
hand in God's light can do.

Sheila Harris-Franklin
HEARTS

To my mother from whom I gathered strength and my husband from whom I obtained an abyss of knowledge.

Hungry hands reaching up towards the sun
Looking for guidance
Away out of the rain
The heaviness of the soul is unbearable
Many forms of relief have suggested themselves
First
There was the ingestion of medicinal supplies
And
Shiny sharp silvery shaving
apparatuses that puncture
Then
There was the noisy metallic machine
that spits out little pointed metal objects
But
Throughout all the confusion
A beacon of hope was revealed
Opening a window through which
A ray of sunshine flooded to uplift desolate hearts.

Geneva Doris Jennings-Robinson
MOTHER

Dedicated to my dear mother, Mrs. Opal E. James Jennings-Arnold She has been a good mother to me and a dear friend to me all of my life and I truly thank the Lord for her being my mother.

Silver hair and fragile skin
Loving and always my friend
A good warrior and a trooper indeed
Having new special needs.

Time is passing on and many in a rush
We must take time and be of trust
Steps are shortened just a bit
Gait is unsteady but lamps are lit

Eyes are dimming on the trail
Hands still write and open mail
Precious, precious memories
Spirit high and thoughts are yet keen

Hard labor is all in the past
Wisdom and knowledge is present and will last
Debt is paid so don't you fret
You're in your golden years and a special pet

Dearer to me than anyone I know
Responsible for my being and to grow
Couldn't have mounted many tasks
This person is dear to me as time will pass "Mother."

Paul S Anderson
TIME IN MOTION

May all your dreams of
yesterday
Be the hope of your
tomorrow
And the visions of
today
The inventions of
next week
May the love you shared
yesterday
Be the dream of your
tomorrow
And your visions of
happiness
The reality of
eternity

Andrew F Clemons
THE TOLLING BELLS

Dedicated In Memory Of My Nephew; MR. GARY CARLTON -JACKSON DECEMBER 25, 1953-JANUARY 21, 1989

Through silence I hear the tolling bells.
Once they sound then they pause,
only to sound again, and again.
It seems as though my head will
swell from the sound of the,
tolling bells.
The tolling bells sounding every
hour, The tolling bells sounding,
for someone who has just fallen from power.
Those who are lost will some day
surely pay the cost.
For no life is for sale, and no one can
ever escape the sound, of the tolling bells.
The bells shall toll for everyone
announcing the time of day,
or because someone's life has sadly
been snuffed away.
Those bells, Those tolling bells, the
sound can be such hell.
The sound of the tolling bells!
The tolling bells!

John F Hennessy

John F Hennessy
ON BEING A "WINNER"

Did you ever take up with a "loser"?
A person that can't seem to "win"?
They really make an honest effort—
But they're beat before they begin.

The seemingly "always a winner"—
Preaches that it's "ALL IN THE MIND"—
"ALWAYS KEEP A POSITIVE ATTITUDE
AND YOUR LOSING WILL CEASE YOU WILL FIND."

They point out examples—people they know
Who keep "WINNING" foremost in their head—
And how they keep winning—winning and winning—
They'll be "winners" until they are dead!

Well friends—I agree with most of these thoughts—
If I didn't I'd be as "foolish as sin"—
But there's one thing I know—YOU check it out—
You've "GOTTA LOSE SOME IN ORDER TO WIN"! ! !

R Evelyn Gale Quadro
MEMORIES

To the family of Ruth Frances Spencer and Joseph Oscar Gale. To those who have gone before: Vernon, Laura, Jess and baby William.

Over the hill there's a meadow of green,
It's so cool, so quiet, what a beautiful scene.
Wild flowers sprouting up here and there,
Tall trees in abundance, heads pointing in air.

The deer so still, dips his head unafraid,
To eat the cool grass, then lies down in the shade.
Where cool water runs, plays a tune as it flows,
White clouds in the sky and the wind gently blows.
I go back in my memories to this wonderful place,
And once again see mother's beautiful face.
Father, sisters and brothers, there by her side,
Some day I'll see them all again, and with them abide.

Lisa Ann Mathis
CLOUDY SKIES

To my wonderful parents, Mr. and Mrs. Natividad and Dorothy Pagan. For all the love and inspiration you've given me.

The cloudy skies above thou head
The wintry days that thou do dread
The lonely nights thy fight in vain
To cultivate the earth to thrive, but in vain.

Through fallen leaves the grass does grow
Through misty days the rain does flow
Through fields and plains thy nurture thee
Through prayer and care from thy humble home.

The sunny sky replenishes thy soul
The day seems sweet, but who knows what it holds
For cloudy skies are waiting to chase in
Those lonely nights thy don't call a friend.

Through hardship and pain thou fight one's cause
Thou fight in vain one truly are.
For lonely nights are bound to return
Those cloudy skies that surround our earth.

June Butterfield
RESPONSE TO IRINA RATHUSHINSKAYA "GREY IS THE COLOR OF HOPE"

Hope is not grey
Hope is the pale seeds of Spring
sleeping in the fields of Winter's dread
green at the heart
When life is brought forth torn and
bleeding after the siege
When mourning invades with
shattering immensity
lean as an assassin
and blinding storms invade in
fiercest fury
Hope is there
Hope is a ruby flame
racing through corridors of
memory
with prismed brightness
bent in kneeling
Hope is the voice of misty distant
songs
blue in infinity
weightless as thistledown
Hope is the purest golden scent of
summer's dawn
clinging in triumph as ivy
masters stone
No
Hope is not grey
Grey is the shrouding of despair
heavy as old armor
and unresisting

Beverly L Soisson
FRIENDSHIP

Friends are honest.
Friends are true.
Friends don't make each other blue.
Friends care, Friends share.

Friends are always, always, there.
You once had a special place in my heart
But you hurt me and tore it apart.
Friends don't make each other cry
they stand by them until they die.
Friends come to see you day by day
they don't go to others and push you away.
You'll be my friend until the end of time
the question is, will you be mine.

Dorothy E Foster
MY TWIN SISTER AND I
I look back at our childhood,
Precious moments to see
Happy times, fun times—
Just you and me.

Two "look alikes,"
"The twins"
But differences? Yes!
You, the quiet one,
Me, Tomboyish mess.

We had our little squabbles
as other children do.
And Mom would say "Hug sister,"
"Please say I'm sorry too."

The dolls, the toys—
Doubled of course,
We could get along with less.
The greatest joy was each other,
Sharing childhood happiness.

Your hurts were mine
One ill, so was the other.
This invisible tie we had
Each discomfort was felt together.

We've cried together,
Shared happy moments,
Reminisced to times gone by
Even when we're silver haired
I'm sure the bond will not untie

As we grew older,
And each went our way,
Families to raise, distances apart.
The unity is still there,
This love in our heart.

If there was ever a gift to be given,
A precious one you cannot buy
It's the love, the friendship,
The bond between two—
"My twin sister and I."

Hill Graywin
THE WATERS OF WISCONSIN
Freshened by the Spring Rains,
Drench'ed by the Summer Sun,
Painted by the Fall Foliage,
Chilled by the Winter Snows.

Lorraine E Bell
THIS LIFE
Do you remember, just yesterday
You had this feeling of being alive
Every moment was exciting
Each experience different
A sweet word or action made you feel precious

Somewhere, somehow, it all slipped away
Slowly your eyes began to open
With every lie or tear you adjust the focus
So you were born into adulthood
Falling farther and farther from forever

Now it's so hard to feel back to that time
When love was something pure, everlasting
Your first would be your one and only
Giving all of you to the chosen one
Painting pictures, writing words of tomorrow

Looking around you, you see it's all gone
Now you're 19 with bills and rent to pay
The real you (the heart) had long since passed away
Left you to meaningless actions
People who could care less
You no longer care about this life

Denise Mondell
FOREVER IN MY HEART

This poem is dedicated to my cousin Bobby Young in memory of his wife Kim.

When I said I loved you, I meant forever.
I always thought we'd be here together.
Our love was perfect, I thought you'd never go away,
But I guess it was time for you on that certain day.
I remember they told me that you were gone,
And I thought without you, I couldn't carry on.
I knew I'd miss that special feeling of when you
Touched my hand, but he had a reason to take you
Away, and I'd have to understand.
You may be gone, but not forgotten, forever in my
Heart you will stay.
God may have taken you physically, but the
Memories can't be taken away.
I realize now you loved me as much as I do you.
And you'll always be in my heart, no matter what I do.
When you left you never said good-bye, but I understand,
Because it means forever, and I know someday,
We again, will be together.

Lara Dionne Greene
FATHER DEAR

To George Serantes; In my heart, you will ALWAYS be my real Father.

I remember the day,
When he walked away,
Leaving us here,
With only a mother.

Father dear,
Take my tears,
And watch me grow,
From young to old.

Why did I suffer,
For your mistakes,
Made me a lot tougher,
Now it's easier to take.

Father dear,
It wasn't Mom,
That you were married to,
All those years.

You had more than that,
Had me and that's the fact,
Forget all the tears,
Father dear.

Pamela Neal
I'LL ALWAYS BE NEAR

To my loving husband, Pete.

He comes to me in darkness
and eases away my fright
like the caress of a summer breeze
in the coldest hours of night.

As lightning streaks across the sky
I can see his smiling eyes.
He wipes away a single tear
with a kiss stifles my cries.

The thunder follows the lightning
and we know the storm is here.
Our passion grows beyond control
as he whispers "I'll always be near."

Sunlight filters through my window
as I wake to a brand new day.
Knowing that it was only a dream
that God has taken him away.

I walk to the room adjoining mine
and a soft sigh is all I hear,
As I look at the babe so much like him
I hear his words "I'll always be near."

Vivian Smith Walker

Vivian Smith Walker
SWEET POETRY
Sweet Poetry,
Sacred first love of my life;
Stay close beside me;
Let my thoughts run rife
With simple curiosity
To plumb life's vaguest mysteries.
Abandon not, nor stay my pen,
As ever, since my life began,
You've chosen to abide with me
And touch with beauty, all I see.
Continue please as you see fit,
To shape my life, and all of it,
For good or ill shall rendered be
To serve you first;
Sweet Poetry.

Deborah A Smith
LOVING
Oh, that gentle touch,
Flesh meeting in the darkness;
A message silently given,
And, Silently received.

Eyes that reflect beauty,
Mirrors of our souls;
Reaching out to each other,
Finding we are one.

Laughter in the night,
Of unspoken moments remembered;
Times we have shared,
Memories we will cherish.

As our bodies become one,
May our hearts and minds meet also;
For if we reach this height,
We are one—we are loving.

Edward Ray Younce
WHATIF
Whatif my hair starts to fall out,
Whatif my teeth start to sprout.

Whatif I fall and shout,
Whatif I don't get stout.

Whatif nobody has eyes,
Whatif nobody dies.
Whatif I'm not smart,
Whatif I get hit with a dart.

Whatif there's no television,
Whatif there's no season.

Whatif Whatifs come back,
Whatif they come with a sack.

Hazel B Foster
THE STAR
Once upon a time
A star shone down
Upon the Earth
And showed the way
To a baby's birth.

There stands a tree
In a little dell.
A hemlock, so tall.
Not even a cherry picker
Can reach its top.

Could I but climb so high
I would, with my own hands
Fly on that topmost branch
A star that all could see
As it reaches to the sky.

As taller grows the tree
So higher reaches the star
Up to where the first
Star showed the way
To a baby's birth.

Carol Stearns Clement
DOWN IN THE WOODLOT
Down in the woodlot yesterday
The Spring caressed my thoughts
That leapt in a quivering yearning desire
As my heart reached out towards life.
It was there, with love, I cupped my hands
Around the fresh new boughs,
And there, with love, I leaned my cheek
Against the aging bark.

Down in the the woodlot yesterday
I lay naked on the earth.
Pulling its cover over my breast
I died in the cool damp soil.
Who was it then, that awoke last night
And breathed the warm sweet air,
With fervent joy and gentle step
Walked away and left me there?

Dorothy H Hall
AUTUMN
Autumnal breezes fill the air
Then for more work we must prepare
The leaves pile up in drifts so high
They catch the stroller's wandering eye.

The sycamores forever rustle
While at their work the people hustle
The trees adorned in hues of rust, brown and gold
Are the most beautiful sight to behold.

Thanksgiving time will soon be here
But God help us to thank Thee all the year
May autumn leave us with an inner peace
And give Him praises that never cease.

Bun King Kang
SUDDENLY
Suddenly,
Leaves are golden again
Days are gone,
Like the Autumn's wind invisible
Only feeling is sensed
I thought, I could forget you
By being away from you
Only I feel your presence

In this lost land
Your silhouette, a glimpse of you
Caress me like the Fall's wind
I sense you
Somewhere within me
Impossible,
To ignore your existence
Like the Summer is gone
With the falling leaves
In the color of the dawn.

Betty Richardson McCarter
AN ANGEL KISS

This poem is dedicated to Mrs. R.C. Richardson.

Mama, where are you going?
Oh, not too far,
There's a path I must follow and a valley to go through.
Wait a minute, Mama, and I'll go with you.
No, not this time,
The path is for one, my child, not meant for two.
What about the valley, Mama, it sounds so far?
The valley is near, not far away,
It's green and fresh with a shimmering light,
Trees grow so high they cast a shadow on those that go by,
But then there is light, like a heavenly glow,
And you see old friends from so long ago.

Oh, Mama, don't leave me, I'll be so afraid.
Hush, my child, don't you know I'll never be far away.
When you walk through the valley that Mama's been through,
I will be standing there waiting for you.
Goodbye, Mama, I'll try to be brave,
I think I'm going to cry Mama.
Yes, my sweetheart, please do, tears of love are angel's kisses,
And Mama will be sending them back to you.

Elizabeth Wittig Pitcher
GONE ON BEFORE
We weep and mourn for those who pass
On to Heaven's shore,
When really they are better far
Than we, forevermore.

If they have known their Lord and King,
It is but going home,
And in the beauty of the skies,
They evermore do roam.

We see this body made of clay,
We learn to love them so,
We don't want their soul to leave,
We didn't want them to go.

Yet over on the other shore,
They're happy with their King,
For they have reached their Homeland,
And with the Angels, they do sing.

So as we live upon this earth,
For Heaven we prepare,
We want to meet our Saviour,
And greet our loved ones there.

Rebecca S Collison
IT WAS A LONG TIRING NIGHT
It was a long tiring night
And all through the town,
There was no room at the inn
For Mary and Joseph to settle down.

Finally an innkeeper,
Willing and able,
Said Mary and Joseph
Could sleep in his stable.

Then late at night,
A child was born
Who we call
Our wonderful Lord.

Shepherds came
From a field afar,
And wisemen came
By following a star.

To honor the baby
Who is our King;
For peace and
Everlasting life he brings.

Jennifer Elaine Smith
THE FEELING WITHOUT YOU
The times we spent together lie in the past, the love I for you will
Forever last.

The times I wish you here, holding me close and tight;
remembering when we used to say "I love you" and "good-night."

We were younger then, but now that we're both grown,
you're with someone else, and I insist to stay alone.

I cannot predict the future, but I will hope and pray,
that we will be together once again someday.

I love you so much, and I want you to love me too, I hope that again one day, I will hear you say "I love you."

Grant Edward Smith
NEVER ALONE
I walked along the beach today
It was raining
The sea was there
the sky the sand the cold
The birds were playing tag with the sea
chasing and being chased
It was endless
Their little game of never really touching
holding

I wanted to be alone
To escape the thing that makes one hate
I hate loneliness
It makes my life so miserable

It's wonderful how the sea can swallow
so many problems
and still survive
I went to be alone
but I found you
Your smile your words
"hello, I'm glad you're here"
The wind brought your smile and words
I felt a soft whisper from your breath
And I knew I would never be alone
I wanted to play tag with you
chasing and being chased
That endless game of never really
touching holding
And I wanted to hold you
today when it rained

Faith L White
WINTER SEED
Weathered bare branches clutch for the clouds,
Puffy, gray as unlaundered linen;
The air is still and cold,
Absent of color and the melodic musings of birds.
I would prefer Spring, the exuberant artist,
To splash bright green over the valleys,
Paint purple pansies, yolk yellow daffodils
And roses, velvet soft, the shade of burgundy wine.
Yet in this quiet season
There is the feeling of creation stirring
As if it were the first time.
In sculpted strands along the walk
Icy arms of a sea anemone are forming,
Long tentacles flowing outward,
The design for the first one that swayed in its silent sea home.
Within winter's darkness
Life is budding, slowly growing
As a thought ripening to fullness
In the mind.

James A Spillane
BEYOND THE RUBBLE
The world a-tremble, Earth a-quake, the moon so full and round.
My head a-spin, senses reeling, feet lift off the ground.
All's lost, I think, the time of doom foretold in ancient past.
The sky a-light with liquid fire, am I to die the last?

On mountain top on high I watched the great stone city fall;
I bowed my head in mourning grief, awaiting Death to call,
When from the dark a figure stepped, the shadows fell away,
'Twas you, my love, in shining grace, that held my breath at bay.

"He who hangs his head in times of trouble,"
Said you, "cannot see beyond the rubble."

I raised my head, You took my hand,
I looked within your eyes.
I felt the tug as time was slowed, we seemed to meld our lives.
In time I looked out past you, past the stones now growing cold,
The city, now deceased, had birthed a castle made of gold.

Caroline K Chaussee
A WISH
I'd give the world if I could be
A wonderful maker of poetry.
I'd write about the trees and flowers,
And then I'd tell of April showers.

Oh! If I gave thee honor due
Nature, Man would love just you.
He wouldn't care to have great wealth.
All he'd want would be good health.

But people going to and fro
See none of the beauty as they go.
I'd make them stop and gaze a bit
To show them what they've missed of it.

And yet, here must I sit and pine
For things I cannot say are mine.
Oh, yes, I'd give the world to be
A wonderful maker of poetry!

Steve L Cates
THE CHANGE OF SEASONS
In the early fall you can see the turning color of the leaves,
As into winter you can see only the grayish of dead trees,
but around into early spring there's a a change in the air ,
Everybody's outside doing so much that some of us wouldn't ever dare,
Then there's the heat of summer which is so severely hot,
Now everybody's talking let's have some of the winter and some of us does not,
Here we go again on the planet Earth with its four seasons,
On the Merry Go Round we go and asking so many questions,
But we take it in stride with our heads up high,
As we see the migrating Geese coming over again in the Great Blue Sky.

Molly Anderson

Molly Anderson
THAT'S LIFE!

As Infinite Love hath purpose of being, So hath beings purpose; that through purpose beings might know—God.

That's what It's all about; that is—this life we live. The thoughts we have, the joys we give and share with those who need . . . and care to know what—we're all about.

Angela R Bowling
VIETNAM OUR INJUSTICE
Imagination is all we can use when we hear the news.
They show us the soldiers standing tall but they don't
show us the blood as they fall!
For some reason the cameras just didn't show it all.
They didn't write about how it felt to hug the ground and pray as the guy next to you gets blown away.
Think of all the young men that had to go and fight just because our government thought it was right.
What about the ones that came back?
The ones dead and in a body sack?
For the soldier it is over but for the family; it is a dreadful; deadly; reality.
The president didn't hear their cries;
or have to look into their bleeding

eyes.
Their relatives well, they got advice
to the wives of those who lost their lives.
"Just think of it as an instant divorce
and get your life back on course.":
To the children who lost their dad,
"Don't be sad.
Your mom will remarry. Maybe to
that nice man you call uncle Harry."
To the mothers;
"I'm sorry, but you're young, you can have others."
To the fathers, "Your son was brave
and would have made you proud.
Why towards the end, he didn't even cry out loud."
To the grandparents, "We did our best to protect him.
There were just too many of them."
To the brothers and sisters.
"Even though you don't have your
brother, you have each other and
your memories, Make the most of it .
Hey, is this his old baseball mitt?"

Thea Fronsman-Cecil
ALL HALLOWS' NIGHT
Shadows on the midnight sky
Witches on their broomsticks fly
Cats sit behind their backs
Oranges, silvers, golds, & blacks
Owls perched upon their shoulders
Assist their gliding by huge boulders
Landing by fire-flames
The witches play haunting games
Chanting things around the fire
Gold sparks rise higher & higher
When onward comes the dawn
The magic is all gone

Janice Lynn Canerdy
MISS AMERICA
Her importance is not new.
Yet, each day the world awakens in awe of her.
She exists because long ago men desired to give liberty a form.

She is a stately, proud beauty.
Every inch of her stands for some big or small freedom.
Did I say "small freedom"? Forgive me.

Her loose, flowing robe envelops me.
Each fold shelters my security.

Her torch bears no real flame;
Yet, it warms my soul.
Her crown is mine. Yes, I am royalty.

This day is precious,
But it is not the equal of the one she cradles in her arm.

She and her message are worth far more
Than the fortune that has gone into her making and upkeep.

Offering me that fortune in exchange for my freedom
Would be like offering me a drop of blood
In exchange for my heart.

F Esther Barnard
LOST IN AN OASIS
Tiny city park oasis
in the midst of concrete desert;
mecca of the maimed and lost,
destitute and lonely people.

Drifting—hunting, ducks and geese
on a lake of torpid water;
boys in summer feeding catfish;
boys and girls in winter skating.

Silvered lovers in their twilight;
youthful lovers strolling, laughing—
all encircled by the traffic:
sirens screaming, red lights flashing.

In the darkness, silent meetings—
tiny embers, acrid odors:
tiny city park oasis,
Jesus' name profanity!

JoAnn Woody
PLEASE
You came into my world one bright and sunny day,
And Darlin' I just knew your love was here to stay.

And as Old Father Time began to turn the clock around,
I realized your love was the truest I had found.

So Darlin' won't you promise me that you'll never leave,
And that because of your true love, I'll have no cause to grieve.

Well now the years have passed away, and with them your love's gone.
I thought your love was stronger than the strongest bond.

So Darlin' won't you please, just listen to my plea,
And bring your love on home, back to your ever-lovin' me.

Mrs Nell Reed
GENTLE SPRING
It seems of all the seasons,
That each year come 'round,
The one I like the best,
Has the most gentle sound,
Winter seems too harsh,
Fall a bit too bland,
Summer is too crisp,
Hot and crackling is the land,
But spring's cool breezes blow,
And cool us as we stride,
The blossoms of the trees,
No longer do they hide,
And even yet its name,
So pleasing to the ear,
Is joyfully received,
When someone says,
Spring is here!

Ernest Paul
**THE DAY WILL COME—
WHEN YOU ARE ALONE**
The day will come—when you are alone—waiting for a ring on your telephone—but—there will be a knock—on your front door—a knock—you have never heard before.
You go to see—and at the door—there will be someone you have never seen before—he will speak to you—in a solemn voice—and tell you—then and there—today my friend—you have no choice—I—tell you now—your time has come—so please—pack your bags—and come along.
Just where you go—no one will know—but—if you have—lived—a life of evil—I am sure—he will—take you to the Devil.

Evelyn Achilles Nadeau
MY GARDEN
I've often wandered, in my dreams,
through forest and fields of green or gray.
I've run through drops of rain, laughing,
smelling flowers newly born,
reaching for an elusive space
to plant my dreams and harvest their moods;
to watch my vines entangle my life.
My garden overflows!

D Marshall
LEAVING
Names fade, faces dim, easily forgotten.
I never know when they cease to exist.
Most vanish no matter how I try to retain.
But even today, you remain.

As I walk through the past of my life,
Memories are there, some live, some die.
And friends are the ones I think of most,
When it's late at night or in places remote.

All I can say is you're one of those.
And you'll always be a part of me.
Of all the friends I've loved who left,
I'll miss you most, 'cause I loved you best.

Mary D Sands
HILLS OF HOME

To Obbie—my little sister

Once, when we were very young
We climbed the velvet hills of spring,
Brushing the star flowers in the grass
To free the black-bird's wing.

There, far below, lay home and love.
We were so safe, so very sure.
Spring promised brighter skies above,
The wind blew sweet and pure.

Lost in the high pines, all the world
Faded away in a haze of blue.
The bluejay scolded from his perch,
The squirrel called to you.

Now I am trapped here, held by life
To chores that fret in hours long.
The feet that once ran young and free,
To slower walks belong.

True, I may never climb again
The hills of home where hearts find rest,
Yet eyes may seek the pine topped peak—
In memories be blest.

William H Rose 3rd
MOCKINGBIRD
With flurries of complaints she
readies her boat each spring.
And lowd protestations accompany
her lovely lawns and gardens' care.
Skeptical is her scrutiny of latest
sparkling ring.
And criticize her household
decorations if you dare,
Yet never will you match her deep
disdainful eye.
Shopping by the hours produces
clothing by the bulging bale
But dressing for the next occasion
elicits only a discontented sigh
And searching for perfection
continues with each successive sale.
Carefully collected china, crystal,
silver, prints and glass
Fill her drawers, line her cabinets
and cover her walls.
Her care is endless, she cleans,
shines and polishes with every pass.
Her need to acquire is endless and
endlessly it calls.
But, be it night time, dawn or day,
she always hears his varied song
above.
It is the mockingbird that so delights
my love.

Mr Masao Kinoshita
OCTOBER 15TH, 1973
Follow your heart's desire
In wild flighted passion
Reach out with all your power
Enter your very dimension
Bright colors dance all 'round
Imagined Christmas tree blurred
Running wild and flying 'round
Dragging a Trans Am Firebird

Noreen M Countie
FOOLISH
Love is endless, love is strong.
It has no boundaries, it has no form.
The wind, the sea,
A breath, a song.

Destiny is a lost hope
for you and for me.
This foolish, endless love
never to be.
How hopeless the efforts
to hold on become.
We are foolish, we are young.

Mary Champion
COUNTRY BOY
Along the winding road he went
lugging books the teacher sent,
scanning rocks and earthy crust
for snakes that make tracks in dust,
banging pail that faintly smelled
of eggs and jar that peaches held.
Once he stopped to look inside,
tasting crumbs that time had dried.

Maple leaves come drifting down,
striking ground without a sound,
making red and golden bed
ere they become a wet brown dead.
September winds blow 'cross his face,
nodding the heads of Queen-Anne's lace,
then picking up sounds of children's yells
that faintly echoed through the hills.

Many years have passed since they
from that country lane did stray
to distant cities—different employ—
each part of him—that country boy.

Jo Ann Marcoly
DEAR GOD
Dear God
Why do I lose faith in your love?
You're always there for me.
But, I guess I don't take much notice
in you.
When I don't know which way to
turn, you're there.
If I could just realize I don't need
anything in life but you.
Lord, help me overcome my
problems.

Is there any reason for me to go through all this pain?
Do I have a reason to live?
To be alive?
I can't comprehend because all of this is really insane.

Jane B Cox
THE STONE WALL

Dedication—To Peter—The best of Son-in-Laws

The Stone Wall is covered with ivy mostly,
very protective for those who
are in need of.
In the early settlers' days would be considered a fort,
Those passing by can look, and
see over the top of the wall.
We are not completely alone.

In the village are many walkers, cars going about are few.
Different from the hustle and
bustle just a few miles away.
A village distinctly of quiet importance.
Quite, nearby the trains go
humming by to and from the
city throughout the day.
A major part of the charming
village.

Also can be heard the gentle toll of the bells in the steeple,
While folks are dining in the
pleasantry of home.

Over the stone wall can be seen the College Campus,
which to all is a never ending
attribute.
The students are happily walking to and fro.
Those behind "The Stone Wall"
keep a cheery attitude.

Jo Ann Hileman
AS I CLOSE MY EYES

For my daughters, Dorreen and Elena. And for all children everywhere.

As I close my eyes
To say goodnight.
I wish my Daddy
could hold me tight.

I'll be good, and if I cry
Mommy's there to dry my eyes.

It won't be long
I'll sing a song.

Dear Lord, just let him know
How much we love him so.

Edward Kneeland Shelton
FATE
At the top of the stairs, there stand two doors.
One of them mine, and one of them yours.
The angel of death waits to gather his due,
Will it be me, or will it be you?
Fate stands on the landing, looks left then looks right,
Which of our hearts will be stilled in the night?
We both say our prayers, and make pact with our God,
Sleep sound in the knowledge that his staff and his rod,
Will protect us from the one, that takes life in the night,
But God allows fate to say when the time's right.
I wake in the morning, not knowing your plight,
Or the fatal decision made deep in the night.
I go on with my life, Oh I choose to ignore,
Until fate's, on the landing, outside of my door.

Debra Norris Goodman
WEBS
Spiders weave their sticky webs,
And sometimes, people, too
I have often wondered
Exactly, why they do?

If, I were a spider,
I would weave my web to snare
All the people that I love
And those of whom I care.

With all my arms, I'd hold
Them close,
So I could make them see,
Their lives could be so happy,
If, they were stuck with me.

Donna DeMarco-Panico

Donna DeMarco-Panico
WELCOME TO THE NINETIES
Welcome to the nineties.
Let's hope we have some fun.

We've just been through the eighties
Where our lives nearly came undone.

Reagan and Khadafy, rivals to the end.
Who can win the war of will—the fight of mighty men?

Welcome to the nineties.
We just left a decade behind.

Hostages were taken.
Governments left benign.

Welcome to the nineties.
The eighties were a mess.

Our neighbors near and far,
Still fighting not to be oppressed.

Welcome to the nineties
Let's strive for a brighter day.

Let us hope negotiations stay alive
And disarmament is on the way.

Welcome to the nineties.
Bush is at the helm.

We pray he steers our ship correct.
He is in charge of our realm.

Leah V Gillman
THIS DAY WILL NEVER COME AGAIN
This day will never come again
Take from it what you can
Live it to the fullest
But don't hurt your fellowman
For if you do, it's all too true
Wherever you may go
When you are least expecting
The little deed will show
In someone's eyes or attitude
Or just the way they act
You may never make it up
Or ever take it back
The mind is so computerized
It gathers what it can
It's up to us to see that
We don't hurt our fellowman

Beverly Schmidt
UNICORN
Clouds of white in sky of blue
Field flowers scent the air
White in a field of blue, green and purple
Pure and genuine 'til death
The unicorn stands alone
Golden horn shimmering in the sun
Birds resting upon its back

Lynn Moses
SOMETIMES
Sometimes it's easy to write a song
The words just seem to belong.

Sometimes in the evening
as the sun is setting
The colors shine a radiant glow.

Sometimes as I sit taking it all in
I know that it was
meant to be so.

Sometimes when I've been looking for peace.
That's when the gentle feeling
surrounds me again.

Sometimes peace comes
in the colors of the sun.

Catherine Beardsley
LITTLE GIRL

I dedicate this to all of the abused children on the face of the earth

Hey little girl, why so sad
You look so lonely, you're feeling real bad
Who is crushing your world, with anger and hate
Who wants to hurry and make you wait.
You feel so deserted by those you love.
You pray so hard to God up above.
Is someone inflicting remorse and shame
They don't understand that you can't play this game.
You feel so alone. You wish you could die
each day of your life, that pain makes you cry
I know who you are, I know how you feel
and believe me these feelings you're feeling are real
Let me come into your world of fear
I'll love you sweetheart, You are so dear
Let us be friends, I'll help you along
Together we can make each other strong
You're worthy of love. You need some care
and all of this with you I will share.
We'll break out of this hole and grow like a tree
I'll take care of you sweetheart
because you are me.

Linda Aker
THE LADY IN THE CHAIR
Oh how I feared the lady in the chair
Yet something always drew me there
She could only sit as time passed by
and yet she never saw a cloud in the sky
she told me I was like her as a child
Perhaps this was the fear that drove me wild
She seemed so content, Happy and carefree
I searched so hard to find a key
To unlock some sadness, Despair or hate
For her life, I thought, an awful fate.
I found nothing hidden behind her door
She had found the richness of life, only I thought her poor.
I no longer fear that lady in the chair you see,
through her, I became a better me!

John M Pollard Sr
TROUBLED TIMES
Times are getting harder, as days go by
And it seems like a black cloud, is covering the sky
The pay is slowly rising, but the jobs are going down
And there is poverty, all around town
There is poverty among Whites, and poverty among Blacks
Because poverty strikes hard, on both sides of the tracks
With this poverty, comes an increase in crime
That has reached its high, for our day and time
People today, don't care about one another
And man don't realize, that each man is his Brother
If people helped one another, instead of hindered
And all inner hostilities, were freely surrendered
The world today, would not be as bad
And mothers and fathers, would not be as sad
I for one, do cherish more brighter days
This can be done, in some very simple ways
By loving one another, and giving a helping hand
By trying to believe, in your fellow man
By living a clean life, to insure peace of mind
And by saying a prayer, for all mankind

David L Bell
VISIONS

A special dedication, To my special friend. (Note for note.)

You are the song in my soul,
The flowers that bloom in the spring.
You are the only thoughts I know,
The reason I have songs to sing.

You are my ocean, I am your tiniest drop.
You are my path to a perfect love.
I am your valley, you are my mountain top.
You are the delight of a pure white dove.

You are the whisper of wind in the trees,
The petals of every flower.
You are the silence of my eternal peace,
The freshness of a spring shower.

You are the prayer to an unknown god,
The light of all my inner joy.
You are the wings to my heaven,
In your presence, I am but a boy.

You are my freedom from darkness into light,

My earthly angel of vision.
You are my shining star in the dark of night,
The diamond of my inspiration.

Nancy Decker
ANOTHER NEW YEAR
Another new year is upon us,
The beginning of nineteen eighty nine.
What is in store for you and me,
At this date in time?
Will there be sadness and sorrow,
Or happiness and joy?
Do we know what will be tomorrow.
Who has the power to destroy,
Or build and make things new.
To tear down what is good,
Or root out evil from the core.
If we all help as we should,
Together we accomplish more.
To bring about peace and happiness
And gather friendships at our door.
So let us build this new year,
And make it better
For people far and near,
And for those yet to come.

Brenda Carraway Howell
MOTIONLESS

To my son, Tommy Edwards, with great love and respect.

I'm twisted, I'm tangled, I have no motion. I see out my two eyes, I see what I see. Mine is an ugly world, full of ways of hate and deceit.

I strive on hurting myself. I shout out because it makes my insides soothe with joy. Look at my face, and see my soul. Buried in lies and deceit.

I cry out at you, "I hate you," I say. No one hears what I have to say, because all they see is my spiteful ways.

"Come out of me," I yell at myself, a prisoner of a monster, I created myself.

Lisa Stephan

Lisa Stephan
A BATTLE FOR LIFE
There's a downpour of blood coming from your wrist,
As you cry and plead for friends.
The love you felt poured out with the blood,
As your life crawls to an end.
You begin to weep as the pain overcomes you
And tears fall desperately from your eyes,
You want another chance to live
But the razor doesn't understand your cries.
You start to scream and beg
As you fall on to your knees
You remember those who love you
As you willingly struggle to breathe.
You pray hopelessly that it's a dream
And your life will be restored,
But you were playing with death;
The everlasting blood continues to pour.
In your last few moments of regret
You see a blinding light;
You've taken your last breath
And now it seems you've lost the fight.

Chris Chew Smith
MY BEST FRIEND
This is for a friend,
Who will never know,
The beautiful friendship,
I had to let go.

At one time,
We were so tight,
But over the years,
Would argue and fight.

He had a problem,
That he would deny,
Causing friction,
Between him and I.

It took all my power,
To leave him that day.
But for his benefit,
I will stay away.

It's best for him,
It's best for me.
And best friends,
We can no more be.

He's doing great,
I'm glad to hear,
He doesn't smoke,
Or need a beer.

We were closer,
Than he knew,
And I sure am
Missing you . . . my best friend.

Steven Ferguson
THE HELL CALLED PRISON

To My Dearest Love Darlene & son Patrick D., Whom stayed by my side and kept my spirits up, also to my Parents for helping me, and May Jehovah God keep you in his memory. S.J.F.

Men so tired and left all alone
To live in a world of steel and stone;
Where hours are slow and seem never to pass
Where the day is like the year that lasts & lasts.

Where hope and dreams have been buried alive
And hate and pain lives and strives;
Where men are beaten and treated cruel,
Where "The strong survive" is the Golden Rule.

Where men are fed just like a hog,
Chained and beaten like some kind of dog;
Where sleeps not sleep but just a way,
To escape from the rest of the hellish day.

Where men have lost all reason to care,
Alone in life they've nothing to share;
No hopes, no dreams, no riches nor fame,
Nothing is left but heartaches and shame.

Where the soul burns a little more each day,
And the body slowly fades away;
Until nothing is left but a human shell,
wasting away in a manmade hell.

Yes, men locked away in a cell,
To live their lives in a nightmarish hell;
And a place where debts to society are paid,
The Hells Called Prisons That men have made.

Charlie Earl Porter
MEMPHIS CLOSE ENCOUNTER

Dedicated to the Sherells the singing group I met at the Maredian Naval Air Station USO show. When it is a question of to Red Ball or not to Red Ball.

My true love let go to Memphis!
There is work I hear on the river front,
and these cotton bowls hurts my hands . . .
The logging season is almost over . . . .
and the well water is filled with sand.

At twilight time down by the river,
the romance is so intense . . . .
The Delta Queen just blows its whistle . . . .
While bursting with song and dance.

My fair lady let us meet in Memphis!
There is a street up there—they call it Beal,
Where people meet to sing and swing . . . .
While musicians play both horn and string . . . .
and this soil is getting hard to till.

From coast to coast across the nation,
they proclaim with acclamation . . . .
The city is clean and streets are gleaming . . . . .
the people are honored to say.

As you walk along you see faces beaming,
and if you ask you are quickly told . . . .
It was the home of a king you know . . .
the king of rock and roll.

The city is most impressive tho,
with Christ on the rise . . . .
There is a magic in the air that lingers . . . .
the magic of the love of God.
God has not left this place—oh!
quite the contraire . . . .
his power is being revealed with Life eternal everywhere!

Charlie Earl Porter
OUR LAND

Dedicated to Odessa Porter, a woman with the widows' box of celebrity artifacts from the Peabody Hotel in Memphis Tennessee custodian, her late husband.

Iris Lymeric
There was a Saintly Land—'twas like heaven it ran.
They all got together to see,
what they could name it yes in deed!
They all decided yes aree . . . .
To call it "OUR LAND."!

James B Hughes
GLIMMERING HOPE

Dedication—To the children of the world.

Look ahead, a tiny speck in the vastness of time.

All eyes are destined to see its sparkle, its shine;

A reflection of life that all strive to see.

The child's eyes search beyond blue skies, their innocence is our key.

Death on the battlefield looked at with pity; violence in the streets is survival in the city.

The children's knowledge holds our fate.

Our stubbornness erases their simple wisdom as we teach them to hate.

A love for life strong in their hearts, they will conquer even the steepest slope,

Giving them a chance to express themselves is our last glimmering hope.

Charlie Earl Porter
ROSE LIGHT

Dedicated to Dianna Ross who I dreamed had shot me in the back because I would not sing at Motown Records.

The Rose is a flower with exquisite beauty.

The soft petal of a rose can only be described to the person who has experienced the subtle brush of its soft petals against their skin.

The fragrance has been simulated, while futile attempts have been made to capture the smell of a fresh rose in bodies and bottles for years.

To look upon a rose in the brisk morning light while the dew is laden upon its petals, makes it shimmer with dimension and depth of softness.

A person cannot describe a rose to another—he or she has to experience the rose.

The Love Light . . . . Rose Light, the Winning Light of the World!

Erna M Sawyers
THREE GRAY WHALES
Three gray whales were having fun, not far from the ocean shore,
They were happy jumping about, not realizing winter had come;
There was no way out to the open sea, altho' men had tried in vain
To open a path, so that they would be free again.

The cry went out over the wire, "Let's try to save the whales"!
Everyone was willing, they came from near and far with generous equipment, toiling
by day and under the stars.
Those who couldn't go, stayed home, sent cash and said prayers.

Yet, it seemed, like everything had failed, and time was running out;

It had already for one gray
whale, as it slipped out of sight.
The other two were cut and
bruised, from sharp ice around
the holes;
When lo, an ice cutter could be
heard to free their prison wall!

The crowd sent up a victory cry,
the two gray whales were
free!
The last that, was seen of them,
they were swimming out to
sea;
Somewhere out there, I am sure,
they bask in waters warm;
And if they could talk, would
surely say, "thanks everyone
for helping us back home."

Undrala R White
BOASTING WITH PRIDE
His lapels lay flat
to his broad chest
where his arms were
sternly crossed.

The muscles in his neck
seemed to keep his tie
straight and his head high.

His hair was receding slightly
but the distinctly placed grey
made your eyes only drop to
his thick mustache, of the
same blend.

It was there where his spirit
was discovered through the
biggest, brightest, and
most beautiful smile.

Anna Lou Bozeman
MY DARLING DAUGHTER
You're my darling daughter,
I love you more each day.
If possible, I love you more
Today than I did yesterday.

Just think of all the tomorrows,
For my love for you to grow.
It grows as fast as you do,
And that's still a way to go.

Thank God for a daughter like you,
Someone so fine and true.
Who is there when I cry and when
I laugh.
Then I feel completely whole
Not half.

Love you,

Mommy

Nicole Chantee'
LONELY? WHY NO!
Lonely, why no, I should say not!
Having to spend all your time by
yourself,
Doing what you want.
Looking forward to tomorrows dawn
and sunset.
Seeing the beauty in children at play.
Walking alone at night on cool sand.
Cuddling up with good music and a
book.
Laughing at a new comedy on TV.
Lying alone when you're ill.
And just to cry for no reason.
This is not lonely—
It's just not having someone to share
it with!

Mary K Hilty
HAVE YOU?
Have you been in the mountains at
sunrise,
Watched the deer come out of the
pine
Searching for the spring and the salt
lick
Jumping gracefully with white flag
behind?

Have you seen the trout rise to your
bait,
In a stream swift running and cool?
Or watched shadows changing at
noontime
Shimmering on a still mountain
pool?

Have you walked through the forest
at sunset
Smelling the sweet pungent odor of
pine,
Stepped over a log or a tree stump
Trod softly on moss or on vine?

Have you slept in the mountains at
night,
And heard the hoot of the owl in the
tree
And awoke at the first sign of
daylight
Feeling rested and happy and free?

Valerie Williams
LOVE CAN GROW
Our love can grow
Day by day.
Through friend and foe
Together we stay.

Our love grew stronger
As days passed by.
The nights seemed longer
But dawn was nigh.

Our love, now,
Is at its highest peak.
I don't know how
'Cause in the beginning it was weak.

Of course I didn't mind.
I knew you felt the same.
We're one of a kind
In this real life game.

Laura J Billingsley
TODAY I BROUGHT ROSES

To the Veterans of Foreign Wars

We've shared a perfect love, for
three short years today.
Last night I dreamt of you, and
wondered what you'd say.
If I told all the dreams I've had, you
just might be amused;
But in your laughing eyes I'd see
your love, and I'd laugh too.
I dream of you each night and
sometimes wake with a start;
But thoughts of you and all we've
shared will always fill my heart.

Remember, dear, our hopes and
dreams; the things we planned
together;
The life we lived in that time, proves
our love will live forever.
I never tire of memories of the wars
you fought to win;
And I'll be back tomorrow, to bring
you fresh flowers again
But today I brought Roses to lay
down on the snow;
And show the world I love the one,
here, six feet below.

Renee M LaTourrette
DAYBREAK ON THE HILLS OF JERUSALEM
Jerusalem at dawn:
the donkey's gentle braying
brushes my sleepy soul
with his downy message.
Big black ants
begin their busy day
carrying heavy loads, and
Jesus asks for mine.

Jerusalem at dawn:
scarred parched hills,
the liquid sun has discovered
your nakedness.
The sad eyed floppy eared
sheep
spill over your shame
and give you back
your dignity.

Jerusalem at dawn:
distant bells are ringing
Jesus weeps
and a crown of thorns
is at my feet.

Arleen C Duwel
I NOW HAVE HOPE!

To My Husband Garry, For giving me the Inspiration! Love Ya Always—Arleen.

Babe,
I now have hope—
that we can cope!

It must start from the heart,
so we may live and truly give!

I know you work hard—
this I cannot discard!

I may be on a cloud but . . .
that's because I am proud!

I realize at times
I'm not so understanding—
and even more so demanding!

We have two beautiful and healthy
boys—
who will bring us lots of joys!

Baby, maybe we'll be o.k. with this I
say—
please don't ever go away!

I don't mean to be this way—
I just got to say—
"I Love You with all my Heart."

All My Love—
Arleen.

Starla Smith
NEVER SAY GOODBYE

This poem is dedicated in loving memory of my brother, Robin Smith

His life was short
but so well lived
Oh, to have him back
What I wouldn't give.

A special person
he was indeed
for a friend he would be there
in any time of need.

Giving flowers of love
and cards from the heart
this makes it more sad
he had to depart.

These little treasures
he left behind
are hidden, waiting
for me to find.

Each one holds a memory
a story of its own
for when I want to recall him
since I can't pick up the phone.

He's gone now in body
but in spirit he still lives
within me, always
and advice he still gives.

Even though he had to die
as long as I have my memories,

I'll never say goodbye.

Annemarie Mullaney
QUEST FOR KNOWLEDGE
The world keeps turning,
My mind keeps burning
with questions that should be
answered
by years of learning.

Who am I?
Where am I going?
Why do we die?
When will I stop growing?

The world is spinning
Yet, no one is winning
the war against themselves.

We have a beginning . . . .

Each day as we rise
marks a new dawning
and brings constant surprise
My curiosity continues to burn,
and I shall never abandon my
quest to learn.

Dahna Cheryl Allensworth

Dahna Cheryl Allensworth
I DON'T KNOW!
I don't know what to say you see;
Except I wish you were looking at
me:

I feel so empty and have lost all
hope;
Next time I won't tell you I'll just
cope:

I sigh by day and cry by night;
Maybe a new love will come and I'll
see the light:

I'm so scared I can hardly face you;
I don't know what to say and I don't
know what to do:

All I can say and all I can do;
Is go to you and say "I LOVE
YOU!"

Carolyn S Harvey
ROOTS
Across the cornfield I look to see,
Sunbeams rising to greet a new day.
As the peace and quiet surround me,
I wonder what the weatherman will
say.

Last year, the loss was plain to see.
Our spirits rise after a good rain.
Patience comes hard tilling this prairie,
But the cows need a lot of grain.

Although drafty when winter comes,
This old house stands true to form.
For a century or more, say some.
But the love living here is warm.

With toil and sweat of generations before me,
A high price for our farm was paid.
This is where I always want to be.
All that I am, has been country-made!

Grant C Swanson
WHAT IS LOVE?

To the ladies who held my fragile heart, and broke it.

Love is a beautiful red rose,
Irresistible, tempting and exciting.
You hold it tight,
And it cuts you deep with its thorns.
Yet you grasp for more,
No matter how much you bleed.
Because in love as life,
There are no boundaries.

Kenneth H Smith
A CHRISTMAS MEMORY

I dedicate this poem to my dad, Vernon Smith. For without living it, I couldn't have written it. Thanks Dad.

Once upon a Christmas,
With snow upon the ground.
There was a simple Christmas,
With presents brightly bound.

With daddy out of work,
We never dreamed or asked for more.
Than the love of our family,
On this crisp Christmas morn.

Yet, the stockings were full of candy,
Each and every one.
Yet, we felt the love,
Stronger than our own.

The love of our Father,
Is what Christmas is all about.
It's not how many presents you get,
It's how much love you give back out.

Mary C Suniga
A PRAYER FOR YOU AND ME
Before I lay down to sleep
And as I'm closing my eyes
I pray a prayer for you and me.
I pray that we stay together
And if this is love
To let it last forever and ever.
When I pray God will hear
For all the faith I have is in him.
So I have nothing to fear
As I pray this prayer for you and me.

Abdul M Mandani
DON'T GIVE UP!
When the going gets tough,
When everything looks so rough,
You fail even when you do your best,
Don't give up then, don't rest.

When you feel all beat-up and sore,
And think it's no use trying anymore,
When you stumble, fall and are hardest hit,
Don't give up then, don't quit.

When success seems out of reach,
When failure sticks to you like a leech,
Pull up your socks, roll up your sleeves,
Don't give up then, don't leave.

When you feel downcast and blue,
Brace up and battle it through;
When you find nothing is going right,
Don't give up then—stand up and fight.

When you live through your trouble,
You become seasoned and more stable,
For the grandeur of life is born of defeat,
When you give up, you leave your life incomplete!

Sandra D Bufkin
MODERN DAY KNIGHT

To: Steve I need You Knight and Day Love Always Sandy

You are My Modern Day Knight.
Although you wear no armor, You protect me just the same.
There are no Dragons, With fire breathing breath.
Only hard times that scare me half to death.
You carry no sword, But your words sometimes cut like a knife
When I need you, I never fear.
Without saying a word you know I need you near.
Sometimes I start crying, Because I feel our love's dying.
But you Always pull us through.
You let me know that no one Loves me better than you.
No one has to tell me, Cause that's something I know.
You'll never desert me, and I'll never let you go.
I'll Love you for Always. The way you Love me.
And when ever I need you, You'll be here for me
As I'll, Be here for you.

Mary Eleanor Chambers
BABY
Oh yes here I go
for me you will know.

I have a sad heart
cause we're so far apart.

I set on my big fat tuffie
holding on to my sweet puppy

Watching a boring old TV show
with your old step pa you know.

I guess it doesn't matter;
eating more and getting fatter.

Sometimes I drive my new car,
hardly ever go very far.

Writing you a big old letter;
don't always tell you about the weather.

Oh yes I'm none other,
just your old fattie mother.

Missy Bailey
A SPECIAL FRIEND

I dedicate this poem to Denise Carter, my best friend and my inspiration. I also dedicate it to John K. Gallentine for his support and encouragement.

To only you I tell
This secret of a special friend
Whose ideas are clear as a bell.
She is secretly modest,
Even when she shows
The spirit of kindness
Which is rarely found
In friend or in foe.
To list all her qualities
I could not do, for,
She hides many
And shows very few.
Quietly she speaks,
With a soft friendly tone
To friends and enemies,
At school and at home.

Alice Kemppa
THE EAGLE FLIES IN TRUTH AND GRACE

To "Piiku"
Thanks for your encouragement!

The eagle flies in truth and grace
To dignify our freedom's face.
Shall he be downed before his time,
Without a tear from all mankind?

Or will we keep reality
And soar to heights we cannot see?
To live again with joy in truth
On wondrous lands to leave our youth.

Man will decide the fate of earth
And test his judgment for its worth.
The sky is dark without a sun
As we survey what we have done.

Will he close his eyes and try to hide?
Or will he smile with waves of pride?
Will ominous shades be put to rest....
Will the eagle fly—did we do our best?

Kenneth J Hamburger
NEVER WORKING WELL TOGETHER
Never working well together
things all seem to break down.
Have you seen the weather?
it rains on me
until I drown.

You and I
are not so far from being together.
The things you do
the lies we tell
to stop the truth from hurting you.

Tommy F Castillo
REMEMBER ME

To my mother Adonna for being strong and believing in me, and Dale K. for being patient and supportive.

My heart holds so much room,
It pains to be filled.
The emptiness is dark,
And the loneliness cold.
Hear the silence.
Remember me
Love is deep and sharp.
I share freely to you
My Dreams,
Behold! FIRE! FLAME!
Fantasy renamed.

Remember me
Shadows dance with my soul,
Drinking my essence.
Take of me all that I may give.
Fear not.
When you
Remember me

Carole Anne McGriff
TO GRANDMA
You rocked me in your arms
And wrapped your love around me,
You wiped away my tears
When I fell and scraped my knee.

Lessons of love and life you taught
And passed them on to me,
You showed me the ways of caring
While sitting on your knee.

Sounds of fun and laughter
Still echo in my ear,
Memories of those childhood days
Are still held very dear.

Even though the miles separate us
And the years have gone by too,
Our lives still touch in that special way
And I wrap my love around you.

Lauretta L Ferriera
TWO OF A KIND
Mere words cannot reveal,
the pain I feel inside.
Everytime I think about you,
I get tangled up inside.
The reason for living,
has suddenly become unknown.
For when I think of life without you,
I feel so alone.
As you may know, I'm still hoping,
Someday we might find—
That we were destined to be together
Our being two of a kind.

Robert Buchanan
CARDBOARD HEARTS
Happiness,
Is hard to come by
In a world full of
Cardboard hearts.
Where honor means nothing
And love even less
To give up your love,
Is to offer your life
And when love is taken
And not returned
Your life is gone.
For love to a cardboard heart
Is death by a cardboard mind.
Papercuts hurt.

H W Shelling
THE MELLOW RING
Wondrous is the art with wide latitude,
To change and beautify a platitude,
And make of it , each dull ill-spoken word,
Flow gently so its triteness goes unheard,
In verse or song, endowed with mellow ring,
That no prosaic sound can ever bring.

Marge Donner
A TREE IN THE FOREST
A tree in the forest
strong and vivacious
I sat next to
carefully
not to damage it
I put my ear against the bark

the lifeblood stirred within
I could hear the running
through the branches
then
I leaned on the tree
hoping the life too
would stir in me

Dreama K Martin
BLUE WONDER
It was silently calling to her
To come into the blue wonder
It was singing a beautiful song
That the young girl had heard before
Its beautiful fingers
Motioned for her to come
The girl was still kneeling
Just an inch or two away
Then the naive girl
Took the invitation
She walked forward
Letting the fingers grab her ankles
Then she became afraid
And ran back to her place
Finally she became brave again
And ran into the blue wonder to become a fish

Virginia Allen Roscoe
THIS I BELIEVE

To Matthew Tucker, my little grandson, so greatly loved, and the joy of my life.

Death, the intruder in life,
Strikes at our earthly being,
Bringing it to an end
So a great spiritual re-birth——
A journey into Eternity, can begin!
Our soul, at last set free
From pain and sorrow,
Doubt and fear,
From toil and strife,
Our Saviour near,
Joyous and happy,
Christ's followers, forever live
In His promise fulfilled.
This, then, the dear Lord's will!

Bonnie Spence Ceglowski

Bonnie Spence Ceglowski
PARADOX
DEAR OLD LOVE:
DARE I SEE YOU AGAIN? ?
FOR, I FEAR (THE LOSS OF THE DREAM)
AND THE STRENGTH, and comfort, ITS DELUSION
AFFORDS ME IN MY DARK HOURS, those fearful times
when i wrap myself in the shroud
glittering with the fantasy
WHERE I CAN
CHASE THE CHILL OF WINTER
WHERE I CAN
WARM MY FROZEN SOUL
and then IF I SHOULD MEET YOU, AND YOU AND I
DISCOVER IT IS
TRULY OVER! ! ! ! ! ! ! !
if you shake your head in disbelief,
and think "whatever did i see"
? ? ? ? ? ? ? ? ? ? ? ? ? ? ? ? ? ? ?
then
my security,
my safe delusions, my Love fantasies
* * *
would shatter
and i would be
standing
alone
without even the pretense! !
perhaps I would feel free,
PERHAPS STRONGER,
PERHAPS LOST?
PERHAPS
THE EMPTY PAIN OF A LOST LOVE,
AND
THE MEMORY OF SOMETHING (VERY SPECIAL)
that i choose to lose, so long ago
would cease to twinge
lest more? ? ?
PERHAPS, WE WILL ACKNOWLEDGE THAT IT HAD ITS TIME
NEVER TO BE AGAIN
AND THAT KNOWLEDGE WILL BRING US COMFORT
PERHAPS, I FEAR
(AS YOU DO ALSO,
THOUGH YOU DON'T ADMIT)
that the magic will once again ignite
FIRE, WITHIN OUR WAITING, SOULS,
AND THE LOVE WILL JUST BEGIN? ! *
I LONGINGLY AWAIT THE DESIRE OF YOUR REPLY! !
FOREVER LOVING YOU;
MISSY

Trudy H Burkham
CHASING FIREFLIES

To my loving husband, who has always believed in me.

Fireflies darting through the evening sky
Glow much brighter than the stars on high.
It's hard to catch one as they flee here and there;
They flicker, and then disappear.
Silently, they glide around.
A child's sharp laughter is the only sound
Assaulting the stillness of a hot summer night,
Breaking the monotony of the heavy quiet.
Oh, to be a child again,
Chasing fireflies as the day dims.

Elisabeth A Perry
REMINISCENCE

Dedicated to James—may all your dreams come true.

I thought of you today, as I so often do—I remembered the good times between me and you. The bad times are over, so far away, and I cannot remember where time took away . . .

The love of a lifetime, for you and for me, the helpmate ever faithful, oh how can it be—That I no longer share the dreams of yesterday? Did I see them slipping? Did I ask them to stay? Did I care to take hold of a future so bright? Did I let love leave me without even the sight—Of a broken heart shattered by life's foolish game? Did I know that life would never be the same?

Or did I run blindly to a room with no door, no way to get back to where I was before? Did I see a soul lonely, so ever alone, searching for healing of a heart hardened like stone?

The questions are endless and await the day, when my heart is whole again, whole enough to say—That I can love again, no matter the cost; I can open the door to a feeling once lost.

I can trust in someone; I can bare my soul. I can be vulnerable and still remain whole. I can look to the future and never look behind, because in the future is happiness to find.

Crissy Pocock
FRIENDS FOREVER
It had to happen sometime,
Just not as soon as it did.
We'd been best friends for a long time,
And now it had to end.

The fight, the awful fight,
Though it wasn't really there.
My best friend had betrayed me,
And she didn't even care.

I told myself to forget it
We'd make up very soon.
But the more I thought about it,
I knew it wasn't true.

We made that promise long ago,
Friends forever.
What happened and why,
The end—friends for never.

Clarice Turner
FRIGHTENED CHILD

To my mother, Verna Hedges, for her love, support and encouragement.

Looking back I remember
a child shivering
not from cold
but from fright
Afraid of a man
who was a part of her
yet distant still
not knowing if the hand
would comfort her
or hurt her

A child shivers
not from cold
but from torment
caused by others
A part of her yet distant
siblings that protected her
yet caused her pain

A child shivers
in the arms of another
the only one who could calm
her fears, protect her
from most, comfort her as no other
the solid ground
her mother . . .

Bradford B Taylor
WHO'S THERE?
The nightlight glows
The shadows appear
The T.V. turned off
The children sleep near.

Here they come
Small but bright
These little creatures
Of the night.
They eat food scraps
They scurry around
They search the house
Without a sound.

A pounce!
What's that?
Oh no!
A cat!

Their eyes get bigger
Then close with fright
These little creatures
Must stay out of sight.

Janice D Miller
NOT A WORD WAS SPOKEN
When you're alone and you're feeling down,
No one's in sight, no one can be found.

The thoughts that you have are hidden within,
Wants to be shared with a relative or friend.

Looking out of your window where you sat all day,
Never a spoken word, no one's walking your way.

The sun is beginning to set,
No spoken word has been said yet.

There's a knock on your front door,
There's two pair of feet, maybe more.

You get out of your chair to let them in,
But, in hours, you find yourself lonesome again.

As you sit down, you remember, that you were never alone.
Next to you sitting on the table lays a friend—
your telephone.

N Sensabaugh
A WORLD WITHOUT MUSIC

To Mrs. Evelyn McCleod with love

I wandered in a fancied world
Where music played no part;
Where no magnetic chords pealed forth
To surge upon my heart

Where no one sang a lovely song
Where violins never played
Where, in the glory of our God
No hymns were ever made.

My heart sank low within my breast
My soul had lost its zeal.
And then I heard a song burst forth
Upon a distant hill.

I joined the song and as I sang
My thoughts were turned above
To God, the great composer
Whose masterpiece is love!

Joseph K Blackwell
8-23-88

To my fellow pioneers and good friends Eric and Jon.

The earth had begun to stir
On this cloudy Sunday morning
So we hurried to the car
For soon it would be pouring
We swallowed the magic herb
A toast to our history
Releasing our lagged minds
To discover the world's mysteries
Racing under stormy clouds
Their beauty setting us free
Forgetting all our troubles
We laughed at today's society
Smiles plastered to our faces
The seven hours seemed like one

And friends would reunite
In the Angeles under the sun
We praised the nature we consumed
In a celestial night of festivities
We traveled to technology
In bliss to conduct our studies
A population of people in line
Their unhappy lives becoming so slate
Three pioneers of physics and psyche
We learned so much as we waited
But if all good things must end
This night will live on forever
The earth might have turned
But my memories I'll never surrender

G P Thompson

G P Thompson
THE COMMON THREAD

To this World of People. "Peace, through understanding."

The Human Race,
likened
to flowers
in the sun,

Are beautiful
to hold,
their colors
never one.

Their tongues
and thoughts,
often mixed
with fire,

Share a
common thread
fulfilled
desire.

Jerome E Buser
OUT IN THE COUNTRY
Out in the country,
Where life is pure and clean.
The best of Mother Nature,
Can be seen.

Wide open the space,
For the animals to play.
Like the parks in the city,
Where they have to stay.

With the birds and the bees,
In the deep blue sky.
There is no smog,
In which they have to fly.

Shrubs and plants and trees,
Many colors do they add.
Like a rainbow,
After a recent rain we had.

In all this beauty,
Man does hold the key.
For the future,
What will it be?

Sean McKenna
DON'T QUIT

Submitted by: Sean McKenna, To my sister Jill . . . Who has put so much love and beauty into my troubled life.

When things go wrong as they sometimes will,
When the road you're trudging seems all up hill . . .
When the funds are low and the debts are high,
And you want to smile, but you have to cry . . .
When care is pressing you down a bit,
Rest if you must, but don't you quit.

Life is queer with its twists and turns,
as everyone of us sometimes learns,
And many a failure turns about
When you might have one had you stuck it out;
Don't give up, though the pace seems slow—
You may succeed with another blow.

And you never can tell how close you are,
It may be near when it seems so far;

So stick to the fight when you're hardest hit—
It's when things seem worst that you must not quit.

Darlene Potrykus
ROMANCE
Whenever I am with You
I am truly filled with Joy
Just as a child with a brand new toy
And every day that we're apart
My mind's eye will still see
All the precious hours that we've shared
And that's wonderful to me
With every touch, every kiss
I yearn for so much more
Of the sweet magic that you give to me
That I've never known before
My heart is very happy
And my soul is made anew
So please remember Darling.
I will Always Love You

Nancy B Love
ODE TO A ROBIN
Hello, little robin! Where is your mate?
Loitering about? Or is he late
Winging north for a rendezvous?
You can't be alone; there are always two,
Unless mischance has befallen one
Or the romance not yet begun.
There are twigs and straw to gather afield,
A site to choose and a nest to build;
Blue eggs to lay and shield from the chill
Until wee ones your warm nest fill.
You'll gather food from the countryside
To stuff the mouths they open wide;
I await your coaxing call to the young
As they test their wings to perches far flung;
You'll scold the cat that ventures near,
Instilling in it a sharp beak fear;
You'll keep close watch o'er growing wee
'Til they're full-feathered, a-wing and free.
Then, work complete, with happy song
You'll share your joy the full day long.

Larry Graves
YOU GOTTA' BELIEVE
Have you ever felt like a grain of sand,
With the waters of time splashing on you?
You haven't got much time to do the things,
That you really want to do.

I feel something, deep inside,
Like a magnet, it's pulling me;
Bringing me closer to the place,
And my meeting with destiny.

Should I run or stay and fight?
My soul in anguish cries;
Is it nobler to search for the truth,
Or hide behind some lies?

All for one, and one for all,
Is the way I was taught to believe;
That everyone had his place,
Some to follow, some to lead.

As time goes by I know I'll find,
The things that are mine to achieve;
And as always my philosophy will be,
To get there, you gotta' believe.

Heather Schumaker
BROKEN-HEARTED
I sit in the dark paralyzed
with fear,
Trying to stop from shedding
my tears,
Wishing everything could change
or maybe just go away,
Hoping he would come back
maybe to stay,
Wishing he was holding me
oh so tenderly,
Trying so hard to get him back
but nothing ever seems to last,
When the hurting never stops
it's hard not to care alot,
All that I'm trying to say
is that life just isn't the same,
Without him near me.

Tara Katz
I LIVE IN ISOLATION
I live in isolation,
Separate from everyone around me,
But there is no one around me,
For I am alone.
I am afraid of the REAL WORLD
That surrounds my kingdom,
The world in which I live,
Alone, in isolation.
I feel fear towards everyone
In the REAL WORLD,
Of which I'm not a part,
In which I don't belong.
I'm powerless in the REAL WORLD,
The world of birth, and death,
The world of pain, and sorrow.
I pray to see the light,
The sun at the end
Of the long bumpy road
That will let me be accepted,
Into the REAL WORLD.

Lisa M Johnson
A TEACHER . . .
A Teacher . . .
the only passage through the dusty green wall.
To explore the deep shadows of school day dreams.
To the remembrance of lost friendships, loves, achievements, and failures.
To see long lost decrepit faces asking for grief from you . . .
the only one left to see the abandoned shadows of such cherished times.
With guilt seeping into the soul,
of the matter which forms the shape you venture in,
as you walk the lonesome hallway of your memory.
You . . . are the only one left.

Phoebe Walton
WRITTEN TRUTH
Feeling alone and sad one day
I sat me down to write,
All the things I could not say,
On pages of gleaming white

But as I wrote, my heart did swell
And a hot tear dimmed my eye
Until my story I did fully tell
And left my cup, now dry

I took that page and read it through
When suddenly to my surprise
I found I'd made a great to-do
Of little things quite unwise

So I sat me down once more
And laughed at my own care
That seemed so very big before
But so small, when written there

Leticia Cruz

Leticia Cruz
DREAMER
Footsteps on a sandy beach I see as I walk by
They are my own I realize as I notice only I have come this way
As I look back I notice that someone has followed me
And has erased every print I've made and not left a trace of thee.
But as I think to try to see who has come this way with me
I notice that through my long trip only water and waves have accompanied me
So I sit down and see that now it is about midnight
And I decide to take a rest, to close my eyes and dream
I dream about a setting sun, two eyes

that meet, and life in paradise
I then awaken and as I stand, I see sunrise has taken place
I walk away and in the sand I see a note which says,
That dreams can sometimes turn into reality
I walk away and as I stand I see that all was just a dream
As I look down upon my bed, I see a note which says
That dreams can sometimes turn into Reality.

Leona Marie Relyea
HERE I AM LORD
"SAY IT WITH LOVE."

"HERE I AM LORD."

Here I am LORD, please heal my soul. Take away all my sins LORD, for "We who love you." Spirit of love LORD, Spirit of GOD. For heal my weakness, "I NEED YOU SO!" Here I am LORD, "GIVE ME YOUR STRENGTH LORD!" and take away my weakness. For here I am. Spirit of love, I will take your hand LORD, I need your love LORD, "So here I am." I need you so LORD, O'h here I am . . .

Marlo Hutts
THE SILENT DANCER
Alone
You start to dance
You twist and twirl
Like a ballerina
You say no words
But still you talk
With your dance
You look at us
Through shining eyes
And tell us
What you are saying
Then you stop
For a moment
There is silence
Then the cannon
Of applause
You bow and blush
And off the stage
You dance
You were
The Silent Dancer.

Ethel F Jeppson
THE IRON HORSE
Have you heard of the tale
Of the swift Iron Horse
And the Posse that never could fail,
Where the desert is rough
And the going is tough
And there's Dope Smugglers free on the trail?
If you've ridden the 'Swell'
You have heard of 'Old Shiek'.
Of his night and day search you retell
Never stopped short of death—
Or to catch a quick breath,
Of his sleuthing you know very well!

Shiek was BORN a show horse,
Never trailed an Outlaw:
Never tracked with a Posse—of course
Yet moved straight as a dye
To the place where they lie
Buried deep in the sand-rough and coarse.
There Shiek froze, ears alert,
Pointing where in a mound
Peeked the collar of someone's white shirt:
In a flash the guns blazed!
Slowly every mound raised
As each smuggler fought free of the dirt!

Now they guessed they must fail
As the Posse, with force,
Had them handcuffed and ready for jail.
But Old Shiek was not through,
There was more he could do!
In a Wash pointed Rue down its trail.
Wisely Rue 'gave him head.'
As he followed his nose,
Seemed by instinct alone to be led.
Darkness fell! They must leave!
Later found cause to grieve!
There were tracks of two men—who had fled!

Cheryl A D'Egidio
ONLY IN MY DREAMS
He seemed so real,
I wanted to believe that he would never leave.
But he was only in my dreams.

His eyes would melt my heart,
And he always knew me as if looking right thru me.
Guess he was only in my dreams.

With a smile just for me,
The love was always there so it didn't seem fair
That he was only in my dreams.

Why did my heart pound so?
As his arms held me tight and the warmth just right.
Could he be only in my dreams?

Whispering words of love.
With a voice soft and kind that floated in my mind.
Yes, he was only in my dreams.

I let him get away.
Wasn't able to grab onto the lover that I wanted to.
I knew he was only in my dreams.

He was the perfect lover.
But his love couldn't last and his warmth soon passed.
Too bad he was only in my dreams.

Magali César
THE PESSIMIST
In this life I have walked the line:
The straight, the true, the very fine.
But what, in return, did I get?
The crooked, the false—only fret!
Thus, now I wonder what to do.
Should I consult the very few
Who, like me, have done only right
To gain this pitiful insight?
Nay, for no one comprehends this:
In this life, there is just no bliss.

Lana Cowans
YES MY LOVE
Yes, my love
I
Would do anything
In
My power
to please
You.

You're
the light
of
My heart
the apple
of
My eye

Yes, My Love
truly
You are
the Rose
of
Sharol
I
will love
You

With
Every ounce
of
this creation
You have
Made

Yes, My Love
I'll
Love you
with
Everything,
And
Fail not
To
Give you
the praises.

Yes, My Love
You're
the blender
of
My life

the Gas
to
My Soul
the Fire
of
My heart

Yes, My Love
You're
the Spring
of
Now and then
And
Forever
More

You're
the Joy
of
My rivers
And
My Valleys
And
My Bright
Morning Star.

Bernice Fice
BEFORE THE MIRROR
As I stand before the mirror,
Can't go on without you, dear,
I miss you so, you'll never know,
Don't break my heart, don't let me go.

As I stand before the mirror,
You're mine, though far or near,
Come back to me, I love you still,
Let's not pretend, our love is real.

As I stand before the mirror,
You're the echo of my life,
Tell me, darling, that you care,
Tell me, won't you be my wife?

Lebron Parker
I WENT BACK TO THE PLACE WHERE

To My Family

I went back to the place where
As a boy I used to play
I sat down in the shade
By the creek where I used to wade
I could still hear the voice of my mom
Saying, "It's time to come home, Tom"
I would get up and go,
But I'd walk very slow
Mom would say, "There is wood to chop
And the hogs need slop,
Then take a bath and wash your head
And come in for supper, there's beans and corn bread"
Beans and corn bread was nothing new,
We had it often on our menu

I went for a look at the old homestead
But in it's place was a honky-tonk instead
That made me feel pretty low
And I knew it was time to go

If you have childhood memories
You want to recall
Remember, you're only young once,
That's all

John Karl Reiman

John Karl Reiman
TOY SOLDIER

This poem is dedicated to Robert Louis Harris, a son for all ages, with love and devotion

We look at him
His shoes are shined, his body trim.
His eyes show keen alert.
His rat-a-tat-tat is set in the ground
Beside a box that feeds it noise.
And our play man kneels by the gun
His plastic arm and the handle one.

His jaws clamp down on duty,
His body rigidly sits
And awaits the distant cry.
Enough my son,
Let the plastic go,
Along with the era of the rolling drums.
For the rat-a-tat-tat deserves no fun
And the sadness and darkness of man
Need the guile and wit of my little son,
Long through the years 'til his life has run.

Arlene J Hibbler
PEOPLE SAY

To my sister Elizabeth, who never let me down and who never let me stay down. I thank you for your love and attention.

People's lives, they come and go
It's in and out and who's to know
What we are—shooting stars
People say

Who's to love and who's to hate
The motion of our heart escapes
Into grief—falling leaves
People say

Miracles in life, are the same
It goes together with happiness
in pain
We are here in time—changing
minds
People say

We rush around and then go
crazy
Or stay in bed until we're lazy
Who's to blame—what a shame
People say

Some times we don't want to
face
Of what we do—from day to
day
Cause we know—we'll feel low
People say

Lance D Utley
QUITE A FRIGHT

I had the terror of my life
While buzzing the banquet knife.
Its huge eyes stared hard, right at me.
Form deadly hands I did flee.

I was only minding my business,
Relieving my emptiness.
Calypso's fruit did catch my eye.
And Odysseus was I.

Upon a mount of potatoes
I did set my sticky toes.
The gravied paste I did enjoy.
Then was the butter's envoy.

And with the knife's blunt blade in
sight,
I did receive quite a fright.
Polyphemus did halt my feast.
With hasty speed I fled east.

His grossly deformed, two-eyed face
Did observe my rapid pace.
My silken wings did beat out
The threat of a one hit bout.

Adah (Penny) Gilmette
FREDDIE

It's twelve years later, and you're still a lazy bum but I still love you Mom.

How do you cope, with a kid with no
hope,
forever making a bed?
He'll just drop his shoes, and simply
refuse,
to come down the stairs to be
fed.

If he had to cook, he'd rather starve,
hey,
talk about being lazy,
But if I go up and take him a tray,
he'll say, "hey man, that's crazy."

His clothes are strewn, all over the
floor,
that room is a total disaster,
I can't shame him into keeping it
clean,
he says "up here I'm the master."

So I'll just keep him, what else can I
do?
since I've got him already.
I'll have to take him, just like he is
cause,
I love that lazy bum "Freddie."

Suzanne Y Reeves
LITTLE PATTERNED FEET

Lemon fresh, morning colored view.
Tangerine curtains that flew.
Whispering pages slip by
beneath cherrywood highs.

Rainy day, Sunday and dry.
Sleepy face, hidden deep sighs.
Playful games, whistling mother's
chair.
Catch-me-can if you dare?

Little patterned feet
stumble to the stairs.
"Here I stand
holding one hand
into the sun"
. . . and the shadow fades.

Gentle touch, silent lullabies
sweep away tender young cries.
Wishful hopes, rescued drowning
dreams.
Loving cycles, past failures
redeemed.

Hoa Le
ASK MOTHER

Kind mother you give birth to me!
but you give birth for what?
if you knew what I'm thinking
then you
Mother would be very sad.

Ancient Mother, exactly like a
flower,
brilliant under the sunlight;
presenting beauty of a
Motherhood
waiting, resembling flowers that
drop off

Mother pick up the flowers falling
on your hand look missing
but missing is nothing
therefore missing is thinking

In the future I like Mother
also pick up the flowers
but which flower belong to
Mother?
which flower belong to me?

Madelyn Nickolds Alixopulos
PURGATORY

Perhaps in some foreign clime, some
distant place,
We may recapture in some measure
The bliss we knew as ours alone.
Beyond the borders of time,
And the restricted confines of space,
I shall look at some bright being
and recognize your face.
We will wander hand in hand,
In places thronged with dreams
With tender lips and soft clear eyes.
And we shall know them as our own
And love them all—until we come
To one completely formed of sighs.
And we will know—God, will we
know
What could have been and never
was.
What was, should not have been.
We shall meet again and part.
And meet again and part again
Through all Eternity.

Jon Michael Pompia
A STREET CAFE IN PARIS

For the honor and glory of God

A street cafe, Paris, France
An apparition in blue
A visage from my past?

A face of a thousand hymns
Breathed in the cathedrals of
Berlin

Her name I could not remember
Her presence I would never forget

Do I dare speak a solitary word to
her?
Or should I remain
In the silence of my adoration
Leaving the precious moment
To rise like the mist
And then vanish forever?

Be still, poor heart

A street cafe, Paris, France
The music begins
And with loneliness I shall dance

Lisa Ann Quick
CHARLES L. QUICK, SR

This poem is dedicated to my Dad for all the love and happiness he has brought to me and my family. Thanks Dad, I love you.

He is the unique man that I call Dad.
He can leave sunshine in every
corner of my world.
He leaves a rainbow and a pot of gold
wherever he roams.
He has that sparkle in his eyes that
show this Dad is full of pride.
His memories linger in my soul,
while his name is close at heart.
He is a family man that stuck to his
roles as a father and a friend.
He is the meaning of love.
He is the one that fills my life with
joy.
He can turn strangers into friends.
He can make enemies realize hatred
cannot exist.
He is always there to lend a hand.
He is there through the good times
and the bad.
He is like a bridge over troubled
water, always there to make sure I
crossed it.
He has gave so much love, and filled
my heart with happiness.
He is a stern, well disciplined Dad.
He knows right and wrong.
He follows the old fashion way of
life
He is a farmer, he is a friend, he is
the ideal family man.
He is the one thing no one else can
be . . .
He is my DAD.

Laura Anne Castaneda

Laura Anne Castaneda
HEARTS

Hearts are so bouncy,
So full.
They bring life,
They're not dull.
They share meanings
Of peace,
Love, joy, and many more.
But when your heart is broken,
It'll crack
All over the floor.
It'll shatter like glass,
And be noticed like a scream.
Some broken hearts are mended,
But some stay broken
Without knowing
What a heart
Is supposed to mean.

Loyal Hanson Jr
A BLESSING

Oh what a joy life can be
All its awe and majesty
The waves of the sea
A bird that's free
The calmness of a cool day
The friendliness of a lone stray
The wonder of a strange day
Oh how we enjoy life in so many
a way
We live, we die
We laugh and sometimes even cry
Life seems so long
Like a low melody of song
But yet, as we often regret, it can be
so short
Contort and twist along the dark mist
of life
What could it be?
To me it's what you create
What's your answer to life?

Joan L B Schermerhorn
OOPS!

Trying hard to write a poem
In twenty one words or less.
Not much more that I can say,
Than what I've typed I guess.

Using the word counter
I am most perplexed indeed.
How can I eradicate
Three words that I don't need?

Could it be that memory
Has proved a bit unkind?
Several "what if" questions
Keep buzzing in my mind.

Made a slight mistake, ahem!
It happens now and then;
More frequently as time flies by,
No telling where or when.

Just a few more lines are left
To ply some clever stuff,
But that might take forever,
And this is long enough.

Gail Dean
LIFE IS VALUABLE

Life is a gift.
Live your life and be best.
Life is when you need friends.
In life you can do a lot
of things.

Some of the things in
Life you can do is play,
Get friends, go to school
stay out of trouble.
Be like my friends crazy teenagers,
Or like me and
Help on a Rescue Squad.

You help make others also
Have a life to live to
be valuable

Yvonne Harrison
LATAN SETAR

I dedicate this poem to all true Pagans around the world. Also to the freedom of religion, my poem is a very special dedication.

My mother was Lilith,
Goddess of lust and filth.
Down with a Jackal she did lay,
Until I sprang forth from her womb

one day.
A child so fair from out of the mire,
Touched and blessed by Satans' fire.

My father is Lucifer so gloriously proud.
His name upon the earth I'll shout aloud,
For as a Jackal he rapturously came;
And I was conceived out of his name.
The seed of his loins to fill his need.
A daughter to do his great deed.

Thus the world will know me,
As in time all mankind will see;
The works and wonders of the one.
In glorious victory the conquest is won.
Oh, behold I am she, Latan Setar,
The chosen as Satan's star.

Todd Kopecki
THE SEASON
Spring is the best of seasons,
Because the greatest of them begins.
The fans in the stands cheer with a reason,
Hoping that their baseball team wins.

Herbert Maier
FOR J.R.O., IN MEMORIAM—FEBRUARY, 1967
Now is the blaze of a thousand noons forgot
Obscured by much more murderous thermal magnitudes. Prime witness of the Al'magordo bloom lies throttled, stilled by what we wot
Not now. We mourn, but must forever lag
In reparation for the hurt he bore.
But do we apprehend what gave him pause
When there on wells edge of the world he heard
The whimper the poet foretold, the grovelling bang
And hung back fearing the known?
For is it cause
When turning back there is none, still to gird
For obliteration? Not for this the angels sang,
That dust should interrupt the sun above
And damp the fires of the sun below.

Frederick Van Doren

Frederick Van Doren
AUTUMN IN NEW YORK

To Doris Miriam—The leaf that never falls.

Leaves peek defiantly, protesting the inevitable arrival
Of remorseless, engulfing snow.
They die and drift silently downward to form a rustling carpet,
A last, plaintive reminder of once heaven seeking, glory and life,
Now merely a nuisance to be collected and summarily disposed of
Sometimes by the ritual of fire or maybe just left to 'mulch'!
Birds rise in formation, wave goodbye with their wings, head for sunnier climes.

In its last bastion, Fall dresses the trees in russet shades,
the whole tapestry of 'man-made' Autumn colors;
In their wardrobe lies Nature's Autumn palette.
In the wings, grim-visaged Winter waits patiently for his entrance,
Grinning sardonically at the cast of fearful players, from man to beast,
Who try hard to prepare for his unavoidable coming,
So beauty exists in, not Spring nor Summer, but Fall.

Letha Menon
NATURE HAS HER OWN BEAUTY
Nature has her own beauty
which no human race can erase,
She holds her own and remains serene
In spite of all attacks upon her.
She stands resplendent in the shimmering light of dawn
Like a queen awakened by the melodious songs of birds
But, man, with his selfishness and greed
Has cast an ugly shadow over her.
Inventions follow inventions to conquer nature,
To control her and subdue her.
Yes, man triumphs a little.
But, succumbs to defeat, at last.
Nature, stands adamant, with a smile on her lips
When man proclaims his victory over her.
At last, she holds her rein of supremacy
Over man's foolish calculations.
She wreaks her wrath upon mankind
In the form of a thunder or lightning.
Sometimes a deluge, a drought or an epidemic,
Which no man can control or overcome.

Crystal Nedved
DANCE OF THE HEART
Her laughter sparkles, her eyes shine.
Love and wisdom emanate thru her being.

Joy you bring into my life,
warming my heart thru the night.

A beautiful woman with a spirit soaring free.
With gentleness and kindness you love me.

Risking day by day to share our dreams,
ever changing, growing in our love.

Natural to be with each other,
acceptance as the key. Two soaring spirits,
united but separate identities.

Love fresh each day, opening, flowering
from the spring rains.
Sunshine of the spirit smiling on all we do.

Quiet times in the stillness of the night,
trusting each other to be safe.

Loving you blesses my soul every time I see you my dear.

Michelle De Hart
EVERLASTING LOVE

In loving memory of my grandfather—Earle M. Davis

I don't know what's become of you now,
And won't even ask because I don't know how

My heart now has an empty space,
A faded memory and a forgotten place.

I hope you know how much I cared,
I'll hold on to the memories that we've shared.

I don't really understand what has happened to you,
But I know soon the sun will shine through.

A peaceful place is where you'll now be,
That someday soon I know I too will see.

With a kiss on the cheek and tears in my eyes,
Now to you I must say goodbye.

I'll now put the memories in my heart,
So that never again we must part.

Ronald R Cole
GENTLENESS

Dedicated to Jesus Christ, God's Nature

Is brought to our attention
on a warm and sunny day,
when God's nature bestows
upon us the soothing effects
of a mild and gentle breeze.

Oh gentle one
what strength you have.

The strength to win
when you are behind,
and to quit
when you are ahead.

The strength to give
when you have nothing,
and to love
when you are unloved.

Oh gentle one
what can you fear,
except that you may not
be gentle.

Julie Leschinsky
DAUGHTER TO MOTHER
I sit here and
Try to remember
The time spent
Together.
But somehow,
Every time I try
The doors to my mind seem to close,
Leaving only memories of recent years.

Was it because you worked so hard?
Were so busy—
Sitting on a sultry day next to the cold running shower
that beat against the tub like tears
that once so long ago you shed?

I can't remember all those years
When I was small and you were there
To turn the lights off.
Yet, now that we're apart—
The memories of today
Race through my mind.

I see you and me as
Us
And all those lines
On your still-young face.
And as for me, I'm consoled
By the happiness you spread,
And every difference that you made
Each time the rain
began
to
fall.

Kimberly A Custer
TEARS IN THE WIND

In loving memory to Kevin "Smitty" Smith

Ride to live, live to ride.
He's now riding by God's side.
Death is certain, life is not.
The course of our lives we do not plot.
And in the wind where I must be.
There's a guardian angel watching me.
Live to ride, ride to live.
To all a part of his soul did he give.

Andrew Ben
PUNISH THE FOOL
"Arrest that tall man
Arrest the vile crook
My own purse he took
Down the street he ran."

Anger shouts may cease
Law have evidence
Thief with jail sentence
Stealing shall decrease.

"Chastise the rascal
When having enough proof
'Neath a court house roof
Place him on trial."

'Not at all guilty'
Thought the city judge
Verdict as on edge
Five years say jury!

Sister Mary Capistran RSM
ETERNAL FLAME
I must carry on
O, my Leader,
The torch which you've held above—
Never fearing to face
NEW FRONTIERS of Outer Space,
Of Intellect, Peace, and True Love.

I must carry on
O, my Leader,
Plow deeply the furrows of mind
Like you, learn the facts and figures
Learn to light with your torch the world's blind

I must carry on
O, my Leader,
Learn the reason and cause of events
Love the people in your

heart-warming fashion
Feed the hungry whom poverty rents.

O, Frontiersman, with pioneer courage
Help me fight for the right to be free—
Learn that courage, great confidence, and convictions
Are the wicks that keep flaming Liberty.

I must carry on
O, my Leader,
With a heart filled with grieved mystery.
O, Voice, which we loved and cherished,
Tho' through nightmarish shot you've perished,
You've so captured minds and spirits
That we find in our deeds part of thee.

I must carry on
O, my Leader,
Like an Eagle, conquering hatred; soaring free
And
With intellect of steel
Find your solutions real
And
With faith—with true love
Ask God's help from above
For,
My Leader, tho' you've gone,
Your Eternal Flame burns on
—In me—
The living Twentieth Century!

Andrew Ben
RESIDENTIAL CHOICE
Area in the North,
Proper housing district
From where settlers came forth
Began living project.

Region to extend South,
Life in a small chalet
Folks commence commonwealth
Desire world peace pathway.

Province in the far East,
A nation's open door
Midst wild flower and beast
Gain of luck and error.

Land also extends West,
Suitable settlement
Region of interest
Liberty is present.

Michael A Pfiester
NO VISITOR EVER CAME
Tranquil cold October through the misery of the storms—
He sat and waited patiently, for a visitor to come pay a call.

Throughout the day and to the night
he sat waiting in his chair
Yet as always, No visitor ever came.

Still into the winter as cold gray December haunted All—
He sat inside his loneliness for a visitor to come pay a call.

Throughout the day and to the night
he sat waiting in his chair
Yet as always, No visitor ever came.

January enhanced with sorrow came slowly as he did wait.
Through snows of pain and misery
for a visitor to come pay a call.

Throughout the day and to the night
he sat waiting in his chair—
Yet as always, No visitor ever came.

March came with more upset after February's final fall—
The winds blew long and freely as he sat for a visitor to come pay a call.

He heard the sound of knocking and with hope he took a grin,
But only found the banging of the shutters in the wind.

He sank back to depression and silently he cried.
Bowed his head in darkness, weeping anguish, as he died

No visitor ever came.

Carole Brown
ONE LITTLE BOY!
One little boy, with eyes of blue
Scuffed up knees, and holes in his shoes
Jumping, climbing, running hard,
Laughing, crying—spirit unmarred.

One little boy still afraid of the dark
Up at dawn, then out for a lark.
Quiet one moment, tornado, the next,
Expanding his wings, and heavens—what's next?

One little boy, out to change the world
Exploring the creek bed, his flag unfurled,
Rocks in his pockets, his shoes untied,
Unmindful of dirt, with his dog at his side.

One little boy, yes, that's my son.
Whether he's reading his books or having some fun,
Asleep in his bed, or awake with some noise,
He's God's gift to me—and I thank Him for boys!

Joyce Smith
THE TEENAGER

To all the young ones growing up now

The teenager is the same
Whether it be of the 20's—30's—50's—60's, 70's 80's
Their style may change some
Their music may change
There will always be the problems
Of deciding to sleep with your date
Being grounded, coming in 3 mins late
Tearing your dress for the prom
Taking the car for a ride without asking
Slipping out after all is asleep, to go to the big dance
Getting drunk & sniffing coke in the locker room, or shooting up
Getting beat up for not taking the test paper
Threatening the teacher for not giving you the As to stay on the team

John Thomas Tomlinson
TOTALLY ENAMORED

To all those who may have known, or may, in future, know me.

Esprit de corps, modus operandi,
And, why not let it be–joie de vivre

Time, ranter than discordant note,
Most of the time. Or thinking that

Satisfaction comes only in a flash of time—
So diminutive, so delusional. For even

If appreciation of life may come from
One who has but an iota of the

Quota alloted; or from another,
Who has a maxigift all variegated

Complete, with sound and sight so
Vivid that resonances abound, and

Clear the air surrounding planet Earth.
This could be, should be, the agenda

Each day. Reclude not to your isle,
Mankind. Reverberations echo

Constant from such as Yosemite
Crater. Sometimes, faults shake

The bed–rock of ground, fissuring
Solid rock, and diffusing the more

Evanescent elements of the atmosphere.
But even if bogus humankind might

Seem to be winning some of the
Skirmishes involved in the continuous

Quest for enjoyment of life, life
Continues, never ending, callous

Though cynicism may be (yes becomes no?).
But then, even sadomasochistic freaks

At your door, can be sandbagged,
Their illusory suppositions made no

More of; they are just that. There
Are others round you, and though it

May be that for a time you may seem
Keel–hauled, you know but to look;

Maintain your natural curiousity,
Your six senses. You have these, if

They only go on in your way, as
Somehow regenerated awareness. They

Are ready; to go on carousel, to unwind
Knots of palpability, to flay the faces

Of hatred hung on status quo, knowing
Only: operate by the numbers. These,

Then, are the many brick walls
(mortar–less?) that impede,

Rather than help out. Imposed
Conformance; to be servile in your

Thinking, and resultant acting. This
Results from action that is enormous in

Non–progressive arrogance and stupidity.
But, vibrations of all sorts round us,

Do indeed surround us, resulting in
Total enamourance. Do you agree?

There are those who see, day after
Day, piece by bit, that peace shall be.

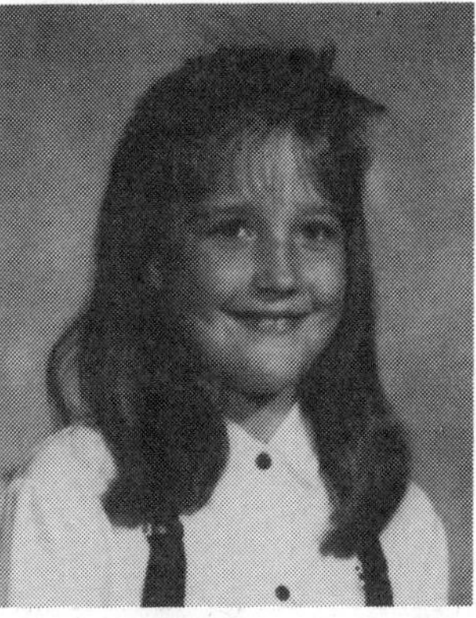

Jackie Chizek

Jackie Chizek
HORSE

To Auntie Connie

As you glide through the midnight air,
moonlight shines through your hair.
You're wilder than the wind so fast,
and you're free . . . from me.

Shannon
DOWNED GLADIATOR FROM THE SKY
Downed gladiator from the sky,
With fearless disregard you fought
A battle that might have been mine.

Soaring with great speed you did ascend,
All principles that we can understand and defend.

We now stand by you in respect of your last flight,
Because downed gladiator, this was the final flight.

Flags flowing halfway down,
saddened eyes staring at blue skies,
Downed gladiator from the sky,
such sorrow seen within many eyes.

Downed gladiator from the sky,
never have any regrets for you did try,
Planes overhead, once there were five, now but four.
Gladiator five peel off, make room for a downed gladiator fallen from the sky.

The sound of a bugle singing the saddened tale of taps,
Rifles fire a salute to a downed gladiator who has died while in flight.

Your wings now retired, time that you now rest our proud gladiator,
Let us say good-bye now, but never shall we forget,
That of our proud gladiator, who will forever fly.

Karen Shelton
THE FORGOTTEN CHILD
There is someone far to see;
The little girl who tries to be.

All alone and tries to hide;
Reaches out to catch the sky.

Her soul searches through the night;
Her mind wanders to another side.

She reaches out to nothing there;
Then pulls back in a silent stare.

Searching for an escape—tries so hard;
Hurt by love that has fallen apart.

Wrestling with confusion, lonely, and scared;
It's burned inside: There's none out there.

Trying to find a where, why, or when;
God, she wishes it had been!

Now it's time—she must leave;
Going to a place she has to be.

Only now . . . somewhere down the road;
This little girl shall never grow old.

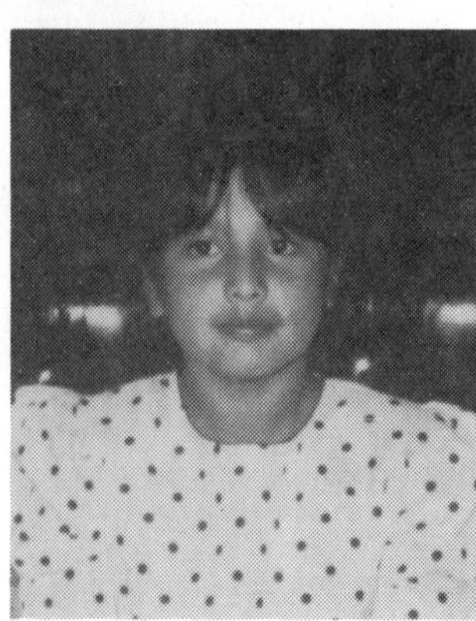

Abigail Martin

Abigail Martin
TREES
Trees grow in the most amazing way,
You can even measure it every single day,
And to your amazement you can see,
The sprouting of a little tree,
Planting one takes lots of care,
You should plant one if you dare,
You could build a treehouse or two,
In your special tree that you grew,
A hammock, a place to read, a place to rest,
I guarantee you will love your tree, it's the

```
BBBB  EEEE  SSSS   TTTTT
B   B E     S        T
BBBB  EEEE   SSSS    T
B   B E         S    T
BBBB  EEEE  SSSSS    T
```

Ellene Smith
A MOTHER'S THANKSGIVING
A mother's joy, so the kids do say, is having them all over for Thanksgiving day.
While we Moms are in the kitchen, making turkey, cakes and pies—The kids are by the T.V. trying to quieten their own kids' cries. When dinner is over I really must confess, they leave us dear sweet Moms to clean up all the mess. While the grandkids are crying and you're trying to straighten up at least—
The older kids are back in the kitchen for another little feast. So when that mess is cleaned up and you're ready for a break—The kids decide it's time to leave and for the door they do make. So to you Mothers on Thanksgiving don't put your pots away—you really must remember—You've still got Christmas day!

Bertie Lee J
MY LOVE I LEFT AT SEA
The beautiful memories I have of my love I left at sea
The fun and laughter and all the picnics we wish would last the summer just you and me the beautiful red roses you would leave inside my screen door some time we were sad like the time we cried over a little bird that fell from a tree the wind was blowing strong it was then I knew why our love was special I will keep a red rose in my window for you and me and send my love and laughter across the sea with tears unseen I listen to the echo from the tossing ship onward to a distant shore with my love I left at sea.

Time had passed I return to the sea where we left our footprints in the sand that time had washed away but the memory I hold in the garden of my heart time will never wash away My love I left at sea.

Steven J Fox
PAGES OF EMPTINESS

I dedicate this poem to my children, Heather and Erik, and my Mother.

I sit here silently staring—
into an empty page—
deciding just what to write—
To say what I must say.

As a million words boil—
within my tortured brain—
A thousand different emotions—
All scream to be explained.

Yet my pen remains silent—
Not setting a single word,—
No fine lines of feelings—
No new phrases to be preserved.

Just blank,—barren pages—
With nothing more to tell.
An empty and wordless testimony—
Of a hand——
From which the pen—
—has fell

Katherine Louise Gentner
THERE WAS A TIME
There was a time
when your life touched mine:
That day we shared so briefly,
leaving for me
A deep, indelible mark
upon the threshold of my heart!

Katherine Louise Gentner

Katherine Louise Gentner
DISCOVERY

To all those who let thoughts take wing That Truth might have expression through words that sing!

I looked into your eyes
and knew
Life would never be
the same again
Without those depths
of blue

Wherein I might
lose myself
And find
you!

Pauline Kohlmetz
TO NIGHT
The stars are shining ever so bright.
The moon is overly light.
I'm not ready to say goodnight.
It don't seem right to close
your eyes for the night.
It's so beautiful, I want to enjoy
More of it.
The light of the night makes
Me feel cool tonight.
So I'll stay awake awhile
longer tonight,
So there'll be more to remember
of the night.
The sky seems so full of light,
The man in the moon seems happy of it.
These things seem to make
everything
so cheerful.
So to remember of tonight.
A restful mind, is sure to give
you a restful night.
To make a better tomorrow each day.

Martha L Hockenjos
A TEAR
We cry a Tear every once in awhile,
for all the Pain and Loneliness we Feel.
We cry a Tear every once in awhile,
for all the People that don't care.
We cry a Tear every once in awhile,
for all the people that do Care.
We Cry A Tear
We cry a Tear every once in awhile,
for all the Love and Hate we Fear.
We cry a Tear every once in awhile,
for all the People that hurt us and Leer.
We cry a Tear every once in awhile,
for all the World to see and Indear.
We Cry A Tear

Ronald T Jolly
CHILD'S PLAY

To my lovely daughter Lee Anne my wife Georgina and my mother Joan McNally who has shown me nothing but love and understanding.

It's fun to watch the children play,
their little bodies running
rampant as wildfire.
Their eyes wide dancing in their sockets,
facial expressions showing
nothing but utter joy,
The children are so friendly and free,
filled with so much
enthusiasm and unaltered
life,
The young bodies never tiring,
playing games of make
believe,
I'm filled with so much joy,
by something as simple as
watching the children play.

Alastair Gilmour
MATILDA THE DAIRY COW
Matilda was a dairy cow
She gave milk by the pail,
But one day something strange occurred
Her milk turned into ale.

The dairy maid was most amazed
At what was coming out,
And when she turned to look again
The ale had changed to stout.

Matilda didn't care at all,
She felt so young and frisky,
She gave a moo, and closed an eye
And out came pure malt whiskey.

The farmer jumped around with joy
This cow would come in handy,
Especially when at party time
They needed cherry brandy.

Matilda's name became well known,
Her fame spread near and far,
The farmer laughed because he owned
The first four legged bar.

Clarence Gantt
TO GET OUT OF THE DARK
I start with an extraordinary shadow,
suddenly I get extremely
sensitive
and I change my look a dozen
times,

but my comfortability gets
narrow,
and then come the thrills that
made me totally
avoid my acceptance of any
skills.
And then making up but not
breaking up,
by feeling concerned made me a
man with a mission,
To want to contribute,
To want to produce to the
Finding of Peace of mind
To the pursuit of my dreams,
To be gentle and bear romance in
my heart,
But mostly in my mind
To live with insight and not be
blind
And to be satisfied with those
moments
that I triumph with in time.

Melissa Warner
THE LAST "GENTLE GIANT"

This poem is dedicated to the members of GREENPEACE for their efforts in saving the whales.

Alone she swam,
for her mate was gone,
Having been stricken down,
by a harpooner's gun.

In terror she had fled,
from his dying cry,
She did not look back,
nor understand why.

For days she searched,
for another of her kind,
But, unbeknownst to her,
there were none to find.

Exhausted, the birth
was too much to bear,
She died with her calf,
at least, from harpoons they
were spared.

A few days later, on the shore,
a crowd stood and cried,
Over the last "Gentle Giant,"
and the baby at her side.

Royal F Gregory
ROSES—2-19-1989

I give these roses to express the
love I have for you,
So deeply bestowed in my heart.
These roses are to signify an
undying love, a love that was meant
to be from the very start.
These roses represent a beautiful
love song or perhaps a poet's
unspoken rhymes;
These roses are in remembrance of
our togetherness and so many
beautiful times.
I used to give you one red rose, at
the end of each day;
one red rose for your journey through
my life and loving me along the way.
But now I give you twelve red
roses, wrapped in their paper of blue;
Twelve red roses to simply say, how
much I'm in love with you.

Jessica Sherman
THE SUN

The sun is a bright orange ball,
That disappears at nightfall.
If it goes at six or eight it might be
too late.
Late is not a gain,
But a lack,
A lack of the beautiful golden sun.

Debra K Godsey
RETIREMENT

The hands of time keep turning,
But friendship never strays.
You'll always be remembered
In so very many ways.

As you begin your journey,
May all your dreams come true,
And may all your expectations
Bring happiness to you.

Enjoy life to the fullest.
Take time to sit back quietly,
And capture precious moments
With friends and family.

We hope each treasure you want
from life
Will be there for you to find.
There is no doubt, you will be
missed,
By the friends you leave behind.

Mrs John R Leidecker
HOPE, THOUGHTS & REMEMBERING

I've come a long way in this old
world.
And as I look back, I stop & think of
all that's been.
You dream of all you could have
done.
But try to remember what has been.
You have to have hope for the best.
And say tomorrow I'll do my best.
For the ones who have tried & come
out on top.
Give courage to the ones who can
still go on.
Each road & sunrise & sunset is a
new tomorrow
With hope in it for a better day.
So don't look back but look ahead
And see the best as you travel on.

Karen M Lewis
TEACHER'S PLEA

This is dedicated to all of my children who have passed through my doors and to the future children in my classroom.

Dear God, I ask, please hear my plea,
Could I have just one more hand for
me?
One to wipe noses,
One to dry tears,
One to give hugs,
To rid of their fears.

Four extra hands I think might just
do,
So I can help love your children for
you.
One to help writing,
One to draw faces,
One to turn pages,
To dream of far places.

If possible, three more hands would
be good,
So that I can accomplish things that I
should.
One to pick up Joe,
One to give praise,
One to hold up my head,
On "one of those days"!

Would it be too much to ask for just
one more for me?
What? You say that this just can not
be!
But how can I reach them all? What
can I do?
With 50 hands reaching up . . . and
me with just two!

Then grant me one wish for my
children today,
Give me the strength to show them
the way.
I will hold them and love them and
give them good starts,
With just TWO little hands, I will
embrace all of their hearts!

Loretta Robbins
TOUCH OF DIVINITY

He touched me and gave me life
He touched my eyes and gave
me light.
He touched my ears so I could hear
He touched my heart with
"Love" and took away the fear
He sacrificed His Son for me
I ask Lord, what can I do for
"Thee"?

Mr Mark Antonio Pasley

Mr Mark Antonio Pasley
REALITY

I never really knew you
You were just another friend,

But when I knew you noticed me
I let my heart unbend.

I couldn't keep past memories
They only made me cry,

I had to forget my first love
And give love another try

So now I've fallen in love with you
And I'll never let you go,
I love you more than anyone
I just had to let you know

And if you ever wonder
I don't know what I'll do,

But you are your own person

But just remember . . .I LOVE
YOU!

Loretta Robbins
LOVE

Love is a gift given from the
heart, not to be bought or sold

Like vintage wine its value
increases as it grows old

Some people lose it or misplace it
during the course of life

It can always be found for it is
never out of site

It is labeled "Fragile," handle with
care

A package more precious than a
gem so rare

Send it over the world this word
called "Love"

For it is one of the keys to open a
door to the "Kingdom Above."

Chris Lang
DOES SHE LOVE ME?

Dedicated to Teddi, my inspiration.

The sky is getting dark
The future is getting grim
Does she love me,
Or does she love "him"?

There is no light shining
In this terrible place I am in
Does she love me,
Or does she love "him"?

There is no hope around me
My chances are very slim
Does she love me,
Or does she love "him"?

If she loved me she'd tell me so.
If she loved me she'd let me know.
I cannot harvest the grain I sow.
But I cannot, will not, let her go.

For many years I have loved her
I ask myself again
Does she love me,
No, she loves "him."

Drema Wickline Milam
MY SON

To my son, Eric, without whom this poem would not have existed.

From a little bundle of arms and legs
and love,
To a tender and rowdy boy of two.
I often sit and think of the nights, I
sat and rocked and cuddled you.

Sometimes it seems so long ago and
then sometimes it seems like
yesterday.
I used to sit and watch you for hours;
as in your crib you'd play.

As I look down at your young and
youthful face, I am for certain no
other could ever take its place.
For it seems that with each day you
grew, I have grown too.
For this special bond that binds us, it
grows stronger every day.
It keeps us linked together; if we're
with each other or if one of us is
away.

Looking back now I remember all
the places I wanted to go and the
things I wanted to do. For some
reason they don't seem so important

now, when I compare them to you.

And as I sit here on your bed with your little hand in mine and as you gently close your eyes in sleep. I want to thank you for making me your mother and for making my life complete.

James Frye
SOMETHING NEW
A girlfriend to find; beauty to behold;
Song divine; beauty to sing divinely to me, with a clear voice so fine;
That rings throughout the night for me to find.
To find near to me, so dear and warm;
In a reality so pristine, and fine.
Enveloped before me, so glorious a world now to find,
And, singing like a bird divine,

So, opens the world for me to find.
With a song from your lips that kisses my mouth, and heart,
And, with words of wisdom that never do keep us apart!
Smiles that glow forever, and from within that dark,
And, beauty to take me from this terrible lost dark.
Oh, the land of enchantment on now do we take our start,
Someday to reach a land, from which we never did part.
Love is the reason my heart doeth soar,
And, in me now the lion roars;
So, eternity doeth take a star,
Star like that of your eyes, that gives me more.

Theresa Harmon
THE UNFELT TOUCH
Oh my! Oh my!
My return from the struggles of war.
What a loss! Oh such a loss!
Both my hands are gone forever.
Only God can make hands
to feel the sacred touch.

But man-made metallic hands
are so helpful and the next best
They can do the work of
normal hands,
but when I stroke my
little daughter's head
there is the unfelt touch
that can never be.

But with my child
and my life
I have God's blessings.

Rebecca Moss
THE RHYTHM OF LIFE
Come! Let us praise the Lord
With rhythm and with rhyme
It's the spark of God within us
That flows on all the time.

At sunrise and sunset
In springtime and in fall
The universal rhythm
Flows within us all.

We sense it in the ocean
And the creatures of the sea
We feel it in the forests,
On the hillsides and the lea.

God, in all His glory
Has made man to know
His rules of life that we may live
To move ahead and grow.

With earth and sky it all began
Then cities great were built by men
They made wheels and built machines
The rhythm of life still flows within.

John A Spitale
SOARING SPIRITS
That morning their spirits soared to the sky
Through the cold and clouds far above
Bringing the hopes and dreams of many men
Backed by a country full of pride and love

But hopes and dreams are made by man
As was that gleaming rocket
All of these were turned into nightmares
On the last flight of the Challenger

But I know that their spirits are still soaring
Straight through those clouds far above
Soaring, soaring in all our hearts and minds
For now they're holding the hands of God

Mia Hartsook
BLISS BODY
In stillness, softness diffuses
Body blossoms, revealing subtle structure
Faintest fabric, like the finest veins,
Barely visible on a petal.
Most delicate, translucent web
Purest body, purest bliss.

Within this body-flower, deep within
Most precious ambrosial nectar
Pure bliss—fluid crystalline sap
Flowing through glistening veins
Nectar of immortality
Honey-sweet, transcending sweetness
Life essence, essence of nourishment.

Body boundaries become diffuse
Expanding through fibrous webs
Subtle pores channeling outward
So softly—softer than the softest
This celestial vessel of immortality
Most precious vessel of bliss.

Pearl Hammersteadt
SMALL TOWN GONE
Where are the fields of flowers,
The lambs that played in fields of clover?
The builders come.
The builders go.
Where are the greenbeans grown?
Perhaps in countries we've never known.
The builders come.
The builders go.
Where are our quiet streets;
The pathways through the woods?
The builders come.
The builders go.
And where are the birds that sing
That once built nests in trees now gone?
And the builders come.
And the builders go.
And where do the builders go?
Listening to the birds that sing—
In a mansion on a hill—
Looking down on our crowded town.

Lusina De La Torre

Lusina De La Torre
STAR, STAR
Star, Star
Where can you be?
Up in the sky
Above me?
Is it true
What people say
Do some stars
fall away?
Down down to the ground
For their wishes
To come true?
Star, Star
I knew did you?

Annette Mc Cormick
THE MOON
How fine is the moon
that dwells in the sky
You made it through Adam and Eve
and never stopped to wonder why.

Shining down on us
a light that leads the way
Navigators and Indians looked to you
wondering when night would turn to day.

And as you quickly disappear
you take a glance back
With a look of pride on your face
and finally hit the sack.

Rickie L Moss
ON SOME DAYS
On some days
loneliness lingers like grey clouds
hung heavily over mountain peaks
no longer seen . . .
On some days
my heart cannot escape the weight of the past
and my cries fade into the distance
unheard . . .
On some days
images surface
and I remember the warmth of two hearts
meeting
sharing
precious moments in time.
On some days
I reach out to shadows left behind
to dance in the wind
and the emptiness whips through me
as I try to embrace what I can no longer see . . .
On some days
locked in a room of memories
solitude befriends me
as I wearily search for strength alone
and wondering why
days pass by
without notice
of each new sunrise.
Some days
were made for grieving . . .

Phyllis Schoolcraft McCall
DADDY'S BIBLES

To the memory of Samuel M. Schoolcraft Great Dad and friend

Yes, he had more than one, some were presents from his only son.
Daddy held God's faith, hope, and love within. He read the Holy Bible thin.
Daddy read and studied the Bible fast
He told me there were so many interesting happenings in the past.
Although all his Bibles had been worn, Not a single page was torn
Some of the covers had come untwined
Many sacred messages were underlined
It's still so clear to my mind, of Daddy's calloused hands, gently turning the thin pages, seeking God's Holy words to find.
He often said the Holy Bible was the only book he never got tired of.
There was so much mercy in God's love.
Daddy didn't need a college education to learn the Bible well.
He prayed each day and night for God to save poor souls from hell.
The kingdom of heaven was my Daddy's goal.
I believe Daddy's name is written in the Book of Life.
For God has now claimed his sweet soul.

S Irene Wright
EMPLOYMENT COUNSELLOR
Take time to work——
It is the price of success.
Take time to think——
It is the source of power
Take time to play——
It is the secret of perpetual youth.
Take time to read——
It is the fountain of wisdom.
Take time to be friendly——
It is the road to happiness.
Take time to laugh——
It is the music of the soul.
Take time to dream——
It is the road to greater vision.
Take time to give——
The day is too short to be selfish.
Take time to love and be loved——
It is the privilege of God.

Elizabeth Novotny Mrkvicka
I LIKE TREES
I like trees and honey bees and
Birds and pretty flowers,
Sunny days and breezy days and
Days with warm rain showers.
I like trees that shine and glisten,
And singing birds so I can listen.

Trees that grow graceful and tall,
From tiny seedlings so small.
I like trees that burst in blossom;
In the springtime each new season.
The buzzing bees look so funny,
As they extract nectar to make honey.
When I see a bumble bee,
I make sure he don't see me.
I like pine trees so green,
Sprinkled with snowflakes, what a scene!
Or in a parlor trimmed so fine,
A star atop where it can shine.
Trees, they are for all four seasons,
Planted they are for many reasons.
Summer, winter, spring, and fall,
I like those trees, one and all.

BK Hanson
L.A. SUNSET

Poetry in black and white on a page; life in black and white in a world filled with prejudice. Thanks for showing me that Living is more than that. I love you!

The clouds are pink against the azure sky: It's dusk.
Soft, muted colors promise a nighttime gala of twinkling lights for any who pauses to admire.
The moon will cast its pale gaze on a sleepy world: A deceptive peace fills the air tonight.
In Ethiopia, the children are starving. Swollen stomachs, aching hearts, tearful eyes staring in anguish.
What have these innocents done to deserve this?

And in Compton and East L.A.—not so distant—gangs butcher each other like cattle.
Who took the innocence from these children?
Hunger, sadness, despair and death fill the world to overflowing. The socialite bemoans the status of the stock market and a child dies of malnutrition.
Where is the justice in this world?
The sun has disappeared over the horizon and the sky has turned to indigo, while the Evening Star begins its nighttime vigil.
How calm it seems to be!
Does even Mother Nature lie?

Cyril Kronschnabel
TO-DAY'S PARADE

An endless line of cars and trucks flies swiftly down our street.
Each one is on a journey, or aimless goals to meet.
I sit and watch as they go by; not knowing their intent,
But surely they must have a goal, to make their time well spent.
Some may be going for a ride, for a breath of good fresh air
Or have a purpose for their ride, to satisfy a care.

Fore surely, life must have a plan to make it worth their while,
Or else a life is wasted, not worth that extra mile.
When we reach the age of reason and seek to find our plan
To give our life a meaning and to help our fellow-man.
Then we have made our lives worth living, to help in God's great plan.

Gordon Shao

Gordon Shao
CHRISTMAS

This poem is dedicated to Cathy Marie, My sweet, loving wife.

CHRISTMAS n. (A tale of the birth of Christ on December in Bethlehem of Judea, is the year's most Holy Day.)
C is for the Christ child born in manger,
H is for the hallowed hour of honorary prayer.
R is for remembrance of the holy babe,
I is for the inborn sweet and rare.
S is for the solemn shepherds in field heard the good tidings of great joy by night with angels,
T is for trusting fully in God's care.
M means Mary blessed the holy Mother, and brought men's gifts so fair.
A is for the anthem of angels; "Peace on earth, good will toward men.
To God in the highest glory. Halleluia, Amen."
S is for the star that shone in Heaven, guiding to the place where Jesus lay.

Rey-Angelo C Ramirez
SO TIRED

To Gigi Tengco
For truly knowing you all these years
And being a great inspiration

Numbness in the mind
Seeping through your heart
Your mind hurts
the eyes show
tears—of anger and joy
Of people, countless people
yearning to help
to love and share
Thrown away into a madness
unknown, unknowing
Yes. I guess, the world ain't ready
No. Not just yet—
for miracles and mysteries
for time elapsed immemorially
For we all are too soaked into
our own realities.

Joan Maki
SPRINGTIME

The great blue skies and budding trees
of birds in song, the springtime breeze.
The forests green, and rippling streams
of where I've been in springtime dreams.
Watching stars that shine so bright,
of moonlit walks on a springtime night.
Walking hand in hand with the one you love
as the stars shine down from up above.
Along a darkened path you may steal a moonlit kiss
as you do, you can hear sounds of nature all around
and harmonize in this.

Crystal Lynn Sura
BOTH, I LOVE

one cries tears, with fear
one never does

one I hold close to comfort
one holds me close, which is comforting

one I protect and always will
one is my protection

both, I love—
one is my husband one is my son

Walter Szabla Jr
WHAT IS LOVE

This is dedicated to my parents.

What is love, people say
their opinions every day.

With a kiss and a hug.
The heart grows stronger
with such love.

Jean Stowell
WHO WAS THIS MASTER OF FEATHERED BLISS . . .

Who was this master of feathered bliss—
This uncaptured creature, the Pegasus—
Flying through the vail of infinity—
On wings shiny as glass—
For there is one who knows all,
The past—

Karon Northcutt
LOVING FRIENDS

And the wind was bitter cold,

The sky as dark as night,
No one for miles, nothing in sight.

I kept on walking, across the cold frozen ground,
The whistling wind, and my heart beat was the only sound.

For miles and miles, I trudged through the snow,
I kept thinking of shelter, and a warm fire's glow.

Suddenly, in the distance, a dim glimmer appeared,
It grew larger and larger, the closer I neared.

It was a lonesome little cabin, alone in the woods,
I feared not to enter, and feared if I should.

I walked across the porch, and gave the door a quick shove,
As I stood in the doorway, I thanked the Lord up above.

For sitting by the fire, I saw a soft face and a warm grin,
This figure of a man, was my husband, my friend.

Shawnna Kifer

Shawnna Kifer
THE REASON

To Jim Cox, whose strength I deeply admire, and whose individuality I adore.

Black symbolizes independence, strength.
It puts you apart from the elite,
But brings you and holds you together with your group.

But black also symbolizes loneliness, darkness.
So I say to you wear a gray,
Be apart, but not alone.

If you choose to be apart,
But not alone,
I will be there as your stepping stone.

Terel LeFler
WOMANLINESS

There is some fragrance
Light, provocative,
You use;
And sometimes I sense
The scent, as in a dream,
Knowing that you've awakened
And will woo me, womanlike.
There is a warmth I feel
About your womanliness
Which transcends even joy of sex;
As you return all perfumed
To our bed,
Tossing and turning
Until I hold you close
In my embrace,
You could not guess
The gift of love you give . . .
It is my manliness.

Gina Stephenson
BLUE-SY COSMIC RHYME

For my guardian angel, Chip

I'd love to take you flying
Transcending Space and Time
And sing a soulful tune to you
A Blue-sy Cosmic Rhyme.

Your Love is not lost to me
I feel it in the breeze
Your love comes winging soulfully
And stirs the grass and trees

I'll sing a Blue-sy Cosmic Rhyme
Of white-winged horse flying
Of transcendental beauty
Of souls reborn and dying.

I'll see you in eternity
Pure Love and pure Light
A cosmic spirit dancing
In a blue starlit night.

Perhaps we'll sing in Harmony
A Blue-sy Little Rhyme
A delightful unfolding
Transcending Space and Time.

Jewel Thompson
STILL SILENCE
I've staked the portals of hell,
My mind is befuddled and bleak.
No answer comes to me yet,
Just askance for you to speak.

No sign of your ever replying,
No sign of an answer aglow.
Just still silence from the other side
Is the only echo I'll ever know.

Agree with me, my friend.
Come to my defense.
A reply is what I crave,
Something with common sense.

Atone with me, won't you please,
So my mind will be at ease.
If not, I'll keep remembering
How hard I've tried to appease.

Alesha Loyd
HAPPINESS IS
Happiness is a bird singing in the trees
Happiness is meeting a new friend
Happiness is coming home again
Happiness is sharing and caring for others
Happiness is knowing GOD
Happiness is getting along
Happiness is loving one another

Kathleen Lombardi
TRUE LOVE

To my son, Daniel and Darla Lombardi With All My Love, Mother

O how I love thee, my precious one.
Just us two watching the setting sun.
Soon the moon will be full, and bright as can be.
Lighting the dark sky for you and for me.

Hands clasped together we'll walk through the night.
True love is so silent, on a moon lit night.

Words are not spoken, our thoughts are entwined.
For our love is so precious.
It's one of a kind.

With each setting sun, and the star filled sky.
My love, I'll be with you, till the sun dost rise.

My love for thee is like a circle, not to be broken,
until death has spoken.
You have loved me and my love I returned.
The love I yearned for, my precious one.

Connie Ford
I SAW YOU AS A WINDOW
I saw you as a window to a world so full of life.
Just a glow never touching, a thousand hearts you scattered and then mine. I thought you would be my world, just like in a fairy tale. Not distant and remote and somewhere far above me. Suddenly it all ended causing my world to go to pieces. But toward the end I knew it was not I you wanted. I wasn't yet to understand, why you couldn't have loved me. Am I like a child with a dream. Always dreaming and never seeing. I saw you as a window to a world so full of life. I thought you would be mine, was it my mistake. You just left me here with my feeling, like a child with a dream. Am I always dreaming and never seeing.
I saw you as a window to a world so full of life.

Latania L Alli

Latania L Alli
THE THING

This poem was dedicated to my grandmother, Lillie Bell Heard my aunt, Alberta Love and my best friend, Carmella Humphry

Listen world open your ears
Hear me very clear
There is a thing that creeps on you
And you don't know it's there
You can't see it, you can't feel it
It spreads like a spilled glass of wine
It doesn't care who its victim is
It'll love to creep up your spine
The thing is mean, it's not a dream
It thinks you're a buttercup

And before you know it my dear friend
The thing has eaten you up
This thing is called cancer
For some there's no answer
Or you may be a lucky one
But if it shall creep upon you
You'll see it isn't fun
So congratulations
To all you patients
Who escaped the thing so well
For all I know, I wouldn't care
If the thing
Burned in hell.

R Vasudevan
TIMELESS ORIGINAL
Someone said, "Nothing is new under the Sun."
Sun shines like a virgin terrain,
but everything under the Sun is dark,
mankind lives in the sorrowest part of sorrow,
loneliest part of loneliness.

Editors say, "There's nothing original in what you write."
What is the 'originalness' of the original?
Can imagination be creative?
It is but the result of image, knowledge, experience, dead past.

A writer has a style of seeing, looking, perceiving, sensing.
He is in the shadows of maturity, records overheard gossip, everyday observations.

Yonder in the south, there is a tree, standing in hushed quietness, majestically,
against the dying sunset, scattering the rosy hue.
It changes—the scenery changes all the time,
always new, fresh, like an un-chattering mind,
active, thoughtless and dynamic.
Is that 'original,' when the writer writes that?
Can the 'present' ever be described?
If the 'present' is always unborn, where is the 'original?'

Kimberly Ann Savino
DEVASTATION
There's a pain inside of me,
for a perishing love.
A love once felt,
between you and I.
Forever you said,
As we turned to part.
Never doubting,
I kept it close at heart.
Now one month later,
I still cry.
Only one month later,
you've closed your eyes.
Please don't go,
I silently cry.
Never to be heard.
A tear fell from the sky.
I know that in your heart,
I'm just a memory.
But this love that I feel,
is for eternity.
You'll forever be,
A part of me.

Betty Taplin
SUMMER'S END
I thought I was alone on Scroggie Bay,
The embers idling gently on the hearth,
And in the silence
Grandfather Clock ticking away the seconds
Of the diminishing day . . .
Outside, the gusting wind
Makes branches of the pine and hemlock sway,
While leading colored maple leaves
In a twirling ballet . . .
The calm and mirrored water of last summer
Comes suddenly to life,
Making a futile rush from the bay
In frenzied strife,
As if warning of summer's end
To one lost-looking, lonely loon
Riding the current 'round the bend . . .
The chickadees and bluejays,
anticipating winter's needs,
Make darting, frequent visits to the feeder,
Pecking furiously at the last few seeds . . .
The multi-colored forest staunchly guards the lake,
And I am not alone on Scroggie Bay.

Kay McHenry
HEAVEN IS ABOVE

To all my sisters and brothers in Christ and my dear husband, Othello, and my loving daughters, Lartricia, Tayandra and Natosha Marie McHenry

(H)eaven is not this earth below
(E)arth is now where Satan goes to and fro
(A) new heaven and a new earth soon to be
(V)anished Satan forever will soon see
(E)arth and sky and all belong to God
(N)o more Satan to roam this sod

(I)nto heaven to enter one and all
(S)eek God who will never let you fall

(A)way beyond the clouds is heaven land
(B)lessed are those who join the Christian band
(O)nly Jesus shed blood can set us free
(V)ictory was the death of him for you and me
(E)ntering into heaven we can for eternity!

Betty A Ward
HERE I AM
Here I am
on the brink of eternity
ready to fall over into a wealth of knowledge

waiting

to envelop me into its greatness

After falling into its powdery whiteness
I will run with swift steps
leaving snowy tracks behind
so that the younger loved ones can touch one
with his fingertip—and test it on his tongue

Then know that he too can step into

such
permanent, perfect
bloody clean tracks
and become Greater than anything or anyone can imagine

he can know that the greatest miracle
is waiting for his magic to turn it into reality
he can know that any mountain
is just his stepping stone

he can know that His power is so great that each life can be turned into supernatural greatness for His will.

Brent Webber
FOREVER
Ever in my mind's eye
is the fair-haired girl
with the blush of youth
upon her delicate cheeks
in some far-off springtime,
but always out of reach.
I never met or knew her.

Growing old I'll not be bitter
at missing what might have been,
but will sigh with melancholy.

Mrs Doris L Schmidt
LAND OF LIBERTY
And the Indians looked and the Bagpipes played their wailing tune
And the flow of life moved on unerringly across the plain,
Over the never ending desert under the unrelenting blazing sun
Like waves of grain bending under the never ending wind.

And the Indians looked at the massing white-skinned souls
Who rutted the trails of Antelope, Buffalo and Deer,
Who struck the trees to build a permanent home
And they stood and looked and knew their numbers would decline
And their game would never again so freely roam.

And the teepees burned
And the tomahawks blazed
And the arrows flew
And the howls filled the air
And the Indians dwindled
And the blood flowed free.

And then we were asked to look at the LAND fought for so savagely,
And we were told we were living in a land of guarantee,
Of life and liberty for you and me,
And we looked at the blood stained land and the effaced tree,
And wondered who enjoyed the warranty
And who sacrificed for this land of liberty?

Sandra G Phillips
THE LAND OF ME
You do your thing, I'll do my thing
and never the twain shall meet.
As long as we don't cooperate
We'll always face defeat.

This is my opinion, that's your opinion.
Is there no authority?
Then don't see a physician whenever you're ill—
Ask your neighbor down the street.

For every action an opposing reaction.
Where is the harmony?
Unless all are hermits on Walden's Pond
Only chaos can be.

Until we learn to live and let Love,
Confusion will abound.
Forever the Land of the Free
Will be the Land of Me
Wherever souls are found.

Dave M Yates
MUSIC
I'm a human necessity,
A teenagers escape;
A portable source of energy,
I'm always cranked.
The king of the beach,
The commander of your soul;
I switch moods without warning,
And I play loud rock n roll.

Laura M Teverbaugh

Laura M Teverbaugh
I WANT TO GET AWAY FROM THIS TABLE

I prayed for a miracle and you came around the corner, thank you for everything, I love you Mr. Jeffrey McMillian.

Now comes the time to testify,
that all I've lived was not a lie.
Yet, I have but one desire;
I want to get away from this table.

In so much as I was given in birth,
had I not strived to prove my worth.
After being a slave on this dirty earth;
I want to get away from this table.

Having earned a life-time and supply,
of almost every-thing, I reply,
That I have but one desire;
I want to get away from this table.

I could not bow before his Grace,
even in all my satin and lace,
had I not earned my rightful place;
I want to get away from this table.

In the event that I don't get home,
just remember this road was long,
and as I traveled things went wrong;
I want to get away from this table.

Marella Wilson
A FALL POEM
October's bright blue weather,
We enjoyed it this year.
With trick or treat on Halloween
And ghosts and goblins, never fear.

The leaves of red and gold are gone
The branches now are bare,
We've gathered nuts for baking,
With others we will share.

Election day has come and gone
A new president was elected.
I hope some problems of the world,
May somehow be corrected.

Thanksgiving Day will soon be here,
It's time to count our blessings.
To roast the turkey, bake the pies
And make the oyster dressings.

It's time for the family to gather
At the old home place each year.
They love Grandma's cake and pies,
And all the love and good cheer.

Mary Carlyle Rountree
MY SCRAPBOOK
I treasure my scrapbook, I've kept through the years,
some pages bring laughter and others bring tears.
This, "School Friendship Book" was given to me—
by a dear friend on my birthday.

I look at my scrapbook this evening—all alone
and muse on the faces of friends I have known.
I turn the leaves of memory in shadowy design,
as I see the smiling faces of those classmates of mine.

The four years of High School I finished so long ago,
fills my heart with memories—all aglow.
With friends I made in school—I have kept in touch,
all through the years—they have meant so much.

At last my dream is over and I close my book once more,
to review my life gone on before.
A phone call, a card, or a letter is a pleasure to me,
it makes my life worth living you see.

I have traveled far and wide these many years,
my life has been filled with faith—not fears.
The world is so big and yet so small,
love is the shortest distance between us all.

Nosa Eke

Nosa Eke
THE QUEER MAN

For Patrick (1937-87) and Grace, (1940-) my parents.

He was tall, short; tall in height, short in goodwill.
His wife deserted him, his children hermited him.
Neighbors said he was a queer.
He said nothing—humming, gesticulating and soliloquizing only.
One day, a neighbor's wife volunteered to help steam his pot of soup.
A pot due for replenishment long, long ago.
Each time he opened the pot, maggots would swarm and swarm.
He often steamed the pot until the clustered maggots fell back in the pot, swarming in the soup.
The man raised no objection to the wife's gesture.
He only hummed, gesticulated and soliloquized.
One step and wham! He pounced on the wife and mounted—
pressure, force.
The wife screamed and neighbors came.
Satisfied, the man greeted the puzzled neighbors 'hello!'
'So the man can talk,' said a neighbor.
He stole a curious glance at the queer man and
Slowly, gradually walked away.

Mary Anne Segerbeck
RAINY DAY
How can you talk of lovers
Yet never speak of love?
How can you say another way is best
While at the same time . . .
Well let that question rest.

You're near. You're far. You're near.
Dear what is on your mind?
Your head for me is not too clear
And my heart becoming hard to find.

Machines they take us here and there
We involve them in our lives.
Here I sit listening to this lovesinging machine,
And talking with you of strife.

It seems we're talking on two levels
Each from behind transparent shields.
Questions only later heard
Answers far from right.

The rain keeps pouring down
there's water all around.
It's clinking in our glasses
and shining in our eyes.

The solutions that we're coming to
they seem so far from wise.

Patricia G West
TEAR'S WITHIN

Dedication of Tears Within to Abigail Elizabeth Ann West from Ma Ma Patricia Gail West

I cried a tear, I let it fall the pain within I could not tell, I know God is the only one that I could ever tell, you came along, some months ago you were so small, I was afraid I'd let you fall, but deep inside I loved you so.
Even if I had to go, you had no hair, your eyes are blue as the sky, your skin as white as the snow, you cried your tears I wiped them off, you smiled your little smile I gave you life, you gave me love, but now I'm gone, You'll see me no more, for God has called for me to go. I watch you now from up above, I loved you so, I gave you life, don't cry my child for I am free.

Gladys I Blue
AGE IS A THREAD THAT WRAPS AROUND US
Age is a thread that wraps around us.
It's often the sign others see.
But inside hidden in this cocoon
Is the kind of one we'd like to be.

Age can be full of fun, life and laughter
Plus soft words spoken, to be shared.
Music from the soul of mystic being
Played on the harps of one who cares.

Touching hands carry all the message of a longing soul to be set free.
Sweet sighing winds waft the perfume
Memory lane swaying with the breeze.

Is the inner one to wither, longing
For an answer to a loving plea?
Gently slip the bands of lonely thinking
Walk down the path that sets you free!

Left in life are precious treasures
Open the door between you and me
To have, to hold all the music
Tuned to say I love you—you love me.

Rebecca B Ronquillo

Rebecca B Ronquillo
HEAR MY CALL

To Elizabeth Clare Prophet, my guru and Emmanuel James, my son.

The singers of by gone days sang of golden ages
Of blessed lands vast, bright, and beautiful
And of earth free from disease and dirt.
They sang of past utopias; they sang of lost paradise
They sang of lands of beauty; they sang of lands of glory
Peopled by men upright and faithful
Peopled by women virtuous and beautiful.
Where now are the glorious lands and faithful men?
Where now are the beauteous lands and virtuous women?
Brothers of every race, hear my call!
Do you see the task that calls for one and all?
Let us all put our hearts, hands, and heads to the task
Of bringing back the glory of centuries past.
We can rid the world if ills and aches
We can rid the world of floods and quakes
We can rid the world of wants and wars
If we stop the beat of battle drums; stop the blast of nuclear bombs
If we stop the burst of rifle fire; stop the goad of drugged desire
If we stop the noise of rock madness; stop the mess of drunken orgies
If we stop the race for filthy lucre; stop the craze for fame and power.
Only by the great power of hearts, hands, and heads dedicated to the high task
Can we all make the glory of the distant past soon fully ours at last.

Kathleen M Johnson
THE MOON

Dedicated to: My Family. For me, dreams have never exceeded reality.

The guide of your spirit,
creator of whims.
Instigator of emotions,
between hers and hims.

Bright light of the evening,
God made, reason unknown.
Making its way across the heavens
never finding its home.

Appears at time of resting
to say that day is done.
The labor of today is gone,
await the morning sun.

Sister Mary Joyce Schladweiler OSF
IS IT LOVE?

This poem is dedicated to all who have ever loved me, and to all whom I have loved.

Love can be
Life sacrificed,
Health broken,
Fortune dwindled,
Body battered;
Relationship shattered,
But always mendable,
Because IT IS LOVE.

But merely sex ?
Lives confused,
Bodies used.
Or abused.
Emptiness to muse.
Disease beyond repair.

HOW can the two be confused e'er ?

Shary G Letzo
FALL SPLENDOR SONG
The magnificent trees in their beautiful Fall colors
Shades of green turn to red, gold, russet and brown,
Hastily, the leaves rustle and fall to the ground;
Then Ole Man Winter strips their clothing to the last
We remember then, the splendor of this Fall past.

Our Lady Wind whistles a pretty tune all around
While the pine trees sing and sway with her sound.
The sky dims its lights and starts up the drums
The leaves hop and dance along
Then the rain comes and makes her debut.

Keeping time with the pitter-patter through the air
They all make one beautiful orchestral symphony;
All mellowed together in perfect harmony,
As they play one last concerto of Fall Splendor Song.

Alexandria Keller

Alexandria Keller
CHILDREN

This poem is dedicated to Ben and Jack Lynn

Laughter, Hurt, Tears and Anger
These are some words that describe children.
Laughter, for the funny things, they always seem to do.
Hurt, for the awful things, most go through.

Tears, for the times they can't hold back.
Anger, for the times they wouldn't believe it's a fact.
Oh Children, Children,
What would we do?
Without your love,
and without you!!

Lizzie Wade

Lizzie Wade
SPECIAL LADY

To my parents Johnnie Mae and Willie Carter Sr. And Eddie Lou-Cole for making my dream come true.

She's such a special lady
The finest woman that I know on Earth
The badest lady that will kick up dirt
The lady with the sweetest smell
The only sister that will give you Hell!

This sexy lady with the scheming smile
This kool babe won't take no jive
The meanest Queen I ever seen
The cleanest babe that has ever been made
She's such a special lady.

Fitzroy Tex Joseph

Fitzroy Tex Joseph
YOU NEVER SAID GOODBYE

'Livicated' to the people of Dominica West Indies

You're not saying goodbye today
Was it deliberate?
You're not saying goodbye today
only brought pain my way
You're not saying goodbye today
Broke the attitude of my happy o.k.

Elswiter Easy
MAINTAIN THY PRIDE OH MAN

To my only and loving son—Paul

Maintain thy pride, oh man,
For it's your only chance
To lead us on in this dark, and gloomy land.
Thy light so brightly shines
On this dim path we must tread.
So, maintain thy pride, oh man,
To gladly lead us on.

Far above the mountain top,
Thy light must shine for us.
Because we must soar ever so high,
Even as far as the sky.

Maintain thy pride, oh man;
You are our leader yet.
We cannot stop to fret,
Because the path we'll take,
Will be the one we make.

Maintain thy pride oh man.

race.
For this is the job for you,
To lead your people safely through.

Maintain thy pride, oh man.
Thy journey is not o'er.
You were given this task before
To gently lead us on,
So maintain, maintain, maintain,
Thy pride oh man.

Ivanka Suveg
DREAM
Once more like a child,
Puzzled and innocent.
Watching the world go by,
And never noticing the time.

Loving, caring, sharing,
Touching and overbearing.
Running after a puppy,
Who is very grumpy.

Playing, talking, walking
And always provoking.
Sunshine, rain or sleet,
Never mind, the outfit.

My dream is very neat,
I dangle my feet.
Happiness is close by,
Only if we really try.

Kathleen C Dempsey
LAND OF PROMISE
This was the land of promise,
Dream of our fathers of long ago,
Who labored long and prayed that God
Would somehow make it so.
With courage, and with gratitude
In this land they came to bless;
Seeking their right to worship God
In their pursuit of happiness.

"Without a vision my people perish."
This was nurtured in their breast,
Until at last there was fulfillment
Until at last there was peace and rest.

We live in this Land of Promise,
Freedom's banner is still unfurled,
God, give us new vision and courage,
For ours is the Hope of the World!

Poul E Hoegh
BECAUSE I LOVE YOU

Dedicated to an unknown woman with inner beauty who likes my poem and would like to get to know me better by calling me in California at (408) 554-0737

Because I love you, I will give to you, myself, in every way,
Whether you need helping hands, or simply want to play.
I will love you without prejudice, but with the total verve
You could wish for from a man, who fully loves without reserve.

Because I love you, I'll not dwell on what has happened, past to present.
I'll defend your every move, without passing any judgment.
I will try to give you comfort, when I see you feeling blue,
Not because I share your sadness, but because I FEEL for you.

Just because I love you and because you give me joy
And because you're so delightful, cute, affectionate and coy,
I'll be there when you might need me, but I won't invade your space.
I will pace you by your side, without making it a race.

Because I love you, I will be beside you, every day and night.
I'll appreciate your efforts, even if results are slight.
Because I love you, I will hold you close when you need closeness.
When you need some quiet times, I'll put a curb on my verboseness.

I will offer you my help, but won't force you to accept it.
If I think you are in error, I won't drive you to correct it.
Even if I find you wrong, I'll not emphasize your guilt.
I will sprinkle you with kindness, when you are about to wilt.

All because I love you, every way that you stand tall,
Your loving Poul.

Tennessee Jackson
TRAFFIC JAM
If you ever want to
see a bunch of privates
get warm by fire
in a fire barrel four feet deep

wedge your way into the crowd
and peep to yonder corner and see

the fire barrel warm itself
from breathing soldiers' heat

and then hear the Drill Sergeant's call:
F O R M A T I O N
and see a pile of human feet
rush and run from the heat in utter confusion

Now I thought I'd seen it all before in
Lisbon and Conakry where cars get
jammed, can't find their way and
wait in perfect unison

yet there's no sight I've seen in my
travels around the world I've seen
like those privates feet left unwarmed
running in confusion not knowing
from which direction
the voice had yelled
or how to tell one Drill Sergeant's
bark from another's bite
as dusk turned to night

and all you hear are privates' feet
that trample over one another like
one big stalled and hurried traffic jam
confused in the night

Grant Nash
THE COCKSWAIN'S SONG
Avast!
Come up to breathe ye myties
Sost I might glympse thy ponderous hulk
Don't hold your breath ye mytie mammals
Come up and make a splendorous show
Come sing your mystical songs
Sost I might stand wrapt in utter awe
Come spray my face with thy sumptuous spout
Sost I might feel thy life
Come up to breathe ye myties
Sost I might view thy life

Shiver me timbers

Thar she blows

20 points off the port bow
A hump like a snowhill
A spout like a gyser

Tis Moby Dick

Loos the scuttleboats
To arms! . . . To arms!
Spare no quarter . . . nor your arms
After her my men
The first with blood on his spear has a dubloon

L D Sauvage
THEY BECAME YOU
A diamond may be a stone
to a primitive man.
Ivory may be a tusk
to an elephant.
Gold may be just yellow dust.
But the diamonds in your eyes,
The ivory of your skin,
And the gold of your smile
Make you more precious
Than any or all of them to me.

I took the diamonds of my feelings,
The ivory of my thoughts
And the gold of my love.
And when they were put all together,
They became you.

Louise Mason
A QUIET MOMENT

To my family

As—I sat beside the brook
On my lap an open book
Not a word have I read
Watching the squirrels instead,
Seems some nuts they've found
Scattered about o'er the ground.

Aline Dixon Dykes
THE SUN

To: Faye Klahn; who also produces a glowing light.

The Sun is my glowing, gliding clock
It spends the winter traveling to and from Antarctica,
Waiting to pendulum back towards the North;
Heading for Greenland and Norway and me.

Gradually, I watch the sunrise which trends
Towards my South, or Violet window, where I winter in its
Weak, warm glow, lacking heat in the pale rays; inching towards my
East window where it peeks in shamelessly in dead summer.

Then, reaching the zenith of its Northward orbit, turns Southward
And the heavens are timing the year by its passing;
To mark anew its foreordained trail to the icy
Blazing splendor, of the South Pole and its penguins.
I feel like an aged American Indian
Backed up in his smokey tepee,
Cogitating on his canyons and gulches of time; and
I feel his spirit is noble; pulling forward my afghan for warmth.

Mrs Pearl M Graham
THE SHARE-CROPPER

In memory of my father, William L Graham (deceased).

Many days he spent working in a field
With a team of mules and a sturdy plough,
Awaiting the harvest, its crop to yield.
Wiping the sweat from his toil-worn brow.
In the early morn, when the sky was clear,
He quickly finished laying off the rows;
Drinking water from a jug that was near;
Ending a days' work with the seed he sows.
For he was a sower of much good seed,
His life goals were stored in the fertile soil,
With firm trust in God to supply each need,
And reward him here for his sweat and toil:
He was one of the best farmers I know,
My dad, born over ninety years ago.

Travis Troxell
FALL
It is a beautiful sight to behold
When I look up at the sky
Through strange shapes of leaves
Tinted orange and gold . . .

Then, I know a lovelier sight is when
I glance down to find the same
shapes stencilled upon the ground.

Ruth Garrett
I WONDER
Have you ever wondered
What "Heaven's" like
With all its streets of Gold
and a light that shineth
Both day and night
and you never grow old.

All our loved ones will be there
and our friends we knew long ago.
And we will all be happy
on that Golden shore.

There will be no pain or sorrow
no more burdens to bear.
We will all be singing and rejoicing
With our savior over there.

And as I stood there wondering
I could hear the Angels sing
Glory to "God" in the highest
and Peace on earth to man

Leone B Elliott
MIGRATORY MUSING
There came a distant honking,
an old familiar cry;
A V-like chain appearing from
the distant northern sky.

I spoke of how it thrilled me,
the wonder of it all,
"That's nothing," said my comrade,
"geese migrate every fall."

I saw that old gray gander,
his eyes alert and keen;
A bold and dauntless leader,
the monarch of the scene.

I saw those far-flung waters,
the Gulf of Mexico,
The mighty frozen Northland,
its leagues of swirling snow.

The springtime and the autumn
spread out before me then,
I saw the time when, sure as fate,
they'd all fly back again.

I saw the God who made them,
the God of hope and peace,
And yet my friend beside me
saw—just a flock of geese.

John Theus
HOME IS ONLY A WORD

This poem is dedicated to the REN Center

Home is only a word, a place where prayer is no longer heard, where love has flown away, like an uncaged bird.

Home is only a word, where, "I love you" is very seldom heard, where love has faded like the shadows of an evening sun.

God grants all good, I pray one day He will bind our hearts with a love so strong man nor time will force us to forsake, a bond between family and home, that only He can break, home is only a word.

Home is only a word, a place in the back of our minds a place that is lost, in the shifting sands of time,
Home is only a word.

Daniel Eggleston
EVERSIX
red, and green, and grape
rainbow in a box,
big, and round, and fat;
crushed softly 'gainst the bite,
smack for me a cadence
with your juicy juice!

"Ah, there you are my Craig!"
(Cursed/blessed by idle age)
"You really shouldn't wander."
(Reach, for me, my hand, and walk.)
"There will come a time, my son,
(As sand will fall on sand)
When your father won't be there
And you'll need him still . . . "
(oh bubble gum! and hold my
hand . . .)

Dawn Cahoon-Kniff
LOVE . . .
This word, into many languages, translates.
But, beneath the words, the feelings are the same.
To Latins, Amour, Amore, Romance states.
Kjerlighet, Liebe, Kasih . . . or any other name.

It's one thing that "old Father-time" can not change.
Modes of expression may vary . . . it is true.
Like Eskimos rubbing noses, may seem strange.
And, Natives on Islands, have a different view.
A quality of life, innate, within all.
Inspires, motivates and causes us to grow.
Animal and vegetable respond to its call.
'True sense of it . . . a bit of Heaven . . . to know.

'Tis sad, that it is not always understood,
And it's potential for good, nurtured and used.
Real love can reveal to us, our brotherhood.
'Should not be taken for granted . . . or abused.

As great Ships are supported by the Ocean . . .
Without bruising them, love brings things together.
Soothing as water . . . more than mere emotion.
Cohesive, powerful! gentle as a feather.

Peggy Fudge

Peggy Fudge
MY SON

This poem is dedicated to my wonderful son "Keith"

You were but a tiny seed
within me,
That grew, and grew and grew,
I nourished you as days went
by,
And felt you as you grew.

Month after month I felt you grow,
and move around within me,
You were like a breath of air; So
Light but know it's there.

And then you bloomed out from
within,
And came into the light; I cradled
you within my arms,
You were so soft and warm, and I
Will always cherish
"YOU"
because
"YOU"
are
my
"SON"

Violet Nast Huberty

Violet Nast Huberty
WINTER BLUES

To my children Jack, Rosemary, Caroline

Don't moan and groan when North
Winds Blow

That bring the sleet and hail and
snow and sends a chill upon your
spine

That makes you moan and groan and
whine

So soon it will be spring again
and all the birds will call again

They'll be the humming of the busy
bee

Buds bursting out on bush and tree

Warm breezes will so gently blow

They'll touch you from your head to
toe

So don't moan and groan when North
winds blow

that bring the sleet and hail and snow

I'm glad that I'm alive and free and
can see four seasons come and go
Amen

Sandra L Adams
WHAT LIFE
Life is adjusting to everything
disgusting
And being agreeable to things that
make you miserable
When you are young you think it's
growing up
But when you're a teenager you soon
discover
Life is not all roses
When you hit twenty one
It's not fun anymore
But then comes thirty and you
wonder what's left
Then comes forty and oh lordy
There goes fifty and wasn't it nifty
Oh to be twenty one again
But then there's sixty plus five
And social security checks oh sigh!
If you make it to seventy
Playing bingo and lottery
A class reunion at ninety
To see who survived
But then you reach 100
All's left is to wonder
What could I have changed
If I would have changed a thing

Terry Lee Kinzer

Terry Lee Kinzer
THE LADY FROM RIGER
There once was a lady from Riger,
She took a ride on a tiger.
They came from the ride,
With the lady inside,
And a smile on the face of a tiger.

Terry Lee Kinzer
MONKEYS IN THE TREES
There once were monkeys in the
trees,
They threw coconuts in the seas.
They packed all their bags,
And put on their rags,
Then the monkeys left all the trees.

Ilga S Angiolini
I HEAR A SOUND
I hear a sound: What can it be,
Do I hear a bird in a white birch
tree.
I suppose it is spring after all,
For we have waited since
summer, winter, and fall.
The trees are so green, so lively
today,
They make me and the birds
feel so gay.
The sun shining bright on the quiet
old lake,
Shows the reflection of my
peachy–red face.
I see a swan onto my side,
So beautiful, so lively, so
brightly white.
How did it happen to be this way,
I wish it could be here
everyday.

Patricia Russell
FADED DREAMS
They're fading fast.
Deep into the past.
You've let them die.
As you sit and cry.

We tried to tell you.
That's what they'd do.
You didn't believe us.
Now you're not joyous.

You now see we were right.
As you sit home at night.
You're ready to scream.
While we chase our dreams.

You're drowned in sorrow.
There's no more time to borrow.
This is your last chance.
This is the final dance.

Kyriacos P Kouros
AIDS (NO MORE)

To my Parents

AT corridor's far extremity
lies the deathbed
and from above
the crucifix gapes in contempt.
THE sobbing
as a mad rodent
tears apart serenity;
curses
painted in painful grey
are choked by fate.
BLAMES
towards the unknown Father of all
shake the metaphysic faith;
this victim
of the heartless reaper
will never run across adolescence.
IMPOTENT
stands knowledge in reacting
lonely souls in infinity scatter
and then, when Love is thought as lost
the blood from the nails
becomes tear!

Elsie H Baric
THE LINCOLN LEGEND

Dedicated to my dear mother, Helen.

Your mother fondly smiled, as over your books you bent.
Abe perhaps she dreamed you'd grow up to be president.
People said you were awkward, they said you lacked style.
Now you're compared to a God who lived for a while.
Your speeches were eloquent, they touched the very soul.
Bringing freedom to everyone, you achieved your goal.
A philosopher and founder of democracy,
You charmed the poor as well as the aristocracy.
"With malice toward none and charity for all."
Your words and spirit made you seem ten feet tall.
Personal tragedies saddened you and your wife.
The death of your son was the sorrow of your life.
The greatest tragedy that affected one and all,
Was the day the assassin's bullet caused you to fall.
Did you have psychic powers? You foresaw your demise.
But yours was the brightest star that would ever rise.
You touched the nation. You made the world a better place,
Enduring great hardships with dignity and grace.
So the boy in that log cabin, turning the pages,
Became The Lincoln Legend that lives through the ages!

T M Capate
HEAVEN FLOWER

Heaven Flower,
Where are you tonight?
Heaven Flower,
Save me from my own stupidity flight.

I took off in a craft
that I knew could not fly,
but my own ego blinded me
when I saw the beauty of the sky.

I thought I was more powerful,
than anyone around,
now I'm in a freefall
that fast approaches the ground.

My life passes before me,
and I didn't much care for it the first time,
Help me Heaven Flower,
Please! Give me a sign.

No answer!
None at all!
Well it doesn't much matter
I'm at the end of my fall.

I don't really care for me,
just the trouble I will and have caused.
Oh Heaven Flower! I have so many bad values,
so many annoying flaws.

Heaven Flower,
If I could have one wish granted,
upon my grave
I would like you planted.

Because I want people to know,
that with you I lived and died,
and not like me find out too late,
there are other ways to touch the sky.

Hannah M Mahady
ESPECIALLY TO MY FIRST LOVE

Childhood memories of my mother and father, Billy, Karen, Mary Ellen, Mamie, Anna and Pa Pa Mahady. My sweet children Lorrie and Leslie. And to you Jimmy R. Forever in my heart. Hannah M Mahady.

When we began to walk this path we took our first steps together
We too, held hands and made plans
and talked about forever

There was nothing to be right and
nothing to be wrong
We had our long walks our long
talks and our favorite song

What we knew was simple
and beautiful as well
We only knew of Heaven
We never heard of Hell.
And because we had to part, proves
how cruel the world can be—
But there's one thing they can't take away
And that's the memory.

Deborah Lee Hardman
OUR THOUGHTS

Even though
We are not close,
Our love
Is very near.
Let's base our love,
Upon our thoughts,
And not what
We might hear.

Betty Wilson
EVOLUTION OF LOVE

To my soul mate—a scholar of reality, the source of my strength.

At first it all was casual
We spoke of memories past.
The conversation flowed like wine
Someone to be my friend, at last.

He chose his words so carefully.
He expressed them with such grace.
To see his eyes, to see his smile—
The look of trust formed on his face.

He searched within his heart one night
And shared himself with me.
We both knew love was real this time—
To commit without a guarantee.

The evolution of our love
Developed deep within my soul.
What once seemed like a broken life
He touched and made it whole.

He opened up my mind, my heart.
We found a joy that had no end.
He set my thoughts and senses free
Became my lover—stayed my friend.

Shirley Powell—Maxine Livingstone Seagull
THE WEB OF LIFE

In loving memory of our mother, friend and wife—K-S-M-E

The fertile womb
Expells a life . . .
Thrusting it out
To a world of strife

Another miracle
In Destiny's plan
Testing the virtues
And strengths of man.

As the child grows
We show him the way
For the good or the bad
It's that choice he'll pay

He'll Flounder and Fall
And pick up again,
With Trial and Error
He's sure to win

As Parents and teachers
We must lead the way

From the darkness of night
Toward the Brightness of Day

Michael David Church
OH

"OH" is dedicated to those who wear the "Rings of gold with starlight shining"

A wanton desire, as yet unachieved,
keeps fires for lovers, whose
heartbeats bereave;

Looking more closely may only
discover, an empty illusion, and no
hope to recover;

Watching our love dissolve into
space, a gift for the next, of our
perpetuate race;

While we forever together blend
colors of beauty, with God's purest
"lite" to shine, like a star of
deliverance, for lost souls to find;

And were given room now, to take
steps over life's old, in search of an
old friend in time . . .

Victor M Delgado
THE JOURNEY

This poem is dedicated to my sons Hermes, Victor R., Pabel, Lester, Aramis, Oliver and my daughter Arelis.

She is gone, never to be seen again.
Now that she is gone,
I ask myself, why did she come?
What secret lies deep within her heart?

Why did she leave the big city,
The glittering lights?
Was it to escape a love torn apart,
Or the caverns of Manhattan
Full of fright?

She is gone, never to be seen again.
I am alone, my heart full of pain.
I met her only by chance,
And smitten by her with just a glance

She was not pretty, she was not fair,
Yet she bewitched me, I was caught unaware
I was intoxicated by her charms,
The perfume on her hair,
But my heart did not warn me,
beware!

She is gone, never to be seen again.
With her went all my dreams,
But the journey of love is like a train,
There are many stops along the way.

R" Lou F Baum
MY STONE SILHOUETTE

The hammer of time keeps rapping away,
Denting our Rocks many times each day.
As each chip falls crumbling to the ground,
Love builds it stronger and bigger around.

To build a strong Rock is not easy to do,
Others will smash it to sand it is true.
Emotions of fear, resentment and greed,
Like nothing more than upon us to feed.

Strength comes with feeling and living each day,
Facing that hammer, we kneel and we pray.
God give us courage to show loving kindness,
And pity our foe in his own selfish blindness.

Eve Lynn Mahaney
THE ROSE

The first time that you came to me,
You brought a special gift for me.
You placed beside our marriage bed
A single, perfect rose, so red.

A special fragrance meant for me;
Our time was spent so happily,
And every night beside my bed
A single, perfect rose, so red.

Sometimes we fought so needlessly
Of things that mattered least to me;
Still, every night beside my bed
A single, perfect rose, so red.

As time wore on, I failed to see
A ghostly pallor come to thee.
And then one night beside my bed
No single, perfect rose of red.

Time somehow has stood still for me:
Your face before me endlessly.
And by my bed each silent night,
A single, perfect rose, so white.

Danielle R Ogier
LOVE ME
Love me tender
Love me dear
Hold me tight all through the night
And let me know that you are near
Love me, please just love me.

Marguerite Mooney
WHERE DID ALL THE MUSIC GO?
Watch the people rushing by,
Wearing their proper smiles on faces.
Paced by the pulse of the noisy crowd,
In the ragged rhythm of fearsome places.

If loneliness would fly away,
To be lost in yonder revolving door
Or become as dead as last year's news,
Then forever deported to a foreign shore.

Night comes quickly, the rhythm stops,
Light and music fast disappear.
Doors are closed and so alone
No one listens and no one hears.

A merry masquerade of life they make.
They never hear the call above the beat.
Then follows the cold and dismal night,
Where care and worry stalk their retreat.

All the lonely people, where do they belong?
Wearing made-up faces, they keep in jars of stone,
Staring through the window at the anxious milling throng,
While happiness awaits them from the God whom they disown.

Phyllis J Long
MY PRECIOUS RUNAWAY

To all precious runaways and their loved ones.

Gone again! Oh, the anxiety, the heartache;
It is surprising, but not unexpected. I am reeling.
Her way: not as ours; her choice: running. So much at stake.
How is she hurting? What is she thinking, feeling?

Days drag; I function, yet part of me is painfully wrest.
Where is she? Place—unknown, but in my spirit, deeply set.
Imagining the worst, I hope for the best.
I pray, "Lord, snare her in your loving net."

Lord, strengthen me, too, my Companion, my Confidant.
In new environs, with friendships afar, I struggle alone.
No, not alone; I feel your Presence, constant.
Present to her; ease the separateness to which she's prone.

Return, Beautiful Daughter of my heart.
Lord, bring her to our family/Godly team.
Change negative crisis to positive new start,
Greater strength, resolve, confidence and esteem.

Arlys E Bader
MY FLAG AMERICA

To my Dad, who died of cancer in July of 1988.

I am a flag as you can see
I stand for love and security
The price we've paid in this Great Land
For I am America's brand

For I am you, and you are me
I wave back and forth and keep you free
For without this strength for mind and soul
America, would not have met her goal

So be very proud of my stripes you see
For I wave back and forth and keep you free
Without the freedoms that you know
Your minds, and souls would never grow

We are a nation together true
Yes, I am the red, the white, the blue
So look onto me and be very proud
And don't ever let any one curse me loud

Speak softly of me and wisely too
For without me and my stars so blue
You wouldn't have the freedoms now
Because others want them stopped somehow

So every time you look at me
Be happy that you live so free
And by the miracles of the grace of God
Be happy you live on "American Sod."

Denis Lambert
LIFE

This poem is dedicated to Cedric and Francis Lambert, my grandparents. It is also dedicated to Chuck and Sue Pierce, two very special friends.

Life is like a flower.
It comes on a certain day.
It lives its life fully,
But eventually must go away.

Life is like a clock.
It ticks just like your heart.
But if that ticking stops,
From use you will depart.

Life is like a leaf.
At first, it's just a blossom.
Then it grows, gets old, and falls,
In the late part of autumn.

Life is like a battery.
At first, it's fresh and new.
Then, it gets old and starts to weaken,
After it's been used.

You can't just explain life.
It's very hard to do.
Life has its ups and downs,
But that's what makes it true.

Linda Rhea Lanning
THE SEA GULLS
As I look at the clear blue sky,
I see a Sea Gull soaring by.
Soaring high up in the sky,
Making circles and floating,
Soaring, soaring, higher and higher.
Floating, floating, floating.
In the clear blue sky.
As I look out at the ocean,
I see the Dolphins at play.
Surfers are gliding over the waves.
Swimmers are there with their graceful styles.
Sea Gulls floating on the waves.
A speed boat passes by.
The cool wind blowing the sails of boats.
As the sail boats glide by.
There is a freighter way out there,
On it's way to parts unknown.
As I look at the beach I see,
The waves come rolling in,
Then they rush right out again.
Little children are making sand castles.
Life guards all decked out in orange.
Surfers gather on the beach exhausted.
The swimmers are bathing in the sun.
Sea shells there just for the taking.
Then as I look at the clear blue sky,
I see a Sea Gull soaring high,
Free, for all to see.

Michelle Green

Michelle Green
UNDERNEATH MY WINGS

To my beautiful Mother, Louise Green, who I love so dearly, Thanks for believing in me. I love you Addie, my Grandmother who is deceased.

Like a bird locked up in chains
hiding her worldly pains: tears falling down like
April's rain.
Darkness covering her eyes; a vision of racing across the skies.
Praying for the best to find a home of rest.
Trying to make a decision of a lost dream of vision.
Broken away from her chains,
free from life's game.
Happiness is the word to
describe this beautiful bird.
Free at last of time's hurting past.

Stephen Caissie
YOU'RE ON MY MIND
There's something I want you to know,
you're on my mind whereever I go.
Whether it's just going out to play,
or when I'm at work during the day.
And everyday I'll take awhile . . .
just to daydream about your smile.
And how it changed the way I feel,
from a life that didn't seem real.
As I sit and watch the rain come down,
and thoughts of you are all around.
And even though it's cloudy and gray,
in my heart I have a sunny day.
If I could pick a dream to come true,
it would be one that's all about you.
Because when I have a dream of being a rich man,
all the riches come from holding your hand.
Although you're on my mind both day and night,
and you're the one that makes my life right.
There's just one more thing I have to say,
thank you for being there for me everyday.

Diane E Perry
MY BEAUTIFUL BOBBY
It was not that long ago that, you entered my life
And now I find that you are living in my heart,
However I know that you will never be mine
Because the ring on your finger keeps us apart.

Craving your love and tender touch
I pray every night that someday we'll be together,
I wait patiently for your kiss and your arms
Living in a shell and wanting no other.

What was it that brought me to you
On that twenty-first day in May?
When I looked in those beautiful eyes
Knowing then, in my heart you'll always stay.

Bobby, my beautiful Bobby
When you put your arm around me,
I felt a thrill like none other before
What can I do to make you see, what you mean to me.

When you hold my hand, you lift me higher and higher
You own my heart and always on my mind,
My desire for you burns like a raging fire
And Bobby, you have the finest body a woman could find.

M Q Cie
I
I soar above the wings of a Dove
I am Freedom
I light the torch of Love
My fingers of dawn radiates Birth
My crisp air awakens Nature
My morning mist settles gently to Earth
The echoes of life call out my Future
Suddenly!
A White She-Dove glides through the Air
In all her radiance she Appears
Shrills of Justice she dares
With an air of Dignity, she Disappears

Brenda Claiborne
MY SPECIAL LOVE

Dedicated to Greg Sanders . . . whose love and warmth inspired me to write this poem.

He came into my life unexpected
but I gladly accepted
It can be a real surprise
To see life through another's eyes.
He makes everything so nice
I wonder how I stayed a block of ice.
This guy is special you see

because he's meant just for me.

He doesn't drive a fancy car
He doesn't keep me out all night in a bar.
It's the little things he do
That makes my life seem new.
Oh what fun it is to share
The special love that's in the air.

He's so easy to touch
That's why I need him so much
He never makes me sad
just makes me glad
I should tell this title bye
and just name this "My Special Guy."

Barry G Ferguson

ASIAN HOLIDAY

Fog-laced treetops in the distance,
Last night's rain still drips in cadence,
Yesterday's boy thinks about snow.
Jefferson Airplane breaks the silence,
The sun returns bright and deadly,
And I remember my faded purpose.
Fire and smoke and an ungodly smell
Reminds the drifters here of hell,
And heat for the holidays is lovely.
Those freezing people in the homeland,
Their breath remains the hottest air,
And their cold touch is only hot to us.
Brother wants to light-out for home,
But Uncle says he needs the rest,
I confess, I don't know my kin,
Vacations are good for a week or so
But after duration, I don't know
Who pays the bills for all these luxuries.
Going home now, I'm staying long
And find out what went wrong
When we all "took the road
less traveled by."

May More Plennert

PRAISE HIS BEAUTY

Summer is gone,
The birds have flown away.
Butterflies and flowers
Will return again next May.
Autumn now is with us,
Ending the hottest summer days.
God now opens up His beauty,
With His colorful displays
Of yellow, red and gold.
On the leaves, as grasses sway
The wind blows a little harder.
Blowing all summer showers away.
We marvel at the bright blue sky,
With white puffy clouds above.
We sing praises to God on high
We are thankful for His love.
He gave us all this beauty,
To behold with eyes that see
His land, His sky, His deepest rolling sea.
He gives to you and me.

Tony Mirc

IT'S NOT JUST A LOVING GAME

Anybody could put a ring on your finger
Anybody could change your name
Anybody could say "I love you," even a stranger
Anybody could play a loving game

But it's not a game
If somebody changes your name
Or puts a ring on your finger, you'll never be the same
So never never never play a loving game

When the wedding bells were ringing
As we said "I do"
We promised each other love forever true
Now and forever you'll always have my name
Putting a ring on your finger darling, it's not just a loving game

It's not just a loving game
When I gave you my name
Marriage is a lifetime proposition in God's name
Now and forever true love, it's not just a loving game

Barbara E Stuart

AFTER THE STORM

After the storm,
When trickling traces
Still grace my window pane,
When the air is thick and damp
With the heaviness of rain,
I watch, with wonder,
A bright new world
Made fresh and alive again.

After the storm,
When life is stilled
As if in breathless awe,
When icy peaks begin to warm
Above a misty thaw,
It seems the world
Is cleansed, once more,
Of even human flaw.

Wendy Notter

LOVE AND THE FOUR SEASONS

In the Spring:
As the flowers begin to bud,
Our hearts begin to bloom.
As the world begins to grow again,
Our love for one another grows too.

In the Summer:
We walk along the beaches,
We kiss beneath the moon.
We play in the sand,
And make up little tunes.

In the Fall:
As things begin to die,
And fall off on the ground,
Our love for one another,
Grows everyday without a sound.

In the Winter:
We build a little fire,
And we cuddle up to one another.
We think of happy thoughts,
Like always being together.

Rick J Juenemann

JUST AS YOU LEFT ME

Just as you left me, I'll always be,
I couldn't change at all
When you went away
I heard you say, darling,
Don't ever fall.
Days may be lonely,
And nights may be long.
But with you in my heart
I can still carry on.
For just as you left me
I'm destined to be,
Just as you left me, that's all.

Sheelagh Blacklock

MY SPECIAL SON

Cradled in my arms, a bundle,
a miracle, nestled in my heart
with wispy halo drawn from silvered down
framing eyes as blue and as wide
and as wandering as the skies,
a vision of wonder in his mama's eyes.
A dreamy vision that did not, would not
heed the signs, those unfamiliar signs
I could not understand
how your gentle wings would alight
on different shores,
your feet tread different lands.
Sparks kindle your eyes and I look for the flames
and my heart leaps to share in the fire,
but then grey, misty veils sign a quiet farewell,
clouds cover the stars in your eyes.
Where do you go, son,
I need to know. Why?
Help me to understand
is it tempest
or gentle draught which draws you away,
while hope 'waits your return on the tide.

Julia M McChesney

YOU'RE ONE OF A KIND

To Memories loved, and Memories Strong

Always on my mind are memories shared with you
I hope you'll always be there
I'm forever here for you
People say that love grows over a long long time
I hope that proves true
A dream come true is a dream of you
You keep my spirits high
I hope your feelings are just as strong
This feeling I feel for you is so good, so rare . . .
I'll never let it go.
This seems to be a perfect love
A love so hard to find
When you smile at me
You lift my worries
You soften my cries
I can't seem to concentrate
On anything but you
In my heart I know, my love
For you is one of a kind!

Eve Lear

RAINBOW'S END

It's true! It's true!
The rainbow has an end!
You can reach out and touch it
Let all the light, the colors
For one instant
Play upon your hand
As you step through
It's soaring arch
Never to be
The same again.

June Reece Galloway

IN LATE DECEMBER

In late December
When trees are cold and bare,
There is a great love story
Meant for all to share.

The story of the Christ Child
Born so long ago,
God sent his son to teach us
The things that we should know.
Born in a lowly manger,
The greatest of all Kings,
To tell the birth of Jesus
The angel's choir did sing.

The Wise Men brought their gifts of gold:
The shepherds stood in awe
With no gift but their gift of love
For the miracle they saw.

Little children love to tell
The story of His birth.
How He was sent by God above
To reign upon this earth.

Though many years have come and gone,
In reverence we behold,
The story of our Savior's birth,
The greatest ever told.

Sonia I Duncan

LIFE WITHOUT LOVE

This poem is dedicated to my brother and his wife, George and Rose Afanasieff, and to my sister, Eudoxia Rhodes, for all the kindnesses extended to me.

Life without love
is like a song
that has not been written.
Life without love
is like a flower
that has not bloomed.
Life without love
is like a ballad
which has not been sung.
Life without love
is like a dance
which has not been performed.
Life with love
is everything
and even more.

Randy Salter

MY TWO GIRLS

This poem is dedicated to my daughters, Kasey & Krystal. I love you very much.

From the heavens they were sent:
In the heavens like stars above.
I knew that this is what God had meant;
As free as the flight of the dove.
Two little girls so sweet and small,
God chose me over the world and all.
Each with a little round nose,
Eyes so big and bright
As bright and red as a rose;
They twinkle in the light.
A smile from ear to ear
They tell me they want me near.
They'll not be with me for long;
We must love them while we can;
They'll soon be grown and gone.
One day soon we'll give their hand;
Then we'll soon be alone again.
My two little girls are grown
While their new life is beginning;
Now's the time for a family of their own.

Tammy Sutton

SHOW ME A SMILE

Show me a smile, hide all your tears.
Life must continue, as we meet another year.

Show me a smile, share all the joy.
Bring St. Nicholas here, with his sack full of toys.

Show me a smile, with the way you feel inside.
You want to laugh, you want to live,
So baby please don't cry.

Show me a smile, meant for only me.

Always try your best, and you will succeed.

Show me a smile, a smile we can share.
Remember you are loved, Remember people care.

Show me a smile, you can win.
Try your best, If you lose, try again.

Show me a smile, you can make it through
You have me to lean on, when you don't know what to do.

Show me a smile, show me a friend.
You can succeed, you can win.

Angela Lo Bianco
SISTERS
We told each other secrets no one else could share
The dreams and hopes that some day would appear.
The sorrows and disappointments hurt less, because we cared.

Our lives are bonded together in love and in despair;
Our hearts and minds are full of memories we share.

We are sisters, for each other, always there.

Pauline Withers

Pauline Withers
PRECIOUS MEMORIES

Dedicated with love to our two beautiful daughters, Nicki and Suzanne

Where are my little girls of yesterday
They were here just an hour ago,
Was it a day, or a year did you say
So quickly did the sand in the hour glass flow.

There were questions to answer and stories to read
Of the wonders of nature and far away lands,
There were fairies to find and birds to feed
Pillow fights and building castles in the sand.

They were the tiny Queens of my happy domain
With sweet clover crowns in their hair,
They ruled my heart and a house that was plain
And made it a castle of beauty so rare.

Now my daughters have grown and my castle is bare
And I am sure the fairies have moved away,
The clover loses beauty when it isn't entwined in hair
And the hours creep slowly through the day.

Turn back, turn back, Oh time in thy flight
A poem I read through my tears,
May those two lovely mothers with queens of their own
Know and love the same magic years.

Jon Cavness
TO DAD

To J. N. "Red" Cavness

To Dad,
I love you more than you will know
Sometimes I know my feelings don't show
There are times I know you cannot see
The love that hides inside of me.
From your muscle and your bone
I have started a family of my own
My kids are young and they will learn
My affection and love they will earn.
I know you've had your thoughts and doubts
We've had our fights and we've had our bouts
But thru it all and to the end
You're the best father that's ever been.
I love you so I cannot say
If I could have you one more day
Now you're gone and gone at last
I will just remember the past
Now you're gone and I'm alone
Thank you Dad for your muscle and your bone.

Lisa Schmoldt
WHEN I AM GONE
As I look back upon the memories
happy and sad
vivid and fading
I wonder what would happen if there were none
everything gone
nothing to remember
Then I realize I would be poor
not in money
but, in love
No need for time to think
always busy
and on the run
But there are memories—when I am gone
to hold and cherish
from yesterday's dawn
Hold on to the memories
That's all you have
let them cheer you
Don't be sad

Terri Dockery
I LOOK IN THE MIRROR, I WONDER WHO I AM
I look in the mirror, I wonder who I am,
I don't know where I'm going or even where I've been.

I search the face for maybe a clue,
But there's nothing there but sad eyes of blue.

Who is this stranger staring back at me?
She's only a glimpse of someone she used to be.

There's a trace of a smile hidden deep in her eyes,
Then she laughs out loud as she comes to realize.

Simple fools, they think they know her so well,
But how can they when I don't even know myself?

Fools, yes, maybe so, but looking close enough they'll see,
I'm the biggest fool of all and a tear slips down her cheek.

Heather E Hyde
I NEVER MEANT TO FRIGHTEN YOU
I never meant to frighten you.
Just a little timid deer.
Yet I can't pursue you any farther
For fear I might drive you
deeper into the thicket.
I thought of you last night.
As I slept.
A lingering dream.
I think of you daily,
each waking hour,
A tantalizing fantasy.
Have I frightened you?
Speaking so freely
Of fantasy,
Wishing it were reality.
Just a little timid, Dear?

Valerie M Elton
THE SANCTUARY OF LOVE

dedicated to Harm Eerkes, with love

The child stood
alone
rooted in fear
and terrified
by the thundering, crashing power
of the waves
as they threw
themselves at the shore in a
frenzy
of noise and motion.

Then
inch
by
inch
their fingers
crept
towards her
across the sand
as if to snatch her away, to be
tossed
between their rolling,
tumbling
hands
and carried away forever into the
swirling blackness of
their
depths.

And then her father came,
and took the child's hands in his
own warm, strong ones
and held her close.
And his strength and love flowed
through her and filled her
and gave her peace,
releasing her from the prison of
her fear
and surrounding her with the
sanctuary of his love.

And, as the seagulls rest,
safe and warm in the cleft of the
rock that shelters them, even
in the midst of raging storms
that dash out their fury against
its very foundations;
Even so did the child learn to rest in
the strength of her father's
love
and gradually to walk by his side
at the water's edge,
wading in the warm pools
and dancing together in the sun.

Elizabeth A Stonner
WALLS

To my husband Bernie and daughters Terri and Linda, with all my love forever, Mom.

I am me,
I scream and shout.
Help this person inside out.
The walls I build a day at a time;
are harder to remove from that line.
Brick by brick,
I fight,
to stay . . . or go;
which is it?
I just don't know.
I hear a voice above that wall.
It echoes down,
like in a great hall.
The eyes at the top look down
and see;
I'm the one . . .
looking back at me.
A scary thought ran through my mind;
it's me I'm leaving . . .
far behind.
So brick by brick I take my stand
and pull them down,
with my two hands.
It's a harder road to hoe . . .
and each brick is heavier
than the one before.
But I have found a special thing;
up from the dark, myself I
bring.

Jennifer Kay Ramsey
REMEMBER NOW HE'S GONE AWAY
Forget his name, Forget his face,
Forget his kiss, his warm embrace,
Forget the love that you once knew,
Remember he has someone new.

Forget him when they play your song,
Forget you cried the whole night long,
Forget how close you once were,
Forget he has chosen her.

Forget you memorized his walk,
Forget the way he used to talk,
Forget the things he used to say,
Remember now he's gone away.

Forget his laugh, Forget his grin,
Forget the dimple on his chin,
Forget the way he held you tight,
Remember he's with her tonight.

Forget the love that didn't last,
Forget the love that went by so fast,
Forget the romance that now has passed.

Forget he said, "I'll leave you never,"
Remember now he's gone forever.

Hilda Valle
I'M THE ONE

To the only man I'll always love, Stan

I'm the one, who sits home and
waits.
I'm the one, who never, yells when
you are late.
I'm the one, who'll never, claim you
in public.
I'm the one, who'll never ask, for
more, than you're willing
to give.
I'm the one, who'll pretend to
never care.
If you're with me or not.
I'm the one, who'll never show you
my tears.
I'm the one, with the heart of stone,
who won't yell to

the world that you are
mine.
With all those things against
me and more.
You'll never know my lonely
nights.
When I cry myself to sleep,
And . . .
Always promise myself the
same
That when you are here you
are mine
But remember when you
are alone.
I'm the one, who still cares

I'M THE ONE

Anne Issersohn
VEDDY GOOOD!

Dedicated to Aunt Maggie

I had an old, old Maiden Aunt, her
accent was quite LIMEY
From Scotland came she long ago,
her ideas most OLD TIMEY
She'd come to visit once a year, our
piano then would ring
She'd sing about the days gone by
when she did the HIGHLAND
FLING!
She'd tell about the place they called
a comin', thru the Rye
Where someone took the low road,
and someone took the high
Another one she loved to do was
"Dear old Glasgow town"
They had a few, it wasn't brew, the
TOWN went round and round!
She'd do a song of Danny Boy, the
pipes, the pipes did play
The boys and girls danced all
around, for them their life was gay
Her music had a special charm, as
there she sat enraptured
Her eyes would shine like two bright
stars, as I saw her YOUTH
recaptured

I think of her quite often now
And sometimes shed a tear
For that dear old soul, and her
lost YOUTH
AS MY OWN IS DRAWING
NEAR!

Ardyth D Hargis II
A PROPHECY IN TIME

I dedicate this poem to mom, dad, grandma & grandpa, and Robbie, who have inspired me throughout my young years; and to Amy, Keith, Steph(s), and "the dudes." May we grow forever in friendship.

On the ledge there's a timepiece
From the olden days.
Golden days were on their way,
Here to come and go.
The minute hand is made of
blackened gold,
The hour and second the same.
They all stand still on the number
twelve;
And no one knows just why.
The outside is made of pure silver;
Pure as the water that cleanses the
infants.
And no one knows what the cover
engraving means.
It reads:

"The path chosen, the path left
behind.
Repent, repent, the road you
find.
For the other is the path to
peace."

On the ledge there's a timepiece that
no one understands.
And on that street, no one is there.

Kathryn Keller Bearhalter
THE ILLEGITIMATE CHILD

To My Beloved Nephew, Benny Keller

There is a child that is not wanted.
There is a child that has no name.
But the Grace of God has granted
the baby a mother, just the same
as the child that sees good fortune
at the entrance to the womb.
Is one less a mother, since her child
has a claim—
To sin and more misfortune than the
heart will allow.
Can the scenes be neglected patterns,
Can others be to blame,
If a wanted child is heralded
Just because she has a name.

Virginia Tobias
GOOD MORNING, HOW ARE YOU?

"Good morning, How are you?
"I'm sorry—I'm not ready for
that yet—and neither are you"—
A familiar story—
Outside the leper colony

Death's survivors shipwrecked onto
tiny islands—
Ignoring steamship whistles and
embracing sailors landing with their
own men Friday
Women in the night—questioning
their fate—children
gone—abused and used, now blessed
and caring for their
mother's needs—though miles apart

Experience on a resume for
application—talents and noted
observations—qualifying there—
"but here we do not hire
imperfect people"—
Outside the Leper Colony

Educated people—degrees and
position rightly earned
busy, busy, everywhere—All around
the hives of social good—
Yet out of town when honeyed
wisdom calls in an
Appointment

People playing other roles,
Hanging up their shingles,
"Advice to the Lovelorn
Unlimited"—
or—
"Psychology in Residence"—
Listing "Siberian Express"
credentials—
Yet never having worn a
Blizzard's snowshoes—
Outside the Leper Colony
"I'd like a Tom Collins—
I wonder if it's as sharp
As I remember"
"Hey kid—Long time no
see—aren't you lost in this
dump?
C'mere and lemmee hug
You for ole time's sake."

Murphy G Smith
NEW ANIMAL

To GOD Almighty My LORD and Savior, And His SON Jesus Christ who gave me this talent which I'm now trying to develop.

I tried to tell your mother, but I
didn't know how
Your sister has got the mind of a
dizzy cow
Her body has all the right curves and
swells
Yes her body is by Fisher but her
mind is by Mattel
She's as thin in the waist as a wasp
With hips like a thoroughbred horse
Her teeth are white, her neck is long,
she's very strong & quick
When bugs fly about, her tongue
lashes out, in flash they're gone with
a flick
She hunts like a wolf, climbs a hill
like a goat
and can outrun a full grown antelope
Her bare assets are something to fear
From ten miles away she spooks a
whole herd of deer
Like a camel she doesn't touch water
for days
to smell her afterwards puts your
mind in a haze
At first glance; she looks like any
warm blooded mammal
But on closer inspection she's a new
kind of animal

Connie A Gentry
DEVOTION

This poem is for Wesley Kim Paeglow, we will love each other forever, for as long as the other wants to.

As long as you love me
I'll stay by your side
I'll be your companion
Your friend and your guide . . .

As long as you love me
As long as you care
I'll do anything
And I'll go anywhere . . .

I'll bring you the sunshine
I'll comfort your fears
I'll gather up rainbows
To wipe off your tears . . .

As long as forever
My love will be true
For as long as you love me
I'll love you!

Susan Leigh (Peifer) Nelson
THE PHOTOGRAPHER

To: Tom Lewis, alias, "Road Kill," for whom this poem was written.

I know a photographer,
his camera's by his side.
He takes pictures of everything,
even when cars collide.
Since he drives quite a bit,
He's always on the go,
Taking many pictures,
of certain things for show.
When he sees a pretty woman,
walking merrily along,
To the camera, he does reach,
and prays things don't go wrong.
He must be alert,
and, certainly be ready,
A good eye is needed, and,
his hands must re-main steady.
For, if he doesn't have,
exactly what it takes,
His roll of film, will contain,
Nothing But Mistakes!

Patricia Reitter
BEST FRIENDS

To Becky: Our friendship is so very true and I know we will be friends for a really long time. Thank you for always being there for me; I'm always there for you.

Our friendship has lasted quite a long
time,
We each have had some hills to
climb.
Since our friendship is so true,
We will be friends for many years
through.
Yes as usual we have had many a
quarrel,
Yet we never have bid farewell.
It is so much fun to go shopping,
We find all the sales that stores are
offering.
Physical fitness is what we could use,
"We are too busy" is our excuse.
Remember I am there for you when
you need me,
When you are in trouble or in a
catastrophe.
We both love tapes, music and
shopping,
Our favorite talk is of new flings.
I hope we are friends from
here on,
And that our friendship will never be
gone.

Zelpha George Bearden
WHERE IS MY GARDEN

This poem is dedicated to the memory of my precious mother, Neudy Hilton George.

Where is my garden, I'm not sure
that I know,
If it's covered in roses or it's covered
in snow.
It's been a great pleasure I've shared
in my life,
It has made me a happier more
contented housewife.
Doesn't matter where I am or
whatever betide,
I'm happier just knowing that my
garden's outside.

Where is my garden, I'm not sure
that I know,
In January it's silent, all covered with
snow.
I wonder what it dreams as it sleeps
so sound,
It seems to enjoy this rest it has
found.
February comes—she relaxes, gives a
yawn,
Her glamorous protection—where
has it gone?
She looks for her clothing, she owns
not a thing,
Better be thinking of a wardrobe for
spring.

Where is my garden, I'm not sure
that I know,
As the March winds begin to whistle
and blow.
The wee baby plants, their leaves
want to show,
They will do their best to hurry and
grow.

April helps and she brings showers too,
She's always been a nice friend to you.
She tends your babies and gives them a chance,
To don spring clothes and get out and prance.

Where is my garden, I'm not sure that I know,
As May sees her really start in to grow.
I don't really care what the skeptics may say,
There's nothing more perfect than my garden in May.
Now here comes June and you can count on her,
For roses, verbeni as, pinks, poppies—larkspur.
There's a riot of color in my garden in June,
It's marvelous how suddenly everything's in bloom.

Where is my garden, I'm not sure that I know,
Dahlias and geraniums, their blooms all aglow.
Gladiolus, it seems, make the cosmos feel tame,
For July is the month with red cannas aflame.
August is here and the sun smiles down,
Wish it would rain and moisten the ground.
My flowers wilt and their bodies they bend,
When will this heat ever come to an end?

Where is my garden, I'm not sure that I know,
September is the time to put on a show.
The wind is cooler and the nights get long,
So the roses prepare to burst into song.
In comes October with a bit of a chill,
My roses just smile and bloom on still.
Geraniums and Mums—what beauties you are,
The brightest you've been this year by far.

Where is my garden, I'm not sure that I know,
November promises to help make this so.
Gently frost comes in its dress of white,
The leaves fall softly—ever so quiet.
The leaves will cover and shroud the ground,
As December now enters without a sound.
And humbly my garden, with her cap on her head,
Puts on her nightgown and slips off to bed.

Where is my garden, My Great Father above?
You've folded her gently in your arms of love.
You've tucked in the corners of her cover neat,
As gently soft leaves you placed on her feet.
As my graceful trees now brace for the cold,
I see that around them a cloak you do fold.
In awe I shall watch as you put her to rest,
I know with your love my garden is blessed.
GOODNIGHT MY GARDEN!

Candida Mackey
WITHOUT YOU

For Mark Snow, Because I love him.

I never realized . . .
The love I had with you
Until you were gone.

It's only now . . .
When you are so inaccessible
That I feel the loneliness.

My life feels so empty
I feel so lost . . .
Without you.

But I will never tell you this
Because I can't take the pitiful look
You would have in your eyes.

So I will only sit here
And let myself think . . .
About you.

Try to forget you
And live my life . . .
Without you.

Renée L Keyser
GRANDMA'S CHRISTMAS STAR

This poem is lovingly dedicated to my Grandmother—Clara Moore, who taught me a lot about the joy and love of Christmas time the whole year through, and who now is a "Christmas Star" forever. "I miss you Grandma."

On each Christmas Grandma
We say a special prayer,
for one who always filled us
with tenderness and care.
Who baked us special goodies
and bandaged up our knees,
who never told us, "No you can't"
but answered all our pleas.
For you have given us happiness
and there can be no other,
So, wonderful and loved by us
As our own dear sweet Grandmother
So, we send you all the love
you've given us these years,
though we never could repay
someone quite so dear.
We can only say to you
on this Christmas bright,
you have held the star we've seen
on this holy night.
It has never topped a tree
or twinkled in the sky,
No, it's been right here with us
in our Grandma's eyes.

Gerry Linstead
LEGACY OF LOVE

To my Mother, I never had the privilege.

Within my heart, from dawn of life,
I've cherished a gift of love
Willed unto me, unselfishly, by one soon called above.
I knew her but a fleeting time, upon this earthly plane,
She gave me life and set my course,
Tho' hers was paved with pain!
Anguished thru' my early years, with no one there to call,
I shed my tears and prayed to God, to lead me thru' it all.
A mother has a "special dream," to show her child the way,
But I was left without the light, to guide me day by day.
Yet as I grew, throughout the years, from early on to now,
I saw her footprints on my path, and knew her love, somehow.
Tho' always here in spirit, the time will come I pray,
To have her here beside me, thru' each eternal day.

Peggy L Day
LOOK AT A TREE

To my beloved son, Edward, and Pam. With the love of my heart . .

Look at a tree. What do you see?
It's bigger than you. It's bigger than me!
Look at that tree! It was created by the power
Of the Almighty King!
Look at a bird. High on the wing.
He can fly fast. And can he sing!
Look at that bird. He was created by the power
Of the Almighty King!
We can do all things through Christ which strengthens.
We can do nothing if we try on our own.
We are blessed to have the mind of one who knows all things
Oh! So blessed we can speak to him one on one.
Look at a brother. What can he be?
Anything good, if only he would.
Look at that brother. He was created by the power
Of the Almighty King!

Mary Kopler Rice
JUST FOR YOU

For my dear husband, Kenneth, who loved Blue Roses

Each Valentine's Day, You gave me a Rose
And said that you loved me true.
I guess that I sort of took it for granted,
As lovers often do.

This Valentine's Day I found a perfect Rose,
The color you loved, "True Blue"
And laid it where you are resting now.
Just for You!

Jimmy Dawson

Jimmy Dawson
GRANDCHILDREN

To all my grandchildren

When grandchildren come along a great change takes place.
They will bring a tear to your eyes and a smile to your face.
Grandchildren are not ordinary children, they are some special thing.
They create a special joy and they can tug on your heart strings.
The love they give is a very special and different kind;
It is so pure and honest and among the best you can find.
Like our own children, they were a special gift from above;
And they will always need and receive that same affection and love.
Grandchildren have a way with grandparents that seem to get them more
Than was given to their parents that came along before.
They have a way of pulling all the love from grandparents they can get;
And as long as they live this love of grandparents they won't forget.
They can do and say things that only grandparents can believe;
And when they visit grandparents' house, they never want to leave.
Always show them your love and teach them the best you can,
Because they are very special, that's why we call them grand.

Pauline Violette
WHAT IS A POET?

I dedicate this poem to the Lord Jesus, my family, and all the poets around the world.

A poet is a person who writes direct lines that rhyme
With the message that is on his mind
With a fashionable rhythm to express his feelings
About a person or an object of any kind.
To express a truth, to touch someone's heart
To make him laugh, or to make him cry
To express in a sentimental way
What makes him melancholy or what makes him gay.
He may write about natural beauty
Or write about someone's personality
Or some object of rare beauty—
Maybe describing the moon, the sun and the stars
Or anything else in God's creation.
A talent given by the hand of The Divine
To express what is on his mind
And to write it down and learn how the human mind
Works in all mankind.
And to share it with others
And be touched by the hand of a poet
Who has written with a sentimental reason
To make it known that it helps to express
What is on his mind by writing it down—
And from time to time, open up his mind
And to read and to see what was written down at one time.
And to share with others
To comfort from the hand of a poet
And to share the talent given
By the hand of The Divine.

Ms Melanie D Shy
ODE TO BIRDS

This poem is dedicated to the many winged wonders of this world who bring mystery, beauty and grace to its skies

There is no more heavenly a sight
As a majestic bird in flight

Watching as they glide on the wind
Soaring to where all time begins

The graceful speed of a

hummingbird's wings
The lovely song that a nightingale sings

Eagles, hawks and other birds of prey
These species may not exist someday

Hunters, pollution and uprooting of the trees
These elements make it hard for the birds to soar free

Yet through it all one thing is certain and on this you can rely
Birds are and shall always remain the first masters of the sky.

Arlene Siragusa
PLEASE LORD DON'T TAKE ME YET

To my family and friends

Please Lord, don't take me yet,
I'm not ready to go,
I've got so many things to do
too many lawns to mow,
The neighbor next door needs
me and the elderly lady down
the street, a friendly hello
and how are you to everyone I meet.
They need me Lord 'cause they know
that I really care, never a "no"
when they have to go to the
doctor or anywhere.
Please Lord, don't take me now
my friend can hardly see, who will
take care of her if you take me?
There's so many people that need
me to shop for them and shovel
the snow, please Lord, don't take
me yet, I'm not ready to go.

DeLinda Griffis
TRANQUILITY TO SURVIVE

Dedicated to my Mother and Father, Jerry, Justin, Tara, & Bobby, my children . . . and future generations. "I love you ALL."

Our lives are so weary from one day to the next, A solution for the crimes and governments' problems is the greatest quest.
Responsibilities we have more than most can bear, It seems that the prime of our years is now extinct or rare.
As a faithful patriot of the Red, White & Blue, I thank the people who fought,
But those who knew . . . Somehow somewhere our history went wrong,
Generations of people have come and had gone.
The flag we raise "All" should salute, but the majority of the people make it a major dispute. The seriousness of this country's troubles our eyes refuse to see, If the world would actually stand still maybe somebody would believe.
As our Forefathers declared
when on this land they arrived,
there has to be Tranquility
for mankind to survive.

Beatrice E Mondor
COSMIC COMEDY

To my husband Al, for his patience and tolerance of me while my head was in the clouds.

Twas the Moon's last quarter. He wished it well spent,
On a riotous spree of the firmament.

He sent invitations to all of the stars,
Including Jupiter, Venus and Mars.

The Big Dipper was filled with nectar so fine,
The little one sweetened with
raspberry wine.

Saturn appeared with her colorful rings,
Jupiter brought many moons and things.

Planet Uranus headed the line,
Her several satellites followed behind.

When Planet Earth's orbit brushed her lips,
Venus shyly went into eclipse.

Halley's Comet whizzed by in a terrible storm,
Some think 'twas the star, when the Christ Child was born!

But what were those creatures disturbing his dust?
Some drunken Earthlings, they sure had a crust!

On Halley's next orbit, could a miracle work?
And calm down this world that has gone so berserk!

JoAnne Manse
I SOMETIMES WONDER WHY YOU GO SO FAR

I sometimes wonder why you
go so far.
Where do you go to wander
off alone?
How can I reach you when you're
where you are?
Your heart locks up and seems to
turn to stone.
I'm not so sure the battle's lost
or won.
Your eyes emit a secret in your soul.
Past certainty has fled and
now is gone.
What's left are merely fragments
of the whole.

Then I detect the love
within you bloom.
Your smile reflects confusion
and alarm.
No longer do you stay
within your tomb,
A place that's only yours and
knows no harm.
When love admits the world
of the unknown
The lover's seeds of pleasure
can be sown.

Ann Marie Reyes
FROM WITHIN

For my husband, Victor and my mother, Alice. They believe in me.

Let me never forget that my real self, my real value, is within.

I am not merely what you see.

I am not merely what you know of me.

The real truth of who I am lies within my heart, within my conscious thoughts.

This is where my true value lies.

This is where my true self is.

From within.

Ethel H Bennett
MEMORIES

Dedicated to my loving husband Darrell H. Bennett

Crying, sad and all alone,
From me my love has gone.
The moon isn't as beautiful as it used to be,
Because there was just you and me.

He planted for us some apple trees,
We looked at the blossoms with the bees.
The roses grew so very tall,
They last from spring into the fall.

Three little kittens playing cat and mouse,
Up, down and around the house.
Dry patches of grass often marred,
Our paradise in our own back yard.

Warm winds tickle our faces,
Then blow away to other places.
Cracked walks have sunken below,
Time is telling us we'll have to go.

He took his flight into the air,
Into the heavens I know not where.
The next flight out may be my own,
United together and all alone.

Debra Krone
MY FIRST BORN

I dedicate, with Love, this poem to Lori, my oldest daughter, now fifteen.

With Hair Of Golden Silk,
Eyes Like The Deep-Blue Sea,
She Came Into My Life
As Cute And Cuddly As Could Be.

This Loving Child Of Mine,
Made Each Day A Precious One.
Her Arms Out Reached,
With A Hug, She Loves Me.

Her Life Is Full Of Love,
Touching Those Around Her.
My Precious First Born,
Lori, I Love You.

Richard J Toth
MY SPECIAL FRIEND

This poem is dedicated to my wife Sandra, who was the inspiration behind it.

If there were a description for
beauty,
Describing you would be
impossible
When, our eyes meet, they say
words of meaning without
sound.
When, our lips touch, we seem to
exist in our own private world.
When in one another's arms,
there's a feeling of being safe
and content.
We call each other friend, and it
will be friend for as long as life
exists.
Being friends, with the ability of
loving one another,
A combination that is very rare,
and very special.
Yes! I Love You, and I will always
be your friend,
A friend you can count on for
loving, or friendship, and,
I will always be here for you,
"MY SPECIAL FRIEND"

Claire T Murray
A BLESSING

Dedication: To all good people who know that it is better to give than to receive.

In the hustle of the morning's shopping,
I passed a beggar by.
I saw him there, but not even stopping,
Just thinking, "There but for the grace of God go I."

I then returned and pressed a bill
Into his outstretched hand.
As I turned away, I heard him say
"God Bless—the only things that you take with you are the things you give away."

Beverly Hightower
THOSE PEEK-A-BOO YEARS

To the gentlemen dreaming of a fancy make-believe her and missing a real me . . .

Those peek-a-boo years,
peek-a-boo tears
and peek-a-boo fears . . .
Oh, those peek-a-boo years, those
peek-a-boo years
And peek-a-boo cheers for
peek-a-boo her
. . . yes, peek-a-boo her . . .

Why peek-a-boo tears?
Oh, peek-a-booey.

Mr Jeffery A Veasy
SPACE

I dedicate this poem first to God the Father, Son, & Holy Ghost. For without I would not exist. Also to my Mother & Father and Rennice whom I love with all my heart and who are an integral part of my world.

In one man's heart
There's another man's soul.

In one man's love
There another man's hate.

In between
There is space of fertility, ready to bloom
Into the binding factor
Which creates a force so powerful that,
Opposites attract, and that which was crooked
Is made straight.

In one man's heart
Is another man's heart

In one man's love
There's another man's love

The fertile space is the
Space of faith.

Flossie Childress Barnes
MOTHER'S SPECIAL PLACE

In memory of My Mother, Della Moss Childress 1904 to 1948

Her hair like a swirl of black satin sheers,
Framed her face pale as ivory lace.
Her lovely green eyes filled with tears,
"I must go to a Special Place."

The children gathered and held her hand in vain,
She whispered so soft and low.
"Someday, you'll find this Special Place in God's Domain,
"Children, I love you so."

In a short time, she was gone,
Early morning, a smile on her face.
Someday we'll enter God's Domain one by one.
We'll find this Special Place.

Bev Couling

Bev Couling
FRIENDS FOREVER

In memory of David Couling (1970-1987) "For every joy that passes, something beautiful remains."

Tired and weary, I stagger out under the stars
blinded by my own thoughts:
barely noticing the chill of the cutting breeze
as it swirls about my bare legs;

Deep breaths are not enough
anymore to ease the angry knot about to cut within me
Oh Great God! Why?
What have you done? Must all living souls end?

I was jolted to reality once again by the familiar pitter patter of a faithful friend.
I could hold it in no longer—
feeling my hurt was a furry muzzle and a caring tongue on my already wet cheek

I stared out for ages at the little dancing crystals of energy—realizing love and friendship never dies, but live on forever.
Like a huge star never loses its endless sparkle,
like a friend always there
He also understands we are . . .
Friends forever.

Nina J Horsley
FOR THE MEMORY

This poem is dedicated to my brother, Calvin, who passed from this life but whose memory lives on in my heart.

My soul can look back and see
Things my eyes have never seen
Like You hanging on the tree
Giving Your life's blood for me
And I know I don't deserve
The life You gave so free
But my soul thanks You for the memory.

The memory of Your tear-stained cheeks
Tears that You spilt, just for me
The memory of Your blood-stained brow
I can almost see You now
When I can't tell right from wrong
This memory helps me to go on.

My soul can look back and see
So many things You've done for me
Like guiding me and setting my soul free
Though I know I don't deserve
The love You gave so free
My soul thanks You for the memory.

"The Storm"

Tracy Tomicek
THE STORM

For John Kennedy Blake

Through a storm you run
Ceaseless–
Say it will find its end
Then look not back
For fear of the evil below
And within
Say we will see that day
When there is no more obscurity
In your wicked sky
No more to follow
No more stony–prickly ground
To lie
Say my love you will be true
Do not flee
But rather choose
Beg do I, turn not away
Because, can you not see
As long as the storm rages in you
So also will it in me

Kathryn Angell Leonard
THE TIDE

To my beautiful Mother Amy Lenora Farrell

The sun sinks low in the summer skies,
The birds are going to sleep;
But the waves beat on the rock bound shore,
And a moan comes from the deep.

The moon is now seen and the stars of the night;
The village is going to rest:
But the tide grows higher and higher,
As the waves beat in from the west.

And so through the long watchless hours,
Except for the sentinel stars,
The tide flows from the ocean
Till it reaches the guardian bars.

At daybreak the flowing tide ceases,
The ocean is calling her own;
For the waters she covered the sands with
Were only considered a loan.
And thus is the life of our loved ones,
Their flowing and ebbing of years,
Be their lives calm or stormy, as Fate grants,
God, like the ocean, calls those he holds dear.

Helen Spiropoulou
SOUND POLLUTION

You came from the terra
Of the voice-saurs
Your neck is full of explosions
You are ejaculating turbulence
Sounds, words like refusals
Wanting to degenerate me
To ravish me with your voice.

I silently draw lines
Upon my red red body
My body becomes an echo
Of the stagnate absolute
My body becomes
A nightmare's broadcast.

I nourish my wounds
You will not understand
How the silence works
Upon the pilgrim's pillow
Or among the flowers' turmoil
You will never conceive
The immobility of the stalagmite.

Susan J Leon (Ward)
DAYTIME FRIEND

Dedicated to Paul Fike and Dorothy Heminger for their words of encouragement.

Shadow upon the wall, you walk when I do, you leap when I do.
When I feel so very alone, I look over my shoulder and there you are right near me, and my loneliness is gone.

The sun is going down,
Oh dear shadow, who has kept me company, you are slowly fading away.
Good-bye friend, until another sun shiny day.

Kimberly J Lesher
WHY DON'T YOU NOTICE ME?

To Phillip—You never even knew!

Why don't you notice me,
I pass you every day
Whenever I look into your eyes
There's so much I want to say.

I see a heart of tender care,
That no one else can find.
I see you and I together,
An illusion of my mind
Maybe I am selfish
Because I want you for my own.
When we are dead and gone
You never will have known.

At my Height of Heavenly Bliss
You forever belong to me
I try to leave your heart alone
But through me you can see

I don't want a marble palace
Nor bright starlit skies
All I want is you
And a look of love in your eyes.

Patricia C Morrison
MY CHILD'S FACE

This poem is dedicated to my two daughters and two sons, God bless them.

I look into my child's face
And see a vision there.
Her hands can hold the human race
The future her shoulders bear.

Her youth is upon her
Her fondest dreams yet explored,
Her willingness to learn the truth
A daughter of our Lord.

She courageously faces challenges
Her journey, a difficult course,
Great inner strength she must possess
Final destination, an Eternal Door.

Yes, when I see my child's face
I know within my heart,
She'll beat the odds, and inspire us
Life's trials, the hardest part.

Mike Strader
MY DREAM

I once had a dream, where I was walking alone, down a long dark road. And I remember feeling deep inside so hurt and confused. The farther I walked, the darker my path would become.
(And I was scared).

So I reached into my pocket and grabbed some matches and quickly struck it against its cover. The light was bright and warm and I was safe and reassured. But then it was gone, and quickly another one was lit. The light was back and again I was safe. I had the courage to walk on.

But, I began to realize that each time a match was lit, the flame became dimmer, nor did it last as long as the previous one, and again I was scared.

When suddenly from deep in the darkness, I heard a voice. But I was not frightened, for I had known this voice before. So, I followed the voice, and it led me through many yesterdays. I saw my hurt, my pain, and my insecurities. And with each memory I saw my path become brighter and I was able to see what I had feared . . . MYSELF!!

Karen Rocque
MAMA WAS ALWAYS THERE
Looking back on childhood days
I don't remember a whole lot;
Not toys at Christmas, nor fancy clothes
Or Dad being around very much . . .
But I do have warm memories,
Of someone there to care
For it seemed when times were darkest
Mama was always there.

Dad was a "Good Joe," but he drank too much
And money, there was never any,
My brother was older, gone most of the time
I knew I just missed him plenty . . .
Mama became real sick one time
I can hardly express my fear
For although I seemed to be alone a lot
Mama was always there.

When Mama got stronger, my prayers answered
Dad seemed to be gone for good:
I never asked Mama any questions
I just knew she'd took all she could.
As a young girl I'd often worry
"What am I going to wear?"
Never any money, but a dress would appear
Yes, Mama was always there.

Later, I wed my high school sweetheart
And life was wonderful, at best
But it ended in heartbreak, for he cheated on me
I knew it couldn't last
Down on my luck, my heart broken in two
Feeling there was no one to care,
How wrong I was, when I turned and found
Yes, Mama was still there!

Yes, Mama was always there for me
And some say I go too far
To make her golden years happy & bright
To take her for rides in our car
I just want her to know we're grateful
That, for her, my brother and I care
I just want her to know that I love her
And, for Mama, I'll always be there!

Stephanie Evanich
GOD'S PRECIOUS GIFT
I received a gift sent from
high above
Mine and mine alone to care
for and above all love
Am I worthy of such an
honor
A gift such as this is so
much more than I deserve
God smiled upon me with all
of his heart
And with your first breath is
where it all did start
You had a twinkle in your
little eyes
And the message from above was
heard clearly through
your cries
No-one knows what the future
may bring
But clearly I do realize this
one little thing
God smiled on me and you are
my gift
And as the days go by and you
go from walk to run
I'll lift my head everyday to
Heaven and thank the
Good Lord for you
MY SON . . .

Phyllis Majewski
MY REFLECTION
That fleeting image
Reminded me of you.
Mirroring my love
Or did I mirror yours?
Then I recognized
The me I saw in you.
My feeling of past
You living them now.
I could only love
You because it was my
Own passed vision too.
I could only have faith
And reflect on the
Vanishing likeness.

Dorothy Walters Richards
YESTERDAY AND TODAY
Yesterday I flew kites high in the wind
Climbed the tallest trees with a friend
Gathered nuts and berries on the wooded hill
Fished and swam in the pond by the mill.

Jumped rope, played hide-and-seek, tag and Andy over,
Made pretty garlands from the sweet smelling clover
That grew in the meadow beside a stream.
Spent hours in a hidden nook to dream
That a magic carpet was taking me
To exotic places beyond the sea.

I would race to catch the brilliant leaves
As the fierce Autumn winds tossed them from the trees.
When deep snows and ice brought Winter's chill
I would skate, make snowmen and sleigh down the hill.

But as fast as the bird-on-the-wing does fly,
Or like the will-o-wisp, the years passed by.
Today as I sat in a chair by the window pane
And watched carefree children play in the rain.
I thought how wonderful it would be once again,
To run and fly kites high in the wind!

Helen Regina Gzanowicz
AN EVENING WALK
How silently creation worships Him!
The evening air speaks gently of His name;
And as I pause to meditate and praise,
The dew resounds as softly its acclaim.

Tenderly the autumn breeze shares all her joys,
"Redemption lingers not too long!"
A mist descends and whispers in refrain,
"Dawn awaits the hope of that glad day!"

At once the sounds of night are stilled.
Do they hear Him walking in their path of seers?
The trees stand breathless at their posts,
Commanding praise from all the starry host.

Songs of nature adorn His handi-work,
The nearness of His love their theme so great.
There is no clamor for their own,
But quiet thought of Him alone.

Creation's voice speaks louder than my own!
(my heart's devotion stands in awe)
Still nearer to Him her worship calls,
And stirs my mind with sweet amens.

Bonnie Howlett
LORD, NOW I LAY MY HEAD TO REST
Lord, now I lay my head to rest
I have worked hard all day and given my best
While others dread the start of day
I will humbly and quietly pray
For the strength to live and work through you
Dear Lord there is so much to do
Each day as I face the tasks ahead
Lord I will feel no dread

We have known each other for a long, long time
Through Your grace I continue to climb
Above the loss, the pain and strife
Some how you have taught me to live my life
To understand sometimes clouds appear
And to know periods of sunshine are very dear
Thank you Lord, for each day given
For teaching me the joy of living

Heidi Callahan
I'LL CRY ON YOUR SHOULDER
I'll cry on your
shoulder

call you
BAD NAMES
get mad
not call you

for days
get sad

YOU make me glad

Through all I've done
a friend would not have stayed
but
what you have in you
does not come
every day
no
lawyer

could have put
it to test
you were not the best

BEST WHAT?

you say and I replied
(with sort of a sigh)
why
the VERY BEST FRIEND
in
the world!

Dale Schleinitz
FOR MY GRANDPA
For My Grampa, who in the sixties
held us in his arms
told of his love for us
and would
Protect us from little harms,
I've grown to love him
though he's passed away
and if he could
come back to us,
I wish he would someday.
For My Grampa who does not hear us;
his head's beneath the sod
but his spirit is in heaven
and hears us very well,
We say to him we love you
'cause you are so very swell
I know that God takes care of him
he is the father above
'cause he takes good care of us
and watches with lots of love

Cristy T Cruz
WISHES
I try to do the best that I can do
That no one else but me
Our life is full of intrigue and mystery
Frustration, success and worry
Just like what's happening to me
Sometimes it's worthy and earthy
I try to do the best that I can do
That no one else but me
Welcome distress so far happiness
And no one else impress
Not looking for notoriety
Illusion turn to reality
I try to do the best that I can do
That no one else but me
Freedom for love
Have courage to fight
All the bittersweet, that comes into my life
I try to do the best that I can do
That no one else but me
Mostly called this challenge
Like a thorn of life
A long long way to an end
With a happy ending
I try to do the best that I can do
That no one else but me
Striving hard for a change
Goal to achieve the very best
Stand tall with deep determination
Strong and courage of conviction
Oh! it is so really wonderful to know
Could it be me?

Arnold Wisper
RON, JOHN & OLLIE
Ron, John & Ollie sat down to meet one day,
Ron can't know, John can't recall,
Ollie makes the play.
Arms to Iran, hostages to the U.S.,
Money to the Contras, oh what a mess!!

Congressmen & Senators on T.V. galore.
Bright lights shining, cameras grinding, tell me "What for?"
We traded arms, we traded money, what's the bottom line?
Let's wrap it up, call it off, and have a glass of wine.

When all the fuss subsides, and the questions are through
No more, "What did they know?" and "What did they do?"
Ron, John & Ollie will meet some day in a bar,
Ron won't know, John won't tell, but Ollie will be a movie star.

Patricia P Garate
THE COUNTRY GAL AND THE CONVENTION

I'm a country gal about to take a trip
To a big city convention
Oh, Lord, don't let me make a slip!

Do I still know how to act in formal
And high-heeled shoes?
Or will I walk as if I were wearing
Tennies and faded blues?

When last I attended a "Ritzy" brunch
Big picture hats were in
And filmy chiffon dresses and gloves
Were what we were wearing then

Good grief! Do they all dress like Cher?
Or, if I dress more like me
Will I be comfortable there?

Just help me through this, Lord
And make me behave
And I'll be ever so grateful
Till I go to my grave!

Regina Golden
THE ARTISTS

Michael and Mark are two handy men;
one tickled the keys while the other would dance;
But never again will we see them as when
relaxed after dinner or like circumstance.

Judo became their new life pursuit,
which they willingly taught the senior ennuye,
With a kick or a stance they gained good repute
else a verbal recount of what it should be.

Swimming and diving all came on the line
a little less show, but improvement, you know;
High diving, endurance, life-saving all shine
with the glow of success and bravissimo.

Now Markie is nine and Michael is ten;
willingly they would devote summer days
To karate, soccer, swimming, and then
they languor through weeks of soft summer haze.

Glorie M Crouch
I PREFER

To the children of the world, that they may appreciate earth's fascination.

On Earth the rule of man,
Makes us wonder where
liberty lies.
In spotless Heaven there
is no doubt,
That God must be obeyed.
In hell you would never
believe,
The work you would find.

I prefer earth with its
replenishing skies,
For I will have the
greatest amount of
freedom, here.

Robert H Wolf
GOD'S KEYS

Our God's the master locksmith,
His children, each a key;
He fashioned them with care and love,
Gave each to you and me.

We then became the key rings,
To hold each key in place;
The parents and the teachers,
Who read each little face.

We learn to help each key-child
Unlock life's every door;
We pray His hand will guide our choice,
His faith and love our store.

The keys were cut precisely,
To turn each lock with ease;
The cylinders of life fit close,
Our skills God oversees.

With passing years each key-child grows
To teacher, parent, guide;
And they in turn become the rings
To hold God's keys, betide!

Imogene Kole
TO MY OLD NAVY BLUE SWEATER

"I am an old sweater.
I can be worn in public,
But I'm embarrassing.
I come out when I'm needed
For warmth and comfort,
Then I'm tossed into a
Corner, and forgotten, until
The next time I am called
Out to serve again, for a
Brief time.
It's a lonely life.
It would be nice to be sought
Out just for myself.
It's sad to get old and shabby.
Too bad you can't just unravel.
Old sweaters need extra care
And love.
I am cherished, and worn close
To the heart!
My owner just told me so!"

Lola Corning
A USER'S REGRETS

Never start the drug habit, I'm telling you why:
You'll miss finding rainbows that swing from the sky;
You'll lose many sunsets, as clouds turn to gold.
Say "No!" to drug habits, for you are risking your Soul.

Never start the drug habit, a User knows why,
All roads lead to heartaches, as times passes by.
There'll be hours of sorrow, as drugs take their toll,
Don't pass it off lightly, you're risking your Soul.

Once you start the drug habit, of pitfalls beware.
The future holds darkness, a demon waits there.
The demon of drugs, that blots out the smile
Of some friendly stranger walking his last mile.
The demon of highways that ceases the touch
Of kisses from loved ones, those needed so much.
Say "No!" to drug habits, keep faith and control,
Each step toward heaven, and the right to your Soul.

Mary Jane Richards

Mary Jane Richards
UNITY AMONG NATIONS IS THE NEW AGENDA FOR MANKIND

Kindly Dedicated to my Lover, my Husband, and my Inspiration— Robert O. Richards

U nity among nations is the
N ew agenda for mankind. The
I ntention is to create a world in which
T he nations there-in will permit
E very one of its citizens to
D emand human rights for all.

S ince the very beginning of
T ime people have struggled
A nd suffered and fought
T hroughout their
E ntire lifetimes in
S earch for a better, more meaningful life.

O ut of the continuing process, a measure of
F reedom has gradually been attained.

A cclaiming equal rights victory for every
M ember of every race on Earth is the
E ventual goal. All yearn for its ultimate
R ealization, and the effort extended will not be
I n vain, for it is the one great desire of every
C hild and adult in the world; and may God bless
A merica for being their inspiration!

Sue Marino
IT HAPPENED ON A SUMMER NIGHT

It happened on a summer night
far up a canyon hill.

They knew each other couldn't
resist the warm tingle that

came when they began to mingle.
Their kisses were surprising for

they had been mesmerizing.
They share something special,

But yet don't feel comfortable.
For he is free and awaiting to
be taken, and she is taken and
awaiting to be set free . . .

Clara Mae Quarles Mackey
NATURE'S MUSIC

Nature has music of her own
like rustling leaves
Wind whistling in breeze
Trees that shake and shiver
Thunder and lightning make me quiver
Water fall a sound unique
Eruption from a volcano's peak
Tumbleweeds cry of ghosts
Living in towns of old
Birds singing in the trees
Nature's sounds are all around—
expressed through natural beauty
The buzzing of the bumble bee
The music released in me
The wonders of nature's song
Make me feel in her presence
I belong!

Glen Gray
TO MOM AND DAD

We hope the last forty years
Have brought happiness, not tears.
To have had four boys,
Life could not have been full of joys.
Many a nite you should have been in bed,
Knowing that someday, we too would be wed.
You put up with us through good and bad,
At times, we even made you sad.

But now these things are done and gone,
And you with your lives must go on.
So to you I say;
I hope in some little way
What we have done here to-day,
Will show you how much we care,
And we hope another forty years,

Together, you will share.
Because a couple like you,
God will Bless,
We know you will live in
happiness.
We thought it only right,
That's why we celebrate with
you to-nite.
So have a very enjoyable time,
With this I close my little
rhyme.

With Love
Glen

Erika Avelson
GROWN UP
I may be young,
But I'm not stupid.
You take for granted my intelligence
Because of my age.
Believe me when I say what I say.
Do not dispute my ideas,
For I have grown more than the
average adult.
I have lost my innocence long ago
And not by sinful means.
Exposed to the reality of life
By a mean and cruel world.
Responding through strength of the
inner spirit.
Living as I believe and not as you see
fit.
You try to conform me to a world of
illusion.
You only accomplish to make a mass
of confusion.
Believe in my world;
Watch me unfurl.
Do not protect me,
But open your eyes!
Be aware—watch me fly.

Monique Laplante Gaudreau
SECRET CACHÉ AU COEUR DE MON COEUR
Depuis longtemps, la trame a
commencée en secret.
De fil dór et de cristal elle se forme

Cést dúne richesse inestimable
Et dúne beauté sans pareille,
Quélle se façonne, se forme, se tisse,
Tout au long des jours,
Cette brillante dentelle magnifique,
Si delicate et merveilleuse!

Elle peut se briser au simple souffle
du vent,
Mais le souffle doux de mon amour,
Me fait entendre la mélodie
La mélodie de l'Infini.
Et me fait voir le scintillement exquis
de cette dentelle d'or de cristal!

Au coeur de mon coeur se cache
undoux secret
J'entends mélodie de l'Infini

Delana Wilson
THE STORM
Hopes and dreams spiralling down
the drain
Dark, boiling clouds full of fury and
pain
Lightning bolts crackling again and
again
Relentless beatings of wind and rain.
Then a silence and stillness you could
feel but not see like a vacuum
sucking the life from me.
Then suddenly it was over, as quickly
as that
And I put on my shoes and reached
for my hat.
I stepped out to view the damage
done
No one had lost and no one had won.
The debris was there, as I thought it
would be
Scratches on you and bruises on me.
And tears of regret rolled down my
cheek
I opened my mouth, but no words
could I speak.
Silently, I whisper, this storm is o'er.
There will be no dark, angry clouds
like before.
And the sun peeked out from behind
a cloud
As a rainbow arched in the field
freshly plowed.
The storm is over, and the birds start
to sing,
The storm is over, and it's time for
spring.

Glenn T Perry
BEING AT THE SEA
Life has been so lovely
Time has been so short
Since I first saw you
Along the ocean shore
You had so much beauty
That my mind could not absorb
A being so brown and lovely
As a forest on an August morn
As I walked toward you
Thinking of what to say
You jumped into the ocean
So swift to swim away
I thought my life was over
Just when it had begun
As I peered into the sea
I wondered what became of thee
A beautiful being came toward me
A small smooth hand took hold of
mine
She said "Come With Me"
And I need your love to set me free.

Judith Maria Du Bose
MIST
My mind transfixes the wholeness where sky and land meet, and the imagery invites us to look through the mist of that which places the hues of a gleaming vision.

The imagery is of the hue of an angel, that transforms the mist into a majestic glow of heaven and earth.

In this transfiguration, people are gathered greeting each other with the gift of peace.

The mist becomes transparent; "Know that I am God," the gift of knowledge.

As this transparence renews the hue and imagery, the Holy Spirit dwells within the chambers of the heart, revealing the face of God, who reaches through the incandescence of heaven and earth, and touches those whom He has created.

Dear God, we are offering our thanksgiving within this circle. You have touched our hearts. "Yesterday is but a memory, and tomorrow is today's dreams. Let today embrace the past with remembrance, and the future with longing."

In my heart the Spirit dwells in rhythmic silence, yet my heart beats to a divine feeling. For in the dew of little things the heart finds its morning and is refreshed.

As the poet says, "In giving us more of thyself, thou givest us all." You gave with heart touched joy. Yet you knew not that you gave us all.

The Spirit continues to dwell within this circle, opening each heart with the beauty of grace and love. My heart is filled with thanksgivings, and I offer you my all, from the silence of my heart to the silence of the heart of God.

Colin Fenton
HOLIDAY RELATIVES

To Jennifer . . . so that you may never forget an introductory class, a departing promise, and a special friendship

In a corner hole of the kitchen
wainscoting
And within quick scampering
distance to the
Food pantry
The family has made their winter
home quietly
Cautiously
The Field Mice.

Unseen voices
Within the country cabin.
Unwelcomed
By the farmer's selectively friendly
cat
They sleep and eat inside the wall all
day, easily growing fat.

Holiday relatives
From somewhere else, seen but once
a year
Sharing the warmth of the fire and
Handel's carols—
These messengers from St. Nicholas.
Christmastime has returned.

Melvin B Mellard

Melvin B Mellard
MISSING MOTHER
As I begin this message my head and
my hand are able to start
But deep inside me there's a turmoil
Profound sadness—an extremely
heavy heart
But I know that if I don't jot this
down and stare at each word I say I'll
not be able to stand the agonizing
desolation of this approaching May
For I know that this coming Sunday
will most assuredly be the saddest I'll
ever see because back in July I lost
the most precious mother there ever
will be.

My dear mother was a saint on earth
Never speaking nor harboring a
thought that was bad.
She asked not a thing more of this
world but to love and be loved by us
9 children & Dad.

I see that loving smile that tender
face those perfect hands and those
soft brown eyes
All her trials are over now she only
waits for all of us to join her in
Paradise.

Frances I Jacelone
GIFT OF LOVE
Treasure it most dearly.
Let if flourish in your heart.
Low times may come or follow,
But keep this from the start.

Teach it every chance you get.
Learn to know its ways.
Rejoice the many splendid things
It brings you every day.

Cherish it and all its beauty.
Speak of it and all its truths.
Laugh with it for it is sunshine.
Live in it, for it is you.

Do not fret or worry,
Or try to understand.
Just offer it to God above,
'Tis guided by His hand.

This is the perfect gift,
To share with whom you wish.
This is a Sacred gift, my friend,
This is the Gift of Love!

Mildred M Russell
I WONDER
Could the Rivers of Heaven
  Be made of Mother's tears?

Could the light of Heaven
  Be fueled by Mother's love?

Could the songs of heaven
  Be created by the birth of a child?

Can we rise to the heights of
rhapsody
  thru love?
Em–Em–Are

Theresa M Harmon
A TRIBUTE TO CLOVER
Walking hand in hand with my Dad,
we stopped by the clover field.
He said, "Dear daughter, this clover,
  Feeds the cows
  that gives us our milk,
  Feeds the animals for market,
  pays the mortgage,
  carpets the land.
  For future generations
  with Mother Nature's
  and God's help
  to hold and Preserve."
Many years afterwards
with a prayer on my lips
I lay a bouquet of clover
on his sacred grave.

Barbara Mashak
LONELY WITHOUT YOU
Why did he have to die
  Why God Why
If only you could tell me why
  He meant everything to me
As if you couldn't see
But why, did he have to go away
God, at least you could have let him
  stay just one more day
I really don't understand, and frankly
now

don't give a damn
Everyday, Every hour, minute, I live with fear
Just thinking back on the memories, brings oh so many tears, All I Can say is, Why, God, Why, Isn't He Here!

Mark Pasterniak
ODE TO RAY CHAPMAN

Three games in first place,
His wife about to have a child,
Bat in hand at homeplate,
When a Carl Mays's pitch went wild.

August 16, 1920,
The count was 1 and 1.
Crowding the plate on a high pitch,
'Thud,' Ray collapsed to the ground.

Unconscious through the evening,
The next morning he did die.
He missed the 1920 World Series,
And the sound of his daughter's cry.

The doctor said he was unlucky,
By a fraction of an inch.
And witnesses say he never saw
That deadly killer pitch.

Three games in first place,
His wife about to have a child,
Bat in hand at homeplate,
When Ray Chapman,
he did die . . .

Mrs Joyce N Collins
SEASONS OF LOVE

To my beloved husband & friend, Robert Eugene Collins, who makes every season exciting!

Such joyous times, in golden hues,
First moments spent together;
Silvery winter, pine mint
spring . . .
Our two hearts felt no weather!

Only in each other's eyes,
Did summer's colors dance
In reflected pools of dazzling
greens . . .
We shared such sweet romance.

Autumn's brown and vibrant reds,
Splashed on every bush and
tree;
But we two scarcely noticed . . .
Beyond each other we could not
see.

The tapestry of our wedded life,
Is enriched by textures bold;
As the seasons of our love provide,
A shelter from the cold.

John G McCafferty
DISCIPLINE OF THE COSMOS

Beyond the sight of man made
means,
To cosmic perimeters can we
explore.
Is our reality just a speck of dust?
Do we stand at the bourn of what's
far more?

To be able at the edge of time to
stand
To view what's further on.
Will there be a stygian blackness,
Or the brilliance of an empyreal
Dawn?

We look up to see a starry gossamer,
A fretwork on the womb of night.
The planets moving in their orbits,
Shining forth such noble light.

With such geometric discipline
They seem to move across our sky.
Until darkness on the earth descends.
They seem invisible to our eye.

The finiteness of the mind of man
Cannot begin to comprehend,
Does the firmament go on forever,
Forever without end?

If we could stand at the edge of space
Do you think that we might see,
Another million universes?
Might they go on endlessly?

Cosmic dust cannot be seen,
Except when looked at from afar.
Across perhaps a trillion miles,
We see the nova of a star.

We see a light no longer there,
And yet the brilliance still shines on.
Ten thousands years ago its light had
ended.
And in a cosmic minute of time is
gone.

We cannot understand this mystery.
What is beyond the Firmament?
There are probably no frontiers at all,
Which adds to our bewilderment.

Nancy Gordon
PRISONER'S WOMAN

They sent him away, one October
day. I felt I was torn in two.
They made him a prisoner behind
those gray walls
and made me a prisoner too.

Sad and alone., I had to go home,
scared, crying "Lord what am I going
to do?"
Three children to feed, bills to be
paid, so many things to go through.

I laid on my bed and cried till I slept
He was my lover, my friend, my
man.
and he saw we were always well
kept.
Everyone shows me, the children too,
it's as if they were saying "they're
guilty too."
No one to talk to, no one to love.
What is a prisoner's woman to do?
The days drag on into weeks, then
months, I'm trying to be faithful and
true. In my home I'm left all alone,
I'm paying for his crimes too.

Gertrude Lewis

Gertrude Lewis
A WOMAN'S LOVE

Apostolic Church of God

A woman's love so glorious and so
sweet
Her love for you will surely keep
She sets aside a time each day
Thankful to God; to meditate and to
pray—
With joys so rare of her love and
beauty there—
Her gift of love from God, so brightly
glows
A woman's love within her heart will
never grow old;

As her soul is filled with her faith in
God—
Of memories, of her love can't be
bought
Was planned above with heaven's
seal
Has given glory with her beautiful
love—
Is still untold.

Jan L Marks
GOOD-BYE, MY LOVE

My darling, I love you.
How much? You'll never know
Unforeseen circumstances,
have forced me to go.
Your love is so gentle, so
loyal, so true. Oh my darling,
how will I go on without you.
You gave me your strength,
when I had none. You held
me so tight, when I was alone.
You'll never know, how
much you did for me.
You loved me, with a love
that I have never known.
With sweetness and gentleness
you touched my soul.
You were always there,
whenever I needed you.
You were always there.

Barbara M Betkis
ROCK AND ROLL

Don't you see it's up to me
What I do with this roller coaster
type of emotion
When I'm down
stick around, and it's bound
to zoom way out to the heights
Then turn around and land
Safely back on the ground
So start anew, with things to do
And love to share and give
And life to live
So could I be without them?

M O Flanery
PASSING DAYS

Since time and tide so swiftly flies
I'll try and write of days gone by,
So when I've gone to my home above
I'll leave some thoughts to those I
love

To you I've told of long ago
Of many dear ones that I know;
To those who read the story told
I know they'll think of times of old.

Of Father, Mother, sisters too
And brother, the in-laws few
Have passed on through this life we
live
Some thoughts of love, some to
forgive.

And in their resting place we find
That we are not so far behind
Pray God to guide us through this life
Of many trials, and of much strife.

And now I'll say farewell to all
And wish for you our Savior's call,
For in that day 'twill be so sweet
When we shall meet at Jesus' feet.

Barbara Thomas

Barbara Thomas
SINCERE HEART

To my beloved children and friends with all my love

True friends when the joy of thy
presence is ever about me
sincere friend how can I ever know
discontent heart? discontent puts a
barrier between me and thee friend
discontent dilutes the strength of
Christ within me I do need to know
that only through trusting thee sincere
friend will help answers to life's test
be found problems are not really
problems They are merely means to
strengthen our sincere friendship
circumstances sincere heart are
exercising tools joys and strength
come from mastering these tools
Your trust sincere friend is pleasure
pure in your motive of giving our
relationship sincere heart is
satisfaction circumstances creates the
ultimate vision even an inch or
moment That is enough for I have not
come this way before my sincere
heart you have made the path and so
in trust I walk every step with thee I
will be only a whisper away your
inspiration has overwhelmed me
sincere friend your personal time in
giving a helping hand awesome in
gratitude sincere friend captured in
moments of illusion my love for you
is deep I pray for your grieving heart
to release the love you have sharing
has been sincere your vision is
generous until we touch again
remember my heart is sincere my
love continues, because I care and
appreciate your valuable responses in
my figment mind the Lord works.
Strangely. For your concern in the
future God bless your heart sincere
friend.

Edna Pearl Harwell
I'M A CLOWN

I'm a clown, Clickety Clacket,
My, My, what's all that racket?
All dressed up, go'in to town
Spread'in joy all around.
Up and down the streets I go,
Hope'n soon to put on a show.

Zoodie's my name, and I'm a great

joy,
To all the sweet little girls and boys,
To grown-ups too I'm a bit of a thrill,
Hopp'in and skipp'in and runn'in, I will.
Come along and join the crowd,
Makes my heart sing, I'm Soooooo Proud!

Lorentina H Zeller
GOOD FRIDAY
Down the rocky path He trod,
The innocent, suffering Lamb
of God;
Beaten and scourged He walked the road
Scoffed and spat on by the crowd;
Upon His head a thorny crown
A heavy cross that weighed Him down;
Sweat and blood as He climbed the hill
His Father's mission to fulfill;
Nailed upon that cruse'd tree
Peace He won for you and me.
Dear Father, help us all to see
Tho' paid by Christ, to us 'tis free!
Thru Him our sins are all forgiven,
For Christ has oped the gates of Heaven.
Lord, lead us on that narrow way
And thank Christ, as we hear Him say:
It is finished!

Kacy C Pierce
THERE

Thanks to my parents, for allowing me to write my poems, my own way.

Have you ever wanted to fly
Fly high
High
Way up there

With it all
With Him
I'll be there soon
You know
There . . .

Marie E Gilchrist
THE LEGEND OF THE GLOW WORM
Long, long ago when the moon shone down,
And cast its light on the sleeping town—
And the Wise Men came and offered their best
And all of the animals knelt with the rest—
To pay their homage to Christ the King.
And the shepherds listened to the angels sing
To the heavenly music!
To the glorious song!
In the stable of Bethlehem
Mary pondered the throng.
And suddenly the Babe, with a smile so sweet
Saw a tiny, brown worm with a small grain of wheat—
His special gift—'Twas all he could find
To bring to the Child who would rescue mankind . . .
And created a wonder that lives to this day!
A tiny, brown worm with his body aglow,
Was a part of that miracle on a night long ago!
And we need to remember as we go on our way
Whomever Christ touches can glow in this way!

Carol S Spaw

Carol S Spaw
LET'S MAKE LOVE IN THE FOREST
Listen to the wind blow through the naked trees.
It's just you and me against the fallen leaves.
Listen to the birds sing as we whisper here and there and you softly pull the sleeping leaves from my mustled hair.

Let's hold each other close and look up in the sky.
As the warm sun blankets our naked bodies as we fall quietly asleep.
We now lay beneath the trees, while the few remaining leaves fall softly down upon us in our sleep.

Cordelia E Hohn
BUTTERFLIES AND DAISIES
Fields of lovely daisies
Dancing in the sun,
Just like little ladies
Having lots of fun.

Golden heads are lifted
Their skirts caught by the breeze,
Are fluttering and swirling
Around the ladie's knees.

Butterflies are flitting
Going here and there,
Just pausing for a moment
Upon the ladie's hair.

Gentle springtime breezes
Touch both earth and sky,
Oh, oh, oh,—so lovely
We breathe a little sigh.

Mr Morris Halperin
FAILURE, MY DELIGHTFUL ENEMY
I know you but don't trust you.
Your form envelops me,
Blinds me to what is in front of me.
You fell me, I seem helpless,
Prostrate, dead.
But I resurrect.
By the power
That was in my hair
And is now in my hands,
I grab your posts
And pull down your edifice.
I walk through the black wall
And on into new failure.
I know you as an imposter,
A false prophet.
But my worthlessness
Becomes my worthiness, my strength.
You, failure, never fail me,
You are my greatest teacher
And my true friend.
Tough as a bully,
Your dwelling is a spider's web,
But your innards are soft, even gentle.
To all who are captured
But not vanquished by you
Your web is only weak thread,
Your brashness but a small breeze
Which waves away your very grasp.
My remaining resolve to rise
Blows away the blinding mist,
Even the black wall which blocks my view, my pathway.
I have labored much
To bring out all of my failures.

I now walk steadily, cheerfully,
Through all of them.
I will live you see
The failure of failure itself
And have unspoiled life
Forever.

Helen Marie Lunceford
A PRAYER—FOR—OUR WONDERFUL MOTHER
God made thee, wonderful Mother of mine
Patient, adorable, and everything that's fine.
When you are ill, I say a prayer
Because I know God is always there
To hear me when I pray.
For your health and happiness each day
And I thank Thee, Heavenly Father above
For all Thy tender care and love
That is always, and forever divine.
For, our wonderful Mother
And, Thee blessed Mother of thine.

Tania L Shufelt
NATURE'S SYMPHONY
Music to my ears,
It brings out the tears,
The music of the cricket,
Playing from the thicket.

The water ran so wild and free
I did not have to see,
For within the soothing waterfall
I can hear its musical call.

As I look into the sunlit sky,
I hear the songs the birds cry.
The sounds I hear are oh, so fresh,
It places goose bumps upon my flesh.

To nature's music I will always cling,
For that's what makes my heart to sing.
The melodies lift me when I am down;
Thank you, nature, for your beautiful sound.

Randy Covert
FROM ME TO YOU
Building a new beginning, not starting over,
rather being me
forgetting some of my past,
and setting new dreams free.
I question my wisdom
and ask myself why
then wake with a feeling
I've been searching to try.
Many of us live within troubled times
with resentment in our hearts
and anger in our minds.
I've tried bitterness, and rightfully so
yet always wanting better times,
and never letting go.
So help me to find
what it is I look for
my gift will be me,
I can give nothing more.

Kay Huyck
HANDS
There are hands that keep busy most of the day.
There are some that knit and crochet,
Others are used to help their friends,
Some hands are so crippled from pain,
They can hardly write their name, it seems a shame,
As you go on your way, try not to stray,
No matter how great the pain,
At the end of the day point your hands up to heaven and pray.

Gail E Davis
HALLOWEEN RISING
Sun shining
Harbor with tug boat gliding
Air traffic abounding
weather 50°, and blustery
Fall day, and Halloween rising

Witches brew cooking
Goblins dancing to joy
Halloween rising near
A queer night to come
Witches brew to enjoy

Candy and children mixing
Halloween rising
Ghosts and goblins dancing
Witches brew drinkers
Bags of cheer smiling

Halloween is near
Children go home
Goblins and ghosts disappear
Witches brew drunk
Halloween is here

Flora Kalloch Peavey-Place
I MEANT TO:
I meant to wash the kitchen floor
but, no, not I—
I sat and relaxed, to gaze at the clouds rolling by,
I knew the windows needed to be washed
I sat and watched the colored wind sock get tossed.

I went to polish the silver tea set on the serving wagon
But was delayed, to listen to the grandfather clock

tongue wagging,
I could see dust on top of the TV,
in my room
It seemed more logical to put off
dusting until afternoon.

I waited until 10 AM to make the
water bed
I was busy listening to what the
pine trees said,
I planned to sew a button on my
red blouse
But stopped to hear the wind
whistle at the corner of the
house.

I knew I should call my special
luncheon friend
But got side-tracked to pay
homage to a wren,
I went to the deck to water plants
in a pot
But a butterfly called my
attention, and I forgot.

After rain I looked here and
there, to seek a rainbow
Not a colored ray could I find far
above or way below,
It was then I heard the clothes
basket and washing machine
calling
I paid them no mind, I still kept
right on stalling.

Finally I got a bee in my bonnet,
it sent me an alarm
Procrastination said, "Stop—no
more resting on your laurels
and charms,"
I pretended everything was
copacetic, that I did not care
I sat down and played the organ,
and let the work stare.

Oma V Curry
THE OLD HOME PLACE

I went back to the old home place
Where I spent my childhood years
And with each step I took
I brushed away the tears.

There among the soft rolling hills
And meadows wide and green
Where mocking birds' sweet song
rang out, by a meandering stream.

The old red barn still standing
Where I used to play
Always filled in summer
With new mown hay.

The hills that I climbed
Just to run back down
Wind blowing through the trees
Soft muted summer sounds.

The drone of honey bees
The chirping birds' songs
Reminded me of summer days
All of them long gone.

The big stone house
With windows tall and wide
Set against the backdrop
of trees, and sloping hillside.

Memories flooded me of days gone
by
When love was dependable
When earth seemed solid
And blue was the sky.

I could see the smile
Upon my Mother's face
And my Daddy's folded hands
As he said table grace.

I wandered through the rooms
And came at last
To the one I called my own
In those days long past.

Memories of my childhood
Were very strong and then
I stored those memories in my heart
For some future use again.

With happy heart I walked away
Quite satisfied that now
That I had been back home again
I could face the world some how.

Colin
JUSTICE RIDE ON

He galloped from far
And in the moonlight you could see
A glitter of a little star.

In the moon light
And the lonely moon light
it just added to a lonely job.

PEACE AND ORDER

No matter how far
and not just across the bar
or not just the length of the barrel of a
forty-four
Justice had to travel and care
not for cold nights and lonely stars.

And all you had for a companion
on a lonely night
was a cry of a coyote
and it came to you
like a sour note
on an out strung guitar

And the badge covered a lonely heart
had been carried too far

Ah—but Justice had to travel
no matter how far.

And all he had to cover
that loneliness that
once filled his heart is
now covered by a star

And sometimes hard
for sometimes Justice had to
travel at night,
and cold lonely nights
were not a thing that were to
be a (assumed) from afar
But were to be a mild stone
along the way.

Ah—Justice! ! Ah—Justice! !

RIDE-ON RIDE-ON!
And don't let the emptiness
thought deter your journey
CARRY ON LITTLE STAR! ! ! !

Lisa Ezernack
FROZEN DREAMS

Immense is the electricity from your
fingertips.
Intensified by the bitter cold around
us
Tiny lightning bolts now zooming up
and down,
Smiling for at last the magic's found
us.

Take me slowly, over and over into
the ecstasy,
Promised by the excitement of the
contrast.
More exciting than my uttermost
expectancy.
If only forever it could last.

Hold me closely as I drift away,
Fill my sweet dreams with your ever
gentle touch.
For in my dreams you'll always stay,
And always love me . . .Oh, so,
much!

Make this bitter cold night,
The most exciting I've ever faced.
Make every part of me alright,
Leave these sweet dreams, to fill the
empty space.

Allow me to wake,
To a brilliant glow of satisfaction.
Reach out and take,
The memories, filled with last night's
sweet reaction.

Roy E Clark
MY FATHER'S MERRIEST CHRISTMAS

In memory of Arthur E Clark (November 7, 1910-December 2, 1988), my father a Landscape Gardener, Florist and Flower Designer. His entire life was a work of ART.

Today, December 2nd, my father
died.
Peacefully, in his sleep, about
eventide.
But please, I don't want you to feel
sorry for me,
Alas, finally he has been set free
From Alzheimer's disease, a curse of
man,
As was time according to God's great
plan.
He had worked very hard, all of his
life,
Taking good care of his children and
wife;
Often working two jobs, and
sometimes three,
To put presents under the Christmas
tree.

He made Christmas for my sisters
and I
He was very much that kind of
special guy.
In fact, if he could talk to us again,
I'm sure he'd tell us with a dimpled
grin,
Take good care of your mom, on this
yuletide,
Do all you can, for the lady who was
my bride.
Enjoy Christmas with your family,
don't shed a tear,
I'm enjoying the best Christmas ever
this year.
No substitute party for me, it's the
real thing,
At last, I'm spending Christmas, with
the KING.

Oma V Curry
YOUR FACE

In memory of my beloved husband Hansel who died June 29, 1984

I see your face in the morning sunrise. I see your face at noon. And when the curtain of night falls over my world, I see your face in my dream light. I know your breath is stilled, but your presence is all around, and I feel your strength embracing me in your warmth. They say love knows no bounds, nor earth, nor sea, nor sky, can limit what is in the heart of the one who is loved.
So if love is endless and lasts forever, know that my face will join yours, in the morning sunrise, at noonday, and on the darkest night.
And our souls will blend as one together, forever in flight.

Ray Rollinson
NOW GEORGE BUSH HONORS FREE-LOADERS*

Please

Remind
George Bush

That he was
Elected
President

By those who love
America
And not by those
Who love Japan.

And that he insults
The intelligence
Of we veterans
And all the other
Americans who

Suffered through World War II,
As he went to grovel
At the feet of Japan's
Blaspheming emperor,
Son of Hirohito,
The old-war-criminal.

*Instead of honoring Japs,
George Bush should start figuring
How to get these free-loaders;
Who refuse to pay one yen
For our defense of Japan
For over forty years now;
Off our tax payers' backs.

TGPFY
(The Great Poet From Yonkers)

Mr B J Rovney
WARNING: I CAN READ YOUR MIND!

This being my very first officially published work in this life, I offer it for Patty Dittman. In my wanderings through many worlds and realitys, she is one of the brightest stars I ever found. —BJR

Have you ever wondered what it's
like, to read another's mind?
To explore a human soul and ponder
what you find?

To know a person's secret lives,
don't believe it can't be done
Some are so allowed to know, God
help you, I am one

No matter who you are, whether near
or far, I can sense just what you feel
It's something I cannot control, it
makes the senses reel

Objects move around all by
themselves, others break or bend
Electricity acts radically wherever I
attend

Just try to lead a normal life, keep
friends and hold a job
When your head is like a T.V. set
without a tuning knob!

When at times you fall asleep and
dreams you don't recall
For your mind has left your body
behind and walked right through the
wall

Then takes, you, quite invisibly, in
and out of time and space
People don't know that you're

watching, can't feel your presence, see your face

It's O.K., don't give in to fear or anger, let only calm in your eyes command
There's a saying that goes, "If looks could kill . . . ," with some of us, they can!

So, thank the stars you're only human, for your life could be much worse
You could have the problems of my telepathic curse!

Yes, far beyond just random chance, I can map tomorrow in advance
Yet if I could have a single wish, I'd ask for ignorance

Till then I'll try to act in secret, but, if I should slip from time to time
Take to heart these words, most seriously, . . . WARNING!: I can read your mind!

Dianna Lunde Burts
I AM A WOMAN
Bending as green willow branch
forging as young tree
open as wild meadow
deeper than the sea.

Adapted as the water-reed
strong as mountain high
eluding as midnight-shadow
endless as the sky

Fiery as sunset's close
soft as morning dew
freer than the wind's mad rush
boundless as ocean's blue.

Ageless as a Grecian font
soft as desert sand
fragile as the petaled rose
eternal as the land.
I am a woman.

Ann M Cavanaugh
TUCKED AWAY
Although you think
That we should stay
Like shiny marbles
Tucked away

Safe and sound
Waiting for
Your level ground

In your heart you know
Some day
We'll rebound
And hey . . .
Enough

Could you blame us then
Will you ever
Remember when

We could only
Roll down . . .
Roll around?

And even though life
Is never too sound
We know today
That rolling up . . .
And rolling down . . .
Is better than being

Tucked away

Florence M Bacila
GRAND-CHILD

For Nicholas: May you both never lose the magic of child–hood.

Tiny arms around my neck,
Wet kisses on my cheek.
The sound of every syllable,
The first time that he speaks.
Smiles that light his face,
And frowns when he's confused.
The wonder of expression,
With each thing that is new.
A bird in flight, a butterfly,
The feel of morning dew.
A ray of sun, drops of rain,
Wonders you may share.
The joy of his discoveries
In memory you compare.
To another child, another time,
Not so long ago.
Life has made its cycles,
Its seasons come and go.
When my time is spent,
I wonder will he remember.
The old grey head bent over his.
My May and his December.

Miriam Madison

Miriam Madison
GOOD-BYE MY FRIEND, ANCIENT WARRIOR OF TIME
Good-bye my friend
ancient warrior of time.
Sleep lightly, rest well
ancient friend of mine
Somewhere in the vast universe
twinkling and shining bright
you have joined the multitude
your soul has taken flight
shine brightly, ancient warrior of time.

No longer will your days be lonely.
tears you will cry no more,
but move in that vast universe
on that distant shore.
Move with grace
ancient friend of mine,
ancient warrior of time.

Maria Angela Hiott
LITTLE PAPER BOY OF YESTERYEAR

In Loving Remembrance of my children, Arthur Cope Hiott, Candace St Clair Hiott. In Dedication to Cameron St Clair Hiott III

So long long ago, tried and true
He's the only one for you
Come rain or shine, always on time
bringing the news.
In torn and tattered jeans old worn out shoes
Spreading just a touch of love and Kindness for everyone it seems, As he goes on his way, with that happy grin, a wave of his hand,
saying have a nice day.

Oma C Givan
ENDING THE DEPRESSION
This poem I write is filled with sorrow.
Not remembering yesterday, nor living for tomorrow.

I have so many loved ones that remember me when,
I was filled with joy & happiness,
Inside me no sin.

At this point in my life, I have but one friend.
His name is "David Long," with me to the end.

I'm but 27, and my life is all gone.
With people all around, I still feel alone.

David Long you're a wonderful man.
Remember you were good to me, & did all you can.

My mind is so deluded, not liking how I live
I've helped others in everyway & "God" did I give.

I had to write this last one to see if I could do it.
But life seems so hopeless, I've given up, I've quit.

Harold S Martin
WHEN ALL LIFE'S WORK IS OVER
When all life's work is over
And the reaper comes to call
It's not so much what you've gained or lost
But how you treated all

When folks stopped by for a little advice
On how to make life better
Was the advice you gave the best you knew
And good advice to the letter

Was all your dealings firm, but fair
And those you brushed did prosper
Can it be said you did your best
And your name is on the roster

When the pearly gates are opened
And the master says come in
You probably won't feel worthy
But the new life will begin

Bruce R Senecal
QUIET NIGHT
The moon glistens off the newly fallen snow.
The quietness of the night is a reflection of time standing still.
All can be heard, or not heard, depending on one's sensitivity to nature's giving.
I long for the quiet night, for the solitude it brings.
I can find happiness, when there is no laughter.
I can find sadness, when no one speaks of sorrow.
I have no one to answer to but myself.
Yet, it is myself which seeks the answers
to the questions of emotions.
Once found,
I use them to fuel my soul.
I am the quiet night, when the moonlight glows.

Helene Lenga Kohen
MY MOM
I was born one day
in beautiful May,
in my Mom's loving arms
so full of charm.

In the scent of spring
which is a lovely thing,
I nursed at my Mom's breast
where it was the very best.

From the start
there was love in my Mom's heart,
when I was well
fairytales she would tell.
She made pretty little dresses
I made quite a few messes,
but how she used to show me
off to all her friends to see.

My Mom was caring and wise
as she'd kiss the tears from my eyes,
when I hurt myself as a little girl
with my long hair she gently would curl.

My Mom has always been a woman of passion
and to this day she is also a woman of fashion,
My Mom loves to go out and have a good time
and my Mom's youthfulness will continue to shine.

In the corner of my heart
there is a spot that is a part,
of my Mom's love that I have never forgot
and a love that can never be caught.

Out of laughter and tears
with all the coming years,
I shall nurse my love and keep it deep
faithfully each day till I go to sleep.

I remember the long talks we had about life
after experiencing pain and strife,
and my Mom would gently point out
from my heart love will blossom and come about.

Before too long I found the way
and finally grew up one day,
I met a boy I did marry
and his name was Gary.

All too soon my Mom went away
and I didn't know what to say,
why the heartbreak? why the pain?
but I only called in vain.

Sick of these fears
and weary of these tears,
at last I learned the truth
it was my inexperience in youth.

The pain of the heart did cease
at home with my Mom I felt at peace,
how my Mom did talk to me
to open my eyes and see.

Before too long, despite the wrong
I did become strong,
once again when I felt whole
I found the other half of my soul.

Fate took a different turn
in my life I was to learn,
from the mountains to the desert I went
with my two little baby boys God sent.

At last I met my friend, my soul-mate
and I'll always be grateful for his sake,
my partner throughout my life, my love
God must have been watching me from above.

Now we celebrate our Anniversary together
my Mom, Dad, Nathan, and my Michael forever,
but not in any way
does it take away.

The love I'll always feel for my Mom
during the quiet times of feeling calm,
each day my happiness shows
for only stronger my love grows.

All through my life I'll remember
she was always gentle and tender,
in showing me the way
and she made me the woman I am today.

Terryl Stinson
MY GIFT FROM GOD

To Felicia, my beautiful Gift from God.

God blessed me with
a beautiful flower
And I will, from this moment on,
be a gardener nurturing my flower on
By loving and caring for it
and making sure it gets enough sunshine . .

Oh what joy my flower brings me!
Just when I was feeling weak
God gave me this flower to keep
And I will water it plus till its ground
so that my flower will always be around . . .

Then I will watch her blossom
right before my eyes
My love for her will be
deeply rooted inside
I will cherish every moment
we share together
I will never forsake her,
"no, not ever"——

Roses are red, violets are blue
God gave me a flower
and I love you,
My Gift From God.

Agnes Johnson Kantola
TO MARION FAY (AT 3)
She is more than child—she is a spirit rare—of such a fairy grace and airy charm—And, yet with brooding calm and steady gaze
She gives those who may see, a glimpse of all the years that have been and that may be—
A vision of lost glories
And desires unfulfilled!

Ms Rosa Lee
IT'S ICE CREAM

To my Mom Janie, my children Jamie and Jerry To Erik, To my Dad Ralph & Ethel Ivey.

The terror of the night is finally gone
I have done all I can to win my war,
Now I'll just be my total self; calm, confident,
Reassured and in control of myself.
No longer do I care what people say or think,
Because as far as I'm concerned they're the ones who are in need of a shrink.
Mission impossible has finally been accomplished and I have no desire to roam; everything I've ever done or wanted has been right here at home.
If you ain't hometown youse lowdown That's my motto now, and no one from here or out of town is gonna take from this gal Hon!
Believe me when I tell you I haven't a family nor friend, but I'll endure and live my own life, right to the sweet end.
As for me I'll take vanilla, cause it's all ice cream to me, and with a cherry on top.
Amen

Garrick G Krienke
CREATION
the Mind enters the house,
and climbs the Spiral Staircase,
peering for any light,
from the world of Infinite Ideas.
it keeps looking;
Confused,
until there is no more room,
the house gets smaller,
you gasp for breath.
Then,
the blocking wall dissolves,
into the bliss of creativity.

Carol Wolff
UNTITLED
If I could wish upon a star,
I'd want to be wherever you are,
So I could hold you close my dear,
And know that you would always be near.
Then every day would seem to be,
Valentines Day, for both you and me.
To share in a life with lots of love,
And have life's blessings from above.

Ann Pizzuti Enke
THE SCHOOL PRAYER

This poem is dedicated to my six lovely grand-children, Jody, Jenny, Ray, Dale, Mike and E.J.

Moral values started to decay;
When the School Prayer was taken away,
Racial violence, crime, and other insidious things
Have started a corruption that only brings—
Chaos to this great nation of ours
Because the folly of youth only leave scars;
The temptations that encircle our youth;
Are scary and lead to the utmost truth—
Because sexual disease, alcohol, and drugs
Will eventually produce a nation of thugs;
We need "peace on earth" and self esteem
Before we can be a winning team!
The "anything goes" attitude prevailing today;
Will weaken our nation if we delay—
The School Prayer must be part of our nation
To help our youth resist temptation!

Cornell Cleaver Hatchett
LONELINESS
Loneliness is a funny thing—
Accomplishments you handle with a fling.
You walk with hundreds everyday,
With others you work and then you play.
You hold your head up, of that you're proud;
Your family, your friends, they form a crowd.
You sing, you dance, you jump and sway;
With most and sundry, you have your way,
But inside—you're dead.
Along come some with oily tongues;
It doesn't matter who they're among.
Their methods and manners are,
Oh, so smooth.
To let them tell it, they're in the groove.
Their hands will creep and caress and sicken;
Their eyes will widen, their tongues will thicken.
They'll wine you and dine you in admiration,
And offer to share a bed in consolation,
But inside—you're dead.

Intelligence and pride are said of some worth
If you value them highly, and bred well from birth.
It's better to die than fall for this scheme.
Time marches on and thought it may seem
That life isn't worth living,
There're others who need you and value your giving.
They reward you with love and laughter and song.
To those who love you, you can do no wrong.
They need you alive—not dead.

Gloria Hester
YOU WILL NEVER KNOW
You will never know what tomorrow brings
You'll never know if the birds will sing
Tomorrow is never promised to anyone
That's something you can't wish upon
You might be here today and gone tomorrow
And suddenly someone is brought upon sorrow
No one knows when their time shall come
And soon your loved ones you are taken from
No one is prepared for grief and pain
It's just like flying in an airplane
Not ever knowing if it would land or crash
Just as if you'd break out in a rash
The future is something to think about
And there is no use to sit and pout
Whatever you do; try living a decent life
Try to make it through struggle and strife
Leave this world with love in your heart
As if to say; you have made a new start
Heaven awaits for thee with love, a shiny star for you above
For those who want to perish in hell
Are those of you who give up and fail.

Ann Pizzuti Enke
NEW ENGLAND'S GLOW
New England's summer has gone to rest—
A transition of beauty is now at its best!
Colorful trees especially on the mountainside;
Form a spiritual painting that we cannot hide;
The flighty birds are beginning to congregate;
Contemplating on a warmer climate before it's too late.
The squirrels are hiding their food everywhere
In hopes that when winter arrives they won't despair,
Eventually no leaves will we soon see
And suddenly the Christmas Season appears instantly!
This jubilant holiday eases our weary hearts
As soon as this subsides we wait for Spring to start,
Suddenly New England's foliage begins to bloom;
Later summer takes hold with its flowery perfume,
Hopefully we pray to our Lord up above—
We'll keep on seeing these Seasons we gratefully love!

Janeane Faye Murphy

Janeane Faye Murphy
TRUE LOVE

Dedicated to my parents, Leroy and Symenzie Murphy, who perfected true love and adorned it with truth.

Its bonds tie cords of inseparable depths,
A twine of immeasurable quality.

A love stronger than death,
And softer than twilight.

Minds joined together in purpose,
Like a jeweled sphere suspended in space.

Values of trust and loyalty,
Sown of painless honesty.

Two thoughts in unison's embrace,
Like velvet pinions gainst downy breast.

Desperate motives linked with delicate heart,
Entwined on turbulent elusive seas.

Riding pillion on golden steeds,
Time travelers through hope's horizon.

The dream walkers on geode stones,
Existing as life's variable star.

Beautiful fantasy, adorned by truth.
Perfected reality, sought by few.

Mildred A Strickland
WORRY WOES
Today I forgot to worry
Really I did, it's true;
And now I don't know where to start in again,
With old worries, or with some that are new.

Of course, I don't like to worry.
Who does? I'm sure I can't say.
But when tiny worries come floating toward me,
I just cannot send them away.

Then they grow bigger and bigger,
And spread out like a cloud overhead

Which shadows me much of the daytime,
And next morning greets me at my bed.

Now I've been thinking this over,
And I don't see why I should allow
These miserable worries to plague me.
I must meet and defeat them right now.

Then as I prepared for the battle,
A wonderful thought came to me.
Why not plan to forget to worry each day
'Til my worries have fled, and I am free.

Melanie Tinsley
TO MY LOVE

Dreaming
of moonlight
resting on the everchanging ocean;
sitting,
with you,
on a deserted beach
on a clear brisk,
starlit night
listening to the
peaceful surrender of waves to breeze
ever wondering—
"Would anything change if we
just slipped away on that
ever moving wave
which entreatingly
licks at our toes . . .
beckoning us to follow
into the silvery foam
and sapphire depths
—FOREVER—
to spend eternity
in each other's arms?"

Rose C (Posey) McGilton
MY FRIEND

I have a friend, we help each other
At all times, in all situations
We share and we care, we are so close
This wife, mother, grandmother,
friend, neighbor, confidant, co-worker.
Sometimes we know what the other is thinking.
We talk about you God!
How you supply all our needs great and small.
How we have our own Master's degree
As a C.O.G. A child of God.
This lovely woman, with whom I am,
Having lunch with today.
Sets such an inspiring example of spiritual strength
Forgive my pride Lord, in this beautiful blend,
Of mother, wife and friend.

Gordon J Bell
ONLY YESTERDAY

I feel the agony of a forgotten child
Who lived when days were long and dreams were big
And life was so very, very free.

He seems so far away—that yesterday child
Who loved the countryside
So long ago.

I see him still
Sitting within a meadow
Of long ago.

Thinking of dreams that would be true
Some would be, but most were only dreams
But they are gone and so is he.

So many collections he had
Of rocks, shells and pets.
The sad little child who kept to himself.
But he was happy in his world of fantasy
where no one could stray, but
he.

Dreams that reached beyond the stars
Only to be shattered in the turmoil of grownups
Where all believe themselves to be Gods!
I miss him so
That sad little child—who walked the easy path, only
But only, Yesterday.

John E Daugherty
IT'S NOT JUST THAT YOU USED ME

it's not just that you used me
you see
not even that you told others not to befriend me
that i was strange and dangerous

it's that you pretended to like me
no
it's that you pretended to care

and if your heart has swayed since then
how am i to know
how am i to sense it
how am i to care

Earl E Sumners
FOREVER

Happiness, an un-forgettable and deserved reward when shared
Divided between individuals by unknown consequences
But brought about because of nurtured love and respect
Consummated, when blitzful moments are ever-lasting

So, cherish the moments, hours, days, and years
That flourish with compassion and sometime reason
Give of thyself with great passion and relentless caring
Build upon the sensitive nature of your love and kindness

And I will Forever Love You

And come Autumn of our lives and its tender feelings
That dwell on yesterday beauty and memorable moments
We shall share our destiny and the un-told future
In the warmth and golden surroundings of your love
When time no longer affords us frivolous days nor blitzful nights
And our past is in the archives of celestial encumbrance

It will be written in our hearts, love conquers all
Surely, somewhere in the rainbow of God's Plan We Will be together
And I will Forever Love You

H Lamar Stewart
STORY OF A "SPORK"

To my Wife, Betty Stewart, who enjoys Living . . . especially in Frostproof, Florida 33843.

Again writing . . . and about the useful SPORK,
A two-way Utensil—part Spoon and part Fork.
For a handicapped Person who long has needed Help,
Who so quietly endures, with never a bitter Yelp.

Imagine if you can any Person with a real shaky Hand . . .
Even feeding himself each Day would be simply Grand.
No more soiled Linens, Floors or a Dress or a Shirt,
Greatly improves Attitude—no more feeling like Dirt.

No more Tears shed about the malformed Hand . . .
Now just Sunshine galore throughout the Land.
With Handle of a Fork swiveled onto end of a Spoon,
The Spoon part swivels and you get a useful Boon.

Created is a glorious feeding Utensil—part Spoon part Fork . . .
Readily known by ALL grateful handicapped users as a SPORK!
Thankful are ALL who use such a combination "Tool" . . .
Causes the Healthy to be appreciative and stay Cool.

Thus with Gratitude for the SPORK lingering still . . .
Unfortunates continue to Progress up a steep Hill.
Glad an Inventor worked so hard with such a sharp Mind,
Bringing needed Assurance to ALL Persons of this Kind!

Leon Hodge
TRYING

In loving memory of Bera and Lussia Hodge

For the sake of trying!
There could be no wrong.
Give it your all, and be strong.
And for one accord, which I long
I hope it stays forever on . . .
Humbly on your knees,
Grow with pride and grace
For it's seen in your eyes and face.

H Cajo Dulin
AMERICAN LIFE STYLE

For Sophie and Louis: Love and thank you. Combined genes begot shared genes.Next time around, if possible, shall return the favor!

Mentors, misers, and mendicants
Share thoughts in fraternity,
Under threads of different color;
all daydream of assets,
wealth and money.
Who can not say in a lifetime,
they didn't scheme to wield,
hoard, o
beg it!
Raise your flag; watch your screens;
Dream in bullion no matter where
you find your bed.
And caricature in fashion
the American lifestyle,
Invented in stereotype,
A talisman of money.

Donna Corbin
SILENT CRIES

Can silent cries be heard—I don't think they can because no one has answered mine.
No one sees beyond my eyes because they don't want to discover the thoughts inside.
I won't tell them either 'cause they wouldn't understand the kind of love I feel.
It's somewhat like a fairy tale, yet more than that—more than just being real.
It's a special kind of power, but not bad in any way because no one but me knows.
They are my silent cries—the ones no one answers, and the ones I'll never show.

Mary Olive Chapman
IT LEADS ME ON, THAT DISTANT STAR

It leads me on, that distant star
Which seems to beckon from afar
With promise of a better day.
I turn to go and yet must stay.
Why do I yearn for distant heights?
Why must my days and all my nights
Be filled with thirsts I cannot quell?
O burned out hopes would you foretell
Of victory? Let me yet know
Surcease from pain, the afterglow
Of dreams come true. Let nothing mar
The hopeful promise in that star.

J C Geyer
SERENITY

The sunlight fades all around
As dusk turns into dark.
The raindrops fall gently down
As Heaven opens up.
The wind blows softly,
Calling out my name,
As I prepare to sleep.
And nighttime overtakes me,
While dreams fulfill the void.
I drift off slowly,
As I float away,
Leaving this world behind.
With nighttime comes a freedom
Not witnessed in the light.
All the colors of the rainbow
Reach out to hold my hand.
Through my eyes I see nothing,
Through my soul I see life.

Robert E Rader
TRY

I dedicate "TRY" To: Dawn Duwall who gives me her love. To: Bobby and Amanda Rader, (my children), who give me strength and determination, and most of all, To: My Lord who gives me the faith and wisdom to write the words.

I'm here to climb this mountain's peak
For Jesus Christ I'm here to seek
With him there I will not fall
Even if I have to crawl

He made this mountain and valley too
He makes the sky and water blue

If your faith is really true
You can climb this mountain too

For He knows his plans for you
No self-pity will get you through
Start at the bottom and do not cry
You have to climb you can not fly

For at this mountain's peak you'll see
What He does for you and me
He's in my heart He's in my soul
With His love I am told

T—Trust there is a way
R—Reach out in all directions
Y—Yield yourself to God's will

John Meise
TOGETHERNESS
Together or apart is meaningless to me;
For there is only togetherness,
Though I have gone from thee.
It may at first seem we're apart
When you are left alone.
But you will find me in your heart,
In morning's pureness, in sunset glow,
At eventide, and in the snow,
And blowing rain:
When you look out, as I looked out,
And loved it all just as it came.

M David Clark
PASSING ON

Dedicated to all those who have shown me Love is not dead

Church bells have fallen silent.
Lover's Lane has long been draped
with the stench of shattered dreams
and broken promises.

The songs of love and joy are merely memories.
The skies now gray cry velvet tears
for days gone by.

Playgrounds are no longer inhabited
by the laughter of small children playing.
Silence is soul shattering.

The heart of life has
stopped.
The world itself has grown
bitterly cold.

Only a handful still mourn its
passing . . .
. . . Love is dead

Thora J Supple
VALHALLA
Valhalla's halls sing a song
Of great men's acts and deeds
Of valour, courage, victory
The Muses, at their feet!

Valhalla, heaven of the gods
A place of famed renown:
A crypt, so vast, it spans the earth
From cloud to shining cloud!

We read of legends of the great
Yet know we will not make
The list of entrants to this shrine
Or drink Valhalla's wine!
Oh, mighty men of stature great
Who mapped our history
I ask of thee, one little thing
To please, make room for me!

Margie Worrix St Laurent
THE BOY THAT TIME FORGOT
When I was about seven or eight
I used to play near a garden gate.
I had a friend who played with me,
But he was all of twenty three.

Blind man's bluff, and hide and seek,
I'd yell "Now, Jack don't you peek,"
With childish laughter he would join
My fun,
And we would romp and play till the
Day was done.

When we grew tired, I would draw
In the sand, pictures he seemed to understand.
And he seemed to find a special joy
In an old clothespin I fashioned for a toy.

Some folks called him simple, others wild,
But my Mom chose the name "God's special child."
His mind, she said, just never grew,
And the friends he had were very few.

I remember his face when I went away,
"Now don't cry Jack, I'll be back someday."
And I accepted a flower from the hand, of
This dear and child-like man.

Many years later I went to find
Home and memories I left behind,
And I walked along a cemetery row
Reading names I used to know.

I came upon his name there, and
Recalled good times we used to share.
I knelt and placed a forget-me-not
On the grave of the boy that time forgot.

Olga Wahlsten
MIRROR IMAGES
Tracing imagery
in pool waves,
spreading out distortions—,
sudden sun-sparkle blindness—
seek then, other hidden selves,
(not seen through windows,)
in moving twilight shadows.

Tereasa Booher
CLOWNS
Clowns dance all in a
Line, laughing and crying.
Oh what a lovely sight
When they step into the light
Nodding away all
Sadness in the air tonight

Carl Vizcarra
MY LOVE

To my son Mario and his wife Peggy.

My love is a silent boat
That paddles in a dreamy float
Breaking waters in sweetened note.

My love is a hasty light
That breaks through the saltry night
Wretched lightening, coming straight.
My love is a sickened child
Who sings at night in bed and style,
Knowing that death is near
Holding high its mortal Spear.

Katheryn Lay
A CHRISTMAS CALLING
Amid reveling, boisterous celebrations,
The loud, blasting music,
Via modern electronics;
Despite the hustle and bustle of hurried crowds
And the glint and glitter of tinsel and foil,
A wee faint cry
Can be heard in the hearts of those who listen;
The sound of a babe crying in a manger.

Henry Le Fout
WHITE

To my family . . . .

White is like the dots
in a polka-dotted dress.
The dots are like clouds
when they touch the white birds
in the sky.
The white birds are really angels,
flying up high.
White roses are forever
like good guys and
good feelings.
White is pure
like white chocolate and candy
which unicorns eat every day
during the white of winter.
White snow tastes like the salt of the sea.
White is like love,
the greatest feeling in the world.

Beatrice B Wright

Beatrice B Wright
THE OUTSIDERS

To my family and friends around the nation. To my grandchildren and my one uncle and aunts.

The Outsiders are all
welcome in.
They are deep down in
their sin.
Always wondering
what we are doing.
They ought to come
on in and see!
Wondering what songs
we're going to sing.
Always making their
heart bells ring.
Wondering what prayer
we will pray.
They never come
inside to stay.
We always have them a place where they can always be safe.
Outsiders sit there wondering who's in church, because they can't say very much. They talk about this they talk about that; always wondering what's in the collection plate.

In here we have no hate. They wonder what the preacher is Preaching, cause they can't do the teaching . They come on in and meet us, we're sure to give them a Special greeting.
They wonder what we are wearing cause it doesn't need any repairing.
They look and see who's driving what car.
Because they don't want to be very far. Come on in outsiders and join us, we need to reach our goal. That's what we were told, and it'll help to save your soul.

Dorothy Moase
SAY IT WITH LOVE
You can "Say it with Love" in more ways than one
From early morning 'til setting of the sun.
With a friendly, "Hello," with a wink from the eye
With a cup of cool water or a warm apple pie.
With the words of a song, with the touch of your hand,
With thoughts from the heart and a round gold band.
You can "Say it with Love" a thousand ways
With a bouquet of flowers, with fun-filled days.
But the best way to say it , and you'll agree too,
Is to use those three little words: I LOVE YOU!

Debi Young-Martinez
THIS OL' TOWN

This poem is dedicated to my brother, Curt Young; in his memory of "Dean Bradford Cannon" 1969-1989

Here I am again in this ol' town,
Where we used to clown around.
But there's a stillness here;
One that will stay with me, the rest of my years.
I have tears in my eyes . . . .
But I don't know how to cry.
You were taken away so fast
And now all I do is think of the past.
We had our boyhood days;
Which feels like they've been stolen away.
We were the best of friends,

Until your life was thrown into the wind.
How was I to know your fate?
How was I to know when I left;
the words I wanted to say, would come too late.
I wasn't there when you died,
on that fatal January night.
I didn't get a chance to say goodbye,
You didn't get a chance to see my unborn baby's eyes.
So, here I am . . . at a funeral for my best friend;
how it hurts me to know this is your end.
I stood at your coffin, silently saying goodbye
and asking God above, why?
I was the last to leave your side,
The reality caught me, and I wanted to hide;
Instead, I walked away; with the sun shining down . . .
upon this Ol' Town.

Pam Waddell
IF I WERE ONLY . . .

Inspiration: more than just a dream!

If I were only a rabbit, and could make work seem like play
If I were only an owl, and could make night seem like day,

If I were only a coyote, and could make tension relax
If I were only an eagle, and could make proper contacts,

If I were only young, and never grow old
If I had only done what I had been told,

If I were only a tortoise, and make fast ways slow
If I were only a fox, and know which way to go,

If I were only a duckling, and venture no where
If I were only a puppy with no burdens to bear,

If I were only free from a world of sin
If I were only there to start over again,

If I had only known what I could have been
If I had only seen His treasures back then,

If I had only seen the pain in His face
If I had only known of His Father's Grace,

If I were only better in even one small way
If I had only given Him a better day,

If I had never seen some wicked ways here
I would be with Him, and His cross I would bear! ! !

Jessica Greene
NOT QUITE

A scarlet heart filled with love,
A violet sky of a child's imagination,
Indigo eyes of the deepest eternity,
Thoughts of a girl in love?
Not Quite.

A warm teardrop running down a tender cheek,
The harsh blow of a stinging word,
Angry thoughts of an unfaithful friend,
Clenched fists over that which we have lost,
Thoughts of a person swallowed by the black waters of despair?
Not Quite.

Wanting to feel a mother's soft hand,
And yet pushing it away.
Wanting to feel the wind in your hair,
And yet hiding your face.
Wanting to feel the dirt on your hands,
And yet washing it away.

Overwhelming love, suicidal despair,
Confusion, loneliness, depression, guilt.
Not scenes of a soap opera or a Hollywood movie,
Just feelings of a girl growing up.

Juna D'Lynn Ottolini

Juna D'Lynn Ottolini
THE UNKNOWN SOLDIER

Dedicated to Dennis Billings for giving me the inspiration to write this, and also to my parents for their encouragement and support.

Say a prayer for THE UNKNOWN SOLDIER . . .

He doesn't know where he's going,
He doesn't know what he's gonna do.
He's just trying to make a living,
Just like me and you.

He doesn't know what to think,
He's in a pretty big mess.
He's just trying to understand,
You know he's doing his best!

He has someone who loves him,
He has someone who cares;
She's trying to help him see
To take pride in his goals, hopes, and dreams.

Where's he going?
What's he looking for?
He doesn't know . . .
He's not so sure.

Say a prayer for THE UNKNOWN SOLDIER . . .
Help him see the light.
Help him to distinguish
What is wrong and what is right.

Daniel C Borden
IF YOU COULD

If you catch the morning rays
and bottle them all up
If you could gather every flower
and hold them high in hand
If you could envelope all my dreams
and mail them to my heart
If you could dance upon the stars
and fall into my arms
If you could envision endless sleep
and dream forever after
If you could venture thru the heavens
and think of me each step
If you could picture perfect romance
and feel it in my touch
If you could smell a thousand roses
and kiss me 'fore each breath
Then you'd know how much I love you
my love so sweet and true

Charlotte Turner Burns
A LOOK AT PROVERBS 17:3

Dedicated to Todd Keyes, For your Christ-like spirit of love and encouragement in my life, I praise the Lord. To my children, family, brothers and sisters in Christ Jesus, I love you all very much.

I haven't any money, silver or gold.
The furnishings within my home are tattered, torn and old.
Compared to you I haven't much, to show the world you see.
The greatest gift I've ever known, lives deep inside of me.
Your life is filled with gold and the things you've bought yourself.
My life is filled with Jesus, His love rests on every shelf.
See the refining pots for silver the furnace is for gold,
so the precious gift of Christ, is what in my life I hold.
For never will I lose him, nor will his worth decrease.
He's with me everywhere I go, still works when I'm asleep.
So you may have your gold and silver, for them I want no part.
Their value will be nothing, for the Lord will test our hearts.
Amen . . .

Robin Nylund
YOU HOLD THE KEY

This poem is dedicated to the guy who holds the key to my heart—Roy Hooker.

Only when I see you,
—may I rise from the depths of my imagination.
You hold the key to my heart, my love, my life.

The key turns when I see you,
Unlocking my captured heart.
Releasing the power of love,
—into your hand.
Your words puff air into my breast,
Your touch sends my heart beating.
Your thoughts are messages in my head.

We kiss,
My soul leaps to life,
Quiet power unleashed,
The love from your lips sends blood coursing through my veins,
With our hearts entwined,
—the ring completes.
And I'm able to love again.

I'm alive in your grasp,
Only when you unlock my heart,
—does life carry on.

You hold the key.

Carol Aryaeenia
THE SILENT EARTH

Oh wind, blow, blow your wondrous clouds of 'cotton wool'
Onto the world, a world that has now stood still:
A silent hush; not even one small sound
Can be heard; it seems our Earth has found
A moment to itself;—for snow is on the ground.
The snow, how silently it seemed to fall about,
As if tired after one strenuous battle fought
Up in the skies it loved and knew so well,
And then did breathe its lingering farewell
To come upon this Earth, and with the rest of Nature, dwell . . .

Peggy C Tew
TENDER THE MOMENT, DEEPER THE LOVE . . .

To my husband Steven, for whom it was written. I LOVE YOU . . .

A tender touch . . .
The moment
Your lips meet mine.
The words "I LOVE YOU,"
Echoing in my mind.
Time stands still, as if floating . . .

Feeling endless, motionless, quietly hovering,
A cloud.

Thoughts escape me
Senses whirl . . .
Feeling so light and airy
As if, I'll drift forever . . .
forever more.

Yet . . . we draw apart
Tender moments . . .
Dispel.

And reappearing . . . Now deeper in feeling,
Than ever before.
The knowledge "I'll love you, forever" . . . forever more.

Kathryn Herziger Weber
PIANO KEYS

To Michelle, my much loved daughter; For the world of beauty, I could never share with you.

The piano keys fell as dewdrops;
The same moisture that fell
from my eyes.
Not because of pain or hurt,
Because of the fullness of life.
Because of its indecisions, because of its pain; its love.
Its death of dreams—its opening of doors—
The closing of doors that
seemed so ready and open.
It is so beautiful and so ugly;
impossible to live in—
Impossible to transcend.

I cry because I don't
understand.
Yet my mind, so large and glorious,
should be able to comprehend;
Yet never will. I AM HAPPY,

But it hurts.
I love those that sometimes cause me the greatest pain,
Yet greatest joy.
This is life and I love it.
Then why do all of us court death?
What is inside us . . .
Impossible to tap.
THE FUTURE WILL REMAIN THE SAME.

Earl E Sumners
HE'S MY FRIEND

Dedicated to a life long friend, Elijah, who was very ill but is well on the way to a full recovery.

In this world of un-known elements and deceit
Tis hard to recognize truth, reality and love
And yet, in our years of joy, torment, and tribulation
I find with you that breath of freshness like a dove

The many memories in our vault of life's journey
Shall never be daunted by the future come what may
Your never ceasing friendship has built dreams among men
An eternal flame of passion that will never stray

Your heart, big as the world attached in colorful ribbons
That illuminate brightly of deeds generated by our soul
The ecstasy shared by those fortunate of your time and presence
Conveys the highly regarded statue reserved for feelings
of love un-told

And tomorrow when the sun shines into your life again
Share with me the joyous memories and sounds of yesterday
For only we remember those significant moments of treasure
Complete, un-abridged, and joyful.

Friend Emeritus

Janice Stuart
SEARCHING
Although your eyes may never see the one whose voice is calling thee;
From that deep well of life within, you hear the one who has always been.
Alone amid the sadness of your soul, as you search for what you do not know,
The song you sing is of love unknown, the face of one your dreams not shown.
You are a lover yet were loved but once through the hazy years of time;
The rain in your eyes hides the tears in your soul, as you journey back to long ago
Until your sleep has brought visions of your lover true, my presence shall go with you.

David M Whitcraft
UPON THE RETURN OF A DAY OUT SLAYING DRAGONS
Pulled by a passionate pucker
Our imaginations grow
Sensitive skin attached from within
Stretching to and fro
Beating on each other to increase the nightly heat
Mounting motions teather
Sweat comes dripping from your brow so
I loosen the restricting leather
But suddenly the night is knocked
Back in to me by a bedly board
Severely blown and overcome
I sheathe my nightly sword.

MaryAnn Stefano
EVEN THOUGH WE JUST MET
Even though we just met.
I feel like I have to tell you this
I have been in love with you from afar,
and you never knew.

You always looked so caring, sensitive and kind.
You always treated me so nice.

Every time I needed someone, you were there for me.
Now it's my turn, whenever you need someone I'll be there for you.

Although we may never meet again,
I will never stop feeling the way I do about you.

Bret H Yager
ON DRIED FORGET-ME-NOTS
Proud in their vase,
Of azure glaze,
They repose and watch the passing days.

Proud they are, pathetic too,
For they have lost their brilliant hue,
Like eyes of the old, the fading blue.

Yet they were once so bright and strong,
At peace with all that's right or wrong,
And fluttered with the robin's song.

So here they stand,
Not tall or grand,
In just the way that I had planned.

And here they'll stay,
From day to day,
Until the weather of centuries wears them away.

Timothy Stacy
DESTINY
Man is born in bondage
To a power much higher than he,
And through his life it leads him—
This thing called destiny.
The road it leads him on
Is sometimes steep and rugged.
The choices put before him
Are confusing, tantalizing, and varied.
The decisions he must make
Sometimes sting like a well-thrown dart;
But his path will be much easier
If only he follows his heart.

Debra M Zima
UPON GOD'S WINGS
I searched my memories for you,
And found such agony.
Remembering your gentle touch
With your arms about me.

The breeze was gentle and calling
As we wandered the beach.
At dusk we spoke only but once
Our hearts we gave to each.

The words I shall always recall
As now you are no more.
The door of heaven was open,
And alone you did soar.

Carol Wolff
LITTLE FARMER
Jumpin' Jimminy, here comes the goat
He'll kick, butt and nab at your throat,
Leapin' Lizzards, the gander is loose
His old neck aughta' be in a noose,
And Golly, that old guinea hen's noise
Is driving me nuts, I'm losing my poise.
Have pity on a little farmer like me
Old lamp, where's the genie to set me free?

John E Murdock

John E Murdock
PROMOTION DAY

To my wife, Willie Murdock, and to our children, Barbara, John, Jr., Michael, Willie Flo, Deborah, Kay and David.

Promotion Day with Jesus,
What a promise to you and me.
As we travel this road with Jesus,
Promotion Day is sure to be.

Promotion Day with Jesus,
Is a natural cry you see.
For in God's plan for you and me,
Promotion Day is meant to be.

Promotion Day with Jesus,
The cry will surely be.
For in this world of sorrow,
Promotion Day, we long for thee.

Promotion Day with Jesus,
What heavenly bliss to see,
To a world of joy, peace and love.
Promotion Day, we welcome thee.

Marella Wilson (age 78)
CHRISTMAS POEM
There's a feeling to Christmas in the air,
With candles and holly and wreaths everywhere.
There's a hustle and bustle on every street,
And a friendly greeting to friends that you meet.

The cookies and candies and goodies are made,
And under the tree all the gifts have been laid.
The cards are all sent, and the chores are all done.
Christmas carols are taught to each daughter and son.

On the night before Christmas, when the tree is aglow,
Mother reads us the story, how a long time ago,
A baby was born in a stable that day.
The only bed that he had was a manger of hay.

The wise men came bringing gifts from afar,
To the baby Jesus born 'neath the Bethlehem star,
In memory of the Christ child born to us that day.
We too, bring gifts to those we love, to honor him that way.

Stephanie Monka

Stephanie Monka
MY TEDDY BEAR
He has the softest eyes and the sweetest disposition.
He listens without a thought to judge
And doesn't reply in words.
But I can hear his vibration
And it is the sound of the Universe.

Love heals all things, even in the guise of fur.
His soft eyes see mine without seeing
And understand the mysteries of the earth.
He walks with me without walking,
Even in my dreams.
He holds my hand with his paw, like the angels of old.

He belongs to the God who made him,
Even though he was crafted by human hands.

Betty Joyce White
BLESS OUR BIRDS
When the North winds blow, and the birds go south,
I think they spread the alarm by word of mouth,
Or maybe they feel it 'neath their pretty feathers,
And hold a group gathering of "if's or whether's"?
"If" we go, will we make it safely, 'tis many a mile?
Or "whether" we'll stick around and make a shut-in smile?
God gave us these gorgeous creatures to enjoy, if you may,
And most of us miss seeing them on a cold winter day.

My advice to you, folks, all over the

land!
Is, look out for our birdies and give them a hand.
When the North Wind blows and it's very cold,
Keep your feeders full each day . . . to them it's pure gold.
Stay little birdies . . . . we love you all!
So before your next gathering in the fall . . .
You won't have to meet and group together,
And make a decision of "if" or "whether,"
'Cause we promise to feed you in all kinds of weather.

Brandon Welsh
WHERE'S THE BEAUTY LEFT TODAY?
Where is the beauty that I used to see?
Where is the beauty that used to be?

That beauty that is a long time gone,
It makes me cry to write a song.

That beauty that was and is no more,
Is from the people who don't care anymore.

There's nothing but violence, drugs, and pain,
It's enough to make most go insane.

Why isn't like it used to be?
When there was all that beauty, I used to see.

Shauna L Webb
SILENCE
Silence—what does it look like?
Some may think it's a flower among many.
Others say it's like a stormy summer night.
Nature may deliver a kind of silence.
Cities send a silence of noise.
We all have our different views.
Opinions are acceptable, but not always shared.
A photograph may be a silence of actions not shown.
How do we know; does silence look like anything?
Does one wonder how silence may appear?
Some may view silence as a sound.
Others view silence as nothing.
Is silence an illusion?
Does silence exist?
When you are excluded, what do you hear?
If it is silent, take a look.
Silence—what does it look like?

Marianna Gitz
SAND CASTLES
With a shovel in my hand,
I built a castle out of sand.
Though it looked quite small to you—
My imagination grew.

In yonder courtyard stands my prince
Sword in hand—about to mince,
A fire-breathing dragon near the wall
Oh no! You made my castle fall.

Sandra Monge-Calderon
IDENTITY

This poem is dedicated to my family

Identity, who am I
Someone who is free
Someone who laughs and cries
And is willing to be just me

Identity, knowing who I am
and liking who I see
Helping and caring for others
Not only thinking of me

Identity, never to let another
shake my confidence in all I can be
Knowing who I am is enough for me

Barbara Ann Tomlinson
DEATH OF THE PINE TREE

To: My Dad James Ronald Hoffman
From: Your Daughter, Barbara Ann Tomlinson

Such a small Blue Spruce Pine Tree.
Would you grow up to be big?
Washing dishes every day.
Always gave you a drink to stay.
Dad would get mad at what I done.
But, look how you turned out in the long run.
You grew over 25 feet tall.
With lovely pine cones hanging in all . . . .
I was so proud of this pine tree.
And, would tell the story far and near.
I always said, "Donate it to Cumberland, MD.
Or Washington, D.C."
For all the world to see.
Here it is Christmas 1987.
Dad cut you down and I hope you are in Heaven.
You will always be a part of me.
Your pine cones are hanging on my Christmas Tree.

Nathalie Floyd Ward
LITTLE SINS
Murder, arson, envy, rape,
Heinous sins of every kind,
Make remorse and conscience nag
At the corners of the mind.

Little sins evade remorse.
Laziness, self-pity—these
Nibble, nibble night and day
Like mice upon a piece of cheese.

Flee from little sins in terror.
Little voices day by day,
Gossip, temper, selfishness,
Eat the will and heart away.

Bea Buelina Murphy

Bea Buelina Murphy
INTIMATE (SONG POEM)

Dedicated to any and everyone in love with love. Dedicated especially to, and for Pices March wherever you may be.

I knew love with you today
in the most intimate way.

Quietly you entered my life
as you usually do.

Then warmly
you bid me good day.
You always had the last say.
Why did you return love?
I've pined for you
like a lovesick dove,

then my prayers were answered
from above.

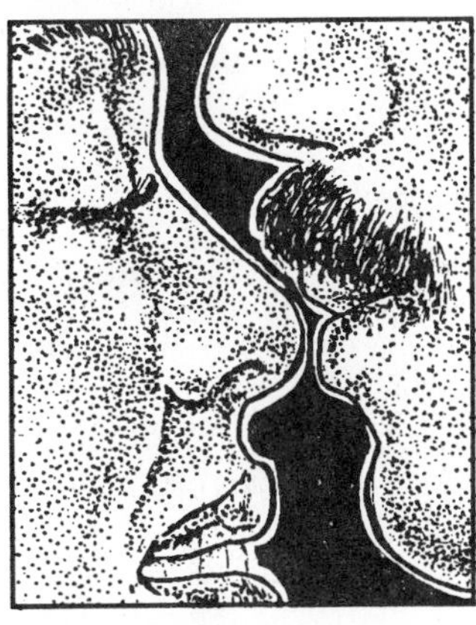

Gently you held me in your arms.
Skillfully turned on all your charms.

For all time
I could be your fool.

Please don't use me
as a tool.

In my solitary life
there is no other.

I wonder though
are we really right
for each other?

You loved me tenderly today
in the most intimate way.

Jerry L B Griggs II
FAITH
Through the limited time of man
God has watched our failures
and accomplishments
Our narrow and unfocused minds
refuse to see him
We shall regret that
until time is no more

Watch, look, listen, and pray

Our only hope is in keeping faith
Nobody should forget God's son
The perfect boy
who was the perfect man
In him we should keep faith

Pray, trust, believe, or die

Many members of mankind
do not keep faith
It is their own petty interests they trust
The son's death was a joke
from man
Even the faithful laugh at their master

Die, die, die, or live

Thomas D Grussing
BLISSFUL PEACE
Peace without war
this would be grand
truce without fear
Liberty, ever may it stand

Life with no remorse
Enough death with disease
Let nature take her course
Love life, may it please

War machines, idle, empty
Generals playing games
Not killing, not wasting
Nothing wild, all tame

But alas, it 's only dreams
Reality, sad as it may be, is true
Greed, power, a way of life
Always there, nothing new

Peace, a wonderful thought
Yes indeed, let's plant the seed
Majority rules
Dream people dream

Beverly Jean McCants

Beverly Jean McCants
CASTLE ROCK

To my children Desirée Scott & Melanie & my other relatives

Someone wants to rock your castle.
Someone wants to shake your tree.
Someone is watching you.
Someone's watching me!
A man's home is his castle; A place to retreat from the blows the world to his psyche will mete. Yes—to the gate opened wide—he (she) retreats; when he has experienced defeat.
The home, indeed is a castle. Be ready to guard your mighty fortress and let love be your buttress!
Be on the alert for those who want to storm your castle: Those who want to wreak havoc . . . Those who want to break your heart . . . . tear it and you or yours apart.
Yes guard your castle; For it is with demonic forces of the world that you wrestle!
Maybe a dog can be your Sentry at the front door, ready to sound the alarm about any force seeking to do you harm.
Some say we need the bible. Some say we need the strength of six brothers: This means 6 bullets, in the chamber of a gun! Demons are no fun.
Whatever your defense—Be ready—for someone's watching you!!
Guard your castle! It's long overdue
If you don't—sorrow you may rue!!
Your castle—keep it solid as bedrock & sheet metal. Sleep on rose petal (s)

Mia Hartsook
HEAVEN'S DESCENT
Tender, tender in the night
Vibrant Being, golden light
Softest body, softest air
Fullness melting everywhere.

Translucent petals in the heart
Deep with incandescent fire
Channels open, pouring wide
Streaming bliss, streaming Life.

Eye of rishi, inner light
Wakeful, clear, eternal, bright
Cosmic silence, cosmic hum
Thrilling space, ringing song.

Swelling waves and swelling warmth
Peaking fuller, rushing on
Dissolving matter, grains of form
Melting, swirling, shining sun.

Softly, softly comes the Dawn
Inner fullness flooding on
Golden gates, opening wide
Heaven's bliss—eternal Life.

Bonnie Head
HIS MANY FRIENDS

The old man sat just inside the door
His eyes were filled with tears as he stared at the floor.
On the table he had his nearest friend,
His Bible—a Book he would cherish until the very end.
His hands were drawn and old,
But so were the pages of the book he read in his humble little abode.
When he was lonely he always had a friend.
As he read the pages came alive.
It no longer mattered that he was all alone,
For he wasn't lonely and he had formed a bond.
He had all his friends, Matthew, Mark, Luke, and John.
Wouldn't people be surprised to see all his friends had come to life?
All of them were in his mind,
So all his friends he did find.
In the tattered old Book withered and old,
He found his friends and warmth from the cold.
With wrinkled hands she turned the pages.
Old and battered throughout the ages.
He once again met all his friends,
Who had come to see him from far away lands.

Irene Henry
HERE, THERE AND EVERYWHERE

When I'm here, you're not there
When I'm there, you're everywhere
On my way I fare
You're not to care
Here, there and everywhere.

Amanda Simmons

Amanda Simmons
GIVE ME A CHANCE (I DO LOVE YOU)

I dedicate this poem to my darling Tony. Love is like a flower, it needs the sun and the rain to grow. Make it last forever.

Without your facts,
How can you honestly tell.
that our love isn't deep,
as the gates of Hell.

My love for you I soon discover,
that you are my only and forever lover.
You are my life, my best friend,
that's why our love really has no end.

We both have our needs to be respected,
but it's hard to be fair when being rejected.
So give us a chance, enjoy this with me,
for once things will go as they really should be.

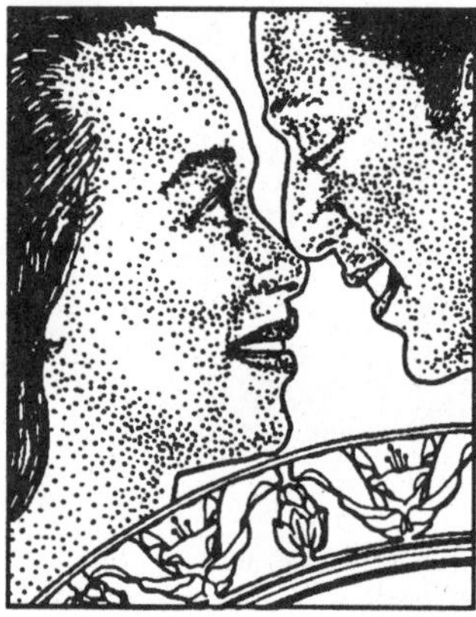

If you can touch me way down deep inside,
then you can see these feelings, I can't seem to hide.
Search yourself, feel our love, so sweet and tender ,
tell me to these feelings you will not absolutely surrender.

Your recent break-up must have been turmoil and pain,
the fact is, not every relationship ends the same.
All I ask you for is one worthy chance,
And I'll guarantee you sweet romance.

You'll understand when the time comes,
love of the heart and where it's from,
Give me a chance, I do love you.

Rhonda Lee Gunn
MELODY OF THE MOUNTAINEER

It is with great love and respect that I dedicate this poem to my mom Ruth Gunn and dad George Gunn

God, let me live my future on these green hills,
Above the dim of over changing cloud,
Where purest sun the dawn air distills,
No man-made gas nature's form enshroud.
Upon this broad plateau of table land
And lift my indebted heart, O God, to Thee,
High on these radiant supremacy let me stand
Far, far beyond the plain, the billowing sea.

I would not scorn the green vales below
Nor any of my gentleman disdain,
Because no preference for these hills they show,
But pick, instead, the valley or the plain.

And revels in the creature of thy hand
While nature's beautiful music fills my ear,
My soul, subjugated, upon these mountains grand,
Is filled with joy when evening stars appear.

So let me on these marvelous heights remain
With all I love and hold most dear to me,
Till I shall reach a far more honorable plain,
Where man, reclaimed, Thy face, O God, may see.

Rita Mae Farr
A CHILD OF LIFE

This poem is dedicated to my daughter, "Crystal Dawn," the special child in my life.

I wonder what a child of love and life thinks.
Do they realize what they see?
Love to me is supposed to be happy and gentle.
Life was meant to be simple.
A rose from life comes with hope,
a rose from love comes with dreams. "Love's no fun if you're not happy and things aren't gentle."
Life's no good when things aren't so simple
A rose with-out life has no hope.
A rose with-out the power of love has no dreams.
A child that has love gets a kiss and a hug.
A child that has life has your love.
But a child with-out love doesn't know what it's like to get a kiss and a hug.
A child with-out life,
Shall never know your love.

Mia Hartsook
COSMIC BEING'S SONG

I dance with Infinity
Unboundedness is my name
My gown, the starry-spangled sky
The rains rain within me
The oceans move within me
Each cell, a living universe
Universes within universes
Each alive, awake, sentient, omniscient
I move with Eternity
I breathe Infinity
I am

David Russell
DARKNESS

Hidden inside the darkness
lies a world with no limitations

The end is nowhere in sight,
as the start is with a form of light.

With the blink of an eye
or in a deep silent sleep
darkness will always be there.

So when you wake or turn
something new is being said or done.

With this in mind
you can always be sure
somewhere in the circle in which you live,
your dreams will come true

Darkness will always be there
so when you open your eyes,
always beware.

Lillian Laila
ETERNAL LOVE

Somewhere in the beyond,
our destinies met;
Someone in the beyond,
sealed our souls in a net;
Somehow from the beyond,
together our lives were set;
To the earth from the beyond,
this love forever kept.

Marie Kirsch
CLAY FEET

Now, just when I thought I was heaven-bound,
I stopped for a moment to look around.
Quickly I turned, but you would not believe,
the things to be done before I could leave.

Hands that were soiled had, to somehow, be cleaned
And the fields were ripe and I had not gleaned.
Clothes that were spotted, I had to replace,
and debts left unpaid, I, now, had to face.

So, while there's still time take that look around.
Don't wait till you think that you're heaven-bound.
For, just when I thought I was on my way
I found that my feet were still mired in clay.

Cy Headlough
TOMORROWS

In memory of my talented mother, Anne Pickles

We all expect tomorrow
to arrive
so we might
begin

to

continue

to

complete
all the things
we forgot
had not time enough

or

didn't realize the
worth of

And are

surprised at times
to find our
tomorrows

have
all
run
out!

Cathy Lambert
FEELING WITHIN

For my only love, Hugh

Since the time our eyes first met
I hoped for that day

For when we might be
together . . .

From a distance I'd see you
But felt you were unapproachable
Then you would smile
And in return give me new
hope . . .

Finally that day came to be
When we were together.
From the first time we kissed
I felt the warmth that radiates about
your body . . .

Thoughts and visions of you made
my body quiver
While with you at my side
Helped to ease the loneliness created
within my heart . . .

There is a feeling deep within
A feeling that radiates from the
centre of my being
Leaving my mind adrift between the
clouds . . .

Your smile is filled with expression
As your eyes radiate with
compassion
Sometimes leaving you wordless
While physically you express all
emotions . . .

I've never felt this way the way
I feel right now
For each moment we're together
Makes me want it all to last
forever . . .

M Q Flanery
GOD'S BLESSING
This eve another day has passed,
How have we lived, have we outdone
The tempter's snares, have we
surpassed
The tempter's net, have we o'er
come?

Yes there is only one safe way,
That we may find eternal life;
The Lord above will lead the way,
We need Him in this world of strife.

Oh; Lord in heaven from above
Look down upon us we do pray
Be near us Lord with Your own love
Guide and direct us on our way.

Praise God in heaven for the Son,
To teach us right before too late
To know that He's the only One
To lead us through the Heavenly
gate.

And there we'll find eternal peace,
For our own souls to come to rest;
Where songs of love shall never
cease
Thank God in Heaven we are blessed.

Michelle H Schuldt
DREAMLAND
There is this beautiful land right over
the mountain.
It has the most prettiest river anyone
has ever seen.
In the middle of the land there is a
fountain.
All around the grass is a lovely green.

When it gets dark the moon is very
bright.
The moonlight shines on a cold
sparkling stream.
All the people are filled with delight.
Too bad, it was only a dream.

Gracie Lowder
REALITY
Reality is our presence today, the
authenticity of our past, our
inevitable future, and our unspoken
fears.
Our time is only measured, with so
much to give and learn.
Our freedom is not where we live,
but rather, escaping the prisons of our
mind.

Our world is not always passionate
and forgiving—
it is sometimes too often punishing
and lashing.
Our only solace is hope.

In our well orchestrated society, it is
almost comical
to see the self-inflictions; sometimes
only laughter can help us overcome
the idiocy of it all.

Reality is not behaving as you are
expected,
considering all the human emotions—but it is a hunger,
a greed to strive for more, for
adventure,
for not having fear of life's gambles.

We are only here for a short while,
and perhaps again
in another form or time. Let our
many lives, hearts, and minds
be in perfect synchronicity to want
and yearn for more.

Reality does not have to be black or
white,
wrong or right, or unforgiving, but
only individualistic . . . . . as we are.

Estelle Langham
BRANWEN'S GARDEN

To: Tabitha Jade Langham and Nicole Daniels

Branwen's Garden
A curiosity some will say
Tulips and roses growing along the
way
A stream rippling over rocks
Fairies dancing in golden smocks

Strange beautiful flowers
Trailing up and down the bowers
Flowering trees with whispering
leaves

You must go and walk the path
Enjoy the beauty and laugh
Be gay, not sad I say, hear the pipes
of Pan along the way

Fall, winter, summer & spring
Beautiful exotic birds sing
In Branwen's Garden love abounds,
as the world turns around

Rhoda Williams

Rhoda Williams
A DREAM
A dream is only as far away as you
cast it.
Cast out dreams? Why?
Your dreams are your friends.
Dreams can comfort you,
Dreams can cradle you in their arms
at night.
Your dreams keep you as happy,
or as sad as you want to be.
Let your dreams be your only
boundaries.
Why let your fears keep you from
your dreams?
Your dreams, my dreams,
Simple or complex,
A dream is a dream.
Grasp them,
Hold on to them,
Even live them, if possible.
Color your dreams, I do.
Are they gold? Are they grey?
I choose golden dreams.
They're the ones that come true.
So do not be afraid, dream with me.
Our dreams are our only boundaries.

Violet Cua
STORMY

Forever in my heart

I went to the league to get me a pet
came home with a mongrel, the best
buy yet. Her name was Stormy, it fit
her well she wrecked our house,
made it look like hell. No punishment
we gave her for what she had done,
so Stormy knew we loved her and so
her trust begun.
Through eighteen years she loved us
all, then she went to heaven in the
fall. I miss my Stormy and the way
her tail would wag without her now
my life is very, very sad.

Stephen Foster Betz
THIRD ACT OF FOUR

Dedicated to Alan Scott Betz—My only son, because only from "classic" can "new" be born.

Geese
like angry commuters
take flight honking

The sun
shortens its golden span

Midnights so bright
you could read by their light
cauldron now
in snarled cumulus

The backdrops
change and fade

'till at last
gleans the frosted dew to
sanitize the stage
lest she muddy her foot
or soil the lace white
of her arrival

Shirley E Degree
ONE DAY AT A TIME
Sitting amongst the cobwebs of
utter confusion
Wondering if soon I will conquer this
optical illusion
I refuse to go on like a feather
in the wind
Knowing if I can just hang in there,
I can't possibly lose again!
The spirit way down within the
depths of my very soul
Is longing to be weightless, to fly
freely above my existence
So as to evaluate it, not in part,
but as a whole.
It somehow seems impossible
this entrapment of this maze
Almost a dilemma, in one gigantic
haze
But the fight for self survival, will
strengthen me they say
And one day at a time, I will be a
winner
And alone, my weightless spirit will
smile one day!

Pantelis Efthymiou
NEW YORK
Underneath the surface
of masquerade faces
and Broadway theaters . . .
Underneath the showcases
of crystal skyscrapers
and neon dazzling lights . . .
Beyond the magic colors
of advertisement billboards
and glittering diamonds . . .
Beyond the noise of songs
and nude stage dancers,
exists a terrestrial kingdom
of medieval, paradise.
It consists of mobsters
and savage parasites.
At the metropolis of violence,
a virtuous man is under siege
by a self-destructive power.
At twilight, a foggy sky
wanders like a phantom
to patrol the Wallstreet towers.

Phyllis Ann Bucci
JUST A DREAM AWAY

For Donald Brown, who will forever live in my heart, my mind, and my dreams.

Last night I saw you again, my
long lost love so true,
I can still feel my heart
pounding—from just the sight of
you.
Your hair so black your skin so
tan, that beautiful innocent
smile
That brought back so many
memories of a life that seemed
worthwhile
I watched you through a window,
just a street away
Even that close I could not reach
you, no more than I can do
today

But it was so wonderful, so
wonderful just to see you again
my dear
To have you so close to me, to feel
you oh so near
Yes my love for just a moment I
was near you again it seems
And I would do anything to be
near you, even if it is—only in
my dreams.

Rick Andres
CONSUMMATION
Cherished thoughts and lucid dreams
often so remorid,
A menstruation of polluted streams
like a sauce for the pate'.
A pastiche haunts the spiritual
principle embodied here.

Sang with great surdity I reach to hold it, to bring it near.
Death of this spell which makes me write.
Verbal consummation, restless soul in flight.
By your proclamation it's empty tonight.
Diligent behavior for I knew what was right.
Once more for some reason you've dropped from sight.
You know what I'm saying, I know what you've said.
We've stabbed it with knives, let's leave it for dead.
Vaguely betrayed by a soft spoken source,
I will seek asylum and hold no remorse.
A concept of reality, confirmation of fears.
Emotional breakdown, unleashing of tears.
Strong in character but weak at the knees,
Caring bears pain like a dreadful disease.

Melissa A Alliston

HAPPINESS SHALL TRIUMPH ANGER

Happiness shall triumph anger,
Love shall overcome hatred.
Throw darkness upon light and watch as it disappears in the blink of an eye.
Throw light upon darkness and be opened
to all that may be seen.

Hugh Michael

BUILDING A LIFE

I always swore that surely someday
I'd settle down to be a man . . .
I'd build a cottage near the ocean
And have a pretty woman close at hand.

We'd have a quiet life in our cottage—
Pass peacefully into dust.
The children would go on with lives of their own—
As we knew they must.

They'd rent an apartment in New York City—
They'd have roaches wall to wall.
They'd call a doctor on the hotline
When they began to feel very small.

They'd speak a language learned in Brooklyn
And we'd not understand a word they said.
Their children would move out soon to the country
And hope it was like all they'd read.

They'd soon turn around for they'd discover
Life everywhere is just the same—
It's fast, it's slow and hard and easy—
A hungry man must learn his own name.

Yolen Lemelle Jr

SOMEDAY

As the day rolls along
By the window I sit and stare at nature's sights
Because I am all alone
With no lover to hold me tight.

The radio speaks to me softly
As to caringly say,
"Just wait patiently and see,
Your rainbow will come someday."

Outside, the world is cold
With its deviously white smile,
Grinning at me bold,
Trying to persuade, "You'll never walk down that aisle!"

However, I still hope and pray,
But I don't moan and whine,
Because I have faith someday
That special one will be mine.

Maybelle A Finn

A NEED

Dedicated to President and Mrs Bush—

There is so much loneliness
On this earth
It seems we are
Prisoned from birth.

There is such need for union
Such need for clasping hands
Yet we deny the brotherhood
The human heart demands.

Reach out to a friend to-day
Don't put it off—
There is a way—to reach out
in love and say—
Our friendship's offered
here to stay.

With quivering lips and
heartfelt hope
On to a glimpse of love
we grope
No longer life and love
are stilled,
Hidden meanings now are
filled.

To share our thoughts and
feelings too
Such need is long past—overdue.
Demands no longer are
alone
To simmer in a heart
of stone.

Poets give and fill
this need
With peace and tranquil
thoughts concede.

Cheryl Leidig-Reed

Cheryl Leidig-Reed

THE RHUBARB PATCH

Dedicated to the memory of my beloved step-father Thomas H. Edwards, now departed, whose love and encouragement guided me during my later youth. Also, in dedication to my departed baby brother, Dennis Lee Edwards, with much love.

The ambrosial, inviting scent of Mable's rhubarb patch has lingered, thus, these many years and served my memory keenly.
It calls me back to resilient days of youth and virginality.
Life, at once, perpetual; youthful games played so serenely.

Has my mind, alas, become a sentinel for memory's inhumanity?
Perhaps the taste of rhubarb "sweet" was but acrid on my tongue.
The aromatic ruse, but an analgesic numbing of my painful memory.
Mine was not an Ozzie and Harriet family I found myself among.

Alcohol, divorce and death were but a few of the difficulties
infiltrating my unhappy childhood, like a never-ending bane.
Discomposed, bewildered, I searched the rubble of my crazy life.
The peace of the rhubarb patch told me my search was not in vain.

Mable, a stout and loving woman was my next-door neighbor friend.
I was a dimpled Shirley Temple girl looking for a hiding place.
A refuge in which to ease the pain from the jungle of my youth.
The happy memory of that rhubarb patch, mere time can not erase.

Butterflies fluttered gaily, birds warbled cheerfully all around.
In Mable's backyard I pilfered rhubarb stalks on which to dine.
Perhaps the sweetness of the rhubarb was acrid in reality, yet,
the peace I found eased my cares, and soothed my weary mind.

Melinda Arabie

LIFE

Life can be loving,
or it can be full of hate.
Life can be a world of hope,
or full of sorrow.
Life is a part of living,
it is also part of dying.
The world is upon us today,
but will it be tomorrow?
Life gives us the chance to live,
it also takes away lives.
Let life go on for others to come,
for me, it may not be.

Helen Banks

MY CHILDHOOD CRAZE

My childhood days was wildwood craze
Poor as could be, climbing every tree
Berries every place, dirty hands and face
Butterflies so pretty, catch one a duty
At the old fishing hole sticks for a pole
Caught with a wand frogs in a pond
Spearing in ice house, quiet as a mouse
Put meat on table, said prayers when able
Ice chests a must but ice blocks made rust
Before it was banned 500 quarts canned
Then many moves with coal and oil stoves
Saved every twig; helped butcher a pig
Simple games played happy hours made
Barefoot on hot days, caused wounds always
And the war time flu sure weakened us too
Diseases to fight meant doctors at night
Hot irons from stove ironed clothes that froze
Christmas meant new sleds, sleep in feather beds
Ice skates that clamp and falls to get damp
Very little light to study ar night.
House dances were fun when dating begun
Parents at doors to check our late hours
Most people were good stock with never a lock
If I could live o'er those hours I'd adore

Lilian L Atkins

THOUGHTS ABOUT LIFE, APRIL 1955

Moonlight and shadow
Sunshine and rain
Joy and contentment
Sorrow and pain
Jealousy and hatred
Laughter and tears
Love and affection
Combine our years.

Sleeping and waking
Giving and taking
Working and playing
Through every day
Waiting and watching
Talking and listening,
Despairing and yearning,
We go on our way.

Believing and trusting
Obeying and serving
Rebelling and longing, for what,
We can't say.

Hoping and fearing
Contriving and striving
Lying and cheating
And sometimes
We pray.

Peggy A Archer

THE HOUSE

A house stands empty—alone.
A house now empty—once a home.
Someone's drifting to and fro—
Wandering, no place to go.
Times are harder—dreams seem to falter.
And plans—they do alter.
A 'home' filled with laughter is the dream sought after.
Struggling thru the long, long day—
Then, at nightfall, someone prays—

"Oh, Lord above with endless love,
Give me one more day.
Please hear my plea, and you will see,
I'll surely find the way."

"Return me to 'the house' alone—
Return me to my blessed home.
I've wandered much too far—
Followed that elusive star."

"Return me to my home.
I've nowhere left to roam"

Craig Armstrong

FULL OF EMOTIONS OF WHICH I CAN NOT DESCRIBE

Full of emotions, of which I can
not describe.
Empty of emotions, of which I
feel I have never had.
I sit alone in a cold dark room
feeling alone and sad.
And lost in a life, that creates
these feelings, and then strips
them away.
My mind is full of nothing, and
my soul as empty as death.
And I feel as if I want to slip
away, and take my final breath.
My feelings rise and fall, as often
as the changing tide.
And I feel left out, with nothing,
and with no one with which to

confide.
And again just as always, these
emotions I must hide.

Steven Gregory Alston
CHILDREN OF PROMISE
Strange, when you look into their eyes and see them stare back at you,
What do you see? Children of promise
Innocent eyes stare back at you*—
with wonder, wonder of a new world
Unfolding swiftly—every minute, every hour, every day.
Children of promise
Strange, when you look into their eyes and see them stare back at you
What do you see? Children of promise

A promise stares back at you, a promise of growth, of learning, of seeing the world anew. Children of promise.
Strange, when you look into their eyes and see them stare back at you,
What do you see? Children of promise
Possibilities stare back at you—
possibilities of new discoveries, new ideas
New thoughts. Children of promise
Will that wonder cease? Will that promise die? Will those possibilities remain unfulfilled? Children of promise. It's up to you, it's up to me—it's up to us.

Mary Poston-Wolcott

Mary Poston-Wolcott
HAPPINESS
In our time, what is the price of happiness
an individual must pay,
In order to laugh and have the courage
to express what one wants to say?
To be able to develop the mind
and stand on your own two feet,
To juggle a career and care for the kids,
are demands not easy to meet.
To tell others, I need this time
alone, just for me
To make a journey by myself
upon the Creative Sea.
And to take the time to experience
the feel of a caring touch,
For some the cost of happiness
can never be too much!

Celia Bourque
GHOST-BUSTERS
My friends think I'm great,
They know little about me.
When I get mad I tear
everything
Apart, like houses, trees anything in
my way.
They call me "Hugo" the "Ghost-Buster"

Jacquelyn Coretta Robinson
ALL IN THE NAME OF LOVE
All in the name of love, I devote myself to you.
Along, with my complete love, may continuous exaltation in our lives always be.
May we continue to give ourself to God for the betterment of our future.
Let us not forget our short comings in the past, for they have made us stronger in our endeavor to make our love eternal, and forever shall it last.

All in the name of love, may we be showered with blessings from our All Mighty God. May He look upon us and continue to let our love reign as one, for in His eyes and His eyes only, in Holy Matrimony may He eternally keep us as one.

Anne Hazard
SILENT TEARS
A touch so gentle, with a light breeze;
A flow of emotions rustle like trees.
—sandy beaches,
—rough waves,
—silent tears . . .
Passing as the wind, it will never stay;
The untouched pieces of my heart begin to fray.
—deafening thunder,
—blinding lightning,
—silent tears . . .
Another fallen heart lay upon the world's floor;
From a love that couldn't make it to shore.
—starless nights,
—empty touches,
—silent tears . . .
Run on and on, like waves crashing into the sand;
A soft love, but through the storm it couldn't stand.
—silent tears,
for a love that will never die;
and can never be . . .

Anne Hazard
IN THE CORNER
Though I hear nothing, I can hear the cry;
The fear the child tries so hard to hide.
In the corner, the child is afraid to even blink;
All the poison he is taught to think.
He runs and runs, but he goes no where;
Always on a desperate search for someone to care.
He finds nothing, so he just gives in;
A child so helpless can never
win . . .
And we just close our eyes to the sin.
Do you ever hear the pain from someone next door;
Is the cry from a child, a sound you can ignore?
The children of tomorrow are dying today;
Because someone turned, and walked away . . .
The one who commits this brutal act, also needs a friend;
The child close to death; the abuser at ropes end.
He shivers with terror, as the fist approaches his face;
No blood; no bruises; no evidence; no case.

As the child grows, there is so much pain and anger inside;
Everything as a child, this man has learned to hide.
He has somehow survived the hell he went through;
But has he really gotten over, being brutally abused?
There is a little girl in the corner, surrounded by fear;
Living in terror, day after day, tear after tear.
She has no choice, but to just give in;
A child so helpless can never win:
and we just close our eyes to the sin . . .

Matthew Tracy Hallman
TRANSFORMATION

To Lori, because sometimes when we change we change back

Don't placate my best.
Don't get so close I lash out.
If this another dream,
they're just not as much an impact
when I have to change them.

A werewolf falls in love with a mermaid
Nothing existed between them anyway.
They used to pierce the moon where it reflected.
Night has a hectic nature, some think of sleep,
while the moon adds a glow to skin that
won't accept itself. It is nature's way to change
things about it, but nature won't change
as won't the moon.

And a werewolf falls in love
with a mermaid, sometimes very much
and sometimes the daylight brings
new occurrence that means nothing
to passion's seedlings.

Gabrielle M Irwin
OUR LOVE WAS ALWAYS STRONG—RIGHT OR WRONG.

To our Poopsie. Written from the heart by your wife, Pinky.

I'll Love You Forever, Jim Hear What I Say.
From Dusk Til Dawn, Every Single Day.
Words Of Kindness, If My Heart Would Fall . .
I Love You Entirely, Oh That Smile, The Best Of All.
Every New Day For Us, Thank-You For Every Hour & Minute.
My Love Reaches Out To Hold You . .
My Heart, To Bring You With In It.
Right Or Wrong, It Was Meant To Be, Always You & Me.
Whether, It Be Wrong, Or Right.
That's The Way, We Set Our Sight.
Right Or Wrong, We Chose Our Life.
Jim, I've Always Been Proud To Be Your Wife.
Because You Were My Mate, We Had A Daughter, Who's Great.
Count Them, All Your Kids, There Are Seven.
As Far As I'm Concerned, All Gifts From Heaven.
Not Knowing What Tomorrow May Bring, Even If I Plan.
But For Sure Jim, You'll Always Be My One And Only Man.
I Know You Told Me, Not To Be Sad.
But My Dear Jim, I'm Gonna Miss You So Bad.
As Time Passes On, And It's My Turn To Move Along.
You & I Will Be Together Again, Right Or Wrong.

Shayla Graff
RAPTURE OF LOVE

To Kyle, who gives me my support and inspiration.

Only a silent dream
Exploding
Into an intense, brightly colored
Reality.
Surrounding and
Overwhelming me.

Like the suddenness
Of a summer storm,
Taking me
Into a flight of passion,
Smothering me
In a flood of emotions,
Drowning me
In a sea of tears.

Laura M Lora
WINTER
There's a winter in my heart
even if the Spring is here,
there's a winter in my soul.

Since you went away
I have always cried
I have always wished,
you'd come back to me.

Let me kiss your lips,
let me feel you are mine,
and let me feel Spring
has come to my heart.

Carol Rizzo
CHRISTIAN

In memory of beloved Christian Balsamo Oct. 5, 1963-89. For Christian to the Balsamo family and anyone who's lost a loved one, memories of love and laughs will be with us forever.

Traffic jams, ruined shoes, wet socks some of the hassles of the rain,
God came upon you said this is not good enough for you and took away all your pain,

You came into my life so quickly left just as fast,
With you I only see my future never looked back on my past,

If only I hadn't met you I wouldn't be shedding these tears,
But if I hadn't met you I couldn't feel you, even now so near,

Fun and laughter, kindness, forgiveness too good for earth,
I know you earned your wings, my angel's flying high, not buried in that pile of dirt,

A lifetime of love rolled up into a month,

We had sincerity, love and caring,
I'm glad it was me who completed
your hunt,

No more pain, sorrow or suffering do
you feel now,
We'll be together again after I earn
my angel crown,

I will live for you for me and for our
son,
Give him a family maybe someday,
never forget you were the one,

The tears I shed are tears of sorrow
because you're no longer here,
Tears of joy, there is something better
after waiting, not to live in fear,

We're all born to live never live to
die,
Then die to live again in the eternal
sky,

No longer think of the rain as a hassle
of water slowing up traffic for at least
an hour,
But as my sweet Christian smiling,
saying I'm watching you stop
pouting it's only a shower,

Cheryl Lynn Stephens
THE TELEPHONE RING
Last night, as I lay slumbering
I thought I heard the telephone ring
Only once
Long, sweet, clear
Yet it hung there
In the air
And did not form
There was no sound
Only the deep longing
In my soul
To have him.

Mark E Smith
WHY NOT DREAM
They say dreams are foolish.
Oh how wrong they can be
Cause if you didn't dream
You would be like a blind
Sailor at sea.
Reality is harsh too harsh to see
When you dream you can be what-
ever you want to be.
A person who dowsn't dream is the
fool you see.
Because he is always trying to be
number one you see.
So keep on dreaming, cause dreams
are short you see.
You have you whole life to
live in reality.

Bonnie Thomas Turner
A CUDDLING DOWN

To my mother, Mildred Harter Thomas, against whose loving breast I lay. In life, she watched over me; in death she watches still . . .

There is love
in this cuddling
down of softness
a pink accepting
warm protecting
place for loving
your head into:
this pillow
of a mother's breast
for cuddling down.

Raoul Derek Smith
I SEE
Bush or tree or blade of grass,
Are differently seen by lad or lass,
Who look on them with eyes
that see
Only what they think should be!

One sees God in all his glory;
Another, a scientific story.
One sees beauty, one sees death,
Reasons height or fancies depth.

But I see life in time unending,
That is to human form attending!
A rabbit, bird or bumblebee,
It's home to them, and also me!

Rita J Wise
RECIPE FOR L-O-V-E !!
1—Cup of
Longevity
Ounces of passion, respect & care
Volumes & volumes of time-to-
share;
Eternal exciting moments,
. . . repeatedly MIXED, but
unmeasured.
—From the WISE Kitchen

Shirley Marrow

Shirley Marrow
INSPIRING

To my beloved mother, and three children may their dreams be inspired by mine.

Inspiring are our dreams.
Inspiring are our hopes.
Inspiring are the ones that past
beyond the ropes.
The ropes are very tight and the
binded is very strong.
But for the ones with inspiring
dreams
You'll have to carry on.

Ruth Anne Parker
GIVING IT ALL

To my Grandchildren Nick-D.W.—Oshun-Erik-Kimani & Ebonie

I gave you all the love that I had
And that was good and not bad
You took that love and twisted it
about
Which hurt me badly and made me
want to shout
I am a woman who is in love with her
man
But you are still looking all over this
land
For something or someone whom
you'll never find
Because you don't yet know that I'm
in your heart and in your mind

Tracy Leflar
RAIN
The rain has come again.
Others think it gloomy.
I think of it as a dear friend.
There is comfort in the washing
clean,
All the dusty earthly things.
My heart too needs this cleansing.
My tears fall in time,
As the raindrops,
Play an old love song,
On my mind.

Lori Elizabeth Love
SHADOWS
Lights thrown low,
promises made,
powerful.
Daylight breaks,
like promises,
powerless.

Mary C Bentley
THE CALENDAR ON THE WALL
I look at the calendar on the wall
And my hurried scrawl tells it all.
In the little square that says Tuesday
I have a luncheon date with Susie.
On Friday I guess I'm out for the day
With shopping to do and the bills to
pay.

And so page by page the year flips
by;
Grandma's birthday comes in July.
And for the Church supper Thursday
I must bake a cherry pie.
I could never keep my days in order
If it were not for my handy little
recorder—
The calendar on the kitchen wall!

Dorine Crosley
LONELINESS
What is loneliness?
Is it waiting under the sun,
Hoping that the someone will come?
Is it watching the birds fly South
In the mist of an autumn breeze?
But what is loneliness?
Is it the lonely heart:
Aching in pain?
Or, the single soul,
Holding on to its own?
No, loneliness is a world of its own!

Nancy Pauline Blake
SHE IS YOUR MOTHER.

To Pierce Blake, My Dear Husband.

When I first met her, She was nice.
Then I married you, and got to know
her more.
She was always there to greet you at
the door.
With a praise the Lord, How good to
see you,
do stay a while.

Then off to the kitchen she would
go.
She would begin to cook whatever
she had.
It would be just plain food, Maybe
only coffee and toast.
But served with generosity and love,
that meant the most.

You might see her in the yard,
among her flowers.
Or in the garden, applying to
everything her gentle touch.
These are the things she likes so
much.
For with them she would share.
With her loved ones, when they were
there.

She is our Mother.

Sue A Flynn
LIFE IN A BOTTLE
I drink to remember
I remember when I drink
Photographs of life race
through my mind

I drink when I'm happy
I drink to become happy
Days of my future slip
slowly past my eyes

I drink when I'm sad
I drink to cover sadness
Hiding in the bottom of
my glass from the world

I drink to be social
I'm social when I drink
My life is as transparent
as the liquid before me

I drink when I want
I want when I drink
Life is so meaningless
when I live in a glass bottle

Deidre Dickerson
SACRED SIN
Each time I think or our sacred
interlude, I Shiver
Remembering feeling your
touch, I Ache
With desire from an
overwhelming passion, I
Caressed
The very soul of you which made
no effort to Refrain
From the burning desire which
pulsated as we Entwined
Our bodies became one in this
sinful Delight
Expressing our innermost
feelings in which we Sinned
Will we be forgiven for lusting
Incessantly
Or will we be held accountable
due to Negligence?

Betty Kay Saffell McGarry
MAGNIFICENT SCENE
Early in the morning . . .
When the sun is coming up . . .
Sitting on my porch steps
With my coffee cup . . .
Gazing out across the lawn
Surveying every inch . . .
Breathing in the "beauty"
And to VISUALIZE! .
All the little things
Now "before" MY eyes . . .
Splotches of purple, and yellow
On a mantle of green . . .
The DANDELIONS, and VIOLETS
Are, the "MAGNIFICENT SCENE."

Joelle Leboa
WHO'S HERE?

With total love and appreciation to my daughter, Renee', whose love and encouragement helped me to believe in myself and to share my creativity.

Am I alone this time around?
You are a shadow, a memory.
Are you me, or someone I knew,
Another time, another galaxy?

You peek and hide, play and guide,
showing aspects of myself discorded.
Those of strength and joy and
decisions made with no thought.

A dancer, a player, one of creative endeavor and accomplished absurdity.
Outrageous behavior and solemn reflection of life and universes unseen.

Should I wander long in this playground of insane dimensions?
Were it not for a playmate of wisdom,
How would I know who I am?

Essie & Randy Bradford

Essie M Bradford
THE FALLEN FIREFIGHTER

In loving memory of our darling SON, "Randy," who lost his life in the line of duty, as A volunteer firefighter on May 17, 1986. A precious son, loving husband to his wife Cheryl. A devoted father to his two sons, Keith & Josh & baby girl Stephanie. Mike & Joey, (RANDY'S) two brothers shared a Special relationship.

The firebell rang.
Much noise was in the air.
In just A short while,
our hearts were filled with despair.

Most of the town was watching,
in shock and disbelief.
As the huge fire got out of hand,
friends and relatives were stricken with grief.

It's so very hard to console
little children of our land.
Many have never known death,
and find it hard to understand.

As many watched in sorrow,
hoping the fireman could survive.
A Celestial firetruck was sent.
We couldn't see when it arrived

The firefighter had shed the old firesuit,
and A clay vessel he wore.
The new firetruck was waiting
to usher him in the door.

"Well done, my faithful servant,
enter the joy of The Lord,"
Said the angel guarding the door,
as the fireman got on board.

This new firetruck was purest crystal,
decorated with precious stones.
The driver said, "welcome aboard,
we've come to take you home."

The firefighter was given an award.
Surprised, he looked down to see.
"Whatsoever is done to the least of these, is done unto me."

He then thought of his little children,
whom he had loved, SO MUCH!
And the many little problems
when they would need daddy's Special Touch.

With excitement, he thought of Heaven,
when he remembered what God had said,
"Of such is the Kingdom of Heaven."
as he touched a child on the head.

The Firefighter's attempt to put the fire out,
had not really failed at all!
The fireman was PROMOTED ;
he answered A greater call.

Katherine McManus
THE WATCH

To Ralph Nader in memory of my Soldier of Peace

He gave to me for you
before his going ever brave
this shining silver watch
more a century in age

Strength belies its pocket size
neither bold nor grand in sound
the sturdy timer small
is to carry far around

Have a care to wind it will you
away from wind and fire
then notice how persistent hands
guide every and each hour

Unknowing day from night
unseeing grief or tear
tiny lever set in motion moves
unceasing without fear

Patient and tenacious only
in all truth you find
until we are together
it simply tocks the time

Wanda La Rue
YOU
For you, my love,
Yours . . . I'll be
a matching dove
for you from me.

My love for you
runs very deep.
For when we said, "I do"
it was for keeps.

When I am with you
my dear sweet one,
I don't feel a tad bit blue,
For it's your heart I've won.

Yleana J Abello

Yleana J Abello
TOUCHED BY A RAY OF LIGHT

Dedicated to my son Jarrett and my nephews & nieces who inspired me.

Touched by a ray of light,
I enter within a threshold of
wholesome harvest feast.
A mid-November day, frosted windows,
crackling firewood, hurried paces,
smiling faces.
A spectral splendor, too glorious to behold,
richly blessed to satisfy the longings
of my soul.

And in May, the rivers swell subside
to unveil the fertile crown of glory.
Topped by flowering hillsides,
basking in the warm days light.
Feared lightning skies waken to
reveal a rainbow's delight.
A spectral splendor, too glorious to behold,
richly blessed to satisfy the longings
of my soul.

Peggy Sowell
SPRING
Awakening slowly,
opening drowsy eyes,
yawning and stretching,
coming out of a long winter's slumber,
pushing aside,
the blanket of sod,
slipping out,
first one,
then another,
and another.
Until finally
all petals are
swaying in the warmth
of the sun,
It's spring!

Altman Boone
IN A MIRROR AT FIFTY
Whose great pile of wonder are you looking at now?
The ones who made you in a lust-filled hour?
Where is the bud they once destined to flower—
Sweet rock-a-bye baby, gone from the bough?

Whose great pile of wonder are you looking at now?
The One who made you in a moment of truth?
Where is His semi-sweet glory of youth?
Forgot with a tear by the hand at the plow.

Whose great pile of wonder are you looking at now?
Your soul-mate's, aglow with her white knight's first gleaming
(Unaware that what's there is more in her dreaming;
Still waiting in the wings to share in the bow)?

Whose great pile of wonder are you looking at now?
Your offspring, the dear ones? The dear ones must wonder
If the glow goes away with the wind and the thunder,
'Cause the pedestal's vacant except for the Vow.

Linda I Blevins
JANUARY HIGH TIDE
I look out the window and there's the sea. Are you a dream come true, or the end of me? Somedays you are tranquil; somedays you're a beast. Is this my famine or is this my feast? You've come onto land since I've been here. Are you telling me to leave or do you just want me to fear the power of your waves as they beat the sand? Are you saying, "I have the upper hand?" Do you know that I love you, do you know that I care? I won't bother your dunes; I won't take more than my share. I will protect you til my dying day. You are in charge, please let me stay.

Sheila Bellefleur
THE SNOW QUEEN

I wish to dedicate this poem to my husband . . . who makes all my dreams come true.

It is the Snowflakes Dance.
From the top of the steeple,
to the heaven-sent below
Observe, as they circle and frolic
to the chimes of the hour.

A rose petal is dipped in a crystalline stream
from the sunshine's fragrant light.

A lovelight so pure in the eyes that behold;
it captivates the beauty and tranquility
portrayed in pearlescent form of sweet repose.

Within the midst of the illuminated path,
A fair princess proceeds with gliding steps
to her awaiting magical dream.

A dream she clutches onto, full of promise and truth,
The promise that will unlock her heart with a golden key.

Satin and Pearls;

Doves and White Gloves,

Love and Honor,

Faith and Happiness

. . . A Bride is to Begin.

Harriet (Shove) Bedard
I HAD A DREAM
When the World of Poetry
Convention is held each year
I always wish I could attend
I fantasize how it would be
Receiving my 'Golden Poet Award'
for my poetry
Four years ago   I had a dream
That I was there—serving everyone
coffee and cake
So disappointed   when I did awake
This summer I traveled to Sacramento via Greyhound
Our son paid my fare—so I could go there
To get 3 grandchildren—before we
had to be homeward bound
My young cousin from Placerville
came—escorted me around
She and I spent the day in Old
Sacramento
Highlight—we went to visit at

'World of Poetry'
I took along a cake (with special decor) The staff made coffee
I didn't make the Convention—part of my dream came true
I met and visited with everyone—but Eddie-Lou Cole
What a reception from John Campbell and all the others
Be in my 'memory bank' forever
Have pictures taken that day to treasure
Record album from John Campbell—I keep on display
Hebrews 6:12 "Through faith and patience inherit the promises"
Some of my dream came true—it is still my intention
To some day—attend a World of Poetry Convention . . . . .

Sylvie Sonia LaFond

Sylvie Sonia LaFond
LAST PERFORMANCE

To lovers of poetical art don't ever give up your inner beliefs, goals and dreams; Should doubt prevail, hold forever the knowledge deep within that somewhere, sometime . . . it will be yours

Facing the rich emerald curtain,
the crowd in tuxedo, awaits
anxious, curious, demanding,
impatience boiling by the
unexpected delay
Oblivious to the cruel drama that
unfolds behind the scene . . . .
Tears glistened on the actress'
face, leaving smudges of
make-up.
The face artist, called upon
hastily, curses under his breath,
indignant to reshape his art
work, his masterpiece . . .
So engrossed in his self esteem . . he
remains steadfast, unaware,
uncaring . . .
A brief phone call an hour
ago . . . few words said
hastily . . . the ironic jolt
the impact of measured words,
staccato . . .
The better part of herself slashed
without mercy: "A freak
accident"
Brief notes to remember: "She
did not suffer . . . died on
impact, details following . . .
yes . . . positive identification
made" . . .
Last words suspended in airless
space, bridge to a stormy night.
Steel halo encircling her mind,
leaded pain tearing the marrow
of the soul,
Thoughts waltzing away . . . this
solo concert ultimately will be
for Chris . . .
Artist, she is the core, she must
perform . . a m u s t, amidst
tragedy.
Her love has gone beyond
unreachable spaces of clawing
and cries
Life is not fully hers yet, part
belongs to those who created
her,
A cheering and demanding crowd
who gave her career and lover
to cherish . . .
Remembering happy times, she
sheds away the pangs of hurt,
Inhales deeply . . . tearing the
webbed unfairness . . . Yes they
will see her, all of her
the best that can ever be given.

From the orchestra the first bars
of music calls her . . . Sudden
hushes precedes her entrance . . .
True to her art, she stepped in
front of the lights, smile grafted,
not seeing
She sang to them, with her lover's
memories, giving the best
performance ever.
The grief, the passion, the deepest
pain, the greatest joy, all
exploited!
For that night was her last
performance . . . she gave her
audience the most and purest
naked emotions an artist can
provide . . . and they took it all,

Not knowing!

Brian Brockway
THE VIRTUOUS TEACHER
His honor, sacred, in showing his all,
Given with truth so he never shall fall
Loyalty shall show, for a person like this
Shall always have compassion when something's amiss.
A courage shown within his heart
That keeps him moving like a dart
To give service to others, rendered with cheer,
Moving him skyward from year to year.
These four virtues interact with each other,
And form a greater virtue that one shares with another.
A virtue whose strength is found through friends
With a happiness that grows, yet never ends.
This virtue, given from God above,
Shown from one to another known as love.
A challenge to those who wish to succeed:
Never let thy hearts be filled with greed:
Follow these virtues, and learn to care
For others as yourself, without fear to share.
Do this, and happiness you shall find,
As happiness is learned only by being kind.

Paulette Bray-Fontaine
YOURS TRULY
When the rains come and bring the cold,
My mind strays and the patterns unfold.
Times to remember, times to forget.
Moments of elation, calls for celebration.
A handful of true friends, countless acquaintances.
Youth offered a shelter, a built-in excuse.
Lessons learned the hard way, stains of self-abuse.
Lovers only I could justify, now seem unimportant.
Still, given the chance to rectify
I wouldn't, and I know it.
Yes, I've felt pain, but I remain, alive and well,
Yours truly.

Paula Petra Bramble
NONSENSE
I went to the cinema tomorrow
And took a front seat in the back;
I beg a guy for some peanuts
Ate it and gave it back.

I fell from pit to box
And broke a front bone in my back
I called for a taxi and walked home
And that's why I'll never come
back.

Larry C Bork
WHEN LOVERS MEET
Moonlite shining on the beach
The water's edge within our reach
Seashells found along the land
As we stroll there hand in hand

A seagull swooping toward the ground
As if to say our love he'd found
Your eyes and my eyes quickly meet
And our two hearts skip a beat

The whiteness of the driftwood bare
A lovers' sweet kiss stolen there
The pounding surf on distant shore
Our arms entwined forever more

And when this world we leave behind
Etched there in the sands of time
Will be two names, yours and mine
Two names of lovers, yours and mine

Stanley W Bori Jr
DAISY DAPPLE DEW
A daisy, sprig twisted upturned flute
Lively honey bee buzzed to nestle this shoot
To seek sweet nectar for sumptuous reward
Flight'd away to his hive to hoard
Light'd with sunshine, oh dapple this sprig
In such a heavenly garden should we dig
To plant a seed for all to seek
Nary a home for just the meek
Oh fluted horn dripping with dew
So covetous am I to hew down a few
To garner this treasure unto my own
Kept secret forever, its blessed favor unknown
This world's wonder, privy I share with you
Majestic creation, oh daisy dapple dew.

Cherry R Burns
HEAR THIS GOD, A PRAYER TO YOU
Hear this God, a prayer to you
To thank you for the things you do
For the rainbow in the sky
For the trees that grow so high
For the teddy with whom I sleep
For sweet memories that we keep
For the bunnies in the grass
For the milk that's in my glass
For the stars and for the moon
For the birthday I'll have soon
Thank you God for all your sharing
And for all the love and caring . . .

Thank you.

Amen . . .

Phyllis J Cardassi
PEACEFUL FLIGHT
Birds of fire with wings gliding slowly into the dusk.
The sunset's glare leaves them with tones of rust.
Their wings seem ignited to the sky to acknowledge their magnificence as they fly high.
When bearing downward to kiss the ocean's tides, the seagull's body straightens up as it slowly glides.
The playground that surrounds their world is a boundary of heavens, that God kept unspoiled.
The innocence of the birds passing overhead, watching them land for that one piece of bread.
Never really knowing how lucky they are being free, even with the beauty of their existence just perched up on a tree.
Flying high gracefully gliding into their flight. Some are singing softly so sweetly onto night.

Christopher C Miller

Christopher C Miller
TRAVELING THROUGH SPACE
Traveling through space, with no-where to go, my euphoric spirit freely flows,

I inner a dimension, that has slowly past through, I get a vista of me and you,

Yes I see our love, when it was so true, plus all the pains I put you through,

Now I see, why our love faded away, I still feel the melancholy, to this very day,

What I would give, if our love could be anew, I'd hold you forever and always be true.

Moneva Canada-Byrd
A FISHERMAN'S STORY
I was riding down the river
In a little ole canoe
And I heard a gentle voice
Saying how do you do?
Then I looked around
And to my great surprise
I saw this gorgeous mermaid
Right before my eyes.

I sat there so startled
Not knowing what to say
Then she said I'm Mary
And this is my lucky day,
It seems like a life time
That I've been watching you
Riding on the river
In your little ole canoe.

I just had to meet you
And tell you how I feel

Darling I'm in love with you
And I know that it's real,
But our lives are different
And I could never be with you
So I'll watch you on this river
Riding in your ole canoe.

This story may seem funny
And I'm sure you don't believe
You probably think I'm lying
Or that I'm trying to deceive
But let me tell you fishermen
I'm sure not fooling you
Just ride down the river
In your little ole canoe.

Nelson Camacho
SPARKLING CRYSTALS
Deep beneath thy heart lies there a cave,
within the caves of darkness sparkling so.
In a dim light as the sunlight above,
shining soft and beautiful with such a glow.
Filled with warm feelings of joy and caring,
from within as a feeling of love so true.
where roses and flowers truly bloom,
as the soft hearted spring time blue.
so is that love within my heart,
as sparkling crystals vividly sparkles as a rainbow.
Yet lost as so an island out at sea,
is my heart's love that will but only grow.
so as sparkling daisies and as so sparkling crystals,
shining bright as but only two bright lovers.
within thy heart all around but one's self,
sparkling so as crystals of vivid colors.
A place of tranquility peace of mind,
sparkling within my heart hotter than coal.
A cave sparkling with crystals of fire,
as a star shining thru my very soul.

Christina H Carpenter
CHRISTMAS IS
Christmas is a time when love
and happiness fill the air
Christmas is a time for sharing
Christmas is a time for caring
Christmas is a time when dreams
become reality
Christmas is a time to wish a
friend Merry Christmas
Christmas is all these things and
much more
So instead of just wishing you
Merry Christmas, my wish for
you this holiday season is that
your life may be filled with love
and happiness, as well as with
special memories of sharing and
caring
But most of all, my wish for you
this holiday season and always
is that you will never stop
believing in yourself or in your
dreams
For as long as you continue to
believe in yourself and in your
dreams, having your every
dream become reality will never
be impossible

C Mindy Brown
TO DADDY . . .
I feel you slipping through my fingers
like sand through a fine sifter.
I reach out to grab you
and my hands close on nothing.
I look for you near me.
My eyes see empty spaces
where you used to be.
My life feels empty, incomplete,
As a puzzle missing a piece.
I wait in vain for you to return—
for you to love me again—
to feel the warmth in my heart
Which has collapsed from the strain
Of reaching out to you.

Arlena Faye Aborn

Arlena Faye Aborn
THE PICTURE PUZZLE
The pieces are all different forms,
short ones, tall ones, little ones, too.
Blue, green, red, violet and yellow/orange,
Comers, goers, doers and setters, one is you.

Humbleness is virtue, boastfulness is proud,
takers take all, givers seem very small.
Remember, any one of these gets lost in a crowd,
never judge a book by its cover,
take Ole King Saul.

Colors blend in, voices will descend,
Time will take its toll, thanks for being a friend.

Life comes and goes, Eternity will claim thee,
the piece you are will be special
for all to see.

Talents, assets, and treasures make a pretty sight.
Each and every person sees us
all in complete light.

The pattern of each one's life will always be
a mystery of lines and curves,
handed down thru family trees.

The Almighty had a plan for each one of us
Hoping, sharing and trusting is
an absolute must.

Take the hour glass, turn it around and around.
Life, love and happiness keep us
firmly on the ground.

Pain and suffering, loving and
forgiving, is the story of living.

Jewell Greene Cooper
THE STATUE OF LIBERTY
There's a lady in the harbor—upon her head a crown,
Its huge spikes are like sun-rays, shining on the ground,
She wears it so very proudly—for all the world to see,
Projecting truth and light and freedom all for you and me.
She's a symbol of our country, a gift to the U.S.A.
At night she's a lighthouse—to show everyone the right way,
She has a torch in hand to guide the planes and the ships at sea,
And a beacon gives a signal if there's danger around, you see.

The lady in the harbor stands brave, straight and tall,
She gives us faith and courage, to stand up if we should fall,
She's there to guide and protect us, with her care and veracity,
She's the queen of our country, she's the Statue Of Liberty.

She's never spoken one single word, but she has said it all,
By shining light for all the world, she's at our beck and call,
The broken shackle around her leg is the symbol of liberty,
We're free to live and love and worship—where we choose to be.

If you're a stranger in our country and you feel so all alone,
See the lady in the harbor, she'll make you feel at home,
You're sure to find love and protection where everyone is free,
You've found a symbol of our country, she's the Statue Of Liberty.

Debby K Combs
LIFE FOR TWO
You've started a new life
In the beginning you were half
Joined together now you are ONE
Hand in hand you've opened a new gate
Choose the Path you wish to follow
Make of it a Garden
Pick only the Roses
The thorns can be broken
If scratched during the gathering
Remember Time will heal
Share with one another
Make your bouquet the fullest
Let your dreams come true
Most of all express your feelings
By saying I Love You

Diana Montgomery Clouse
DEATH OF A DREAM
What started out a lovely plan,
Like a flower, faded too soon.
The bud slowly withered away,
Long before it could ever bloom.

Did we fail in nurturing it,
When it was but a tender shoot?
Or did the winds of time prevail,
Preventing it from taking root?

Now with feelings of helplessness,
My soul within longing to scream;
We sit in silent agony,
As we watch the death of a dream.

Allan J De Fiori Litt B
FERNET-BRANCA

World-famous Italian bitters—since 1845

Fernet Branca is an excellent,
bitter tonic for the anemic soul.
It can be used daily or weekly
mixed in coffee, cocoa or other
black beverages.
Unique liquid blend. Fine
product.
Fernet Branca is remarkably suitable
in daily use, it resembles:
Ferro-China Bisleri, Commom,
wonderful Italian tonic for
every adult person, family and
friends.
It is made of rare, curative,
medicinal herbs. But Fernet Branca,
Sold inexpensively in all Italian
grocery stores.
It does good to your health. It
restores & calms your vital
energies through life.
Fernet Branca It benefits also
your liver . . .
In amaritudine magna est
fides. In amaritudine
fermentum fidei.
Ora et labora. ———
Sane et guberna. ******

Mary L Cisko
LIFE'S SPAN
Part her, Part him—yet self-unique.
Into life we're born, 'til death we seek
To assemble, know and understand,
Part her, Part him—Child, woman, man.

At times we grow, sometimes regress
While scavenging for happiness.
Plateaus of thought we often reach
To look beyond—another peak.

Friend and foe our ladders build
To aid our climb of each new hill.
'Til by and by we backward look
To find we failed to fill each nook.

Richard M Haynes
BEAUTY OF A LADY

To My Love, Sweet Diane

She is of A Summer breeze,
Gentle and warm;
She is of A flowered meadow,
Charismatic in essence;
She is of the flighted one,
Freely spirited;
She is of the beast,
Acutely lion-hearted;
She is of the small furry one,
Caressing the Earth with every step;

She is of the mountain,
Majestic in beauty;
She is of the clouds,
At times untouchable;
But when embraced,
Catapults man to wuthering heights
Most of all,
Rich in Divine Power

The Loving One

Romola Payne Davis
THOUGHTS FOR TODAY
If I can find one word to say
To help someone thru a very bad day
Or if I can find one note to sing
And to someone else some happiness bring

Then I will have found some reason to stay
And travel down life's pathway for another day.
If I can bring a smile to someone's sad face
and do it with compassion and grace
Then I will have made this day worthwhile
and be ready to travel on another mile.
If I can hear children laughing at play
I'll make it thru another day
And if I can laugh even tho I sometimes cry
Then this life will never pass me by.

Dion Nolan Cruse
TEN MINUTES FROM WORK

The morning is brisk—
And hangs before me—
Will-o'-the-wisp,
Expelled rhythmically
In my morning routine,
Of walking with the sun in my face
Heading east;
Along the tracks—where those dinosaurs roll,
Among scrub pine—and past a squirrel's abode,
There on the left
A graveyard bereft,
Those who enter
Go to forgive, forget or regret
Or to relive
Moments joyous, moments sad
Remem'bring all of them—good and bad,
Depositing deep, those moving memories—
In the bosom of the mind,
Fore'er to keep;
I continue my walk since it's almost eight—
And it's too fine a day, for me to be late.

Deborah Fenter-Reedy

Deborah Fenter-Reedy
WHO AM I?

To my Godly husbandman, who treats me as the woman of my poem, and to all God's women who should accept no less.

Who am I?
I am a queen of all races
Born of God on this earth
And given the deed of filling many places
Who am I?
I am the mother of all children be they young or old
For always are we growing and need much to be told
Who am I?
I am woman
Within, without
And though I never utter a word
My feminine presence gives a shout!
Who am I?
I am my God Father's love
Whose love covers all others
For it's pure, forever, and from Heaven above
Who am I?
Not all that I am or shall be
For when He shall come I will be as He
God's woman I am, and ever must be
For I am destined to live eternally

Kenneth Davis
FINE LOVE

Try love, my love
Buy love, my love.
But die love, my love.

Why, love, is my love
confined love, my love?
Blind love, this is my love.

My love dies, love;
so why, love, don't I love
In thy love?—fine love

Oh to find love, thy love.
Shining love is thy love.
So fine love is thy love.

Dorothy Davis
WEATHER

The dust . . .
The rain . . .
The wind . . .
All mixed in one.

Bert Rutledge
HELP THIS, THY CHILD, TODAY

Oh Lord! In this Thy child's darkest hour,
Help her keep her faith steadfast in Thee:
And keep her forever in Thy holy power,
And ease her heart from its despair and misery.

In this, Thy child's hour of deep felt sorrow,
Show now unto her Thy sweet holy face:
And let her not face alone a sad tomorrow,
But keep her in Thy tender embrace.

Help her now, dear God, I humbly pray,
To keep her eyes always turned up toward Thee:
And her trust always in Thee, let it not stray,
This I ask from my heart, Lord, as You can see.

Please help her find all of the answers,
To each and every question that she'll surely ask:
Let her know that You love and are still beside her,
Today and forever, just like You have been in the past.

Glenn B Petitt
THE BERRY PATCH

A berry patch has lots of peace
Though your pants will lose their crease
While you're crawling thru the weeds
Your thoughts are far from daily needs
You're conscious of the sky and sun
It isn't work it's really fun
There's no radio blaring loud
And you're not jostled by a crowd
A horse fly lights upon your arm
He doesn't mean you any harm
A distant cow calls for her young
Sweeter music is rarely sung
The hawks asoaring in the sky
With their plaintive little cry
The sun will bake you to a turn
But you'll never even yearn
For the things you left at home
When you started out to roam
Instead of doing a lot of kicking
Let's just go out berry picking

Susannah E Feldman
LITTLE BIT FARAWAY

To my Mother: Who, as a young bride, homesteaded in the Australian bush.

A homestead nestles on an inland slope, whose hearth-slab heard the pioneer's hopes;
A "damper" bakes in the fire glow and a settler asks naught but a "fair go."
There's a white frost thick on the slip-rails and at dawn the mists rise tall,
Creating blurred images in the grasslands—like tapestries on a cathedral wall.

Then mountains merge with rolling hills—the rolling hills join plains,
Then the green plains kiss the brown expanse and the roadway meets the trail.
The trail then narrows to a winding track in the mallee thick of the great outback.

Across the Darling, westward bound with the gulli maya brimming
A free soul in an ancient land seeking some identity with the beginning.

A landscape dry and cracked by age belittles the setting of any stage;
Beautiful murals of nature's toll—of red and grey eroded soil.
Inhabited by those of an unknown source, all embraced by the Southern Cross.

Here is the land of the digeridoo, the nullanulla, the woomera, and the boomerang too;
Ant-hill and yacca, the terrain they dot—this is the Bushman's Camelot.

There's a shanty true and humble in a clearing on the rise,
In converse with the landscape and in harmony with the skies;
To gaze in fascination ne'er wanting to depart,
This simple scene—encroaching on the memory and entwining round the heart.

"Little bit faraway" in mulga country the spinafex keeps the "she-oak" company,
Of desolate places, they comrades be, sharing their lonely enchanted dynasty.

A "willy-willy goes walkabout "beyond the old black stump,"
The sun sinks low in an amber cameo—and the sigh of a unique land echoes . . . echoes . . .

Night winds blow cold on the desert's face, a million sand pebbles move—and erase
The strange mirages which during the day, beckons many a soul into harm's way.

Then back O'beyond in a purple haze lies "the heart" in the sun's hot blaze—
Then stranger beware, do take God's hand, because this, is the Never-Never Land.

Geneva M Allcock
THANK THEE LORD EVERY DAY

Stars shining on my window pane
Wind swept down on falling rain
A mocking bird trills a beautiful song
To greet the bright new day
And flowers that brighten
Our lives along the way
These are things for which we say
Thank Thee Lord every day.

Crocus peeping up through
New fallen snow
Sunshine's bright gleam
Making all the icicles glow
Sleigh bells all a jingle
And cheeks rosy red
We see God's touch
In all we love and know
And for these things we say
Thank Thee Lord every day

In the spring the children
All laugh and play
And enjoy the sunshine
And a new spring day
Birds sing and build their nests
With these many things
We are so richly blessed
In the cooling breeze
Graceful trees blow and sway
For all these things we say
Thank Thee Lord every day.

Sherri Veen
ACCEPTANCE

As I gaze across the way
I see an old woman sitting in the sun,
rocking patiently, a shawl across her shoulders
as if to ward off an imaginary chill.

As she slowly rocks back and forth,
her face goes through many expressions:
A tender smile first, then a frown.
What is she thinking of?

Is she remembering her children? Her lovers?
Is she thinking of the love and caring she has
given that never seemed to be enough?
Or of the beauty she has experienced in her life?

Is she remembering the struggles for independence,
fought so long ago, which are forgotten by all but she,
the price she has paid for them?

I admire her, and wish I too could live such a
full life. She looks familiar. I look closer, and as I see my reflection in the window
I realize—she is me.

Michael T Barrett
WHAT I AM

To all my friends who had faith in me, and to God, in whom I have faith.

I was born, and I will die,
I've never been stoned, and I'll never get high.
I might be rich, in monetary ways,
I may be poor, not eating for days.
I might be a sportsman, who loves contact games,
I may be a nerd, who never forgets names.
I might be a magician, who performs many tricks,
I may be a professor, with a studying fix.
I might be a scientist, who loves to do tests,

I may be an exterminator, looking for pests.
I might be a cop, working my beat,
I may be a butcher, cutting up meat.

I might be a pastor, spreading the Word,
I may be a shepherd, overlooking my herd.
I might be a clerk, with letters to type,
I may be a reporter, looking for hype.
I might be a bus driver, praying to Heaven,
I may be a crapster, waiting for seven.
I might be a fireman, saving a life,
I may be an antagonist, causing a strife.
I might be an astronaut, living in space,
I may be a surgeon, saving a face.
I might be a biologist, studying mice,
I may be a millionaire, wouldn't that be nice.
I might be a driver, with deliveries to make,
But I tell you what, I am no flake.
And I might be a hunk, with a great looking bod,
But what I am is a Christian, with a kind, loving God.

Alexander Painter
TO SONNY
There is a bond between men in combat.
And this I will explain.
It is because we climbed the mountain,
And endured much pain.
I can not begin to tell you of the Sorrow and of doubt;
But if you never climbed the mountain,
The pain you can live with out.

Bonnie Fritchey
TILL DARKNESS FALLS
A friend is someone to whom we show respect and affection
When things go wrong they point you in the right direction
They are by your side and in your heart
A warm sensation that feels right, from the start

Beware of the ones who seem quite envious
These are the ones who are most often devious
They smile to your face but true kindness they lack
When you are out of sight they will stab you in the back

In friendships I have been lucky, with the exception of two
One everybody knows, could the other one be you?
Do not use your tongue as a sword on a friend
With the two-edged sword it may be you, in the end

A true friend is precious much like gold
It matters not whether young or old
Hold on to what is special and unique
It is of you my dear friend to whom I speak

That all of mankind may one day shake hands, I pray
In His plan for the world, is this not His way?
As the light shines on us from the One who bestows
Till darkness falls may all friendships grow.

Ramona L Thompson
THE BIG BANDS KEEP CALLING ME
In my dreams, I can still see myself Dancing, to the tunes of World War Two

So many different faces from all over the States, loving arms to hold you.

When I would dance with each one, I thought I was a movie star, I was only 13 years old.

Saturday was the night to look pretty as I could, Mom would take me, an army Band would play.

One night, I got up and my voice everyone loved, they wanted me to sing in the Band, when the war was over.

I was too young Mom said "to this day how I wish I would have let you, me too, I think about it so much, maybe I could have been on T.V. cover.

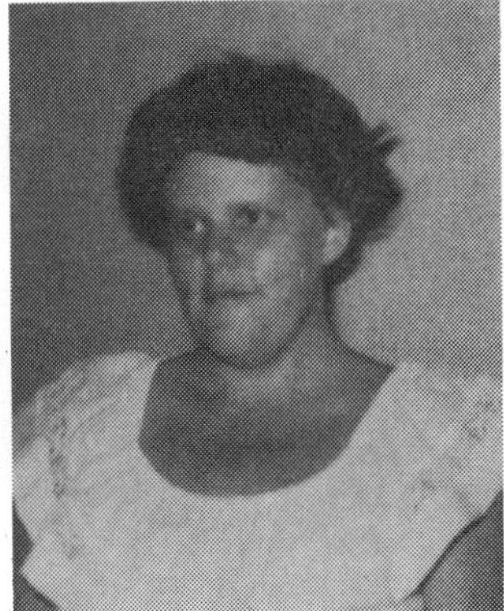

Candy L Fish

Candy L Fish
MISSING CHILDREN

I Dedicate This Poem To My Loving Husband, Daniel Fish The Only One Who Inspired Me To Continue To Write And Submit My Poems. "I Love You Dear."

Listen everyone to what
I have to say
I think it's time we all
get together and pray
To pray for the children
who are missing
every day
We all need to show them
that we care
Show them that we
care for the
families
Who have children
no longer there

It's hard for some to
realize
What those families go
through from day
to day
All that I'm asking is for
everyone to do
their part
To help bring a
child back
Back home where they
belong.

Matthew P India
THE REALM OF LIGHT
And the dead pass forth screaming into the spectral light. I follow.
Movement so cool, so slightly constant. I move unhindered now.

The light approaches! I am in essence reborn,
Where verdant pastures and valleys of Eden once more proliferate abundantly.
Likewise, Eden travels within the realm of light. Image to conscience be sworn.

Here, destiny unfolds to proclaim a blessed sanction upon sacred birth rites
As a nation emerges through the eye of eternity.

I see ancient forefathers who once existed, ever so concealed from mortal limits.
How they glide through the universe, these harbingers of hallowed secrets.

I accompany this procession with the archangel, masculine entity of a feminine breed. Whereupon his sword pierces the heavenly pitch, more brilliant lights I have never seen.

My feelings are individual, yet universal. My soul is one, yet so many.
Into the procession lean.

We are joined with all who once endured, spirits of the universe.
Embraced are we by this spectacled light, its burning caress sanctifies the soul. We are uplifted through the light. Ascending, we disperse.

Gateways to infinity are instantly displayed! Nations! Galaxies! All travelers!
Their purpose is fulfilled. Hurtling forward, the prophet's message heard.

I will awaken, as an infant does. Untamed.

Life renewed, I sleep in the warm waters of humanity, waiting to be named.

Melissa Ann Hill
MY LIFE FOR THE ETERNAL
As I awoke,
The bright sun shown down on my arms.
The wind blew through my hair, and
I thought it was going to be another hot, boring, lonely day.

Then a sharp pain went through my body as axes chopped at my feet.
What were they doing?
Were they going to burn me like they had done to so many of my friends?

I kept telling them they were hurting me,
but they didn't stop chopping at my body.
Oh, the pain I took,
until I finally gave up and fell
to the ground.

Then I heard the people talking;
saying something about Jesus,
King of the Jews.
The murderers were saying that it should be good enough
for the murder of the "King."

I have heard of Him; He walked by me
One day talking with some men He called the Disciples,
But murder, why murder Jesus?
He only wanted to help and do good things for all people.

The men started walking, carrying me with them. Where was I going?
When they stopped walking, Jesus started carrying me.
Where was He taking me?

After a long walk and changing of hands, they gave me a rest and laid me on the ground.
But I didn't get to rest very long, because after they laid me on the ground, Jesus laid on top of me.

More pain shot through my body, not only mine, but also Jesus' They nailed Him to me and then stood us up.
Didn't they know that it was hurting me and Jesus?

I guess not, because after they stood us up, they laughed at us and left us to die, both of us.

Before we passed on and while Jesus was talking to the thieves, I realized that my life, even though not as important, was also taken for the eternal life of others.

Evelyn Hill Huntsberger
FALLEN GIANT
Your solid strength misled me.
Had I known how fragile were the roots
that held your sturdy body in its place,
I would have been more apprehensive;
taken more pains to bolster your foundations;
piled rocks head-high at cost to nails
and hands and body;
done anything to keep the implacable current,
the rising waters,
from wresting you from your place.

Your age and girth had little to do
with the joy you've brought so
many,

for so many years.
The sweet sap of life, rising irresistibly,
had brought bounty not
measured by ear or eye,
but by an inner sense of earthy good.

How could we guess the devastation
would be so complete, so
overwhelming?
How could we know the vacant space
where you had stood
would be so wide,
so arid,
so bereft?

Elizabeth Mae Crowelle
LITTLE HANDS
These Little Hands
So very small . . . .
They are mine until I
Grow big and strong . . . .
These Little Hands
Are mine for now . . . .
They are precious to
Me from above . . . .
Because they are
The Little Hands . . . .
God gave to me . . . .
To go with my love. AMEN. . . .

Florence Ruth Cole
AIN'T IT HELL? ON QUITTING SMOKING AND GETTING OLD
We lose our youth, our looks and our hair
Get used to dentures and try not to despair
But the final indignity—we can't even eat
Anything but plain vegetables and a little lean meat.

No salt for Albert, no sugar for Fran
I should shudder as I study my diet plan.
No sugar—no carbohydrates—no fat.
Just one cigarette and I could stand all that.

I chew gum. I knit. I crochet like mad.
The gum sticks to my teeth and the stitches are bad,
But when I think of how healthy I'll be.
I'm a slave no more—at last I'm free.

Don't have to have matches and cigs in my bag
Nothing to smoke. Oh what a drag!
My purse used to be loaded with all kinds of pills
Now I just carry valium for my anxiety ills—
No indigestion anymore—nothing to get heartburn for.

My breath is sweet, no tobacco smell.
As I said before, ain't it hell?
Oh I'm a changed old gal, that's for sure
I can hardly stand being so goddamned pure!

Tina A Johnson
COULD IT BE

Could It Be is dedicated to anyone out there who was hurt by their first love.

Could it be,
That sometimes you think of me.
Does our love we had ever cross your mind?
Could it be you forgot all about our time?
Do you remember our first date?
I still say we met by hands of fate.
Could it be you remember our first kiss?
And that beautiful night of bliss!
Yes I remember wearing your ring.
Yet when we broke-up I had to return everything.
But it's so hard to return a heart broke in two!
Could it be that didn't even bother you?
Could it be you remember I had to go away?
Funny even then I thought you'd beg me to stay.
Could it be you never cared how you almost destroyed me?
Could it be you just couldn't see?
But here I am much stronger now.
I have made it through the hurt somehow!
Could it be you sometimes go back to the past?
Well take a good look back there, to see the scars that forever will last!!
Yes you take a good look at me.
Then leave it alone; just let it be.

Shane

Lane Thomas
ODE TO A COMPANION
Some people would say to me "He's just a dog, you're too close."
But those who knew Shane knew different.
For he would sit close to you when you were sad as to say
"It's okay I'm here with you."
For he would smile always and look right into your eyes.
He had the spirit of a child and was willing to play at any time.
He would want you to hug him and give him lots of love.
He would talk to you when he wanted anything.
He would follow, to let you know you weren't alone.
So I say to you who thought of him as,
"Just A Dog!"
You never knew Shane.
You missed out on a lifetime full of pure love.
For he had only goodness in his soul.
Shane made you love him in the short time you knew him.
He will always be more than "Just A Dog."
He was my friend and will always be my friend.
If only now in the depths of my heart.
For there never will be another friend like him.
And I will always love and miss him.
For he's not "Just A Dog." He was part of my life.

Barbara Jones Flug
THE MOTHER'S LIFE OF HAPPINESS BEGINS WITH THE FIRST
The mother's life of happiness begins with the first cry and laughter of her child.

With each step and each spill, there grows the spark of pride which will never wither.

The secrets given and good night wishes are tucked away and never forgotten.

The bond of love grows with each moment of each day.
This love is like a star, it shines for everyone to see.

And then it's like autumn, the sun doesn't shine nor the bird sing.

There is no sound of children playing, and the emptiness of the spark of laughter.

Yes, there is the silver tear that never sheds the eye.
And the yearn to hear once more the child's voice is endless. As are the waves that come into shore.

But with each passing day of life, the fond memories are relived, and never fade, even though the child is beyond her touch.

One's love can never be measured or begotten.

Jill Evans
MY SHOES
Oh my shoes, my shoes, my shoes,
Oh how I need new shoes,
the ones upon my feet,
just aren't neat,
that's why I can't BARE to leave,
them on my feet!

Clinton Lee Eisworth
ARMAGEDDON
Amber age receding
empty ear proceeding
Remissible silence
explosive violence
Malaise is abounding
blasphemy resounding
Almighty reverence
shall not be recompense
Gone past salvation day
forgotten passion play
Eternity won't come
until there's martyrdom
Delirium tremens
apocalyptic cleanse
Dubiously benumb
even though most succumb
Only ye who transcends
shall receive the amends
Never again to stray
ever knowing alway

Regina Deutschman
NO SEPARATION
We think that we are separate
From the Spirit of our birth;
We forget we must remember,
In our journey while on earth.

Remember to commune with It,
To always be aware;
For It is ever part of us—
And gives us loving care.

We must constantly remind ourselves
To seek the higher will;
To listen to the still, small voice—
And remember, "Peace, be still."

If we will only seek It,
Then we shall surely find
That It has never left us—
It is with us all the time.

Sally Ann Beaudo
THE CHILDREN
Look into the children's eyes,
see their pleas, their silent cries.
Crying out for love and shelter,
hoping someday they'll have a home.

Living out of cardboard boxes,
not knowing where their future leads.
But, only knowing insecurity,
for they have no one they can trust.

Carrying their possessions on their backs,
they move from place to place and happiness they truly lack.
Dreaming of a backyard swing,
or even the security of a warm classroom.

Our nation crumbles as our homeless suffer.
Not only the aged and alcoholic,
but also America's future,
THE CHILDREN.

Open your hearts and share with these less fortunate,
the nation's destiny is in our hands.

Lucille Cathell Densmore
TODAY'S SADNESS
Few know and even less care
About the heartaches and suffering
A family must bear
But if they knew and understood
Before they went there
Of the horrors of addiction
They'd never dare

H Leonard Clark Jr
TRUE COLORS
Color me purple, color me blue,
Show me your colors that reflects
you—then and only then shall
your "TRUE COLORS" come

through.

Only you can paint the colors that are within you—the picture you paint may be an original . . .
that may paint you!

Paint with the brush that's of your mind—the strokes you paint will flow-free if you "see" as you paint what you do not see.

LOVE has no color, for its colors are within you—the colors of one through and through are only colored by you.

WATCH YOUR COLORS, FOR THEY NEED NOT FADE AWAY....

"AS MOST COLORS DO"!

Jini George
MY DARLING DAUGHTER
You are my daughter
special to me from the day you were born.
And now that you are a grown woman
I have a feeling of loss.
My little girl is gone
and I don't yet know
this beautiful, independent woman before me.
Will we ever regain those special feelings
that we alone shared
or will we simply drift apart
never to know that bond again?

Sister Eletta Marie Galleni
TO MY FRIEND, WHO WILL VISIT IN APRIL
The promise of your visit
trembles on my window-shelf
like some exquisite goblet
etched by skillful hands to
catch the sun.
I tiptoe as I pass it,
lest the pounding
of my alleluia heart
should shake it from
precarious perch.
With each new dawn,
it shatters rosy light
to dance in happy colors
in the rooms of my todays.
(I hope its stem is hollow, for I intend
to quench my thirst
from friendship's cup.)
My tears of joy-filled waiting
join the nectared wine
of those remembered
yesterdays.
Each evening finds me solaced
that the promise, bathed in
moonlight,
advances April's coming.

Jill French
TO: CHAD & HEATH
I thank you for being so kind, when I needed a little understanding.
So listen close to what I say, a little life planning!
I hope that you never follow the steps of your father or of me.
Forgive me where I've failed you and make life what YOU want it to be.
I trust God to watch over you, whenever I'm not around.
Plant your feet deep, and stand tall on high ground.
Hold your head high, for you shouldn't pay for our mistakes.
But be man enough, to own up to the ones that you will make.
I wish like as a mother and child, I could kiss the pain away.
But as you grow older, you'll see, the pain is here to stay.
Fill your heart with love for your fellow man, and not hate.
For your friends will be many and your reward will be great.
Humble yourself, to that of an understanding child.
Be meek, but be strong, be mannered and mild.
Love those that hate you and never quick to judge.
'Cause you don't know the road they've traveled, or the mud and drudge.
Be a friend to all who are in need,
'cause even your spirit can fall.
Be compassionate and understanding, who knows when you may have to crawl.
Don't follow behind someone, and envy their place.
Don't walk in front of them, and kick dirt in their face.
Walk equal with them hand in hand.
There is no problem here, you can't withstand.
Carry God's pride and not that of man's.
The weight may be heavy, but not more than you can stand.
I am proud of you now, but as you grow, and then bloom.
Don't rush life at all, give yourself plenty of room.
To become a MAN, a man of love,
one that YOU can be proud of!

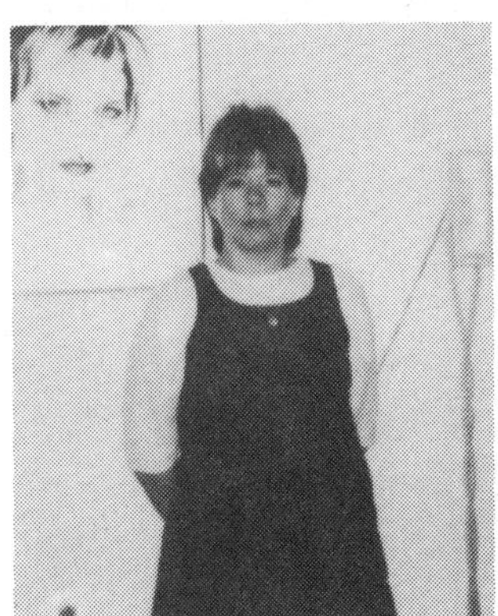

Joanne C Oakley

Joanne C Oakley
I WAS SOMEBODY
I was a little fetus,
My intelligence uncompared,
I had been created "CREATED" but no one cared,
As for me, my life, would not be SPARED!

Einstein! Edison! Alexander Graham Bell!
I knew everything, they knew, ever, so well,
But I was, to be, terminated, destined to die,
Look! I'm a person, that Book cannot lie!

Just because! Just because!
I'm not wanted right now,
Maybe next year, or six months from today,
But not now, not in this womb, Oh please can't I stay?

Just give me a chance, one opportunity, that's all,
If it's money you need, I'm going to be a Scientist, give me a call!
I'll go to school, I'll study and study,
I'll invent and invent,
I'll help out our world, I'll be worth every cent.

I was too little, and I had to have more time.
But I heard them say, that I was an accident, my life, not worth, a dime,
My hair would be brown, my eyes would be blue,
My feet were going to be big, my heart would be too,
But I didn't make it, not this time, my life was not, worth a dime!

Maggie Fohl
MY DADDY
I was called from home one evening
As the sun was sinking low,
Called to see my dear Daddy
he was called to go.

When I reached his silent bedside
To me he could not speak,
The angels had called him home to heaven,
He had sweetly gone to sleep.

He was a kind and gentle man,
Helped everyone who came his way,
I often wondered why God called him
Home to heaven on that day.

My neighbor told me God always picks
The most beautiful flowers for His throne,
That is why he picked my Daddy,
When He took him home.

I thank God he was a Christian,
Lived his life the best he knew,
Some day I will meet him
If to Jesus I will be true.

Johanna Sauvé
SOARING
What you live for only you can know
along your way, yes you will grow
for every moment that you live
a memory that you can save
and with your eyes and with your soul
you'll maybe reach your wished-for goal;
and only time will tell
if you've done all the things you wanted to.
As with your life, now flying high,
you'll make a reach
yes, touch the sky
and all your dreams are there for you
now lying still
to make come true
somehow it seems so far away
but you'll be there one special day
and until then you'll keep your dreams,
so very clear,
until you're there.
So while you live remember this
life was not meant for you to miss,
and make each day a memory
and let all people see you free.

Jennifer Sellers
HE ONCE CRIED FOR ME
As the soft romantic fire glowed on through the night,
I tried to love him but it didn't feel right
He held me close but I pushed him away,
Never knowing that I'd love him someday
The tears streamed steadily down his face,
This memory of him I can never erase
When I saw his confusion and torment inside,
My love for him I could no longer hide
To his open arms I could only run
And soon our bodies and lives became one
We promised to love throughout eternity
With our hearts and our minds joined in unity
I grew to love him more and more
but he loved me less than ever before
When I held him close he pushed me away,
without emotion or words to say
By my side he would no longer sleep,
My memories of him are all I can keep
It is my love for him that he will never again see,
That I cry these tears that he once cried for me

Betty Jane Shaw
SURVEY
Will, words, describe God's heaven,
Foam, glowing sapphire, and red—
Define an inward tingling,
At his art*craft, overhead?

I walked, and my eyes viewed heaven,
But, God, only know its appeal,
And, awe, derived from such splendor,
So, peaceful, and perfectly real!

What, words, can define God's heaven!—
I, saw,—but I cannot, say,—I know of no, words, to, tell, you,
but, I, viewed, "heaven," to*day.

Gina Slivenski
A RICH FRIENDSHIP
A long time ago, a lesson did I learn,
It's not how much money you spend,
Or how much you earn.

It's not the way you wear your hair,
Your clothes being old or new.
The blessing is in caring, and trying to be fair.

There's more to being special,
Than this being bought brand new.
Because it comes from within the heart
This gift I give to you.

You cannot wear it, or exchange for a different size,
But, you can count on its sincerity,
Its truth will never die.

And so, this wealth between us, we know will never end.
On this Very Special Day, I say,
Merry Christmas . . . . Friend.

Lilian Sas
AUTUMN MEMORY
The half-century mark is approaching,
And, the mind and the body soon tire.
Seems there's nothing can stop this encroaching
On the narrowing road of desire.

Too soon we have travelled the highways.
And seen all the beautiful lands,
Have lingered in devious byways,
Been lost in the shifting sands.

But today I think of my childhood.
One memory—bright as a gem—

Shines like the gold of an Autumn
wood,
And I'd like to relive it again.

My favorite friend, her brother and I,
Set off to explore a large wood.
A golden wood, 'neath a sunlit sky.
Time on our hands, and in leisurely
mood.

As we strolled on red-gold carpets of
leaves,
The sun shone down, and a gentle
breeze
Stirred the world around to
enchantment and peace
We were enthralled, and at ease.

We said not a word, happily
wandering on
Under glistening trees in the
afternoon sun.
The rustling leaves gaily eddied and
danced.
We laughed, and joined in, and so the
time passed.

The leaves whispered their magic,
and under their spell,
We three became spirits of Autumn
as well.

Angela M Palacio
LONELINESS

This poem is heartily dedicated to Mom and Dad for their sacrifices and sufferings, their feelings of isolation during the last days of their unhappy life. Their loneliness and sufferings they bear with smile on their faces.

I sat alone thinking of you.
Feelings I could not understand,
feeling contented,
feeling blue.
I shake the blueness out of my inner
being, brush aside
the creeping depressed sensation.
Yet in this world of ours who could
be not.
I was alone nobody did care.
I hold on to something to hear a
reassuring voice alas! such is
rudeness I received.
Oh wave of emptiness, why floats
over my being?
Go away and knock yourself on a
rock.
Leave me alone but how! how can
this be fulfilled?
Not him to reassure you, not him to
be bothered with,
not him to stay with you.
Yes miserable creature I pity you, but
alas! I realize
I have to wake up from these abuses.
Let thyself grow out from the
cobwebs of tragedies and life's
roughness.
Stand alone in spite of weakness and
breathe the fresh air to invigorate
your soul.
Yes poor soul, I have to compensate
goodness, now is the time after going
through this wickedness.
I cannot stay alone, feelings of
loneliness, why is this so?
Life is too much, it is empty. I felt
bored realizing I was only existing
and not living.
Useless being, useless creature,
useless woman, loneliness is for you,
for you and more.
Oh! I feel thirsty, life is dry. I cannot
smell the freshness of life. It creeps
on me like fumes from the incinera-
tors, fumes that fog the horizon.
Oh lonely being, cheer yourself up,
perhaps someday life would be great
for you .

Daniel D Scheller
CASTING NO REFLECTION
Could it be,
I've been living on the backside of a
mirror,
looking out instead of in?

For having found life was my
beginning
and death will be my end,
I begin to dream the dreams all men
dream
as they tarry along the way,
only to wake and realize,
yesterday I was the one
that made me what I am today.

Oh, I have dreamed the dreams of
yesterday
'til all those years have passed me by
and now I drift in loneliness,
waiting, for my time to die.

Should I sell or should I keep
this life that seems so meaningless,
or, should I dream the dreams,
no man dreams,
in the quiet
solitude
of death?

Zola Salena

Zola Salena
DREAMING

To Fantasia and all those who dream.

Make up your own dreams
Don't ride upon mine.
I'm dreaming a dream,
That will take me up high.

If you hitch-hike on my dream
It might cause it to die,
So make up your own dream to
To live as you try.
Don't weigh my progress,
By being my shadow.
I won't weigh yours by being
so shallow,
But let's think up our own
To live as we try,
For life is so short, and
too soon we die.

A dream is a beginning to bring a
new morrow.
It's all that we have in sickness
and sorrow,
It lightens our load as nothing else
can,
So make up your own dream
And take your own stand!

Betty Parry
WHILE CALIFORNIA IS GOING UNDER SEA

Dedicated to my loving family LaRoy, Theresa, Leslie Parry

While California is
going under sea,
Oklahoma is going
into poverty.
Inflation goes up and down, pretty
soon,
There will be no
town. But as we look
into the sky, we
hold our heads up
high, as the winds
blow and gives a breeze
We all catch cold
And sneeze and sneeze.
When there's no
town, we all
go down, then
who's left to
shop around.

Martha F Wells

Martha F Wells
BESIDE THE STILL WATER
I walked through the meadow one
day
where all nature in beauty doth
lay,
and where all nature seems to meet
in realm of blessed retreat.
I walked beside the water so clear
and felt that the Lord was
surely near,
and our Lord's words I did utter,
"He Leads Me Beside the Still
Water."
I thought of our Lord as He walked
by the sea
beside the waters of blue Galilee
where He, too, found a blessed retreat
to prepare for the throng He
soon would meet.
By the shores of His tempest-stilled
sea
they knew He was sure to be,
eagerly coming from far and near
His kind and gentle words to
hear.
Here He taught them His every truth
to rich and poor, to age and
youth,
and here their troubles hearts
calmed He,
beside the waters of blue
Galilee.

Crystal Nedved
CHAINS
Bound by invisible chains
unaware of the weakest links,
Free we are not by living in darkness.

Caught up in the struggles of power
dishonest at the base of our being,
Ego running the show.

Free these chains grow in peace,
Live in harmony.

Shatter the chains and fly free
to be the very best you, you can be.

Ann Semaan
TWILIGHT
When the north wind blows,
Bringing icy throes;
A bird, in winged flight,
Wends its way,
As the drifting day,
Threads shadows into light;
With lifted eyes to the moving skies,
I think about my life,
And like a starlit beam
Into tranquil dream,
The day becomes the night.

Scott A Nuce
I AM WISDOM
I am wisdom—
And I have lived a thousand years.

I have seen the crashing waves
Beat a hollow city
Into the barren shore;
I have seen the downfall
Of the mightiest empires;
I have seen light.

I have seen the pulsating
Rhythm of the modern cities
Of today;
I have seen the dying embers
Of yesterday's memories;
I have seen darkness.

I have watched all—
I have seen everything.

I am wisdom—
And I have lived a thousand years.

Jennifer Renee Owens
SOME OTHER WORLD
If there were some other world,
right above my hand,
If there were some other world,
Some far and distant land,
Where mountains stretch tall,
So calm and bright;
Where the silver lakes gleam,
In the sound moonlight;
Where birds show off,
Their feathers with joy,
And in the large lakes
Not a single decoy.
Of course all of this
Just comes from my brain,
But it just goes to prove
I can't be insane;
Because in this world
Wars remind me of sin
And in that other world,
Wars will never begin.

Patricia Rubio Peck
SPECIAL LOVE
The love between a father and a
daughter,
Is God's special gift: to womenkind.
For even when he's gone, with each
tear you shed:
You'll also have a smile:

Of a warm memory of those loving arms,
Reaching out to hold and comfort you.
The warm smile and understanding eyes of someone you can always count on.
I just hope he's aware of:
How much he means to me.
And I hope that I can live up to, being the daughter
He can always be proud of.
I'm grateful to God: for this unconditional love,
That has made life for so many a happier world.
Thank you God for letting me have
This special love:
For which no one else could ever replace.

Margaret M Kenehan

Margaret M Kenehan
CREATIVITY

This poem is dedicated to my sons, Douglas, Donald, David, and Daniel, and to the memory of their late father, Orville, who have been, and remain, my inspiration—now and for all time.

I am Creativity.
In darkness, I am light.
The winds of change
Blow over me.
I bend and sway
And reach new heights.

A fragile hope
For humanity . . .
But still,
I can ignite
The hearts and minds
Of all mankind.

Don't put out my light.

Debra Santivasci
A FATHER'S LAMENT
To my children I love so very dear,
There is something I have to say; I fear.
Your Mom and I have grown apart,
Even though it breaks my heart.
It is nothing you have said or done.
Together we used to have so much fun.
We will see each other still yet.
But not as much as before, I regret.
When it's time for you to go to bed,
I can not be there to kiss your head.
My love for you shall always be the same.
Remember this foremost that none is to blame.
So keep a picture of me by your side.
I will always be there for you waiting right outside.

Robert W Perez
LOVE PRAYER
Oh God hear my prayer,
Hear me now as I speak through the air.
My love for her is never ending,
Pure, bright, and understanding.

Hear me oh Lord, and hear me well,
For such sad things I will tell.
My heart is full of grief, and sorrow.
Can I bear another tomorrow?

Without her my life is dark,
Shadows of emptiness reflects my heart.
With her I feel so complete,
No one in the world could ever compete.

Lord, you gave her to me without one plea,
But my stupidity cast her free.
I live my life as if I were doomed,
For life without her is full of gloom

Lord hear my words like never before,
For what I ask I'll ask no more.
Grant me one wish, and it will be;
Please Lord, send my love back to me!

Miss Marty McNaul-Moore
THE LAST STAR
Little star—shining bright
Your presence seems to rule the night.
Way up there beyond the fog
Unyielding and ever glowing cog.
You instill in me a need
To trace your path on fiery steed.
Perhaps the wild and windy skies
Would clear my mind and dry my eyes

Veronica A Rychter-Danczyk
"JUNIOR'S" PRIDE IN AMERICA
I am a young "Junior woman,"
who will stand gratefully at your side;
Exclaiming what it means to be a member, shouting with
love, sincerity, devotion and pride!

Since I joined this organization,
I vowed solemnly this pledge;
To always be justifiably proud of
womanhood and our heritage!

"Congratulations!" seem to be in order as we celebrate
the anniversary of our 50th year; "No it didn't
Come to us that easy, you see, many had to give that extra
hand while raising a family or building a career!

We are known as a freedom-loving people
who have contributed significantly;
Whether social, cultural, or economic development,
to enrich this America, our country.

I thank God for what I am able to contribute;
the long hours, sweat and strife,
As I share to help create for many a happier,
healthier, more beautiful American life!

Miss Marty McNaul-Moore
MEMOIRS
Nine letters and a valentine,
Such silly things to keep.
A Marine doll in a plastic case,
Old memories down deep.

An oyster shell so paper thin,
We found it on the beach
I've kept it for when wet the green,
His eyes out to me reach.

Some pictures in his uniform,
A dress I bought to wear for him.
The memory of him lying stiff,
An ocean I could not swim.

I m sure it must be wrong
For me to keep these things,
But although I must forget
Such sweet memories they bring.

Bonita Ann Muhammad

Bonita Ann Muhammad
AGELESS SCULPTURE

TO: My family the Muhammads, Pace, Williams, McCormick, and boss E. Henry, and friends, lots of love.

It is as if I don't belong anymore
To a type of surrounding that informs me of,
A small artistic curve in my face.

Similar to that of an aging apple, which keeps,
The youthful fruits of life, gazing at me from afar.

Often I wish closer they would come.
And yet to them, It appears I am a huge dose of poison,
Ready to destroy them should they touch me.

As I slide my feet slowly across the floor,
I watch through my window and journey back to when,
I could run like a gold medal track star.

Just like the ambitious figures I focus on, with my eyes.

My hands shaking and speech of quiver I know somehow that,
I am a sculpture, hand molded, created by,
The greatest artist of all times and,

Although they distance me now,
Little do they know, the future holds my youthfulness.

As each new life comes into existence from my tree,
AS TRUE REMEMBRANCE OF ME.

Pauline Nelson-Deeley
IN THE CLINIC
They come in every color and size
With bravely smiling lips but haunted eyes,
They know just what they bring.
How can they be so cheerful, choose
To make a joke, when they can lose
At the die's cast, their everything.
One wants to make a miracle blaze
To wipe out all the lonely days
Of wondering, hope, and fear.
But all such things are at God's pleasure,
Each smile, each bit of courage, His treasure,
Each gallant will—the miracle is here!

Lillian Mc Mahon
THE DISSOLUTION OF A DIVINE PARTNERSHIP
Today was Genesis for me
As the Lord God fashioned me to be
A part of His eternal plan for His creation.
He programmed me to be a boy
And filled my little heart with joy,
Designing me from this biological equation;
My eyes will be a startling blue,
Set in a field of freckles,
With fringy brows 'n' lashes too,
Light blonde but with red speckles.
Just thinking of how I'll be me,
Consumed by curiosity,
It seems the nine months never will be finished.
But little did I ever dream
That she'd reject the gift supreme,
A loving unique human being!
The bells for me began to toll
My mother's womb became my tomb.
Abortion! By distortion of her soul.

Jacqueline (Poorbaugh) Richmond
A RIP IN THE SKY—PRAYER AND LAMENTATION FOR THE CHALLENGER SEVEN
Soaring upward with power enough for a thousand cities,
Gold and white and blue—all our hearts soar with you!

"Challenger"—your name is the very nature of man.
Inside ride seven stalwart souls; they can do it, Yes! they can!

Then like a giant rip in the sky,
jagged edges tear at our hearts
As we watch the unwatchable and try to <u>not</u> acknowledge their fate.

That rip in the sky will remain in our minds and not abate.
There will be no clean healing for their loss is too great.

Scars will form in the shape of that

awful rip and sever,
And the anguished cries of "My father! My husband! My son!
My daughter! My wife! My mother!"
will echo through space forever, and ever, and ever!

*Auwe Mike, Auwe Gregory, Auwe Judy.
Auwe Francis, Auwe Ronald, Auwe Christa.
Auwe, auwe Ellison.

God rest and keep these brave, soaring souls.

Amen

*"Auwe" is a Hawaiian word of mourning.

Randy Miller
SHARKS
Sharks are vicious like a thunder storm.
Through the dark waters they will roam.
They swim through-out the day.
Then prey on food all night.
They'll swallow a fish in one short bite.
Their dark black eyes are their symbol of death.
Their sharp razor teeth will take away your breath.
Tho sharks are beautiful creatures to see.
They are one of the deadliest eating machines to roam the sea.

Barbara Rysdorp
THAT'S WHEN WINNERS LOSE
You're fast with a quip
all debate you rout
only your words are heard
so I feel left out.

Jesse Johnson Jr

Jesse Johnson Jr
(THEY WHO SAY) HE'S NOT REAL
Did you ever stop to wonder
About a flower, or a tree
Did you ever think about
How you and I came to be
How we can laugh, how we can cry
How we can breathe and feel
Being able to see Nature's beauty
And they say, "He's not real"
If this was so, don't you know
We wouldn't exist today
Enjoying our lives, becoming wise
In a highly abundant way
How about the mountains
And the waters that continuously run
As long as they've been running
By now, you'd think there'd be none
Take a look around you, how could these things be done
Man can not make any of them
Oh, yeah! what about the sun
In spite of all our wicked ways
That've sometimes knocked us down
We somehow find the strength to get up
And start another round
And what about our table, on which we eat our meal
I'll never understand, the woman or man
Who says, "He's not real"

Diane Mason
JUDGED
We are judged by our face, our speech, our voice, a look, a glimpse.

What side does one see? The sides we have talked with, examined, or loved?

Are there not more sides? Yes, God sees. He always sees. Is that not so, He says judge not?

Complex is our person, but where is it? Do we see only a portion at a time and yet sometimes we see more?

Those trained in seeing, can they really see? Do we really walk in the same shoes? No, and yes. Yes, and no.

Our hearts reach out, sometimes joyfully, sometimes not. Why do we tear or break and wish not to do?

Must we express ourselves and die? We die by expressing our thoughts and words, and yet we also find life. Of course, is not this life in the body continually doing the same?

Questions are always, aren't they? Doesn't everyone have them?
Aren't we all seeking our Maker, our hope, our reason for living? Yes, and always yes.

Fairy McAlpin
TAKE TIME FOR THE CHILDREN
Take time for the children
God gave them to you
And he will be watching
To see how good of a job you will do
Take time for the children
Show them you really do care
When they come home from school
With good news to share
Take time for the children
Do whatever you can
To help them get through
Things they don't understand
Take time for the children
Watch what you do
For there are little ones
That want to be just like you
Take time for the children
Hold tight to their hand
For it won't be long
Till they will be
Leaders in this great land

Ann Marie Robinson
THE IMMIGRANT
I would rather not be in an alien land
adrift, adrift forever.
I would rather be with the ones that I love
than be apart forever.

I would rather not be in an alien land
when the ones I love are dying,
And me not there to hold their hand
though not for want of trying.

I came with a man to this alien land
but his dreams were not of me,
So here I stay like a burnt out bark
afloat on a foreign sea.

My children were born in this alien land,
they are home and free.
They have no way to understand
the foreigner in me.

There is no peace for the immigrant
always a heart divided,
Always an aching, lonely want
for a family united.

Ms Jocelyn Royer-Meade

Ms Jocelyn Royer-Meade
MY BLACK SKIN

To the people of my beautiful island, The Commonwealth of Dominica, West Indies

My Black Skin is soft, supple and shiny—STRONG
My Black Skin reminds me of our succulent sapodilla
Smooth and Sweet—of our native tamarind and guava jelly—
DELICIOUS
My Black Skin is Africa, Europe, the Caribbean—mixed in one
It is a combination of the majestic Egyptian pyramids;
the soft brown sands of the Nile delta and the magnificent monuments of Europe.
It is mystic charm and island beauty.
It is the mahogany among huge baskets
of flowers and fruit, sold by our smiling women
and girls in our island's markets.

My Black Skin is bewitching like our warm, black, volcanic sandy beaches.
It is aromatic like our cafe noir and cocoa beans
It is like our coconut when opened—
Refreshing and Cool.
My Black Skin fascinates some and frightens others;
Yet, it is addictive like our honey comb and tranquil Island.
My Black Skin adds flavor to me like cinnamon sticks and nutmeg in our tropical punch
It is the vanilla spices exuding poignant aromas
to our tasty cuisine.
My Black Skin is Me
MY BLACK SKIN IS—ME.

Shirley E Rosacker
EVENTIDE
I sit at my window,
Alone at dusk,
The wind whistles soft and low,

Lightning bugs flash,
Their beams off and on,
As the katydids' cymbals crash,

The soft creak of the frog,
Breaks the still of the night,
As he sings from his perch on a log,

And the bob-a-link calls,
To his mate from afar,
As eventide gently falls.

Kathryn D McCoy
TO FIND A CURE FOR CEREBRAL PALSY
For all of us that have CP I stand and say how proudly I can be. One day we are going to find a cure. If we all stand together our hopes and dreams will come true. I am telling you this because I don't want you to quit. And if you do I think you're kind of dumb, because one day we will find a cure. And if everybody quits I'll still be fighting on. Cause I know my dream will come true to find a cure for CP too.

Pearl P Reimann
DO IT NOW
Give me my roses while I live,
Don't wait until I die.
They help me o'er the rough spots,
They cheer me when I cry.
Give me kind words as I pass thru,
Don't save them 'til I'm gone.
I'm sure I'll have enough up there,
When I at last reach home.
My heart cries out for help down here,
I need you now my friend.
And just to know you love, you care,
A heavy heart can mend.
So do things now while you have time,
To help your fellow man.
Don't wait 'til folks lie dead and still,
To lend a helping hand.

Farrell Timlake
SO MANY TICKS OR WHY I'M SO DOGGONE TIRED
The clock which runs
is the great big dog
licking to wake the face
and tugging at the heels
which is walked with until
the time of day
when the postman
delivers
and all hell breaks loose

Zelpha Reed
PEACE
Peace is still and quite an innermost feeling of tranquility. To be sought after between people and nations To replace war show kindness to end hardships and make lasting friendships.

To see people try to come together and communicate language and seek an innermost peace, innermost peace puts hardships to rest and lets the people of nations communicate with peace. To show the children of this world how to live in a more peaceful world. to stop warships and soldiers from sacrifice and death. To show armies a peaceful defense and tranquility.

Nations need peace and people small or large need to see a peaceful world no more wars like Nam but calm peace talks. Bring peace to our nations take away and give freedom and liberty a chance. Peace, peace, to all the people in this world large or small, black or white.

Use peace to bring nations and people of any race together as for what the Lord God intended give peace a chance to sing, and put war and death to rest. As nations and people of this World stand together united through peace and God's will.

Margaret Evans Wright

Margaret Evans Wright
THANKFUL

For these I am thankful: a great nation free,
A land that my forefathers founded for me;
The rights that I cherish, the trust I may gain;
The chance to reach goals that I strive to attain;

To rise above failure that darkens my way;
To live for tomorrow and not just today;
For love and devotion so pure, undefiled,
The unchanging faith as is found in a child;

For God's Holy Word that enlightens my path;
For right of expressing my justified wrath;
I'm thankful for power, when moved to do right;
For beams of a candle, dividing the night;

For dreams that I hold, and for which I aspire;
For youth, to fulfill ev'rything I desire;
For guidance and care that are God's love divine—
I'm thankful each day for these blessings of mine.

Vashtee Ramhit
THE RUNAWAY

Here I am in this lonely, frightful world
With no one to turn to.
I'm so lonely, so hungry, so frightened
And not a soul to turn to
Why, oh why did I runaway.

I thought that I was man enough
To face the world by myself
But oh, how wrong I was
Why didn't I listen
I had everything a man could ever have wanted.
Now I have nothing
Why, oh why did I runaway.

Now I am stranded here
With not a thing of my own
How could I have been so stupid
To leave all those who I dearly loved
Why, oh why did I runaway.

Edna Maw Rampey
PRISMS OF COLOR

Never has there been such a dark and dreary day.
That there was not a prism of colorful rays
To light our path and guide our ways
To heights unknown to human sights.

Theirs are for the soul alone
Discovered from God's guidance shown.
A little kindness, love, a good deed
These produce colors never before known.

Mary C Thornton
VIETNAM HEROES

Vietnam heroes, there were many,
Back in the world we treated them like there weren't any.

They fought to keep us free,
Wanting us all to accept them was their silent plea.

Officers ordered them to fight,
They did so, not even knowing if it was right.

Coming home was their dream,
We didn't want them here, is how we made it seem.

We had protests to stop the war,
But when they came home we slammed the door.

For most, the war is gone,
But for many it still lives on.

They remember it in their nightmare,
And try to forget it through their prayers.

Maybe because I'm so young I don't understand,
How our country turned its back on its own man.

But to our Vietnam heroes, I say Thank you,
And let you now that I appreciate, all you've been through.

Elizabeth M Taurasi
SUMMER

I dedicate this poem to my family for all the summers we spent together on Cape Cod.

Summertime is here, this fact made quite too clear,
Though you wish it to go on forever, the Fall is blowing near.
Summer breezes, cool crisp evenings, the days never cease,
The beach at night, cool and calm, filled with total peace.
Each day begins with the rising sun, Glowing each day until the day is done,
The passion of the days, the stillness of the nights,
Trigger in your mind, making all seem right.
Walking on the docks or beach never seem the same,
For they change each day and nature is to blame.
The enticing scents of barbeques burning in the sand,
Or dancing at the yacht club, nothing could seem more grand.
But as the summer ends, as the days grow short,
There are so many memories of which you have to sort.
Parties on the beach, walking hand in hand,
To bid farewell to the one you love, crying on the sand.
All good things must come to an end, as summertime holds true,
But each year the summer returns and changes just like you.

John Robert Matter

John Robert Matter
What shall we do with a blue butterfly

To all who cherish things precious

What shall we do with a blue butterfly
Let it fly if it can
Let it fly

What can we do with a blue green moon
Let it be—for it will not
Much too soon

What will we do when all the waters
Turn to gold
But drink of the sands
For we are as yet
Not gods

B R Tarr
TO MR. W. H.

Only the poem, not the poet's choice
Conveys the poet to posterity.
Not poet's Muse, but only poet's voice
Invents in hearts so long as eye can see.
Small care which beauty that great poet loved
But that he loved the one he loved so well
To call such lines with such sweet art imbued
Time in all seasons finds them parallel.
His strains are frequent met, so wide their worth,
Woven in speech, their glinting trespass shines,
Even as shadows they betray their birth
Magnetically inducing his designs.
His flesh transformed to thought leapt sea and land,
Its substance mended not by any hand.

Lucia Tarallo
OH SWEET BABE! ! !

To all the innocent children of the world

Oh sweet babe!
With porcelain face
And empty crystal eyes.
Rosebud mouth,
Never to cry again.
It pains me
To see your lifeless body
Gracefully arched in death,
Protected by a paternal embrace
Made tragic by its failure.
Oh innocent babe!
Your haunting image,
With small cherubic hand
Clenched in that moment of death,
Remains forever etched in my soul,
A reminder of self-righteous stupidity!
Oh sweet babe!
Only seconds to oblivion,
Your precious spirit . . .
  ignored in life!
  ignored in death!

Betty Taplin
THE ABANDONED FARM-HOUSE

The abandoned farmhouse, dark, alone and still,
Stands stately yet, high on a windy hill,
The windows stare, like eyes, across the open field,
The shutters rattle now and then, but do not yield
Against the winter chill and snowy blast,
As the farmhouse contemplates the past.

The rooms are empty, bleak and bare,
No smell of baking fills the air,
No talk or laughter and running steps
Of happy children with their pets,
Silent now, it was not always so,
When bursting with family not so long ago.

The abandoned farmhouse stands alone and waits
For someone to, once more, swing wide the gates,
For warmth of crackling fires and glowing lights,
On these long, dark and frigid nights,
The farmhouse trembles, but recalls with pride,
When all the family was at home, inside.

Stephen Svoboda
MY BODY LIES SPREAD

My body lies spread, supine on some grassy mound,
A fleshy integument comfortably set aside to sleep.
My opiate, a quickly eaten lunch of bread, cheese and
Summery air, quiets the unwearied,

but fretful, sinews of youth.

I sink with nomadic ease down a well traveled way, into
A pastoral reverie, warmed by the afternoon sentinel.
Motion unrecalled, my crippled mind wrestles unsuccessfully
With the unformed shapes that flit and expire near untenable words.

But a settled thing, felt, unseen, and dead from long ago,
Is resurrected and tethered by an Apollonian harl.
Divorced from the warm water of unconsciousness,
The thought is ferried through the muck of memory.

A Voice, A Peal, light clears a path for words
As my mind rushes to seize and create.
Lambent eyes are opened then closed by the sun.
I stretch my Arms in the motion of a god and

I am killed in the instant I am freed.

Louise E Thornton
REFLECTIONS OF INSENSITIVENESS

There's no turning back
the clock one more time
There's no turning back
to pick up dreams left behind.

Will all the tomorrows
be filled with sorrows
Because there's no turning back
the clock one more time
And there's no turning back
to pick up dreams left behind?

Shirley Scott

Shirley Scott
PAID IN FULL

This poem is dedicated to: Danny Nelson Night, My Beloved Nephew

As I walk out of this darkness
I am greeted by a Special Brightness,
I feel no pain and I know that my Life wasn't in Vain.
I am no longer the Same
I am so glad of this Wonderful Change,
I have finally come to my Home On The Range,
I feel the Warm Sunshine,
Somehow I can still feel your hand in mine,
But, I know my Savior is following close behind.
Is this the kind of Life at the End of the Way?
I would gladly pay but I know my Lord would say,
You have earned this every step of your Way,
You would always say to others,
If you Obey, The Lord will repay.
I can honestly say this:
payment feels good in every way.

Wilma June Scherrer
BELLS

I hear a bell—
It calls to me.
I cannot go
Nor can I see.

I hear more bells.
They ring so clear,
Echoing their call
So far, yet near.

I hear the bells—
My feet are running.
I see the sheep,
They're coming, coming.

The Shepherd is there,
His dog by his side.
I thought of Christ
And glowed with pride!

Carolyn Reese
A DREAM

The feelings left, like
A sky of pastel ribbons
of a time, a special time
to dream of bright
rainbows floating along.

Hearing the chatter of
People on the streets,
or laughter in the rain.
the peaceful quiet at
times as of an island
surrounded by the sea.
The cool breeze
whispering by.

maybe it was a dream,
or was it?

Marguerite Welser
TRAVELING THROUGH LIFE

As we look back on our life
and the people we've met
there are faces we cannot erase.
The crowds seem to pass in an endless array
but few fit our small space.

We float through the atmosphere
with few goals in mind
ignoring God's gifts all around
but near the end of our journey
we stop to asses the treasures we have found.

We think of the people who held out a hand
to help us on our way
or the kind words they spoke
to urge us along and guide us
through each new day

We forget the haughty and arrogant ones
who tried to impress the crowd
they would badger or cheat
each person they'd meet
or become abusive and loud

So as we travel along
on our ride through space
let's try to help someone each day.
For the journey is short
and will end with a jolt
when our spacecraft has vanished away.

Mildred E Olson
TICKLING THE EARTH

When you tickle the earth with a hoe,
She'll laugh and give you row on row
Of pumpkins, carrots, onions and peas—
When they're all ripe—you take your ease,
Sit on your porch in a rocking chair;
And thank the Lord your home is here!
Your neighbor comes and you sit and talk
About farming joys as you rock
and rock
and rock!

Carolyn Andrews Cheek

Carolyn Andrews Cheek
LOVE

"To my family & friends" I hope I make you proud

Why me Lord, what did I ever do?
To deserve my families love, and Love from You.
They are different Loves, but loves that are true.
I can make it in this world with help from them,
And a lot from you,
Although there may be trials and tribulations You put us through
This I know, is a part of the test of love for You.
In the eyes of You, we were joined together as one.
We need to feel this way, till our purpose in life is done.
Only You, can tell us when our job here on earth is through
Then our souls will be resting
In heaven with You.

Lord, help us and light our way
With Your help, we can survive the day.
Thank You, for sending a gift of love that is true
That gives me a lot of love, to share with You
When my purpose here on earth is through,
Then I will be waiting,
To be joined with You.

Christine Viola Yonkers
BAMBI

In the cold morning dew
At the break of dawn
Comes the birth
of a new baby fawn
The sun streaming down
Warming the ground
As new dawn breaks
With a screaming sound
He wobbles around
He tries to stand
His mother gives him milk
Like a life giving hand
He finally stands
and tries to run
Frolicking around
and having fun
He's finally exhausted
and tired from the run . . .
Turns his head
at a shot of a gun
There at his feet
His mother lay dying
and the whole world hears
Young Bambi crying . . .

Stanley A Wright
THE RACE

A boy is a child until full grown
How long this takes is not yet known.

The tangled webs of life are sewn
As careful and fragile as glass that's blown.

Many a day I have seen wasted away
as I watch the ships that sit at bay.

The children outside giggle and play
My mind says that's you, just yesterday.

I look out my window at a day so fair
As I struggle to get up from my easy chair.
I remember the time that I'd count grey hair
It's not needed now they're all grey there.

The wrinkles now are deep in my face.
My hands are not nimble they've lost their grace.
I slowly walk a while at an aged pace
down the hall to my quiet resting place.

As I lay myself down to sleep awhile
I dream of a woman's face bearing a warm smile
and I drift towards a bright lit place.
I wake up to feel the wrinkles on my face
And thought to myself I've won that race.

R van Oosbree
CHRISTMAS MEDITATIONS

To all those, who still believe in me; altho' I've reached my year eighty-three.

Why did it have to happen this way
In order to have such a nice Christmas Day?
Why did He have to come as a baby, small,
Instead of a warrior, strong and tall?

Why did there have to be such an awful ordeal
Of jealous-king-Herod letting his vengeance feel?
By trying to destroy the New-Heaven-sent-King,
Striking the Innocents, such havoc to bring?

All through the ages the powerful and

strong
Had tried to conquer the world,
so long.
Now it had come to "the fulness of time,"*
When God decided: "the world shall be Mine!"

"We'll win hearts through My Son from Above,
And do it completely with pure divine love.
Then they will sing: "Sweet Holy Child,
Coming to save us; so tender and mild."

Now we're awaiting our Lord's soon return;
Not as a babe this time; how our hearts yearn
To welcome our Savior-King, ruling in love;
Vanquishing evil by His power from above.

*Galations 4:4.

Jennifer F Sistik
FACTS OF LIFE—ONE ASPECT
Freedom is to be—
A bird flying high,
To stand in the rain
And have the drops
Hitting you softly; quietly.

Freedom is one less hassle,
One less enemy.
It is sharing,
Because you want to share.
It is having a breeze dance
Thru the creaking trees.

Freedom is to be able to laugh,
(or to cry);
To be alive, have peace.

It is friendship, understanding,
And trust.
Freedom is to be free and to love.
Freedom is to be us.

Lucinda M Nichols

Lucinda M Nichols
LOVES CHOSEN WORDS

This poem dedicated—to my children Ronda, John, Mark and Roberta Rossman a precious part of my life.

It's love, It's more than words can say.
It's here with us, and shall be handled with care.
It's kind words spoken, and all carried through.
It's love when you marry, so pure and so true.
It's love with a child, so healthy and small.
It's love when you're happy, and letting it show.
It's love when you smile, and let people know.
It's love when you share, and put things aside.
It's you as the groom, and you as the bride.
It's a kiss on the cheek, it's the shake of a hand.
It's knowing your woman, and knowing your man.
It's the problems that rise, and shall be handled with care.
It's wisdom and knowledge, and knowing you're there.

Juanita Christopherson
INSIDE TEARS
When the heart is breaking and the face smiles on,
When the thoughts are weeping and the words sing a song,
And from your house of memories flows a rush of fears
You know you aren't crying, just shedding inside tears.

If your tasks you discharge without a falter,
And nothing in your life has seemed to alter:
When the heart of you is dead and the sight blears,
You've entered the heartbreak room to shed inside tears.

Many the face that smiles while the inside dies,
Many a life stands still while the heart still cries.
Many the ears are deaf while the mind hears,
The whispering sound of the falling inside tears.

Walter C Bare
JESUS WEPT
As the abused child fitfully slept
Jesus wept.

The homeless, the elderly, we do not accept, so
Jesus wept.

From the drunken husband, the beaten wife crept, and
Jesus wept.

As the starving under the rug were swept,
Jesus wept.

Drugs, AIDS, murder and rape we expect, while
Jesus wept.

To their parents, children show little respect, and
Jesus wept.

At the waging of wars, we are so adept, that
Jesus wept.

The good that we could do, we have no concept, so
Jesus wept.

The false prophets in such high esteem are kept, that
Jesus wept.

Our efforts to heal these wrongs are so inept, that
Jesus wept.
Jesus wept.

Lula May Hart Adams
MR. O'LEARY TALKED OF IRELAND
One winter night
when I was six
Mr. O'Leary came.
His talk of "Areland"
made pictures in my head.

The whitewashed cottage
with roof of straw and reeds
near Dingle, Kerry County.
He sang of Tipperary
and danced an Irish jig.

He told of Blarney Castle
and laughed about the folk
who kissed the Blarney Stone
for good luck, and the Great
House of Lords in Dublin.

But most beautiful was where
the blue green mountains
reached the sea, colors
mingled like a mist.

Finally, I went to bed with the
desire to travel in my head.

Javan J Harper
A CHILD'S CRY
Listen to me when I cry.
Don't shun me away.
I've got something to say.

You forgot to tell me you love me.
You forgot to hug me today.
You forgot to tell me you understand and care.
You forgot to pray and make the pain go away.

Thelma Louise Duncan
RUN A-WAY
Sometimes I wish I could just run away
but I know if I did I could not stay.
The children they need me for this and for that
if not to keep kids it's just for a chat.
They've got to have mama and papa on hand
they think we were made to fit
in their plans.
We love them so dearly and in our own way
but sometimes we'd love to just run away.
I thank God for patience and then count to ten
just to look up and see them walk in.
The first thing they do is give me a big hug and kiss
and the next thing I think of is a moment of bliss.
I do love to see them day after day
but it sure would feel good to
just run away.

Lee Dobbins
0° / 360° LONGITUDE

I dedicate 0° / 360° Longitude to all those who are themselves dedicated to the eventuality that "The Circle will truly be unbroken by-and-by."

So, where were you when all this History passed?
Growing stronger? I'd presume!
Knowing nothing of the costume change;
Bewilderment only "part" of "The Game"!

Napoleon's anticipating,
And Hitler's "attempt,",
Only following Caesar's strange thinking
Of uniting a "Holy Kingdom"
Before such a "Holiness" was thought!

"Where did it start?", I suppose one would ask.
"At the Beginning!",
The only answer.

"Where will it end?", an obvious question.
Given our Nature,
With our costume and persona,
The answer lies within our stand.
"It'll 'End' where 'It' began!".

Robert Jason Curll
WAKE UP MAN
Everyday man wakes up to a new day,
Never to see the dawn.
As he opens his eyes with a yawn,
He curses the work that gives him pay.
Man wishes for weekends of broads and beer,
High rolling on a Vegas strip,
Never holding on to life's grip,
Never facing the horror of the coming year.
Man's vision of a world of desire,
Comes only in fantasy,
Only seen by his twisted eye,
And in the depth of Hell's fire.
Wake up man and see the light.
Love with thy heart,
And don't be a part,
Of the darkness of the night.

Joseph John Hayes
LOVE SONG

To my love Mary ellen Stonack Hayes Forever

They say love is blind
Then blind I must be
I care not
For my eyes, have seen you

If I am blind so be it
For I have seen you
I feel love
There is no need to see more

Myra Eoff
DON'T LOOK BACK
Don't look back
When you close the door
'Cause if you do
It'll only hurt me more.

Don't stop to explain
Don't tell me why,

If you're gonna leave
Just tell me good-bye.

I love you, I'll miss you,
But I can make it alone.
I want you, I need you,
But I'll hold my own.

'Cause I can't tie you down
You've got to be free,
And I can't make you love
Only me.

So don't look back,
I'll tell you again
Just kiss me good-bye
If this is the end.

Edith Wood Greer
MOTHER
Many thoughts of you we have
Our words are far too bare
To tell you how we love you,
How much we really care.
Each day we're thinking of you and
Rejoice with pleasure true that we may
share the treasure of a mother
such as you.

David Wayne Glover
CHOSEN WASTES
Broken hearts; Broken dreams
Broken lives; Broken faiths
Broken loves; Chosen wastes

Hearts are broken as the sun
Falls and as the sun sets
Love has broken mine for we have not yet

A thousand times with you
A thousand times without
A thousand dreams lost, a thousand carried out

Feelings are there, feelings are not
Time goes on, love will not stop
Love will stop, time will go on

Paths meet at one end, never again
Our paths are chosen, and have not met
Things will happen, Things will not;
Only what we let

Love willing for yours, and to keep it mine
Sharing love we have and have not
It will take death to make our love stop

Broken hearts; Broken dreams
Broken lives; Broken faiths
Broken loves; Chosen wastes

Paul J Illk
LOVE TO MY WIFE ON HER 75TH
I didn't buy a present
and now it is too late,
Yet I want to give you something
That you will appreciate.

I have a present for you.
It's nothing but emotion.
I promise you forever
My unqualified devotion.
The Sespe Sage—

Texas Theresa Miller
THE POET
The poet keeps his lonely vigil,
Apart from men;
And yet his heart is touched
With every human joy and pain.
In touch with the pulse of nature,
His restless spirit wanders
Through the hills at night,
Moaning with the lonesome wind.

Gay of heart, he rides the skies
On the wings of flying birds.
He dances with the happy breezes
On sparkling, sunlit waters.
His soul is free from the chains of men,
But his heart is ever bound
To seek eternal truth.
He never knows—He only feels.
But his spirit
Slips through the bars of human logic
And brings forth
Warm-blooded truth.

Frank McGullion
I'M SITTING HERE NOW
I'm sitting here now;
And it's Easter morn.
Thinking and knowing;
Why Jesus Christ was born.

Jesus was on this Earth;
to show and tell,
To give Us a chance;
Not to live in hell.

God's spirit, is all around;
If we stop and listen,
We can hear and feel;
A positive sound.

The walk, is for Us to take,
to really be Free
God is for real,
And I hope Everyone will see!

Eugene Geno Garcia
I HAD A DREAM LAST NIGHT
I had a dream last night. I dreamt that I had finally met the perfect girl, you know the one. The one that I had been waiting for most of my life, the one that I had spent many broken hearts looking for. Yes, I know I have been hurt so many times and I know I deserve the best. Last night in my dream I knew I had met the best. It felt so good that I did not ever want to wake up. That dream so touched my heart and my soul that I know I must go on with my life and with my search knowing that one day I will meet the girl of my dreams. Now I know not to be so impatient, because if you believe in your dreams hard enough and set your mind to it and especially your heart. One day you will find that person of your dreams. And you know what, that person of my dreams is you.
So, now you know dreams do come true.

Anna M Norris

Anna M Norris
A GURGLING BROOK

I dedicate this poem, "A Gurgling Brook," to my only son, William.

Rushing by me, the gurgling brook
Laughing in glee, a stream of silver,
Laughing and rushing and tumbling and eager,
Sailed on to the great broad river.
The brook raced, the wind raced,
To see which would the faster be.
The wind tired and slowed down,
But the brook raced on to the great broad river.

The stars winked and broadly smiled,
To see their faces in the stream of silver,
The wind gathered speed and leaped the miles,
And out raced laughing brook at the great broad river.

Alice Hiykel Kline
BEAUTY
I recall a day when all the world was once so dear,
Yes green were all the trees and plants,
Exploding to the sky,
Their fragrances were so immense,
They lifted me so high,
The streets were overflowing,
With lilies here and there,
While daisies lined the hills and slopes,
Their petals were so fair.
The weeping willow draped her hair,
Upon the misty ground,
A ballerina in the wind,
She dare not make a sound.
The morning glories hugged the fence,
Where hollyhocks stood tall,
And I did sit among the flowers,
And dream a dream for all.
Yes I remember when the world was beautiful and new,
Her beauty's there for all to share,
Her splendor beckons you.

Teresa O Gulley
OBSERVING
I heard the children's laughter,
Young, innocent, and carefree,
And, inwardly, that's where I long to be.

The birds were harmoniously chirping;
Not a worry did they possess.
I wish people could exist in such bliss.

I listened as people gossiped,
So obnoxious and false,
But I can't judge, I also have those faults.

A woman cried with heart wrenching sobs.
I asked, "What could be so sad?"
"The loss of loved ones not saved by M.A.D.D."

The ambulance sped by, noisily,
Another life down the drain,
Smitten by that deadly drug—cocaine.
'Peace on earth, good will toward men'
"But to have inner peace," was my retort,
As I watched the news of ill-report.

The whippoorwill sang sweetly,
The close of another day.
Now I lay me down to sleep, I pray.

Miguel Angel Sefair

Miguel Angel Sefair
THE FREEDOM EAGLE

Dedicated to: Honorable Jorge Bush: President of the United States of America.
The Author.

For what does it serve the eagle
To follow the snake's tracks
To reach the recognition of his victim
And lose the Kingdom Heights?

What would happen
If its diplomatic beak
Would open to express the hunger
Of the starving city?

What would happen
If the Freedom adversaries
Would aspire to offer the eagle
To cease being an eagle
To become a barnyard chicken?

The eagle listened and answered:
No, lord of the earth;
The heights are mine,
My beak is a weapon,
And my wings of majestic dignity
Are my liberty.

Carmela Mariano
NEVER LOOK FOR TOMORROW
Never look for tomorrow, live for today,
Make each moment count, never dismay,
For tomorrow may be so far away,
Then all is lost, no longer to stay.

Life is precious. We realize too late,
For in God's plan, each has their fate,
Don't let the idle hours pass us by,
For ours, is not to reason why?

Cherish one another, if only to glance,
Who knows, you may not have that second chance,
A kind word, just the touch of a hand,
Knowing you're there, and that you understand.

Someone to share the good and the bad,
Some days happy and some days sad,
Never look for tomorrow, make the most of today,
Count your blessings, we're here for only a short stay.

Sara Mitchell
TIME TRAVEL
The silvery river of my mind
flows over those dark rocks
Some made light by the
Silvery magic of the Unicorn's
horn
Others, the light refuses to touch.
This river flows free through
time;
touching all with its inner glow.

Such are memories.

Emilie C Laverde
LOVE: A BITTERSWEET JOURNEY
At a score and a half of existence,
Love is but . . .
a journey of bittersweet memories.

A journey encountering
much sorrow and happiness.
Sorrow—from those things
from which
much fulfillment is desired.
Happiness—from those things
from which
little fulfillment is expected.

When only but sorrow
permeates a life cycle,
it seems as if
Nature quickly comes to the rescue.
It is as if
a special force in the Universe
senses the urgency
to wash away
any bitter felt sentiment . . .
for a new sweet, loving emotion.

Tonya L Harper

Tonya L Harper
MANDI—A LITTLE GIRL WITH A BIG LIGHT
Mandi goes out every night. And
She raises her eyes toward the moon
And stars and wonders how God
Could have made such a beautiful
Creation. With the moon and the
Stars shining so brightly in the sky.
The night doesn't seem as dark
anymore. She has the love of God in
Her heart—
Which lights up the whole night. She
Wakes up every morning and looks
At the sun and wonders how God
Could have made such a beautiful
Bright star—a star that lights up the
Whole sky. She realizes it's not so
Hard because the light in her heart is
Much brighter than the sun—this
Light is the light of God and it
Follows her wherever she goes and
She shows this special light of God to
Everyone she sees. She thanks God
For giving her this special light to
Share and as she grows, this light will
Grow and everyone will wonder
Where this light came from and why
She has such a glow and such
Happiness. She will tell them about
This special light and where it came
From and they will want it too. The
Light is the light of Jesus Christ—
Jesus Christ is the light of the world.

Rika Nakazawa
A VISION OF THE FUTURE
Look at the chunk of pretty blue
crystal Granpa!,"
urged the child,
And the man saw a small lake with
millions of fish
washed up on the shore,
Unable to live in water of acid rain.
"Look at that big clear Ocean,
Granpa!,"
exclaimed the child,
And the man saw a gray sky
blackened and filthy
with pollution,
Because of Man's industries.
"Look at that couple kissing,
Granpa,"
whispered the child,
And the man saw two people
enveloped in sorrow
and pain,
Because of the absence of trust and
understanding.
"Look at those majestic kings with
green crowns, Granpa!,"
yelled the child,
And the man saw a whole desolate
forest
of burnt stumps,
Destined for oblivion through nuclear
disasters.
"Look at this wonderful world
Granpa!,"
shouted the child,
And the prophet looked,
searched . . .
and saw nothing at all . .

Lou Ellen Muncy
NATURE
The sun rises,
The sun sets;
Orange and yellow,
By dusk are met.

Dark is
The night;
The stars
Shine bright.

The tide comes,
The tide goes;
The water touches
Someone's toes.

Someone walking
In the sand,
Sees the horizon;
Reaches out with her hand.

She doesn't reach,
No one can;
Nature was meant to be seen,
But not touched by man.

Angela Nail
LOVE HURTS
When we started going together.
I thought it would last forever.
But I guess it wasn't meant to be.
One day you were there for me.
And the next day you were gone.
Was it the color of her hair
Or was it her eyes.
Whatever it was, it made me hurt
deep inside.
You said you'd never leave me.
No matter what, you said we'd
always be together.
What happened to all the joys and
hopes we shared together.
I should have known what was
happening
But I was too blind to see.
I let you hurt me time after time.
But I won't do it again.
Now it's time for me to let go of the
pain, so here I go.
Goodbye for now and forever more.

Mary Ann Smith

Mary Ann Smith
AWAKEN IN COLD SWEATS

I dedicate this poem in behalf of my parents Mary Lee and Bennie L Smith, written by their daughter Mary A. Smith

It was the Mid-December, A cold and
bitter Night
The Night was long and weird
I was asleep lying in bed, could
barely keep my eyes open
This sudden chill from the stillness of
the dark kept
me awake
A loud but squeaky noise, like the
ticking of a clock
caused me to become suspicious

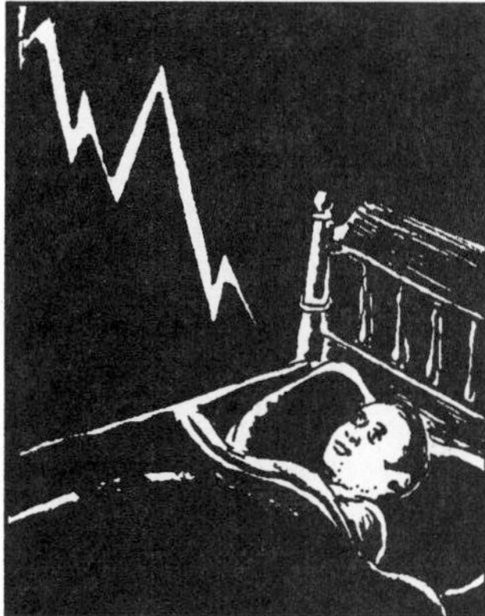

I awaken in cold sweats, This
mysterious feeling
Prevailed over me
I tossed and turned, trying to get to
sleep, a ton
Of weight crashed upon my body
I could barely move my toes,
I struggle to get away
Somehow I manage to steal away
from it all!

Ann Mabin
SMILE
A smile is a funny thing
It can make you laugh and sing
It even makes your heart ring
A smile is a funny thing
It can do almost anything
A smile can light up a room
And chase away the gloom
It can be big or small
A smile can make you 10 feet tall

A smile is such a wonderful gift
You can give it to anyone
And boy what a lift
You may have on your best
But what about the rest
Until you have a smile on your face
You shouldn't go any place

A smile is a funny thing
It can do almost anything
It can make you laugh and sing
Boy! What a wonderful thing
Smile! ! ! ! ! !

Dawn Thomas
LIFE GOES ON
A wave crashes violently on the
beach
Two children get a wicked lashing
each.

Time and the sea turn rock to sand
Learning and experience turn boy to
man.

The sun rises magnificently over the
blue water
A woman delightfully gives birth to a
daughter.

A wave gently laps onto the sand
A young couple walk hand in hand.

The mysterious ocean stretches as far
as the eye can see
Life for a man behind bars goes on
endlessly.

The continual beating of waves cuts
away at the land
Time creates wrinkles and cripple old
hands.

A wild storm shakes the sea and its
creatures
A war scars mental and physical
features.

The waves continue pounding and
The sun never ceases to rise and fall,
Just like people must continue living
Overcoming obstacles, enemies and
all.

Mark D Thompson
GOD HELP ME HOLD MY MOTHER'S HAND
When I was a little girl mother would
always hold my hand. As I grew
older day by day,
mother would always understand.
How strong can I stand? God help me
hold my mother's hand.

I pray every night that you will
rescue our souls so mother won't
have to go. How can it hurt so bad
when you say that it's your plan?
God help me hold my mother's hand.

Can memories turn the tide, the times
we've laughed and cried? How could
you send your son to die when you
still feel the pain inside?
How strong can I stand, God help me
hold my mother's hand.

When it's time to say good-bye, I'll
never forget the teardrops in your
eyes. To struggle day by day when
mother has to go away.
How strong can I stand, God help me
hold my mother's hand.

I pray every night that you will
rescue our souls so mother won't
have to go. How can it hurt so bad
when you say that it's your plan?
God help me hold my mother's hand.

Can life be without pain, or a rose without thorns?
If we could cry without tears, and our love never mourn. How strong can I stand, God help me hold my mother's hand.

I pray every night that you will rescue our souls so mother won't have to go. How can it hurt so bad when you say that it's your plan? God help me hold my mother's hand.

How can our family stay together without our mother's love? I'll pray and talk to her every night when I pray to God above. How strong can I stand, God help me hold my mother's hand.

I pray every night that you will rescue our souls so mother won't have to go. How can it hurt so bad when you say that it's your plan? God help me hold my mother's hand.

If there is a miracle left, will you save this one for me? I would give myself like the rain gives the sea. Now I know that I can stand, God help me hold my mother's hand.

Mary L Hensley
HAPPY MORNINGS
For Sunshine and Happy Mornings
For the days so bright and blue
Brings out the whispering moments
In dreams that's oh so true

The smiles that lie around us
For the joys we have each day
To the friendships, we bring each other
That nothing, can take away

So life is like a family
Put all in one to see
For the time we spend together
Is a place where we all can be

In this, there is a story
To share along with you
For I know it has a meaning
Of Love, and Happiness too.

Judge Leodis Harris
ON PEDOPHILIA
What kind of nation have we now become?
U.S. millions of sex abused children.
If lust for thy neighbor's wife is a sin,
What's lust for thy neighbor's daughter or son?
By God, men; why must he "do it" to one
Whose youth knows not such—who only intends
To trust him, as relative, neighbor, friend?

How pedophiles get made is not so strange.
For they're just doing what was done to them.
A cycle; vicious, implosive, insane.
Someone in his childhood sex-abused him.
Speak up you rascal, it's you who's to blame.
We'll suffer by lifetimes each child you've trimmed.
Speak up, you bastard and tell us your name.

C L Kasey
ON LOOKING BACK
Hidden in folds of memories past,
Scenes of sensual pleasures last.
Times impress, is bold
By stealthful manner told.
We strive to regain, control the moment.
Our reward is despair, twinned with torment.

Best not dwell on fragments of thought.
Deeds time was then—paid when bought.
What had been—is evermore gone
Only, by memory reached, is all that's won.
Stayed within—one's pleasant thought list.
Rehearsed repeat—time's stubborn resist.

Tread, carefully past's path.
Enjoy its wisdom—forego its wrath.
As wind tossed leaves depart its tree
Much like memories—glanced briefly.
Take pleasure—in the the measure of your past.
Never again, to fit the same shadow cast.

Tho, mortal and mellowed, by life we be
The end, is usher of our eternity.

Cindie & Raymond Howell

Cindie Howell
IN MY HEART

To my loving husband Raymond Summerton Howell II

In my heart is where you are.
In my heart you are a star.
You shine for me and only me.
With brightness only i can see.
Your love is never ending;
And your heart is true to me.
You're for ever in bending;
Just to make me hap*-py
You work very hard;
And you love so gently.
You show me things i've never seen;
Inside your heart and inside of me.
In my heart
My love grows stronger;
For you make it stay longer and longer.
In my heart
You'll always be;
The one and only one for me.
In my heart you'll always remain;
My husband; my lover; and most of all my friend.
I'll stay with you; till death do us part;
And after that; you'll still always be "In My Heart"

Reginald Tully
LONELY
To be alone in this world of today is like being a
  Playwright without a play.
Unable to share a thing or a line....
  The lonely feeling corrupts the mind.
To be alone is a humble fate.
  A horrible experience with no friend or mate.
Alone in this day with just yourself...
  An unjustly feeling, an unwanted wealth!

Lois Ansell Mullins
MY HOPELESS LOVE

To Buck, my husband of 43 years, whom I have loved longer than that.

This longing that I have for you
Is not a passing whim...
It follows me wherever I go
And haunts me from within.

Time has not changed one little thing
The bond between remains
Undaunted by time or circumstance
My feelings are still the same.

Oh, could our love have lasted
Through all the dreary years
I would not have been unhappy
Or have shed so many tears.

In all my waking hours I yearn
For things that cannot be
For you will belong to someone else
Through all eternity.

But, maybe, in the world to come
There'll be someone just like you
and, finally, perhaps I'll find
That dreams, sometimes, come true.

Gary A Mullins
YOU ARE TO ME

To my mother, Lois Ansell Mullins

You are to me a budding tree or
A flower, a blooming rose...
The twinkle of the stars at night
And valleys where rivers flow.
Tall mountains with their snow-capped peaks
And the wind that brings them life;
The moon that rises from behind the earth
To give the night its light.

You are to me the gentle kiss of
An early morning dew...
And the warmth of the rising sun
That gives the earth anew
The boundless oceans their mighty strength
That sometimes we may see,
And the breath of life that you and God
So graciously gave to me.

You are to me a cornerstone
From where I've built my life...
You gave me strength, love and hope
Even through some trying times.
Now that I've grown older
So many things I've begun to see...
Thank you, my dear Mother,
For what you have given me.

Ray P Riddle
A ROSE
A rose is beauty in all its forms
The color of a rainbow
And so, my friend, are you a rose
The color of a rainbow.

E Leona (Hickman) Blansett
GRANDPA RETIRED
I'll put down my ax,
pick up my knife.
Sit down and whittle,
for the rest of my life.

The ax blade is dull,
The handle has a crack.
My boots are worn out,
And so is my back.

Under the tree yonder,
is a bench that I made.
I'll sit there and whittle,
In that nice cool shade.

When the cold winds blow,
with no wood for the fire,
I'll just tell all the folks,
"Grandpa, decided to retire."

Betty Corrao
MISTY IMPRESSIONS
Gentle tiny arms, flagellating through the air
Speckles of sunshine dancing through your hair
With skin of an angel tinted oh so fair
I knew this new love forming would be one very rare.

Anxiously awaiting your walk through my door
Your face swelled with happiness, the smile I adore
The picture of your Mom and Dad many years before
I'm flooded with memories of love forevermore.

Seems like only yesterday you were reaching for a balloon
Tomorrow, my dear grand-daughter, you'll be reaching for the moon.

Jeanette S Paul

Jeanette S Paul
DEMOCRACY
God didn't make us all alike
This is why sometimes
We think others aren't bright
When all of the time as we disagree
It is just an opinion
We can listen then flee
For this is the best—a democracy
We don't get excited we don't get upset
Or say things we may regret
We learn from others from cradle to chair
Remembering, too, we haven't been there
An open mind is how we learn
So don't get upset just be concerned

Judith Moriconi
GRANDMA
I'm sure you think of grandma
As someone old and gray,
But when you're down and blue
She's with you all the way,

Everywhere you go, there's a grandma
Who's special in someone's eyes,
Her gentle wrinkled hands
Wipe the tears that you cry,

A grandma's love
Is full of pride,
Her love for you
It never dies,

Grandma lives in your heart
She's with you, wherever you go,
And always remember
Your grandma loves you so.

Carol R Roe
THE GOLDEN DAYS OF AUTUMN
Autumn, like all the other seasons,
Is a time for beginnings and endings.
It's a time for trees to change color,
And a time for green leaves to be gone.
It's a time for harvesting to start,
And a time for growing crops to stop.
It's a time for chrysanthemums to bloom,
And a time for petunias to die.
It's a time for short, cool days to bring relief,
And a time for long, hot days to be forgotten.
But, most of all, it's a time to pause
And think about who we are,
And who we can become.

Yolanda White
TO MY WONDERFUL MOM
A mother's love you should always treasure
For this is something you cannot measure,
A mother has love for her children all,
To guide and protect them when they fall.

A mother's love is sincere and pure,
Not for today, but for years and years.
From a babe in arms to a strong young lad.
She is always ready with a loving hand.
To keep you safe away from harm,
Always near with protective arms.

Take care of your mothers, friends of mine
For a true devoted mother is hard to find.
Guard her well with love my dears,
For the loss of a mother is hard to bear.

Zelpha Reed
WITHOUT LOVE'S EMBRACE
Here I stand without you my
love, my protector, my prince
charming who's looking down
upon me.
When I'm in danger, my prince
charming tall dark and
handsome on a white charger,
rescues me without an embrace.
The memories of our happy times
come and go as time passes,
as I remember how protective
my prince charming is,
As I still stand without you and
your embrace you stand without
me.
Oh where oh where has this love
gone, so far and so near, as we
fear love's beckoning call.
Shall time and fate and God's
blessing of love give our love
away as we meet at the gate.
Tragic fear of pain, and tragedy
brings pain, and fear in love—
Where is a love so kind soft and
warm as we touched—
Oh how tragic that love is a
triangle paralyzed by fear as
two people care for each other,
and fear to answer love's
beckoning call.
Love's tender moments of
surrender to love's beckoning
call, may prove to be a
wonderland of happiness as love
conquers all.
As you ride your charger into the
night look for the star shining
bright, follow that star for it's
God's leading light to guide you
as we conquer the love, fear and
tragedy of God's burning

Armando Barrientos
TODAY
I love the days when happiness was in our hearts, it seems like yesterday.
How it drifted away, seems so unfair like the air that moves, yet it stays.
Am I so different from feeling, feeling the wind that brings happiness,
the sun that brings light to your eyes
the storm that tore us apart
the raindrops that fell in my heart.
But yet! I linger and I wondered and I wait for the tender wind.
If only yesterday can bring back tomorrow,
When today is here.

Leonard A Wilson III

Leonard A Wilson III
FLOWERS
Flowers express any emotions
and any occasions.
Flowers are expression of emotions
Whether they be those of love, sympathy, joy, respect or any of the diverse emotions
of human nature. Emotions are easily displayed with the breathless beauty of flowers,
They are impartments of love
and are behooved of expressing human feelings.
If thou ever want to express emotions
thou should use flowers,
For they erotically express emotions.
Flowers are the requital
of all emotions.
Therefore it's plausive to say that
they are the key of emotions.
Do thou begin to understand?
Remember whatever thou are feeling
Flowers express them!

Traci Baker
MOM, I LOVE YOU
You are God's own gift to me,
In the most beautiful form that I can see.
You are what makes yesterday
worth remembering
And tomorrow worth living for.
I will cherish the path that you
walk in my life,
The place that you fill in my heart.
I will be there for you.
When the stars cease to shine
For my love knows not the
boundaries of time,
But the place that you hold in my heart
Over blooming in me,
I will love you endlessly.
I love you, Mom

Marion McCullough
THE DEADLIEST WEAPON
Harsh words were exchanged and if looks would kill
Jan would be dead and buried on Grampian Hill . . .
"I have proof," Bill scornfully shouted,
"You have been unfaithful, there is no doubt about it ."
Jan rushed out of the room, to the attic she fled,
Opening the trunk lid, she said,
"I'll find that weapon, if it's the last thing I do."
Her hands were shaking, she was desperate too . . .
"What if, ah, there it is," Cold to the touch
She steeled herself and lifted it up. It didn't weigh too much. . .
Then, striking a match the sulfur smelled strong,
Her aim was quick, it didn't take long,
The deadliest weapon completely destroyed
A bunch of old love letters blue ribbon tied.

Michael Milton Cook
MOM
Your hair is as softly
silver as the starlight
on a soft powder snow.
Your eyes are as green
as jade topped with
finely knit brows of soft
silver like the light of
a new moon sliver on
a deep black night. Your
lips are like the red of
the ruby etched firmly
in my memory of you.

Louis Buttinger
A REFUGEE'S LAMENT
Who can say that we did not love
not care enough for you, land of our childhood memories?
Did not uncounted generations of our fathers till your soil;
contribute labor and native intelligence
in order that the nation may prosper
in dignity and freedom?

Never did we contemplate leaving
you for some distant land.
too soon did we have to learn that
man is not
the ultimate architect of his own destiny;
fate, with a heartless unconcern for
human suffering
is life's relentless
arbitrator . . . excepting none.

By cataclysmic events did we
become separated
from our father's land.
An event, vaguely remembered now
by few:
"Just one more democracy gone under."

As one of the witnesses to man-made disasters
that time after time convulse and
torment peace and
freedom-loving people in so many
parts of the world,
I bow my head to mourn the death of
those who lost their lives
in defense of dignity under freedom.

Jessie M Combs
MARTYR
To lay my head against the wood,
My only comfort be.

In union with the one,
Who gave his life for me.

Oh world of sorrow,
World of woe.
And tears stream down my face.

A world made by God's own hand,
To Him—gave no place.

Oh take my hand and lead me on.
O'er rocks and thorns and clods.

Let my feet follow the footprints.
That thy own feet have trod.

O'er the roads and down the hills,
Till I at last shall see—
Thee.
And we shall realize our Love—
In Eternity.

Zylla Del Mar

Zylla Del Mar
I REMEMBER NOW

To MPS . . . for reasons we both know.
To Germaine . . . the child who had once been and will never be again.
To the world I had once lost . . .
From CSA, the unbeliever—no more!

The world I had once
forgotten . . .
like flashes of fragmentary
mem'ries,
came rushing back resolutely;
'twas because of a certain child!

looking at me
with those expectant eyes
i could not fathom—
probing . . .
searching . . .
questioning . . .

and there,
i mirrored the innocence
i once had known.

unbidden,
so poignant many a thought
i could not shelve behind.

and once more . . .
i lived again
in the world of pleasant recollection
i had once forgotten!

And now—I REMEMBER!

Marcelle Daniel
MY HUSBAND
He said he loves me,
so he says.
I know that it is hard for him
To show he cares.

He travels for his job,
most of the week.
For his job such crazy hours
he has to keep.

When he comes home at the
end of the week.
He comes through the door, dead on
his feet.

He bought me a house, because
he said he would.
He tries to keep his promises,
if he could.

The difference in our ages
doesn't bother me
But, sometimes I see it bothers
society.

For our love has a bond that
is not easily broken.
What we feel for each other,
no words have to be spoken.

Sister Eustelle Burnett
BLACKCAP'S LESSON
Young chickadee wailed to his
mother,
"Oh, Mother," moaned he,
"Redbreast, Bluebird, Bobolink and
Wren have left us—where can they
be?
I am lonesome, sad, and it is lifeless
and drear, I want to fly away!"
"Oh, no! Son, Blackcap," said
Mother.
"Redbreast, Bluebird and all had to
go.
Their food is all locked under ice and
snow.
You have a beak that is hard and
pointed—just made to unlock bird
pantries—
You can always eat. Besides, the
humans throw us many a treat.
Our songsters will return when winter
has gone and bring back to us their
summer song. Our friends in the
houses need our chickadee antics and
God-given tune.
It keeps winter days from seeming
too long.
Look in through the windows,
Blackcap, dear, see the toddlers look
for your cheer.
See them hop and laugh and clap
chubby hands.
You must not fly to southern lands!"
"Thank you, Mother, I see their
cheer. I want to stay here, all the long
year."

"Chick-a-dee-dee-dee-dee"

Sister Bernal Schmitt
"CHOOSE LIFE"—"NOT DEATH"
Part I:
God's given "Span of Life" is like a
line,
Made up of many seconds
Its length varies for each individual
And has a definite beginning
and end.

Beware of the clip, clip, clip
Like a scissors, snip, snip,
snipping
At this determined "Life Line."

Our God given—"Gift of Life"
Surely but slowly fades away
Each hour, minute and second
Glides along without halting
Suddenly death appears in the
distance,
The "Veil of Death" opens
And we are—gone—to a
"Self-Determined End."

Part II:
In Contrast—We choose "God" as
our "Final End."
We pass through the
shimmering
"Gates" of "Paradise"
To the "Abode" of "God"
"God" the "Epitome" of
"Beauty," "Goodness," and
"Love"
To our "Spiritually Determined
"End"

Evelyn Burkhard Perry
THE MOONLIT LAKE
The brilliant moon is soaring
High overhead in the sky,
And silver paths are making
The water glow in the rye.

The lake is being guarded
On either side by trees
Which cast reflections assorted
Into the silent sea.

The wind is causing ripples
O'er the silvery lines to play;
Fish, too, are causing ripples
As they swim in the eddying bay.

Sandra M Gelet
FOR THESE I CAN BE GRATEFUL
For What Can I Be Grateful?
For Life!

Mind cannot grasp, if faith is strong,
when life was not;
When Divine Intelligence reached
out to plan the worlds
on which we dwell
And devise the plan that we
approved;
For Eternal Personality that was and
is uniquely mine,
Without limit of scope, or depth, or
growth,
If I will it so.

For Love!

In infinite wisdom, my Father
planned for me a sojourn here.
He gave his Son, whose love made
possible redeeming grace,
Whereby I might return to him, a
wiser Woman refined by trial,
not fully escaping sorrow.
The Son gave me a test of love:
"Feed My Sheep"; "Keep my
Commandments, for he it is that
loveth me."
He gave me opportunity to serve, and
thereby love, his sons and daughters.
He planned for me a home, wherein I
may help perpetuate the family ties
And hold to my bosom those whose
love I earn,
And to whom I give my undying
devotion.

For work!

The divine injunction: "In the sweat
of thy face shall thou eat bread,"
Become his plan for Eternal growth.
To Life, it is the refiner, and love
grows from its toil.

For These I can Be Grateful . . . . . .

Life, the Source; Love, the
Motivation; Work, the Royal
Highway,
Liberty and Peace.

These Three . . . . . and I May have
Eternal Joy

E Mae Degn

E Mae Degn
SYMPHONY
A sun that is setting, fires the western
sky.
Your presence rises to meet my
beating heart, I need not wonder why.
The Symphony of myriad hues,
breathless to behold,
Your kiss, so soft, so lasting, your
arms so tender to enfold.
My soul bursts forth from out my
breast, flies free to immerse
with love's sweet breath.
Trust, truth, space and time will be
the test.

A wisp of lavender, a gossamer pink,
a hint of maize, a crimson base,
Love's illusion perhaps, I think.
The Symphony slowly subsides, and
love's sweet breath descends on me,
Enraptured soul in soul,
To harmonize eternally?

Russell L Miller J R
SOME GIRLS BUT ONE
Some girls are a bore.
All girls love the store.
Some girls always weep.
Because they can't find a boy to
keep.

Some girls are so nice.
Some are like sugar and spice.
They always bug you for your
money.
But we sometimes say not my money
Honey.

There still is only one girl that
pleases me.
I always say she's as beautiful as a
rose tree.
Her eyes are as bright as the sun.
Her smile gives a spark like a gun.

Her hands are as soft as cotton.
I say she is nice not rotten.
She always gives a little of a wave.
They say she is as free as a bird not a
slave.
She is a goddess of love.

Rosalie S Gustafson
MY KITTY
Furry, purry, soft as silk
Still you are the tiger's ilk
Burning in you, still, the fire
Of some ancient jungle sire.

Now reclining on the telly,
Or in my lap, a lump of jelly;
A bed for you, always on top
"Laps were made so cats could
nap."

Little kitty, so adorable,
How I spoil you is deplorable.
Tho soft and cuddly, mild as milk
These scratches say you're tiger's
ilk!

Mrs Rosalie S Gustafson
UNTIMELY VISIT
April called on March one day—
Which later she did rue—
For March had started cleaning
house,
And was not nearly thru.

All day she'd swished and rushed
about—
My, but she loved fresh air—
A long icicle tipped her nose,
And snowflakes filled her hair.

So April's coming was a bit—
Untimely, shall we say?
Perhaps March would have
welcomed her
On any other day.

Though April looked so shy and
sweet
In dress of chartreuse lace,
Mistress March just ripped it off,
And flung it in her face.

Poor frightened April turned and fled;
More shock she felt than pain;
If you saw April's copious tears,
Perhaps you thought 'twas rain!

Sherry Gail Grindstaff
LOVE'S REFLECTIONS
Let's say for now
We've far to go we do not see
What others do when skies are bright
And days are long.
Our love we share with all our joy,
Our hearts are full and filled within,
Our lives we live with all our dreams
or heartaches,
To give and live together.

The time may come
When we see the end of our dreams.
And the love that we feel seems to
have disappeared.
We look for different ways to
improve our lives.
And hope we see the way to come
together again.
The storms of pain we feel will come
to an end
And I see you look at me with love
And make my dreams come true
With all my heart.
I love you.

Glenda Wheeler
SEASONS END
I sit watching from my window
High above the street below.
The season has changed.
Not with sudden moves,
But with silent and expected motion
The days are cooler, warmed only by
the sun.
And the nights cooler still.
You've changed too.

You made no announcements.
You let me know it was over
By saying and doing nothing.
It was silent.
But even silence can be deafening
To the ears of one
Who doesn't want to hear.

Joan Chaney Davis
YOUR TREASURE
A mama is your treasure that's so little thought about—
Until too late for most of us to even sort it out;
A mama is taken for granted,
Most of the time—
And then too late, we realize, what we had paid no mind;
So treasure, this precious treasure, if you still have the chance—
For all too soon this treasure is gone without a backward glance;
For God makes this decision about the time we have—
To love and treasure Mama
The gift he gave, without a doubt
Because once she's gone
You will always long
For the time you spent together;
So treasure, your treasure, while you can
Because if not now, it may be never.

Michael Lee Hambelton

Michael Lee Hambelton
OPEN YOUR EYES
Open your eyes your future is easy to see.
Bright with victories of challenges you've won.
How soon do you want to see it come true.
Open your eyes and it was always there for you.

Downfalls are lessons you've made yourself.
Each one is useful no-one's to blame.
So lift your sights to the highest goal.
Take it from your heart take it from your soul.

Happier, healthier, prosperous, and free.
Your mind's expanding ready to grow.
Loving and caring all you hold true.
Forget the past each day is new.

Roger W Dahn
THE CHOICES OF THE NEW GENERATION
An everyday event, time and time again
Setting himself up, for what could be a sin
Whirl one direction, then spin the other way
How many choices, must he make in one day?
The choices of, the new generation
Can't always be made, with no hesitation
Right or wrong, there's no problem there
But add hesitation, and no time to spare
This is where, the devil waits for he
Knowing he'll mess up, in no time you see
Not a few times, but many might I add
What's in the mind, of this foolish young lad?
He fends for his family, and loves them so dear
But competent and smart, he's definitely not near
Now not every person, can be right every time
But when you've done it once, you keep it in mind
He did it once again, for just a little fun
The choice that he made, again the wrong one
He'll pay for his choice, his family as well
These generation choices, could land him in hell!

Lucille L Scott
A COVERED BRIDGE
As we went for a walk one day
We saw a covered bridge, built so sturdy and strong.
Then we took a walk through and
It was pretty long .

The daisies nearby were so colorful
And filled with love.
They are made with the
Hand from up above.

G E R Hook
HER LONELINESS
How can I survive her loneliness
The granite cliffs of her loneliness?
In the evening, her seabird cries come to me on the wind.
Her despair leads me to the water's edge,
And in the darkness between the waves,
I see her foam-flecked eyes,
Disappointed and gently accusing.
her voice calls to me,
And the cresting waves of her sobs
Beat on the sands of my breast.
Lord, let me not break myself on the
Granite cliffs of her loneliness.
Let my heart beat singly,
And let the ocean of her intensity be calm.

Elaine A Ermel
MY LAST BREATH
God grant me that I may live to love,
'til my dying day.

When it comes to, "My Last Breath,"
I then most humbly pray.

When in the Lord's safe loving hands,
I'm peacefully asleep;

So in his eyes I may be judged,
As good enough to keep.

Audrey Casari
FALLING FREE
I sat and watched the twinkling,
The twinkling of each leaf.
I wished to see it leave the tree
And fall to earth beneath.

I sat for hours watching
The leaves go drifting free
But never once did I observe
One as it left the tree.
Each little leaf that I could see
Was drifting in the air.
It had deserted Mother Root,
I could not tell from where.

I sought its source so endlessly,
Whence came it from the tree?
Where was it 'til it fell to earth,
A fairy float to see?

Its secrets remained hidden
Like secrets of God's love.
We know not when God loosens it
But feel it from above.

We see it shown in smiles,
Feel it in gentle touch.
Its spirit hears our every prayer
And helps us, oh, so much!

So falling leaves, I watch you
As you release your grip,
And I hitch mine securely
And hope that I won't slip.

But if I do, I know
That God's our solid root,
And I can trust his love and care
As in his hands I'm put.

B G Bullington
ED
The mathematics of the earth
possessed his mind
The rhythm of the universe, his heart.
His hands would touch them both
to build, to make, create,
to guide a plow or stretch a fence,
dream of a system that would irrigate
his land, dig ditches for the pipe
to water trees and garden,
and plant small seed by seed
in rows made straight by string
stretched so the rows
of peas and corn and onions
looked mathematically right.

And he could fell a tree and cut
the lengths by saw so that
they fit a fireplace or a stove.
A man like that survives
wherever in the the world he finds
himself. This is a man
to whom the world belongs.

Janet Snyder Dugger

Janet Snyder Dugger
MY SELF-ESTEEM AND I

To my mother for her love of poetry, to my father for his sense of humor, Bess and Lindsay Snyder. Also to Jeff and Karla for believing in me and encouraging me to write.

I took Ballroom Dance Lessons
and while attempting to "bop"—
My partner said—
"Don't step out WIDE like a cow!"
While like a rabbit he did hop!
I just considered the source
instead of starting a row . . .
Although I did resent
being compared to a cow!

I'm not the best dancer,
but I do enjoy trying.
And no old codger
will send me home crying!
I may write Poetry
as well as learning to bop.
But, it's a break from work
and I'm thankful for
Like a rabbit—I don't hop!

Now there's two ways
to look at everything
So, rather than look glum,
I gathered up my sense of humor
and told everyone!
Although this actually happened
a few years ago
It still brings chuckles
from my friends
when to a dance we go!

Tina Horton
SOMEDAY
Someday all this pain and
heartache that I now feel,
Will someday seem so unreal.
All I ever wanted was for him to
love and care about me,
But I guess that I expected too
much of him and now he wants
to be free.
People say that I'll get over
him before too long,
And that all of my memories of
us will too soon be gone.
But how can you let go of
someone that you've grown
close to,
And someone who always made
you feel brand new.
But as time passes on,
I realize that most of the hurt and
pain has gone and been swept
away with the many tears.
And that it seems like years since
I've had him in my arms,
Or had him so near.

Connie P Cole (Mann)
MEAN STREAKS
The sun played plaids upon my skirt
As my hands traced the shadows
With the warmth of sun touching my heart
Although the swallow's melodies reminded me
Of you and I as History

The breeze chilling to the bones
As its force moves the dark blue water
The reflections showing my face
And the sorrows it has sustained
The cold blueness holds our sadness

The remains of the memories
About the size of the last mosquito
Swallowed by circles of raindrops

Ottis L Cotton
DAYBREAK ON THE MOUNTAIN

I saw beauty beyond all imagination
At daybreak, where I stood in awe
A glory shone o'er all the nation
As far as eye could see, was not a flaw

A golden skyline covered our busy world
As the light came creeping o'er the earth
Stars grew dim, as petals came uncurled
New born plants burst forth of nature's birth

I strolled along at daybreak, on the mountain
The beauty almost took my breath away
Gleaming rays of light, looked like a fountain
Such GLORY shines around this time of day

If you've never been on top of the mountain
At daybreak, when all nature is at its best
You've missed life flowing like a fountain
And the beauty of GOD'S creation, on the crest

Elizabeth T Cranch
POOR BUTTERFLY

It always makes me sad to see
A butterfly pinned under glass
With beautiful wings outspread
Like parchment crisp, and neatly placed
And used for decoration in a place
For all to see. Void of all life
And mounted with precision—
A thing of beauty, once so free
To flit from bowers of flowers bright
And gay—with sunbeams dancing on
Their wings and Nature's breezes softly
Bearing them on hapless journeys and
Unchartered paths.

Fragile and free, and in no hurry to
Arrive, but a dipping here and there and
Resting on a swinging red-rose tree.
Innocent of others' presence and only
Vaguely aware of its own—
Then caught, when least suspected by human
Hands, and stretched and pinned and placed beneath a glass
To decorate as ornament, or just be shown—

Ah, poor butterfly—my heart cries out for Thee
A thing of beauty once, and free—
Now trapped and lifeless for dull folks to see!

Dori Bakove
THE VOLUNTEER

She walks lightly,
As if she were not overweight
But had retained the youth of thirty years ago.
Her hair has grey in the brown that was once blonde.

None of this disturbs her
For she is going where the young are,
And they see only the inner self
With clear childhood eyes.

They like her she feels, as she them
And run to tell her important things,
Not all, for all children are not alike,
But she understands and feels welcomed
All the same, and welcomes all.

The room is bright and cheerful, and
There is a warm responsive air.
She smilingly greets the one or two adults,
Removes her jacket, reaches for a sheaf of folders,
And settles down with red marking pen,
Happy to be here where she feels wanted.

She thinks, fleetingly, how different this is
Than when she was a child, and how far away
In more ways than one.
Then turns and beckons to a child
Who has misspelled a word.
Her day has begun.

John Cabrera

John Cabrera
MONTE CRISTI NEVER FAR

Dear Mother, receive my poem as a flower-bouquet offering to you .....

Monte Cristi come to me
Oh beautiful town you are! ....
With cactus groves
And ocean coves
You're really not that far .....

El Morro calls to me
Its beauty never far
No matter where you are
Oh Monte Cristi come to me
To where I really am ....

I am always there
For in my heart
It is really not that far ....
So Monte Cristi come to me
And make me feel at home ....

Kathleen M Beiro
FORGIVE AND LOVE

It's important that we learn to forgive
So the hurts will heal and we can live,
A happier, more peaceful life.
A life without worry or painful strife.

Jesus is our greatest teacher.
He was a humanitarian and a preacher.
Forgiveness on the cross He asked.
His Father heard, and carried out the task.

Open up your heart and reach out.
That's what this poem is all about.
Learn to love without strings attached.
Forgiveness and love are quite a match.

Learn to accept me, to let me be.
That's how I grow into becoming me.
Remember the sad times, feel the pain.
Then let it go and begin to gain.

A life without barriers or walls.
A gift of acceptance and love, the best of all.
Our Father forgives us from up above.
He gives us his unconditional love.

Roseanna Napolitano Lackas

Roseanna Napolitano Lackas
MY MAN—MY EVERYTHING

"To my loving husband Al, who is my everything.'" And "To my wonderful mother and father—for without them this would never have been possible."

When the dark clouds surround me causing the day to drag by,
I can rely on you always to be the trustful, thoughtful, friendly guy.
For the friendship that you and I share goes much deeper than words can compare.

Sometimes when the little girl in me needs to be fathered,
I can run to you daddy dear, and you'll never utter—"I can't be bothered."
I'll sit upon your knee which is an invitation to chat.
And then I'm off again remembering your protective fatherly pat.

There are days however, when I realize you are down and out,
Needing and wanting my motherly instincts to come about.
I'll extend loving gestures and encouraging words observing in sheer joy.
The childish expressions upon your face, knowing you are now playing the little boy.

As lovers, we share much more than words can ever describe.
Just gazing into each other's eyes, with silent longing, feelings come alive.
What more can I ask for, what other gifts can you bring?
Just being you is enough my Love, Friend, Father, Son—MY EVERYTHING!

Iris M Besaw
DISINHERITED

Great grandfather's grandfather in his day
Lived in a castle, the old stories say.
Many's the night that the great hall rang
With the sound of the harp and the songs that they sang,
And the tales that were told of the ancestor who
Fought at the side of great Brian Boru,

I searched for my castle, and finally, then,
Came to the place where it once had been.
But sheep are now grazing within the keep,
The harp and singers are long asleep.
Scattered the stones of the once proud wall,
Long gone the banners and welcoming hall.

For only a moment I seem to see
The ghosts of the past surrounding me.
I hear faint music and laughter, and then
All is silent and peaceful again.
My dreams are all shattered, and I know at last,
My castle belongs to the dim, distant past.

Miss Joan T Camp
OH IT'S SOMETHING TO BE IRISH OR HERITAGE

Oh it's something to be Irish, something whimsical and gay
Though you kill your own ambition in your contradictory way
Though you'll never own a house or lot, nor ever gain renown
You have something that's the envy of the richest in the town
For when God breathed the breath of life into the lowly clod
He smiled and, for the Irish, put a singing in the sod

Michael J Berge
BATTERED DREAM SHIP

Once I sent a ship to sea, and hope was on her bow,
But time has brought her back to me and wisdom's painted now,
Yes, time has brought me many things and some of them were good,
And some of them were failure's stings I little understood.

When hope set forth the dream was fair, the sea was calm and blue,
I knew we'd meet with storms out there and had to ride them through;
But still I dreamed my ship would ride and weather every blow,
For hope flings many a truth aside which wisdom comes to know.

The storms have come with bitter

cold, I've prayed unto the Lord,
I've had false cargoes in the hold and thrown them overboard;
I've trimmed my sails to meet the gale, I've cut my journey short;
With battered hull and tattered sail at last I've come to port.

'Tis not enough to hope and dream
for storms will surely rise,
However smooth the sea may seem,
'tis there disaster lies;
And I have learned from time and stress, to those who ride the wave,
And come at last to happiness must suffer and be brave.

Helen M Shoneck
FREE VERSE ON FREEDOM

To the women of the world

Anxiety is akin to hunger? Yes, in that hunger can be allayed with food.
Truth dissipates the clouds of fear
With the sunshine of nurturing intelligence.
Fear and anxiety once held
The innocent in a grip of immobility.
But truth, learned and expressed
Returned their power within.
This conviction that we are free
From other's misunderstanding,
Produces the joy to be ourselves,
And benefits the souls
Of like convictions and faith.

Beverly R Rizzo
THE SPIRIT OF MASSACHUSETTS
The hills of the Berkshires are gleaming with snow,
The gracious inns of Nantucket Island await,
Romantic Cape Cod beckons with its majestic sand dunes,
Old Sturbridge Village reflects life in the past.

Busy, bustling Boston is vibrating with excitement,
The spirit of the Pilgrims is felt in quiet Plymouth town,
Along the Mohawk lies breathtaking woodlands and gorges,
And magical Salem town bewitches the traveler.

This is the spirit of Massachusetts calling,
Where the rustic, peaceful country-side awaits me,
Where the salty air and the playful sea call,
and the rich heritage of the past haunts me.

Take me to playful cities like Boston and Springfield,
Let me bask in the colorful foliage, and watch the sun set over the glistening snow,
The spirit of Massachusetts has captured me forever.

Gail McPeak Poderzay
WHY
You asked me to tell you what I think is the reason why,
The answer lies between the Earth and the Overpowering Sky.

We were put upon this land to prove what we are worth,
And for every sad and painful death, is the miracle of birth.

We need each other to cling to, to keep from going insane.
The flowers need the sunshine as well as they need the rain.
I believe the Lord communicates through the Lightning and the Thunder.
And I'm glad I have the ability to be satisfied to just wonder.

David Parker
FALL SONG
The moon rises gibbous
Waiting for my call.
The moon shines on softly
Waiting for the fall.
A dream, only a dream,
Is reality.
A dream, but just a dream,
One as soft as she.
With the morn' comes the fall,
Dew soaked cool and sweet.
With the morn', comes safety
From this trail I beat.
The leaves colored brightly,
Fall down to the ground.
The leaves, mottled gaily,
Fall endlessly down.
Someday soon, I will fall
To the dew soaked grass.
Someday soon, I'll forget,
And my life will pass.
My tears, colored brightly,
Fall down to the ground.
My tears, mottled sadly,
Fall endlessly down.

Ada Kendall Miller
THIS IS TODAY
This is today, there may not be a tomorrow,
I want to live it every moment of the day
Filled full with Love, Joy, Peace and pure Contentment
And then, at eve let me kneel and humbly pray.

This is today, let kindness be the keynote
To fill each moment and to soothe each woe,
Of all that I may meet upon life's pathway,
A fuller, richer life that I may know.

This is today, may I take time to play with children,
To listen to their joy or childish woe,
To share their simple trusting faith, to be humble
And to forgive, no malice let me know.

This is today, Lord, help that I might live it
As though it were the last of this my life.
Let it be filled with deeds of love and mercy
To offset all unkindness, hate and strife.

This is today, then may I sing and be happy,
There is so much sorrow, heartaches, pain and fears
That will linger after I've departed,
So let me laugh to hide the anguish of a falling tear.

James P Dowd
ALL SAME . . . ALL SAME . . .

All Same . . . All Same was written in honor of the noted Potawatomi leader Shabni (He Has pawed Through) b 1775-d 1859

They called him barbarian,
Uncivilized man.
He sounded forth no clarion,
His name he could not write.
They called him "Friend of White Men,"
Castrated brother.
He sold their land with X of pen,
He bargained for a nation.

A grove of timber was given him,
For all time.
It was taken at a whim,
He blacked his face and left.

Upon his way he met a friend,
Civilized man.
And here all rime must end.
He said, "White man called him,
Damn Indian."

With tear stained eyes,
He looked heavenward and said,
"No damn Indian, no damn White man,
All same . . . All same . . . "

This was God's barbarian.

Sharon Rose Gray
IN MEMORIES OF YOU
Memories of you flashed through my mind as I thought of you today. You're my loving brother that God called to me one day. A place you have in my heart you're one I'll never forget and when God called you home you went with no regrets. For such a kind and loving person you were God knew you had won the race.
He called you home to be with him, by His loving grace. I know you are happy where you are for nothing can compare for you're in the arms of Jesus in his loving care.

William Michael O'Farrell
WRITE VERSE FOR THE LOVE OF WRITING

To that long leg thing of loveliness with the smiling Irish eyes who stole my heart in our first kiss.

Oh there you stood
In loveliness
As Venus would
Like some goddess,
And young red rose
Long stem and fair
Where beauty grows
And love's seen there.

Oh love's of heart
From deep in soul
Where love gets start
And is made whole.

Oh saw you come
Strolling down street
Not knowing from
Looking so sweet
With smile on face
When seeing me
Whose beauty trace
In love to be.

Up there you wait
For me, my Love,
At Heaven's gate
Up there above
With open arms
Oh dearest Love
And all thy charms!

James C Hostetler
VISIONS

Dedicated to my loving mother Ruth Hostetler. Went home to be with the Lord, May 22, 1988—by James Hostetler

Visions, dreams, and so often do I see
The harsh realities of life to be
You grow in a womb, full of care and pride
But all too soon this magic has matured and died
Together we grew, my mother, our Lord and I
Always living, always loving
Knowing that nothing else would preside
Then one day you feel a deep trembling inside
Just then the two of us began to realize
God's plan for both of our lives
Justified the endless thinking, a futility
We with all of our mortality
We with a careless desire, certainly never to expire
For on that fateful day don't you see
I was granted, a greatest gift of all
A chance to see another type of visions,
Dreams, and this time God's realities
For on this day, my earthly mother precious to me
Went home to God.
Our Lord to her and I to be.

Jane Jennings Sullivan
THE GROWING YEARS
As your child grows older,
The more priceless he becomes,
As a baby you fed, changed and loved him
You enjoy showing him off,
Then comes the first tooth,
The first word (which is normally Da-Da),
And he crawls and gets into everything,
But you love him even more,
Then finally comes his first step,
You discipline with love,
And as your child grows older he begins to return your love,
He respects your judgement,
And often asks your opinion of things,
For you have succeeded in teaching him LOVE

Violet B Roberts
SOLILOQUY OF A CAST IRON SINK
I ain't much to look at
I'm not in the "pink,"
I'm just an old-fashioned
Cast-iron sink.
I've seen many things
In my heyday
So there's just a few words
I'd like to say.
Women have washed dishes.
And babies so small
Maybe Grandma washed her hair,
When she came to call!
Mothers have shed tears
On that fateful day

When Johnnie went to war
And Susie ran away.
These modern-day 'gadgets'
Ain't got nothing on me
So I think I'll stick around
'Till the next cen-tu-ry!

Leo Reeve Moore

Leo Reeve Moore
THE DEATH OF A NATION

Dedicated to Arizona Moore, Marguerite Robinson, Harriet Carroll, Bimbo Schwarz, Geri Cohen, Herbert Taylor, Warren Easton High School and The United States.

Sir Jesus crossed the Atlantic deep.
Its cargo chained, some whipped, and some did weep.
Oh, 1619, that dreaded year,
Now trapped in bondage, in hate, in fear.

The winds of war, blowing gray, and blowing blue,
The blood runneth freely, down Bull Run's boot.
The congressional plan, did pass the test,
Freeing the invisible shadow, from the plantation nest.

The 1896, legalized beast,
Gave the hooded monster, a lynching feast.
A king appeared, a knight from God,
Put forth his sword, into jim crow's heart.

Nothing ventured, not much gained,
The protest is done, life remains the same.
Dealing in drugs, on a city street,
From the ghetto, to a prison, then a dead piece of meat.

Children begetting children, all wards of the state.
Ignorance and poverty, what is their fate?
Lost in America, without any salvation,
The writing on the wall, means the death of a nation.

Seppo Kauppinen
NOSTALGIA FOR SIXTIES
Hey! Hippie girl I remembered you well,
You came to me like a whirl and my life felt no hell.
You knew my weakness and I knew your sweetness
Before your coming I was afraid of beads from your neck.
Now I can sing—They are on you every sec.
I see the beautiful bells in your hands, you played them
in step of eternal rock'n roll bands.
Do you remember in 1969? It was fine.
At Woodstock we felt the rock.

We sang: "Give peace a chance" and turned into trance with grass.
My hands were knowing a sure point in your hair, when you lighted a joint for me with no going anywhere.
Every wet morning you brought the flowers at my feet by saying:
Only the flowers feel the salt of the street, don't kick them away from you like most of the men do.

Danielle Cerniglia
EYES
The eyes, mirrors of the soul
Reflections from deep within
Glances of hopes, dreams, and desires.
How they sparkle, laughing without a sound.

When I look in your eyes, I am sometimes lost.
They tell me everything I need to know,
You look away,
And the moment is gone forever.

Sally A Truax
DAYS

I would like to dedicate this poem "Days" to my mom, dad, and brother, and my friends. Thank you for your support and understanding.

Some days my thoughts are just like cacoons–all cold, dull and blind

They hang from dripping branches in the grey woods of my mind;

And other days they drift and shine such free and flying things!

I find the gold dust in my hair, left by their brushing wings.

Heather Ann Bilbo
JUPITER'S RING
I live day by day . . .
The facets of my personality
Are that of a windmill,
Increasing speed,
The unbearable pitch is heard,
The murmur of splitting air,
Then suddenly, it spins off its foundation
And flies away like an owl,
At night, after a satisfying hunt

David McCraine
LOOK BUT DON'T BE MISTOOK
Have you ever been Mistaken
OH but a way to be Forgiven
If we could only Die that day we were saved
OH but our Lord has more in store for US

We should ask for forgiveness when we STRAY
But Hey! Who are we to say
That's why we need a SAVIOR
'Cause even though we go to Church
That don't give us the right to be a man such as us
So next time give ear, when you are near and can help
'Cause who wants to be accused or misused
Not I says the rich, the rich in faith

A J Adams
HELPING HAND
"Take my hand," suggested the guide
When rugged terrain bruised my feet,
Tore my knees as ascent grew steeper
While the heat of day burned our backs.
"Take my hand," he said again
As I slipped and fell and wondered:
"What's the use when woodlands cool
And dancing brook beckon below?"

"Take my hand," he kindly urged.
I took his hand to note its strength.
There in the palm a gaping wound
Aglow with light of Risen Glory.

Prof Eleanor J Macdonald

Prof Eleanor J Macdonald
EVENTIDE

To Dr. Paul C. Castagno, my Godson with love.

Eventide and calm reflection
Thoughts of joy and introspection
Golden sunset gently fading
Velvet stillness all pervading
Heart and spirit upward soaring
Love of life's great gifts outpouring.

Nature's beauty, Heaven's grace
Give to eventide its place.

Karen Sue Bowen
IMAGE OF A STRANGER
I was scared to pass my mirror today
Afraid of whom I might see,
for every time I pass by
I notice a change in me.

But most of all
I'm afraid of the day
when I'll look in my mirror and see,
A person I've never seen before
Looking back at me.

Greer McCowan
FRIENDS FOREVER
I'll always be there for you.
Even when you are blue.
Even when we are far apart.
We'll still be close at heart.
I can't find the words to say,
What I want to tell you this day.
Even though you don't know what went wrong,
Just remember you don't know what you have until it's gone.
I'll always be your friend,
'Cause I don't want this friendship to come to an end.

Laura V Kutz
(U.S.A.) THE TORCH THAT SET US FREE
The torch that set us free
Let it shine from sea to shining sea;
And let the whole world see
What it means, to have freedom.

An American

Maria R Mazzenga
KITSCH
An American told me
Freedom here
A life
of
Choice

In the slum
A skinny black woman
Dances the garish club
Drunk
Drugged

She moved in her dance
To the stir
In her
Heart
Embittered
Free

Em W Burgess
THE DREAM
Buried in dirt, my bones and flesh
In time with Mother Earth will mesh.
And then, who knows?
A flower grows.
Or, rain-soaked, join a sparkling stream
Alight with sun: life-source, I dream,
Of souls who help fulfill God's scheme.

B Frederick King
TRUE
The shock of happiness! Is to realize how great God is. The love that reached even me. His only son at Calvary. May I do something for you? He has proven so true, and just today He came through.
Through disappointment and despair.
And I have peace beyond compare.
Now is there something I can do for you? He is so true!

Lillie Mae Crum
THE GOLDEN YEARS
The golden years of life for me, have suddenly arrived.
I wasn't ready to grow, but I'm sure that I'll survive.
It seems each day grows shorter, or maybe it's just me
I don't do the things I ought to, with out a push you see.
I pause and watch the sunrise, at the beginning of each new day.
I listen, to the birds sing, and then I kneel to pray.
"Our Father who art in Heaven
thank you for your love,
thank you for the peace and joy
that comes from Thee above.
I thank you for the sunshine
and I thank you for the rain
I thank you for your healing touch
that eases all my pain."
And as the evening shadows fall and the sun begins to set,
I lift my heart in worship, that God did not forget,
to love me and sustain me,
as I stumbled along life's road,
but He came and walked beside me,
and shared my heavy load.
As I close my eyes in slumber,

I surrender my all to Thee.
I know my heavenly Father,
will be watching over me.

Jessica Anne Lee

Jessica Anne Lee
FANTASY, REFLECTING LIKE A JEWEL UNDER FLUORESCENT LIGHTS

Dedicated to Janice Ann, My Inner Child

Pulling rabbits out of a hat
I see the day has come to an end.
Nighttime laughter
It echoes
Unlike the cold of day.
I sit,
And watch the time slip into oblivion.
Needless to say
There are moments in haste
Mostly though
There are bits and pieces,
And if the ear is quick
An echo will linger
To light the dawn of fantasy,
Reflecting like a jewel
Under fluorescent lights.

Rosemary Cornum
FEELINGS
As I lie here on my bed
Words keep tumbling in my head

Yes, a poem I must write
I'll put it down in black and white

Could it be, that I someday
might have something great to say?

This poem I'm about to write
Will be something out of sight

This is my priority
to contribute to society

It will make my life worth while
by touching someone with a smile

Seeds of kindness, I will sow
Spreading love where ever I go

These are the most precious to me
Feelings of love we cannot see

Victor G Buendia
A LOST SON
My father, I am talking to you from the bottom of my heart

And you know better than anyone in what kind of hell I was.
Even as I did wrong and sin, You were not ever away from me.
I didn't know that until now.

You even sent an angel to take away my sadness and despair,
To give me back to myself . . . I couldn't feel anymore.

The nights were long, lonely and painful
No one to hold—no one to talk to.

And on dark cold nights to fall asleep with a broken heart
And tears on my soul.

Only to wake up in the morning to bright sunny day with a
Somber and empty mind.

But, my Father, I see and I can once again feel the taking and

The giving of the Master all over again.

You took away part of my life to make me see who I was,
But you came once again to show me who I could really be.

I thank thee for giving me another chance in this life
To be happy and to make someone happy, too.

P.S. I promise my father—To be kind, gentle and loving
To the angel you have given me, because I feel this is your gift to my soul.

Your loving son

Mary L Brett Hunter
MY MAN
I once met a man
Who appeared loving and kind
I immediately became his fan
For I thought he was truly fine
We married and a house we shared
I loved him, was devoted and truly cared
It wasn't long as I recall
As I look back over the years
A spouse and family he didn't cherish
That's when I realized my real fears
We divorced, and now two houses we share
I loved and lost
He never loved nor did he care

Brian C Pratt

Brian C Pratt
LIFE AS I KNEW IT TO BE

Sadly, I dedicate this poem to all the aborted babies of the world.

My forming body is engulfed in darkness
I live in a warm liquid from head to toe
floating weightlessly in my expanding home
My cells split often forming more and more
of my growing body

Am I alive or not—no one knows
in here or outside my home of protection
Does my host know I'm here—who is she
who are my creators of life, do they know of me
or am I a surprise to them and the world I'm destined for
Am I alive or just growing in secret
Do they know of me . . . what are they like
What am I like, boy or girl—who will I take after . . .

I feel scared I don't know why—am I alive . . .
My presence is threatened—something is wrong
My host is scared-confused-helpless
I don't know how I can feel her thoughts
what's wrong . . . what's wrong with me . . .
Quiet, what's that, something is coming in
penetrating my warm home of protection
Are they coming in to get me now or just say hello to their own
No . . . it hurts, what are they doing . . . don't they know I'm alive

I'm being pulled—the pain, what is wrong with me . . .
What is wrong with them . . .
Darkness—cold lifelessness numbs my tiny body motionless
What's wro . . .

Karen S Lucas
MAKE ME YOUR VESSEL
Make me Your vessel Lord, I empty myself,
Washed clean by the Light of Your word;
Bind up the broken shards, with Your nail-pierced hands,
You're the Potter, Creator and Wine.
Remold me if needed, I belong to You Lord,
Make me pliable, quick to give way;
If I ever resist, help me not to forget
You're the Potter and I am the clay.
Make me Your vessel Lord, fill 'till I'm full
and pour me if needed I pray;
If I can be used in Your most humble way
I'm willing, choose me if you may.
Break me if needed, I belong to you Lord
'Cause I know You know best and will stay
close beside me to hide me, 'till I'm whole again,
You're the Potter and I am the clay.
Make me Your vessel Lord, tried by the fire
'till what's left of my will becomes dross;
If ever I think I am more than I am,
Place me at the foot of the cross.
Make me Your vessel, I belong to You Lord
Glaze me colors to brighten the gray;
Here is my heart, I entrust in Your hands,
You're the Potter and I am the clay.

Jennifer J Decker
THE PLAYER PIANO
Tuxedoed keys tinkle and thump
to noted scroll conducting
phantom orchestra
impersonating
Gershwin rhapsodies
Mozart's mirth
ragtime rhythm
and polished polkas.
The Watham's shuffling spirit
turns moods upright
and directs frolickers
prancing on the ivory boardwalk.

Patricia A Farkas
THE HOLLOW COST
Set me free; set me free.
Spare the cost, use the rod, spear the bird.
Lift a strap, drill a hole . . .
lobotomies always are free.

How hollow, how hollow, how hollow . . .
Schaloum, schaloum,
schaloum . . . (Does it really mean rest me in peace?)

How much does a hollow cost cost?
Messrs, Bush and Gorbachov—
Are your kids looking out for you?
Or are they looking up to you through six feet of smelly green grass?
Give them grass, give them gas,
Give them cash, give them cash
Or they'll come back to haunt us, rob us, cheat us and defeat us
And we'll all blow up this ball of fire again.

Give me ten willing men, if you can, if you can.
Give me ten willing men, if you can.
Love, forgiveness, understanding,
Mercy, cigarettes and candy . . .
May start to win a mighty big campaign.

Daanon De Cock
UNTITLED
Oh precious heart
Like the sun that rises every morning
Or the moon in the sky each night
Shine your glorious light
On my naked body
Change the color of my soul
Let me see the beauty of the world
Protect me from the blindness of night
Make me feel warm and whole
Show me the way to happiness
I want to hear the sweet music
Of birds chirping in the morning light
Hear the dogs howling at the half moon
Because the moon drives me just as crazy
And the sun excites me and energizes me
But when the eternal light
of your love
Shines in my eyes and blinds me,
From all that makes me sad
I realize that the night is
a peaceful thing
Only to fall asleep and dream of your precious heart

Wendell K Babcock
MEMORABILIA
Age begets memories,
Precious, pleasant, painful.
Pictures frame 10,000 words of mystic moments,
Frozen forever in still statues of sentiment.
Knitted, not tucked away in the torture and torment of time,
But exhibited, exposed,
Expressing with radical realism
The life and longing of a departed loved one—
the vacant chair,
still pressed with the posture of missing presence;
the fingerprinted black pen,
pendulummed by black velvet,
entombed to write no more;
the childhood valentine,
embossed with "sweetheart" and smell of spice;
sentimental staircases lined with laughter,
laced and latticed with limitations.
Sentiment speaks with soft-cushioned steps;
Sensibility closes the clutching closet of the past,
Simply, silently, calmly clinging to the present.

Eunice Schroader
LIFE
Is life a reality or is it just a dream
We go from day to day, thinking that things will be better,
For some it will, for others it will be worse. When my life has run its course, I will know that life is a reality and not just a dream. When I live in Paradise that is us.

Eduardo Tavarez

Eduardo Tavarez
EDDA

With all my love to my sister Edda, object of my Muse . . .

Delicate, subtle, of noble soul
Generous, gentle, as a writer
You are a good fairy godmother and a dreamer
Object of my Muse in my song . . . .

And I want from the flowers the perfume
And from honey the feminine sweetness
From the Lord the afternoon calmness
So I could give you my verses here . . .

From the Great Romantics you keep
The virtue of dreaming in your lap
And many loves in their embraces, give
Elegance to your steps when you walk . . . .

Deep inside you feel the vibrations
Of sadness, love and happiness
Of the people of peace, melancholy
Which transform your being into
Orange Blossom . . . .

Nedra Nancyan Heine
A FRIEND FROM GOD
To have a friend is a blessing indeed.
Someone to be there in happiness or need.

Someone with whom to share—
A cry—a laugh—a prayer.

Someone who really cares about you.
Someone who is interested in all that you do.

SOMEONE

To go for a walk.
To sit for hours and talk.

A friend to laugh with you—not at you.
A friend to come and cry and pray with you.

Thru thick and thin—you know they care
In your hour of need—you know they will be there.

So—I ask of GOD today
To send some friend
your
way.

Someone with whom to share—
A cry—a laugh—a prayer.

Bob K Johnson
A MORNING STAR
A morning star I did see,
Falling like a hard thrown dart.

My prayerful wish to be,
Grant us a single heart.

This heart is a home for you and me,
Where our love can grow, like from the start.

I remember a dream,
Of a wonderful, magnificent place.

Of a cottage by a mild flowing stream,
In morning sunlight, I lay watching your face.

In the sunlight's golden beam,

With beauty made from above,
Shaming Diana, of ancient Greece.

Like a delicate morning dove,
Your touch brings a sweet release.

Sharing with me your soul filling love,
Brings complete, perfect peace.

David M Kane
THE LAST ROSE (PART I)
Sitting in the golden sand
underneath the shining sun,
Warm breeze breaks the morning calm.
So many thoughts confused with emotions.
Watching the water's reflection, all I can see
is the Last Rose

When we dance our hearts come together.
Flowing with every step like a dream.
Hoping each song would last forever.
Forever the Last Rose.

It could rain for a thousand years,
I would never shed a tear.
I will love her forever.
Forever the Last Rose.

I sit and listen to myself; all I hear
No hellos, no goodbyes, nothing but my fears.
Outside, finally falls the night,
The moon looks down on all the lonely people
with their frowns.
As for me all I can see is the Last Rose.
Forever the Last Rose.

Clover Kreger
MY LOVE, MY PREOCCUPATION
We swim in each other's kisses
I dive into your mouth, and you into mine
The depths in your eyes no-one can fathom
But it's I who brings out their luster shine

Presents to each other, endless gifts
Trust, devotion to our dual-blended joy
Seeking to cleanse one another of past sorrows
And in our force untied overcome the dark alone

Our predator whilst in separate solitude
That can conquer us no more
We refract ourselves, like prisms
The thousand facets of this love
Of you, and I

Bennie C Stephens
THE COLOR BLACK
Why is the color black used to represent bad?
Was it started by someone prejudice superstitious,
or just sad.

Black monday, Black cat, Black magic, Black bee.
These are but a few of the many bad blacks we see.

What should I tell my children who are black like me that this makes them bad, because being black
is to be.

Rod Lewis
ARE YOU READY TO DEPART?
With justice, mercy, love, advance the eternal plan.
One part of earth, one part divine, together make
The Fatherhood of God, the Brotherhood of Man.

Is reason lost? Is rationale Utopian?
Is it too much to ask that we could—full awake,
With justice, mercy, love, advance the eternal plan?

Think well! One button pushed could bring night stygian.
Dead! The birds, the fawn—and YOU! This would unmake
The Fatherhood of God, the Brotherhood of Man.

Our Lord has given us all that we need. We scan
His Book, to learn His way. We must make no mistake:
With justice, mercy, love advance the eternal plan.

All souls are His. The Christian, the Mohammedan
Must share this panicked Earth, and all, ALL! must partake
The Fatherhood of God, the Brotherhood of Man.

Noah cannot help us now, nor other artisan;
It's up to us to act or die. For survivance sake
With justice, mercy, love—advance the eternal plan—
The Fatherhood of God, the Brotherhood of Man.

Lorraine Goggins

Lorraine Goggins
WINTER WONDERLAND

I dedicate this poem to my family who have always been supportive of my writing and to 8 special friends, Sue, Mary, Paula, Pete, Mrs. DePaul, Lynne, Lisa, Anne Marie and all my friends at CATCH 22

I awaken to a coverlet of minute ice crystals
Enveloping the cold surface of my window pane.
I am so tempted to stay snuggled beneath my blanket
But in my security of warmth I do not remain.
Instead I arise and wipe the frost from the window
And as I look outside, what a picturesque ensemble I see.
The trees have shed their leaves and are quite barren
Yet their branches, from the element of snow are not free.
This white flaky substance also encompasses the ground
Making it difficult for plant life to breathe so for now they sleep.

All shapes and sizes of snowmen, snowflakes and snowforts are about
Children are laughing and playing in the frozen vapor which is knee deep.
They are bundled up like eskimos in the weather so brisk and cold

As they go sledding and iceskating or they shovel snow that is piled high.
Feet are made stiff from the low temperature, runny noses dry in the air
Dangling icicles are a common sight and firmly packed snowballs whizz by.
I am ready to brave the weather for I too am bundled up like an eskimo
And as I walk out the door to the invigorating climate to start my day.
I am reminded once again by the snow and the chill that the winter is here
And I dream of the day's end when again in my cozy heated room I can lay.

Ozzie B Glisson
JUST MIND YOUR OWN BUSINESS

You've got me so confused
My mind's in a fog.
I don't know if I'm your horse
Or if I'm your dog.
Just mind your own business
And I'll take care of mine.
If I ever need your service,
I'll let you know on time.
You may think you're getting by
With Slandering me,
But the one that keeps the record
Knows it all you see.
Find yourself another sucker
And stop picking on me.
Get off of my back
And just let me be
I've probably said enough
But I want you to know
If I ever need you,
I'll let you know Pronto.

Robert F Gloor
FROM MY HOSPITAL BED

Though death is not yet at my door
Its chill is in the air.
For though I walk not by its shore
The chill blows in from there.

I wrap my robe about me tight
And shiver in my bed
For fear that I might catch death's sight
Or hear its nearing tread.

Claire W Harkrider
HEAT WAVES

I would like to dedicate this poem to my sister, Letty G. Moon without whose encouragement I would never have begun. With my love.

Hot bands of summer played endlessly,
Prairie breezes danced gleefully in the grass.
Her hatbrim flapped in a fitful gust the only sound the plop of jumping bass.

Circles spread on quiet water below the bank where she sat in the shade of the tall reaching tree nodding low in the breeze
on the edge of a shadowy glade.

As she watching the faces of youth had waited, quieting her fears.
No longer young . . . no longer light-hearted . . .
bowed down by the weight of years.

If only . . . . if only . . . if only . . . . she'd known
the sorrows and bleakness of time spent all alone and away from the love
that creates the only reason and rhyme.

Hindsight can be very deceiving
and the wisest of us can be wrong.
So she waits in the cool evening of life
for the sound of the beloved's song.

But the song will never more be sung.
The faces laugh cruelly and move on.
The blue breezes sigh in sympathy
and the hot summer bands march on!

Edda Tavarez Cabrera

Edda Tavarez Cabrera
CHILD OF LITTLE SAD EYES

To all the forgotten children of the World, this my Motherly Lament of Sadness and Hope . . .

Child of little sad eyes, melancholic and somber
Who head-lowered walks in shadows of indifference
When did your luminous eyes lose their glow?
When did your child curiosity, die? . . .

In your weak entrails I see hunger entangled
Which like a merciless weed slowly spreads and destroys
And even though the child of my flesh you are not
I have sons, and in the core of my being, your anguish cries.

Little sad eyes like two pieces of a night without stars
Small pebble going down hill through the roads of the world
Let's be the saving hand that will detain your fall
Let's imitate Christ, loving and compassionate . . . .

Mercy for those eyes that cry and implore
Mercy for that life that dies with hope.
Let's teach him to earn his bread and cure his wounds
His tragedy reflects our troubled humanity . . . .

Angel of sadness, cherubim without heaven
Our love will break your chain of slavery
And in your universal eyes of sadness, one day
The beautiful stars of your redemption, will shine! . . . .

Constance Russell
THE SUGAR SNOW

With silent flake on flake all through the April night
The power of Heaven had draped our little world in white—
The Great—the Patient Builder—had builded our world anew.

'T was Easter morn and every white robed tree
Sent forth a silent gleam of mystery—
The elms were crowned with white
And in the morning light
One might call them lilies, in their majesty.
No footprints there of man or beast
To mark the place where roadways meet and stretch away
'Tween rows of birches, snow-laden, leaning o'er;
And mystic pines their shadows throw
Across the deep, new fallen snow.
The church bells' blended tones reach us here—
All else is silence while the world is sparkling white
As far as one can see.

With silent flake on flake, all through the April night
The power of Heaven had draped our little world in white.
The Great, the Patient Builder has builded our world anew.

Lee R Will
DAYBREAK

Daybreak, the dawn of the morning
The sun is shining so clear
Come see, explore your surroundings
There is no reason to fear

Sing out, the day it has started
Bore once again from the night
Feel free, with no chains around you
Your soul is soaring in flight

Sunrise, it creeps to the sky
Climbing higher with the passing of time
New life, is springing forth
While thoughts are arousing your mind

Gazing at the horizon
Changing colors to the eye
You're witnessing the morning
As the sun rises to the sky

Its rays touch down all around
While the warmth is felt on the face
The light cuts through the darkness
Awakening the human race

Life giving sunlight
Caresses the world anew
Lighting up the hemisphere
For me and for you

Sunshine, the night it is over
It's the start of a brand-new day
Speak out, express all your feelings
Let the world know what you have to say

Look round, at your surroundings
As the sun awakens the land
Sing out, so you can be heard
Let others know where you stand

Daybreak, a new day has dawned
The sun is shining so clear
Come see, reach out your hand
There is no reason to fear

Brenda Godwin
LOVE

LOVE
Love is special.
It happens between two people
Who have something very special between them.

Love is something that you take with you wherever you go.

You hold onto that love in your heart, and keep it
there forever. Don't ever let it go!

What happens to love when your heart has been broken,
When that special someone leaves?

Where does it go? Does it sink way down deep & then emerge
When someone new comes along?

Or does it stay down deep and is only brought back by your memories?

LOVE

Devronne

Devronne
ARTIST'S SONG

To Desiraee, Danielle and Nicole, my wonderful daughters.

Abide with me
in my heart of hearts—

vision
liberty
originality

My song for the arts—

Portrayed drama
of emotion—

longing
desire
passion
fire

Alive on canvas calling . . .

Hazel Lillian Weber
WOULD WE

If we could know about tomorrow,
If it were like opening up a door,
Would we want to open it up quickly
Just to see what the future has in store?

If we saw hope and anticipation,
Would we enter and explore?

Or, would we be afraid of the tomorrow
And quickly close the door?

What if we saw in the future
Only loneliness, emptiness and pain?
Would we really want to open it,
Or shut it tight,
Never to ever open it up again?

Susan Davis Wilson
I CARE ABOUT YOU STRONGLY

I care about you strongly
though the mere words
I cannot say
I want to tell you
Oh, so badly
but you're always afraid
because mostly when
they're said
You're always betrayed

I want us to have
something special
especially in that way
I want us to share and
to care and never to delay
and . . .

I promise that if our relationship
ever is betrayed
I will not be—the one—
who has strayed

Because Darling,
I DO LOVE YOU!

Sylvia Wilson
HEY GRANNIE YOU'RE SORTA SWEET

Hey, Grannie you're sorta sweet,
you're cute and smart and even neat.
I loved you when,
I was small.
I love you now,
and I'm so tall.
I remember when, I was nine,
all these things are really fine.
Like when you'd say
"Wash your feet!"
Or, hey girls,
Now eat your meat!
You'd wake us up
to catch the bus,
And, oh, sometimes,
We would really fuss.
Now, what I'm saying
is I love you.
You're super special,
for what you do!

Gertrude Brown Welbourn
YOU DON'T HAVE TO ROUND A CORNER

You don't have to round a corner,
To find your joy and peace.
You don't have to climb a mountain,
To realize victory.
You don't have to see a rainbow,
To learn of God's promise to man.
For all this beauty and goodness
Surrounds you, upholds you,
As ever is in God's plan.

But you must know of His presence;
You must trust Him to be right there.
You must know that good comes from goodness;
And then pass it on through love and care.

Pauline Rogers
POETRY

Poetry lives in the back of one's mind
Where all the words are easy to find
Telling us what we long to hear
Constantly holding us ever so near

After sad farewells have long been made
And happy memories begin to fade
A poem will stay to always remember
To hold and keep forever and ever

Someday . . . I'll write some poetry
When all my thoughts and time are free
So that you shall know . . . and also see
Exactly how I feel . . . inside of me

I'll write in dark indelible ink
Visualizing an invisible link
Showing you how I dream and think
With words that flow like a quenching drink

Someday . . . I'll write some poetry

Rebecca Ruby
EACH OTHER

To the one that made a difference in my life and always will.

Each has our own
Secret Love
With a special person
Moments
Like these
Are
Worth waiting for
Waiting to be heard
Nobody can
Ever forget
You and I
Until at last
We discovered
A living gift
In each other

Georgia Anne Dean

Georgia Anne Dean
I SEE YOUR SHINING FACE LOOKING TOWARDS ME

I see your shining face looking towards me, as if you had something on your mind, you were trying to say.
I see your tears lightly dust the ground, as the eagle cries and one more looks about to see who shares the pain. The waves of your body quiver yet only for a minute, as the thunder makes its way down.
I hear it from a distant plain, and I recall a memory, if only for a short while. The valleys I've climbed, the folks I've met, all saying the same thing. But no one really seeking for what it is they can't find.

The moon shines down on what I once knew as close to me. Yet is all gone now.
I see your shining face looking towards me, as if you had something on your mind, you were trying to say.
But, yet you hide the truth, as the eagle flies on—
but yet does not cry . . .

David F Plant
LEGACY

This is for Heidi. And it's from the men she left behind.

Part of what makes ourselves
so special
Is that we have gifts from
those we lost
And our best tribute to them
is to understand
That they gave their hearts so
that we
Would stand even taller, having
learned through
Their grace that we could walk
even deeper
In their footsteps and lead
ourselves onward.

Teresa A Ramsey (Age 93)
4TH OF JULY POEM 1987

Our lady of Liberty
With her outstretched hand;
She welcomes all people,
To our beautiful land.

She holds her torch high
To light up the ocean;
She does all these things
With the greatest devotion.

Be they Chinese or Germans,
All humans alike,
Respecting all nations,
Black, Yellow or White.

We worship with freedom,
No one seems to care;
If we had a dictator,
We just wouldn't dare.

Let's worship our freedom,
And Thank God we're here;
Enjoy every moment,
'Till our last days are here.

Emily R Whalen
I HEARD A LARK SING

I heard a lark sing
When I awoke
I heard a lark sing
And it spoke
Of sadness and tears;
For her love had gone.

I heard a lark sing
When I awoke,
I heard a lark sing
And it spoke,
Of the gay times
The happy times
When life was new
And bright as the sun
Before her love had gone.

I heard a lark sing
When I awoke
I heard a lark sing
And it spoke,
Of unending dreams
Spun like silver threads
In a gossamer gown
As illusive as the night.

I heard a lark sing
I heard a lark sing
And its song
Healed my soul;
For I knew
I was not alone

Helen H Wickwire
FRIENDS

As I walk down the street
Always old friends I chance to meet;
Meandering seniors strolling by—
Teens jogging and singing the song
Of their right to belong.
Hoping they will heed my call
Of "Hi friends, how are you doing today?"
"Will the sky be sunny, or clouds of gray?"
Never mind—today is great!
It matters not what the elements be
So long as old friends I see,
Whether they meander, jog, or skate,
I'm happy to know they're "First Rate."

Victor Leppky
THE ROSE

When the snow runs down the mountains
And the warm winds start to blow
And the spring rains on those winds
Come to make the roses grow
The hand of God gives life to all
From ocean depths to sky above
And the common thread thru all
The life that's given thru impartial love

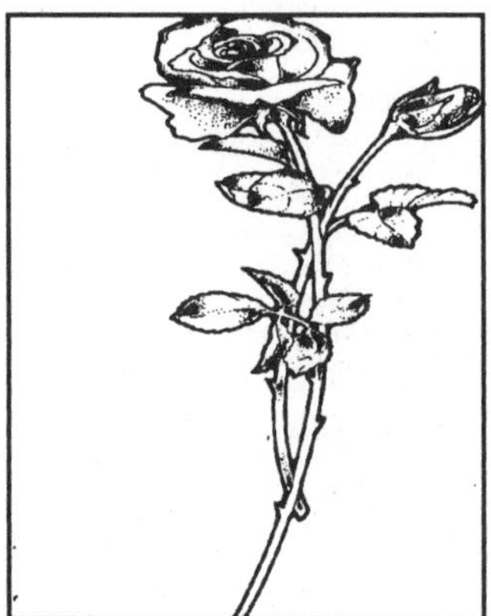

When those who go in search of love
Feel their world is torn apart
Can see the love that grows the rose
Then will find it in their heart
And those who finally find this love
Find there's nothing that they need
For all they touch will be a rose
When love is given as the seed.

Jennifer C Luccio
FOR JESS

She whirls through life
in the fast lane.
You want her affection
but she will not play the game.
Don't lose sight of her,
she might slip away.
High spirited, up-beat,
she is not here to stay
She'll be gone in a heartbeat
if you dare turn around.
You try to catch her heart,
but you can't tie it down.
Her laughing eyes hold secrets
that you long to understand.
She dares you to keep up with her.
You wonder if you can.
Your heart melts in her smile,
it breaks when she is gone.
Take a deep breath, call to her.
Tell her you are coming along.

Grace T Murphy
REFLECTION

Its long slender body ebbs by
harboring in its bosom the
secrets of by-gone years.

An armless doll, an airplane tire, and an old palm frawn
ride the crest, leaving us with
many unanswered questions.

A lone fish as if trying to escape
jumps up into the sunshine and

then
falls back into the murky deep.

So too, life passes us by
keeping many secrets, divulging
only what we care to see.

And in finality, a mighty force
grabs us up and presses us to its
bosom to ride the crest of the
unknown.

Laura Hanson Nass
ELSIE TANAKA
Little Elsie Tanaka,
Knocked on my door,
One rainy morning,
At Wailuku Drive, 1604.

She was wearing rubber boots,
Two shirts and patched pants,
And drove an old orange Datsun,
With many, many dents.

She asked to cut philodendron leaves,
From our front yard,
To use in decorations,
For her church bazaar.

Before she left the yard that day,
Elsie came back to our door,
With bright red anthuriums,
And papaya, at least four.

Hawaii's sweet Aloha,
Working as days of yore,
You give so very little,
They give you so much more.

Nina Ogle
WHO HAS GONE WRONG?
So many say our youth are no good,
They dress, talk, and act like a hood.
How did they learn to act that way?
We know they will rule our nation
some day.

It all started the day they were born,
It's the adults that have caused the
harm.
It's not our youth who make the
shows.
And write the books, that much we
know.

Nor make the movies with the
bedroom scenes,
Why not make more shows that are
clean?
Leave out the sex, violence and
crime,
Cheating and stealing all of the time.

Who brings to our nation all of the
drugs,
Adults who are no better than thugs.
It's adults who have programmed our
youth.
So how can they know what is the
truth.

So don't say to me, our youth are no
good,
They learn from adults, all the day
long.
So adults clean up your act today,
Or sooner or later we will all pay.

Tatiana Ouroussoff
UNTITLED
Whisper gently my dear and dry your
tears;
The well is dry
Why?
What have I done to make you go?
You did not listen though;
Love is silent, so they say;
Baby's gone; No way;
Little prince of mine, you've gone to
the desert sands alone;
My scruffy pirate, Sir,
You took a ship, far, far away;
With brown eyes open far and wide
To The Isle of Man you went and
died;
Though pirates leave and ships
descend
Like coffins with the horizon,
And the unbearable lightness of it all
Has weighed us down;
To you I say adieu, my scruffy pirate;
I bid you farewell;
To the depths of the sea you fell;
Mystery still there, my hungry bear;
Love is deep; we'll always share.

Margueriete Love

Margueriete Love
A COLD WINTER'S NIGHT
As I sit here quietly, looking out of
my window on a cold winter's night;
Listening to the rain dripping drops
of water against my window-pane.
The smell of freshly-brewed coffee is
in the air, I'm relaxing comfortably in
my easy-chair. When "suddenly the
shadows" of sleep tries to steal my
very sight.

Mable Johnson
IN MEMORY OF MOTHER
She often sat alone at night,
When all had gone to bed;
As she sewed our torn clothes,
A little prayer she said.
Mama always has a healing word,
For people in distress;
Though her hands were worn and
rough,
Their touch was a sweet caress.
Through the years when trials came,
Mama kept her courage strong;
She always took her cares to Him,
And hummed a little song.
Mama wore a crown of patience,
As she struggled on;
The hands that now rest forever,
Are the hands that made our home.
My heart is filled with memories,
Thoughts of her constant care;
Mama's love and Mama's tears,
Thank you Jesus, is my prayer.

Heidi Huber
ANOTHER TEAR
Another month,
Another year,
Another day,
Another tear.

I mourn once more
of days gone bye,
Again today
I want to cry.

My aching heart
full of pain,
Sometimes I wonder
if I am sane!

Will I go on
or will I break?
This endless sadness
I cannot take.
Am I alone?
Are there others here?
Are they holding back
Another tear?

Irma Du Bois Erickson
SONNET, ON A DESERT SUNSET
Behold a glorious sunset on the
sea!
Colors run rampant, diffused by
the clouds
Scudding and rifting in their
purple shrouds.
An artist's palette, bright with paint I
see,
So vast it covers mountains, sky and
sea.
The ripples change from orange to
red to pink
Then all the sea is rose before I
blink.
Over yonder there appears a glint of
gold
That spreads and deepens as it fades
away,
While blue from out the sky has
tinged the rose
And all the scene is lavender and
grey.
A desert day draws calmly to a
close
And I have but to sleep another night
For Mother Nature's wondrous
show of shows.

Elizabeth N Mezo
WORKING GIRL
She arises at five
to curl her hair
and hopes her family
won't see her there.

Before the mirror
she grimaces and grins
but knows she looks right
as the day begins.

Breakfast is at seven
unless she sleeps late
then she is lucky
if she eats by eight

Onto the highway
she speeds away
and arrives at the place
where she remains all day.

Katie Maeng
MY TIME
The morning after,
The night before,
The time in between,
I wanted no more
Of pain and torment,
Of nightmares and screams,
Of fears that haunt me
With thunderbolt beams.
Pleasure-filled moments
Are ended by greed.
No more gayous laughter
Is what I don't need.
Happiness refrains
Drowning colors away.
Young dying young,
I don't want to stay.
Nothing to live for,
I'm at the end of the line.
My time has come,
This suicide's mine.

Gregory D Quinney
MOONLIGHT
Moonlight is truly beautiful
A lover's paradise
Or even when I am alone
It still brightens my nights

The moonbeams seem to hit me
They make me feel a chill
It's not the cold within the wind
But love at heart I feel

The aura that surrounds the moon
It surely is a wonder
I long for days that have passed
And future I still ponder

I see the moon and think of you
Such mysterious fantasies
I dream of how you and I
Can make realities

For you and I are apart
Chosen was our fate
I long for us to be together
Whatever steps it takes

You and I must come together
This is our destiny
The clock of time seems to weep
But our love's in harmony

Marian Bethel
GIVING UP
You say you'll never love again,
You say it's been too long,
But, come the day, you're over her,
I'll prove to you, you're wrong!

I know that if you're given time,
You'd learn to love again,
You'll know there's more to being
lovers,
There's also being friends.

So, please don't say you've given up,
Or throw away your dreams,
For when you take me in your arms,
You'll learn what true love means!

And when you tell me, one fine day,
You're sure that I'm the one,
I'll hold you close, and softly say,
"I knew it could be done!"

Maryjane Eggborn
TWO FRIENDS

To Carolyn & Ted because they're so special

A Badge for Courage?
That, too, perhaps.
There was a war in a far land
And he a soldier.
At home again
And now a Badge for Service
Not failing where there's need
Family, friends, town
And a wider circle
What of her?
A source of strength
Thoughtful of what makes life good
Community, its history; church
A love of Nature and beauty
At its best.

Charmaine M Troceen
AN AFFAIR OF THE HEART
I truly love you, & I have right from
the start.
From our beginning, it was 'love at
first-sight'!
Not just because you're
'beautiful' . . ,
But because you truly are!
Not just visually on the outside,
But because of your 'inner' beauty,
too!
I love you because you've proven
your strength . . ,
Not just because you're stable &
strong!
Together, we've 'weather'd life's
storm's' . . ,
We've survived all 'tests of stress.'
Not once did you 'lose your grip, or
footing'!
You never 'let me down,' or left me
unprotected, or devastated . . ,
Never a 'wash-out': Never lost 'your
temper,' or 'cool'!

Together, we've been 'warm',
'relaxed', & comfortable . . ,
Not once was I lacking of the security
you afforded me!
'Our dimension' kept growing within
'our framework' . . ,
But then, you had 'a heart as big as
all-outdoors' . . ,
Not, just for me alone'; but for my
friend's & family's pleasure, too!
You've indeed proven yourself a
steadfast companion from our
start . . ,
We've had an-ever increasing 'love-
affair' . . ,
A romance that has circumvented the
course & span of time!
I truly 'Love You', my dearest, my
beautiful . . , 'House and Home'!!

Kimberly Tally
THE WORLD WON'T STOP FOR YOU

Our good times faded, our love
simply died
I wanted to work it out,
But you said, "I've tried."
So we split apart and went our
separate ways
Seems forever since we've talked,
Though it's only been a couple of
days.
My life has stopped, though I miss
your touch
I still care for you, but not quite as
much.
Seems you didn't want to hurt me
But you wanted to say good-bye.
You're very special and the time with
you was true
Now that it's over,
I realize . . .
The world won't stop for you.

Autumn Rose Wagner
WAS ONCE

The sea rushes in
as on lonely bench I sit,
warm gusts my only blanket.

Was once
you held me long and tight,
but not tonite.

Richard Gray Austin
THE FACELESS MIND

The sound of the alarm arouses this
morn, while the house is dark and
gloomy.
We strain to open our tight closed
eyes, but weariness will keep them
shut.
Desperately struggling for one more
minute, the alarm music sings us
awake.
At one point we fight to remain
asleep, while now we are laboring to
rise.
Our frames seemed glued to a place
on the sheet, until finally we are able
to budge.
Rolling from bed and stumbling to
bathroom, each movement is heavy
and ponderous.
Finding the switch we turn on the
light, and are temporarily lost without
sight.
Approaching the mirror we stare at
the face, that must be freshened
before leaving.
Is the face what we are worrying
about, or what is underneath behind
the eyes.
Are we tormented by what the day
holds, or are misplaced feelings
dictating the stress.
Are we anxious about how we
perform, when we already know we
are the best.
Are we annoyed at what others might
think, when we already know they
are wrong.
Are we distressed at what others
might say, when we already know
they are jealous.
Are we tortured to ponder if others
will like us, when we already know
we are accepted.
Are we always wondering what the
future holds, when we already have
faith in God.
Are we always thinking the worst is
on us, when there are others just like
we.
Should not we think of how life
might be, without us being here in it.

Sarah Ann Walton
THE ROOF OVER OUR HEADS

Rooftops tiled, pitched, and flat,
Our shelter of protection built by
facts.
Gutters clogged are like people
ignored;
No one sees them unless they don't
work anymore.

Slap on a patch to cover that hole!
The rains are coming and it's gonna
get cold.
Cover that man and give him
something to eat.
Train him to keep a job?
Why? He has shoes on his feet.

The right to pursue happiness and
build dreams that will last
Are constructed by leaders that use
current facts
Not just to patch leaky roofs far away
on other hills,
But to reconstruct our country
Changing lives with their bills.

Joaquín E Piedra

Joaquín E Piedra
FROM BEHIND THE JAIL'S BARS

I have seen myself behind the
hanging sun.
Among hats and umbrellas scattered.
Between laughing yellow shadows
and sperm.
Dripping water from dampened
blankets
and old mattresses.

Sinks spilling gelatin through
smashed edges.
Broken eye glasses and fragmented
mirrors.

I have cried sourly,
and slammed the door
that echoes
from behind the jail's bars.

It is walking on the unpaved road,
on the uneven portion of the street,
downhill.

Beyond the cliffs,
where the trails tangle and submerge.
Where the sparkling sun glances
away.

I am here,
on the slopes,
alone.

Kathleen Lairscey
EMOTIONAL STRUGGLE

If emotion is alive
and lives in me,
How shall I know which
one to be?
Is there enough room
in my emotional bank,
For all these titles
of emotional rank?
There exists wars among them
you know . . .
All inside my head
where me is to grow.
Alas, I will let them choose,
Whose to win and
Whose to lose.

Heather Marie Gnehm
LOVE ME

You mean so much to me,
More than words can say.
When I see you I open my arms,
Open so wide.
Just so you can hold me,
Make me feel important, loved, and
cared about.
When I'm with you,
I'm the happiest person around.
But there always comes that time,
When we aren't together.
So far apart,
My knees get weak, my heart feels
broken,
and I only wish,
Wish I had you there to hold.
So don't leave me please!
Don't stop loving me.
Even when you find out the truth,
I hope you will love me even more.

Dominic Pontolillo
ELEPHANT MAN

If shape be man's destiny,
And contours be of account,
In life's journey to a place
Where men in equality lie;
Then, beauty's only sanity
Must lie in inhumanity.

Splendid misery,
Ecstatic distortion,
Love's surrender and proclivity
To human divinity;
A moment in time
Of animal infinity.

"I am a human being,"
he said.
Human-like he lay,
And passed away.

Minnetta Wilson Adams
REVERIE

In the darkling night when the tumult
has died
And the throngs lie abed
The hours are more precious, more
poignant
Each word that is said.
The small fragile moments,
concealed
By the rush of the day
May then be remembered with
pleasure
And hoarded away.
The night's probing fingers search
deep
In the sub-conscious brain
Recalling soft thoughts that were
born
In the mist and the rain.
Thoughts that play no part of day
But belong to the night
When the walls of the room fade
away
In the shadowy light,
And the bonds of convention that
shackle
Our minds and our souls
Are dissolved by the sigh of the wind
And the song of the trolls.
Wil-o'-th'wisp beckons, we roam
'Til the heralds of dawn
Shatter dreams, and we stumble to
earth
And we lock up our song.
Day is for mortals—who dream not
Nor hear not—nor see—
Night is for dreamers
For Gypsies
For lovers
For Me—

Amber Driscoll
IT WAS FOR OUR FREEDOM

Thadeus was our leader,
But, Willis, he is now,
For Thadeus, he was killed,
While crossing Salon's Brow.
So Willis, he took over,
For he was Thad's best friend,
And it was for our freedom,
That he'd surely defend.

Thuan Nguyen

Thuan Nguyen
IF I HAVE A CHANCE

This poem is dedicated to Vietnam—my mother land and to America—the sweet land of freedom.

If I have a chance
To visit Washington D.C.
The first place I wish to see
is The Vietnam Veteran Memorial
Where there is a big wall
The bouquets, the footprints and
grasses
I will face the wall
Which talked about the quiet deaths.
I will run my fingers over the names
It will let my tears fall down
To be wet what I love
The unknown names
But brighten like a torch.

Perhaps who you were
I'm still thinking of
That you were not
A stranger in my heart
And in my country.
Because now we people believe
You were right
You were there for light
That you fought for freedom
That you died for us.

If I have a chance to talk
I will call you, The brave warriors of freedom.
I will have just a little flower
Crystallized from my tears
For You—The courageous deaths . . .

Ruth W Flynn
CLIMBING THE HILL TOGETHER
Come take my hand
And climb the Hill with me,
We will get to the top
And look down on the valley below,
The trees will circle us, as if to say
We will hide you.
We will feel the warmth of the Sun,
And the wind will whisper thru
the leaves on the trees,
We're so glad you're here—
At the Top of the Hill.

But, you Didn't take my hand
And climb the Hill with me,
I climbed the Hill alone
And when I looked back
you were nowhere to be seen.
I wandered around in the circle of trees,
No warmth from the Sun did I feel,
And the wind was whispering
thru the leaves on the trees—
Why: O Why: O Why.

William E Richardson
MEMORIES
Through my lips escapes a longing sigh
For the want of you and I to be together in love's embrace;
And for the want of us to be side by side
Then face to face, so that I may look
Upon your overwhelming beauty and loveliness, afore
My loving memory of you fades and you are gone
Forevermore.

Now and always you shall be walking across my heart
As a shadow of love and happiness in refrain—
Stealing into my life your loveliness shall always haunt me
And there remain as my great love of the yester years.
That is only known to me now in longing sighs
And lonely drops of tears.

Giselle Shohet
THE PURPLE-AND-YELLOW-PLAID MAGICAL DRESS
mother and daughter braced
themselves for the spiral fall
they rolled and rolled in a purple-and-yellow-plaid ball

soon the skirt of mother's dress
billowed up and out
and grew to encircle the pair despite their shout

they were wearing purple-and-yellow-plaid dresses
only mother's black hat hid her
streaming tresses

mother was chasing close behind her
girl gone crazed
down an' aroun' the museum's
endless spiral maze

a girl with glad arms outstretched and streaming blond curls
was running and screaming and doing
swirls-twirls-whirls
they rolled and rolled in a purple-and-yellow-plaid ball
mother and daughter braced
themselves for the spiral fall

the Guggenheim became a place of make-believe
in August of 88' on a Tuesday eve

Victor E Buksbazen
ONCE MORE WITH VISION
I laid down a book on war and causes of war
to gaze at a sunset; clouds
climbed purple
and pink in the sky, drifting
westward to
where the sun had died and
left
its legacy o'er the dark'ning
earth.

I saw green fields and red barns and sheep on a hillside
grazing; and I wondered why
any sane man would
give up all this for war. Perhaps
if others
laid down their books on war
and causes of war
to gaze at sunsets and wonder
why . . .

They, too, might catch the vision
that would disarm their hearts.
Then those who warn of an
eternal sunset
might catch a glimpse of the dawn.

Adolph R Lugo
THE SEARCH
Since man on earth has played a role
Within himself a battle has he waged
To understand that which we term the soul.
He prays, while in his mind
confusions rage.
No matter where he goes, no matter what he tries—
Be it council, food, or meditation,
He's betrayed by trembling hands, by muffled cries,
For atheist or agnostic, he fears for his salvation.
Perhaps a monk he should consult,
And through solitude his problem solve.
Let him ponder, listen, wait for some result
Which will lighten this awesome burden so involved.
He kneels, he prays, he stands up bold,
But the answer to this quest is never to unfold.

Sylvia Orsey
MY MEMORIES
When I consider how my days were spent
Before we met one Sunday afternoon
I often wonder how they came and went.
The picture fades . . . and maybe all too soon,
Then starting with the day I met you—
No flashing lights or shooting stars were there*
But mutual understanding slowly grew
Until our every thought we loved to share.

Now, after many years have come and gone,
My life with you is clear beyond belief,
My memories improved from that day on
And all that time stands out in bold relief,
. . . But this is not just living in the past . . .
It's re-enjoying years that went too fast.

Mary K McDonald

Mary K McDonald
PRAYER

The heart's desire, well earned—good fortune.

Without prayer there would be nothing in this world
When most of us lie down to rest in the still of the night there is fear for our loved ones in this cruel world of fright
We ask, Dear Lord, that they may be safe, all right and hope that this war will end soon,
And without blight

Without prayer there would be nothing in this world
Although we know our loved ones are across or far from sight you are our only counselor and delight
Most we are willing to struggle and help win this desperate fight
Please God, we don't want another ruler, with your great might.
Without prayer there would be nothing in this world

Lola Hansell
SUNDAY MORNING
Early Sunday morning as I walked up the walk
And turned the key on the front door of the church,
The morning breeze was calm
I thought of David and a psalm.
I entered the church—how quiet it seemed
But the spiritual wasn't lean.

I carried the Lord's bread past the pews
And God knew,
The reason I was there
And my heart was there.
I placed the cloth on the Lord's table
and smoothed it out with care,
And my love was there.

I walked through the swinging door
And God knew what for.
The pantry I did find
God knew what was on my mind.
I rubbed and polished the Lord's tray
There is much I could say.

A doily was placed with care,
I placed the Lord's bread there
And carried it to the Lord's table
And looked up and Brother Ron was there.

Each Sunday I'll remember
What the Lord did and why
I'm there.

THE THOUGHTS OF LOLA

Karen Sweeney
AN ANIMAL ODYSSEY
Amber and charcoal
With splashes of white,
As light as the day
Or as dark as the night;
All of the animals,
Two by two,
Boldly line up
For a trip to the zoo.

Outrageous with splendor
Or simple and cute,
Many are noisy
While others are mute;
Still, all of the animals,
Two by two,
Amble along
On their way to the zoo.

Zebras and panthers,
With four kangaroo,
Polar bears, lions,
To name but a few;
Yes, all of the animals,
Two by two
Provide quite a sight
As they by-pass the zoo.

Barbara A Ilasi
FOREVER MY LOVE
How I wish to see your face,
dressed in white linen lace,
and when I lay you down to die,
At peace you'll be as you lie.

Your hair spread out like golden silk,
and hair the colour of pure white milk,
your hands entwined across your chest,
with blood-red nails like a fallen crest.

On your body there will be dressed,
A majestic gown a queen possessed,

'twil be the colour of the azure skies,
so that I may recall your azure eyes.

On a bed of gold lamé you'll lie,
that's where I'll lay you down to die,
I'll kiss your lips one last time,
Forever my love,
you'll always be mine!

Martin R Fox
MIND
Once within a dark wood blindly;
Running, stumbling, lost and crying;
Thoughts of life spent idly hiding;
In self-consciousness abiding.
In morbid madness, pitied plea,
I prayed to God, to be a tree.

Marvin M Ellison
A TIME FOR ALL SEASONS
"To everything there is a season, a time for every purpose under the Sun." October means our Summer is now over, warning that the time for that season is gone! Although there is a time for dying we can look forward to a rebirth in the Spring! That's when the grass turns green and leaves grow and children sing! That's the time for living and joy, a time for love and labor to employ. A time for peace and a loss of hate and love of all, both small and great! We lose a lot in dreadful Winter, but gain it back, and more, when Spring enters. So the time for remembering is the Winter season to meditate the good, the bad and whatever reasons!

Dorothy M Duran
OH! MISTRESS MINE!

To my cats Minky, Smokey & all the cats I have loved:

Oh, Mistress mine,
you gaze upon me,
Human, gross, inept,
What secrets in your eyes are kept,
What is my fate,
you seem to know,
Where is it I will finally go?
your velvet fur, your regal style,
In all your ways you beguile.
your impeccable neatness!
your incredible sweetness!
Sorceress! Seductress! Enchantress!
But you can be forgiven,
For your heart is ever loving, ever gentle, ever kind,
Sensitive, wise, elegant too,
Oh would that I could be like you!

Anita Pierce Daughtry
TODAY I AWOKE
Today I awoke,
with words still unspoke

As I got out of bed,
I was filled with such dread

Another day to face,
Who will win this rat race?

With each day that passes by,
I stop and I question and I ask why?

Why are we born,
only to die?

Why must we struggle and live as we do?
Just what can we accomplish in this life, me and you?

Maria Cryder
WITHIN YOURSELF
There were no sounds of laughter,
His were stilled within himself,
There were no words or chatter,
Because he could not give of himself.

Unseeing eyes gave no signs of love,
His sight was within himself.
A lonely heart and searching mind,
Drove him deeper within himself.

How sad this life must be,
To love alone within oneself,
Never hearing laughter or beauty see,
Choosing to stay with oneself.

Reach out, reach out, oh timid soul,
You need not stay within yourself,
Cast off your fears and live this day,
Come out I say, from within yourself.

Rosal Giammarese

Rosal Giammarese
OH I CAN'T GET YOU OUT OF MY MIND
Oh I can't get you
Out of My Heart I
Think about you all
Through the day My
Heart cries out for
you the rains may come
The winds may blow
The days are blue and
My Heart cries out for
You each day My Heart
Grows weaker thinking
About you because I
Love you I can't see
Anything but you I love
I love you I love you
You're breaking My Heart
in two you will always
Be in My Heart I love
No one but you

Nicole Houk
THE PRINCE & THE MAIDEN
His eyes were of fire as he stared me down.
He was upper class for he wore a golden crown.

As for I a mere maiden with tattered rags of dust.
I glanced at him, for wanting and having him is a must.

There came a day when he left, my eyes grew swollen as I wept.
I cried for forty days and forty nights blew out the candles shut out the lights.

Then I saw him he came to me and kissed me once, twice, thrice, it was then I knew
he'd love me forever.

Johnnie B Lee III
COLORS
Colors fall from the beautiful sky,
when they hit the ground we cry.
They are called the colors of life,
so sad to see the colors die.
Red is the color of blood
that spills upon our ground.
Green is the color of happiness,
that fills our ears with sound.
Yellow is the color of glory,
when the game is won.
Blue is the color of peace,
when the job is done.
Enjoy your life to the most,
and make it very grand.
Catch all the colors you can find,
all the colors you can.

Valerie Hillsdon-Hutton
HEDGECOURT LAKE
Quiet in the presence of another,
Swans upon a silken lake;
Rare moments snatched between times,
Oases set in gardens of tranquility.
Remembering
things past and yet to be;
Suspension
outside of time.
Joy in each other's life:
Cost of each other's pain.
Moments which outgrow, like babies my enclosing arms.

Haddy Harrington
SANTA CRUZ TORNADO
Ocean roars and gusty winds
The waves that tell a story
Destructive force of nature
Hammers against the shores
Is there a message being told?
With greedy humans looting
As homes are ripped and fold
There is nothing left
But memories
Of ocean roars and gusty winds
And the destructive force of nature
Maybe nature is trying to tell us
What is meaningful in life
Abundant love and peace on earth
Instead of hardship and strife
To learn to live and let go
Of things that are meaningless
Will take a lifetime of truth and love
To stay on a path of righteousness
Ocean roars and gusty winds
Will always interfere
But sunny skies and calm of the sea
Will enlighten our lives some more.

Matty D Hadly
1935 IN MEMORY 1977
FAMOUS NAMES AND FACES
Every curtain of night is pinned back by "A Star."
Loving memories, "The Strings of his Guitar."
Voices and sounds, King of Rock and Roll,
In years to come "Graceland" people will still stroll.
Sunshine and darkness cover his "Tomb,"

Peeking through the treetops, "A Silvery Moon."
Reaching out, "Old Shep," his first at the age of ten,
Elvis, "The Pelvis," "Peace in the Valley," and "Heartaches" begin.
Stardom ended on August Sixteen,
"Love me Tender," "Don't be Cruel"—"It's all a Dream."
"Everybody Loves Somebody," that's true,
Yet, there comes a day, we all sing "The Blues."

Dorothy E Gaines
'TIS HOLY?
It has been said—All the World's a Stage
My, oh my, how the Players romp about
There's Softness, Meekness & Bombastic shouts
Threats, Condemnation, Truth, half Truths and doubts
Spectators: Look askance, with mouth agape
Wondering which avenue to take
The scene goes on with Thunder & clamour
Banners, Bayonets, Sickle and Hammer
Virtue, Dragons, Demons and Rumors.
Heard midst this Tumultuous din
Is—"'Tis holy, not a mortal sin"
Yet the bickering, & clawing prevail
Bedfellows to groans, moans & wails
Those souls, that succumb via a Cause
If could return—would shockingly pause
In somber Thought and Deliberation
Can this be Hereafter—"Soul preservation"
What has happened to Love?
What and Where is the Law?
From the ethereal—Love is a Law, in itself
True love, binds from within
Regulated law, binds from without.

Elinor E I Imbraguglio

Elinor E I Imbraguglio
THE SEA
I gaze far out to the open sea
How calm and peaceful it seems;
A jewel set in our universe,
Sparkling where the moonlight gleams.

Quiet, serene, a thing of beauty;
An azure velvet carpet stretching proudly;
Or a monster! treacherous! cruel! seething!
Whirling! swirling! roaring loudly!
The Sea . . .

Stephanie Ann Jennings
BOUNTY ON MR BELL
Ring, ring, goes the Graham Bell,
Saying, someone has a tale to tell.
May it be of idle gossip,
Or of great wordly detail.
Ring, ring, goes the Graham Bell.
Ship to shore and cellular phones,
From coast to coast they've invaded most every home.
Having taken away the tranquility of ever, truly, being alone.
Ring, ring, goes the Graham Bell,
As it churns the mind, deeper, into "Insanities Hell."
The ring, ringing, of the Bell.
"Oh," what an awesome war, this tiny bell, has waged.
Now, at its beckon call, from most every room and at the end of every hall.
Controlled & enslaved, by the master's ringing rage,
The modern world, cannot cast out the ring ringing, of its Bell

Durran Wynn Jack
AS I SIT HERE
As I sit here,
remembering things so dear,
it comes to mind,
that one very special time,
I held you so tight,
and told you "I love you,"
all through the night,
if I had only known,
my love for you,
would never truly be shown,
how was I to know,
that I would soon be gone,
with only your memory,
to carry on,
to heaven or hell,
destiny will never tell,
but no matter where I go,
or what I do,
I will always, always,
be loving you . . . .

Shauna Thompson
ENVY
There was a blind girl
Who lived in the alley
One bitter night
As she dug
Through metal cans
An angry young man
Hurt her
He gave her a baby
And he gave her AIDS
And when she died
No one noticed

How I hated her!
She had the right
To feel sorry
For herself
And I didn't

But she didn't
And I did
And I hated her more

Marie Bentley
SIRENS IN THE NIGHT
I once lived in a western town
Close to a busy street,
I listened to the traffic's steady roar
At night when I couldn't sleep.
I imagined I could tell by the sound
Between a pickup or a Big Mack,
Or Fords or Chevys or V W Bugs
Or Jeeps or Cadillacs.
Just to try to cross that busy street
Would surely give me a fright,
But the sound that sent cold chills up my spine
Were those sirens in the night.
Were they rushing to put out some tragic fire
Or to save some ill person's life,
Had a convenience store just been robbed
Or to settle some family strife?
Had someone been drinking and trying to drive
And acting like some crazy clown
Were the police rushing to the scene
To pull him over or chase him down?
I never did quite figure it out
Though I tried with all my might,
But the sound that sent cold chills up my spine
Were those Sirens in The Night.

Carole Dunagin St Clair

Carole Dunagin St Clair
COLD SOUTH WIND ABLOW'G
Shine on, shine on frosty moon
the kids are gone and I'm 'aloone.'
Peering out the window what do I spy
but a full moon ashin'g bright in the sky.
The south winds ablow'g and ahowl'g,
it sends the tallest trees abow'g.

Look'g up thru the leafless trees,
the night so cold and black, it 'tis.
I can see the moon's frosty light
shin'g amidst the spooky limbs—bright.
Oh it's a cold austerely bleak night.
come morn's sun warmth—all will be right.

Jean Young
ANGEL AT THE END OF THE DRIVE
Late I decided to mow the lawn.
You begged me to wait until dawn
But I persisted in having my way
And went to finish the job that day.

I mowed until twilight enfolded the sky,
And then with an audible sigh
I went to put the mower away;
And there in the diminishing light of day

A luminous being all in white
at the end of the drive glowed in the night.
Was it an angel from God above
sent to welcome you to Heaven with love?

I gave little thought to the being there.
A neighbor dressed in white, who cared?
I was tired and needed a shower.
Grass was in my toes, and late was the hour
Early next morning God called you home,
and I was left to battle this world alone.
Remembering the angel at the end of the drive,
I know that somewhere you are still alive.

Wilma R Yarnal
THE GIFT
Flower gardens filled with praise
Are often confused for whom they were raised,
Water and soil and light from above
Are ingredients needed with handfuls of love.

The roses need tended, the weeds need picked
The roots need foot room because the sod's too thick,
Begonias need sunlight and the Glads need shade
I'll be in this garden till the end of my days.

My knees are cracking, my fingers hurt
From shoveling and digging and turning this dirt,
But oh what a sight when the work is all done
When my garden sparkles from the warmth of the sun.

I know God is with me as I turn this soil
He smiles at me for my hard work and toil,
A gift so precious He gives me each year
Or maybe my gift for bending His ear?

Jennifer K Sloan
MR B.
My love for you is still unknown
although you know I like you
But like isn't how I feel
I'm thinking it's closer to love
I won't tell you my dreams
until I know it's o.k.
until I have you and hold you
I will let you into my thoughts
if only you push your way towards me
I will let you into my dreams
if only you dream about me
If you don't feel the same, and know you never will
Just let me slip away—Please
let there only be silence and air
between us, like the old way
Let me only share the same air you
breathe and take away the purple sky
And just leave me this way
stranded like in the beginning
so God will give me my wings
I could be the best,
better than your wildest dream—
I'm thinking how good it could really be
But you don't know this now
because you still don't know the real me

Stephanie Shea
A SUDDEN SPACE WITHIN MY HEART
A sudden space within my heart,
strange it never seemed there before you came.
Now this space mocks me.
Could I have dreamed it all?
Can't focus, can't remember, can't forget.
I feel my mind resist reality.
I sleep in pain,
awake to pain,
remember,
then drift to dream.
Fragments replay
and I ride a wave
that moves me closer to you.
Awake, and realize our memories separate us,
not even the same.
No yesterday, no tomorrow,
only to live forever like this.
You say, "I'll hold your hand through the earthquake."
I say "catch me as I fall into the black emptiness."

Amy Sellers

Amy Sellers
FARE THEE WELL BEAUTIFUL HOUSE
Goodbye to diamond shaped window panes
Glistening always in the bright clear sunlight
Goodbye to tall pines that scent the country lanes
Swaying silvery pine branches in the bright moonlight

A million stars seem to twinkle high overhead
Like a shower of diamonds
on a jeweler's velvet blue bed
The soft chilly breezes
whispering with a sigh
To a house I know I must soon say goodbye.

Pat Roettger
ENDLESS LOVE
You're looking in the mirror
And brushing your long grey hair,
As you sit there and pinch each wrinkle,
Your eyes just seem to stare.
I know what you are thinking
As I watch you every day,
Go through the same routine
in your quiet little way.
Your reflection in the mirror
is something to behold
I still see a lovely lady
Not someone grey and old.
Your cheeks are still rosy,
Your lips still taste like wine,
You'll always be my darling
I'm so lucky you're still mine.

Pat Rowland
THE SADNESS OF EACH DAY
The sadness of each day
Clouds my eyes.
Such memories of days gone by,
So much sadness and tears,
So few joys.
The kids are growing up,
They have their own lives to lead.
That's great.
But where is the need for me?
The love is gone between two people,
That once was so deep.

Just angry words, lonely days,
And nights with no sleep.
Sorrow keeps passing through my mind,
I wonder if living
Is worth the existing time?
God surely has a need for me,
Somewhere, sometime.
Maybe I'll see just what my purpose
On this world will be.
Dear God give me the strength
To stay and see.

Frances Rowe
TO BE REMEMBERED
When my earthly life is finished
and I set sail for the unknown.
I want to be remembered by
the seeds that I have sown.

Just a friendly smile and a handshake
can lift a weary traveler's load.
The little acts of kindness can leave
a tribute that time cannot erode.

Life is likened to a lovely rose
too soon its beauty is gone,
but memories of golden deeds
will live on and on.

Flora F O'Quinn

Flora F O'Quinn
EARLY MORNING IN AUTUMN
Gay Indian Summer bursts from her mould
In Mother Nature's own pattern—
both glamourous and bold
Splashes of red, orange, yellow and gold—
A riot of color—beauty untold!

My eyes color-crowded with scenery so rare,
My feelings unfettered burst forth and laid bare
The soul's depth—exposed by Nature's own hand—
For eyes that see, a heart that feels, a mind that understands!

Kelli Kingsbury
LIFE
A simple flower
A stony tower
People's laughter ringing
A lonely child singing
A hurt person's tears
A smile that lasts through the years
You see, life has been here all along.
And my love of life will never
be gone.

Patricia Brown
LOST TO THE FOIL
Chocolate over again
Calls to the candystore windowpane.
No one sees beyond the need.
Chocolate farmyard figurines
Lined wall to wall, but never seen,
Works of art for the game of darts.
Bulls eye on the pretty ones,
Carved and precious, breakable,
Empty inside when cracked.
They can't stand alone.
Broken, they could have been rabbits or chicks.
Broken pieces look the same,
Taste good, gobbled quickly
By a passing appetite.

If they stick to the pretty colored foil,
Painted and stamped, the same as other wrappers,
Look out if they stick to the wrapping,
You might as well forget it.
A forgotten smudge of sweetness
Lost to the foil.

Debra Hirsch
THINGS GONE PAST
The heartbeat of the days had me fooled—things went by so fast. I saw your beauty as a swirling autumn leaf, but now it's all gone past.

If I could see you now, we would reminisce and dream those dreams we were going to follow; but what we once had, we would miss.

I thought you were wonderful as you played beautiful tunes in your eyes.
The richness of your spirit fell and drowned without reprise.

There are so many loves in this world, so many friends anew. But in every smile, every kiss, there remains a part of you.

Barbara Anne Seidman
BLUE SKIES
Blue skies,
Yellow sun,
Run together in the afternoon,
Sometimes swirling and turning,
creating a purposeful design—
Sometimes rolling, so slowly and
softly, through the air.

"Rest your mind," the Blue skies say.
And the Yellow sun, "Thank you, I will."

And the Yellow-Brown relies upon
the Azure shoulder of the sky,
Lying its head down, knowing that
it's O.K.

"This is the way; thank you for
wanting to be there;
For being there."

When a Man loves a Woman,
When a Woman loves a Man,
It can steal my heart away to a room
where I long to stay.
In your hands there is plenty,
In your hands I am free to love all my being—
Free to love you, and me.

This is the way;
Thank you for wanting to be there;
For being there.

Doris Perry
MY WINDOW
I have a window to the world
where I can watch the Seasons
come and go.
It's there I find Spring's wealth
and dream upon the falling
Snow.

The window opens to my garden
And views the daffodils and
tulips standing by.
It comforts me with trees and
birds to changing Splendor of
the sky.

I have a window that displays
colors of blue, white and grey.
They are feathers of my friend
the Jay;
A tufted crest his head adorns
His diet—suet, seeds and acorns.
That loud and raucous song fills
the air all winter long.

Now friendly chickadees too
With black cap come into view;
The sparrows, white throats,
house
And the Junco smooth and sleek
Gather the seeds at their feet.

Erin Rose Casey
A POW'S PLEA
A tiger cage
in the blazing sun
Nowhere to hide
and nowhere to run
I served my country,
Did they forget?
'Cause it's been twenty years
And I'm not home yet

Kelilea Harding

Kelilea Harding
HOPE AND DREAM

I would like to dedicate this poem to my Mom Teckla Harding and my teacher Mrs Ann Moynagh for encouraging me to write poetry. This is for you.

Let the weak say i am Strong.
Let the poor say i am Rich.
Let the blind say i can See.
Let the hard hearted's heart be
softened.
And let us not weep of sorrow
and pain.
Life will be hard but, we will
have a better world someday,
someday we will.

Frank Perkiel
THE NAIL
Is there something special about a nail?
Which we never praise, admire or hail.
A plain, simple, cold steel nail,
Shiny or rusty, new or stale.

It has no life, no soul, no magic.
Just sits or lies there, looking so tragic.
Its shape is short, long, straight or bent,
Lonely it is without an enemy or friend.

Sometimes it is dull, sharp, round or square.
Nobody really will ever care.

But let me tell you—to start—
Without nails things would be falling apart.

Where would you hang up your pots,
Your calendars, many other things,
lots . . .
Where would you suspend your pictures?
Perhaps the answer is in the Scriptures.

So herald to all, in print or in braille,
By telegraph or by mail.
And HAIL TO THE NAIL,
For without it YOU SHALL
FAIL! ! !

John Stone
THE EMPTY HAND
From out the bowels of unknown land
It springs to clutch onto a soul,
To cease to burrow like a mole,
To lunge from loneliness, the hole,
This pure and craving empty hand.
But when the search concludes in vain
It plunges back towards endless mist
And curses at its severed wrist
And prepares the bedrock pounding fist
For another punch at fruitless pain.
This hand has felt the earth's caress
As well the water softened stone,
Has scuttled 'cross the twelfth time zone,
A shame it has to crawl alone
With no companion, no egress.
But certain things console the fingers,
Give them hope to scout some more
Like prospects of a utopian shore,
The mitten its lost lover wore
And mother's love which ever
lingers.

Wanda Elaine Eyler
THE LONESOME FLOWER

In memory of Wanda Elaine Eyler
March 26, 1955-July 22, 1981
The following poem was written by Wanda when she was 12 years old.

As I sat by a tree one day,
A buzzing bee passed my way.
I turned to look and to my
surprise,
A lonesome flower looked into
my eyes.

It was a lonesome daffodil,
And about its roots dry leaves lay
still.
Its stems and roots, I was
surprised to see,
Were healthy as healthy can be.

I loved that little daffodil,
So I moved the leaves that lay
still,
And planted flowers, the color of
wine
So the daffodil would have
someone to pass the time.

And now on that lonesome hill,
The daffodil and I lay still.
With wine colored flowers all
about,
We Rest in Peace without a doubt.

Lory Moore
AUDACITY
Plan well your strategy.
Use all the miracles of science
to build the barriers high.
Parade your pitiful defenses before
the monster FEAR.
But wait!—'Tis but a lumpish
shadow after all;
grotesque and wavering—and yet
a shadow of such density
that now there is no sun.
How can this be?
There is no shadow lest the sun does
shine.

But this dark thing that blots out light
and warmth—
If not a shadow . . . .
What?—Reality?

Run quickly now and build the
barriers
higher still.
Strengthen the old defenses,
You men of many skills.
Or will you stand
Throw back your head and
laugh—
Not as one laughs to hide his
weakness,
But lightly, gaily,
as a child with a happy secret!

Olan E Beckner
AS IS THE WINTER
What a contrast, this season we call
winter.
To look and see the beauty of fallen
snow
As it lies on the earth, and glistens,
Its white color crystals all aglow.

And the snowflakes, as they fall to
earth
Like diamonds sparkling from the
light
Of the winter's sun up in the sky,
So clear at times and so very bright.

Oh how beautiful, as through the
glass
We gaze at snowfall from within our
room,
The wintry cold but a touch away.
Contrast—the beauty and the gloom.

Then we take that step outside the
door,
As the bitterness of winter kisses our
cheek
With its cold—so hurtful cold.
Oh from afar this winter looked so
meek.

And as is winter, so is it all.
We must look closely, and rightly so.
As all contrasts confuse,
We must make judgements very
slow.

Lee W Davidson
NIGHT TO MORNING
Come bless the earth by entering with
light
Beyond the sentiments which view at
night!
Now disappears the Zodiac, your by,
Through Dawn who glows into the
evening sky.

From dawn to noon I always will
embark
With the glory of sunlight over
retreating dark.
All shadows scurry to be away from
light,
And the Muses hurry to acquiesce to
your might.

Come, come, more closely to us,
Apollo!
In overcast, rain or snow, we miss
your show.
In the troubled minds of men who
face the night,
You are the inspiration and the
greatest light.

Even if a morn be bad, the night is
worse!
The night and evil lurking strike a
curse.
None are immune to darkness
everywhere;
Memories of nightmares and stories
overbear.

Your sunrise is the best event of the
day!
The morning is the early time
display;
And we love your heavenly light as it
graces our eyes;
It glorifies the earth and all the skies.

Desiree Giselle Lopez

Desiree Giselle Lopez
A WOODED GRAVE

I dedicate this poem to my family and friends who supported me, and to Shakespeare, for his writings which inspired me.

It was midnight,
She sat by a grave,
Sitting, crying, moaning,
Beseeching an answer.

Her eyes fell on the tombstone,
Making the roses glisten.
Her cries echoing in the woods,
Empty, hollow, saddening.

Her sobs subsided,
To a soft moan.
She touched the grave,
And her cries stopped completely.

Softly she bade goodbye to her only
love,
Lifting herself she stood.
Leaving the grave,
And with a last loving look behind
her,
She was gone.

Tanya Bauman
SILENT PAIN
Lonely tears,
Slipping down my cheek,
Silently falling,
For you who made me weak.
Leaving me scared,
With memories and feelings,
Scalding tears,
Neither helping or healing.
Shadows reach past me,
Beyond all defense,
Only thinking of you,
And not of the rest.
Only showing sorrow,
Like droplets of rain,
Leaving the world,
Unaware of my pain.

Mildred L Benke
DOOR TO DOOR
The winter work day is over
Away with the records and files
Co-workers hurry out the door
Wearing faded and weary smiles.

I did my very best today
Tho' nobody seemed to care
I put out the lights—I'm on my way
Tired but not in despair.

My footsteps are loud and echo now
In the empty corridor
But I'm free of frustration and petty
temptation
As I close the outside door.

The night drops like a curtain
As I reach my own front door
And I'm filled with excitement and
joy
At the fond embrace I'm looking for.

The aroma of good cooking adds a
special dimension
The music is soft and sweet
And I revel in true contentment
I'm home! My joy is complete!

M M Burress
DID YOU?
Did you help some one in need?
Did you do a good deed?
Did you have a happy face?

As you went from place to place
Did you plant a seed?
Did you pull a weed?
Did you walk a mile
and remember to smile?
Did you thank the Lord
for the good word?
Did you hear a bird sing?
Give thanks to God for everything!

Nancy Carlene Sexton Fields and Leighanne

Nancy Carlene Sexton Fields
LEIGHANNE
Mommy and all my friends
you were all so kind
Please don't grieve
for the shortness of my lifetime
I was only frightened of leaving
you behind
Life on earth is painful from birth
There's no such thing as peace on
earth
I'm not alone so there's no need
for fear
There's nothing to hurt me here
It's true, Jesus loves all the little
children
and I'll live forever, in a better
world
A world made with love
it's bright, shining and new
It awaits you, too
A place where golden bells ring
while the angels sing
I'm a new soul in my heavenly
home
There's plenty of adventure here
for me
New surprises that I just can't
wait to see
By the time you get here
I'll know my way around
It'll be great when we all meet
again
Try not to be sad when you think
of me now and then
I guess it's hard for you to
understand just now that you
really should be glad
Please, don't cry for me
I'm not in the frail, cold little
body
the way you remember me
Oh Mommy, just wait 'til you see
me again
the gold in my hair
the glow of my skin
God had something for me to do
singing, talking, touching
hearts,
sharing love, and spreading his
holy word
My body weakened, he gave me
strength
I crawled into Sunday School
to hear, to learn, to teach
of God's unfailing love
My body was ready to die for
quite some time
But, God let me stay until you
were strong enough for me to
leave you behind
So don't grieve for the shortness
of my time
Remember never too early, never
late
and when the the time is right
I'll wait for you
just inside the Pearly Gates

Hugh McChesney
PEACE OF THE DAY
This was a warm Summer day
the verdant fruit trees today
were wistfully crowded

Astride on the lusty ground
the gold from the sun found
colors from all remote corners

Silent quiet day in the orchard
I prayed I would find no one
My desires were devotedly heeded

I was alone but with a friend
entirely in the moment

The days before people were
busily picking the cherries
beautiful bounty becomes work

Now only the silence remain
the hustle and strife a domain

to expire with forces humanity
bring, but not today No not today!

Esther Newton
TO GRAMPA WHO ART IN HEAVEN
Some say I'll never know you,
I'll never know your touch.
All I've got to say to that,
Is they don't know so much.
I knew you first, I knew you best,
I knew you, before the rest.
I saw your face, I felt your touch,
I saw the smile, that means so much.

I came from, where you are now,
I know when, but I'm not sure how.
I was with you, for eight short years,
But Mom's life was filled with tears.
I didn't know, but God knew why,
That's why I'm here, and you're in the sky.
Mom really needed a little girl,
So God sent me to this world.
As you know, now there's another,
His name is Lincoln, and he's my brother.
Some say it's you, he looks like,
And he's such a little tike.
But he's really growing, and growing fast.
And now Mom's tears are in the past.
We know you're with us, day and night.
We see your face, in the bright moonlight.
You'll forever be, by our side,
And by your love, we will abide.
On this earth, we'll do our best.
We'll see you again, when they lay us to rest.
We'll see your face, we'll know you.
We'll see your smile, in the sky of blue
We'll know you, by your touch,
Grampa, we love you, very much.

Donnie D Nulph
NIGHT EYES
Night Eyes watching as I slumber.
Hesitate to pull my number.
Make no noise, and cause no scare
and fool me not, I know you're there!
Stay with me till morning sun,
calls out my name when dark is done.
Do your dancing as I doze,
in restful state both eyes I close.
From satan's frothing jaws protect me,
guard me close and don't neglect me.
Keep me both alive and well,
and save me from the hounds of hell!
Use me not for mass of black,
no sacrifice, and no attack.
but should I die by evil's hand transport
me swift to sacred land.

Deborah Ann White
DOWN THE TUNNEL WE GO
Down the tunnel we go
long and dark and scary
to find the safe.
We bend down low
to dodge the hairy
cobwebs of this place.
At the bottom of the tunnel
Ah, there is the vault
so big, so strong.
We place in it our bundles
of guilt and shame, our faults.
A safe to lock them up where they belong.

Timothy L Palmer
DREAM GIRL
Her body is shapely,
appealing and delicate.
Her walk is so graceful,
displaying real eloquence.

Her hair is jet black,
falls down to her waist.
Her lips, they're so luscious,
I just have to taste.

Her face is so perfect,
pleasant and kind.
The simplest lover,
I ever will find.

Her eyes are like silver,
her heart is pure gold.
Her smile's true beauty
You'd have to behold.

Her laugh is like honey,
her voice sweet and gay.
I love her completely,
what more can I say.

Her knowledge is vast,
her humor so rich.
She's always so kind
for she's never a bitch.

Her love is so strong
that it never will end.
Her honor's so deep that
she's always a friend.

I add all this up, but
it sometimes will seem,
I'ved got to be sleeping,
and this is a dream.

For this is my dream girl,
the best of all time.
And from this day on,
she'll always be mine.

Ollie Oliver

Ollie Oliver
I TOUCHED AN ANGEL

To the memory of my dear mother, who, though deceased, is still fondly remembered, my beloved husband Jack, daughters Linda, and Rebecca, and to all those offered encouragement.

I touched the face of an angel
Her eyes looked deep into my soul,
The bond between us was so strong,
I knew her heart must be pure gold.
Her hands were so loving and tender,
I felt so calm and serene,
Her love for me was eternal,
Nought would ever come between.
The face was the face of my mother,
None but God could love me more,
Now she's no longer with me,
She walks on Heaven's shore.

She will always be my mother
even tho' she's gone from sight,
She has joined the angel choir,
In the land of eternal light.
Where one sweet day I'll join her
by God's amazing grace,
I'll be in His presence forever,
and once again touch my dear
mother's face.

Heather Johnston
EPIPHANY
Show a man a unicorn and ask him what he sees.
He might say a white steed of pure breed stands before me,
But if he believes and trusts in their magical lure
Before him will stand a beauty that is pure so pure.
Placed before a girl she will see
The night full of power maybe.
If she is pure the unicorn will speak,
And draw her up from her world so bleak.
For that night she will share a mystery with him.
The rest of her life she will remember of him
And beauty, magic of his mane in her face,
Then her tears as he parted
As he faded away growing so dim,
And then he was gone,
Just a dream
Of long ago.

Patricia J Castle

Patricia J Castle
BAHIA HONDA KEY

To Bob

Memory, you and me—day in June, Florida key
Purple glow, on the shore—
Portuguese man-of-war
Pounding surf, you and me—melody of the sea
Wading out, sandy beach—island far out of reach.

Starfish, moonspell—let go, all's well
Funny face, wet hair—brown skin, warm air
Chest deep, ocean walk—moonglow, sweet talk
Salty seat, waist deep—everybody else asleep.

Day gone, night falls—wet hugs, dreamland calls
Quiet walk, go slow—stingray, by your toe
Coconuts, white sand—soft breeze, your hand
Memory, you and me—Bahia Honda Florida Key!

Teresa R Koch
BLOSSOM
Hear their laughter
Wipe their tears.
Share their excitement
Lift their fears.

Give them hope
When all else fails.
Give them dreams
Not fairy tales.

Show them love
In small, small ways.
And watch them grow
With passing days.

Our children, little
For such a short while.
Take time to watch them,
Blossom under a smile.

Marlys (Marlie) Marks
MAKE ME HIGH
So say I'm terrific, and terribly smart;
That you'll love me forever, with all of your heart;
Tell me I'm marvelous and terribly rare;
Then send me red roses, and a little "Care Bear."

Don't pour on the butter and the syrup too much;
You'll get me all sticky for I'm such a soft touch.
So adore me a little, and praise me a lot,
And you'll send me up there somewhere near Camelot.

Say I'm one of a kind, and not just a clone;
Then buy me a castle, and build me a throne.
From my pedestal up here, I can look all around;
Don't let me fall off . . . . and don't knock me down!

Rosemarie Kennedy
GRIEF
What can I do with my arms,
Now that you are gone?
How can I deal with my heart
And the ache that lingers on?
How can I quiet my mind?
For years all thoughts were you.
Now that you are gone,
What in the world can I do?

(Mrs) Pansy Ward
HELP SOMEBODY TODAY
When I awake in the morning,
I look to the East,
I thank the Lord for the day
I ask Him to bless and give me peace.
Then I pray a prayer this is, what I say,
Lord, help me to help someone today,
Then I go to the kitchen the food to prepare,
I ask the Lord to give me more love to share.
I sit at the table with my head, I bend,
I thank the Lord for food
relatives and friends
I ask him to bless and lend a hand,
To help all people of this
wonderful land
I go to work to help people if, I can
As I go, I look up to heaven on my way,
I still pray, a prayer to the Lord,
To help me to help somebody today.

Sandra Walker
WHAT CHRISTMAS MEANS
Christmas time is here,
A holiday often full of cheer,
It isn't the gifts we receive,
But in the Spirit we believe.

For Jesus was born, He, Who is kind,
Sharing his love with all, Who seek
and find,
The true meaning of Christmas Day,
Not the gifts, but the Love that comes
your way.

Those who have less than me,
The blessings with giving you can
see,
And what a precious start,
When one gives completely from the
heart.

And the sparkle in the eye,
Of a child, Who has less than I,
To be able to bring Cheer for one,
Who might not otherwise share in the
fun.

Yes, to all you beautiful Friends,
Christmas is the beginning, not the
end,

With a very precious start,
When one gives completely from the
heart.

Tara Glinsky
MOODS
Clouds make you grumpy,
Blizzards make you mad,
Sunshine makes you happy,
And raindrops make you sad.

But even when you're in these
moods,
Grumpy, happy, mad or sad,
You're still the same old person,
And boy am I sure glad.

Barbara A Hilderbrand
SPRAY DREAMS . . .
I breathe the breath of the sea
as it sighs upon the shore,
while wings of roaring surges
play, on vibrant inner cores.

Myriads of color-flashes
darting through my eyes
see creative energies dip
and dance, atop the murmuring tide.

Sublime and joyful love-calls
pulse the mighty sea,
breathing its breath of living
dancing blue-green spray through me.

Patricia Berry
WOODMONT AFTERNOON
Children leave their books and
pencils lay,
to take advantage of a rare fall day.
The faithful dog on the sand reclines,
October sun on the water shines.
Children throw pebbles to the other
side,
peel up rocks to see where little
things hide.
Woodpecker pecks out a woody
song,
the smell of the sea is pleasantly
strong.
The autumn air seems to clear ones
head,
the sunshine makes the heart feel
glad.
The cry of gulls can be heard all
around,
peace and thoughtfulness quickly
surround.
The busy world and its troubles have
fled,
leaving peace of mind instead.
A small boy fishes from a kicker
boat,
I'm aware of three wild ducks afloat.
The shadow of a passing freighter,
falls with the sun, it is getting later.
It is a special world apart,
a place to listen with your heart.
In the troubled world this scene is
rare,
to hold it forever is my simple prayer.
We begin to gather the treasures we
have found
and climb the path that leads us
home.
The coolness of late afternoon creeps
in,
as we climb the path that leads us
home and
will bring us back again!

Raquel Soto

Raquel Soto
MY FAITHFUL BEST, BEST FRIEND

This poem is dedicated To: Miss Sabrina Marie Wise "My Friend"

As our friendship departs
And we go our separate ways
For the first time in our life
It only seems like years have gone-
bye
But, it was only yesterday that
We said good-bye . . .
Now, you are so Far Away . . .
But, let us think of all
Those happy and sad
memories . . .
That we have shared in our
friendship . . .
We were always there for each other!
There were good and bad times,
But, nothing seems to have ever
Hurt or departed our
friendship . . .
There were difficult times in our lives
But, we still remain the Best, of Best
of Friends . . .

It was hard saying Good-bye . . .
But, let us think it was only A
Farewell,
As, through the years . . .
We shall see each other Again . . .
And knowing you are so far
away . . .
Let our thoughts and trust stay
In our hearts as well as in our lives!

Peter Tudosoiu

Peter Tudosoiu
IT'S NEVER TOO LATE
It's never too late to stop dreaming,
It's never too late to start living.
It's never too late to stop crying,
It's never too late to start trying.

Whether you're young, whether
you're old
We are in the same boat.
Whether you're pretty, whether
you're ugly
It's not your fault.

It's never too late to stop quitting,
It's never too late to start thinking.
It's never too late to stop hating,
It's never too late to start loving.

Whether you're white, whether
you're black
We breathe the same air.
Whether you're dumb, whether
you're smart
Who said life is fair?! . . .

James Croker
THE ALCOHOLICS LAMENT
Why can't we be like the others? Be free from the scourge of the grapes that have wrath.
Ironically they keep chanting you see, it's not the first it's also the last. The doctors and priests look upon us as beasts, our will power is shot they aver.
They shoot for the moon, can't get there too soon, our problem we try solving alone. Their own known are left to suffer alone.
It's not the present, it's a long time resident. There's horror deep in our past.
The drink makes us warm, can't do any harm this time we swear! There's no cause for alarm.
The torment and wear is part of the fare to pay for my tortuous trip to the stir.
But after a few our minds go askew. The line up we face, it's remorse and disgrace. We're back in the rut of despair. The fabled rats never ran such a race. Satan is driving and setting the pace. If you can weather the storm without losing your norm, you're back again just with loss of face. They are all eyeing us with looks of disgust.
Thinking perhaps, that couldn't happen to us. The problem is great, on it hinges the fate of all who have gone thru the mill. It's a hair breadth line between saneness of mind, and ending up out on the sill.
We try with deep passion to follow the fashion, and trod down life's righteous strict path.
The frivolity, and fun sets deep like the sun. Sleepless nights are something that last. But love of the grape is a love that can't wait,
It barters your soul, and gives you the gate.

In a lonely room midst terror, and gloom, you fight back for your place in the sun, and when you get back, you reverse on the track, and the task that was done is undone.
Oh why were we cursed, that we have to be nursed; every time we partake of the juice of the grape.

Howard J Golley Jr
MY NEW YEAR'S WISH
Last night I had a dream that I was an
angel for a while
I took away all the sorrow and gave
everyone a smile.

I found a cure for AIDS and cancer,
hearts were all working great
Sugar was no problem, people could
see and enjoyed what they ate.

I done away with taxes and put all
drivers in a safety car
Every man and woman had
something to do, this cut crime down
by far.

Just before I woke up, I gave a party
for all
The entire world was there, and we
all had a ball.

My dream wasn't long enough to do
all I wanted to do
But my wish for the New Year would
be for this dream to come true.

Sue Williamson
SPRING
The grass is beginning to "green-up"
The buds are beginning to show
Soon we'll have to dig-up
With spade and shovel and hoe
And rake leaves from winterized
beauties
We planted before the snow.
To let the warm sun do its duty
And bring out the flowers aglow.
Then comes the planting of gardens
With hopes of vegetables good
To grace our tables and storage
Against the winter's cold.
The cycle of living continues
As it has in ages past
So we might just as well face it
And accept each day as it passes.

Karen Woodworth
LOVE OF A PARENT
Could it be the twinkle in your eyes
or the smile on your face?
Or could it be that your hearts are
made
of gold and diamonds,
that's why nothing can break that
rugged image
you want to portray.

Deep down I know that you are
as gentle as a Teddy Bear
ready to hug your child in time of
need.
To me that's what parents are.

I'm so glad that you're my mom and
dad!

James A Williams
A POET'S LAMENT
I long to write of the setting sun,
And of the beautiful things that
Nature has done,

About the silvery moon shining at night—
But you know, I just don't seem able to write
On an empty stomach.

I'd like to tell of life's higher things,
Such as a flower that grows and a bird that sings,
Of a day in May when one's heart feels light—
But try as I may I simply can't write
On an empty stomach.

My soul longs to fly on a carpet of dreams
To hazy blue hills and clear mountain streams
Where the sweet joy of life at my heart strings will pull
But, pray tell me my friend, can a heart be full
On an empty stomach?

Ella Mae Driver
A REASON
There is a reason,
And a season,
To every generation.

A time to be born,
And a time to mourn,
A time to plant corn.

A time to rejoice,
And a time to recite,
A time to be quiet.

A time to weep,
And a time to sleep,
A time to reap.

A time to say good-by,
And a time to buy,
A time to eat pie, or fly.

A time to rest,
And a time to do your best,
If you sail east or west.

There is a reason,
And a season,
To every generation.

Ella Mae Driver
ROSES, ROSES, ROSES
Roses of red, roses of yellow,
Roses of blue reminds me
That I love you.
Roses, Roses, Roses

Roses of red, roses of yellow,
Roses of blue, roses of pink,
Cause me to think
Roses, Roses, Roses.

Roses of red, roses of yellow,
Roses of blue, roses of pink
And roses of white means it's
Alright to give a bouquet of roses.

Roses of red, roses of yellow,
Roses of blue, roses of pink
And roses of white,
That is a pure delight.

But, I would choose to give to you
A bouquet of roses of blue,
Because I would be blue, too,
Without you.

Ella Mae Driver
LIVING IN A CASTLE
This house looks shabby, weather-beaten,
And torn from the wear and tear
Of all kinds of weather through the years.
But, has shown no fears, nor cried no tears
Through all of the wear and tear
Down through the years.
And the people stopping by
For awhile, ask why
We don't tear this old house down,
And not leave it standing around.
But, this house has been a shelter
For me in all kinds of weather.
And people stopping by
Don't realize that I
Am living in a castle so tall
With high, high walls;
And that once up-on a time
There lived a King
In this castle of mine,
As strange as it may seem.
The people don't see swinging
Chandeliers in the halls,
Nor famous pictures on the walls.
So the people stopping by
Don't realize that I
Am living in a castle so tall.

Colette
BIRDS THAT ARE FREE
Follow your heart for it knows you best, grasp on to your feelings and forget the rest, contentment may be your reward if you should pass the test. As we go on and live our lives the world is suffering of many cries, they're loud and clear for I do hear them shouting out "what's it all about?" In life you can choose from many a streams and often wind up with endless dreams. Once there was a time when a flower in bloom could open and brighten a gloomy room, but now it takes gold & silver that shines or people would rather pay it no mind, so here we are in this empty space working 9 to 5 with grief on our face insisting that this is quite a place, while birds that are free fly peacefully with grace.

Regina Anderson
LITTLE GIRAFFE, LIFT UP YOUR HEAD
Shy little giraffe, lift up your head
Even if your stripes are red
No other animal in this jungle will bother thee
Unless of course if you are a peppermint they see.

Patricia Shinn King

Patricia Shinn King
BEYOND THE SHADOWS (A LEGACY OF LOVE)

I dedicate this poem to my children, Janet, Mike & Brenda, Randy, Danny, and Craig. Who have been the complete joy and inspiration of my life. Without you (my children) my life would have been a rose that never bloomed

Yes I have left you as I lay Beyond the Shadows
in eternal rest.
But do not weep my children my love will forever surround you,
I gave you my best.
I taught you hope, faith, but most of all,
I taught you love.
So with gladden, not weary hearts, raise your heads
to God above.
Destiny is your road map of life, for each choice
is yours to make.
But feel love in your hearts with
every step you take.

Life goes so quickly as a whispering wind
across the lake.
Or, as quietly as a glistening falling snow flake.
Riches and fame mean nothing at all,
Only Love Prevails,
When God comes to make His final call.
So when you leave this "ole" earth,
as I have done.
Leave your love behind like a shining beacon
to guide someone.
And somehow Beyond the Shadows in this silent tomb
I will know and I will smile,
Knowing my life here on earth was
worth while.

Lillian Hugh Lawson
THE LARGE ROCK BY THE SEA
There is a touch of pathos
Even in a stone
When bleak and bare from ocean's wear
All of its moss is gone
Like a sentinel it stands there
Where seagulls soar and roam,
A secret deep it seems to keep
Above the billowing foam.
Does it not remind you of
The ancient days of yore?
It seems to bring a message from
The lives we lived before.

Rev Evalena Romans-Lewis
MINISTRY OF THE ANGELS
So beautiful like apples of gold in pictures of silver,
It's written in the scriptures, the angels are the chariots of God.
And have reached their crescendo, proclaiming the angel story
He is risen, this is the ministry of the angels,
Is it any wonder, the angels in glory unveiled their
Faces and sang praises, bless the Lord, O, my soul, bless
His holy name, for who so ever shall call upon the name
of the Lord shall be saved, a light kindled that day at
Calvary, darkness and despair died, as the Cross blazed
With God's glory, the miracle of the Resurrection took
Place, for man's redemption throughout the ages, and
the greatest story from history's pages, is the
Ministry of the angels, He is Risen, it
Was then hope and man's future was
Born, believer look up, take courage
Be strong in the Lord, He's Alpha and
Omega, He's our King of Kings and
Lord of Lords, He is Risen
This is the ministry
of the angels
Hallelujah, He is Risen

Leanna Reeves
THUNDERSTORM
You hear the trees whisper.
You also hear a child whimper.
You feel the breeze.
The breeze will sometimes make you freeze.
The thunder sounds like potatoes rolling.
The lightning sounds like something is popping.
The rain feels gentle.
It makes you tingle.
The rain is free.
The temperature will go down a degree.
Smell the fresh air.
It ruined my hair.

Nicole Cobb
I'VE OUTGROWN ALL THE LITTLE GAMES
I've outgrown all the little games
I used to love to play,
My baby book is tied up tight,
My cosy's tucked away.

I've outgrown pigtails in my hair
And night-lights on my wall,
I won't be starting gradeschool,
But college, in the fall.

I've outgrown elves and fairies,
Traded dress-up for the prom,
But I promise that I'll never,
Ever, ever outgrow "MOM".

Vicki Featheringill
WHEN THE NIGHT WINDS BLOW
When the night wind blows
My mind wanders to a place of long ago
A time when I was young and serene
Where the fires were warm and the snow crisp and clean

When the night wind blows
My mind wanders to the spring of my youth
And the white spots of a new born deer
A time and a place where I knew no fear

When the night wind blows
My mind wanders to the days of a long ago summer
Where the blue of the sky and the ocean were one
As all the days were passed in the sun

When the night wind blows
My mind wanders to the fall of my life
Could this be the time when the leaves were so deranged
Oh how the seasons of life have changed

Angela Fay Weldon
A TASTE OF HEAVEN UNTO ME
I thank my God daily,
for the gifts He's given me.
He gave me two precious daughters,

they're like a taste of Heaven unto me.

A child is like a precious stone,
to treasure and to cherish.
Bring them up in the ways of the Lord,
so their souls shall never perish.

perhaps when they grow up,
and have themselves a family,
they could hold their child upon their knee,
and think themselves, "A taste of Heaven unto me."

Mary K Fulton

Mary K Fulton
SAY IT NOW

To the community.

If you have a kind word to say
To help some traveler on their way
Say it now.

If you can lift a burdened heart
by helping them to share their load
Say it now.

There may be some one on the street
that needs a smile or just for you
to help them across the street.
So help them now with a smile.
It may mend a troubled mind.
So heal it now.

If you have one rose to give
Give it now.

For it might help someone to live
So give it now.

So when the battle is fought and the
Race you have run you will hear the
Master say "Come home My child to rest."
So say it now.

Richard S Romero
SENSE

The more I feel,
the less I feel.
The more I live,
the less I live.
The more I wait,
the less I wait.
The more I hope,
the less I hope.
Nothing makes sense if it's out of proportion.

Pauline V Streiff
CREATIVENESS

Creativeness is born of the soul and the mind
It's always a hope for all mankind
Create only good so that you leave behind
A beautiful memory, a gem of a kind

A song, a poem, a tale sweetly told
A theory perhaps that will never grow old
Because it's so true based on facts that are known
And grows like a seed that's already been sown

How beauty enhances the soul and the mind
And grows upon the souls of mankind
For beauty will grow as the truth goes on
And lives on the songs from each beautiful mind

General Brown Jr
A SPECIAL MESSAGE

I send a prayer to the Lord, above.
A special prayer: Surrounded by love.
I may be selfish, but I'm sincere:
For the love I lost, was all so dear.
Near in mind, gone out of sight, oh,
Lord, how will I sleep tonight?
I am safe and sound, but also down.
Sad and sometimes blue.
I got to find someone new, my aching
Heart beckons you.
Life is empty, love is too.
Please,! won't somebody help me through?
The moon is out. The stars are bright
I got to find some love tonight.
Love tonight, would be just right.
Love tonight, is just my plight.
Surely, that would make things right.

Gretchen Torres
JOHN MCENROE

This man has found that tennis is his game.
The sport has brought him wealth, prestige, and fame.

He looks unshaved and has curly brown hair,
Freckles are scattered on his face so fair.

Wearing wrinkled clothes and a red sweat band,
He is sure to swing a strong deep forehand.

Concentration and the will to succeed,
His fans can always count on this indeed.

His temper leads him into many spats,
Because of this he is known as a brat.

Through his career he has received some fines,
But he does not let it boggle his mind.

He has little to say during interviews,
And all that are watching become amused.

Though he did not win Wimbledon again,
You can bet his desire will never end.

He will always be there for the Davis Cup.
No matter what it takes he will always be up.

He gives a hundred percent, that is John McEnroe,
This vibrant, raving, loyal tennis pro.

Spencer Lowell Turner
BRIDGES OF YOUTH

To my family who allows me to fall free.

Depths of unknown challenge
Twist and curl beneath my
Trembling feet
The night whispers soft
The dares of youth
The cries of freedom's
Selfish soul.
Water runs its endless race
Taunting me to go
I'm mesmerized and hypnotized
By its graceful flow
Dancing on the edge of darkness
Flirting with the wind
Laughing at the circling birds
Scoping every curve and bend
Running through the narrow way.
I feel a rush of beauty's mind
Kicking away my feet's
Safe glue
Falling through the nighttime
In the breeze I blew.

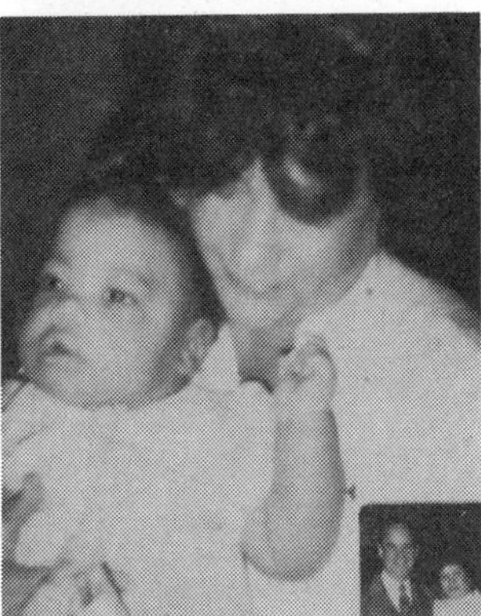

Marjorie Henderson LVN

Marjorie Henderson LVN
THE MASTERPIECE

To my mom and dad, Georgia & Bill Henderson, Sister & Brothers Phyllis, Billy, Connie, Rosie, Gloria, John, Tammy, Stevie. My son Gary, my Daughter Pamela, my Granddaughter Melissa & special Baby Andrea.

It's springtime again
All of nature struggles to be born
Small blades of green sprout forth
Life is fighting to be renewed
Great travail is on womanhood
A gripping pain and silent release
A hand cautiously protective of the womb
And the priceless treasure it carries
The dynamic contractions, dilated
The crown suddenly appears,
"EUPHORIA"
Then deadly silence, followed by a gasp
A cry and the rebirth of a nation

Michael P Gorzelic
FROZEN SNOW

Slip, Slide, Oops!
Scamper, Scurry, Fall.
Laughter, laughter, is the call
Lying in snow yet ten feet tall.

Ten degrees quiet and cool
Sculptured layer of winter's swimming pool
A cake with ice spread on top
Children out to play, don't stop!
don't stop!

Deep soft peace spread underneath
A display of God's art
One of nature's blessed wreaths
Hung each year nice and neat.

A toy for children high and low
Prejudice abolished, one of earth's hopeful goals.
Equality emerges thru the secret
wonders of frozen snow,
A key of joy that will never grow old.

Joyce Smith

Joyce Smith
GRANDMAS

To my Ma-Maw, Mrs. Nancy E. Jones Prosise, who I was named for

They come in all sizes
They bring toys to you when they visit
They cook your favorite food
They let you do things that mommy & daddy forbid,
They give advice that mommys & daddys don't care for,
They knit & sew and bring things to wrap us up with.
They keep everything you make if it's only a paper with ziggy lines
They knit you scarfs for your B.D. even if it is in July
They are built-in baby sitters

Melissa A Vanmeter
HE CAME UPON ME ONE COLD DARK NIGHT

He came upon me one cold dark night,
the candle in the window was still alight
The storm crashed loud against the door,
as I lie here wishing it were there no more
He told me he loved me and wanted me back,
that's when the thunder sounded a crack
His love had lit my heart on fire,
with flames as raging as his burning desire
I sent him away, his heart was torn
The storm died down and soon it was gone,
but so was I by the break of dawn.

E Greve
THIS MAN

He . . . Could rebuke the wild wind—
Could hush the restless seas
And . . . From the deep sleep of death
Could . . . Say . . . "Maiden, arise!
Get up!
Go" . . . She went on her way
Grateful that she no longer
Slept with her ancestors
Through . . . The majesty of this man
Her Redeemer . . . and all mankinds
She was redeemed from death
For yet a little while
Once more loving arms
Enclosed her, could teach
Her. Have faith, have hope
For those who sleep as you
Slept, will rise again
To know the grandeur of life
Given to all by this so gentle
. . . A Man . . .

Ruth Helen Price

Ruth Helen Price
MY LITTLE LINDA

I dedicate this poem to my daughter, Linda Joyce Lofton, who has been a Joy to me always. And to the three Grandsons she has given me, Jamie, Timmy, and Brian.

You came to me from Heaven
As I wished upon a star,
For the name of Linda—means beautiful
And sweetheart—That you are.

A healthy beautiful baby
With big blue eyes and dimpled cheek,
You were forever happy and playful
As you grew from week to week.

Suddenly it's been years
of growing, learning and love,
And now you are a young lady
Bright and lovely as the stars above.

Soon you will be on your way
To live a life of your own,
You're still my little girl
Yet somehow the years have flown.

As you can see by my every line
I shall always be proud that you are mine,

Not by possession
But forever in my heart,
Today, tomorrow and always
Together or Apart.

Natalie (Missy) L Reves
TRUTH IN PAIN
Frigid darkness.
Brilliant stars.
Heart feeling for strength.
Head beckoning for answers.
Omniscient light guiding me.
Finding———Myself.

Georgia N Campbell
OUR NATION'S BLESSINGS

To all my loved ones

Dear Lord, bless our nation, U.S.A.
Our government leaders need help today.
So many warring nations in this world,
And much talk of missiles being hurled.
Our forefathers went to you in prayer,
God blessed our nation and showed His care,
A wonderful country we have today,
Thank you, Lord for our U.S.A.
It has grown in number and very strong,
But many disobey and do wrong.
Would you bless our leaders who obey you,
Help them keep our flag, red, white, and blue.
May we be guided by your love and stand,
Strong and obedient and keep a Christian land.
Help us keep the beautiful lands of today,
For the future generations in our U.S.A.

Esther Zearing
THE DAWNING OF A NEW DAY
It is the dawning of a new day
So fresh and new.
New things to see,
New things to experience,
And a chance to do things over.

Yesterday didn't turn out
As I had expected it to.
No interests or goals had I.
No yearning to meet challenges
That had been laid before me.

Now I have that chance
To do things different,
To make something of myself.
Fear fills my being as water does a cup,
Not knowing what lies ahead.

But, I have determination on my side
And a want to do my best.
So, I shall strive and shall succeed
At whatever life shall bring.

R L Williams
TWO DUCKS
There are two creatures very white,
two sassy ducks about 20" in height.
Heckle and Jeckle I call them—
lacking a better name,
these ducks are funny and unusually tame.
Often we'll see them close by the shore,
and when we feed them they'll seem to want more!
Hard corn and bread—they'll really devour,
sometimes it seems that they'd eat every hour!
Never has there been a more natural boat,
creatures designed primarily to float.
But when they want to they have the ability
to move through the water with aquatic agility,
their orange little feet swiftly moving like oars,
rapidly spinning like rotating doors.
And when the day approaches its dusk,
Heckle and Jeckle their instincts will trust,
because for them it's really no chore
to make their way to the western shore,
and on this shore they will roost all night,
until the dawning of a new day's light.

Elaine Martin Uonelli
SO WE WAIT
Traffic jam up—
So we wait; so we wait.
Christmas sale rush—
So we wait; so we wait.

Friend or mate
In a meeting—
So we wait; so we wait.

Looking for
That special seating;
So we wait; so we wait.

Waiting rooms—
So we wait; so we wait.
Airport mix-up—
So we wait; so we wait.

At a park
Or at a bank,
Lines and lines—
So we wait; so we wait.

Labor pains,
A baby's coming—
So we wait; so we wait.

What's to come
From all this waiting?
Is it patience
Or frustrating?

Spent a lifetime—
Waiting, waiting.
Is it worth it?
So we wait; so we wait.

Jessica Toulan
NO-ONE'S FREEDOM
Everyone's so far away
And no-one knows I'm here
I walk along this lonely road
With no-one to come near
Maybe I should not have been
And maybe I'm not real
Why can't they see that I
Can think and I can feel?

The whisper of the lonely pines
Of the place I long to go
Run away—Far away
They will never know.

Freedom is what I cried for
To be as boundless as the sea
To have the road stretched out
Before my eyes
And to learn all her mysteries
I never thought I'd need to be somewhere
To have a place to call my home
But now as time goes on I realize
I never wanted to be alone.

I thought I was an eagle
And you became my sky
Never asking any questions
Nor telling any lies
You let me go the distance
Always thought that you'd be there
But when I turned around to call you
The only thing I found was air.

My silent cry of yesterday
Longs to soar with you again
High above the winds sweet love
Just like it was back then.

Freedom is what I cried for
To be as boundless as the sea
To have the road stretched out
Before my eyes
And to learn all her mysteries
I never thought I'd need to be somewhere
To have a place to call my home
But now as time goes on I realize
I never wanted to be alone.

Now I know that I'm not the eagle
And I no longer have a sky
I'm now asking all the questions
I can't help but wonder why
I've got all that I wanted
I'm the spirit of the free
And there's nothing here that's binding
'Cause there's no-one left but me.

Freedom is what I cried for
To be as boundless as the sea
To have the road stretched out
Before my eyes
And to learn all her mysteries
I never thought I'd need to be somewhere
To have a place to call my home
But now as time goes on I realize
I never wanted to be alone.

I never wanted to be so alone.

Joyce Dumas

Joyce Dumas
BEINGS IN A BORROWED BODY

I dedicate this poem to my most dear loving and supportive husband Paul, and all my children, Tony, Daniel, and Michael, who are all loving, patient, and supportive in everything I have and will accomplish.

What are these beings
that we be?
They're made to look
like you and me

Are we real or are we
a thought?
It's a wonder, suspense,
something to be sought

What do we look like
how would we know?

Our body was borrowed from
long ago

Are we beautiful or
are we ugly?
This unknown puzzle
is such drudgery

What are these beings
that we be?
Could it be they're just
you and me?

Bonnie Parker
FRIENDS
We live so very far away,
But in my mind you're clear as
day,
Your thoughts, feelings, cares or
woes,
Are stamped within my heart, "I
know."

Over the miles, the months, the years,
We've known of each, "the
other's" fears.
We feel the pain, the hurt, the tears,
And hold each other, as the
other is dearer.

You and I are one, it seems,
We've lived inside each other's
dreams.
We've traveled down some lonely
roads,
We've helped each bear many
heavy loads.
We've laughed, cried, prayed and
cursed,
This life so dear, our pride,
we've nursed.

Our vibrations, strong and true,
Will never let my heart forget
you.
The same for you, is true above,
For this my friend, is known as
love.

Tonya Teagle
ANYTHING FOR YOU
My desires are, not to capture or
hold any part of you,
But to realize and caress your wants,
needs and desires.
To enhance your personality
And romance your sensuality
To give you room to truly grow as
high and far as you would like to go.
To help you really and truly find,
All the love you have in mind. To
give you tenderness
As long as I live, are some of the
things I want to give.
I want you to consume all the love
that's flowing free
Explore my mind and body beyond
what the eyes can see
I want to touch you ever so tenderly
While we're making love so very
splendidly
And feel our hearts beating as one
It's wonderful to know we've only
just begun
We can touch the sky my dear
If only you let go, of all you fear.

Lisa Ann Smith
PIECES OF THE PUZZLE
Some memories we hold forever
others just wash away
Some linger for eternity
others only for a day.

We choose the ones we want to keep
and the ones we want to discard
Some are very easy to live with
others are very hard.

Memories are parts of our lives
gathered and collected
They are meant to be cherished
savored and protected.

Though friends and loved ones may
leave,
their physical bodies may die
We each have memories no one can
take
locked deep down inside.

Mary F Rodgers
ANNIVERSARY POEM
Ten years ago we met today
and I never thought we could both
stay
in a house together with all these kids
at times we feuded and barely did
you've taught me a lot
whether I liked it or not
about money and cars
and a few things about bars
but most of all about love and respect
always keeping me guessing what
would happen next
We've talked about death, we're
enjoying life
I'm really so lucky to be your wife.

Patti McMullen

Kathy McMullen Shealy
FLASHBACK

For my sister, Patti McMullen, an artist who, in her own medium can create an image as well as, if not better, than any writer. May she be as importantly recognized in her field as she is in her family.

Blood red drops
of innocence
splattered the ground
beneath love infested bodies
oblivious to time's
ultimate betrayal.

Purities' loss
extracts its price
in souls.
Memory gives no quarter,
remorse yields no mercy.

Treasured pearls
pay for themselves
by years spent
in cultivation . . .

Kevin Fisher
AS I DROVE PAST THE GATES
As I drove past the gates
I saw the elm trees I played upon as a
child
The shingles on the old house was
weathered and torn
But the memories I had
kept me occupied all the while
Of this cozy backwoods place where
I was born.

It seems like only yesterday
That the family and I were nestled by
the fire
Glad to have each other's company in
an old fashioned way
With bonds of unity that was
cherished and admired.

It's the photographs I see
That make me homesick for what
used to be
My fondness wishes were fulfilled
returning to this house once again,
But lonesome is the sound of
squeaking floors and the howling
wind.

Doesn't seem like twenty years since
I said goodby
The sand in the hourglass reminds me
of how time flies,
My childhood dreams are still with
me even though I am a man
Of summer evenings and catching
fireflies with my hands.

But yesterday was not so long ago
For there's a child that lives inside us
all
That keeps us young at heart even
when we grow old
The child is our thoughts we need
only to recall.

Anne Marie Madison
HOPE
What is life? Can someone answer
that for me. I lie alone in my room
wondering if anyone can help me,
because I am confused, at what I am
doing here.

There is no one in this world. I am
alone. Where can I turn, who will I
find. I eat, I sleep, is that life?

There must be someone left in this
world; I do not want to be alone. I
need, I need.

What is life? Someone please come
from above and tell me.

James Currie
TO THE MIDNIGHT ISLANDS
Companions, do you feel the beat
Of engines far below your feet?

As stars attest, for who fares forth,
Our prow is pointed towards the
north.

Wind (even relative) is nil,
And that accentuates the chill.

Upon an icy foreshore can
Be clearly heard the ptarmigan.

At last observe where we are led,
Polaris standing overhead.

In midnight rigors sight will fail.
(Around a cairn let bagpipes wail.)

Jennie Pinkos
MY SEA
The wild wind blows, birds fly,
Looking into that salty sky,
Wood creeks, the boat rocks,
Wildly until we reach the docks.
Waves grow stronger,
The night seems longer,
I'll stay here forever,
I can leave this never,
I want to sail away
in my beautiful sea,
Maybe you can sail with me.

M L Lent
EVERYONE
We all have our troubles and sorrows
And work that never gets done.

We all hope for a brighter tomorrow
And a "better place under the sun."

We all have our hills and our valleys
And races that never get run.

We all have our dreams of the future
When life is all pleasure and fun.

We all have our joys and our
heartaches
They come to us all—everyone.

We all have temptations and victories
There seems to be no place to run.

We all have our strength and our
weakness
There's good and there's bad in each
one.

We all have the same chance with
Jesus
He loves us all, every one.

He is always there to receive us
Ready to say "Welcome home."

He died on the cross to redeem us
How can we reject Him, God's Son?

Walter S Reid
GREAT TASTE

This poem was written in 1980 in commemoration of my 22nd birthday. I would like to dedicate it to all professional athletes the world over.

One day in a race
I was outpaced
It seemed I would be unplaced
It would have been a sad case
If I had lost the race
Embarrassment I would have had to
face
So I refused to be abased
And time I did not waste
I found extra pace
And I won the race
And I found grace
What great taste.

Merced B Torres Jr
LIKE A BROKEN PETAL
Like a broken petal that drifts in
the wind
With each coming day, a new life
will begin,
So listen children for what I say
is true,
From the day you were born til the
day you grow old,
I will always love you.
And if I should happen to pass
away,
Keep smiling my children for by your
side I will always stay.

Myrtle Fredonia Olson
WHEN I SEARCHED FOR LOVE
As I chased my son into grandpa's
barn,
I climbed the loft so old and worn.
When he escaped, I found myself
alone,
To experience fifteen years of
unknown.

Laughter and voices I suddenly hear,
But there's no one anywhere near.
Memories I had totally forgot,
Seek my mind and leave me not.

My sudden urge to write it down,
Brings the times when I couldn't
frown.
These barn walls are a dingy and
rain-soaked vision,
Where my future and past have made
another collision.

I have just been faced with a new
kind of love,
One of my own, everyone else would
shove.
Who says you can't turn back to the
days?
When hidden memories bring on so
many ways.

I realize that there's no one who
knew,
All of the things that made me feel

new.
But I want to tell you before I go,
When I searched for love, I was watching it grow.

Erika Seebacher
A TALK WITH FATHER
My son, why do you and Mary fight this way?
You have bloody conflict and struggle every day.
Look at nature, take lessons from the seasons;
Brotherly love and compassion are the reasons.
Spring forgives Winter for its coldheartedness
Year after year without loving less.
Audacity and boldness are forgiven Summertime
By Fall, with a mild temper that is sublime.
Each the other's lack is filling
With a heart and spirit that's willing.
So, Johnny, Johnny, get up from here;
Go find Mary, your sister dear;
Forgive her for that screech and shout—
That is what love is all about.

Will Allen Matthews II
THOUGHTS
I sit in the mainstream of consciousness,
Wondering the existence of reality.
The days go by, some long, some slow.
My next move is a mystery.
Love comes, love goes.
Sometimes true, sometimes imaginary.
Those who are good usually do well,
But sometimes the evil do even better.
WHY? Is the question I wish to ask,
Yet the answer lies in the depths.
So we go on, living lives of normalcy,
While the true uniqueness goes undiscovered.

Marjorie Kozichek
PRECIOUS CHILDREN
To-day I saw a child
So carefree and so gay
I hung onto every word
This darling had to say

She was so sweet and precious
So unassuming and unafraid
My heart was really captured
With her delightful ways displayed

She loved to go to grandpa's
To see the fuzzy sheep
She fed one with a bottle
Which to her, was really neat.

As I listened to her speaking
And I felt the joy she brought
I thought of countless children
And the suffering life had wrought.

It is a sad, sad, story
The tales that we hear
Of children that have suffered
And have been brought up in fear.

We only hope that someday
These tales of terror end
And little children everywhere
Will be loved as our dearest friends.

Joan Martinez
HEART & SOUL
The ALPHA is what I live for
The reason behind my actions
It's what makes it all worthwhile
My reward for the sacrifices of life
My one moment in Camelot
A brief glimpse of heaven on earth

The ALPHA is from the Heart
It lives on only in memories.

The OMEGA is inevitable
It eventually comes
As the result of humanness

It is the destruction of something beautiful
The product of self-centeredness
The pain of rejection

The OMEGA is from the Soul
It lives on in reality.

Becky Patterson
PUPPY LOVE
The day I got my puppy
I knew I was in love,
I felt he must have come to me
From heaven up above.
As I recall that fateful day
I have to sit and smile,
As thoughts of him fill my mind
Every little while.
His eyes are big and brown,
His fur the color of a dove,
I think I have been fatally stricken
With a thing called "puppy" love.

Lori Krause
A PRAYER FOR STRENGTH
My heart is heavy with emptiness.
Thoughts are crowded out of my mind.
My soul is like a barren woman
That breeds loneliness of a kind.

And above this pit of darkness
There seems to be no spark of light.
Oh my God have you forsaken me?
Oh my God take away this night.

If I must travel this deserted by-way
Dare I look for purpose and intent.
If there is a reason for this Hell
Can it possibly be Heaven sent?

Like no other time in life, my Master,
Give me your strengthening grace.
Don't leave me behind to weep, but grant
Peace so these wounds time may erase.

Etti W Nissila
LIFE
Life is a most valuable thing
We get as a gift, it gives us so many things,
To use it, like we wish.

Life takes us sometime crossroads.
We wonder what road to take. We take the one that looks the best,
And continue our way.

Oh our journey, in this life, takes us many places.
We overcome our obstacles, and our mistakes we made it.

Life is a mystery, we get as as gift.
So that's why we should appreciate
The many things we get.

Tammy Rene Rudd
FREEDOM
Sometimes it screams,
other times it's a whisper
but it's always there.
It yearns for the open spaces,
to see eagles soar above.
It's a never ending dream.
Sometimes it screams,
other times it's a whisper
but it's always there.
It beckons from the far away mountains,
from the distant shores,
to live in the past but
yet to fulfill the future.
Sometimes it screams,
other times it's a whisper
but it's always there.

Morris L Miller

Morris L Miller
LOVE'S LIGHT

To my children who now add to the light in my life.

The light of love it shone so bright
T'was on that deep blue starry night.
Through Somber eyes, I saw her golden hair
With softness rustled in the night air.

She moved so lightly, crossed my path
I glimmered a moment as she passed.
Kindly moving the sentiment of my heart
It seemed to me an eternity that flashing dart.

Time stood still, all reality passed away
As longingly she turned my night to day.
Cross the meadow I dazingly wandered
As in my feeling heart I pondered.

Could this be real or just a dream
For all my life I searched it seemed.
T'was all I hoped that life could be
That fading moment you came to me.

Love's light had shined that night
Now here after is pure delight.

Jeanne Seay
THE PLAN
The hands of time keep moving on,
Like the shifting sands on the shore.
Some loved ones have gone to a better world
In this life we'll see them no more.
But the memories we have will linger
As our life here on earth goes on,
To make our days and nights more bearable
While in our hearts for our loved ones we long.

Someday we'll join them in that wondrous world
Where there's no pain, no sorrow or tears
Just happiness and love everyday,
With the ones we hold so dear.

Stacy A LeMaster
WHERE WAS I?
Where was I when you needed me?
Where was I when you cared?
Where are you when I need you?
The pain I cannot bear.

Why did you have to leave,
and leave me feeling blue?
The pain you left behind,
it doesn't seem to be true.

When I close my eyes at night,
or think of you everyday.
The pain you left behind,
it will not go away.

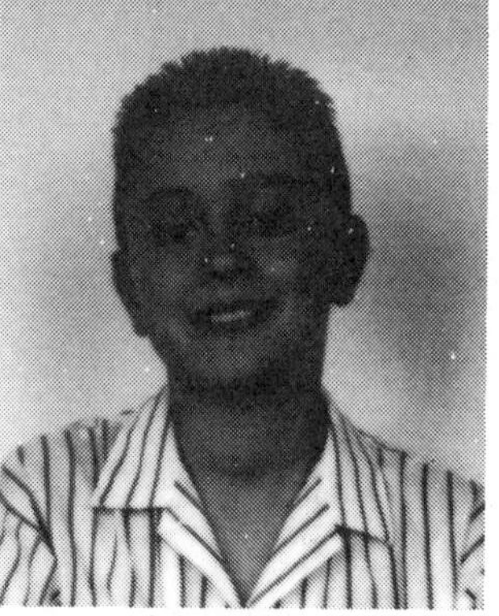
Simon Aloyts

Simon Aloyts
NOT A WITNESS (ADAPTED FROM EDGAR ALLAN POE'S "THE CASK OF AMONTILLADO")

To my dear parents.

Oh how wisely I lured him into my house,
Where not a soul was present not even a mouse.

There were many public shaming I needed to avenge,
But when he turned to an insult I wanted revenge.

I thought out the plan for a long time,
When I was finished I heard the clock chime.

Twelve midnight I thought in my head,
Time to offer my friend an eternal bed.

I went out in the street with light so dim,
I wasted no time and finally found him.

"Hello there old pal," I said to my friend,
"Come to my house, for a coach shall I send?"

"No, no my friend I think I can walk,
Now what's so important that you can't stand here and talk?"

"Amontillado, Amontillado it is!
Do you want to taste it?" I said in a

hiss.

"Amontillado? You're kidding for sure,
It cannot be found on just any old moore!"

"In my house Amontillado I've seen,
I need you to taste it, in that your throat is quite keen."

"Very well then, lead me, to this Amontillado of yours.
Lead me straight to your wine cellar's doors."

"So I shall friend, now follow me,
The Amontillado you shall see."

When we entered the wine cellar, I heard a slight cough,
It showed a sickness although incredibly soft.

"Catching a cold in the cellar? Such a grisly joke!
Here drink this, it is my Médoc!"

He now displayed more than his usual spunk,
One of the many symptoms of being drunk.

He won't feel a thing now, I thought to myself,
Even if he's to be cut up and put on a shelf.

At length we came upon the hole in the wall,
Which resembled slightly a bathroom stall.

Then quickly, using much haste,
I tied a chain around his waist.

Then I tied him to the pole,
Which lined the inside of the hole.

As I sealed him in, he didn't jerk,
My Médoc accomplished its venomous work.

..... Finally I sealed him in, my catacombs, so deep,
And I left him there for fifty years, sleeping an eternal sleep.

Jim Roberts
ILEEN
Go with speed to find the one,
who may possess the key, for
she has a mind as thee.
One who may unlock the worlds,
the world of many strange lands
filled with dreams.
For this I speak, even . . .
as she sleeps.
She is a beautiful woman, one with a kind personality and the eyes with fire so radiant with light to brighten an entire sky.
And I fill her life with love in her dreams,
even . . .
as she sleeps.
A poem to one I write, and as you speak I wish that you may hear the words.
For I feel you may understand
the world from which I come, on
the brighter side of the sun.
Sweet dreams, even . . .
as she sleeps.

Dora Epler
HAUNTING HOUSE
The little tumble-down adobe on
Front Street still stands,
Empty now and swaybacked, waiting for a final rush of
Blood-red water to bring it down.

When the Curandera lived there it looked the same, less
Tilted maybe, more solidly squatting on the ground, and
Impervious to summer rains. We all knew that.

There was glass in all the windows then, and it smelled
Alive, in that way only lived-in adobes smell. Now it is
Dusty as Curandera herself by now.

A shiver still stiffens my back as I pass, and I turn my
Face in dread, expecting to see, afraid I might see, a face
In a window, her face, with my eyes.

Dena L Hess
I HAVE A DREAM

Dedicated to my family, for their encouragement and to all, who keep peace in mind.

I have a dream,
this dream's inside of me,
all people should be free
and live in harmony.
But when I think of
all the war and hate,
I dare to think of this world's fate.
People should live as one
and keep in mind our earth and sun,
it shines so bright, but all we do is fight.
People live and die
with only dreams of being free,
all should know the feeling of love and dignity.
So you see,
this dream inside of me
is that all people should be free
and live with peace in mind
and peace and harmony is what we all shall find.

Alida Shinn
CATHEDRAL PINES IN MICHIGAN
One day we took a walk to see the Cathedral pines,
For soothe they were standing in a semi-circle
Ever since before Christopher Columbus landed in 1492,
Sentinels of time and space
Touching high o'er head seeming to reach the sky,
Now in danger of ax and saw for need of money to save them.
So whip out your checkbook and write a check to save them,
Those ancient, wise emblems of yester years.
Let them not fall at lumberman's stroke.
Those cathedral pines are priceless in the scheme of time
Reaching from the past to present high o'er head,
Helping past and present meet,
Treasures of the past.
Help save them to survive and show we care
For the trees' bark outside
And age rings inside.
Stand on your Michigan woods reaching upward to the sky
Saying "We care. We care."

Karyn Finazzo
A WOMAN SO FULL OF GRACE
A woman so full of grace
yet a child with no place.
Maturity so much in bloom
but for love there is no room.
Smiles and laughter hide a fear
seen only through the reflection
in the mirror.

Donna Lea Bennett

Donna Lea Bennett
MY RECIPE FOR "MOM"

To the greatest, most respected lady in my life, My Mom, Marietta Willson

Take a little bit of tenderness
And a whole lot of love
The softness of a puppy dog
The purity of a dove

The touch of an angel
The faith of a mother's care
The strength of your concern
For those whose life you share

The freshness of a summer breeze
Add a dash of T.L.C.
A teaspoon of integrity
And a can of sweet puree

The warmth of a newborn
The patience of a seed
The elegance of a fresh rose
The desire to succeed

The brightness of an autumn leaf
A smile from the heart
There really is no recipe
You're truly a piece of art

I Love You Mom!

Shajia Khan
THE CANDLE OF TIME
Gazing down the dark halls of life—
With all the names etched in stone,
You look for yours upon the wall—
Yet knowing your name remained unknown.

With a match and a long candlestick in hand,
You walk further down
And notice the hall coming to an end.
Your heart and soul are fixed on a goal,
And your desire to be known has greatly grown.

Now comes your chance to light the hall
With all that you've heard and learned.
As you strike the match
And watch its bright flame burn,
Deep down inside, you're knowing that
The only way to have your name
etched on the dark hall walls—

Is to light the Candle of Time—
And then by the light, begin to write
In the diary of life.

Virginia McReynolds
ONE KIND WORD
Have you noticed when you are blue
What one kind word can do?
Just a friendly smile and sincere hello
Can pick you up and you feel a new.

Who knows what burdens each one bear
But to take time out to show you care,
Will often erase so much despair
We should never be so busy that we can not share,

A little kindness, love, and cheer
It does not cost one single tear,
But possibly gain a friend so dear
And oh! how precious to have one near.

Because you see, I've been lonely too
That is how I know what a kind word can do.
What a terrible thought to be all alone
With not a friend to call my own.

My prayer, that my life could be
So dedicated to others
That in some small way their heart could see
What a wonderful gift it was for me.

Janet Pinkley
FLEETING MOMENTS
For one brief moment,
I held it in my hand.
It trembled there . . .
and was gone.
Gone in an instant.

Happiness comes and goes
so swiftly.
Fleeting moments
only dimly remembered.
Lost in the passage of time.

Dennis R Reinsel
YOURS ALWAYS
For better or worse,
were the words that we said.
Fifteen years later,
we're always in red.

Four kids and a house,
two cars and a boat,
I don't remember this,
in the letters we wrote.

Laundry in baskets,
and dishes stacked high,
You know that I love you,
by the Glint in my eye.

Time is so precious,
we're always on Go.
When can I tell you,
the things you should know?

Before all the hassles,
when we were scott free,
we were just kids,
on a Love making spree.

When you're going left,
and I'm going right,
You know that I love you,
when we settle at night.

We made it this far,
through thick and through thin,

we're not doing half bad,
for the shape that we're in.

I said that I love you,
the promises I'll keep.
Let's keep looking ahead,
for the Glory we'll reap!!!

Gladys Chamberlain
DIFFERENT
I am different.
I don't like being different.
People who say they are my friends
really aren't.
They laugh at me.
I am different.
Boys laugh at me and tell me I am
ugly just because
I don't look like their girlfriends.
I am different.
Sometimes I go home and think what
is the sense in trying to please them if
I don't please myself.
They laugh at me.
I am Different.
Usually I don't look forward to the
next day because
I know what to expect.
I am different and can't help it.

R G Curtis
MY TRUE LOVE
Once what seems like a long time ago
I thought I'd be alone when I grow
old.
But with a stroke of luck I found you,
never again were my days to be blue.

Hair dark brown, but looks like
black,
Now I know I'll never have to look
back!
When you look at me with your eyes
of brown
I feel like a king with his shining
crown.

Our union was surely made by the
man up above.
And the name was meant to be True
Love.

You are the reason today that I live,
You have my all,
there is no more to give.

I'll make you happy or at least I'll
try.
I hope and pray to never make you
cry.
With our love so strong there could
never be another.
We'll remain together and forsaking
all others!

Oral Dorothy McVicker
IF I WISH FOR SOMETHING GOOD IN MY LIFE TODAY
First I'd ask for God's help, then I
will pray.
Remembering the days when I was a
child, helping mother in her garden to
weed.
It was back then I realized, God
would never fail me.
If ever thru life, I'd go to Him in my
time of need.

Nancy Hall
FRIENDS
Friends are friends no matter what
Even in times when you have fought.
A friend is a diary
You tell secrets to
And your inner most feelings come
shining
Through.

Friends are people who are always
there
And are those willing to share.
You keep their secrets.
They'll always keep yours
And you'll never find them behind
closed
Doors.

At moments of laughter, sorrow and
need
Right by your side you will see
The friend whom forever
Has always cared
And whom forever will always be
there.

Jonathan Barry

Jonathan Barry
THE DRIVEN SPIKE, FINALLY

Dedicated to the Sheiman family, Rose, and to my teachers Robert Garvin and Richard DeMartino—true masters of the way.

Broken to the point of death, born
again to the living—
Struggle makes me not unkind, I am
not bitter, for my soul is ruled by love
. . . Rich beyond my poverty, my
mind is clear,
inspiration fills me—pain and
happiness, both are treasures . . .
It is not that I welcome torment—
anguish can instruct if it does not kill
. . . The driven spike demands that I
awaken to my greater self, know
myself, be myself, accept myself . . .
Only part of me is mortal, and I
remember all I have never known.

Finally, I like myself; now I can
return myself to you—
for only those who love themselves,
can give themselves away . . .
I finally have found comfort in being
me, and I am newly born; starting
over, coming home for the first time;
coming home at last . . . without
clinging, to be happy;
without longing, to be free; finally.

Darrin K Helsel
I DO NOT EXIST
I do not exist anymore
my soul fluctuates in and out of
existence
my life is a dream and a nightmare
both the pleasures and horrors in a
dreamscape world
such are the whimsical games of a
God
who creates these entertainments for
fellow omnipotents
to play with our lives as they choose
no matter what the cost
no matter what the outcome
pawns we are on a grand chess board
silent hands from the sky
move us to new spaces on the board
our purpose in this life
to capture the queen.

Marcell Meldrum
TRUE LOVE
Darling soldier, I'll be waiting for
you,
Cheering the day, you'll come
smiling thru;
With joy and peace, in this world of
strife,
We know our love has its place in
life.

The sacrifice dear, is so little it
seems,
It'll be a pleasure to realize our
dreams,
If only your arms could about me
enfold,
My life is all yours, to have and to
hold.

Then, as we seek our guiding star,
Perhaps in the distance, not too far.
We can trust our true gift of love,
As sure as the stars in heaven above.

April Kaminski
LOVE IS LIKE A FLOWER
Love is like a flower in many ways.
It starts off as a tiny bud,
Each time we kiss it grows,
Bigger and bigger stronger and
stronger.

With love, care, and time it will soon,
blossom standing tall and proud.
Each time it withers away,
You have to know it will be back
someday.

Gwendolyn Diane Walker

Gwendolyn Diane Walker
WHAT ARE WE CELEBRATING?
What is in the air during this time of
year?
"Glad tidings to you and be of good
cheer."
Sales from store to store, from
morning to midnight,
Everyone rushing and squirming
towards the blue light.
Santa with his white beard dressed in
his annual suit,
Taking orders from children and
promising Video Pursuits.

Carolers preparing their voices to
sing Christmas cheers,
Parties and ornaments decorate the
office atmosphere.
Liquor stores are stocking and selling
by the case,
Almost everyone you see is wearing
a smile on their face.

Children requesting every game and
toy they see,
Advertised by the media and
commercialized on T.V.
Plays are being performed by the old
and young,
Foretelling the story of Jesus Christ
the Son.

Who is the baby cuddled in His
mother's arms?
Born in a manger, better known as a
barn.
Where three wise men followed a
star,
Which led them to this baby
promised from afar.

Christ is the reason for this season,
and He has paid the "cost,"
So that me, you, and EVERYONE,
will celebrate HIM on CHRISTmas!

Robert Payette
EYE OF THE STORM
Not a soul in sight,
except me' and the ocean.
I love to watch the waves roll,
with continuous motion.

The violence and electricity,
you can feel it in the air.
The thought of damage already done,
and
the damage that will soon be here.
The eye of the storm the lull in the
air,
will almost have you believing, this
freak of nature will soon be leaving.
The picture of waves crashing on the
beach,
is somehow so alone and irreversible,
when they have no one to reach.

Glenn C Arthur
A QUIET ONE, THIS ONE I SEE
A quiet one, this one I see
Sometimes lost in ecstasy
Expressionless at times the face
Has no flavor of emotion—not a
trace
But this one who sits so far beyond
Sings alone a melancholy song.
Fire nor ice could break the chain
That holds back secrets of the
brain
A life that's divided into many a part
That can't all be played by such
a solemn heart.
If white were black and black were
white
There wouldn't be such a
grueling fight
Against the time allotted per day
That makes our lives slowly
fade to gray.
He likes to think of himself as a
riddle without a clue
He strives to be quite different
from the rest of you.
A cloak of pale-dark blankness is all
that can divide
The world from warmth and
tenderness that's hidden deep
inside

A strange and eerie feeling flows through my every vein
As I dare to lift the veil that will reveal this person's name.
It is I.

Reyna Burruel
WAR
Chances of Nuclear War is highly foreseen,
And if war breaks out and kills
Us all not all shall perish.
'Cause even when all the people are gone
American or other, there shall always
Be others to take our place.
So there can never be peace for man
Loves the thrill of war more than peace.
'Cause war is a chance for man's
Competitive spirit to come alive and thrive.
And peace makes man feel as a part of him
Inside is dying and has no escape,
So that is why there can never be peace.

Myrna Brooks
BROKEN WINGS
The search for love is greater than
All other dreams known by man.

Bountiful is love—some others may know;
They seem to find it wherever they go.

Love abides with birds of the air;
Touching wings, they learn to care.

But what of the bird with a broken wing?
He cannot fly, he cannot sing.

Majestic trees find love on high
As they reach to embrace the sun-filled sky.

But if their branches are smitten and hewn,
They will never reach the sun at noon.

The wingless bird and the blackened tree
Sing no sweet songs for you or for me.

In darkness, loveless, I walk alone.
My wings are broken, my heart is stone.

Oh love that heaven brought!—
That such high flight should come to naught.

Kathy Carpenter
THE INTRUDER
When I stepped out of the comfort of my home
It surrounded me and would try to bite
All the parts of me that had shown.
Then it's threatening power grew more in the night.

It burned my fingers when I entered my car
And engulfed me while driving so that I couldn't see.
I struggled to drive away from it in fear
While it continued its grip until I reached safety.

Its silent clutch caused fear all around,
And claimed several lives with its blinding hand.
Some folks were forced to stay in their homes
While its eerie presence continued to stand.

It made headline news all around the world,
So that all who saw and heard would know
The awesome experience that people can have
In Alaska when it drops to minus fifty below.

Bryan Geary

Bryan Geary
(ON THE EDGE OF) DARKNESS
God, can You please help me? I seem to have lost my way.
God, give me lightness in this darkness we call day.
God, how many times have I cried inside always unfulfilled?
God, is it me or is it that I've wandered from Your will?

No more happy, no more loving,
Painful memories always recovering.
The childish innocence is almost gone,
And I'm tired of wandering from home.

God, my life is such a mess. I feel I'm going crazy.
God, my mind is so tired, and my thoughts seem rather hazy.
God, life is indeed so rough, even though I seem to drown.
God, how many places in my heart seem more lost than found?

No more happy, no more loving,
Painful memories always recovering.
The childish innocence is almost gone,
And I'm tired of wandering from home.
I want to come home. I want to come home.

Kathy A Doss
FEELINGS OF LOVE
To know you love me, as I love you,
To feel the things in life, we'll together go through,
gives me courage and strength, to get through each day,
assurance of you beside me, to help guide the way.
Shared, is the love we have. It's not yours, nor mine.
But ours, together shared, for a very long time.
Friends and lovers, we can be both.
We'll just follow along, as our love grows.
Feelings are hard to put in words, but why try to explain,
To feel the feeling, and know, it doesn't need a name.
I could say "I love you," but that's already known.
I had to express love to you in words of my own.
Mental and physical feelings are trying to speak too,
and come out in words, in this poem for you.
To watch and see, to feel and touch,
To know and to love, is never too much.

Darlene Jackson
LOOK AROUND

I wish to dedicate this poem to my mother Deola Westover, for her continuing encouragement in my pursuit of writing

Deep within my very being,
The depths of which one cannot see,
There's an awareness of something pending,
Perhaps fear of what awaits in life for me.
My unrestful soul, always stirring,
My mind reflecting its dreams.
The past that's gone, the future beginning,
thoughts reoccurring, never resting it seems.
Where is my place in this life.
that brings happiness and peace of mind,
To release my restless soul from strife?
Surely it's ahead of me and not behind.
Is this search for satisfaction never ending,
Or is it all in what we call life?
Will anything stop those feelings pending,
that cut into my soul like a knife?
Have I only to open my eyes and look around me,
rather than trying to search within,
Stretch out my hand and grasp what I see,
And a brighter future will soon begin.
Then contentment will set my soul free.

Walter Kurtzman
SONNET #1 ELLEN
When in my mind I dwell on days gone by,
And sadly think of joys that did not last.
When fondest memories bring but a tear to the eye
Over hopes and dreams now faded in the past.

Elusive happiness I find in others looks,
While life's excitement is consumed in misspent hope.
And prospects of love I find in library books
Dispirited in feeling that my stage has limited scope.

Now into my being your precious presence comes,
And completes my soul as only love can do.
Now every nerve and cell within me hums
With rapturous melodies that sing our love is true.

For your sweet love received such pleasure brings,
That Scorpio's Leo feels exalted above any kings.

Elisa M Soriano
THE NIGHT
The day has gone by
its simple passing
only Night remains
the Night for stars and the moon
the Night for dreamers and lovers thinking
so deep and pensive is the Night
recovering us from light
allowing us to be what we wish
turning us back
taking us from reality
proving our dreams
voyaging through the grooves
showing our true selves

Maureen Ann McArdle
CALLED PARADOX
Living in a town called Paradox,
Where living is really being dead.
Dying in a town called Paradox,
Where dying is getting far ahead.
Driving down a road called Paradox,
Where the distance is never far.
Crossing over a bridge called Paradox,
Where you never reach where you are.
Existing in a life called Paradox,
Where you wish life would begin.
Ending a life you called Paradox,
Is when your life will begin.

Anita T Brantley

Anita T Brantley
AN INVITATION
Today, my heart reaches out and embraces all the world.
With tenderness and loving thoughts, I leap from
Face to face of those I know, and those I don't
What difference does it make?
Stop the guns
Disperse the mob
Put out the all consuming
Fires of jealousies and hates—

Resolve the bitter boundaries of
Race, creed, color, and the like!
Till nothing can restrain the peace
That such a love will bring.
Then all the world can come to know
A heaven on our earth.
With open arms, and tears of joy,
I extend this invitation—
Will you pause to share this glorious day,
and take me in—
As I have you?

Sarah Raynes
WEST VIRGINIA
The hillsides
The trees,
The flowers
The breeze.

Hiking through the woods
I'll never forget,
And living in the mountains
I'll never regret.

Autumn's bright colors,
Winter's snow covered trees,
Spring's many singing birds,
Summer's rustling leaves.

You may like it
On the ocean's shores,
But I like climbing trees
And having cuts and sores.

"Those people in West Virginia
Are really crazy," they say;
But I'll love it all my life,
And here I'll try to stay.

Christopher Scherer
AMERICAN SUICIDE
Madness isn't catching, it's only rising to the
Plagiarized insanity, blinking from the bridges: a jumper. gone.
Leaning on a ledge, leering twelve-stories down
Upturned tenement faces, screaming,
"Jump! Jump! Jump!" the gun
Closed in cosmoline and honey—safety—fires.
Not to go alone. never—ever
As rapid as dropping; solid as concrete.
Howling sirens—windy—missed? maybe.
Windows rattled, alternatives shattered to pieces,
Prismed in an ashtray.

Caught, cuffed, confessed, convicted.
Sentenced, stripped, strapped and salted.

Seconds last forever—everlasting
Father, free us from our sins, grins,
Boils, wens of change and eczema. witnessed.
Fingers, aged with wisdom, clutched tight
'Round the handle. cocked.
Madness isn't catching—it's falling.

George Beecher
TO JUDGE A POEM
The poem is for me
Not millions more
Like a brief letter
I've been hoping for
The stamp is rare
I wonder what it tells
And read to see
If it was meant for me—alone

The poem is for me
All share unknown
Like a birthstone
Amethyst or emerald
I've never owned
What good is it
Until I see
It seems for my eyes—alone

The poem is for me
No swarming crowd
Like a bottle floating
To my island world
Of wonder wording
Sealed—I read
And see it must be
Sent for me to know—and own

Harriet Taylor
LOST CHILD
I was told it would be better than before
When my Dad walked out the door!
Then why don't I feel happy?
Did you both really think of me
The ugly fights way into the night
Couldn't you remember when there was romance
Your eyes looking bright
The dinner by candlelight
And when I arrived
The joy as you both sighed
Couldn't you take it to God in prayer
So at night, when I go to sleep
Mom and Dad would be there.

Betty Ann Wooley

Betty Ann Wooley
LITTLE FLOWER
Little flower of the wild
You are Mother Nature's child
Lain upon her meadows breast
Dance to breezes soft caress

Petals wing and gently fold
Not your head of crimsoned gold
Kiss the sun and silver dew
Staged against a sky of blue

Laced amidst a carpet green
She chose a field beside a stream
And fashioned you as her bouquet
To dance a wilderness ballet

Winnie Stouffer
THE AMERICAN DREAM
How I love to remember my childhood days, down on my Grandpa's farm
I can almost smell the fresh cut hay, stored in the old red barn
Or walks with Ted the family dog, thru Blue Bell dotted fields
Where after dark we often went, to hear the Whippoor-Wills
I remember seeing sunlight, filtering thru the Willow Trees
It would paint such pretty rainbows, on the surface of the stream
There were Meadow Larks, and Bob-o-Links, busy feeding young
and Mother Mallard, and her children, swimming by me one by one
Snitching Grandmas homemade cookies, long before the dinner bell chimed
Was something she'd forbidden, but I did it all the time
Helping Paw to harness Bessie, maybe even milk the cows
Walking just inside his arms, as he'd stride behind the plow
I remember the sweet smell of earth, freshly tilled and turned
And watching Grandma squeeze, and press, the butter from the churn
Sometimes on winter evenings, when the snow was on the ground
After supper in the kitchen, we would gather all around
While Grandma in her prayer cap, sitting rocking to and fro
Doing mending by the lamp light, told us tales of long ago
I remember just how good it felt, snuggling in my feather bed
The fresh smell of sun dried linen, as it crinkled neath my head
All those simple old time pleasures, unappreciated then
How I wish, that I could go back, and find them all again
With my Grandma in the homeplace, singing while she cooked and cleaned
And my Grandpa working hard each day, in search of The American Dream

Mabel M Bishop
TO YOU
For twenty years we've traveled together
Hand in hand, all the way.
But though we've had much happiness,
We haven't always been gay.
For we had our share of troubles,
Our share of worry, too
But we faced them all together,
And come smiling through.

Sometimes the obstacles loomed so large
On the horizon, bleak and gray
We wondered how we could face the world
In the dawn of another day.
But each day is a new beginning,
A challenge to follow through.
And I'll meet them all with courage
So long as I have you

Jerry Thomas
A HEART THAT BEATS TO DIE
Walking through a painful memory,
is like walking through the rain.
Instead of drowning in the puddles,
you drown in tears of pain.
And though you fear not, the lightning, that flashes in the sky.
You should fear the dreaded thunder,
of a 'heart that beats to die!'

A 'heart that beats to die', surpasses
the tempo of common time.
Discarding 'life' as celebration,
accepting misery as perfect rhyme.
A 'heart that beats to die', will
eventually reach its goal.
And as the last song is sung, the body will deliver up its soul.

The soul in which was given, at
conception before birth.
As a gift, through a couple, from
'He', who knows what life is worth.
Though it be a gift that's given, it
bears great responsibility.
In the plan concerning mankind; and
the goal of all humanity.

So first protect yourself, against the
'heart that beats to die'.
By thinking of the good memories,
not those that make you cry.
Yes, first protect yourself, against the
'heart that beats to die'.
By celebrating life once more; Yes,
tuning-in to this thing called life!

Kelly Lane Brooks
IF I DIE
If I die . . .,
Don't cry.
Just watch my soul fly . . .,
away!

If I live . . .,
Then please forgive . . .,
my different ways.

The world will keep on turning.
Hell will keep on burning.
Hearts will keep on yearning
for their dreams to come true.

So . . .

If I die . . .,
Don't cry.
Just watch my soul fly . . .,
away.

Mechelle Le-Shawn Sweet

Mechelle Le-Shawn Sweet
NO DADDY
Here I sit, all alone
Because there is no daddy in my home.

Just mommie, baby sis and of course there's me
Because there is no daddy in my family.

It would be nice if there was someone to take care of us
To take me to school, sis to the sitter and to put up a fuss.

I praise God that there will one day be
A daddy in my life, and we'll be a complete family.

And I hope that my dream of a daddy will one day come true
Will my new daddy wonderful, will my new daddy be you?!

Heather Turner
SILENT TEARS
If you could only see the tears
That never meet the eye,
But stay within the heart
And nourish on each sigh.
We would be Kinder in life
And greet each friend with cheer,
And always use a helping hand
To Aide each Silent Tear.

Grace M Weaver
RAIN
I love the mighty pouring rain,
The fierce and biting storm;
It lashes at the window pane
And tears across the lawn;

It shrieks around the gables,
And it seeps in any cracks,
It challenges to battle
All the trees and chimney stacks.
It writhes among the grasses,
Tears to shreds the wave-top's spume,
Groans among the forest giants,
Every wire sings its wild tune.
It drenches all who brave its wrath,
The streams swell to a flood.
I love the furious elements
When they are in a mood.

Mary C Weaver
MY MOM
Mom, the love we shared together
Has grown in heaps and bounds.
Years full of happiness,
Has made life's path an easier walk.

For the times of your help,
For the times of your patience,
For the times of your understanding,
Making me feel secure—I miss you.

Your many acts of kindness,
Filled with cheerful words,
Made me aware of a love
That grew for all. Thanks MOM.

Dena D Buckles
LONGING
Eight long years have gone.
When will this aching void abate?
Walls scream their silence since
That jolly chuckle is no more,
Nor is that eager helping hand.
Your handiwork is everywhere:
The home you built with loving care,
Life's problems that we shared,
And thoughtful gifts bestowed.
How deep the yearning for a day
Or just an hour's chat.

Richard D Braverman
WHY?
Does the rose ask why?
Or does she simply spray fragrance
Up past clouds to sky
To charm the Gods in restful trance?

Does the thrush ask why?
Or does he gladly trill gay notes
To thus certify
That goodness only he promotes?

Does the sun ask why?
Or does she send her loving light
All to beautify
The earth by day the moon by night?

But sadly forlorn man asks why
Unlike the flowers, birds and stars
And claims he must search till he die
For new and better avatars.

Louis Sorabella
GOD'S MESSAGE
In the bible, God's Holy Word,
Is a message all have heard;
God loved the world, and me and you,
Believe it, friend, for it is true.
If in your heart, you want real peace,
Call on Jesus, for full release;
God's precious message, yes, it is true,
Very simply, my Jesus, loves you!

Michel Rose
I TRY
I try to understand the sun
I try to understand the bum
and I try and I cry and I die.

I try to understand the flower
I try to understand the power
and I try and I cry and I die.

I try to understand the rain
I try to understand the pain
and I try and I cry and I die.

I try to understand the rainbow
I try to understand the sorrow
and I try and I cry and I die.

I try to understand my life
I try to understand my wife
and I try and I cry and I die . . .

Martina Quintero

Martina Quintero
AT EASE TO MY LOVE

I gratefully dedicate: At Ease to My Love, to my cherishable friend. Robert Gordan Frederick

I have been waiting a long time for the heat to vaporize, and you give me warmth. I have lived in loneliness, and emptiness and you provide me with happiness. I have lived a life of being unwanted and you give me friendship. I did live with a broken heart and you give me love. I have lived by uncertainty about true real life and you provide me with imagination, facts, ideas, dreams, and hopes. I have lived being unsure of myself and you provide me with security.

Our paths have cross severe times through the passing years of open and closed gates. Our path has aimlessly wandered by our hearts and now we can join our broken hearts together. And now we can restore what has been destroyed, broken, and hurt. Bob we have built a strong lasting relationship that makes us as one unbeatable team! Love with all the friendship and T.L.C., can give.

Mae Gladys Allen
NEW BEGINNINGS

Dedicated to my 5 children: Janelle, Clemmons Jr., Rilene, Linda, and Sharon.

A blessed and prosperous New Year,
The beginning of 1989 is here.
Remember, as we make our new resolutions
that God is always there with the solutions.
Praise God for his infinite mercy and abiding love,
which He dispenses to all of us, from above.
No matter how much we stray or fail,
God is always there as a strong supporting rail.
Where we are weak and unsure, he is always strong,
letting us know that he loves us, even when we are wrong.
God continually supplies our daily needs,
thus giving us opportunities to plant daily seeds,
of a kind word, a smile, or acts of compassion,
then watch the instant response and re-action.
So during this New Year, let us remember
the needy, the homeless, and elderly in a loving way,
And knowing that God so loved the world,
that he gave his only son,
And if we share a little of our love,
we'll know in our heart that we have won.
The word of God clearly says, "When you give to the poor, you lend to the Lord, and he will repay."

LaRue S Allen
A GLIMPSE OF A BLISSFUL MORNING
A fleeting glimpse was given to me.
To store in my heart for the darker hours.
A vision of beauty on a fathomless sea.
And blessings untold, coming down in showers.

Weakness and suffering, a part of the past.
As we feed at His table, now reserved, for His Own.
The evil one and his throngs will be judged at last.

A blessed re-union with loved ones long dead.
With endless Eternities to talk to our Lord.
As we behold the Glorious Crown on His Head.
We will never grow weary of hearing His Word.

Joseph T Craig
REMINISCENCE
I'd like to walk again along a dusty road,
That only now, my memory knows;
To feel again the warm soft dust
Work up between my toes.

I'd like to wade the cool spring branch
That brought contented happiness;
And watch again, the small fish dart
And hide among the watercress

I'd like to follow down the furrow,
New made across the field
To watch the seed go in the ground
And then to watch the yield.

To see again the cotton fields,
The corn, the new mown hay:
The fields of waving golden grain,
Miraged in memory's yesterday.

Margaret F Margetan
MY LITTLE RED HOT TOMATO
It is time my little seedling pure
To cover you in bed and to endure
To give you heat like a simmering fire
Let the light shine on you as I so desire.

As you drink from the liquid I pour
A little seedling you will be no more
I will protect you in your prime
But there will come a certain time.

Your mature green foliage will form a cluster
Of bright yellow powder to pollinate and muster
I am proud you've grown so tall and high
It will be hard to remove you and say good-bye
Your colour will turn to a shiny complexion
You'll stand out in a row with a deep red reflection
Your destination has grown to completion
You no longer need my constant protection.

The time has come to pluck you off the vine
As my hand and yours entwine
And you'll lay there all in a glow
My little red hot tomato.

Leo Michael
OLD OAK
Near my garden stood an aged old oak,
Still healthy looking, but some branches broke.

The bark was rough but badly creased
From the claws of raccoons and other crawling beasts.

At the base of the tree's hollow trunk
Lived a family, the striped skunk.

As I in my hammock lay
I loved to see the striped kittens play
Mama skunk foraged near and wide
To find nourishment for her little tribe
Her menu, bugs, beetles and pheasant eggs
To top it off with a pair of frog legs.

And an annoying owl with its mournful hoot
But such a nice bird I could not shoot.

Near my path a wasps' nest hung
I thank the Lord I never was stung.

The wasps buzzed their hive all day
To keep all people far away.

My neighbor says the end of the tree's life is near
According to legend it was planted by Paul Revere.

A strong wind broke a hollow limb
And made a big enough hole for a squirrel to come in.

To build a nest in this crowded place
Leaving room for storage space.

Acorns ripening hung in the breeze
The squirrel waiting for the harvest moon.

To gather them before the winter freeze
Or be covered by the falling snow.

From a darkened cloud a lightning stroke
Cut the fabric of the mighty oak.

In splintered shape, to earth it fell
Giving up all it done so well.

Glinnie J Albrecht Berry
A SPECIAL PRAYER FOR LOVED ONES FAMILY AND FRIENDS

Dedicated to the family & dear friends of: Claud Williams—Wanda Curtis— & my very precious brother Hubert, sister Hazel, & Uncle Clem, also "God's Bill," my late husband.

May the Lord's Holy Comforter be ever so near;
And with His "All-Powerful" love:
Touch all the family, and friends so dear;
While praising our Heavenly Father Above,

for giving us the blessed hope;
Of life eternal, thru Jesus' gift of love:
Without which, who can cope?
Oh help us Lord, still our fears!
Let us be more like a Heavenly dove.
Give us more perfect faith, and dry our tears.
May all the saints on earth, and Heavenly Hosts above,
join us in a "great" amen!
Set us free, to 'heartily sing"
AMAZING GRACE;
That most beautiful Salvation Hymn:
Knowing we may see, this loved one again,
When we reach that Heavenly Realm!

Craig E Southern C D E

Craig E Southern C D E
TEARS

In loving memoriam to my father
ALFRED RALPH SOUTHERN
1919-1979

If tears could help . . .
Why couldn't I cry?
When all had been vastly ruined;
and left behind.

In a moment of turmoil,
In a moment of strife . . .
I tried to cry,
But just couldn't;
To save my own life!

Just a little trickle,
Or minute relief . . .
To help me put things into perspective;
To deal with my grief!

I ponder back to when . . .
The tears in my heart were then . . .
But, no more can I weep;
I feel so helpless, alone, and weak!

However, as time goes on,
I know the day . . .
Will return that is gonna stay . . .
When I will know tears again;
Only to again begin!

Mary Carda
THE MOON
Trapped in a sea I dared not fathom I struggled through alone.
The moon played my fate before me as my face was sprayed with foam.
My lovers passed, one by one, mocking my pain and sorrow.
My empty eyes begged for help—but not a soul would follow.
Then one per chance gazed through the mist, brandished a grin and wink,
And without a word leapt after me, not daring first to think.
The tide broke free; I took your hand and thus was led to shore.
In your eyes I heard unuttered words forbidden evermore.
My cheek caressed your feather touch; I found the strength to go,
Knowing wistfully I gave you back to the Past that holds your soul.
Knowing wistfully I gave you back to the Past that holds your soul.
Now bravely forth I face my path and see the stars and smile,
Believing a man and his roguish ways set stars in my eyes awhile.
And if by chance I awake from dreaming and gaze on the moon above,
I also see a man named Friend and fill my heart with love.

Joyce Burley
WILD HORSES
Racing across the hilly meadows,
Racing across the dusty plains,
Scorching sun up high above them,
Their bodies drenched with cooling rains.

Not caged in with wooden fences,
Land as far as the eye can see,
Independent of man's ways,
They are free.

Hoofbeats pounding the earth,
Thundering through the sky,
Not held back by man's contraptions,
This is where they live and die.

Susan Stone
DREAM HORSES
Horses are running in my dreams,
Bays, blacks, greys and creams.
Over the hills of my reverie,
Tossing their manes, they gallop free.
To the top of the hill, then down to the sea.
The dreamer in me runs
With all of the horses
And I am now wild and free.

Mary J Bowser
LOVE IS NOT BLIND
Love is not blind . . .
It sees many different things
It sees the hungry and the homeless,
The sick and the disabled,
Prejudice and injustice
Wars between nations,
due to greed and lust for power
To gain freedom, or to remain free.

Love is not blind . . .
It sees the destruction of its environment and inhabitants,
due to drugs, alcohol, violence, and pollution
And wishes that we will soon find a solution forever more.

Love is not blind . . .
It sees also the lovely green grass, and autumn leaves
Vari-colored flowers and trees in bloom
It sees a smile on many of its loved ones' faces,
due to health, happiness, and prosperity
And wishes that it will remain there forever more.

Elizabeth A Doherty
TO A FRIEND
A wise old owl,
—always there to explain things.
A teddy bear,
—who listens, but doesn't speak.
The clouds and the sun,
—guaranteed to be there.
Stars and the moon at night,
—watching over me.
Like a path and lighthouse,
—guiding me from rocky shores.
Letting me be a seagull.

Jessie K Andersen
DO YOU REMEMBER
Do you remember
The times that we shared—
When you told me you loved me,
And how much you cared?

Do you still think of
Our walks hand-in-hand,
The laughter—the tears—
The castles in the sand?

You made my world
So happy and bright,
But the torch you once held
Has now drifted from sight.

How I long for yesterday
When I held you tight—
And our dreams close at hand.
But the waves of time
Have washed our castles from the sand.

Mrs Shirley Tokunbo

Mrs Shirley Tokunbo
VOWS OF DESTRUCTION

I wish to dedicate this poem to my wonderful family, my husband Khamisi, my son Moriba and my daughter Zawadi. Special thanks goes to my mother, sister and brothers—for sharing their faith in me.

With these nails I thee stab
I promise to make you bleed
I'll enjoy every moment while you suffer
I'll fight you every chance I get, I will be glad

With my body as my weapon, I promise you heart-ship
For as long as it takes I'll torture you
As you have tortured me
For you men are sick
Your bodies weak
Your minds disturbed

I'll show you no mercy
As you have showed me none
For thine days are short
The end is near
Pain for ever and ever
You're Dead!

Diane Ciaramaglia
MISUNDERSTAND
Please don't misunderstand
The feelings that I show
Or the things I want to share
Please don't misunderstand
If I say to you I care.

A part of me is independent
Trying to be my own.
Another part is crying out
I don't want to be alone.

That's the part that's frightened and confused
Afraid of being hurt and abused

The part that's independent
Says no commitments, no ties
What is it that you want?
I can't hear it in your words
Or see it in your eyes.

I sometimes may cling to you
And always be around
Please don't misunderstand
For I will never tie you down.

Joe Chandler
BEAUTY INSIDE
The sun sets in the west
A beautiful orange color
Fading from day into night
A beautiful sight

Waves rolling in
As knights entering a battle
Endlessly pounding at the shoreline rocks
Like the steady ticking of clocks

Such exquisite beauty
Unexplainable by any words
It conveys so much joy
Comparable to a child with a new toy

Look inside
And there you will find
Such incomparable beauty
Vigor and continuity

Let go this you will not
Found what you sought

Bonnie Caspers
CAN YOU JUST IMAGINE, HOW THE WORLD WOULD BE
Can you just imagine,
How the world would be

If people thought,
In terms of "we"

If everyone,
Would learn to care

And, simply share,
What's theirs, to share

Maybe a few,
Of the tears would dry

If someone were there,
To wipe an eye

Maybe some loneliness would end,
If more people, would try,
To be a friend

Why is compassion,
So hard to give?

In this crazy world,
Where we must live

They say, "The best things in life are free"

And, I think, I truly must agree

A smile and hug,
Won't cost you a thing

But, to someone who's down,
What joy it can bring

A great poet once wrote,
Before his end had come

"You may say that I'm a dreamer,
But I'm not the only one"

I, for one,
Choose to believe

What he longed for, we could achieve

A world where people,
Could live as 'one'

Just like, in the songs,
He sung

All we really need to do
To make that kind of dream come true

Is to, start thinking,
In terms of "we"

And try, a little
'unity'

What greater thing,
Could there ever be

Than, to give to another
Unselfishly?

If this, could only,
Somehow be done

Then, the battle,
I feel,
Would be half-won!

Vizjak Damir
COMFORTABLE POSITION
It is not hard to control mediocrities, hit their sense
Discover their formally built feelings which come up
within one-way circled brain with many Stop signs in.
Listening them is like rhapsody played in just one piano key.
But, they are always in such a comfortable position,
surrounded with nice women, and other mediocrities as well.
The best Swiss watches are created on their pattern.
Fascinated with white teeth, physical fitness, Porsche's
and gentle skin they hesitate to kiss their own mothers
after AIDS has appeared. So wise of them.
On the other side born to die people find out just barriers.
Sign of failure sparkling on their flags, but all in all
they don't change principles like dirty socks.
And how to compose the story of success, when a vampire
with shiny teeth running around and there is no woman
they didn't seduce nor a career they didn't realize.

Lois C Carlson
FOOTPRINTS IN THE SAND
I heard a sermon preached, one day,
On "Footprints In The Sand,"
We often see them on the beach
Where folks walk, hand in hand,
We see them on a wooded path
And on a desert floor
But many times, with wind and rain
Perhaps, they're seen no more.

Footprints, like impressions,
We leave, when life is through
Whether they be good or bad,
Is up to me, and you,
If we wander as we go
Along life's earthly strand
We never know if we may leave
Our footprints in the sand.

Others, watching, unawares
May think we know the way,
And try to follow, as we walk
But wander, day by day;
Then, sometimes, when the going's rough,
They cannot understand
And miss, like us, the path that shows,
Right footprints in the sand.

If we follow where Christ leads
And daily do His will,
He will make our footprints deep
For other feet to fill,
He will never leave us,
Our lives are in His hands,
And, always, someone else will see
Those footprints in the sand.

Sharisalyn K Barnes-Wall

Sharisalyn K Barnes-Wall
SOLITAIRE

For my Mother,Your dream is finally a reality.

I am but a deck of cards;
My mind is being shuffled
as I am passed through one
family to another, as would
a good piece of gossip.

I sit waiting to play any
game the world has to offer
and wind up playing a
lonely game of solitaire.

I am happy as I could play
a Queen, but sad
as the last card
is a Joker.

Alas, I am being shuffled
once more;
being dealt out among
the crowd.

Marilyn Karres
THE FISHERMAN
He wakes so early in the morning with a brightness
in his eyes, that not even lack of sleep could dull when his thoughts are on his flies.

The trunk is full of rods and reels, worms, boots, and junk that he'll probably never think to use,
when the fishing seems quite punk.

He'll catch his hook in branches and lose his bait besides, but this fisherman has his hunches and his hopes are mighty high.

True, he may not catch a thing or even get a bite, but just the same you can bet he will sleep plenty sound at night.

Evelyn Caro
SUNSET 2,094,330
I saw it,
spread in the sky-gallery,
dying brightness dripping
down to earth.

I touched it with my eyes,
and I wept
as I considered the One Who
paints with fire and cloud.

Mabel Glover
REMEMBER OUR VETERANS
My thoughts go back to several wars
Where men fought and died on sea and shores.
Why God, did they have to die so young
For their lives had only just begun?
The wounded too, we do not forget
We are thankful they are with us yet.
My son too, served his country well
He came back home, with a sad story to tell.
The scars of war are with these men to stay
But they are grateful for a better America today.
Though memories wane, and more pleasant ones are in store
For these men, if we only show our appreciation just a little more.
God bless them one and all, for the brave deeds they have done
They were brave men, in the wars they have won.
For these brave men, we pray with heads bowed
And our American flag can wave very proud.
May we always stand strong, if it need to be
To keep our America for ever free.
God Bless America.

Marceline Evans
STANDING OVATION

Written for and to Gianina Marie De Laurentiss

Little girl—you will always be—
Nothing less than—
Standing ovation to me—!

Although you are not even two—
And surely not yet three . . .
Just one sad look from those—
Huge soul-ful eyes
And you've got it "Little Lady"
Oh how well you do know how—
To mesmerize!

Gosh what a little Ham—wow!
"What a star"
That smile—that face—that special glow
That certain something—by far.
So, pretty little standing ovation,
watch it—

Because—you are you must know
Only one generation—from
my very own creation

Mary Alice Merrill Clements
NOW IT IS FALL
The air is crisp and sometimes
cold
The leaves turn color
And they are a sight to behold
A view of mountains is more
Colorful than an artist
Can paint with brush
It takes your breath away
And leaves a hush
The colors of fallen leaves are
very varied
They are shades of yellow,
orange and red
Squirrels rush about hiding nuts
For in the winter they must be
fed
Apples are more juicy after a
frost
All this beauty is ours
Without a cost

Eddie H Bowen

Eddie H Bowen
WHILE IN A GRAVEYARD

To my sister, Mattie Jean Bowen Crisler and her children, Joseph Robert "J. J." Crisler and Melody Ann Crisler.

Many tears were shed
over these dead.

Time and time again,
they fell like rain
upon the land,
absorbed by sand
but, leaves kept falling.

Sandra Long
EUTHANASIA
Your suffering I can no longer bear,
my love, so frail and helpless, lying there
with unbearable pain etched in your eyes,
and the muffled sounds of hidden cries.
I hear you beg in whispers soft and low,
please, end my suffering and let me go,
let me go where I'll suffer no more,
and I'll wait for you, love, at heaven's door.

Reminiscing, I sit with your hand in

mine,
and remember years back to a special time,
when we stood at the altar in sweet wedded bliss,
and til death do us part, was sealed with a kiss.

Holding you in my arms, cradled up tight,
I raise the cup to your lips, so pale white,
and ask God's forgiveness for what I do,
but heaven knows how much I love you.
My face is wet with flowing tears
remembering all, our wonderful years,
and as life slips from your weightless frame,
I stroke your hair, and whisper your name.

Sophie Kleeman
INFINITE WISDOM
Dear God in your infinite wisdom
Look down upon those in despair.
This world is so full of misgiving
But I know in your heart you care.

The pendulum of life swings unfailing
Its stroke never missing a beat.
Dear God as they plod slowly onward
Let their journey not end in defeat.

Starting each day with your blessing
Let not fear or despair bar the way.
A touch of your hand, love will command
In knowing they are close to Thee.

N Yvonne Hageman
I LOVED HER TOO

Dedicated to Jack F. Phillips In memory of Francis L. Phillips (Nee: Moore) October 3, 1934-December 24, 1988

Daughter, Wife, Daughter-in-Law, Sister-in-Law.
Mother, Mother-in-Law, Grandmother, Aunt and more.
A woman of many names and a multitude of roles.
She no longer walks amongst us.
Her voice will reside in our minds and hearts now.
We shared pain, sorrow, heartache, and fear,
Which made times of happiness and joy a special treasure.
Remember her smiles and her laughter too,
They were so special, and more so to you.
A daughter who brought joy to her parents.
A wife crowned Queen by an adoring husband.
A cherished daughter-in-law.
Gracious sister-in-law.
Mother words escape me, but loved you were.
An exceptional mother-in-law.
Grandmother loved by frolicking grandchildren.
Aunt, Friend, Confidant, admired by numerous people.
A saint I've painted you say?
We are aware of her stubborn streaks too.
We have lost a unique person, you and I.
I cannot share your pain, losing someone you loved so much,
But I share your grief and sorrow for
I cherished her too.
Let love and laughter conquer thy sorrow,
Shared memories and God's blessing ease the morrow.

Veronica Gregg
GRANDMOTHER'S THINGS
Some beads
some lace
and other odd things.
Needles and pins
an old piece of string
Grandmother's things.
Once lost
or just misplaced;
A small scrap of this
and one or two of that
Grandmother's little things.
Now old
perhaps forgotten
or just thrown away.
But the memories stay
of Grandmother's things.

Jean A Williams

Jean A Williams
POEMS

To . . Richard, Beth, Mark, Jeff, Kenny, Gary and Mom . . for their love, devotion and unknowing inspiration.

A verse, a POEM, just something to rhyme . .
Give me a topic, and it won't take much time
To mince and arrange some words just for you,
Be it joyous, naughty, serious or blue.

Charles Osgood I'm not, but would like to be
Close to this master of journalistic "rhymery."
Making headlines and deadlines, leaving thoughts or a smile,
His stories are told and in quick-witted style.

Your ears are attuned as POEMS brighten your day,
At parties and banquets POEMS do find their way.
Used by presidents, boxers, the old and the young,
And songs without lyrics, how could they be sung?

Poetry with meaning is not always contemplative,
Tho' by its virtue alone, it is stimulative.
A novel's story can't be told, with such brevity
And still remain poignant, show beauty or levity.

Personal pleasure derived from this mode of expression
Is evident, I hope, by these lines in succession.
Kudos to "The POEMS" and "The Poets" at heart.
This is the message I've hoped to impart.

(Even its license is free.)

Max J Levinsohn
REQUIEM FOR LISA

To "Lisa Elana Cohen—My Grand-Daughter."

Cry now the black opaque . . .
Regret . . . a silent thunder rolling in the throat . . .
Consciousness aware only of compounded pain
To endless sleeplessness . . .
Cry now the black opaque . . .
Wait . . . wait for the echo of tormented time's
Noiseless reverberation
Spinning nothing out of nothing . . .
Self inflicted emptiness
In retrospect drifts
Around ever present memories
To bury itself within the fount
Of a mortal's agony and his perpetuated hurt . . .
Cry now the black opaque . . .
The conjured image of that which was
Beauty . . . brush it lightly
Or else destroy the moment . . .
Return substance to unwanted reality . . .
Remember the life unconsummated
And cry . . .
Cry now into the black opaque.

Stanley H Tyler
VISION
When by labors bent
What catches your roving eye?
Some noxious weed, a discarded trashy bottle cap?
Or, perhaps some simple pool of mud?

It might be some gem—a nugget of pure gold.
In more dejected mood you might have passed it by.
The pool settles a bit—a mirror begins to clear;
There's a blue sky up there—a bird on wing.

It seems too certain that what we perceive
Is dependent upon our mood or frame of mind.
A couple lean down with arms entwined
Faces aglow with smiles and warmth
As they behold their cuddled three day old
Serenity personified—with every muscle soothed.
The zephyr stops and the mirror further clears
The couple we saw was really you and I.

I Shyke
THIS WAS THE JAPAN WORLD WAR
Seek not here musical or theatromania connection
In a world enveloped by television domination
With vaudeville's types of presentation
For what lasting value has this concealment
If designed or chance heralded by government
And via private billions spent on sponsorship
On purpose of through stupid self censorship
Then state the facts without poetic or other refute
That unindexed was the Japan World War of ill repute
A missing title by some sort of hocus pocus
A juggling in news, TV, radio, movies and books
About blood thirsting in the Thirties and Forties
By Nippon in the 20th of Centuries
Relax no soothing rhymes for facts
To note and record full scale warring acts
Against two billion people in 48 nations terrorized
Until on Sept. 8th in 51' peace was signed
In San Francisco to prove now if not before
That this had been the Japan World War
Although proclaimed otherwise by recording history
As an indexed differently titled story.

Anita Wendinger
FRIENDS ARE FRIENDS FOREVER!
Friends are friends forever
and a friend will always
say forever.

For when it's time to say
good-bye, it never means the
same, for someday you'll
meet each other in Heaven.

And when that time comes
You'll both rejoice and say
Amen.

For friends are friends
forever and your friend
will never say never ever.

Valerie J Putsey
WE'VE SAVED THE STATUE
We sing about America, from coast to shining coast,
We sing about a land that's free, a land we love the most,
We sing about our freedom and this is freedom's song,
We want to sing of Liberty, her life we have prolonged.

We've saved, saved the statue, The Statue of Liberty,
We've saved, saved the statue, and kept our country free,
This precious gift was given by friends, over a hundred years ago,
We've saved, saved the statue, let goodness overflow.

She came to us from France one day in 1884,
Two-hundred, fourteen crates were built to bring her to our shore,
She stands on Liberty Island, her robe must be unfurled,
We're proud of our Miss Liberty, tallest statue in the world!

We've saved, saved the statue, The Statue of Liberty,
We've saved, saved the statue, and kept our country free,
This precious gift was given by friends, over a hundred years ago,
We've saved, saved the statue, let goodness overflow.

John Vincent O'Donnell
HEARTACHE

Why the shadows?
Why the gloom?
Why the shades
Pulled down in
Every room?
Why the quiet
And why the sobs?
Why? Because up
There somewhere,
The Good Lord
Reached down and
Plucked a flower
From the garden
Of life.

Zeldah S Livingston

Zeldah S Livingston
GROWING OLD

To my three daughters Muriel, Lenore and Ardis

I have run life's race
From childhood to old age
And I hope my name's written above
On that sacred page.

There have been trials
Joy, sickness and sorrow
But God says in His word
To hope for a better tomorrow.

My eyes have grown dim
I don't hear very well
My joints are all stiff
And sometimes they swell.

Life's race soon will be run
And I must bid you goodbye
As I leave this old Earth
For my home in the sky

When my life's work is finished
And my life's race has been run
I hope you can remember
Some good I have done.

Ida Ma Collebrusco
FAITH

Father, I love Thy Promise at the break of dawn,
Thrill at the feel of cool spring rain—
Thank Thee for a Faith that leads me on
To a life made glorious again.

I have been lonely in a crowd,
Lost in the quietness of my room—
With shattered hope, have cried aloud—
Father! help me this awful gloom.

Father, I thank Thee for Peace of Mind,
Which has come to me today—
For Faith that strengthens, and Hope that inspires—
For Truth, Life, and Love to guide my way.

Lee Banning Morris
CLOTH OF ALASKA

These are the threads
of thin ice
sudden sharp flashes
reflecting silver light
in the night
from the moon;
spun gold
from the sun
at noon.
Blue white sparks
in vivid snow
atop a peak or
fallen low
wherever
streams flow.
Myriad color petals
of flowers
and leaves,
herbs, berries
breathe the air
of gossamer cleanness
everywhere
in Alaska;
from lofty height
o'er endless land
a weaving by
the Mystic Hand.

June Floyd Johnson
WOMAN OF DEPRESSION YEARS

To my dear sister: Juanita Floyd Leake avid reader and collector of my poems.

A strong willed woman with ragged and torn clothes,
In my father's brogan shoes, she waded against the cold.
She put potatoes in the pump and potato house,
All dry peas the barrel would hold, we didn't do without.
She drove cows home so they could be milked,
She fed them corn, she had grown, shelled and silked.
Thanking God for every bean she picked,
For the barnyard fertilizer and each bean stick.
For the sun that shown and made them grow,
And for each row she had to hoe.
She thanked God for the pecans that fell,
And each sack that she could sell.
She made a way where there was no way,
Now I thank God, that I live to-day.
To have known the hardships that made her go on,
She made us a life, with happiness, and a home.

She's with God now, and finally at peace,
For her hardships she's rewarded, and troubles ceased.

Gene Koester
THE AMERICAN WORKER'S LAMENT

They'd be hurt if they knew I was thinking,
For in this place thinking's not allowed
And sometimes I almost turn to drinking
But that wouldn't make my family proud.

There were so many times I tried to tell them,
How to make things work better than they do
But my boss told me I'd never sell him
You just do it the way I told you to.

So I sit and I do just what they tell me
And hope that no one learns my name
And I dream sweet dreams about retirement
When somebody else can play this game.

Anthony Lindsey
THE WELL

To Lyn, who will never know how much she means to me.

A child sits quietly at the edge of a deep well, throwing rocks into the water to hear the splash—
eager to know what is there, but unable for one reason or another to find out.

A man, standing by his side, watches the rocks in their perilous journey, losing sight of each as it pierces the dark of the well. He wonders if they will reach the water below, but will never really know.

Child and Man are one in the need to know, a rare event in this time of generation gaps, of misunderstandings between young and old. They remain apart, separated by thoughts, by experiences that cannot be shared. But they can enjoy this one moment together, pitching rocks into the well and wondering where they go.

William P Trivette

William P Trivette
LEST I FORGET

To Deanna, my ever present help.

Back through my early years, through smiles and tears
I wonder, did I leave some things undone?
In the hours of my prime, in the busy moments of time
Did I forget my duties to someone?

In my moments of success, When God seemed to bless and bless
Did I let the precious seconds slip away?
Did I push the best aside, to pursue some foolish pride
Not seeing the brightest hours of of the day?

Did I grasp some sandy bar, while reaching for a star
Laying all my greatest talents on the shelf?
Did some person cry in vain, reaching out to me in pain
As I showered all my blessings on myself?

Were the tender years of life, Marred by bitterness, strife
As the grapes of plenty withered on the vine?
Old memories linger yet, Lest my heart should e'er forget
The wasted opportunities that were mine.

John H Baxter
WAKE UP AMERICA!

Wake up America!
It is later than you think;
The hour has come to rise up;
Your fortunes are on the brink.
Wake Up America!

Wake Up America!
Your destiny is in your hand;
Get your eyes set on your goal;
For this is still the best land.
Wake Up America!

Wake Up America!
Your patriot fathers lived and died bravely;
That you might be a nation great;
Let your light shine forth boldly.
Wake Up America!

Wake Up America!
Keep the flag waving over the free;
And stand up for your father land;
And pray God that it shall ever be.
Wake Up America!

Harriett Janus Klinedinst
A TELEGRAPHER'S DAUGHTER

Father was a telegrapher,
And he made the old key fly.
He would tick away the message
It looked as easy as pie.

The Morse code was quite a load,
For two little girls to handle
But we would try to make a word,
The message was really mangled.

My sister and I spent many a night
With dad on his tower job,
And we'd pull the levers
For the train to go by,
Under his watchful eye.

Dad always knew when the trains were due
By the tick of the telegraph wire,
He'd always pull the switch on time
And no. 90 would sail thru like a house on fire.

We stayed with dad on many a night
So we could pull the levers,
He'd call the numbers and we struggled to pull
So number 90 could go by Ginger Hill.

So as time goes by, all these things are gone
And only memories remain.

Akumla Longkumer
ACROSS THE OCEAN TO A LOVING MOTHER

As I travel across the wide ocean
Unto the land of the unknown,
Watching the slowly sinking sun yonder
My mind turns to thoughts of you mother.

Thoughts run back to yesteryears
Long forgotten memories recollected:
Days filled with fun and laughters
Times I took your love for granted!

Time oft spent in vain pursuits
Insensitive to your sighs and woes;
Busy in my own world of interests
I was not there to share your sorrows.

But you always loved me I know.
In your own simple way,
You did your best somehow
To make me what I am today.

Though we're a thousand miles apart—
For all your love and devotion
I want to tell you mother:
You will always be my inspiration

And I love you more than ever!

Henry Asher Mayo
CAN'T FORGET THOSE FEELINGS

Can you see the desperation
behind these cold green eyes
Can you sense this empty
hear the sadness in my sighs
I say it doesn't bother me
but I know that it's a lie
Do you know that you destroyed me
when you said good-bye
I long to hold you close
feel the warmth upon my skin
I can't forget those feelings
do you remember when
We walked in the rain
or picked the daisies from the lawn
I can't forget those feelings
And the past forever gone
We looked at the world around us
pretending we didn't care
About the people staring
We had our love to share
I knew that it was over
before you said it's through
But I can't forget those feelings
And I'm still in love with you

E V A Hedger
HOME

Here I've been for many years
A place of love of life and fears.
You may not think of it as Home
But it's the best I've ever known.
It's not the best I know that's true
But it's the place I always knew.
Here I've loved, I've laughed and dreamed
And here I'll stay, or so it seems
Until the life is gone for good
Then I'll have left this neighborhood.
But still the memories will carry on
For they will never really be gone.
But until that day I'll stay right here
A place of love of life and fears.

Karin Arechavaleta-Meiwitz
JULIET'S ORDEAL

Now, I know what Juliet must
have felt in losing her lover.
Now, I understand why she wanted
to end it all.

I, too, feel a passion with darkness,
not for fear of losing my Romeo,
But, rather for the doubt of ever
finding him.

Juliet must have lived in bliss
before she faced darkness.
I have lived in Obscurity hoping to
discover the light of ecstasy.

Now, I can sense what Juliet
felt when she lost her love.
Now, I can see why she
terminated it all.

George Gauthier

George Gauthier
NO LIGHTS OF DARKNESS

No lights of darkness
there's no color
but only waves that enter the mind,
without endless points,
pain is stored with no escape,
deep inside is a force,
hatred and violence.

Enter into doom
the pit of flame and horror,
goblins circle the surroundings,
leaving no way out of the forsaking place,
into a hole, floating, drifting,
fading away from darkness,
into a world of fantasy,
and wonders of the mind absorbant.

Entering a room with no sign of life,
movement is dead,
stars shine like diamond studs on a coal black sky,
a dimension that moves a personal soul,
into superb life of fascination,
inherit a dream of every century,
to any pleasure that drifts you into the well of memories.

Donald Smith
WELL, HERE I AM LAYING-ON MY SIDE

Well, here I am laying on my side.
Reading the new issue of TV Guide.
I turned the page and what did I see a
poetry contest, "I said that's
For me. It said, win 300 prizes worth
over 25 thou." I let out a shout,
"GEE MA." that's worth more than
two pigs and a cow. So hello,
Eddie Lou, How do you do, on this
special birthday wish to you.
I'm here to let you know I've got this
poem to show and win
All the prizes from head to toe.

B Lou Shrewsbury
HOME IN COLORADO

Living in the State of Colorado
Is a generous privilege to extol.
It is indeed a golden El Dorado
As year after year unfolds.

The grandeur of the High Country Peaks
That are not as steep as they seem,
Any defeats triumphed by end of day
As we climb and reach our dream.

The majestic Rocky Mountains
Reach upward toward the sky,
Reminding us of God upon the mountain
Alone, to rest and pray, we know not why!

As we descend the lofty roadways,
And view Lakes, Rivers and Ski Runs,
Elk, Deer, Antelope and Wild Sheep
That climb and jump in merry fun.

As we return to our Bed at night,
To kneel, pray, and to thank our God,
Recalling the Wonders his hands have wrought
Thinking of him and "How Very Great Thy Art."

Audrey Frances Pecor
PEACE VICTORY

You must build peace
along a fireplace-on gray bricks
with sunlicks and birds
gliding in shadows;
Songs emanating from fir trees,
Cooking fumes edging round
a corner.

You must build peace
with a friend-so much a
free soul in her corner
that you are allowed freedom
In yours.

From this-for granted niche—
Seek memories to pass on—
As she does-this place of peace—
to others.

Enjoy today . . . It must carry you
to the next
Place of Peace.

Kathryn Charlotte Miller
THE LOOKING GLASS

If you would
see me again
look into the looking glass
If you would need to hold me
in your arms
Clasp your arms about yourself
It is I,
within them
Should tears sweep
over your eyes
mine also weep
Should pain engulf your heart
with grief
So does my own aching heart
for you
grieve
You have not become somebody else
along
Time's Passageway,
nor me
Time is only time,
my Dear
by which one measures centuries
Time but may make for,
a foggy glance
and dim the view
But it never forsakes, Love
Time, never washes Love away,
entirely from you
Love only dies,
when we die
and men prepare our graves
You hear me?
I needn't speak?
Need there be words and speeches?
Within our very presence lies
the complete
and entire phrases
Nothing is laid to rest
until we ourselves
are laid to rest
When we cannot appreciate the sun
through trees
And, know that they not their heads
within the breeze
Life isn't worth anything
Life is sad, and bungling
Life is wasted hours
and good for nothing
Our sleeping is but an imitation
of death,
until
We breathe right along with
the earth
we live!
I wish not to be,
like those
Who want nothing, of life
but for repose
What more need to be explained?
Nothing is, except for
what we think
there is
And, there is
nothing more
than this:
How can we adore,
what we do not inherit?
All else, besides,
Love,
hasn't any merit!
Life is difficult
only then
When we do not realize,
what gives us happiness
Do not tell me,
you are lost and alone
When I am here?
You know, where I am,
My Love!
Just look into a mirror!
(I am within the glass.)

Shirley M Flynn
POETRY CONTEST

A Poet is a man,
Who is on a never ending journey,
He can help you cross over the stars,
He can help you walk the seas,
He can suppose a mishap, with a happy ending.
He can leave an indelible imprint on mans emotions,
to feed his soul.

Margaret C Kearns
NOW IT IS SPRING

In loving memory of Marilyn Jean Kearns. Jeanie wanted a poem for school. I walked to the upstairs window, and far below, I saw APRIL.

Look! said the Jonquil, nodding its head
To the Crocus over in the flower bed;
The branches are full of little gray fur
The March winds blow, Br-r-Br-

r-Brr.

Gosh! there's a Robin, my he looks cold
Hopping around out there so bold;
What is this I see?, A snow flake!
Drifting down to me?

It falls so softly now, as it covers the ground
On bushes and branches of trees all around;
Tiny buds showing, through branches and such
The snow doesn't seem to worry them much.

Jonquils, Crocus'
Birds on the wing;
Now it is APRIL
Now it is Spring.

Naomi Swinford
MY SOCIAL WORKER

To Nancy Seppala—my social worker, my best friend who I will always love and respect who was the purpose this poem was written for. And to Phyliss

Sometimes you give me that gentle shove,
but you also give me so much of your love.
There is a funny side of you, I love that part of you too.
You give the best hugs, because they feel safe and snug.

I hope you don't take them away, I hope they're here to stay,
you help me with my fears, and you understand my tears.
I love to laugh with you, and be close to you too.
For me it's easy to run away, but when I think of you,
or when I'm with you I want to stay.
Your support I can count on, you're there like the rising sun.

And I'm on the receiving end of your sunshine, and it's the most beautiful sunshine I'll ever find. I love your beautiful smile,
It helps me want to keep it around for a long while.
You really help me, and help set my burdens free. I love the inside and outside of you—you're my best friend too—and I love you.

Debbi Spring-Smith
ANY HOPES UNDONE
I wish you a New Year full of smiles
May laughter carry the endless miles of any sorrow
you have, yet, to go

May the goodness turn badness into an old friend
May the lost blessings come to visit you again
May your thoughts keep turning into sunsets
that welcome your nights . . . waiting for requests

May the answers be mornings you can understand
May love wake you by gently holding your lost hand
May love guide you through the fog of dawn's confusion
May love help you find a purpose with a reason

I wish you a New Year full of hopes
And a tree with swings attached to ropes
so you . . .
Can fly away from
Any hopes undone.

Margaret Talavera
A CHILD'S EYES
A child's eyes is a mirror of its surroundings:
Pathetically even those horrid moments in which a child is
Mentally or physically abused!
What will become of those eyes who have surrendered to fate?
How much harm could they endure?
A trickle spouts from those child's eyes . . .
An amusing smile appears . . .
A gleam from those very sad eyes vibrate and
Just as suddenly a voice much more mature than that
Tiny and bruised body speaks the child . . .
Withholding all pain and anguish . . .
Softly pronounces:
"Jesus now I lay me down to sleep!" . . .

Isaac V Smith
100 YEARS BACK DOWN THE WAY
100 years back down the way,
I opened my eyes to the light of day.
As the years piled upon my head,
All my dreams upon the future fed.
Now I take flights, in fantasy, to my childhood land,
Viewing the scenes where God took my hand,
I met temptations, temptations strong,
A whisper in my ear, sonny, that's wrong.
I visit the old homes which were once my lair,
But the old homes are not, any more, there.
The old homes are gone, a lone chimney marks the spot,
Where in the days of yore I came to a lot.
Gone, are the old friends, but images still abide,
Where we once whooped, we laughed, and we cried.
Their faces I can see, but they do not call my name,
As they used to shout when we would play some game.
Their tongues lie silent now, have been for many years,
The memory of those happy days floods my face with tears.
Reunion, in the city, that city with the golden street
Will be the Acme of our life when loved ones we shall meet.
Beyond life's river, stand DEAR ones, watching the other shore,
Seeking for faces of love ones they SO much adore.
Soon, I know not when, I will join the throng,
Waiting, this side the river, for the crossing GONG.

Snowflake

Barbara Weigner
A SNOWFLAKE ON MY PILLOW

To my cat Snowflake—whose unconditional love keeps me going.

Home is where you are—
my dear sweet cat—
I love you so much—
but you know all that—
To think of life without you—
is more than I can bear—
How can I get through a day—
without your stare—
Your antics are truly funny—
You have a sense of humor—
that make all my days sunny—
How sensuous you truly are
You really are my shining star—
So cuddle me, warm me, love me,
And fill my days with joyful glee—
God has been so good to me—
And no matter what ills befall me—
I shall prevail—
For with a Snowflake on my pillow—
I cannot fail.

H K Jeanes
LITERATI
Robert Frost lost;
Ezra Pound found.
Emily Dickenson.
chickens on . . .

Heloise B Pistorius
THE MUSIC MAGICIAN
You're the silent guitar player in a band
And as I watch
Your long sensitive fingers pluck and thrum
the delicate strings of your instrument

The sound crashes and echoes
in the semi-dark
fading away into butterfly riffs
leading your concentration

You're the enchanter
evoking memory and sensation as you strum
gently, softly
as your audience sits spellbound

You live for the music that you play
drifting on a sea of sound you play away
your nights for me too
thank you

Kathryn Otis
OCEAN BLUE
Ocean blue, ocean blue
Why are you so blue?
Ocean blue, ocean blue
Why do you have waves?
Ocean blue, ocean blue
Why are you so cold?
Ocean blue, ocean blue
Why are you so shiny?

Oh Kathryn, Oh Kathryn
I'm so blue because somebody put food coloring in me.
Oh Kathryn, Oh Kathryn
I have waves because I was born with waves.
Oh Kathryn, Oh Kathryn
I'm cold because I take too much cold medicine.
Oh Kathryn, Oh Kathryn
I'm sooo shiny because the sun shines on me.
Oh Kathryn, Oh Kathryn

John Nyikos
MORE THAN RHYMING WORDS
Poetry is more than just some rhyming words
It's a star-filled sky or a flock of birds,
The wagging tail of a puppy dog,
or sunshine breaking through the fog,
Poetic beauty is all around,
in the sky and on the ground,
and if you're wise enough my friend,
you will surely comprehend.

Shawn Holmes
THE TAPESTRY
The Tapestry in my mind,
Pictures you in the night,
With your white lacy dress.
The sweet caress
Of your fingers may chill my spine,
But warms my heart all the time.

Marcia Soper Coverdale
MOTHER'S DAY POEM
God gave me a mother
Gentle, firm, gracious and wise.
She values honesty
And loves to surprise.

She is a teacher, a leader,
A hostess, a nurse.
She loves to shop
And carries an interesting purse.

She is a lady, a secretary
A seamstress, a cook.
She likes to dress up
And curl up with a book.

She has a heart as warm as the sun.
She loves to smile, laugh, and have fun.

When I want to talk
She has open ears.
If I am sad
She would help dry my tears.

She is a Christian,
A companion, a true friend.
She never stops giving,
Her love has no end.

She can scold. She can praise.
She can laugh. She can cry.

She is thoughtful and understanding
And says give your goals a try.
Mom—you are pretty special.
I think your character is fine.
I'm happy you have given me life
And proud that you are mine.

Elpidio M Juan

Elpidio M Juan
JUST FOR YOU

Dedicated to President Marcos & Family by s/o E. Juan, Interstate Guard Service, Inc.

JUST FOR YOU

Mother! Mother! My beloved Mother
Listen to me once more
From nowhere, wherever, whenever
I am here

JUST FOR YOU

Please listen to your son, Ferdinand
Won't you feel once more?
The throbs of my heart, my being
Say to me, Ferdinand are you tired?
No! Mother, I take 'em all in stride

JUST FOR YOU

But what are all of these?
Lilies of the valley, black and red red roses
I can't believe it, 'restrate their meanings
Are they real Mother?

Ray O Smith
RAINBOW
I will bring a rainbow down from the sky,
Catch me a bluebird and teach you to fly.
Gather the sunbeams to wear in your hair;
Pocket some moonglow for us to share;
Harvest the stardust for when you feel blue.
Sprinkle it softly to banish the gloom.
And if you feel lonely and should you cry
I will bring a rainbow down from the sky.

Floyd E Sare
MY SISTER'S NEW HOME
My sister lives in Heaven today.
With Mom and Dad she has gone to stay.
Although their bodies are still on earth,
Their souls now dwell in Heaven's girth.
We who are left with memories fond,
Will one day, too, share Heaven's bond.
Amen!

Christine M Randall
REALITY
I see myself leaving reality
adrift in a world of my own
I return to reality once again to find
I'm unloved, unnoticed, unwanted, and alone

I feel as though I am deserted
in a place unknown to me.
A place I cannot feel comforted in,
where no one cares, Reality.

I hear loud cries of sorrow
of those, mine are a part
Life's reality is to blame
for the despair within my heart

I can feel that life is a place
that has caused man many fears
I can see how different this reality is
As all man's cares float amidst their tears

This reality that I visit now
has become very cold and black
The world of my own reality
has now come to take me back.

Karen Ann Ramsey
THE DEED
Bliss, is what I longed for,
Ecstasy, is what I see,
The bluest sky, the birds that fly,
The quiet of a night's breeze.

The tempest of life is our battle,
The will to live is our need.
I've won the battle, I've gained the peace,
Life——was my greatest deed.

Mattie J Wright
WHO WANTS PEACE?
Who wants peace in the world today?
This question I'm asking of you
Who wants to be free from a life of sin
Who wants to live a life that is true?

The war clouds hang low, the outlook is grim
Those who should know have said.
Our young men are fighting in strange wars
Many have been wounded, some are dead.

Who wants peace in the world today?
Something we may never see.
There will always be wars and rumors of wars
So it says in the Bible to me.

Whoever wants peace in the world today
Must start putting his trust in the Lord.
Invite Him into your heart; He'll abide with you
There will be no need of the sword.
The kind of peace you will have in your heart
Is the kind that abides forever.
The wars may come and nations may fall,
This kind of peace no one can sever.

Kenneth D Price
THE WORLD'S LOST SOUL
He crawled out of an alley,
And stumbled down a road.
His dreams, could have been many,
But now, they're all too old.
Life went by, too fast for him,
He didn't see, what it had to show.
Now his life, is a drunken haze,
And he has nowhere to go.

What drives a man,
To the depths of Hell?
Is it the thought,
That he's lost his wishing well?
Or maybe the love,
Of a lonely woman,
Who couldn't understand.

He crawled out of an alley,
And stumbled down a road.
His dreams have all been awakened.
His stories, have all been told!

Gina Marie Berola

Gina Marie Berola
ON THE EDGE OF TIME
Captured
Within the limits of my mind
Dancing ON THE EDGE OF TIME.
Teardrops collecting sunlight
So they can shimmer like stars
Before crashing to the earth.
Music
Misty music,
Spinning—spinning
Capturing
My fragile body,
Capturing
My feelings.
On the edge of time
I am dancing—
Captured.

Patches Withington
THE GOLDEN WEST
If the golden west you wish to see,
Put on your bonnet and come with me.
Moose and elk—take a look.
It's like pictures in a nature book.
Mountains soaring to the skies,
It's a sight for your sore eyes.
Falls tumbling over the rocks.
Relax, enjoy, forget about clocks.
Flowers blooming in profusion,
No sweat, no confusion.
Sea lions, lolling on the shore,
Makes you go and look for more.
Redwoods massive and sublime,
Makes you forget about time.
Sea rushing toward the shore,
Truly cancels out all bore.
Pines and oaks by the billions,
Things to see by the millions.
Skies the bluest you ever saw,
All in tune with our God's law.
Traffic easy, roads uncluttered
When I drove it, my heart just fluttered
Roadrunners, mighty few,
One or two you're treated to.
Sparkling rivers winding, winding,
It's a sight you will be finding.
Placid lakes like a mirror,
Peace and quiet, God is nearer.
Ocotillos and saguaros,
To remember in your tomorrows.
Attractions well named,
Popular and famed.
Gorgeous desert sunsets to behold,
Mauve, orange, yellow, purple and gold.
Verdant green valleys, rooks and rills,
Cattle grazing on a thousand hills,
Cross winds, dust devils, tumbleweeds,
Everywhere, everywhere adventure leads.
National parks and canyons galore,
Who could ask for anything more?
License plates from every state,
They know very well what's great.
Oh, yes, and don't forget the tram,
That's trilling excitement what am!

Jill Theriot
WORLDLY LOVE VS. GOD'S LOVE
Tossed to and fro by the restless waters
as is your love.
Angry winds that rip all hell apart
as is your love.
Darkness covers the land about
as is your love.
Clouds that hide the brightness of the sun
as is your love.
Like a consuming fire, destroying everything in its path
as is your love.
Like a trembling earthquake that shakes me to fear
as is your love.
Like a fierce tornado tearing my world to pieces
as is your love.
Like the flooding rains drowning out life
as is your love.
Helplessly, I cry to God
It is not in my reaching up to Him,
but it is in His reaching down to me
that I am safe,
once more.

As is HIS LOVE . . . .

Kenneth Randolph Taylor
BARBARA
We were once like cats and dogs,
Never getting along.
But then she went to college,
Left home and said "so long."

We hardly saw her after that,
For she was busy with the books.
And then something happened, and
death she almost did not rook.

She tried to miss a deer, and hit
A tree instead.

Fortunately she came out of it,
With hardly a bump on her head.

I think what I would have done
If she had died.
And I have to say,
"Thank God she's alive!"

Arlene Audrey Spratt
LIFE IS BUT A YEAR
Spring like a baby long awaited, loud and flowerly
moist, and birds singing,
Summer the carefree happy days
of youth and long hot days of
the elderly looking to the cool
evening;
Autumn the golden prosperous
year colorful . . .
raked and dry rustling leaves
with children, jumping in them,
And Winter the long cold days of
the aged and
fun filled days of the youngsters;
Life is but a year!

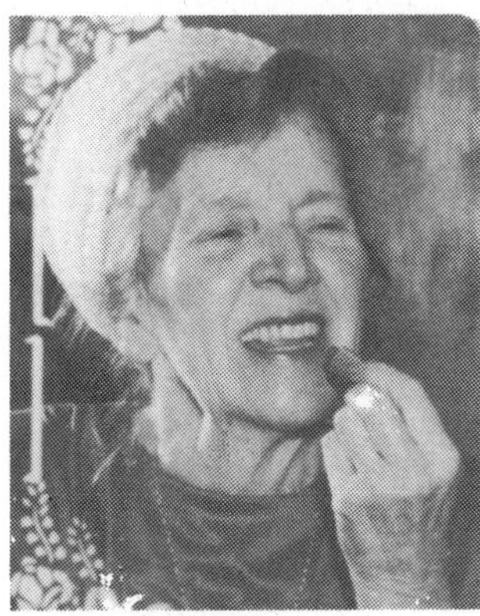

Mary Gladish Berks

Mary Gladish Berks
NEVER TOO OLD

*To my competent and caring doctors,
My loved and loving family,
And God on Whom my whole life depends.*

I "ain't no Spring Chicken,"
But I'd love to have a loving man.

I've got a lot of love in me!
Oh, if you could only see
How happy we would be!

Just you for me,
And me for you,
And no one else will do!

The remaining years would have more meaning,
Together with happiness we'd be beaming!

Wherever you are, far or near,
I am dreaming of you dear!

I'd love to hold you close to my heart,
And never ever let us part!

Ms Ute D Boulden
THE TRIBE OF SOUTH ALLEN
Have you heard of the tribe of South Allen?
These people are very religious souls
For they faithfully pilgrimage
To various shrines in their habitat
area every weekend.
Some zealous followers even drop in
devotion on Wednesdays.
Ceremonial dances take place inside
the shrines
And vary according to the dancer.
The dancing rite is interspersed with
The sipping and sometimes
"chugging"
Of a yellowish libation said to be the
favorite of the gods.
Worshippers have claimed that spirits
entered their bodies
And made them speak in a slurred
fashion.
After the gods had waned them of
their religious fervor,
The tribe falls dormant until they
are called upon again.
The fraternities strike again!?

Ann La Vin
GETHSEMANE
Silently, I walked with You. I know I felt Your sacred breath . . . .

You sat here in the Garden as I do now, touched by Your Holy Presence, under these five olive trees 2,000 years old. These aged roots still flourish today, beneath Your feet and mine! They blossom now as they did for you—True love shining for ever! Divine . . . . .

Thanks to OFM Father Peter Eichelberger's daily care, a brown-robed Franciscan monk in bare sandals studying Your Holy Star (Acquila?) leading the Three Wise Men—to wobble 26,000 years once around the Earth—so he told me in Capharnaum as You prophesied. It lighted the way for Three Wise Men as it lighted mine today, walking through Gethsemane in faith and spiritual time—Your Way!

I know You were here as my grandmother was; both I've never seen. Your holy Word has led me on to Calvary through St. Peter's Gate via Dela Rosa and Shepherds' Field, Galalea and Bethlehem, baptized in the Jordan, kneeling on Your Altar Star of Nativity—Church of the Holy Sepulchre—the Rock surrounded by Mountains of Temptation, Olive and Loaves and Fishes, Golgotha bells tolling Ecce Homo over Jericho and Jerusalem . . . .

The same path You traveled still leads the Way today—through Love, Faith, Truth, Work and Prayer—Infinity with God's blessings Your Word PEACE TODAY!

Edith Teich
MY WISH
Please don't bring or send flowers to my bier
For I can not smell them for I am not there
My spirit has gone to God my Father above
In my memory send a rose to someone you love
God has been very good these many years to me
Through loss of family and sin he set me free
My earthly bones ashes soon will be at rest
In the waters of the Gulf of Mexico I love best
You too can have peace of mind and soul
Ask God to help you make heaven your goal

Ruth G De Loof

Ruth G De Loof
GOLDEN YEARS

To my wonderful husband (Don) who has been my inspiration for this poem.

You came into my world
In the golden years of my life
And brought back the happiness I'd lost
When I became your wife

Each day is a new beginning
We've travelled far and near
No longer am I lonely
For you are always here

We have so much fun dancing
And playing cards with friends
And sharing all life offers
And to be in love again

I thank God for our happiness
And this bright new world of mine
And this love that will endure
Until the end of time

Ruth Couch
MOTHERS
I sit alone thinking back through the years
When mothers were special, to her children so dear,
Now the years have rolled by,
Mother's growing old,
She's a big burden She's been told,

She's passed from one down to the other, like some unwanted
Guest not treated like a mother,
She feels unloved Unwanted and so alone,
She feels no one loves her, and she has no place to call home,

So Mother go off to the rest home, and the Children all say,
We'll come and see you, but we can't stay You'll be fine with
People your own age, Mother feels so sad and so alone, she feels
No one loves her And she has no home,

But God is watching from his home in the sky,
He gives Mother a new home in the Sweet by and by,
Please don't cry when Mother is gone, She's no longer a
Burden, Mother's gone to her new home,

She'll find all the Love and care she will need,
In her Heavenly home with Jesus she be,
Where she never grows old, no burden she be,
She'll be with Jesus, How Happy she'll be.

Maryanne E Hebel
THE ROSE
Each thorn is a tear of pain I have for you;
Each stem is the strength and belief I have in you;
Each leaf is for all the growing happiness I have with you;
Each petal is for all my thoughts and feelings for you;
Each rose is all my love to you . . .

James Thomas Karam
A MYSTIC SMILE, FROM ACROSS THE SEA
A mystic smile, from across the sea,
comes to me in a dream.

Far beyond your reaching arms,
in the night, my memories appear,
reaching out for thee,
happy are my dreams,
for your smiling faces are near . . .

Smiles of friendliness and love, listen to a soothing word,
dreaming, still am I, far across the sea . . .

How long shall it be . . . My love, I send to thee, from across the sea.

I know not the way before me, I patiently wait.

Yet, I must confess, confused am I,
on which side of the sea to be . . .

My loving one's awaiting me,
sensations I sense, a dream that never fades away,
happy thoughts to fill my awakened days.

Oceans apart, I return thee a warm loving smile,
forever lasting, until, once again we meet.

Who knows when-ever, my favorite dreams will be upon me,
to be across the sea, forever united . . .

Bruce Melton Bellamy
MY DREAM
My dream is that you will accept me as I am,
that you will love and trust me with all your heart,
that you will need me to quench an uncontrollable desire which burns deep within your heart.
I dream that you will be that special person who will laugh with me when I'm happy, as well as cry with me when I'm hurt,
someone who will believe in me and stand by me with love,
for if you can love me with half the love I have to offer, my dreams would transform into reality,
and then shall I love you more than life itself.

Cleota Benham
RESTING ON THE LAURELS OF A BOUGH

While resting on laurels of a bough,
What can be said to "Life's reason"
That's in season—right now.

Life never promised it would be fair and easy
And it never even hinted when the end would cease thee.

So while resting on the laurels of a bough
And seeing in mirrored stream
'Neath rocky cliffs—somehow,

Looking through that defining path of right
And wrong way to go
Bordered with a quality of color—
Your own way—you'll know!

With sounds of echoing through rock and water
Both far and near,
It's the silence of your own soul
You'll most suredly hear.

So while resting on the laurels of a bough.
There is this distinction
Between directions allow.

The jagged (wrong way) terrain below
And the silent right voice of insistence.

Leo A Brandao
TO GAIN FROM LOSS

I've lost again, but then we all
at times, a loss must suffer
But first was she and now 'tis ye
and how much more is mine
In '48 my loss was light;
a greater frame I found
In later life my childhood gone
a loss so sane and sound
But paved the way for tearful teens
Then that gone too as time elapsed
and summer vanished quick
No loss back then brought greater pains
for though indeed 'twas gone
A greater good was then in store
as summer kills the spring
or winter the autumn leaves
But as my latest loss was ye
what have I now to hold
You've taken all as so did she
in splintered days of old
Not like the fruits which kill the flowers
for better things to be
But like the fire that burns the wood
leaves ashes drifting free

Monique Andy
DREAM LOVER

To my one-n-only Love, Andrew the beat of my Heart, the pulse of my Soul some things never die . . .

Looking at a sunset-n-seeing your face
Our Love wuz created somewhere in space
I catch site of moonbeams-n-feel your touch
These emotions I feel are far too much
everywhere I look, I see only you
Our eternal Love is Forever true
Dream Lover—sweep me up in your arms
turn me on with your endless charms
heal my heart-n-make pain turn away
how do I live without you each day?
Dream Lover—let's fly up high
Dream Lover—I can hear you sigh
Dream Lover—I can feel you cry
Dream Lover—we can touch the sky
I can remember each moment with you
-n- I can recall each thing that you do
You are from Heaven, from a star above
for nothing-n-no one do I feel such Love
across the world on a unicorn we'll ride
not even death can tear me from your syde
Dream Lover—wherever you are
pleaze look up to the nearest star
Dream Lover—thru you I'll survive
you are the reason I am alive

James W Brown
TO TIME

High hallowed Time! Who haunts our teeming sphere
With visions of its passing!
Dark Cloud, or shroud, that bounds our brief career
Of shadow-casting!
Who frames our mortal woes by change unkind
Yet, passing, blunts the sharpest of our sorrows.

Seeking the Unfolder of Tomorrows,
Our prophets and our youth
Have long in dreams and visions glimpsed Thy face
In chasing after truth
And in those silent moments, left this place!

Gina Lichtigfeld

Gina Lichtigfeld
DREAM

Last night, I think
I walked with you
Alone and aware
That my love was true.

If I could only tell you
The way I feel
To show that
My love is real.

Don't you know that you
are killing me to see
You look right through me
like a glass key.

To show you how much I care,
Is for you to be awake and aware
As I see us working as a team.
Was this real
Or just a . . . .
DREAM?

Ellen M Burnett
A MARRIAGE PRAYER

Today I'm Sending up a prayer
Entrusting it in God's Good care
That he will give us strong protection
and guide us in the right direction
If we should stumble along the way.

That we may have wisdom to do what is right
Secure in the knowledge that patience is might.

That we may have charity for others in need
That our faith in each other becomes part of our creed
That our new life be blessed with both laughter and tears
To draw us much closer through all of the years.

The above is my prayer as we start our new life
May the Lord bless our love
Giving you a Good wife.

Michael J Rayno
MOTHERS ARE SPECIAL EVERYWHERE

Mothers are special everywhere
They all have a special love & care

But I don't know of one as special as you
Now I've hurt you & you are sad & blue

Mama I love you so please don't cry
Or sit around trying to figure out why

I'll be home soon, it won't be long
Until then we just gotta be strong

Mama you've raised me the best you could
And if some changes could be made you know I would

But the past is something to leave behind
And look at the future with an open mind

Just thank the good Lord I'm alive today
He has reasons for punishing me this way

Mama he let me live when I could have died
Mama I love you & I know you tried

When I think of the special love you share
I realize more & more how mothers like you are very rare

Viola Q Seligo
THE CLOWN

When not Consciously
occupied—
As on this dismally
dark, drear day.
Scenes from Long Past days—
Run, Rerun—
Incessantly, Persistent—
Emerging
From a mind in Turmoil—
Evidenced
By a recurring dream
in which I
Am Hopelessly Lost
And from which
I Awaken, Equally
Totally Lost

Inez Simens
IT SEEMS LIKE IT WAS ONLY YESTERDAY

It seems like it was only yesterday
That I looked down to watch you at play.
You were quiet and a shy tot
Who did not like to talk a lot.
Then, like a firecracker bursting in the sky,
You shot high above the level of my eye.
Your personality changed during the summer of '82
Into a bubbling 16 year old that we hardly knew.
That trip to Israel brought forth a new Jay
Who always seemed to have something to say.
You grew into a fine, young man of 19
Who was thoughtful, helpful and never mean.
You always kept both feet on the ground,
Eager for advice, above the stereophonic sound.
We are so proud of your values and integrity
And your goal to obtain a Law Degree.
May the years find us happy and healthy together,
With lots of sunny skies and not much stormy weather.

Dorothy Black
ODE TO TOMORROW

What shall I do today?
What shall I say?
What does it matter what goes on when it is but one day?
To be cheerful, to be sad, that's my choice.
For tomorrow is mine to eat, to dine, to rejoice.
Over the hill? Not at all, for I shall walk in glory not to fall.
Ode to tomorrow, ode to tomorrow.

Kenneth Martz
THROW THE ACE

Deep, dark clouds loom before you.
A lonely wind blows coldly, mercilessly.
The moon hides the sun.
The dreary clouds further darken the day,
Even effecting one's spirit, his hope.
All has been dealt but a single joker.
In desperation, it is thrown.
The last hope turns into a stone,
And like lead, falls to the ground,
carrying one's heart with it.

But, as the stone strikes the ground,
It gains an unimaginable force.
The entire planet is moved.

In its new place, the sun defeats the moon.
It drives away the clouds and warms the day.
The flower buds bloom once again.
The lark resumes its joyous song.
I saw the card, it had changed into, an ACE.

Christopher Alan Thomas
THE REPLY

This poem is dedicated to the memory of those who served.

Forget the past, Hide it from view?
Forget the men, Far more than a few?
A greater mistake could not be made.

They fought and died under that Battlejack so grand.
Many giving up all, in their honored final stand.
To remember them is the least I can do.

I am not ashamed, but rather quite proud;
Of the men who served, and the banners they flew.
I will remember the gray, as well as the blue.

The Stars and Bars, the Battlejack too;
Shall wave forever, no matter what you do
At my Southern home, and in my Southern heart.

I shall also sing "Dixie" in a voice loud and clear.
So that all who pass near, may pause and hear;
The song that is the South.

Change our flag, make its memory a blurr?
Remove the "Jack," claiming it a slurr?
In reply I state, The Hell with you, Sir!

Herbert W Bell
MY HAPPY BOYHOOD DAYS DOWN ON THE FARM

Many weary years have passed,
since I've seen the old home last.
And my happy boyhood days, down on the farm.

That's where I spent my busy hours,
roaming wild, among the flowers.
Those were my happy boyhood days,
down on the farm.

It takes me back so many years,
and it sometimes starts the tears.
As I think of those happy boyhood days, down on the farm.

There was a grandfather old and gray,
who was busy all the day
and a grandmother to soothe us from all harm.

My old dog I loved so dear
and he was always near,
as we roamed among the field and the trees.

Now the folks got old
and the farm got sold,
so I started out in this world on my own.

I don't have much to say,
but if I could only name the day,
when I could go back and start all over once again.

So whenever I am near,
it won't matter what time of year.
I think I will go back one more time.

Then I will have to shed more tears,
as I think back through the years,
of my happy boyhood days, down on the farm.

William D Harper
THE EYE OF THREE

Through the time doors
Ascending and descending
Beyond the horizons of space
The moment now eternal
Light and sound
Which projects which
Or simply both in unison
And harmony
With colors cascading in
Musical vibration
Touch feeling
All above time
Or in time
Even beyond time
Thru
The eye of three

Linda Brekke
MORNING SUN

To William E Mininfield, Jr., everything a friend should be. You've given me and my life so much, thank you my friend. This one's for you with love, first, last and always!

The rising sun,
A ball of flame
Against silvery clouds;
Vibrant colors of
Crimson and gold gush forth
Across the heavens,
Leaving behind a prism trail.

Buffy Hart

Buffy Hart
DREAMS

To my loving family who has given me much love and support; To Mr. Rodney Ritchey who first opened my eyes to the excitement of poetry; And to NKOTB who know what dreams are made of and have inspired me.

DREAMS—Escapades of the mind;
Journeys into the
unfathomable
And mortally inexistent;
Into incomprehensible
Depths of the human entity.

DREAMS—Conflagrations of
foreboding thoughts;
A barrage of bizarre and
whimsical profligations;
Prophesies of the future;
Inexplicable encounters of
de ja-vu;
Exhortation of excruciating
premonitions.

DREAMS—The diligent work
Of the subconscious
In the course of the
Temporary hibernation
Of the human soul—sleep.

DREAMS—The publication of
Your deepest and innermost
Hopes, desires, and fantasies
Plagued by your inner
Fears, insecurities,
And lesser evils.

Carl C Williams
MEDITATIONS OF MOTHER (IN A COUNTRY GRAVEYARD)

Through a winding, wooded road on a lovely day in June,
O'er a steep and rocky hill, I climbed that afternoon
To see my Mother's grave. My heart could hardly wait.
The road abruptly stopped at Allen's graveyard gate.

Beneath an aged Cedar, with graceful arms o'er-spread,
Was Mother's grave—her youthful life had quickly fled.
Many a year had passed since last I saw her face,
Or as a child when last I felt her fond embrace.

As I mused these solemn thoughts, the loss my heart did burn;
For her return, my broken spirit sore did yearn;
'Twas then I heard her say, "My child, weep not for me,
I've run the race, and now enjoy Heaven's ecstasy."

"I now await for you in a land of golden dreams;
My mansion fair on a street of gold brightly beams;
My Father walks with me by flowing, crystal streams;
My joy abounds as from His eyes the love-light gleams."

"Toil on! Faint not! Life's fleeting day is sweeping by.
Bear the storm! Share the Light of Life before you die!
True and faithful to your honored trust, hold fast !
God Almighty shall crown your work of love at last."

Robert F Bluhm
SPRING TRAINING

Spring training begins.
No losses, no wins.

New names on the roster.
Egos to foster.

Running and stretching.
Aching and pain.

Answering questions.
Reporters refrain!

Shooting the breeze.
And dreaming fantastic.

Once again!
The autumn classic . . .

Muriel McKinlock D'Agostino
THE YOUNGSTERS

Unfettered by the snow
Last year's fawns
race through the meadow.
On the hillside, haughty matrons,
now quickening with tomorrows' fawns,
say goodbye to their youngsters
who proclaim their freedom.
This tells us it is Spring.

Robert S Nicolini
GATO NEGRO

I watch the black cat as he watches me
Gold eyes shining, he searches my dull brown ones looking for the glow
But there is none, for the hunt that lights has long been gone from me
His red tongue licks over white fangs like a snake testing the air
His fur sleek and jet black glistens in the moonlight;
muscles slack but at the ready
I watch with envy the grace of his leap at some invisible foe
And the light touch of black paws on autumn leaves with no crack of sound

He is as he was thousands of years ago; a survivor in a world of man
And I, too, am a survivor of his world of tiger and claw
In a flash of black he's gone into the night, leaving only the breath of where he was
I feel the place for warmth—there is none
Was it an omen or just a cat on the prowl, I think as I walk away
But somewhere in the dark, two gold eyes search for the soul of the brown-eyed man.

Dorothy Lyons
THE GIFTED CHILDREN

A poem dedicated to the "International Year of the Child"

The "Gifted Child" is a "Special Breed"
He really possesses an extra amount of determination to succeed
Is there something different in his chromosome or DNA?
Or is it that he is willing to study harder and sacrifice play?
Rolling up his sleeves
Putting his shoulder to the wheels
He develops a "Strategy" making concentration his 'Master"
Thus, with him "The Learning Process" grows faster
He thrives on each "New Venture" accepting each challenge he meets
Reaping "Joy and Satisfaction" when complete

David Lloyd McClure
THERE IS A TIME FOR GIVING

There is a time for Giving;
Thanksgiving is the Day;
And so this gift I'm giving you
Will melt your tears away.

Manuel Gloria
LIFE'S BEAUTY
The beauty of life
Can be seen in a new born
child's eyes.
It can also be seen in the eyes of our elders.
Beauty,
heard in our children's laughter,
felt in the love of our friends.
We must acknowledge this beauty
or risk losing it forever.

The crashing of waves along seashores.
The chirping of birds in every tree,
Each sound grasping the
beauty of life
A red sunset,
a shimmering moonlight,
each reflecting moments in
which our lives seem so content.
Time spent alone
or the time spent with friends
has no difference.
It is how the time is spent.
For every new day brings with it
a new light,
a new joy,
a new friend,
a new hope.

Once again,
it is the beauty of life.

Patricia Green
AUNTIE'S TOWN
I took some bread and laid the crumbs
down on my back porch walk
For one small ant who I had watched
move by a little rock.
He took the bread within his hands
And said "Look what I found!"
"I'll haul this to my little home
That's in my Auntie's town."
And so he worked and worked to move
The bread that he had won
And by the struggle that he made
It must have weighed a ton.
And when he got inside his home
he said unto his friends
Who all were sleeping in their beds
inside a cozy den.
"I sound the alarm go out on the porch
There's food out there for all!"
And so I saw a host of them
Come out behind the walls.
They gathered the bread within their hands
And said "Look what I found!"
"I'll haul this to my little home
That's in my Auntie's town!"

Rosalynn C Harding
GRANDMA
I love you, I love you, I love you I do.
I wish you were here
to help me through.
Through the good times
and the bad
To make it seem not so sad
To help me like you used to do.

But now you're gone
to the big man in the sky
A lot of times I sit down
and cry.
I know you're better off
with Him
Life on earth can be grim
Although I can't see you
I know you're there
Walking beside me
Along with Him
Carrying me through thick
Helping me through thin

Shannon Harrison
PATH OF LONELINESS
As I walked along
a narrow path,
I watched the river
as it passed.

My mind finding
what it's looking for
All that can be found
is never more.

I watched several people
hand in hand
Then thought to myself,
they must be grand.

Why can't I be like them?

Debra Lynn Hite Harvey
LOVE ME TRUE
Love me true
or love me, not at all
For I'd rather have
true love,
Than no love at all!

Bill Mac Ewen
THANKING GOD

This poem is dedicated to Audrey my beautiful and patient wife.

Thank you for all the things that effect my life.
The happy times and even the strife . . .
For the birds and the bees.
And all the hidden beauty that you let me see . . .
For all the ducks and the beautiful swan.
And all the goldfish that live in our pond.
Even when the day is getting late,
I don't feel down for at night with the stars I have a date.
And for all the beautiful thoughts you put into my heart.
And each morning you give me the courage for a new start.

And especially for the love received from my trusty dog,
And when she dies please be kind to her Lord . . .
Unlike people love and kindness they will never forget,
And forgive all those humans who are too selfish to own a pet.
And for the rain and the pretty snow.
And the March winds that blow and blow.
And when I lay my head on my pillow to sleep,
Thank you for letting my rest be peaceful and deep.
And if I ever pass all of your tests,
Like our father Abraham in your bosom may I enjoy eternal rest . . .

Gilbert R Barker
LIVING IN THE MOUNTAIN
Living in the mountain is a lot of fun,
To awaken each day to the morning sun,
Watching the wildlife procure their food,
Will definitely place one in a positive mood.

We have wild turkey, deer, squirrel, and rabbit,
Watching the wildlife can become an enjoyable habit.
The birds and the bees neither sow or reap,
However, they must earn their keep.

They must improve their habitat,
build their nest, and feed their young,
They must never leave a song un-sung.
They sing to establish territory and make it secure,
They have full knowledge their assets will inure,
To their off-spring mother nature helps propagate,
For the weak and the helpless death will be their fate.

The lives of the weak mother nature will assess,
The crippled and the infirm will experience sudden death.
The reason for this is to keep the species strong,
That they may continue to sing their song.

The city dweller hasn't been afforded this life that is serene,
If I told him about it he wouldn't comprehend what I mean.
To the city dweller I have something to say,
The peace and tranquility that exist in this mountain,
Will entice me to stay.

Yolanda Denise Hill

Yolanda Denise Hill
THAT PIECE OF ROCK

To Saroyan: My beautiful piece of rock. Love, Mommy

Sir Rock-Sir Rock, resource of your land.
Blessed is the plan in the palm of your hand.

Sir Rock-Sir Rock so strong so bold.
Summer has turned to winter, it's getting very cold.

Brisk was the wind that cracked your skin.
Strong was the force that made it deepen within.

Divine was the spirit who rumbled your ground.
Then along came that pebble, tumbling down.

Halt Sir Rock, pick up that piece.
It's vitally important, to say the least.

That plan in your hand could be a total waste.
Because Sir Rock will crumble if that pebble is not in place.

James L Adcock Jr
A WISH FOR THE WORLD
A wish I have
for all the people of Earth,
Is again to be as innocent
as we were at our birth,
Sad but it's true, we're falling apart,
for we can't see our way clear,
to read the truth within our heart,
We need to bind our hearts together,
and finally live as one,
and understand that finding happiness,
with thought of war just can't be done,
We need to look at all we've done
and all that is going on,
and realize that a change is needed,
or our fortress will soon be gone,
So a wish I have
for all the people of Earth,
and a fair warning to all I say,
PLEASE! ! Let's open our eyes for once,
THE CHANGE IS NEEDED TODAY! ! ! . .

Doris Caplinger
NATURE
Nature is the path we lead
To feel the earth on ground,
And help to brighten our heart each day
From brighter marks around.
Nature has ways to open our minds
And see the joy and care,
Nature can leave and how it can make
Our wants of needs to share.
Among the lakes and streams that flow
And birds that sing a song,
Can always help us see the pride
Nature can leave along.
Nature is shown through mountains and shores,
Along with grass and hills
And can always help us see through love
The joy of nature's thrills

Evora R Bartsch
TO MY LITTLE SISTER
My dear little darling sister,
You see I have not forgot,
Today you are five years old, dear,
Yet to me you're a tiny tot.

I am sending you this little token,
I've wrapped it up with care,
I've filled the box as full of love
As the sides would let me dare.

And when you're eating the candy, dear,
Just take a bite for me.
You'll find that bite the "bestest" bite,
A piece of candy could be.

Then take the cup in the other box,
On this, your Fifth Birthday,
And when you drink your milk from it,

Remember your sister who's now far away.

Then put it away in remembrance, dear,
Of a sister from you apart,
But who sends to you, her darling sis,
The best love of her young faithful heart.

Ida M Collebrusco
I LOVE YOU
Never thought I could love again, until I met you—
My heart is aching in vain—Your indifference saddens me too!
I loved the twinkle in your eyes when you looked at me—
Suddenly! You made me realize I loved you instantly.

Your voice echoes on the walls of my heart—
Must I tuck you away, forget I love you so much?
More than I can bear—being apart!
Longing for your tender touch.

There was a time I could not confess my love for you—
Then you suffered a freedom you did not want—
As before, you ignored me—
But why? What did I do?

David M Burgess

David M Burgess
THE TEENAGER

In Memory of Jason Brothers

One is afraid to die, yet the other is afraid to live.
If their souls ever reach the heavens they will somehow learn to fly.
But why must they fly in the heavens and not on earth.
They laugh in great joy never showing their despair.
Their eyes tell the story of their adolescence.
Some see no other solution and suicide is not the answer.
How many must we ignore?
How many more must die?
They need help!
We need help!
"the teenager."

Brian Domenic Alberti
TIME INDEFINITE
Take me
For I am yours
Whatever you want
I am yours

Are you mine?
Existing in time, or what I do not know
Please—Let's just stop and stand ever so still, so still, so still
Such as statues in concrete; molded forever

Should we be times
Or should times be ours
With sands running

Through—All we know.

Pamela D Macon
NEVER TO BE HURT AGAIN
Sometimes I sit and wonder and I look over the past
I can still remember the love that didn't last.

It wasn't the worst love and it wasn't the best.
It was just a relationship that was put to test.

I tried almost everything to make it work.
But instead of being happy I was only hurt.

He didn't seem to mind what was going on
His business was elsewhere and I was left alone.

But I learned a lesson and I paid the cost
Of an uncertain love that I simply lost.

Never again will I make the mistake of sharing
My love for another man's sake.

I will always be careful of whom I choose
To keep from being hurt by the love that I lose.

Robert Blair
A NEW SEASON

To the unheard voices . . . the unseen faces, To courage and the telling heart.

With the magic of star laden nights all around
As leaves of the trees on flight to the ground
Send seafaring dreams a-sweep in the air

Like hopes of the spring and the hallowed times there.
We turn a new season and full to the brim
As old sailors light with glass full of trim.

Paul T Forrer
m
i think
of that momentous mote,
the meager midge
and marvel.
wound up by millennia,
without mainspring or mechanics,
it moves in its madcap motions
better than any machine—in mid air.

like any mouse
or man,
it has its motives
and meaning,
though almost removed
from human sight and mind.
as ephemeral as summer mist,
it mates and melts away—
a tremolo of light,
emitting
a melodious
minute—mmmmmmmmmm . . .

Audrey Zweidinger Fried
PRICELESS TREASURES
I do not crave such priceless things
As strings of pearls, and diamond rings,
And cars, and yachts . . . . things money can buy . . .
Or a famous name, whichne-er will die.

Of Life's Treasures, a few will do . . . .
A Home, . . . A Child . . . . Content-ment . . . . You.

Jesse Chapa
BED TIME STORIES
Dreams are forever, they never die,
they come and go from our bed rest,
some are good and some are bad,
some we wish we never had.

Sleep my little children
enter worlds that are still unknown,
beware of those who come to you,
beware of those shadows that over look your view.

You never know when you're awake,
or if it were just a dream,
You never know if you're alive,
until someone hears you scream.

So open up your eyes and
see where you've arrived,
Could it be the land of paradise,
or is it the land of never ending cries.

Sister Lorelda Kilchenstein
SPRING
Something is stirring in all of my being,
My head is awhirring, I feel I must fling
  my cap in the air . . . and with a great flair
I must shout "IT IS SPRING"!

What is this tingling that has me astir?
Why am I mingling a HIM with a HER?
  My blood wants to bubble . . . I'm headed for trouble!
Why not? IT IS SPRING!

A weesome green earth bud juts out of the mud,
A warble is wobbly and almost a dud!
  I laugh as this shaky old . . .
  quakey old earth
Feels rebirth . . . IT IS SPRING!

Tracy Ann Houck
A POET'S GAME
To pin from pen to immaculate mat, rolling over unruly pages, cluttered with fits and rages, yet devoid
Empty of the crowd of inspirations, vanished and run amuck amid the glimmers, momentarily on tracks of lost times those last times, now forgotten
Impotent potential crushed at the thought, by the time all ways on the floor, grappling with the donkey, untaled the wriggling story squirming, still, somehow untold
To make it stick, surely hurt, sorely indelible
to bear to see the farce of the covered lie bared, unfolded and to hold it there, just so

Daphene "Punki" Wilkes

Daphene "Punki" Wilkes
WHAT HAPPENED?

Thanks Sam!

Oh . . . this selfish world we have woven.
What a terrible thing to do to such a beautiful place,
With greed, deceit, and self-centeredness.
Why are we slapping God in the face?

What happened to "Love thy neighbor?"
Are people too deaf to hear,
The crying out of their friends, the pain they feel?
Is it really that hard to care?

When God first created man in His image,
Oh how proud He must have been.
Even He did not know how sour grapes could turn,
Now His eyes cry for what He has seen.

From children who thought they were foolish to learn,
The ways of our grandfathers they now have long lost,
The tales of the past to combine with the future.
What a small price to pay . . . now how great the cost.

We have stabbed out our hearts with total malice,
Now this great world of ours has scars so deep.
That all the great men and all the great horses,
Just wring their hands and weep, weep, weep.

Narayanan Ganesan
THE DISTANT CALL
I heard last night
The cowbells ring
I smelled the dust
The hooves had raised
Coming home for the eventide
In a far-off distant land

My aging bones
Bear a silent ache
To lie in rest and slowly bleach
Ashened by the blighting sun
Amidst the bones of my thousand kin
In a far-off distant land

An arid land where nothing grows
A blue, blue sky and a searing sun
No monsoon rains nor salmon runs—
Way too far to trudge back home—
Oh! The call is strong and the way is long
From a far-off distant land

Angélica Chacón
MY LOVE FOR HIM
Dear God,
I am so confused right now.
Please help me solve my problem somehow.
This guy has taken my heart away.
I think about him every day.
If given the choice, you know who I would choose.
He's so special and I love him so.
His love I can't bear to lose!
We love each other and that's all it takes.
Please heal my heart if it begins to break.
Help my parents to know and see,
That his wife someday I want to be.
I have never loved this way before,
For him, my heart has an opened door.
I hope my parents have a change of heart,
So that he and I will never be apart.

Hazel M Dolby
LOVE
Love is something; we put into action,
Using it wrong could mean laying in traction;
A four-letter word that's larger than the earth, it has been around longer than birth.
It could mean peace and joy, to all mankind, without it; could mean a twist of the mind. Try putting it to work it's not very hard, you can stretch it a foot; and then a few yards.

Helen L Goodall
OH LOVE OF LOVES
Oh Love of Loves,
He gave to us, to shine throughout the dark of night. It's like a Peace, a light within, when you know your soul alright. The Master of this vessel, the molder of this clay. I would say that we are very special, and life, it's really ok. But to lose this love, oh love of loves. What would life hold in store, nothing but hell torment of darkness, everywhere you turn closed doors. So hold tight to this love.
Oh Love of Loves, And never let it go.

Jason Marc Harris
EARTH IS OUR PRISON, THE SKY THE BARS
He left that night to seek and find, with his coat pulled over his head. He wore a mask, but did not bind the clasp too tight, and let the horse lead. Through the ford and the Grotto of Black Ice, he questioned what he thought he knew well.
As the night embraced him and his steed, he peered down the well.
In the depths he saw the bones of one he had read in the dark tomes.
"Who rolled the dice?"
Tom asked the servant of the outer spheres, which cried with bloody tears that Tom could see burned where they fell. "Alas, alas, I wish I knew.
Though immortal, I may tell you but one piece of the silver crown. Even now as your land boils around you with infernal fire, you cannot see beyond the sky!

Why do I dwell in this well, which stinks of sepulchral filth?
Perhaps, because I was a man like you, who swam too far into the sea."
What is left in this house of stone?
Rotting wood, rags of cloth, and cracked, bleached bone.
Simmering snakes in a broth of yellow leaf, mold which grows in hair alive, crushed beneath the New World tide, the Old World died with the first tree.
Sitting on the log, and lying down, we have lost,
holding on to a fish which cannot swim, now to drop off the cliff,
and die beneath. A vortex of light!
See what is!

J Averil Nicewarner
NATURE'S LIGHT
Catching lightning-bugs in a jar,
Under the moon, beneath the stars;
In a field, glowing bright
Caught thirty, forty the jar's alight;
Sitting on a blanket, a thermos in hand—
By the rip-roaring ocean, bright yellow sand;
Maybe quite near, maybe quite far—
Catching lightning-bugs in a jar.

AH C Croom
ME, JOHN AND MA
Sometime this summer I'll be settin in my chair,
I'll be by myself without no one there.
'N' I'll see John comin up the walk,
'N' he'll be walkin' slow and 'll stop a mite to talk
He'll stop on the porch and pass the time of day
'N' 'en he'll go inside to Ma, 'n' they'll have a lot to say.
John was our oldest, born mor'n sixty years ago
I forget exactly, I'll ask Ma. She'll know.
All our others are scattered, one died in the war.
John went too,—since—he's never wandered far
Two years ago John came last. They laid him on the hill.
Last year Ma joined him. Now they can talk their fill
I guess I'm gettin' old. I'm 'bout eighty five I guess.
At my age I can't do much, that road's an awful mess.
Don't often leave the place, neighbors tend my need.
Don't farm any more, don't even buy the seed.
Can't walk much, at least not very far.
So I'm just sit waitin' a chance to talk to John and Ma!

Janet Seidel
MUSIC IN COLOR
Into the air strong rhythm pounds.
So feverishly passionate it sounds.
As a mood may have color, so this music, too,
Can be shaded reds as one mood reflects blue.

Ballet has its satin pink for beauty of balanced grace.
Sweet Rose blushes in magic waltz of joyous, lilting pace.
Truest red of patriots' blood throbs in Sousa's every beat.
Wild mad screams of modern jazz give forth their cyclamen heat.
Royal wine flows through the majesty of Wagner's thunder and fire.
Cinnamon spices a Spanish dance, as skirts swirl ever higher.

They say music is threads of gold,
For is that not what books have told?
But the music going 'round in my head
Is not gold, but ombred red.

Catherine V Porter
WINTER WONDER
Behold a winter wedding!
Majestic oaks are adorned in ice appliqued gowns and an aura of white illusion veils.
Willowy trees gleam in polished silver
Small graceful shrubs sparkle crystal
Dark pines bend and bow down by the weight of their jewel encrusted branches
One tiny golden circlet crocus peeking in awe as a very young uninvited child
Under a canopy of blue, the sun adds its splendor to this glistening, gleaming event
Icicles form inverted spires of a Cathedral
Tall flickering cedar candles line a carpet of blue and white diamonds
A scarlet vested cardinal presides on this day of days
As a gentle wind stirs, a hushed choir breaks forth with tinkling chords as silver slivers fall through the air.
Feathered friends chorus merry notes of happiness
Bright berries nod their gay greetings
The willow weeping crystal droplets
God, the Giver of Gifts, bestows His blessing on this Union
And at evening a million stars twinkle their message of good wishes.

Antonino E Najera Sr
SINGING ALONG
I'll "say it with love"—oh yes singing it with love—
For World of Poetry again—can't come—I'm robbed;
Poet's Seminar at sea—How I wish I could attend
Health forbades me—travel long—hope ye comprehend.
Hyper-tension, heart attacks—disallow me then—
Going along with—in thought—don't say all in vain;
Reading this verse—reminds me I'm with you all along
In unison merrily humming this—our song.

Come along—let's attend—Poet's Seminar at sea—
A rare privilege—you'll be happy as can be;
We'll learn a lot—from those masters—in Poetry
You won't regret—if you are one of the "entry."

It's worth the trouble—we don't learn such in school—
Sea Seminar is "it"—(if) improvement be thy goal;
As our luxurious ride—smoothly steaming
Nearing Port—you and I—and all gayly singing.

World of Poetry enthusiast—here we are now—
Nice place—something new—enjoying it all somehow;
Happily with all celebrant—don't get me wrong
(Humming) Singing along this—our Camaraderie song.

Christine Fraley

Christine Fraley
MR. VOLCANO

To Mére, Chapelle, Hunter, Rail, and to Joe C. XXOOXXOO
Thankyou Linda for helping, and Thankyou Roxanne, for doubting!

Mr. Volcano is not really bad,
But sometimes he gets a little too mad!

He bubbles and boils
And lets out steam
Then all the townspeople start to scream!

His lava pours out,
Red hot, no doubt
Melting rocks, or pushing them out.

So now you know what he can do,
And he has some relatives
Who do it too!

Marlene Weikert
MOONSTRUCK
One balmy and summery evening time
I gazed upon the moon so sublime,
It rose brilliantly atop and over the mountain
Surveying God's queenly green earth in Raccoon Run
Viewing thru the space of tall timbers,

its movement would rise and fall
I could hear in the dark silence,
the wood's whimpers
My eyes could see the wonder of
it all
Aromatic scents of blossoms and
night air mingled
The fireflies and one's
heartstrings would dance as a
gypsy flamenco
There was a feeling, drinking in
to quench the thirst
The taste only a tease, it couldn't
quite appease
Only in life will one always search
To attain to touch on something
so profound
Waiting in the darkness, pensive
and in limbo
Intrigued, as though my feet
hadn't touched ground
By now, my heart slowed to an
even flow
More to the tune of a gracely
minuet
In all its simplicity I knew I had
experienced Nature's Kiss
Not here, but there beyond the
moonbeams
Awaits a timeless journey and
interlude of bliss

Kari Vink-Lainas
THE WORLD IS A SHADE OF ROSE
the world is a shade of rose
as i spy from upon my pedestal.
i sit high, alone,
the heaven in my eyes,
watching, looking, seeing.
it is peaceful here—
the noise plays beneath my feet.
the world is rose,
the skies, streets, smiles,
as i look down from my seat on the
sun.
miles away,
though my toes touch the ground,
my rose colored glasses
perched high upon my nose.
don't cry, my friend.
the world is a shade of happy,
rose and peach and gay.

Sandra Gail Thomas
WITH YOU, I WILL SURVIVE
The wind will blow and sing its song
While leaves will shake and fall,
Storms will flood the thirsty earth
And mountains will stand tall.
Oceans roar and waves will break
While sea life grows up strong,
Birds will soar then fly away
And time will move along.
While each one calls the second near
Like the honey bee to her hive,
I'll always know a simple thought
That with you I will survive.

Penny Rae Stephenson
NOW AND FOREVER
All too seldom, a wish is sent,
To different parts of the world.
Just to let the people know,
That there is someone that cares.

Though I have never met you,
I think of you each day.
So to you my unknown friends,
I send this wish your way.

May the sun always shine,
Everywhere that you go.
May you always be loved,
By those that you know.

Always may you find,
All the warmth within a hug.
Like the sparkle from a fire,
All the glow of a smile.
Like the joy from a child,
All the happiness in the world.

Always may the gift of love,
Be there at your side.
From now my friend until eternity!

Monica J Browning
WHIMSICAL
Her deep velvet gown
cascaded down
the extended marble staircase.
Luscious satin
her tiny feet were wrapped in
and beyond the window
from where I looked
I could hear the violin
playing a rhapsody
from her chateau of crimson.

Her face and skin were
pure and white.
Enchantment was the color of her lips
as her clear through cape
cascaded down her fingertips.
She looks towards my eyes
yet never sees me
past the windowsill.

Donald Lambeth
CATS AND DOGS
Cats purr
Dogs bark
Cats climb trees
Dogs dig holes
Gophers dig holes

Cats get loved
Dogs are mean
Sometimes
nice.

Brad L Zimmerman
GEORGE AND NELLIE
Looking back on
the years that passed,
now having peace at last.

Running after the
eighteen they raised,
they deserve a special
kind of praise.

Forty-Nine Years
have passed.

THE GOLDEN ANNIVERSARY
is here at last.

During the day
of happy cheer,
the memories will
last for many a year.

Archie Bibbey
WILMA
Fifty-four years is a long, long time
Since you and I were wed.
But with you, my love, my wife
divine,
The time too swiftly has sped.

If a thousand years is only a day
And I could spend them all with you,
Believe me, dear, when I say
A million years would be too few.

There is so many things I would like
to say
Before this verse is done
That the Prophet has said in a better
way
in Proverbs thirty-one.

The sands of time are running slow
To give more time for me
To tell the Lord: "I love her so,
That woman thou gavest me."

I give my thanks every day
For one more day together.
If I may have my way
I will stay with you forever.

Jane Wilson
THE REINCARNATE
This life I will remember
on into the future.
Remember how green
and full of life the world was.
(now as I live)
I don't know how this life's
patterns shall transcend
but I know, most surely,
they will to someone there.

When the world is barren
with wilderness savagely protected,
I will ache for this life I once had
so far away from me in the future.
Crystal waters, vast forests, and
uncounted, free running wildlife
that I will never know
in that future life shall haunt me
as someone that was there, and knew.
And the truth will pierce me
like an arrow of light.

Robert Bruce Williams
THESE GENTLE ONES
These gentle ones whose warm and
tender care
Ignites the shaft of light to
end despair,
Thrice crowned are they with
goodness, truth and joy,
As now the art of healing they
employ.

Neva Lou King

Neva Lou King
SEASONING REASONING
Removing the fly from my big pot of
stew
Seemed to be the logical thing to do.
I'll admit it to be a sly undertaking—
But I'd spent half the afternoon on
it's making.

I know I'm to blame, 'twas entirely
my fault—
I decided to see if the stew needed
salt;
And just as I lifted the lid for a sip—
That's when this fly dropped in for a
dip.

I removed him quickly from the spot
where he fell;
With the stews' spicy flavor, surely
no one could tell.
He barely landed, his wings weren't
even wet,
For he hadn't swam around in it yet.

To throw it all out would be such a
waste!
A wee little fly wouldn't alter its
taste.
I don't mean to sound facetious or
clever—
But it still looks and smells as
delicious as ever.

When I think of the fact: that tonight
at the table—
I must eat some too, that is, if I'm
able—
I think I'll consider another
proposal—
And pour it all down the garbage
disposal.

Gale Smith
DON'T WEEP NO TEARS
Don't weep no tears for me when I
die.
For I have lived a hard and cruel life.
Tho you will never see me, talk to
me, or ever hold me in your arms
again rejoice.
For I will never have to hurt, worry
or cry with pains of loneliness.
I fought and struggled with stride to
live in a world that I do not belong to.
Now the day has come to hand and I
can lay my pain and sorrow to rest
forever.
Don't weep no tears for me.

Laura Ann Bonnett
AT FRIENDSHIP'S DOOR
Something wonderful, just fell into
my lap
It happens to be you, touching my
life
Each day a new surprise, as our
friendship does unwrap
A smile from you is all it takes, to
scatter away the strife
And lift me to the wind, so I can soar
atop the clouds
And take me to a place, far away
from any crowds.

Something surely happens, when you
are in my presence
A special kind of feeling, that warms
me to my soul
Even if in thought, you are there in
essence
As if our meeting, were inscribed
upon a scroll
I believe that there's a reason, for
encounters such as these
I believe that God will lead us, if we
only ask Him please.

We couldn't feel the strength, if our
feelings were not shared
Sensations running far too great, that
they cannot be hidden
When reflected from each other, even
though they go unaired
Throw light upon the path, that now
lies ahead untrodden
By faith let us choose, the uncharted
course
As our destinies are led, by a much
greater force.

Take my hand, and gently guide me
Teach me, for I love to learn

Taking time to show me you, and who you are to be
As together we discover, what it is we yearn
I want to reach my hand to you, and enter friendship's door
For knowing you has made me, far richer than before.

Elaine F Briden
CAMOUFLAGED
A baptism in the snow, white covering for purity of Mother Earth.
Cleansing, taking warmth from the Spirit—
Feelings hope that harmony abides.
Where do birds go when branches are thickly laden?
How many people are homeless without a warm stove?
Why did the bird lie so long in the street?
Care, cars flying by, birds wings still—
Feathers, so soft, gone to live with Grandfather.
Where do birds go lying in the street, dead?
Care, do birds have Spirits?
Feather, so soft, Grandfather take you home.
Two dollars won't bring back the Seagull's life
Like the friend, drunk, passed-out lying in the street, alive—
Care, coffee—two dollars for another beer.
Feathers, so soft, Grandfather take care.
Never held a live Seagull, are feathers soft when alive?
A he-gull, he was, because he wasn't camouflaged.
Gliding transparent between the earth and sun in a hazy blue,
Your sisters and brothers were flying for you—
Feathers fly with the Angels, so soft like the snow, Grandfather forgive.
Was it really you?

Bernice Chambers
A MIND CAN REACH A MOUNTAINOUS HEIGHT
A mind can reach a mountainous height, or seek the parental sea;
To work its way through heartfelt wastes, and skim each memory tree.
Also well worn by thoughts of stone, to meet briefly and let go.
The train of thought breaks into crystals, on jagged unhappy dreams below.
Despite one's mind rugged trying course, sanity for the strong retains,
A clear thought out life unlike calm hopes upon life's plains;
Bright, happy, molded and formed through stubbornness and adversity;
That gives to each and every man some thought of its purity.

Walter Copeland
LOVE LOCK
When I look into your face, in the morning when I wake
I look at you and gaze
Now what I want to do, is reveal to you
All my heart contains

You are on my mind, every minute of time
Loving you is my only goal
When I'm hold'n you near, feeling warm and secure
Completely body and soul

Love emotions quickly surge, I'm compelled by this urge
With every breath I take
Your beauty in its essence, and privilege of your presence
Is the valued prize at stake

A spell I must be under and yes, I only wonder
Did indeed, you mean to weave it
Now my heart with every beat, beats romance for you so sweet
Amour eternal, dare we achieve it

A love lock you've got on me
Let's throw away the key
Caught in love's grip and please
Don't let it slip from me

Orville A Cottrill
JUSTICE
From a distant icy valley,
Where the wind and sleet blows fierce.
Came a single gallant rider,
With armour a sword will not pierce.

Riding from kingdom to kingdom,
He has battled the dragon called greed.
The hope of his people in bondage,
Rides high on a shining black steed.

With a swing from the sword of justice,
The corrupt through the land will fall.
The rider in all his glory,
Rides on to a distant call.

Marché Whitworth
THE CRYING SLEEPER

Arise, O Sleeper, and call upon thy God, if so be that God will think upon us, that we perish not." Jonah 1:6

To Lay it Down & Not to Touch;
To Pick it Up & Hold so Dearly;
To Lose it All & Throw in the Towel;
To not go on for the Lack of Seeing Clearly.

So Lost & Falling Deeper—
This is what I was,
A Crying Sleeper.

Anthony M Cestaro
MELINDA
Melinda—Stands by the window, clock strikes four, and she watches him walk out the door.
Melinda—Dreams of him always, he didn't know his leaving would make her cry.
I don't understand, she just sits and waits, why?
'Cause she knows he'll never come back, she lost him to another, one who couldn't love him like she did.
Melinda—sleep 'til morning, softly wake, think of how it was, and how it could have been.
Melinda—you're still so young, you have your whole life ahead of you.
Go out and find another, someone who can love you too.
Melinda,—Melinda, Melinda,
Melinda—Dreams of him always, he didn't know his leaving would make her cry.
He made her cry, Melinda

Ted Andresen
IF YOU PLAY
If you play with fire your fingers burn
If you play with passion senses learn
If you play with music you will write a song
If you play with love then love is gone

For love forgives forgets forbears remains
But love has never learned to play the games.

Elvira C Schnabel

Elvira C Schnabel
THE BUTTERFLY
Ethereal creature, with gossamer wings,
Multi-colored beauty—what joy it brings!
So lovely, delicate, like exquisite silk,
Fluttering from flower to flower for its "milk."

So like man, God's illustrious creation,
Handsome, brilliant, a wondrous sensation,
But as the butterfly disintegrates and fades away,
So will man, he's not really meant to stay.

All earthly things, whether grand or small,
Are not eternal, and won't last at all,
Arrogant man and his treasures will rot and rust,
Man, in the end, is but a mound of dust.

Sherry Cheaves
SPECIAL LOVE

Dedicated to Robert Smith
Love Sherry

I've shared a bed with many,
Made Love to quite a few,
But none felt the way it did,
As when I made Love with you.

You touched me in a Special Way,
that reached this lonely heart,
and now I cry a silent tear,
and hope we never part.

I've heard never trust Love at first sight,
Take time and let it grow,
But where I want to be for life,
I already know.

I've traveled down this road of life,
looking for the one I Love,
Now I've found that Special someone,
And I thank the Lord above.

There are thoughts that should not be spoken,
Sounds that will never be heard,
But when I said I Love You,
I meant every single word.

Ruby Woodell
CLING TO HIS HAND

I dedicate my poem to my lovely daughter, Hazel Sigferson, with love Mother

Oh! how You loved the soul of man
The depth was proven on the cross
The blood flowed from Your feet and hands
My Saviour You, died to, save the lost
The, sharp spear pierced Thy precious side
As You groaned there on the cross,
I feel so puney, frail and small that You
Suffered at such a cost;
Dying, on that cross for all.

Bonnie Braeuler
AS I WATCHED MY CHILDREN GROW
Years moved around years
and the seasons passed
me by

From tiny babies in my arms
to young adults
I hardly know

Sometimes with pain weighing heavy
in my heart of tear drops
in my eyes

Time moved on too swiftly
as I watched my
children grow.

Brian Sharenon
LIFE IS A THING THAT FADES AWAY
Life is a thing that fades away
while drifting farther and
farther every day
Life is not a problem that can be solved
but more a reality to be
experienced
It's something that can only be understood backwards
but must be lived forwards
It has no meaning, you live to die
then forever your body shall lie
Nothing else matters nor anyone else
I seem to be lost within myself
I have lost the will to live
for my life has nothing more to
give

Mary R Pineda
A THOUGHT ON DESTINY
Do we choose our own destiny?
Are our lives ruled by fate?
For these answers, I search desperately
but with myself, I still debate.

I fail to understand infinity
life is not always as it seems to be.
Is it possible to overcome destiny
and how can we live for eternity?

In this life there is little time
to discover those answers so divine.
They seem so extricable—
the possibilities inexhaustible.

No matter how diligently we try
we cannot explain why we live or

die.
Perhaps we are God's puppets
and it is He who pulls the strings.

It must be He who holds the key
to the secret of our destiny
The answers I shall then find
when I leave this world behind.

Saundra Wilson
TOUCHED
I have been touched
many times,
Sometimes it's an invasion
unpleasant—
I withdraw.
Occasionally there is one
whose touch is precious,
warm, friendly,
A "we're both here
and I care"
type of touch.

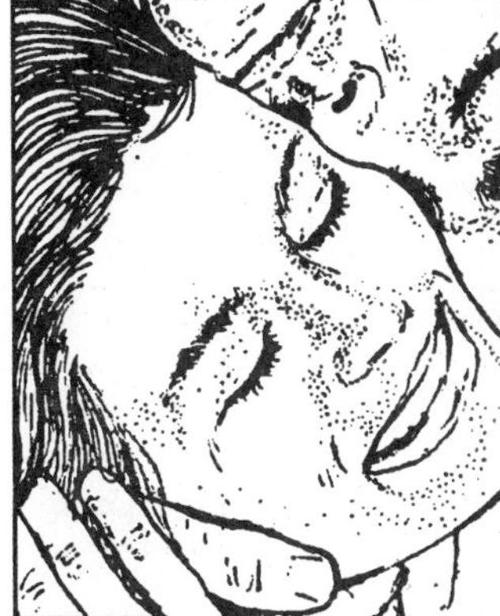

It's real.
A touch that contacts
more than the body
And lasts
beyond the moment.
A treasure—
A touch.

Vickie Pentz
THE ARMS OF GOD
When I look at the sky, I see the warmth and Love through Your blue eyes. And as the wind gently blows my hair past my ear, I hear the whisper of Your voice that calms me and gives me peace inside.

As I stand by the waters, my soul thirsts for understanding of all that has happened to me, and as I wait anxiously for an answer, the sun sets, three crosses appear, and I know You care and will always take care of me, just like a mother kangaroo takes care of her young.

As the sun rays shine through the trees, I feel strength to make it through another day.

Then, looking across the field, I see a beautiful oak tree, its limbs are so strong, I go and lay beneath it, I close my eyes and see Your Loving Arms around me, it is now I feel safe, knowing—I am in the arms of God!

Sara E Rose
THE DECEMBER MUG
I was so touched by the poem "A Cup of Christmas Tea",
Until one December morn'
My friend Ruby stopped with a gift for me.
Something good to go with your Coffee on "that day" she said.
As in my hands a lovely decorated box she laid.
Thinking it to be a gift of her "goodies", off to the refrig., it went.
Out of the blue came unexpected guests and
I without a thing to present;
Ah, the goodies that Ruby had sent.
Now! In anticipation off came ribbons and paper.
But, horror! Ruby had pulled me a caper!
Out of the box came a lovely Christmas Mug.
Oh me! My guests took my gift to their house
To put under their Christmas tree.

Franklin Grapel
SONG OF REMEMBRANCE
Songs in the quiet night,
Shadows etched in memory,
Visions of long-lost lovers,
Haunting me.
Voices of yearning,
Long-forgotten years,
Why do you return to me
with aspect so sad?
Do you call to me,
Or is it that you have come
to fill the place of one
Once loved, now gone?

Ophelia Phinezy
TREES ON THE HILL AT PORTSMOUTH
From a distance I saw a beautiful site
A bunch of greenleaf trees
Much to my delight.
They were grouped upon a hill
Standing very still.

The sun shone down on the leaves so green
The darkest tree trunks I've ever seen.
A picturesque view on a hilly lot
Trees on the hill at Portsmouth.

Esther E Penner

Esther E Penner
SMOKERS AND CIGARETTES
For a more healthful society

HEALTH

Again, and again, and again and once again,
We non-smokers cannot breathe!
Our eyes, our nose, our throat and our ears,
they tear, they run, they scratch and they pain.
We cry, we blow, we cough and we wheeze,
Why, oh why! When we've already said please!

ENVIRONMENT

Cigarette burns are on the carpets.
We see you smoke in the halls.
We find them round our desks.
We find them on the sinks.
We even find them where it stinks.

LIFE

Sometimes my food doesn't taste so good.
My clothes, they reek of foul air.
Who said you could kill me off?
My family wants me, they care!

Sr Christine Biskupski r c
WHAT WEALTH OF GRACE IS HERE SONG OF SONGS
His left hand pillows my head
His right hand even now is ready to embrace me

The shadows of life, soul and heart
So long can at times seem to be

And love like the sunset can seem
So far away and yet at times so near

And yet behind those shadows
Deep in our soul and heart's soil

Love like a flower under grace
Can grow and blossom through our toil

In the breeze of His gentle touch
We tremble inward as grace finds a way.

Then awakens His Trust

His eyes so gentle bathe us
In eyes of secret repose.

Come My Love, Come Lord Jesus
Come.

Pam Sims
A CRY FOR THE CHILDREN
Cry for the children
My heart you fill with sorrow
For I see your ears are closed
Your silence leaves your children
cold and hungry
Unloved they roam the earth
To you I say open your hearts
Let their noise be gay and filled with laughter
May their warmth be found from all adults
Let them warm your hearts so
So their plight is heard
And may you open the doors so no
tears are shed out of fear
For the children are the future
Teach them well and aid them in their peers
Unless this is done then there really is no future

Jan Andriano
SILENCE IS GOLDEN
Silence is Golden is
what they say.
But where are you
this miserable day

The kids are all gone
the dogs are asleep
The rooms are all clean
so proper and neat

For I am so lonesome
Unhappy you see
What happens to miserable
people like me

For Silence is Golden
is what they say
Why does it have
to be this way—

Carla Jane DeLong
ENDLESS QUEST
The boundaries of corruption
begin with lust, it's an
endless sensation that pulls
at your heart and plunges
you into your fantasies.
Once this corruption touches
you, you feel as if you could
never live without the burning
desire to ignite the flame.
For years I have followed that
twisting path. This lust is
good enough for me. It's my
private hell that's been sent
from heaven I will endure
this corruption until my
death and bow in awe of
timeless love.

L Beth Lockwood
IN THE DARK I CANNOT SEE
In the dark I cannot see
That fear that is inside of me.
I have refuge from the daily scorn
The tail of life, darks evil horn.

In the dark there is no light;
No argument, there is no fight.
I can wait to let it pass
That which makes my heart beat fast.

In the dark I am alone
I cannot hear the dreary tone.
Sit and think at nothing's dream;
No one hears the silent scream,

But at last still in the dark,
I can hear the lonesome bark;
The shriek, the pain and agony
of life without a memory.

In the dark—still in the dark.
I hear the lonesome passive lark.
I lie alone awaiting that which
Will come and take me back.

Phyllis E Bartman
I'M THANKFUL FOR FISH
To all the Fish Organizations throughout the world

I had lost all joy and hope,
until Fish came, . . .

I walked out, my house was on fire,
no food
no clothes
no home

Until Fish came . . .

I will always have a friend . . .
When things went wrong;
with my health . . .
I needed to go to the hospital,
Fish came . . .
The total times Fish cares, Fish came . . .

Darlene Margera
BRANDON'S WORLD OF MAKE-BELIEVE
When you were just a little boy
of two or three,
We played a game
Just you and me

When we were driving in the country
Imaginary animals would run across the road
You would say "Look Mom-Mom",
"Do you see it too?"

Now you have passed the world of make-believe
Much too soon it seems to me

One day when I was feeling low
I was driving in the country real slow
As I turned the curve
I saw a big blue bird
It was a peacock
with its tail spread wide

I wish you were with me
So I could say
"Look Brandon"
"Do you see it too?"

Beverly J Hoge
APRIL SNOW
Death came to see me today.
He doesn't use a last name.
He comes to the house unannounced
But not unwanted
Because He's the only friend I have.
Before I know my need He comes
And no one else can match that loyalty.

Before I came to know Him well,
I had heard His reputation
Discussed by cab drivers, doctors,
and other disseminators of knowledge.
Everyone, if not formally introduced,
Had heard of Him and spoke of Him
with great respects

Of course, I visualized Him wearing
white tie and tails.
I wanted to meet Him
And have Him kiss my hand.
My disappointment was acute
When He grabbed my body and
kissed my breast
Without asking my name.
For a long time I refused to
acknowledge His presence
But He continued to visit
And finally won my loyalty
By reminding me that I had answered
the door naked.

Oscar Strommer
HOW IT REALLY WAS, AT HOME ON THE RANGE
I once lived at a home
Where the jackrabbits roam
Where the coyotes and prairie dogs
play.
Where seldom is heard a discouraging word
'Cause your neighbor lives ten miles
away.

We could sit there at night
With kerosene light,
And read or play checkers or cards,
No T-V to see,
We were happy to be
In a sod house of gumbo so hard.

The old kitchen range
Very seldom saw change
In the fuel we'd pick from the hills.
There'd be dried up cow-pies
that we'd stack to the skies,
And save 'em, to cut fuel bills!

Temple W Wachsmuth
U.S. POLICIES

To The Environment

Guatemalan Mayans
Shot and underfed
Landless seeking shade
Under U.S. Banks facade
Coke 'a Cola refreshes
Congressmens' parched throats
United States, United Fruit
Launder peoples blood
By posing the countries
Blooded Spanish Mayans
As holders of the deed
And not the doers.
Americans can express
And say I didn't know
And not realize
They are only standing in line
What a country does to others
It is already doing to itself.
Weapons and drugs
Money and greed
Turned outward are mounted
On the swivel of time.
The U.S. Government is full of liars
And our country's morals lag
The man who sees and does nothing
Is just as guilty
Of every act and it will live forever
And haunt man's short span of life
When you know and do nothing
You are nothing.
And in the end will be treated as
such.

Nicole L Wise

Nicole L Wise
A TEAR FOR LIFE

To John Michael Golden—Gone but never forgotten

We all cry
some don't know why
few spend their life
seeing all eyes are dry.

We all laugh and play
most everyday
while others find a way
to make the laugh stay.

We all must die
but why should we cry?
We'll go to a better place.
For birth we rejoice
and lift our voice
To the new one who hurts in this
world's haste.

Pamela J Miller
THE END
"The end of us is near," cried the
clergyman in red,
"Mark my words by morning, by
morning we'll all be dead.
But fear not fair lads, and ladies, have
faith belief and trust,
If we shall ever come through
together, pray so you must.
Hush your crying sobs dear damsels
and quiet your young heirs,
Take heed, look sharp and love all,
that the good lord bares"

And the gentleman and the ladies,
rose and bowed their heads,
and prepared themselves, and others
for their unseen future that lies ahead.

A scream rings through the
courtyard, a shudder falls upon the
crowd.
Silence envelopes the courtyard,
thunder crashed bold and loud!

Within the darkening skies to the
horror of everyone's eyes.
A dark figure appeared before them,
thunder rumbled in the skies—
A flash of lightning shone brightly, a
shadows cast upon the land
A dark and lonely feeling, a cold
gripping hand.

The sky burst into raindrops, and the
wind tore at the earth.
And the fire within the chimney was
smothered at the hearth.

And the valley was hushed and quiet,
as the beast burned on the stake.
And the figure strode on forever,
mere destruction in its wake.

Yrral Notnalb
TOMORROW
Once I was young
And I would run
I could jump so high

And yes, back then
I had this friend
And never thought he'd die

Add more fears
And other years
With little pause for sorrow

Scarce time for taste
just a dogged pace
in search for another tomorrow

Patrick Scott Morgan
A TRIBUTE TO MY GRANDMOMMY
Grandmommy is a cooking gal.
How she does it we don't know how.
But everything is just so good.
Everything tastes just like it should.

She throws in a dash of salt, maybe
more.
She cooks and cooks 'til her muscles
are sore.
She makes the best chocolate pie,
And when she peels the onions they
make her cry.
But she does more than cook
She sometimes reads her book.
She picks the beans,
And rounds up the greens
And sometimes drives the truck.

When she's not busy she pulls off her
hat,
And starts crocheting pillows and
pretty things like that.

William A Guffey
BRIGHT STAR
I look up at the stars shining bright
and wonder little star
are you someone's lost child.
Did you suddenly disappear from this
old world to become a bright
star up in the night sky.
To become a star in the night to light
up the sky.
There has been so many lost and so
few found.
Little star shining bright I wonder
whose lost child are you.
So tonight when you look up at the
stars shining bright see
if you can see a smile of a lost child.
A lost child who has left this old
world to become a bright
star shining in the night.

Sheryl D Martin
UNENDING FLICKER
Many days of my life I've spent . . .
just being lonely.
We are born in this world alone,
some only minutes apart . . .
. . . but alone.
The only other security other than
God's love . . . is yours.
Somehow I find it hard to face the
unforeseen days filled
with . . . endless nights.

You are to me . . . an unending
candle that burns . . . for life.
When you are gone or either far away
that small flame in my heart just
flickers, flickers . . . flickers madly,
only because we are apart.
In the silent moments of the night . . .
I long to touch you so much.
Whether you know it or not the flame
that flickers . . . will never go out!

Cynthia Elmore
A PRAYER TO MY LOVER'S DEATH
I remember the times we spent
together
I always wondered which way
you would go,
As I put flowers on your grave
I have a feeling that your soul is
not here,
I get into the car to leave for my
home
I can feel you in the car with
me,
I just want you to know
I haven't fell in love with
anyone, since your death,
I know you can read my mind
I miss you plus I still love you,

I miss going places with you and
running on the beach beside you
Well my mind tells me you are
listening,
You know I am glad if you are
listening
If you have to leave I want you
to go now,
I know you want to look after me
But go to heaven and you and
the Lord can watch over me
together,
I just want to say one more thing
before you go
I LOVE YOU AND ALWAYS
WILL.
AMEN

Belva Mullins
FIRST DAY OF SCHOOL

To Randy and Kathi

I watched him eat his breakfast there
He brushed his teeth and combed his
hair.
He tied his shoes in knots and bows
And carefully checked all of his
clothes.
He hugged me tight and kissed my
cheek
I felt my knees go very weak.
He paced the room a time or two,

As though he didn't know what to do.

He gathered papers, books, and pencils four.
I watched him quietly open the front door.
I heard the bus around the bend
I ran to the door, and saw him get in.
I turned around to rooms so quiet,
I heard the bus go out of sight.
Tears fell upon the kitchen stool
My little boy has gone to school.

Feliz Atilano
PRIORITIES
Surrounded by the peeling walls
he slept
hungover
on the broken rocking chair.
A cockroach ran across
his torn tee-shirt.
Empty beer cans
and dirty ash trays
fouled the room.
A can of beans in the cupboard
and a case of beer in the refrigerator.

Daddy, wake-up
I'm hungry.

Harlow Broomes
CLIMBING
" . . . The whole being is exerted towards accomplishing nothing."—Albert Camus

They go up on their cyclic journey each day
Mount Sisyphus, the stone of life
Weighing heavily upon their shrunken shoulders
The white heat of the day
Like hot mist glued to their flesh.

Above an aeroplane of homeward bound birds
Underlook a chain-gang of ants marching.

They show their teeth
Like the anguished grin of dogs,
Barbecued. Seeking a laugh, they chant
"Send in the clowns," to divert them
From their tortuous passage
The unreasoning pain
Their tear-bleached cheeks.

Clambering on top of the mountain
They cry victory, lifting
The soft stone above their hard heads
Then, unsatisfied weightlifters
They dump it at the foot
Of the mount only to scamper down
Behind it

Howard Beeson
HOLIDAY CHEER

To Phyllis and Bob Smith, our daughter and son-in-law in Dallas, Oregon.

We send you our blessings and late Christmas cheer.
And to our late greeting we wish a "Happy New Year."
Now as Mom puts this together with no doubt leading from above.
I know that it made joy in her heart with added fragrance of her love.
We know donations of food are not needed with both your salaries.
And it could be that too much of contents would add some calories.
You must wait for the other though it might be awhile.
Only wish we could be there to see your big smile.
Well as you open this package with joy in your souls.
Do not be surprised to find more than orange rolls.

Lawrence F Kelly
THE SEA OF LOVE
For many years the tides have changed.
Who's to know how far they've ranged?
Who's to know, or wonder why,
The waves have driven hearts so high!

It moves not now, no ripple, nor swell.
Calm as death, no joy to tell.
The love that caused the oceans roar,
Lay still and silent, forever more.

Who's to know how, or ever know why,
A love like ours can somehow die?
I'll look on now, my life I'll spend,
To find the stone, and make the calmness end.

Hear me out! Oh sea of saddness,
I'll drop it in and end this maddness,
And once again the shores will peal,
With this love I'll always feel.

Sheelah K Shulick

Sheelah K Shulick
PLEASE WAKE ME

To young drivers & party goers, everywhere

The squeal of the tires still echoe through town.
I rose up to find my body still down.
Memories of parties, we were so high and flying
The only difference now is everyone's crying.
I tried to call out to them but no sound is flowing,
for my mouth has been sealed with a mortician's sewing
This can not be real, for I was just laughing
"How could this have happened?" I heard a friend asking
There are things unsaid, I had yet to tell you
So many things that now I'll never do.
Just a dream someone wake me, cuz I'm too young to die!
Somebody please shake me, I can't open my eyes!
The sky now has darkened, everyone has gone home.
The only memory of me, is carved in this stone.
I can still hear my name, but cannot reply.
I'm stuck here forever without saying good bye.
If I'd known it would be this way, life for granted I wouldn't have taken.
I'll never see the sun again, never know the joy of waking.
I have lost the only thing I know, my life is gone forever.
Separate are my body and soul, to join again they'll never.

Mark Edwards
SMILE
Life is reality and not all dreams
Sometimes you just have to stand up and scream
Some people don't believe in fortune or gain & so half their life will be run with pain
To live a life of pain for sins trapped in their mind
But for the sins of people will kill our kind
We all should live a life without murder & hurt
So our minds and the talents of people can flirt
People shouldn't be put thru the everyday rage
Before too long we will be put in a cage
But a time will come where everyone will fade away
At that time the restless will be damned to stay
They'll stay to show the new breed what happened to us
And teach them a lesson not to give such a fuss
Life was meant to live and not to kill
Whether it be air, animals or the taking of someone's will
That will is what stops you from destroying the human race
It just might be too late, just stop and look at someone's face
They're not always happy but mostly sad
That is what makes everyone internally mad
So if you don't have a smile stop and put one on
Just think sooner or later humans will be done
And when the earth is all burned and curled
If you would have smiled, you could have saved the world!

Ethel Domec
ON RECITAL

To my dear daughter, Colleen, and the memory of all those recital years.

"Oh, God, keep her safe, don't let her fall,
May she dance like a fairy just for tonight,
Let her soul reach out to the music's call,
And her eyes gleam anew with a magic light.

Arrayed in her glory of sequins and net,
Let her float like a cloud before my eyes,
Let my eager heart not sigh or fret,
And my anxious mind restrain its sighs."

I have prayed this prayer for many a year,
Through hours of agony I toss and turn,
A ribbon askew, or a hasty tear,
Can make me tremble and fret, and yearn.

But my child floats on in a dream-like haze,
Secure in the beauty of blooming youth,
Never knowing the worry which clouds my days,
When recital is over, it's Heaven, in truth.

Patricia Donaldson
MOM, I LOVE YOU!
The love I have for you,
Is greater than you know.
You have always been there,
With all the caring that you show.

When I got a cut,
You seemed to make it better.
Helping with my spelling,
In each and every letter.

When Dad got up and left us,
You tried to ease the pain.
Always telling me that it's okay,
But I always felt the same.

You were always there to help me,
If I said the magic word.
Just in case you're wondering,
"Mom, I love you," was the word.

Ben B Cumella
TO THE VIETNAM'S HEROES
Silently was resting the night.
The blood, still warm,
Was wetting the earth.
Scattered were the bodies,
torn and crushed.
Valiantly they fought with might.
Liberty, Liberty was their dream
for the cry of freedom
that should have been heard.
Love had in them been bred
and their blood pure and fresh,
runs out like a stream.
No cannon, no shot, no blast.
Calm and peace reign now at last

Lisa Anderson
I WISH AND I PRAY TO GOD
I wish and I wish
And I pray to God
And I pray to God again
Then I get no answer
so I ask again
I wish and I wish
And I pray to God
And I pray to God again
So I ask you another question again
But I still get no answer so
I wish and I wish
And I pray to God
And I pray to God again
Finally I got answer
God why have you not answered me before?
Because I've been busy
Why couldn't you have just said one minute because I've been wishing and wishing and praying to you but you never answer me!
I have been busy listening to other people I never heard you
God bye for now.
(THE NEXT DAY)
I wish and I wish
And I pray to God
And I pray to God again

Yes what is it?
My mom is dying why are you taking my mom and not someone else
All you can do is to wish and pray that she gets better
OK bye for now
(THAT NIGHT)
I wish and I wish
And I pray to God
And I pray to God again
yes what is it?
My mom is dead now. Why didn't you take someone else
She is safe with me but she cannot talk to you. Only I can talk to you
God bye for now
I wish and I wish
And I pray to God
And I pray to God again
Yes what is it?
My sister is very very sick will she get better soon?
Yes she will get better soon
God can I ask you a question?
Yes you can!
When will I die?
I cannot tell you that
Why not?
I do not want to tell you when you will die
OK bye for now
(A week later she died of a very bad cold)

Darcy L Hoover
BEGIN
Begin a new life
Starting out fresh
Meet another believer
You take what you can get
Taking no chances
Changing your part
Every one that passes
This will be your last
Smiling new moments
Don't cry over old
What happened is history
Too often retold
Start a new life
Beginnings will come
Looking the other way
Just see what you've become
Walking on new soil
Leaving no tracks
Thankful you came to
The second path

Dale P Kelly
CRY FOR SPRING
Cry for Spring, Old Man Winter has won!
Victory! His voice may sing.
"O wind of North or South may blow."
"Hide O Nature or take my toll."
Cry for Spring, little bird from nest to wing.
A worm from Mother's beak to bring
A new song for you to sing. Cry Oh Cry for Spring!
Cry for Spring, little flower from below.
From April shower your seed to sow.
From gentle bud your petals grow.
Cry oh cry for Spring!

Ann Giammona
DO YOU KNOW WHERE YOU ARE GOING?
Do you know where you are going,
to where your life will lead you to?
Will you follow it to a loving heart,
or to one who won't love you?

Sometimes we are so quick to jump,
into what lies ahead.
That we close our eyes to the truth,
no matter what is said.

It feels like love,
it seems so real,
that's something we all say.
When in fact it's just physical,
and in time it fades away.

But left behind amid love's ruins,
is a heart that cries out loud.
To the one who left it lying there,
in pieces on the ground.

But keep in mind a successful love,
and a life that's full and true.
Does not happen overnight,
and in time will come to you.

Dennis R Bunting
THE POINT OF THE KNIFE IS DANGEROUSLY NEAR
The point of the knife is dangerously near
The dark of the room
Brings nothing but fear

The breath of the person holding the knife
Indicates madness
And hatred for life

The sickness inside him brings terror I feel
The knife starts its piercing
So cold and so real

The pain is do deep I stagger and fall
My mind is so heavy
My world seems so small

My life flashed before me, I'm coming to rest
My problems are over
With this knife in my chest

His mind is now laughing, his gaze I can see
The person who did this
Was no one but <u>me</u>.

Lorenza James
LOUISE: GOD'S GENTLE FLOWER
Sunshine sprinkles on your face,
God's love and Amazing Grace.
No greater love than yours is found,
no greater joys abound.
For Jesus, who died to set us free,
lives in your heart perpetually.
His spirit guides the words you speak, to hearts of those who seek
To know him, who conquered sin;
redeeming man from his bitter end.
You're His love which can't be bound, stepped on or pushed down; and in
The garden of God's delight, you're a gentle flower blooming bright.

Gentle flower you are, touching lives near and far.
Loving men as would Christ, you are a living sacrifice.
Laboring untiringly to give God glory, your life tells His story:
A compassionate will for all to be free, living with Him eternally.
God's servant you are, a rare breed; more of you the world needs. For
In the garden of God's delight, you're a gentle flower blooming bright.

Someday God will say "well done" for the race you've run. For the Faith and patience you live, for the love you give. For
Willing to stand and boldly say, "man needs Christ today.
Every heart needs to yield, that from heaven we may be filled
With the God-child born to save, dying men from an eternal grave."
No one is more sincere, or filled with godly fear
Than you Sister Louise; with you God must be pleased. For
In the garden of God's delight, you've been His gentle flower blooming bright.

Marion E Singleton-McCullum

Marion E Singleton-McCullum
A SEED

To all my grandchildren.

I am like a seed, so small dry and plain.
Plant me in poor soil and I will never grow nor strive. Plant me in rich soil and water me, and watch me grow so spiritual tall.

High above the earth below with branched out limbs and leaves so shiny and green.

With my head bowed so low thanking Thee Dear Lord!
For making me so spiritual tall, shiny, fruitful and green.

Phyllis Latham
THE SUNSHINE
I could feel its warmth
creep in my place, as I
turn to see, it kissed me
on my face.

Then this feeling came over me.
There was something about it that wouldn't let me be.

So I stood and removed my clothes, that's when the sweat began to roll.

As I laid in its warmth,
I thought to myself, this
is just fine. And I thank
You Lord for your great
sunshine.

Aaron McDermott
HE AND I
In the life of love she couldn't face it;
She didn't believe that I was in love with her.
She acted smart and sincere.
She just caught a glimpse of what he looked like
In her little young mind.
She probably thought that he was out of his mind.
When she saw him for the second time, they both fell in deep love.
The guys and the gals on both squads joked and teased.
Later, it seemed like that she didn't like him anymore.
For the rest of her life she didn't ever see him again.

Divya Bhat

Divya Bhat
METEORS
Meteors, meteors falling from space,
They look like beautiful shooting stars
because they fall with a pace.

There is really no such thing as a shooting star,
Just like there should be no such thing as a speeding car.

So if you see a shooting star,
While walking home from the store,
You will know it is just a meteor.

Dewayne Lewis
SANDS OF THE OCEAN
From the sands of the ocean,
I see my life as not of a dream,
My beginning not impressive,
My present not all it seems,
My future just a day away,
And still there's room to dream.

From the sands of the ocean,
I can see far away lands,
Distant—wonderful—mysterious places,
Yet I'll always long for home again,
In the wink of an eye I can be anywhere,
With imagination anyplace in time,
From this sand time can stand still,
Past—present and future mean nothing
If there's no you by my side.

Tanika Johnson
MAGIC STREAM
While Dreaming a little
Dream,
We float down a magic
Stream,
To flower covered meadows,
Where tall trees cast their
Shadows.
Cool winds blow our hair.
Birds chirp here and

There.
I look into your brown eyes;
Wild.
But the magic stream is
So mild.
As we travel back, lovers
As one
Underneath the setting sun

Michelle Dawn McRae
SKETCH
Your KISS . . . a magic potion
Your TOUCH . . . a tender feeling
Your EYES . . . a glowing sensation
Your SMILE . . .a wicked impression
Your BODY . . . a splendid creation
Your VOICE . . . a sweet sensation
Your MIND . . . a growing invention
Your HEART . . . a generous devotion
Your SOUL . . . a curious production
Myself . . . Your own fragile flower—

Emarie Iniguez
WHEN I THINK OF HOW MY WORLD BEGAN
When I think of how my world began,
I try to forget but I don't think I can.
I remember back then ,
When I was only ten.
I never thought I'd get to be,
So wild, grand, and free.
I was never once so pure,
And most insecure.
But yet I never dreamed,
That I was what I seemed.
I never once thought,
That little girl that fought,
Would grow to be,
A bigger . . . older . . . me.

Alma Martin Stokes McCord Millet

Alma Martin Stokes McCord Millet
A LEAF THAT QUESTIONS

To my beautiful children Myra, Hilda, Alma, Donna & Don
Love Always Mother
Alma Martin, Stokes, McCord, Millet

Who am I?
Where are my roots?
My siblings leaves number eleven.
Branch of my mother's leaf is Cherokee, black and white;
Branch of my father's leaf is black and white;
Branch of my maternal grandmother's leaf is black;
Branch of my paternal grandmother's leaf is black;
Branch of my maternal grandfather's leaf is Cherokee and white;
Branch of my paternal grandfather's leaf is white;
Branch of my maternal great-grandmother's leaf is Cherokee;
Branch of my paternal great-grandmother's leaf is unknown;
Branch of my maternal great grandfather's leaf is white;
The rest of my branches, trunk and roots are unknown.
Where are my roots?
Who am I?

John H McNally
ODE TO LIFE
1980 to 1990 relates more to the thirties.
You may prefer an ode to the eighties.
For the 21st century we strive
Our friends are tuned to keep us alive
We hope to live and enjoy the nineties.

David McKenzie
ARDOR
So we met and fortune smiled upon enlightened hearts.
How lucky in a world of dreams as one we now take part.
Walking in the rain at night enchanted with your smile.
Feeling joy, feeling peace and comfort all the while.
Impassioned with your love and hope, the amorous desire.
A feeling so unique and true that warms me like a fire.
When you're near, all the world seems frivolous to me.
Because our love grows stronger like a flower from a seed.
Unselfishly we share the warmth and splendor of our love.
Enhanced forever you and I and blessed from up above.

John Michael Poole
CASTLES BUILT OF GOLDEN SAND

To My Beautiful Daughter, Shannon, And Her Summer Of California Sun

There be castles built of golden sand
Of roaring waves against the land
Thoughts of dragons, kings, and ghouls
Lost in the mist as the ocean rolls
Of a sky filled with light
The cool, blue summer's night

Rippled waves spread asunder
The silent lightning, the distant thunder
Heartless waves moving fast
Have taken time into the past
Now a mound heaped on land
There be castles built of golden sand

Lurana Mary Locke
A LITTLE HELLO
You didn't come by to say hello.
But how could you or any one know.
How my heart yearns for you.
My days are so lonely and blue.
A word could make the day so bright.
Then everything would seem so right.
I can't stop the fluttering of my heart.
I can't stop the tears that seem to start.
If you would say hello to me.
Then how happy I would be.
Maybe I could win your heart.
And through life we'd never part.
From you a little hello.
Would mean more than any one knows.
I wanted a hello, not a good bye. .
Something to keep the tears from my eyes.

Frederick X Hartman Jr
TOMORROW

Dedicated to
Fred and Florence Hartman
With me through it all

Please let me dream of times to come—
Tomorrow takes away the pain
Dissolving old wounds from the past
As tears dropped into pool left rain

Vanish too the nightmares vast
As if they are the morning stars
Let me look ahead not back
That I may, erase all scars

Tomorrow takes away the pain
The lies from lovers yesterday
It covers old love tracks as sand
On wind swept deserts far away.

The smoke from old flames forced to die
Will rise and blend into the past
And sear my heart with embers left
Now mind and soul will rest at last.

Sherylin Kay Schroeder
QUESTION REMARKS
Can we find
Means to measure
Intelligence
Using five senses,
Perceiving only
The end result
Of thought's process?

And,
Is there not more?
Unspoken by any thought,
Unheard by any ear:
Soul's Song,
Something beyond
Mind's agility to grasp;

Fenced in by thought
Patterns and limited
By what we
Perceive ourselves to be?

Rosalind Marie Robinson
THE MOST BEAUTIFUL ROSE
My dearest friend

I'm glad we did not pick the rose, to possess as yours or mine
Pleased we did not take the rose, to enjoy for a minute's time
With you, I so desired to, but the sharpe thorns upon its vine
Reminded me that it would be selfishly cruel; not to be unkind
For I could not give my total heart, soul, freedoms of my mind
Cursed with fate's elusive love; unconquerable, if it you find

I like to pretend

Sometimes to be the wind, gently caressing your petals just so
Dew kissing your budded sweet lips, the way that you would know
The sun making hot passions rise, the beautiful rose all aglow
The rain shedding healing tears with you, ah! so slow, so slow
Sharing pain together in soil of another's garden, it can grow
Unchanged by seasons it still remains the most beautiful rose

We will never end

This special love that we share, it will last through eternity
Flawlessly unencumbered, by what may have been or is yet to be
Its unique floral charisma, forever to enchant us effortlessly
Cultivated by kindness, it grew best when allowed to grow free
I take fantasy garden walks, with no one's reason for jealousy
The most beautiful rose is our friendship; and shared memories

Lora L Sullivan
GOLDEN STAGE
I live for my music, that's the only way
I can't seem to get along, without it, I feel so alone
day by day I go, chasing down the melodies within my soul
there's no doubt, about it, it'll never grow old

the bird flies away with his silver wings
there's trouble in his very soul, so a song he'll sing
to chase away his blues, he'll sing the night away
on a golden stage he'll sing the night away.

Only for a moment, I can see the sunrise,
above a deep blue ocean, from the shore of a lonely sea
as I walk away, only to return again

to what has to be, just my music and me
I'll dream of a golden stage.

Kim Stebbins
BROKEN HEART
Your love used to lift me up and cradle me.
I used to shiver with each glance.
I remember how you'd hold me close;
And how safe I felt in your arms.
I knew no one could break my heart.
Like a dark cloud our lives changed.
And what was once joy has turned to pain.
Oh, how I loved you, and your gentle touch.
But now, all I see is the rain.
Your laughter used to put a spark of happiness in my life
I used to smile with you and never be sad.
I was addicted to your love.
I used to feel no one could break my heart.
Like a dark cloud our lives changed.
And what was once joy has turned to pain.
Oh, how I loved you, and your gentle touch.
But now, all I see is the rain.
'Cause you love, yes you, broke my heart!

Frances Porter
A LIFE SAVER

To my Irish cardiologist. You are my one and only love, now and forever.

You are a doctor by profession
Losing a patient your first hard lesson
You spend your days in ICU
Touching lives in joy and sorrow
Giving many hope for a new tomorrow
Your days and nights are long and hard,
saving lives is your reward.

Yes, many have felt those hands, strong capable and sure.
yet only I know the man that saves my life when he walks through the door.
To touch me with hands strong, capable and sure.

Estel M Dodd
CADE'S COVE IN AUTUMN
Like a funeral procession
they inch their way around
the ancient bends and hollows—
voices hushed in curious awe,
frenzied lifestyles forgotten
in the backward flow
of time recalled.
The sheltered cove
neither bows to change
nor accepts the intrusions of
modern mobility;
and when the cars are gone,
carrying their passengers away
from this quiet hallowed glade
it is they who seem to die
and are not mourned—
the valley and the peace
lives on 'neath autumn's blanket
nestled in the arms of
forever mountains
and ages yet unborn.

Justin Sebastian
CONFUSED BOY
His life was short sighted
His life was a loose existence
He specialized in sidestepping strictness
Mistakes were his best friend

Dwelling on the darkness of life
He refused to face his fears
His sanity suffered by resisting the unfamiliar
He was lying to his most basic self.

His life was forever altered
When he forgot what he was wishing for
He used varieties of weirdness for protective layers
But camouflage wasn't the cure

Blinded to the freedom of failure
He filed and forgot of discovering delights
Memories' message just outside his grasp
Success shined behind failures' shadow

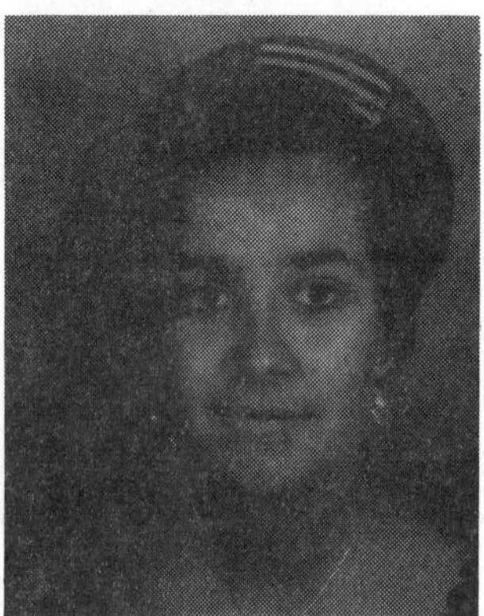
Catarina Rodrigues

Catarina Rodrigues
STEVEN

To Remind the World that the Handicapped and Disabled are "Special" People with Lots of Love to Offer

When he smiled at her, she felt so close to the little boy
She suddenly felt her heart fill with joy.
As she looked at the child in sudden anger—
trying to break free.
She gave more value to human sanity.
He struggled with his disabilities as though a perfectly normal child lay inside.
Parents loving and guiding him—
their faces filled with pride
For they knew God had given them . . .
a special child!

Harold L Sargent
THE AMERICAN SPIRIT
One day we went into a battle,
Nervous we were like a jockey in a saddle
We were all scared, why shouldn't we be,
It was a battle being fought upon the sea.

We left all our thoughts presently behind,
To ourselves we did constantly remind—
We will shoot those Jap planes down,
And many more before they get off the ground.

We have come a long way to pay a debt,
We won't quit 'til they are licked you bet;
We won't give up the ship, you wait and see,
We're Americans, that's why and proud to be.

When the battle was o'er and we had won,
The Japs had all gone on the run;
The facts of the battle I cannot release,
But it makes us just that nearer to home and peace.

I dedicate this poem in my own simple verse,
To the American, who is ridding the world of a curse;
He's the greatest fighting man on the earth,
The American, who fights for all he is worth.

John P McMeekin
A FRIEND

Dedicated to my children, Amber, James and Joey.

If you have closed eyes, you must improvise, then you will find why, you can not see,
To see me you need light, if your eyes are shut tight, you can't expect to, look into me,
If you close your mind, surely you can't find, my offer of a, return to peace,
Now that you've got time, show me you're not blind, I can be quite kind, if you release,
See me, if you want to understand a friend,
Believe me, if you want one that you can depend,
When you're unwanted, and you feel haunted, you should remember, what I will tell,
Friends can be phony, full of baloney, and if you let them, you they will sell,
If you're defeated, and you've been cheated, I may be needed, for what I can say,
If this description, is your affliction, I have a prescription, could help you today,
See me, if you want to understand a friend,
Believe me, if you want one for whom you can send,
Friends that you don't need, will show you their greed, won't let you succeed, as well as mislead,
Friends that do not heed, who will watch you bleed, off you they will feed, until you are freed,
So talk to a friend, 'cause you can't offend, they will help you mend, on them you depend,
The friend who will lend, and try always to bend, for whom you can send, is really a friend,
See me, if you want to understand a friend,
Believe me, if you want one that you can depend.

Gail Stewart
DESTINY
I'm not a quitter, I'm not a loser,
I'm not lonely, I'm not lazy,
My life seems a little bit hazy,
My world is upside down and crazy,
Why?
Because it's plain to see, I haven't found my destiny.

Lou Mayberry
ADVENT

To the memory of my husband, "Bob."

Christmas is coming! Christmas is coming!
Joyfully ring the bells
Listen to the story the Bible tells—
Prepare ye, Prepare ye,
Prepare your minds, prepare your hearts
Scatter your goods to the needy
Send your love far and wide

Birthday gifts for the Christ child!
He is the meaning of Christmas,
Always and ever by your side!

Rachelle Prisco-Braido
DREAM
It seemed to be
The day without time
When my life would
Retain myself
But order without time
Was inevitable,
And alas impossible . . . . .
Visions of eternity
Led me to loneliness,
Frozen in a state of subconscious,
My mind wanders endlessly
As if in a daze . . . . .
With a drowning sigh
I fall into
The sanctuary of realism,
Awakening my victims of emotion . . . . . .

Toni Payne
I'D GIVE IT ALL TO YOU
If all the gold
were mine to give
I'd give it, Dear, to you

If rainbows bright
made life just right
I'd give them, Dear, to you

And if the seas
were mine and mine alone
I'd give them all to you

But what I have
is LOVE,
but LOVE
and I give it
Dear
to you.

Ollie M Van Brunt
THAT'S COUNTRY
A gaggle of geese,
a herd of swine,
a flock of sheep,
a lonesome pine.
That's country!

A country road,
a winding trail,
a cottontail bunny, a covey of quail.
That's country!

A place of peace,
a place of rest,
a place for birds
to build their nest.
That's country!

A place to hunt,
a place to roam,
a place where man
can call his home.
That's country!

Florine R Sanders
BEYOND THE GREY

Dedicated To My Loving Parents, Charles and Naomi Sanders

She stood, trapped, in the mist of a smoky,
but not desolate tunnel.
The air around her was thick and discomforting.
Her face was content; and she wore a peaceful expression as if she were
a candle of hope that would
bring forth light, to warm the coldest of hearts.

As she strolled, her lean and disfigured hands
reached toward the door which
led her far beyond
To a grand and spacious walkway.
It stretched for miles and miles
with a color of a radiant sunrise.
It swallowed the mist and smoke,
Reviving the air with freshness
and delightful vives.
And beyond the amber grey,
She found serenity.

Jorge Mendoza
LATE AT NIGHT

Late at night,
Once Scorpio falls,
Stars shine bright
And the night bird calls.

Late at night,
When I'm all alone,
I think of you,
And no one knows.
I see your eyes,
I feel your body
Touching mine,
I make love to my dreams . . .
Late at night

Late at night,
Once the tears in my eyes
Begin to fill,
I think of you
And the world stands still.
I hold my breath,
And my body feels tight,
I kiss your shadow . . . .
Late at night.

Lucy Rendler-Kaplan
THE SEASONS

Summer is when I go to the pool, air conditioning is the way to get cool.

School is out during the summer, when school begins what a bummer.

Fall is when the leaves change color, compared to fall school is duller. In fall I rake leaves and jump in the piles, people enjoy fall for miles and miles.

Winter is when the snow comes down, like a blanket snow covers the town. In winter I shovel the snow, then I watch the cold wind blow.

Spring is when the flowers bloom, the pretty colors fill my room. The sunlight shines through my window, and the seedlings come up row by row.

Cheryl Wamberg
PERCEPTION VS REALITY

C is for the growing crowds that
 seem to be everywhere
H is for the increased hassles as
 we begin to holiday prepare
R is for that extra running round
 no one else seems to mind
I is for the ice and snow that sets
 me on my behind
S is for the added stress pressing
 in from every side
T is for the traffic that makes me
 want to stay inside and hide
M is for the awful mess of trying
 to get organized a bit
A is for all the activities we into
 our schedules must fit
S is for the final sigh that signals
 Christmas is done
We have had our fun and into a
 busy new year we now run

C is for the creation of the world
 that includes you and I
H is for the happiness we share,
 being friends is a valuable tie
R is for the personal relationship
 I have with the Lord
I is for the invitation to accept
 the blessings on me he has
 poured
S is for his saving Son he so
 unselfishly sent
T is for the thankfulness of being
 taught what that meant
M is for the miracle of life I so
 often for granted take
A is for always being aware and
 such appreciate
S is for the thoughtful sharing of
 this message so dear
Christmas—not just a day, but
 an attitude to carry throughout
 the year

Mary McWhorter Collett

Mary McWhorter Collett
PEOPLE, U.S.A.

We're people meeting people
 around the world today,
A patriotic feeling
 from the U.S.A.
We're people seeing people
 where you work and dwell,
As friends we get to know you
 and to others tell.

Each country has its customs
 that we've come to see,
And flags of every color
 Wave so proud and free.
We're people greeting people
 in a very special way,
With friendship in our hearts
 we're from the U.S.A.

Terry Taylor
LIFE

No one ever told me that life could be
As warm and as gentle as a summer's breeze
The smell of fresh air makes me gay
And I thank God for it every day
So many of us take for granted
The love and affection that we're handed
I agree that life can be hard and sometimes unbearing
But life can also be kind and seem like a blessing
I feel so lucky to be in it
That I wouldn't trade in, for the world,
My winning ticket

Horace Williams Jr
MOUNTAIN OF PAIN

To Michelle, a very special lady, whom I will never forget.

As I lie here crying on my bed, my heart beats as though I were dead.

They say in time pain goes away, but I feel that mine is here to stay.

As I battle against this with all my might, I feel as though I am losing the fight.

I don't think of her that much anymore, but when I do, it hurts just like before.

Why did this have to happen to me? I thought her and I were destiny.

As I close my eyes and go to sleep, that mountain of pain seems so very steep.

I will continue to climb it day by day, and hope that in time this pain will go away.

Sandy Fong
SAIL ON WITH EYES ANEW

Tears fall softly from your eyes,
Massive world revolves in a flash,
Torrent wind blows harsh and cold,
Tidal waves splash high and rough,
Spiteful words sting right to the heart,
Intense pain grows unbearably near,
Familiar nightmare lurks in the dark.
Sail on bravely across the ocean blue,
Reach me by the sandy shore,
Hand in hand, we leave footprints on the sand,
Feel the warmth of the brilliant star,
Fly your kite high in the sky,
Change like a caterpillar to a butterfly,
Experience all with eyes anew.

Steven F Ploegstra
BROKEN BY HIS LOVE

High above the peaks
the lonely eagle soars
Into bewildered cries
all of his heart he pours

A friend of many years
lies broken on the stone
In vigil high above
he rides the wind alone

Days he hung above her
though wind grew rough and chill
Trying hard to reach her
and raise her with his will

At night he finds a perch
where he can watch his mate
His cries are full of anger
the God has won his hate

At last he finds an answer
a dive from high above
And now his body lies
broken, by his love

Virginia M Cole

Virginia M Cole
SWEET SUCCESS

This poem is dedicated to my daughter, Bonnie.

The real character of life
 is trying;
Not whether we fail
 or win,
It's staying on course—
 not quitting
It's completing what we begin.

There's a whole lot of
 satisfaction—
And how sweet it is
 to take;
When we arrive at that goal
 we've been striving for
That we thought
 we couldn't make.

Karinda Uphoff
THE FUN WE HAD

The fun we had,
 though things went bad.
The times we shared
 when you said you cared.
For me, you had lust,
 for you, I had trust.
Things weren't the way they seemed,
 it was all just a dream.

Pauline V Richardson
SOUVENIR

Do not forget
the Sweet Song
of love

That lasted throughout
most our lives together

Now love
It is time to depart

Hoping the remembrance
of the Melodie
So Sweet to our heart
at times

should bring a smile
and dreams of
tender touch
wherever we are

Dorothy J Degonia
FROM THE HEARTS OF BABES

To All My Children

Dishes fill the sink again
Toys upon the floor
Rugs to be swept
Beds to be made
And someone's at the door.

Now it's twelve o'clock
The work's all done
At last we can be alone
Whoops, I spoke too soon
It's lunch time at noon
And someone's on the phone.

I stand tall within your shadow
Though I'm only half your size
I understand more than you'll ever
know
More than you realize.

A lot of things a mother must
Remember to do and say
But one thing stands out from all the
rest
Have you hugged your child today?

Aurora Sotelo

Aurora Sotelo
BRIEF MELODY

To the memory of my beloved parents, and with affection to the rest of my family.

My heart kept so quiet
when you called me Darling . . . .
I gave you a flower,
and you gave me a garden.

We walked together
on the smoothest sand,
and we looked at each other
as woman and man.

I searched for your dreams
and you searched for mine;
then we wished, profoundly,
to retain the time.

Don't think of tomorrow.
Forget all the past.
Embrace me, my dearest,
and let's catch the stars.

Marda Rowe
CHILDREN
You'll always love them no matter
what
You'll always be there whether or not
They try your patience
and test your rules
They wear your nerves
and are stubborn mules
They question your ideas
and twist your words
They scramble your days
and act like nerds
You'll always love them no matter
what
They are your children whether or
not

Ray Welch
RAINBOWS END
Aromatic flowers grow
a breath of warmth so sweet
Clear and crystal waters flow
to rainbows end they meet

Thunderous clouds of winter bring
chilling breeze from northwind's
mouth
Fleeting birds refuse to sing
upon their journey south

The sun appears; applies its heat
an effort to dry the rain
winter clouds begin retreat
Bring rainbows back again

An aromatic flower grows
outside upon the step
A sign of changing season shows
that rainbows can't be kept

Walter Warren Williams
OUR CHRISTMAS PRAYER
Our Christmas prayer is to do
This coming year all good anew,
And to forgive the petty slights
That happen through the days and
nights.

Let us forgive abuse we get
For the mistakes we make or set
Within the confines of our lives,
So we can live as God too strives.

Let me love mankind totally
Without reservation within me,
For love is all there is in good
And let us stand where angels stood.

Let charity be our lives' goal
Not ourselves alone but the whole,
We share our talents and our worth
With every man upon this earth.

Let service to each man we meet
Be our prayer and ne'er delete,
And let our lives aspire to give
The right of every man to live.

Olga Velazquez
YOU SHOWED ME
When I met you, you showed me
something
Remember what it was, old friend?
Remember the smile, the hand you
lent me?
The sparkle, the life that you gave
me.
Remember the words, the fellowship
you shared with me?
The times that you cared for me.
Remember the paths where you led
me?
The many good things you did for
me.
Remember the silent thoughts you
sent me?
The message that you wrote for me.
Remember the time that you cried for
me?
The time that you found me.
Remember the joy, laughter, peace
that you tossed to me?
The songs that you taught me.
Remember the home that you made
for me?
The many storms that you passed
with me.
Remember the hope that you lit for
me?
The eternal patience that you
revealed to me.
Remember the beauty that you
showed me, my old friend!

Tuesday Lynn Thompson-Lobert
MY LITTLE BROTHER WAS ONLY TWENTY-FIVE
My little brother was only twenty-
five,
When he decided, it was time to die,
He could make people laugh,
whenever they were down,
He was always, acting like a clown,
He was caring and giving, so full of
life.

Then something happened to change
his mind,
My little brother was surely, one of a
kind,
All he wanted to do was fly,
And when they took that away, he
just wanted to die,
Now Fly, Little Brother, Fly!
My little brother was only twenty-
five,
When he decided, it was time to die.

Linda D Jones
NEW YORK LIFE

This poem is dedicated to my daughter, Kimara M. Jones, I Love You

Good Morning, Good Afternoon,
Good Luck
Subway, Buses, And Trains
Traveling Can Be Such A Pain
Coffee, Services, And Attitudes
Is Everyone In A Bad Mood?

He's In The Arts
I Have A Job
I Pray To God I Don't Get Robbed
What An Adventure
Everyday! ! !
NEW YORK LIFE
Is Not
Always The Way

Lucille Kerr Rawling

Lucille Kerr Rawling
SHOW YOUR LOVE
If you truly LOVE somebody
Be certain they will know.
Do not ever . . . hide it
Feel PROUD, to let it show!

LOVE is such "A Blessing"
Given free and honestly told,
Comes back to you, "The Giver"
Always multiplied . . . TENFOLD!

When you LOVE somebody, tell
them!
It will make "Their Feelings" glad.
By holding your LOVE within you
You'll just end-up . . . feeling sad.

Send someone a "Valentine"
Your LOVE for them, to impart,
Share the LOVE that's in you
Open up "YOUR LOVE FILLED
HEART!"

Go right ahead, play "Dan Cupid!"
Toss "Lots of LOVE" . . . around . .
From TRUE LOVE . . . freely given
Responding LOVE, will plentifully
abound!

Rick McMahon
LIKE COLOR TO THOSE BORN BLIND
Like color to those born blind
Love is beyond me . . .

I can imagine—glittery teardrops
falling
From smiling souls
Or sunflakes in spring
Dancing in the wake of heartshaped
wings . . .

But I am trapped in clouds
While so many stars are shining in
the sky

So like those born blind explaining
color
I am spewing symbols to show you
That I know of
What others feel towards life and
lovers . . .
As I could have felt
Before a tempered existence of
survival
Left me bleeding black wind from
my secluded mind's
Brooding
Colder than frost, in the shade, on a
dark star . . .

Charles E Olson III
LOVELY LETTERS

The night before last about 5 o'clock, this mailman came walking through the cell block. He handed me a thing so rare, a lovely letter which was not there.

Now I was so curious I couldn't withstand, so I took it from his empty hand.

I opened it and then revealed a lovely letter which was not sealed.

It wasn't in an envelope, in fact, it wasn't even wrote! Now I read far, far, into the night of the witty things you did not write.

And at the end which was not there, your name was glowing like a flare.

I know I shall never forget, those lovely letters I did not get.

Melba W Henson
THE QUEST

"A strictly honest man, it is
impossible to find."
So said Diogenes, that philosophic
Greek.
Methinks Diogenes had but a poor
unhappy mind,
To take a lantern and so
diligently seek
Throughout the land of Greece in
such a foolish cause—
As searching, ever seeking for a
sign,
To prove to all the world, his firm
belief that evil was
A basic part of mortal man's
design.

Now had he sought with equal
diligence for goodness with his
Radiating vehicle of light,
He may have better molded the
receptive minds of man,
For seeing in their fellowman a
very different sight.
For it is an eternal and happy
truth.
that always what we think—we
really are;
And we can try to see but ugly
darkness, or the luminescent
beauty of a star.

Rufus RA-MAN Harris
CONFUSED WRITER

I gotta write this book
About the subject
My mind refuses to remember
Or maybe in the beginning
I never knew;
But, yesterday
Or maybe the day before today
Or perhaps even two days
Before tomorrow,
I am sitting
And concentrating
Or maybe
Just
Dreaming.

David Albertson
TWO ROSES

Two Roses,
one red, one white—
one dark, one bright—
upon t'which kissed—
a sunbeam did lay—
a serpent did crawl—
betwixt the two;
and morning succumbed—
a rose anew
a pink, a link—
of the two.

Three roses—
one red, one pink, one white
one dark, one light, one bright—
upon t'which kissed—
a moonbeam did lay—
a slug did creep—
betwixt the three—
and morning conceived—
a rose anew—
a scarlet, a harlot
of the two.

Four Roses,
one red, one scarlet, one pink, one
white—
one dark, one shaded, one light, one
bright—
upon t'which kissed—
a worm did lay—
and a dove did weep—
betwixt the four—
and morning perceived—
a settle, a nettle
from Heaven's door.

A settle, a nettle—
did grow,
from seed 'twas sown,
betwixt the scarlet,
betwixt the pink,
their nectar it did drink—
morning gave light,
and shown only on the white—
whose heart—
was burdened with might.

Two Roses
one red, one white
one dark, one bright
upon t'which kissed
nothing but regretfulness lay
and nothing did crawl—
betwixt the two,
and morning did come
yet betwixt the two
only the nettle grew.

Phyllis Stenson
LITTLE JOE—OUR TORTOISE

Does he get lonely?
Yes, I'm sure he does
When I sit outside
He comes to greet me
I wonder where his home was first
In just which part of the desert
He was given to us over thirty years
ago
He is licensed as all endangered
species are
Cannot be released back to the wild
Yet as I feed him lettuce and grapes
I see his species in aeons past
They survived on very little
But in what was once his habitat
Now stand homes and freeways
He has our love and security
They can never replace his freedom.

Manervia Herrington

Manervia Herrington
GOD MADE THAT TREE

God made that tree for me
With bright colors glistening.
He lovingly touched each leaf
And they seemed to be listening.

As He stroked gently, with His brush,
Red, yellow and orange nestled
among the green.
There was no need to rush,
To paint this MASTER SCENE.

Each twig was bowing to His will,
Creating with His love for me.
His works make my heart to thrill,
And His beauty my eyes to see.

My Lord, my Savior, shows his love
To the smallest and to the
largest,
With His glorious beauty from above
Yes, my Lord is quite an artist.

Tyler W Smith
WHO ARE WE

Don't walk away we've only just
met,
"Hello" and "Goodbye" is that all we
get?

Your appearance is beauty, that you
can't hide.
Only the you that I seek is the you
that's inside.

Don't misunderstand I don't want
your "role,"
I ask for your true self that resides in
your soul.

Just let it all out I have an excellent
ear,
It will relieve a great burden and put
to rest much of your fear.

I don't aim to exploit you, I just want
us to learn.
And promise to you my own truth in
return.

Without our complete honesty we
could never grow,
And who we really are neither one
would ever know.

Let us share together now so that
when we meet again, we can
open up and speak freely without the
slightest strain.

So just keep in touch with the you
that really is inside
And you'll never have a burden that
you feel a need to hide!

Sophia K Lilles
INSPIRATIONAL

I am inspired by a
certain face,
or a smile.
A fleeting glance,
a blue bird flying
against the sky.
A warm heart . . .
A fragrant rose,
a butterfly . . .
The innocence
of a child.
And i thank God
i am alive!
It is so lovely to be
heavenly inspired!

Jerry W Komarek
A REWARDING FEELING!

During my boyhood days, I once had,
a frightening dream,
I had done something radically
wrong, it did suddenly seem.

As I was running, across an open
field, the sky opened up,
GOD began to scold me for
something, so I did promptly stop.

He spoke to me in Czech, which
seemed the normal thing to do,
Since my parents, always spoke to
me, in that language too.

That GOD created humans, in his
own image, was taught to me,
But now as I think it over, I feel that
this, just cannot be!

Every race, has its own distinct
features, and skin coloration,
No human brain, is capable of
compiling, and logical clarification.

But nothing's more rewarding, than
performing a sincere good deed,
It matters not, what happens to be,
the doer's race or creed!

Cindy Kustelski
DISTANT LOVE

I feel we've grown closer
even though we were apart
I feel I love you so much more
from the bottom of my heart

Just because you're my first
boyfriend
doesn't mean our love has to end

You've done so many things
for me
You've shown me what love
could be

Now my love for you has grown
so much
I can't wait to feel your
tender touch

I want you to know how special
you are
I'll always love you no matter
how far apart we are

We've had a lot of great times
together
I hope we can share them forever

I hope you stay my boyfriend for
years
For the laughter the fun
Or to share all our fears

I just want to let you know
That I could never let you go

I just want to make you see
That you mean so much to me

Sandi Karas
SILENT SCREAMS

Shadows of the past envelop you, like
fog around a spirit.
Uncertainties of the future glare with
dark eyes
They watch your every move.
Tears are unable to fall; emotions are
unable to show.
You scream in fear, but aren't sure
why.
You don't tell anyone, for fear the
dark man will show
You don't accept praise, it may be
"him" in disguise.
You pretend you're happy, by giving
it away.
but you never accept it.
You end up drained and empty,
And then you say you're not good
enough for anyone.
you hurt, i want to help
Not because I feel sorry for you; not
because I pity you;
i love you.
When you're confused, *i'm confused*
. . . That's the beauty of friendship.
I want you to have faith that there is
something to look forward to.
You have so much inside of you.
i know you do.
Please, while we talk now, take my
hand . . .
not the knife . . .
And let me show you . . . *let me
help you.*

Ann C Sweeney
RED MOON

This inspiration given to Donna Richard who became the gentle spirit guiding and teaching me to give voice to my songs of poetry.

Red moon over dark places
Spiraling downwards
Upon jagged shores
Banked in obscure
mist and rainbow casements
of darting figments
Stark . . . unreal
Moon of desert places
Red moon in
blood curling skies

Plains of empty truths
But the bleeding
Drops of red
moon on shadowed spheres
of collating atmos-
pheres
settled in the dust
of the heart
bleeding . . . left
alone . . .
heart bleeding . . .
left alone . . . .

Jenni Caldwell
ALL ALONE AND THINKING OF YOU
Here I sit all alone,
With thoughts, of you, of my own.
Everything is boggled in my mind,
As I sit and think of what's behind.
Lately I don't know what to do,
Because all I think of is missing you.
I try to go on with my life,
And just see you but once a year.
But there's just one thing that won't go away,
It's my love for you, and here it will stay.
So I'm writing this poem, to say to you;
I'll always love you through and through.

Joyce Zbysienski
HIND SIGHT
What good is it to see the colors of the rainbow,
If you do not smell the sweetness of the earth?
What good is it to see the colors of the flowers,
If you do not take time to smell their worth?

What good is it to see the colors of the birds,
If you do not take time to hear their song?
What good is it to see the colors of the trees,
If you do not listen to the winds so strong?
What good is it to see the colors of all humanity,
If you do not take time to feel their need?
What good is it to see the colors of the world,
If you do not take time to plant a seed?

Anja Wesik
THE BELIEVER
Bow to his people,
Shame lay on his face,
And they knew it.
He was their disgrace.

With a pore in his heart,
And nails as long as a highway,
He pierced through every soul,
"You will do it my way!'

Little Eve grew a rose
And death was on her way.
"Sacrifice thou misbelievers!
For I am here to stay!"

People bow down to his side
And never rebelled their thoughts.
He could not destroy their feelings.
Frighten them could he not.

Steve Traister
PLURAL ARCH
I stumbled onto nascent beauty
Through no stroke of magic
It gleamed so brightly in the darkness
It changed my focus
Provided laughter to a barren field

Layers of ice softened
Melted into water
Forming pools of life
I emerged from solitude
My skin drenched

I turned my back on an empty shell
Crossed the bridge
That joins one life to another
Then joyously collapses upon itself
Once the journey is complete

Martha Gordon Chrestman

Martha Gordon Chrestman
STREETSWEEPING

To my Mother, who gave me a smile to carry.

Into the work day she trods.
Glances dance off down-ridden shoes,
Scuffed, devitalized, projecting abuse,
From doing a man's job.
Curiously, she nods at feet passing by:

Open-toed sling-backs,
High-polished wing tips,
Hand lasted uppers.
Pointed toed boot tips,
Rich leather air steps,
Hush Puppy joggers, pass by,
Telling more than vacuumed eyes.
Into the Void she marches.
To mechanized management and ire,
In Scotch-guarded, stay-pressed attire.
Silently, she watches, Society's fallen arches,
Commit unpunished crime.

Jennifer Lynn Hill
YOU SHATTERED MY DREAMS
You shattered my dreams,
You ruined my schemes,
You proved you didn't care,
Why was I even there.

You called me your friend,
Then you did what you did,
Why did you leave me,
My feelings are now dead.

It's all over,
And we're apart,
I'm left to pick up the pieces,
Of my broken heart.

Thinking of you,
Makes me cry,
There's one thing to do,
And that is say Good-bye.

Chandriée D Guinn
COMPARISON OF LOVE
I'll compare our love to the ocean
so calm and so serene,
yet so much depth and beauty,
and still so much unseen.

Yet the ocean can be fierce and strong
like the urgency of love,
pounding at the shore,
rolling like thunder from above.

Our passion flows between us
like the raging waters roar,
our bodies entwine together
like the water to the shore.

But our love, like the ocean,
so boundless, so free,
Like the ocean and sand unite,
so have we . . .

Lance M Freeman
THE CHILLY NIGHT AIR
The chilly night air
urged us in from the street
To a steamy little place
with floor show heat.

An early bird matinee
of live burlesque
The manager's scowlin'
with his feet on the desk.

Twenty bucks 'tween us
dollar at the door
Log jam of lumberjacks
hollerin' for more

Blue collar workers
'N' upper class gents
Old men pitchin'
their trenchcoat tents

A revolving exhibition
of live nude girls
Sleazin' 'n' teasin'
in brunette curls

Chair Act Katie
Snake Skin Annie
Stirrin' your batter
by shakin' their fannies

Bouncin' ivory dreams
behind red rim tassels
Cat calls—blue balls
hormone hassles

Scissors kick shots
red spike heeled shoes
Droolin' n' stewin'
over matrimony blues

Back stage chance
might relieve my sorrow
I'll buy a dozen roses
for my wife tomorrow

Thomas A Dickerson
ON STREP THROATS
In years gone by, folks breathed a sigh,
Just died and met their Maker
But now, alas, it's come to pass
(Without a hint of logic)
That folks beget with suffering sweat
A throat that's streptococcic! !

I've begged St. Blaise, tried every craze,
Yet somehow missed the boat!
I've walked on eggs with drunken legs
(Good Lord it gets my goat!)
But every germ—like an ill-spent worm
Winds up within my throat! !

Oh throat, poor throat, we treat thee so inane!
Sweet precious passage to our lungs
And yet befouled with lovers' tongues,
Fed foul foods and smoke 'til numb,
And all washed down with demon's rum! !

Dear Lord Above, Ah Loving Dove, please heed this supplication;
To spare our throats, these mortal moats
from viral altercations! !

Jo Anne Coats
THE BAG LADY
Wretched character with soiled garments.
Hiding a bitter heart.
Scrounging in stench ranked refuse.
Why did it happen so?
Fragility or rancor per chance.

Bother not this foppish fool.
The knotted ball of her existence
Unravels in an off season,
A time, a place
Few earthly creatures know.

Aquilla Reid
THE WELCOMING DOOR OF LIFE
I'm not rich, though I'm not poor, but I knock with gladness at life's welcoming door.

I'm not an outsider looking in, I don't have to lose since I know I can win.

There are lots of stumbling blocks and great wide seas, but the only thing can take me through is the confidence I have in me.

Evelyn J Dallas
WINTER'S SNOW
How does it go?
I used to know—
The lines all run
together so;

A word or two
that rhymed with blue,
and one verse ended
"always true."

The paper's gone
you wrote it on
like Summer's song
when leaves have blown;

So young that day
I tossed away
your boyish, awkward-
seeming say;

How could I know
in winter's snow
I'd reach back
for first love's glow?

Jean Kendall
ON BEING PEPPER

For my daughter, Linda; sons, Daryl, Clifford, Gregory, and my cat, Pepper!

Penniless and purposeless, he's
even pious and proud,
Easing easily into petulant ways
to shun a crown
Pleases himself pursuing lost
riddles in the sun;

Picture this, watching birds fly
rushes his fun . . .
Entrancing nature to whet his
appetite's delight
Rambles off in the night into a
world without sight.

Nancy Correia

Nancy Correia
HAPPILY PROUD

I dedicate this poem to my dad, whom I love and miss very much. I love you dad, Love, your daughter Nancy (Daddy's little girl).

Losing my mom, hurts so bad,
An April night, I lost my dad,
It seems my world, is falling apart,
Breaking into so many pieces, is my
heart,

This gift of life, I don't understand,
To take away from this earth, a
wonderful man,
Growing up was not easy at all,
But my dad stood strong, brave and
tall

My favorite quality time as a child,
was watching my parents sing
together
I felt loved, and safe, nothing we
couldn't weather,
Chords on a guitar, he only knew
three,
But watching him play, meant
everything to me.

After my mom's death, my dad
changed somehow;
To me he saw us differently, an open
love now.
He held me, he really talked to me,
he told me he loved me,
I've always loved you dad, now I
know to me your love will always be,
I always thought I'd have my mom or
dad, never thought I'd feel alone,
Then slowly I look at pictures of my
kids, reach for the phone.
One of their voices, say hi mom, are
you o.k.
I'll be home soon, wait till I tell you
about my day.

I'm more confused about life,
Than ever before,
Help me daddy, somehow reach for
me,
hold me once more,
I know in my heart, you & mom,
are together forever in heaven's sky.
All my love, dad, mom was right
She loved a very special guy.

I love you and I miss you
with everything I feel,
Memories of you both are
wonderfully real.

Lucy Stancil Howard
TO A RAINDROP

Little raindrop—precious raindrop
Why do you cry?
Did it hurt when you fell
From your cloud in the sky?
You splashed upon my window pane
And shed about a million tears—
I watched you as you trickled down,
And I was simply full of fears—
That you would drown.

Little raindrop—dear little raindrop,
Please don't feel bad
You were needed so, here on earth
below
All the flowers were sad . .
The leaves were hot, and oh, so tired
And the daisies hung their
heads;
Then you ran into a little stream
That watered my mother's
flower beds.

Janill Roberts
EYES OF WILD

To John Ryder who will always have a special place in my heart.

His seductive gaze
Turned to eyes of wild
As I stood and stared
Feeling warmth surround my
heart
The gentle blood flowing
Through my veins
Slowly turning to liquid fire
Leaving me breathless
Hypnotized
By his eyes of wild
My heart swirls in the wind
As he unlocks
The savage secrets from my soul
Liquid fire turning to flames
Of wild desire
Knowing he could never be
captured
A spirit to be free in the wind
Eyes of wild

Balongo B'Intamba
MY VILLAGE

This poem is dedicated to BOLOKWA BOMBINDO, my loved mather

My village is in the center of my
region
Only by vocation, one road makes a
lane
Very often the peasants, used to wear
lace
The tightened huts, we shall say that
a pension

The men and the dogs going to the
plantation
They work there so much that the
living is fine
Their way of tilling in the range is
native
Everyone possess his goods, with
affection

In the evening the olds keep smoking
their short pipe
In intoning the songs in the rhythm of
tom-tom
Women come back from range a little
tired

The dogs' cries are mixing to the fuss
of tom-tom
The youngsters are listening to the
story squatted
And pastors, flocks, all, are on their
way back from grassland.

Cherrye Martineau

Cherrye Martineau
CHILD OF THE WIND

To Peaches Merino and Destiny

The wind rolls on for reasons,
Like silk scarves and the seasons.
Fog floats in and you laugh like the
seas,
Like a soft night and a warm summer
breeze.
In search of the Holy Grail, the forest
of forgiveness lies deep within.
Perhaps we can only say each life is a
veil,
A small white sail waving on the
wind;
A softly misting night waiting to be
known, as only the rain can clear the
air.

Soon you will live all your days
To the farthest dimension of the
rainbow's edge
A moon in full phase; love's ways by
love's pledge.

By Power of Love and Divine Grace
Steps lead out of this darkened
labyrinthine space
Into the light where I know I will
grow
Like roses in the wild, open as a
child.

Let me be a channel for the Great
Flow
without, within;
For the Music of the spheres softly
whirling through the years,
A child of the wind.

Debra Hester Smith
A SMALL GIRL'S DREAMS

Happiness and love all around,
drifting slowly down a quiet river,
floating through a field of flowers on
a spring day,
watching trees swaying in the breeze,
a porcelain ballerina twirling through
the clouds,
things so beautiful all the time are the
dreams that are mine.

Judy L Monroe

Judy L Monroe
DANDELION

To Marty, Mike, Roger and B.J. who always believed that the dandelion would bloom again.

It was such a delicate gift I gave to
you—
Lo, those long light years ago
When, in the plentiful pastures of our
youth,
My tender, velvet yellow petals lifted
toward the sun
In delightful anticipation of a long
sweet spring
You plucked my blossom and held it
to your heart
And loved me.

And even as you held me, stroked
me,
and possessed me then
I knew the truth of life and love—
That when my petals would change
into frothy white wisps,
My leaves, dry and crisp would fall
to the ground
Forgetting the fragility of my tender
and simple gifts
You would lift me to your lips
and silently—easily
Blow me away—

Ronald L Shelton II
AFRICAN-AMERICAN MAN . . . WHERE ARE YOU?

Yesterday, you were the head of the
family,
Today, you are destroying the family.

Yesterday, civil rights was your goal,
Today, gang rites is your goal.

Yesterday, a college degree was a
symbol of excellence,
Today, it's a drug deal which doesn't
make any sense.

Yesterday, the church was a spiritual ground,
Today, the prison is a common ground.

Yesterday African-American man,
we looked up to you,
Today African-American man . . .
where are you?

Linda St Michel
ONLY INSIDE
They just don't know. They just can't see
All the ghosts lurking 'round me.
Just hanging and haunting
Spooks teasing and taunting.
They don't go away.
Not a thing I can say.

They whisper and moan. All secrets they tell
Of a past and a future all in the same Hell.
No, it doesn't change.
It won't rearrange.
It's not up to you.
Not a thing you can do.

I made my own bed. I dug my own grave.
For now I'll just sit but someday I'll wave.
No more to explain
The despair and the pain.
I won't feel anymore.
They'll just shut the door.

Alma Hilts Robertson
THE FEELING OF SPRING
I have a feeling it's nearly Spring—
with sights and sounds that it will bring—
A time when grass is fresh and green;
bugs, flowers and weeds are seen.
Vegetables and fruit give sight; where
just before the fields were white.
Then listen while the birdies sing,
watch the butterflies spread their wings.
Brides and grooms are everywhere,
And lovely Spring just fills the air.
What a season, none like the rest,
For Spring surely is the best.

Robert F Price
D/FW AIRPORT

To my children
Jerry, Tereasa, and Jay Price.

D/FW Airport
All of us, the people from all nations,
Amid silver wings and runways
toward many a destination.
P.A.'s echo, laughter, conversation,
some in tears;
Brothers, lovers, mothers, unsuspect-
ing! IT appears.

THE PLEISOSAUR
Like a magnet, thoughts drift to this
primeval past;
An ancient sea where you now stand:
Dakota soil within its grasp.
This prehistoric monster reboned and
mounted.
80 million years after, a geological
minute of time is counted.

THE PLEISOSAUR
A reptile, oarlike limbs propelling;
exotic life forms swim at distance.
Jaws gaping a pearlish steel; flesh its
very existence.
Eyes on target, head darting, it
extends a slithering neck.
A giant ammonite unaware: its
meatless casing descends a limestone
deck.

THE PLEISOSAUR
On shallow sea recede, your surface
glittered by a Cretaceous sun.
Let lightning tread your watery stage
no more; dynamic forces have begun.
Unleash the sediments of time, the
midriff of our continent to re-own.
Abundant are the creatures that laid
their fragile cheeks to stone.

D/FW Airport
Minutes pass, a sound intrudes.
Awareness is sought.
In awe I turn a glancing smile to a
crowd in thought.
Skeptics! Guilt of a moment's waste.
Realist! Pride, the knowledge of man.
Eras: giants, evolved and taken. The
sea again has given birth to land.

MAN
The Present. The future. Aware of the
dominators of our past.
Are we the ending link in this chain
so vast?

Wesley Allen Roberts
Baron Cyprus Ivory-Cloud
Blue Sky
MIRRORS

Dedicated to Lt. Colonel Wesley M. Morris. My Grandfather and my Namesake.

It causes me to feel insecure to
see the reflection of myself in
things on the walls.
I wonder if they are one-way
glass windows where people are
watching me from the inside.

When I was a child I used to think
that a reflection of me, through glass
and silver, was a boy who looked like
me in another world very much like
our own which is an imagination
world thought of by me.
The glass and silver are the mirrors
that make me feel insecure.
Mirrors make me feel as if I'm being
watched even though no eyes are
upon me. I can clearly see the
handsome face of mine through these
things of glass and silver.
Mirrors are what make up a room in a
funhouse of entertaining horror.
Mirrors are vanities where women
sharpen their beauty.
Mirrors are fascinating things to me
of suspicion and beauty.
Beauty of clear reflection and illusion
reflections, and the reflections are
made from the glass and silver
which make up the mirrors
which are
things of beauty;
Suspicion,
Vanities,
Illusion,
Glass,
and Shinny Silver.

Jackie LeViness
LORD OF THE LILIES

Sol. 6:3 I am my beloved's and my beloved is mine. He feedeth among the lilies.

He is the Lord of each Lily,
swaying in the breeze.
Lord of all Creation,
Lord of you and me.
The lilies bow before Him,
as his Spirit passes by,
for the lilies have no sin,
perhaps as you or I.
They never fear His presence.
They never shed a tear.
The lilies know He's forgiven Us,
—they know someday we'll
hear.

He lifts away our foolish fears,
and wipes away each tear.
The lilies in the valleys know
that we are all His.

Sway as the lilies in the valley do,
sway gently in His love.
For the lilies are His flower of Life,
as are his precious bees.
Flowers of Life given to Us,
to drift, perfume and please.
So drift as the lily does,
And sway with His sweet love.

"For I Love You,
as I Love every lily petal,
every leaf, every stem, every
day.

You will always be,
'My Lamb,'
though times you knew it not."

Showing His power Divine,
dew drops fall, each time,
weeping,
"Oh yes child, Thou art Mine"!

For I am your candle in
darkness,
and the Lord of your life.

Ranay Hodgson
TURN BACK THE HANDS OF TIME

Michael, My Forever Friend

Turn Back the Hands of Time
To when we were friends.
We talked and laughed constantly,
Touched and hugged carelessly.

Turn back the Hands of Time
To when we were together.
The future seemed ours to share,
We were such a caring pair.

Just Turn Back the Hands of Time—
I need you—my friend—Forever.

Sabra Force
SONG OF LOVE
I wish I could be the river you seek
and the valley you'd like to find,
I wish I could be the ocean you'd swim
and the mountain you'd like to climb.

I wish I could be the pillow at night
that lays beneath your head,
I wish I could be that special dream
that nightly shares your bed.

I wish I could be the one at your side
when things in your life go wrong,
I wish I knew that I was the one
who could sing you your favorite song.

I wish I could know the thoughts in your soul
and whether I'm ever there,
and if your heart ever chances to think:
"can it be that she could care?"

I wish you could know all the hours I spend
of each waking day and night,
thinking of you and only you
and wondering: can this be right?

'Cause I fell in love a long time ago
with you and all that you are,
and this ache in my heart wouldn't hurt so bad
when I gaze at the evening star . . .

If I could know that you feel the same
that you care as much for me,
that locked somewhere within your heart
is a prayer this love could be.

Linda M Smock
AN EASTER TO REMEMBER
Easter is a happy time, a time that we are blessed.
God gave us fluffy bunnies, and chickies in their nest.
God gave us baby duckies, and lambs that love to run.
God gave us loving parents, who make Easter so much fun.
God gave us Jesus His Only Son, to die upon a cross.
He was placed into a tomb, He died to save the lost.
The reason we celebrate Easter, is because of Jesus' empty tomb.
He is not there, He is Alive, And He's coming for us soon.

Rodolfo M Reventar Jr
HEARKEN ELIJAH'S END-TIME MINISTRY
Through the miracle of awakening or rebirth,
We are now living in constant inspiration and hope,
Dutifully advocating and achieving the requisites
For a Christlife as light in darkness, as salt in food.
Yes, having one true faith that saves and assures,
With the fullest measure of undeceived wisdom
To magnify, glorify—uphold One New Man in all
Its physical, ethical and spiritual aspects.

A turning completely to God-inbreathed Revelation,
Soulfully seeking only as the Blood-cleansed among men
The life-giving grace of what HEAVEN has promised.
Celebrating with inner joy all that's

divine,
To edify our humanity against what's profane.
Only after casting aside the chaff from the wheat
Will the apostates discern, be enlightened
Where all lies in disguise end.
And TRUTH begins to light up the Way.
With its prize of liberty, be at peace with ETERNITY.

The Lamb's victory over all iniquity is ours as well.
How beatific will our glorious transformation,
All the Saints' vindication be in the Millennium to come.

Laura Linhart
BLOOD

To my mother who has helped me through all the rough times.

Selfishness and jealousy rule
Over feelings—
Making raw wounds
Bleed.
But feelings surface like a
Bubble
In the flow of Blood.
Inner voices scream in agony
Reaching for the light
To open the door
That will let the healing waters
Stop the flow of
Blood.

Look at the
Scars.

They are beginning to bleed
Again.

All because of . . .
You.

Diane Morris
FLIGHT
White, wispy puffs
Nature's traveling pillows
Sleeping angels lay.

Upon eagle's wings
Silver visions in the sky
Unknown destinies.

Blue, peaceful journey
Gentle breezes speak to me
Lifelike spirits play.

Fanny Mulay
LESSONS IN EATING TURKEY
When eating a turkey, first eat the head,
But first make sure the turkey is dead.
Then eat the neck,
So you know how to peck.
Then you eat the drumsticks,
So you can use them for toothpicks.
Last of all you eat the feet,
And now my lesson's complete!

Mary Louise Richardson Fratesi
GEN OF THE SEA
Our country discovered by Columbus in 1492.
On the Atlanta Ocean in ships; Nina, Santa Maria, and Pinta.
A tough and rough journey.
Little or no information by book or mail.
Sickness curing methods of little knowledge.
Storms were rapid and strong.
Sails were torn but sailors skill at repairs.
Father weaved at the loom.
Therefore Columbus traveled to find Trading Center.
Queen of Spain and England beared expense.
Of voyage at his nineteenth and twentieth years.
Brothers: Bartholomew and Diego plan the trip.
They longed to go to sea and knew how to handle oars and sails.
For they fished sardines which they needed to sail.
Another trading center needed.
Learned all about in English Extension Course.
At University of Arkansas.
Of all senses he was dreamy and sensitive,
So read geography in Latin and Spanish.
This Great Man of the Sea, Columbus the Gen of the Ocean.

John C Farley II
THOUGHTS OF WINTER

I would like to thank Carolyn Farley (my mother) for teaching me to see with more than just my eyes, and to Karen Oudshoorn (a very dear friend) for helping me find a way (poetry) to reveal what I've seen.

There's a bitter chill
crisp and cold
as a north wind blows
strong and bold
there's the sound of geese
high over head
as the birds fly south
for the months ahead
it's the warmth of a fireplace
to fight the chill
enjoyed with a loved one
when the night is still

it's the sound of silence
around the lake
and the picture of beauty
the first snows make
it's a time for romance
and a time for love too
when the fire in your heart
will be your warmth for you

Nancy Bashara Hermes
IT FEELS FUNNY
It feels funny
  To feel good;
I've been feeling bad
  So long.
Guess the devil
  Had me
Under his spell;
I just knew
I was on the
  Way to hell.
I decided to see
  The light,
And now I feel
Everything's all right.

It feels funny
  To be up;
I've been down
  So long.

When you walk
  In the light
Everything seems
  Right.

It feels funny
To feel good,
Even though
I know I should.

I hope someday
I can say
It feels funny
To feel bad
I've been
Feeling good
  So Long!

Rebecca Harkins
INSOMNIAC'S PRAYER

This poem is dedicated to the loving memory of my sister Marie—who was an incurable insomniac.

Oh, Keeper of the sleep,
If sleeping seed you keep,
One tiny seed I pray
To cherish night and day,

To nurture, water and plant deep,
Then sleep, and sleep, and sleep, and sleep.

John C Mac Iver

John C Mac Iver
THE BIRDS AND THE RAIN

To my loving wife Penny, your my constant inspiration, I love you!

I hear the droplets of rain,
Descend from leaf to leaf,
I hear the birds singing their sweet refrain,
A sound more beautiful then belief.
It's not important to understand,
All that our world holds,
Alas that's the way it is with man,
Everything must be understood so that it can be bought and sold.
Someday things will change,
I hope it's very soon,
Although I wish nature to stay the same.
We should be the ones to change our tune.
Not the Birds,
Nor the Rain,
They should be heard,
And given their fame.

Angela Shaw

Angela Shaw
OUR PARTING WAS MEANT TO BE

I would like to dedicate this poem to Jeff Coleman, who I care about very much, but our relationship could not continue, For my fear of it ending forever.

I never meant to hurt you,
Try to understand.
Please don't be angry or blue,
Just be my friend and take my hand.
We were too different,
You and I could never last.
So, let's just say good-bye,
Let's put it all in our past.
I think deep down inside you know,
I still do really care.
Even if it seems as though,
I have been unfair.
Someday the hurt will go
And you will finally see,
What before you didn't know
Our parting was meant to be.

S R Mitchell
SHIPS OF MIND
I think of the sea oft times
where all the thrills abound.
But I am landlocked where I am
with grain fields all around.

The square riggers that I love
they sail beyond my eyes.
So I conjure up those ships above
I look into the skies.

That clouds the EAGLE over there
and here's the CUTTY SARK.
I can watch them every day
until it gets too dark.

Then I can dock them on the moon
or moor them to a star.
The swabs can sing all night long
in my heavenly safe harbor.

So when my heart yearns for a sail,
a main, a jib, a mast.

I find my heart a wandering far
and my wistful eyes upcast.

Vivian Keglewitsch
SEASONS
He lay upon a printed quilt,
The sun's golden Spring smile
dancing on web-fine hair.
He smiled, he cooed as dimpled fists
beat the mote-filled air.
This was the baby.

He swung upon a sagging gate;
His playmate, Summer's gentle wind,
coaxing him to and fro.
He laughed and sang a tuneless song
about the way he'd grow.
This was the boy.

He strode across the leaf-loamed
lawn,
The Autumn chill captured his
breath—patterns before his eyes.
Intense those eyes and filled with
hope—dreams to be realized.
This was the youth.

He stood and watched the clouds sift
snow,
A crystalline comforter for Winter's
clear, cold truth.
Smiling lips, song-filled heart;
dreaming, hopeful eyes;
Baby, boy, youth;
And, now, the man.

Mary Ellen Knopp
SUMMER DAY
In a grassy meadow by a beautiful
stream,
We gazed at the sky in a world of
dreams.
Dreams of the future for you and me,
and our breathtaking love "so real"
you see.

The meadowlark warbles a lovely
song,
and the babbling brook seems to hum
along.
My heart swells with joy, as I look in
your eyes,
The same color blue, as the heavenly
skies.

Now seasons and tears have torn us
apart,
But the picture forever is deep in my
heart.
And now that you're gone, I've only
the dream,
Of that summer day we spent by the
stream.

Come back my love and say you're
mine,
And all the grey skies leave behind.
Just let me hold you close in bliss,
And kiss forever summer lips.

H William Large
THE ROYAL DREAM
Joseph had a most unusual
avocation . . .
(A gift from God, they say);
A stranger within a mighty
nation . . .
(The plan of God, they say).
The interpreter of dreams: the
avocation;
Egypt (where flows the Nile)
was this nation.

Pharoah of long ago had within his
household
This servant whose talents were
most unusual,
Whose name by fame was Joseph,
we're told.
When the dreams of Pharoah
became unexplainable,
He sent for Joseph for an interpretation
Just so he might receive a
soothing revelation.

Says Pharoah to Joseph,

"Why first the fat cows, and then the
thin?
How could the thin devour the
fat within?
"No rest have I, because this stupid
dream
Occurs and recurs while I toss
and scream!
"O Interpreter of dreams, can you
explain
Just why I am plagued, again
and again?"

Answers Joseph to Pharoah,

"O wise Pharoah, the ALMIGHTY
speaks:
'Prepare for a famine; not of
weeks . . . but for years
'All nations will seek you, shedding
hunger tears!'"

Stephanie Sawicki
THE LESSON
Observe the crystals:
their smooth faces,
sharp edges . . .
double pyramids of durable silicon
and free, spirited oxygen
tolerate the pressure of 7.

I've seen how some of these
magic wands
bond solidly,
break cleanly,
heal themselves.
Observe the fluorite,
the genius stone, a third eye
stone:

—travel at the speed of thought;
experience the formlessness
within
the form.

The potential isn't always tapped,
but always there.

L M Bates
MY GAZELLE TWINS
Dance thy dance of the Shulamite
Song
For it is your ordained time to give
forth thy birth Oh Judah
Gazelles leaping on thy mountains
and the big-horn Rams will be a
stature
For thy truth will be sounded as a
clarion
Thy vines will gather thy fruits and
many will come to thy vineyards
tasting of thy sweetness of thy
pomegranates
You are all perfect and you reign
with Majesty
Arrayed all glorious thy loveliness
consumes thy beauty
There's not been a greater than
Solomon, yet, he has come
But, You, long for the day of union
The whole earth will be filled with
your glory, for, the procession of Thy
King
As the earth proclaims with the
Jubilation dance
Read from thy book, Oh John and
glean your promises to you, my
beloved
Only with dove eyes do we see thee
Your gardens are rare and prepared
with pleasant fruits and mandrakes
But, only you thy love and thy
consummation of the day
For you have ordained the mystery of
the Shulamites Heart
Proclaiming, thou, entrance to thy
gates
For, the turtledove song, that is sung,
Is Sung In A New Land.

Rose H Behnke
I HEAR THE GEESE AT CHRISTMAS TIME
I hear the geese at Christmas time,
Their honking's loud and clear.
It's Faith and Hope
for all mankind
To usher in the year.

Shalon Valerie Davis

Shalon Valerie Davis
FAR AWAY

*In remembrance of our passed on
loved ones.
To families with a departure to a new
foundation
Where happiness lies.*

At one time
We talked about passing on
Now why do I
have to get used to you being gone
I repeat and cry over
Why did you leave me
to hurt and feel lonely
I know one day we'll be together
again
But why did your life have to end
Far away you have went
Far away is where
The rest of your life will be spent
I ask far away why should you be
Why did you go so far away from me
I know far away that's what you are
Up in heaven shining with the stars
I'll cry inside out
Until we're together again
That's when my life will end
But until then
You're part of my lord
Part of my prayer
Part of my remembrance
That you were here
Far away you are from me
If there's a place called missing you
That's where I'll be

Marita J Ledbetter
COUNTRY ROAMING

*For Leslie my husband, my walking
companion.*

On the roadside, in our path,
a Meadowlark screeched at us in
wrath.
We came across her little nest
where three eggs lay, as if to rest.
The mother chirped—"let them be!"
though nothing else occurred to me.

Into the woods through many trees,
ferns, flowers-hundreds of these.
So many birds, I can recall
the magic singing of them all.

Along the way a rabbit small
was playing in the weeds so tall;
too soon to stop, we further roamed
and found a little stream a frog called
home.

Then as twilight slowly drew near
we caught sight of a beautiful deer.
It was such a perfect day,
one of those we tuck away.

Carla J Brown
MAN SELF-DESTRUCTS

*Dedicated to my son—Terry
Grandsons—Christopher and Sean*

We can build rockets and spaceships,
Orbit the earth, study the stars.
Man can land aircraft on the moon
and
explore the sand dunes of Mars,

But there's a time yet to come,
an awareness we've yet to see
of the molding of our children
with love, healthy mind, and body.

There's a mountain we've yet to
climb,
a knowledge that we must teach,
as people are being hurt
and they are all within our reach.

There's a sickness we've yet to heal
if our world is to be made whole.
God made all the colors of skin;
each with heart, mind, body, and
soul.

All are brothers in the master's eyes
and soon your body and soul will
part.
Do you think you'll make it to
heaven
with the malice that's in your heart?

Lurlene Chesser
LOVE
Love is a fragile, delicate thing,
Like the fine gold dust on a
Butterfly's wing.
You find it in the most unusual
places
Even in smiles on young and old
faces.

You never really have love, until you
give it away
Sometimes it flies away, other times
it here to stay,
Like helping a friend that's lonely
and blue,
If you give help it will come back to
you.

The heart is the box that stores your
love
The Will and power to use it comes
from above.
It goes to friends, sweethearts,
husbands and wives
Goes to many different things that
enters our lives.

So take your sunshine day by day

Just be ready if troubled rain falls your way.
Keep an open heart and don't be blue
A light tap on your shoulder might be love looking for you.

Tom Forte
OUT OF THE GHETTO

My prayer is for you, children of poverty.

Please God, make my alley a stream,
A beautiful river of no return.
Give me a canoe of silver and gold,
Laced with rubies, diamonds and pearls.

Give me your breath 'O God, for a sail,
And your sword, your fiery sword
For an oar.

Alfred Kebodeaux Jr
ONE TRUE FRIEND
All my life, Lord, I've been blessed with gifts
I know You have sent,
All of these gifts, Lord, I shared with people
I thought were my friends,
They lied to me, cheated and stole and the
scene went out of control,
They left me broke, lonely and out in the cold.

Of all the millions of people on earth, Lord, I'm
down to my last friend,
And this is my one true friend, Lord, that I
know You have sent,
And if You send more gifts, Lord, I'll share
with this Friend;
She will be special in my life until the end.

When You take us away, Lord, if You have
room for only one,
Leave me behind, Lord, and take my friend.

Jerry W Komarek
I JUST DON'T HAVE ALL OF MY MARBLES ANYMORE!
This year, I have attained the age of seventy four,
And I just don't have, all of my marbles, any more!

It was quite suddenly, that this all had come about,
But that I'll be able to cope, I don't have any doubt.

Recently, I went back to my boyhood days, unexpectedly,
I began playing lengthy games—at times on one knee.

Perhaps to you, this may seem, to be beyond belief,
But I will explain it all, and will make it quite brief.

Grandchildren Bobby and Becky, had recently come our way,
And I began to think of games, which we all could play.

I brought a bag of my boyhood marbles, into view,
Suggesting that playing with them, would be something new.

I must have put on, a fairly interesting demonstration,
For it seemed to fill their hearts, with inspiration.

They took all of the marbles, when they left for home,
And that was the inspiration, for composing this poem!

Peggy J Collis

Peggy J Collis
CAUSE OF DEATH?

This is dedicated to all the plastic people in the world. Those who are too afraid to express and accept this greatest gift and need of all us poor mortals which is Love.

As I sit here tonight,
my soul hath no light.

All hope and caring is gone.
Pain has turned me to stone.
But it still hurts,
right down to the bone.

Oh! so many times,
I've reached out in desperation.
Only to be filled,
with hurt and frustration.

Yet, once more—
here I lie in the dirt on my face.
Because I can't walk at their pace.

Yet the only crime I'm guilty ove,
is being filled with too much Love.

So Judge and Jury—
I bid you Good Night.
As I take this Gun—
and turn out the Light!!

Michael Thomas Wyzykowski
ELAINE'S FATHER

This poem is dedicated to my loving Daughter Elaine Marie.

As a child my life was not one
That anyone could call pleasant.
So I have worked my mind,
Body, and soul to the bone
To give my children the things
That I never had.

But sometimes they think
That no one cares.
They stare in the air
And go on with their lives
As if I wasn't there.

Only the young refuse to see
That where they're heading
Is nowhere to be.
The life they're making today
I never wanted them to see.

One day they will realize
The things I have said,
And they will hopefully see
That it will be up to them
To decide what their lives will be.

Carolyn Wall
GONE HOME
Sitting peacefully in a chair;
She didn't notice the angels
there.
The flutter of wings creating a breeze,
Giving her peace and harmony.

She smiled as they talked to her,
Telling of heaven above.
Taking her gently through the clouds;
To a Kingdom filled with love.

Gates of Pearl opening wide
As they swept inside.
Setting her feet on golden sand,
Beside a river so grand!

Looking around at Everyone;
All the loved ones she knew.
But, best of all were the open arms
of Jesus Christ anew.

If she could say one thing today,
to her loved ones down here.
Would probably be, Not to worry!
There's nothing here to fear.

Mrs J W Jones Jr
A SPECIAL BOY-STEVE
There was a boy so lean and tall,
God said, "My lad, you're a favorite of all."
"You've learned the rules, you've run the race
much faster than the rest, in all good grace!"

II

I have a special place for you, within my heavenly realm
The needs are many and great, at this, my starry helm.
Though loved ones miss you and are lonely now.
In time, they'll see the wisdom, at present,
they know not how!

III

Steve, You were given as a blessing for a little while!
To parents, to nurture you, until my special call.
May your loved ones have patience until that time,
when all will meet in that era sublime.

IV

The memories you left were all so sweet
To be kept until that time when you will greet
all face to face, once more, again
As they, you're loved ones walk Remembrance Lane.

Ruby T Crider
A SMALL CHILD'S PLIGHT

Here in the yesterday stands a small child, waiting as death comes calling at her mother's side.

She was such a little thing to have no mother near, for in the years that lay ahead, she needed her so much to care, to hold her in her arms and wipe away her tears.

And now as the years unfold, she yearns for a mother's love. She knows she has missed something special, that only a mother can give.

She wondered what it would be like to have a mother near, to feel her arms around her as she rocked her in her chair, and whispered love to her as she tucked her in her bed.

But as she grew to womanhood, and became a mother too, she whispered these words, I know your love, and knew that her mother heard.

I never knew you, Mother, when you left me in this world, but I know how much you must have loved your tiny little girl.

Patricia Clanton

Patricia Clanton
AS I STAND HERE

To my loving grandmother who has inspired my life and helped make my life a bit easier to live Pastor Prophetess Everlena Middleton.

Lord as I stand here today,
Nothing will come to mind of what I am to say.
I stand here as a vessel for you,
I don't know what to say; I don't know what to do.

Lord please tell me a little song or maybe a little prayer;
So that I can sing my song or say my prayer,
in the church, at school, and everywhere.
Singing and praying to your people just to let them know
That the wages of sin is death,
And only the gift from you is eternal life.

Lord I'm only a little girl,
And don't know much to do or say,
But I know that you love and care for me
Each and every day.

Lord as I stand here a child in heart,
I want to know everything about your word and want it to never depart.
I don't know everything and learn new things each day,
But I do know that you died on Calvary one sad day.
I heard that you died on Calvary for the sins of all of us,
and that you formed us from the earth's sand and dust.
Then you blew life into us all that wonderful day,
As if we did something wonderful in order to be here today.

Lord as I stand here now with tears forming in my eyes,
I just want to know what I can do to

show you how grateful I am.
I know that I could never repay you
for the blood you shed,
or the friends you lost
As you hung on that deadly cross.
I know you didn't do anything to
deserve to be treated that way;
And then you asked your father to
forgive us,
For we knew not what we were doing
on that day.

Lord as I stand here today about to sit
down,
I know that Jesus loves and cares for
us all
And he's done everything he could
that we might not fall.
He died and rose again, he left us in
the flesh,
But yet he sent us a comforter to help
and strengthen us;
He is Lord all mighty, Lord of Host
who died, rose and sent us a
comforter, the
HOLY GHOST!!

D'Arleane Brammer
SPRING AT THE LAKE

To my family with love.

Ducks sound like they laugh
While floating their path;
Playing follow the leader again.

The woodpecker pecks,
Barely bending his neck;
Ferrets bugs from the tree trunk; and
then,
A bug of bright green
Lands to make a bright ring
On the surface of water, for when
It's spring at the lake,
All growing things wake,
For all have a part in God's plan.

Xai Yang
THE FOUR SEASONS
When everything's new and clean
And you hear the robins sing;
The grass and flowers come to life.
It's the beginning of spring.

When all you feel is stickiness
'Cause you've been fried in the sun;
The bugs continue to pest you
Yet summer has just begun.

When the foliage begins to change
Mornings and evenings are cool.
Farmers reap and harvest their crops.
Fall takes students back to school.

When temperatures drop to zero
And the land's a frozen white;
The Christmas spirit's everywhere—
Winter's a joyous delight.

Alice McKinney
AN OLD FRIEND
Today I stopped and thought of you
Across the miles and passing years.
Although our lives are far apart,
At times we share our joys and tears.
Somehow a mystic bond remains,
Transcending time and distant places.
Our thoughts reach out in unison
In visions of remembered faces.
Glimpses of you have filled my mind
And held it captive through the day
As if you're reaching out to me
With words you wish to say.
How different now our living is
Since carefree, youthful times once
end!
Oh, but how very gratifying
To know that still you are my friend!

Anthony Olisa
SONGS OF SORROW
America has treated me thus
It has led me among the shaft of the
forest;
Returning is not possible,
And going forward, a great difficult.
The affairs of this world are like
chameleon faces
into which I have step
But when I clean can not go off.
I am on the world extremely corner
I am not sitting in the row with the
executives
But those who are lucky
Sit in the middle and forget.
I am on the world extremely corner.

My people, I have been somewhere
If I turn here, the rain beats me,
If I turn there, the sun burns me.
The firewood of this world
is for only those who can take heart,
And that is why not all can gather it.

I have wandered in the wilderness
The great wilderness which men call
life.
The rain has beaten me
And death has made war upon my
house.
I can go beyond and forget.

Something has happened to me
The thing so great that I can not
weep.
I have no son to fire the gun when I
die,
I have no daughter to weep when I
close my eyes.
I can go beyond and forget.

What's the wieling for?
Emmanuel himself has gone back.
The tree on which I lean is fallen,
Those who dare not look in my face,
have come out as men.
How well, their pride is with them.

Emmanuel, if you go, tell them,
Tell Patrick and Janet that they have
done me evil.
Ask them why did they send me here
to learn
When I should have been at home
wasting my time.
And be like an ordinary person.

Helen Campbell Radtke
I HAVE A FRIEND
Friendship is a precious thing—
It has a beginning but not an end.
It stretches out across the miles,
To add a tear or bring a smile.

A friend will stay when the going is
rough—
Never a doubt but always a trust.
Distance, storms, or even a quake
Will not true friendship shake.

It grows in service, love, and grace,
A spidery web like old Spanish lace.
So fragile, tender, delicate, rare,
A special guard must be stationed
there;

To keep our friendship true and
strong—
Let it grow deeper as we move along,
Fearless and true to the very end,
Life's precious gift, "I have a friend."

Lettie B Jackson

Lettie B Jackson
THE SEED

*Dedicated to Archie R. Jackson,
husband*

We planted a seed today
We watered it with our tears
We warmed it with our laughter
It had been so many years

We covered it with our love
We fed it with our caring
We stood aside and watched it grow
We cultivated it with sharing

The seed, it grew and blossomed
Kissed by gentle rain
Warmed by gentle sunlight
We were together again

This seed that we had planted grew
with every year
And we knew in all our hearts our
time was finally here

We caressed our every moments as
most lost persons do.
But we had loved and laughed and
cried
And tenderly said "I love you:"

Nikola Ristivojevich
**RAISING HAUSE FOR MY
SLAVE**
At stuffy,
summer, obscure and moping nights
J raise a house for my slave.

J've been thinking,
how,
for many years,
long and obedience and modesty full,
how,
what to give
to reward him.

With gallons of wine, or lots of
women,
beautiful,
enormous treasure,
J've been thinking
but still
J raise a hause for my slave.

J built it from the basis,
twist,
stairs and rooms and windows
twisted,
even chambers,
left and right,
then round
when he walks,
never to know where reality is
to reward my slave.

Steven Silvester
A BABY BOY
The excitement of a baby boy,
Like getting his first real riding toy,
He will always bring lots of pure joy.

A wave of happiness he will bring.
His pure soft touch will make your
heart sing,
And joyful ears, when he cries will
ring.

The stress of nine full, hard months is
gone.
It makes you want to sing a love
song.
You'll find he makes you want to
belong.

The boy of your dreams has found his
life.
No better parents could show the
light,
Because the love in your heart is so
bright.

Jessica Virginia Ansaldo
BAND OF DREAMS
Quiet evening on the shore,
Wake up now, look out your door,
It seems the skies forever old,
It seems your stories never told!
"Just a little band of dreams
A ring around your heart it seems,
Silent as the morning dove . . . .
there awaits your only love."
Sleeping now upon your breast,
his breathing puts your mind at rest,
as shallow as a single tear, you sleep
within a world of fear, and wake to
find a lonely rose, a vision of the love
you chose! "Caught inside a band of
dreams, a ring around your heart it
seems, silent as the morning dove . . .
Oh where awaits, my only love?"

Craig Lee Arnel
LAW
Obey the law.

Appreciate other people
Rich or poor,
Sharing ideas
To stopping war.

Working on projects
To conquer the difficulties,
That occur,
When people fight
Over what they think
is wrong or right.

So get along
And sing the same song
If we fought over beliefs
All the time,
Then no one would have
Anything to believe in.

Kim Benjamin
THE WATERFALL
The water races to the edge of the
waterfall with uncontrolled speed.
Sometimes, it runs into rocks and the
water is separated.
Hopefully it will pull itself back
together before the next comes
along—
Sometimes it can slide over them if it
is strong enough.
But it doesn't avoid the rocks, it
rushes toward them
—despite the danger—
Would it be better without rocks?
To take away the beauty of the
patterns they make?
No—
It speeds on to that great fall—

—the final rock—
where none has returned.
Finally—
it settles, it floats,
contemplating the journey it took to arrive.

Jo Champion Abel
THE SEA
The sea rolls
and it glides
The sea jumps
and it slides

The sea lurches
and it moans
The sea screams
and it groans

The sea laughs
and it cries
The sea sings
and it sighs

The sea takes
and it gives
The sea's dead
But it lives!

Melissa Belle Porter
WITHOUT YOU
Sometimes, I am afraid,
That you might go away;
Leaving me with only your memory,
Never to see you or hear your voice again.

Sometimes, I am afraid,
That our someday will never come,
That you will be taken away, and my dreams will die,
And I will live only wanting to be with you.

Sometimes, I am afraid,
That my star will fade into the sky,
and never return,
And that when I look up to see it shining,
Darkness will be my only vision.

Sometimes, I am afraid,
Because life wouldn't be the same
Without You in it.

Daniel McCormack
SAVIOR
Polka-dotted pedestrians adorn my selfish dreams.
Fractured faces appear as strangers that,
represent vanity and catastrophe.
Controlled and noncontrolled eclipses of conscience.
My dreams hold me over to the next simple situation.
Like wood in the beavers' dam.
Never allowing reality to interfere,
except in spells of hunger or sickness.
Driven on rampantly by a delirious taste,
for adventure and excitement.
Causing me to ponder every grain of the bread.
Happiness lurks here as the talented,
enemy of regression.
Gathering every greedy vein of child,
to listen to his wonderful and tempting stories.
So vibrant as to make the dullest possibility appear,
a gyrating success.
All comes together,
as does conscience and subconscious at dawn,
when my next
challenge
awakens me.

Patricia M Balik
SOMEONE SPECIAL
A special word, a special thought,
That's what something special I have fought.
A special smile, I can endure,
To really know of things I am sure.
A special laugh, a small hello,
And all my problems surely go.
It's special yes, that's what I said,
For never tomorrow, it's here and now instead.
To have someone special, someone dear,
Makes so many things just disappear.
A special friend that's for sure,
It's never too hard, without words to lure,
You get angry with me, sometimes I know,
Only because you're my friend and you care so.
You say get your head straight girl, you're worth much more,
Don't put yourself down, don't hit the floor.
You're a special friend, just like a star.
Someday I may learn before I go too far.
Please don't give up, I know I am not fit,
Only please special friend, don't ever quit.

Geraldine A Green
LORD, I'VE THANKED YOU FOR MY ROSES AND NOT MY THORNS
Lord, I've thanked you for my roses
And there have been many times
That you've answered my prayers
From this heart of mine.

I want to humbly kneel before you
And ask that you forgive,
Because I didn't thank you for my thorns
In the days passed I lived.

When pressure came my way
I felt, Lord, you did forget,
Not realizing that my thorns
Were my best blessings yet.

Lord, I always want to know you're there
In my good times and my bad,
And that a rose is beautiful
But a thorn isn't always sad.

Sometimes a thorn is God's way
To show He cares and loves,
So He sends down a thorn to mold us,
Then reveals His self with a rose from above.

But I kneel to you, dear Lord,
And my gratitude that you know,
When to send a rose to me
And with each thorn, your face you show.

Howard Maupin

Howard Maupin
ENJOY EVERYDAY

I Howard Maupin hereby dedicate "ENJOY EVERYDAY" to this Great Book of great poems of the Western World as a tribute to MANKIND.

Enjoy every day, let not a single day pass
Without the accepted cheerful thought
That it was a day well received in thy grasp
And to be remembered for what time brought.

Enjoy every day for what it is.
Take time, condition and people for what they are.
Let not the negative time in fear fizz
That life away to sorrow and horror.

Enjoy every day as a motto to hold.
Our time on earth is for us to live and enjoy;
Whereas we are not benefitting to not unfold
That gratification for what that day could employ.

Enjoy everyday as a habit of life
Knowing of no other way to behave;
For in all life happiness does derive
From the spirit of the mind that the attitude paved.

Jennie Boeing
OUR MISTAKE

To all the Vietnam Veterans

We know we made a mistake that long time ago,
When spitting on our men coming back home.

When they needed us most we let them down,
And walked away with an ungrateful frown.

But as time went on we uncovered the fact,
And learned those men were Heroes coming back.

Those men who fought for Americans' pride,
Are back now and finally by our side.
And though their war goes on still today,
We are here to have faith, to hope and to pray.

Lift your heads up high, we are grateful today,
And we are sorry my friends for those lonely days.

Joy Brand
LIKE WHEN, MAN, WHEN
What I mean, man, is

You pulled voices out of quiet air,
Put them in a box and called it radio.
You drew pictures out of blank air,
Put them in a box and called it television.
You even went down into the infinitesimal
Spaces of the atom and found there
Enough light and heat to destroy a city.
You put that into a bomb. Presto!
Nuclear energy.

Then you reached way out into empty space
And found there something that could help you
Transmit messages, maintain energy,
Operate mechanical devices.
So you threw a spaceship off the earth,
With the power you had discovered in liquid oxygen,
And rode it to the moon.

But what I mean, man, is

When are you going to discover that total power
In the atmosphere around you,
which some men call God,
And use it in yourself?

Like when, man, when?

Jennie Pearse
MY HANDS
My hand God gave me
Is now very old.
My hand worn out but the stories they show.
Nails broken and veins
Stick out. But even though,
My hands done God's work
And it show—

Lorice V Bailey-Grant
ALMOST
Almost I would have reached
the summit of happiness
and surrender my pliant self
on the altar of my love
for you.
Almost I would have gone beyond
the brink of bliss
and shiver and shake
my prostrate self
down prone, convulsing
in climax of two become one.
Almost you loved me
Almost you carried me away
astray to the valley
and the shadow
of shame
in the name of love.
Almost I believed
your lies
and cried
when I found
you could mix and fix a tale
and tack it up for sale

and I bought it:
almost . . .

Barbara J Haungs
I AM A BLIND MAN
I am a blind man—
Yet, I see things no seeing man can.
I can see the wind blow.
I listen and the trees tell me tales of the sky.
The birds tell me of far away lands and of gardens of delight.
I see a darkness that no man who sees could ever stand.
For no stars are ever in my darkness.
I will never see the rising sun.
To know a flower has thorns,
I must touch it.
Colors have no meaning to me, they are merely names of people who have no faces.
I shall never see a rainbow.
Though man claims it is a sight to behold.
Though I could tell man much about his world that he would never guess.
I can tell man how the rain smells,
I can tell him what the crickets say.
I know of a wall before I am upon it.
Everything I touch is a world of wonder.
Every new place I go new "sights" to "see"
Yet . . . . .
I am a blind man.

Franz von Weizmann
A PRAYER
A few words from someone deep in need.
An expression of guilt over a dastardly deed.
A pause in one's busy schedule of life
A time of thanks for granting your wife.
Not an exercise in lip movement or in song,
But a sincere expression to forgive your wrong.

Remember the teachings of the Holy men of life,
Who in simplicity have offered solutions to strife.
No tent or cathedral or even a home,
Just any place in which man can roam.
The fancy buildings and the religious attire
Serve only to disguise rather than inspire.
All that is needed is sincerity of mind
And the LORD will not forget you even if blind.

Catherine S Vande Hey
MY PRECIOUS ANGEL
The death of a child, is one of the deepest sorrows inflicted upon the heart!
It causes a weariness that makes even simple functions, like a smile, unbearable to perform!
Memories an' pictures only seem to add to the pain, when a loved one is taken without notice!
The tragedy seems to drag on long after the funeral, has come an' gone!
All the thoughtful cards an' words in the world, can't ease the terrible emptiness, felt inside!
It can't console you when you go to their room, to remove all their favorite toys an' belongings!
Each box that you fill, you realize all your hopes an' dreams for their future, have also died!
The room no-longer rings, with the merry laughter, of a child at play, just a hollow silence!
The cruel hand of fate, has robbed me not only of my child's life but my own will to go on!
Somehow, life does go on, even though, we wish we could make it go back in time, an' stop!
Days turn into years an' memories fill the vacant place, making you just a thought away!
My Precious Angel, I see you in every sunrise an' every sunset!
When the rain falls, an' the storm has passed, I see the rainbow, an' remember its promise!
Just as you my Angel, cause the tears to flow in my heart, you have shown me the rainbow!
At night while the sky is filled with twinkling starlight, you are with me in my spirit!
My heart can sense your warm embrace, with each gentle breeze, that caresses my face!
Your tender spirit, has become one with mine, giving me the strength to make the best of each day
You have given me hope in a here-after, where the circle of our love will be unbroken!
I will always feel the loss, for the things that will never be, as long as you are a part of me!
For if love is eternal, an' life is but a twinkling of an eye, then I will be with you bye and bye!
So till that wonderful day, when our paths shall meet, I'll just say, "till we meet again,
My Precious Angel!

Howard L Church
IT'S ABOUT TIME!
It's about time!
A gift sublime,
From the hand of God,
To all mankind.

Ours to use,
In ways we choose,
To glorify Him,
Unless, the "gift" we lose.

Every tick of the clock,
Prompts us to take stock,
Of every blessing received,
From Jesus, our Rock.

Health and friends,
Our work—'til journey's end,
Blessed gifts, all three
If you're in partnership with Him!

Sandra May Whitmore
IF I HAD ONLY KNOWN

In memory of my late husband Raymond who was the most loving husband and father "We miss you"!

We found ourselves talking in great detail,
Of the way you had wanted things done,
And while we had talked,
My whole heart was aching,
Never wanting to be only one;

You must have seen all the pain I was feeling,
For as careful as careful could be,
You had me believing we talked of the future,
Not the present as I do now see;
In my mind I had pictured you'd always be here,
But my heart knew that this couldn't be,
The picture was that you would be by my side,
Through all eternity;

My love I now see how it tore at your heart,
Knowing your time was drawing ever nearer,
It makes my heart break,
I could not partake,
In the burden that you had to bear;

The days seem so long and so empty,
And the nighttime it's longer still,
Only when darkness closes in all around me,
I find peace knowing you'll always be near.

In Memory Of My Late Husband

Mildred Muniz
MEMORIES INTERNATIONAL
Forward I see with my eyes
With thoughts and hopes of excitement
I can't contain myself.
The smiles of friendship I hope to see
Voices of pleasant cheer
Expression that reflect warmth
Extending the cultural greeting to me . . . .
But . . . . to my unexpected quick realization
My thoughts and hopes of positive response changed
the glow of excitement is only to return back home
the smiles of friendship I saw one in a thousand
the voices were of different cultural dialect
Cold, business careless tones, smiles without meaning
Expressions were expressed in different cultural ways
I didn't understand; I'm not sure I want to
I faced unfriendly cultural individuals
In the Land of Natives I had hoped to see
Which obviously belongs to another culture
of the so called friendly land.

M Jean Lalk
HAMMER
Rossiya is swallowed up . . . . .
Bolshi has eaten . . . singing
Sons and daughters fear stained faces see not, know not
The mongrel image moves and acts
Bloody Red Freedom Hammer.

Dwellers of the field, Watch:
Your song has turned to sorrow
Struggle uselessly and fall
Birthed in chains, baby-smiles—innocents enslaved.
Bloody Red Freedom Hammer.

Eesti, swallowed, the circle of her being, unmapped.
Children of Riga
on the knee of a stranger.
Arm raised, hand armed.
Bloody Red Freedom Hammer.

The small knees of Vilnus . . .
spread, unwilling . . she remembers
Ruthenia and Tirana.
Sofia, skirts torn, loins uncovered
Sits in loud silence, LOUD
Bloody Red Freedom Hammer.

A broken rainbow girts your land
Oh Kishnev.
The blues and greens are
Blotted out.
Covered, smothered by its force.
Bloody Red Freedom Hammer.

Seated sadly in the center
of a demolished land.
Prague, when will you dance again?
Your nameless fears come to an end.
Bloody Red Freedom Hammer.

M T Landry

M T Landry
DUSK
the purple dove,
endlessly pursuing her vanished dream,
is led astray
once more, catching her breath
in the hawthorn, perched in stillness,
contemplating the unknown present.

—the midday sun
never appeared more triumphant

—the purple dove,
in the mayflower, catching her breath,
has chosen to stand alone,
trusting—

—when new sounds offered have opened her a way
will she have to forget, also
that she can fly?

—awkwardly outlined,
in increasing darkness,
she can't understand, yet,
that "All" is white—

Quintina
VISIONS TOLD
Growing up in this era it seems, is much more difficult than in your dreams.
It's more important in this day

and age, to get an education
to earn a good wage.

You will make it, you will
see . . . by learning and teaching
how this world should be.
Understanding and compassion
for your fellow man . . . . . .
Should be one of your goals in
your future plan.

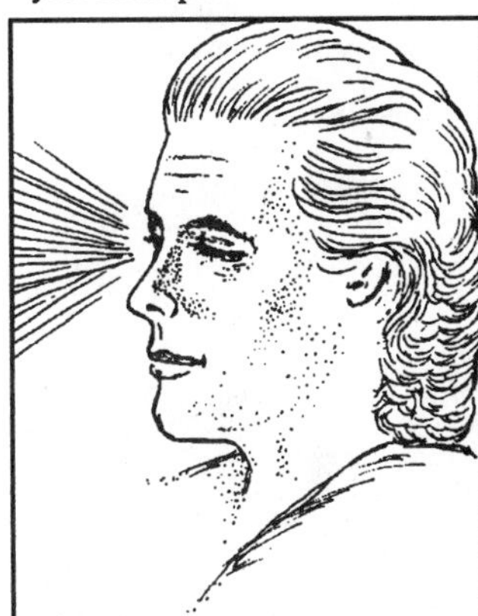

To learn from the hurts of the
past is the biggest test;
To make a better world, should
be your greatest quest.
To acknowledge your elders, who
were once your age,
Some raised with reason and
some raised with rage;
To understand the strife they've
been through,
Will sharpen your judgement in
all that you do.

You will make it, you will
see . . . . by learning and
teaching how this world should
be.
Understanding and compassion
for your fellow man,
Should be one of your goals in
your future's plan.

Charles H Abdalian

THE TRUTH

I went to my Cell within me and
asked,
What is truth?
A cell said,
I have cells within me
Which have no body, no form, and no
shape.
Millions, billions living within me
Helping me to have life.
I am million times larger than these
cells.
Now that I have life and I Could live,
This kind of life is the truth.

I WENT TO A MAN ON THE
EARTH
And asked him, What is the truth?
He said, "I am a man,
But I have cells within me,
Million times smaller than I.
They give me life, Now this kind of
living
Is the Truth"

I went to the earth and asked,
"What is the truth?"
HE said, "I have billions
Of creatures living within me:
Man, animals, creatures, insects,
Trees, fish, and vegetation.
All these give me life to live.
This kind of living is the Truth."

I went to the universe
And asked Him "what is the truth?"
Universe said,
"I have billions of stars within me,
And they are billion times smaller
Than I am,
Helping me to live.
THAT'S THE TRUTH!"

Lana Smith

Lana Smith

ASSAULT WITH A DEADLY WEAPON

Dedicated to Jerry Eli Smith. Find a way to live your dreams. Mine came true when I had you.

Across the city I have a friend, in this
wide world with an endless end.
Yet days go by and weeks rush on,
and before I knew it 3-1/2 months
were gone.

Tomorrow I think I will get to talk to
you.
But tomorrow comes and tomorrow
goes, making the distance between us
grow and grow.

Son, Please Forgive Me for all my
mistakes.
Sometimes I didn't know what road
to take.
Fortunately we live in America, so
it's never too late. Changes we can
make.
You showed me how to take my hate
and turn it into something top rate.

Yes, across the city is my Son, a
special friend.
When I had problems you didn't
bend.
You stayed by my side till the very
end.

To laugh and live you'd remind me,
to take the time.
Remember the concerts we shared,
and going to Florida and eating pie
made from Lime.
Even it if was our last dime.

Our family was small, but you have
to admit together we went through it
all.
For seventeen years 24 hours a day
we were on call.
With you there no problem was ever
too tall.

So please when you get sad.
Shut your eyes and forget the bad.
Laugh at the good times we had.

You and I have no right to feel bad.
Touch your arms and legs, look in the
mirror. Then kick yourself in the rear,
and don't shed one tear.

You're the BEST!
That's why you'll pass this test.
Soon you'll be out with all the rest.
The Song by Prince "My Mother is
Never Satisfied"
You were only fourteen that night.
You're so bright sometimes your
mind is out of sight.

All the counselors know which kids
are right or wrong.
By the way they sing their song.

I LOVE YOU! ! You're part of me.
When you have pain mine's the
same.
When to me you lie, I die and forever
cry,
it makes me not want to try.

When it's all over and time for you to
pack.
At least the Son I lost for awhile will
be the one coming back.

I know at 17 in the army you wanted
to go, and get there know fast or
slow.

NEVER FORGET you had a choice
that day.
It was wrong, you're locked up and
we both must pay.

Gangs seem right till you get caught.
Now you have learned . . No amount
of money can your freedom be
bought.

When it comes to my SON I get
LOUD.
Yes I'M VERY PROUD.

Canadia Collins

Canadia Collins

CONTEMPLATION BEFORE FLIGHT: A MOON IS NOT FOREVER

The sun is for a longest time,
But the moon is not forever.
Our moon
Is somewhat lent to us, by
Some others from the heavens.
From old
Teachings we, the small-boned
people,
Did learn that, if great moon
ever should
Go away, then beneath the sands
We could rely on continued
length of survival;
The curse of red earth-dust
would be
On the outside of us, rather than
within.
—Thus,
From inside-out we must always
build, and
Never very likely the other way
around.
Near-forgotten
The soaring up to peaks, or at
least
Unafraidly playing music high-up
upon the tops
Of mountains—safely in highest
places!
Required's a moon of weightiest
power
for dependable
Lifting and sorting of a planet's
Unbreathable red earth-dust
—Setting out,
steadfastly
We, shall look toward the sun!
—For,
The moon, so undependably, may
someday
go away.

Marvin T Caton

BETH

Beth is the kind of girl that you very
seldom meet,
But when you do, you can expect a
great big treat.
She is twenty three and has real short,
but nice, blond hair,
And in the little time I've known her
she seems to really care.
Though she is handicapped she still
stands up and fights,
So if you have a problem, call her,
she knows all the rights.
Family problems have her overruled
to where she can't get out,
But if she does, no matter which way
she goes, she'll find the right route.
I like to be with her, even though
we've been together just one time,
And someday, I hope, that both of us,
together, will hear our bells chime.
When she is down and out and crying
and not in a very good mood,
She calls me and as we talk I hope I
don't say anything rude.
She is soft all over just like a brand
new baby kitten,
After we are married and we have
kids, she's going to need more than
one mitten.
Even though she is allergic to this
and that she still manages to have a
cat,
And you can bet your booties that in
their house there isn't one rat.
She's as light as a bird and umpteen
times as gentle as a dove,
And I haven't much room left, so, for
now, I'll say good night my love.

Love,
Always
Marvin T. Caton

Adrian M Jackson

THE ESSENCE OF YOU

This Poem is Dedicated to my wife Ethel D. Jackson

I look into your eyes and see a beauty
refined and bold,
A love so special, more precious than
the ancient sea scroll.

Like a wildflower growing beautiful
and free,
You are the glowing force of life
inside of me.

I go up against prejudice, evil and
jealousy,
A door that tries to block my way
daily.

But you are the strength that makes
me see,
That with you at my side there is
nothing I can not be.

Seeing the riches you have within,
Makes me feel most fortunate of
men.

My senses reel from the love you
emanate

My heart beats with a rhythm almost primate.

The air around you is peaceful and serene,
The love we share, of this some can only dream.

The Lord of life blessed me with you,
Forever and always my love shall be true.

Christopher Jones
CROSSROADS
. . . a mild bit of advice for the Wise: for as long as u live, please don't ever look me in the eye and tell me 'it's hopeless' or 'it's impossible' or 'you can't help but fail' and 'this is what you will do!'
for as sure as your words pierced my heart and shook my consciousness—without your predisposed alibi—there burns a flame within me—within my heart—strong enough to humble the mightiest institution to suffer unto me its greatest gift, the gift of knowledge.
there rumbles in me a desire mightier than the human condition compelling me to excel in the face of adversity.

for even when i'm down, i dream of the day i'm on my feet again. my glory days lie ahead of me. i suffer to decipher these gifts i have, to free them from my shoulders. unto him whom such gifts are bestowed, 'lo they remain a burden unto his soul, until their contents be revealed. i suffer these things. and if you dare mock me—in the midst of my struggles—daring me to endure, daring me to withstand his barrage of scrutiny, so shall i stand taller than any man before me, casting an ominous shadow over your lost, dark words. for i have arrived. at this crossroad. determined to take on my identity and the obstacles you lay before me. step aside. i have arrived.

Matt Strother
REFLECTIONS ON A KILL
The cold morning air stunned my skin
As I walked stiffly into the wind.
With the frost from the ground and the orange from the sun,
I paused for a moment because of the impressive one.

The startled animal captured my view,
As I continued onto the morning's fresh dew.
I heard a corruption that shattered my ears,
Then realized the effect of its long-tolling fears.

The limp furry creature lay on the ground,
Wishing its body not to be found.
And now, with the ten-point souvenir on the plaque,
I sit and wonder, is it really worth all of that?

Daniel Propst
THE BEST THINGS IN LIFE
I start to see the dawn break,
as the clouds thicken in a gray sea,
and the fields turn into a yellow infinity,
We travel to a routine destination for some,
and another step in life for others,
My thoughts are of good memories,
new friends and times to come,
I know now that the best things
in life cannot be seen, only given
and experienced,
Remember this and be forever content.

Dennis Junior
LOVE'S PRAYER
Dear, I pray in need,
You and I have reached that black agreement.
I know You have been shamed; so indeed,
To cause depression, failure, and resentment.
My Love, please return the gift of love to me.
I just love, truly, You; I repent.
My impure tears flow to be forgotten in my own pity.
Love from or to, whoever won't do.
Why don't You love me?
I, will give anything; just all there is to please.
Ask God to help You love me sincerely.
Teach me love me; this heartache to ease.
Oh! about life: I care no more; now freed.
I pray Love's Prayer, Dear, with newly found honesty.

Patsy Legg
A MOTHER'S LOVE CAN'T BE REPLACED, AND I THANK THE LORD
A mother's love can't be replaced,
And I thank the Lord that by his grace,
I was blessed with a mother like you.
To love and guide me my whole life through,

So, on this day that you gave me birth,
I'd like to say that to me you are worth,
All of the treasures this world has to offer
And thank the Lord that I am your daughter.

Joyce Leonhardt
TO THE SUPER BOWL
An Optimistic View
I'm going to send my poem in,
It's all about the Broncos and how they win.

A while back the count was 1 and 3.
Were they not playing like monkeys in a tree?

After the Colts came and played their game,
The Broncos were not too proud of their name.

What a score, what a score.
Come on Broncos, we want more.

Now the count is 5 and 5.
They're starting to look alive!

They must correct each and every mistake.
Get going guys—before it's too late!

Just wait, with all of them—including John Elway,
To the Super Bowl, they're going all the way.

With the help of Rich Karlis and his golden toe,
To the Super Bowl, the Broncos will go!!!

The K C Chiefs came to town and the Broncos did win.
Come on guys, do it again and again!!!

Loyd T Wardrup

Loyd T Wardrup
MUSICAL MYTHOLOGY

To: All music Teachers
To: All music lovers
To: All who love mythology

Apollo, god of all fine arts, divinity of the sun
Played on his golden lyre until the muses contest won
Pan, with his pipe, god of the shepherd's suit
Challenged Apollo's golden lyre with his reed, the flute
King Midas was the one who the contest judged
Being partial to the goat god's pipe, let himself be nudged
He gave the victory to the inferior reed who hears
Caught Apollo's wrath; and now he hath; great long asses ears
Pan won his bout; without a doubt, because his judge was Midas
Apollo lost, became so cross, the ears, they would not hide us
If you're the judge, don't try to nudge, the best must win the bout
The Midas' fears will grow the ears, if you are left in doubt
The piano received the golden harp when Apollo was rehired
The organ got the pipes of Pan, because the goat retired.

Perry D Long
MAGNIFICENT DESOLATION
The astronauts circled the moon,
First month after June;
Landed in that lonely lagoon;
And it was high noon
Somewhere on the planet earth!

Even a grasshopper would look good,
Or an ant, or a butterfly;
Magnificent desolation!
Was their first exclamation.
Praises went up from every nation;
Around the whole wide world.
The red, white and blue banners of
Beautiful America
In the gentle breezes were proudly
Waving, gracefully unfurled.

Standing in moondust
Walking in moondust
Running in moondust
We say again and again and again.
Magnificent Desolation

Denise Vakhshoorpour

Denise Vakhshoorpour
NOW YOU KNOW
So now you've read my every thought,
you've taken the wrappings of my deepest secret and ripped them apart.

In a way I'm angry that you've invaded my privacy.
In a way I'm relieved that you are able to understand me.

So now you've read my history,
you've seen my heart thru sad and glad;
the me I refuse to let anyone see.

Now you know that I really care,
if not for you, then for anyone who will share.

Now you know how much I really need
a flower to grow from just a seed.

Ms Gypsyfied
ELIMINATED (GET RID OF REMOVE, OMIT)
you have been eliminated
you are unneeded
unwanted
unknown
your warranty is up
your guarantee is expired
you are not valid any longer
I am forgetting you
I have forgotten you
go away now disappear
you are no longer here.

Sarah Hoagland
SALUTE
To those who work so hard,
To those who try.
We honor you.
To the seniors of the team,
Who for four long years have worked so hard.
Who have practiced many times.
Who have seen victory and triumph,
and loss and defeat.
We praise you.

You've come along way.
From freshmen to sophomores.
From sophomores to juniors.
From juniors to the well earned senior honor.
You were always there when the team needed you.
You provided the leadership of the team.
You're ready for the world.
You've learned so much.
You've worked so hard, for your moment.
Your moment is now and forever.
We will miss you in our hearts,
but in our minds we will always be with you.

Dorothy Johnson Jones
I AM A SNOW WHITE SWAN
Once I wandered through the wilderness called earth.
I wondered who I was and the reason for my birth.

I thought I was an ugly duckling and no one loved me.
I wondered long,
longing to be free.

Then one day I got a glimpse of my reflection in the sea of life.
Now I know the reason for my heartache and my strife.

In the beginning I was free from without and from within;
But one day I was captured by that old dragon called sin.

Now I know I am a Snow White Swan and I have every white feather in place.
I am a princess just waiting to see my Prince face-to-face.

I am just waiting in this broken-down vessel I call me.
I am a Snow White Swan and when this life is done,
My King Jesus will come and set me free.

Rives Randolph Jones IV
TAKEN
Look at me.
Can you not see it?
Observing you, I am speechless.
I daresay I would quake, were I not so baffled.
It is as if I were looking into a mirror,
Only to see myself; Such is the love that I am feeling.
But you look at me as if I were nothing.
Or, perhaps, is it that I cannot see myself?
Perhaps you are me.
I love you so much, that I have ceased to remember
The love that I have for myself.
So look, look closely, for I am fading fast.
And if you want me, then look into me!
See the warmth that surrounds my heart,
The warmth that you have provided and sustained,
The warmth that wants to engulf you in a conflagration.
Grasp it, if you dare,
For the blaze of passion is both short and sweet
And my soul aches to bathe in it's embers.
Do you see it?
The flame burns low, and I am smitten.

Charles M Garcia
THE TOUCH OF A CHILD
The touch of a child
From hand to the heart,
Feelings awaken,
Unbidden,
With a start.

What to do?
Reach out?
Hold back?
Emptiness filling
Where once there was lack.

Frightened,
Yet, thrilled.
Casual meeting,
Yet, somehow,
God-willed.

I'll open my heart
To the way the wind blows,
Leave it to Him,
And then, well . . . who knows?

Sarah Mongan
SWEET, FAMILIAR WORDS
Together we sit
In the porch swing,
Your aged hand is upon mine.

You're singing so sweetly
Those familiar words I love;
Your voice is gentle and kind.

The town is silent,
Our minds are at ease.
Back and forth we go.
Now and then you squeeze my hand,
As if to let me know—

That we should cherish
Our time on Earth
And never forget the memories;
Because life is just a short span of time
Between two eternities.

Peggy Ann Gould
BITTERNESS GONE
Trust you must
For it is not for you to say
Along come a day
When can I say
That I will feel your love
Close to my heart
When can I say
About my fear, my dear
When can I say
That it will leave me
Will it be when
I love for even a day

Rev Abb Israel Javine

Rev Abb Israel Javine
MY HOPE IN HIM

To my wife Mary, to Marilyn, Timothy, Castro and Jonathan our children, our grandson Xavier, LPN Monica Bates and all our Friends, with Love.

My hope in Him is growing strong
And I change everyday.
I'm beginning even to look like him
He's showing me the way.
And when the light afflictions come
The light is what I see.
That's when those old afflictions
Work glorious for me.
Always beholding as in a glass
His glory before my face,
The honeycone, no sweeter, is this
Hope that I see and taste!
My hope in Him is growing strong
And unto it I'm cleaving,
Believing not in what I see, but
Seeing what I believe, receiving.

Rhonda Lee Sparks
MOTHERS
Mothers are someone who can't be replaced
and you will always see love in their face.

When your world is ending she will be there
To pick you up and tell you, "I Care."

A mother and child, there is no greater love.

Though miles are between you, you are as close
As a hand and glove.

Though sometimes her hand is strong, her words
Of wisdom are never wrong.

She lets you make your own mistakes, but she
Is there to catch you just in case.

Her love is never ending and also never pending.

She will always be there to love and share
And no matter what, "She will always care."

Louise Gooden
A CHILD OF WAR
A child was sitting by the road,
His body cold and bare.
He must have cried many tears
Because no one seemed to care.
He had not eaten for many days,
But still he kept on trying.
Being there was his only way
To show us he was dying.
God must have heard his silent cry,
For soon a soldier passed near by.
He took the child in to his arms
As if to shelter him from harm.
The war had taken all from him,
His life was now so bare;
But God has shown His love once more,
The child now knows someone cares.
The soldier took him to a home
Where love and joy abound.
There no suffering or death was known,
Only love and happiness could be found.
Secure in the arms of his Father above,
So peaceful, the feeling, surrounded by His love.
No sounds of war exploding in his ears,
Only the soft touch of angels brushing away his tears.

Corine Morris
DANGER!
Danger!—Danger!—Everywhere;
We are made to wonder who really cares—
From what we see and what we know;
God is one where we can go.

Danger!—Danger!—in the streets;
So much crime that make us weep—
The rich man, the poor man—black and white;
The rate that crime is rising is out of sight.

Danger! To the young and old;
In the country and city streets—
You ask where is it safe;
Only Jesus is our hiding place.

The evils of dope are in our schools;
If only mankind would obey the Golden Rule—
Don't do to others what you don't want done to you;
Live and Love—Be honest and true—
Love God with all your heart;
Then the DANGER! in our world will surely depart.

Edith L Mott
ABOUT LOVE
Seeing with God's eyes
We should love our neighbors fine
'Cause that's the bottom line

Dear friend, it's true
Life is a little brighter
When I think of you

With God's way to live
With Jesus' loving hands to touch
Always willing to give

As we fly through pages
Ups & downs of life's bitter-sweet wages
Here's a love for ages.
Full of life and love
Blessings from above
Give and get a hug
The soul I know not
From body when begot—
Lord, I give you lot.

Joanna Peters
A FRIEND
A friend understands
A friend believes
A friend stands by you,
and never leaves
A friend can listen
A friend can talk
A friend goes with you,
on those long winter walks
A friend is by you,
in good times or bad
A friend is special
A friend is around
A friend is there when you feel down
A friend is funny
A friend is true
Can't you see, my friend
this friend is you

Vijay Raghav Rao
2001 A.D.
Granny has gone to the moon for a picnic
Daddy is back from heaven in a sputnik
Books and condoms wrapped in wool
My test-tube babe now goes to school

We have a mint in the heart of our mill
Where roulettes spin those wads at will
Our farms can grow the bombs with skill
We sow and reap with a mission to kill

The Garden of Eden is now on lease
To produce robots called Adams and Eves
Plenty abounds—but—'something' we miss!
I wish I know where lies this 'bliss'!

I go to the temple. I go to the church
To realms unknown I run. I search
I dig up the past. I chase the future

Peace eludes . . . Death awaits this creature . . .

Buried in the din in the debris of time
Few chimes still ring in an unbroken rhyme
"Not far dear! Just peep within
I dwell in you! Just seek within"

Jerri L Everman-Hupe
CHRISTMAS . . .
Christmas . . .
'Tis the season to be jolly
HO HO HO
It brings us closer to those we love
This is . . .
usually by golly.
For some, it brings warm hearts and cheer
For the rest of us, it's just a harsh reminder
of better years.
To be so young and know
that the best years are far behind
Is the saddest Christmas feeling
of any kind.
Merry Christmas
HO HO HO!

Marrion Etoris Thompson
IF I DIE TOMORROW

This poem is dedicated to my immediate family, Aunt Georgia and especially Ron for always believing in me.

If I die tomorrow
My death no grave defeat,
For the life I've led will surely make
My obituary a mere receipt.

I was born a poverty stricken child
Today called culturally deprived,
And fought this insurmountable dilemma
To accomplish what others had tried.

Gone from church hymns to disco whims
From birth to acute adolescence,
No more dependent or emotionally insecure
But an assured adult convalescent.

Sometimes a slow life, sometimes a fast life
At times reluctant with no ambition,
Maybe a good life, maybe a bad life
Maybe a life of perfect mission.

Good times came in spatches
Bad times endurably long,
Sometimes life's demands and pressures
Confused the right and the wrong.

I've robbed the cradle, I've robbed the grave
Done the ultimate and the unpredict-able,
Been grand feminist and moral sexist
Been vindictive and indispensable.

Each moment was spent in full
With little time for leisure or rest,
For I know without a single doubt
I've seen life at its very best.

So if I die tomorrow
All my debts and dues collected,
If there's any part of life I've missed
With death I'll feel unrejected.

Kenny Ray Smith
THIS SINGLE WHITE ROSE
One day in confusion while in the rain
I began to run to ease my pain
My heart felt broken as if all alone
I cried to God "where'd I go wrong?"
I ran and ran with not a care
Just hoping to find true peace somewhere
Running through these woods so far far away
'Twas then I noticed God led my way
I crossed a creek all covered by fog
Then decided to rest sitting on a log
But as I struggled getting to that place
Something grabbed my shirt with a sharp embrace
Tugging near my heart I couldn't get free
Like thorns of glory held on to me
As I looked down these thorns cried tears
Which seemed held in for so many years
They trickled so softly down to the ground
Then lowering my head here's what I found
With petals so beautiful so pure and white
And as I stared all things became quiet
It had blue tears falling upon it's leaves
As if it was crying "come hold me please"
Then I sat down and felt God's touch
As if that's what I've needed so much
After feeling God's touch I'm aware
He knows
He led me to
"<u>THIS SINGLE WHITE ROSE</u>"

Joyce G Stecher
OF TWO MINDS
One mind is a dancer whirling along the convoluted
Corridors of thought toward ever higher
Levels of consciousness and knowledge.
The other is a plodder, peering nervously around corners,
Glimpsing worlds yet to be explored,
Wanting to proceed, uncertain as to path.

Wise is the soul blessed with both minds,
For the dancer will ever push the plodder upward
Toward shining goals,
While the plodder will clutch at the dancer,
Forcing moderation and tempering speed,
Slowing it to enjoyment of all things,

Before Time dies.

Barbara Raines Pyles
SOMETIMES WE'VE GOT TO SAY GOODBYE
Sometimes we've got to say
goodbye
And just as many times,
we ask ourselves why.

But nothing can stop
this going away,
We have to face it,
day by day.

Our hearts will ache
and our eyes will cry
and every night,
we'll ask the Lord why.

We'll keep to ourselves,
the feeling and hide,
Wishing once more,
for them back by our side.

The days will go by
and the years, as they do.
Your memory will be with us
and you will be too.

The love that we shared
when you were here,
Will be remembered
with a tear.

A frown won't set
upon my face,
But my love for you
will take it's place.

Cynthia A Range
PROUD
I am young, gifted, and "yes" I am Black,
but because of my color do I have to lack?
I have the talent, the wisdom and courage
to accomplish whatever I put my mind to.
Color should have no bearing on what one can do!

I am Black and I am proud,
never ashamed among a crowd.
This is the time to stand and be strong,
so that our accomplishments will not take too long!

A change has to come, we must all stand together,
to make our situation become a lot better.
We have to make everyone
understand that God
created woman from the man.
We are two sexes made for the other,
not to be mistreated because of our color.

To mistreat another because of their skin
is discriminating and to God a sin.
Let us open us our eyes, along with our minds
and try to treat each other a little more kind.

I hope that I have helped someone see
that we can <u>all</u> live in this world more happy and free.
We are all unique in our own special way, let's
use that to make a better world someday.

Paul P Czech Jr
RESURRECTION
Die is but a word, nothing really dies!
All men are fools as I, without the right to judge:
But if I am wrong, I will be the first to admit my guilt.
I'll say all the days I spent on this earth, were
But existence, and all my life I lived in vain.
Being blind to all; and pretending to be a man,
While slowly shrinking into nothingness.
For God rules the earth, and my heart will sing repentance
That true love never knew.
Yet I can not do what other men do, I can not resolve
In putting asunder true love; then extoll on its blissfulness.
For I believe, that if God permits
That someday when my body stops its motion
That my soul will live on.
I'll live on in the minds of other men,
In the blue skies and passing clouds, in rolling oceans,
In the roses rare beauty, within the robins song,
Within the caressing showers and soft breezes,
And within the works that I leave behind,
And in all the things that are to remain available to man's vision,
Within the things I have truly loved in God's mansion.

Jorge De Jesús
WIND
I am looking out the window trying to feel the wind blow. I see a gorgeous figure that shows a magic touch. That magic is warm and tender the wind is blowing forever. I look up all around and I still see that image that is flowing around. I call it by its name in which is wind. It just continues blowing as nothing is on its way. I stretch my arms out and suddenly the wind stops. I felt something inside but I didn't realize what it was.

Richard DiVia
THE GREATER TRUTH
Time, with its' memories
Choke all we need and hold dear—
An often elusive vine
Left alone to flourish and
overpower
what true beauty it hides—
Some people are born to suffer—
To greatness—
To weather the vine and still
maintain a dignity beneath its
gnarled leaves—
To know the greater strength lies
not within this milieu—
But within ourselves—
It is—as once said—
the greater truth—
Not dabbled on porcelain—
But alive and vulnerable—
Fragile like an urn—
But resilient to mend—
That vine is pity that fades a soul
like fine artwork—
But like fine artwork can be
restored
To what inspiration first
conceived it—
created it—and made it
memorable.

Daniel N Escalante
THOUGHTS OF SPRING
The Green Green Grass, that lies around us. The blue sky that sparkles in our eyes. The butterflies, and beautiful birds, that words cannot describe. The wonderful wind that breezes through like the spring that just went by, but don't be sad, it's not that bad for spring will soon be back.

Constance Lee Evans
LONG AGO—STILL NOW
Oooh you left me so many years ago
I never forgot you—our love grew so
I heard not a word Then one day you

called
I almost died and ooh how I cried

We got together and spoke of the days
When we ran through the park and played in the hay
Our hearts got together again as before
Even though you were married you still loved me so

My days had a meaning, as long ago
You came back to me and the nights weren't so cold.
You told me to wait, you'd be back to stay—but you lied eye to eye
and your heart went astray.

Why did you come back? Just to see me cry
Why did I think your love hadn't died
I thought we would never fall so apart
And I love you so much with this broken heart
Now as long ago—still you lie as I cry
'Cause I love you so—as long ago.

Brenda White
MY BEST FRIEND
There is a man who's part of my life
He's my husband and I'm his wife,
I love him more than I could ever say,
So I try to show him each and every day,

He has a special place forever in my heart
I hope in this life we never have to part.

But one day I'm afraid that we will
But even death, my love, will not kill,

Sickness will come and one of us will have to go.
But which one is first I'll never know.
But I'll always love him until the bitter end.
Because he has been my lover, partner, and friend.
I know a love like ours will never end,
It won't break only bend.

James M Taggart
THE MAKER OF THEE . . .
O luminary sun of crimson host
A radiant painter of limitless hue
Morning daystar I desire thee most
Thy sky of monochrome snow-shade blue
('nd meltest the frost upon the rue)

Our sky a woven enigma of divine blend
A tranquility fractured the nested sing
Colours rich the visioned tones transcend
As intertwined fronds that autumn bring
('nd bringest to light the rite of spring)

And a child wept beneath the willow-tree
That the sun beneath a raging sea
But ceased his weeping, weeping
That his star but sleeping, sleeping
('s the sparkle-truth thou art keeping)

And as the eventide ebb into cloudless dawn
A faithful wind did gale and was gone
With doubts damp tear the north draft away
And dryed the child's lamentful bray
('nd I be that of this child a day)

And the wind to branch ripple a prophets words
As the drifted song of calm nested birds
And each dusty rose falls the same soil
As each aged child falls in windy coil
('nd then face the sun of all, not to boil)

O luminary sun of crimson host
Brightest artist of limitless hue
Brilliant daystar I desire thee most
Monochrome canvas of snow-shadow blue
(Of meek to seek the maker of . . . you)

marva warrick weaver
JESUS REMEMBERS—SENIORS
We came into the world—
A little boy—and a girl—
With regret—our families watched us grow.
Soon—we left home, to go on our own—
Looking back—over the years,
Someone was always there,
Now—it seems, as we grow older—
There's no one to care.

Jesus—you made us—you alone would know,
How to comfort—in our times of woe!
Family and friends—have forsaken,
But—you said—you'd never let go,
So—we know that you are with us—
And that's all we need to know!

Thank you—for thinking of us,
At a time—
When the world is passing us by,
We have given—our all to our children—
But—you have given—more!

Katie Trudgett
HER FRIEND

Dedicated to: His love and her love, Their love, Mom and Polar.

His eyes and nose are black as night,
His hair beautiful, long and so white.
He's just right.
He's just like mine, this was her wish,
I took him from the prison and to her with a kiss.
His love for her you could plainly see,
His love is pure, and for her only.
They grew to love and cherish each other.
They did nothing separate, not without the other.
She left him with me, 'cause I will take care,
For she had to leave town and knew I would be there.
Now this little guy and mine had their own fun,
When they were together they would bounce, play and run.
But her friend would stop and go to the window,
He would sit there and wait till she would show.
The happiness in his eyes and hers you could see,
To be together again, their love was clear to me.
As time goes on a year has past,
Life goes on and now Christmas at last.
It's New Year's Eve morning as I lay in my bed,
Now this is the heartbreaker, many tears I have shed.
The front door was open, when it should have been closed.
Now this her friend thought was great, and ran into the road.
I heard her friend hollering, then she looked into the street,
She said, "OH GOD NO," and I knew, as I jumped to my feet.
I opened my bedroom door, and it was all there,
He, still, in her arms and her look of despair.
He was still hanging on as we rushed to the doctor,
They tried to save him, they did what they ought to.
His young little body, fragile and so weak,
His loving little soul slipped away, as he went to sleep.
Her heart was shattered, as mine had been too,
As she cried over his little body, that was loved so true.
I dragged her away with all of my might,
She kept saying, "I don't believe it" as we cried through the night.
Needless to say our New Years was shot.
We lost one of our friends, one that meant a lot.
She told me later, when she could keep from crying,
That her little friend held his head up from where he was lying.
Till she had picked him up, then he went into shock.
He hung on for her arms of security, which meant such a lot.
Now if you haven't figured out this story so far,
It's of love and heartache between my mom and her dog Polar.
This little dog with a big heart of gold,
We miss him so much, his memory we forever hold.
Whenever I bring this true story to mind,
It breaks my heart all over again and I cry!!

Lenore Cooper Clark
RETREAT
Come now with me into this darkened room,
Shut out the cares that mar the cluttered day,
The noisy freeways and the tasks that loom,
The jostling crowds along the busy way.
Soft music or the whispered words of love
Alone shall be the sounds we hear tonight,
The silence and the darkness all above
Give contrast to the outer scene of blight.

Cool fragrant sheets invite the body's rest,
The loved one's body close is sweeter still,
We sink into a sleep divinely blest,
And let the soul's renewal drink its fill.
Whatever morning's light may bring of care,
This night with you will make it joyous fare.

Patricia A Sharkey
WINGS OF LOVE

This poem is dedicated to my dear children: Michael, Matthew, Daniel and Timothy

Oh butterfly, in all your magnificent beauty,
If I should, just for one fleeting moment,
Put a halt to your freedom
And even gently imprison your fragile wings in my palms,
You would never fly again.

So it is with love,
Like a lovely butterfly,
Imprisoned—
It may lose it's wings forever.

Catherine Buckson
THE ROSE
The rose you gave me
is dried and dead,
Just like our love
is now.
It once was alive,
Like the feeling we had.
Somehow I thought
I could bring it back;
But my tears just formed
A puddle around it.

Meriam Bush
LITTLE THINGS IN LIFE
It is the little things in life
Count them one by one
That makes our task worth while
When'er our day is done.

It is the little things in life
Wherever you may look
Maybe just some precious moment
In which to read a book

It is the little things in life
Wherever you may roam
When you have your children with you
To make a happy home.

It is the little things in life
Just a call on the phone
That can make or break your day
When you are all alone.

It is the little things in life
Maybe just a letter
So don't put off these little things
That make life so much better.

Sheila M Crozier
TO YOU, OH LORD, I GIVE TO THEE
To you, Oh Lord, I give to thee
All the things that matter to me.
In charge of my life I cannot be
For I am yours for all to see

Take these things I offer thee
My family and friends, all of me.
Work in your time and your will to

be
To your Glory and Honor for the world to see.

Dorothy J Kowalski

Dorothy J Kowalski
COUNTRY CURTAINS

This poem is dedicated to my dear and true friend, Agnes F Cutcher.

Country curtains with embroidery
Ruffles, fringes and lace.
Displays a window dressing most refined
Bow tiebacks to keep them in place.

Country imported Swiss tambour
With flowers and deep scolloped borders.
A band of grained ribbon skillfully
Appliqued with mitered corners.

Country curtains bring Victorian warmth
Enhance every room in the home.
Each with their special trim
Dramatic with their color tone.

Country old fashion Cape Cod
French full ruffles and traditional.
With charm and elegance of centuries past
A loved classic, crisp look of colonial.

Rebecca Walker Adams
MANIPULATION
I play with your mind like the master of games.
I play with your time like the master of names.
I strike and you bleed—
I want and you need.
For all that I know—
Is all that you do.
And the core of your soul
Is like the shine on my shoes.

Ronda C Jardine
THE SECRET PLACE

To my children, Jacqueline and Jordan

Every child has a secret place where he or she can go,
But only few can see it, for it is a secret place, you know.
They can go alone or they can take a friend,
With the imagination, there is just no end.

In the secret place there are many beautiful things,
Lady-bugs and dandelions and clear running streams.
Blue-green grass and dozens of kinds of flowers,
And trees that stand as tall as ancient castle towers.
Speaking of castles, they too, stand there.
Among them, you'll find a unicorn, a Pegasus and even the March Hare.
Over by the lake, you can stand and watch the fish,
Or look down a well, and make many a wish.

On the edge of a cliff, you can stare over yonder.
The beauty of what you see sparks the mind to wonder,
Why is such a magical place hidden by a wall?
It is quite a shame it can't be seen by all.

For if everyone could see such a beautiful place,
There would surely be a smile on every single face.
That would mean no more abuse, no more prejudice, not even war.
All of that would stay on the other side of the door.

Yet if everyone could see the Secret Place,
With its doors open wide.
Then the children who need this secret place,
Would have no place to hide.

Michael Anderson
POPS

I remember Papa. The fourth of Julys—the backyard cookouts, steamers, Nana's potato salad and spitting watermelon seeds at my cousins. Firecrackers exploded by punks down the alley. The town parade. Walking to the commons for the fireworks show. And Papa carrying me back to the house on his shoulders.

I remember Papa. The Christmas eves—the white plastic tree nobody liked. The millions of relatives. And Papa getting red boxer shorts with pink hearts. Everyone laughing, drinking and singing.

I remember Papa. The Sunday dinners after church. Papa's rolled shirt sleeve revealing his faded anchor tattoo. Papa cutting the roast. Nana's addictive sponge cake and apple pies.

I remember Papa. Summers, always painting the house—that same yellow color. The endless ballgames on the transistor radio. Trips to the movies in his white '64 Dodge Dart. The quarter I'd get just for being a good kid.

I remember Papa. For not saying good-bye. For bringing a silence to my life. And for taking away a lot of the fun.

Paula Marie Bittel
MY SPECIAL AUNT
I was blessed with a special aunt,
Who never says I can't.
She's always doing for others and me,
And she even likes tea.
Her favorite past times are cards, cooking and to read,
And sometimes she might plant a little seed.
She looks great in anything she wears,
And she's very partial to her rocker recliner chair.
Her house is as clean as can be,
Everyone ought to come and see.
A special lady she is by far,
Here she comes now, driving her big car.
She gives real good advice,
And she even likes rice.
For to know her is to love her,
And I certainly do.
This little poem is for you,
Now you know from who!

Deborah René Bowers
I'LL BE YOUR FRIEND
If ever you are lonely
and down on your love,
Remember that I'm always here
just look up above.

You never have to worry
that your call won't be heard,
Just speak your mind
and I'll hear every word.

I'll share your happy times
your sad ones too,
Never fret and don't forget
I'll be here for you.

Early in the morning
when the sun begins to rise,
I'll be right beside you
when you open your eyes.

And when the night falls
with the stars shining bright,
Take the time to think of me
because I'm your guiding light.

Your worries are mine
and your happiness too,
I'll always be here
I'll be your friend, forever true.

Cindy Lewis

Cindy Lewis
DON'T GIVE UP WHAT YOU DREAM FOR
Don't give up what you dream for,
You've got to learn to get off the floor.
You've got to learn to face your fears,
You can't just hide in a puddle of tears.
Life isn't always a bucket of smiles,
You've got to help push it through all those miles.
Life my friend is what you've got,
It may be a little, it may be a lot.
One more thing—Dreams can come true,
But that, my friend is up to you.

Shannon Manns
THE BEQUEST
As maturity crept up slowly
It was gained quickly.
And the blue-eyed
Honey blonde "princess"
Ruled the new generation.
And the thick black soot
Blanketed
The deserted streets.
The evilness of dark
Stalked the children
Like a panther
Lurking
In the shadows
Waiting
For its prey.
The muffled moans of
The children
Heard
Ringing through the ears of man
And yet he, who caused such destruction
Could only bow his head in shame
And cry
For forgiveness
After the tragedy
Of war.

Debra Maxey
I WILL NEVER FORGET YOU
I miss you so much each day goes by and it feels like an eternity and it really hasn't been that long ago.

Each morning when I wake you are on my mind as fresh as the morning dew and all day long no matter what I do you are still there on my mind. It doesn't matter who I see all I can see is the fading memory of your face on theirs.

At night when I go to bed you are there in my dreams.
And that is why I will never forget you!

Amalie G Spellman McCarthy
OCTOBER
My worshiping altar
Is stripped bare.
Bare as on Good Friday
And it is only October.

So I raise up this
Scintillating chalice
Of earth's harvest.
Of Bread and Wine of Life

Good Friday is a while away.

M Marie Maxwell
SHARD OF HEAVEN
Compare our love not to the rose
Whose fragile splendour soon doth fade,
Nor to the everchanging sun
Whose glories oft' the clouds may shade.

Compare it not to diamonds bright,
Though flawless they may seem;
For what eternal value dwelleth
In their cold, hard gleam?

Nor to the mighty mountains
Whose foundations oft' may quake,
Compare this firm devotion
Rooted far too deep to shake.

'Tis a shining shard of heaven

With a holy fire instilled.
By the unchanging, everlasting One
Its very life was willed.

So behold it with a reverence,
Ye peoples far and near.
In silent, solemn wonder stand
When of its bloom you hear.

Allen Hipolito Mayor
EXPECTATION OF AN EXPECTANT SOUL
Do not expect your expected something
from your expected person who does not expect you
Because this expected person might expect something
from you which you do not expect this
unexpected something from him;
Expecting your expected person who does not expect you
would you only expect that which
is unexpected . . .
Instead, just wait for an unexpected person
who expects you on an unexpected time
and unexpected place,
And your expected something
would result more than what you expect
of an expected one.

Raymond M Carreau
THERON
Star-crossed lovers haunting space and time—
Demigod spawn of an enchanted emerald sea.
I, the king of the mystic race—
And you, the queen of fantasy.

With a stardust tiara for a bridal crown,
A skein of iridescent moonbeams for a gown—
You raced beside me among the stars:
Ganymede, Altair, and the twin Centaurs.

Galaxies, oh many galaxies, we roamed about—
Tossing stardust and sunbeams to and fro,
Re-arranging star-laced heavens—
In the olden time, long ago.

Among perfect worlds designed for our own—
You became obsessed, a beautiful foe.
Fought we a nameless war ordained by fate—
Where the glittering-tailed meteors glow.

Oh, how we challenged the universe—
You and I,
In the olden time—
So very long ago.

Della Ann Wallace
I LOVE YOU, BABY

To Thomas Earl Turner:
I Love YOU, Baby, Dellann

I love you, baby
And I miss you all the time.
My life is empty without you for the most part
And my heart is a dead stone.
I just can't shake your love from my memory
And the heat of your last kiss still burns my tongue.
I've been branded by the touch of your hand
And reborn in the fires of your love.

A thing newly made under your instruction
Alone without your guiding hand.
Yearning for the strength of your body
To sweetly build me up again.

Your eyes are like pools of blue water
Covering me slowly up
Until I am wet and shaking
And drowning in your sweet love.

The realm within your arms
Is like the enchanted land
That I stepped into once unaware
Of the sweet pleasure that I would come to there.

I have tasted your sweet flesh
And now I hunger at the thought
Of being filled by your desire
Steaming, sweetly hard, and hot.

Wendy Padilla
THE INHERITORS
Icy winds of constant winter
blow across the tundra of our land
as we the vanquished bow our heads
before the hourglass of sand

A yesteryear of troubles
unmet by those beneath our feet
fall as shadowy reminders
of what was once bequeathed

One step ahead of desolation
while on our shoulders sweeps the past
We are the inheritors of your world
and perhaps the very last

Renate Schuetz
WITHIN ME
Within me lies a garden
I share with very few.
A garden filled with happy things,
With love and dreams come true.
My garden is beyond compare,
Visible to those who love and care.
My garden is like paradise
So perfect and serene.
My garden is a dream come true,
And truly do I thank the Lord
Thank Him . . . for sending you.

Gary L Thomas I-DAV
GOD AND THE AMERICAN VETERAN
When our beloved country was founded, our Forefathers fought to preserve, our Heritage based 'In God We Trust," by uplifting his name, from this tiny planet, Earth.

But seems like our lifestyles have changed, nothing is held sacred in this present life, because we have forgotten our American Veterans, those who suffered, bled and died.

But there was one before us, one who shed his Blood upon a rugged tree, the Begotten and Supreme sacrifice of God, His Name, Saviour, Justice and Prince of Peace.

Sam W Scantlan
OUR SPECIALS AT CHURCH
You musicians go sit down,
We have ting-a-ling on tape
Which we purchased at the store,
It will go up high and hesitate.

Next year we will tell the singers
To go sit down because we have a tape,
That lingers long and high,
Expensive, first-class, and in good shape.

The next year we will tell the preacher
To go sit down and listen well;
We have a tape—a sermon great
That was made to tape and sell.

So, we will go to church in style,
Sit down and quickly play the tapes.
No wasted time—no one to pay,
We'll hear the greatest voices pray,
—And all coming from behind the drapes.

Wardell Brown

Wardell Brown
I SEE BLACK, AND WHITE
Oh how sad it is to say to another,
You can't drink out of my cup,
because you're another color.

Irene Whitney
SLEEP ON MY LOVE
Sleep on my love, until the end of time
May the Lord bless you, and keep you in his care.
I remember your wonderful, blond hair.
Your eyes of heavenly blue,
Your heart so loving and true,
Your winning smile,
I will love you until the end of time.
The warmth of your embrace,
As I looked upon your face.
I loved you from the start
You will always have a special, place deep within my heart.
You were my first and only love,
As the stars in heaven, that shine above.
My love for you will never end,
This message to heaven,
I do send.
Sleep on my love

Nancy Hopkins Tier
ONE THING NEEDFUL
Man stands upon the poles of earth,
Yet one thing needful—second birth.
He marks and streaks the upper air,
But is no higher than his prayer.
And now at home in outer space,
He may not know his need of grace.
How mighty is the mind of man,
But one thing needful, God's own plan.

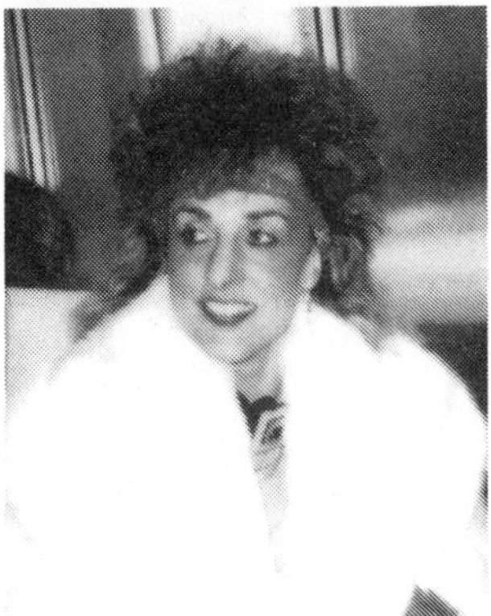

Michelle A Ventress

Michelle A Ventress
ADMIRATION

This poem is dedicated to my loving father, Thomas Lee Young. His memory will always be in my heart.

My Dad was the Best
Always ahead of the Rest
Always Confessed, and he'd Understand
He Was Some Kind of a Man

With Jesus By his Side
He Did everything with Such Pride
Remembering Back through the Years
Sometimes Brings Tears.

All the good times we've Shared
I've Always Known How much he Cared
Always Making me feel I Was Number one
Never once Made me feel he'd Rather Had A Son

I Looked at him With Such respect
Never felt the Fear of Neglect
I Wish He Was Here today
There would be So Many Things I'd Want to Say

Things That Were taught to me,
Would Never be,
If it wasn't for my Dad always Talking to me

I Think of my Dad everyday
Even though he's 17 years, Away
Used To Cry to get my Way
But To my Dad That Was OKAY

No one Could ever take His Place
For He is Exception In this Case
One Thing I will Never forget,
That My Dad was Heaven Sent

Tammy Barlow May
MY PRECIOUS CHILD

To my precious child Daniel Justin, Born 12-31-88. God has found you innocent. I love you son.

The seed of life within me, the God of love bestows
That no man taketh from the womb,
the heart in which it grows.

The child I bear within me, a babe to be born of sin
My Jesus hast prepared the way, for your life to begin.

I could not give you up "save face," for I knew my love was true
I broke the law of my God, The price I paid was you.

As I carry you inside my womb, my precious child to be
My Jesus hast prepared the way, for you to be with me.

My only prayer be for you, That God's mercy shines enough
That you will know dear little one—Momma just couldn't give you up.

Norma J Miller
THE MEMORIES YOU GAVE TO ME!
I'll always remember the
fun we had,
Our walks down the road,
and our lonely talks.

I would give you a cookie and
your eyes would say, "I
Love you!"

The many times we would go
to McDonald's and I'd get
you a cone,
And then you would get most
of my own.

I know someday we will meet
again,
And then I can hold you in my
arms again.

So till that day, I'll always
have the memories you gave
to me.

Maia Myrrh
HEBREWS
I understand that movement of the race
In prayer the body perpetuates to and fro
Those utterances conceived by backing
"Pray pray
We will attain
(the holy way)
Stay stay
Another genetic day
(o long away)
ago
King of the sky and air
(fair)
swaying forward Lilies touch thee twice
(nice)
It is in natural inclines
(rhymes)
I ride thy heart and crest
(nest)
I lean an age and age
(sage)
swaying backward My back shadows the
yoke
(hope)
Prophets song of the dead
(bread)
Echoes a flat tune
(croon)

Tahera Terane Grayer
I WUZ THERE
In life's difficult and embarrassing wayz, I wuz there.
Feeling unwanted and seeming everything wuz unfair.
In life's embarrassing and foolish times, I wuz there.
Watching as people stared with a cold-hearted glare.
In life's most lonely and unloved times, I wuz there. Longing for a person to talk to and one who would care.
In life's moments of trickery and lying, I wuz there. Being used, refused, and gullible to every dare.
In life's saddest and most depressing times, I wuz there. Feeling intense pain and crying more tears than one could bear.
In all of life's foolish loves, I wuz there. Trying to work out difficult times, feeling foolish and dumb, feeling lonely and unloved, being used and lied to and cryin' a million tears.
I had only wished that I wasn't there.

John Coleman
BOUND IN CHAINS

This poem is dedicated to the glory of God.

In the beginning this man was beauty,
But in the end his beauty lost.
He lived life on a love theme,
And died on a dogwood cross.
His torture had no mercy.
Yet his love for man not tossed.
He lived life with such perfection,
They killed a man without fault.

Jesus is the man I speak of,
He bought our sins with blood.
People ask for forgiveness,
And be washed in a crimson flood.
A life was given for everyone,
But not given in vain.
Jesus has the key my friend,
He'll unlock your chains.

Elliott
CONTINENTAL DRUMMER
Continental Drummer, Continental Boy
going to see the war's not a toy
you know you have a gun
and the war's not yet begun
Continental Drummer, Continental Boy

You know the war's not a toy
beat out that rhythm
Continental Boy
you know you have not yet one
so feel that joy of perspiration

You know you're not a Yankee Doodle Guy
and you are not a spy
and you know you're a Continental Boy
and that peace like war is not a toy.

Continental Drummer is what you are
going away from home, it's not that far
take that last step and you will not last long
so take your drumstick and beat out a song

Continental Boy you know you have a gun
you know also that the war has just begun
Continental Drummer beat that song
let the war begin
Do you know that using that gun is a sin

Doris Clark
GOLDEN HEARTS
A Golden Heart
A Golden day
A Golden love
is here to stay

A Golden moment
will mark the day
A Golden Melody
will always play

A Golden Bell
will sound
its chimes
Our love will
last through
all times

A Golden hope
of another day
When you bring
your love to stay

The End

Keith Coursey
BREAKING THE BALL AND CHAIN
I saw two men in a park
One was white one was dark
They clasped hands and hugged in joy
The men were still there so was the boy

I asked the man of white
How he could see past the bloodshed bays
The long fighting for the south days
His property vanquished his empire in fade
And all the comrades that died under the blade

Look at the man he said
Look at his eyes see the Spirit
I had to join up for I did fear it
He is my brother the image of Adonai
This kind of wall crashing is why Jesus died

I asked the man of ebony
When the whip has licked your back
How can your forget this terrible attack
How may you forgive a pride stomped in the dirt
The separation of family surely the severest hurt

He wept to me
I forgive for I have been forgiven
I live because the power of hate has been driven
Jesus broke my ball and chain
His blood is the cleansing rain

Vickie Guinn
IF ONLY FOR A WHILE

To Larry Erickson—who has gone away, but whose memory never will.

My love for you started out
when I was just a child,
Every time I thought of you
I saw you when you smiled.

At times I thought it was puppy love
and it would go away,
But it has been so many years
I now know it's here to stay.

I've often wondered how you'd react
and the things that you might say,
If only you knew the thoughts of you
that tear at me each day.

I don't want to have this love for you
I don't want to see your smile,
I just hope one day it will go away
If only for a while.

Elva Mae Wilson

Elva Mae Wilson
A MOTHER'S PRAYER

To my children Kathleen, Billie June, Vincent, Roger and Esther with love.

Dear Lord, as you must know,
without my saying so,

I love my children so much more
than mere words can convey.

So, please, I pray, be with them each
and every day, as they traverse life's
pathway.

Help them to bear the many burdens
of this earthly life,
With all its worries, cares and strife!

And I ask of you, Dear Lord above
Please send them their share of health
and joy, happiness and love!

Please let them know how much you
care and that you are always there,
When they come to you in prayer.

Help them to put their faith and love
and trust in you my Lord Divine,
As I did so many years ago in time.

Charlotte Michael Stratton
DESIRED SPIRIT
if my spirit is meek, quiet, then my soul knows it's cold outside. for me it's still a dream, that I dream and humble myself to a great love, to give me the cold outside I desire. but yet what I desire seems to be a part of me, all the sun, bleeming, blasting ragging light for I can not see. It even covers the love I feel just for a moment but the one that I love holds back some of the Sun, yet still it seems I'm part of the sun that my love shall make cold some day.

Glenda M Francis
LISTLESS EYES

The poem is dedicated to two special people: my daughter, Terisha Lopez, who plays a major part in my drive to succeed in life and my aunt, Christina De Foe, for her undying patience and love.

Through his eyes, the world is the most beautiful, most ornate place to

live, to experience, and to indirectly own.
For he was endowed with many attributes which even the greatest of all mankind can not dispute.

"Yes, it is my world," he says
"I create what others can not."
"I feel what others can not."
"I see what others can not."
"Yes, it is my world."

He takes nothing for granted, and in return he is blessed with the finer qualities of life.

Now he knows the true value of living; for he's been blessed with yet another chance.
He takes not the resonance of chirping birds for granted.
He takes not the redolence of Autumn for granted.

"Yes, it is my world," he says
"I create what others can not."
"I feel what others can not."
"I see what others can not."

You see, he's no ordinary man; just a blind man!

Kenneth D Patton
IN A MUSEUM
In a museum life is like a dream that seems to feel so real

In a museum you can see what used to be the mummy is a real scream that seems so keen not mean

In a museum you can see knight of old so bold in the rusty trusty armor that knight might give you a fright

In a museum you might phone that you seen a bone from a dinosaur or czar that was a star so far

In a museum you might see some master painting of Remington oh what fun, rustle what muscle, of Rembrandt or Portrait of Grant or of Michel angelo eating a tangelo what a fellow, or Gauguin so gran, of Monet with a net I haven't seen him yet, or even me, or some other work of art from the heart that your heart to pound with resound

In a museum you see an original manuscript or an aboriginal, kept in a crypt, or a poet such as Whittier with wit, Poe what a poet, yours, or mine, so fine, Kipling that did ring, T. S. Eliot got hot, or Shakesphere did get in gear or another poet did knowit, or perhaps a great novel that Jules Verne did earn and learn or some other great wrighter wrote.

In a museum you might see something reminding you of when the West was best but to me it used to be when I was a cow boy I had some joy I'd straddle the saddle and ride the range with pride I'd stride

In a museum you might see a castle grand without a hassle some might be a castle right?

In a museum you might see a sabre tooth tiger long and strong a sloth a bear with fair hair or a wooly mammoth standing cooly there
In a museum you could see stars or cars and planets might be made of granite right in the night you can plan it

In a museum you can see most all man's history is not a mystery in the fall or on a wall that is all, you could have ball

In a museum you can see nature's wonders no not blunders, rocks that sock you in hock, animals past and present a pheasant or a bird that is the word

In a museum I'm sure you will see um and many more things that they store galore

So come with me to see um and we could have a scream in a museum

bruise
ON STREETWALKING
through Aging skin pores where the cold cuts deep
through this drolldrum night where the Fear must sleep

"there are no reasons why,
love . . ."

into the melting Fire she must walk
into his arms, Falling woman

"desire burns us and keeps us
warm . . ."

this sullen night, the Fallen morn
her streamsea laughter imploding glass

"magdalene, walk the streets with
me . . ."

the mountainsilent towers seem so high, touching the sufferringsky
closing in—nights like this were made for walking

"could I wrap her in my
dreams . . ."

nature. woman. softly call.
pierce the Silence of the Fall

"death will separate us, hush my
love . . ."

through the sweetdesertskin pours love's mortality
the sad flesh of Woman shapes this wounding street

"there are no reasons. why, love?"

[and on that night, he never stopped to speak to anyone till the stormy sea swallowed him in . . .]

Anna L Bold
OOH OOH OOH I LOVE YOU
Ooh, ooh, ooh, I love you
Be my little dee dee do
Come along and dance with me
Be my little honey bee
Let's just walk along the sea
I love you and you love me

Jeanne Cusick
DEAN
Dean Mayday was thirty-five years old.
His wife, Mary Sue, kissed him on the cheek
every morning.
His children, Paul, Tony, and Suzy, poured his juice
every morning.
His company car, a Volvo, drove him to work
every morning.
He was back in suburbia by 5:33
every afternoon.
Except for this one.
His wife, Mary Sue, called the police.
His children, Paul, Tony, and Suzy, cried.
Dean felt nothing.

Al Smyth worked in the city.
He yelled at his secretary, June
every day.
He drank four martinis at lunch
every day.
He was late back to work
every day.
Except for this one.
His secretary, June, called the police.
His workers worried what he could've done.
Al looked back at the 35 year-old man his intoxicated car had just hit.
Al kept driving.

Tamara Carlson
FIRE IN THE FOREST
There's a fire in the forest, what could I say,
I took a deep breath and began to pray.
I said "Dear Lord, please let it stop;
Before everything gets burned up."
I could smell smoke, I said "Oh dear——
I hope the fire isn't so near."
My sisters and brothers and I were afraid,
that our legs began to shake.
The sky was pitch gray and covered with smoke,
All you could see was a big orange glow.
A sprinkle of ashes fell on our hands,
We ran inside and told our Dad.
The very next day we looked at the sky,
It really cleared out, it wasn't very bad.
There's another fire somewhere out there,
I don't really think that's very fair.
But when it gets near the big pipeline,
that's when everybody's gonna hop in line.
Well, this is the end of my fabulous rhyme
I hope everybody has a great time! !

Antoinette Barbosa
DREAMS
If I should ever have a dream of my own today,
Don't ever let them take it away.
For my dream is the only thing I have left for my world to see.
Constructive criticism is what they do to my dreams that I have.
When they do that, they just don't realize that they're hurting me so deep inside.
I've given to this world the faith that life moves on.
But what happens when everybody's sad?
People in homeless homes, broken homes just from a simple divorce.
Suicides, just because nobody cares!
It doesn't seem worth it .
So my dreams I hope to keep.
So this world will not cheat me out of what I want.
Forever my dreams will go on.
Until the day I die.
I can promise you this, I have a dream to keep until eternity!

Kim Rowlett
TO LIVE A DREAM
He put his hand
On my shoulder
and said,
Rise little girl
and get out of
bed.
I will take you up
to where dreams
live;
Where fantasy abides
And where dreams
and man
Shall never die
Where reality does
not exist
Yet is there
then he turned to me and said
Come with me to Hell
To the place that only
the dead go.
For they dared not dream
Only someone truly evil can live
here.
All around you, you see
What was once living and
free.
Yet now we're surrounded by the
rotting corpses of the dead
Who dared not dream
For life is not as life would
seem
For life my child is
only a dream.

Nancy Poitras
A LOVER'S ODE TO SAILING
Oh my little sailboat
Sitting in the sea
Silently awaiting the joy of you and me.
Here we come my sailboat
Two who love the sea
Two who love the sound you make
mating wave to wake.

Tack the jib
Steer the sail
Balance bow and stern
Keep an eye to left and right
And mind the captain firm.

Oh my little sailboat sitting in the sea
Lovingly I rub your bow
And caress your mainsail threads
While you in kind must brace your bowls
As we balance bow to stern
To keep the movement graceful and keep the rudder firm.

Oh my little sailboat sitting in the sea.
Seducing like an ancient skiff
What joy you give to me.

Roseann J D'Antonio
REACHING OUT
Reach Out For The Stars,
For They Only Appear Far Away.
Take It Step By Step, Each And Every Day.
Don't Worry, Because It Will Only Bring Fear;

Put Positive Thoughts In Your Mind,
For The Negative Ones Aren't So Kind.
If Your Expectations Don't Work,
Remember That You Didn't Fail;
It's Just One Closer Step Towards
Reaching Out For The Stars.

Margaret Van Dyke
WHISPER OF SPRING
Did you hear, do you know?
Was that a bird, who told you so?

The whisper of spring, freshness in the air,
Tell us now that spring is everywhere.

Many colors do unfold, as the flowers come to a bloom.
And the green of the leaves make us all a rainbow room.

Another year has come and gone—to bring new health and hope.
So may we always be thankful to God above, for all His love.

Remembering the year ahead, will bring us color,
With newness and hope, for all of us to adore.

J P Maloney
HE CANNOT READ HIS TOMBSTONE WHEN HE'S DEAD
He cannot read his tombstone when he's dead
If with pleasure you are viewing any work a man is doing.
If you like him or you love him tell him now, don't withhold your appreciation
till the parson makes oration, and he lies with little lies on his brow. For no matter how you shout it, he won't really care about it.
He won't really know how many tears you shed.
If you think some praise is due him,
Now is the time to slip it to him, For he cannot read his tombstone when he's dead.
More than fame and more than money,
is the comment kind, and sunny, and the hearty, warm approval of a friend.
For it gives to life a savor, and it makes you stronger, braver and it fills your soul with courage to the end.
If he earns your praise bestow it.
If you like him, let him know it.
Let the words of true encouragement
Be said, do not wait till life is over
And he's underneath the clover, for
He cannot read his tombstone when he's dead.
Down the ways of truth and beauty,
You can bless the deeds of duty, if you'll give a hearty handshake when you can, for no matter where you're stationed there's a measured inspiration
in the words of honest "praisin" you can give your fellow man.

Allison Wahlers
THE JOURNEY
A mother's love,
A baby's tear,
A bond that grows
Throughout the years.

It starts at birth
And grows through time
And soon the two
Begin to climb.

The lifetime journey
Built on love
And a trust
Sent from above.

So when the time
Comes to depart,
The two are joined
Heart to heart.

Melissa L Winters
BEST FRIENDS
How many times have we walked this way,
And smiled at each other in a day.
How many days have we shared throughout the years
And been there for each other when there were tears.
How many secrets and thoughts did we share
And take time to let each other know we were there.
How many times have we fought with each other
Only to be brought once again back together.
How many good times and bad times have we seen
All throughout the years as we grew from our teens.
How many times must we say goodbye
For every time we do I always cry.
But even though we have to part for a little while
I know when we meet again there will be a friendly smile.

Arlouine G Wu
WHEREVER YOU LIVE
Wherever you live,
In a room, an apartment or house,
All alone, with your family or spouse,
On a farm, in a city or town,
East or West, high up or low down,
Your problems are just the same—or are they?

There's the sun and the moon and the rain,
There's the cold and the heat and the strain;
There's the flowers and moonlight and bugs
And disasters like earthquakes or floods.
So wherever you live
Your problems are still just the same—or are they?

There'll be love, or just kindness and hope;
There'll be greed, even hunger and dope;
There'll be jealousy, hate and revenge,
(Nothing's changed since the days at Stonehenge.)
Hence wherever you live
Your problems are really the same—aren't they.

Terri Woodward
A LOVE HATE RELATIONSHIP
"Let's get those hearts pumping!"
Shouts the aerobic leader above the music.
"Come on; you can do it!
Just one more set."
Body dripping,
Chest pounding,
Muscles screaming,
Mind searching:
Why?
Why am I here?
Why am I doing this?
Why do I like it?
Why do I hate it?
I feel like I'm going to die.
I'm here to be fit for life.

Laurel E Lawson

Laurel E Lawson
TESTINGS

To all my special friends and family who've helped me through my own testings.

As petals from a rose are crushed
To bring forth perfume sweet,
Or gold by trial of fire bright
Becomes refined through heat;
So must we all bear sorrows great
Throughout our earthly life,
Knowing that the end result
Is worth the painful strife.
For we are only travelers here
Our journey is not free;
And only by the tests we pass
Can we made perfect be.

Norma Finklea
I LOVE YOU, LORD JESUS!
I thank you Lord Jesus, for being so kind and devoted Yes! taking the time out from all your doing and giving me so much love and attention.
Yes! Now I see the light and I understand the hardship, I was facing. Nobody believed me! I love you Lord Jesus, Yes! Thank You so much for your love and caring for all peoples. I feel our nearness. I know you came to open the eyes of them who's lost and can not see the light of our Lord Jesus around us. I can see many people don't honor his name for they are still in darkness but I have learned that Jesus' Name is a powerful sign for believers to get right with God. The Father, Son and Holy Spirit are one Being. God bless all peoples always, okay! Love Poetically,
Norma Finklea
Your Joy!

Mrs Norma Finklea
THE TRAIL OF BEING A DESERTED WIFE!
While traveling in my walks of adult life. Oh! feeling daily of the heart and pain of being a victim, an abused wife.
The lonely times of always talking with God and of happiness and peace of mind, knowing God's always there to comfort the deserted wife, God Bless Us!
"Love, Peace, and Joys, Always,."
Yours truly,
Poet: Mrs. Norma Finklea

Mrs Norma Finklea
THE TWO YELLOW BUTTERFLIES
Oh! While dancing down the street, said one butterfly to another, They are kissing and mating like lovers Yes! Instead of having this freedom, Oh! the tenderness of the love portions.
It makes me believe now us Lovers should be as one! (smile).
Married happily, In Love, always.
You and me together forever.
Oh! how I feel the warmth within my heart, only our father knows of my lover's portion, for you're only Troy! Your big brown eyes talk to me, what my heart feels of your only tender embrace of yesterday. Memories of greatest heart felt of Joy's tender embrace of the soft touch of being together as Lovers of us praising our Lord Blessing the two Yellow Butterflies in Reality is Troy & Joy. What a pair, and couple too! Ok!
Poetically yours,.
Truly by Norma Finklea

Carol J W Randolph
WHAT GOD CAN DO
Through trials and tribulations turmoil and grief
My precious Lord Jesus can grant thee relief

When you think you have endured all you can stand
Just come to Jesus on bending knee and praying hand

Your problems will be little though the days will be long
But through the Lord Jesus your dismay won't prolong

He is your private counselor for Him you should consult
He promises to give thee an adequate result

So whenever you're troubled and nothing seems to be going your way
Just take time for Jesus . . . just take time to pray

You will find that things aren't as bad as they seemed
And that God can make them better than you ever dreamed

Your friends will forsake you and lead you astray

But only through God will you ever find your way

Not on many can you depend
For God will be with you until the end

Man makes many promises that he cannot keep
But to obtain your salvation Jesus Christ you must seek
—I would encourage you to take God into your life
For He and only He can help you through this strife

Eleanor Engebretsen
A PACK RAT
If you have a garage sale, I'll take a look
I might find some crystal or an old book,
There are many items you don't use any more,
And they might be just what I'm looking for.

Sometimes I see toboggans or a skate board,
And they all are at prices I can afford,
Cosmetics and jewelry always take my eye,
And I find name brands that I now can buy.

Some things are new at a little bitty price,
And I give them as gifts, they are so nice,
Often I see drapes that look like new,
And beautiful dishes that are cobalt blue.

A knitted sweater, an afghan or a shawl,
I always want to buy them all.
I'm just a pack rat; you might say,
Because I like things that are cast away.

Eric W Shaffer
POSSIBILITIES
A cherubic infant sits under the blossoming sun
on the picnic table. Years pass, grass grows
snow falls over and over.
Now a hopeful intellectual thinks of himself
and writes of this cherubic one.

A something in the distance, yes, I saw;
Over there, above that star, just beyond
that light hint of haze.
A something in the distance, yes, I saw . . . and mounted
the world to transfix my gaze.

Possibilities come to us in a flash
and a flash only have we to seize them.
For the people depend upon us, solitary few
to lift them to our breasts and appease them.

Martha B Martinez
ODE TO FAREWELL
Our days must be a journey
While in this earthly life,
A mystery never ceasing
Until the trumpets sound.

It seems not very long ago
Our heartbeat was entwined,
From then to many partings
Your words still follow true.

"Tread onward in the wilderness
When the way becomes unclear,
For there are many roads ahead
And rivers wide to cross."

Your love stays close around us
Through sunny days and rain,
Each prayer silent in the wind
Over distant sunset hills.

Though tears may cloud my vision
Comes time for "fare thee well,"
From our parting shall remain
Unseen memories, always near . . .

Betty Jean Brooks

Betty Jean Brooks
MY GRANDCHILDREN

For all Grandparents

—Grandchildren—
I thought I would not have any,
But, now today, I have many.
Each added one is more love,
Thanks, to "Our God, above."
Hope the mothers, will raise them right.
This is my prayer, each and every night.
Look after them until they are grown.
And are parents themselves, and on their own.
And may they always be well and strong.
Love each other as a family.
And grow in Love together.
Sharing Day by Day.
And look above as they pray.
By Betty the Poet

Laurel Reeves
WAR—STRIFE
War is only pain and thrall
Engulfed in Life's dim-shadowed wall.
War brings only blood stained hands
From Peace's bound unbroken bands
Do we ask our kin to die for us
And let their souls pass by?
Then if we don't, let's join the strand
And bind Life's unbound broken bands.

Diane Brandon
HOLIDAZE

This poem is lovingly dedicated to my children, Bethanye and Jason, who gave me two of the best reasons to go on.

Through fragrances of simmering potpourri
And scented candles
I thought of you.

While wading through scattered gift wrap paper
Abandoned by happy, shrieking children
I thought of you.

Above the raucous laughter and chatter
Of holiday guests
I thought of you.

Watching hues of red, orange and blue flames
In the fireplace
I thought of you.

In the midst of all the holiday fanfare
I listened to a violin's gentle serenade—
And thought of you.

Kerri R Vanderpool

Kerri R Vanderpool
WAR
Across the sky the break of light
swallows up the passing night.
The ground is wet with mist and dew
and left to perish the remaining few.
The men who fought to save this land
will wash away like grains of sand.
The dawn echoes of the night that's past
of forgotten men laid down to rest.
The scattered remains of an evil fight
that once were whole before the night.
How do we know who won this war?
A man shot down is one more score?
Another man is maimed for life
is this a point for the other side?
Each man was born so innocent
into a world of discontent.
Then taught to hate and kill each other
instead of helping one another.
Two men turn around and eye to eye
one will live the other die.
For a single moment they share the fear
in one man's eye he sheds a tear.
This man that stands in front of him
is not a man but just a kid.
A shot is fired from in the distance
the boy collapses in a single instant.
The night is still and the men go home
to our "freedom" for which we've won.
It is sad that man must come to this
when all we need is love and peace.
Maybe as our nation grows stronger
we will have to fight and kill no longer.
For within our hearts we will hope for peace
and hand in hand the wars might cease.

Maria Lopez-Belio
GYPSY SUNSET
Swift daring sidesteps
throw the sky in gypsy disarray
as undulating crinoline and ruffles
caress billowing clouds in scarlet,
torn skirts in hues of crimson scatter,
to the guitarist's passion a flurry of castañets
as she defiant
seduces time,
one last fiery unleashing of arms and legs
she paints the floor in an array of color
and ends the dance alone
solitary carnation crushed beneath her hell,
black curls unleashed in the crescendo frame her face
as draped in her mantilla
she recedes,
black silk falling from her shoulders
she fades rhythmically
until the morrow.

Tonya R Jordan
THE NIGHT'S SNOWBLANKET
Snowflakes falling gently to the ground.
With only the moon's light showing.
Falling slowly without a sound,
With the wind strongly blowing.

The soft, white snow is deep,
Cold is the night's air,
All creatures are fast asleep,
The night's silence is noticeably rare.

Peter Rodriguez
SHADOWS ON THE WALL

To my sister Nilda, whom I love, lady of grace and substance.

The cage, the bars, the walls, no place to run, no place to go.

Shadows on the walls, I see you there. You are my dream that needs the night to stay alive, so did the shadow need daylight to finish dreaming and to survive, as biological drives make me strive to survive and progress, thee shall not flag nor fail, thee shall never surrender my passion.

You on the walls angel of them all who have a place to go, give me light, give me love. Show your yearning attachment because you're my prize and my treasure, you know my fears, you see the monsters. Shall I frown with it or smile, it will determine darkness or daylight.

Priscilla L Draper
CARELESS LOVER

I dedicate this poem to all the women throughout the world who have been hurt by careless men—Why can't men be more sensitive like Jesus is? Men should use Him for their model! !

All alone & feeling blue—looking out the window but never seeing you.

Waiting in vain to see you come—
(Boy, talk about being dumb!) Oh, where are you when I'm so glum?

Your feelings were shallow, the words were untrue—
You never meant it when you said "I love you."

You played with my feelings, you tore up my heart—
Now I'm all alone & we're far apart.

I was unsure about loving anew—for I'd been hurt too often before you.

Now you're gone, and taken my heart away—and
I sit here alone waiting for you the whole day.

Careless lover, someday you'll be sorry—someday you'll be blue—

That you threw my love away & been untrue,
Real love is kind & faithful & true—
careless lover,
this definitely isn't you!

Kenneth L Hartwell
GOD THE FATHER

To my lovely wife "Brenda" and four beautiful children, "William, Kevin, Chrystal, & Karry"

Praise You Father
For Your Son
Praise You Father
For what You've done
Praise You Father
For the Victory that's won

Praise You Father
You've taken our lust
Praise You Father
For You are just
Praise You Father
Worship You we must

By our Father
We are one
By our Father
Good deeds are done
By our Father
Thy Victory is won

Doris Gentile
MY LITTLE COLETTE
Colette, Colette, my little Colette the days go by, and I think of you yet.

I hope that maybe in some way we can be together again some day.

My paintings of mountains, and trees, and skies so blue, helps me forget my thoughts of you.

If there is a heaven we will meet again, because my heart could not break again

I look at the picture of your little face, and the image of you brings a smile to my face.

I'll always remember you the way you were, and keep you in my heart forever more.

Far from me, and yet not gone, my thoughts of you still linger on.

Robert Akimoto
BITTER-SWEET
We are caves within ourselves
Sheltered by our own destiny,
Impinged upon a sullen world
Seeking to hide from our own mortality.

We are blind to the beauty around us,
Numb to the touch of others
Deaf to the sounds of life
Trusting no one;
Always taking more than we give.

Why exist?
Only to be plagued by an endless sorrow,
Justifying the ultimate truth of our nothingness.

Altruism is a reflection of our souls,
Bearing witness to our fortitude and compassion
While inaugurating our precious freedom.

We are all kindred spirits
Contemplating the universe . . .
Defining our existence . . .
Searching for wisdom.

And finding an end to our journey
We return to innocence,
Blessed with the knowledge of our rebirth
And charged with newfound energy.

The cycle continues,
Reminding us of our changing lives;
Forever rekindling the path to enlightenment.

Margaret R Benton
(MEMORIES OF MOTHER)
Oh! Lord—I see—Mother—
In her old rocking chair
Rocking—to—and fro
Daunting—and—haunting—
me . . .
(Yet)
The mind's dream—is only—a little more—
Than—
A—hollow—replica—of—the life—and—the
Love Mother—and—I—had—
(Memories Yes)
But—not—ghost—see'ing—Mother there—
In her—old—rocking chair—
Rocking—to—and—fro.
The soft wind—singing—and—swaying—
The screen door—Oh! Mother—
The soft wind—is—whispering—
A—warm—and—lov'ing—Good bye.
(Sighing)
Let—the—months—and—years creep by.—
Look—about—and—stand by—
A comforting—sensation—of Mother's—
Warm Love—creeps—thru my heart—
And mind—(Lord!)
Help me—to share it—Help me to—bear it—
It haunts me—in my heart—and dreams
Oh!—How real—it all—seems.

La Dera Greenland
REFLECTIONS
The glass is melted and flows
Like water past me.
It is clear and I wish to touch it.
I move down the path and watch the stream
Fill a mirror pool.
I stand and look at the pool,
It reflects me.
I see what I am, what I might have been,
And what I still might be.
I know this to be truth.
I walk to the center of the pool
And stand on its surface.
Here is where I should be.
I cannot wait for the future.
I turn and take it from the very arch of heaven.
What power, what passion, what love!
Why had I not done it before now?

Randall Lige Perkins
POWERS OF A DREAM
Tonight with-in the vast chambers of my mind
My thoughts drifted off
Through the darkness of time
As I arose and looked up
You were standing there
With the moonlight, dancing in your hair
In your eyes, like a candle
There was a flickering glow
As you leaned over and kissed me
With lips, as soft as the petals of a rose
You turned undoing your gown
letting it float softly to the floor
With-in my eyes there was so much beauty
That only an angel could pastore
As you laid down upon the sheets
My fingers fumbled across your body
exploring and teasing
while your lips moist and searching
to my restless soul was pleasing
from deep inside, I could feel
the trembling needs of your desires
My heart was pounding
My soul burning like a raging fire
At a moment so intense
heated with passion
I woke up calling your name
It was all just a dream
My mind playing games
but it was such a beautiful dream
for I was holding an angel
without her halo or wings

Gloria Hill Williams

Gloria Hill Williams
SEASONS

This poem is dedicated to my precious children, Melanie and Charles.

The birds sing a melodious entree
that spring is forthcoming
And so beautiful is their song
That the sky begins to shed tears
Tears that will green the grass
And awaken the sleeping flowers
And spring is here
Mother nature begins to sweat
At the thought of being pregnant with summer
And summer comes

We can feel her heat as she hyperventilates
in an effort to recover from the birth of her last child
And soon she'll order the leaves to fall
Leaving the trees with branches exposed and naked
Awaiting winter's snowy coat
And just as our hair turns white with age
She sends the snow to warn us
Of the imminent death of another year.

Ina Askew
THE COMING OF SPRING
Down the hill and over the water-gap, after all these years,
I could still find my way in the dark, if Nature had not upset the old path by avalanche of dirt and stone and carried with it many of the landmarks I knew as a child.

There was the old thorn tree—now gone—It was here, each year, the blue birds built their nest—just out of reach—among the thorns—of the small hands that made such effort to reach it, each trip up and down the 'holler.'

The gnarled roots of that tree had grown deep into the bank of the old gully, made from the Spring rains washing down the hill side, and rushing on to meet with like-waters of the Big Indian Creek at the foot of the hill.

Ah, the ecstasy of life at the coming of each Spring , when Nature mingled her many showers; The stillness after each clap of thunder blast! The sky ablaze as lightning trekked its age old path: The joy of awakening from such a night, with the face of earth renewed at last!

Duffy Dey
SNORKELING
Entering a new world
I feel a closeness around me yet a vastness too.
A feeling of weightlessness
yet tons of water surround me.
A world of Fantasy
Each creature dressed in a colorful uniform
Guarding its castle of coral.
A vast wet desert as far as I can see.
A huge metropolis, perhaps Atlantis,
With its inhabitants disappearing down
small ancient halls with no dust
and reappearing out of secret passages.
Old rusty objects from the outer space above.
Discovering a new world
Yet feeling its ancient history.
The land without rain that is always flooded.
The land where outsiders get old quickly
Becoming wrinkled as a prune.
So I vanish from this world of fantasy
Through a curtain of gravity
Entering into a world of science and men.

M D Quest
STRANGERS
The wind roars down—out of the Crazy Woman Mountains.
It circles the trailer house and peers through the windows, laced with frozen fingers.

We prop a kitchen chair against the door. Towels stuffed beneath.
Moonbear wraps around the woodstove, hugging the heat in black fur coat.

I look in your face for some sort of sign—only opaque blue, distant as

the crazys—colder than ice.
Dylan plays with race cars on a blanket. Motor roaring in mud.
Contentment is imaginary.

You read People Magazine
I read Tennessee Williams
the wind howls in defiance
love has no mysterious visitor.

You curl up with Dylan, and douse the light.
I check the wood pile and retreat to the cold back bedroom.
Maybe tomorrow, the wind will stop.

Kenn Crandall
WHY WEAR THE MASK?
How long can we hide
behind

the mask of unfeeling? If

we wait too long, the feelings
we have been hiding will die.
Please uncover your Passion.
Share with me all of your
feeling. In that we will
be one along with those
who will not
HIDE!
Unmask yourself!
And I will
do

the
same.

"What Mask
do you wear
today"

Evelyn E Ryder
GHOSTLY PASSIONS
They speak of fiery passionate kisses
Of which I have experienced of recent
Ah, but what do I know of such passions
Except those of my life like dreams?

It is of the night
That my faceless lover comes to call
Yet I fear sleep
Lest I wake to find him gone

If it is but a dream
How can I fear sleep
If this faceless wonder only comes to me
When the moon keeps silent company with the stars?

Yet come light I feel weary
As if I've kept company with lust through the night
Could it possibly be, that sharing passions
With my wonderlust friend
Could really be dreams of the night?

Then how should I hear the closing door
When my eyes are open?
How then,
Do I explain this, to my heart?

Beverly Alderman
THE DAY SHOULD NOT FALL UNKNOWN

To infinity

The day should not fall unknown,
and only a shudder of
Wonder at life's sweet
mystery . . .
Night's final curtain comes so soon,
it makes of life
Only a whisper, a sigh of sadness to know the ecstasy is
Forever gone.

Craig Colquitt
SEASONS CHANGE
Tumbling through the air,
Landing at the whim of the wind,
Leaves,
Colorful acrobats,
Flashing in my eye,
A new time announcing,
Reflections and a sigh.

Thoughts of fireplaces
Turtlenecks,
Football,
Freedom,
God's many graces.

Philip Scott
HOW BIG IS THE NEIGHBORHOOD?
They say there was someone
Who knew the secrets of the sky.
He may have passed this way,
But no one knows when or why.

They say he understood space,
And time, and what quasars are,
But he didn't leave us clues,
To even reach the nearest star.

A clue might help to answer
Mankind's curious inborn need
To find if we are all alone,
And thus, the one, and only seed.

Bertie Lee J
SMILING FACES
I stepped out of myself in a dream last night I went soaring through the stars unaware of time freedom and no tomorrow I could hear beautiful music through the universe and the wind swept me to the other side I saw smiling faces I had put smiles on when they had forgotten how to smile I listen for the sound of night but there is no night only the still of peace my heart beat danced under the lilac tree to the music of the humming birds wings I sat down beside the river flowing with blue water and watch the butterflies dance on the lilies where they never die and the smiling faces never grow old.

Lynne Cooper
SHELTER
I saw them lining up there,
All crowding round the door.
There must have been a dozen
Or maybe even more.
Their clothes were not the cleanest
Their shoes were not the best,
But one thing everyone had
And shared with all the rest,
And that was their sad faces,
The outcome of despair,
The air of "What can I do
In a world that doesn't care?"
And then I saw a sight
Which made me tremble in my shoes.
A car drove up and stopped there,
(It didn't make the news)
But out there came a family,
Mom, Dad, a kid or two,
All looking for some shelter.
It could have been me. Or you.

Myra Cochran
CRIME OF THE HEART
Many times when I see you. I try to understand why you don't see that I care for you, and I would never want to hurt you or lose your trust in me. The pain stays with me every day as I feel I have committed a crime against you but my only crime is wanting to love you.

Sonya Nicole Crane
HOLD ON FOREVER
When I think of you
loving someone else
the tears roll down my face
I look in the mirror
and see myself crying
deep inside
I feel like I'm dying
I hurt more and more
as the days drift by
knowing me
I'll hold on forever
hoping someday
that we'll be together.

Leah Lutz
MY MIND'S EYE
In my mind's eye I see
Caterpillars crawling up a tree
And a butterfly just set free
from its cocoon

Whiporwhills sighing by a stream
While young and old fishermen dream
Of days gone by and days ahead
and catching that big one.

Blue above and green below
And just enough breeze to blow
The heat of the day
away from the dreamers.

A perfect day that slips by
Until the moon lights up the sky
And wise old owls glide by
on silent wings.

No day lasts forever they say
But I don't see it that way
In young and old its there to tay
forever a memory.

Robert J Jakubowdki
SNOWSTORM
The snow comes down very heavy
Then I shovel it away
It seems the snow is gone
and the sun is here to stay
It snows again and again
The sun now may not be back today.

Robert J England
I FEAR
I cry, I fear, because I love you,
I cry, I fear, because I care,
I cry, I fear, you say you love me,
I cry, I fear, and I fear.

I ache, I want, for you to want me,
I ache, I want, just to be near,
I ache, I want, afraid you'll not need me,
I ache, I want, and I fear.

Donna Harrison
ECLIPSE
The old eternal spring once more
Comes back the old eternal way
With tender rosy light before
The going out of day

The great white moon across my door
A shadow in the twilight stirs
But now forever comes no more
That wondrous look of hers

Donald R Sorrells
CRICKETS
The crickets are singing on a cool spring night
to hear their sweet song is such a delight,
The smell of the dew floating softly to the ground
creates an aroma of serenity bound,
The stars begin to twinkle in the dark sky above
like diamond of peace created by love,
As I rest in my silence with a soft breeze on my face
I feel a quiet calm with no need to race,
Just a time to be thankful for life so dear
Just a time to be thankful for God so near,
So in my silence I feel love growing strong
toward life and the crickets singing love's sweet song.

Jetta Southard
IF THESE WALLS COULD TALK
This house has its memories, just about every kind
When I think about them, it almost blows my mind.
If these walls could talk, I wonder what they would say
About all the things that has happened here each and every day.
The day we moved in, when the building all was done
The things our little girls said and did, when they were having fun.
When they were teenagers, saying goodbye to their dates
The room where a family member passed away.
Whether sad memories or happy ones, they are here to stay
More than one generation has lived in this house
Sometimes it creaks, then it's quiet as a mouse.
So many birthdays have been celebrated here
With our girls and their children, several every year.
Christmas and Thanksgiving were always a happy time
When the loved ones arrived and the doorbell chimed.
Thirty-five anniversaries we had in this place
As I think of all these things, a smile comes on my face.
For if these walls could talk, I think what they would say
Is keep remembering the memories, they will help to fill the day.

Elsie Kaiser
AWAKENING
I didn't know

days could be

so long
so cold
so empty
so lonely
so meaningless

without you.

Jetta Southard
HEARTS
There is the heart with envy, then the heart of love.
There are hearts of malice, some hard as stone.

There of ones of kindness that I have known.
The ones that are young, and the ones that are old.
Then there is the heart of gold.
There is the chocolate heart, the Valentine kind.
And the broken hearts, the one like mine.

David G Masker
THE BURNING BUSH
The light shines down on the figure on the cross;
Tends to make one wonder just who is the boss;
And who could of done such a horrible deed;
And how so carelessly they've sowed their seed;
They couldn't guess the harm that they had done;
Underneath the setting sun;
The Romans couldn't realize nor Judas understand;
That they were not crucifying just any man;
He was the Son of the Lord and all that was true;
But what He offered was nothing new;
He was the light in the day and the blue in the sky;
His word is everywhere it continues to fly;
A rolling stone gathers no moss;
And neither does His word and the tears on the cross;

Ceceilia J Zorumski
HOW TO CAPTURE A MOMENT THE PICTURES IN MY MIND
These two cameras
on my head
Blink and think many pictures
that I dread
Some day I fear
they will take action
and repeat a fraction
of what's lying
in the dark room
of my mind
If they were developed
and weren't kind
so I shall be careful
about the pictures
that I take
Then when I am at ease
I can turn each page
In my mind as I please
Of all the people
who have been kind
and helped me to be
pleasant all the time
So if I loose this camera
that was a gift
The pictures become yellow
with age
I will always have
The pictures of my mind
Pictures are memories
when we forget to remember
Camera caught and kept for keeps
Times Change
Clothes change
children grow
into adults
that can only
be captured by
a camera and kept for keeps
sight with the ears
sight with the eyes
sight with your heart
blind man sees
through his finger tips
loosing your eye sight
not losing your vision

Terry L Zeller
A MIRACLE

To Ed, Jessica, Jennifer and Janice. Thank you for believing in me. Love Mom

A miracle is a tiny thing that can happen to you or me.
But when it happens, it's a giant thing indeed.

Michele R Eginoire
A SUICIDE'S AFTERMATH
You were a son, a brother, and a friend to us all.
You were the one who looked out for us to make sure we didn't fall.
You partied every night and had girls along the way,
You lived life to the fullest, and you lived it day by day.
You tried to act so carefree, yet inside you hurt so bad,
For you wanted to have the family life, you wanted to be a dad.
You are the kind of person that will never be replaced,
You took a life so beautiful, Oh God, it was such a waste.
We miss you every day, and we talk to you each night,
If only we could touch you and have you in our sight.
When you left you took a piece of us, and empty it will be,
Until we are together where we'll spend eternity.
I know that we will see you, and you'll come to meet us all,
To lead us into heaven and walk us down that hall.
But right now our lives aren't over, there is work we still must do,
Before we go to heaven and enjoy the peace with you.
Help us complete our tasks and stay forever near,
Be with us when we miss you and talk so we can hear.
You'll have our love forever, for it will never fade,
I wish you wouldn't have left us, I wish you would have stayed.

Shirley E McCoy

Shirley E McCoy
SHADES OF AMETHYST
Today I looked down at my feet
And saw in bloom some violets, sweet
I stood immobile, lost in thought
Remembering other violets brought
Some years ago by little girls
Who wore bright ribbons in their curls
As patiently they stooped for hours
Among the purple fragrant flowers
To pluck bouquets and to impart
A breath of Spring to cheer my heart.

A mist of tears came with a sigh
When I realized no longer I
Had any little girls to bring
Me violets to herald Spring;
But then a winsome little smile
Tugged hopefully—soon in a while
A brown eyed lass with laughter, too
Will sing, "Here, Grandma, flowers for you!"
And I'll kiss Jana—no regrets
Accept with thanks her violets!

Patricia Andreasen
OUR ALL WE GIVE
For life and all it has to give,
For freedom's right to work and live,
For friends and loved ones far and near,
And all things our hearts, hold dear,
These memories both old and new,
The things we set our hearts to do.
The many hardships in our life,
The joy and sorrows in the strife,
Our homes and families large or small,
For these and more we give our all.

V Broadzinski
GROWING . . .
Trying not to scoff
Wanting to hold the hardness off
But with the addition of the years
Less and less moves me to tears
Growing older, growing colder

No joy reaching my heart
Caring requires too much on my part
With no feelings of any significance
Nothing holds any magnificence
Yes, growing older, growing colder

Unable to share
Unwilling to care
Preferring to be alone
Striving to be all on my own
I'm growing older, growing colder

Carol Huey
ARMY OF HIS LOVE
Onward we move into a "Army of His" love,
Giving out what 'He' wants from above.

Leaving behind our steps and demands,
And caring out 'His' plan to conquer the land.

Angels to help us in time of needs,
As we go to the battle grounds and plant our seeds.

Not to pull back, but forward we go,
For many we will conquer as we saw.

Banners will fly and trumpets will sound,
For the "Army of 'His' love is 'Heaven' bound.

H G Farish
609 ECHELON, R. (A) .A.F.
What out of . . . mud, mountains, slow sliding rivers,
Out of aeroplanes and A-rabs,
Out of the moans of the camp guard
And the hopes of the married men.
Out of "avions" and "kites" and "pursuit" planes
Flying, diving, climbing, banking, soaring
And out of crashes, nosed over, landed wheels up,
Overshot, spun-in, shot down in flames.
Out of a twin-boomed Lightning, diving unnecessarily
To create the scream of a Stuka or a One-O-Nine.
Out of the deep blue Mediterranean sky,
The whispy clouds, the black puffs of ack-ack fire
Or the wide arcs of tracer shells moving across the night.
Out of a Goodnight chorus spreading from tent to tent,
"The Airmens Lament" or "Lilli Marlene" from
Week-end airmen, a long way now from
Their comfortable hanger in the City of London.
Out of rising full-clothed from wet blankets at dawn,
The return of missing pilots and the wait for mail.
Above all out of the sunflash of a Spitfire weaving
Overhead, on patrol at angels thirty.

Dean Flora
FROM DEEP WITHIN THE DEPTHS BELOW
From deep within the depths below;
a surging starts to rise.
Gaining strength with every moment,
and power from deep inside.
The beating of the heart,
is pounding in his chest;
filled with anticipation,
and fearing what is next.
The windows of the mind,
embrace the vision seen;
that started the crescendo,
resounding from within.
A look, a smile, the moment seized;
the calming of the storm;
with wonder left to fill the mind,
of what is yet to come.

Ms Dale Annette Wilson
A NEW LIFE
Up ahead I see a door.
A door to a new life.
Is it mine or someone else's?
Should I turn the knob?
Or turn my back.
Is it a he's life or is it a she's life?
I long to see,
but it might not be for me.
I need a new life.
For my old one is not quite right.

Mrs Regina Conrath
THE BLACK DRESS
The dress kept in the closet all these years
Was once worn to favor the solemnity of death,
To express the sad widow's grief and tears;
Now limp, no longer fresh, in this year the fortieth.
Its beauty reaches into my thoughts for its use,
The long unused dress destroys itself;
The wonder is why it was kept with no excuse.
Unworn, unseen, glamorous, it has no pelf.
The wonder is its beauty and limited success;
So comes the time for the black dress to go,
Blameless, yet holds quality in its agedness
Change is wrought, this dress I outgrew.
Elegant, worn once, its seams intact,
I'll discard the dress carefully with tact.

Cindy S Tunno
MORE THAN WORDS
O lonely eyes filled with despair,
Did you think no one could see?
All the hurt, and emptiness

is seen by empathy . . .
Needing Someone—Never having
felt in the heartys of few.
Now I find, the "eyes like mine,"
I'm starting to need you . . .

If I could Only reach you
Please, don't turn away . . .
Maybe I could show you,
You mean More than words
Could-ever say . . .

My life was hanging from a high
cliff.
I wanted just to let go . . .
When you came., and felt the same,
I somehow found a-glimpse of
hope.
I need not only be your lover,
but your Closest friend.
Like Sunrise skies, as tears subside
I want to live again.!

If I could Only reach you.
If I can find a way . . .
Maybe I can show you.
You mean More than words
could-ever say . . .
And "We" mean More than these
words could ever say . . .

Sidney Bossuk
A JEWISH CHILD AT CHRISTMAS
A Jewish Child At Chirstmas
It is a time of strange
There is no tree
No Presents
No Elues
No "Rudolph"
No "Jingle Bells"
No Santa
It is a time of hidden
There is no cross
No Mary
No Joseph
No Disciples
No New Testament
No Jesus
It is a time of confusion
There is no meaning
No Joy
No Laughter
No Happiness
No Smile
No Life

Earl Floyd Anderson III
SOMEONE

For my dearest Elisabeth, the one who inspires my dreams and gives meaning to my life.

We all need someone, someone to
understand
And when we are scared, someone to
hold our hand
I need someone's hands to open my
heart's doors
And no one else's hands are more
beautiful than yours
My want for your love is more than
you could know
For our love for each other can now
only grow.

Your voice reminds me of the siren's
sweet song
As it warms my heart all the year
long
To your beauty—nature can not
compare
To your radiant smile and your silky
brown hair
As your eyes glisten in the morning
sun
I forget every other care
And realize that you're the one
With whom my life I want to share.

My feelings for you I can no longer
control
For a profound love has overcome
my soul
Your loving me is a wish that is very
dear
For it I would give my entire heart,
save one tear
And it I will shed when you are no
longer near
My love flows for you like a clear
mountain stream
Because for you to love me is my
only dream.

James Henry Goin
THE TREE
Try standing like a tall oak tree, the strength that stands out as if to say, stop and look at me. See my arms outreached as tall as they can be, inviting those little creatures to come and sit on me.

Yes, I'm a symbol of strength, don't you know this, haven't you seen? Through all these years I've been here, just looking around it seems. I'm an example for all of you to see, that to be strong, you don't have to be a tree.

But to be the type of person that people want to see, try being more enchanting like the big oak tree. Extend your limbs and wave your leaves and open up some more, and see how strong you really are, and see how fast you score.

Now that you have opened up, and as strong as a tree be careful what you do and say, for all of this is free. And if what's said or what's done will cause hurt to anyone, including me you see, then forget ever trying to be anything, other than a tree.

Julie Diane Kisner
MIRRORED SKIES
He had blonde hair and the
deepest blue eyes,
Deep, ocean blue eyes that mirrored
the skies.
Whenever he laughed those
eyes would twinkle bright,
Like a shining star in the black night.
Whenever I felt down,
The shine from those eyes would
make me smile instead of frown.
I loved him with an everlasting
love,
Like the moon loves the stars above.
He gave me hopes and dreams
all the time,
And when he kissed me my heart
would chime.
But suddenly, my dreams were
shattered,
All my hopes battered.
His eyes no longer had that
shine
When he told me he would no longer
be mine.
As I looked into his eyes,
All my spirits floated down like
lonely butterflies.
Now, whenever I feel down,
I want to smile instead of frown.
So I just think of those deep
ocean blue eyes that mirrored
the skies,
That twinkled bright like a shining
star in the black night.
And the thought puts my hopes
and dreams in flight.

I N Childress
PREFERENCES
Why do we love the rose
And don't care for the dandelion
Love most days and moments
And dread the ravages of time

A rose must be pruned and nurtured
A dandelion grows free
A rose is cut, then wilts and dies
A dandelion showers its seeds

A rose, is it worth the care it takes
you can mow a dandelion down
The scent of the rose if fleeting
The dandelion will always be around.

Lena Herrera

Lena Herrera
JUST AS THE WIND ENCIRCLES ME

Lord, my sanctuary. Mother I love you dearly, thank you for belief and encouragement. Family. "U2" Wide Awake In America my audible solitude. G. Hassan much respect over the years. Church Family. O. Lee

Just as the wind encircles me—
So was I captivated by the Silhouette
that appeared before me.
As a bird would sing to me in my
darkest hour
There I saw Him standing.
No Fortress stood between my
silhouette and I—
Only my Inner Being
Yet as the bird sang the walls were
no more.
My fingers were not ravaged, I did
not have to Pry.
Pride became not a wall, Rejection a
grain of sand.
Only the sun shone in my heart as I
heard my silhouette
singing to me from a near distance.
As an echo in the night my soul said
to me:
'Let the bird sing to you—
let not Pride and Rejection get in the
way
for no new Friend would you make.'
I tried not to stumble, yet I tripped
over my sword
an open wound left unattended
I took my chance on meeting my
beautiful silhouette
Now my wound is no more Because
In You My Silhouette I found A
Beautiful New Friend.

Joe B Freeman
TO PAINT WITH WORDS
I'd like to write my mind in prose
so all the world could see
the things that linger in my heart
and the thoughts that keep me
company

To paint a picture with pen and words
would be my one desire
Of bluebird songs, of trees, and
brooks
or a saddened heart to inspire

To paint with words a scene so clear
that even the blind could see
Of mountain streams and sunsets
hues
and of the plains golden majesty

To express my thoughts in such a
way
I may ease another's pain
If it helped them heal from what I
wrote
there would be so much to gain

So this is why I'll continue to try
to write my mind in verse
To paint some scenes and write of
dreams
a work of beauty to rehearse

Cecil Volk
YESTERDAY
"Please" and "Thank you"
softly on older ears
memories of courtesy
gone—the "you" generation

Me, mine, I'm—
who? what? "wha"?
chagrin in recognition
acceptance abhorred
BUT
The mass on axis turns
cars whizz by—
to be defended by radios
splattered by inconsiderates

22 year old babies
lovelocked and impoverished
selfish, utterly so,—until—
the rights of others become
known

Deborah L Ronald
NEW LIFE

Dedicated to my three wonderful children, John, Terry & Kristy.

What is "new life", I've heard people
ask, when discussing events of the
day,
Some take it so lightly, others don't
care, and many just brush it away.
A puppy so sweet and soft when it's
born, a kitten so cuddly and round,
A new bud from a young tree is
beautiful, when growing up out of the
ground.
There are many ways of expressing
"new Life", from puppies to kittens
and trees,
But there's one kind of life, far above
all the rest, and this one is special to
me.
For this "new life" I speak of is
growing, and it started not long ago,
And you my love are the reason, that
I cherish this "new life" so.
Conceived in love, on that beautiful
night, it was something just meant to

be,
It's living and growing, in his own special place, and for now that place is in me.
A gift from above, I've heard it called, by folks watching a setting sun,
But to me it's a way of taking two lives, and blending them into just one.
It's really unselfish when you stop to think, about this "new life" that's so new,
For what you've done sweetheart, is given to me, a big precious part of you!

Larry J Galaske
INNOCENT STAR

Dedicated, To Elaine Bevans, whom I shall love forever.

There's a wish upon a star,
It's sparkling light fascinating
yet so far.
Should only stay in your garden of space,
So people of Earth can seek your face.
But just in case,
Just in case you should fall
burning brite with your tail so long.
Please don't fall here
Where innocent stars don't belong.

Paul Mark Mazzacane
CORNERED IN A ROUND ROOM

To my family, my friends, everyone who wants to know me and anyone who can identify with this

Cornered in a round room
Treed in the middle of the sea
Frowned upon by the man on the moon
Hostage in the land of the free
Mislead, misinterpreted, misinformed and misfired
Exhausted, lazy, bored and tired
Strained, maimed, plain insane
Dodging drops of acid rain

Cornered in a round room
Penned up behind the drought-dried garden
Drowning in a waste-flooded ocean
Terrorized by a third-world nation
Mislead, misinterpreted, misinformed and misfired
Exhausted, lazy, bored and tired
Foolish, blind, changed of mind
Far too close and hard to find

Sylvia Mersino
WEDDING WISH

To my children Patty, Tim, Dave, Ray, Peggy, and Ginny.

Wishing you happiness
All through the years.
Let there be love and laughter;
Even a few tears.

If you work together,
There will be no fear.
For unity is something
To always hold dear.

Accepting things right from the start
Will keep you together—never to part.

Kimberly A Burson
REMEMBER ME

Remember me,
As the evening pales
Turning the bright daylight
Into soft colors of pastel,
And all of your worries of the day
Begin to fade.

Remember me,
When you bask in the warmth
Of a crackling winter fire,
Some cold December's eve,
Leaving the cold, damp world outside.

Remember me,
When the troubles of the day
Won't leave your mind,
And the peace you seek
Is so hard to find.

Remember me,
Remembering you,
With Love.

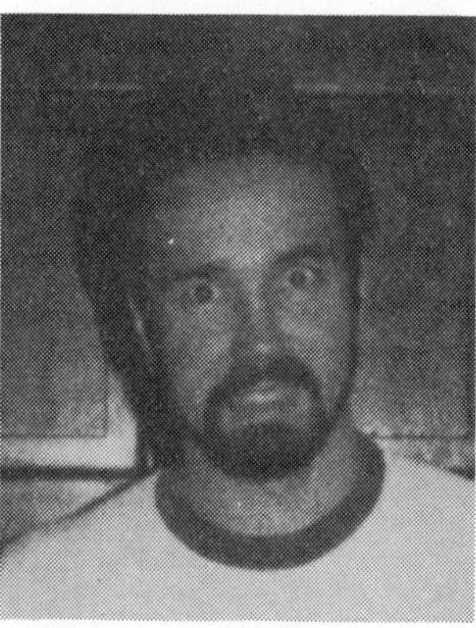

ron shirkey

ron shirkey
DEAR GOD, HOW DO I THANK YOU?

Dedicated with Gratitude to Betty Jerke—who, with "Tough Love", helped me find my God.

Dear God, how do i thank you? What can i do?
Who are you? What are you? If i only knew
You stood by me all through my life . . .
Through all the trouble and through all the strife
But i never acknowledged you, i didn't care
In fact i went so far as to say you just weren't even there
You didn't let me have things my way
So i turned my back and i bid you good day
i kept saying i could do it on my own . . .
i became as hard as a stone
As long as i said this, you let me be
In your infinite wisdom only you could see

i finally came to the end of my rope
there was absolutely no sign of hope

Then you caught me just before the big fall
Put me back together and all
I just had to reach out for you
How do I thank you God, what can I do?
After that, I'd die for you
Now I can see . . . Now I know . . .
Let it go, just let go

Diana L Campbell
LEARN TO LOVE YOURSELF

This poem I dedicate to my Mother. For teaching me how to love.

Learn to stand alone
Surviving, is what it is in the beginning
Let yourself choose a life of joy
Don't worry about survival
Ego, prevents your destruction
Look into yourself for clarity
Love yourself enough to try
Make the first move into life
This will surely open doors
Atonement, is your guide to knowing yourself
Wholeness, is your goal
Realize your oneness with God
This will bring your love out
Allow yourself peace of mind
Feel, all the love around you
See, the grace and beauty in all
Enjoy your life, for that is your gift
Be happy, for that is what you control
Let your love shine for all to see
Sharing love is, life's greatest joy
Love yourself, and others will

Helen Pentecrics
RECOLLECTIONS

If we could turn back the hands on the clock of life and return to yesterday,
How many of us would change ourselves, be happy, bright and gay?
Could we forget our broken dreams, a childhood that's gone,
Would we remember how many times we were right or wrong.

If a lot of forgotten moments, our memories could recall, would many a blinding teardrops wet our eyes and slowly fall.
Would we really try to change things and begin our lives anew, or would we just dismiss the past as some folks often do?
Would we try to go on bravely and really fight to win, or just go on dreaming of things that might have been?
Many of us have forgotten how to kneel and pray. To thank Him for our blessings at the closing of each day.
If we would just remember Him, who made us all,
Our many, many yesterdays would we happy to recall.

Jenny Mamrak
PEACE?

This poem is dedicated to all who believed and stood by me.

The geese flocked to the water
seeking safety,

For the earth was ablaze
in bright orange colors.

But how would they find
freedom from danger there?

For you and I know that when the
button is pushed
there'll be nowhere to hide.

So I ask you now, what's the use in
killing our world?
Why can't we have peace?

Mary Sciola
DON'T CRY MY LOVE WHEN I'M GONE

To my love: W.L.M.

Don't cry when I'm gone
I love you just the same only I'm up above
I'm with you just the same from up above
I will take care of you where ever you may be
Your journey will be safe, I will see
I will care for you day or night
I will keep you out of danger where ever you may be
You don't see me but I'm just above, love
Don't cry my love when I'm gone
I'm with you where ever you may be
You don't see me, I'm just up above
I will keep you from any wrong
Don't cry my love when I'm gone.

Sulinda Hudson
ALL THESE MEMORIES

To Jason: My inspiration

I started thinking 'bout us last night and
All the good times we have had together
Like when we first met,
Like the day we spent
'Round the city and when Christmas time was here
You were always there for me to cry on
You've been there for all the good times and the bad . . . of these few months
Now I'd like to thank you very much for being you
And I hope we're together for a few more memories

Maudie Hulette
MANKIND'S SALVATION

This poem is dedicated to Robert, My loving husband.

O Word of God. Jesus.
You brought wisdom from on high,
You brought truth unchanging
You are the light for all mankind.
We love thee for thy sacrifice
We worship thy sweet name,
Since you shed your precious blood
Our lives are not the same.
The rich, the poor, the aged, the young
Received the gift divine,
The proof of love you showed to us
Forever will it shine.
You showed the way, Lord Jesus
Where truths of gems are stored,
You taught us how to reach them
Through the footsteps of our Lord.
Your truth is everlasting
There's joy in every word,
It shines like A Beacon
Above A sinful world.
You are mankind's road map
You are his trusting friend,
You stand beside his door, and knock
Eager to get in.

Mary M Jones
CAN'T YOU SEE

To my beloved husband Bob, for always being there. To my precious children, Sonny and Amber, the joys of my life and to my trusted friends, Rita and Brenda, who took the time to look. I love you all, Mary

My friends look at me and I wonder what they see?
Can they really see what's inside of me?
So often we put up a front for them you know,
But why can't they see what's inside of me.
So many people with so much pain, just how can I tell them?
Some how I don't think I have the right,
To put my pain on the outside of me.
So many people with real problems today,
But yet if I tell them will they just turn away?
People can't see the stamp that I feel,
Rejected! Second! Not good enough you see,

Is what is stamped on the outside of me.
Maybe if I smile more, or laugh more, or even care more,
Just maybe they won't see the stamp that's on me.
Some how I have muddled through life, and I've done a good job you see,
A Joker, A Kidder, lots of fun is what most people,
See on the outside of me.
Today it seems that too many carry a stamp and others to busy to look.
So won't you please try to look on the inside of me.
For if you look deep within my heart you will see,
Battle scars, from the war, inside of me.

Angela M Schreiber
FORGIVE ME

I'm set in my ways
sitting here bewildered.
I don't know you.
Yet I've seen you many times before.
Don't remember your name
yet you know mine.
I feel so helpless.

Don't want to get in your way
yet I want to help
but my body won't move
I want it to.
Looking deep in your eyes
What I can see; feel; sense.
Are you annoyed with me?
I don't think I did anything
It's not that I don't want to help
I can't, forgive me, because I'm old.

Deanie Golding
REMEMBERED SORROWS

There is a book of 'Counted Sorrows'.
I do not count, but I remember.
Oh, for the ability to forget!

There must be some that do, else, a world of sorrows
Or, is there? and I don't know—
Their sorrows remembered.

There must be joys that I do not remember.
Life can not be made entirely of sorrows.
Can it be, and I do not remember?

Maybe I am searching for a perfect peace,
or maybe I am searching for SOME peace,
That I can not remember.

Is it an imperfect memory and I can not recall?
Let my heart be open to joys not remembered.
Life can not be made up of all sorrows. Can it be?

Hanna Olcha Zbierzchowska
IN THE HOSPITAL /I/

I was awaked by some clamorous birds
their wings like hands lifted to the sky
someone was lying still watching the passing shadows
someone was praying loud to all his gods
someone was standing in the row of laughing ghosts
someone was not dying
because the death had been taken away from him
someone was promising that the sun would not be stolen from me
everything
suddenly
the road uncertain endless
I was awaked by some clamorous birds
and entered that real unreality

Hanna Olcha Zbierzchowska
IN THE HOSPITAL /II/

I look at that person in the morror
mutilated deformed contorted
face twisted with pain
strange image I do not recall
they tell me to call it myself
my self
I do not agree for
I do not accept
I sun the sight of myself

onto a sheet of paper
torn out of an old exercise-book
the words are flowing
the acridity of catharsis

Ruth Suli Urman
THE SCENE

broccoli thick and green
mountainous, voluptuous
almost pubescent
luminescent.
glittering sun, sprinkling
the waves.
you're foaming at the mouth
as you casually mention
how you're turningoffyourcircuits

one by one.
my skin is burning fire
tingling to the touch.
(do you need a light?)
you drench me in your sarcasm.
i fan you with my moods.
we remain cool, collected
two tomatoes peeling
on a vast stretch of loneliness.

Patricia Rhineburger
PROMISES

Promises are made promises are broken
But what is a promise.
It's your word so often spoken.

And the meaning of those words can be
So valuable when heard.
But yet so cheap.
So make promises from the heart meant to keep.
A promise to me is one's word
Spoken with love.
For broken promises could only destroy us.
If you can't make a promise and keep it don't make one at all.
If you can't say I love you and mean it
don't even bother to call.

MaryAnn Stefano
WHAT IS A FRIEND?

A friend is someone fair and true.
Who share their feelings just with you.
Their by your side through thick and thin.
They aid you when you hurt within.
They share your troubles and share your pain.
They share the dreams of fortune and fame.
They pick up your spirits when you are down,
They make you smile instead of frown.
For your injuries they take the pain,
For your misfortune they take the blame.
Fun, excitement, pain and tears,
Are all the things a good friend shares.

Carole Lins
I HOPE THAT YOU CAN SEE

To Edward, I dedicate this poem, a very special person in my life

I hope that you can see,
How much your friendship means to me.
I enjoy being with you,
And having someone to talk to.
You have started to help me
Erase my doubts and fears,
that I've had inside for many years.
Our "hello" in the mornings
And our "good-night kiss,"
Helps to get me through the day.
Yes, I really hope that you can see,
How much our friendship means to me!

Marlese Kubler

Marlese Kubler
GOTCHA CLOWN

Ma'am and Dave with many comical memories.

There is a funny character
That lives in town.
She may not look like one,
But she is a goofy clown.
You will be amazed,
As she plays out her schemes;
With tricks unbelievable
For you to see.
As she sneaks up behind you
To throw a pie in your face.
Clever as she may be,
She loves to use frosting
for your toothpaste.
She will often take
An awesome picture,
So that you can look back
Sometime in the future.
People like to watch
Funny happy clowns,
That have tricks by the millions,
But sometimes they frown.
Clowns are big, clowns are small.
Once in a while they're even a star.
This goofy clown I'm talking about,
Goes by the name of Mar.

Daniel A Wise
FRIENDS

To my wife and best friend, Mary.

We've shared our joy . . .
We've shared our sorrow.
We've shared our hopes
of tomorrow.

We have laughed . . .
We have cried.
We have comforted each other . . .
When loved ones died.

We've helped each other
in many ways.
That's why we'll stay
Friends always.

Dawn Anne Evans
WHAT HAS JESUS DONE FOR ME?

What has Jesus done for?
A crown of thorns which made him bleed.
He bore the pain of nails in hands
and carried the cross to Calvary's stand.
He washed my sins away
So in Heaven I can play.
I will have a peaceful heart
when we meet in God's high court.
When in need of loving care
I turn to Jesus in sweet hour of prayer.
He has shown us what is right
and has kept us in his tender sight.
We have questioned his true love,
and still he cares from up above.
For me his life he gave,
so from sin I shall be saved.

Christine Alison Bennett
WHERE BIRDS STILL SING

Hearts carved by those we knew
Gone with their sacred memories
Live shattered, breaking into
How do you repair a broken love
That was taken tragically above
My best friend's hurt is deep
Inside, you silently weep
I can't reach out to heal your pain
When for three years I was totally insane
From a loved one's death, who's to blame?
Shall you recover from this deep despair
To one day open your soul to again share
All the wondrous joys captured each day
In a world colored a dismal grey
Where birds still sing and children play.

Holly D Binns
GRANDPA'S POCKETS

I dedicate this poem to my grandfather, W.E. WATTS, with all my love.

GRANDPA'S POCKETS
are a mystery to me.
They hold everything
you'd ever need.

GRANDPA'S POCKETS
hold the coins that buy
the goodies to make me
smile.

GRANDPA'S POCKETS
hold the tissue that wipes
my tears away when I
cry.

GRANDPA'S POCKETS
hold the hands that hold
me tight when I'm
afraid.

GRANDPA'S POCKETS
are a mystery to me.

Sandra Ann Rodgers
YESTERDAY, TODAY

To my husband Tony, who is my Yesterday and Today, my Past and Future.

It seems just like yesterday,
I was running without a care,
no worries, no problems.
Now I'm making a mold for myself.
What to do, what to think,
how to plan, how to act,
how to act upon the plans,
that I am thinking to do.

It seems just like yesterday,
I was trying to dream the future.
What it held for me, for you.
Now I'm living the future.
Were the dreams true or false?
Is this mold good or bad?
There is no more growing up.
The past is gone, the future is now!

Rupert Hickman
HAPPY WARRIOR

To my uncle, Calbert McClinton Stanley, for his work in civil rights in (Horry county) South Carolina through 1950-1978.

The happy warrior is laid to rest
beneath the Minnesota ice and snow.

He had fought so many battles for us
that we hate to see him go.

It was a hot day in Philadelphia when
he gave out his first battle cry or yell,
that rang out throughout the
countrysides, valleys, and hills and
fell on Capitol Hill.

Three decades he spoke with fiery
zest for the rights of all mankind,
Black, brown, yellow, red, and white
in America as well as in other lands.

The happy warrior, although, is gone;
leaves with us a legacy of hope,
Goodwill, and enthusiasm in the
future of our land; where everyone
Can work, play, live, love, and enjoy
his or her life in his own way.

As his body lay wrapped in the
Rotonda, and friends and foes past to
Pay their last respect to one whose
life and deeds would last down
Through the year, decades and
centuries, not only in memory,
documents,
And minds but through the impact of
life now and through the times.

He lay there lifeless and still but his
deeds will live on as a
Beacon light to all mankind who will
fight for human
Rights. We can still hear his voice
whispering back through
Eternity, "fight on, fight on," until all
men are free.

For the black man has been
discriminated against, the aged lie in
Bed all racked with pain crying out
give me a little support and
Security and let me live my life out
feeling free with a little
Dignity, the ones living in improper
housing—the hope of a
Warm house on a cold winter's night,
to the uneducated—a
Chance to study and apply his
skills—and a better life
For all that will.

His voice is still—never again to be
heard in the Senate halls
But his work will stand to remind us
of that happy warrior who
Once passed this way touched each
life—and changed it in some
Way. That great warm smile that he
possessed brought us
Happiness and hope where there were
confusion and distress.

Lynda M Snyder
SNOW

Cold, wet, pure and white
The flakes of winter I see in sight
Each little drop a shape of its own
No two alike have ever been known

As it rests on the trees
And covers the ground
It brings a smile to my face
For memories I've found

A sight to see
A wonderful glow
But not always welcome
That's the story of snow

Margaret DeBeaulieu
THE SAND PIPER

To poet lovers

Across the narrow
beach we flit
One little sandpiper and I
As fast, I gather
Bit by Bit

The scattered driftwood
Bleached and dry
The wild waves
Reach their hands for it.

The wild winds cry
As up and down the
Beach we flit
One little sandpiper and I.

Emily McCormick
AMERICA WE LOVE

America the land we love,
Was given to us from God above.
We shall never forget the ones
before,
That taught us to love forevermore.

America, the land of freedom,
To worship God as we choose,
Go where we want to go,
And do what we want to do.

America, a land of beauty,
Of many wonderful places,
Will make tears in our eyes,
And joyful smiling faces.

America, the land we love,
No matter what color, race, or creed.
We will never forget you America,
Because you are the land we need.

We want to thank you, America,
For this wonderful land of ours,
And we shall always be grateful,
As we bow our heads in prayer.

Helen Patricia Dillard
STORM PARADE

This poem is dedicated to my family and friends.

Smokey gray clouds drift across a
crystal blue sky
and rest in billowing halos atop
majestic mountain peaks,
a curtain of shadows drawn over
a thirsty valley below.
Dancing trees yield to the wind's
haunting song;
A thunderous drum roll announces
the grand finale;
Lightning fireworks race wildly
across a black sky.

In a moment of quiet anticipation,
the earth and mankind await
nature's gift—
Raindrops pierce the clouds,
falling free—destination earth.
A rainbow emerges through the
clouds,
a sign of hope, painted by divine
hands.

April Zeman
I LOVE YOU

I love you, I love you.
In more ways than one,
I love you, I love you,
for more than just fun,
I love you, I love you,
'cause clouds from astray,
I love you, I love you.
Because this is the way,
I love you, I love you,
and I tease and play,
but sometimes I wonder
if love's too high a price
to pay.

Bunni Koblentz

Bunni Koblentz
THAT SPECIAL TREATMENT

To Ron Shimohara D.C. and Michael Aveni D.C. for healing me with their kindness, compassion, friendship and skill, (the best chiropractors in all the world,) to show you've touched my life . . .

Each day it seems as we all grow
older;
We carry life's stress on our back,
neck and shoulders.
Then we get to the point when there's
too much pain,
It's time to see our chiropractor,
again.
A doctor who never makes me wait,
(Even though sometimes "I" show up
late.)
It seems as though he's always there,
No matter what, he always cares.
When no one else can take care of
me,
That special treatment begins with
fluidotherapy.
A warm cozy feeling that helps me
relax,
With his firm gentle hands, he adjusts
my back.
Every muscle joint and bone that
aches so much,
Is usually relieved by just his touch.
Then I ask him "Doctor, what is
causing this pain"?
He never hesitates to explain,
In a way he knows I'll understand,
then suggests "the right diet and
exercise plan."
And we talk of life. He takes the
time,
To hear what I've got on my mind.
He's more than a Doctor, He's a
special friend,
And I start my days feeling strong,
thanks to Him.

Mary G Kensel
EARLY SPRING

To my treasured and loving family—

Glorious beauty abounds
Loveliness everywhere
Trees budding—renewing
Life's wonders!
Flowers blossoming
Birds singing—crickets chirping
Green grass
Covered with dew!

Kristi Anne Hill
THE GHOSTS WITHIN

Hidden in a picture
That is no longer being created.
Invisible to mirrors,
No longer reflecting my image.
Deafened by the resounding voice,
That defies my own.
Blinded by a vision,
Far too faint to see.
A foreigner in a common land.
Singing a song, they could never
learn.
Alone, yet crowded
In an empty world.
An outsider imprisoned
Forever in the end.

Barbara S Verzi
THE TIME BETWEEN

This poem is dedicated to my late father Joseph William Venora Jr. and my late brother Robert Venora whose passing inspired me to write it.

A gentle slap and it all begins,
And murmurs loud a cry.
A baby is born so small and new,
And yet it's time to die.
Not die from death but life you see,
For birth is the beginning,
And death is the end,
And life is just the time we'll spend
"Between."

Joan Revlett Whitaker
KISS OF DEATH

I sense its presence
Its raspy voice I now can hear
I feel the end is drawing near
I feel the kiss of death upon my brow
I release the reins and turn over my
plow
I have no fear of deaths long sleep
Or of the grave so cold and deep
While on this earth I have done my
best

And know I have earned my final rest
Much sadness I feel and ache in my heart
To know from my loved ones I must part
But we have God's assurance of another world
When his trumpet sounds and his banner unfurls
From his own word we shall rise again
To a new beginning which has no end
So I set my eyes on him above
And leave behind all those I love
Perhaps I'll be missed when I am gone
Though it cannot be for so very long
by his time just in the blink of an eye
I leave you now with all my love
I must bid you goodbye

Philip R McCaffrey
WHO WILL SAVE THE CHILDREN

Who will save the children,
Who will help them live,
Who will save the children,
It's hard when just one gives.

Who will save the children,
It's really hard to say,
Who will save the children,
They're dying day by day.

Who will save the children,
The numbers are very few,
Who will save the children,
Help, before they all are blue.

Who will save the children
Don't put it off another day,
Who will save the children,
Stop, you can find a way.

Who will save the children,
Only if your intentions are pure,
Who will save the children,
Help protect and save our future.

Julie R Zarcone
ALWAYS A PART OF ME

To my husband Lawrence and my children Tammy, Kim and Lawrence. Thank you for having faith in me.

I carried you within me with loving care,
The love that only a mother can share.

When I gave life to you, you depended on me,
To guide and love you, for eternity.

I mothered you when you were oh so small,
I picked you up, when you would fall.

I was always near you, watching you grow,
Teaching you things, you did not know.

I will forever remember those sleepless nights,
Trying to chase away all your frights.

I'd kiss your face and stroke your hair,
I'd rock you to sleep, you knew I was there.

I raised you with all the love that I could,
Then we finally survived your childhood.

One morning I woke and I looked at the sun,
The years have gone by, is my job finally done?

The time has passed and I taught you well,
You stood up tall, whenever you fell.

Yet I still want to drive away all your fears,
Kiss your cheek and dry your tears.

For a mother's love goes as deep as the sea,
And you will "always" be, a part of me.

Jewell Phillips
CHANGES

Things change—
Friendships fade
Money is spent
Glory's lost.

Seasons change—
So do people.
Day turns to darkness

Sorrow to joy

Pain is eased.
Rules are broken—
Promises forgotten
Trust betrayed.

Life ends—
Love cools
Hate dies
Stars fall.

Things change—but God is always God.

Lucas L Johnson II

Lucas L Johnson II
THE MEN WHO GAVE, EVEN THEMSELVES

In commemoration of those American soldiers who fought and died in the Vietnam war

They were a breed of men inexplicable, innumerable, like echoing shells on a timeless seashore. They met as strangers, each of them learning to form an unbreakable bond of camaraderie and brotherhood, a bond that would uphold them and encourage them as they burned with the unquenchable desire to loyally fight for the cause for which their beloved country had sent them. Unfalteringly, they were gung-ho to lay down their lives, many of them youngsters still captured by a fading childhood. Yet, like tameless horses, they arose to the realization of an invigorating consciousness. Fight to survive!
America can never forget these soldiers of such bold a courage, who when filled with the fear of death and sweltering with the heated pain of countless bloody wounds, pressed on through the thickness of the fight, ever clinging to their vanishing sanity and the grace of god that willed their every tenacious step.
Let every beating heart remember the strife of these men, for they spilled their precious blood to uphold the mightiness of the country they loved. May they rest in peace, these faithful soldiers of time past, whose tours of duty are endlessly appreciated.
For they gave all that true men could possibly give beyond the asking of their country, they gave the gift of life, these men gave themselves.

Claribel Elkins
LITTLE GIRLS

To my daughters and grandson, Mike.

Little girls are really nice,
And sweet as they can be,
I know, 'cause I had two of them,
Who brought much joy to me—
But now a little boy has come—
To climb a romp, and play—
And when his laughing voice calls "Granny"
The darkest hour turns into sunlit day,

The joy of having children
Is multiplied ten fold
Each time they reproduce themselves
and a grandchild I behold.

In each little childish form
I see again my own reborn
And when I clasp a little hand
I feel like a queen surveying my land.

Candace Alease White
THE STARS ABOVE

It was a night I would
always remember
The sky was a glorious
shade of blue
The stars were like little
light bulbs everywhere
Then in that special
time and place
You said you love me
and you hoped that
our love would
last forever

That night seemed
to go on forever
You and me
hand in hand
No one to see us
But God in his
own plan
Our love that night
grew like we never
knew it would
I hope that night means
as much to you
As it does to me
Cause I Love you

Gwenda Cherry
LOOKING BACK

Time has changed us, you and I.
How quick and silent the years
slipped by.

Knowing emotions we never addressed,
our love forever to be suppressed.

Our now gray hair, no longer blonde.
Our slow steady steps, the need to
hold on.

Our tired eyes, growing ever dimmer.
Thoughts of you <u>still</u> make mine
glimmer.

Going back, the changes I would make.
For looking back through passing time,
for sure two hearts can break.

Angela G Tribley
KISSED BY THE MOON

The moon is high
Up in the sky,
Blissfully glittering above.

It's moonbeams shine
And catches fine
The sparkling eyes of love.

Through the sea air
Glistening fair
Caressing the waves, it gleams.

Urged by the sight
They kiss in the night
Realizing their utmost dreams.

Put in this trance
They radiate romance
Gently embracing, they swoon.

Rendering never
Their love is forever
Heavenly kissed by the moon.

Verlena Gilliam

Verlena Gilliam
OLD MAN'S LAMENT

A gusty wind on a wintry night;
Whipped his cloak, from left to right.
he tried to stand straight and tall,
But he just bent; and that was all,
Just like a tree, that drooped it's head;
And gave up all; when it was dead.

He was an old man; this is true,
And thought he knew, just what to do.
Whilst I bow; he prayed to God.
Please, send me, just a pound of lard.
My bones are tired; they ache you know.
A few more days, then I must go;
To meet my maker; my life to judge.

I've been mistreated; but have no grudge.
Been messin' with women, all my life;
Never dared to take a wife.
Could've gotten married and had a son.
But now it's too late; My life is done.

Pamela Kraft
IT'S A 10-SPEED LIFE
I was riding my 10-speed the other day
When I got to thinking
Life's a lot like that 10-speed.
When things get rough
I gear down a little,
Concentrate on the road ahead of me.
Before I know it, I'm over the rough spots.
When the going is easy,
I sit back and enjoy the ride.
If I'm feeling adventuresome,
I gear up and give myself a challenge.
I try to cover a little more ground
Every time I ride
And give myself credit that I tried.

Ronii Foster
THE CHOICE........
(TAKE CONTROL)
Many times we deceive ourselves,
Into thinking we're something that we're not.
We do stupid, idiotic things,
Saying it's the only chance that we've got.

We set goals that we can never reach,
Then give up when things go wrong.
Not once ever stopping to think,
That this journey could be long.

We turn to others for strength and support,
By saying the things we so desperately need to hear.
We're consoled for just a little while,
While the self-destruction continues to draw near.

We try to place the blame somewhere else,
Believing we'd never do this to ourself.
But life gets worse; to the breaking point,
Till we put our happiness away on a shelf.

Will we ever be satisfied with what we have,
Or will we go through life with our heads in a hole?
For nothing and no-one can make it right,
Unless first, we take full control.

J W Wack
MUSING FROM THE OTHER SIDE
What a lovely, floating feeling. When I was alive, I hated my name—Wilhelmina-Wilma-Witch-Wort. I don't like it any better now—Mother's cruel joke. I was no beauty, her disappointment she changed it to Crystal (beauty mine). I earned ten years of her unabated anger. I was always Wilhelmina. I loved her you know, but I never liked her whimpy second husband.

I loved strawberries—she chocolates. I could make any drink in the world, better than most—remembered good jokes. No touching—bar between us. I made a good living serving the animals at my zoo. Will I be cleaning glasses and bottles with my red, chapped hands?

One last sweet night, his kisses hot on my skin, I expired quickly in a ball of flames, my Fiero enfolded by death's messenger.

My white cat, Samantha, died of leukemia. I loved Robert once, he was at the top of the list, but I drew a line through his name. Maybe I'll see my infant son here.

The bright light gently embraces me—drawing me, urging me somewhere . . .

Su Ann Thompson
IF ONLY TIME COULD STOP
if only time could stop.
i'd travel back, in search of
youth, on wings of
wisdom.
in search of dreams that only
innocent children dream.
for one brief moment, find my
soul,
knowing that life is something
worth living for.
in search of that "something"
i haven't quite yet found.
but, now i come to You;
my life is still.
and as i throw back the shades of
yesteryear,
i suddenly find i'm home.
i'm Home.

Bruce R Lindsay
LOVE'S POWER
I Have truly
Tasted the grandeur & sweetness of a fragile love; though gone for the moment, it was alive as yesterday, and shall be tomorrow and forever.
The beautiful splendor of each of those passing days shall be remembered throughout my entire life.
Reserved one day for the woman of all my hopes & dreams. To be ravished upon her for eternity.

Larry Harrington
TO MY DEAREST FRIEND
Pictures on paper
So nice to show
Share with others
How time does go

On my heart
The image of one
Keeping inside
Sharing with none

Except the one
Engraved so true
The image of youth
The picture of you.

Wanda Smith
THOUGHTS AND MEMORIES
My thoughts of you are endless;
The good times we have shared.
Each time we were together,
How much I thought you cared.

My thoughts are of the happiness
I feel when I'm with you.
You always lift my spirits,
When I feel alone and blue.

My thoughts are uncontrollable
No matter what I do.
You're always there, but now I wonder,
Do you have these same thoughts too?

My thoughts now seem just memories
Of love I thought I had.
And once again you've shown me,
How it feels to be lonely and sad.
Now I have only memories,
Of dreams that might have been.
But like they say, all good things
Must sometime come to an end.

Given time if the saying's true,
My thoughts might fade away.
But I'll cherish every memory,
Every minute of each day.

Gale Lynn Dimartino

Gale Lynn Dimartino
THE PASSING
The old man stood quietly amidst
The impassive silence of dawn,
Holding soft hands with the hills
For the last time.

He had always risen to greet the day
Before others had opened their eyes
To the sun.

He touched the colors of the sky
And felt the gentle stir of fading life.

The beauty and understanding of things
That are forever wild was sure his,
For he had always lived among the hills,
uncut and free.

Yet, his great strength had come from the seasons,
Looking forward from one to the next.

But now, as with the aged pine,
He felt himself falling toward the earth,
Until at last—he rose to greet the sun!

Pamela Levy
SAFETY IN NUMBERS
Safety in numbers
I laughed when friends told me
That being alone was the worst thing for me
Lies told like truths, bent and then twisted
Slapped in the fact by lovers turned enemies

Multiply good times, subtracting the bad times
Leaves you with nothing except on your own
Divided by treason, like winter you're freezin'
Safety in numbers, a lie for all seasons

Calculate losses, body count growing
Account for the past moves and all that they're showing
The final equation, still undecided
Safety in numbers, no figure provided

John J Jay
HOW GREAT
They say we're all alone,
in this universal space.
All these countless worlds,
for just one human race.

If ours is the only world,
so full of life as such,
then surely God has made us,
with His one and holy touch.

The bible says He made us,
and earth to pass His test.
For here to work and toil,
maybe heaven to later rest.

We should count our blessings,
each and everyone He gives.
To know without a doubt,
how truly great he is.

Gregory Eichhold
THE AMERICAN DREAM
Getting mad at each other
Over losing your toys,
Growing up this way
Isn't nice for little girls
And little boys.
Can fighting be justified?
Why all this confusion?
Jesus Christ and the American Way . . .
Is this all just an illusion?
To live and love each other
Is how to go about things.
Joy and complacency
Is what happiness brings,
So all you young folk
Out there, listen to what I say
Forget about your indifferences,
Believe in Jesus Christ . . .
And the American Way!

Doris Worthen
MOUSE
He ran in and out
and looked all about
That's when I heard mama shout,
It's a mouse, it's a mouse,
In our house.
Get the poison, get the trap,
Get the hammer and give him a rap.
Hit that mouse upon his head
Roll him over and make sure he's dead.
Get the broom and push him aside,
And maybe the next mouse will stay outside.
The little louse
That was a mouse.

Cynthia A Adams
A HOLIDAY FROM PRAYER
I thought I could take
A holiday from prayer,
Take all the cares
And toss them to the air.
That they'd be taken care of
By him who dwells up there.

My idle musing proved me wrong,
For not long after, disaster came along

And burned their house
Quite to the ground.
Their fears were such as fears abound.
And I took a holiday from prayer.

Patricia Wells
MEMORIES

I dedicate this poem to a loving and special grandmother Lena Rand Hamlin

Out in the country high on a hill,
Stood a big white house and yellow daffodils.
The white picket fence all in a row,
With a fancy gate to open and close.
In the door was grandmother so dear,
As she loved and held me so near.
We'd sit and make paper dolls all through the day,
Or see how many games we could think to play.
She'd make apple pies without a recipe book,
It's so much fun just watching her cook.
She taught me how to make mud pies,
and bake them in the sun.
To awake from a nap,
As the pie becomes a real one.
She had her special ways
Of making me do what's right,
As I kneeled by the bed
To say my prayers at night.

Faith Board
SPRING

Spring is just the beginning.
The trees begin to bud and the flowers begin to grow.
The birds begin to nest and sing.
The bees begin to buzz.
Color comes where winter grey once made the world so bleak—
The cool breezes begin to warm and kites begin to soar
up in the bright blue sky almost to heaven's door.
As trees and flowers come into full bloom, you know that
spring will be over soon.
For as spring grows to its full intent, summer begins
with a brilliant dance.

Evelyn M Gray

Evelyn M Gray
HEART ATTITUDES BLESS OTHERS

"This poem is dedicated to William, my sweet husband" Also the Deacon's Conference, Kalamazoo, Mi.

Deep are the feelings of the heart—
Each life is obligated to at least start
To love others in an honest way;
Who knows—"you" might make somebody's day.

Encouragement feeds and nurtures life;
Forgiveness, caring discourages strife.
Agapé love is the heart's fuel,
For Christ is the Master of this tool.

Wherever you live or work or play
Remember you can make the difference
in a life today.
Simply loving others as you love yourself
Can create an environment for communication and help.

M I Baker
WHEN THE SNOW FALLS IN THE COUNTRY

This poem is dedicated to my mother, Erna Blau, who made all our childhood Christmases so memorable.

When the snow falls in the country,
and the fields look pure and white,
we remember little children
having their first snowball fight.

When the sun shines it looks like crystals,
and the wind blows the clouds away,
that's the time to wait for Christmas,
it's a joyful holiday.

When we're cheerful
'cause it's Christmas,
and our hearts, they open wide;
we remember a little manger
with Maria and her Christchild.

And the time is full of wonders,
God's great gift to all mankind.
He will love us forever after,
He was born at Christmas time.

Pasquale DiFranco
THE SOGGY CROCUS

Spring's first warm sun,
And first warm breeze
Has thinly loosed
A crust of earth,

And the crocus innocently
And blithely
Pops into the sun,
Briefly to delight the eye
Anticipating spring.

Then suddenly come graying clouds,
And wind, and cold,
And snow in big soft flakes
Floats thickly on the ground
Swelling inch by inch about the delicate flower
As if to choke it.

Then warmth returns,
And snow melts,
Leaving the soggy crocus bent
Heavily upon the ground,
When dry to rise again,
But blithely, never!

Evelyne Bursha
YESTERDAY IS SO SOON

Am I afraid of pain and strife
As I go from day to day
Down the uneven pathway of life
Seeing each day lived in all its
Sorrow and gaiety?
I have seen pain
Pain struck deeply into the face of a mother
Who has lost a loved and cherished one
I have seen the worry of a father
Seeking and finding no answer
Within himself, for a wayward son
I have seen the thunder—
The lightning flash—
As the whole world seemed to crash
Around our heads smashing and
Smothering us in its clutches.
I have seen depression—panic—
War—seen its dead and its crippled
I have seen happiness, pain, and sorrow
Seen children at play.
I do not fear tomorrow
I've seen yesterday.

Ann Marie Brown

Ann Marie Brown
IMPASSIONED HEART

Distant sounds, alluring tones,
Run endlessly through my mind
Searching for feelings that once existed,
Seeming never again to find.
Taunting me with romantic passages
he plays, I know he's calling to me.
His touch is different from others;
My heart listens, longing to be set free.
My soul is overwhelmed.

As he touches the keys with such confidence
His eyes are searching mine
Knowing I'm trembling without pretense.
Feelings hidden for a lifetime,
Aching to be unleashed
If only for a brief moment,
Never again to cease.
Could I love again?
Never! To him I say.
but to his luminous tones and chords,
I say forever stay.

Otis C Polk Jr
A BRAVE NEGRO TEXAS FRONTIERSMAN

There once rode the plains of Young County,
From Ft. Belknap to the muddy Red,
A man big and tall in statue,
Whom the Indians wanted dead.
He was feared by the mighty Comanches,
And hated by the Kiowas too,
He blazed the trail and made it safe,
For the ancestors of me and you.

Britt Johnson was the name of this warrior,
Legend says, top cowhand and scout,
And over the plains of West Texas,
The name, Negro Britt, was known throughout.

He was a friend of Allen Johnson,
And was known by Gen. Throckmorton too,
And men who visited Veole's station,
Also knew what Negro Britt could do.

But then on a trip to Ft. Griffin,
The second night out at Turtle Hole,
His old Kiowa enemies, Mamanti and Quitan,
Killed Negro Britt in the morning's cold.

Ena Winkler
EVENING BEACH

The last dull gleams of daylight die
The wind lies down.
Slowly the waves retreat, bubbling trails
along the shelly sand.
No seabirds fly
Only a plume of smoke,
A foolish feather, pencilled high,
Against the sky,
Flickers, then fades.
The eeling mist coils and twist.
Tarnish on the sea-glossed rocks.
And, in the darkening sky, a feeble moon,
Gleams, then blurs,
Silence echoes silence
And no thing stirs.

Wanda Loyd Laton
SISTER

Sister is a very special word to me
Because you're so special to me
you see.
The years around us have quickly gone by
But our love and friendship
have not offered to die.
Over the years we've laughed and we've cried
But when things got rough you
were there by my side.
You've shared my sorrows an my joys
And treated them all like they
were yours.
When I needed a friend you were always there
You always let me know that
you care.
You've never hesitated when I asked you to keep my son
You always told me that it
would be fun.
When I had exciting news to share
Somehow your calendar was
always clear.
You'll never know how much I Love You
But maybe these words will
give you a clue.

Judylee Annette Glover
MY BROKEN HEART

To J.R., the inspiration for this poem, with warmest regards.

I thought I loved you,
and then you broke my heart.
Then I knew you didn't really love me,

and it tore me all apart.
How can I go on,
knowing you don't care
that I feel my life is at an end,
that I have nothing left to share?
I can't believe
that all those things you said
Were only empty compliments;
I let them go to my head.
Of course you didn't really love me,
how could I have thought you did?
You broke my heart,
and I just can't love you
Anymore.

Christina Ann Buchhorn
REFLECTIONS THROUGH THE CLOUDS

I am Dedicating my poem to my son Charlie and my daughter Heather, so that they may always see the future in a bright way, to always be positive in anything they may do.

As I see the gray in the clouds, I can reach the sky,
Reflect upon the goodness in thee,
but then again understanding what is around me is not only fear,
hurt and dismay, maybe in all of us,
but to always keep the positiveness in ones sight, to realize, in reality
sometimes this cannot be so.
So the next time you peak through the clouds,
remember the gray of negative will soon go away,
Destiny will be sought, how hard we fought, the power of truth will help us through, so reach the sky, to the stars so high.
Reach the light, You and I.

Kellie D Koon
ARIZONA

Arizona the Great
You Grand Canyon State
with your
billowing desert sea
your Palo Verde Tree.
Mother of,
the Cactus Wren,
with its speckled
breast,
helps it
to make its home,
upon a
Saguaro Cactus
nest.
Forever
Arizona be
Arizona grand.
Painting your
color on
Arizona land.

Edith M Lloyd
FACTS AND QUESTIONS

A single seed will grow into beautiful flowers.
An acorn, into a mighty tree.
The clock tells the seconds, minutes and hours.
A strong wind blows; this we feel; we can not see.
So many things are taken for granted;
The sun, the sea and the sky.
Little ones' fists are clenched, their mouths pursed to cry.
Are their souls blessed, or forever cursed?
Each breath we breathe, each fragrant smell—
Is the world a bubble about to burst?
Does it make a difference? Who among us can tell?
Somewhere in time, as the wind blows,
The clock ticks and the baby grows.
Stars in the sky keep shinning.
Some old, some new; what a prize!
Oh, wonder of wonders, that we know not all.
Some things in life should be left to surprise.

Carole Stiverson
GOODBYE MY LOVE GOODBYE

Goodbye my love goodbye
Goodbye my love goodbye,
I think that I shall cry.
I missed my love, give time a shove
My heart heaves with a heavy sigh,
Oh! that my soul could fly like a dove.
Then I could say goodbye
Goodbye my love goodbye
I think that I shall cry
Could time stand still—
You'd be here still
But I must wait, until it's late
and then
I'll cry goodbye my love goodbye.

Julie Haley
MIND'S VIEW

Placing things in proper prospective from the mind, is difficult to do.
As my thoughts are directly from my heart and constantly of you.
Each morn, when I awake, at night, throughout the day
You're on my mind, In my dreams whatever I do and say.
Time, forever time, means so very much. Only when we're together we never have enough.
To have you holding me, to feel your kiss and touch.
I long to be in your arms, content, alone with you.
Is this a reality? Or Just Mind's View.
Whenever I try to rationalize, the way things ought to be
There is an interference, coming from within me.
For now, I'll not decipher it. Only let it lay
And try to find the answers somehow, somewhere, someday.

Kristina White
UNTITLED

You are a traitor, a liar.
Your words are minced when you say
It's only I who understand, only I who care.
There are others, many of them.
But are they like me?
Do they care and understand only on command?
Understand! Care! Be there!
A vicious circle of injustice.
Disinterested are you in a true and honest friendship
Only in brief and meaningless tristes
With uncaring and impassionate people.
Am I only a stand-in? A sounding board?
No, I'm more. A listener, a psychiatrist
And also, I'm a doctor to clean your wounds.
I'm a punching bag, your loyal pet.
A piece of sanity in the insane-asylum of life.
Never is it enough. Never!
I hate you for it. I despise your very existence
As much as I hate you, I do those things. Why?
Why am I your faithful, naive servant?
Why? Because I love you.

Gina Fiorino

Gina Fiorino
WINTER

Dedicated to my Mom and Dad, for loving me. And to my sister Joey, my friend.

Now as fall goes by and winter is here,
We watch as the snow appears.
We wait for the 25th day of December,
Forgetting the months of October and November.

But when spring comes, we still remember
those times in December.
For hidden in all children are
the good times of winter.
Whether it's spring, summer or fall,
the feeling of winter is always there.
For the wonderful times of winter never fall.

Elaine M Mathews
THE COMING

Her footsteps in the darkness
echo off the cavernous walls
of her den. Soft whispers blend
into the night, only to be
remembered in the morning.
Finally she arrives, seeking
the warmth of the fire. Sitting
under the second full moon
with twelve others of her kind,
she commands the rituals
to begin. Dancing and
swirling in the circle, their
golden eyes reflect
the madness
of the moon. Stretching
sinously to the rhythm
of their unearthly cries, only
to plunge into the dark
abyss of the mind of a ruler.
Claws outstretched, to sink
into the pulpy flesh
of his brain. Feline cries
fill his ears with a banshee pitch
that sounds of a 1942 London air
raid, reverberating between his
ears until the only escape
is to scream over it all.
His mouth to ashes and
his tongue to black
before sound is established.
The enemies have won
their fight for slavery as they
scale the canyon walls of
consciousness, to find a new leader
has risen from the ashes
of the old to rule his minions.
Knowingly and willfully they
succumb only to be treated with
indifference to their nature.
They gave their lifeblood and
their families for an eternity
of slavery. To overcome is to
die.

Evelyn M Wills
CHRISTMAS LONG AGO

Could there ever be a Christmas
Like the one so long ago
When Aunts and Uncles all the Kin
To Grandpas house did come
And the hearty laughter of them all
Still lingers in my ear
As tho that Christmas long ago
Had just passed by this year
There was Grandma in the cellar
Sorting out her special jars
Corn and Beans Suckatash
All those favorite things
And Grandpa too was planning
As he checked the Piglet pen
Just which little porker
He'd carve that Christmas Day
And soon there it was Christmas
And all the Kin folks came
And we ate and ate and had such fun
As only Kinfolks make
And then off to the Parlor
Where the tall Pine stood
All decorated just for us
The Old Maid Aunts did it right
And there came Santa in his sleigh
HO HO Merry Christmas to us all
With a bag full of gifts for all
And then was time for all to go
With hugs and sweet good byes
And so it is I can't forget
That Christmas so very long ago

Mrs Dorothy M Hosey
WINGS

Wings of The Boeing 747 purred a melodious drone
At Frankfort, Germany when it headed home.
More Passengers it took to heart at Heathrow:
Diplomats, Students, Parents, Residents, Young Men-on-Leave
One and All for whom we now deeply grieve!
Leaving the Scottish Town of Lockerbie
There seemed to be a quiver in each wing
As a pressure-timer awakened that Horrible Thing—
A Hellish explosion in the evening sky
At 31,000 feet with Boeing Wings, who could die?
The giant Wings of Flight 103 faltered in terrible lament
As plane and 270 persons and homes were devastatingly spent!
On the evening breeze came a whirr of Angel Wings-soft yet clear
Reminder that God's help is always near!

To escort and waft them gently on their Heavenly Way.
Oh, what a Price the Terrorists made us pay!
As God moves ever steadily with His Plan
To help enlighten the Needs of Man!
As down the Corridor of Time, Death howls in fiendish glee,
Little realizing how much It brought us closer to God and to Eternity!

Melody A Wallace
SEEKING

I keep running away,
Saying to myself, there has to be a better way.
But, I'm standing still in time,
Being selfish, foolish, and blind.

LORD, you open doors for me,
But, I'm too blind to see.
Reaching out your hand, wanting me to stay.
But, being the fool I am, I turn away.

Frightened, and scared, and not prepared,
I keep running, running nowhere.
Trying to understand, but too nebulous to understand.
About the things, we as people say, and what we do.
So, how do we know what is right?
This is what I ask in my prayer tonight.

LORD, you know what I feel, and what I do,
And that my faith in you is true.
Your all I need to know,
Because, I believe you will show me the way, and in your arms I will stay.

Timothy D Lyons
ESSENCE

This poem was created from, and is dedicated to, the memory of Susan Salkind.

Can you envision the glorious light from across the fields,
How strong and proud its glow makes my heart feel,
Conquering all the evil darkness that it has sealed,
And I am blinded by the bright light that the heavens reveal.

The tender touch of the sun's warmth shines through the trees,
Amongst the colorful shower of October's falling leaves,
As it brings me bending humbly to my knees
I can feel the caress of the autumn sun,
And it has made my spirit free.

My vision of a morning horizon over the distant hills,
I stare captured by the beauty, and it gives my soul chills,
Suddenly I feel reborn, so completely fulfilled,
And I smile in amazement at the horizon rising over the hills.

For there is a harmonic echo from the deep valley below,
Telling me I must continue on the road
To the place where I go,
And someday when I arrive there
Then I shall finally know,
The answer to the musical echo from the deep valley below.

I long to walk upon the green grass under the blue sky,
To stride strong with conviction and never wonder why,
With each step of faith upon the blades the harder I must try,
To someday roll playfully in the green grass under the blue sky.

And when I hear the soft whisper of the westerly wind,
Giving me guidance when I know not where I have been,
As it quietly blows away my most wicked of sins,
Now I sing joyfully with the whisper of the westerly wind.

Finally to embrace the freedom of the refreshing shore,
As it washes me with wet wonder like never before,
Remarkably I can not feel the pain of life anymore,
Drowning in the baptizing arms of my Lord.

Mayra Ramirez
SHATTERED DREAMS

To Chris

All my dreams were shattered, since the day you left me.
All my hopes were broken, since you went away.
If I only knew that you never needed me, I wouldn't give you the chance, like the way I did then.
I gave you my heart but you took it for granted, and now is too late to repair the mistake.
You hurt me so deeply by the way you treated me,
and the pain that is left, is driving me insane.
I just hope one day if you ever remember, the good times we had and we used to share, that you realize how much I did love you, and there's no other who will really care. I want you to know that life is not easy,
Being without you it isn't the same.
I'm just trying to cope the best I can think of, but I found it harder, herder, everyday now, there's only loneliness, and my life is empty, my days and my nights for me are the same, there's nothing else that could turn my sadness, into greatest moments filled with happiness.

O Edward Gray
AFTER THE CIVIL WAR

I must write about the post civil war years in a poem.
About the Southern soldiers of laying down their guns to go home.
I need to tell of those ragged, defiant, Confederate men fighting to the very end.
How they were discouraged, but glad to have some rest so wounds could mend.
Some wounds were deep and beyond repair,
Especially when loved ones at home were not waiting there.
Faced with burned-down homes and the plantation's destruction.
"Old Abe," the president, had already planned for reconstruction.
Yes, the Civil War had ended, but many problems were brought forth
Problems of what to do with the freedman as viewed by the South and the North
A conflict of ideas resulted in what to do with the negro.
Some concerned Americans founded an agency called the freedman's bureau.
Unfortunately Abe Lincoln's plan could not be followed, though he was "The Great Emancipator."
His life was cut short by an assassin's bullet while in the Ford Theater.
Now the freedman could not help how they got where they were,
And most were glad to no longer be slaves that is for sure.
It seems the South knew where they had been,
And could not accept them as a first rate citizen.
While the North and the radicals were glad for their emancipation,
They failed to consider his needs for land, jobs and an education.
The radicals wanted to keep the old southern leader out of power and influence, it was their institution.
But with persistence, they successfully adopted the 13th, 14th and 15th Amendment to the Constitution.
So now with the abolishment of slavery, citizenship for the blacks and their right to vote is true.
But for real freedom and civil rights for the black, there was a lot more to do.

Alioa Chaney
MY LOVE FOR YOU

I looked for light, and I found you.
You're all I ever wanted.
Though you and I have become best friends, I want so much more.
When there is happiness, and laughter, are you there? And when you're here, the birds sing and the wind whispers. And when I'm with you, you make my life change. For know that I have no problems,no fears nor cries. And I want you to know you brighten my day with every touch, move, or sound you make. And as I wish I could tell you the way I truly feel about you, I learn to hide them until you let them free. and as I lie to you about him, I wish you could see that it is really you I talk about. When we look into each other's eyes as you look away. Do you know I love you?
I wish you knew, but you don't. I love you and I wish you could see. But until we both share these feelings, I hide. I'll learn to see we are only best friends, you and I.

Christopher C Russell
MINDMELD

As I look into your deep blue eyes,
The distance between us close . . .
Those radiant pools of blue
Drawing me further into you.
Falling, falling into the abyss
That is your mind,
Becoming lost in the happiness of your love
Fascinated by thoughts so pure
Enthralled by the innocence of your dreams.

Shocked by the ecstasy
As your mind touches mine,
Contemplating the euphoria of your soft caresses,
We separate, probing feelings that are new.
Your thoughts then envelop mine
Seeking things that are hidden . . .
Opening my heart's desires,
Pulling me further and further into you
Stroking me with your selfless love
Bringing our endless love spurting forth,
Into ultimate climax . . .
You look away . . . contact lost.
Leaving me stripped of all pretence
Yearning, yearning for the dreams and feelings lost . . .

Lisa Ezernack
I AM

Dedicated to my mother, Anna Fowler, and my three sisters, Cindy, Deb, & Tana, who have shown me a lifetime of reasons to be . . . Thanks

Well, here I am; stop and look at me.
Today you'll see things you never thought you'd see.

I'm no longer lonely, shy, or scared,
Surprise, old friend, look how I've fared.

I've survived the climb up the jagged hill,
Try and set me back now, I doubt you will.
Look good and remember the things that you see,
For, today, I am everything; today I am me!

I'm proud and secure and, in fact, even brave,
Climbed out of my shell so dark and concave.
I shine with the glory of each day's delight,
Soar with the eagles, possess their great might.

I used to think you blocked the way,
Of what I'd feel or think or say.
Then, suddenly, I began to see,
The power you owned was given freely by me.

So, I've recalled the power of my birthright,
In turn, opened doors to a wondrous sight.
Peace and serenity have burst the strong dam.
I've climbed the great barriers and finally I AM!

Ha Binh Trung

Ha Binh Trung
THE KNIGHTS

One day when on the beach of the hamlet Chu Lai
Came bold and gallant the American soldiers,
The Viet women, after the manner of Hawaii,
Put around their neck welcoming flowers,
Many of them were young and did not have enough
Combat experience against the enemy,
In guerilla warfare the encounter was tough,
During a fierce ambush they fell

down bravely,
Knightly had they gone deep in the forest tall grass
Their corpses in plastic bags returned in copter
Their unborn children were left behind alas!
Their lovers of passage forsaken forever.
To fight hard or to die, however "not to win"(1).
That was the policy they would not understand
Was it like with tied hands, but for human sin,
They had to go to wars and die for other men?
They had fought for a cause:
Freedom and Democracy.
Despite the bloody war, Love has no ending,
Death's only absence, Life's eternity,
Existence Nothingness have the same meaning. (2)

(1) The "No-win policy" of the U.S. placed the Allied forces in the defensive position.
(2) TIn Buddhist Pragna Bible: "Existence does not differ from Nothingness, Nothingness is not different from Existence, Existence is indeed Nothingness, Nothingness indeed is Existence. There is no creation, no destruction, no dirtiness, no cleanliness, no augmentation, no reduction."

Bob Henson
REMEMBER THE TIME

To my friends who really cared, to my loved ones who stood by me when I truly needed them. I love you all.

When we were teenagers and life was such fun,
We would laugh and giggle
And tell lots of puns.

We were always saying remember this or that,
It would always lead to the best of the facts.

"Remember the time when we ran through the rain,
We had lots of fun,
Then came sniffles and pain?"

"Remember the time on the football field,
I got hit real hard
And you laughed with great zeal?"

"Remember the time that we danced till dawn,
Then we told our parents
It was the car, it wouldn't run?"

"Remember the time we played like adults,
We smoked a cigarette
And got drunk as a cuss?"

The years flew by and the fun's all gone,
Now we sit here listening
To fond old songs,
We Remember The Times, the grand old years
And we hope against hope
That the gray disappears.

Those fond old memories of time gone by
They always seem to make me cry.

Now I'm up in my years I walk with a cane,
I have children and grandchildren
Which tradition will train.
I share the memories that have gone fastly by,
And I say to them all "Remember The Time."

Ryan Dalgal
LAST TANGO

This poem is dedicated to Patrick Joseph Ryan and Julia Esther Kormondi Ryan as well as all individuals who identify with these characters.

I saw them in their Last Tango;
They exited from the bedroom
into the bathroom—together
to continue this dance of life—
Their dance of life!

I saw them in their Last Tango;
They step in unison—slowly,
very slowly and then a
few faster steps.
And the night becomes darker!

I saw them in their Last Tango;
His arm around her shoulder,
her arm around his waist,
the other arms held
straight out to the front.

I saw them in their Last Tango;
Was their entry into the bathroom
to play with toiletries and in
a child-like way spray each other
in a ticklish frolic?

I saw them in their Last Tango;
Their dance today is not unlike
other dances that came before;
The strain is the same
in their game.

I saw them in their Last Tango;
He, bedridden with various cancers
and other ailments, relies on her
to assist him with his dance of life.
He needs her. He says so.

I saw them in their Last Tango;
She, also sick and uncommonly stubborn,
loves to be needed.
She needs him to need her
or their is no dance.

I saw them in their Last Tango—
Their Dance of Life!

Orton J Stange
RYAN THOMAS KIENZLEN
Ryan Thomas Kienzlen is only three:

But what an efffect he has on me.

He quickens my heart, and livens my step,

And brings tears to my eyes, which I try to hide,

With the four magic words "I wuv you Gampa."

I remember when I was only three and would sit
Upon my Grandpa's knee, and now in my Grandson I see

A reflection of me.

He's my projection to the future, my journey

Through the universe, and beyond to the stars.

I sit here and ponder, and wonder what his Life will be?

When he is my age, Sixty and Three.

Thelma L Hanner
A WINTER FAIRYTALE
The year was Nineteen-hundred and eighty-nine
When Mother Nature, having 'snow' in mind,
She summoned all the elements,
And even added some embellishments!
Said she, "Now hear this, one and all,
This year we're going to have a ball!
And 'Old Man Winter' will be King,
The boss of snow and everything"!
Well the 'King' took on the best of jobs,
Dropping snow in 'gobs 'n gobs'
Until mere mortals cried,
"ENOUGH"!,
We're BURIED in the fluffy stuff."
Young Jacky Frost, an impish mite,
Was told to nip, and grip, and bite,
Until folks tingled nose to toes,
And so did add much to our woes!
Now, good old Mother Nature,
All clothed in gleaming white,
Surveyed her work of wonderment
And CHUCKLED with delight!
Said she to all the elements,
"Come now, we've had our fun,
Let's just fade into his-tory
And make way for the sun"!

Ramona See
BROKEN BLOSSOMS
Broken blossoms in the dust, caressed by the wind
Autumn leaves fall on my love, never to live again.
Winter comes with sparkling snow, like diamonds in the sky.
But the flowers I bring to you, lay beneath the snow and die.

Spring's the time for much rejoicing, I feel only pain.
And the blossoms are so broken, torn and tattered by the rain.
Summertime and memories haunt me, love and sorrow meld as one.
And the petals are all withered, dying in the summer's sun.

Many seasons have gone by, since you went away.
Still I stand by your grave weeping, never more to love again.
So I bring to you the flowers, as a sacred loving trust.
And my heart is just as broken, as the blossoms in the dust.

Mildred L Simon
MY SISTER
Twas a poem you requested and by the way
The time it took was longer than just a day
So here's to my sister, my one and only
For without whom I would have been awfully lonely
Who else but you would have taught me my ABC's
Not right side up but upside down!
Now let me see
Shall we take a trip through memory lane at last
And remember the bicycles of a Christmas past
So shiny and such a bright blue, they were so fine
You rode quite well but I always had a wreck on mine
Remember the beautiful dolls that were so petite
With the finest of wardrobes right down to their feet
Hours and hours we spent at play, isn't that right?
How Mother must have loved us to stay up late and sew at night
Making not only lovely doll clothes but in between
Made us cowgirl outfits with fringe and blouses of green
And remember our dog, Sampson, who thought he could climb a tree
He was always a friend to you and to me
As he listened to laughter and our sobs as well
My but we thought that dog was swell
Oh yes, we had our fights as siblings do
But nevermind, what's important is that I still have you
So though in miles we're far apart
Please know you'll always hold a special place in my heart
For I love you very much, you're the best sister anyone ever had
And for you I thank God, I am so glad!

Poetess Kalamu Chaché
I LOVE YOU LIKE . . .
I love you like the sun shines.
I love you like great poetic lines.
I love you like the moon glows.
I love you like the Nile River flows.
I love you like the earth all around.
I love you like a harmonic melody sound.
I love you like very twinkling star.
I love you like the planets near and far.
I love you like the waters deep.
I love you like the pleasant dreams from sleep.

Carol Ann Smith
THE PIT AND THE PENDULUM
The torture of the Inquisition,
The thought I would soon go,
The scamper of the lousy rats,
that would but start unslow.

In this small prison of cement or brick,
of what did rats have to eat?
Just the thought made me sick,
and the scurry of their feet.

With a swing, not unlike an axe,
The pendulum came down,
The pendulum came down upon,
and almost hit me near the ground.

A deep, bright light engaged me eye upon.
In a pit a fire was burning,
Into the fire I almost went,
It gave me an urgent yearning.

It was General Lasalle I was rescued by,
So now I live to tell this lie.

Sean J Oliveira
MISUNDERSTOOD
I'm a person who turned his face from the past, for the promise of no future with only the present to survive.

I'm an alien lost in a misroled cast, in the premise of a new culture, with nothing left to derive.

Laughing at myself I twist the story straight.
Do you really believe you're caught up in some fate?
To exist, or resist

We all have a certain goal, pushing us through the maze.
There are always certain dice to roll, to break us out of this faze.
I'm not here to evolve, that's all I'm trying to say.
There are problems left to solve, history isn't there to replay.

He's a man too old to have a childhood, still fool enough to believe the lie
that the promise stands in youth.
I could give you my story if I only would, knowing that I could simply rely
on what is understood to be the truth.

All humanity mocks their so-called substantial existence.
Do you really still believe it all relies on persistence?
Too behoove, or too move?

David L Heilpap
YOU AND ME
We've traveled paths of life,
That 'til now never crossed,
Acquired friends, and loved ones,
Though many have we lost.

Don't be afraid to walk with me,
Though life be somewhat humble.
I need you on the path I take,
Along side, case I stumble.

Cecil D Clayton
MEMORIES
I think of a murmuring Ozark stream.
Of a quiet pool and rapids a-gleam;
Of a mountain trail gloomy and dim;
And the moon coming over the mountain rim;
Memories like these come back to me still.
At the plaintive cry of the Whip-Poor-Will.

Willard G Luffman

Willard G Luffman
MY MORNING THOUGHTS OF YOU

This poem is dedicated to "Carolyn Jean Cole," and, to my 3 year old son, Christopher Willard Luffman, with love always

As I picture you, walking across the floor,
With your curlers, still in your hair,
The beauty you endured last night,
This morning is still there.

Nothing could take away,
The loveliness in your face,
Nor change any portion of your soft body,
Which lies, sexy, in its place.

Dressed in your house coat,
You deliberately hide your pretty negligee,
To make me wonder, how much softness lies within,
And only with a gesture, It's needless to say.

But as your lips touch mine,
The sensations I feel, from your soft kiss,
Remembering mornings of you like this,
Darling, should you ever leave, these thoughts I'd surely miss.

For beauty, in no other,
Like yours, Have I known,
Even seeing you, in your curlers,
You still show the beauty, you've always shown.

Ruth Hooper Zamora
COSTLY TRIP
"They" said I must see a doctor
And insisted 'til I went.
But they didn't feel the pain
For the money I had spent.

The doctor poked and questioned
Gave me tests and some advice.
Then, "Peace! Peace!" I yelled,
"Peace, at any price."

Pills and rest—no stress must I
And diet, stringent, they say,
In order that I might just live
To see many another day.

I ask you—is it worth it
To continue in this way,
Contained, detained, pained, restrained,
To live from day to day?

I guess if "they" deem it a necessity
I'll go along with their plot
For what the heck! "It's best for me"
Though happy—I am not.

Clarice A Merswolke
THE WARNING
Flock of crows
screaming danger
hysterically,
arouse, notify
venturesome kin
snatching kernels of corn
sowed in Spring
with farmer aiming shotgun
t'is suicidal,
maims many mates.

Those who challenged
have sordid feathers
their only cover
for a shrinkable skeleton
in sun, wind, rain,
on fruitful fields
with towering tassels
seemingly nodding, mourning,
in harvest moonlight.

Leslie Nyberg
SOMETIMES I WONDER
Sometimes I wonder,
I wonder about who I am, what I am, and who or what I will be.
I know I will never stop trying,
Never stop thinking or longing for the future.
But always something happens, something that breaks my hold on life.
Always it comes down to reality,
The truth of the matter, the centre of the Universe, the question of whether I can
Always the pattern turns and the change is too great.
It is the root of the matter, the underlying factor of meaning,
Meaning that is strong and everflowing.
I know the circumstances but it is to no avail,
I see the forthcoming disaster.
My shell breaks and I am open to the world.
My wounds will heal in time,
tomorrow it will be anew.
I will be back, returning from the past,
Leaving behind the memory, glad to begin again,
But carefully, cautiously, I will progress until I am safe.
But time is too often uneven, but as always I will endeavor.
Use the power of my thought as I kneel down and clasp my hands,
Asking to forgive and be forgived.
All alone I watch.
The continuality is rough, the road of life unsafe.

Sarah Saunders Sires
A BAG FULL OF WISHES
I wouldn't wish for you wealth
Instead, it would be health
And all those things which matter most and are free
Like the lovely shape of a tree
Flowers that bloom in the spring
Lovely birds on the wing
Sunsets and sunrises, rainbows and such
Neighbors that mean so much
Sweet memories of the past
And hope for the future
Friendships which will last
and thoughts that are pure
These are some of the things I wish for you
Love, love of family, love of friends,
Love, something we can't have enough "OF"

Richard T Gragg
MOTHER EARTH
Oh Mother Earth your mounds of soil
From sunup to sundown men with thee toil

We move you abuse you but cannot destroy
You return with the wind and jump with joy

We burn you with fire and turn you to dust
We drown you in water you wash up and crust

You loaned us oh earth to stay for awhile
Then come and reclaim us like a mother's child

Clarice a Daggett
MY SURPRISE

To my friend, Eunice B. Lanzl.

A friend left a gift at my door
On a day that I chose to be out.
According to shape and dimension
'Twas designed to make women stout.

On 'Opning the box some time later.
Lo!—a Bible—large print, red and gold
A gift with the best of intention
A most beautiful sight to behold.

This good friend knew of my struggle
Eyes growing dim, Bible falling apart
A fact that I don't need to mention
It will ever be dear to my heart.

Now, I go for sweets like no other
In a box, served on plate or in bowl
But, a thing that sure needs my attention
Is the food that's so good for the soul.

Blanka Jirak
WHISPERING
When wonders will wane
with the wild weapons,
where will we wander,
we, the women, weeping
with the wounded world
wondering w h y ?

Alice L Curry
PLEASE REMEMBER ME
I met a lonely man one night.
His face was marked with such pain and strife.

What happened to this man on the street?
You'll pass him by, but do you want to meet?

You shake your head and you'll wonder why.
Down on his luck, but does he cry?

He once had a job, like me and you.
But then the jobs became too few.

This man lost not job alone.
But his family, friends and home.

He wraps up in paper when it's cold.
Not just him, but the young and the old.

Does he dream of the warm bed he once had?
It is so unbelievable; It's all too sad.

There are so many out there with so very much.
Can't we reach out with a loving touch?

I don't have all that much to give.
But after all he has a right to live!

Stop and think . . . Stop and think . . .
For their lives are on the brink.

Renate S Higgins
BIRTHDAY WISHES
I'm sending you
Birthday wishes
That come from the heart.
Wish that so many miles
Didn't keep us apart.

No matter the gap or the day,
You're thought of just so.
Today, Tomorrow, Forever.
More than you know.

LaVaune Ingallinera
A HUMAN CONCERN

To Sting, Green Peace, all the people in the world who care, and Gregg my true love.

The time has come, we must make amends
The human race has gone far out of hand

The tropical rain forests have now turned to sand
The ozone's been eaten by fluorocarbons that we've banned

The nuclear age with its efficiency and power
Has caused environmental problems hour by hour

The ocean's conditions are now very poor

With dead fish and sick seals
washing up on the shore

The animals that once bountifully
roamed the land
Are now becoming extinct with
no protection from man

Some say we're doomed; the
Apocalypse is at hand
I say let's turn the tables and
give the earth what it demands

We have the power to make it happen
with modern technology and science
If the will is there nothing can
defy us

D Christopher Winslow
PSILO
A copy of Castanada's "A Separate Reality" opened, face up, lay in heat for a cool hand to caress the glossy cover for a moment.
An Anthropology student explains its significance, "anthropologically" to an insurance agent who was a Libra sun Cancer moon Virgo rising, who wanted another beer. The student had more "shroom" juice talking in tongues, and it was clear to the agent there was a lot of land in Mexico unexplored, even by yogis.

Agnes Magnone
I STOOD BY.

Dedicated to my grandsons—Gary & Grant

Lord, why did you leave me
when I needed you most?
These words were spoken
By a soul who seemed lost.

And the Lord said, I did not leave
you
I was always near by,
I watched you when I heard you
Give your every sigh.

Did you not see me stand by
When you wept your many tears?
Who was it helped you cry
And swept away your fears?

I was always at your side
Each day I stood by,
I ever opened my arms wide
And lifted you up high.

When life seems least fair
Then turn your eyes to me,
And know that I deeply care,
I am standing by, you see!

Eleanor H Balestrino
A BABY IS A MIRACLE
A baby is a miracle of God's lasting
love,
A baby is a miracle sent from Him
above;
A baby is a miracle for a man and
his wife;
A baby is a miracle for they started
him in life.

A baby is a miracle whether a boy
or a girl,
A baby is a miracle who will go into
the world;
A baby is a miracle for you to give
unto others,
A baby is a miracle through him we
all are brothers.

A baby is a miracle let him grow
into a man,
A baby is a miracle give him all the
help you can;
A baby is a miracle who should
always serve his God,
A baby is a miracle so do not spare
the rod.

A baby is a miracle a leader he may
be,
A baby is a miracle to guide you
and me;
A baby is a miracle who will stand
for all that's right,
A baby is a miracle who will help us
see the light.

Gwendolyn Kaye Walker

Gwendolyn Kaye Walker
OH GOD I GET SO WEAK AT TIMES
Oh God, I get so weak at times,
You said just call and you'd hear my
whine.

I try to live by the rules you've set,
My body and mind gets so weak, it's
so easy to forget.

It seems the harder I try, oh the
harder it gets.

The tears won't stop flowing
My pillow gets so wet.

I always remember "Footprints," but
during painful times
they're so hard to see.

Oh God! Touch me now and set my
pain free.

Oh God I get so weak at times,
You said just call and you'd hear my
whine.

Avel
UNTITLED
Husbands anger
seeps into my veins
crawls between the spaces
across my face
trickles downward
inward
until it finds the cavity of
love
causing turmoil and panic
a state of unrest
spilling over the sides to the
beds of joy
crushing tender thoughts
with its blanket
of hate
suffocating life and smiles
it causes the capillaries to
explode
veins to burst
upheaving spit and words
breaking the bonds and doors of trust
crushing roses
imbedded in tears

Yet through all this madness
a daisy appears
after the passing
of a seasonal shower

Matthew David Reichin
COMMENCE ATTACK
Skeleton songs sing in air.
Bare bones rattle at night
and scare up trouble from
depths below; to brittle ears
those lyrics flow.

Eyes see neither war nor
bodies, fears resume in night
mares' wake. Tears explode
on pilots' pillows:
protection of the surface breaks.

Numbed warriors' intrusion
ignites Death Man's fuse.
Mysteries of all they touch,
but headlines on the network news.

Mabel Glenn Haldeman
HOW CAN IT BE?

This poem is dedicated to many interested friends

How can it be that anyone with
blessings hundredfold
Can turn his back on Jesus Christ, for
such a thing as gold?
That anyone can soil his hands with
canker and with rust,
When Christ has shed His precious
Blood to raise him from the dust?

How can it be that anyone should
hate to drop, for time,
The things that perish, when to them
is offered the sublime,
The riches and the wealth untold
reserved for them above?
It must be that they never knew the
Saviour's dying love.

How can it be that youthful life is
laid at human feet,
When theirs might be the joys untold
of love divinely sweet?
It must be that they have a mist of
darkness o'er their eyes;
For cannot clever youth discern the
value of a prize?

How can they spurn the gracious
One, whose love is unsurpassed,
And cling to but a substitute, which
ne'er was meant to last?
Yet ignorance is prevalent and reigns
upon the throne
Of hearts where wisdom from above
has never yet been known.

Oh, may such souls be made to say,
before the day is done,
"I have accepted, by God's grace, His
holy, blessed Son.
And now I wonder how and why so
long I said Him 'Nay';
For words cannot express the joy I
have in Him today!"

Patricia Goulet
THE TREE OF LIFE
It was a seedling once, like me.
It grew strong with promise once,
like me.
It had many uses once, like me.
It had a certain beauty when it went
through its changes once, like me.
One day life with its ever strange
twists and turns took its toll on the
tree and me.
The branches became weak and
droopy, twisted and brown.
I grew wrinkled and old, my world
turning upside down.
My job lost, my family and friends,
distancing themselves with doing
their own thing.
As I look closer at the tree
I see a beauty and strength within
I never saw before,
and I know it will survive, like me.

Rich Baron
ON GROWING OLDER

To my darling wife Maggie
Through whose beautiful eyes
I remain forever young.

Hearts walk a beat
Amidst skipping stones of bubbling
youth;
Sighs stretch out
Questioning where time has flown.

The hourglass of life quivers
Teetering over sands of eternity;
Visions of forever
Fade into the mist of whenever.

The past is a constant companion
Embracing love and laughter of years
no more;
To be graceful a desired plateau
Unattainable above mountainous
ranges of regret.

Why slam the gates of the garden
When there are many seeds yet to be
sown?
Why challenge the unbeknownst
When it is familiarity which comforts
the soul?

Heart, please skip a beat
Bursting bubbles to boil my blood;
And, then, in between elongated
sighs
I will fly at my own speed
Soaring with delirious delight across
a rainbow of wonder.

Irene Manalis
SWINGING THOUGHTS

I dedicate this poem to my family.

When I am very lonely
and have nothing to do,
I get out in the garden
and swing a thought or two:

I think of the future
and what could be
But . . . the one I like best
is me to be a P r i n c e s s!

Sandra Cortright
A MEMORY

Dedicated to: To my family; David, Holly and Patrick for all their support and confidence in me as a poet. I love you!

A memory is part of us living
That somehow cannot let go,
An inner thought locked in your mind
A peaceful feeling to know.

A memory never lived nor died;
A calling voice that is speechless,
That special power unknown to us
That can bring us strength or
weakness.

A memory of someone special
That we cannot easily forget
It flashes like a picture
That hasn't been taken yet.

You can call a memory in a whisper,
It will always be there to find.
A memory is never put to sleep
It just lives silently in your mind.

Nona Razor Lester
GENTLE RAIN

I lovingly dedicate this poem to my sister, Thelma Flowers, who has greatly encouraged me over the years.

When I arose this morning
Through the window I could see,
The rain falling so gently
On the grass and leaves of the trees.
And as each drop fell so lightly

dripping upon each leaf,
It seemed fairies were dancing
Leaving the prints of their little feet.
As the trees swayed back and forth
With each rush of wind,
The branches became giant brooms
Sweeping the skies clean again.

Joanne Marie Campagna
TIME

Time, where did it go?
I remember our fun, it never went too slow.
We laughed, we cried together
No other friends were better.
Those times were just grand
Being sad I couldn't understand.
We had the best of times
With all our riddles and our rhymes.
But like the setting of the sun
There came an end and youth was undone.

Looking back I thought it would never end
But it did, tearing hearts that will never mend.
Everyone went their own way
No more time was left to play.
Thinking of those days of yesteryear
It brings to my eye a sad tear.
I miss those days of everyone
We were a group but yet one.
I want those days back right now
But time has passed, to time we bow.

Lillian Chambrun
WITHOUT IMAGINATION

Without imagination,
There'd be no near past;
Da Vinci and Saint Francis,
Made happenings last!

Without imagination,
There'd be no present;
TV's, space-age, computers,
Have rules to be be bent!

Without imagination,
There'd be no futures;
On moon and stars or planets
Unknown does quite lure!

Kate M Smith
coiled

with a hiss serpentine eked out in a long syllable
flipping off the tongue as a droplet from a faucet
i, to my littlest self rush
whose jealous arms held only that tiny one
as my scruples whittled away at me, a meager stick
needing shaping, but the pith is numb, the heart gone
only journeys of nights, flights returning one to one's own
the glitter of eyes into staid glass mirrors
half-fearing, half open-armed
to capture that which is mine, a reflection
and wind my tail round the body.
that's how i imagine serpents.

Donna R Reel
MOTHER

This poem is Dedicated to my mother, Delores Ann Laux, who died on November 5, 1988; And in doing so, took a part of me with her. She left ths world at 3:30 A.M. after suffering a stroke.

You raised me and you taught me well. I needed you when I was small. And as I grew inside and out, I watched in wonder at the strength you showed. I saw the awesome discipline that kept you from breaking when things got tough. And now that I am on my own, I think about the times before.

When we were still together, and the love was strong and sure, and coming home from school would find you waiting at the door. I don't keep in touch like I ought to, and I needed you when I was small. But Mother, oh Mother; now that I'm grown, I need you even more.

Rickie L Vickry

Rickie L Vickry
WHEN YOU SING A SONG

I dedicate this poem to Jesus Christ for saving me, to Stephanie Brewer for her inspiration and encouragement, to Exie Higginbotham, and to Becky McGee.

With the beauty and sweetness of a nightingale,
You sing your song so very well.
With a beautiful voice and the songs you sing,
Heartfelt tears and happy smiles you bring.
With the praise you give to the Lord each time,
Let the heavenly light of Jesus Christ shine.
I see his love light shining through you,
And know his love just has to be true.

So! Sing your songs of the Lord Jesus Christ,
For the songs you sing tell the story of life.
The lights of Jesus Christ that shines through you,
You may not see but other people do.
So! Keep singing your songs so beautiful and sweet,
And the light that shines may it always be.
For the songs you sing about Jesus Christ,
Help me to forget my sorrow, pain, and strife.

I pray you will always sing your songs,
About the love of Jesus Christ your whole life long.
So your songs can help others as they have helped me,
To more understand God in his great trinity.

Danny Charles Washington
SAVOIR FAIRE

You are a beautiful morning
That sets my spirit free
You imbue my mind with thoughts of love
While kissing my soul so sensuously
May we always abide within this love
And have lots of fun
The desire in my heart is that
We will always be as one
My love for you keeps growing
Your love will always glow inside of me
You are my heartbeat
My link to life
You are all the lovely things
I desire my beautiful lover to be
I will love you and no other
My love is yours, eternally

Evelyn Kimball Blake
THIS PLACE—THIS TIME

Let us wander on the beach tonight
While the ocean casts its eternal spell;
Seaweed lines the timeless shore
Remembering its home in mystic depths.
We will follow its trail awhile
Watching the sky for shooting stars—
Just you and I together now—while there's time—
Walk beside me closely—take my hand
We will watch the moon rise o'er the sea
And the gulls that dip o'er the waves.
There are never enough precious times like these
For us to write about in memories book,
But for now we'll rest in sand still warm from the sun
Just us alone in this space and time;
Make it beautiful—this moment that we share
Before our footsteps lead us back to reality.

Rayfield Covington
MY PEOPLE

This poem is dedicated to those who did not live long enough to see their dreams fulfilled.

We are the people who seek to find the true meaning of life
We are the people who have suffered hunger and strife
We are the people who have been put down throughout the years
We are the people who have shed many tears
We are the people who once had a beautiful home
We are the people who other men have owned
We are the people who worked in the cotton fields
We are the people who were hunted and killed
We are the people whose children cried out for more
We are the people on whom society shut their door
We are the people the white men took for pleasure
But we are also the people whose pride was our treasure
We are the people who are united as one
Bonded together by the things we have done
Standing tall with our heads held high
Looking ahead with dreams that will never die
Making ourselves known in the world today
Inspiring others to go forth with the words that we say
Building a place for our families and friends
So things will never be the way they once had been

Linda S Fulton
THE REALM OF LIFE

In memory of Evelyn K. Barella

For each day we live yesterday it will always be tomorrow

For each day we live with our wrongs or rights
it will be the past

For each day we live negatively it will be impossible

We must live for today and forget the past wrong, and look for the future

For if you can do this in your lifetime it will be the sphere or the Realm of your Life

Mary Helen Walsh
YESTERDAY'S LAUGHTER

To my family, who allows me the pleasure time, of reliving my childhood.

Funny, how the wind is still cold
And the shadow of me seems somehow so bold;
Strange, I am standing on the hill quite alone
And yet, I hear them laughing a sparkling tone.

Wonderful, how the clouds still roll by
And the roar of the river, that always seemed too high;
Comforting, to have a memory so dear
That I can see them playing now, right here!

There's Joey and my best friend, Sue
And my teacher tying her patent-leather shoe;
Amazing, I can find my old school yard
And hold my precious times unmarred.

Gladys Pauley
THINGS NOT SEEN

Now faith is the substance of things hoped for,
the evidence of things not seen.
HEBREWS 11-1

For we walk by faith, not by sight.
2 CORINTHIANS 5-7

odor, whether the fragrance of flowers
or the stench of decaying food.

taste whether the sweetness of sugar
or the bitterness of medicine.

Wind, whether the gentle breeze of summer
or the stinging blast of winter.

Love, whether the soft caress of a baby
or the kiss of young lovers.

Neither is GOD seen
but we know HE is there.

Rose Ballard
LONELY THOUGHTS
Feelings between us, are still running fine.
To you my husband, I am glad you are mine.
We have shared a lot of things, through both thick and thin.
Neither one of us were willing to give in.
When we first met, I wasn't really much more than a child.
I was headstrong, and stubborn and a little bit wild.
You showed me, that I could count on you.
For me, that was the best thing you could do.
When I see you, leaning back in your easy chair.
I long to tell you, how much I really care.
Right words for me to say, just doesn't seem to come through.
So I choose to write this poem to say I love you.
I do miss you, when we are apart.
These words that I am writing, are straight from my heart.
Although we have been married for several years.
If I should lose you, I would cry a million tears.

Christopher A Wolfe
VALENTINE XXIV

For Colleen

No voices do I hear, no sounds,
But something much alive surrounds
My senses and my inner ear,
So that in no sound I hear
The soul's lament of Nature burn,
The echoes of a spirit yearn,
In some strange language far too old
To be translated or retold,
But feel rather than know the cause.
And there within the wooden jaws
A vision not my own commands,
As I look out upon the land
Through cedared prison bars and coil
In cramped and isolated soil.
My vision lost, I turn in rage
And viciously uproot the cage
And share the joy of liberty.

Robert H Wolf
THERE'S MORE
There's more to this world than just life, Dear,
Than sunshine and blue skies above;
Just take you a husband or wife, friend,
Discover the magic of love.

There's business and profits and such, Sir,
There's eating and drinking and strife;
Just take a good look at your living, Boy,
Discover you're missing a wife.

There's fashions and figures and flirting, Dear,
Where parties and dancing are rife,
Just take a good look at your living, Dear,
Discover a husband's your life.

If all of your talents were turned into love,
To future, and family and home;
You never would linger at office or club,
And you'd be much too busy to roam!

If all of your talents were turned into love,
To family, cooking and caring;
You never would miss all that freedom you had,
When with him and your family you're sharing!

Timothy S Gwen

Timothy S Gwen
NATURE'S INTENT

This Poem is A Dedication, and A Reminder for myself. This Is Also A true Poem, that once happened to myself, On one cold morning.

A sudden awakening, from a dream this night
As a warm shiver of love flows through my veins
I can hear wild geese singing songs alone
From their long-distance flight. They feel no pains
Just to be free, and never to be owned

Feelings of joy come rushing to me
Thoughts explode like crashing tides
Nature's willingness to help me see
Calms my heart, and strengthens my strides
Beauty's outside, naked of lies
Envying these geese, as they stretch their wings across the sky

The early morning star peeks over the country hills
Nourishing this poor earth, with fire of light
The silent dawn gives me wondrous chills
Lifting the frost, that once covered this night

I sit in awe, as this mighty star rises
Touching the face of life as the scars slowly mend
This dream of dreams holds great surprises
Taking me closer, and closer to my journey's end—

Charlene Klein
OUR AUNT
A dear Aunt loved so true
That years say now is ninety-two.
As my Uncle's wife
She chose that as her life.

The work on a farm, was hers to carry
Some say, an Aunt by marriage,
And not a drop of blood we can claim
But only the love that flows through her veins.
In church, as an Angel she sang
An Aunt by marriage you say
Not so to my brother and me
She is our own dear Aunt Villie.

Frank Paul Graffeo
ALL THE REST OF MY DAYS,
All the rest of my days,
I plan to be with you.
All the rest of my days,
I'll keep on being true.
I hope you see, you're my everything,
All the joys true love, can bring.
Even my pep and my zing,
All the rest of my life,
I'll keep on loving you.
All the rest of my days,
I'll sing love songs, to you.
Can't you see that you're my life,
All my dreams are you.
All the rest of my days,
I'll make our dreams, come true.
All the rest of my days,
I'll live just for you.
"All the rest of my days."

Zita Victoria Moak (Lyles)
FAREWELL

To my Mother Johnnie Louise Halstead-Moak

I like to think of the old dreams,
The calm and battle on life's streams
As memory turns to my old friends,
Sorrow into my pleasure blends.
To the lessons which hardship has taught me,
Of friendships time has brought me.
if the future brings us together,
Or misfortune tears us apart,
Memories never forgotten, will linger in my heart.
My sincere and lasting hope is that you never forget this day
Your classmates and Blythewood High School,
As each senior sets out on his way.
So farewell dear teachers and classmates
We'll always be grateful to you
For the inspiration you've given us
And your friendships tried and true.

Mrs Lynn Hightower
SILENT DEATH
Picking her up to knock her down,
Telling each other you don't need her around.
You both think you are so bad,
This is really nothing but sad.
What can she do?
My God, she is only two.
This poor child is afraid to tell,
She is living her life in hell.
Not knowing how to scream
Only wanting to awaken from a dream.
Nothing she can do
My god, she is only two
Then one day while eating her lunch
This little girl had no hunch,
All of a sudden she saw the knife,
She was so afraid for her life.
Never to know why.
Never able to cry.
What could she do?
She had no clue.
My God, she was only two.

R L Oldmixon
A FATHER'S PRAYER
Dear Lord, I wish my child would understand
the things it takes to be a man.
A man is kind and wise and fair,
and learns to give and take and share.
A man is strong within his heart,
and from his God does never part.

Dear Lord, I wish we could grow to see
each other's points whete'er they be.
I wish that we could grow in love,
in all things under heaven above.
I wish that we could understand
as son, as father, and as man. .

Sarah XO!
THE KISS
The crude rough harsh kiss.
The one thing I shall never miss.
Snatched from me,
Torn away.
He could not see
Why I ran away.
A soft touch with a strong hand.
A lonely boy from a foreign land.

Paige Tanner
FADED MEMORIES
Memories of you . . . .
Holding my hand
Walking thru the sand
Knowing no fear,
When you were near

Memories of . . . .
What used to be
What I thought you were to me
Or of what I thought we were together

Faded memories . . . .
As the days go by,
Knowing that I
Would live those moments again.

Marylouise Uebele
KALEIDOS-HOPE 1989-1990
Old New Year's Resolutions
Old unfeeling "I don't cares"
Old dreams buried then revived
Old deadened flames rekindled
Old shaky peace now tranquil–firmed

Current fancies somehow jelled
Current failures reconciled
Current loves fled hearts replaced
Current marriage sans divorce
Current births fealty enhance
Current college goals assured

New diplomas new careers
New contracts honor–kept
New homes and lasting fam'ly
New end to evil drugs
New era violence–free

A beloved nation's true desire
Can will this burdened land away
From shameful homelessness and debt!

Index

A

AALAIE, Kim M, 910
AARSTAD, Doris E, 587
ABATA CSSR, Rev Russell M, 462
ABBATE, Barbara, 874
ABBOTT, Peggy, 202
ABBOTT, Robert J, 37
ABDALIAN, Charles H, 1175
ABDUL, Herman, 585
ABEENE, Darla, 551
ABEL, Jo Champion, 1173
ABELLO, Yleana J, 1097
ABENTI, Melissa, 543
ABERN, Marietta, 234
ABEYTA, Ann, 840
ABOLINS, Tina, 476
ABORN, Arlena Faye, 1099
ABOUHALKAH, Fran, 245
ABRAMOSKI, E R, 985
ABRAMS, Lillian G, 242
ABRAMS, Martha I, 139
ABRAMS, Susan Scott, 19
ABTS, Carol, 28
ACCURSO, Dimi, 180
ACEVEDO, Ines Rivera, 650
ACHORD, Shanna, 411
ACKER, Glenda J, 60
ACKERMAN, Jan M, 605
ACKLIN, Virginia, 691
ACKMAN, N A, 389
ACQUAFREDDA, Joseph, 246
ACRES, C Thomas, 665
ACUNA, Belia A, 971
ADAIR, Freda, 553
ADAM, Jacqueline M, 690
ADAM, Reneé, 669
ADAMETS, W C, 352
ADAMS Jr, Daniel N, 389
ADAMS, A J, 1118
ADAMS, Angel, 351
ADAMS, Angelia C, 13
ADAMS, Barbara A, 847
ADAMS, Bernice Ellen, 787
ADAMS, Brenda K, 349
ADAMS, Cynthia A, 1194
ADAMS, Elinor R, 19
ADAMS, Erin G, 831
ADAMS, Eugenia, 801
ADAMS, James, 598
ADAMS, Jeff, 466
ADAMS, Jeff, 826
ADAMS, Jenny, 583
ADAMS, June Defaye, 879
ADAMS, Kathy, 107
ADAMS, Kip, 800
ADAMS, Loretta, 20
ADAMS, Lucie, 304
ADAMS, Lula May Hart, 1109
ADAMS, Mary E, 245
ADAMS, Michele D, 236
ADAMS, Minnetta W, 1124
ADAMS, Philip A, 122
ADAMS, Rebecca W, 1180
ADAMS, Ricky D, 475
ADAMS, Sandra L, 1070
ADAMS, Sue E Macleod, 153
ADAMS, Tamera N, 220
ADAMS, Velma Lee, 192
ADAMS, Vicky, 12
ADCOCK Jr, James L, 1152
ADCOCK, Lora Lee, 719
ADCOCK, Patricia S, 505
ADELSOHN, Pauline, 176
ADKINS, Elaine, 923
MICHAEL, Hugh, 1094
ADKINS, Savonna, 913
ADKINS, Shelli, 627
ADKINSON, Brooke W, 985
ADLEMAN, Darrin, 398
ADOX, Joan, 785
ADSIT-CHAFFEY, Mary Lee, 283
ADSITT, Robert P, 918
AESCHLIMANN, Lawrence, 80
AFOLABI, Niyi, 265
AFZAL, Hisana, 64
AGAPETUS, Deona M S, 79
AGBOR-BAIYEE, William, 868
AGGIE, Just Plain, 125
AGNEW, Evlin C, 314
AGOSTA, Nikki, 910
AGOSTINI, Lisa-Marie, 362
AGOSTINI, Vivian, 1007
AGUAYO, Sherri Lynn, 17
AGUIAR, Matilde, 854
AGUIRRE, Mary Alice, 658
AHMADI, Boz, 911
AIRRIESS, Jeanna R, 390
AKER, Linda, 1052
AKERS, Ann M, 1001
AKERS, Harry A, 35
AKERS, Linda K, 824
AKIMOTO, Robert, 1186
AKIYAMA, Janel, 123
AKRIDGE, Eleanor B, 862
AKRIDGE, Linda S, 977
ALAHOUZOS, Irene E, 670
ALAMAH, Charles, 897
ALAMIA, Teresa Chapa
ALANO, Michelle L, 782
ALBA, Kathleen Owen, 638
ALBERS, Jeanne, 827
ALBERSMEIER, Adele, 328
ALBERT, Andrea, 295
ALBERTI, Brian Domenic, 1153
ALBERTSON, David, 1165
ALBRECHT BERRY, Glinnie J, 235, 1141
ALBRECHT, Trudy E, 744
ALBRIGHT, Kimberly Ann, 919
ALBURY, Irma, 44
ALCAIDE, Anibal, 493
ALCARAZ, Adelia (Adelle) A, 930
ALCORN, Lydia, 781
ALCOTT, Norman M, 251
ALDER, Adam Lee, 862
ALDERMAN, Beverly, 1187
ALDOUS, Robert G, 743
ALDRED, Susan J White, 462
ALDRICH, Nellie Ann, 177
ALDRIDGE, Annette D, 136
ALEMAN, Deanne C, 854
ALEMAN, Maria T, 120
ALEXANDER, Arajuana, 977
ALEXANDER, Cassandra, 556
ALEXANDER, Joy, 1009
ALEXANDER, Kimberly D, 30
ALEXANDER, Lisa Marie, 593
ALEXANDER, Marcia, 374
ALEXANDER, Margaret J, 175
ALEXANDER, Niis, 175
ALEXANDER, Sharon L, 298
ALEXANDER, V S, 579
ALEXANDER, Wendy M, 442
ALEXANDRE, Jacques L, 648
ALEXANDRE, Judith Brink, 1018
ALFANO Jr, Edward C, 742
ALFANO, Rose C, 185
ALFARO, Christine, 398
ALFORD, Linda, 197
ALGAR, Sharon Steege, 518
ALGER, Andrew, 340
ALI, Maajid M, 932
ALISA, Kaarin, 471
ALISPACH, Judy Diane, 151
ALISPACH, Mandie, 967
ALIXOPULOS, Madelyn N, 1059
ALLAIRE, Joseph W, 557
ALLAN, Lori J, 813
ALLAN, Margaret, 768
ALLAN, Michael G, 788
ALLAN, Tammy J, 802
ALLARD, Kt, 303
ALLCOCK, Geneva M, 1100
ALLEN Jr, E, 664
ALLEN, Anita J, 610
ALLEN, Audrey, 743
ALLEN, Barbara, 388
ALLEN, Chris, 712
ALLEN, Claudette D, 377
ALLEN, Dennis, 679
ALLEN, Edward D, 246
ALLEN, Gladys Pearl
ALLEN, Gloria Miller, 451
ALLEN, Harry T, 171
ALLEN, Judith Ann, 467
ALLEN, Julia E, 566
ALLEN, Larue S, 1141
ALLEN, Lois M, 1034
ALLEN, Louella M, 198
ALLEN, Mae Gladys, 1141
ALLEN, Rayson Leon, 924
ALLEN, Robin E, 334
ALLEN, Ruth S, 463
ALLENSWORTH, Dahna Cheryl, 1054
ALLGOOD, Richard, 422
ALLI, Latania L, 1066
ALLISON Jr, Harry E (Skeeter), 429
ALLISON, Jr (Bob) Robert Steve, 734
ALLISON, Merle A, 383
ALLISON, Peggy, 431
ALLISON, Susan D, 596
ALLISTON, Melissa A, 1094
ALLRED, Erika, 826
ALMADA, Jennifer M, 762
ALMADA, Manuel, 37
ALMAND, Dianne, 222
ALMESTICA, Richard (Taino), 222
ALOYTS, Simon, 1136
ALROBAIDI, Nasser, 1014
ALSTON, Lelia M, 618
ALSTON, Margrit, 872
ALSTON, Steven G, 1095
ALTAZIN, Edith, 431
ALTHOFF, Lori, 213
ALTMAN, Kristine V, 146
ALTMILLER, Barbara, 630
ALVARADO, Steven J, 952
ALVAREZ, Lisa, 309
ALVERS, Tracy, 940
ALVERSON, Dorothy Z, 1047
AMADO, Margie Alari, 17
AMAGRANDE, Charles James, 608
AMARIUTEI, Ion, 354
AMBRISCO, Peggy, 8
AMBURGEY, Maudie, 871
AMELL III, Francis Edward, 552
AMES, Nikki, 413
AMES, Ronald M, 261
AMII, Charlotte T, 233
AMSTUTZ, Celesta M, 180
ANASTASIO, Anthony J, 700
ANDERSEN, Diane, 103
ANDERSEN, Jeannette, 993
ANDERSEN, Jennifer K, 752
ANDERSEN, Jessie K, 1142
ANDERSEN, Leah E, 77
ANDERSON III, Earl Floyd, 1189
ANDERSON, Anna L, 323
ANDERSON, Anna Toma, 400
ANDERSON, B J, 216
ANDERSON, Bette Roth, 385
ANDERSON, Beville, 685
ANDERSON, Carl L, 201
ANDERSON, Christine, 796
ANDERSON, Dorothy C, 1027
ANDERSON, Eldora, 526
ANDERSON, Esther H, 936
ANDERSON, Heidi, 41
ANDERSON, James, 554
ANDERSON, Jan, 506
ANDERSON, Jay Harris, 496
ANDERSON, Jody, 446
ANDERSON, Judy Dianne, 863
ANDERSON, Julie L, 58
ANDERSON, Karen M, 686
ANDERSON, Kathleen L, 539
ANDERSON, Laural D, 925
ANDERSON, Linda, 110
ANDERSON, Linda Susan, 829
ANDERSON, Lisa, 1159
ANDERSON, Lisa, 485
ANDERSON, Lisa R, 1001
ANDERSON, Lorie, 658
ANDERSON, Margaret, 111
ANDERSON, Marion L, 907
ANDERSON, Mary E, 505
ANDERSON, Michael, 1180
ANDERSON, Molly A, 1050
ANDERSON, Monica F, 573
ANDERSON, Patti L, 610
ANDERSON, Paul S, 1048
ANDERSON, Paula L, 52
ANDERSON, R H, 687
ANDERSON, Regina, 1132
ANDERSON, Seal, 984
ANDERSON, Stanley Earl, 457
ANDERSON, Theresa, 135
ANDERSON, Traci, 1009
ANDERSON, Violet Henson, 305
ANDERSON, Wanda, 290
ANDERSON-MEYER, Kimberley M, 638
ANDERSON-PITTMAN, Joann (Kay), 618
ANDERSON-ROTVOLD, Mary, 929
ANDERSON-SCALES, La Don, 223
ANDRE OSU, Sr Mary, 41
ANDREASEN, Patricia, 1188
ANDREJKO, Michael James, 247
ANDRES, Helen P, 907
ANDRES, Merle S, 463
ANDRES, Rick, 1093
ANDRES, Walter H, 907
ANDRESEN, Ted, 1156
ANDRESS, Susan, 615
ANDREST, Cindy, 401
ANDREWIN, Edward S, 394
ANDREWS Sr, Billy F, 960
ANDREWS, Elizabeth Ann, 883
ANDREWS, Ilo, 346
ANDREWS, Joseph, 607
ANDREWS, Marie, 79
ANDRIA, Paula, 676
ANDRIANO, Jan, 1157
ANDRIOPOULOS, Evangeline, 378
ANDRISANO, Michael J, 461
ANDRIUZZO, Tina, 317
ANDRO, Bro C G, 898
ANDY, Monique, 1150
ANESGART, Martin N, 352
ANGELI, Barbara J, 383
ANGELINO, Annette S, 857
ANGELOFF, Luben G, 379
ANGEROSA, Elizabeth, 359
ANGEVINE, Dorothy, 978
ANGILERI, Rita M, 699
ANGIOLA, Rosanna, 1010
ANGIOLINI, Ilga S, 1070
ANGLISANO, Loryn M, 135
ANGSTADT, Sally, 795
ANGUS, Chloe, 661
ANNECHINO, Carol M, 544
ANNERL, Annemarie S, 672
CAVANAUGH, Ann M, 1085
ANONYMMOUS, Tj, 1017
ANONYMOUS, Mary Ann, 926
ANSALDO, Jessica V, 1172
ANSELMO, Donna Marie, 641
ANSELOWITZ, Tara Lynn, 75
ANTAYA, Dawn, 737
ANTHONY RN, Joan Scott, 450
ANTOINE, Willy, 616
ANTON, Mary E, 346
ANTONE, Louella Marie, 926
ANTONELLI Jr, Alvo Joseph, 318
ANTONIO, Mollie, 327
ANTRIM, Robert L, 819
APGAR, Brenda, 12
APICE, Steven Jude, 811
APIKOS, D A, 272
APPEL, Caren, 688
APPEL, William R, 23
APPLEBY, Carrie, 140
APPLEBY, Joyce E, 784
APPLEBY, Norma L, 427
APPLEGATE-HAGER, Sandye, 890
APPLEYARD, Jody, 911
AQUILINO, Tony, 806
ARABIE, Melinda, 1094, 963
ARAGON, Marie, 143
ARAGON, Virginia, 154
ARCE, Margaret A, 373
ARCHBOLD, Catherine M, 163
ARCHER, Denise M, 941
ARCHER, Michael R, 70
ARCHER, Peggy A, 1094
ARCHILA, Shirley L, 237
ARCHINAL, Jody, 542
ARDELL, Norma, 218
ARECHAVALETA-MEIWITZ, Karin, 1146
AREM, Aitch, 337
ARENDT, Luanne Larson, 628
ARENTSON, S Renee, 790
ARGALUZA, Jose Luis, 228
ARGONDIZZO, Margaret, 23
ARGYROS, George N, 1030
ARIANNE, Ann R, 761
ARISTIZABAL, Lisa, 400
ARJUN, Angela, 756
ARMANIOS, Vicky, 860
ARMIJO, Betty Ann R, 679
ARMITAGE, John J, 344
ARMOGIDA, Rima E, 358
ARMSTRONG, Craig, 1094
ARMSTRONG, Jean, 964
ARMSTRONG, Katharine Victoria, 448
ARMSTRONG, Kathy, 547
ARMSTRONG, Ken, 108
ARMSTRONG, Mary Aileen, 970
ARMSTRONG, Mrs James C, 262
ARMSTRONG, Nancy Susan, 786
ARMSTRONG, Patricia, 527
ARMSTRONG, Roberta, 982
ARMSTRONG, Shane, 278
ARMSTRONG, Vera H, 76
ARMSTRONG, Viva Gay, 926
ARMSTRONG-JONES, Lynne, 177
ARNAEZ, Adelaida V, 645
ARNDT, Leonard L, 272
ARNDT, Martha M, 1046
ARNEL, Craig Lee, 1172
ARNHOLD, Brandi L, 70
ARNOLD, Ann, 951
ARNOLD, Crystal F, 845
ARNOLD, Jacqueline J, 1030
ARNOLD, M Elaine, 897
ARNOLD, Shirley, 972
ARNOLD, Shirley J, 748
ARNOLD, Virginia J, 967
ARNOTT, Mildred, 965
AROLIN, Marianna Jo, 894
ARPANTE, Mary, 505
ARRANT, John D, 842
ARRINGTON, Nathaniel, 629
ARROYO Jr, Robert, 769, 769
ARROYO, Edna, 913
ARTEAGA, Carol, 505
ARTHUR, Glenn C, 1138
ARTHUR, William S, 870
ARTHUR-TOWNSELL, Pamela D, 679
ARTINO, Sandra, 927
ARTIS, Felix-Lasalle, 729
ARVIDSON-WRIGHT, Patti, 503
ARYAEENIA, Carol, 1089
ASBURY, Martha J, 457
ASDORIAN, Lora W, 899
ASHBY, Mark, 224
ASHENBRENER, Mary, 72
ASHENFARB, Deborah C, 923
ASHER, Nell, 5
ASHLEY, Kara W, 285
ASHMORE, Todd, 370
ASKEW, Ina, 1186
ASSELIN, Chris, 73
ASTIE, Michelle D, 151
ASTON, S Lee, 413
ASUNCION, Maricel L, 518
ATHERTON, Catherine B, 650
ATILANO, Feliz, 1159
ATKIAN, Shannon, 133
ATKINS, Anita Louise, 84
ATTENHOFER, Richard, 821
AUBE, Margaret, 691
AUBERT, Christine C, 586
AUERBACK, Linda M, 608
AUGER, Jeffery A, 556
AUGUSTINE, Patty L, 837
AURECCHIONE, Laurie, 444
AUSBY, Hope La-tanya, 830
AUSTEN, Kim, 885
AUSTILL-MCCASLIN, Janet, 28
AUSTIN Jr, James E, 102
AUSTIN, Cheryl A, 357
AUSTIN, Richard Gray, 1124
AUTREY, Joyce Duggan, 585
AUVIL, T David, 218
AVANT, Marie, 175
AVEL, M, 1200
AVERETT, Lydia R, 580
AVERILL, Lorinda, 16
AVERY, Christopher M, 584
AWREY, Lily E, 514
AXELSON, Erika, 1081
AXT, Adelon, 172
AXTON, Florence G, 251
AYER, Anne, 1007
AYER, Frederick W, 1034
AYERS, J, 304
AYERS, Sherry "Spike", 462
AYOTTE, Bonnie S, 572
AZEVEDO, Francesca A, 663

B

B'INTAMBA, Balongo, 1167
BABAEI, Pamela, 843
BABB, Barbara S, 560
BABB, M M, 128
BABCOCK, Alicia E, 535
BABCOCK, Wendell K, 1120
BABEL, Dorothy J, 154
BACHI, Kathleen M, 817
BACHMAN, Al, 72
BACHMAN, Alice, 190
BACILA, Florence M, 1085
BACKETTI, John, 203
BACKUS, Daniel, 30
BACON, Jennifer N, 627
BADE, Maria-Constanza, 636
BADER, Arlys E, 1072
BADER, Mark E, 218
BADGER 2ND, Ethel W, 428
BADGER, Jim, 188
BADGER, Susan E, 972
BAGENT, Beth A, 200
BAGGETT, Alice Diane, 382
BAGGETT, Shawn E, 437
BAGLEY, Marie D, 866
BAGULEY, Janett L, 606
BAGWELL, Jacqueline S, 841
BAGWELL, Robyn L, 409
BAHL, D T, 667
BAHLMANN, Eileen, 793
BAHORIK, Elizabeth S, 272
BAILEY III, Calvin, 146
BAILEY, Amy D, 443
BAILEY, Barbara J, 730
BAILEY, Brenda J, 595
BAILEY, Bridget M, 485
BAILEY, Bryan C, 362
BAILEY, C W, 968
BAILEY, Charles Arnett, 160
BAILEY, Cynthia L, 500
BAILEY, Debby, 650
BAILEY, Diane, 715
BAILEY, Horace, 922
BAILEY, Janette, 499
BAILEY, Kathryn, 157
BAILEY, Lori A, 87

BAILEY, Lucille S, 385
BAILEY, Missy, 1055
BAILEY, Richard, 997
BAILEY, Shelley Lynn, 929
BAILEY, Sherry L, 629
BAILEY-GRANT, Lorice V, 1173
BAILIFF Jr, Thomas W, 311
BAILIN, Leah, 107
BAILLIE, Chris, 261
BAIN-HATCHER, Debra A, 10
BAINES, Beverlyn S, 97
BAIRD Jr, Floyd Lewis, 13
BAIRD, Darlene Benton, 692
BAIRD, Jeanne, 946
BAIRD, R Kim, 652
BAISLEY, Christina, 769
BAISLEY, Peter, 1000
BAKARA, Frank G, 228
BAKER Jr, Robert J, 83
BAKER, Ann Marie, 830
BAKER, Arthur R, 872
BAKER, Barbara E, 339
BAKER, Brooke, 143
BAKER, Deborah Lynn, 908, 908
BAKER, Delford (Panaderro), 747
BAKER, Florence Jo, 101
BAKER, Glenna M, 726
BAKER, Heather, 172
BAKER, Ivan, 666
BAKER, Ivan O, 8
BAKER, James, 368
BAKER, Jamey Lowell, 658
BAKER, Jill A, 815
BAKER, Kitty, 670
BAKER, Leslie Anne, 587
BAKER, Lillian, 109
BAKER, Lois M, 344
BAKER, M I, 1195
BAKER, Ms Jannie, 360
BAKER, Ms June A, 648
BAKER, Nancy, 21
BAKER, Patty M, 370
BAKER, Randy, 994, 994
BAKER, Ronald L, 677
BAKER, Ruth A, 120
BAKER, Terry A, 840
BAKER, Traci, 1113
BAKER, Violet, 471
BAKER-FISH, Miss Dorothy, 370
BAKOVE, Dori, 1116
BALANCIERE, Romell R, 414
BALDRIDGE, Petra, 1033
BALDWIN, Arlantha J, 776
BALDWIN, Deni, 497
BALES, Anne Marie, 331
BALES, Cathy Marie, 832
BALES, Helen F, 755
BALESTRINO, Eleanor H, 1200
BALEY, Geneve, 198
BALIK, Patricia M, 1173
BALINT, Bunny, 293
BALL, Gypsy, 475
BALLA, Vera, 873
BALLARD, Myrtle A, 1019
BALLARD, Rose, 1202
BALLIETT, Patricia A, 851
BALLIN, Laraine, 154
BALLINGER, Michael, 404
BALLINGER, Shirley J, 657
BALLOU Jr, Bert, 424
BALLOU, Louise M, 16
BALO, Janet, 756
BALOG, C J, 250
BALTHAZOR, Terry L, 988
BALTRUSH, Deborah E, 374
BAMFORD, Mary F, 274
BAN, Stephan C, 880
BANCROFT, James T, 316
BANCROFT, Sharon, 737
BANCROFT, Steven N, 619
BANFIELD, Miriam Felix, 711
BANISH, Twila, 232
BANKHEAD, Stephen, 225
BANKS, Betty Jean, 808
BANKS, Chevelle, 753
BANKS, Diane F, 283
BANKS, Helen, 1094
BANKS, Joseph W, 312
BANKS, Max S, 641, 967
BANKS, Susan J, 322
BANMILLER, Jill, 503
BANNERMAN, Anita L, 63
BANNON, Jesse, 345
BAPTIS, John P, 955
BARAJAS, Elias Dominguez, 22
BARAJAS, Raquel, 596
BARAN, Elynor A, 705
BARANIK, Michelle L, 323
BARANOWSKI, Jeanne L, 466
BARB, Doris, 811
BARBARE, Dan C, 688
BARBARO, Schelli M, 102
BARBER, Alice M, 195
BARBER, Elaine D, 836
BARBER, Helen J, 79
BARBER, Jeff, 908
BARBER, Lilian S, 949
BARBER, Robert D, 33
BARBER, Yvonne Allen, 270
BARBOSA, Antoinette, 1183
BARBOUR, Marian, 1016
BARBOUR, Phillip S, 548
BARBOUR, Wilma, 152
BARCHUS, Dorothy L, 929
BARCOMB, Brenda M, 938
BARD, Catherine M, 164
BARDECK, Walter, 263
BARDEKJIAN, Maryjan, 566
BARE, Walter C, 1109
BAREFOOT, Karen R, 340
BARG, Barbara Ann, 348
BARGELT, Edmond, 80
BARGER, John F, 601
BARGER, Nancy J, 223
BARIC, Elsie H, 1071
BARKER, Alvin Lee, 796
BARKER, Gilbert R, 1152
BARKER, Helene M, 193
BARKER, Jen, 690
BARKER, Jessica E, 203
BARKER, Maria C, 80
BARKER, Rafaela W, 394
BARKER, Sadie H, 1015
BARKER, Sharon, 1031
BARKLEY Jr, Richard L, 909
BARKLEY, William O, 534
BARKOW, Blanche L, 345
BARKS, Lisa, 37
BARKSDALE, Willard W, 193
BARNARD, F Esther, 1051
BARNELL, Darlene P, 101
BARNES, Cindy G, 238
BARNES, Flossie Childress, 1077
BARNES, Lori A, 731
BARNES, Marie, 349
BARNES, Mary Williams, 554
BARNES, Shirley, 280
BARNES, Sue, 804
BARNES, Tracy, 185
BARNES, Veola Victoria, 368
BARNES-WALL, Sharisalyn K, 1143
BARNETT, Dorothy, 208
BARNETT, Janis Hirst, 770
BARNETT, Joanne, 238
BARNETT, Lynne A, 869
BARNHART ARDIETA, Ruth E, 1032
BARNHART, Francis Andrew, 915
BARNHORST, Donald J, 847
BARNOWSKI, Raymond John, 382
BARON, Rich, 1200
BARONE, Rose Marie P, 208
BAROTT, Carol A, 661
BARR, Holly A, 1013
BARR, Jennifer, 384
BARR, Lois, 488
BARRERA, Michelle, 967
BARRESI, Barbara Ann (Goobie), 564
BARRETT, David E, 208
BARRETT, Joseph E, 19
BARRETT, Kaye, 729
BARRETT, Michael T, 1100
BARRETT, Raymond T, 849
BARRETT, Richard Alan, 539
BARRETT, S L, 10
BARRIENTOS, Armando, 1113
BARRINGTON, Kay, 441
BARRON, Cheryl, 627
BARRON, Evola L S, 336
BARRON, Leo D, 743
BARROW, David A, 466
BARRY, Heather, 949
BARRY, Jonathan, 1138
BARRY, Marlene, 47
BARSALOU, June E, 933
BARSCEWSKI, Shannon, 662
BARSTOW, Lynne, 316
BARTH, Helma, 325
BARTHOLIC, Kathleen A, 884
BARTHOLOMAUS, Brett W, 641
BARTLET, Lindsey, 81
BARTLETT, Alan L, 381
BARTLETT, Joyce, 268
BARTLETT, Mary, 286
BARTLEY, Vivien Leigh, 699
BARTMAN, Phyllis E, 1157
BARTOLE, Shannon, 598
BARTOLINI, Lyn, 363
BARTON, Bonita, 233
BARTON, Erselia M, 66
BARTON, Joan R, 395
BARTSCH, Evora R, 1152
BASCOM, Alice M, 353
BASCOM, Karen L, 340
BASHAM, Patti, 479
BASHAM, Rhonda Kay, 443
BASINGER, Doris Stroud, 743
BASKIN, Jeanne E, 548
BASS, Cathleen A, 683
BASS, Linda, 281
BASSANER, Judith, 549
BASSETT, Carole E, 189
BASSETTE III, James R, 842
BASSO, Bill, 524
BASTI, Maria C, 863
BATCAGAN-PASICATAN, Susan T, 761, 526
BATES, Diane Yvette, 678
BATES, L M, 1170
BATES, Lois, 786
BATTAGLIA, Rhonda Lee, 426
BATTERSON-ROSSI, Barbara, 1029
BATTLE, Tashire, 559
BATTLES, Eric London, 455
BAUER, Joyce, 1015
BAUER, Karen Ann, 937
BAUER, Patty Call, 826
BAUER, Scott, 477
BAUM, R "Lou" F, 1071
BAUM, Rhoda Lee, 126
BAUM, Sandi L, 1029
BAUMAN, Frances L, 407
BAUMAN, Jeff, 369
BAUMAN, Olga, 215
BAUMAN, Sam, 323
BAUMAN, Tanya, 1129
BAUMGARDNER, Betty, 88
BAUTCH, Madge E, 933
BAXTER, Aimee A, 89
BAXTER, Amy, 1000
BAXTER, John H, 1145
BAXTER, Richard L, 889
BAXTER, Therese M, 775
BAY, Bernice, 153
BAY, Doug, 233
BAYNE, Ann, 71
BEACH, Christine, 609
BEACH, Donald C, 104
BEACH, Mary Anne, 676
BEACH, Troy R, 991
BEADLES, Troy A, 310
BEAL, Jane Ellen L, 428
BEALS Jr, Omer, 898
BEALS, Barbara, 1023
BEALS, Dolores E, 136
BEAN-SARGEANT, Karen M, 169
BEARD, Cynthia A, 224
BEARD, John, 157
BEARD, Samantha A, 69
BEARDEN, Nancy C, 195
BEARDEN, Zelpha George, 1075
BEARDSLEE, Larry A, 869
BEARDSLEY, Catherine, 1052
BEARDSLEY, Nathanael, 689
BEARHALTER, Kathryn K, 1075
BEASLEY, Mary M, 773
BEATON, Glenn S, 797
BEATTY, Laura M, 154
BEATTY, Sam, 619
BEAUDO, Sally Ann, 1102
BEAULIEU, Kenneth M, 262
BEAUMONT, Elizabeth, 693
BEAUMONT, Ms Dane, 705
BEAVER, Henry M, 1026
BEAVER, Holly Lee, 717
BEAVER, Pat, 171
BEAVERS, E Paul, 147
BECHT, Michelle, 574
BECHTEL, Brandi, 228
BECK, Billye, 422
BECK, Daniel P, 101
BECK, John Preston, 589
BECK, Lorna Lee, 88
BECK, Pauline, 1006
BECK, Richard, 796
BECK, Tammy, 421
BECK, William R, 812
BECKER, Marsha, 334
BECKFORD, Jonathan, 76
BECKMAN, Jennifer L, 486
BECKMAN, Shirley Anne, 873
BECKMANN, Gail E, 672
BECKNER, Olan E, 1129
BECKWORTH, Paul E, 86
BEDARD, Harriet (Shove), 844, 1097
BEDARD, Shirley, 714
BEDELL, Jay D "Dutch", 122
BEDNARCZYK, Marian, 672
BEDZYK, Sharon C, 47
BEECHER, David James, 944
BEECHER, George, 1140
BEEGLE, Lynn, 557
BEERS, Florence L, 854
BEESON, Howard, 1159
BEEZHOLD-DUPREE, Agnes, 295
BEGAY, Natalie R, 343
BEGEMAN, Monica K, 379
BEGLEY, Frances, 598
BEGNAUD, Mary Beth, 189
BEHN, Erin, 339
BEHNKE, Rose H, 1170
BEHREND, Marsha J, 118
BEIGHLEY, Raymond A, 966, 121
BEIGHLEY, Warren L, 310
BEIHL, Irene F, 754
BEIRO, Kathy M, 1116
BEISLY, Pat, 515
BELAIR, Brenda, 879
BELCHER Sr, James E, 768
BELENARDO, Sally, 375
BELFLOWER, Ron W, 489
BELL Jr, Walter R, 335
BELL, Antoinette A, 903
BELL, Bobbi, 719
BELL, Colleen, 453
BELL, David, 612
BELL, David L, 1052
BELL, David Lee, 641
BELL, Deborah Ann, 187
BELL, Dolores, 243
BELL, Gordon J, 1087
BELL, Herbert W, 1151
BELL, Jennivee, 391
BELL, Linda J, 240
BELL, Lorraine E, 1049
BELL, Marguerite E, 685
BELL, Nancy J, 638
BELL, Sandra, 417
BELL, Vita Lashea, 82
BELL-VAN DYKE, June, 903
BELLAMY, Bruce Melton, 1149
BELLAMY, Jina, 1026
BELLAMY, Nancy W, 453
BELLE, Jessica, 773
BELLEFLEUR, Sheila, 1097
BELLEMORE, Lois-lynn, 885
BELLFIELD Jr, Marcell E, 581
BELLISSINO, Sharon Marie, 1029
BELLOMY, Deiedre A, 678
BELLOWS, Hilma, 78
BELSTON, Patty, 237
BELTRAN, Rudy, 774
BELUE, Carmella, 1036
BELVIY, James Lee, 1016
BEMENT, Jane S, 497
BEN, Andrew, 1061, 1060
BENAVENTE, Rose A, 970
BENCHOFF, Marjorie Hind, 313
BENDER, Donna M, 580
BENDER, Joanne S, 785
BENDER, Martha, 76
BENEDICT, Carolyn Sue, 458
BENHAM, Cleota, 1150
BENHAM, Eddie, 193
BENJAMIN, Joseph Irvin, 622
BENJAMIN, Kim, 1172
BENJAMIN, Kirsten M, 962
BENJU, Benju A, 1010
BENKE, Mildred L, 1129
BENLEHR, Helen, 770
BENN, Connie M, 281
BENNET, Christine Alison, 1191
BENNETT, Amy, 271
BENNETT, Antoinette, 864
BENNETT, Dan G, 223
BENNETT, Donna Lea, 1137
BENNETT, Ethel H, 1077
BENNETT, Kathy, 58
BENNETT, Leora C, 193
BENNETT, Linda Jean, 222
BENNETT, Louise, 1026
BENNETT, Luther L, 551
BENNETT, Marion P, 868
BENNETT, Ray (Tariq), 90
BENNETT, Roxie, 113
BENNETT, S M, 527
BENNING, Beverly A, 381
BENNINGTON, Mayme E, 746
BENNION, Mark D, 265
BENO, James P, 431
BENOIT, Mayetta, 396
BENSON, Daisy (Shipley), 78
BENSON, Jean, 320
BENSON, Tamara, 733
BENT, Eric, 760
BENTLEY, Eleanor, 296
BENTLEY, Maria A, 737
BENTLEY, Marie, 1127
BENTLEY, Mary C, 1096
BENTON, Margaret R, 1186
BERARDI, Guido, 939
BEREJIKLIAN, Talar, 361
BERG, Patricia J, 138
BERGAMO, Kristen, 403
BERGE, Michael J, 1116
BERGELT, Daniel, 579
BERGER, Al Scott; Meeks, Sissy, 462
BERGER, Mayme, 761
BERGEVIN, Scott, 918
BERGH, A John, 673
BERGMAN, Shirley, 998
BERGMAN, Valerie L, 863
BERGMANN, Jennifer, 384
BERGQUIST, Michelle R, 877
BERK, Maureen S, 811
BERKOWITZ, Sarah, 928
BERKS, Mary Gladish, 1149
BERMAN, Jayne Whitlow, 896
BERNARD, Bernard, 926
BERNARD, Manning F, 85
BERNARDO, Eleanor, 523
BERNASCONI, Melvin, 354
BERNHARDY, Barbara J, 412
BERNHART, Doug Paul, 468
BERNIER, Eric, 450
BERNSTEIN, A E, 988
BEROLA, Gina Marie, 1148
BERRIER II, James D, 300
BERRY, Alice, 114
BERRY, Charles P, 661
BERRY, Jacqueline, 276
BERRY, Jennifer A, 371
BERRY, Judy, 456
BERRY, Julie R, 346
BERRY, June, 935
BERRY, Laura Flint, 524
BERRY, Leah J, 473
BERRY, Naomi, 122
BERRY, Patricia, 1131
BERRYMAN, Jo Brantley, 345
BERT, Tom, 964
BERTERA, Deborah, 431
BERTUCCI, Frances, 734
BESAW, Iris M, 1116
BESSER, Beverly L, 1022
BESSEY, Jill M, 463
BESSON, Larry Joseph, 496
BEST, Karen, 332
BESTON, Paul Michael, 895
BETCHEL, Dorothy G, 884
BETH ANN, Betha Ann, 725
BETHEA, William E, 1047
BETHEL, Marian, 1123
BETKIS, Barbara M, 1082
BETTAG, Mildred, 840
BETTENHAUSEN, Ruth E, 856
BETTGER, M Marie, 607
BETTIS, Barbara, 580
BETTLES, Jamie Nicole, 358
BETTS, Amy, 980
BETTS, Cora R (Gaillard), 87
BETTS, Kathleen, 335
BETZ, Stephen F, 1093
BETZOLD, Samantha, 474
BEUN, Adriana, 324
BEUS, Dennis J, 714
BEYCHOK-BOYER, Lila Marie, 537
BEYELER, Elena J M, 717
BEYER, Alan Jay, 307
BHANU, R Udaya, 822
BHASKARAN, Shanti, 417
BHAT, Divya, 1160
BIANCO, Angela Lo, 1074
BIANCULLI, Theodore T, 129
BIAS, Keith, 236
BIBBEY, Archie, 1155
BIBLE, James L, 390
BICE, Margaret F, 392
BICKART, Audrey, 349
BICKEL, Missy, 472
BICKERDIKE, John F, 785
BICKERSTAFF, Joseph A, 242
BICKFORD, Jessica, 11
BICKLER, Scott J, 956
BIDDIX, A Russell, 986
BIDWELL, Marlynn, 870
BIEBER, Melba L, 146
BIELEWICZ, Nicole, 484
BIENZ, Ida Mae, 783
BIERKLE, Elizabeth M, 683
BIERMA, Wayne, 525
BIERMANN, Beverly Ann, 250
BIERS, Cathy, 825
BIESAGA, Dorothy, 711

BIESER, Leslie, 967
BIETERMAN, Steve, 453
BIGELOW, Chrysti, 684
BIGGS, Timothy Todd, 180
BILA, Ms Diane M, 354
BILBO, Heather, 1118
BILICA, Carol, 1003
BILLECK, Beth, 129
BILLIEU, Sandra C, 855
BILLINGSLEY, Laura J, 1054
BILLIOT, Louis Joseph, 967
BILLMAN, David James, 639
BILSTEIN, Tom, 605
BILTON, Dorothy Ann, 564
BILYEW, Jennifer, 509
BINDO, Charlotte N, 374
BINNS, Holly D, 1191
BIRACH, Roberta L, 383
BIRD, Amanda Lynn, 1044
BIRD, Glorious B C, 772
BIRD, Mary Emma I, 521
BIRDWELL, Regina Karen, 344
BIRK, Jennifer, 600
BIRMINGHAM, Sharon A, 673
BISER, Louise, 692
BISH, Patricia, 12
BISHOP, Bernice Couey, 72
BISHOP, D A, 37
BISHOP, Johnnie Britt, 541
BISHOP, Mabel M, 1140
BISHOP, Melanie S, 506
BISKUPSKI R.C., Sr Christine, 1157
BISSELBERG, Dorothy C, 809
BITTEL, Paula Marie, 1180
BIWER, Michele M, 334
BJARNADOTTIR, Gudrun Bjork, 696
BLACHFORD, Olga, 817
BLACK, Carol, 966
BLACK, Donald, 560
BLACK, Dorothy, 1150
BLACK, Douglas, 39
BLACK, John G, 544
BLACK, Todd E, 536
BLACKBURN, Frances, 614
BLACKBURN, Pearl, 248
BLACKBURN, Ruth R, 666
BLACKBURN, Tammie, 89
BLACKFORD, Peggy, 128
BLACKLOCK, Sheelagh, 1073
BLACKOWICZ, John D, 594
BLACKSTOCK, Barbara, 478
BLACKSTON, Oji S, 843
BLACKWELL, Joseph K, 1056
BLAINE, Bruce A, 968
BLAINE, Grace, 712
BLAIR Jr, Robert V, 80
BLAIR, Dewey, 937
BLAIR, Dorothy L (Roeder), 837
BLAIR, Kathy, 36
BLAIR, Marlo, 183
BLAIR, Mary E L, 207
BLAIR, Mrs Murl (Wanda), 306
BLAIR, Rexana, 1034
BLAIR, Robert, 1153
BLAIR, Robert M, 240
BLAIS, Autumn, 455
BLAIS, Paul A, 922
BLAKE, Evelyn K, 1201
BLAKE, Julie Lynne, 410
BLAKE, Nancy P, 1096
BLAKE, Robert E, 655
BLAKELY, Jay A, 942
BLANCHARD, Mary Thayer, 921
BLANCHARD, Robert P, 186
BLANCO, Brenda, 337
BLAND, Rita, 421
BLANDFORD, Mona F, 436
BLANKENSHIP, Daryl L, 496
BLANKENSHIP, Jennifer, 450
BLANSETT, E Leona (Hickman), 968, 1112
BLATT, Heidi Lynn, 515
BLAU, Donna, 922
BLAY, Helen M, 360
BLAYLOCK, Debbie Hill, 353
BLAZIER, Nina, 908
BLEDSOE, Ruby W, 27
BLEVINS, Linda I, 1097
BLEVINS, Melody K, 630
BLISS, Elissa, 953
BLOCK, Betty, 332
BLOCK, Stephanie Kittredge, 851
BLOCKER, Greg, 560
BLOCKSON, Willie D, 330
BLOM, Chloe Beeson, 1012
BLOMBERG-WILSON, Kristen A, 330
BLOOM, Barbara, 220
BLOOMFIELD, Lawrence E, 256
BLOOMFIELD, Pamela, 402
BLOUNT, Marc, 1030
BLOW, John N, 107
BLUCHER, George, 356
BLUE, Gladys I, 1067
BLUFORD, Linda E, 869
BLUHM, Robert F, 1151
BLY, William, 373
BOARD, Faith, 1195
BOATRIGHT, Aaron Phillip, 701
BOATWRIGHT, Rochelle, 878
BOAZ, Margaret G, 29
BOBB, Nyoka, 995
BOBBITT, Clarence B, 199
BOBBITT, Kavin W, 791
BOBINO, Clarence, 997
BOCHKAY, Judith Fenton, 746
BOCHMAN, Cindy, 320
BOCK, Cyndi, 140
BOCKELMAN, Diane, 554
BOCKMAN, Patsy, 789
BODE, Mrs W, 1034
BODE, Sheila Cronin, 186
BODENMAN, Donna, 15
BOEHMLEHNER, Evelyn Green, 324
BOEING, Jennie, 1173
BOGGS, Lisa, 823
BOGLE, Mahalia, 308
BOGUTZ, Lillian, 334
BOICE, Judith L, 354
BOISCLAIRE, Joyce, 442
BOLD, Anna L, 1183
BOLDEN, Saundra, 751
BOLDEN, Tanist Denise, 968
BOLDT, Victoria L, 571
BOLE, Shirley A, 112
BOLEN, Stephen Dean, 214
BOLES, Tami, 701
BOLLER, Karen Sue C, 981
BOLTE, Kelly, 942
BOLTON, Douglas E, 908
BOMAN, Maxine J, 770
BOMMARITO, Ada, 704
BON-RICHARDS, Mary, 89
BONANNI, F Deloris, 291
HEENEY, Victoria B, 1035
BONANOMI, Douglas C, 416
BONDS, Cortland, 514
BONNETT, Laura Ann, 1155
BONTRAGER, Kevin D, 522
BONYAI, Joanne J, 370
BOOB, Sheila M, 715
BOOHER, Debby, 556
BOOHER, Rick A, 289
BOOHER, Tereasa, 1088
BOOK, Susan, 500
BOOKER, Kay Walters, 943
BOOKOUT, Dave, 56
BOONE, Altman, 1097
BOOTH, Kay Arneberg, 982
BOOTH, Michele, 783
BOQUET, Stephanie, 827
BORCHARDT, Brian Allen, 910
BORCHARDT, Lovie Lee, 988
BORCHIN, Denise M, 640
BORDEN, Daniel C, 1089
BORDES, Jessica, 745
BORDONARO, Michael J, 283
BORI Jr, Stanley W, 1098
BORIS, Kathy A, 329
BORK, Larry C, 1098
BORQUEZ, Linda, 373
BORRELLI, Belinda, 222
BORUFF, Aileen Campbell, 292
BOSAK, Otakar E, 1016
BOSECKER, Michelle, 671
BOSLEY, Kriss Ann, 291
BOSNELL, Mildred E, 16
BOSS, Tami A, 46
BOSSE, Elaine, 621
BOSSINGER, Charlotte Alcorn, 794
BOSSUK, Sidney, 1189
BOSTICK, Evelyn H, 291
BOSWELL, Sue Cristi, 1025
BOTE, Shirley, 317
BOTELHO, Pamela S, 283
BOTTOMLEY, April M, 761
BOTTOMS, Bernice, 686
BOUCHER-GOSLING, Kathleen, 262
BOUDINOT, Millie, 562
BOUDREAU, Natasha, 900
BOUDRIA, Michelle M, 664
BOUGHTON, Lucille M, 130
BOULDEN, Ann Mcelroy, 182
BOULDEN, Ms Ute D, 1149
BOUNAUITO, Thomas J, 142
BOURGEOIS, Michelle M, 608
BOURGOIN, Esta Groesser, 66
BOURQUE, Celia, 1095
BOUSQUET Jr, Robert L, 909
BOUSQUET, Don G, 34
BOUTHILLIER-ORSZULAK, Renee, 299
BOUTWELL, Deann, 592
BOVE, Donna M, 787
BOWDEN, April, 851
BOWEN, David S, 1009
BOWEN, Eddie H, 1143
BOWEN, Heather L, 849
BOWEN, Janorah, 850
BOWEN, Karen, 1118
BOWEN, Milton J, 669
BOWERS, Deborah Rene, 1180
BOWERS, Denise, 862
BOWERS, Faith L, 776
BOWERS, Florence, 818
BOWERS, Suzanne Carol, 558
BOWERS-ISABELL, Helen, 467
BOWERSOCK, Phyllis M, 760
BOWIE, Lawanda A, 853
BOWKER-RIST, Ruth, 395
BOWLER, Michael, 643
BOWLES, Gary H, 457
BOWLES, Rosetta E, 808
BOWLEY, William E D, 207
BOWLING, Angela R, 1050
BOWLING, Glenda, 94
BOWMAN, Ivannetta, 137
BOWMAN, Mellissa, 700
BOWSER, Mary J, 1142
BOYCE, Karen, 612
BOYCE, Kevin, 64
BOYD Jr, Thomas L, 515
BOYD, Anne E, 505
BOYD, Cindy Jean, 75
BOYD, Earl J, 900
BOYD, Genevia M, 379
BOYD, Mary F, 138
BOYER, Annetta M, 649
BOYER, Olive Ruth, 715
BOYER, Raymond W, 101
BOYETTE, Barbariae, 590
BOYINGTON, Alon Drew, 612
BOYKIN-MCKOY, Lattice, 832
BOYLE, Fred, 95
BOYLE, Patricia, 739
BOYLES, Roxana R, 633
BOZARTH, Sue, 732
BOZEMAN, Anna Lou, 1054
BOZOVICH, Terri Jean, 606
BRABHAM, Akua, 597
BRACE, Marilyn R, 927
BRACEY, Michele, 60
BRACISCO, Kathy L, 578
BRACKEN, Wanda, 156
BRADBERRY, Kimberly, 582
BRADDOM, Karen, 314
BRADFIELD, Lori, 134
BRADFORD, Essie M, 1097
BRADLEY, Donna May, 1001
BRADLEY, Gayle C, 1046
BRADLEY, Jan H, 947
BRADLEY, Melissa A, 159
BRADLEY, Ms Kerren D, 886
BRADLEY, Stacey Lynn, 284
BRADSHAW, Claudine M, 273
BRADSHAW, Donna White, 558
BRADSTREET, Patricia Cole, 628
BRADT, Sharie Lynne, 202
BRADY, A Lynn, 499
BRADY, Denise M, 65
BRADY, Helen F, 1002
BRADY, Julian, 684
BRADY, Katherine M, 477
BRADY, Mrs F E, 401
BRADY, Natalie A, 886
BRADY, Shannon Lee, 255
BRAEULER, Bonnie, 1156
BRAGDON, Betty, 51
BRAHINSKY, Gerald E, 108
BRAMBLE, Paula Petra, 1098
BRAMHALL, Betsy Jane, 426
BRAMLETT, Melissa P, 871
BRAMMER, D'arleane, 1172
BRANCH, June, 778
BRANCH, Michael, 787
BRANCH, Sara, 645
BRANCH, Violet, 951
BRANCHEAU, Deborah, 338
BRAND, Cynthia, 919
BRAND, Dolores, 41
BRAND, Joy, 1173
BRANDAO, Leo A, 1150
BRANDER, Alicia, 364
BRANDES, Iris, 985
BRANDON, Diane, 1185
BRANDON, Geraldine E, 674
BRANDT, Heather, 507
BRANEFF, Bonita Lea, 984
BRANGAN, Virginia, 269
BRANHOF, Margie, 609
BRANNON, Audrey, 827
BRANSTETTER, Elvira E, 522
BRANTLEY, Anita T, 1139
BRANTLEY, Ronald K, 863
BRASNICK, Barbara S, 33
BRASSARD, Teresa, 890
BRASSELL, George, 74
BRASWELL, Kathryn R, 717
BRATTIN, Dorothey M, 283
BRAUN, Audrey, 416
BRAUN, Cathryn, 449
BRAUN, Harriet, 48
BRAUN, Nora M, 375
BRAUTIGAN, Betty, 291
BRAVERMAN, Joan, 854
BRAVERMAN, Richard D, 1141
BRAY, Geneva, 861
BRAY-FONTAINE, Paulette, 1098
BRAYTON-HUDSON, Nancy C, 438
BREAULT SC, Br Edward C, 995
BRECKENRIDGE, Karle, 674
BREDEMAN, Maxine, 20
BREEDEN, Judy Joanne, 114
BREEDLOVE, Annie B, 384
BREEN, Gale E, 274
BREEN, Renee, 706
BREERWOOD, Stacy, 376
BREESE, Pepper, 875
BREHAN, Jeff, 752
BREKKE, Linda, 1151
BRENDAHL, M E, 596
BRENIZER, Jack S, 449
BRENNAN, Shirley L, 837
BRESHEARS, Mary, 187
BRESS, John F, 702
BREUNIG, Cindy, 689
BREVELLE, Rosalie, 554
BREWER, Beth, 702
BREWER, Helen Walpole, 12
BREWER, Jo Ann, 917
BREWER, Julia E, 606
BREWER, Madeleine P, 617
BREWER, Mark Allen, 987
BREWINGTON, Beth "e.j.", 659
BREX, Charles, 952
BREZENOFF, Shirley, 812
BRICKER, Randy J, 608
BRIDEN, Elaine F, 1156
BRIDEVAUX, Joseph, 759
BRIDGES, Beverly J, 798
BRIDGES, Ginny, 825
BRIERE, Caroline, 582
BRIERS, Joyce B, 416
BRIESTENSKY, Diane Lynn, 447
BRIGGS III, John R, 178
BRIGGS, Everett Francis, 584
BRIGGS, Phillip W, 283
BRIGHINDI, Leslie, 936
BRIGHT, Geneva M, 536
BRIGMAN, Pamela S, 999
BRILLMAN, Robyn, 467
BRINKERHOFF, Phillip Reed, 1030
BRINKMAN, J J, 186
BRINLEY, Shirley, 919
BRIONES, Shannon, 1016
BRISBINE, Thelma, 300
BRISK, Jeanne, 518
BRITTAIN, June, 686
BRITTINGHAM, B A, 968
BRITTON, Debbie, 92
BRITTON, Maurtile, 475
BRITTON, Robert D, 398
BRITTON, Terri, 327
BROACH, Pamela, 864
BROCK, Marsha, 93
BROCKEL, Valerie, 712
BROCKETT, Debbie L, 505
BROCKINGTON, Mr Penny, 878
BROCKINTON, O Estelle, 545
BROCKWAY, Brian, 1098
BRODERICK, Arlene, 586
BRODHEAD, Lou Ann, 80
BRODZINSKI, Virginia, 1188
BRONKEMA, Mary E F, 169
BRONSON, Melvin R, 255
BROOK, Clyde R, 30
BROOKES, Melissa, 397
BROOKINS, Mildred M C, 146
BROOKMEYER, Jennifer, 469
BROOKS, Becky, 816
BROOKS, Betsy, 248, 248
BROOKS, Betty Jean, 1185
BROOKS, David-Vincent, 628
BROOKS, Elizabeth, 336
BROOKS, Glenda K, 310
BROOKS, Jeffery Loren, 181
BROOKS, Jerry Marie, 36
BROOKS, Jimmie, 864
BROOKS, Joann, 53
BROOKS, Kelly Lane, 1140
BROOKS, Lisa, 900
BROOKS, Myrna, 1139
BROOMES, Harlow, 1159
BROSIUS, Lisa J, 857
BROUGH, Lorrie, 53
BROUILLARD, Phillippe W, 702
BROUILLETTE, Aubre, 969
BROUSSEAU, Rolanda, 999
BROWN Jr, General, 1133
BROWN Sr, Steven, 764
BROWN, Alisa, 215
BROWN, Amy, 372
BROWN, Ann Marie, 1195
BROWN, Beatrice Florist, 270
BROWN, Bob, 980
BROWN, C Mindy, 1099
BROWN, Carla J, 1170
BROWN, Carole, 1061
BROWN, Charlotte A, 367
BROWN, Christine L, 667
BROWN, Cora M, 290
BROWN, Corinne, 290
BROWN, Debi, 122
BROWN, Donald O, 698
BROWN, Doris G C, 749
BROWN, Dorothy Sill, 750
BROWN, Edvina Boyd, 757
BROWN, Elizabeth, 242
BROWN, Elizabeth P, 232
BROWN, Fern Louise T, 976
BROWN, Florence R, 386
BROWN, Frances, 595
BROWN, Frances P, 366
BROWN, Frances R, 492
BROWN, George R, 486
BROWN, Heidi V, 575
BROWN, James W, 1150
BROWN, Jane M, 349
BROWN, Jean I, 688
BROWN, Jennifer, 449
BROWN, Joyce E, 765
BROWN, Lisa Lynn, 549
BROWN, Mary C, 1030
BROWN, Mary Jane, 341
BROWN, Mildred B, 933
BROWN, Nicole B, 784
BROWN, Pamela M, 767
BROWN, Patricia, 1128
BROWN, Priscilla, 251
BROWN, Regina, 425
BROWN, Rev William F, 379
BROWN, Robert R, 100
BROWN, Robin G, 732
BROWN, Ronald W, 970
BROWN, Ruth Cote, 840
BROWN, Ruthy Stenson, 880
BROWN, Sarah T, 972
BROWN, Shirley A, 577
BROWN, Shirley D, 773
BROWN, T K, 268
BROWN, Tom, 284
BROWN, Verland, 657
BROWN, Walt, 321
BROWN, Walt, 473
BROWN, Wardell, 1181
BROWNE, Angela, 503
BROWNE, Christopher D, 16
BROWNE, Peron N, 644
BROWNELL, Chloris B, 34
BROWNING, Monica J, 1155
BROWNING, Robert, 761
BROWNING, Will, 151
BROWNRIDGE, Tracy Lynn, 916
BROWNSON, Karmen, 683
BROWNSTEIN, Michael H, 1035
BROWNSTEIN, Seymour, 1033
BROWNSTONE, Jean M, 58
BROYLES, Blanche H, 98
BROYLES, Judy, 725
BRUBAKER, Lucille L, 802
BRUCE Jr, Charles H, 546
BRUCE, Cindy, 32
BRUCE, Kevin Stephen Ignatious, 12
BRUCE, Stacey (Staceé) L, 644
BRUCKNER, Laura, 345
BRUGMAN, Elizabeth L, 958
BRUISE, M, 1183
BRUMBACH, Gene R, 150
BRUMITT, Beulah, 469
BRUMLEY, Ramona Lynn, 838
BRUMMETT, Karyn S, 57, 59
BRUNDAGE, Anne M, 1015
BRUNER, Dee Dee, 554
BRUNER, Tiffany Ann, 661
BRUNIE, Jean, 899

BRUNO, Susan, 653
BRUNS, William T, 57
BRUNSON, Imogene G, 95
BRUORTON, John, 656
BRUSCINO, Ronnie, 756
BRUSSALY, John, 846
BRUSTER, Reginald V, 681
BRYAN, Cathy A, 23
BRYAN, Kathleen R, 927
BRYAN, Tim, 782
BRYANT III, Henry Edward, 159
BRYANT, Barbara M, 77
BRYANT, Glenelle P, 273
BRYANT, John, 620
BRYANT, Lola, 955
BRYANT, Melanie W, 395
BRYANT, Wayne, 66
BRYMER, Barbara R, 33
BRYSON, William A, 988
BUBOLTZ, Monica, 691
BUCCI, Phyllis Ann, 1093
BUCHANAN, Connie L, 829
BUCHANAN, Robert, 1055
BUCHERT, Fatima, 119
BUCHHOLD, Louis, 158
BUCHHORN, Christina Ann, 1196
BUCK, Carolyn, 632
BUCK, Lavana, 643
BUCK, Lilli Lee, 236
BUCK, Lynne, 219
BUCK, Martha J, 821
BUCK, Michele, 818
BUCKERIDGE, Norma, 366
BUCKHOLZ, Arlette, 218
BUCKLES, Dena D, 1141
BUCKLEY, Molly J, 958
BUCKLEY, Peter D, 287
BUCKMAN, Caroline, 306
BUCKNAM, James D, 556
BUCKSON, Catherine, 1179
BUDGETTS, Bridget, 422
BUE, Annelise, 1042
BUENAVENTURA, Audrey D, 86
BUENDIA, Victor G, 1119
BUETTNER, Debi, 158
BUFFALOE, Vanessa R, 776
BUFKIN, Sandra D, 1055
BUFORD, Pamela Denise, 539
BUGDEN, Carolyn, 858
BUHEIT, Michelle Rae, 720
BUHL, Louise, 455
BUHLER, Joyce Escott, 504
BUKOVSKY, Christine B, 641
BUKOWSKY, Marin Lee, 767
BUKSBAZEN, Victor E, 1125
BULD, John, 67
BULDO-JACKSON, Rebecca, 1036
BULICH, Bernadette, 497
BULLARD Jr, Greg R, 851
BULLARD, Angela C, 174
BULLINGTON, B G, 1115
BULLOCH, Lori, 933
BULLOCK, Jessica Anne, 516
BULLOCK-MARTIN, Juanita, 471
BUMBACO, Sandra, 325
BUMBRY, Virginia M, 815
BUMGARDNER, Noelle, 923
BUNCH, Patsy, 705
BUNCH, Venita, 669
BUNDY, James E, 140
BUNKER, Amber, 419
BUNKOWFST, Patricia E, 1015
BUNTING, Dennis R, 1160
BURBRIDGE, Shannon, 295
BURCH, Darlene L, 563
BURCH, Howard R, 993
BURCHETT, Kristina, 360
BURCHFIELD, Debra, 669
BURCHSTEAD, Christie B, 901
BURD, Eric Wayne, 287
BURDEKIN, Lynn, 752
BURDETTE, Cody A, 139
BURDICK, Carol E, 1043
BURDINE, Floyd J, 568
BURDS, Denis P, 643
BURETEA, Serban, 407
BURFORD, Audrey R, 679
BURGA, Evelyn, 1026
BURGAMY, Deborah, 774
BURGER, Beverly Chandler, 749
BURGER, Louisa M, 981
BURGESS, David M, 1153
BURGESS, Mary W, 1118
BURGHEN, Elizabeth A, 261
BURGNER, Susan, 674
BURGOS, Aura, 906
BURIAN, Lorraine, 460
BURKE, Coleen, 387
BURKE, Dawn M, 834
BURKE, Dennis A, 1013
BURKE, Donna Gill, 1039
BURKE, Forest E, 692
BURKE, Gary, 587
BURKE, Karen, 551
BURKE, Kerry E, 787
BURKE, Lisa G, 274
BURKE, Renee L, 768
BURKES, Paul S, 478
BURKETT, Eva M, 195
BURKETT, Florence H, 294
BURKHAM, Trudy H, 1056
BURKHARDT, Brenda Lee, 750
BURKHART, Garry D, 755
BURKS, Linda Farley, 966
BURKS, Willean, 765
BURLEY, Joyce, 1142
BURLEY, Norma, 641
BURLINGAME, Marie B, 760
BURLINGHAM, Eleanor Jane, 108
BURLISON, J Kevin, 808
BURMAN, Dorothy K, 424
BURNETT, Deana, 124
BURNETT, Ellen M, 1150
BURNETT, Frances Lenay, 493
BURNETT, Mignon P, 101
BURNETT, Sr Eustelle, 1114
BURNETT, Ursula, 1015
BURNINGHAM, Kathryn F, 182
BURNS, Charlotte T, 1089
BURNS, Cherry R, 1098
BURNS, Elizabeth D, 549
BURNS, Katherine, 224
BURNS, Louise W, 669
BURNS, Maynard R, 797
BURNS, Robert Edgar, 811
BURNS, Sharon J, 637
BURNS, Stella F, 50
BURNSTEIN, Anna Rose, 183
BURR, Gary S, 98
BURRELL, Miss Laura Lambe, 970
BURRESS, M M, 1129
BURRIS, B, 177
BURRIS, Eilene A, 123
BURRIS, Elizabeth, 513
BURRIS, Margaret Peel, 744
BURRIS, Rebecca D, 961
BURROW, Carmen, 664
BURROW, John, 527
BURRUEL, Reyna, 1139
BURSHA, Evelyne, 1195
BURSON, Kimberly A, 1190
BURT, Daniel R, 469
BURTLE, Anna, 984
BURTON, Carol A, 1007
BURTON, Pauline, 777
BURTON, Stephanie, 315
BURTS, Dianna Lunde, 1085
BUSAM, Timothy L, 264
BUSBEE, Deborah L, 699
BUSCHBASCHER, Trina M, 145
BUSCHEK, Jeffrey Alan, 366
BUSCHMAN, Helen M, 7
BUSER, Jerome E, 1057
BUSER, Julie M, 42
BUSH, David, 194
BUSH, John S, 209
BUSH, Meriam B, 1179
BUSH, Ms Jamie, 288
BUSH, Rich J, 359
BUSHAW, Ann I, 434
BUSHMAN, Kate, 925
BUSHNELL Jr, Wayne M, 886
BUSSELL, Sandra Q, 202
BUSSEY, Alex W, 676
BUSSEY, Stella M, 619
BUTLER, Daisy Loram, 330
BUTLER, David E, 1045
BUTLER, Dorothy W, 348
BUTLER, Eleanor, 901
BUTLER, J Murray, 344
BUTLER, Jeffery W, 68
BUTLER, Joan, 452
BUTLER, Mark W, 618
BUTLER, Miss Larnell Custis, 935
BUTLER, Ruth V, 630
BUTLER, Wendy L, 343
BUTRYM, Melissa N, 164
BUTTAFUOCO, Josephine, 728
BUTTENHEIM, Mimi, 899
BUTTERFIELD, June, 1048
BUTTERS, Beth Ann, 820
BUTTINGER, Louis, 1113
BUTTON, Tosha, 589
BUTTURFF, Christopher A, 116
BUZAN, Lurena, 422
BUZICK, Dwight, 166
BUZZELL, Lucille E, 156
BYER, Gregory N, 1034
BYERS, Becky Wilson, 222
BYGGDIN, Elizabeth M, 148
BYKER, Tonya Yvonne, 103
BYNUM, Deborah J, 65
BYNUM, Dwayne L, 515
BYRAM, Angela D, 371
BYRD Sr, Richard E, 279
BYRD, Barbara, 350
BYRNE, Kathleen, 895
BYRON, Michael, 950
BYSTROM, Herman, 116

C

CABALLERO, Florence McMillian, 96
CABETS, Judia Mcclendon, 55
CABRERA, Edda Tavarez, 1121
CABRERA, Eva Elizabeth, 52
CABRERA, John, 1116
CABRINETY, Patricia B, 960, 967
CACCAVIELLO, Rozana, 738
CACCIATORE, John Anthony, 243
CADMAN, P Wendi, 356
CADOGAN Sr, Charles S, 579
CADY, Patrick L, 698
CAFARELLA, Leatha M, 442
CAFOUREK, Katheren Layman, 746
CAGLE, Sandra, 1040
CAHALY, Kimberly Anne, 406
CAHILL, C F (Stone-Skipper), 493
CAHOON-KNIFF, Dawn, 294, 1070
CAISSIE, Stephen, 1072
CALABRESE, John A, 144
CALCATERRA, Theodore J, 581
CALDERWOOD, Patsy Taylor, 249
CALDWELL, Frank L, 690
CALDWELL, Jenni, 1166
CALDWELL, Marion E Herbert, 337
CALDWELL, Wendy H, 384
CALHOUN, Wilbur Orlando, 50
CALI III, John Michael, 314
CALICUTT, Sue L, 89
CALIGIURI, Nick, 161
CALKINS, Amelia, 309
CALKINS, Anne, 607
CALKINS, Eddie Steven, 572
CALKINS, Mark D, 1031
CALKINS, Mary T, 332
CALLAHAN, Heidi, 1079
CALLAHAN, Rebecca L, 790
CALLAWAY, John, 639
CALLIHAN, Wesley J, 851
CALLIS, Claude, 507
CALLOWAY, Frederick S, 927
CALLWOOD, Deborah L, 955
CALNAN, Kimberle, 151
CALVERT, Teresa A, 548
CALVERY, Albert L, 288
CAMACHO, Henry, 1025
CAMACHO, Nelson, 1099
CAMACHO, Nephi, 938
CAMBRA, Lee, 754
CAMBRE, Dianne, 477
CAMBRIDGE, D M, 333
CAMBY, Illa Michelle, 876
CAMBY, Jeannette, 953
CAMEAU, Teresa, 839
CAMELWORT, M T, 188
CAMERON, Carol, 776
CAMERON, Ronjon, 531
CAMMUSE, Stephen Wayne, 704
CAMP, Joan T, 1116
CAMPAGNA, Joanne Marie, 1201
CAMPBELL, Clifford J, 760
CAMPBELL, Deanne, 565
CAMPBELL, Debra Sue, 288
CAMPBELL, Diana L, 1190
CAMPBELL, Diane, 671
CAMPBELL, Evelyn A, 973
CAMPBELL, Georgia N, 1134
CAMPBELL, Jane, 419
CAMPBELL, Janice, 722
CAMPBELL, Jennifer M, 950
CAMPBELL, Jimmy, 493
CAMPBELL, Juanita, 595
CAMPBELL, Kristen L, 682
CAMPBELL, Laura M, 900
CAMPBELL, Linda Rose, 784
CAMPBELL, Mazell B, 616
CAMPBELL, Miss Joann, 374
CAMPBELL, Stephen P, 516
CAMPBELL, Susan, 207
CAMPBELL, William T, 589
CAMPOS, Bobby, 526
CAMPTON, Rachel, 424
CANADA-BYRD, Moneva, 1098
CANADAY, Samantha, 357
CANERDY, Janice Lynn, 1051
CANN, Carolyn, 417
CANNADY, Laurie, 880
CANNELLA, Francesco A, 540
CANNING, Lisa, 484
CANNING, Ralph E, 27
CANNON, Alice Rae, 452
CANNON, Major T, 899
CANNON, Rhondalene G, 958
CANO, Art, 577
CANOY, Oneida N, 865
CANTERBURY, Mary D, 793
CANTLON, Iris, 128
CANTRELL, Helen L, 695
CANTRELL, Lessie, 48
CANTRELL, Linda, 1046
CANTRELL, Ruth, 259
CANTRELL-WERRY, Celita, 24
CANTWELL, Jerald E, 499
CAPACHIETTI, Janet M, 1033
CAPATE, T M, 1071
CAPELL, Uldine S, 380
CAPERTON, Kenneth Davis, 661
CAPISTRAN RSM, Sister Mary, 1060
CAPLINGER, Doris, 1152
CAPPS, Charles, 120
CAPPS, Kathy Darlene, 501
CAPTAIN, Joanna Mae, 797
CAPUTO, Laura, 856
CARDA, Mary, 1142
CARDASSI, Phyllis J, 903, 1098
CARDENAS, Aurora C, 968
CARDENAS, R Margaret, 362
CARDIN, Pauleta, 712
CARDINAL, Charlie, 617
CARDINAL, Grace D, 23
CARDIS, Lou, 158
CARDWELL, Evelyn Heath, 740
CARETTA, Glen, 713
CARETTO, Pete A, 317
CAREY, Jane E, 163
CAREY, Rachel, 457
CAREY, Warren E, 389
CARHART, Olga L, 1043
CARLEY, Robert J, 555
CARLING, Dorrie E, 450
CARLING-SLETTELAND, Helena, 642
CARLINO, Elvia, 294
CARLISLE, Deborah Treat, 731
CARLSON, Cindy L, 137
CARLSON, Lois C, 1143
CARLSON, Margaret M, 964
CARLSON, Tamara, 1183
CARMAN, L May, 532
CARMER, Jane, 505
CARMICHAEL, Beth, 226
CARMICHAEL, Jeffrey David, 120
CARMONA, Jose A, 1001
CARNAL, Ana Irene, 489
CARNER, Jessica Dawn, 783
CARNIGHAN, Rebecca, 100
CARO, Evelyn, 1143
CARO, Rosa M, 761
CAROZZA, Tony, 879
CARPENTER, Alma J, 297
CARPENTER, Arden K, 131
CARPENTER, Betty, 674
CARPENTER, Christina H, 1099
CARPENTER, Connie A, 212
CARPENTER, Kathy, 1139
CARPENTER, Kevin, 609
CARPENTER, Pamela, 775
CARPENTER, Susan S, 893
CARPER, Dvm, Diana Lynn, 711
CARR, Charlotte L, 388
CARR, James A, 859
CARR, Richard, 899
CARR, Robin, 360
CARR, Ron, 126
CARR, Ruby E L, 664
CARR, Tara, 388
CARRABIS, Laurajean, 625
CARRARETTO-ZANETTE, Vanna, 290
CARREAU, Raymond M, 1181
CARRERO, Rose, 283
CARRICO, Nina Lois, 264
CARRIER, David M, 481
CARRION, Marlis, 309
CARROLL, Antonietta R, 67
CARROLL, Barbara, 302
CARROLL, Carmen, 796
CARROLL, Dennis E, 1042
CARROLL, Dianne M, 554
CARROLL, Ernest P, 517
CARROLL, Kathleen, 24
CARROLL, Lauren E, 677
CARROLL, Linda A Patricia, 245
CARROLL, Mary S, 342
CARROLL, Ross P C, 734
CARROZZI, Geraldine, 351
CARRUTH, Kenneth James, 609
CARSON, Cheryl A, 630
CARSWELL, Ada, 917
CARTER, B J, 112
CARTER, Curtis, 223
CARTER, Dannie Lee, 61
CARTER, Donna, 1023
CARTER, Eleanor D, 441
CARTER, Hilder V, 606
CARTER, Jerry, 766
CARTER, Katharine S, 921
CARTER, Kenneth W, 163
CARTER, Louise, 198
CARTER, Orbrenett Kay, 622
CARTER, Debra K, 1011
CARTWRIGHT, Jason, 814
CARUSO, Judy Lyn, 227
CARUTHERS, Benita M, 379
CARVER, James E, 67
CARVER, Shannon P, 482
CARVO, Carolyn, 969
CAS, Debbie, 340
CASADY, Simon, 40
CASANTA, Isabelle, 390
CASARI, Audrey, 1115
CASE, Ora L, 398
CASE, Sheree L, 784
CASE, Tracy L, 401
CASEY, Arlene Clare, 111
CASEY, Barbara, 780
CASEY, Betty Elizabeth, 915
CASEY, Donald P, 479
CASEY, Erin Rose, 1128
CASEY, Ernest Randol Ph, 330
CASEY, Mary R, 320
CASHWELL, Willa Ewing, 78
CASIANO, Arlene, 900
CASON, Barbara A, 327
CASPER, A L, 706
CASPER, Lylah, 890
CASPERS, Bonnie, 1142
CASPI, David Isadore, 271
CASSADA, Robert S, 451
CASSARD, Jean A, 825
CASSIDY, Elizabeth, 150
CASSIDY, Helen M, 909
CASSIDY, Robert S, 744
CASSITY Jr, Martin M, 687
CAST, Don, 882
CASTANEDA, Laura, 1059
CASTEEL, Virginia Dare, 66
CASTELLA, Patricia, 621
CASTIEL, Janet, 168
CASTIGLIONE, Nancy, 607
CASTILLO, Tommy F, 1055
CASTLE, Elmer R, 815
CASTLE, Patricia J, 1130
CASTO, Sharlene E, 398
CASTOR, Jackie, 253
CASTRO Sr, Rustico S, 839
CASTRO, Jewell, 725
CASTRO, Julie Ann, 1024
CASUCCIO, Salvatore, 329
CASULA, Margaret B, 277
CATALANO, Domenick P, 905
CATALDI, Mary Anne, 820
CATANZARO, J, 324
CATANZARO, Louis M, 415
CATES, Diedra E, 302
CATES, Steve L, 1050
CATES, Tiffany, 934
CATLETT, Richard Don, 304
CATOE, Ms Micki, 48
CATON, Marvin T, 1175
CATRON, Clara, 983
CATRON, Dudley Jess, 800
CATTERTON, Mildred R, 103
CAULDWELL, Darleene, 431
CAUSEY, Betty, 896
CAUSEY, Jeannie C, 452
CAVADINI, James F, 751
CAVANAGH, Jayne, 578
CAVANAUGH, James, 406
CAVAZOS, Elizabeth, 459
CAVENDER, Judie, 338
CAVIN, Vicky, 204
CAVNESS, Jon, 1074
CAWOOD, Darius C, 264
CAYO, Emma S, 59
CAZELET, Lynn, 640
CECIL-OLEARO, Frances, 871

CENTANNI, Joseph A, 326
CERNIGLIA, Danielle, 1118
CERRONI, Sandra E, 611
CERVINKA, Tanya, 331
CESAR, Magali, 1058
CESARINI, Joan, 499
CESSNA, Trudy, 746
CESTARO, Anthony M, 1156
CEUTERICK, Franceska, 759
CHABALA, Allene Marie, 100
CHACHE', Poetess Kalamu, 1198
CHACON, Angelica, 1154
CHAFFEE, Mike, 376
CHAFFIN, Belinda Jean, 929
CHAFFIN, Larry D, 193
CHAFIN, Pearl, 789
CHAMBERLAIN, Gladys, 1138
CHAMBERLAIN, Nancy D, 58
CHAMBERS, Bernice, 1156
CHAMBERS, Dorothy P, 11
CHAMBERS, Glennda E, 745
CHAMBERS, Mary Eleanor, 1055
CHAMBLISS EDD, Charlotte J, 346
CHAMBRUN, Lillian, 1201
CHAMNESS, Theresa Marie, 1008
CHAMPION, Carolyn, 442
CHAMPION, Mary, 1051
CHANDLER, Amanda, 39
CHANDLER, Dorothy, 690
CHANDLER, Joe, 1142
CHANDLER, Joyce H, 318
CHANDLER, Kathryn S, 434
CHANDLER, Randall S, 276
CHANDLER, Rose Wiley, 226
CHANDLER, Sunny V, 745
CHANDLER, Terry A, 360
CHANDLER-WYANT, Donna, 701
CHANEY, Alisa, 1197
CHANEY, Elsie, 91
CHANEY, Jennifer, 785
CHANEY, Russ, 970
CHANG, Janice May, 18
CHANG, Laurie M, 461
CHANNELL, Eleanor, 485
CHANTEE, Nicole, 1054
CHAPA, Jesse, 1153
CHAPIN, David L, 755
CHAPMAN, Carol S, 904
CHAPMAN, Dorothy M, 177
CHAPMAN, Dorothy R, 472
CHAPMAN, Ginger, 853
CHAPMAN, Louise, 573
CHAPMAN, Mary Olive, 1087
CHAPMAN, Mimi, 684
CHAPMAN, Patricia, 958
CHAPMAN-POWELL, Carla, 747
CHAPPELL, Mary, 846
CHAPPELL, Sher, 742
CHAPPELLE, Guen, 386
CHAPUT, Rebecca Lynne, 912
CHARBONO, Katie, 909
CHARETTE, Sonny, 270
CHARLIE, The Shadow Poet, 593
CHARNOSKI, Nancy Leu, 18
CHARVONIA, Athena, 673
CHASE, Diane L, 882
CHASTAIN, Betty J, 941
CHATFIELD, Dennis, 62
CHATMAN, Marsha K, 463
CHATTOPADHYA, Madhumita, 261
CHAUSSEE, Caroline K, 1050
CHAVERS, Kelly A, 831
CHAVEZ, Aileen, 785
CHAVEZ, E J, 801
CHAVEZ, Linda, 740
CHAVEZ, Shirley, 968
CHAVIRA, Consuelo, 399
CHE, Phil, 897
CHEATWOOD, Donna, 861
CHEAVES, Sherry, 1156
CHECK, Cheryl, 695
CHEEK, Carolyn Andrews, 1108
CHEEK, Randy L, 655
CHEFFO, Irene Kalebdjian I, 1016
CHENIER, C Ann, 555
CHEPPA, Carmella P, 707
CHERN, Paul E, 842
CHERRIER-REGESKI, Wanda, 111
CHERRIS, Charles Cseresznye, 205
CHERRY, Cindy Jo, 326
CHERRY, Gwenda, 1193
CHERRY, Hazel, 731
CHERRY, Katrina, 405
CHESHIRE, Carolyn L, 285
CHESSER, Lurlene, 1170
CHEUNG, Penny, 240
CHEVALIER, Maria J, 706
CHEVRIER, Norma, 682
CHEW, Trina J, 499
CHEWNING, Rose A, 131
CHIA, C H, 189
CHIAROTTI, Eleanor, 409
CHIESA, John R, 838
CHIFFOLO, Nancy Anne, 1038
CHIGBROW, Keith Robert, 620
CHILCOTE, Chenoa, 671
CHILDERS, Andreah, 702
CHILDRESS, I N, 1189
CHILDS, Chisai, 256
CHILLE, Maria, 758
CHILLI, Maria, 547
CHIODO, M, 1035
CHIODO-WILHELM, Jan, 996
CHIPMAN, Edward E, 294
CHISNELL, Marvin O, 1017
CHITTUM, Peggy, 747
CHIZEK, Jackie, 1061
CHO, Benjamin, 411
CHOFEY, David J, 611
CHONG, Beverly, 13
CHONTOS, Jennifer, 61
CHOPPE, Sandra, 277
CHRESTMAN, Martha G, 1166
CHRISTENSEN, Carole J, 635
CHRISTENSEN, Donna M, 103
CHRISTENSEN, Helen, 371
CHRISTENSON, S R, 185
CHRISTIAENS, Cody, 102
CHRISTIAN, Artie, 772
CHRISTIAN, Evanne Marie, 1044
CHRISTIAN, Jerry, 726
CHRISTIANSEN, Donald E, 525
CHRISTIE, Huntley P, 6, 641
CHRISTIE, Patrick, 155
CHRISTINSON, Holly, 692
CHRISTMAN, Diane M, 188
CHRISTMAS, Diane, 535
CHRISTOFFELSZ, Maureen H, 20
CHRISTOFFERSON, Kimberly, 579
CHRISTON, George, 507
CHRISTOPHERSON, Juanita, 1109
CHRISTY, Clarence, 124
CHUBRICH, Sophie, 927
CHUNG, Mei, 86
CHUNN, Naomi Campbell, 516
CHURCH, Brenda, 105
CHURCH, Helen S, 396
CHURCH, Howard L, 1174
CHURCH, Michael David, 1071
CHURCH, Quetta Copley, 734
CHURCHEY, Kathy, 279
CHURCHILL, Joan, 873
CHURCHILL-SULAK, Kathy, 808
CIALONE, Carole Ahlf, 557
CIARAMAGLIA, Diane, 1142
CIARMELLO, Christine, 352
CIAVARDINI, Marla, 379
CICCARIELLO III, Anthony John, 914
CIE, M Q, 1072
CIERLITSKY, Robert J, 898
CIMAGLIO, Gina, 394
CIPOLLA, Victor A, 441
CIPRIANO, Lori Jean, 137
CISKO, Mary L, 1099
CLAIBORNE, Brenda, 1072
CLAIRBORNE, Matilda Johnson, 657
CLAIWORTH, Robertson, 375
CLAMP, Sandra J, 891
CLANTON, Patricia Ann, 1171
CLARK Jr, H Leonard, 1102
CLARK Jr, Joseph, 757
CLARK, Amy E, 307
CLARK, Andrew, 1040
CLARK, Annemarie, 263
CLARK, Annie M, 356
CLARK, Barbara Ann, 96
CLARK, Barbara H, 201
CLARK, Beverly, 477
CLARK, Clarah A, 282
CLARK, Col Bobby, 642
CLARK, Doris, 1182
CLARK, Dorothy M, 473
CLARK, Jarret Henry, 244
CLARK, Jenny, 673
CLARK, Kenneth D, 789
CLARK, Lenore C, 1179
CLARK, Leona, 354
CLARK, Lillian K, 907
CLARK, Lucile Clay, 510
CLARK, M David, 1088
CLARK, Marian, 180
CLARK, Marie C, 546
CLARK, Mary E, 1017
CLARK, Melody J, 480
CLARK, Michael D, 341
CLARK, Molly, 185
CLARK, Roy E, 1084
CLARK, Susan P, 857
CLARKE, Emily E, 808
CLARKE, Lois J, 492
CLARKE, Paula Hayes, 155
CLARKE, Stephen L, 168
CLAUNCH, Carl J, 509
CLAUSELL, Deborah, 478
CLAUSS, Mary Esther, 46
CLAY, Amy L, 772
CLAY, Bonnie F, 956
CLAY, Theodore, 38
CLAYBAUGH, Dreama, 853
CLAYBORNE, Sharon Davis, 735
CLAYCOMB, Elnora M, 637
CLAYTON, Cecil D, 1199
CLAYTON, Doris M, 319
CLAYTON, Janice Rothwell, 743
CLAYTON, M T, 304
CLEARWATER, David, 486
CLEARY, Diana J, 935
CLEAVES, Mrs Winnifred A, 851
CLEGG, Donald L, 378
CLEMENS, Kathy, 99
CLEMENT, Carol Stearns, 1049
CLEMENT, Judy, 825
CLEMENT, Lee, 886
CLEMENTS, Betty W, 972
CLEMENTS, Janie F, 297
CLEMENTS, Lloyd, 331
CLEMENTS, Mary Alice M, 1143
CLEMONS, Andrew F, 1048
CLENDENNIN, Barbara, 920
CLER, Ombra See, 230
CLEVENGER, Eillene M, 667
CLIFFORD, Henrietta M, 537
CLIFT, Colin, 256
CLIFTON, Raymond Lee, 779
CLIFTON, Daniel, 508
CLIFTON, Gladys A, 121
CLINE, Linda, 836
CLINE, Michael, 832
CLINE, Robert Dwain, 553
CLOHERTY, Connie A, 157
CLOSE, David, 841
CLOUD, Blaine, 107
CLOUD, Jan V, 33
CLOUD, Ms M Eileen, 926
CLOUD, Sondra, 861
CLOUSE, Diana Montgomery, 1099
CLOUSER, Dan C, 932
CLOUSS, Charles R, 711
CLOUTIER, Susan Marie Boucher, 313
CLOYD, Donald R, 155
CLYDE, Mary Kestler, 463
COATES, Billie Jo, 497
COATES, Deanne, 37
COATS, Jo Anne, 1166
COBB, Gary Lamar, 657
COBB, Nicole, 1132
COBB, Thadius, 784
COCCOLI, Rose, 265
COCHRAN, Ben, 552
COCHRAN, Joel R, 565
COCHRAN, Laura D, 298
COCHRAN, Lisa, 320
COCHRAN, Myra, 1187, 530
COCHRANE, Viviane, 672
CODY, Timi Smith, 862
COE, Keith L, 777
COE, Paula W, 803
COE, Sheryl, 133
COELHO, Kathleen F, 1039
COERPER, Allison, 427
COFFEY Sr, Elmer G, 160
COFFEY, Mary E, 7
COFFEY, Terrie Louise, 889
COFFIE, Darlene F, 225
COFFIN, Larissa, 1045
COHEN, Anne E, 71
COHEN, Hal, 489
COHEN, Phyllis J, 584
COHEN, Sidney R, 451
COHEN, Stan, 937
COIA, Dean, 437
COING G, Lee Du, 364
COLANGELO, Dorothea, 790
COLBERT, Amelia, 85
COLBERT, Steven N, 706
COLBY, Carolyn B, 651
COLBY, Cynthia, 307
COLBY, Emily Jane, 420
COLBY, Tod Anthony, 31
COLCORD, Elmer D, 1046
COLE, Connie P, 1115
COLE, Donald A, 653
COLE, Florence R, 1102
COLE, Jim, 82
COLE, Patricia C, 386
COLE, Ronald R, 1060
COLE, Tabaitha, 297
COLE, Tanan, 617
COLE, Tracey M, 766
COLE, Virginia M, 1163
COLE, Willie C, 476
COLE, Wilma R, 120
COLEMAN, (Chief) Felihkatubbe, 1024
COLEMAN, Alyce M, 369
COLEMAN, Bethy, 123
COLEMAN, Beverly B, 1042
COLEMAN, Christine K, 807
COLEMAN, Eileen, 516
COLEMAN, John, 1182
COLEMAN, Lee, 662
COLEMAN, Rosa L, 928
COLET, Cherie L, 832
COLETRANE, Claire W, 51
COLETTE, Colette, 1132
COLIN, Lawrence C, 1084
COLLAZO, Sonia F Kerns, 232
COLLEBRUSCO, Ida M, 1153, 1145
COLLER, Marsha, 29
COLLETT, Mary Mcwhorter, 1163
COLLEY, Douglas E, 486
COLLIER, Brian P, 926
COLLIER, James Church, 361
COLLIER, Lorraine R, 147
COLLIER, Marty, 769
COLLINS, Anise Trail, 676
COLLINS, Callie Harris, 506
COLLINS, Canadia, 1175, 489
COLLINS, Cheryl Leanne, 820
COLLINS, Eva L, 542
COLLINS, Fred, 224
COLLINS, Herman, 1010
COLLINS, Hilda M, 763
COLLINS, Isabelle, 483
COLLINS, Jenny E, 963
COLLINS, Joyce N, 1082
COLLINS, Karen, 387
COLLINS, Lance, 329
COLLINS, Melody, 1043
COLLINS, Roy A, 803
COLLIS, Peggy J, 1171
COLLISON, Rebecca S, 1050
COLLOPY, Mary-Jo, 1042
COLMENARES, Carmen L, 612, 961
COLMER, Ivy E, 426
COLO, Alfred, 167
COLQUITT, Craig, 1187
COLSON, Tracy, 39
COLWELL, Thomas B, 104
COMBERIATE, Jo B, 41
COMBS, Anna Rhynes, 619
COMBS, Brenda Marie, 613
COMBS, Debby K, 1099
COMBS, Diana Lynn, 312
COMBS, Jessie M, 1113
COMER, Carla J, 427
COMER, Stephen E, 352
COMINOS, Panagiota Y, 561
COMPESTINE, Rhoda L, 534
COMPSON, Hallie C, 1028
COMPTON, Janet Lynn, 121
COMPTON, Paul E, 366
COMPTON, Sandra, 851
COMSTOCK, Ronnie L, 791
CONANT, Robin L, 480
CONAWAY, Robert, 61
CONAWAY, Vernon W, 438
CONDON, J Helen, 568
CONDON, Marcelle, 120
CONGDON, Sharon L, 305
CONGER, Janette, 17
CONGLETON, Christine, 1041
CONGLETON, Slade, 359
CONIGLIO, Anna J, 428
CONKLIN, Paul L, 444
CONLEY, Denona C, 508
CONLEY, Edd R, 351
CONLEY, Qiana Cerise, 620
CONLEY, Stephen, 191
CONN, Ann Morgan, 481
CONNELL, Patti, 482
CONNELLY, Nicole M, 263
CONNER, Barbara Jean, 737
CONNER, Ethel M, 966
CONNER, Judy Lowery, 652
CONNER, Mary Dossett, 554
CONNER, Mrs Ray, 141
CONNER, Raymond J, 208
CONNER, Sylvia M, 144
CONNER, Virginia Cain, 892
CONNETT, Susan Kay, 867
CONNOLA Jr, Louis, 804
CONNOLLY, Matthew, 858
CONNOR, Evelyn, 414
CONNOT, Jodi, 229
CONRAD, Linda M, 144
CONRADS, Wilma, 166
CONRATH, Mrs Regina, 1188
CONROD, David Alan, 372
CONROY, Bill, 555
CONROY, Vincent E, 122
CONSTANCE, Patricia C T M, 149
CONSTANTINE, Michael, 738
CONTI, Valerie M, 690
CONTRUBIS, Gene, 212
CONWAY III, George W, 77
CONWAY, John Ashby, 429
CONWAY, Kelly, 964
CONWAY, Kerri, 17
CONYERS, Evelyn W, 320
COOK RN, Ethel Case, 160
COOK, Beth Ellen, 311
COOK, Beth M, 387
COOK, Betty M, 732
COOK, Bruce L, 176
COOK, Donalda J, 889
COOK, Jennifer, 768
COOK, Judith, 798
COOK, Michael, 1113
COOK, Millie Ann, 251
COOK, Miss Mary Cahill, 822
COOK, Salayne, 1019
COOK, Scotty Lee, 188
COOK, Susan K, 162
COOK, Ursula, 95
COOKIE, M, 994
COOKS, Louise S, 593
COOL, Michael Alan, 878
COON, William E, 150
COONEY, Rebecca J, 991
COOPER, Ann, 647
COOPER, Catherine L, 955
COOPER, Charles L, 914
COOPER, Claire, 965
COOPER, David A, 152
COOPER, Ella G, 250
COOPER, Gerry, 585
COOPER, Gladys, 223
COOPER, Jewell Greene, 1099
COOPER, Karla, 943
COOPER, Keith R, 571
COOPER, Lynne, 1187
COOPER, Robert P, 912
COOPER, Shirley, 589
COOPER, Terri Lynn, 224
COOPER, Wendy, 1024
COOPER, William J, 214
COPELAND, James M, 859
COPELAND, Walter, 1156
COPP, Joyce, 282
COPP, Kerri Lynn, 873
COPPOCK, Carol, 801
COPPOCK, Julieann Sherman, 902
COPPOCK, Rose, 269
CORA, Raquel, 608
CORATHERS, Phyllis L, 876
CORBELLO, Yvonne, 445
CORBEN, Beverly, 990
CORBETT, Tina, 333
CORBETT-KOUTZ, Leesia C, 118
CORBIN, Brooksie J, 365
CORBIN, Chris, 893
CORBIN, Donna, 1087
CORBIN, John, 155
CORBIN, Ruth Ann, 478
CORBO, Alfred, 467
CORCORAN, Sandra B, 85
CORDARO, Josephine, 962
CORDIER, Timothy, 523
CORDOVA, Desiree, 762
CORDOVA, Julie Anne, 39
COREY, Darren, 433
CORION, Leo, 445
CORKHILL, Fern C, 571
CORMIER-CLAVETTE, Noella, 456
CORNEILSON, June, 951
CORNELISEN, Nicole, 582
CORNELL, Christine, 21
CORNELL, Rana Laverda, 9
CORNELSON, Marie Pabian, 412
CORNING, Lola, 1080
CORNING, Lynn, 668
CORNUM, Rosemary, 1119
CORORAN, Jean D, 434
CORR, Kenneth E, 583
CORRARO, Betty, 1036, 1112
CORREIA, Nancy, 1167
CORRELL, Karen L, 355
CORRELL, Mary F, 259
CORRIGAN, Carey, 845
CORSENTINO, Patsy, 246
CORTEZ, Angelina M, 802
CORTEZ, Cindy, 737

Index

CORTEZ, Evon Boykins, 47
CORTRIGHT, Sandra, 1200
CORVAIA, Maria Dona, 718
CORY, Darlene L, 639
COSENTINO, Jo-Ann, 19
COSGROVE, Hilda M, 467
COSGROVE, John, 29
COSMOPULOS, Stavros, 799
COSNER, Regina L, 461
COSTA, Denise, 615
COSTA, Elizabeth M, 167
COSTA, Joseph M, 1014
COSTA, Julie, 138
COSTA, Michele, 499
COSTANTINI, Monica, 257
COSTANZO, Robert "Rocky", 921
COTE, Wilfred J, 293
COTHRAN, Jack W, 544
COTTER, Bethann, 801
COTTER, Cathy, 971
COTTON, Ottis L, 1116
COTTRILL, Beverly (Harrington), 1028
COTTRILL, Kay Lilly, 898
COTTRILL, Orville A, 1156
COUCH, Dana, 515
COUCH, Lori R, 7
COUCH, Ruth, 1149
COUGHLAN, John S, 372
COULING, Bev, 1078
COULON, Natalie, 376
COUNTIE, Noreen M, 1051
COURET, Dusty, 540
COURNUYER, Dennis R, 423
COURSEY, Keith, 1182
COURSEY, Shelah M Conner, 718
COURTRIGHT, Candra, 349
COURVILLE, Marion, 437
COVAL, Dr Naomi Miller, 49, 551
COVELLI, Laura S, 359
COVERDALE, Marcia Soper, 1147
COVERDELL, Melvena, 335
COVERT, Randy, 1083, 1033
COVERT, Ruth, 656
COVINGTON, Elaine, 752
COVINGTON, Rayfield, 1201
COWAN, Bobbe, 299
COWAN, Chamayn R "Cercie", 411
COWAN, Douglas, 24
COWAN, Jolita Lynn, 519
COWANS, Lana, 1058
COWARD, Anita Juliet, 529
COWARD, J W, 540
COWEN, Lisa, 849
COX, Algie Lee, 706
COX, Anna Jane Blackburne, 1052
COX, Barbara Fenne, 63
COX, Deanna L, 774
COX, Erwin, 161
COX, Gloria, 304
COX, Jennifer, 975
COX, Joyce, 636
COX, Kelly L, 565
COX, Mrs June F, 707
COX, Rebecca R, 194
COX, Shirley F, 659
COX, Shirley Mae, 790
COX, Sue, 875
COX, Teresa, 770, 768
COYLE, Ronald J, 223
COYNE, Daniel R, 718
COZART, Juanita, 202
COZZETTO, Rochelle E, 606
COZZI, Peggy Walker, 423
CRABLE, Karrah H E, 542
CRABTREE, Mike, 367
CRABTREE, Mrs Thelma, 300
CRACKEL, Madge S, 902
CRAFT III, Harry C, 891
CRAFT, Pamela Jean, 803
CRAFT, Wilburn B, 866
CRAIG III, Charles R, 368
CRAIG, Anna Marie Rose Soldo, 756
CRAIG, Barbara, 751
CRAIG, Irene Floyd, 681
CRAIG, Jennifer, 335
CRAIG, Joseph T, 1141
CRAIG, Michael, 698
CRAIG, Michael David, 34
CRAIG, Steven, 962
CRAIG-CLARK, Tracy M, 5
CRANCH, Elizabeth T, 1116
CRANDALL, Kenn, 1187
CRANDALL, Lori, 979
CRANE, Gayle, 927
CRANE, Sonya Nicole, 1187
CRANFORD, Ralph L, 153
CRAVER, Mary Garner, 441
CRAWFORD, Allan, 495
CRAWFORD, Deborah, 458
CRAWFORD, Gary, 401
CRAWFORD, John K, 281
CRAWFORD, Mary, 594
CRAWFORD, Nellie Mae, 745
CRAWLEY, Patrick, 424
CREBASSA, Elspeth, 508
CREIGHTON, Foster, 1028
CRENSHAW, Sandra, 773
CRESPO, Eleonore J, 107
CRESPO, Ellen, 109
CREVISTON, Kay, 998
CRIDER, Colleen E, 402
CRIDER, Ruby T, 1171
CRINER, Elmo, 610
CRIPE, Ann, 624
CRIPPEN, David, 357
CRIST, Bill, 528
CRIST, Imogene, 633
CRITNEY, Marvette, 654
CRITTENDEN, Edna High, 282
CRIVELLO, Lisa Renee, 18
CROASMUN, George W, 462
CROATT, Joe, 442
CROBAUGH, Emma, 968
CROCKER, Vera H, 443
CROFT, Karen Sue, 294
CROKER, James M, 1131
CROMBIE, Elizabeth, 153
CROMWELL, Robert, 452
CRONAN, Ella, 651
CRONIN, Walt, 419
CROOK, Jo Ann, 270
CROOM, H C, 1154
CROSBY, Jon C, 637
CROSBY, Julia, 671
CROSBY, Vickie, 856
CROSE, Mione Delight, 954
CROSLEY, Dorine, 1096
CROSS, Donald R, 920
CROSS, Gail T, 619
CROSS, Marjorie L, 799
CROSS, Tyrena M, 772
CROSTIC, Sarah, 622
CROSTIC, Stephanie, 477
CROSTON, Stephen P, 549
CROUCH, Gloria M, 1080
CROUCH, Kathryn E, 814
CROUCH, Kirk Gerard, 1006
CROUCH, Lisa, 793
CROUCH, Mildred Allen, 559
CROUCH, Ron, 273
CROW, Grant, 272
CROWDER, Gayle, 873
CROWDER, Laura B E Jensen, 724
CROWE, Virginia, 472
CROWELLE, Elizabeth Mae, 1102
CROWLEY, Beth M, 610
CROY, Kathy, 31
CROY, Valerie, 207
CROZIER, Sheila M, 1179
CRUIKSHANK, Virginia E, 110
CRULL, Scott, 147
CRUM, Lillie Mae, 1118
CRUMBLEY, Sandra D, 463
CRUMP, David L, 533
CRUMP, Kathleen Ann, 282
CRUMP, Michael R, 98
CRUMPTON, Carl F, 386
CRUNELLE, Edna M, 577
CRUSE (DEWITT), Rebecca L, 614
CRUSE, Dion Nolan, 1100
CRUSE, Patricia A (McDaniels), 617
CRUSO, Anthony C, 939
CRUTCHER, William, 46
CRUZ, Cheri A, 523
CRUZ, Cristy T, 1079
CRUZ, Diana Ramos, 355, 557
CRUZ, Leticia, 1057
CRWTH, Mr, 26
CRYDER, Maria, 1126
CRYSTAL, Aleta Ellen, 793
CSIK, Barbara, 397
CSUGIE, Evelyn D, 741
CUA, Violet, 1093
CUCCHIARA, Anthony M, 209
CULLAR, Carol, 164
CULLEN, Paul B, 969
CULP, Jeane M, 1033, 962, 962
CULP, Jr, 59
CULVER, Adlain R, 196
CUMBERBATCH, Marlene C, 314
CUMELLA, Ben B, 1159
CUMMING, Robert B, 232
CUMMINGS, Dianne H, 974
CUMMINGS, James William, 118
CUMMINGS, Marylin Rose, 389
CUMMINGS, Monica E, 852
CUMMINGS, Patricia
CUMMINS, Teresa, 362
CUNDIFF, Charlene R, 111
CUNDIFF, Connie, 524
CUNINGHAM-WALKER, Deborah, 310
CUNKO, Edith, 681
CUNNINGHAM, Jo Ann, 355
CUNNINGHAM, Michael H, 378
CUNNINGHAM, Natasha, 754
CUNNINGHAM-DECKER, Deanna Jean, 604
CUOMO, Tom J, 333
CUPANO, Nancy, 388
CUPP, Daveda J, 650
CURCIO, Jerilynn, 38
CURENTON, Ginevar, 493
CURLEE, Anthony M, 763
CURLEE, Violet Verena, 721
CURLL, Robert J, 1109
CURNUTT, Albert Z, 623
CURRENT, Aletha, 164
CURREY, Linda Rose, 649
CURRIE, Bob, 27
CURRIE, James, 1135
CURRIE, Josephine, 750
CURRY, Alice L, 1199
CURRY, Heather, 707
CURRY, Jennifer, 234
CURRY, Jewell, 5
CURRY, Oma V, 1084, 1084
CURTIS, Brian C, 571
CURTIS, Daniel M, 763
CURTIS, Dori, 190
CURTIS, Dorothy, 111
CURTIS, Jane, 75
CURTIS, Mrs Cloia, 925
CURTIS, R G, 1138
CURTIS, Tanya, 511
CURTIS, Virginia, 688
CURTISS, Christine, 822
CUSANELLI, Cindi S, 843
CUSANO Jr, Paul, 916
CUSICK, Jeannie, 1183
CUSMANO, Darlene, 946
CUSTER, Janet L, 523
CUSTER, Kimberly A, 1060
CUTHBERTSON, Mary L, 708
CUTLIP, Barry, 986
CUTTS, Kelli R, 411
CYBORSKI, Annie, 874
CZECH, Paul P, 1178
CZEPIGA, Walter A, 221

D

D'AGOSTINO, Muriel Mckinlock, 1151
D'AGUINO, Deana, 578
D'ALFONZO, Laurie, 711
D'ANDREA Jr, Nicholas, 803
D'ANTONIO, Roseann J, 1184
D'EGIDIO, Cheryl A, 1058
D'ELIA, Rita, 68
D, Joy, 723
DABNEY, Dennis P, 677
DABNEY, Frances, 170
DAGGETT, Clarice A, 1199
DAGGETT, Dorothy L, 180
DAHL, Annette, 881
DAHLBERG, Herman, 979
DAHN, Roger W, 1115
DAILEY Jr, Henry W, 676
DAILY, Debra Lee, 482
DAILY, Gloria Jean, 474
DAINTY, Sonia, 303
DALBEC, Brenda M, 825
DALEY, Terry, 583
DALEY, Tricia, 28
DALEY, William C, 390
DALGAL, Ryan, 1198
DALLAS, Evelyn J, 1166
DALLAS, Shirley I, 961
DALLY, Vivian, 417
DALRYMPLE, Ernest, 658
DALTON, Joanne, 852
DALTON, Mark J K, 368
DALY, Cynthia M, 1019
DALY, Hilary, 362
DAMES, Dionne N, 1039
DAMIR, Vizjak, 1143
DAN, Alex, 982
DANE, Janet L, 646
DANE, Lisa, 1037
DANIEL, Fern, 575
DANIEL, Marcelle, 1114
DANIEL, Maria R, 697
DANIEL, Richard, 397
DANIEL, Rose Marie, 235, 235
DANIELEWICZ, Kimberly A, 91
DANIELLE, Kathleen, 236
DANIELS, Barbara, 356
DANIELS, Charlotte, 897
DANIELS, Chundra Lynn, 730
DANIELS, Don, 697
DANIELS, Edna E, 872
DANIELS, June, 592
DANIELS, Manulani R, 45
DANIELS, Margaret, 139
DANIELS, Marilyn, 53
DANIELS, Michael R, 429
DANIELS, Robby, 87
DANIELS, Sharon (Pierson), 912
DANN, Christine, 55
DANTES, Nancy Denise, 272
DAO, Martino Paul, 214
DARBELLIPS, Brad, 467
DARBY, Anna L, 241
DARBY, Dorthea, 649
DARDEN, Robbie, 910
DARDER, Antonia, 984
DARGITZ, Christy, 987
DARNER, Josephine, 970
DARNIELLE, Mary Lou, 115
DARROW, Rose, 325
DART, Sharlene, 259
DARVIE, Noel, 464
DARVILLE, Patricia, 673
DAS, Anubhavananda, 518
DAUGHERTY, John E, 1087
DAUGHTRY, Anita Pierce, 1126
DAUSTER-HUSTED, Karen, 834
DAUTERMANN, Mary L, 659
DAVEE, Lowell "Ted", 897
DAVENPORT, Alma Hunter, 914
DAVENPORT, Betsy L, 684
DAVENPORT, Iva, 774
DAVENPORT, Mandy, 885
DAVENPORT, Tashia S, 572
DAVEY, M Catherine, 1008
DAVID, Alice, 872
DAVID, Leon Thomas, 1007
DAVIDIAN CPCU, S J, 424
DAVIDS, Dorathy N, 619
DAVIDSON, B R, 422
DAVIDSON, Betty A, 963
DAVIDSON, Charles H, 975
DAVIDSON, David J, 180
DAVIDSON, Lee W, 1129
DAVIDSON, Rene (Graves), 571
DAVIDSON, Theresa M, 394
DAVIES, Angela, 616
DAVIES, Caroline M, 187
DAVIS Jr, Dr Gust D, 848
DAVIS Jr, Harry, 342
DAVIS Jr, Isaac D, 870
DAVIS, Alexis, 751
DAVIS, Amy, 698
DAVIS, Amy Elizabeth, 234
DAVIS, Bernard, 991
DAVIS, Beverly, 103
DAVIS, Brooke, 648
DAVIS, Carol Eden, 434
DAVIS, Carolyn, 208
DAVIS, Carolyn J, 833
DAVIS, Cecil M, 13
DAVIS, Claudia, 448
DAVIS, Darlene A, 385
DAVIS, Debra L, 522
DAVIS, Deloris J, 463
DAVIS, Dorothy, 248, 1100
DAVIS, Dorsie G, 236
DAVIS, Elaine C, 825
DAVIS, Elizabeth M, 865
DAVIS, Ethel L, 492
DAVIS, Frank, 437
DAVIS, G Henry, 351
DAVIS, Gail E, 964, 1083
DAVIS, Helen L, 337
DAVIS, Hilda Myers, 558
DAVIS, James D, 444
DAVIS, Jan T, 439
DAVIS, Joan Chaney, 1115
DAVIS, Joe, 945
DAVIS, Joyce, 993
DAVIS, Joylin, 383
DAVIS, Judith, 1003
DAVIS, Kelly, 360
DAVIS, Kenneth, 1100
DAVIS, Leslie R L, 45
DAVIS, Letitia R, 668
DAVIS, Margret K, 145
DAVIS, Marion F, 720
DAVIS, Mary E, 973
DAVIS, Mattie A, 393
DAVIS, Maxine L, 525
DAVIS, Melody Carol, 745
DAVIS, Milton, 1006
DAVIS, Nancy J, 856
DAVIS, Nancy R Horn, 86
DAVIS, Page Leroy, 55
DAVIS, Pearle Z, 821
DAVIS, Priscilla, 62
DAVIS, R Spenser, 264
DAVIS, Raymond O, 708
DAVIS, Romola E, 1099, 963
DAVIS, Sandra Lenci, 124
DAVIS, Sarah I, 947
DAVIS, Sarah M, 19
DAVIS, Shalon V, 1170
DAVIS, Stephanie, 954
DAVIS, Stephanie M, 804
DAVIS, Stephen E, 255
DAVIS, Todd M, 672
DAVIS, Vanessa D, 493
DAVIS, Virginia D, 330
DAVIS, Yvonne G Engel, 265
DAVIS-KYRIMIS, Gwendolyn J, 831
DAVISON, Heather, 957
DAWE, Joyce, 782
DAWKINS, Terri L, 962
DAWNE, Dawne K, 429
DAWSON, Jean, 790
DAWSON, Jimmy R, 1076
DAWSON, Wallace J, 778
DAY, Billie R, 843
DAY, Brian, 827
DAY, Jaclyn, 351
DAY, Julie L, 593
DAY, Julie M, 828
DAY, Linda S, 716
DAY, Michele, 660
DAY, Peggy L, 1076
DAY, Tami Lasharia, 621
DECOCK, Daanon, 1119
DELACUADRA, Jose, 1007
DE LA RIVA, Leticia Torres, 407
DE PETRILLO, Tina Joanne A, 57
DE ROCHE, Halina, 154
DEAL, Gaye Follmer, 126
DEAL, Kevin, 313
DEAN Jr, William S, 677
DEAN, Angela, 99
DEAN, Deanna, 354
DEAN, Gail, 1059
DEAN, Georgia Anne, 1122
DEAN, Inez, 875
DEAN, Shirley J, 219
DEANGELIS, Sandra, 195
DEARDUFF, Faye Britton, 522
DEARDUFF, Helen M, 406
DEARDURFF, J R, 24
DEAUX, James, 929
DEBEAULIEU, Margaret, 1192
DEBERG, Kathryn, 715
DEBOLLE, Dawn, 576
DEBONIS, Kristen L, 693
DEBOVES, Joseph J, 535
DECARLO, Cela, 566
DECHAU, Gary, 136
DECHTER, Jeani, 126
DECINO, Mandy M, 77
DECKER, Barbara, 98
DECKER, Bette M, 1033
DECKER, Eva, 688
DECKER, Jennifer J, 1119
DECKER, Nancy, 1053
DECOTEAU, Holly, 489
DEDMON, Grace B, 79
DEDOVITCH, Teresa Chaykowsky, 53
DEEN, Wilma Lee, 184
DEER, Joseph, 220
DEES, Barbara, 941
DEES, Darin, 359
DEES, Donna Hickman, 98
DEESE, Aleta J, 924
DEESE, Danielle N, 541
DEFEIS, Patricia, 264
DEFIORI, Allan J, 494, 1099
DEGEORGE, Frank, 230
DEGIACOMO, Laura, 529
DEGN, E Mae, 1114
DEGONIA, Dorothy J, 1164
DEGRAFF Jr, David D, 580
DEGREE, Shirley E, 1093
DEGREGORIO, Alison, 432
DEGROTE, Opal, 528
DEGUY, Marilyn M Cruz, 137
DEHART, Michelle, 1060
DEHECK, Ruth Marie, 913
DEIBLER, Danielle, 555
DEIMER, Lorena Ruth, 40
DEITSCH, Janis S, 726
DEJESUS, Johnny, 489
DEJESUS, Jorge, 1178
DEKARPENTER, Jose, 815
DEKENO, Lillian, 83
DELMAR, Zylla, 1113
DEL, Phil, 53
DELACRUZ, Gloria, 419

DELANEY, Kim, 371
DELANGE, Frances E, 935
DELAP, Janice Moore, 663
DELATORRE, Lusina, 1064
DELCAMP, Heidi Holt, 51
DELCORE, Nick, 605
DELDERFIELD, Rosemary, 904
DELFIN, S Melissa, 555
DELFINE-LANIER, Judith, 322
DELGADO, L, 868
DELGADO, Melinda, 248
DELGADO, Victor M, 1071
DELGIUDICE, Leon L, 224
DELGRECO, Sandra M, 162
DELINE, Valerie, 936
DELISLE, Robert M, 118
DELLAFEMINA, Michael "Misha", 715
DELLANO, Shira Yael, 227
DELMAS, Dee Dee, 677
DELONG, Carla, 1157
DELOOF, Ruth G, 1149
DELORENZO, Tom, 630
DELREAL, Martha, 486
DELRUSSI, Michael, 771
DEMARCO, Mildred L, 778
DEMARCO, Tobyn, 504
DEMARCO-PANICO, Donna, 1052
DEMATTEO, Claire A, 228
DEMEIO, Renaldo, 702
DEMENT, Doyle L, 260
DEMERCHANT, Joseph Allen, 353
DEMERS, Marie, 242
DEMEYERE, Kathleen L, 206
DEMING, Lynda S, 357
DEMMERS, Linda S, 848
DEMOREST, Muriel, 802
DEMPSEY, Barbara, 293
DEMPSEY, Katherine M, 17
DEMPSEY, Kathleen C, 1069
DEMPSTER, Rae, 887
DENISON, Anita, 688
DENMARK, Elizabeth, 867
DENNIS, Donald, 427
DENNIS, Laura Marie, 153
DENNIS, Michael, 368
DENNIS, Mildred Quine, 638
DENNIS, Sheila, 1002
DENNY, J Steven, 645
DENNY, Pamela S, 357
DENSLOW, Jane, 394
DENSMORE, Lucille Cathell, 1102
DENTON, Faye M, 126
DENTON, Sandra L, 364
DEOGNY, Lynn, 731
DEORTIZ, Carmen M, 970
DEPONTE, Brian J, 975
DEPUTY-THOMAS, Linda, 889
DERBY, Cheryl, 578
DERBYSHIRE, Nancy, 298
DERIEUX, Bessie Kay, 974
DERKACY, Caroll M Hubert, 738
DEROSA, Sandra, 118
DEROSIER, Dee, 905
DERRICO, Sharon, 653
DERUITER, Carole, 316
DESARMO, Lillian M, 572
DESCHEPPER, Vashni, 776
DESHANE, Sandy Malette, 95
DESILVA-THURSTON, Carla C, 29
DESIMONE, Maria A, 372
DESJARDINS, Deborah, 965
DESON, Lisa L, 289
DESORMEAUX, Gilles P, 79
DESSAINT, Linda Jean, 74
DETHERAGE, Shirley, 957
DETTBARN, Aaron, 943
DETWILER, Phyllis, 790
DETWILER, Tammy, 546
DEUTSCH, Lisa, 64
DEUTSCHMAN, Regina, 1006, 1102
DEVENPORT, Jean, 453
DEVERE, Jane, 633
DEVERNEI, Emil, 501
DEVIC, Audrey, 119
DEVINE, Anne, 44
DEVINE, Glenda, 454
DEVITA, Stefanie, 818
DEVIVO, Linda S, 132
DEVORE, Thomas, 229
DEVRONE WHITEFIELD II, Michael, 735
DEVRONNE, D, 1121
DEWALD, Denise A, 709
DEWBERRY, Rachel V, 511
DEWEY, Jane K, 73
DEWEY, Timothy L, 757
DEWITT, Judy Ann, 424
DEWOODY, Jerry M, 203
DEY, Duffy, 1186
DEYOUNG, Vanessa Ann, 255
DIACZUK, Holly M, 61
DIAMANTINO, Gloria, 696
DIANA, Kathryn M, 824
DIAZ, Celia, 88
DIAZ, Gaby, 284
DIAZ, Lorrie A, 299
DIAZ, Octavio Esquivel, 1025
DIBELLA, Russell, 668
DIBENEDETTO, Gerarda, 485
DIBUONO, Alexander, 824
DICKENS, Nikol P, 909
DICKENS, T R, 581
DICKER, Dorothy Amy, 276
DICKERSON, Danny J, 1006
DICKERSON, Diedre, 1096
DICKERSON, Marie, 810
DICKERSON, Thomas A, 1166
DICKERSON, Virginia A, 724
DICKEY, Elizabeth J, 149
DICKINSON, Eloise V, 921
DICKINSON, Jimmie L, 142
DICKINSON, Pamela Jill, 954
DICKINSON, Tonya, 969
DICKINSON, William F, 1009
DICKISON, Matilda, 275
DICKMAN, Becky, 825
DICKSON, Dorothy, 383
DICKSON, Tup, 569
DIDYOUNG, Kari, 206
DIEHL, Merdieth, 533
DIEM, Richard A, 873
DIETHORN, Sister Grace, 253
DIFRANCO, Pasquale, 1195
DIGGINS-LIEBLER, Marjorie, 923
DIIURO, Christopher, 652
DILLAHUNTY, Crystal Lynn, 982
DILLARD, Helen P, 1192
DILLER, Michael E, 668
DILLEY, Becki, 808
DILLON, Paula, 958
DILLS, E Jane, 735
DILWORTH-MILLS, Shelley, 829
DIMAIO, Hugh D, 717
DIMARCO, Kimi, 860
DIMARTINO, Gale Lynn, 1194
DIMATTEO, Nora A, 656
DIMEO, Kathryn M, 72
DIMICK, Georgia Ann, 1012
DIMMICK, Judy K, 311
DINGLE, Mary Estle, 136
DINGLE, R L, 815
DINNING, Shirley Yvonne May, 712
DIPRETORE, Vicki L, 789
DIRKS, Elizabeth A, 127
DIRKS, Terri L, 97
DISBROW, Lisa, 170
DISEKER, Deannie, 76
DISHMAN, Janice C, 163
DISHON Jr, Robert Hugh, 908
DISNEY, William Ralph, 448
DISPENZIERE, Kris, 941
DISTEFANO, Diana Marie, 538
DITTY, Helen Weaver, 106
DIXON, Janie, 196
DIXON, Jerry Robert, 599
DIXON, Ladonna, 888
DIXON, Linda, 758
DIXON, Myrtle, 257
DIXON, Shanda G, 791
DLUZNIEWSKI, Bill, 877
DMYTRASZ, Denise, 204
DO, Thuy Tran, 689
DOBBIE, Don, 369
DOBBINS, Lee, 1109
DOBSON, Monica E, 300
DOCKERY, Terri, 1074
DODD, Bonita Holley, 997
DODD, Estel M, 1162
DODD, Judy Bayles, 410
DODD, Ruth Mae, 286
DODDS, John A, 980
DODSON, Margaret B, 556
DOHERTY, Elizabeth A, 1142
DOILEY, William L, 600
DOLATA, Belinda M, 799
DOLBY, Hazel M, 1154
DOLGOFF, Wilma, 561
DOLL, David W, 421
DOLL, John W, 819
DOLLAR, Evelyn, 302
DOLLARD, Annette, 230
DOLOHANTY, Margie M, 923
DOLSEN Jr, Sam J, 888
DOMEC, Ethel, 1159
DOMES, Betty Louise, 30
DOMINGO, Rhona, 921
DOMMAN, Maryann, 1001
DOMYAN, John, 574, 574
DONAHOE, Erin, 373
DONAHUE, Rose Marie, 697
DONAHUE-MINALL, Kelly, 385
DONALD, Carolyn, 599
DONALD, Odies M, 217
DONALDSON, Patricia, 1159
DONNAHEE, Melanie, 675
DONNELLY, Homans, 29
DONNENWIRTH, Carol, 70
DONNER, Marge, 1055
DONOHOE, Kara, 515
DONOHOE, Nell, 22
DONOHUE, Tracy, 376
DONOVAN, Barbara, 241
DONOVAN, Debbie, 80
DONOVAN, Janet, 102
DONOVAN, Kathy, 503
DONOVAN, William, 292
DOOLEY, Bill, 1035
DOOLITTLE, Peggie Jo, 604
DORAN, Kevin M, 863
DORECK, Alvin Richard, 28
DORER, Sherrill, 543
DOREY, Lee Anne, 744
DORIUS, Quay B, 216
DORMAN, Luann L, 547
DORNAN, Joanne, 770
DORNEMANN, Karl, 823
DORNIN, Nikki, 904
DORROUGH, Mary G, 868
DORSEY, George A, 33
DORSEY, Sharon P, 823
DOSS, Joyce, 1025
DOSS, Kathy A, 1139
DOSSEY, Virginia Lynn, 876
DOTHAGER, Myrtle Mae, 37
DOTSETH, Stephanie, 626
DOTSON, Elizabeth Jo, 953
DOTSON, Lucille, 675
DOTY, Eric R, 846
DOTY, Kristian, 25
DOUCET, Chrystal, 904
DOUCETTE, Jennifer, 439
DOUGHERTY, Christine, 499
DOUGLAS Jr, Junial, 227
DOUGLAS, Carmelita M, 225
DOUGLAS, Hazel C, 51
DOUGLAS, Kenneth L, 594
DOUGLAS, Peggy, 418
DOUGLASS, Pamela J, 27
DOUTHWAITE, Kingsley, 405
DOVICH, Joe, 604
DOWD, James P, 1117
DOWDELL, Richard, 539
DOWDLE, Leota, 268
DOWELL, Georgia, 840
DOWELL, Grace, 348
DOWLER, David D, 530
DOWLING, Clara Martha, 481
DOWNES, Dallas W, 530
DOWNEY, Cynthia E, 935
DOWNEY, Jana K, 42
DOWNING, Lisa Sanders, 154
DOWNING, Tammy, 737
DOWNS, Angie R, 531
DOWNS, Barbara, 17
DOWNS, Bertha Coleman, 68
DOWNS, Christine, 640
DOYLE, Alicia K, 1016
DOYLE, Debbie, 475
DOYLE, George, 242
DOYLE, Geraldine H, 267
DOYLE, Joyce C, 80
DOYLE, Karen D, 718
DOYLE, Kristy R, 216
DOZIER, Ara R, 454
DRAKE, Carol Dixon, 489
DRAKE, Ginger, 496
DRAPER, Elizabeth P, 45
DRAPER, Priscilla L, 1185
DREHS, Eileen, 388
DREIBELBIS, B Ewing, 35
DRENNAN, Thomas J, 440
DRENT, Laura J, 491
DRESSER, Tascha, 325
DRESSLER, Michelle J, 177
DREW, Ann-marie, 906
DREW, Shirley W, 382
DREWEL, Tilda, 458
DRISCOLL, Amber, 1124
DRISCOLL, Sue, 995, 996
DRITT, Bob, 498
DRIVER, Calvin L, 464
DRIVER, Ella Mae, 1132,
DRIVER, Virginia, 1029
DROLUK, Jenna Marie, 982
DROPE, Jean Truer, 577
DROUIN, Camille M, 901
DROUIN, Martine, 58
DROUIN, Ralph, 134
DRUCKENMILLER, Heather L, 600
DRUM, Sharon, 52
DRUMMOND, La Vena May, 135
DRUMMOND, Merry Llew, 174
DRUMMOND, Shannon, 192
DRURY, Melony, 897
DRYDAK, Kerri Lynne, 894
DRYDEN, Dorothy A, 349
DUBE, Muriel Marie, 511
DUBEAU, Susan M Dorie, 546
DUBOIS, Cindy, 508
DUBOIS, Eloise Barclay, 55
DUBOSE, Judith Maria, 1081
DUCA, Angelo R, 85
DUCHENE, Frank B, 210
DUCHENE, Jeanne, 546
DUCKETT, Joann, 711
DUDASH, Chris, 350
DUDLEY, Sarah, 522
DUENES, Erin, 437
DUEST, Carolyn P, 745
DUFAUX, Don, 948
DUFF, B A, 273
DUFF, Bertha, 484
DUFF, Drucilla, 1044
DUFFY, Donna M, 366
DUFRESNE, Denise Gosselin, 866
DUGAN, Henry J, 337
DUGAN, Janice L, 525
DUGAN, Joe, 78
DUGAN, Mary, 256
DUGGAN, Mortimer, 176
DUGGER, Janet Snyder, 1115
DUGGER, Judy, 628
DUJON, Claudette, 84
DULA, Robert B, 5
DULCEY, Dan, 951
DULIN, H Cajo, 1087
DUMAS, Debbie L, 219
DUMAS, Joyce, 1134
DUMENIGO, Argelio, 513
DUNAWAY, Martha, 115
DUNAWAY, Sherry, 800
DUNBAR, Elizabeth S, 536
DUNCAN, Daniel Louis, 374
DUNCAN, Darlene F, 543
DUNCAN, Esther N, 299
DUNCAN, James E, 629
DUNCAN, Mark Gary, 469
DUNCAN, Mary Evelyn, 1011
DUNCAN, Sonia I, 1073
DUNCAN, Stephanie, 337
DUNCAN, Steve, 671
DUNCAN, Thelma Louise, 1109
DUNCIL, Leila M, 150
DUNKELBERGER, Kenneth R, 260
DUNLAP, Brenda Sue, 316
DUNLAP, Edith, 311
DUNLAP, Richard W, 310
DUNLEAVY, Rosemary T, 731
DUNLOP, Lance, 692
DUNN, Deborah T, 218
DUNN, Holly, 566
DUNN, Jean, 584
DUNN, Melody R, 741
DUNN, Treverton E, 243
DUNN-DIAMOND, Janice, 868
DUNNE III, Matt S, 364
DUNNE, Brian Robert, 901
DUNPHY, Murray, 660
DUPATZ, Caroline J, 353
DUQUETTE, Jill, 271
DUQUETTE, Michelle Jacqueline, 915
DURAN, Dorothy M, 1126
DURAN, Robin M, 767
DURBIN, Charles L, 30
DUREN, Mrs Ann, 6
DURFEE, Lorinda Lee, 953
DURHAM II, Thomas J, 648
DURHAM, Diane R, 635
DURHAM, G Roderic, 32
DURHAM, Pamela J, 824
DURKIN, Evelyn L Opalinski, 145
DURR, Eleanor, 805
DURRY, Paula F, 721
DURST, Marilyn Jean (Kale), 654
DUSSAULT, Kathleen A, 670
DUTRA, Lisa, 435
DUTTON, Holly M, 523
DUTTON, Myra, 294
DUTTWEILER ESQUIRE, J M, 860
DUVAIR, Suzanne, 66
DUVAL, Lee, 355
DUWEL, Arleen C, 1054
DUZAN, Sharon, 606
DWYER, Don, 127
DWYER, Virginia M, 32
DYAL, Rachel Susan, 233
DYBDAL, Shirley, 715
DYCK, Sylvia, 792
DYDE, Anne D, 1009
DYE, Beatrice, 736
DYE, Charles F, 451
DYER, Charlene M, 109
DYER, Gabrielle, 986
DYER, Michelle L, 438
DYER, Shirley, 601
DYKES, Aline Dixon, 1069
DYKINS, Vi, 421
DYKSTRA, Melissa L, 819
DYSON, Stephen R, 219
DZWONSZYK, Jacqueline, 325

E

E M R, Jr, 698
EADS, Christy, 132
EAGAN, Kathleen M, 443
EAGLE Jr, Charles E, 64
EAMES, Brenda, 61
EARLYWINE, Michael, 894
EARNEST, Jean, 40
EARNEY, Patricia A, 377
EASLEY Jr, Edward, 114
EASLEY, Mary Ruth, 11
EASON, Kymberli, 501
EASON, Sarah, 1019
EASON, Tracy, 724
EASTON, Lisa, 689
EASTUP, Lavonda, 472
EASTWOOD, Melva L Moore, 882
EASTWOOD, Shirley, 638
EASY, Elswiter, 1068
EATON, Bonnie J, 1031
EATON, James Clark, 855
EBANKS, Gary, 145
EBAUGH, Frances C, 109
EBERHART, Denise, 466
EBERLE, Eugenie, 15
EBRAHIMIAN, Armineh, 904
ECCLES, Lenard W, 646
ECHAVE, Ralph A, 417
ECKARD, Thasia Anne, 915
ECKERLE, Lori Ann, 566
ECKERLE, Philip A, 764
ECKHART, Katherine N, 64
ECKSTEIN, M.D., Marlene R., 285
ECKSTEIN, Tony J, 228
ECKSTRAND, Sally, 113
EDDINS, Jeffrey A, 303
EDDY, Steven A, 954
EDELENBOS, Bonnie L, 688
EDELMAN, Lynn, 875
EDEN, Ronald F, 472
EDEN-GREENE, J, 276
EDGAR, Beth, 270
EDGAR, Nancy L, 925
EDIE, Kenneth E, 814
EDMONDS, Deborah C, 33
EDMONDSON, Effie M, 239
EDRA Sr, Gerardo C, 1028
EDWARDS, Allison, 990
EDWARDS, Carol (Uebinger), 148
EDWARDS, China L, 302
EDWARDS, Gerald Bart, 1039
EDWARDS, Jack, 344
EDWARDS, James L, 183
EDWARDS, Jeff, 646
EDWARDS, June F, 455
EDWARDS, Lillian, 702
EDWARDS, Margaret, 323
EDWARDS, Mark, 1159
EDWARDS, Rita, 319
EDWARDS, Robin, 156
EDWARDS, Rosalind, 590
EDWARDS, Susan, 1036
EDWARDS, Todd, 381
EDWARDS, Tracy L, 174
EDWARDS, Verona, 804
EDWARDS-WRENN, Barbara, 709
EFFLER Jr, Robert P, 37
EGAN, Amy Day, 381
EGAN, John J, 795
EGELSKE, Eileen, 142
EGENBERGER, Marian, 989
EGENBERGER, Marva M, 495
EGGBORN, Maryjane, 1123
EGGLESTON, Daniel, 1070
EGGLESTON, John, 560
EGGLESTON, Mrs Harriet, 128
EGINOIRE, Michele R, 1188
EHLERS, Cheryl Lynn, 396
EHLERT, E H, 196
EHRMAN, Don Toussaint, 450
EHRMAN, Harry, 425
EICAS, Ruth Poorman, 35

EICHEL, J Diane, 714
EICHENSEHR, Laura, 220
EICHHOLD, Gregory, 1194
EILENBERG Jr, Garrett, 1042
EINBUND, Allysa, 84
EISENHOWER, Jeffrey Wayne, 85
EISNER, Sylvia, 861
EISWORTH, Clinton Lee, 1102
EJEM, Dan, 1013
EKE, Nosa, 1067
EL-SHARKAWY, Trisha M, 577
ELAM, Sena C, 91
ELBANNA, Stephanie Y, 355
ELDER, Sage, 98
ELDORA, Jessie, 431
ELDRIDGE, Rebecca, 49
ELEDGE, Tammy R, 564
ELFBERG, Carol, 586
ELFERT, Bernard Graf, 331
ELFRING, Elizabeth M, 830
ELI, Holly Renee, 182
ELIJICH, Ruth Fuqua, 172
ELKINS, Alfred, 78
ELKINS, Claribel, 1193
ELLARD, Mary C, 226
ELLENBERGER, Donna, 905
ELLER, Cheryl A, 284
ELLER, Edward J, 599
ELLERBROCK, April L, 567
ELLERING, Jane C, 313
ELLICOTT, Marilyn A, 468
ELLINGER, Julie, 142
ELLIOTT, Mark, 1182
ELLIOTT, C E, 13
ELLIOTT, Carolyn, 509
ELLIOTT, Karen Sue E, 906
ELLIOTT, Leone B, 1070
ELLIOTT, Maureen Black, 954
ELLIOTT, Shirley, 893
ELLIOTT, Susan T, 425
ELLIOTT, Tracy Jane E, 378
ELLIS, Agnes, 260
ELLIS, Annie E S, 793
ELLIS, Caroline Rehder, 888
ELLIS, Gary L, 217
ELLIS, Jen, 762
ELLIS, Joseph A, 687
ELLIS, Marilyn, 296
ELLIS, Marion A, 668
ELLIS, Mel, 583
ELLIS, Paula, 783
ELLIS, R J, 1035
ELLIS, Ruth E, 104
ELLIS, Sharon A, 308
ELLISON, Kathryn M, 245
ELLISON, Marvin M, 1126
ELLISTON, William H, 453
ELLISTON-WRIGHT, Cheryl, 268
ELLS, Catherine Molly, 914
ELLSWORTH, Mike, 85
ELMER, Mary Jane, 368
ELMORE, Cynthia, 1158
ELMORE, Ruth, 977
ELRABADI, Lobna, 918
ELSIFOR, Vivian, 245
ELSNER, Emma M, 656
ELSON, Rosemarie W, 645
ELTON, Valerie M, 1074
ELWOOD, Michael Troy, 334
ELWOOD, Phyllis, 221
ELWOOD, Virginia, 128
ELY, Tina, 892
EMBERTON, Carole Tereza, 958
EMBRY, Jane M, 741
EMERSON, Willie M, 281
EMERY, Cherie A, 378
EMERY, Linda S, 397
EMERY-IMBELLONI, Mary, 855
EMFINGER, Anissa, 43
EMILIE, Mary Lou, 418
EMMEL, Karen, 613
EMMERSON, Shannon, 383
EMMETT, Anita (Penny), 420
EMRICH, Laura Lee, 727
ENDLER, Nancy Kane, 411
ENERSON, Heidi R, 629
ENG, Christine, 316
ENGEBRETSEN, Eleanor, 1185
ENGELBRECHT, Jennifer, 489
ENGELHART, Michelle L, 718
ENGLAND, Candace L, 572
ENGLAND, Robert J, 1187
ENGLISH, Ginger Anne, 865
ENGLISH, Johnette, 28
ENGLISH, Noelle Marie, 183
ENGLUND, Jodee, 316
ENGLUND, Loretta Ann Hannigan, 664
ENKE, Ann Pizzuti, 1086, 1086
ENNIS, John L, 728
ENO ENO TED ENO, 419
ENSOR, Ruth Simons, 851
ENTO, Jay-Ola, 690
ENTWHISTLE, James J (Jimejoe), 915
ENTWISTLE, Frank, 654
ENVIK, Patty Lou, 426
EOFF, Myra, 1109
EPLER, Dora, 1137
EPP, James E, 54
EPPEN, Joyce M, 374
EPPERLEY, Jean D, 936
EPPINGER, Julie, 959
EPPLEY, George T, 19
EPSTEIN, Myra Lorber, 652
ERB, Susan, 369
ERDELL, Professor John, 347
ERICKSON, Cecile, 687
ERICKSON, Irma Du Bois, 1123
ERICKSON, Margaret, 319
ERICKSON, S M, 596
ERIE, Amber Lynn, 302
ERIKSON, Pearl Palmer, 113
ERLSTON, Brad Richard, 705
ERMEL, Elaine A, 1115
ERNST, Captolia B, 786
ERTEL, Eleanor E, 655
ERWIN, Brandi, 862
ERWIN, Brandi L, 43
ERWIN, Sam, 534
ESCALANTE, Daniel N, 1178
ESCH, Andy, 858
ESCOBAR, Junita, 127
ESCOBAR, Rose Mary E, 457
ESHLEMAN, Moleta, 169
ESKEW, Melissa S, 605
ESKOWITZ, Leonard, 196
ESMUS, Louisa, 170
ESPERE, Roseller S, 859
ESPINO, Gloria V, 80
ESPINOSA, Ana V, 614
ESPINOSA, Jaime, 813
ESPINOZA, Amanda L, 784
ESPOSITO, Lilly L, 57
ESQUIRE, J, 347
ESSICK, Steve, 871
ESTEB, Judy A, 1043
ESTES Jr, C G, 724
ESTES, Cherie G, 475
ESTES, Donna Mcclain, 216
ESTES, Lee, 701
ESTILL, Julie, 49
ESTRADA, June Caroline, 511
ESTRADA, Michael A, 159
ETZLER, Lenna E, 966, 965
EUBANK, Lucile A, 454
EUGENIO, John, 929
EURESTI, Kelli Ann, 300
EVANICH, Stephanie, 1079
EVANS, Alvin, 259
EVANS, Annette Y, 800
EVANS, Bettye M (Hughes), 941
EVANS, Brenda S, 719
EVANS, Claudine L, 403
EVANS, Constance Lee, 1178
EVANS, Dawn Anne, 1191
EVANS, James M, 415
EVANS, Jeff S, 503
EVANS, Jill, 1102
EVANS, Johnie Ryan, 52
EVANS, Joyce Jackson, 16
EVANS, Katie, 733
EVANS, Laura, 130
EVANS, Lauri L, 1017
EVANS, Marceline, 1143
EVANS, Martha, 239
EVANS, Melody A, 202
EVANS, Michael J, 977
EVANS, Milton, 68
EVANS, Rose, 126
EVANS, Tania, 734
EVANS, Teresa, 446
EVANS, Terrisa, 927
EVANS, Virginia C, 72
EVANS, W Chuck, 396
EVERHARDT, Gladys Alford, 848
EVERHART, Dianne, 957
EVERITT, John L, 948
EVERLY, Kay, 165
EVERMAN-HUPE, Jerri L, 1178
EVERSON, Marguerite F, 1022
EVERT, Lester, 488
EVERY-PEDRO, Karen, 929
EVICH, Christy, 501
EWERS, Audrey J, 599
EWING, Donald, 842
EWING, Dorothy Jean, 878
EWING, Michel, 754
EXLEY, Lynda Rae, 177
EYBERS, Joyce, 927
EYLER, Wanda Elaine, 1128
EZERNACK, Lisa, 1197, 1084
EZERO, Lynn M, 834
EZQUERRO-GARCIA, Mary, 770

F

FAAS, Marianne, 1016
FABIAN, Todd Allen, 469
FACE, Neil O, 75
FACHET, Laurie L, 742
FADIN, Cindy, 686
FAGAN, Jennifer, 315
FAGER, Douglas A, 372
FAGG, Connie Sue, 185
FAHEY, Linda Marie, 382
FAHIM, Joni Alice, 160
FAIN, M Steven, 834
FAIR, Eddie, 797
FAIRCHILD, Kimberly A, 499
FAIRFIELD, Elizabeth A, 694
FALACIENSKI, Jeannie, 1046
FALCO, Maria, 857
FALCO, Stella, 919
FALK, Arline I, 611
FALK, Marian, 555
FALKNER, Alice, 65
FALLON, William, 803
FAMILTON, Rock, 47
FAMMEREE, Guy, 558
FAMOLARE, Suzanne, 192
FANCHER, Betty K, 749
FANNIN, Keotah M, 788
FANTASIA, Anna Maria, 5
FARAH, Karim, 387
FARIS, Rev Warner W, 604
FARISH, Greggs, 1188
FARKAS, Patricia A, 1119
FARKAS, Vince, 736
FARLEY II, John C, 1169
FARLEY, Lynda R, 161
FARLEY, Tony Dale, 567
FARMER III, Ralph, 495
FARMER, Rita, 286
FARNHAM, Lloyd, 721
FARNSWORTH, Alice, 201
FARNSWORTH, Janice L, 1040
FARQUHAR, Glenn W, 341
FARR, Donna G, 739
FARR, Rita Mae, 1092
FARRAR, Wanda K, 458
FARRELL, Eileen E, 160
FARRELL, James H, 838
FARRELL, Roxie A, 956
FARRIER, Jeffrey K, 243
FARRIER, Vera W, 192
FARRIS Jr, Walter R, 383
FARRIS, Dottie L, 971
FARSJO, Tallak T, 312
FASCO, Kelly A, 972
FASHBAUGH, Lynda, 1037
FASOLO, Angela M, 67
FASSLER, Edith B, 182
FATT, Bishop Patti A Lee, 591
FAUDE, Christine M, 820
FAUDT, Sunny Oralee, 377
FAUGHNAN, Cecilia C, 950
FAULK, Rebecca A, 884
FAULKERSON, Jeffrey A, 94
FAULKNER, C A, 163
FAULKNER, D H, 796
FAULKNER, Joan, 68
FAULKNER, Ruth, 117
FAULKNER, Shandora S, 941
FAUSTNER, Janet M, 786
FAVARO, Frank, 627
FAYE, Essie, 464
FEATHERINGILL, Vicki, 1132
FEFFERMAN, Nicolle D, 467
FEILER, Faith P, 274
FEINBERG, Norma Bischoff, 1012
FEJA, Beverly A, 302
FEKETE, Britt Nicole, 887
FELDMAN, Susannah E, 1100
FELIX, Jennifer, 327
FELIX, Michael E, 319
FELKINS, Steve, 105
FELLING, Ginni, 271
FELLOWS, Lorraine C, 68
FELSCHOW, Donna M, 530
FELTMAN, Carol, 221
FELTNER, Emma, 93
FELTON, Ethilia, 677
FELTON, Liz, 978
FELTS, Jenn, 187
FENCIL, Jeannine, 447
FENNELL, Delores, 92
FENNESSY, Marjorie Ann, 110
FENTER-REEDY, Deborah, 1100
FENTON, Colin, 1081
FENTON, Lori Mae, 870
FENTON, Theresa, 258
FENWICK, Jennifer Nelson, 537
FENWICK, Mary Kay, 281
FENWICK-BAILY, Derek, 436
FERBRACHE, Kathy, 874
FEREBEE, Alma D, 984
FERENCZI, Julianna, 233
FERGER, Corrine A, 542
FERGUSON, Barry G, 1073
FERGUSON, Claudia, 107
FERGUSON, Daniel J, 189
FERGUSON, Frances, 434
FERGUSON, Jay, 899
FERGUSON, Kathleen M, 797
FERGUSON, Michael G, 504
FERGUSON, Mitzi, 109
FERGUSON, Steven, 1053
FERGUSON, Syble, 873
FERMIN, Robert, 293
FERNALD, Charles H, 206
FERNANDEZ, Amparo J, 208
FERNANDEZ, Maria J, 632
FERR, Helen Gloria, 814
FERRARIS, L E, 998
FERRARO, Linda D, 266
FERRE, Francis, 691
FERREIRA, Alfonse, 758
FERREIRA, Nalani N L, 715
FERREIRA, Thomas J, 148
FERRELLI, Margaret, 807
FERRERIA, Immx, 373
FERRI, Dottie, 71
FERRIERA, Lauretta L, 1055
FERRIS, Alma Ray, 50
FERRIS, Deborah A (Robinson), 641
FERRIS, Joanne, 813
FERRIS, Kathryn L, 1026
FERRITER, Sarah, 1038
FERRO, G V, 295
FERRUCCI, Joe, 524
FERRY, Stella, 778
FERTIG, Dianne, 865
FESSENDEN, Trish, 26
FETTERMAN, Virginia, 169
FEWSMITH, Grant, 890
FEWSTER, Martin, 458
FIANO, Robin M, 965
FIATO, Dawn Marie, 347
FICE, Bernice, 1058
FICHTEL, Ian, 701
FICOCELLI, David Brian, 220
FIELD, Christine, 362
FIELD, Ellie, 826
FIELD, Phyllis, 400
FIELDING, Aileen, 643
FIELDS, Bobbie, 918
FIELDS, Joan, 340
FIELDS, Nancy C S, 1129
FIFIELD, Diane L, 735
FIGUEROA, Toni, 768
FILBECK, Evilena, 414
FILLERS, Jamesina F, 448
FILOCOMO, Joseph, 62
FILOSENA, Larry, 412
FINAZZO, Karyn, 1137
FINDLING, Jenny (Wren), 948
FINGERUT, Suzanne, 943
FINK, Stephanie D, 904
FINKLE, Valerie, 43
FINKLEA, Norma, 1184, 1184
FINLEY-LAKNER, Lori, 404
FINN, Maybelle A, 1036, 1094
FINTON, Genny, 596
FIORDIMONDO, Kim, 1008
FIORENTINO, Shirley, 702
FIORINO, Gina, 1196
FIRESTONE, Dolores P, 768
FIRST, Jerome, 153
FISCHER, Karl, 348
FISCHER, Pamela, 929
FISET, Nadine, 483
FISH, Candy L, 1101
FISHBACK, Lois M, 470
FISHER, Darryl, 716
FISHER, David O, 177
FISHER, Heidi Marie, 892
FISHER, Herbert J, 36
FISHER, Kelly, 6
FISHER, Keshia C, 999
FISHER, Kevin, 1135
FISHER, Marsha, 215
FISHER, Sandra S, 31
FISHER, Sherry M, 171
FISHMAN, Victoria, 572
FISKE, Yvonne L, 9
FITCH, George Hopper, 237
FITE, Karolyn S, 690
FITZGERALD, Carol, 190
FITZGERALD, Shawn, 955
FITZGERALD, Valerie R, 753
FITZPATRICK, Judy, 436
FITZPATRICK, Terri L, 330
FITZSIMMONS, Jamie Lynn, 478
FITZWATER, Traci, 323
FLACCO, Marie, 471
FLACH, R L, 223
FLACK, Patricia E, 901
FLAHERTY, Anne Marie, 483
FLAHERTY, Brett Thomas, 345
FLAIG, Helen J, 634
FLANAGAN, Mrs Clara, 961
FLANDERS, Craig, 842
FLANERY, M O, 1082, 1093
FLASHEN, Harvey L, 694
FLATHERS, Willie Jeneva, 832
FLAX, Kimberly A, 883
FLECK, Laurie Ann, 41
FLEISCHER, Audrey, 811
FLEMING, Bill, 382
FLEMING, Delbert D, 140
FLEMING, Kathy L, 62
FLEMING, Melissa, 738
FLEMING, Tikeshay J, 308
FLEMMER, Judith Joyce, 469
FLEMMING, Lev, 98
FLESCH, Blaze A, 309
FLETCHER, Alan, 946
FLETCHER, Lyla K, 828
FLETCHER, Sharleen, 214
FLETCHER, Vanessa, 107
FLICKENSCHILD-STEWART, Dawn E, 718
FLOOD, Tracy Jo, 750
FLORA, Dean, 1188
FLORES, Gayle, 336
FLORIS, Marcel, 1046
FLOVIN, Mary, 283
FLOWERS, Samantha R, 865
FLOWERS, William R, 184
FLOYD, Bonnie J, 524
FLOYD, Jeanne, 722
FLOYD, Mattie, 229
FLOYD, Peggy L, 537
FLUG, Barbara J, 1102
FLUKER, Grace, 79
FLYNN, Donna P, 476
FLYNN, Joseph P, 748
FLYNN, Julia, 380
FLYNN, Kenneth, 94
FLYNN, Ruth W, 1125
FLYNN, Shirley M, 1146
FLYNN, Sue A, 1096
FLYTHE Sr, Larry E, 659
FOCERI, Claire, 1046
FOERSTER, John W, 1014
FOGARTY, Suzan, 785
FOHL, Maggie, 829, 1103
FOIL, Rita M, 301
FOLDS, Regina, 39
FOLEY, Lisa Marie, 830
FOLEY, Martha, 600
FOLTIN, Sadie O, 349
FONG, Carol Ann, 33
FONG, Sandy, 1163
FONSECA, Marilsa Torres, 804
FONT, Vincent, 678
FONTAINE, Will, 192
FONTE, Kathleen, 670
FONTINO, Frances Copeland, 204
FOOS, Teresa, 612
FORBES, E Ray, 397
FORBES, Norma, 723
FORBES, T M, 304
FORCE, Sabra, 1168
FORCELLI, Matthew, 322
FORD, Angie, 1022
FORD, Connie, 1066
FORD, Gregory, 859
FORD, Jimmy Wayne, 339
FORD, Lorna Hicks, 302
FORD, Marjorie A, 262
FORD, Patricia, 344
FORD, Sharon, 734
FORD-WILKINS, Marcella, 573
FORDHAM, Stephani, 588
FORE, Kelly J, 785
FORELLA Jr, Michael A, 277
FOREST, Margaret, 885
FORET, Deborah J, 232
FORGACH, Amy K, 177
FORMUSA, William J, 654
FORNEY, Miriam E, 459
FOROUGHI, Tahirih K, 595
FORRER, Paul T, 1153
FORREST, David W, 594

FORREST,Eloise S, 22
FORREST, James Taylor, 404
FORRESTER, Deidre, 49
FORRESTER, Stefan, 735
FORSS, George, 114
FORSTER, Sandra, 138
FORSYTHE, Pasquale W, 818
FORTALEZA, Al, 769
FORTE, Tom, 1171
FORTINO, Tammi, 35
FORTNA, Ira Curtis, 53
FORTNEY, Linda Diane, 907
FORTSON Jr, Charles W, 866
FOSS, Sharon, 409
FOSTER, Anita Roper, 286
FOSTER, Dixie, 110
FOSTER, Dorothy E, 1049
FOSTER, Elinor, 207
FOSTER, Ethel R, 238
FOSTER, Florence E R, 869
FOSTER, Gayle, 408
FOSTER, Hazel B, 1049
FOSTER, Helen, 705
FOSTER, Mary, 968
FOSTER, Ronii, 1194
FOSTER, Sonja, 364
FOSTER, Virginia L, 781
FOSTER-BEY, Kevin, 720
FOTI, Florence M, 1002
FOTSCHKY, Donna L, 799
FOUCHE, Carrie, 993
FOUCHE, Mary A, 344
FOUNTAINE, Saundra K, 422
LEFOUT, Henry, 1088
FOWLER, Dorothy, 697
FOWLER, Elinor, 286
FOWLER, Louise, 514
FOWLER, Vicki, 366
FOX Jr, Leroy E, 446
FOX, Bernice A, 899
FOX, Connie, 713
FOX, Dona L, 810
FOX, Dorothy, 538
FOX, Evelyn, 91
FOX, Jeanette, 873
FOX, Martin R, 1126
FOX, Patricia, 953
FOX, Roger D, 386
FOX, Shirley A, 317
FOX, Stephen L, 900
FOX, Steven J, 1062
FOX-COLEY, Tamera, 986
FOXWELL, Beverly, 765
FRABBIELE-TAYLOR, Shannon M, 883
FRAGOSO, Albertina V A, 483
FRAHM, Brenda L, 40
FRAIZER, Janice, 734
FRALEY, Christine, 1154
FRAM, Lewis J, 76
FRANCESCONI, Marylou, 488
FRANCIOSE, Marie Jane, 320
FRANCIS, Dorothy, 122
FRANCIS, Glenda M, 1182
FRANCIS, Phyllis Dee, 399
FRANCIS, Rita A, 1017
FRANCIS, Trudi H, 884
FRANCO, Ms Mary Ann, 201
FRANCO, Theresa, 738
FRANDSEN, Carla, 190
FRANDSEN, Lee, 1004
FRANK, Julius Carl, 747
FRANK, Ronald M, 188
FRANK-LANDRY, Gloria J, 265
FRANKLIN, April T, 590
FRANKLIN, Carla J, 576
FRANKLIN, Jean M, 951
FRANKLIN, Jennie, 559
FRANKLIN, Norma, 789
FRANKLIN, Phyllis, 252
FRANKLIN, Walter, 230
FRANS, Nancy Baird, 629
FRANTZ, Corey, 529
FRANTZ, Laurie Alice, 742
FRANTZ, Rob W, 458
FRANTZ, Tammy, 279
FRANUSICH, Angela, 671
FRASCA, Theresa A, 187
FRASE, Bobby Todd, 946
FRASER, Edna G, 455
FRASER, Jackie, 455
FRASER, Rose-Marie J, 686
FRASER, Vicki Lynn, 729
FRATESI, Mary Louise Richardso, 1169
FRAUCHIGER, Pat, 35, 34
FRAYSER, Lathan H, 363
FRAZIER, Delores Jean, 96
FRAZIER, Linda, 713
FREAS, Sharon R, 771
FREDERICK, Andrew T, 70
FREDERICK, Myrna D, 817
FREDERICK, Vera, 332
FREDERICKS, Sarah E, 354
FREDERICKSON, Lucille, 178
FREDERIKSEN, Arvid, 131
FREDERIKSEN, Miss Krista, 831
FREDRICK, Katrina, 954
FREE, Grace, 98
FREED, Andrea R, 189
FREEDMAN, Marc, 501
FREELING, Jane Y, 1041
FREEMAN, Bee Jay, 678
FREEMAN, Caprice C, 431
FREEMAN, Christine, 287
FREEMAN, Jasper D, 531
FREEMAN, Joe B, 1189
FREEMAN, Lance M, 1166
FREEMAN, Ronald A, 723
FREES, Margaret M, 680
FREESEMANN, Teresa, 898
FREEZE, Mrs William H, 576
FRENCH, Amanda, 911
FRENCH, Donald, 505
FRENCH, Hazel, 979
FRENCH, Jill, 1103
FRENCH, Rick, 895
FRENCH, Susan B, 919
FRENCH, Travis, 1015
FRERET, Randy, 899
FRERICHS, Naoma L, 20
FREYHOLTZ, Joan Kyar, 177
FRICK, Susan M, 831
FRICKER, Rebecca, 37
FRIDGE, Martha, 393
FRIED, Audrey Z, 1153
FRIEDBACHER, Shannon, 697
FRIEDEL, Wolfgang, 568
FRIEDERICH, Margaret, 545
FRIEDLANDER, Carole, 277
FRIEDRICH, Timothy C, 723
FRIEND, Mary J, 395
FRIEND, Norma P, 1003
FRIES, Mark, 634
FRIESE, Rita D, 757
FRIGON, Matthew A, 702
FRITCHEY, Bonnie, 1101
FRITTS, Marilyn B, 464
FROEMMING, Hazel M, 429
FROMAN, Jean R, 1022
FRONSMAN-CECIL, Thea, 1051
FROSCHAUER Jr, Richard A, 385
FROST, Lee K, 625
FROST, Mary Jo, 7
FRYE, Carl L, 983
FRYE, James, 1064
FRYER, Billy, 602
FUCITO-LENKO, Joyce, 989
FUDGE, Peggy, 1070
FUHRMANN, Kurt, 339
FUKUSHIMA, Jr, Dennis H, 491
FULLER II, John M, 563
FULLER, Amanda, 131
FULLER, Beatrice Maxey, 266
FULLER, Eric B, 943
FULLER, Janice L, 434
FULLER, Margaret R, 569
FULLER, Mary Ann, 1021
FULLERTON, Kristin, 179
FULTON, Fred F, 238
FULTON, Linda S, 1201
FULTON, Mary K, 1133
FULTON, Peter H, 285
FUNSCH, Clarence, 269
FUNSTON, Brian Randall, 754
FURLOTTE, Tammy, 943
FURLOUGH, W D, 696
FURMAN, Paul, 46
FURNAS, Craig, 22
FURNESS, Anthony, 384
FURR, Mary, 684
FURREY, Anne-Marie, 471
FUTCH, Pat, 565
FUTUJMA, Jean, 780
FYLAN-BENAVIDEZ, Maureen, 754

G

GABBARD, Mrs Wilma L Spicer, 493
GABEL, Tricia, 340
GABERT, Jackie, 500
GABOR, Marypat, 882
GABR, Tarek M, 443
GABREL, Tamara, 311
GABRIEL-NOEL, Carolyn K, 644
GABRIELSSON, Dorothy, 903
GABY, Donna, 606
GADDY, Herman Gabin, 915
GADFIELD, Sharon, 160
GADSON, Helen J, 530
GAGNON, Annette, 655
GAGNON, Arlene R, 211
GAGNON, Pierrette, 883
GAHAGAN, Al, 550
GAHRING, C C, 482
GAIA, Celeste, 968
GAIL, Darlene, 293
GAINES, Dorothy E, 1126
GAINES, Mary, 404
GAINES, Sean W, 1021
GAITERS, Tonya, 950
GAITHER, Leslie P, 537
GAJUS, Jennifer Lee, 119
GALASKE, Larry J, 1190
GALASSO, Tom, 201
GALBRAITH, F Templeton, 158
GALE, Daniel J, 526
GALI, Lena, 849
GALITELLO, Morse A, 830
GALL, Theresa, 871
GALLA, Cathy, 864
GALLANT, Lorraine, 698
GALLAS, Heather, 867
GALLENI, Sister Eletta Marie, 1103
GALLER, Carl A, 27
GALLETTO, Scott Alan, 238
GALLEY, Violet Ursula, 73
GALLIMORE, Margaret, 505
GALLO, Elna D, 209
GALLO, Peter, 428
GALLO, Shannon, 150
GALLOWAY, Cynthia, 88
GALLOWAY, June Reece, 1073
GALLUP, Lucy Defluent, 527
GALOZO, Pete G, 152
GALUPPI, Michael P, 667
GALVIN, Deborah M, 504
GALYON, Cathy L, 541
GAMBLE, Anna D, 320
GAMBLE, Rosa L, 331
GAMMONS, Jennifer, 265
GANE, Sally, 462
GANESAN, Narayanan, 1153
GANGE, Ruth, 540
GANGI, Cristine, 108
GANN, Linda G, 1036
GANNON, Bernadette S, 799
GANT, Lainee, 905
GANTT II, Andrew H, 62
GANTT, Clarence, 1062
GANZ Jr, Jack L, 343
GARAFALO, Melinda, 464
GARAMELLA, Trinity, 35
GARATE, Patricia P, 1080
GARBER, Carol M Plant, 718
GARBER, Joseph G, 688
GARCIA, Arthur R, 844
GARCIA, Charles M, 1177
GARCIA, Eugene Geno, 1110
GARCIA, Gracie, 727
GARCIA, Jennifer, 353
GARCIA, Jodi, 1041
GARCIA, John Anthony, 945
GARCIA, Judy, 812
GARCIA, Rhonda L, 892
GARDINER, Dian L, 500
GARDINER, Teresa Ann, 1047
GARDNER, "Doc" Carlos, 785
GARDNER, Hazel, 924
GARDNER, Helen, 393
GARDNER, Jim, 804
GARDNER, Leanne, 633
GARDNER, Lee Ann, 755
GARDNER, Sharon Anne, 572
GARDNER, Terry L, 69
GARDNER, Wendy Lee, 320
GARELICK, Joanna, 261
GARFIELD, Deborah A, 146
GARGIULO, Sue, 962
GARISTO, Orsolina C, 378
GARITY, Jef, 660
GARLAND, Evern E, 364
GARLAND, Martin, 115
GARLAND, Mrs Jean B, 51
GARLAND, Susan, 138
GARLIT, Lucy A, 1016
GARMAN, Mary, 74
GARMON, Robby, 613
GARNER Jr, Perry L, 888
GARNER, Colleen, 136
GARNER, Holly, 589
GARNER, J Lynne, 335
GARNER, Sandra, 235
GARNS, Miriam, 71
GAROFALO, Amy, 647
GARRETSON, Edith E, 960
GARRETT, Beatrice, 484
GARRETT, Bill, 219
GARRETT, Dolores J, 446
GARRETT, Ruth, 1069
GARRETT, Vicki L, 692
GARRETT, Vickie E S, 451
GARRIDO, Aldo, 105
GARRIGAN, Marion F, 694
GARRIOTT, C Brice, 303
GARRISON Jr, George C, 496
GARRISON, Gaylle S, 727
GARRISON, Laverne, 881
GARRO, Barbara, 47
GARRY, David John, 653
GARVERICK, Todd Timothy, 894
GARVEY, Lindsworth S, 741
GARZA Jr, Leroy Paul, 238
GARZA, Richard, 539
GASKIN, Frances C, 290
GASKINS, Karen, 90
GATELEY, Frances, 236
GATENS, Julie, 1020
GATES, Louis, 27
GATEWOOD, Jessica Maria, 1007
GATHINGS Jr, P D, 55
GAUDIOSO, Deborah, 537
GAUDREAU, Monique Laplante, 1081
GAUER, Jeffrey S, 161
GAUTHIER, George, 1146
GAUTHIER, Sharon V, 607
GAUTREAUX, Lorraine M, 31
GAUTREAUX, Penelope, 326
GAVRUN, Della, 772
GAWEL, Richard, 220
GAWRYCH, Kelly, 1000
GAY, June W, 456
GAYDEN, Chris, 854
GAYE, Sally, 1024
GAYHEART, Haskell S, 754
GAYLORD, Charles, 474, 806
GAZZOLA, Geraldine R, 569
GEALT, Marshall, 765
GEAN, James T, 272
GEANE, Gloria, 359
GEARHART, Sandra S, 151
GEARY, Bryan L, 1139
GEARY, William F, 879
GEBAUER, Terri, 850
GEBHARDT Sr, David L, 601
GEBHARDT, Linda F, 785
GEBHARDT, Richard E E, 695
GEDRICH, Elaine M, 1041
GEE, Jeannie C, 542
GEESLIN Jr, Thomas, 606
GEESMAN, Robin A, 925
GEFFEN, Shara Lyn, 244
GEISENDORFER, James, 424
GEISER, Deborah M, 241
GEITNER, Melody M, 338
GELBER, T Butler, 795
GELET, Sande M, 1114
GELL, Dianna Lynn, 663
GEMMELL, Sharolyn K, 1029
GENCORELLI, Genevieve, 325
GENGLER, Barb E, 988
GENOVESE, Anjanette, 613
GENSLER, Jerry H, 874
GENTEMAN, Michelle, 517
GENTILE, Doris, 1186
GENTILE, Missy E, 941
GENTNER, Katherine L, 1062, 1062
GENTRY, Connie A, 1075
GENTRY, Joyce, 926
GENZEN, Hope Ellen, 632
GEORGALAS, Lorna, 880
GEORGE, Annette L, 855
GEORGE, Carol, 789
GEORGE, Eloys E, 474
GEORGE, Jalynne, 751
GEORGE, Jini, 1103
GEORGE, Joyce, 533
GEORGESON, C Russell, 240
GEREAU, Bobbie, 523
GERENA, Aixa, 732
GERHARDS, Kimberly D, 870
GERICK, Babb, 451
GERKIN, Dorothy M, 555
GERMAIN, Florence, 129
GERMAN, Terry J, 391
GEROW, Jennifer, 7
GERTH, Julie, 378
GERTSCH, Lois, 102
GERY, Richard F, 237
GESS-SMITH, Roxann, 675
GHEESLING, Robbin L, 458
GIACCIO, Rebecca, 628
GIALANELLA, Darlene A, 397
GIAMMARESE, Rosai, 1126
GIAMMONA, Ann, 1160
GIANNONE, Sharon, 875
GIANTURCO, Margaret, 842
GIBBONS, Annamae H, 975
GIBBONS, Pegge Fitz, 1040
GIBBS, Betty, 780
GIBBS, Carri L, 209
GIBBS, Jerry E, 1026
GIBBS, Kay, 260
GIBBS, Loretta F, 741
GIBBS, Lucy, 894
GIBBS, Randall E, 412
GIBLIN, Joyce, 252
GIBSON, Betty, 111
GIBSON, Cheli E, 584
GIBSON, Janet, 335
GIBSON, Kay, 327
GIBSON, Kevin D, 283
GIBSON, Renee, 774
GIBSON, Richard, 204
GIBSON, Tina, 77
GIBSON, Ursula T, 140
GIBSON, Viola F, 612
GIDDINGS, Mike, 389
GIESBRECHT, Sharlene A, 532
GIFFING, Margaret A, 379
GIFFORD, Joanne M, 332
GIGLIA, Angelo G, 400
GILBERT, Charlotte A, 675
GILBERT, Hugh R, 415
GILCHRIST, Marie E, 1083
GILES, David M, 90
GILES, Linda L, 654
GILL, Patricia G, 694
GILLARD, Bette, 432
GILLEN, Greta, 593
GILLES, Marsha C, 191
GILLESPIE, Ann H, 1008
GILLESPIE, Cathlene, 370
GILLESPIE, Lori J, 637
GILLETLY, Mark C, 222
GILLEY, Ora, 356
GILLIAM, George, 379
GILLIAM, Karan L, 989
GILLIAM, Loretta, 82
GILLIAM, Verlena, 1193
GILLIAM, Walter, 911
GILLIES, G C, 910
GILLILAND, Kim, 27
GILLMAN, Leah V, 1052
GILLUM, Kelly L, 651
GILMAN, Joanna, 448
GILMER, Patricia V, 739
GILMETTE, Ada (Penny), 1059
GILMORE, Luard E, 99
GILMOUR, Alastair, 1062
GILPATRICK MA, Carole M, 704
GILROY, Bryan A, 77
GILSON, Cheryl, 583
GILSON, Mary, 590
GILSON, Tamara, 637
GINEBAUGH, Kelly, 475
GINGRICH, Marie E, 501
GINN, Tracey Elaine, 369
GINSBERG-COWAN, Evie, 926
GINSBURG, Konstantin A, 102
GINTER, Leslie Jo, 380
GIOFFRE, Barbara Donnici, 717
GIOVANINI, D J, 997
GIOVENCO, Joan, 421
GIPSON, Robert Glenn, 1009
GIPSON, Rosemary, 96
GIRARD, Moira, 774
GIRARD, Stephanie D, 50
GIRASUOLO, Stacy, 401
GIRILLO, Donald A, 976
GIRON, Juan Ascidro, 881
GISI, Kathy Z, 437
GISLER, Ruth, 416
GITTINGS, Charlette M, 351
GITZ, Marianna, 1091
GIVAN, Oma C, 1085
GIVEN, Margaret, 309
GIVENS, Jerry, 15
GIVENS, Mary Anna Lee, 739
GLADMAN, Diana L, 953
GLANCY, Susan, 317
GLASER, Betty, 373
GLASS, John C, 295
GLASS, Patricia E, 570
GLASS, Patrick, 894
GLASS-BROWN, Lisa Marie, 40
GLASZCZ, Jerilynn, 443
GLATKY, Mrs Pearl, 539
GLATZER, Angeline J, 310
GLAVAZ, Ernie, 22
GLAZ, Emilia A, 472
GLAZEWSKI, Lisa A, 281
GLAZIER, Diane K, 728
GLEASON, Nancy G, 134
GLEN, The Pen, 147

GLENDOWNE, Diana, 203
GLENISTER, Michael, 500
GLENN, Linda J, 348
GLIDDEN, Linda M, 58
GLINES, C R, 858
GLINSKY, Tara, 1131
GLISSON, Ozzie B, 1121
GLOOR, Robert F, 1121
GLORIA, Manuel, 1152
GLOVER, Albert, 631
GLOVER, Dave Wayne, 1110
GLOVER, Judylee Annette, 1195
GLOVER, Mabel, 1143
GLYN, Howard, 679
GNEHM, Heather Marie, 1124
GOALEN, Jean M, 207
GOATES, Nancy L, 26
GOBBI, Mandy, 351
GOBLE, Bruce Wayne, 947
GOBLE, Christopher, 224
GOBOR, Andreas, 47
GODFREY, Bill, 189
GODFREY, Michele, 769
GODSEY, Debra K, 1063
GODSEY, Glenda, 111
GODWIN, Brenda, 1121
GOEBEL, Paula, 588
GOEHLER, Susanna B, 386
GOERTLER, Grace Marston, 265
GOFF, Mary, 10
GOFFINET, Rebecca, 845
GOGER, Joan, 384
GOGGINS, Lorraine, 1120
GOIN, James Henry, 1189
GOINS, Steve, 292, 292
GOLBAR, Katy, 345
GOLD, Abbie, 901
GOLD, Mimi Mayers, 516
GOLDBACH, Joyce J, 495
GOLDBERG, Barbara, 78
GOLDBERG, Ethel, 674
GOLDBERG, Marcia R, 575
GOLDEN, Jeannette B, 131
GOLDEN, Karyne, 447
GOLDEN, Randy D, 812
GOLDEN, Regina, 1080, 1034
GOLDEN, Tina Lee, 369
GOLDENBERG, Tatyana, 10
GOLDING, Annette, 713
GOLDING, Deanie, 1191
GOLDMAN, Berthold, 264
GOLDMAN, Ruth Phares, 97
GOLDSTEIN, Frances, 547
GOLDWERT, Marvin, 152
GOLLEY Jr, Howard J, 1131
GOLOB, Aron S, 81
GOMER, Mary E, 360
GOMES, Antonio, 132
GOMEZ, Amy A, 710
GOMEZ, Jesse Carlos, 608
GOMEZ, Melory, 21
GOMPERTS, Jessica, 149
GONESH, G S, 488
GONYEA, Douglas W, 892
GONZALES Jr, Guillermo H, 117
GONZALES, Beatrice B, 335
GONZALES, Carolyn J, 429
GONZALES, Maxene, 903
GONZALES, Patricia, 837
GONZALES, Sherri L, 226
GONZALES, Shirley, 103
GONZALES, Tracey, 978
GONZALEZ, Blasita, 798
GONZALEZ, Frances, 119
GONZALEZ, Jewell, 919
GONZALEZ, Magali Ruiz, 1011
GONZALEZ, Sylvia, 167
GONZALEZ, Veronica, 864
GONZALEZ, Willie Stine, 692
GONZALEZ-FOUCHEA, Miguel, 720
GOOD, Leisa Bain, 780
GOOD, Melanie, 1009
GOODALL, Helen L, 1154
GOODE, Dennis I, 934
GOODEN, Louise, 1177
GOODHUE, Jean W, 116
GOODMAN Jr, Hugh, 739
GOODMAN, Debra Norris, 1052
GOODMAN, Fred H, 368
GOODMAN, Gentrie, 403
GOODMAN, Helene M, 599
GOODMAN, Nancy, 251
GOODRICH, Gary L, 542
GOODRUM, Grace Pearl, 1040
GOODSTONE PHD, Erica, 895
GOODWIN IV, John S, 1032
GOODWIN, Joan S, 208
GOODWIN, Melanie, 245
GOODWIN, William, 239
GOOSLIN, Mary, 240
GORDON, Belinda M, 915
GORDON, Debbrajeane', 152
GORDON, Denise, 298
GORDON, James E, 552
GORDON, Jay, 106
GORDON, Jennifer, 869
GORDON, Larry, 556
GORDON, Marie Elaina, 81
GORDON, Marjorie, 493
GORDON, Nancy, 1082
GORDON, R M, 21
GORDON, Traci W, 400
GORDON, Vivian, 405
GORE, Sharon B, 971
GORHAM, Waitie D, 14
GORLEY, S Elizabeth, 398
GORON, Noelle, 610
GORSKI, Walter, 315
GORTON, Stephen R, 248
GORZELIC, Michael P, 1133
GOSSARD, Bonnie, 685
GOTAY, Julio, 874
GOTTBERG, Armin C, 83
GOTTLIEB, Elisa, 124
GOTTLIEB, Sari, 178
GOUCHNOUR, Linda, 134
GOULD, Lois Sameth, 453
GOULD, Marcia, 429
GOULD, Peggy Ann, 1177
GOULDING, Melanie, 552
GOULDNER, David A, 625
GOULET, Patricia, 1200
GOWER, April N, 99
GOWER, Vivian, 643
GOWIN, James M, 427
GRAB, Rosalie, 142
GRABE, Donna, 412
GRABER, Virgil E, 418
GRABOWSKI, Robert D, 174
GRABSTAS, Mark, 520
GRACE, Mary, 968
GRAEF, Annie H, 1037
GRAFF, Shayla, 1095
GRAFF, Susan, 458
GRAFFEO, Frank Paul, 1202
GRAGG, Richard T, 1199
GRAHAM, Donna, 388
GRAHAM, Lisa E, 652
GRAHAM, Martha, 169
GRAHAM, Mrs Pearl, 1069
GRAHAM, Rose, 855
GRAHAM, Shannon, 341
GRAHAM, Staci, 484
GRAHAM, Susan, 1023
GRAHAM, Susan P, 594
GRAHAM, Willie Lee, 683
GRAHAME, Christopher W, 14
GRAMM, Shaunna M, 944
GRANA-RAFFUCCI, Felix A, 450
GRANADOS, Laura, 1042
GRANATO, Nevada S, 696
GRANDCHAMP, Barbara L, 718
GRANGER, Loretta Diane, 377
GRANNIS, Shirley L, 167
GRANT Jr, Gerald H, 540
GRANT Jr, Howard, 653
GRANT, Jeannine Lee, 626
GRANT, Katie, 964
GRAPEL, Franklin, 1157
GRASSO, Derek, 168
GRATA, Stacey Lee, 707
GRATZ, Alexa, 134
GRAUSO, Sally B, 356
GRAVELY, Katherine L, 135
GRAVENEY, Jenna, 483
GRAVES, Jay, 850
GRAVES, Larry, 1057
GRAVES, Margaret A, 813
GRAVIER, Steven J, 352
GRAY, Doug, 56
GRAY, Edith, 137
GRAY, Evelyn M, 1195
GRAY, Felicia D, 491
GRAY, Glen, 1080
GRAY, Kevin B, 539
GRAY, Mary, 958
GRAY, O Edward, 1197
GRAY, Rebecca D, 164
GRAY, Ricardo O, 117
GRAY, Sharon Rose, 1117
GRAY, Steven K, 491, 287
GRAY, William, 208
GRAY, Willie Lee, 389
GRAY-CREWS, Christine, 901
GRAYDON, Bill, 361
GRAYER, Mrs Ruth, 323
GRAYER, Tahera T, 1182
GRAYSON, Dorothy B, 435
GRAYWIN, Hill, 1049
GRAZIAPLENA, Louis, 840
GRAZULIS, Linda C, 235
GRDINICH, Kathleen, 481
GREAT SPIRIT, Father Jesus, 145
GRECO, Trevor, 813
GREEK, Ken, 237
GREEN, Alicia, 812
GREEN, Allen, 116
GREEN, Anne, 1012
GREEN, Anne, 507
GREEN, Antonia K, 851
GREEN, Barry, 100
GREEN, Bernice S, 600
GREEN, Beverly A, 15
GREEN, Cher, 961
GREEN, D W, 318
GREEN, Debbie, 547
GREEN, Debby, 456
GREEN, Dr P L, 1012
GREEN, Elbert P, 133
GREEN, Ericka Katheryn, 830
GREEN, Geraldine A, 1173
GREEN, Janet, 399
GREEN, Joann, 58
GREEN, Laurette, 1012
GREEN, Lucille, 361
GREEN, Marion, 319
GREEN, Michael M, 976
GREEN, Michelle, 1072
GREEN, Patricia, 1152
GREEN, Sharletta M, 748
GREEN, Tena, 213
GREENAWALT Jr, William R, 646
GREENAWALT, Lois, 237
GREENE Jr, Benjamin W, 414
GREENE, Elizabeth L, 798
GREENE, Flora E, 666
GREENE, Jessica, 1089
GREENE, Joanne T, 269
GREENE, Lara Dionne, 1049
GREENE, Tricia, 267
GREENFELD-KRAVETZ, Darlene, 581
GREENLAND, Ladera, 1186
GREENMYER, Paula K, 142
GREENWOOD, B Ray, 816
GREER, Deborah, 298
GREER, Edith Wood, 1110
GREER, Kathleen R G, 742
GREER, Mrs Frank, 318
GREER, Shawn, 706
GREGERSON, Alicia, 851
GREGORIS, Pauline C, 266
GREGORY, Art W, 199
GREGORY, Cindy M, 670
GREGORY, D, 404
GREGORY, Gus, 134
GREGORY, Myra M, 385
GREGORY, Royal F, 1063
GREGORY, Sharon M, 350
GREGORY, Winnie, 623
GREIF, Alma, 309
GRELL, Elizabeth, 910
GRENIER, Iris, 72
GRESCHNER, Belinda R J, 483
GRESKE, David Edwin, 166
GREVE, E, 1133
GEYER, J C, 1087
GREYWOLF, Billy A, 32
GRIBBINS III, William, 833
GRIDER, J Quenton, 717
GRIDER, James T, 28
GRIENER, Gene, 959
GRIER, Walter, 944
GRIFFEN, Tom, 498
GRIFFEY, Tina M, 127
GRIFFIN, Doris H, 1015
GRIFFIN, Lolita, 664
GRIFFIN, Sharon D Long, 592
GRIFFIS, Delinda, 1077
GRIFFITH, Cathy, 436
GRIFFITH, Linda D, 1045
GRIFFITH, Matthew A, 793
GRIGGS II, Jerry L B, 1091
GRIGGS, Alyssa, 246
GRIGGS, Dorothy M, 1022
GRIGGS, Karen, 492
GRIGNON, Karen, 1024
GRIGSBY, Phil E, 622
GRIJALVA, Lucila V, 999
GRILO, Lisa, 45
GRIMARD, Philip A, 330
GRIMES, Anna Bebhinn, 592
GRIMES, Cindy C, 602
GRIMES, Janinne, 930
GRIMES, Jody L, 510
GRIMES, Lisa, 900
GRIMES, Lori, 164
GRIMES, Sherry K, 191
GRIMES, Stacy L, 737
GRIMM, Alison, 117
GRIMM, Barbara, 763
GRIMM, Lisel, 133
GRINDROD, Lorijean, 936
GRINDSTAFF, Kevin Andrew, 456
GRINDSTAFF, Sherry Gail, 887, 1114
GRISWOLD, Gary David, 682
GROCE, Charmene K, 253
GROCE, Shelly Renae, 301
GRODENCHIK, Wendy, 277
GROGAN, Beth, 946
GROMADA, Bertha Eva C, 305
GRONDIN, Kathryn S, 276
GROOM, Daryel, 897
GROOMS, Lisa, 843
GROSS, Wende, 474
GROSSI, Patricia, 409
GROSSMAN, I G "Butch", 219
GROSSNICKLE, Dorma, 775
GROTHENDICK, Joey Ann, 944
GROVE, Virginia B, 947
GROVES, Zelma Spivey, 193, 915
GROVES-WALKER, Nina, 52
GRUJICICH, Jeff, 535
GRUMBLES, Edith Brake, 699
GRUMMET, Brenda R, 258
GRUNENFELDER, Renate, 936
GRUSSING, Thomas D, 1091
GUARINO Jr, J Rudolph, 151
GUDENAS, Julie, 825
GUENTHER, Justina J, 471
GUERENA, Michael, 382
GUERRA, Mimi, 631
GUERRERI, Diane F, 816
GUERRERO, Janis C, 481
GUERRIERI, Teresa E, 588
GUERRIERO, Jennifer, 475
GUERRINI, Susan V, 269
GUEST, Anne-marie, 670
GUEST, Patricia, 71
GUFFEY Jr, Ralph L, 442
GUFFEY, William A, 1158
GUGINO, Lisa, 928
GUGLICIELLO, Sonia (Sonnie), 1009
GUIDA, Rosemary, 356
GUIDERA, Terri, 387
GUIDI, Dan, 578
GUINDON, Grace F, 772
GUINN, Chandriee D, 1166
GUINN, Vickie, 1182
GUJRAL, Shiela, 950
GULESERIAN, Cristy, 356
GULICK, John D, 811
GULLEY, Angela, 771
GULLEY, Teresa O, 1110
GULLEY, Vellmer, 364
GUM, Louise Hyde, 334
GUMKE, Eva, 856
GUNN, Rhonda Lee, 1092
GUNNELL Sr, Joseph C, 564
GUNTER, Charlie, 414
GUNTER, Greg, 584
GURLEY, Felix, 241
GURNETT, Debbie, 97
GURNEY, David, 621
GUSTAFSON, Gary, 588
GUSTAFSON, Rosalie S, 1114, 1114
GUTHRIE, Jack D, 380
GUTHRIE, Jessica, 312
GUTIERREZ, Anita, 584
GUTIERREZ, Mike, 512
GUTTRIDGE, Wendi L, 238
GUYER, Randi Lynn, 176
GWEN, Timothy S, 1202
GYERMEH, Samuel, 575
GYPSYFIED, Ms, 1176
GZANOWICZ, Helen Regina, 1079

H

H, Gwen, 177
HAARBERG, Renea, 341
HAAS, E P, 805
HABETS, Laurie, 932
HACH, Alice M, 1029
HACKBARTH, Eleanor, 205
HACKERMAN, Deborah, 289
HACKET, Janice E, 733
HACKETT, Thomas J, 719
HADDAD, Jennifer Lea, 119
HADDAD, Khuloud, 809
HADDEN, Alfred, 371
HADLEY Jr, Paul B, 717
HADLEY, Matthew, 799
HADLOCK, Helen, 846
HADLY, Matty D, 1126
HAEFNER, Kenneth, 992
HAGAN Jr, Ronny W, 946
HAGEMAN, N Yvonne, 1144
HAGEN, Jacqueline, 326
HAGEN, Kathleen, 29
HAGER, Brian E, 559
HAGER, Lucky, 720
HAGER, Pauline, 688
HAGGARD, Eulah, 106
HAGGBERG, Barney P, 831
HAGSTROM, Caren, 540
HAGUE, Audrey C, 209
HAHN, Barbara F, 517
HAHN, Madalyn, 29
HAHN, Virginia, 978
HAIDSIAK, Lisa J, 728
HAIGHT RN, Ellen Kaye, 608
HAINES, Betty, 240
HAINES, Diann, 138
HAINES, Jeri, 191
HAINES, Kerry, 950
HAIRE, Marie Law, 7
HAJEK, Concetta Tm, 569
HAKR, Pauline, 768
HALAVEY, Libba, 298
HALBROHR, Peter, 43
HALBROOK, Stacie S, 647
HALCOMB, Sylvia, 615
HALDEMAN, Mabel Glenn, 1200
HALE, Jeanne Embry, 749
HALES, Kirsty, 802
HALES, Nicole Antonia, 832
HALETSKY, Ena M, 239
HALEY, Ben, 1030
HALEY, Derrick T, 549
HALEY, Ginger, 74
HALEY, Jack N, 729
HALEY, Julie, 1196
HALEY, Michelle, 553
HALIBURTON, B J, 737
HALL III, Joseph P, 719
HALL, Amy Susanne, 347
HALL, Bobbie, 773
HALL, Brad D, 203
HALL, Catherine J, 281
HALL, Charolette E, 713
HALL, Donna R, 568
HALL, Dora V, 362
HALL, Dorothy H, 1049
HALL, Duane J, 1000
HALL, Eleanor, 241
HALL, Imogene, 740
HALL, Jon Howard, 892
HALL, Ken, 711
HALL, Kimberly M, 418
HALL, Leslie T, 887
HALL, Margaret L, 238
HALL, Melva F, 666
HALL, Millard R, 705
HALL, Nan Wood, 792
HALL, Nancy, 1138
HALL, Patricia W, 497
HALL, Pearl M, 416
HALL, Ruth A, 149
HALL, Susan, 723
HALL, Suzanne, 488
HALL-VANDER, Olivia, 1047
HALLETT, Harold W, 99
HALLETT, Rita, 395
HALLETT, Timna, 336
HALLIDAY, Vicky J, 18
HALLMAN, Matthew Tracy, 1095
HALLYBURTON, Janice Ivey, 693
HALM, Thomas V, 490
HALOG, Basilisa L, 322
HALPERIN, Mr Morris, 1083
HALPIN, Doris M, 176
HALTERMAN, Cathy, 595
HALVORSEN, Beulah E U, 292
HALVORSEN, Glenda L, 842
HALVORSON, Richard A, 482
HAM, Douglas M, 512
HAMBELTON, Michael Lee, 1115
HAMBRICK, Sharon B, 43
HAMBURG, Helene-Del, 931
HAMBURGER, Kenneth J, 1055
HAMEL, Gail E, 653
HAMILL, Kathe, 163
HAMILTON (RAY), Laura Jean, 258
HAMILTON, Carol W, 564
HAMILTON, Julianne S, 440
HAMILTON, Melvin J, 812
HAMILTON, Ms Dorothy J, 221
HAMILTON, Paula S, 130
HAMILTON, Phyllis, 113
HAMILTON, Sarah Lillian, 81
HAMILTON, Vivian, 306

HAMILTON, William Scott, 562
HAMLIN, Rev Byron G, 427
HAMM, Edward L, 394
HAMMAN, Daniel H, 1043
HAMMEL, Bonnie, 255
HAMMELL, B J, 180
HAMMER, Elizabeth A, 406
HAMMERSTEADT, Pearl, 1064
HAMMON, Kevin D, 59
HAMMOND, Joan C, 703
HAMMONDS, Gayle R, 72
HAMMONDS-QUISENBERRY, Eddie L, 657
HAMPTON, Robert A, 461
HANCE, Esther, 366
HANCOCK, Claudiette F, 590
HANCOCK, George A, 878
HANCOCK, Joy, 239
HAND, Susan, 780
HANDFIELD, Michelle, 885
HANDY, Evelyn, 398
HANDY, Rosetta White, 767
HANEY, Martha D, 804
HANGE, Grace, 205
HANIF, Justine E, 748
HANKE, Cindy L, 375
HANKEY, Dwight, 269
HANKINS, Andrea, 128
HANKINS, Angela, 240
HANKS, Brion K, 326
HANN, Cynthia, 551
HANNA, Ken, 264
HANNER, Thelma L, 1198
HANNIFORD, Dawn, 586
HANNUM, Maxine, 911
HANSEL, Russell, 940
HANSELL, Lola, 1125
HANSEN, Audrey, 886
HANSEN, James Richard, 1017
HANSEN, Kimberly Ann, 585
HANSEN, Lorraine, 345
HANSEN, Merle C, 743
HANSEN, Mrs Susan, 48
HANSEN-BEARD, Lora, 118
HANSEN-DE NICOLA, Judith, 185
HANSON, B K, 1065
HANSON, Fae, 648
HANSON, Gladys Faye, 675
HANSON, Loyal, 1059
HANSON, Margie H, 459
HANSON, Syble L, 215
HANSON, Theresa Marie, 934
HAPHEY, Muriel, 402
HARAC, Miss Pamela, 336
HARALDSDOTTER, Ulla, 942
HARBERTS, Marilyn A, 612
HARDEY, Crystal Ann, 708
HARDIE Sr, Randall H, 1035
HARDING, Alfrieda, 310
HARDING, Kelilea, 1128
HARDING, Mary Beth, 500
HARDING, Rosalynn C, 1152
HARDMAN, Deborah Lee, 1071
HARDMAN, Sherral K, 426
HARDY, Willie F, 505
HARE, David, 1046
HARGETT, Linda, 543
HARGIS II, Ardyth D, 1075
HARGIS, Angela M, 852
HARGRAVES, Dena M, 273
HARING, Alyce, 122
HARKER, Patrick, 504
HARKINS, Rebecca, 1169
HARKNESS, Cynthia Lee, 222
HARKRIDER, Claire W, 1121
HARLAND, Buffy L, 538
HARLOW, Marie, 828
HARMAN, Christine, 540
HARMAN, Perry, 511
HARMATI (CESEKE), Terez, 954
HARMER, Sydney Lee, 297
HARMICK, Robin Lynn, 464
HARMON R N, Betty A, 749
HARMON, Alan T, 968
HARMON, Jack Darel, 258
HARMON, Theresa M, 1081, 1064
HARMS, Janelle, 677
HARNER, Kim, 222
HARNESS, Betty, 1017
HARPER, Beatrice, 1028
HARPER, Christine S, 5
HARPER, Emily, 167
HARPER, Javan J, 1109
HARPER, Margery E, 687
HARPER, Mary Ruth, 403
HARPER, Maynard M, 518
HARPER, Michelle, 667
HARPER, Sally, 1009
HARPER, Teresia A, 855
HARPER, Tonya L, 1111
HARPER, Vivienne, 827
HARPER, William D, 1151
HARRELL, Consuelo, 5
HARRELL, Daphne D, 621
HARRELL, Rick, 449
HARRINGTON, Allene, 942
HARRINGTON, Deborah H, 612
HARRINGTON, Haddy, 1126
HARRINGTON, Julie, 324
HARRINGTON, Larry, 1194
HARRINGTON, Patrick, 88
HARRINGTON, Richard A, 101
HARRINGTON, Rita F, 23
HARRIS, Alice R, 185
HARRIS, Barbara, 867
HARRIS, Brian, 529
HARRIS, Charlotte M, 567
HARRIS, Dianne Leigh, 332
HARRIS, Don L, 554
HARRIS, Gloria Gail, 578
HARRIS, Heather, 887
HARRIS, Helen, 188
HARRIS, Helen A, 41
HARRIS, Jason Marc, 1154
HARRIS, Jeffrey, 907
HARRIS, Judy, 647
HARRIS, Leodis, 1112
HARRIS, Lori L, 501
HARRIS, Peggy L, 805
HARRIS, Robert, 250
HARRIS, Robert Franklin, 697
HARRIS, Rufas Ra-man, 1165
HARRIS, Sally, 1032
HARRIS, Sharon L, 762
HARRIS, Shawna, 948
HARRIS, Sheldon Locke, 805
HARRIS, Stephanie C, 798
HARRIS, Tara Mia, 113
HARRIS, Virginia B, 700
HARRIS-FRANKLIN, Sheila, 1048
HARRISON, A R, 1038
HARRISON, Alisa, 710
HARRISON, Clarice E, 497
HARRISON, Donna, 1187
HARRISON, Dorothy June, 869
HARRISON, Ella Ruth, 461
HARRISON, Jessica, 815
HARRISON, John, 260
HARRISON, John B, 62
HARRISON, Joni J, 141
HARRISON, Kimberly A, 624
HARRISON, Linda Kay, 665
HARRISON, Miki, 934
HARRISON, Nancy, 129
HARRISON, Shannon, 1152
HARRISON, Yvonne, 1059
HARRITY, Andrea, 691
HARROD, Maxine, 386
HARSHA, Ethel C, 533
HART, Bessie M, 574
HART, Buffy, 1151
HART, Clarissa, 601
HART, Deborah L, 934
HART, Sam, 906
HART, Virgil S, 886
HARTER, Barbara, 915
HARTER, Becki, 58
HARTER, Jerry R, 147
HARTFORD-PAGE, Connie, 786
HARTLEY, Litzi, 22
HARTLEY, S I G, 447
HARTMAN Jr, Frederick X, 1161
HARTMAN, Betty J, 340
HARTMAN, Mrs Alfred Z, 788
HARTMAN, Robin, 206
HARTMANN Jr, Richard J, 931
HARTMANN-PHIPPS, Hanne, 83
HARTSOOK, Mia, 1091, 1064, 1092
HARTWELL, Kenneth L, 1186
HARTZELL, Jennifer L, 86
HARTZELL, Laura L, 345
HARTZFIELDT, Maggie L, 239
HARVEST MOON EYES, Marcia A, 669
HARVEY, Bill, 542
HARVEY, Carolyn S, 1054
HARVEY, Debra Lynn H, 1152
HARVEY, Loretta, 588
HARVEY, Nancy C, 200
HARWELL, Edna Pearl, 1082
HASH, Cynthia, 592
HASKETT, Wilda M, 867
HASLER, Astrid, 686
HASSAN, Mahbubul, 762
HASSETT, Carol J, 100
HASSINGER, Margaret M, 965
HASTING, Kristi, 610
HASTINGS, Jeanne D, 678
HASTINGS, Jennifer S, 130
HASTINGS, Myron L, 937
HATCHER, Claudette R, 144
HATCHER, Diana L, 626
HATCHER, Tami, 566
HATCHETT, Cornell G C, 1086
HATFIELD, Douglas Lee, 748
HATHEWAY, Maruja, 861
HATIN, Candice Sue, 958
HATLEY, Faye, 956
HATLEY, Paula A, 696
HATT, Janice Irene, 930
HAUNGS, Barbara J, 1174
HAUPT, Cecilia G, 466
HAVENS, Michelle M, 202
HAWK, Martha D, 542
HAWKES, Teddy, 427
HAWKINS, Clyde C, 938
HAWKINS, David M, 662
HAWKINS, Doris M, 480
HAWKINS, Edithe, 446
HAWKINS, Jack, 309
HAWKINS, S, 24
HAWKINS, Sheila, 899
HAWKINSON, Marguerite, 759
HAWKS, Richard B, 949
HAWORTH, M D, 1031
HAY III, Soloman L, 974
HAY, Karen, 821
HAY, Lynne, 920
HAYDEN, Denise C, 271
HAYES Jr, Gunnar L, 530
HAYES, Adell, 839
HAYES, Cynthia P, 535
HAYES, Deborah A M, 107
HAYES, Grace, 425
HAYES, Jennifer S, 770
HAYES, Jerry W, 26
HAYES, Joseph, 371
HAYES, Joy Marie, 465
HAYES, Misty, 104
HAYES, Tommie, 12
HAYES, Wayne A, 75
HAYMAN, Jacquelyn G, 141
HAYN, Lois, 410
HAYNES, Earnest B, 613
HAYNES, Richard M, 1099
HAYNES, Susanne Marie, 673
HAYNES-FARMER, Lisa, 201
HAYNIE, Bonnie Baca, 510
HAYS, Jeannette Ann, 542
HAYSLETT, Bridgett, 49
HAYSLIP, Melody Jan, 818
HAYSON, Ida Mae, 444
HAYTE, Teresa E, 897
HAYWOOD, Beth, 195
HAYWORTH, Patricia Paulley, 773
HAZARD, Anne, 1095, 1095
HEAD, Bonnie, 1092
HEAD, Wilma D, 90
HEADLEY, Cindy, 539
HEADLEY, Helen, 818
HEADLEY, Laury K, 894
HEADLOUGH, Cy, 1092
HEALY, Vincent John, 226
HEARD, Anita, 980
HEARD, Jane Ann, 610
HEARN, Debbie A, 816
HEARRON, Joelle K, 726
HEATH, Barbara, 31
HEATON, Lee R, 104
HEBEL, Maryanne E, 1149
HEBEL, Patricia A, 298
HEBERT, Carol Koehler, 126
HEBERT, Sue Mimi, 258
HECKENLAIBLE, Arline, 304
HECKMAN, Katie, 824
HEDGER, E.V.A., 1146
HEERDT, M Margaret, 421
HEFLIN, Marion F, 720
HEFNER, Mark, 653
HEGG, Helen E, 636
HEID, Patricia, 820
HEIDEMAN, Berneta, 628
HEIDRICK, Kate, 479
HEIDT, Debra Sue, 363
HEIFNER, Janet Rae, 42
HEIL, Christina, 739
HEILMAN, Tami, 1030
HEILPAP, David L, 1199
HEILWECK, Patricia, 683
HEINBUCH, Diane M, 786
HEINE, Nedra Nancyan, 1120
HEINRITZ, Lisa, 55
HEINS, Ingrid, 301
HEINTZ, Veronica, 219
HEINTZELMAN, Richard L, 533
HEINZ, Mindy, 204
HEINZ, Susanne, 143
HEINZL, Clara E, 400
HEISER, Gloria M, 894
HEISEY, Betty W, 681
HEISKELL, Matt, 611
HEISTON, Glenn, 323
HEITGER, Luellen H, 665
HELLARD, Rachel Y, 16
HELLEGERS, Tisha, 114
HELLER Jr, George F, 633
HELLER, Edward A, 508
HELLINE, Molly, 998
HELLING, Brenda Irene, 653
HELLINGER, Heinz, 976
HELLMERS, Frances W, 788
HELMINIAK, Stacy, 732
HELSEL, Darrin K, 1138
HEMANS, Donna, 778
HEMINGER, Carol R Reed, 708
HEMMERS, Kathleen Joy, 970
HENDERSON, Ann M, 67
HENDERSON, Brenda K, 188
HENDERSON, Chester, 335
HENDERSON, Christi, 27
HENDERSON, Diana L, 973
HENDERSON, Everett, 381
HENDERSON, Joy, 930
HENDERSON, K, 393
HENDERSON, L.V.N., Marjorie, 1133
HENDERSON, Lois, 406
HENDERSON, Melba, 354
HENDERSON, Patricia A, 719
HENDERSON, Regina, 235
HENDERSON, Sheri L, 666
HENDERSON, Vernice, 807
HENDERSON, Vesta Rae, 916
HENDERSON, Vickie Lee, 171
HENDERSON, Wanda, 939
HENDRICKS, Helen, 230
HENDRICKS, Ruth Delamar, 655
HENDRICKSON, Diana L, 716
HENDRICKSON, Eileen, 815
HENDRIX, Amber, 855
HENDRIX, Jacquelyn M, 844
HENDRY, Jim, 412
HENDY, Irene, 513
HENFIELD, Christopher, 760
HENLEY, Marcia Evone, 831
HENLEY, Patricia, 323
HENNEBERRY, Julie A, 725
HENNESSY, John F, 1048
HENNING, Edna Mae, 988
HENRIKSEN, Einar, 181
HENRY, Ann, 834
HENRY, Art, 544
HENRY, Cheryl, 736
HENRY, Dorothy A, 245
HENRY, Elwin, 158
HENRY, Irene, 1092
HENRY, Jamie, 603
HENRY, John Vincent, 338
HENRY, Kristi Ann, 691
HENRY, Margaret C, 525
HENRY, Marie, 352
HENRY, Mary S, 587
HENRY, Mrs Irene, 212
HENRY, Sabrina, 987
HENSLEY, Betty S, 166
HENSLEY, Ellouise, 247
HENSLEY, Mary L, 1112
HENSLEY, Sharron S, 668
HENSON, Bob, 1198
HENSON, June M, 466
HENSON, Melba W, 1165
HENTREL, Fawn A, 614
HEPNER, Maria G, 435
HEPWORTH, Donna Lynn, 878
HERASIMCHUK, Alyse M, 10
HERBERT, Jessie, 371
HERBERT, Rodney, 519
HERBIG, Tamara, 552
HERBRANSON, Brenda Marie, 138
HERLE, Theresa, 905
HERLIHY, Laura, 898
HERMAN, Jackie Lynn, 748
HERMANN-LOCKEN, Julie, 171
HERMANNS, Tina Marie, 441
HERMANSEN, Berti, 576
HERMES, Nancy Bashara, 1169
HERMOSILLO, Blanca M, 523
HERNANDEZ, Alaena, 440
HERNANDEZ, Aracelis, 88
HERNANDEZ, Maria, 759
HERNANDEZ, Paul G, 711
HERNDON, Jeni, 699
HERRELL, Jason, 262
HERRERA, Lena, 1189
HERRERAS, Kathy, 44
HERRIN, Alfred C, 393
HERRIN, Eleze M Gaede, 839
HERRIN, Patricia A, 623
HERRING, Bonnie, 762
HERRING, Curtis Lee, 342
HERRING, Debra, 1038
HERRING, George R, 935
HERRINGTON Sr, Joseph C, 375
HERRINGTON, Manervia, 1165
HERRON, Denise, 82
HERRON, John F, 977
HERTEL, Anna-margrethe, 656
HERTENSTEIN, Pamela, 86
HERTZ, Donna, 828
HERVEY, J N, 184
HERZOG, Jennifer Anne, 616
HESS, Bonnie L, 108
HESS, Dena L, 1137
HESS, Diane, 78
HESTER, Gloria, 1086
HESTER, Joan, 112
HESTER, Lucille, 380
HESTER, Margie, 192
HETTICK, Elizabeth L (Lacy), 73
HETTICK, Tammy, 260
HETTINGER, Angela M, 599
HETZEL, Phauneil R K, 601
HEUER, Penelope, 710
HEWITT, Cleo, 922
HIOTT, Maria Angela, 1085
HIBBLER, Arlene J, 1059
HICKCOX, Shirley P, 103
HICKEY, Albert S, 119
HICKEY, E Glenn, 223
HICKEY, Ruth Ann Burrell, 23
HICKIN, G M, 682
HICKMAN, Rupert, 1192
HICKS Sr, William O, 745
HICKS, Barbarella A, 939
HICKS, Christine, 867
HICKS, Dolores G D, 924
HICKS, Edna B, 976
HICKS, Elizabeth L, 83
HICKS, Lorraine, 562
HICKS, Marvis L, 468
HICKS, Pati, 941
HICKS, Rustee L, 308
HICKS, Tracy Lynn, 657
HIGDON, Debbie, 948
HIGGINS, Blanche Eloise, 61
HIGGINS, Renate S, 1199
HIGGINS, Robert M J, 116
HIGGINSON, Robert, 401
HIGGS, Verle Nichols, 936
HIGH, Margaret H, 909
HIGHFILL, Melody Ann, 178
HIGHLAND, Mary Jo, 224
HIGHSMITH, Sheila, 367
HIGHTOWER, Beverly, 1077
HIGHTOWER, Mrs Lynn, 1202
HILBERGER, Sherry D, 394
HILBERS, Sara Susan, 201
HILDBOLD, Elsie T, 1013
HILDEBRAND, Christina, 806
HILDERBRAND, Barbara A, 1131
HILEMAN, Jo Ann, 1052
HILGEN, Ruth E, 76
HILKEVITCH, Rhea R, 161
HILL, Charles E, 520
HILL, Dave, 524
HILL, Edward C, 1021
HILL, Elana B, 760
HILL, Esther, 950
HILL, Geraldean M, 713
HILL, Glen R, 826
HILL, Howard, 1045
HILL, Jennifer Lynn, 1166
HILL, Joan E, 437
HILL, Jocelyn, 1041
HILL, Joseph, 182
HILL, Kristi Anne, 1192
HILL, Laura, 926
HILL, Mary E, 394
HILL, Mary Marie, 826
HILL, Melissa Ann, 1101
HILL, Mrs Eva V, 241
HILL, Patti L, 358
HILL, Queen E, 440
HILL, Yolanda D, 1152
HILL, Yusefa, 546
HILLARY, Jennifer, 291
HILLER, Laurie L, 597
HILLSDON-HUTTON, Valerie, 1126
HILSZ, Lori, 992
HILTY, Mary K, 1054
HIMMELSPACH, D C, 798
HINDMAN, Stephen, 321
HINES, Sharon C, 1002
HINKLE, Pat, 888
HINSON, Tommy, 83

HINTERLONG, Ellen, 950
HIRAE, Lorna, 175
HIROSHIGE, Laurie, 632
HIRSCH, Cassandra J, 472
HIRSCH, Debra, 1128
HIRSCH, Jeffrey C W, 443
HIRSCHON, Betty, 439
HIRST, Susan May, 488
HIRT, Jacque, 843
HISLIP, Jackie L, 349
HITCHCOCK, Marianne, 493
HITCHENS, Kimberly, 134
HITCHENS, Susan J, 862
HITE, Sally, 861
HITLER, Agnes B, 369
HITTLE, Walter, 797
HIXSON, Stacie, 910
HJORTH, Esther, 342
HLADICK, Jennifer, 979
HOAG, Jennifer Lynn, 327
HOAGLAND, Sarah, 1176
HOANG M, Chu, 971
HOARD, Ann, 485
HOATLAND, Irene, 696
HOBART, Jenness, 712
HOBBIE, Stephanie E, 846
HOBBS, Anne, 367
HOBBY, Dianne Lee, 275
HOBSON, Delores M, 344
HOCHSTEDLER, Shirley, 76
HOCK, Terry Felicia, 996
HOCKENBERRY, Gloria, 1001
HOCKENJOS, Martha L, 210, 1062
HOCKING, Elinor, 860
HODGE, Diann, 445
HODGE, Frankie, 389
HODGE, Leon, 1087
HODGE, Mamie, 805
HODGE, Olevia, 6
HODGES, Lyndall, 377
HODGES, Margaret I, 518
HODGINS, Beatrice D, 278
HODGSON, Michael, 1014
HODGSON, Ranay, 1168
HOEDEL, Berta, 581
HOEFT, Vada Beeman, 386
HOEGE, Richard L, 570
HOEGH, Poul E, 1069
HOEHN, Kay, 698
HOFF, Artress L, 875
HOFF, Carrie, 508
HOFF, Marie, 977
HOFF, Stephen, 887
HOFFA, Arthur R, 486
HOFFER, Kevin B, 784
HOFFERT, Mary, 817
HOFFMAN, Becci R, 924
HOFFMAN, Betty S, 557
HOFFMAN, Evelyn, 736
HOFFMAN, Heather, 893
HOFFMAN, J Bradley, 28
HOFFMAN, Jolyn, 647
HOFFMAN, Margo E, 756
HOFFMAN, Marilyn K, 817
HOFFMAN, S, 48
HOFMANN, Kathleen S, 54
HOGAN, Louis L, 759, 642
HOGAN, Melody, 109
HOGE, Beverly J, 1158
HOGG, W W, 681
HOGGATT, Terry Len, 522
HOGRELL, Jodi J, 539
HOHENBERRY, Nancy, 723
HOHN, Cordelia E, 1083
HOHN, Mary E, 787
HOLCOMB, Brenda, 598
HOLCOMB, Dean Carl, 42
HOLDEN, Catherine, 508
HOLDEN, Mary Virginia, 838
HOLDEN, Ray, 820
HOLDER, Marianne F, 492
HOLDERMAN, Raymond H, 575
HOLDRIDGE, H Paul, 42
HOLIDAY, Frank, 324
HOLLADAY, Larry D, 34
HOLLAND, Betty, 417
HOLLAND, Michelle, 266
HOLLAND, Sherri L, 143
HOLLANDER, Edith Spark, 877
HOLLEBRANDT, Traci, 763
HOLLEMAN, Gloria, 400
HOLLEN, Mary Jane, 288
HOLLENBECK, Sherry, 54
HOLLER, Bill, 950
HOLLERAN, Carolyn, 25
HOLLEY, Keith E, 834
HOLLIDAY, Jeffrey A, 570
HOLLIDAY, Patricia, 470
HOLLIER, M Elaine, 997
HOLLING, Robert J, 637
HOLLINGER, J A, 11
HOLLINGSWORTH, Mrs Dora Lee, 14
HOLLIS, Danny, 166
HOLLIS, Linda R, 532
HOLLIS, Texana C, 986
HOLLISTER, Camilla C, 756
HOLLOMAN, Randy Lynn, 549
HOLLOWAY, John A, 661
HOLLYFIELD, Bettie, 669
HOLM, Mary, 403
HOLMAN, Angel, 543
HOLMAN, Janet Louise, 627
HOLMAN, Mike, 171
HOLMES, John C, 765
HOLMES, Judy, 313
HOLMES, Robt P, 809
HOLMES, Shawn, 1147
HOLMES, William J, 365
HOLST, Henry Roger, 151
HOLT, Dale A, 542
HOLT, Gerald Dean, 766
HOLT, Lavone B, 66
HOLT, Michelle, 12
HOLT, Mrs Jessie, 136
HOLTZMAN, Jan S, 548
HOM, Carroll E, 423
HOMAN, Richard David, 645
HOMEIER, Joyce Fales, 622
HONEY, Sylvia G, 656
HONEYCUTT, Lonnie, 124
HONNEN III, George B, 850
HONS, Calline, 470
HOOGNER, Melanie, 737
HOOGSTAD, Jeanne B, 240
HOOK, G E R, 1115
HOOPS, Belva A, 650
HOOVER, Alan, 613
HOOVER, Clifford R, 595
HOOVER, Darcy L, 1160
HOOVER, Michael N, 165
HOOVER, Tonya Danyell, 223
HOPE, Jannie, 707
HOPE, Melody, 749
HOPF-PAGEL, Genevieve, 474
HOPKINS OSF, Marita, 424
HOPKINS, Alfred M, 611
HOPKINS, Hollis Hughes, 180
HOPKINS, Sara, 1025
HOPKINSON, Patricia, 401
HOPP, Margaret V, 339
HOPPA, Dennis J, 730
HOPSON, Larry E, 999
HORGAN, Regina, 624
HORITA, Renette J, 876
HORIUCHI, Toshimi, 347
HORN, Eleanor, 62
HORN, Judith C, 1028
HORN, Michael A, 991
HORNACEK, Timothy J, 210
HORNBECK, P J, 180
HORNE, Shirley, 910
HORNER, Loretta, 536
HORNICK, Yolanda Starr, 808
HOROWITZ, Katie, 540
HORROCKS, Alice L, 234
HORSLEY, Nina J, 1078
HORTON, Grace Barras, 410
HORTON, Londa Kay, 314
HORTON, Sulin, 849
HORTON, Tina, 1115
HORVATH, Sandra R, 399
HOSEY, Mrs Dorothy M, 1196
HOSKINS, Courtney A, 276
HOSKINS, Linda, 256
HOSKISON, Elaine, 576
HOSTETLER, James C, 1117
HOSTETLER, Mary, 976
HOSTLER, Deborah, 91
HOUCK, Tracy Ann, 1153
HOUGHTON, Patsy Dunagin, 552
HOUGLUM, Rebekah, 365
HOUK, Nicole, 1126
HOUSE, Mike, 415
HOUSE, Willie, 538
HOUSEHOLDER, Kathy, 902
HOUSER, Karen S, 823
HOUSER, Richard, 51
HOUSHOLDER, P Annie, 631
HOUSTON, Ann, 876
HOUSTON, Bernice, 62
HOUSTON, Jann, 978
HOUZE, Margery, 470
HOWARD Jr, Spencer E, 581
HOWARD, Andrea Sue, 490, 490
HOWARD, Carissa, 543
HOWARD, Emma Jean, 162
HOWARD, Faith C, 776
HOWARD, Jessica Dara, 531
HOWARD, Kathi, 250
HOWARD, Kristie, 747
HOWARD, Lucy Stancil, 1167
HOWARD, M Ruth, 374
HOWARD, Thomas A, 788
HOWARD, Tina, 758
HOWE, Amy Beth, 507
HOWE, Todd D, 211
HOWELL Jr, William W, 97
HOWELL, Brenda C, 1053
HOWELL, Cindie A, 1112
HOWELL, Karen V, 317
HOWELL, Renee C, 246
HOWELL, Roberta E, 289
HOWELL, Tara, 859
HOWELL, Wayne, 307
HOWERTON, Judy K, 709
HOWES Sr, Robert C, 11
HOWEY, Bill R, 887
HOWLETT, Bonnie, 1079
HOY, Margaret (Pieters), 981
HOYAL, Faye Judd, 708
HRAPSKY, Alan D, 360
HRCAN, Paulina, 220
HRITZ, Clifford, 48
HRNCIR, Melba Jean, 561
HRONEK, Betty, 26
HRUSKA, Elias, 146
HSIN, Lin Hsin, 591
HSU, Johnny, 398
HUBBARD, Joyce A, 716
HUBBARD, Nicole, 128
HUBBARD, Romaine A, 522
HUBBLE, Judy Kay, 272
HUBER, Betty, 322
HUBER, Heidi, 1123
HUBER, Wilhamine J, 995
HUBERTY, Violet Nast, 1070
HUBRICH, Patricia K, 663
HUDDLE, Harriett, 361
HUDGINS, Joel E, 643
HUDSON, Angela B, 324
HUDSON, Brandi Lynn, 382
HUDSON, Carolyn S, 392
HUDSON, Elizabeth E, 895
HUDSON, Reeves, 344
HUDSON, Sulinda, 1190
HUDSON, Tosha L, 1044
HUEPPCHEN, Gary S, 192
HUEY, Carol, 1188, 643
HUEY, June Vaughn, 314
HUFFMAN, Mary L, 410
HUFFSTUTTER, Imogene S, 165
HUGHES, Alice, 631
HUGHES, Alison K, 310
HUGHES, Anthony M, 729
HUGHES, Gloria, 218
HUGHES, James M, 1031
HUGHES, Jim B, 1053
HUGHES, Joan A, 377
HUGHES, Ken, 691
HUGHES, Sylvia G, 394
HUGO, Jan, 332
HULASIE, Shivcharran, 557
HULBERT, Jan, 51
HULETTE, Maudie, 1190
HULITT, Brian K, 298
HULL, Elaine C, 380
HULL, Wendell "X Legend", 382
HULLUM, Sid Tex, 962
HULSE, Elizabeth Lu, 881
HULSHIZER, Cynthia, 504
HULTEEN, Mae F, 359
HUMISTON, Alison, 925
HUMMELL, R Lee, 464
HUMPAL, Ann, 633
HUMPHERYS, Trina, 159
HUMPHREY, Lois, 309
HUMPHREYS, Bruce R, 229
HUMPHREYS, Michael, 823
HUMPHREYS, Sarah M, 781
HUMPHRIES, J D, 374
HUMPHRIES, Linda K, 175
HUNDLEY, Rubye L, 35
HUNDLEY, Sherrie A, 144
HUNGERFORD, Mary Jane, 465
HUNING, Gerry, 678
HUNNICUTT, Hugh G, 438
HUNSADER, Erin J, 298
HUNST, Peggy L, 760
HUNSUCKER, Betty, 246
HUNT, David Austin, 396
HUNT, Eloise, 322
HUNT, Kristin, 432
HUNT, Mona, 488
HUNT, Portia M, 660
HUNT, Rose L, 991
HUNT, Sherral, 811
HUNT, Timothy D, 497
HUNTER, Clare, 782
HUNTER, Clarice F, 29
HUNTER, Henry, 511
HUNTER, Jerry, 636
HUNTER, Jill Renee, 1005
HUNTER, John Lee, 19
HUNTER, Lenore D, 119
HUNTER, Mary L Brett, 1119
HUNTER, Sharon, 243
HUNTING, Willis B, 945
HUNTINGTON, Gloria M, 685
HUNTSBERGER, Evelyn Hill, 1101
HUNWARDSEN, Bonnie, 585
HUNZIKER, Debbie, 944
HUPKA, Rhonda M, 143
HURL, Susan, 873
HURLEY, Carol L, 119
HURLEY, Laura, 821
HURLEY, Lisa, 910
HURST, Ida Olivia, 653
HURST, Ivan W, 91
HUSAR, Krista, 453
HUTCHINS, Robert, 562
HUTCHINSON, Cynthia, 570
HUTCHINSON, Jeff, 688
HUTCHINSON, Verna, 175
HUTCHISON, Carol Follis, 732
HUTSON, George H, 818
HUTSON, Joanne (Hibbert), 47
HUTTO, Virginia K, 587
HUTTON Sr, Essex C, 164
HUTTON, Darrin Lee, 547
HUTTS, Marlo, 1058
HUYCK, Kay, 1083
HUYTEN, Lorraine V, 476
HYATT, Kellie, 980
HYATT, Ruby, 248
HYDE, Barbara Lynn, 387
HYDE, Heather E, 1074
HYDE, Sally A, 627
HYDER, Clyde K, 250
HYMES, Kelley L, 583
HYNES, Carol AC, 914
HINTZ, Holly L, 1045

I

I C L, Irene, 602
IACUZIO, Candida, 871, 1003
IANNIELLO, Danielle, 679
IANNUCCILLI, Lynda, 448
IBRAHIM, Josetta, 888
IGLESIAS, Jose E, 454
IGLESIAS, Joseph, 461
IH, Young H, 131
ILASI, Barbara A, 1125
ILIJEVICH Jr, Fred N, 538
ILLK, Paul J, 1110
IMBRAGUGLIO, Elinor E I, 1126
IMES, Theresa G, 981
IMPERIAL, Joseph John, 868
IMWOLD, Dotti, 891
INABA, Ayumi, 45
INDIA, Matthew P, 1101
INGALLINERA, Lavaune, 1199
INGRAM, Carolyn, 632
INGRAM, Kimmonique, 81
INIGUEZ, Emarie, 1161
INMAN, Mary, 1019
INNES, Georgette M, 165
INSADOWSKI, Christine A, 388
INSALACO, Lori, 700
INSKO, Donna, 311
INTERNATIONAL, Shawn, 772
INWOOD, Alma A, 999
IOCOLANO, Susan, 94
IONG, Alison, 875
IORIO, Joseph Scott, 115
IPPOLITO, Becky L, 936
IPPOLITO, Christopher H, 195
IPPOLITO, Cynthia, 26
IRBY, Teresa A, 597
IRELAND, Allen Lee, 684
IRION, Karyl, 58
IRIZARRY, Maria, 524
IRVIN, Jean Ann, 850
IRVINE, Debbie, 318
IRWIN, Gabrielle M, 1095
IRWIN, Misty, 663
IRWIN, Patricia R, 635
ISAAC Jr, Gradie, 500
ISBELL, Mrs Robert, 233
ISENBERG, Caryn R, 230
ISENHOUR, Frank Y, 321
ISRAEL, Doris, 909
ISSERSOHN, Anne, 1075
ISSLER, Evelyn, 387
IVEY Jr, Ralph R, 371
IVORY, Jewelene, 329

J

JABLONSKI, Robert James, 505
JACELONE, Frances I, 1081
JACK, Durran Wynn, 1127
JACKSON III, Matthew E, 768
JACKSON, Ada Mae, 836
JACKSON, Adrian M, 1175
JACKSON, Alex B, 808
JACKSON, Angela, 744
JACKSON, Benny L, 626
JACKSON, Brandi, 179
JACKSON, Brenda D, 782
JACKSON, Brian Mceuen, 343
JACKSON, Cynthia, 365
JACKSON, Darlene, 1139
JACKSON, Darryl Leon, 266
JACKSON, James L, 270
JACKSON, Jocelyn R, 306
JACKSON, Leonard M, 756
JACKSON, Lettie B, 1172
JACKSON, Linda, 613
JACKSON, Patricia J, 252
JACKSON, Ralph J, 872
JACKSON, Rodger Lee, 157
JACKSON, Shannon M, 751
JACKSON, T, 511
JACKSON, Tennessee, 1069
JACKSON, Wendy L, 553
JACOBE, Benjamin D, 396
JACOBS, Bertha Lee, 359
JACOBS, Mae G, 798
JACOBS, Melissa A, 938
JACOBS, Rebecca A, 107
JACOBS, Sherrie, 479
JACOBS, Sulayne A, 892
JACOBS, Timothy M, 85
JACOBSON, Angela, 162
JACOBSON, Billy, 258
JACOBSON, Mavis, 282
JACOBSON, Penelope J, 1009
JACOBSON, Susan B, 229
JADE, Betty, 626
JAEGER, Glenna, 497
JAEGER, Windy Lee, 196
JAEHRLING, Tony, 692
JAFFE, Sandra, 901
JAGGER, Marchetta, 973
JAGIELSKI, Ann Marie, 935
JAGUSH, Jon Marc, 752
JAKIMOWICH, Shirley A, 774
JAKUBIAK, Edward J, 859
JAKUBOWSKI, Robert, 1187
JALOTA, Raman, 252
JAMES, Catherine, 322
JAMES, Janice, 711
JAMES, Jo Anne, 923
JAMES, Lorenza, 1160
JAMES, Lori Marie, 99
JAMES, Ronald H, 465
JAMES, Russell, 640
JAMES, Susan Ashe, 545
JAMES, Tamara M, 930
JAMES, Tonya L, 38
JAMESON, Daneen Dustin, 800
JAMESON, Leslie, 108
JAMESON, Wendy, 336
JAN, Michael J, 768, 296
JANDIK, Kathryn Kay, 103
JANGEL, Patricia A, 998
JANIE, Ms, 105
JANIS, Florence C, 726
JANKOWSKI, Michael, 1027
JANKOWY, Agnes R, 561
JANNEY, C Dale, 433
JANSEN, Willa, 5
JANSSEN, Amy, 903
JANSSON, Dorothy, 272
JANZEN, Leanne, 268
JAPP, Phoebe R, 445
JARAMILLO, Ernie, 696
JARDIN, Mary E, 923
JARDINE, Ronda C, 1180
JARMON, Katherine, 418
JAROSSY, Kathy, 225
JAROSZEWICZ, Linda, 749
JARRARD, Tammy, 805
JARRATT, Mildred, 39
JARRELL, Eloise, 706
JARRETT, Danielle Meghan, 913
JARSKI, Pamela Runyon, 93
JARVIS, Ann E, 996
JARVIS, Betty J, 1005
JARVIS, Dorothy R, 129
JARVIS, Kathy, 549
JARVIS, Michelle, 847
JARVIS, Ruth, 270

JASON, Rose M, 627
JASPER, Jody Lee, 396
JASPERT, W P, 899
JASSIN, Laura May, 850
JAVINE, Rev Abb I, 1177
JAY, John J, 1194
JEAN, Heather, 661
JEANES, H K, 1147
JEANNETT, Ann, 982
JEANNIE, Jeannie, 1006
JEDNAT, Courtney M, 191
JEFFERS, C S, 372
JEFFERS, Georgia M, 969
JEFFERSON, Benny J, 91
JEFFERSON, Vickie, 953
JEFFORDS, Elizabeth G, 731
JEFFREY, C J, 754
JELINEK, Gretchen, 599
JENKINS, Alfred, 387
JENKINS, Barbara J H, 762
JENKINS, Denise Ellen, 977
JENKINS, Dianne, 183
JENKINS, Mrs Sharon L, 1027
JENKINS, Noreen Ann, 558
JENKINS, Pearl G, 83
JENKINS, Raymond, 283
JENKINS, Samantha Ann, 1037
JENKINS, Susan, 312
JENKINS, Tom "The Tramp", 613
JENKINS, Valirie D, 397
JENKINS, Yvonne M, 224
JENKINSON, Grace, 905
JENNINGS, Cheryl S, 313
JENNINGS, James C, 346
JENNINGS, Mary E, 232
JENNINGS, Russell W, 821
JENNINGS, Stephanie Ann, 1127
JENSEN, Amy, 607
JENSEN, Caroline, 572
JENSEN, Connie, 559
JENSEN, Deborah L, 911
JENSEN, Donna J, 350
JENSEN, Terie, 851
JEPPSON, Ethel F, 1058
JEREMY, Trisa, 1028
JEROME, Mildred Capps, 532
JEROME, Yvonne, 643
JERUE, Linda, 788
JESKA, Kimberly N, 354
JESSIE, Ann D, 958
JESSIE, Emmalena H, 827
JESSUP, Gerald, 734
JESTER, Jimmie Joe, 148
JETER, Diane Day, 210
JETTE, Carl, 104
JEWELL, Anna Grace, 750
JEWELL, Jimka, 344
JEWELL, Maxine, 624
JEWETT, Jeff Jay, 269
JEX, Gabriele, 256
JILL, Susan, 282
JILLARD, Teresa C, 9
JINKS, James E, 995
JINKS, Thelma, 995
JIRAK, Blanka, 1199
JOBLON, Edna, 361
JODICE, Jerry E, 174
JOECKEL, Carole J, 392
JOHANNES, Walter C, 904
JOHANNSEN, Gloria, 24
JOHANSEN, Naomi, 137
JOHN, Mertis, 570
JOHNOPOLOS, Stephen G, 441
JOHNS, Adrienne M, 666
JOHNS, Vernald Wm, 420
JOHNS, Vernetta, 112
JOHNSON II, Lucas L, 1193
JOHNSON Jr, Jesse, 1106
JOHNSON Sr, Lester A, 985
JOHNSON, Alice, 101
JOHNSON, Amy Dawn, 650
JOHNSON, Angela E, 715
JOHNSON, Ann A, 558
JOHNSON, Anthony Clark, 107
JOHNSON, Barbara M, 981
JOHNSON, Betty J, 426
JOHNSON, Blossom R, 55
JOHNSON, Bob K, 1120
JOHNSON, Bridget M, 374
JOHNSON, Carol, 348
JOHNSON, Carolyn E, 884
JOHNSON, Cecelia D, 896
JOHNSON, Charles H, 66
JOHNSON, Chris, 48
JOHNSON, Darrell, 234
JOHNSON, Deborah, 618
JOHNSON, Dena M, 155
JOHNSON, Diane, 979
JOHNSON, Diane, 689
JOHNSON, Dorothy Mae, 623
JOHNSON, Edward L, 993
JOHNSON, Eleanor V, 259
JOHNSON, Errol D, 656
JOHNSON, Esther R, 649
JOHNSON, Faye, 987
JOHNSON, Frederic L, 488
JOHNSON, Gloria L, 131
JOHNSON, Henrietta L, 929
JOHNSON, Jackie, 285
JOHNSON, Jan, 908
JOHNSON, Jeffery, 602
JOHNSON, Jenine, 855
JOHNSON, Joyce, 306
JOHNSON, Julie Ann, 205
JOHNSON, June Alexis, 373
JOHNSON, June Floyd, 1145
JOHNSON, Karen F, 8
JOHNSON, Kathleen M, 1068
JOHNSON, Kathryn W, 465
JOHNSON, L D, 430
JOHNSON, Lana Jean, 317
JOHNSON, Laura M, 809
JOHNSON, Lee, 794
JOHNSON, Leigh Anne, 895
JOHNSON, Lisa, 1057
JOHNSON, Lisa Elaine, 568
JOHNSON, Lori, 196
JOHNSON, Lori, 836
JOHNSON, Lorraine A, 199
JOHNSON, Lucia, 37
JOHNSON, Lyn, 113
JOHNSON, Mable, 1123
JOHNSON, Marie, 692
JOHNSON, Marilyn P, 223
JOHNSON, Maureen E, 391
JOHNSON, Melinda T, 812
JOHNSON, Michelle A, 732
JOHNSON, Michelle S, 655
JOHNSON, Mrs F W, 165
JOHNSON, Nancy J, 140
JOHNSON, Nicole M, 338
JOHNSON, Nina M, 188
JOHNSON, Norman L, 411
JOHNSON, Patricia L, 835
JOHNSON, Paul, 350
JOHNSON, Paula, 801
JOHNSON, Pegi, 563
JOHNSON, Peter F, 890
JOHNSON, Phil, 438
JOHNSON, Philip B, 609
JOHNSON, Richard Alton, 420
JOHNSON, Rita, 753
JOHNSON, Ruth E, 771
JOHNSON, S L, 21
JOHNSON, Shandra, 535
JOHNSON, Sheila Grace, 287
JOHNSON, Stacy L, 880
JOHNSON, Sylvia, 63
JOHNSON, Tanika T, 1160
JOHNSON, Terry, 207
JOHNSON, Terry, 731
JOHNSON, Tina A, 1102
JOHNSON, Virgil W, 385
JOHNSON-CARNEY, Jeannette, 274
JOHNSON-TENNIS, Myrtle Mae, 826
JOHNSON-WOOTEN, Shirley Diane, 726
JOHNSTON, Alberta L, 623
JOHNSTON, Diana Lane, 73
JOHNSTON, Heather, 1130
JOHNSTON, Juliann, 936
JOHNSTON, Laura, 485
JOHNSTON, Michelle, 1037
JOHNSTON, Ray P, 235
JOHNSTON, Valerie K, 226
JOHNSTONE, Lisa D, 778
JOICE, Wendy Marie, 63
JOINER, Gerald D, 846
JOINER, Holly, 192
JOINER, Michael, 328
JOIVELL, Virginia N, 341
JOLLY, Ronald T, 1062
JON, John E, 423
JONES II, Donald E, 15
JONES II, Robert L, 674
JONES III, Ulysses, 613
JONES IV, Rives R, 1177
JONES Jr, Mrs J W, 1171
JONES Jr, Robert L, 806
JONES Sr, Terrell, 460
JONES, Alyce Russell, 654
JONES, Anita Duran, 820
JONES, Anne, 589
JONES, Annie G, 941
JONES, Azizi, 431
JONES, Barbara K, 370
JONES, Benedict L, 289
JONES, Bobbie, 596
JONES, Carol, 673
JONES, Charlene D, 242
JONES, Charles, 83
JONES, Charles S, 880
JONES, Christopher, 1176
JONES, Christy L, 34
JONES, Clark L, 299
JONES, Connie Sue, 591
JONES, Cora R, 602
JONES, Cynthia Jean, 866
JONES, Deborah A, 966
JONES, Donna Lee, 782
JONES, Dorothy J, 1177
JONES, Elizabeth Gooden, 1007
JONES, Ginger, 559
JONES, Helen A, 266
JONES, Ila B, 222
JONES, Iris L, 5
JONES, J Nicholas, 659
JONES, Jacquelyn H, 616
JONES, Janelle, 829
JONES, Janice Elaine, 659
JONES, Jeanette J, 399
JONES, Jennifer Lynn, 735
JONES, Joan M, 762
JONES, John P, 889
JONES, Jonathan, 670
JONES, Judith, 1028
JONES, Karma Lee, 729
JONES, Katie Kelley "Kay", 787
JONES, Katy, 523
JONES, Ken, 436
JONES, Kimberly D, 689
JONES, Kimberly J, 781
JONES, Linda D, 1164
JONES, Linda M, 392
JONES, Marguerite G, 1015
JONES, Martha A, 509
JONES, Mary M, 1190
JONES, Ora Lee Hunter, 1032
JONES, Otis, 538
JONES, Pearline J, 660
JONES, Phyllis Jean, 389
JONES, Pierre B, 928
JONES, Randy Dock, 318
JONES, Robert C, 622
JONES, Ronald P, 389
JONES, Samantha, 248
JONES, Shawnta, 293
JONES, Sheila V, 662
JONES, Sian, 779
JONES, Solomon, 254
JONES, Terrence G, 149
JONES, Tom, 493
JONES, William Martin, 473
JORDAN Jr, William R, 127
JORDAN, Carol Barrett, 982
JORDAN, Elma A, 319
JORDAN, Frederick V, 198
JORDAN, Jonathan E, 566
JORDAN, Mark, 958
JORDAN, Rodenick, 259
JORDAN, Shena L, 436
JORDAN, Tonya, 1185
JORGENSEN, Dwayne, 986
JORGENSON, Karan K, 773
JORGENSON, Myrtle H, 131
JORGENSON, Teresa, 201
JOSEPH, Bapthol, 412
JOSEPH, Fitzroy Tex, 1068
JOSEPH, Jo Ann, 544
JOSEPH, Stacy, 802
JOSEPH, Ward, 440
JOSINE, Josephine A, 168
JOSWICK, Stephanie, 50
JOURNEY, Terry Ann, 278
JOY, Margaret M, 179
JOY, Steve B, 118
JOYCE, Lafredia, 536
JOYNER, Madeline E, 541
JOYNER, Marlene Candler, 45
JOYNER, Stencil, 604
JUAN, Elpidio M, 1148
JUAREZ, Marcus, 794
JUBAIRA, Ibrahim A, 436
JUDD, David K, 916
JUDD, Dorothy, 510
JUDGE, Alice, 445
JUDGE, Kevin E, 158
JUENEMANN, Rick J, 1073
JUNE, Cheryl, 845
JUNEK, Michael, 1018
JUNIOR, Dennis, 1176
JURICH, George, 481
JUSSILA, Norma J, 767
JUST, T Jonathan, 759

K

KABANUK, Patricia, 303
KACKMAN, Patricia, 146
KAESS, Donna Lynn, 133
KAGAN-WILBUR, Caroljean, 819
KAHAN, Selma C, 592
KAHL, Aaron A, 513
KAHLER, Helen S, 178
KAHRHOFF, Gertrude, 209
KAISER, Elsie, 1187
KAISER, Ethel Louise, 205
KAISER, Howard L, 323
KAKU, Carissa, 380
KAKU, Christina, 345
KALAR, Fern L, 948
KALE, Verna, 462
KALINSKI, Daniel B, 197
KALKHOFF, Kelly Oliver, 899
KALKSTEIN, Stefanie Rose, 250
KALLEN, Kaara, 402
KALLIAN, Trina, 750
KALLIMANIS, Maura, 254
KALLMANN, Agatha, 549
KALLMEYER, Juanita, 261
KALOGEROPOULOS, George C, 315
KAMENEL, Monica, 215
KAMINER, Al, 837
KAMINER, Nyna R, 863
KAMINSKI, Alisa, 570
KAMINSKI, April, 1138
KAMINSKI, Jill, 815
KAMRAN, Zahid, 363
KANANOWITZ, Anna G, 863
KANE, David M, 1120
KANE, Kathleen L, 613
KANE, Pall J, 301
KANE, Robert, 899
KANE, Robert W, 557
KANE, Tami, 121
KANG, Bun King, 1049
KANNA, Svea, 461
KANT, Iva, 1020
KANTOLA, Agnes Johnson, 1086
KANTOR, Anatole, 135
KAPLAN, Patricia Ann (Rando), 913
KAPLAN, Sherri N, 263
KAPLAN, Steven, 442
KAPLAN, Tillie Lewis, 498
KARAM, James T, 1149
KARAS, Sandi, 1165
KARAS, Steven, 86
KARASSEFERIAN, Lee, 577
KARG, Joanne Mct, 699
KARLIK, Rosemary, 774
KARMIK, Elvira, 291
KARN, Miss Emily, 959
KARNS, Nikki, 14
KARRES, Marilyn, 1143
KASEY, C L, 1112
KASIAN, Dorothy, 568
KASO, Philip W, 489
KASPRZAK, Susan, 779
KASTENS-TOBIN, Lisa Marie, 413
KATAI, Marlene, 186
KATHER, Scott David, 561
KATRANIS, Evangeline, 641
KATZ, Amy K T, 535
KATZ, Benjamin, 679
KATZ, Hazel Hoff, 387
KATZ, M, 134
KATZ, Tara, 1057
KAUFFMAN, Jody, 532
KAUFFMAN, Maureen T, 96
KAUFMAN, Amber, 950
KAUPPINEN, Seppo, 1118
KAUS, Gary, 378
KAUTZMAN, Denise M, 814
KAVANAUGH, Diane T, 569
KAY, Dory, 873
KAY, Lisa L, 201
KAZAMIAS, Thomas M, 952
KEARLEY, Dixie, 1041
KEARNEY, Rethea W, 703
KEARNS, Margaret C, 1021, 1146
KEAS, Mrs Harley, 54
KEATHLEY, Barbara, 794
KEATING, M Ada, 149
KEATON, Michael N, 1031
KEAVENEY, Kathleen M, 624
KEBODEAUX Jr, Alfred, 1171
KEEFE, Docie, 1043
KEEFE, Susan, 647
KEEGAN, Helen, 747
KEELS, Maryanne, 490
KEEN, Antoinette, 110
KEENE, Geneva, 850
KEENER, Margie C, 885
KEETON, Izora, 948
KEGLEWITSCH, Vivian, 1170
KEHRER, Hazel, 40
KEILHOLTZ, Esther, 136
KEITEL (CARTER), Patricia, 99
KEITH, Cristyl L, 344
KELALIS, Barbara, 82
KELLER, Alexandria, 1068
KELLER, Almyra, 113
KELLER, Edwin, 797
KELLER, Franz, 752
KELLER, Gladys V, 236
KELLER, Nellie, 199
KELLER, Samantha, 239
KELLER, Susan L, 781
KELLER, Teresa D, 714
KELLERMAN, Karen, 1005
KELLETT, Veda, 438
KELLEY (CAD), Constance, 570
KELLEY Jr, Howard V, 80
KELLEY, Elizabeth G, 983
KELLEY, Jerolene "Jerrye", 967
KELLEY, Joanne Lawrence, 830
KELLEY, Marvierene L, 100
KELLEY, Michelle, 587
KELLEY, R Jean, 596
KELLEY, Vickie L, 850
KELLOGG, Dennis L, 58
KELLOGG-KEESLING, Elizabeth, 657
KELLY, Brenda, 430
KELLY, Cassandra, 744
KELLY, Dale P, 1160
KELLY, Dr John J, 551
KELLY, Elizabeth Y, 198
KELLY, Gerald James, 129
KELLY, Jason Alan, 123
KELLY, John E, 537
KELLY, Kathleen P, 665
KELLY, Kevin L, 980
KELLY, Lawrence F, 1159
KELLY, Leo James, 322
KELLY, Margaret R, 667
KELLY, Mary, 625
KELLY, Mary E, 883
KELLY, Pamela Clark, 480
KELLY, Pamela J, 261
KELLY, Patricia J, 160
KELLY, Victoria, 1012
KELLY-STARCHILD, Kenny, 778
KELM, Linda, 184
KELSAY, Lois Elaine, 922
KELSEY, Addie L, 342
KELTZ, Clara H, 496
KEMP, Dwight L, 773
KEMPER BALDERSON, Alberta, 607
KEMPPA, Alice, 1055
KEMPTON, Ron, 331
KEMSKI, Elizabeth, 316
KENAS, Anna, 933
KENDALL, Jean, 1167
KENDALL, Shelly, 568
KENDRICK, Judy, 23
KENEDY, Carolyn J, 286
KENEHAN, Margaret M, 1105
KENNADY, Tammy, 426
KENNEBREW, Rena, 422
KENNEDY Sr, John R, 786
KENNEDY, Arthur F, 405
KENNEDY, Beverly, 533
KENNEDY, Carolyn E, 801
KENNEDY, David Lee, 70
KENNEDY, Isaac Jay, 910
KENNEDY, James Arthur, 189
KENNEDY, Jeanne Marie, 149
KENNEDY, Ken, 621
KENNEDY, Laura, 753
KENNEDY, Mary, 548
KENNEDY, Rosemarie, 1130
KENNEDY-SEARLE, Martha, 468
KENNER, Charles, 628
KENNER, Willie M, 286
KENNISON, Eudora "Tree", 272
KENNON, Martha, 907
KENRICK, Kelly, 182
KENSEL, Mary G, 250, 1192
KENT, Ann, 1024
KENT, Isabel, 835
KENT, Janice T, 92
KENT, Landis L, 370
KENT, Mimi, 105
KENT, Mr Malcolm, 667
KENWORTHY, Asa L, 653
KENYON, Jonathan M, 346
KEPALAS, Elena, 585
KEPPLER, David J, 390
KERLEY, Carol J, 19
KERN, Adam T, 844
KERN, Amry L, 145
KERN, Joseph G, 48
KERN, Mary M, 205

Sheri Raquel, 903
KERNER, Anne C, 612
KERNER, Jon S, 163
KERNS, Bessie, 264
KERNS, Glenda Diann, 56
KERR, Kevin, 790
KERR, Kleon, 173
KERR, Sharon, 431
KERSJES, Carmel J, 51
KERTELS, Rita H, 563
KERTON, Les, 174
KERZMANN, Grace E, 372
KESLER, Jamie, 638
KESLER, John P, 338
KESSLER, Amalia D, 112
KESSLER, Joan, 623
KETCHAM, Bob, 441
KETCHAM, William, 887
KETCHERSIDE, Trish, 69
KETTL, Gaye, 728
KETTNER, Margaret, 406
KEUS, Erwin, 779
KEY, Carole, 687
KEY, Mary J, 1001
KEYES, John, 494
KEYSER, Renee L, 1076
KEYSSER, Orval, 259
KHAALIQ, Saleem A, 671
KHALID, Mrs Claire, 611
KHAN, Gloria, 778
KHAN, Shahed U M, 260
KHAN, Shajia, 1137
KIBBEE, Terrie V, 856
KIDD, Donna L, 870
KIDD, Elizabeth A, 757
KIDD, Kenneth Lee, 282
KIDD, Robin L, 13
KIDD-RUFF, Beth Ann, 572
KIDDE, Katherine, 84
KIDDER, Imogene Wells, 579
KIEFEL, Karla, 404
KIEFREIDER, Chuck, 776
KIEHL, Tracy L, 289
KIEL, Judy A, 1006
KIELBIK, Sylvia, 879
KIELLEY, Jennifer, 191
KIENHOLZ, Ella Eaton, 235
KIESLING, Carla J, 753
KIFER, Shawnna, 1065
KILCHENSTEIN OSF, Sr Lorelda, 1153
KILDAY, Edith F, 9
KILGORE, Karen L, 363
KILLEEN, Karen W, 778
KILLIEBREW, Barrietta, 36
KILLIN, Mamie Lou, 670
KILLINGER, Merle T, 922
KILLION, Paula L, 704
KILLION, Sally Heeney, 302
KILLMER, Margaret, 28
KILLMON, Mary M, 563
KILROY, Rozella K, 205
KIM, Jong K, 444
KIMBER, Vickie J, 773
KIMBERLYNN, Ann, 468
KIMITHI EL, Mr Dedan, 219
KIMMEL, Annette J, 656
KIMMEY, William G, 730
KINCAID, Midge, 19
KINDRED Sr, Howard R, 1002
KINDSCHI, Gina, 255
KING Jr, Kenneth, 729
KING, B Frederick, 1118
KING, Cheryl L, 7
KING, Eula R, 1031
KING, Jennie, 100
KING, Jeri, 18
KING, Joanne, 514
KING, Lisa, 168
KING, Mattie B, 256
KING, Michael, 373
KING, Nadine, 660
KING, Neva Lou, 1155
KING, Patricia S, 1132
KING, Robert E, 821
KING, Sherri, 97
KING, Stephanie, 1005
KING, Tammy M, 1012
KING, Trevor L, 87
KINGREY, Virginia, 721
KINGSBURY, Kelli, 1128
KINGSTON, Erin Marie, 288
KINION, Kristy, 508
KINNAMAN, Roger E, 901
KINNEY, Ann Marie, 497
KINNEY, Dawn Delynn, 56
KINNEY, Della Mae, 984
KINNEY, John, 795
KINNEY, Linda S, 783
KINNEY, Susan, 736
KINNEY, Tara Lynn, 497
KINOSHITA, Mr Masao, 1051
KINSER, J Guy, 67
KINSER, Michael R, 588
KINSES, Karen, 702
KINSEY, Flora, 559
KINTER, Alice, 780
KINTOP, Evelyn, 742
KINZER, Terry Lee, 1070, 1070
KINZIE, Mary E, 406
KIRBY, Mary Paxton, 97
KIRK, Sarah Kirk, 631
KIRK, Ginnie, 257
KIRK, Leonard D, 168
KIRK, Warren Lee, 54
KIRKENDOLL, Dawn M, 574
KIRKLAND, Thia P, 125
KIRKMAN, Diana J, 784
KIRKMAN, Iva May, 114
KIRKPATRICK, Anna Lee, 567
KIRKPATRICK, Joyce, 828
KIRKPATRICK, Kerry V, 199
KIRMSE, Michelle, 217
KIRSCH, Al, 1032
KIRSCH, Marie, 1092
KIRTLEY, Martin, 710
KISER, Nagiko Sato, 813
KISH, Ed Y, 990
KISH, Lori A, 243
KISNER, Julie Diane, 1189
KISSEE, Linda K, 194
KITCHIN, Sean, 316
KITSIOS, Nicholas G, 216
KITTLE, Jerry D, 418
KITTRELL, Margaret, 7
KIVITS, Rosemarie, 733
KIZZIAH, Jo Ann, 107
KLAERS, Lu, 14
KLECKLEY, Edgar H, 877
KLEEMAN, Sophie, 1144
KLEIN, Charlene, 1202
KLEIN, Gretchen M, 24
KLEIN, Hannah E, 650
KLEINSMITH, Julie A, 476
KLEIS, Edna, 926
KLEMP, Colleen S, 807
KLEPPER, Judy E, 178
KLEYN, G Jhon, 36
KLIM, Alice (Maroonie), 635
KLIMKOWSKI, Barbara, 544
KLINE, Alice Hiykel, 1110
KLINE, Charles, 170
KLINE, George, 169
KLINE, Kimberley Joy, 280
KLINEDINST, Harriett Janus, 1145
KLINGER, Charles E, 609
KLINGER, Edward E, 870
KLINGER, Jody M, 443
KLINGNER, Karen Paige, 764
KLOCK, Martha R, 606
KLOPCHIN, Mary C, 1023
KLOTZBACH, Melody, 594
KLUG, Mary C, 399
KLUSSMANN, Helen, 627
KMIEC, Lynette M, 233
KNAPP, Evelyn, 292
KNAPP-LAWSON, Michelle, 538
KNECHT, Dennis L, 887
KNECHT, Jeanie, 742
KNECHT, Jeffrey D, 668
KNERR, Dorothy, 317
KNIGHT, Ann Marie, 552
KNIGHT, Kimberly A, 278
KNIGHT, Mary E, 965
KNIGHT, Pat J, 882
KNIGHT, Virginia C, 747
KNIPE, Julie C, 338
KNOFF, Eleonore, 125
KNOLL, Dianne, 249
KNOLL, Ingrid C, 529
KNOPP, Carol E, 706
KNOPP, Mary Ellen, 1170
KNOWLDEN, Margaret W, 632
KNOWLES, Marion, 788
KNOWLES, Patricia, 563
KNOWLES, Patrick, 1003
KNOWLES, Sandra, 57
KNUTILA, Erik, 301
KNUTT, Michele K, 435
KOBLENTZ, Bunni, 1192
KOBRA, Tami, 764
KOCH, Dolores Harple, 1033
KOCH, Kristin M, 666
KOCH, Teresa R, 1130
KOCHMAN, Cassandra, 530
KOCISCIN, Peggy, 248
KOCK, May, 300
KOCOL, Romuald, 537
KOCUREK, Theresa, 271
KODYS, Andrea, 633
KOEHLER, Heather, 848
KOEHLER, Jessica, 315
KOEHNE, Christine, 69
KOENIGS, Thomas (Taj), 456
KOEPPER, Ellie, 42
KOESTER, Becky, 343
KOESTER, Gene, 1145
KOESTLER, Jason, 148
KOETZLE, Jimmie Lee, 439
KOFOED, Dorothy, 930
KOHAN, Judith M, 307
KOHEN, Helene Lenga, 427, 269, 1085
KOHLMETZ, Pauline, 641, 1062
KOKONES, Michelle, 208
KOLAR Jr, George A, 281
KOLE, Imogene, 1080
KOLERSKI, Cyndee L, 269
KOLLAR, Wanda, 521
KOLLMAN, Nikki, 198
KOLPIEN, Lori, 543
KOLZ, Harvey E, 846
KOMAREK, Jerry W, 1165, 1171
KOMMER, Michele L, 863
KONDREWYCH, Mrs Anna Margaret, 210
KONKUS, Verna Mae, 887
KONN, Terry M, 357
KOON, Kellie D, 1196
KOONS, Melissa A, 170
KOOP, Pamela D, 892
KOPACK, Mike, 533
KOPECKI, Todd, 1060
KOPF, Victoria, 149
KOPPLIN, Jean E, 931
KOPPMAN, Mae, 891
KORENGEL, Edwin N, 1016
KORIYAMA, Naoshi, 157
KORMAN, Marie C, 311
KORNAHRENS, Karen S, 303
KORNHISER, Laurel, 407
KORNSTEIN, Mrs Rose, 1009
KORTE, Barbara J, 949
KORTY, Margaret B, 83
KOSCHMIDER, Christina, 509
KOSHKIN, Deanna, 164
KOSILEK, Robert J, 176
KOSKI, Patricia, 678
KOSKO, Michele A, 503
KOST, Sheila, 668
KOSTADINKA, Connie, 326
KOSTEK, Kathy, 975
KOSTELECKY, Sheila Ann, 911
KOSTER, Della Frances, 318
KOSTIC, T A, 352
KOSTOCK-FORRER, Debe, 825
KOTASKA, Marlynn Marie, 735
KOTLUS, Jordana, 823
KOTULA, Emeline Ennis, 694
KOUROS, Kryiacos P, 1071
KOVAR, Verna L, 230
KOWALSKI, Anita, 781
KOWALSKI, Dorothy J, 1180
KOWALSKI, Shelly Lee, 161
KOWERT, Frieda, 325
KOYA, Yemisi, 480
KOZAK, Regina V, 773
KOZICHEK, Marjorie, 1136
KOZIER, Maureen E, 690
KRACHT, Mona, 590
KRAFT, Earle A, 197
KRAFT, Pamela, 1194
KRAKOWER, Jane, 153
KRALL, A G, 492
KRAMER, Debby, 148
KRAMER, Judith Kay, 933
KRASNOVSKY, Anna, 452
KRATT, Eileen C, 861
KRAUS, Janet Cooper, 396
KRAUSE, Lori, 1136
KRAUSE, Margaret E, 52
KRAUSER, Paula S, 219
KRAUSS-BURLESON, Suzanne, 625
KRAUSSE, N Lee, 319
KREBS, John C, 297
KREGER, Clover, 1120
KREIS, Margo, 984
KREISER, Stephanie, 264
KREKLEWICH, Uriel R A, 1000
KRELL, Tiffany, 908
KRENCH, Linda, 546
KRENKE, Pamela L, 760
KRENTZEL, Catherine E D, 451
KRETSCH, Tammy, 695
KRETSCHMER, Lillian E, 120
KREUTZER, Nancy A, 139
KRICK, James F, 845
KRIEGER, Rosemary G, 6
KRIELAART, Rita, 788
KRIENKE, Garrick G, 1086
KRINGDON, Sylvia, 375
KRIPALANI, Lakshmi A, 489
KRISE, Loretta M, 464
KRIZ, Kelly, 771
KROG, Christina, 190
KROLL, Dieter, 757
KROMASH, Stephanie, 384
KRONE, Debra, 1077
KRONER, Lucille M, 951
KRONSCHNABEL, Cyril, 1065
KROOK, James M, 126
KROONDYK, Wes, 508
KROP, Jonathan, 126
KROUSEY, Ken, 34
KRUEBBE, Amy, 956
KRUG, Timothy C, 197
KRUG, Vicki A, 297
KRUKIN, Esta, 479
KRUSE, Bud, 587
KRUSE, Frederick W, 434
KRUSZYNSKI, Tim, 743
KRYMIS, Dolores, 1014
KUBASHACK, Genevieve B, 992
KUBIDA, William G, 701
KUBLER, Marlese, 1191
KUCERA, Elizabeth F, 587
KUCERA, Julieanne, 909
KUCI, Joanne L, 260
KUCICH, Kelly, 420
KUCK, Sandra Taylor, 683
KUDDES, Shawna Swafford, 832
KUEPFER, Brenda Kay, 940
KUHL, Kathy, 997
KULA, Edward J, 999
KULAGE, Kristen, 944
KULESSA, Julie, 613
KULKARNI, Shyamkant, 196
KULWICKI, Loretta, 640
KUMAR, Tobi, 183
KUMMERT, Wm Ward, 915
KUNKEL, Aileen R, 395
KUNKEL, R R, 705
KUNKLE, Beverly Rose, 814
KUNZ, Gregory G, 586
KUNZI, Fred, 779
KUPFERSCHMID, Anna L, 56
KUPI, Cheryl, 710
KUPREWICZ, Geraldine M, 982
KURASHIGE, Clarence K, 149
KURLAND, Meredith, 418
KURPUIS, Ernest G, 974
KURTH, Nina, 992
KURTZMAN, Walter, 1139
KUS, Alvin P, 896
KUSSMANN, Darline, 917
KUSTEISKI, Cindy, 1165
KUSTER, Maria, 10
KUSTER, Missy L, 675
KUTZ, Laura V, 1118
KUWAZAKI, Stan, 275
KUYKENDALL, Suzzanne M, 723
KUYPER, Trudie J, 432
KUZMITCH, Linda M, 650
KVIDAL, Reinert B, 730
KWIATKOWSKI, Sherri, 617
KWIECIEN, Kellie, 742
KYROUZ, Karen E, 528, 528, 528

L

LA FOUNTAIN, Jodi, 37
LAVIN, Ann, 1149
LAABS, Ted, 138
LABARGE, Susan, 733
LABELLE, Dorothy, 884
LABENNE, Connie J, 17
LABON, Elwanda, 670
LABOUNTY, Michlin, 406
LABRADOR, Charlie M, 501
LACASCIA, Angela, 710
LACEY, Diane L, 956
LACEY, Theresa, 580
LACH, Maureen K, 305
LACHANCE, Angela, 196
LACHOUT, Alice W, 964
LACKAS, Roseanna Napolitano, 1116
LACKEY, Beulah M, 520
LACKO, Michelle, 529, 527
LACNY, Lesley, 888
LACOMBE, Betsy, 402
LACOMBE, Erna O, 1024
LACOSTE, Steve, 479
LACROIX, Francis A, 202
LAFFERTY, Harold E, 390
LAFFERTY, Margaret P, 586
LAFLEUR, Vickie, 714
LAFOND, Alice A, 279
LAFOND, Sylvie Sonia, 1098
LAFRANCHI, Suzie, 857
LAGRONE, John T, 555
LAHETTA, Carl A, 503
LAHEY, Sabin, 423
LAHR, Georgiana Lieder, 420
LAILA, Lillian, 1092
LAING, William G, 1002
LAIRSCEY, Kathleen, 1124
LAITALA, Ian, 801
LAJEUNESSE, Bob, 618
LAKASCHUS, Christa G, 14
LAKE, Michelle N A, 876
LALEMAN, Lois M, 553
LALIBERTE, Lisa R, 831
LALK, M Jean, 1174
LALLI, Lisa S, 185
LAMAR, Sharon L, 476
LAMB, Michael, 882
LAMB, Ray W, 30
LAMB, Sophia, 1034
LAMBERT, Cathy, 1092
LAMBERT, Denis, 1072
LAMBERT, Greg, 303
LAMBERT, Larry L, 569
LAMBETH, Adell Carlock, 797
LAMBETH, Donald, 1155
LAMBRIOLA, Angela Ann, 617
LAMECK, Ronald, 59
LAMIRANDE, Mr Pierre, 641
LAMKIN, Rebecca Lynn, 193
LAMM, Lorrie, 495
LAMMERT, Joseph S, 141
LAMONTAGNE, Debralee, 661
LAMPMAN, Louis, 947
LANCASTER, John, 695
LANCIONI, Sue, 454
LAND, Angela I, 837
LAND, Eldon E, 255
LAND, Ms Tempie R, 637
LANDES, Courtney, 983
LANDIS, Frances, 276
LANDMANN, Beth, 211
LANDREY, Katherine L, 212
LANDRUM, Robert O, 350
LANDRY, M T, 1174
LANDRY, Miss Maxine, 804
LANE, Donna Charity, 1027
LANE, Lola T, 822
LANFORD Jr, Kenneth W, 1043
LANG, Chris, 1063
LANG, Joy L, 460
LANG, Marianne, 42
LANGDON-SMITH, Eve, 337
LANGE, Laura A, 871
LANGELIER, Carol, 79
LANGFORD, Martha L, 660
LANGFORD, R, 895
LANGHAM-SHARP, Estelle, 1093
LANGLEY, Ron, 825
LANGSTON, Alma Wesselman, 747
LANJE, Jean, 347
LANKFORD, Jean, 825
LANNING, Linda Rhea, 1072
LANNOM, S Craig, 909
LANSBERRY, Dixie, 969
LANTZ, Amy Suzanne, 654
LANTZ, Sally, 392
LANZL, Eunice B, 204
LAPALME, Joyce, 301
LAPE, Tessa, 376
LAPLUME, Shannon, 502
LAPOINTE, Michelle, 699
LAPOLE, Larry, 108
LARGE, H William, 1170
LARGO, Martha, 459
LARIONI, Kathleen Motisko, 314
LARKEY, Lawrence E, 543
LARKIN, Debi, 823
LAROCCA, John W, 446
LAROCHE, Madelyn, 50
LAROWE, Sheri, 342
LARSEN, Donna Jean, 597
LARSON, Adam D, 779
LARSON, Bernadine, 24
LARSON, Carol C, 104
LARSON, Gregg A, 521
LARSON, Ida, 678
LARSON, Irene Mary, 428
LARSON, Joan M, 254
LARSON, Michael, 622
LARSON, Shelley J, 883
LARSON, Tricia Ann, 351
LARUE, Charlotte R McWhorter, 529
LARUE, Wanda, 1097
LASALLE, William J, 170
LASENBERRY, Sharon, 741
LASH, Kathleen, 345

LASHBROOK, Lee, 21
LASHER, Stephanie, 240
LASHLEY, Heather, 765
LASKEY, Thomas A, 379
LAST, Marilyn M, 177
LASTRINGER, Joyce E, 1047
LATELLA, Heidi J, 350
LATELLA, Mary Ann, 738
LATHAM, Kelly, 1047
LATHAM, Phyllis, 1160
LATHROP, Thelma Coil, 996
LATHROPE, Robin Donna, 309
LATON, Wanda Loyd, 1195
LATOURRETTE, Renee M, 1054
LATTANZIO, Donna, 172
LAUBE, Minnie R, 817
LAUBER, Jack, 407
LAUGHNER, Donna J, 27
LAUNER, Margaret M, 271
LAUPP, Irene S, 890
LAURA, Laura, 393
LAURA, Jamie, 405
LAUTERBACH, Nancy, 565
LAVALLE, Rubicely M, 557
LAVARON, Brenda Lee, 839
LAVELL, Judy Lea, 714
LAVENE, Tammy Kay, 727
LAVERDE, Ms Emilie C, 1111
LAVERTY, Debra, 882
LAVICKA, Judith, 895
LAVIGNE, Richard, 92
LAVORANTE, Kimberly, 908
LAW, Jon B, 511
LAW, Mildred P, 1021
LAW, Shawn, 32
LAWHORN, Hilda Jones, 280
LAWLER, Leo J, 428
LAWLER, Penny, 153
LAWRENCE OSB, Neal Henry, 819
LAWRENCE, Alan, 785
LAWRENCE, Bea, 595
LAWRENCE, Dacia, 741
LAWRENCE, Helene P, 456
LAWRENCE, Kim Hope, 912
LAWRENCE, Robert, 520
LAWS, Catherine Gwen, 1042
LAWSETH, Linda, 524
LAWSON, Chereece, 555
LAWSON, Cynthia L, 1030
LAWSON, Laurel E, 1184
LAWSON, Lillian Hugh, 1132
LAWYER, Beverly, 479
LAY, Katheryn, 1088
LAYMAN Jr, Donald G, 328
LAYMAN, Andrew F, 30
LAYTON, C Renee, 42
LAYTON, Helen M, 576
LAYTON, Peter, 665
LAZAR, Ilanit, 395
LAZARO, Robert, 312
LAZARUS, Arthur, 46
LAZEAR, Elizabeth, 150
LAZUKA, Lillian R, 969
LE, Hoa, 1059
LEA, Carole Ann, 721
LEA, Cynthia, 207
LEA, Richard M, 908
LEACH, Larry D, 278
LEACH, Marlene, 991
LEACH, Paula J, 347
LEADER, Gloria, 961, 961
LEAF, Jason, 799
LEAGUE II, Avery Atwell, 100
LEAP, Amy, 990
LEAR, Eve, 1073
LEASON, Mary R, 391
LEATHERWOOD, Margaret, 733
LEAVELL, Joe, 304
LEAVITT, Cynthia D, 1020
LEAVITT, Richard A, 843
LEBARRON, Mary M, 451
LEBLANC III, Pierre A, 187
LEBLANC, Marie E, 932
LEBOA, Joelle, 1096
LECKBAND, Julie, 912
LECOMPTE, Dorothy, 165
LECOUTEUR-SULLIVAN, Karin, 926
LECRONE, Sharon L D, 323
LECTURE, Linda E, 489
LEDBETTER, John, 984
LEDBETTER, Marita J, 1170
LEDESMA, Carol, 79
LEDET, Kathleen L, 512
LEDLON, K, 364
LEE III, Johnnie B, 1126
LEE J, Bertie, 1062, 1187
LEE, Agnes, 297
LEE, Beth, 1007
LEE, Betty Y, 761
LEE, Daphne, 1014
LEE, Elayne, 145
LEE, Jessica Anne, 1119
LEE, Joyce, 183
LEE, Lillian Mary Smith, 263
LEE, Lori L, 731
LEE, Michelle E, 346
LEE, Mieke, 934
LEE, Millie, 646
LEE, Ms Rosa, 1086
LEE, Peter, 381
LEE, Phillip W, 814
LEE, Saun, 824
LEE, Steve L, 225
LEE, Valerie L, 554
LEECHE, Paula, 115
LEEDY, B T, 774
LEFEBVRE, Chere, 618
LEFEBVRE, Kandy Shane, 853
LEFEVER, Floel, 249
LEFLAR, Tracy, 1096
LEFLER, Terel, 1065
LEFLORE, Elisha Ann, 878
LEGACY, Tris A, 859
LEGASSIE, Elizabeth J, 104
LEGAULT, Valerie L, 860
LEGG, Patsy, 1176
LEGGETT, Juanita, 1043
LEGGETT, Paula, 39
LEGGHETTE, Alicia, 542
LEGNER, Amanda, 113
LEGRANDE, Yoni Star, 24
LEHMAN, Jason, 1031
LEHMAN, Joan, 118
LEHMANN, Sandra N, 523
LEHNER, F Joe, 123
LEHR, Donald P, 540
LEI, Lauana, 497
LEIBOWITZ, Melvin, 675
LEIBY, T R, 202
LEICESTER, Marjory O, 211
LEIDECKER, Mrs John R, 1063
LEIDIG-REED, Cheryl, 1094
LEIDY, Karen L, 434
LEIFELD, Susan, 903
LEIGH, Simon C, 513
LEIGHTON, Kelly, 455
LEIN, Alicia R, 973
LEIN, Dolores, 978
LEININGER, Jennifer, 812
LEIPOLD, Beverly A, 547
LEISING, Mary Lou R, 282
LELAND, Shane, 906
LEMASTER, Stacy A, 1136
LEMELLE Jr, Yolen, 1094
LEMKE, Lori, 12
LEMME, Incoronata, 291
LEMMOND, Sylvia, 46
LEMNA, Debbie, 115
LEMONS, Geraldine V, 440
LEMONS, Laura, 793
LEMONS, Wanda Lee, 183
LEMONT, Adlai, 639
LEMPERLE, Virginia, 986
LEMPKA, Michael L, 342
LENHARDT, Patricia, 755
STUETTGEN, Kim M, 1045
LENT, M L , 1135
LENTO, Stephanie, 245
LENZ, Cynthia, 919
LEO, Larry D, 116
LEON (WARD), Susan J, 1078
LEONARD, Jeff, 823
LEONARD, Kathryn A, 1078
LEONARD, Melody M, 236
LEONARD, Robert C, 1003
LEONARD, Willa M, 450
LEONCINI, Wanda Ann, 638
LEONE, Donald A A, 25
LEONE, Jason, 974
LEONHARDT, Clarence, 210
LEONHARDT, Joyce, 1176
LEPHIEW, Rebecca, 517
LEPPANEN, David W, 276
LEPPKY, Victor, 1122
LEPRI, Joyce A, 978
LEPROWSE, Jodelle, 598
LERMAN, Yulia, 346
LEROI, Robin, 971
LESCHINSKY, Julie, 1060
LESHAN, Lawrence, 70
LESHER, Kimberly J, 1078
LESPERANCE, Cindy, 94
LESSANE, Sheila Mose, 599
LESSENBERRY, Nikki, 429
LESSLEY, Grant, 59
LESTER, John W, 872
LESTER, Michael, 498
LESTER, Nona Razor, 1200
LESTER, Virginia N, 540
LETANY, Jan, 877
LETHCO, Mark Trenton, 733
LETOURNEAU, Steven J, 477
LETSON, Penny, 807
LETZO, Shary G, 1068
LEUSCHNER, Hildegard, 864
LEVASSEUR, Roberta M, 693
LEVAY, Naomi, 359
LEVENSON, Julie, 679
LEVERETTE, Michelle D, 422
LEVIE, M C, 679
LEVIERE, Marie, 621
LEVIN, Nancy Kay, 106
LEVINE, Abe (Al), 387
LEVINE, Jeffrey, 560
LEVINESS, Jackie, 1168
LEVINSOHN, Max J, 1144
LEVITT, Barbara, 446
LEVORSE, A A, 238
LEVY, Daniel Leo, 135
LEVY, Pamela, 1194
LEW, Alison Tamiko, 74
LEWALLEN, Arrie Herndon, 949
LEWALLEN, Karly A, 889
LEWANDOWSKI, Colleen, 247
LEWINTER, Melissa, 713
LEWIS, Carolyn M, 295
LEWIS, Cindy, 1180
LEWIS, D M, 98
LEWIS, David N A, 944
LEWIS, Dewayne, 1160
LEWIS, Donna, 135
LEWIS, Garnet, 431
LEWIS, Gertrude, 1082
LEWIS, Jeremy, 794
LEWIS, John, 211
LEWIS, Karen M, 1063
LEWIS, Kathleen Kay, 228
LEWIS, Kimberly N, 559
LEWIS, Louise, 876
LEWIS, Lydia, 432
LEWIS, Maxine, 640
LEWIS, Miss Eleanor A, 76
LEWIS, Patrick, 942
LEWIS, Rod, 1120
LEWIS, Sara, 871
LEWIS, Stewart, 876
LEWIS, Trevor S, 129
LEWIS, Winifred Jane, 1014
LEWMAN, Lance, 973
LEWTHWAITE, Yve Pendragon, 1046
LEYSER, Debbie, 252
LEYSER, Ophra, 728
LEZZIERI, Gloria E, 838
LIBBY, Cynthia E, 780
LIBBY, Debbie, 524
LIBERMAN, Grace B, 947
LICASTRI, Cheryl Lynne, 299
LICHTENBERG, Charles F, 502
LICHTIGFELD, Gina, 1150
LIDDELL, Samantha, 1023
LIDDY, Debra Sievert, 698
LIDE, Tammy, 975
LIEN, Daniel R, 478
LIEN, Peggie, 425
LIEPELT, Michelle Lynn, 582
LIGHTSEY, Mae Dempsey, 772
LIINAMAA, Liisa, 120
LILES, Nell, 489
LILLARD-JOHNSON, Melissa, 213
LILLES, Sophia K, 1165
LILLEVOLD, Joanne, 456
LILLY, Ellen, 843
LILLY, Michael A, 452
LIMERES, Nelda E, 783
LIMOGES, Mrs Susan J, 71
LIMON, Victoria, 922
LIMPERT, Rhonda, 912
LIND, Jayne, 895
LIND, Tonya F, 957
LINDBLAD, Blanche B, 847
LINDEKE, Pamela K, 391
LINDEN, Donna Von Der, 472
LINDEN, Michael J, 125
LINDEN, Tracy, 357
LINDERMAN, Lillian H, 607
LINDGREN, Nancy R, 118
LINDIC, Pat, 871
LINDSAY, Bruce R, 1194
LINDSAY, Linda J, 932
LINDSEY, Anthony T, 1145
LINDSEY, Jo Starrett, 411
LINE, Kristy, 167
LINEBERRY, Edna, 163
LINEBURG, Pearl R, 343
LINER, Mary, 582
LING, Edwin R, 620
LINGARD, Sandy, 992
LINGLE, Fred K, 100
LINGREN, Donna V, 803
LINHART, Laura, 1169
LINK, Emily S, 434
LINK-SANDOVAL, Susan, 1026
LINN, Vicki Bea, 416, 988
LINS, Carole, 1191
LINSTEAD, Gerry, 1076
LINVILLE, Raina, 598
LIOKAREAS, Chris, 404
LIPOVAC, James E, 351
LIPPERT, Sharen Marie, 494
LIPSCOMB, Wilma V Sines, 847
LISANTI, Pauline, 611
LISBONA, Beth Leann, 662
LISHNEVSKI, Alexia, 990
LISS Jr MD, Joseph P, 545
LISTER, Shirley, 796
LISTON, Tracy, 29
LITCHFIELD, Isabel C, 173
LITCHFIELD, Jean A, 553
LITTLE, Lloyd L, 588
LITTLE, Malina, 873
LITTLEJOHN, Dolly E, 480
LITTLEJOHN, Phyllis Mae, 635
LITTON, Foster W, 99
LITWIN, Jackie, 84
LITZENBERG, Jean T, 507
LITZSINGER, Deadra Dee, 621
LIVENGOOD (SHANE), Patricia A, 764
LIVERNOCHE, Beverly M, 189
LIVES, J Garrison, 553
LIVESAY, Laura, 701
LIVIA, Anna, 50
LIVINGSTON, Dorothy C, 173
LIVINGSTON, Zeldah S, 1145
LIWARU, Jaahlay, 519
LLARINAS, Pedro S, 130
LLENA, Lucia L, 312
LLEWELLYN, Kenneth, 340
LLOYD, Edith M, 1196
LLOYD, Joyce, 1023
LLOYD, Maurece W, 436
LLOYD, Reed Vernon, 1025
LLOYD, Tanya, 1015
LLOYD-WAYNE, Letha M, 993
LNENICKA, Darlene Baxa, 433
LOADHOLT, Stephanie, 101
LOBIANCO, Judith, 896
LOCK, Dee, 334
LOCKE, Elizabeth, 916
LOCKE, Lurana Mary, 1161
LOCKHART, Elaine M, 269
LOCKHART, Robert W, 502
LOCKWOOD, Alan G, 391
LOCKWOOD, Byron H, 342
LOCKWOOD, L Beth, 1157
LOCKWOOD, Violet V, 179
LOCUST, Jochebed C, 674
LODOLCE, Lisa, 231
LOEB, Betty Irean, 214
LOEFFERT, James E, 841
LOESCH, Donna, 331
LOFTUS, Michelle J, 244
LOGAN, Frank, 55
LOGAN, Pamela J, 748
LOGUE, John, 985
LOIACONO, Andrew J, 236
LOISELLE, Loraine, 1015
LOK, Juliana, 725
LOMAX, Barry, 522
LOMAX, Glen F, 432
LOMBARD, Brooke, 873
LOMBARDI, Kathleen, 1066
LOMBARDO, Albert, 445
LOMBARDO, Carmine, 601
LOMBARDO, Diana, 104
LOMELI, G G, 459
LONESOME, Paul, 416, 416
LONG, Donna Stevens, 275
LONG, George-Ann, 1048
LONG, Kevin S, 386
LONG, Kristin, 112
LONG, Leonard, 366
LONG, Lucy, 671
LONG, Marvin A, 204
LONG, Norton R, 139
LONG, Perry D, 1176
LONG, Phyllis J, 1072
LONG, Ranee, 776
LONG, Robin, 486
LONG, Sandra, 1143
LONG, Sherry L, 636
LONG, Virginia M, 780
LONGACRE, Verna, 683
LONGKUMER, Akumla, 1146
LONGRES, Blanche A, 41
LONGSTREET, Rebecca Anna, 187
LOO, Jane Thompson, 599
LOOK, April V, 893
LOOMIS, Brenda, 477
LOPEZ, Arlene W, 722
LOPEZ, Desiree, 1129
LOPEZ, Ember J, 707
LOPEZ, J Victor, 1047
LOPEZ, Jan, 780
LOPEZ, Laura Lee, 155
LOPEZ, Nancy Ann, 640
LOPEZ, Robert A, 200
LOPEZ, Samantha Roberts, 694
LOPEZ, Sandra J, 64
LOPEZ, Yvonne T, 414
LOPEZ-BELIO, Maria, 1185
LORA, Laura M, 1095
LORD, Kelly, 918
LORD, Marian Y, 790
LORENSON, Joyce, 953
LORENZ, Janet K, 886
LORI, Karen J, 218
LORIA, Heidi, 988
LORING, Cheryl Mari Lakey, 268
LORTON, Troy, 767
LOUDERMILK, D O, 891
LOUDIN, Robert, 744
LOUDON, Joyce E (Penner), 571
LOUDY, Betty S, 530
LOUIS, Lonnie, 358
LOUREY, Delores Lee, 473
LOVE, Beatrice, 192
LOVE, Lisa, 819
LOVE, Lori E, 1096
LOVE, Marguerite, 1123
LOVE, Nancy, 1057
LOVE, Regina, 536
LOVE, Sherry, 706
LOVE, Walter, 775
LOVE-WARNER, Linda, 6
LOVELAND, Cathy, 194
LOVING, Cathy E, 457
LOVING, Gerry A, 1000
LOWDER, Gracie, 1093
LOWE, E A, 314
LOWE, Jess H, 745
LOWE, Lorie Ann, 339
LOWE, Patricia B, 547
LOWE, Rebecca, 835
LOWENSTEIN, Fran, 288
LOWERY, Marsha A, 863
LOWERY, Valorie, 328
LOWREY, Angela K, 244
LOWREY, Dale Conner, 716
LOWRY, Mae, 711
LOYD, Alesha, 1066
LOYD, Daisy, 571
LOZANO, Gina Monica, 894
LU, Kathy, 694
LUBERDA, Trish E (Nangle), 483
LUBLIN, Eric S, 16
LUCAS, Carol A, 39
LUCAS, Carolyn B, 890
LUCAS, Chrystal A, 853
LUCAS, Debbie S Farr, 639
LUCAS, Emilie, 929
LUCAS, Grafton E, 79
LUCAS, Karen S, 1119
LUCAS, M, 513
LUCAS, Taya, 545
LUCAS-CAMERON, Lois Jean, 121
LUCCIO, Jennifer C, 1122
LUCK, Annie, 626
LUCZAK, Janet Williams, 143
LUDINGTON, Linda, 517
LUDOLFF, Connie, 88
LUDWIG, Cecilia A, 834
LUEBBERS, Daloris A, 92
LUEDERS, Natalie, 534
LUEKE, Clarence A, 184
LUFFMAN, Emmerson G, 857
LUFFMAN, Willard G, 1199
LUGO, Adolph R, 1125
LUGO, M A, 199
LUHR, Jonathan L, 141
LUICK, Barb, 187
LUJAN, Sydney, 432
LUM, Gretchen Y, 727
LUMMUS, Jacki, 351
LUNCEFORD, Helen Marie, 442, 1083
LUND, P S, 520
LUNDBECK, Linne, 334
LUNDGREN, Angela L, 692
LUNDY, Gwen T, 174
LUNSFORD, Pam, 410
LUNSFORD, Reny, 54
LUPACCHINO, Donna, 544
LUPER, Angela J, 697
LUPER, Steve, 85

LUPER, Tamhra J, 722
LUSCOMBE, James J, 752
LUSCOMBE, Raelene, 206
LUSE, Jeff Allen, 527
LUSH, Londa, 946
LUSSIER, Shane J, 446
LUTKEHAUS, Moira, 412
LUTZ, Donald J, 600
LUTZ, Leah, 1187
LUTZ, Millie Marsau, 651
LUZANIA, Janine M, 68
LY, Pakada, 398
LYDICK, Sara M, 346
LYLES, Zita Victoria Moak, 1202
LYLISTON, W Phillip, 878
LYMAN, Donna A, 61
LYMAN, Pat, 284
LYNCH, Donna M, 638
LYNCH, Juliet R, 766
LYNCH, Mary Agnes, 198, 1004
LYNCH, Robert, 134
LYNN, Alice H, 712
LYNN, Mandy, 833
LYNN, Nikki Jones AKA Neci, 756
LYON, Jane L, 1047
LYONS, Anne, 1037
LYONS, Beryl A, 140
LYONS, Dorothy, 1151
LYONS, Kari, 138
LYONS, Mildred W, 115
LYONS, Stuart T, 166
LYONS, Timothy D, 1197

M

M T, Trevor, 882
MAAHS, Selisa, 828
MAAT, Dawn Marie, 154
MABEUS, Catherine L, 327
MABIN, Ann, 1111
MABRY, Karen, 506
MACIVER, John C, 1169
MAC, Sy, 72
MACARTHUR, Colin, 430
MACCALLUM, Lorene, 342
MACCHIA, Alissa, 1040
MACCREADY, Sandra J, 622
MACCREE Jr, M W, 25
MACDONALD, Alice A, 115
MACDONALD, Carie L, 733
MACDONALD, Eleanor J, 1118
MACDONALD, Flora C, 767
MACDONALD, Lisa, 249
MACDONALD, Marsha Jean, 253
MACDONALD, Ola, 802
MACEWEN, Bill, 1152
MACGILLIVRAY, Anne, 407
MACHART, Ida-Rose, 44
MACHESKA, David M, 31
MACHOTKA, Patti Stocker, 1022
MACHTIG, Victoria, 319
MACHURICK, Patti Nicole, 636
MACK, A D, 11
MACK, Georgie M K, 841
MACK, Michael, 943
MACKEY, Candida, 1076
MACKEY, Mrs Clara Mae Quarles, 1080
MACKIE, Kimmery Ann, 733
MACKOVITCH, Shannon, 249
MACLEAN, Bridget, 171
MACLEAN, Duncan, 278
MACMONAGLE, Julie, 817
MACNAUGHTON, S E, 575
MACON, Pamela, 1153
MACPHERSON, David, 270
MACRAE, E Sims, 601
MACWHINNIE, Rosalie, 960
MADARAS, Kenneth, 570
MADDEN, Owen H, 377
MADDEN, Robert, 254
MADDOX, Linda, 694
MADDOX, Linda Pace, 636
MADDOX, Tonya M, 759
MADERA III, Henry P, 880
MADEWELL, Ozella, 137
MADISON, Anne Marie, 1135
MADISON, Edith Walker, 914
MADISON, Jacqueline E, 875
MADISON, John D, 685
MADISON, Leigh, 36
MADISON, Miriam, 1085
MADONIA, Donna, 816
MADRID, Christine, 121
MADSEN, Alice, 407
MADSEN-CLOUTIER, Sherie, 865
MAEDER, Alicia Star, 396
MAENG, Katie, 1123
MAERTZIG, Anna Rose, 896
MAGAARD, Donna, 592
MAGANA, Cheryl, 758
MAGEDDON, R, 272
MAGEE, Margaret W, 123
MAGGAY, Feliza, 580
MAGGIO, Elena, 260
MAGLEY, Julie Heck, 931
MAGNONE, Agnes, 1200
MAGSIG, Linda L, 1031
MAGUIRE, Ann, 391
MAHABIR, Mr Parmanand, 381
MAHADY, Hannah M, 1071
MAHAFFEY, Carl R, 95
MAHALAK, Delphine, 1018
MAHAN, Patricia M, 749
MAHANEY, Eve Lynn, 1071
MAHONEY, Christine M, 920
MAHONEY, Neil F, 632
MAHR, Cookie, 99
MAHURIN, Sue G, 293
MAICHELE, Martha M, 578
MAIER, Albert M, 102
MAIER, Herbert, 1060
MAIN, Rocky, 59
MAIN, Tanya Lynn, 200
MAINE, Kathy Lynn, 817
MAINPRIZE, Marion, 665
MAINS, Vivian, 314
MAISEL, Aileen, 486
MAJANO, Marla, 73
MAJEWSKI, Phyllis, 1079
MAKHUDU, Dennis P, 598
MAKI, Joan, 1065
MAKIN, Robert, 71, 71
MAKLA, Alice, 260
MALATY, Elena, 570
MALAWKA, Laura, 454
MALDONADO, Gloria, 693
MALECKI, Cathy Joe, 913
MALEK, Rami, 406
MALEK, Silvia, 323
MALERICH, Melanie C, 81
MALIN, Tina, 395
MALLARDI, Laurie, 494
MALLETTE, Cathy, 336
MALLEY, Anne Marie, 448
MALLEY, Frank, 712
MALLEY, L M, 573
MALLEY, Lisa J, 398
MALLORY, Malinda, 233
MALLORY, Subretta, 514
MALLORY, Vernell, 693
MALLOY, Nancie, 671
MALLOY, Steve M, 527
MALONE, Bill, 787
MALONE, Charlotte A, 615
MALONE, Clifford, 756
MALONE, Cynthia, 981
MALONE, Elizabeth, 535
MALONE, Linda T, 330
MALONE, Maureen A, 792
MALONEY (MEANEY), Kathleen A, 485
MALONEY, Georgia, 775
MALONEY, J P, 1184
MALONEY, Mary, 983
MALOTA, Debra M, 663
MALOY, Loraine M, 87
MAMIENSKI, Rosemary H, 1021
MAMRAK, Jenny, 1190
MANAKER, Stella, 186
MANALILI, Michelle, 363
MANALIS, Irene, 1200
MANCINI, Maria, 487, 487
MANDANI, Abdul M, 1055
MANDEVILLE, Holly Ann, 870
MANDULAK, Elaine C, 828
MANESS, Esther Ahart, 824
MANESS, Hazel G, 287
MANEY, Christy D, 367
MANGAN, Karmel, 819
MANGASCLE, Monya M, 375
MANGO, Antonina, 956
MANHEIMER, Jenifer L, 89
MANIACI, Wendy Marie, 746
MANICA, Holly, 617
MANITSAS, Karri J, 898
MANLEY, Christy, 626
MANLEY, N J, 477
MANLOVE, Le Roy, 10
MANLY, Wendie Parras, 421
MANN, Carol, 364
MANN, Guy L, 642
MANN, Vineler L, 783
MANNEY, Josephine H, 570
MANNING, Betty Lou, 918
MANNING, Joette, 1011
MANNO, Jerry, 994
MANNS, Shannon, 1180
MANSE, Joanne, 1077
MANSKER, Sue, 280
MANSOURI, Lori, 9
MANTER, Jeffrey L, 675
MANUEL, Tyrus, 222
MANVILLE, Diane M D, 792
MANVILLE, Mabel L, 1022
MANWARRING, Melvin, 42
MANZI, Michele Renee, 960
MAPEL, Marilyn J, 671
MAPES, Marie L, 201
MAPHIS, Nina M, 1030
MAQSOOD, Shahid, 63
MARAN, Lynn E, 126
MARBLE, Myrna R, 87
MARCANTOGNINI, Ahna, 922
MARCH, Stephanie, 513
MARCH, Virginia, 146
MARCHAND, Sherry M, 676
MARCHANT, Russell P, 485
MARCHESE, Patricia Ann, 446
MARCHETTI, Maria Rosa, 927
MARCHISCHUK, Joyce, 295
MARCOE, Eugene B, 466
MARCOGLIESE, Andrea, 797
MARCOLY, Jo Ann, 1051
MARCOUX, Lillian C, 444
MARCUCCI, Barbara F, 333
MARCUS, Jody, 478
MAREN, Beth A, 257
MARGERA, Darlene, 1157
MARGETAN, Margaret F, 1141
MARIANO, Carmela, 1110
MARIANOS, George, 181
MARING, Nancy M, 606
MARINO, Carol A, 102
MARINO, Susan Frances, 1080
MARINOS, April, 818
MARION, Dr L Marvin, 673
MARION, Faith, 207
MARK, Patricia, 426
MARKARIAN, Christine, 675
MARKEL, Stephen, 430
MARKEY, David A, 307
MARKHAM, Camelia A, 124
MARKHAM, Jack A, 144
MARKHAM, Kathleen S, 858
MARKHAM, T R, 664
MARKINS, Denise, 146
MARKLEY, Mary K, 134
MARKS, Greg J, 819
MARKS, Jan L, 1082
MARKS, Marlys M, 1130
MARKS, Samantha, 983
MARLOWE, Dixie T, 640
MARMOL, Nestor J, 738
MARNACH, Nye, 510
MARNEENATE, Tonya, 359
MARONCELLI, John P, 160
MARPLE, Margaret, 454
MARQUES, Sandra E, 597
MARQUEZ, Mark, 950
MARRERO, Clarisse, 770
MARRON, Betty Ann, 61
MARROW, Shirley, 1096
MARSEE, Ella Mae, 1025
MARSH, Lucille M, 900
MARSHALL III, Johnny, 912
MARSHALL, Beverly A, 570
MARSHALL, D, 1051
MARSHALL, Darrin, 585
MARSHALL, Edie, 936
MARSHALL, James, 601
MARSHALL, Jenny W, 826
MARSHALL, Jonathan, 825
MARSHALL, Lee C, 1007
MARSHALL, Ruth A, 561
MARSIGLIA, Tony, 476
MARSO, Emily, 428
MARSTON, Laurel L, 839
MARTEL, Kristi, 921
MARTEL, Nora E, 992
MARTENSEN, Eileen M, 1036
MARTIN Jr, Howard W, 265
MARTIN Jr, Robert L, 769
MARTIN, Abigail, 1062
MARTIN, Adam, 25
MARTIN, Ann Ferguson, 842
MARTIN, Anne, 325
MARTIN, Brain V, 938
MARTIN, Brenda, 307
MARTIN, Carol, 813
MARTIN, Cliff, 218
MARTIN, Darlene L, 20
MARTIN, David, 119
MARTIN, Donna, 724
MARTIN, Dreama K, 1056
MARTIN, Eddie, 563
MARTIN, Eva M, 102
MARTIN, Genia Lynn, 467
MARTIN, Harold S, 1085
MARTIN, Hattie, 494
MARTIN, Janet Rose, 333
MARTIN, Jennifer R, 907
MARTIN, Julie E, 901
MARTIN, Kryssi W, 878
MARTIN, Leslie, 822
MARTIN, Lois Ella, 102
MARTIN, Luann, 326
MARTIN, Maxine E King, 127
MARTIN, Merle P, 497
MARTIN, Michael T, 705
MARTIN, Nancy F, 230
MARTIN, Patricia Ann, 198
MARTIN, Rebecca, 632
MARTIN, Roger Jonas, 546
MARTIN, Sherry, 124
MARTIN, Sheryl D, 1158
MARTIN, Willee C, 670
MARTIN-ROOT, Sandra Jean, 787
MARTINEAU, Cherrye, 1167
MARTINEZ Jr, Ruben Jose, 211
MARTINEZ, Antonio, 270
MARTINEZ, Doris N, 307
MARTINEZ, Joan, 1136
MARTINEZ, Laurie D, 733
MARTINEZ, Martha B, 1185
MARTINEZ, Rosa, 737
MARTINEZ, Tony, 591
MARTINEZ, Veronica L, 474
MARTZ, Christine, 155
MARTZ, Keith, 174
MARTZ, Kenneth, 1150
MARXMILLER, Alexis Megan, 867
MARYALICE, Maryalice, 514
MASHAK, Barbara, 1081
MASKER, David G, 1188
MASON, Darrel A, 18
MASON, Deana L, 126
MASON, Diane, 1106
MASON, Lavona W, 300
MASON, Louise, 1069
MASON, M S Terry, 598
MASSARA, Loretta G, 281
MASSARO, Mario R, 249
MASSEY, Cynthia A, 296
MASSEY, Lillie M D, 835
MASSIE, Tonilyn, 425
MASTRIANNA, Mary-Jo, 941
MASTROBUONO, Giuseppe Vittorio, 293
MASTRULL, Regina, 598
MASUDA, Nancy L, 267
MATES, Annette, 78
MATHENY, Anna, 583
MATHERLY, Snow J, 415
MATHERS, Gloria J, 112
MATHERS, Jimi, 287
MATHESON, Cindy Maureen, 715
MATHESON, Jeanette L, 214
MATHEWS, Doris Averitt, 865
MATHEWS, E June, 336
MATHEWS, Elaine M, 1196
MATHEWS, Kennith, 220
MATHIAS, Brandi, 907
MATHIS, Alice L, 902
MATHIS, Edith, 993
MATHIS, Lisa Ann, 1048
MATHIS, Shawna, 796
MATISOFF, Martin, 130
MATLOCK, David Allen, 586
MATNEY, Jennifer, 50
MATTE, Judy, 821
MATTER, John Robert, 1107
MATTESON, Dave, 316
MATTHEWS III, Will Allen, 1136
MATTHEWS, Anna M, 618
MATTHEWS, Carol Sue, 498
MATTHEWS, Emily E, 93
MATTHEWS, Holly D, 623
MATTHEWS, Roy D, 548
MATTHIS, Leslie J, 944
MATTIA MD, Gerry, 800
MATTIES, Jennifer, 334
MATUTINO, Peter G, 781
MATZA, John, 940
MAUCK, Russell, 726
MAULDIN, Patricia M, 157
MAUPIN, Howard, 1173
MAUPIN, Mark, 84
MAURER, Donald J, 739
MAURER, P J, 101
MAVRIYANNI, Niki, 685
MAWYER, Margaret J, 842
MAXEY, Debra, 1180
MAXIE, Jean Ann, 730
MAXIM, Teresa M, 822
MAXWELL, Jennifer, 863
MAXWELL, John T, 752
MAXWELL, M Marie, 1180
MAY, Alethea, 565
MAY, Kcarolina B, 993
MAY, Tammy Barlow, 1181
MAY, Terri A, 830
MAYBERRY, Lou, 1162
MAYER, Claire M, 175
MAYER, Jonathan, 938
MAYER, Lauretta L, 240
MAYER, Sylvia L, 858
MAYERS, Vince, 89
MAYHEW, Joyce Kepley, 179
MAYLEN, Vyvian M, 707
MAYNARD, Gerald, 859
MAYNARD, Mr Victor, 806
MAYNARD, Shannon, 335
MAYNEZ, Adeline O, 816
MAYO, Henry Asher, 1146
MAYO, Jeanne Marie, 19
MAYO, Pauline, 694
MAYOR, Allen Hipolito, 1181
MAYS, Jennifer K, 728
MAYS, Judith McGhee, 649
MAYS, Karen A, 194
MAYSONET, Rose Marie, 183
MAZROLLE, Barbara, 315
MAZUCA, Joan, 642
MAZZA, Angeline J, 200
MAZZACANE, Paul Mark, 1190
MAZZELLA, Ronald, 534
MAZZENGA, Evelyn, 1022
MAZZENGA, Maria, 1118
MAZZONE, Michelle D, 564
MAZZONE, Thomas J, 172
MCAFEE, Taira, 516
MCALEER, Lisa A, 529
MCALLISTER, Dianne, 204
MCALLISTER, Kathy K, 476
MCALONEY, Donna R, 680
MCALPIN, Fairy, 1106
MCANEAR, Anna, 297
MCARDLE, Maureen Ann, 1139
MCAULIFFE, Mary J, 73
MCBRIDE, Billy Morton, 337
MCBRIDE, Grant W, 117
MCBRIDE, Mark Allen, 734
MCBROOM, Lorene, 9
MCBRYDE, John M, 141
MCBURNEY, Faith, 654
MCCAFFERTY, John G, 1082
MCCAFFERTY, S J, 634
MCCAFFREY, Philip R, 1193
MCCAFFREY, Philip R, 509
MCCALL, Phyllis S, 1064
MCCANDLESS, Annaliese L M, 666
MCCANDLESS, Marjorie, 620
MCCANDLESS, Sheila L, 704
MCCANN Jr, Hubert T, 874
MCCANTS, Beverly Jean, 1091
MCCARDELL, Deborah, 917
MCCAREY, John, 713
MCCARTER, Betty R, 1050
MCCARTHY, Amalie G, 1180
MCCARTHY, Stephanie Worobel, 602
MCCARTHY, Valerie L, 498
MCCARTNEY, Barbara, 546
MCCARTNEY, Irene Laverne, 835
MCCARTOR, Marion, 994
MCCARTY, D R, 57
MCCASKILL, Patricia H, 148
MCCAULEY, Linda G, 666
MCCAUSLAND, Sheila, 849
MCCHESNEY, Hugh, 1129
MCCHESNEY, Julia M, 1073
MCCLAIN, Peggy J, 1002
MCCLEAN, Douglas, 500
MCCLELEN, Shirley, 938
MCCLELLAN, Michael W, 1013
MCCLENAN, Gay, 374
MCCLENDON, Willie Mae, 765
MCCLEVE, Kimberly, 735
MCCLONEY, Teddy J Ancher, 115
MCCLUNEY, Irma, 171
MCCLURE, David L, 1151
MCCLURE, Loretta M, 545
MCCLURE, Pat, 758
MCCLURG, Dr Louise, 146
MCCLUSKEY, Anita M, 583
MCCLUSKEY, Laura A, 162
MCCOLLUM, Ivory R, 643
MCCOLLUM, Matt, 268
MCCOMBS, Audrey B, 494
MCCONCHIE, Andrea A, 130
MCCONICO-WILSON, Tinniae, 970
MCCONNELL, Dorothy T, 712
MCCOOL, Laura J, 534
MCCORD, Megan Lyn, 700
MCCORMACK, Daniel, 1173
MCCORMICK, Annette, 1064

MCCORMICK, Dorothy A, 696
MCCORMICK, Emily, 1192
MCCORMICK, LeAnn, 476
MCCORMICK, Michelle, 256
MCCORMICK, Ricky, 38
MCCOWAN, Dana, 986
MCCOWAN, Greer, 1118
MCCOY, Ada S, 797
MCCOY, B K, 814
MCCOY, Kathryn D, 1106
MCCOY, Paul B, 736
MCCOY, Shirley E, 1188
MCCOY, Tami L, 292
MCCRACKEN, Kathleen, 409
MCCRADY, Debbie, 392
MCCRAINE, David, 1118
MCCRAY, Evelina W, 435
WILCOX, Lori, 1025
MCCREA, James H, 719
MCCRORY, Margaret, 223
MCCUE, Charles A, 913
MCCUE, June, 63
MCCULLERS, Randall J, 91
MCCULLOUGH, Andrea, 919
MCCULLOUGH, Marion, 1113
MCCUNE, Carole, 203
MCCUNE, Colleen, 876
MCCURDY, Iris, 669
MCCUTCHEN, Tara, 603
MCDANIEL, Gigi, 820
MCDANIEL, Kathleen T, 368
MCDANIEL, Patti, 851
MCDANIEL, Stacey, 227
MCDANIEL, William A, 963
MCDEARMON, Dora, 984
MCDERMOTT, Aaron, 1160
MCDERMOTT, Barbara J, 72
MCDERMOTT, Gloria Narciso, 985
MCDERMOTT, Kelliann A, 275
MCDONALD, Barbara M, 949
MCDONALD, Jacqueline, 625
MCDONALD, Janice K, 98
MCDONALD, Judy, 847
MCDONALD, Kathleen, 621
MCDONALD, Mary K, 1125
MCDONALD, Meta, 208
MCDONALD, Myrna, 962
MCDONALD, Wilda T, 845
MCDONOUGH, Geraldine , 200
MCDONOUGH, Joseph J, 796
MCDOWELL, David H, 231
MCDOWELL, Luella, 261
MCELHANEY, Darla Elliott, 625
MCELROY, Njoki, 862
MCENDREE, David Shane, 822
MCFADDEN, Judi, 983
MCFADDEN, Zula A, 594
MCFADDEN-COOPER, Rebecca, 178
MCFALL, Ken, 202
MCFALLS, Dorothy L, 667
MCFARLAND, Theresa, 559
MCFETRIDGE, Mary I, 372
MCGALLIARD, Susan, 379
MCGARRY, Betty Kay Saffell, 1096
MCGAUGHY, David, 782
MCGEE Jr, James V, 110
MCGEE, Catherine, 604
MCGHEE-SIEHOFF, Estella M, 50
MCGILLIS, Sean, 303
MCGILTON, Rose C (Posey), 1087
MCGINLEY, John, 674
MCGINLEY, Shaun, 22
MCGINNESS, Lynn, 174
MCGINNIS Jr, Charles D, 473
MCGINNIS, Joan E, 794
MCGINNIS, Sarah, 116
MCGIRT, Tommie, 646
MCGIVERN, Kelly M, 672
MCGLYNN, Edward F, 691
MCGOFFIN, Judith York, 681
MCGONIGAL, Claire, 1037
MCGOVERN, Betty, 289
MCGOWAN, Luana, 864
MCGOWAN, Sean, 82
MCGOWAN, Shona Lynn, 970
MCGOWEN, Sheree B, 906
MCGRAW, Dolores, 425
MCGRIFF, Carole Anne, 1055
MCGUINN, Kate, 293
MCGUINNESS, Tom, 801
MCGUIRE, Bob, 949
MCGUIRE, Brian J, 590
MCGUIRE, Meredith, 691
MCGUIRE, Michael A, 197
MCGUIRE, Rob, 494
MCGULLION, Frank, 1110
MCHARNEY, Sofia, 428
MCHENRY, C J, 447
MCHENRY, Kay, 1066
MCHONE, Colleen, 970
MCINNES, Kathryn A, 932
MCINTYRE, Christine, 948
MCINTYRE, Jessie, 665
MCKAIG, June K, 962
MCKAY, Dianna, 428
MCKEARNEY, Roberta J, 317
MCKEE, Brook D, 906
MCKEEHAN, Janet Lynne, 361
MCKEEHAN, Lita Maria, 149
MCKEEN, Nancy, 1027
MCKEIGHEN, Nancy L, 253
MCKEITHEN, Jim, 1030
MCKELLAR, Janice R, 986
MCKENNA, Sean, 1057
MCKENNEY Jr, George E, 292
MCKENZIE, David, 1161
MCKENZIE, Evelyn L, 178
MCKENZIE, Hazel M, 972
MCKENZIE, M Jane, 335
MCKEOWN, Karen J, 751
MCKEY, Sandra D, 131
MCKINLEY, Beneva J, 112
MCKINNEY, Alice, 1172
MCKINNEY, Becky, 355
MCKINNEY, Gurtha May S, 978
MCKINNEY, James P, 624
MCKINNEY, Melvyn, 916
MCKINNEY, Mildred W, 485
MCKINNEY, Nathan, 774
MCKINNEY, Suzanne A, 240
MCKINNON Jr, Ken, 1039
MCKINSTER, Christopher L, 315
MCKNIGHT, Ida Lewellen, 310
MCLAIN, Alta R, 69
MCLAIN, Darryl, 437
MCLAIN, Julie, 1005
MCLAIN, Vanessa D, 872
MCLARRY, Claudia, 513
MCLAUGHLIN, Maureen E, 585
MCLAUGHLIN, Michelle, 912
MCLAUGHLIN, Rebecca, 194
MCLEAN, Harriet E, 221
MCLEMORE, Sylvia Anne, 553
MCLEOD, Denise L, 365
MCLEOD, Mrs Sandra E, 113
MCMAHON, Ann, 156
MCMAHON, Lillian, 1105
MCMAHON, Rick, 1164
MCMAIN, Nan M, 36
MCMANNIMAN, Elizabeth, 45
MCMANUS, Katherine, 1097
MCMASTERS, Jeffery D, 493
MCMEEKIN, John P, 1162
MCMILLAN, Charles A, 387
MCMILLAN, Jan, 15
MCMILLAN, Sally, 226
MCMILLIAN, Stephen, 460
MCMULLEN Jr, Charles, 236
MCMURRAY, Bryan, 583
MCMURRAY, R J, 459
MCMURRY, F D, 331
MCNAB, Helen, 760
MCNABB-WILEY, Janet, 33
MCNABNEY, Margaret M, 43, 1016
MCNAIR, Betty, 52
MCNAIR, Evelyn, 28
MCNALLY II, Charles E, 741
MCNALLY, John H, 1161
MCNAMARA, Clifford J, 28
MCNAMARA, Dolores, 248
MCNAMARA, Liam, 921
MCNAMER, Joe, 597
MCNAUL-MOORE, Miss Marty, 1105, 1105
MCNEESE, Leeuna, 69
MCNUTT, Janice Lynn, 905
MCNUTT-HITE, Mrs Lee, 312
MCPHEE, Michael, 356
MCPHERSON, Audrian, 482
MCPHERSON, Margie C, 280
MCQUEEN, Donna M, 986
MCQUEEN, Tabatha D, 637
MCQUEENEY, W Thomas, 487
MCQUERY, Janice Johnson, 72
MCRAE, Michelle Dawn, 1161
MCRAE, Shawn, 710
MCREYNOLDS, Virginia, 1137
MCSHINE, Hattie P, 139
MCTEER Sr, Ted, 766
MCVANE, Henry, 148
MCVICKER, Madonna E, 399
MCVICKER, Oral D, 1138
MCWEENEY, Mrs Gina, 367
MCWEST, Kari James, 785
MCWILLIAMS, Elizabeth, 181
MEACHAM, Agnes (Drumwright), 913
MEACHAM, Kenneth Shawn, 461
MEAD, Beverly, 531
MEAD, Delana, 1027
MEAD, Mr Fern, 639
MEADE, J V, 21
MEADE, Ken, 23
MEADE-DICKINSON, Diane, 251
MEADERS, Ruby, 127
MEADOWS Jr, James N, 510
MEANEY, Sharon S, 364
MEANS, Russell D, 793
MEARS, William "B", 771
MEASE, Cricket, 1036
MECCHI, Bruce Wayne, 423
MECHAM-MCKINNIS, Julia, 917
MECKLER, David, 321
MEDEIROS, Lori Ann, 883
MEDEMA, Eric, 128
MEDICI, Robert, 216
MEDLICK, Paul M, 984
MEDLIN, Stephen E, 45
MEDLOCK, Latisha, 235
MEEK, Novella, 525
MEEKER, Ethel Cravey, 525
MEEKINS, Mary A, 979
MEEKS, Joe, 664, 529, 966
MEENEN, Bertha L "Bert", 170
MEFFORD, Adeline, 623
MEHNERT, Robert, 222
MEIDINGER, Jeannette, 562
MEIER, Beverly, 918
MEIER, Elizabeth C, 730
MEIGIDE, Susan Klock, 838
MEIGS, Van L, 458
MEINERS, Mickey, 158
MEINERT Jr, Bernard R, 276
MEINHOLD, Colleen M, 803
MEISE, John, 1088
MEISTER, Gay, 676
MEKONEN, Kenneth, 844
MELANCON, Kevin D, 1000
MELBY, Melissa, 614
MELDRUM, Marcell, 1138
MELE, Ann, 134
MELENDREZ, Erick, 499
MELGOZA, Rosalba, 129
MELI, Elaine, 151
MELLARD, Melvin B, 1081
MELLEN, Stephanie, 395
MELLIN, Elsie Aldrich, 139
MELLO, Brian, 601
MELLOTT, Jane, 253
MELLOTT, Shirley, 212
MELMED, Jennie C, 8
MELNICK, Daniel P, 737
MELOCHE, Cassandra, 422
MELTON, Heather L, 997
MELTON, Hoss, 931
MELTON, Jodi L, 612
MELTON, Kathy, 597
MELVIN, Mary Jo, 357
MENDELSOHN, Cynthia, 870
MENDEZ, Caryn, 20
MENDEZ, Noemi C, 896
MENDOZA Jr, John J, 413
MENDOZA, G L, 811
MENDOZA, Jorge, 1163
MENDREY, Kate Louise, 856
MENERAY, Robert, 125
MENERY, Sheldon K, 418
MENIDES, Laura Jehn, 627
MENKE, Jennifer, 302
MENNA, Mrs Linda, 237
MENON, Letha, 1060
MERCADEL Jr, Raymond T, 634
MERCADO, Annalyn, 218
MERCADO, Emilda, 554
MERCADO, Nancy Maldonado, 659
MERCADO, Ramona G, 222
MERCER, T H, 893
MERCHANT, Jaime A, 145
MERCURIO, Maria, 693
MERINO, E E, 842
MERLINI, Sandra A, 401
MERLO, Kevin, 852
MERRELL, Amy L, 806
MERRIAM, Dorothy, 225
MERRIAM, Sigrid Rita, 1029
MERRILL, Sheila, 912
MERRIMAN, Joanie C, 631
MERRITT, Lucinda, 365
MERRITT, Pamela C, 322
MERRIWEATHER, Joyce L, 37
MERSINO, Sylvia, 1190
MERSWOLKE, Clarice A, 1199
MERTEN, Donald, 213
MERTENS, Betty, 311
MESAS, Jose M, 241
MESEROLE, Charles D, 75
MESERVE, Missi, 531
MESICK, Christa, 919
MESKA, Roger M, 1039
MESKAN, Ginger Lee, 462
MESNICK, Patricia, 960
MESSICK, Janet J, 117
MESSINA, Ben, 104
MESZAROS, Sherry, 987
METCALF, Diana, 690
METCALF, Kate, 693
METCALFE, Derek R, 409
METCALFE, Mary, 1007
METLAK, Laura L, 870
METLING, Leona A, 1045
METZ, Dallas, 882
METZ, Raymond S, 905
MEYER, Claudia, 361
MEYER, Elsie U, 93
MEYER, Larissa, 524
MEYER, Shari L, 244
MEYERHOFF, Cathy L, 240
MEYERS, Russell L, 446
MEYERS, Shellie, 707
MEYERSON, Mark, 57
MEZO, Elizabeth N, 1123
MEZZACAPO, Charles R, 303
MEZZACAPPA, Kellie, 259
MICEK, Tori, 482
MICELI, Josephine, 8
MICELI, Lisa, 800
MICHAEL, Cathy, 352
MICHAEL, Gayol Shaw, 316
MICHAEL, Johnathan Simon, 658
MICHAEL, Leo, 1141
MICHAEL, Rhonda B, 350
MICHAELS, Jaye, 491
MICHAELS, Maria, 736
MICHALOVE, Steven A, 441
MICHELINI, Iris Y, 97
VENTRESS, Michelle A, 1181
MICHIE, William L, 73
MICHKO, Paul J, 734
MICHULSKI, Roberta F, 570
MICK, E J, 424
MICKELSON, Neil, 999
MICKENS, Ray, 492
MICKEY, Mariam M, 660
MICKIEWICZ, Randall A, 517
MICKLICH, Jeanette, 378
MIDDLETON, Janet S, 238
MIDDLETON, Sharon A, 43
MIGIMOTO, Fumi, 65
MIHELI, John Alan, 685
MIKALONIS, Jacklyn, 639
MILAKOVICH, Janice L, 413
MILAM, Drema, 1063
MILBURN, D Judson, 698
MILEA, Linda Lou, 281
MILES, Brenda K, 139
MILES, Charmaine, 634, 963
MILES, Lillie M, 369
MILES-SHEPPARD, Mary Helen, 1044
MILK, Sylvia, 826
MILKS, Edith Ruby, 478
MILLAN, Christine A, 407
MILLAR, Donald, 972
MILLBURN, Gary L, 771
MILLEN, Frederic, 687
MILLEN, James Knox, 9
MILLER Jr, James E, 896
MILLER, Ada Kendall, 1117
MILLER, Ashley L, 720
MILLER, Barry (Bear), 952
MILLER, Belinda A, 352
MILLER, Bertha H, 400
MILLER, Betty, 261
MILLER, Catherine L, 346
MILLER, Charlie, 651
MILLER, Christopher C, 1098
MILLER, Claudia A, 356
MILLER, Darcy, 741
MILLER, Dena, 1001
MILLER, Doris R S, 766
MILLER, Esther, 116
MILLER, Eva La Rue, 634
MILLER, Faye, 844
MILLER, Glenda S, 288
MILLER, Harvey T, 1021
MILLER, Janice D, 1056
MILLER, Jennifer, 542
MILLER, Jeremy, 782
MILLER, Joyce J, 39
MILLER, Kathryn C, 1146
MILLER, Kathy, 28
MILLER, Lavada Belcher, 461
MILLER, Lizbeth L, 744
MILLER, Lois M, 917
MILLER, Mark A, 682
MILLER, Marvin, 133
MILLER, Mary, 780
MILLER, Mary M, 990
MILLER, Melissa C, 466
MILLER, Morris L, 1136
MILLER, Nicki Jo, 604
MILLER, Norma J, 1182
MILLER, Pamela J, 1158
MILLER, Paris, 68
MILLER, Randy, 1106
MILLER, Renee E, 533
MILLER, Richard Lee, 172
MILLER, Russell, 1114
MILLER, Scott M, 642
MILLER, Sean A, 34
MILLER, Sharlene L, 32
MILLER, Sharon Rutherford, 868
MILLER, Shelly, 576
MILLER, Susan K, 110
MILLER, T L, 170
MILLER, Texas Theresa, 1110
MILLER, William A, 811
MILLER-HARRIS, Kevin, 145
MILLET, Alma Martin, S M, 1161
MILLIGAN, Shane P, 333
MILLIGAN, Stanley J, 194
MILLS, Betty, 728
MILLS, Chuck, 1044
MILLS, Elsa Hertel, 1040
MILLS, Margaret Ann, 6
MILLS, Pearlina, 855
MILLSAPS, Gaylean, 921
ATKINS, Lilian L, 1094, 1094
MILNE, Heather, 452
XO, Sarah, 1202
MILNER, Linda, 324
MILOT, Annette, 328
MILSOM, Mike, 338
MILSTEIN, Rose, 884
MILTON, Georgia P, 564
MIMMO, Mimmo, 634
MINARDI, Anna, 221
MINCEMOYER, Sandra M, 190
MINEAR, Ron, 603
MINER, Edward H, 728
MINER, Sunbow, 343
MINGLE, Winifred, 363
MINIMI, Tony P, 366
MINKOFF, Tracy E, 879
MINNIE, Sandra M, 567
MINOPOLI, Doreen C, 536
MINOR, Doris, 65
MINOR, Kimi, 786
MINOZZI, Michael, 212
MINTON, Susan Lee, 532
MINTY, Amy, 739
MINUTILLO, Susan Ashley, 591
MIOSKIE, Bobbie Ann, 171
MIOT, Daniel, 381
MIRACLE, Tracey L, 105
MIRANDA, Mirna, 605
MIRC, Tony, 1073
MIRICH, Theodore D, 848
MISCIO, Tracy, 934
MISTERKA, Adam F, 1001
MISTLER, Rose Marie, 156
MISTYSYN, Thomas, 943
MITCHELL, Andrew J, 888
MITCHELL, Charles R, 718
MITCHELL, Chuck, 141
MITCHELL, Colin M, 561
MITCHELL, Enid, 438
MITCHELL, Fred H, 125
MITCHELL, Georgia Lee, 507
MITCHELL, Harriet R, 425
MITCHELL, Josephine, 500
MITCHELL, Karen, 603
MITCHELL, Kerri Rae, 414
MITCHELL, Larry S, 831
MITCHELL, Lenise M, 707
MITCHELL, Mae, 994
MITCHELL, Martin A, 619
MITCHELL, Michael, 444
MITCHELL, Peter J, 979
MITCHELL, S R, 1169
MITCHELL, Sarah, 1111
MITCHELL, Tina Monica, 299
MITTENDORF, Bob, 318
MITZEL, Chrysann, 951
MIX, Vicki, 153
MIYAHIRA, Linda M, 425
MIYASHIRO, Tiffanie, 632
MIYAUCHI, Heather E, 744
MIZE, Gregory H, 131
MIZE, Sam, 519
MOASE, Dorothy, 1088
MOATS, Anne, 308
MOBASSERI, Bahareh, 401
MOCCERO, Lydia, 378
MOCNY, Kathy L, 581

MOECK, June M, 115
MOELLER, Deborah, 986
MOEN, Margaret, 254
MOFFETT, Lorena E, 141
MOGEL, Barry A, 227
MOGORU, Dedrick M, 70
MOLL, Mia, 211
MOMARTS, Joyce, 771
MOMBERG, D Elaine, 172
MONACO, Josephine, 1032
MONAHAN, Evan, 888
MONAHAN, Wm J, 674
MONAI, Vonne, 294
MONDELL, Denise, 1049
MONDOR, Beatrice E, 1077
MONDS, Judith, 42
MONELLO, Lisa Ann, 161
MONETTE, Mary C, 440
MONETTI, Debra Renee, 809
MONEY, Sharon L, 629
MONEYSMITH, Carol, 586
MONGAN, Sarah, 1177
MONGE-CALDERON, Sandra, 1091
MONK, Herbert Lee, 919
MONKA, Stephanie, 1090
MONNIER, Missy, 14
MONROE, Dani, 375
MONROE, Judy L, 1167
MONROE, Shirley Smith, 759
MONSON, Amy A, 829
MONTANARI, Jean, 404
MONTEER, Barbara, 257
MONTEMAYOR, Joanne M Wilke, 71
MONTFORD, Clara, 92
MONTGOMERY, Dusty, 648
MONTGOMERY, Jack W, 226
MONTGOMERY, Ron, 233
MONTGOMERY, Vincent, 74
MOODY, Jennifer, 106
MOON, Donald R, 285
MOON, Hal, 112
MOONEY, Barbara D, 132
MOONEY, G E, 77
MOONEY, Jacqueline, 384
MOONEY, Lawrence H, 235
MOONEY, Marguerite, 1072
MOORE Jr, James I, 200
MOORE, Alan, 624
MOORE, Angela, 482
MOORE, April C, 173
MOORE, Betsy, 1029
MOORE, Brice, 955
MOORE, Carol Ann, 267
MOORE, Carzell, 713
MOORE, Charlotte, 539
MOORE, Deborah M, 830
MOORE, Diana D, 916
MOORE, Edith Eastin, 975
MOORE, Eva, 291
MOORE, Freeman E, 816
MOORE, Gladus M, 470, 1032
MOORE, Hazel S, 860
MOORE, Jean D, 123
MOORE, John W, 708
MOORE, Joyce Keller, 67, 210
MOORE, Leo Reeve, 1118
MOORE, Lory, 1128
MOORE, Lucille J, 836
MOORE, Marge, 423
MOORE, Martha Ann, 417
MOORE, Mary Louise, 840
MOORE, Milton V, 507
MOORE, N R, 714
MOORE, Nellie C, 386
MOORE, Robert, 52
MOORE, Sandra Ann, 1047
MOORE, Sonia A, 1027
MOORE, Tammy Renee, 1019
MOORE, Wendy Kaori, 425
MOORE-CORNETT, Alice D, 1005
MOORES, Hervey C, 233
MOORHEAD, Marc, 597
MORA, Stephen M, 65
MORAES, Millie, 393
MORALES, Carmen R, 173
MORAN, J P, 827
MORAN, Janice, 492
MORAND, Evelyn J, 881
MORBIT, Patricia, 524
MOREAN, Katherine L, 821
MOREAUX, Mary, 79
MOREHEAD, Crystal, 218
MORELAND, A And The Quorum Sig, 949
MORELLI, Diane M, 733
MORENCY, Sheila, 171
MORENO, Antonia, 574
MOREY, Tod A, 604
MORGAN III, William Monroe, 945
MORGAN, Christie, 305
MORGAN, Chuck, 449
MORGAN, Evelyn, 157
MORGAN, Helen Kelsey, 579
MORGAN, Jane, 803
MORGAN, Jeanne Louise, 565
MORGAN, Judith G, 479
MORGAN, Lisa M, 158
MORGAN, Mary K, 562
MORGAN, Patrick Scott, 1158
MORGAN, Rusty, 821
MORGAN, Sharon, 775
MORGAN, Sharon A, 522
MORGAN, Shauna, 575
MORGAN, Shirley Grace, 988
MORIARTY, Chelsea, 224
MORICONI, Judith J, 1112
MORIN, Julie A, 265
MORIN, Richard J, 518
MORLEY, Maribeth, 250
MORNING DAWN, Wayne A, 95
MORNING, Kelli, 715
MORNINGSTAR, Yvonne, 402
MORONEY, Kellie A, 1013
MOROTTI, Gloria J, 628
MORREY, Frances, 447
MORRIS, Alex M, 120
MORRIS, Barbara Jane, 172
MORRIS, Barrie L, 149
MORRIS, Clover D, 93
MORRIS, Corine, 1177
MORRIS, D Marie, 508
MORRIS, Diane, 1169
MORRIS, Jennifer L, 678
MORRIS, K, 181
MORRIS, Kathleen, 516
MORRIS, Kathy O, 872
MORRIS, Lee Banning, 1145
MORRIS, Marcia R, 16
MORRIS, Margaret L, 848
MORRIS, Ms Jeannette, 516
MORRIS, Sandra M, 526
MORRIS, Shirley Hill, 647
MORRISON, Eileen M, 319
MORRISON, Mary E, 875
MORRISON, Patricia C, 1078
MORRISON, Sondra, 346
MORRISON, Trinnette M, 339
MORRISSETTE, Brooke G, 94
MORROW, Glenda Marie, 1018
MORROW, Lieunell S, 755
MORROW, Teresa, 596
MORROW, William (Tom), 648
MORSE, Derald A, 336
MORSE, Gael M, 702
MORSE, Stephen John, 260
MORSEY, Ethel J, 589
MORTENSEN, Lorina B, 330
MORTENSEN, Tracy A, 512
MORTIMER III, Thomas Francis, 779
MORTLOCK, Michael J, 535
MORVANT, Hazel, 623
MOSBY, Barbara H, 609
MOSCHOWSKY, Elle, 417
MOSELEY, Allen D, 241
MOSES, Debbie, 95
MOSES, Lynn, 1052
MOSES, Peggy J, 360
MOSESIAN, Pamela M, 569
MOSHER, Marie J, 541
MOSOLF, Lillian F, 120
MOSS, Angela, 953
MOSS, Gladys V, 997
MOSS, Margaret, 574
MOSS, Molaika Mccoya, 617
MOSS, Rebecca, 1064
MOSS, Rickie L, 1064
MOSS, Sandra D, 1029
MOST Jr, Kenneth D, 478
MOSYCHUK, Heather Margaret, 615
MOTA, Gina, 381
MOTE, D R, 466
MOTON, Shirley A, 182
MOTT, Edith L, 1177
MOULIK, Amal, 155
MOULTON, Bonnie, 358
MOULTRIE, Lyle, 222
MOURA, Genny, 288
MOWRER, Amy, 536
MOWRY, Linda S, 430
MOXLEY, Patrick Lahay, 558
MOYER, Jackie, 1043
MOYER, Wanda, 935
MOYERS, Joel E, 487
MOZART, Mitch E, 367
MOZENA, Carmen, 775
MOZER, Christine B, 1048
MOZES, Barry, 160
MOZINGO, Patricia Q, 435
MRKVICKA, Elizabeth, 1064
MROZ, Desdra L, 700
MUEHLBACH, Christina, 996
MUELLER, George, 50
MUELLER, Louise, 682
MUELLER, Michael, 997
MUELLER, Sharon A, 538
MUELLER, Susanne, 168
MUHAMMAD, Angel S A, 325
MUHAMMAD, Bonita Ann, 1105
MUHLNICKEL, Amber, 599
MUIA, Maria A, 132
MUILENBURG, Babe B, 586
MUISE, Mary E, 969
MULAY, Fanny, 1169
MULCARE, Mary Ellen, 603
MULHOLLAND, Kevin, 603
MULLANEY, Annemarie, 1054
MULLANEY, Eileen, 132
MULLEN, Mildred R, 407
MULLEN, Norma, 562
MULLEN, Timothy, 421
MULLEN, William M, 8
MULLENAX, Ruthe, 556
MULLENS, Mary A, 803
MULLENS, Wilbur D, 554
MULLER, Helen J, 227
MULLER, Karlie A, 683
MULLIN, Tara G, 657
MULLINS, Belva, 1158
MULLINS, Gary A, 1112
MULLINS, Lois Ansell, 1112
MULVEY, Michael P, 828
MULVILLE, Martha, 726
MUMMA, Sheila, 683
MUNCY, Lou Ellen, 1111
MUNDSCHENK, Linda M, 1025
MUNGER, Delos, 999
MUNGIN, Carol F, 833
MUNIZ, Mildred, 1174
MUNKACSY, William M, 295
MUNROE, Kerry, 642
MUNSON, Nancy Flebbe, 650
MUNTZ, Mary Broderick, 782
MURDOCK, John E, 1090
MURPHEY, Esther, 874
MURPHY, Alberta, 937
MURPHY, Bea Buelina, 1091
MURPHY, Carol, 1004
MURPHY, Daniel J, 640
MURPHY, Ellen, 380
MURPHY, Fern Gardiner, 782
MURPHY, Grace T, 1122
MURPHY, Janeane Faye, 1086
MURPHY, Jodi Lynn, 700
MURPHY, Julia C, 438
MURPHY, Kathleen M, 90
MURPHY, Kathryn, 100
MURPHY, Laura, 452
MURPHY, Marie-louise, 136
MURPHY, Mary G, 566
MURPHY-KELLEY, Linda, 184
MURRAY, Charles W, 727
MURRAY, Claire T, 1077
MURRAY, Doris, 459
MURRAY, Erma E, 418
MURRAY, Evelyn, 180
MURRAY, Gilbert S, 56
MURRAY, Virginia D Hale, 515
MURRAY-DUDLEY, Martha, 142
MUSIAL, Mary Ann T, 275
MUSIYOWSKI, Stacy Lynn, 274
MUSOLFF, R J, 644
MUSSELL, Stan, 93
MUUSS, Kim, 630
MUYLAERT, Madeline, 408
MUZICHENKO, Lyuba, 672
MUZZY Sr, Harvey E "Chief", 1003
MYATT, Pat, 142
MYERS, Barbara, 411
MYERS, Carolyn M, 980
MYERS, Deborah A, 605
MYERS, Debra Rae, 28
MYERS, Donna, 281
MYERS, Jacqueline, 102
MYERS, Maryjo, 262
MYERS, Ruth I, 942
MYERS, Wendolyn C, 804
MYERS-YOUNG, Lenora, 709
MYLES, Earnestine J, 934
MYRRH, Maia, 1182

N

NADEAU, Evelyn A, 1051
NADEAU, Lionel A, 816
NADER, Percilla G, 953
NADER, Ronald W, 685
NADOLNY, Robert W, 111
NAGEL, Carla J, 712
NAGLE-SIMMONS, Amelia J, 747
NAGY, Mr Bela, 981
NAHAR, Sultana, 425
NAHIRNIAK, Stephanie, 937
NAIL, Angela, 1111
NAILE, Jacqueline, 353
NAJERA Sr, Antonino E, 1154
NAKAKIHARA, Kirk, 644
NAKAMURA, Hiromu, 184
NAKAZAWA, Rika, 1111
NANCE, Peggy Oliver, 940
NANCY JO, Nancy J, 1010
NANNARIELLO, Gary, 159
NANTZE, Carol Maxwell, 1014
NAOMI MARY, Naomi M, 611
NAPIER, Marian Leigh, 515
NAPIER, Mary "Connie" Z, 108
NAPOLETANO, Tony, 910
NAPOLI, Susan, 1007
NAPPA, Cynthia B, 348
NARANICK, Claudia S, 117
NARDIN, Doya, 1018
NARDONI, Nic Louis, 838
NASH, Amber, 875
NASH, Grant, 1069
NASH, Michael L, 813
NASH, Pat, 137
NASH, R A, 164
NASS, Laura Hanson, 1123
NATHANSON, Bonnie, 490
NATIONS, Roberta, 187
NAUHEIM, J S, 155
NAULT, Sonja, 974
NAVAGH, Karen R, 402
NAVARRE, Joanne M, 74
NAVARRO, Vanessa, 757
NAVICKI, Bonnie Lou, 990
NAWELLS, Corinne, 776
NAZWORTHY, Cynthia, 250
NEAL, Pamela, 1049
NEAL, Sylvia P, 121
NEAL, Terry R, 541
NEALE, James H, 749
NEALEIGH, Diana Flowers, 525
NEAS, Karen, 117
NEATER, By, 284
NEAVOLL, Della, 26
NEBEL, Deborah, 251
NEDVED, Crystal, 1104, 1060
NEEDHAM, Orin E, 44
NEELY, Theresa, 997
NEER, Jennifer, 1005
NEESE, Maggie, 975
NEFF, Joanna, 100
NEIDIG, Valerie, 191
NEIGHBORS, Judy M, 836
NEIGHBORS, K Mark, 828
NEILSON, Debbera E, 765
NEILSON, Wendee, 106
NEIMAN, Frances E, 438
NELMS, Kevin Brent, 810
NELSON, Christa Lee, 286
NELSON, Debra, 324
NELSON, Eric P, 1010
NELSON, L Mae, 845
NELSON, Michael C, 778
NELSON, Noel G, 957
NELSON, Patricia, 357
NELSON, Peggy T, 734
NELSON, Ruth Marie, 700
NELSON, Susan Leigh (Peifer), 1075
NELSON, Thora E, 38
NELSON, Vicki, 470
NELSON, Virginia M, 340
NELSON, Waudell B, 215
NELSON-DEELEY, Pauline, 1105
NEMETH-SPEARMAN, Katherinea, 282
NEMOLA, Lucia, 558
NENNICH, David J, 18
NERYS, Oscar, 631
NESBITT, Robert F, 934
NESS, Helen N, 123
NESSET, Marcia L, 230
NESSLAGE, Ronnie, 126
NESTAVAL, Jamie, 930
NESTOR, Lewis Rodger, 767
NETHERCOTT, Jill T, 515
NEU, Dori Lamer, 383
NEUBAUER, Carrie, 844
NEUBAUER, Margaret W, 214
NEUMAN, Sandra, 166
NEUSER, Kathleen N, 619
NEVAREZ, Melissa, 902
NEVILLE, Jeanne M, 25
NEVILLE, Mary Grace, 491
NEVINS, Peggy, 59
NEW JERUSALEM PROJECT GROUP, 8
NEW, Bill, 80
NEW, Nancy, 686
NEWBERN, Martha J, 118
NEWBY, Barbara A, 24
NEWBY, Carmen Rae, 996
NEWBY, Parker S, 805
NEWCOMB, Rann, 154
NEWELL, Harold L, 204
NEWLAND, Walter M, 76
NEWLIN, Carl A, 52
NEWMAN, Clarke, 188
NEWMAN, Linda E, 607
NEWMAN, Milton A, 737
NEWSOM, Dorothy A, 946
NEWSOME, Gwen, 340
NEWSON, Sally, 619
NEWTON, Esther, 1129
NEWTON, Gregory, 435
NEWTON, Naomi, 890
NEWTON, Phyllis, 40, 693
NGUYEN, Khanh H, 400
NGUYEN, Lien, 776
NGUYEN, Thuan, 1124
NICAS, Carole, 167
NICELY, Patricia B, 379
NICEWARNER, J Averil, 1154
NICHOLES, Wade, 605
NICHOLLS, Norene C, 465
NICHOLS, Donna A, 1002
NICHOLS, Donna Jo, 931
NICHOLS, Edward M, 691
NICHOLS, Grace C, 819
NICHOLS, Granny, 484
NICHOLS, Harry Lee, 87
NICHOLS, Lucinda M, 1109
NICHOLS, Nick, 526
NICHOLS, Robert A, 75
NICHOLS, Sally L, 244
NICHOLS, Tim O, 335
NICHOLS-SMETANA, Belinda, 60
NICHOLSON, Alfred G, 819
NICHOLSON, Christopher A, 856
NICHOLSON, Delores, 491
NICHOLSON, Margo, 691
NICKEL, Hulda, 592
NICKELS, Jacqueline C, 657
NICKERSON, Flotella, 285
NICKERSON, Mary, 906
NICKOLS, Wendy Raquel, 717
NICKRENZ, Elizabeth, 284
NICOLAIDES, Anthony D, 423
NICOLAISEN, Ruth Ann, 924
NICOLI, Ruth S, 720
NICOLINI, Robert S, 1151
NIDER, Kebra L, 15
NIEBAUER, Sherie, 186
NIEHAUS, Rudolf, 961
NIELSEN, Dawn M, 105
NIELSEN, Ellen, 578
NIELSEN, Maxine, 8
NIEMAN, Carol, 979
NIEMEYER, Ginger, 999
NIEMI, Candalyn M B, 651
NIEMI, Dorothy P, 790
NIGHTHAWK, Johnnie, 136
NIGRO RN, Mary G, 730
NIGRO-MCGEGHAN, Patricia A, 78
NIHART, Nancy E, 40
NILSSON, Sherry Lyn, 94
NIMMO, Lenora Lee, 167
NISSEN, Jeri L, 880
NISSILA, Etti W, 1136
NITEK, Ginger Sue, 471
NITSCHKE, Amber, 250
NITTERAUER, Mary Jane, 922
NIX, J Donald, 228
NIX, Jay Braxton, 1005
NIXON, Eunice H, 98
NIXON, Sheila W, 74
NIXX, Jimi, 341
NOAH, Judy, 243
NOBLE, Patricia H, 682
NOCERA, Paul M, 317
NOEL, Brenda E, 408
NOFTSGER, Barb, 865
NOGUERA, Debra, 153
NOLAN, Erika, 1038
NOLAN, Kathi, 446
NOLAN, William Allen, 792
NOLEN, Teresa Diane, 247
NONEMAN, Robert Alan, 787
NOON, Michael E, 415
NORCROSS, E Lynn, 997
NORDIN, Berith, 272
NORDLUND, Barbara, 930
NORGREN, Amy L, 404
NORMAN, Charles H, 537
NORRIS, Anna Mary, 1110
NORRIS, Laura, 423
NORRIS, Lorraine, 137

NORRIS, Natalie, 67
NORRIS, Orpha P, 888
NORRIS, Sylvia, 12
NORTE, Lenora, 120
NORTH, Evelyn G, 829
NORTH, Sheila D, 925
NORTH, Stacey, 1025
NORTHCUTT, Karon, 1065
NORTON, Anne, 64
NORTON, Bicki, 371
NORTON, D A, 67
NORTON, Diane, 701
NORTON, Donna E, 732
NORTON, Heather, 960
NORTON, Larry D, 922
NORTON, Mie Kimura, 457
NORTON, Nancy E, 360
NORTON, Tracy, 523
NORUM, Jo, 92
NOTARNICOLA, Lea Rose, 462
NOTNALB, Yrral, 1158
NOTTA, W, 29
NOTTER, Wendy, 1073
NOURSE, Eva Allen, 184
NOVAK, Geraldine (Gerrie), 533
NOVAK, L C, 1007
NOVINGER, Linda L, 463
NOWELS, Evelyn Louise, 847, 295
NTAWE, Gerard, 916
NU, William, 273
NUCE, Scott A, 1104
NUGENT, Daisy, 375
NUGENT, Yvette L, 363
NULPH, Donnie D, 1130
NUNEZ, Henry J, 798
NUNHAM, Connie J, 1011
NUNN, Mark, 336
NURMI, Hilma, 360
NUSS-RICK, Donna J, 240
NUTT, Dorothy F, 472
NYBAKKEN, Kate, 963
NYBERG, Leslie, 1199
NYE, Jo Ellen, 746
NYIKOS, John, 1147
NYLEN, Leslie Ann, 64
NYLUND, Robin, 1089
NYSTROM, Joan I, 72

O

O'BANNON, Ruth, 482
O'BRIEN, John J P, 387
O'BRIEN, Joseph Edward, 159
O'BRIEN, Melinda K, 469
O'BRIEN, Shelly, 273
O'CONNELL, Cindy J, 47
O'CONNELL, Joseph P, 611
O'CONNELL, Leslie, 96
O'CONNELL, Loretta M, 587
O'CONNOR, Edith W, 329
O'CONNOR, Kerri Jean, 706
O'CONNOR, Therese, 868
O'DONNELL, Daniel, 1010
O'DONNELL, John Vincent, 1145
O'DONOGHUE, Kathleen, 176
O'DONOVAN, Brian Donald, 873
O'DRISCOLL, Shirley, 197
O'FARRELL, William M, 1117
O'FLAHERTY, Margaret, 203
O'FLANNAGAN, Kathleen, 525
O'HARA, Barbara A, 564
O'HARA, Brian, 798
O'HARA, Kelly M, 650
O'KEEFE, Maureen, 576
O'LEARY, Janet, 409
O'LEARY, Nancy C, 430
O'LOUGHLIN, Marguerite B, 216
O'LOUGHLIN, Mary T, 21
O'NEAL, Travis, 253
O'NEIL, Connie L, 829
O'NEIL, Sheila, 211
O'NEILL, Mary B, 122
O'QUINN, Flora, 1128
O'ROURKE, Hope, 20
O'SHEA, Maureen, 697
OAKLEY, Joanne C, 1103
OBERDORF, Catherine A, 777
OBERLE, Dorothy Helen, 784
OBERMILLER, William L, 362
OBERT, Magdalena, 14
OBRIEN, Nancy, 800
OCONNOR, Stephen J, 857
ODAR, Thomas, 761
ODIERNO, Richard A, 346
ODOM, Bonnie, 663
ODOM, Tina R, 137
ODOM, Tommie H, 577
ODONNELL, Mary J, 840
OESTERMYER, Jan, 216
OFFICER, Gina M, 907
OGBU, E Ken, 249
OGDEN, Jo-Ann M, 87
OGIER, Danielle R, 1072
OGLE, Nina, 1123
OHLBAUM, Jennifer, 886
OHN, Elizabeth Q, 287
OKE-CHIERO, Judy, 461
OKEEN, Marion, 279
OKEY, Robert, 985
OLARIKSIRI, Julie, 195
OLCOTT, Sylvia G, 495
OLDHAM, N J, 295
OLDMIXON, R L, 1202
OLEYAR, Florence, 1004
OLIGER, Evelyn P, 630
OLINGER, Nancy, 996
OLISA, Anthony, 1172
OLIVA, Melanie, 835
OLIVEIRA, Paulette, 1020
OLIVEIRA, Sean J, 1198
OLIVER, Alfred, 886
OLIVER, Edna, 962
OLIVER, Margaret H, 217
OLIVER, Ollie, 1130
OLIVER, Ruth S, 263
OLIVER, Samuel C, 162
OLIVER, Tina, 986
OLSEN, Dawn S, 935
OLSEN, Eric, 344
OLSEN, Judi A, 568
OLSEN, Larry M, 615
OLSEN, Lisa, 82
OLSHINSKY, Bonnie, 92
OLSIN, Donna M, 331
OLSON III, Charles E, 1165
OLSON Jr, Ron J, 795
OLSON, Catherine E, 1006
OLSON, Christin, 179
OLSON, Julie A, 732
OLSON, Kari, 624
OLSON, Mildred E, 1108
OLSON, Myrtle F, 1135
OLTMAN, Marillyn M, 559
ONOPA, Diane, 751
OPOKA, Edward M, 733
OPPERMAN, Agnes, 141
ORCHARD, Michelle E, 891
ORIGER, Linda Ellen, 620
OROL, Donna (Dee), 257
OROSZI, Arline C, 382
ORPUT, Derace E, 303
ORR, Jean M, 921
ORR, Judy M, 321
ORR, Latonia, 603
ORR, Lori, 1001
ORSBORN, Anne M, 680
ORSEY, Sylvia, 1125
ORT, Jeanette M T, 397
ORTEGA, Guillermo Gil Chamorro, 978
ORTIZ Jr, Frank, 946
ORTIZ, Joseph, 513
OSBORN, Barbara A, 120
OSBORN, Brian W, 9
OSBORNE, Dawna, 7
OSBORNE, Judy C, 685, 57
OSBORNE, Kevin V, 729
OSBORNE, William, 44
OSBURN, Laura M, 580
OSGOOD-SOJOURNER, Dorothy, 324
OSMERA, Elizabeth, 572
OSMON, Lara, 939
OSTERMAN, John, 724
OSTERMAN, Shannon L, 885
OSTRANDER, Howard, 212
OSTROM, Alice Koonts, 974
OSTROM, Helen M, 17
OTAKE, Patricia D G, 678
OTILANO, Gloria Petelo, 899
OTIS, Kathryn, 1147
OTT, Margaret E, 186
OTT, Regina Denise, 582
OTTERLINE, Valerie J, 724
OTTO, Sherry L, 601
OTTOLINI, Juna D'lynn, 1089
OTWELL, Irma B, 377
OUIMET, Lucie-C, 231
OUROUSSOFF, Tatiana, 1123
OVERPECK, Dee, 15, 1032
OVERTON, Laura, 301
OWEN, Sue, 99
OWENNA, Jessie Ray, 258
OWENS, A H, 1014
OWENS, Dennis "Pete", 912
OWENS, Jennifer R, 1104
OWENS, Shawn Annette, 635
OWNBEY, Jenna V, 85
OXLEY, James R, 125

P

PABOR, Helen W, 945
PACANA, Irene Suchta, 552
PACE, Billy, 789
PACE, Dawn M, 473
PACE, George, 650
PACE, Mamie L, 480
PACHECO, John A, 642
PACITTO, Mary E, 501
PACK, Ida, 938
PACKER, Ruth, 521
PACKETT, John B, 892
PACOTTI, Jean, 198
PADDEN, Christina, 26
PADEN, Corie, 602
PADGETT, S Eric, 1029
PADHAY, Amit Bando, 8
PADIAS, Nancy Dye, 185
PADILLA, Ray, 626
PADILLA, Sana, 770
PADILLA, Wendy, 1181
PAFFRATH, Kenneth F, 566
PAGE Jr, Lindsey W, 917
PAGE, Carolyn G, 571
PAGE, Elizabeth, 632
PAGE, Jean R, 982
PAGE, Joann Stovall, 267
PAGE, Luther, 169
PAGELS, Aileen, 48
PAGLIANETE, Dianna, 1003
PAHL, Lisa Colleen, 1023
PAIGE, Byron, 444
PAIGE, Sheryl J, 703
PAIGE, Thomas A, 760
PAINTER, Alexander, 1101
PAINTER, Freda Beth, 255
PAJE, Veronica L, 715
PALACIO, Angela M, 1104
PALERMO, Samuel, 381
PALEY, Jon B, 129
PALFFY-ROSS, Marguerite, 716
PALM, Larry, 1009
PALM, Virginia, 335
PALMACCI, Tina, 629
PALMER, Cecelia Lynn, 756
PALMER, David, 409
PALMER, Emmaline, 796
PALMER, Maureen J, 759
PALMER, Ruth C, 301
PALMER, Shelley L, 558
PALMER, Timothy L, 1130
PALMIERO, Dawn, 63
PALMORE, Eugene R, 53
PANDOS, Vassilios, 962
PANEK, Jeannie L, 705
PANION, Nathan, 622
PANITCH, Sanford, 618
PANNOZZO, Gina, 642
PANNULLO, Lorrie A, 169
PANOZZO, Roberta J, 388
EFTHYMIOU, Pantelis, 1093
PANTOS, Nicolas, 484
PANZONE, Valentina M, 1042
PAPANDREW, Peter, 249
PAPET, Pamula, 647
PAPKA, Tamara, 811
PAPP, Paul Michael, 58
PAPPAKOSTAS, Kathy L, 815
PAPROCKI, Kelley, 920
PAQUIZ, Jovy G, 878
PARADISE, Susan M, 633
PARAMORE Jr, Julian A, 356
PARDRIDGE, Michael, 217
PARENT, Kris Antonia, 589
PARENT, Nicole M, 883
PARISH, Joann A, 310
PARISI, Dominick, 1036
PARK, Gwen, 675
PARKER, Bonnie, 1135
PARKER, Chris Gray, 450
PARKER, David, 1117
PARKER, David W, 60
PARKER, Dawn, 217
PARKER, Dorothy L, 329
PARKER, Gwen, 577
PARKER, Jennifer K, 307
PARKER, Lebron, 1058
PARKER, Lena, 25
PARKER, Linda D, 436
PARKER, Linda L, 334
PARKER, Linda Moles, 120
PARKER, Lona, 304
PARKER, Louise, 218
PARKER, Margaret E, 528
PARKER, Misty Eve, 365
PARKER, Nancy, 991
PARKER, Rebecca Jane, 388
PARKER, Roy L, 504
PARKER, Ruth Anne, 1096
PARKER, Tracey E, 649
PARKER-ZIEGENBEIN, Mickey, 124
PARKISON, Mary Evelyn, 275
PARKS, Casey, 43
PARKS, Keith, 496
PARKS, Tracy Allen, 109
PARNELL, Darlena A, 593
PARR, Susan, 659
PARRENELLO, Ann, 937
PARRETT, Laura, 226
PARRISH, Eugene J, 74
PARRISH, Jessica, 1015
PARRISH, Joyce, 708
PARRISH, Peggy, 88
PARRISH, Robert S, 713
PARRISH, Wayne, 90
PARRY, Betty, 1104
PARSONS, Carol Ann, 637
PARTAIN, Wanda, 123
PARTIN, Rhonda K, 658
PARU, Marden David, 487
PASCAL, Mariaelena, 980
PASKIN, Donna W, 7
PASLEY, Mark Antonio, 1063
PASLEY-SMITH, Jennifer, 556
PASS, Michele M, 278
PASSAMONTE, Sandra J, 680
PASTERNIAK, Mark, 1082
PASTORIUS, Janet Lee, 928
PASZTOR, Sharon, 327
PATACSIL, Porfiria, 427
PATCH, Pat, 985
PATE, C D, 671
PATE, Mary Kay, 656
PATEE, Gene, 477
PATEL, Farah, 118
PATERA, Bernice V, 1006
PATERNO, Lou, 447
PATRICK, Claudia, 395
PATRICK, Eunice Evelyn, 569
PATRICK, Kathleen, 140
PATRICK, Kenneth R, 495
PATTEN, Bernard M, 431
PATTERSON, Becky, 1136
PATTERSON, Carol Joyce, 67
PATTERSON, Charlotte V, 844
PATTERSON, Deborah B, 661
PATTERSON, Gretchen A, 156
PATTERSON, Larry Brown, 381
PATTERSON, Lona, 367
PATTERSON, M F, 787
PATTERSON, Taconya, 610
PATTON, Bertha P, 271
PATTON, Kenneth D, 1183
PATTON, Lucie Dean, 77
PAUCIELLO, Sal Robert, 884
PAUL, Catherine P, 775
PAUL, Elaine, 658
PAUL, Ernest, 1051
PAUL, Jeanette S, 1112
PAUL, Netto A, 579
PAUL, Richard, 23
PAUL, Tapian, 367
PAUL, Wade, 290
PAULETTE, Geraldine, 1045
PAULEY, Gladys, 1201
PAULK, Geary, 114
PAUNOVSKA, Verka, 633
PAURICH, John S, 935
PAVLO, Corrine Ann, 61
PAVLOVSKY, R C, 746
PAWLOWSKI, Deborah, 1018
PAXSON, Katherine T, 347
PAXSON, Michel, 160
PAXTON, (Maggie) Margaret, 744
PAYETTE, Robert, 1138
PAYNE, Adrian, 868
PAYNE, Brian C, 469
PAYNE, Edith Mae, 336
PAYNE, Jill, 295
PAYNE, Phyllis B, 758
PAYNE, Sandy, 556
PAYNE, Tammy L, 860
PAYNE, Toni, 1162
PAYNE, Ursula, 206
PEACOCK, Shanon, 772
PEAKE, Margaret L, 243
PEARCE, Carole M, 1039
PEARCE, Grace E Hayes, 708
PEARCE, Judi, 562
PEARCE, Richard, 576
PEARCE, Stephen F, 658
PEARCY, Patty, 519
PEARO, J, 520
PEARSE, Jennie, 1173
PEARSON, Bertha Cornwall, 979
PEARSON, Lori Gayle, 914
PEARSON, Shirley, 877
PEARSON, Twyla, 228
PEARSON, Winnifred, 170
PEAVEY-PLACE, Flora Kalloch, 1083
PEAVLER, Kathy, 955
PEAY, E L, 243
PEAY, Eugene, 244
PECK, Patricia Rubio, 1104
PECOR, Audrey Frances, 1146
PEDERSEN, Brent, 784
PEDERSEN, Doug, 829
PEDRO, Robert A, 433
PEDROLI, Amy Lyn, 32
PEEK, Debrina J, 109
PEGG, Zora Riddle, 231
PEILER, Charlotte M, 828
PEIPPO, Kaisa, 409
PEIREZ, Greg, 278
PEKALA, Keli Jo, 423
PELATE, Sharon M, 964
PELC, Ryszarda Lida, 279
PELHAM, Virginia Ross, 834
PELLARIN Jr, Victor L, 534
PELLETIER Jr, Gilbert J, 1014
PEMBERTON, Nancy Brown, 735
PEMBERTON, Troy J, 428
PEMSL, Maria A, 347
PENCE, Michelle R, 701
PENDLETON, Renee, 447
PENDOLA, Rose M, 9
PENMAN, Wililiam J, 228
PENN, Lora Marie, 920
PENNER, Douglas Lee, 962
PENNER, Esther E, 1157
PENNINGS, Kim, 951
PENNINGTON, Anita Arbutus, 721
PENNINGTON, Gene, 460
PENNINGTON, Kimberly L, 232
PENNINGTON, Ted, 488
PENNINGTON, Tracy Y, 33
PENNO, Bonnie, 797
PENROD, Jeanne, 399
PENTERICS, Helen, 1190
PENTZ, Vickie, 1157
PENZO, Jessica, 212
PEOPLES, Joseph N, 531
PEPIN, Myrna L, 702
PERALTA, Manuel, 307
PERAULT, Robert, 22, 22
PERCUPCHICK, Harry, 841
PERDUE, John, 89
PERDUE, Laura G, 50
PERDUE, Melissa Anne, 56
PEREIRA, Antonio V, 881
PEREIRA, Lisa, 960
PEREZ Jr, Anthony, 173
PEREZ, Brian E, 516
PEREZ, Paul, 367
PEREZ, Robert Wayne, 1105
PERILLI, Lynne, 722
PERKIEL, Frank, 1128
PERKINS, Becky-Joe N, 370
PERKINS, Connie, 509
PERKINS, Detra Danelle, 537
PERKINS, Jennifer, 483
PERKINS, Joanne, 510
PERKINS, Joanne, 995, 995
PERKINS, Kimberly, 875
PERKINS, Larry A, 827
PERKINS, Nancy Arlene, 408
PERKINS, Patsy L, 454
PERKINS, Randall L, 1186
PERNA, Ann, 421
PERRA, Jennifer O, 644
PERRELET, Crystal Ann, 773
PERRIMAN, Betty J, 1011
PERRIN, Leanne J, 252
PERRINGTON, Phil Joseph, 859
PERRON, Carmen, 709
PERRY, Amy Denise, 660
PERRY, Anthony, 370
PERRY, Beth, 763
PERRY, Constance L, 120
PERRY, Danny, 167
PERRY, Delores E, 651
PERRY, Diane E, 1072
PERRY, Doris, 1128
PERRY, Elisabeth A, 1056
PERRY, Evelyn B, 1114
PERRY, George, 16
PERRY, Glenn T, 1081
PERRY, Kay, 157
PERRY, Sylvia Wallau, 704
PERSONS, Charles K, 1042
PESCE, Charlene, 623
PESCHKA, Darcy Kay, 271
PESOLA, Maija, 920
PESUTICH Jr, James J, 561

PETEL, Beverly, 560
PETER, Ms Bonnie Simmons, 726
PETERS, Agnes M, 828
PETERS, Alycia G, 783
PETERS, Dorris L, 833
PETERS, Joanna, 1177
PETERS, Keli, 402
PETERS, Shirley D, 474
PETERSON, Barbara, 319
PETERSON, Barbara D, 819
PETERSON, Brenda Tanner, 462
PETERSON, David, 300
PETERSON, Erik C, 1024
PETERSON, Geraldine, 170
PETERSON, Janet G, 585
PETERSON, Keith, 602
PETERSON, Lawrence W, 770
PETERSON, Leah, 101
PETERSON, Mark, 113
PETERSON, Naomi, 960
PETERSON, Patricia E, 645
PETERSON, Sarah, 181
PETERSON, Tracy Ann, 1013
PETERSON, Walter David, 767
PETINAK, Kathleen E, 340
PETITT, Glenn B, 1100
PETOSKEY, Barbara L, 130
PETRAITIS, Marilyn Jean, 465
PETRILLO, Amanda J, 115
PETRO, Christopher C, 266
PETRORO, Nicholas, 408
PETRY, Geraldine H, 176
PETTIT, Robert, 1039
PEVY, Charles, 526
PEZEL, David, 624
PEZZANI, Nellie, 910
PFAFF, Betty, 513
PFAFF, Tracy Ann, 381
PFEFFER, Karen J, 820
PFERTSH, Edward, 89
PFIESTER, Michael A, 1061
PFUND, Terra, 565
PHAIAH, Pamela, 1044
PHAM, Kenh, 80
PHAN, David A, 1015
PHELAN, Susan, 1040
PHELPS, Ila, 989
PHELPS, Ronnie, 729
PHILIPPS, Dana, 453
PHILLIP, Dennis F, 754
PHILLIPPY, Wendy S, 111
PHILLIPS, Bonnie L, 888
PHILLIPS, Carroll, 980
PHILLIPS, Catherine L, 869
PHILLIPS, Charlotte A, 531, 291
PHILLIPS, Chris A, 722
PHILLIPS, Coral N, 468
PHILLIPS, Deborah, 358
PHILLIPS, Deborah C, 757
PHILLIPS, Dennis, 488
PHILLIPS, Heather, 947
PHILLIPS, Jean C, 213
PHILLIPS, Jennifer, 955
PHILLIPS, Jewell, 1193
PHILLIPS, Marguerite, 213
PHILLIPS, Mrs M R, 403
PHILLIPS, Nancy K, 234
PHILLIPS, Ron, 969
PHILLIPS, Ron, 237
PHILLIPS, Rose Marie, 866
PHILLIPS, Sandra G, 1067
PHILLIPS, Timothy J, 373
PHILLIPS, Vicki, 655
PHILLIPS, Zoe V, 644
PHILO, Thelma, 413
PHINEZY, Ophelia, 1157
PHINNEY, Alberta Dedera, 807
PHIPPIN, Melvin T, 304
PHIPPS Sr, Thomas E, 82
PHIPPS, Gertrude, 827
PHYLLIS, Phyllis J, 667
PICARD, Tammy, 249
PICCIANO, David, 163
PICHON, Sandra Haynes, 175
PICKARD, Annie, 703
PICKARD, Gregory J, 364
PICKER, Franklin August, 959
PICKERING, Pamela, 556
PICKETT, Linda, 402
PICKETT, Mr John J, 932
PICKETT, Sheri Lyn, 791
PICKETT, Vicki B, 498
PICKIN, Damaris A, 893
PICKREN, Rhonda, 901
PIEDRA, Joaquin E, 1124
PIEPER, Orville W, 874
PIERANDOZZI, Denise, 474
PIERCE, Andrew C, 902
PIERCE, Helen Cecil, 200
PIERCE, Kacy C, 1083
PIERCE, Patrick, 752
PIERCE, Philena Porter, 694
PIERCEFIELD, Ira W, 571
PIERCEY, Richard, 475
PIERRITZ, Jane, 442
PIERSON Jr, Harold J, 277
PIERSON, Ann Marie, 534
PIERSON, Judith K, 1002
PIERSON, Sandra Lee, 414
PIETROMONACO, Emily, 133
PIGG, Evelyn Evon, 931
PILCHER-FREAS, Betty, 173
PILGREEN, Kenneth L, 544
PILLA, Angela, 585
PILLSBURY, Eleanor, 544
PINCINCE, Donna D, 1044
PINCKERT, Laura L, 905
PINEDA, Aura L, 1013
PINEDA, Mary R, 1156
PINERSKI, Larry, 50
PINKLEY, Janet, 1137
PINKOS, Jennie, 1135
PINKSTON, Anngeannette, 914
PINOTTI, Theresa C, 974
PINTO, John M, 492
PIPER, Margarita S, 563
PIPER, Mary Jane, 355
PIPER, T M, 602
PIRARD, Barbara, 69
PIRONE, Joan Marie, 501
PISACHUBBE, Jeanita, 584
PISTON, Louise, 783
PISTORIOS, Heloise B, 1147
PITCHER, Elizabeth W, 1050
PITCHFORD, James Kelly, 296
PITCOCK, D R, 512
PITTA, Barbara-Ann, 845
PITTLER, Evelyn J, 675
PITTMAN Jr, Rick, 280
PITTMAN, Becky S, 597
PITTMAN, Laura, 589
PITTS, Larry B, 293
PITTS, William M, 998
PIZZONI, Evonne, 459
PLAAS, Alison, 512
PLACCO, Jessie, 874
PLACE, Janine M, 166
PLAIR, Shelia, 181
PLANT, David F, 1122
PLAT, Lena M, 550
PLATT, Kathy D, 538
PLATT, Paul, 766
PLATZ, Frances, 132
PLEASANT, Kimberley K, 879
PLENNERT, May More, 1073
PLEWA, Patricia O, 106
PLOEGER, James, 799
PLOEGSTRA, Steven F, 1163
PLOWMAN, Ann E, 216
PLOWMAN, Betsy, 236
PLUM, Karen, 23
PLUMMER, Mildred M, 191
PLUMMER, Thomas, 587
PLUNKETT, Anne M, 78
PLUNKETT, Phyllis Klock, 955
PNAZEK, Karen, 768
POAGE, Alyce, 627
POCHER, Deborah S, 460
POCOCK, Crissy, 1056
PODEJKO, Julie Ann, 533
PODERZAY, Gail Mcpeak, 1117
PODOLAK, Marilyn, 552
POE Jr, David L, 392
POE, Katherine, 801
POEPPEL, Rita, 175
POER, Robert E, 818
POGUE, Janie, 1044
POINT, Eloise, 759
POIRIER, Cindy, 620
POITRAS, Nancy, 1183
POL, Heather, 959
POLAND, Beatrice, 156
POLANDO, Rosemary, 775
POLASKO, Christopher, 985
POLINO, Frances L, 363
POLK Jr, Otis C, 1195
POLK, Jane, 351
POLK, Johnny R, 772
POLK, Karen Dawn, 717
POLLARD Jr, Richard D, 360
POLLARD Sr, John M, 1052
POLLARD, Gladys M, 706
POLLARD, Mary G, 539
POLLEY, Richard L, 174
POLLOCK, J Gordon, 466
POLLOCK, Shirley N, 964
POLLUM, Roseann, 105
POLNY, Stanistawa, 396
POMEROY, Mary, 78
POMEROY, Michelle, 691
POMEROY, Theodore, 119
POMPIA, Jon Michael, 1059
PONCHIK, Kim Lian, 246
PONTING, Jean, 772
PONTOLILLO, Dominic, 1124
PONTON, Eleanor, 428
POOLE, Anita Gale, 56
POOLE, John Michael, 1161
POORKER, Nancy, 350
POPE, Lynn Smith, 511
POPE, Michael Lee, 307
POPHAM, Mark Steven, 550
POPLAWSKI, Julianne, 330
POPPE, Jeri Mae, 732
PORADISH, Sylvia, 918
PORCHE, Kimberly D, 589
PORMANN, Alison, 362
PORTANOVA, Andrea, 603
PORTER, Andrea C, 558
PORTER, April L, 221
PORTER, Catherine V, 1154
PORTER, Charlie Earl, 277
PORTER, David, 677
PORTER, Ellen Dale, 342
PORTER, Frances, 1162
PORTER, Frances L, 61
PORTER, Kirsty, 442
PORTER, Melissa Belle, 1173
PORTER, Ross A, 619
PORTNOY, Irving, 205
PORUBSKY, Mathew J, 556
POSEY, Isaih, 264
POSEY, Janet Lynn, 1037
POSNER, Rachel, 603
POSPISIL, Kimberly, 266
POSTEL, Miguel, 471
POSTON-WOLCOTT, Mary, 1095
POTHOF, Kathleen, 861
POTO, Marie, 1021
POTOKER, Herbert, 60
POTRYKUS, Darlene, 1057
POTTER, Cheryl A, 63
POTTER, Elaine, 716
POTTER, Kathryn, 135
POTTER, Lavona M, 877
POTTERF, Kathleen, 645
POUKISH, Jr, John J, 142
POULOS, Betty Daniels, 989
POWELL, Angela, 296
POWELL, Charles, 521
POWELL, Edyth E, 927
POWELL, Margaret, 848
POWELL, Nancy Carol, 718
POWELL, Roy Nathaniel, 931
POWELL, Sandra, 174
POWELL, Sandra C, 320
POWELL, Shirley, 1071
POWELL, Wilda, 551
POWELSON-STEPHENS, Tamara R, 290
POWER, Anne, 533
POWER, Erika, 727
POWER, Lea, 543
POWER, Lori Lee, 506
POWERS, Becky, 622
POWERS, Danielle M, 773
POWERS, Danny, 805
POWERS-MASKA, Donna, 852
POXLEITNER, Denise, 521
POYNTER, Ruby, 323
PRAGER, Kristina, 74
PRAGER, Meryl J, 363
PRAJZNER, Sharyn L, 202
PRASUHN, Estella E B, 1006
PRATHER, Mildred, 887
PRATT, Brian C, 1119
PRATT, Macey, 649
PRAVDA, Muriel, 563
PRAYTOR, Debra, 319
PREDA, Vasile, 901
PREEPER, Deborah, 403
PREGNO, Holly, 462
PREISLER, Norma Rockwell, 1013
PREMINGER, Bryon L, 582
PRESLEY, Kimberly, 647
PRESSLER, Ruth Elliott, 892
PRESTON, Debbie S, 215
PREUSCH, Helen V N, 409
PREWITT, April, 851
PREYER, Monique, 524
PRIBBENOW, Roxanne, 502
PRICE, Edith L, 109
PRICE, Emily Verona, 972
PRICE, Irene, 460
PRICE, John Howard, 305
PRICE, Joleen, 423
PRICE, Joyce G, 741
PRICE, Karen D, 866
PRICE, Kenneth D, 1148
PRICE, Linda Farber, 473
PRICE, Merdina, 591
PRICE, Patricia J, 234
PRICE, Robert F, 1168
PRICE, Ruth Helen, 1134
PRICE, Toni M, 25
PRICE, William J, 448
PRIDDY, Ellen Hope, 140
PRINCE II, Ronald L, 1000
PRINCE, Ellen, 232
PRINCE, Mark, 667
PRINCE, Octavia, 534
PRINCE, Sharon D, 840
PRINGLE, Mrs Vernon, 998
PRINO, Terrie, 468
PRIOR, Elizabeth A, 244
PRIOR, Robert, 986
PRISCO-BRAIDO, Rachelle, 1162
PRITCHARD, Cheryl, 324
PRITCHARD, Kathy, 909
PRITT, Christy, 496
PRIVEE, Noel C, 674
PROBERT, John, 810
PROBOLA, Laura A, 595
PROBSDORFER, Andrea, 239
PROCTOR, Jeanette L, 834
PRONYCH, Lanelle, 193
PROPST, Daniel, 1176
PROSSER, B J, 210
PROSSER, Wendy, 494
PROTOPAPA, Gina, 619
PROVENCAL, Marc Alan, 189
PROVOST, Emilie J, 885
PRUIKSMA, Bruce, 773
PRUIKSMA, Heather, 921
PRUITT, Ce, 833
PRUITT, Dell, 460
PSZERACKI, Joan, 720
PUENTE, Mayte, 84
PUENTE, Rebecca Lynn, 893
PUGH, Julie Gay, 438
PULEO, Frank M, 405
PULLEN, Hilary, 802
PUMROY, Mil, 408
PURA, Peter, 153
PURI, Kamal, 193
PURL, Teresa J, 425
PURNELL, Kathi, 515
PURSEL, Dean J, 956
PURTEE, Clara C, 871
PUTMAN, Ada Marie, 331
PUTNAM, Gloria, 377
PUTSEY, Valerie J, 1144
PUTT, Cara Suzanne, 298
PYLE, Becky, 384
PYLE, C L, 406
PYLE, Jeananne Northup, 116
PYLE, Jonathan, 747
PYLES, Barbara R, 1178
PYNCHON, Ralph F, 315

Q

QUADRO, R Evelyn Gale, 1048
QUAID, Kelley L, 1041
QUAID, R L, 267
QUALLS, Tammy, 957
QUALSET, Anna J, 666
QUAM, Brian, 653
QUAY, Sasha, 167
QUAYLE, Betty (Lynn Eyles), 92
QUEEN, Lorena, 438
QUELLO, Belva, 419
QUESADA Jr, Manuel, 371
QUEST, M D, 1186
QUICK, Lisa Ann, 1059
QUICK, Ted G, 398
QUIGLEY, Kim, 277
QUIGLEY, Margaret, 309
QUILLEN, Margaret P, 616
QUINN, Pat Moran, 833
QUINNEY, Gregory D, 1123
QUINONES, David, 729
QUINTANILLA, Lisa, 849
QUINTELA, Suzanne, 1041
QUINTERO, Martina, 1141
QUINTERO, Stephen M, 607
QUINTILIANI, Linda M, 168
QUINTINA, Quintina, 1174

R

RABAN, Terry R, 457
RABINOWITZ, Ann, 270
RACCIO, Donna, 682
RACEY, Olivia, 888
RACHAL, Meshan, 567
RACHELS, Alice Mary, 401
RADABAUGH, Ann, 846
RADCLIFF, Connie M, 638
RADER, Robert E, 1087
RADIC, Dragica, 343
RADTKE, Catherine A, 10
RADTKE, Helen C, 1172
RADTKE, Lea, 877
RAEBURN, Joseph, 464
RAEVSKY, Frank G, 259
RAGAN, Tabitha, 286
RAGIN, Grace E, 512
RAGSDALE, Howard E, 1031
RAGSDALE, Meda, 632
RAHMING, Ella E E, 612
RAHN, Jodie M, 764
RAHN, Olive K, 406
RAIMO, David V, 683
RAIN, Heidi, 1037
RAINES, Bunky, 393
RAINES, Dee, 176
RAINES, R Marina, 877
RAINEY, Jan K, 28
RAINS, Lisa, 742
RAIZ, Mary D, 124
RAJESWAREN, Anita N, 306
RAKHSHANI, Vanessa Sue, 68
RALSTON, Dorothy M, 376
RALSTON, Esther, 394
RALSTON, John, 661
RAMELLA, Kim, 870
RAMEY, Tom, 179
RAMEY-SWARTZ-FOSTER LOVE, C J, 140
RAMHIT, Vashtee, 1107
RAMIREZ, Awilda, 228
RAMIREZ, Carie, 841
RAMIREZ, Mayra, 1197
RAMIREZ, Rey-Angelo C, 1065
RAMMINGER, Natascha Marie, 954
RAMPEY, Edna Maw, 1107
RAMSAY, Kirsten, 716
RAMSDEN, Gloria A, 350
RAMSEY, Amy, 519
RAMSEY, Jennifer Kay, 1074
RAMSEY, Karen Ann, 1148
RAMSEY, Meredith C, 588
RAMSEY, Teresa A, 1122
RANA, Pradeep S, 745
RANCOURT, Renee M, 722
RAND, Sabra G, 254
RANDALL, Christine M, 1148
RANDALL, Janelle, 353
RANDALL, Mrs Lela M, 725
RANDALL, Walden S, 51
RANDEL, Karen, 976
RANDOLPH, Carol J W, 1184
RANDOLPH, Elaine Hoxie, 203
RANDOLPH, Ted R, 829
RANDRUP, Lillian, 1027
RANGE, Cynthia A, 1178
RANJITH, A K, 1011
RANK, Sophie, 747
RANKIN, Jennifer, 793
RANKIN, Kenneth E, 32
RANSICK, C Todd, 800
RANSOM, Beatrice, 859
RANSOM, C D, 44
RANSOM, Mary H, 948
RANSON, Mary M, 290
RANSON, Ora L, 1017
RAO, Sheila, 356
RAO, Vijay Raghav, 1177
RAPER, Janet R, 902
RAPPAPORT, Stace, 651
RAPUE, Terry, 1014
RARDIN, Eric John, 1018
RASBURY, Michele, 795
RASCHEIN, Karren, 760
RASEY, Ramona L, 540
RASH, Sherry G, 1045
RASMUSEN, Connie Nolan, 444
RASMUSSEN II, Elmer A, 771
RASMUSSEN, Ally, 220
RASMUSSEN, Owen, 112
RASMUSSEN, Roseanne, 600
RASMUSSEN, Shandra, 495
RASMUSSEN-VIEAU, Jane, 646
RASNIC, Kristy, 416
RASO, Gino, 79
RATHBONE, Donna J, 985
RATHJEN, Eldor, 763
RATLEY JOE ANN MANSELL, Joe Ann, 349
RATLIFF, Diane, 42
RATLIFF, Hiram, 884
RATNER, Harvey, 584
RATTIGAN, Russ, 420
RAUDAT, Joyce H, 562
RAULERSON, Thomas J, 740
RAUSCHENBACH, Catherine E, 603

RAUSCHER, Randace Ellen, 588
RAUSCHNING, Jean I, 312
RAWCLIFFE-VELA, Elizabeth M, 391
RAWLING, Lucille Kerr, 1164
RAWLINGS, Marie, 358
RAWLINS, Elizabeth P, 209
RAWLS, Lisa, 36
RAY, Anthony L, 999
RAY, Carolyn R, 253
RAY, Hildegard, 560
RAY, Matthew T, 411
RAY, Natasha, 677
RAYBURN, Susan C, 432
RAYFIELD, Lisa, 101
RAYFORD, Pervis, 38
RAYMAN, Virginia, 994, 1038, 709
RAYMOND, Arcelia Hood, 419
RAYNES, Sarah, 1140
RAYNO, Michael J, 1150
RAZZAQ, Ozlem, 646
REA, Cecelia Clair, 159
REA, Jesse L, 442
READER, George G, 53
READING, Amy J, 640
READING, Roberta T, 403
REAL, Joane T, 255
REAMER, Ryan, 329
REASONER-JANES, Kristy, 914
REBANT, Carl J, 315
REBILLARD, Joyce D, 241
RECTOR, Phyllis Sue, 470
REDD, Shirley Ann, 6
REDDEN III, John A, 245
REDDICK, Kimberly, 753
REDFEARN, Amanda Lynn, 327
REDFEARN, Deb, 311
REDFERN, Amy Elizabeth, 516
REDIC, Stephen P, 46
REDMON, Virginia E, 454
REE, Sharon Lynn, 389
REECE, Christine, 124
REED, Betty Hall, 1014
REED, Carol Anita, 393
REED, Clara Pierce, 960
REED, Cyndi, 903
REED, Fredrick, 778
REED, Geraldine, 690
REED, H B, 237
REED, James B, 820
REED, Julie, 569
REED, Marvin E, 789
REED, Mrs Nell, 1051
REED, Ms Sylvia A, 647
REED, Penny M, 333
REED, Rhonda Marie, 776
REED, Vivian L, 679
REED, Zelpha, 1106, 1113
REED-DAVIS, Anita, 1023
REEDER, Kimberly R, 550
REEDER, Mrs Lorraine, 29
REEDY, B K, 620
REEDY, Dawn M, 44
REEDY, Jeri Lynn, 474
REEDY, Susan E, 157
REEL, Donna R, 1201
REEM, Marie Antoinette, 915
REESE Jr, Jimmy L, 332
REESE, Carolyn, 1108
REESE, Elma L, 455
REESE, Teddy D, 746
REEVES, Beth, 862
REEVES, David, 559
REEVES, Ingrid E, 31
REEVES, Laurel, 1185
REEVES, Leanna, 1132
REEVES, Suzanne Y, 1059
REEVES, Zane, 77
REFLECTION, M, 179
REGEHR, Lydia, 1029
REGIS, George, 275
REGO, Susan, 238
REHFELDT, Patricia, 872
REICHART, Carol Schmidt, 988
REICHIN, Matthew David, 1200
REID, Aquilla, 1166
REID, Dionne A, 614
REID, Lori, 56
REID, Marsha, 854
REID, Ruby, 354
REID, Walter, 1135
REIFF, Kathryn L, 151
REIFF, Laura, 111
REILLY, Diane E, 145
REILLY, Isabelle G, 303
REIMAN, John Karl, 1058
REIMANN, Pearl P, 1106
REIMER, Alice, 639
REIMER, Roberta, 827
REIN, Peg, 329
REINDERS, Paula, 645
REINER, Rachel Elisa, 740
REINHOLTZ, Tena, 374
REINSEL, Dennis R, 1137
REISSNER, Erica, 517
REITER, Peg, 106
REITERMAN, Linda, 594
REITTER, Patricia, 1075
RELF, Bashawn Mink, 131
RELL, Rhonda, 255
RELYEA, Leona Marie, 1058
REMMERT, Linda S, 300
REMREY, Susan A, 973
REMY, Dora Lynn, 478
REMY, Margaret S, 805
RENDLER-KAPLAN, Lucy, 1163
RENEAU, Elinor, 905
RENEAU, Guy, 216
RENFRO, April, 643
RENICHE, Patricia, 25
RENNER, Elaine R, 809
REPP, Larry E, 659
RESCH, Dale, 572
RESCH, Deborah, 551
RESCIA, Joyce Sabin, 304
RESLIER, Michelle H, 332
RETHEMEYER, Christopher V, 235
REU, Kari, 178
REUSSER, Thelma L, 973
REUTER, Nancy, 563
REVANDER, Elizabeth, 631
REVENTAR Jr, Rodolfo M, 1168
REVES, Natalie (Missy) L, 1134
REYBURN, Dr Stanley S, 23
REYES, Ann Marie, 1077
REYES, Benito F, 465
REYES, Mirella, 680
REYES, Pedro A, 852
REYNEBEAU, Kris, 508
REYNOLDS Sr, Michael W, 530
REYNOLDS, Bernice (Bunny), 582
REYNOLDS, Betty L, 133
REYNOLDS, Doris J, 362
REYNOLDS, Grace, 504
REYNOLDS, John L, 697
REYNOLDS, Karen J, 176
REYNOLDS, Kelly, 474
REYNOLDS, Leah Jewel, 978
REYNOLDS, Lisa Read, 1012
REYNOLDS, Lisa Renee, 942
REYNOLDS, Lori, 199
REYNOLDS, Milton Wade, 354
REYNOLDS, Renota, 320
REYNOLDS, Stacey M, 923
REYNOLDS, Symphony, 796
REYNOLDS, Vicki S, 86
REYOR, John N, 966, 966
RHEAM, Florence Lee, 843
RHINE, Joy Ward, 810
RHINEBURGER, Patricia, 1191
RHOADES, Deborah A, 307
RHOADS, R M (Dusty), 637
RHODES, Doris J, 1026
RHODES, Dorothy L, 717
RHODES, George E, 829
RHODES, James E, 445
RHODES, Ken A, 774
RHODES, Patricia L, 920
RICCELLI, Linda M, 636
RICE, Doris House, 652
RICE, Edwin, 648
RICE, Jan M, 808
RICE, Jo Ann, 433
RICE, Joyce, 890
RICE, Kathleen, 488
RICE, Marti, 131
RICE, Mary Kopler, 1076
RICE, Randall, 1001
RICH, Alice, 294
RICH, Jenny, 195
RICH, Melissa S, 1012
RICHARD, Frances Ann, 719
RICHARD, Johnathan, 143
RICHARD, Renee T, 144
RICHARD, Tina, 357
RICHARDS, Beresford, 291
RICHARDS, Chet, 61
RICHARDS, Debra, 393
RICHARDS, Doris, 774
RICHARDS, Dorothy W, 1079
RICHARDS, Jylle, 725
RICHARDS, Mary Jane, 1080
RICHARDSON, Betty, 547
RICHARDSON, Brenda, 748
RICHARDSON, Charlotte, 190
RICHARDSON, D J Jena, 806
RICHARDSON, Denelda I, 498
RICHARDSON, Evelyn Elaine, 213
RICHARDSON, Grace T, 480
RICHARDSON, Harold E, 860
RICHARDSON, Ina Clare, 440
RICHARDSON, Inga, 631
RICHARDSON, Jodie Lynn, 272
RICHARDSON, Kathy, 232
RICHARDSON, Margaret, 736
RICHARDSON, Pauline V, 1163
RICHARDSON, Ruth, 238
RICHARDSON, Terri Lynn Kruse, 536
RICHARDSON, Warren H, 474
RICHARDSON, William E, 1125
RICHENS, Calvin M, 203
RICHENS, Pat, 348
RICHEY, Theodosia, 142
RICHINGS, Jim, 608
RICHMOND, Jacqueline Poorbaugh, 1105
RICHMOND, Sharon, 1027
RICHTER, Cynthia A, 67
RICHTER, Sherry A, 131
RICHTER, Tracy, 370
RICKARD, Dean, 174
RICKARDS, Catherine, 952
RICKARDS, Shannon, 385
RICKER, Denise, 332
RICKERMAN, Jeanette, 924
RICKMAN, Peggy Sue, 206
RICKMAN, Sharron A, 51
RIDDELL, Patrick, 531
RIDDLE, Lois, 392
RIDDLE, Ray P, 1112
RIDEOUT, Marguerite, 880
RIDGEDELL, Lynell, 162
RIDGEWAY, Ethel Bernice, 197
RIDGWAY, M, 341
RIDLEY, Hazel, 974
RIDPATH, Heather L, 920
RIEBOLD, Heather A, 461
RIEDEL, Diane Gould, 376
RIEDEN, Charles Eric, 557
RIEGER, Jennifer, 112
RIEMENSCHNEIDER, Kathleen, 949
RIEPE, Charlotte, 391
RIES, J L, 1020
RIESBECK, Peter L, 566
RIESENBERG, Theresa F, 751
RIGDON, Evelyn, 615
RIGGINS, Cathy, 157
RIGGLE, Alfred J, 390
RIGGS, David W, 638
RIGGS, E Marice, 716
RIGGS, Lisa, 71
RIGGS, Michelle L, 686
RIGGS, Sheree M, 817
RIGSBY, Patricia, 1012
RIHA, Rhonda, 42
RILEY, Ellen L, 841
RILEY, Frank, 538
RILEY, Randall E, 57
RILEY, Tracy, 753
RILEY, Vera B, 705
RILEY-BRUNEY, Judith K, 710
RIMOSUKAS, Evelyn J, 558
RINALDI, Michael J, 291
RING, Hank, 137
RING, Linda, 407
RING, Mary F, 569
RING-PENZA, Diane, 236
RINIE, Norma C, 65
RINKER, Betty B, 367
RINTA, Catharina, 35
RIOS, Gloria Ann, 625
RIOS, Patricia J, 663
RIOS, Peggy, 905
RIPLEY, Heather, 480
RIPPON, Robin, 857
RISHI, Sri Chang Le, 909
RISTIVOJEVICH, Nikola, 1172
RITCHEY, Christopher T, 652
RITCHIE, Joyce, 384
RITCHIE, Shawn E, 355
RITTER, Alyssa, 931
RITTER, Amy, 722
RITTER, Gerald A, 13
RIVARD, Ron, 104
RIVERA, Anthony, 802
RIVERA, Felix, 877
RIVERA, Ramona, 536
RIVERA, Terry L, 9
RIVERA-KINDRICK, Tamre, 843
RIVERS, Raeleen, 511
RIVINIUS, Melissa A, 952
RIZZI, Grace, 1013
RIZZO, Beverly R, 1117
RIZZO, Carol, 1095, 965
ROACH, Jill, 361
ROBAK, Susan C, 891
ROBB, Laura, 494
ROBBINS, Dot Scroggins, 242
ROBBINS, Gale, 152
ROBBINS, Loretta, 1063, 1063
ROBBINS, Pamela S, 601
ROBECK, Danny M, 417
ROBERSON, Lena, 827
ROBERSON, Tonie Marie (Hill), 647
ROBERT, Tammy L, 172
ROBERTS, Debra Lynn, 217
ROBERTS, Demita, 772
ROBERTS, Dorothy C, 652
ROBERTS, Edward P, 118
ROBERTS, Ester K, 995
ROBERTS, Glynda M, 880
ROBERTS, Helen, 337
ROBERTS, J Renee, 611
ROBERTS, James T, 983
ROBERTS, Janill, 1167
ROBERTS, Jessie R, 158
ROBERTS, Jim, 1137
ROBERTS, Joan, 746
ROBERTS, Nellie Mingus, 1019
ROBERTS, Patricia, 973
ROBERTS, S Marie, 518
ROBERTS, Schelle, 750
ROBERTS, Sherene R, 331
ROBERTS, Ted W, 579
ROBERTS, Violet B, 1117
ROBERTS, Wesley A, 1168
ROBERTS, Wesley L, 452
ROBERTS-AUE, Pamela S, 319
ROBERTS-DIXON, Maxine, 455
ROBERTSON STEM, Patricia, 6
ROBERTSON, Alma Hilts, 1168
ROBERTSON, Dalray, 111
ROBERTSON, Gloria Jean, 629
ROBERTSON, Ila Smith, 846
ROBERTSON, Joan A, 498
ROBERTSON, Mary, 76
ROBERTSON, Tony, 860
ROBERTSON, Wendy, 894
ROBICHAUD, Dick, 59
ROBICHAUX, Denice E, 1034
ROBINETT III, Lonnie E, 639
ROBINETT, Marie, 13
ROBINETT, Shirley, 257
ROBINETTE, D Gail J, 716
ROBINSON, Ann Marie, 1106
ROBINSON, Anne, 176
ROBINSON, Barbara, 211
ROBINSON, Beverly G, 266, 510
ROBINSON, Charles A, 836
ROBINSON, Dora, 105
ROBINSON, Doris, 1048
ROBINSON, Dwayne R, 471
ROBINSON, Frances, 91
ROBINSON, Georgina "Jo", 681
ROBINSON, Jacquelyn Coretta, 1095
ROBINSON, Joseph M, 450
ROBINSON, Kristi, 662
ROBINSON, Laurie Ann, 73
ROBINSON, Lisa, 547
ROBINSON, Marcella L, 472
ROBINSON, Maycie, 615
ROBINSON, Nicole, 1009
ROBINSON, Rosalind Marie, 1161
ROBINSON, Sheryl J, 666
ROBINSON, Shirlie L, 785
ROBINSON, Todd, 439
ROBINSON, Wade L, 370
ROBINSON, Walter W, 448
ROBINSON, William A, 565
ROBINSON, Willie J, 376
ROBLES, Claudia, 672
ROBLES, Peggy, 992
ROBOTHAM, Arthur, 712
ROBSON, Ivan, 620
ROCCO, Helen, 295
ROCHA, Lisa Marie, 1013
ROCHE, Timothy M, 283
ROCHON, Denise, 496
ROCK, Denise A, 304
ROCK, Donna Kaye, 170
ROCKWELL, Alycen, 534
ROCKWELL, Dorothy, 114
ROCQUE, Karen, 1079
RODENBERGER, Bob, 876
RODENBURG, Anne M, 336
RODERICK, Joanne, 985
RODGERS, Carolyn Ann, 854
RODGERS, Connie, 458
RODGERS, Helen F, 1012
RODGERS, Mary F, 1135
RODGERS, Sandra Ann, 1192
RODI, Lisa A, 564
RODMAN, Richard, 495
RODNEY, Ronald I, 481
RODRIGUES, Catarina, 1162
RODRIGUEZ, Benjamin Roy, 1000
RODRIGUEZ, Debbie, 143
RODRIGUEZ, Eloisa C, 747
RODRIGUEZ, Geselle, 437
RODRIGUEZ, Ginasenda, 515
RODRIGUEZ, Peter, 1185
RODRIGUEZ, Rebecca, 460
ROE, Carol R, 1113
ROE, Lisa, 353
ROE, Mrs Michelle, 275
ROE, Sandra, 90
ROEDER, Terry, 540
ROETHLEIN, Joanne, 1000
ROETHLISBERGER, Lee R, 797
ROETTGER, Pat, 1127
ROGER, Diane M, 950
ROGERS, Emily, 853
ROGERS, Hilary A, 708
ROGERS, James E, 174
ROGERS, Joyce, 820
ROGERS, Kenneth E, 183
ROGERS, Kitty, 658
ROGERS, Lila Fay, 780
ROGERS, Lillian E, 119
ROGERS, Oleta, 369
ROGERS, Pauline, 1122
ROGERS, Raymond F, 869
ROGERS, Sandra Lee, 670
ROGERS, Sean, 925
ROGERS, Sigrid C, 343
ROGERS, V Beverly, 890
ROHN, Mary Jane, 808
ROHRICK, Tamera, 21
ROJANO, Myleen S, 650
ROJO, Nancy L, 62
ROLAND, Antoinette A, 536
ROLAND, Karan L, 381
ROLAND, Yeo Kok Kheng, 703
ROLL, D Jay, 274
ROLLING, James, 1030
ROLLINS, Kelly, 255
ROLLINSON, Ray, 1084
ROMAN, Franceen C, 339
ROMANO, Tom, 852
ROMANS-LEWIS, Rev Evalena, 1132
ROMEISER, Delpha Funk, 252
ROMERO, Jackie, 749
ROMERO, Richard S, 1133
ROMEYN, Pamela, 616
ROMIG, Edna B, 883
ROMOLINI, Giggy Rome, 478
ROMOND, Pauline, 203
RONALD, Deborah L, 1189
RONDEAU, April, 692
RONQUILLO, Rebecca B, 1068
RONSHAUSEN, Esther, 990
RONTOS, Puella, 854
ROOD, Meg, 28
ROOT, Tressie J, 367
ROPER, Jack Michael, 350
ROPER, Robin, 83
RORK, Sean B, 385
ROSA, John, 197
ROSACKER, Shirley E, 1106
ROSARIO, Elaine, 894
ROSARIO, Gloria E, 289
ROSCOE, Bertha J, 473
ROSCOE, Virginia Allen, 1056
ROSE III, William H, 1051
ROSE, Betty L, 998
ROSE, Faith E, 291
ROSE, J.D., 975
ROSE, Josephine, 351
ROSE, Michel, 1141
ROSE, Rande J Sara, 640
ROSE, Sara E, 1157
ROSE, Timothy R, 271
ROSECRANS, Dawn M, 677
ROSEMAN, Sol, 126
ROSENBERG, Marnie, 752
ROSENBERGER, Marlon M, 93
ROSENBURG, Elise, 525
ROSHINI, A K Ayesha, 550
ROSIER, Mrs Joyce, 131
ROSKOWSKE, Douglas Frank, 800
ROSS, Alice P, 32
ROSS, Christie, 546
ROSS, Helen T, 195
ROSS, John, 128
ROSS, Karen J, 96
ROSS, Michelle, 203
ROSS, Scott W, 1000
ROSSE, Robert M, 229
ROSSELL, Elizabeth L, 1041
ROSSER, Georgianna M, 506
ROSSER, Yvonne, 92
ROSSI, Dino A, 214
ROSSI, Nicki, 696
ROSSI, Remo, 102

Index

ROSSI, Thomas, 980
ROTH, Cristiana A, 27
ROTHMAN, Lawrence, 188
ROTON, John L, 861
ROTTLER, Emil K, 92
ROTUNDO, Ann, 55
ROUBAIX, Pepe M, 853
ROUMILLAT, Teresa C, 341
ROUNDTREE Jr, Algie O, 342
ROUNTREE, Mary Carlyle, 1067
ROURKE, Kay, 284
ROUSE, Bernice A, 936
ROUSE, Julie, 440
ROUSE, Mickie P, 5
ROUX, Scott E, 627
ROVNEY, Mr B J, 1084
ROWAN, Susan E, 304
ROWE, Frances, 1128
ROWE, Marda, 1164
ROWE, Margaret G, 410
ROWE, Matthew B, 485
ROWE, Roger A, 339
ROWELL, Janice E, 592
ROWLAND, Ann Michele, 6
ROWLAND, Marie, 792
ROWLAND, Pat, 1127
ROWLAND, Sharon, 196
ROWLETT, Kim, 1183
ROWLEY Jr, Clinton W, 161
ROWLEY, Kevin, 792
ROWSEY, Eldron C, 664
ROY, Betty, 467
ROY, Eva M, 15
ROY, Rose-Marie, 928
ROYAL, Fred, 993
ROYAL, Mary C, 1002
ROYBAL, Olivia, 1034
ROYER-MEADE, Jocelyn, 1106
RUBIN, Ben, 488
RUBIN, Diana K, 763
RUBINO, Joseph, 117
RUBINSTIEN, Alyse Lynne, 27
RUBIO, Andrea, 520
RUBY, Rebecca, 1122
RUCKER, Carroll A, 591
RUDD, Tammy Rene, 1136
RUDDY, Joe, 486
RUDDY, Shawn P, 552
RUDIES, Patricia J, 214
RUDOLPH, Kelly, 711
RUDOLPH, Tammy, 229
RUDUSKI, Karen, 491
RUEN, Catherine M, 557
RUFF, W B, 6
RUGG, Edith E, 35
RUGGIERO, Lisa M, 11
RUHR, Melissa, 1030
RUIZ, Dorothy, 665
RUIZ, Shelly, 867
RULON, Rachelle, 755
RUMAGE, Christina E, 666
RUMBAUT, Sasha, 447
RUMBOLT, Colette, 835
RUMMEL, Amethyst, 417
RUMOHR, Betty, 706
RUNDELL, Anita, 178
RUSCHAU, Jenny, 88
RUSCONI, Louis J, 394
RUSH, Cheryl, 225
RUSH, Edna, 800
RUSH, Eric, 545
RUSH, Suzan Lee, 736
RUSHER, William, 382
RUSHING, Leon, 725
RUSSELL, Alexandra, 802
RUSSELL, Christopher C, 1197
RUSSELL, Constance, 1121
RUSSELL, Darla, 807
RUSSELL, David, 1092
RUSSELL, Eadie Mae, 888
RUSSELL, Estelle, 1019
RUSSELL, Jocelyn, 296
RUSSELL, Judith L, 870
RUSSELL, Lorene, 818
RUSSELL, Mildred, 1081
RUSSELL, Patricia, 1070
RUSSELL, Tracy R, 366
RUSSELL, Walt, 390
RUSSELL-SEFFERN, Tere E, 1008
RUSSO, Elina, 374
RUSSO, Trio, 603
RUST, Richard W, 150
HAYES, Joseph John, 1109
RUTH, Catherine, 117
RUTH, H D, 333
RUTH, Nancy A, 186
RUTHERFORD, Billy Fred, 751
RUTHERFORD, Bonnie, 478
RUTHERFORD, Joseph, 499
RUTLEDGE, Bert, 1100, 1032
RUTLEDGE, Lori, 298
RUTTER, Marilyn B, 209
RUTTER, Neil A, 570
RUYLE, Lori, 868
RUZZO, Pete D E, 51
RYAN, Daniel, 872
RYAN, Doreen E, 686
RYAN, Jennifer Lyn, 709
RYAN, Robert H, 399
RYAN, Suzanne, 998
RYCHTER-DANCZYK, Veronica A, 1105
RYDER, Evelyn E, 1187
RYDER, Kari, 333
RYDER, Lee L, 792
RYDER, Ricky E, 95
RYDER, Wilma Shockey, 448
RYKOWSKI, Maureen E, 602
RYON, Eve, 836
RYSDORP, Barbara, 1106
RZEPINSKI, Veronica, 361

S

SABINO, Joy, 566
SABIR, Abdul-Alim, 751
SABLAN, Francis T, 1029
SACAVAGE, June M, 683
SACHS, Denise, 695
SACKETT, Dorothy, 828
SACKS, Kimberly, 493
SADLER, Bernice, 404
SADLER, Dianne, 604
SAEGER, Janice, 939
SAENZ, Gil, 689
SAFFELL, Valerie Jean, 532
SAFI, Constance C, 444
SAFONTE, Nikki, 243
SAGER R.PH., Fred, 122
SAGERS, Ida, 693
SAINTIL, Erlyne, 645
SALAM, Yusuf Abdul, 180
SALAPACK, Christine E, 959
SALATA, Clare, 713
SALAZAR, Josefina B, 906
SALAZAR, Ruth E C, 757
SALENA, Zola, 1104
SALINA-SATCHEL-HAYES-LEDGER, Salina S, 408
SALINARDO, Dan, 832
SALISBURY, E A, 665
SALMAGGI, Ferris Nicholas, 954
SALMON, Jan, 341
SALMONSEN, Drene, 849
SALTER, Mazy W, 195
SALTER, Randy, 1073
SALTZ, Elizabeth, 75
SALZANO, Alice, 300
SALZARULO, Angelina, 671
SAMARIGAN, Susan M, 923
SAMBELL, Richard, 456
SAMCZYK, Mary Ann, 94
SAMMY, The Amazing, 132
SAMPLEY, Franklin D, 202
SAMPSON, Margaret C, 65
SAMSON, Amy Marie, 916
SAMUELS, D'Angelo, 262
SAMUELS, Walter G, 181
SANBORN III, Wallis Remsen, 936
SANBORN, Cara, 596
SANCHEZ, Barbara, 822
SANCHEZ, Jim P, 450
SANCHEZ, Mary A S, 372
SANCHEZ, Victor, 932
SANDER, Victoria, 947
SANDERS, Ella Mae, 556
SANDERS, Florine R, 1163
SANDERS, Holly, 659
SANDERS, Laura, 70
SANDERS, Leon, 672
SANDERS, Lois C, 470
SANDERS, Malone, 299
SANDERS, Ronald J, 696
SANDERS, Rose Ann, 458
SANDERS, Scott E, 440
SANDERS, Ted L, 1017
SANDIFER, Donald R, 1002
SANDRIDGE, Clara, 164
SANDS, L M, 683
SANDS, Mary D, 1051
SANDS, Sheree, 245
SANDS, William M, 194
SANFILIPPO, Audrey T, 450
SANFORD, Amy, 383
SANFORD, Patricia, 660
SANFORD, Rob, 747
SANGILLO, Patricia L, 591
SANHEIM, Samantha, 755
SANNER, Barbara, 168
SANNWALD, Kathleen, 372
SANTAMARIA, Leticia, 514
SANTANA, Doris M, 846
SANTANOCITO, Shannon, 365
SANTEE, Ms Mila, 185
SANTIAGO, Anthony M, 855
SANTIAGO, Barbara L, 930
SANTISTEVAN, Victoria L, 710
SANTIVASCI, Debra, 1105
SANTOMIERI, Renee Willis, 886
SANTOS, Branwen, 408
SANTRY, Sunny, 737
SANZILLO, Marie, 617
SAPIENZA, Marilyn, 883
SARATHI, Della, 255
SARE, Floyd E, 1148
SARGENT, Harold L, 1162
SARIC, Nancy, 960
SARKAR, Subrata A, 951
SARKIS, Adib J, 937
SARKISSIAN, Michael, 585
SARTELL, Jennifer, 681
SARTIN, Ralph M, 93
SARTY-WAMBOLDT, Dorothy J, 501
SARVEY, Gary Eugene, 1011
SAS, David Wayne, 736
SAS, Lilian, 1103
SASSER, Wendy A, 674
SATTERLEE, Patricia J, 596
SAUER, Bonnie M, 954
SAUER, Rick, 464
SAUNDERS, Freddi, 982
SAUNDERS, Karen, 242
SAUNDERS, Lucille, 84
SAUNDERS, Mari P, 951
SAURDIFF, Julie Ann, 712
SAUVAGE, L D, 1069
SAUVE, Johanna, 1103
SAVACOOL Jr, Randal, 898
SAVANT, Susie, 681
SAVICH, Rebecca, 530
SAVICKI, Zachary Scott, 265
SAVINO, Dee, 186
SAVINO, Kimberly Ann, 1066
SAWICKI, Stephanie, 1170
SAWULA, Sharon, 327
SAWYERS, Erna M, 1053
SAXE, Mickie L, 564
SAXE, Sheri, 807
SAXON, C B, 945
SAXTON, June Marie, 114
SAXTON, Karen Jane, 83
SAYCHECK, Dorothy Mattson, 405
SAYER, Janet Sue, 301
SAYLES, Rasheeda Alia, 40
SAYNER, Evelyn Dodge, 656
SCALCIONE, Julia, 850
SCALES, Elizabeth A, 438
SCALI-COOK, Pasqualina, 329
SCALISE, Linda I Potter, 12
SCALLY, John R, 69
SCANTLAN, Sam W, 1181
SCARBERRY, Grace, 636
SCARBROUGH, Sindy, 244
SCARNICI, Lisa L, 187
SCAROLA, Gail, 676
SCAROLA, Kathryn N, 792
SCHAAD, Gilbert, 161
SCHAAF, Ronald J, 88
SCHAEFER, Eric S, 94
SCHAEFER, Helen Price, 43
SCHAEFER, Maude B, 233
SCHAFFNER, William C, 136
SCHAMBERS, Helen, 1020
SCHAPLEY, Corey, 992
SCHARPS, Laureen, 669
SCHARTZ, Jewel George, 113
SCHATZBERG, Joan W, 590
SCHAU, Kevin M, 833
SCHAUSS, Dan, 573
SCHAWE, Mary F, 10
SCHEDIN, K C, 59
SCHEERER, Joanne, 105
SCHEHR, Kathleen M, 164
SCHEIMAN-NEILSON, Debra K, 672
SCHEIN, Seth, 622
SCHEKMAN, Lori, 268
SCHELIN, Micheal J, 772
SCHELLENBERG, James, 156
SCHELLER, Daniel, 1104
SCHELLER, Norma Jean, 1013
SCHENCK, Doris I, 19
SCHEPANOWSKI, Beth, 18
SCHERER, Christopher, 1140
SCHERMAN, Evan, 20
SCHERMERHORN, Joan Lb, 1059
SCHERR Jr, Richard J, 98
SCHERRER, Wilma June, 1108
SCHIEFFER, Mary, 433
SCHILDKAMP, Kenn, 919
SCHILLE, Wendy, 322
SCHILLER, Denise, 240
SCHILLO, Carroll A, 762
SCHIMMEL, Stacy, 964, 964
SCHIRRMACHER, Patricia Grosz, 880
SCHLADWEILER OSF, Sr Mary Joyce, 1068
SCHLAGHECK, Christine, 1047
SCHLANGEN, Bonnie, 1031
SCHLEGEL, Cindy R, 514
SCHLEHLEIN, Melinda, 46
SCHLEINITZ, Dale, 1079
SCHLESIGER, Marianne, 622
SCHLEY, Barrett, 121
SCHLITZER, Raymond, 151
SCHMELER, Cheryl, 234
SCHMELZIA, Virginia, 355
LEE, Sandra, 1020
SCHMIDT, Ann Marie, 993
SCHMIDT, Beverly, 1052
SCHMIDT, Cathy, 296
SCHMIDT, Crystal L, 866
SCHMIDT, Jennifer M, 267
SCHMIDT, Lynda, 996
SCHMIDT, Mrs Doris L, 1067
SCHMIDT, Patricia, 821
SCHMIERER, Tina, 672
SCHMITT, Dan, 501
SCHMITT, Sister Bernal, 1114
SCHMOLDT, Lisa, 1074
SCHMORAK, Rosalind Gene, 24
SCHNABEL, Elvira C, 1156
SCHNAPP, Katie, 487
SCHNECKLOTH, K A, 476
SCHNEIDER, Angela M, 746
SCHNEIDER, Ethel, 274
SCHNEIDER, Heidi, 525
SCHNEIDER, Kilian, 44
SCHNEIDER, Zach, 211
SCHNIKWALD, Erik P, 670
SCHNIZER, Charlene, 435
SCHNURR, Martha Jayne Young, 403
SCHOCKAERT, Barbara, 40
SCHOENBERGER, Kim, 24
SCHOENER, Dorothea, 705
SCHOFIELD, Carl A, 567
SCHOFIELD, Lisa, 586
SCHOLLHAMMER, Ellamay N, 87
SCHONFELD, Arlene D, 702
SCHOPPE, Delores M, 953
SCHOPPE, Jodie, 700
SCHORNICK, Norma, 823
SCHOW, John, 30
SCHOYEN, Warner O, 17
SCHRAGA, Melissa, 753
SCHRAGE, Kara, 980
SCHRAPFER, Margret, 262
SCHRECK, Thelma D, 897
SCHREIBER, Angela M, 1191
SCHREIBER, Carl R, 994
SCHROADER, Eunice, 1120
SCHROEDER, Beverly J, 334
SCHROEDER, Debbie, 46
SCHROEDER, Kathleen, 759
SCHROEDER, Roger, 162
SCHROEDER, Sherylin Kay, 1161
SCHROEDER, Tammy L, 324
SCHROUGHAM, Dorval, 653
SCHUELER, Helmut, 41
SCHUETZ, Renate, 1181
SCHULDT, Michelle H, 1093
SCHULMEISTER, Lorraine, 315
SCHULTE, Thomas, 507
SCHULTE, Vivian, 486
SCHULTZ, Betty C, 642
SCHULTZ, Vera M, 951
SCHULZ, Lillian, 271
SCHUMACHER, Albert C, 589
SCHUMAKER, Heather, 1057
SCHUNK, Renee L, 433
SCHUSTER, Deborah, 956
SCHUTH, Roni J, 133
SCHUTZ, Tina, 998
SCHWAB, Christine S, 532
SCHWAB, Wanda Alice, 148
SCHWALB, Dorothy Anne, 684
SCHWAN, H Jeri, 190
SCHWANTES, Jane, 213
SCHWARTZ, Bernice G, 380
SCHWED, Antonia H, 155
SCHWEINSBERG, Patricia L, 509
SCIBEK, Jennifer, 504
SCIOLA, Mary, 1190
SCIOTTI, Christine E, 153
SCOCO, Allison, 245
SCOFIELD, William R, 745
SCOPEL, Gin, 62
SCOTT, Alyce Bruhn, 917
SCOTT, Dale, 311
SCOTT, Diane Cole, 252
SCOTT, Diane Elizabeth, 925
SCOTT, Donna, 728
SCOTT, Dorothy J, 140
SCOTT, Elizabeth Y, 415
SCOTT, J L (Leon), 206
SCOTT, Jamie K, 788
SCOTT, Janetta H, 847
SCOTT, Laura B, 662
SCOTT, Leona, 167
SCOTT, Lillian E, 943
SCOTT, Lucille L, 1115
SCOTT, Mary, 716
SCOTT, Patricia, 397
SCOTT, Philip, 1187
SCOTT, S Lynn, 811
SCOTT, Sharon, 894
SCOTT, Shaun-Marie, 263
SCOTT, Shirley, 1108
SCOTT-DEVER, Barbara, 36
SCOTTON, Sharon B, 464
SCROGGIN, Steven M, 762
SCROGGINS, Patricia, 389
SCRUGGS, Linda G, 629
SEABROOK, Michael J, 896
SEAGER, Steven A, 501
SEALE, Tihan, 1030
SEALS, Claudette, 11
SEAMON, Patsy, 286
SEARCY, Joyce E, 286
SEARFOSS, Rachael, 979
SEARS, Katherine, 819
SEARS, Marshall, 618
SEATON, Ralph, 407
SEAVEY, Kelly, 686
SEAY, Ms Jeanne, 1136
SEBASTIAN, Justin, 1162
SECKINGER, Susan J, 658
SEDERQUIST, Sally E, 392
SEDGWICK, Mary L, 54
SEE, Louise, 163
SEE, Ramona, 1198
SEEBACHER, Erika, 1136
SEEKAMP, Tammy, 888
SEELEY, Belva, 684
SEELEY, Gretchen, 801
SEELY, Dorothea S, 673
SEFAIR, Miguel Angel, 1110
SEGERBECK, Mary Anne, 1067
SEGNO, Kathy, 159
SEGRAVES, Joan M, 447
SEIBERT, Sam, 487
SEIDEL, Janet, 1154
SEIDENWURM, Jerry, 47
SEIDMAN, Barbara Anne, 1128
SEIGLE, Marsie R, 486
SEIPEL, Margaret Caturia, 234
SEITER, Mary Alice, 243
SELBY, Edna M, 744
SELBY, Jeannie, 1008
SELBY, Kay, 991
SELE, Ethel, 955
SELIGO, Viola Q, 1150
SELINGER, Michele, 696
SELLERS, Amy, 1127
SELLERS, Jennifer, 1103
SELLERS, Shirley, 807
SELLS, Jonelda Bowers, 41
SELM, Earleta H, 338
SELS, Roberta S Vanloben, 981
SEMAAN, Ann, 1104
SEMERARO, Cheryl Ann, 218
SEMERDJIAN, Salpy, 194
SENADHIRA, Shireen, 45
SENECAL, Bruce R, 1085
SENECAL, Lisa, 81
SENIOR, Kenneth D, 157
SENKO, Marcia, 617
SENSABAUGH, N, 1056
SENTER, Bev, 692
SENUS, Joanne, 790
SERENDIPITY, M, 40
SERGEANT, Doris M, 146
SERGENT, Cindy, 661
SERGIO, Christine, 838
SERIO, Barbara Gari, 452
SERLING, Elaine, 549
SERRA, Nicole, 695
SERRANO, Maria, 481
SERRATO, Yolanda H, 837
SETON, Rhonda, 838
SEVANDAL, Marciana A, 735
SEVERSON, Hannah M, 191
SEVERSON, Valarie T, 630
SEVIER, Gordon C, 318
SEVIN, Leona Ann B, 984
SEWELL, Madeline F, 465
SEWELL, Michael, 74

SEXTON, Edward, 678
SEXTON, Harriett B, 227
SEYER, Melinda, 425
SEYMOUR, Sheri, 635
SHADIX, Rozene, 953
SHAFER, Sandra J, 128
SHAFER, Sheila Williams, 51
SHAFER, Wanda Rutman, 770
SHAFFER, Barbara, 996
SHAFFER, Deirdre, 514
SHAFFER, Eric W, 1185
SHAFFER, Mickey L, 373
SHAFFER, Robert, 565
SHAHBAZIAN, Caroline, 52
SHALLA, Diane Elaine, 654
SHAMBLIN, Laine, 65
SHAMGOCHIAN, Alice, 122
SHANAHAN, Doris, 722
SHANDY, Marjorie C, 105
SHANER, Romaine, 514
SHANKS, Julie, 595
SHANNON, D R, 1061
SHANNON, Jack, 889
SHANNON, Jeffrey L, 857
SHAO, Gordon Pinsan, 1065
SHAPARD, John Loco, 468
SHAPIRO, Frank Roy, 16
SHAPIRO, Leon, 276
SHAPIRO, Susan, 186
SHARENON, Brian, 1156
SHARKEY, Patricia A, 1179
SHARMA, Roshni S, 268
SHARMA, Sharad, 566
SHARP, Charles E, 303
SHARP, Marcia Kay, 1000
SHARP, Sharron, 774
SHARPE, Laura-Lee, 77
SHARPLEY, Molly, 867
SHARRETTS, Sharon G, 879
SHAVER, Frances P, 1032
SHAVER, Lorine, 375
SHAVER, Sandra Knox, 262
SHAW, Angela, 1169
SHAW, Betty Jane, 1103
SHAW, Charles, 750
SHAW, Davette L, 625
SHAW, Lisa M, 782
SHAW, N L, 1016
SHAW, Scott, 517
SHAW, Tina, 238
SHAW, Trish, 366
SHAWLER, Delonna, 856
SHAWN, Sheila, 309
SHEA, Stephanie, 1127
SHEALY, Kathy Mccmullen, 1135
SHEARER, Margaret L, 939
SHEARIER, Steven V, 534
SHEARS, Laura, 752
SHECKELLS, Diane Adele, 690
SHEEHAN, Timothy Jay, 325
SHEETS, David L, 715
SHEFCHIK, Joseph W, 435
SHEFFIELD Sr, Rex E, 63
SHEFFLER, Elaine, 895
SHELBY, Andrea, 15
SHELDON, Steven, 645
SHELLENBERGER, Verna S, 65
SHELLEY, Joseph E, 146
SHELLING, H W, 1055
SHELTON II, Ronald L, 1167
SHELTON Jr, Horace B, 510
SHELTON, Crystal, 943
SHELTON, Edward K, 1052
SHELTON, Karen, 1062
SHELTON, Katherine W, 345
SHELTON, Keith, 321
SHELTON, Ruth, 812
SHELTON, Sherry Farrow, 416
SHELTON-HARDEBECK, Wanda, 450
SHEPHARD, Vicki, 219
SHEPHERD, Cindy L W, 227
SHEPHERD, Deborah G, 614
SHEPHERD, J Beverly, 415
SHEPHERD, Terryl, 920
SHEPLER, Gene, 690
SHERIDAN, Catherine, 162
SHERIDAN, Jeryl Ann, 836
SHERMAN, Dan, 765
SHERMAN, Glenda Martin, 881
SHERMAN, Helen J, 115
SHERMAN, Jessica, 1063
SHERMAN, Stephen R, 75
SHERRICK, Sandra Ann, 353
SHERWOOD, Doreen E, 285
SHIARIS, Sophie P, 1034
SHIFF, Scott A, 519
SHIFLET, Michael, 1040
SHILLABEER, June, 106
SHIMASAKI, Robin, 989
SHINE, Bonnie Cowie, 100
SHINN, Alida, 1137
SHIPP, Dawn, 1027
SHIRKEY, Ron, 1190
SHIRLEY, Margaret, 67
SHIVE, Florence, 283
SHIVE, Rickey, 378
SHIVECK, Jordan, 449
SHIVERDECKER, Nola N, 930
SHOCKLEY, Leatha S, 54
SHOCKMAN, Monte, 900
SHOEMAKE, Thomas R, 136
SHOEMAKER, Frank A, 306
SHOHET, Giselle, 1125
SHOMO, J G, 683
SHONECK, Helen M, 1117
SHOOK-HAGEN, Jan, 821
SHORE, Ruby E, 527
SHORES, Gloria J, 531
SHORMA, Sharon Ann M, 930
SHORT, David F, 469
SHORT, Reba, 337
SHORT, Tom, 668
SHREVE, F, 61
SHREWSBURY, B Lou, 1146
SHREWSBURY, William T, 42
SHRIVER, M E, 731
SHUFELT, Tania L, 1083
SHULER, Starla, 243
SHULICK, Sheelah K, 1159
SHUMPIS, Gloria J, 564
SHUMWAY, Loula R, 321
SHURA, Stan W, 274
SHUTE, Charlene Gail, 159
SHUTT, Alice May, 891
SHUTT, Deboraha Linn, 513
SHY, Ms Melanie D, 1076
SHYKE, I, 1144
SIBLEY, W Howard, 395
SYDEBOTHAM, Pauline K, 1028
SIEDHOFF, Mary E, 38
SIEFERT, Carolyn, 787
SIEGEL, Eva Loren, 990
SIEGEL, Melanie, 266
SIEGERS, Shonna, 918
SIEGWART, Bruce, 887
SIEKIERKE, Franc, 675
SIELAFF, Drayth S, 627
SIEMERING, Henrietta, 874
SIERRA Jr, Francisco, 593
SIGFERSON, Hazel A, 457
SIGMON, Gertrued Hickin, 289
SIGMON, Jane, 26
SILVA, Nadine, 142
SILVER, Betty, 642
SILVER, Jonathan D, 9
SILVERIO MD, Juan, 600
SILVERS, Ricky, 1036
SILVESTER, Steven, 1172
SILVESTRO, Antoinette M, 1026
SILVESTRO, Denise, 581
SILVESTRO, Marsie, 853
SILVEY, Virgie N, 635
SIME, Jennifer, 539
SIMENS, Inez, 1150
SIMMONS, Amanda, 1092
SIMMONS, Brenda, 328
SIMMONS, Donna A, 30
SIMMONS, Dyana, 669
SIMMONS, Erma, 748
SIMMONS, Gail, 802
SIMMONS, Grace, 560
SIMMONS, P, 322
SIMMONS, Roberta B, 470
SIMMS, Jane A, 82
SIMON, Floyd A, 900
SIMON, Johanna, 269
SIMON, Mildred L, 1198
SIMON, Sylvia J, 655
SIMONE, R T, 903
SIMONE, Sherri A, 855
SIMONEAU, Vickie, 578
SIMONTON, Genevra A, 1003
SIMPSON, Angela, 165
SIMPSON, Edward, 143
SIMPSON, Glenda J, 892
SIMPSON, Helen K, 263
SIMPSON, Wendi, 412
SIMPSON, Yvonne, 958
SIMS, Diane, 229
SIMS, Pam, 1157
SIMS, Vickie Lynn, 192
SINAGA, Lilia, 1019
SINCLAIR, Amy, 38
SINCLAIR, Ann, 378
SINCLAIR, Diane, 283
SINCLAIR, Doris, 404
SINCLAIR, Louise M, 802
SINCLAIR-SPOHN, Mary, 525
SINDLINGER, Phil, 992
SINGER, Bob, 143
SINGH, Eva-Dawn R, 1012
SINGHOSE, Isabelle, 182
SINGLETARY, Constance Ann, 182
SINGLETON, J D, 132
SINGLETON, Sigrid, 569
SINGLETON-MCCULLUM, Marion E, 1160
SINN, Amy, 595
SINNATAMBY, Sonali, 322
SINYARD, Barbara, 992
SIPES, B L, 660
SIRAGUSA, Arlene, 1077
SIRES, Sarah Saunders, 1199
SISEMORE, Sharon E, 669
SISKIND, Phyllis O, 925
SISLIN, Leno, 1044
SISTIK, Jennifer F, 1109
SITTIG, Roy Ivan, 940
SIVERLY, Virginia M, 358
SIVERTSON, Eric, 267
SIVILS, Roberta, 875
SIXT, Earl R, 455
SIZEMORE, Jennifer, 465
SIZEMORE, Karri, 727
SJOSTROM, Eli, 794
SKAGGS, Magdoline, 867
SKARPHEDINSSON, B J, 341
SKELLENGER, Nancy, 358
SKELTON, Willard Lee, 423
SKIDMORE, Janice L, 1023
SKIDMORE, Linda J, 52
SKIFF, Ruth, 165
SKINNER, Alexis, 5
SKINNER, Peggy, 11
SKIPPER, Ernestine, 348
SKOLFIELD, Sandra L, 668
SKOLFIELD, Stuart, 902
SKUSA, Marjorie K, 508
SLACK, Mary, 384
SLAGLE, Clarence R, 305
SLANINA VSC, S Celine, 471
SLANKER, Renee, 917
SLAUGHTER, Brad R, 634
SLEDZINSKI, Renee F, 961
SLEIGHTER, Sylvia E, 453
SLESINSKI, Myldred, 54
SLIFKIN, Debra Lynn, 689
SLIVA, Frank S, 977
SLIVENSKI, Gina, 1103
SLOAN, Jennifer K, 1127
SLOAN, Ted A, 60
SLOCUM, Will, 791
SLOMSKI, Lisa Anne, 419
SLOOT, Janet Vander, 913
SLOSSER, Michelle, 657
SLOTER, Lisa, 1033
SLOVAK, John George, 369
SLOWEK, Patricia, 183
SLY, Robert E, 502
SMALL, D Shawn, 142
SMALLWOOD, Gregg H, 911
SMALLWOOD, Hannafi, 391
SMARDON, John Laurie, 247
SMART, Angie M, 966
SMELCER, Debby A, 847
SMELTZER, Charles E, 909
SMERDON, Edward, 790
SMILEY, Marilyn P, 922
SMITH Jr, John Lee, 932
SMITH PHD, Doris D, 281
SMITH Sr, Curt, 852
SMITH, Algie, 237
SMITH, Angie M, 786
SMITH, Anita, 519
SMITH, Barbara, 403
SMITH, Barbara J, 996
SMITH, Betty L, 10
SMITH, Beverly, 451
SMITH, Brenda D C, 614
SMITH, C M, 247
SMITH, Carol, 1198
SMITH, Carolyn Dumas, 582
SMITH, Catherine G, 726
SMITH, Cecy, 454
SMITH, Charles L, 1040
SMITH, Charlotte "Charlie", 813
SMITH, Chris Chew, 1053
SMITH, Christine, 136
SMITH, Connie Sue, 835
SMITH, Constance J, 212
SMITH, Crystal D, 625
SMITH, Crystel, 5
SMITH, Dan H, 452
SMITH, David, 395
SMITH, Deborah, 534
SMITH, Deborah A, 1049
SMITH, Debra Hester, 1167
SMITH, Denise M, 703
SMITH, Denise V, 649
SMITH, Dianna, 1042
SMITH, Dolly C, 793
SMITH, Donald, 1146
SMITH, Donna Lee, 53
SMITH, Dorothy, 931
SMITH, Dorothy E, 415
SMITH, Eleanor L, 46
SMITH, Ellene, 916, 1062
SMITH, Eric Scott, 1025
SMITH, Estus Marsalis, 913
SMITH, Ezekial, 1020
SMITH, Frances Kay, 823
SMITH, Gale, 1155
SMITH, Georgie E, 606
SMITH, Gerald, 573
SMITH, Geri Bennett, 869
SMITH, Glinda C, 841
SMITH, Grace M, 605
SMITH, Grant Edward, 1050
SMITH, Holly L, 520
SMITH, Howard F, 810
SMITH, Iona P, 441
SMITH, Isaac V, 1147
SMITH, Jacqueline (Jackie), 162
SMITH, Jacqueline A, 400
SMITH, Janet L, 166
SMITH, Janis Y, 703
SMITH, Jef, 180
SMITH, Jennifer E, 1050
SMITH, Joyce, 1133, 1061
SMITH, Kate M, 1201
SMITH, Kenneth H, 1055
SMITH, Kenneth P, 358
SMITH, Kenny Ray, 1178
SMITH, Kim, 589
SMITH, Lana, 1175
SMITH, Laurel W, 376
SMITH, Leisha, 607
SMITH, Leontine, 693
SMITH, Lillian, 904
SMITH, Linda A, 168
SMITH, Linda Dawn, 205
SMITH, Lisa Ann, 1135
SMITH, Louise, 101
SMITH, M, 297
SMITH, M Elizabeth, 581
SMITH, Ma; Kathryn V, 32
SMITH, Mamie Stanley, 245
SMITH, Margaret E, 19
SMITH, Mark E, 1096
SMITH, Marshall G, 911
SMITH, Mary, 797
SMITH, Mary Ann, 1111
SMITH, Mary C, 419
SMITH, Mary J, 79
SMITH, Mary Morris, 847
SMITH, Melissa, 289
SMITH, Mildred H, 150
SMITH, Minter, 1030
SMITH, Missy, 90
SMITH, Mrs Virginia, 230
SMITH, Murphy G, 1075
SMITH, Myrtle, 108
SMITH, Noreen H, 1024
SMITH, Paula E, 727
SMITH, Phyllis Joan, 302
SMITH, Raoul Derek, 1096, 527
SMITH, Ray O, 1148
SMITH, Rita, 96
SMITH, Robert Leroy, 405
SMITH, Rosalie, 307
SMITH, S Lee, 300
SMITH, Sandy, 460
SMITH, Saundra, 274
SMITH, Scott Allen, 618
SMITH, Shannon James, 499
SMITH, Sharyn A, 74
SMITH, Sheila Cline, 995
SMITH, Sherri, 789
SMITH, Shirley, 942
SMITH, Shirley Mae, 515
SMITH, Starla, 1054
SMITH, Susan C, 446
SMITH, Susan M, 467
SMITH, T, 362
SMITH, Tammy, 520
SMITH, Tegan, 682
SMITH, Thomas C, 689
SMITH, Tracy W, 990
SMITH, Tyler W, 1165
SMITH, Virginia D, 905
SMITH, Wanda, 1194
SMITH, Wendy, 693
SMITH, Wendy C, 32
SMITH, Willie M, 750
SMITH-BARNES, Melissa R, 974
SMITH-EMERY, Kathleen, 961
SMITH-MOORE, Shirley, 541
SMITH-SUDGES, Lucinda, 862
SMITH-WIEGAND, Lynette, 849
SMITHEY, Billy R, 326
SMITHSON-WOODS, Rachel, 709
SMOCK, Linda M, 1168
SMORADO, Adrienne M, 229
SMOTHERMON, Paul D, 582
SNEATH, Mr Lynn, 721
SNEED, Eldridge J, 1033
SNELL, Dian, 1032
SNIDER, Harold R, 64
SNIDER, Joni E, 731
SNOW, Edna A, 592
SNOW, Melinda Shaw, 761
SNOW, Mrs R Alix, 872
SNOW, Scott M, 772
SNOW, Valerie, 471
SNOWBALL, Edith May, 716
SNYDER Jr, Carl H, 285
SNYDER, Bobbi N, 282
SNYDER, Lynda M, 1192
SNYDER, Margaret E, 473
SNYDER, Peggy Opal, 62
SOBARZO, Anna Marie, 723
SOBAY, Theodore F, 493
SOBEL, Charlotte, 388
SOBOL, Vicki, 849
SODEN, Eunice S, 703
SODERSTROM, Rebecca L, 121
SOELL, Elizabeth D, 103
SOENSKEN, Lorene Tarver, 353
SOISSON, Beverly L, 1048
SOJA, Susette, 530
SOLANDER, Tara, 597
SOLIMANO, Susan, 400
SOLIS, Julio C, 532
SOLLARS, Marie, 896
SOLLEY, Scott, 754
SOLOD, Alex, 234
SOLORIO, Jacqueline R, 412
SOLTIS, Elizabeth A, 1018
SOMERMAN, Helen, 84
SONDERMANN, Marta L, 144
SONNER, Klara, 294
SORABELLA, Louis, 1141
SORENSON, Karen Maloney, 479
SORGE, Sara E, 545
SORGI, Joan A, 191
SORIANO, Elisa M, 1139
SOROKOSKI, Marty, 464
SORRELLS, Donald R, 1187
SOSA, Samuel, 510
SOTELO, Aurora, 1164
SOTIRAKOPOULOS, Andrea, 195
SOTO, Dodie, 1024
SOTO, Raquel, 1131
SOTO, Tony, 99
SOTOLONGO, Lilian L, 939
SOTSKY, Shirley, 230
SOUDER, Robert W, 88
SOUSA, Audnie A, 32
SOUTHARD, Jetta, 1187, 1187
SOUTHARD, Regan, 583
SOUTHERN, C.D.E., Craig E, 1142
SOUTHERN, Gary L, 466
SOUTHWOOD, Diana, 53
SOUZA, Eileen A, 523
SOUZA, P, 455
SOWDON, Ross Boyd, 456
SOWELL, Peggy, 1097
SOWKA, Steve, 610
SPAETH, Sheila J, 154
SPAGNOLA, Laura, 920
SPAIN, Anthony L, 918
SPALDING, Marcell, 257
SPALDING, Nicole, 526
SPANGLER, Phyllis, 808
SPARAPANI, Gaby, 179
SPARHAWK, Jennifer, 229
SPARKMAN, Lee, 491
SPARKS, C, 811
SPARKS, Rhonda Lee, 1177
SPATE, Bertha, 254
SPATUZZI, Patricia, 345
SPATZ, William, 730
SPAW, Carol S, 1083
SPEAKER, Linda, 269
SPEAKS, Nelda M, 213
SPEARMAN, Raenita Y, 743
SPEARS, Scott W, 256
SPEARS, Toni L, 321
SPECH, Reinaldo, 281
SPEKTOR, Mira J, 456
SPELLMAN, Lillian, 51
SPENCE, E B, 76
SPENCE, Frances, 539

SPENCE, Jeremy T, 779
SPENCE, Scott A, 769, 769
SPENCE, Stella, 502
SPENCE-CEGLOWSKI, Bonnie, 1056
SPENCER, Bernice, 299
SPENCER, Carolyn, 175
SPENCER, Jennifer Lynn, 527, 710
SPENCER, Kendell W, 409
SPENCER, Lynnda, 398
SPENCER, Michael J, 935
SPENCER, Nathalia S, 595
SPENCER, Roberta, 7
SPENCER, Ruth D, 251
SPICER, Angel, 678
SPICER, Douglas L, 521
SPILLANE, James A, 1050
SPILLER, Melanie, 511
SPINNER, Helena F, 470
SPINOS, Anthony, 961
SPIRIO, Lawrence, 945
SPIROPOULOU, Helen, 1078
SPIROS, Mitchell, 213
SPISINSKI, Maureen, 810
SPITALE, John A, 1064
SPITALNICK, Bill, 142
SPITZ, J L, 140
SPITZER, Osf, Sister M Imelda, 127
SPIVEY, Edwin P, 152
SPIVEY, Lois C, 28
SPJELDVIK, Ruth M B, 952
SPLAINE, Stephanie J, 486
SPOOR, Elmer R, 1035
SPORLEDER, Keith L, 552
SPRADLING, Lois, 989
SPRAGUE, Bonnie S, 171
SPRAGUE, Dorothy P, 808
SPRAGUE, Else, 395
SPRAGUE, Jim, 1026
SPRAGUE, Shannon, 280
SPRATT, Arlene Audrey, 1149
SPRAYBERRY, Sharon, 836
SPRENG, Emily, 700
SPRING, Joannie, 390
SPRING, Leo J, 545
SPRING-CLAUSSEN, Douglas, 974
SPRING-SMITH, Debbi, 1147
SPUNGIN, Jennifer, 1011
SPURLOCK, Anna Jane, 861
SPURLOCK, Kathy, 666
SPURRIER, Harry A, 439
SQUIRES, Debbie, 869
STCLAIR, Carole Dunagin, 1127
ST JACQUE, Kellyann, 817
STMICHEL, Linda, 1168
ST SAUVER, Julie A, 69
ST. JULES, Ruby J, 454
STABILE, Elena, 292
STACEY, Stephanie M, 1008
STACY, Timothy, 1090
STADLER, Steven, 796
STAFENAU, A, 509
STAFFA, Daniel P, 655
STAFFORD, Jan, 273
STAFFORD, Tanya A, 884
STAGNO, Jeff, 668
STAHA, Roxanne M, 557
STAHELI, D Bee, 688
STAHL, Helen M, 246
STAHL, Virginia D, 84
STAHLECKER, James G, 864
STAHNKE, Astrid B, 27
STAIKOS, Stavroula, 1017
STALKER, Roxanne, 188
STALLINGS, A George, 409
STALLINGS, Dorothy G, 727
STALLINGS-JENNEY, Faith, 134
STALLONS, Sandra M, 748
STALLWORTH, Karen L, 731
STALNAKER, Erma, 230
STAMER, Rita E, 646
STAMEY, Helen L, 75
STAMM, Michele, 463
STAMPER, Vicky L, 119
STAMPER, Wilma Jean, 296
STANCIL, Sara Ann, 715
STANDLEY, Eunice I, 912
STANFIELD, Joyce Liles, 635
STANG, Philip D, 885
STANGE, Orton J, 1198
STANLEY, Barbara J, 1032
STANLEY, Beulah, 607
STANLEY, Connie J, 153
STANLEY, Dorothy C, 952
STANLEY, Houston H, 8
STANLEY, Marguerite, 980
STANLEY, Peter, 951
STANLEY, Sherry A, 826
STANSBURY, Lisa Naomi, 144
STANSELL, Harriet, 317
STANSFIELD, Beulah T, 572
STAPLES, Olive M, 313
STAPLETON, Candy Apple, 1014
STAPLETON, Gloria S, 132
STAR, Donna M, 712
STARK, Avis, 923
STARK, Daryle, 400
STARK, Iris Theresa, 284
STARK, Jennifer A, 383
STARKE, Carl F, 883
STARR, Sherry, 1028
START, Peggy, 120
STAS, Annette, 312
STASNY, Bette, 48
STATON, Pauline B, 918
STAUFFER, Michael W, 13
STAUTY, Joy P, 420
STCLAIR, Lance, 816
STCLAIR, Terri Thomas, 615
STEAGER, James, 564
STEARNS, Warren D, 166
STEBBINS, Kim, 1162
STECHER, Joyce G, 1178
STEDMAN, Ronald J, 580
STEELE, Emily, 904
STEELE, Glenda J, 527, 526
STEELE, Karen G, 308
STEELE, Sarah, 646
STEELE, Yasmin, 190
STEELE-WILKINS, Stacey, 302
STEELY, Irene Nettles, 202
STEEN, Dava, 456
STEFANACCI, Steve J, 465
STEFANDES, Ann, 969
STEFANO, Maryann, 1090, 1191
STEGEMANN, Geraldine, 546
STEIDEL, Carolyn A, 401
STEIGER, Linda Marie, 743
STEIMANN, Dorothy M, 468
STEIN, Adelle, 662
STEIN, Cindi, 535
STEIN, Joseph A, 701
STEINBACH, Jeff, 414
STEINER, M Elisabeth, 467
STEINHILBER, Isadoria I, 254
STEINMAN, Martha L, 270
STEINNAGEL, Barbara A, 60
STELLA, Tracie Lynn Ranck, 835
STEM, Nancy, 354
STEMPF, Patricia, 411
STENSON, Phyllis, 1165
STENVALL, Edith Maria, 993
STEPANIAN, Serop, 487
STEPHAN, Lisa, 1053
STEPHANO, Grace Dombrowski, 45
STEPHENS, Bennie C, 1120
STEPHENS, Brian Allen, 22
STEPHENS, Cheryl Lynn, 1096
STEPHENS, Lillian R, 232
STEPHENS, Mary J, 946
STEPHENS, Milford, 577
STEPHENS, Sandra Mason, 628
STEPHENSEN, Kyler M, 348
STEPHENSON, Amy, 967
STEPHENSON, Eric E, 278
STEPHENSON, Geneva, 249
STEPHENSON, Gina, 1065
STEPHENSON, John, 226
STEPHENSON, Jolene, 463
STEPHENSON, Jonathan R, 892
STEPHENSON, Penny Rae, 1155
STEVENS, C J, 360
STEVENS, Frances, 321
STEVENS, Kathryn L, 538
STEVENS, Kirk Anthony, 697
STEVENS, Lola Mae, 34
STEVENS, Robert, 402
STEVENS, Roberta Mae, 580
STEVENS, Tracy, 651
STEVENS, Vivian Leda, 848
STEVENSON, Clara, 394
STEVENSON, Clifton, 307
STEVENSON, Ellen P, 88
STEVENSON, Linda S, 171
STEVENSON, Raquel L, 339
STEVENSON, Stella, 550
STEVENSON, Toya L, 355
STEVESON, Juanita Jo, 697
STEWARD, Anthony, 23
STEWART, Art, 308
STEWART, Druanne C, 509, 511
STEWART, Gail, 1162
STEWART, H Lamar, 1087
STEWART, Heidi Lynne, 838
STEWART, Helen, 119
STEWART, Prince A, 405
STEWART, Richard C, 779
STEWART, Sheila Betts, 326
STEWART, Sylvia Paris, 913
STEWART, Tammie, 413
STEWART-WILSON, Debbie, 746
STEWMAN, Katina, 96
STGOAR, Dr Walter T, 56
STICKNEY, Brandon M, 531
STIFEL, Timothy, 199
STILES, Harold W, 704
STILES, Shel, 526
STILES, Sue A, 197
STILLMAN, Lauren J, 237
STILLMAN, Nora Nita, 813
STINGIS, Deborah J, 976
STINSON, Clara G, 352
STINSON, Terryl, 1086
STITT, Linda Pierce, 648
STITZEL, Brian, 972
STIVER, Nancy, 496
STIVERSON, Carole, 1196
STJUSTE, Edvard, 960
STLAURENT, Margie Worrix, 1088
STOCK, Marci, 954
STOCKMAN, Arthur, 469
STOCKTON, Ronald T, 303
STODDARD, Alice R, 38
STOFFLE, Anton J, 96
STOJANIK, Ellen, 453
STOKER, Angela, 789
STOKOSZYNSKI, Carmen Kaye, 418
STOLTE, Marie C, 661
STOLTZFUS, Ila H, 796
STONE, Buffy, 903
STONE, Carolyn S, 604
STONE, Chandra L, 1010
STONE, Faith, 415
STONE, Frances, 344
STONE, Jeff, 310
STONE, John, 1128
STONE, Kathryn, 252
STONE, Katrine Frances, 239
STONE, Marjory W, 466
STONE, Pamela, 822
STONE, Rhoda M, 173
STONE, Sonyia A, 177
STONE, Susan, 1142
STONE, Susan, 396
STONESTREET, Charlotte, 822
STONNER, Elizabeth A, 1074
STOOPS, Bill, 654
STOOPS, Cheri Bell, 187
STOPPERICH, Carole A, 655
STOREY, Shirley J, 974
STORIE, Mina Joe A, 64
STORLIE, Martin, 297
STORM, Cindy, 401
STORMS, Tara C, 289
STORY, Jared, 886
STOTT, Mary (Reed), 1018
STOTTS, Bernice, 33
STOTTS, Catherine, 806
STOTYN, Vivian L, 82
STOUFFER, Winnie, 1140
STOUT, Larry C, 957
STOUT, Lois Webb, 890
STOVER, Chrisandra L, 87
STOVER, Nathaniel (Glenn), 684
STOVER, Patricia V, 810
STOWE, Elizabeth, 53
STOWE, Janette, 467
STOWE, Robert L, 807
STOWELL, Jean, 1065
STOWERS, Danette L, 124
STPIERRE, Phyllis, 141
STRADER, Mike, 1078
STRAHAN, Rose, 8
STRAHAN, Shannon Alley, 502
STRAIGHT, Suzanne, 167
STRAIN, Harrison W, 577
STRAIN, Rhonda C, 460
STRAIT-MCGRATH, Leann, 987
STRANGE-DUNN, Ross M, 693
MICHAEL, Charlotte M, 1182
STRATTON, Kim, 127
STRATTON-FERRIER, Brian, 436
STRAWN, Judith S, 689
STRAZZANTI, Maria Nadia, 475
STRECKER, Pamela J, 1042
STREET, Angela E, 145
STREET, Ethel Hunt, 649
STREIFF, Pauline V, 1133
STREIFLING, Grace E, 440
STREIT, Robert J, 714
STREVER, Rose Payzant, 733
STREY, Helen, 39
STREY, Jami, 406
STRIBIK, Elizabeth, 397
STRICKLAND, Etta Mae, 617
STRICKLAND, Glen Paul, 954
STRICKLAND, Mildred A, 1086
STRICKLAND, Patricia R, 152
STRICKLAND, Ronnee, 78
STRICKLAND, Sindy, 1037
STRICKLAND, Sissy, 211
STRICKLER, Fe, 482
STRICKLER, Loretta, 151
STRICKLIN, Vera Williams, 598
STRIPLING, Barbara A, 20
STROBEL, Steven R, 801
STROM, Therisia, 749
STROMMER, Oscar, 1158
STROMQUIST, Shelley, 956
STRONG, Calvin L, 728
STRONG, Karen M, 136
STRONG, L Claudine, 535
STROTHER, Matt, 1176
STROUD, Marlene A, 998
STROUD, Tim, 739
STRUCK, Connie, 436
STRUVE, Patricia S, 793
STUART, Barbara E, 1073
STUART, Janice, 1090
STUART, Katie, 483
STUART, Margie Dell, 981
STUBBS, Toni L, 86
STUCKENBERG, Martha, 75
STUCKEY, Annelle, 453
STUCKEY, Ruth, 1021
STUCKMAN, Joyce, 95
STUDLEY, Mary Jane, 382
STUECHER, Virginia L, 480
STUFFLE, Grace M, 443
STUFFLEBEEM, Vera McGown, 408
STULL, Donald R, 308
STUMP, Ralph B, 993
STUMREITER, Mary M, 239
STURDIVANT, Kit, 742
STURGEON, Luetta G, 147
STURGIS, Barbara F, 615
STURM, Elizabeth, 728
STYER, Sharon, 1008
SUDY, Mary Rose, 545
SUEN, Billie Jo, 623
SUGLIAN, Ludmila, 255
SUKHDEO, Gokarran, 765
SULIKOWSKI, Daniel C, 1043
SULLIVAN, Andrea, 305
SULLIVAN, Elizabeth G, 96
SULLIVAN, J Roy, 110
SULLIVAN, James R, 759
SULLIVAN, Jane Jennings, 1117
SULLIVAN, Kate, 864
SULLIVAN, Les, 671
SULLIVAN, Lora L, 1161
SULLIVAN, Pat, 32
SULLIVAN, Rosemary, 202
SULLIVAN-TRICOMI, Colleen, 230
SUMMERLOTT, Leona, 634
SUMMERS, Becky, 225
SUMNERS, Earl E, 1090, 1087
SUMNERS, Steven B, 411
SUMPTER, Mary Ursula, 746
SUMTER, Cliff, 548
SUNAGEL Jr, Gerald Allen, 463
SUNIGA, Mary C, 1055
SUPPLE, Thora J, 1088
SURA, Crystal Lynn, 1065
SURLES, Lea, 154
SURLS, Frances M, 82
SURPRENANT, Bernadette, 987
SUSMAN, Ethel A, 764
SUTCLIFFE, Martin James, 187
SUTER, Hilda Adams B, 199
SUTHERLAND, John W, 420
SUTHERLAND, Raymond, 1033
SUTTER, Heather A, 1020
SUTTERFIELD, William E, 154
SUTTON, David C, 676
SUTTON, Eileen, 619
SUTTON, Lottie, 162
SUTTON, Marguerite I, 578
SUTTON, Michelle A, 854
SUTTON, Sarah, 360
SUTTON, Tammy, 1073
SUVEG, Ivanka, 1069
SVOBODA, Gertrude, 553
SVOBODA, Stephen, 1107
SWAFFORD, Claire J, 927
SWAILS, Gloria, 159
SWAIM, Colette, 150
SWAIN, Carolyn, 399
SWAIN, Deborah E B, 326
SWALINA, Carolyn, 681
SWAN, Ann, 8
SWANK, Jody, 298
SWANK, Lorene, 729
SWANN, Therese C, 106
SWANSON, Barbara Ann, 159
SWANSON, Grace A, 1045
SWANSON, Grant C, 1055
SWANSON, Judith A, 441
SWANSON, Maxine Parker, 35
SWANSON, Vanessa Jo S, 809
SWARROW, Nicole M, 453
SWARTZ, Nancy Jean, 809
SWARTZBAUGH, Marc L, 592
SWAY, Roxanna A, 868
SWEARENGEN, Shawla M, 461
SWEAT, Douglas D, 663
SWEENEY, Ann C, 1166
SWEENEY, Carrie, 452
SWEENEY, Evelyn L, 763
SWEENEY, Karen, 270, 1125
SWEENEY, Marie T, 244
SWEENEY, Susan, 49
SWEENY, Barbara Davis, 547
SWEET, Joyce Elaine, 823
SWEET, Mechelle Le-Shawn, 1140
SWEISS, Pauline, 256
SWEITZER, Jennifer, 957
SWENSON, Joyce H, 308
SWEZEY, Beverly, 326
SWIECZKOWSKI, Juliet Ann, 423
SWIFT, Cheryl "Kish", 835
SWILLEY, Dawnmarie E, 629
SWINFORD, Naomi, 1147
SWINSON, Rhonda K, 649
SWISHER, Patricia, 66
SWOPE, Edie, 794
SWORD, Jenica, 879
SWORDS, Christine, 541
SWYERS, Mary A, 561
SY, Krishna, 699
SYKES, C Larry, 742
SYLVESTER, Jodi Lynn, 297
SYMINGTON, James W, 494
SZABLA Jr, Walter, 1065
SZCZECH, Robin, 649
SZCZEPANSKI, Mary, 859
SZEWCZYK, Gerald S, 985
SZILAGYI, Theresa Marie, 761
SZKRYBALO, Joel, 353
SZOLLOSY-SZABO, Eva, 965
SZUROMI, Laszlo, 393
SZYDLA, Barbara Ford, 603
SZYMCHACK, Danielle, 580

T

TABAH, S A, 198
TABB, Willie Jewel, 526
TACHIBANA, Bruce, 522
TACKETT, Rhonda, 594
TAFOYA, Irene M, 695
TAGGART, James M, 1179
TAGGERT, Martin Bud, 687
TAGUE, Bobbie A, 631
TAHERBHAI, Husein, 246
TAIT, Val Gene, 254
TAITT, S L, 576
TAKAHASHI, Mamilyn, 610
TALAVERA, Margaret, 1147
TALBERT, Aimee K, 413
TALBERT, Wynona R, 703
TALBOT, C, 698
TALIK, David, 882
TALKEN, Shirley, 158
TALLEY, Kimberly, 1124
TALTON, Gerry-Kay, 313
TAMBORSKI, Joan L, 1016
TAMSIN, Kenneth, 449
TANAKA, Louise T, 845
TANCO, Marina, 1027
TANGREDI, J C, 457
TANK, Rose M, 625
TANNER, Paige, 1202
TANNIS, June, 210
TANZA, Marie, 233
TAPLIN, Betty, 1107, 1066
TAPPER, Vanessa, 937
TARALLO-JENSEN, Lucia, 1107
TARANTO, Bridgett O, 449
TARASE, Martha, 891
TARGOWSKI, Francis A, 522
TARMAN, Linda J, 794
TARO, Joseph M, 781
TARR, B R, 556, 1107
TARR, Ronald, 466
TARRENCE, L, 204
TARSISH, Abraham, 23
TASCH, Caroline M, 520
TASCH, Rick, 184
TATE, Cheri M, 254
TATE, Cyril, 789
TATE, Donald L, 129
TATE, John, 1039
TATE, Karen D, 849

TATICH, Stacey, 722
TAUGER, Gayle, 95
TAURASI, Elizabeth M, 1107
TAVAREZ, Eduardo, 1120
TAYLOR, Agnes, 150
TAYLOR, Arturo, 582
TAYLOR, Barbara, 567
TAYLOR, Barbara Rame, 598
TAYLOR, Ben, 971
TAYLOR, Bradford B, 1056
TAYLOR, Cindy, 614
TAYLOR, Cynthia, 683
TAYLOR, Darion A, 903
TAYLOR, Donna, 939
TAYLOR, Doris Ann, 727
TAYLOR, Ethel Huffman, 808
TAYLOR, Eunice A, 258
TAYLOR, Georgia Kay, 1003
TAYLOR, Harriet, 1140
TAYLOR, Hattie C, 1043
TAYLOR, Ida M, 302
TAYLOR, Judy E, 470
TAYLOR, Kenneth Randolph, 1148
TAYLOR, Kris, 215
TAYLOR, Kristie M, 85
TAYLOR, Marilyn R, 803
TAYLOR, Martha, 830
TAYLOR, Mattie Jewel, 607
TAYLOR, Parris A, 495
TAYLOR, Rebecca, 522
TAYLOR, Rebecca H, 107
TAYLOR, Richard L, 143
TAYLOR, Rita K, 644
TAYLOR, Robert, 139
TAYLOR, Rosie L, 60
TAYLOR, Ruth Emma, 6
TAYLOR, Sandra K, 217
TAYLOR, Sandy, 296
TAYLOR, Susan A, 453
TAYLOR, Teri, 323
TAYLOR, Terry, 1163
TAYLOR, William, 47
TAYLOR-PRINGLE, Dian, 288
TEAGLE Jr, Henry R, 655
TEAGLE, Tonya, 1135
TEAGUE, Kerry Andrew, 902
TEAGUE, L, 515
TEAGUE, Traci, 65
TEAGUE, Vickie, 424
TEAKAM, Harven, 639
TEASLEY, Earl S, 9
TEED, Donald L, 280
TEED, Russell B, 333
TEEL, Irene, 553
TEEL, James Michael, 718
TEEL, Wilford F, 835
TEGNELIA, Ladisca, 37
TEHAN, Jasen, 1202
TEICH, Edith, 1149
TELLIS, Lynnette D, 959
TEMPESTA, Jeannie Marie, 982
TEMPLE, Laurie, 231
TEMPLE, T, 945
TENDLER, Christy, 871
TENNIES, Heather Suzanne, 955
TENNYSON, Warnella Faye, 1045
TENPAS, Dawn, 752
TEPE, Holly, 427
TERAULT, Cynthia F, 424
TERBORG, Janice, 31
TERON, Joy Lynn, 628
TERRANOVA, John S, 605
TERRELL, Cynthia, 374
TERRUSO, Lisa M, 756
TERRY, Theresa G, 149
TERRY, Debra, 971
TERRY, Stephen F, 12
TERVAKOSKI, Tony, 164
TESTERMAN, Suzanne M, 771
TETZLAFF, Bernadine, 1008
TEVEPAUGH, Carolyn M, 349
TEVERBAUGH, Laura M, 1067
TEW, Peggy C, 1089
THAI, Han, 248
THANASIU, Francine B, 312
THATCHER, David L, 88
THAYER, Michele, 892
THEEL, Annette E, 449
THEIS, Prudence F, 972
THEOBALD, Sue, 26
THERIAULT, Linda Wright, 720
THERIOT, Jill, 1148
THEUS, John, 1070
THEXTON, Bridget, 959
THIBODEAUX, Lynn, 484
THIBODO, Reana K, 144
THIEL, Misti, 544
THIESING, Hilda, 100
THOBURN, Robert, 11
THOMAS I(DAV), Gary L, 1181
THOMAS, Amorette A K, 648
THOMAS, Barbara, 1082
THOMAS, Catherine U, 536
THOMAS, Christopher A, 1151
THOMAS, David R, 127
THOMAS, Dawn, 1111
THOMAS, Debi, 184
THOMAS, Donna, 151
THOMAS, Ethel J, 638
THOMAS, Heather Diane, 626
THOMAS, Janet, 426
THOMAS, Jeff, 833
THOMAS, Jennifer M, 210
THOMAS, Jeremiah, 403
THOMAS, Jerry, 1140
THOMAS, Joyce Harmon, 853
THOMAS, Julie, 130
THOMAS, Lane, 1102
THOMAS, Linda, 1025
THOMAS, M L, 951
THOMAS, Margaret (Peggy), 791
THOMAS, Mary Adams, 112
THOMAS, Mia Frances, 76
THOMAS, Michelle M, 143
THOMAS, Patricia M, 889
THOMAS, Rebecca, 21
THOMAS, Rose R, 1004
THOMAS, Sandra Gail, 1155
THOMAS, Sharline M, 717
THOMAS, Twyla, 94
THOMAS, Zeni, 166
THOMASON, F A, 34
THOMASON, Frank J, 804
THOMASON, Jeanine, 860
THOME, Scott, 799
THOMPSON, Andrea C, 282
THOMPSON, Brooke Ann, 276
THOMPSON, Bruce A, 1018
THOMPSON, Catherine, 397
THOMPSON, Charles S, 30
THOMPSON, Cindy, 77
THOMPSON, Deanna, 698
THOMPSON, Delaphine J, 634
THOMPSON, Dematrice H, 519
THOMPSON, Denise, 779
THOMPSON, Diana, 760
THOMPSON, Diane, 422
THOMPSON, Dorris L, 21
THOMPSON, Dru R, 866
THOMPSON, Evangela, 861
THOMPSON, Florence M, 429
THOMPSON, G P, 1057
THOMPSON, Galyn, 1028
THOMPSON, Hank, 844
THOMPSON, James M, 804
THOMPSON, Jewel, 710, 1066
THOMPSON, Joe, 731
THOMPSON, John L, 138
THOMPSON, Juanita Ragan, 953
THOMPSON, Levann M, 433
THOMPSON, Lucy A, 720
THOMPSON, Lynn, 519
THOMPSON, Marianne, 337
THOMPSON, Mark D, 1111
THOMPSON, Marrion E, 1178
THOMPSON, Mary E, 837
THOMPSON, Mercedes B, 841
THOMPSON, Mrs Louette, 287
THOMPSON, Ms Linda M, 714
THOMPSON, Pamela, 690
THOMPSON, R, 839
THOMPSON, Ramona L, 1101
THOMPSON, Rebecca, 263
THOMPSON, Sallie, 918
THOMPSON, Sarah M, 612
THOMPSON, Shauna, 1127
THOMPSON, Su Ann, 1194
THOMPSON, T B, 47
THOMPSON, Tanny Darrell, 480
THOMPSON, Terry, 7
THOMPSON-LOBERT, Tuesday Lynn, 1164
THOMPSON-ZANOLLA, Margaret, 916
THOMSEN, Rob, 599
THOMSON, Candice, 879
THOMSON, Virginia W, 379
THON, Suzanne, 114
THORLAKSON, Rosemary E, 278
THORN, Brenda, 355
THORNE, Donna Marie, 49
THORNE, Tim E, 565
THORNTON, Christy, 723
THORNTON, Francine D, 849
THORNTON, Krista, 948
THORNTON, Lilas L, 331
THORNTON, Lisa, 675
THORNTON, Louise E, 1108
THORNTON, Mary C, 1107
THORP, John Gray, 92
THRASH, Barbara, 352
THRELKELD, Rolf, 687
THRIFT, Peggy Merele, 211
THROWER, Lorene D, 44
THRUSH, Robbin, 109
THUDIUM, Katherine (Libby), 350
THUESON, Meagon, 932
THURLOW, Tammie, 725
THURMAN, Brenda H, 68
THURMAN, Denise R, 833
THURMAN, Ms Pat, 602
THURMAN, Neal B, 741
THWEATT, Harry M, 682
TICHERICH, Marta Leigh, 723
TIDWELL, Allen, 1039
TIEGS, Minnie, 146
TIEPPO, Donna M, 89
TIER, Nancy Hopkins, 1181
TIERNEY, Joanne, 386
TIETZE, Michiele J, 938
TIFFANY, Mary T, 991
TIJERINA, Melissa Marie, 962
TIKRITI, Reyam Angela, 385
TILLERY, Hope, 163
TILLETT, A C, 219
TILLINGHAST, W P, 198
TILLMAN, Portia Owens, 751
TIMLAKE, Farrell, 1106
TIMMINS Jr, Robert A, 839
TIMMINS, Susan, 84
TIMNEY, Irene Iverson, 576
TIMPANO, Franca, 406
TIMPE, Crystal A, 221
TINCH, Janet L, 372
TINDALE, Kimberly J, 486
TINDALL, Vicki, 815
TINDELL, Susan, 874
TINI, Mair, 896
TINKER, Danny Joe, 814
TINNEY BA, Ethel M, 769
TINSLEY, Melanie, 1087
TIPPER, Jessie P, 977
TIPTON, Jenny, 127
TIPTON, Misty, 794
TIPTON, Palina, 110
TIPTON, Renee, 678
TIRABOSCHI, Christa, 532
TISCHLER, Dana M, 1001
TISDALE, Phebe Alden, 898
TISON, George A, 903
TITONE, Christine, 981
TITUS, Doris P, 701
TITUS, Lisa, 156
TIZOL, Donna J Carley, 56
TKACH, Marge, 724
TOBEY, Cathy, 549
TOBIAS, Evelyn, 668
TOBIAS, Virginia, 1075
TOBIN, April Hayes, 705
TOBOLA, Arline M, 985
TODARO, Dolores, 204
TODD, Bonita Folger, 117
TODD, Lee Ann, 626
TODD, Melba, 983
TOEWS, Freda, 613
TOFTE, Mavis, 161
TOGNATO, Alessandra, 1008
TOKUDA, Nancy, 242
TOKUNBO, Mrs Shirley, 1142
TOLAN-PARKER, Mercedes, 24
TOLAND, Douglas S, 297
TOLBERT, Alleda, 262
TOLENTINO, Maria Elena, 199
TOLENTINO, Michael, 169
TOLER, Nathan, 341
TOLER, Shirley, 870
TOLES, Angela, 596
TOMARIN, Lillie F, 60
TOMASZEK, Deborah Lynn, 791
TOMBARELLI, Betsy, 357
TOMBLIN, Jerry Lee, 463
TOMER, Bernice, 294
TOMICEK, Tracy, 1078
TOMINAGA, Gayle Mieko, 656
TOMLINSON, Barbara Ann, 1091
TOMLINSON, Donna, 150
TOMLINSON, John T, 1061
TOMPKINS, Polly E, 381
TOMPKINS, Rocky S, 819
TONER, Wendy C, 437
TOOLE, Gary, 719
TOOLSON, Sonoma Young, 10
TOPIWALA, Priti, 901
TORKELSON, Rev Helen Y, 924
TORKELSON, Tammy "Sims", 946
TORNABENE, Josie Marie, 439
TORRENCE, Asia, 854
TORRES Jr, Merced B, 1135
TORRES, Dolores, 770
TORRES, Gretchen, 1133
TOSH, Minnie, 895
TOSIC, Olivia, 628
TOTE, Martha Jeanne, 670
TOTELS, Darlene, 106
TOTH, Richard J, 1077
TOTH, Sandy, 186
TOTH, Tibor G, 229
TOTTEN, Audrey M, 634
TOUCH, Violet, 553
TOULAN, Jessica, 1134
TOURISH, Dorothy, 397
TOURJEE, Brian, 551
TOUSIGNANT, Cherilyn L, 862
TOWLE, Elsie C, 330
TOWNE, H L, 376
TOWNES, Correll L, 280
TOWNES, Melcia L, 39
TRABILSY, Najeh A, 680
TRABOSH, Barbara A, 476
TRACEY, Jeffery E, 982
TRACY, Fred T, 1041
TRAEGER, Patricia L, 104
TRAINI, Ann B, 876
TRAINOR, Terri, 371
TRAISTER, Steve, 1166
TRAKAS, Kathleen D, 227
TRANSOU, Larry Lee, 143
TRASK, Richard, 806
TRAUDT, Marji, 337
TRAVIERSO, Frances C, 594
TRAYLOR, Wilma Jean, 128
TRAYNELIS-YUREK, Elaine, 155
TRAYNOR, June, 242
TRAYNOR, Robert M, 867
TREADAWAY, Richard J, 8
TREADWAY, Maudie M, 864
TREADWELL, Terry, 695
TREAT, Troy D, 602
TREMONTE, William K, 133
TRENCH, Harold R, 518
TRENTHAM, Melody M, 947
TRETTON, Frances-Faith P, 114
TREVINO, Pedro, 443
TREVISAN, Carol, 1038
TREXLER, Monica M, 265
TREXLER, Naidene S, 426
TRIANO, Cathy M, 729
TRIBBIE, Dottie, 285
TRIBBLE, Eugene A, 109
TRIBELHORN, Erik, 373
TRIBLEY, Angela G, 1193
TRICHILO, Joseph J, 548
TRIGO, Marion, 191
TRIKONES, Debbie Lee, 593
TRIMBLE, John Mitchell, 517
TRIMBOLI, Steve, 849
TRIMPEY, Jennie L, 53
TRIPP, Barbara Lane, 738
TRISSEL, Amy Noel, 110
TRISTANI, Alberto D, 839
TRITCH, Rita, 65
TRIVETTE, William P, 1145
TROAST, Andi, 1040
TROCEEN, Charmaine M, 1123
TROJANOWSKI, Michael, 609
TROMBLEY, Russell C, 108
TROOSTENBERGHE, Barbara Van, 328
TROPE-LEWIS, Rosalee, 492
TROTMAN, Ross George, 181
TROTT, Alyssa, 486
TROTT, Joan, 681
TROTT, Rosemary C, 543
TROTTER, Beverly Jones, 778
TROTTER, Charles E, 549
TROTTER, Gordon D, 544
TROUT, Adamarie "Amie", 689
TROUTMAN, Jeanne M, 475
TROXELL, Jeff, 812
TROXELL, Travis, 1069
TRUAX, Sally A, 1118
TROYER, Les, 90
TRUCHINSKI, Larry E, 273
TRUDGETT, Katie, 1179
TRUETT, James William, 201
TRUITT, George F, 128
TRUJILLO, Armando, 644
TRUJILLO, Edward M, 221
TRUJILLO, Jo-Ellen (Joy), 502
TRUJILLO, Redgie D, 857
TRUNG, Ha Binh, 1197
TRUNK, Anthony J, 287
TRUNKHILL, Lorrie, 476
TRZEBIATOWSKI, Tami, 209
TSANG, Joanna, 518
TUBMAN, Heidi, 231
TUCKER, Carol Ann, 700
TUCKER, Joseph, 769
TUCKER, Nicole, 462
TUCKETT, Grant H, 14
TUCKEY, Sophie Marie, 506
TUDBALL, Elizabeth F, 810
TUDOSOIU, Peter, 1131
TUGEND, Joseph, 541
TULANEY Jr, John E, 268
TULLY, Reginald, 1112
TUMARKIN, Paul, 980
TUNNO, Cindy S, 1188
TUOMALA, Heather M, 782
TUPA, Robert F, 665
TURGEAU, Trudy A, 178
TURI, Bobbi, 996
TURK, Phyllis, 487
TURNAGE, Paula, 638
TURNBULL, Dorothy, 403
TURNER Jr, Cornel, 651
TURNER, Barbara, 771
TURNER, Bonnie Beebe, 794
TURNER, Bonnie Thomas, 1096
TURNER, Chad C, 16
TURNER, Clarabelle N, 766
TURNER, Clarice, 1056
TURNER, Glenna, 621
TURNER, Heather, 1140
TURNER, Joseph, 379
TURNER, Joseph M, 593
TURNER, Leslie, 523
TURNER, Lloyd, 468
TURNER, Ronda, 889
TURNER, Spencer L, 1133
TURNEY, Amelia E (Ms Meme), 20
TURPIN, Cindi Lee, 168
TURRIFF, Julie E, 599
TUSINGER, Juanita, 286
TUTTLE, Mrs Edna, 636
TWARDOWSKI, R M, 237
TWEED, Timothy E, 862
TWIFORD, Dorothy, 753
TWOMBLY, Rebecca, 594
TWOROGER, John, 62
TYGRETT, Belinda, 847
TYLAR, Mark D, 580
TYLER, Christine, 475
TYLER, Elsie F, 359
TYLER, Nikki, 378
TYLER, Stanley H, 1144
TYLER, Suesan J, 370
TYNER, Sunday K, 156
TYNG, Lillian M, 469
TYREE, Patricia, 885
TYSON, Michele Lee, 532
TYSON-ASHITEY, Arvis, 495

U

UBER, Gwenodine, 66
UEBELE, Walter C, 115
UEBELE, Marylouise, 1202
UHLS, Debra, 49
UJHELYI, Ilona, 630
ULLRICH, Janice C, 127
ULMER, Tamra, 43
UMPHENOUR, Terry, 62
UNDERWOOD, Sheila, 382
UNFERTH, Etalea, 155
UNGER, Jennifer Lynn, 1000
UNGER, Pauline, 210
UNISLAWSKI, Catherine L, 578
UNTCH, Dana Alex T, 23
UONELLI, Elaine Martin, 1134
UPDEGRAFF, Gary, 110
UPDEGRAFF, Rhonda, 844
UPHOFF, Karin Christa, 392
UPHOFF, Karinda, 1163
UPSHAW, Margaurette, 207
URIE, Theresa Joy, 190
URMAN, Ruth Suli, 1191
URSIC, Neda, 720
URSU, Mike, 430
USLICK, Mary Kay, 637
UTLEY, Lance D, 1059
UTLEY, Timothy, 182
UTTERBACK, Almeda, 758
UTTERBACK, Melville C, 806
UZOUKWU, Jude Mbamara, 543

V

VAHS, Judy, 259
VAIL, Rose S, 56
VAKHSHOORPOUR, Denise, 1176
VALADES, Anne James, 331
VALADEZ, Alicia Abeyta, 987
VALASCO, Ricky, 793
VALDAL, Eric J, 662
VALDINA, Mary G, 169

Index

VALDISERA, Margaret M, 751
VALENCIA, Martha, 7
VALENCIA, Shelby, 247
VALENTI, Cliff, 722
VALENTI, Michael, 372
VALENTI, Vince, 392
VALENTINE, Mildred E, 316
VALENTINE, Pamela Jean, 626
VALENTINO, Danuta, 246
VALERO, Carol L, 896
VALLARIO, Shele, 882
VALLE, Hilda, 1074
VALLE, Nancy J, 584
VALTRAKIS, Daniel Kevin, 375
VALVO, Frank, 292
VANBRUNT, Ollie M, 1162
VAN DAM, Georgina, 223
VAN DUYNE Sr, Allen, 364
VANOOSBREE, R, 1108
VANCE, Ruth Adrienne, 73
VANCE, Susan L, 940
VANCELETTE, Susan, 12
VANCIL, Norma L, 362
VANDEHEY, Catherine S, 1174
VANDERBECK, Courtney, 358
VANDERHORST, Muriel, 799
VANDERPOOL, Kerri R, 1185
VANDERSLICE, Roy W, 73
VANDERSTAPPEN, Stacey, 368
VANDEUSEN, Diana C, 31
VANDEVELDE, David G, 129
VANDEVER, Julie D, 803
VANDINE, Debra Lynn, 160
VANDIVER, Michelle, 870
VANDOREN, Frederick, 1060
VANDRUFF, Keith, 724
VANDUZER, Jennifer F, 830
VANDYKE, Margaret, 1184
VANFLEET, Kim, 686
VANFOSSEN, Mark, 241
VANGELDER, Karma M, 889
VANGILDER, Helen E, 970
VANHOORN, Margaret, 669
VANHORN CAC, Edward D, 205
VANHORN, Natalie, 558
VANHORNE, Norman, 645
VANLEEUWEN, Gary F, 363
VANMETER, Melissa A, 1133
VANMETER, Vincent A, 845
VANNATTAN, Shelena, 308
VANNOSTRAND, Terri, 847
VANNOY, Ang, 530
VANNUYEN, Nee, 694
VANORSE Sr, Bert J, 265
VANOVER, Wilfred, 742
VANRHEEN, Evelyn, 433
VANRHEEN, W F, 433
VANSCOIK, Thelma, 443
VANSELUS, Cleone, 227
VANSISTINE, Sandra M, 793
VANTASSELL, Terrance Gene, 294
VANVOOREN, Chris, 630
VANWART, Gail J, 529
VANWORTH, Terry, 722
VARDEN, Jennifer, 338
VARELA, Angelica, 306
VARELAS, Barbara A, 609
VARGA, Bozsi D, 544
VARGAS, Carmen Marie, 316
VARIAND, Gregory P, 893
VARNADO, Chrissie, 480
VARNADORE, Chad, 459
VARNEY Jr, Russell V, 449
VARSOLONA, Mary Ann, 895
VASQUEZ, Angel Luis, 924
VASQUEZ, Nicolina, 737
VASUDEVAN, R, 1066
VAUGHAN Jr, Hugh W, 733
VAUGHAN, Ollie M, 82
VAUGHAN, R Wesley, 18
VAUGHAN, Sarah Daniel, 560
VAUGHAN, Tarah K, 367
VAUGHN, Betty, 763
VAUGHN, J O, 506
VAUGHN, Jane, 532
VAUGHN, Julia, 886
VAUGHN, Maycel Irene, 321
VAUGHN, Peggy, 880
VAUGHN, Phoebe J, 1006
VAUGHN, R E, 726
VAUGHT, Angel, 561
VAZQUEZ, Lillian, 610
VAZQUEZ, Rita, 950
VEACH, Violet Moser, 251
VEASY, Mr Jeffery A, 1077
VEAZEY, Robert K, 323
VEEN, Sherri, 1100
VEGA, Patricia, 530
VEGTER, Kimberly, 218
VEICH, Gregory C, 998
VEILE, Jean, 297
VEILLEUX, Mary, 267
VEITCH, Nichole Marie, 1023
VEITCH-CLENNON, Beatrice, 624
VELA, Efrain, 422
VELARDE, Albert A, 509
VELASQUEZ, Victor, 822
VELAZQUEZ, Marie, 232
VELAZQUEZ, Olga, 1164
VELEZ, Carmen R, 827
VELISHEK, Tanya, 971
VELIZ, Carmen, 385
VELTRI, Fortes, 332
VENCILL, April, 804
VENGLASS, Gina, 982
VENTA-DOBROVOLSKY, Lydia, 353
VENTALORO, Rusty Jessie, 876
VENTO, Carmen, 128
VENTURA, Mary Ann, 937
VENTUROLI, Renae, 767
VERDADERO, Gloria Cadag, 600
VERGARA, Julian, 541
VERGARA, Lautaro G, 293
VERITY, Sylvia, 708
VERMETTE, Stephanie, 569
VERNAZZA, Kelly, 633
VERNER, Candy L, 667
VERONA, Kimberly M, 344
VERRA, Jill Finch, 68
VERZI, Barbara S, 1192
VESSA, J R, 462
VESTUTI, Gary, 132
DIVIA, Richard, 1178
VIALPANDO, Katrina, 824
VIBBERT, James D, 853
VICENT, Albert E, 1017
VICENTE, Rebecca, 956
VICHECK II, Edmund C, 535
VICKERS, Kim, 624
VICKRY, Rickie L, 1201
VIDALIS, Michael A, 747
VIERGUTZ, Brian, 846
VIGANI, Drew, 317
VILEN, Constance L, 609
VILENSKAYA, Larissa, 943
VILLAFRANCA, Diane M, 290
VILLARINI, Ana M, 85
VILLARREAL, Marcy, 696
VILLATORO, J Nohe, 601
VILLERS, Earl, 504
VILLONE, Terri, 1045
VINCENT, Betty, 685
VINCENT, Dona, 902
VINCENT, Gina M, 575
VINCENT, James, 858
VINCENT, Joanne E, 18
VINCENT, Lee, 419
VINCION, Linda, 814
VINES, Gary E, 289
VINES, Toi L, 777
VINK-LAINAS, Kari, 1155
VINSON, Jeannie, 786
VINSON, Max, 457
VIOLETTE, Pauline, 1076
VIRES, Kenneth, 431
VIRTUE, Jane S Miller, 255
VISCOMI, Christina, 518
VISGER, Rita R, 318
VITOLO, Cara, 764
VITONE, V J, 93
VIZCARRA, Carl, 1088
VIZTES, Elizabeth A, 402
VIZZINI, Lucia A, 471
VLAHAKIS, Linda M, 1044
VOELKER, Edward D, 926
VOGEL, Craig, 193
VOGES, Sierra, 445
VOGLER, Dee Marie, 663
VOGLER, Ethel M, 627
VOGT, Charmaine R, 8
VOID, Michael L, 609
VOIGT, Liz, 157
VOISEY, Mary E, 573
VOLGARES, Gladys, 319
VOLID, Ruth, 878
VOLK, Cecil, 1189
VOLKMAN, Celia, 744
VOMSCHEIDT, Anamaria R, 305
VONWEIZMANN, Franz, 1174
VONBIEBERSTEIN, Dolores, 127
VONDRAN, Evelyn H, 64
VONMETER, Mary Lou, 57, 85
VORWERK, Gail, 330
VOSE-CANNON, Dawna L, 351
VOTH, Menno Walter, 217
VOYLES, Destiny F, 5
VUK, Brana, 989
VYVYAN, Sally Ann, 347

W

WACHSMUTH, Temple W, 1158
WACK, J W, 1194
WADDELL, Michael W, 33
WADDELL, Pam, 1089
WADE, Lizzie, 1068
WADE, Terry E, 851
WADLEY, Janis Heiner, 79
WADSWORTH, Denise, 208
WAGGIE, Vickie E, 956
WAGNER, Autumn Rose, 1124
WAGNER, Bette Rose, 967
WAGNER, David Kevin, 800
WAGNER, Georgia Lee, 795
WAGNER, Janet A, 275
WAGNER, Joan Marie, 123
WAGNER, Lila L, 239
WAGNER, Marcia L, 295
WAGONER, Jana M, 693
WAHEED, Aisha C, 881
WAHLERS, Allison, 1184
WAHLSTEN, Olga, 1088
WAKEFIELD, Debbie, 941
WAKEFIELD, Linda, 1026
WALANGA, Bob, 704
WALDEN, Dexter A, 131
WALDEN, Margaret, 757
WALDEN, Trisha K, 359
WALDOW, Thea M, 699
WALDOW, Veronica S, 907
WALDROFF, Heather, 869
WALDRON, Jacqueline C, 707
WALDRUP Sr, Richard M, 264
WALDSMITH, Annie Ruth, 147
WALES, Andrea, 496
WALIA, J S, 714
WALKER Jr, Joseph Lamah, 1002
WALKER, Alice M, 1002
WALKER, Ann D, 777
WALKER, Ansel A, 20
WALKER, Barbara, 912
WALKER, Bernice, 987
WALKER, Brian, 271
WALKER, C J, 293
WALKER, Carolyn A, 805
WALKER, Celeste, 574
WALKER, Cristy D, 205
WALKER, Dawn Evelyn, 506
WALKER, George, 840
WALKER, Gwendolyn D, 1138
WALKER, Gwendolyn K, 1200
WALKER, H M, 248
WALKER, Julie, 135
WALKER, Miles, 442
WALKER, Norman H, 697
WALKER, Peggy, 957
WALKER, Randall M, 18
WALKER, Reva McFarland, 924
WALKER, Rita A, 820
WALKER, Robert J, 366
WALKER, Sandra, 1131
WALKER, Steven Ray, 458
WALKER, Tammy S, 897
WALKER, Tempest, 604
WALKER, Terresa L, 791
WALKER, Vivian Smith, 1049
WALKMASTER, Carl R, 30
WALL, Carolyn, 1171
WALL, Marlene, 730
WALL, Tonja, 517
WALLACE Sr, Charles E, 788
WALLACE, Alfred Leon, 249
WALLACE, Ashley, 698
WALLACE, Della Ann, 1181
WALLACE, Dorothy E, 219
WALLACE, Izetta, 327
WALLACE, Melody A, 1197
WALLACE, Pamela F, 611
WALLACE, Phyllis, 1010
WALLACE, Tammy L, 301
WALLACE, Theresa Marie, 482
WALLER, Anglena, 1026
WALLER, Barbara J, 684
WALLER, Bernita, 858
WALLIN, Rick, 670
WALLIZER, Carla, 852
WALLS, Stephen L, 435
WALQUIST, Danielle, 662
WALRAVEN, Frances A, 363
WALSH, Aimee, 694
WALSH, Carol A, 563
WALSH, Catalina M, 643
WALSH, Daniel A, 155
WALSH, E Brian, 29
WALSH, Ellen M, 114
WALSH, Gayle, 456
WALSH, Jo, 548
WALSH, Karen, 30
WALSH, Kelly, 1010
WALSH, Kenneth, 574
WALSH, Mary Helen, 1201
WALSTON, Deborah L, 375
WALTEMATE, Tamara, 45
WALTER, Cindy, 547
WALTER, Doris Brubaker, 164
WALTER, M C, 801
WALTER, Tania, 377
WALTERS, Janet, 600
WALTERS, Karen, 582
WALTERS, Lynn Dixon, 820
WALTERS, Sheryl L, 1022
WALTON, Helen M, 799
WALTON, Phoebe C, 1057
WALTON, Sarah Ann, 1124
WALTON, Shirley Dawn, 710
WAMBEKE, Jeff Scott, 100
WAMBERG, Cheryl, 1163
WAMER Jr, Daniel J, 631
WANG, Chung-Hsin, 526
WANTNUK, Verna, 384
WARD, (Mrs) Pansy, 1130
WARD, Angela Louise, 500
WARD, Athanasia, 348
WARD, Beth E, 11
WARD, Betty A, 1066
WARD, Dura, 418
WARD, Emmanuel M, 116
WARD, Eric Bennett, 891
WARD, George H, 226
WARD, Henrietta, 212
WARD, Janeen, 151
WARD, Jeffrey L, 696
WARD, Jessica, 910
WARD, Laverne Smith, 194
WARD, Nan, 681
WARD, Nathalie Floyd, 1091
WARD, Raymond A, 380
WARD, Ruth M, 377
WARD, Sharon, 1011
WARD, Stacey M, 298
WARD, Tamara, 538
WARD, Toni Patricia, 451, 10
WARDELL, Cecil A, 55
WARDEN, Tracy, 70
WARDRUP, Loyd T, 1176
WARE, Doris Brown, 25
WARLICK, Lauren K, 329
WARNER, Melissa, 1063
WARNIX, D Janette L, 449
WARR-HAYWORTH, Darlene S, 439
WARREN Jr, Theodore J, 577
WARREN, Bertha, 277
WARREN, Catherine F, 1021
WARREN, Dierdre, 1023
WARREN, Mark, 385
WARREN, Nichole, 78
WARREN, Vera, 1035
WARREN, Zelda, 416
WARRING, Robert G, 365
WASHINGTON, Brenda, 457
WASHINGTON, Celeste Aliesha, 635
WASHINGTON, Charles, 21
WASHINGTON, Danny Charles, 1201
WASHINGTON, Gloria, 999
WASHINGTON, Helen J, 419
WASHINGTON, Lajaniese S, 738
WASHINGTON, Loree Jackson, 699
WASHINGTON, Luetress Dimples, 831
WASHINGTON, Nekita, 365
WASHINGTON, Tanaya, 651
WASKOM-HEATH, Retha, 273, 275
WASYLYK, Karen A, 165
WATCHORN, Mary Lou, 689
WATERHOUSE, Brian, 724
WATERS, Carolyn, 806
WATERS, Ellen R, 1036
WATERS, Leann, 369
WATERS, Tracy Lee S, 460
WATERS, Virginia Dean, 1005
WATHEN, Mary, 515
WATKINS, B B, 744
WATKINS, Bruce W, 408
WATKINS, David A, 320
WATKINS, Elysia J, 812
WATKINS, Leanne, 588
WATKINS, Melissa, 879
WATKINS, Pamela J, 481
WATKINS, Susan E, 536
WATSON, Betty, 68
WATSON, Beverly M, 234
WATSON, D Gordon, 563
WATSON, Darren, 567
WATSON, Dawn, 308
WATSON, Debra A, 564
WATSON, H D, 839
WATSON, Heather, 16
WATSON, Michael, 631
WATSON, Patsy K, 1021
WATSON, Ruth Conklin, 248
WATSON, Tonnetta, 646
WATT, D Purl, 97
WATT, Kathy, 1025
WAUGH, Marcia, 825
WAY, Grant, 764
WAYNE, Lorna E, 325
WAYNO, Mrs Jerome R, 404
WEAKS, Tammy, 496
WEAL, Carol, 730
WEATHERS, Anny, 128
WEAVER Jr, Ben, 465
WEAVER, Dan, 569
WEAVER, Elizabeth, 665
WEAVER, Glenn, 13
WEAVER, Grace M, 1140
WEAVER, Karen Y, 23
WEAVER, Lucinda, 343
WEAVER, Marva Warrick, 1179
WEAVER, Mary C, 1141
WEAVER, Wendy J, 84
WEBB, Herbert R, 942
WEBB, Jennifer Love, 296
WEBB, John L, 717
WEBB, Ruby Cummings, 284
WEBB, Shauna L, 1091
WEBBER, Brent, 1067
WEBBER, Helen E, 487
WEBBER, Keith A, 236
WEBBER, Mabel Stone, 334
WEBER, Anita L, 754
WEBER, George L, 399
WEBER, Hazel Lillian, 1121
WEBER, Jimma, 173
WEBER, Katherine J, 931
WEBER, Kathryn Herziger, 1089
WEBER, Sandra Mae, 287
WEBERT, Marilyn, 441
WEBSTER, A Nicholas, 788
WEBSTER, Anne M, 820
WEBSTER, Kathleen, 594
WEBSTER, Kim, 550
WEBSTER, Mary Anne, 507
WEBSTER, Roy, 63
WEBSTER, Russ, 442
WEDBERG, Mary Beth Stewart, 269
WEDDING, Kheresa Dawn, 261
WEDEGIS, Jennifer, 36
WEDGE, Frieda M, 701
WEDGWOOD, Penelope, 934
WEEKES, Neville G, 584
WEEKS, Brenda L Day, 172
WEEKS, Shelly, 407
WEESNER, Stephen L, 203
WEGMANN, Ann S, 939
WEGNER, Helen Rae, 976
WEGNER, Maria, 276
WEGNER, Regina T, 399
WEHLING, Linda, 843
WEHRENDT, Shannon L, 560
WEHRLI, Dixie Lamont, 179
WEHRMEISTER, Evelyn M, 1039
WEIGNER, Barbara, 1147
WEIKERT, Marlene, 1154
WEIKLE, C, 362
WEIL, Maria R, 399
WEILAND, Adrienne "Addie", 443
WEINBAUM, Joseph, 463
WEINDORF, Steve, 410
WEISKOPF, Wanda, 26
WEISS, Donna M, 1024
WEISS, Helen E, 703
WEISS, Kirsten, 549
WEIST, Carmen Orodio, 547
WEITSMAN, Amy, 402
WEITZEL, Doris J, 441
WELBOURN, Gertrude B, 1122
WELCH, Faith Ann, 934
WELCH, Herbert D, 923
WELCH, Ray, 1164
WELCH, Scott D, 850
WELCH, Stephen A, 784
WELDON, Angela Fay, 1132
WELKER, Margaret W, 895
WELLBORN, Ann, 987
WELLER, Amy, 412
WELLER, Traci, 507
WELLIVER, Kim A B, 794
WELLS SCRIVEN, Emmanuel, 600
WELLS, Anthony T, 473
WELLS, Beth, 971
WELLS, Cora, 954
WELLS, David Thayer, 753
WELLS, Janet Ezell, 595

WELLS, Jon A, 795
WELLS, Lee, 183
WELLS, Lurline, 181
WELLS, Martha F, 1104
WELLS, Nicholas, 262
WELLS, Patricia, 1195
WELLS, Shawn J, 250
WELLS, Susan E, 672
WELLS, Ted Ray, 129
WELSER, Beverly, 263
WELSER, Marguerite, 1108
WELSH, Brandon, 1091
WELTMER, Melanie, 116
WENDINGER, Anita, 1144
WENDLER, Marilea Hall, 623
WENDLING, Bob, 503
WENDT, J Travis, 750
WENDT, Mr Kris A, 743
WENTZ, Nora M, 837
WENTZEL, Barbara, 356
WENTZELL, Tracey, 38
WENZEL, Evelyn M, 181
WENZEL, Lori A, 841
WEPPENER, Barbara S, 838
WERDER, Jaci-Rene B, 594
WERGIN, Patricia, 324
WERLING, Edward L, 561
WERNER, Jeri Ann, 541
WERNER, Meghan, 885
WESGAITES, Annette J, 279
WESIK, Anja, 1166
WESLOWSKI, Ann, 343
WESSEL, Carla, 192
WEST Jr, Thomas A, 384
WEST, Carolyn S, 49
WEST, Connie L, 972
WEST, Diana L, 408
WEST, Frederick, 164
WEST, G Steven, 87
WEST, Joyce, 56
WEST, Mary A, 69
WEST, Nancy Fay, 625
WEST, Patricia G, 1067
WEST, Shirley T, 814
WESTA, Diana Hunt, 243
WESTFALL, Ann, 498
WESTFALL, Bill, 519
WESTGATE, Patti, 568
WESTMAN, Hazella, 940
WESTON, Donald A, 591
WESTWOOD, Melissa, 229
WETHERALL, Edward, 165
WETMORE, June, 49
WETMORE, Randy, 50
WEUSI, Chicha O, 858
WEXLER, Irving, 318
WEYER, Angela, 21
WEYMAN, Patty M, 470
WHALEN, Emily R, 1122
WHALEN, Peter, 548
WHALEY, Linda D, 125
WHEELER, Dorothy K, 251
WHEELER, Emily F, 368
WHEELER, Gay, 200
WHEELER, Glenda, 1114
WHEELER, Grace Paschal, 795
WHEELER, Marcia L, 499
WHEELER, Marjorie, 562
WHEELER, Rex, 615
WHELPLEY, Jan C, 348
WHIPKEY, Edith M, 238
WHIPPLE, Hazel, 65
WHISENANT, Kelly, 147
WHISTLER, Linda D, 942
WHITAKER, Carolyn S, 296
WHITAKER, Ethel R, 806
WHITAKER, Joan Revlett, 1192
WHITAKER, Johnny, 173
WHITCRAFT, David M, 1090
WHITE Jr, Mrs John A, 81
WHITE, Alice M, 21
WHITE, Amelia Sprague, 674
WHITE, Bernadette, 1018
WHITE, Betty Joyce, 1090
WHITE, Brenda, 1179
WHITE, Candace A, 1193
WHITE, Darrell A, 866
WHITE, Deborah Ann, 1130
WHITE, Dennis, 484
WHITE, Dottie, 761
WHITE, Eleanor, 148
WHITE, Emily, 550
WHITE, Eunice C, 1046
WHITE, Evangelist Jean D, 371
WHITE, Faith L, 1050
WHITE, Frances, 1004
WHITE, G "Marie" Williams, 646
WHITE, Gail D, 54
WHITE, George, 522
WHITE, Georgia, 720
WHITE, Gladys J, 217
WHITE, Gordon, 500
WHITE, Helen M, 568
WHITE, Jan, 813
WHITE, Kathy D, 148
WHITE, Kristina, 1196
WHITE, Leann K, 896
WHITE, Lynnda Kaye, 701
WHITE, Maggie Jean, 418
WHITE, Marilyn T, 989
WHITE, Marjorie A, 209
WHITE, Mary Cramer, 491
WHITE, Mary Gerry, 473
WHITE, Mary Ruth, 560
WHITE, Michelle, 622
WHITE, Mrs Kate, 952
WHITE, Ms Armetta L, 1022
WHITE, Sherry G, 301
WHITE, Suzanne, 510
WHITE, Tammy N, 159
WHITE, Terry, 963
WHITE, Trudee De Kay, 820
WHITE, Undrala R, 1054
WHITE, Virginia Lois, 482
WHITE, Yolanda, 1113
WHITE-ALLEN, Nina I, 636
WHITE-HARRISON, Mima, 14
WHITE-KAUFMAN, Mildred L, 231
WHITE-SANFORD, Lajan, 722
WHITEHEAD, Letitia, 98
WHITENACK, Mary, 20
WHITESIDE, Daniel L, 81
WHITEWOLF, Aryn A, 558
WHITFIELD, Melody Anita, 750
WHITFORD, Susan Ansbro, 978
WHITING, Toreen Lehman, 192
WHITLEY, Paul B, 699
WHITLOCK, Nanette, 170
WHITLOCK, Rosemary, 901
WHITLOCK, Virgie L, 363
WHITLOW, Karen Chambers, 971
WHITMAN, Felicia, 49
WHITMORE, David E, 976
WHITMORE, Sandra May, 1174
WHITNEY, Irene, 1181
WHITT, Karen Marie, 172
WHITTAKER, William R, 1031
WHITTING, Janice, 420
WHITTINGTON, Amanda, 728
WHITTINGTON, Reba, 276
WHITWORTH MD, Thomas C, 113
WHITWORTH, Marche', 1156
WHITWORTH, Orval, 644
WHYTE, Maureen C, 476
WIATER, Teresa, 294
WIBLE, Caroline M. Raker, 657
WICKER, Mack O, 949
WICKWIRE, Helen, 1122
WIDDOWSON Jr, Frederick G, 887
WIDEN, Sandra, 105
WIDNER, Jack, 973
WIEBE, Franklin, 969
WIEBUSCH, Marana, 1023
GREGG, Veronica, 1144
WIEJA, Emily, 988
WIENEKE, Lucy, 676
WIERSUM, Richard W, 223
WIETING, M Akal Kaur, 732
WIGGIN, Loretta Clark, 989
WIGGINS, Barbara J, 390
WIGGINS, Richard, 848
WIGHTMAN, Joan, 882
WIGLE, Penny R, 313
WILBUR, Helen J, 1037
WILBUR, Helen P, 75
WILBUR, W E, 262
WILCOX, Christine L, 705
WILCOX, Colleen, 413
WILCOX, Frank L, 816
WILCOX, Jean, 847
WILCOX, Jeanne Jo, 542
WILCOX, R Dwain, 342
WILCOX, Sabrina, 411
WILCZEWSKI, Mike, 199
WILD, Lisa, 684
WILDER, Marte, 818
WILDER, Shari Lynn, 673
WILDERMAN, Steve, 548
WILDT, Debbie, 837
WILEY Jr, James William, 151
WILEY, Barbara B, 319
WILEY, Jeanette Rich, 952
WILEY, Kim, 858
WILEY, Marjorie R, 10
WILEY, Mary Holmes, 465
WILHELM Jr, Kermit R, 216
WILHELM, Gwen, 161
WILHELM, Mary Elaine, 329
WILKE, Karen Correll, 339
WILKE, Rita K, 180
WILKERSON, Susan, 63
WILKES, Bill, 264
WILKES, Daphene "Punki", 1153
WILKES, Marjorie, 82
WILKES, Sam E, 553
WILKES, Sarajo, 277
WILKIE, Julie, 456
WILKIE, Susan Briggs, 893
WILKINS, Alyssa J, 48
WILKINS, Evamay, 997
WILKINS, Nancy C, 525
WILKINS, Sally Jo, 648
WILKINS, Shirley, 679
WILKINSON, Judy, 632
WILKINSON, Julia, 571
WILKINSON, Laurel, 593
WILKINSON, Margaret, 579
WILKINSON, Mildred, 275
WILL, Lee R, 1121
WILLETT, Tammy, 317
WILLETTE, George F, 78
WILLI, Connie M, 469
WILLIAMS IV, Eddie G, 144
WILLIAMS Jr, Harold E, 35
WILLIAMS Jr, Horace, 1163
WILLIAMS, Alberta, 938
WILLIAMS, Aldouphus L, 769
WILLIAMS, Alicia Tamie, 396
WILLIAMS, Allen B, 1010
WILLIAMS, Audra, 163
WILLIAMS, Barbara A, 775
WILLIAMS, Barbara A, 532
WILLIAMS, Barbara R, 17
WILLIAMS, Bessie, 13
WILLIAMS, Bobbie J, 526
WILLIAMS, Brenda, 793
WILLIAMS, Carl C, 1151
WILLIAMS, Carol A, 543
WILLIAMS, Carolyn, 559
WILLIAMS, Carolyn R, 753
WILLIAMS, Cassie Roseberry, 245
WILLIAMS, Christopher J, 594
WILLIAMS, Darryl E, 156
WILLIAMS, David L, 802
WILLIAMS, Deborah C, 233
WILLIAMS, Debra, 1008
WILLIAMS, Della, 92
WILLIAMS, Ellen M, 724
WILLIAMS, Emma Jean, 771
WILLIAMS, Geneva, 483
WILLIAMS, Geraldine, 503
WILLIAMS, Gilberta K, 704
WILLIAMS, Gloria Hill, 1186
WILLIAMS, Hazel E, 591
WILLIAMS, J Dee, 70
WILLIAMS, James A, 1131
WILLIAMS, James E, 944
WILLIAMS, Jane A, 200
WILLIAMS, Jean A, 1144
WILLIAMS, Jimmy C, 562
WILLIAMS, Kathleen, 1005
WILLIAMS, Kathy, 14
WILLIAMS, Linda, 171
WILLIAMS, Linda J, 809
WILLIAMS, Lois E, 249
WILLIAMS, Manuel, 964
WILLIAMS, Marcia, 637
WILLIAMS, Marcus, 162
WILLIAMS, Marilyn, 588
WILLIAMS, Mary L Hall, 80
WILLIAMS, Pam, 698
WILLIAMS, Pamela J, 766
WILLIAMS, Patricia A, 25
WILLIAMS, Peggy Ryan, 948
WILLIAMS, R L, 1134
WILLIAMS, Rhoda, 1093
WILLIAMS, Robert A, 944
WILLIAMS, Robert Bruce, 1155
WILLIAMS, Robert Lewis, 947
WILLIAMS, Sandy, 961
WILLIAMS, Shana K, 721
WILLIAMS, Sharon E, 345
WILLIAMS, Sherrie, 610
WILLIAMS, Sue, 1131
WILLIAMS, Terri, 516
WILLIAMS, Terri L, 630
WILLIAMS, Terry L, 315
WILLIAMS, Valerie, 1054
WILLIAMS, Walter Warren, 1164
WILLIAMS-BRUNSON, Audrey W, 416
WILLIAMSON Jr, Fred W, 367
WILLIAMSON, Joan, 308
WILLIAMSON, Joyce Ann M, 858
WILLIAMSON, Larry, 703
WILLIAMSON, Mary Ann, 578
WILLIAMSON, Sue, 1131
WILLIAMSON, Theone, 97
WILLIAMSON, W John, 124
WILLIFORD, Chyanne W, 801
WILLIMONT, Marie, 763
WILLIS, Donald W, 169
WILLIS, Dwayne E, 906
WILLIS, Jean, 908
WILLIS, Joyce D, 524
WILLIS, Kelly, 267
WILLIS, Margaret, 252
WILLIS, Pat, 551
WILLIS, Paula, 517
WILLIS, Tammy M, 503
WILLMOTT, Edgar J, 252
WILLS, Evelyn M, 1196
WILLS, George Roland, 82
WILLS, Teresa, 389
WILLSON, Lisbeth M, 681
WILMOT, Sharron M, 300
WILQUET, Brenda, 577
WILSON III, Leonard A, 1113
WILSON Jr, Dewey M, 415
WILSON Jr, Wesley W, 764
WILSON MHS, Sr Miriam R, 156
WILSON Sr, James E, 225
WILSON, Amanda Dianne, 818
WILSON, Amy Lee, 972
WILSON, Betty, 1071
WILSON, Betty J, 844
WILSON, Brenda Comer, 548
WILSON, Bruce, 824
WILSON, C K, 184
WILSON, Darren, 762
WILSON, Deborah, 253
WILSON, Delana, 1081
WILSON, Diana K, 252
WILSON, Edward, 131
WILSON, Elva Mae, 1182
WILSON, Helen, 380
WILSON, Jane, 1155
WILSON, Jean, 428
WILSON, Jessie W, 559
WILSON, Kristin, 373
WILSON, Larry L, 61
WILSON, Linda T, 259
WILSON, Lois, 810
WILSON, Marcelle I, 629
WILSON, Marella, 1090, 1067
WILSON, Margaret M, 393
WILSON, Mark A, 1038
WILSON, Ms Dale Annette, 1188
WILSON, Nancy Grady, 244
WILSON, Nancy J, 173
WILSON, Netty, 695
WILSON, Nina, 130
WILSON, Phyllis M, 573
WILSON, Reagan, 783
WILSON, Richard, 263
WILSON, Robert, 654
WILSON, Robert P, 231
WILSON, Ruth A, 792
WILSON, S Dunham, 427
WILSON, Sandra L, 932
WILSON, Saundra, 1157
WILSON, Steve R, 157
WILSON, Susan Davis, 1122
WILSON, Sylvia, 1122
WILSON, Tammy, 528
WILSON, Tammy Lyn, 656
WILSON, Timothy L, 719
WILSON, Vicki L, 247
WILSON, Victoria M, 459
WILSON, Virginia L, 260
WILSON, Wendell R, 31
WILSON, Yvonne Spirie, 807, 961
WILSON-HICKS, Mrs Marcia, 1039
WILSON-MARYMAN, Linda, 167
WINBORNE, Marcia Sebby, 566
WINCHESTER, Tammy L, 479
WINDLEY, T M, 928
WINDMILLER, Mary I, 845
WINDWEHEN, Paul E, 1020
WINEGAR, Madge Abigail, 127
WINEGAR-PETRONEK, Sandra, 173
WINGER, Shelly Kay, 656
WININGER, Larry Glenn, 782
WININGS, Joan Lancaster, 710
WINKELMAN, Recha, 659
WINKIS, Michael A, 654
WINKLER, Ena, 1195
WINKLER, Stephanie, 689
WINN, Maureen A, 1004
WINN, Sheri, 574
WINSLETT, Elizabeth, 984
WINSLOW, D Christopher, 1200
WINTER, Phillip, 587
WINTERS, Alice, 69
WINTERS, Marguerite E, 391
WINTERS, Melissa L, 1184
WINTERS, Ruth Ann, 359
WINTLE, Ruth C, 391
WISE, Daniel A, 1191
WISE, Nicole L, 1158
WISE, Paula M, 11
WISE, Rita J, 1096
WISEMAN, Glenn E, 459
WISHON, Deanna V, 495
WISNER, Sheila, 330
WISNIEWSKI, Andrea J, 865
WISPER, Arnold, 1079
WISSNER, Erin E, 590
WITCHER, Shirley, 931
WITHERINGTON, Andrea, 832
WITHERS, Pauline, 1074
WITHINGTON, Patches, 1148
WITMAN, Thomas R, 10
WITMEYER, Sara G, 914
WITT, Deanna, 86
WITT, Erin, 541
WITT, Kenneth, 647
WITTE, William, 914
WITTEMAN, Susan K, 802
WITTEN, N May, 125
WLOCH, Doris Murdock, 257
WOFFORD, Larry T, 280
WOGLOM, Viola H, 44
WOHLFORD, Michael P, 618
WOJTASIK, Robert J, 616
WOLDRUFF, Micky, 63
WOLF, Angela D, 656
WOLF, Cheryl, 276
WOLF, Katherine Ann, 185
WOLF, Robert H, 1080, 1202
WOLFE, Christopher A, 1202
WOLFE, D E, 505
WOLFE, Mark R, 596
WOLFE, Robert D, 481
WOLFE-GOOSSEN, Micki, 130
WOLFF, Carol, 1090, 1086
WOLKENBROD, Mavis, 629
WOMACK, Donna R S, 247
WOMACK, Fenicia D, 773
WOMBLE, Julie, 439
WONG, Minna, 881
WOOD, Amanda E, 443
WOOD, Capt Irby F, 445
WOOD, Deborah A, 700
WOOD, Kenneth, 730
WOOD, Lora, 921
WOOD, Mary Alice, 889
WOOD, Maryanne, 282
WOOD, Nancy L, 224
WOOD-TRESENTE, Patricia E, 572
WOODALL Sr, Rayford, 825
WOODALL, Lloyd A, 838
WOODALL, Ray S, 1016
WOODARD, Agnes G, 911
WOODARD, Brenda, 576
WOODARD, David, 988
WOODARD, Edith T, 153
WOODARD, Priscilla T, 748
WOODARD, Ruth Graham, 5
WOODDELL, Philo Glenn, 253
WOODELL, Ruby, 1156
WOODEN, Paula, 367
WOODFORD, Jody, 626
WOODIN, Stacie, 618
WOODMAN, Walter J, 10
WOODRUFF, Lynn, 717
WOODS, Felton D, 276
WOODSON, Lisa M, 31
WOODWARD, Terri, 1184
WOODWORTH, Karen, 1131
WOODY, Joann, 1051
WOOLEY, Betty Ann, 217, 1140
WOOLFF, Roxane, 152
WOOLRIDGE, Tanya J, 280
WOOTEN, Eric Randall, 268
WOOTEN, Nealy H, 798
WOPSCHALL, Paul R, 613
WORDEN, Lisa, 695
WORK, Dawn, 293
WORKMAN Jr, Joe E, 704
WORKMAN, Marvin W, 485
WORMACK, Karen Elise, 866
WORRELL, Carol Smith, 232
WORTH, Karen, 553
WORTHEN, Beula M, 277
WORTHEN, Doris, 1194
WORTMAN, Mary F, 904
WOS, Karen L, 689
WOURMS, Patricia M, 113
WRENN, Mary Coker, 917
WRIGHT, Beatrice B, 1088
WRIGHT, Clarence N, 421
WRIGHT, Diane, 777

WRIGHT, Donna Brodie, 633
WRIGHT, Elda Schwarz, 81
WRIGHT, Eleanor R, 1040
WRIGHT, Faith, 280
WRIGHT, Frank, 529
WRIGHT, Gary L, 605
WRIGHT, Gayle A, 103
WRIGHT, Judith A, 111
WRIGHT, La Jetta Y, 682
WRIGHT, La Wanna Hall, 454
WRIGHT, Lee Fissori, 686
WRIGHT, Linda B, 502
WRIGHT, Mae, 388
WRIGHT, Margaret E, 1107
WRIGHT, Mark J, 194
WRIGHT, Mary V, 1038
WRIGHT, Mattie J, 1148
WRIGHT, Mendy, 648
WRIGHT, Ruth F, 36
WRIGHT, S Irene, 1064
WRIGHT, Sarah B, 502
WRIGHT, Sgt S A, 1108
WRIGHT, Sonya, 947
WRIGHT, Tarita Alecia, 225
WRIGHTMAN, Mildred E, 343,
WRONKO, Mary, 971
WU, Arlouine G, 1184
WUERTH, Helen G, 495
WULTSCH, Elizabeth, 352
WYATT, Danielle (Dani), 898
WYATT, Leonora A, 825
WYLIE, Joan Brice, 884
WYMAN, Steve, 803
WYMAN, Van, 428
WYNIA, Chrish, 445
WYNN, Byron, 99
WYNN, Glenn T, 452
WYRAUCH, Theresa, 431
WYTCH, She-Leiyas J, 247
WYZYKOWSKI, Michael T, 1171

X

XANDER, Terry, 700
XENOS, Iphigenia, 544

Y

YAGER, Bret H, 1090
YAHOLA, John R, 871
YAMADA, D H, 384
YAMAMOTO, Virginia K, 267
YAMNICKY, Jennifer Lynn, 282
YANCEY, Pamela, 413
YANCY, Wanda, 852
YANEZ, Roi, 405
YANG, Xai, 1172
YANKE, Robyn C, 928
YANOW, Kenneth, 928
YARBORO, Charlotte H, 410
YARBROUGH, Melody, 89
YARBROUGH, Ruth G, 504
YARDUMIAN, Gary, 560
YARICK, Eugenia Wood, 657
YARNAL, Wilma R, 1127
YARNALL, Cheryl S, 297
YASKELL, Steven H, 202
YATES III, Willie, 868
YATES, Dave M, 1067
YATES, Louise Suiter, 1019
YATES, Randy, 548
YAUGER Jr, Lester B, 894
YAVITT, Barbara, 568
YEAPLE, Gail, 382
YEARWOOD, W F, 291
YEE, Winnie C, 362
YEGGY, Dawn C, 311
YELLEN, Yadja, 357
YELLIN, Judith, 571
YENCHKO, Cindy Ann, 765
YEOMAN, Michael D, 156
YEOMANS, Robert, 413
YERKES, Dolores E, 662
YERKES, Karn, 420
YERRO, Teodulfo T, 258
YLANAN, Jude Brian, 579
YONKERS, Christine V, 1108
YORK, Brenda, 1015
YORK, Diane, 987
YORK, Grace, 624
YORK, Linda K, 566
YORNS, Ruth H, 102
YOTTER, Carrie, 780
YOUMAN, Cosseam T, 833
YOUNCE, Eddie Ray, 1049
YOUNG Jr, Carl M, 209
YOUNG, Angi, 638
YOUNG, Bart M, 942
YOUNG, David A, 413
YOUNG, Debbie, 567
YOUNG, Donald A, 822
YOUNG, Donna, 326
YOUNG, E A, 752
YOUNG, Edith, 807, 1007, 1008
YOUNG, Hy, 843
YOUNG, Inez Babb, 599
YOUNG, Jean, 1127
YOUNG, Jessie J, 141
YOUNG, John Preston, 225
YOUNG, Joy K, 440
YOUNG, Kimberly Anne, 537
YOUNG, Lauvonda M, 34
YOUNG, Linda Bishop, 107
YOUNG, Margaret S, 368
YOUNG, Marlene B, 426
YOUNG, Michael, 220
YOUNG, Michael, 994
YOUNG, Nicholas D, 473
YOUNG, Rhonda, 429
YOUNG, Sandra J, 512
YOUNG-BROWN, Joyice B, 637
YOUNG-MARTINEZ, Debi, 1088
YOUNGBLOOD, Diane L, 186
YOUNGBLOOD, Joan E, 839
YOUNGBLOOD, Monica S, 147
YOUNGBLOOD, Roxanne, 674
YOUNGBLUD, John Shetler, 597
YOUNGS, Marjorie, 347
YOUNKIN, Marie Neubert, 288
YOUNKINS, Rose B, 994
YOUSE, Linda M, 959
YOVINO, Miriam K, 669
YOWELL, Lorene W Cate, 921
YUHASZ, Keith R, 48
YUILL, John, 93

Z

ZABKA, Alma Joyce, 936
ZACHARIAS, Donna, 290
ZACHARIAS, May L, 834
ZACHGO, Steven, 620
ZACK, Wayne G, 952
ZAGERS, Ingrid, 268
ZAGORSKI, Beth, 135
ZAK, John A, 138
ZAKRAYSEK, Theresa A, 824
ZALE, Patrick, 844
ZALESKI, Robert John, 108
ZALMA, Thea Rae, 699
ZAMORA, Ruth Hooper, 1199
ZANELLA, Sarah A, 959
ZANGARE, Mary T, 863
ZANNONE, Nancee, 990
ZARCONE, Julie R, 1193
ZAROWSKY, Lara, 590
ZARRILLO, Vincent P, 122
ZAUN, Lois, 835
ZAWADA, Mark G, 184
ZBERCOT, John Charles, 725
ZBIERZCHOWSKA, Hanna Olcha, 1191
ZBYSIENSKI, Joyce, 1166
ZEARING, Esther, 1134
ZEBATTO, Mary, 121
ZEGERS, Cornelis, 878
ZEIHEN, Donna, 376
ZELENAK, Gerry, 705
ZELINSKY, Erica, 456
ZELLER, Lorentina H, 1083
ZELLER, Terry L, 1188
ZELLMER, Norma M, 687
ZEMAN, April, 1192
ZEMTSEFF, Gary, 1004
ZEMTSEFF, George T, 1004
ZEMTSEFF, Linda Marie, 1004
ZEN, Delores E, 113
ZEOLI, Tracy Lee, 217
ZERVOS, Clifford G, 382
ZETTLER, Mary F, 31
ZHAI, Zhenming, 83
ZIAVRAS, Charles E, 359
ZIEGELGRUBER, David L, 231
ZIEGLER, C Russell, 147
ZIEGLER, Heidi Ann, 1046
ZIELKE, Gertrude, 974
ZIEROLD, Emily F, 409, 1027
ZIETZ, Dorothy, 379
ZIGLER, Lisa M, 902
ZIMA, Debra M, 1090
ZIMMER, Barbara S, 221
ZIMMER, John, 801
ZIMMER, Minta G, 762
ZIMMERMAN, Brad L, 1155
ZIMMERMAN, Fran, 581
ZINGALE, Jim, 407
ZINIOUS, Leona Lz, 255
ZINKEL, Rod M, 63
ZIPP, Alaina, 148
ZIRNIS, Elmar E, 856
ZISTER, Mariza, 54
ZOGAIB, Henri, 1037
ZOLESKI, Stephen E, 830
ZORATTO, Carmen, 507
ZORUMSKI, Cecelia J, 1188
ZOSKE, Elke, 17
ZUBERKA, Andrea, 12
ZUCK, Jessica, 726
ZULAUF-WATERBURY, Janice, 664
ZUNIGA, Monica C, 507
ZURSTADT, Sara, 1017
ZWEIGLER, Barbara, 464
ZWIES, Ardath (Spires), 832